2017 Directory of California Wholesalers and Service Companies

Published January 2017 next update January 2018

WARNING: Purchasers and users of this directory may not use this directory to compile mailing lists, other marketing aids and other types of data, which are sold or otherwise provided to third parties. Such use is wrongful, illegal and a violation of the federal copyright laws.

CAUTION: Because of the many thousands of establishment listings contained in this directory and the possibilities of both human and mechanical error in processing this information, Mergent Inc. cannot assume liability for the correctness of the listings or information on which they are based. Hence, no information contained in this work should be relied upon in any instance where there is a possibility of any loss or damage as a consequence of any error or omission in this volume.

Publisher
Mergent Inc.
444 Madison Ave
New York, NY 10022

©Mergent Inc All Rights Reserved
2017 Mergent Business Press
ISSN 1080-2614
ISBN 978-1-68200-345-9

TABLE OF CONTENTS

Summary of Contents & Explanatory Notes 4
User's Guide to Listings 6

Products & Services Section
SIC Numerical Index 9
SIC Alphabetical Index 11
Firms Listed by SIC 13

Alphabetic Section
Firms listed alphabetically by company name 1265

Geographic Section
County/City Cross-Reference Index 1614
Firms Listed by Location City 1619

SUMMARY OF CONTENTS

Number of Companies 28,172
Number of Decision Makers 84,863
Minimum Number of Employees 50

EXPLANATORY NOTES

How to Cross-Reference in This Directory

Sequential Entry Numbers. Each establishment in the Products & Services Section is numbered sequentially (P-00000). The number assigned to each establishment is referred to as its Entry Number. To make cross-referencing easier, each listing in the Products & Services, Alphabetic and Geographic Sections includes the establishment's entry number. To facilitate locating an entry in the Products & Services Section, the entry numbers for the first listing on the left page and the last listing on the right page are printed at the top of the page next to the Standard Industrial Classification (S.I.C.) description.

Source Suggestions Welcome

Although all known sources were used to compile this directory, it is possible that companies were inadvertently omitted. Your assistance in calling attention to such omissions would be greatly appreciated. A special form on the facing page will help you in the reporting process.

Analysis

Every effort has been made to contact all firms to verify their information. The one exception to this rule is the annual sales figure, which is considered by many companies to be confidential information. Therefore, estimated sales have been calculated by multiplying the nationwide average sales per employee for the firm's major SIC/NAICS code by the firm's number of employees. Nationwide averages for sales per employee by SIC/NAICS codes are provided by the U.S. Department of Commerce and are updated annually. All sales—sales (est)—have been estimated by this method. The exceptions are parent companies (PA), division headquarters (DH) and headquarter locations (HQ) which may include an actual corporate sales figure—sales (corporate-wide) if available.

Types of Companies

Descriptive and statistical data are included for companies in the entire state. These comprise manufacturers, machine shops, fabricators, assemblers and printers. Also identified are corporate offices in the state.

Employment Data

This directory contains companies with 50 or more employees. The employment figure shown in the Products & Services Section includes male and female employees and embraces all levels of the company: administrative, clerical, sales and maintenance. This figure is for the facility listed and does not include other plants or offices. It should be recognized that these figures represent an approximate year-round average. These employment figures are broken into codes A through E and used in the Alphabetic and Geographic Sections to further help you in qualifying a company. Be sure to check the footnotes at the bottom of the page for the code breakdowns.

Standard Industrial Classification (SIC)

The Standard Industrial Classification (SIC) system used in this directory was developed by the federal government for use in classifying establishments by the type of activity they are engaged in. The SIC classifications used in this directory are from the 1987 edition published by the U.S. Government's Office of Management and Budget. The SIC system separates all activities into broad industrial divisions (e.g., manufacturing, mining, retail trade). It further subdivides each division. The range of manufacturing industry classes extends from two-digit codes (major industry group) to four-digit codes (product).

For example:

Industry Breakdown	Code	Industry, Product, etc.
*Major industry group	20	Food and kindred products
Industry group	203	Canned and frozen foods
*Industry	2033	Fruits and vegetables, etc.

*Classifications used in this directory

Only two-digit and four-digit codes are used in this directory.

Arrangement

1. The **Product & Services Section** contains complete in-depth corporate data. This section lists companies under their primary SIC. SIC codes are in numerical order with companies listed alphabetically under each code. A numerical and alphabetical index precedes this section.

> IMPORTANT NOTICE: It is a violation of both federal and state law to transmit an unsolicited advertisement to a facsimile machine. Any user of this product that violates such laws may be subject to civil and criminal penalties, which may exceed $500 for each transmission of an unsolicited facsimile. Mergent Inc. provides fax numbers for lawful purposes only and expressly forbids the use of these numbers in any unlawful manner.

2. The **Alphabetic Section** lists all companies with their full physical or mailing addresses and telephone number.

3. The **Geographic Section** is sorted by cities listed in alphabetic order and companies listed alphabetically within each city.

USER'S GUIDE TO LISTINGS

PRODUCT & SERVICES SECTION

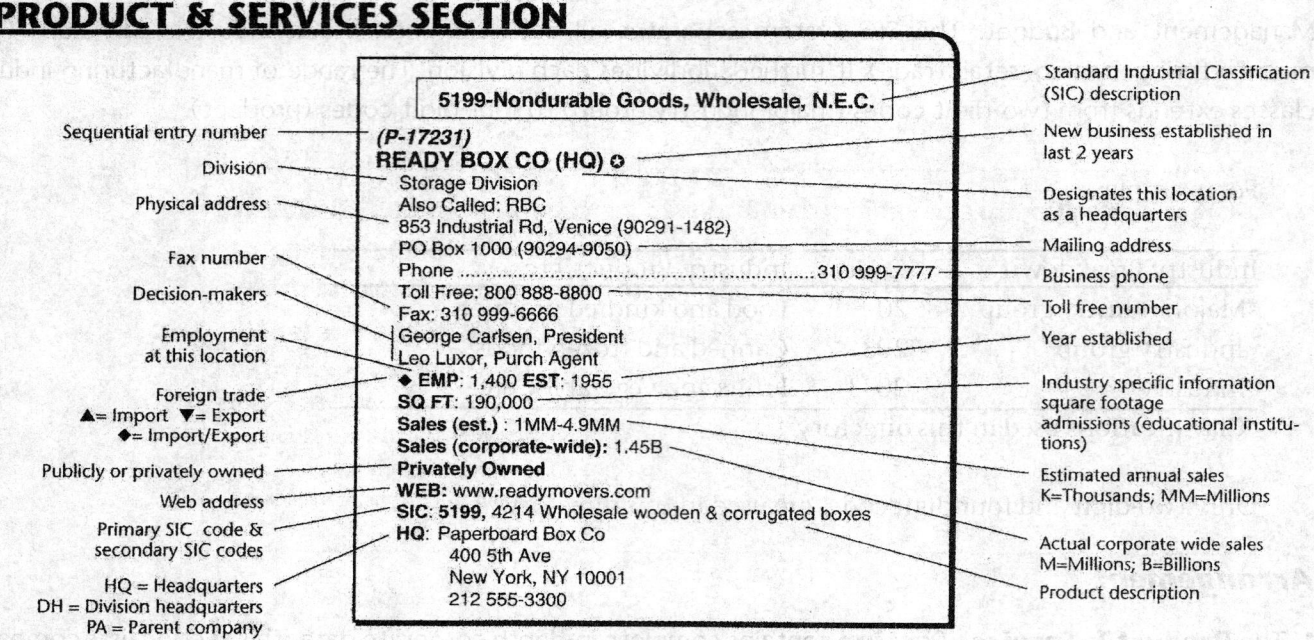

ALPHABETIC SECTION

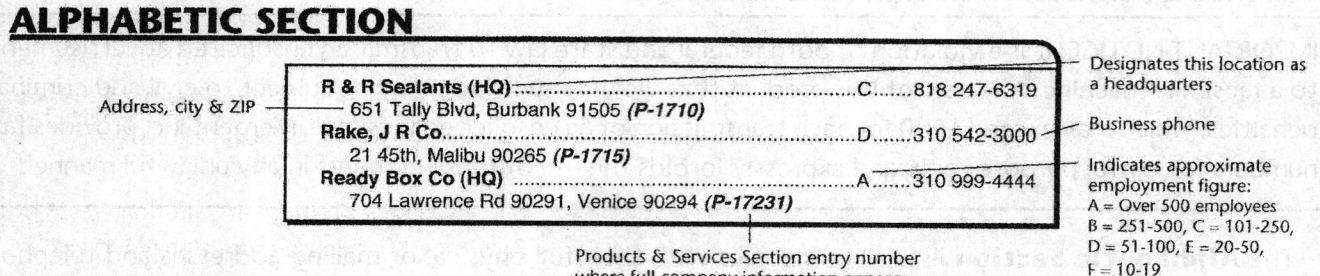

GEOGRAPHIC SECTION

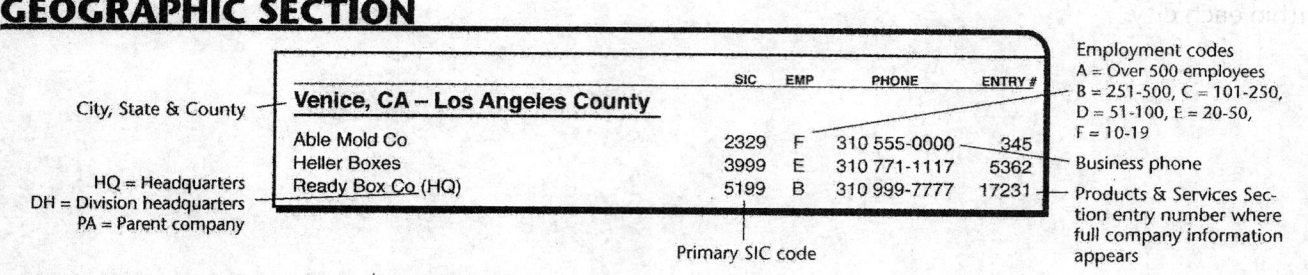

NUMERICAL INDEX of SIC DESCRIPTIONS
ALPHABETICAL INDEX of SIC DESCRIPTIONS

PRODUCTS & SERVICES SECTION
Companies listed alphabetically under thier primary SIC
In-depth company data listed

ALPHABETIC SECTION
Company listings in alphabetical order

GEOGRAPHIC INDEX
Companies sorted by city in alphabetical order

SIC INDEX

PRDTS & SVCS

ALPHABETIC

GEOGRAPHIC

California
County Map

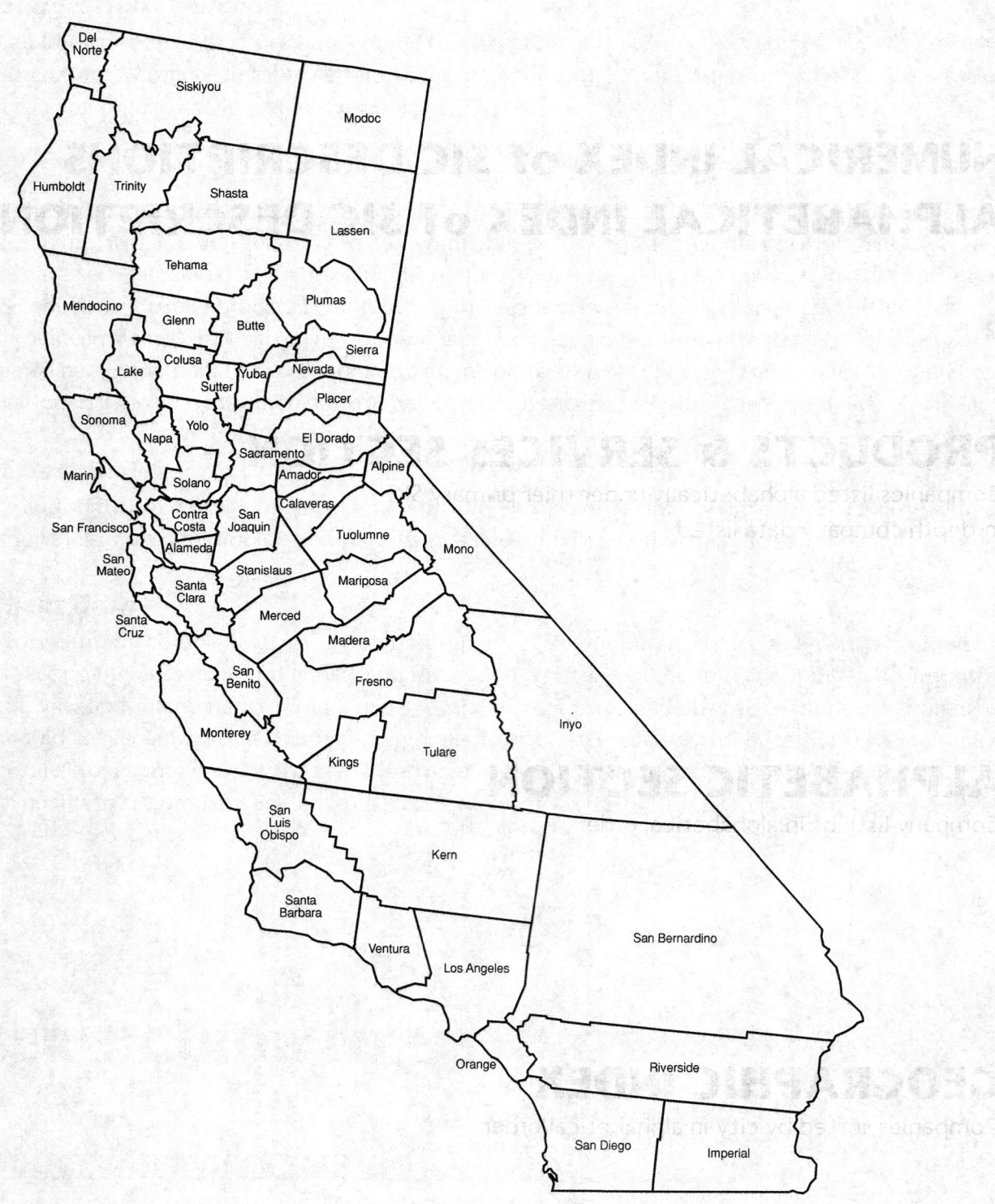

SIC INDEX

Standard Industrial Classification Numerical Index

SIC NO	PRODUCT

01 AGRICULTURAL PRODUCTION-CROPS
0111 Wheat
0112 Rice
0115 Corn
0131 Cotton
0132 Tobacco
0134 Irish Potatoes
0139 Field Crops, Except Cash Grains, NEC
0161 Vegetables & Melons
0171 Berry Crops
0172 Grapes
0173 Tree Nuts
0174 Citrus Fruits
0175 Deciduous Tree Fruits
0179 Fruits & Tree Nuts, NEC
0181 Ornamental Floriculture & Nursery Prdts
0182 Food Crops Grown Under Cover
0191 Crop Farming, Misc

02 AGRICULTURAL PRODUCTION-LIVESTOCK AND ANIMAL SPECIALTIES
0211 Beef Cattle Feedlots
0212 Beef Cattle, Except Feedlots
0213 Hogs
0214 Sheep & Goats
0241 Dairy Farms
0252 Chicken Egg Farms
0253 Turkey & Turkey Egg Farms
0254 Poultry Hatcheries
0259 Poultry & Eggs Farms, NEC
0279 Animal Specialties, NEC
0291 Animal Production, NEC

07 AGRICULTURAL SERVICES
0711 Soil Preparation Svcs
0721 Soil Preparation, Planting & Cultivating Svc
0722 Crop Harvesting By Machine
0723 Crop Preparation, Except Cotton Ginning
0742 Veterinary Animal Specialties
0751 Livestock Svcs, Except Veterinary
0752 Animal Specialty Svcs, Exc Veterinary
0761 Farm Labor Contractors & Crew Leaders
0762 Farm Management Svcs
0781 Landscape Counseling & Planning
0782 Lawn & Garden Svcs
0783 Ornamental Shrub & Tree Svc

08 FORESTRY
0811 Timber Tracts
0851 Forestry Svcs

09 FISHING, HUNTING, AND TRAPPING
0971 Hunting & Trapping

10 METAL MINING
1041 Gold Ores

12 COAL MINING
1221 Bituminous Coal & Lignite: Surface Mining
1241 Coal Mining Svcs

13 OIL AND GAS EXTRACTION
1311 Crude Petroleum & Natural Gas
1381 Drilling Oil & Gas Wells
1382 Oil & Gas Field Exploration Svcs
1389 Oil & Gas Field Svcs, NEC

14 MINING AND QUARRYING OF NONMETALLIC MINERALS, EXCEPT FUELS
1422 Crushed & Broken Limestone
1429 Crushed & Broken Stone, NEC
1442 Construction Sand & Gravel
1446 Industrial Sand
1474 Potash, Soda & Borate Minerals
1481 Nonmetallic Minerals Svcs, Except Fuels
1499 Miscellaneous Nonmetallic Mining

15 BUILDING CONSTRUCTION-GENERAL CONTRACTORS AND OPERATIVE BUILDERS
1521 General Contractors, Single Family Houses
1522 General Contractors, Residential Other Than Single Family
1531 Operative Builders
1541 General Contractors, Indl Bldgs & Warehouses
1542 General Contractors, Nonresidential & Non-indl Bldgs

16 HEAVY CONSTRUCTION OTHER THAN BUILDING CONSTRUCTION-CONTRACTORS
1611 Highway & Street Construction
1622 Bridge, Tunnel & Elevated Hwy Construction
1623 Water, Sewer & Utility Line Construction
1629 Heavy Construction, NEC

17 CONSTRUCTION-SPECIAL TRADE CONTRACTORS
1711 Plumbing, Heating & Air Conditioning Contractors
1721 Painting & Paper Hanging Contractors
1731 Electrical Work
1741 Masonry & Other Stonework
1742 Plastering, Drywall, Acoustical & Insulation Work
1743 Terrazzo, Tile, Marble & Mosaic Work
1751 Carpentry Work
1752 Floor Laying & Other Floor Work, NEC
1761 Roofing, Siding & Sheet Metal Work
1771 Concrete Work
1781 Water Well Drilling
1791 Structural Steel Erection
1793 Glass & Glazing Work
1794 Excavating & Grading Work
1795 Wrecking & Demolition Work
1796 Installation Or Erection Of Bldg Eqpt & Machinery, NEC
1799 Special Trade Contractors, NEC

40 RAILROAD TRANSPORTATION
4011 Railroads, Line-Hauling Operations
4013 Switching & Terminal Svcs

41 LOCAL AND SUBURBAN TRANSIT AND INTERURBAN HIGHWAY PASSENGER TRANSPORTATION
4111 Local & Suburban Transit
4119 Local Passenger Transportation: NEC
4121 Taxi Cabs
4131 Intercity & Rural Bus Transportation
4141 Local Bus Charter Svc
4142 Bus Charter Service, Except Local
4151 School Buses
4173 Bus Terminal & Svc Facilities

42 MOTOR FREIGHT TRANSPORTATION AND WAREHOUSING
4212 Local Trucking Without Storage
4213 Trucking, Except Local
4214 Local Trucking With Storage
4215 Courier Svcs, Except Air
4221 Farm Product Warehousing & Storage
4222 Refrigerated Warehousing & Storage
4225 General Warehousing & Storage
4226 Special Warehousing & Storage, NEC
4231 Terminal & Joint Terminal Maint Facilities

44 WATER TRANSPORTATION
4412 Deep Sea Foreign Transportation Of Freight
4424 Deep Sea Domestic Transportation Of Freight
4449 Water Transportation Of Freight, NEC
4481 Deep Sea Transportation Of Passengers
4489 Water Transport Of Passengers, NEC
4491 Marine Cargo Handling
4492 Towing & Tugboat Svcs
4493 Marinas
4499 Water Transportation Svcs, NEC

45 TRANSPORTATION BY AIR
4512 Air Transportation, Scheduled
4513 Air Courier Svcs
4522 Air Transportation, Nonscheduled
4581 Airports, Flying Fields & Terminal Svcs

46 PIPELINES, EXCEPT NATURAL GAS
4613 Refined Petroleum Pipelines
4619 Pipelines, NEC

47 TRANSPORTATION SERVICES
4724 Travel Agencies
4725 Tour Operators
4729 Passenger Transportation Arrangement, NEC
4731 Freight Forwarding & Arrangement
4783 Packing & Crating Svcs
4785 Fixed Facilities, Inspection, Weighing Svcs Transptn
4789 Transportation Svcs, NEC

48 COMMUNICATIONS
4812 Radiotelephone Communications
4813 Telephone Communications, Except Radio
4822 Telegraph & Other Message Communications
4832 Radio Broadcasting Stations
4833 Television Broadcasting Stations
4841 Cable & Other Pay TV Svcs
4899 Communication Svcs, NEC

49 ELECTRIC, GAS, AND SANITARY SERVICES
4911 Electric Svcs
4922 Natural Gas Transmission
4923 Natural Gas Transmission & Distribution
4924 Natural Gas Distribution
4925 Gas Production &/Or Distribution
4931 Electric & Other Svcs Combined
4932 Gas & Other Svcs Combined
4939 Combination Utilities, NEC
4941 Water Sply
4952 Sewerage Systems
4953 Refuse Systems
4959 Sanitary Svcs, NEC
4961 Steam & Air Conditioning Sply
4971 Irrigation Systems

50 WHOLESALE TRADE¨DURABLE GOODS
5012 Automobiles & Other Motor Vehicles Wholesale
5013 Motor Vehicle Splys & New Parts Wholesale
5014 Tires & Tubes Wholesale
5015 Motor Vehicle Parts, Used Wholesale
5021 Furniture Wholesale
5023 Home Furnishings Wholesale
5031 Lumber, Plywood & Millwork Wholesale
5032 Brick, Stone & Related Construction Mtrls Wholesale
5033 Roofing, Siding & Insulation Mtrls Wholesale
5039 Construction Materials, NEC Wholesale
5043 Photographic Eqpt & Splys Wholesale
5044 Office Eqpt Wholesale
5045 Computers & Peripheral Eqpt & Software Wholesale
5046 Commercial Eqpt, NEC Wholesale
5047 Medical, Dental & Hospital Eqpt & Splys Wholesale
5048 Ophthalmic Goods Wholesale
5049 Professional Eqpt & Splys, NEC Wholesale
5051 Metals Service Centers
5052 Coal & Other Minerals & Ores Wholesale
5063 Electrl Apparatus, Eqpt, Wiring Splys Wholesale
5064 Electrical Appliances, TV & Radios Wholesale
5065 Electronic Parts & Eqpt Wholesale
5072 Hardware Wholesale
5074 Plumbing & Heating Splys Wholesale
5075 Heating & Air Conditioning Eqpt & Splys Wholesale
5078 Refrigeration Eqpt & Splys Wholesale
5082 Construction & Mining Mach & Eqpt Wholesale
5083 Farm & Garden Mach & Eqpt Wholesale
5084 Industrial Mach & Eqpt Wholesale
5085 Industrial Splys Wholesale
5087 Service Establishment Eqpt & Splys Wholesale
5088 Transportation Eqpt & Splys, Except Motor Vehicles Wholesale
5091 Sporting & Recreational Goods & Splys Wholesale
5092 Toys & Hobby Goods & Splys Wholesale
5093 Scrap & Waste Materials Wholesale
5094 Jewelry, Watches, Precious Stones Wholesale
5099 Durable Goods: NEC Wholesale

51 WHOLESALE TRADE¨NONDURABLE GOODS
5111 Printing & Writing Paper Wholesale
5112 Stationery & Office Splys Wholesale
5113 Indl & Personal Svc Paper Wholesale
5122 Drugs, Drug Proprietaries & Sundries Wholesale
5131 Piece Goods, Notions & Dry Goods Wholesale
5136 Men's & Boys' Clothing & Furnishings Wholesale
5137 Women's, Children's & Infants Clothing Wholesale
5139 Footwear Wholesale
5141 Groceries, General Line Wholesale
5142 Packaged Frozen Foods Wholesale
5143 Dairy Prdts, Except Dried Or Canned Wholesale
5144 Poultry & Poultry Prdts Wholesale
5145 Confectionery Wholesale
5146 Fish & Seafood Wholesale
5147 Meats & Meat Prdts Wholesale
5148 Fresh Fruits & Vegetables Wholesale
5149 Groceries & Related Prdts, NEC Wholesale

SIC INDEX

SIC NO	PRODUCT
5153	Grain & Field Beans Wholesale
5154	Livestock Wholesale
5159	Farm-Prdt Raw Mtrls, NEC Wholesale
5162	Plastics Materials & Basic Shapes Wholesale
5169	Chemicals & Allied Prdts, NEC Wholesale
5171	Petroleum Bulk Stations & Terminals
5172	Petroleum & Petroleum Prdts Wholesale
5181	Beer & Ale Wholesale
5182	Wine & Distilled Alcoholic Beverages Wholesale
5191	Farm Splys Wholesale
5192	Books, Periodicals & Newspapers Wholesale
5193	Flowers, Nursery Stock & Florists' Splys Wholesale
5194	Tobacco & Tobacco Prdts Wholesale
5198	Paints, Varnishes & Splys Wholesale
5199	Nondurable Goods, NEC Wholesale

60 DEPOSITORY INSTITUTIONS

- 6011 Federal Reserve Banks
- 6021 National Commercial Banks
- 6022 State Commercial Banks
- 6029 Commercial Banks, NEC
- 6035 Federal Savings Institutions
- 6036 Savings Institutions, Except Federal
- 6061 Federal Credit Unions
- 6062 State Credit Unions
- 6081 Foreign Banks, Branches & Agencies
- 6082 Foreign Trade & Intl Banks
- 6091 Nondeposit Trust Facilities
- 6099 Functions Related To Deposit Banking, NEC

61 NONDEPOSITORY CREDIT INSTITUTIONS

- 6111 Federal Credit Agencies
- 6141 Personal Credit Institutions
- 6153 Credit Institutions, Short-Term Business
- 6159 Credit Institutions, Misc Business
- 6162 Mortgage Bankers & Loan Correspondents
- 6163 Loan Brokers

62 SECURITY AND COMMODITY BROKERS, DEALERS, EXCHANGES, AND SERVICES

- 6211 Security Brokers & Dealers
- 6221 Commodity Contracts Brokers & Dealers
- 6231 Security & Commodity Exchanges
- 6282 Investment Advice
- 6289 Security & Commodity Svcs, NEC

63 INSURANCE CARRIERS

- 6311 Life Insurance Carriers
- 6321 Accident & Health Insurance
- 6324 Hospital & Medical Svc Plans Carriers
- 6331 Fire, Marine & Casualty Insurance
- 6351 Surety Insurance Carriers
- 6361 Title Insurance
- 6371 Pension, Health & Welfare Funds
- 6399 Insurance Carriers, NEC

64 INSURANCE AGENTS, BROKERS, AND SERVICE

- 6411 Insurance Agents, Brokers & Svc

65 REAL ESTATE

- 6512 Operators Of Nonresidential Bldgs
- 6513 Operators Of Apartment Buildings
- 6514 Operators Of Dwellings, Except Apartments
- 6515 Operators Of Residential Mobile Home Sites
- 6519 Lessors Of Real Estate, NEC
- 6531 Real Estate Agents & Managers
- 6541 Title Abstract Offices
- 6552 Land Subdividers & Developers
- 6553 Cemetery Subdividers & Developers

67 HOLDING AND OTHER INVESTMENT OFFICES

- 6712 Offices Of Bank Holding Co's
- 6719 Offices Of Holding Co's, NEC
- 6722 Management Investment Offices
- 6726 Unit Investment Trusts, Face-Amount Certificate Offices
- 6732 Education, Religious & Charitable Trusts
- 6733 Trusts Except Educational, Religious & Charitable
- 6794 Patent Owners & Lessors
- 6798 Real Estate Investment Trusts
- 6799 Investors, NEC

70 HOTELS, ROOMING HOUSES, CAMPS, AND OTHER LODGING PLACES

- 7011 Hotels, Motels & Tourist Courts
- 7021 Rooming & Boarding Houses
- 7032 Sporting & Recreational Camps
- 7033 Trailer Parks & Camp Sites
- 7041 Membership-Basis Hotels

72 PERSONAL SERVICES

- 7211 Power Laundries, Family & Commercial
- 7212 Garment Pressing & Cleaners' Agents
- 7213 Linen Sply
- 7215 Coin Operated Laundries & Cleaning
- 7216 Dry Cleaning Plants, Except Rug Cleaning
- 7217 Carpet & Upholstery Cleaning
- 7218 Industrial Launderers
- 7219 Laundry & Garment Svcs, NEC
- 7221 Photographic Studios, Portrait
- 7231 Beauty Shops
- 7241 Barber Shops
- 7251 Shoe Repair & Shoeshine Parlors
- 7261 Funeral Svcs & Crematories
- 7291 Tax Return Preparation Svcs
- 7299 Miscellaneous Personal Svcs, NEC

73 BUSINESS SERVICES

- 7311 Advertising Agencies
- 7312 Outdoor Advertising Svcs
- 7313 Radio, TV & Publishers Adv Reps
- 7319 Advertising, NEC
- 7322 Adjustment & Collection Svcs
- 7323 Credit Reporting Svcs
- 7331 Direct Mail Advertising Svcs
- 7334 Photocopying & Duplicating Svcs
- 7335 Commercial Photography
- 7336 Commercial Art & Graphic Design
- 7338 Secretarial & Court Reporting Svcs
- 7342 Disinfecting & Pest Control Svcs
- 7349 Building Cleaning & Maintenance Svcs, NEC
- 7352 Medical Eqpt Rental & Leasing
- 7353 Heavy Construction Eqpt Rental & Leasing
- 7359 Equipment Rental & Leasing, NEC
- 7361 Employment Agencies
- 7363 Help Supply Svcs
- 7371 Custom Computer Programming Svcs
- 7372 Prepackaged Software
- 7373 Computer Integrated Systems Design
- 7374 Data & Computer Processing & Preparation
- 7375 Information Retrieval Svcs
- 7376 Computer Facilities Management Svcs
- 7377 Computer Rental & Leasing
- 7378 Computer Maintenance & Repair
- 7379 Computer Related Svcs, NEC
- 7381 Detective & Armored Car Svcs
- 7382 Security Systems Svcs
- 7383 News Syndicates
- 7384 Photofinishing Labs
- 7389 Business Svcs, NEC

75 AUTOMOTIVE REPAIR, SERVICES, AND PARKING

- 7513 Truck Rental & Leasing, Without Drivers
- 7514 Passenger Car Rental
- 7515 Passenger Car Leasing
- 7519 Utility Trailers & Recreational Vehicle Rental
- 7521 Automobile Parking Lots & Garages
- 7532 Top, Body & Upholstery Repair & Paint Shops
- 7533 Automotive Exhaust System Repair Shops
- 7534 Tire Retreading & Repair Shops
- 7536 Automotive Glass Replacement Shops
- 7538 General Automotive Repair Shop
- 7539 Automotive Repair Shops, NEC
- 7542 Car Washes
- 7549 Automotive Svcs, Except Repair & Car Washes

76 MISCELLANEOUS REPAIR SERVICES

- 7622 Radio & TV Repair Shops
- 7623 Refrigeration & Air Conditioning Svc & Repair Shop
- 7629 Electrical & Elex Repair Shop, NEC
- 7631 Watch, Clock & Jewelry Repair
- 7641 Reupholstery & Furniture Repair
- 7692 Welding Repair
- 7699 Repair Shop & Related Svcs, NEC

78 MOTION PICTURES

- 7812 Motion Picture & Video Tape Production
- 7819 Services Allied To Motion Picture Prdtn
- 7822 Motion Picture & Video Tape Distribution
- 7829 Services Allied To Motion Picture Distribution
- 7832 Motion Picture Theaters, Except Drive-In
- 7833 Drive-In Motion Picture Theaters

79 AMUSEMENT AND RECREATION SERVICES

- 7911 Dance Studios, Schools & Halls
- 7922 Theatrical Producers & Misc Theatrical Svcs
- 7929 Bands, Orchestras, Actors & Entertainers
- 7933 Bowling Centers
- 7941 Professional Sports Clubs & Promoters
- 7948 Racing & Track Operations
- 7991 Physical Fitness Facilities
- 7992 Public Golf Courses
- 7993 Coin-Operated Amusement Devices & Arcades
- 7996 Amusement Parks
- 7997 Membership Sports & Recreation Clubs
- 7999 Amusement & Recreation Svcs, NEC

80 HEALTH SERVICES

- 8011 Offices & Clinics Of Doctors Of Medicine
- 8021 Offices & Clinics Of Dentists
- 8031 Offices & Clinics Of Doctors Of Osteopathy
- 8041 Offices & Clinics Of Chiropractors
- 8042 Offices & Clinics Of Optometrists
- 8049 Offices & Clinics Of Health Practitioners, NEC
- 8051 Skilled Nursing Facilities
- 8052 Intermediate Care Facilities
- 8059 Nursing & Personal Care Facilities, NEC
- 8062 General Medical & Surgical Hospitals
- 8063 Psychiatric Hospitals
- 8069 Specialty Hospitals, Except Psychiatric
- 8071 Medical Laboratories
- 8072 Dental Laboratories
- 8082 Home Health Care Svcs
- 8092 Kidney Dialysis Centers
- 8093 Specialty Outpatient Facilities, NEC
- 8099 Health & Allied Svcs, NEC

81 LEGAL SERVICES

- 8111 Legal Svcs

83 SOCIAL SERVICES

- 8322 Individual & Family Social Svcs
- 8331 Job Training & Vocational Rehabilitation Svcs
- 8351 Child Day Care Svcs
- 8361 Residential Care
- 8399 Social Services, NEC

84 MUSEUMS, ART GALLERIES, AND BOTANICAL AND ZOOLOGICAL GARDENS

- 8412 Museums & Art Galleries
- 8422 Arboreta, Botanical & Zoological Gardens

86 MEMBERSHIP ORGANIZATIONS

- 8611 Business Associations
- 8621 Professional Membership Organizations
- 8631 Labor Unions & Similar Organizations
- 8641 Civic, Social & Fraternal Associations
- 8651 Political Organizations
- 8699 Membership Organizations, NEC

87 ENGINEERING, ACCOUNTING, RESEARCH, MANAGEMENT, AND RELATED SERVICES

- 8711 Engineering Services
- 8712 Architectural Services
- 8713 Surveying Services
- 8721 Accounting, Auditing & Bookkeeping Svcs
- 8731 Commercial Physical & Biological Research
- 8732 Commercial Economic, Sociological & Educational Research
- 8733 Noncommercial Research Organizations
- 8734 Testing Laboratories
- 8741 Management Services
- 8742 Management Consulting Services
- 8743 Public Relations Svcs
- 8744 Facilities Support Mgmt Svcs
- 8748 Business Consulting Svcs, NEC

89 SERVICES, NOT ELSEWHERE CLASSIFIED

- 8999 Services Not Elsewhere Classified

SIC INDEX

Standard Industrial Classification Alphabetical Index

SIC NO	PRODUCT

A

6321 Accident & Health Insurance
8721 Accounting, Auditing & Bookkeeping Svcs
7322 Adjustment & Collection Svcs
7311 Advertising Agencies
7319 Advertising, NEC
4513 Air Courier Svcs
4522 Air Transportation, Nonscheduled
4512 Air Transportation, Scheduled
4581 Airports, Flying Fields & Terminal Svcs
7999 Amusement & Recreation Svcs, NEC
7996 Amusement Parks
0291 Animal Production, NEC
0279 Animal Specialties, NEC
0752 Animal Specialty Svcs, Exc Veterinary
8422 Arboreta, Botanical & Zoological Gardens
8712 Architectural Services
7521 Automobile Parking Lots & Garages
5012 Automobiles & Other Motor Vehicles Wholesale
7533 Automotive Exhaust System Repair Shops
7536 Automotive Glass Replacement Shops
7539 Automotive Repair Shops, NEC
7549 Automotive Svcs, Except Repair & Car Washes

B

7929 Bands, Orchestras, Actors & Entertainers
7241 Barber Shops
7231 Beauty Shops
0211 Beef Cattle Feedlots
0212 Beef Cattle, Except Feedlots
5181 Beer & Ale Wholesale
0171 Berry Crops
1221 Bituminous Coal & Lignite: Surface Mining
5192 Books, Periodicals & Newspapers Wholesale
7933 Bowling Centers
5032 Brick, Stone & Related Construction Mtrls Wholesale
1622 Bridge, Tunnel & Elevated Hwy Construction
7349 Building Cleaning & Maintenance Svcs, NEC
4142 Bus Charter Service, Except Local
4173 Bus Terminal & Svc Facilities
8611 Business Associations
8748 Business Consulting Svcs, NEC
7389 Business Svcs, NEC

C

4841 Cable & Other Pay TV Svcs
7542 Car Washes
1751 Carpentry Work
7217 Carpet & Upholstery Cleaning
6553 Cemetery Subdividers & Developers
5169 Chemicals & Allied Prdts, NEC Wholesale
0252 Chicken Egg Farms
8351 Child Day Care Svcs
0174 Citrus Fruits
8641 Civic, Social & Fraternal Associations
5052 Coal & Other Minerals & Ores Wholesale
1241 Coal Mining Svcs
7215 Coin Operated Laundries & Cleaning
7993 Coin-Operated Amusement Devices & Arcades
4939 Combination Utilities, NEC
7336 Commercial Art & Graphic Design
6029 Commercial Banks, NEC
8732 Commercial Economic, Sociological & Educational Research
5046 Commercial Eqpt, NEC Wholesale
7335 Commercial Photography
8731 Commercial Physical & Biological Research
6221 Commodity Contracts Brokers & Dealers
4899 Communication Svcs, NEC
7376 Computer Facilities Management Svcs
7373 Computer Integrated Systems Design
7378 Computer Maintenance & Repair
7379 Computer Related Svcs, NEC
7377 Computer Rental & Leasing
5045 Computers & Peripheral Eqpt & Software Wholesale
1771 Concrete Work
5145 Confectionery Wholesale
5082 Construction & Mining Mach & Eqpt Wholesale
5039 Construction Materials, NEC Wholesale
1442 Construction Sand & Gravel
0115 Corn
0131 Cotton
4215 Courier Svcs, Except Air

6159 Credit Institutions, Misc Business
6153 Credit Institutions, Short-Term Business
7323 Credit Reporting Svcs
0191 Crop Farming, Misc
0722 Crop Harvesting By Machine
0723 Crop Preparation, Except Cotton Ginning
1311 Crude Petroleum & Natural Gas
1422 Crushed & Broken Limestone
1429 Crushed & Broken Stone, NEC
7371 Custom Computer Programming Svcs

D

0241 Dairy Farms
5143 Dairy Prdts, Except Dried Or Canned Wholesale
7911 Dance Studios, Schools & Halls
7374 Data & Computer Processing & Preparation
0175 Deciduous Tree Fruits
4424 Deep Sea Domestic Transportation Of Freight
4412 Deep Sea Foreign Transportation Of Freight
4481 Deep Sea Transportation Of Passengers
8072 Dental Laboratories
7381 Detective & Armored Car Svcs
7331 Direct Mail Advertising Svcs
7342 Disinfecting & Pest Control Svcs
1381 Drilling Oil & Gas Wells
7833 Drive-In Motion Picture Theaters
5122 Drugs, Drug Proprietaries & Sundries Wholesale
7216 Dry Cleaning Plants, Except Rug Cleaning
5099 Durable Goods: NEC Wholesale

E

6732 Education, Religious & Charitable Trusts
4931 Electric & Other Svcs Combined
4911 Electric Svcs
7629 Electrical & Elex Repair Shop, NEC
5064 Electrical Appliances, TV & Radios Wholesale
1731 Electrical Work
5063 Electrl Apparatus, Eqpt, Wiring Splys Wholesale
5065 Electronic Parts & Eqpt Wholesale
7361 Employment Agencies
8711 Engineering Services
7359 Equipment Rental & Leasing, NEC
1794 Excavating & Grading Work

F

8744 Facilities Support Mgmt Svcs
5083 Farm & Garden Mach & Eqpt Wholesale
0761 Farm Labor Contractors & Crew Leaders
0762 Farm Management Svcs
4221 Farm Product Warehousing & Storage
5191 Farm Splys Wholesale
5159 Farm-Prdt Raw Mtrls, NEC Wholesale
6111 Federal Credit Agencies
6061 Federal Credit Unions
6011 Federal Reserve Banks
6035 Federal Savings Institutions
0139 Field Crops, Except Cash Grains, NEC
6331 Fire, Marine & Casualty Insurance
5146 Fish & Seafood Wholesale
4785 Fixed Facilities, Inspection, Weighing Svcs Transptn
1752 Floor Laying & Other Floor Work, NEC
5193 Flowers, Nursery Stock & Florists' Splys Wholesale
0182 Food Crops Grown Under Cover
5139 Footwear Wholesale
6081 Foreign Banks, Branches & Agencies
6082 Foreign Trade & Intl Banks
0851 Forestry Svcs
4731 Freight Forwarding & Arrangement
5148 Fresh Fruits & Vegetables Wholesale
0179 Fruits & Tree Nuts, NEC
6099 Functions Related To Deposit Banking, NEC
7261 Funeral Svcs & Crematories
5021 Furniture Wholesale

G

7212 Garment Pressing & Cleaners' Agents
4932 Gas & Other Svcs Combined
4925 Gas Production &/Or Distribution
7538 General Automotive Repair Shop
1541 General Contractors, Indl Bldgs & Warehouses
1542 General Contractors, Nonresidential & Non-indl Bldgs
1522 General Contractors, Residential Other Than Single Family
1521 General Contractors, Single Family Houses

8062 General Medical & Surgical Hospitals
4225 General Warehousing & Storage
1793 Glass & Glazing Work
1041 Gold Ores
5153 Grain & Field Beans Wholesale
0172 Grapes
5149 Groceries & Related Prdts, NEC Wholesale
5141 Groceries, General Line Wholesale

H

5072 Hardware Wholesale
8099 Health & Allied Svcs, NEC
5075 Heating & Air Conditioning Eqpt & Splys Wholesale
7353 Heavy Construction Eqpt Rental & Leasing
1629 Heavy Construction, NEC
7363 Help Supply Svcs
1611 Highway & Street Construction
0213 Hogs
5023 Home Furnishings Wholesale
8082 Home Health Care Svcs
6324 Hospital & Medical Svc Plans Carriers
7011 Hotels, Motels & Tourist Courts
0971 Hunting & Trapping

I

8322 Individual & Family Social Svcs
5113 Indl & Personal Svc Paper Wholesale
7218 Industrial Launderers
5084 Industrial Mach & Eqpt Wholesale
1446 Industrial Sand
5085 Industrial Splys Wholesale
7375 Information Retrieval Svcs
1796 Installation Or Erection Of Bldg Eqpt & Machinery, NEC
6411 Insurance Agents, Brokers & Svc
6399 Insurance Carriers, NEC
4131 Intercity & Rural Bus Transportation
8052 Intermediate Care Facilities
6282 Investment Advice
6799 Investors, NEC
0134 Irish Potatoes
4971 Irrigation Systems

J

5094 Jewelry, Watches, Precious Stones Wholesale
8331 Job Training & Vocational Rehabilitation Svcs

K

8092 Kidney Dialysis Centers

L

8631 Labor Unions & Similar Organizations
6552 Land Subdividers & Developers
0781 Landscape Counseling & Planning
7219 Laundry & Garment Svcs, NEC
0782 Lawn & Garden Svcs
8111 Legal Svcs
6519 Lessors Of Real Estate, NEC
6311 Life Insurance Carriers
7213 Linen Sply
0751 Livestock Svcs, Except Veterinary
5154 Livestock Wholesale
6163 Loan Brokers
4111 Local & Suburban Transit
4141 Local Bus Charter Svc
4119 Local Passenger Transportation: NEC
4214 Local Trucking With Storage
4212 Local Trucking Without Storage
5031 Lumber, Plywood & Millwork Wholesale

M

8742 Management Consulting Services
6722 Management Investment Offices
8741 Management Services
4493 Marinas
4491 Marine Cargo Handling
1741 Masonry & Other Stonework
5147 Meats & Meat Prdts Wholesale
7352 Medical Eqpt Rental & Leasing
8071 Medical Laboratories
5047 Medical, Dental & Hospital Eqpt & Splys Wholesale
8699 Membership Organizations, NEC
7997 Membership Sports & Recreation Clubs
7041 Membership-Basis Hotels
5136 Men's & Boys' Clothing & Furnishings Wholesale
5051 Metals Service Centers

SIC INDEX

SIC NO	PRODUCT
1499	Miscellaneous Nonmetallic Mining
7299	Miscellaneous Personal Svcs, NEC
6162	Mortgage Bankers & Loan Correspondents
7822	Motion Picture & Video Tape Distribution
7812	Motion Picture & Video Tape Production
7832	Motion Picture Theaters, Except Drive-In
5015	Motor Vehicle Parts, Used Wholesale
5013	Motor Vehicle Splys & New Parts Wholesale
8412	Museums & Art Galleries

N

SIC NO	PRODUCT
6021	National Commercial Banks
4924	Natural Gas Distribution
4922	Natural Gas Transmission
4923	Natural Gas Transmission & Distribution
7383	News Syndicates
8733	Noncommercial Research Organizations
6091	Nondeposit Trust Facilities
5199	Nondurable Goods, NEC Wholesale
1481	Nonmetallic Minerals Svcs, Except Fuels
8059	Nursing & Personal Care Facilities, NEC

O

SIC NO	PRODUCT
5044	Office Eqpt Wholesale
8041	Offices & Clinics Of Chiropractors
8021	Offices & Clinics Of Dentists
8011	Offices & Clinics Of Doctors Of Medicine
8031	Offices & Clinics Of Doctors Of Osteopathy
8049	Offices & Clinics Of Health Practitioners, NEC
8042	Offices & Clinics Of Optometrists
6712	Offices Of Bank Holding Co's
6719	Offices Of Holding Co's, NEC
1382	Oil & Gas Field Exploration Svcs
1389	Oil & Gas Field Svcs, NEC
1531	Operative Builders
6513	Operators Of Apartment Buildings
6514	Operators Of Dwellings, Except Apartments
6512	Operators Of Nonresidential Bldgs
6515	Operators of Residential Mobile Home Sites
5048	Ophthalmic Goods Wholesale
0181	Ornamental Floriculture & Nursery Prdts
0783	Ornamental Shrub & Tree Svc
7312	Outdoor Advertising Svcs

P

SIC NO	PRODUCT
5142	Packaged Frozen Foods Wholesale
4783	Packing & Crating Svcs
1721	Painting & Paper Hanging Contractors
5198	Paints, Varnishes & Splys Wholesale
7515	Passenger Car Leasing
7514	Passenger Car Rental
4729	Passenger Transportation Arrangement, NEC
6794	Patent Owners & Lessors
6371	Pension, Health & Welfare Funds
6141	Personal Credit Institutions
5172	Petroleum & Petroleum Prdts Wholesale
5171	Petroleum Bulk Stations & Terminals
7334	Photocopying & Duplicating Svcs
7384	Photofinishing Labs
5043	Photographic Eqpt & Splys Wholesale
7221	Photographic Studios, Portrait
7991	Physical Fitness Facilities
5131	Piece Goods, Notions & Dry Goods Wholesale
4619	Pipelines, NEC
1742	Plastering, Drywall, Acoustical & Insulation Work
5162	Plastics Materials & Basic Shapes Wholesale
5074	Plumbing & Heating Splys Wholesale
1711	Plumbing, Heating & Air Conditioning Contractors
8651	Political Organizations
1474	Potash, Soda & Borate Minerals
0259	Poultry & Eggs Farms, NEC
5144	Poultry & Poultry Prdts Wholesale
0254	Poultry Hatcheries
7211	Power Laundries, Family & Commercial
7372	Prepackaged Software
5111	Printing & Writing Paper Wholesale
5049	Professional Eqpt & Splys, NEC Wholesale
8621	Professional Membership Organizations
7941	Professional Sports Clubs & Promoters
8063	Psychiatric Hospitals
7992	Public Golf Courses
8743	Public Relations Svcs

R

SIC NO	PRODUCT
7948	Racing & Track Operations
7622	Radio & TV Repair Shops
4832	Radio Broadcasting Stations
7313	Radio, TV & Publishers Adv Reps
4812	Radiotelephone Communications
4011	Railroads, Line-Hauling Operations
6531	Real Estate Agents & Managers
6798	Real Estate Investment Trusts
4613	Refined Petroleum Pipelines
4222	Refrigerated Warehousing & Storage
7623	Refrigeration & Air Conditioning Svc & Repair Shop
5078	Refrigeration Eqpt & Splys Wholesale
4953	Refuse Systems
7699	Repair Shop & Related Svcs, NEC
8361	Residential Care
7641	Reupholstery & Furniture Repair
0112	Rice
5033	Roofing, Siding & Insulation Mtrls Wholesale
1761	Roofing, Siding & Sheet Metal Work
7021	Rooming & Boarding Houses

S

SIC NO	PRODUCT
4959	Sanitary Svcs, NEC
6036	Savings Institutions, Except Federal
4151	School Buses
5093	Scrap & Waste Materials Wholesale
7338	Secretarial & Court Reporting Svcs
6231	Security & Commodity Exchanges
6289	Security & Commodity Svcs, NEC
6211	Security Brokers & Dealers
7382	Security Systems Svcs
5087	Service Establishment Eqpt & Splys Wholesale
7829	Services Allied To Motion Picture Distribution
7819	Services Allied To Motion Picture Prdtn
8999	Services Not Elsewhere Classified
4952	Sewerage Systems
0214	Sheep & Goats
7251	Shoe Repair & Shoeshine Parlors
8051	Skilled Nursing Facilities
8399	Social Services, NEC
0711	Soil Preparation Svcs
0721	Soil Preparation, Planting & Cultivating Svc
1799	Special Trade Contractors, NEC
4226	Special Warehousing & Storage, NEC
8069	Specialty Hospitals, Except Psychiatric
8093	Specialty Outpatient Facilities, NEC
7032	Sporting & Recreational Camps
5091	Sporting & Recreational Goods & Splys Wholesale
6022	State Commercial Banks
6062	State Credit Unions
5112	Stationery & Office Splys Wholesale
4961	Steam & Air Conditioning Sply
1791	Structural Steel Erection
6351	Surety Insurance Carriers
8713	Surveying Services
4013	Switching & Terminal Svcs

T

SIC NO	PRODUCT
7291	Tax Return Preparation Svcs
4121	Taxi Cabs
4822	Telegraph & Other Message Communications
4813	Telephone Communications, Except Radio
4833	Television Broadcasting Stations
4231	Terminal & Joint Terminal Maint Facilities
1743	Terrazzo, Tile, Marble & Mosaic Work
8734	Testing Laboratories
7922	Theatrical Producers & Misc Theatrical Svcs
0811	Timber Tracts
7534	Tire Retreading & Repair Shops
5014	Tires & Tubes Wholesale
6541	Title Abstract Offices
6361	Title Insurance
0132	Tobacco
5194	Tobacco & Tobacco Prdts Wholesale
7532	Top, Body & Upholstery Repair & Paint Shops
4725	Tour Operators
4492	Towing & Tugboat Svcs
5092	Toys & Hobby Goods & Splys Wholesale
7033	Trailer Parks & Camp Sites
5088	Transportation Eqpt & Splys, Except Motor Vehicles Wholesale
4789	Transportation Svcs, NEC
4724	Travel Agencies
0173	Tree Nuts
7513	Truck Rental & Leasing, Without Drivers
4213	Trucking, Except Local
6733	Trusts Except Educational, Religious & Charitable
0253	Turkey & Turkey Egg Farms

U

SIC NO	PRODUCT
6726	Unit Investment Trusts, Face-Amount Certificate Offices
7519	Utility Trailers & Recreational Vehicle Rental

V

SIC NO	PRODUCT
0161	Vegetables & Melons
0742	Veterinary Animal Specialties

W

SIC NO	PRODUCT
7631	Watch, Clock & Jewelry Repair
4941	Water Sply
4489	Water Transport Of Passengers, NEC
4449	Water Transportation Of Freight, NEC
4499	Water Transportation Svcs, NEC
1781	Water Well Drilling
1623	Water, Sewer & Utility Line Construction
7692	Welding Repair
0111	Wheat
5182	Wine & Distilled Alcoholic Beverages Wholesale
5137	Women's, Children's & Infants Clothing Wholesale
1795	Wrecking & Demolition Work

PRODUCTS & SERVICES SECTION

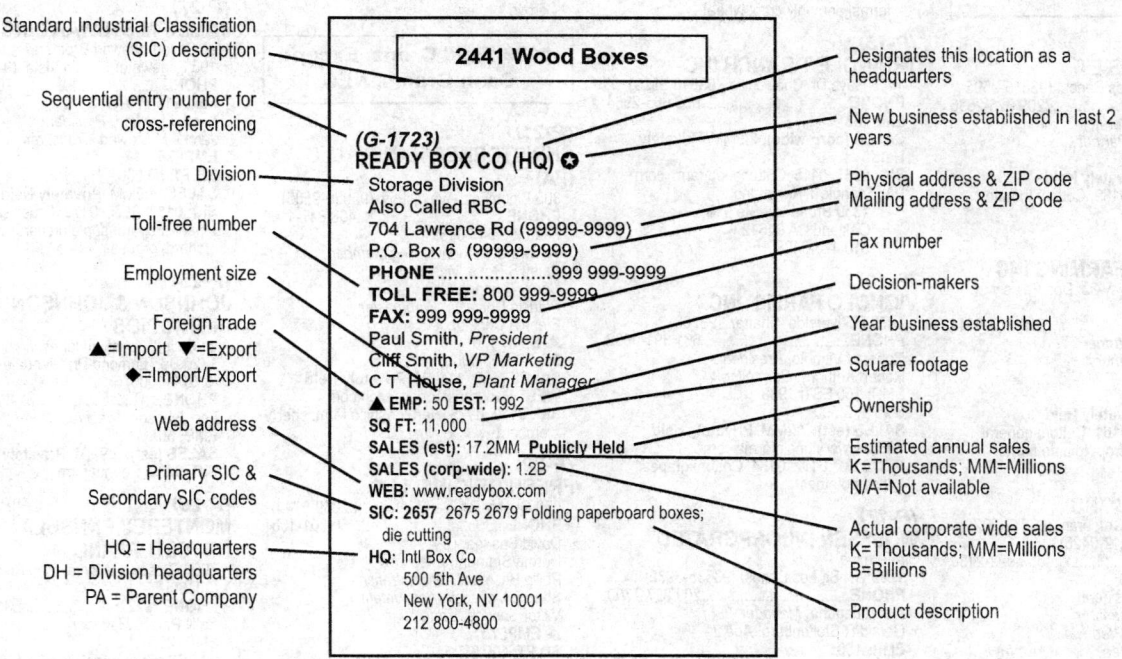

- Companies in this section are listed numerically under their primary SIC Companies are in alphabetical order under each code.
- A numerical and alphabetcal index precedes this section.
- **Sequential Entry Numbers.** Each establishment in this section is numbered sequentially. The number assigned to each establishment's Entry Number. To make cross-referencing easier, each listing in the Product's & Services, Alphabetic and Geographical Section includes the establishment's entry number. To facilitate locating an entry in this section, the entry numbers for the first listing on the left page and the last listing on the right page are printed at the top of the page next to the Standard Industrial Classification (SIC) description.
- Further information can be found in the Explanatory Notes starting on page 5.
- See the footnotes for symbols and abbreviations.

IMPORTANT NOTICE: It is a violation of both federal and state law to transmit an unsolicited advertisement to a facsimile machine. Any user of this product that violates such laws may be subject to civil and criminal penalties which may exceed $500 for each transmission of an unsolicited facsimile. Harris InfoSource provides fax numbers for lawful purposes only and expressly forbids the use of these numbers in any unlawful manner.

0111 Wheat

(P-1)
JOE MULLER AND SONS
15810 County Road 95, Woodland (95695-9222)
PHONE.................................530 662-0105
Fax: 530 662-8488
Frank Muller, *Partner*
Thomas Muller, *Partner*
Teresa Lee, *Office Mgr*
Marie L Muller, *Financial Exec*
Louie Muller, *Manager*
EMP: 85
SALES (est): 10.2MM **Privately Held**
WEB: www.joemuller.com
SIC: 0111 0115 0161 Wheat; corn; tomato farm

(P-2)
T & P FARMS
1241 Putnam Way, Arbuckle (95912)
P.O. Box 83 (95912-0083)
PHONE.................................530 476-3038
Fax: 530 476-3445
Perry Charter, *Partner*
Tom Charter, *Partner*
Shelby Nation, *Bookkeeper*
EMP: 100 EST: 1976

SALES (est): 12.3MM **Privately Held**
SIC: 0111 0112 0181 0161 Wheat; rice; seeds, vegetable: growing of; tomato farm; general farms, primarily crop; food crops grown under cover

0112 Rice

(P-3)
ANDERSON FARMS INC
Also Called: Andco Farms
4600 2nd St, Davis (95618-9446)
P.O. Box 1410 (95617-1410)
PHONE.................................530 753-5695
Fax: 530 756-8252
John B Anderson, *President*
EMP: 100 EST: 1965
SQ FT: 8,000
SALES (est): 3.2MM **Privately Held**
SIC: 0112 0161 Rice; tomato farm

(P-4)
CATTAIL FARMS INC
3970 Cr95b, Knights Landing (95645)
P.O. Box 1024 (95645-1024)
PHONE.................................916 207-6580
Sawyer Y Monckton, *CEO*
EMP: 99
SALES: 35K **Privately Held**
SIC: 0112 Rice

(P-5)
MCFADDEN FARM
16000 Powerhouse Rd, Potter Valley (95469-8771)
PHONE.................................707 743-1122
Fax: 707 743-1126
Eugene McFadden, *Owner*
Linda Jackson, *Office Mgr*
Patty Boatwright, *Bookkeeper*
Andrea Caldwell, *Manager*
EMP: 50
SQ FT: 1,000
SALES: 1.5MM **Privately Held**
WEB: www.mcfaddenfarm.com
SIC: 0112 0172 0139 2099 Rice; grapes; herb or spice farm; food preparations

(P-6)
SUN WEST WILD RICE FACILITY
Vance Ave, Biggs (95917)
P.O. Box 305 (95917-0305)
PHONE.................................530 868-5188
Fax: 530 868-5195
Ralph Velasquez, *Manager*
EMP: 50
SALES (est): 1MM **Privately Held**
SIC: 0112 Rice

0115 Corn

(P-7)
JOE HEIDRICK ENTERPRISES INC
36826 County Road 24, Woodland (95695-9355)
PHONE.................................530 662-2339
Fax: 530 662-1715
Joe Heidrick, *President*
EMP: 50
SQ FT: 1,500
SALES (est): 5.8MM **Privately Held**
SIC: 0115 0111 0161 0139 Corn; wheat; tomato farm; alfalfa farm

(P-8)
SIMONI & MASSONI FARMS
2510 Taylor Ln, Byron (94514)
P.O. Box 399 (94514-0399)
PHONE.................................925 634-2304
Fax: 925 634-2728
Diane Simoni, *Partner*
Anthony Massoni, *Partner*
Paul Simoni, *Partner*
Sherry Wollfenbarger, *Admin Sec*
Sherry Wolfenbarger, *Info Tech Mgr*
EMP: 50
SALES: 5MM **Privately Held**
SIC: 0115 Corn

0131 Cotton

(P-9)
AL BARCELLOS ET
17599 Ward Rd, Los Banos (93635-9595)
PHONE.................................209 826-2636
Aaron Barcellos, *Partner*
Arnold Barcellos, *Partner*
EMP: 50
SALES: 2MM Privately Held
SIC: 0131 0161 0139 Cotton; tomato farm; alfalfa farm

(P-10)
CLARK BROS FARMING INC
19772 State Highway 33, Dos Palos (93620-9621)
PHONE.................................209 392-6144
Norman L Clark, *Partner*
Allan W Clark, *Partner*
EMP: 50
SQ FT: 5,000
SALES: 8MM Privately Held
SIC: 0131 0191 0161 Cotton; general farms, primarily crop; tomato farm

(P-11)
GILKEY FARMS INC
2411 Whitley Ave, Corcoran (93212-2025)
P.O. Box 426 (93212-0426)
PHONE.................................559 992-2136
Fax: 559 992-8266
Donald Gilkey, *President*
Charles Gilkey, *Treasurer*
Brent Gilkey, *Vice Pres*
Kirk Gilkey, *Vice Pres*
Matt Gilkey, *Vice Pres*
EMP: 60
SQ FT: 4,500
SALES (est): 5.1MM Privately Held
SIC: 0131 0139 0111 0119 Cotton; alfalfa farm; hay farm; wheat; safflower farm

(P-12)
J G BOSWELL COMPANY
21101 Bear Mountain Blvd, Bakersfield (93311-9412)
P.O. Box 9759 (93389-9759)
PHONE.................................661 327-7721
Fax: 661 834-2427
Dave Cosyns, *Manager*
EMP: 200
SALES (corp-wide): 625.3MM Privately Held
SIC: 0131 0111 0724 Cotton; wheat; cotton ginning
PA: J. G. Boswell Company
101 W Walnut St
Pasadena CA 91103
626 356-7492

(P-13)
J G BOSWELL COMPANY
Also Called: Ranching Shop
28001 S Dairy Ave, Corcoran (93212)
P.O. Box 877 (93212-0877)
PHONE.................................559 992-5141
Fax: 559 992-8550
Paul Athorp, *Branch Mgr*
Hugh Bello, *Manager*
EMP: 500
SALES (corp-wide): 625.3MM Privately Held
SIC: 0131 0724 0182 Cotton; cotton ginning; food crops grown under cover
PA: J. G. Boswell Company
101 W Walnut St
Pasadena CA 91103
626 356-7492

(P-14)
STONE LAND COMPANY (PA)
Also Called: Stone Ranch
28521 Nevada Ave, Stratford (93266)
PHONE.................................559 947-3185
Fax: 559 945-9442
Jack G Stone, *President*
Sally Moreno, *Corp Secy*
William Stone, *Vice Pres*
Amie Stone, *Office Mgr*
▲ EMP: 100
SQ FT: 2,000

SALES: 1MM Privately Held
WEB: www.jgslc.com
SIC: 0131 0191 0111 Cotton; general farms, primarily crop; wheat

(P-15)
TRIANGLE T RANCH INC
4408 Hays Dr, Chowchilla (93610-8929)
PHONE.................................559 665-2964
EMP: 68
SALES (corp-wide): 2.5MM Privately Held
SIC: 0131 0115 Cottonseed farm; corn
PA: Triangle T Ranch Inc
1330 Broadway Ste 915
Oakland CA 94612
510 428-0428

(P-16)
VIGNOLO FARMS INC
1270 E Riverside, Shafter (93263)
PHONE.................................661 391-0682
Robert J Vignolo, *President*
Robert Anthony, *Controller*
EMP: 150 EST: 1938
SQ FT: 2,500
SALES (est): 7.2MM Privately Held
WEB: www.vignolofarms.com
SIC: 0131 0172 0134 Cotton; grapes; Irish potatoes

(P-17)
WOLFSEN INCORPORATED
Sjr Farming
1269 W I St, Los Banos (93635-3930)
PHONE.................................209 827-7700
Albert Laguna, *Manager*
Gerald R Stoltenberg, *Agent*
EMP: 150
SALES (corp-wide): 18.2MM Privately Held
WEB: www.wolfsenic.com
SIC: 0131 Cotton
PA: Wolfsen Incorporated
1269 W I St
Los Banos CA 93635
209 827-7700

0132 Tobacco

(P-18)
PAX LABS INC
660 Alabama St Fl 2, San Francisco (94110-2008)
PHONE.................................510 828-8174
James Thomas Monsees, *President*
Scott Dunlap, *Chief Mktg Ofcr*
EMP: 80
SQ FT: 8,000
SALES (est): 45MM Privately Held
SIC: 0132 Tobacco

0134 Irish Potatoes

(P-19)
GIUMARRA FARMS INC
11220 Edison Hwy, Edison (93220)
PHONE.................................661 395-7000
Fax: 661 364-0232
Salvadore Giumarra, *President*
William Butler, *CFO*
EMP: 100
SQ FT: 15,000
SALES: 7MM Privately Held
SIC: 0134 0174 0161 0175 Irish potatoes; orange grove; carrot farm; plum orchard

(P-20)
JOHNSTON FARMS
13031 E Packinghouse Rd, Edison (93220)
PHONE.................................661 366-3201
Fax: 661 366-6534
Tari Johnston, *Principal*
Terry Henderson, *Principal*
Dennis B Johnston, *Principal*
Gerald Johnston, *Principal*
Kevin Johnston, *Principal*
▲ EMP: 65 EST: 1953
SQ FT: 100,000

SALES (est): 6.9MM Privately Held
WEB: www.johnstonfarms.com
SIC: 0134 0174 Irish potatoes; orange grove

0139 Field Crops, Except Cash Grains, NEC

(P-21)
CHRISTOPHER RANCH LLC (PA)
305 Bloomfield Ave, Gilroy (95020-9565)
PHONE.................................408 847-1100
Fax: 408 847-0139
William Christopher, *Mng Member*
Patsy S Ross, *Vice Pres*
Corey Tennant, *CIO*
Patricia Destasio, *Webmaster*
Frank A Christopher,
▲ EMP: 170
SQ FT: 220,000
SALES (est): 114MM Privately Held
WEB: www.christopher-ranch.com
SIC: 0139 0175 Herb or spice farm; cherry orchard

(P-22)
FRESH ORIGINS LLC
570 Quarry Rd, San Marcos (92069-9744)
PHONE.................................760 801-1087
David Sasuga, *CPA*
Norma Stamant, *Executive*
Philip Bosman, *Administration*
Sharon McIntosh, *Accountant*
Victor Sasuga, *Prdtn Mgr*
▲ EMP: 75
SQ FT: 400,000
SALES (est): 9.9MM Privately Held
WEB: www.freshorigins.com
SIC: 0139 Herb or spice farm

(P-23)
GARLIC COMPANY
18602 Zerker Rd, Bakersfield (93314-9747)
PHONE.................................661 393-4212
Fax: 661 393-9340
John Layous, *Managing Prtnr*
Joe Lane, *Partner*
Gordan Cook, *CFO*
Dan Prentice, *Executive*
Bill Lane, *Plant Mgr*
▲ EMP: 125
SQ FT: 150,000
SALES: 53.8MM Privately Held
WEB: www.thegarliccompany.com
SIC: 0139 2099 0191 Herb or spice farm; food preparations; general farms, primarily crop

(P-24)
GENE M ACCITO
331 Pelican Pl, Yuba City (95993-7100)
P.O. Box 3322 (95992-3322)
PHONE.................................530 674-3179
Gene M Accito, *Owner*
EMP: 80
SALES (est): 1.6MM Privately Held
SIC: 0139 Food crops

(P-25)
HAYDAY FARMS INC
15500 S Commercial St, Blythe (92225-2750)
P.O. Box 1226 (92226-1226)
PHONE.................................760 922-4713
Fax: 760 922-6579
Atsuya Ichida, *President*
Dale Tyson, *Vice Pres*
◆ EMP: 75
SQ FT: 2,160
SALES: 17.4MM Privately Held
SIC: 0139 0722 0723 Hay farm; hay, machine harvesting services; field crops, except cash grains, market preparation services

(P-26)
HERB THYME FARM INC
7909 Crossway Dr, Pico Rivera (90660-4449)
PHONE.................................603 542-3690
Mary Lord, *Principal*
EMP: 70

SALES (est): 1.4MM Privately Held
SIC: 0139 Herb or spice farm

(P-27)
JAMES M STEWART INC
Also Called: Stewart Brothers
195 Edgewater Dr, Rio Vista (94571-2009)
PHONE.................................707 374-6369
Fax: 916 775-1163
Scott J Stewart, *President*
James M Stewart, *Treasurer*
EMP: 75
SQ FT: 50,000
SALES: 4.5MM Privately Held
SIC: 0139 0175 0172 Grass seed farm; pear orchard; apple orchard; cherry orchard; grapes

(P-28)
JOHNSON & JOHNSON PISTACCIOS
Also Called: Johnson/Johnson
1720 Ben Lomond Dr, Glendale (91202-1006)
PHONE.................................818 242-7853
Lee Johnson, *President*
EMP: 50
SALES (est): 2.9MM Privately Held
SIC: 0139 Peanut farm

(P-29)
MONTEREY PNNSULA HRTCLTURE INC
7909 Crosswite Drve, Pico Rivera (90660)
PHONE.................................310 884-5911
Sally Perez, *Manager*
EMP: 200
SALES (corp-wide): 50.9MM Privately Held
WEB: www.herbthyme.com
SIC: 0139 Herb or spice farm
PA: Monterey Peninsula Horticulture, Inc.
360 Espinosa Rd
Salinas CA 93907
831 449-3440

(P-30)
PAN AMERICAN AGRICULTURE CORP
583 Ojai St, Fillmore (93015-9732)
PHONE.................................805 524-1489
Reza Safavi, *President*
EMP: 55
SQ FT: 6,000
SALES (est): 3MM Privately Held
WEB: www.panamericanagriculture.com
SIC: 0139 Herb or spice farm

(P-31)
QUAIL H FARMS LLC
5301 Robin Ave, Livingston (95334-9317)
P.O. Box 247 (95334-0247)
PHONE.................................209 394-8001
J Michael Hennigan, *Mng Member*
Robert Hamaguchi, *Controller*
Larelle Miller, *Sales Mgr*
Jackie E Smith,
▼ EMP: 505
SALES (est): 51.8MM Privately Held
SIC: 0139 Sweet potato farm

(P-32)
RICHARD IEST DAIRY INC
13507 Road 17, Madera (93637-9040)
PHONE.................................559 673-2635
Richard C Iest, *President*
Marisela Macias, *General Mgr*
EMP: 99
SALES: 950K Privately Held
SIC: 0139 Field crops, except cash grain

(P-33)
ROCKET FARMS INC
Also Called: Green House, The
297 Wilshire Rd, Oceanside (92057-3902)
PHONE.................................760 439-6515
Don Bowden, *Manager*
EMP: 70
SALES (corp-wide): 40.9MM Privately Held
WEB: www.herbthyme.com
SIC: 0139 0191 Herb or spice farm; general farms, primarily crop

PRODUCTS & SERVICES SECTION

0161 - Vegetables & Melons County (P-56)

PA: Rocket Farms, Inc.
360 Espinosa Rd
Salinas CA 93907
831 442-2400

(P-34)
YAGI BROS INC
Also Called: Yagi Bros Produce
5614 Lincoln Blvd, Livingston (95334-9642)
P.O. Box 515 (95334-0515)
PHONE...................209 394-7311
Blaine Yagi, *President*
Ben Yagi, *Vice Pres*
George Yagi, *Admin Sec*
Duane Hutton, *Manager*
EMP: 55
SQ FT: 31,000
SALES: 1.5MM Privately Held
WEB: www.yagibros.com
SIC: 0139 Sweet potato farm

0161 Vegetables & Melons

(P-35)
ABE-EL PRODUCE
42143 Road 120, Orosi (93647-9714)
PHONE...................559 528-3030
Fax: 559 528-6772
Franklin Abe, *Partner*
Herbert Abe, *Partner*
Kelly Abe, *Controller*
Kelly Abe-Hayashi, *Controller*
EMP: 350 **EST:** 1964
SALES: 7MM Privately Held
SIC: 0161 0174 Vegetables & melons; citrus fruits

(P-36)
ACE TOMATO COMPANY INC
777 N Pershing Ave Ste 1a, Stockton (95203-2153)
PHONE...................209 982-0734
Fax: 209 982-0235
Kathleen Lagorio Janssen, *CEO*
Tom McMillen, *CFO*
Dean Janssen, *Corp Secy*
Henry K Cole, *Vice Pres*
EMP: 60
SQ FT: 300,000
SALES (est): 4.2MM Privately Held
SIC: 0161 0723 Tomato farm; vegetable packing services

(P-37)
AMERICAN FARMS LLC
1107 Harkins Rd, Salinas (93901-4435)
P.O. Box 599 (93902-0599)
PHONE...................831 424-1815
Fax: 831 757-0657
David Gill,
Steven Gill,
Forest Whitten, *Real Est Agnt*
EMP: 100
SQ FT: 3,000
SALES (est): 29.6MM Privately Held
WEB: www.americanfarms.net
SIC: 0161 0139 Vegetables & melons; lettuce farm; cauliflower farm; broccoli farm; feeder crops
PA: Mesa Packing Llc
510 Broadway St
King City CA 93930
831 385-9173

(P-38)
BALOIAN PACKING CO INC (PA)
Also Called: Baloian Farm
446 N Blythe Ave, Fresno (93706-1003)
P.O. Box 11337 (93772-1337)
PHONE...................559 485-9200
Fax: 559 268-7651
Edward Baloian, *Ch of Bd*
Timothy Baloian, *President*
Yosh Kamine, *General Mgr*
Emily Baloian, *Admin Sec*
David Cuadros, *Controller*
▲ **EMP:** 64
SQ FT: 35,000
SALES (est): 24.5MM Privately Held
WEB: www.baloianpacking.com
SIC: 0161 0723 Broccoli farm; pepper farm, sweet & hot (vegetables); cucumber farm; squash farm; vegetable packing services

(P-39)
BALOIAN PACKING CO INC
Also Called: Baloian Farms
3138 W Whites Bridge Ave, Fresno (93706-1125)
PHONE...................559 441-7043
Glen Yemoto, *Branch Mgr*
Pamela Angulo, *Finance*
Peter Baloian, *Safety Dir*
Luis Corella, *Sales Staff*
Richard Cowden, *Sales Staff*
EMP: 86
SALES (corp-wide): 24.5MM Privately Held
SIC: 0161 0723 Broccoli farm; pepper farm, sweet & hot (vegetables); cucumber farm; squash farm; vegetable packing services
PA: Baloian Packing Co., Inc.
446 N Blythe Ave
Fresno CA 93706
559 485-9200

(P-40)
BLACK DOG FARMS OF CALIFORNIA
530 W 6th St, Holtville (92250-1023)
P.O. Box 57 (92250-0057)
PHONE...................760 356-2951
Fax: 760 356-4614
Kenneth Peterson, *President*
Dora Saikhon, *Shareholder*
Carol Saikhon, *Vice Pres*
Carmen Lizaola, *Human Res Dir*
EMP: 150
SQ FT: 4,000
SALES (est): 15.3MM Privately Held
WEB: www.blackdogfarms.com
SIC: 0161 Vegetables & melons

(P-41)
BOLTHOUSE FARMS
3200 E Brundage Ln, Bakersfield (93304)
PHONE...................661 366-7205
William Bolthouse, *Owner*
Bob Borda, *Marketing Mgr*
Douglas Bynum, *Director*
◆ **EMP:** 2300
SALES (est): 24.3MM
SALES (corp-wide): 7.9B Publicly Held
SIC: 0161 Carrot farm
HQ: Wm. Bolthouse Farms, Inc.
7200 E Brundage Ln
Bakersfield CA 93307
661 366-7205

(P-42)
BOSKOVICH FARMS INC
4224 Pleasant Valley Rd, Camarillo (93012-8533)
P.O. Box 1352, Oxnard (93032-1352)
PHONE...................805 987-1443
Fax: 805 484-1056
Ken Mumford, *Manager*
Martha Mayorga, *Executive*
Bridget Boskovich, *Marketing Staff*
EMP: 300
SALES (corp-wide): 98.9MM Privately Held
WEB: www.boskovichfarms.com
SIC: 0161 0115 Vegetables & melons; corn
PA: Boskovich Farms, Inc.
711 Diaz Ave
Oxnard CA 93030
805 487-2299

(P-43)
BRAGA FRESH FAMILY FARMS INC
33750 Moranda Rd, Soledad (93960)
PHONE...................831 675-2154
Rodney Braga, *President*
EMP: 500
SALES (est): 10.8MM Privately Held
SIC: 0161 Lettuce & leaf vegetable farms

(P-44)
C & G FARMS INC
Also Called: AMARAL RANCHES
25453 Iverson Rd, Chualar (93925)
P.O. Box 2216, Gonzales (93926-2216)
PHONE...................831 679-2978
Carlos Amaral, *President*
George Amaral, *Admin Sec*
Mike Amaral, *Controller*
▼ **EMP:** 200 **EST:** 1996
SQ FT: 2,000
SALES: 43.6MM Privately Held
WEB: www.cgfarms.com
SIC: 0161 Lettuce & leaf vegetable farms; broccoli farm; cabbage farm

(P-45)
CALGENE LLC
37437 State Highway 16, Woodland (95695-9353)
PHONE...................530 753-6313
Fax: 530 753-1510
Nordine Chiekh,
Gerald Steiner, *Exec VP*
Michelle Bowman,
EMP: 120
SQ FT: 71,000
SALES (est): 5.1MM
SALES (corp-wide): 13.5B Publicly Held
WEB: www.monsanto.com
SIC: 0161 0171 5191 8731 Tomato farm; strawberry farm; seeds: field, garden & flower; agricultural research; agricultural research, commercial; food research; commercial nonphysical research
PA: Monsanto Company
800 N Lindbergh Blvd
Saint Louis MO 63167
314 694-1000

(P-46)
CALIFORNIA VEGETABLE SPC INC
Also Called: California Endive Farm
15 Poppy House Rd, Rio Vista (94571-1201)
P.O. Box 638 (94571-0638)
PHONE...................707 374-2111
Fax: 707 374-2063
Alexandre Pierron-Darbonne, *CEO*
Richard Collins, *President*
Luc Darbonne, *CEO*
Jose Arias, *Vice Pres*
Howard Hoffman, *Vice Pres*
▲ **EMP:** 70
SQ FT: 11,000
SALES (est): 8MM Privately Held
WEB: www.endive.com
SIC: 0161 Endive farm

(P-47)
CALIFORNIA WATERCRESS INC (PA)
550 E Telegraph Rd, Fillmore (93015-9667)
P.O. Box 874 (93016-0874)
PHONE...................805 524-4808
Alfred C Beserra, *President*
Teresa Beserra, *Admin Sec*
EMP: 65
SQ FT: 1,000
SALES: 5MM Privately Held
SIC: 0161 Vegetables & melons

(P-48)
CAPAY INCORPORATED (PA)
Also Called: Capay Fruits and Vegetables
3880 Seaport Blvd, West Sacramento (95691-3449)
PHONE...................916 303-7145
Fax: 530 796-3344
Thaddeus Barsotti, *CEO*
Freeman Barsatti, *Principal*
Moyra Barsotti, *Admin Sec*
Yvonne Zerpuche, *Manager*
EMP: 89
SALES (est): 17.4MM Privately Held
WEB: www.capay.com
SIC: 0161 Vegetables & melons; melon farms

(P-49)
CERUTTI BROS INC
26118 Mcclintock Rd, Newman (95360-9746)
P.O. Box 550 (95360-0550)
PHONE...................209 862-2249
Fax: 209 862-2770
Patrick Cerutti, *CEO*
EMP: 60
SALES: 950K Privately Held
SIC: 0161 Vegetables & melons

(P-50)
CHRISTENSEN & GIANNINI LLC
1588 Moffett St Ste B, Salinas (93905-3365)
PHONE...................831 449-2494
Sam Daoro,
Shelley Daroro, *Partner*
Dirk Giannini, *Partner*
Lori Giannini, *Partner*
Renea Wood, *Controller*
EMP: 54
SALES (est): 6.3MM Privately Held
SIC: 0161 Vegetables & melons

(P-51)
CHRISTOPHER RANCH LLC
Also Called: California Produce
1690 Freitas Rd, San Juan Bautista (95045-9530)
PHONE...................831 636-8722
Fax: 831 636-8741
Steve Moss, *Manager*
EMP: 65
SALES (corp-wide): 114MM Privately Held
WEB: www.christopher-ranch.com
SIC: 0161 Rooted vegetable farms
PA: Christopher Ranch, Llc
305 Bloomfield Ave
Gilroy CA 95020
408 847-1100

(P-52)
CHURCH BROTHERS LLC (PA)
19065 Portola Dr Ste C, Salinas (93908-1250)
P.O. Box 509 (93902-0509)
PHONE...................831 796-1000
Fax: 831 796-1061
Tom Church,
Jay Brown, *CFO*
Chris Vear, *Prdtn Mgr*
Steve Church,
Amy Harbon, *Manager*
EMP: 75
SQ FT: 1,000
SALES (est): 34MM Privately Held
SIC: 0161 Lettuce farm; spinach farm

(P-53)
COAST FARMS INC
645 Laguna Rd, Camarillo (93012-8523)
P.O. Box 3297 (93011-3297)
PHONE...................805 383-0455
Roy Chikasawa, *President*
Don Chikasawa, *Treasurer*
Martha Chikasawa, *Admin Sec*
EMP: 100
SALES (est): 3MM Privately Held
SIC: 0161 Vegetables & melons

(P-54)
COSTA SONS
36817 Foothill Rd, Soledad (93960-9656)
PHONE...................831 678-0799
Tony Costa, *CEO*
David Costa, *Co-Owner*
Diane Costa, *Co-Owner*
Elsie Costa, *Co-Owner*
Michael Costa, *Co-Owner*
EMP: 50 **EST:** 1958
SALES (est): 2.8MM Privately Held
WEB: www.costafarmsinc.com
SIC: 0161 Vegetables & melons; broccoli farm; cauliflower farm; celery farm

(P-55)
DAN AVILA AND SONS
2718 Roberts Rd, Ceres (95307-9627)
PHONE...................209 495-3899
Daniel Avila, *Owner*
EMP: 60
SALES: 16MM Privately Held
SIC: 0161 0139 Watermelon farm; sweet potato farm

(P-56)
DARRIGO BROSCOOF CALIFORNIA (PA)
Also Called: Andy Boy
21777 Harris Rd, Salinas (93908-8609)
P.O. Box 850 (93902-0850)
PHONE...................831 455-4500
Andrew A D'Arrigo, *Ch of Bd*
John C D'Arrigo, *President*
E John Culligan, *Corp Secy*

0161 - Vegetables & Melons County (P-57)

Angela Salinas, *Analyst*
Chad Amaral, *VP Opers*
EMP: 50
SQ FT: 13,000
SALES (est): 241.6MM **Privately Held**
SIC: 0161 Broccoli farm; carrot farm; lettuce farm; celery farm

(P-57)
DIMARE ENTERPRISES INC (PA)
Also Called: Dimare Company
1406 N St, Newman (95360-1309)
P.O. Box 517 (95360-0517)
PHONE 209 827-2900
Fax: 209 862-0103
Thomas F Dimare, *President*
Linda Klein, *CFO*
Paul J Dimare, *Treasurer*
Desiree Mendonca, *Manager*
EMP: 250
SQ FT: 20,000
SALES (est): 57.5MM **Privately Held**
WEB: www.dimare-ca.com
SIC: 0161 0174 Vegetables & melons; citrus fruits

(P-58)
DOBLER & SONS LLC
174 Struve Rd, Moss Landing (95039-9661)
P.O. Box 1660, Watsonville (95077-1660)
PHONE 831 724-6727
Carl Dobler, *Mng Member*
Craig Dobler,
Kenneth Dobler,
Michael Dobler,
Steven Dobler,
EMP: 350
SALES (est): 38.2MM **Privately Held**
WEB: www.doblerandsons.com
SIC: 0161 Cabbage farm; lettuce farm

(P-59)
DONALD VALPREDO FARMING INC
Also Called: Db Custom Farming
2101 Mttler Frontage Rd E, Bakersfield (93307-9649)
PHONE 661 858-2245
Fax: 661 858-2558
Donald Valpredo, *President*
Tito Martinez, *Opers Mgr*
EMP: 60
SALES (est): 8.2MM **Privately Held**
WEB: www.valpredofarms.com
SIC: 0161 Tomato farm; onion farm

(P-60)
DRESICK FARMS INC (PA)
19536 Jayne Ave, Huron (93234)
P.O. Box 1260 (93234-1260)
PHONE 559 945-2513
Fax: 559 945-9627
Michael L Dresick, *CEO*
Jan Dresick, *Vice Pres*
EMP: 50 **EST:** 1974
SQ FT: 3,500
SALES (est): 33.4MM **Privately Held**
WEB: www.dresickfarms.com
SIC: 0161 Lettuce farm; cantaloupe farm; tomato farm; rooted vegetable farms

(P-61)
ED SILVA (PA)
Also Called: Silva Farms
21 River Rd, Gonzales (93926)
P.O. Box Z (93926-0669)
PHONE 831 675-2327
Ed Silva, *Owner*
▼ **EMP:** 80
SQ FT: 30,000
SALES (est): 42MM **Privately Held**
WEB: www.edsilva.com
SIC: 0161 Broccoli farm; cabbage farm; lettuce farm

(P-62)
FAUROT RANCH
703 Hall Rd, Royal Oaks (95076-5712)
PHONE 831 722-1346
Fax: 831 722-8956
Rodgers Faurot, *Owner*
EMP: 50
SALES (est): 2.5MM **Privately Held**
SIC: 0161 Lettuce & leaf vegetable farms; rooted vegetable farms

(P-63)
FREITAS BROTHERS
Hwy 1, Guadalupe (93434)
P.O. Box 895 (93434-0895)
PHONE 805 343-3134
Eric Freitas, *Partner*
Jon Freitas, *Partner*
Heidi Parson, *Manager*
▼ **EMP:** 50
SQ FT: 1,500
SALES (est): 3.2MM **Privately Held**
WEB: www.freitasfarms.com
SIC: 0161 Vegetables & melons

(P-64)
FRESH LEAF FARMS LLC (HQ)
1250 Hansen St, Salinas (93901-4552)
PHONE 831 422-7405
Mann Packing, *Partner*
Anthony Costa Sons, *Partner*
Joe Nucci, *President*
Tom Koster, *VP Sales*
Alicia Blanco, *Marketing Mgr*
EMP: 50
SALES (est): 16.8MM
SALES (corp-wide): 147.1MM **Privately Held**
SIC: 0161 Lettuce & leaf vegetable farms
PA: Mann Packing Co., Inc.
1333 Schilling Pl
Salinas CA 93901
831 422-7405

(P-65)
FRESH VENTURE FARMS LLC
1181 S Wolff Rd, Oxnard (93033-2105)
PHONE 805 754-4449
Robert Boelts,
EMP: 80
SQ FT: 4,000
SALES (est): 8MM **Privately Held**
SIC: 0161 0191 Vegetables & melons; general farms, primarily crop

(P-66)
GEORGE AMARAL RANCHES INC
25453 Iverson Rd, Gonzales (93926-9403)
P.O. Box 3035 (93926-3035)
PHONE 831 679-2977
Fax: 831 679-0270
George Amaral, *President*
Mike Amaral, *Accountant*
▼ **EMP:** 100
SQ FT: 3,000
SALES (est): 50.6MM **Privately Held**
WEB: www.amaralranches.com
SIC: 0161 Lettuce & leaf vegetable farms; broccoli farm; cabbage farm; celery farm

(P-67)
GEORGE CHIALA FARMS INC
Also Called: Chiala, George Packing
15500 Hill Rd, Morgan Hill (95037-9516)
PHONE 408 778-0562
Fax: 408 779-4034
George Chiala Sr, *President*
Alice Chiala, *CFO*
George Chiala Jr, *Vice Pres*
Soheila Guerin, *Executive*
Gina Fitch, *Accountant*
EMP: 120
SQ FT: 14,000
SALES (est): 51.8MM **Privately Held**
WEB: www.gcfarmsinc.com
SIC: 0161 0723 Vegetables & melons; vegetable crops market preparation services

(P-68)
GILLS ONIONS LLC
1051 Pacific Ave, Oxnard (93030-7254)
PHONE 805 240-1983
Fax: 805 271-1932
Steve Gill, *Mng Member*
Darlene Gonzales, *Human Res Mgr*
Ericca Trost, *Regl Sales Mgr*
Teri Trost, *Regl Sales Mgr*
Jessica Ortega, *Sales Staff*
▲ **EMP:** 55
SALES (est): 27MM **Privately Held**
WEB: www.gillsonions.com
SIC: 0161 Onion farm

(P-69)
GIUSTI FARMS LLC
1800 Higgins Canyon Rd, Half Moon Bay (94019-2573)
PHONE 650 726-9221
Fax: 650 726-9553
Aldo Giusti,
John Giusti,
EMP: 50
SQ FT: 145
SALES (est): 2.1MM **Privately Held**
SIC: 0161 Artichoke farm; pea & bean farms; brussels sprout farm

(P-70)
GIVENS JOHN
Also Called: Givens Farms
1133 N Fairview Ave, Goleta (93117-1822)
PHONE 805 964-4477
John Givens, *Owner*
EMP: 70
SALES (est): 1.9MM **Privately Held**
SIC: 0161 Vegetables & melons

(P-71)
GOLDEN ACRES FARMS
87770 62nd Ave, Thermal (92274-9263)
P.O. Box 371 (92274-0371)
PHONE 760 399-1923
Fax: 760 399-1326
Joe Kitagawa, *President*
Kiyoko Kitagawa, *Corp Secy*
EMP: 50
SQ FT: 500
SALES (est): 2.8MM **Privately Held**
SIC: 0161 Vegetables & melons

(P-72)
HALF MOON FRUIT & PRODUCE CO (PA)
Also Called: Giovannetti Equipment Sales
211 Court St, Woodland (95695-3114)
PHONE 530 662-1727
John B Giovannetti, *President*
Harold Dickerson, *Corp Secy*
Ronald Giovannetti, *Vice Pres*
EMP: 50
SQ FT: 60,000
SALES (est): 6.5MM **Privately Held**
SIC: 0161 0112 0131 0111 Vegetables & melons; lettuce farm; rice; cotton; wheat; barley farm; alfalfa farm

(P-73)
HENRY HIBINO FARMS
106 Rico St, Salinas (93907-2101)
PHONE 831 757-3081
Fax: 831 757-0176
Henry Hibino, *Owner*
EMP: 75
SQ FT: 20,000
SALES (est): 6.2MM **Privately Held**
SIC: 0161 Vegetables & melons

(P-74)
IWAMOTO & GEAN FARM
Also Called: Harry's Berries
2064 Olga St, Oxnard (93036-2715)
PHONE 805 659-4568
Fax: 805 981-9925
Kaz Iwamoto, *General Ptnr*
Mariko Gean, *Partner*
Richard Gean, *Partner*
Yoshiko Iwamoto, *Partner*
EMP: 70
SALES (est): 5.3MM **Privately Held**
SIC: 0161 0171 Vegetables & melons; strawberry farm

(P-75)
J MARCHINI & SON INC
8736 Minturn Rd, Le Grand (95333-9711)
PHONE 559 665-9710
Joseph Marchini, *Branch Mgr*
EMP: 185
SALES (corp-wide): 25.6MM **Privately Held**
SIC: 0161 Rooted vegetable farms
PA: J. Marchini & Son, Inc.
8736 Minturn Rd
Le Grand CA 95333
559 665-2944

(P-76)
JAY FISHER FARMS INC
2251 W Central Ave, Lompoc (93436)
PHONE 805 735-1598
Fax: 805 736-0912
Elmer Fisher, *President*
Patricia Fisher, *Corp Secy*
EMP: 50
SALES (est): 1.7MM **Privately Held**
SIC: 0161 0181 Vegetables & melons; flowers grown in field nurseries

(P-77)
KELOMAR INC
3949 Austin Rd, Brawley (92227-9702)
PHONE 760 344-5253
Fax: 760 344-6072
Michael W Morgan, *President*
Joseph Johnson, *CFO*
Anna Kortson, *Admin Asst*
EMP: 120
SQ FT: 3,000
SALES (est): 8.3MM **Privately Held**
WEB: www.kelomar.com
SIC: 0161 Vegetables & melons

(P-78)
LA GRANDE FARM
P.O. Box 370 (95987-0370)
PHONE 530 473-5923
Ron La Grande, *Partner*
Mike La Grande, *Partner*
EMP: 70
SQ FT: 8,000
SALES (est): 3.9MM **Privately Held**
SIC: 0161 0191 0111 Tomato farm; general farms, primarily crop; wheat

(P-79)
LUCKY FARMS INC
1194 E Brier Dr, San Bernardino (92408-2838)
P.O. Box 985, Loma Linda (92354-0985)
PHONE 909 799-6688
Fax: 909 796-6599
Wen S Liaou, *President*
Gary Liaou, *Vice Pres*
Cyndi Arista, *Manager*
EMP: 60
SQ FT: 28,000
SALES (est): 7.9MM **Privately Held**
WEB: www.luckyfarms.com
SIC: 0161 Vegetables & melons

(P-80)
MICHAEL W MORGAN
3949 Austin Rd, Brawley (92227-9702)
PHONE 760 344-5253
Michael W Morgan, *Owner*
EMP: 50
SALES (est): 2.4MM **Privately Held**
SIC: 0161 Vegetables & melons

(P-81)
MIKAELIAN & SONS INC
10368 Avenue 400, Dinuba (93618-9558)
PHONE 559 591-6324
Mike Mikaelian, *President*
Carol Mikaelian, *Corp Secy*
EMP: 120 **EST:** 1953
SALES: 1MM **Privately Held**
SIC: 0161 0175 0172 Watermelon farm; deciduous tree fruits; grapes

(P-82)
MURANAKA FARM
11018 W Los Angeles Ave, Moorpark (93021-9744)
P.O. Box 189 (93020-0189)
PHONE 805 529-0201
Fax: 805 529-4527
Greg EMI, *President*
Chiaki Harami, *Corp Secy*
Luis Salazar, *Opers Staff*
EMP: 230
SALES (corp-wide): 148.6MM **Privately Held**
WEB: www.muranakafarm.com
SIC: 0161 Lettuce & leaf vegetable farms
PA: Muranaka Farm
11018 E Los Angeles Ave
Moorpark CA 93021
805 529-6692

PRODUCTS & SERVICES SECTION

0171 - Berry Crops County (P-107)

(P-83)
NEIL BASSETTI FARMS
41715 Espinosa Rd, Greenfield (93927-6101)
P.O. Box 429 (93927-0429)
PHONE 831 674-2040
Maryanne Martinus, *Partner*
Adrienne Bassetti, *Partner*
Patrick Bassetti, *Partner*
Allison Fierro, *Partner*
Mary Ann Martinus, *Partner*
EMP: 50
SALES (est): 5.7MM **Privately Held**
WEB: www.nbassetti.com
SIC: 0161 Vegetables & melons

(P-84)
OCEAN MIST FARMING COMPANY (PA)
Also Called: Ocean Mist Farms
10855 Ocean Mist Pkwy A, Castroville (95012-3232)
PHONE 831 633-2144
C Edward Boutonnet, *CEO*
Ed Bouponnet, *President*
Dorian Richards, *CFO*
Tom Bengard, *Treasurer*
Les Tottino, *Bd of Directors*
EMP: 150
SQ FT: 2,000
SALES (est): 48.5MM **Privately Held**
SIC: 0161 Lettuce & leaf vegetable farms; artichoke farm

(P-85)
OCEANVIEW PRODUCE COMPANY
3000 E Hueneme Rd, Oxnard (93033-8112)
PHONE 805 488-6401
Fax: 805 986-2204
David H Murdock, *President*
EMP: 60
SALES (est): 3.6MM **Privately Held**
SIC: 0161 5148 Celery farm; lettuce farm; fresh fruits & vegetables

(P-86)
OPAL FRY AND SON
Also Called: Fry, Opal W & Son Farming
Maricopa Hwy, Bakersfield (93307)
PHONE 661 858-2523
Jack Fry, *Partner*
George Fry, *Partner*
EMP: 50
SQ FT: 400
SALES (est): 2.4MM **Privately Held**
SIC: 0161 0131 Vegetables & melons; cotton

(P-87)
PAYNE BROTHERS RANCHES
13330 County Road 102, Woodland (95776-9119)
PHONE 530 662-2354
William A Payne, *Partner*
Robert B Payne, *Partner*
EMP: 100
SALES (est): 4.7MM **Privately Held**
WEB: www.paynefarms.com
SIC: 0161 0191 Tomato farm; general farms, primarily crop

(P-88)
PFYFFER ASSOCIATES INC
2611 Mission St, Santa Cruz (95060-5702)
P.O. Box 879 (95061-0879)
PHONE 831 423-8572
Fax: 831 423-6057
Ernie Bontadelli, *President*
Steve Bontadelli, *Vice Pres*
Charlie Bontadelli, *Principal*
EMP: 50
SALES (est): 3.2MM **Privately Held**
SIC: 0161 Brussels sprout farm

(P-89)
RICHTER BROS INC
22474 Karnak Rd, Knights Landing (95645-9405)
PHONE 530 735-6721
Fax: 530 735-6959
Henry Richter Jr, *President*
Amelia Richter, *Treasurer*
David Richter, *Director*
EMP: 80
SQ FT: 2,300
SALES (est): 7MM **Privately Held**
WEB: www.richterbros.com
SIC: 0161 0111 0173 0115 Tomato farm; wheat; walnut grove; corn; rice

(P-90)
ROBERT CECCHINI INC
Also Called: Cecchini & Cecchini
5301 Orwood Rd, Brentwood (94513-5245)
P.O. Box 1150, Discovery Bay (94505-7150)
PHONE 925 634-4400
Robert L Cecchini, *President*
EMP: 100 EST: 1933
SALES (est): 8.2MM **Privately Held**
SIC: 0161 0115 0111 0139 Asparagus farm; corn; wheat; alfalfa farm

(P-91)
ROYAL PACKING DCF
Also Called: Doll Fresh Vegetable
32839 S Lassen Ave, Huron (93234)
P.O. Box 938 (93234-0938)
PHONE 559 945-2537
Jack Shiyomura, *Manager*
EMP: 60
SALES (est): 1.8MM **Privately Held**
SIC: 0161 Lettuce farm

(P-92)
SAN MIGUEL PRODUCE INC
Also Called: Cut N Clean Greens
4444 Navalair Rd, Oxnard (93033-8298)
PHONE 805 488-6461
Roy I Nishimori, *CEO*
Jan Berk, *Vice Pres*
James Pingel, *Info Tech Mgr*
Cora Reedy, *Accounting Mgr*
Scott Ripple, *Purch Mgr*
◆ **EMP:** 160
SQ FT: 25,000
SALES (est): 45.8MM **Privately Held**
WEB: www.cutnclean.com
SIC: 0161 0723 4212 Vegetables & melons; vegetable packing services; farm to market haulage, local

(P-93)
SANTA BARBARA FARMS LLC (PA)
1200 Union Sugar Ave, Lompoc (93436-9740)
PHONE 805 736-9776
Fax: 805 735-4186
Robert M Witt, *CEO*
Charles Witt, *COO*
RC Gerber, *CFO*
▲ **EMP:** 66
SQ FT: 2,800
SALES (est): 33.9MM **Privately Held**
WEB: www.oceanviewflowers.com
SIC: 0161 0181 Vegetables & melons; florists' greens & flowers

(P-94)
SCARBOROUGH FARMS INC
731 Pacific Ave, Oxnard (93030-7322)
P.O. Box 1267 (93032-1267)
PHONE 805 483-9113
Fax: 805 247-1803
Ann Stein, *President*
Wayne G Jansen, *President*
Brandon Stein, *Opers Staff*
Jeff Stein, *Sales Mgr*
Elvia Alvarado, *Sales Staff*
EMP: 150
SALES (est): 19.6MM **Privately Held**
SIC: 0161 Vegetables & melons

(P-95)
SEASHOLTZ JOHN
1355 M St, Firebaugh (93622-2338)
PHONE 559 659-3805
EMP: 196
SALES (corp-wide): 36.6MM **Privately Held**
SIC: 0161 Vegetables & melons
PA: Seasholtz, John
4965 N Crystal Ave Ste A
Fresno CA 93705
559 229-0453

(P-96)
SUN AND SANDS ENTERPRISES LLC (PA)
Also Called: PRIME TIME INTERNATIONAL
86705 Avenue 54 Ste A, Coachella (92236-3814)
PHONE 760 399-4278
Fax: 760 399-4172
Carl Sam Maggio,
Kathy Jones, *Administration*
Amy Dorchuck, *Accounting Mgr*
Jim Detty, *Credit Mgr*
Patricia McManus, *Controller*
▲ **EMP:** 64
SQ FT: 7,500
SALES (est): 123.9MM **Privately Held**
WEB: www.primetimeproduce.com
SIC: 0161 Lettuce farm; snap bean farm (bush & pole); cantaloupe farm; watermelon farm

(P-97)
TANIMURA ANTLE FRESH FOODS INC (PA)
1 Harris Rd, Salinas (93908-8608)
P.O. Box 4070 (93912-4070)
PHONE 831 455-2950
Fax: 831 455-3913
Rick Antle, *President*
Ken Silveira, *COO*
Vic Feuerstein, *CFO*
Vic Goochey, *CFO*
Mike Antle, *Exec VP*
◆ **EMP:** 100
SQ FT: 135,000
SALES (est): 602MM **Privately Held**
WEB: www.taproduce.com
SIC: 0161 0182 0723 2099 Lettuce farm; celery farm; cauliflower farm; food crops grown under cover; vegetable packing services; food preparations

(P-98)
TEIXEIRA FARMS INC
2600 Bonita Lateral Rd, Santa Maria (93458-9798)
PHONE 805 928-3801
Allan Teixeira, *President*
Chris Wong, *CFO*
Glenn Teixeira, *Treasurer*
Marvin Teixeira, *Vice Pres*
Dean Teixeira, *Admin Sec*
EMP: 188
SALES (est): 13.9MM **Privately Held**
WEB: www.teixeirafarms.com
SIC: 0161 Broccoli farm; cabbage farm; cauliflower farm; celery farm

(P-99)
TERRA FIRMA FARM CORP
Also Called: Terra Firma Farms
4713 Baker Rd, Winters (95694-9613)
P.O. Box 836 (95694-0836)
PHONE 530 795-2473
Fax: 530 795-1631
Paul Underhill, *CEO*
Paul Holmes, *Treasurer*
Hector Melendes, *Admin Sec*
EMP: 50
SQ FT: 800
SALES: 1.4MM **Privately Held**
WEB: www.terrafirmafarm.com
SIC: 0161 0174 0173 0175 Rooted vegetable farms; citrus fruits; tree nuts; deciduous tree fruits

(P-100)
THORKELSON RANCHES
13218 Elm Ave, Patterson (95363-9627)
PHONE 209 892-9111
Merlin Thorkelson, *Partner*
Clay Thorkelson, *Partner*
EMP: 150
SQ FT: 10,000
SALES (est): 2.5MM **Privately Held**
SIC: 0161 Vegetables & melons; tomato farm

(P-101)
UESUGI FARMS INC (PA)
1020 State Highway 25, Gilroy (95020-8074)
PHONE 408 842-1294
Fax: 408 842-1326
Joseph Aiello, *President*
Dennis Humphries, *Vice Pres*
Diane Zent, *Financial Exec*
Virginia Haro, *Accounting Mgr*
Greg Churchill, *Sales Mgr*
EMP: 66 EST: 1979
SALES (est): 47.9MM **Privately Held**
SIC: 0161 Vegetables & melons

(P-102)
WM BOLTHOUSE FARMS INC (DH)
7200 E Brundage Ln, Bakersfield (93307-3016)
PHONE 661 366-7205
Jeff Dunn, *President*
Harleen Singh, *CFO*
Marty Buck, *Treasurer*
Todd Putnam, *Chief Mktg Ofcr*
Scott Laporta, *Exec VP*
▲ **EMP:** 2250
SQ FT: 700,000
SALES: 617.1MM
SALES (corp-wide): 7.9B **Publicly Held**
SIC: 0161 2099 0723 Carrot farm; onion farm; ready-to-eat meals, salads & sandwiches; crop preparation services for market
HQ: Bolthouse Holding Corp.
7200 E Brundage Ln
Bakersfield CA 93307
310 566-8350

0171 Berry Crops

(P-103)
APTOS BERRY FARMS INC
730 S A St, Oxnard (93030-7138)
PHONE 831 726-3256
Garland Reiter, *CEO*
Joseph M Reiter Jr, *President*
EMP: 70
SQ FT: 5,000
SALES (est): 4.4MM **Privately Held**
SIC: 0171 Strawberry farm; raspberry farm

(P-104)
B & E FARMS INC
Also Called: Ito Farms
9112 Mcfadden Ave, Westminster (92683-6533)
PHONE 714 893-8166
Bill Ito, *President*
Ed Ito, *Vice Pres*
EMP: 50
SQ FT: 2,000
SALES (est): 3.4MM **Privately Held**
SIC: 0171 Strawberry farm

(P-105)
BLAZER WILKINSON LP
19040 Portola Dr, Salinas (93908-1213)
P.O. Box 7428, Spreckels (93962-7428)
PHONE 831 455-3700
John Wilkinson, *General Ptnr*
Scott Blazer, *Partner*
Paige Hufford, *Accounting Mgr*
Kiana Amaral, *Controller*
EMP: 300
SQ FT: 25,000
SALES (est): 16.5MM **Privately Held**
SIC: 0171 Strawberry farm

(P-106)
CARDENAS BROS FARMING COMPANY
1141 Tama Ln, Santa Maria (93455-1127)
PHONE 805 928-1559
Alberto Cardenas, *President*
Delfina Cardenas, *Vice Pres*
EMP: 100
SALES (est): 4.7MM **Privately Held**
SIC: 0171 Strawberry farm

(P-107)
CJJ FARMING INC
125 W Mill St, Santa Maria (93458-4325)
PHONE 805 739-1723
Fax: 805 739-9093
Juan Cisneros, *President*
Jesus Cisneros, *Admin Sec*
EMP: 50

0171 - Berry Crops County (P-108)

SALES (est): 3.1MM Privately Held
SIC: 0171 0161 Strawberry farm; squash farm; broccoli farm; lettuce farm; romaine farm

(P-108)
CONROY FARMS INC
520 Maulhardt Ave, Oxnard (93030-8914)
P.O. Box 1467, Camarillo (93011-1467)
PHONE..................805 981-0537
Fax: 805 482-0100
Michael P Conroy, *President*
Willaine Conroy, *Chairman*
Alice Menchaca, *Manager*
EMP: 325
SQ FT: 700
SALES: 3MM Privately Held
SIC: 0171 Strawberry farm

(P-109)
DARENSBERRIES LLC
Also Called: D B Specialty Farms
714 S Blosser Rd, Santa Maria (93458-4914)
P.O. Box 549 (93456-0549)
PHONE..................805 937-8000
Fax: 805 928-4774
Daren Gee, *Owner*
Nancy Machut, *Manager*
EMP: 250
SQ FT: 1,500
SALES (est): 13.1MM Privately Held
SIC: 0171 Strawberry farm

(P-110)
ETCHANDY FARMS LLC
4324 E Vineyard Ave, Oxnard (93036-1056)
PHONE..................805 983-4700
Michael Etchandy,
EMP: 99 **EST:** 2014
SQ FT: 400
SALES (est): 1.1MM Privately Held
SIC: 0171 Strawberry farm

(P-111)
FARMHILL LLC
1800 San Juan Rd, Aromas (95004-9027)
P.O. Box 1119, Mount Shasta (96067-1119)
PHONE..................831 726-1986
Fax: 831 726-2650
Thomas P Driscoll, *President*
Josh Pappe, *CEO*
Nancy Driscoll, *Vice Pres*
EMP: 100
SALES (est): 3.3MM Privately Held
SIC: 0171 Strawberry farm

(P-112)
FRESHWAY FARMS LLC
2165 W Main St, Santa Maria (93458-9739)
P.O. Box 5369 (93456-5369)
PHONE..................805 349-7170
Paul M Allen, *Mng Member*
EMP: 150 **EST:** 2014
SALES: 22MM Privately Held
SIC: 0171 0161 Strawberry farm; broccoli farm

(P-113)
GAMA BERRY FARMS LLC
730 S A St, Oxnard (93030-7138)
PHONE..................805 483-1000
Garland Reider, *CEO*
EMP: 60 **EST:** 2012
SALES (est): 928.5K Privately Held
SIC: 0171 Berry crops

(P-114)
GUY GEORGE
Also Called: King George Cabbage
315 2nd St Ste A, Watsonville (95076-5112)
P.O. Box 40 (95077-0040)
PHONE..................831 728-2410
Guy George, *Partner*
EMP: 50
SALES (est): 883.1K Privately Held
WEB: www.guygeorge.com
SIC: 0171 0161 Strawberry farm; cabbage farm; lettuce farm

(P-115)
JAL BERRY FARMS LLC
1767 San Juan Rd, Aromas (95004-9028)
PHONE..................831 763-7200
Jose Lopez,
Luz Rodriguez, *Human Res Mgr*
Robert F Dunaven Jr,
Hernando Ramirez,
EMP: 99
SALES (est): 6.4MM Privately Held
SIC: 0171 Berry crops

(P-116)
KUSUMOTO FARMS
6535 Stonehill Dr, San Jose (95120-1619)
PHONE..................408 927-8348
Mel Kusumoto, *Owner*
EMP: 90
SALES (est): 3.8MM Privately Held
SIC: 0171 Strawberry farm

(P-117)
LACUESTA FARMING INC
1141 Tama Ln, Santa Maria (93455-1127)
PHONE..................805 349-1940
Fax: 805 349-1940
Fernando Contreras, *President*
Dalila Contreras, *Corp Secy*
EMP: 100
SALES (est): 4.6MM Privately Held
SIC: 0171 Strawberry farm

(P-118)
LASSEN CANYON NURSERY INC
14735 Big Springs Rd, Weed (96094-9665)
PHONE..................530 938-4720
Kenneth Elwood, *President*
EMP: 100
SALES (corp-wide): 52MM Privately Held
WEB: www.lassencanyonnursery.com
SIC: 0171 Strawberry farm
PA: Lassen Canyon Nursery, Inc.
1300 Salmon Creek Rd
Redding CA 96003
530 223-1075

(P-119)
LASSEN CANYON NURSERY INC
11651 Palm Ln, Ripon (95366)
PHONE..................209 599-7777
Kenneth Elwood, *President*
EMP: 100
SALES (corp-wide): 52MM Privately Held
WEB: www.lassencanyonnursery.com
SIC: 0171 Strawberry farm
PA: Lassen Canyon Nursery, Inc.
1300 Salmon Creek Rd
Redding CA 96003
530 223-1075

(P-120)
LASSEN CANYON NURSERY INC (PA)
1300 Salmon Creek Rd, Redding (96003-9641)
P.O. Box 992400 (96099-2400)
PHONE..................530 223-1075
Fax: 530 223-6754
Elizabeth Elwood Ponce, *CEO*
Kenneth Elwood Jr, *President*
William Welty, *Plant Mgr*
Tony Boyes, *Foreman/Supr*
Mel Fernandez, *Marketing Staff*
▼ **EMP:** 125
SQ FT: 3,000
SALES (est): 52MM Privately Held
WEB: www.lassencanyonnursery.com
SIC: 0171 5141 5191 Berry crops; raspberry farm; strawberry farm; groceries, general line; hay

(P-121)
MARIZ BERRY FARMS
1650 E Gonzales Rd, Oxnard (93036-3700)
PHONE..................805 981-9908
Victor Lopez, *Partner*
Donald Driscoll, *Partner*
Keith Ford, *Partner*
EMP: 105 **EST:** 1997

SALES (est): 3.9MM Privately Held
SIC: 0171 Strawberry farm

(P-122)
MENDOZA FARMS INC
527 W Fesler St Apt A, Santa Maria (93458-4052)
PHONE..................805 352-1070
Hector Mendoza, *President*
Alex Mendoza, *Partner*
EMP: 50
SALES (est): 1.6MM Privately Held
SIC: 0171 Strawberry farm

(P-123)
MORGAN FARM LLC
201 Vista Dr, Watsonville (95076-1754)
P.O. Box 758 (95077-0758)
PHONE..................831 726-5120
Jason Morgan, *President*
EMP: 70
SALES: 3MM Privately Held
SIC: 0171 7389 Strawberry farm;

(P-124)
NORTH RIVER RANCH LLC
3601 W Pendleton Ave, Santa Ana (92704-3814)
PHONE..................714 556-6244
George Murai,
Mark Murai, *Partner*
Triple M Packing, *Partner*
EMP: 50
SQ FT: 25,000
SALES (est): 7MM Privately Held
SIC: 0171 Strawberry farm; raspberry farm

(P-125)
ORANGE COUNTY PRODUCE LLC
11405 Jeffrey Rd, Irvine (92602-0503)
PHONE..................949 451-0880
Matthew K Kawamura, *Mng Member*
Blanca Bermudez, *Human Resources*
John Kubo, *Marketing Staff*
Arthur Kawamura,
Matthew Kawamura, *Mng Member*
EMP: 100
SQ FT: 1,000
SALES (est): 47.1MM Privately Held
SIC: 0171 Strawberry farm

(P-126)
PENDLETON FARMS
307 Wilshire Rd, Oceanside (92057-2902)
P.O. Box 522, San Luis Rey (92068-0522)
PHONE..................760 754-2359
Donald Stickles, *Owner*
EMP: 55
SALES (est): 2.3MM Privately Held
SIC: 0171 Strawberry farm

(P-127)
RED BLOSSOM SALES INC
865 Black Rd, Santa Maria (93458-9701)
PHONE..................805 349-9404
Ruben Trevino, *Manager*
EMP: 500
SALES (corp-wide): 141.5MM Privately Held
SIC: 0171 Strawberry farm
PA: Red Blossom Sales, Inc.
400 W Ventura Blvd # 140
Camarillo CA 93010
805 686-4747

(P-128)
REITER AFFL COMPANIES LLC
124 Carmen Ln Ste A, Santa Maria (93458-7768)
PHONE..................805 925-8577
Mario Pena, *Manager*
Sandra Orozco, *Managing Prtnr*
EMP: 86
SALES (corp-wide): 54.6MM Privately Held
SIC: 0171 Berry crops
PA: Reiter Affiliated Companies, Llc
730 S A St
Oxnard CA 93030
805 483-1000

(P-129)
REITER AFFL COMPANIES LLC
Also Called: Reiter Berry Watsonville
140 Westridge Dr, Watsonville (95076-6602)
PHONE..................831 786-4244
EMP: 74
SALES (corp-wide): 54.6MM Privately Held
SIC: 0171 Raspberry farm
PA: Reiter Affiliated Companies, Llc
730 S A St
Oxnard CA 93030
805 483-1000

(P-130)
RINCON PACIFIC LLC
1312 Del Norte Rd, Camarillo (93010-8502)
PHONE..................805 986-8806
Kenneth Hasegawa,
EMP: 100
SALES (est): 11.6MM Privately Held
SIC: 0171 Strawberry farm

(P-131)
RIO MESA FARMS LLC
75 Sakata Ln, Watsonville (95076-5132)
P.O. Box 1359 (95077-1359)
PHONE..................831 728-1965
Mary Gregg, *Administration*
EMP: 99
SALES (est): 3.1MM Privately Held
SIC: 0171 Strawberry farm

(P-132)
SANTA PAULA BERRY FARMS LLC
1650 E Gonzales Rd, Oxnard (93036-3700)
PHONE..................805 981-1469
Keith W Ford,
EMP: 50
SALES (est): 2.5MM Privately Held
SIC: 0171 Strawberry farm

(P-133)
SIERRA CASCADE BLUEBERRIES
12753 Doe Mill Rd, Forest Ranch (95942)
P.O. Box 613 (95942-0613)
PHONE..................530 894-8728
John Carlon, *Owner*
John Carlo, *Owner*
EMP: 50
SALES: 300K Privately Held
SIC: 0171 Blueberry farm

(P-134)
SOLIMAR FARMS INC
1312 Del Norte Rd, Camarillo (93010-8502)
PHONE..................805 986-8806
Glen Hasegawa, *President*
Ken Hasegawa, *Vice Pres*
Susan Josue, *Office Mgr*
Carol Elrod, *Bookkeeper*
EMP: 80
SQ FT: 2,000
SALES (est): 16MM Privately Held
SIC: 0171 Strawberry farm

(P-135)
SUPERIOR BERRY FARMS LLC
730 S A St, Oxnard (93030-7138)
PHONE..................805 483-1000
David Mulder,
EMP: 60
SALES (est): 750.3K Privately Held
SIC: 0171 Strawberry farm

(P-136)
T T MIYASAKA INC
209 Riverside Rd, Watsonville (95076-3656)
PHONE..................831 722-3871
Tim Miyasaka, *President*
EMP: 400
SQ FT: 500
SALES (est): 10.8MM Privately Held
SIC: 0171 Strawberry farm

PRODUCTS & SERVICES SECTION

0172 - Grapes County (P-163)

(P-137)
UYEDA FARM
656 Lakeview Rd, Watsonville (95076-2228)
P.O. Box 1045, Freedom (95019-1045)
PHONE.................................831 722-6345
Norman Uyeda, *Owner*
Darrell Uyeda, *Owner*
EMP: 50
SALES (est): 1.1MM **Privately Held**
SIC: 0171 Strawberry farm

(P-138)
UYEMATSU INC
1004 E Lake Ave, Watsonville (95076-3406)
PHONE.................................831 724-2200
Richard Uyematsu, *President*
Alan Uyematsu, *Vice Pres*
EMP: 65
SQ FT: 1,650
SALES (est): 4.9MM **Privately Held**
SIC: 0171 Strawberry farm

0172 Grapes

(P-139)
7TH STANDARD RANCH COMPANY
Also Called: Sun Pacific Farming
33374 Lerdo Hwy, Bakersfield (93308-9782)
PHONE.................................661 399-0416
Berne Evans, *Partner*
Robert Reniers, *Partner*
Ernie Villagra, *Information Mgr*
Richard Peters, *Finance Mgr*
Ernie Larson, *Controller*
EMP: 500
SQ FT: 140,000
SALES (est): 13.6MM **Privately Held**
SIC: 0172 4222 Grapes; refrigerated warehousing & storage

(P-140)
ALEXANDER DELU
15175 N Devries Rd, Lodi (95242-9217)
PHONE.................................209 334-6660
EMP: 80
SALES (est): 2.8MM **Privately Held**
SIC: 0172 0722

(P-141)
ANTHONY VINEYARDS INC (PA)
5512 Valpredo Ave, Bakersfield (93307-9178)
P.O. Box 9578 (93389-9578)
PHONE.................................661 858-6211
Fax: 661 858-6166
Domenick T Bianco, *President*
Paul A Loeffel, *CFO*
Robert O Bianco, *Senior VP*
Justin McGowan, *Administration*
Tom Karle, *Sales Executive*
▼ **EMP:** 50
SQ FT: 125,000
SALES: 38.5MM **Privately Held**
WEB: www.anthonyvineyards.com
SIC: 0172 0174 Grapes; grapefruit grove; tangerine grove

(P-142)
BAZAN MARIO AG SERVICES & VINE
Also Called: Bazan Mrio Vinyrd Mgmt AG Svcs
1984 Yountville Cross Rd, Yountville (94599-1291)
P.O. Box 864, NAPA (94559-0864)
PHONE.................................707 945-0718
Fax: 707 945-0718
Mario Bazan, *Owner*
Lori Valdivia, *Controller*
▲ **EMP:** 62 **EST:** 1997
SALES: 1.3MM **Privately Held**
SIC: 0172 Grapes

(P-143)
BEDROSIAN FARMS INC
8333 S Sunnyside Ave, Fowler (93625-9659)
P.O. Box 219 (93625-0219)
PHONE.................................559 834-5981
Ernest Bedrosian, *President*
Kenneth Bedrosian, *Vice Pres*
Krikor Bedrosian, *Vice Pres*
Karen Shea, *Admin Asst*
EMP: 50
SALES (est): 3.2MM **Privately Held**
SIC: 0172 Grapes

(P-144)
BROCCHINI FARMS INC
27011 S Austin Rd, Ripon (95366-9627)
PHONE.................................209 599-4229
Robert Brocchini, *President*
Steve Brocchini, *Principal*
Ingrid Redway, *Manager*
EMP: 50
SALES (est): 4.8MM **Privately Held**
WEB: www.brocchinifarms.com
SIC: 0172 0173 0139 Grapes; almond grove; alfalfa farm

(P-145)
CHAPPELLET VINEYARD
1581 Sage Canyon Rd, Saint Helena (94574-9628)
PHONE.................................707 286-4219
Fax: 707 963-7445
Donn Chappellet,
Andrew Opatz,
EMP: 50
SALES (est): 2.3MM **Privately Held**
SIC: 0172 Grapes

(P-146)
CIRCLE K RANCH
8640 E Manning Ave, Selma (93662-9763)
PHONE.................................559 834-1571
Fax: 559 834-2258
Melvin Kazarian, *General Ptnr*
Ronald Kazarian, *Partner*
Charles Kazarian, *Info Tech Mgr*
Melissa Fulton, *Bookkeeper*
EMP: 60 **EST:** 1971
SQ FT: 25,000
SALES (est): 3.4MM **Privately Held**
WEB: www.circlekranch.com
SIC: 0172 Grapes

(P-147)
CLARBEC INC
Also Called: Madrone Vineyard Management
19368 Orange Ave, Sonoma (95476-6249)
PHONE.................................707 996-4012
Rebecca Jenkins, *Principal*
Clarence A Jenkins Jr, *President*
Isaac Jenkins, *Manager*
EMP: 50
SQ FT: 1,600
SALES (est): 3.6MM **Privately Held**
SIC: 0172 Grapes

(P-148)
CLENDENEN VINEYARD MGT LLC
9235 W Dry Creek Rd, Healdsburg (95448-9134)
P.O. Box 69 (95448-0069)
PHONE.................................707 473-0881
Fax: 707 433-5176
John Clendenen,
Catherine Clendenen,
EMP: 60 **EST:** 1993
SALES (est): 3.6MM **Privately Held**
SIC: 0172 Grapes

(P-149)
DELMART FARMS INC
30988 Riverside Cntrl Vly, Shafter (93263)
PHONE.................................661 746-2148
Robert J Vignolo, *President*
Jane Vignolo, *Vice Pres*
EMP: 100
SQ FT: 1,000
SALES (est): 2.3MM **Privately Held**
SIC: 0172 0131 0134 0724 Grapes; cotton; Irish potatoes; cotton ginning

(P-150)
DIRT FARMER & CO INC
9725 Los Guilicos Ave, Kenwood (95452)
P.O. Box 638 (95452-0638)
PHONE.................................707 833-2054
Keith Kunde, *President*
EMP: 53
SALES (est): 500K **Privately Held**
SIC: 0172 0761 Grapes; farm labor contractors

(P-151)
DOMAINE CARNEROS LTD
1240 Duhig Rd, NAPA (94559-9713)
P.O. Box 5420 (94581-0420)
PHONE.................................707 257-0101
Fax: 707 257-3020
Eileen Crane, *CEO*
Robert Aldridge, *CFO*
Scott Rounds, *Technology*
Claire Galobic, *Accountant*
Kristen Guiducci, *Controller*
▲ **EMP:** 80
SQ FT: 50,000
SALES (est): 8.7MM **Privately Held**
WEB: www.domainecarneros.com
SIC: 0172 2084 Grapes; wines

(P-152)
DRAKE LARSON RANCHS
Also Called: Larson, Drake Sales
89780 Ave 60, Thermal (92274)
P.O. Box 355 (92274-0355)
PHONE.................................760 399-5494
Fax: 760 399-0062
Drake Larson, *Partner*
Pamela Larson, *Partner*
EMP: 200
SQ FT: 3,000
SALES (est): 3.9MM **Privately Held**
SIC: 0172 0161 4222 Grapes; vegetables & melons; refrigerated warehousing & storage

(P-153)
E & J GALLO WINERY
Also Called: J Vineyards & Winery
11447 Old Redwood Hwy, Healdsburg (95448-9523)
PHONE.................................707 431-5400
Joseph Gallo, *CEO*
Martin Jwines, *Prdtn Dir*
Emilie Eliason, *Mktg Dir*
Scott Zapotocky, *Director*
Samantha Veader, *Assistant*
EMP: 52
SALES (corp-wide): 4.1B **Privately Held**
SIC: 0172 2084 Grapes; wines
PA: E. & J. Gallo Winery
600 Yosemite Blvd
Modesto CA 95354
209 341-3111

(P-154)
GALLEANO ENTERPRISES INC
4231 Wineville Ave, Mira Loma (91752-1412)
PHONE.................................951 685-5376
Donald Galleano, *President*
Charlene Galleano, *Vice Pres*
EMP: 100
SALES (est): 3.5MM **Privately Held**
SIC: 0172 Grapes

(P-155)
GIUMARRA VINEYARDS CORPORATION
Also Called: Giumarra Winery
1122 O Edison Hwy, Bakersfield (93304)
P.O. Box 1969 (93303-1969)
PHONE.................................661 395-7071
Barry Douglas, *Manager*
EMP: 55
SALES (corp-wide): 162.4MM **Privately Held**
SIC: 0172 Grapes
PA: Giumarra Vineyards Corporation
11220 Edison Hwy
Edison CA 93220
661 395-7000

(P-156)
GIUMARRA VINEYARDS CORPORATION (PA)
11220 Edison Hwy, Edison (93220)
P.O. Box 1969 (93303-1969)
PHONE.................................661 395-7000
Fax: 661 366-7134
Randy Giumarra, *VP Sales*
William Butler, *CFO*
Craig Bowers, *Info Tech Mgr*
Kenneth Witham, *Asst Controller*
Jeffrey Giumarra, *Controller*
▼ **EMP:** 500 **EST:** 1946
SQ FT: 10,000
SALES: 162.4MM **Privately Held**
SIC: 0172 2084 2086 Grapes; wines; fruit drinks (less than 100% juice): packaged in cans, etc.; tea, iced: packaged in cans, bottles, etc.

(P-157)
H & R GUNLUND RANCHES INC
3510 W Saginaw Ave, Caruthers (93609-9568)
PHONE.................................559 864-8186
Russell P Gunlund, *President*
EMP: 220
SALES (est): 5.4MM **Privately Held**
SIC: 0172 Grapes

(P-158)
JACK NEAL & SON INC
360 Lafata St, Saint Helena (94574-1410)
PHONE.................................707 963-7303
Fax: 707 967-3542
Mark J Neal, *President*
Tina Galambos, *Vice Pres*
Aj Prez, *Manager*
EMP: 200
SQ FT: 20,000
SALES (est): 14.9MM **Privately Held**
SIC: 0172 Grapes

(P-159)
JAKOV P DULCICH & SONS
31956 Peterson Rd, Mc Farland (93250-9606)
PHONE.................................661 792-6360
Fax: 661 792-6529
Jakov Dulcich, *Owner*
Nick Dulcich, *Vice Pres*
Mayra Contreras, *Executive*
Delia Armstrong, *Financial Exec*
Delia Hillard, *Manager*
▲ **EMP:** 250
SALES (est): 25.6MM **Privately Held**
SIC: 0172 Grapes

(P-160)
JANE MCCLURG
4584 E Floral Ave, Selma (93662-9624)
PHONE.................................559 834-3080
Jane McClurg, *Owner*
EMP: 75
SALES (est): 3.7MM **Privately Held**
SIC: 0172 Grapes

(P-161)
KANDARIAN AGRI ENTERPRISES
Also Called: Agrichem
116 W Adams Ave, Fowler (93625-9614)
P.O. Box 278 (93625-0278)
PHONE.................................559 834-1501
Fax: 559 834-1582
Eugene Kandarian, *President*
Yvonne Kandarian, *Vice Pres*
EMP: 180
SQ FT: 6,500
SALES (est): 11.2MM **Privately Held**
SIC: 0172 4213 5191 Grapes; contract haulers; chemicals, agricultural; fertilizer & fertilizer materials; pesticides

(P-162)
KARAM BATH
1673 W Kamm Ave, Caruthers (93609-9797)
PHONE.................................559 864-3868
Karam Bath, *Owner*
EMP: 50 **EST:** 1983
SALES (est): 982.7K **Privately Held**
SIC: 0172 Grapes

(P-163)
KAUTZ VINEYARDS INC (PA)
Also Called: Kautz Ironstone Vineyards
1894 6 Mile Rd, Murphys (95247-9543)
PHONE.................................209 728-1251
Fax: 209 728-1275
John K Kautz, *CEO*
Stephen Kautz, *President*
Kurt Kautz, *Treasurer*
Gail Kautz, *Vice Pres*
Bruce L Rohroer, *Director*
◆ **EMP:** 100
SQ FT: 75,000
SALES (est): 14.7MM **Privately Held**
WEB: www.ironstonevineyards.com
SIC: 0172 5812 Grapes; eating places

0172 - Grapes County (P-164)

PRODUCTS & SERVICES SECTION

(P-164)
KLEIN FOODS INC
Also Called: Rodney Strong Vineyards
11455 Old Redwood Hwy, Healdsburg
(95448-9523)
P.O. Box 6010 (95448-6010)
PHONE.....................707 431-1533
Fax: 707 433-0939
Thomas B Klein, *President*
Tobin Ginter, *CFO*
Jean Brennan, *CTO*
Carmen Castaldi, *VP Sales*
Erica Odden, *Marketing Staff*
▲ **EMP:** 100
SQ FT: 20,000
SALES (est): 26.5MM Privately Held
WEB: www.rodneystrong.com
SIC: 0172 2084 5182 Grapes; wines; wine & distilled beverages

(P-165)
KVL HOLDINGS INC (PA)
Also Called: Saint Nicolas Vineyard
37700 Foothill Rd, Soledad (93960-9620)
P.O. Box C (93960-0167)
PHONE.....................831 678-2132
Nicholaus Hahn, *CEO*
EMP: 50
SQ FT: 30,000
SALES (est): 21.1MM Privately Held
SIC: 0172 2084 6719 Grapes; wines; investment holding companies, except banks

(P-166)
LAMANUZZI & PANTALEO LLC (PA)
11767 Road 27 1/2, Madera (93637-9108)
PHONE.....................559 432-3170
Fax: 559 275-5892
Frank P Pantaleo, *Owner*
Karol Ryals, *Accountant*
Ron Netz, *Controller*
Ron Nitz, *Controller*
Tina Baer,
▲ **EMP:** 64
SQ FT: 1,000
SALES: 30.8MM Privately Held
SIC: 0172 4222 Grapes; warehousing, cold storage or refrigerated

(P-167)
LANGETWINS INC
1298 E Jahant Rd, Acampo (95220)
PHONE.....................209 339-4055
Fax: 209 339-9014
Randy Lange, *President*
Brad Lange, *CFO*
Charlene Lange, *Vice Pres*
Susan Lange, *Admin Sec*
EMP: 75
SALES (est): 6.7MM Privately Held
WEB: www.langetwins.com
SIC: 0172

(P-168)
LANZA VINEYARDS INC
Also Called: Wooden Valley Farms
4756 Suisun Valley Rd, Fairfield (94534-3114)
PHONE.....................707 864-0730
Fax: 707 864-6038
Richard Lanza, *President*
Adrienne Lanza, *Corp Secy*
Kenneth Lee Lanza, *Vice Pres*
Lawrence Dean Lanza, *Vice Pres*
Mario Richard Lanza Jr, *Vice Pres*
EMP: 50
SQ FT: 1,300
SALES (est): 5.2MM Privately Held
WEB: www.woodenvalley.com
SIC: 0172 2084 Grapes; wines

(P-169)
M CARATAN INC
33787 Cecil Ave, Delano (93215-9597)
PHONE.....................661 725-1777
Chris Caratan, *Principal*
Denise Smith, *Sales Mgr*
Claire Caratan, *Marketing Staff*
Ryan Debuskey, *Marketing Staff*
Lauren Olcott, *Marketing Staff*
EMP: 105
SALES (corp-wide): 17.2MM Privately Held
SIC: 0172 Grapes

PA: M. Caratan, Inc.
33787 Cecil Ave
Delano CA 93215
661 725-2566

(P-170)
MCCUTCHEON ENTERPRISES INC
604 W Nebraska Ave, Fresno (93706-9280)
P.O. Box 188, Caruthers (93609-0188)
PHONE.....................559 864-3200
Mike D Mc Cutcheon, *President*
EMP: 100
SQ FT: 4,200
SALES: 550K Privately Held
SIC: 0172 0173 Grapes; pistachio grove

(P-171)
MIRABELLA FARMS INC
5551 S Orange Ave, Fresno (93725-9505)
PHONE.....................559 237-4495
Paquerette Markarian, *President*
Philip Markarian, *Treasurer*
Joseph Markarian, *Vice Pres*
EMP: 75
SALES (est): 2.2MM Privately Held
WEB: www.mirabellafarms.com
SIC: 0172 Grapes

(P-172)
NESTOR ENTERPRISES LLC
13852 E Peltier Rd, Acampo (95220-9342)
PHONE.....................209 727-5711
Fransico Ilayala,
EMP: 50
SALES (est): 2.8MM Privately Held
WEB: www.nestorenterprises.com
SIC: 0172 Grapes

(P-173)
OAK RIDGE WINERY LLC
6100 E Hwy 12 Victor Rd, Lodi (95240)
PHONE.....................209 369-4768
Rudy Maggio,
Darwin Schnell, *Regional Mgr*
John White, *Area Mgr*
Nicholas Karavidas, *General Mgr*
Scott Parker, *Controller*
▲ **EMP:** 50
SALES (est): 6.2MM Privately Held
WEB: www.oakridgewinery.com
SIC: 0172 Grapes

(P-174)
ONEILL BEVERAGES CO LLC (PA)
Also Called: O'Neill Vintners & Distillers
101 Larkspur Landing Cir, Larkspur (94939-1746)
PHONE.....................844 825-6600
Jeffrey B O'Neill, *CEO*
Mike Drobnick, *Senior VP*
Brian James, *Vice Pres*
Kyle Makki, *Executive*
Joan Lasky, *Executive Asst*
▲ **EMP:** 63
SQ FT: 5,000
SALES (est): 23MM Privately Held
SIC: 0172 2084 Grapes; wines

(P-175)
PANDOL & SONS
401 Road 192, Delano (93215-9598)
PHONE.....................661 725-3755
Cheri Diebel, *CEO*
Jack V Pandol, *Partner*
Lucy Pandol, *Partner*
Steve Pandol III, *Partner*
Sherry Dibdel, *CFO*
EMP: 50 **EST:** 1930
SQ FT: 10,000
SALES: 13.9MM Privately Held
SIC: 0172 0723 Grapes; fruit (fresh) packing services

(P-176)
R H PHILLIPS INC (DH)
Also Called: R H Phillips Vineyard
26836 County Road 12a, Esparto (95627-2139)
PHONE.....................530 757-5557
Fax: 530 662-2880
John Giguiere, *Ch of Bd*
Vance Schram, *CFO*
Pat Kane, *Vice Pres*

Steven Crosta, *Manager*
EMP: 245
SQ FT: 4,500
SALES (est): 9.8MM
SALES (corp-wide): 6.5B Publicly Held
SIC: 0172 2084 5182 Grapes; wines; wine & distilled beverages
HQ: Constellation Brands Canada, Inc.
441 Courtneypark Dr E
Mississauga ON L5T 2
905 564-6900

(P-177)
RICHARD BAGDASARIAN INC
65500 Lincoln St, Mecca (92254-6500)
P.O. Box 698 (92254-0698)
PHONE.....................760 396-2168
Fax: 760 396-2801
Nicholas L Bozick, *CEO*
Michael Bozick, *President*
Darrell Billings, *CFO*
Tim Graven, *CFO*
Bobbie Bozick, *Exec VP*
▲ **EMP:** 60
SQ FT: 40,000
SALES (est): 13.7MM Privately Held
WEB: www.bagdasarianinc.com
SIC: 0172 0174 Grapes; citrus fruits

(P-178)
RICHARDS GROVE SARALEES VINYRD
1998 Jones Rd, Windsor (95492-7758)
PHONE.....................707 837-9200
EMP: 65
SQ FT: 10,333
SALES (est): 1.7MM Privately Held
WEB: www.saraleesvineyards.com
SIC: 0172

(P-179)
RIOS FARMING COMPANY LLC
3851 Chiles Pope Vly Rd, Saint Helena (94574-9588)
PHONE.....................707 965-2587
Fax: 707 965-9354
Manuel Rios,
Shelia Rios, *Manager*
EMP: 140
SQ FT: 1,500
SALES (est): 6.1MM Privately Held
SIC: 0172 0762 Grapes; vineyard management & maintenance services

(P-180)
ROBERT ALVES FARMS INC
Also Called: Alves, Robert L
10642 E Dinuba Ave, Selma (93662-9783)
PHONE.....................559 896-3309
Fax: 559 896-2401
Robert Alves, *Owner*
Rita Garza, *Bookkeeper*
EMP: 70
SALES (est): 3.6MM Privately Held
SIC: 0172 Grapes

(P-181)
RON D & SHELLEY N HORN
3719 E Floral Ave, Fresno (93725-9651)
PHONE.....................559 834-2118
Ronald Horn, *Owner*
EMP: 50
SALES (est): 877.1K Privately Held
SIC: 0172 Grapes

(P-182)
SAN BERNABE VINEYARDS
53001 Oasis Rd, King City (93930-9667)
PHONE.....................831 385-4897
Fax: 831 385-0667
Claude Hoover, *President*
Dorothy Indelicato, *Treasurer*
Frank Indelicato, *Admin Sec*
Don Allen, *Controller*
EMP: 65
SQ FT: 15,000
SALES: 4.5MM
SALES (corp-wide): 46.5MM Privately Held
WEB: www.winequest.com
SIC: 0172 2084 Grapes; wines; brandy & brandy spirits
PA: Delicato Vineyards
12001 S Highway 99
Manteca CA 95336
209 824-3600

(P-183)
SANDRINI FARMS
29794 Schuster Rd, Mc Farland (93250-9784)
PHONE.....................661 792-3192
Mae Sandrini, *Owner*
EMP: 60
SALES (est): 1MM Privately Held
SIC: 0172 Grapes

(P-184)
SCHEID VINEYARDS CAL INC
305 Hilltown Rd, Salinas (93908-8902)
PHONE.....................831 385-4801
Fax: 831 385-0136
Kurt Gollnick, *Branch Mgr*
Bob Piotrowski, *Regional Mgr*
Jose Rosales, *Prdtn Mgr*
Pete Garibay, *Maintence Staff*
Shawn Veysey, *Director*
EMP: 90
SALES (corp-wide): 57.9MM Publicly Held
WEB: www.scheidvineyards.com
SIC: 0172 5813 Grapes; drinking places
HQ: Scheid Vineyards California Inc.
305 Hilltown Rd
Salinas CA 93908
831 455-9990

(P-185)
SCHEID VINEYARDS INC
1201 Morningside Dr Ste 1, Manhattan Beach (90266-4763)
PHONE.....................310 545-4757
Kurt Gollnick, *COO*
EMP: 105
SALES (corp-wide): 57.9MM Publicly Held
SIC: 0172 Grapes
PA: Scheid Vineyards Inc.
305 Hilltown Rd
Salinas CA 93908
310 301-1555

(P-186)
SCHEID VINEYARDS INC (PA)
305 Hilltown Rd, Salinas (93908-8902)
PHONE.....................310 301-1555
Fax: 831 455-9998
Scott D Scheid, *President*
Alfred G Scheid, *Ch of Bd*
Kurt J Gollnick, *COO*
Michael S Thomsen, *CFO*
Heidi M Scheid, *Treasurer*
EMP: 65
SQ FT: 6,700
SALES (est): 57.9MM Publicly Held
SIC: 0172 2084 Grapes; wines

(P-187)
SCHEID VINEYARDS INC
373 Healdsburg Ave, Healdsburg (95448-4137)
PHONE.....................707 433-1858
Cameron Lyeth, *Branch Mgr*
EMP: 108
SALES (corp-wide): 57.9MM Publicly Held
SIC: 0172 Grapes
PA: Scheid Vineyards Inc.
305 Hilltown Rd
Salinas CA 93908
310 301-1555

(P-188)
SCHRAMSBERG VINEYARDS COMPANY
1400 Schramsberg Rd, Calistoga (94515-9624)
PHONE.....................707 942-4558
Fax: 707 942-4336
Hugh Davies, *President*
Jack Bittner, *Bd of Directors*
William P Davies, *Bd of Directors*
Matthew Levy, *Executive*
Roslyn Ewing, *Social Dir*
▲ **EMP:** 50
SQ FT: 20,000
SALES (est): 6.4MM Privately Held
WEB: www.schramsberg.com
SIC: 0172 Grapes

PRODUCTS & SERVICES SECTION
0174 - Citrus Fruits County (P-213)

(P-189)
STAGECOACH VINEYARDS
1345 Hestia Way, NAPA (94558-2105)
PHONE..............................707 255-5459
Fax: 707 259-1198
Jan Krupp, *Partner*
Joshua Syrah,
▲ EMP: 100
SALES (est): 6.7MM Privately Held
WEB: www.stagecoachvineyard.com
SIC: 0172 Grapes

(P-190)
TREASURY WINE ESTATES AMERICAS
Also Called: Meridian Vineyards
7000 E Highway 46, Paso Robles (93446-7390)
PHONE..............................805 237-6000
Fax: 805 239-5715
Jim Schaefer, *Manager*
Lisa Kruse, *Vice Pres*
Steve Chase, *Analyst*
Jim Lunt, *Plant Mgr*
Pamela Haste, *Director*
EMP: 120
SALES (corp-wide): 1.7B Privately Held
WEB: www.stclement.com
SIC: 0172 2084 Grapes; wines, brandy & brandy spirits
HQ: Treasury Wine Estates Americas Company
555 Gateway Dr
Napa CA 94558
707 259-4500

(P-191)
V SANGIACOMO & SONS
Also Called: Sangiacomo Vineyards
21543 Broadway, Sonoma (95476-8205)
PHONE..............................707 938-5503
Fax: 707 938-0739
Victor F Sangiacomo, *Partner*
Angelo C Sangiacomo, *Partner*
Lorraine J Sangiacomo, *Partner*
EMP: 180
SQ FT: 1,200
SALES (est): 13MM Privately Held
WEB: www.sangiacomo-vineyards.com
SIC: 0172 Grapes

(P-192)
VINCENT B ZANINOVICH SONS INC
Also Called: V B Z
20715 Ave 8, Richgrove (93261)
PHONE..............................661 720-9031
John V Zaninovich, *CEO*
Vincent Zaninovich, *President*
Andrew Zaninovich, *Vice Pres*
Tom Nguyen, *Technology*
▼ EMP: 200
SQ FT: 15,450
SALES (est): 15MM Privately Held
SIC: 0172 Grapes

(P-193)
VINCENT V ZANINOVICH & SONS
2480 E Washington St, Earlimart (93219-9694)
PHONE..............................661 849-2613
INA Zaninovich, *Partner*
Estate of Vincent V Zaninovich, *Partner*
EMP: 99
SALES (est): 3.5MM Privately Held
SIC: 0172 0139 0131 Grapes; alfalfa farm; cotton

0173 Tree Nuts

(P-194)
AGRESERVES INC
Also Called: Deseret Farms of California
6100 Wilson Landing Rd, Chico (95973-8902)
PHONE..............................530 343-5365
Fax: 530 891-8037
Travis Reid, *Branch Mgr*
EMP: 75

SALES (corp-wide): 169.1MM Privately Held
WEB: www.dlandi.com
SIC: 0173 0175 Almond grove; walnut grove; prune orchard
HQ: Agreserves, Inc.
79 S Main St Ste 1100
Salt Lake City UT 84111
801 715-9100

(P-195)
CANDOR-AGS INC (PA)
9491 N Fort Washington Rd # 102, Fresno (93730-0660)
PHONE..............................559 439-2365
David Brian Mahaffy, *CEO*
EMP: 52
SALES (est): 61.2MM Privately Held
SIC: 0173 Tree nuts

(P-196)
CHARANJIT SINGH BATTH
Also Called: Batth Farms
5434 W Kamm Ave, Caruthers (93609-9400)
PHONE..............................559 864-9421
Fax: 559 864-9421
Charanjit Singh Batth, *Owner*
EMP: 90
SQ FT: 1,200
SALES (est): 6MM Privately Held
SIC: 0173 0175 0172 2034 Almond grove; prune orchard; grapes; raisins

(P-197)
DE BENEDETTO FARMS INC
Also Called: D'Best Produce
1547 N Marks Ave, Fresno (93722-5723)
P.O. Box 9760 (93794-9760)
PHONE..............................559 276-2400
Maurice De Benedetto, *President*
Mark De Benedetto, *Shareholder*
Mathew De Benedetto, *Shareholder*
Maury De Benedetto, *Shareholder*
Maurice Debenedetto, *Agent*
EMP: 80
SQ FT: 2,000
SALES (est): 4.1MM Privately Held
SIC: 0173 Pecan grove; almond grove

(P-198)
DOUGLAS & JAYNE STARN
6621 Blue Gum Rd, Hughson (95326-9684)
PHONE..............................209 883-4886
Douglas Starn, *Partner*
Jayne Starn, *Partner*
EMP: 53
SALES (est): 1.1MM Privately Held
SIC: 0173 Almond grove

(P-199)
ED THOMING & SONS INC
33600 S Koster Rd, Tracy (95304-8996)
PHONE..............................209 835-2792
John Thoming, *President*
James L Thoming, *Vice Pres*
EMP: 100
SQ FT: 800
SALES (est): 4.4MM Privately Held
SIC: 0173 0175 Almond grove; deciduous tree fruits

(P-200)
FARMERS INTERNATIONAL INC
1260 Muir Ave, Chico (95973-8644)
PHONE..............................530 566-1405
Fax: 530 566-1408
Don Wada, *CEO*
Mohnish Seth, *Principal*
Chad Bales, *Accounting Mgr*
▼ EMP: 50
SALES (est): 9.3MM Privately Held
WEB: www.farmersinternational.com
SIC: 0173 Almond grove

(P-201)
FRAZIER NUT FARMS INC
10830 Yosemite Blvd, Waterford (95386-9637)
PHONE..............................209 522-1406
Fax: 209 874-9638
Jim Frazier Jr, *President*
Heidi Frazier-Slacks, *Corp Secy*
Steve Slacks, *Vice Pres*
▼ EMP: 50

SALES (est): 4.8MM Privately Held
SIC: 0173 Walnut grove

(P-202)
INTERNATIONAL ALMOND EXCHANGE
144 W Lake Ave, Watsonville (95076-4573)
PHONE..............................831 728-4534
Jagjit Tut, *CEO*
Rajveer Tut, *Vice Pres*
▼ EMP: 50
SQ FT: 653,400
SALES: 1MM Privately Held
SIC: 0173 Almond grove

(P-203)
KEENAN FARMS INC
31510 Plymouth Ave, Kettleman City (93239-9721)
P.O. Box 99, Avenal (93204-0099)
PHONE..............................559 945-1400
Fax: 559 945-1414
Robert M Keenan, *CEO*
Manny Guerrero, *Vice Pres*
Charles J Keenan III, *Vice Pres*
Catherine Underwood, *Office Mgr*
Bob Keenan, *Info Tech Mgr*
◆ EMP: 100
SALES (est): 23.2MM Privately Held
SIC: 0173 2068 Pistachio grove; nuts: dried, dehydrated, salted or roasted

(P-204)
MARIANI NUT COMPANY INC (PA)
709 Dutton St, Winters (95694-1748)
P.O. Box 809 (95694-0809)
PHONE..............................530 795-3311
Fax: 530 795-2681
Jack Norman Marlani, *CEO*
Martin Mariani, *Treasurer*
Dennis Mariani, *Vice Pres*
Cori Smith, *Accounting Mgr*
Marty Mariani, *CPA*
◆ EMP: 110
SQ FT: 30,000
SALES (est): 48.3MM Privately Held
WEB: www.marianinut.com
SIC: 0173 Walnut grove; almond grove

(P-205)
MARIANI NUT COMPANY INC
1709 Deutton, Winters (95694)
P.O. Box 809 (95694-0809)
PHONE..............................530 795-1272
Jack McDowel, *Director*
EMP: 100
SALES (corp-wide): 48.3MM Privately Held
WEB: www.marianinut.com
SIC: 0173 Walnut grove
PA: Mariani Nut Company, Inc.
709 Dutton St
Winters CA 95694
530 795-3311

(P-206)
MARIANI NUT COMPANY INC
12 Baker St, Winters (95694-1704)
P.O. Box 808 (95694-0808)
PHONE..............................530 795-2225
Jef McDowell, *Manager*
EMP: 70
SALES (corp-wide): 48.3MM Privately Held
WEB: www.marianinut.com
SIC: 0173 Walnut grove
PA: Mariani Nut Company, Inc.
709 Dutton St
Winters CA 95694
530 795-3311

(P-207)
MARTINI INC
Also Called: R Marchini' Enterprises
12006 Le Grand Rd, Le Grand (95333-9708)
PHONE..............................209 389-4566
Fax: 209 389-4084
Richard Marchini, *President*
Judy Marchini, *Treasurer*
EMP: 50
SQ FT: 1,200
SALES (est): 3.1MM Privately Held
SIC: 0173 0191 Almond grove; general farms, primarily crop

(P-208)
RAMOS ORCHARDS
9192 Boyce Rd, Winters (95694-9625)
P.O. Box 488 (95694-0488)
PHONE..............................530 795-4748
Fax: 530 795-4148
Fred Ramos, *Owner*
EMP: 67
SQ FT: 9,600
SALES (est): 3.5MM Privately Held
SIC: 0173 0175 Walnut grove; prune orchard

(P-209)
RICHARD SWANSON INC
17659 Swanson Rd, Delhi (95315-9636)
P.O. Box 244 (95315-0244)
PHONE..............................209 632-3883
Timothy Swanson, *President*
Erline Swanson, *Treasurer*
Richard Swanson, *Vice Pres*
EMP: 60
SALES (est): 1.5MM Privately Held
SIC: 0173 0175 0252 Almond grove; peach orchard; chicken eggs

(P-210)
WONDERFUL ORCHARDS LLC (PA)
Also Called: Paramount Farming
6801 E Lerdo Hwy, Shafter (93263-9610)
PHONE..............................661 399-4456
Fax: 661 399-1735
Craig Cooper,
Elaine Tensley, *Office Mgr*
Paula Opperman, *Admin Asst*
Thomas Champieux, *Technician*
Andy Bayless, *Project Mgr*
▲ EMP: 150
SQ FT: 10,000
SALES (est): 144.6MM Privately Held
SIC: 0173 0179 Almond grove; olive grove

(P-211)
WONDERFUL ORCHARDS LLC
Also Called: Wonderfulpistachiosandalmonds
13646 Highway 33, Lost Hills (93249-9719)
P.O. Box 400 (93249-0400)
PHONE..............................661 797-6400
Fax: 661 392-6519
Dennis Elam, *Branch Mgr*
Mike Doiron, *Prdtn Mgr*
EMP: 150
SALES (corp-wide): 144.6MM Privately Held
SIC: 0173 0191 Almond grove; general farms, primarily crop
PA: Wonderful Orchards Llc
6801 E Lerdo Hwy
Shafter CA 93263
661 399-4456

0174 Citrus Fruits

(P-212)
ACEMI NURSERY INC
3626 N Howard Ave, Kerman (93630-9619)
PHONE..............................559 842-7766
Alvaro Garcia, *President*
Carmen Garcia, *Vice Pres*
EMP: 80
SALES: 5MM Privately Held
SIC: 0174 Citrus fruits

(P-213)
AIRDROME ORCHARDS INC (PA)
610 E Gish Rd, San Jose (95112-2792)
PHONE..............................408 297-6461
Fax: 408 297-2504
Charles Fumia, *CEO*
John Fumia Jr, *CFO*
Anthony Buldo, *Vice Pres*
Paul Buldo, *Vice Pres*
Tony Buldo, *Vice Pres*
▼ EMP: 50
SQ FT: 30,000
SALES (est): 9.2MM Privately Held
SIC: 0174 0175 Orange grove; pear orchard

0174 - Citrus Fruits County (P-214)

(P-214)
BADGER FARMING COMPANY INC
150 W Pine St, Exeter (93221-1613)
PHONE..............................559 592-5520
Fax: 559 592-2042
Oleah Wilson, *President*
James Wilson, *President*
Richard Pescosolido, *Agent*
EMP: 60
SALES (est): 2.6MM **Privately Held**
SIC: 0174 Citrus fruits

(P-215)
BERESFORD CORP
582 Market St Ste 912, San Francisco (94104-5310)
PHONE..............................415 981-7386
Christopher D Lange, *President*
EMP: 145
SALES (est): 8.3MM **Privately Held**
SIC: 0174 Citrus fruits

(P-216)
CALIFORNIA CITRUS COOPERATIVE
859 Center St, Riverside (92507-1408)
PHONE..............................951 683-4045
Larry Topham, *Manager*
Jim Guthrie, *Sales Staff*
Allen Washburn, *Manager*
EMP: 65
SQ FT: 2,000
SALES (est): 5.5MM **Privately Held**
SIC: 0174 Grapefruit grove; orange grove

(P-217)
GRIFFITH FARMS
504 N Kaweah Ave, Exeter (93221-1200)
PHONE..............................559 592-1009
Fax: 559 592-2364
Dennis Griffith, *Partner*
Roger Smith, *Info Tech Dir*
Deborah McGrew, *Manager*
Dave Tomlinson, *Manager*
EMP: 60
SQ FT: 1,800
SALES (est): 4.7MM **Privately Held**
WEB: www.griffithfarms.com
SIC: 0174 Citrus fruits

(P-218)
HAMILTON FAMILY RANCH
2562 Doville Ranch Rd, Fallbrook (92028-9138)
PHONE..............................760 728-1358
Dorothy Hamilton, *Partner*
Alexander Hamilton, *Partner*
Meade Hamilton, *Partner*
Michelle Hamilton, *Partner*
EMP: 70
SALES (est): 1MM **Privately Held**
SIC: 0174 Lemon grove

(P-219)
HRONIS INC A CALIFORNIA CORP (PA)
10443 Hronis Rd, Delano (93215-9556)
PHONE..............................661 725-2503
Kosta Hronis, *President*
Pete Hronis, *Vice Pres*
Shelley Molica, *Office Mgr*
Ruben Galaviz, *Manager*
▼ EMP: 64
SQ FT: 150,000
SALES (est): 42.6MM **Privately Held**
WEB: www.hronis.net
SIC: 0174 0172 Citrus fruits; grapes

(P-220)
MARLAND CO LP
444 S Flower St Ste 1200, Los Angeles (90071-2977)
PHONE..............................213 614-6171
Chirstopher Martin, *Partner*
Oliver Santos, *Admin Sec*
EMP: 50
SQ FT: 200
SALES (est): 843.4K **Privately Held**
SIC: 0174 Orange grove

(P-221)
PADILLA FARM LABOR INC
20486 Road 196, Lindsay (93247-9426)
PHONE..............................559 562-1166
David Padilla, *President*
Rosie Padilla, *Corp Secy*
EMP: 200
SALES (est): 6.4MM **Privately Held**
SIC: 0174 Orange grove

(P-222)
S SURABIAN & SONS
225 W Tulare St, Dinuba (93618-2630)
P.O. Box 7 (93618-0007)
PHONE..............................559 591-5215
Fax: 559 591-7675
Albert Surabian, *Owner*
Mike Flora, *Manager*
EMP: 120
SQ FT: 15,000
SALES: 460K **Privately Held**
SIC: 0174 Citrus fruits

(P-223)
SATICOY LEMON ASSOCIATION
Also Called: Saticoy Fruit Exchange
7560 Bristol Rd, Ventura (93003-7027)
P.O. Box 46, Santa Paula (93061-0046)
PHONE..............................805 654-6500
John Elliott, *Branch Mgr*
EMP: 100
SALES (corp-wide): 155.7MM **Privately Held**
SIC: 0174 Lemon grove
PA: Saticoy Lemon Association
103 N Peck Rd
Santa Paula CA 93060
805 654-6500

(P-224)
WONDERFUL CITRUS PACKING LLC
Also Called: Fillmore Farm Management
2707 W Telegraph Rd, Fillmore (93015-9647)
PHONE..............................805 525-3818
EMP: 100
SALES (corp-wide): 2.1B **Privately Held**
WEB: www.paramountcitrus.com
SIC: 0174 Citrus fruits
HQ: Wonderful Citrus Packing Llc
1901 S Lexington St
Delano CA 93215
661 720-2400

(P-225)
WONDERFUL COMPANY LLC
Also Called: Paramount Citrus
1901 S Lexington St, Delano (93215-9207)
PHONE..............................661 720-2400
Fax: 661 720-2502
Freddie Hernandez, *Manager*
Etienne Rabe, *Vice Pres*
Julia Carabajal, *Admin Asst*
Molly Villarreal, *Admin Asst*
Matthew Mitchell, *Network Enginr*
EMP: 273
SALES (corp-wide): 2.1B **Privately Held**
SIC: 0174 3911 Citrus fruits; jewelry, precious metal
PA: The Wonderful Company Llc
11444 W Olympic Blvd # 210
Los Angeles CA 90064
310 966-5700

(P-226)
YOUNG DOWLIN L
Also Called: Young's Nursery
101 Clay St, San Francisco (94111-2033)
PHONE..............................760 397-4104
Fax: 760 397-4514
Dowlin L Young, *Owner*
Daisy Young, *Co-Owner*
EMP: 50
SQ FT: 1,000
SALES: 2.5MM **Privately Held**
SIC: 0174 Citrus fruits

0175 Deciduous Tree Fruits

(P-227)
ANTHONY BOTELHO
382 Olympia Ave, San Juan Bautista (95045-9501)
PHONE..............................831 623-4228
Anthony Botelho, *Owner*
EMP: 60 EST: 1998
SALES (est): 1.2MM **Privately Held**
WEB: www.botelhoforsupervisor.com
SIC: 0175 Apple orchard

(P-228)
ASHLEY LANE CHERRY ORCHARDS LP
500 N Jack Tone Rd, Stockton (95215-9725)
P.O. Box 659, Linden (95236-0659)
PHONE..............................209 546-0426
Henry J Foppiano, *Partner*
Diane Lechich, *Administration*
EMP: 50 EST: 2014
SALES (est): 1.7MM **Privately Held**
SIC: 0175 Cherry orchard

(P-229)
BT HOLDINGS INC
Also Called: Quercus Ranch
4150 Soda Bay Rd, Kelseyville (95451)
P.O. Box 548 (95451-0548)
PHONE..............................707 279-4317
Mark Navone, *Owner*
David Weiss, *President*
EMP: 50 EST: 1979
SQ FT: 120,000
SALES (est): 500K **Privately Held**
SIC: 0175 0172 Pear orchard; grapes

(P-230)
CLARENCE UNRUH FARMS INC
14242 S Mccall Ave, Selma (93662-9472)
P.O. Box 308, Kingsburg (93631-0308)
PHONE..............................559 896-9499
Clarence Unruh, *Owner*
Mary-Jo Unruh, *Co-Owner*
EMP: 100
SALES: 3MM **Privately Held**
SIC: 0175 0172 0173 Nectarine orchard; plum orchard; grapes; plantain grove

(P-231)
DENIZ PACKING INCORPORATED
21801 Avenue 16, Madera (93637-8608)
PHONE..............................559 673-0066
Fax: 559 673-1359
Johnny Deniz, *President*
Karen Helton, *Treasurer*
Brian Deniz, *Vice Pres*
Johnny A Deniz, *Office Mgr*
Cindy Schafer, *Admin Sec*
EMP: 50
SQ FT: 2,000
SALES: 3MM **Privately Held**
SIC: 0175 0172 0723 0173 Peach orchard; plum orchard; nectarine orchard; grapes; fruit (fresh) packing services; almond grove

(P-232)
ENNS PACKING COMPANY INC
Also Called: Enns Farms
1911 Bergren Ct, Kingsburg (93631-2705)
PHONE..............................559 897-7700
Melvin Enns, *President*
Kenneth Enns, *Treasurer*
Eugene Enns, *Principal*
Mike Enns, *Admin Sec*
James Stewart, *Manager*
EMP: 50
SQ FT: 4,200
SALES: 36.9K **Privately Held**
SIC: 0175 4222 0723 Deciduous tree fruits; storage, frozen or refrigerated goods; fruit (fresh) packing services

(P-233)
FARMINGTON FRESH SALES LLC (PA)
7735 S Highway 99, Stockton (95215-9623)
P.O. Box 30667 (95213-0667)
PHONE..............................209 983-9700
Fax: 209 983-1825
Ernie Pascua, *CEO*
Natalie Hamilton, *Accountant*
Gary Goodrich, *Controller*
Joel Harris, *Opers Staff*
Garrett Rajkovich, *
EMP: 69
SQ FT: 132,000
SALES: 25.8MM **Privately Held**
WEB: www.farmingtonfresh.com
SIC: 0175 4731 Apple orchard; pear orchard; agents, shipping

(P-234)
HAMLOW RANCHES INC
4018 Swanson Rd, Denair (95316-9733)
P.O. Box 898 (95316-0898)
PHONE..............................209 632-2873
Karen Hamlow, *CEO*
EMP: 50 EST: 1951
SALES (est): 1.5MM **Privately Held**
SIC: 0175 0173 Peach orchard; almond grove

(P-235)
HB ORCHARDS CO INC
9909 State Highway 70, Marysville (95901-9413)
P.O. Box 5370 (95901-8531)
PHONE..............................530 743-5121
George Hatamiya, *President*
Roy Hatamiya, *Treasurer*
Robert Hatamiya, *Admin Sec*
EMP: 61
SALES (est): 1.8MM **Privately Held**
SIC: 0175 0173 Peach orchard; prune orchard; almond grove; walnut grove

(P-236)
HILDRETH FARM INCORPORATED
1520 Rddick Cunningham Rd, Ukiah (95482-9638)
PHONE..............................707 462-0648
Michael L Hildreth, *President*
Susan Hildreth, *Vice Pres*
EMP: 56
SALES (est): 2.3MM **Privately Held**
SIC: 0175 0172 Pear orchard; grapes

(P-237)
J & P SOLARI
6302 Foppiano Ln, Stockton (95212-9407)
PHONE..............................209 931-1765
Joe S Solari, *Partner*
Joseph Solari I I I, *Partner*
Phillip Solari, *Partner*
Raymond Solari, *Partner*
EMP: 100
SALES (est): 1.2MM **Privately Held**
SIC: 0175 0173 0811 Cherry orchard; walnut grove; almond grove; timber tracts

(P-238)
JEFF W BOLDT FARMS
Also Called: Jeff Boldt Farms
12725 S Smith Ave, Kingsburg (93631-9719)
PHONE..............................559 897-0859
Jeff Boldt, *President*
Brenda Boldt, *CEO*
Tamara Boldt, *Director*
Taylor Boldt, *Director*
EMP: 74
SALES: 1.2MM **Privately Held**
SIC: 0175 Deciduous tree fruits

(P-239)
KINGSBURG APPLE PARTNERS LP
10363 Davis Ave, Kingsburg (93631-9539)
P.O. Box 456 (93631-0456)
PHONE..............................559 897-5132
Colleen Jackson, *Ltd Ptnr*
Susan Jackson Diepersloot, *Ltd Ptnr*
Brent Jackson, *Ltd Ptnr*
Becky Stark, *Controller*
▼ EMP: 100
SQ FT: 140,000
SALES (est): 6.4MM **Privately Held**
WEB: www.kingsburgorchards.com
SIC: 0175 Apple orchard; pear orchard

(P-240)
KOZUKI FARMING INC
16518 E Adams Ave, Parlier (93648-9718)
PHONE..............................559 646-2652
EMP: 60
SALES: 2.2MM **Privately Held**
SIC: 0175 0172

PRODUCTS & SERVICES SECTION **0181 - Ornamental Floriculture & Nursery Prdts County (P-264)**

(P-241)
MALLOY ORCHARDS INC
925 Koch Ln, Live Oak (95953-9602)
PHONE..................530 695-1861
Fax: 530 695-3428
William A Filter Jr, *President*
EMP: 200
SALES (est): 4.1MM **Privately Held**
SIC: 0175 0173 0761 Peach orchard; prune orchard; walnut grove; farm labor contractors

(P-242)
MICHELI FARMS INC
6005 Highway 99, Live Oak (95953-9749)
PHONE..................530 695-9022
John Micheli, *President*
Justin Micheli, *Admin Sec*
Janette Coprider, *Manager*
EMP: 50
SQ FT: 108,000
SALES (est): 2.4MM **Privately Held**
WEB: www.lomocold.com
SIC: 0175 0173 Peach orchard; prune orchard; walnut grove

(P-243)
MIKE JENSEN FARMS
13138 S Bethel Ave, Kingsburg (93631-9216)
PHONE..................559 897-4192
Fax: 559 897-1305
Mike Jensen, *Owner*
Charlie Brandt, *General Mgr*
EMP: 200
SQ FT: 14,000
SALES (est): 6.3MM **Privately Held**
SIC: 0175 2033 2099 Apricot orchard; nectarine orchard; peach orchard; plum orchard; fruits: packaged in cans, jars, etc.; food preparations

(P-244)
MONTPELIER ORCHARDS MGT CO INC
Montpelier Nut Company
4931 S Montpelier Rd, Denair (95316-9663)
PHONE..................209 883-4079
Fax: 209 874-5129
Lupe Dalvinos, *Manager*
EMP: 50
SALES (corp-wide): 8.2MM **Privately Held**
SIC: 0175 Deciduous tree fruits
PA: Montpelier Orchards Management Company, Inc.
1131 12th St
Modesto CA 95354
209 577-2804

(P-245)
NISSHO OF CALIFORNIA INC
89055 64th Ave, Thermal (92274-9607)
PHONE..................760 727-9719
Abel Bustamante, *Manager*
Walter May, *Manager*
EMP: 373
SALES (corp-wide): 73MM **Privately Held**
SIC: 0175 Deciduous tree fruits
PA: Nissho Of California, Inc.
1902 S Santa Fe Ave
Vista CA 92083
760 727-9719

(P-246)
NTY FRANCHISE COMPANY LLC
18645 Brookhurst St, Fountain Valley (92708-6709)
PHONE..................714 964-3488
EMP: 75
SALES (corp-wide): 30.7MM **Privately Held**
SIC: 0175 Deciduous tree fruits
PA: Nty Franchise Company, Llc
4350 Baker Rd Ste 350
Minnetonka MN 55343
952 923-1223

(P-247)
PETERSON FAMILY INC
38694 Road 16, Kingsburg (93631-9106)
PHONE..................559 897-5064
Vernon E Peterson, *Owner*
EMP: 100
SALES (est): 5.4MM **Privately Held**
WEB: www.peterson.org
SIC: 0175 0174 Deciduous tree fruits; citrus fruits

(P-248)
PHILLIPS FARMS
33771 Road 156, Visalia (93292-9153)
PHONE..................559 798-1871
Fax: 559 798-0594
Douglas Phillips, *Owner*
Bobby Chavez, *Finance Mgr*
EMP: 50
SALES (est): 3.9MM **Privately Held**
SIC: 0175 0723 Deciduous tree fruits; fruit (fresh) packing services

(P-249)
SCHEU MANUFACTURING CO
Also Called: National Riverside Co
8855 Baker Ave, Rancho Cucamonga (91730-5042)
P.O. Box 250, Upland (91785-0250)
PHONE..................909 981-5343
Fax: 909 982-2851
Paul Biallas, *Manager*
Phil Chiazza, *Controller*
EMP: 80
SALES (corp-wide): 7.5MM **Privately Held**
SIC: 0175 3567 4225 3634 Deciduous tree fruits; heating units & devices, industrial: electric; general warehousing & storage; electric housewares & fans; refrigeration & heating equipment; heating equipment, except electric
PA: Scheu Manufacturing Co.
297 Stowell St
Upland CA 91786
909 982-8933

(P-250)
SMITH RANCH
1671 Campbell Rd, Live Oak (95953-9707)
PHONE..................530 695-2521
Dale Smith, *Partner*
Dean Smith, *Partner*
Gail Hebert, *Principal*
EMP: 50
SALES (est): 3.2MM **Privately Held**
SIC: 0175 0173 Peach orchard; prune orchard; walnut grove

(P-251)
VIRGINIA SARABIAN
Also Called: Sarabian Farms
2816 S Leonard Ave, Sanger (93657-9754)
PHONE..................559 493-2900
Fax: 559 493-2909
Michael Sarabian, *Owner*
Sarkis Sarabian, *Owner*
Virginia Sarabian, *Owner*
Maddie Alcazar, *COO*
Michelle Novella, *COO*
EMP: 50
SQ FT: 1,200
SALES: 15MM **Privately Held**
SIC: 0175 0172 4222 2033 Nectarine orchard; peach orchard; plum orchard; grapes; warehousing, cold storage or refrigerated; fruits: packaged in cans, jars, etc

0179 Fruits & Tree Nuts, NEC

(P-252)
AGRILAND HOLDING INC
23400 Road 24, Chowchilla (93610-9558)
PHONE..................559 665-2100
James Maxwell, *President*
Sandra Bain, *Admin Sec*
Jarl Hansen, *Manager*
Charles Lowe, *Manager*
EMP: 85
SQ FT: 7,500
SALES (est): 2.9MM **Privately Held**
SIC: 0179 0173 Fig orchard; tree nuts

(P-253)
CHIQUITA FRESH NORTH AMER LLC
1440 E 3rd St, Oxnard (93030-6106)
PHONE..................954 924-5642
Junior Cutrale, *Mng Member*
EMP: 300
SQ FT: 1,500
SALES (est): 50MM **Privately Held**
SIC: 0179 Banana grove

(P-254)
DOLE FOOD COMPANY INC (HQ)
1 Dole Dr, Westlake Village (91362-7300)
PHONE..................818 874-4000
Fax: 818 879-6650
David H Murdock, *Ch of Bd*
Johan Linden, *President*
Johan Malmqvist, *CFO*
Roberta Wieman, *Exec VP*
Yoon J Hugh, *Senior VP*
◆ EMP: 188
SALES (est): 1.1B
SALES (corp-wide): 10B **Privately Held**
WEB: www.dole.com
SIC: 0175 0174 0175 0161 Pineapple farm; banana grove; citrus fruits; deciduous tree fruits; lettuce farm; celery farm; cauliflower farm; broccoli farm; fruits; vegetables; fruit juices: fresh; fruit juices: packaged in cans, jars, etc.
PA: Dfc Holdings, Llc
1 Dole Dr
Westlake Village CA 91362
818 879-6600

(P-255)
DOLE HOLDING COMPANY LLC
1 Dole Dr, Westlake Village (91362-7300)
PHONE..................818 879-6600
David H Murdock, *Ch of Bd*
EMP: 74999
SALES: 57.6MM
SALES (corp-wide): 521.8MM **Privately Held**
SIC: 0179 0174 0175 0161 Pineapple farm; banana grove; citrus fruits; deciduous tree fruits; lettuce farm; celery farm; cauliflower farm; broccoli farm; fruits; vegetables; fruit juices: fresh; fruit juices: packaged in cans, jars, etc.
PA: Dhm Holding Company, Inc
1 Dole Dr
Westlake Village CA 91362
818 879-6600

(P-256)
HENRY AVOCADO CORPORATION (PA)
2355 E Lincoln Ave, Escondido (92027-1298)
P.O. Box 300867 (92030-0867)
PHONE..................760 745-6632
Fax: 760 745-5043
Philip Henry, *President*
Jerry Miller, *CFO*
Betty Guerrero, *Vice Pres*
Rick Opel, *Vice Pres*
Lori Deaver, *Office Mgr*
▲ EMP: 70
SQ FT: 35,000
SALES: 180.2MM **Privately Held**
SIC: 0179 4213 Avocado orchard; trucking, except local

(P-257)
IRVINE VALENCIA GROWERS
11501 Jeffrey Rd, Irvine (92602-0503)
PHONE..................949 936-8000
Peter Changala, *President*
Brian Thompson, *Treasurer*
EMP: 75
SQ FT: 10,000
SALES (est): 2.9MM **Privately Held**
SIC: 0179 0723 Avocado orchard; fruit (fresh) packing services

(P-258)
MUNGER BROS LLC
Also Called: Munger Farm
786 Road 188, Delano (93215-9508)
PHONE..................661 721-0390
Baldev K Munger,
Kewel K Munger,
Leslie Jiles, *Manager*
EMP: 600
SQ FT: 50,000
SALES: 10MM **Privately Held**
SIC: 0179 Avocado orchard

(P-259)
ROYAL MEDJOOL DATE GARDEN
1203 Perez Rd, Bard (92222)
P.O. Box 930 (92222-0930)
PHONE..................760 572-0524
Fax: 760 572-2292
Stephen P Shadle, *Partner*
Ida Choules, *Partner*
David Nelson, *General Mgr*
EMP: 75
SQ FT: 8,000
SALES (est): 1.5MM **Privately Held**
WEB: www.royaldates.com
SIC: 0179 8611 Avocado orchard; business associations

(P-260)
SUN GARDEN DATE GROWERS LP
1455 Hagberg Rd, Bard (92222)
P.O. Box 190 (92222-0190)
PHONE..................760 957-0396
Fax: 760 572-0577
Glenn Mc Collum, *Partner*
Jack Thein, *Partner*
EMP: 50
SALES (est): 1.4MM **Privately Held**
SIC: 0179 Date orchard

(P-261)
SUNDANCE NATURAL FOODS COMPANY
2231 Willowbrook Dr, Oceanside (92056-2506)
P.O. Box 5358 (92052-5358)
PHONE..................760 945-9898
Fax: 760 945-9899
K Jacob Hoffnagle, *CEO*
Mary Hahlbohm, *Treasurer*
Maya Schultze, *Executive*
EMP: 50
SQ FT: 40,000
SALES (est): 6.6MM **Privately Held**
WEB: www.sundancenaturalfoodscompany.com
SIC: 0179 0723 Avocado orchard; fruit (fresh) packing services

(P-262)
WILLIAM C ARTERBERRY
40147 Calle Roxanne, Fallbrook (92028-9701)
PHONE..................760 728-9096
William Arterberry, *Owner*
Lana Dominguez, *Office Mgr*
EMP: 62
SALES (est): 1.1MM **Privately Held**
SIC: 0179 Avocado orchard

0181 Ornamental Floriculture & Nursery Prdts

(P-263)
3-WAY FARMS (PA)
428 Browns Valley Rd, Watsonville (95076-0330)
PHONE..................831 722-0748
Fax: 831 722-8977
Delbert Herschbach, *President*
Lorraine Stern, *Treasurer*
Rosemarie Herschbach, *Admin Sec*
EMP: 50
SALES (est): 3.8MM **Privately Held**
SIC: 0181 3999 Ornamental nursery products; flowers, artificial & preserved

(P-264)
AZALEA & ROSE CO
1420 N Campus Ave, Upland (91786-2317)
PHONE..................909 949-2442
Mike Tolle, *President*
EMP: 50
SALES (est): 751.9K **Privately Held**
SIC: 0181 Roses, growing of

0181 - Ornamental Floriculture & Nursery Prdts County (P-265)

PRODUCTS & SERVICES SECTION

(P-265)
BALL HORTICULTURAL COMPANY
400 Obispo St, Guadalupe (93434-1632)
PHONE................805 343-2723
John Sorell, *Branch Mgr*
EMP: 117
SALES (corp-wide): 761.1MM Privately Held
SIC: 0181 Bulbs & seeds
PA: Ball Horticultural Company
622 Town Rd
West Chicago IL 60185
630 231-3600

(P-266)
BALL TAGAWA GROWERS
819 Zenon Way, Arroyo Grande (93420-5855)
P.O. Box 2440, Pismo Beach (93448-2440)
PHONE................805 481-7526
Fax: 805 481-7452
Randy Tagawa, *Partner*
Ann Ball, *Partner*
EMP: 50
SQ FT: 120,000
SALES (est): 1MM Privately Held
SIC: 0181 Nursery stock, growing of

(P-267)
BARCELO ENTERPRISES INC
4400 Macarthur Blvd # 980, Newport Beach (92660-2054)
PHONE................760 728-3444
Antonio C Barcelo Sr, *President*
Antonio Barcelo Jr, *Vice Pres*
Rosa H Barcelo, *Vice Pres*
Pam McElwain, *Controller*
▲ **EMP:** 100
SALES (est): 7.1MM Privately Held
WEB: www.alivingfossil.com
SIC: 0181 Ornamental nursery products

(P-268)
BAY CITY FLOWER CO (PA)
2265 Cabrillo Hwy S, Half Moon Bay (94019-2250)
P.O. Box 186 (94019-0186)
PHONE................650 726-5535
Fax: 650 720-2004
Harrison Higaki, *Ch of Bd*
Naomi Higaki, *Shareholder*
Sam Hasegawa, *CFO*
Jeanne Watson, *Production*
Sandee Loeffler, *Mktg Dir*
▲ **EMP:** 75
SQ FT: 2,000
SALES (est): 67.7MM Privately Held
WEB: www.baycityflower.com
SIC: 0181 Plants, potted: growing of

(P-269)
BAY CITY FLOWER CO
1450 Cabrillo Hwy S, Half Moon Bay (94019-2243)
PHONE................650 712-8147
Harrison Higaki, *Principal*
EMP: 224
SALES (corp-wide): 67.7MM Privately Held
SIC: 0181 Plants, potted: growing of
PA: Bay City Flower Co.
2265 Cabrillo Hwy S
Half Moon Bay CA 94019
650 726-5535

(P-270)
BLX GROUP INC
71534 Sahara Rd, Rancho Mirage (92270-4340)
PHONE................760 776-6622
Fax: 760 776-6626
Timothy Blixseth, *President*
EMP: 95
SALES (est): 4.5MM Privately Held
SIC: 0181 Nursery stock, growing of

(P-271)
CALIFORNIA PAJAROSA
133 Hughes Rd, Watsonville (95076-9458)
PHONE................831 722-6374
Fax: 831 722-1316
John Furman, *President*
Albert Furman, *Shareholder*
Betty Mitchell, *Shareholder*
Alan Mitchell, *Vice Pres*
EMP: 52
SQ FT: 17,000
SALES (est): 1.6MM Privately Held
SIC: 0181 Roses, growing of; flowers grown in field nurseries

(P-272)
CAMFLOR INC
2364 Riverside Rd, Watsonville (95076-9430)
PHONE................831 726-1330
Daniel Campos, *President*
Zandra Campos, *CFO*
Gil Campos, *Info Tech Mgr*
Jose Campos, *Financial Exec*
Carlos Cardoza, *Sales Mgr*
▲ **EMP:** 110
SALES (est): 3.5MM Privately Held
WEB: www.camflor.com
SIC: 0181 Ornamental nursery products

(P-273)
COLOR SPOT NURSERIES INC
420 Espinosa Rd, Salinas (93907-8894)
PHONE................831 444-0523
Fax: 831 449-5077
Michael F Vukelich, *Manager*
EMP: 270
SALES (corp-wide): 5.4B Privately Held
WEB: www.colorspot.com
SIC: 0181 Plants, potted: growing of
HQ: Color Spot Nurseries, Inc.
27368 Via Ste 201
Temecula CA 92590

(P-274)
COLOR SPOT NURSERIES INC
Also Called: Color Spot Lodi
5400 E Harney Ln, Lodi (95240-6903)
PHONE................209 369-3018
Fax: 209 333-0250
David Barrett, *President*
Bob Strange, *Executive*
John Gigounas, *Agent*
Jeffrey P Widman, *Agent*
EMP: 60
SALES (corp-wide): 5.4B Privately Held
WEB: www.colorspot.com
SIC: 0181 5193 Plants, potted: growing of; flowers & florists' supplies
HQ: Color Spot Nurseries, Inc.
27368 Via Ste 201
Temecula CA 92590

(P-275)
DAVE WILSON NURSERY INC (PA)
Also Called: Dwn
19701 Lake Rd, Hickman (95323-9706)
P.O. Box 429 (95323-0429)
PHONE................209 874-1821
Fax: 209 874-1920
Robert B Woolley, *CEO*
Dennis Tarry, *President*
Dave Wilson, *Principal*
Mary Tarry, *Credit Mgr*
EMP: 50
SQ FT: 8,000
SALES (est): 17.7MM Privately Held
SIC: 0181 Nursery stock, growing of

(P-276)
DLT GROWERS INC
13131 S Bon View Ave, Ontario (91761-8226)
PHONE................909 947-8198
Fax: 909 923-3125
Jaime Delatorre, *President*
Ricardo Delatorre, *Vice Pres*
Salvador Gonzalez, *Sales Staff*
Sal Latorre, *Manager*
EMP: 50
SQ FT: 400
SALES (est): 3.6MM Privately Held
SIC: 0181 5193 Plants, foliage & shrubberies; flowers & nursery stock

(P-277)
DO RIGHTS PLANT GROWERS
540 Glade Dr, Santa Paula (93060-1617)
PHONE................805 525-2155
Fax: 805 525-2076
Dudley Arthur Davis, *CEO*
Diane Davis, *Vice Pres*
Ramon Ibarra, *Accounts Mgr*
EMP: 100
SQ FT: 42,000
SALES (est): 8.4MM Privately Held
WEB: www.dorights.com
SIC: 0181 Bedding plants, growing of; flowers grown in field nurseries; nursery stock, growing of; plants, potted: growing of

(P-278)
DUARTE NURSERY INC
23456 E Flood Rd, Linden (95236-9429)
PHONE................209 887-3409
Jim Duarte, *Manager*
EMP: 350
SQ FT: 1,558
SALES (corp-wide): 85MM Privately Held
WEB: www.duartenursery.com
SIC: 0181 Nursery stock, growing of
PA: Duarte Nursery, Inc.
1555 Baldwin Rd
Hughson CA 95326
209 531-0351

(P-279)
DUARTE NURSERY INC (PA)
Also Called: Duarte Properties
1555 Baldwin Rd, Hughson (95326-9522)
PHONE................209 531-0351
Fax: 209 531-0352
John Duarte, *President*
Anita Duarte, *Treasurer*
Jeff Duarte, *Vice Pres*
Shirley Brooks, *Administration*
Jena Dotson, *VP Finance*
EMP: 50
SALES (est): 85MM Privately Held
WEB: www.duartenursery.com
SIC: 0181 Ornamental nursery products

(P-280)
EUROAMERICAN PROPAGATORS LLC
32149 Aquaduct Rd, Bonsall (92003-4807)
PHONE................760 731-6029
John Rader, *COO*
Gerald Church, *COO*
Todd Waterman, *Officer*
Tom Foley, *Executive*
Roy Lillywhite, *Executive*
▲ **EMP:** 375
SQ FT: 60,000
SALES (est): 46.6MM Privately Held
WEB: www.euroamprop.com
SIC: 0181 Ornamental nursery products

(P-281)
EVERGREEN DISTRIBUTORS INC (PA)
Also Called: Evergreen Nursery
13650 Carmel Valley Rd, San Diego (92130-5624)
P.O. Box 503130 (92150-3130)
PHONE................858 481-0622
Fax: 858 481-5649
Mark L Collins, *President*
Deborah Robertson, *Corp Secy*
Michael Chamberlin, *Vice Pres*
Wally Kearns, *Project Mgr*
James Carpenter, *VP Opers*
▲ **EMP:** 50 EST: 1980
SQ FT: 3,000
SALES (est): 39.6MM Privately Held
SIC: 0181 Nursery stock, growing of

(P-282)
FRANTZ WHOLESALE NURSERY LLC
12161 Delaware Rd, Hickman (95323-9602)
PHONE................209 874-1459
Fax: 209 874-1929
Michael Frantz,
Stephanie Boyd, *Office Mgr*
Dan Gerdis, *Opers Mgr*
Mitzi Frantz,
▲ **EMP:** 150
SALES (est): 8MM Privately Held
WEB: www.frantznursery.com
SIC: 0181 Nursery stock, growing of

(P-283)
GALLUP & STRIBLING ORCHIDS LLC
Also Called: Gallup and Stribling Holdings
3450 Via Real, Carpinteria (93013-3047)
PHONE................805 684-1998
Fax: 805 684-3227
Alexander L Stribling, *CEO*
Michael E Pfau, *Admin Sec*
Gayle Teague, *Accountant*
Jim Stribling, *CPA*
Nancy E Welty, *Controller*
▲ **EMP:** 50
SQ FT: 1,400,000
SALES (est): 3MM Privately Held
SIC: 0181 Flowers grown in field nurseries

(P-284)
GLAD-A-WAY GARDENS INC (PA)
2669 E Clark Ave, Santa Maria (93455-5815)
P.O. Box 2550 (93457-2550)
PHONE................805 938-0569
Brian Caird, *President*
Lance Runels, *Vice Pres*
Erin Caird, *Admin Sec*
Sharon King, *Administration*
Lorena Nol, *Human Resources*
▲ **EMP:** 170
SQ FT: 15,000
SALES (est): 13.9MM Privately Held
WEB: www.gladaway.net
SIC: 0181 Flowers grown in field nurseries

(P-285)
GOLD COAST FARMS LLC
32701 Road 204, Woodlake (93286-9625)
PHONE................559 564-6316
Jim Means, *Manager*
EMP: 50
SALES (est): 1.4MM Privately Held
SIC: 0181 Nursery stock, growing of

(P-286)
GRAND VIEW GERANIUM GRDNS INC
18307 Central Ave, Carson (90746-4017)
PHONE................310 217-0490
Fax: 310 217-0536
EMP: 60
SQ FT: 2,500
SALES (est): 3.2MM Privately Held
WEB: www.gvgeranium.com
SIC: 0181

(P-287)
GROVER LANDSCAPE SERVICES INC
6224 Stoddard Rd, Modesto (95356-9198)
PHONE................209 545-4401
Fax: 209 545-3315
Mark Grover, *President*
Lorraine Grover, *Corp Secy*
Ruth Jupe, *Accounting Mgr*
EMP: 100 EST: 1970
SQ FT: 10,850
SALES: 13.5MM Privately Held
SIC: 0181 0782 0783 0781 Ornamental nursery products; landscape contractors; tree trimming services for public utility lines; landscape planning services

(P-288)
HERITAGE LAND COMPANY INC
Also Called: Delta Growers
111 N Zuckerman Rd, Stockton (95206)
P.O. Box 487 (95201-0487)
PHONE................209 444-1700
Dennis Gardenmeyer, *CEO*
EMP: 50
SALES (est): 4.4MM Privately Held
SIC: 0181 Sod farms

(P-289)
HMCLAUSE INC (DH)
555 Codoni Ave, Modesto (95357-0507)
PHONE................530 747-3700
Fax: 209 527-8684
Matthew M Johnston, *President*
Andre Cariou, *Vice Pres*
Gerry Hawkins, *Info Tech Dir*
Dwayne Robertson, *Controller*
Andr Cariou, *VP Sales*
◆ **EMP:** 133 EST: 1856

▲ = Import ▼ = Export
◆ = Import/Export

PRODUCTS & SERVICES SECTION
0181 - Ornamental Floriculture & Nursery Prdts County (P-313)

SQ FT: 200,000
SALES (est): 79.2MM **Privately Held**
WEB: www.harrismoran.com
SIC: 0181 Seeds, vegetable: growing of
HQ: Groupe Limagrain Holding
Rue Henri Moudor
St Beauzire 63360
475 828-101

(P-290)
HMCLAUSE INC
42 Glenshire Ln, Chico (95973-1093)
PHONE..............................530 713-5838
EMP: 70 **Privately Held**
SIC: 0181 Seeds, vegetable: growing of
HQ: Hm.Clause, Inc.
555 Codoni Ave
Modesto CA 95357
530 747-3700

(P-291)
HOLLAND AMERICA FLOWERS LLC
808 Albert Way, Arroyo Grande (93420-5828)
PHONE..............................805 343-4004
Benno Dobbe, *CEO*
Cees Dobbee, *Manager*
Jane Riffle, *Accounts Mgr*
▲ **EMP:** 83
SQ FT: 1,700
SALES (est): 6.5MM
SALES (corp-wide): 15MM **Privately Held**
SIC: 0181 Flowers grown in field nurseries
PA: Holland America Bulb Farms, Inc.
1066 S Pekin Rd
Woodland WA 98674
360 225-6575

(P-292)
J ROBERT ECHTER
Also Called: Robert J Echter Foxpoint Farms
1150 Quail Gardens Dr, Encinitas (92024-2365)
PHONE..............................760 436-0188
Robert J Echter, *Owner*
Robert Echter, *Owner*
Rhonda Kavanaugh, *Administration*
EMP: 50 **EST:** 2015
SALES (est): 789.9K **Privately Held**
SIC: 0181 Ornamental nursery products

(P-293)
JOHANNES FLOWERS INC
4990 Foothill Rd, Carpinteria (93013-3085)
PHONE..............................805 684-5686
Fax: 805 566-2199
Johannes A P Persoon, *President*
Madalenne Leanoard, *Vice Pres*
Jan Persoon, *Vice Pres*
Wilbert Q J Persoon, *Vice Pres*
Nancy Vaughn, *Bookkeeper*
▲ **EMP:** 60 **EST:** 1970
SALES (est): 4.4MM **Privately Held**
WEB: www.johannesflowers.com
SIC: 0181 5992 Flowers grown in nurseries; florists

(P-294)
KAWAHARA NURSERY INC
698 Burnett Ave, Morgan Hill (95037-9022)
P.O. Box 1358 (95038-1358)
PHONE..............................408 779-2400
Fax: 408 779-6850
David Kawahara, *President*
John Kawahara, *Vice Pres*
Monica Nicasio, *HR Admin*
Karen Knoll, *Manager*
▲ **EMP:** 240 **EST:** 1947
SALES (est): 11.8MM **Privately Held**
WEB: www.kawaharanursery.com
SIC: 0181 5193 Nursery stock, growing of; flowers & florists' supplies

(P-295)
KENDALL FARMS LP
4230 White Lilac Rd, Fallbrook (92028-8802)
PHONE..............................760 731-0681
Fax: 760 731-5205
Jason Kendall, *Managing Prtnr*
Troy Conner, *General Mgr*
Tony Mungo, *Admin Asst*
Katia McLauglin, *Prdtn Mgr*
Christy York, *Sales Dir*
EMP: 50
SALES (est): 4.2MM **Privately Held**
WEB: www.kendall-farms.com
SIC: 0181 Flowers grown in field nurseries

(P-296)
KITAYAMA BROS INC
481 San Andreas Rd, Watsonville (95076-9524)
P.O. Box 537, Brighton CO (80601-0537)
PHONE..............................831 722-2912
Michael Deardorff, *President*
Stuart Kitayama, *General Mgr*
EMP: 80
SALES (corp-wide): 9.4MM **Privately Held**
SIC: 0181 5193 Flowers grown in field nurseries; flowers & florists' supplies
PA: Kitayama Bros., Inc.
540 E Bridge St Ste A
Brighton CO 80601
303 659-8005

(P-297)
KITAYAMA BROTHERS INC
Also Called: Kitayama Flowers
481 San Andreas Rd, Watsonville (95076-9524)
PHONE..............................831 722-8118
Fax: 831 722-4133
Winston Moore, *Branch Mgr*
EMP: 73
SALES (corp-wide): 5MM **Privately Held**
SIC: 0181 5261 5193 Flowers grown in field nurseries; roses, growing of; nurseries & garden centers; flowers & florists' supplies
PA: Kitayama Brothers, Inc
540 E Bridge St Ste A
Brighton CO 80601
303 659-8000

(P-298)
L E COOKE CO
26333 Road 140, Visalia (93292-9452)
PHONE..............................559 732-9146
Fax: 559 732-3702
David Henry Cox, *CEO*
Ron Ludekens, *President*
Phillip Cox, *Admin Sec*
Kathy Reed, *Controller*
Ernie Adamakis, *Sales Mgr*
▲ **EMP:** 200
SQ FT: 6,000
SALES (est): 8.8MM **Privately Held**
WEB: www.lecooke.com
SIC: 0181 Nursery stock, growing of

(P-299)
LA VERNE NURSERY INC
3653 Center St, Piru (93040)
P.O. Box 410 (93040-0410)
PHONE..............................805 521-0111
Richard Wilson, *CEO*
Beatriz Dera, *Manager*
EMP: 90
SQ FT: 16,000
SALES (est): 4.9MM **Privately Held**
SIC: 0181 Ornamental nursery products; fruit stocks, growing of

(P-300)
MARATHON LAND INC (PA)
2599 E Hueneme Rd, Oxnard (93033-8112)
P.O. Box 579, Port Hueneme (93044-0579)
PHONE..............................805 488-3585
Jurgen Gramckow, *President*
EMP: 125
SQ FT: 3,000
SALES (est): 8.8MM **Privately Held**
WEB: www.sod.com
SIC: 0181 Sod farms

(P-301)
MARTINEZ FARMS INC
2440 Cactus Rd, San Diego (92154-8007)
PHONE..............................619 661-6571
Fax: 619 661-7118
Richard Martinez, *President*
Jose Martinez, *Ch of Bd*
EMP: 400
SALES (est): 14.5MM **Privately Held**
WEB: www.certseedpotato.com
SIC: 0181 Nursery stock, growing of

(P-302)
MATSUI NURSERY INC (PA)
1645 Old Stage Rd, Salinas (93908-9737)
PHONE..............................831 422-6433
Fax: 831 422-2387
Toshikiyo Matsui, *President*
Doug Brothers, *Vice Pres*
Clint Bishop, *Business Mgr*
Heather Butts, *Natl Sales Mgr*
Hillary Fish, *Marketing Mgr*
▲ **EMP:** 63 **EST:** 1967
SQ FT: 3,000,000
SALES (est): 18.9MM **Privately Held**
SIC: 0181 Ornamental nursery products

(P-303)
MONROVIA NURSERY COMPANY (PA)
Also Called: Monrovia Growes
817 E Monrovia Pl, Azusa (91702-6297)
P.O. Box 1385 (91702-1385)
PHONE..............................626 334-9321
Fax: 626 334-3126
Miles R Rosedale, *CEO*
William B Usrey, *President*
Richard Van Landingham, *President*
Dennis Conner, *Vice Pres*
Sylvia Lopez, *Executive*
▲ **EMP:** 567
SQ FT: 50,000
SALES (est): 487.5MM **Privately Held**
WEB: www.monrovia.com
SIC: 0181 5193 5261 Nursery stock, growing of; flowers & florists' supplies; nurseries & garden centers

(P-304)
MYRIAD FLOWERS INTERNATIONAL
4601 Foothill Rd, Carpinteria (93013-3097)
PHONE..............................805 684-8079
Fax: 805 684-7959
Harry Van Wingerden, *President*
Michelle Van Wingerden, *Vice Pres*
Erik Van Winderden, *Executive*
Erik Wingerden, *Office Mgr*
▲ **EMP:** 65
SQ FT: 2,000
SALES (est): 5MM **Privately Held**
WEB: www.myriadflowers.com
SIC: 0181 Flowers grown in field nurseries

(P-305)
NAUMES INC
3792 Feather River Blvd, Olivehurst (95961-9688)
PHONE..............................530 743-2055
Fax: 530 743-5107
Bob Cosey, *General Mgr*
Stephanie Nicholson, *General Mgr*
Mary Rodriguez, *Director*
EMP: 50
SQ FT: 66,646
SALES (corp-wide): 167.8MM **Privately Held**
WEB: www.naumes.com
SIC: 0181 0723 4731 Fruit stocks, growing of; fruit (farm-dried) packing services; agents, shipping
PA: Naumes, Inc.
2 W Barnett St
Medford OR 97501
541 772-6268

(P-306)
OCEAN BREEZE INTERNATIONAL
Also Called: Mobis Wholesale
3910 Via Real, Carpinteria (93013-1266)
PHONE..............................805 684-1747
Fax: 805 684-0235
Rene Van Wingerden, *President*
June Van Wingerden, *Vice Pres*
▲ **EMP:** 60
SQ FT: 900,000
SALES (est): 10.4MM **Privately Held**
WEB: www.oceanbreezeintl.com
SIC: 0181 Flowers: grown under cover (e.g. greenhouse production)

(P-307)
OCEAN VIEW FLOWERS LLC
1105 Union Sugar Ave, Lompoc (93436-9737)
PHONE..............................800 736-5608
Robert M Witt,
Roseann Strand, *Marketing Staff*
John Donati,
EMP: 175
SALES (est): 220.3K **Privately Held**
SIC: 0181 Florists' greens & flowers; florists' greens cultivated: growing of

(P-308)
OLIVE HILL GREENHOUSES
3508 Olive Hill Rd, Fallbrook (92028-8296)
P.O. Box 1510 (92088-1510)
PHONE..............................760 728-4596
Fax: 760 728-1420
George A Godfrey, *Owner*
William McGregor, *Technology*
Shelley Demitsas, *Human Res Dir*
Denise Godfrey, *Mktg Dir*
▲ **EMP:** 100
SQ FT: 2,000
SALES (est): 7.7MM **Privately Held**
WEB: www.olivehill.net
SIC: 0181 Ornamental nursery products

(P-309)
PACIFIC EARTH RESOURCES (PA)
Also Called: Pacific Sd/Pcfic Arbor Nrsries
305 Hueneme Rd, Camarillo (93012-8522)
PHONE..............................805 986-8277
Fax: 805 488-1549
Richard Rogers, *Owner*
Elizabeth Rogers, *Partner*
Jill George, *MIS Staff*
EMP: 80
SQ FT: 8,000
SALES (est): 26.6MM **Privately Held**
SIC: 0181 Sod farms; nursery stock, growing of

(P-310)
PLANT SOURCE INC
2029 Sycamore Dr, San Marcos (92069-9753)
PHONE..............................760 743-7743
Fax: 760 743-7998
Steve Pyle, *President*
Harriette Gomez, *Human Res Mgr*
▲ **EMP:** 50
SALES (est): 14.2MM **Privately Held**
SIC: 0181 Plants, foliage & shrubberies

(P-311)
PLUG CONNECTION INC
2627 Ramona Dr, Vista (92084-1634)
PHONE..............................760 631-0992
Tim Wada, *President*
Bradley Rhoads, *CFO*
James Peterson, *Vice Pres*
Christine Labrador, *Creative Dir*
Nathaniel Williams, *Systs Prg Mgr*
▲ **EMP:** 80
SQ FT: 350,000
SALES (est): 5.3MM **Privately Held**
WEB: www.plugconnection.com
SIC: 0181 Bedding plants, growing of

(P-312)
PYRAMID FLOWERS INC
3813 Doris Ave, Oxnard (93030-4706)
PHONE..............................805 382-8070
Fax: 805 382-8075
Fred Van Wingerden, *President*
Edith Van Wingerden, *Vice Pres*
Sara Miranda, *Office Admin*
Marius Leemhuis, *Prdtn Mgr*
Marcos Van Wingerden, *Prdtn Mgr*
▲ **EMP:** 120
SQ FT: 900,000
SALES (est): 16.2MM **Privately Held**
WEB: www.pyramidflowers.com
SIC: 0181 Flowers grown in field nurseries

(P-313)
RICHARD WILSON WELLINGTON
Also Called: Colorama Wholesale Nursery
1025 N Todd Ave, Azusa (91702-1602)
PHONE..............................626 812-7881
Fax: 626 969-0481
Richard Wilson, *Owner*
Katie Giannone, *Manager*
▲ **EMP:** 100
SQ FT: 70,000

0181 - Ornamental Floriculture & Nursery Prdts County (P-314)

PRODUCTS & SERVICES SECTION

SALES (est): 10.7MM **Privately Held**
SIC: 0181 5193 Nursery stock, growing of; nursery stock

(P-314)
RIVER RIDGE FARMS INC
3135 Los Angeles Ave, Oxnard (93036-1010)
PHONE.................805 647-6880
Fax: 805 647-1325
Rieuwert Jan Vis, *President*
Donna Vis, *Mktg Dir*
Larry Muro, *Accounts Mgr*
▲ EMP: 95
SQ FT: 440
SALES (est): 12MM **Privately Held**
SIC: 0181 5193 Flowers grown in field nurseries; flowers: grown under cover (e.g. greenhouse production); plants, potted

(P-315)
ROCKET FARMS INC (PA)
360 Espinosa Rd, Salinas (93907-8895)
P.O. Box 3756 (93912-3756)
PHONE.................831 442-2400
Charles Kosmont, *CEO*
Mark Clark, *Vice Pres*
Bartley Clark, *Purch Mgr*
Rannel Santiago, *Sales Mgr*
▲ EMP: 106
SQ FT: 1,500,000
SALES (est): 40.9MM **Privately Held**
SIC: 0181 Flowers: grown under cover (e.g. greenhouse production)

(P-316)
ROSE THOMPSON COMPANY
949 Cassou Rd, San Marcos (92069-9715)
PHONE.................760 736-6020
Fax: 760 736-6029
David Thompson, *President*
Scott Thompson, *Corp Secy*
Karen Thompson, *Vice Pres*
Chris Beck, *Office Mgr*
Joe Blair, *Technology*
EMP: 54
SQ FT: 1,704
SALES (est): 2.6MM **Privately Held**
WEB: www.thomprose.com
SIC: 0181 Ornamental nursery products

(P-317)
SAN GABRIEL NURSERY AND FLOR (PA)
632 S San Gabriel Blvd, San Gabriel (91776-2798)
PHONE.................626 286-0787
Fax: 626 286-0047
Margie Yoshihashi, *President*
Mary Swanton, *Treasurer*
Saburo Ishihara, *Vice Pres*
Dianne Yoshimura, *Admin Sec*
Ichiro Yoshihashi, *Manager*
EMP: 73
SQ FT: 5,000
SALES (est): 4.8MM **Privately Held**
WEB: www.sgnursery.com
SIC: 0181 Nursery stock, growing of

(P-318)
SIERRA GOLD NURSERIES INC
5320 Garden Hwy, Yuba City (95991-9499)
PHONE.................530 674-1145
Fax: 530 674-1007
Jack Poukish, *CEO*
Brian Berg, *Vice Pres*
Ellen Berg, *Vice Pres*
Jaco Pokish, *General Mgr*
Margaret Mitchell, *CIO*
▲ EMP: 86
SQ FT: 2,500
SALES (est): 10.6MM **Privately Held**
WEB: www.sierragoldtrees.com
SIC: 0181 Nursery stock, growing of

(P-319)
SIERRA-CASCADE NURSERY INC (PA)
472-715 Johnson Rd, Susanville (96130-8727)
PHONE.................530 254-6867
Steve Fortin, *President*
Randy Jertberg, *COO*
Robert Akeson, *Vice Pres*
Robert Murie, *Vice Pres*

Justin Whitaker, *Info Tech Mgr*
▼ EMP: 400
SQ FT: 2,600
SALES (est): 133.7MM **Privately Held**
SIC: 0181 Nursery stock, growing of

(P-320)
SUN VALLEY GROUP INC (PA)
3160 Upper Bay Rd, Arcata (95521-9690)
PHONE.................707 822-2885
Leendert De Vries, *President*
Robert Jenkins, *CFO*
David Aronovici, *Executive*
Gail Brett, *Creative Dir*
Debbie Hartman, *Regional Mgr*
▲ EMP: 350
SQ FT: 8,700
SALES (est): 124.6MM **Privately Held**
WEB: www.thesunvalleygroup.com
SIC: 0181 Flowers: grown under cover (e.g. greenhouse production); flowers grown in field nurseries; bulbs, growing of

(P-321)
SUNRISE RANCH
3623 Etting Rd, Oxnard (93033-5813)
PHONE.................805 488-0813
George Mimaki, *Partner*
Lori Kamei, *Partner*
Bryan Mimaki, *Partner*
EMP: 90
SQ FT: 750
SALES (est): 5.7MM **Privately Held**
SIC: 0181 Flowers grown in field nurseries

(P-322)
SUPERIOR SOD I LP
17821 17th St Ste 165, Tustin (92780-2172)
P.O. Box 1911, Tehachapi (93581-5911)
PHONE.................909 923-5068
Fax: 661 822-5978
Michael Considine, *Partner*
Richard H Considine, *Partner*
Trudy Considine, *Partner*
Peter Moore, *Partner*
EMP: 125
SQ FT: 1,400
SALES (est): 6.4MM **Privately Held**
WEB: www.superiorsod.com
SIC: 0181 0782 Sod farms; lawn & garden services

(P-323)
TOPSTAR FLORAL INC
4255 W Gonzales Rd, Oxnard (93036-7786)
PHONE.................805 984-7972
Fax: 805 984-5362
Steve Van Wingerden, *President*
Alfredo Martinez, *Sales Executive*
Don Marek, *Director*
EMP: 50
SQ FT: 6,500
SALES (est): 4.2MM **Privately Held**
WEB: www.topstarfloral.com
SIC: 0181 Flowers grown in field nurseries

(P-324)
W J GRIFFIN INC
Also Called: Por La Mar Nursery
905 S Patterson Ave, Santa Barbara (93111-2407)
P.O. Box 6354 (93160-6354)
PHONE.................805 683-5639
Fax: 805 967-3266
Brian Caird, *CEO*
Dan Jauchen, *Vice Pres*
Christy Lockwood, *Controller*
Christy Nockward, *Manager*
▲ EMP: 250
SQ FT: 200,000
SALES (est): 36.5MM **Privately Held**
WEB: www.miniroses.com
SIC: 0181 Plants, potted: growing of

(P-325)
WEST COAST TURF (PA)
42540 Melanie Pl, Palm Desert (92211-5127)
P.O. Box 4563 (92261-4563)
PHONE.................760 340-7300
Fax: 760 360-7345
John M Foster, *President*
Joe Foster, *Vice Pres*
Doreen Aldape, *Admin Sec*

Jennifer Huether, *Info Tech Mgr*
EMP: 50
SQ FT: 2,000
SALES (est): 41.5MM **Privately Held**
WEB: www.westernsod.com
SIC: 0181 Sod farms

(P-326)
WEST FLOWER GROWERS INC
3623 Etting Rd, Oxnard (93033-5813)
PHONE.................805 488-0814
Fax: 805 488-9433
Bryan H Mimaki, *President*
George Mimaki, *General Mgr*
EMP: 70
SALES (est): 2.5MM **Privately Held**
SIC: 0181 Ornamental nursery products

0182 Food Crops Grown Under Cover

(P-327)
CHANNEL ISLNDS VGTBLE FRMS INC (PA)
595 Victoria Ave, Oxnard (93030-4710)
PHONE.................805 984-1910
Steve Nishimori, *President*
Karen Nishimori, *Vice Pres*
Aide Ahumada, *Office Mgr*
Kourtney Nishimori, *Manager*
EMP: 60 EST: 1994
SQ FT: 2,000
SALES (est): 5.9MM **Privately Held**
SIC: 0182 Vegetable crops grown under cover

(P-328)
COUNTRYSIDE MUSHROOMS INC
11300 Center Ave, Gilroy (95020-9257)
PHONE.................408 683-2748
Donald W Hordness, *President*
Lewis Di Cecco, *Vice Pres*
EMP: 70
SALES (est): 7MM **Privately Held**
SIC: 0182 Mushrooms grown under cover

(P-329)
FITZ FRESH INC
211 Lee Rd, Watsonville (95076-9447)
P.O. Box 1450, Freedom (95019-1450)
PHONE.................831 763-4440
Fax: 831 722-7109
Patrick J Fitz, *President*
Holly Pedemonte, *Manager*
▲ EMP: 50
SQ FT: 2,000
SALES (est): 5MM **Privately Held**
WEB: www.fitzfresh.com
SIC: 0182 Mushrooms grown under cover

(P-330)
FUJI NATURAL FOODS INC (HQ)
13500 S Hamner Ave, Ontario (91761-2605)
P.O. Box 3728 (91761-0973)
PHONE.................909 947-1008
Fax: 909 947-7260
Ikuzo Sugiyama, *President*
Duke Takayama, *CFO*
▲ EMP: 72
SQ FT: 65,000
SALES: 11.1MM
SALES (corp-wide): 7.8MM **Privately Held**
SIC: 0182 Bean sprouts grown under cover
PA: Taiyo Shokuhin Kogyo K.K.
2618-6, Naegicho
Tatebayashi GNM 374-0
276 722-551

(P-331)
GREENHEART FARMS INC (PA)
902 Zenon Way, Arroyo Grande (93420-5807)
P.O. Box 1510 (93421-1510)
PHONE.................805 481-2234
Fax: 805 481-7374
Hoy Buell, *CEO*
Leo Wolf, *Treasurer*
Henry Katzenstein, *Vice Pres*
Melody Fair, *Info Tech Mgr*
Jennifer Alexander, *Accounting Dir*

▲ EMP: 133
SQ FT: 225,000
SALES (est): 45.9MM **Privately Held**
WEB: www.greenheartfarms.com
SIC: 0182 Vegetable crops grown under cover

(P-332)
GROWERS TRANSPLANTING INC (HQ)
360 Espinosa Rd, Salinas (93907-8895)
P.O. Box 3756 (93912-3756)
PHONE.................831 449-3440
Fax: 831 443-0254
Charles I Kosmont, *CEO*
Leslie Surber, *CFO*
Kevin Doyle, *Vice Pres*
Bill Rover, *Vice Pres*
Dale Cox, *Controller*
▲ EMP: 83 EST: 1981
SQ FT: 4,000,000
SALES (est): 34MM
SALES (corp-wide): 50.9MM **Privately Held**
WEB: www.growerstrans.com
SIC: 0182 Vegetable crops grown under cover
PA: Monterey Peninsula Horticulture, Inc.
360 Espinosa Rd
Salinas CA 93907
831 449-3440

(P-333)
HOKTO KINOKO COMPANY (HQ)
2033 Marilyn Ln, San Marcos (92069-9756)
PHONE.................760 774-8453
Katsumi Shigeta, *CEO*
Kazumi Ikeda, *Vice Pres*
Koji Morofuji, *General Mgr*
Aki Natscubara, *Admin Asst*
Tasuku Omura, *Marketing Mgr*
▲ EMP: 110
SALES: 17MM
SALES (corp-wide): 521.1MM **Privately Held**
SIC: 0182 Mushrooms grown under cover
PA: Hokuto Corporation
138-1, Minamihori
Nagano NAG 381-0
262 433-111

(P-334)
HOLLANDIA PRODUCE LP
1545 Santa Monica Rd, Carpinteria (93013-3067)
P.O. Box 1327 (93014-1327)
PHONE.................805 684-8739
Fax: 805 684-9363
Pete Overgaag, *Partner*
Laura Rose, *Executive Asst*
Elizabeth Seyle, *Controller*
Jake Overgaag, *Sales Staff*
▲ EMP: 160
SQ FT: 16,000
SALES (est): 38.7MM **Privately Held**
WEB: www.hollandiaflowers.com
SIC: 0182 Vegetable crops grown under cover

(P-335)
MONTEREY MUSHROOMS INC
Also Called: Monterey Mushrooms-Morgan Hill
642 Hale Ave, Morgan Hill (95037-9221)
P.O. Box 818 (95038-0818)
PHONE.................408 779-4191
Fax: 408 778-0367
Clark Smith, *Branch Mgr*
Rosa Garcia, *Human Res Dir*
Jim Adams, *Purchasing*
EMP: 350
SQ FT: 5,000
SALES (corp-wide): 815.5MM **Privately Held**
WEB: www.montereymushrooms.com
SIC: 0182 2034 Mushrooms grown under cover; dehydrated fruits, vegetables, soups
PA: Monterey Mushrooms, Inc.
260 Westgate Dr
Watsonville CA 95076
831 763-5300

PRODUCTS & SERVICES SECTION

0191 - Crop Farming, Misc County (P-360)

(P-336)
MONTEREY MUSHROOMS INC (PA)
260 Westgate Dr, Watsonville (95076-2452)
PHONE..................................831 763-5300
Fax: 831 763-0700
Shah Kazemi, *President*
Ray Selle, *CFO*
Joe Caldwell, *Vice Pres*
Michael O'Brien, *Vice Pres*
Terry Marler, *Executive*
▲ EMP: 50
SALES (est): 815.5MM **Privately Held**
WEB: www.montereymushrooms.com
SIC: 0182 Mushrooms grown under cover

(P-337)
MONTEREY MUSHROOMS INC
777 Maher Ct, Royal Oaks (95076-9014)
PHONE..................................831 728-8300
Fax: 831 728-9504
Wayne Batista, *Branch Mgr*
Edward Stoll, *Human Res Mgr*
EMP: 501
SALES (corp-wide): 815.5MM **Privately Held**
WEB: www.montereymushrooms.com
SIC: 0182 Mushrooms grown under cover
PA: Monterey Mushrooms, Inc.
260 Westgate Dr
Watsonville CA 95076
831 763-5300

(P-338)
MOUNTAIN MEADOW MUSHROOMS INC
26948 N Broadway, Escondido (92026-8315)
PHONE..................................760 749-1201
Fax: 760 749-1697
Bob Crouch, *President*
Elizabeth Crouch, *Vice Pres*
Roberto Ramirez, *Vice Pres*
Manuel Zuniga, *Vice Pres*
Shelley Steffen, *Safety Mgr*
EMP: 72
SQ FT: 110,000
SALES (est): 8.2MM **Privately Held**
SIC: 0182 Mushrooms grown under cover

(P-339)
NORTH SHORE GREENHOUSES INC
Also Called: North Shore Living Herbs
82900 Johnson St, Thermal (92274-9319)
PHONE..................................760 397-0400
Leonardus Overgaag, *President*
Suzette Overgaag, *Vice Pres*
Serena Letterman, *Executive Asst*
Veronica Portillo, *Accountant*
Henry Bolanos, *Controller*
▲ EMP: 83
SALES (est): 10.1MM **Privately Held**
WEB: www.northshoregreenhouses.com
SIC: 0182 Food crops grown under cover

(P-340)
PLEASANT VALLEY FLOWERS INC
3132 E Pleasant Valley Rd, Oxnard (93033-4112)
PHONE..................................805 986-2776
Fax: 805 986-2018
Lane Devries, *President*
Laura Gonzalez, *Office Mgr*
Vickie Rossi, *Credit Mgr*
Frank Dipen, *Manager*
▲ EMP: 335
SQ FT: 7,500
SALES (est): 9.1MM
SALES (corp-wide): 124.6MM **Privately Held**
WEB: www.pleasantvalleyflowers.com
SIC: 0182 Food crops grown under cover
PA: The Sun Valley Group Inc
3160 Upper Bay Rd
Arcata CA 95521
707 822-2885

(P-341)
PREMIER MUSHROOMS LP (PA)
2880 Niagara Ave, Colusa (95932)
P.O. Box 888 (95932-0888)
PHONE..................................530 458-2700

John Ashbaugh, *Partner*
Rex Pugh, *CFO*
▲ EMP: 51
SQ FT: 10,000
SALES (est): 42.3MM **Privately Held**
SIC: 0182 Mushrooms grown under cover

(P-342)
PREMIER MUSHROOMS LP
2847 Niagara Ave, Colusa (95932)
P.O. Box 888 (95932-0888)
PHONE..................................530 458-2700
Jose Flores, *Plant Mgr*
EMP: 165
SALES (corp-wide): 42.3MM **Privately Held**
SIC: 0182 Mushrooms grown under cover
PA: Premier Mushrooms, L.P.
2880 Niagara Ave
Colusa CA 95932
530 458-2700

(P-343)
ROYAL OAKS ENTERPRISES INC
Also Called: Royal Oaks Mushroom
15480 Watsonville Rd, Morgan Hill (95037-5921)
P.O. Box 447 (95038-0447)
PHONE..................................408 779-2362
Don Hordness, *President*
Deanne Arellano, *President*
Linda Abdella, *Treasurer*
Joseph Andrighetto, *Vice Pres*
Don Hordeness, *Vice Pres*
EMP: 50
SQ FT: 1,600
SALES (est): 3.6MM **Privately Held**
SIC: 0182 Mushrooms grown under cover

0191 Crop Farming, Misc

(P-344)
ALONZO FARMS INC
7481 Batavia Rd, Dixon (95620-9762)
PHONE..................................707 678-5282
Gerald Alonzo, *President*
Kathleen Alonzo-Barr, *Corp Secy*
Donald Alonzo, *Vice Pres*
Alfred C Alonzo, *Assistant VP*
EMP: 75 EST: 1947
SALES (est): 2.4MM **Privately Held**
SIC: 0191 General farms, primarily crop

(P-345)
ARNAUDO BROS TRANSPORT INC (PA)
Also Called: Arnaudo Bros Trucking
16505 S Tracy Blvd, Tracy (95304-9436)
PHONE..................................209 835-0406
Steve Arnaudo, *President*
Leo Arnaudo, *Vice Pres*
Edna Rossi, *Office Mgr*
Ed Arnaudo, *Admin Sec*
EMP: 65 EST: 1947
SQ FT: 1,200
SALES (est): 9MM **Privately Held**
SIC: 0191 4212 General farms, primarily crop; local trucking, without storage

(P-346)
BABE FARMS
1293 W Stowell Rd, Santa Maria (93458-9709)
PHONE..................................805 928-3728
Fax: 805 349-2806
Judith Lundberg, *Branch Mgr*
EMP: 107
SALES (corp-wide): 60.6MM **Privately Held**
SIC: 0191 General farms, primarily crop
PA: Babe' Farms
1485 N Blosser Rd
Santa Maria CA 93458
805 925-4144

(P-347)
BOWLES FARMING CO INC
11609 Hereford Rd, Los Banos (93635-9514)
PHONE..................................209 827-3000
Fax: 209 826-1134
Phillip Bowles, *President*
Cannon Michael, *Vice Pres*

EMP: 50
SALES (corp-wide): 4.8MM **Privately Held**
WEB: www.bfarm.com
SIC: 0191 General farms, primarily crop
PA: Bowles Farming Co Inc
716 Montgomery St Ste 1
San Francisco CA 94111
415 421-4800

(P-348)
BUTTON & TURKOVICH
24604 Buckeye Rd, Winters (95694-9001)
PHONE..................................530 795-2090
Fax: 530 795-3331
Tony Turkovich, *Partner*
Estate of Robert L Button, *Partner*
EMP: 100
SQ FT: 1,500
SALES (est): 6.6MM **Privately Held**
SIC: 0191 General farms, primarily crop

(P-349)
CAPTIVA VERDE FARMING CORP
78080 Calle Amigo Ste 201, La Quinta (92253-8965)
PHONE..................................760 771-3333
Jeffrey J Ciachurski, *CEO*
David Pratt, *COO*
Chris Thompson, *CFO*
Mike Boyd, *Director*
EMP: 110
SALES (est): 89K **Privately Held**
SIC: 0191 General farms, primarily crop

(P-350)
CB NORTH LLC
480 W Beach St, Watsonville (95076-4555)
PHONE..................................831 786-1642
Richard Dahl,
Jeffrey Conner,
Beth Potillo,
Bob Ritts,
EMP: 1000
SALES (est): 10.4MM **Privately Held**
SIC: 0191 General farms, primarily crop

(P-351)
COELHO WEST CUSTOM FARMING
26979 S Butte Ave, Five Points (93624)
P.O. Box 434 (93624-0434)
PHONE..................................559 884-2566
Anthony P Coelho Jr, *President*
EMP: 58
SALES (est): 4.7MM **Privately Held**
SIC: 0191 General farms, primarily crop

(P-352)
CRYSTAL ORGANIC FARMS LLC
6900 Mountain View Rd, Bakersfield (93307-9627)
PHONE..................................661 845-5200
Jeff Meger, *President*
Abigail Oledo, *Administration*
EMP: 946 EST: 2003
SALES (est): 11.4MM
SALES (corp-wide): 1.8B **Privately Held**
SIC: 0191 General farms, primarily crop
PA: Grimmway Enterprises, Inc.
14141 Di Giorgio Rd
Arvin CA 93203
661 854-6250

(P-353)
DAN R COSTA INC
17239 Louise Ave, Escalon (95320-8732)
PHONE..................................209 234-2004
Fax: 209 234-2001
Dan R Costa, *President*
Shirley Costa, *Corp Secy*
EMP: 250
SALES: 3.5MM **Privately Held**
WEB: www.dannysfalldecor.com
SIC: 0191 0115 0723 General farms, primarily crop; corn; vegetable packing services; fruit (fresh) packing services

(P-354)
DELTA BREEZE FARMING INC
Also Called: Courtland Farming
11566 State Highway 160, Courtland (95615-9732)
PHONE..................................916 775-2055
Mahinder S Shaliwal, *President*
Mahinder S Dhaliwal, *President*
Tawnya Dhaliwal, *Corp Secy*
Fernando Vellanoweth, *Advisor*
EMP: 210
SQ FT: 4,000
SALES: 1.8MM **Privately Held**
SIC: 0191 General farms, primarily crop

(P-355)
DICK ANDERSON & SONS FARMING
Also Called: Vasto Valle Farms
15900 W Dorris Ave, Huron (93234)
P.O. Box 10 (93234-0010)
PHONE..................................559 945-2511
Richard Anderson, *President*
Robert Anderson, *Corp Secy*
Craig Anderson, *Vice Pres*
EMP: 135
SQ FT: 1,000
SALES (est): 10.4MM **Privately Held**
SIC: 0191 General farms, primarily crop

(P-356)
DON GRAGNANI FARMS
Also Called: Universal Custom Farming Co
12910 S Napa Ave, Tranquillity (93668)
P.O. Box 128 (93668-0128)
PHONE..................................559 693-4352
Fax: 559 693-2172
Donald Gragnani, *Partner*
Irene Gragnani, *Partner*
Jerry Gragnani, *Partner*
Jeanne Gragnani-Lloyd, *Partner*
Martha Alejo, *Manager*
EMP: 80
SQ FT: 3,000
SALES (est): 10MM **Privately Held**
WEB: www.gragnanifarms.com
SIC: 0191 General farms, primarily crop

(P-357)
DW BERRY FARMS LLC
3960 N Rose Ave, Oxnard (93036-1820)
P.O. Box 1029 (93032-1029)
PHONE..................................805 795-8403
Dean Walsh, *Mng Member*
EMP: 300 EST: 2010
SALES: 13MM **Privately Held**
SIC: 0191 General farms, primarily crop

(P-358)
E K T FARMS
105 Logan St, Watsonville (95076-2709)
P.O. Box 794 (95077-0794)
PHONE..................................831 724-0832
Edward J Kelly, *Co-Owner*
Jean Kelly, *Co-Owner*
EMP: 220
SALES (est): 11.3MM **Privately Held**
SIC: 0191 General farms, primarily crop

(P-359)
ELKHORN BERRY FARMS LLC
262 E Lake Ave, Watsonville (95076-4718)
PHONE..................................831 722-2472
Lario Ageas, *General Mgr*
▲ EMP: 95
SALES (est): 6.4MM **Privately Held**
SIC: 0191 0171 General farms, primarily crop; strawberry farm

(P-360)
GENE WHEELER FARMS INC
220 W Avenue H6, Lancaster (93534-1636)
P.O. Box 10029 (93584-2029)
PHONE..................................661 951-2100
Fax: 661 723-7260
Gene Wheeler, *President*
Edi Rush, *Manager*
▼ EMP: 250
SALES: 26.2MM **Privately Held**
WEB: www.GeneWheelerfarms.com
SIC: 0191 General farms, primarily crop

0191 - Crop Farming, Misc County (P-361) — PRODUCTS & SERVICES SECTION

(P-361)
GRIMMWAY ENTERPRISES INC
Also Called: Premiere Packing
6301 S Zerker Rd, Shafter (93263)
P.O. Box 81498, Bakersfield (93380-1498)
PHONE 661 399-0844
Randy Mower, *Vice Pres*
EMP: 400
SALES (corp-wide): 1.8B **Privately Held**
SIC: 0191 0174 General farms, primarily crop; citrus fruits
PA: Grimmway Enterprises, Inc.
14141 Di Giorgio Rd
Arvin CA 93203
661 854-6250

(P-362)
GRIMMWAY FARMS
2105 Anderholt Rd, Holtville (92250-9798)
PHONE 760 356-2513
Fax: 760 356-2547
Rancho Riddle, *Owner*
EMP: 70
SALES (est): 1.4MM **Privately Held**
SIC: 0191 General farms, primarily crop

(P-363)
HALL COMPANY
44328 W Nees Ave, Firebaugh (93622-9647)
PHONE 209 364-0070
Tim Hall, *Partner*
Laurie Hall, *Partner*
EMP: 70
SALES (est): 7.8MM **Privately Held**
WEB: www.orolomaranch.com
SIC: 0191 General farms, primarily crop

(P-364)
HAMMONDS RANCH INC
47375 W Dakota Ave, Firebaugh (93622-9516)
PHONE 209 364-6185
Fax: 559 364-6191
James M Hammonds, *President*
William E Hammond, *Chairman*
Mary Hicks, *Corp Secy*
Michelle Cole, *Accounts Mgr*
EMP: 100 EST: 1929
SQ FT: 3,500
SALES (est): 11.1MM **Privately Held**
SIC: 0191 General farms, primarily crop

(P-365)
HANSEN RANCHES
7124 Whitley Ave, Corcoran (93212-9669)
P.O. Box 398 (93212-0398)
PHONE 559 992-3111
Fax: 559 992-2107
James Hansen, *Partner*
Edward Halverstadt, *CFO*
Gary Oneal, *Manager*
EMP: 60
SQ FT: 4,000
SALES: 20.6MM **Privately Held**
SIC: 0191 General farms, primarily crop

(P-366)
HARRIS FARMS INC
Also Called: Harris Farm Horse Division
27366 W Oakland Ave, Coalinga (93210-9627)
Rural Route 1 Box 400 (93210-9222)
PHONE 559 884-2203
Dave McGlothlin, *Sales/Mktg Mgr*
Charlotte Wrather, *Agent*
Thurman Carey, *Editor*
EMP: 50
SALES (corp-wide): 5B **Privately Held**
WEB: www.harrisfarms.com
SIC: 0191 0752 General farms, primarily crop; boarding services, horses: racing & non-racing
PA: Harris Farms, Inc.
29475 Fresno Coalinga Rd
Coalinga CA 93210
559 884-2435

(P-367)
HARRIS FARMS INC
Subway
24505 W Dorris Ave, Coalinga (93210-9667)
PHONE 559 935-0717
Jonathan Farrington, *General Mgr*
Francis Fuente, *CIO*
Steve Warren, *Human Res Dir*
Dave McGlothlin, *Plant Mgr*
Kirk Doyle, *Opers-Prdtn-Mfg*
EMP: 340
SALES (corp-wide): 5B **Privately Held**
WEB: www.harrisfarms.com
SIC: 0191 7011 5813 5812 General farms, primarily crop; hotels & motels; drinking places; eating places
PA: Harris Farms, Inc.
29475 Fresno Coalinga Rd
Coalinga CA 93210
559 884-2435

(P-368)
HARRIS FARMS INC
23300 W Oakland Ave, Coalinga (93210-9804)
PHONE 559 884-2477
Fax: 559 884-2267
John Harris, *President*
Mike Casey, *Human Res Mgr*
Maury Ellefson, *Manager*
David McGlothlin, *Manager*
EMP: 300
SALES (corp-wide): 5.6B **Privately Held**
WEB: www.harrisfarms.com
SIC: 0191 0182 0161 General farms, primarily crop; food crops grown under cover; vegetables & melons
PA: Harris Farms, Inc.
29475 Fresno Coalinga Rd
Coalinga CA 93210
559 884-2435

(P-369)
HIGARD FARMS LLC
6 Quail Run Cir, Salinas (93907-2345)
PHONE 831 753-5982
Gary Higl,
EMP: 96
SALES (est): 1.8MM **Privately Held**
SIC: 0191 General farms, primarily crop

(P-370)
J & J FARMS
36245 W Ashlan Ave, Firebaugh (93622)
P.O. Box 155 (93622-0155)
PHONE 559 659-1457
Bill Jones, *Owner*
Stephen Fessler, *CFO*
EMP: 50
SALES (est): 3.8MM **Privately Held**
SIC: 0191 General farms, primarily crop

(P-371)
J & S FARM
803 W Kimball Ave, Visalia (93277-6567)
PHONE 559 308-0294
Sasha Gonzales, *Principal*
James B Reese, *Principal*
EMP: 60
SALES (est): 591.5K **Privately Held**
SIC: 0191 General farms, primarily crop

(P-372)
J CRECELIUS INC
Also Called: Montetisea Framing
5043 N Montpelier Rd, Denair (95316-9608)
P.O. Box 579 (95316-0579)
PHONE 209 883-4826
Jim Crecelius, *President*
Robert McClain, *CFO*
EMP: 100
SALES (est): 2.2MM **Privately Held**
SIC: 0191 0173 General farms, primarily crop; tree nuts

(P-373)
J M TELFORD FARMS
3280 N Academy Ave, Sanger (93657-9345)
PHONE 559 875-4955
Jerri Telford, *Co-Owner*
EMP: 50
SALES (est): 1.2MM **Privately Held**
SIC: 0191 General farms, primarily crop

(P-374)
JACOBS FARM/DEL CABO INC
390 Swift Ave Ste 8, South San Francisco (94080-6221)
PHONE 650 827-1133
Fax: 650 827-2032
Ted Witt, *Manager*
Lissett Ortega, *Manager*
Hector Rodriguez, *Manager*
EMP: 75
SALES (corp-wide): 77.9MM **Privately Held**
SIC: 0191 General farms, primarily crop
PA: Jacobs Farm/Del Cabo, Inc.
2450 Stage Rd
Pescadero CA 94060
650 879-0580

(P-375)
JOHN GRIZZLE FARMING
1395 Bonds Corner Rd, Holtville (92250-9736)
PHONE 760 356-4381
Fax: 760 356-2577
John Grizzle, *Owner*
Imala Rodriguez, *Owner*
EMP: 50
SALES (est): 4.1MM **Privately Held**
SIC: 0191 0212 General farms, primarily crop; beef cattle except feedlots

(P-376)
JOSE VRAMONTES
Also Called: V and V Farms
14345 N Highway 88, Lodi (95240-9312)
PHONE 209 810-5384
Jose Vramontes, *Owner*
EMP: 50
SALES: 700K **Privately Held**
SIC: 0191 General farms, primarily crop

(P-377)
KG BERRY FARMS LLC
1660 Philbric Rd, Santa Maria (93454-8027)
P.O. Box 1087 (93456-1087)
PHONE 805 680-6751
Kevin John Guggia, *Mng Member*
Nicole Lea Guggia,
EMP: 115
SQ FT: 1,000
SALES (est): 5.4MM **Privately Held**
SIC: 0191 General farms, primarily crop

(P-378)
KIRSCHENMAN ENTERPRISES INC
10100 Digiorgio Rd, Bakersfield (93307)
P.O. Box 27, Edison (93220-0027)
PHONE 661 366-5736
Wayne Kirschenman, *CEO*
Norma Rapp, *Admin Sec*
▼ **EMP:** 60
SQ FT: 25,000
SALES (est): 10.1MM **Privately Held**
SIC: 0191 General farms, primarily crop

(P-379)
L & J FARMS CARACCIOLI LLC
27905 Corda Rd, Gonzales (93926)
P.O. Box H (93926-0239)
PHONE 831 675-7901
Fax: 831 675-7907
Phil Caraccioli,
Gary Caraccioli,
EMP: 50
SALES (est): 4.5MM **Privately Held**
SIC: 0191 General farms, primarily crop

(P-380)
LION RAISINS INC
Also Called: Lion Brothers Farms-Newstone
12555 Road 9, Madera (93637-9089)
P.O. Box 1350, Selma (93662-1350)
PHONE 559 662-8686
Fax: 559 622-8689
Jeff Bergeron, *Manager*
EMP: 200
SALES (corp-wide): 84.3MM **Privately Held**
WEB: www.lionraisins.com
SIC: 0191 General farms, primarily crop
PA: Lion Raisins, Inc.
9500 S De Wolf Ave
Selma CA 93662
559 834-6677

(P-381)
LONE OAK FARMS
13866 4th Ave, Hanford (93230-8800)
PHONE 559 583-1277
Fax: 559 583-6706
Bernard Teveld, *Owner*
EMP: 50
SALES (est): 2.8MM **Privately Held**
SIC: 0191 General farms, primarily crop

(P-382)
LS FARMS LLC
29794 Schuster Rd, Mc Farland (93250-9784)
PHONE 661 792-3192
Antonette Anich, *Mng Member*
EMP: 500
SALES: 11.4MM **Privately Held**
SIC: 0191 General farms, primarily crop

(P-383)
LUCICH SANTOS FARMS
12631 Rogers Rd, Patterson (95363-8511)
P.O. Box 637 (95363-0637)
PHONE 209 892-6500
Peter Lucich, *Partner*
David Santos, *Partner*
EMP: 120
SQ FT: 20,000
SALES (est): 8.5MM **Privately Held**
SIC: 0191 General farms, primarily crop

(P-384)
MOON MOUNTAIN FARMS LLC
3846 E Telegraph Rd, Fillmore (93015-9779)
PHONE 805 521-1742
Les Blake, *Mng Member*
EMP: 50
SALES (est): 1.6MM **Privately Held**
SIC: 0191 General farms, primarily crop

(P-385)
OSCAR VALERO
Also Called: Valero Labor
1685 Jones St, Woodland (95776-6380)
PHONE 530 668-4342
Oscar Valero, *Owner*
EMP: 50
SALES: 100K **Privately Held**
SIC: 0191 General farms, primarily crop

(P-386)
RAINBOW RANCHES INC
13650 Copus Rd, Bakersfield (93313-9676)
PHONE 661 858-2266
Fax: 661 858-6427
Michael Andrews, *CEO*
Marina Quintana, *Admin Sec*
EMP: 210
SALES (est): 6.9MM **Privately Held**
SIC: 0191 General farms, primarily crop

(P-387)
RANCHO LAGUNA FARMS INC
2410 W Main St, Santa Maria (93458-9712)
P.O. Box 6617 (93456-6617)
PHONE 805 925-7805
Larry Ferini, *President*
Tracy Ferini, *Vice Pres*
Jason Marchant, *Administration*
EMP: 59
SALES (est): 2.2MM **Privately Held**
WEB: www.lagunaproduce.com
SIC: 0191 General farms, primarily crop

(P-388)
RED BLOSSOM SALES INC
Also Called: Red Blossom Farms
9 Harris Pl, Salinas (93901-4586)
PHONE 831 751-9169
Michelle Huber, *Manager*
EMP: 503
SALES (corp-wide): 141.5MM **Privately Held**
SIC: 0191 General farms, primarily crop
PA: Red Blossom Sales, Inc.
400 W Ventura Blvd # 140
Camarillo CA 93010
805 686-4747

(P-389)
ROCKET FARMS HERBS INC
7909 Crossway Dr, Pico Rivera (90660-4449)
P.O. Box 398104, San Francisco (94139-8104)
PHONE 562 205-1900
Don Barnett, *CEO*
Dale Cox, *Controller*

▲ = Import ▼ = Export ◆ = Import/Export

PRODUCTS & SERVICES SECTION

0214 - Sheep & Goats County (P-416)

EMP: 493
SALES (est): 36.7MM **Privately Held**
SIC: 0191 General farms, primarily crop

(P-390)
SAFARI HARVSTG & FARMING LLC
313 Plaza Dr Ste B12, Santa Maria (93454-6931)
PHONE..................805 925-2600
Robert T Sheehy,
Ellie Elenes, *Admin Sec*
Jose Gallardo, *Supervisor*
EMP: 300
SALES (est): 10.4MM **Privately Held**
SIC: 0191 0722 General farms, primarily crop; crop harvesting

(P-391)
SCHULTE RANCHES
Also Called: Dos Pueblos Ranch
Rr 1 Box 228, Goleta (93117-9700)
PHONE..................805 563-0821
Fax: 805 968-4822
Rudolph Schulte, *Owner*
EMP: 70
SQ FT: 600
SALES (est): 1.8MM **Privately Held**
SIC: 0191 0179 General farms, primarily crop; avocado orchard

(P-392)
SERIMIAN M S D L RANCH
Also Called: D & L Produce
10463 S Del Rey Ave, Selma (93662-9706)
PHONE..................559 896-1517
Donald Serimian, *Partner*
Lionel Serimian, *Partner*
EMP: 50 EST: 1961
SALES (est): 1.1MM **Privately Held**
SIC: 0191 General farms, primarily crop

(P-393)
SHELDON RANCHES
25140 Burr Dr, Lindsay (93247-9786)
P.O. Box 668 (93247-0668)
PHONE..................559 562-3978
Charles H Sheldon, *President*
Traci Sheldon, *Manager*
EMP: 60
SALES (est): 2.8MM **Privately Held**
SIC: 0191 General farms, primarily crop

(P-394)
SUN WORLD INTERNATIONAL LLC
5701 Truxtun Ave Ste 200, Bakersfield (93309-0651)
P.O. Box 80298 (93380-0298)
PHONE..................661 392-5000
Fax: 661 631-4189
Merrill N Dibble, *President*
David Hostetter, *CFO*
Ron Schuh, *Treasurer*
Michael J Aiton, *Senior VP*
David Fenn, *Senior VP*
▲ EMP: 450
SALES (est): 57.6MM **Privately Held**
WEB: www.sun-world.com
SIC: 0191 General farms, primarily crop
PA: Sun World International, Inc.
16351 Driver Rd
Bakersfield CA 93308

(P-395)
SWANTON BERRY FARMS INC
25 Swanton Rd, Davenport (95017-9742)
P.O. Box 308 (95017-0308)
PHONE..................831 425-8919
Fax: 831 466-0952
James Cochran, *President*
Lisa Timberger, *Bookkeeper*
EMP: 50
SALES (est): 3.3MM **Privately Held**
SIC: 0191 General farms, primarily crop

(P-396)
TAPIA FARMS
8425 W Ave 8, Rosamond (93560)
PHONE..................661 256-4401
Charlie Tapia, *Owner*
EMP: 50
SALES (est): 1.6MM **Privately Held**
WEB: www.tapiafarms.com
SIC: 0191 General farms, primarily crop

(P-397)
TERRA LINDA FARMS 1
17625 S Marks Ave, Riverdale (93656-9559)
P.O. Box 758 (93656-0758)
PHONE..................559 867-3400
Joe Coelho, *Partner*
EMP: 50
SALES (est): 1.6MM **Privately Held**
SIC: 0191 General farms, primarily crop

(P-398)
TERRANOVA RANCH INC
16729 W Floral Ave, Helm (93627)
P.O. Box 130 (93627-0130)
PHONE..................559 866-5644
Diego Lissi, *President*
Don Cameron, *Vice Pres*
Marsha Cantu, *Office Mgr*
Annette Bauer, *Info Tech Mgr*
Jenice Vrintead, *Controller*
EMP: 50
SQ FT: 5,000
SALES (est): 5.8MM **Privately Held**
SIC: 0191 0172 General farms, primarily crop; grapes

(P-399)
THOMPSON FAMILY FARMS LLC
16478 Beach Blvd Ste 391, Westminster (92683-7860)
PHONE..................714 848-7536
Robert Thompson, *Mng Member*
EMP: 50
SALES (est): 739.4K **Privately Held**
SIC: 0191 General farms, primarily crop

(P-400)
V&V FARM LABOR CONTRACTOR
18396 S Wagner Ave, Ripon (95366-9720)
PHONE..................209 599-4834
Jose Villanueva, *President*
EMP: 50
SALES (est): 2MM **Privately Held**
SIC: 0191 General farms, primarily crop

(P-401)
VAN GRONINGEN & SONS INC
15100 Jack Tone Rd, Manteca (95336-9729)
PHONE..................209 982-5248
Fax: 209 983-9014
Robert Van Groningen, *President*
Monica Kuil, *CFO*
Dan Van Groningen, *Vice Pres*
Dan Vangroningen, *Vice Pres*
Paul Hiemstra, *Plant Mgr*
▼ EMP: 360
SQ FT: 3,000
SALES (est): 57.6MM **Privately Held**
WEB: www.vgandsons.com
SIC: 0191 0762 General farms, primarily crop; farm management services

(P-402)
VAQUERO FARMS INC
43405 W Panoche Rd, Firebaugh (93622-9720)
PHONE..................559 659-2790
Fax: 559 659-0924
Havier Rodriguez, *Manager*
EMP: 60
SQ FT: 150
SALES (corp-wide): 7.5MM **Privately Held**
SIC: 0191 General farms, primarily crop
PA: Vaquero Farms, Inc.
2800 W March Ln Ste 330
Stockton CA 95219
209 476-0002

(P-403)
VICTORIA ISLAND FARMS
16021 E Hwy 4, Holt (95234)
P.O. Box 87 (95234-0087)
PHONE..................209 465-5609
Eileen Nichols, *Owner*
▲ EMP: 70 EST: 1998
SQ FT: 1,484
SALES (est): 6.1MM **Privately Held**
SIC: 0191 General farms, primarily crop

(P-404)
VINO FARMS INC
1451 Stanley Ln, NAPA (94559-9760)
PHONE..................707 258-2729
Jin Ledbetter, *Principal*
EMP: 174
SALES (corp-wide): 68.4MM **Privately Held**
SIC: 0191 General farms, primarily crop
PA: Vino Farms, Inc.
1377 E Lodi Ave
Lodi CA 95240
209 334-6975

(P-405)
VINO FARMS INC
51375 S Netherlands Rd, Clarksburg (95612-5019)
PHONE..................916 775-4095
Fax: 916 775-4097
John Ledbetter, *Owner*
Mike Harder, *Design Engr*
EMP: 116
SALES (corp-wide): 68.4MM **Privately Held**
SIC: 0191 General farms, primarily crop
PA: Vino Farms, Inc.
1377 E Lodi Ave
Lodi CA 95240
209 334-6975

(P-406)
WILLOW FARMS LLC
9452 Telephone Rd Pmb 142, Ventura (93004-2600)
PHONE..................805 647-0720
George Ito,
EMP: 60
SALES (est): 1.9MM **Privately Held**
WEB: www.willowfarms.com
SIC: 0191 General farms, primarily crop

0211 Beef Cattle Feedlots

(P-407)
BRANDT CO INC
Also Called: Brandt Cattle
7015 Brandt Rd, Calipatria (92233-9761)
PHONE..................760 348-2295
Fax: 760 348-2290
William Brent, *Manager*
EMP: 53
SALES (corp-wide): 9.8MM **Privately Held**
WEB: www.brandtco.com
SIC: 0211 0139 Beef cattle feedlots; alfalfa farm; grass seed farm
PA: Brandt Co., Inc.
299 W Main St
Brawley CA 92227
760 344-3430

(P-408)
JR SIMPLOT COMPANY
3265 W Figarden Dr, Fresno (93711-3912)
P.O. Box 28955 (93729-8955)
PHONE..................559 439-3900
EMP: 178
SALES (corp-wide): 4.5B **Privately Held**
SIC: 0211 Beef cattle feedlots
PA: J.R. Simplot Company
999 W Main St Ste 1300
Boise ID 83702
208 336-2110

(P-409)
MENDES CALF RANCH
13356 Avenue 168, Tipton (93272-9749)
PHONE..................559 688-4708
Fax: 559 688-1023
Victor Mendes, *Owner*
EMP: 90
SALES: 3MM **Privately Held**
SIC: 0211 Beef cattle feedlots

0212 Beef Cattle, Except Feedlots

(P-410)
FULLMER CATTLE NTHRN CAL LLC
16600 Hellman Ave, Corona (92880-9722)
PHONE..................909 597-3274
Que J Fullmer,
Que Fullmer, *Owner*
EMP: 120
SQ FT: 100,000
SALES (est): 4.7MM **Privately Held**
SIC: 0212 Beef cattle except feedlots

(P-411)
M & T CALF RANCH
Also Called: Tuls Cattle
14998 Avenue 192, Tulare (93274-9074)
PHONE..................559 686-7663
Fax: 559 686-7662
Sid Tuls, *Partner*
Mike Frings, *Partner*
Jason Tuls, *Partner*
EMP: 60
SQ FT: 1,800
SALES (est): 1.8MM **Privately Held**
SIC: 0212 Beef cattle except feedlots

(P-412)
ROBINSON & SONS
Also Called: Robinson and Enterprises
293 Lower Grass Valley Rd # 201, Nevada City (95959-3120)
PHONE..................530 265-5844
Lowell Robinson, *Partner*
Neil Robinson, *Partner*
EMP: 70
SQ FT: 2,000
SALES (est): 1.3MM **Privately Held**
WEB: www.timrobinson.com
SIC: 0212 Beef cattle except feedlots

(P-413)
SWEETBRIER DEVELOPMENT
151 Silliman Rd, Watsonville (95076-9459)
PHONE..................831 722-5577
Fax: 831 722-0191
Carlos Fear, *Principal*
Gloria Chillon, *Manager*
John Siletto, *Manager*
EMP: 50
SALES (est): 2.7MM **Privately Held**
SIC: 0212 Beef cattle except feedlots

(P-414)
WESTERN MEAT PROCESSORS INC
Also Called: Agri-Feed Industries
502 E Barioni Blvd, Imperial (92251-1776)
P.O. Box 728 (92251-0728)
PHONE..................760 355-1175
Philip E Bauer, *Principal*
EMP: 50
SALES (est): 4.2MM **Privately Held**
SIC: 0212 0723 Beef cattle except feedlots; grain milling, custom services

0213 Hogs

(P-415)
LINDA TERRA FARMS (PA)
5494 W Mount Whitney Ave, Riverdale (93656-9329)
PHONE..................559 867-3473
John Coelho, *CEO*
EMP: 170
SQ FT: 1,014
SALES (est): 20.2MM **Privately Held**
SIC: 0213 0182 0172 Hogs; fruits grown under cover; grapes

0214 Sheep & Goats

(P-416)
ETCHEGARAY FARMS LLC
32324 Famoso Rd, Mc Farland (93250)
P.O. Box 964, Visalia (93279-0964)
PHONE..................661 393-0920
Sam Etchegaray,

0241 - Dairy Farms County (P-417) — PRODUCTS & SERVICES SECTION

EMP: 50
SQ FT: 8,000
SALES (est): 634.9K Privately Held
SIC: 0214 0172 0179 0174 Lamb feedlot; grapes; avocado orchard; grapefruit grove

0241 Dairy Farms

(P-417)
B & R TEVELDE
2911 Hanford Armona Rd, Hanford (93230-9379)
PHONE..............................559 583-1277
Bernard Tevelde, *Owner*
Nico Slabber, *Principal*
EMP: 52
SALES: 950K Privately Held
SIC: 0241 0111 Dairy farms; wheat

(P-418)
BLAKE ALEXANDRE
Also Called: Alexandre Ecodairy Farms
8371 Lower Lake Rd, Crescent City (95531-9749)
PHONE..............................707 487-1000
Fax: 707 487-1001
Blake Alexandre, *Owner*
Stephanie Alexandre, *Co-Owner*
Meagan Curtis, *Manager*
EMP: 50
SALES (est): 10.8MM Privately Held
WEB: www.ecodairyfarms.com
SIC: 0241 7389 Milk production;

(P-419)
BOSMAN DAIRY
6802 Avenue 120 A, Tipton (93272-9525)
PHONE..............................559 752-1012
Fax: 559 752-7001
Clarence Bosman, *Partner*
Frank Bosman, *Partner*
EMP: 130 EST: 1959
SALES (est): 13.2MM Privately Held
SIC: 0241 Dairy farms

(P-420)
CASE VLOTT CATTLE
Also Called: Vlot Brothers
20330 Road 4, Chowchilla (93610-9489)
P.O. Box 309 (93610-0309)
PHONE..............................559 665-7399
Case Vlott, *Owner*
Dirik Vlot, *President*
Ellie Vlot, *Manager*
EMP: 50
SALES (est): 2MM Privately Held
SIC: 0241 Dairy farms

(P-421)
COSTA VIEW FARMS
Also Called: Costa View Farms Shop
16800 Road 15, Madera (93637-9445)
PHONE..............................559 675-3131
Fax: 559 673-3177
Darryl Azevedo, *Partner*
Linda Azevedo, *Partner*
Teresa Carr, *Partner*
William Carr, *Partner*
Dimas Costa, *Partner*
▲ **EMP:** 50
SALES (est): 9MM Privately Held
SIC: 0241 Dairy farms

(P-422)
CURTI FAMILY INC
3235 Avenue 199, Tulare (93274-8909)
PHONE..............................559 688-8323
Phillip A Curti, *President*
Preston Nicholas Curti, *Shareholder*
Phillip Justin Curti, *Corp Secy*
EMP: 54
SALES (est): 6.3MM Privately Held
SIC: 0241 Dairy farms

(P-423)
CURTIMADE DAIRY INC
Also Called: Curti's Dairy
Road 24, Tulare (93274)
PHONE..............................559 688-8323
Ben Curti, *President*
EMP: 50
SALES (corp-wide): 38.5MM Privately Held
SIC: 0241 Milk production
PA: Curtimade Dairy, Inc.
18337 Road 24
Tulare CA
559 992-5866

(P-424)
FOSTER DAIRY FARMS (PA)
Also Called: Crystal Creamery
529 Kansas Ave, Modesto (95351-1515)
PHONE..............................209 576-3400
Fax: 209 576-3437
Frank Otis, *President*
Mark Shaw, *CFO*
Tom Foster, *Vice Pres*
Luis Miranda, *Vice Pres*
Jeff Sussman, *Vice Pres*
EMP: 800
SALES (est): 433.7MM Privately Held
SIC: 0241 Milk production

(P-425)
FRANK J GOMES DAIRY A CALIFO
Also Called: F and A Farms
5301 Deangelis Rd, Stevinson (95374-9726)
PHONE..............................209 669-7978
Frank J Gomes, *Partner*
Albert Xavier, *Partner*
Stacy Peck, *Manager*
EMP: 58
SALES (est): 8.5MM Privately Held
SIC: 0241 Dairy farms

(P-426)
GALLO CATTLE CO A LTD PARTNR
Also Called: Joseph Farms Cheese
10561 State Highway 140, Atwater (95301-9309)
P.O. Box 775 (95301-0775)
PHONE..............................209 394-7984
Fax: 209 394-2392
Michael Gallo, *CEO*
Micah Gallo, *Partner*
Tiffanie Gallo, *Partner*
Linda Jelacich, *Partner*
Marv Bennett, *CFO*
EMP: 500
SQ FT: 6,000
SALES (est): 53.1MM Privately Held
SIC: 0241 2022 Dairy farms; cheese, natural & processed

(P-427)
HIGH PLAINS RANCH LLC (PA)
2911 Hanford Armona Rd, Hanford (93230-9379)
PHONE..............................559 583-1277
Bernard Te Velde, *Mng Member*
EMP: 120
SQ FT: 2,000
SALES (est): 17.4MM Privately Held
SIC: 0241 Dairy farms

(P-428)
HOLLANDIA DAIRY INC (PA)
622 E Mission Rd, San Marcos (92069-1999)
PHONE..............................760 744-3222
Fax: 760 744-2789
Arie H Dejong, *President*
Peter De Jong, *Vice Pres*
Rudy De Jong, *Vice Pres*
Bert Ton, *Vice Pres*
EMP: 185
SQ FT: 20,000
SALES (est): 47.5MM Privately Held
WEB: www.hollandiadairy.com
SIC: 0241 Dairy farms; milk production

(P-429)
IEST FAMILY FARMS
Also Called: Richard Iest Dairy
14576 Avenue 14, Madera (93637-8922)
PHONE..............................559 674-9417
Fax: 559 675-1448
Richard Iest, *Partner*
Danny Iest, *Partner*
Gerrlyn Iest, *Partner*
Bryant Elkins, *General Mgr*
Linda Wedel, *General Mgr*
EMP: 70
SALES (est): 10.4MM Privately Held
SIC: 0241 Dairy farms

(P-430)
JAMES J STEVINSON A CORP (PA)
Also Called: Anchor J Dairy
25079 River Rd, Stevinson (95374-9724)
P.O. Box 818, Newman (95360-0818)
PHONE..............................209 632-1681
Robert Kelley, *President*
Kevin F Kelley, *Treasurer*
George Kelley, *Vice Pres*
Leone Jones, *Admin Sec*
EMP: 50
SQ FT: 1,500
SALES: 5MM Privately Held
SIC: 0241 0191 Dairy farms; general farms, primarily crop

(P-431)
MADDOX DAIRY LLC
3899 W Davis Ave, Riverdale (93656-9417)
PHONE..............................559 867-3545
Stephen Maddox,
Julia Maddox Chow, *CFO*
EMP: 73
SALES (est): 873.6K Privately Held
SIC: 0241 Dairy farms

(P-432)
MADDOX DAIRY A LTD PARTNERSHIP (PA)
3899 W Davis Ave, Riverdale (93656-9417)
PHONE..............................559 867-3545
Steven Maddox, *Partner*
Douglas Maddox, *Partner*
Patrick Maddox, *Partner*
Julia Maddox, *Controller*
EMP: 60
SQ FT: 8,700
SALES (est): 10.2MM Privately Held
SIC: 0241 Milk production

(P-433)
MADDOX DAIRY A LTD PARTNERSHIP
Also Called: Ruann Dairy
7285 W Davis Ave, Riverdale (93656-9735)
PHONE..............................559 867-4457
Patrick Maddox, *Manager*
EMP: 50
SALES (corp-wide): 10.2MM Privately Held
SIC: 0241 Milk production
PA: Maddox Dairy, A Limited Partnership
3899 W Davis Ave
Riverdale CA 93656
559 867-3545

(P-434)
MADDOX DAIRY A LTD PARTNERSHIP
12863 W Kamm Ave, Riverdale (93656-9231)
PHONE..............................559 866-5624
Steve Maddox, *Partner*
EMP: 70
SALES (corp-wide): 10.2MM Privately Held
SIC: 0241 Milk production
PA: Maddox Dairy, A Limited Partnership
3899 W Davis Ave
Riverdale CA 93656
559 867-3545

(P-435)
MAPLE DAIRY LP
15857 Bear Mountain Blvd, Bakersfield (93311-9413)
PHONE..............................661 396-9600
Fax: 661 396-9626
John Bos, *Partner*
A J Bos, *Partner*
EMP: 75
SALES (est): 9.5MM Privately Held
SIC: 0241 Dairy farms

(P-436)
NIELSENS CREAMERY (PA)
Also Called: Hoffman Farms
21346 Road 140, Tulare (93274-9363)
P.O. Box 579 (93275-0579)
PHONE..............................559 686-4744
Fax: 559 686-2355
Chase Hoffman, *Partner*
Marion N Hoffman, *Partner*
Merilyn Johnson, *Manager*
EMP: 50
SQ FT: 11,000
SALES (est): 4MM Privately Held
SIC: 0241 Milk production

(P-437)
ORGANIC PASTURES DAIRY CO LLC
7221 S Jameson Ave, Fresno (93706-9386)
PHONE..............................559 846-9732
Fax: 559 842-8061
Mark L McAfee, *Mng Member*
Amanda MBA, *Financial Exec*
Laura Huntington, *Controller*
Kaleigh Lutz, *Marketing Mgr*
Bob Atthowe, *Sales Staff*
EMP: 50
SALES (est): 32.4MM Privately Held
SIC: 0241 Dairy farms

(P-438)
P H RANCH INC
Also Called: Veldhuis Dairy
6335 Oakdale Rd, Winton (95388-9648)
PHONE..............................209 358-5111
Fax: 209 358-0422
Ray Veldhuis, *President*
Jeanette Veldhuis, *Corp Secy*
Ray Veldhuis Jr, *Vice Pres*
Patricia Mello, *Manager*
EMP: 50
SALES (est): 6.2MM Privately Held
WEB: www.phranch.com
SIC: 0241 Milk production

(P-439)
VELDHUIS NORTH DAIRY
12465 Lee Rd, Ballico (95303-9714)
P.O. Box 239 (95303-0239)
PHONE..............................209 394-5117
Fax: 209 394-4154
Eric Veldhuis, *Managing Prtnr*
EMP: 50
SQ FT: 696
SALES (est): 2.3MM Privately Held
SIC: 0241 Milk production

(P-440)
VLOT BROTHERS TRUCKING CO INC
Also Called: Vlot Brothers Dairy
3197 Avenue 21, Chowchilla (93610-9294)
P.O. Box 309 (93610-0309)
PHONE..............................559 665-7399
Fax: 559 665-7601
Dirk J Vlot, *Partner*
Case Vlot, *Partner*
Valerie Vlot, *Partner*
Luci Melina, *Manager*
EMP: 80
SALES (est): 9.8MM Privately Held
SIC: 0241 Dairy farms

(P-441)
WITHROW CATTLE
Also Called: Withrow Dairy
5301 Pleasant Grove Rd, Pleasant Grove (95668-9752)
PHONE..............................916 780-0364
Shane Johnson, *Manager*
EMP: 65
SALES (corp-wide): 2.6MM Privately Held
WEB: www.withrowdairy.com
SIC: 0241 Dairy farms
PA: Withrow Cattle
5301 Pleasant Grove Rd
Pleasant Grove CA 95668
916 780-0364

(P-442)
ZONNEVELD DAIRIES INC
1560 Cerini Ave, Laton (93242-9700)
PHONE..............................559 923-4546
Fax: 559 923-9523
John Zonneveld Jr, *President*
Frank Zonneveld, *Corp Secy*
EMP: 60
SALES (est): 9MM Privately Held
WEB: www.cainhibbard.com
SIC: 0241 Dairy farms

PRODUCTS & SERVICES SECTION

0291 - Animal Production, NEC County (P-464)

(P-443)
ZONNEVELD FARMS
1560 Cerini Ave, Laton (93242-9700)
PHONE.................................559 923-4546
Andrew Zonneveld, *Partner*
Craig Wierenga, *Project Mgr*
EMP: 99
SALES (est): 3.5MM **Privately Held**
SIC: 0241 0191 Dairy farms; general farms, primarily crop

0252 Chicken Egg Farms

(P-444)
DEMLER EGG RANCH
28198 Gromer Ave, Wasco (93280-9558)
P.O. Box 207 (93280-0207)
PHONE.................................661 758-4577
David Demler, *Partner*
Sharman Demler, *Partner*
EMP: 50
SALES (est): 1.4MM **Privately Held**
SIC: 0252 Chicken eggs

(P-445)
FOSTER FARMS LLC
770 N Plano St, Porterville (93257-6329)
PHONE.................................559 793-5501
Fax: 559 784-7506
Paul Bravinder, *Manager*
Christa Brown, *Financial Exec*
Fatima Lopes, *Sales Staff*
Chris Jones, *Maintence Staff*
Gustavo Gomez, *Supervisor*
EMP: 300
SQ FT: 81,000
SALES (corp-wide): 1.9B **Privately Held**
SIC: 0252 2015 Chicken eggs; poultry slaughtering & processing
PA: Foster Farms, Llc
1000 Davis St
Livingston CA 95334
970 874-7503

(P-446)
GEMPERLE ENTERPRISES
Also Called: Gemperle Farms
10218 Lander Ave, Turlock (95380-9627)
PHONE.................................209 667-2651
Fax: 209 667-4366
Steve Gemperle, *Mng Member*
▼ **EMP:** 90
SQ FT: 8,000
SALES (est): 8.4MM **Privately Held**
SIC: 0252 5144 Chicken eggs; eggs

(P-447)
NORCO RANCH INC (DH)
Also Called: Norco Ranch Inc.
12005 Cabernet Dr, Fontana (92337-7703)
PHONE.................................951 737-6735
Fax: 951 737-9405
Creig Williardson, *President*
Michael Lemire, *Controller*
Carl Forshage, *Manager*
Rita Cabot, *Accounts Mgr*
EMP: 350
SQ FT: 120,000
SALES (est): 45.5MM
SALES (corp-wide): 14.9B **Privately Held**
WEB: www.norcoeggs.com
SIC: 0252 Chicken eggs
HQ: Moark, Llc
28 Under The Mountain Rd
North Franklin CT 06254
951 332-3200

(P-448)
VALLEY FRESH FOODS INC
Nest Best Egg Company
3600 E Linwood Ave, Turlock (95380-9109)
P.O. Box 370, Rochester WA (98579-0370)
PHONE.................................209 669-5600
Duane Olsen, *Branch Mgr*
EMP: 61
SALES (corp-wide): 1.5B **Privately Held**
SIC: 0252 2048 Chicken eggs; prepared feeds
PA: Valley Fresh Foods, Inc.
3600 E Linwood Ave
Turlock CA 95380
209 669-5600

(P-449)
VALLEY FRESH FOODS INC
Also Called: Rainbow Farms
1220 Hall Rd, Denair (95316-9617)
P.O. Box 910, Turlock (95381-0910)
PHONE.................................209 669-5510
Fax: 209 668-3562
Danny O'Day, *Manager*
Mark Oldenkamp, *Vice Pres*
Gail Campbell, *Admin Asst*
Sarah Snyder, *Administration*
Victor Madeiros, *CTO*
EMP: 100
SQ FT: 1,216
SALES (corp-wide): 1.5B **Privately Held**
SIC: 0252 2015 Started pullet farm; poultry slaughtering & processing
PA: Valley Fresh Foods, Inc.
3600 E Linwood Ave
Turlock CA 95380
209 669-5600

0253 Turkey & Turkey Egg Farms

(P-450)
BOSS POULTRY
4068 Avenue 404, Dinuba (93618-9778)
PHONE.................................559 897-7507
Kenneth F Boss, *Owner*
EMP: 50
SALES (est): 2.2MM **Privately Held**
SIC: 0253 Turkey farm

(P-451)
DIESTEL TURKEY RANCH
14111 High Tech Dr C, Jamestown (95327)
P.O. Box 4314, Sonora (95370-1314)
PHONE.................................209 984-0826
Fax: 209 984-0243
Tim Diestel, *Owner*
Joan Diestel, *Co-Owner*
Boris Marroquin, *Technology*
Pam Thomson, *Manager*
EMP: 150
SALES (est): 5.9MM **Privately Held**
SIC: 0253 2015 Turkey farm; poultry slaughtering & processing

(P-452)
DIESTEL TURKEY RANCH (PA)
22200 Lyons Bald Mtn Rd, Sonora (95370-8772)
P.O. Box 4314 (95370-1314)
PHONE.................................209 532-4950
Fax: 209 532-5059
Dave Harmer, *CFO*
David Harmer, *CFO*
Joan Diestel, *Vice Pres*
Heidi Diestel, *Principal*
Jason Diestel, *Principal*
EMP: 91
SQ FT: 5,000
SALES (est): 33.7MM **Privately Held**
SIC: 0253 Turkey farm

(P-453)
SWANSON FARMS
5213 W Main St, Turlock (95380-9413)
P.O. Box 2367 (95381-2367)
PHONE.................................209 667-2002
Fax: 209 667-1624
Richard E Swanson, *President*
Larry Pickering, *Vice Pres*
Scott Tyson, *Office Mgr*
Chris Endsley, *MIS Dir*
Michael Mason, *Analyst*
EMP: 65 **EST:** 1942
SQ FT: 5,000
SALES (est): 4.5MM **Privately Held**
WEB: www.associatedfeed.com
SIC: 0253 0173 Turkey farm; almond grove

0254 Poultry Hatcheries

(P-454)
FOSTER POULTRY FARMS (PA)
Also Called: Foster Farms
1000 Davis St, Livingston (95334-1526)
P.O. Box 457 (95334-0457)
PHONE.................................209 394-6914
Fax: 209 394-6329
Ron M Foster, *President*
Donald Jackson, *President*
Leslie Cardoso, *COO*
Caryn Doyle, *CFO*
Regina King, *Treasurer*
◆ **EMP:** 250
SQ FT: 40,000
SALES (est): 4.3B **Privately Held**
WEB: www.fosterfarms.com
SIC: 0254 2015 5812 0173 Poultry hatcheries; chicken hatchery; chicken slaughtering & processing; turkey processing & slaughtering; chicken restaurant; almond grove; animal feeds; local trucking, without storage

(P-455)
FOSTER POULTRY FARMS
Also Called: Foster Farms
1307 Ellenwood Rd, Waterford (95386-8702)
PHONE.................................209 394-7901
Jay Husman, *Manager*
Janice Cardoza, *Supervisor*
EMP: 50
SQ FT: 68,316
SALES (corp-wide): 4.3B **Privately Held**
WEB: www.fosterfarms.com
SIC: 0254 Poultry hatcheries
PA: Foster Poultry Farms
1000 Davis St
Livingston CA 95334
209 394-6914

(P-456)
FOSTER POULTRY FARMS
843 Davis St, Livingston (95334-1525)
P.O. Box 457 (95334-0457)
PHONE.................................209 394-7901
Richie King, *Branch Mgr*
EMP: 3000
SALES (corp-wide): 4.3B **Privately Held**
WEB: www.fosterfarms.com
SIC: 0254 2015 Poultry hatcheries; poultry, processed
PA: Foster Poultry Farms
1000 Davis St
Livingston CA 95334
209 394-6914

(P-457)
FOSTER POULTRY FARMS
Also Called: Foster Turkey Live Haul
1033 S Center St, Turlock (95380-5568)
PHONE.................................209 668-5922
Dean Williams, *Manager*
Scott Strickland, *Foreman/Supr*
EMP: 50
SALES (corp-wide): 4.3B **Privately Held**
WEB: www.fosterfarms.com
SIC: 0254 Poultry hatcheries
PA: Foster Poultry Farms
1000 Davis St
Livingston CA 95334
209 394-6914

(P-458)
FOSTER POULTRY FARMS
900 W Belgravia Ave, Fresno (93706-3909)
PHONE.................................559 265-2000
Jessi Amezcua, *Branch Mgr*
EMP: 567
SALES (corp-wide): 4.3B **Privately Held**
WEB: www.fosterfarms.com
SIC: 0254 2015 5812 0173 Poultry hatcheries; chicken hatchery; chicken slaughtering & processing; turkey processing & slaughtering; chicken restaurant; almond grove; animal feeds; local trucking, without storage
PA: Foster Poultry Farms
1000 Davis St
Livingston CA 95334
209 394-6914

(P-459)
INGENUE INC
Also Called: Q C Poultry
6114 Scott Way, Commerce (90040-3518)
P.O. Box 17238, Anaheim (92817-7238)
PHONE.................................323 726-8084
Fax: 323 726-8085
Don Kurz, *CEO*
Nick Macis, *President*
Phil Fisher, *Principal*
Joseph Wassel, *Principal*
Michelle Macis, *Admin Sec*
EMP: 100
SQ FT: 10,000
SALES (est): 7.8MM **Privately Held**
SIC: 0254 5144 Poultry hatcheries; poultry products

0259 Poultry & Eggs Farms, NEC

(P-460)
REICHARDT DUCK FARM INC
3770 Middle Two Rock Rd, Petaluma (94952-4625)
PHONE.................................707 762-6314
Fax: 707 778-1500
John T Reichardt, *President*
Kathy Shaw, *CFO*
▼ **EMP:** 95
SQ FT: 1,296
SALES (est): 3.6MM **Privately Held**
WEB: www.reichardtduckfarm.com
SIC: 0259 Duck farm

0279 Animal Specialties, NEC

(P-461)
BELCAMPO GROUP INC
65 Webster St, Oakland (94607-3720)
PHONE.................................510 250-7810
Anya Fernald, *CEO*
Nate Morr, *COO*
EMP: 70 **EST:** 2011
SALES (est): 3.7MM **Privately Held**
SIC: 0279 2011 2015 5812 Domestic animal farms; beef products from beef slaughtered on site; poultry slaughtering & processing; family restaurants; office management

(P-462)
SAN BERNARDINO MTNS WILDLIFE
Also Called: Wildhaven Ranch
29450 Pine Ridge Dr, Cedar Glen (92321)
P.O. Box 1782, Lake Arrowhead (92352-1782)
PHONE.................................909 226-6189
Diane Dragotto Williams, *CEO*
EMP: 50 **EST:** 1995
SALES: 125K **Privately Held**
SIC: 0279 Bird sanctuaries

(P-463)
WILDLIFE WAYSTATION
14831 Little Tjunga Cyn Rd, Sylmar (91342-5906)
PHONE.................................818 899-5201
Fax: 818 890-1107
Martine Colette, *President*
Alfred J Durtchi, *General Mgr*
Peggy Summers, *Admin Sec*
EMP: 50
SQ FT: 800
SALES (est): 2.3MM **Privately Held**
WEB: www.wildlifewaystation.org
SIC: 0279 Bird sanctuaries

0291 Animal Production, NEC

(P-464)
BOOTH RANCHES LLC
440 Anchor Ave, Orange Cove (93646-2200)
PHONE.................................559 626-4472
Otis Booth Jr, *Branch Mgr*
Edgar Rodriguez, *Manager*
EMP: 78
SALES (corp-wide): 18MM **Privately Held**
SIC: 0291 General farms, primarily animals
PA: Booth Ranches Llc
12201 Avenue 480
Orange Cove CA 93646
559 626-4732

0291 - Animal Production, NEC County

(P-465)
E & T FOODS INC
Also Called: Monrovia Ranch Market
14827 Seventh St, Victorville (92395-4023)
P.O. Box 661912, Arcadia (91066-1912)
PHONE...................760 843-7730
Fax: 760 843-8060
Franco Duenas, *Branch Mgr*
EMP: 320
SALES (corp-wide): 54.7MM Privately Held
SIC: 0291 General farms, primarily animals
PA: E & T Foods, Inc.
328 W Huntington Dr
Monrovia CA 91016
626 357-5051

(P-466)
HALEAKALA RANCH LLC
9923 Tyler Rd, Gerber (96035-9767)
PHONE...................530 529-6651
Daniel James Davidson, *Mng Member*
▼ EMP: 50
SALES (est): 1.2MM Privately Held
SIC: 0291 General farms, primarily animals

(P-467)
INTEGRAL SENIOR LIVING LLC
12979 Rncho Pnsqitos Blvd, San Diego (92129)
PHONE...................858 484-3801
Fax: 858 538-1330
EMP: 57
SALES (corp-wide): 19.4MM Privately Held
SIC: 0291 General farms, primarily animals
PA: Senior Integral Living Llc
2333 State St Ste 300
Carlsbad CA 92008
760 547-2863

(P-468)
LAGUNA BCH GOLF BNGLOW VLG LLC
Also Called: Ranch At Laguna Beach, The
31106 Coast Hwy, Laguna Beach (92651-8130)
PHONE...................949 499-2271
Mark Christy, *Principal*
Kurt Bjorkman, *General Mgr*
EMP: 50
SALES (est): 3MM Privately Held
SIC: 0291 General farms, primarily animals

(P-469)
MIGUEL RAMOS
196 San Andreas Rd, Watsonville (95076-9522)
PHONE...................831 761-9941
Miguel Ramos, *Owner*
EMP: 60
SALES (est): 2.9MM Privately Held
WEB: www.miguelramon.com
SIC: 0291 General farms, primarily animals

(P-470)
R RANCH MARKET
1112 Walnut Ave, Tustin (92780-5607)
PHONE...................714 573-1182
Jubira Martinez, *Owner*
EMP: 709
SALES (est): 5MM
SALES (corp-wide): 114.8MM Privately Held
SIC: 0291 General farms, primarily animals
PA: R-Ranch Market, Incorporated
13985 Live Oak Ave
Irwindale CA 91706
626 814-2900

(P-471)
RAVA RANCHES INC
700 Airport Rd, King City (93930-2501)
P.O. Box 1600 (93930-1600)
PHONE...................831 385-3285
Jerry J Rava Sr, *President*
EMP: 50 EST: 1987
SALES (est): 4.8MM Privately Held
SIC: 0291 General farms, primarily animals

(P-472)
RIO BRAVO RANCH SHOP
15701 Highway 178, Bakersfield (93306-9500)
PHONE...................661 872-5050
Jim Nickel, *Partner*
George Nickel Jr, *General Mgr*
EMP: 50
SALES (est): 845.6K Privately Held
SIC: 0291 General farms, primarily animals

(P-473)
SEE-GRINS INC
Also Called: See Grins Rv's and Farm Land
7900 Arroyo Cir, Gilroy (95020-7314)
PHONE...................408 683-4652
Randy Scianna, *President*
EMP: 52
SALES (est): 5.7MM Privately Held
SIC: 0291 General farms, primarily animals

0711 Soil Preparation Svcs

(P-474)
BIO INDUSTRIES INC
2060 Montgomery Rd, Red Bluff (96080-4613)
PHONE...................530 529-3290
Ben Sale, *President*
EMP: 50
SQ FT: 400
SALES (est): 100K Privately Held
SIC: 0711 Soil preparation services

(P-475)
JR SIMPLOT COMPANY
Also Called: Simplot Growers Solutions
35836 W Bullard Ave, Firebaugh (93622-9714)
P.O. Box 725 (93622-0725)
PHONE...................559 659-2033
Johnny Valov, *Branch Mgr*
EMP: 50
SALES (est): 4.7B Privately Held
SIC: 0711 Fertilizer application services
PA: J.R. Simplot Company
999 W Main St Ste 1300
Boise ID 83702
208 336-2110

(P-476)
MEE INDUSTRIES INC
16021 Adelante St, Irwindale (91702-3255)
PHONE...................626 359-4550
John Mee, *Principal*
EMP: 68
SALES (corp-wide): 21.2MM Privately Held
WEB: www.meefog.com
SIC: 0711 Soil preparation services
PA: Mee Industries Inc.
16021 Adelante St
Irwindale CA 91702
626 359-4550

0721 Soil Preparation, Planting & Cultivating Svc

(P-477)
CALIFORNIA VALLEY LAND CO INC (PA)
Also Called: Woolf Enterprises
18036 Gale, Huron (93234)
P.O. Box 219 (93234-0219)
PHONE...................559 945-9292
Stuart P Woolf, *President*
John L Woof, *Vice Chairman*
Michael T Woolf, *Treasurer*
John L Woolf, *Vice Ch Bd*
Jason Puchdu, *Manager*
EMP: 93
SQ FT: 4,500
SALES (est): 53.3MM Privately Held
SIC: 0721 Planting services; crop cultivating services; crop protecting services

(P-478)
CHUCK JONES FLYING SERVICE (PA)
Also Called: Aerial Applicators
216 W Hamilton Rd, Biggs (95917-9793)
P.O. Box 497 (95917-0497)
PHONE...................530 868-5798
Fax: 530 868-1428
Dale Jones, *President*

Lori A Jones, *Treasurer*
Alan Jones, *Vice Pres*
EMP: 50
SQ FT: 25,000
SALES (est): 3.2MM Privately Held
SIC: 0721 Crop dusting services

(P-479)
GERAWAN FARMING PARTNERS INC
15749 E Ventura Ave, Sanger (93657-9657)
P.O. Box 67 (93657-0067)
PHONE...................559 787-8780
Dan Gerawan, *President*
EMP: 300
SALES (est): 11.6MM Privately Held
SIC: 0721 0172 Tree orchards, cultivation of; grapes

(P-480)
JOHN H KAUTZ FARMS
5490 Bear Creek Rd, Lodi (95240-7213)
PHONE...................209 334-4786
Fax: 209 339-1689
John H Kautz, *Co-Owner*
Gail Kautz, *Owner*
EMP: 50 EST: 1952
SQ FT: 3,000
SALES (est): 6.3MM Privately Held
SIC: 0721 Orchard tree & vine services

(P-481)
OAKRIDGE LANDSCAPE INC (PA)
28064 Avenue Stanford K, Valencia (91355-1159)
PHONE...................661 295-7228
Fax: 661 295-7230
Jeffrey E Myers, *CEO*
Len Poloniato, *VP Finance*
EMP: 51
SALES (est): 41.5MM Privately Held
WEB: www.oakridgelandscape.com
SIC: 0721 0781 Irrigation system operation, not providing water; landscape services

(P-482)
S & S RANCH INC
Also Called: Stamoules Produce Company
904 S Lyon Ave, Mendota (93640-9735)
PHONE...................559 655-3491
Fax: 559 655-2425
Pagona Stefanopoulos, *CEO*
Athanasios Stefanopoulos, *Vice Pres*
Ellena Stefanopoulos, *Admin Sec*
Kevin Dees, *Info Tech Mgr*
▼ EMP: 85
SQ FT: 500
SALES (est): 8.8MM Privately Held
SIC: 0721 Planting services; crop cultivating services; crop protecting services

(P-483)
SEAMAN NURSERIES INC
336 Robertson Blvd Ste A, Chowchilla (93610-2867)
PHONE...................559 665-1860
William Seaman, *President*
EMP: 70
SALES (est): 6.3MM Privately Held
SIC: 0721 0762 5261 Orchard tree & vine services; farm management services; nurseries

(P-484)
SUNRIDGE NURSERIES INC
441 Vineland Rd, Bakersfield (93307-9556)
PHONE...................661 363-8463
Fax: 661 366-4251
Craig Stoller, *CEO*
Glen Stoller, *Ch of Bd*
Terrie Stoller, *Corp Secy*
EMP: 70
SQ FT: 60,000
SALES (est): 14MM Privately Held
WEB: www.sunridgenurseries.com
SIC: 0721 Vines, cultivation of

(P-485)
THIARA SUKHWANT
Also Called: Thiara Orchards
1537 Atkinson Ct, Yuba City (95993-9679)
PHONE...................530 673-1581
Sukhwant Thiara, *Owner*

Ravi Thiara, *Principal*
EMP: 50 EST: 1964
SALES (est): 2.7MM Privately Held
SIC: 0721 Tree orchards, cultivation of

(P-486)
TRAVERS TREE SERVICE INC
1811 Lomita Blvd, Lomita (90717-1905)
P.O. Box 411 (90717-0411)
PHONE...................310 545-5816
Richard Travers, *President*
Don Lorenzen, *Vice Pres*
Susan Travers, *Admin Sec*
Mary Keyse, *Manager*
EMP: 50
SQ FT: 2,000
SALES (est): 4.7MM Privately Held
SIC: 0721 Orchard tree & vine services

(P-487)
VISTA VERDE FARMS INC
7124 Whitley Ave, Corcoran (93212-9669)
P.O. Box 398 (93212-0398)
PHONE...................559 992-3111
Jim Hansen, *President*
Kendell W Gardner, *Corp Secy*
Jess Hansen, *Vice Pres*
EMP: 70
SQ FT: 3,000
SALES (est): 3.1MM Privately Held
SIC: 0721 0173 Crop planting & protection; almond grove

0722 Crop Harvesting By Machine

(P-488)
A & G GROVE SERVICE
32731 Mesa Lilac Rd, Escondido (92026-4402)
P.O. Box 1752, Fallbrook (92088-1752)
PHONE...................760 728-5447
Angel Huerta, *Owner*
EMP: 100
SALES (est): 6.1MM Privately Held
SIC: 0722 Crop harvesting

(P-489)
ANTHONY HARVESTING INC
401 S Vanderhurst Ave, King City (93930-2934)
P.O. Box 608 (93930-0608)
PHONE...................831 385-6460
Scott Anthony, *President*
Cindy Beal, *Office Mgr*
EMP: 110
SALES (est): 7.1MM Privately Held
SIC: 0722 Crop harvesting

(P-490)
BARNES AND BERGER
1091 S Intake Blvd, Blythe (92225-8209)
PHONE...................760 922-6136
Fax: 760 922-6136
Euell Barnes, *Partner*
Duane Berger, *Partner*
Beverly Siegal, *Regional Mgr*
Beverly Sidel, *Office Mgr*
EMP: 50
SQ FT: 8,900
SALES (est): 3MM Privately Held
WEB: www.barnesandberger.com
SIC: 0722 Cotton, machine harvesting services

(P-491)
BYRD HARVEST INC
Also Called: Byrd Produce
192 Guadalupe St, Guadalupe (93434-1514)
P.O. Box 60 (93434-0060)
PHONE...................805 343-1608
Fax: 805 343-2794
Joe George, *President*
Barbara Stanley, *Treasurer*
Chad Smith, *Vice Pres*
EMP: 300 EST: 1964
SQ FT: 5,000
SALES (est): 22.6MM Privately Held
SIC: 0722 Field crops, except cash grains, machine harvesting services

PRODUCTS & SERVICES SECTION
0723 - Crop Preparation, Except Cotton Ginning County (P-515)

(P-492)
DANELL CUSTOM HARVESTING LLC
8265 Hanford Armona Rd, Hanford (93230-9344)
PHONE.................................559 582-1251
Rance Danell,
EMP: 150
SALES (est): 12.5MM **Privately Held**
SIC: 0722 Crop harvesting

(P-493)
DARR & PITCAIRN AG INC
16674 Wasco Ave, Wasco (93280-7404)
PHONE.................................661 758-5156
Mike Pitcairn, *Partner*
Jim Darr, *Partner*
EMP: 50
SQ FT: 2,400
SALES (est): 2.7MM **Privately Held**
SIC: 0722 5083 6799 Cotton, machine harvesting services; tractors, agricultural; investors

(P-494)
EARLIBEST ORANGE ASSN INC
622 Spruce Rd, Exeter (93221)
PHONE.................................559 592-2124
Fax: 559 592-2023
Rodger B Jensen, *President*
James M Burkhart, *Treasurer*
David A De Lorenzo, *Vice Pres*
EMP: 75
SQ FT: 75,000
SALES (est): 1.9MM
SALES (corp-wide): 10B **Privately Held**
WEB: www.dole.com
SIC: 0722 0723 Fruit, machine harvesting services; fruit crops market preparation services
HQ: Dole Food Company, Inc.
   1 Dole Dr
   Westlake Village CA 91362
   818 874-4000

(P-495)
JJ VALENCIA HARVESTING INC
15433 W Telegraph Rd, Santa Paula (93060-3061)
P.O. Box 527 (93061-0527)
PHONE.................................805 525-8467
Eduardo Z Valencia, *CEO*
EMP: 58
SALES (est): 1.9MM **Privately Held**
SIC: 0722 Crop harvesting

(P-496)
LOPEZ HARVESTING
24079 Avenue 196, Strathmore (93267-9633)
PHONE.................................559 568-2553
Danny Lopez, *Owner*
EMP: 80
SALES (est): 2.1MM **Privately Held**
SIC: 0722 Crop harvesting

(P-497)
LOS DOS VALLES HARVSTG & PKG
2365 Westgate Rd, Santa Maria (93455-1045)
P.O. Box 1942 (93456-1942)
PHONE.................................805 739-1688
Felipe C Zepeda, *President*
Bailey Bridges, *E-Business*
EMP: 150
SQ FT: 4,500
SALES (est): 11.4MM **Privately Held**
SIC: 0722 0723 Vegetables & melons, machine harvesting services; vegetable packing services

(P-498)
NOBLESSE OBLIGE INC
Also Called: Eight Star Equipment
2015 Silsbee Rd, El Centro (92243-9671)
PHONE.................................760 353-3366
Alex Abatti Jr, *President*
Tim Castelli, *CFO*
David Wells, *CFO*
Sid Swarthout, *Admin Sec*
EMP: 1200
SALES (est): 21.2MM **Privately Held**
WEB: www.noblesseoblige.com
SIC: 0722 Combining services; cotton, machine harvesting services; hay, machine harvesting services; vegetables & melons, machine harvesting services

(P-499)
PREMIUM PACKING INC
Also Called: Premium Harvesting
449 Harrison Rd, Salinas (93907-1617)
P.O. Box 4500 (93912-4500)
PHONE.................................831 443-6855
Fax: 831 443-6945
Jesus Alderete Jr, *President*
Marlene Alderete, *Corp Secy*
Ronnie Alderete, *General Mgr*
EMP: 130
SALES (est): 13.4MM **Privately Held**
WEB: www.premiumpacking.com
SIC: 0722 7361 Crop harvesting; labor contractors (employment agency)

(P-500)
R & G ENTERPRISES
155 N D St, Porterville (93257-3620)
P.O. Box 230 (93258-0230)
PHONE.................................559 781-1351
Val B Guzman, *Partner*
Jose M Rios, *Partner*
EMP: 200
SQ FT: 1,500
SALES: 3MM **Privately Held**
SIC: 0722 0761 Crop harvesting; farm labor contractors

(P-501)
RC PACKING LLC
26769 El Camino Real, Gonzales (93926-9405)
PHONE.................................831 675-0308
Fax: 831 675-9015
Dennis Capraro, *Mng Member*
EMP: 300
SALES (est): 27.2MM **Privately Held**
WEB: www.rcpacking.com
SIC: 0722 Crop harvesting

(P-502)
TRI VALLEY VEGETABLE HARVSTG
123 N Depot St, Santa Maria (93458-3907)
P.O. Box 1969 (93456-1969)
PHONE.................................805 928-2727
Robert Espinola, *President*
Ronald Burke, *Treasurer*
EMP: 80
SQ FT: 600
SALES (est): 5.7MM **Privately Held**
SIC: 0722 Vegetables & melons, machine harvesting services

(P-503)
VALLEY PRIDE INC
86120 Tyler Ln, Coachella (92236-3123)
PHONE.................................760 398-1353
Fax: 760 398-3079
Tom Spulding, *Manager*
Merced Zepeda, *Manager*
Mercedes Zepeda, *Manager*
EMP: 60
SALES (corp-wide): 2.2MM **Privately Held**
WEB: www.valleyprideinc.com
SIC: 0722 Crop harvesting
PA: Valley Pride, Inc.
   10855 Ocean Mist Pkwy D
   Castroville CA 95012
   831 633-5883

0723 Crop Preparation, Except Cotton Ginning

(P-504)
ADOBE PACKING COMPANY (PA)
367 W Market St, Salinas (93901-1423)
P.O. Box 4026 (93912-4026)
PHONE.................................831 753-6195
Fax: 831 758-5630
Jose G Esquivel, *President*
Basil Mills, *Shareholder*
Roger Mills, *Shareholder*
Mary Esquivel, *Treasurer*
Susan Mills, *Vice Pres*
EMP: 225
SQ FT: 2,500
SALES (est): 12.4MM **Privately Held**
WEB: www.millsfamilyfarms.com
SIC: 0723 4783 Vegetable packing services; packing & crating

(P-505)
AGRO-JAL FARMS INC
257 Kathleen Ct, Santa Maria (93458-4953)
P.O. Box 1862 (93456-1862)
PHONE.................................805 928-2682
Fax: 805 346-2461
Abel O Maldonado Jr, *President*
Frank Maldonado, *Vice Pres*
EMP: 100
SALES (est): 8.4MM **Privately Held**
SIC: 0723 Vegetable crops market preparation services; vegetable precooling services

(P-506)
ALL STAR SEED (PA)
Also Called: Eight Star Commodities
2015 Silsbee Rd, El Centro (92243-9671)
PHONE.................................760 482-9400
Fax: 760 337-8005
Alex Abatti Jr, *President*
Tim Castelli, *CFO*
Sid Swarthout, *Vice Pres*
Estella Soto, *Executive*
Rick Bush, *Manager*
◆ **EMP:** 57
SALES (est): 73.4MM **Privately Held**
WEB: www.abatti.com
SIC: 0723 Seed cleaning

(P-507)
ALLDRIN BROTHERS INC
Also Called: Alldrin Brothers Almonds
584 Hi Tech Pkwy, Oakdale (95361-9371)
PHONE.................................855 667-4231
Fax: 209 667-0463
Gary Alldrin, *President*
Grant Neil Alldrin, *Mktg Dir*
Ron Salado, *Marketing Staff*
Karen Pyatt, *Manager*
◆ **EMP:** 50
SQ FT: 5,000
SALES (est): 8.6MM **Privately Held**
WEB: www.alldrinbros.com
SIC: 0723 Almond hulling & shelling services

(P-508)
ANDERSEN & SONS SHELLING INC
4530 Rowles Rd, Vina (96092)
P.O. Box 100 (96092-0100)
PHONE.................................530 839-2236
Fax: 530 839-2502
Karl Andersen, *CEO*
Pat Andersen, *President*
Franklin Andersen, *Vice Pres*
Michael Andersen, *Vice Pres*
Jeff West, *Controller*
◆ **EMP:** 100
SALES (est): 17.9MM **Privately Held**
SIC: 0723 Crop preparation services for market

(P-509)
ANDERSON NUT COMPANY
Also Called: Gustine Mini Storage
3050 S Hunt Rd, Gustine (95322)
P.O. Box 445 (95322-0445)
PHONE.................................209 854-6820
Fax: 209 854-6088
Brian Anderson, *Partner*
Dan Anderson, *Partner*
◆ **EMP:** 50
SQ FT: 26,500
SALES: 5MM **Privately Held**
SIC: 0723 Walnut hulling & shelling services

(P-510)
BAIRD-NEECE PACKING CORP
60 S E St, Porterville (93257-4721)
P.O. Box 791 (93258-0791)
PHONE.................................559 784-3393
Fax: 559 784-7773
Dick Neece, *President*
Kelly Neece, *Opers Staff*
Donna Swacker, *Manager*
EMP: 180
SQ FT: 37,249
SALES (est): 16.5MM **Privately Held**
WEB: www.bairdneece.com
SIC: 0723 Fruit (fresh) packing services

(P-511)
BLUE BANNER COMPANY INC (PA)
2601 3rd St, Riverside (92507-3310)
P.O. Box 226 (92502-0226)
PHONE.................................951 682-6183
Fax: 951 686-6209
Thomas L Mazzetti, *CEO*
Vincent Mazzetti, *Officer*
Martin Diaz, *Vice Pres*
EMP: 50
SQ FT: 38,650
SALES (est): 8.4MM **Privately Held**
SIC: 0723 0174 Fruit (fresh) packing services; citrus fruits

(P-512)
BLUE DIAMOND GROWERS
4800 Sisk Rd, Modesto (95356-8730)
PHONE.................................209 545-6221
Fax: 209 545-6215
Bruce Mickelson, *Manager*
Steve Van Duyn, *Bd of Directors*
Tom Weaver, *Personnel Exec*
Jim Sahaj, *Plant Mgr*
Bill Weavers, *Plant Mgr*
EMP: 200
SALES (corp-wide): 1.4B **Privately Held**
WEB: www.bluediamond.com
SIC: 0723 2068 Almond hulling & shelling services; nuts: dried, dehydrated, salted or roasted
PA: Diamond Blue Growers
   1802 C St
   Sacramento CA 95811
   916 442-0771

(P-513)
BOGHOSIAN RAISIN PKG CO INC
726 S 8th St, Fowler (93625-2506)
P.O. Box 338 (93625-0338)
PHONE.................................559 834-5348
Fax: 559 834-1419
Phillip Boghosian, *CEO*
Philip Boghosian, *CEO*
Peter Boghosian, *Corp Secy*
Cheryl Kennedy, *Executive Asst*
Vicky Barbago, *Accountant*
◆ **EMP:** 60
SQ FT: 11,000
SALES (est): 18.9MM **Privately Held**
WEB: www.boghosianraisin.com
SIC: 0723 Fruit (farm-dried) packing services; fruit drying services

(P-514)
BORG PRODUCE INC
1601 E Olympic Blvd # 103, Los Angeles (90021-1940)
P.O. Box 21008 (90021-0008)
PHONE.................................213 305-6621
David Sullivan, *President*
Andrew Miller, *Executive*
Linda Chen, *Admin Sec*
Evon Clemens, *Controller*
Bryan Nakagawa, *Sales Mgr*
▲ **EMP:** 110
SALES (est): 8.6MM **Privately Held**
SIC: 0723 Vegetable crops market preparation services; vegetable packing services; fruit crops market preparation services; fruit (fresh) packing services

(P-515)
BOSKOVICH FARMS INC (PA)
711 Diaz Ave, Oxnard (93030-7247)
P.O. Box 1352 (93032-1352)
PHONE.................................805 487-2299
Fax: 805 487-5189
George S Boskovich Jr, *CEO*
Philip J Boskovich Jr, *President*
Loy Durham, *QA Dir*
Andrew Costales, *Info Tech Mgr*
Linda Grayson, *Controller*
▲ **EMP:** 205
SQ FT: 7,000

0723 - Crop Preparation, Except Cotton Ginning County (P-516)

PRODUCTS & SERVICES SECTION

SALES (est): 98.9MM **Privately Held**
WEB: www.boskovichfarms.com
SIC: 0723 5812 0161 Crop preparation services for market; eating places; rooted vegetable farms; lettuce & leaf vegetable farms

(P-516)
CAL CITRUS PACKING CO
111 N Mount Vernon Ave, Lindsay (93247-2438)
P.O. Box 637 (93247-0637)
PHONE..................559 562-2536
Fax: 559 562-4477
Jerry Luallen, *President*
Lori Leer, *Marketing Staff*
Henry Howison, *Manager*
▼ EMP: 68
SQ FT: 30,000
SALES (est): 5.3MM **Privately Held**
WEB: www.calcitruspacking.com
SIC: 0723 Fruit (fresh) packing services

(P-517)
CALIFORNIA ARTICHOKE & VEGETAB
Also Called: Ocean Mist Farms
10855 Ocean Mist Pkwy, Castroville (95012-3232)
PHONE..................831 633-2144
Edward Boutonnet, *President*
Albert Pieri, *Shareholder*
Don Reasons, *Treasurer*
Dale Huss, *Vice Pres*
John Pattullo, *General Mgr*
EMP: 60
SALES (est): 16MM **Privately Held**
WEB: www.oceanmist.com
SIC: 0723 Vegetable packing services

(P-518)
CARMEL VALLEY PACKING INC
26965 Encinal Rd, Salinas (93908-9539)
P.O. Box 3723 (93912-3723)
PHONE..................831 771-8860
Fax: 831 443-8353
Oscar Gardea, *President*
EMP: 150
SALES: 3MM **Privately Held**
SIC: 0723 Vegetable packing services

(P-519)
CARUTHERS RAISIN PKG CO INC (PA)
12797 S Elm Ave, Caruthers (93609-9711)
PHONE..................559 864-9448
Fax: 559 864-3849
Don Kizirian, *President*
Gina Elsea, *CFO*
Raul Garcia, *Corp Secy*
Hans Gunland, *Vice Pres*
Gregg Weaver, *Regional Mgr*
◆ EMP: 68
SQ FT: 4,000
SALES (est): 19.6MM **Privately Held**
WEB: www.caruthersraisin.com
SIC: 0723 Fruit (farm-dried) packing services

(P-520)
CECELIA PACKING CORPORATION
24780 E South Ave, Orange Cove (93646-9426)
PHONE..................559 626-5000
Fax: 559 626-7561
James J Cotter, *CEO*
David G Roth, *President*
Randy Jacobson, *Sales Staff*
◆ EMP: 130
SQ FT: 55,000
SALES (est): 15.9MM **Privately Held**
SIC: 0723 Fruit (fresh) packing services

(P-521)
CHOOLJIAN & SONS INC (PA)
Also Called: DEL REY PACKING CO
5287 S Del Rey Ave, Del Rey (93616-9700)
P.O. Box 160 (93616-0160)
PHONE..................559 888-2031
Fax: 559 888-2715
Gerald Chooljian, *CEO*
Courtney Chooljian, *Corp Secy*
Kathleen Merlo, *Vice Pres*

Gerlad Chooljian, *Agent*
▼ EMP: 69
SQ FT: 14,400
SALES: 29.5MM **Privately Held**
SIC: 0723 Fruit (farm-dried) packing services

(P-522)
CORONA - COLLEGE HEIGHTS ORA
8000 Lincoln Ave, Riverside (92504-4343)
PHONE..................951 359-6451
Fax: 951 689-5115
John Demshki, *President*
Susan Justin, *Controller*
Brad Tilden, *Plant Mgr*
▼ EMP: 300 EST: 1905
SQ FT: 180,000
SALES (est): 35.3MM **Privately Held**
WEB: www.cchcitrus.com
SIC: 0723 Fruit (fresh) packing services

(P-523)
CRISP WAREHOUSE INC
Also Called: Crisp California Walnuts
20500 Main St, Stratford (93266-9758)
P.O. Box 490, Lemoore (93245-0490)
PHONE..................559 947-9221
James R Crisp, *President*
Stacie Annon, *CFO*
◆ EMP: 67
SQ FT: 50,000
SALES (est): 5.5MM **Privately Held**
SIC: 0723 Walnut hulling & shelling services

(P-524)
DESERT VALLEY DATE INC
86740 Industrial Way, Coachella (92236-2718)
PHONE..................760 398-0999
Fax: 760 398-1514
George Kirkjan, *President*
Tamara Kirkjan, *Vice Pres*
◆ EMP: 50
SQ FT: 42,000
SALES (est): 9.7MM **Privately Held**
WEB: www.desertvalleydate.com
SIC: 0723 Crop preparation services for market

(P-525)
DOLE FRESH VEGETABLES INC
16199 9th St, Huron (93234)
PHONE..................559 945-2591
Luis Perez, *Principal*
EMP: 118
SALES (corp-wide): 10B **Privately Held**
SIC: 0723 Crop preparation services for market
HQ: Dole Fresh Vegetables, Inc.
2959 Salinas Hwy
Monterey CA 93940
831 422-8871

(P-526)
DOLE FRESH VEGETABLES INC
32655 Camphora Rd, Soledad (93960-9600)
PHONE..................831 678-5030
Fax: 831 678-5391
Sheila Lee, *Manager*
Luis Gonzalez, *Technical Staff*
Tom Mack, *VP Opers*
EMP: 210
SQ FT: 1,664
SALES (corp-wide): 10B **Privately Held**
SIC: 0723 Fruit (fresh) packing services
HQ: Dole Fresh Vegetables, Inc.
2959 Salinas Hwy
Monterey CA 93940
831 422-8871

(P-527)
EARTHBOUND FARM LLC (DH)
1721 San Juan Hwy, San Juan Bautista (95045-9780)
PHONE..................831 623-7880
Kevin C Yost, *President*
Myra Goodman, *Exec VP*
Sarah Lacasse, *Executive*
Blaine Sutliff, *Administration*
Elsie Gularte, *Accounting Mgr*
◆ EMP: 995
SQ FT: 15,000

SALES (est): 189.8MM
SALES (corp-wide): 3.8B **Publicly Held**
SIC: 0723 2037 2099 Vegetable packing services; fruit crops market preparation services; frozen fruits & vegetables; food preparations
HQ: Earthbound Holdings Iii, Llc
1721 San Juan Hwy
San Juan Bautista CA 95045
831 623-7880

(P-528)
ECO FARMS AVOCADOS INC (PA)
28790 Las Haciendas St, Temecula (92590-2614)
PHONE..................951 694-3013
Steve Taft, *CEO*
Norman Traner, *Corp Secy*
Eric Thurston, *Sales Staff*
▲ EMP: 55
SQ FT: 20,000
SALES (est): 14.6MM **Privately Held**
SIC: 0723 Vegetable packing services

(P-529)
EXETER PACKERS INC (PA)
Also Called: Sun Pacific Packers
1250 E Myer Ave, Exeter (93221-9345)
P.O. Box 217 (93221-0217)
PHONE..................559 592-5168
Fax: 559 592-3308
Berne H Evans III, *CEO*
Robert Reniers, *President*
Ernie Larsen, *CFO*
Toby Lewis, *CFO*
◆ EMP: 230
SQ FT: 70,000
SALES (est): 131.9MM **Privately Held**
SIC: 0723 Fruit (fresh) packing services

(P-530)
EXETER PACKERS INC
Also Called: Euclid Parking
23744 Avenue 181, Porterville (93257-9579)
PHONE..................559 784-8820
Lenard Shelton, *General Mgr*
EMP: 150
SALES (corp-wide): 146.6MM **Privately Held**
SIC: 0723 Fruit (fresh) packing services
PA: Exeter Packers, Inc.
1250 E Myer Ave
Exeter CA 93221
559 592-5168

(P-531)
EXETER-IVANHOE CITRUS ASSN
901 Rocky Hill Dr, Exeter (93221-1322)
PHONE..................559 592-3141
Fax: 559 592-5936
Kevin Riddle, *President*
Terry Orr, *General Mgr*
Westbrook Edwards, *Director*
EMP: 75
SQ FT: 30,000
SALES (est): 11MM **Privately Held**
WEB: www.exetercitrus.com
SIC: 0723 Fruit (fresh) packing services

(P-532)
FIENO INC
11583 Big Canyon Ln, San Diego (92131-4308)
PHONE..................760 352-2996
Fax: 760 352-4455
Chris B Jackson, *President*
Mary A Jackson, *Vice Pres*
EMP: 55
SALES (est): 3.4MM **Privately Held**
SIC: 0723 Hay baling services

(P-533)
FISHER RANCH LLC
10610 Ice Plant Rd, Blythe (92225-2757)
PHONE..................760 922-4151
Fax: 760 922-3080
Dana B Fisher Jr,
Meloni Carnes, *Manager*
Mike George, *Manager*
EMP: 99
SALES: 20.7MM **Privately Held**
SIC: 0723 Field crops, except cash grains, market preparation services

(P-534)
FOWLER PACKING COMPANY INC
Also Called: Telemarketing
8570 S Cedar Ave, Fresno (93725-8905)
PHONE..................559 834-5911
Fax: 559 834-3336
Dennis Parnagian, *CEO*
Randy Parnagian, *Treasurer*
Kenneth Parnagian, *Vice Pres*
Derrick Bender, *VP Bus Dvlpt*
Philip Parnagian, *Admin Sec*
EMP: 125
SQ FT: 6,300
SALES (est): 57.6MM **Privately Held**
WEB: www.fowlerpacking.com
SIC: 0723 4783 5148 Fruit (fresh) packing services; packing & crating; fresh fruits & vegetables

(P-535)
GILLETTE CITRUS COMPANY
10175 S Anchor Ave, Dinuba (93618-9204)
PHONE..................559 626-4236
Fax: 559 626-0804
Jay Gillette, *Partner*
Dean Gillette, *Partner*
Mark Gillette, *Partner*
Jim Lamb, *Finance Mgr*
Greg Gillette, *Manager*
EMP: 60
SQ FT: 14,000
SALES (est): 4.8MM **Privately Held**
SIC: 0723 Fruit (fresh) packing services

(P-536)
GOLDEN VALLEY CITRUS INC
19875 Meredith Dr, Strathmore (93267-9691)
P.O. Box L (93267-4012)
PHONE..................559 568-1768
Fax: 559 568-1769
Martine Mittman, *President*
Gerald Denni, *Vice Pres*
Sergio Erives, *Manager*
Marilou L Marin, *Manager*
EMP: 75
SQ FT: 25,000
SALES (est): 13.2MM **Privately Held**
SIC: 0723 Fruit (fresh) packing services

(P-537)
GRIDLEY PACKING INC
1366 Larkin Rd, Gridley (95948-9708)
PHONE..................530 846-3753
Fax: 530 846-0657
James D Sanderson, *President*
Becky Sanderson, *Vice Pres*
▲ EMP: 150
SQ FT: 25,800
SALES (est): 2MM **Privately Held**
SIC: 0723 Fruit (fresh) packing services

(P-538)
GRIMMWAY ENTERPRISES INC
6101 S Zerker Rd, Shafter (93263-9611)
P.O. Box 81498, Bakersfield (93380-1498)
PHONE..................661 393-3320
Bob Grimm, *Principal*
Dave Eagle, *Manager*
EMP: 233
SALES (corp-wide): 1.8B **Privately Held**
SIC: 0723 Vegetable packing services
PA: Grimmway Enterprises, Inc.
14141 Di Giorgio Rd
Arvin CA 93203
661 854-6250

(P-539)
GRIMMWAY ENTERPRISES INC
Also Called: Grimmway Frozen Foods
830 Sycamore Rd, Arvin (93203-2132)
P.O. Box 81498, Bakersfield (93380-1498)
PHONE..................661 854-6250
Fax: 661 854-6223
Brandon Grimm, *Manager*
Shawna Uwaine, *Purchasing*
EMP: 400
SALES (corp-wide): 1.8B **Privately Held**
SIC: 0723 Vegetable packing services
PA: Grimmway Enterprises, Inc.
14141 Di Giorgio Rd
Arvin CA 93203
661 854-6250

PRODUCTS & SERVICES SECTION
0723 - Crop Preparation, Except Cotton Ginning County (P-562)

(P-540)
GRIMMWAY ENTERPRISES INC
Also Called: Grimmway Farms
11412 Malaga Rd, Arvin (93203-9641)
P.O. Box 81498, Bakersfield (93380-1498)
PHONE.................................661 854-6200
Gary Giragosian, *Manager*
Hector Pacheco, *Opers Mgr*
Michael Riccomini, *Manager*
Alberto Felix, *Supervisor*
EMP: 100
SALES (corp-wide): 1.8B **Privately Held**
SIC: 0723 Vegetable packing services
PA: Grimmway Enterprises, Inc.
14141 Di Giorgio Rd
Arvin CA 93203
661 854-6250

(P-541)
GRIMMWAY ENTERPRISES INC
Also Called: Grimmway Farms
6900 Mountain View Rd, Bakersfield (93307-9627)
P.O. Box 81498 (93380-1498)
PHONE.................................661 845-5200
Fax: 661 845-5262
Bob Grimm, *Owner*
Steve Martinez, *CFO*
Brian Spaulding, *Senior VP*
Gary Bumgarner, *Info Tech Dir*
Dave Conaway, *Network Tech*
EMP: 200
SALES (corp-wide): 1.8B **Privately Held**
SIC: 0723 Vegetable packing services
PA: Grimmway Enterprises, Inc.
14141 Di Giorgio Rd
Arvin CA 93203
661 854-6250

(P-542)
GROWER DIRECT NUT COMPANY INC
2288 Geer Rd, Hughson (95326-9614)
PHONE.................................209 883-4890
Fax: 209 883-1896
Aaron Martella, *President*
Kevin Chiesa, *COO*
Lucio Salazar, *Vice Pres*
Jennifer Martella, *Admin Sec*
Rosie Ochoa, *Human Res Mgr*
◆ **EMP:** 50
SALES (est): 37.4MM **Privately Held**
WEB: www.grower-direct.com
SIC: 0723 Walnut hulling & shelling services

(P-543)
GROWERS STREET COOLING LLC
1080 Growers St, Salinas (93901-4445)
P.O. Box 2162 (93902-2162)
PHONE.................................831 424-2929
Fax: 831 424-4523
Ronald Mondo, *Mng Member*
Sherrie Ceja, *Manager*
Bill Lorentz, *Manager*
EMP: 53
SQ FT: 20,000
SALES (est): 8MM **Privately Held**
SIC: 0723 Vegetable precooling services

(P-544)
GUERRA NUT SHELLING COMPANY
190 Hillcrest Rd, Hollister (95023-4944)
P.O. Box 1117 (95024-1117)
PHONE.................................831 637-4471
Fax: 831 637-1358
Frank Guerra, *President*
Jeff Guerra, *CFO*
Connie Flores, *Executive*
▼ **EMP:** 55
SQ FT: 20,000
SALES (est): 7.8MM **Privately Held**
WEB: www.guerranut.com
SIC: 0723 Walnut hulling & shelling services

(P-545)
HARRIS WOOLF ALMONDS
Also Called: Harris Woolf California Almond
26060 Colusa Ave, Coalinga (93210-9245)
PHONE.................................559 884-1040
Stuart Woolf, *President*
Hortencia Solorio, *Executive*
Phillip Mariscal, *Sr Ntwrk Engine*
David Silva, *Info Tech Mgr*
Stehen Nazaroff, *Controller*
◆ **EMP:** 150
SQ FT: 110,000
SALES (est): 15.2MM **Privately Held**
WEB: www.harriswoolfalmonds.com
SIC: 0723 2096 Tree nut crops market preparation services; almond hulling & shelling services; potato chips & similar snacks

(P-546)
HILLMAN HOLDINGS LLC (PA)
116 W Cedar Ave, Tulare (93274-5348)
P.O. Box 1379 (93275-1379)
PHONE.................................559 685-6100
Scott Hillman,
Honere Foster,
Bret Hillman,
Kurt Killman,
EMP: 420 EST: 2000
SALES (est): 36.7MM **Privately Held**
SIC: 0723 Feed milling custom services

(P-547)
HILLTOP RANCH INC
13890 Looney Rd, Ballico (95303-9710)
PHONE.................................209 874-1875
Fax: 209 874-1877
David Harrison Long, *CEO*
Brad Filbrun, *CFO*
Christine Long, *Vice Pres*
Dave Long Jr, *Vice Pres*
Dexter Long, *Vice Pres*
▼ **EMP:** 175
SQ FT: 134,800
SALES (est): 48.1MM **Privately Held**
WEB: www.hilltopranch.com
SIC: 0723 5441 Almond hulling & shelling services; candy, nut & confectionery stores

(P-548)
HILLTOWN PACKING CO INC
9 Harris Pl A, Salinas (93901-4586)
PHONE.................................831 784-1931
Fax: 831 772-7109
Chris Huntington, *President*
Louis Huntington Sr, *Shareholder*
Louis Huntington Jr, *Treasurer*
▼ **EMP:** 300
SALES (est): 30.3MM **Privately Held**
SIC: 0723 Vegetable packing services

(P-549)
INDEX FRESH INC (PA)
3880 Lemon St Ste 210, Riverside (92501-3355)
PHONE.................................909 877-0999
Fax: 909 877-1999
Dana L Thomas, *President*
Giovanni Cavaletto, *COO*
Merrill Causey, *CFO*
Ana Pelaez, *Vice Pres*
Kevin Thron, *Vice Pres*
▼ **EMP:** 52
SQ FT: 40,000
SALES (est): 28.3MM **Privately Held**
WEB: www.indexfresh.com
SIC: 0723 Crop preparation services for market

(P-550)
ITO PACKING CO INC
1592 11th St Ste H, Reedley (93654-2939)
P.O. Box 707 (93654-0707)
PHONE.................................559 638-2531
Fax: 559 638-2282
Craig Ito, *President*
Janet Ito, *Vice Pres*
Tracy Ito, *Vice Pres*
Bobby Ikemyia, *Planning*
Stephanie Ito, *Accounting Mgr*
▲ **EMP:** 200 EST: 1940
SQ FT: 400,000
SALES (est): 33.2MM **Privately Held**
SIC: 0723 Fruit (fresh) packing services

(P-551)
J G BOSWELL COMPANY
Also Called: Processing Office
710 Bainum Ave, Corcoran (93212-9603)
P.O. Box 457 (93212-0457)
PHONE.................................559 992-2141
Ross Hall, *Vice Pres*
Giselle Kina, *Vice Pres*
Jackqueline Leslie, *Vice Pres*
Delta Merideth, *Vice Pres*
Michel Tony, *Vice Pres*
EMP: 100
SALES (corp-wide): 625.3MM **Privately Held**
SIC: 0723 Crop preparation services for market
PA: J. G. Boswell Company
101 W Walnut St
Pasadena CA 91103
626 356-7492

(P-552)
JLG HARVESTING INC
27 Zabala Rd, Salinas (93908-7702)
P.O. Box 5205, Yuma AZ (85366-2461)
PHONE.................................831 422-7871
Jose Luis Garcia, *President*
EMP: 400
SALES (corp-wide): 25.7MM **Privately Held**
SIC: 0723 Crop preparation services for market
PA: Jlg Harvesting, Inc.
1450 S Atlantic Ave
Yuma AZ 85365
928 329-7548

(P-553)
KERN RIDGE GROWERS LLC
25429 Barbara St, Arvin (93203-9748)
P.O. Box 455 (93203-0455)
PHONE.................................661 854-3141
Robert Giragosian,
Zak Karlan, *Opers Mgr*
Brad Coleman, *Sales Staff*
Scott Moore, *Manager*
▼ **EMP:** 500
SQ FT: 53,000
SALES (est): 44.2MM **Privately Held**
WEB: www.kernridge.com
SIC: 0723 5148 Vegetable packing services; vegetables, fresh

(P-554)
KIRSCHENMAN PACKING INC
12826 Edison Hwy, Edison (93220)
PHONE.................................661 366-5736
Wayne Kirschenman, *President*
Paul Sandoval, *Shareholder*
Herb Spitzer, *Vice Pres*
EMP: 120
SQ FT: 25,000
SALES (est): 4.4MM **Privately Held**
SIC: 0723 Vegetable packing services

(P-555)
KLINK CITRUS ASSOCIATION
Also Called: Klink Citrus Exchange
32921 Road 159, Ivanhoe (93235-1455)
P.O. Box 188 (93235-0188)
PHONE.................................559 798-1881
Fax: 559 798-0182
Eric Meling, *CEO*
EMP: 170
SQ FT: 50,000
SALES (est): 20.2MM **Privately Held**
SIC: 0723 Fruit (fresh) packing services

(P-556)
LIMONEIRA COMPANY (PA)
1141 Cummings Rd Ofc, Santa Paula (93060-9783)
PHONE.................................805 525-5541
Fax: 805 525-8761
Harold S Edwards, *President*
Gordon E Kimball, *Ch of Bd*
Gus Gunderson, *COO*
Joseph D Rumley, *CFO*
Joseph Rumley, *CFO*
◆ **EMP:** 158 EST: 1893
SALES: 100.3MM **Publicly Held**
WEB: www.limoneira.com
SIC: 0723 0174 0179 6531 Fruit (fresh) packing services; citrus fruits; lemon grove; orange grove; avocado orchard; real estate agents & managers; real estate leasing & rentals; commodity investors

(P-557)
LO BUE BROS INC
Also Called: Lo Bue Bros East
713 E Hermosa St, Lindsay (93247-2204)
PHONE.................................559 562-6367
Fax: 559 562-4746
Fred Lobue, *Branch Mgr*
EMP: 200
SALES (corp-wide): 41MM **Privately Held**
WEB: www.lobuebros.com
SIC: 0723 5148 0174 Fruit (fresh) packing services; fresh fruits & vegetables; citrus fruits
PA: Lo Bue Bros., Inc.
201 S Sweetbriar Ave
Lindsay CA 93247
559 562-2548

(P-558)
MAGARRO FARMS
3 Sterling, Irvine (92618-2517)
PHONE.................................949 859-6506
John Magarro, *Owner*
EMP: 80
SQ FT: 30,000
SALES (est): 3.5MM **Privately Held**
SIC: 0723 0171 Fruit precooling services; strawberry farm

(P-559)
MANN PACKING CO INC (PA)
1333 Schilling Pl, Salinas (93901-4535)
P.O. Box 690 (93902-0690)
PHONE.................................831 422-7405
Lorri Koster, *CEO*
Michael Jarrod, *President*
William Beaton, *CFO*
Richard Ramsey, *Chairman*
Rick Russo, *Exec VP*
EMP: 450
SQ FT: 90,000
SALES (est): 147.1MM **Privately Held**
WEB: www.broccoli.com
SIC: 0723 4783 0722 Vegetable packing services; packing & crating; crop harvesting

(P-560)
MARIANI NUT COMPANY
709 Dutton St, Winters (95694-1748)
PHONE.................................530 662-3311
Gary Sutton, *Partner*
Dennis Mariani, *Partner*
Jack Mariani, *Partner*
Deanna Reed, *Benefits Mgr*
EMP: 99
SALES (est): 973.1K **Privately Held**
SIC: 0723 Tree nuts (general) hulling & shelling services

(P-561)
MARIANI PACKING CO INC (PA)
500 Crocker Dr, Vacaville (95688-8706)
PHONE.................................707 452-2800
Fax: 707 452-2973
Mark A Mariani, *CEO*
George Sousa Jr, *Vice Chairman*
Forrest Chandler, *CFO*
Marian Ciabattari, *Corp Secy*
Craig Mackley, *Exec VP*
◆ **EMP:** 275 EST: 1982
SALES (est): 131.9MM **Privately Held**
WEB: www.marianifruit.com
SIC: 0723 2034 5148 Fruit (farm-dried) packing services; fruit drying services; dried & dehydrated fruits; fresh fruits & vegetables

(P-562)
MELVIN T WHEELER & SONS
Also Called: Wheeler, M T Trucking & Custom
5301 Woodland Ave, Modesto (95358-9593)
PHONE.................................209 526-9770
Fax: 209 526-4819
Melvin T Wheeler, *Owner*
EMP: 55
SALES (est): 9.6MM **Privately Held**
SIC: 0723 4212 0139 Alfalfa cubing services; animal & farm product transportation services; hay farm

0723 - Crop Preparation, Except Cotton Ginning County (P-563)

(P-563)
MILLER MILLING COMPANY LLC
2201 E 7th St, Oakland (94606-5301)
PHONE..................510 536-9555
David Hegewald, *Vice Pres*
EMP: 50
SALES (est): 879.9K **Privately Held**
SIC: 0723 Flour milling custom services

(P-564)
MONARCH NUT COMPANY LLC
Also Called: Munger Farms
786 Road 188, Delano (93215-9508)
PHONE..................661 725-6458
Fax: 661 725-5408
Kamie Munger, *Mng Member*
Albert Arkush, *CFO*
David Munger,
◆ **EMP:** 250 **EST:** 1986
SQ FT: 20,000
SALES (est): 47.8MM **Privately Held**
WEB: www.mungerfarms.com
SIC: 0723 Tree nuts (general) hulling & shelling services

(P-565)
MOONEY FARMS
1220 Fortress St, Chico (95973-9029)
PHONE..................530 899-2661
Fax: 530 846-5109
Mary Mooney, *President*
Steve Mooney, *Vice Pres*
Richard Munkes, *Controller*
▲ **EMP:** 50
SQ FT: 100,000
SALES (est): 30.2MM **Privately Held**
WEB: www.mooneyfarms.com
SIC: 0723 2034 2033 Fruit crops market preparation services; dried & dehydrated fruits; canned fruits & specialties

(P-566)
MORADA PRODUCE COMPANY LP
500 N Jack Tone Rd, Stockton (95215-9725)
P.O. Box 659, Linden (95236-0659)
PHONE..................209 546-0426
Fax: 209 546-0427
Henry Foppiano, *Partner*
Sandy Haswell, *Controller*
Linda Jenkins, *Manager*
▲ **EMP:** 1500
SQ FT: 98,000
SALES (est): 57.6MM **Privately Held**
SIC: 0723 Fruit (fresh) packing services; vegetable packing services

(P-567)
NATIONAL CUSTOM PACKING INC
13526 Blackie Rd, Castroville (95012-3212)
PHONE..................831 724-2026
Fax: 831 633-0207
Jonathon Thornton, *President*
Fred J Haas, *Ch of Bd*
Ron Marker, *CFO*
Louise McNary, *Corp Secy*
Nenita Victory, *QC Mgr*
EMP: 50
SQ FT: 12,000
SALES (est): 5.1MM
SALES (corp-wide): 299.6MM **Privately Held**
WEB: www.nationalpacking.com
SIC: 0723 Crop preparation services for market
PA: The Vps Companies Inc
310 Walker St
Watsonville CA 95076
831 724-7551

(P-568)
NEWSTAR FRESH FOODS LLC
126 Sun St, Salinas (93901-3751)
PHONE..................831 758-7800
Brian McLaughlin, *Controller*
William Han, *General Mgr*
John Aguina, *Administration*
Glenn Adler, *QA Dir*
Lisa LI, *Engineer*
EMP: 100

SALES (corp-wide): 85.1MM **Privately Held**
WEB: www.newstarfreshfoods.com
SIC: 0723 Vegetable crops market preparation services
PA: Newstar Fresh Foods, Llc
850 Work St Ste 101
Salinas CA 93901
831 758-7800

(P-569)
NEWSTAR FRESH FOODS LLC (PA)
850 Work St Ste 101, Salinas (93901-4378)
P.O. Box 5999 (93915-5999)
PHONE..................831 758-7800
Mark Drever, *CEO*
Susan Ajeska, *Vice Pres*
Mitch Secondo, *Vice Pres*
Ken Schoenthal, *Executive*
Alejandro Fimbres, *Program Mgr*
▼ **EMP:** 200
SQ FT: 1,300,000
SALES (est): 85.1MM **Privately Held**
WEB: www.newstarfreshfoods.com
SIC: 0723 2099 Vegetable crops market preparation services; ready-to-eat meals, salads & sandwiches

(P-570)
NORALCO INC
Also Called: H Naraghi Farms
20001 Mchenry Ave, Escalon (95320-9614)
P.O. Box 602, Denair (95316-0602)
PHONE..................209 551-4545
Haslem Naraghi, *President*
◆ **EMP:** 125
SQ FT: 120,000
SALES (est): 3.1MM **Privately Held**
SIC: 0723 5145 Almond hulling & shelling services; walnut hulling & shelling services; nuts, salted or roasted

(P-571)
NUNES COOLING INC
925 Johnson Ave, Salinas (93901-4327)
P.O. Box 1585 (93902-1585)
PHONE..................831 751-7510
Frank R Nunes Jr, *President*
Mike Scarr, *CFO*
EMP: 50
SALES (est): 4.8MM **Privately Held**
SIC: 0723 Vacuum cooling

(P-572)
OLAM AMERICAS INC (DH)
25 Union Pl Ste 3, Fresno (93720)
PHONE..................559 447-1390
Gregory C Estep, *CEO*
Siva Subramanian, *Vice Pres*
Thomas Betancourt, *Warehouse Mgr*
Pallavi Shah, *Manager*
◆ **EMP:** 1000
SALES (est): 782.3MM
SALES (corp-wide): 19.8B **Privately Held**
SIC: 0723 Crop preparation services for market
HQ: Olam Us Holdings Inc
2077 Convention Ctr 150
College Park GA 30337
404 209-2676

(P-573)
PEARL CROP INC (PA)
Also Called: Linden Nut
1550 Industrial Dr, Stockton (95206-3929)
PHONE..................209 808-7575
Halil Ulas Turkhan, *President*
Hulya Dayac, *Shareholder*
Jim Tropp, *CFO*
Jackie Aboona, *Admin Sec*
◆ **EMP:** 75 **EST:** 2007
SQ FT: 126,000
SALES (est): 1MM **Privately Held**
SIC: 0723 Crop preparation services for market

(P-574)
PHELAN & TAYLOR PRODUCE CO
1860 Pacific Coast Hwy, Oceano (93445)
P.O. Box 458 (93475-0458)
PHONE..................805 489-2413
Fax: 805 489-0191
John Taylor, *President*

EMP: 150
SQ FT: 20,000
SALES (est): 5.9MM **Privately Held**
SIC: 0723 0161 4213 Crop preparation services for market; vegetables & melons; trucking, except local

(P-575)
R & N PACKING CO
47920 W Nees Ave, Firebaugh (93622-9593)
P.O. Box 130, Turlock (95381-0130)
PHONE..................209 364-6101
Fax: 209 364-6172
Leo Rolandelli, *President*
Dian Ruiz, *Manager*
EMP: 250
SALES (est): 7.5MM **Privately Held**
SIC: 0723 Vegetable packing services

(P-576)
RAMCO ENTERPRISES LP
Also Called: Ramco Employment Services
520 E 3rd St Ste B, Oxnard (93030-0182)
PHONE..................805 486-9328
Jesse Espinoza, *Branch Mgr*
EMP: 740
SALES (corp-wide): 85MM **Privately Held**
SIC: 0723 Crop preparation services for market
PA: Ramco Enterprises, L.P.
320 Airport Blvd
Salinas CA 93905
831 758-5272

(P-577)
READY ROAST NUT COMPANY LLC (PA)
Also Called: Madera Quality Nut
2805 Falcon Dr, Madera (93637-9287)
PHONE..................559 661-1696
Thomas Finn, *Mng Member*
Tom Finn, *Managing Dir*
Rosario Reyes, *QA Mgr*
Vern Simmons, *Controller*
Vern Brannum, *Production*
◆ **EMP:** 75
SQ FT: 144,000
SALES (est): 16.2MM **Privately Held**
SIC: 0723 Tree nut crops market preparation services

(P-578)
RED TOP RICE GROWERS
3200 8th St, Biggs (95917)
P.O. Box 477 (95917-0477)
PHONE..................530 868-5975
Fax: 530 868-5064
John Adams, *President*
Doug Rudd, *Corp Secy*
Steve Cribari, *Vice Pres*
Sharon Protine, *Manager*
EMP: 50 **EST:** 1958
SALES (est): 5.9MM **Privately Held**
SIC: 0723 Rice drying services

(P-579)
REDLANDS FOOTHILL GROVES
304 9th St, Redlands (92374-3404)
PHONE..................909 793-2164
Fax: 909 798-0669
Robert Knight, *Plant Mgr*
Manuel Martnas, *General Mgr*
Espie Estrada, *Personnel*
EMP: 50
SQ FT: 48,000
SALES (est): 6.3MM **Privately Held**
SIC: 0723 Fruit (fresh) packing services

(P-580)
REDWOOD EMPIRE PACKING INC
8801 Old River Rd, Ukiah (95482-9659)
PHONE..................707 462-5521
Randall Ruddick, *President*
EMP: 150
SALES (est): 8.5MM **Privately Held**
SIC: 0723 Fruit (fresh) packing services

(P-581)
S STAMOULES INC
Also Called: Stamoules Produce Co
904 S Lyon Ave, Mendota (93640-9735)
PHONE..................559 655-9777
Fax: 559 655-2511

Peggy Stefanopoulos, *President*
Chrisopher S Stefanopoulos, *Treasurer*
Danny Stefanopoulos, *Vice Pres*
Tom Stefanopoulos, *Vice Pres*
Elena Stefanopoulos, *Admin Sec*
▼ **EMP:** 1000
SQ FT: 40,000
SALES (est): 100MM **Privately Held**
WEB: www.stamoules.com
SIC: 0723 Fruit (fresh) packing services; vegetable packing services

(P-582)
SAN JOAQUIN FIGS INC
Also Called: Nutra-Figs
3564 N Hazel Ave, Fresno (93722-4912)
P.O. Box 9547 (93793-9547)
PHONE..................559 224-4492
Fax: 559 224-4926
Keith Jura, *President*
Mary Jura, *Corp Secy*
Dan Mortenson, *Administration*
John Boylan, *Safety Mgr*
Heather Hildebrant, *QC Mgr*
◆ **EMP:** 50
SQ FT: 18,000
SALES (est): 9.4MM **Privately Held**
WEB: www.nutrafig.com
SIC: 0723 Fruit (fresh) packing services

(P-583)
SATICOY LEMON ASSOCIATION (PA)
Also Called: Saticoy Fruit Exchange
103 N Peck Rd, Santa Paula (93060-3099)
P.O. Box 46 (93061-0046)
PHONE..................805 654-6500
Fax: 805 654-6510
Glenn A Miller, *President*
Jerry Pogorzelski, *CFO*
Jima Garrett, *Admin Sec*
Lee Raymond, *Manager*
Laura Cossey, *Supervisor*
▲ **EMP:** 100 **EST:** 1933
SALES (est): 155.7MM **Privately Held**
SIC: 0723 Fruit crops market preparation services

(P-584)
SATICOY LEMON ASSOCIATION
600 E 3rd St, Oxnard (93030-6001)
P.O. Box 46, Santa Paula (93061-0046)
PHONE..................805 654-6543
Kevin Colvard, *Plant Mgr*
EMP: 130
SALES (corp-wide): 155.7MM **Privately Held**
SIC: 0723 Fruit crops market preparation services
PA: Saticoy Lemon Association
103 N Peck Rd
Santa Paula CA 93060
805 654-6500

(P-585)
SEED DYNAMICS INC
1081b Harkins Rd, Salinas (93901-4406)
P.O. Box 6069 (93912-6069)
PHONE..................831 424-1177
Fax: 831 424-0174
David Holly, *CEO*
Curtis J Vaughan, *COO*
Mel Bachman, *Risk Mgmt Dir*
Deanna Locke, *Manager*
EMP: 53
SQ FT: 34,000
SALES (est): 6.4MM **Privately Held**
WEB: www.seeddynamics.com
SIC: 0723 3999 Crop preparation services for market; seeds, coated or treated, from purchased seeds

(P-586)
SIMONE FRUIT CO INC
8008 W Shields Ave, Fresno (93723-9657)
PHONE..................559 275-1368
Fax: 559 275-0860
Mauro Simone, *President*
Margaret Simone, *Admin Sec*
▼ **EMP:** 100
SQ FT: 2,400
SALES (est): 2.3MM **Privately Held**
SIC: 0723 2034 0179 Fruit (fresh) packing services; fruits, dried or dehydrated, except freeze-dried; fig orchard

PRODUCTS & SERVICES SECTION
0723 - Crop Preparation, Except Cotton Ginning County (P-608)

(P-587)
SUMA FRUIT INTL USA INC
1810 Academy Ave, Sanger (93657-3739)
PHONE 559 875-5000
Fax: 559 875-1301
Ralph Hackett, *CEO*
Sabrina Hatton, *Office Mgr*
Eric Myers, *Engineer*
▼ EMP: 50
SQ FT: 60,000
SALES (est): 3.3MM **Privately Held**
SIC: 0723 Fruit (fresh) packing services
HQ: Del Monte Fresh Produce N.A., Inc.
 241 Sevilla Ave Ste 200
 Coral Gables FL 33134
 305 520-8400

(P-588)
SUN PACIFIC MARICOPA
Also Called: Maricopa Packers
31452 Old River Rd, Bakersfield (93311-9621)
PHONE 661 847-1015
Bern Evans, *Managing Prtnr*
Linda Spencer, *Accountant*
EMP: 400
SQ FT: 450,000
SALES (est): 23.2MM **Privately Held**
SIC: 0723 Fruit (fresh) packing services

(P-589)
SUN RICH FRESH FOODS USA INC (HQ)
515 E Rincon St, Corona (92879-1391)
PHONE 951 735-3800
Brian Tieszen, *President*
Carl Svangtun, *President*
Neville Israel, *CFO*
Gary Burton, *Project Mgr*
Wendalin Marrero, *Personnel*
▲ EMP: 60
SQ FT: 33,000
SALES (est): 23.2MM
SALES (corp-wide): 77.2MM **Privately Held**
SIC: 0723 Fruit (fresh) packing services
PA: Sun Rich Fresh Foods Inc
 22151 Fraserwood Way
 Richmond BC V6W 1
 604 244-8800

(P-590)
SUN WORLD INTERNATIONAL INC (PA)
16351 Driver Rd, Bakersfield (93308-9733)
P.O. Box 80298 (93380-0298)
PHONE 661 392-5000
Keith Brackpool, *Ch of Bd*
Timothy J Shaheen, *CEO*
David Fenn, *Vice Pres*
Nancy Cervantes, *Assistant*
◆ EMP: 1500
SQ FT: 160,000
SALES (est): 428.6MM **Privately Held**
SIC: 0723 0172 0174 0175 Vegetable crops market preparation services; vegetable packing services; grapes; citrus fruits; deciduous tree fruits; date orchard; mango grove; melon farms; pepper farm; sweet & hot (vegetables)

(P-591)
SUN WORLD INTERNATIONAL INC
52200 Industrial Way, Coachella (92236-2705)
P.O. Box 1028 (92236-1028)
PHONE 760 398-9300
Fax: 760 398-9498
Dave Margulas, *General Mgr*
Jesse Calderon, *Manager*
EMP: 500 **Privately Held**
SIC: 0723 Fruit (fresh) packing services
PA: Sun World International, Inc.
 16351 Driver Rd
 Bakersfield CA 93308

(P-592)
SUNKIST GROWERS INC
531 W Poplar Ave, Tipton (93272-9646)
P.O. Box 3720, Ontario (91761-0993)
PHONE 909 983-9811
Fax: 909 933-2409
Owen Belletto, *Branch Mgr*
Ted Leaman, *Vice Pres*
Don Conley, *Network Enginr*
Richard D Heck, *Research*
Henry A Affelds, *Engineer*
EMP: 221
SALES (corp-wide): 1.1B **Privately Held**
WEB: www.sunkist.com
SIC: 0723 5149 2099 Fruit crops market preparation services; juices; food preparations
PA: Sunkist Growers, Inc.
 27770 N Entertainment Dr # 120
 Valencia CA 91355
 818 986-4800

(P-593)
SUNKIST GROWERS INC
531 W Poplar Ave, Tipton (93272-9646)
P.O. Box 3720, Ontario (91761-0993)
PHONE 559 752-4256
Owen Belletto, *Vice Pres*
EMP: 221
SQ FT: 25,000
SALES (corp-wide): 1.1B **Privately Held**
WEB: www.sunkist.com
SIC: 0723 Fruit crops market preparation services
PA: Sunkist Growers, Inc.
 27770 N Entertainment Dr # 120
 Valencia CA 91355
 818 986-4800

(P-594)
TALLEY FARMS
2900 Lopez Dr, Arroyo Grande (93420-4999)
P.O. Box 360 (93421-0360)
PHONE 805 489-2508
Fax: 805 489-5201
Brian Talley, *President*
Todd Talley, *Treasurer*
Rayn Talley, *Vice Pres*
Rosemary Talley, *Admin Sec*
Jeff Halfpenny, *Sales Staff*
EMP: 175
SQ FT: 2,000
SALES (est): 28.5MM **Privately Held**
SIC: 0723 0161 Vegetable packing services; vegetables & melons

(P-595)
TANIMURA & ANTLE INC
Also Called: Salad Time Farms
4401 Foxdale St, Baldwin Park (91706-2161)
P.O. Box 4070, Salinas (93912-4070)
PHONE 831 424-6100
Randy Sipled, *Manager*
EMP: 400
SALES (corp-wide): 602MM **Privately Held**
WEB: www.taproduce.com
SIC: 0723 Vegetable packing services
PA: Tanimura & Antle Fresh Foods, Inc.
 1 Harris Rd
 Salinas CA 93908
 831 455-2950

(P-596)
TAYLOR FARMS CALIFORNIA INC (HQ)
150 Main St Ste 500, Salinas (93901-3462)
P.O. Box 1649 (93902-1649)
PHONE 831 754-0471
Fax: 831 754-0743
Bruce Taylor, *Owner*
Alec Leach, *President*
Tanya Mason, *President*
Thomas Bryan, *CFO*
Ed St Clair, *Business Dir*
EMP: 50
SALES (est): 295.3MM
SALES (corp-wide): 3B **Privately Held**
SIC: 0723 Vegetable crops market preparation services
PA: Taylor Fresh Foods, Inc
 150 Main St Ste 400
 Salinas CA 93901
 831 676-9023

(P-597)
TAYLOR FRESH FOODS INC (PA)
150 Main St Ste 400, Salinas (93901-3442)
P.O. Box 1649 (93902-1649)
PHONE 831 676-9023
Bruce Taylor, *CEO*
Nicole Devincenzo, *Officer*
Glen Fry, *Vice Pres*
Ron Guzman, *Vice Pres*
Drew Burnham, *Info Tech Dir*
▲ EMP: 150
SQ FT: 2,500
SALES: 3B **Privately Held**
SIC: 0723 Vegetable crops market preparation services

(P-598)
TELESIS ONION CO
21484 S Colusa, Five Points (93624)
PHONE 559 884-2441
Dan Garcia, *Manager*
EMP: 50
SALES (corp-wide): 13.7MM **Privately Held**
SIC: 0723 Vegetable packing services
PA: Telesis Onion Co
 3265 W Figarden Dr
 Fresno CA 93711
 559 884-2441

(P-599)
TRINITY FRUIT PACKING COMPANY
18700 E South Ave, Reedley (93654-9711)
PHONE 559 743-3913
David E White, *President*
▲ EMP: 250
SQ FT: 300,000
SALES: 12MM **Privately Held**
SIC: 0723 Fruit (fresh) packing services

(P-600)
VALLEY FIG GROWERS
2028 S 3rd St, Fresno (93702-4156)
PHONE 559 237-3893
Fax: 559 237-3898
Gary Jue, *President*
Paul Mesple, *Chairman*
Jim Wegley, *Bd of Directors*
Linda Cain, *Vice Pres*
Michael N Emigh, *Principal*
EMP: 50 EST: 1959
SQ FT: 100,000
SALES (est): 27.5MM **Privately Held**
WEB: www.valleyfig.com
SIC: 0723 2033 Fruit (fresh) packing services; fruits & fruit products in cans, jars, etc.

(P-601)
VASQUEZ BROTHERS INC
Also Called: Central Coast Packing
157 Kidder St, Soledad (93960-3021)
P.O. Box 625 (93960-0625)
PHONE 831 678-8894
Fax: 831 678-3009
Carlos Vasquez, *President*
Arturo Vasquez, *Vice Pres*
Nancy Vasquez, *Manager*
EMP: 100
SQ FT: 10,000
SALES (est): 8.9MM **Privately Held**
WEB: www.centralcoastpacking.com
SIC: 0723 Vegetable packing services

(P-602)
VENTURA COUNTY LEMON COOPS
Also Called: Ventura Pacific Co
P.O. Box 6986, Oxnard (93031-6986)
PHONE 805 385-3345
Donald Dames, *President*
Milton Daily, *Ch of Bd*
Mark Jacobs, *CFO*
Jim Waters, *Treasurer*
James H Gill, *Admin Sec*
EMP: 80 EST: 1943
SQ FT: 87,000
SALES (est): 11.4MM **Privately Held**
WEB: www.venturapacific.net
SIC: 0723 Fruit crops market preparation services

(P-603)
WAWONA PACKING CO LLC
12133 Avenue 408, Cutler (93615-2056)
PHONE 559 528-4000
Fax: 559 528-1944
Brent Smittcamp, *Mng Member*
Tara Sondergaard, *Office Mgr*
Georgia Griffin, *Bookkeeper*
Mark Berlinger, *Sales Dir*
Ben Vived, *Sales Associate*
▼ EMP: 1400
SQ FT: 16,000
SALES (est): 57.6MM **Privately Held**
WEB: www.wawonapacking.com
SIC: 0723 Fruit (fresh) packing services

(P-604)
WONDERFUL CITRUS PACKING LLC
5286 S Del Rey Ave, Del Rey (93616-9700)
PHONE 661 720-2400
EMP: 50
SALES (corp-wide): 2.1B **Privately Held**
WEB: www.paramountcitrus.com
SIC: 0723 0174 Fruit (fresh) packing services; citrus fruits
HQ: Wonderful Citrus Packing Llc
 1901 S Lexington St
 Delano CA 93215
 661 720-2400

(P-605)
WONDERFUL CITRUS PACKING LLC (HQ)
Also Called: Paramount Citrus Packing Co
1901 S Lexington St, Delano (93215-9207)
PHONE 661 720-2400
Craig B Cooper,
Mary Gutierrez, *Credit Mgr*
Kevin Adams, *Controller*
◆ EMP: 273
SQ FT: 400,000
SALES (est): 181.8MM
SALES (corp-wide): 2.1B **Privately Held**
WEB: www.paramountcitrus.com
SIC: 0723 0174 2033 Fruit (fresh) packing services; orange grove; lemon grove; fruit juices: fresh
PA: The Wonderful Company Llc
 11444 W Olympic Blvd # 210
 Los Angeles CA 90064
 310 966-5700

(P-606)
WONDERFUL CITRUS PACKING LLC
36445 Road 172, Visalia (93292-9193)
PHONE 559 798-3100
Fax: 559 798-1033
David Smith, *Manager*
EMP: 89
SALES (corp-wide): 2.1B **Privately Held**
WEB: www.paramountcitrus.com
SIC: 0723 0174 Fruit (fresh) packing services; orange grove
HQ: Wonderful Citrus Packing Llc
 1901 S Lexington St
 Delano CA 93215
 661 720-2400

(P-607)
WONDERFUL CITRUS PACKING LLC
Also Called: Paramount Citrus
13293 Famoso Rd, Mc Farland (93250)
PHONE 661 387-1288
EMP: 50
SALES (corp-wide): 2.1B **Privately Held**
SIC: 0723 Fruit (fresh) packing services
HQ: Wonderful Citrus Packing Llc
 1901 S Lexington St
 Delano CA 93215
 661 720-2400

(P-608)
WONDERFUL CITRUS PACKING LLC
710 Del Norte Blvd, Oxnard (93030-8963)
PHONE 805 988-1456
Tom Hooten, *Manager*
EMP: 60
SALES (corp-wide): 2.1B **Privately Held**
WEB: www.paramountcitrus.com
SIC: 0723 0174 Fruit (fresh) packing services; citrus fruits
HQ: Wonderful Citrus Packing Llc
 1901 S Lexington St
 Delano CA 93215
 661 720-2400

0723 - Crop Preparation, Except Cotton Ginning County (P-609)   **PRODUCTS & SERVICES SECTION**

(P-609)
YOUNGSTOWN GRAPE DISTRS INC
1625 G St, Reedley (93654-3435)
P.O. Box 271 (93654-0271)
PHONE....................916 635-2200
Fax: 559 637-4480
Michael J Forrest, *CEO*
Brian Forrest, *General Mgr*
▲ EMP: 206
SQ FT: 100,000
SALES (est): 27MM **Privately Held**
SIC: **0723** Fruit (fresh) packing services

0742 Veterinary Animal Specialties

(P-610)
ACC
Also Called: Advance Critical Care of La
9599 Jefferson Blvd, Culver City (90232-2917)
PHONE....................310 558-6100
Amy Gram, *Administration*
Shannon Brown, *Mktg Coord*
EMP: 84
SALES (est): 2.3MM **Privately Held**
SIC: **0742** Veterinary services, specialties

(P-611)
ADOBE ANIMAL HOSPITAL INC
4470 El Camino Real, Los Altos (94022-1003)
PHONE....................650 948-9661
Fax: 650 948-1465
Dave M Ross, *President*
Jerry Berg, *Vice Pres*
Paul Eccles, *Practice Mgr*
Summer Holmstrand, *Practice Mgr*
Barry Riddle, *Technician*
EMP: 100
SQ FT: 6,577
SALES (est): 8.6MM **Privately Held**
SIC: **0742** Animal hospital services, pets & other animal specialties

(P-612)
ADVANCED CRITICAL CARE EMERGE
20051 Ventura Blvd Ste I, Woodland Hills (91364-2646)
PHONE....................818 887-2262
Howard Liberson, *CEO*
Richard J Mills, *President*
EMP: 100
SALES (est): 2.2MM **Privately Held**
SIC: **0742** Animal hospital services, pets & other animal specialties

(P-613)
ADVANCED VETERINARY CARE CTR
15926 Hawthorne Blvd, Lawndale (90260-2644)
PHONE....................310 542-8018
Fax: 310 542-8098
Bonnie Mc Garr, *Owner*
Dr- J Hemker, *Admin Asst*
EMP: 56
SALES (est): 1.9MM **Privately Held**
WEB: www.advancedveterinarycarecenter.com
SIC: **0742** Animal hospital services, pets & other animal specialties

(P-614)
ANIMAL CARE CENTER
Also Called: Constance Dehaan Dvm
6470 Redwood Dr, Rohnert Park (94928-2326)
PHONE....................707 584-4343
Constance Dehaan, *Partner*
EMP: 60
SALES (est): 1.1MM **Privately Held**
SIC: **0742** Veterinarian, animal specialties

(P-615)
ANTECH DIAGNOSTICS INC (HQ)
17672 Cowan Bldg B, Irvine (92614-6845)
PHONE....................800 745-4725
Robert L Antin, *CEO*
Bob Anton, *President*
Kevin Bloss, *President*
Tomas Fuller, *CFO*
Stephen Elliott, *Vice Pres*
▲ EMP: 50
SALES (est): 194.2MM
SALES (corp-wide): 2.1B **Publicly Held**
SIC: **0742** Veterinary services, specialties
PA: Vca Inc.
12401 W Olympic Blvd
Los Angeles CA 90064
310 571-6500

(P-616)
BRADSHAW VETERINARY CLINIC
Also Called: Allison, Amanda Dvm
9609 Bradshaw Rd, Elk Grove (95624-9490)
PHONE....................916 685-2494
Fax: 916 685-8351
Michael Johnson, *Ch of Bd*
Thomas Zehnder, *President*
Scott Maynard, *Controller*
EMP: 75
SQ FT: 8,000
SALES: 3MM **Privately Held**
SIC: **0742** **0741** Veterinarian, animal specialties; veterinarian, livestock

(P-617)
CONTRA COSTA VET MED EMRGCY CL
1145 Turtle Rock Ln, Concord (94521-3526)
PHONE....................925 798-5830
Fax: 925 798-4982
Peter Mangold, *President*
EMP: 50
SQ FT: 3,500
SALES (est): 1.3MM **Privately Held**
SIC: **0742** Veterinary services, specialties

(P-618)
CRUZ VETERINARY HOSPITAL
2585 Soquel Dr, Santa Cruz (95065-1937)
PHONE....................831 475-5400
Macy Nichols, *Owner*
Terry Cullison, *Manager*
EMP: 80
SALES (est): 1.1MM **Privately Held**
SIC: **0742** Animal hospital services, pets & other animal specialties

(P-619)
HAPPY PET CO
Also Called: Very Important Pet Vaccine Svc
5813 Skylane Blvd, Windsor (95492-6836)
PHONE....................707 586-8660
Will Santana, *CEO*
Ken Pecoraro, *CFO*
Ivan Ayres, *Manager*
EMP: 50
SQ FT: 1,700
SALES (est): 1.1MM **Privately Held**
WEB: www.vipvaccine.com
SIC: **0742** Veterinary services, specialties

(P-620)
JAMES I MILLER
Also Called: J I Miller
17659 Chatsworth St, Granada Hills (91344-5602)
PHONE....................818 363-7444
James I Miller, *Owner*
EMP: 50 EST: 2001
SALES (est): 515K **Privately Held**
SIC: **0742** Veterinarian, animal specialties

(P-621)
MARINE MAMMAL CENTER (PA)
2000 Bunker Rd, Sausalito (94965-2697)
PHONE....................415 339-0430
Fax: 415 289-7333
Jeffrey Roger Boehm, *CEO*
Hanna Scardina, *Volunteer Dir*
Marci Davis, *COO*
Jennifer Morrow, *Officer*
Annie Caporaso, *Store Mgr*
EMP: 50
SQ FT: 25,000
SALES: 11.5MM **Privately Held**
SIC: **0742** **8299** **8733** Animal hospital services, pets & other animal specialties; arts & crafts schools; noncommercial biological research organization

(P-622)
MUELLER PET MEDICAL CENTER
Also Called: Mueller Grooming & Pet Sups
7625 Freeport Blvd, Sacramento (95832-1084)
PHONE....................916 428-9202
Ken Schenck, *President*
Margit Spencer, *Practice Mgr*
John Else, *Administration*
Michael Reget,
Cynthia W Slosser,
EMP: 50 EST: 1955
SQ FT: 4,000
SALES (est): 1.8MM **Privately Held**
WEB: www.muellerpmc.com
SIC: **0742** **5999** Animal hospital services, pets & other animal specialties; pets & pet supplies

(P-623)
NATIONAL VETERINARY ASSOCIATES (PA)
29229 Canwood St Ste 100, Agoura Hills (91301-1503)
PHONE....................805 777-7722
Fax: 805 496-2222
Greg Hartmann, *CEO*
Thomas Sawicki, *COO*
R James Woloshyn, *CFO*
Craig Frances, *Bd of Directors*
Carol Henry, *Chief Mktg Ofcr*
EMP: 118
SQ FT: 5,000
SALES (est): 708.1MM **Privately Held**
SIC: **0742** Veterinary services, specialties

(P-624)
NICHOLAS B MACY DVM
2585 Soquel Dr, Santa Cruz (95065-1937)
PHONE....................831 475-5400
Nicholas Macy, *Owner*
Jay Stone, *Co-Owner*
EMP: 70 EST: 1950
SALES (est): 979.7K **Privately Held**
SIC: **0742** Veterinarian, animal specialties

(P-625)
TONY LA RUSSAS ANIMAL RES FND
2890 Mitchell Dr, Walnut Creek (94598-1635)
P.O. Box 30215 (94598-9215)
PHONE....................925 256-1273
Elena Bicker, *Exec Dir*
Gaye McDuff, *Volunteer Dir*
Marie Bardando, *COO*
Launda Damerel, *Finance*
Stephanie Erickson, *Opers Staff*
EMP: 70
SQ FT: 37,000
SALES (est): 3.4MM **Privately Held**
WEB: www.arf.net
SIC: **0742** **8699** Veterinary services, specialties; animal humane society

(P-626)
VCA ANIMAL HOSPITALS INC
Also Called: VCA Lmis Bsin Vterinary Clinic
3901 Sierra College Blvd, Loomis (95650-7943)
PHONE....................916 652-5816
Robert Antin, *CEO*
Tomas Fuller, *CFO*
Neil Tauber, *Senior VP*
Stephen Speredelozzi, *Manager*
EMP: 50
SALES (est): 1MM **Privately Held**
SIC: **0742** Veterinary services, specialties

(P-627)
VCA ANIMAL HOSPITALS INC
4299 E Ramon Rd, Palm Springs (92264-1422)
PHONE....................760 778-9999
Mary Nightingale, *Principal*
EMP: 54
SALES (est): 1.9MM **Privately Held**
SIC: **0742** Veterinary services, specialties

(P-628)
VCA ANIMAL HOSPITALS INC (HQ)
Also Called: VCA TLC Animal Hospital
12401 W Olympic Blvd, Los Angeles (90064-1022)
PHONE....................310 571-6500
Robert Antin, *President*
Tomas Fuller, *Treasurer*
Neil Tauber, *Vice Pres*
Jynelle Castillo, *Marketing Staff*
Catherine Brown,
EMP: 118
SQ FT: 3,200
SALES (est): 29.4MM
SALES (corp-wide): 2.1B **Publicly Held**
SIC: **0742** Veterinary services, specialties
PA: Vca Inc.
12401 W Olympic Blvd
Los Angeles CA 90064
310 571-6500

(P-629)
VCA ANTECH INC
12401 W Olympic Blvd, Los Angeles (90064-1022)
PHONE....................310 207-0781
Bob Antin, *President*
EMP: 211
SALES (est): 300.8K
SALES (corp-wide): 2.1B **Publicly Held**
SIC: **0742** Animal hospital services, pets & other animal specialties
HQ: Vicar Operating, Inc.
12401 W Olympic Blvd
Los Angeles CA 90064
310 571-6500

(P-630)
VCA INC
1818 S Sepulveda Blvd, Los Angeles (90025-4314)
PHONE....................310 473-2951
Todd Tams, *Administration*
Nelson Weiss, *Med Doctor*
EMP: 80
SALES (corp-wide): 2.1B **Publicly Held**
WEB: www.vcawoodlands.com
SIC: **0742** Veterinarian, animal specialties
PA: Vca Inc.
12401 W Olympic Blvd
Los Angeles CA 90064
310 571-6500

(P-631)
VCA INC
Also Called: VCA-Asher Animal Hospital
2505 Hilltop Dr, Redding (96002-0505)
PHONE....................530 224-2200
Annette Hixenbau, *Director*
Larry Correia,
Chris Elton, *Director*
EMP: 55
SALES (corp-wide): 2.1B **Publicly Held**
WEB: www.vcawoodlands.com
SIC: **0742** Veterinary services, specialties
PA: Vca Inc.
12401 W Olympic Blvd
Los Angeles CA 90064
310 571-6500

(P-632)
VICAR OPERATING INC (HQ)
Also Called: Veterinary Centers America VCA
12401 W Olympic Blvd, Los Angeles (90064-1022)
PHONE....................310 571-6500
Fax: 310 571-6700
Robert Antin, *President*
Michael Everett, *President*
Arthur Antin, *COO*
Elizabeth Ho, *Officer*
Jeff Sonnenberg, *Senior VP*
EMP: 188 EST: 1985
SALES (est): 58.1MM
SALES (corp-wide): 2.1B **Publicly Held**
WEB: www.vcaantech.com
SIC: **0742** Veterinary services, specialties
PA: Vca Inc.
12401 W Olympic Blvd
Los Angeles CA 90064
310 571-6500

PRODUCTS & SERVICES SECTION

0761 - Farm Labor Contractors & Crew Leaders County (P-658)

(P-633)
WEST RIVERSIDE VETERINARY HOSP
5488 Mission Blvd, Riverside (92509-4514)
PHONE..................951 686-2242
Michael Butchko, *President*
Ruby Butchko, *Vice Pres*
EMP: 50
SALES (est): 1.6MM **Privately Held**
WEB: www.drbutchko.org
SIC: 0742 Animal hospital services, pets & other animal specialties

(P-634)
WILSHIRE ANIMAL HOSPITAL
2421 Wilshire Blvd, Santa Monica (90403-5876)
PHONE..................310 828-4587
Fax: 310 453-1452
Natoional Pet Care Center, *Owner*
Lisa Keno, *Bd of Directors*
Reni Westmoreland, *Administration*
Pernilla Edstrom,
Michelle Jack,
EMP: 50
SQ FT: 2,000
SALES (est): 1.8MM **Privately Held**
SIC: 0742 Animal hospital services, pets & other animal specialties

0751 Livestock Svcs, Except Veterinary

(P-635)
AMERICAN BEEF PACKERS INC
13677 Yorba Ave, Chino (91710-5059)
PHONE..................909 628-4888
Lawrence Miller, *President*
Rafael Santamaria, *CFO*
Henry Wong, *Sales Mgr*
EMP: 250
SALES: 200MM **Privately Held**
SIC: 0751 2011 5147 Slaughtering: custom livestock services; beef products from beef slaughtered on site; meats & meat products

0752 Animal Specialty Svcs, Exc Veterinary

(P-636)
BEAR RIVER VETERINARY CLINIC
6998 Eric Ln, Wheatland (95692-9768)
P.O. Box 1204 (95692-1204)
PHONE..................530 633-2957
Fax: 530 633-9155
Thomas D Morrow, *Owner*
EMP: 76
SALES: 450K **Privately Held**
SIC: 0752 Grooming services, pet & animal specialties

(P-637)
CANINE CMPNONS FOR INDPENDENCE (PA)
2965 Dutton Ave, Santa Rosa (95407-5711)
P.O. Box 446 (95402-0446)
PHONE..................707 577-1700
Fax: 707 528-0146
Paul Mundell, *CEO*
John D Miller, *Ch of Bd*
Alan Feinne, *CFO*
Anne Gittinger, *Vice Pres*
Juergen Rottler, *Vice Pres*
EMP: 71
SQ FT: 40,000
SALES: 23MM **Privately Held**
SIC: 0752 Training services, pet & animal specialties (not horses)

(P-638)
DEDICATION & EVERLASTING LOVE
Also Called: D E L T A Rescue
6021 Shannon Valley Rd, Acton (93510-1190)
P.O. Box 9, Glendale (91209-0009)
PHONE..................661 269-4010
Fax: 818 269-5049
Leo Grillo, *President*
EMP: 60
SALES: 5.9MM **Privately Held**
SIC: 0752 Shelters, animal

(P-639)
GUIDE DOGS FOR BLIND INC (PA)
Also Called: G D B
350 Los Ranchitos Rd, San Rafael (94903-3606)
P.O. Box 151200 (94915-1200)
PHONE..................415 499-4000
Fax: 415 499-4035
Chris Benninger, *CEO*
Cathy Martin, *CFO*
Kenneth Stupi, *CFO*
Janet Benjamin, *Officer*
Sue Dishart, *Officer*
EMP: 170 EST: 1942
SALES: 43.3MM **Privately Held**
WEB: www.guidedogs.com
SIC: 0752 8299 Animal training services; educational service, nondegree granting: continuing educ.

(P-640)
HANGTOWN KNNEL CLB PLCRVLLE CA
100 Placerville Dr, Placerville (95667-3910)
P.O. Box 2176 (95667-2176)
PHONE..................530 622-4867
Pam Bectel, *President*
Joe Barnes, *Corp Secy*
EMP: 75
SALES: 110K **Privately Held**
SIC: 0752 Training services, pet & animal specialties (not horses)

(P-641)
HUMANE SOCIETY SILICON VALLEY
Also Called: Pet Pourri
901 Ames Ave, Milpitas (95035-6326)
PHONE..................408 262-2133
Carol Novello, *CEO*
Christine B Arnold, *Exec Dir*
Katherine Stella, *Controller*
Kay McCleery, *Director*
EMP: 80
SQ FT: 3,000
SALES: 13.7MM **Privately Held**
SIC: 0752 Shelters, animal

(P-642)
LAEC INCORPORATED
Also Called: Equestrian Center
480 W Riverside Dr, Burbank (91506-3209)
PHONE..................818 840-9063
Tim Behunin, *President*
George Chatigny, *General Mgr*
Kenneth Mowry, *Admin Sec*
Robin Cohen, *Controller*
EMP: 75
SALES (est): 2.3MM **Privately Held**
WEB: www.la-equestriancenter.com
SIC: 0752 7999 Boarding services, horses: racing & non-racing; horse shows

(P-643)
OJAI RAPTOR CENTER
370 Baldwin Rd, Ojai (93023-9705)
PHONE..................805 649-6884
Kimberly Stroud, *Director*
EMP: 70 EST: 2011
SALES (est): 208.6K **Privately Held**
SIC: 0752 Shelters, animal

(P-644)
PETCO ANIMAL SUPPLIES INC (DH)
10850 Via Frontera, San Diego (92127-1705)
PHONE..................858 453-7845
Fax: 858 677-3033
James M Myers, *Ch of Bd*
Brad Weston, *President*
James Lampassi, *CEO*
Bruce Hall, *COO*
Michael M Nuzzo, *CFO*
◆ EMP: 500
SQ FT: 164,000
SALES (est): 8B
SALES (corp-wide): 317.9K **Privately Held**
WEB: www.petco.com
SIC: 0752 5199 5999 Grooming services, pet & animal specialties; pet supplies; pet supplies
HQ: Petco Holdings, Inc. Llc
10850 Via Frontera
San Diego CA 92127
858 453-7845

(P-645)
SONOMA COUNTY HUMANE SOCIETY
Also Called: Hssc
5345 Highway 12, Santa Rosa (95407-6401)
P.O. Box 1296 (95402-1296)
PHONE..................707 542-0882
Scott Anderson, *Director*
Susan Holzer, *Human Resources*
Don Malone, *Director*
EMP: 50
SALES (est): 1.6MM **Privately Held**
SIC: 0752 Shelters, animal

(P-646)
TOWN CATS MORGAN HILL RESCUE
195 San Pedro Ave Ste B, Morgan Hill (95037-5141)
P.O. Box 1828 (95038-1828)
PHONE..................408 779-5761
Rosi Mirko, *Director*
Petrica Aberu, *Director*
Petrica Guthrie, *Director*
Albert Mirko, *Director*
EMP: 50
SALES: 1.8MM **Privately Held**
WEB: www.towncats.org
SIC: 0752 Shelters, animal

0761 Farm Labor Contractors & Crew Leaders

(P-647)
AGSOURCE SERVICES LLC
222 N Garden St Ste 400, Visalia (93291-6328)
PHONE..................559 735-9700
Fred Lagomarsino, *Mng Member*
EMP: 50
SALES (est): 2.4MM **Privately Held**
SIC: 0761 Farm labor contractors

(P-648)
ALICIA ARROYO INC
Also Called: Arroyo Labor Contracting Svc
800 Johnson Cyn Rd 4, Gonzales (93926)
P.O. Box 846 (93926-0846)
PHONE..................831 675-2850
Fax: 831 675-0560
Alicia Arroyo, *President*
Debra Arroyo, *Treasurer*
Michael Arroyo, *Vice Pres*
EMP: 250
SQ FT: 500
SALES (est): 7MM **Privately Held**
SIC: 0761 Farm labor contractors

(P-649)
ANDRES BERMUDEZ
Also Called: Bermudez Brothers
121 E Grant Ave Ste 4, Winters (95694-1770)
PHONE..................530 795-1000
Fax: 530 795-1536
Andres Bermudez, *Owner*
EMP: 100
SQ FT: 200
SALES (est): 2.4MM **Privately Held**
WEB: www.andresbermudez.com
SIC: 0761 Farm labor contractors

(P-650)
ARMANDO GONZALEZ CONTRACTING
32380 Elmo Hwy, Mc Farland (93250-9616)
P.O. Box 1540 (93250-0140)
PHONE..................661 792-3785
Armando Gonzalez, *Owner*
EMP: 300
SALES (est): 3.6MM **Privately Held**
SIC: 0761 Crew leaders, farm labor: contracting services

(P-651)
ASIAN LEGAL WORKFORCE
1046 Rudder Ln, Foster City (94404-3821)
PHONE..................650 703-2190
Carlos G Umali, *Principal*
EMP: 75
SALES: 100K **Privately Held**
SIC: 0761 Farm labor contractors

(P-652)
AZCONA HARVESTING LLC
44 El Camino Real Unit A, Greenfield (93927-5637)
P.O. Box 3310 (93927-3310)
PHONE..................831 674-2526
Fax: 831 674-9156
Nick Azcona,
Cheryl Sellen, *Controller*
Pier Azcona,
EMP: 200
SQ FT: 1,000
SALES: 17.2MM **Privately Held**
SIC: 0761 Farm labor contractors

(P-653)
AZTEC HARVESTING
1075 N Broadway, Blythe (92225-1664)
P.O. Box 1080 (92226-1080)
PHONE..................760 922-7348
Fax: 760 922-7348
Charles Garcia, *President*
Marilyn Garcia, *Vice Pres*
Steve Garcia, *Vice Pres*
Tina Garcia, *Admin Sec*
EMP: 800
SALES: 5MM **Privately Held**
SIC: 0761 4212 0722 Farm labor contractors; local trucking, without storage; crop harvesting

(P-654)
BORJON ISCANDER
Also Called: Bvls
18586 Highway 49, Plymouth (95669)
P.O. Box 252 (95669-0252)
PHONE..................209 245-6289
Iscandor Borjon, *Owner*
Elana Borjon, *Co-Owner*
EMP: 250
SALES (est): 123.5K **Privately Held**
SIC: 0761 Farm labor contractors

(P-655)
COASTAL HARVESTING INC
503 S Palm Ave, Santa Paula (93060-3364)
PHONE..................805 525-6250
EMP: 300
SALES (est): 10.2MM **Privately Held**
SIC: 0761

(P-656)
EDWARDO Z GARCIA
Also Called: Z Garcia Farm Labor
380 Tucker St, Arvin (93203-1527)
PHONE..................661 854-5414
Edwardo Z Garcia, *Owner*
EMP: 250
SALES (est): 4.3MM **Privately Held**
SIC: 0761 Crew leaders, farm labor: contracting services

(P-657)
ELIOCO PRODUCE INC
Also Called: Preferred Produce
26490 Encinal Rd, Salinas (93908-9708)
P.O. Box 5700 (93915-5700)
PHONE..................831 424-5450
Robert Elliott, *President*
EMP: 105
SQ FT: 1,400
SALES (est): 7.3MM **Privately Held**
SIC: 0761 Farm labor contractors

(P-658)
ELISEO ESPARZA DELGADILLO
88 Wildflower Dr, Galt (95632-2329)
P.O. Box 431 (95632-0431)
PHONE..................209 745-3937
Eliseo E Delgadillo, *President*
EMP: 50

0761 - Farm Labor Contractors & Crew Leaders County (P-659)

SALES (est): 2.8MM Privately Held
SIC: 0761 Farm labor contractors

(P-659)
EZ LABOR & HARVESTING INC
1624 Main St, Brawley (92227-9508)
PHONE..................................760 344-6693
Ray Hannon, *President*
EMP: 100
SALES (est): 8.5MM Privately Held
SIC: 0761 Crew leaders, farm labor: contracting services

(P-660)
F & F CONTRACTING INC
4145 W Alamos Ave, Fresno (93722-3939)
PHONE..................................559 276-2418
Frank Echeverrie, *President*
EMP: 200
SQ FT: 500
SALES (est): 10.2MM Privately Held
SIC: 0761 Farm labor contractors

(P-661)
FIVE STAR PACKING LLC
437 W 5th St, Holtville (92250-1167)
P.O. Box 838 (92250-0838)
PHONE..................................760 356-4103
Marc Heraz,
John A Heraz, *Manager*
EMP: 737
SQ FT: 900
SALES (est): 14.7MM Privately Held
SIC: 0761 Farm labor contractors

(P-662)
FRANK BARRAZA
Also Called: Barraza Farm Labor Contractor
147 E Alamo, Calipatria (92233)
P.O. Box 864 (92233-0864)
PHONE..................................760 348-7363
Fax: 760 348-7264
Frank Barraza, *Owner*
EMP: 99
SALES (est): 3.6MM Privately Held
SIC: 0761 Farm labor contractors

(P-663)
GOMEZ FARM LABOR CONTG INC
62610 Monroe St, Thermal (92274-9059)
PHONE..................................760 399-1994
Jose J Gomez, *President*
Erma Gomez, *Office Mgr*
George Gomez, *Admin Sec*
EMP: 100
SQ FT: 900
SALES (est): 4.4MM Privately Held
SIC: 0761 Farm labor contractors

(P-664)
GONZALES SALVADOR LABOR CONTRS
217 4th St, Galt (95632-1955)
PHONE..................................209 745-2223
Salvador Gonzalez, *President*
Theresa Gonzalez, *Treasurer*
EMP: 100
SALES (est): 3.6MM Privately Held
SIC: 0761 Crew leaders, farm labor: contracting services

(P-665)
HALL AG ENTERPRISES INC
Also Called: Hall AG Services
759 S Madera Ave, Kerman (93630-1744)
PHONE..................................559 846-7360
Brad Hall, *President*
Loraine Garcia, *Corp Secy*
Mike Hooser, *Vice Pres*
Mike Van Hooser, *Vice Pres*
Stacy Hampton, *Manager*
EMP: 200
SALES (est): 5.4MM Privately Held
SIC: 0761 7361 Farm labor contractors; labor contractors (employment agency)

(P-666)
HARO & HARO ENTERPRISES INC
115 W Walnut St Ste 4, Lodi (95240-3541)
PHONE..................................209 334-2035
Fax: 209 334-2173
Emelia Haro, *President*
Jose Haro, *Principal*

EMP: 1000
SALES (est): 12.6MM Privately Held
WEB: www.haroandharo.com
SIC: 0761 Farm labor contractors

(P-667)
J A CONTRACTING INC
2209 W Tulare Ave, Visalia (93277-2137)
P.O. Box 2109, Tulare (93275-2109)
PHONE..................................559 733-4865
Juan Ayala, *President*
Javier Diaz, *Opers Mgr*
EMP: 300
SQ FT: 1,500
SALES (est): 9MM Privately Held
WEB: www.jacontracting.net
SIC: 0761 Farm labor contractors

(P-668)
JACOBS TREE SPECIALIST INC
2209 W Tulare Ave, Visalia (93277-2137)
P.O. Box 684, Lemoore (93245-0684)
PHONE..................................559 639-7138
Gregorio Jacobo, *President*
EMP: 50
SALES: 900K Privately Held
SIC: 0761 Farm labor contractors

(P-669)
JESUS A NAVA FARM LABOR
1698 Jones St Ste 1, Brawley (92227-1776)
P.O. Box 1767 (92227-1353)
PHONE..................................760 344-8084
Fax: 760 344-6984
Jesus A Nava, *Owner*
EMP: 100 EST: 1984
SALES (est): 1.9MM Privately Held
SIC: 0761 Farm labor contractors

(P-670)
JJ RIOS FARM SERVICES INC
4890 E Acampo Rd, Acampo (95220-9601)
P.O. Box 550 (95220-0550)
PHONE..................................209 333-7467
Fax: 209 333-3715
EMP: 80
SQ FT: 4,800
SALES: 2MM Privately Held
WEB: www.jjrios.com
SIC: 0761

(P-671)
JORGE PIMENTAL DIAZ
348 Manzanita Dr, Delano (93215-4675)
PHONE..................................661 344-5139
Jorge Pimental Diaz, *Owner*
EMP: 120
SALES (est): 5.7MM Privately Held
SIC: 0761 Farm labor contractors

(P-672)
KREGER INC
3520 W Howard Ave, Visalia (93277-4058)
PHONE..................................559 884-2585
Patrick L Kreger, *President*
EMP: 700
SALES (est): 6.3MM Privately Held
WEB: www.kreger.com
SIC: 0761 7361 Farm labor contractors; labor contractors (employment agency)

(P-673)
MARIN LABOR SERVICES
277 Country View Ct, Santa Paula (93060-3015)
PHONE..................................805 525-7730
Juan Llamas, *Owner*
EMP: 200
SALES (est): 3.9MM Privately Held
SIC: 0761 Crew leaders, farm labor: contracting services

(P-674)
MAYORAL BROS
420 Hillcrest Cir, Dixon (95620-3722)
PHONE..................................707 693-9111
Rosendo Mayoral, *Owner*
Ricardo Mayoral, *President*
Hector Mayoral, *CFO*
EMP: 400
SALES (est): 223.3K Privately Held
SIC: 0761 Farm labor contractors

(P-675)
MOUNTAIN VIEW AG SERVICES INC
13281 Avenue 416, Orosi (93647-9405)
P.O. Box 674 (93647-0674)
PHONE..................................559 528-6004
Leonard Hutchinson, *President*
Sonya Hutchinson, *Corp Secy*
EMP: 1200
SQ FT: 800
SALES (est): 6.2MM Privately Held
SIC: 0761 Farm labor contractors

(P-676)
MOYA JUAN FARM LABOR SERVICES
Also Called: Moya Farm Labor Services
7919 S Alta Ave, Reedley (93654-9538)
PHONE..................................559 638-9498
Fax: 559 638-2527
Rosa Moya, *President*
Juan Moya, *Vice Pres*
EMP: 150
SALES (est): 9.1MM Privately Held
SIC: 0761 Farm labor contractors

(P-677)
PALO ALTO VINEYARD MGT LLC
50 Adobe Canyon Rd, Kenwood (95452-9044)
P.O. Box 1399 (95452-1399)
PHONE..................................707 996-7725
Fax: 707 833-2997
Beverly Ordaz,
Jesus Ordaz,
EMP: 90 EST: 1997
SQ FT: 1,000
SALES (est): 4.8MM Privately Held
SIC: 0761 Farm labor contractors

(P-678)
PETE SANTELLAN
Also Called: Santellan Farm Labor Contr
176 S Valencia Blvd Ste C, Woodlake (93286-1723)
PHONE..................................559 564-3748
Pete Santellan, *Partner*
Ruben Santellan, *Partner*
EMP: 150
SALES (est): 2.5MM Privately Held
SIC: 0761 Crew leaders, farm labor: contracting services

(P-679)
PYRAMID PRODUCE INC
12826 Edison Hwy, Bakersfield (93307)
P.O. Box 27 (93302-0027)
PHONE..................................661 366-5736
Fax: 661 366-3825
Wayde Kirschenman, *CEO*
Norma Rapp, *Treasurer*
EMP: 250
SALES (est): 4.3MM Privately Held
SIC: 0761 Farm labor contractors; crew leaders, farm labor: contracting services

(P-680)
R AND R LABOR INC
710 Kirkpatric Ct, Hollister (95023-2817)
PHONE..................................831 638-0290
Fax: 831 638-0310
Ramiro Rodriguez Jr, *President*
Jose Rodriguez, *Vice Pres*
Elda Garcia, *Executive*
EMP: 300
SALES (est): 9.1MM Privately Held
SIC: 0761 Farm labor contractors

(P-681)
R MORA FARM LABOR
930 5th St, Wasco (93280-1348)
PHONE..................................661 746-2858
Roberto Mora, *Owner*
EMP: 50
SALES: 300K Privately Held
SIC: 0761 Farm labor contractors

(P-682)
RANCHO SALINAS PACKING INC
2376 Alisal Rd, Salinas (93908-9718)
P.O. Box 5307 (93915-5307)
PHONE..................................831 758-3624
Fax: 831 758-3659
Gilberto Jimenez, *President*

EMP: 150
SQ FT: 500,000
SALES: 2MM Privately Held
SIC: 0761 Crew leaders, farm labor: contracting services

(P-683)
SALAZAR LABOR CONTRACTING
957 Sugarloaf Dr, Escondido (92026-2364)
P.O. Box 460448 (92046-0448)
PHONE..................................760 746-0805
Joe Salazar, *Owner*
EMP: 60
SALES (est): 2.1MM Privately Held
SIC: 0761 Farm labor contractors

(P-684)
SALVADOR MARTINEZ
2049 N Newcomb St, Porterville (93257-9284)
PHONE..................................559 781-5150
Salvador Martinez, *Owner*
EMP: 120
SALES (est): 1.3MM Privately Held
SIC: 0761 Farm labor contractors

(P-685)
SEIU LOCAL 1021
447 29th St, Oakland (94609-3510)
P.O. Box 2077 (94604-2077)
PHONE..................................510 350-9811
Damita Davis-Howard, *Director*
EMP: 165
SALES (est): 43.1MM Privately Held
SIC: 0761 Farm labor contractors

(P-686)
SOUTHERN MNTRREY CNTY LBOR SUP
Also Called: Southern Mntrey Cnty Labor Sup
44 El Camino Real Unit A, Greenfield (93927-5637)
P.O. Box G (93927-0105)
PHONE..................................831 674-2727
Nick Azcona, *President*
Pier Azcona, *Vice Pres*
Robin L Kubicek, *Agent*
EMP: 100
SQ FT: 1,000
SALES (est): 3.2MM Privately Held
SIC: 0761 Crew leaders, farm labor: contracting services

(P-687)
VALLEY PRIDE INC (PA)
10855 Ocean Mist Pkwy D, Castroville (95012-3232)
PHONE..................................831 633-5883
Fax: 831 633-9218
Joseph T Pezzini, *President*
Troy Boutonnet, *Vice Pres*
EMP: 399
SQ FT: 1,500
SALES (est): 2.2MM Privately Held
WEB: www.valleyprideinc.com
SIC: 0761 Crew leaders, farm labor: contracting services

(P-688)
VELAZQUEZ PACKING INC
124 N I St, Lompoc (93436-6721)
P.O. Box 488 (93438-0488)
PHONE..................................805 735-6477
Fax: 805 737-1769
Raul Velasquez Jr, *President*
EMP: 100
SALES (est): 2.8MM Privately Held
SIC: 0761 Farm labor contractors

0762 Farm Management

(P-689)
AG-WISE ENTERPRISES INC (PA)
5100 California Ave # 209, Bakersfield (93309-0716)
P.O. Box 9729 (93389-9729)
PHONE..................................661 325-1567
Bruce Berreta, *President*
Ed Ray, *CFO*
EMP: 150
SQ FT: 4,400

PRODUCTS & SERVICES SECTION
0762 - Farm Management Svcs County (P-715)

SALES (est): 35.9MM **Privately Held**
SIC: 0762 Farm management services

(P-690)
AGRI-CAL VENTURE ASSOCIATES
Also Called: AM Cor Capital
52300 Enterprise Way, Coachella (92236-2707)
PHONE.................760 398-9520
Fax: 760 398-9530
Robert A Wright, *President*
Fred Behrens, *CEO*
EMP: 110
SALES (est): 1.2MM **Privately Held**
SIC: 0762 Farm management services

(P-691)
AGRI-WORLD COOPERATIVE
31545 Donald Ave, Madera (93636-1475)
PHONE.................559 673-1306
Kevin Avilas, *General Mgr*
EMP: 50
SQ FT: 1,500
SALES (est): 3.7MM **Privately Held**
SIC: 0762 Farm management services

(P-692)
ANTHONY VINEYARDS INC
52301 Enterprise Way, Coachella (92236-2708)
PHONE.................760 391-5400
Robert Bianco, *Owner*
Paul Loeffel, *CFO*
EMP: 70
SALES (corp-wide): 38.5MM **Privately Held**
SIC: 0762 Vineyard management & maintenance services
PA: Anthony Vineyards Inc
5512 Valpredo Ave
Bakersfield CA 93307
661 858-6211

(P-693)
ARTHUR KUNDE & SONS INC
Also Called: Kunde Estate Winery
9825 Sonoma Hwy, Kenwood (95452)
PHONE.................707 833-5501
Jim Mickelson, *President*
Arthur Kunde Jr, *President*
William Kunde, *Corp Secy*
Cindy Vandergoot, *Controller*
Antonio Zamudio, *Manager*
▲ EMP: 50
SQ FT: 2,000
SALES (est): 3.6MM **Privately Held**
WEB: www.kunde.com
SIC: 0762 2084 Vineyard management & maintenance services; wines, brandy & brandy spirits

(P-694)
BIANCHI AG SERVICES INC
3056 Colusa Hwy, Yuba City (95993-8931)
PHONE.................530 923-7675
Jim Bianchi, *Branch Mgr*
EMP: 84
SALES (corp-wide): 51.5MM **Privately Held**
SIC: 0762 Farm management services
PA: Bianchi Ag. Services, Inc.
1210 Richvale Hwy
Richvale CA 95974
530 882-4575

(P-695)
CLIMATE CORPORATION (HQ)
201 3rd St Ste 1100, San Francisco (94103-3149)
PHONE.................415 363-0500
David Friedberg, *CEO*
Greg Smirin, *COO*
Colleen McCreary, *Officer*
Nick Koshnick, *Vice Pres*
Jeff Palmer, *Vice Pres*
EMP: 74
SALES: 38.1MM
SALES (corp-wide): 13.5B **Publicly Held**
SIC: 0762 Farm management services
PA: Monsanto Company
800 N Lindbergh Blvd
Saint Louis MO 63167
314 694-1000

(P-696)
CUMMINGS-VIOLICH INC
Also Called: Cummings-Vlich Inc-Orchard MGT
1750 Dayton Rd, Chico (95928-6968)
PHONE.................530 894-5494
Fax: 530 891-4946
Dan Cummings, *President*
Paul Violich, *CFO*
EMP: 80
SQ FT: 3,400
SALES (est): 7.3MM **Privately Held**
WEB: www.cvinc.ws
SIC: 0762 Farm management services

(P-697)
E & J GALLO WINERY
Also Called: Livingston Ranch
5953 Weir Ave, Livingston (95334-9509)
PHONE.................209 394-6271
Alan Reynolds, *Manager*
Jonathon Meikle, *Business Anlyst*
Don Jarvis, *Purch Agent*
EMP: 100
SALES (corp-wide): 1.9B **Privately Held**
WEB: www.gallo.com
SIC: 0762 2084 Vineyard management & maintenance services; wines
PA: E. & J. Gallo Winery
600 Yosemite Blvd
Modesto CA 95354
209 341-3111

(P-698)
E & M AG SVC INC A CAL CORP
2446 W Border Links Dr, Visalia (93291-4316)
P.O. Box 7208 (93290-7208)
PHONE.................559 627-2724
Matt Bakke, *President*
Evett Bakke, *Vice Pres*
EMP: 50
SALES (est): 5.9MM **Privately Held**
SIC: 0762 Farm management services

(P-699)
EASTSIDE MANAGEMENT CO INC
1131 12th St Ste C, Modesto (95354-0813)
PHONE.................209 578-9852
Steven Zeff, *President*
EMP: 148
SALES (corp-wide): 13.8MM **Privately Held**
SIC: 0762 Farm management services
PA: Eastside Management Company, Inc.
1518 K St
Modesto CA 95354
209 578-9852

(P-700)
ECO FARM FIELD INC
28790 Las Haciendas St, Temecula (92590-2614)
PHONE.................951 676-4047
Steven Taft, *President*
Norman Traner, *Corp Secy*
▲ EMP: 75
SQ FT: 20,000
SALES (est): 2.8MM **Privately Held**
SIC: 0762 6519 0722 4212 Farm management services; real property lessors; crop harvesting; local trucking, without storage

(P-701)
ENTERPRISE VINEYARDS
16600 Norrbom Rd, Sonoma (95476-4780)
P.O. Box 233, Vineburg (95487-0233)
PHONE.................707 996-6513
Philip Coturri, *President*
Arden Kremer, *Vice Pres*
Ditty Vella, *Administration*
James Drummond, *Manager*
EMP: 50
SALES (est): 4.7MM **Privately Held**
SIC: 0762 Vineyard management & maintenance services

(P-702)
ENZENNAUER VINEYARD MANAGMENT
18501 Ida Clayton Rd, Calistoga (94515-9537)
P.O. Box 1776, Healdsburg (95448-1776)
PHONE.................707 433-0532
Phillip Enzennauer, *President*
Liz Langerman, *Manager*
EMP: 58
SALES (est): 1MM **Privately Held**
SIC: 0762 Vineyard management & maintenance services

(P-703)
ESPARZA ENTERPRISES INC
251 W Main St Ste G&F, Brawley (92227-2201)
PHONE.................760 344-2031
Luis Esparza, *Branch Mgr*
EMP: 459
SALES (corp-wide): 56.6MM **Privately Held**
SIC: 0762 Farm management services
PA: Esparza Enterprises, Inc.
3851 Fruitvale Ave Ste A
Bakersfield CA 93308
661 831-0002

(P-704)
FREY FARMING & TPSRY VINEYARDS
2203 Fallen Leaf Dr, Santa Maria (93455-5736)
PHONE.................805 937-1542
Jeff Frey, *Owner*
EMP: 90 EST: 1997
SALES (est): 1.3MM **Privately Held**
SIC: 0762 Vineyard management & maintenance services

(P-705)
GLESS RANCH INC (PA)
18541 Van Buren Blvd, Riverside (92508-9261)
PHONE.................951 780-8458
Fax: 951 780-5895
John J Gless, *CEO*
EMP: 50 EST: 1961
SALES (est): 14.1MM **Privately Held**
WEB: www.glessranch.com
SIC: 0762 Orchard management & maintenance services

(P-706)
LASSEN LAND CO
320 E South St, Orland (95963-9111)
P.O. Box 607 (95963-0607)
PHONE.................530 865-7676
Fax: 530 865-8012
Roderick Minkler, *President*
Betty Minkler, *Admin Sec*
Monte Buckhold, *Controller*
Bill Minkler, *Director*
EMP: 50 EST: 1969
SQ FT: 6,000
SALES (est): 8.2MM **Privately Held**
WEB: www.lassenland.com
SIC: 0762 Farm management services

(P-707)
MESA VINEYARD MANAGEMENT INC
2570 Prell Rd, Santa Maria (93454-9110)
P.O. Box 6565 (93456-6565)
PHONE.................805 925-7200
Fax: 805 928-7481
Callado Rodolfo, *Manager*
EMP: 75
SALES (corp-wide): 16.5MM **Privately Held**
SIC: 0762 Vineyard management & maintenance services
PA: Mesa Vineyard Management Inc
110 Gibson Rd
Templeton CA 93465
805 434-4100

(P-708)
MESA VINEYARD MANAGEMENT INC (PA)
110 Gibson Rd, Templeton (93465-9510)
P.O. Box 789 (93465-0789)
PHONE.................805 434-4100
Fax: 805 434-4850
Dana Merrill, *President*
Sarah Wilcoxson, *Admin Asst*
Paul Cuellar, *Accountant*
Bill Erickson, *Controller*
Matthew Merrill,
EMP: 75
SQ FT: 3,200
SALES (est): 16.5MM **Privately Held**
SIC: 0762 Vineyard management & maintenance services

(P-709)
MITCHELL VINEYARDS LLC
Also Called: Mitchell Vineyard Management
1831 Sarahs Way, Saint Helena (94574-9506)
Rural Route 1831 Sarahs Way (94574)
PHONE.................707 963-7050
Anthony B Mitchell,
EMP: 90
SALES (est): 4.5MM **Privately Held**
SIC: 0762 Vineyard management & maintenance services

(P-710)
MONTEREY PACIFIC INC (PA)
Also Called: McIntyre Vineyards
169 The Crossroads Blvd, Carmel (93923-8645)
PHONE.................831 678-4845
Fax: 831 678-4846
Steven McIntyre, *CEO*
Kimberly McIntyre, *Corp Secy*
Jackie King, *Sales Staff*
Sherry Richardson, *Manager*
Jackie Skinner, *Manager*
▲ EMP: 50
SQ FT: 3,000
SALES (est): 9.9MM **Privately Held**
WEB: www.montereypacific.com
SIC: 0762 Farm management services

(P-711)
NISSEN VINEYARD SERVICES INC
1226 Spring St, Saint Helena (94574-2024)
PHONE.................707 963-3480
Peter G Nissen, *President*
Anne Nissen, *Vice Pres*
EMP: 60
SQ FT: 1,760
SALES (est): 6.7MM **Privately Held**
SIC: 0762 Vineyard management & maintenance services

(P-712)
OXFORD FARMS INC
Also Called: Meyers Farming
901 N St Ste 103, Firebaugh (93622-2241)
P.O. Box 457 (93622-0457)
PHONE.................559 659-3033
Marvin Meyers, *President*
Gregory Meyers, *Vice Pres*
EMP: 50
SQ FT: 250
SALES (est): 2.1MM **Privately Held**
SIC: 0762 Farm management services

(P-713)
P C A FARM MANAGEMENT LLC
1901 S Lexington St, Delano (93215-9207)
PHONE.................661 720-2400
David Krause,
EMP: 700
SQ FT: 10,000
SALES (est): 5.8MM **Privately Held**
SIC: 0762 Farm management services

(P-714)
PENTERMAN FARMING CO INC
3851 Chiles Pope Vly Rd, Saint Helena (94574-9588)
PHONE.................707 967-9977
Brian Penterman, *President*
EMP: 60
SALES (est): 3.4MM **Privately Held**
SIC: 0762 Farm management services

(P-715)
PEREZ CONTRACTING LLC
12620 Snow Rd, Bakersfield (93314-8021)
PHONE.................661 399-2700
Fax: 805 239-8076
Greg Perez, *Mng Member*
Margaret Perez,
EMP: 150

0762 - Farm Management Svcs County (P-716)

SALES (est): 4.6MM **Privately Held**
SIC: **0762** Farm management services

(P-716)
PINA VINEYARD MANAGEMENT LLC
7960 Silverado Trl, NAPA (94558-9343)
P.O. Box 373, Oakville (94562-0373)
PHONE.................................707 944-2229
Davie Pina, *Owner*
Johnny White, *COO*
Randy Pina, *Network Mgr*
Omar Cruz, *Human Resources*
EMP: 50
SQ FT: 290
SALES (est): 6.4MM **Privately Held**
WEB: www.pinavineyards.com
SIC: **0762** 0723 2084 Vineyard management & maintenance services; crop preparation services for market; wines, brandy & brandy spirits

(P-717)
REDWOOD EMPIRE VINEYARD MGT
22000 Geyserville Ave, Geyserville (95441)
P.O. Box 729 (95441-0729)
PHONE.................................707 857-3401
Fax: 707 857-1673
Kevin W Barr, *President*
Linda Barr, *Corp Secy*
Nancy Barr, *Corp Secy*
EMP: 100
SALES (est): 9.9MM **Privately Held**
WEB: www.revm.net
SIC: **0762** 0172 Vineyard management & maintenance services; grapes

(P-718)
RICHARD DE BENEDETTO
Also Called: De Benedetto AG
26393 Road 22 1/2, Chowchilla (93610-9624)
PHONE.................................559 665-1712
Fax: 559 665-7059
Richard De Benedetto, *Owner*
Janelle Eggert, *Office Spvr*
EMP: 75
SALES (est): 3.7MM **Privately Held**
SIC: **0762** Farm management services

(P-719)
RICHARD DE BENEDETTO
Also Called: De Benedetto Orchards
26393 Road 22 1/2, Chowchilla (93610-9624)
PHONE.................................559 665-1712
Richard De Benedetto, *Owner*
Janelle Eggert, *Supervisor*
EMP: 60
SQ FT: 4,000
SALES (est): 3.2MM **Privately Held**
SIC: **0762** 0179 0173 0181 Fig orchard; almond grove; nursery stock, growing of; tree nuts, machine harvesting services

(P-720)
ROBERT YOUNG FAMILY LTD PARTNR
Also Called: Robert Young Vineyards
4950 Red Winery Rd, Geyserville (95441-9573)
PHONE.................................707 433-3228
Robert Young, *Partner*
Susan Sheehy, *Partner*
Fred Young, *Partner*
James Young, *Partner*
Joann Young, *Partner*
EMP: 60
SQ FT: 5,078
SALES (est): 3.3MM **Privately Held**
WEB: www.ryew.com
SIC: **0762** Vineyard management & maintenance services

(P-721)
ROTHFLEISCH RANCHES INC
129 S El Cerrito Dr, Brawley (92227-2203)
PHONE.................................760 344-1819
Joseph Rothfleisch, *President*
Kacie Cox, *Manager*
Allison Mainas, *Manager*
EMP: 60
SALES (est): 2.7MM **Privately Held**
SIC: **0762** Farm management services

(P-722)
S & J RANCHES LLC
39639 Avenue 10, Madera (93636-8845)
P.O. Box 3347, Pinedale (93650-3347)
PHONE.................................559 437-2600
Fax: 559 437-2606
James M Burkhart,
Jim Burkhart,
Kevin Olsen,
EMP: 60
SQ FT: 5,133
SALES (est): 2.1MM
SALES (corp-wide): 2.1B **Privately Held**
WEB: www.paramountcitrus.com
SIC: **0762** 0723 Farm management services; citrus grove management & maintenance services; orchard management & maintenance services; fruit (fresh) packing services
HQ: Wonderful Citrus Packing Llc
    1901 S Lexington St
    Delano CA 93215
    661 720-2400

(P-723)
SIERRA PACIFIC FARMS INC (PA)
Also Called: Somis Pacific AG Management
43406 Business Park Dr, Temecula (92590-5526)
P.O. Box 1537 (92593-1537)
PHONE.................................951 699-9980
Fax: 951 695-7593
Scott A McIntyre, *CEO*
Debbie McIntyre, *CFO*
Carey Calendar, *Manager*
EMP: 68
SQ FT: 3,000
SALES (est): 20.9MM **Privately Held**
SIC: **0762** Farm management services

(P-724)
SUN PACIFIC FARMING COOP INC (PA)
Also Called: Allied Farming Company
1250 E Myer Ave, Exeter (93221-9345)
P.O. Box 1125 (93221-7125)
PHONE.................................559 592-7121
Fax: 559 592-3544
Berne H Evans III, *President*
Bob Reniers, *Corp Secy*
Jeanne Wilkerson, *Officer*
Jeannie Wilkinson, *Officer*
Mireya Zepeda, *Hum Res Coord*
EMP: 500
SQ FT: 70,000
SALES (est): 122.8MM **Privately Held**
SIC: **0762** Citrus grove management & maintenance services

(P-725)
T AND M AGRICULTURAL SVCS LLC
493 Dowdell Ln, Saint Helena (94574-1441)
P.O. Box 122 (94574-0122)
PHONE.................................707 963-3330
Samuel Turner,
Sam E Turner, *Sales Executive*
Dianne Martinez,
EMP: 120
SALES (est): 4.9MM **Privately Held**
SIC: **0762** Vineyard management & maintenance services

(P-726)
T AND W FARMS
18000 Old River Rd, Bakersfield (93311-9513)
PHONE.................................661 396-7203
Maynard Troost, *Principal*
Brian Wind, *Partner*
EMP: 50
SQ FT: 1,195
SALES (est): 2.9MM **Privately Held**
SIC: **0762** Farm management services

(P-727)
UNITED BIOSOURCE LLC
303 2nd St Ste 700, San Francisco (94107-1366)
PHONE.................................415 293-1340
Mike Borkowski, *Branch Mgr*
Vicky Wilkinson, *Business Mgr*
EMP: 80
SALES (corp-wide): 101.7B **Publicly Held**
SIC: **0762** Farm management services
HQ: United Biosource Llc
    920 Harvest Dr Ste 200
    Blue Bell PA 19422
    215 591-2880

(P-728)
VALLEY FARM MANAGEMENT INC
37500 Foothill Rd, Soledad (93960-9507)
PHONE.................................831 678-1592
Richard R Smith, *President*
Alice Smith, *Treasurer*
James E Smith, *Vice Pres*
Jason Smith, *Admin Sec*
EMP: 100
SQ FT: 2,880
SALES (est): 9.1MM **Privately Held**
SIC: **0762** Vineyard management & maintenance services

(P-729)
VIMARK INC
Also Called: Vimark Vineyards
19500 Geyserville Ave, Geyserville (95441-9310)
P.O. Box 576 (95441-0576)
PHONE.................................707 857-3588
Krishik Hicks, *Manager*
EMP: 60
SALES (corp-wide): 65.1MM **Privately Held**
SIC: **0762** Vineyard management & maintenance services
PA: Vimark, Inc.
    101 D St Fl 2nd
    Santa Rosa CA
    707 542-3134

(P-730)
VINO FARMS INC (PA)
1377 E Lodi Ave, Lodi (95240-0840)
PHONE.................................209 334-6975
Fax: 209 369-8765
James D Ledbetter, *President*
John K Ledbetter, *CFO*
Kimberly Bronson, *Exec VP*
Craig Ledbetter, *Vice Pres*
Marissa Ledbetter, *Vice Pres*
EMP: 50
SQ FT: 6,000
SALES (est): 68.4MM **Privately Held**
SIC: **0762** 8748 Farm management services; agricultural consultant

(P-731)
VINO FARMS INC
10651 Eastside Rd, Healdsburg (95448-9490)
PHONE.................................707 433-8241
Fax: 707 433-8245
Roy Davis, *Manager*
EMP: 100
SALES (corp-wide): 68.4MM **Privately Held**
SIC: **0762** Vineyard management & maintenance services
PA: Vino Farms, Inc.
    1377 E Lodi Ave
    Lodi CA 95240
    209 334-6975

(P-732)
VYBORNY VINEYARD MANAGEMENT
7327 Silverado Trl, Rutherford (94573)
P.O. Box 367 (94573-0367)
PHONE.................................707 944-9135
J Alex Vyborny, *President*
Thomas Gore, *Vice Pres*
James M Decker, *Admin Sec*
▲ EMP: 99
SQ FT: 16,000
SALES (est): 4.5MM **Privately Held**
WEB: www.vyborny.com
SIC: **0762** Vineyard management & maintenance services

(P-733)
WEST COAST GRAPE FARMING INC
800 E Keyes Rd, Ceres (95307-7539)
P.O. Box 488 (95307-0488)
PHONE.................................209 538-3131
Fred Franzia, *President*
John Franzia, *Vice Pres*
Joseph Franzia, *Admin Sec*
EMP: 2500
SQ FT: 2,093
SALES (est): 53.1MM **Privately Held**
SIC: **0762** Farm management services

(P-734)
WEST COTTON AG MANAGEMENT INC
15900 W Dorris, Huron (93234)
P.O. Box 10 (93234-0010)
PHONE.................................559 945-2511
Bob Anderson, *President*
Richard Anderson, *Ch of Bd*
Craig Anderson, *Admin Sec*
EMP: 200
SQ FT: 1,000
SALES (est): 4.4MM **Privately Held**
SIC: **0762** Farm management services

(P-735)
WHITE HILLS VINEYARD RANC
8385 Graciosa Rd, Santa Maria (93455-6105)
PHONE.................................805 934-1986
Dale Hampton, *President*
EMP: 58
SALES (est): 2.6MM **Privately Held**
SIC: **0762** Vineyard management & maintenance services

0781 Landscape Counseling & Planning

(P-736)
A GROWING CONCERN LANDSCAPES
17382 Gothard St, Huntington Beach (92647-6203)
PHONE.................................714 843-5137
Fax: 714 843-5138
Douglas Neal, *Owner*
EMP: 82
SALES (est): 5.8MM **Privately Held**
WEB: www.growingconcern.com
SIC: **0781** Landscape services

(P-737)
ABSHEAR LANDSCAPE DEVELOPMENT
3171b Rippey Rd, Loomis (95650-9504)
P.O. Box 1817 (95650-1817)
PHONE.................................916 660-1617
Fax: 916 660-1586
Barry Abshear, *Owner*
EMP: 50
SALES (est): 1.8MM **Privately Held**
WEB: www.abshearlandscapes.com
SIC: **0781** Landscape services

(P-738)
AMERICAN LANDSCAPE INC
Also Called: American Golf Construction
7013 Owensmouth Ave, Canoga Park (91303-2006)
PHONE.................................818 999-2041
Gary Peterson, *President*
Pamela Edmiston, *Vice Pres*
Mike Hayes, *General Mgr*
Jamie Tsui, *Admin Sec*
Jim Maddox, *Human Res Dir*
▲ EMP: 250
SQ FT: 14,000
SALES (est): 39.3MM **Privately Held**
SIC: **0781** Landscape services

(P-739)
AMERICAN LANDSCAPE MANAGEMENT (PA)
Also Called: Custom Lawn Services
7013 Owensmouth Ave, Canoga Park (91303-2006)
PHONE.................................818 999-2041
Mickey Strauss, *President*

PRODUCTS & SERVICES SECTION
0781 - Landscape Counseling & Planning County (P-762)

Gary Peterson, *Vice Pres*
Angelica Godfrey, *Info Tech Mgr*
Jason Strauss, *Marketing Staff*
James Maddox, *Agent*
EMP: 125
SQ FT: 14,000
SALES (est): 27.9MM **Privately Held**
SIC: 0781 Landscape services

(P-740)
AMERINE SYSTEMS INCORPORATED
10866 Cleveland Ave, Oakdale (95361-9709)
PHONE..................209 847-5968
Fax: 209 847-9082
Gary Amerine, *President*
Josh Malcom, *Office Mgr*
Ronald Amerine, *Admin Sec*
Mel Richars, *Administration*
Mary Walser, *Sales Executive*
EMP: 50
SQ FT: 20,000
SALES (est): 6.7MM **Privately Held**
WEB: www.amerinesys.com
SIC: 0781 5084 5083 Landscape services; pumps & pumping equipment; irrigation equipment

(P-741)
AZTECA LANDSCAPE
4073 Mennes Ave, Riverside (92509-6722)
PHONE..................951 369-9210
Raquel Ortiz, *Principal*
EMP: 85 **Privately Held**
SIC: 0781 Landscape services
PA: Azteca Landscape
1180 Olympic Dr Ste 207
Corona CA 92881

(P-742)
BARAZANI OUTDOORS INC
14101 Valleyheart Dr # 104, Sherman Oaks (91423-2864)
PHONE..................818 701-6977
Aviva Barazani, *CEO*
Al Guadagno, *Principal*
Greg Moralia, *Mktg Dir*
EMP: 75
SALES (est): 2.4MM **Privately Held**
SIC: 0781 Landscape counseling & planning

(P-743)
BELLAVISTA LANDSCAPE SVCS INC
340 Twin Pines Dr, Scotts Valley (95066-3951)
PHONE..................831 461-1761
Fax: 831 440-0832
Thomas Moore, *President*
Chris Moore, *Vice Pres*
Matt Moore, *VP Mktg*
Brian Moore, *Manager*
Nicole Spencer, *Associate*
EMP: 65
SQ FT: 4,000
SALES (est): 3.3MM **Privately Held**
SIC: 0781 Landscape services

(P-744)
BRIGHTVIEW COMPANIES LLC
2447 Stagecoach Rd, Stockton (95215-7929)
PHONE..................209 993-9277
EMP: 105
SALES (corp-wide): 914MM **Privately Held**
SIC: 0781 Landscape services
HQ: Brightview Companies, Llc
24151 Ventura Blvd
Calabasas CA 91302
818 223-8500

(P-745)
BRIGHTVIEW COMPANIES LLC
201 Longden Ave, Irwindale (91706-1329)
PHONE..................626 574-3940
Richard Perder, *President*
EMP: 105
SALES (corp-wide): 914MM **Privately Held**
SIC: 0781 Landscape services
HQ: Brightview Companies, Llc
24151 Ventura Blvd
Calabasas CA 91302
818 223-8500

(P-746)
BRIGHTVIEW LANDSCAPE DEV INC (DH)
24151 Ventura Blvd, Calabasas (91302-1449)
PHONE..................818 223-8500
Fax: 818 222-8307
Thomas Donnelly, *CEO*
Thomas C Donelly, *President*
Kenneth L Hutcheson, *President*
Andrew J Brennan, *COO*
Pamela L Stark, *Vice Pres*
◆ **EMP:** 50
SQ FT: 25,000
SALES (est): 625MM
SALES (corp-wide): 914MM **Privately Held**
SIC: 0781 Landscape counseling & planning
HQ: Brightview Companies, Llc
24151 Ventura Blvd
Calabasas CA 91302
818 223-8500

(P-747)
BRIGHTVIEW LANDSCAPE DEV INC
2890 E Miraloma Ave, Anaheim (92806-1803)
PHONE..................714 414-0914
EMP: 54
SALES (corp-wide): 914MM **Privately Held**
SIC: 0781 Landscape services
HQ: Brightview Landscape Development, Inc.
24151 Ventura Blvd
Calabasas CA 91302
818 223-8500

(P-748)
BRIGHTVIEW LANDSCAPE SVCS INC
20551 Corsair Blvd, Hayward (94545-1005)
PHONE..................510 723-0690
Tom Stoutt, *Branch Mgr*
Tony Fargnoli, *Manager*
EMP: 50
SALES (corp-wide): 914MM **Privately Held**
SIC: 0781 Landscape services
HQ: Brightview Landscape Services, Inc.
24151 Ventura Blvd
Calabasas CA 91302
818 223-8500

(P-749)
BRIGHTVIEW LANDSCAPE SVCS INC
8500 Miramar Pl, San Diego (92121-2530)
PHONE..................858 458-1900
Patrick Ceatter, *Manager*
EMP: 200
SALES (corp-wide): 914MM **Privately Held**
SIC: 0781 Landscape services
HQ: Brightview Landscape Services, Inc.
24151 Ventura Blvd
Calabasas CA 91302
818 223-8500

(P-750)
BRIGHTVIEW LANDSCAPE SVCS INC
4677 Pacheco Blvd, Martinez (94553-3625)
PHONE..................925 957-8831
Martin Becker, *Manager*
EMP: 80
SALES (corp-wide): 914MM **Privately Held**
SIC: 0781 Landscape services
HQ: Brightview Landscape Services, Inc.
24151 Ventura Blvd
Calabasas CA 91302
818 223-8500

(P-751)
BRIGHTVIEW LANDSCAPE SVCS INC
1960 S Yale St, Santa Ana (92704-3929)
PHONE..................714 546-7843
Dave Hanson, *Manager*
Jeff Mutch, *Vice Pres*
Robert Johnson, *Opers Mgr*
EMP: 100
SALES (corp-wide): 914MM **Privately Held**
SIC: 0781 0782 Landscape services; lawn & garden services
HQ: Brightview Landscape Services, Inc.
24151 Ventura Blvd
Calabasas CA 91302
818 223-8500

(P-752)
BRIGHTVIEW LANDSCAPE SVCS INC
5745 Alder Ave, Sacramento (95828-1107)
PHONE..................916 381-1121
John Bianco, *Manager*
Randy Stephens, *Purchasing*
EMP: 100
SALES (corp-wide): 914MM **Privately Held**
SIC: 0781 Landscape services
HQ: Brightview Landscape Services, Inc.
24151 Ventura Blvd
Calabasas CA 91302
818 223-8500

(P-753)
BRIGHTVIEW LANDSCAPE SVCS INC
7039 Commerce Cir Ste B, Pleasanton (94588-8006)
PHONE..................925 373-9500
Doug Lape, *Manager*
EMP: 80
SALES (corp-wide): 914MM **Privately Held**
SIC: 0781 0782 Landscape services; lawn & garden services
HQ: Brightview Landscape Services, Inc.
24151 Ventura Blvd
Calabasas CA 91302
818 223-8500

(P-754)
BRIGHTVIEW LANDSCAPE SVCS INC
17813 S Main St Ste 105, Gardena (90248-3542)
PHONE..................310 327-8700
Andrea Musick, *Manager*
Larry Hall, *Marketing Staff*
Tim Gravatt, *Accounts Mgr*
Uriel Rojas, *Accounts Mgr*
Tom Cutrono, *Contractor*
EMP: 110
SQ FT: 1,530
SALES (corp-wide): 914MM **Privately Held**
SIC: 0781 0782 Landscape services; landscape contractors
HQ: Brightview Landscape Services, Inc.
24151 Ventura Blvd
Calabasas CA 91302
818 223-8500

(P-755)
BRIGHTVIEW LANDSCAPES LLC
144 Malbert St Ste A, Perris (92570-8384)
PHONE..................951 657-4603
Terry Mahoney, *Branch Mgr*
EMP: 56
SALES (corp-wide): 914MM **Privately Held**
SIC: 0781 Landscape services
HQ: Brightview Landscapes, Llc
2275 Res Blvd Ste 600
Rockville MD 20850
301 987-9200

(P-756)
BRIGHTVIEW LANDSCAPES LLC
2420 Cougar Dr, Carlsbad (92010-8804)
PHONE..................760 929-8509
Trey Dupont, *Manager*
EMP: 100
SALES (corp-wide): 914MM **Privately Held**
SIC: 0781 Landscape services
HQ: Brightview Landscapes, Llc
2275 Res Blvd Ste 600
Rockville MD 20850
301 987-9200

(P-757)
BRIGHTVIEW LANDSCAPES LLC
9090 Birch St, Spring Valley (91977-4107)
PHONE..................619 644-8584
Larry Neuhoff, *Manager*
EMP: 80
SALES (corp-wide): 914MM **Privately Held**
SIC: 0781 Landscape services
HQ: Brightview Landscapes, Llc
2275 Res Blvd Ste 600
Rockville MD 20850
301 987-9200

(P-758)
CICILEO LANDSCAPES
4565 Hollister Ave, Santa Barbara (93110-1709)
P.O. Box 60912 (93160-0912)
PHONE..................805 967-3939
Fax: 805 967-7910
Michael J Cicileo, *President*
Desiree Cicileo, *Executive*
Michael Denton, *Manager*
EMP: 50
SALES (est): 4.5MM **Privately Held**
WEB: www.cicileolandscapes.com
SIC: 0781 0782 Landscape planning services; garden maintenance services

(P-759)
COASTAL MIRAGE LANDSCAPES
26362 Via De Anza, San Juan Capistrano (92675-4723)
PHONE..................949 496-7070
Fax: 949 492-5448
Joe A Malagon, *President*
Rachel Malagon, *Vice Pres*
EMP: 60
SQ FT: 700
SALES (est): 2.6MM **Privately Held**
WEB: www.coastalmirage.com
SIC: 0781 Landscape services

(P-760)
COMET BUILDING MAINTENANCE INC
21 Commercial Blvd Ste 12, Novato (94949-6109)
P.O. Box 2163, San Rafael (94912-2163)
PHONE..................415 383-1035
Fax: 415 383-1935
Richard J Brasile, *CEO*
Bob Basile, *Manager*
EMP: 70
SQ FT: 1,800
SALES (est): 4.5MM **Privately Held**
SIC: 0781 7349 Landscape services; janitorial service, contract basis

(P-761)
DESERT CNCPTS LDSCPG MAINT INC
79469 Country Club Dr I, Bermuda Dunes (92203-1206)
PHONE..................760 200-9007
Fax: 760 200-9014
Julio Castro, *President*
Frank Castro, *Vice Pres*
Antonio Zepeda, *Manager*
EMP: 120
SQ FT: 1,100
SALES (est): 3.4MM **Privately Held**
WEB: www.desertconcepts.net
SIC: 0781 Landscape services

(P-762)
DL LONG LANDSCAPING INC
5475 G St, Chino (91710-5233)
PHONE..................909 628-5531
Fax: 909 628-0970
David L Long, *President*
EMP: 100
SQ FT: 1,550

0781 - Landscape Counseling & Planning County (P-763)

SALES: 6.9MM **Privately Held**
WEB: www.dllong.com
SIC: 0781 Landscape architects

(P-763)
DREAMSCAPE LDSCP & MAINT INC
7192 Mission Gorge Rd, San Diego (92120-1131)
P.O. Box 900069 (92190)
PHONE 619 583-4439
Fax: 619 287-5023
Thomas Bjorstrom, *President*
Lisa Yoshinaga, *Office Mgr*
Jayme Wessels, *Opers Staff*
EMP: 50
SQ FT: 1,200
SALES: 6MM **Privately Held**
SIC: 0781 0782 Landscape planning services; landscape contractors

(P-764)
EDAW INC
401 W A St Ste 1200, San Diego (92101-7905)
PHONE 619 233-1454
Michael Downs, *Branch Mgr*
Mike Stahmer, *Controller*
Colleen Johnston, *Manager*
EMP: 80
SALES (corp-wide): 17.9B **Publicly Held**
WEB: www.edaw.com
SIC: 0781 8748 8712 Landscape counseling & planning; business consulting; architectural services
HQ: Edaw, Inc.
300 California St Fl 5
San Francisco CA 94104
415 955-2800

(P-765)
EDAW INC
2020 L St Ste 400, Sacramento (95811-4267)
PHONE 916 414-5800
Fax: 916 414-5850
Curtis Alling, *Manager*
EMP: 100
SALES (corp-wide): 17.9B **Publicly Held**
WEB: www.edaw.com
SIC: 0781 8711 8712 8748 Landscape architects; engineering services; architectural services; business consulting
HQ: Edaw, Inc.
300 California St Fl 5
San Francisco CA 94104
415 955-2800

(P-766)
ELS INVESTMENTS
Also Called: Environmental Ldscp Solutions
8380 Rovana Cir, Sacramento (95828-2527)
PHONE 916 388-0308
Darryl Alan Thompson Jr, *President*
Shawna Thompson, *Vice Pres*
EMP: 110 EST: 2008
SQ FT: 7,200
SALES (est): 15.7MM **Privately Held**
SIC: 0781 1771 Landscape services; concrete work

(P-767)
FC LANDSCAPE INC
43216 Madison St, Indio (92201-1944)
PHONE 760 347-6600
Francisco Corona, *President*
Marie Martinez, *Manager*
EMP: 75
SALES (est): 2.5MM **Privately Held**
SIC: 0781 Landscape services

(P-768)
GARDEN VIEW INC
417 E Huntington Dr, Monrovia (91016-3632)
PHONE 626 303-4043
Fax: 626 355-3543
Mark Meahl, *President*
Diana Shows, *Regional Mgr*
Diana Showes, *Office Mgr*
EMP: 50
SQ FT: 1,500
SALES: 4MM **Privately Held**
SIC: 0781 0782 Landscape architects; garden services; landscape contractors

(P-769)
GOTHIC LANDSCAPING INC
Also Called: Gothic Grounds Mgmt
27413 Tourney Rd Ste 200, Valencia (91355-5606)
PHONE 661 257-5085
Fax: 661 294-3790
Ron Georgio, *President*
Matt Burr, *CTO*
Leah Randall, *Controller*
EMP: 500
SALES (corp-wide): 131.6MM **Privately Held**
WEB: www.gothiclandscape.com
SIC: 0781 0782 Landscape services; lawn & garden services
PA: Gothic Landscaping, Inc.
27502 Avenue Scott
Valencia CA 91355
661 257-1266

(P-770)
HAROLD JONES LANDSCAPE INC
40 W Cochran St Ste 206, Simi Valley (93065-1607)
PHONE 805 582-7443
Fax: 805 582-0953
Constance Wilson, *President*
Heather Cole, *Manager*
EMP: 50
SALES (est): 3.3MM **Privately Held**
SIC: 0781 Landscape counseling & planning

(P-771)
HART HOWERTON LTD (PA)
1 Union St Fl 3, San Francisco (94111-1223)
PHONE 415 439-2200
Fax: 415 439-2201
Dave Howerton, *CEO*
Roland Aberg, *Vice Pres*
A J Tinson, *Vice Pres*
Kenny Powers, *Office Mgr*
Diane Nielson, *Executive Asst*
EMP: 90
SQ FT: 20,000
SALES (est): 11.2MM **Privately Held**
SIC: 0781 8712 Landscape architects; architectural services

(P-772)
HERITAGE LANDSCAPE INC
7949 Deering Ave, Canoga Park (91304-5009)
PHONE 818 999-2041
William Leighton Knell, *President*
Cherly Knotts, *Manager*
EMP: 130
SALES (est): 3.1MM **Privately Held**
SIC: 0781 0782 Landscape services; landscape contractors

(P-773)
HUPPE LANDSCAPE COMPANY INC (HQ)
9350 Viking Pl, Roseville (95747-9713)
PHONE 916 784-7666
Fax: 916 784-7733
Chris Huppe, *President*
Gina Huppe, *Admin Sec*
EMP: 68
SQ FT: 215,000
SALES (est): 6.4MM
SALES (corp-wide): 116.6MM **Privately Held**
SIC: 0781 0782 Horticulture services; lawn & garden services
PA: Jensen Corporate Holdings, Inc.
1983 Concourse Dr
San Jose CA 95131
408 446-1118

(P-774)
I PWLC INC
408 Olive Ave, Vista (92083-3438)
P.O. Box 3557 (92085-3557)
PHONE 760 630-0231
Richard Ruiz, *CEO*
Erika Roa, *Administration*
EMP: 90
SQ FT: 1,000
SALES (est): 4.6MM **Privately Held**
SIC: 0781 Landscape services

(P-775)
KEVIN PERSONS INC
Also Called: Ground Maintenance Services
2977 Los Feliz Dr, Thousand Oaks (91362-3411)
P.O. Box 879, Newbury Park (91319-0879)
PHONE 805 371-8746
Fax: 805 498-9497
Kevin Persons, *President*
Jennifer Rice, *Project Mgr*
EMP: 50
SALES (est): 5MM **Privately Held**
SIC: 0781 Landscape services

(P-776)
LANDCARE USA LLC
216 N Clara St, Santa Ana (92703-3518)
PHONE 714 245-1465
Fax: 714 245-1466
Rory Malone, *Branch Mgr*
EMP: 86
SALES (corp-wide): 200MM **Privately Held**
SIC: 0781 Landscape architects
PA: Landcare Usa L.L.C.
5295 Westview Dr Ste 100
Frederick MD 21703
301 874-3300

(P-777)
M F COMMERCIAL LANDSCAPE SVCS
1821 Reynolds Ave, Irvine (92614-5713)
PHONE 949 660-8655
Mark Fitt, *President*
Joann Fitt, *Corp Secy*
Tim Skeen, *Vice Pres*
Irene Thavisay, *Accountant*
EMP: 91
SQ FT: 8,400
SALES (est): 5.6MM **Privately Held**
SIC: 0781 Landscape services

(P-778)
MALIBU CANYON LDSCP & MAINT
2046 Tierra Rejada Rd, Moorpark (93021-9769)
PHONE 805 523-2676
David S Bateman, *President*
Brooke D Bateman, *CFO*
D Brooke Bateman, *CFO*
Lee A Tarbet, *Admin Sec*
EMP: 55
SQ FT: 1,500
SALES (est): 2MM **Privately Held**
WEB: www.malibulandscape.com
SIC: 0781 Landscape counseling & planning

(P-779)
MASUDAS LANDSCAPE SERVICES
423 Salmar Ave, Campbell (95008-1413)
PHONE 408 379-7100
Ken Masuda, *Owner*
EMP: 100
SALES (est): 7.2MM **Privately Held**
SIC: 0781 Landscape architects

(P-780)
MEDALLION LANDSCAPE MGT INC (PA)
10 San Bruno Ave, Morgan Hill (95037-9214)
P.O. Box 1768 (95038-1768)
PHONE 408 782-7500
Fax: 408 779-8698
John Gates, *CEO*
Joyce Dawson, *President*
Roger Green, *President*
Ildefonso Fonsie Bettencourt, *COO*
Robert Rosenberg, *CFO*
EMP: 65
SALES (est): 23.3MM **Privately Held**
WEB: www.mlmi.com
SIC: 0781 Landscape counseling services; landscape planning services

(P-781)
MURATA ROCKEY LANDSCAPING
15417 Cornet St, Santa Fe Springs (90670-5533)
PHONE 562 921-3210
Fax: 562 921-3670
Rockey Murata, *President*
Andie Murata, *Corp Secy*
EMP: 60 EST: 1951
SQ FT: 10,000
SALES (est): 4.5MM **Privately Held**
SIC: 0781 Landscape services

(P-782)
NATURES IMAGE INC
20361 Hermana Cir, Lake Forest (92630-8701)
PHONE 949 680-4400
Fax: 949 705-5850
Michelle M Caruana, *CEO*
John Caruana, *Vice Pres*
Walt Smith, *Executive*
Ason Walters, *Executive*
Scott Watson, *Manager*
EMP: 95
SQ FT: 13,800
SALES (est): 13MM **Privately Held**
WEB: www.naturesimage.net
SIC: 0781 0782 Landscape counseling & planning; landscape contractors

(P-783)
OUTSIDE LINES INC
20331 Irvine Ave Ste E7, Newport Beach (92660-0223)
PHONE 714 637-4747
John Wickham Zimmerman, *CEO*
Hugh F Hughes, *President*
Jack Larsen, *Vice Pres*
Thomas Real, *Vice Pres*
Sarah D'Ambrosio, *Office Mgr*
EMP: 50
SALES (est): 16.7MM **Privately Held**
WEB: www.otl-inc.com
SIC: 0781 Landscape counseling & planning

(P-784)
PACIFIC COAST LDSCP MGT INC
3960 Holway Dr, Byron (94514)
P.O. Box 757 (94514-0757)
PHONE 925 513-2310
Fax: 925 513-2911
Alvaro Beltran, *President*
Robin Rowley, *Office Mgr*
Kathy Reed, *Administration*
EMP: 60
SALES (est): 7.6MM **Privately Held**
WEB: www.pacificcoastlandscape.net
SIC: 0781 0782 Landscape services; lawn & garden services; garden services; landscape contractors

(P-785)
PACIFIC RESTORATION GROUP INC
325 E Ellis Ave, Perris (92570-8413)
P.O. Box 429 (92572-0429)
PHONE 951 940-6069
John Richards, *President*
Daniel Richards, *CFO*
Patricia Richards, *Admin Sec*
EMP: 50
SQ FT: 10,000
SALES (est): 5.3MM **Privately Held**
SIC: 0781 Landscape services

(P-786)
PARKER LANDSCAPE DEV INC
6251 Sky Creek Dr Ste A, Sacramento (95828-1027)
PHONE 916 383-4071
Fax: 916 383-3926
Timothy J Parker, *President*
Conney Parker, *Admin Sec*
Daniel Parker, *Accounts Mgr*
EMP: 50
SALES (est): 4.5MM **Privately Held**
SIC: 0781 Landscape services

(P-787)
PIERRE LANDSCAPE INC
5455 2nd St, Irwindale (91706-2072)
PHONE 818 373-0023

PRODUCTS & SERVICES SECTION
0782 - Lawn & Garden Svcs County (P-811)

Harold Young, *CEO*
Joseph Lowden, *President*
Monty Khouri, *CFO*
Natalie Prado, *Accountant*
Norma Perine, *Asst Mgr*
EMP: 200
SQ FT: 9,425
SALES (est): 16.5MM **Privately Held**
SIC: 0781 Landscape architects

(P-788)
PLATINUM LANDSCAPE INC
50885 Washington St # 110, La Quinta (92253-2836)
PHONE.................................760 200-3673
Christopher Johnson, *President*
Cherie Johnson, *Vice Pres*
Valerie Garcia, *Manager*
EMP: 60
SALES: 1.5MM **Privately Held**
WEB: www.platinumlandscape.com
SIC: 0781 Landscape services

(P-789)
PRO PONDS WEST INC
Also Called: Pacific Outdoor Living
8309 Tujunga Ave Unit 201, Sun Valley (91352-3216)
PHONE.................................818 244-4000
Fax: 714 434-7663
Terry Morrill, *CEO*
Jerry McMahon, *Principal*
EMP: 100
SALES (est): 3.2MM **Privately Held**
SIC: 0781 Landscape services

(P-790)
PROFESSNAL LDSCP SOLUTIONS INC
6108 27th St Ste C, Sacramento (95822-3711)
PHONE.................................916 424-3815
Michael E Parker, *President*
Chad Bush, *Vice Pres*
Penny Parker, *Admin Sec*
EMP: 50
SQ FT: 11,000
SALES (est): 3.5MM **Privately Held**
SIC: 0781 Landscape services

(P-791)
RANCHO DEL ORO LDSCP MAINT INC
4167 Avenida De La Plata, Oceanside (92056-6032)
P.O. Box 4608 (92052-4608)
PHONE.................................760 726-0215
Uriel Espinoza, *President*
Richard Kirk, *CFO*
Albertano Cardenas, *Vice Pres*
EMP: 73
SQ FT: 1,400
SALES (est): 3.8MM **Privately Held**
WEB: www.rancho.sdcoxmail.com
SIC: 0781 Landscape services

(P-792)
REGENT ASSISTED LIVING INC
Also Called: Regent Court
2325 St Pauls Way, Modesto (95355-3309)
PHONE.................................209 491-0800
Fax: 209 491-0814
Karen Schemper, *Manager*
EMP: 53
SALES (corp-wide): 27.4MM **Privately Held**
WEB: www.regentassistedliving.com
SIC: 0781 Landscape services
PA: Regent Assisted Living, Inc.
121 Sw Morrison St # 950
Portland OR 97204
503 227-4000

(P-793)
RELIABLE CONCEPTS CORPORATION
954 Chestnut St, San Jose (95110-1504)
PHONE.................................408 271-6659
Fax: 408 271-6659
Daniel Montes, *President*
Cristina Ruiz, *Executive*
Linda Corsbie, *Manager*
Pedro Cisneros, *Supervisor*
Amado Pacheco, *Supervisor*
EMP: 70
SQ FT: 6,000
SALES (est): 4.5MM **Privately Held**
WEB: www.rcc-bgm.com
SIC: 0781 Landscape services

(P-794)
SAN DIEGO LAND SYSTEMS
8720 Miramar Pl, San Diego (92121-2551)
PHONE.................................858 558-0542
Fax: 858 558-6419
Stewart C Frederick, *President*
Yvette Deboer, *Office Mgr*
Damon Follen, *Opers Mgr*
Mike Hedekin, *Sales Dir*
EMP: 50
SQ FT: 11,700
SALES (est): 5.4MM **Privately Held**
WEB: www.landsystems.biz
SIC: 0781 Landscape services

(P-795)
SAN VAL CORP (PA)
Also Called: San Val Alarm System
72203 Adelaid St, Thousand Palms (92276-2321)
P.O. Box 12860, Palm Desert (92255-2860)
PHONE.................................760 346-3999
Robert L Sandifer, *President*
Sharon L Sandifer, *Admin Sec*
EMP: 425
SALES (est): 27.7MM **Privately Held**
WEB: www.cvwebs.com
SIC: 0781 7381 Landscape services; burglary protection service

(P-796)
SHOOTER & BUTTS INC
3768 Old Santa Rita Rd, Pleasanton (94588-3457)
PHONE.................................925 460-5155
Fax: 925 460-8485
James E Butts, *President*
Keith Hollon, *Manager*
Jamie Matthews, *Manager*
EMP: 50
SQ FT: 1,800
SALES (est): 5.1MM **Privately Held**
WEB: www.shooterandbutts.com
SIC: 0781 Landscape services

(P-797)
SIERRA LANDSCAPE & MAINT INC
3760 Morrow Ln Ste A, Chico (95928-8873)
PHONE.................................530 895-0263
Catherine S Gurney, *President*
Maria Gomez, *Office Mgr*
Lynette Derosa, *Controller*
EMP: 52
SQ FT: 8,000
SALES (est): 4.3MM **Privately Held**
WEB: www.sierralandscapeinc.com
SIC: 0781 Landscape services

(P-798)
SLADE INDUSTRIAL LANDSCAPE INC
8838 Zelzah Ave, Sherwood Forest (91325-3139)
P.O. Box 571960, Tarzana (91357-1960)
PHONE.................................818 885-1916
David Slade, *President*
Sylvia Slade, *Corp Secy*
Jon D Cantor, *Agent*
EMP: 55
SALES (est): 4.4MM **Privately Held**
SIC: 0781 0782 Landscape planning services; landscape contractors; garden maintenance services; lawn services

(P-799)
SWA GROUP (PA)
2200 Bridgeway, Sausalito (94965-1750)
P.O. Box 5904 (94966-5904)
PHONE.................................415 332-5100
Fax: 415 332-0719
Gerdo Aquino, *CEO*
Kevin Shanley, *President*
Scott Cooper, *CFO*
Wendy Simon, *Treasurer*
Jessica Reyes, *Admin Mgr*
EMP: 60 **EST:** 1957
SQ FT: 12,000
SALES (est): 46.8MM **Privately Held**
SIC: 0781 Landscape architects

(P-800)
TERRA PACIFIC LANDSCAPE (PA)
1627 E Wilshire Ave, Santa Ana (92705-4504)
PHONE.................................714 567-0177
Fax: 714 567-0179
Rich Wingard, *President*
Kim Quezada, *Admin Asst*
Brenda Polk, *Manager*
EMP: 89
SQ FT: 6,000
SALES (est): 33.3MM **Privately Held**
WEB: www.terrapac.com
SIC: 0781 Landscape services

(P-801)
TOG LANDSCAPING INC
Also Called: Evergreen Landcare
5057 W Washington Blvd, Los Angeles (90016-1450)
P.O. Box 19789 (90019-0789)
PHONE.................................323 549-3150
Timothy Gilmore, *President*
David Myers, *Exec Dir*
Diane Gilmore, *Director*
EMP: 80
SALES (est): 6.4MM **Privately Held**
SIC: 0781 Landscape counseling & planning

(P-802)
VALENCIA TREE LANDSCAPE
321 N Quarantina St, Santa Barbara (93103-3228)
P.O. Box 4554 (93140-4554)
PHONE.................................805 965-4244
Fax: 805 965-5099
Rossendo Valencia, *Owner*
EMP: 50
SALES (est): 1.9MM **Privately Held**
SIC: 0781 Landscape services

(P-803)
VALLEYCREST LDSCP MAINT VCC
24121 Ventura Blvd, Calabasas (91302-1449)
PHONE.................................800 466-8510
Jon Pinkus, *President*
Aaron Pinkus, *Vice Pres*
Lillian Pinkus, *Vice Pres*
EMP: 50 **EST:** 1951
SQ FT: 6,000
SALES (est): 2MM
SALES (corp-wide): 23.1MM **Privately Held**
SIC: 0781 Landscape services
PA: Nortex Wholesale Nursery, Inc.
7700 Northaven Rd
Dallas TX 75230
214 363-5316

0782 Lawn & Garden Svcs

(P-804)
AD LAND VENTURE LP
3217 Fitzgerald Rd, Rancho Cordova (95742-6813)
P.O. Box 1087, Folsom (95763-1087)
PHONE.................................916 853-9015
Fax: 916 853-9016
Gregory Houck, *Partner*
Sherri Strom, *Controller*
EMP: 100
SQ FT: 8,000
SALES (est): 14MM **Privately Held**
SIC: 0782 Landscape contractors

(P-805)
ALL COMMERCIAL LANDSCAPE SVC
5213 E Pine Ave, Fresno (93727-2110)
PHONE.................................559 453-1670
Fax: 559 454-8478
Jack Murray, *President*
Carol Osborn, *Corp Secy*
Tom Delny, *Vice Pres*
EMP: 50
SQ FT: 22,500
SALES (est): 4.3MM **Privately Held**
WEB: www.acls.bz
SIC: 0782 Lawn & garden services; lawn services

(P-806)
ALVIZIA LANDSCAPE CO LLC
2520 Cactus Rd, San Diego (92154-8009)
PHONE.................................619 661-6557
Fax: 619 661-0030
Jose Alexander Jr, *President*
Velda Pacheco, *Vice Pres*
EMP: 160
SQ FT: 1,151
SALES (est): 6.2MM **Privately Held**
SIC: 0782 Landscape contractors

(P-807)
AMERICAN LANDSCAPE MANAGEMENT
Also Called: Custom Lawn Services
1607 Los Angeles Ave I, Ventura (93004-3237)
PHONE.................................805 647-5077
Fax: 805 647-7112
Armondo Bello, *Manager*
Arturo Perez, *Manager*
EMP: 50
SALES (corp-wide): 27.9MM **Privately Held**
SIC: 0782 0783 0781 Lawn & garden services; ornamental shrub & tree services; landscape planning services
PA: American Landscape Management Inc
7013 Owensmouth Ave
Canoga Park CA 91303
818 999-2041

(P-808)
ARAGON COMMERCIAL LDSCPG INC
530 Stockton Ave, San Jose (95126-2463)
PHONE.................................408 998-0600
Fax: 408 998-2617
Scott Tabler, *President*
Julie Tabler, *Manager*
EMP: 135
SQ FT: 7,000
SALES (est): 7.7MM **Privately Held**
SIC: 0782 0781 Lawn & garden services; landscape services

(P-809)
ARREOLAS COMPLETE LDSCP SVC
Also Called: Arreolas Complete Ldscp Svc
8671 Morrison Creek Dr # 100, Sacramento (95828-1862)
PHONE.................................916 387-6777
Fax: 916 387-6777
Humberto Arreola, *Owner*
EMP: 50
SQ FT: 10,000
SALES (est): 2.4MM **Privately Held**
SIC: 0782 Lawn & garden services

(P-810)
ARTISTIC MAINTENANCE INC
16092 Construction Cir E, Irvine (92606-4401)
PHONE.................................949 733-8690
Rudy Moracco, *Manager*
EMP: 150
SALES (corp-wide): 29.5MM **Privately Held**
SIC: 0782 Landscape contractors; garden maintenance services
HQ: Artistic Maintenance, Inc.
23676 Birtcher Dr
Lake Forest CA 92630
949 581-9817

(P-811)
AZTEC LANDSCAPING INC (PA)
7980 Lemon Grove Way, Lemon Grove (91945-1820)
PHONE.................................619 464-3303
Fax: 619 464-3305
Genaro Garcia, *President*
Rafael Aguilar, *Treasurer*
Ramon Aguilar, *Vice Pres*
Suzana Michel, *Accountant*
Alexandra Aguilar, *Director*
EMP: 180
SQ FT: 30,000

0782 - Lawn & Garden Svcs County (P-812)

SALES (est): 22.2MM Privately Held
WEB: www.azteclandscaping.com
SIC: 0782 0783 7349 Lawn & garden services; ornamental shrub & tree services; janitorial service, contract basis

(P-812)
BENCHMARK LANDSCAPE INC
12575 Stowe Dr, Poway (92064-6805)
PHONE.................................858 513-7190
Fax: 858 513-7191
John A Mohns, President
Carrie Craig, Vice Pres
Craig Mohns, Vice Pres
Bill Hoffman, General Mgr
Sharon R Mohns, Admin Sec
EMP: 220
SQ FT: 18,000
SALES (est): 26.8MM Privately Held
WEB: www.benchmarklandscape.com
SIC: 0782 Landscape contractors

(P-813)
BENNETT ENTERPRISES A CA
Also Called: Bennett Landscape
25889 Belle Porte Ave, Harbor City (90710-3393)
PHONE.................................310 534-3543
Fax: 310 534-3176
Sean Bennett, President
Robin Larson, Controller
Joe B Manalastas, Manager
EMP: 90
SQ FT: 10,500
SALES (est): 6.7MM Privately Held
SIC: 0782 Landscape contractors

(P-814)
BLOSSOM VALLEY CNSTR INC
1125 Mabury Rd, San Jose (95133-1029)
P.O. Box 611537 (95161-1537)
PHONE.................................408 993-0766
Mark Collishaw, President
Robert Jimenez, CEO
Kathrin Hoffnagle, Treasurer
Tim Corboline, Webmaster
Jonathan Miley, Bishop
EMP: 60
SQ FT: 5,000
SALES (est): 4.5MM Privately Held
SIC: 0782 Landscape contractors

(P-815)
BRIGHTVIEW COMPANIES LLC
11555 Coley River Cir, Fountain Valley (92708-4224)
PHONE.................................714 437-1586
George Magana, Regional Mgr
Michael Kramer, Engineer
Vicky Harris, Accountant
Sandy Troncoso, Hum Res Coord
Ann Hopkinson, Purch Agent
EMP: 132
SALES (corp-wide): 258.8MM Privately Held
SIC: 0782 Landscape contractors
PA: Brightview Companies, Llc
    2275 Research Blvd
    Rockville MD 20850
    240 683-2000

(P-816)
BRIGHTVIEW LANDSCAPE DEV INC
13571 Vaughn St, San Fernando (91340-3001)
PHONE.................................818 838-4700
Greg Motschenbacher, Branch Mgr
Mike Roberts, Sales Executive
Tadd Russikoff, Contractor
EMP: 60
SALES (corp-wide): 914MM Privately Held
SIC: 0782 0781 Landscape contractors; landscape services
HQ: Brightview Landscape Development, Inc.
    24151 Ventura Blvd
    Calabasas CA 91302
    818 223-8500

(P-817)
C J VANDERGEEST LDSCP CARE INC
2476 Palma Dr Ste G, Ventura (93003-5760)
PHONE.................................805 650-0726
Fax: 805 650-7216
Joanne Smith, President
Dusty Smith, Vice Pres
Patricia Carr, Manager
EMP: 84
SQ FT: 2,000
SALES (est): 3.7MM Privately Held
SIC: 0782 Landscape contractors

(P-818)
CACHO LANDSCAPE MAINTENANCE CO
711 Truman St, San Fernando (91340-3314)
P.O. Box 922764, Sylmar (91392-2764)
PHONE.................................818 365-0773
Fax: 818 365-1466
Eddie Cacho, President
Diana Cacho, CFO
Genaro Gutierrez, Vice Pres
Rosie Armenta, Office Mgr
EMP: 50
SQ FT: 3,184
SALES (est): 3.3MM Privately Held
SIC: 0782 Lawn & garden services

(P-819)
CAL-WEST NURSERIES INC
138 North Dr, Norco (92860-1637)
PHONE.................................951 270-0667
Fax: 909 270-0903
Michael Whiting, President
Christene Smialkowski, Administration
Marc Keck, Project Mgr
Manuel Garcia, Maint Spvr
Jerry Gonzalez, Maint Spvr
EMP: 150
SQ FT: 1,700
SALES (est): 14.9MM Privately Held
WEB: www.calwestlandscape.com
SIC: 0782 0181 Landscape contractors; nursery stock, growing of

(P-820)
CALIFORNIA LDSCP & DESIGN INC
Also Called: CA Landscape and Design
273 N Benson Ave, Upland (91786-5614)
PHONE.................................909 949-1601
Fax: 909 981-9368
Joseph Ciaglia Jr, CEO
Roger Lovingood, Manager
EMP: 120
SQ FT: 1,500
SALES (est): 17.4MM Privately Held
WEB: www.callandscape.com
SIC: 0782 Landscape contractors

(P-821)
CARSON FRANK LDSCP & MAINT INC
Also Called: CARSON LANDSCAPE INDUSTRIES
9530 Elder Creek Rd, Sacramento (95829-9306)
PHONE.................................916 856-5400
Frank M Carson, President
Kathy Pipis, Admin Sec
EMP: 200
SQ FT: 36,000
SALES: 14.1MM Privately Held
SIC: 0782 Landscape contractors

(P-822)
CENTRESCAPES INC
165 Gentry St, Pomona (91767-2184)
PHONE.................................909 392-3303
Fax: 909 392-3308
Mark Marcus, President
Grace Loya, Corp Secy
EMP: 88
SQ FT: 7,000
SALES (est): 7.7MM Privately Held
WEB: www.centrescapes.com
SIC: 0782 Landscape contractors

(P-823)
CHAMPAGNE LANDSCAPE NURS INC
3233 N Cornelia Ave, Fresno (93722-4606)
P.O. Box 9755 (93794-9755)
PHONE.................................559 277-8188
Fax: 559 277-8292
Robert Champagne, President
Gail Champagne, Treasurer
Robert N Champagne, Vice Pres
Courtney Woody, Admin Sec
Janzen Wong, Director
EMP: 87
SALES (est): 5.3MM Privately Held
SIC: 0782 0781 Garden maintenance services; landscape architects

(P-824)
CIELO AZUL INC
Also Called: Blue Skies Landscape Maint
7986 Dagget St, San Diego (92111-2321)
P.O. Box 17026 (92177-7026)
PHONE.................................858 565-8344
Fax: 858 565-8398
Pedro Navarro Jr, President
Natali Navarro, Treasurer
Julie Navarro, Admin Sec
EMP: 75
SALES (est): 4.1MM Privately Held
WEB: www.blueskieslandscape.com
SIC: 0782 Landscape contractors

(P-825)
CITY II ENTERPRISES INC
Also Called: Flora Terra Landscape MGT
845 Earle Ave, San Jose (95126-3404)
PHONE.................................408 275-1200
Fax: 408 275-1201
Gene E Ebertowski, President
Kimberly Garcia, Corp Secy
EMP: 50
SQ FT: 40,000
SALES (est): 3.3MM Privately Held
WEB: www.floraterra.com
SIC: 0782 Lawn & garden services

(P-826)
CLEARY BROS LANDSCAPE INC
4931 Pacheco Blvd, Martinez (94553-4324)
PHONE.................................925 335-9335
EMP: 69
SALES (corp-wide): 18MM Privately Held
SIC: 0782 Lawn & garden services
PA: Cleary Bros. Landscape, Inc.
    521 Diablo Rd
    Danville CA 94526
    925 838-2551

(P-827)
COHEN RICHARD LDSCP & CNSTR
20795 Canada Rd, El Toro (92630-7702)
PHONE.................................949 768-0599
Fax: 949 768-9051
Richard Cohen, President
Linda Cohen, Treasurer
EMP: 50 EST: 1976
SQ FT: 1,000
SALES (est): 2.6MM Privately Held
WEB: www.richardcohenlandscape.com
SIC: 0782 Landscape contractors

(P-828)
COMMON GROUND LDSCP MGT INC
725 Lenzen Ave, San Jose (95126-2734)
P.O. Box 20850 (95160-0850)
PHONE.................................408 278-9847
William Jauch, President
Tris Jauch, Treasurer
Lillian Askew, Administration
EMP: 50
SQ FT: 20,000
SALES: 2MM Privately Held
SIC: 0782 Landscape contractors

(P-829)
COMPLETE LANDSCAPE CARE INC
13316 Leffingwell Rd, Whittier (90605-4136)
PHONE.................................562 946-4441
Tom Murray, President
Tammy Murray, Manager
Bob Fisher, Accounts Mgr
EMP: 57
SQ FT: 26,000
SALES (est): 4.6MM Privately Held
WEB: www.completelandscapecareinc.com
SIC: 0782 1711 Landscape contractors; irrigation sprinkler system installation

(P-830)
D & H LANDSCAPING INC
4221 Appian Way, El Sobrante (94803-2203)
P.O. Box 57, Pinole (94564-0057)
PHONE.................................510 223-6597
Fax: 510 223-7854
David Treas, President
Irma Smallen, Admin Sec
Farrin White, Webmaster
Shelly Bouzidin, Manager
EMP: 60
SALES (est): 4.7MM Privately Held
WEB: www.dandhlandscaping.com
SIC: 0782 0781 Lawn care services; landscape planning services

(P-831)
D AND S LANDSCAPING INC
26901 Hansen Rd, Tracy (95377-8847)
PHONE.................................925 455-4630
Fax: 925 656-4684
Ben Hansen, Principal
EMP: 130
SALES (est): 5.9MM Privately Held
SIC: 0782 Landscape contractors

(P-832)
DANS LANDSCAPE SERVICE INC
718 Aleppo St, Newport Beach (92660-4122)
PHONE.................................714 241-9591
Fax: 714 241-0805
Dan Seminario, President
Myrna Seminario, Vice Pres
Natanio Bonganoy, General Mgr
Jesus Castro, Manager
EMP: 65
SQ FT: 16,000
SALES: 3.3MM Privately Held
WEB: www.danslandscapeservice.com
SIC: 0782 Lawn & garden services

(P-833)
DAVID OLLIS LANDSCAPE DEV INC
450 Kansas St Ste 104, Redlands (92373-1481)
PHONE.................................909 307-1911
David Ollis, President
Criss Campbell, Manager
EMP: 50
SALES (est): 4.9MM Privately Held
WEB: www.davidollis.com
SIC: 0782 Landscape contractors

(P-834)
DE LA TORRE LANDSCAPE & MAINT
656 Paseo Grande, Corona (92882-2837)
P.O. Box 3018 (92878-3018)
PHONE.................................951 549-3525
Fax: 951 549-3565
Robert De La Torre, President
Socorro De La Torre, Vice Pres
Veronica De La Torre, Admin Sec
Veronica Dela Torre, Controller
EMP: 230
SQ FT: 1,108
SALES (est): 8.5MM Privately Held
SIC: 0782 Lawn & garden services

(P-835)
DECKER LANDSCAPING INC
13265 Bill Francis Dr, Auburn (95603-9022)
PHONE.................................916 652-1780
Christopher Decker, President

PRODUCTS & SERVICES SECTION
0782 - Lawn & Garden Svcs County (P-859)

Dan McElvin, *CFO*
Tom Decker, *Vice Pres*
John Decker, *Division Mgr*
Karen Seeker, *Human Res Mgr*
EMP: 75
SQ FT: 2,500
SALES (est): 8.7MM **Privately Held**
SIC: 0782 0781 Landscape contractors; landscape architects

(P-836)
DEL CONTES LANDSCAPING INC
41900 Boscell Rd, Fremont (94538-3196)
PHONE.....................510 353-6030
Fax: 510 353-6036
Tom Del Conte, *CEO*
Mario Camacho, *Division Mgr*
Aron Stunk, *Finance Mgr*
Delane Vergara, *Manager*
Ross Holton, *Accounts Mgr*
EMP: 100
SQ FT: 960
SALES (est): 10.4MM **Privately Held**
WEB: www.dclandscaping.com
SIC: 0782 Landscape contractors

(P-837)
DEMARIA LANDTECH INC
2789 High Mead Cir, Vista (92084-1830)
PHONE.....................858 481-5500
Fax: 858 966-1789
John Demaria, *Owner*
EMP: 50
SALES (est): 1.2MM **Privately Held**
WEB: www.demarialandtech.com
SIC: 0782 Landscape contractors

(P-838)
DESERT HAVEN ENTERPRISES (PA)
43437 Copeland Cir, Lancaster (93535-4672)
P.O. Box 2110 (93539-2110)
PHONE.....................661 948-8402
Fax: 661 258-4125
Jenni C Moran, *CEO*
Roberta Terry, *CFO*
Kathleen Miller, *Program Dir*
EMP: 536
SQ FT: 15,000
SALES: 7.6MM **Privately Held**
WEB: www.deserthaven.org
SIC: 0782 8331 Lawn & garden services; work experience center

(P-839)
DESERT HAVEN ENTERPRISES
43437 Copeland Cir, Lancaster (93535-4672)
P.O. Box 2110 (93539-2110)
PHONE.....................661 948-8402
Jennie Moran, *Branch Mgr*
EMP: 278
SALES (corp-wide): 7.6MM **Privately Held**
WEB: www.deserthaven.org
SIC: 0782 8331 Lawn & garden services; job training & vocational rehabilitation services
PA: Desert Haven Enterprises
 43437 Copeland Cir
 Lancaster CA 93535
 661 948-8402

(P-840)
DIABLO LANDSCAPE INC
1655 Berryessa Rd, San Jose (95133-1082)
PHONE.....................408 487-9620
Fax: 408 487-9621
EMP: 80
SQ FT: 38,000
SALES (est): 6.9MM
SALES (corp-wide): 32.2MM **Privately Held**
WEB: www.diablolandscape.com
SIC: 0782
PA: The Celtis Group Inc
 1655 Berryessa Rd Ste A
 San Jose CA
 408 487-9620

(P-841)
DIVERSCAPE INC
Also Called: Diversified Landscape Co
21730 Bundy Canyon Rd, Wildomar (92595-8780)
PHONE.....................951 245-1686
Fax: 951 926-7440
Vicki Moralez, *President*
Paul Moralez, *President*
Eric Ellis, *Purchasing*
Helen Leutt, *Manager*
EMP: 90
SALES: 9.5MM **Privately Held**
WEB: www.diversifiedlandscape.com
SIC: 0782 1611 Garden maintenance services; landscape contractors; general contractor, highway & street construction

(P-842)
DMA GREENCARE CONTRACTING INC
3000 E Coronado St, Anaheim (92806-2602)
PHONE.....................714 630-9470
Fax: 714 630-9471
Dennis Aldridge, *CEO*
Darin Doucette, *Vice Pres*
Tim Keller, *Purchasing*
EMP: 50
SQ FT: 5,000
SALES (est): 8.2MM **Privately Held**
SIC: 0782 Landscape contractors

(P-843)
DOMINGUEZ LANDSCAPE SVCS INC
8376 Rovana Cir, Sacramento (95828-2527)
P.O. Box 292727 (95829-2727)
PHONE.....................916 381-8855
Fax: 916 381-4796
Robert Dominguez, *President*
Bonnie J Dominguez, *Vice Pres*
Bonnie Dommguez, *Admin Sec*
Loreen Chapman, *Manager*
EMP: 78
SQ FT: 7,200
SALES (est): 5.1MM **Privately Held**
SIC: 0782 Landscape contractors

(P-844)
DOOSE LANDSCAPE INCORPORATED
785 E Mission Rd, San Marcos (92069-1903)
PHONE.....................760 591-4500
Fax: 760 591-4549
Robert J Doose, *President*
Shelley Nolet, *Treasurer*
Tom Doose, *Vice Pres*
Susan Daugherty, *Admin Sec*
EMP: 85
SQ FT: 11,300
SALES (est): 6.1MM **Privately Held**
WEB: www.dooselandscape.com
SIC: 0782 Landscape contractors

(P-845)
DULEYS LANDSCAPE INC
28876 Topaz Rd, Tollhouse (93667-9712)
PHONE.....................559 855-5090
Fax: 559 855-3315
Robert Duley, *President*
Debbie Duley, *Vice Pres*
EMP: 50
SALES (est): 3.3MM **Privately Held**
SIC: 0782 Landscape contractors

(P-846)
DWIW INC
Also Called: Land Scapes
700 W 16th St, Costa Mesa (92627-4303)
PHONE.....................949 574-7147
John Duley, *President*
Pam Duley, *Vice Pres*
EMP: 50
SQ FT: 5,000
SALES (est): 2MM **Privately Held**
WEB: www.dwiw.com
SIC: 0782 Landscape contractors

(P-847)
ELITE LANDSCAPING INC
2972 Larkin Ave, Clovis (93612-3986)
PHONE.....................559 292-7760
Guy Stockbridge, *President*
Jill Stockbridge, *CFO*
EMP: 150
SQ FT: 20,000
SALES (est): 7.2MM **Privately Held**
WEB: www.elitelandscapinginc.com
SIC: 0782 Landscape contractors

(P-848)
EMERALD LANDSCAPE SERVICES
1041 N Kemp St, Anaheim (92801-2518)
PHONE.....................714 844-2200
John C Croul, *President*
Pam McIntyre, *Controller*
Pam Mc Entire, *Consultant*
EMP: 70
SALES (est): 4.5MM **Privately Held**
SIC: 0782 0781 Landscape contractors; landscape planning services

(P-849)
ENHANCED LANDSCAPE MGT INC
1938 E Thousand Oaks Blvd, Thousand Oaks (91362-2913)
PHONE.....................805 557-2737
Fax: 805 557-2738
Gregory Epstein, *President*
EMP: 65
SALES (est): 3.8MM **Privately Held**
SIC: 0782 0721 Lawn & garden services; crop related entomological services (insect control)

(P-850)
ESQUIRE LANDSCAPE INC
8380 Miralani Dr Ste B, San Diego (92126-4304)
PHONE.....................858 530-2949
Fax: 619 697-4064
William A Behl, *President*
Lisa Derby, *Manager*
EMP: 50
SQ FT: 1,500
SALES (est): 2MM **Privately Held**
SIC: 0782 Landscape contractors

(P-851)
EXCEL LANDSCAPE INC
710 Rimpau Ave Ste 108, Corona (92879-5724)
P.O. Box 77995 (92877-0133)
PHONE.....................951 735-9650
Jose Alfaro, *President*
▲ **EMP:** 120
SQ FT: 1,200
SALES (est): 9.2MM **Privately Held**
WEB: www.excellandscape.com
SIC: 0782 Lawn care services; garden maintenance services

(P-852)
EXECUTIVE LANDSCAPE INC
2131 Huffstatler St, Fallbrook (92028-8861)
P.O. Box 1075 (92088-1075)
PHONE.....................760 731-9038
Fax: 760 731-9036
Edwin Earle, *CEO*
Walter Earle, *Treasurer*
Kathleen D Earle, *Vice Pres*
Rachel Pslieger, *Manager*
EMP: 230
SQ FT: 1,800
SALES (est): 24.2MM **Privately Held**
WEB: www.executivelandscapeinc.com
SIC: 0782 Landscape contractors

(P-853)
FENDERSCAPE INC
Also Called: Proscape Landscape
1446 E Hill St, Signal Hill (90755-3527)
PHONE.....................562 988-2228
Fax: 562 988-5998
David Fender, *President*
Linda Fender, *Treasurer*
Dan Juarez, *Office Mgr*
Lori Martin, *Administration*
Nikki Dagel, *Controller*
EMP: 127
SQ FT: 1,893
SALES (est): 1MM **Privately Held**
SIC: 0782 Landscape contractors

(P-854)
FS COMMERCIAL LANDSCAPE INC (PA)
5151 Pedley Rd, Riverside (92509-3937)
PHONE.....................951 360-7070
Fax: 951 360-7075
G John Wood, *President*
EMP: 75
SQ FT: 1,500
SALES (est): 9.3MM **Privately Held**
WEB: www.fslandscapes.com
SIC: 0782 Landscape contractors

(P-855)
GACHINA LANDSCAPE MGT INC
1130 Obrien Dr, Menlo Park (94025-1411)
PHONE.....................650 853-0400
Fax: 650 853-0430
John P Gachina, *CEO*
Stacie Callaghan, *Business Dir*
Diane Giacchino, *Branch Mgr*
Sylvia Espinoza, *Admin Asst*
Silvia Espinoza, *Administration*
EMP: 269
SQ FT: 12,000
SALES (est): 32.8MM **Privately Held**
WEB: www.gachina.com
SIC: 0782 Landscape contractors

(P-856)
GARDENERS GUILD INC
2780 Goodrick Ave, Richmond (94801-1110)
PHONE.....................415 457-0400
Fax: 415 457-2373
Kevin Davis, *President*
Mike Davidson, *Vice Pres*
Ismael Polanco, *Admin Asst*
Gloria Young, *Accountant*
Ginny Kuhel, *Director*
EMP: 140
SQ FT: 25,000
SALES (est): 18.5MM **Privately Held**
WEB: www.gardenersguild.com
SIC: 0782 Landscape contractors

(P-857)
GATEWAY LANDSCAPE CNSTR INC
6735 Sierra Ct Ste A, Dublin (94568-2656)
PHONE.....................925 875-0000
Fax: 925 449-1344
Corey Pontrelli, *President*
David J Garcia, *Vice Pres*
EMP: 75
SQ FT: 3,000
SALES (est): 5.9MM **Privately Held**
WEB: www.gatewaylci.com
SIC: 0782 1711 Landscape contractors; irrigation sprinkler system installation

(P-858)
GOTHIC LANDSCAPING INC (PA)
Also Called: Gothic Ground Management
27502 Avenue Scott, Valencia (91355-3965)
PHONE.....................661 257-1266
Jon S Georgio, *President*
Ronald Georgio, *Vice Pres*
Perry Jones, *Vice Pres*
Mike Georgio, *Principal*
Michelle Schiff, *Executive Asst*
EMP: 200
SQ FT: 5,000
SALES (est): 131.6MM **Privately Held**
WEB: www.gothiclandscape.com
SIC: 0782 Landscape contractors; lawn services

(P-859)
GRANTS LANDSCAPE SERVICES INC
3046 Orange Ave, Santa Ana (92707-4248)
PHONE.....................714 444-1903
Fax: 714 444-1687
Kenneth Grant, *Vice Pres*
Harold Grant, *Vice Pres*
EMP: 75
SQ FT: 4,000
SALES: 1.6MM **Privately Held**
SIC: 0782 Landscape contractors

0782 - Lawn & Garden Svcs County (P-860) — PRODUCTS & SERVICES SECTION

(P-860)
GREEN AGAIN LDSCPG & CON INC
851 Charter St, Redwood City (94063-3004)
PHONE 650 368-9304
Fax: 650 368-9320
Frederick C Nurisso, *President*
Ralph Earlywine, *Manager*
EMP: 55
SQ FT: 1,400
SALES (est): 1.4MM **Privately Held**
WEB: www.greenagain.com
SIC: 0782 Landscape contractors

(P-861)
GREEN SCENE LANDSCAPE INC
21220 Devonshire St # 102, Chatsworth (91311-8224)
PHONE 818 280-0420
Scott Cohen, *CEO*
Lisa Cohen, *Vice Pres*
Jason Byrne, *Bookkeeper*
EMP: 58
SQ FT: 1,100
SALES (est): 1.7MM **Privately Held**
WEB: www.greenscenelandscape.com
SIC: 0782 Landscape contractors; lawn care services

(P-862)
GREENBRIER LAWN TREE EXPRT CO
3616 Bancroft Dr, Spring Valley (91977-2116)
PHONE 619 469-8720
Fax: 619 469-8748
Bill Gibson, *President*
Elsa Garaygordobil, *Admin Asst*
EMP: 60
SQ FT: 6,000
SALES (est): 2.5MM **Privately Held**
SIC: 0782 Landscape contractors

(P-863)
GROWING COMPANY INC
4 Wayne Ct Ste 3, Sacramento (95829-1305)
PHONE 916 379-9088
Bruno Sandoval, *President*
Anne Sandoval, *Vice Pres*
Gualberto Cardenas, *Area Spvr*
Modesto Gonzalez, *Area Spvr*
Linda Cardenas, *Human Res Dir*
EMP: 100
SQ FT: 10,000
SALES (est): 10.8MM **Privately Held**
WEB: www.thegrowingcompany.net
SIC: 0782 Landscape contractors; garden maintenance services

(P-864)
GS BROTHERS INC (PA)
2215 N Gaffey St, San Pedro (90731-1238)
PHONE 310 833-1369
Alan M Gaudenti, *President*
Robert M Gaudenti, *Corp Secy*
EMP: 190
SQ FT: 7,000
SALES (est): 21.9MM **Privately Held**
SIC: 0782 Landscape contractors

(P-865)
HABITAT RSTRATION SCIENCES INC (PA)
1217 Distribution Way, Vista (92081-8817)
PHONE 760 479-4210
Mark Girard, *President*
June Collins, *President*
EMP: 65
SALES (est): 11.9MM **Privately Held**
SIC: 0782 Landscape contractors

(P-866)
HABITAT RSTRATION SCIENCES INC
Also Called: Restoration Resources Hrs
3888 Cincinnati Ave, Rocklin (95765-1312)
PHONE 916 408-2990
Mark Girard, *President*
Victor Navarrete, *Project Mgr*
EMP: 50
SALES (corp-wide): 11.9MM **Privately Held**
SIC: 0782 Landscape contractors

PA: Habitat Restoration Sciences, Inc.
1217 Distribution Way
Vista CA 92081
760 479-4210

(P-867)
HARVEST LANDSCAPE ENTPS INC
Also Called: Harvest Landscape Maintenance
1290 N Hancock St Ste 202, Anaheim (92807-1986)
P.O. Box 3877, Orange (92857-0877)
PHONE 714 283-4298
Stephen G Schinhofen, *CEO*
Shelley Fajardo, *CFO*
Don Saunders, *Marketing Staff*
EMP: 160
SALES (est): 18.3MM **Privately Held**
SIC: 0782 Landscape contractors

(P-868)
HEAVILAND ENTERPRISES INC
2180 La Mirada Dr, Vista (92081-8815)
PHONE 760 598-7065
Fax: 760 598-1733
Thomas J Heaviland, *CEO*
Ernie Pile, *COO*
Gloria Alas, *Human Res Dir*
Jim Allen, *Purchasing*
EMP: 190
SQ FT: 2,500
SALES (est): 13.1MM **Privately Held**
WEB: www.heaviland.net
SIC: 0782 1542 Landscape contractors; commercial & office buildings, renovation & repair

(P-869)
HEMINGTON LANDSCAPE SVCS INC
4170 Business Dr, Cameron Park (95682-7230)
PHONE 530 677-9290
Fax: 530 677-0590
Mark E Hemington, *President*
Jill Hemington, *Corp Secy*
Lori Grant, *HR Admin*
Harvey Dhillon, *Manager*
EMP: 100
SALES (est): 7.1MM **Privately Held**
WEB: www.hemington.com
SIC: 0782 Landscape contractors

(P-870)
HORT TECH INC
78355 Darby Rd, Bermuda Dunes (92203-9661)
P.O. Box 3284, Palm Desert (92261-3284)
PHONE 760 360-9000
Fax: 760 360-1800
Bryan Jensen, *President*
Linda Gurrola, *Admin Sec*
EMP: 160
SQ FT: 8,000
SALES (est): 7MM **Privately Held**
SIC: 0782 Landscape contractors

(P-871)
IKES LANDSCAPING & MAINTENANCE
2700 Tiber Ave, Davis (95616-2958)
PHONE 530 758-1698
Eric Aichwalder, *President*
Don Kearney, *Vice Pres*
Aletha Aichwalder, *Admin Sec*
EMP: 80
SQ FT: 2,000
SALES (est): 3MM **Privately Held**
SIC: 0782 5992 Landscape contractors; lawn care services; plants, potted

(P-872)
IRRI-SCAPE CONSTRUCTION INC
20182 Carancho Rd, Temecula (92590-4348)
PHONE 951 694-6936
Fax: 951 694-0799
Robert Smith, *President*
EMP: 100
SQ FT: 1,500
SALES (est): 6.4MM **Privately Held**
SIC: 0782 Landscape contractors

(P-873)
J REDFERN INC
Also Called: Golden State Landscaping
164 N L St, Livermore (94550-2118)
P.O. Box 2091 (94551-2091)
PHONE 925 371-3300
John E Redfern, *President*
Nca Land, *Marketing Staff*
Nancy Robins, *Manager*
EMP: 108
SALES (est): 7.7MM **Privately Held**
WEB: www.jredfern.com
SIC: 0782 Landscape contractors

(P-874)
J VITALE LANDSCAPE & MAINT
8801 Cottonwood Ave, Santee (92071-4460)
PHONE 619 938-2435
Jim Vitale, *President*
EMP: 90
SALES (est): 7MM **Privately Held**
SIC: 0782 Landscape contractors

(P-875)
JAMES H COWAN & ASSOCIATES INC
29243 Pacific Coast Hwy, Malibu (90265-3917)
PHONE 310 457-2574
Fax: 310 457-0752
Clark J Cowan, *President*
Kendall Whitney, *Admin Sec*
EMP: 95
SQ FT: 3,500
SALES (est): 9MM **Privately Held**
WEB: www.jhcowan.com
SIC: 0782 Landscape contractors

(P-876)
JENSEN CORP LANDSCAPE CONTR
1983 Concourse Dr, San Jose (95131-1708)
PHONE 408 446-4881
John Vlay, *CEO*
Shamina Edwards, *Admin Sec*
EMP: 150 EST: 2008
SALES (est): 10MM **Privately Held**
SIC: 0782 1521 Landscape contractors; single-family housing construction

(P-877)
JENSEN CORPORATE HOLDINGS INC (PA)
1983 Concourse Dr, San Jose (95131-1708)
PHONE 408 446-1118
John Vlay, *CEO*
Paul Johnson, *CFO*
Quang Trinh, *CFO*
Donald Defever, *Division Pres*
Glenn Berry, *Vice Pres*
EMP: 117 EST: 1969
SQ FT: 13,000
SALES (est): 116.6MM **Privately Held**
WEB: www.jensencorp.com
SIC: 0782 Landscape contractors

(P-878)
JENSEN LANDSCAPE SERVICES INC
Also Called: Jensen Corp Landscape Contrs
1983 Concourse Dr, San Jose (95131-1708)
PHONE 408 446-1118
John Vlay, *CEO*
Anthony Whalls, *President*
Paul Johnson, *CFO*
Glenn Berry, *Vice Pres*
Frederick Loo, *Controller*
EMP: 165
SALES (est): 8MM
SALES (corp-wide): 116.6MM **Privately Held**
WEB: www.jensencorp.com
SIC: 0782 Landscape contractors
PA: Jensen Corporate Holdings, Inc.
1983 Concourse Dr
San Jose CA 95131
408 446-1118

(P-879)
JLP LANDSCAPE CONTRACTING
901 7th St, Santa Rosa (95404-4255)
PHONE 707 526-6285
Fax: 707 526-2301
John Prior, *President*
Alicia Lene Ruppell Prior, *Treasurer*
Alicia Ruppell, *Vice Pres*
EMP: 50
SQ FT: 2,000
SALES (est): 3.1MM **Privately Held**
SIC: 0782 0781 Landscape contractors; landscape planning services

(P-880)
JMA INVESTMENTS LTD
Also Called: Ahrens Landscape & Maintenance
9265 Beatty Dr, Sacramento (95826-9702)
P.O. Box 279199 (95827-9199)
PHONE 916 685-1355
Fax: 916 369-7264
Jeff Ahrens, *President*
Michele Ahrens, *Vice Pres*
EMP: 99
SQ FT: 2,000
SALES (est): 14MM **Privately Held**
SIC: 0782 Lawn care services

(P-881)
JPA LANDSCAPE & CNSTR INC
256 Boeing Ct, Livermore (94551-9258)
P.O. Box 1292, Pleasanton (94566-0129)
PHONE 925 960-9602
Ed Morrissey, *President*
Jody Morrissey, *Treasurer*
Sharon Evans, *Human Res Mgr*
Jason Kuhlwein, *Opers Mgr*
Frances Morrissey, *Marketing Staff*
EMP: 75
SQ FT: 9,000
SALES (est): 3.9MM **Privately Held**
WEB: www.jpalandscape.com
SIC: 0782 Landscape contractors

(P-882)
JRA LANDSCAPE INC
1010 W Whites Bridge Ave, Fresno (93706-1328)
P.O. Box 9789 (93794-9789)
PHONE 559 276-1726
Fax: 559 276-2913
John Alsdorf, *President*
EMP: 60
SQ FT: 1,200
SALES (est): 4.7MM **Privately Held**
SIC: 0782 Landscape contractors

(P-883)
KIRKPATRICK LDSCPG SVCS INC
43752 Jackson St, Indio (92201-2540)
P.O. Box 10430 (92202-2542)
PHONE 760 347-6926
Fax: 760 347-4846
Steven Kirkpatrick, *President*
Sandy Eggleston, *Controller*
EMP: 200
SQ FT: 5,000
SALES (est): 10.9MM **Privately Held**
SIC: 0782 Lawn care services; garden maintenance services

(P-884)
KITSON LANDSCAPE MGT INC
5787 Thornwood Dr, Goleta (93117-3801)
PHONE 805 681-9460
Fax: 805 681-9460
Sarah Kitson, *President*
David Fudurich, *Treasurer*
Brent Kitson, *Vice Pres*
Susan Ellis, *Office Mgr*
Sally Kitson, *Admin Sec*
EMP: 80 EST: 1969
SQ FT: 52,272
SALES (est): 4.9MM **Privately Held**
WEB: www.kitsonlandscape.com
SIC: 0782 Landscape contractors

PRODUCTS & SERVICES SECTION
0782 - Lawn & Garden Svcs County (P-910)

(P-885)
L A SWIKARD INC
Also Called: Terra Firma Landscape Company
9520 Candida St, San Diego (92126-4540)
PHONE..................................858 408-3700
Fax: 858 408-2396
Larry A Swikard, *President*
Cindy A Swikard, *CFO*
EMP: 225 EST: 1981
SQ FT: 20,000
SALES (est): 14.4MM **Privately Held**
SIC: 0782 Landscape contractors

(P-886)
L BARRIOS & ASSOCIATES INC
302 E Fthill Blvd Ste 101, San Dimas (91773)
P.O. Box 3948 (91773-7948)
PHONE..................................626 960-2934
Henry Barrios, *President*
EMP: 50 EST: 1955
SALES (est): 3.3MM **Privately Held**
SIC: 0782 1711 Landscape contractors; lawn services; irrigation sprinkler system installation

(P-887)
LAND SERVICES LANDSCAPE CONTRS
901 Brown Rd, Fremont (94539-7089)
PHONE..................................510 656-8101
Fax: 510 656-8103
John Ahner, *President*
Kari E Wood, *Office Mgr*
EMP: 80
SQ FT: 11,000
SALES (est): 3MM **Privately Held**
SIC: 0782 Landscape contractors

(P-888)
LANDCARE USA LLC
Also Called: Trugreen
216 N Clara St, Santa Ana (92703-3518)
PHONE..................................949 559-7771
Kenny Stites, *Branch Mgr*
EMP: 80
SALES (corp-wide): 200MM **Privately Held**
SIC: 0782 Lawn care services
PA: Landcare Usa L.L.C.
5295 Westview Dr Ste 100
Frederick MD 21703
301 874-3300

(P-889)
LANDCARE USA LLC
Also Called: Trugreen
770 Metcalf St, Escondido (92025-1667)
PHONE..................................760 747-1174
Brett Horan, *Branch Mgr*
EMP: 80
SALES (corp-wide): 200MM **Privately Held**
SIC: 0782 Lawn care services
PA: Landcare Usa L.L.C.
5295 Westview Dr Ste 100
Frederick MD 21703
301 874-3300

(P-890)
LANDCARE USA LLC
Also Called: Trugreen
1196 Patricia Ave, Simi Valley (93065-2809)
PHONE..................................805 520-9394
Noe Alcaraz, *Branch Mgr*
EMP: 125
SALES (corp-wide): 200MM **Privately Held**
SIC: 0782 Lawn care services
PA: Landcare Usa L.L.C.
5295 Westview Dr Ste 100
Frederick MD 21703
301 874-3300

(P-891)
LANDCARE USA LLC
930 Shiloh Rd Bldg 44-B, Windsor (95492-9664)
PHONE..................................707 836-1460
Fax: 707 836-1470
Scott Hall, *Branch Mgr*
EMP: 60

SALES (corp-wide): 200MM **Privately Held**
SIC: 0782 Lawn care services
PA: Landcare Usa L.L.C.
5295 Westview Dr Ste 100
Frederick MD 21703
301 874-3300

(P-892)
LANDCARE USA LLC
1315 W 130th St, Gardena (90247-1503)
PHONE..................................310 719-1008
Fax: 310 323-4780
Don Cully, *Branch Mgr*
EMP: 56
SALES (corp-wide): 200MM **Privately Held**
SIC: 0782 Landscape contractors; lawn services
PA: Landcare Usa L.L.C.
5295 Westview Dr Ste 100
Frederick MD 21703
301 874-3300

(P-893)
LANDCARE USA LLC
4134 Temple City Blvd, Rosemead (91770-1550)
PHONE..................................310 354-1520
Joe Espinoza, *Branch Mgr*
EMP: 56
SALES (corp-wide): 200MM **Privately Held**
SIC: 0782 Landscape contractors; lawn services
PA: Landcare Usa L.L.C.
5295 Westview Dr Ste 100
Frederick MD 21703
301 874-3300

(P-894)
LANDCARE USA LLC
5248 Governor Dr, San Diego (92122-2800)
PHONE..................................858 252-0658
EMP: 56
SALES (corp-wide): 200MM **Privately Held**
SIC: 0782 Landscape contractors; lawn services
PA: Landcare Usa L.L.C.
5295 Westview Dr Ste 100
Frederick MD 21703
301 874-3300

(P-895)
LANDCARE USA LLC
Also Called: Trugreen
1323 W 130th St, Gardena (90247-1503)
PHONE..................................310 354-1520
Dave Evans, *Branch Mgr*
Conrado Sigala, *Area Mgr*
Adam Budnik, *Manager*
EMP: 170
SALES (corp-wide): 200MM **Privately Held**
SIC: 0782 7342 Lawn care services; disinfecting & pest control services
PA: Landcare Usa L.L.C.
5295 Westview Dr Ste 100
Frederick MD 21703
301 874-3300

(P-896)
LANDCARE USA LLC
Also Called: Trugreen
3213 Fitzgerald Rd, Rancho Cordova (95742-6813)
PHONE..................................916 635-0936
Kevin Arnett, *Branch Mgr*
Michael Gard, *Administration*
EMP: 100
SALES (corp-wide): 200MM **Privately Held**
SIC: 0782 Lawn care services
PA: Landcare Usa L.L.C.
5295 Westview Dr Ste 100
Frederick MD 21703
301 874-3300

(P-897)
LANDCARE USA LLC
Also Called: Trugreen
5248 Governor Dr, San Diego (92122-2800)
PHONE..................................858 453-1755

Fax: 858 453-0569
Craig Gerber, *VP Finance*
Jasmine Sutherland, *Administration*
Jim Clifford, *Manager*
Krista Jimenez, *Manager*
EMP: 112
SALES (corp-wide): 200MM **Privately Held**
SIC: 0782 Lawn care services
PA: Landcare Usa L.L.C.
5295 Westview Dr Ste 100
Frederick MD 21703
301 874-3300

(P-898)
LANDCARE USA LLC
Also Called: Trugreen
7755 Deering Ave, Canoga Park (91304-5653)
PHONE..................................818 346-7552
Fax: 818 313-8531
Raul Sanchez, *Branch Mgr*
EMP: 150
SALES (corp-wide): 200MM **Privately Held**
SIC: 0782 Lawn care services; landscape contractors
PA: Landcare Usa L.L.C.
5295 Westview Dr Ste 100
Frederick MD 21703
301 874-3300

(P-899)
LANDCARE USA LLC
Also Called: Trugreen
85 Old Tully Rd, San Jose (95111-1910)
PHONE..................................408 727-4099
Jeff Kunkel, *Branch Mgr*
EMP: 75
SALES (corp-wide): 200MM **Privately Held**
SIC: 0782 Lawn care services
PA: Landcare Usa L.L.C.
5295 Westview Dr Ste 100
Frederick MD 21703
301 874-3300

(P-900)
LANDCO
7333 Clybourn Ave, Sun Valley (91352-5143)
PHONE..................................818 612-0118
Martin Stowell, *Owner*
▲ EMP: 100
SALES (est): 5.4MM **Privately Held**
SIC: 0782 Landscape contractors

(P-901)
LANDESIGN CNSTR & MAINT INC
1328 Airport Blvd, Santa Rosa (95403-1009)
P.O. Box 2326 (95405-0326)
PHONE..................................707 578-2657
Fax: 707 578-2658
John Fitzgerald, *Owner*
Denise Fitzgerald, *Co-Owner*
EMP: 90
SQ FT: 1,000
SALES: 5MM **Privately Held**
SIC: 0782 Landscape contractors

(P-902)
LANDSCAPE DEVELOPMENT INC (PA)
28447 Witherspoon Pkwy, Valencia (91355-4174)
PHONE..................................661 295-1970
Gary Horton, *CEO*
Jenny Lunde, *CFO*
Tim Myers, *CFO*
Tom McDaniel, *Bd of Directors*
Casper Correll, *Vice Pres*
▲ EMP: 350
SALES (est): 77.3MM **Privately Held**
WEB: www.landscapedevelopment.com
SIC: 0782 5039 Lawn & garden services; landscape contractors; soil erosion control fabrics

(P-903)
LAWNMAN II INC
4300 82nd St Ste C, Sacramento (95826-4730)
PHONE..................................916 739-1420
Fax: 916 739-1430

Burnie Lenau, *President*
▲ EMP: 60
SQ FT: 3,000
SALES: 3MM **Privately Held**
WEB: www.lawnmansac.com
SIC: 0782 Landscape contractors

(P-904)
LAZAR LANDSCAPE DESIGN & CNSTR
2884 Ettie St, Oakland (94608-4009)
PHONE..................................510 444-5195
Fax: 510 444-5198
Gary Lazar, *Owner*
Patti Hyland, *Finance Mgr*
EMP: 55
SALES (est): 2.8MM **Privately Held**
WEB: www.lazarlandscape.com
SIC: 0782 Landscape contractors

(P-905)
LEONARD ANTHONY VALENTI INC
9110 Marcella Ave, Gilroy (95020-9716)
P.O. Box 1179 (95021-1179)
PHONE..................................408 848-9688
Leonard A Valenti, *President*
EMP: 60
SALES (est): 4.7MM **Privately Held**
SIC: 0782 7349 1742 Landscape contractors; building maintenance, except repairs; plastering, drywall & insulation

(P-906)
LIBERTY LANDSCAPING INC
5212 El Rivino Rd, Riverside (92509-1807)
PHONE..................................951 683-2999
Fax: 951 683-2591
Alejandro Casillas, *President*
Rose Casillas, *Vice Pres*
EMP: 100 EST: 1998
SALES: 7.7MM **Privately Held**
SIC: 0782 Landscape contractors

(P-907)
MACKENZIE LANDSCAPE A CAL CORP
33380 Bailey Park Blvd, Menifee (92584-9585)
PHONE..................................951 679-5477
Fax: 909 679-1687
Michael Mackenzie, *President*
Judy Mackenzie, *CFO*
EMP: 100
SQ FT: 1,500
SALES (est): 2.6MM **Privately Held**
SIC: 0782 Landscape contractors; highway lawn & garden maintenance services

(P-908)
MARIPOSA LANDSCAPES INC (PA)
Also Called: Mariposa Horticultural Entps
15529 Arrow Hwy, Irwindale (91706-2002)
PHONE..................................623 463-2200
Fax: 626 960-8477
Terry Noriega, *President*
Antonio Valenzuela, *Vice Pres*
Ren Flugel, *General Mgr*
James Olsen, *Opers Staff*
Teresa Lu, *Manager*
EMP: 54
SQ FT: 2,000
SALES (est): 46.9MM **Privately Held**
WEB: www.mariposahorticultural.com
SIC: 0782 Garden maintenance services; lawn care services; landscape contractors

(P-909)
MARTINA LANDSCAPE INC
811 Camden Ave, Campbell (95008-4103)
PHONE..................................408 871-8800
Fax: 408 968-0943
Joe Martina, *President*
Martha Hernandez, *Office Mgr*
EMP: 80
SQ FT: 2,000
SALES (est): 5MM **Privately Held**
SIC: 0782 Landscape contractors

(P-910)
MEDLIN DEVELOPMENT
320 Tropicana Ranch Rd, Colton (92324-3605)
PHONE..................................909 825-5296

0782 - Lawn & Garden Svcs County (P-911) — PRODUCTS & SERVICES SECTION

Mike Medlin, *President*
Lynn McMahon, *Treasurer*
Lee Ann Hollands, *Vice Pres*
EMP: 50
SQ FT: 1,800
SALES (est): 1.5MM **Privately Held**
SIC: 0782

(P-911)
MIDORI LANDSCAPE INC
Also Called: Midori Landscaping
3231 S Main St, Santa Ana (92707-4405)
PHONE...............................714 751-8792
Fax: 714 751-4167
Naga Hamamoto, *President*
Ruth Horner, *Human Res Mgr*
Al Gamatero, *Manager*
Walt Takeda, *Manager*
EMP: 80
SQ FT: 8,200
SALES (est): 5.3MM **Privately Held**
SIC: 0782 Landscape contractors

(P-912)
MIKE MCCALL LANDSCAPE INC
4749 Clayton Rd, Concord (94521-2936)
PHONE...............................925 363-8100
Fax: 925 363-8148
Mike McCall, *President*
Mark Tate, *COO*
Nana David, *Human Res Mgr*
Garrett McCall, *Purch Dir*
Marie Haffner, *Sales Executive*
EMP: 140
SQ FT: 1,000
SALES (est): 12.3MM **Privately Held**
WEB: www.mikemccalllandscape.com
SIC: 0782 Landscape contractors

(P-913)
MISSION LANDSCAPE SERVICE
952 E Francis St, Ontario (91761-5630)
PHONE...............................909 947-7290
Fax: 909 947-7291
David Dubois, *Owner*
Rocco Campanozzi, *Vice Pres*
Stacey Garnham, *Pharmacy Dir*
Manuel Menchaca, *Foreman/Supr*
Stephen Natalo, *Sr Project Mgr*
EMP: 80
SALES (est): 3.4MM **Privately Held**
SIC: 0782 Landscape contractors

(P-914)
MISSION LDSCP COMPANIES INC
536 E Dyer Rd, Santa Ana (92707-3737)
P.O. Box 15026 (92735-0026)
PHONE...............................714 545-9962
Fax: 714 668-0119
David Dubois, *CEO*
Kristen Parkins, *President*
Beth Du Boise, *Treasurer*
Beatrice Campos, *Vice Pres*
Raul Salazar, *Regional Mgr*
EMP: 200
SQ FT: 11,000
SALES (est): 18.5MM **Privately Held**
WEB: www.missionlandscape.com
SIC: 0782 Landscape contractors

(P-915)
MONUMENT CONSTRUCTION INC
Also Called: Techcon
16200 Vineyard Blvd # 100, Morgan Hill (95037-7164)
PHONE...............................408 778-1350
Paul Maxwell Swing, *CEO*
Kevin Lanning, *Shareholder*
Christopher Farrar, *CFO*
Diane Swing, *CFO*
Vanessa Gonzales, *Office Mgr*
EMP: 70
SQ FT: 2,500
SALES (est): 8.1MM **Privately Held**
SIC: 0782 Landscape contractors

(P-916)
MPL ENTERPRISES INC
Also Called: Mike Parker Landscape
2302 S Susan St, Santa Ana (92704-4421)
PHONE...............................714 545-1717
Fax: 714 545-4843
Michael Parker, *President*
EMP: 90
SQ FT: 2,000
SALES (est): 5MM **Privately Held**
WEB: www.mikeparkerlandscape.com
SIC: 0782 Landscape contractors

(P-917)
N V LANDSCAPE INC
24400 Walnut St Ste D, Newhall (91321-2855)
P.O. Box 55188, Santa Clarita (91385-0188)
PHONE...............................661 286-8888
Jeff Brown, *President*
Holly Brown, *Corp Secy*
EMP: 60
SALES (est): 1.5MM **Privately Held**
WEB: www.nvlandscape.com
SIC: 0782 Landscape contractors

(P-918)
NATIVE SONS LANDSCAPING INC
25 Beta Ct Ste L, San Ramon (94583-1245)
PHONE...............................925 837-8175
Mike Hertel, *President*
Louise Hertel, *Vice Pres*
Cory Langelier, *Controller*
EMP: 50
SQ FT: 1,800
SALES (est): 4.5MM **Privately Held**
WEB: www.nativesons.net
SIC: 0782 0781 Landscape contractors; landscape counseling & planning

(P-919)
NEW EARTH ENTERPRISES INC
3790 Manchester Ave, Encinitas (92024-4935)
PHONE...............................760 942-1298
Fax: 760 942-8675
James R Williams, *President*
Carlos Delval, *Vice Pres*
Jessie Wilhoite, *Vice Pres*
EMP: 60
SQ FT: 192
SALES (est): 3.3MM **Privately Held**
SIC: 0782 Landscape contractors

(P-920)
NEW IMAGE LANDSCAPE COMPANY
3250 Darby Cmn, Fremont (94539-5601)
PHONE...............................510 226-9191
Brian Takehara, *President*
Elodia Criado, *Human Res Mgr*
Guillermo Ruvalcaba, *Opers Mgr*
Jessica Atkins, *Mktg Coord*
C Culbertson, *Accounts Mgr*
EMP: 55
SQ FT: 4,000
SALES (est): 3.6MM **Privately Held**
WEB: www.newimagelandscape.com
SIC: 0782 Lawn & garden services

(P-921)
NEW VIEW LANDSCAPE INC
24860 Calabasas Rd, Calabasas (91302-1429)
PHONE...............................818 222-8972
Fax: 818 222-8977
Lance Lortscher, *President*
Mike Stell, *Treasurer*
EMP: 60
SQ FT: 1,200
SALES (est): 3.2MM **Privately Held**
WEB: www.newviewlandscape.com
SIC: 0782 Garden maintenance services; turf installation services, except artificial

(P-922)
NEW WAY LANDSCAPE & TREE SVCS
7485 Ronson Rd, San Diego (92111-1507)
PHONE...............................858 505-8300
Fax: 858 505-8305
Randy Newhard, *CEO*
Kathryn Dejong, *President*
Bob Rogers, *President*
Dan Suhovecky, *CFO*
Kristine Duncan, *Treasurer*
EMP: 175
SQ FT: 6,400
SALES (est): 22.5MM **Privately Held**
WEB: www.newwaypro.com
SIC: 0782 Landscape contractors

(P-923)
NIEVES LANDSCAPE INC
1629 E Edinger Ave, Santa Ana (92705-5001)
PHONE...............................714 835-7332
Fax: 714 641-8475
Gregorio Nieves, *President*
Patricia White, *Admin Sec*
Ann Cashman, *Manager*
EMP: 150
SALES (est): 12.6MM **Privately Held**
SIC: 0782 Landscape contractors

(P-924)
NITTANY LION LANDSCAPING INC
Also Called: NI Services
14770 Firestone Blvd # 203, La Mirada (90638-5917)
PHONE...............................714 635-1788
Sam Aldrich, *President*
Don G Abbey, *Ch of Bd*
Mayra Mejia, *Accountant*
EMP: 63 **EST:** 1994
SQ FT: 7,300
SALES (est): 6.5MM **Privately Held**
SIC: 0782 Landscape contractors

(P-925)
NORTHWEST LANDSCAPE MAINT CO
283 Kinney Dr, San Jose (95112-4433)
PHONE...............................408 298-6489
Warren Nakamura, *President*
Douglas Nakamura, *Corp Secy*
Paul Nakamura, *Vice Pres*
EMP: 50
SQ FT: 4,808
SALES (est): 2.5MM **Privately Held**
WEB: www.northwestlandscapemc.com
SIC: 0782 Landscape contractors

(P-926)
OCONNELL LANDSCAPE MAINT INC
4600 Leisure Village Way, Oceanside (92056-5147)
PHONE...............................760 630-4963
Fax: 760 630-4963
Glen Foreman, *Branch Mgr*
EMP: 50
SALES (corp-wide): 145.8MM **Privately Held**
SIC: 0782 Landscape contractors
PA: O'connell Landscape Maintenance Inc.
23091 Arroyo Vis
Rcho Sta Marg CA 92688
949 589-2007

(P-927)
PAC WEST LAND CARE INC
Also Called: Pacific West Tree Service
408 Olive Ave, Vista (92083-3438)
P.O. Box 99 (92085-0099)
PHONE...............................760 630-0231
Barry Blue, *President*
Kevin Cesare, *Manager*
EMP: 130
SQ FT: 3,000
SALES (est): 4.4MM **Privately Held**
SIC: 0782

(P-928)
PADILLA LANDSCAPE INC
181 Sand Creek Rd Ste B, Brentwood (94513-2209)
P.O. Box 196 (94513-0196)
PHONE...............................925 513-9353
Joseph R Padilla, *President*
Rita Padilla, *Vice Pres*
Danielle Padilla, *Administration*
EMP: 52
SALES (est): 2.1MM **Privately Held**
SIC: 0782 Landscape contractors

(P-929)
PARK LANDSCAPE MAINTENANCE
529 W 4th Ave, Escondido (92025-4037)
PHONE...............................760 317-2550
EMP: 80
SALES (corp-wide): 12.9MM **Privately Held**
SIC: 0782 Landscape contractors
PA: Park Landscape Maintenance Inc
22421 Gilberto Ste A
Rcho Sta Marg CA 92688
949 546-8300

(P-930)
PARK LANDSCAPE MAINTENANCE (PA)
Also Called: Park Landscape Maint 1-2-3-4
22421 Gilberto Ste A, Rcho STA Marg (92688-2104)
PHONE...............................949 546-8300
Robert Morrison, *President*
Tom Tracy, *Shareholder*
Mike Tracy, *CEO*
Tom England, *CFO*
EMP: 300
SQ FT: 10,000
SALES (est): 12.9MM **Privately Held**
SIC: 0782 Lawn care services; lawn services; landscape contractors

(P-931)
PARK WEST RESCOM INC
22421 Gilberto, Rcho STA Marg (92688-2104)
PHONE...............................949 546-8300
Michael S Tracy, *CEO*
Bart Ryder, *President*
EMP: 101
SQ FT: 10,000
SALES (est): 4.9MM **Privately Held**
SIC: 0782 Landscape contractors

(P-932)
PARKWOOD LANDSCAPE MAINT INC
16443 Hart St, Van Nuys (91406-4608)
PHONE...............................818 988-9677
Fax: 818 988-4934
David Melito, *President*
EMP: 95 **EST:** 1988
SQ FT: 1,500
SALES (est): 5.5MM **Privately Held**
WEB: www.parkwoodlandscape.com
SIC: 0782 Landscape contractors

(P-933)
PENNEY LAWN SERVICE INC
Also Called: Penny Lawn Service
4000 Allen Rd, Bakersfield (93314-9091)
PHONE...............................661 366-3777
Fax: 661 587-4787
EMP: 100
SQ FT: 1,275
SALES (est): 8MM **Privately Held**
SIC: 0782

(P-934)
PETALON LANDSCAPE MGT INC
1766 Rogers Ave, San Jose (95112-1109)
PHONE...............................408 453-3998
Fax: 408 453-3997
Rudy Sotelo, *CEO*
John Linn, *President*
Noreen Prado, *Manager*
EMP: 65
SQ FT: 5,000
SALES (est): 5.5MM **Privately Held**
SIC: 0782 Landscape contractors

(P-935)
PINELANDS PRESERVATION INC
4501 Auburn Blvd Ste 201, Sacramento (95841-4213)
PHONE...............................609 703-0359
Christopher Carlino, *CEO*
Jason Maltezo, *Administration*
EMP: 60
SALES (est): 1.9MM **Privately Held**
SIC: 0782 8741 Landscape contractors; management services

(P-936)
PLANTASIA INC
Also Called: Plantasia Landscaping
2550 Via Tejon Ste 3f, Palos Verdes Estates (90274-6809)
PHONE...............................310 375-0387
Fax: 310 375-2587
Alex Colovic, *President*

PRODUCTS & SERVICES SECTION

0782 - Lawn & Garden Svcs County (P-963)

EMP: 75 EST: 1973
SALES (est): 5.9MM Privately Held
SIC: 0782 1629 Landscape contractors; irrigation system construction

(P-937) PLOWBOY LANDSCAPES INC
2190 N Ventura Ave, Ventura (93001-1343)
P.O. Box 1802 (93002-1802)
PHONE..................805 643-4966
Fax: 805 648-5571
Douglas Wasson, President
Robert Mooney, General Mgr
Juanita Crawford, Administration
Mimi Camacho, Bookkeeper
Cyndi Brinker, Purchasing
EMP: 55
SQ FT: 3,500
SALES (est): 4.9MM Privately Held
WEB: www.plowboyinc.com
SIC: 0782 Landscape contractors

(P-938) PRO SCAPE INC
510 Venture St, Escondido (92029-1212)
PHONE..................760 480-1544
Fax: 760 480-0784
Michael Helms, President
Jay Helms, Vice Pres
Aleah Helms, Admin Sec
EMP: 50
SQ FT: 2,600
SALES (est): 2.5MM Privately Held
SIC: 0782 Landscape contractors; garden maintenance services

(P-939) PROCIDA LANDSCAPE INC
8465 Specialty Cir, Sacramento (95828-2523)
PHONE..................916 387-5296
Fax: 916 387-5298
John Procida Jr, President
EMP: 160
SQ FT: 15,000
SALES (est): 10.3MM Privately Held
SIC: 0782 Lawn care services; lawn services; garden planting services

(P-940) R NAVARRO LANDSCAPE SERVICES
359 West Rd, La Habra Heights (90631-8048)
PHONE..................562 690-6414
Raul Navarro, President
Dana Navarro, Vice Pres
EMP: 60
SALES (est): 3.1MM Privately Held
SIC: 0782 Landscape contractors

(P-941) RANCHO CALIFORNIA LANDSCAPING
13801 S Western Ave, Gardena (90249-2517)
PHONE..................310 768-1680
Fax: 310 768-1626
Sal Mora, President
Ramon Sandoval, Opers Staff
Mike Barajas, Supervisor
EMP: 50
SQ FT: 33,610
SALES (est): 3.5MM Privately Held
WEB: www.ranchocalifornia.biz
SIC: 0782 Landscape contractors

(P-942) RANCHO WEST LANDSCAPE
39140 Pala Vista Dr, Temecula (92591-7213)
PHONE..................951 301-3979
Fax: 951 694-0584
Greg Duncan, Owner
Jerry Horan, Office Mgr
EMP: 50
SALES (est): 5.5MM Privately Held
SIC: 0782 Landscape contractors

(P-943) RELIABLE GARDENS INC
7837 Burnet Ave, Van Nuys (91405-1046)
PHONE..................818 904-9801
Fax: 818 904-0537
Steven Selden, CEO
Debra Selden, CFO
Laurie Levavi, Vice Pres
EMP: 60 EST: 1959
SALES (est): 4.2MM Privately Held
SIC: 0782 Garden planting services; garden maintenance services; landscape contractors; lawn services

(P-944) RESCOM SERVICES INC
2575 Fortune Way Ste E, Vista (92081-8413)
PHONE..................760 930-3900
Fax: 760 407-0175
Mark Sutton, President
Michael Smith, CFO
EMP: 92
SQ FT: 2,500
SALES (est): 6.2MM Privately Held
WEB: www.rescomservices.com
SIC: 0782 Lawn & garden services

(P-945) RESIDENT GROUP SERVICES INC (PA)
Also Called: Rgs Services
1156 N Grove St, Anaheim (92806-2109)
PHONE..................714 630-5300
Fax: 714 630-1330
James M Gilly, President
Michael K Hayde, CEO
Christy Hernandez, Admin Asst
Michael Schmidt, Sales Executive
Evette Poole, Manager
EMP: 149
SQ FT: 15,000
SALES (est): 20.5MM Privately Held
WEB: www.rgsservices.com
SIC: 0782 Landscape contractors

(P-946) RMT LANDSCAPE CONTRACTORS INC
421 Pendleton Way, Oakland (94621-2122)
PHONE..................510 568-3208
Rick Deherrera, President
Julie Briggs, Vice Pres
Sally Lipska, Admin Sec
Danika Briggs, Admin Asst
Lissette Eppler, HR Admin
EMP: 50
SQ FT: 12,000
SALES (est): 5.4MM Privately Held
WEB: www.rmtlandscape.com
SIC: 0782 Landscape contractors

(P-947) S G D ENTERPRISES
Also Called: Four Seasons Landscaping
14937 Delano St, Van Nuys (91411-2123)
PHONE..................818 782-3455
Stephen G Darrison, President
Marilyn Darrison, Manager
EMP: 50
SQ FT: 1,800
SALES (est): 5.2MM Privately Held
SIC: 0782 6512 6513 Landscape contractors; nonresidential building operators; apartment building operators

(P-948) SANSEI GARDENS INC
3250 Darby Cmn, Fremont (94539-5601)
PHONE..................510 226-9191
Fax: 510 226-1298
Brian Takehara, President
Reed Kelly, VP Opers
Lydia Creata, Manager
EMP: 110
SQ FT: 3,000
SALES (est): 10.6MM Privately Held
WEB: www.sanseigardens.com
SIC: 0782 Landscape contractors

(P-949) SCOTTS PLANT SERVICE CO
6206 Carver Rd, Modesto (95356-9177)
P.O. Box 3723 (95352-3723)
PHONE..................209 545-0903
Scott Reis, President
EMP: 67
SALES (est): 350K Privately Held
SIC: 0782 Landscape contractors

(P-950) SCYENCE INC
Also Called: Echo Landscape
2401 Grant Ave Lot B, San Lorenzo (94580-1807)
P.O. Box 20926, Castro Valley (94546-8926)
PHONE..................510 481-8614
Fax: 510 481-5386
Troy Deherrera, President
Danielle Scheid, Controller
EMP: 60
SQ FT: 1,600
SALES (est): 2.5MM Privately Held
WEB: www.scyence.com
SIC: 0782 Landscape contractors

(P-951) SERPICO LANDSCAPING INC
1764 National Ave, Hayward (94545-1722)
PHONE..................510 293-0341
Sharon Serpico Hanson, CEO
Rick Oliver, COO
Richard Hanson, Admin Sec
Lorrie Jackson, Manager
EMP: 50
SQ FT: 1,000
SALES (est): 6MM Privately Held
WEB: www.serpicolandscaping.com
SIC: 0782 Lawn & garden services

(P-952) SHASTA LANDSCAPING INC
1340 Descanso Ave, San Marcos (92069-1306)
PHONE..................760 744-6551
Leonard R Hogan, CEO
Daniel Hogan, President
Susan Hogan, CFO
Debara Prescott, Corp Secy
EMP: 75
SQ FT: 6,000
SALES (est): 3.9MM Privately Held
WEB: www.shastalandscaping.com
SIC: 0782 Landscape contractors

(P-953) SHORELINE LAND CARE INC
Also Called: Landcare Logic
7348 Trade St Ste B, San Diego (92121-3434)
PHONE..................858 560-8555
Craig Gerber, CEO
Brett Gerber, Managing Prtnr
John Crawford, COO
Jalin Gerber, Business Dir
Michelle Ferraro, Administration
EMP: 64 EST: 2007
SALES (est): 3.9MM Privately Held
SIC: 0782 Landscape contractors

(P-954) SIERRA VIEW LANDSCAPE INC
Also Called: Restoration Resources
3888 Cincinnati Ave, Rocklin (95765-1312)
PHONE..................916 408-2990
Fax: 916 408-2999
EMP: 50
SALES (est): 7MM Privately Held
SIC: 0782

(P-955) SILVERWOOD LANDSCAPE CNSTR INC
2209 S Lyon St, Santa Ana (92705-5305)
PHONE..................714 427-6134
Steven Paul Lancaster, President
Marsha Lancaster, CFO
EMP: 50
SALES (est): 5.3MM Privately Held
SIC: 0782 Landscape contractors

(P-956) SOTO COMPANY INC
34275 Camino Capistrano A, Capistrano Beach (92624-1917)
PHONE..................949 493-9403
Fax: 949 493-6265
Joe Soto, President
Carol Soto, Corp Secy
Jessica Solis, Admin Mgr
EMP: 75
SQ FT: 4,000
SALES (est): 3.2MM Privately Held
WEB: www.sotocompany.com
SIC: 0782 Landscape contractors

(P-957) SOUTHWEST LANDSCAPE INC
2205 S Standard Ave, Santa Ana (92707-3036)
P.O. Box 15611 (92735-0611)
PHONE..................714 545-1084
Fax: 714 545-2109
Dan Hansen, President
Sandra Hansen, Corp Secy
Robert Hansen, Vice Pres
EMP: 80
SQ FT: 7,800
SALES (est): 6.3MM Privately Held
WEB: www.southwestlandscapeinc.com
SIC: 0782 Landscape contractors

(P-958) SPECIALIZED LANDSCAPE MGT SVCS
Also Called: SLM Services
4212 Peast Los Angeles, Simi Valley (93063)
PHONE..................805 520-7590
Rene Emeterio, President
Wendy Emeterio, Corp Secy
EMP: 77
SALES (est): 3.4MM Privately Held
SIC: 0782 Landscape contractors

(P-959) SPECTRUM CARE LANDSCPE MNGMNT
Also Called: Spectrum Care Landscaping
23282 Del Lago Dr, Laguna Hills (92653-1308)
PHONE..................949 454-6900
Fax: 949 454-6910
Roland Tittle, CEO
Kelly Goetz, Software Dev
EMP: 300
SQ FT: 8,000
SALES (est): 21MM Privately Held
WEB: www.spectrumcarelandscape.com
SIC: 0782 4971 0781 Landscape contractors; irrigation systems; landscape counseling & planning

(P-960) STONE TREE LANDSCAPE CORP
5757 Wilshire Blvd # 505, Los Angeles (90036-3628)
PHONE..................323 965-0944
Fax: 323 934-9269
Jerome Steinbaum, President
EMP: 50
SALES (est): 1.1MM Privately Held
SIC: 0782 Landscape contractors

(P-961) SUNSET LANDSCAPE MAINTENANCE
27201 Burbank, El Toro (92610-2500)
PHONE..................949 455-4636
Fax: 949 457-1823
James Roughan, President
Claudia Roughan, Corp Secy
Scott Morff, VP Opers
EMP: 100
SQ FT: 6,300
SALES (est): 5.9MM Privately Held
SIC: 0782 Lawn & garden services

(P-962) TED COOPER/COOPER INDUSTRIES
P.O. Box 36007 (95158-6007)
PHONE..................408 358-3060
Ted Cooper, Owner
EMP: 50
SALES (est): 1.6MM Privately Held
WEB: www.coopindustries.com
SIC: 0782 1799 Landscape contractors; parking facility equipment & maintenance

(P-963) TRANSPORTATION CALIFORNIA DEPT
1490 George Dr, Redding (96003-1460)
PHONE..................530 225-3349
Frank Herrman, Manager
EMP: 70 Privately Held
SIC: 0782 Highway lawn & garden maintenance services

0782 - Lawn & Garden Svcs County

HQ: California Dept Of Transportation
1120 N St
Sacramento CA 95814

(P-964)
TREE SCULPTURE GROUP
Also Called: Tarra Landscape
463 Roland Way, Oakland (94621-2014)
PHONE.....................510 562-4000
Fax: 510 562-4020
Craig Lundin, *President*
Paulette Roddy, *Executive*
Dan Dachauer, *Manager*
EMP: 60
SALES (est): 3.6MM **Privately Held**
WEB: www.treesculpture.com
SIC: 0782 Landscape contractors

(P-965)
TREEBEARD LANDSCAPE INC
9917 Campo Rd, Spring Valley (91977-1609)
P.O. Box 2777 (91979-2777)
PHONE.....................619 697-8302
Fax: 619 697-0820
Tim Hillman, *President*
Craig Des Lauriers, *Vice Pres*
EMP: 100
SQ FT: 2,500
SALES (est): 6.5MM **Privately Held**
SIC: 0782 Garden maintenance services; lawn services

(P-966)
TROPICAL PLAZA NURSERY INC
9642 Santiago Blvd, Villa Park (92867-2521)
PHONE.....................714 998-4100
Fax: 714 998-4788
Leslie T Fields, *President*
Mike Feilds, *Vice Pres*
Deloris Segura, *Manager*
EMP: 100
SQ FT: 5,000
SALES (est): 2.6MM **Privately Held**
SIC: 0782 Landscape contractors

(P-967)
TRU GREEN LANDCARE INC
5248 Governor Dr, San Diego (92122-2800)
PHONE.....................602 276-4311
David M Flott, *President*
Acquannita Castaneda, *Officer*
Joseph Hanks, *Vice Pres*
John Horne, *Branch Mgr*
David Schlott, *Opers Mgr*
EMP: 450
SQ FT: 3,000
SALES (est): 7.6MM
SALES (corp-wide): 2.5B **Publicly Held**
WEB: www.landcareusa.com
SIC: 0782 Landscape contractors
HQ: Landcare Usa, Inc
2603 Augusta Dr Ste 1300
Houston TX 77057
713 692-6371

(P-968)
TRUGREEN LIMITED PARTNERSHIP
Also Called: Tru Green-Chemlawn
393 Watt Dr Ste B, Fairfield (94534-4207)
PHONE.....................707 864-5594
Fax: 707 864-5599
Christopher Reed, *Manager*
Martin Becker, *Branch Mgr*
EMP: 70
SALES (corp-wide): 4B **Privately Held**
SIC: 0782 Lawn care services
HQ: Trugreen Limited Partnership
1790 Kirby Pkwy Forum Ii Ste 300
Forum Ii
Memphis TN 38138
901 681-1800

(P-969)
TRUGREEN LIMITED PARTNERSHIP
Also Called: Tru Green-Chemlawn
1130 Palmyrita Ave # 300, Riverside (92507-1714)
P.O. Box 1359, Rancho Cucamonga (91729-1359)
PHONE.....................951 683-0144
Fax: 951 683-0705
Jeff Martinau, *Manager*
EMP: 50
SALES (corp-wide): 4B **Privately Held**
SIC: 0782 Lawn care services
HQ: Trugreen Limited Partnership
1790 Kirby Pkwy Forum Ii Ste 300
Forum Ii
Memphis TN 38138
901 681-1800

(P-970)
ULTIMATE LANDSCAPE MGT CO
700 E Sycamore St, Anaheim (92805-2831)
PHONE.....................714 502-9711
James Bernd, *President*
EMP: 50
SALES (est): 3.6MM **Privately Held**
SIC: 0782 Landscape contractors

(P-971)
ULTIMATE LANDSCAPING MGT
700 E Sycamore St, Anaheim (92805-2831)
PHONE.....................714 502-9711
Fax: 714 502-9611
James Berne, *President*
Lindsey Hughes, *Office Mgr*
Angelica Herrera, *Accounts Mgr*
EMP: 80
SALES (est): 4.2MM **Privately Held**
SIC: 0782 Landscape contractors

(P-972)
UNITED LANDSCAPE RESOURCE INC
Also Called: Botanica Landscapes
5411 Colusa Hwy, Yuba City (95993-9311)
P.O. Box 569 (95992-0569)
PHONE.....................530 671-1029
Fax: 530 671-3326
Bill Lucich, *President*
Edmund Clavel III, *President*
Tim Corey, *COO*
Candice Lucich, *Corp Secy*
EMP: 65
SQ FT: 2,000
SALES: 3.7MM **Privately Held**
WEB: www.botanica.net
SIC: 0782 Landscape contractors; lawn care services

(P-973)
UNITED PACIFIC SERVICES INC
251 Imperial Hwy Ste 450, South Gate (90280)
PHONE.....................562 691-4600
Fax: 562 691-8839
Gus K Franklin, *President*
Susan K Franklin, *Vice Pres*
EMP: 50 EST: 1999
SQ FT: 8,000
SALES (est): 6.3MM **Privately Held**
WEB: www.united-pac.com
SIC: 0782 Landscape contractors

(P-974)
VALLEY LANDSCAPING & MAINT INC
12900 N Lwer Scramento Rd, Lodi (95242)
PHONE.....................209 334-3659
Fax: 209 339-0047
Don Oliver, *President*
Lori Peck, *Treasurer*
Jed Phelps, *Vice Pres*
Lorne Trescott, *Controller*
Anna Gordon, *Human Res Mgr*
EMP: 120
SQ FT: 5,000
SALES (est): 7.5MM **Privately Held**
SIC: 0782 Landscape contractors

(P-975)
VENCO WESTERN INC (PA)
2400 Eastman Ave, Oxnard (93030-5187)
PHONE.....................805 981-2400
Fax: 805 981-2450
Linda Del Nagro Burr, *President*
Bill Barrett, *Manager*
EMP: 150
SQ FT: 15,000
SALES (est): 15MM **Privately Held**
WEB: www.vencowestern.com
SIC: 0782 Landscape contractors

(P-976)
VINTAGE ASSOCIATES INC
Also Called: Vintage Nursery
78755 Darby Rd, Bermuda Dunes (92203-9621)
P.O. Box 5250, La Quinta (92248-5250)
PHONE.....................760 772-3673
Gregory Gritters, *President*
Paul Stetz Jr, *Store Mgr*
Lori Nelson, *Admin Asst*
Eric Schmidt, *Opers Mgr*
Gary Conner, *Manager*
EMP: 160
SQ FT: 1,000
SALES (est): 12.8MM **Privately Held**
SIC: 0782 5193 5261 Landscape contractors; nursery stock; nurseries

(P-977)
W B STARR INC
20602 Canada Rd, Lake Forest (92630-8100)
PHONE.....................949 770-8835
Fax: 949 770-8839
William B Starr, *President*
Martha L Starr, *Vice Pres*
EMP: 65
SQ FT: 10,000
SALES (est): 3.6MM **Privately Held**
WEB: www.wbstarr.com
SIC: 0782 Garden maintenance services

(P-978)
WATKIN & BORTOLUSSI INC
726 Alfred Nobel Dr, Hercules (94547-1805)
PHONE.....................415 453-4675
Phillip Bortolussi, *President*
Peggy Bortolussi, *Vice Pres*
Steven Seikel, *Controller*
EMP: 60
SQ FT: 1,000
SALES (est): 3.3MM **Privately Held**
SIC: 0782 Landscape contractors

(P-979)
WENDT LANDSCAPE SERVICES INC
Also Called: Pacific Coast Sweeping
29714 Avenida De Las, Rancho Santa Margari (92688)
PHONE.....................949 589-8680
Fax: 949 589-8946
Richard Wendt, *President*
Jill Wilyard, *Office Mgr*
Shawn Wendt, *Marketing Staff*
EMP: 70
SQ FT: 6,600
SALES (est): 3.5MM **Privately Held**
SIC: 0782 Landscape contractors

(P-980)
WM VANDERGEEST LANDSCAPE CARE
3342 W Castor St, Santa Ana (92704-3908)
PHONE.....................714 545-8432
Fax: 714 545-0738
Allan M Curr, *President*
Sherry Curr, *Treasurer*
Chris Curr, *Vice Pres*
EMP: 100 EST: 1974
SQ FT: 10,000
SALES (est): 3.4MM **Privately Held**
SIC: 0782 Landscape contractors

(P-981)
WURZEL LANDSCAPE MAINTENANCE
Also Called: Canyon Way Nursery
3214 Oakdell Rd, Studio City (91604-4221)
PHONE.....................818 762-8653
Marc W Wurzel, *Partner*
Doris Wurzel, *Partner*
EMP: 50
SALES (est): 2.3MM **Privately Held**
SIC: 0782 Garden maintenance services; landscape contractors

(P-982)
YEAR ROUND LANDSCAPE MAINT INC
15189 Sierra Bonita Ln, Chino (91710-8904)
PHONE.....................909 597-7734
Larry M Sweeden, *President*
Melanie Reiley, *Office Mgr*
EMP: 50
SQ FT: 5,700
SALES (est): 3.4MM **Privately Held**
SIC: 0782 Lawn & garden services; garden maintenance services

0783 Ornamental Shrub & Tree Svc

(P-983)
ARBORWELL INC (PA)
2337 American Ave, Hayward (94545-1807)
PHONE.....................510 881-4260
Alvin Foye Sortwell, *President*
Brad Carson, *CFO*
Dennis Shanagher, *Corp Secy*
Andy Lavelle, *Vice Pres*
Ann B Sortwell, *Vice Pres*
▲ EMP: 74
SQ FT: 5,000
SALES (est): 37.7MM **Privately Held**
WEB: www.arborwell.com
SIC: 0783 Ornamental shrub & tree services

(P-984)
ASPLUNDH TREE EXPERT CO
Also Called: Utility Tree Services
6100 Francis Botello Rd C, Goleta (93117-3259)
PHONE.....................805 964-9216
Alex Ramos, *Business Mgr*
EMP: 99
SALES (corp-wide): 6.7B **Privately Held**
WEB: www.asplundh.com
SIC: 0783 Tree trimming services for public utility lines
PA: Asplundh Tree Expert Co.
708 Blair Mill Rd
Willow Grove PA 19090
215 784-4200

(P-985)
ASPLUNDH TREE EXPERT CO
10730 Campbell Ave, Riverside (92505-1314)
PHONE.....................951 352-3144
Steven Asplundh, *Branch Mgr*
EMP: 103
SALES (corp-wide): 6.7B **Privately Held**
SIC: 0783 Ornamental shrub & tree services
PA: Asplundh Tree Expert Co.
708 Blair Mill Rd
Willow Grove PA 19090
215 784-4200

(P-986)
ASPLUNDH TREE EXPERT CO
2055 N Ventura Ave, Ventura (93001-1308)
PHONE.....................805 641-0528
Tony Ortiz, *Branch Mgr*
EMP: 94
SALES (corp-wide): 6.7B **Privately Held**
SIC: 0783 Ornamental shrub & tree services
PA: Asplundh Tree Expert Co.
708 Blair Mill Rd
Willow Grove PA 19090
215 784-4200

(P-987)
ASPLUNDH TREE EXPERT CO
Also Called: Asplundh Construction Co.
6101 Gateway Dr, Cypress (90630-4841)
PHONE.....................714 893-2405
Fax: 714 740-9424
Joseph Guerrero, *Branch Mgr*

EMP: 150
SALES (corp-wide): 6.7B **Privately Held**
WEB: www.asplundh.com
SIC: 0783 Ornamental shrub & tree services
PA: Asplundh Tree Expert Co.
708 Blair Mill Rd
Willow Grove PA 19090
215 784-4200

(P-988)
BROOKER ASSOCIATES
16372 Cnstr Cir E 5, Irvine (92618)
PHONE....................................949 559-4877
Ray Duval, *Branch Mgr*
EMP: 52
SALES (corp-wide): 5.4MM **Privately Held**
WEB: www.brookerassociates.com
SIC: 0783 1721 1542 Planting services, ornamental bush; spraying services, ornamental bush; commercial painting; commercial & office buildings, renovation & repair
PA: Brooker Associates
2331 E Lambert Rd
La Habra CA 90631
714 773-9490

(P-989)
CLS LANDSCAPE MANAGEMENT INC
4711 Schaefer Ave Unit A, Chino (91710-5544)
PHONE....................................909 628-3005
Fax: 909 464-1021
Kevin L Davis, *President*
Laura Hanson, *Office Mgr*
Kimberly Davis, *Admin Sec*
Crissy Coscia, *Manager*
EMP: 325
SQ FT: 2,500
SALES: 16.3MM **Privately Held**
WEB: www.clslandscape.com
SIC: 0783 0782 Ornamental shrub & tree services; lawn & garden services

(P-990)
DAVEY TREE SURGERY COMPANY
6915 Eastside Rd Ste 94, Anderson (96007-9401)
PHONE....................................530 378-2674
Fax: 530 378-1673
Dennis Dodson, *Manager*
Dennis Dotson, *Manager*
EMP: 60
SALES (corp-wide): 821.9MM **Privately Held**
SIC: 0783 Surgery services, ornamental tree
HQ: Davey Tree Surgery Company
2617 S Vasco Rd
Livermore CA 94550
925 443-1723

(P-991)
DAVEY TREE SURGERY COMPANY (HQ)
2617 S Vasco Rd, Livermore (94550-8322)
P.O. Box 5015 (94551-5015)
PHONE....................................925 443-1723
Fax: 925 443-1751
Karl J Warnke, *CEO*
R Douglas Cowan, *President*
David Adante, *CFO*
Howard Bowles, *Senior VP*
Rita Packard, *Comms Mgr*
EMP: 873
SQ FT: 5,000
SALES: 12.4MM
SALES (corp-wide): 821.9MM **Privately Held**
SIC: 0783 Ornamental shrub & tree services; tree trimming services for public utility lines; surgery services, ornamental tree
PA: The Davey Tree Expert Company
1500 N Mantua St
Kent OH 44240
330 673-9511

(P-992)
DAVEY TREE SURGERY COMPANY
1914 Mission Rd Ste N, Escondido (92029-1116)
PHONE....................................760 975-0225
EMP: 100
SALES (corp-wide): 821.9MM **Privately Held**
SIC: 0783 Surgery services, ornamental tree
HQ: Davey Tree Surgery Company
2617 S Vasco Rd
Livermore CA 94550
925 443-1723

(P-993)
GREAT SCOTT TREE SERVICE INC (PA)
10761 Court Ave, Stanton (90680-2435)
PHONE....................................714 826-1750
Fax: 714 826-1753
Scott Griffiths, *President*
Jacob Griffiths, *Vice Pres*
Dan Doble, *Info Tech Dir*
EMP: 50
SQ FT: 28,675
SALES (est): 7.6MM **Privately Held**
WEB: www.gstsinc.com
SIC: 0783 Pruning services, ornamental tree

(P-994)
LEONARD CHAIDEZ INC
Also Called: Leonard Chaidez Tree Service
2298 N Batavia St, Orange (92865-3106)
P.O. Box 29, Anaheim (92815-0029)
PHONE....................................714 279-8173
Fax: 714 279-8133
Leonard Chaidez, *President*
Deborah Foushee, *Admin Sec*
Jamie Lance, *Manager*
EMP: 60
SQ FT: 2,000
SALES (est): 3.5MM **Privately Held**
SIC: 0783 0781 8748 0782 Ornamental shrub & tree services; landscape services; environmental consultant; lawn & garden services

(P-995)
ORIGINAL MOWBRAYS TREE SVC INC
17332 Millwood Dr, Visalia (93292-9577)
PHONE....................................559 798-0530
Gloria Mowbray, *Branch Mgr*
EMP: 164
SALES (corp-wide): 12MM **Privately Held**
SIC: 0783 Ornamental shrub & tree services
PA: The Original Mowbray's Tree Service Inc
1845 Bus Ctr Dr Ste 215
San Bernardino CA 92408
909 383-7009

(P-996)
PACIFIC SLOPE TREE COOP INC
11201 State Rte One 201, Point Reyes Station (94956)
P.O. Box 400 (94956-0400)
PHONE....................................415 663-1300
Fax: 415 663-1303
Thomas Kent, *President*
Elan Whitney, *Corp Secy*
EMP: 50
SALES: 4MM **Privately Held**
WEB: www.pacificslopetree.com
SIC: 0783 Ornamental shrub & tree services

(P-997)
RAUL ACEVEDO
Also Called: Ace Reforestation
1638 W Castle Ave, Porterville (93257-9277)
PHONE....................................559 791-1304
Raul Acevedo, *Owner*
EMP: 50
SALES: 500K **Privately Held**
SIC: 0783 0782 Ornamental shrub & tree services; lawn & garden services

(P-998)
SP MCCLENAHAN CO
Also Called: McClenahan S P Co Tree Service
1 Arastradero Rd, Portola Valley (94028-8012)
PHONE....................................650 326-8781
Fax: 650 854-1267
James M Mc Clenahan, *President*
Joshua McClenahan, *Risk Mgmt Dir*
Shannon Gutierrez, *Administration*
Miguel Berumen, *Reverend*
EMP: 56
SQ FT: 5,000
SALES (est): 5.3MM **Privately Held**
SIC: 0783 Ornamental shrub & tree services; planting, pruning & trimming services

(P-999)
TONY GOMEZ TREE SERVICE
700 N Johnson Ave Ste H, El Cajon (92020-2521)
PHONE....................................619 593-1552
Fax: 619 401-8320
Antonio Gomez, *Owner*
Cindy Gomez, *Office Mgr*
EMP: 60
SALES (est): 2.7MM **Privately Held**
SIC: 0783 Ornamental shrub & tree services

(P-1000)
TREEPEOPLE INC
12601 Mulholland Dr, Beverly Hills (90210-1332)
PHONE....................................818 753-4600
Fax: 818 753-4625
Walt Burkley, *Ch of Bd*
Andy Lipkis, *President*
Tom Hansen, *COO*
Gwyn Quillen, *Treasurer*
Paul Bergman, *Admin Sec*
EMP: 50
SQ FT: 21,000
SALES: 3.9MM **Privately Held**
WEB: www.treepeople.org
SIC: 0783 8641 Planting, pruning & trimming services; environmental protection organization

(P-1001)
UTILITY TREE SERVICE INC (DH)
1884 Keystone Ct Ste A, Redding (96003-4870)
PHONE....................................530 226-0330
Fax: 530 226-5269
Scott Asplundh, *President*
Joseph P Dwyer, *Corp Secy*
Brent D Asplundh, *Vice Pres*
Carl Asplundh III, *Vice Pres*
Gregg Asplundh, *Vice Pres*
EMP: 50
SALES (est): 8.9MM
SALES (corp-wide): 6.7B **Privately Held**
SIC: 0783 Tree trimming services for public utility lines

(P-1002)
WEST COAST ARBORISTS INC
11405 Nardo St, Ventura (93004-3201)
PHONE....................................805 671-5092
Lorenzo Perez, *Owner*
EMP: 244
SALES (corp-wide): 293.2MM **Privately Held**
SIC: 0783 Ornamental shrub & tree services
PA: West Coast Arborists, Inc.
2200 E Via Burton
Anaheim CA 92806
714 991-1900

(P-1003)
WEST COAST ARBORISTS INC
21718 Walnut Ave, Grand Terrace (92313-4437)
PHONE....................................909 783-6544
Patrick Mahoney, *President*
EMP: 50
SALES (corp-wide): 325.8MM **Privately Held**
SIC: 0783 Ornamental shrub & tree services

PA: West Coast Arborists, Inc.
2200 E Via Burton
Anaheim CA 92806
714 991-1900

0811 Timber Tracts

(P-1004)
BOETHING TREELAND FARMS INC
2923 Alpine Rd, Portola Valley (94028-7546)
PHONE....................................650 851-4770
Fax: 650 841-4252
Richard Hanley, *Branch Mgr*
EMP: 700
SALES (corp-wide): 84.2MM **Privately Held**
WEB: www.boethingtreeland.com
SIC: 0811 5193 0181 Tree farm; nursery stock; nursery stock, growing of
PA: Boething Treeland Farms, Inc.
23475 Long Valley Rd
Woodland Hills CA 91367
818 883-1222

(P-1005)
BOETHING TREELAND FARMS INC (PA)
23475 Long Valley Rd, Woodland Hills (91367-6006)
PHONE....................................818 883-1222
Fax: 818 316-2098
Bruce Edgar Pherson, *CEO*
Marjorie Boething Arnold, *Shareholder*
Sally Boething Hilton, *Shareholder*
Cathy Boething Pherson, *Shareholder*
Marji Boething, *CFO*
EMP: 60
SQ FT: 1,500
SALES (est): 84.2MM **Privately Held**
WEB: www.boethingtreeland.com
SIC: 0811 5261 Tree farm; nurseries

(P-1006)
BOETHING TREELAND FARMS INC
Also Called: Boething Treeland Nursery
20601 E Kettleman Ln, Lodi (95240-9756)
PHONE....................................209 727-3741
Fax: 209 592-4970
Seilpe Gomez, *Branch Mgr*
Constance Cook, *Manager*
EMP: 175
SALES (corp-wide): 84.2MM **Privately Held**
WEB: www.boethingtreeland.com
SIC: 0811 Tree farm
PA: Boething Treeland Farms, Inc.
23475 Long Valley Rd
Woodland Hills CA 91367
818 883-1222

(P-1007)
BRIGHTVIEW TREE COMPANY
Also Called: Specimen Contracting
9500 Foothill Blvd, Sunland (91040-1857)
PHONE....................................661 305-3312
Tadd Russikoff, *Manager*
EMP: 115
SALES (corp-wide): 914MM **Privately Held**
WEB: www.vctree.com
SIC: 0811 Tree farm
HQ: Brightview Tree Company
24151 Ventura Blvd
Calabasas CA 91302
818 223-8500

(P-1008)
BRIGHTVIEW TREE COMPANY
Also Called: Environmental Industries
3200 W Telegraph Rd, Fillmore (93015-9623)
PHONE....................................805 524-3939
Fax: 805 524-4354
Susan Flores, *Branch Mgr*
EMP: 160
SALES (corp-wide): 914MM **Privately Held**
WEB: www.vctree.com
SIC: 0811 0782 Tree farm; lawn services

0811 - Timber Tracts County (P-1009)

PRODUCTS & SERVICES SECTION

HQ: Brightview Tree Company
24151 Ventura Blvd
Calabasas CA 91302
818 223-8500

(P-1009)
BRIGHTVIEW TREE COMPANY
8501 Calaveras Rd, Sunol (94586-9434)
PHONE..................925 862-2485
Fax: 925 862-2935
John Serviss, *Branch Mgr*
Nancy Kennedy, *Office Mgr*
EMP: 100
SALES (corp-wide): 914MM Privately Held
WEB: www.vctree.com
SIC: 0811 Tree farm
HQ: Brightview Tree Company
24151 Ventura Blvd
Calabasas CA 91302
818 223-8500

(P-1010)
BRIGHTVIEW TREE COMPANY
28915 E Funck Rd, Farmington (95230-9567)
P.O. Box 289 (95230-0289)
PHONE..................209 886-5511
Fax: 209 886-5508
Gina Mortenson, *Manager*
John Serviss, *Branch Mgr*
EMP: 85
SQ FT: 784
SALES (corp-wide): 914MM Privately Held
WEB: www.vctree.com
SIC: 0811 Tree farm
HQ: Brightview Tree Company
24151 Ventura Blvd
Calabasas CA 91302
818 223-8500

(P-1011)
GREEN DIAMOND RESOURCE COMPANY
900 Riverside Rd, Korbel (95550)
P.O. Box 68 (95550-0068)
PHONE..................707 668-4446
Fax: 707 668-3710
Neal Ewald, *Manager*
Jack Blakely, *General Mgr*
Patrick Boland, *Network Mgr*
Neil Cheatum, *Software Dev*
EMP: 100
SALES (corp-wide): 456.8MM Privately Held
SIC: 0811 0851 Timber tracts; forestry services
HQ: Diamond Green Resource Company
1301 5th Ave Ste 2700
Seattle WA 98101
206 224-5800

(P-1012)
PINERY LLC
13701 Highland Valley Rd, Escondido (92025-2300)
P.O. Box 2484, Rancho Cucamonga (91729-2484)
PHONE..................858 675-3575
Philip C Guardia,
Susan Gaven, *Controller*
Cheryl Guardia,
▲ EMP: 60
SQ FT: 2,800
SALES (est): 4.5MM Privately Held
SIC: 0811 Christmas tree farm

(P-1013)
WEYERHAEUSER COMPANY
800 Pier T Ave, Long Beach (90802-6236)
PHONE..................562 983-6709
EMP: 77
SALES (corp-wide): 7B Publicly Held
SIC: 0811
PA: Weyerhaeuser Company
33663 Weyerhaeuser Way S
Federal Way WA 98104
253 924-2345

0851 Forestry Svcs

(P-1014)
CALIFORNIA SILVER-AGRICULTURE
831 Ash Ave, Lindsay (93247-1449)
PHONE..................559 562-3795
Raul L Acevedo, *Owner*
EMP: 50
SALES: 50K Privately Held
SIC: 0851 Forestry services

(P-1015)
FORESTRY AND FIRE PROTECTION
Also Called: Shasta-Trinity Ranger Unit
875 Cypress Ave, Redding (96001-2719)
PHONE..................530 225-2418
Fax: 530 225-2039
Mike Chuchel, *Manager*
Hope Barton, *Personnel*
EMP: 150 Privately Held
WEB: www.calopps.org
SIC: 0851 Fire prevention services, forest
HQ: Forestry And Fire Protection California Department Of
1416 9th St Ste 1535
Sacramento CA 95814
916 653-7772

(P-1016)
R C O REFORESTING INC
1332 Fairlane Rd Ste A, Yreka (96097-8504)
P.O. Box 1370 (96097-1370)
PHONE..................530 842-7647
Fax: 530 841-1257
Roberto C Ochoa, *President*
Tammie Ochoa, *Office Mgr*
EMP: 50
SALES: 1.2MM Privately Held
SIC: 0851 Reforestation services; fire prevention services, forest

(P-1017)
REDDING TREE GROWERS CORP
18985 Avenue 256 Apt A, Exeter (93221-9558)
PHONE..................559 594-9299
Francisco Acevedo, *President*
Amelia Acevedo, *Vice Pres*
EMP: 100
SALES: 2MM Privately Held
SIC: 0851 Reforestation services

(P-1018)
UNITED STATES FOREST SERVICE
17696 State Highway 89, Hat Creek (96040-9431)
P.O. Box 220, Fall River Mills (96028-0220)
PHONE..................530 335-4103
Fax: 530 335-4518
Carol Chandler, *Director*
EMP: 50
SALES (est): 722.9K Privately Held
SIC: 0851 Forestry services

(P-1019)
USDA FOREST SERVICE
100 Forni Rd, Placerville (95667-5310)
PHONE..................530 626-1546
Lawrence Crabtree, *Principal*
Nikki Esposito, *MIS Dir*
EMP: 53 Publicly Held
SIC: 0851 Forestry services
HQ: Usda Forest Service
201 14th St Sw
Washington DC 20024

0971 Hunting & Trapping

(P-1020)
DUCKS UNLIMITED INC
Also Called: Western Regional Office
3074 Gold Canal Dr, Rancho Cordova (95670-6116)
PHONE..................916 852-2000
Fax: 916 852-2200
Rudy Rosses, *Director*
Clay Rogers, *President*
Matt Fenoff, *Managing Dir*
Cathy Sanders, *Admin Asst*
Anna Thompson, *Admin Asst*
EMP: 50
SALES (corp-wide): 178.4MM Privately Held
WEB: www.ducks.org
SIC: 0971 Wildlife management
PA: Ducks Unlimited, Inc.
1 Waterfowl Way
Memphis TN 38120
901 758-3825

1041 Gold Ores

(P-1021)
BARRICK GOLD CORPORATION
Also Called: Mc Laughlin Mine
26775 Morgan Valley Rd, Lower Lake (95457-9411)
PHONE..................707 995-6070
Pat Purtell, *Branch Mgr*
Patrick Purtell, *Div Sub Head*
EMP: 100
SALES (corp-wide): 10.2B Privately Held
WEB: www.barrick.com
SIC: 1041 Gold ores
PA: Barrick Gold Corporation
161 Bay St Suite 3700
Toronto ON M5J 2
416 861-9911

(P-1022)
GOLDEN QUEEN MINING CO LLC
Also Called: Golden Queen Mining Co Inc
15772 K St, Mojave (93501-1709)
P.O. Box 1030 (93502-1030)
PHONE..................661 824-4300
Fax: 661 824-1071
Thomas Clay, *Ch of Bd*
Robert Walish, *President*
Andree St-Germain, *CFO*
Curtis Campbell, *Manager*
EMP: 95
SQ FT: 2,500
SALES: 70MM Privately Held
SIC: 1041 Gold ores

(P-1023)
MERIDIAN GOLD INC
Also Called: Royal Mountain King
4461 Rock Creek Rd, Copperopolis (95228)
P.O. Box 190 (95228-0190)
PHONE..................209 785-3222
Edgar Smith, *Branch Mgr*
EMP: 160
SALES (corp-wide): 1.8B Privately Held
SIC: 1041 Gold ores
HQ: Meridian Gold Inc.
4635 Longley Ln Ste 110
Reno NV 89502

1221 Bituminous Coal & Lignite: Surface Mining

(P-1024)
CHEVRON MINING INC
Moly
67750 Bailey Rd, Mountain Pass (92366)
PHONE..................760 856-7625
Fax: 760 856-2344
Allen Randle, *Branch Mgr*
John Burba, *Vice Pres*
Robert Noll, *Vice Pres*
William Schramm, *Comptroller*
John Benfield, *Opers Mgr*
EMP: 400
SALES (corp-wide): 138.4B Publicly Held
SIC: 1221 Surface mining, bituminous
HQ: Chevron Mining Inc.
116 Invrneco Dr E Ste 207
Englewood CO 80112
303 930-3600

1241 Coal Mining Svcs

(P-1025)
GREKA INC
1791 Sinton Rd, Santa Maria (93458-9708)
P.O. Box 5489 (93456-5489)
PHONE..................805 347-8700
Andy Devegvar, *President*
Randeep Grewal, *CEO*
EMP: 150
SQ FT: 3,000
SALES: 40MM Privately Held
SIC: 1241 1081 Coal mining services; metal mining services

(P-1026)
RIO TINTO MINERALS INC
Also Called: Reno Tenco
14486 Borax Rd, Boron (93516-2017)
PHONE..................760 762-7121
Xiaoling Liu, *CEO*
Preston Chiaro, *President*
Hugo Bague, *Principal*
Donald Lohse, *QA Dir*
Robert Vargas, *Business Anlyst*
◆ EMP: 150
SALES (est): 21.2MM
SALES (corp-wide): 34.8B Privately Held
SIC: 1241 Coal mining services
HQ: U.S. Borax Inc.
8051 E Maplewood Ave # 100
Greenwood Village CO 80111
303 713-5000

(P-1027)
TAFT PRODUCTION COMPANY
950 Petroleum Club Rd, Taft (93268-9748)
PHONE..................661 765-7194
Daniel S Jaffee, *President*
EMP: 95
SALES (est): 7.5MM
SALES (corp-wide): 262.3MM Publicly Held
WEB: www.oildri.com
SIC: 1241 1081 Coal mining services; metal mining services
PA: Oil-Dri Corporation Of America
410 N Michigan Ave # 400
Chicago IL 60611
312 321-1515

1311 Crude Petroleum & Natural Gas

(P-1028)
BENTLEY-SIMONSON INC
1746 S Victoria Ave Ste F, Ventura (93003-6190)
PHONE..................805 650-2794
James Bentley, *Ch of Bd*
Theodore Bentley, *Ch of Bd*
Clifton O Simonson, *President*
Petter Romming, *Vice Pres*
Tim Hilf, *Manager*
EMP: 100
SQ FT: 1,000
SALES (est): 4.6MM Privately Held
SIC: 1311 Crude petroleum & natural gas production

(P-1029)
BETA OPERATING COMPANY LLC
Also Called: Beta Offshore
111 W Ocean Blvd Ste 1240, Long Beach (90802-4645)
PHONE..................562 628-1526
Dickie Hunter, *CEO*
Steven Jaffe, *Administration*
Homer Teran, *Administration*
George Romero, *Engineer*
Veronica Banuelos, *Accountant*
EMP: 66
SQ FT: 15,000
SALES (est): 22.1MM
SALES (corp-wide): 22.2MM Privately Held
SIC: 1311 Crude petroleum production; natural gas production

PRODUCTS & SERVICES SECTION
1311 - Crude Petroleum & Natural Gas County (P-1052)

PA: Rise Energy Partners, Lp
909 Lake Carolyn Pkwy # 200
Irving TX 75039
972 556-2950

(P-1030)
BP WEST COAST PRODUCTS LLC
22600 Wilmington Ave, Carson (90745-4307)
PHONE..................310 816-8787
R Stager, Maintence Staff
EMP: 310
SALES (corp-wide): 222.8B Privately Held
SIC: 1311 Crude petroleum & natural gas
HQ: Bp West Coast Products Llc
4519 Grandview Rd
Blaine WA 98230
310 549-6204

(P-1031)
BP WEST COAST PRODUCTS LLC
1306 Canal Blvd, Richmond (94804-3556)
PHONE..................510 231-4724
Fred Glueck, Vice Pres
EMP: 310
SQ FT: 4,550
SALES (corp-wide): 222.8B Privately Held
SIC: 1311 Crude petroleum production
HQ: Bp West Coast Products Llc
4519 Grandview Rd
Blaine WA 98230
310 549-6204

(P-1032)
BP WEST COAST PRODUCTS LLC
Also Called: BP Arco
4 Centerpointe Dr, La Palma (90623-1074)
PHONE..................714 670-5400
Max Min, Manager
EMP: 310
SALES (corp-wide): 222.8B Privately Held
SIC: 1311 Crude petroleum production
HQ: Bp West Coast Products Llc
4519 Grandview Rd
Blaine WA 98230
310 549-6204

(P-1033)
BREITBURN ENERGY PARTNERS I LP
707 Wilshire Blvd # 4600, Los Angeles (90017-3612)
PHONE..................213 225-5900
Randall H Breitenbach, President
EMP: 81
SALES (est): 2.6MM
SALES (corp-wide): 1.1B Privately Held
SIC: 1311 Crude petroleum & natural gas
PA: Breitburn Energy Partners Lp
707 Wilshire Blvd # 4600
Los Angeles CA 90017
213 225-5900

(P-1034)
BREITBURN GP LLC
707 Wilshire Blvd # 4600, Los Angeles (90017-3501)
PHONE..................213 225-5900
Halbert S Washburn, CEO
EMP: 833
SALES (est): 19.2MM
SALES (corp-wide): 1.1B Privately Held
SIC: 1311 Crude petroleum & natural gas
PA: Breitburn Energy Partners Lp
707 Wilshire Blvd # 4600
Los Angeles CA 90017
213 225-5900

(P-1035)
CABINDA GULF OIL CO INC
6001 Bollinger Canyon Rd, San Ramon (94583-2324)
P.O. Box 5046 (94583-0946)
PHONE..................925 842-1000
R H Matzke, President
Charles Baumhauer, Info Tech Mgr
Fernando Mario, VP Info Tech Mgr
Karen Draper, Technology
David Spence, Technology
▼ EMP: 327
SALES (est): 29.4MM
SALES (corp-wide): 138.4B Publicly Held
WEB: www.chevrontexaco.com
SIC: 1311 Crude petroleum production
PA: Chevron Corporation
6001 Bollinger Canyon Rd
San Ramon CA 94583
925 842-1000

(P-1036)
CALIFORNIA RESOURCES CORP
1320 4th St, Los Osos (93402-1206)
PHONE..................661 763-6107
EMP: 207
SALES (corp-wide): 2.4B Publicly Held
SIC: 1311 Crude petroleum production
PA: California Resources Corporation
9200 Oakdale Ave Fl 9
Chatsworth CA 91311
888 848-4754

(P-1037)
CALIFORNIA RESOURCES CORP
5000 Stockdale Hwy, Bakersfield (93309-2650)
PHONE..................661 395-8000
Fax: 661 322-7457
EMP: 207
SALES (corp-wide): 2.4B Publicly Held
SIC: 1311 Crude petroleum & natural gas
PA: California Resources Corporation
9200 Oakdale Ave Fl 9
Chatsworth CA 91311
888 848-4754

(P-1038)
CALIFORNIA RESOURCES CORP
111 W Ocean Blvd Ste 800, Long Beach (90802-7930)
PHONE..................562 624-3400
EMP: 138
SALES (corp-wide): 2.4B Publicly Held
SIC: 1311 Crude petroleum & natural gas
PA: California Resources Corporation
9200 Oakdale Ave Fl 9
Chatsworth CA 91311
888 848-4754

(P-1039)
CALIFORNIA RESOURCES CORP
270 Quail Ct Ste 100, Santa Paula (93060-9205)
PHONE..................310 208-8800
Steven Prow, Manager
EMP: 207
SALES (corp-wide): 2.4B Publicly Held
SIC: 1311 Crude petroleum production; natural gas production
PA: California Resources Corporation
9200 Oakdale Ave Fl 9
Chatsworth CA 91311
888 848-4754

(P-1040)
CALIFORNIA RESOURCES PROD CORP
3450 E 5th St, Oxnard (93033-2100)
PHONE..................805 483-8017
EMP: 83
SALES (corp-wide): 2.4B Publicly Held
SIC: 1311 1382
HQ: California Resources Production Corporation
11109 River Run Blvd
Bakersfield CA 93311
661 869-8000

(P-1041)
CALIFORNIA RESOURCES PROD CORP (HQ)
Also Called: Vintage Production California
11109 River Run Blvd, Bakersfield (93311-8957)
PHONE..................661 869-8000
Todd A Stevens, Principal
Richard Oringderff, President
Todd Stevens, CEO
Chris Aledo, Manager
EMP: 125
SALES (est): 113.8MM
SALES (corp-wide): 2.4B Publicly Held
WEB: www.oxy.com
SIC: 1311 1382 Crude petroleum production; oil & gas exploration services
PA: California Resources Corporation
9200 Oakdale Ave Fl 9
Chatsworth CA 91311
888 848-4754

(P-1042)
CHEVRON USA INC
6001 Bollinger Canyon Rd, San Ramon (94583-5737)
P.O. Box 6017 (94583-0717)
PHONE..................925 842-0855
Fax: 925 827-6546
Kim Smith, Branch Mgr
John Watson, Ch of Bd
Robert Cody, CIO
Elaine Petkovich, Accountant
Rita Rose, Human Resources
EMP: 100
SALES (corp-wide): 138.4B Publicly Held
SIC: 1311 2911 Crude petroleum & natural gas; petroleum refining
HQ: Chevron U.S.A. Inc.
6001 Bollinger Canyon Rd D1248
San Ramon CA 94583
925 842-1000

(P-1043)
E & B NTRAL RESOURCES MGT CORP (PA)
1600 Norris Rd, Bakersfield (93308-2234)
PHONE..................661 679-1714
Fax: 661 679-1797
Steve Layton, President
Frank J Ronkese, CFO
Jeff Blesener, Senior VP
Joyce Holtzclaw, Vice Pres
Jeff Jones, Vice Pres
EMP: 65
SALES: 326.3MM Privately Held
WEB: www.ebresources.com
SIC: 1311 Crude petroleum & natural gas

(P-1044)
FREEPORT-MCMORAN OIL & GAS LLC
1200 Discovery Dr Ste 500, Bakersfield (93309-7038)
PHONE..................661 322-7600
Fax: 661 395-5371
Kiran Leal, Manager
Tate Enterline, Administration
Osama Karaman, Engng Exec
Betty Walker, Manager
EMP: 60
SALES (corp-wide): 15.8B Publicly Held
SIC: 1311 Crude petroleum & natural gas
HQ: Freeport-Mcmoran Oil & Gas Llc
700 Milam St Ste 3100
Houston TX 77002
713 579-6000

(P-1045)
IRON HORSE INSURANCE CO
6001 Bollinger Canyon Rd, San Ramon (94583-2324)
PHONE..................925 842-1000
David J O'Riley, CEO
James D Lyness, President
M J Barry, Vice Pres
P Joy, Admin Sec
EMP: 900
SALES (est): 14.4MM
SALES (corp-wide): 138.4B Publicly Held
WEB: www.texaco.com
SIC: 1311 Crude petroleum production
HQ: Texaco Inc.
6001 Bollinger Canyon Rd
San Ramon CA 94583
925 842-1000

(P-1046)
LINNCO LLC
5201 Truxtun Ave, Bakersfield (93309-0421)
PHONE..................661 616-3900
David D Wolf, Exec VP
Danielle D Murphy, General Mgr
Harold Smith, Database Admin
Ben Mendes, Project Engr
Walter Ayers, VP Human Res
EMP: 1434
SALES (corp-wide): 150.3MM Publicly Held
SIC: 1311 Crude petroleum & natural gas
PA: Linnco, Llc
600 Travis St Ste 5100
Houston TX 77002
281 840-4000

(P-1047)
OXY USA INC
9600 Ming Ave Ste 300, Bakersfield (93311-1365)
PHONE..................661 869-8000
Gary O Lee Jr, Credit Mgr
EMP: 125
SALES (corp-wide): 12.7B Publicly Held
SIC: 1311 Crude petroleum & natural gas
HQ: Oxy Usa Inc
1001 S County Rd W
Odessa TX 79763
432 335-0995

(P-1048)
PETROLEUM SALES INC
2066 Redwood Hwy, Greenbrae (94904-2467)
PHONE..................415 945-1309
Stephanie Shimk, Branch Mgr
EMP: 70
SALES (corp-wide): 33.3MM Privately Held
SIC: 1311 Crude petroleum & natural gas
PA: Petroleum Sales Inc
1475 2nd St
San Rafael CA 94901
415 256-1600

(P-1049)
QUANTUM TECHNOLOGIES INC
25242 Arctic Ocean Dr, Lake Forest (92630-8821)
PHONE..................949 399-4500
Dean K Aoki, CEO
Alan Niedzwiecki, President
Bradley J Timon, CFO
Mark Arold, Vice Pres
Neel Sirosh, Principal
EMP: 140
SALES (est): 38.2MM Privately Held
SIC: 1311 Crude petroleum & natural gas

(P-1050)
SAMEDAN OIL CORPORATION
Also Called: Noble Energy
1360 Landing Ave, Seal Beach (90740-6525)
PHONE..................661 319-5038
EMP: 336
SALES (corp-wide): 310.9MM Privately Held
SIC: 1311 Crude petroleum production; natural gas production
PA: Samedan Oil Corporation
1001 Noble Energy Way
Houston TX 77070
580 223-4110

(P-1051)
STRAND ENERGY COMPANY
Also Called: Breitburn Energy Co
10350 Heritage Park Dr, Santa Fe Springs (90670-3787)
PHONE..................562 944-9580
Robert Erlandson, Supervisor
EMP: 265
SALES (corp-wide): 362.1MM Privately Held
SIC: 1311 Crude petroleum & natural gas
PA: The Strand Energy Company
515 S Flower St Ste 4800
Los Angeles CA 90071
213 225-5900

(P-1052)
VAQUERO ENERGY INCORPORATED
15545 Hermosa Rd, Bakersfield (93307-9477)
PHONE..................661 363-7240
Fax: 661 366-2959
Ken Hunter, President
Wyatt Shipley, Manager
EMP: 50 EST: 2007

1381 - Drilling Oil & Gas Wells County (P-1053) — PRODUCTS & SERVICES SECTION

SALES (est): 651.5K **Privately Held**
SIC: **1311** Crude petroleum production

1381 Drilling Oil & Gas Wells

(P-1053)
AERA ENERGY LLC (HQ)
10000 Ming Ave, Bakersfield (93311-1301)
P.O. Box 11164 (93389-1164)
PHONE.................................661 665-5000
Fax: 661 665-5065
Christina S Sistrunk, *President*
Andrew Hoyer, *Chief Mktg Ofcr*
Robert C Alberstadt, *Senior VP*
Brent D Carnahan, *Senior VP*
Lynne J Carrithers, *Senior VP*
EMP: 800
SALES (est): 2.1B
SALES (corp-wide): 421.1B **Publicly Held**
WEB: www.aeraenergy.com
SIC: **1381** Directional drilling oil & gas wells

(P-1054)
AERA ENERGY LLC
25401 Highway 33, Fellows (93224-9790)
P.O. Box 397 (93224-0397)
PHONE.................................661 768-3100
Fax: 661 665-3222
Gene Voiland, *Manager*
EMP: 50
SALES (corp-wide): 421.1B **Publicly Held**
WEB: www.aeraenergy.com
SIC: **1381** Directional drilling oil & gas wells
HQ: Aera Energy Llc
   10000 Ming Ave
   Bakersfield CA 93311
   661 665-5000

(P-1055)
AERA ENERGY LLC
Also Called: Aera Energy South Midway
29235 Highway 33, Maricopa (93252-9793)
PHONE.................................661 665-3200
Andy Anderson, *Manager*
Bob Alberstadt, *Senior VP*
Sheila Moore, *Administration*
Mitchell Aera, *Engineer*
Joshua Whittle, *Buyer*
EMP: 60
SALES (corp-wide): 264.9B **Publicly Held**
WEB: www.aeraenergy.com
SIC: **1381** Directional drilling oil & gas wells
HQ: Aera Energy Llc
   10000 Ming Ave
   Bakersfield CA 93311
   661 665-5000

(P-1056)
ALUMATEC INC
18411 Sherman Way, Reseda (91335-4319)
PHONE.................................818 609-7460
Francesco Chinaglia, *President*
Yazmin Ibarlucea, *Treasurer*
Laura Chinaglia, *Admin Sec*
Massimiliano Nava, *Director*
EMP: 80
SALES (est): 7.1MM **Privately Held**
WEB: www.alumatec.com
SIC: **1381** Drilling oil & gas wells

(P-1057)
ELYSIUM JENNINGS LLC
1600 Norris Rd, Bakersfield (93308-2234)
PHONE.................................661 679-1700
Steve Layton,
EMP: 200
SALES (est): 8.1MM
SALES (corp-wide): 326.3MM **Privately Held**
SIC: **1381** Drilling oil & gas wells
PA: E & B Natural Resources Management Corporation
   1600 Norris Rd
   Bakersfield CA 93308
   661 679-1714

(P-1058)
EXCALIBUR WELL SERVICES CORP (PA)
22034 Rosedale Hwy, Bakersfield (93314-9704)
PHONE.................................661 589-5338
Fax: 661 589-1089
Stephen Layton, *President*
Frachsco Galesi, *President*
Gordon Isbel, *Vice Pres*
Gordon Isbell, *General Mgr*
Mary Telupessy, *Business Mgr*
EMP: 81
SALES (est): 44.8MM **Privately Held**
SIC: **1381 1389** Drilling oil & gas wells; fishing for tools, oil & gas field

(P-1059)
GOLDEN STATE DRILLING INC
3500 Fruitvale Ave, Bakersfield (93308-5106)
PHONE.................................661 589-0730
Fax: 661 589-0147
Philip F Phelps, *President*
James Phelps, *Treasurer*
Velma Phelps, *Vice Pres*
Marsha Weaver, *Office Mgr*
Joey Rocha, *Engineer*
EMP: 75
SALES (est): 10.6MM **Privately Held**
WEB: www.gsdrilling.com
SIC: **1381** Drilling oil & gas wells

(P-1060)
NABORS WELL SERVICES CO
1025 Earthmover Ct, Bakersfield (93314-9529)
PHONE.................................661 588-6140
Tom Jaquez, *Manager*
EMP: 160 **Privately Held**
SIC: **1381** Drilling oil & gas wells
HQ: Nabors Well Services Co.
   515 W Greens Rd Ste 1000
   Houston TX 77067
   281 874-0035

(P-1061)
PAUL GRAHAM DRILLING & SVC CO
2500 Airport Rd, Rio Vista (94571-1034)
P.O. Box 669 (94571-0669)
PHONE.................................707 374-5123
Fax: 707 374-6821
Kevin P Graham, *President*
Jill Graham, *CFO*
Clarence Santos, *Vice Pres*
Eddie Woodruff, *General Mgr*
Chris Clouser, *Engineer*
EMP: 170
SQ FT: 30,000
SALES: 30MM **Privately Held**
SIC: **1381 7389 7359** Drilling oil & gas wells; crane & aerial lift service; industrial truck rental

1382 Oil & Gas Field Exploration Svcs

(P-1062)
DCOR LLC (PA)
290 Maple Ct Ste 290, Ventura (93003-9144)
P.O. Box 3401 (93006-3401)
PHONE.................................805 535-2000
Bill Templeton, *General Mgr*
Andrew Prestridge, *President*
Alan C Templeton, *CFO*
Greg Cavette, *Vice Pres*
Dennis Conley, *Vice Pres*
EMP: 76
SALES (est): 171.2MM **Privately Held**
WEB: www.dcor.com
SIC: **1382** Oil & gas exploration services

(P-1063)
DCOR LLC
290 Maple Ct Ste 290, Ventura (93003-9144)
PHONE.................................805 576-1200
Stephanie Rice, *Branch Mgr*
EMP: 56
SALES (corp-wide): 171.2MM **Privately Held**
SIC: **1382** Oil & gas exploration services
PA: Dcor, L.L.C.
   290 Maple Ct Ste 290
   Ventura CA 93003
   805 535-2000

(P-1064)
DEMENNO KERDOON
2000 N Alameda St, Compton (90222-2799)
PHONE.................................310 537-7100
Fax: 310 639-2946
Shane Bamelin, *Principal*
Jim Tice, *Principal*
Jim Ennis, *Director*
Mike Patterson, *Director*
EMP: 125
SQ FT: 11,614
SALES (est): 28.4MM **Privately Held**
WEB: www.demennokerdoon.com
SIC: **1382** Oil & gas exploration services

(P-1065)
NATIONS PETROLEUM CAL LLC
9600 Ming Ave Ste 300, Bakersfield (93311-1365)
PHONE.................................661 387-6402
Phil Sorvet,
Doug Wright, *Manager*
EMP: 60
SALES (est): 3.5MM
SALES (corp-wide): 1.2MM **Privately Held**
SIC: **1382** Oil & gas exploration services
PA: Nations Petroleum Company Ltd
   255 5 Ave Sw Suite 750
   Calgary AB T2P 3
   403 206-1420

(P-1066)
QRE OPERATING LLC
707 Wilshire Blvd # 4600, Los Angeles (90017-3501)
PHONE.................................213 225-5900
Alan L Smith, *Mng Member*
EMP: 229
SALES (est): 585.1K
SALES (corp-wide): 1.1B **Privately Held**
SIC: **1382** Oil & gas exploration services
HQ: Qr Energy, Lp
   707 Wilshire Blvd # 4600
   Los Angeles CA 90017

(P-1067)
R W LYALL & COMPANY INC (DH)
2665 Research Dr, Corona (92882-6918)
P.O. Box 2259 (92878-2259)
PHONE.................................951 270-1500
Fax: 909 270-1600
Jeffrey W Lyall, *President*
Jennifer Fritchle, *COO*
Bruce Lange, *COO*
Tony Mauer, *CFO*
▲ EMP: 168
SQ FT: 70,000
SALES (est): 49.8MM
SALES (corp-wide): 3.3B **Publicly Held**
WEB: www.rwlyall.com
SIC: **1382** Oil & gas exploration services
HQ: Burndy Llc
   47 E Industrial Park Dr
   Manchester NH 03109
   603 626-3730

1389 Oil & Gas Field Svcs, NEC

(P-1068)
BAKER HUGHES INCORPORATED
3901 Fanucchi Way E, Shafter (93263-9539)
PHONE.................................661 831-7686
Fax: 661 834-4575
Richard Mounts, *Manager*
Eralda Bustamante, *Executive*
Garren Hodge, *Facilities Mgr*
Stephanie Destrampe, *Manager*
EMP: 70
SALES (corp-wide): 15.7B **Publicly Held**
WEB: www.bjservices.com
SIC: **1389** Oil field services
PA: Baker Hughes Incorporated
   2929 Allen Pkwy Ste 2100
   Houston TX 77019
   713 439-8600

(P-1069)
BAKER PETROLITE CORPORATION
5125 Boylan St, Bakersfield (93308-4511)
PHONE.................................661 325-4138
Doug Thomas, *Manager*
Bob Misuraca, *Plant Mgr*
Lawrence Chau, *Manager*
EMP: 60
SALES (corp-wide): 15.7B **Publicly Held**
WEB: www.bakerpetrolite.com
SIC: **1389** Oil field services
HQ: Baker Petrolite Llc
   12645 W Airport Blvd
   Sugar Land TX 77478
   281 276-5400

(P-1070)
BSIA NATURAL RESOURCES CO
4475 Dupont Ct Ste 4, Ventura (93003-7745)
PHONE.................................805 650-2794
Clifton O Simonson, *President*
EMP: 50
SALES (est): 3.9MM **Privately Held**
SIC: **1389** Oil & gas field services

(P-1071)
CL KNOX INC
Also Called: Advanced Industrial Services
34933 Imperial St, Bakersfield (93308-9579)
PHONE.................................661 837-0477
Fax: 661 833-9312
Leslie Knox, *President*
Chris Knox, *Corp Secy*
Sheila Rogers, *Manager*
EMP: 80 EST: 1992
SALES (est): 10.6MM **Privately Held**
SIC: **1389 8742** Oil field services; industrial consultant

(P-1072)
CUMMINGS VACUUM SERVICE INC
Also Called: Cummings Transportation
19605 Broken Ct, Shafter (93263-9583)
PHONE.................................661 746-1786
Pam Cummings, *President*
Ted Cummings, *Vice Pres*
Shiloh Smith, *Engineer*
EMP: 60
SQ FT: 3,000
SALES (est): 6.3MM **Privately Held**
SIC: **1389** Oil field services

(P-1073)
DWAYNES ENGINEERING & CNSTR
3655 Addie Ave, Mc Kittrick (93251)
P.O. Box 116 (93251-0116)
PHONE.................................661 762-7261
Fax: 661 762-7246
Dwayne Emfinger, *President*
Karen Nakashima, *Office Mgr*
Terry Jamesson, *Executive Asst*
EMP: 78
SALES (est): 7.8MM **Privately Held**
WEB: www.dwayneseng.com
SIC: **1389** Construction, repair & dismantling services

(P-1074)
ENGINEERED WELL SVC INTL INC
3120 Standard St, Bakersfield (93308-6241)
P.O. Box 309 (93302-0309)
PHONE.................................866 913-6283
Paul Sturgeon, *CEO*
John E Powell Jr, *Principal*
EMP: 125 EST: 2009
SALES (est): 46.8MM **Privately Held**
SIC: **1389** Oil field services

▲ = Import ▼ = Export
◆ = Import/Export

PRODUCTS & SERVICES SECTION
1389 - Oil & Gas Field Svcs, NEC County (P-1097)

(P-1075)
ETHOSENERGY FIELD SERVICES LLC (DH)
Also Called: Wg
10455 Slusher Dr Bldg 12, Santa Fe Springs (90670-3750)
PHONE..................................310 639-3523
Rob Duby, *President*
Patricia Lelito, *CFO*
Mike Fieldhouse, *Vice Pres*
Nicole Roberts, *Executive*
Mary Ros, *General Mgr*
EMP: 75
SALES (est): 27.9MM
SALES (corp-wide): 5B **Privately Held**
WEB: www.woodgroupgts.com
SIC: 1389 8711 3462 Oil consultants; industrial engineers; pump, compressor & turbine forgings

(P-1076)
FIELD FOUNDATION
15306 Carmenita Rd, Santa Fe Springs (90670-5606)
P.O. Box 4236, Cerritos (90703-4236)
PHONE..................................562 921-3567
Irwin Field, *Owner*
EMP: 50 **EST:** 1948
SALES: 24.3K **Privately Held**
SIC: 1389 Oil sampling service for oil companies

(P-1077)
GENE WATSON CONSTRUCTION A CA
801 Kern St, Taft (93268-2734)
PHONE..................................661 763-5254
Gene Watson, *Ltd Ptnr*
Patricia Watson, *Ltd Ptnr*
Dave Artoffer, *Finance*
EMP: 530
SALES (est): 11.2MM **Privately Held**
WEB: www.gwc-ltd.com
SIC: 1389 1382 Oil field services; oil & gas exploration services

(P-1078)
GRAYSON SERVICE INC
4004 Enos Ln, Bakersfield (93314-9884)
PHONE..................................661 589-5444
Fax: 661 589-5447
Carol A Grayson, *President*
Cheryl Grayson, *Vice Pres*
EMP: 150
SALES (est): 6.3MM **Privately Held**
SIC: 1389 Servicing oil & gas wells

(P-1079)
HALLIBURTON ENERGY SVCS INC
Also Called: Halliburton Service Division
801 S 2nd St, El Centro (92243-3451)
P.O. Box 2478 (92244-2478)
PHONE..................................760 353-2710
Billy Rex, *Branch Mgr*
EMP: 87 **Publicly Held**
SIC: 1389 Cementing oil & gas well casings
HQ: Halliburton Energy Services, Inc.
10200 Bellaire Blvd
Houston TX 77072
713 839-3950

(P-1080)
HALLIBURTON ENERGY SVCS INC
34722 7th Standard Rd, Bakersfield (93314-9435)
PHONE..................................661 393-8111
Fax: 661 399-3915
Dennis Lovett, *Branch Mgr*
Doug Keller, *Treasurer*
Bob Freeman, *Exec Dir*
EMP: 87 **Publicly Held**
SIC: 1389 Oil field services
HQ: Halliburton Energy Services, Inc.
10200 Bellaire Blvd
Houston TX 77072
713 839-3950

(P-1081)
HILLS WLDG & ENGRG CONTR INC
Also Called: Hwe Mechanical
22038 Stockdale Hwy, Bakersfield (93314-8889)
PHONE..................................661 746-5400
Debora M Hill, *Vice Pres*
Robert Hill, *Shareholder*
EMP: 92
SALES (est): 7.1MM **Privately Held**
SIC: 1389 Testing, measuring, surveying & analysis services

(P-1082)
HIRSH INC
Also Called: Better Mens Clothes
860 S Los Angeles St # 900, Los Angeles (90014-3319)
PHONE..................................213 622-9441
Mistie Banks, *General Mgr*
Stanley Hirsh, *President*
EMP: 50
SALES (est): 1.1MM **Privately Held**
SIC: 1389 Lease tanks, oil field: erecting, cleaning & repairing

(P-1083)
HUNTING ENERGY SERVICES INC
Also Called: Hunting-Vinson
4900 California Ave 100a, Bakersfield (93309-7024)
PHONE..................................661 633-4272
Bobby Ford, *Branch Mgr*
EMP: 76
SALES (corp-wide): 810.5MM **Privately Held**
WEB: www.hunting-inc.com
SIC: 1389 Oil field services
HQ: Hunting Energy Services, Inc.
2 Northpoint Dr Ste 400
Houston TX 77060
281 820-3838

(P-1084)
HVI CAT CANYON INC
2617 E Clark Ave, Santa Maria (93455-5815)
PHONE..................................805 621-5800
Randeep S Grewal, *President*
Ken Miller, *CFO*
Susan Whalen, *Vice Pres*
Flavio Parigi, *Credit Mgr*
EMP: 125
SALES (est): 9.6MM **Privately Held**
SIC: 1389 Oil field services

(P-1085)
JERRY MELTON & SONS CNSTR
Also Called: Jerry Melton & Sons Cnstr
100 Jamison Ln, Taft (93268-4329)
PHONE..................................661 765-5546
Fax: 661 765-7696
Jerry W Melton, *President*
Karen Melton, *Treasurer*
Judy Melton, *Vice Pres*
Steven Melton, *Admin Sec*
EMP: 85
SALES (est): 11.6MM **Privately Held**
WEB: www.jerrymelton.com
SIC: 1389 Oil & gas wells: building, repairing & dismantling; grading oil & gas well foundations

(P-1086)
MMI SERVICES INC
4042 Patton Way, Bakersfield (93308-5030)
PHONE..................................661 589-9366
Fax: 661 589-2080
Steve McGowan, *President*
Mel McGowan, *CEO*
Eric Olson, *Vice Pres*
Roxanne Campbell, *Info Tech Dir*
Matthew Kennedy, *Safety Mgr*
EMP: 250
SQ FT: 4,500
SALES (est): 46.6MM **Privately Held**
WEB: www.mmi-services.com
SIC: 1389 Oil field services

(P-1087)
NABORS WELL SERVICES CO
2567 N Ventura Ave C, Ventura (93001-1201)
PHONE..................................805 641-0390
Paul Smith, *Manager*
EMP: 90 **Privately Held**
SIC: 1389 Oil field services
HQ: Nabors Well Services Co.
515 W Greens Rd Ste 1000
Houston TX 77067
281 874-0035

(P-1088)
NABORS WELL SERVICES CO
7515 Rosedale Hwy, Bakersfield (93308-5727)
PHONE..................................661 589-3970
Fax: 661 589-5276
Alan Pounds, *Manager*
Dusty Keeler, *Opers Mgr*
Ron C Cleveland, *Manager*
EMP: 270 **Privately Held**
SIC: 1389 1382 Servicing oil & gas wells; oil & gas exploration services
HQ: Nabors Well Services Co.
515 W Greens Rd Ste 1000
Houston TX 77067
281 874-0035

(P-1089)
NABORS WELL SERVICES CO
19431 S Santa Fe Ave, Compton (90221-5912)
PHONE..................................310 639-7074
Bernie Fish, *Manager*
Gary Kaufman, *Human Res Mgr*
Paul Harper, *Purch Agent*
EMP: 230 **Privately Held**
SIC: 1389 Gas field services
HQ: Nabors Well Services Co.
515 W Greens Rd Ste 1000
Houston TX 77067
281 874-0035

(P-1090)
OIL WELL SERVICE COMPANY (PA)
10840 Norwalk Blvd, Santa Fe Springs (90670-3826)
PHONE..................................562 612-0600
Fax: 562 424-8026
Jack Frost, *President*
Connie Laws, *Treasurer*
Richard Laws, *Vice Pres*
Matt Hensley, *Admin Sec*
EMP: 105
SQ FT: 9,000
SALES (est): 94MM **Privately Held**
WEB: www.ows1.com
SIC: 1389 Oil field services

(P-1091)
PACIFIC PROCESS SYSTEMS INC (PA)
7401 Rosedale Hwy, Bakersfield (93308-5736)
PHONE..................................661 321-9681
Jerry Wise, *CEO*
Robert Peterson, *CFO*
Alan George, *Corp Secy*
Greg Fry, *Project Mgr*
Dominador Tomate, *Purch Mgr*
▼ **EMP:** 90
SQ FT: 7,000
SALES (est): 252.7MM **Privately Held**
WEB: www.pps-equipment.com
SIC: 1389 7353 5082 Testing, measuring, surveying & analysis services; oil field equipment, rental or leasing; oil field equipment

(P-1092)
PC MECHANICAL INC
2803 Industrial Pkwy, Santa Maria (93455-1811)
PHONE..................................805 925-2888
Fax: 805 925-6168
Lew Parker, *President*
Brandon Burginger, *COO*
Rachel Saxon, *Officer*
Mary Parker, *Exec VP*
Mitch Caron, *Vice Pres*
EMP: 50
SQ FT: 67,000
SALES (est): 9.3MM **Privately Held**
WEB: www.pcmechanical.com
SIC: 1389 Oil field services

(P-1093)
PROS INCORPORATED
3400 Patton Way, Bakersfield (93308-5722)
P.O. Box 20996 (93390-0996)
PHONE..................................661 589-5400
Robert Lewis, *President*
Lori Bulier, *Manager*
EMP: 58
SALES (est): 24.4MM **Privately Held**
SIC: 1389 Oil field services

(P-1094)
SCHLUMBERGER TECHNOLOGY CORP
Also Called: Schlumberger Well Services
2841 Pegasus Dr, Bakersfield (93308-6896)
PHONE..................................661 864-4750
Fax: 661 642-2065
Paul George, *Manager*
Martine Hernandez, *Admin Sec*
Alejandro Pena, *Opers Mgr*
EMP: 70 **Privately Held**
SIC: 1389 1382 Construction, repair & dismantling services; oil & gas exploration services
HQ: Schlumberger Technology Corp
100 Gillingham Ln
Sugar Land TX 77478
281 285-8500

(P-1095)
SCHLUMBERGER TECHNOLOGY CORP
Schlumberger, Well Completions
12131 Industry St, Garden Grove (92841-2813)
PHONE..................................714 379-7332
Gene Barnett, *Systems Mgr*
Osman Kuyucu, *Executive*
Tim Ramey, *Safety Mgr*
Arthur Berg, *Sales Executive*
EMP: 51 **Privately Held**
SIC: 1389 3561 Oil & gas wells: building, repairing & dismantling; pumps & pumping equipment
HQ: Schlumberger Technology Corp
100 Gillingham Ln
Sugar Land TX 77478
281 285-8500

(P-1096)
SOLI-BOND INC
4230 Foster Ave, Bakersfield (93308-4559)
PHONE..................................661 631-1633
Fax: 661 631-1677
Dwight Hartley, *President*
EMP: 50
SALES (corp-wide): 59MM **Privately Held**
SIC: 1389 Oil field services
PA: Soli-Bond, Inc.
2377 2 Mile Rd
Bay City MI 48706
989 686-2540

(P-1097)
TOTAL-WESTERN INC (HQ)
8049 Somerset Blvd, Paramount (90723-4396)
PHONE..................................562 220-1450
Paul F Conrad, *CEO*
Mary A Pool, *CFO*
Leonard Crespo, *Vice Pres*
Earl Grebing, *Vice Pres*
John Young, *Vice Pres*
EMP: 50
SQ FT: 13,000
SALES (est): 114.1MM
SALES (corp-wide): 278.7MM **Privately Held**
WEB: www.total-western.com
SIC: 1389 Oil field services; construction, repair & dismantling services; excavating slush pits & cellars; grading oil & gas well foundations
PA: Bragg Investment Company, Inc.
6251 N Paramount Blvd
Long Beach CA 90805
562 984-2400

1389 - Oil & Gas Field Svcs, NEC County (P-1098)

PRODUCTS & SERVICES SECTION

(P-1098)
TRUITT OILFIELD MAINT CORP
1051 James Rd, Bakersfield (93308-9753)
P.O. Box 5066 (93388-5066)
PHONE.................................661 871-4099
Fax: 661 399-6399
Kimberly Sue New, *President*
Steve New, *Vice Pres*
EMP: 300
SQ FT: 3,000
SALES (est): 46.6MM **Privately Held**
SIC: 1389 Oil field services

(P-1099)
TRYAD SERVICE CORPORATION
5900 E Lerdo Hwy, Shafter (93263-4023)
PHONE.................................661 391-1524
Fax: 661 399-3663
James Varner, *President*
Estate of Burl G Varner, *Shareholder*
Tony Courtis, *Vice Pres*
Danny Seely, *Vice Pres*
Paul Herzberg, *Purch Mgr*
▲ **EMP:** 90
SALES (est): 10.8MM **Privately Held**
SIC: 1389 Oil & gas wells: building, repairing & dismantling

1422 Crushed & Broken Limestone

(P-1100)
SPECIALTY MINERALS INC
Minerals Technology
6565 Meridian Rd, Lucerne Valley (92356)
P.O. Box 558 (92356-0558)
PHONE.................................760 248-5300
Fax: 760 248-6707
Doug Mayger, *Branch Mgr*
Darin Lindsey, *General Mgr*
Douglas Mayger, *General Mgr*
Jay Rosse, *Engineer*
Kathy Garten, *Business Mgr*
EMP: 150
SALES (corp-wide): 1.8B **Publicly Held**
WEB: www.specialtyminerals.com
SIC: 1422 Crushed & broken limestone
HQ: Specialty Minerals Inc.
622 3rd Ave Fl 38
New York NY 10017
212 878-1800

(P-1101)
SYAR INDUSTRIES INC
885 Lake Herman Rd, Vallejo (94591-8324)
P.O. Box 2540, NAPA (94558-0524)
PHONE.................................707 643-3261
Fax: 707 552-1973
Mike Burneson, *Manager*
Julie Yeoman, *Executive*
EMP: 100
SALES (corp-wide): 91.1MM **Privately Held**
WEB: www.syar.com
SIC: 1422 5211 Crushed & broken limestone; cement
PA: Syar Industries, Inc.
2301 Napa Vallejo Hwy
Napa CA 94558
707 252-8711

1429 Crushed & Broken Stone, NEC

(P-1102)
SAN RAFAEL ROCK QUARRY INC (HQ)
Also Called: Dutra Materials
1000 Point San Pedro Rd, San Rafael (94901-8312)
PHONE.................................415 459-7740
Bill Toney Dutra, *CEO*
Harry Stewart, *COO*
Michael Cole, *Purch Mgr*
David Grummitt, *Marketing Staff*
EMP: 70
SALES (est): 52.6MM
SALES (corp-wide): 162.7MM **Privately Held**
SIC: 1429 1629 Basalt, crushed & broken-quarrying; marine construction

PA: The Dutra Group
2350 Kerner Blvd Ste 200
San Rafael CA 94901
415 258-6876

1442 Construction Sand & Gravel

(P-1103)
GRANITE ROCK CO (PA)
350 Technology Dr, Watsonville (95076-2488)
P.O. Box 50001 (95077-5001)
PHONE.................................831 768-2000
Fax: 831 768-2403
Thomas H Squeri, *CEO*
Bruce G Woolpert, *Vice Chairman*
Mary E Woolpert, *Chairman*
Rodney Jenny, *Exec VP*
Greg Diehl, *Vice Pres*
EMP: 100
SQ FT: 10,000
SALES (est): 1.2B **Privately Held**
WEB: www.graniterock.com
SIC: 1442 3273 5032 2951 Gravel mining; construction sand mining; ready-mixed concrete; sand, construction; stone, crushed or broken; asphalt & asphaltic paving mixtures (not from refineries); highway & street paving contractor; concrete block & brick

(P-1104)
GRANITE ROCK CO
Also Called: AR Wilson Quarry
Quarry Rd, Aromas (95004)
P.O. Box 699 (95004-0699)
PHONE (95004-0699)...........831 768-2300
Bruce Wollepert, *President*
EMP: 100
SALES (corp-wide): 1.2B **Privately Held**
WEB: www.graniterock.com
SIC: 1442 2951 Gravel mining; asphalt paving mixtures & blocks
PA: Granite Rock Co.
350 Technology Dr
Watsonville CA 95076
831 768-2000

(P-1105)
HANSEN BROS ENTERPRISES (PA)
Also Called: Hbe Rental
11727 La Barr Meadows Rd, Grass Valley (95949-7722)
P.O. Box 1599 (95945-1599)
PHONE.................................530 273-3100
Fax: 530 272-5401
Orson Hansen, *President*
Frank Bennallack, *Treasurer*
Helen Hansen, *Vice Pres*
Sue Peterson, *Vice Pres*
John Smith, *Admin Asst*
EMP: 70
SQ FT: 20,000
SALES (est): 45.4MM **Privately Held**
WEB: www.gohbe.com
SIC: 1442 3273 1794 7359 Gravel mining; ready-mixed concrete; excavation work; equipment rental & leasing

(P-1106)
LEGACY VULCAN CORP
San Bernardino Division
2400 W Highland Ave, San Bernardino (92407-6408)
PHONE.................................909 875-1150
Darryl Charleson, *Sales/Mktg Dir*
Randy Riberdy, *Manager*
EMP: 50
SALES (corp-wide): 3.4B **Publicly Held**
WEB: www.vulcanmaterials.com
SIC: 1442 3273 Sand mining; ready-mixed concrete
HQ: Legacy Vulcan, Llc
1200 Urban Center Dr
Vestavia AL 35242
205 298-3000

(P-1107)
LEGACY VULCAN CORP
Also Called: Mission Vly Rock Asp & Rdymx
5745 Mission Center Rd, San Diego (92108-4300)
P.O. Box 3098 (92163-3098)
PHONE.................................858 547-9459
Pat Coughlin, *Manager*
Barry Coley, *Office Mgr*
Ms Gerry Wood, *Personnel*
EMP: 90
SALES (corp-wide): 3.4B **Publicly Held**
WEB: www.vulcanmaterials.com
SIC: 1442 3273 2951 Gravel mining; common sand mining; ready-mixed concrete; asphalt paving mixtures & blocks
HQ: Legacy Vulcan, Llc
1200 Urban Center Dr
Vestavia AL 35242
205 298-3000

(P-1108)
LEGACY VULCAN CORP
Also Called: Pleasanton Asphalt Sand & Grav
501 El Charro Rd, Pleasanton (94588)
PHONE.................................925 373-1802
Don Kahler, *Branch Mgr*
Mike Drummond, *Manager*
EMP: 53
SQ FT: 73,379
SALES (corp-wide): 3.4B **Publicly Held**
WEB: www.vulcanmaterials.com
SIC: 1442 Gravel mining
HQ: Legacy Vulcan, Llc
1200 Urban Center Dr
Vestavia AL 35242
205 298-3000

(P-1109)
WEST COAST AGGREGATE SUPPLY
Also Called: Aggregate West Coast
92500 Airport Blvd, Thermal (92274)
P.O. Box 790 (92274-0790)
PHONE.................................760 342-7598
Marvin Struiksma, *President*
EMP: 50
SALES (est): 5.4MM **Privately Held**
SIC: 1442 Common sand mining

1446 Industrial Sand

(P-1110)
PREMIER SILICA LLC
31302 Ortega Hwy, San Juan Capistrano (92675)
P.O. Box 249 (92693-0249)
PHONE.................................949 728-0171
Fax: 949 728-0321
Mike Miclette, *Branch Mgr*
EMP: 53
SALES (corp-wide): 4.8B **Publicly Held**
SIC: 1446 Silica sand mining
HQ: Premier Silica Llc
5205 N O Connor Blvd # 200
Irving TX 75039
972 444-9001

(P-1111)
PW GILLIBRAND CO INC
4537 Ish Dr, Simi Valley (93063-7667)
P.O. Box 1019 (93062-1019)
PHONE.................................805 526-2195
Fax: 805 522-4031
Celine Gillibrand, *CEO*
Richard Valencia, *President*
Jim Costello, *Corp Secy*
Tim McGuire, *Sales Dir*
EMP: 75
SQ FT: 11,000
SALES (est): 24.8MM **Privately Held**
WEB: www.pwgcoinc.com
SIC: 1446 Grinding sand mining; foundry sand mining

1474 Potash, Soda & Borate Minerals

(P-1112)
PACIFIC COAST MINES INC
26877 Tourney Rd, Valencia (91355-1846)
PHONE.................................661 287-5400

Preston Chiaro, *President*
Glenn I Swartz, *Treasurer*
Jim Gude, *Officer*
Tom Albanese, *Vice Pres*
Lawrence F Bellotti, *Vice Pres*
EMP: 200
SQ FT: 10,000
SALES (est): 148.1K
SALES (corp-wide): 34.8B **Privately Held**
WEB: www.boraxfr.com
SIC: 1474 1481 Borate compounds (natural) mining; mine exploration, nonmetallic minerals
HQ: U.S. Borax Inc.
8051 E Maplewood Ave # 100
Greenwood Village CO 80111
303 713-5000

1481 Nonmetallic Minerals Svcs, Except Fuels

(P-1113)
IMERYS MINERALS CALIFORNIA INC
Also Called: Imerys Filtration Minerals
2500 Miguelito Canyon Rd, Lompoc (93436)
PHONE.................................805 736-1221
Kenneth Schweibert, *Manager*
Robert Rees, *Sales Staff*
EMP: 346
SALES (corp-wide): 1.2MM **Privately Held**
SIC: 1481 3295 Nonmetallic mineral services; minerals, ground or treated
HQ: Imerys Minerals California, Inc.
2500 San Miguelito Rd
Lompoc CA 93436
805 736-1221

1499 Miscellaneous Nonmetallic Mining

(P-1114)
DICAPERL CORPORATION (DH)
Also Called: Grefco Dicaperl
23705 Crenshaw Blvd, Torrance (90505-5236)
PHONE.................................610 667-6640
Ray Perelman, *CEO*
Glenn Jones, *President*
Mike Cull, *Treasurer*
Barry Katz, *Senior VP*
▼ **EMP:** 90
SQ FT: 5,000
SALES (est): 9.4MM
SALES (corp-wide): 47.1MM **Privately Held**
SIC: 1499 3677 Perlite mining; filtration devices, electronic
HQ: Grefco Minerals, Inc
1 Bala Ave Ste 310
Bala Cynwyd PA
610 660-8820

(P-1115)
IMERYS FILTRATION MINERALS INC (DH)
1732 N 1st St Ste 450, San Jose (95112-4579)
PHONE.................................805 562-0200
Fax: 805 562-0298
Douglas A Smith, *CEO*
John Oskan, *President*
Leslie Zimmer, *CFO*
Fred Weber, *Treasurer*
Paul Woodberry, *Vice Ch Bd*
◆ **EMP:** 50
SQ FT: 11,600
SALES (est): 848.1MM
SALES (corp-wide): 1.2MM **Privately Held**
SIC: 1499 Diatomaceous earth mining
HQ: Imerys Usa, Inc.
100 Mansell Ct E Ste 300
Roswell GA 30076
770 645-3300

PRODUCTS & SERVICES SECTION
1521 - General Contractors, Single Family Houses County (P-1140)

(P-1116)
IMERYS MINERALS CALIFORNIA INC (DH)
2500 San Miguelito Rd, Lompoc (93436-9743)
P.O. Box 519 (93438-0519)
PHONE.................................805 736-1221
Fax: 805 736-1222
Douglas A Smith, *President*
John Oskam, *CEO*
John Leichty, *CFO*
Jack Murray, *Vice Pres*
Bruno Van Herpen, *Vice Pres*
▼ EMP: 70
SQ FT: 11,600
SALES (est): 711.7MM
SALES (corp-wide): 1.2MM **Privately Held**
SIC: **1499** 3295 Diatomaceous earth mining; minerals, ground or treated
HQ: Imerys Filtration Minerals, Inc.
1732 N 1st St Ste 450
San Jose CA 95112
805 562-0200

(P-1117)
MONARCHY DIAMOND INC
550 S Hill St Ste 1088, Los Angeles (90013-2417)
PHONE.................................213 924-1161
Rajnikumar Patel, *President*
EMP: 425
SALES (est): 12.3MM **Privately Held**
SIC: **1499** Gem stones (natural) mining

1521 General Contractors, Single Family Houses

(P-1118)
A & W MAINTENANCE
7573 Cibola Trl, Yucca Valley (92284-3255)
PHONE.................................310 619-8694
Alesia Ellis, *Owner*
EMP: 54
SQ FT: 3,400
SALES (est): 1.6MM **Privately Held**
SIC: **1521** 7349 Townhouse construction; building maintenance, except repairs

(P-1119)
A I T DEVELOPMENT CORP
Also Called: Mega Builders
21021 Devonshire St # 102, Chatsworth (91311-2362)
PHONE.................................818 407-5533
Alon A Toker, *President*
Isabell Toker, *Corp Secy*
EMP: 66
SQ FT: 3,300
SALES (est): 4MM **Privately Held**
SIC: **1521** General remodeling, single-family houses

(P-1120)
A M ORTEGA CONSTRUCTION INC
58 Kellogg St, Ventura (93001-1732)
PHONE.................................951 360-1352
Archie Maurice Ortega, *Branch Mgr*
EMP: 52
SALES (corp-wide): 50.6MM **Privately Held**
SIC: **1521** Single-family housing construction
PA: A. M. Ortega Construction, Inc.
10125 Channel Rd
Lakeside CA 92040
619 390-1988

(P-1121)
A W PROPERTIES WEST LLC
16236 San Dieguito Rd # 310, Rancho Santa Fe (92091-9802)
P.O. Box 9296 (92067-4296)
PHONE.................................858 832-1462
Fax: 858 756-7594
Danny Hampel,
Jayme Doan, *Human Resources*
Lindsey Greene, *Real Est Agnt*
EMP: 68
SALES (est): 3.8MM **Privately Held**
SIC: **1521** Single-family housing construction

(P-1122)
ALL AXIS ENTERPRISE INC
4408 Market St Ste E, Oakland (94608-3456)
PHONE.................................510 451-1200
T Anderson, *CEO*
EMP: 99
SALES (est): 950K **Privately Held**
SIC: **1521** Single-family housing construction

(P-1123)
ALLSTATE CONSTRUCTION CO
1364 Londonderry Pl, Los Angeles (90069-1335)
PHONE.................................310 652-6942
Morris Bardoff, *President*
EMP: 50
SALES (est): 4.5MM **Privately Held**
SIC: **1521** General remodeling, single-family houses

(P-1124)
ALPHA-WINFIELD CONTRACTORS INC
Also Called: Winfield Construction
1096 Yerba Buena Ave, Emeryville (94608-3836)
PHONE.................................510 652-4712
Kenneth J Winfield, *President*
EMP: 100
SQ FT: 1,200
SALES (est): 7.4MM **Privately Held**
SIC: **1521** 1542 New construction, single-family houses; general remodeling, single-family houses; commercial & office buildings, renovation & repair

(P-1125)
AMERICAN DREAM
300 Portinao Cir, Sacramento (95831-2952)
PHONE.................................916 613-4917
Conway Phillips, *Principal*
EMP: 60
SALES (est): 500K **Privately Held**
SIC: **1521** Single-family housing construction

(P-1126)
AMERICAN SOLAR SOLUTION INC
6400 Laurel Canyon Blvd # 400, North Hollywood (91606-1564)
PHONE.................................877 946-8855
Nicki Zvik, *President*
Shay Yavor, *COO*
Jerry Goldman, *Principal*
Julihta Gershomov-Rivas, *General Mgr*
EMP: 70
SALES (est): 5.4MM **Privately Held**
SIC: **1521** 1711 1522 General remodeling, single-family houses; solar energy contractor; residential construction

(P-1127)
AMERICAN TECHNOLOGIES INC (PA)
Also Called: ATI
210 W Baywood Ave, Orange (92865-2603)
PHONE.................................714 283-9990
Fax: 714 283-9995
Gary Moore, *President*
Steven Pace, *CFO*
Doug Fairless, *Exec VP*
Jeff Moore, *Exec VP*
Bruce Ehlers, *Vice Pres*
▲ EMP: 128
SQ FT: 57,000
SALES (est): 180.8MM **Privately Held**
WEB: www.amer-tech.com
SIC: **1521** 1541 1742 1731 Single-family housing construction; industrial buildings & warehouses; plastering, drywall & insulation; electrical work; painting & paper hanging; plumbing, heating, air-conditioning contractors

(P-1128)
AMERICAN TECHNOLOGIES INC
Also Called: American Restoration Services
2688 Westhills Ct, Simi Valley (93065-6234)
PHONE.................................818 700-5060
Fax: 818 700-5065
Doug Waters, *Branch Mgr*
Julie Marcus, *Office Mgr*
Vicky Flores, *Admin Asst*
Joanne Kelley, *Admin Asst*
Allen Brush, *Project Mgr*
EMP: 99
SALES (corp-wide): 180.8MM **Privately Held**
WEB: www.amer-tech.com
SIC: **1521** 1799 Single-family home remodeling, additions & repairs; repairing fire damage, single-family houses; asbestos removal & encapsulation; decontamination services
PA: American Technologies Inc.
210 W Baywood Ave
Orange CA 92865
714 283-9990

(P-1129)
ARRAND PROPERTIES LLC
5032 Westside Dr, San Ramon (94583-9125)
P.O. Box 2212, Dublin (94568-0221)
PHONE.................................925 289-1032
Celia Arrand,
Ali Adams,
EMP: 50 EST: 2013
SALES (est): 2.3MM **Privately Held**
SIC: **1521** 1522 1541 General remodeling, single-family houses; hotel/motel & multi-family home renovation & remodeling; renovation, remodeling & repairs: industrial buildings

(P-1130)
ARYA GROUP INC
Also Called: Arya Design Group
10490 Santa Monica Blvd, Los Angeles (90025-5033)
PHONE.................................310 446-7000
Fax: 310 446-9120
Ardie Tavangarian, *President*
Mini King, *Manager*
EMP: 50
SQ FT: 3,000
SALES (est): 8.3MM **Privately Held**
SIC: **1521** 1542 New construction, single-family houses; commercial & office building, new construction

(P-1131)
AUSTIN BUILDERS
151 1/2 N Yale Ave, Fullerton (92831-4509)
PHONE.................................714 879-1100
Robert Austin, *Owner*
EMP: 50
SALES (est): 3.1MM **Privately Held**
WEB: www.austinbuilders.com
SIC: **1521** New construction, single-family houses

(P-1132)
AUSTIN CONSTRUCTION
330 L P Ranch Rd, Templeton (93465-8739)
PHONE.................................805 610-0622
Brian Wayne Austin, *Principal*
EMP: 50
SALES (est): 2.5MM **Privately Held**
SIC: **1521** Single-family housing construction

(P-1133)
BEEN ENTERPRISES
755 N Peach Ave Ste F11, Clovis (93611-7259)
PHONE.................................559 298-8864
Fax: 559 298-0163
Clyde E Been, *Partner*
David Been, *Partner*
EMP: 75
SALES (est): 3.5MM **Privately Held**
SIC: **1521** 0782 New construction, single-family houses; landscape contractors

(P-1134)
BILL BROWN CONSTRUCTION CO
242 Phelan Ave, San Jose (95112-6109)
PHONE.................................408 297-3738
William E Brown, *President*
Sandra Jaimes, *Controller*
Pee Janovich, *Opers Mgr*
EMP: 70
SQ FT: 1,650
SALES (est): 4.5MM **Privately Held**
WEB: www.bbrownconstruction.com
SIC: **1521** 1794 1791 Single-family housing construction; excavation work; structural steel erection

(P-1135)
BLU HOMES INC
1245 Nimitz Ave, Vallejo (94592-1024)
PHONE.................................415 625-0809
William M Haney III, *CEO*
EMP: 151
SALES (corp-wide): 61.6MM **Privately Held**
SIC: **1521** Single-family housing construction
PA: Blu Homes, Inc.
1245 Nimitz Ave
Vallejo CA 94592
617 275-2339

(P-1136)
BLU HOMES INC
1245 Nimitz Ave Bldg 680, Vallejo (94592-1024)
PHONE.................................707 674-5368
William Haney III, *President*
EMP: 275
SALES (est): 46.4MM **Privately Held**
SIC: **1521** Single-family housing construction

(P-1137)
BOLIN BUILDERS INC
3848 Berkesey Ln, Valley Springs (95252-9506)
P.O. Box 1437 (95252-1437)
PHONE.................................209 772-9721
Benton Bolin, *President*
Thelma Bolin, *Corp Secy*
William Bolin, *Vice Pres*
EMP: 50 EST: 1998
SALES (est): 4.3MM **Privately Held**
SIC: **1521** New construction, single-family houses

(P-1138)
BREHM COMMUNITIES (PA)
1935 Camino Vida Roble # 200, Carlsbad (92008-5568)
PHONE.................................760 448-2420
Fax: 858 448-2421
Forrest W Brehm, *President*
Anna Martineuz, *Executive Asst*
Tim Godfrey, *VP Opers*
EMP: 64
SQ FT: 5,984
SALES (est): 10MM **Privately Held**
SIC: **1521** New construction, single-family houses

(P-1139)
BRIECK RESTORATION INC
13750 Danielson St, Poway (92064-8889)
PHONE.................................858 679-9928
Dorothy Ledesma, *CEO*
Leilani Santos, *Executive*
Leanne Ledesma, *Controller*
EMP: 50
SALES (est): 3MM **Privately Held**
SIC: **1521** Single-family home remodeling, additions & repairs

(P-1140)
BROOKFELD STHLAND HOLDINGS LLC
Also Called: Brookfield Residential
3200 Park Center Dr # 1000, Costa Mesa (92626-7163)
PHONE.................................714 427-6868
Edrian Soley,
Allison Bevrouty, *Manager*
Erin Livermore, *Asst Sec*
EMP: 160
SALES (est): 25.7MM
SALES (corp-wide): 14.9B **Privately Held**
SIC: **1521** Single-family housing construction
HQ: Brookfield Homes Corporation
3201 Jermantown Rd # 150
Fairfax VA 22030
703 270-1400

1521 - General Contractors, Single Family Houses County (P-1141)

PRODUCTS & SERVICES SECTION

(P-1141)
BROOKFIELD HOMES OF CALIFORNIA
Also Called: Brookfield 1996 California
12865 Pointe Del Mar Way # 200, Del Mar (92014-3860)
PHONE.................................858 481-8500
Steven Doyle, *President*
Richard Whitney, *CFO*
Mary Peddy, *Office Mgr*
Judy Fisher, *Manager*
EMP: 50 **EST:** 1996
SALES (est): 3.7MM **Privately Held**
SIC: 1521 Single-family housing construction

(P-1142)
BROOKFIELD HOMES PACIFIC INC (DH)
12865 Pointe Del 200, Del Mar (92014)
PHONE.................................858 481-8500
Fax: 858 794-6185
Steven Doyle, *CEO*
Larry Cortes, *CFO*
Sabrina Kanner, *Senior VP*
Dan Kindbergh, *Senior VP*
John Moore, *Senior VP*
EMP: 81
SQ FT: 14,000
SALES (est): 39.5MM
SALES (corp-wide): 14.9B **Privately Held**
WEB: www.onewfc.com
SIC: 1521 Single-family housing construction
HQ: Brookfield Office Properties Inc
181 Bay St Suite 330
Toronto ON M5J 2
416 369-2300

(P-1143)
BRUCE OLSON CONSTRUCTION INC
7320 River Rd, Olympic Valley (96146)
P.O. Box 1518, Tahoe City (96145-1518)
PHONE.................................530 581-1087
Fax: 530 587-4612
Bruce W Olson, *CEO*
EMP: 145
SQ FT: 3,000
SALES (est): 12.5MM **Privately Held**
SIC: 1521 Single-family housing construction

(P-1144)
BX CONSTRUCTION LLC
11671 Sterling Ave Ste K, Riverside (92503-4971)
PHONE.................................951 509-9412
Aofan Wang,
Annie Naguillan,
EMP: 60
SQ FT: 1,100
SALES: 795K **Privately Held**
SIC: 1521 6552 6799 New construction, single-family houses; land subdividers & developers, residential; real estate investors, except property operators

(P-1145)
C W DRIVER INCORPORATED
2248 N 1st St, San Jose (95131-2022)
PHONE.................................650 308-4001
Mike Castillo, *Senior VP*
Josie Rushton, *Assistant*
EMP: 78
SALES (corp-wide): 259MM **Privately Held**
SIC: 1521 Single-family housing construction
PA: C. W. Driver, Incorporated
468 N Rosemead Blvd
Pasadena CA 91107
626 351-8800

(P-1146)
CALATLANTIC GROUP INC
Also Called: Standard Pacific Homes
5750 Fleet St Ste 200, Carlsbad (92008-4709)
PHONE.................................760 476-0104
Brian L Utsler, *Regional Mgr*
EMP: 140

SALES (corp-wide): 3.5B **Publicly Held**
WEB: www.standardpacifichomes.com
SIC: 1521 Single-family housing construction
PA: Calatlantic Group, Inc.
15360 Barranca Pkwy
Irvine CA 92618
949 789-1600

(P-1147)
CALATLANTIC GROUP INC
Southern Cal Inland Empire Div
355 E Rincon St Ste 300, Corona (92879-1372)
PHONE.................................951 898-5500
Fax: 951 372-8510
Douglas Krah, *Manager*
EMP: 53
SALES (corp-wide): 3.5B **Publicly Held**
SIC: 1521 Single-family housing construction
PA: Calatlantic Group, Inc.
15360 Barranca Pkwy
Irvine CA 92618
949 789-1600

(P-1148)
CALATLANTIC GROUP INC
13200 Fiji Way, Marina Del Rey (90292)
PHONE.................................310 821-9843
EMP: 59
SALES (corp-wide): 2.4B **Publicly Held**
SIC: 1521
PA: Calatlantic Group, Inc.
15360 Barranca Pkwy
Irvine CA 92618
949 789-1600

(P-1149)
CALHOUN CONSTRUCTION INC
150 Flocchini Cir, Lincoln (95648-1700)
PHONE.................................916 434-8356
Robert F Calhoun, *CEO*
Thomas Calhoun, *President*
Katrina Gallagher, *Manager*
EMP: 175 **EST:** 2001
SALES (est): 13.9MM **Privately Held**
WEB: www.calhounconstruction.org
SIC: 1521 Single-family housing construction

(P-1150)
CALIFORNIA PREFERRED BLDRS INC
20335 Ventura Blvd # 422, Woodland Hills (91364-2444)
PHONE.................................818 402-3345
Jacob Sherf, *President*
EMP: 50
SALES (est): 4.4MM **Privately Held**
SIC: 1521 New construction, single-family houses

(P-1151)
CARROLLCO INC
4054 W Ashcroft Ave, Fresno (93722-3973)
P.O. Box 13039 (93794-3039)
PHONE.................................559 396-3939
Benjamin Carroll, *CEO*
Tara Baltis, *Bookkeeper*
EMP: 50
SQ FT: 10,000
SALES (est): 2.9MM **Privately Held**
SIC: 1521 0782 Single-family home remodeling, additions & repairs; landscape contractors

(P-1152)
CENTEX HOMES INC
27101 Puerta Real Ste 300, Mission Viejo (92691-8589)
PHONE.................................949 453-0113
Bryan Swindell, *Branch Mgr*
EMP: 200
SALES (corp-wide): 5.9B **Publicly Held**
WEB: www.centexhomes.com
SIC: 1521 New construction, single-family houses
HQ: Centex Homes, Inc.
2728 N Harwood St
Dallas TX 75201
800 777-8583

(P-1153)
CENTEX HOMES INC
250 Commerce Ste 100, Irvine (92602-1341)
PHONE.................................949 453-0113
Fax: 949 453-8994
Richard Douglass, *Branch Mgr*
EMP: 108
SALES (corp-wide): 5.9B **Publicly Held**
WEB: www.centexhomes.com
SIC: 1521 New construction, single-family houses
HQ: Centex Homes, Inc.
2728 N Harwood St
Dallas TX 75201
800 777-8583

(P-1154)
CLARK/MCCARTHY A JOINT VENTURE
18201 Von Karman Ave # 800, Irvine (92612-1000)
PHONE.................................714 429-9779
W Carter Chappell, *Principal*
Richard Heim, *Partner*
Margie Rosario, *Principal*
Michael Chatlin, *Accountant*
Moly Huddleston, *Manager*
EMP: 1250
SALES (est): 35.6MM **Privately Held**
SIC: 1521 Single-family housing construction

(P-1155)
CLASSIC RESIDENTIAL INC
1597 Murray Ave, El Cajon (92020-5655)
PHONE.................................619 818-5793
Jason Beckman, *Principal*
EMP: 67
SALES: 500K **Privately Held**
SIC: 1521 Single-family housing construction

(P-1156)
CLYDE MILES CNSTR CO INC
1110 Burnett Ave Ste C, Concord (94520-5611)
PHONE.................................925 427-4473
Clyde E Miles, *President*
EMP: 100 **EST:** 1994
SALES (est): 8.7MM **Privately Held**
SIC: 1521 Single-family housing construction

(P-1157)
COASTLINE CNSTR & AWNG CO INC
5742 Research Dr, Huntington Beach (92649-1617)
PHONE.................................714 891-9798
John W Almquist, *President*
EMP: 100
SQ FT: 1,600
SALES (est): 9.2MM **Privately Held**
SIC: 1521 Mobile home repair, on site

(P-1158)
COLONY STRWOOD HOMES PARTNR LP
1999 Harrison St Fl 24, Oakland (94612-3520)
PHONE.................................510 250-2200
Frederick C Tuomi, *CEO*
Charles D Young, *COO*
Arik Prawer, *CFO*
EMP: 820
SALES (est): 1.1MM
SALES (corp-wide): 271.8MM **Privately Held**
SIC: 1521 Single-family home remodeling, additions & repairs
PA: Colony Starwood Homes
8665 E Hartford Dr # 200
Scottsdale AZ 85255
480 362-9760

(P-1159)
CONSTRUCTION CUSTOMER SERVICE
1320 N Hancock St Ste A, Anaheim (92807-1991)
PHONE.................................714 701-1858
Fax: 714 701-1868
Jackie Roth, *President*
EMP: 50

SQ FT: 3,600
SALES (est): 2.9MM **Privately Held**
WEB: www.constructionserviceinc.com
SIC: 1521 8711 7361 Single-family housing construction; building construction consultant; labor contractors (employment agency)

(P-1160)
CORONEL CONSTRUCTION INC
2328 Venice Dr, Delano (93215-9241)
PHONE.................................661 725-4400
Samuel Coronel, *President*
Ramona Coronel, *Treasurer*
EMP: 85
SALES (est): 6.4MM **Privately Held**
SIC: 1521 Single-family housing construction

(P-1161)
COUNTY OF RIVERSIDE
Facilities Mgmt
3133 Mission Inn Ave, Riverside (92507-4199)
PHONE.................................951 955-4800
Fax: 951 955-4828
Michael Sylvester, *Director*
Keith Beecher, *Administration*
Timothy Morris, *Info Tech Mgr*
Jesse Sarmiento, *Info Tech Mgr*
Steve Selbert, *Maint Spvr*
EMP: 325 **Privately Held**
SIC: 1521 9532 7349 Single-family housing construction; urban & community development; ; building maintenance services
PA: County Of Riverside
4080 Lemon St Fl 11
Riverside CA 92501
951 955-1110

(P-1162)
CUSTOM BUILDING PRODUCTS INC
7711 Center Ave Ste 500, Huntington Beach (92647-3076)
PHONE.................................562 598-8808
Fax: 626 965-1477
Thomas Nieto, *Manager*
EMP: 50
SALES (corp-wide): 342.4MM **Privately Held**
WEB: www.custombuildingproducts.com
SIC: 1521 3546 3423 New construction, single-family houses; power-driven handtools; hand & edge tools
PA: Custom Building Products, Inc.
7711 Center Ave Fl 5
Huntington Beach CA 92647
800 272-8786

(P-1163)
CUSTOM DESIGN CO INC
20969 Ventura Blvd # 217, Woodland Hills (91364-6617)
PHONE.................................818 507-5959
Fax: 818 507-0906
Mina Hamedani, *President*
Jalil Hamedani, *Vice Pres*
EMP: 50
SQ FT: 5,000
SALES (est): 4.4MM **Privately Held**
SIC: 1521 1542 1751 Single-family housing construction; general remodeling, single-family houses; nonresidential construction; cabinet & finish carpentry

(P-1164)
DE MATTEI CONSTRUCTION INC
1794 The Alameda, San Jose (95126-1729)
PHONE.................................408 295-7516
Mark De Mattei, *President*
John Hinton, *CFO*
Anna Arde, *Accounting Mgr*
▲ **EMP:** 60
SQ FT: 5,000
SALES (est): 10.6MM **Privately Held**
WEB: www.demattei.com
SIC: 1521 1542 Single-family housing construction; commercial & office building contractors

PRODUCTS & SERVICES SECTION

1521 - General Contractors, Single Family Houses County (P-1188)

(P-1165)
DENNIS ALLEN ASSOCIATES (PA)
201 N Milpas St, Santa Barbara (93103-3201)
PHONE.....................805 884-8777
Fax: 805 884-0043
Dennis W Allen, *President*
Brenda Allen, *Vice Pres*
Ian Cronshaw, *Vice Pres*
Bryan Henson, *General Mgr*
Jennifer Cushnie, *Admin Sec*
EMP: 95
SALES (est): 35.1MM **Privately Held**
WEB: www.dennisallenassociates.com
SIC: 1521 1542 General remodeling, single-family houses; new construction, single-family houses; commercial & office buildings, renovation & repair; commercial & office building, new construction

(P-1166)
DENNIS HYDE CONSTRUCTION INC
6212 Patton Way, Bakersfield (93308-2750)
PHONE.....................661 393-1077
Dennis Hyde, *President*
Julie Hyde, *Vice Pres*
EMP: 60
SALES (est): 5.5MM **Privately Held**
SIC: 1521 Single-family housing construction

(P-1167)
DEWHURST & ASSOCIATES
7533 Girard Ave, La Jolla (92037-5102)
P.O. Box 574 (92038-0574)
PHONE.....................858 456-5345
Fax: 858 454-0180
Donald Dewhurst, *Chairman*
Doug Dewhurst, *President*
Dave Dewhurst, *CEO*
Dan Sehlhorst, *Architect*
Teresa Tucker, *Manager*
EMP: 70
SQ FT: 1,200
SALES: 6.5MM **Privately Held**
WEB: www.dewhurst.com
SIC: 1521 New construction, single-family houses

(P-1168)
DOMUS CONSTRUCTION & DESIGN
Also Called: Statewide
8864 Fruitridge Rd, Sacramento (95826-9708)
PHONE.....................916 381-7500
Maksim R Yurtsan, *CEO*
Anna Kutsar, *Admin Sec*
EMP: 50 **EST:** 2008
SALES (est): 6.4MM **Privately Held**
SIC: 1521 Repairing fire damage, single-family houses

(P-1169)
E & E CO LTD
Also Called: Jla Home
2222 E Beamer St, Woodland (95776-6226)
PHONE.....................530 669-5991
EMP: 550
SALES (corp-wide): 219.7MM **Privately Held**
SIC: 1521 Single-family housing construction
PA: E & E Co., Ltd.
45875 Northport Loop E
Fremont CA 94538
510 490-9788

(P-1170)
EBC INC (PA)
Also Called: Ellis Building Contractors
219 Manhattan Beach Blvd, Manhattan Beach (90266-5324)
PHONE.....................310 753-6407
Brad Ellis, *President*
Patricia Ellis, *Admin Sec*
EMP: 95
SALES: 922K **Privately Held**
SIC: 1521 1542 New construction, single-family houses; commercial & office building, new construction

(P-1171)
EMERCON CONSTRUCTION INC (PA)
2906 E Coronado St, Anaheim (92806-2501)
PHONE.....................714 630-9615
Fax: 818 630-6071
Richard Anderson, *President*
Joan E Anderson, *Exec VP*
Frank Brady, *Exec VP*
Phil Roberts, *Marketing Staff*
Alan Lavine, *Superintendent*
EMP: 50
SQ FT: 30,000
SALES (est): 11MM **Privately Held**
WEB: www.emercon.com
SIC: 1521 Single-family housing construction

(P-1172)
EXCEL CONTRACTORS INC
Also Called: Progressin Drywall
348 E Avenue K8 Ste B, Lancaster (93535-4514)
PHONE.....................661 942-6944
Fax: 661 942-1781
John Rockey, *President*
Rose Rockey, *Vice Pres*
Jarrett Lemmon, *Project Mgr*
EMP: 100
SALES (est): 8.4MM **Privately Held**
SIC: 1521 1742 1542 Single-family home remodeling, additions & repairs; new construction, single-family houses; drywall; commercial & office building, new construction; commercial & office buildings, renovation & repair

(P-1173)
F R GHIANNI ENTERPRISES INC
Also Called: F R Ghianni Drywall Cnstr Co
1937 Friendship Dr Ste A, El Cajon (92020-1137)
PHONE.....................619 279-1073
Fax: 619 562-5313
Frank R Ghianni, *President*
Debby Weklem, *Admin Sec*
EMP: 100
SQ FT: 1,600
SALES (est): 5.6MM **Privately Held**
SIC: 1521 1771 1742 Single-family housing construction; concrete work; drywall

(P-1174)
FIELDSTONE COMMUNITIES INC
Also Called: Fieldstone Co, The
5465 Morehouse Dr Ste 250, San Diego (92121-3778)
PHONE.....................858 546-8081
Andrew Murphy, *Manager*
EMP: 50
SALES (corp-wide): 22.9MM **Privately Held**
WEB: www.fieldstone-homes.com
SIC: 1521 New construction, single-family houses
PA: Fieldstone Communities, Inc.
16 Technology Dr Ste 125
Irvine CA 92618
949 790-5400

(P-1175)
FIELDSTONE COMMUNITIES INC
16 Technology Dr Ste 125, Irvine (92618-2325)
PHONE.....................949 790-5400
Frank S Foster, *President*
Neah Bruck, *Manager*
EMP: 50
SALES (est): 4.8MM **Privately Held**
SIC: 1521 New construction, single-family houses

(P-1176)
FORT HILL CONSTRUCTION (PA)
12711 Ventura Blvd # 390, Studio City (91604-2491)
PHONE.....................323 656-7425
Fax: 323 654-0531
George Peper, *President*
Gordon Foote, *CFO*
James Kweskin, *Vice Pres*
Mike Mc Grail, *Vice Pres*
Scott Schuster, *Office Mgr*
▲ **EMP:** 70 **EST:** 1971
SQ FT: 4,000
SALES (est): 14.6MM **Privately Held**
WEB: www.forthill.com
SIC: 1521 Single-family housing construction

(P-1177)
FROMER INC
22225 Acorn St, Chatsworth (91311-4724)
PHONE.....................818 341-3896
Kim Fromer, *President*
Guy Zimmerman, *Vice Pres*
EMP: 70
SQ FT: 1,200
SALES (est): 6MM **Privately Held**
SIC: 1521 1522 Single-family housing construction; multi-family dwelling construction

(P-1178)
FRONTIER LAND COMPANIES
Also Called: Frontrs-Frnters Land Companies
10100 Trinity Pkwy # 420, Stockton (95219-7238)
PHONE.....................209 957-8112
Fax: 209 957-3618
Thomas Doucette, *President*
George K Gibson, *Vice Pres*
EMP: 50
SQ FT: 3,000
SALES (est): 7.2MM **Privately Held**
SIC: 1521 8742 6552 Single-family housing construction; real estate consultant; subdividers & developers

(P-1179)
G I L C INC
585 W Beach St, Watsonville (95076-5123)
P.O. Box 50085 (95077-5085)
PHONE.....................831 724-1011
David Wats, *President*
EMP: 50 **EST:** 1922
SALES (est): 4.6MM **Privately Held**
SIC: 1521 Single-family housing construction

(P-1180)
GALLAHER CONSTRUCTION INC
220 Concourse Blvd, Santa Rosa (95403-8210)
PHONE.....................707 535-3200
William P Gallaher, *President*
Joe Lin, *CFO*
Cynthia J Gallaher, *Admin Sec*
EMP: 50
SQ FT: 11,000
SALES: 30MM **Privately Held**
WEB: www.dflow.com
SIC: 1521 6552 New construction, single-family houses; land subdividers & developers, residential; land subdividers & developers, commercial

(P-1181)
GAMUT CONSTRUCTION COMPANY INC
9340 Santa Anita Ave # 105, Rancho Cucamonga (91730-6149)
PHONE.....................909 948-0500
Fax: 909 483-1640
Mark Scarlatelli, *President*
Mark Scalatelli, *President*
Michelynn Scalatelli, *Corp Secy*
James White, *Vice Pres*
EMP: 75
SQ FT: 2,500
SALES (est): 6.5MM **Privately Held**
SIC: 1521 6799 Single-family housing construction; general remodeling, single-family houses; real estate investors, except property operators

(P-1182)
GENE A GARCIA CONSTRUCTION
1663 E Poppy Hills Dr, Fresno (93730-4510)
PHONE.....................559 352-6173
Gene Aaron Garcia, *Principal*
EMP: 50 **EST:** 2010

SALES (est): 371.9K **Privately Held**
SIC: 1521 New construction, single-family houses

(P-1183)
GENERATION CONTRACTING & EMERG
13685 Stowe Dr Ste B, Poway (92064-8824)
PHONE.....................858 679-9928
Fax: 858 679-9948
Dorothy Ledesma, *President*
Paul Brieck, *Admin Sec*
EMP: 50
SQ FT: 9,940
SALES (est): 4.6MM **Privately Held**
WEB: www.contractorforlife.com
SIC: 1521 1542 Single-family home remodeling, additions & repairs; nonresidential construction

(P-1184)
GOLDEN ARROW CONSTRUCTION INC
Also Called: Five Star Labor
21213 Hawthorne Blvd B, Torrance (90503-5595)
PHONE.....................310 523-9056
Jill Bird, *President*
John Williams, *Manager*
EMP: 206
SQ FT: 2,000
SALES: 3MM **Privately Held**
SIC: 1521 7361 Single-family housing construction; employment agencies

(P-1185)
GRANTS CUSTOM CABINETS
7310 Kingsbury Rd, Templeton (93465-8304)
PHONE.....................805 466-9680
Grant Moore, *Owner*
EMP: 185
SALES (est): 4.5MM **Privately Held**
SIC: 1521 General remodeling, single-family houses

(P-1186)
GRANVILLE HOMES INC
1396 W Herndon Ave # 101, Fresno (93711-7126)
PHONE.....................559 268-2000
Fax: 559 436-1659
Darius Assemi, *CEO*
Farid Assemi, *President*
Derek Hayashi, *CFO*
Steve Rau, *Admin Sec*
Loren Spohr, *Admin Asst*
EMP: 60
SQ FT: 5,000
SALES (est): 17.9MM **Privately Held**
WEB: www.sommervilleestates.com
SIC: 1521 New construction, single-family houses

(P-1187)
GREYSTONE HOMES INC
6121 Bollinger Canyon Rd # 500, San Ramon (94583-5287)
PHONE.....................925 242-0811
Dale Billy, *President*
EMP: 250
SALES (corp-wide): 9.4B **Publicly Held**
SIC: 1521 Single-family housing construction
HQ: Greystone Homes, Inc
25 Enterprise
Aliso Viejo CA 92656
949 349-8000

(P-1188)
HAMBURGER HOME
3701 Wilshire Blvd # 900, Los Angeles (90010-2804)
PHONE.....................213 637-5000
Sandra Cohen, *Principal*
EMP: 155
SALES (corp-wide): 19MM **Privately Held**
SIC: 1521 Single-family housing construction
PA: Hamburger Home
7120 Franklin Ave
Los Angeles CA 90046
323 876-0550

1521 - General Contractors, Single Family Houses County (P-1189)

(P-1189)
HINERFELD-WARD INC
8931 Ellis Ave Ste B1, Los Angeles (90034-3336)
PHONE.....................310 842-7929
Tom Hinerfeld, *President*
Peter Borrego, *Vice Pres*
Joe Lerman, *Office Admin*
EMP: 70
SALES (est): 5.7MM **Privately Held**
WEB: www.hinerfeld-ward.com
SIC: **1521** Single-family housing construction

(P-1190)
HOMES BY SHABBIR KAZI
19631 Yorba Linda Blvd B, Yorba Linda (92886-3500)
PHONE.....................714 524-4131
Shabbir Kazi, *Owner*
EMP: 50
SALES (est): 2.8MM **Privately Held**
SIC: **1521** New construction, single-family houses

(P-1191)
HOWARD CDM
Also Called: Howard Construction
3750 Long Beach Blvd, Long Beach (90807-3310)
PHONE.....................562 427-4124
Martin D Howard, *President*
William G Burkett, *CFO*
Steven C Phillips, *Exec VP*
Sonya Rodriguez, *Office Mgr*
Christopher Duvali, *Project Mgr*
◆ EMP: 50
SQ FT: 7,000
SALES (est): 12.8MM **Privately Held**
WEB: www.howardcdm.net
SIC: **1521** Single-family housing construction

(P-1192)
JDF CONSTRUCTION INC
1114 E Truslow Ave, Fullerton (92831-4626)
PHONE.....................714 526-1120
John Fitzmaurice, *President*
▲ EMP: 50
SALES (est): 3.2MM **Privately Held**
SIC: **1521** Single-family housing construction

(P-1193)
JF SHEA CONSTRUCTION INC
17400 Clear Creek Rd, Redding (96001-5113)
P.O. Box 494519 (96049-4519)
PHONE.....................530 246-4292
Fax: 530 246-9940
Ed Kernaghan, *Vice Pres*
Laura Vuolo, *Vice Pres*
EMP: 60
SALES (corp-wide): 2B **Privately Held**
WEB: www.jfshea.com
SIC: **1521** New construction, single-family houses
HQ: J.F. Shea Construction, Inc.
655 Brea Canyon Rd
Walnut CA 91789
909 595-4397

(P-1194)
JF SHEA CONSTRUCTION INC
Also Called: Shea Homes
2 Ada Ste 200, Irvine (92618-5325)
PHONE.....................949 526-8792
Bob Yoder, *President*
Steven Seemann, *Vice Pres*
EMP: 75
SALES (corp-wide): 2B **Privately Held**
WEB: www.jfshea.com
SIC: **1521** Single-family housing construction
HQ: J.F. Shea Construction, Inc.
655 Brea Canyon Rd
Walnut CA 91789
909 595-4397

(P-1195)
JF SHEA CONSTRUCTION INC
Shea Business Properties
675 Brea Canyon Rd Ste 8, Walnut (91789-3065)
PHONE.....................909 594-0998
Bill Gaboury, *President*
Robert O Dell, *Treasurer*
Dennis Poulton, *Vice Pres*
Edmund H Shea, *Vice Pres*
Roger Standley, *Controller*
EMP: 50
SQ FT: 1,500
SALES (corp-wide): 2B **Privately Held**
WEB: www.jfshea.com
SIC: **1521** New construction, single-family houses
HQ: J.F. Shea Construction, Inc.
655 Brea Canyon Rd
Walnut CA 91789
909 595-4397

(P-1196)
JF SHEA CONSTRUCTION INC
Also Called: Shea Homes
6130 Monterey Hwy Ofc, San Jose (95138-1797)
PHONE.....................408 225-1475
Alfonso Garcia, *Manager*
EMP: 344
SQ FT: 3,500
SALES (corp-wide): 2B **Privately Held**
WEB: www.jfshea.com
SIC: **1521** New construction, single-family houses
HQ: J.F. Shea Construction, Inc.
655 Brea Canyon Rd
Walnut CA 91789
909 595-4397

(P-1197)
JF SHEA CONSTRUCTION INC
Also Called: Shea Homes
2580 Shea Center Dr, Livermore (94551-7547)
PHONE.....................925 245-3660
Layne Marceau, *President*
Leigh Tedlie, *Administration*
David Miller, *CIO*
Alex Baird, *Project Mgr*
Rick Bross, *Project Mgr*
EMP: 150
SALES (corp-wide): 2B **Privately Held**
WEB: www.jfshea.com
SIC: **1521** New construction, single-family houses
HQ: J.F. Shea Construction, Inc.
655 Brea Canyon Rd
Walnut CA 91789
909 595-4397

(P-1198)
JOSE CORONA
Also Called: Corona Mill Works & Cab Work
5572 Edison Ave, Chino (91710-6936)
PHONE.....................909 606-3168
EMP: 79
SQ FT: 4,000
SALES (est): 6.9MM **Privately Held**
SIC: **1521**

(P-1199)
JUAN LOPEZ
Also Called: All Types of Baseboard
3065 Beyer Blvd Ste B106, San Diego (92154-3499)
PHONE.....................619 428-3138
Fax: 619 428-1038
Juan Lopez, *Owner*
EMP: 100
SALES (est): 4.6MM **Privately Held**
SIC: **1521** 1542 Single-family housing construction; commercial & office building contractors

(P-1200)
K HOVNANIAN COMPANIES CAL INC (PA)
Also Called: K Hovnanian
400 Exchange Ste 200, Irvine (92602-1340)
PHONE.....................949 222-7700
Nicholas Pappas, *President*
EMP: 65
SALES (est): 103.4MM **Privately Held**
SIC: **1521** Single-family housing construction

(P-1201)
KATELLA PROPERTY SOLUTIONS INC
10801 6th St Ste 212, Rancho Cucamonga (91730-5987)
PHONE.....................909 896-4489
Reegis Christian, *President*
Danielle Whitton, *Vice Pres*
EMP: 50
SALES (est): 5.2MM **Privately Held**
SIC: **1521** 7349 1542 6411 Single-family home remodeling, additions & repairs; building maintenance services; commercial & office buildings, renovation & repair; insurance adjusters

(P-1202)
KB HOME GRATER LOS ANGELES INC (HQ)
10990 Wilshire Blvd # 700, Los Angeles (90024-3913)
PHONE.....................310 231-4000
Bruce Karatz, *CEO*
Leonard Leichnitz, *Vice Pres*
Jacqueline Sargent, *Info Tech Mgr*
Julie Richland, *Recruiter*
Ray Irani, *Director*
EMP: 90
SQ FT: 40,000
SALES (est): 59.7MM
SALES (corp-wide): 3B **Publicly Held**
SIC: **1521** 1522 Single-family home remodeling, additions & repairs; multi-family dwelling construction
PA: Kb Home
10990 Wilshire Blvd Fl 5
Los Angeles CA 90024
310 231-4000

(P-1203)
KERRY MCCAFFREY CNSTR INC
3720 Wally Allen Rd, Lincoln (95648-9744)
PHONE.....................916 645-1388
Kerry McCaffrey, *CEO*
EMP: 81
SALES (est): 7.5MM **Privately Held**
SIC: **1521** New construction, single-family houses

(P-1204)
LACONSTRUCTORA CO INC
2030 Broadway, Oceanside (92054-6516)
PHONE.....................760 439-7686
Fabio Marchi, *President*
EMP: 50 EST: 1997
SALES (est): 1.9MM **Privately Held**
SIC: **1521** New construction, single-family houses

(P-1205)
LARGO CONCRETE INC
1650 Hotel Cir N, San Diego (92108-2816)
PHONE.....................619 356-2142
EMP: 116
SALES (corp-wide): 93.6MM **Privately Held**
SIC: **1521** Single-family housing construction
PA: Largo Concrete, Inc.
2741 Walnut Ave Ste 110
Tustin CA 92780
714 731-3600

(P-1206)
LENNAR HOMES CALIFORNIA INC (DH)
Also Called: Lennar Builders
25 Enterprise Ste 400, Aliso Viejo (92656-2712)
PHONE.....................949 349-8000
Fax: 949 349-0781
Stuart Miller, *CEO*
Caroline Koschel, *General Mgr*
Linda Fitzpatrick, *Personnel Exec*
Bob Tummolo, *VP Opers*
EMP: 124
SQ FT: 12,000
SALES (est): 135.5MM
SALES (corp-wide): 9.4B **Publicly Held**
SIC: **1521** 6552 New construction, single-family houses; subdividers & developers
HQ: Lennar Homes Inc
730 Nw 107th Ave Ste 300
Miami FL 33172
305 559-4000

(P-1207)
M & R WOOD PRODUCTS INC
13312 Ranchero Rd 150, Oak Hills (92344-4812)
PHONE.....................909 460-1865
Michael Tognari, *CEO*
Bob Lodolo, *COO*
Rory Baker, *CFO*
EMP: 50
SQ FT: 7,000
SALES (est): 3.6MM **Privately Held**
WEB: www.mrwp.com
SIC: **1521** New construction, single-family houses

(P-1208)
M K S CONSTRUCTION INC
Also Called: Schetter Electric
471 Bannon St, Sacramento (95811-0203)
P.O. Box 1377 (95812-1377)
PHONE.....................916 446-2521
Frank Schetter, *President*
EMP: 152
SQ FT: 7,800
SALES (est): 6.3MM **Privately Held**
SIC: **1521** Single-family housing construction

(P-1209)
MACARTHUR TRANSIT COMMUNITY
345 Spear St Ste 700, San Francisco (94105-6136)
P.O. Box 190220 (94119-0220)
PHONE.....................415 989-1111
Susan Johnson, *Vice Pres*
EMP: 200
SALES (est): 1.1MM **Privately Held**
SIC: **1521** Single-family housing construction
PA: Bridge Economic Development Corporation
345 Spear St Ste 700
San Francisco CA 94105

(P-1210)
MACHADO & SONS CNSTR INC
1000 S Kilroy Rd, Turlock (95380-9589)
PHONE.....................209 632-5260
Manuel B Machado, *President*
Mary Machado, *Admin Sec*
EMP: 50
SALES (est): 12.9MM **Privately Held**
WEB: www.machadoandsons.com
SIC: **1521** 1542 1771 1541 New construction, single-family houses; commercial & office building, new construction; patio construction, concrete; industrial buildings & warehouses

(P-1211)
MAI CONSTRUCTION INC
50 Bonaventura Dr, San Jose (95134-2104)
PHONE.....................408 434-9880
Fax: 408 434-0598
Roger Mairose, *Ch of Bd*
Mike Mairose, *President*
Barry Paxton, *Vice Pres*
Julie MAI, *Executive*
Debbie Squires, *VP Finance*
EMP: 50
SQ FT: 38,036
SALES (est): 12.1MM **Privately Held**
WEB: www.maiindustries.com
SIC: **1521** Single-family housing construction

(P-1212)
MARCHBROOK BUILDING CO
Also Called: Grupe Co
3255 W March Ln Ste 400, Stockton (95219-2352)
PHONE.....................209 473-6084
Frank A Passadore, *President*
Greenlaw Grupe Jr, *CEO*
Donald Benioff, *CFO*
EMP: 60
SALES (est): 2.7MM **Privately Held**
SIC: **1521** New construction, single-family houses

▲ = Import ▼=Export
◆ =Import/Export

PRODUCTS & SERVICES SECTION
1521 - General Contractors, Single Family Houses County (P-1236)

(P-1213)
MARK R EGGEN CONSTRUCTION INC
3910 Calle Andalucia, San Clemente (92673-2606)
PHONE................949 661-2674
Mark Eggen, *President*
EMP: 50
SALES: 7.5MM **Privately Held**
SIC: 1521 Single-family housing construction

(P-1214)
MATRIX GROUP INTERNATIONAL INC
1520 W Cameron Ave, West Covina (91790-2713)
PHONE................626 960-6205
David Voyticky, *President*
Joseph Voyticky, *Treasurer*
EMP: 70
SALES (est): 2.5MM **Privately Held**
SIC: 1521 Single-family housing construction

(P-1215)
MCCLONE CONSTRUCTION COMPANY
4340 Product Dr, Cameron Park (95682-8492)
PHONE................703 433-9406
Fax: 530 677-3984
Scott McClone, *Branch Mgr*
Steve Donley, *Vice Pres*
Kevin Miller, *Vice Pres*
John Salluce, *Vice Pres*
Kim Wagner, *Office Mgr*
EMP: 62
SALES (corp-wide): 149.8MM **Privately Held**
SIC: 1521 Single-family housing construction
PA: Mcclone Construction Company
5170 Hillsdale Cir Ste B
El Dorado Hills CA 95762
916 358-5495

(P-1216)
MCMILLIN COMMUNITIES INC
Also Called: Temeku Hills
41687 Temeku Dr, Temecula (92591-3909)
PHONE................951 506-3303
Sonia Howard, *Branch Mgr*
EMP: 944
SALES (corp-wide): 119.8MM **Privately Held**
SIC: 1521 Single-family housing construction
PA: Mcmillin Communities, Inc.
2750 Womble Rd Ste 200
San Diego CA 92106
619 561-5275

(P-1217)
MCMILLIN CONSTRUCTION SVCS LP
2750 Womble Rd, San Diego (92106-6114)
PHONE................619 477-4170
Mark McMillin, *CEO*
Gary Arnold, *President*
Gary Beason, *CFO*
Joe Shiely, *Exec VP*
Karen Brassfield, *CIO*
EMP: 50
SQ FT: 29,000
SALES (est): 2.4MM **Privately Held**
SIC: 1521 Single-family housing construction

(P-1218)
MERCEDES DIAZ HOMES INC
7239 Washington Ave # 100, Whittier (90602-1432)
PHONE................562 698-7479
Mercedes Diaz, *President*
Ramon Diaz, *Vice Pres*
Debbi Hernandez, *Human Res Mgr*
EMP: 50
SALES (est): 7.4MM **Privately Held**
SIC: 1521 General remodeling, single-family houses

(P-1219)
MERITAGE HOMES CORPORATION
15937 Cusano Pl, Bakersfield (93314-6658)
PHONE................661 829-6739
EMP: 79
SALES (corp-wide): 2.5B **Publicly Held**
SIC: 1521 New construction, single-family houses
PA: Meritage Homes Corporation
8800 E Raintree Dr # 300
Scottsdale AZ 85260
480 515-8100

(P-1220)
MICHAEL BRUINGTON
9 Soledad Dr Ste E, Monterey (93940-6036)
PHONE................831 663-1772
Michael Bruington, *Exec VP*
EMP: 50
SALES (est): 4.2MM **Privately Held**
SIC: 1521 Single-family housing construction

(P-1221)
MID COAST BUILDERS SUPPLY INC
Also Called: New Mid Coast Builders
624 Calle Plano, Camarillo (93012-8528)
P.O. Box 3290 (93011-3290)
PHONE................805 484-3157
Fax: 805 484-0499
Ray E Cook, *President*
EMP: 140 EST: 1975
SQ FT: 5,000
SALES: 2.9MM **Privately Held**
WEB: www.midcoastbuilders.com
SIC: 1521 New construction, single-family houses

(P-1222)
MIDSTATE CONSTRUCTION CORP
1180 Holm Rd Ste A, Petaluma (94954-7120)
PHONE................707 762-3200
Fax: 707 762-0700
Roger Nelson, *President*
Jim Debolt, *CFO*
Monica Nelson, *Bd of Directors*
Wesley Barry II, *Vice Pres*
Patrick Draeger, *Vice Pres*
EMP: 80
SQ FT: 18,928
SALES (est): 32.7MM **Privately Held**
SIC: 1521 1541 1542 New construction, single-family houses; general remodeling, single-family houses; industrial buildings, new construction; renovation, remodeling & repairs: industrial buildings; commercial & office building, new construction; commercial & office buildings, renovation & repair

(P-1223)
MIKE ROVNER CONSTRUCTION INC
1758 Junction Ave Ste C, San Jose (95112-1022)
PHONE................408 453-4061
EMP: 152 **Privately Held**
SIC: 1521
PA: Mike Rovner Construction, Inc.
5400 Tech Cir
Moorpark CA 93021

(P-1224)
MILLENIA DEVELOPMENT
929 Bettina Way, San Jacinto (92582-2507)
PHONE................951 660-5691
Brett Stucker, *Owner*
EMP: 50
SALES: 2MM **Privately Held**
SIC: 1521 Single-family housing construction

(P-1225)
MJD CONSTRUCTION CORP
Also Called: M J D Concrete Works
28244 Dorothy Dr, Agoura Hills (91301-2605)
PHONE................818 575-9864
Fax: 818 575-9865
Mathias Di Cecco, *President*
Matt Dicecco, *Agent*
EMP: 60
SQ FT: 1,500
SALES (est): 7.4MM **Privately Held**
SIC: 1521 Single-family housing construction

(P-1226)
NICHOLAS LANE CONTRACTORS INC
1157 N Red Gum St, Anaheim (92806-2515)
PHONE................714 630-7630
Scott N Shaddix, *President*
Jo Ann Shaddix, *Corp Secy*
Veronica Gonzales, *Assistant*
EMP: 400
SQ FT: 5,000
SALES: 26MM **Privately Held**
WEB: www.nicholaslane.com
SIC: 1521 1542 New construction, single-family houses; commercial & office buildings, renovation & repair

(P-1227)
OLSON COMPANY LLC (PA)
Also Called: Olson Homes
3010 Old Ranch Pkwy # 100, Seal Beach (90740-2750)
PHONE................562 596-4770
Fax: 562 596-4703
Steve Olson,
Karen Hoover, *President*
Leslie Keller, *President*
Scott Laurie, *COO*
Mario Urzua, *CFO*
EMP: 99
SALES (est): 46.9MM **Privately Held**
SIC: 1521 Single-family housing construction

(P-1228)
OMNIGEN
Also Called: Handyman Connection
1740 W Katella Ave Ste G, Orange (92867-3434)
PHONE................714 288-0077
Fax: 714 288-2883
Rich Panitz, *President*
Linda Panitz, *Vice Pres*
Rich Patatz, *Manager*
EMP: 50
SQ FT: 1,000
SALES (est): 3.3MM **Privately Held**
WEB: www.omnigen.com
SIC: 1521 Single-family home remodeling, additions & repairs

(P-1229)
PACIFIC BAY PROPERTIES (PA)
4041 Macarthur Blvd # 500, Newport Beach (92660-2512)
PHONE................949 440-7200
Malcolm S McDonald, *President*
EMP: 50
SALES (est): 9.2MM **Privately Held**
SIC: 1521 Single-family housing construction

(P-1230)
PACIFIC DESIGN DIRECTIONS INC
Also Called: Pacific Interior Design
8171 E Kaiser Blvd, Anaheim (92808-2214)
PHONE................714 685-7766
Fax: 714 685-7799
Susan S Stoneburner, *President*
Kristen S Stolle, *Division Mgr*
Kristen Stoneburner, *Manager*
EMP: 50
SQ FT: 8,600
SALES: 15.3MM **Privately Held**
WEB: www.pacdesign.com
SIC: 1521 1731 7389 8712 Single-family housing construction; general electrical contractor; interior designer; architectural services

(P-1231)
PAGLIA & ASSOCIATES CNSTR
Also Called: Protech Construction
2651 Saturn St, Brea (92821-6703)
PHONE................714 982-5151
Vince Paglia, *President*
Kimm Paglia, *CFO*
Patrick Flynn, *Project Mgr*
J J Macdonald, *Project Mgr*
Norbert Nowak, *Project Mgr*
▲ EMP: 65
SQ FT: 6,500
SALES: 13.1MM **Privately Held**
WEB: www.protechconst.com
SIC: 1521 1542 New construction, single-family houses; commercial & office building, new construction

(P-1232)
PARAY DEVELOPMENT CORP
2030 Ardath Ave, Escondido (92027-3703)
PHONE................760 685-2462
Paul Raymond, *CEO*
Quincy Raymond, *General Mgr*
EMP: 180
SQ FT: 40,000
SALES: 55MM **Privately Held**
SIC: 1521 New construction, single-family houses

(P-1233)
PENINSULA CUSTOM HOMES INC
1401 Old County Rd, San Carlos (94070-5202)
PHONE................650 574-0241
Fax: 650 574-0273
Richard L Breaux, *CEO*
Bryan Murphy, *President*
Heline Grignon-Boulon, *Human Res Mgr*
Dianne Dalton, *Manager*
EMP: 60 EST: 1979
SALES (est): 10.5MM **Privately Held**
WEB: www.pchi.net
SIC: 1521 New construction, single-family houses

(P-1234)
PERENNIAL ENGRG & CNSTR INC
Also Called: Dm Construction Services
2907 Tech Ctr, Santa Ana (92705-5657)
PHONE................714 771-2103
David Peter Solomos, *CEO*
Doug Clark, *Corp Secy*
Mark Caviston, *Principal*
EMP: 350
SALES (est): 22.8MM **Privately Held**
SIC: 1521 8712 Single-family housing construction; architectural engineering

(P-1235)
PETERSEN BUILDERS INC
7706 Bell Rd Ste A, Windsor (95492-8546)
PHONE................707 838-3035
Fax: 707 838-4981
Talbert Petersen, *President*
Rex Petersen, *Treasurer*
Dwight Petersen, *Admin Sec*
Angella Cranse, *Accountant*
▲ EMP: 50
SQ FT: 1,300
SALES (est): 7.2MM **Privately Held**
SIC: 1521 1522 1542 1541 New construction, single-family houses; multi-family dwellings, new construction; commercial & office building, new construction; school building construction; food products manufacturing or packing plant construction

(P-1236)
PINNACLE BUILDERS INC
1911 Douglas Blvd Ste 85, Roseville (95661-3811)
PHONE................916 372-5000
Raymond Gregorich Jr, *President*
Howard Horrocks, *Vice Pres*
Liz Burek, *Finance Dir*

1521 - General Contractors, Single Family Houses County (P-1237)

PRODUCTS & SERVICES SECTION

EMP: 300
SQ FT: 3,000
SALES (est): 11.5MM **Privately Held**
WEB: www.pinnaclebuildersinc.com
SIC: **1521** 1542 1751 1522 New construction, single-family houses; commercial & office building, new construction; carpentry work; residential construction

(P-1237)
PORTER CONSTRUCTION CO INC
18931 Portola Dr Ste A, Salinas (93908-1295)
PHONE...................831 455-3020
Daniel Porter, *President*
Debra Porter, *Corp Secy*
EMP: 240
SALES (est): 11.2MM **Privately Held**
SIC: **1521** 1542 New construction, single-family houses; commercial & office building, new construction

(P-1238)
PRIMECARE QUALITY HM CARE INC
2372 Morse Ave, Irvine (92614-6234)
PHONE...................949 681-3515
Alex H Tsai, *President*
Hao Yu Tsai, *President*
EMP: 99
SALES (est): 3.6MM **Privately Held**
SIC: **1521** New construction, single-family houses

(P-1239)
PULTE HOME CORPORATION
6210 Stoneridge Mall Rd, Pleasanton (94588-3268)
PHONE...................925 249-3200
Fax: 925 485-3690
Can Carrol, *Manager*
Hallie Mullen, *VP Mktg*
Jessica Mayorga, *Manager*
Scott Weide, *Real Est Agnt*
EMP: 65
SQ FT: 12,000
SALES (corp-wide): 5.9B **Publicly Held**
SIC: **1521** New construction, single-family houses
HQ: Pulte Home Corporation
   3350 Peachtree Rd Ne
   Atlanta GA 30326
   248 647-2750

(P-1240)
QUALITY GROUP HOMES INC
Also Called: Consortium For Community Svcs
250 Dos Rios St Ste A1, Sacramento (95811-0442)
PHONE...................916 930-0066
Sarah Thomas, *Director*
EMP: 184
SALES (corp-wide): 8.6MM **Privately Held**
SIC: **1521** New construction, single-family houses
PA: Quality Group Homes, Inc.
   4928 E Clinton Way # 108
   Fresno CA 93727
   559 255-8519

(P-1241)
R J DAILEY CONSTRUCTION CO
401 1st St, Los Altos (94022-3607)
PHONE...................650 948-5196
Robert J Dailey, *President*
Christine Dailey, *Corp Secy*
Roger Allen, *Director*
EMP: 70
SQ FT: 2,000
SALES (est): 11.1MM **Privately Held**
SIC: **1521** New construction, single-family houses; general remodeling, single-family houses

(P-1242)
REDHORSE CONSTRUCTORS INC
36 Professional Ctr Pkwy, San Rafael (94903-2703)
PHONE...................415 492-2020
Fax: 415 492-2016
David J Warner, *President*
Jay Blumenfeld, *General Mgr*
Lauren Battung, *Administration*
Don Reinhardt, *Administration*
Alex Hayes, *Project Mgr*
EMP: 75
SQ FT: 3,500
SALES (est): 37.8MM **Privately Held**
WEB: www.redhorseconstructors.com
SIC: **1521** General remodeling, single-family houses; new construction, single-family houses

(P-1243)
REGIONAL CONNECTOR CONSTRS
1995 Agua Mansa Rd, Riverside (92509-2405)
PHONE...................951 368-6400
Patty Macias, *Office Mgr*
EMP: 50
SALES (est): 2MM **Privately Held**
SIC: **1521** New construction, single-family houses

(P-1244)
REYNEN & BARDIS CONSTRUCTION (PA)
10630 Mather Blvd, Mather (95655-4125)
PHONE...................916 366-3665
Fax: 916 364-3570
Chris Bardis, *President*
Dennis Lillard, *CFO*
Jeannie Ramirez, *Executive Asst*
John Reynen, *Admin Sec*
Ann Fraire, *Real Est Agnt*
EMP: 120
SALES (est): 48.3MM **Privately Held**
WEB: www.rbhome.us
SIC: **1521** 6552 New construction, single-family houses; land subdividers & developers, residential

(P-1245)
RICHMOND AMERICAN HOMES
16600 Sherman Way Ste 180, Van Nuys (91406-3725)
PHONE...................818 908-3267
Fax: 818 374-5150
Bob Shiota, *Exec VP*
EMP: 50
SALES (corp-wide): 1.8B **Publicly Held**
SIC: **1521** Single-family housing construction
HQ: Richmond American Homes
   5171 California Ave # 120
   Irvine CA 92617
   949 467-2600

(P-1246)
RICHMOND AMERICAN HOMES
5171 California Ave # 120, Irvine (92617-3036)
PHONE...................949 467-2600
EMP: 50
SALES (corp-wide): 1.8B **Publicly Held**
SIC: **1521** Single-family housing construction
HQ: Richmond American Homes
   5171 California Ave # 120
   Irvine CA 92617
   949 467-2600

(P-1247)
RIDGESIDE CONSTRUCTION INC
Also Called: Ridgeside Finishing
4345 E Lowell St Ste A, Ontario (91761-2223)
P.O. Box 1237 (91762-0237)
PHONE...................909 218-7593
Dan Zita, *President*
Kevin Hammond, *Vice Pres*
EMP: 65
SALES (est): 125.2MM **Privately Held**
SIC: **1521** Single-family housing construction

(P-1248)
ROBERT MORKEN CONSTRUCTION
1300 Regency Way Ste 59, Kings Beach (96143)
PHONE...................530 386-1512
Robert Morken, *President*
EMP: 50
SALES: 10MM **Privately Held**
SIC: **1521** 1542 New construction, single-family houses; commercial & office building, new construction

(P-1249)
RYLAND HMES INLND EMPIRE CSTMR
Also Called: Home Building
1250 Corona Pointe Ct # 100, Corona (92879-2099)
PHONE...................951 273-3473
Fax: 951 273-3472
Linda Edwards, *President*
Coleen Burnette, *Manager*
Karen Carter, *Manager*
EMP: 80
SALES (est): 6.9MM **Privately Held**
SIC: **1521** Single-family housing construction

(P-1250)
S TAYLOR CONSTRUCTION INC
23905 Clinton Keith Rd, Wildomar (92595-7897)
PHONE...................310 291-4505
Steve Taylor, *President*
EMP: 103
SALES: 1MM **Privately Held**
SIC: **1521** Single-family housing construction

(P-1251)
SAVOY CONTRACTORS GROUP INC
Also Called: Ritz Companies
8905 Research Dr, Irvine (92618-4237)
PHONE...................949 753-1919
Fax: 949 753-1955
Robert Ritz Sadeghi, *Ch of Bd*
Janet Bryant, *Office Mgr*
Dena Ortiz, *Office Mgr*
Robert Sadeghi, *Senior Mgr*
Mariangela Bonk, *Director*
EMP: 175
SQ FT: 2,000
SALES (est): 14.3MM **Privately Held**
WEB: www.theritzcompanies.com
SIC: **1521** 7349 Single-family housing construction; building maintenance services

(P-1252)
SEARS HOME IMPRV PDTS INC
9586 Dist Ave Ste F, San Diego (92121)
PHONE...................858 790-7721
Jerry Hanosh, *Branch Mgr*
EMP: 52
SALES (corp-wide): 25.1MM **Publicly Held**
SIC: **1521** General remodeling, single-family houses
HQ: Sears Home Improvement Products, Inc.
   1024 Florida Central Pkwy
   Longwood FL 32750
   407 767-0990

(P-1253)
SELIG CONSTRUCTION CORP
337 Huss Dr, Chico (95928-8209)
PHONE...................530 893-5898
M Scott Selig, *President*
Kendra Hudson, *Financial Exec*
▲ EMP: 50
SALES (est): 5.8MM **Privately Held**
WEB: www.seligconstruction.com
SIC: **1521** General remodeling, single-family houses

(P-1254)
SHAPELL INDUSTRIES LLC
Also Called: Shapell's Home Center
11280 Corbin Ave, Northridge (91326-4120)
PHONE...................818 366-1132
Nathan Shapell, *Ch of Bd*
EMP: 50
SALES (corp-wide): 4.1B **Publicly Held**
WEB: www.shapell.com
SIC: **1521** Single-family housing construction
HQ: Shapell Industries, Llc
   8383 Wilshire Blvd # 700
   Beverly Hills CA 90211
   323 655-7330

(P-1255)
SHEA HOMES AT MONTAGE LLC
655 Brea Canyon Rd, Walnut (91789-3078)
PHONE...................909 594-9500
EMP: 81 EST: 2013
SALES: 3.6MM
SALES (corp-wide): 2B **Privately Held**
SIC: **1521** Single-family housing construction
HQ: Shea Homes Limited Partnership, A California Limited Partnership
   655 Brea Canyon Rd
   Walnut CA 91789

(P-1256)
SHEA HOMES LMTD PARTNERSHIP A (HQ)
655 Brea Canyon Rd, Walnut (91789-3078)
PHONE...................909 594-9500
Jim Shontere, *Partner*
John F Shea LP, *Partner*
Robert Odell, *Treasurer*
Bruce Verker, *CIO*
Steve Rilee, *Info Tech Dir*
EMP: 50
SQ FT: 29,000
SALES: 1.1B
SALES (corp-wide): 2B **Privately Held**
WEB: www.highlandsranch.com
SIC: **1521** Single-family housing construction
PA: J. F. Shea Co., Inc.
   655 Brea Canyon Rd
   Walnut CA 91789
   909 594-9500

(P-1257)
SHEEHAN CONSTRUCTION INC
477 Devlin Rd Ste 108, NAPA (94558-7511)
PHONE...................707 603-2610
Steve Mosiman, *President*
Tom Sheehan, *Vice Pres*
EMP: 500
SALES (est): 42.2MM **Privately Held**
WEB: www.sheehanconstruction.com
SIC: **1521** Single-family housing construction

(P-1258)
SHIMMICK CONSTRUCTION CO INC
16481 Scientific Bldg 2, Irvine (92618-4355)
PHONE...................510 777-5000
Trina Clay, *Principal*
Justin Watkins, *Engineer*
Taylor Casaccia, *Business Mgr*
William Corn, *Opers Mgr*
Robert Knapp, *Superintendent*
EMP: 676
SALES (corp-wide): 319.6MM **Privately Held**
SIC: **1521** Single-family housing construction
PA: Shimmick Construction Company Incorporated
   8201 Edgewater Dr Ste 202
   Oakland CA 94621
   510 777-5000

(P-1259)
SHIMMICK CONSTRUCTION CO INC
6535 Calaveras Rd, Sunol (94586-9530)
PHONE...................925 862-1901
EMP: 193
SALES (corp-wide): 319.6MM **Privately Held**
SIC: **1521** Single-family housing construction
PA: Shimmick Construction Company Incorporated
   8201 Edgewater Dr Ste 202
   Oakland CA 94621
   510 777-5000

▲ = Import ▼ = Export
◆ = Import/Export

PRODUCTS & SERVICES SECTION
1521 - General Contractors, Single Family Houses County (P-1284)

(P-1260)
SIGNATURE INTERIORS INC
1587 E Bentley Dr Ste 101, Corona (92879-1788)
PHONE.....................................951 340-2200
Fax: 951 340-3366
John French, *President*
Jody French, *Shareholder*
Leah Ortiz, *Controller*
Jennifer Ashman, *Purch Agent*
Marisa Gonzalez, *Manager*
EMP: 310
SQ FT: 15,000
SALES (est): 14.6MM **Privately Held**
WEB: www.signatureinteriorsinc.com
SIC: **1521** Single-family housing construction

(P-1261)
SKYVA CONSTRUCTION INC
5781 Old Antelope N Rd, Antelope (95843-3962)
P.O. Box 8094, Citrus Heights (95621-8094)
PHONE.....................................916 726-4999
Fax: 916 726-4929
Vladimir Andrichuk, *President*
EMP: 50
SALES (est): 4.6MM **Privately Held**
WEB: www.skyvaconstruction.com
SIC: **1521** Single-family housing construction

(P-1262)
SMA BUILDERS INC
16134 Leadwell St, Van Nuys (91406-3424)
PHONE.....................................818 994-8306
Shawn Antin, *President*
Diana Antin, *Vice Pres*
EMP: 50
SALES (est): 8.5MM **Privately Held**
SIC: **1521** Single-family housing construction

(P-1263)
STEVEN N LEDSON
Also Called: Ledson Winery & Vineyards
7335 Sonoma Hwy, Santa Rosa (95409-6269)
P.O. Box 653, Kenwood (95452-0653)
PHONE.....................................707 537-3810
Steven N Ledson, *Owner*
Amy Ackerman, *Executive*
Karla Reed, *Human Res Dir*
EMP: 60
SALES (est): 5.9MM **Privately Held**
SIC: **1521 2084** Single-family housing construction; wines

(P-1264)
STOCKER & ALLAIRE INC
21 Mandeville Ct, Monterey (93940-5745)
PHONE.....................................831 375-1890
Fax: 831 375-1480
David Stocker, *President*
David Allaire, *CFO*
EMP: 50
SQ FT: 3,200
SALES (est): 9.2MM **Privately Held**
WEB: www.stockerallaire.com
SIC: **1521** General remodeling, single-family houses

(P-1265)
STRUCTURE CNSTR & DEV INC
Also Called: Structure Cnstr & Rmdlg Co
4420 Hotel Circle Ct, San Diego (92108-3411)
PHONE.....................................619 846-2555
Dean Patel, *CEO*
EMP: 99
SALES (est): 4.5MM **Privately Held**
SIC: **1521** Single-family housing construction

(P-1266)
SUMMERHILL CONSTRUCTION CO
Also Called: Summerhill Homes
3000 Executive Pkwy # 450, San Ramon (94583-4255)
PHONE.....................................925 244-7520
Roger Menard, *President*
EMP: 50
SQ FT: 45,000
SALES (est): 4.2MM
SALES (corp-wide): 62.6MM **Privately Held**
WEB: www.summerhillhomes.com
SIC: **1521** New construction, single-family houses
HQ: Summerhill Homes Llc
3000 Executive Pkwy # 450
San Ramon CA 94583
925 244-7500

(P-1267)
SUPERIOR CONSTRUCTION INC
265 N Joy St Ste 100, Corona (92879-0601)
P.O. Box 1148 (92878-1148)
PHONE.....................................951 808-8780
Fax: 951 808-8787
Kenneth Day, *President*
Don Mc Lellan, *Sls & Mktg Exec*
Don McLellan, *Sls & Mktg Exec*
EMP: 100
SQ FT: 3,000
SALES (est): 9MM **Privately Held**
SIC: **1521 1542** New construction, single-family houses; commercial & office building, new construction

(P-1268)
SUPPORT FOR HOME INC
1333 Howe Ave Ste 206, Sacramento (95825-3362)
PHONE.....................................530 792-8484
Bert Cave, *Principal*
Carlotta Sanchez, *Principal*
EMP: 50
SALES (est): 3.3MM **Privately Held**
SIC: **1521** Single-family housing construction

(P-1269)
SWINERTON BUILDERS INC
2300 Clayton Rd Ste 800, Concord (94520-2166)
PHONE.....................................925 602-6400
Jeffrey Hoopes, *CEO*
Gary Rafferty, *President*
Linda Schowalter, *CFO*
Charlene Atkinson, *Principal*
EMP: 81
SALES (est): 24.4MM **Privately Held**
SIC: **1521** New construction, single-family houses

(P-1270)
T B PENICK & SONS INC
41892 Enterprise Cir S, Temecula (92590-4822)
PHONE.....................................951 719-1492
EMP: 203
SALES (corp-wide): 139.2MM **Privately Held**
SIC: **1521** General remodeling, single-family houses
PA: T. B. Penick & Sons, Inc.
15435 Innovation Dr # 100
San Diego CA 92128
858 558-1800

(P-1271)
THOMPSON/BROOKS INC
151 Vermont St Ste 9, San Francisco (94103-5184)
PHONE.....................................415 581-2600
Fax: 415 581-2601
Judith A Thompson, *CEO*
R Bruce Clymer, *President*
Clifton B Shoolroy, *CFO*
Greg Hall, *Vice Pres*
EMP: 50
SQ FT: 5,000
SALES (est): 9.3MM **Privately Held**
WEB: www.thompsonbrooks.com
SIC: **1521 1542 1541 1531** Single-family housing construction; general remodeling, single-family houses; nonresidential construction; industrial buildings & warehouses; operative builders

(P-1272)
TIMBER WORKS CONSTRUCTION INC
7031 Roseville Rd Ste A, Sacramento (95842-1670)
PHONE.....................................916 786-6666
Scott D Robbins, *President*
EMP: 125 EST: 2008
SALES (est): 13.5MM **Privately Held**
SIC: **1521 1542** Single-family housing construction; nonresidential construction

(P-1273)
TOLL BROTHERS INC
Also Called: Toll Brothers Division Office
6800 Koll Center Pkwy # 320, Pleasanton (94566-7053)
PHONE.....................................925 855-0260
Fax: 925 855-9927
Rick Nelson, *Branch Mgr*
EMP: 60
SALES (corp-wide): 4.1B **Publicly Held**
WEB: www.tollbros.com
SIC: **1521** New construction, single-family houses; townhouse construction
PA: Toll Brothers, Inc.
250 Gibraltar Rd
Horsham PA 19044
215 938-8000

(P-1274)
TORRES GENERAL INC
9484 Mission Park Pl, Santee (92071-5610)
PHONE.....................................619 448-8900
Fax: 619 448-8955
Carlos Torres Jr, *President*
Maria Morfin, *Financial Exec*
EMP: 100
SALES (est): 7.5MM **Privately Held**
SIC: **1521** Single-family housing construction

(P-1275)
TURNER CONSTRUCTION COMPANY
555 S Flower St Ste 4220, Los Angeles (90071-2438)
PHONE.....................................213 891-3000
Fax: 213 486-9857
Michael O'Brien, *Senior VP*
John Hook, *Purch Mgr*
EMP: 70
SALES (corp-wide): 506.6MM **Privately Held**
SIC: **1521** Single-family housing construction
HQ: Turner Construction Company Inc
375 Hudson St Fl 6
New York NY 10014
212 229-6000

(P-1276)
US BEST REPAIR SERVICE INC
Also Called: US Best Repairs
2004 Mcgaw Ave, Irvine (92614-0911)
PHONE.....................................888 750-2378
Mark Zaverl, *CEO*
Kyle Keller, *COO*
Jeff Bougher, *Vice Pres*
Samuel Tucci, *Business Mgr*
Don Frank, *Manager*
EMP: 101
SALES (est): 14.3MM **Privately Held**
WEB: www.usbestrepairs.com
SIC: **1521 1522 1542** Single-family home remodeling, additions & repairs; remodeling, multi-family dwellings; commercial & office buildings, renovation & repair

(P-1277)
VALLEYWIDE CONSTRUCTION INC
284 W Lester Ave, Clovis (93619-3788)
PHONE.....................................559 834-6212
Christina Birdsell, *President*
John Birdsell, *Treasurer*
EMP: 150
SQ FT: 5,000
SALES (est): 6.8MM **Privately Held**
SIC: **1521 1751** New construction, single-family houses; framing contractor

(P-1278)
VAN ACKER CNSTR ASSOC INC
1060 Redwood Hwy Frntg Rd, Mill Valley (94941-1613)
PHONE.....................................415 383-5589
Fax: 415 383-5597
Gary Van Acker, *President*
Pamela Blier, *Vice Pres*
Matt Evilsizer, *Project Mgr*
Allison Ewald, *Project Mgr*
Neema Haghshenas, *Project Mgr*
EMP: 134
SQ FT: 15,000
SALES (est): 24.6MM **Privately Held**
WEB: www.vanacker.com
SIC: **1521** New construction, single-family houses

(P-1279)
VASONA MANAGEMENT INC
Also Called: Vasonic Construction
37390 Central Mont Pl, Fremont (94538)
PHONE.....................................510 413-0091
Fax: 510 413-0097
Dan Scharnow, *Vice Pres*
EMP: 80
SALES (corp-wide): 31MM **Privately Held**
WEB: www.vasonamanagement.com
SIC: **1521** Single-family housing construction
PA: Vasona Management, Inc.
18 E Main St
Los Gatos CA 95030
408 354-4200

(P-1280)
VENTURA STREETS DEPT
Also Called: City Hall
336 San Jon Rd, Ventura (93001-3233)
PHONE.....................................805 652-4515
Fax: 805 653-6655
Ron Calkins, *Director*
EMP: 100 EST: 1998
SALES (est): 3.1MM **Privately Held**
SIC: **1521 1611** General remodeling, single-family houses; highway & street construction

(P-1281)
WARMINGTON RESIDENTIAL CAL INC
3090 Pullman St, Costa Mesa (92626-5901)
PHONE.....................................714 557-5511
James Warmington Jr, *President*
Mike Riddlesberger, *CFO*
Matt Tingler, *Vice Pres*
EMP: 150
SALES (est): 23MM **Privately Held**
SIC: **1521** Single-family housing construction

(P-1282)
WATSON ME INC
26871 Henry Rd, Fellows (93224-9794)
PHONE.....................................661 768-1717
EMP: 94
SQ FT: 1,088
SALES (est): 51.7MM **Privately Held**
SIC: **1521** New construction, single-family houses
PA: Watson Me Inc
801 Kern St
Taft CA 93268
661 763-5254

(P-1283)
WEST COAST ARBORISTS INC
8524 Commerce Ave Ste B, San Diego (92121-2670)
PHONE.....................................858 566-4204
EMP: 244
SALES (corp-wide): 293.2MM **Privately Held**
SIC: **1521 0783** Single-family home remodeling, additions & repairs; ornamental shrub & tree services
PA: West Coast Arborists, Inc.
2200 E Via Burton
Anaheim CA 92806
714 991-1900

(P-1284)
WEST HILLS CONSTRUCTION INC
423 Jenks Cir Ste 101, Corona (92880-2540)
PHONE.....................................800 515-5270
Ross L Wood, *President*
Rusty Wood, *Vice Pres*
EMP: 50
SQ FT: 7,500

1521 - General Contractors, Single Family Houses County (P-1285)

PRODUCTS & SERVICES SECTION

SALES: 7.1MM **Privately Held**
SIC: **1521** 4911 1623 1731 New construction, single-family houses; electric services; communication line & transmission tower construction; electrical work; operative builders; power plant construction

(P-1285)
WESTCOR CONSTRUCTION OF CAL
2351 W Lugonia Ave Ste D, Redlands (92374-5014)
PHONE.................................909 796-8900
Michael A Coronado, *President*
Kevin R Booth, *CFO*
James D Hammer, *Treasurer*
Robert Keele, *General Mgr*
Feliciano Sanchez, *Controller*
EMP: 120
SQ FT: 4,600
SALES: 13.9MM
SALES (corp-wide): 30.5MM **Privately Held**
SIC: **1521** Single-family housing construction
PA: Westcor Construction
5620 Stephanie St
Las Vegas NV 89122
702 433-1414

(P-1286)
WOOD CASTLE CONSTRUCTION INC
770 W Golden Grove Way, Covina (91722-3255)
PHONE.................................626 966-8600
Fax: 626 966-9100
Daniel Toro, *President*
Victor Quintana, *Treasurer*
Julio Toro, *Vice Pres*
EMP: 50
SALES (est): 5.9MM **Privately Held**
SIC: **1521** Single-family housing construction

(P-1287)
XL CONSTRUCTION CORPORATION
9245 Laguna Springs Dr # 135, Elk Grove (95758-7991)
PHONE.................................916 282-2900
Eric Raff, *Branch Mgr*
EMP: 191
SALES (corp-wide): 175.6MM **Privately Held**
SIC: **1521** Single-family housing construction
PA: XL Construction Corporation
851 Buckeye Ct
Milpitas CA 95035
408 240-6000

(P-1288)
ZOHAR CONSTRUCTION INC
Also Called: Quality Construction
4272 Pasadero Pl, Tarzana (91356-5218)
P.O. Box 4522, Valley Village (91617-0522)
PHONE.................................818 609-7473
Zohar Haykeen, *President*
EMP: 100 EST: 2011
SALES (est): 4.4MM **Privately Held**
SIC: **1521** Single-family housing construction

1522 General Contractors, Residential Other Than Single Family

(P-1289)
ALL-PRO REMODELING
706 N Tustin St, Orange (92867-7149)
PHONE.................................714 288-1314
Fax: 714 288-1347
Dale Terry, *President*
John Johnston, *General Mgr*
John Ston, *General Mgr*
Eric Johnson, *Manager*
▲ EMP: 56
SQ FT: 5,000
SALES (est): 6.5MM **Privately Held**
WEB: www.allproremodeling.com
SIC: **1522** Hotel/motel & multi-family home renovation & remodeling

(P-1290)
AMES CONSTRUCTION INC
14427 Meridian Pkwy, March ARB (92518-3014)
PHONE.................................951 697-9094
Jeff Geist, *President*
EMP: 303
SALES (corp-wide): 1B **Privately Held**
SIC: **1522** 1521 1611 1542 Residential construction; single-family housing construction; highway & street construction; nonresidential construction
PA: Ames Construction, Inc.
14420 County Road 5
Burnsville MN 55306
952 435-7106

(P-1291)
APEX DEVELOPMENT INC
23679 Calabasas Rd # 764, Calabasas (91302-1502)
PHONE.................................818 887-0400
Anthony A Nowaid, *President*
Maria Noble, *Controller*
EMP: 138
SALES (est): 9MM **Privately Held**
SIC: **1522** 1521 1541 1542 Residential construction; single-family housing construction; industrial buildings & warehouses; nonresidential construction; highway & street construction; bridge, tunnel & elevated highway

(P-1292)
APPLIED MATERIALS INC
3340 Scott Blvd, Santa Clara (95054-3101)
PHONE.................................408 727-5555
Fax: 408 986-7775
Gary E Dickerson, *President*
Aron Rosenfeld, *Info Tech Dir*
Sean Herbert, *Software Engr*
Haoyi Chen, *Technician*
Suhas Bhoski, *Engineer*
EMP: 77 EST: 2013
SALES (est): 7.3MM **Privately Held**
SIC: **1522** Hotel/motel & multi-family home construction

(P-1293)
ARNEL DEVELOPMENT COMPANY
3146 Tiger Run Ct Ste 108, Carlsbad (92010-6696)
PHONE.................................760 599-6111
Carol Cole, *Principal*
EMP: 62
SALES (corp-wide): 16.6MM **Privately Held**
SIC: **1522** Residential construction
PA: Arnel Development Company
949 S Coast Dr Ste 600
Costa Mesa CA 92626
714 481-5000

(P-1294)
ASHWOOD CONSTRUCTION INC
5755 E Kings Canyon Rd # 110, Fresno (93727-4744)
PHONE.................................559 253-7240
Fax: 559 253-7244
Michael J Conway Jr, *President*
EMP: 50
SQ FT: 1,200
SALES (est): 12.1MM **Privately Held**
WEB: www.ashwoodco.com
SIC: **1522** Multi-family dwellings, new construction

(P-1295)
AXIS SERVICES INC
Also Called: Axis Construction
2566 Barrington Ct, Hayward (94545-1133)
PHONE.................................510 732-6111
Fax: 510 732-6222
Bizhan Mahallati, *CEO*
Parisa Mahallati, *Vice Pres*
Conor Meyers, *Vice Pres*
Thomas Ordmandy, *Project Mgr*
Harlan K AIA, *Technology*
EMP: 110
SQ FT: 10,000
SALES (est): 17.3MM **Privately Held**
WEB: www.axisconstruction.com
SIC: **1522** Residential construction

(P-1296)
BILL BROWN CONSTRUCTION CO
242 Phelan Ave, San Jose (95112-6109)
PHONE.................................408 297-3738
Fax: 408 297-3848
William Brown, *President*
EMP: 100
SALES (est): 14.7MM **Privately Held**
SIC: **1522** Residential construction

(P-1297)
BLH CONSTRUCTION COMPANY
21031 Ventura Blvd # 200, Woodland Hills (91364-6517)
PHONE.................................818 905-3837
Charles Brumbaugh, *CEO*
Brian Holland, *COO*
EMP: 150
SALES (est): 27.1MM **Privately Held**
WEB: www.blhconstruction.com
SIC: **1522** Apartment building construction

(P-1298)
BROWN CONSTRUCTION INC
1465 Entp Blvd Ste 100, West Sacramento (95691)
P.O. Box 980700 (95798-0700)
PHONE.................................916 374-8616
Fax: 916 374-8616
Ron Brown, *President*
Matt Carota, *CFO*
Kathryn Mc Guire, *Treasurer*
Matt Defazio, *Vice Pres*
Liz McCapes, *Vice Pres*
EMP: 71
SQ FT: 11,000
SALES: 198MM **Privately Held**
WEB: www.brown-construction.com
SIC: **1522** 1542 Apartment building construction; nonresidential construction

(P-1299)
BRUCE OLSON CONSTRUCTION INC
7320 River Rd, Tahoe City (96145)
P.O. Box 1518 (96145-1518)
PHONE.................................530 581-1087
Bruce Olson, *President*
Susan Kolak, *Bookkeeper*
EMP: 90
SQ FT: 3,050
SALES (est): 5.3MM **Privately Held**
WEB: www.bruceolsonconstruction.com
SIC: **1522** Residential construction

(P-1300)
CALATLANTIC GROUP INC
Also Called: Standard Pacific Homes
15360 Barranca Pkwy, Irvine (92618-2215)
PHONE.................................949 789-1600
Ernie Bitto, *IT/INT Sup*
EMP: 60
SALES (corp-wide): 3.5B **Publicly Held**
WEB: www.standardpacifichomes.com
SIC: **1522** Residential construction
PA: Calatlantic Group, Inc.
15360 Barranca Pkwy
Irvine CA 92618
949 789-1600

(P-1301)
CJ CONSTRUCTION & DEV INC
78206 Varner Rd Ste D, Palm Desert (92211-4136)
PHONE.................................760 247-6868
Lloyd James, *President*
EMP: 52
SQ FT: 2,200
SALES: 5MM **Privately Held**
SIC: **1522** Apartment building construction

(P-1302)
CKL CONSTRUCTION INC
967 W Hedding St, San Jose (95126-1257)
PHONE.................................408 244-7042
Fax: 408 249-0372
Cortland C Lanning Jr, *President*
Tanya Camarena, *Manager*
EMP: 300
SQ FT: 3,133
SALES (est): 16.9MM **Privately Held**
SIC: **1522** 1611 Condominium construction; general contractor, highway & street construction

(P-1303)
COBALT CONSTRUCTION COMPANY
2259 Ward Ave Ste 200, Simi Valley (93065-1880)
PHONE.................................805 577-6222
Fax: 805 249-7599
Darin Kruse, *CEO*
John Beaudion, *CTO*
Matt Bryson, *Info Tech Mgr*
Eduardo Garcia, *Technology*
Andrew Persons, *Project Engr*
▲ EMP: 70
SQ FT: 43,000
SALES (est): 32.5MM **Privately Held**
SIC: **1522** 8711 1542 Multi-family dwellings, new construction; construction & civil engineering; commercial & office building, new construction; specialized public building contractors

(P-1304)
COUNTRY BUILDERS INC
Also Called: Country Builders Construction
5915 Graham Ct, Livermore (94550-9710)
PHONE.................................925 373-1020
Fax: 925 373-1019
Weldon Offill, *President*
Keith Offill, *CFO*
Iris Garcia, *Manager*
EMP: 150
SQ FT: 5,000
SALES (est): 14.7MM **Privately Held**
WEB: www.countrybuilders.com
SIC: **1522** Apartment building construction; remodeling, multi-family dwellings

(P-1305)
COVE BUILDERS INC
3329 W Castor St, Santa Ana (92704-3907)
PHONE.................................714 436-2973
Ed Holmes II, *President*
Timothy Reynolds, *Treasurer*
Pierre J Baptiste, *Superintendent*
EMP: 120
SALES (est): 7.9MM **Privately Held**
SIC: **1522** 1542 Residential construction; nonresidential construction; single-family housing construction

(P-1306)
DANCO BUILDERS INC
5251 Ericson Way Ste A, Arcata (95521-9274)
PHONE.................................707 822-9000
Fax: 707 822-9596
Daniel J Johnson, *President*
Kendra Johnson, *Shareholder*
Kirk Heberly, *Vice Pres*
Bill Bowman, *Project Mgr*
Collen O Sullivan, *Manager*
EMP: 100
SQ FT: 15,000
SALES (est): 16.2MM **Privately Held**
WEB: www.dancobuilders.com
SIC: **1522** 1542 Apartment building construction; commercial & office building contractors

(P-1307)
DINYARI CONSTRUCTION INC
500 Phelan Ave, San Jose (95112-2506)
PHONE.................................408 289-5400
Toll Free:.................................888 -
Fax: 408 289-5596
Farbod Buck Dinyari, *President*
Katayoon Dinyari, *Vice Pres*
Daniel Perez, *Sales Staff*
EMP: 50
SQ FT: 12,000
SALES (est): 5.5MM **Privately Held**
WEB: www.dinyari.com
SIC: **1522** 1542 Residential construction; commercial & office building contractors

1522 - General Contractors, Residential Other Than Single Family County (P-1332)

(P-1308)
DOUGLAS ROSS CONSTRUCTION INC
1875 S Bascom Ave # 2400, Campbell (95008-2356)
PHONE..................408 429-7700
Fax: 650 470-4701
J Douglas Ross, *President*
Andrew Maurer, *CFO*
Jeffrey Jelniker, *Vice Pres*
Scott Small, *Vice Pres*
Brianne Lynch, *Executive Asst*
EMP: 55
SQ FT: 7,158
SALES (est): 12.4MM **Privately Held**
SIC: **1522** Residential construction; hotel/motel & multi-family home renovation & remodeling

(P-1309)
EDEN HOUSING INC
22645 Grand St, Hayward (94541-5031)
PHONE..................510 582-1460
John Gaffney, *CEO*
Linda Mandolini, *President*
Jan Peters, *COO*
James Kennedy, *Bd of Directors*
Mary Lucero-Dorst, *Associate Dir*
EMP: 150
SQ FT: 10,000
SALES: 13.5MM **Privately Held**
SIC: **1522** Multi-family dwellings, new construction

(P-1310)
FAIRFIELD DEVELOPMENT INC (PA)
Also Called: Ffd II
5510 Morehouse Dr Ste 200, San Diego (92121-3722)
PHONE..................858 457-2123
Christopher E Hashioka, *President*
Paulette Green, *President*
Greg Pinkalla, *COO*
James A Hribar, *CFO*
James L Bosler, *Chairman*
▲ EMP: 225
SALES (est): 372MM **Privately Held**
WEB: www.westbrook-apts.com
SIC: **1522** Multi-family dwelling construction

(P-1311)
G B GROUP INC (PA)
8921 Murray Ave, Gilroy (95020-3633)
PHONE..................408 848-8118
Fax: 408 848-8119
Gregory D Brown, *CEO*
Mark Greening, *President*
Jeffery Dame, *President*
Regan L Brown, *Corp Secy*
Pat Falconio, *Exec VP*
EMP: 79
SQ FT: 4,300
SALES (est): 56.6MM **Privately Held**
WEB: www.gbgroupinc.com
SIC: **1522 1542** Hotel/motel & multi-family home renovation & remodeling; condominium construction; nonresidential construction

(P-1312)
HAMMER DOWN DAVILA CNSTR
Also Called: Hdd Construction
2338 W Erie St, Caruthers (93609-9529)
P.O. Box 642 (93609-0642)
PHONE..................559 864-2001
Fax: 559 864-4718
David Davila, *Owner*
EMP: 85 EST: 1998
SQ FT: 2,400
SALES (est): 5MM **Privately Held**
SIC: **1522** Residential construction

(P-1313)
HEIDI CORPORATION
Also Called: Donald J Schefflers Cnstr
15815 Amar Rd, City of Industry (91744-2107)
PHONE..................626 333-6317
Fax: 626 855-3428
Donald J Scheffler, *President*
▲ EMP: 75
SQ FT: 15,000
SALES (est): 10.1MM **Privately Held**
SIC: **1522** Residential construction

(P-1314)
HURLEY CONSTRUCTION INC
1801 I St Ste 200, Sacramento (95811-3000)
PHONE..................916 446-7599
Fax: 916 444-9843
Peter H Geremia, *CEO*
Steven Eggert, *Vice Pres*
Christine Baltzell, *Accountant*
Julie Goldfine, *Controller*
Trisha Malone, *Manager*
EMP: 80
SQ FT: 2,500
SALES (est): 12.6MM **Privately Held**
WEB: www.antonllc.com
SIC: **1522** Multi-family dwellings, new construction

(P-1315)
IMPERIAL CONTRACTING
30 Waterworks Way, Irvine (92618-3107)
PHONE..................949 333-6460
Kevin Finkle, *Branch Mgr*
EMP: 94
SALES (corp-wide): 44.3MM **Privately Held**
SIC: **1522** Residential construction
PA: Imperial Contracting
16573 N 92nd St Ste 125
Scottsdale AZ 85260
480 892-9157

(P-1316)
JAMES E ROBERTS-OBAYASHI CORP
20 Oak Ct, Danville (94526-4006)
PHONE..................925 820-0600
Fax: 925 820-1993
Larry R Smith, *CEO*
Gina Sakamoto, *Officer*
Obayashi Corporation, *Principal*
Gary Fettke, *Project Mgr*
Jeanine Kaufman, *Project Mgr*
EMP: 110 EST: 1978
SQ FT: 4,000
SALES (est): 34.2MM **Privately Held**
WEB: www.jerocorp.com
SIC: **1522 1542** Multi-family dwellings, new construction; commercial & office building, new construction

(P-1317)
JAMES MCCUTCHEON
17521 Walker Basin Rd, Caliente (93518-1407)
PHONE..................661 867-1810
Mg Taylor, *President*
EMP: 50
SALES (est): 4.5MM **Privately Held**
SIC: **1522** Residential construction

(P-1318)
JWC CONSTRUCTION INC (PA)
Also Called: Jon Wayne Construction
2580 Fortune Way, Vista (92081-8441)
PHONE..................760 727-2494
Fax: 760 727-2637
Jon Wayne, *CEO*
Karen Wang, *Controller*
David Dillon, *Manager*
EMP: 50
SQ FT: 7,000
SALES (est): 25.7MM **Privately Held**
SIC: **1522 1521** Residential construction; new construction, single-family houses

(P-1319)
JWC CONSTRUCTION INC
4570 Campus Dr, Newport Beach (92660-8809)
PHONE..................949 252-2107
William V Gennusa, *Principal*
EMP: 50
SALES (corp-wide): 23.4MM **Privately Held**
SIC: **1522 1521** Residential construction; new construction, single-family houses
PA: Jwc Construction, Inc.
2580 Fortune Way
Vista CA 92081
760 727-2494

(P-1320)
K&M CONSTRUCTION
642 Pine Ave, Pacific Grove (93950-3347)
PHONE..................831 643-2819
Kevin Ralph, *Partner*
EMP: 70
SALES (est): 3.3MM **Privately Held**
SIC: **1522** Residential construction

(P-1321)
KB HOME SOUTH BAY INC
5000 Executive Pkwy # 125, San Ramon (94583-4210)
PHONE..................925 983-2500
Chris Apostolopoulos, *CEO*
Robert Freed, *President*
Patrick Coyle, *Vice Pres*
Joe Gregorich, *Vice Pres*
Andrew Kusnick, *Vice Pres*
EMP: 140
SQ FT: 5,500
SALES (est): 17.2MM
SALES (corp-wide): 3B **Publicly Held**
SIC: **1522 1521** Residential construction; single-family housing construction
HQ: Kb Home Greater Los Angeles Inc.
10990 Wilshire Blvd # 700
Los Angeles CA 90024
310 231-4000

(P-1322)
KERN 2008 CMNTY PARTNERS LP
Also Called: Desert Oaks Apartments
1219 N Plaza Dr, Visalia (93291-8837)
PHONE..................559 651-3559
Terry Coyne, *General Ptnr*
Sarah Todd, *Manager*
EMP: 85
SALES (est): 950K **Privately Held**
SIC: **1522** Residential construction

(P-1323)
LAKE MERRITT HOTEL ASSOCIATES
1800 Madison St, Oakland (94612-4638)
PHONE..................510 832-2300
Fax: 510 832-7150
Randall C Berger, *Partner*
Cheryl Berger, *Partner*
Johanna Stein, *Manager*
EMP: 50 EST: 1990
SQ FT: 44,155
SALES (est): 3.4MM **Privately Held**
WEB: www.lakemerritthotel.com
SIC: **1522 7011** Apartment building construction; hotels & motels

(P-1324)
MARK SCOTT CONSTRUCTION INC
241 Frank West Cir # 200, Stockton (95206-4012)
PHONE..................209 982-0502
Mark Scott, *Owner*
EMP: 74
SALES (corp-wide): 55MM **Privately Held**
PA: Mark Scott Construction, Inc.
2835 Contra Costa Blvd
Pleasant Hill CA 94523
925 944-0502

(P-1325)
MILLSAP DEGNAN & ASSOC INC
4280 Redwood Hwy Ste 10, San Rafael (94903-2600)
PHONE..................415 472-4244
Fax: 415 472-4258
Steve Millsap, *CEO*
Doug Degnan, *President*
Amy Schauf, *Controller*
EMP: 60
SALES (est): 5.5MM **Privately Held**
WEB: www.millsapdegnan.com
SIC: **1522 1771 8711** Residential construction; concrete work; engineering services

(P-1326)
NANCY SMITH CONSTRUCTION INC
47 Yorkshire Dr, Oakland (94618-2021)
PHONE..................510 923-1671
Ronald Smith, *President*
Christy Smith, *Treasurer*
Randal Smith, *Vice Pres*
EMP: 50
SALES (est): 15.3MM **Privately Held**
SIC: **1522** Apartment building construction

(P-1327)
NIBBI BROS ASSOCIATES INC
Also Called: Nibbi Bros Concrete
180 Hubbell St, San Francisco (94107-2219)
PHONE..................415 863-1820
Robert L Nibbi, *President*
Larry Nibbi, *CEO*
Richard Fedick, *CFO*
Mike Nibbi, *Vice Pres*
EMP: 150
SALES (est): 17.7MM **Privately Held**
SIC: **1522 1542** Residential construction; custom builders, non-residential

(P-1328)
OC LIGHTHOUSE CONSTRUCTION
1901 Carnegie Ave Ste 1j, Santa Ana (92705-5504)
PHONE..................949 797-0151
John W Severens, *CEO*
Robert Gallegher, *President*
Jack Sezerens, *President*
Cheryl Severens, *Admin Sec*
EMP: 50 EST: 1994
SQ FT: 4,000
SALES (est): 1.5MM **Privately Held**
SIC: **1522** Residential construction

(P-1329)
OLEN RESIDENTIAL REALTY CORP (HQ)
Also Called: Olen Companies, The
7 Corporate Plaza Dr, Newport Beach (92660-7904)
PHONE..................949 644-6536
Igor M Olenicoff, *President*
Petricia Stone, *Accountant*
Linda Davis, *Manager*
EMP: 70
SALES (est): 57.6MM **Privately Held**
SIC: **1522** Multi-family dwellings, new construction

(P-1330)
PARKHURST TERRACE
100 Parkhurst Cir, Aptos (95003-9657)
PHONE..................831 685-0800
Cheryl Digrazia, *Principal*
EMP: 70
SALES (est): 4MM
SALES (corp-wide): 41.9K **Privately Held**
SIC: **1522** Apartment building construction
HQ: Midpen Property Management Corporation
303 Vintage Park Dr # 250
Foster City CA 94404
650 356-2900

(P-1331)
PRC BUILDERS INC
26616 Mission St, San Juan Capistrano (92675-3122)
PHONE..................949 529-7011
David P Fitts, *President*
Jason Pammer, *Vice Pres*
EMP: 90 EST: 1997
SALES: 12MM **Privately Held**
SIC: **1522** Residential construction

(P-1332)
PRIDE INDUSTRIES
Cbc Base Bldg 19 43rd St, Port Hueneme (93041)
PHONE..................805 985-8481
Fax: 805 984-9518
Dennis Carter, *Branch Mgr*
EMP: 140
SALES (corp-wide): 279.8MM **Privately Held**
SIC: **1522** Residential construction

1522 - General Contractors, Residential Other Than Single Family County (P-1333)

PA: Pride Industries
10030 Foothills Blvd
Roseville CA 95747
916 788-2100

(P-1333)
PROJECT FROG INC
99 Green St Ste 200, San Francisco (94111-1400)
PHONE..................................415 814-8500
Fax: 415 814-8501
Ann Hand, *CEO*
Mark Miller, *President*
Greg Saunders, *CFO*
Brian Holte, *Exec VP*
Oscar Alvarez, *Vice Pres*
▲ EMP: 55
SALES (est): 22MM **Privately Held**
SIC: 1522 Residential construction

(P-1334)
PSLQ INC
28910 Rancho California R, Temecula (92590-1870)
PHONE..................................951 795-4260
John P Swensen, *President*
Lee Quigley, *Vice Pres*
Danny Perez, *Manager*
EMP: 75
SQ FT: 800
SALES (est): 11.3MM **Privately Held**
SIC: 1522 0781 Residential construction; landscape services

(P-1335)
RDR BUILDERS LP
Also Called: Rdr Production Builders
1806 W Kettleman Ln Ste F, Lodi (95242-4316)
PHONE..................................209 368-7561
Ron Dos Reis, *Partner*
Mark Barbieri, *Partner*
Ed Dos Reis, *Partner*
Ron Dos-Reis, *President*
Mark Elstob, *CFO*
EMP: 85
SQ FT: 1,400
SALES: 18MM **Privately Held**
SIC: 1522 1542 Multi-family dwellings, new construction; hotel/motel & multi-family home renovation & remodeling; commercial & office building, new construction; commercial & office buildings, renovation & repair

(P-1336)
REEGS INC
Also Called: Monterey Construction Company
88 Monterey Salinas Hwy A, Salinas (93908-8976)
PHONE..................................831 455-7931
Richard Benjamin Rega, *President*
EMP: 65
SALES (est): 2.7MM **Privately Held**
SIC: 1522 Residential construction

(P-1337)
REGIONAL INVESTMENT & MGT LLC
4640 Admiralty Way # 1050, Marina Del Rey (90292-6642)
PHONE..................................310 821-1945
Alicia Miller,
Mia Cramer, *Opers Staff*
EMP: 50
SALES (est): 3.5MM **Privately Held**
SIC: 1522 6798 Multi-family dwellings, new construction; real estate investment trusts

(P-1338)
SAARMAN CONSTRUCTION LTD
683 Mcallister St, San Francisco (94102-3111)
PHONE..................................415 749-2700
Fax: 415 749-2709
Jeffrey M Saarman, *President*
Steven P Saarman, *CEO*
Michael Lunny, *Senior VP*
Benjamin Tsai, *Vice Pres*
Paul Saarman, *General Mgr*
EMP: 250
SQ FT: 4,500
SALES (est): 36.7MM **Privately Held**
WEB: www.saarman.com
SIC: 1522 1521 Condominium construction; apartment building construction; general remodeling, single-family houses; new construction, single-family houses

(P-1339)
SHEA HOMES VANTIS LLC
655 Brea Canyon Rd, Walnut (91789-3078)
PHONE..................................909 594-9500
EMP: 81
SALES (est): 3.5MM
SALES (corp-wide): 2B **Privately Held**
SIC: 1522 Apartment building construction
HQ: Shea Homes Limited Partnership, A California Limited Partnership
655 Brea Canyon Rd
Walnut CA 91789

(P-1340)
STERLING CONSTRUCTION
17661 Greenwood Way, Jamestown (95327-9733)
PHONE..................................209 984-5594
Fax: 209 984-0628
Rusty Jantz, *Owner*
Vivian Jantz, *Partner*
▲ EMP: 50
SALES (est): 3.8MM **Privately Held**
SIC: 1522 Multi-family dwellings, new construction

(P-1341)
STRATHAM HOMES INC
2201 Dupont Dr Ste 300, Irvine (92612-7509)
PHONE..................................949 833-1554
Ali Razi, *President*
David Lamb, *Shareholder*
Mehrdad Rassekh, *Shareholder*
Scott Lehman, *Superintendent*
EMP: 100
SQ FT: 7,000
SALES: 30MM **Privately Held**
SIC: 1522 Residential construction

(P-1342)
SWINERTON INCORPORATED
2300 Clayton Rd Ste 800, Concord (94520-2166)
PHONE..................................925 689-2336
Fax: 925 677-0296
Lawrence Mathews, *Branch Mgr*
Dexter Cheng, *Technology*
Sean Saulsbury, *Technology*
Jose Cruz, *Human Resources*
Jack Dettis, *Manager*
EMP: 97
SALES (corp-wide): 2.8B **Privately Held**
SIC: 1522 8741 Residential construction; construction management
PA: Swinerton Incorporated
260 Townsend St
San Francisco CA 94107
415 421-2980

(P-1343)
T G CONSTRUCTION
139 Nevada St, El Segundo (90245-4209)
PHONE..................................310 321-5900
Steve Pavone, *President*
▲ EMP: 50
SALES (est): 3.7MM **Privately Held**
SIC: 1522 Residential construction

(P-1344)
THOMPSON BUILDERS CORPORATION
250 Bel Marin Keys Blvd A, Novato (94949-5727)
PHONE..................................415 456-8972
Paul Thompson, *President*
F Joseph Hass, *Vice Pres*
Carrie Bush, *Admin Asst*
Mike Pahland, *Project Mgr*
Chris Tiem, *Project Mgr*
▲ EMP: 169
SQ FT: 6,000
SALES: 72.1MM **Privately Held**
WEB: www.westbaybuilders.com
SIC: 1522 1542 Multi-family dwelling construction; commercial & office building, new construction

(P-1345)
TONNER HILLS HSING PARTNERS LP
17701 Cowan Ste 200, Irvine (92614-6840)
PHONE..................................949 263-8676
Laura Archuleta, *Partner*
EMP: 50
SALES (est): 4.6MM **Privately Held**
SIC: 1522 Apartment building construction

(P-1346)
TOSCANA HOMES LP
Also Called: Toscana Country Club
300 Eagle Dance Cir, Palm Desert (92211-7440)
PHONE..................................760 772-7227
William Bone, *Partner*
Nancy Hayes, *Controller*
Paul Leby, *Manager*
EMP: 50
SQ FT: 6,000
SALES (est): 3.5MM **Privately Held**
WEB: www.sunrisemis.com
SIC: 1522 Residential construction

(P-1347)
TOTAL SOURCE ENVIROMENTAL INC
Also Called: TSE
306 W El Norte Pkwy Ste 5, Escondido (92026-1960)
PHONE..................................619 822-8518
Robert Lizik, *President*
EMP: 50
SALES (est): 3.5MM **Privately Held**
SIC: 1522 Apartment building construction

(P-1348)
TOTAL-WESTERN INC
2811 Fruitvale Ave Ste A, Bakersfield (93308-5947)
PHONE..................................661 589-5200
Fax: 661 589-7874
Jeff Jordan, *Manager*
Ed Harper, *Manager*
Bill Reynolds, *Manager*
EMP: 80
SALES (corp-wide): 278.7MM **Privately Held**
WEB: www.total-western.com
SIC: 1522 1542 Residential construction; nonresidential construction
HQ: Total-Western, Inc.
8049 Somerset Blvd
Paramount CA 90723
562 220-1450

(P-1349)
V DEVELOPMENT INC
Also Called: Capital Builders
550 Harvest Park Dr Ste A, Brentwood (94513-4058)
PHONE..................................925 634-8890
Manuel Vierra, *President*
Kelly Moore, *Human Resources*
EMP: 75
SQ FT: 2,300
SALES: 5MM **Privately Held**
SIC: 1522 Residential construction

(P-1350)
WERMERS MULTI-FAMILY CORP (PA)
5120 Shoreham Pl Ste 150, San Diego (92122-5959)
PHONE..................................858 535-1475
Thomas W Wermers, *President*
Jeff Bunker, *President*
Tom Wermers, *CEO*
Richard Lemmel, *CFO*
Bart Harmann, *Vice Pres*
EMP: 100
SQ FT: 7,000
SALES: 59MM **Privately Held**
WEB: www.wermerscontractors.com
SIC: 1522 Hotel/motel & multi-family home construction

(P-1351)
WESTERN NATIONAL PROPERTIES (PA)
Also Called: Arkebauer Properties
8 Executive Cir, Irvine (92614-6746)
P.O. Box 19528 (92623-9528)
PHONE..................................949 862-6200
Fax: 949 862-6496
David Stone, *Ch of Bd*
Rex Delong, *President*
Michael K Hayde, *President*
Jeffrey R Scott, *CFO*
Debra Meute, *Vice Pres*
▲ EMP: 129
SQ FT: 37,000
SALES (est): 71.5MM **Privately Held**
WEB: www.wng.com
SIC: 1522 6513 6512 6531 Apartment building construction; apartment building operators; nonresidential building operators; real estate agents & managers

(P-1352)
WL BUTLER INC
204 Franklin St, Redwood City (94063-1929)
PHONE..................................650 361-1270
Fax: 650 361-8657
William Butler, *CEO*
Frank York, *President*
David A Nevens Jr, *COO*
Gina Henson, *CFO*
Gina Tankersley, *Vice Pres*
EMP: 250
SQ FT: 5,500
SALES (est): 28.7MM **Privately Held**
SIC: 1522 Residential construction

(P-1353)
WM ONEILL LATH AND PLST CORP
P.O. Box 60352 (94088-0352)
PHONE..................................408 329-1413
William O'Neill, *President*
Sandra O'Neill, *Admin Sec*
EMP: 50 EST: 2009
SALES (est): 4.3MM **Privately Held**
SIC: 1522 Residential construction

(P-1354)
ZASTROW CONSTRUCTION INC
Also Called: Reliance Company
3267 Verdugo Rd, Los Angeles (90065-2035)
PHONE..................................323 478-1956
Mark Zastrow, *President*
Patti Eldridge, *Treasurer*
Kai Wilson, *Vice Pres*
EMP: 115 EST: 1976
SQ FT: 2,000
SALES (est): 11.9MM **Privately Held**
SIC: 1522 Multi-family dwelling construction; multi-family dwellings, new construction

1531 Operative Builders

(P-1355)
ALBERT D SEENO CNSTR CO INC
4021 Port Chicago Hwy, Concord (94520-1122)
P.O. Box 4113 (94524-4113)
PHONE..................................925 671-7711
Albert D Seeno Jr, *CEO*
Richard B Seeno, *Principal*
Thomas A Seeno, *Principal*
Nancy Cassidy, *Human Res Mgr*
EMP: 80
SQ FT: 30,000
SALES (est): 28.2MM **Privately Held**
WEB: www.seenohomes.com
SIC: 1531 Speculative builder, single-family houses

(P-1356)
BARA CONSTRUCTION SERVICES
2678 Bishop Dr Ste 116, San Ramon (94583-4455)
PHONE..................................925 790-0130
Selina Singh, *Principal*
EMP: 50
SQ FT: 1,500
SALES (est): 4.6MM **Privately Held**
SIC: 1531 1799 1711 ; ; coating, caulking & weather, water & fireproofing; heating systems repair & maintenance; heating & air conditioning contractors

▲ = Import ▼=Export
◆ =Import/Export

PRODUCTS & SERVICES SECTION
1531 - Operative Builders County (P-1379)

(P-1357)
CALATLANTIC GROUP INC (PA)
Also Called: CALATLANTIC HOMES
15360 Barranca Pkwy, Irvine (92618-2215)
PHONE.................................949 789-1600
Larry T Nicholson, *President*
Scott D Stowell, *Ch of Bd*
Peter G Skelly, *COO*
Jeff J McCall, *CFO*
Wendy L Marlett, *Chief Mktg Ofcr*
EMP: 55
SQ FT: 39,000
SALES: 3.5B **Publicly Held**
WEB: www.standardpacifichomes.com
SIC: 1531 1521 6162 6541 Operative builders; single-family housing construction; mortgage brokers, using own money; title & trust companies

(P-1358)
CALATLANTIC GROUP INC
3825 Hopyard Rd Ste 195, Pleasanton (94588-8529)
PHONE.................................925 847-8700
Fax: 925 730-1397
Glen Martin, *Manager*
Lloyd McKibbin, *Treasurer*
Jim Berson, *VP Mktg*
Carl Metz, *VP Sales*
Maggie Beattie, *Marketing Staff*
EMP: 50
SQ FT: 5,000
SALES (corp-wide): 3.5B **Publicly Held**
WEB: www.standardpacifichomes.com
SIC: 1531 1521 Operative builders; single-family housing construction
PA: Calatlantic Group, Inc.
15360 Barranca Pkwy
Irvine CA 92618
949 789-1600

(P-1359)
CALATLANTIC GROUP INC
Also Called: Ryland Homes
5740 Fleet St Ste 200, Carlsbad (92008-4704)
PHONE.................................760 931-4414
Fax: 760 603-8005
Karen Carter, *Manager*
EMP: 55
SALES (corp-wide): 3.5B **Publicly Held**
WEB: www.ryland.com
SIC: 1531 Speculative builder, single-family houses
PA: Calatlantic Group, Inc.
15360 Barranca Pkwy
Irvine CA 92618
949 789-1600

(P-1360)
CAPITAL PACIFIC HOLDINGS INC
4100 Macarthur Blvd # 150, Newport Beach (92660-2069)
PHONE.................................951 279-2447
Laura Godwin, *General Mgr*
EMP: 50
SALES (corp-wide): 46.3MM **Privately Held**
WEB: www.cph-inc.com
SIC: 1531 Speculative builder, single-family houses
PA: Capital Pacific Holdings, Inc.
4100 Macarthur Blvd # 315
Newport Beach CA 92660
949 622-8400

(P-1361)
DE ANZA SQUARE SHOPPING CENTER
1306 S Mary Ave 1370, Sunnyvale (94087-3130)
PHONE.................................408 738-4444
Rosanna Callegari, *Principal*
EMP: 99
SALES: 950K **Privately Held**
SIC: 1531 Operative builders

(P-1362)
DONALD LAWRENCE FULBRIGHT CO
Also Called: Donald Lawrence Company
32557 Road 138, Visalia (93292-9381)
P.O. Box 2622 (93279-2622)
PHONE.................................559 625-0762
Fax: 559 625-0784
Donald Fulbright, *President*
Jeffrey Englund, *Treasurer*
Mary Fulbright, *Vice Pres*
Lisa Jones,
EMP: 62
SQ FT: 1,700
SALES (est): 4.8MM **Privately Held**
SIC: 1531 Speculative builder, single-family houses

(P-1363)
DR HORTON INC
2280 Wardlow Cir Ste 100, Corona (92880-2879)
PHONE.................................951 272-9000
Steve Fitzpatrick, *Branch Mgr*
EMP: 50
SALES (corp-wide): 10.8B **Publicly Held**
WEB: www.drhorton.com
SIC: 1531 Operative builders
PA: D.R. Horton, Inc.
301 Commerce St Ste 500
Fort Worth TX 76102
817 390-8200

(P-1364)
FIELDSTONE COMMUNITIES INC (PA)
16 Technology Dr Ste 125, Irvine (92618-2325)
PHONE.................................949 790-5400
William H McFarland, *CEO*
Peter Ochs, *Ch of Bd*
Frank Foster, *President*
David Langlois, *Exec VP*
Jim Hanson, *Senior VP*
EMP: 130
SQ FT: 15,000
SALES (est): 22.9MM **Privately Held**
WEB: www.fieldstone-homes.com
SIC: 1531 Operative builders

(P-1365)
GREENBRIAR HOMES COMMUNITIES
4340 Stevens Creek Blvd, San Jose (95129-1102)
PHONE.................................510 497-8200
Fax: 408 984-7060
Carol M Meyer, *Ch of Bd*
Gilbert M Meyer, *President*
Judy Pasco, *Vice Pres*
Magda Fowler, *Accountant*
EMP: 100
SQ FT: 12,000
SALES (est): 8.3MM **Privately Held**
SIC: 1531 Operative builders

(P-1366)
GREENLAND US CONSULTING INC
515 S Figueroa St # 1703, Los Angeles (90071-3301)
PHONE.................................213 362-9300
Ifei Chang, *CEO*
EMP: 99 **EST:** 2013
SALES (est): 4.2MM **Privately Held**
SIC: 1531

(P-1367)
GRUPE DEV COMPANYNORTHERN CAL
3255 W March Ln Ste 400, Stockton (95219-2352)
P.O. Box 7576 (95267-0576)
PHONE.................................209 473-6000
Fritz Unruh, *CEO*
EMP: 119
SQ FT: 7,000
SALES: 5.6MM
SALES (corp-wide): 82.9MM **Privately Held**
WEB: www.grupe.com
SIC: 1531 Speculative builder, single-family houses; speculative builder, multi-family dwellings; condominium developers
PA: The Grupe Company
3255 W March Ln Ste 400
Stockton CA 95219
209 473-6000

(P-1368)
HOOPA MODULAR BUILDING ENTP
4415 Dogwood Ln Apt C, Redding (96003-2552)
PHONE.................................530 244-2421
Craig Roseberg, *Manager*
Craig Rosenberg, *Manager*
EMP: 75
SALES (corp-wide): 3MM **Privately Held**
WEB: www.hoopamodular.com
SIC: 1531 Operative builders
PA: Hoopa Modular Building Enterprise
151 Cal Pac Rd
Hoopa CA 95546
530 625-4551

(P-1369)
HWN MARIPOSA ASSOCIATES LLC
11150 Santa Monica Blvd # 760, Los Angeles (90025-3380)
PHONE.................................310 478-8757
Thomas B Wilson,
EMP: 99
SALES (est): 3.3MM **Privately Held**
SIC: 1531 Operative builders

(P-1370)
INLAND VALLEY CNSTR CO INC
18382 Slover Ave, Bloomington (92316-2363)
PHONE.................................909 875-2112
Fax: 909 875-5401
Kenneth Caruso, *President*
Kelly Bird, *Treasurer*
Stacy Veggin, *Treasurer*
Terina Prague, *Manager*
EMP: 75
SQ FT: 4,000
SALES (est): 21.2MM **Privately Held**
WEB: www.inlandvalleyconst.com
SIC: 1531 Operative builders

(P-1371)
K B HOME COASTAL
10990 Wilshire Blvd Fl 7, Los Angeles (90024-3907)
PHONE.................................310 231-4000
Jeff Nezger, *President*
Domenico Cecere, *CFO*
William Hollinger, *CFO*
Kelly Allred, *Vice Pres*
Cory Cohen, *Vice Pres*
▲ **EMP:** 90
SQ FT: 13,346
SALES (est): 12.7MM
SALES (corp-wide): 3B **Publicly Held**
WEB: www.kbhome.com
SIC: 1531 Operative builders
PA: Kb Home
10990 Wilshire Blvd Fl 5
Los Angeles CA 90024
310 231-4000

(P-1372)
KAUFMAN AND BROAD LIMITED
Also Called: Kaufman & Broad
10990 Wilshire Blvd Fl 7, Los Angeles (90024-3907)
PHONE.................................310 231-4000
Bruce Karatz, *Ch of Bd*
Jeff Mezger, *COO*
Dom Cecere, *CFO*
Victoria Sulinas, *Admin Asst*
Gary Moore, *Manager*
EMP: 151
SALES (est): 7.6MM
SALES (corp-wide): 3B **Publicly Held**
WEB: www.kbhomesutah.com
SIC: 1531 Operative builders
PA: Kb Home
10990 Wilshire Blvd Fl 5
Los Angeles CA 90024
310 231-4000

(P-1373)
KB HOME (PA)
10990 Wilshire Blvd Fl 5, Los Angeles (90024-3902)
PHONE.................................310 231-4000
Jeffrey T Mezger, *President*
Glen Longarini, *President*
Amy McReynolds, *President*
Jeff J Kaminski, *CFO*
Nick Franklin, *Exec VP*
EMP: 100
SALES: 3B **Publicly Held**
WEB: www.kbhome.com
SIC: 1531 6351 6162 Operative builders; speculative builder, single-family houses; condominium developers; speculative builder, multi-family dwellings; surety insurance; mortgage guarantee insurance; credit & other financial responsibility insurance; mortgage bankers & correspondents

(P-1374)
LENNAR CORPORATION
25 Enterprise Ste 400, Aliso Viejo (92656-2712)
PHONE.................................949 349-8000
Jonathan Jaffe, *COO*
Gary Hildabrand, *Executive*
Marc Chasman, *Div Sub Head*
Jenny Masters, *Comms Dir*
Brian Seveland, *Telecom Exec*
EMP: 100
SALES (corp-wide): 9.4B **Publicly Held**
WEB: www.lennar.com
SIC: 1531 Operative builders
PA: Lennar Corporation
700 Nw 107th Ave Ste 400
Miami FL 33172
305 559-4000

(P-1375)
LENNAR HOMES INC
3788 Edington Dr, Rancho Cordova (95742)
PHONE.................................916 517-4950
Brenda Coementson, *Principal*
EMP: 101
SALES (corp-wide): 9.4B **Publicly Held**
SIC: 1531 Operative builders
HQ: Lennar Homes Inc
730 Nw 107th Ave Ste 300
Miami FL 33172
305 559-4000

(P-1376)
LENNAR HOMES INC
980 Montecito Dr 302, Corona (92879-1792)
PHONE.................................951 739-0267
Maureen Johnson, *Manager*
Patty Lollis, *Sr Corp Ofcr*
Gary Glazer, *Vice Pres*
Monica Smith, *Controller*
Todd Palmaer, *VP Human Res*
EMP: 200
SALES (corp-wide): 9.4B **Publicly Held**
SIC: 1531 Operative builders
HQ: Lennar Homes Inc
730 Nw 107th Ave Ste 300
Miami FL 33172
305 559-4000

(P-1377)
LEWIS COMPANIES (PA)
1156 N Mountain Ave, Upland (91786-3633)
PHONE.................................909 985-0971
Richard A Lewis, *President*
William Francke, *Vice Pres*
Goldy S Lewis, *Principal*
Randall W Lewis, *Principal*
Robert E Lewis, *Principal*
EMP: 200
SALES (est): 59.4MM **Privately Held**
WEB: www.lewishomes.com
SIC: 1531 Operative builders

(P-1378)
LYON PROMENADE LLC
4901 Birch St, Newport Beach (92660-2114)
PHONE.................................949 252-9101
William Lyon,
Joanna Lizarraga, *Office Mgr*
Frank T Suryan,
EMP: 50
SALES (est): 2.8MM **Privately Held**
SIC: 1531 Operative builders

(P-1379)
MANOR BELL L P
790 Sonoma Ave, Santa Rosa (95404-4713)
PHONE.................................707 526-9782

Jose Luis Caballero,
Charles A Cornell,
EMP: 99
SALES (est): 5.1MM **Privately Held**
SIC: 1531 Condominium developers

(P-1380)
NEW HOME COMPANY INC (PA)
85 Enterprise Ste 450, Aliso Viejo (92656-2680)
PHONE..................949 382-7800
H Lawrence Webb, *Ch of Bd*
Tom Redwitz, *COO*
John M Stephens, *CFO*
Wayne Stelmar, *CIO*
EMP: 51 **EST:** 2009
SQ FT: 18,700
SALES: 430.1MM **Publicly Held**
SIC: 1531 Operative builders

(P-1381)
PACIFICA REFLECTIONS
Also Called: Pacifica Crossroads
405 Reflections Cir, San Ramon (94583-5203)
PHONE..................925 275-9800
Fax: 925 275-9802
Tracy Dalton, *Principal*
EMP: 50
SALES (est): 5.4MM **Privately Held**
SIC: 1531 Condominium developers

(P-1382)
PORTER RANCH DEVELOPMENT CO
8383 Wilshire Blvd # 1000, Beverly Hills (90211-2439)
PHONE..................323 655-7330
Nathan Shapell, *Partner*
I N S Corporation, *Partner*
EMP: 85 **EST:** 1976
SALES (est): 4MM **Privately Held**
SIC: 1531 Speculative builder, single-family houses

(P-1383)
RYLAND HOMES OF TEXAS INC
15360 Barranca Pkwy, Irvine (92618-2215)
PHONE..................805 367-3800
EMP: 201
SALES (est): 11.6MM **Privately Held**
SIC: 1531 Operative builders

(P-1384)
STANDARD PACIFIC OF TEXAS INC
15360 Barranca Pkwy, Irvine (92618-2215)
PHONE..................949 789-1621
Scott Stowell, *President*
Steve Scarborogh, *President*
Michael Cortney, *Bd of Directors*
Ronald Jacobs, *Bd of Directors*
Keith Koeller, *Bd of Directors*
EMP: 93
SALES (est): 11.2MM
SALES (corp-wide): 3.5B **Publicly Held**
WEB: www.standardpacifichomes.com
SIC: 1531 Operative builders
PA: Calatlantic Group, Inc.
   15360 Barranca Pkwy
   Irvine CA 92618
   949 789-1600

(P-1385)
STRAUB - BRUTOCO A JOINT VENTR
202 W College St Ste 201, Fallbrook (92028-2970)
PHONE..................760 414-9000
Richard Straub, *Partner*
Robert Mhyre, *Partner*
Michael J Murphy, *Partner*
EMP: 150
SQ FT: 17,000
SALES (est): 4.5MM **Privately Held**
SIC: 1531 1541 ;; industrial buildings & warehouses; industrial buildings, new construction; prefabricated building erection, industrial

(P-1386)
TRI POINTE HOMES INC (HQ)
19520 Jamboree Rd Ste 300, Irvine (92612-2429)
P.O. Box 57088 (92619-7088)
PHONE..................949 438-1400
Douglas F Bauer, *CEO*
Barry S Sternlicht, *Ch of Bd*
Thomas J Mitchell, *President*
Michael D Grubbs, *CFO*
Tom Grable, *Division Pres*
EMP: 151
SALES: 1.7B
SALES (corp-wide): 2.4B **Publicly Held**
SIC: 1531 Speculative builder, single-family houses
PA: Tri Pointe Group, Inc.
   19540 Jamboree Rd Ste 300
   Irvine CA 92612
   949 438-1400

(P-1387)
US HOME CORPORATION
Also Called: US Home
980 Montecito Dr 302, Corona (92879-1792)
PHONE..................951 817-3500
Mike Lutz, *Branch Mgr*
EMP: 50
SALES (corp-wide): 9.4B **Publicly Held**
WEB: www.ushome.com
SIC: 1531 Speculative builder, single-family houses
HQ: U.S. Home Corporation
   10707 Clay Rd
   Houston TX 77041
   305 559-4000

(P-1388)
VAN DAELE DEVELOPMENT CORP
Also Called: Van Daele Homes
2900 Adams St Ste C25, Riverside (92504-8312)
PHONE..................951 354-6800
Fax: 951 354-2996
Michael B Van Daele, *CEO*
Jeff Hack, *President*
Barbara Koenig, *Project Mgr*
Marie Dorries, *Assistant*
Millie Polk, *Assistant*
EMP: 110
SQ FT: 6,000
SALES (est): 3.3MM **Privately Held**
WEB: www.vandaele.com
SIC: 1531 Speculative builder, single-family houses

(P-1389)
VILLA LA ESPERANZA LP
3533 Empleo St, San Luis Obispo (93401-7334)
PHONE..................805 781-3088
John Fowler, *Managing Prtnr*
Robin Bush, *Accounting Mgr*
EMP: 99 **EST:** 2015
SALES (est): 2.6MM **Privately Held**
SIC: 1531 Cooperative apartment developers

(P-1390)
WARMINGTON HOMES (PA)
3090 Pullman St, Costa Mesa (92626-7936)
PHONE..................714 434-4435
Fax: 714 641-9337
Timothy P Hogan, *President*
James P Warmington, *Ch of Bd*
Michael McClellan, *President*
Greg Oberling, *President*
Jack Schwellenbach, *President*
▲ **EMP:** 120
SQ FT: 40,000
SALES (est): 129.3MM **Privately Held**
SIC: 1531 Speculative builder, single-family houses

(P-1391)
WARMINGTON HOMES
15615 Alton Pkwy Ste 150, Irvine (92618-7302)
PHONE..................949 679-3100
EMP: 96

SALES (corp-wide): 129.3MM **Privately Held**
SIC: 1531 Speculative builder, single-family houses
PA: Warmington Homes
   3090 Pullman St
   Costa Mesa CA 92626
   714 434-4435

(P-1392)
WARMINGTON HOMES
2400 Camino Ramon Ste 234, San Ramon (94583-4350)
PHONE..................925 866-6700
Larry Riggs, *Exec VP*
EMP: 159
SALES (corp-wide): 129.3MM **Privately Held**
SIC: 1531 Speculative builder, single-family houses
PA: Warmington Homes
   3090 Pullman St
   Costa Mesa CA 92626
   714 434-4435

(P-1393)
WILLIAM LYON HOMES (PA)
4695 Macarthur Ct Ste 800, Newport Beach (92660-1863)
PHONE..................949 833-3600
Matthew R Zaist, *President*
William H Lyon, *Ch of Bd*
Colin T Severn, *CFO*
Tom Bui, *Vice Pres*
Gary Haddy, *Vice Pres*
EMP: 151
SALES: 1.1B **Publicly Held**
WEB: www.lyonhomes.com
SIC: 1531 Operative builders; speculative builder, single-family houses

---
1541 General Contractors, Indl Bldgs & Warehouses

(P-1394)
2H CONSTRUCTION INC
2653 Walnut Ave, Signal Hill (90755-1830)
PHONE..................562 490-2897
Fax: 562 424-5578
Daniel E Hume, *CEO*
Sean Hitchcock, *President*
Ronald Compton, *Vice Pres*
Rebecca Anacleto, *Administration*
Greg Harris, *Project Engr*
EMP: 51
SQ FT: 9,000
SALES (est): 18.4MM **Privately Held**
WEB: www.2hconstruction.com
SIC: 1541 1542 Industrial buildings, new construction; commercial & office building, new construction

(P-1395)
5 STAR POOL PLASTER INC
7275 National Dr Ste A, Livermore (94550-8868)
PHONE..................209 599-3111
Juan C Munoz, *President*
Luz Munoz, *Vice Pres*
Christopher Newton, *Vice Pres*
EMP: 53 **EST:** 2008
SALES (est): 7.2MM **Privately Held**
SIC: 1541 1521 Renovation, remodeling & repairs: industrial buildings; single-family home remodeling, additions & repairs

(P-1396)
ACME CONSTRUCTION COMPANY INC
1565 Cummins Dr, Modesto (95358-6401)
P.O. Box 4710 (95352-4710)
PHONE..................209 523-2674
Fax: 209 523-0213
Philip Mastagni, *President*
Judith Boydston, *CFO*
Ron Kettelman, *Vice Pres*
Michael A Mastagni, *Vice Pres*
Nella Mastagni, *Admin Sec*
EMP: 75
SQ FT: 12,000

SALES (est): 21.4MM **Privately Held**
WEB: www.acmeconstruction.com
SIC: 1541 1542 Industrial buildings & warehouses; commercial & office building, new construction

(P-1397)
ADIR INTERNATIONAL LLC
Also Called: La Curacao
4444 Ayers Ave, Vernon (90058-4317)
PHONE..................213 639-7716
Russell Yeager, *Branch Mgr*
EMP: 232
SALES (corp-wide): 484.7MM **Privately Held**
SIC: 1541 Industrial buildings & warehouses
PA: Adir International, Llc
   1605 W Olympic Blvd # 405
   Los Angeles CA 90015
   213 639-2100

(P-1398)
ALSTON CONSTRUCTION CO INC (PA)
8775 Folsom Blvd Ste 201, Sacramento (95826-3725)
PHONE..................916 340-2400
Fax: 916 340-0565
Paul David Little, *CEO*
Carl Panattoni, *Shareholder*
Adam Nickerson, *CFO*
Dave Fazekas, *Exec VP*
Dan Hudson, *Exec VP*
EMP: 100
SQ FT: 36,000
SALES: 642.5MM **Privately Held**
WEB: www.panconinc.com
SIC: 1541 1542 Industrial buildings & warehouses; commercial & office building contractors

(P-1399)
ANGELES CONTRACTOR INC (PA)
8461 Commonwealth Ave, Buena Park (90621-4170)
PHONE..................714 523-1021
Young W Kang, *President*
Ray Yoo, *Vice Pres*
Kaylie Park, *Accountant*
Grace Cho, *Controller*
Steve Spooner, *Superintendent*
EMP: 78
SQ FT: 30,000
SALES (est): 34.4MM **Privately Held**
WEB: www.angelescontractor.com
SIC: 1541 Industrial buildings & warehouses

(P-1400)
AQUATIC DESIGNING INC
Also Called: North Coast Fabricators
4801 West End Rd, Arcata (95521-9242)
PHONE..................707 822-4629
Paula E Crowley, *President*
Tim Crowley, *COO*
Jim Galzie, *General Mgr*
Jessica Whitwell, *Administration*
EMP: 50 **EST:** 1979
SQ FT: 12,000
SALES (est): 15MM **Privately Held**
SIC: 1541 1542 7699 Prefabricated building erection, industrial; commercial & office buildings, prefabricated erection; industrial machinery & equipment repair

(P-1401)
ARNTZ BUILDERS INC
19 Pamaron Way, Novato (94949-6214)
PHONE..................415 382-1188
Donald M Arntz, *CEO*
Brian Proteau, *President*
Thomas Artz, *Corp Secy*
Allen Arntz, *Info Tech Mgr*
Edrianne Elliot, *Project Mgr*
EMP: 50
SQ FT: 3,500
SALES (est): 18.7MM **Privately Held**
SIC: 1541 1542 Industrial buildings, new construction; renovation, remodeling & repairs: industrial buildings; commercial & office building, new construction; commercial & office buildings, renovation & repair

PRODUCTS & SERVICES SECTION
1541 - General Contractors, Indl Bldgs & Warehouses County (P-1423)

(P-1402)
BAGHOUSE PARTS & SERVICES INC
600 W Freedom Ave, Orange (92865-2537)
PHONE 800 584-4720
Samuel Dalsanto, *CEO*
EMP: 156
SQ FT: 10,000
SALES: 5MM **Privately Held**
WEB: www.baghouseparts.com
SIC: 1541 5075 Industrial buildings, new construction; air pollution control equipment & supplies

(P-1403)
BCM CONSTRUCTION COMPANY INC
2990 State Highway 32 # 100, Chico (95973-8632)
PHONE 530 342-1722
Fax: 530 342-1768
Kurtis Carman, *President*
Nancy Chinn, *Treasurer*
Matt Bowman, *Vice Pres*
Scott January, *Vice Pres*
Kate Wetmore, *Administration*
EMP: 50
SQ FT: 1,700
SALES (est): 17.7MM **Privately Held**
WEB: www.bcmconstruction.com
SIC: 1541 Industrial buildings, new construction

(P-1404)
BEAR VLY FBRCATORS STL SUP INC
22060 Bear Valley Rd, Apple Valley (92308-7209)
P.O. Box 1412 (92307-0026)
PHONE 760 247-5381
Fax: 760 240-6062
Judy Carlos, *President*
Tony Carlos, *Vice Pres*
EMP: 60
SQ FT: 25,000
SALES (est): 11.7MM **Privately Held**
SIC: 1541 1791 5051 Renovation, remodeling & repairs: industrial buildings; structural steel erection; steel

(P-1405)
BECK INTERNATIONAL INC
Also Called: Beck Group, The
9641 Sunset Blvd, Beverly Hills (90210-2938)
PHONE 310 281-2980
EMP: 300
SALES (corp-wide): 596.8MM **Privately Held**
WEB: www.beckarchitecture.com
SIC: 1541 1542 Industrial buildings & warehouses; nonresidential construction
PA: Beck International, Inc.
1807 Ross Ave Ste 500
Dallas TX 75201
214 303-2200

(P-1406)
BLACH CONSTRUCTION COMPANY (PA)
2244 Blach Pl Ste 100, San Jose (95131-2041)
PHONE 408 244-7100
Fax: 408 244-2220
Mike Blach, *President*
Juan Barroso, *Vice Pres*
Gaye Landau, *Vice Pres*
Daniel Rogers, *Vice Pres*
Ken Treadwell, *Vice Pres*
EMP: 80
SQ FT: 24,000
SALES (est): 62.1MM **Privately Held**
WEB: www.blach.com
SIC: 1541 1542 Industrial buildings & warehouses; commercial & office building, new construction

(P-1407)
BOMEL CONSTRUCTION CO INC (PA)
8195 E Kaiser Blvd, Anaheim (92808-2214)
PHONE 714 921-1660
Kent Matranga, *CEO*
Lisa Matranga, *CFO*
Lisa McGinnis, *CFO*
Shawn Devine, *Vice Pres*
James Ure, *Vice Pres*
EMP: 51
SQ FT: 8,000
SALES (est): 125.3MM **Privately Held**
WEB: www.bomelconstruction.com
SIC: 1541 Industrial buildings & warehouses

(P-1408)
BRANNON INC
Also Called: Smith Electric Service
1340 W Betteravia Rd, Santa Maria (93455-1030)
PHONE 805 621-5000
Fax: 805 621-5050
Michael Brannon, *President*
Gary Smith, *Bd of Directors*
Larry Brannon, *Vice Pres*
Steve Fredette, *Vice Pres*
Joyce Gardner, *General Mgr*
EMP: 150
SQ FT: 10,000
SALES (est): 61MM **Privately Held**
WEB: www.smith-electric.com
SIC: 1541 1711 1731 1542 Industrial buildings, new construction; plumbing, heating, air-conditioning contractors; fire sprinkler system installation; fire detection & burglar alarm systems specialization; general electrical contractor; nonresidential construction

(P-1409)
C OVERAA & CO
Also Called: OVERAA CONSTRUCTION
200 Parr Blvd, Richmond (94801-1191)
PHONE 510 234-0926
Fax: 510 237-2435
Jerry Overaa, *CEO*
Christopher Manning, *President*
Roy Samuelsz, *Officer*
Elizabeth Brown, *General Mgr*
Erin O Disman, *Info Tech Mgr*
EMP: 350 EST: 1907
SQ FT: 20,000
SALES (est): 158.5MM **Privately Held**
WEB: www.overaa.com
SIC: 1541 Industrial buildings, new construction

(P-1410)
C OVERAA & CO/BAYVIEW
200 Parr Blvd, Richmond (94801-1120)
PHONE 510 234-0926
Gerald Overaa, *Principal*
EMP: 99 EST: 2013
SALES (est): 4.4MM **Privately Held**
SIC: 1541 Industrial buildings & warehouses

(P-1411)
CALIFORNIA SHTMTL WORKS INC
1020 N Marshall Ave, El Cajon (92020-1829)
PHONE 619 562-7010
Robin Hoffos, *President*
Joe Isom, *Vice Pres*
▲ **EMP:** 90 EST: 1913
SQ FT: 15,000
SALES (est): 45.8MM **Privately Held**
WEB: www.califsheetmetal.com
SIC: 1541 3444 Renovation, remodeling & repairs: industrial buildings; sheet metalwork

(P-1412)
CENTIMARK CORPORATION
1420 S Archibald Ave, Ontario (91761-7626)
PHONE 909 652-9280
Jong S Lee, *Manager*
Jeff Johnson, *Manager*
EMP: 50
SALES (corp-wide): 605.3MM **Privately Held**
WEB: www.centimark.com
SIC: 1541 Industrial buildings, new construction
PA: Centimark Corporation
12 Grandview Cir
Canonsburg PA 15317
724 743-7777

(P-1413)
CHALMERS CORPORATION
Also Called: C.E.G. Construction
7901 Crossway Dr, Pico Rivera (90660-4449)
PHONE 562 948-4850
Fax: 562 948-1735
Tracy John Chalmers, *CEO*
James N Devling, *CFO*
Christina Barba, *Manager*
EMP: 55
SQ FT: 45,000
SALES (est): 19.2MM **Privately Held**
WEB: www.cegconstruction.com
SIC: 1541 8742 Industrial buildings & warehouses; management consulting services

(P-1414)
CLARION CONSTRUCTION INC
21067 Commerce Point Dr, Walnut (91789-3052)
PHONE 909 598-4060
Fax: 909 598-5517
Kelly Owen, *President*
Jay Cook, *CFO*
Bruce Kidd, *Vice Pres*
Karen Snider, *Vice Pres*
Dana Spann, *Vice Pres*
EMP: 50
SQ FT: 10,000
SALES (est): 13.3MM **Privately Held**
SIC: 1541 Industrial buildings & warehouses

(P-1415)
CLARK CNSTR GROUP-CALIFORNIA
18201 Von Karman Ave # 800, Irvine (92612-1092)
PHONE 714 754-0764
Richard M Heim, *President*
Brandi Corbin, *Hum Res Coord*
Kimberly Wicks, *Purch Agent*
EMP: 450 EST: 2012
SALES (est): 35.5MM
SALES (corp-wide): 4.1B **Privately Held**
SIC: 1541 1542 Industrial buildings & warehouses; nonresidential construction
HQ: Clark Construction Group, Llc
7500 Old Georgetown Rd # 15
Bethesda MD 20814
301 272-8100

(P-1416)
CONEJO PACIFIC TECHNOLOGIES
1560 Newbury Rd Ste 1, Newbury Park (91320-3448)
PHONE 805 498-5315
Scott Connelly, *President*
EMP: 65
SQ FT: 100
SALES (est): 4.3MM **Privately Held**
SIC: 1541 0782 Industrial buildings & warehouses; landscape contractors

(P-1417)
DENVER D DARLING INC
Also Called: Darco Construction
8402 Katella Ave, Stanton (90680-3215)
PHONE 714 761-8299
Denver D Darling, *President*
Wayne Darling, *Vice Pres*
Ron Neilsen, *Project Mgr*
EMP: 75
SQ FT: 10,000
SALES (est): 11MM **Privately Held**
WEB: www.darcoconstruction.com
SIC: 1541 1771 Industrial buildings, new construction; concrete work

(P-1418)
DEVCON CONSTRUCTION INC (PA)
690 Gibraltar Dr, Milpitas (95035-6317)
PHONE 408 942-8200
Fax: 408 262-2342
Gary Filizetti, *President*
Keith Offill, *CFO*
Brett Sisney, *CFO*
Jonathan Harvey, *Vice Pres*
Daisy Pereira, *Vice Pres*
EMP: 320
SQ FT: 45,000
SALES: 1.2B **Privately Held**
WEB: www.devcon-const.com
SIC: 1541 Industrial buildings, new construction

(P-1419)
DPR CONSTRUCTION
5010 Shoreham Pl Ste 100, San Diego (92122-6900)
PHONE 858 646-0757
Peter Salvati, *Director*
Christy Daly, *Office Mgr*
Liz Foster, *Project Engr*
Landry Watson, *Sales Associate*
Anna Bickford, *Manager*
EMP: 300
SALES (corp-wide): 2.9B **Privately Held**
WEB: www.dprconstruction.com
SIC: 1541 1542 Industrial buildings & warehouses; commercial & office building contractors
PA: Dpr Construction, Inc.
1450 Veterans Blvd
Redwood City CA 94063
650 474-1450

(P-1420)
DPR CONSTRUCTION INC
1510 S Winchester Blvd, San Jose (95128-4334)
PHONE 408 370-2322
Fax: 408 370-2422
Jim Carter, *Manager*
Raymond Castillo, *Project Mgr*
Walter Eng, *Project Mgr*
Michael Galea, *Superintendent*
Matthew Lawson, *Superintendent*
EMP: 50
SALES (corp-wide): 2.9B **Privately Held**
WEB: www.dprconstruction.com
SIC: 1541 1542 Industrial buildings & warehouses; nonresidential construction
PA: Dpr Construction, Inc.
1450 Veterans Blvd
Redwood City CA 94063
650 474-1450

(P-1421)
DPR CONSTRUCTION INC (PA)
1450 Veterans Blvd, Redwood City (94063-2617)
PHONE 650 474-1450
Fax: 650 474-1451
Douglas E Woods, *CEO*
Alison Lyons, *President*
Michele Leiva, *CFO*
Ron J Davidowski, *Treasurer*
James F Dolen, *Exec VP*
▲ **EMP:** 500
SQ FT: 36,300
SALES: 2.9B **Privately Held**
WEB: www.dprconstruction.com
SIC: 1541 1542 Industrial buildings & warehouses; commercial & office building contractors

(P-1422)
DPR CONSTRUCTION A GEN PARTNR
1450 Veterans Blvd, Redwood City (94063-2617)
PHONE 650 474-1450
Douglas E Woods, *President*
Michele Leiva, *CFO*
Ron J Davidowski, *Corp Secy*
James F Dolen, *Exec VP*
Michael Ford, *Exec VP*
EMP: 2300
SQ FT: 36,300
SALES: 2.6B
SALES (corp-wide): 2.9B **Privately Held**
SIC: 1541 Industrial buildings & warehouses
PA: Dpr Construction, Inc.
1450 Veterans Blvd
Redwood City CA 94063
650 474-1450

(P-1423)
EXCEL CONSTRUCTION SVCS INC (PA)
1950 Raymer Ave, Fullerton (92833-2513)
PHONE 714 680-9200
Fax: 562 921-0510
Karen Latzlaff, *CEO*
Dan Jurado, *President*

1541 - General Contractors, Indl Bldgs & Warehouses County (P-1424)

PRODUCTS & SERVICES SECTION

Todd London, *Vice Pres*
EMP: 54
SQ FT: 12,000
SALES (est): 31.5MM **Privately Held**
SIC: 1541 Industrial buildings & warehouses

(P-1424)
FRIZE CORPORATION
16605 Gale Ave, City of Industry (91745-1802)
PHONE.................................626 369-6088
Fax: 626 336-5329
James N Frize, *President*
Brad Daugherty, *Project Mgr*
Jon Oleinick, *Project Mgr*
Carlos Marquez, *Site Mgr*
Paul Nevarez, *Safety Mgr*
EMP: 80
SQ FT: 25,000
SALES (est): 22.5MM **Privately Held**
WEB: www.frizecorp.com
SIC: 1541 1542 Industrial buildings & warehouses; commercial & office building contractors

(P-1425)
FULLMER CONSTRUCTION
1725 S Grove Ave, Ontario (91761-4530)
PHONE.................................909 947-9467
Fax: 909 947-2970
Robert A Fullmer, *President*
Loyd McGhee, *COO*
Gene Fulmer, *CFO*
Ray Stromback, *CFO*
Gered Yetter, *CFO*
◆ **EMP:** 120
SQ FT: 20,000
SALES (est): 65.4MM **Privately Held**
SIC: 1541 Industrial buildings & warehouses

(P-1426)
GARYS CARPETING INC
182 Granite St Ste 102, Corona (92879-1288)
PHONE.................................951 272-8210
Fax: 909 272-9009
Gary Suarez, *President*
Suzzane Suarez, *Vice Pres*
EMP: 55
SQ FT: 10,000
SALES (est): 8.9MM **Privately Held**
SIC: 1541 Industrial buildings & warehouses

(P-1427)
GEORGE RICHARD
P.O. Box 712002, Santee (92072-2002)
PHONE.................................619 805-6751
George Richards, *President*
EMP: 60
SALES (est): 2.5MM **Privately Held**
SIC: 1541 Renovation, remodeling & repairs: industrial buildings

(P-1428)
GERDAU REINFORCING STEEL (DH)
3880 Murphy Canyon Rd # 100, San Diego (92123-4410)
PHONE.................................858 737-7700
Fax: 619 286-3603
Christopher Ervin, *Vice Pres*
Steven Fellows, *Treasurer*
Howard Bennion, *Vice Pres*
Jennifer Martin, *Risk Mgmt Dir*
Kimberli Clement, *Office Mgr*
EMP: 50
SALES (est): 459.2MM **Privately Held**
WEB: www.pcsgp.com
SIC: 1541 Steel building construction
HQ: Gerdau Ameristeel Us Inc.
4221 W Boy Scout Blvd # 600
Tampa FL 33607
813 286-8383

(P-1429)
GERDAU REINFORCING STEEL
5425 Industrial Pkwy, San Bernardino (92407-1803)
PHONE.................................909 713-1130
Fax: 909 713-1131
Lee Albright, *Manager*
EMP: 65 **Privately Held**
SIC: 1541 Steel building construction

HQ: Gerdau Reinforcing Steel
3880 Murphy Canyon Rd # 100
San Diego CA 92123
858 737-7700

(P-1430)
GHIRINGHLLI SPCIALTY FOODS INC
101 Benicia Rd, Vallejo (94590-7003)
PHONE.................................707 561-7670
Mike Ghiringhelli, *President*
Ed Ferrero, *Vice Pres*
Margee Longnecker, *Office Mgr*
Matt Kyne, *Buyer*
EMP: 145
SQ FT: 1,000
SALES (est): 47MM **Privately Held**
WEB: www.gfoods.net
SIC: 1541 Food products manufacturing or packing plant construction

(P-1431)
GOEBEL MECHANICAL INC
501 Lakeville Cir E, Petaluma (94954-5736)
P.O. Box 157 (94953-0157)
PHONE.................................707 778-2340
Gregory D Goebel, *President*
Duane D Goebel, *CFO*
Joanne R Goebel, *Admin Sec*
EMP: 60
SQ FT: 2,500
SALES (est): 4.2MM **Privately Held**
SIC: 1541 Industrial buildings & warehouses

(P-1432)
GRIMMWAY ENTERPRISES INC
Grimmway Farm
12020 Malaga Rd, Arvin (93203-9527)
PHONE.................................661 854-6240
Fax: 661 854-6244
Ron Black, *Manager*
John Maricich, *Manager*
Mike Blakley, *Supervisor*
EMP: 100
SALES (corp-wide): 1.8B **Privately Held**
SIC: 1541 1542 Industrial buildings & warehouses; nonresidential construction
PA: Grimmway Enterprises, Inc.
14141 Di Giorgio Rd
Arvin CA 93203
661 854-6250

(P-1433)
H C OLSEN CNSTR CO INC
710 Los Angeles Ave, Monrovia (91016-4250)
PHONE.................................626 359-8900
Fax: 626 359-1131
Linda Jacqueline Pearson, *CEO*
Karl Pearson, *Corp Secy*
Paul Inciti, *CTO*
Linda Graybill, *VP Finance*
Paul Hudson, *Sr Project Mgr*
EMP: 75 **EST:** 1946
SQ FT: 12,800
SALES (est): 27.4MM **Privately Held**
WEB: www.hcolsen.com
SIC: 1541 Industrial buildings, new construction

(P-1434)
HAL HAYS CONSTRUCTION INC (PA)
4181 Latham St, Riverside (92501-1729)
PHONE.................................951 369-1008
Hal Hays, *President*
E Denise Hays, *CFO*
Pedram Afshar, *Project Engr*
Evelyn Nevarez, *Accounting Mgr*
Lori McDaniels, *Finance*
EMP: 113
SQ FT: 28,400
SALES: 75.3MM **Privately Held**
WEB: www.halhays.com
SIC: 1541 1542 1623 1629 Industrial buildings & warehouses; commercial & office buildings, renovation & repair; water, sewer & utility lines; dams, waterways, docks & other marine construction; highway & street paving contractor; concrete work

(P-1435)
HAMANN CONSTRUCTION
1000 Pioneer Way, El Cajon (92020-1923)
PHONE.................................619 440-7424
Fax: 619 440-8914
Jeffrey C Hamann, *CEO*
Gregg Hamann, *Treasurer*
Eric Sobocinski, *Info Tech Mgr*
Sarah Jacobson, *Manager*
EMP: 75
SQ FT: 15,000
SALES (est): 17.7MM **Privately Held**
WEB: www.hamannco.com
SIC: 1541 Industrial buildings, new construction

(P-1436)
HASKELL COMPANY (INC)
478 Lindbergh Ave, Livermore (94551-9553)
PHONE.................................925 960-1815
EMP: 185
SALES (corp-wide): 923.1MM **Privately Held**
SIC: 1541 Industrial buildings, new construction
HQ: The Haskell Company Inc
111 Riverside Ave
Jacksonville FL 32202
904 791-4500

(P-1437)
HERRERO BUILDERS INCORPORATED (PA)
2100 Oakdale Ave, San Francisco (94124-1516)
PHONE.................................415 824-7675
Fax: 415 824-7674
Mark D Herrero, *Ch of Bd*
Rick Herrero, *President*
James Totoritis, *CFO*
Stephanie Roberson, *Officer*
Craig Braccia, *Vice Pres*
▲ **EMP:** 128
SQ FT: 10,000
SALES (est): 84MM **Privately Held**
WEB: www.herrero.com
SIC: 1541 Industrial buildings, new construction

(P-1438)
HUGO ALONSO INC
Also Called: Alonso Construction
2820 Via Orange Way Ste J, Spring Valley (91978-1742)
PHONE.................................619 660-5395
Hugo Alonso, *President*
Norma Alonso, *Corp Secy*
Tom Fox, *Vice Pres*
Jessica Cervantes, *Admin Asst*
EMP: 50
SQ FT: 13,000
SALES (est): 11.1MM **Privately Held**
WEB: www.hugoalonsoinc.com
SIC: 1541 1721 Industrial buildings & warehouses; industrial painting

(P-1439)
JACKSON CONSTRUCTION (PA)
155 Cadillac Dr, Sacramento (95825-5403)
PHONE.................................916 381-8113
Fax: 916 381-0212
John Jackson Jr, *President*
Don Hanson, *CFO*
Lynda Jackson, *Corp Secy*
Eric J Edelmayer, *Vice Pres*
Bill Fargo, *Vice Pres*
EMP: 50 **EST:** 1974
SQ FT: 10,000
SALES (est): 19.1MM **Privately Held**
WEB: www.jacksonprop.com
SIC: 1541 1542 6552 6531 Industrial buildings & warehouses; nonresidential construction; land subdividers & developers, residential; real estate agents & managers

(P-1440)
JH BRYANT JR INC (PA)
17217 S Broadway, Gardena (90248-3117)
PHONE.................................310 532-1840
Fax: 310 327-1458
Barbara Bryant, *CEO*
John Bryant III, *President*
Howe Rich, *CFO*
Joseph Perez, *Vice Pres*

Aaron Smith, *Project Mgr*
EMP: 50
SQ FT: 6,500
SALES (est): 13MM **Privately Held**
WEB: www.jhbryant.com
SIC: 1541 Industrial buildings & warehouses

(P-1441)
JULIUS STEVE CONSTRUCTION INC
230 Calle Pintoresco, San Clemente (92672-7503)
PHONE.................................949 369-7820
Fax: 949 369-7821
Leigh Thornburg Julius, *CEO*
Pete Ferrarini, *President*
Marcie Miller, *Executive*
Chris Hinck, *Project Dir*
Colleen Pierce, *Project Dir*
EMP: 50
SQ FT: 6,700
SALES: 12.9MM **Privately Held**
WEB: www.stevejuliusconstruction.com
SIC: 1541 Industrial buildings & warehouses; industrial buildings, new construction

(P-1442)
KAJIMA CONSTRUCTION SVCS INC
Also Called: Kajima International
250 E 1st St Ste 400, Los Angeles (90012-3820)
PHONE.................................323 269-0020
Nori Ohashi, *Branch Mgr*
Rob Stein, *Vice Pres*
Philip Holmes, *Info Tech Mgr*
Brett Anderson, *Project Mgr*
Howard Craig, *Project Mgr*
EMP: 50
SALES (corp-wide): 14.8B **Privately Held**
SIC: 1541 1542 8712 Industrial buildings, new construction; commercial & office building, new construction; house designer
HQ: Kajima Construction Services, Inc.
3475 Piedmont Rd Ne Ste 1
Atlanta GA 30305
404 564-3900

(P-1443)
KAZARIAN/JEWETT INC
Also Called: Kcb Builders
6621 Pcf Cast Hwy Ste 120, Long Beach (90803)
PHONE.................................562 594-5927
K C Kazarian, *President*
Bill Jewett, *Treasurer*
Barbara Kazarian, *Vice Pres*
EMP: 50
SALES: 2MM **Privately Held**
SIC: 1541 1542 Industrial buildings & warehouses; commercial & office building contractors

(P-1444)
KEMP BROS CONSTRUCTION INC
10135 Geary Ave, Santa Fe Springs (90670-3253)
PHONE.................................562 236-5000
Fax: 562 236-5010
Greg S Solaas, *President*
Steven Solaas, *President*
Steve Rosenfield, *Vice Pres*
Mark Rettig, *Business Dir*
Luis Cevallos, *Project Mgr*
EMP: 50
SQ FT: 15,500
SALES (est): 16.3MM **Privately Held**
SIC: 1541 1542 Industrial buildings & warehouses; hospital construction

(P-1445)
KENDRICK CONSTRUCTION SERVICES
Also Called: Kendrick Co The
3010 Old Ranch Pkwy # 470, Seal Beach (90740-2789)
PHONE.................................562 546-0200
Gregory T Hook, *President*
Randy Kendrick, *Shareholder*
Liz Gloriani, *CFO*

1541 - General Contractors, Indl Bldgs & Warehouses County (P-1465)

Jud Leibee, *CFO*
Sandra Combee, *Admin Sec*
EMP: 55
SQ FT: 3,500
SALES (est): 6.4MM **Privately Held**
WEB: www.kendrickconstruction.com
SIC: 1541 1542 Industrial buildings & warehouses; nonresidential construction

(P-1446)
KERNEN CONSTRUCTION
2350 Glendale Dr, McKinleyville (95519-9205)
P.O. Box 1340, Blue Lake (95525-1340)
PHONE..............................707 826-8686
Fax: 707 826-1888
Kurt Kernen, *Partner*
Scott Farley, *Partner*
Walt Hurst, *Project Mgr*
EMP: 60
SQ FT: 120
SALES (est): 15MM **Privately Held**
WEB: www.kernenconstruction.com
SIC: 1541 1542 Industrial buildings, new construction; renovation, remodeling & repairs: industrial buildings; commercial & office building, new construction; commercial & office building, renovation & repair

(P-1447)
LEDCOR CMI INC
6405 Mira Mesa Blvd # 100, San Diego (92121-4120)
PHONE..............................602 595-3017
David W Lede, *CEO*
EMP: 5000
SALES (est): 158.5MM **Privately Held**
SIC: 1541 1611 1629 1623 Industrial buildings & warehouses; highway & street construction; mine loading & discharging station construction; industrial plant construction; pipeline construction; condominium construction; communication services

(P-1448)
LEVY PRMIUM FDSRVICE LTD PRTNR
Also Called: Levy Cncessions At Staples Ctr
1111 S Figueroa St, Los Angeles (90015-1300)
PHONE..............................213 742-7867
Jeffrey Rosenbaugh, *Manager*
EMP: 70
SALES (corp-wide): 9.7MM **Privately Held**
WEB: www.cafespiaggia.com
SIC: 1541 Industrial buildings & warehouses
PA: Levy Premium Foodservice Limited Partnership
980 N Michigan Ave # 400
Chicago IL 60611
312 664-8200

(P-1449)
MA STEINER CONSTRUCTION INC
8999 Greenback Ln Fl 2, Orangevale (95662-4650)
PHONE..............................916 988-6300
Martin Steiner, *President*
Darlene Bycroft, *Manager*
EMP: 64
SALES (est): 13.5MM **Privately Held**
SIC: 1541 1794 1542 1611 Industrial buildings, new construction; excavation & grading, building construction; commercial & office building, new construction; highway & street construction; general contractor, highway & street construction

(P-1450)
MILES CONSTRUCTION GROUP INC
27226 Via Industria, Temecula (92590-3751)
PHONE..............................951 260-2504
Adam Miles, *President*
S Parkinson, *Corp Secy*
G King, *Vice Pres*
EMP: 50
SQ FT: 8,000

SALES: 3.7MM **Privately Held**
SIC: 1541 1542 Industrial buildings & warehouses; industrial buildings, new construction; steel building construction; warehouse construction; commercial & office building, new construction

(P-1451)
MILLIE AND SEVERSON INC
3601 Serpentine Dr, Los Alamitos (90720-2440)
P.O. Box 3601 (90720-0399)
PHONE..............................562 493-3611
Fax: 562 598-6871
Scott Feest, *President*
Robert E Wissmann, *Senior VP*
John Grossman, *Vice Pres*
Mark Huber, *Vice Pres*
Mike McIsaac, *Project Mgr*
EMP: 75 EST: 1945
SQ FT: 15,000
SALES: 288.6MM
SALES (corp-wide): 288.7MM **Privately Held**
WEB: www.mandsinc.com
SIC: 1541 Industrial buildings, new construction; renovation, remodeling & repairs: industrial buildings; steel building construction; warehouse construction
PA: Severson Group Incorporated
3601 Serpentine Dr
Los Alamitos CA 90720
562 493-3611

(P-1452)
MINSHEW BROTHERS STL CNSTR INC
12578 Vigilante Rd, Lakeside (92040-1112)
P.O. Box 1000 (92040-0902)
PHONE..............................619 561-5700
Fax: 619 561-4758
James Minshew, *President*
Daniel P Minshew, *Treasurer*
John M Minshew, *Vice Pres*
Brian T Johnson, *Controller*
EMP: 105
SQ FT: 22,000
SALES (est): 25.9MM **Privately Held**
SIC: 1541 1791 Steel building construction; structural steel erection

(P-1453)
MODERN BUILDING INC
3083 Southgate Ln, Chico (95928-7427)
P.O. Box 772 (95927-0772)
PHONE..............................530 891-4533
Fax: 530 891-6834
L Gage Chrysler, *CEO*
Gary Fowler, *Corp Secy*
James Seegert, *Vice Pres*
Sandy Karatakeli, *Office Mgr*
Debbie Barnett, *Admin Asst*
EMP: 50
SQ FT: 5,000
SALES (est): 22.7MM **Privately Held**
WEB: www.modernbuildinginc.com
SIC: 1541 1542 Industrial buildings & warehouses; commercial & office building, new construction

(P-1454)
OLTMANS CONSTRUCTION CO (PA)
10005 Mission Mill Rd, Whittier (90601-1739)
P.O. Box 985 (90608-0985)
PHONE..............................562 948-4242
Fax: 562 695-2939
Joseph O Oltmans II, *Ch of Bd*
John Gormly, *President*
Dan Schlothan, *CFO*
Tom Augustine, *Vice Pres*
Greg Grupp, *Vice Pres*
▼ **EMP:** 85
SQ FT: 33,000
SALES (est): 317MM **Privately Held**
WEB: www.oltmans.com
SIC: 1541 1542 Industrial buildings, new construction; renovation, remodeling & repairs: industrial buildings; commercial & office building, new construction; commercial & office building, renovation & repair

(P-1455)
ORANGE COAST BUILDING SERVICES
2191 S Dupont Dr, Anaheim (92806-6102)
PHONE..............................714 453-6300
Fax: 714 453-6301
Kevin W Franklin, *President*
Jim Ongaro, *Vice Pres*
Cheryl Matsumiya, *Controller*
EMP: 115
SQ FT: 6,000
SALES (est): 26.6MM **Privately Held**
WEB: www.ocbsonline.com
SIC: 1541 1542 Industrial buildings, new construction; commercial & office building contractors

(P-1456)
OUT OF SHELL LLC
Also Called: Ling's
9658 Remer St, South El Monte (91733-3033)
PHONE..............................626 401-1923
Fax: 626 401-1925
Alice Liu,
Bing Yang,
Harry Wong, *Manager*
EMP: 200
SALES (est): 24.4MM **Privately Held**
SIC: 1541 Food products manufacturing or packing plant construction

(P-1457)
PARSONS PROJECT SERVICES INC
100 W Walnut St, Pasadena (91124-0001)
PHONE..............................626 440-4000
Charles Harrington, *CEO*
Todd K Wager, *President*
EMP: 131
SALES (est): 5.2MM **Privately Held**
SIC: 1541 Industrial buildings & warehouses

(P-1458)
PCL INDUSTRIAL SERVICES INC
1500 S Union Ave, Bakersfield (93307-4144)
PHONE..............................661 832-3995
Joe W Carrieri, *CEO*
Gary L Basher, *Corp Secy*
Gordon Panas, *Exec VP*
Roberta A Kerchinski, *Finance Dir*
Cheri Kiser, *Accountant*
EMP: 300
SALES (est): 78.4MM **Privately Held**
SIC: 1541 Industrial buildings & warehouses

(P-1459)
R Q CONSTRUCTION INC
3194 Lionshead Ave, Carlsbad (92010-4701)
PHONE..............................760 477-1199
George H Rogers III, *CEO*
Michael D Patterson, *President*
Craig Shadle, *CFO*
Donald M Rogers, *Vice Pres*
Mary Baker, *Admin Sec*
EMP: 140
SQ FT: 8,000
SALES (est): 41.5MM **Privately Held**
SIC: 1541 Industrial buildings & warehouses

(P-1460)
R Q CONSTRUCTION LLC
Also Called: Rqc
3194 Lionshead Ave, Carlsbad (92010-4701)
PHONE..............................760 631-7707
George H Rogers III, *CEO*
Craig Shadle, *CFO*
Mary Baker, *Admin Sec*
Christina Clemm, *Admin Sec*
EMP: 170
SALES (est): 73.9MM **Privately Held**
SIC: 1541 1611 Industrial buildings & warehouses; general contractor, highway & street construction

(P-1461)
RORE INC (PA)
5151 Shoreham Pl Ste 260, San Diego (92122-5962)
PHONE..............................858 404-7393
Gita Murthy, *CEO*
Kim Zakar, *Vice Pres*
Annie Rossimiller, *Accountant*
Nandita Murthy, *Controller*
Sheryl Jenkins, *Marketing Staff*
EMP: 68
SQ FT: 3,500
SALES: 16MM **Privately Held**
WEB: www.roreinc.com
SIC: 1541 4959 1542 Renovation, remodeling & repairs: industrial buildings; toxic or hazardous waste cleanup; commercial & office building, new construction; commercial & office building, renovation & repair

(P-1462)
SHAWS STRCTURES UNLIMITED INC
Also Called: Shaw Construction
2573 W Cambridge Ave, Fresno (93705-4737)
PHONE..............................559 275-3475
Paul W Shaw, *President*
Gloria Shaw, *Vice Pres*
Mildred Shaw, *Vice Pres*
EMP: 50
SQ FT: 7,850
SALES (est): 6.6MM **Privately Held**
SIC: 1541 1542 1791 Prefabricated building erection, industrial; commercial & office buildings, prefabricated erection; religious building construction; structural steel erection

(P-1463)
SHIMS BARGAIN INC
Also Called: JC Sales
7030 E Slauson Ave, Commerce (90040-3621)
PHONE..............................323 726-8800
Andy Kim, *Manager*
EMP: 210
SALES (corp-wide): 182.8MM **Privately Held**
SIC: 1541 Industrial buildings & warehouses
PA: Shims Bargain, Inc.
2600 S Soto St
Vernon CA 90058
323 881-0099

(P-1464)
SIERRA BAY CONTRACTORS INC
4021 Port Chicago Hwy # 150, Concord (94520-1122)
PHONE..............................925 671-7711
Fax: 925 825-4021
Albert D Seeno Jr, *President*
Robert Coburn, *Vice Pres*
Thomas A Seeno, *Vice Pres*
Nancy Caity, *Human Res Mgr*
Nancy Cassity, *Human Res Mgr*
EMP: 50 EST: 1997
SQ FT: 2,000
SALES (est): 5.4MM **Privately Held**
WEB: www.sierrabayinc.com
SIC: 1541 6221 Industrial buildings & warehouses; commodity contracts brokers, dealers

(P-1465)
SILMAN VENTURE CORPORATION (PA)
Also Called: Silman Construction
1600 Factor Ave, San Leandro (94577-5618)
PHONE..............................510 347-4800
Tom Mangin, *CEO*
Rick Silva, *COO*
EMP: 125 EST: 2007
SQ FT: 17,000
SALES: 40MM **Privately Held**
SIC: 1541 Industrial buildings, new construction

1541 - General Contractors, Indl Bldgs & Warehouses County

(P-1466) STANTRU RESOURCES INC
Also Called: Stantru Reinforcing Steel
11175 Redwood Ave, Fontana (92337-7137)
P.O. Box 310189 (92331-0189)
PHONE..................................909 587-1441
Ida Ichen, *President*
William M Klorman, *Manager*
EMP: 83
SALES (est): 6.1MM **Privately Held**
SIC: **1541** 1542 Industrial buildings, new construction; pharmaceutical manufacturing plant construction; commercial & office building, new construction; school building construction; institutional building construction

(P-1467) STEELTECH CONSTRUCTION SVCS
4081 E La Palma Ave Ste G, Anaheim (92807-1701)
PHONE..................................714 630-2890
Fax: 714 630-3568
Edward Campbell, *President*
EMP: 100
SQ FT: 2,200
SALES: 5MM **Privately Held**
SIC: **1541** Industrial buildings & warehouses

(P-1468) SWINERTON BUILDERS (HQ)
Also Called: Swinerton MGT & Consulting
260 Townsend St, San Francisco (94107-1719)
PHONE..................................415 421-2980
Jeffrey C Hoopes, *Ch of Bd*
John T Capener, *President*
Gary J Rafferty, *President*
Randall Brinkhoff, *CFO*
Linda G Schowalter, *CFO*
▲ EMP: 200
SQ FT: 300,353
SALES: 2.8B
SALES (corp-wide): 2.8B **Privately Held**
SIC: **1541** 1522 1542 Industrial buildings, new construction; steel building construction; hotel/motel, new construction; commercial & office building, new construction; commercial & office buildings, renovation & repair; specialized public building contractors
PA: Swinerton Incorporated
   260 Townsend St
   San Francisco CA 94107
   415 421-2980

(P-1469) SWINERTON BUILDERS
Swinerton Renewable Energy
16798 W Bernardo Dr, San Diego (92127-1904)
PHONE..................................858 622-4040
Fax: 858 622-4044
Don Adair, *President*
Brian McCarthy, *Executive*
Michelle Alford, *Admin Asst*
Jesse Blake, *Webmaster*
Bob Danielson, *Project Mgr*
EMP: 65
SALES (corp-wide): 2.8B **Privately Held**
SIC: **1541** 1522 Industrial buildings & warehouses; residential construction
HQ: Swinerton Builders
   260 Townsend St
   San Francisco CA 94107
   415 421-2980

(P-1470) T B PENICK & SONS INC (PA)
15435 Innovation Dr # 100, San Diego (92128-3443)
PHONE..................................858 558-1800
Fax: 858 558-1881
Marc E Penick, *CEO*
Frank Klemaske, *President*
Timothy Penick, *President*
Byron Klemaske, *Exec VP*
Jamie Awford, *Vice Pres*
EMP: 151
SQ FT: 30,000
SALES: 139.2MM **Privately Held**
WEB: www.tbpenick.com
SIC: **1541** 1542 Industrial buildings & warehouses; nonresidential construction

(P-1471) TAISEI CONSTRUCTION CORP (HQ)
970 W 190th St Ste 920, Torrance (90502-1063)
PHONE..................................714 886-1530
Fax: 714 886-1546
Tetsuo Tawada, *CEO*
Takashi Uchida, *Treasurer*
Richard Aman, *Exec VP*
Tom Fadgen, *Data Proc Dir*
Joe Megia, *VP Finance*
▲ EMP: 52
SQ FT: 15,000
SALES (est): 44.6MM
SALES (corp-wide): 13.2B **Privately Held**
SIC: **1541** 1542 Industrial buildings & warehouses; nonresidential construction
PA: Taisei Corporation
   1-25-1, Nishishinjuku
   Shinjuku-Ku TKY 160-0
   333 481-111

(P-1472) TCB INDUSTRIAL INC (PA)
2955 Farrar Ave, Modesto (95354-4118)
PHONE..................................209 571-0569
Fax: 209 577-3735
Dave Raybourn, *CEO*
Bruce Elliott, *CFO*
EMP: 55
SALES (est): 61.3MM **Privately Held**
WEB: www.Tcbindustrial.net
SIC: **1541** Industrial buildings & warehouses

(P-1473) TEKTETCO
Also Called: Tribal Tektet
5251 Ericson Way, Arcata (95521-9273)
PHONE..................................707 822-9000
Daniel Johnson,
Terry Wilson,
EMP: 65 EST: 2009
SALES (est): 3MM **Privately Held**
SIC: **1541** 1542 1522 Industrial buildings, new construction; commercial & office building, new construction; hotel/motel, new construction; multi-family dwellings, new construction

(P-1474) TORRES CONSTRUCTION CORP (PA)
7330 N Figueroa St, Los Angeles (90041-2547)
PHONE..................................323 257-7460
Fax: 323 257-8044
Martha McGowin, *President*
Mael Torres, *Treasurer*
Esteban Torres, *Vice Pres*
Rod McGallian, *Project Mgr*
Nick Porter, *Project Mgr*
EMP: 76
SQ FT: 7,500
SALES (est): 39MM **Privately Held**
WEB: www.torresconstruction.com
SIC: **1541** Industrial buildings & warehouses

(P-1475) TRI-TECH RESTORATION CO INC
3301 N San Fernando Blvd, Burbank (91504-2531)
PHONE..................................818 565-3900
Fax: 818 565-3999
Armine Bakmazian, *President*
Michael Boyd, *Admin Sec*
Shant Kavarian, *Info Tech Mgr*
Emil Dilanian, *Project Mgr*
Lucine Soulakhian, *Cust Mgr*
EMP: 70
SQ FT: 35,000
SALES: 8MM **Privately Held**
WEB: www.tritechrestoration.com
SIC: **1541** Industrial buildings & warehouses

(P-1476) TRILOGY RIO VISTA
Also Called: Shea Homes
1200 Clubhouse Dr, Rio Vista (94571-9801)
PHONE..................................707 374-1100
Fax: 707 374-1124
Steve Hextell, *Vice Pres*
Jason Hughes, *General Mgr*
EMP: 60
SALES (est): 7.6MM **Privately Held**
SIC: **1541** Industrial buildings, new construction

(P-1477) UNIVERSAL DUST COLLECTOR
Also Called: UDC
1041 N Kraemer Pl, Anaheim (92806-2611)
PHONE..................................714 630-8588
George G Shaffer, *President*
Theresa A Shaffer, *CEO*
Deborah Huerta, *Corp Secy*
Jeff Brown, *Vice Pres*
Curtis Schendel, *Vice Pres*
EMP: 90
SQ FT: 30,000
SALES: 28MM **Privately Held**
WEB: www.udccorporation.com
SIC: **1541** Industrial buildings & warehouses

(P-1478) WATSON CONTRACTORS INC
3185 Longview Dr, Sacramento (95821-7214)
PHONE..................................916 481-6293
Greg Watson, *President*
EMP: 65
SALES (est): 4.1MM **Privately Held**
WEB: www.watsonroofing.com
SIC: **1541** Renovation, remodeling & repairs: industrial buildings

(P-1479) WESTPORT/BERGER A JOINT VENTR
4333 E Live Oak Ave, Arcadia (91006-5531)
PHONE..................................626 447-2448
Joanne Apodaca,
Vincent Wile,
EMP: 208
SQ FT: 200
SALES (est): 5.9MM **Privately Held**
SIC: **1541** 1522 Steel building construction; apartment building construction

---

1542 General Contractors, Nonresidential & Non-indl Bldgs

(P-1480) A RUIZ CNSTR CO & ASSOC INC
1601 Cortland Ave, San Francisco (94110-5716)
PHONE..................................415 647-4010
Fax: 415 285-9243
Antonio Ruiz, *President*
Wayne McIntosh, *Vice Pres*
Henrietta Ruiz, *General Mgr*
Victor Alvarez, *Project Mgr*
Victor Godinez, *Project Mgr*
EMP: 50
SQ FT: 10,000
SALES (est): 16.7MM **Privately Held**
WEB: www.aruizconstruction.com
SIC: **1542** Commercial & office building contractors

(P-1481) AARDEX INC
1550 E Main St, Santa Maria (93454-4819)
PHONE..................................805 928-7600
Shane Fowleror, *President*
EMP: 60
SALES (est): 3.4MM **Privately Held**
SIC: **1542** Commercial & office building, new construction

(P-1482) ABHE & SVOBODA INC
880 Tavern Rd, Alpine (91901-3810)
PHONE..................................619 659-1320
David Grant, *Manager*
Daniel Markwell, *Project Mgr*
Jim Ness, *Sr Project Mgr*
Frank Orbach, *Director*
EMP: 94
SALES (corp-wide): 1.7MM **Privately Held**
SIC: **1542** Commercial & office building, new construction
PA: Abhe & Svoboda, Inc.
   18100 Dairy Ln
   Jordan MN 55352
   952 447-6025

(P-1483) ACCESS PACIFIC INC
755 E Washington Blvd, Pasadena (91104-5009)
PHONE..................................626 792-0616
Tomas Torres, *President*
EMP: 50 EST: 2009
SALES (est): 13.1MM **Privately Held**
SIC: **1542** Nonresidential construction

(P-1484) AFA CONSTRCTN GRP/CAL INC JV
2040 Peabody Rd Ste 400, Vacaville (95687-6694)
PHONE..................................707 446-7996
Ralph Hodges, *President*
Olivia Trudell, *Vice Pres*
EMP: 80
SALES (est): 4.3MM **Privately Held**
SIC: **1542** Nonresidential construction

(P-1485) AHTNA GOVERNMENT SERVICES CORP
3100 Beacon Blvd, West Sacramento (95691-3483)
PHONE..................................916 372-2000
Chris Smith, *President*
Roy Phares, *Executive*
Chris Whitaker, *Data Proc Staff*
David Fengler, *Technology*
Dan Graham, *Technology*
EMP: 60
SALES (corp-wide): 220.1MM **Privately Held**
WEB: www.ahtnagov.com
SIC: **1542** Nonresidential construction
HQ: Ahtna Government Services Corporation
   3100 Beacon Blvd
   West Sacramento CA 95691
   916 372-2000

(P-1486) AIS CONSTRUCTION COMPANY
1811 W Betteravia Rd, Santa Maria (93455-1044)
P.O. Box 4209, San Luis Obispo (93403-4209)
PHONE..................................805 928-9467
Fax: 805 566-6534
Andy Sheaffer, *President*
Clif Leonard, *Controller*
Marissa Nibokin, *Manager*
EMP: 85
SQ FT: 4,000
SALES (est): 15.3MM **Privately Held**
WEB: www.aisconstruction.com
SIC: **1542** Commercial & office building contractors

(P-1487) AK CONSTRUCTORS INC
1828 Railroad St, Corona (92880-2512)
PHONE..................................951 280-0269
Kenneth G Dougher, *President*
Micheal Harrington, *Corp Secy*
Andrew Donegan, *Vice Pres*
Megan Freeman, *Admin Asst*
Cathy Baglio, *Administration*
EMP: 50
SALES (est): 19.6MM **Privately Held**
WEB: www.akconstructors.com
SIC: **1542** Commercial & office building, new construction

PRODUCTS & SERVICES SECTION **1542 - General Contractors, Nonresidential & Non-indl Bldgs County (P-1509)**

(P-1488)
ALLEN L BENDER INC
2798 Industrial Blvd, West Sacramento (95691-3888)
PHONE..................................916 372-2190
Fax: 916 372-2243
Blake Bender, *President*
Brian Bender, *CFO*
Jennifer Bittner-Bender, *Bd of Directors*
Bruce Miller, *Project Mgr*
Richard L Thurn, *Agent*
EMP: 120 EST: 1956
SQ FT: 22,000
SALES (est): 17.1MM Privately Held
WEB: www.allenbender.com
SIC: 1542 8711 Nonresidential construction; engineering services

(P-1489)
ALTEN CONSTRUCTION INC
720 12th St, Richmond (94801-2365)
PHONE..................................510 234-4200
Robert Andrew Alten, *CEO*
Amy Stegemiller, *Bd of Directors*
Shannon M Alten, *Vice Pres*
EMP: 80
SQ FT: 14,000
SALES (est): 40.8MM Privately Held
WEB: www.altenconstruction.com
SIC: 1542 Commercial & office building, new construction

(P-1490)
ANDERSON BURTON CONSTRUCTION
1510 Oxley St Ste G, South Pasadena (91030-5745)
PHONE..................................626 441-2464
EMP: 99
SQ FT: 500
SALES (est): 2.9MM Privately Held
SIC: 1542 Commercial & office buildings, renovation & repair

(P-1491)
ANDREW L YOUNGQUIST CNSTR INC
3187 Red Hill Ave Ste 200, Costa Mesa (92626-3454)
PHONE..................................949 862-5611
Andrew L Youngquist, *Ch of Bd*
James Lefler, *President*
Richard Lee Youngquist, *Vice Pres*
EMP: 90
SQ FT: 10,319
SALES (est): 9.5MM Privately Held
WEB: www.alyconstruction.com
SIC: 1542 1522 8741 Commercial & office building contractors; residential construction; construction management

(P-1492)
ARAGON CONSTRUCTION INC
5440 Arrow Hwy, Montclair (91763-1604)
PHONE..................................909 621-2200
Joseph E Aragon, *President*
Regina Aragon, *General Mgr*
Jamie Williams, *Administration*
John Halbach, *Project Mgr*
EMP: 55
SALES (est): 29.9MM Privately Held
SIC: 1542 Institutional building construction; commercial & office buildings, renovation & repair; shopping center construction; specialized public building contractors

(P-1493)
ASR CONSTRUCTORS INC
Also Called: Contractors Complete Surety
33891 Mission Trl, Wildomar (92595-8431)
PHONE..................................951 779-6580
Fax: 951 779-6588
Alan Lee Rigotti, *President*
Stacey Rigotti, *Corp Secy*
EMP: 270
SQ FT: 3,000
SALES (est): 47.5MM Privately Held
SIC: 1542 Nonresidential construction

(P-1494)
AT YOUR SVC HTG & COOLG LLC
333 H St Ste 5000, Chula Vista (91910-5561)
PHONE..................................602 550-6946
Joe Lizarraga, *Manager*
EMP: 66
SALES: 950K Privately Held
SIC: 1542 Nonresidential construction

(P-1495)
B C C S INC (PA)
Also Called: South Bay Construction Company
1711 Dell Ave, Campbell (95008-6904)
PHONE..................................408 379-5500
Fax: 408 379-3256
Richard Furtado, *Partner*
Jerri Kroen, *CFO*
Wayne Smith, *Vice Pres*
Linda Lipsius, *Office Mgr*
Kaitlin Lockhart, *Admin Asst*
EMP: 63
SQ FT: 10,100
SALES (est): 90.7MM Privately Held
WEB: www.sbci.com
SIC: 1542 Commercial & office buildings, prefabricated erection

(P-1496)
BALFOUR BEATTY CNSTR LLC
2335 Broadway Ste 300, Oakland (94612-2495)
PHONE..................................510 903-2060
Alison Stevens, *Project Mgr*
EMP: 186
SALES (corp-wide): 10.4B Privately Held
SIC: 1542 Nonresidential construction
HQ: Balfour Beatty Construction, Llc
  3100 Mckinnon St Fl 10
  Dallas TX 75201
  214 451-1000

(P-1497)
BALLIET BROS CONSTRUCTION CORP
390 Swift Ave Ste 14, South San Francisco (94080-6221)
PHONE..................................650 871-9000
Fax: 650 952-5682
Robert F Balliet, *President*
Michael Warren, *Vice Pres*
Mareth Vedder, *Admin Sec*
EMP: 50
SQ FT: 9,000
SALES (est): 2.1MM Privately Held
WEB: www.ballietbros.com
SIC: 1542 1522 2434 2431 Commercial & office buildings, renovation & repair; remodeling, multi-family dwellings; wood kitchen cabinets; trim, wood

(P-1498)
BARNHART-BALFOUR BEATTY INC (DH)
Also Called: Balfour Beatty Construction
10620 Treena St Ste 300, San Diego (92131-1141)
P.O. Box 270399 (92198-2399)
PHONE..................................858 635-7400
Fax: 858 635-7401
Robert Van Cleave, *Ch of Bd*
Eric Stenman, *President*
Glynna Hoekstra, *Exec VP*
Arthur Lee Barnhart, *Exec Dir*
Martin Gabey, *Project Mgr*
◆ EMP: 100 EST: 1983
SQ FT: 22,000
SALES (est): 162.9MM
SALES (corp-wide): 10.4B Privately Held
WEB: www.balfourbeattyus.com/southwest
SIC: 1542 8741 Commercial & office building, new construction; specialized public building contractors; construction management
HQ: Balfour Beatty Construction, Llc
  3100 Mckinnon St Fl 10
  Dallas TX 75201
  214 451-1000

(P-1499)
BCCI CONSTRUCTION COMPANY (PA)
Also Called: Bcci Builders
1160 Battery St Ste 250, San Francisco (94111-1216)
PHONE..................................415 817-5100
Fax: 415 995-6026
Michael Scribner, *President*
Hisham Mushasha, *CFO*
Bill Groth, *Senior VP*
Michael Dean, *Vice Pres*
William Groth, *Vice Pres*
EMP: 140
SQ FT: 15,121
SALES (est): 92.2MM Privately Held
WEB: www.bcciconst.com
SIC: 1542 Commercial & office buildings, renovation & repair

(P-1500)
BECHTEL ENTPS HOLDINGS INC
50 Beale St Bsmt 1, San Francisco (94105-1819)
P.O. Box 193965 (94119-3965)
PHONE..................................415 768-6745
Dan Chao, *Director*
Leslie Woodside, *Info Tech Dir*
Paul Unruh, *Director*
EMP: 430
SALES (est): 14.5MM Privately Held
SIC: 1542 4581 Nonresidential construction; airport
PA: Aterra Limited
  31 Gelliswick Road
  Milford Haven

(P-1501)
BEL ESPRIT BUILDERS INC
20902 Bake Pkwy Ste 100, Lake Forest (92630-2175)
PHONE..................................949 709-3500
David K Jackson, *President*
Debra Jackson, *Admin Sec*
Michael Grambusch, *Opers Mgr*
EMP: 50
SALES (est): 6.9MM Privately Held
SIC: 1542 Nonresidential construction

(P-1502)
BELMONT BRUNS CONSTRUCTION INC
1125 Mabury Rd, San Jose (95133-1029)
P.O. Box 612707 (95161-2707)
PHONE..................................408 977-1708
Fax: 408 294-1078
Mark A Collishaw, *CEO*
Paul J Helvik, *Vice Pres*
Jack Collishaw, *Admin Sec*
EMP: 55
SALES (est): 15.4MM Privately Held
SIC: 1542 1541 Commercial & office building, new construction; commercial & office buildings, renovation & repair; industrial buildings & warehouses

(P-1503)
BENNATHON CORP (PA)
Also Called: Tudor Cnstr & Restoration
10291 Iron Rock Way, Elk Grove (95624-1301)
PHONE..................................916 405-2100
Fax: 916 405-2170
David Urman, *President*
Tony Huynh, *CFO*
Peter Jones, *Vice Pres*
Al Kladiva, *Vice Pres*
EMP: 50
SQ FT: 30,000
SALES (est): 18.2MM Privately Held
SIC: 1542 1541 1521 Commercial & office buildings, renovation & repair; renovation, remodeling & repairs; industrial buildings; repairing fire damage, single-family houses

(P-1504)
BERGMAN KPRS LLC (PA)
2850 Saturn St Ste 100, Brea (92821-1701)
PHONE..................................714 924-7000
Fax: 909 627-5425
Mark C Bergman,
Tom Shirley, *Project Mgr*
Chris Sneed, *Project Mgr*
Trey Reese, *Engineer*
Holly Beatty, *Controller*
EMP: 125
SQ FT: 7,500
SALES (est): 52.5MM Privately Held
WEB: www.thebergman.com
SIC: 1542 Restaurant construction; shopping center construction

(P-1505)
BERNARDS BROS INC
3633 Inland Empire Blvd # 860, Ontario (91764-4922)
PHONE..................................909 941-5225
Rick Fochtman, *Branch Mgr*
EMP: 117
SALES (corp-wide): 165.5MM Privately Held
SIC: 1542 Commercial & office building, new construction
PA: Bernards Bros. Inc.
  555 1st St
  San Fernando CA 91340
  818 898-1521

(P-1506)
BIG LGUE DREAMS CONSULTING LLC
2100 S Azusa Ave, West Covina (91792-1507)
PHONE..................................626 839-1100
Jeffrey Odekirk, *Principal*
John Willie, *Manager*
EMP: 66
SALES (corp-wide): 37.8MM Privately Held
SIC: 1542 Stadium construction
PA: Big League Dreams Consulting, Llc
  16333 Fairfield Ranch Rd
  Chino Hills CA 91709
  909 287-1700

(P-1507)
BLAZONA CONCRETE CNSTR INC
525 Harbor Blvd Ste 10, West Sacramento (95691-2246)
PHONE..................................916 375-8337
J Dennis Blazona, *CEO*
Karen Blazona, *Vice Pres*
Angie Famlila, *Accountant*
Charissy Nelson, *Controller*
EMP: 100
SALES (est): 22.2MM Privately Held
WEB: www.blazona.com
SIC: 1542 Commercial & office building contractors

(P-1508)
BOGART CONSTRUCTION INC
9980 Irvine Center Dr # 200, Irvine (92618-4365)
PHONE..................................949 453-1400
Fax: 949 453-1414
Brad K Bogart, *President*
Yvon Belgabillo, *Office Admin*
Noel Amand, *Project Mgr*
Daniel Stone, *Project Mgr*
Megan Diblasi, *Project Engr*
EMP: 55
SQ FT: 10,000
SALES: 38.7MM Privately Held
WEB: www.bogartconstruction.com
SIC: 1542 Commercial & office building contractors

(P-1509)
BRADDOCK & LOGAN SERVICES INC
4155 Blackhawk Plaza Cir # 201, Danville (94506-4613)
P.O. Box 5300 (94526-1076)
PHONE..................................925 736-4000
Fax: 925 648-5700
Joseph E Raphel, *CEO*
Thomas Thompson, *Officer*
Missy Castaneda, *Regional Mgr*
Kari Cartner, *Administration*
Jim Demartini, *Finance*
EMP: 200
SALES (est): 43.7MM Privately Held
SIC: 1542 1522 Nonresidential construction; residential construction

1542 - General Contractors, Nonresidential & Non-indl Bldgs County (P-1510)

(P-1510)
BRADY-FORTITUDE
3710 Ruffin Rd, San Diego (92123-1812)
PHONE.................................858 496-0500
Mark Owens, *Supervisor*
EMP: 99
SALES (est): 3.9MM **Privately Held**
SIC: 1542 Commercial & office building, new construction

(P-1511)
BROWARD BUILDERS INC
1200 E Kentucky Ave, Woodland (95776-5906)
PHONE.................................530 406-1815
Dennis Broward, *President*
Randy Cantrell, *Vice Pres*
Anne Jensen, *Office Mgr*
Shawn Appleton, *Project Mgr*
EMP: 100
SQ FT: 7,000
SALES: 50.3MM **Privately Held**
WEB: www.browardbros.com
SIC: 1542 1531 School building construction; cooperative apartment developers

(P-1512)
BROWNCO CONSTRUCTION CO INC
1000 E Katella Ave, Anaheim (92805-6617)
PHONE.................................714 935-9600
Fax: 714 935-9666
Scot Alan Brown, *President*
Jeff Radtke, *Vice Pres*
Christine Moananu, *Admin Asst*
Michael Campbell, *Project Mgr*
Carla Marquez, *Persnl Mgr*
EMP: 87
SQ FT: 15,000
SALES (est): 23.7MM **Privately Held**
WEB: www.browncoinc.com
SIC: 1542 Nonresidential construction

(P-1513)
BUILD GROUP INC
457 Minna St Ste 100, San Francisco (94103-2914)
PHONE.................................415 777-4070
Ross Edwards Jr, *President*
Todd C Pennington, *President*
Jason Berry, *CFO*
David Grigg, *Plan/Corp Dev D*
John Santori, *Business Dir*
▲ EMP: 80 EST: 2006
SQ FT: 8,000
SALES: 390.5MM **Privately Held**
SIC: 1542 Commercial & office building contractors

(P-1514)
BURCH CONSTRUCTION COMPANY INC
405 Maple St Ste C-101, Ramona (92065-1890)
P.O. Box 395 (92065-0395)
PHONE.................................760 788-9370
Fax: 760 788-0325
Nancy Burch, *CEO*
Mitchell Burch, *President*
Meredith Schuler, *Admin Sec*
EMP: 50
SQ FT: 4,000
SALES (est): 12.1MM **Privately Held**
SIC: 1542 Commercial & office building, new construction

(P-1515)
BYCOR GENERAL CONTRACTORS INC
6490 Marindustry Dr Ste A, San Diego (92121-5297)
PHONE.................................858 587-1901
Scott Kaats, *CEO*
Richard A Byer, *President*
Terry Holum, *Project Mgr*
Richard Maxa, *Project Mgr*
Tamela Cross, *Project Engr*
EMP: 90
SQ FT: 10,041
SALES: 76.6MM **Privately Held**
WEB: www.bycor.com
SIC: 1542 Commercial & office building, new construction; commercial & office buildings, renovation & repair

(P-1516)
C & C CONSTRUCTION INC
7941 E Hidden Lakes Dr, Granite Bay (95746-9539)
PHONE.................................916 434-5280
Fax: 916 434-5288
Paul Cavaghan, *CEO*
Denise Caton, *Vice Pres*
Sarah Summers, *Project Mgr*
Sherry Angel, *Manager*
EMP: 50
SQ FT: 12,800
SALES (est): 10.1MM **Privately Held**
SIC: 1542 Commercial & office building contractors

(P-1517)
C W DRIVER INCORPORATED (PA)
468 N Rosemead Blvd, Pasadena (91107-3010)
PHONE.................................626 351-8800
Dana Roberts, *President*
Bessie Kouvara, *CFO*
John Janacek, *Senior VP*
Robert Maxwell, *Senior VP*
Steven S Nelson, *Vice Pres*
EMP: 60 EST: 1919
SQ FT: 14,000
SALES (est): 259MM **Privately Held**
WEB: www.cwdriver.com
SIC: 1542 Commercial & office building, new construction

(P-1518)
CAHILL CONTRACTORS INC (PA)
425 California St # 2200, San Francisco (94104-2207)
PHONE.................................415 986-0600
Fax: 415 986-4406
John E Cahill Jr, *CEO*
Chuck Palley, *President*
Darrell Diamond, *Corp Secy*
Mark Zaleski, *Vice Pres*
Theresa Amos-Chapman, *Executive Asst*
▲ EMP: 121 EST: 1974
SALES: 233MM **Privately Held**
WEB: www.cahill-sf.com
SIC: 1542 Commercial & office building, new construction

(P-1519)
CAL-PACIFIC CONSTRUCTION INC
1009 Terra Nova Blvd, Pacifica (94044-4308)
PHONE.................................650 557-1238
John Wah Chan, *President*
Kennedy Chan, *CEO*
Gilbert Lee, *Project Engr*
EMP: 50
SQ FT: 4,500
SALES (est): 9.1MM **Privately Held**
SIC: 1542 1521 Commercial & office building contractors; general remodeling, single-family houses

(P-1520)
CALICO BUILDING SERVICES INC
15550 Rockfield Blvd C, Irvine (92618-2791)
PHONE.................................949 380-8707
Fax: 949 380-7336
Ron Strand, *President*
Orlando Fernandez, *Vice Pres*
Christopher Guidry, *Vice Pres*
Thomas Miquelon, *Vice Pres*
Guy Reza, *Business Dir*
EMP: 185
SQ FT: 1,700
SALES (est): 45.1MM **Privately Held**
WEB: www.calicoweb.com
SIC: 1542 Nonresidential construction

(P-1521)
CALIFORNIA STRL CONCEPTS INC
14431 Ventura Blvd # 587, Sherman Oaks (91423-2606)
PHONE.................................661 257-6903
Sean McGroarty, *President*
EMP: 85 EST: 2006
SALES: 20.1MM **Privately Held**
SIC: 1542 Commercial & office building, new construction

(P-1522)
CAPTURED SEA INC
5901 Warner Ave, Huntington Beach (92649-4659)
PHONE.................................714 856-3358
Fax: 562 592-9005
Dave Wooten, *President*
Ibeta Vecere, *Manager*
EMP: 60
SQ FT: 24,000
SALES (est): 5.9MM **Privately Held**
WEB: www.capturedsea.com
SIC: 1542 Nonresidential construction

(P-1523)
CELLO & MAUDRU CNSTR CO INC
2505 Oak St, NAPA (94559-2226)
P.O. Box 10106 (94581-2106)
PHONE.................................707 257-0454
Fax: 707 257-2854
William F Maudru, *CEO*
Clint Simpson, *Regional Mgr*
Bill Maudru, *CTO*
Doug Pederson, *Project Mgr*
Bill Schaeffer, *Project Mgr*
EMP: 50
SQ FT: 2,000
SALES (est): 26.1MM **Privately Held**
WEB: www.cello-maudru.com
SIC: 1542 1521 Commercial & office building, new construction; commercial & office buildings, renovation & repair; new construction, single-family houses; general remodeling, single-family houses

(P-1524)
CENTURY VISION DEVELOPERS INC
3000 Oak Rd Ste 360, Walnut Creek (94597-7782)
P.O. Box 907, Concord (94522-0907)
PHONE.................................925 682-4830
Kenneth Hofmann, *Shareholder*
Albert Shaw, *Shareholder*
EMP: 50
SALES (est): 9.5MM **Privately Held**
SIC: 1542 6512 Commercial & office building, new construction; commercial & industrial building operation

(P-1525)
CHARLES PANKOW BLDRS LTD A CAL (PA)
199 S Los Robles Ave # 300, Pasadena (91101-2452)
PHONE.................................626 304-1190
Rik Kunnath, *Ch of Bd*
Kim Lum, *Partner*
Dick Walterhouse, *COO*
Kim Petersen, *CFO*
Lindsey Gray, *Project Engr*
EMP: 50
SQ FT: 40,000
SALES (est): 208.4MM **Privately Held**
WEB: www.pankow.com
SIC: 1542 Commercial & office building contractors

(P-1526)
CHARLES PANKOW BLDRS LTD A CAL
1111 Broadway Ste 200, Oakland (94607-4171)
PHONE.................................510 893-5170
Fax: 510 893-5199
Scott Anderson, *Manager*
Ricky Phillips, *Superintendent*
EMP: 450
SALES (corp-wide): 208.4MM **Privately Held**
SIC: 1542 Commercial & office building contractors
PA: Charles Pankow Builders, Ltd., A California Limited Partnership
199 S Los Robles Ave # 300
Pasadena CA 91101
626 304-1190

(P-1527)
CIRKS CONSTRUCTION INC
Also Called: Kdc Construction
3300 Industrial Blvd, West Sacramento (95691-5028)
PHONE.................................916 362-5460
Ryan Ferris, *Branch Mgr*
Dale Nelson, *Superintendent*
EMP: 142
SALES (corp-wide): 93.5MM **Privately Held**
SIC: 1542 Nonresidential construction
PA: Cirks Construction Inc.
2570 E Cerritos Ave
Anaheim CA 92806
714 632-6717

(P-1528)
CLAIM JUMPER RESTAURANT
Also Called: Cwn Management
27845 Snta Margarita Pkwy, Mission Viejo (92691-6701)
PHONE.................................949 461-7170
Fax: 949 461-7175
Robert Ott, *Owner*
Kady Pray, *General Mgr*
EMP: 110 EST: 1997
SALES (est): 8MM **Privately Held**
SIC: 1542 5813 5812 Restaurant construction; drinking places; eating places

(P-1529)
CLARK & SULLIVAN BUILDERS INC
2024 Opportunity Dr # 150, Roseville (95678-3026)
PHONE.................................916 338-7707
Fax: 916 338-7701
B J Sullivan, *President*
Kevin Stroupe, *CFO*
Ted Foor, *Project Engr*
EMP: 150
SQ FT: 5,000
SALES (est): 17.5MM
SALES (corp-wide): 75.6MM **Privately Held**
SIC: 1542 1541 Commercial & office building, new construction; industrial buildings, new construction
PA: C.S. General, Inc.
905 Industrial Way
Sparks NV 89431
775 355-8500

(P-1530)
CLARK CNSTR GRUP-CALIFORNIA LP
18201 Von Karman Ave, Irvine (92612-1000)
PHONE.................................714 429-9779
Richard M Heim, *CEO*
Mark Eames, *Vice Pres*
Gwen Burrow, *Executive Asst*
Michael Chatlin, *Manager*
EMP: 393
SQ FT: 5,000
SALES (est): 2MM
SALES (corp-wide): 4.1B **Privately Held**
WEB: www.clarkus.com
SIC: 1542 Commercial & office building, new construction
HQ: Clark Construction Group, Llc
7500 Old Georgetown Rd # 15
Bethesda MD 20814
301 272-8100

(P-1531)
CLUNE CONSTRUCTION COMPANY LP
201 Mission St Ste 1300, San Francisco (94105-1887)
PHONE.................................415 395-7245
Bob Dahlstrom, *President*
Steve Wallenberg, *Partner*
Emmett Glynn, *CFO*
EMP: 149
SALES (est): 3.5MM
SALES (corp-wide): 341.6MM **Privately Held**
SIC: 1542 Commercial & office building contractors
PA: Clune Construction Company, L.P.
10 S Riverside Plz # 2200
Chicago IL 60606
312 609-3635

PRODUCTS & SERVICES SECTION
1542 - General Contractors, Nonresidential & Non-indl Bldgs County (P-1555)

(P-1532)
CODDING CONSTRUCTION CO
1400 Valley House Dr # 100, Rohnert Park (94928-4935)
P.O. Box 5800, Santa Rosa (95406-5800)
PHONE.................707 795-3550
John Gordon, *CEO*
Reginald E Bayley, *Corp Secy*
Rick Freeman, *Vice Pres*
EMP: 50
SQ FT: 5,000
SALES: 14.2MM
SALES (corp-wide): 21.6MM **Privately Held**
WEB: www.codding.com
SIC: 1542 Commercial & office building contractors
PA: Codding Enterprises Lp
1400 Valley House Dr # 100
Rohnert Park CA 94928
707 795-3550

(P-1533)
CONNECT YOUR HOME LLC
Also Called: Dish Systems
1 Park Plz Ste 600, Irvine (92614-5987)
PHONE.................949 777-0100
Brookhollow Marketing, *Principal*
Laurie Wade, *Finance*
Michael Grier, *VP Mktg*
EMP: 90
SQ FT: 14,000
SALES (est): 11MM **Privately Held**
SIC: 1542 Commercial & office building contractors

(P-1534)
CONTRACTOR WAREHOUSE
5950 N Paramount Blvd, Lakewood (90805-3710)
PHONE.................562 633-1428
Fax: 562 633-8555
Greg Inshinsha, *Manager*
EMP: 52
SALES (est): 5.6MM **Privately Held**
SIC: 1542 Commercial & office building contractors

(P-1535)
DAL CAIS INC
5101 Florin Perkins Rd, Sacramento (95826-4817)
PHONE.................916 381-8080
Tim Obrian, *President*
Phyllis O'Brien, *Corp Secy*
EMP: 80
SQ FT: 24,000
SALES (est): 5.5MM **Privately Held**
WEB: www.dalcais.com
SIC: 1542 6552 Commercial & office building, new construction; subdividers & developers

(P-1536)
DANCO BUILDERS NORTHWEST
5251 Ericson Way Ste A, Arcata (95521-9274)
PHONE.................707 822-9000
Dan Johnson, *President*
Colleen O'Sullivan, *Manager*
EMP: 65
SALES: 950K **Privately Held**
SIC: 1542 Nonresidential construction

(P-1537)
DAVLOR COMPANY
Also Called: Davlor Constructio Corp
12 Oakbrook, Trabuco Canyon (92679-4722)
P.O. Box 892799, Temecula (92589-2799)
PHONE.................949 244-9748
Dave Fenton, *Owner*
EMP: 94
SALES (est): 5.6MM **Privately Held**
SIC: 1542 Commercial & office building contractors

(P-1538)
DEL AMO CONSTRUCTION
23840 Madison St, Torrance (90505-6009)
PHONE.................310 378-6203
Fax: 310 378-4663
Steve Donahue, *CEO*
Ed Hong, *CFO*
Susan Donahue, *Corp Secy*
Jason Cave, *Vice Pres*
Harry Donahue, *Vice Pres*
EMP: 55
SQ FT: 4,000
SALES (est): 33.4MM **Privately Held**
SIC: 1542 1771 Commercial & office building, new construction; concrete work

(P-1539)
DESIGNED MBL SYSTEMS INDS INC
800 S 2nd St, Patterson (95363)
P.O. Box 367 (95363-0367)
PHONE.................209 892-6298
Fax: 209 892-5018
David W Smith, *President*
Edward Smith, *Vice Pres*
EMP: 130
SQ FT: 100,000
SALES (est): 26.9MM **Privately Held**
WEB: www.dmsi-inc.com
SIC: 1542 2451 3448 2452 Design & erection, combined: non-residential; mobile classrooms; mobile buildings: for commercial use; prefabricated metal buildings; prefabricated wood buildings

(P-1540)
DIANI BUILDING CORP (PA)
351 N Blosser Rd, Santa Maria (93458-4219)
P.O. Box 5757 (93456-5757)
PHONE.................805 925-9533
Michael J Diani, *President*
Lowell Ledgerwood, *Treasurer*
Jeffrey Neal, *Senior VP*
Peter Hemesath, *Vice Pres*
Jason Diani, *Admin Sec*
EMP: 58
SQ FT: 11,000
SALES (est): 36.5MM **Privately Held**
SIC: 1542 Commercial & office building, new construction

(P-1541)
DIEDE CONSTRUCTION INC
12393 N Hwy 99, Lodi (95240-7269)
P.O. Box 1007, Woodbridge (95258-1007)
PHONE.................209 369-8255
Steven L Diede, *President*
Lillian Diede, *Corp Secy*
Bruce J Diede, *Vice Pres*
Wayne J Diede, *Vice Pres*
Esther Snider, *Office Mgr*
EMP: 100
SQ FT: 23,000
SALES (est): 66.2MM **Privately Held**
SIC: 1542 1771 1761 Commercial & office buildings, renovation & repair; foundation & footing contractor; roof repair

(P-1542)
DIVISION THREE CNSTR SVCS
30620 Plumas St, Lake Elsinore (92530-6915)
PHONE.................951 609-3043
Steve Fisher, *President*
Randy Kendrick, *Shareholder*
Janet Richards, *Office Mgr*
EMP: 80
SALES (est): 5.7MM **Privately Held**
SIC: 1542 Commercial & office building contractors

(P-1543)
DMC CONSTRUCTION INCORPORATED
2110 Del Monte Ave, Monterey (93940-3712)
PHONE.................831 656-1600
Dan McAweeney, *President*
Dan Mc Aweeney, *President*
EMP: 80
SQ FT: 3,500
SALES: 41MM **Privately Held**
SIC: 1542 1541 School building construction; hospital construction; commercial & office building, new construction; renovation, remodeling & repairs; industrial buildings; industrial buildings, new construction

(P-1544)
DON KINZEL CONSTRUCTION INC
4300 Easton Dr Ste 2, Bakersfield (93309-9420)
PHONE.................661 322-9105
Fax: 661 322-1702
Donald Kinzel, *President*
▲ **EMP:** 93
SQ FT: 2,700
SALES: 4.6MM **Privately Held**
SIC: 1542 1521 Nonresidential construction; new construction, single-family houses

(P-1545)
DPR CONSTRUCTION INC
2480 Natomas Park Dr # 100, Sacramento (95833-2979)
PHONE.................916 568-3434
Fax: 916 568-3442
Trish Timothy, *Manager*
Mark Cirkcina, *Regional Mgr*
Matthew Arroyo, *Project Mgr*
Alex Panici, *Engineer*
Kat Koon, *Accountant*
EMP: 300
SALES (corp-wide): 2.9B **Privately Held**
WEB: www.dprconstruction.com
SIC: 1542 Commercial & office building, new construction
PA: Dpr Construction, Inc.
1450 Veterans Blvd
Redwood City CA 94063
650 474-1450

(P-1546)
DPR CONSTRUCTION INC
4665 Macarthur Ct Ste 100, Newport Beach (92660-1825)
PHONE.................949 955-3771
Jim Washburn, *Regional Mgr*
Greg Trujillo, *Sr Project Mgr*
Andrew Fisher, *Manager*
Bill Francis, *Supervisor*
EMP: 50
SALES (corp-wide): 2.9B **Privately Held**
WEB: www.dprconstruction.com
SIC: 1542 Nonresidential construction
PA: Dpr Construction, Inc.
1450 Veterans Blvd
Redwood City CA 94063
650 474-1450

(P-1547)
EAGLE LATH & PLASTER INC
4350 Warehouse Ct, North Highlands (95660-5809)
PHONE.................916 925-1435
Robert P Milani, *President*
Tom Lingel, *Controller*
EMP: 100 **EST:** 2010
SQ FT: 10,000
SALES: 10MM **Privately Held**
SIC: 1542 Commercial & office building contractors

(P-1548)
ELEVEN WESTERN BUILDERS INC
2862 Executive Pl, Escondido (92029-1524)
PHONE.................760 796-6346
Fax: 760 796-6360
Rick Backus, *President*
Claudia M Backus, *Admin Sec*
Tamara Backus, *Admin Sec*
Jasen Boyens, *Project Mgr*
Doug Child, *Project Mgr*
EMP: 100
SQ FT: 20,000
SALES (est): 76MM **Privately Held**
SIC: 1542 Commercial & office building, new construction

(P-1549)
EMS CONSTRUCTION INC
12185 Dearborn Pl, Poway (92064-7111)
PHONE.................858 679-8292
Charles S Speck, *President*
Sean Speck, *President*
Marybeth Edwards, *Vice Pres*
EMP: 75
SALES (est): 12.7MM **Privately Held**
SIC: 1542 Nonresidential construction

(P-1550)
ENVIRONMENTAL CONSTRUCTION INC
21550 Oxnard St Ste 1050, Woodland Hills (91367-7126)
PHONE.................818 449-8920
Farid Soroudi, *CEO*
Zia Abhari, *President*
Imessa Bejanian, *Accountant*
Beverly Parks, *Manager*
EMP: 90
SQ FT: 2,500
SALES (est): 32.3MM **Privately Held**
SIC: 1542 Commercial & office building contractors

(P-1551)
ERICKSON-HALL CONSTRUCTION CO (PA)
500 Corporate Dr, Escondido (92029-1517)
PHONE.................760 796-7700
Fax: 760 796-7750
Dave Erickson, *CEO*
Mike Hall, *COO*
Mike Conroy, *CFO*
Julia Hope, *Executive Asst*
Kelly Thomas, *Admin Asst*
EMP: 75
SALES (est): 42MM **Privately Held**
WEB: www.ericksonhall.com
SIC: 1542 Commercial & office building contractors

(P-1552)
F & H CONSTRUCTION (PA)
1115 E Lockeford St, Lodi (95240-0878)
P.O. Box 2329 (95241-2329)
PHONE.................209 931-3738
Fax: 209 931-4427
Charles Allen Ferrell, *President*
Dan Blackburn, *Partner*
Stephen Seibly, *Corp Secy*
Harold Erwin Jones, *Vice Pres*
Karen Ley, *Admin Asst*
EMP: 75
SQ FT: 8,000
SALES: 75.4MM **Privately Held**
SIC: 1542 1541 Commercial & office building, new construction; industrial buildings, new construction

(P-1553)
FINE LINE GROUP INC
457 Minna St, San Francisco (94103-2914)
PHONE.................415 777-4070
Fax: 415 543-8249
John S Santori, *Ch of Bd*
Robert M Helmers, *Exec VP*
EMP: 50
SQ FT: 7,000
SALES (est): 7.1MM **Privately Held**
WEB: www.finelinegroup.com
SIC: 1542 Commercial & office buildings, renovation & repair

(P-1554)
FRANK SCHIPPER CONSTRUCTION CO
Also Called: Fscc
610 E Cota St, Santa Barbara (93103-3166)
PHONE.................805 963-4359
Fax: 805 963-1270
Frank Schipper, *President*
Arlan Schipper, *Vice Pres*
Paul Wieckowski, *Vice Pres*
Erwin Villegas, *Project Mgr*
Megan Barnhart, *Controller*
EMP: 50
SQ FT: 2,200
SALES (est): 14.2MM **Privately Held**
SIC: 1542 Commercial & office buildings, renovation & repair; commercial & office building, new construction

(P-1555)
GENERATION CONSTRUCTION INC
15650 El Prado Rd, Chino (91710-9108)
P.O. Box 991 (91708-0991)
PHONE.................909 923-2077
Fax: 909 923-2527
Antwan De Paul, *President*
Diana Simons, *Office Mgr*
EMP: 150

1542 - General Contractors, Nonresidential & Non-indl Bldgs County (P-1556)

SALES (est): 34.1MM **Privately Held**
SIC: 1542 Commercial & office buildings, renovation & repair

(P-1556)
GRAHAM-PREWETT INC
2773 N Bus Park Ave # 101, Fresno (93727-8662)
PHONE...................................559 291-3741
Fax: 559 291-5082
Sean Prewett, *President*
Gary Graham, *Vice Pres*
Lee Shelby, *Controller*
Stacy Novela, *Human Res Dir*
Cynthia Sayer, *Manager*
EMP: 50
SQ FT: 2,000
SALES (est): 15.3MM **Privately Held**
WEB: www.grahamprewett.com
SIC: 1542 Commercial & office building contractors

(P-1557)
GRANI INSTALLATION INC (PA)
5411 Commercial Dr, Huntington Beach (92649-1231)
PHONE...................................714 898-0441
Fax: 714 373-1381
Gregory A Grani, *CEO*
EMP: 100
SQ FT: 6,000
SALES (est): 43.2MM **Privately Held**
SIC: 1542 1742 Commercial & office buildings, renovation & repair; acoustical & ceiling work

(P-1558)
GREEN VALLEY CORPORATION (PA)
Also Called: Swenson, Barry Builder
777 N 1st St Fl 5, San Jose (95112-6350)
PHONE...................................408 287-0246
Fax: 408 998-1737
C Barron Swenson, *President*
Lee Ann Woodard, *CFO*
Steven W Andrews, *Senior VP*
Ronald L Cot, *Senior VP*
David A Gibbons, *Senior VP*
EMP: 50 **EST:** 1961
SQ FT: 12,000
SALES (est): 99.4MM **Privately Held**
WEB: www.barryswensonbuilder.com
SIC: 1542 1522 6512 Commercial & office building, new construction; multi-family dwelling construction; commercial & industrial building operation

(P-1559)
GSF ENTERPRISES INC
Also Called: Gsf Builders
610 S Jefferson St Ste L, Placentia (92870-6635)
PHONE...................................714 524-9500
John Dunbar, *CEO*
Bob Mangold, *CFO*
Gary Viano, *Vice Pres*
EMP: 75
SQ FT: 1,500
SALES (est): 19.9MM **Privately Held**
WEB: www.woodframers.com
SIC: 1542 Nonresidential construction

(P-1560)
H/S DEVELOPMENT COMPANY LLC
4800 Stockdale Hwy # 205, Bakersfield (93309-2636)
PHONE...................................661 327-0912
Stephen W Hair,
John T Sessions,
Carol Ward, *Manager*
EMP: 72
SALES (est): 7MM **Privately Held**
SIC: 1542 Nonresidential construction

(P-1561)
HARDISTY CONSTRUCTION ADMINIST
410 W 30th St Ste A, National City (91950-7269)
PHONE...................................619 245-6828
Fax: 619 474-4445
John T Hardisty, *President*
Wade Lindsay, *Vice Pres*
Melanie Langston, *Office Mgr*
EMP: 70
SALES (est): 9MM **Privately Held**
SIC: 1542 1521 1522 Nonresidential construction; single-family housing construction; residential construction

(P-1562)
HARPER CONSTRUCTION CO INC (PA)
2241 Kettner Blvd Ste 300, San Diego (92101-1769)
PHONE...................................619 233-7900
Fax: 619 233-1889
Jeffrey A Harper, *CEO*
Jeff Harper, *CEO*
Ron Harper, *Chairman*
Stephen Marble, *Vice Pres*
Nancy Firenze, *Admin Asst*
EMP: 55
SQ FT: 17,000
SALES (est): 232.2MM **Privately Held**
SIC: 1542 1521 Commercial & office building contractors; single-family housing construction

(P-1563)
HARRIS CONSTRUCTION CO INC
5286 E Home Ave, Fresno (93727-2103)
PHONE...................................559 251-0301
Fax: 559 251-8645
David P Parkes, *President*
Robert Willis, *COO*
Richard F Spencer, *Chairman*
Mike Spencer, *Vice Pres*
Greg Bacchetti, *Executive*
▲ **EMP:** 150 **EST:** 1914
SQ FT: 6,000
SALES (est): 74.9MM **Privately Held**
SIC: 1542 1541 Hospital construction; commercial & office building, new construction; food products manufacturing or packing plant construction

(P-1564)
HARVEY INC
Also Called: Harvey General Contracting
9455 Ridgehaven Ct # 200, San Diego (92123-1649)
PHONE...................................858 769-4000
Stephen Harvey, *CEO*
Debra Gillespie, *CFO*
Paul J Pietsch, *Vice Pres*
EMP: 125
SALES: 30.9MM **Privately Held**
SIC: 1542 Commercial & office building contractors

(P-1565)
HATHAWAY DINWIDDIE CNSTR CO
275 Battery St Ste 300, San Francisco (94111-3378)
PHONE...................................415 986-2718
Greg Cosko, *CEO*
Paul Gregory Cosko, *President*
Stephen W McCoid, *Exec VP*
Gordon D Smith, *Senior VP*
Greg Burg, *Vice Pres*
EMP: 400
SQ FT: 21,000
SALES (est): 158.5MM **Privately Held**
WEB: www.hdcco.com
SIC: 1542 Commercial & office building, new construction; commercial & office buildings, renovation & repair
PA: Hathaway Dinwiddie Construction Group
  275 Battery St Ste 300
  San Francisco CA 94111

(P-1566)
HATHAWAY DINWIDDIE CNSTR GROUP (PA)
275 Battery St Ste 300, San Francisco (94111-3378)
PHONE...................................415 352-1501
Fax: 415 956-5669
Greg Cosko, *CEO*
David Miller, *CFO*
Stephen E Smith, *Senior VP*
Stephen W McCoid, *Vice Pres*
Travis Leach, *Administration*
EMP: 60
SQ FT: 18,000
SALES (est): 196.8MM **Privately Held**
SIC: 1542 Commercial & office building contractors

(P-1567)
HENSEL PHELPS CONSTRUCTION CO
5251 Viewridge Ct Ste 120, San Diego (92123-1613)
PHONE...................................858 266-7979
Scott Schilling, *Manager*
Melia Ellis, *Administration*
EMP: 60
SALES (corp-wide): 3.1B **Privately Held**
SIC: 1542 Commercial & office building contractors
PA: Hensel Phelps Construction Co.
  420 6th Ave
  Greeley CO 80631
  970 352-6565

(P-1568)
HENSEL PHELPS CONSTRUCTION CO
226 Airport Pkwy Ste 150, San Jose (95110-1024)
PHONE...................................408 452-1800
Jon W Ball, *Vice Pres*
Tina Wells, *General Mgr*
Richard Franssen, *Info Tech Mgr*
Charles J Chiparo, *Project Mgr*
Dana Napper, *Engineer*
EMP: 200
SALES (corp-wide): 3.1B **Privately Held**
WEB: www.henselphelps.com
SIC: 1542 1541 Nonresidential construction; industrial buildings & warehouses
PA: Hensel Phelps Construction Co.
  420 6th Ave
  Greeley CO 80631
  970 352-6565

(P-1569)
HENSEL PHELPS CONSTRUCTION CO
9404 Genesee Ave Ste 140, La Jolla (92037-1353)
PHONE...................................619 544-6828
Thom Diersbock, *Branch Mgr*
Robin Freeman, *General Mgr*
Bill Welch, *Manager*
EMP: 70
SALES (corp-wide): 3.1B **Privately Held**
SIC: 1542 Nonresidential construction
PA: Hensel Phelps Construction Co.
  420 6th Ave
  Greeley CO 80631
  970 352-6565

(P-1570)
HENSEL PHLPS GRNTE HNGR JV
18850 Von Kamon 100, Irvine (92612)
PHONE...................................949 852-0111
Cuyler R McGinley, *Vice Pres*
John A Franich, *Vice Pres*
Paul Ligocki, *Manager*
EMP: 200
SALES: 300MM **Privately Held**
SIC: 1542 1629 Nonresidential construction; heavy construction

(P-1571)
HILBERS INC
Also Called: HILBERS CONTRACTORS & ENGINEER
1210 Stabler Ln, Yuba City (95993-2620)
PHONE...................................530 673-2947
Fax: 530 674-4141
Kurt G Hilbers, *President*
Glenn Hilbers, *Treasurer*
Susan P Growney, *Vice Pres*
Larry E Hilbers, *Vice Pres*
Tom Jones, *Vice Pres*
EMP: 75
SQ FT: 6,790
SALES: 110.6MM **Privately Held**
WEB: www.hilbersinc.com
SIC: 1542 1541 Commercial & office building contractors; industrial buildings, new construction

(P-1572)
HOLBROOK CONSTRUCTION INC
9814 Norwalk Blvd Ste 200, Santa Fe Springs (90670-2992)
PHONE...................................714 523-1150
Laurence A Holbrook, *President*
Richard Holbrook, *CFO*
Lisa Garcia, *Controller*
Patty Granados, *Human Res Mgr*
EMP: 75
SQ FT: 3,000
SALES (est): 4MM **Privately Held**
WEB: www.holbrookconstruction.net
SIC: 1542 Nonresidential construction

(P-1573)
HOUALLA ENTERPRISES LTD
Also Called: Metro Bldrs & Engineers Group
2610 Avon St, Newport Beach (92663-4706)
PHONE...................................949 515-4350
Fax: 626 403-6074
Fouad Houalla, *President*
Aref Mikati, *CFO*
Shelly Irvine, *Admin Asst*
Mustafa Mubaidin, *Project Mgr*
Raife Alameddine, *Controller*
▲ **EMP:** 85
SQ FT: 1,200
SALES (est): 28.9MM **Privately Held**
SIC: 1542 Commercial & office building, new construction; specialized public building contractors

(P-1574)
HPM CONSTRUCTION LLC
17911 Mitchell S, Irvine (92614-6015)
PHONE...................................949 474-9170
Karen Price, *President*
Cuyler McGinley, *Corp Secy*
Cindy McMackin, *Vice Pres*
Hensel Phelps Construction,
Morrow-Meadows Corporation,
EMP: 100 **EST:** 2012
SALES: 300MM
SALES (corp-wide): 3.1B **Privately Held**
SIC: 1542 Nonresidential construction
PA: Hensel Phelps Construction Co.
  420 6th Ave
  Greeley CO 80631
  970 352-6565

(P-1575)
HUTCHISON CORPORATION
Also Called: Inner Space Constructors Div
6107 Obispo Ave, Long Beach (90805-3799)
PHONE...................................310 763-7991
Fax: 310 763-4381
Robert J Hutchison, *Ch of Bd*
Linda Mc Dannold, *Corp Secy*
Stephen Mc Dannold, *Vice Pres*
Norma Herrera, *Executive*
Dave Hardt, *Project Mgr*
EMP: 80
SQ FT: 50,000
SALES (est): 22.2MM **Privately Held**
SIC: 1542 1742 1521 Nonresidential construction; commercial & office building, new construction; acoustical & ceiling work; single-family housing construction

(P-1576)
I WMI
17100 Pioneer Blvd # 230, Artesia (90701-2776)
PHONE...................................562 977-4906
David T Gajdzik, *President*
Chris Gajdzik, *CFO*
EMP: 280
SALES: 40MM **Privately Held**
SIC: 1542 Commercial & office building contractors

(P-1577)
J B COMPANY
1825 Bell St Ste 100, Sacramento (95825-1020)
PHONE...................................916 929-3003
EMP: 70
SQ FT: 24,000
SALES (est): 5.8MM **Privately Held**
SIC: 1542 1541

PRODUCTS & SERVICES SECTION
1542 - General Contractors, Nonresidential & Non-indl Bldgs County (P-1599)

(P-1578)
J M C INTERNATIONAL LLC
1470 W Herndon Ave # 100, Fresno (93711-0552)
PHONE..................559 256-1300
Paul Owhadi,
EMP: 50
SQ FT: 14,000
SALES: 22MM Privately Held
SIC: 1542 1522 Commercial & office building contractors; residential construction

(P-1579)
J R ROBERTS CORP (HQ)
7745 Greenback Ln Ste 300, Citrus Heights (95610-5866)
PHONE..................916 729-5600
Fax: 916 729-5666
Robert Olsen, CEO
Robert C Hall Jr, President
Mike Vinks, Vice Pres
Erne Sanchez, Executive Asst
EMP: 100 EST: 1979
SQ FT: 9,000
SALES (est): 28.2MM
SALES (corp-wide): 391.5MM Privately Held
SIC: 1542 Commercial & office building, new construction
PA: S.D. Deacon Corp.
  7745 Greenback Ln Ste 250
  Citrus Heights CA 95610
  916 969-0900

(P-1580)
J R ROBERTS ENTERPRISES INC
7745 Greenback Ln Ste 300, Citrus Heights (95610-5866)
PHONE..................916 729-5600
Robert F Olsen, Ch of Bd
Robert C Hall Jr, President
James F Reilly, Corp Secy
Erne Sanchez, Executive Asst
EMP: 110
SALES (est): 11.6MM Privately Held
WEB: www.jrroberts.com
SIC: 1542 1522 Commercial & office building contractors; multi-family dwellings, new construction; remodeling, multi-family dwellings

(P-1581)
JACOBS FACILITIES INC
4435 First St Pmb 338, Livermore (94551-4915)
PHONE..................925 423-7564
Arlene Emmert, Branch Mgr
EMP: 90
SALES (corp-wide): 12.1B Publicly Held
SIC: 1542 Commercial & office building, new construction
HQ: Jacobs Facilities Inc.
  1111 S Arroyo Pkwy # 415
  Pasadena CA 91105
  626 578-3500

(P-1582)
JAYNES CORPORATION CALIFORNIA
111 Elm St Fl 4, San Diego (92101-2649)
P.O. Box 26841, Albuquerque NM (87125-6841)
PHONE..................619 233-4080
Fax: 619 234-4090
Donald Power, CEO
Wayne Davenport, Corp Secy
Rick Marquardt, Exec VP
Richard Cohen, Senior VP
Kathrn Pfaff, Office Mgr
EMP: 105
SALES (est): 15.8MM
SALES (corp-wide): 162.9MM Privately Held
WEB: www.janescorp.com
SIC: 1542 Nonresidential construction
HQ: Jaynes Corporation
  2906 Broadway Blvd Ne
  Albuquerque NM 87107
  505 345-8591

(P-1583)
JOHN F OTTO INC
Also Called: OTTO CONSTRUCTION
1717 2nd St, Sacramento (95811-6214)
PHONE..................916 441-6870
Carl Barrett, President
Carol Otto, Corp Secy
Rick McVey, Vice Pres
Allison Otto, Vice Pres
Elease Terry, Vice Pres
EMP: 120 EST: 1958
SQ FT: 10,000
SALES: 142.7MM Privately Held
WEB: www.ottoconstruction.com
SIC: 1542 1541 Commercial & office building, new construction; industrial buildings, new construction

(P-1584)
JOHN M FRANK CONSTRUCTION INC
Also Called: John M Frank Service Group
913 E 4th St, Santa Ana (92701-4748)
PHONE..................714 210-3600
Fax: 714 210-3610
John M Frank, CEO
Laurie Dawson, Admin Sec
Lillian Xie, Controller
Myra Maniel, Manager
EMP: 80
SALES (est): 23MM Privately Held
WEB: www.cscconcreteservices.com
SIC: 1542 5411 5812 Commercial & office building, new construction; commercial & office buildings, renovation & repair; supermarkets; family restaurants; restaurant, lunch counter

(P-1585)
JOHN PLANE CONSTRUCTION INC
661 Hayne Rd, Hillsborough (94010-7006)
PHONE..................415 468-0555
Fax: 415 468-0540
John Plane, President
Paul Grech, Vice Pres
Betty Sullivan, Receptionist
EMP: 120
SQ FT: 4,500
SALES: 8.7MM Privately Held
WEB: www.johnplane.com
SIC: 1542 Commercial & office building contractors

(P-1586)
JR CONSTRUCTION INC
8123 Engineer Rd, San Diego (92111-1907)
PHONE..................858 505-4760
Ramon B Camacho, President
EMP: 70
SALES (est): 14.8MM Privately Held
WEB: www.jrconstruction.net
SIC: 1542 Nonresidential construction

(P-1587)
JUNE A GROTHE CONSTRUCTION INC
Also Called: J G CONSTRUCTION
15632 El Prado Rd, Chino (91710-9108)
PHONE..................909 993-9400
June A Grothe, CEO
Gordon Baker, COO
Brian Villeneuve, CFO
Wally Clark, Vice Pres
Michael Crawford, Vice Pres
EMP: 65
SQ FT: 15,500
SALES: 32.9MM Privately Held
SIC: 1542 Shopping center construction

(P-1588)
KADENA PACIFIC INC
3421 Gato Ct Ste A, Riverside (92507-6819)
PHONE..................951 990-7865
Fred Neff, President
Cherly Parris, CFO
Scott Bailey, Treasurer
Beverly Bailey, Admin Sec
Rossie Soriano, Administration
EMP: 50
SALES (est): 4.9MM Privately Held
WEB: www.kadenapacific.com
SIC: 1542 Nonresidential construction

(P-1589)
KARSYN CONSTRUCTION INC
2740 N Sunnyside Ave, Fresno (93727-1330)
PHONE..................559 271-2900
Fax: 559 271-2908
Joseph C Parker, President
Judith Parnell, CFO
Kristin Parker, Corp Secy
Kay Porba, Office Mgr
EMP: 60
SQ FT: 5,000
SALES (est): 14.2MM Privately Held
WEB: www.karsyn.com
SIC: 1542 Commercial & office building, new construction

(P-1590)
KEENAN HOPKINS SUDER & STOWELL
Also Called: Khss Contractors
5109 E La Palma Ave Ste A, Anaheim (92807-2066)
PHONE..................714 695-3670
Doug Downing, Manager
EMP: 100
SALES (corp-wide): 291.1MM Privately Held
SIC: 1542 1742 Nonresidential construction; drywall
PA: Keenan, Hopkins, Suder & Stowell Contractors, Inc.
  5109 E La Palma Ave Ste A
  Anaheim CA 92807
  714 695-3670

(P-1591)
KIE-CON INC
3551 Wilbur Ave, Antioch (94509-8530)
PHONE..................925 754-9494
Fax: 925 754-0624
Allen Kung, President
Jamie Sisk, Business Mgr
EMP: 90
SALES (est): 21.4MM
SALES (corp-wide): 20.9B Privately Held
SIC: 1542 Commercial & office building contractors
HQ: Kiewit Corporation
  3555 Farnam St Ste 1000
  Omaha NE 68131
  402 342-2052

(P-1592)
KIEWIT CORPORATION
4650 Business Center Dr, Fairfield (94534-6890)
PHONE..................707 439-7300
Richard Raine, Branch Mgr
Wesley Lucey, Superintendent
EMP: 80
SALES (corp-wide): 20.9B Privately Held
SIC: 1542 Nonresidential construction
HQ: Kiewit Corporation
  3555 Farnam St Ste 1000
  Omaha NE 68131
  402 342-2052

(P-1593)
KIEWIT CORPORATION
Also Called: Measure of Excellence Cabinets
12700 Stowe Dr Ste 180, Poway (92064-8883)
PHONE..................858 208-4285
Chantal Brand, Branch Mgr
David Collentine, Manager
EMP: 80
SALES (corp-wide): 20.9B Privately Held
SIC: 1542 Commercial & office building contractors
HQ: Kiewit Corporation
  3555 Farnam St Ste 1000
  Omaha NE 68131
  402 342-2052

(P-1594)
KIEWIT CORPORATION
10704 Shoemaker Ave, Santa Fe Springs (90670-4040)
PHONE..................907 222-9350
EMP: 80
SALES (corp-wide): 20.9B Privately Held
SIC: 1542 Nonresidential construction
HQ: Kiewit Corporation
  3555 Farnam St Ste 1000
  Omaha NE 68131
  402 342-2052

(P-1595)
KLASSEN DEVELOPMENT INC (PA)
2021 Westwind Dr, Bakersfield (93301-3015)
PHONE..................661 327-0875
Fax: 661 327-5933
Jerry D Klassen, President
Bob Klassen, COO
Troy Fringer, CFO
Ed Childres, Vice Pres
Mark Delmarter, Vice Pres
EMP: 70
SQ FT: 7,981
SALES (est): 36.2MM Privately Held
WEB: www.klassencorp.com
SIC: 1542 Commercial & office building contractors

(P-1596)
KOLL COMPANY LLC (PA)
17755 Sky Park Cir # 100, Irvine (92614-6400)
PHONE..................562 948-5296
Fax: 949 250-4344
Gerald O Yahr, Mng Member
Don Koll, CEO
Jim Micell, CFO
Christy Daprato, Vice Pres
Kevin Deighan, Vice Pres
EMP: 60
SQ FT: 52,000
SALES (est): 63.2MM Privately Held
WEB: www.koll.com
SIC: 1542 6552 6531 8741 Commercial & office building contractors; subdividers & developers; real estate managers; management services

(P-1597)
KPRS CONSTRUCTION SERVICES INC (PA)
2850 Saturn St Ste 110, Brea (92821-1701)
PHONE..................714 672-0800
Fax: 714 672-0871
Joel H Stensby, President
Lev Rabinovich, Treasurer
Jeanette Koga-Horen, General Mgr
Paul Kristedja, Admin Sec
Frank Chien, Info Tech Dir
EMP: 95 EST: 1995
SQ FT: 31,000
SALES (est): 55MM Privately Held
WEB: www.kprsinc.com
SIC: 1542 8711 Nonresidential construction; building construction consultant

(P-1598)
KRIKORIAN PREMIERE THEATRE LLC
410 S Myrtle Ave, Monrovia (91016-2812)
PHONE..................626 305-7469
Ted Goldbeck, Branch Mgr
Todd Cummings, Vice Pres
EMP: 86
SALES (corp-wide): 62.3MM Privately Held
WEB: www.krikorianmetroplex.com
SIC: 1542 Nonresidential construction
PA: Krikorian Premiere Theatre Llc
  2275 W 190th St
  Torrance CA 90504
  310 856-1270

(P-1599)
LAMON CONSTRUCTION COMPANY INC
871 Von Geldern Way, Yuba City (95991-4215)
P.O. Box 632 (95992-0632)
PHONE..................530 671-1370
Fax: 530 671-2970
Henry S Lamon, President
Steve Ithurum, Vice Pres
Ken Northon, Vice Pres
Kristy Miller, Office Mgr
EMP: 50 EST: 1952
SQ FT: 2,500

1542 - General Contractors, Nonresidential & Non-indl Bldgs County (P-1600)

SALES: 7.8MM **Privately Held**
WEB: www.lamonconstruction.com
SIC: **1542** Commercial & office building, new construction

(P-1600)
LEDESMA & MEYER CNSTR CO INC
9441 Haven Ave, Rancho Cucamonga (91730-5844)
PHONE....................909 297-1100
Joseph M Ledesma, *CEO*
Kris Meyer, *President*
Leah Cariker, *Office Mgr*
Jeff Carter, *Superintendent*
Jeff Jaso, *Superintendent*
EMP: 55
SALES (est): 8.1MM **Privately Held**
SIC: **1542** School building construction

(P-1601)
LEVEL 10 CONSTRUCTION LP
1050 Entp Way Ste 250, Sunnyvale (94089)
PHONE....................408 747-5000
Dennis Giles, *President*
Jim Evans, *CFO*
EMP: 220 EST: 2011
SQ FT: 12,000
SALES: 200MM **Privately Held**
SIC: **1542** Commercial & office buildings, renovation & repair

(P-1602)
LMC HOLLYWOOD HIGHLAND
Also Called: Lennar Multi Family Community
95 Enterprise Ste 200, Aliso Viejo (92656-2611)
PHONE....................949 448-1600
Todd Farrell, *CEO*
EMP: 500 EST: 2013
SALES (est): 22MM **Privately Held**
SIC: **1542** Commercial & office building contractors

(P-1603)
LUSARDI CONSTRUCTION CO
6376 Clark Ave, Dublin (94568-3036)
PHONE....................925 829-1114
Kurt Evans, *Manager*
EMP: 200
SALES (corp-wide): 129.4MM **Privately Held**
SIC: **1542** Commercial & office building contractors
PA: Lusardi Construction Co.
1570 Linda Vista Dr
San Marcos CA 92078
760 744-3133

(P-1604)
M & M INTERIORS INC
3410 La Sierra Ave Ste F, Riverside (92503-5205)
PHONE....................951 279-9535
Fax: 951 279-2372
Mark A Maes, *President*
Mark Maes, *President*
Juanita Trigo, *Financial Exec*
EMP: 200
SQ FT: 8,000
SALES: 6MM **Privately Held**
WEB: www.mnminteriors.com
SIC: **1542** 1742 Commercial & office building contractors; drywall

(P-1605)
M P M & ASSOCIATES INC
19625 Ventura Blvd # 100, Tarzana (91356-7111)
PHONE....................818 708-9676
Parviz Danesh, *General Mgr*
EMP: 100
SQ FT: 9,000
SALES: 2MM **Privately Held**
WEB: www.mpmassociates.com
SIC: **1542** Commercial & office building, new construction; shopping center construction

(P-1606)
MALLCRAFT INC
2225 Windsor Ave, Altadena (91001-5306)
P.O. Box 91983, Pasadena (91109-1983)
PHONE....................626 765-9100
EMP: 50
SQ FT: 5,000
SALES (est): 13.6MM **Privately Held**
WEB: www.mallcraft.com
SIC: **1542** Commercial & office building contractors

(P-1607)
MARK DIVERSIFIED INC
650 Howe Ave Ste 1045, Sacramento (95825-4700)
PHONE....................916 923-6275
David Mark, *President*
Cecil J Mark, *Officer*
EMP: 50
SQ FT: 16,000
SALES: 30MM **Privately Held**
SIC: **1542** 1541 Commercial & office building, new construction; industrial buildings, new construction

(P-1608)
MARK SCOTT CONSTRUCTION INC (PA)
Also Called: M S
2835 Contra Costa Blvd, Pleasant Hill (94523-4221)
P.O. Box 4658, Walnut Creek (94596-0658)
PHONE....................925 944-0502
Fax: 925 944-0908
Mark A Scott, *CEO*
Troy Brincat, *CFO*
Michael Barham, *Project Mgr*
Scott Blanchette, *Project Mgr*
Arnie Corral, *Project Mgr*
EMP: 50
SQ FT: 16,000
SALES (est): 55MM **Privately Held**
WEB: www.msconstruction.com
SIC: **1542** Commercial & office building, new construction

(P-1609)
MATT-COLOMBO A JOINT VENTURE
9814 Norwalk Blvd Ste 100, Santa Fe Springs (90670-2997)
PHONE....................562 903-2277
Paul Matt, *Partner*
Faron Vandissel, *Manager*
EMP: 99
SALES: 950K **Privately Held**
SIC: **1542** Nonresidential construction

(P-1610)
MATTHEW BURNS
Also Called: Act Associates
617 Flower Dr, Folsom (95630-4816)
PHONE....................209 676-4940
EMP: 60
SALES (est): 6.2MM **Privately Held**
SIC: **1542** 0851

(P-1611)
MCCARTHY BLDG COMPANIES INC
20401 Sw Birch St Ste 200, Newport Beach (92660-1796)
PHONE....................949 851-8383
Fax: 949 756-6846
Nicholas Sandersfeld, *Business Dir*
Barbara Copeland, *Administration*
Brett Bickford, *Project Mgr*
Stacey Newman, *Project Mgr*
Alejandro Rodriguez, *Project Engr*
EMP: 347
SALES (corp-wide): 2.7B **Privately Held**
SIC: **1542** 1541 Institutional building construction; commercial & office building, new construction; industrial buildings, new construction
HQ: Mccarthy Building Companies, Inc.
1341 N Rock Hill Rd
Saint Louis MO 63124
314 968-3300

(P-1612)
MCCARTHY BLDG COMPANIES INC
Southern California Division
20401 Sw Birch St Ste 300, Newport Beach (92660-1798)
PHONE....................949 851-8383
Randy Highland, *Branch Mgr*
EMP: 75
SALES (corp-wide): 2.7B **Privately Held**
WEB: www.mccarthy.com
SIC: **1542** Nonresidential construction
HQ: Mccarthy Building Companies, Inc.
1341 N Rock Hill Rd
Saint Louis MO 63124
314 968-3300

(P-1613)
MICON CONSTRUCTION CAL INC
1616 Sierra Madre Cir, Placentia (92870-6626)
PHONE....................714 666-0203
Gene F Holle, *President*
Donald A Napolitano, *Vice Pres*
Rashmi Shah, *Bookkeeper*
EMP: 54
SQ FT: 9,000
SALES (est): 10.4MM **Privately Held**
WEB: www.miconconstruction.com
SIC: **1542** 1771 0782 Nonresidential construction; concrete work; landscape contractors

(P-1614)
MORENO-MENCO PACIFIC JV
Also Called: Moreno General Engineering
15110 Keswick St, Van Nuys (91405-1134)
PHONE....................760 747-4405
Jenna Lockstedt, *Principal*
David Archuletta, *Principal*
Oscar Mendoza, *Principal*
Artour Gevoian, *Sr Project Mgr*
EMP: 50
SALES (est): 3.3MM **Privately Held**
SIC: **1542** 1541 Commercial & office building, new construction; industrial buildings, new construction

(P-1615)
MTM & THOMASVILLE CO
16035 Phoenix Dr, City of Industry (91745-1624)
PHONE....................626 934-1112
Howard Lee, *Owner*
Cecilia Son, *General Mgr*
EMP: 51
SALES (est): 2.4MM **Privately Held**
SIC: **1542** Nonresidential construction

(P-1616)
MURPHY-TRUE INC
Also Called: Jim Murphy & Associates
464 Kenwood Ct Ste B, Santa Rosa (95407-5709)
PHONE....................707 576-7337
Jim M Murphy, *CEO*
Leighton J True III, *Vice Pres*
Thomas Anderson, *Project Mgr*
Aaron Jacobs, *Project Mgr*
Audrey Giroux, *Marketing Mgr*
EMP: 60
SQ FT: 5,000
SALES: 35.1MM **Privately Held**
SIC: **1542** 1521 Commercial & office building, new construction; new construction, single-family houses

(P-1617)
NATIONAL CONSTRUCTION & MAINT
Also Called: NCM
1955 W 9th St, San Bernardino (92411-2007)
PHONE....................909 888-7042
Fax: 951 943-1144
John Omar Blanco, *CEO*
EMP: 50
SQ FT: 600
SALES (est): 17.6MM **Privately Held**
SIC: **1542** Nonresidential construction

(P-1618)
NEUBAUER-JENNISON INC
53 Sierra Manor Rd, Mammoth Lakes (93546)
P.O. Box 3579 (93546-3579)
PHONE....................760 934-2511
Fax: 760 934-4644
John Neubauer, *President*
Greg Jennison, *Treasurer*
EMP: 50

SALES (est): 5.9MM **Privately Held**
SIC: **1542** 1521 Nonresidential construction; single-family home remodeling, additions & repairs

(P-1619)
NEXT VENTURE INC
Also Called: Sierra Group
560 Rverdale Drv Glendale, Glendale (91204)
PHONE....................818 637-2888
Fax: 818 637-2111
Carl Frommer, *President*
Scott Martin, *CFO*
Richard Freeman, *Exec VP*
Warren Markar, *Admin Asst*
Jorge Corrales, *Project Mgr*
EMP: 55
SQ FT: 7,000
SALES: 14MM **Privately Held**
SIC: **1542** Commercial & office buildings, renovation & repair

(P-1620)
NMN CONSTR SOLANA GENERATING
3002 Dow Ave Ste 526, Tustin (92780-7250)
PHONE....................714 389-2104
Jim Cochran, *President*
EMP: 50
SALES (est): 224.7K **Privately Held**
SIC: **1542** Commercial & office building contractors

(P-1621)
NOVO CONSTRUCTION INC (PA)
1460 Obrien Dr, Menlo Park (94025-1432)
PHONE....................650 701-1500
James C Fowler, *CEO*
Jim Fowler, *President*
Doug Ballou, *Executive*
Chuck Flynn, *Executive*
Tom Smoll, *Executive*
EMP: 85
SQ FT: 10,000
SALES: 553.8MM **Privately Held**
WEB: www.novoconstruction.com
SIC: **1542** Commercial & office building contractors

(P-1622)
NOVO CONSTRUCTION INC
608 Folsom St, San Francisco (94107-1305)
PHONE....................650 701-1500
Fax: 415 576-1801
James Fowler, *President*
Russell Woods, *President*
Paul Cornett, *Executive*
Rob Volpentest, *Business Dir*
Nicole Reverdy, *Admin Asst*
EMP: 58
SALES (corp-wide): 553.8MM **Privately Held**
WEB: www.novoconstruction.com
SIC: **1542** Commercial & office building contractors
PA: Novo Construction, Inc.
1460 Obrien Dr
Menlo Park CA 94025
650 701-1500

(P-1623)
OLIVER & COMPANY INC
1300 S 51st St, Richmond (94804-4628)
PHONE....................510 412-9090
Fax: 510 412-9095
Steven Henri Oliver, *CEO*
Jeffrey Shields, *CFO*
Josh Oliver, *Vice Pres*
Jeff Shields, *Vice Pres*
Nicole Sprague, *Executive Asst*
▲ EMP: 90
SQ FT: 6,302
SALES (est): 43.1MM **Privately Held**
WEB: www.oliverandco.net
SIC: **1542** Nonresidential construction

(P-1624)
PAAT & KIMMEL DEVELOPMENT INC
5450 Riverside Dr, Chino (91710-4206)
PHONE....................909 315-8074
Victor Paat, *CEO*
EMP: 60 EST: 2014

1542 - General Contractors, Nonresidential & Non-indl Bldgs County (P-1648)

SALES: (est): 11.8MM **Privately Held**
SIC: **1542** Commercial & office building, new construction

(P-1625)
PACIFIC BUILDING GROUP (PA)
9752 Aspen Creek Ct # 100, San Diego (92126-1082)
PHONE.................................858 552-0600
Gregory A Rogers, *CEO*
James Roherty, *President*
Lisa Hitt, *CFO*
William Hansen, *Vice Pres*
Ron Maize, *Vice Pres*
EMP: 83
SQ FT: 17,880
SALES: 52MM **Privately Held**
WEB: www.pacificbuildinggroup.com
SIC: **1542** Commercial & office building contractors; commercial & office building, new construction

(P-1626)
PACIFIC ENGINEERING BUILDERS
1009 Terra Nova Blvd, Pacifica (94044-4308)
PHONE.................................650 557-1238
John Chan, *President*
Kennedy Chan, *Treasurer*
Chan Kennedy, *Treasurer*
Ada Lee, *Admin Sec*
EMP: 85
SALES: (est): 8.2MM **Privately Held**
SIC: **1542** Commercial & office buildings, renovation & repair

(P-1627)
PACIFIC STTES ENVMTL CNTRS INC
11555 Dublin Blvd, Dublin (94568-2854)
P.O. Box 11357, Pleasanton (94588-1357)
PHONE.................................925 803-4333
Robert E McCarrick, *CEO*
Ernie Lampkin, *Treasurer*
Kevin Krause, *Program Mgr*
Keith Wayne, *Area Mgr*
Matt McCarrick, *Office Mgr*
EMP: 50
SQ FT: 2,000
SALES: (est): 13.3MM **Privately Held**
WEB: www.pacificstates.net
SIC: **1542** 1791 1794 8744 Nonresidential construction; storage tanks, metal; erection; excavation & grading, building construction;

(P-1628)
PACIFICORE CONSTRUCTION INC
1342 Bell Ave Ste 3a, Tustin (92780-6440)
PHONE.................................657 859-4500
Jeff Austin, *CEO*
Scott Austin, *President*
Kathy Arslan, *Project Engr*
Vicky Omae, *Controller*
Bob Cassman, *Marketing Staff*
EMP: 50 EST: 2011
SQ FT: 2,500
SALES: 15.4MM **Privately Held**
SIC: **1542** Commercial & office building, new construction

(P-1629)
PAMCO CONSTRUCTION SERVICES
211 Granite St Ste H, Corona (92879-6560)
P.O. Box 70207, Riverside (92513-0207)
PHONE.................................951 279-1962
Paul Bailey, *CEO*
Andre Bishop, *Owner*
EMP: 50
SALES: (est): 4.5MM **Privately Held**
SIC: **1542** Commercial & office building, new construction

(P-1630)
PARAMOUNT BLDG SOLUTIONS LLC
4741 Pell Dr, Sacramento (95838-2048)
PHONE.................................916 564-4102
Glen Kucera, *Branch Mgr*
EMP: 279

SALES: (corp-wide): 154.2MM **Privately Held**
SIC: **1542** Commercial & office building contractors
PA: Paramount Building Solutions, Llc
10235 S 51st St Ste 185
Phoenix AZ 85044
480 348-1177

(P-1631)
PARKCO BUILDING COMPANY
3190 Airport Loop Dr F, Costa Mesa (92626-3403)
PHONE.................................714 444-1441
W Adrian Hoyle, *President*
Eric Loyd, *Sr Project Mgr*
EMP: 99
SALES: (est): 9.2MM **Privately Held**
SIC: **1542** 1771 1799 Commercial & office building, new construction; garage construction; foundation & footing contractor; erection & dismantling of forms for poured concrete

(P-1632)
PARSONS GVRNMENT SVCS INTL INC
Also Called: Parsons Global Services Inc.
100 W Walnut St, Pasadena (91124-0001)
PHONE.................................626 440-6000
Thomas L Roell, *President*
Curtis A Bower, *Exec VP*
Gary L Stone, *Senior VP*
J Zlatoper, *Vice Pres*
Laura York, *Executive Asst*
EMP: 268 EST: 1969
SALES: 408.1MM
SALES: (corp-wide): 7.9B **Privately Held**
SIC: **1542** Commercial & office building, new construction
PA: The Parsons Corporation
100 W Walnut St
Pasadena CA 91124
626 440-2000

(P-1633)
PCL CONSTRUCTION SERVICES INC
500 N Brand Blvd Ste 1500, Glendale (91203-3938)
PHONE.................................818 246-3481
Dale Kain, *Manager*
Doug Schell, *Executive*
Silas Eudy, *Branch Mgr*
Greg Tan, *Project Mgr*
Bryan Hamilton, *Director*
EMP: 191
SQ FT: 17,619
SALES: (corp-wide): 3.8B **Privately Held**
SIC: **1542** Commercial & office building contractors
HQ: Pcl Construction Services, Inc.
2000 S Colorado Blvd 2-500
Denver CO 80222
303 365-6500

(P-1634)
PENWAL INDUSTRIES INC
10611 Acacia St, Rancho Cucamonga (91730-5410)
PHONE.................................909 466-1555
Fax: 909 466-1565
Carmen Angulo, *Financial Exec*
Kevin Griffin, *Opers Staff*
▲ EMP: 100
SQ FT: 65,000
SALES: (est): 21.8MM **Privately Held**
WEB: www.penwal.com
SIC: **1542** 3999 8742 3993 Shopping center construction; advertising display products; management consulting services; signs & advertising specialties

(P-1635)
PERRY COAST CONSTRUCTION INC
Also Called: WEST COAST CONSTRUCTION
6770 Central Ave Ste B, Riverside (92504-1443)
PHONE.................................951 774-0677
Robert Perry, *President*
Erin Perry, *Treasurer*
Britney Perry, *Admin Sec*
EMP: 105
SQ FT: 10,000

SALES: 9.7MM **Privately Held**
SIC: **1542** Nonresidential construction; restaurant construction

(P-1636)
PHILMONT MANAGEMENT INC
3450 Wilshire Blvd # 850, Los Angeles (90010-2211)
PHONE.................................213 380-0159
Monica Nam, *President*
Cindy Rhee, *Manager*
EMP: 99
SQ FT: 6,000
SALES: 5MM **Privately Held**
SIC: **1542** Commercial & office building, new construction

(P-1637)
PINNACLE CONTRACTING CORP
21800 Burbank Blvd # 210, Woodland Hills (91367-6470)
PHONE.................................818 888-6548
Mark Tieman, *CEO*
Mark A Tieman, *President*
Iral Meyerhoff, *CFO*
Michael Grossman, *Chairman*
Susan Berson, *Vice Pres*
EMP: 50
SQ FT: 3,500
SALES: (est): 12.5MM **Privately Held**
WEB: www.pincon.com
SIC: **1542** Commercial & office buildings, renovation & repair

(P-1638)
PINNER CONSTRUCTION CO INC (PA)
1255 S Lewis St, Anaheim (92805-6424)
PHONE.................................714 490-4000
Fax: 714 490-4016
John Pinner, *President*
Dirk Griffin, *CFO*
R Pinner, *Treasurer*
Justin Davis, *Vice Pres*
Johnny R Pinner, *Vice Pres*
▲ EMP: 75
SQ FT: 6,700
SALES: 112.5MM **Privately Held**
WEB: www.pinnerconstruction.com
SIC: **1542** Commercial & office building, new construction; hospital construction; stadium construction

(P-1639)
PLATINUM CONSTRUCTION INC
865 S East St, Anaheim (92805-5356)
PHONE.................................714 527-0700
Darrin W Streilein, *President*
EMP: 100
SALES: (est): 18.9MM **Privately Held**
SIC: **1542** 1541 1742 Commercial & office building contractors; steel building construction; plastering, drywall & insulation

(P-1640)
PREFERRED CONSTRUCTION CO INC
5199 E Pacific Coast Hwy, Long Beach (90804-3309)
PHONE.................................714 630-3004
Thomas Cordova, *President*
▲ EMP: 60
SQ FT: 4,000
SALES: (est): 8.5MM **Privately Held**
SIC: **1542** Commercial & office building contractors

(P-1641)
PRS/ROEBBELEN JV
4811 Tunis Rd, Sacramento (95835-1007)
PHONE.................................916 641-0324
EMP: 50
SALES: (est): 5.2MM **Privately Held**
SIC: **1542**

(P-1642)
QUIRING CORPORATION
Also Called: Quiringeneral
5118 E Clinton Way # 201, Fresno (93727-2094)
PHONE.................................559 432-2800
Fax: 559 432-6614
Paul K Quiring, *President*

Greg Quiring, *Treasurer*
Eileen Martin, *Vice Pres*
Kerry Haverty, *Executive*
Dennis Fischer, *Info Tech Mgr*
EMP: 62
SQ FT: 4,000
SALES: (est): 18.7MM **Privately Held**
WEB: www.quiring.com
SIC: **1542** Commercial & office building, new construction

(P-1643)
QUIRING GENERAL LLC
Also Called: Construction
5118 E Clinton Way # 201, Fresno (93727-2088)
PHONE.................................559 432-2800
Greg A Quiring, *Mng Member*
Paul Quiring, *CEO*
John Wood, *CFO*
Greg Quiring, *Mng Member*
Tony Fortney, *Superintendent*
EMP: 80
SQ FT: 6,200
SALES: 46MM **Privately Held**
SIC: **1542** Commercial & office building, new construction

(P-1644)
R J M CONSTRUCTION INC
224 Donna Dr, Redlands (92374-5526)
PHONE.................................909 794-8853
Belinda Marin, *Corp Secy*
Roger Marin, *President*
EMP: 50
SALES: (est): 3.4MM **Privately Held**
SIC: **1542** Commercial & office building contractors

(P-1645)
RANCHWOOD CONTRACTORS INC
923 E Pacheco Blvd, Los Banos (93635-4327)
PHONE.................................209 826-6200
Greg Hostetler, *President*
Catherine Hostetler, *Corp Secy*
EMP: 80
SQ FT: 3,500
SALES: (est): 14.6MM **Privately Held**
SIC: **1542** 1521 Commercial & office building, new construction; new construction, single-family houses

(P-1646)
RANSOME COMPANY
1933 Williams St, San Leandro (94577-2303)
P.O. Box 2177 (94577-0217)
PHONE.................................510 686-9900
Fax: 510 686-9906
Myles Oberto, *Ch of Bd*
Geoff Raaka, *President*
Peter Scott, *Vice Pres*
Gary Gonzales, *Manager*
EMP: 50
SALES: 8MM **Privately Held**
WEB: www.ransomeco.com
SIC: **1542** Nonresidential construction

(P-1647)
RED ONE - PSI JOINT VENTR LLC
310 W Murray Ave, Visalia (93291-4937)
PHONE.................................559 772-8264
Reynaldo Ruiz, *Partner*
Angelina Derossett, *Manager*
EMP: 50 EST: 2015
SALES: (est): 2.4MM **Privately Held**
SIC: **1542** 1541 Commercial & office buildings, renovation & repair; hospital construction; school building construction; renovation, remodeling & repairs: industrial buildings

(P-1648)
REEVE-KNIGHT CONSTRUCTION INC
128 Ascot Dr, Roseville (95661-3422)
PHONE.................................916 786-5112
Fax: 916 786-5113
Robert H Reeve, *CEO*
Joe E Knight, *President*
Cynthia Knight, *Treasurer*
M Kathy Reeve, *Admin Sec*

1542 - General Contractors, Nonresidential & Non-indl Bldgs County (P-1649)

Christine Tadlock, *Admin Asst*
EMP: 75
SQ FT: 9,200
SALES (est): 45.7MM **Privately Held**
WEB: www.reeve-knight.com
SIC: **1542** Commercial & office building, new construction; commercial & office buildings, renovation & repair

(P-1649)
RHC EQUIPMENT LLC
5237 Mallard Estates Rd, Chico (95973-9524)
PHONE.................530 892-1918
Randy Hill, *Manager*
EMP: 50
SALES: 85K **Privately Held**
SIC: **1542** Nonresidential construction

(P-1650)
RMA - ECC A JOINT VENTURE LLC
2707 Saturn St, Brea (92821-6705)
PHONE.................714 985-2888
Raheel Mohammad,
Mary Nguyen,
Sarah Weaver, *Manager*
Lauren Tarzjani, *Assistant*
EMP: 99
SALES: 25MM **Privately Held**
SIC: **1542** Nonresidential construction

(P-1651)
RMR CONSTRUCTION COMPANY
2424 Oakdale Ave, San Francisco (94124-1581)
PHONE.................415 647-0884
Fax: 415 647-0319
Ray Reinertson Jr, *President*
Robert Reinertson, *Vice Pres*
Marie Reinertson, *Admin Sec*
Cindy Reinertson, *Controller*
EMP: 140 EST: 1979
SQ FT: 12,000
SALES (est): 31.7MM **Privately Held**
SIC: **1542** Commercial & office buildings, renovation & repair

(P-1652)
RMS GROUP INC
17802 Mitchell N, Irvine (92614-6004)
PHONE: 714 373-4882
Fax: 714 373-4772
Russel W McDaniel, *President*
Margaret Nativo, *Office Mgr*
EMP: 75 EST: 2000
SQ FT: 14,000
SALES (est): 8.7MM **Privately Held**
SIC: **1542** Commercial & office building, new construction

(P-1653)
ROBERT CLAPPER CNSTR SVCS INC
Also Called: RC Construction Services
2223 N Locust Ave, Rialto (92377-4113)
PHONE.................909 829-3688
Robert W Clapper, *President*
Rebecca Clapper, *Corp Secy*
Howard Brissette, *Project Mgr*
Joe Garcia, *Project Mgr*
Rich Negley, *Project Mgr*
EMP: 100
SALES: 35MM **Privately Held**
WEB: www.rcconstructionservices.com
SIC: **1542** Commercial & office building, new construction

(P-1654)
ROEBBELEN CONSTRUCTION INC
1241 Hawks Flight Ct, El Dorado Hills (95762-9648)
PHONE.................916 939-4000
Hans J Roebbelen, *CEO*
Kenneth Roebbelen, *President*
Dennis Daniell, *CFO*
Robert McLean, *Officer*
David Thuleen, *Exec VP*
EMP: 80
SQ FT: 25,000
SALES (est): 18.8MM **Privately Held**
SIC: **1542** 1541 Commercial & office building contractors; industrial buildings & warehouses

(P-1655)
ROEBBELEN CONTRACTING INC
1241 Hawks Flight Ct, El Dorado Hills (95762-9648)
PHONE.................916 939-4000
Kenneth Wenham, *CEO*
Terrence J Street, *President*
Kenneth Debruhl, *COO*
Robert McLean, *COO*
Dennis Daniel, *CFO*
EMP: 350
SQ FT: 28,000
SALES (est): 158.5MM **Privately Held**
SIC: **1542** 1541 8741 Commercial & office building, new construction; industrial buildings & warehouses; construction management

(P-1656)
RUDOLPH AND SLETTEN INC (HQ)
Also Called: TUTOR PERINI
1600 Seaport Blvd Ste 350, Redwood City (94063-5575)
PHONE.................650 216-3600
Fax: 650 599-9030
Martin B Sisemore, *President*
Norma Swinger, *CFO*
Dan Dolinar, *Exec VP*
Paul Aherne, *Vice Pres*
Nevan Elam, *Vice Pres*
EMP: 100 EST: 1960
SQ FT: 47,000
SALES: 940.3MM
SALES (corp-wide): 4.9B **Publicly Held**
WEB: www.rsconstruction.com
SIC: **1542** 1541 Nonresidential construction; industrial buildings & warehouses
PA: Tutor Perini Corporation
15901 Olden St
Sylmar CA 91342
818 362-8391

(P-1657)
S J AMOROSO CNSTR CO INC (PA)
390 Bridge Pkwy, Redwood City (94065-1061)
PHONE.................650 654-1900
Fax: 650 654-9002
Dana McManus, *Ch of Bd*
Gilbert J Amoroso, *President*
Robert Erskine, *Vice Pres*
Mike Cleveland, *Executive*
Sandra Bagoje, *Executive Asst*
EMP: 330
SQ FT: 22,500
SALES (est): 184.7MM **Privately Held**
SIC: **1542** Commercial & office building contractors

(P-1658)
SAN JOSE CONSTRUCTION CO INC (PA)
1210 Coleman Ave, Santa Clara (95050-4397)
PHONE.................408 986-8711
Fax: 408 986-0278
John Dimanto, *President*
Jean Dimanto, *CFO*
Erin Conte, *Officer*
Jonathan Guzman, *Project Engr*
Patti Hibbard, *Accountant*
EMP: 57
SQ FT: 14,500
SALES (est): 48.8MM **Privately Held**
WEB: www.sanjoseconstruction.com
SIC: **1542** Commercial & office building, new construction

(P-1659)
SAVANT CONSTRUCTION INC
13830 Mountain Ave, Chino (91710-9014)
P.O. Box 636 (91708-0636)
PHONE.................909 614-3000
John L Aldridge, *President*
Lonnie Truett, *CFO*
Brad Hastings, *Corp Secy*
Darren Nowicki, *Vice Pres*
Richard Zerillo, *Vice Pres*
EMP: 52
SQ FT: 36,000
SALES (est): 20.8MM **Privately Held**
WEB: www.savantconst.com
SIC: **1542** Commercial & office building, new construction

(P-1660)
SC BUILDERS INC (PA)
910 Thompson Pl, Sunnyvale (94085-4517)
PHONE.................408 328-0688
Fax: 408 328-0684
Samuel B Abbey, *CEO*
Chris Smither, *Vice Pres*
Jessica Brasil, *Administration*
Jessica Jones, *Administration*
Jennifer Nishita, *Administration*
EMP: 64
SALES (est): 44.3MM **Privately Held**
WEB: www.scbuilders.com
SIC: **1542** 1611 8711 Custom builders, non-residential; general contractor, highway & street construction; building construction consultant

(P-1661)
SD DEACON CORP (PA)
7745 Greenback Ln Ste 250, Citrus Heights (95610-5865)
PHONE.................916 969-0900
Steven D Deacon, *CEO*
Bob Miller, *Partner*
Richard Smith, *President*
Brett Mykrantz, *Exec VP*
Pete Snook, *Principal*
EMP: 100
SQ FT: 5,000
SALES: 391.5MM **Privately Held**
WEB: www.deacon.com
SIC: **1542** Commercial & office building, new construction

(P-1662)
SD DEACON CORP
17880 Fitch, Irvine (92614-6002)
PHONE.................949 222-9060
John Steffens, *Manager*
EMP: 60
SALES (corp-wide): 391.5MM **Privately Held**
WEB: www.deacon.com
SIC: **1542** Commercial & office building, new construction
PA: S.D. Deacon Corp.
7745 Greenback Ln Ste 250
Citrus Heights CA 95610
916 969-0900

(P-1663)
SERVICE FIRST CONTRS NETWRK
2510 N Grand Ave Ste 110, Santa Ana (92705-8754)
PHONE.................714 573-2200
Mark Bucher, *CEO*
Frank Vanderberg, *President*
Stan Hatch, *Treasurer*
Gary Bucher, *Admin Sec*
EMP: 50
SQ FT: 6,500
SALES (est): 13.6MM **Privately Held**
SIC: **1542** 1522 6512 Commercial & office building contractors; residential construction; nonresidential building operators

(P-1664)
SEVERSON GROUP INCORPORATED (PA)
3601 Serpentine Dr, Los Alamitos (90720-2440)
P.O. Box 3601 (90720-0399)
PHONE.................562 493-3611
Jonathan Edward Severson, *President*
Brian Cresap, *Treasurer*
Scott Feest, *Vice Pres*
Robert Severson, *Vice Pres*
Eugene Flynn, *Research*
EMP: 60
SQ FT: 15,000

SALES (est): 288.7MM **Privately Held**
WEB: www.millieseverson.com
SIC: **1542** 1541 Commercial & office building, new construction; hospital construction; institutional building construction; industrial buildings, new construction

(P-1665)
SHAWMUT WOODWORKING & SUP INC
Also Called: Shawmut Design and Cnstr
11390 W Olympic Blvd Fl 2, Los Angeles (90064-1607)
PHONE.................323 602-1000
Leonard Porzio, *Principal*
Terry McIntyre, *Business Dir*
Shawnta Larkin, *Administration*
Rosanna Cipriani, *Manager*
EMP: 145
SALES (corp-wide): 957.6MM **Privately Held**
SIC: **1542** Commercial & office building contractors; commercial & office building, new construction
PA: Shawmut Woodworking & Supply, Inc.
560 Harrison Ave Ste 200
Boston MA 02118
617 338-6200

(P-1666)
SIERRA PACIFIC WEST INC
2125 La Mirada Dr, Vista (92081-8830)
P.O. Box 231640, Encinitas (92023-1640)
PHONE.................760 599-0755
Fax: 760 632-5438
Sandra L Brown, *CEO*
Tom Brown, *President*
Frank Pantajo, *Purch Mgr*
Jonathan Fenton, *Manager*
Michell Joyner, *Manager*
EMP: 56
SALES (est): 16.5MM **Privately Held**
WEB: www.sierrapacificwest.com
SIC: **1542** 1611 Nonresidential construction; highway & street construction

(P-1667)
SIGMA SERVICES INC (PA)
2140 Eastman Ave Ste 200, Ventura (93003-7786)
PHONE.................805 642-8377
Vivian Solodkin, *President*
Louie Valenzuela, *CFO*
Louie Valenzuela, *CFO*
Benjamin Valenzuela Jr, *Vice Pres*
Kim Thomas, *Admin Asst*
EMP: 60
SQ FT: 4,200
SALES (est): 21MM **Privately Held**
WEB: www.sigmaconstruction.net
SIC: **1542** 6531 7349 1731 Commercial & office building contractors; real estate managers; janitorial service, contract basis; electrical work; facilities support services

(P-1668)
SILVER CREEK INDUSTRIES INC
2830 Barrett Ave, Perris (92571-3258)
PHONE.................951 943-5393
Brett D Bashaw, *CEO*
Micheal Rhodes, *Corp Secy*
Bill Bonnett, *Administration*
EMP: 175
SQ FT: 25,000
SALES (est): 89.5MM **Privately Held**
WEB: www.silver-creek.net
SIC: **1542** 2452 Nonresidential construction; prefabricated wood buildings; prefabricated buildings, wood

(P-1669)
SILVERLINE CONSTRUCTION INC
1421 W 132nd St, Gardena (90249-2105)
PHONE.................310 464-8314
Michael Murphy, *CEO*
Richard Ernst, *Project Mgr*
EMP: 220
SALES (est): 32.1MM **Privately Held**
WEB: www.pyramidbuilders.com
SIC: **1542** Commercial & office building contractors

PRODUCTS & SERVICES SECTION
1542 - General Contractors, Nonresidential & Non-indl Bldgs County (P-1691)

(P-1670)
SIMMONS CONSTRUCTION INC
19252 Flypath Way, Bakersfield (93308)
PHONE.....................................661 636-1321
Fax: 661 636-1323
Charles J Simmons, *President*
Evalee Simmons, *Vice Pres*
Brenda Maniates, *Administration*
EMP: 50
SALES: 17.8MM **Privately Held**
SIC: 1542 Commercial & office building, new construction

(P-1671)
SINANIAN DEVELOPMENT INC
18980 Ventura Blvd # 200, Tarzana (91356-3228)
PHONE.....................................818 996-9666
Fax: 818 705-7914
Antranik Sinanian, *CEO*
Harry Sinanian, *Shareholder*
Sinan Sinanian, *President*
Andy Sinanian, *Co-President*
EMP: 70
SQ FT: 4,000
SALES (est): 35MM **Privately Held**
SIC: 1542 1522 6552 Nonresidential construction; residential construction; subdividers & developers

(P-1672)
SKYLINE COML INTERIORS INC (PA)
Also Called: Skyline Construction
731 Sansome St Fl 4, San Francisco (94111-1723)
PHONE.....................................415 908-1020
Fax: 415 908-1030
David Hayes, *CEO*
Rick Militello, *President*
Randy Scott, *Senior VP*
Howard Fish, *Vice Pres*
Lana Fastovich, *Accountant*
EMP: 80
SQ FT: 9,000
SALES: 136MM **Privately Held**
WEB: www.skylineconst.com
SIC: 1542 Commercial & office buildings, renovation & repair

(P-1673)
SNYDER LANGSTON L P
Also Called: Snyder Langston
17962 Cowan, Irvine (92614-6026)
PHONE.....................................949 863-9200
Fax: 310 863-1087
Stephen Jones, *Ch of Bd*
John Rochford, *President*
Paul Pfeiffer, *CFO*
Jo-E Immel, *Vice Pres*
Lee Watkins, *Vice Pres*
EMP: 91
SQ FT: 16,000
SALES (est): 53.5MM **Privately Held**
WEB: www.snyderlangston.com
SIC: 1542 8742 1522 Commercial & office building, new construction; real estate consultant; residential construction

(P-1674)
SO CALIFORNIA VENTURES LTD
1101 Richfield Rd, Placentia (92870-6790)
PHONE.....................................714 524-0021
John T Palazzo, *President*
EMP: 80
SALES (est): 8.2MM **Privately Held**
SIC: 1542 Commercial & office building contractors

(P-1675)
SOLPAC INC
Also Called: Soltek Pacific
2424 Congress St, San Diego (92110-2819)
PHONE.....................................619 296-6247
Stephen W Thompson, *CEO*
Dave Carlin, *President*
Heather Wiley, *COO*
Kevin Cammall, *Officer*
John Myers, *Senior VP*
EMP: 124
SQ FT: 7,386
SALES (est): 59.8MM **Privately Held**
SIC: 1542 Commercial & office building, new construction; commercial & office buildings, renovation & repair

(P-1676)
SPAN CONSTRUCTION & ENGRG INC (PA)
1841 Howard Rd, Madera (93637-5122)
PHONE.....................................559 661-1111
Fax: 559 233-1818
King F Husein, *CEO*
George Goddard, *President*
Firoz Mohamed Husein, *CEO*
Marilyn Clayton, *Executive Asst*
Douglas M Standing, *Admin Sec*
▼ EMP: 85
SQ FT: 120,000
SALES (est): 54.2MM **Privately Held**
WEB: www.spanconstruction.com
SIC: 1542 1541 1791 Commercial & office buildings, prefabricated erection; agricultural building contractors; industrial buildings, new construction; structural steel erection

(P-1677)
SPECTRUM CONSTRUCTION INC
427 College Blvd, Oceanside (92057-5441)
PHONE.....................................760 631-3450
Paul Sears, *CEO*
EMP: 50
SALES (est): 3.8MM **Privately Held**
SIC: 1542 Commercial & office building contractors

(P-1678)
STREAMLINE FINISHES INC
26429 Rancho Pkwy S # 140, Lake Forest (92630-8330)
PHONE.....................................949 600-8964
William Seidel, *President*
EMP: 80 EST: 2004
SQ FT: 6,000
SALES (est): 13.9MM **Privately Held**
SIC: 1542 Commercial & office building contractors

(P-1679)
SUFFOLK CONSTRUCTION CO INC
550 S Hope St, Los Angeles (90071-2627)
PHONE.....................................949 453-9400
Fax: 949 453-9495
Barbara Hescock, *Director*
Jeffrey Gouveia Jr, *COO*
Mike Azarela, *Exec VP*
Kimberly Steimle, *Exec VP*
Michael Beaumier, *Vice Pres*
EMP: 90
SALES (corp-wide): 2.5B **Privately Held**
WEB: www.suffolkconstruction.com
SIC: 1542 Commercial & office building contractors
PA: Suffolk Construction Company, Inc.
65 Allerton St
Boston MA 02119
617 445-3500

(P-1680)
SUMMER SYSTEMS INC
28942 Hancock Pkwy, Valencia (91355-1069)
PHONE.....................................661 257-4419
Fax: 661 257-2640
Don London, *President*
Connie London, *Admin Sec*
Mary Insolo, *Manager*
EMP: 80
SQ FT: 20,000
SALES (est): 22.8MM **Privately Held**
WEB: www.summersystemsinc.com
SIC: 1542 Nonresidential construction

(P-1681)
SWINERTON BLDRS PACIFIC R
16798 W Bernardo Dr, San Diego (92127-1904)
PHONE.....................................619 954-8011
Mark Payne, *Principal*
EMP: 65
SALES (est): 8.6MM **Privately Held**
SIC: 1542 Nonresidential construction

(P-1682)
SWINERTON BUILDERS
865 S Figueroa St # 3000, Los Angeles (90017-3009)
PHONE.....................................213 896-3400
Fax: 213 896-0027
Gust Soteropolus, *Branch Mgr*
Dave Callis, *Vice Pres*
Blanca Banda, *Project Mgr*
Paul Banuelos, *Project Mgr*
Jaime Pace, *Project Mgr*
EMP: 100
SALES (corp-wide): 2.8B **Privately Held**
SIC: 1542 1541 Nonresidential construction; industrial buildings & warehouses
HQ: Swinerton Builders
260 Townsend St
San Francisco CA 94107
415 421-2980

(P-1683)
SWINERTON BUILDERS HC
Also Called: Hmh Builders
15 Business Park Way # 101, Sacramento (95828-0959)
PHONE.....................................916 383-4825
Gary J Rafferty, *Ch of Bd*
Eric M Foster, *President*
Leonard J Bischel, *CFO*
Frank Foellmer, *Exec VP*
Linda J Schowalter, *Senior VP*
EMP: 150
SQ FT: 25,000
SALES: 19.8MM
SALES (corp-wide): 2.8B **Privately Held**
WEB: www.hmh.com
SIC: 1542 Commercial & office building, new construction; hospital construction; institutional building construction
PA: Swinerton Incorporated
260 Townsend St
San Francisco CA 94107
415 421-2980

(P-1684)
SWINERTON INCORPORATED (PA)
260 Townsend St, San Francisco (94107-1719)
PHONE.....................................415 421-2980
Fax: 415 433-0943
Jeffrey C Hoopes, *CEO*
Gary J Rafferty, *President*
Linda G Showalter, *CFO*
Phyllis Smith, *Treasurer*
Randall Brinkhoff, *Officer*
▲ EMP: 200
SQ FT: 66,943
SALES: 2.8B **Privately Held**
SIC: 1542 1541 6531 1522 Nonresidential construction; industrial buildings & warehouses; real estate managers; residential construction

(P-1685)
TASLIMI CONSTRUCTION CO INC
1805 Colorado Ave, Santa Monica (90404-3411)
PHONE.....................................310 447-3000
Fax: 310 447-0432
Shidan Taslimi, *President*
Mehran Taslimi, *Vice Pres*
Susanne Taslimi, *Admin Sec*
Thomas Aldrich, *Project Mgr*
Mona Chamian, *Project Mgr*
EMP: 66
SQ FT: 8,500
SALES (est): 25MM **Privately Held**
SIC: 1542 Commercial & office building, new construction; commercial & office buildings, renovation & repair

(P-1686)
TAYLOR BAILEY INC
355 Lafata St Ste E, Saint Helena (94574-1413)
PHONE.....................................707 967-8090
Mike Digiulio, *President*
Robert Covey, *Vice Pres*
Gerald Eastman, *Vice Pres*
EMP: 60
SQ FT: 2,000
SALES (est): 10.5MM **Privately Held**
WEB: www.baileyandtaylor.com
SIC: 1542 Agricultural building contractors

(P-1687)
TAYLOR STRUCTURES INC
905 Cotting Ln Ste 100, Vacaville (95688-8777)
PHONE.....................................707 499-6870
Fax: 707 449-6875
Ridley Taylor, *President*
Scott Taylor, *Vice Pres*
EMP: 75
SQ FT: 3,000
SALES (est): 8.9MM **Privately Held**
SIC: 1542 Commercial & office building, new construction

(P-1688)
TCG BUILDERS INC
Also Called: Core Group, The
890 N Mccarthy Blvd # 100, Milpitas (95035-5127)
PHONE.....................................408 321-6450
Fax: 408 321-6455
Andrew W Meade, *CEO*
Timothy Tempel, *President*
Jillian Dressel, *Corp Secy*
Robert Wagle, *Vice Pres*
Rosy Tattersall, *Administration*
EMP: 50
SQ FT: 6,000
SALES (est): 15.5MM **Privately Held**
SIC: 1542 Commercial & office building contractors; commercial & office buildings, renovation & repair

(P-1689)
TECHNO COATINGS INC
795 Debra St, Anaheim (92805)
PHONE.....................................714 774-4671
Michael Birney, *President*
Tom Puett, *Project Mgr*
Rebecca Williams, *Director*
Brent Bergman, *Manager*
EMP: 150
SALES (corp-wide): 109.2MM **Privately Held**
WEB: www.technocoatings.com
SIC: 1542 1629 1721 1799 Commercial & office buildings, renovation & repair; blasting contractor, except building demolition; painting & paper hanging; wallcovering contractors; coating of concrete structures with plastic; coating of metal structures at construction site; waterproofing
PA: Techno Coatings, Inc.
1391 S Allec St
Anaheim CA 92805
714 635-1130

(P-1690)
TEMALPAKH INC
Also Called: Works Floor & Wall, The
979 S Gene Autry Trl, Palm Springs (92264-3464)
PHONE.....................................760 770-5778
Gerald A Flowers, *CEO*
Michael Collins, *Vice Pres*
Rusty Harling, *Admin Sec*
Blake Hudson, *Controller*
Azalea Rodriiguez, *Manager*
EMP: 65
SQ FT: 13,000
SALES (est): 13.9MM **Privately Held**
SIC: 1542 5713 5211 Commercial & office buildings, renovation & repair; floor covering stores; tile, ceramic

(P-1691)
THE NEVELL GROUP INC (PA)
Also Called: N G I
3001 Entp St Ste 200, Brea (92821)
PHONE.....................................714 579-7501
Fax: 714 579-7588
Michael J Nevell, *President*
Bryan Bodine, *CFO*
Therese Belisle, *Exec VP*
Bruce Pasqua, *Senior VP*
Greg Thomas, *Vice Pres*
EMP: 250
SQ FT: 35,000
SALES: 102.6MM **Privately Held**
SIC: 1542 Commercial & office building, new construction

1542 - General Contractors, Nonresidential & Non-indl Bldgs County (P-1692)

(P-1692)
TILLER CONSTRUCTORS PARTNR INC
306 W Katella Ave Ste A, Orange (92867-4755)
PHONE.................................714 771-5600
Fax: 714 771-1850
Lin Lindstedt, *President*
Carry Evert, *Vice Pres*
Kerry Evert, *Vice Pres*
Richard Andrews, *Project Mgr*
Howard Meyers, *Marketing Staff*
EMP: 64
SQ FT: 4,000
SALES (est): 24.6MM **Privately Held**
WEB: www.tillerconstructors.com
SIC: 1542 Institutional building construction; commercial & office building contractors

(P-1693)
TOTAL BUILDING CARE INC
21228 Norwalk Blvd, Hawaiian Gardens (90716-1021)
PHONE.................................562 467-8333
Yong A Kim, *CEO*
Yong Kim, *CEO*
Colin Oconnell, *Vice Pres*
Rachel Boid, *Manager*
EMP: 70
SALES (est): 10.3MM **Privately Held**
WEB: www.totalbuildingcare.com
SIC: 1542 Nonresidential construction

(P-1694)
TRENDEX CORPORATION
9353 Eton Ave, Chatsworth (91311-5810)
PHONE.................................818 407-9600
Fax: 818 610-3303
William Vincent, *President*
Janet Ayers, *Corp Secy*
Michelle Orawa, *Manager*
EMP: 60
SQ FT: 3,500
SALES: 11MM **Privately Held**
SIC: 1542 1742 Commercial & office building contractors; drywall

(P-1695)
TRICORP CONSTRUCTION INC (PA)
Also Called: Tricorp Hearn Construction
1030 G St, Sacramento (95814-0823)
PHONE.................................916 779-8010
Steve Hunter, *President*
Tony Moayed, *Vice Pres*
Jeannine H Long, *Business Dir*
Ken Cohen, *Principal*
Sandy Williamson, *Controller*
EMP: 60
SQ FT: 10,000
SALES (est): 33.6MM **Privately Held**
WEB: www.tricorpconstruction.com
SIC: 1542 1521 Commercial & office building contractors; single-family housing construction

(P-1696)
TRITON STRUCTURAL CONCRETE INC
15435 Innovation Dr # 225, San Diego (92128-3445)
PHONE.................................858 866-2450
Tim Penick, *President*
Mitch Miller, *Project Mgr*
Khanna Tsymuk, *Project Mgr*
Patrick Sullivan, *Project Engr*
Mary Ann Wilson, *Controller*
EMP: 250
SALES: 57.5MM **Privately Held**
SIC: 1542 Commercial & office building, new construction

(P-1697)
TRUEBECK CONSTRUCTION (PA)
Also Called: Bnb Norcal
201 Redwood Shores Pkwy # 125, Redwood City (94065-1134)
PHONE.................................650 227-1957
David C Becker, *President*
Brad Bastian, *Shareholder*
Jeff Nielson, *Shareholder*
Sean Truedale, *Vice Pres*
Christy Crissi, *Manager*
EMP: 61
SQ FT: 6,000
SALES (est): 11.9MM **Privately Held**
SIC: 1542 Commercial & office building contractors; custom builders, non-residential

(P-1698)
TURELK INC
Also Called: Turelk San Diego
11622 El Camino Real # 100, San Diego (92130-2049)
PHONE.................................858 633-8085
Michael Turi, *Branch Mgr*
EMP: 85
SALES (corp-wide): 110MM **Privately Held**
SIC: 1542 Commercial & office buildings, renovation and repair
PA: Turelk, Inc.
3700 Santa Fe Ave Ste 200
Long Beach CA 90810
310 835-3736

(P-1699)
TURNER CONSTRUCTION COMPANY
1211 H St, Sacramento (95814-1910)
PHONE.................................916 444-4421
Fax: 916 444-9214
Donna Afflerdach, *Branch Mgr*
Frank D Zovi, *General Mgr*
EMP: 75
SALES (corp-wide): 506.6MM **Privately Held**
WEB: www.tcco.com
SIC: 1542 Nonresidential construction
HQ: Turner Construction Company Inc
375 Hudson St Fl 6
New York NY 10014
212 229-6000

(P-1700)
TURNER CONSTRUCTION COMPANY
300 Frank H Ogawa Plz # 510, Oakland (94612-2040)
PHONE.................................510 267-8100
Fax: 510 267-8118
Danny Cooke, *Branch Mgr*
Michael Brian, *General Mgr*
EMP: 50
SALES (corp-wide): 506.6MM **Privately Held**
WEB: www.tcco.com
SIC: 1542 8742 6531 Commercial & office building, new construction; management consulting services; real estate agents & managers
HQ: Turner Construction Company Inc
375 Hudson St Fl 6
New York NY 10014
212 229-6000

(P-1701)
TURNER CONSTRUCTION COMPANY
75 Hawthorne St Ste 2000, San Francisco (94105-3919)
PHONE.................................415 705-8900
Dan Wheeler, *Branch Mgr*
EMP: 60
SALES (corp-wide): 506.6MM **Privately Held**
WEB: www.tcco.com
SIC: 1542 Nonresidential construction
HQ: Turner Construction Company Inc
375 Hudson St Fl 6
New York NY 10014
212 229-6000

(P-1702)
TURNER CONSTRUCTION COMPANY
15378 Ave Of Science # 100, San Diego (92128-3451)
PHONE.................................858 320-4040
Fax: 858 558-4408
Richard C Bach, *Senior VP*
Ron Rudolph, *Executive*
Richard Jimenez, *CTO*
Dan McGuckin, *Manager*
EMP: 61
SALES (corp-wide): 506.6MM **Privately Held**
WEB: www.tcco.com
SIC: 1542 Nonresidential construction
HQ: Turner Construction Company Inc
375 Hudson St Fl 6
New York NY 10014
212 229-6000

(P-1703)
TURNER CONSTRUCTION COMPANY
1211 H St, Sacramento (95814-1910)
PHONE.................................916 444-4421
Frank Daizoi, *Branch Mgr*
EMP: 60
SALES (corp-wide): 506.6MM **Privately Held**
WEB: www.tcco.com
SIC: 1542 8741 Commercial & office building contractors; management services
HQ: Turner Construction Company Inc
375 Hudson St Fl 6
New York NY 10014
212 229-6000

(P-1704)
TUTOR PERINI CORPORATION (PA)
15901 Olden St, Sylmar (91342-1051)
PHONE.................................818 362-8391
Ronald N Tutor, *Ch of Bd*
James A Frost, *President*
Gary G Smalley, *CFO*
Michael R Klein, *Vice Ch Bd*
Mark Caspers, *Exec VP*
♦ EMP: 160 EST: 1894
SALES: 4.9B **Publicly Held**
WEB: www.perini.com
SIC: 1542 8741 1611 1791 Commercial & office building contractors; construction management; concrete construction: roads, highways, sidewalks, etc.; structural steel erection; concrete reinforcement, placing of; construction & civil engineering

(P-1705)
TUTOR PERINI CORPORATION
15901 Olden St, Sylmar (91342-1051)
PHONE.................................818 362-8391
Ronald N Tutor, *Ch of Bd*
Robert Band, *President*
Michael J Kershaw, *CFO*
William B Sparks, *Treasurer*
James Frost, *Exec VP*
EMP: 7733
SQ FT: 46,000
SALES (est): 158.5MM **Privately Held**
SIC: 1542 1611 1622 Specialized public building contractors; commercial & office building contractors; highway & street construction; bridge, tunnel & elevated highway

(P-1706)
TUTOR PERINI CORPORATION
530 Bush St, San Francisco (94108-3623)
PHONE.................................415 638-6941
EMP: 86
SALES (corp-wide): 4.9B **Publicly Held**
SIC: 1542 Commercial & office building contractors
PA: Tutor Perini Corporation
15901 Olden St
Sylmar CA 91342
818 362-8391

(P-1707)
TUTOR-SALIBA CORPORATION (HQ)
15901 Olden St, Sylmar (91342-1051)
PHONE.................................818 362-8391
Fax: 818 367-5379
Ronald N Tutor, *CEO*
Jack Frost, *COO*
William B Sparks, *CFO*
Naseeb Saliba, *Exec VP*
John D Barrett, *Senior VP*
♦ EMP: 100
SQ FT: 20,000
SALES: 30MM
SALES (corp-wide): 4.9B **Publicly Held**
WEB: www.tutorsaliba.com
SIC: 1542 1629 7353 1799 Commercial & office building, new construction; subway construction; cranes & aerial lift equipment, rental or leasing; rigging & scaffolding; subdividers & developers
PA: Tutor Perini Corporation
15901 Olden St
Sylmar CA 91342
818 362-8391

(P-1708)
UNITED SEAL COATING SLURRYSEAL
3463 State St Ste 522, Santa Barbara (93105-2662)
PHONE.................................805 563-4922
Luis Rodriguez, *President*
Justin Rodriguez, *Treasurer*
Al Rodriguez, *Vice Pres*
Michelle Rodriguez, *Admin Sec*
EMP: 57
SQ FT: 2,500
SALES: 12.2MM **Privately Held**
WEB: www.unitedpavinginc.com
SIC: 1542 1522 7363 2951 Commercial & office building, new construction; residential construction; truck driver services; asphalt paving mixtures & blocks

(P-1709)
USS CAL BUILDERS INC
8051 Main St, Stanton (90680-2452)
PHONE.................................714 828-4882
Allen Othman, *CEO*
Jennifer Hotrum, *President*
Arlene Bautista, *Office Mgr*
Eric Othman, *Admin Sec*
Stephen Park, *Project Engr*
EMP: 135
SQ FT: 15,000
SALES (est): 83.9MM **Privately Held**
SIC: 1542 Specialized public building contractors

(P-1710)
VANCREST CONSTRUCTION CORP
7171 N Figueroa St, Los Angeles (90042-1279)
PHONE.................................323 256-0011
John T Van Dyke, *President*
Jim Van Dyke, *Vice Pres*
EMP: 50
SQ FT: 2,000
SALES (est): 10.2MM **Privately Held**
SIC: 1542 Commercial & office buildings, renovation and repair

(P-1711)
W L BUTLER CONSTRUCTION INC (PA)
204 Franklin St, Redwood City (94063-1929)
PHONE.................................650 361-1270
William L Butler, *CEO*
Frank York, *President*
Dave Fister, *Vice Pres*
David Fister, *Vice Pres*
Gina Tankersley, *Vice Pres*
EMP: 50
SQ FT: 13,500
SALES (est): 106.4MM **Privately Held**
SIC: 1542 Commercial & office building, new construction; commercial & office buildings, renovation and repair

(P-1712)
W M KLORMAN CONSTRUCTION CORP
23047 Ventura Blvd, Woodland Hills (91364-1133)
PHONE.................................818 591-5969
Fax: 818 591-5926
William M Klorman, *President*
Tom Brull, *President*
Doug Fowler, *Vice Pres*
Ida Chen, *Controller*
EMP: 65
SQ FT: 4,000

PRODUCTS & SERVICES SECTION

1611 - Highway & Street Construction County (P-1733)

SALES: 50MM **Privately Held**
WEB: www.klorman.com
SIC: 1542 1521 Commercial & office building, new construction; new construction, single-family houses

(P-1713)
WEBCOR CONSTRUCTION LP (DH)
Also Called: Webcor Builders
1751 Harbor Bay Pkwy # 200, Alameda (94502-3001)
PHONE 510 748-1900
Jes Pedersen, *CEO*
Julia Gray, *COO*
Rich Lamb, *COO*
Tim Lutz, *CFO*
Matthew Reece, *CFO*
EMP: 71
SALES (est): 63MM
SALES (corp-wide): 15.1B **Privately Held**
WEB: www.webcor.com
SIC: 1542 Commercial & office building contractors
HQ: Obayashi Usa, Llc
  577 Airport Blvd Ste 600
  Burlingame CA 94010
  650 952-4910

(P-1714)
WEINSTEIN CONSTRUCTION CORP
15102 Raymer St, Van Nuys (91405-1143)
PHONE 818 782-4000
Fax: 818 789-3373
Itzcik Weinstein, *President*
Ilana Nisnevich, *Human Res Mgr*
EMP: 50
SALES (est): 7.9MM **Privately Held**
WEB: www.weinsteinconstruction.com
SIC: 1542 1521 Commercial & office building, new construction; new construction, single-family houses

(P-1715)
WEST COAST CONTRACTORS INC
2320 Courage Dr Ste 111, Fairfield (94533-6743)
PHONE 541 267-7689
Fax: 707 435-1010
Alan Bond, *President*
Sharon Newcomer, *CFO*
Mark Dietlin, *Vice Pres*
James Latner, *Vice Pres*
Wai Zah, *Exec Dir*
EMP: 130
SQ FT: 15,000
SALES (est): 16.4MM **Privately Held**
WEB: www.westcoastcontractors.com
SIC: 1542 Specialized public building contractors; school building construction; commercial & office buildings, renovation & repair

(P-1716)
WHITING-TURNER CONTRACTING CO
250 Commerce Ste 150, Irvine (92602-1345)
PHONE 949 863-0800
Fax: 949 863-0864
Len Cannatelli, *Vice Pres*
Murray Hestley, *Vice Pres*
Suzanne Slonaker, *Admin Asst*
Ryan Barry, *Project Mgr*
John Caine, *Project Mgr*
EMP: 50
SALES (corp-wide): 5.7B **Privately Held**
WEB: www.whiting-turner.com
SIC: 1542 1541 Nonresidential construction; industrial buildings & warehouses
PA: The Whiting-Turner Contracting Company
  300 E Joppa Rd Ste 800
  Baltimore MD 21286
  410 821-1100

(P-1717)
WIER CONSTRUCTION CORPORATION
16884 Old Survey Rd, Escondido (92025-3601)
PHONE 760 743-6776
Fax: 760 746-5224
Cathy Wier, *President*
Brian Wier, *Vice Pres*
Renee Carman, *Property Mgr*
EMP: 50
SQ FT: 10,000
SALES (est): 8.9MM **Privately Held**
WEB: www.wierconstruction.com
SIC: 1542 Specialized public building contractors

(P-1718)
WIMER CONSTRUCTION
10855 Wimer Country Rd, Sunland (91040-1348)
PHONE 818 848-0400
Rick Wimer, *Owner*
EMP: 50
SALES (est): 4.2MM **Privately Held**
WEB: www.wimerconstruction.com
SIC: 1542 Commercial & office building contractors

(P-1719)
WR CHAVEZ CONSTRUCTION INC
Also Called: Wr Chavez Company
12125 Kear Pl Ste A, Poway (92064-7131)
PHONE 858 375-2100
Fax: 858 375-2108
Wilfred R Chavez, *President*
Debbie L Chavez, *Treasurer*
Sherri Smeal, *Office Mgr*
EMP: 80
SQ FT: 15,000
SALES: 21.5MM **Privately Held**
SIC: 1542 1721 Commercial & office building, new construction; commercial painting

(P-1720)
XL CONSTRUCTION CORPORATION (PA)
851 Buckeye Ct, Milpitas (95035-7408)
PHONE 408 240-6000
Fax: 408 240-6001
Eric Raff, *President*
Dave Beck, *Exec VP*
Mario Wijtman, *Exec VP*
David Beck, *Vice Pres*
Alan Laurlund, *Vice Pres*
EMP: 109
SALES (est): 175.6MM **Privately Held**
WEB: www.xlconst.com
SIC: 1542 Commercial & office building, new construction; commercial & office buildings, renovation & repair

(P-1721)
ZUMWALT CONSTRUCTION INC
5520 E Lamona Ave, Fresno (93727-2276)
PHONE 559 252-1000
Fax: 559 252-1005
Kurt E Zumwalt, *President*
Teri Zumwalt, *Admin Sec*
Rodney Benedict, *Project Mgr*
Bob Webb, *Project Mgr*
Nicole Lewis, *Marketing Staff*
EMP: 100
SQ FT: 2,000
SALES: 22.8MM **Privately Held**
WEB: www.zumwaltconst.com
SIC: 1542 1522 Nonresidential construction; residential construction

---
1611 Highway & Street Construction

(P-1722)
A CSG-NOVA JOINT VENTURE
3960 Industrial Blvd # 500, West Sacramento (95691-3496)
P.O. Box 1505 (95691-1505)
PHONE 916 371-7303
Shelli Moreda, *Manager*
Scott Victor, *Co-Venturer*
EMP: 99
SALES (est): 3MM **Privately Held**
SIC: 1611 1623 1629 Airport runway construction; concrete construction: roads, highways, sidewalks, etc.; oil & gas pipeline construction; levee construction

(P-1723)
ADOPT-A-HIGHWAY MAINTENANCE
Also Called: Adopt-A-Beach
3158 Red Hill Ave Ste 200, Costa Mesa (92626-3416)
PHONE 800 200-0003
Peter Morin, *CEO*
Patricia Nelson, *President*
Dan Day, *CFO*
Dennis Day, *Admin Sec*
EMP: 104
SQ FT: 6,000
SALES (est): 17.5MM **Privately Held**
WEB: www.adoptabeach.com
SIC: 1611 4959 Highway & street maintenance; sanitary services

(P-1724)
AECOM ENERGY & CNSTR INC
Also Called: Washington Group
2850 Carmel Valley Rd, Del Mar (92014-3800)
P.O. Box 1129 (92014-1129)
PHONE 858 481-9502
EMP: 359
SALES (corp-wide): 17.9B **Publicly Held**
WEB: www.wgint.com
SIC: 1611 Highway & street construction
HQ: Aecom Energy & Construction, Inc.
  6200 S Quebec St
  Greenwood Village CO 80111
  303 228-3000

(P-1725)
ALL AMERICAN ASPHALT (PA)
Also Called: All American Agrigate
400 E 6th St, Corona (92879-1521)
P.O. Box 2229 (92878-2229)
PHONE 951 736-7600
Fax: 909 736-7646
Mark Albert Luer, *President*
Mark Luer, *President*
Robert Bradley, *Officer*
Kim McGuire, *Branch Mgr*
Jim Harnetiaux, *CIO*
EMP: 60
SALES (est): 200.8MM **Privately Held**
WEB: www.allamericanasphalt.com
SIC: 1611 5032 Highway & street paving contractor; brick, stone & related material

(P-1726)
ALL AMERICAN ASPHALT
All American Service and Sup
1776 All American Way, Corona (92879-2070)
P.O. Box 2229 (92878-2229)
PHONE 951 736-7617
Kim McGuire, *Manager*
EMP: 150
SALES (corp-wide): 200.8MM **Privately Held**
WEB: www.allamericanasphalt.net
SIC: 1611 Highway & street paving contractor
PA: All American Asphalt
  400 E 6th St
  Corona CA 92879
  951 736-7600

(P-1727)
ALL AMERICAN ASPHALT
Camco Construction Supply
1776 All American Way, Corona (92879-2070)
PHONE 951 736-7617
Kim McGuire, *Branch Mgr*
Bill Anthlam, *Manager*
Pat Clure, *Manager*
Dennis Jones, *Manager*
Randy Meador, *Manager*
EMP: 150
SALES (corp-wide): 200.8MM **Privately Held**
WEB: www.allamericanasphalt.net
SIC: 1611 Highway & street paving contractor
PA: All American Asphalt
  400 E 6th St
  Corona CA 92879
  951 736-7600

(P-1728)
AMERICAN ASP REPR RSRFCING INC (PA)
24200 Clawiter Rd, Hayward (94545-2216)
P.O. Box 3367 (94540-3367)
PHONE 510 723-0280
Fax: 510 723-0280
Allan A Henderson, *CEO*
Steve Aguirre, *COO*
Kim Henschel, *Vice Pres*
Keely Sleek, *Controller*
Larry Lockhart, *Manager*
EMP: 51
SALES (est): 29.9MM **Privately Held**
SIC: 1611 Resurfacing contractor

(P-1729)
AMERICAN ASPHALT SOUTH INC
14436 Santa Ana Ave, Fontana (92337-7141)
P.O. Box 310036 (92331-0036)
PHONE 909 427-8276
Alan Henderson, *President*
Kim Henschel, *Vice Pres*
Jeff Petty, *Vice Pres*
Lyle Stone, *Admin Sec*
Rich Elecsion, *Manager*
EMP: 65
SALES (est): 12.8MM **Privately Held**
WEB: www.americanasphaltsouth.com
SIC: 1611 Highway & street maintenance

(P-1730)
AMERICAN PAVING CO
315 N Thorne Ave, Fresno (93706-1444)
P.O. Box 4348 (93744-4348)
PHONE 559 268-9886
Fax: 559 268-0662
Steve Poindexter, *President*
Richard Nemmer, *Ch of Bd*
Christopher Hickey, *Vice Pres*
Ross Jenkins, *Admin Sec*
John Leonardo, *Accountant*
EMP: 50
SQ FT: 9,000
SALES: 6.4MM
SALES (corp-wide): 31.9MM **Privately Held**
WEB: www.americanpavingco.com
SIC: 1611 1771 Highway & street paving contractor; curb construction; sidewalk contractor
PA: Lyles Diversified, Inc.
  1210 W Olive Ave
  Fresno CA 93728
  559 441-1900

(P-1731)
AMS PAVING INC (PA)
11060 Rose Ave, Fontana (92337-7051)
PHONE 909 357-0711
William Edwin Hawkins, *CEO*
Norma Swanson, *CFO*
Jorge Alcaraz, *Manager*
EMP: 50
SQ FT: 4,000
SALES (est): 18.6MM **Privately Held**
WEB: www.amspaving.com
SIC: 1611 Surfacing & paving

(P-1732)
ANNUZZI CONCRETE SERVICE INC
85 Elmira St, San Francisco (94124-1910)
PHONE 415 468-2795
Fax: 415 468-0503
Carmello Annuzzi, *President*
Jack Annuzzi, *Vice Pres*
EMP: 50
SQ FT: 5,000
SALES (est): 6.5MM **Privately Held**
SIC: 1611 Concrete construction: roads, highways, sidewalks, etc.

(P-1733)
ANVIL BUILDERS INC
1475 Donner Ave, San Francisco (94124-3614)
PHONE 415 397-4925
Hien Manh Tran, *President*
Alan Guy, *COO*
Richard Leider, *Corp Secy*
Ann Hauer, *Controller*
EMP: 100

1611 - Highway & Street Construction County (P-1734)

PRODUCTS & SERVICES SECTION

SQ FT: 1,000
SALES: 28MM **Privately Held**
SIC: 1611 1623 General contractor, highway & street construction; water, sewer & utility lines

(P-1734)
ARCHER WESTERN CONTRACTORS LLC
9915 Mira Mesa Blvd # 230, San Diego (92131-7003)
PHONE..................858 715-7200
Tim Gerken, *CFO*
EMP: 52
SALES (corp-wide): 3.4B **Privately Held**
WEB: www.walshgroup.com
SIC: 1611 Highway & street construction
HQ: Archer Western Contractors, Llc
  2410 Paces Ferry Rd Se # 600
  Atlanta GA 30339
  404 495-8500

(P-1735)
ARGONAUT CONSTRUCTORS
1236 Cent Ave, Santa Rosa (95401)
P.O. Box 639 (95402-0639)
PHONE..................707 542-4862
Michael D Smith, *CEO*
Michael A Smith, *Vice Pres*
Flora Echavarren, *Manager*
EMP: 175 EST: 1957
SQ FT: 10,000
SALES: 28.1MM **Privately Held**
WEB: www.argonautconstructors.com
SIC: 1611 1623 Highway & street paving contractor; oil & gas pipeline construction

(P-1736)
ATKINSON CONSTRUCTION INC
18201 Von Karman Ave # 800, Irvine (92612-1092)
PHONE..................303 410-2540
John O'Keefe, *President*
Curt Hamilton, *Project Engr*
Marc Hartman, *Engineer*
EMP: 450
SALES (est): 39.3MM
SALES (corp-wide): 4.1B **Privately Held**
SIC: 1611 1622 Highway & street construction; bridge, tunnel & elevated highway
HQ: Clark Construction Group, Llc
  7500 Old Georgetown Rd # 15
  Bethesda MD 20814
  301 272-8100

(P-1737)
AVAR CONSTRUCTION INC
GMI
47375 Fremont Blvd, Fremont (94538-6521)
PHONE..................510 354-2000
EMP: 79
SALES (corp-wide): 25MM **Privately Held**
SIC: 1611 Highway & street construction
PA: Avar Construction, Inc
  47375 Fremont Blvd
  Fremont CA 94538
  510 354-2000

(P-1738)
BASIC RESOURCES INC (PA)
928 12th St Ste 700, Modesto (95354-2330)
P.O. Box 3191 (95353-3191)
PHONE..................209 521-9771
Fax: 209 579-9502
Jeffrey Reed, *CEO*
Wendell Reed, *President*
John Henriksen, *Vice Pres*
Marty Cortwright, *Admin Sec*
Leatha Wilson, *Admin Sec*
▲ EMP: 50
SALES (est): 244.2MM **Privately Held**
SIC: 1611 3273 2951 3532 Highway & street paving contractor; ready-mixed concrete; asphalt & asphaltic paving mixtures (not from refineries); mining machinery; construction machinery

(P-1739)
BEADOR CONSTRUCTION CO INC
26320 Lester Cir, Corona (92883-6399)
PHONE..................951 674-7352
David A Beador, *President*
Joe Beador, *General Mgr*
Melissa Holst, *Office Mgr*
Lisa Perry, *Controller*
EMP: 80
SQ FT: 1,415
SALES (est): 18.3MM **Privately Held**
SIC: 1611 General contractor, highway & street construction

(P-1740)
BECHO INC
15901 Olden St, Sylmar (91342-1051)
PHONE..................818 362-8391
Tim Smith, *President*
Louis Lucido, *President*
William B Sparks, *Treasurer*
Steve Pavoggi, *Vice Pres*
Jim Tripp, *Vice Pres*
▲ EMP: 60
SQ FT: 8,000
SALES: 9.4MM **Privately Held**
WEB: www.bechoinc.com
SIC: 1611 1622 1799 Highway & street paving contractor; bridge construction; shoring & underpinning work

(P-1741)
BENS ASPHALT & MAINT CO INC
Also Called: Medina Construction
2537 Rubidoux Blvd, Riverside (92509-2142)
PHONE..................951 248-1103
Fax: 951 248-1105
George Abernathy, *Branch Mgr*
EMP: 50
SALES (corp-wide): 24.4MM **Privately Held**
WEB: www.bensasphalt.com
SIC: 1611 Highway & street maintenance
PA: Ben's Asphalt & Maintenance Company, Inc.
  2200 S Yale St Ste A
  Santa Ana CA 92704
  714 540-1700

(P-1742)
BNBUILDERS
Also Called: B N B
201 Redwood Shores Pkwy, Redwood City (94065-1134)
PHONE..................650 227-1957
Bradley Bastian, *President*
Tim O'Brien, *Treasurer*
Jeffrey Nielsen, *Vice Pres*
Perry Sunders, *Manager*
EMP: 59
SALES (est): 14.9MM **Privately Held**
SIC: 1611 General contractor, highway & street construction

(P-1743)
BRUTOCO ENGRG & CNSTR INC
1272 Center Court Dr # 101, Covina (91724-3667)
PHONE..................909 350-3535
Fax: 951 822-9661
Michael J Murphy, *President*
Mike Fenley, *Senior VP*
John Glanville, *Vice Pres*
Ron Neal, *Vice Pres*
Paul Sullivan, *Vice Pres*
EMP: 200
SQ FT: 5,000
SALES (est): 48.8MM **Privately Held**
WEB: www.brutoco.net
SIC: 1611 1629 1622 General contractor, highway & street construction; dams, waterways, docks & other marine construction; bridge construction; highway construction, elevated

(P-1744)
BURTCH TRUCKING INC
Also Called: Burtch Construction
18815 Highway 65, Bakersfield (93308-9794)
P.O. Box 80546 (93380-0546)
PHONE..................661 399-1736
Fax: 661 399-3356
Brenn Burtch McGowan, *President*
Linda Kay Burtch, *Principal*
Tom Cook, *General Mgr*
Sandy Debondt, *Office Mgr*
Jeanette Vanheel, *Manager*
EMP: 53 EST: 1979
SQ FT: 4,000
SALES (est): 10.9MM **Privately Held**
WEB: www.burtchconstruction.com
SIC: 1611 Surfacing & paving; highway & street paving contractor

(P-1745)
CALIFORNIA PAVEMENT MAINT INC
Also Called: Rayner Equipment Systems
9390 Elder Creek Rd, Sacramento (95829-9326)
PHONE..................916 381-8033
Fax: 916 381-3703
Gordon L Rayner, *CEO*
Richard Rayner, *President*
Mick Marchini, *Vice Pres*
Bruce Taylor, *Vice Pres*
Connie Morotti, *Executive*
EMP: 123 EST: 1979
SQ FT: 24,300
SALES: 14MM **Privately Held**
WEB: www.cpmamerica.com
SIC: 1611 Highway & street paving contractor

(P-1746)
CHIEF TRNSP & ENGRG CONTRS INC
Also Called: Chief Engineering Co
32220 Terra Cotta St, Lake Elsinore (92530-7315)
P.O. Box 677 (92531-0677)
PHONE..................951 258-6607
Jose Aceituno Jr, *CEO*
EMP: 78
SALES (est): 10.3MM **Privately Held**
SIC: 1611 Highway & street construction

(P-1747)
CHRISP COMPANY (PA)
43650 Osgood Rd, Fremont (94539-5631)
P.O. Box 1368 (94538-0136)
PHONE..................510 656-2840
Robert P Chrisp, *CEO*
David Morris, *Vice Pres*
Roger Weisbrod, *Vice Pres*
Stephanie Acosta, *Office Mgr*
Camie Olsen, *Controller*
EMP: 144
SQ FT: 8,000
SALES (est): 95MM **Privately Held**
WEB: www.chrispco.com
SIC: 1611 Highway signs & guardrails

(P-1748)
CITY OF EL CENTRO
307 W Brighton Ave, El Centro (92243-3004)
PHONE..................760 337-4505
Fax: 760 337-3172
Terry Heagan, *Principal*
Leticia Salcido, *Finance*
John Edney, *Council Mbr*
Jason Jackson, *Council Mbr*
Efrain Silva, *Council Mbr*
EMP: 200 **Privately Held**
SIC: 1611 Highway & street construction
PA: City Of El Centro
  1275 W Main St
  El Centro CA 92243
  760 337-4510

(P-1749)
CITY OF ENCINITAS
Also Called: Street Maintenance Department
160 Calle Magdalena, Encinitas (92024-3721)
PHONE..................760 633-2850
Fax: 760 436-3592
Larry Watt, *Branch Mgr*
Blair Knoll, *Buyer*
Rob Tobin, *Supervisor*
EMP: 50 **Privately Held**
WEB: www.cityofencinitas.org
SIC: 1611 Highway & street maintenance
PA: City Of Encinitas
  505 S Vulcan Ave
  Encinitas CA 92024
  760 633-2600

(P-1750)
CITY OF LA MESA
Also Called: Lamesa City Public Works
8152 Commercial St, La Mesa (91942-2926)
PHONE..................619 667-1450
Fax: 619 466-5984
Eric Johnson, *Superintendent*
EMP: 50 **Privately Held**
SIC: 1611 Highway & street maintenance
PA: La Mesa, City Of (Inc)
  8130 Allison Ave
  La Mesa CA 91942
  619 463-6611

(P-1751)
CITY OF MILL VALLEY
Also Called: Department of Public Works
26 Corte Madera Ave, Mill Valley (94941-1830)
PHONE..................415 388-4033
Don Hunter, *Manager*
Leah Emerson, *Officer*
Sheryl Patton, *Officer*
Bob Hughes, *General Mgr*
Anne Montgomery, *City Mgr*
EMP: 120 **Privately Held**
WEB: www.donnadacuti.org
SIC: 1611 Highway & street maintenance
PA: City Of Mill Valley
  26 Corte Madera Ave
  Mill Valley CA 94941
  415 388-4033

(P-1752)
COMMERCIAL COATING COMPANY INC
Also Called: Commercial Paving
2809 W Avenue 37, Los Angeles (90065-3620)
P.O. Box 65557 (90065-0557)
PHONE..................323 256-1331
Fax: 323 256-2273
Adrian Loera, *President*
William Emerson, *Treasurer*
EMP: 52
SQ FT: 10,000
SALES (est): 13.9MM **Privately Held**
SIC: 1611 Resurfacing contractor

(P-1753)
COUNTY OF ALAMEDA
Also Called: Public Works Dept
399 Elmhurst St, Hayward (94544-1307)
PHONE..................510 670-5455
Fax: 510 293-0960
Daniel Woldesenbet, *Director*
Tyrone McKim, *Info Tech Mgr*
Roberta Davies, *Human Resources*
Denise Fetty, *Human Resources*
Margret Elliott, *Manager*
EMP: 300 **Privately Held**
WEB: www.co.alameda.ca.us
SIC: 1611 9199 Highway & street paving contractor; general government administration;
PA: County Of Alameda
  1221 Oak St Ste 555
  Oakland CA 94612
  510 272-6691

(P-1754)
COUNTY OF CONTRA COSTA
Also Called: Administration of Public Works
255 Glacier Dr, Martinez (94553-4825)
PHONE..................925 313-2000
Fax: 925 313-2333
Julia Bueren, *Director*
Barry Schamach, *Database Admin*
EMP: 250
SQ FT: 29,865 **Privately Held**
SIC: 1611 Highway & street maintenance
PA: County Of Contra Costa
  625 Court St Ste 100
  Martinez CA 94553
  925 957-5280

(P-1755)
COUNTY OF GLENN
Also Called: Planning and Public Works Agcy
777 N Colusa St, Willows (95988-2211)
P.O. Box 1070 (95988-1070)
PHONE..................530 934-6530
Dan Obermyer, *Manager*
Douglas Holvik, *Exec Dir*
Parker Hunt, *Accounting Mgr*

PRODUCTS & SERVICES SECTION
1611 - Highway & Street Construction County (P-1777)

Talat N Peri, *Personnel Exec*
Sheryl Thur, *Recorder*
EMP: 125 **Privately Held**
WEB: www.countyofglen.net
SIC: 1611 Highway & street maintenance
PA: County Of Glenn
516 W Sycamore St Fl 2
Willows CA 95988
530 934-6410

(P-1756)
COUNTY OF IMPERIAL
Also Called: Public Works
304 E 4th St, Imperial (92251-1725)
PHONE.................................760 355-1748
Fax: 760 355-4438
Willy Riven, *Manager*
Brad Poiriez, *Executive*
Blanca Acosta, *Administration*
EMP: 60 **Privately Held**
WEB: www.imperialcounty.net
SIC: 1611 Concrete construction: roads, highways, sidewalks, etc.
PA: County Of Imperial
940 W Main St Ste 208
El Centro CA 92243
760 482-4556

(P-1757)
COUNTY OF LOS ANGELES
Also Called: Public Works, Dept of
38126 Sierra Hwy, Palmdale (93550-4607)
PHONE.................................661 947-7173
Mark Caddick, *Manager*
EMP: 130 **Privately Held**
WEB: www.co.la.ca.us
SIC: 1611 9621 Highway & street maintenance; regulation, administration of transportation;
PA: County Of Los Angeles
500 W Temple St Ste 375
Los Angeles CA 90012
213 974-1101

(P-1758)
COUNTY OF LOS ANGELES
Also Called: Public Works, Dept of
1525 Alcazar St Bldg 1, Los Angeles (90033-1001)
PHONE.................................626 458-1700
Robert Scharf, *Director*
EMP: 250 **Privately Held**
WEB: www.co.la.ca.us
SIC: 1611 9511 Highway & street maintenance; sanitary engineering agency, government;
PA: County Of Los Angeles
500 W Temple St Ste 375
Los Angeles CA 90012
213 974-1101

(P-1759)
COUNTY OF MERCED
Public Works Dept Rd
715 Martin Luther King Jr, Merced (95341-6041)
PHONE.................................209 826-2253
Fax: 209 722-7690
Dana Hertfelder, *Director*
Matthew Fell, *Info Tech Mgr*
EMP: 50 **Privately Held**
SIC: 1611 Concrete construction: roads, highways, sidewalks, etc.
PA: County Of Merced
2222 M St
Merced CA 95340
209 385-7511

(P-1760)
COUNTY OF MONTEREY
Also Called: Monterey County Public Works
168 W Alisal St Fl 3, Salinas (93901-2487)
PHONE.................................831 755-4800
Fax: 831 755-4958
Yaz Emrani, *Director*
EMP: 300 **Privately Held**
WEB: www.montereycountyfarmbureau.org
SIC: 1611 Highway & street construction
PA: County Of Monterey
168 W Alisal St Fl 3
Salinas CA 93901
831 755-5040

(P-1761)
D A MCCOSKER CONSTRUCTION CO
Also Called: Independent Construction Co
3911 Laura Alice Way, Concord (94520-8544)
P.O. Box 5307 (94524-0307)
PHONE.................................925 686-1958
Fax: 925 686-1499
Brian Clay McCosker, *President*
David A Mc Cosker, *Ch of Bd*
Sharon McCosker, *Office Mgr*
Brian Cartmell, *Admin Sec*
Dan Schuetz, *Safety Mgr*
EMP: 50
SALES (est): 22.3MM **Privately Held**
SIC: 1611 Surfacing & paving; grading; highway & street paving contractor

(P-1762)
D W POWELL CONSTRUCTION INC
8555 Banana Ave, Fontana (92335-3019)
PHONE.................................909 356-8880
Fax: 909 356-1299
Doyle W Powell, *President*
Michael Powell, *General Mgr*
Suzanne Powell, *Admin Sec*
Tara Steinman, *Manager*
EMP: 50
SQ FT: 2,000
SALES (est): 8MM **Privately Held**
SIC: 1611 General contractor, highway & street construction

(P-1763)
DENNIS M MCCOY & SONS INC (PA)
32107 Lindero Canyon Rd # 212, Westlake Village (91361-4255)
PHONE.................................818 874-3872
Fax: 307 685-3166
Dennis McCoy, *CEO*
Morgan McCoy, *President*
EMP: 50
SQ FT: 3,000
SALES (est): 21.7MM **Privately Held**
WEB: www.mccoyandsons.com
SIC: 1611 Grading

(P-1764)
DESILVA GATES CONSTRUCTION LP
7700 College Town Dr # 230, Sacramento (95826-2303)
PHONE.................................916 386-9708
Edwin O Desilva, *Branch Mgr*
EMP: 74 **Privately Held**
SIC: 1611 General contractor, highway & street construction
PA: Desilva Gates Construction L.P.
11555 Dublin Blvd
Dublin CA 94568

(P-1765)
DESILVA GATES CONSTRUCTION LP (PA)
11555 Dublin Blvd, Dublin (94568-2854)
P.O. Box 2909 (94568-0909)
PHONE.................................925 361-1380
Fax: 925 803-4260
Edwin O Desilva, *President*
David Desilva, *Exec VP*
Richard B Gates, *Exec VP*
J Scott Archibald, *Vice Pres*
Scott Archibald, *Vice Pres*
EMP: 100
SALES (est): 139MM **Privately Held**
WEB: www.desilvagates.com
SIC: 1611 1794 1542 General contractor, highway & street construction; excavation & grading, building construction; nonresidential construction

(P-1766)
DISNEY CONSTRUCTION INC
859 Cowan Rd 3, Burlingame (94010-1204)
PHONE.................................650 689-5149
Richard L Disney, *President*
Linda A Lowe, *CFO*
Jackie Dagenais, *Admin Mgr*
Tim Bennett, *General Mgr*
Seth Scribner, *Project Mgr*
EMP: 60
SALES: 30MM **Privately Held**
SIC: 1611 Highway & street construction

(P-1767)
DOUMIT COMMUNICATION INC
25 Cadillac Dr Ste 134, Sacramento (95825-8358)
PHONE.................................916 362-3519
Samir Doumit, *President*
Geralee Doumit, *Corp Secy*
EMP: 58 **EST:** 1996
SALES (est): 6.5MM **Privately Held**
SIC: 1611 7389 General contractor, highway & street construction;

(P-1768)
DRYCO CONSTRUCTION INC (PA)
42745 Boscell Rd, Fremont (94538-3106)
PHONE.................................510 438-6500
Fax: 510 438-6510
Daren R Young, *President*
David Henke, *CFO*
William McCrea, *Vice Pres*
Kevin Mitchell, *Vice Pres*
Rafael Torres, *Vice Pres*
EMP: 117
SQ FT: 3,700
SALES (est): 96.8MM **Privately Held**
WEB: www.dryco.com
SIC: 1611 1721 5211 Surfacing & paving; pavement marking contractor; lumber & other building materials

(P-1769)
EBS GENERAL ENGINEERING INC
1320 E 6th St Ste 100, Corona (92879-1700)
PHONE.................................951 279-6869
Fax: 951 279-6832
Joe Nanci, *President*
Tom Nanci, *Controller*
Kathy Fairweather, *Human Res Mgr*
Cathy Fairweather, *Manager*
EMP: 80
SQ FT: 4,000
SALES (est): 14.5MM **Privately Held**
SIC: 1611 Highway & street construction

(P-1770)
ED SAFETY SERVICES INC
1040 W Kettleman Ln # 388, Lodi (95240-6056)
PHONE.................................209 333-0807
EMP: 112
SALES (est): 12.7MM **Privately Held**
SIC: 1611

(P-1771)
FOOTH THE / EASTE TRANS CORRI
125 Pacifica Ste 100, Irvine (92618-3324)
PHONE.................................949 754-3400
Fax: 949 453-8865
Michael Kraman, *CEO*
Amy Potter, *CFO*
Tracy Bowman, *Controller*
EMP: 70
SQ FT: 10,000
SALES (est): 175.1MM **Privately Held**
SIC: 1611 Highway & street construction

(P-1772)
GCI CONSTRUCTION INC
1031 Calle Recodo Ste D, San Clemente (92673-6269)
PHONE.................................714 957-0233
Terry Gillespie, *President*
Floyd Bennett, *Corp Secy*
Richard Tirrell, *Vice Pres*
Sandy Child, *Controller*
EMP: 50
SQ FT: 3,000
SALES (est): 9.2MM **Privately Held**
SIC: 1611 Highway & street construction

(P-1773)
GHILOTTI BROS INC
525 Jacoby St, San Rafael (94901-5370)
PHONE.................................415 454-7011
Fax: 415 583-8198
Dante W Ghilotti, *CEO*
Michael M Ghilotti, *President*
Daniel Y Chin, *CFO*
Thomas G Barr, *Vice Pres*
Dominic Nuccio, *Vice Pres*
EMP: 290 **EST:** 1914
SQ FT: 86,249
SALES (est): 110.6MM **Privately Held**
WEB: www.ghilottibros.com
SIC: 1611 1794 1623 Surfacing & paving; grading; highway & street paving contractor; excavation work; water, sewer & utility lines

(P-1774)
GHILOTTI CONSTRUCTION CO INC
600 S Napa Junction Rd, American Canyon (94503-1277)
PHONE.................................707 556-9145
Fax: 707 556-9682
Mark Bower, *Branch Mgr*
EMP: 119
SALES (corp-wide): 150.2MM **Privately Held**
WEB: www.ghilotti.com
SIC: 1611 1623 General contractor, highway & street construction; underground utilities contractor
PA: Ghilotti Construction Company, Inc.
246 Ghilotti Ave
Santa Rosa CA 95407
707 585-1221

(P-1775)
GOLDEN STATE BRIDGE INC
1227 E South St, Orland (95963-9100)
PHONE.................................530 865-8400
Jeff Sides, *Branch Mgr*
EMP: 83
SALES (corp-wide): 60.7MM **Privately Held**
SIC: 1611 General contractor, highway & street construction
PA: Golden State Bridge, Inc.
3701 Mallard Dr
Benicia CA 94510
925 372-8000

(P-1776)
GRAHAM CONTRACTORS INC
860 Lonus St, San Jose (95126-3713)
P.O. Box 26770 (95159-6770)
PHONE.................................408 293-9516
Fax: 408 293-3633
Gerald Graham Jr, *President*
Reed Graham, *Vice Pres*
John Waiters, *General Mgr*
Cassandra Sander, *Accountant*
Tom Weisner, *Manager*
EMP: 50
SQ FT: 1,200
SALES (est): 10.4MM **Privately Held**
WEB: www.grahamcontractors.com
SIC: 1611 Highway & street paving contractor

(P-1777)
GRANITE CONSTRUCTION COMPANY (HQ)
585 W Beach St, Watsonville (95076-5123)
P.O. Box 50085 (95077-5085)
PHONE.................................831 724-1011
James H Roberts, *President*
Laurel Krzeminski, *Exec VP*
Christopher S Miller, *Exec VP*
Richard A Watts, *Senior VP*
Kathleen Schreckengost, *Senior Mgr*
EMP: 200 **EST:** 1922
SQ FT: 39,000
SALES: 1.2B
SALES (corp-wide): 2.3B **Publicly Held**
WEB: www.graniteconstructioncompany.com
SIC: 1611 1622 Highway & street construction; general contractor, highway & street construction; bridge construction; tunnel construction
PA: Granite Construction Incorporated
585 W Beach St
Watsonville CA 95076
831 724-1011

1611 - Highway & Street Construction County (P-1778)

(P-1778)
GRANITE CONSTRUCTION COMPANY
3005 James Rd, Bakersfield (93308-9179)
P.O. Box 5127 (93388-5127)
PHONE..................................661 399-3361
Fax: 661 399-3598
Bruce McGowan, *Branch Mgr*
Dennis Wesley, *Marketing Mgr*
EMP: 200
SALES (corp-wide): 2.3B **Publicly Held**
WEB: www.graniteconstruction.com
SIC: **1611** Highway & street construction
HQ: Granite Construction Company
585 W Beach St
Watsonville CA 95076
831 724-1011

(P-1779)
GRANITE CONSTRUCTION COMPANY
Also Called: Southern California Regional
38000 Monroe St, Indio (92203-9500)
PHONE..................................760 775-7500
Fax: 760 775-8227
Jay McQuillen, *Manager*
Kurt Davis, *Foreman/Supr*
Claes Bjork,
James Bradford,
Gary Cusumano,
EMP: 393
SALES (corp-wide): 2.3B **Publicly Held**
WEB: www.graniteconstructioncompany.com
SIC: **1611** 1771 Highway & street construction; concrete work
HQ: Granite Construction Company
585 W Beach St
Watsonville CA 95076
831 724-1011

(P-1780)
GRANITE CONSTRUCTION COMPANY
21541 E Bear Mtn Blvd, Arvin (93203)
PHONE..................................661 854-3051
Fax: 661 854-3051
Mike Hosley, *Branch Mgr*
Nic Brown, *General Mgr*
EMP: 67
SALES (corp-wide): 2.3B **Publicly Held**
WEB: www.graniteconstruction.com
SIC: **1611** Highway & street construction
HQ: Granite Construction Company
585 W Beach St
Watsonville CA 95076
831 724-1011

(P-1781)
GRANITE CONSTRUCTION COMPANY
Also Called: Palmdale Area
213 E Avenue M, Lancaster (93535-5335)
PHONE..................................661 726-4447
Fax: 661 726-4460
Steve Bridge, *Branch Mgr*
Todd Hill, *Div Sub Head*
Bill Case, *Branch Mgr*
James Inglis, *Manager*
Carolyn Luke, *Manager*
EMP: 150
SQ FT: 12,716
SALES (corp-wide): 2.3B **Publicly Held**
WEB: www.graniteconstruction.com
SIC: **1611** Highway & street paving contractor
HQ: Granite Construction Company
585 W Beach St
Watsonville CA 95076
831 724-1011

(P-1782)
GRANITE CONSTRUCTION COMPANY
715 Comstock St, Santa Clara (95054-3403)
PHONE..................................408 327-7000
Fax: 408 327-7099
Pat Traberso, *Manager*
Melinda Luong, *Executive*
Philip Lee, *Safety Dir*
EMP: 182
SQ FT: 22,902

SALES (corp-wide): 2.3B **Publicly Held**
WEB: www.graniteconstruction.com
SIC: **1611** 1622 1629 General contractor, highway & street construction; bridge construction; dams, waterways, docks & other marine construction
HQ: Granite Construction Company
585 W Beach St
Watsonville CA 95076
831 724-1011

(P-1783)
GRANITE CONSTRUCTION COMPANY
2716 S Granite Ct, Fresno (93706-5455)
PHONE..................................559 441-5700
Fax: 559 441-5789
Todd Hill, *Manager*
EMP: 225
SALES (corp-wide): 2.3B **Publicly Held**
SIC: **1611** General contractor, highway & street construction
HQ: Granite Construction Company
585 W Beach St
Watsonville CA 95076
831 724-1011

(P-1784)
GRANITE CONSTRUCTION INC
2095 Us Highway 111, El Centro (92243-9731)
PHONE..................................760 337-3030
Jeff Mercer, *Manager*
EMP: 120
SALES (corp-wide): 2.3B **Publicly Held**
WEB: www.graniteconstruction.com
SIC: **1611** Highway & street construction
PA: Granite Construction Incorporated
585 W Beach St
Watsonville CA 95076
831 724-1011

(P-1785)
GRANITE CONSTRUCTION INC (PA)
585 W Beach St, Watsonville (95076-5123)
P.O. Box 50085 (95077-5085)
PHONE..................................831 724-1011
Fax: 775 358-0372
James H Roberts, *President*
William H Powell, *Ch of Bd*
Christopher S Miller, *COO*
Laurel J Krzeminski, *CFO*
Michael F Donnino, *Senior VP*
EMP: 250
SALES: 2.3B **Publicly Held**
WEB: www.graniteconstruction.com
SIC: **1611** 1622 1629 1442 Highway & street construction; general contractor, highway & street construction; bridge construction; tunnel construction; dam construction; canal construction; land leveling; construction sand & gravel

(P-1786)
GRANITE CONSTRUCTION INC
5 Justin Ct, Monterey (93940-5733)
P.O. Box 720, Watsonville (95077-0720)
PHONE..................................831 657-1700
Fax: 831 657-1711
Kurt Kniffin, *Principal*
EMP: 67
SALES (corp-wide): 2.3B **Publicly Held**
WEB: www.graniteconstruction.com
SIC: **1611** Highway & street construction
PA: Granite Construction Incorporated
585 W Beach St
Watsonville CA 95076
831 724-1011

(P-1787)
GRANITE CONSTRUCTION INC
4291 Bradshaw Rd, Sacramento (95827-3805)
PHONE..................................916 855-4495
Ryan Bingle, *Manager*
Sandy Smithers, *Executive Asst*
Amy Tobia, *Administration*
Brian Kotaska, *MIS Mgr*
Kelly Mitchell, *Business Mgr*
EMP: 67
SALES (corp-wide): 2.3B **Publicly Held**
WEB: www.graniteconstruction.com
SIC: **1611** Highway & street construction

PA: Granite Construction Incorporated
585 W Beach St
Watsonville CA 95076
831 724-1011

(P-1788)
GRANITE CONSTRUCTION INC
15560 County Rd 87, Esparto (95627)
PHONE..................................530 787-2012
EMP: 67
SALES (corp-wide): 2.3B **Publicly Held**
WEB: www.graniteconstruction.com
SIC: **1611** Highway & street construction
PA: Granite Construction Incorporated
585 W Beach St
Watsonville CA 95076
831 724-1011

(P-1789)
GRANITE CONSTRUCTION INC
1324 S State St, Ukiah (95482-6414)
PHONE..................................707 467-4100
Dan Schuster, *Manager*
Pat Clancy, *Info Tech Mgr*
Pat Traverso, *Manager*
EMP: 67
SALES (corp-wide): 2.3B **Publicly Held**
WEB: www.graniteconstruction.com
SIC: **1611** Highway & street construction
PA: Granite Construction Incorporated
585 W Beach St
Watsonville CA 95076
831 724-1011

(P-1790)
GRANITE CONSTRUCTION INC
25485 Iverson Rd, Gonzales (93926-9403)
PHONE..................................831 763-5595
Eric Gaboury, *Manager*
EMP: 67
SALES (corp-wide): 2.3B **Publicly Held**
WEB: www.graniteconstruction.com
SIC: **1611** Highway & street construction
PA: Granite Construction Incorporated
585 W Beach St
Watsonville CA 95076
831 724-1011

(P-1791)
GRANITE CONSTRUCTION INC
1800 Felton Quarry Rd, Felton (95018-9153)
PHONE..................................831 335-3445
Eric Gaboury, *Manager*
EMP: 67
SALES (corp-wide): 2.3B **Publicly Held**
WEB: www.graniteconstruction.com
SIC: **1611** Highway & street construction
PA: Granite Construction Incorporated
585 W Beach St
Watsonville CA 95076
831 724-1011

(P-1792)
GRANITE ROCK CO
1900 Quarry Rd, Aromas (95004)
P.O. Box 699 (95004-0699)
PHONE..................................831 768-2330
Fax: 831 768-2380
Carey Wong, *Branch Mgr*
EMP: 151
SALES (corp-wide): 1.2B **Privately Held**
SIC: **1611** Surfacing & paving
PA: Granite Rock Co.
350 Technology Dr
Watsonville CA 95076
831 768-2000

(P-1793)
GRANITE ROCK CO
Also Called: Pavex Construction Company
355 Blomquist St, Redwood City (94063-2701)
PHONE..................................650 869-3370
John Franich, *Manager*
EMP: 300
SALES (corp-wide): 1.2B **Privately Held**
WEB: www.graniterock.com
SIC: **1611** Highway & street paving contractor
PA: Granite Rock Co.
350 Technology Dr
Watsonville CA 95076
831 768-2000

(P-1794)
GRIFFITH COMPANY (PA)
3050 E Birch St, Brea (92821-6248)
PHONE..................................714 984-5500
Thomas L Foss, *CEO*
Jim Waltze, *Ch of Bd*
Jaimie Angus, *COO*
Gordon Csutak, *CFO*
Dave Diaz, *Vice Pres*
EMP: 60 EST: 1922
SQ FT: 100,000
SALES (est): 194.3MM **Privately Held**
SIC: **1611** Highway & street construction

(P-1795)
GRIFFITH COMPANY
1128 Carrier Parkway Ave, Bakersfield (93308-9666)
P.O. Box 70157 (93387-0157)
PHONE..................................661 831-7331
Fax: 661 831-0113
Rus Grigg, *Manager*
Jerry Eyraud, *Sales Executive*
EMP: 60
SALES (corp-wide): 194.3MM **Privately Held**
SIC: **1611** Surfacing & paving
PA: Griffith Company
3050 E Birch St
Brea CA 92821
714 984-5500

(P-1796)
GRIFFITH COMPANY
12200 Bloomfield Ave, Santa Fe Springs (90670-4742)
PHONE..................................562 929-1128
Fax: 562 864-8970
Dan Magrew, *Manager*
Gordon Csutak, *Vice Pres*
Jim Coury, *Division Mgr*
Elvira Arellano, *Admin Asst*
Jill Kiefer, *Admin Asst*
EMP: 60
SQ FT: 4,036
SALES (corp-wide): 194.3MM **Privately Held**
SIC: **1611** 1622 General contractor, highway & street construction; bridge construction; tunnel construction
PA: Griffith Company
3050 E Birch St
Brea CA 92821
714 984-5500

(P-1797)
GRIFFITH COMPANY
1128 Carrier Parkway Ave, Bakersfield (93308-9666)
PHONE..................................661 392-6640
Walt Weishaar, *Branch Mgr*
EMP: 60
SALES (corp-wide): 194.3MM **Privately Held**
SIC: **1611** General contractor, highway & street construction
PA: Griffith Company
3050 E Birch St
Brea CA 92821
714 984-5500

(P-1798)
HARDY & HARPER INC
1312 E Warner Ave, Santa Ana (92705-5416)
PHONE..................................714 444-1851
Fax: 714 444-2801
Daniel Thomas Maas, *CEO*
Fred T Maas Sr, *Director*
EMP: 50 EST: 1946
SQ FT: 3,000
SALES (est): 17MM **Privately Held**
WEB: www.hardyandharper.com
SIC: **1611** Highway & street construction

(P-1799)
HERITAGE CONSTRUCTION
Also Called: Service Contractors Network
18001 Irvine Blvd, Tustin (92780-3338)
PHONE..................................714 573-2223
Frank Vandenburg, *President*
Gary Bucher, *Admin Sec*
Frank Andenburg, *Administration*
EMP: 65 EST: 1997

PRODUCTS & SERVICES SECTION
1611 - Highway & Street Construction County (P-1823)

SALES (est): 4.1MM Privately Held
SIC: 1611 General contractor, highway & street construction

(P-1800)
HILLCREST CONTRACTING INC
1467 Circle City Dr, Corona (92879-1668)
P.O. Box 1898 (92878-1898)
PHONE.................................951 273-9600
Fax: 909 273-9608
Glenn J Salsbury, *President*
E G Lindholm, *Vice Pres*
Jason Jones, *Project Mgr*
Darcy Searle, *Project Mgr*
EMP: 75
SQ FT: 11,600
SALES (est): 19MM Privately Held
SIC: 1611 General contractor, highway & street construction

(P-1801)
INTERNATIONAL PAVING SVCS INC
Also Called: I P S
1199 Opal Ave, Mentone (92359-1284)
P.O. Box 10458, San Bernardino (92423-0458)
PHONE.................................909 794-2101
Brent Rieger, *President*
EMP: 80 EST: 2007
SALES (est): 12.7MM Privately Held
SIC: 1611 Surfacing & paving

(P-1802)
J B BOSTICK COMPANY INC (PA)
2870 E La Cresta Ave, Anaheim (92806-1816)
PHONE.................................714 238-2121
Fax: 714 238-2142
James B Bostick, *President*
Joyce Stevens, *CFO*
Jerry Hamlin, *Vice Pres*
Cari Bachman, *Marketing Staff*
Carl Bostick, *Sales Staff*
EMP: 75
SQ FT: 2,870
SALES (est): 34.9MM Privately Held
WEB: www.jbbostick.net
SIC: 1611 1771 Grading; highway & street paving contractor; concrete work

(P-1803)
JACOBSSON ENGRG CNSTR INC
77590 Enfield Ln, Palm Desert (92211-0404)
P.O. Box 14430 (92255-4430)
PHONE.................................760 345-8700
Fax: 760 345-8799
Dan Jacobsson, *President*
Ingeborg Jacobsson, *Treasurer*
Fran Brown, *Office Mgr*
Donna Munoz, *Human Res Mgr*
EMP: 75
SQ FT: 9,000
SALES (est): 12.5MM Privately Held
WEB: www.jacobssoninc.com
SIC: 1611 Highway & street construction

(P-1804)
JAMES MCMINN INC
21801 Barton Rd Ste B, Grand Terrace (92313-4402)
PHONE.................................909 514-1231
Jim McMinn, *President*
Rick Monge, *Vice Pres*
Michelle Spence, *Controller*
John Herzog, *Superintendent*
EMP: 50 EST: 2005
SALES (est): 12MM Privately Held
SIC: 1611 Grading

(P-1805)
JOHN BENWARD COMPANY INC
21750 8th St E Ste B, Sonoma (95476-9803)
PHONE.................................707 996-7809
Fax: 707 996-2028
John Benward, *President*
Earl G Broderick, *Vice Pres*
Donna Blue, *Prdtn Mgr*
EMP: 50
SQ FT: 6,400

SALES (est): 11.4MM Privately Held
WEB: www.benwardco.com
SIC: 1611 Surfacing & paving

(P-1806)
JOHN BRINK GENERAL CONTRACTOR
1760 W Lake Blvd Ste 3, Tahoe City (96145)
P.O. Box 1902 (96145-1902)
PHONE.................................530 583-2005
Fax: 530 583-4405
John Brink, *Owner*
Keri Campbell, *Manager*
EMP: 50 EST: 1974
SALES (est): 4MM Privately Held
SIC: 1611 General contractor, highway & street construction

(P-1807)
KAD PAVING COMPANY
Also Called: Kad Engineering
32147 Dunlap Blvd Ste K, Yucaipa (92399-1757)
P.O. Box 9150, Redlands (92375-2350)
PHONE.................................909 790-3366
Donald S Wheeler Jr, *President*
Mary Bedolla, *Manager*
EMP: 52
SQ FT: 11,000
SALES (est): 8.3MM Privately Held
SIC: 1611 Surfacing & paving

(P-1808)
KEC ENGINEERING
200 N Sherman Ave, Corona (92882-7162)
P.O. Box 909 (92878-0909)
PHONE.................................951 734-3010
Fax: 951 735-2041
James Elfring, *President*
Timothy Stephens, *CFO*
Les Card, *Vice Pres*
Matthew Card, *Vice Pres*
Scott Pfeiffer, *Vice Pres*
EMP: 110
SQ FT: 9,600
SALES (est): 21.8MM Privately Held
WEB: www.kecengineering.com
SIC: 1611 Highway & street construction

(P-1809)
KIEWIT INFRASTRUCTURE WEST CO
1111 Broadway, Oakland (94607-4139)
PHONE.................................510 452-1400
William Silver, *Branch Mgr*
Duc Le, *Engineer*
EMP: 54
SALES (corp-wide): 20.9B Privately Held
SIC: 1611 Highway & street construction
HQ: Kiewit Infrastructure West Co.
4004 S 60th St
Omaha NE 68117
402 342-2052

(P-1810)
KIEWIT INFRASTRUCTURE WEST CO
3200 Busch Rd, Pleasanton (94566)
PHONE.................................925 462-1088
Fax: 925 462-6545
Allan Kung, *General Mgr*
EMP: 80
SALES (corp-wide): 20.9B Privately Held
WEB: www.kiecon.com
SIC: 1611 Highway & street construction
HQ: Kiewit Infrastructure West Co.
4004 S 60th St
Omaha NE 68117
402 342-2052

(P-1811)
KIEWIT INFRASTRUCTURE WEST CO
10704 Shoemaker Ave, Santa Fe Springs (90670-4040)
PHONE.................................562 946-1816
Ken Riley, *Manager*
Jack Clapp, *Project Mgr*
EMP: 125
SQ FT: 12,514

SALES (corp-wide): 20.9B Privately Held
WEB: www.kiecon.com
SIC: 1611 1542 1541 Highway & street construction; nonresidential construction; industrial buildings & warehouses
HQ: Kiewit Infrastructure West Co.
4004 S 60th St
Omaha NE 68117
402 342-2052

(P-1812)
KIEWIT INFRASTRUCTURE WEST CO
12700 Stowe Dr Ste 180, Poway (92064-8883)
PHONE.................................858 486-3410
Fax: 858 486-3941
Mike Lowe, *Manager*
EMP: 51
SALES (corp-wide): 20.9B Privately Held
WEB: www.kiecon.com
SIC: 1611 Highway & street construction
HQ: Kiewit Infrastructure West Co.
4004 S 60th St
Omaha NE 68117
402 342-2052

(P-1813)
KIEWIT PACIFIC CO
Also Called: Kie Con
3551 Wilbur Ave, Antioch (94509-8530)
PHONE.................................925 754-9494
John Burke, *Manager*
Gus Brannan, *Manager*
EMP: 50
SQ FT: 4,320
SALES (corp-wide): 20.9B Privately Held
WEB: www.kiecon.com
SIC: 1611 Highway & street construction
HQ: Kiewit Infrastructure West Co.
4004 S 60th St
Omaha NE 68117
402 342-2052

(P-1814)
LARRY JACINTO CONSTRUCTION INC
9555 N Wabash Ave, Redlands (92374-2714)
P.O. Box 615, Mentone (92359-0615)
PHONE.................................909 794-2151
Larry Frankland Jacinto, *CEO*
Steve Hopkins, *CFO*
Dennis Drexler, *Vice Pres*
Scott Dickerson, *Marketing Staff*
EMP: 80
SQ FT: 8,500
SALES (est): 21.5MM Privately Held
SIC: 1611 Grading; highway & street paving contractor; sidewalk construction

(P-1815)
LEGACY PARTNERS LIMITED INC
Also Called: Legacy Paving
738 W Washington Ave A, Escondido (92025-1692)
PHONE.................................760 747-2711
EMP: 53
SALES (est): 4.4MM Privately Held
WEB: www.legacypaving.com
SIC: 1611

(P-1816)
LUND EQUIPMENT LP
5302 Roseville Rd, North Highlands (95660-5036)
PHONE.................................916 344-5800
Walter Martinez, *Principal*
EMP: 50
SALES (est): 5.6MM Privately Held
SIC: 1611 General contractor, highway & street construction

(P-1817)
M F MAHER INC
Also Called: Maher M F Concrete Cnstr
490 Ryder St, Vallejo (94590-7217)
PHONE.................................707 552-2774
Fax: 707 552-0328
Malcolm F Maher, *President*
Janice K Maher, *Corp Secy*
Ronald Maher, *Vice Pres*
Steve Maher, *Executive*
Kim Johnson, *Controller*

EMP: 70
SQ FT: 4,000
SALES (est): 10.8MM Privately Held
WEB: www.mfmaher.com
SIC: 1611 General contractor, highway & street construction

(P-1818)
MACRO-Z-TECHNOLOGY COMPANY (PA)
Also Called: M Z T
841 E Washington Ave, Santa Ana (92701-3878)
PHONE.................................714 564-1130
Fax: 714 564-1144
Bryan J Zatica, *CEO*
Violet Torres, *General Mgr*
Christina Fabela, *Safety Mgr*
John Newlin, *QC Mgr*
Jackie Bach, *Marketing Staff*
EMP: 97
SQ FT: 3,000
SALES (est): 47.6MM Privately Held
SIC: 1611 1542 8711 Concrete construction: roads, highways, sidewalks, etc.; commercial & office building contractors; engineering services

(P-1819)
MAMCO INC (PA)
Also Called: ALABBASI
764 Ramona Expy Ste C, Perris (92571-9716)
PHONE.................................951 776-9300
Marwan Alabbasi, *CEO*
Elizabeth Alabbasi, *President*
Rumzi Alabbasi, *Vice Pres*
EMP: 62
SQ FT: 2,200
SALES (est): 29.6MM Privately Held
SIC: 1611 General contractor, highway & street construction

(P-1820)
MANERI TRAFFIC CONTROL INC
Also Called: Mtc
47423 Rainbow Canyon Rd, Temecula (92592-5952)
PHONE.................................951 695-5104
Maria Maneri, *Owner*
EMP: 70
SQ FT: 900
SALES (est): 9.1MM Privately Held
SIC: 1611 7389 Highway & street sign installation; flagging service (traffic control)

(P-1821)
MANHOLE ADJUSTING CONTRS INC
9500 Beverly Rd, Pico Rivera (90660-2135)
PHONE.................................323 725-1387
Fax: 323 558-8001
John Corcoran, *President*
Maria E Corcoran, *Vice Pres*
Aung Win, *Controller*
Hane Tok, *Personnel Exec*
EMP: 50
SALES (est): 10.8MM Privately Held
SIC: 1611 General contractor, highway & street construction; highway & street paving contractor

(P-1822)
MARATHON GENERAL INC
1728 Mission Rd, Escondido (92029-1111)
PHONE.................................760 738-9714
Fax: 760 738-7091
Mark Miller, *President*
Steven Gallant, *CFO*
Donald Tolen, *Vice Pres*
EMP: 80
SQ FT: 3,000
SALES (est): 18.5MM Privately Held
WEB: www.maragen.com
SIC: 1611 Grading; highway & street paving contractor

(P-1823)
MARTIN BROTHERS CONSTRUCTION (PA)
20 Light Sky Ct, Sacramento (95828-1016)
PHONE.................................916 381-0911
Fax: 916 381-0611

1611 - Highway & Street Construction County (P-1824)

PRODUCTS & SERVICES SECTION

Felipe Martin Sr, *President*
EMP: 60
SQ FT: 9,600
SALES (est): 23.3MM **Privately Held**
SIC: **1611** 1794 1541 1795 Highway & street construction; surfacing & paving; excavation work; excavation & grading, building construction; industrial buildings, new construction; demolition, buildings & other structures

(P-1824)
MATICH CORPORATION (PA)
1596 E Harry Shepard Blvd, San Bernardino (92408-0197)
P.O. Box 10, Highland (92346-1010)
PHONE.................................909 382-7400
Fax: 909 824-2360
Stephen A Matich, *CEO*
Martin A Matich, *Chairman*
Randall Valadez, *Treasurer*
Patrick A Matich, *Exec VP*
Robert M Matich, *Exec VP*
EMP: 60 EST: 1954
SQ FT: 10,000
SALES (est): 64MM **Privately Held**
WEB: www.matichicm.com
SIC: **1611** 2951 General contractor, highway & street construction; asphalt paving mixtures & blocks

(P-1825)
MESA CONTRACTING CORPORATION
22845 Savi Ranch Pkwy D, Yorba Linda (92887-4625)
PHONE.................................714 974-7300
Fax: 714 974-0149
Ronald Gene Smith, *CEO*
Ron McAmis, *Corp Secy*
Bill Bates, *Vice Pres*
EMP: 120
SQ FT: 4,518
SALES (est): 17.9MM **Privately Held**
SIC: **1611** Grading

(P-1826)
MGB CONSTRUCTION INC
91 Commercial Ave, Riverside (92507-1111)
PHONE.................................951 342-0303
Emily Beach, *President*
Emilly Beach, *President*
EMP: 150
SALES (est): 17MM **Privately Held**
SIC: **1611** Highway & street paving contractor

(P-1827)
MIDSTATE BARRIER INC
Also Called: MBI
3291 S Highway 99, Stockton (95215-8032)
P.O. Box 30550 (95213-0550)
PHONE.................................209 944-9565
Clark Ebinger, *President*
Dale R Breen, *Vice Pres*
Stephen V Gifford, *Vice Pres*
EMP: 75
SQ FT: 20,000
SALES: 20MM **Privately Held**
WEB: www.hwysfty.com
SIC: **1611** Highway signs & guardrails; guardrail construction, highways

(P-1828)
MILLERS CUSTOM WORK INC
471-825 Diane Dr, Susanville (96130-7742)
P.O. Box 1300 (96130-1300)
PHONE.................................530 257-4207
Fax: 530 257-7160
James C Miller, *President*
Darrel E Miller, *Treasurer*
Robert D Miller, *Admin Sec*
EMP: 60 EST: 1952
SQ FT: 1,670
SALES: 2.9MM **Privately Held**
WEB: www.millercustom.com
SIC: **1611** Highway & street paving contractor; grading

(P-1829)
MORRO BAY PUBLIC WORKS
Also Called: City of Morro Bay
955 Shasta Ave, Morro Bay (93442-1934)
PHONE.................................805 772-6261
Fax: 805 772-6268
Janice Peters, *Mayor*
Scot Graham, *Planning Mgr*
Rick Algert, *Business Mgr*
Joe Woods, *Business Mgr*
Karen Sweeny, *Manager*
EMP: 100
SALES (est): 7.5MM **Privately Held**
SIC: **1611** Highway & street construction

(P-1830)
MUSE CONCRETE CONTRACTORS INC
8599 Commercial Way, Redding (96002-3902)
PHONE.................................530 226-5151
Fax: 530 226-5155
Boyce Muse, *President*
Joan Muse, *CFO*
Corring Bepler, *Office Mgr*
EMP: 94
SALES (est): 17MM **Privately Held**
WEB: www.museconcrete.com
SIC: **1611** 1771 Concrete construction: roads, highways, sidewalks, etc.; concrete work; curb construction

(P-1831)
MYERS & SONS CONSTRUCTION LP
4600 Northgate Blvd # 100, Sacramento (95834-1121)
PHONE.................................916 283-9950
Clinton C Myers, *Partner*
Clinton W Myers, *Partner*
Jenna Carlson, *Human Resources*
EMP: 250
SALES (est): 144.8MM **Privately Held**
SIC: **1611** Highway & street construction

(P-1832)
NATIONAL PAVING COMPANY INC
4361 Fort Dr, Riverside (92509-6784)
P.O. Box 3649 (92519-3649)
PHONE.................................951 369-1332
Richard J Lindholm, *President*
Lawrence Spicher, *CFO*
Savannah Vendejas, *Admin Sec*
Therry Carroll, *Controller*
Jennifer Mossman, *Prdtn Mgr*
EMP: 78
SQ FT: 4,000
SALES (est): 15.3MM **Privately Held**
WEB: www.nationalpaving.com
SIC: **1611** Highway & street paving contractor

(P-1833)
NEHEMIAH CONSTRUCTION INC
12150 Tributary Ln P, Rancho Cordova (95670)
PHONE.................................707 746-6815
EMP: 50
SQ FT: 2,500
SALES: 98.4K **Privately Held**
WEB: www.nehemiahconst.com
SIC: **1611**

(P-1834)
NICHOLAS GRANT CORPORATION
Also Called: Daley
12570 Highway 67, Lakeside (92040-1159)
PHONE.................................619 390-3900
Fax: 858 642-9269
John Daley Jr, *President*
Mark Thunder, *Exec VP*
Abraham Ramirez, *General Mgr*
Myrna Alvarez, *Controller*
Frank Herrera, *Foreman/Supr*
▲ EMP: 100
SALES (est): 19.1MM **Privately Held**
SIC: **1611** Highway & street construction

(P-1835)
NORTH BAY CONSTRUCTION INC
431 Payran St, Petaluma (94952-5908)
P.O. Box 751389 (94975-1389)
PHONE.................................707 283-0093
Fax: 707 765-6417
John E Barella, *President*
Will Earnshaw, *Vice Pres*
Steve Geney, *Vice Pres*
Rick Vercelli, *Manager*
EMP: 80
SQ FT: 7,000
SALES (est): 9.6MM **Privately Held**
WEB: www.nbcinc.net
SIC: **1611** 1623 Highway & street paving contractor; grading; sewer line construction

(P-1836)
O C JONES & SONS INC (PA)
1520 4th St, Berkeley (94710-1748)
PHONE.................................510 526-3424
Fax: 510 526-0990
Kelly Kolander, *President*
Robert Pelascini, *Ch of Bd*
Beth Yoshida, *CFO*
Rob Layne, *Vice Pres*
Heidi Faria, *Admin Asst*
EMP: 150 EST: 1924
SQ FT: 80,000
SALES (est): 114.3MM **Privately Held**
WEB: www.ocjones.com
SIC: **1611** Grading; highway & street paving contractor

(P-1837)
OGRADY PAVING INC
2513 Wyandotte St, Mountain View (94043-2311)
PHONE.................................650 966-1926
Fax: 650 966-1946
Thomas M O'Grady Jr, *President*
Robert Taylor, *Managing Prtnr*
Durin Celine, *CFO*
Celine Duran, *Corp Secy*
Shelley McGee, *Officer*
EMP: 110
SQ FT: 3,200
SALES (est): 21.4MM **Privately Held**
WEB: www.ogradypaving.com
SIC: **1611** Surfacing & paving; grading

(P-1838)
ORTIZ ASPHALT PAVING INC
382 E Orange Show Rd, San Bernardino (92408-2414)
P.O. Box 401370, Hesperia (92340-1370)
PHONE.................................951 966-7060
Bruce Kevin Ortiz, *President*
Candace Arsay, *Manager*
EMP: 50
SQ FT: 1,000
SALES: 17MM **Privately Held**
SIC: **1611** Highway & street paving contractor

(P-1839)
ORTIZ ENTERPRISES INCORPORATED (PA)
6 Cushing Ste 200, Irvine (92618-4230)
PHONE.................................949 753-1414
Fax: 949 753-1477
Patrick Ortiz, *President*
Jill Ortiz, *Vice Pres*
Cary B Purves, *Vice Pres*
Doug Dawson, *Project Mgr*
Juan Ramirez, *Project Mgr*
EMP: 50
SQ FT: 12,000
SALES (est): 31.5MM **Privately Held**
SIC: **1611** Highway & street construction

(P-1840)
PAINTED HILLS POWER
15234 Painted Hills Rd, Whitewater (92282-2902)
PHONE.................................760 406-1771
David Erskine, *Owner*
EMP: 50
SALES (est): 452.8K **Privately Held**
SIC: **1611** 7389 Highway & street sign installation;

(P-1841)
PALP INC
Also Called: Excel Paving Co
2230 Lemon Ave, Long Beach (90806-5124)
P.O. Box 16405 (90806-0995)
PHONE.................................562 599-5841
Fax: 562 591-7485
Curtis P Brown, *CEO*
George McRae, *Senior VP*
Bruce Flatt, *Vice Pres*
Michelle Drakulich, *Admin Sec*
Tony Fratangelo, *Project Mgr*
EMP: 225 EST: 1976
SQ FT: 11,000
SALES (est): 49.5MM **Privately Held**
WEB: www.palp.com
SIC: **1611** 8711 Highway & street paving contractor; grading; engineering services

(P-1842)
PAPICH CONSTRUCTION CO INC (PA)
800 Farroll Rd, Grover Beach (93433-2748)
P.O. Box 2210, Pismo Beach (93448-2210)
PHONE.................................805 473-3016
Jason William Papich, *President*
April Papich, *Admin Sec*
Chris Centeno, *Project Mgr*
Megan Keenan, *Manager*
EMP: 100
SQ FT: 3,500
SALES (est): 65.6MM **Privately Held**
WEB: www.papichconstruction.com
SIC: **1611** General contractor, highway & street construction

(P-1843)
PARSONS CORPORATION
100 W San Fernando St # 450, San Jose (95113-2233)
PHONE.................................626 440-2000
Joe Scarano, *Manager*
Julia Hawkinson, *Project Mgr*
EMP: 63
SALES (corp-wide): 7.9B **Privately Held**
SIC: **1611** Highway & street construction
PA: The Parsons Corporation
100 W Walnut St
Pasadena CA 91124
626 440-2000

(P-1844)
PAVE-TECH INC
2231 La Mirada Dr, Vista (92081-8828)
PHONE.................................760 727-8700
Rudy Zavalani, *CEO*
Larry Keepers, *Shareholder*
Debbie Bruce, *Manager*
Anna Keepers, *Manager*
EMP: 50
SALES (est): 15.9MM **Privately Held**
SIC: **1611** Highway & street paving contractor

(P-1845)
PENA GRADING & DEMOLITION INC
Also Called: Pena Trucking
11253 Vinedale St, Sun Valley (91352-3217)
PHONE.................................818 768-5202
Orestes Pena, *President*
Irma Pena, *Vice Pres*
EMP: 50
SQ FT: 8,000
SALES (est): 8.3MM **Privately Held**
SIC: **1611** Grading

(P-1846)
PETER KIEWIT SONS INC
1925 Wright Ave Ste C, La Verne (91750-5847)
PHONE.................................909 962-6001
Rohit Shard, *Branch Mgr*
EMP: 177
SALES (corp-wide): 20.9B **Privately Held**
SIC: **1611** Highway & street construction
PA: Peter Kiewit Sons', Inc.
3555 Farnam St Ste 1000
Omaha NE 68131
402 342-2052

PRODUCTS & SERVICES SECTION
1611 - Highway & Street Construction County (P-1869)

(P-1847)
QUAIL ENGINEERING INC
Also Called: Pacific Exteriors
11372 Trask Ave Ste 110, Garden Grove (92843-2605)
PHONE..................714 636-0612
Mark Kabarsky, *President*
▲ EMP: 50
SQ FT: 480
SALES (est): 4.4MM **Privately Held**
SIC: 1611 Grading

(P-1848)
R & R MAHER CNSTR CO INC
1324 Lemon St, Vallejo (94590-7250)
P.O. Box 3129 (94590-0668)
PHONE..................707 552-0330
Fax: 707 552-4841
Richard V Maher, *President*
Jearlene Brown, *CFO*
Bradley V Maher, *Vice Pres*
Bradley Maher, *Vice Pres*
Richard D Maher, *Vice Pres*
EMP: 55
SQ FT: 1,600
SALES: 5.5MM **Privately Held**
SIC: 1611 Concrete construction: roads, highways, sidewalks, etc.

(P-1849)
REEVES TRACTOR SERVICE INC
5455 Blue Ridge Dr, Yorba Linda (92887-4234)
P.O. Box 702 (92885-0702)
PHONE..................714 692-4020
Jeffrey G Reeves, *President*
Laurie Reeves, *Manager*
EMP: 60
SALES (est): 4.5MM **Privately Held**
SIC: 1611 Grading

(P-1850)
REMEDIATION CONSTRUCTORS INC
Also Called: Remcon
751 Wakefield Ct, Oakdale (95361-7761)
PHONE..................209 847-9186
Fax: 209 847-9189
Stephen B Christensen, *President*
Mark A Gordine, *Vice Pres*
Chester Mallory, *Vice Pres*
Joanna Fondse, *Human Res Mgr*
Tina Micheletti, *Director*
EMP: 80
SQ FT: 6,000
SALES (est): 5.4MM **Privately Held**
SIC: 1611 8711 Surfacing & paving; engineering services

(P-1851)
RICK HAMM CONSTRUCTION INC
201 W Carleton Ave, Orange (92867-3607)
PHONE..................714 532-0815
Fax: 714 532-1078
Rick Hamm, *President*
Llana Hamm, *Corp Secy*
Erin Sweeney, *Manager*
EMP: 90
SQ FT: 25,000
SALES (est): 21.1MM **Privately Held**
WEB: www.rickhamm.com
SIC: 1611 1771 1791 1741 General contractor, highway & street construction; patio construction, concrete; precast concrete structural framing or panels, placing of; masonry & other stonework; stone masonry; concrete block masonry laying; erection & dismantling of forms for poured concrete

(P-1852)
RJ NOBLE COMPANY (PA)
15505 E Lincoln Ave, Orange (92865-1015)
P.O. Box 620 (92856-9020)
PHONE..................714 637-1550
Fax: 714 637-6321
Michael J Carver, *President*
James N Ducote, *CFO*
Craig Porter, *Vice Pres*
Jim Merva, *Info Tech Dir*
Kori Ingstad, *Project Mgr*
EMP: 145 EST: 1950
SQ FT: 5,500
SALES (est): 70.6MM **Privately Held**
WEB: www.rjnoblecompany.com
SIC: 1611 Highway & street paving contractor

(P-1853)
ROMERO GENERAL CNSTR CORP
Also Called: ROMERO CONSTRUCTION
2150 N Centre City Pkwy, Escondido (92026-1347)
PHONE..................760 489-8412
Fax: 760 489-1460
Keith Reilly, *President*
Jeff Rohring, *CFO*
Troy Greer, *Vice Pres*
Reilly Keith, *Director*
Brian Dvorak, *Superintendent*
EMP: 175
SQ FT: 3,500
SALES (est): 49.1MM **Privately Held**
WEB: www.romerogc.com
SIC: 1611 Highway & street paving contractor

(P-1854)
ROY E LADD INC
Also Called: Ladd Construction Co
3724 Sunlight Ct, Redding (96001-0173)
PHONE..................530 241-6102
Fax: 530 241-5492
Craig Wiseman, *President*
Tom Capener, *Treasurer*
Mark Christopher, *Director*
Eric Ladd, *Vice Pres*
Bill Schoonmaker, *Vice Pres*
EMP: 50
SQ FT: 3,000
SALES: 20MM **Privately Held**
SIC: 1611 1622 Highway & street construction; bridge construction

(P-1855)
SAN JOAQUIN HILLS TRANSPORTTN (PA)
Also Called: Transprttion Corridor Agencies
125 Pacifica Ste 100, Irvine (92618-3324)
P.O. Box 53770 (92619-3770)
PHONE..................949 754-3400
Fax: 949 754-3467
Michael Kraman, *CEO*
Linda Lindholm, *Executive*
Kathleen Loch, *Executive*
Lance Maclean, *Executive*
Jim Rhodes, *Info Tech Dir*
EMP: 57
SQ FT: 17,000
SALES: 151.2MM **Privately Held**
SIC: 1611 General contractor, highway & street construction

(P-1856)
SECURITY PAVING COMPANY INC
Also Called: Valley Base Materials
13170 Telfair Ave, Sylmar (91342-3573)
PHONE..................818 362-9200
Fax: 818 767-3169
Michael L Mattivi, *CEO*
Albert Mattivi, *President*
Thomas J Mattivi, *Vice Pres*
EMP: 100
SQ FT: 4,000
SALES (est): 46.5MM **Privately Held**
SIC: 1611 Highway & street construction

(P-1857)
SEQUEL CONTRACTORS INC
13546 Imperial Hwy, Santa Fe Springs (90670-4821)
PHONE..................562 802-7227
Thomas S Pack, *CEO*
Abel Magellanes, *Vice Pres*
Vicki Norieda, *Admin Sec*
EMP: 50
SQ FT: 80,000
SALES (est): 7.9MM **Privately Held**
SIC: 1611 Highway & street construction

(P-1858)
SHELTON CONSTRUCTION COMPANY
5628 Spinnaker Bay Dr, Long Beach (90803-6806)
PHONE..................714 903-7853
William Shelton, *President*
Michelle Spence, *Office Mgr*
EMP: 60
SQ FT: 3,200
SALES (est): 6MM **Privately Held**
WEB: www.sheltonconst.com
SIC: 1611 Grading

(P-1859)
SIGNATURE PAINTING & CNSTR INC
1565 3rd Ave, Walnut Creek (94597-2604)
PHONE..................925 287-0444
Brian Mitchell, *President*
Erik Oller, *Vice Pres*
Christian Cupolo, *Project Mgr*
Mike Witter, *Manager*
Charlie Johnson, *Superintendent*
EMP: 50
SALES (est): 7MM **Privately Held**
SIC: 1611 General contractor, highway & street construction

(P-1860)
SKANSKA USA CVIL W CAL DST INC (DH)
1995 Agua Mansa Rd, Riverside (92509-2405)
PHONE..................951 684-5360
Richard Cavallero, *CEO*
Michael Cobelli, *COO*
Joseph Nogues, *CFO*
Michael Aparicio, *Exec VP*
Lisa Picard, *Exec VP*
EMP: 700
SQ FT: 15,000
SALES: 396.5MM
SALES (corp-wide): 17.5B **Privately Held**
SIC: 1611 1622 1629 8711 General contractor, highway & street construction; bridge construction; highway construction, elevated; dam construction; engineering services; asphalt paving mixtures & blocks
HQ: Skanska Usa Civil Inc.
7520 Astoria Blvd Ste 200
East Elmhurst NY 11370
718 340-0777

(P-1861)
SKANSKA USA CVIL W CAL DST INC
88200 Fargo Cnyn Rd, Coachella (92236)
P.O. Box 1510, Indio (92202-1510)
PHONE..................760 342-8004
EMP: 352
SALES (corp-wide): 17.5B **Privately Held**
SIC: 1611 1522 General contractor, highway & street construction; residential construction
HQ: Skanska Usa Civil West California District Inc.
1995 Agua Mansa Rd
Riverside CA 92509
951 684-5360

(P-1862)
SKANSKA-RADOS A JOINT VENTURE
11390 W Olympic Blvd, Los Angeles (90064-1619)
PHONE..................213 978-0600
Kent Percy, *Partner*
Michael Witz, *Partner*
Kristin Darby, *Safety Mgr*
EMP: 70
SALES (est): 950K **Privately Held**
SIC: 1611 Highway & street construction

(P-1863)
SOUTH COAST STONE PAVING
Also Called: Hillside Contractor
2618 N Baker St, Santa Ana (92706-1511)
PHONE..................714 835-0258
David Lopez, *Principal*
EMP: 65
SALES (est): 5.6MM **Privately Held**
SIC: 1611 Highway & street construction

(P-1864)
STEVE MANNING CONSTRUCTION INC
5211 Churn Creek Rd, Redding (96002-3914)
P.O. Box 491660 (96049-1660)
PHONE..................530 222-0810
Fax: 530 222-4908
Steve Manning, *President*
Arlene T Litsey, *Treasurer*
Kolet Willey, *Office Mgr*
Bill Spoon, *Project Mgr*
Heidi Hankins, *Financial Exec*
EMP: 115
SQ FT: 2,200
SALES (est): 19.2MM **Privately Held**
SIC: 1611 Highway & street construction

(P-1865)
STEVENS CREEK QUARRY INC (PA)
12100 Stevens Canyon Rd, Cupertino (95014-5443)
PHONE..................408 253-2512
Richard A Voss, *President*
Richard Voss, *President*
Bob Romano, *President*
Diana Voss, *Admin Sec*
Pat Hennigan, *Sales Mgr*
EMP: 60
SALES (est): 20.5MM **Privately Held**
WEB: www.scqinc.com
SIC: 1611 7353 1442 General contractor, highway & street construction; highway & street maintenance; heavy construction equipment rental; construction sand mining

(P-1866)
STRONGHOLD ENGINEERING INC (PA)
2000 Market St, Riverside (92501-1769)
PHONE..................951 684-9303
Fax: 951 684-9329
Beverly A Bailey, *President*
Scott Bailey, *Managing Prtnr*
Cheryl Parris, *CFO*
Ashley Powell, *Office Mgr*
Dan Rasmussen, *General Counsel*
EMP: 58
SQ FT: 21,000
SALES (est): 120.3MM **Privately Held**
SIC: 1611 General contractor, highway & street construction

(P-1867)
SUDHAKAR COMPANY INTERNATIONAL
1450 N Fitzgerald Ave, Rialto (92376-8621)
PHONE..................909 879-2933
Fax: 909 879-2939
Ashok Sudhakar, *President*
Betty Bogle, *Vice Pres*
Robyn Stroup, *Accounting Staf*
EMP: 100 EST: 1998
SQ FT: 16,000
SALES: 21MM **Privately Held**
WEB: www.sudhakarco.com
SIC: 1611 Highway & street sign installation; highway reflector installation

(P-1868)
SUKUT CONSTRUCTION LLC
4010 W Chandler Ave, Santa Ana (92704-5202)
PHONE..................714 540-5351
Michael Crawford, *Principal*
Joe Philbin, *Principal*
Mike Zanaboni, *Principal*
Paul Kuliev, *Finance*
EMP: 99 EST: 2014
SALES (est): 4.9MM **Privately Held**
SIC: 1611 1623 1629 Highway & street construction; grading; water, sewer & utility lines; pipe laying construction; earthmoving contractor

(P-1869)
SULLY-MILLER CONTRACTING CO (DH)
Also Called: Blue Diamond Materials
135 Sstate College Ste 400, Brea (92821)
PHONE..................714 578-9600
Fax: 714 578-2850
Dave Martinez, *President*

1611 - Highway & Street Construction County (P-1870)

Tim Orchard, *CFO*
Scott Bottomley, *Vice Pres*
Russ Caruso, *Vice Pres*
Mike Edwards, *Vice Pres*
EMP: 340
SALES (est): 141MM
SALES (corp-wide): 78.4MM **Privately Held**
WEB: www.thebluediamond.com
SIC: 1611 Highway & street construction
HQ: Sully-Miller Holding Corporation
135 S State College Blvd # 400
Brea CA 92821
714 578-9600

(P-1870)
SUPERIOR PAVING COMPANY INC
Also Called: United Paving Company
1880 N Delilah St, Corona (92879-1892)
PHONE 951 739-9200
Fax: 714 739-2400
Sabas Trujillo, *CEO*
Jorge Alcaraz, *Opers Staff*
Tracie Moran, *Mktg Dir*
EMP: 85
SQ FT: 3,000
SALES (est): 21.6MM **Privately Held**
WEB: www.united-paving.com
SIC: 1611 Surfacing & paving; highway & street paving contractor

(P-1871)
SUPERIOR READY MIX CONCRETE LP
Also Called: Srm Contracting & Paving
7192 Mission Gorge Rd, San Diego (92120-1131)
PHONE 619 265-0955
Fax: 619 583-3147
Brent Cooper, *Branch Mgr*
Bill Butler, *General Mgr*
Wayne Mello, *Project Mgr*
Steve Lobaugh, *Superintendent*
EMP: 50
SALES (corp-wide): 204.1MM **Privately Held**
WEB: www.superiorrm.com
SIC: 1611 Surfacing & paving
PA: Superior Ready Mix Concrete L.P.
1508 Mission Rd
Escondido CA 92029
760 745-0556

(P-1872)
TEAM GHILOTTI INC
2531 Petaluma Blvd S, Petaluma (94952-5523)
PHONE 707 763-8700
Glen Ghilotti, *President*
Glen C Ghilotti, *President*
Monica Bourdens, *Office Mgr*
EMP: 50
SQ FT: 5,900
SALES (est): 9MM **Privately Held**
WEB: www.teamghilotti.com
SIC: 1611 Highway & street construction

(P-1873)
TELFER OIL COMPANY (PA)
Also Called: Western Oil & Spreading
211 Foster St, Martinez (94553-1029)
P.O. Box 709 (94553-0151)
PHONE 925 228-1515
Fax: 925 229-3955
Michael S Telfer, *Owner*
John Telfer, *Owner*
Ken Chambless, *CFO*
Daniel Frankel, *Vice Pres*
EMP: 55
SQ FT: 5,000
SALES (est): 78.5MM **Privately Held**
WEB: www.telfercompanies.com
SIC: 1611 2951 4213 4212 Highway & street paving contractor; resurfacing contractor; paving mixtures; liquid petroleum transport, non-local; local trucking, without storage

(P-1874)
TNT GRADING INC
Also Called: T-N-T Grading
529 W 4th Ave B, Escondido (92025-4037)
PHONE 760 736-4054
EMP: 95
SQ FT: 2,500
SALES (est): 5.5MM **Privately Held**
WEB: www.tntgrading.com
SIC: 1611

(P-1875)
TORO ENTERPRISES INC
2101 E Ventura Blvd, Oxnard (93036-8951)
P.O. Box 6285 (93031-6285)
PHONE 805 483-4515
Fax: 805 483-3635
Sean Castillo, *President*
Buffy Castillo, *Shareholder*
Teresa Ortega, *Shareholder*
Reuben Ortega, *Vice Pres*
Monica Ramirez, *Accountant*
EMP: 67
SALES (est): 22.4MM **Privately Held**
WEB: www.toroenterprises.com
SIC: 1611 Concrete construction: roads, highways, sidewalks, etc.

(P-1876)
TRANSPORTATION CALIFORNIA DEPT
Also Called: Maintenance Department
611 Payran St, Petaluma (94952-5910)
PHONE 707 762-6641
John Peterson, *Manager*
EMP: 110 **Privately Held**
WEB: www.caltip.org
SIC: 1611 9621 Highway & street maintenance; regulation, administration of transportation.
HQ: California Dept Of Transportation
1120 N St
Sacramento CA 95814

(P-1877)
TRANSPORTATION CALIFORNIA DEPT
Also Called: Caltrans Eastern Reg Rd Maint
1940 Workman Mill Rd, Whittier (90601-1414)
PHONE 562 692-0823
Fax: 562 692-7903
Edward Toledo, *Manager*
John Janson, *Manager*
EMP: 200 **Privately Held**
WEB: www.caltip.org
SIC: 1611 9621 Highway & street maintenance; regulation, administration of transportation.
HQ: California Dept Of Transportation
1120 N St
Sacramento CA 95814

(P-1878)
TRANSPORTATION CALIFORNIA DEPT
Also Called: Caltrans
2019 W Texas St, Fairfield (94533-4461)
P.O. Box 8 (94533-0084)
PHONE 707 428-2031
Fax: 707 428-2022
E L Poplin, *Branch Mgr*
EMP: 150 **Privately Held**
WEB: www.caltip.org
SIC: 1611 9621 Highway & street maintenance; regulation, administration of transportation.
HQ: California Dept Of Transportation
1120 N St
Sacramento CA 95814

(P-1879)
UNIVERSAL ASPHALT CO INC
10610 Painter Ave, Santa Fe Springs (90670-4091)
P.O. Box 2548 (90670-0548)
PHONE 562 941-0201
Fax: 562 941-4080
Daniel M Houck, *President*
Richard Houck, *Project Mgr*
EMP: 50
SQ FT: 22,000
SALES (est): 7MM **Privately Held**
SIC: 1611 Highway & street paving contractor

(P-1880)
VALLEY DEMO INC
1016 Meredith Dr, Bakersfield (93304-6124)
PHONE 661 900-4818
Jesus Fernandez, *President*
EMP: 98
SALES (est): 950K **Privately Held**
SIC: 1611 Highway & street construction

(P-1881)
VANCE CORPORATION
2271 N Locust Ave, Rialto (92377-4113)
PHONE 909 355-4333
Fax: 909 355-4339
Verner E Thomas, *CEO*
Darrel L Lohman, *CFO*
EMP: 50
SQ FT: 10,000
SALES (est): 10.6MM **Privately Held**
SIC: 1611 General contractor, highway & street construction

(P-1882)
VSS INTERNATIONAL INC (HQ)
Also Called: V S S
3785 Channel Dr, West Sacramento (95691-3421)
P.O. Box 981330 (95798-1330)
PHONE 916 373-1500
Fax: 916 373-1438
Jeffrey Reed, *President*
Ron Bolles, *Treasurer*
Wendell Reed, *Treasurer*
John Shoden, *Treasurer*
Alan Berger, *Vice Pres*
▲ **EMP:** 62
SQ FT: 5,000
SALES (est): 45.5MM
SALES (corp-wide): 244.2MM **Privately Held**
SIC: 1611 3531 2951 Highway & street paving contractor; construction machinery; asphalt paving mixtures & blocks
PA: Basic Resources Inc
928 12th St Ste 700
Modesto CA 95354
209 521-9771

(P-1883)
WESTERN PAVING CONTRACTORS INC
15533 Arrow Hwy, Irwindale (91706-2002)
PHONE 626 338-7889
Fax: 626 338-3799
Enrique Castillo, *CEO*
Henry Castillo, *President*
Gina Alvarez, *Office Mgr*
Sean Hughes, *Project Mgr*
Ferry Soendjojo, *Controller*
EMP: 65
SQ FT: 3,200
SALES (est): 21.8MM **Privately Held**
SIC: 1611 Surfacing & paving; grading

(P-1884)
WESTERN RIM CONSTRUCTORS INC
621 S Andreasen Dr Ste B, Escondido (92029-1904)
PHONE 760 489-4328
Ray C Samuelson, *President*
Sandra Roth, *Manager*
EMP: 50
SALES (est): 10.2MM **Privately Held**
WEB: www.westernrim.net
SIC: 1611 General contractor, highway & street construction

(P-1885)
WR FORDE ASSOCIATES
984 Hensley St, Richmond (94801-2117)
PHONE 415 924-3072
Fax: 510 215-9867
Donald J Russell, *Partner*
Dale Robbins, *Treasurer*
Molly Forde, *Executive*
Kathy Massara, *Office Mgr*
Candice Russell, *Admin Asst*
EMP: 55
SQ FT: 4,500
SALES: 8.5MM **Privately Held**
SIC: 1611 1622 1794 Grading; bridge construction; excavation & grading, building construction

1622 Bridge, Tunnel & Elevated Hwy Construction

(P-1886)
AMERICAN BRDGE/FLUOR ENTPS INC
1390 Willow Pass Rd, Concord (94520-5200)
PHONE 510 808-4623
Robert Luffy, *President*
David Degney, *Exec VP*
Douglas Fuller, *Vice Pres*
Donald Jones, *Vice Pres*
▲ **EMP:** 80
SALES (est): 14MM **Privately Held**
SIC: 1622 Bridge construction

(P-1887)
AMERICAN CIVIL CONST
Also Called: American Civil Constrs W Coast
2990 Bay Vista Ct Ste D, Benicia (94510-1195)
PHONE 707 746-8028
Fax: 707 746-0936
Jeffrey Foerste, *President*
Clifford Barber, *Vice Pres*
David Wilkerson, *Vice Pres*
EMP: 75
SQ FT: 19,000
SALES (est): 13.4MM
SALES (corp-wide): 102.6MM **Privately Held**
WEB: www.wcbridge.com
SIC: 1622 1611 Bridge, tunnel & elevated highway; bridge construction; surfacing & paving
PA: American Civil Constructors Holdings, Inc.
4901 S Windermere St
Littleton CO 80120
303 795-2582

(P-1888)
COUNTY OF SACRAMENTO
Also Called: Municipal Svcs Agency
9700 Goethe Rd Ste D, Sacramento (95827-3558)
PHONE 916 875-2711
Thor Lude, *Chief*
Jason Spackman, *Admin Asst*
Katie Beland, *Human Res Mgr*
EMP: 100 **Privately Held**
WEB: www.sna.com
SIC: 1622 9199 Bridge, tunnel & elevated highway; general government administration;
PA: County Of Sacramento
700 H St Ste 7650
Sacramento CA 95814
916 874-5544

(P-1889)
FLATIRON WEST INC
2100 Goodyear Rd, Benicia (94510-1216)
PHONE 707 742-6000
Richard Tradinski, *Manager*
Todd Bennett, *General Mgr*
Peggy Cross, *Office Mgr*
Jonathan Krause, *E-Business*
Tina Krause, *E-Business*
EMP: 150
SALES (corp-wide): 778.5MM **Privately Held**
SIC: 1622 1629 Bridge construction; industrial plant construction
HQ: Flatiron West, Inc.
1770 La Costa Meadows Dr
San Marcos CA 92078
760 916-9100

(P-1890)
FLATIRON WEST INC
16341 Chino Corona Rd, Chino (91708-9233)
PHONE 909 597-8413
Thomas J Rademacher, *Ch of Bd*
EMP: 95
SALES (corp-wide): 778.5MM **Privately Held**
SIC: 1622 1611 Bridge, tunnel & elevated highway; highway & street construction

PRODUCTS & SERVICES SECTION
1623 - Water, Sewer & Utility Line Construction County (P-1912)

HQ: Flatiron West, Inc.
1770 La Costa Meadows Dr
San Marcos CA 92078
760 916-9100

(P-1891)
FLUOR DANIEL CONSTRUCTION CO (DH)
3 Polaris Way, Aliso Viejo (92656-5338)
PHONE.....................949 349-2000
Paul Buckham, *President*
Michael Steuert, *CFO*
Kendra Miller, *VP Human Res*
Ronald Peterson, *QC Dir*
Michael Pardon, *Manager*
EMP: 500
SALES: 3.3MM
SALES (corp-wide): 18.1B **Publicly Held**
SIC: 1622 Bridge, tunnel & elevated highway
HQ: Fluor Enterprises, Inc.
6700 Las Colinas Blvd
Irving TX 75039
469 398-7000

(P-1892)
GRANITE CONSTRUCTION COMPANY
5335 Debbie Rd, Santa Barbara (93111-2001)
P.O. Box 6744 (93160-6744)
PHONE.....................805 964-9951
Fax: 805 964-7661
Bruce McGowan, *Manager*
Brian Larninan, *Personnel Exec*
EMP: 169
SQ FT: 65,396
SALES (corp-wide): 2.3B **Publicly Held**
WEB: www.graniteconstruction.com
SIC: 1622 Bridge, tunnel & elevated highway
HQ: Granite Construction Company
585 W Beach St
Watsonville CA 95076
831 724-1011

(P-1893)
HAZARD CONSTRUCTION COMPANY
6465 Marindustry Dr, San Diego (92121-2536)
P.O. Box 229000 (92192-9000)
PHONE.....................858 587-3600
Klaus Guttau, *Vice Pres*
Noli Gavino, *Treasurer*
Rick McDonald, *Info Tech Mgr*
Bonnie Atkinson, *Data Proc Staff*
Barbara Larsen, *Human Res Dir*
EMP: 100 **EST:** 1926
SQ FT: 37,000
SALES (est): 43.6MM **Privately Held**
WEB: www.hazardconstruction.com
SIC: 1622 1611 Bridge construction; highway & street construction; grading; surfacing & paving; highway & street paving contractor

(P-1894)
JOHANN B GAROVI
Also Called: Garovibridge
109 Pinheiro Cir, Novato (94945-6817)
PHONE.....................415 898-1801
Johann B Garovi, *Owner*
Alexander Garovi, *Plant Mgr*
EMP: 50
SALES (est): 5MM **Privately Held**
SIC: 1622 Bridge, tunnel & elevated highway

(P-1895)
KIEWIT INFRASTRUCTURE WEST CO
12700 Stowe Dr Ste 180, Poway (92064-8883)
PHONE.....................360 693-1478
R Michael Phelps, *President*
EMP: 60
SALES (corp-wide): 20.9B **Privately Held**
SIC: 1622 Bridge, tunnel & elevated highway
HQ: Kiewit Infrastructure West Co.
4004 S 60th St
Omaha NE 68117
402 342-2052

(P-1896)
MCM CONSTRUCTION INC (PA)
6413 32nd St, North Highlands (95660-3001)
P.O. Box 620 (95660-0620)
PHONE.....................916 334-1221
Fax: 916 334-8355
James A Carter, *President*
H McGovern, *Vice Pres*
Harry D McGovern, *Vice Pres*
Kevin Wood, *Vice Pres*
Dan Shaw, *Executive*
EMP: 70
SQ FT: 5,000
SALES: 150MM **Privately Held**
WEB: www.mcmconstructioninc.com
SIC: 1622 Bridge construction

(P-1897)
MCM CONSTRUCTION INC
19010 Slover Ave, Bloomington (92316-2459)
PHONE.....................909 875-0533
Fax: 909 875-2243
Nella Flores, *Branch Mgr*
Dan Shaw, *Sales Dir*
EMP: 150
SALES (corp-wide): 150MM **Privately Held**
WEB: www.mcmconstructioninc.com
SIC: 1622 Bridge construction
PA: M.C.M. Construction, Inc.
6413 32nd St
North Highlands CA 95660
916 334-1221

(P-1898)
R M HARRIS COMPANY INC
1000 Howe Rd Ste 200, Martinez (94553-3446)
PHONE.....................925 335-3000
David R Harris, *CEO*
Mark Snapp, *Admin Sec*
EMP: 100
SQ FT: 4,500
SALES (est): 17.6MM **Privately Held**
SIC: 1622 1611 Bridge, tunnel & elevated highway; highway & street construction

(P-1899)
SEMA CONSTRUCTION INC
6 Orchard Ste 150, Irvine (92618-4534)
PHONE.....................949 330-4300
Steve Mills, *Manager*
EMP: 90
SALES (corp-wide): 411.1MM **Privately Held**
SIC: 1622 Bridge, tunnel & elevated highway
PA: Sema Construction, Inc.
7353 S Eagle St
Centennial CO 80112
303 627-2600

1623 Water, Sewer & Utility Line Construction

(P-1900)
A & H COMMUNICATIONS INC
1791 Reynolds Ave, Irvine (92614-5711)
PHONE.....................949 250-4555
Brian Elliott, *President*
Dexter Flipen, *CFO*
Greg Elliott, *Vice Pres*
Brett Howard, *Vice Pres*
C B Howard, *Agent*
EMP: 250
SQ FT: 4,500
SALES (est): 19.7MM **Privately Held**
SIC: 1623 Cable laying construction

(P-1901)
ADVANCED NETWORK TECH INC
7950 Cherry Ave Ste 107, Fontana (92336-4023)
PHONE.....................909 428-9030
Frederick C Young, *CEO*
Anna Baird, *Corp Secy*
EMP: 100

SALES (est): 24.4MM
SALES (corp-wide): 912.6MM **Publicly Held**
WEB: www.blackbox.com
SIC: 1623 4812 1731 Telephone & communication line construction; radio telephone communication; communications specialization
PA: Black Box Corporation
1000 Park Dr
Lawrence PA 15055
724 746-5500

(P-1902)
ARB INC
2235 N Ventura Ave, Ventura (93001-1311)
P.O. Box 1772 (93002-1772)
PHONE.....................805 643-4188
Fax: 805 643-7268
David Cox, *Branch Mgr*
EMP: 50
SALES (corp-wide): 1.9B **Publicly Held**
WEB: www.arbinc.com
SIC: 1623 Oil & gas pipeline construction
HQ: Arb, Inc.
26000 Commercentre Dr
Lake Forest CA 92630
949 598-9242

(P-1903)
ARB INC
50 Quint St, San Francisco (94124-1424)
PHONE.....................415 206-1015
Chris Slack, *Branch Mgr*
Chris Sigua, *Administration*
EMP: 50
SALES (corp-wide): 1.9B **Publicly Held**
SIC: 1623 1542 Water, sewer & utility lines; oil & gas line & compressor station construction; water & sewer line construction; pipeline construction; nonresidential construction; garage construction
HQ: Arb, Inc.
26000 Commercentre Dr
Lake Forest CA 92630
949 598-9242

(P-1904)
ARIZONA PIPE LINE COMPANY (PA)
17372 Lilac St, Hesperia (92345-5162)
P.O. Box 401865 (92340-1865)
PHONE.....................760 244-8212
Fax: 760 244-0963
Lowell D Moyers, *CEO*
Nina Moyers, *CEO*
Tom Seals, *Corp Secy*
Phyliss Moyers, *Vice Pres*
Connie Borden, *Executive*
EMP: 400 **EST:** 1979
SQ FT: 5,000
SALES: 98.8MM **Privately Held**
SIC: 1623 Pipeline construction

(P-1905)
ARIZONA PIPE LINE COMPANY
1745 Sampson Ave, Corona (92879-1864)
PHONE.....................951 270-3100
Fax: 909 270-3101
John Guzlow, *Vice Pres*
Steve Lords, *CFO*
John Gulzow, *Vice Pres*
Janea McDonald, *Administration*
Alan Hart, *Project Mgr*
EMP: 200
SALES (corp-wide): 98.8MM **Privately Held**
SIC: 1623 8711 Water, sewer & utility lines; engineering services
PA: Arizona Pipe Line Company
17372 Lilac St
Hesperia CA 92345
760 244-8212

(P-1906)
AT&T SERVICES INC
Also Called: SBC
720 Western Ave, Glendale (91201-2301)
PHONE.....................818 242-4102
Fax: 818 502-9039
Mary Bermeir, *Manager*
Mary Bernier, *Manager*
EMP: 50

SALES (corp-wide): 146.8B **Publicly Held**
WEB: www.dsdllc.com
SIC: 1623 Telephone & communication line construction
HQ: At&T Services, Inc.
208 S Akard St Ste 110
Dallas TX 75202
210 821-4105

(P-1907)
BALI CONSTRUCTION INC
9852 Joe Vargas Way, South El Monte (91733-3108)
PHONE.....................626 442-8003
Fax: 626 442-8315
Ted Polich III, *President*
Michael E Brooks, *CEO*
Gilbert Moreno, *CFO*
Priscilla Moynier, *Office Mgr*
Kevin Delate, *Project Mgr*
EMP: 100
SQ FT: 7,000
SALES: 23.7MM **Privately Held**
WEB: www.baliconstruction.com
SIC: 1623 Underground utilities contractor

(P-1908)
BASILE CONSTRUCTION INC
7952 Armour St, San Diego (92111-3718)
PHONE.....................858 278-2739
Fax: 858 586-7809
Allen Basile, *President*
Dawn Basile, *Admin Sec*
Lisa Hitt, *Controller*
Jackie Larison, *Accounts Mgr*
EMP: 50
SQ FT: 1,200
SALES: 10.7MM **Privately Held**
WEB: www.basile-dig.com
SIC: 1623 Water, sewer & utility lines; water & sewer line construction

(P-1909)
BESS TESTLAB INC
2461 Tripaldi Way, Hayward (94545-5018)
PHONE.....................408 988-0101
Fax: 408 988-0103
Juan Jose Bohorquez, *President*
Brandy Molina, *Manager*
Francisco Rojas, *Manager*
Giovanni RHO, *Agent*
EMP: 50
SALES (est): 9.2MM **Privately Held**
WEB: www.besstestlab.com
SIC: 1623 Water, sewer & utility lines

(P-1910)
BILL NLSON GEN ENGRG CNSTR INC
Also Called: Bill Nelson GEC
2741 E Malaga Ave, Fresno (93725-9399)
PHONE.....................559 439-1756
Bill Nelson, *President*
Jeff Nelson, *Vice Pres*
Kristin Nelson, *Admin Sec*
EMP: 60
SQ FT: 1,200
SALES (est): 11.9MM **Privately Held**
SIC: 1623 Water, sewer & utility lines

(P-1911)
BLOIS CONSTRUCTION INC
3201 Sturgis Rd, Oxnard (93030-8931)
P.O. Box 672 (93032-0672)
PHONE.....................805 485-0011
James B Blois, *President*
Steve Woodworth, *CFO*
Dan Schultz, *Vice Pres*
Gloria Magallames, *Executive*
Tod Decker, *General Mgr*
EMP: 150
SQ FT: 10,000
SALES: 22MM **Privately Held**
WEB: www.bloisconstruction.com
SIC: 1623 Underground utilities contractor

(P-1912)
BROCK G AND L CNSTR CO INC
4145 Calloway Ct, Stockton (95215-2400)
PHONE.....................209 931-3626
Lynne Brock, *President*
Gary Brock, *Vice Pres*
David Brock, *Project Mgr*
EMP: 50
SQ FT: 5,800

1623 - Water, Sewer & Utility Line Construction County (P-1913)

SALES (est): 9.5MM Privately Held
SIC: 1623 Water, sewer & utility lines

(P-1913)
BURTECH PIPELINE INCORPORATED
102 2nd St, Encinitas (92024-3203)
PHONE.................................760 634-2822
Fax: 760 634-2415
Dominic J Burtech, *President*
Julie Burtech, *Vice Pres*
Ryan Miller, *General Mgr*
Tina Carriera, *Controller*
Adam Vandervort, *Sr Project Mgr*
EMP: 70
SQ FT: 3,000
SALES (est): 24.1MM Privately Held
WEB: www.burtechpipeline.com
SIC: 1623 Water main construction; sewer line construction; pipe laying construction

(P-1914)
C P CONSTRUCTION CO INC
105 N Loma Pl, Upland (91786-5620)
P.O. Box 1206, Ontario (91762-0206)
PHONE.................................909 981-1091
Fax: 909 981-6704
Charles Pfister Jr, *President*
Charles Michael Pfister, *Corp Secy*
John Blough, *Vice Pres*
Mark E Pfister, *Vice Pres*
Russel Pfister, *Vice Pres*
EMP: 50
SQ FT: 4,000
SALES: 13MM Privately Held
SIC: 1623 Sewer line construction; pipeline construction

(P-1915)
CAL SIERRA CONSTRUCTION INC
5904 Van Alstine Ave 1, Carmichael (95608-5327)
PHONE.................................916 416-7901
Fax: 916 485-3906
Joel Lucich, *President*
Greg Lucich, *Corp Secy*
Marco Lucich, *Vice Pres*
Christa Kelly, *Administration*
EMP: 80
SQ FT: 3,800
SALES (est): 12.6MM Privately Held
WEB: www.calsierra.net
SIC: 1623 8711 Water, sewer & utility lines; pipeline construction; sewer line construction; engineering services

(P-1916)
CASS CONSTRUCTION INC (PA)
1100 Wagner Dr, El Cajon (92020-3047)
P.O. Box 309 (92022-0309)
PHONE.................................619 590-0929
Fax: 619 590-1202
Jimmie Nelson, *Ch of Bd*
Kyle P Nelson, *President*
Jerry Gaeir, *Vice Pres*
Laura Nelson, *Vice Pres*
Angelina Parravano, *Vice Pres*
EMP: 105
SQ FT: 5,700
SALES (est): 109.2MM Privately Held
WEB: www.cassconstruction.com
SIC: 1623 1611 Underground utilities contractor; grading

(P-1917)
CATANIA HIJAR CORPORATION
Also Called: Teldata
11487 Woodside Ave, Santee (92071-4724)
PHONE.................................800 400-3401
Doug Catania, *President*
Robb Hijar, *Vice Pres*
EMP: 103
SQ FT: 14,000
SALES (est): 10.6MM Privately Held
SIC: 1623 1731 Cable laying construction; telephone & telephone equipment installation; communications specialization; safety & security specialization; access control systems specialization

(P-1918)
CDM CONSTRUCTORS INC
9220 Cleveland Ave # 100, Rancho Cucamonga (91730-8560)
PHONE.................................909 579-3500
Joyce Jackson, *Branch Mgr*
Steven E Wolosoff, *Research*
Heinz Redmann, *Mfg Staff*
Philip Blakeley, *Manager*
Luis Leon, *Manager*
EMP: 90
SALES (corp-wide): 1.2B Privately Held
SIC: 1623 Water, sewer & utility lines
HQ: Cdm Constructors Inc.
75 State St Ste 701
Boston MA 02109
617 452-6000

(P-1919)
CH2M HILL CONSTRUCTORS INC
2485 Natomas Park Dr # 600, Sacramento (95833-2975)
PHONE.................................916 920-0212
Craig Eldrich, *Branch Mgr*
Andy Cramer, *Manager*
EMP: 270
SALES (corp-wide): 5.4B Privately Held
SIC: 1623 8711 Water, sewer & utility lines; engineering services
HQ: Ch2m Hill Constructors, Inc.
9189 S Jamaica St
Englewood CO 80112
720 286-2000

(P-1920)
CITY HANFORD PUBLIC IMPRV CORP
900 S 10th Ave, Hanford (93230-5234)
PHONE.................................559 585-2550
Gary Misenhimer, *Branch Mgr*
Lou Camara, *Deputy Dir*
EMP: 96 Privately Held
SIC: 1623 9199 Water, sewer & utility lines;
PA: City Of Hanford Public Improvement Corporation
315 N Douty St 321
Hanford CA 93230
559 585-2515

(P-1921)
CMAC CONSTRUCTION COMPANY
Also Called: Cmac Cnstr Refinery & Pipeline
1450 Santa Fe Ave, Long Beach (90813-1248)
PHONE.................................562 435-5611
Fax: 562 495-0871
Michael L Mc Fadden, *CEO*
Debra Loveall, *General Mgr*
Michael McFadden, *General Mgr*
Debbra Lovall, *Manager*
EMP: 55
SQ FT: 3,000
SALES (est): 11.6MM Privately Held
WEB: www.cmac.us
SIC: 1623 Pipeline construction

(P-1922)
CONSTRUCTION SPECIALTY SVC INC
Also Called: C S S
4550 Buck Owens Blvd, Bakersfield (93308-4948)
P.O. Box 9429 (93389-9429)
PHONE.................................661 864-7573
Daniel I George, *President*
Denise George, *CFO*
Steve Fenton, *Controller*
EMP: 53
SQ FT: 1,000
SALES (est): 16.7MM Privately Held
WEB: www.CSSIncorp.biz
SIC: 1623 3271 Pipeline construction; concrete block & brick

(P-1923)
CORETCO INC
Also Called: Colich & Sons
547 W 140th St, Gardena (90248-1509)
PHONE.................................323 770-2920
Tom Colich, *Partner*
John Colich, *Partner*
Ted Anderson, *Agent*

EMP: 160
SQ FT: 4,500
SALES (est): 8.8MM Privately Held
SIC: 1623 8711 Sewer line construction; engineering services

(P-1924)
D S S COMPANY
655 W Clay St, Stockton (95206-1722)
P.O. Box 6099 (95206-0099)
PHONE.................................209 948-0302
Fax: 209 948-1640
David C Barney, *CEO*
Phillip R Dunn, *President*
Steve McPeak, *Project Mgr*
EMP: 50
SQ FT: 5,000
SALES (est): 9.8MM
SALES (corp-wide): 4.1B Publicly Held
WEB: www.dsscompany.com
SIC: 1623 1611 Sewer line construction; general contractor; highway & street construction
HQ: Knife River Corporation
1150 W Century Ave
Bismarck ND 58503
701 530-1400

(P-1925)
DALEO INC
7190 Forest St, Gilroy (95020-6612)
PHONE.................................408 846-9621
Fax: 408 846-9611
David Levisay, *President*
Susan Levisay, *Corp Secy*
Debbie Christian, *Accounts Mgr*
EMP: 54
SALES (est): 10.8MM Privately Held
WEB: www.daleoinc.com
SIC: 1623 Cable television line construction

(P-1926)
DBI SERVICES INC
5560 Tech Cir, Moorpark (93021-1794)
PHONE.................................805 523-7114
Derek Crombie, *President*
Bruce Sakamogo, *Shareholder*
EMP: 70
SALES (est): 8.1MM Privately Held
SIC: 1623 Telephone & communication line construction

(P-1927)
DIVERSIFIED UTILITY SVCS INC
3105 Unicorn Rd, Bakersfield (93308-6858)
P.O. Box 80417 (93380-0417)
PHONE.................................661 325-3212
Fax: 661 325-3340
Leigh Ann Anderson, *CEO*
Cody Anderson, *Shareholder*
William Mitchell, *Shareholder*
Steven S Anderson, *CFO*
Steve Hill, *Business Mgr*
EMP: 272
SALES (est): 74.4MM Privately Held
SIC: 1623 Water, sewer & utility lines

(P-1928)
ELECTRIC TECH CONSTRUCTION INC
1910 Mark Ct Ste 130, Concord (94520-1280)
PHONE.................................925 849-5324
Dean Balough, *CFO*
Kathryn Balough, *Admin Sec*
EMP: 80
SQ FT: 5,000
SALES (est): 14.5MM Privately Held
SIC: 1623 1731 Telephone & communication line construction; electrical work

(P-1929)
ERNEST E PESTANA INC
Also Called: Pestana Construction
84 W Santa Clara St # 580, San Jose (95113-1812)
PHONE.................................408 432-8110
Ernest E Pestana, *President*
EMP: 100
SALES (est): 11.9MM Privately Held
SIC: 1623 Water, sewer & utility lines

(P-1930)
FISHEL COMPANY
647 Young St, Santa Ana (92705-5633)
PHONE.................................714 668-9268
Jeong Jeon, *Branch Mgr*
EMP: 86
SALES (corp-wide): 301.8MM Privately Held
SIC: 1623 Underground utilities contractor
PA: The Fishel Company
1366 Dublin Rd
Columbus OH 43215
614 274-8100

(P-1931)
FLOYD JOHNSTON CNSTR CO INC
2301 Herndon Ave, Clovis (93611-8911)
PHONE.................................559 299-7373
Fax: 559 323-9446
EMP: 75
SQ FT: 6,000
SALES (est): 13.5MM Privately Held
SIC: 1623 Water main construction; sewer line construction; pipeline construction

(P-1932)
GD NIELSON CONSTRUCTION INC
147 Camino Oruga, NAPA (94558-6215)
PHONE.................................707 253-8774
Diann Nielson, *President*
George S Nielson, *Corp Secy*
David Craighead, *Project Mgr*
Sue Branson, *Controller*
EMP: 60
SALES (est): 13.8MM Privately Held
WEB: www.nielsoninc.com
SIC: 1623 1629 1799 Sewer line construction; drainage system construction; boring for building construction

(P-1933)
GENERAL PRODUCTION SVC CAL INC
Also Called: G P S
1333 Kern St, Taft (93268-9700)
P.O. Box 344 (93268-0344)
PHONE.................................661 765-5330
Fax: 661 765-4860
Charles Beard, *CEO*
Oreste Risi, *President*
Don Schock, *Top Exec*
Charles Rhoades, *Controller*
Chuck Rhodes, *Controller*
EMP: 180
SALES (est): 60.6MM Privately Held
SIC: 1623 Oil & gas pipeline construction

(P-1934)
GEO TELECOM
252 Woodcrest Ln, Aliso Viejo (92656-2134)
PHONE.................................949 362-0921
Peter Skerlos, *Owner*
EMP: 50
SALES (est): 3.6MM Privately Held
SIC: 1623 Transmitting tower (telecommunication) construction

(P-1935)
GRANIT-BAYASHI 2 A JOINT VENTR ◆
585 W Beach St, Watsonville (95076-5123)
PHONE.................................831 724-1011
EMP: 60 **EST:** 2016
SALES (est): 1.5MM Privately Held
SIC: 1623 Water & sewer line construction

(P-1936)
GSE CONSTRUCTION COMPANY INC (PA)
6950 Preston Ave, Livermore (94551-9545)
PHONE.................................925 447-0292
Fax: 925 447-0962
Orlando Gutierrez, *CEO*
Steve Mazza, *Vice Pres*
Sue Gutierrez, *Admin Sec*
Martin Wibbernhorst, *Manager*
Dennis Gutierrez, *Asst Sec*
EMP: 140
SQ FT: 23,400

PRODUCTS & SERVICES SECTION

1623 - Water, Sewer & Utility Line Construction County (P-1957)

SALES (est): 66.3MM Privately Held
SIC: 1623 1542 Water & sewer line construction; pipe laying construction; pipeline construction; nonresidential construction

(P-1937)
HCI INC (HQ)
Also Called: H C I
3166 Hrseless Carriage Rd, Norco (92860-3612)
P.O. Box 5389 (92860-8097)
PHONE 951 520-4202
Steven G Silagi, *President*
Stephen Young, *CFO*
Rakesh Garach, *Bd of Directors*
Brian Clarke, *Vice Pres*
Bob Warwick, *General Mgr*
▼ EMP: 300 EST: 1981
SQ FT: 100,000
SALES (est): 85MM Privately Held
SIC: 1623 Communication line & transmission tower construction
PA: Lombardy Holdings, Inc.
    3166 Hrseless Carriage Rd
    Norco CA 92860
    951 808-4550

(P-1938)
HENKELS & MCCOY INC
2840 Ficus St, Pomona (91766-6501)
PHONE 925 493-7800
Fax: 909 451-2591
John B Henkels Jr, *Branch Mgr*
EMP: 66
SALES (corp-wide): 1.3B Privately Held
SIC: 1623 Water, sewer & utility lines
HQ: Henkels & Mccoy, Inc
    985 Jolly Rd
    Blue Bell PA 19422
    215 283-7600

(P-1939)
HERMAN WEISSKER INC (HQ)
1645 Brown Ave, Riverside (92509-1859)
PHONE 951 826-8800
Fax: 951 321-4780
Luis Alberto Armona, *CEO*
Ron Politte, *President*
Marty Mayeda, *CFO*
Kieth Nelson, *Office Mgr*
EMP: 92 EST: 1959
SQ FT: 12,000
SALES (est): 118MM
SALES (corp-wide): 280.6MM Privately Held
WEB: www.hermanweissker.com
SIC: 1623 8711 1731 Water, sewer & utility lines; engineering services; electrical work
PA: Meruelo Enterprises, Inc.
    9550 Firestone Blvd # 105
    Downey CA 90241
    562 745-2300

(P-1940)
HP COMMUNICATIONS INC
13341 Temescal Canyon Rd, Corona (92883-4980)
PHONE 951 572-1200
Fax: 951 266-8080
Nicholas Goldman, *President*
Chris Dotinga, *Shareholder*
Ahmad Olomi, *Exec VP*
Chris Price, *Vice Pres*
Hank Goldmann, *Business Dir*
EMP: 240 EST: 1998
SQ FT: 400
SALES (est): 158.5MM Privately Held
SIC: 1623 Communication line & transmission tower construction

(P-1941)
HPS PLUMBING SERVICE INC
3100 E Belle Ter, Bakersfield (93307-6830)
PHONE 661 324-2121
Fax: 661 322-5648
Leslie Denherder, *President*
Jay Buenviaje, *Project Mgr*
EMP: 300
SALES (est): 21.2MM Privately Held
WEB: www.hpsmechanical.com
SIC: 1623 1711 Water, sewer & utility lines; plumbing contractors

(P-1942)
INSITUFORM TECHNOLOGIES LLC
19000 Macarthur Blvd, Irvine (92612-1438)
PHONE 714 724-2324
Elva Alatorre, *Branch Mgr*
EMP: 50
SALES (corp-wide): 1.3B Publicly Held
SIC: 1623 Pipeline construction
HQ: Insituform Technologies, Llc
    17988 Edison Ave
    Chesterfield MO 63005
    636 530-8000

(P-1943)
IRBY CONSTRUCTION COMPANY
100 W Keystone Rd, Brawley (92227-9741)
PHONE 760 344-4478
Fax: 760 344-4651
Pat Shouse, *Manager*
EMP: 66
SALES (corp-wide): 7.5B Publicly Held
WEB: www.irbyconst.com
SIC: 1623 Electric power line construction
HQ: Irby Construction Company
    318 Old Highway 49 S
    Richland MS 39218
    601 709-4729

(P-1944)
IRISH COMMUNICATION COMPANY (DH)
2649 Stingle Ave, Rosemead (91770-3326)
P.O. Box 457 (91770-0457)
PHONE 626 288-6170
Gregory C Warde, *CEO*
Dan Mitchell, *President*
Pat D Furnare, *Chairman*
Dennis Brackney, *Vice Pres*
Randy Dale, *Vice Pres*
EMP: 100
SQ FT: 9,000
SALES (est): 58.8MM
SALES (corp-wide): 65.8MM Privately Held
WEB: www.irishteam.com
SIC: 1623 8748 1731 Telephone & communication line construction; telecommunications consultant; communications specialization
HQ: Irish Construction
    2641 River Ave
    Rosemead CA 91770
    626 288-8530

(P-1945)
IRISH CONSTRUCTION (HQ)
2641 River Ave, Rosemead (91770-3392)
P.O. Box 579 (91770-0579)
PHONE 626 288-8530
Fax: 626 288-6170
Gregory C Warde, *Ch of Bd*
Ken West, *President*
William E Wilbanks, *President*
Randall W Dale, *Corp Secy*
Lonnie Gentry, *Vice Pres*
EMP: 150 EST: 1947
SQ FT: 15,000
SALES (est): 58.8MM
SALES (corp-wide): 65.8MM Privately Held
WEB: www.irishconstruction.com
SIC: 1623 Water, sewer & utility lines
PA: Manhattan Capital Corp
    2641 River Ave
    Rosemead CA 91770
    626 288-8530

(P-1946)
IRISH CONSTRUCTION
19490 Monterey St, Morgan Hill (95037-2606)
PHONE 408 612-8440
Fax: 408 782-7891
Sue Nakagawa, *Manager*
EMP: 100
SQ FT: 18,004
SALES (corp-wide): 65.3MM Privately Held
WEB: www.irishconstruction.com
SIC: 1623 1799 Water, sewer & utility lines; athletic & recreation facilities construction

HQ: Irish Construction
    2641 River Ave
    Rosemead CA 91770
    626 288-8530

(P-1947)
IRISH CONSTRUCTION
1028 Marchy Ln, Ceres (95307-6649)
PHONE 209 576-8766
Ron McMillan, *President*
EMP: 63
SALES (corp-wide): 65.3MM Privately Held
SIC: 1623 Water, sewer & utility lines
HQ: Irish Construction
    2641 River Ave
    Rosemead CA 91770
    626 288-8530

(P-1948)
IRISH CONSTRUCTION
1329 Sweetwater Ln, Spring Valley (91977-4147)
P.O. Box 580, San Marcos (92079-0580)
PHONE 619 713-1991
Fax: 760 744-3188
Dave Watson, *Manager*
EMP: 60
SALES (corp-wide): 65.8MM Privately Held
WEB: www.irishconstruction.com
SIC: 1623 1622 Water, sewer & utility lines; bridge, tunnel & elevated highway
HQ: Irish Construction
    2641 River Ave
    Rosemead CA 91770
    626 288-8530

(P-1949)
J & M INC
3826 Depot Rd, Hayward (94545-2722)
PHONE 510 782-3434
Manuel Marques III, *President*
Michael Marcus, *Vice Pres*
EMP: 100
SALES (est): 7.8MM Privately Held
SIC: 1623 Sewer line construction

(P-1950)
J & M INC
6700 National Dr, Livermore (94550-8804)
PHONE 925 724-0300
Fax: 925 782-5532
Manuel Marques III, *CEO*
Matt Cox, *Manager*
Steve Stoddard, *Manager*
EMP: 50
SQ FT: 2,000
SALES (est): 18.8MM Privately Held
SIC: 1623 1629 Water, sewer & utility lines; drainage system construction

(P-1951)
JMB CONSTRUCTION INC
132 S Maple Ave, South San Francisco (94080-6302)
PHONE 650 267-5300
Margaret P Burke, *President*
Pam Burns, *Office Mgr*
Colin Larkin, *Info Tech Mgr*
Barry Boylan, *Project Engr*
Stephen Campbell, *Project Engr*
▲ EMP: 100
SALES (est): 35.5MM Privately Held
SIC: 1623 Water & sewer line construction

(P-1952)
JR FILANC CNSTR CO INC (PA)
740 N Andreasen Dr, Escondido (92029-1414)
PHONE 760 941-7130
Mark E Filanc, *CEO*
Harry S Cosmos, *President*
Kevin Elliotts, *CFO*
Vincent L Diaz, *Vice Pres*
Jim Cunningham, *Broker*
EMP: 100 EST: 1952
SQ FT: 13,200
SALES (est): 152.4MM Privately Held
WEB: www.filanc.com
SIC: 1623 1629 Pumping station construction; waste water & sewage treatment plant construction

(P-1953)
K S FABRICATION & MACHINE INC
Also Called: KS Fabrication & Machine
6205 District Blvd, Bakersfield (93313-2141)
P.O. Box 41630 (93384-1630)
PHONE 661 617-1700
Fax: 661 396-8561
Kevin S Small, *CEO*
Becky Scott, *CFO*
EMP: 150
SALES (est): 44MM Privately Held
SIC: 1623 Water, sewer & utility lines

(P-1954)
K T A CONSTRUCTION INC
1920 Cordell Ct Ste 105, El Cajon (92020-0900)
PHONE 619 562-9464
Fax: 619 562-1685
Paul Michael Henderson, *CEO*
Mike Henderson, *President*
Marilyn L Henderson, *Vice Pres*
Brin Browne, *Manager*
EMP: 62
SQ FT: 5,200
SALES (est): 18.1MM Privately Held
SIC: 1623 Sewer line construction; water main construction

(P-1955)
KANA PIPELINE INC
1639 E Miraloma Ave, Placentia (92870-6623)
PHONE 714 986-1400
Dan Locke, *President*
Helen Troy, *General Mgr*
Chris Christiansen, *Project Mgr*
Rizwan Rana, *Project Mgr*
Derek Woodland, *Project Mgr*
EMP: 100
SQ FT: 55,000
SALES (est): 41.6MM Privately Held
WEB: www.kanapipeline.com
SIC: 1623 1629 Water main construction; sewer line construction; drainage system construction

(P-1956)
KENNEDY PIPELINE COMPANY
61 Argonaut, Laguna Hills (92656-1423)
P.O. Box P.O. Box 16711 (92653)
PHONE 949 380-8363
Fax: 949 380-0172
Stuart P Trumble, *Owner*
Michael Trumble, *President*
Mark Trumble, *Vice Pres*
Linda Johnson, *Office Mgr*
Felix Parra, *Manager*
EMP: 80
SQ FT: 20,000
SALES (est): 14.5MM Privately Held
WEB: www.kennedypipeline.com
SIC: 1623 Oil & gas pipeline construction

(P-1957)
KOBELCO COMPRESSORS AMER INC (HQ)
1450 W Rincon St, Corona (92880-9205)
PHONE 951 739-3030
Fax: 951 739-3029
Takaaki Hayata, *CEO*
Diane Cabrera, *Executive Asst*
Mohamad A Gauhar, *CTO*
Toshi Takanami, *Project Mgr*
Sherish Akula, *Project Engr*
◆ EMP: 260
SALES (est): 173.9MM
SALES (corp-wide): 15.5B Privately Held
WEB: www.kobelcoedti.com
SIC: 1623 3563 Oil & gas line & compressor station construction; air & gas compressors; air & gas compressors including vacuum pumps
PA: Kobe Steel, Ltd.
    2-2-4, Wakinohamakaigandori, Chuo-Ku
    Kobe HYO 651-0
    782 615-111

1623 - Water, Sewer & Utility Line Construction County (P-1958)

(P-1958)
KS INDUSTRIES LP (PA)
Also Called: K S I
6205 District Blvd, Bakersfield
(93313-2141)
P.O. Box 41630 (93384-1630)
PHONE.................................661 617-1700
Kevin Small, *CEO*
Doug Erickson, *Vice Pres*
Jerry Janzen, *CIO*
Art Medrano, *Purch Mgr*
Allan Faughn, *VP Opers*
EMP: 2000
SQ FT: 20,000
SALES (est): 275.9MM Privately Held
WEB: www.ksilp.com
SIC: 1623 Water, sewer & utility lines

(P-1959)
LARKIN LEASING INC
674 N Batavia St, Orange (92868-1221)
PHONE.................................714 528-3232
William Larkin, *President*
Tim Larkine, *Director*
EMP: 80
SQ FT: 15,000
SALES (est): 6.1MM Privately Held
SIC: 1623 Underground utilities contractor

(P-1960)
LIGHTBEAM POWER COMPANY GRIDLE
100 Century Center Ct # 100, San Jose
(95112-4535)
PHONE.................................800 696-7114
John Fong,
Brendan Beasley,
John Gann,
EMP: 51
SALES (est): 1.7MM Privately Held
SIC: 1623 Electric power line construction

(P-1961)
LIGHTBEAM PWR GRIDLEY MAIN LLC
100 Century Center Ct # 100, San Jose
(95112-4535)
PHONE.................................800 696-7114
John Fong,
Brendan Beasley,
John Gann,
EMP: 51
SALES (est): 4.6MM Privately Held
SIC: 1623 Electric power line construction

(P-1962)
LINKUS ENTERPRISES LLC
5595 W San Madele Ave, Fresno
(93722-5068)
PHONE.................................559 256-6600
Horacio Guzman, *CEO*
EMP: 125
SALES (corp-wide): 140.7MM Privately Held
SIC: 1623 Telephone & communication line construction
PA: Linkus Enterprises, Llc
18631 Lloyd Ln
Anderson CA 96007
530 229-9197

(P-1963)
LINKUS ENTERPRISES LLC (PA)
18631 Lloyd Ln, Anderson (96007-8459)
PHONE.................................530 229-9197
Horacio Guzman, *CEO*
John Daily, *COO*
Dant Morris, *Vice Pres*
Jon Warren, *VP Finance*
Toni Lauritzen, *Accounts Mgr*
EMP: 151
SQ FT: 3,200
SALES (est): 140.7MM Privately Held
SIC: 1623 5731 4813 Telephone & communication line construction; antennas, satellite dish;

(P-1964)
LOMBARDY HOLDINGS INC (PA)
3166 Hrseless Carriage Rd, Norco
(92860-3612)
P.O. Box 6019 (92860-8034)
PHONE.................................951 808-4550
Fax: 951 808-4299
Marc Laulhere, *CEO*
Pam Laulhere, *Admin Sec*
EMP: 200
SQ FT: 80,000
SALES: 85MM Privately Held
SIC: 1623 5211 Telephone & communication line construction; cable television line construction; electrical construction materials

(P-1965)
MARGATE CONSTRUCTION INC
25007 Figueroa St, Carson (90745-6316)
P.O. Box 4507 (90749-4507)
PHONE.................................310 830-8610
Fax: 310 830-9276
Charles T Riegelhuth, *President*
Betty Finlay, *Manager*
C Thomas, *Agent*
EMP: 150 EST: 1965
SQ FT: 3,000
SALES (est): 9.4MM Privately Held
SIC: 1623 1541 Pumping station construction; industrial buildings & warehouses

(P-1966)
MATRIX SERVICE INC
500 W Collins Ave, Orange (92867-5510)
PHONE.................................714 289-4419
Fax: 714 289-6699
William Sullivan, *Manager*
John Barron, *Purch Mgr*
EMP: 113
SALES (corp-wide): 1.3B Publicly Held
WEB: www.matrixservice.com
SIC: 1623 Water, sewer & utility lines; oil & gas line & compressor station construction; oil & gas pipeline construction; telephone & communication line construction
HQ: Matrix Service Inc.
5100 E Skelly Dr Ste 700
Tulsa OK 74135
918 838-8822

(P-1967)
MCELVANY INC
13343 Johnson Rd, Los Banos
(93635-9704)
PHONE.................................209 826-1102
Fax: 209 826-5431
Charles McElvany, *President*
Holli McElvany, *Corp Secy*
Isaac McElvany, *Vice Pres*
Helen McElvany, *Principal*
EMP: 52
SQ FT: 1,200
SALES (est): 10.8MM Privately Held
WEB: www.mcelvany.com
SIC: 1623 1629 Sewer line construction; land preparation construction

(P-1968)
MCGUIRE AND HESTER (PA)
9009 Railroad Ave, Oakland (94603-1245)
PHONE.................................510 632-7676
Fax: 510 562-5209
Michael R Hester, *CEO*
Louis Roessler, *Treasurer*
Robert Doud, *Exec VP*
Kevin Hester, *Area Mgr*
Andrew Vasconi, *Division Mgr*
EMP: 243
SQ FT: 27,652
SALES (est): 129.2MM Privately Held
WEB: www.mcguireandhester.com
SIC: 1623 7353 Underground utilities contractor; heavy construction equipment rental

(P-1969)
METROCELL CONSTRUCTION INC
4711 Chino Ave, Chino (91710-5130)
PHONE.................................909 627-1502
James H Culwell, *President*
Christine Culwell, *Manager*
EMP: 50
SALES: 12.3MM Privately Held
SIC: 1623 Transmitting tower (telecommunication) construction

(P-1970)
MGE UNDERGROUND INC
816 26th St, Paso Robles (93446-1243)
P.O. Box 4189 (93447-4189)
PHONE.................................805 238-3510
Fax: 805 238-1975
Michael Joe Goldstein, *President*
Kelly Fiscalni, *Admin Sec*
Summer Golstein, *Admin Sec*
Matt Cruzat, *Project Mgr*
Tiffany Hickey, *Human Resources*
EMP: 85
SQ FT: 780
SALES: 18MM Privately Held
WEB: www.mgeunderground.com
SIC: 1623 Underground utilities contractor

(P-1971)
MLADEN BUNTICH CNSTR CO INC
1500 W 9th St, Upland (91786-5636)
PHONE.................................909 920-9977
Mladen Buntich Jr, *Ch of Bd*
Lee Rocsncr, *Vice Pres*
Lee Roesner, *Vice Pres*
Mladen Griffith, *Executive*
Scott Peterson, *Admin Sec*
EMP: 60
SQ FT: 4,000
SALES (est): 24.7MM Privately Held
WEB: www.buntich.com
SIC: 1623 Sewer line construction; pipeline construction

(P-1972)
NOVA GROUP INC
185 Devlin Rd, NAPA (94558-6255)
P.O. Box 4050 (94558-0450)
PHONE.................................707 257-3200
Ronald M Fedrick, *President*
Scott R Victor, *President*
Walt Birdshaw, *CFO*
Carole L Bionda, *Vice Pres*
Walter M Birdsall, *Vice Pres*
▲ EMP: 150
SQ FT: 15,000
SALES: 1.4MM
SALES (corp-wide): 7.5B Publicly Held
SIC: 1623 Water, sewer & utility lines
PA: Quanta Services, Inc.
2800 Post Oak Blvd # 2600
Houston TX 77056
713 629-7600

(P-1973)
NOVA GRP INC -OBAYASHI CORP A
185 Devlin Rd, NAPA (94558-6255)
P.O. Box 4050 (94558-0450)
PHONE.................................707 265-1116
Ronald M Fedrick, *Manager*
EMP: 50
SALES: 32MM Privately Held
SIC: 1623 Pipeline construction

(P-1974)
NOVA-CPF INC
7411 Napa Vallejo Hwy, NAPA
(94558-7501)
P.O. Box 4050 (94558-0450)
PHONE.................................707 257-3200
Charles Fedrick, *President*
Elbert C Lewey, *Treasurer*
David W Fedrick, *Vice Pres*
Ronald Fredrick, *Principal*
EMP: 200
SQ FT: 11,000
SALES (est): 9.3MM Privately Held
SIC: 1623 Underground utilities contractor

(P-1975)
ORION CONSTRUCTION CORPORATION
2185 La Mirada Dr, Vista (92081-8830)
PHONE.................................760 597-9660
Fax: 760 597-9661
Richard Dowsing, *CEO*
Mark Dowsing, *Vice Pres*
Robert Wilson, *Info Tech Mgr*
Rob Wilson, *Opers Mgr*
Tammy Luna, *Accounts Mgr*
EMP: 80
SQ FT: 7,000
SALES (est): 32.6MM Privately Held
WEB: www.orionconstruction.com
SIC: 1623 1629 1542 Water, sewer & utility lines; industrial plant construction; non-residential construction

(P-1976)
PACIFIC SOUTHWEST CNSTR & EQP
2308 Shaylene Way, Alpine (91901-3174)
PHONE.................................619 445-5190
Thomas L Scanlan, *President*
Kristina Scanlan, *Vice Pres*
EMP: 65
SALES (est): 4.9MM Privately Held
SIC: 1623 Underground utilities contractor

(P-1977)
PACIFIC W SPACE CMMNCTIONS INC
Also Called: P W C
900 W Gladstone St, San Dimas
(91773-1734)
PHONE.................................909 592-4321
Sheryl F Patton, *CEO*
Joanna Patton, *CFO*
Betty Fonteno, *Corp Secy*
Rich Patton, *Vice Pres*
EMP: 69 EST: 1981
SQ FT: 2,000
SALES (est): 15.7MM Privately Held
SIC: 1623 Communication line & transmission tower construction

(P-1978)
PAULEY CONSTRUCTION INC
81529 Industrial Pl, Indio (92201-2014)
PHONE.................................760 347-7608
EMP: 73
SALES (corp-wide): 2.6B Publicly Held
SIC: 1623 Communication line & transmission tower construction
HQ: Pauley Construction, Llc
2021 W Melinda Ln
Phoenix AZ 85027
623 581-1200

(P-1979)
PAULUS ENGINEERING INC
2871 E Coronado St, Anaheim
(92806-2504)
PHONE.................................714 632-3322
Ronald Paulus, *President*
Jason Paulus, *Vice Pres*
Michelle Obermeier, *Asst Controller*
EMP: 60
SQ FT: 40,000
SALES (est): 11.5MM Privately Held
WEB: www.paulusengineering.com
SIC: 1623 Sewer line construction; pipeline construction

(P-1980)
PEARCE SERVICES LLC
Also Called: Cross Rock
90 Wellsona Rd, Paso Robles
(93446-7642)
P.O. Box 1708 (93447-1708)
PHONE.................................805 237-7480
Fax: 805 237-7484
Scott Hutchins, *President*
Matt Gillette, *Exec VP*
Kaylee Palmer, *Office Mgr*
EMP: 50 EST: 1998
SQ FT: 2,800
SALES (est): 24.3MM Privately Held
WEB: www.psixbox.com
SIC: 1623 Communication line & transmission tower construction
PA: Willcrest Partners, Llc
100 Spear St
San Francisco CA 94105
415 816-0086

(P-1981)
PRESTON PIPELINES INC (PA)
133 Bothelo Ave, Milpitas (95035-5325)
PHONE.................................408 262-1418
Fax: 408 262-1870
Michael D Preston, *President*
Ron Bianchini, *COO*
Bob Chance, *CFO*
John Soares, *CFO*
Dave Heslop, *Vice Pres*
EMP: 150
SQ FT: 12,000
SALES (est): 155MM Privately Held
WEB: www.prestonpipelines.com
SIC: 1623 Pipeline construction

PRODUCTS & SERVICES SECTION
1623 - Water, Sewer & Utility Line Construction County (P-2003)

(P-1982)
PRESTON PIPELINES INC A CAL
133 Bothelo Ave, Milpitas (95035-5325)
PHONE...................................408 262-6989
Michael Preston, *President*
EMP: 300
SQ FT: 1,000
SALES (est): 12.1MM **Privately Held**
SIC: 1623 Pipeline construction

(P-1983)
PRIMORIS SERVICES CORPORATION
26000 Commercentre Dr, Lake Forest (92630-8816)
PHONE...................................949 598-9242
Peter J Moerbeek, *Principal*
EMP: 455
SALES (corp-wide): 1.9B **Publicly Held**
SIC: 1623 Water, sewer & utility lines
PA: Primoris Services Corporation
    2100 Mckinney Ave # 1500
    Dallas TX 75201
    214 740-5600

(P-1984)
QUAGGA CORPORATION
90 Blue Ravine Rd 200a, Folsom (95630-4715)
PHONE...................................916 357-5129
Fax: 916 357-5193
Ken Apperson, *CEO*
AZ Phoenix, *Senior Partner*
Scott Knorp, *President*
Tim Keester, *COO*
Randy Olsen, *CFO*
EMP: 75
SQ FT: 4,300
SALES (est): 9.9MM
SALES (corp-wide): 5.7B **Publicly Held**
WEB: www.quagga.com
SIC: 1623 5065 Communication line & transmission tower construction; communication equipment
HQ: Paetec Communications, Inc.
    600 Willowbrook Office Pa
    Fairport NY 14450
    585 340-2500

(P-1985)
QUALITY TELECOM CONSULTANTS (PA)
Also Called: Quality Techniques Engrg Cnstr
3740 Cincinnati Ave, Rocklin (95765-1204)
P.O. Box 807, Loomis (95650-0807)
PHONE...................................916 315-0500
Scott Duncan, *President*
Candice Northam, *Treasurer*
Jacob Duncan, *Vice Pres*
Osh Duncan, *Admin Sec*
Donna Burns, *Accounting Mgr*
EMP: 89
SALES (est): 23.8MM **Privately Held**
WEB: www.qualitytelecomconsultantsinc.com
SIC: 1623 1731 4899 8748 Communication line & transmission tower construction; communications specialization; communication signal enhancement network system; telecommunications consultant

(P-1986)
RANCHO CALIFORNIA WATER DST (PA)
Also Called: Rcwd
42135 Winchester Rd, Temecula (92590-4800)
P.O. Box 9017 (92589-9017)
PHONE...................................951 296-6900
Fax: 951 676-0615
Stephen J Corona, *President*
Ralph Daily, *President*
Bennet Drake, *President*
Jeff Armstrong, *CFO*
Philips Forbes, *Treasurer*
EMP: 145
SQ FT: 71,000
SALES: 64.7MM **Privately Held**
WEB: www.ranchowater.com
SIC: 1623 Water, sewer & utility lines

(P-1987)
RANGER PIPELINES INCORPORATED
1790 Yosemite Ave, San Francisco (94124-2622)
P.O. Box 24109 (94124-0109)
PHONE...................................415 822-3700
Fax: 415 822-3703
Thomas Hunt, *President*
Mary Shea-Hunt, *Corp Secy*
Peter Cuddihy, *Vice Pres*
Irene Ishihara-Rivas, *Controller*
Glenele Oberrich, *Manager*
EMP: 101
SQ FT: 20,000
SALES (est): 39.3MM **Privately Held**
SIC: 1623 Water, sewer & utility lines

(P-1988)
REC SOLAR COMMERCIAL CORP
3450 Broad St Ste 105, San Luis Obispo (93401-7214)
PHONE...................................844 732-7652
Fax: 805 528-9701
Matt Walz, *CEO*
Tom Giovanni, *CFO*
Art Villa, *Vice Pres*
Ted Walsh, *Vice Pres*
Kristin Ochs, *Executive Asst*
EMP: 160 EST: 2013
SALES (est): 122.8MM
SALES (corp-wide): 23.4B **Publicly Held**
SIC: 1623 Water, sewer & utility lines
PA: Duke Energy Corporation
    400 S Tryon
    Charlotte NC 28285
    704 382-3853

(P-1989)
ROBERT HEELY INC
Also Called: Robert Heely Construction
236 W Forest Ave, Coalinga (93210-1930)
PHONE...................................559 935-0570
Fax: 559 935-5049
Neal Franklin, *Manager*
Trina Dewitt, *Manager*
EMP: 60
SALES (corp-wide): 121.6MM **Privately Held**
WEB: www.robertheely.com
SIC: 1623 8741 Oil & gas pipeline construction; construction management
PA: Robert Heely, Inc.
    5401 Woodmere Dr
    Bakersfield CA 93313
    661 617-1400

(P-1990)
S E C C CORPORATION
16224 Koala Rd, Adelanto (92301-3915)
PHONE...................................760 246-6218
Manuel Armenta, *Manager*
EMP: 53
SALES (corp-wide): 22.8MM **Privately Held**
SIC: 1623 Transmitting tower (telecommunication) construction
PA: S E C C Corporation
    14945 La Palma Dr
    Chino CA 91710
    909 393-5419

(P-1991)
S E PIPE LINE CONSTRUCTION CO
11832 Bloomfield Ave, Santa Fe Springs (90670-4693)
PHONE...................................562 868-9771
Fax: 562 868-4677
Charles Rikel, *President*
James Doulames, *Vice Pres*
Thomas Tustin, *Admin Sec*
Chris Rikel, *Manager*
EMP: 100
SQ FT: 5,000
SALES (est): 41.6MM **Privately Held**
SIC: 1623 Gas main construction; electric power line construction; oil & gas pipeline construction

(P-1992)
SAM HILL & SONS INC
Also Called: WMS Transportation
2627 Beene Rd, Ventura (93003-7203)
P.O. Box 5670 (93005-0670)
PHONE...................................805 620-0828
Fax: 805 644-2813
Ronald Hill, *President*
Scott Anderson, *Vice Pres*
Bobby Cardoza, *Vice Pres*
Spencer Hill, *Technology*
EMP: 50
SQ FT: 1,000
SALES (est): 9MM **Privately Held**
WEB: www.samhillandsons.com
SIC: 1623 Underground utilities contractor

(P-1993)
SANCO PIPELINES INCORPORATED
727 University Ave, Los Gatos (95032-7610)
PHONE...................................408 377-2793
Fax: 408 377-7405
David R Schrader, *President*
Don Drexel, *Vice Pres*
EMP: 50 EST: 1956
SQ FT: 3,000
SALES (est): 21.6MM **Privately Held**
WEB: www.sancopipelines.com
SIC: 1623 Water, sewer & utility lines

(P-1994)
SCHILLING PARADISE CORP
697 Greenfield Dr, El Cajon (92021-2983)
PHONE...................................619 449-4141
Jeff Platt, *President*
Michael Manos, *Principal*
Chris Colgan, *Superintendent*
EMP: 175
SALES (est): 17.1MM **Privately Held**
SIC: 1623 1731 Underground utilities contractor; general electrical contractor

(P-1995)
SOLCOM INC
Also Called: Solcom Communications Inc
24801 Huntwood Ave, Hayward (94544-1813)
PHONE...................................510 940-2490
Tony McMenamin, *President*
EMP: 999
SALES: 50MM **Privately Held**
SIC: 1623 Telephone & communication line construction

(P-1996)
SOLCOM GROUP INC
28835 Mack St, Hayward (94545-1215)
PHONE...................................510 940-2490
Fax: 510 940-2491
▲ EMP: 60
SQ FT: 6,000
SALES (est): 8.3MM **Privately Held**
WEB: www.solcom.com
SIC: 1623

(P-1997)
SOLEX CONTRACTING INC
42146 Remington Ave, Temecula (92590-2547)
PHONE...................................951 308-1706
Fax: 951 308-1856
Jerry Allen, *President*
Keith Schultz, *Project Mgr*
Valerie Wallace, *Controller*
Ben Long, *Safety Mgr*
EMP: 70
SQ FT: 12,000
SALES (est): 31.8MM **Privately Held**
SIC: 1623 1542 1541 Communication line & transmission tower construction; commercial & office building, new construction; renovation, remodeling & repairs: industrial buildings

(P-1998)
SPIESS CONSTRUCTION CO INC
Also Called: Scci
1110 E Clark Ave Ste 210, Santa Maria (93455-5155)
P.O. Box 2849 (93457-2849)
PHONE...................................805 937-5859
Fax: 805 934-4432
Scott A Coleman, *President*
Barry L Matchett, *Vice Pres*
Bill Geiser, *Project Mgr*
Jeff Davidson, *Controller*
Laura Jevne, *Manager*
EMP: 60
SQ FT: 5,000
SALES (est): 33.2MM **Privately Held**
WEB: www.sccitanks.com
SIC: 1623 Sewer line construction; water main construction

(P-1999)
SPINIELLO COMPANIES
1441 E 9th St, Pomona (91766-3834)
PHONE...................................909 629-1000
Priscilla Moyer, *Manager*
Abby Cruz, *Project Engr*
EMP: 100
SALES (corp-wide): 229.3MM **Privately Held**
SIC: 1623 Water, sewer & utility lines
PA: Spiniello Companies
    354 Eisenhower Pkwy # 1200
    Livingston NJ 07039
    973 808-8383

(P-2000)
SRD ENGINEERING INC
3578 E Enterprise Dr, Anaheim (92807-1627)
PHONE...................................714 630-2480
Fax: 714 630-2484
Deborah Denton, *CEO*
EMP: 65
SQ FT: 5,000
SALES (est): 9MM **Privately Held**
SIC: 1623 Water & sewer line construction

(P-2001)
STATE PIPE & SUPPLY INC
Also Called: Westcoast Pipe Lining Div
2180 N Locust Ave, Rialto (92377-4166)
PHONE...................................909 356-5670
Fax: 909 356-4229
Kenneth Walker, *Manager*
Steve Hernandez, *Sales Staff*
Frank Luna, *Sales Staff*
Ivan Vukosav, *Sales Staff*
EMP: 50
SALES (corp-wide): 1.7B **Privately Held**
WEB: www.statepipe.com
SIC: 1623 3312 Pipe laying construction; blast furnaces & steel mills
HQ: State Pipe & Supply, Inc.
    183 S Cedar Ave
    Rialto CA 92376
    909 877-9999

(P-2002)
T C CONSTRUCTION COMPANY INC
10540 Prospect Ave, Santee (92071-4591)
PHONE...................................619 448-4560
Fax: 619 258-9751
Terry W Cameron, *CEO*
Austin Cameron, *President*
Jack Gieffels, *CFO*
Derek Franken, *Vice Pres*
Darren Tharp, *Vice Pres*
EMP: 150
SQ FT: 16,000
SALES: 61.5MM **Privately Held**
SIC: 1623 1611 Underground utilities contractor; highway & street paving contractor

(P-2003)
TRITON TOWER INC (PA)
3200 Jefferson Blvd, West Sacramento (95691-5418)
PHONE...................................916 375-8546
Kevin Wingard, *President*
Mike Monroe, *Treasurer*
Rex Avakian, *Admin Sec*
Justene Grewal, *Accounting Mgr*
Felis Risling, *Manager*
EMP: 51
SALES: 2.5MM **Privately Held**
SIC: 1623 Transmitting tower (telecommunication) construction

1623 - Water, Sewer & Utility Line Construction County (P-2004)

(P-2004)
TURN AROUND COMMUNICATIONS INC
4400 Temple City Blvd, El Monte (91731-1011)
P.O. Box 6121 (91734-2121)
PHONE.................................626 443-2400
Sayeid Kouhkan, *President*
Renee Bubetz, *Executive Asst*
Carlos Schettini, *Director*
EMP: 170
SQ FT: 23,683
SALES: 7.6MM **Privately Held**
SIC: 1623 Telephone & communication line construction

(P-2005)
UNITED POWER CONTRACTORS INC
405 Maple St Ste A-103, Ramona (92065-1890)
PHONE.................................760 735-8028
Andres A Canales, *President*
Jerome Reuben Rodriguez, *CEO*
Mark Walken, *Senior VP*
Reuben Rodriguez, *Vice Pres*
EMP: 117 **EST:** 2007
SALES (est): 21.8MM **Privately Held**
SIC: 1623 Water, sewer & utility lines; electric power line construction

(P-2006)
UTAH PACIFIC CONSTRUCTION CO
40940 Eleanora Way, Murrieta (92562-5946)
PHONE.................................951 677-9876
Fax: 951 677-6742
Craig R Young, *President*
Brian Keeline, *Vice Pres*
Jason Bent, *Safety Mgr*
Paula Durnford, *Manager*
Ann Young, *Manager*
EMP: 50
SQ FT: 5,000
SALES (est): 8.3MM **Privately Held**
SIC: 1623 Sewer line construction; water main construction; pipeline construction

(P-2007)
UTI LEAK SEEKERS
Also Called: Uti Underground Technology
1398 Monterey Pass Rd, Monterey Park (91754-3619)
PHONE.................................323 724-0081
Lisa Pickareela, *Manager*
EMP: 70
SALES (est): 2.5MM **Privately Held**
SIC: 1623 Underground utilities contractor

(P-2008)
VADNAIS TRENCHLESS SVCS INC
26000 Commercentre Dr, Lake Forest (92630-8816)
P.O. Box 5166 (92609-8666)
PHONE.................................858 550-1460
Paul Vadnais, *CEO*
EMP: 606 **EST:** 2014
SALES: 166.7MM
SALES (corp-wide): 1.9B **Publicly Held**
SIC: 1623 1622 Water, sewer & utility lines; tunnel construction
PA: Primoris Services Corporation
  2100 Mckinney Ave # 1500
  Dallas TX 75201
  214 740-5600

(P-2009)
VADNAIS TRENCHLESS SVCS INC
2130 La Mirada Dr, Vista (92081-8815)
PHONE.................................858 550-1460
Paul Vadnais, *CEO*
Jesse Mangan, *CFO*
Jeff Anderson, *Vice Pres*
▲ **EMP:** 100
SALES (est): 24.3MM **Privately Held**
WEB: www.vadnaiscorp.com
SIC: 1623 Water & sewer line construction

(P-2010)
VALVERDE CONSTRUCTION INC
10918 Shoemaker Ave, Santa Fe Springs (90670-4533)
PHONE.................................562 906-1826
Joe Valverde, *President*
Ahron Valverde, *Materials Mgr*
EMP: 50
SALES (corp-wide): 28.1MM **Privately Held**
SIC: 1623 Underground utilities contractor
PA: Valverde Construction, Inc.
  10918 Shoemaker Ave
  Santa Fe Springs CA 90670
  562 906-1826

(P-2011)
VCI CONSTRUCTION LLC (HQ)
1921 W 11th St Ste A, Upland (91786-3508)
PHONE.................................909 946-0905
Fax: 909 946-0924
John Xanthos, *President*
Vic Marovish, *CFO*
Logan Teal, *Vice Pres*
Patrick Davies, *Division Mgr*
Debbie Villegas, *Office Mgr*
EMP: 100
SQ FT: 29,500
SALES: 68MM
SALES (corp-wide): 2.6B **Publicly Held**
WEB: www.vcicom.com
SIC: 1623 Underground utilities contractor
PA: Dycom Industries, Inc.
  11780 Us Highway 1 # 600
  Palm Beach Gardens FL 33408
  561 627-7171

(P-2012)
W A RASIC CNSTR CO INC (PA)
4150 Long Beach Blvd, Long Beach (90807-2650)
PHONE.................................562 928-6111
Peter L Rasic, *CEO*
Walter Rasic, *Vice Pres*
Zorkita Paschall, *Office Mgr*
Randall Kulkarni, *CTO*
Randall Beck, *Info Tech Mgr*
EMP: 151
SQ FT: 8,500
SALES (est): 186.9MM **Privately Held**
WEB: www.warasic.com
SIC: 1623 Sewer line construction; water main construction

(P-2013)
W M LYLES CO (HQ)
1210 W Olive Ave, Fresno (93728-2816)
P.O. Box 4378 (93744-4378)
PHONE.................................951 973-7393
Fax: 559 441-1290
Richard E Amigh, *President*
Stan Simmons, *Senior VP*
Ken Strosnider, *Vice Pres*
Scott Audrey, *Admin Sec*
Joe Scerbo, *Project Mgr*
EMP: 50
SQ FT: 6,200
SALES: 241.8MM
SALES (corp-wide): 31.9MM **Privately Held**
WEB: www.wmlyles.com
SIC: 1623 Pipeline construction; underground utilities contractor
PA: Lyles Diversified, Inc.
  1210 W Olive Ave
  Fresno CA 93728
  559 441-1900

(P-2014)
WATER & SEWER SERVICE
7051 Dublin Blvd, Dublin (94568-3018)
PHONE.................................925 828-8524
Fax: 925 875-2286
Berrt Michalzzyk, *General Mgr*
EMP: 80
SALES (est): 2.7MM **Privately Held**
SIC: 1623 Water, sewer & utility lines

(P-2015)
WATKINS CONSTRUCTION CO INC
Also Called: Johnston Vacuum Tank Service
112 E Cedar St, Taft (93268-9708)
P.O. Box 243 (93268-0243)
PHONE.................................661 763-5395
Fax: 661 763-1936
Eddie Watkins Sr, *President*
Mary King, *Manager*
EMP: 60
SQ FT: 4,800
SALES (est): 10.9MM **Privately Held**
WEB: www.watkinsconstructionco.com
SIC: 1623 Oil & gas pipeline construction

(P-2016)
WDC EXPLRTION WELLS HOLDG CORP
1300 National Dr Ste 140, Sacramento (95834-1981)
PHONE.................................916 419-6043
Fax: 916 928-5720
Robert L Ruck, *CEO*
Ray Imbsen, *CFO*
Raymond Imbsen, *CFO*
Kelly Lee, *Accounting Mgr*
Oscar Navarro, *Finance*
EMP: 203
SQ FT: 8,788
SALES (est): 20.2MM **Privately Held**
SIC: 1623 1629 Pumping station construction; waste water & sewage treatment plant construction

(P-2017)
WEST STATES SKANSKA INC
1995 Agua Mansa Rd, Riverside (92509-2405)
PHONE.................................970 565-4903
Curtis Brotten, *President*
Don McCallan, *Purch Mgr*
Chris Eastin, *VP Mktg*
Alaina Kimmey, *Mktg Dir*
David W Sitton, *Manager*
EMP: 150
SQ FT: 800
SALES (est): 9.8MM
SALES (corp-wide): 17.5B **Privately Held**
SIC: 1623 1541 Water, sewer & utility lines; industrial buildings & warehouses
HQ: Skanska Usa Civil West Rocky Mountain District Inc.
  1995 Agua Mansa Rd
  Riverside CA 92509
  970 565-8000

(P-2018)
WEST VALLEY CNSTR CO INC (PA)
580 E Mcglincy Ln, Campbell (95008-4999)
PHONE.................................408 371-5510
Fax: 408 371-3604
Kevin Kelly, *CEO*
David Barnes, *CFO*
Jeff Azevedo, *Vice Pres*
Jeff Boss, *Vice Pres*
Mike Cadei, *Vice Pres*
EMP: 150 **EST:** 1958
SQ FT: 9,000
SALES (est): 159.5MM **Privately Held**
WEB: www.westvalleyconstruction.com
SIC: 1623 Water main construction

(P-2019)
WHITTIER EQUIPMENT RENTALS
11832 Bloomfield Ave, Santa Fe Springs (90670-4610)
PHONE.................................562 863-0641
Charles Rikel, *President*
T C Tustin, *Treasurer*
James Doulames, *Vice Pres*
EMP: 85
SQ FT: 5,000
SALES (est): 3.9MM **Privately Held**
SIC: 1623 Pipeline construction

1629 Heavy Construction, NEC

(P-2020)
AMERICAN CIVIL CONSTRS LLC
3701 Mallard Dr, Benicia (94510-1246)
PHONE.................................707 746-8028
Pete Wells, *Manager*
Sharon McAdams, *Engineer*
Candace Rider, *Controller*
Bill Allison, *Manager*
EMP: 150
SALES (corp-wide): 102.6MM **Privately Held**
WEB: www.americancivilconstructors.com
SIC: 1629 0783 0181 Land preparation construction; earthmoving contractor; golf course construction; dam construction; spraying services, ornamental bush; removal services, bush & tree; sod farms
HQ: American Civil Constructors Llc
  4901 S Windermere St
  Littleton CO 80120
  303 795-2582

(P-2021)
ANDERSON PCF ENGRG CNSTR INC
1390 Norman Ave, Santa Clara (95054-2047)
PHONE.................................408 970-9900
Fax: 408 970-9975
Peter E Anderson, *CEO*
Matthew Mirenda, *Vice Pres*
Ann Anderson, *Admin Sec*
Justin Chow, *Project Mgr*
Bonnie Giordina, *Manager*
EMP: 100
SQ FT: 3,000
SALES (est): 49.1MM **Privately Held**
WEB: www.andpac.com
SIC: 1629 1623 Dams, waterways, docks & other marine construction; pumping station construction; underground utilities contractor

(P-2022)
ARB INC (HQ)
26000 Commercentre Dr, Lake Forest (92630-8816)
PHONE.................................949 598-9242
Fax: 949 454-7190
Brian Pratt, *President*
Alfons Theeuwes, *CFO*
John P Schauerman, *Corp Secy*
Timothy Healy, *Vice Pres*
Larry Jansen, *Vice Pres*
▲ **EMP:** 140
SQ FT: 50,000
SALES: 330.2MM
SALES (corp-wide): 1.9B **Publicly Held**
WEB: www.arbinc.com
SIC: 1629 1623 Industrial plant construction; waste disposal plant construction; waste water & sewage treatment plant construction; water, sewer & utility lines; oil & gas line & compressor station construction; water & sewer line construction; pipeline construction
PA: Primoris Services Corporation
  2100 Mckinney Ave # 1500
  Dallas TX 75201
  214 740-5600

(P-2023)
AUBURN CONSTRUCTORS INC
730 W Stadium Ln, Sacramento (95834-1130)
PHONE.................................916 924-0344
Fax: 916 924-1800
Dean Bailey, *President*
Bill Franceschini, *Corp Secy*
Kevin Couper, *Vice Pres*
David Ewing, *Branch Mgr*
Susan Dettloff, *Manager*
EMP: 80
SQ FT: 5,500
SALES: 55.9MM **Privately Held**
WEB: www.auburnconstructors.com
SIC: 1629 Industrial plant construction; waste water & sewage treatment plant construction

PRODUCTS & SERVICES SECTION
1629 - Heavy Construction, NEC County (P-2045)

(P-2024)
BELECTRIC INC (HQ)
951 Mariners Island Blvd, San Mateo
(94404-1558)
PHONE..................510 896-3940
David Taggart, *President*
Judith Pham, *Draft/Design*
Cary Croopnick, *Engineer*
Diane Padilla, *Finance*
Vivek Phanse, *Director*
◆ EMP: 64
SQ FT: 29,198
SALES (est): 22.8MM
SALES (corp-wide): 360.9MM **Privately Held**
SIC: 1629 Power plant construction
PA: Belectric Holding Gmbh
Wadenbrunner Str. 10
Kolitzheim 97509
938 598-040

(P-2025)
BEMUS LANDSCAPE INC
1225 Puerta Del Sol # 500, San Clemente
(92673-6312)
P.O. Box 74268 (92673-0143)
PHONE..................714 557-7910
William Howard Bemus, *President*
Jonathon Parry, *Corp Secy*
Martine Bemus, *Vice Pres*
Kirk Hinshaw, *Vice Pres*
Wish Corneluas, *Controller*
EMP: 300
SQ FT: 7,000
SALES (est): 40.7MM **Privately Held**
WEB: www.bemuslandscape.com
SIC: 1629 0782 Drainage system construction; landscape contractors

(P-2026)
BILL PAPICH CONSTRUCTION INC
800 Farroll Rd, Grover Beach
(93433-2748)
PHONE..................805 489-9420
Jason Papich, *President*
Marcia Papich, *Corp Secy*
Tiana Andruss, *Administration*
EMP: 50
SALES (est): 5.6MM **Privately Held**
SIC: 1629 Blasting contractor, except building demolition

(P-2027)
BRIGHTSOURCE ENERGY INC (PA)
1999 Harrison St Ste 2150, Oakland
(94612-3500)
PHONE..................510 550-8161
Fax: 510 550-8165
H David Ramm, *CEO*
Richard Kelly, *Ch of Bd*
Jack Jenkins-Stark, *CFO*
Arnold Goldman, *Chm Emeritus*
Joe Desmond, *Senior VP*
▲ EMP: 85
SQ FT: 5,000
SALES (est): 137.3MM **Privately Held**
WEB: www.brightsourceenergy.com
SIC: 1629 Power plant construction

(P-2028)
BRIGHTVIEW COMPANIES LLC (DH)
24151 Ventura Blvd, Calabasas
(91302-1449)
PHONE..................818 223-8500
Rofer Zino, *CEO*
Roger Zino, *CEO*
Andrew Brennan, *COO*
Gareth Asten, *CFO*
Mark Lanteigne, *CFO*
◆ EMP: 175
SQ FT: 25,000
SALES (est): 3.8B
SALES (corp-wide): 914MM **Privately Held**
WEB: www.valleycrest.com
SIC: 1629 0782 0781 Golf course construction; lawn & garden services; landscape services; landscape planning services

HQ: Brightview Landscapes, Llc
2275 Res Blvd Ste 600
Rockville MD 20850
301 987-9200

(P-2029)
BRIGHTVIEW GOLF MAINT INC
405 Glen Annie Rd, Santa Barbara
(93117-1427)
PHONE..................805 968-6400
Richard Hasah, *Manager*
EMP: 50
SALES (corp-wide): 914MM **Privately Held**
SIC: 1629 Golf course construction
HQ: Brightview Golf Maintenance, Inc.
24151 Ventura Blvd
Calabasas CA 91302
818 223-8500

(P-2030)
BRIGHTVIEW GOLF MAINT INC (DH)
Also Called: Valleycrest Golf Crse Mint Inc
24151 Ventura Blvd, Calabasas
(91302-1449)
PHONE..................818 223-8500
Burton Sperber, *Ch of Bd*
Richard A Sperber, *Ch of Bd*
Gregory Pieschala, *President*
Andrew Mandell, *CFO*
Michael L Dingman, *Chairman*
EMP: 100
SQ FT: 80,000
SALES (est): 140.5MM
SALES (corp-wide): 914MM **Privately Held**
SIC: 1629 Golf course construction
HQ: Brightview Companies, Llc
24151 Ventura Blvd
Calabasas CA 91302
818 223-8500

(P-2031)
BRIGHTVIEW LANDSCAPE DEV INC
8450 Miramar Pl, San Diego (92121-2528)
PHONE..................858 458-9900
Vince Germann, *Manager*
Stuart Sperber, *Vice Chairman*
Pamela Stark, *Vice Pres*
Michael Lyons, *General Mgr*
Lee Moody, *MIS Mgr*
EMP: 300
SQ FT: 16,050
SALES (corp-wide): 914MM **Privately Held**
SIC: 1629 Irrigation system construction; land preparation construction
HQ: Brightview Landscape Development, Inc.
24151 Ventura Blvd
Calabasas CA 91302
818 223-8500

(P-2032)
BRIGHTVIEW LANDSCAPE DEV INC
11555 Cley Rver Cir Ste A, Fountain Valley (92708)
PHONE..................714 546-7975
Fax: 714 546-9524
Gins Garmann, *Manager*
Thomas C Donnelly, *Branch Mgr*
Jeff Mutch, *Sales Staff*
Eric Wilson, *Manager*
EMP: 450
SALES (corp-wide): 914MM **Privately Held**
SIC: 1629 0781 Irrigation system construction; land preparation construction; landscape services
HQ: Brightview Landscape Development, Inc.
24151 Ventura Blvd
Calabasas CA 91302
818 223-8500

(P-2033)
BYROM-DAVEY INC
13220 Evnng Crk Dr S # 103, San Diego (92128-4103)
PHONE..................858 513-7199
Fax: 858 513-7198
Steve V Davey, *Owner*
Joanne Caspersen, *Treasurer*

Christine Butler, *Vice Pres*
Raul Gilbert, *Vice Pres*
Eric Jennings Sr, *Vice Pres*
EMP: 50
SQ FT: 2,200
SALES (est): 13.5MM **Privately Held**
WEB: www.byromdavey.com
SIC: 1629 1611 Land preparation construction; athletic field construction; highway & street construction

(P-2034)
C A RASMUSSEN INC (PA)
28548 Livingston Ave, Valencia (91355-4171)
PHONE..................661 367-9040
Charles A Rasmussen, *President*
D I C K Greenburg, *CFO*
Tim Macdonald, *Vice Pres*
Mike Medema, *Vice Pres*
Doug Misley, *Vice Pres*
EMP: 50
SQ FT: 20,000
SALES (est): 87.7MM **Privately Held**
WEB: www.carasmussen.com
SIC: 1629 1611 Earthmoving contractor; grading

(P-2035)
CAL WEST UNDERGROUND INC
951 6th St, Norco (92860-1442)
PHONE..................951 371-6775
Jeffrey M Abernathy, *President*
Wendy Davidson, *Office Mgr*
EMP: 63
SQ FT: 1,200
SALES (est): 10.2MM **Privately Held**
SIC: 1629 Trenching contractor

(P-2036)
CANTEL MEDICAL CORP
140 Mason Cir, Concord (94520-8549)
PHONE..................925 609-6328
EMP: 95
SALES (corp-wide): 664.7MM **Publicly Held**
SIC: 1629 Waste water & sewage treatment plant construction
PA: Cantel Medical Corp.
150 Clove Rd Ste 36
Little Falls NJ 07424
973 890-7220

(P-2037)
CARL J WOODS CONSTRUCTION INC
Also Called: Woods C J Engineering Contrs
1321 Gray Ave, Yuba City (95991-3204)
PHONE..................530 673-7877
Fax: 530 673-7439
Carl J Woods, *President*
William Woods, *Vice Pres*
EMP: 50
SQ FT: 600
SALES (est): 3.4MM **Privately Held**
SIC: 1629 1611 Marine construction; airport runway construction

(P-2038)
CATTRAC CONSTRUCTION INC
15030 Slover Ave, Fontana (92337-7237)
PHONE..................909 355-1146
Fax: 909 355-4410
Stephanie A Jacinto, *CEO*
Greg Dineen, *Vice Pres*
Mark Richardson, *Manager*
Bruce McBride, *Supervisor*
Bill Thomas, *Supervisor*
EMP: 60
SQ FT: 5,000
SALES (est): 13.8MM **Privately Held**
WEB: www.cattrac.com
SIC: 1629 7353 4213 Earthmoving contractor; earth moving equipment, rental or leasing; trucking, except local

(P-2039)
CE ALLENCOMPANY INC
2109 Gundry Ave, Long Beach (90755-3517)
PHONE..................562 989-6100
C E Peter Allen, *President*
Tim Parker, *VP Opers*
Porcia Siedler, *Manager*
EMP: 50
SQ FT: 1,277

SALES (est): 8.2MM **Privately Held**
SIC: 1629 7353 Industrial plant construction; oil equipment rental services

(P-2040)
CENTRAL VALLEY AG GRINDING
Also Called: Central Valley AG Transload
5509 Langworth Rd, Oakdale (95361-7909)
PHONE..................209 544-9246
Michael Barry, *President*
Ryan Hogan, *CFO*
Paul Konzen, *Admin Sec*
EMP: 93
SALES (est): 6.1MM
SALES (corp-wide): 34.5MM **Privately Held**
SIC: 1629 0723 Railroad & railway roadbed construction; field crops, except cash grains, market preparation services
PA: Central Valley Ag Grinding, Inc.
5707 Langworth Rd
Oakdale CA 95361
209 869-1721

(P-2041)
CITY OF LIVERMORE
Also Called: Water Resources Division
101 W Jack London Blvd, Livermore (94551-7632)
PHONE..................925 960-8100
Fax: 925 960-8105
Darren Greenwood, *Manager*
EMP: 50 **Privately Held**
SIC: 1629 Waste water & sewage treatment plant construction
PA: City Of Livermore
1052 S Livermore Ave
Livermore CA 94550
925 960-4020

(P-2042)
DIVECON SERVICES LP
1180 Eugenia Pl Ste 100, Carpinteria (93013-2000)
PHONE..................805 488-6428
Theodore K Roche IV, *President*
Joe Copper, *CFO*
Jack W Cover, *Vice Pres*
Scott White, *Office Mgr*
EMP: 145
SQ FT: 10,000
SALES (est): 9.8MM **Privately Held**
SIC: 1629 Dams, waterways, docks & other marine construction; marine construction

(P-2043)
DOD CONSTRUCTORS A JV
185 Devlin Rd, NAPA (94558-6255)
PHONE..................707 265-1100
Ronald Fedrick, *CEO*
Scott Victor, *President*
Walter Birdsall, *CFO*
Carole Bionda, *Vice Pres*
EMP: 99 EST: 2013
SALES (est): 2.6MM **Privately Held**
SIC: 1629 Dams, waterways, docks & other marine construction

(P-2044)
DOD FUELING CONSTRUCTORS A JV
185 Devlin Rd, NAPA (94558-6255)
PHONE..................707 265-1100
Ronald Fedrick, *Principal*
Walter Birdsall, *CFO*
Carole Bionda, *Principal*
Chris Mathies, *Principal*
Scott Victor, *Principal*
EMP: 99 EST: 2013
SALES (est): 2.5MM **Privately Held**
SIC: 1629 Dams, waterways, docks & other marine construction

(P-2045)
DOD MARINE CONSTRUCTORS A JV
185 Devlin Rd, NAPA (94558-6255)
PHONE..................707 265-1100
Ronald Fedrick, *Partner*
Carole Bionda, *Partner*
Walter Birdsall, *Partner*
Chris Mathies, *Partner*

1629 - Heavy Construction, NEC County (P-2046)

PRODUCTS & SERVICES SECTION

Scott Victor, *Partner*
EMP: 99 **EST:** 2013
SQ FT: 18,000
SALES (est): 2.5MM **Privately Held**
SIC: 1629 Dams, waterways, docks & other marine construction

(P-2046)
DUTRA DREDGING COMPANY (HQ)
2350 Kerner Blvd Ste 200, San Rafael (94901-5595)
PHONE 415 721-2131
Bill T Dutra, *CEO*
EMP: 60
SQ FT: 2,000
SALES (est): 12MM
SALES (corp-wide): 162.7MM **Privately Held**
WEB: www.dutragroup.com
SIC: 1629 Dredging contractor
PA: The Dutra Group
2350 Kerner Blvd Ste 200
San Rafael CA 94901
415 258-6876

(P-2047)
DUTRA GROUP (PA)
Also Called: Dutra Dredging
2350 Kerner Blvd Ste 200, San Rafael (94901-5595)
PHONE 415 258-6876
Bill T Dutra, *CEO*
Harry Stewart, *COO*
James Hagood, *CFO*
Jim Haygood, *CFO*
Denise Dutra, *Business Dir*
▲ **EMP:** 100
SQ FT: 22,000
SALES (est): 162.7MM **Privately Held**
SIC: 1629 8711 1429 Marine construction; dredging contractor; earthmoving contractor; civil engineering; igneous rock, crushed & broken-quarrying

(P-2048)
DUTRA MANSON JV
1000 Point San Pedro Rd, San Rafael (94901-8312)
PHONE 415 258-6876
Harry K Stewart, *Director*
Wilson Hackworth, *CFO*
Jim Haygood, *CFO*
Stephen Lewis, *Info Tech Dir*
Gerard Raalte, *Senior Engr*
EMP: 60
SALES (est): 7.4MM **Privately Held**
SIC: 1629 Marine construction

(P-2049)
ESOLAR INC (DH)
3355 W Empire Ave Ste 200, Burbank (91504-3160)
P.O. Box 10189 (91510-0189)
PHONE 818 303-9500
Fax: 818 303-9501
John Van Scoter, *CEO*
Bill Gross, *President*
Linda Heller, *CFO*
Dale Rogers, *Exec VP*
Rick Huibregtse, *Senior VP*
▲ **EMP:** 78
SALES (est): 20.3MM
SALES (corp-wide): 184.6MM **Privately Held**
SIC: 1629 Power plant construction

(P-2050)
FORD CONSTRUCTION COMPANY INC
300 W Pine St, Lodi (95240-2022)
PHONE 209 333-1116
Fax: 209 333-8597
Richard Piombo, *Treasurer*
Nicholas B Jones, *President*
Burt Young, *COO*
David S Snyder, *General Mgr*
Scott Davis, *Technical Staff*
EMP: 100
SQ FT: 8,500
SALES (est): 20.5MM **Privately Held**
WEB: www.ford-construction.com
SIC: 1629 1623 Dam construction; earthmoving contractor; water & sewer line construction

(P-2051)
FOUNDATION CONSTRUCTORS INC (PA)
81 Big Break Rd, Oakley (94561-3081)
P.O. Box 97 (94561-0097)
PHONE 925 754-6633
Fax: 925 625-5783
Dermot Noel Fallon, *CEO*
Pete Brandl, *President*
Nikki Sjoblom, *Corp Secy*
Don Hilton, *Vice Pres*
Mike Lindsay, *Vice Pres*
▲ **EMP:** 100
SQ FT: 6,000
SALES (est): 74MM **Privately Held**
SIC: 1629 Pile driving contractor

(P-2052)
FOUNDATION PILE INC
8375 Almeria Ave, Fontana (92335-3283)
PHONE 909 350-1584
Derek Halecky, *CEO*
Peter Brandl, *President*
Nikki Sjoblom, *CFO*
Dermot Fallon, *Vice Pres*
Mike Lindsay, *Vice Pres*
EMP: 100 **EST:** 1978
SALES (est): 9.7MM
SALES (corp-wide): 74MM **Privately Held**
SIC: 1629 1794 Pile driving contractor; excavation & grading, building construction
PA: Foundation Constructors, Inc.
81 Big Break Rd
Oakley CA 94561
925 754-6633

(P-2053)
GHILOTTI CONSTRUCTION CO INC (PA)
Also Called: Gcc
246 Ghilotti Ave, Santa Rosa (95407-8152)
PHONE 707 585-1221
Fax: 707 585-0129
Richard W Ghilotti, *CEO*
Diana Britting, *Manager*
EMP: 151
SQ FT: 9,000
SALES (est): 150.2MM **Privately Held**
WEB: www.ghilotti.com
SIC: 1629 Land preparation construction

(P-2054)
GRANITE CONSTRUCTION COMPANY
Also Called: Northern California Regional
4001 Bradshaw Rd, Sacramento (95827-3800)
PHONE 916 855-4400
Fax: 916 369-0429
Wayne Cornelius, *Manager*
Tim Gruber, *Human Res Mgr*
Randy Kremer, *Opers-Prdtn-Mfg*
Will Jackson, *Director*
EMP: 61
SQ FT: 1,364
SALES (corp-wide): 2.3B **Publicly Held**
WEB: www.graniteconstructioncompany.com
SIC: 1629 1611 Land preparation construction; highway & street construction
HQ: Granite Construction Company
585 W Beach St
Watsonville CA 95076
831 724-1011

(P-2055)
HANS TECHNOLOGIES INC
1300 Clay St Ste 600, Oakland (94612-1427)
PHONE 510 464-8018
Jerry Moseley, *President*
Craig Johns, *Vice Pres*
Kenneth Norcross III, *Vice Pres*
Weiping Xia, *Vice Pres*
James Li, *Admin Sec*
▲ **EMP:** 58
SQ FT: 6,500
SALES: 13.5MM **Privately Held**
SIC: 1629 Waste water & sewage treatment plant construction

(P-2056)
HAT CREEK CNSTR & MTLS INC (PA)
24339 State Highway 89, Burney (96013-9615)
PHONE 530 335-5501
Fax: 530 335-5510
Robert Thompson, *President*
Perry Thompson, *Corp Secy*
Howard A Lakey Jr, *Vice Pres*
Weston Hutchings, *Opers Mgr*
Shandy Spooner, *Manager*
EMP: 50
SALES (est): 16.9MM **Privately Held**
WEB: www.hatcreekconstruction.com
SIC: 1629 1771 1521 5032 Earthmoving contractor; concrete work; single-family housing construction; sand, construction; highway & street construction

(P-2057)
IRWIN INDUSTRIES INC (HQ)
1580 W Carson St, Long Beach (90810-1455)
PHONE 310 233-3000
Fax: 310 834-9402
Ricardo B Teamor, *CEO*
Al Storer, *CFO*
Rhonda Smith, *Office Mgr*
Ruby Bolls, *Admin Asst*
Betty Harden, *Admin Asst*
EMP: 700
SQ FT: 13,000
SALES: 300MM
SALES (corp-wide): 566.1MM **Privately Held**
WEB: www.irwinind.com
SIC: 1629 1731 1796 7353 Power plant construction; electric power systems contractors; power generating equipment installation; heavy construction equipment rental; nonresidential construction
PA: Park Corporation
6200 Riverside Dr
Cleveland OH 44135
216 267-4870

(P-2058)
IRWIN INDUSTRIES INC
610 W Hueneme Rd, Oxnard (93033-9012)
PHONE 805 874-3050
Wade Marby, *Manager*
Carlos Avelar, *COO*
Karen Gonzales, *Persnl Dir*
Jim Everett, *QC Mgr*
Ed Curtis, *Supervisor*
EMP: 150
SALES (corp-wide): 566.1MM **Privately Held**
SIC: 1629 Power plant construction
HQ: Irwin Industries, Inc.
1580 W Carson St
Long Beach CA 90810
310 233-3000

(P-2059)
JACOBS ENGINEERING GROUP INC
1111 S Arroyo Pkwy, Pasadena (91105-3254)
P.O. Box 7084 (91109-7084)
PHONE 626 578-3500
Iain Macdonald, *Associate Dir*
Robert Sands, *Program Mgr*
Larry Patrick, *Area Mgr*
William Zeigler, *Admin Mgr*
Wanda Reid, *Admin Asst*
EMP: 89
SALES (corp-wide): 12.7B **Publicly Held**
SIC: 1629 Industrial plant construction
PA: Jacobs Engineering Group Inc.
155 N Lake Ave
Pasadena CA 91101
626 578-3500

(P-2060)
JACOBS FIELD SVCS N AMER INC
3161 Michelson Dr Ste 500, Irvine (92612-4405)
P.O. Box 6025, Cypress (90630-0025)
PHONE 949 224-7585
Brandy Marquez, *Branch Mgr*
Frank Joyce, *Contract Mgr*
EMP: 250

SALES (corp-wide): 12.1B **Publicly Held**
WEB: www.jemcidecatur.com
SIC: 1629 Earthmoving contractor
HQ: Jacobs Field Services North America, Inc.
5995 Rogerdale Rd
Houston TX 77072
832 351-6000

(P-2061)
JACOBS TECHNOLOGY INC
Room 117a Bldg 227, Mountain View (94035)
P.O. Box 336, Moffett Field (94035-0336)
PHONE 650 604-3784
Michael D Weiss, *Manager*
EMP: 121
SALES (corp-wide): 12.1B **Publicly Held**
SIC: 1629 Industrial plant construction
HQ: Jacobs Technology Inc.
600 William Northern Blvd
Tullahoma TN 37388
931 455-6400

(P-2062)
JAMES-TIMEC INTERNATIONAL
155 Corporate Pl, Vallejo (94590-6968)
PHONE 707 642-2222
Anthony Marquez, *Manager*
Lou Hall, *Vice Pres*
Armando Perez, *Controller*
EMP: 50
SALES (corp-wide): 3B **Privately Held**
SIC: 1629 Industrial plant construction; oil refinery construction
HQ: James-Timec International, Inc
2315 W Main St
Baytown TX 77520
281 471-3209

(P-2063)
JOHN S MEEK COMPANY INC
14732 S Maple Ave, Gardena (90248-1934)
PHONE 310 830-6323
John S Meek, *President*
Jeremiah Jilk, *Manager*
EMP: 60
SQ FT: 5,000
SALES (est): 20.1MM **Privately Held**
WEB: www.johnsmeek.com
SIC: 1629 Dams, waterways, docks & other marine construction

(P-2064)
K G WALTERS CNSTR CO INC
195 Concourse Blvd Ste A, Santa Rosa (95403-8217)
P.O. Box 4359 (95402-4359)
PHONE 707 527-9968
Fax: 707 527-0244
Walt Johnson, *President*
David A Backman, *Senior VP*
Thomas Crotty, *Vice Pres*
Valerie Carmichael, *Admin Sec*
EMP: 55 **EST:** 1974
SQ FT: 4,000
SALES: 24MM **Privately Held**
WEB: www.kgwalters.com
SIC: 1629 Waste water & sewage treatment plant construction

(P-2065)
MARCH INTERNATIONAL INC
Also Called: Wall Tech
1249 S Dmnd Bar Blvd 20, Diamond Bar (91765-4122)
PHONE 909 821-5128
Frank Tilton, *CFO*
EMP: 50
SALES (est): 1.8MM **Privately Held**
SIC: 1629 Canal construction

(P-2066)
MCDONOUGH-WESTERN RIM JV
8942 Creekford Dr, Lakeside (92040-3702)
PHONE 619 749-5339
Robert C McDonough, *Partner*
Ray Samuelson, *Partner*
EMP: 50
SALES (est): 2.1MM **Privately Held**
SIC: 1629 Heavy construction

PRODUCTS & SERVICES SECTION
1629 - Heavy Construction, NEC County (P-2089)

(P-2067)
MILCO CONSTRUCTORS INC
3930b Cherry Ave, Long Beach (90807-3727)
P.O. Box 2150 (90801-2150)
PHONE.....................562 595-1977
Fax: 562 424-2347
Charles Miller, *President*
Duane C Miller, *Corp Secy*
Robert Griffin, *Vice Pres*
Larry Cianciola, *Controller*
EMP: 50
SQ FT: 17,000
SALES (est): 8.8MM **Privately Held**
WEB: www.milcoconstructors.com
SIC: **1629** Industrial plant construction

(P-2068)
MITCH BROWN CONSTRUCTION INC
14200 Road 284, Porterville (93257-9374)
PHONE.....................559 781-6389
Fax: 559 781-2358
Mitchell F Brown, *President*
Elizabeth Brown, *Corp Secy*
EMP: 60
SALES (est): 5.2MM **Privately Held**
SIC: **1629** Earthmoving contractor

(P-2069)
MONTEREY MECHANICAL CO (PA)
Also Called: Contra Costa Metal Fabricators
8275 San Leandro St, Oakland (94621-1972)
PHONE.....................510 632-3173
Fax: 510 632-0732
Milton C Burleson, *CEO*
Jim Troup, *President*
Paul Moreira, *CFO*
Masami Ikeda, *Info Tech Dir*
Don Hughes, *Project Mgr*
▲ EMP: 50
SQ FT: 40,000
SALES (est): 86.9MM **Privately Held**
WEB: www.montmech.com
SIC: **1629** 1711 1761 3444 Waste disposal plant construction; waste water & sewage treatment plant construction; mechanical contractor; boiler setting contractor; boiler maintenance contractor; sheet metalwork; sheet metalwork; fabricated structural metal; nonresidential construction

(P-2070)
NORDIC INDUSTRIES INC
1437 Furneaux Rd, Olivehurst (95961-7404)
PHONE.....................530 742-7124
Fax: 530 742-7124
Jens Karlshoej, *President*
Inge Karlshoej, *Corp Secy*
Katti Clark, *Office Admin*
Todd Lemmons, *Project Mgr*
Peter Brown, *Engineer*
EMP: 60
SQ FT: 5,000
SALES (est): 15.9MM **Privately Held**
WEB: www.nordicind.com
SIC: **1629** 4212 4213 Dam construction; levee construction; local trucking, without storage; trucking, except local

(P-2071)
NOVA BRINK A JOINT VENTURE
185 Devlin Rd, NAPA (94558-6255)
PHONE.....................707 265-1100
Ronld Fedrick, *Partner*
Brent Albrechts, *Partner*
Carole Bionda, *Partner*
Scott Victor, *Partner*
EMP: 99
SQ FT: 18,000
SALES (est): 6.9MM **Privately Held**
SIC: **1629** 1623 1622 Dams, waterways, docks & other marine construction; water, sewer & utility lines; tunnel construction

(P-2072)
NOVA GROUP INC
Also Called: Ngi Construction
185 Devlin Rd, NAPA (94558-6255)
P.O. Box 4050 (94558-0450)
PHONE.....................707 265-1100
Fax: 707 257-2774
Ronald M Fedrick, *President*
Scott R Victor, *President*
Scott Victor, *COO*
Art Mendoza, *Officer*
Carole Bionda, *Vice Pres*
EMP: 200 EST: 1957
SQ FT: 11,000
SALES (est): 112.3MM **Privately Held**
SIC: **1629** 1623 1622 5172 Marine construction; waterway construction; underground utilities contractor; tunnel construction; aircraft fueling services

(P-2073)
NOVA LANE CONSTRUCTORS A JV
185 Devlin Rd, NAPA (94558-6255)
PHONE.....................707 265-1100
Ronald Fedrick, *CEO*
Carole Bionda, *Principal*
Walter Birdsall, *Principal*
Chris Mathies, *Principal*
Scott Victor, *Principal*
EMP: 99
SALES (est): 6.5MM **Privately Held**
SIC: **1629** Dams, waterways, docks & other marine construction

(P-2074)
PARSONS CORPORATION (PA)
100 W Walnut St, Pasadena (91124-0001)
PHONE.....................626 440-2000
Fax: 626 440-2630
Charles L Harrington, *Ch of Bd*
James R Shappell, *Vice Chairman*
John A Scott, *President*
George L Ball, *CFO*
Shelley Green, *Treasurer*
◆ EMP: 2000
SQ FT: 900,000
SALES (est): 7.9B **Privately Held**
SIC: **1629** 1611 8711 8741 Chemical plant & refinery construction; highway & street construction; industrial engineers; chemical engineering; management services

(P-2075)
PARSONS CORPORATION
1 Centerpointe Dr, La Palma (90623-1052)
PHONE.....................714 736-6826
EMP: 175
SALES (corp-wide): 7.9B **Privately Held**
SIC: **1629** Dams, waterways, docks & other marine construction
PA: The Parsons Corporation
100 W Walnut St
Pasadena CA 91124
626 440-2000

(P-2076)
PATRICKS CONSTRUCTION CLEAN-UP
7851 14th Ave, Sacramento (95826-4301)
PHONE.....................916 452-5495
Fax: 916 452-9592
Patricio Mercado, *Owner*
EMP: 100
SALES (est): 8.2MM **Privately Held**
SIC: **1629** Land clearing contractor

(P-2077)
POWERPLANT MINT SPCIALISTS INC
2900 Bristol St Ste H202, Costa Mesa (92626-7917)
PHONE.....................714 427-6900
Jim McEachern, *CEO*
Richard G Engel, *President*
J Alexandra Barretto, *Vice Pres*
Dave Gatti, *Vice Pres*
Michael Medock, *Vice Pres*
EMP: 200
SQ FT: 3,300
SALES (est): 20.6MM **Privately Held**
WEB: www.pmsipower.com
SIC: **1629** Dams, waterways, docks & other marine construction

(P-2078)
RE LA MESA LLC
300 California St Fl 8, San Francisco (94104-1416)
PHONE.....................415 675-1500
Arno Harris,
Greg Wilson,
EMP: 100
SALES (est): 11.1MM **Privately Held**
SIC: **1629** Land leveling

(P-2079)
RE MOHICAN LLC
300 California St Fl 8, San Francisco (94104-1416)
PHONE.....................415 675-1500
Greg Wilson, *Treasurer*
EMP: 70
SALES: 575K **Privately Held**
SIC: **1629** Heavy construction

(P-2080)
RE SANTA CLARA LLC
300 California St Fl 8, San Francisco (94104-1416)
PHONE.....................415 675-1500
Arno Harris, *CEO*
EMP: 95
SALES (est): 2.6MM **Privately Held**
SIC: **1629** Heavy construction

(P-2081)
SAN DIEGO HBR EXCURSIONS INC
1050 N Harbor Dr, San Diego (92101-3316)
P.O. Box 120751 (92112-0751)
PHONE.....................619 234-4111
Fax: 619 595-1062
Arthur E Engel, *President*
Karen Spencer, *Controller*
Jay Malone, *Manager*
Josh Gaylord, *Port Captain*
Scot Rockman, *Accounts Exec*
EMP: 100
SALES: 15MM
SALES (corp-wide): 16.3MM **Privately Held**
SIC: **1629** Harbor construction
PA: Star & Crescent Boat Company
1311 1st St
Coronado CA 92118
619 234-4111

(P-2082)
SCHWAGER DAVIS INC
198 Hillsdale Ave, San Jose (95136-1398)
PHONE.....................408 281-9300
Guido A Schwager, *President*
Michael Williams, *Vice Pres*
Lee Larsen, *Project Mgr*
Mario Salice, *Project Mgr*
Lori Rosell, *Controller*
▲ EMP: 116
SQ FT: 12,000
SALES (est): 46.3MM **Privately Held**
SIC: **1629** 1622 Railroad & railway roadbed construction; bridge construction

(P-2083)
SHIMMICK CONSTRUCTION CO INC (PA)
8201 Edgewater Dr Ste 202, Oakland (94621-2023)
PHONE.....................510 777-5000
Fax: 510 777-5099
Paul Cocotis, *Ch of Bd*
Paul Camaur, *President*
Scott Fairgrieve, *CFO*
Christian Fassari, *Exec VP*
Jeffrey Lessman, *Exec VP*
EMP: 151
SQ FT: 30,000
SALES (est): 319.6MM **Privately Held**
SIC: **1629** 1623 Earthmoving contractor; sewer line construction

(P-2084)
SIGMA INVESTMENT HOLDINGS LLC
2288 Villa Heights Rd, Pasadena (91107-1141)
PHONE.....................626 398-3098
Geoffrey G Ren, *Mng Member*
Jason LI, *Engineer*
Asong Fu,
Chauan Ren,
Guang Ren,
▼ EMP: 50
SQ FT: 3,178
SALES: 50MM **Privately Held**
SIC: **1629** Industrial plant construction

(P-2085)
SKANSKA USA CIVIL WEST ROCKY M (DH)
Also Called: Skanska Rocky Mountain Dst
1995 Agua Mansa Rd, Riverside (92509-2405)
PHONE.....................970 565-8000
Curtis Broughton, *Senior VP*
Larry Casey, *Senior VP*
David Sitton, *Vice Pres*
Ericc Taylor, *Vice Pres*
Tammy Hampton, *General Mgr*
EMP: 70
SQ FT: 22,500
SALES (est): 84.8MM
SALES (corp-wide): 17.5B **Privately Held**
SIC: **1629** 1611 1711 Dam construction; general contractor, highway & street construction; mechanical contractor
HQ: Skanska Usa Civil Inc.
7520 Astoria Blvd Ste 200
East Elmhurst NY 11370
718 340-0777

(P-2086)
SLATER INC
11045 Rose Ave, Fontana (92337-7051)
P.O. Box 759 (92334-0759)
PHONE.....................909 822-6800
Fax: 909 822-7647
Phillip S Slater, *CEO*
Edward Johnson, *CFO*
Steve David, *Vice Pres*
EMP: 97
SQ FT: 6,000
SALES (est): 13.4MM **Privately Held**
WEB: www.slaterinc.com
SIC: **1629** 8711 Drainage system construction; engineering services

(P-2087)
SOLAR MILLENNIUM LLC
1111 Broadway Ste 400, Oakland (94607-4165)
PHONE.....................510 524-4517
Uwe T Schmidt, *CEO*
Josef Eichhammer, *CEO*
John Clapp, *CFO*
Steven Brewer, *Ch Credit Ofcr*
Paulie Pan, *Controller*
EMP: 55
SQ FT: 22,000
SALES (est): 3.1MM
SALES (corp-wide): 3.6MM **Privately Held**
WEB: www.solarmillennium.de/index.lang2.html
SIC: **1629** Power plant construction
PA: Solar Trust Of America Llc
3201 Entp Pkwy Ste 490
Cleveland OH

(P-2088)
SOLTIS GOLF INCORPORATED
8579 Cottonwood Ave, Fontana (92335-2918)
P.O. Box 1309, Upland (91785-1309)
PHONE.....................909 822-7000
Christopher Soltis, *President*
EMP: 75
SALES (est): 7MM **Privately Held**
WEB: www.soltisgolf.com
SIC: **1629** Golf course construction

(P-2089)
TEAM WEST CONTRACTING CORP
1611 Jenks Dr, Corona (92880-2514)
PHONE.....................951 340-3426
Jerry R Pacheco, *President*
Michael Eliefson, *Officer*
Bryan Girard, *Officer*
Stephen Girard, *Officer*
Angela Rayfield, *Marketing Staff*
EMP: 92
SQ FT: 7,200
SALES (est): 7.2MM **Privately Held**
SIC: **1629** 1799 Railroad & railway roadbed construction; fence construction

1629 - Heavy Construction, NEC County (P-2090)

PRODUCTS & SERVICES SECTION

(P-2090)
THOMAS CRANE AND TRCKG CO INC
18851 Stewart Ln, Huntington Beach (92648-1520)
P.O. Box 640 (92648-0640)
PHONE.................................562 592-2837
Fax: 714 847-0082
Michael Thomas, *CEO*
John Thomas, *Principal*
Mike Thomas, *Principal*
Linda Thomas, *Admin Sec*
Susan Zee, *Manager*
EMP: 50 **EST:** 1962
SQ FT: 800
SALES (est): 8.7MM **Privately Held**
SIC: 1629 4212 Oil refinery construction; light haulage & cartage, local

(P-2091)
TIMEC ACQUISITIONS INC (HQ)
155 Corporate Pl, Vallejo (94590-6968)
PHONE.................................707 642-2222
Pat McMahon, *President*
Gary Green, *COO*
Dennis Turnipseed, *CFO*
Dennis Truet, *Vice Pres*
EMP: 850
SQ FT: 25,000
SALES (est): 200.2MM
SALES (corp-wide): 3B **Privately Held**
SIC: 1629 Industrial plant construction; chemical plant & refinery construction
PA: Broadspectrum Pty Ltd
L 10 111 Pacific Hwy
North Sydney NSW 2060
294 641-000

(P-2092)
TIMEC COMPANIES INC (DH)
155 Corporate Pl, Vallejo (94590-6968)
PHONE.................................707 642-2222
Fax: 707 558-8372
Denis Turnipseed, *President*
Brian Lapid, *Technology*
Armando Perez, *Controller*
Sherry Andrews, *Payroll Mgr*
Brent Babow, *General Counsel*
EMP: 350
SQ FT: 80,000
SALES (est): 200.2MM
SALES (corp-wide): 3B **Privately Held**
SIC: 1629 1799 Industrial plant construction; chemical plant & refinery construction; oil refinery construction; welding on site
HQ: Timec Acquisitions Inc
155 Corporate Pl
Vallejo CA 94590
707 642-2222

(P-2093)
TUTOR PERINI/ZACHRY/PARSONS
1401 Fulton St Ste 400, Fresno (93721-1645)
PHONE.................................559 385-7025
James Frost, *Partner*
Carol Einfalt, *Partner*
EMP: 99
SQ FT: 15,000
SALES (est): 5.9MM **Privately Held**
SIC: 1629 Railroad & railway roadbed construction

(P-2094)
URS/CONTRACK-PACER FORGE JV
600 Montgomery St Fl 26, San Francisco (94111-2728)
PHONE.................................415 774-2700
EMP: 106
SALES (corp-wide): 4.5MM **Privately Held**
SIC: 1629 Waste water & sewage treatment plant construction
PA: Urs/Contrack-Pacer Forge Jv
3320 E Goldstone Way
Meridian ID 83642
208 386-8032

(P-2095)
VISTA STEEL CO INC
331 W Lewis St, Ventura (93001-1394)
PHONE.................................805 653-1189
Fax: 805 652-1873
John Swaffar, *Branch Mgr*
Alfred Bruni, *Vice Pres*
EMP: 50
SALES (corp-wide): 9.8MM **Privately Held**
SIC: 1629 3449 Dams, waterways, docks & other marine construction; miscellaneous metalwork
PA: Vista Steel Co Inc
6100 Francis Botello Rd C
Goleta CA 93117
805 964-4732

(P-2096)
WINDROW EARTH TRANSPORT INC
14032 Santa Ana Ave, Fontana (92337-7035)
PHONE.................................909 355-5531
Bruce Degler, *President*
Rob Maroney, *CFO*
Kim Pugmire, *Vice Pres*
Sheila Hornak, *Sales Staff*
EMP: 50
SQ FT: 1,100
SALES: 40MM **Privately Held**
SIC: 1629 Earthmoving contractor
PA: Pro Loaders, Inc.
14032 Santa Ana Ave
Fontana CA 92337
909 355-5531

(P-2097)
WOOD BROS INC
14147 18th Ave, Lemoore (93245-9741)
P.O. Box 216 (93245-0216)
PHONE.................................559 924-7715
William S Wood, *CEO*
Donald T Wood, *Corp Secy*
Jerry Ghiglia, *General Mgr*
Cindy McKay, *Accountant*
Bryon Barros, *Foreman/Supr*
EMP: 100
SQ FT: 30,000
SALES (est): 32.9MM **Privately Held**
SIC: 1629 Dredging contractor

1711 Plumbing, Heating & Air Conditioning Contractors

(P-2098)
20/20 PLUMBING & HEATING INC
7343 Orangewood Dr Ste B, Riverside (92504-1053)
PHONE.................................951 396-2020
Thomas Lew Baker, *CEO*
Rebecca Rice, *Opers Staff*
EMP: 200
SALES (est): 19.9MM **Privately Held**
SIC: 1711 Plumbing, heating, air-conditioning contractors

(P-2099)
A & A MECHANICAL CONTRACTORS
2943 Daylight Way, San Jose (95111-3194)
PHONE.................................408 225-1321
Fax: 408 225-4686
George A Reppas, *President*
Arthur G Reppas, *Ch of Bd*
Michael Reppas, *CFO*
Sam Lopez, *Office Mgr*
EMP: 85
SQ FT: 32,000
SALES (est): 4.5MM **Privately Held**
SIC: 1711 Warm air heating & air conditioning contractor

(P-2100)
A & D FIRE PROTECTION INC
Also Called: A & D General Contracting
11465 Woodside Ave Fl 1, Santee (92071-4725)
PHONE.................................619 258-7697
Fax: 619 258-5683
Andrew R Otero, *President*
Rose Pullaro, *Admin Asst*
Jeff Jukes, *Info Tech Mgr*
Larry Bouchard, *Project Mgr*
Owen Curtis, *Project Mgr*
EMP: 80
SQ FT: 10,000
SALES (est): 21MM **Privately Held**
WEB: www.adcompaniesinc.com
SIC: 1711 1542 Fire sprinkler system installation; nonresidential construction

(P-2101)
A A A FURNACE AC CO
1712 Stone Ave Ste 1, San Jose (95125-1387)
PHONE.................................408 293-4717
Jim Rendo, *President*
EMP: 60
SALES (est): 4.3MM **Privately Held**
SIC: 1711 Warm air heating & air conditioning contractor

(P-2102)
A C RENTALS LLC
8540 Production Ave Ste A, San Diego (92121-2263)
PHONE.................................858 271-8571
Eric A Clayton, *Principal*
EMP: 50
SALES (est): 1.8MM **Privately Held**
SIC: 1711 Warm air heating & air conditioning contractor

(P-2103)
A O REED & CO
4777 Ruffner St, San Diego (92111-1578)
P.O. Box 85226 (92186-5226)
PHONE.................................858 565-4131
Fax: 858 292-6958
Steve Andrade, *President*
John Norling, *President*
Clyde Blyleven, *CFO*
Craig Koehler, *CFO*
Alan Rings, *Senior VP*
EMP: 400
SQ FT: 55,000
SALES (est): 154.7MM **Privately Held**
WEB: www.aoreed.com
SIC: 1711 Plumbing, heating, air-conditioning contractors

(P-2104)
AAA DRAIN PATROL
Also Called: Preferred Plumbing and Drain
3437 Myrtle Ave Ste 440, North Highlands (95660-5147)
PHONE.................................916 348-3098
Kathleen Graves, *Owner*
EMP: 50
SALES (est): 2.2MM **Privately Held**
SIC: 1711 Plumbing contractors

(P-2105)
ACCO ENGINEERED SYSTEMS INC
1133 Aladdin Ave, San Leandro (94577-4311)
PHONE.................................510 346-4300
Fax: 510 347-1317
Ron Krassensky, *Manager*
Juan Sandoval, *Area Spvr*
Jose Mendoza, *QA Dir*
Mike Dawes, *Design Engr*
Mark Azzarello, *Project Mgr*
EMP: 200
SALES (corp-wide): 765MM **Privately Held**
WEB: www.accoair.com
SIC: 1711 7623 Process piping contractor; solar energy contractor; ventilation & duct work contractor; warm air heating & air conditioning contractor; air conditioning repair
PA: Acco Engineered Systems, Inc.
6265 San Fernando Rd
Glendale CA 91201
818 244-6571

(P-2106)
ADEE PLUMBING AND HEATING INC (PA)
5457 Crenshaw Blvd, Los Angeles (90043-2496)
PHONE.................................323 296-8787
Fax: 323 299-8139
Jack Stephan Sr, *President*
Jack Stephan Jr, *Vice Pres*
Russell Stephan, *Admin Sec*
Jack Dean, *Manager*
EMP: 64
SQ FT: 18,000
SALES (est): 10.4MM **Privately Held**
SIC: 1711 Plumbing contractors; warm air heating & air conditioning contractor

(P-2107)
ADROIT ENERGY INC
Also Called: Sunwater Solar
1135 Garnet Ave Ste 32, San Diego (92109-2990)
PHONE.................................858 483-3568
James Backman, *CEO*
EMP: 51 **EST:** 1986
SALES (est): 1.5MM **Privately Held**
SIC: 1711 Plumbing, heating, air-conditioning contractors; solar energy contractor

(P-2108)
ADVANTAGE PLUMBING GROUP INC
3331 Orangewood Ave, Los Alamitos (90720-3813)
P.O. Box 733 (90720-0733)
PHONE.................................714 898-6020
Faramaiz Meshkinpour, *President*
Mahin Meshkinpour, *CFO*
EMP: 67
SALES (est): 5.2MM **Privately Held**
SIC: 1711 5074 Plumbing, heating, air-conditioning contractors; water purification equipment

(P-2109)
AEGIS ENTERPRISES INC
Also Called: Aegis Fire Systems
500 Boulder Ct Ste A, Pleasanton (94566-8311)
PHONE.................................925 417-5550
Fax: 925 417-5554
Thomas J McKinnon, *President*
Timothy Higgins, *Vice Pres*
Deborah Almeida, *Opers Mgr*
Mike Sweeney, *Sales Staff*
Micah Hood, *Maintence Staff*
EMP: 100
SALES (est): 18.6MM **Privately Held**
SIC: 1711 Fire sprinkler system installation

(P-2110)
AG AIR CONDITIONING & HTG INC
Also Called: AG Heating and AC
14620 Keswick St, Van Nuys (91405-1203)
PHONE.................................818 988-5388
Fax: 818 781-3333
Yuval Giron, *CEO*
Yitchak Giron, *President*
Abe Eloud, *Accounts Mgr*
EMP: 50
SALES: 3.6MM **Privately Held**
SIC: 1711 Warm air heating & air conditioning contractor

(P-2111)
AIR CONTROL SYSTEMS INC
1940 S Grove Ave, Ontario (91761-5615)
PHONE.................................714 572-6880
Robert Leotaud, *President*
Pat McAuley, *Human Resources*
Marc Leotaud, *Accounts Mgr*
EMP: 50
SQ FT: 4,000
SALES: 15MM **Privately Held**
SIC: 1711 1731 Warm air heating & air conditioning contractor; ventilation & duct work contractor; electrical work

(P-2112)
AIR MECHANICAL INC
608 S Vicki Ln, Anaheim (92804-3207)
PHONE.................................714 995-3947
Wallace Fox, *Principal*
EMP: 62
SALES (corp-wide): 21.2MM **Privately Held**
SIC: 1711 Plumbing, heating, air-conditioning contractors
PA: Air Mechanical, Inc.
16411 Aberdeen St Ne
Anoka MN 55304
763 434-7747

1711 - Plumbing, Heating & Air Conditioning Contractors County (P-2133)

(P-2113)
AIR SYSTEMS INC
940 Remillard Ct Frnt, San Jose (95122-2684)
PHONE..................408 280-1666
Fax: 408 280-0741
Arthur Williams, *CEO*
Marty Cull, *Executive*
Rebecca Macias, *Admin Asst*
Kim Staffiery, *Admin Asst*
Monica Jackson Brown, *Administration*
▲ EMP: 500
SALES: 158.5MM **Privately Held**
SIC: 1711 7623 Plumbing contractors; refrigeration service & repair

(P-2114)
AIR SYSTEMS SACRAMENTO INC
10381 Old Placerville Rd # 100, Sacramento (95827-2558)
PHONE..................916 368-0336
Fax: 916 368-0337
Garry Westover, *CEO*
Kathleen Westover, *President*
Jim Meurer, *Vice Pres*
Craig Medley, *General Mgr*
Justin Iodence, *Project Mgr*
EMP: 130
SQ FT: 10,000
SALES: 35MM **Privately Held**
WEB: www.airsystems1.com
SIC: 1711 7623 Mechanical contractor; warm air heating & air conditioning contractor; ventilation & duct work contractor; plumbing contractors; refrigeration service & repair

(P-2115)
AIRCO MECHANICAL INC
Also Called: AMI Manufacturing
8210 Demetre Ave, Sacramento (95828-0919)
PHONE..................916 381-4523
Wyatt Jones, *CEO*
Bruce Stimson, *CFO*
Larry R Cook, *Vice Pres*
Dean Schouweiler, *Vice Pres*
Stuart Thompson, *Department Mgr*
EMP: 250
SQ FT: 105,000
SALES (est): 112.1MM **Privately Held**
WEB: www.aircomech.com
SIC: 1711 8711 Plumbing, heating, air-conditioning contractors; engineering services

(P-2116)
AIRE-RITE AC & RFRGN INC
15122 Bolsa Chica St, Huntington Beach (92649-1025)
P.O. Box 3419 (92605-3419)
PHONE..................714 895-2338
Fax: 714 893-8641
Donald Langston, *President*
Carol Langston, *Corp Secy*
David Langston, *Vice Pres*
Linda Hubbard, *Technical Staff*
Linda Hubeard, *Manager*
EMP: 97
SQ FT: 22,000
SALES: 16.6MM **Privately Held**
WEB: www.airerite.com
SIC: 1711 Refrigeration contractor

(P-2117)
ALDOC INC
304 N Townsend St Ste D, Santa Ana (92703-3539)
PHONE..................714 836-8477
P S Meckley, *President*
Philip Shurman Meckley, *President*
EMP: 60
SALES (est): 5.1MM **Privately Held**
SIC: 1711 Plumbing contractors

(P-2118)
ALISO MECHANICAL INCORPORATED
29736 A De Las Bandera, Rancho Santa Margari (92688)
PHONE..................949 544-1601
Christopher H Loftus, *CEO*
Jeffrey T Loftus, *President*
EMP: 150

SQ FT: 8,000
SALES (est): 9.3MM **Privately Held**
WEB: www.alisoair.com
SIC: 1711 Warm air heating & air conditioning contractor

(P-2119)
ALL AREA PLUMBING INC
5742 Venice Blvd, Los Angeles (90019-5016)
PHONE..................323 939-9990
Fax: 323 939-9262
Robert Felix, *President*
Beni Monaco, *CFO*
EMP: 235
SQ FT: 3,000
SALES: 1.1MM **Privately Held**
WEB: www.allareaco.com
SIC: 1711 Plumbing, heating, air-conditioning contractors

(P-2120)
ALL TMPERATURES CONTROLLED INC
9720 Topanga Canyon Pl, Chatsworth (91311-4134)
PHONE..................818 882-1478
George Mego, *President*
Kathy Gomes, *Executive*
Cheryl Piper, *Technology*
Nancy Miller, *Financial Exec*
Tony Iannolo, *Manager*
EMP: 72 **EST:** 1978
SQ FT: 13,481
SALES (est): 16.8MM **Privately Held**
SIC: 1711 Warm air heating & air conditioning contractor

(P-2121)
ALLAN AUTOMATIC SPRINKLER CORP
3233 Enterprise St, Brea (92821-6239)
PHONE..................714 993-9500
Fax: 714 993-5708
Jim Charrette, *Vice Pres*
Dom Guzzo, *Manager*
Nigel Mills, *Manager*
EMP: 80
SQ FT: 40,000
SALES (est): 10.6MM
SALES (corp-wide): 6.7B **Publicly Held**
WEB: www.allansocal.com
SIC: 1711 5084 Fire sprinkler system installation; industrial machinery & equipment
HQ: Shambaugh & Son, L.P.
7614 Opportunity Dr
Fort Wayne IN 46825
260 487-7777

(P-2122)
ALLIED FIRE PROTECTION
555 High St, Oakland (94601-3989)
PHONE..................510 533-5516
Fax: 510 533-0913
Ted Vinther, *President*
Linda Lequieu, *Office Mgr*
Fritz Descovich, *Project Mgr*
EMP: 150
SQ FT: 29,000
SALES (est): 26.2MM **Privately Held**
WEB: www.alliedfire.com
SIC: 1711 Sprinkler contractors

(P-2123)
ALPHA MECHANICAL INC
4990 Greencraig Ln Ste A, San Diego (92123-1673)
PHONE..................858 278-3500
Boris Barshak, *Branch Mgr*
Cort Clifford, *Business Mgr*
Renee Poulson, *Human Resources*
EMP: 106
SALES (corp-wide): 37.4MM **Privately Held**
SIC: 1711 Plumbing, heating, air-conditioning contractors
PA: Alpha Mechanical, Inc.
4885 Greencraig Ln
San Diego CA 92123
858 278-3500

(P-2124)
ALPHA MECHANICAL INC (PA)
4885 Greencraig Ln, San Diego (92123-1664)
PHONE..................858 278-3500
Fax: 858 278-3510
Boris Barshak, *CEO*
Renee Larzalere, *CFO*
Liz Moore, *Accountant*
Nicole Lynch, *Controller*
Cathy Fillmore, *Manager*
EMP: 79
SQ FT: 8,000
SALES (est): 37.4MM **Privately Held**
SIC: 1711 Plumbing, heating, air-conditioning contractors

(P-2125)
AMERICAN AC DISTRS LLC
Also Called: Florida Conditioning
16900 Chestnut St, City of Industry (91748-1012)
PHONE..................407 850-0147
John Staples,
Kevin Lentz, *General Mgr*
John Graham, *Hub Mgr*
Tara Qualls, *Hub Mgr*
John Scarsi,
▲ EMP: 92
SALES (est): 6.1MM **Privately Held**
SIC: 1711 Heating & air conditioning contractors

(P-2126)
AMERICAN CONTRACTORS INC
404 W Blueridge Ave, Orange (92865-4204)
PHONE..................714 282-5700
Fax: 714 282-5710
Gilbert L Wiggam, *CEO*
Christopher Wiggam, *Vice Pres*
Lou Assuras, *Controller*
Sue Assuras, *Controller*
EMP: 65
SQ FT: 11,000
SALES: 14.4MM **Privately Held**
SIC: 1711 1623 Plumbing contractors; sewer line construction; water main construction

(P-2127)
AMERICAN INCORPORATED
Also Called: American Air
1345 N American St, Visalia (93291-9334)
PHONE..................559 651-1776
Corwyn Oldfield, *CEO*
Frank Saucedo, *CFO*
Lois Oldfield, *Vice Pres*
Deanna Menezes, *Executive*
Alan Bettencourt, *Admin Asst*
EMP: 425
SQ FT: 115,000
SALES: 75MM **Privately Held**
SIC: 1711 1542 1541 1731 Warm air heating & air conditioning contractor; refrigeration contractor; plumbing contractors; commercial & office building contractors; industrial buildings & warehouses; electrical work

(P-2128)
AMERICAN LEAK DETECTION INC
304 N Townsend St Ste D, Santa Ana (92703-3539)
PHONE..................714 836-8477
Fax: 714 836-9976
Steve Lee, *Manager*
Dan Tre, *Director*
Jerry Mason, *Manager*
Maria Strobelt, *Manager*
EMP: 50
SALES (corp-wide): 26.1MM **Privately Held**
SIC: 1711 Plumbing contractors
PA: American Leak Detection, Inc.
888 E Research Dr Ste 100
Palm Springs CA 92262
760 320-9991

(P-2129)
AMERICAN RESIDENTIAL SVCS LLC
Also Called: AMERICAN RESIDENTIAL SERVICES L.L.C.
9895 Olson Dr Ste A, San Diego (92121-2841)
PHONE..................858 457-5547
Bonnie Bakken, *General Mgr*
Jan Zamisch, *Vice Pres*
Peggy Foreman, *Executive*
Matt Harmon, *General Mgr*
Sue Beckett, *Personnel Exec*
EMP: 80
SALES (corp-wide): 2.8B **Privately Held**
WEB: www.ars.com
SIC: 1711 Plumbing, heating, air-conditioning contractors
PA: American Residential Services Llc
965 Ridge Lake Blvd # 201
Memphis TN 38120
901 271-9700

(P-2130)
AMERICAN RESIDENTIAL SVCS LLC
Also Called: AMERICAN RESIDENTIAL SERVICES L.L.C.
15707 S Main St, Gardena (90248-2506)
PHONE..................310 637-1454
Daniel Dunduenabad, *Manager*
EMP: 50
SALES (corp-wide): 2.8B **Privately Held**
WEB: www.ars.com
SIC: 1711 Plumbing, heating, air-conditioning contractors
PA: American Residential Services Llc
965 Ridge Lake Blvd # 201
Memphis TN 38120
901 271-9700

(P-2131)
AMERICAN RESIDENTIAL SVCS LLC
Also Called: ARS of San Diego-8112
6162 Nncy Rdge Dr Ste 100, San Diego (92121)
PHONE..................858 677-5445
Fax: 858 677-5476
Kevin Kellington, *General Mgr*
James McMahon, *CFO*
Myriam Roblebo, *Accounting Mgr*
EMP: 60
SALES (corp-wide): 2.8B **Privately Held**
WEB: www.ars.com
SIC: 1711 Plumbing, heating, air-conditioning contractors
PA: American Residential Services Llc
965 Ridge Lake Blvd # 201
Memphis TN 38120
901 271-9700

(P-2132)
AMERICAN RESIDENTIAL SVCS LLC
P.O. Box 1592 (92022-1592)
PHONE..................858 292-4452
Fax: 858 593-1669
Ray Olsen, *Branch Mgr*
EMP: 59
SALES (corp-wide): 2.8B **Privately Held**
SIC: 1711 Plumbing, heating, air-conditioning contractors
PA: American Residential Services Llc
965 Ridge Lake Blvd # 201
Memphis TN 38120
901 271-9700

(P-2133)
AMERICAN RESIDENTIAL SVCS LLC
Also Called: Atlas Heating
1965 Kyle Park Ct, San Jose (95125-1029)
PHONE..................650 856-1612
EMP: 60
SALES (corp-wide): 2.8B **Privately Held**
SIC: 1711 Plumbing, heating, air-conditioning contractors
PA: American Residential Services Llc
965 Ridge Lake Blvd # 201
Memphis TN 38120
901 271-9700

1711 - Plumbing, Heating & Air Conditioning Contractors County (P-2134)

(P-2134)
AMERICAN RESIDENTIAL SVCS LLC
Also Called: Rescue Rotter
1520 W Linden St, Riverside (92507-6808)
PHONE.................................951 341-9371
Fax: 951 341-0004
Dave Slott, COO
EMP: 55
SALES (corp-wide): 2.8B Privately Held
WEB: www.ars.com
SIC: 1711 Plumbing contractors
PA: American Residential Services Llc
965 Ridge Lake Blvd # 201
Memphis TN 38120
901 271-9700

(P-2135)
AMERICAN RESIDENTIAL SVCS LLC
Also Called: Rescue Rooter Bay Area North
825 Mahler Rd, Burlingame (94010-1603)
P.O. Box 4036 (94011-4036)
PHONE.................................650 652-1050
Fax: 650 537-1100
Larry Dehart, General Mgr
James McMahon, CFO
Jordon Brand, Manager
Larry Hart, Manager
EMP: 59
SALES (corp-wide): 2.8B Privately Held
WEB: www.ars.com
SIC: 1711 Plumbing contractors
PA: American Residential Services Llc
965 Ridge Lake Blvd # 201
Memphis TN 38120
901 271-9700

(P-2136)
AMERICAN RESIDENTIAL SVCS LLC
Also Called: Rescue Rooter
29196 Simms Ct, Hayward (94544-6911)
P.O. Box 3098 (94540-3098)
PHONE.................................510 657-7601
Chris Peterson, Manager
EMP: 70
SALES (corp-wide): 2.8B Privately Held
WEB: www.ars.com
SIC: 1711 Plumbing contractors
PA: American Residential Services Llc
965 Ridge Lake Blvd # 201
Memphis TN 38120
901 271-9700

(P-2137)
AMERICAN RESIDENTIAL SVCS LLC
Also Called: Rescue Rooter
740 N Hariton St, Orange (92868-1314)
PHONE.................................714 634-1826
Dave Krol, Manager
Renee Michelle, Executive
EMP: 100
SALES (corp-wide): 2.8B Privately Held
WEB: www.ars.com
SIC: 1711 Plumbing contractors
PA: American Residential Services Llc
965 Ridge Lake Blvd # 201
Memphis TN 38120
901 271-9700

(P-2138)
AMERICAN RESIDENTIAL SVCS LLC
Also Called: Rescue Rooter
12507 San Fernando Rd, Sylmar (91342-5023)
PHONE.................................818 833-6677
Darl Coopper, General Mgr
EMP: 60
SALES (corp-wide): 2.8B Privately Held
WEB: www.ars.com
SIC: 1711 Warm air heating & air conditioning contractor
PA: American Residential Services Llc
965 Ridge Lake Blvd # 201
Memphis TN 38120
901 271-9700

(P-2139)
AMERICAN RESIDENTIAL SVCS LLC
Also Called: ARS of San Diego Hvac
8949 Kenamar Dr Ste 110, San Diego (92121-2435)
PHONE.................................858 277-2606
Fax: 858 689-9248
Chip Julin, Branch Mgr
EMP: 59
SALES (corp-wide): 2.8B Privately Held
SIC: 1711 Plumbing, heating, air-conditioning contractors
PA: American Residential Services Llc
965 Ridge Lake Blvd # 201
Memphis TN 38120
901 271-9700

(P-2140)
AMERICAN SOLAR DIRECT INC
217 N Sunset Ave, City of Industry (91744-3524)
PHONE.................................626 435-9211
Kristen Coleman, Office Mgr
EMP: 100
SALES (corp-wide): 45.9MM Privately Held
SIC: 1711 1731 Solar energy contractor; electrical work
PA: American Solar Direct Inc.
11766 Wilshire Blvd # 500
Los Angeles CA 90025
424 214-6700

(P-2141)
AMGREEN SOLAR AND ELECTRICS
1367 Venice Blvd, Los Angeles (90006-5519)
PHONE.................................213 388-5647
Minseon Ko, CEO
Sharon Ko, Administration
EMP: 50
SALES (est): 2.2MM Privately Held
SIC: 1711 1731 Solar energy contractor; lighting contractor

(P-2142)
AMPAM PARKS MECHANICAL INC
1060 N Wilmington Blvd, Wilmington (90742-3207)
PHONE.................................310 835-1532
Charles E Parks III, CEO
James C Wright, CFO
John D Parks, Vice Pres
Charles Parks, Info Tech Dir
Alfalfa Bargy, Project Mgr
▲ EMP: 800
SQ FT: 16,000
SALES (est): 158.5MM Privately Held
WEB: www.parksmechanical.com
SIC: 1711 Plumbing contractors

(P-2143)
AMS AMERICAN MECH SVCS MD INC
2116 E Walnut Ave, Fullerton (92831-4845)
PHONE.................................714 888-6820
Charles S Knight, General Mgr
EMP: 54
SALES (corp-wide): 2.8B Privately Held
SIC: 1711 Mechanical contractor
HQ: Ams American Mechanical Services Of Maryland, Inc.
13300 Mid Atlantic Blvd
Laurel MD 20708
301 206-5070

(P-2144)
ANDERSON ROWE & BUCKLEY INC
2833 3rd St, San Francisco (94107-3532)
PHONE.................................415 282-1625
Fax: 415 282-0752
Robert E Buckley III, President
Hans Raich, Corp Secy
Richard I Buckley Jr, Vice Pres
Darrin Sheridan, Manager
EMP: 95
SQ FT: 40,000
SALES (est): 24.9MM Privately Held
SIC: 1711 Plumbing, heating, air-conditioning contractors

(P-2145)
ANDERSON AIR CONDITIONING LP
2100 E Walnut Ave, Fullerton (92831-4845)
PHONE.................................714 998-6850
Fax: 714 888-2697
Edward Dunn, General Ptnr
Mitchell J Haynam, Partner
Melissa Stewart, General Mgr
Linda Luft, Human Res Mgr
EMP: 60
SALES (est): 12.8MM
SALES (corp-wide): 35.5MM Privately Held
SIC: 1711 Warm air heating & air conditioning contractor
PA: American Mechanical Services Of Maryland, L.L.C.
13300 Mid Atlantic Blvd
Laurel MD 20708
301 206-5070

(P-2146)
APEX MECHANICAL SYSTEMS INC
7440 Trade St Ste A, San Diego (92121-3412)
PHONE.................................858 536-8700
Fax: 858 536-8777
Randall E Melhouse, CEO
Edward Draper, Shareholder
Blaine Stratton, Shareholder
David R Draper, CFO
Kathy Draper, Admin Sec
EMP: 79
SALES (est): 18.3MM Privately Held
SIC: 1711 Mechanical contractor

(P-2147)
APPRENTICE & JOURNEYMEN TRAINI
7850 Haskell Ave, Van Nuys (91406-1907)
PHONE.................................818 464-4579
Leroy Riffel, Director
EMP: 99
SALES (est): 950K Privately Held
SIC: 1711 Plumbing contractors

(P-2148)
AQUALINE PIPING INC
Also Called: Plumbing
2108 Bering Dr Ste C, San Jose (95131-2029)
PHONE.................................408 745-7100
Joshua B Moores, CEO
Chrystal L Steele, Vice Pres
EMP: 75
SALES (est): 10.8MM Privately Held
SIC: 1711 7389 Plumbing, heating, air-conditioning contractors;

(P-2149)
ARISE CONSTRUCTION INC
Also Called: Arise Solar
5390 E Pine Ave, Fresno (93727-2113)
PHONE.................................559 449-8989
Paul Rutkowski, CEO
Glenn Siemens, CEO
Molly Wisser, Manager
EMP: 52
SALES (est): 6.7MM Privately Held
SIC: 1711 Solar energy contractor

(P-2150)
ARRAYCON LLC (PA)
1143 Blumenfeld Dr # 200, Sacramento (95815-3919)
PHONE.................................916 925-0201
Rick Lavezzo, Mng Member
Dan Hubiak,
Angela Lavezzo, Director
EMP: 50 EST: 2010
SQ FT: 50,000
SALES (est): 31.1MM Privately Held
SIC: 1711 8748 Solar energy contractor; business consulting

(P-2151)
ARS AMERICAN RESIDENTIAL (HQ)
Also Called: Southcoast Heating and Air
2373 La Mirada Dr, Vista (92081-7863)
PHONE.................................760 941-7000
Ed Dunn, President
EMP: 50

SQ FT: 18,000
SALES (est): 14.5MM
SALES (corp-wide): 37MM Privately Held
SIC: 1711 Warm air heating & air conditioning contractor
PA: American Mechanical Services Of Maryland, L.L.C.
13300 Mid Atlantic Blvd
Laurel MD 20708
301 206-5070

(P-2152)
ARTIC MECHANICAL INC (PA)
10440 Trademark St, Rancho Cucamonga (91730-5826)
PHONE.................................909 980-2539
Daniel Hallisey, President
Pattie Mackie, Controller
Megan Hallisey, Sales Staff
EMP: 77
SQ FT: 15,500
SALES (est): 22.7MM Privately Held
WEB: www.arcticmechanical.com
SIC: 1711 Heating & air conditioning contractors

(P-2153)
ASI HASTINGS INC
Also Called: Asi Heating, Air and Solar
4870 Vewridge Ave Ste 200, San Diego (92123)
PHONE.................................619 590-9300
Philip Justo, President
Kenneth Justo, Vice Pres
Maria Calcwin, General Mgr
EMP: 120
SQ FT: 2,000
SALES (est): 23MM Privately Held
WEB: www.asihastings.com
SIC: 1711 Plumbing, heating, air-conditioning contractors; solar energy contractor

(P-2154)
ASSOCIATE MECHANICAL CONTRS
622 S Vinewood St, Escondido (92029-1925)
PHONE.................................760 294-3517
Richard Reinholz, President
Laura Reinholz, Admin Sec
Jackie Vonbank, Admin Asst
Bob Chamberland, Project Mgr
Don Leidner, Project Mgr
EMP: 70
SALES (est): 20MM Privately Held
SIC: 1711 Plumbing, heating, air-conditioning contractors

(P-2155)
AYOOB & PEERY PLUMBING CO INC
975 Indiana St, San Francisco (94107-3007)
PHONE.................................415 550-0975
Fax: 415 550-0915
Peter Vincent McHugh, CEO
John Mangiante, Vice Pres
Lydia Lui, Office Mgr
Bud Lewis, Project Mgr
EMP: 80
SQ FT: 20,000
SALES (est): 17.2MM Privately Held
WEB: www.ayoobpeery.com
SIC: 1711 Mechanical contractor

(P-2156)
B Z PLUMBING COMPANY INC
1901 Aviation Blvd, Lincoln (95648-9557)
PHONE.................................916 645-1600
Fax: 916 645-1606
William J Zmrzel, President
Diane Zmrzel, Corp Secy
Carlie Nicodemus, Office Admin
Tom Brownell, Sales Mgr
Jennifer Todd, Director
EMP: 120
SQ FT: 12,000
SALES (est): 7.5MM Privately Held
WEB: www.bzplumbing.com
SIC: 1711 Plumbing contractors

1711 - Plumbing, Heating & Air Conditioning Contractors

(P-2157)
BAKERSFIELD KITCHEN & BATH
3529 Pegasus Dr, Bakersfield (93308-6856)
PHONE..................661 836-2284
Don Chminowski, *President*
Darryl Hubbard, *Manager*
EMP: 80
SALES (est): 3MM **Privately Held**
SIC: 1711 Plumbing contractors

(P-2158)
BARR ENGINEERING INC
12612 Clark St, Santa Fe Springs (90670-3950)
PHONE..................562 944-1722
Fax: 562 944-1343
Peter Buongiorno, *President*
Pamela Price-Recchia, *Corp Secy*
Mike Buongiorno, *Vice Pres*
Pamela Recchia, *Executive*
Dorothy Laney, *Technical Staff*
EMP: 82 **EST:** 1958
SQ FT: 12,200
SALES (est): 14.9MM **Privately Held**
WEB: www.barrengineering.com
SIC: 1711 Warm air heating & air conditioning contractor

(P-2159)
BAY CITY MECHANICAL INC
4124 Lakeside Dr, Richmond (94806-1941)
PHONE..................510 233-7000
Fax: 510 233-7042
Helge Theiss-Nyland, *President*
Bobbie Amos, *CFO*
Chris Cochrane, *Corp Secy*
Crystal Rougeau, *Admin Asst*
John Swahn, *VP Opers*
EMP: 150
SQ FT: 6,000
SALES (est): 33.5MM **Privately Held**
WEB: www.baycitymech.com
SIC: 1711 Heating & air conditioning contractors

(P-2160)
BAYVIEW ENGRG & CNSTR CO INC
5040 Rbert J Mathews Pkwy, El Dorado Hills (95762-5702)
PHONE..................916 939-8986
Robert Ellery, *CEO*
Pete Ellery, *Vice Pres*
Bart Wood, *Vice Pres*
EMP: 80
SQ FT: 6,000
SALES: 9MM **Privately Held**
SIC: 1711 8711 Boiler setting contractor; engineering services

(P-2161)
BDS PLUMBING INC
2125 Youngs Ct, Walnut Creek (94596-6319)
PHONE..................925 939-1004
Brett M Stom, *President*
Dawn L Stom, *Corp Secy*
EMP: 100
SQ FT: 400
SALES (est): 10.8MM **Privately Held**
SIC: 1711 Plumbing contractors

(P-2162)
BELL PRODUCTS INC
722 Soscol Ave, NAPA (94559-3014)
P.O. Box 396 (94559-0396)
PHONE..................707 255-1811
Fax: 707 255-1908
Paul D Irwin, *President*
Stan Foltz, *Corp Secy*
Boone Bell, *General Mgr*
Casey Clark, *Project Mgr*
Nichole Egger, *Project Mgr*
EMP: 74
SQ FT: 24,400
SALES: 20.3MM **Privately Held**
WEB: www.bellproducts.com
SIC: 1711 Ventilation & duct work contractor; warm air heating & air conditioning contractor; mechanical contractor

(P-2163)
BENICIA PLUMBING INC
265 W Channel Rd, Benicia (94510-1146)
P.O. Box 1095 (94510-4095)
PHONE..................707 745-2930
Fax: 707 745-0967
William J Cawley Jr, *CEO*
Doug Kuznik, *President*
Karen Ramey, *Corp Secy*
William J Cawley III, *Vice Pres*
Heidi Bucher, *Controller*
EMP: 55
SQ FT: 10,000
SALES (est): 13MM **Privately Held**
WEB: www.beniciaplumbing.com
SIC: 1711 Plumbing contractors

(P-2164)
BERNEL INC
Also Called: Vfs Fire Protection Services
501 W Southern Ave, Orange (92865-3217)
PHONE..................714 778-6070
Fax: 714 778-6090
Randy Roland Nelson, *CEO*
Kevin Berthoud, *Vice Pres*
EMP: 105
SQ FT: 7,800
SALES (est): 17.7MM **Privately Held**
SIC: 1711 7382 Fire sprinkler system installation; security systems services; fire alarm maintenance & monitoring

(P-2165)
BFP FIRE PROTECTION INC
17 Janis Way, Scotts Valley (95066-3537)
PHONE..................831 461-1100
Fax: 831 461-0433
Chris Amos, *President*
Rick Fischer, *CFO*
EMP: 60
SQ FT: 6,400
SALES (est): 14MM **Privately Held**
SIC: 1711 8711 Fire sprinkler system installation; engineering services

(P-2166)
BIANCHI PLUMBING CO INC
2130 March Rd Ste D, Roseville (95747-9309)
P.O. Box 417307, Sacramento (95841-7307)
PHONE..................916 772-7364
Paul Bianchi, *President*
Hubert Dampierre, *Treasurer*
Patrick Alexandre, *Exec VP*
Christian Boireau, *Exec VP*
Marc Boudier, *Exec VP*
EMP: 180
SQ FT: 10,000
SALES (est): 11.1MM **Privately Held**
WEB: www.bianchiplumbing.com
SIC: 1711 Plumbing contractors

(P-2167)
BILL HOWE PLUMBING INC
Also Called: Am-PM Sewer & Drain Cleaning
9085 Aero Dr Ste B, San Diego (92123-2378)
PHONE..................800 245-5469
Fax: 619 276-5022
William Howe, *President*
Tina Howe, *Vice Pres*
Hector Godinez, *Opers Spvr*
Bill Howe, *Opers Mgr*
Amber Baynard, *Marketing Staff*
EMP: 85
SQ FT: 21,000
SALES (est): 25.4MM **Privately Held**
WEB: www.billhowe.com
SIC: 1711 Plumbing contractors; septic system construction

(P-2168)
BLOCKA CONSTRUCTION INC
4455 Enterprise St, Fremont (94538-6306)
PHONE..................510 657-3686
Fax: 510 657-3688
Bob Blocka, *President*
Jean Blocka, *CFO*
Chad Blocka, *Project Mgr*
Danny Dang, *Project Mgr*
Lori Magruder, *Project Mgr*
EMP: 70
SQ FT: 7,300

SALES: 27.5MM **Privately Held**
WEB: www.blockainc.com
SIC: 1711 1731 Mechanical contractor; general electrical contractor

(P-2169)
BLUE MOUNTAIN CNSTR SVCS INC
Also Called: Blue Mountain Air
707 Aldridge Rd Ste B, Vacaville (95688-9561)
PHONE..................707 820-2323
Fax: 707 451-8111
Gregory S Owen, *President*
Jennifer Carollo, *Vice Pres*
Michael Spier, *Vice Pres*
Tina Miller, *General Mgr*
Vicki Nash, *Controller*
▲**EMP:** 200
SQ FT: 37,000
SALES (est): 80MM **Privately Held**
WEB: www.bluemountainair.net
SIC: 1711 Heating & air conditioning contractors

(P-2170)
BROADWAY MECH - CONTRS INC
873 81st Ave, Oakland (94621-2509)
PHONE..................510 746-4000
Fred Nurisso, *President*
Jill Demar, *Executive Asst*
Krystal Nzoiwu, *Admin Asst*
Frank Yankey, *Info Tech Dir*
Neil Hagge, *Design Engr*
EMP: 150
SALES (est): 51.1MM **Privately Held**
WEB: www.broadwaymechanical.com
SIC: 1711 Plumbing, heating, air-conditioning contractors

(P-2171)
C & L REFRIGERATION CORP
479 Nibus, Brea (92821-3204)
P.O. Box 2319 (92822-2319)
PHONE..................800 901-4822
Fax: 714 990-0605
Ronald J Cassell Jr, *CEO*
Larry Jaslove, *Vice Pres*
Denise Lowe, *Controller*
Margaret Cassell, *Manager*
Barbara Thompson, *Manager*
EMP: 150 **EST:** 1978
SQ FT: 18,000
SALES: 31.2MM **Privately Held**
SIC: 1711 Refrigeration contractor; warm air heating & air conditioning contractor

(P-2172)
CALIFORNIA COMFORT SYSTEMS USA
7740 Kenamar Ct, San Diego (92121-2425)
PHONE..................858 564-1100
Kenneth Hoving, *CEO*
Roger Well, *President*
William George, *Vice Pres*
Trent McKenna, *Vice Pres*
Bo Macaraeg, *General Mgr*
EMP: 399
SALES (est): 95.6MM
SALES (corp-wide): 1.5B **Publicly Held**
SIC: 1711 Heating & air conditioning contractors
PA: Comfort Systems Usa, Inc.
     675 Bering Dr Ste 400
     Houston TX 77057
     713 830-9600

(P-2173)
CALIFORNIA COML SOLAR INC
Also Called: Calcom Solar
635 S Atwood St, Visalia (93277-8302)
PHONE..................559 667-9200
Dylan Dupre, *CEO*
Jason Smith, *President*
Crystal Breshbars, *Accountant*
EMP: 56
SQ FT: 7,000
SALES (est): 18.9MM **Privately Held**
SIC: 1711 Solar energy contractor

(P-2174)
CALIFORNIA UNITED MECH INC (PA)
2185 Oakland Rd, San Jose (95131-1574)
PHONE..................408 232-9000
Tom Sosine, *CEO*
Dirk Durham, *Vice Chairman*
Jon Gundersen, *President*
Jerry Patterson, *CFO*
Blaine Flickner, *Vice Pres*
EMP: 330
SQ FT: 40,000
SALES (est): 93.5MM **Privately Held**
WEB: www.umi1.com
SIC: 1711 Mechanical contractor

(P-2175)
CAN-AM PLUMBING INC
151 Wyoming St, Pleasanton (94566-6277)
PHONE..................925 846-1833
Fax: 925 846-2243
Ronald Capilla, *President*
Karl Kyriss, *CFO*
Martin Ogara, *CFO*
Michael Capilla, *Vice Pres*
Rebecca Jose, *Human Res Mgr*
EMP: 250
SQ FT: 16,000
SALES (est): 13.2MM **Privately Held**
WEB: www.canamplumbing.com
SIC: 1711 Plumbing contractors

(P-2176)
CASPIAN COMMERCIAL PLBG INC
711 Ivy St, Glendale (91204-1003)
PHONE..................818 649-2500
Anahit Alexandrian, *President*
EMP: 65
SALES (est): 7.7MM **Privately Held**
SIC: 1711 Plumbing contractors

(P-2177)
CERTIFIED AIR CONDITIONING INC
7912 Armour St, San Diego (92111-3718)
PHONE..................858 292-5740
Fax: 858 292-0570
Brian Lynch, *President*
Terry Erickson, *Vice Pres*
Harold Meek, *Manager*
▲**EMP:** 150
SQ FT: 1,140
SALES: 13.6MM **Privately Held**
WEB: www.certifiedair.net
SIC: 1711 Warm air heating & air conditioning contractor

(P-2178)
CFP FIRE PROTECTION INC
17461 Derian Ave Ste 114, Irvine (92614-5820)
PHONE..................949 338-4280
Matt Krofcheck, *President*
Josh Hobgood, *Corp Secy*
EMP: 60
SQ FT: 2,000
SALES (est): 5.5MM
SALES (corp-wide): 400.9MM **Privately Held**
SIC: 1711 Plumbing, heating, air-conditioning contractors; fire sprinkler system installation
PA: Mx Holdings Us
     153 Technology Dr Ste 200
     Irvine CA 92618
     949 727-3277

(P-2179)
CH STONE PLUMBING CO INC
Also Called: C H Stone
13170 Spring St, Baldwin Park (91706-2284)
PHONE..................626 962-5001
Fax: 626 962-5505
David K Dean, *CEO*
Nancy Brink, *Shareholder*
Sharon Yokaitis, *Shareholder*
Joseph Saenz, *Vice Pres*
Linda S Collins, *Admin Sec*
EMP: 55 **EST:** 1948
SQ FT: 9,500
SALES (est): 5.8MM **Privately Held**
WEB: www.chstone.com
SIC: 1711 Plumbing contractors

1711 - Plumbing, Heating & Air Conditioning Contractors County (P-2180)

(P-2180)
CIRCULATING AIR INC (PA)
7337 Varna Ave, North Hollywood (91605-4009)
PHONE.................................818 764-0530
Fax: 818 982-2571
Joseph Gallagher, *CEO*
Susan Gallagher, *President*
Marcy Ahlstrom, *CFO*
Pudlewski Mike, *CIO*
Tom Crossman, *Info Tech Dir*
EMP: 100
SQ FT: 13,000
SALES (est): 38.5MM **Privately Held**
WEB: www.circulatingair.com
SIC: 1711 Mechanical contractor

(P-2181)
CITYWIDE PLUMBING HEATING
9825 Carroll Centre Rd, San Diego (92126-6508)
PHONE.................................619 231-2022
John Taylor, *Principal*
EMP: 50
SALES (est): 5.6MM **Privately Held**
SIC: 1711 Plumbing, heating, air-conditioning contractors

(P-2182)
CLAY DUNN ENTERPRISES INC
Also Called: Air-TEC
1606 E Carson St, Carson (90745-2504)
P.O. Box 5444 (90749-5444)
PHONE.................................310 549-1698
Fax: 310 549-8329
Clayton N Dunn, *President*
Ladonna Troullier, *Admin Asst*
Drew Mallad, *Info Tech Mgr*
Allan Ford, *Project Mgr*
Mary L Hufeld, *Project Mgr*
EMP: 120
SALES (est): 29.1MM **Privately Held**
WEB: www.airtecperforms.com
SIC: 1711 Warm air heating & air conditioning contractor

(P-2183)
CMA FIRE PROTECTION (PA)
Also Called: Rlh Fire Protection
4300 Stine Rd Ste 800, Bakersfield (93313-2354)
P.O. Box 42470 (93384-2470)
PHONE.................................661 322-9344
Terrence J Olson, *CEO*
Michael Hardcastle, *Ch of Bd*
Jason Norton, *President*
Margaret McCarty, *Treasurer*
Clifford Arthurs, *Vice Pres*
EMP: 75
SQ FT: 8,000
SALES (est): 31.8MM **Privately Held**
WEB: www.rlhfp.com
SIC: 1711 1542 Fire sprinkler system installation; nonresidential construction

(P-2184)
COAST WEST PLUMBING INC
182 E Liberty Ave Ste A, Anaheim (92801-1020)
PHONE.................................714 446-8686
Fax: 714 446-8989
Dennis Burk, *President*
Linda Burk, *Vice Pres*
Gregg Groves, *Vice Pres*
David Keffe, *Vice Pres*
Bob Haggard, *Manager*
▲ **EMP:** 135
SQ FT: 8,000
SALES (est): 6.6MM **Privately Held**
SIC: 1711 Plumbing contractors

(P-2185)
COMFORT AIR INC
1607 French Camp Tpke, Stockton (95206-1960)
P.O. Box 1969 (95201-1969)
PHONE.................................209 466-4601
Fax: 209 466-2639
Steven J Evans, *President*
Gregory A Gaut, *Vice Pres*
Paulette Gaut, *Admin Sec*
Lawburn Nixon, *Manager*
EMP: 75 **EST:** 1946
SQ FT: 7,000
SALES: 11MM **Privately Held**
WEB: www.comfortairinc.com
SIC: 1711 Warm air heating & air conditioning contractor

(P-2186)
COMFORT SYSTEMS USA INC
4189 Santa Ana St Ste D, Ontario (91761-1557)
PHONE.................................909 390-6677
Joe Nichter, *Branch Mgr*
EMP: 83
SALES (corp-wide): 1.5B **Publicly Held**
SIC: 1711 Plumbing, heating, air-conditioning contractors
PA: Comfort Systems Usa, Inc.
675 Bering Dr Ste 400
Houston TX 77057
713 830-9600

(P-2187)
COMFORT SYSTEMS USA INC
5056 Coml Cir Ste E, Concord (94520)
PHONE.................................925 827-0578
Don Meixsell, *Branch Mgr*
EMP: 83
SALES (corp-wide): 1.5B **Publicly Held**
SIC: 1711 Plumbing, heating, air-conditioning contractors
PA: Comfort Systems Usa, Inc.
675 Bering Dr Ste 400
Houston TX 77057
713 830-9600

(P-2188)
CONFORTI PLUMBING INC
6080 Pleasant Valley Rd C, El Dorado (95623-4257)
P.O. Box 1090 (95623-1090)
PHONE.................................530 622-0202
Marvin Collins, *President*
Jan Zygalinski, *CFO*
EMP: 1020
SQ FT: 1,000
SALES (est): 65.8MM **Privately Held**
WEB: www.confortiplumbing.com
SIC: 1711 Plumbing contractors

(P-2189)
CONTROL AIR CONDITIONING CORP (PA)
5200 E La Palma Ave, Anaheim (92807-2019)
PHONE.................................714 777-8600
Fax: 714 777-8631
Kendrick Ellis, *President*
Eileen Ellis, *Corp Secy*
Stan Ellis, *Vice Pres*
Mike Pence, *Vice Pres*
Mike Mulree, *Project Mgr*
EMP: 150 **EST:** 1978
SALES (est): 103.2MM **Privately Held**
WEB: www.controlaircorp.com
SIC: 1711 Warm air heating & air conditioning contractor

(P-2190)
CONTROL AIR CONDITIONING SVC
5200 E La Palma Ave, Anaheim (92807-2019)
PHONE.................................714 777-8600
Kendrick Ellis, *President*
Greg Rummler, *CFO*
Stanley Ellis, *Vice Pres*
George Scholten, *Principal*
EMP: 51
SALES (est): 4.3MM **Privately Held**
SIC: 1711 Plumbing, heating, air-conditioning contractors

(P-2191)
COREY DELTA CONSTRUCTORS INC
261 Arthur Rd, Fairfield (94533)
PHONE.................................925 370-9808
John T Weatherford, *CEO*
Jake Witkowski, *Safety Mgr*
Dave Markham, *Manager*
EMP: 88
SALES (est): 5.4MM
SALES (corp-wide): 56MM **Privately Held**
SIC: 1711 Mechanical contractor
PA: U.C.I. Construction, Inc.
261 Arthur Rd
Martinez CA 94553
800 245-6750

(P-2192)
COSCO FIRE PROTECTION INC
1075 W Lambert Rd Ste D, Brea (92821-2944)
PHONE.................................714 989-1800
Barry Fielding, *Branch Mgr*
Editha Ajero, *Manager*
EMP: 193
SALES (corp-wide): 400.9MM **Privately Held**
SIC: 1711 Fire sprinkler system installation
HQ: Cosco Fire Protection, Inc.
29222 Rancho Viejo Rd # 205
San Juan Capistrano CA 92675
714 974-8770

(P-2193)
COUNTYWIDE MECH SYSTEMS INC
1400 N Johnson Ave # 114, El Cajon (92020-1651)
PHONE.................................619 449-9900
Paul Duke, *President*
David Cimpl, *CFO*
Mike McDowell, *Exec VP*
Celeste Recchia, *Info Tech Mgr*
Robert Nelson, *Project Mgr*
EMP: 136
SQ FT: 5,000
SALES (est): 52.8MM
SALES (corp-wide): 523.3MM **Privately Held**
SIC: 1711 Plumbing, heating, air-conditioning contractors
HQ: Payne & Jones
100 King
Overland Park KS 66225
913 469-4100

(P-2194)
COUTS HEATING & COOLING INC
1693 Rimpau Ave, Corona (92881-3202)
PHONE.................................951 278-5560
Jeff Lemke, *Branch Mgr*
EMP: 62
SALES (corp-wide): 26.6MM **Privately Held**
SIC: 1711 Heating & air conditioning contractors
PA: Couts Heating & Cooling, Inc.
1693 Rimpau Ave
Corona CA 92881
951 278-5560

(P-2195)
CRITCHFELD MECH INC STHERN CAL
1821 Mcgaw Ave, Irvine (92614-5733)
PHONE.................................949 390-2900
Mike Pearlman, *CEO*
EMP: 100
SALES: 27MM **Privately Held**
SIC: 1711 Warm air heating & air conditioning contractor

(P-2196)
CRITCHFIELD MECHANICAL INC
4085 Campbell Ave, Menlo Park (94025-1006)
PHONE.................................650 321-7801
Fax: 650 321-1798
Joe Critchfield, *Chairman*
Jason Tran, *Project Engr*
Kevin Fielding, *Sr Project Mgr*
EMP: 409
SALES (corp-wide): 222.1MM **Privately Held**
SIC: 1711 Mechanical contractor
PA: Critchfield Mechanical, Inc.
1901 Junction Ave
San Jose CA 95131
408 437-7000

(P-2197)
CYPRESS CREEK HOLDINGS LLC
3250 Ocean Park Blvd, Santa Monica (90405-3208)
PHONE.................................310 581-6299
Matthew McGovern,
Jon Buttles,
EMP: 100
SALES (est): 2.1MM **Privately Held**
SIC: 1711 Solar energy contractor

(P-2198)
D & J PLUMBING INC
4341 Winters St, Sacramento (95838-3031)
PHONE.................................916 922-4888
Fax: 916 922-3437
Steve Waldron, *President*
Geri Richards, *Shareholder*
John Richards, *Shareholder*
Randy Golden, *Vice Pres*
EMP: 100
SQ FT: 5,000
SALES (est): 10.1MM **Privately Held**
SIC: 1711 Plumbing contractors

(P-2199)
D W NICHOLSON CORPORATION (PA)
24747 Clawiter Rd, Hayward (94545-2225)
P.O. Box 4197 (94540-4197)
PHONE.................................510 887-0900
Fax: 510 783-5736
John L Nicholson, *Principal*
Kevin Fleckenstein, *Vice Pres*
Anne Curtis, *Executive Asst*
Lisa Kaloostian, *Admin Asst*
Gonzalo Alliende, *Project Mgr*
EMP: 132
SQ FT: 12,000
SALES (est): 49.1MM **Privately Held**
WEB: www.dwnicholson.com
SIC: 1711 1731 8711 1796 Mechanical contractor; general electrical contractor; engineering services; millwright; residential construction; industrial buildings & warehouses

(P-2200)
D/K MECHANICAL CONTRACTORS INC
3870 E Eagle Dr, Anaheim (92807-1706)
PHONE.................................714 970-0180
Fax: 714 630-8989
Gary Brubaker, *President*
Don Giarratano, *Vice Pres*
Donald Warner, *Technical Staff*
EMP: 200
SALES (est): 18.7MM **Privately Held**
WEB: www.dkmechanical.com
SIC: 1711 Plumbing contractors; warm air heating & air conditioning contractor

(P-2201)
DAART ENGINEERING COMPANY INC
1598 N H St, San Bernardino (92405-4318)
PHONE.................................909 888-8696
Fax: 909 888-9626
Timothy C Cantwell, *President*
James D Dunn, *Corp Secy*
Robert Pfeifer, *Admin Sec*
Deanne Page, *Controller*
EMP: 70
SQ FT: 8,000
SALES: 8.3MM **Privately Held**
WEB: www.daarteng.com
SIC: 1711 Fire sprinkler system installation

(P-2202)
DAVID SHAPOSHNICK INC
1787 Savannah Way, San Marcos (92069-9526)
P.O. Box 1567 (92079-1567)
PHONE.................................760 758-6090
Arlene Shaposhnick, *President*
David Shaposhnick, *Vice Pres*
Jeff Shaposhnick, *Vice Pres*
EMP: 60
SQ FT: 8,000
SALES (est): 5.9MM **Privately Held**
WEB: www.shaposhnick.com
SIC: 1711 Plumbing contractors

1711 - Plumbing, Heating & Air Conditioning Contractors County (P-2227)

(P-2203)
DC SOLAR SOLUTIONS INC
4901 Park Rd, Benicia (94510-1190)
PHONE.....................925 203-1088
Jeffrey Paul Carpoff, *President*
EMP: 50
SALES (est): 11.6MM **Privately Held**
SIC: 1711 Solar energy contractor

(P-2204)
DE HART PLUMBING HTG & A INC
311 Bitritto Way, Modesto (95356-9292)
PHONE.....................209 523-4578
Fax: 209 523-4587
Rod Dehart, *President*
Gary Johnson, *Administration*
Eric Fleck, *Project Mgr*
Eric Drobnick, *Controller*
Jeff Painter, *Director*
EMP: 50
SALES: 9.7MM **Privately Held**
WEB: www.dehartinc.com
SIC: 1711 Plumbing contractors

(P-2205)
DESERT MECHANICAL INC
Also Called: Dmi
15870 Olden St, Sylmar (91342-1241)
PHONE.....................702 873-7333
Fax: 818 362-0866
Casey M Condron, *President*
Joseph Guglielmo, *Senior VP*
Andre Burnthon, *Vice Pres*
Alex L Hodson, *Vice Pres*
Dan Naylor, *Vice Pres*
EMP: 1100
SQ FT: 25,000
SALES: 43.4MM
SALES (corp-wide): 4.9B **Publicly Held**
WEB: www.lvdph.com
SIC: 1711 Plumbing contractors
PA: Tutor Perini Corporation
   15901 Olden St
   Sylmar CA 91342
   818 362-8391

(P-2206)
DON BRANDEL PLUMBING INC
15100 Texaco Ave, Paramount (90723-3916)
PHONE.....................562 408-0400
Fax: 562 633-5129
Greg Brandel, *President*
Dennis Castaldo, *Exec VP*
Jim Brandel, *Vice Pres*
Charron Castaldo, *Admin Sec*
Catherine Taylor, *Controller*
EMP: 50
SQ FT: 20,000
SALES (est): 10.6MM **Privately Held**
WEB: www.brandelplumbing.com
SIC: 1711 Plumbing contractors

(P-2207)
DONALD P DICK AC INC (PA)
Also Called: Mr Cool
1444 N Whitney Ave, Fresno (93703-4513)
PHONE.....................559 255-1644
Fax: 559 255-0598
James B Dick, *President*
David B Dick, *Vice Pres*
Jennifer Perea, *Office Admin*
Jeffrey Dick, *Admin Sec*
Bill Hanner, *VP Sales*
EMP: 50
SQ FT: 30,000
SALES (est): 13.1MM **Privately Held**
WEB: www.mrcool4ac.com
SIC: 1711 Warm air heating & air conditioning contractor

(P-2208)
DRAIN DOCTOR
480 Aldo Ave, Santa Clara (95054-2304)
PHONE.....................408 970-3800
John Lin, *President*
Chris Choi, *Human Res Mgr*
EMP: 50
SALES (est): 4.2MM **Privately Held**
SIC: 1711 8748 Plumbing contractors; business consulting

(P-2209)
DRAIN PATROL
7764 Arjons Dr, San Diego (92126-4391)
PHONE.....................858 560-1137
Scot Buck, *Manager*
EMP: 64
SALES (est): 5.3MM **Privately Held**
SIC: 1711 1623 Plumbing contractors; sewer line construction

(P-2210)
DYNAMIC PLUMBING COMMERCIAL
7343 Orangewood Dr Ste B, Riverside (92504-1053)
PHONE.....................951 343-1200
Thomas L Baker, *President*
EMP: 84
SALES (est): 8.3MM **Privately Held**
SIC: 1711 Plumbing, heating, air-conditioning contractors

(P-2211)
DYNAMIC PLUMBING SYSTEMS INC
5920 Winterhaven Ave, Riverside (92504-1048)
PHONE.....................951 343-1200
Fax: 951 270-0795
Thomas L Baker, *CEO*
Daisy Duncan, *Accounting Mgr*
Brenda Fieri, *Manager*
EMP: 306 EST: 1999
SQ FT: 33,000
SALES (est): 42.6MM **Privately Held**
SIC: 1711 Plumbing, heating, air-conditioning contractors

(P-2212)
E L PAYNE HEATING COMPANY
Also Called: Payne, E L Company
226 S Lucerne Blvd, Los Angeles (90004-3727)
PHONE.....................310 275-5331
Gordon Payne Jr, *President*
Gordon Payne Sr, *Ch of Bd*
EMP: 50
SQ FT: 1,200
SALES (est): 4.9MM **Privately Held**
SIC: 1711 Heating & air conditioning contractors

(P-2213)
EAGLE SYSTEMS INTL INC
Also Called: Synergy Companies
28436 Satellite St, Hayward (94545-4863)
PHONE.....................510 259-1700
Steven R Shallenberger, *President*
Russell Jacobsen, *CFO*
David C Price, *General Mgr*
Rebecca McCafferty, *Office Mgr*
Eleanor Urive, *Office Mgr*
EMP: 325
SQ FT: 6,962
SALES (est): 30.9MM **Privately Held**
SIC: 1711 1731 1742 1793 Plumbing, heating, air-conditioning contractors; general electrical contractor; plastering, drywall & insulation; glass & glazing work

(P-2214)
ECONO AIR CONDITIONING INC
3366 E La Palma Ave, Anaheim (92806-2814)
PHONE.....................714 630-3090
Mike Richard, *CEO*
EMP: 50
SALES (est): 2MM **Privately Held**
SIC: 1711 Warm air heating & air conditioning contractor

(P-2215)
EDGEWATER PLUMBING OF BENICIA
5143 Port Chicago Hwy, Concord (94520-1207)
PHONE.....................707 747-9204
Fax: 707 747-0861
Richard M Klauber, *Ch of Bd*
Steve Wilkerson, *President*
Lisa Wilkerson, *Corp Secy*
EMP: 50
SQ FT: 12,000

SALES (est): 5.5MM **Privately Held**
SIC: 1711 6531 Plumbing contractors; real estate leasing & rentals

(P-2216)
ELECNOR INC
4331 Schaefer Ave, Chino (91710-5451)
PHONE.....................909 993-5470
Jose Castellanos, *CEO*
Alberto Garcia, *Vice Pres*
Ivan Guillermo Ballesteros, *Principal*
Mathew Steinbacher, *Project Mgr*
Leonardo Sancho, *Engineer*
▲ EMP: 422 EST: 2003
SQ FT: 5,000
SALES (est): 29MM
SALES (corp-wide): 12.7MM **Privately Held**
SIC: 1711 Solar energy contractor
HQ: Elecnor Sa
   Calle Marques De Mondejar 33
   Madrid 28028
   914 179-900

(P-2217)
EMCOR FCLITIES SVCS N AMER INC
9505 Chesapeake Dr, San Diego (92123-1304)
PHONE.....................858 712-4700
David Rastolich, *Vice Pres*
Sam Luk, *Project Leader*
Ted Donald, *Project Mgr*
EMP: 230
SALES (corp-wide): 6.7B **Publicly Held**
SIC: 1711 Heating & air conditioning contractors
HQ: Emcor Facilities Services Of North America, Inc.
   306 Northern Ave Ste 5
   Boston MA 02210
   617 482-0100

(P-2218)
ENERGY ENTERPRISES USA INC
Also Called: Canopy Energy
6736 Vesper Ave, Van Nuys (91405-4635)
PHONE.....................424 339-0005
Lior Agam, *CEO*
Heather Pollock, *Project Mgr*
EMP: 100
SQ FT: 6,000
SALES: 50MM **Privately Held**
SIC: 1711 Solar energy contractor

(P-2219)
ENERGY STORE OF CALIFORNIA INC
Also Called: Qc Wall Systems
14958 Venado Dr, Rancho Murieta (95683-9322)
PHONE.....................916 825-8751
Dennis M Barsam, *President*
W Joe Mitchell, *Vice Pres*
Ashley Harrower, *Managing Dir*
Janell Christian, *Controller*
EMP: 100
SALES: 3.5MM **Privately Held**
SIC: 1711 1742 Heating & air conditioning contractors; drywall

(P-2220)
ENVIRONMENTAL SYSTEMS INC (PA)
3353 De La Cruz Blvd, Santa Clara (95054-2633)
PHONE.....................408 980-1711
Fax: 408 980-0714
V C Enfantino, *President*
Patricia Enfantino, *Vice Pres*
Tracey Enfantino, *General Mgr*
Lisa Enfantino, *Office Mgr*
Eugene L Enfantino, *Admin Sec*
EMP: 85
SQ FT: 13,800
SALES: 26.2MM **Privately Held**
SIC: 1711 7623 3444 Mechanical contractor; ventilation & duct work contractor; plumbing contractors; refrigeration service & repair; sheet metalwork

(P-2221)
ESS LLC
Also Called: Evergreen Solar Services
23151 Alcalde Dr Ste C1, Laguna Hills (92653-1460)
PHONE.....................888 303-6424
Jacob Stephens, *President*
EMP: 100
SALES: 30.8MM **Privately Held**
SIC: 1711 Solar energy contractor

(P-2222)
F J HOOVER PLUMBING INC
Also Called: Pipeline Plumbing
2259 Hamner Ave, Norco (92860-2608)
PHONE.....................951 360-8262
Pamela Reno-Kemp, *President*
Hank Kemp, *Vice Pres*
James Dean Potts, *Principal*
EMP: 53
SQ FT: 1,500
SALES (est): 4.9MM **Privately Held**
SIC: 1711 Plumbing contractors

(P-2223)
FAMAND INC
1604 Airport Blvd, Santa Rosa (95403-8204)
PHONE.....................707 255-9295
Charlie Butts, *Branch Mgr*
Stan Butts, *President*
Walt Yocum, *Vice Pres*
EMP: 76
SALES (corp-wide): 40.4MM **Privately Held**
SIC: 1711 Plumbing, heating, air-conditioning contractors
PA: Famand, Inc.
   1512 Silica Ave
   Sacramento CA 95815
   916 988-8808

(P-2224)
FAULT LINE PLUMBING
7640 National Dr, Livermore (94550-8809)
PHONE.....................925 443-6450
Fax: 925 443-6650
Sean Collins, *President*
Karrie Collins, *Corp Secy*
Milani Lindgren, *Manager*
EMP: 50
SALES (est): 8.3MM **Privately Held**
SIC: 1711 Plumbing contractors

(P-2225)
FERREIRA SERVICE INC (PA)
2600 Old Crow Canyon Rd # 100, San Ramon (94583-1660)
PHONE.....................925 831-9330
Fax: 510 783-3375
Susan Ferreira, *CEO*
Albert Ferreira, *President*
Raymond Ferreira, *COO*
EMP: 65
SQ FT: 10,000
SALES (est): 10.3MM **Privately Held**
WEB: www.ferreira.com
SIC: 1711 Mechanical contractor

(P-2226)
FIDELITY HOME ENERGY INC (PA)
2235 Polvorosa Ave # 230, San Leandro (94577-2249)
PHONE.....................858 220-7784
Bradley A Smith, *CEO*
Cary Williams, *Accounting Mgr*
Hall Lunde, *Controller*
Terri Rivers, *Human Res Dir*
Scott Johnson, *Marketing Mgr*
EMP: 73
SQ FT: 12,000
SALES: 20.7MM **Privately Held**
WEB: www.thesungate.com
SIC: 1711 1522 Solar energy contractor; remodeling, multi-family dwellings

(P-2227)
FIRE SPRINKLER SYSTEMS INC (PA)
705 E Harrison St Ste 200, Corona (92879-1398)
P.O. Box 2378 (92878-2378)
PHONE.....................951 688-0336
Fax: 909 272-2535

1711 - Plumbing, Heating & Air Conditioning Contractors County (P-2228)

PRODUCTS & SERVICES SECTION

Harold Roger, *President*
Michael Kerby, *CFO*
Fernando Lescano, *Engineer*
Ralph Tolomei, *Controller*
Jackson Maley, *Manager*
EMP: 89
SALES (est): 28.1MM **Privately Held**
WEB: www.fireinc.net
SIC: 1711 Fire sprinkler system installation

(P-2228)
FISCHER INC
1372 W 26th St, San Bernardino (92405-3029)
PHONE...................909 881-2910
Fax: 909 881-5761
Michael G Fischer, *President*
EMP: 70
SQ FT: 1,600
SALES (est): 8.7MM **Privately Held**
SIC: 1711 Plumbing contractors

(P-2229)
FRESCHI AIR SYSTEMS INC
Also Called: Freschi Service Experts
715 Fulton Shipyard Rd, Antioch (94509-7557)
PHONE...................925 827-9761
Fax: 925 754-2352
John R Freschi Jr, *President*
EMP: 55
SQ FT: 5,000
SALES (est): 6.7MM
SALES (corp-wide): 317.8MM **Privately Held**
WEB: www.lennoxinternational.com
SIC: 1711 3444 Warm air heating & air conditioning contractor; sheet metalwork
HQ: Service Experts Llc
   3820 American Dr Ste 200
   Plano TX 75075

(P-2230)
FRESNO PLUMBING & HEATING INC (PA)
Also Called: Ace Hardware
2585 N Larkin Ave, Fresno (93727-1357)
PHONE...................559 294-0200
Fax: 559 294-0300
Larry Kumpe, *CEO*
Dean Kumpe, *Corp Secy*
Dalon Hankins, *Systs Prg Mgr*
Dave Holman, *Project Mgr*
Marilyn Lulejian, *Bookkeeper*
EMP: 180
SQ FT: 20,000
SALES (est): 24.7MM **Privately Held**
WEB: www.fphinc.com
SIC: 1711 5251 Plumbing contractors; hardware; door locks & lock sets; tools, hand; tools, power

(P-2231)
FRONTIER MECHANICAL INC
Also Called: Frontier Plumbing
6309 Seven Seas Ave, Bakersfield (93308-5133)
PHONE...................661 589-6203
Fax: 661 589-8220
Rick Palmer, *President*
Brenda Palmer, *Shareholder*
Debbie Caywood, *Admin Mgr*
Cathy Johnson, *Administration*
EMP: 93
SQ FT: 120,000
SALES (est): 14.4MM **Privately Held**
WEB: www.frontier-plumbing.com
SIC: 1711 1521 Plumbing, heating, air-conditioning contractors; new construction, single-family houses

(P-2232)
FW SPENCER & SON INC
Also Called: Brisbane Mechanical
99 S Hill Dr, Brisbane (94005-1274)
PHONE...................415 468-5000
Fax: 415 648-4579
William D Spencer, *President*
Virgina Sevilla, *CFO*
Andrew Anderson, *Vice Pres*
Kevin Coyne, *Vice Pres*
Dan Everett, *Vice Pres*
EMP: 200
SQ FT: 140,000
SALES (est): 38.6MM **Privately Held**
SIC: 1711 Plumbing contractors; warm air heating & air conditioning contractor

(P-2233)
GCL SOLAR ENERGY INC
1 Market St Steuart To, San Francisco (94105)
PHONE...................415 362-2601
Peng Fang, *CEO*
Mac Moore, *Business Dir*
Emma Ye, *Admin Sec*
Esther Clayson, *Human Res Dir*
K Pickering, *Human Resources*
▲ **EMP:** 54
SALES (est): 9.2MM **Privately Held**
SIC: 1711 Solar energy contractor
PA: Gcl Solar Energy Technology Holdings Limited
   Rm 1703b-1706 17/F International Commerce Ctr
   Tsim Sha Tsui KLN
   252 683-68

(P-2234)
GENEA ENERGY PARTNERS INC
2600 Michelson Dr Ste 720, Irvine (92612-6527)
PHONE...................714 694-0536
Jon Haahr, *Chairman*
David Balkin, *President*
Joseph Nugent, *President*
Keith Voysey, *CEO*
Michal Pasula, *CFO*
EMP: 85
SQ FT: 10,000
SALES (est): 7.8MM **Privately Held**
WEB: geneaenergy.com
SIC: 1711 Mechanical contractor

(P-2235)
GENERAL ENGINEERING WSTN INC (PA)
Also Called: Thermal Air
1140 N Red Gum St, Anaheim (92806-2516)
PHONE...................714 630-3200
Stephen Weiss, *CEO*
Joseph Urban, *President*
Roger C Pettitt, *Agent*
EMP: 60
SQ FT: 10,000
SALES (est): 12.1MM **Privately Held**
SIC: 1711 Heating & air conditioning contractors; ventilation & duct work contractor

(P-2236)
GENERAL UNDERGROUND
701 W Grove Ave, Orange (92865-3213)
P.O. Box 29830, Anaheim (92809-0194)
PHONE...................714 632-8646
Fax: 714 632-0579
Robert Anderson, *CEO*
Terry Householder, *President*
Karla Distrola, *Vice Pres*
Carol Sallivan, *Admin Sec*
EMP: 110
SQ FT: 8,000
SALES (est): 18.3MM **Privately Held**
WEB: www.gufpinc.com
SIC: 1711 Fire sprinkler system installation

(P-2237)
GEO H WILSON INC
250 Harvey West Blvd, Santa Cruz (95060-2127)
P.O. Box 1140 (95061-1140)
PHONE...................831 423-9522
Fax: 831 423-9903
James E Wilson, *CEO*
Richard J Wilson, *President*
Thomas G Akrop, *Treasurer*
Thomas E Wilson, *Vice Pres*
Tom Lackovic, *Info Tech Dir*
EMP: 85
SQ FT: 37,000
SALES (est): 25.5MM **Privately Held**
SIC: 1711 Plumbing, heating, air-conditioning contractors

(P-2238)
GEORGE M ROBINSON & CO (PA)
1461 Atteberry Ln, San Jose (95131-1409)
PHONE...................510 632-7017
Fax: 510 638-5466
John P Joyce, *President*
Ned Raudsep, *Treasurer*
Dick Goranson, *VP Sales*
EMP: 100
SQ FT: 20,000
SALES (est): 6.2MM **Privately Held**
WEB: www.geomrobinson.com
SIC: 1711 3498 Fire sprinkler system installation; fabricated pipe & fittings

(P-2239)
GRAYCON INC
232 S 8th Ave, City of Industry (91746-3200)
PHONE...................626 961-9640
Fax: 626 961-9041
Joseph F Klein, *CEO*
Miles Felix, *Controller*
Maria J Schaeffer, *Controller*
Sharon Payne, *Manager*
EMP: 50
SQ FT: 12,000
SALES (est): 9MM **Privately Held**
WEB: www.graycon.net
SIC: 1711 Ventilation & duct work contractor; warm air heating & air conditioning contractor

(P-2240)
GREATER SAN DIEGO AC CO INC
3883 Ruffin Rd Ste C, San Diego (92123-4813)
PHONE...................619 469-7818
Randy Baillargeon, *President*
Vanessa Tantay, *Manager*
Sazanne Hirko, *Accounts Mgr*
EMP: 52
SQ FT: 8,500
SALES (est): 11.5MM **Privately Held**
WEB: www.gsdac.com
SIC: 1711 Heating & air conditioning contractors; ventilation & duct work contractor

(P-2241)
GROWITH INC
Also Called: Mr Rooter
1069 Camero Way, Fremont (94539-3785)
PHONE...................805 650-6650
Aung Oo, *CEO*
EMP: 68
SALES (est): 2.1MM **Privately Held**
SIC: 1711 Plumbing contractors

(P-2242)
H L MOE CO INC (PA)
Also Called: Keefe Plumbing Services
526 Commercial St, Glendale (91203-2861)
PHONE...................818 572-2100
Fax: 818 240-1844
Martha Tennyson, *CEO*
Michael C Davis, *President*
Robert Francis, *Vice Pres*
Jeff Hachey, *Vice Pres*
Richard Herrea, *Vice Pres*
EMP: 130
SALES (est): 48.4MM **Privately Held**
WEB: www.hlmoeco.com
SIC: 1711 Plumbing contractors

(P-2243)
HALDEMAN INC
2937 Tanager Ave, Commerce (90040-2761)
PHONE...................323 726-7011
Tom Haldeman, *Ch of Bd*
Mark O Donnell, *President*
Jeff Dandridge, *CFO*
Sue Haldeman, *Treasurer*
Holt Dandridge, *Vice Pres*
EMP: 50
SQ FT: 45,000
SALES (est): 3.8MM **Privately Held**
WEB: www.haldeman.com
SIC: 1711 Mechanical contractor

(P-2244)
HELIOPOWER (PA)
25747 Jefferson Ave, Murrieta (92562-6903)
PHONE...................951 677-7755
Ian Rogoff, *Ch of Bd*
Roy Douglas, *President*
Scott Gordon, *CEO*
MO Rousso, *COO*
Vicki Zelfer, *Treasurer*
EMP: 75
SQ FT: 11,500
SALES (est): 33.1MM **Privately Held**
SIC: 1711 Solar energy contractor

(P-2245)
HORIZON SOLAR POWER INC
3570 W Florida Ave, Hemet (92545-3518)
PHONE...................844 765-2780
Zachary Allman, *Manager*
EMP: 82
SALES (corp-wide): 21.2MM **Privately Held**
SIC: 1711 Solar energy contractor
PA: Horizon Solar Power, Inc.
   7100 W Florida Ave
   Hemet CA 92545
   951 926-1176

(P-2246)
HPS MECHANICAL INC (PA)
3100 E Belle Ter, Bakersfield (93307-6830)
PHONE...................661 397-2121
Les Denherder, *President*
Scott Denherder, *Vice Pres*
Chad Kinsey, *Associate Dir*
Jamie Ramos, *Executive Asst*
Renee Denesha, *Administration*
EMP: 130
SALES (est): 32MM **Privately Held**
SIC: 1711 Plumbing contractors

(P-2247)
HUMPHREY PLUMBING INC
880 S Kilroy Rd, Turlock (95380-9570)
PHONE...................209 634-4626
Fax: 209 667-2457
Justin Humphrey, *President*
Robin Humphrey, *Corp Secy*
EMP: 75
SQ FT: 7,500
SALES (est): 9.5MM **Privately Held**
SIC: 1711 Plumbing contractors

(P-2248)
ICOM MECHANICAL INC
477 Burke St, San Jose (95112-4101)
P.O. Box 975 (95108-0975)
PHONE...................408 292-4968
Fax: 408 292-4968
Donald George Isaacson, *CEO*
Dane Littleton, *President*
Elizabeth Wozniak, *CFO*
Missy Cain, *Senior VP*
Alan Glace, *Vice Pres*
EMP: 225
SQ FT: 24,000
SALES (est): 59.9MM **Privately Held**
WEB: www.icominc.com
SIC: 1711 Plumbing, heating, air-conditioning contractors; mechanical contractor

(P-2249)
INCOM MECHANICAL INC
975 Transport Way Ste 5, Petaluma (94954-6860)
PHONE...................707 586-0511
Charles J Lacoti, *President*
Gabrielle Candrian, *Treasurer*
Jeff Lacoti, *Vice Pres*
Phil Lacoti, *Vice Pres*
EMP: 65
SQ FT: 7,000
SALES (est): 11MM **Privately Held**
WEB: www.incommechanical.com
SIC: 1711 Plumbing contractors; mechanical contractor

(P-2250)
INDUSTRIAL COML SYSTEMS INC
Also Called: San Marcos Mechanical
1165 Joshua Way, Vista (92081-7840)
PHONE...................760 300-4094
Fax: 760 599-0535
Robin Sides, *President*

PRODUCTS & SERVICES SECTION — 1711 - Plumbing, Heating & Air Conditioning Contractors County (P-2274)

Matt Harbin, *Vice Pres*
Cindy Sides, *Admin Sec*
Jason Johnson, *Controller*
EMP: 160
SQ FT: 15,000
SALES (est): 46.2MM **Privately Held**
SIC: 1711 Ventilation & duct work contractor; warm air heating & air conditioning contractor

(P-2251)
INNOVATIVE MAINT SOLUTIONS INC
Also Called: IMS
125 Main Ave, Sacramento (95838-2041)
PHONE 916 568-1400
Fax: 916 679-0963
Roy L Hill, *CEO*
Roy A Hill, *COO*
Dennis Dalton, *CFO*
Mike Mayo, *Vice Pres*
Ron Joung, *Info Tech Mgr*
EMP: 115
SQ FT: 5,400
SALES: 9.7MM **Privately Held**
WEB: www.imsfacilityservices.com
SIC: 1711 0781 1731 7349 Heating & air conditioning contractors; landscape services; lighting contractor; janitorial service, contract basis

(P-2252)
INTECH MECHANICAL COMPANY INC
7501 Galilee Rd, Roseville (95678-6905)
PHONE 916 797-4900
Fax: 916 797-4901
EMP: 100
SQ FT: 7,000
SALES (est): 20.5MM **Privately Held**
WEB: www.intech-mech.com
SIC: 1711

(P-2253)
INTECH MECHANICAL COMPANY LLC
7501 Galilee Rd, Roseville (95678-6905)
PHONE 916 797-4900
Richard B Chowdry,
Julie Chowdry, *Corp Secy*
Cheryl Rogers, *Controller*
Michael Friesen,
Gary Myers,
EMP: 150
SQ FT: 39,775
SALES: 36.4MM **Privately Held**
SIC: 1711 8711 Plumbing contractors; heating & air conditioning contractors; mechanical contractor; process piping contractor; heating & ventilation engineering

(P-2254)
INTEGRATED MECH SYSTEMS INC
2390 Bateman Ave, Duarte (91010-3312)
PHONE 626 446-1854
Fax: 626 446-1855
John P Lynch, *CEO*
Vachik Armenian, *Shareholder*
Jack Lynch, *Shareholder*
Kevin Stiver, *Shareholder*
Louella Abud, *Accounting Mgr*
EMP: 50
SQ FT: 4,500
SALES (est): 15.5MM **Privately Held**
WEB: www.integratedmechanical.com
SIC: 1711 Plumbing, heating, air-conditioning contractors

(P-2255)
IRON MECHANICAL INC
721 N B St Ste 100, Sacramento (95811-0332)
PHONE 916 341-3530
Terrance Risse, *President*
Judy Gomes, *Office Mgr*
Terry Im, *Project Mgr*
Mark Risse, *Project Mgr*
Brendin Barbour, *Project Engr*
EMP: 97
SQ FT: 3,000
SALES (est): 22.6MM **Privately Held**
SIC: 1711 Plumbing, heating, air-conditioning contractors

(P-2256)
J & J AIR CONDITIONING INC
1086 N 11th St, San Jose (95112-2927)
PHONE 408 920-0662
Fax: 408 920-8087
Jerry Hurwitz, *Owner*
Susan Borkin, *Treasurer*
Donna Ellison, *Office Mgr*
Pam York, *Admin Asst*
Lisa Woo, *Info Tech Mgr*
EMP: 60
SQ FT: 10,000
SALES (est): 16.7MM **Privately Held**
WEB: www.jjair.com
SIC: 1711 Warm air heating & air conditioning contractor; ventilation & duct work contractor

(P-2257)
J M CARDEN SPRINKLER CO INC
2909 Fletcher Dr, Los Angeles (90065-1479)
PHONE 323 258-8300
Fax: 323 255-2895
Michael Carden, *President*
Carroll B Carden, *Corp Secy*
Richard Wallace, *Vice Pres*
Mark Berru, *Technology*
Harry Heck, *Technology*
EMP: 60
SQ FT: 48,000
SALES (est): 9.7MM **Privately Held**
WEB: www.jmcfire.com
SIC: 1711 Fire sprinkler system installation

(P-2258)
J P ALLEN CO (PA)
Also Called: Perry, Joseph Allen
924 W Glenoaks Blvd, Glendale (91202-2752)
PHONE 818 848-1952
Joseph A Perry, *Owner*
EMP: 50
SQ FT: 4,000
SALES (est): 7.7MM **Privately Held**
WEB: www.jpallen.com
SIC: 1711 1731 1542 Plumbing contractors; heating & air conditioning contractors; general electrical contractor; nonresidential construction

(P-2259)
J R PIERCE PLUMBING COMPANY
14481 Wicks Blvd, San Leandro (94577-6711)
PHONE 510 483-5473
Fax: 510 483-1808
Richard Pierce, *President*
EMP: 100
SQ FT: 4,000
SALES (est): 15.6MM **Privately Held**
SIC: 1711 Plumbing contractors

(P-2260)
JACKSON & BLANC
7929 Arjons Dr, San Diego (92126-4301)
PHONE 858 831-7900
Fax: 858 527-1502
Kirk Jackson, *CEO*
John Fusca, *President*
Art Aguinaldo, *Purch Agent*
John A Hofmann, *Sales Executive*
John Mueller, *Manager*
▲ **EMP:** 110
SQ FT: 36,000
SALES (est): 41.1MM **Privately Held**
WEB: www.jacksonandblanc.com
SIC: 1711 Heating & air conditioning contractors

(P-2261)
JCT COMPANY LLC
Also Called: Aliso Air Conditioning & Htg
29736 Avenida&Bandera, Rancho Santa Margari (92688)
PHONE 949 589-2021
Fax: 949 589-6413
Jeffrey Loftus,
Monika Hall, *Department Mgr*
Shawn Cooney, *Sales Associate*
Richard Sheets, *Sales Staff*
Kc Fowler, *Manager*
EMP: 50
SALES (est): 6MM **Privately Held**
SIC: 1711 Heating & air conditioning contractors

(P-2262)
JEFF TRACY INC
Also Called: Land Forms Landscape Cnstr
15375 Barranca Pkwy A110, Irvine (92618-2203)
PHONE 949 582-0877
Jeff Thomas Tracy, *CEO*
Jon Gilmer, *President*
Brian Olsen, *President*
Sandy Wallace, *CFO*
Anna B Tracy, *Admin Sec*
EMP: 50
SQ FT: 1,608
SALES (est): 6.1MM **Privately Held**
SIC: 1711 0782 Irrigation sprinkler system installation; landscape contractors

(P-2263)
JPI DEVELOPMENT GROUP INC
41205 Golden Gate Cir, Murrieta (92562-6991)
PHONE 951 973-7680
Fax: 951 728-1848
Brad Janikowski, *President*
Dan Janikowski, *Vice Pres*
Lillian Hughes, *Manager*
EMP: 60
SQ FT: 6,000
SALES (est): 8.3MM **Privately Held**
SIC: 1711 Plumbing contractors

(P-2264)
JR PERCE PLBG INC SACRAMENTO
3610 Cincinnati Ave, Rocklin (95765-1203)
PHONE 916 434-9554
Fax: 916 434-9092
Dennis Pierce, *President*
Jessica Schanrock, *Manager*
EMP: 150 **EST:** 1927
SQ FT: 11,000
SALES (est): 39.1MM **Privately Held**
SIC: 1711 Plumbing contractors

(P-2265)
K & S AIR CONDITIONING INC
Also Called: K&S
143 E Meats Ave, Orange (92865-3309)
PHONE 714 685-0077
Fax: 714 685-1280
Steven Patz, *President*
Renee Patz, *Vice Pres*
Roger Mortensen, *General Mgr*
Kevin Patz, *General Mgr*
David Brown, *Personnel Exec*
EMP: 140
SQ FT: 18,000
SALES: 24.1MM **Privately Held**
SIC: 1711 Warm air heating & air conditioning contractor

(P-2266)
KEN STARR INC
Also Called: Home Comfort USA
3154 E La Palma Ave Ste B, Anaheim (92806-2808)
PHONE 714 632-8789
Ken Starr, *President*
Paul Buono, *Vice Pres*
EMP: 80
SQ FT: 9,000
SALES: 14MM **Privately Held**
SIC: 1711 Plumbing, heating, air-conditioning contractors

(P-2267)
KEY AIR CNDITIONING CONTRS INC
10905 Laurel Ave, Santa Fe Springs (90670-4513)
PHONE 562 941-2233
Richard Rivera, *President*
Robert Donat, *Vice Pres*
Ed Rohrbacker, *Vice Pres*
Lee Sandahl, *Vice Pres*
Larry Stikeleather, *Vice Pres*
EMP: 53
SQ FT: 35,000
SALES (est): 11.1MM **Privately Held**
SIC: 1711 Plumbing, heating, air-conditioning contractors

(P-2268)
KINCAID INDUSTRIES INC
31065 Plantation Dr, Thousand Palms (92276-6623)
PHONE 760 343-5457
Scott Kincaid, *CEO*
M S Mills, *CFO*
Elmer Angadol, *Branch Mgr*
Mike Perezchica, *General Mgr*
Michele Dunphy, *Controller*
EMP: 75
SQ FT: 7,000
SALES (est): 15.2MM **Privately Held**
WEB: www.kincaidplumbing.com
SIC: 1711 Plumbing contractors

(P-2269)
KINETIC SYSTEMS INC
7 Marconi, Irvine (92618-2701)
PHONE 949 770-7364
Fax: 949 770-7416
Hal Brey, *Manager*
Albert Huynh, *IT/INT Sup*
EMP: 50
SALES (corp-wide): 301.4K **Privately Held**
SIC: 1711 Mechanical contractor
HQ: Kinetic Systems, Inc.
48400 Fremont Blvd
Fremont CA 94538
510 683-6000

(P-2270)
KINETICS MECHANICAL SVC INC
6691 Brisa St, Livermore (94550-2505)
PHONE 925 245-6200
Ralph E Dorotinsky, *President*
Craig Kirk, *Vice Pres*
EMP: 100
SQ FT: 10,000
SALES: 16.3MM **Privately Held**
SIC: 1711 Plumbing, heating, air-conditioning contractors

(P-2271)
L A SERVICES INC
Also Called: George Brazil Plbg Htg & AC
9405 Jefferson Blvd, Culver City (90232-2915)
PHONE 310 838-0408
Michael N Diamond, *President*
Goldyne Diamond, *Corp Secy*
Kenneth E Barbura, *Vice Pres*
EMP: 50
SQ FT: 4,000
SALES (est): 4.6MM **Privately Held**
SIC: 1711 Plumbing, heating, air-conditioning contractors

(P-2272)
L J KRUSE CO
920 Pardee St, Berkeley (94710-2626)
P.O. Box 2900 (94702-0900)
PHONE 510 644-0260
Fax: 510 849-9909
David J Kruse, *President*
Karen Lown, *CFO*
Andrew S Kruse, *Exec VP*
Janell Yates, *Vice Pres*
Rob Harper, *Project Mgr*
EMP: 60
SQ FT: 14,000
SALES (est): 13.2MM **Privately Held**
WEB: www.ljkruse.com
SIC: 1711 Plumbing contractors

(P-2273)
L&H AIRCO LLC
2530 Warren Dr, Rocklin (95677-2167)
PHONE 916 677-1000
EMP: 80
SALES (est): 1.6MM **Privately Held**
SIC: 1711 5084 Mechanical contractor; instruments & control equipment

(P-2274)
LADELL INC
Also Called: Johnson Air
605 N Halifax Ave, Clovis (93611-7270)
PHONE 559 650-2000
Steve Johnson, *President*
Tom Johnson, *Vice Pres*
Ryan Calvert, *VP Sales*
Tammy Weber, *Manager*
EMP: 50

1711 - Plumbing, Heating & Air Conditioning Contractors County (P-2275)

PRODUCTS & SERVICES SECTION

SQ FT: 38,000
SALES (est): 5.8MM Privately Held
WEB: www.ladell.com
SIC: 1711 Warm air heating & air conditioning contractor

(P-2275)
LAWSON MECHANICAL CONTRACTORS (PA)
6090 S Watt Ave, Sacramento (95829-1302)
P.O. Box 15224 (95851-0224)
PHONE.................................916 381-6704
Fax: 916 381-5073
Rodney Lawson, *President*
David Lawson, *Corp Secy*
Rod Barbour, *Vice Pres*
Nick Davis, *Systs Prg Mgr*
Daniel Bonner, *Technology*
EMP: 100 EST: 1947
SQ FT: 31,000
SALES (est): 29.1MM Privately Held
WEB: www.lawsonmechanical.com
SIC: 1711 Plumbing contractors; heating & air conditioning contractors; mechanical contractor

(P-2276)
LDI MECHANICAL INC
3760 Happy Ln, Sacramento (95827-9731)
PHONE.................................916 361-3925
Fax: 916 381-7601
Shane Moser, *Manager*
Michael Diaz, *Network Enginr*
EMP: 50
SALES (corp-wide): 94.3MM Privately Held
SIC: 1711 Mechanical contractor
PA: Ldi Mechanical, Inc.
1587 E Bentley Dr
Corona CA 92879
951 340-9685

(P-2277)
LDI MECHANICAL INC (PA)
1587 E Bentley Dr, Corona (92879-1738)
PHONE.................................951 340-9685
Fax: 951 340-9688
Lloyd Smith, *President*
Robert Sylvester, *CFO*
Bridgett Robinson, *Chief Mktg Ofcr*
Mike Smith, *Senior VP*
Robert Smith, *Senior VP*
EMP: 144
SQ FT: 38,000
SALES (est): 94.3MM Privately Held
WEB: www.ldimechanical.com
SIC: 1711 Heating & air conditioning contractors

(P-2278)
LED GLOBAL LLC
1010 Wilshire Blvd, Los Angeles (90017-5662)
PHONE.................................917 921-4315
Saila Smith,
EMP: 100
SALES: 10MM Privately Held
SIC: 1711 Solar energy contractor

(P-2279)
LEGACY MECH & ENRGY SVCS INC
3130 Crow Canyon Pl # 410, San Ramon (94583-1346)
PHONE.................................925 820-6938
Fax: 925 820-6258
Richard Almini, *President*
Chip Eskildsen, *Vice Pres*
Jack Larkin, *Vice Pres*
Bill Longbotham, *Vice Pres*
Linda Jardin, *General Mgr*
EMP: 100
SQ FT: 4,000
SALES (est): 24.1MM Privately Held
WEB: www.legacymechanical.com
SIC: 1711 Heating & air conditioning contractors

(P-2280)
LESCURE COMPANY INC
3667 Mt Diablo Blvd, Lafayette (94549-3739)
P.O. Box 968 (94549-0968)
PHONE.................................925 283-2528
Fax: 925 283-1630
Michael Lescure, *President*
Allen Lescure, *Vice Pres*
Percy James, *Project Mgr*
Tom Burpee, *Controller*
Thomas Durte, *Controller*
EMP: 70
SQ FT: 10,000
SALES (est): 12.1MM Privately Held
WEB: www.lescurecompany.com
SIC: 1711 Plumbing contractors; mechanical contractor; warm air heating & air conditioning contractor

(P-2281)
LIMBACH COMPANY LP
Also Called: Western Air & Refrigeration
12442 Knott St, Garden Grove (92841-2832)
PHONE.................................714 653-7000
Fax: 714 653-7030
Charlie Bacon, *CEO*
John T Jordan Jr, *CFO*
Robert C Morgan, *Vice Pres*
Olivia Gonzales, *Office Mgr*
Porther May, *Manager*
EMP: 167
SALES (est): 33.6MM
SALES (corp-wide): 286.4MM Publicly Held
SIC: 1711 Mechanical contractor
HQ: Limbach Company Llc
31 35th St
Pittsburgh PA 15201
412 359-2173

(P-2282)
LITE SOLAR CORP
3553 Atlantic Ave, Long Beach (90807-5606)
PHONE.................................562 256-1249
Ranbir Sahni, *CEO*
EMP: 150
SALES (est): 14.1MM Privately Held
SIC: 1711 Solar energy contractor

(P-2283)
LOUIS LUSKIN & SONS INC
6004 Venice Blvd, Los Angeles (90034-2233)
PHONE.................................323 938-5142
Fax: 323 938-7335
Martin Luskin, *President*
Robert Luskin, *Treasurer*
Ron Esthel, *Agent*
EMP: 53
SQ FT: 7,000
SALES (est): 3.2MM Privately Held
SIC: 1711 Plumbing contractors

(P-2284)
LOVAZZANO MECHANICAL INC
189 Constitution Dr, Menlo Park (94025-1106)
PHONE.................................650 367-6216
Bruce Lovazzano Sr, *CEO*
Bruce Lovazzano Jr, *President*
Gary Lovazzano, *Treasurer*
EMP: 70
SQ FT: 3,100
SALES (est): 12.2MM Privately Held
SIC: 1711 Plumbing, heating, air-conditioning contractors

(P-2285)
LUPPEN AND HAWLEY INC
6330 N Point Way, Sacramento (95831-1067)
PHONE.................................916 456-7831
Fax: 916 456-0517
John O'Connor, *President*
Terrence O'Connor, *Vice Pres*
John Oconnor, *Vice Pres*
Terrence Oconnor, *Vice Pres*
Greg O'Connor, *Admin Sec*
EMP: 110 EST: 1920
SQ FT: 30,000
SALES (est): 14.3MM Privately Held
WEB: www.luppenandhawleyinc.com
SIC: 1711 1731 Plumbing contractors; warm air heating & air conditioning contractor; electrical work

(P-2286)
LYLES MECHANICAL CO
5014 E University Ave # 101, Fresno (93727-1661)
PHONE.................................559 237-2200
John Sloan, *CEO*
Michael Elkins, *CFO*
Joshua Wilkinson, *Vice Pres*
John Leonardo, *Admin Sec*
John Driscoll, *IT/INT Sup*
EMP: 125
SALES: 17.4MM
SALES (corp-wide): 31.9MM Privately Held
SIC: 1711 Mechanical contractor
PA: Lyles Diversified, Inc.
1210 W Olive Ave
Fresno CA 93728
559 441-1900

(P-2287)
M & L PLUMBING CO INC
3540 N Duke Ave, Fresno (93727-7896)
PHONE.................................559 291-5525
Fax: 559 291-5636
Fred C Ede III, *President*
Fred C Ede, *President*
EMP: 50
SQ FT: 6,000
SALES: 5MM Privately Held
SIC: 1711 Plumbing contractors

(P-2288)
M & M PLUMBING INC
6782 Columbus St, Riverside (92504-1118)
PHONE.................................951 354-5388
Robert Malcom, *President*
Glenn Malcolm, *Principal*
EMP: 80
SALES (est): 6.2MM Privately Held
SIC: 1711 Plumbing contractors

(P-2289)
MARELICH MECHANICAL CO INC (HQ)
24041 Amador St, Hayward (94544-1201)
PHONE.................................510 785-5500
Keith R Atteberry, *President*
Chad Johnston, *Vice Pres*
Terry J Kvochak, *Vice Pres*
William Mosely, *Vice Pres*
Andrew Ostrowski, *Vice Pres*
EMP: 65
SQ FT: 40,000
SALES (est): 48.9MM
SALES (corp-wide): 6.7B Publicly Held
WEB: www.marelich.com
SIC: 1711 1623 3822 Plumbing, heating, air-conditioning contractors; mechanical contractor; pipeline construction; auto controls regulating residntl & coml environmt & applncs
PA: Emcor Group, Inc.
301 Merritt 7 Fl 6
Norwalk CT 06851
203 849-7800

(P-2290)
MASTERSERV INC
Also Called: Mastersev
560 Library St, San Fernando (91340-2524)
PHONE.................................818 356-4602
Fax: 818 408-4106
George Anderson, *President*
Cindy Anderson, *Corp Secy*
EMP: 50
SQ FT: 3,500
SALES (est): 6.3MM Privately Held
WEB: www.masterservinc.com
SIC: 1711 1731 Plumbing, heating, air-conditioning contractors; general electrical contractor

(P-2291)
MDDR INC
Also Called: Econo Air
555 Vanguard Way, Brea (92821-3933)
PHONE.................................714 792-1993
Fax: 714 695-6685
Michael Richards, *President*
Rhonda Richards, *Admin Sec*
EMP: 110
SALES (est): 19.8MM Privately Held
WEB: www.e-conoair.com
SIC: 1711 1731 Heating & air conditioning contractors; electrical work

(P-2292)
MEMEGED TEVUOT SHEMESH (PA)
Also Called: Titan Solar
6711 Valjean Ave, Van Nuys (91406-5819)
PHONE.................................866 575-1211
Ofir Haimoff, *Owner*
Mori Ben, *General Mgr*
EMP: 152 EST: 2011
SQ FT: 20,000
SALES (est): 36MM Privately Held
SIC: 1711 5074 Solar energy contractor; heating equipment & panels, solar

(P-2293)
MESA ENERGY SYSTEMS INC (HQ)
Also Called: Emcor Services
2 Cromwell, Irvine (92618-1816)
PHONE.................................949 460-0460
Fax: 949 460-8833
Robert A Lake, *President*
Steve Hunt, *CFO*
Kip Bagley, *Exec VP*
Michael Ecshner, *Vice Pres*
Charles G Fletcher Jr, *Vice Pres*
EMP: 210
SQ FT: 55,000
SALES (est): 137.8MM
SALES (corp-wide): 6.7B Publicly Held
SIC: 1711 7623 Warm air heating & air conditioning contractor; refrigeration service & repair
PA: Emcor Group, Inc.
301 Merritt 7 Fl 6
Norwalk CT 06851
203 849-7800

(P-2294)
MESA ENERGY SYSTEMS INC
4668 N Sonora Ave Ste 102, Fresno (93722-3970)
PHONE.................................559 277-7900
Michael Echsner, *Branch Mgr*
Kal Hassanieh, *Vice Pres*
Matt Baker, *Opers Staff*
EMP: 60
SALES (corp-wide): 6.7B Publicly Held
SIC: 1711 Heating & air conditioning contractors
HQ: Mesa Energy Systems, Inc.
2 Cromwell
Irvine CA 92618
949 460-0460

(P-2295)
MESA ENERGY SYSTEMS INC
16130 Sherman Way, Van Nuys (91406-3907)
PHONE.................................818 756-0500
Fax: 818 756-1090
Craig Lacko, *Manager*
Wayne Lacher, *Director*
EMP: 104
SALES (corp-wide): 6.7B Publicly Held
SIC: 1711 Warm air heating & air conditioning contractor
HQ: Mesa Energy Systems, Inc.
2 Cromwell
Irvine CA 92618
949 460-0460

(P-2296)
MONSTER MECHANICAL INC
90 Railway St, Campbell (95008-3007)
P.O. Box 1250 (95009-1250)
PHONE.................................408 727-8362
Fax: 408 827-0169
Jeffery Miller, *President*
Jeniffer Miller, *Manager*
EMP: 60
SQ FT: 10,000
SALES (est): 6.7MM Privately Held
WEB: www.monstermechanical.com
SIC: 1711 Plumbing, heating, air-conditioning contractors

1711 - Plumbing, Heating & Air Conditioning Contractors County (P-2319)

(P-2297)
MOUNTING SYSTEMS INC
820 Riverside Pkwy, West Sacramento (95605-1500)
PHONE.....................................916 374-8872
Fax: 916 287-2269
Kasim Ersoy, *President*
◆ **EMP:** 51
SALES (est): 7.1MM
SALES (corp-wide): 308.6MM **Privately Held**
SIC: 1711 Plumbing, heating, air-conditioning contractors
HQ: Mounting Systems Gmbh
Mittenwalder Str. 9a
Rangsdorf
337 085-290

(P-2298)
MUIR-CHASE PLUMBING CO INC
Also Called: M C
4530 Brazil St Ste 1, Los Angeles (90039-1000)
PHONE.....................................818 500-1940
Don Chase, *President*
Jay Chase, *Vice Pres*
Grant Muir, *Vice Pres*
James M Muir, *Vice Pres*
Gail Comstock, *Admin Sec*
EMP: 90 **EST:** 1975
SQ FT: 5,000
SALES (est): 26.9MM **Privately Held**
WEB: www.muirchase.com
SIC: 1711 7699 Plumbing contractors; sewer cleaning & rodding

(P-2299)
MULTI MECHANICAL INC
1210 N Barsten Way, Anaheim (92806-1822)
PHONE.....................................714 632-7404
Fax: 714 632-7302
Brandon Abblitt, *CEO*
Fred Capinpin, *Controller*
EMP: 75
SALES (est): 12.5MM **Privately Held**
WEB: www.multimechanical.com
SIC: 1711 Heating & air conditioning contractors; warm air heating & air conditioning contractor

(P-2300)
MUNI-FED ENERGY INC
192 N Marina Dr, Long Beach (90803-4601)
PHONE.....................................714 321-3346
Phil Bowman, *President*
Clay Sandidge, *Treasurer*
Abbey Lam, *Principal*
EMP: 50 **EST:** 2011
SALES (est): 2.9MM **Privately Held**
SIC: 1711 8748 Solar energy contractor; systems analysis & engineering consulting services

(P-2301)
MURRAY PLUMBING AND HTG CORP
8520 Production Ave, San Diego (92121-2292)
PHONE.....................................858 952-8795
EMP: 327
SALES (corp-wide): 136.5MM **Privately Held**
SIC: 1711 Plumbing contractors
PA: Murray Plumbing And Heating Corporation
18414 S Santa Fe Ave
E Rncho Dmngz CA 90221
310 637-1500

(P-2302)
MURRAY PLUMBING AND HTG CORP (PA)
Also Called: Murray Company
18414 S Santa Fe Ave, E Rncho Dmngz (90221-5612)
P.O. Box 9061, Compton (90224-9061)
PHONE.....................................310 637-1500
Kevan Steffey, *CEO*
Jim Deflavio, *President*
John Odom, *President*
Barbara Braymajor, *CFO*
Douglas Orban, *Branch Mgr*
EMP: 151
SQ FT: 26,000
SALES (est): 136.5MM **Privately Held**
SIC: 1711 Plumbing contractors; warm air heating & air conditioning contractor

(P-2303)
N V HEATHORN INC
Also Called: N V H
1155 Beecher St, San Leandro (94577-1251)
PHONE.....................................510 569-9100
Fax: 510 569-0349
Edward W Heathorn, *President*
David A Heathorn, *CFO*
Norman T R Heathorn, *Principal*
Lisa Heathorn, *Administration*
Jon Hill, *Project Mgr*
EMP: 59
SQ FT: 57,500
SALES (est): 13.9MM **Privately Held**
WEB: www.nvheathorn.com
SIC: 1711 1629 Warm air heating & air conditioning contractor; plumbing contractors; ventilation & duct work contractor; waste water & sewage treatment plant construction

(P-2304)
NATIONAL AIR INC
Also Called: National Air and Energy
2053 Kurtz St, San Diego (92110-2014)
PHONE.....................................619 299-2500
Fax: 619 299-2592
Jared M Wells, *CEO*
Tom Larsen, *Manager*
Jane Poulsom, *Manager*
EMP: 110
SQ FT: 10,500
SALES (est): 32.1MM **Privately Held**
SIC: 1711 Warm air heating & air conditioning contractor

(P-2305)
NOVA PLUMBING INC
3111 W Central Ave, Santa Ana (92704-5302)
PHONE.....................................714 556-6682
Rod Robbins, *President*
Kathryn Taylor, *Vice Pres*
EMP: 105
SQ FT: 13,000
SALES (est): 5.3MM **Privately Held**
SIC: 1711 Plumbing contractors

(P-2306)
NU FLOW AMERICA INC (PA)
7710 Kenamar Ct, San Diego (92121-2425)
PHONE.....................................619 275-9130
Fax: 619 275-7110
Cameron Sean Manners, *President*
Steven Howe, *President*
Bill Turner, *Regional Mgr*
Dennis Persaud, *General Mgr*
Laurie Maya, *Human Resources*
EMP: 61
SQ FT: 15,488
SALES (est): 33.2MM **Privately Held**
WEB: www.nuflowtech.com
SIC: 1711 3317 Plumbing contractors; steel pipe & tubes

(P-2307)
O C MCDONALD CO INC
1150 W San Carlos St, San Jose (95126-3440)
P.O. Box 26560 (95159-6560)
PHONE.....................................408 295-2182
Fax: 408 295-0626
James Mc Donald, *President*
Dean Ziemer, *Purchasing*
EMP: 150 **EST:** 1906
SQ FT: 10,500
SALES (est): 53.8MM **Privately Held**
WEB: www.ocmcdonald.com
SIC: 1711 3585 3541 3444 Mechanical contractor; refrigeration & heating equipment; machine tools, metal cutting type; sheet metalwork; plumbing fixture fittings & trim

(P-2308)
OHAGIN MANUFACTURING LLC
210 Classic Ct Ste 100, Rohnert Park (94928-1660)
PHONE.....................................707 872-3620
Greg Daniels, *President*
Bruce Montoya, *Natl Sales Mgr*
Jake Carlson, *Marketing Staff*
EMP: 50 **EST:** 2013
SALES (est): 4.3MM **Privately Held**
SIC: 1711 Ventilation & duct work contractor

(P-2309)
OHAGINS INC
210 Classic Ct Ste 100, Rohnert Park (94928-1660)
PHONE.....................................707 303-3660
Fax: 707 588-5772
Carolina O'Hagin, *CEO*
Greg Daniels, *CEO*
Mark Marquez, *COO*
Peter Iozzia, *Controller*
Mike Fulton, *Manager*
▲ **EMP:** 60
SQ FT: 57,000
SALES (est): 6.6MM **Privately Held**
WEB: www.ohaginvent.com
SIC: 1711 Heating & air conditioning contractors

(P-2310)
ON-TIME AC & HTG INC (PA)
Also Called: Service Champions
7020 Commerce Dr Ste C, Pleasanton (94588-8023)
PHONE.....................................925 444-4444
Fax: 925 598-1827
Keviin J Comerford, *President*
John Cristiano, *CEO*
Gary Potts, *CFO*
Dan Michie, *Vice Pres*
Debbie Gonzales, *Controller*
EMP: 102
SALES (est): 27MM **Privately Held**
SIC: 1711 Warm air heating & air conditioning contractor

(P-2311)
ONTARIO REFRIGERATION SVC INC (PA)
Also Called: Ontario Refrigeration,
635 S Mountain Ave, Ontario (91762-4114)
PHONE.....................................909 984-2771
Fax: 909 988-7522
Phillip C Talleur, *President*
Mark Gambetti, *General Mgr*
Scott Gray, *General Mgr*
Bryant McGrath, *Info Tech Mgr*
Keri Vargas, *Controller*
EMP: 54 **EST:** 1971
SQ FT: 5,300
SALES (est): 45.8MM **Privately Held**
SIC: 1711 Heating & air conditioning contractors

(P-2312)
ORANGE COUNTY SERVICES INC
Also Called: George Brazil Plbg Htg & AC
3022 N Hesperian St, Santa Ana (92706-1151)
PHONE.....................................714 541-9753
Mike Jones, *General Mgr*
EMP: 50
SALES (corp-wide): 1.4MM **Privately Held**
SIC: 1711 1731 Plumbing, heating, air-conditioning contractors; electrical work
PA: Orange County Services Inc
9405 Jefferson Blvd
Culver City CA 90232
310 515-1001

(P-2313)
ORANGE PACIFIC PLUMBING INC
801 Panorama Rd, Fullerton (92831-1029)
PHONE.....................................714 992-4547
Fax: 714 630-0652
Steven Hartshorn, *President*
Bonnie Hartshorn, *Corp Secy*
Emily Buff, *Manager*
EMP: 66
SQ FT: 5,000
SALES (est): 3.9MM **Privately Held**
WEB: www.orangepacific.com
SIC: 1711 Plumbing contractors

(P-2314)
ORIGINAL SID BLACKMAN PLBG INC
1160 S 2nd St, El Centro (92243-3446)
PHONE.....................................760 352-3632
Fax: 760 352-8272
Thomas Blackman, *President*
Michael Wickline, *Admin Sec*
Frances Sevy, *Controller*
EMP: 68
SALES: 8.2MM **Privately Held**
WEB: www.blackmanplumbing.net
SIC: 1711 Plumbing contractors

(P-2315)
PACIFIC PRODUCTION PLUMBING (PA)
1584 Pioneer Way, El Cajon (92020-1638)
PHONE.....................................951 509-3100
Fax: 951 509-3132
Daniel Whitt, *President*
Kim Whitt, *Treasurer*
Bruce Magellan, *Vice Pres*
Tobin Whitt, *Vice Pres*
Wes Whitt, *General Mgr*
EMP: 50
SQ FT: 3,000
SALES (est): 48.9MM **Privately Held**
SIC: 1711 Plumbing contractors

(P-2316)
PACIFIC RIM MECH CONTRS INC
1701 E Edinger Ave Ste F2, Santa Ana (92705-5028)
PHONE.....................................714 285-2600
Fax: 714 285-2601
John Heusner, *Manager*
Brent Koch, *Opers Staff*
Dennis Dykes, *Manager*
EMP: 61
SALES (corp-wide): 112.2MM **Privately Held**
WEB: www.prmech.com
SIC: 1711 Mechanical contractor
PA: Pacific Rim Mechanical Contractors, Inc.
7655 Convoy Ct
San Diego CA 92111
858 974-6500

(P-2317)
PACIFIC RIM MECH CONTRS INC (PA)
7655 Convoy Ct, San Diego (92111-1103)
PHONE.....................................858 974-6500
Fax: 858 974-6501
Joseph Mucher, *CEO*
Eric Bader, *CFO*
Colin Cook, *Vice Pres*
Randy Foco, *Vice Pres*
John Heusner, *Vice Pres*
EMP: 400
SQ FT: 50,000
SALES: 112.2MM **Privately Held**
WEB: www.prmech.com
SIC: 1711 Plumbing, heating, air-conditioning contractors

(P-2318)
PAN-PACIFIC MECHANICAL LLC (PA)
18250 Euclid St, Fountain Valley (92708-6112)
PHONE.....................................949 474-9170
Fax: 949 474-4274
Cindy Lanette McMackin, *CEO*
Steve Sylvester, *CFO*
Ryan Cavanaugh, *Vice Pres*
Pat George, *Vice Pres*
Jon Houchin, *Vice Pres*
▲ **EMP:** 150
SQ FT: 60,000
SALES: 257.7MM **Privately Held**
WEB: www.panpacplumbing.com
SIC: 1711 Plumbing contractors

(P-2319)
PAN-PACIFIC MECHANICAL LLC
1205 Chrysler Dr, Menlo Park (94025-1134)
PHONE.....................................650 561-8810

1711 - Plumbing, Heating & Air Conditioning Contractors County (P-2320)

PRODUCTS & SERVICES SECTION

Tom Sakurai, *Manager*
EMP: 283
SALES (corp-wide): 257.7MM **Privately Held**
SIC: 1711 Plumbing contractors
PA: Pan-Pacific Mechanical Llc
18250 Euclid St
Fountain Valley CA 92708
949 474-9170

(P-2320)
PAN-PACIFIC MECHANICAL LLC
Also Called: Pan-Pacific Plumbing & Mech
11622 El Camino Real, San Diego (92130-2049)
PHONE.....................858 764-2464
EMP: 567
SALES (corp-wide): 257.7MM **Privately Held**
SIC: 1711 Plumbing, heating, air-conditioning contractors
PA: Pan-Pacific Mechanical Llc
18250 Euclid St
Fountain Valley CA 92708
949 474-9170

(P-2321)
PINASCO PLUMBING & HEATING INC
Also Called: Pinasco Mechinical
2145 E Taylor St, Stockton (95205-6337)
P.O. Box 55287 (95205-8787)
PHONE.....................209 463-7793
Fax: 209 463-3224
Tom Pinasco, *President*
John Pinasco, *Treasurer*
Joseph Pinasco, *Admin Sec*
Sue Smith, *Manager*
EMP: 50
SQ FT: 1,000
SALES (est): 8MM **Privately Held**
SIC: 1711 Plumbing contractors; fire sprinkler system installation; warm air heating & air conditioning contractor

(P-2322)
PIPE RESTORATION INC
Also Called: Ace Duraflo Pipe Restoration
3122 W Alpine St, Santa Ana (92704-6912)
PHONE.....................714 564-7600
Larry Gillanders, *CEO*
Mike Carper, *Exec VP*
EMP: 50 **EST:** 2001
SQ FT: 6,000
SALES (est): 7.8MM **Privately Held**
WEB: www.restoremypipes.com
SIC: 1711 Plumbing contractors

(P-2323)
PLUMB TECH INC
1242 E Maple Ave, El Segundo (90245-3258)
PHONE.....................310 322-4925
Greg Misic, *President*
Jim Gonzales, *Vice Pres*
EMP: 57
SALES (est): 2.6MM **Privately Held**
SIC: 1711 Plumbing contractors

(P-2324)
PLUMBING LIMITED INC
Also Called: Greenes Plumbing
5270 E Pine Ave, Fresno (93727-2111)
PHONE.....................559 453-0690
Fax: 559 453-0691
Jack Green, *Owner*
Tami Green, *CFO*
Sherri Green, *Treasurer*
Sammy R Murphy, *Agent*
EMP: 50
SQ FT: 3,750
SALES (est): 5MM **Privately Held**
SIC: 1711 Plumbing contractors

(P-2325)
PLUMBING PIPING & CNSTR INC
5950 Lakeshore Dr, Cypress (90630-3371)
PHONE.....................714 821-0490
Fax: 714 995-0352
Bruce Cook Jr, *President*
William Collins, *Manager*
Mike Mclsaac, *Manager*
EMP: 100
SQ FT: 12,600

SALES (est): 28.9MM **Privately Held**
WEB: www.1ppc.com
SIC: 1711 Plumbing, heating, air-conditioning contractors

(P-2326)
PPC ENTERPRISES INC
Also Called: Premier Plumbing Company
5920 Rickenbacker Ave, Riverside (92504-1042)
PHONE.....................951 354-5402
Fax: 951 371-4711
Jeffrey Geiger, *President*
Dawn Geiger, *CFO*
EMP: 125
SQ FT: 10,000
SALES (est): 15.3MM **Privately Held**
SIC: 1711 Plumbing contractors

(P-2327)
PRECISE AIR SYSTEMS INC
5467 W San Fernando Rd, Los Angeles (90039-1014)
P.O. Box 39609 (90039-0609)
PHONE.....................818 240-1737
Toll Free:...........................877 -
Fax: 818 240-1551
Fred Khachekian, *President*
Greg Khachekian, *Executive*
Shakeh Petrosian, *Info Tech Mgr*
Dzila Dornian, *Manager*
Greg Khachekin, *Manager*
EMP: 72
SQ FT: 3,200
SALES (est): 17.1MM **Privately Held**
WEB: www.preciseairsystems.com
SIC: 1711 Heating & air conditioning contractors

(P-2328)
PRIBUSS ENGINEERING INC
523 Mayfair Ave, South San Francisco (94080-4509)
PHONE.....................650 588-0447
Fax: 650 588-8592
Bayardo Chamorro, *President*
John Pribuss, *CFO*
Michelle Lamlin, *Vice Pres*
Mark Walsh, *General Mgr*
Rick Bergamaschi, *Project Mgr*
EMP: 70
SQ FT: 16,000
SALES (est): 21MM **Privately Held**
WEB: www.pribuss.com
SIC: 1711 7623 Warm air heating & air conditioning contractor; fire sprinkler system installation; refrigeration service & repair

(P-2329)
PRO-CRAFT CONSTRUCTION INC
31597 Outer Highway 10 B, Redlands (92373-8626)
PHONE.....................909 389-7990
Timothy McFayden, *President*
Susan Mc Fayden, *CFO*
Susan McFayden, *CFO*
Kimberly Ballard, *Office Mgr*
Jill Elliott, *Human Resources*
EMP: 60
SALES (est): 19.6MM **Privately Held**
SIC: 1711 Plumbing contractors

(P-2330)
PRODUCTION PLUS PLUMBING INC
2472 Grand Ave, Vista (92081-7804)
PHONE.....................760 597-0235
Fax: 760 597-0210
Robert Labaron, *President*
Bob Gural, *Sales Mgr*
Kevin Plowman, *Manager*
EMP: 124
SALES (corp-wide): 13.8MM **Privately Held**
WEB: www.productionplusplumbing.com
SIC: 1711 Plumbing contractors
PA: Production Plus Plumbing, Inc.
312 Dawson Dr
Camarillo CA
760 597-0235

(P-2331)
PROGRESSIVE POWER GROUP INC
12552 Western Ave, Garden Grove (92841-4013)
PHONE.....................714 899-2300
Ross A Butcher, *CEO*
Don Hughes, *CFO*
Chris Hammerstone, *Principal*
Chris Staskewicz, *Principal*
Travis Mashin, *General Mgr*
EMP: 50
SQ FT: 12,000
SALES (est): 11.1MM **Privately Held**
SIC: 1711 5211 Solar energy contractor; solar heating equipment

(P-2332)
PURONICS RETAIL SERVICES INC
5775 Las Positas Rd, Livermore (94551-7819)
PHONE.....................925 456-7000
Scott A Batiste, *CEO*
Mark H Cosmez II, *CFO*
EMP: 60
SQ FT: 25,000
SALES (est): 4.6MM **Privately Held**
SIC: 1711 Plumbing contractors

(P-2333)
QUALITY PLUMBING ASSOCIATES
28 Quail Run Cir Ste F, Salinas (93907-2350)
PHONE.....................831 775-0655
Armando Pena, *Principal*
EMP: 55
SALES (est): 5.2MM **Privately Held**
SIC: 1711 Plumbing contractors

(P-2334)
R & R MECHANICAL CONTRS INC
9330 Stevens Rd Ste A, Santee (92071-5639)
PHONE.....................619 449-9900
Randall A Signore, *President*
Richard Signore, *Vice Pres*
Rose Signore, *Admin Sec*
Denise Robbins, *Controller*
Pam Demo, *Personnel Exec*
EMP: 100 **EST:** 1998
SQ FT: 13,900
SALES (est): 9.8MM **Privately Held**
WEB: www.countywidems.com
SIC: 1711 Heating & air conditioning contractors

(P-2335)
R A SCHREIBER PLUMBING
2358 Tavern Rd, Alpine (91901-3107)
P.O. Box 1315 (91903-1315)
PHONE.....................619 659-3101
Fax: 619 659-3106
R A Schreiber, *Owner*
EMP: 50 **EST:** 1986
SALES: 8MM **Privately Held**
SIC: 1711 Plumbing contractors

(P-2336)
R B SPENCER INC
1188 Hassett Ave, Yuba City (95991-7212)
PHONE.....................530 674-8307
Fax: 530 674-9333
Robert B Spencer, *President*
Brigit Spencer, *CFO*
Tom Dodd, *Project Mgr*
Darrin Thomas, *Manager*
EMP: 52
SQ FT: 8,000
SALES (est): 9.6MM **Privately Held**
WEB: www.rbspencerinc.com
SIC: 1711 Warm air heating & air conditioning contractor

(P-2337)
RA HUGHES ENTERPRISES IN
9316 Abraham Way, Santee (92071-2861)
PHONE.....................619 390-4880
Ra Hughes, *Owner*
EMP: 50
SALES (est): 1.7MM **Privately Held**
SIC: 1711 Septic system construction

(P-2338)
RAM MECHANICAL INC
3506 Moore Rd, Ceres (95307-9402)
PHONE.....................209 531-9155
Fax: 209 531-9171
James A Frias, *President*
Gary Broadwell, *Vice Pres*
Neil Hodgson, *Vice Pres*
Tom Bawdon, *Project Mgr*
Greg Peden, *Project Mgr*
EMP: 60
SQ FT: 22,500
SALES: 15MM **Privately Held**
WEB: www.ram-mechanical.com
SIC: 1711 8711 3599 3535 Mechanical contractor; engineering services; custom machinery; conveyors & conveying equipment

(P-2339)
RANDO AAA HVAC INC
Also Called: A A A Furnace Company
1712 Stone Ave Ste 1, San Jose (95125-1309)
PHONE.....................408 293-4717
Fax: 408 287-8534
Jim Rando, *President*
Marrissa Rando, *Principal*
EMP: 50
SQ FT: 5,000
SALES (est): 7.9MM **Privately Held**
SIC: 1711 3444 3433 Heating & air conditioning contractors; ventilation & duct work contractor; sheet metalwork; heating equipment, except electric

(P-2340)
RAWLINGS MECHANICAL CORP (PA)
11615 Pendleton St, Sun Valley (91352-2502)
P.O. Box 703 (91353-0703)
PHONE.....................323 875-2040
Fax: 818 875-2047
Robert S Bratton, *President*
Rex Horney, *Vice Pres*
Patricia Wood, *Admin Sec*
Ken Burton, *Project Mgr*
Amado Deleon, *Controller*
EMP: 65
SQ FT: 22,000
SALES: 21MM **Privately Held**
SIC: 1711 Mechanical contractor

(P-2341)
RCR PLUMBING AND MECH INC (PA)
Also Called: Rcr Companies
12620 Magnolia Ave, Riverside (92503-4636)
PHONE.....................951 371-5000
Fax: 951 893-3558
Robert Richey, *President*
EMP: 150
SQ FT: 35,000
SALES: 46MM **Privately Held**
SIC: 1711 Plumbing, heating, air-conditioning contractors; plumbing contractors; sprinkler contractors

(P-2342)
RE MILANO PLUMBING CORP
4881 Sunrise Dr Ste B, Martinez (94553-4304)
P.O. Box 1383 (94553-7383)
PHONE.....................925 500-1372
Leigha M Ramirez, *CEO*
Robert Romeo, *President*
Elvis Sahnic, *Treasurer*
EMP: 20
SQ FT: 7,000
SALES: 4MM **Privately Held**
SIC: 1711 Plumbing contractors

(P-2343)
RECURRENT ENERGY LLC (HQ)
300 California St Fl 7, San Francisco (94104-1415)
PHONE.....................415 956-3168
Fax: 415 675-1501
David Brochu, *CEO*
Mitchell Randall, *President*
Stacy Colby-King, *Senior VP*
Luke Dunnington, *Senior VP*
Steve Finno, *Senior VP*

EMP: 51
SQ FT: 7,500
SALES (est): 28.5MM
SALES (corp-wide): 3.4B Privately Held
WEB: www.renewableenergyworld.com
SIC: 1711 Solar energy contractor
PA: Canadian Solar Inc
545 Speedvale Ave W
Guelph ON N1K 1
519 837-1881

(P-2344)
REGENCY FIRE PROTECTION INC
7651 Densmore Ave, Van Nuys (91406-2043)
PHONE.................................818 982-0126
Jay Zohar Rapaport, *President*
Tal Dagan, *Vice Pres*
Sue Romero, *Manager*
EMP: 60
SQ FT: 7,500
SALES (est): 11.4MM Privately Held
WEB: www.regencyfire.com
SIC: 1711 7382 Fire sprinkler system installation; burglar alarm maintenance & monitoring; fire alarm maintenance & monitoring; protective devices, security

(P-2345)
RELIABLE ENERGY MANAGEMENT INC
7201 Rosecrans Ave, Paramount (90723-2501)
PHONE.................................562 984-5511
Fax: 562 984-5515
George R Garcia, *President*
Judy Garcia, *Exec VP*
Isabel Garibay, *Office Mgr*
Bethy Skode, *Manager*
EMP: 80
SQ FT: 6,000
SALES (est): 15.8MM Privately Held
WEB: www.relenergy.com
SIC: 1711 Plumbing, heating, air-conditioning contractors

(P-2346)
RENOVA ENERGY CORP
75181 Mediterranean, Palm Desert (92211-9094)
PHONE.................................760 568-3413
Vincent Battaglia, *Ch of Bd*
Dixie Faber, *CFO*
Lea Goodsell, *Exec VP*
Lea Waki, *Vice Pres*
Isaac Gamez, *Project Mgr*
EMP: 50
SQ FT: 5,200
SALES (est): 15.6MM Privately Held
WEB: www.renovasolar.com
SIC: 1711 Solar energy contractor

(P-2347)
RESIDENTIAL FIRE SYSTEMS INC
8085 E Crystal Dr, Anaheim (92807-2523)
PHONE.................................714 666-8450
Fax: 714 666-2978
Ty Maley, *President*
Ruben Hernandez, *Treasurer*
Cesar Anchondo, *Vice Pres*
Jack Maley, *Admin Sec*
EMP: 75 EST: 2000
SQ FT: 6,200
SALES (est): 19.5MM Privately Held
WEB: www.residentialfiresys.com
SIC: 1711 5063 Fire sprinkler system installation; signaling equipment, electrical

(P-2348)
RITCHIE PLUMBING INC
11320 Lombardy Ln, Moreno Valley (92557-5739)
PHONE.................................949 709-7575
Fax: 949 709-7575
Lance Ritchie, *President*
Elizabith Julson, *Office Mgr*
Kathleen Jenkins, *Controller*
Michelle Cuthbert, *Purch Mgr*
Johnny Forsberg, *Sales Mgr*
EMP: 120
SQ FT: 7,500
SALES (est): 6.7MM Privately Held
WEB: www.ritchieplumbing.com
SIC: 1711 Plumbing contractors

(P-2349)
ROBINSON COMPANY CONTRS INC
Also Called: Robinson Electric
8871 Troy St, Spring Valley (91977-2638)
PHONE.................................619 697-6040
Fax: 619 463-2577
Thomas Petree, *CEO*
Donna Garrett, *Office Mgr*
Spencer Tilton, *Director*
EMP: 52
SQ FT: 1,200
SALES (est): 9.1MM Privately Held
WEB: www.robinsonelectric.com
SIC: 1711 6513 Warm air heating & air conditioning contractor; apartment building operators

(P-2350)
RODDA ELECTRIC INC (PA)
380 Carrol Ct Ste L, Brentwood (94513-7353)
PHONE.................................925 240-6024
Fax: 925 240-0624
Raymond Rodda, *CEO*
Jeff Taylor, *Project Mgr*
Craig Rodda, *Technology*
Rob Roy, *Purch Mgr*
Brenda Estrada, *Physician Asst*
EMP: 58
SQ FT: 21,000
SALES (est): 29.4MM Privately Held
SIC: 1711 1731 Solar energy contractor; general electrical contractor

(P-2351)
ROUNTREE PLUMBING AND HTG INC
1659c Industrial Rd, San Carlos (94070-4112)
PHONE.................................650 298-0300
Fax: 650 298-0333
Stephen Singewald, *President*
Pat Singewald, *Corp Secy*
Carmen Ruiz, *Executive Asst*
Debbie Ray, *Accounts Mgr*
EMP: 60
SQ FT: 10,000
SALES (est): 11.4MM Privately Held
WEB: www.rountreeinc.com
SIC: 1711 Plumbing contractors; warm air heating & air conditioning contractor

(P-2352)
RPM MECHANICAL - A JOINT VENTR
2919 E Victoria St, Compton (90221-5614)
PHONE.................................858 565-4131
Kevan Steffey, *President*
Bonnie Mosemak, *Assistant*
EMP: 100
SALES (est): 7.2MM Privately Held
SIC: 1711 Plumbing contractors

(P-2353)
RT/DT INC
Also Called: Thomas Plumbing
1777 Vineyard Dr, Antioch (94509-8501)
PHONE.................................925 757-1981
Fax: 925 757-1172
Robert Thomas, *President*
Dante M Thomas, *Corp Secy*
EMP: 65
SQ FT: 6,000
SALES (est): 4.8MM Privately Held
SIC: 1711 Plumbing contractors

(P-2354)
RUSSELL MECHANICAL INC
3251 Monier Cir Ste A, Rancho Cordova (95742-6812)
PHONE.................................916 635-2522
Fax: 916 635-0867
Danny L Russell, *President*
Cliff Wilcox, *Exec VP*
Steve Russell, *Vice Pres*
Karen Russell, *Principal*
Pat Wanner, *General Mgr*
EMP: 90
SQ FT: 22,000
SALES (est): 18.9MM Privately Held
SIC: 1711 1799 7389 3441 Mechanical contractor; welding on site; design services; fabricated structural metal

(P-2355)
S S W MECHANICAL CNSTR INC
Also Called: Ssw
670 S Oleander Rd, Palm Springs (92264-1502)
P.O. Box 3160 (92263-3160)
PHONE.................................760 327-1481
Fax: 760 325-5045
Sean Wood, *President*
W T Hayes, *Vice Pres*
James Wood, *Project Mgr*
Cary Miller, *Purch Dir*
Josh Cardiff, *Foreman/Supr*
EMP: 140
SQ FT: 7,000
SALES (est): 23.9MM Privately Held
WEB: www.sswmechanical.com
SIC: 1711 Plumbing contractors

(P-2356)
SABER PLUMBING INC
325 Market Pl, Escondido (92029-1302)
PHONE.................................760 480-5716
Fax: 760 781-3583
Glenn Phil Napierskie II, *President*
Annette Mott, *Admin Mgr*
Daniel Smith, *Design Engr*
Chuck Manzanares, *Project Mgr*
Joe Cribben, *Engineer*
EMP: 60
SQ FT: 12,500
SALES (est): 11.1MM Privately Held
WEB: www.saberplumbing.com
SIC: 1711 Plumbing contractors

(P-2357)
SAHARGUN PLUMBING INC
Also Called: Sahargun Mechanical
2216 Stewart St, Stockton (95205-3232)
PHONE.................................209 474-2611
Fax: 209 462-7808
Roger Vincelet, *President*
Patrick Coon, *COO*
Lou Stewell, *Senior VP*
Lou Stillwell, *Senior VP*
Terry Libbon, *Director*
EMP: 70
SQ FT: 12,000
SALES (est): 9.3MM Privately Held
SIC: 1711 Mechanical contractor

(P-2358)
SAN BENITO HTG & SHTMTL INC
1771 San Felipe Rd, Hollister (95023-2543)
P.O. Box 321 (95024-0321)
PHONE.................................831 637-1112
Fax: 831 637-4068
Robert Rodriguez, *President*
Enrique T Rodriguez, *Treasurer*
Araceli Rodriguez, *Vice Pres*
Priscilla Rodriguez, *Vice Pres*
Haydee Soto, *Controller*
EMP: 85
SQ FT: 12,000
SALES (est): 9.4MM Privately Held
SIC: 1711 1761 Warm air heating & air conditioning contractor; sheet metalwork; roofing contractor

(P-2359)
SAWYERS HEATING & AC
5272 Jerusalem Ct Ste D, Modesto (95356-9278)
PHONE.................................209 416-7700
Fax: 209 543-6078
Derek Sawyer, *President*
Weston Sawyer, *Admin Sec*
Roger Vandertop, *Controller*
Amie Matinez, *Manager*
EMP: 75
SQ FT: 10,000
SALES (est): 8MM Privately Held
SIC: 1711 Warm air heating & air conditioning contractor

(P-2360)
SCHMIDT FIRE PROTECTION CO INC
4760 Murphy Canyon Rd # 100, San Diego (92123-4334)
PHONE.................................858 279-6122
Fax: 858 279-3583
John J Durso, *President*
Greg Konold, *Vice Pres*
Leonard Moore, *General Mgr*
Matt Bowler, *Project Mgr*
Tony Legaspi, *Project Mgr*
EMP: 72
SQ FT: 13,800
SALES (est): 14.1MM Privately Held
WEB: www.schmidtfireprotection.com
SIC: 1711 Fire sprinkler system installation

(P-2361)
SCORPIO ENTERPRISES
Also Called: Airemasters Air Conditioning
12556 Mccann Dr, Santa Fe Springs (90670-3337)
PHONE.................................562 946-9464
Fax: 562 944-6258
Charles Everett Thompson, *CEO*
Linda Thompson, *Vice Pres*
Bruce Middleton, *Project Mgr*
Tracy Segovia, *Accounts Mgr*
▼ EMP: 55 EST: 1974
SQ FT: 14,800
SALES (est): 12.5MM Privately Held
WEB: www.airemasters-ac.com
SIC: 1711 Heating & air conditioning contractors

(P-2362)
SDG ENTERPRISES
Also Called: Century West Plumbing
822 Hampshire Rd Ste H, Westlake Village (91361-2850)
PHONE.................................805 777-7978
Fax: 805 777-7737
Nick Simili, *President*
Vincent Simili, *CFO*
Vincent Dipinto, *Vice Pres*
Robert Garcia, *Vice Pres*
Toni Ellis, *Manager*
EMP: 100
SQ FT: 3,000
SALES (est): 12.5MM Privately Held
SIC: 1711 Plumbing, heating, air-conditioning contractors

(P-2363)
SEEMS PLUMBING CO INC
5400 W Rosecrans Ave Lowr, Hawthorne (90250-6686)
PHONE.................................310 297-4969
Fax: 310 297-4828
Ed Hutcherson, *President*
Adrian Fernandez, *Human Resources*
EMP: 50
SALES (est): 6.1MM Privately Held
SIC: 1711 Plumbing contractors

(P-2364)
SERVI-TECH CONTROLS INC (PA)
2480 S Cherry Ave, Fresno (93706-5004)
PHONE.................................559 264-6679
Fax: 559 264-0841
Glenn Johnson, *President*
Janelle R Silva, *Treasurer*
Arthur Johnson, *Vice Pres*
Esther Gregory, *Controller*
EMP: 53
SQ FT: 4,500
SALES (est): 11.2MM Privately Held
WEB: www.servi-techcontrols.com
SIC: 1711 Warm air heating & air conditioning contractor; ventilation & duct work contractor

(P-2365)
SHELDON MECHANICAL CORPORATION
26015 Avenue Hall, Santa Clarita (91355-1241)
PHONE.................................661 286-1361
Fax: 661 287-9083
Dan Boute, *President*
Beverly Nisenson, *Treasurer*
Stanley Nisenson, *Vice Pres*
Grant Schaffer, *Vice Pres*
Chrystal Bout'e, *Admin Sec*
EMP: 80
SQ FT: 45,000
SALES (est): 18.8MM Privately Held
SIC: 1711 Heating & air conditioning contractors; warm air heating & air conditioning contractor

1711 - Plumbing, Heating & Air Conditioning Contractors County (P-2366)

(P-2366)
SHERWOOD MECHANICAL INC
6630 Top Gun St, San Diego (92121-4112)
PHONE..................858 679-3000
Fax: 858 200-1050
Mitch Roberts, *President*
James Robert, *COO*
Bill Smyth, *CFO*
Eric Fox, *Systs Prg Mgr*
Kim Norbeck, *Manager*
EMP: 100
SALES (est): 19.8MM Privately Held
WEB: www.sherwoodmechanical.com
SIC: 1711 Mechanical contractor

(P-2367)
SILICON VALLEY MECHANICAL INC
2115 Ringwood Ave, San Jose (95131-1725)
P.O. Box 10415, Southport NC (28461-0415)
PHONE..................408 943-0380
Blaine Flickner, *CEO*
Brian Pyle,
EMP: 67
SALES (est): 26.3MM Privately Held
SIC: 1711 Heating & air conditioning contractors

(P-2368)
SIMPLEXGRINNELL LP
1868 Palma Dr, Ventura (93003-6300)
PHONE..................805 642-0366
EMP: 64 Privately Held
SIC: 1711 Plumbing, heating, air-conditioning contractors
HQ: Simplexgrinnell Lp
 4700 Exchange Ct
 Boca Raton FL 33431
 561 988-7200

(P-2369)
SIMPLEXGRINNELL LP
3077 Wiljan Ct Ste B, Santa Rosa (95407-5764)
PHONE..................707 578-3212
John Becker, *Branch Mgr*
EMP: 61 Privately Held
WEB: www.simplexgrinnell.com
SIC: 1711 Sprinkler contractors
HQ: Simplexgrinnell Lp
 4700 Exchange Ct
 Boca Raton FL 33431
 561 988-7200

(P-2370)
SMART ENERGY SOLAR INC
Also Called: Smart Energy USA
1641 Comm St, Corona (92880)
PHONE..................951 273-9595
Leo Joaquin Bautista, *Principal*
EMP: 120
SALES (est): 14MM Privately Held
SIC: 1711 Solar energy contractor

(P-2371)
SOLAR COMPANY INC
20861 Wilbeam Ave Ste 1, Castro Valley (94546-5832)
PHONE..................510 888-9488
Fax: 209 274-9116
Mark Danenhower, *President*
Eric Piekarczyk, *COO*
Duane Redman, *CFO*
Nicole Wonderlin, *CFO*
Bruce Greenidge, *Technology*
EMP: 90
SQ FT: 4,000
SALES: 28MM Privately Held
SIC: 1711 Solar energy contractor

(P-2372)
SOLAR ENERGY LLC
21600 Oxnard St Ste 1200, Woodland Hills (91367-4949)
PHONE..................818 449-5816
EMP: 80 **EST:** 2009
SALES (est): 7.2MM Privately Held
SIC: 1711

(P-2373)
SOLAR SERVICE CENTER INC
34859 Frederick St # 113, Wildomar (92595-7007)
PHONE..................951 928-3300
EMP: 73
SALES (corp-wide): 22.8MM Privately Held
SIC: 1711 Solar energy contractor
PA: Solar Service Center Inc.
 1622 Illinois Ave Ste 18
 Perris CA 92571
 888 760-7652

(P-2374)
SOLAR SERVICE CENTER INC (PA)
1622 Illinois Ave Ste 18, Perris (92571-9375)
Po Box P.O. Box 13003
PHONE..................888 760-7652
Cole B Williams, *President*
Lidia Gonzalez, *Comptroller*
Pete Corrao, *Manager*
EMP: 52
SQ FT: 25,000
SALES (est): 22.8MM Privately Held
SIC: 1711 Solar energy contractor

(P-2375)
SOLARCITY CORPORATION
249 E Avenue K8 Ste 111, Lancaster (93535-4518)
PHONE..................888 765-2489
EMP: 110
SALES (corp-wide): 399.6MM Publicly Held
SIC: 1711 Solar energy contractor
PA: Solarcity Corporation
 3055 Clearview Way
 San Mateo CA 94402
 650 638-1028

(P-2376)
SOLARCITY CORPORATION (PA)
3055 Clearview Way, San Mateo (94402-3709)
PHONE..................650 638-1028
Lyndon R Rive, *CEO*
Elon Musk, *Ch of Bd*
Toby Corey, *President*
Michael Mullen, *President*
Tanguy Serra, *President*
EMP: 616
SQ FT: 68,025
SALES: 399.6MM Publicly Held
WEB: www.solarcity.com
SIC: 1711 Solar energy contractor

(P-2377)
SOLECON INDUSTRIAL CONTRS INC
1401 Mcwilliams Way, Modesto (95351-1125)
PHONE..................209 572-7390
Jeffrey Grover, *President*
Allen Layman, *Treasurer*
Elaine Grover, *Vice Pres*
Will Grover, *Vice Pres*
Dave Hedrick, *Vice Pres*
EMP: 70
SQ FT: 15,000
SALES: 11.9MM Privately Held
WEB: www.soleconindustrial.com
SIC: 1711 Plumbing contractors

(P-2378)
SOLEEVA ENERGY INC
448 Kato Ter, Fremont (94539-8332)
PHONE..................408 396-4954
Ahmad Qazi, *CEO*
Ralph Ahlgren, *President*
EMP: 55
SQ FT: 17,000
SALES (est): 5MM Privately Held
SIC: 1711 Solar energy contractor

(P-2379)
SOURCE RFRGN & HVAC INC (PA)
800 E Orangethorpe Ave, Anaheim (92801-1123)
PHONE..................714 578-2300
Bradley Norman Howard, *CEO*
Steve Cook, *President*
Hal Kolp, *President*
Andrew Mandell, *COO*
Scott Rosner, *CFO*
EMP: 250
SALES (est): 428.5MM Privately Held
WEB: www.sourcerefrigeration.com
SIC: 1711 1731 Plumbing, heating, air-conditioning contractors; electrical work

(P-2380)
SOUTH CHINA SHEET METAL INC
Also Called: General Restaurant Equipment
1740 Albion St, Los Angeles (90031-2520)
PHONE..................323 225-1522
Kam C Law, *CEO*
T K Yeung, *Vice Pres*
▲ **EMP:** 65
SQ FT: 24,000
SALES (est): 7.3MM Privately Held
WEB: www.generalrestaurant.com
SIC: 1711 3589 3444 Ventilation & duct work contractor; refrigeration contractor; commercial cooking & foodwarming equipment; sheet metalwork

(P-2381)
SOUTH COAST MECHANICAL INC
2283 E Via Burton, Anaheim (92806-1222)
PHONE..................714 738-6644
James Reynolds, *CEO*
Zoltan Bulgozdi, *President*
Suzanne Griffin, *Controller*
Kim Bates, *Traffic Dir*
John Shirley, *Foreman/Supr*
EMP: 75
SQ FT: 19,000
SALES (est): 20.5MM Privately Held
WEB: www.southcoastmechanical.com
SIC: 1711 Mechanical contractor

(P-2382)
SOUTH VALLEY PLUMBING INC
3750 Charter Park Dr F, San Jose (95136-1356)
PHONE..................408 265-5566
Fax: 408 265-2509
Robert Walker III, *President*
Lynn Jones, *Manager*
EMP: 150
SQ FT: 19,000
SALES (est): 10.7MM Privately Held
SIC: 1711 Plumbing contractors; fire sprinkler system installation

(P-2383)
SOUTHLAND INDUSTRIES (PA)
7390 Lincoln Way, Garden Grove (92841-1427)
PHONE..................800 613-6240
Fax: 949 756-3236
Theodore D Lynch, *Ch of Bd*
Charles M Allen, *COO*
Chuck Allen, *COO*
Kevin J Coghlan, *CFO*
Jon Spallino, *CFO*
EMP: 50
SQ FT: 9,000
SALES: 362.5MM Privately Held
WEB: www.southlandind.com
SIC: 1711 Plumbing, heating, air-conditioning contractors

(P-2384)
SOUTHLAND INDUSTRIES
7421 Orangewood Ave, Garden Grove (92841-1420)
PHONE..................714 901-5800
Fax: 714 901-5811
Chris Taylor, *Manager*
Victor Sanvido, *Senior VP*
Randee Guerry, *Vice Pres*
Phoebe Stowe, *General Mgr*
Chris Lanahan, *Systs Prg Mgr*
EMP: 200
SALES (corp-wide): 362.5MM Privately Held
WEB: www.southlandind.com
SIC: 1711 Plumbing, heating, air-conditioning contractors
PA: Southland Industries
 7390 Lincoln Way
 Garden Grove CA 92841
 800 613-6240

(P-2385)
STERLING PLUMBING INC
3111 W Central Ave, Santa Ana (92704-5302)
PHONE..................714 641-5480
Rodney Robbins, *President*
Leslie Schaefer, *CFO*
Kyro Hudson, *Engineer*
Sonya Farthing, *Manager*
EMP: 100
SALES (est): 16.7MM Privately Held
WEB: www.sterlingplumbinginc.com
SIC: 1711 Plumbing, heating, air-conditioning contractors

(P-2386)
STRATEGIC MECHANICAL INC
4661 E Commerce Ave, Fresno (93725-2204)
PHONE..................559 291-1952
Lonnie F Petty, *President*
Donn Petty, *Treasurer*
Chad Petty, *Admin Sec*
Ken McNeal, *Engineer*
Katherine Aldrich, *Controller*
EMP: 120
SQ FT: 60,000
SALES: 26MM Privately Held
SIC: 1711 Mechanical contractor

(P-2387)
SUNBELT CONTROLS INC
735 N Todd Ave, Azusa (91702-2244)
PHONE..................626 610-2340
Jim Boyd, *Branch Mgr*
John Kaasa, *Bd of Directors*
Bob Hamill, *Vice Pres*
David Ramirez, *Design Engr*
Madeline Simon, *Design Engr*
EMP: 60
SALES (corp-wide): 765MM Privately Held
SIC: 1711 Plumbing, heating, air-conditioning contractors
HQ: Sunbelt Controls, Inc.
 6265 San Fernando Rd
 Glendale CA 91201
 818 244-6571

(P-2388)
SUNGEVITY INC (PA)
66 Franklin St Ste 310, Oakland (94607-3734)
PHONE..................510 496-5500
Fax: 510 496-5501
Danny Kennedy, *President*
Amanda Duisman, *CEO*
David Dunlap, *COO*
Ken Schwarz, *CFO*
Gagan Sandhu, *Chief Mktg Ofcr*
EMP: 75
SALES (est): 92.1MM Privately Held
SIC: 1711 8713 Solar energy contractor; surveying services

(P-2389)
SUNPOWER CORPORATION SYSTEMS (DH)
Also Called: Powerlight
1414 Harbour Way S # 1901, Richmond (94804-3606)
P.O. Box 3821, Sunnyvale (94088-3821)
PHONE..................510 260-8200
Fax: 510 540-0552
Thomas L Dinwoodie, *CEO*
Daniel S Shugar, *President*
Peter Aschenbrenner, *Exec VP*
Lisa Bodensteiner, *Exec VP*
Charles D Boynton, *Exec VP*
◆ **EMP:** 100
SQ FT: 5,000
SALES (est): 56.8MM
SALES (corp-wide): 9.8B Publicly Held
WEB: www.powerlight.com
SIC: 1711 Solar energy contractor
HQ: Sunpower Corporation
 77 Rio Robles
 San Jose CA 95134
 408 240-5500

1711 - Plumbing, Heating & Air Conditioning Contractors County (P-2412)

(P-2390)
SUNRISE PLUMBING & MECH INC
5259 Cherry Ave, Long Beach (90805-6259)
PHONE 562 424-0332
Fax: 562 790-8590
Richard Hubbel, *CEO*
Garnet Hubbel, *Principal*
Richard Humble, *Manager*
EMP: 50
SALES (est): 7.2MM Privately Held
SIC: 1711 Plumbing contractors

(P-2391)
SUNRUN INSTALLATION SVCS INC
2300 Zanker Rd Ste F, San Jose (95131-1114)
PHONE 408 746-3062
EMP: 2000
SALES (corp-wide): 304.6MM Publicly Held
SIC: 1711 Solar energy contractor
HQ: Sunrun Installation Services Inc.
775 Fiero Ln Ste 200
San Luis Obispo CA 93401
805 528-9705

(P-2392)
SUPERIOR AUTOMATIC SPRNKLR CO
4378 Enterprise St, Fremont (94538-6305)
PHONE 408 946-7272
Fax: 408 263-5366
Bob Lawson, *President*
Peter Hulin, *President*
Marci Kearney, *Vice Pres*
Robert Lawson, *Vice Pres*
John Horne, *Project Mgr*
EMP: 100 EST: 1973
SQ FT: 15,000
SALES: 22.6MM Privately Held
WEB: www.superior-fire.com
SIC: 1711 Fire sprinkler system installation

(P-2393)
TAO MECHANICAL LTD
4023 1st St, Livermore (94551-4911)
PHONE 925 447-5220
Fax: 925 447-5264
Mitchell Ibsen, *President*
EMP: 50
SQ FT: 16,250
SALES (est): 8.3MM Privately Held
SIC: 1711 Plumbing contractors

(P-2394)
TARPY HEATING AND AIR
Also Called: Tarpy Plumbing Heating and Air
9723 Roe Dr, Santee (92071-1451)
PHONE 619 820-4580
Paul Tarpy, *President*
Jenee Tarpy, *Treasurer*
Dustin Thogmartim, *General Mgr*
EMP: 50 EST: 2007
SQ FT: 2,100
SALES: 3MM Privately Held
SIC: 1711 Heating & air conditioning contractors

(P-2395)
THERMAL MECHANICAL INC
425 Aldo Ave, Santa Clara (95054-2322)
P.O. Box 4730 (95056-4730)
PHONE 408 988-8744
Fax: 408 988-0233
Richard Rood, *CEO*
David Rood, *President*
Rob Moyer, *Project Mgr*
Boris Zalan, *Technology*
Charles Zuniga, *Purch Agent*
EMP: 77
SQ FT: 30,000
SALES: 20.7MM Privately Held
WEB: www.thermalmech.com
SIC: 1711 Mechanical contractor

(P-2396)
THERMALAIR INC (HQ)
1140 N Red Gum St, Anaheim (92806-2516)
PHONE 714 630-3200
Stephen C Weiss, *CEO*
William Reece, *President*
Rich Perez, *Exec VP*
Ginger Knecht, *Office Mgr*
Barry Doyle, *Manager*
EMP: 67 EST: 1948
SQ FT: 8,500
SALES (est): 10.6MM
SALES (corp-wide): 12.1MM Privately Held
WEB: www.thermalair.com
SIC: 1711 Heating & air conditioning contractors; ventilation & duct work contractor; refrigeration contractor
PA: General Engineering Western, Inc.
1140 N Red Gum St
Anaheim CA 92806
714 630-3200

(P-2397)
THORPE DESIGN INC
410 Beatrice St Ct Ste A, Brentwood (94513)
P.O. Box 1149 (94513-3149)
PHONE 925 634-0787
Fax: 925 634-5975
James Thorpe, *President*
Renee Thorpe, *Treasurer*
Corey Gray, *Department Mgr*
Kevin Hooper, *Department Mgr*
Paul Ramirez, *Department Mgr*
EMP: 60
SQ FT: 500
SALES (est): 13.2MM Privately Held
WEB: www.thorpedesign.com
SIC: 1711 Fire sprinkler system installation

(P-2398)
TODD PLUMBING INC
1701 Clancy Ct, Visalia (93291-5256)
P.O. Box 7629 (93290-7629)
PHONE 559 651-5820
Jim Todd Jr, *CEO*
Jim Todd Sr, *President*
Lisa Todd, *Corp Secy*
EMP: 120
SQ FT: 33,000
SALES (est): 19.5MM Privately Held
SIC: 1711 Plumbing contractors

(P-2399)
TONOPAH SOLAR ENERGY LLC
520 Broadway Fl 6, Santa Monica (90401-2420)
PHONE 310 315-2200
Kevin Smith,
EMP: 60
SALES (est): 4.5MM Privately Held
SIC: 1711 Solar energy contractor

(P-2400)
TRILOGY PLUMBING INC (PA)
1525 S Sinclair St, Anaheim (92806-5934)
PHONE 714 441-2952
Dennis Burk, *President*
Linda Burk, *Vice Pres*
David Keefe, *Director*
Michael McManus, *Director*
EMP: 225
SQ FT: 18,000
SALES (est): 33.5MM Privately Held
WEB: www.trilogyplumbing.com
SIC: 1711 Plumbing contractors

(P-2401)
TRUE AIR MECHANICAL INC
4 Faraday, Irvine (92618-2714)
PHONE 949 382-6337
Mont Flora, *COO*
Scott Flora, *President*
Kaycee Stack, *Principal*
EMP: 180
SALES (est): 11.2MM Privately Held
SIC: 1711 Plumbing, heating, air-conditioning contractors

(P-2402)
UNIVERSITY MARELICH MECH INC
1000 N Kraemer Pl, Anaheim (92806-2610)
PHONE 714 632-2600
Scott Baker, *Senior VP*
Walter S Baker, *CEO*
John R Wycoff, *CFO*
John Ellis, *Vice Pres*
Steve Ruelas, *Controller*
EMP: 150
SQ FT: 24,384
SALES (est): 21.1MM
SALES (corp-wide): 6.7B Publicly Held
WEB: www.umm-inc.com
SIC: 1711 Plumbing, heating, air-conditioning contractors
PA: Emcor Group, Inc.
301 Merritt 7 Fl 6
Norwalk CT 06851
203 849-7800

(P-2403)
UNIVERSITY MECHANICAL & (DH)
Also Called: Spira-Loc
1168 Fesler St, El Cajon (92020-1812)
PHONE 619 956-2500
Fax: 619 956-2319
Steve Shirley, *President*
Peter Novak, *CFO*
John Modjeski, *Senior VP*
Steve Thompson, *Vice Pres*
Cheryl Morris, *Administration*
EMP: 151
SQ FT: 47,000
SALES (est): 103.1MM
SALES (corp-wide): 6.7B Publicly Held
WEB: www.umec-ca.com
SIC: 1711 1623 8741 Mechanical contractor; plumbing contractors; warm air heating & air conditioning contractor; pipeline construction; construction management

(P-2404)
VALLEY CLARK PLBG & HTG CO INC (PA)
Also Called: Clark Plumbing Co
7640 Gloria Ave Ste L, Van Nuys (91406-1800)
PHONE 818 782-1047
Fax: 818 994-4956
Robert J Brunald, *President*
Traci Brunald, *Vice Pres*
Megan Pereyra, *Manager*
EMP: 50
SQ FT: 8,000
SALES (est): 8.4MM Privately Held
WEB: www.clarkplumbing.com
SIC: 1711 Plumbing, heating, air-conditioning contractors

(P-2405)
VALLEY PROCESS SYSTEMS INC
3567 Benton St Ste 341, Santa Clara (95051-4404)
PHONE 408 261-1277
Kenneth D Salazar, *CEO*
Heather Hessel, *Office Mgr*
Carla Oliveira, *Admin Asst*
EMP: 66
SQ FT: 3,200
SALES (est): 8.4MM Privately Held
WEB: www.valleyprocessinc.com
SIC: 1711 Process piping contractor

(P-2406)
VALS PLUMBING AND HEATING INC
413 Front St, Salinas (93901-3690)
PHONE 831 424-1633
Fax: 831 754-5514
Ray Spears, *President*
Valerio L Roberti, *Chairman*
Laura Roberti, *Vice Pres*
Delia Morales, *Manager*
EMP: 60
SQ FT: 12,500
SALES (est): 11.1MM Privately Held
SIC: 1711 5999 Warm air heating & air conditioning contractor; plumbing contractors; plumbing & heating supplies

(P-2407)
VENVEST BALLARD INC
3030 Myers St, Riverside (92503-5526)
PHONE 951 276-9744
George E Donaldson, *CEO*
George McNeil, *CFO*
Tara Haddad, *Accountant*
Sylvia McNeil, *Accounts Mgr*
EMP: 100
SALES (est): 14.7MM Privately Held
SIC: 1711 1731 Plumbing, heating, air-conditioning contractors; general electrical contractor

(P-2408)
VILLARA CORPORATION (PA)
Also Called: Walk Through Video
4700 Lang Ave, McClellan (95652-2023)
PHONE 916 646-2700
Fax: 916 646-2201
Gary Beutler, *CEO*
Tom Beutler, *Vice Pres*
Rob Penrod, *Vice Pres*
Scott Sahota, *Vice Pres*
Alex Long, *Info Tech Dir*
▲ EMP: 482
SALES (est): 183.8MM Privately Held
WEB: www.beutlerhvac.com
SIC: 1711 Heating & air conditioning contractors

(P-2409)
VILLARA CORPORATION
Also Called: Comfort Zone
9828 Bus Park Dr Ste A1, Sacramento (95827-1739)
PHONE 916 364-9370
Gary Beutler, *Branch Mgr*
EMP: 65
SALES (corp-wide): 183.8MM Privately Held
SIC: 1711 Heating & air conditioning contractors
PA: Villara Corporation
4700 Lang Ave
Mcclellan CA 95652
916 646-2700

(P-2410)
VILLARA CORPORATION
Also Called: Beutler Heating & AC
332 E Wetmore St, Manteca (95337-5741)
PHONE 209 824-1082
Fax: 209 824-1085
Glen Hartsough, *General Mgr*
Rob Penrod, *Chief Engr*
Scott Eagle, *Opers Staff*
Justin Sahota, *Sales Staff*
Stacy Moak, *Corp Counsel*
EMP: 65
SALES (corp-wide): 183.8MM Privately Held
WEB: www.beutlerhvac.com
SIC: 1711 Heating & air conditioning contractors
PA: Villara Corporation
4700 Lang Ave
Mcclellan CA 95652
916 646-2700

(P-2411)
VILLARA CORPORATION
Also Called: Beutler Heating & Air
4700 Lang Ave, McClellan (95652-2023)
PHONE 916 646-2222
Dana Coates, *Branch Mgr*
Andre Coetser, *Info Tech Mgr*
Ali Cakus, *Opers Staff*
EMP: 65
SALES (corp-wide): 183.8MM Privately Held
SIC: 1711 Plumbing, heating, air-conditioning contractors
PA: Villara Corporation
4700 Lang Ave
Mcclellan CA 95652
916 646-2700

(P-2412)
W L HICKEY SONS INC
190 Commercial St, Sunnyvale (94085-4507)
P.O. Box 61209 (94088-1209)
PHONE 408 736-4938
Fax: 408 736-4955
Edward Hickey, *CEO*
Michael N Hickey, *President*
Donald Calcany, *CFO*
Ed Calcany, *CFO*
Deborah Lopez, *General Mgr*
EMP: 150 EST: 1904
SQ FT: 10,000
SALES (est): 27.6MM Privately Held
WEB: www.wlhs.com
SIC: 1711 Plumbing contractors

(PA)=Parent Co (HQ)=Headquarters (DH)=Div Headquarters
✪ = New Business established in last 2 years

1711 - Plumbing, Heating & Air Conditioning Contractors County (P-2413)

(P-2413) WALTER ANDERSON PLUMBING INC
Also Called: Anderson Plbg Htg A Condition
1830 John Towers Ave, El Cajon (92020-1134)
PHONE.................................619 449-7646
Fax: 619 449-0312
Mary Jean Anderson, *CEO*
Kyle Anderson, *Vice Pres*
Debbie William, *General Mgr*
Bryan Rominger, *Sales Staff*
EMP: 125
SQ FT: 10,000
SALES (est): 19.1MM **Privately Held**
WEB: www.walterandersonplumbing.com
SIC: 1711 Plumbing, heating, air-conditioning contractors; plumbing contractors

(P-2414) WAYNE MAPLES PLUMBING & HTG
317 W Cedar St, Eureka (95501-1698)
PHONE.................................707 445-2500
Rodney Maples, *Partner*
Dale Maples, *Partner*
Mike Maples, *Partner*
Roger Maples, *Partner*
EMP: 55 EST: 1960
SQ FT: 7,000
SALES (est): 7.3MM **Privately Held**
WEB: www.maplesplumb.com
SIC: 1711 1623 Plumbing contractors; warm air heating & air conditioning contractor; underground utilities contractor

(P-2415) WEST COAST AC CO INC
1155 Pioneer Way Ste 101, El Cajon (92020-1964)
PHONE.................................619 561-8000
Fax: 619 561-3743
David Dudley, *CEO*
James Clower, *Vice Pres*
Colin Fisher, *Vice Pres*
Aaron Whitwer, *Project Mgr*
Brett Marshall, *Superintendent*
EMP: 150
SQ FT: 24,000
SALES (est): 40.1MM **Privately Held**
WEB: www.wcac.com
SIC: 1711 Warm air heating & air conditioning contractor

(P-2416) WESTATES MECHANICAL CORP INC
734 Whitney St, San Leandro (94577-1118)
PHONE.................................510 635-9830
Nigel Cowan, *CEO*
Daniel Loeffler, *Senior VP*
Renee Loefler, *Administration*
William Bird, *Director*
EMP: 60
SQ FT: 20,000
SALES (est): 11.4MM **Privately Held**
WEB: www.westatesmechanical.com
SIC: 1711 Fire sprinkler system installation

(P-2417) WESTERN ALLIED MECHANICAL INC
1180 Obrien Dr, Menlo Park (94025-1411)
PHONE.................................650 326-8290
Fax: 650 321-4946
Angela Simon, *CEO*
Robert Dills, *Shareholder*
Peter Kelly, *Shareholder*
Richard Taipale, *Shareholder*
James A Muscarella, *President*
EMP: 175
SALES (est): 59.9MM **Privately Held**
SIC: 1711 3444 Plumbing, heating, air-conditioning contractors; sheet metalwork

(P-2418) WESTERN STATES FIRE PROTECTION
3720 Industry Ave Ste 107, Lakewood (90712-4135)
PHONE.................................562 731-2961
Fax: 714 572-4418
Wesley Sue, *Manager*
Barbara Head, *Manager*
EMP: 59
SALES (corp-wide): 2.4B **Privately Held**
SIC: 1711 Fire sprinkler system installation
HQ: Western States Fire Protection Company Inc
7026 S Tucson Way
Centennial CO 80112
303 792-0022

(P-2419) WESTERN STATES FIRE PROTECTION
4740 Northgate Blvd # 150, Sacramento (95834-1150)
PHONE.................................916 924-1631
Fax: 916 924-1637
Jack White, *Manager*
Jeff Daane, *Vice Pres*
Darlene Johnstone, *Marketing Staff*
Lana Donahue, *Sales Staff*
Tom Hill, *Manager*
EMP: 80
SALES (corp-wide): 2.4B **Privately Held**
SIC: 1711 Fire sprinkler system installation
HQ: Western States Fire Protection Company Inc
7026 S Tucson Way
Centennial CO 80112
303 792-0022

(P-2420) WILMOR & SONS PLUMBING & CNSTR
8510 Thys Ct, Sacramento (95828-1007)
PHONE.................................916 381-9114
Fax: 916 381-9121
Terry Wilson, *President*
Gary Morrissette, *CEO*
EMP: 80
SQ FT: 6,000
SALES (est): 11.1MM **Privately Held**
WEB: www.wilmorplumbing.com
SIC: 1711 Plumbing contractors

(P-2421) WMI
17100 Pioneer Blvd # 230, Artesia (90701-2776)
PHONE.................................562 977-4950
Michael Chacon, *Vice Pres*
EMP: 99
SALES: 950K **Privately Held**
SIC: 1711 Plumbing contractors

(P-2422) XCEL MECHANICAL SYSTEMS INC
1710 W 130th St, Gardena (90249-2004)
PHONE.................................310 660-0090
Kevin Michel, *President*
Chris Puppe, *Technology*
Scott Burson, *Opers Mgr*
Scott Harrell, *Manager*
EMP: 175
SQ FT: 10,000
SALES: 51.4MM **Privately Held**
WEB: www.xcelmech.com
SIC: 1711 Mechanical contractor

(P-2423) ZERO ENERGY CONTRACTING INC
13850 Cerritos Corporate, Cerritos (90703-2467)
PHONE.................................626 701-3180
Michael Murphy, *Ch of Bd*
Paul Hanson, *CEO*
Jerry Suk, *CFO*
EMP: 125
SQ FT: 8,000
SALES (est): 74MM **Privately Held**
SIC: 1711 Solar energy contractor

(P-2424) ZERO ENERGY CONTRACTING LLC
13850 Cerritos Corporate, Cerritos (90703-2467)
PHONE.................................626 701-3180
Michael Murphy, *CTO*
Joe Power, *Director*
Janette Alcantar, *Manager*
Patrick Sweeting, *Manager*
EMP: 93
SALES (est): 6.9MM **Privately Held**
SIC: 1711 Solar energy contractor

1721 Painting & Paper Hanging Contractors

(P-2425) A-1 ELITE PAINTING INC
56409 Yuma Trl, Yucca Valley (92284-3614)
PHONE.................................760 365-6702
Charles Soffel, *President*
Ted Decicco, *Partner*
Glen Soffel, *Partner*
John Wright, *Partner*
Sharon Soffel, *Corp Secy*
EMP: 50
SALES: 2MM **Privately Held**
SIC: 1721 Painting & paper hanging

(P-2426) ADVANCED INDUSTRIAL SVCS INC
Also Called: Advanced Industrial Svcs Cal
7831 Alondra Blvd, Paramount (90723-5005)
PHONE.................................562 940-8305
Rex Johnston Jr, *President*
Johanna Felix, *Office Mgr*
EMP: 85
SALES (est): 12.1MM **Privately Held**
SIC: 1721 Industrial painting

(P-2427) ANNA CORPORATION
Also Called: Jfp Company
2078 2nd St, Norco (92860-2804)
PHONE.................................951 736-6037
Fax: 951 736-8743
Anna L Degiacomo, *President*
Jaime Flores, *Vice Pres*
EMP: 50
SQ FT: 6,500
SALES (est): 3.2MM **Privately Held**
SIC: 1721 Commercial painting

(P-2428) ARCHITECTURAL COATINGS INC
1565 E Edinger Ave, Santa Ana (92705-4907)
PHONE.................................714 701-1360
Sally K Rimmer, *President*
EMP: 50
SALES (est): 4.5MM **Privately Held**
SIC: 1721 Residential painting; commercial painting

(P-2429) ARENA PAINTING CONTRACTORS INC
525 E Alondra Blvd, Gardena (90248-2903)
PHONE.................................310 316-2446
Wilson Grant, *CEO*
Guy Grant II, *President*
EMP: 100
SQ FT: 10,000
SALES (est): 11.5MM **Privately Held**
SIC: 1721 Painting & paper hanging

(P-2430) ARMSTRONG INSTALLATION SERVICE
Also Called: Armstrong Construction Co
4575 San Pablo Ave, Emeryville (94608-3325)
PHONE.................................408 777-1234
Fax: 510 655-1972
Mitchell Fine, *CEO*
Arthur Levine, *CFO*
Mitch Armstrong, *Executive*
Nora Fanning, *HR Admin*
EMP: 75
SQ FT: 8,000
SALES (est): 6.4MM **Privately Held**
WEB: www.armstrong1234.com
SIC: 1721 1761 1793 Exterior residential painting contractor; interior residential painting contractor; exterior commercial painting contractor; interior commercial painting contractor; roofing, siding & sheet metal work; glass & glazing work

(P-2431) BORBON INCORPORATED
7312 Walnut Ave, Buena Park (90620-1760)
PHONE.................................714 994-0170
Fax: 714 994-0641
David Morales, *President*
Nicole Fiorentino, *Manager*
EMP: 120
SQ FT: 7,400
SALES (est): 12.5MM **Privately Held**
WEB: www.borbon.net
SIC: 1721 Residential painting; wallcovering contractors

(P-2432) C & O PAINTING INC
1500 N 4th St, San Jose (95112-4606)
PHONE.................................408 279-8011
Fax: 408 279-3032
Rick Ohlund, *President*
Chanel Ohlund, *Manager*
EMP: 50
SQ FT: 6,000
SALES (est): 4.4MM **Privately Held**
WEB: www.candopainting.com
SIC: 1721 Commercial painting; commercial wallcovering contractor

(P-2433) C B B Z S INC
Also Called: Shapiro Ben Basat Painting
7015 Valjean Ave, Van Nuys (91406-3915)
PHONE.................................818 908-1900
Fax: 818 908-9428
Zvi Shapiro, *President*
Chaim B Basat, *Vice Pres*
Raz Bronspein, *Manager*
EMP: 55
SQ FT: 5,500
SALES (est): 3.5MM **Privately Held**
SIC: 1721 Interior commercial painting contractor

(P-2434) CAL/PAC PAINTINGS & COATINGS
608 N Eckhoff St, Orange (92868-1004)
PHONE.................................714 628-1514
Dave Bedillion, *President*
Mike Stevenson, *CFO*
Lee Ann Green, *Controller*
EMP: 95
SQ FT: 2,000
SALES (est): 5.9MM **Privately Held**
WEB: www.calpacpainting.com
SIC: 1721 Residential painting

(P-2435) CERTIFIED COATINGS COMPANY
2320 Cordelia Rd, Fairfield (94534-1600)
PHONE.................................707 639-4414
David Joseph Brockman, *CEO*
Pamela Langan, *Admin Sec*
EMP: 100
SQ FT: 8,000
SALES: 27.5MM
SALES (corp-wide): 256.7MM **Privately Held**
SIC: 1721 Industrial painting
PA: Muehlhan Ag
Schlinckstr. 3
Hamburg 21107
407 527-10

(P-2436) CRAMER PAINTING INC
4080 Mission Blvd, Montclair (91763-6011)
PHONE.................................909 397-5770
Fax: 909 397-5776
Steven L Cramer, *President*
Robert Sylvester, *Vice Pres*
Michele Lewis, *Office Mgr*
Anne McWeeney, *Admin Sec*
EMP: 50
SQ FT: 6,800
SALES (est): 3.4MM **Privately Held**
WEB: www.cramerpainting.com
SIC: 1721 Commercial painting

1721 - Painting & Paper Hanging Contractors County (P-2460)

(P-2437)
D C VIENT INC (PA)
1556 Cummins Dr, Modesto (95358-6412)
P.O. Box D (95352)
PHONE..................................209 578-1224
Fax: 209 521-9337
Darlene Vient, *President*
Danielle Bell, *Shareholder*
Douglas J Vient Jr, *Corp Secy*
Douglas C Vient, *Vice Pres*
EMP: 100
SQ FT: 12,000
SALES (est): 32.6MM **Privately Held**
WEB: www.dcvient.com
SIC: 1721 Commercial painting

(P-2438)
D P S INC
Also Called: Empire Community Painting
1682 Langley Ave, Irvine (92614-5620)
PHONE..................................714 564-7900
Jason Reid, *President*
Nancy Meloni, *CFO*
Tracy Meneses, *CFO*
Jeff Gunhus, *Vice Pres*
Matt Stewart, *Vice Pres*
EMP: 91
SQ FT: 1,000
SALES: 2.8MM
SALES (corp-wide): 93.2MM **Privately Held**
WEB: www.nsgmail.com
SIC: 1721 Painting & paper hanging
PA: National Services Group, Inc.
1682 Langley Ave
Irvine CA 92614
714 564-7900

(P-2439)
DAPCON INC
877 Commercial St, San Jose (95112-1411)
PHONE..................................408 573-7200
Fax: 408 573-7400
Fernando Silva, *President*
Albert Gomes, *Vice Pres*
Lucia Silva, *Vice Pres*
EMP: 80
SQ FT: 6,000
SALES (est): 3.4MM **Privately Held**
WEB: www.dapconinc.com
SIC: 1721 1742 Residential painting; commercial painting; drywall

(P-2440)
DUGGAN & ASSOCIATES INC
1442 W 135th St, Gardena (90249-2218)
PHONE..................................323 965-1502
Fax: 323 965-1506
Chris M Duggan, *President*
Becky Derry, *Office Mgr*
Cullum Nelson, *Project Mgr*
Stephanie Alcocer, *Marketing Staff*
▼ EMP: 65
SQ FT: 10,000
SALES (est): 6.6MM **Privately Held**
SIC: 1721 Interior commercial painting contractor; commercial wallcovering contractor

(P-2441)
EMPCC INC
Also Called: Empire Community Painting
1682 Langley Ave Fl 2, Irvine (92614-5620)
PHONE..................................714 564-7900
Jason Reid, *President*
Tracy Meneses, *CFO*
Jeff Gunhus, *Vice Pres*
Matt Stewart, *Vice Pres*
Spencer Pepe, *Admin Sec*
EMP: 59
SQ FT: 1,000
SALES: 1.1MM
SALES (corp-wide): 21.1MM **Privately Held**
SIC: 1721 Painting & paper hanging
PA: Mjp Empire, Inc.
1682 Langley Ave Fl 2
Irvine CA 92614
714 564-7900

(P-2442)
EUROPEAN PAVING DESIGNS INC
1474 Berger Dr, San Jose (95112-2701)
PHONE..................................408 283-5230
Randy Hays, *CEO*
Robyn Cerutti, *CFO*
Ismael Cortez, *Admin Asst*
Liz Schooler, *Administration*
Denton Bullard, *Project Engr*
EMP: 55
SQ FT: 3,000
SALES (est): 5.2MM **Privately Held**
SIC: 1721 Pavement marking contractor

(P-2443)
FREEDOM PAINTING INC
8822 Calmada Ave, Whittier (90605-2006)
PHONE..................................562 696-0785
Gerald Lundgren, *President*
Roselina Lundgren, *Corp Secy*
Beverly Lundgren, *Vice Pres*
Stacey Lundgren, *Executive*
Darren Lundgren, *Supervisor*
EMP: 50
SQ FT: 8,000
SALES: 4MM **Privately Held**
SIC: 1721 Painting & paper hanging

(P-2444)
GENERAL COATINGS CORPORATION
9349 Feron Blvd, Rancho Cucamonga (91730-4516)
PHONE..................................909 204-4150
Craig Kinsman, *Owner*
Nick Bompensiero, *Superintendent*
EMP: 250
SALES (corp-wide): 106.4MM **Privately Held**
SIC: 1721 Painting & paper hanging
PA: General Coatings Corporation
6711 Nancy Ridge Dr
San Diego CA 92121
858 587-1277

(P-2445)
GENERAL COATINGS CORPORATION
600 W Freedom Ave, Orange (92865-2537)
PHONE..................................858 587-1277
Craig Kinsman, *Branch Mgr*
EMP: 250
SQ FT: 7,047
SALES (corp-wide): 106.4MM **Privately Held**
WEB: www.gencoat.com
SIC: 1721 Painting & paper hanging
PA: General Coatings Corporation
6711 Nancy Ridge Dr
San Diego CA 92121
858 587-1277

(P-2446)
GENERAL COATINGS CORPORATION (PA)
6711 Nancy Ridge Dr, San Diego (92121-2231)
PHONE..................................858 587-1277
Fax: 858 587-2122
Craig A Kinsman, *CEO*
Andrew Fluken, *Vice Pres*
Hector Cueva, *Project Mgr*
Gary Vittori, *Project Mgr*
Holly Hirsch, *Project Engr*
EMP: 250
SQ FT: 14,000
SALES (est): 106.4MM **Privately Held**
WEB: www.gencoat.com
SIC: 1721 1799 Painting & paper hanging; waterproofing

(P-2447)
GENERAL COATINGS CORPORATION
1220 E North Ave, Fresno (93725-1930)
PHONE..................................559 495-4004
Lee Morrison, *Principal*
EMP: 250
SALES (corp-wide): 106.4MM **Privately Held**
SIC: 1721 1799 Painting & paper hanging; coating of concrete structures with plastic
PA: General Coatings Corporation
6711 Nancy Ridge Dr
San Diego CA 92121
858 587-1277

(P-2448)
GEORGE E MASKER INC
Also Called: Masker Painting
7699 Edgewater Dr, Oakland (94621-3028)
PHONE..................................510 568-1206
Fax: 510 638-2530
Alan Bjerke, *President*
Newt Millward, *Project Mgr*
Robert Turney, *Project Mgr*
Javier Ayala, *Superintendent*
Paul Kendig, *Supervisor*
EMP: 100
SQ FT: 18,000
SALES (est): 10.1MM **Privately Held**
WEB: www.maskerpainting.com
SIC: 1721 Exterior commercial painting contractor; interior commercial painting contractor

(P-2449)
GIAMPOLINI & CO
Also Called: Giampolini/Courtney
1482 67th St, Emeryville (94608-1016)
PHONE..................................415 673-1236
Fax: 415 775-3077
Greg Quilici, *President*
Patrick Roland, *CFO*
Tom Quilici, *Vice Pres*
James Patrick Roland, *Principal*
EMP: 225
SQ FT: 9,720
SALES (est): 18.2MM **Privately Held**
WEB: www.giampolini.com
SIC: 1721 1542 1742 Exterior commercial painting contractor; interior commercial painting contractor; commercial & office buildings, renovation & repair; plastering, drywall & insulation

(P-2450)
GOLD COAST DESIGN INC
7667 Vickers St, San Diego (92111-1525)
PHONE..................................619 574-0111
Fax: 858 974-0011
David L Gash, *CEO*
Kathleen Gash, *Vice Pres*
EMP: 80
SQ FT: 7,331
SALES (est): 5.5MM **Privately Held**
SIC: 1721 Painting & paper hanging

(P-2451)
GONZALES PAINTING CORP
14437 Meridian Pkwy, Riverside (92518-3007)
PHONE..................................951 214-6400
John J Gonzales, *President*
EMP: 90
SALES (est): 3MM **Privately Held**
SIC: 1721 Interior residential painting contractor; exterior residential painting contractor; interior commercial painting contractor; exterior commercial painting contractor

(P-2452)
GPS PAINTING WALLCOVERING INC
1307 E Saint Gertrude Pl C, Santa Ana (92705-5228)
PHONE..................................714 730-8904
Eliot Schneider, *President*
David Cuevas, *Sr Project Mgr*
Michelle Palacios, *Manager*
Alison Tatum, *Manager*
EMP: 110
SALES (est): 9.6MM **Privately Held**
WEB: www.gpspainting.com
SIC: 1721 Painting & paper hanging

(P-2453)
GUZMANS PAINTING
2772 Bay Tree Dr, Fairfield (94533-7070)
PHONE..................................707 428-3727
Efrin Guzman, *Owner*
EMP: 50
SALES (est): 1.2MM **Privately Held**
SIC: 1721 Painting & paper hanging

(P-2454)
HARRIS & RUTH PAINTING CONTG (PA)
2107 W San Bernardino Rd, West Covina (91790-1007)
PHONE..................................626 960-4004
Fax: 626 338-3584
Terry Cairy, *President*
Mark Heydorff, *COO*
Kathleen Boyer, *Office Admin*
Bruce Boyer, *Admin Sec*
Gayle Peura, *Controller*
EMP: 70
SQ FT: 1,000
SALES: 8.3MM **Privately Held**
WEB: www.harris-ruthpainting.com
SIC: 1721 Commercial painting; industrial painting

(P-2455)
J C FRENCH & COMPANY
2984 1st St Ste L, La Verne (91750-5675)
PHONE..................................909 596-1423
Sandra Perry, *President*
John C French, *CFO*
Robert French, *Corp Secy*
August Jacobson, *Senior VP*
Ann French, *Manager*
EMP: 60 EST: 1977
SQ FT: 12,000
SALES (est): 4.5MM **Privately Held**
WEB: www.jcfrench.com
SIC: 1721 Painting & paper hanging

(P-2456)
J M V B INC
Also Called: Spc Building Services
12118 Severn Way, Riverside (92503-4804)
P.O. Box 614, Orange (92856-6614)
PHONE..................................714 288-9797
Fax: 714 288-9799
Benjamin J Rodriguez, *President*
EMP: 80 EST: 1993
SALES (est): 4.8MM **Privately Held**
SIC: 1721 Painting & paper hanging

(P-2457)
J P CARROLL CO INC
5707 Milton Ave, Whittier (90601-2420)
PHONE..................................323 660-9230
Fax: 323 660-9238
H B Fitzpatrick, *Ch of Bd*
Kevin Fitzpatrick, *President*
Rebecca Derry, *Vice Pres*
Barbara Fitzpatrick, *Admin Sec*
Jun Oro, *Controller*
EMP: 60
SQ FT: 25,000
SALES (est): 4.1MM **Privately Held**
WEB: www.jpcarrollco.com
SIC: 1721 Residential painting; commercial painting; wallcovering contractors

(P-2458)
JD MILLER CONSTRUCTION INC
506 W Graham Ave Ste 202, Lake Elsinore (92530-3600)
PHONE..................................951 471-3513
Jeff Mosher, *CEO*
Jeffery D Miller, *President*
Sunny Janssen, *Manager*
EMP: 50
SALES (est): 8MM **Privately Held**
SIC: 1721 Painting & paper hanging

(P-2459)
JEFFCO PAINTING & COATING INC
1260 Railroad Ave, Vallejo (94592-1012)
P.O. Box 1888 (94590-0655)
PHONE..................................707 562-1900
Fax: 707 562-1907
Steve Jeffress, *President*
Gene Glockner, *CFO*
Todd Anderson, *Vice Pres*
Rich Dreyer, *Vice Pres*
Jeff Dortch, *Project Mgr*
EMP: 100
SALES (est): 11.2MM **Privately Held**
WEB: www.jeffcoptg.com
SIC: 1721 3471 Industrial painting; sand blasting of metal parts

(P-2460)
JERRY THOMPSON & SONS PNTG INC
3 Simms St, San Rafael (94901-5414)
PHONE..................................415 454-1500
Stephen G Thompson, *President*

1721 - Painting & Paper Hanging Contractors County (P-2461)

Dennis J Thompson, *Corp Secy*
Ed Conlon, *Vice Pres*
Eric Foster, *Vice Pres*
Ben Amaya, *Project Mgr*
EMP: 140
SALES (est): 13MM **Privately Held**
SIC: 1721 Painting & paper hanging

(P-2461)
JOHNSON & TURNER PAINTING CO
8241 Electric Ave, Stanton (90680-2640)
PHONE..................714 828-8282
Fax: 714 828-1035
Dale Bodwell, *President*
Michelle Bodwell, *Office Mgr*
Jim Chester, *Superintendent*
▲ **EMP:** 50 **EST:** 1955
SQ FT: 6,000
SALES: 4.8MM **Privately Held**
SIC: 1721 Painting & paper hanging

(P-2462)
LAWRENCE B BONAS COMPANY
3197 Arprt Loop Dr Ste C, Costa Mesa (92626)
PHONE..................714 668-5250
Fax: 714 668-5251
Guy A Bonas, *President*
Doris A Bonas, *Treasurer*
EMP: 75
SQ FT: 7,200
SALES (est): 4.5MM **Privately Held**
SIC: 1721 Painting & paper hanging; wallcovering contractors

(P-2463)
LIVING COLORS INC
16026 Rayen St, North Hills (91343-4814)
PHONE..................818 893-5068
Raymond Sponsler, *President*
Paula Sponsler, *Treasurer*
Daniel Barton, *Sales Executive*
EMP: 60
SALES (est): 3.5MM **Privately Held**
WEB: www.livingcolorsinc.com
SIC: 1721 Residential painting

(P-2464)
M C BUILDER CORP
1251 Montalvo Way Ste L, Palm Springs (92262-5497)
PHONE..................760 323-8010
Ernest Castro, *Owner*
EMP: 50
SQ FT: 2,800
SALES (est): 3.1MM **Privately Held**
SIC: 1721 Commercial painting; residential painting

(P-2465)
MC PAINTING (PA)
2525 Ramona Dr, Vista (92084-1632)
PHONE..................760 599-8000
Kerry Lynn Lewis, *CEO*
Michael Lewis, *President*
EMP: 170
SALES (est): 13.4MM **Privately Held**
WEB: www.mcppainting.com
SIC: 1721 Painting & paper hanging

(P-2466)
MEYER COATINGS INC
606 N Eckhoff St, Orange (92868-1004)
PHONE..................714 467-4600
Fax: 714 467-4606
Diana Meyer, *CEO*
Scott Meyer, *President*
Veronica Santoyo, *Vice Pres*
Kylie Suica, *Admin Asst*
John Beltran, *Project Mgr*
EMP: 50
SQ FT: 4,800
SALES (est): 5.7MM **Privately Held**
WEB: www.meyercoatings.com
SIC: 1721 Commercial painting

(P-2467)
MICKEY WALL PAINTING INC
2470 Acme Ct, Turlock (95380-9564)
P.O. Box 3302 (95381-3302)
PHONE..................209 669-0557
Fax: 209 669-0357
Mickey Wall, *President*
Kathy Wall, *CFO*
Christina Lanjoni, *Manager*
EMP: 50
SQ FT: 6,000
SALES (est): 3.8MM **Privately Held**
WEB: www.mickeywallpainting.com
SIC: 1721 Residential painting; exterior residential painting contractor; interior residential painting contractor

(P-2468)
MIKE CHAMPLIN
Also Called: Mike Champlin Painting
4374 Contractors Cmn, Livermore (94551-7544)
PHONE..................925 961-1004
Fax: 925 961-1005
Mike Champlin, *Owner*
EMP: 100
SALES (est): 6MM **Privately Held**
SIC: 1721 Painting & paper hanging

(P-2469)
NAVAL COATING INC
3475 E St, San Diego (92102-3335)
PHONE..................619 234-8366
Alan Lerchbacker, *President*
Don Vargo, *Human Res Dir*
EMP: 149
SQ FT: 50,000
SALES (est): 17MM **Privately Held**
WEB: www.navalcoating.com
SIC: 1721 1799 Industrial painting; exterior cleaning, including sandblasting

(P-2470)
NORCAL PAINTERS INC
Also Called: Certapro Painters
60 29th St 241, San Francisco (94110-4929)
PHONE..................415 566-6800
Terrance Ladd, *President*
George Irving, *General Mgr*
EMP: 53
SALES (est): 2.9MM **Privately Held**
SIC: 1721 Painting & paper hanging

(P-2471)
NORTH ORANGE COAST PNTG INC
3969 Sierra Ave, Norco (92860-1390)
P.O. Box 520 (92860-0520)
PHONE..................951 279-2694
Fax: 951 279-9510
EMP: 100
SALES (est): 5MM **Privately Held**
SIC: 1721

(P-2472)
P B C PAVERS INC
Also Called: Peterson Bros Construction
1560 W Lambert Rd, Brea (92821-2826)
PHONE..................714 278-0488
Fax: 714 278-0487
Robert Peterson, *President*
Eldin Peterson, *Vice Pres*
Orlando Davila, *General Mgr*
Doug Clayton, *Business Mgr*
Val Payne, *Controller*
▲ **EMP:** 80
SALES (est): 7.1MM **Privately Held**
SIC: 1721 Pavement marking contractor

(P-2473)
PETERSON PAINTING INC
5750 La Ribera St, Livermore (94550-9204)
PHONE..................925 455-5864
Fax: 925 455-5867
Raymond Peterson, *President*
John Peterson, *Vice Pres*
EMP: 350
SQ FT: 10,000
SALES (est): 15.8MM **Privately Held**
WEB: www.petersonpainting.com
SIC: 1721 Residential painting

(P-2474)
PILOT PAINTING & CONSTRUCTION
5555 Corporate Ave, Cypress (90630-4708)
P.O. Box 6377, Anaheim (92816-0377)
PHONE..................714 229-5900
Steve Gilkey, *President*
EMP: 60
SQ FT: 7,856
SALES (est): 3.3MM **Privately Held**
SIC: 1721 Residential painting

(P-2475)
PREMIER COMMERCIAL PAINTING
17150 Newhope St Ste 405, Fountain Valley (92708-4268)
PHONE..................714 546-3692
Robert Black, *President*
EMP: 50
SALES (est): 1.9MM **Privately Held**
SIC: 1721 Painting & paper hanging

(P-2476)
PRIMECO PAINTING & CNSTR
1107 S Cleveland St, Oceanside (92054-5109)
PHONE..................760 967-8278
Brett Musgrove, *President*
Stacey Musgrove, *Admin Sec*
Linda Smith, *Manager*
Sandy Young, *Accounts Mgr*
EMP: 90
SQ FT: 2,100
SALES (est): 7.4MM **Privately Held**
WEB: www.primecopainting.com
SIC: 1721 1542 Painting & paper hanging; commercial & office building contractors

(P-2477)
PS2 (PA)
17903 S Hobart Blvd, Gardena (90248-3613)
PHONE..................310 243-2980
Peter Schmit, *President*
Peter Short, *Admin Sec*
EMP: 68
SQ FT: 2,000
SALES (est): 11.6MM **Privately Held**
SIC: 1721 Painting & paper hanging

(P-2478)
PYRAMID PAINTING INC
2925 Bayview Dr, Fremont (94538-6520)
PHONE..................650 903-9791
Craig Ruybalid, *President*
EMP: 50
SQ FT: 6,240
SALES (est): 4.2MM **Privately Held**
WEB: www.pyramidpainting.com
SIC: 1721 Exterior commercial painting contractor; interior commercial painting contractor

(P-2479)
R & A PAINTING INC
11730 Sheldon Lake Dr, Elk Grove (95624-9649)
P.O. Box 292730, Sacramento (95829-2730)
PHONE..................916 688-3955
Fax: 916 688-5988
Antonio Rodrigues, *President*
Cidalia Rodrigues, *Corp Secy*
EMP: 60
SALES (est): 2.5MM **Privately Held**
SIC: 1721 Commercial painting; residential painting

(P-2480)
R-BROS PAINTING INC
707 W Hedding St, San Jose (95110-1533)
PHONE..................408 291-6820
Fax: 408 291-6828
Rod Rodriquez, *President*
Paulina Tran, *Office Mgr*
Scott Allen, *Accounting Mgr*
Jennifer Wade, *Controller*
▲ **EMP:** 50
SQ FT: 3,000
SALES (est): 5.8MM **Privately Held**
WEB: www.rbrothers.com
SIC: 1721 Commercial painting

(P-2481)
RANDALL MC-ANANY COMPANY
4935 Mcconnell Ave Ste 20, Los Angeles (90066-6756)
PHONE..................310 822-3344
Fax: 310 301-4924
Timothy Mc Anany, *President*
Nancy Mc Anany, *Corp Secy*
Bill Dinh, *District Mgr*
Steve Forsythe, *Purch Mgr*
Timothy J McAnany, *Agent*
EMP: 60
SQ FT: 8,500
SALES: 5.5MM **Privately Held**
WEB: www.rmcompany.com
SIC: 1721 Commercial painting; commercial wallcovering contractor

(P-2482)
RC WENDT PAINTING INC
21612 Surveyor Cir, Huntington Beach (92646-7068)
PHONE..................714 960-2700
Fax: 714 969-6871
Robert C Wendt, *President*
Jeri Wendt, *Corp Secy*
Scott Wendt, *Vice Pres*
Jim Montgomery, *General Mgr*
EMP: 110
SALES (est): 7MM **Privately Held**
WEB: www.wendtcompanies.com
SIC: 1721 Residential painting; commercial painting

(P-2483)
REDWOOD PAINTING CO INC
620 W 10th St, Pittsburg (94565-1806)
P.O. Box 1269 (94565-0126)
PHONE..................925 432-4500
Fax: 925 432-6129
Charles Duke Del Monte, *CEO*
George Del Monte, *Exec VP*
EMP: 110
SQ FT: 19,000
SALES (est): 11.1MM **Privately Held**
WEB: www.redwoodptg.com
SIC: 1721 Commercial painting; industrial painting

(P-2484)
RJP CONSTRUCTION & PAINTING (PA)
22600 Lambert St Ste 807, Lake Forest (92630-1620)
PHONE..................949 707-5449
Fax: 949 707-5849
Raymond J Puzio, *President*
Sophia Patricko, *Office Mgr*
▲ **EMP:** 100
SQ FT: 2,400
SALES: 9.1MM **Privately Held**
WEB: www.rjpinc.net
SIC: 1721 Residential painting; commercial painting

(P-2485)
ROBERT MEUSCHKE COMPANY INC
Also Called: RMC Painting & Restoration
1039 Edwards Rd, Burlingame (94010-2318)
PHONE..................650 342-3993
Bob Meuschke, *President*
Andy Smith, *Admin Sec*
EMP: 50
SQ FT: 1,200
SALES (est): 2.1MM **Privately Held**
WEB: www.rmcpainting.com
SIC: 1721 Exterior commercial painting contractor; interior commercial painting contractor

(P-2486)
RODIN & CO INC
7411 Laurel Canyon Blvd # 10, North Hollywood (91605-3160)
PHONE..................818 358-3427
Fred Rodin, *President*
Rowena Rodin, *Admin Sec*
EMP: 60
SQ FT: 4,400
SALES (est): 4.2MM **Privately Held**
WEB: www.rodincompany.com
SIC: 1721 Painting & paper hanging; wallcovering contractors

(P-2487)
RTE ENTERPRISES INC
Also Called: Color Concepts
21530 Roscoe Blvd, Canoga Park (91304-4144)
PHONE..................818 999-5300
Fax: 818 999-5651
Ron Evenhaim, *President*
EMP: 100
SQ FT: 2,000

SALES (est): 5.3MM **Privately Held**
WEB: www.colorconcepts.net
SIC: **1721** **1742** Painting & paper hanging; plastering, drywall & insulation

(P-2488)
S W P T X INC
Also Called: Student Works Painting
1682 Langley Ave, Irvine (92614-5620)
PHONE..................714 564-7900
Matthew Stewart, *President*
EMP: 120
SALES (est): 2.9MM
SALES (corp-wide): 93.2MM **Privately Held**
WEB: www.nsgmail.com
SIC: **1721** Painting & paper hanging
PA: National Services Group, Inc.
   1682 Langley Ave
   Irvine CA 92614
   714 564-7900

(P-2489)
SANDERS & WOHRMAN CORPORATION
709 N Poplar St, Orange (92868-1013)
PHONE..................714 919-0446
Fax: 714 919-0447
John Thomas Wohrman, *President*
Todd Wohrman, *Treasurer*
Raymond Wohrman, *Project Mgr*
Terra Pawell, *Accountant*
Stephen Stewart, *Manager*
EMP: 150
SQ FT: 12,000
SALES (est): 15MM **Privately Held**
WEB: www.swpainting.com
SIC: **1721** Painting & paper hanging; industrial painting

(P-2490)
SCHAPER CONSTRUCTION INC (PA)
1177 N 15th St, San Jose (95112-1422)
PHONE..................408 437-0337
Fax: 408 437-0339
Leon Schaper, *CEO*
Curtis Schaper, *Vice Pres*
Greg Sipe, *General Mgr*
Phil Adams, *Controller*
Stacii Schneider, *Controller*
EMP: 90
SQ FT: 8,400
SALES (est): 37.6MM **Privately Held**
WEB: www.schaperco.com
SIC: **1721** **1611** **1542** Exterior residential painting contractor; interior residential painting contractor; general contractor, highway & street construction; nonresidential construction

(P-2491)
SCHAPER CONSTRUCTION INC
211 Granite St Ste G, Corona (92879-6560)
PHONE..................951 808-1140
Greg Atteberry, *Project Mgr*
EMP: 55
SALES (corp-wide): 37.6MM **Privately Held**
SIC: **1721** Painting & paper hanging
PA: Schaper Construction, Inc.
   1177 N 15th St
   San Jose CA 95112
   408 437-0337

(P-2492)
SOCAL COATINGS INC
2820 Via Orange Way Ste J, Spring Valley (91978-1742)
PHONE..................619 660-5395
Fax: 619 660-5397
Norma Alicia Alonso, *CEO*
John Thomas Fox, *Vice Pres*
EMP: 50 EST: 2014
SALES (est): 2.5MM **Privately Held**
SIC: **1721** Painting & paper hanging

(P-2493)
STEGER INC
1938 N Batavia St Ste L, Orange (92865-4140)
PHONE..................714 974-4383
Fax: 714 974-4384
Michael Steger, *President*
Chris Knorr, *Project Mgr*
EMP: 50
SALES (est): 3.8MM **Privately Held**
WEB: www.steger.com
SIC: **1721** Residential painting; commercial painting

(P-2494)
STEVE BEATTIE INC
Also Called: Steve Beattie Painting
1766 Westridge Rd, Los Angeles (90049-2516)
PHONE..................310 454-1786
Steve Beattie, *President*
Patricia H McGuire, *CEO*
EMP: 60 EST: 1986
SALES (est): 4.5MM **Privately Held**
SIC: **1721** Residential painting

(P-2495)
STEWART PAINTING INC
1351 Brookdale Ave, Mountain View (94040-3025)
P.O. Box 4880 (94040-0880)
PHONE..................650 968-3706
Fax: 650 968-6856
Bruce Stewart, *President*
Donna Stewart, *Corp Secy*
EMP: 57
SALES (est): 3MM **Privately Held**
SIC: **1721** Residential painting

(P-2496)
STUDENT WORKS PAINTING INC
1682 Langley Ave, Irvine (92614-5620)
PHONE..................714 564-7900
Spencer Pepe, *President*
Mathew Stewart, *Treasurer*
Matthew Stewart, *Treasurer*
Josh Daniels, *Vice Pres*
Carl Dice, *Vice Pres*
EMP: 300
SALES (est): 6.1MM
SALES (corp-wide): 93.2MM **Privately Held**
WEB: www.nsgmail.com
SIC: **1721** Residential painting
PA: National Services Group, Inc.
   1682 Langley Ave
   Irvine CA 92614
   714 564-7900

(P-2497)
T & R PAINTING CONSTRUCTION
7116 Valjean Ave, Van Nuys (91406-3901)
PHONE..................818 779-3800
Fax: 818 994-2633
Robin Rapaport, *President*
EMP: 110
SALES (est): 4.2MM **Privately Held**
WEB: www.tandrweb.com
SIC: **1721** Residential painting; commercial painting

(P-2498)
TRANS WORLD MAINTENANCE INC
Also Called: S A S
1590 Rollins Rd, Millbrae (94030)
PHONE..................650 455-2450
Theodore Siotos, *President*
Ted Siotos, *Vice Pres*
Costandinos Siotos, *Principal*
Alexandra Siotos, *Admin Sec*
EMP: 71
SQ FT: 5,700
SALES (est): 772.7K **Privately Held**
SIC: **1721** **8742** **1542** Residential painting; construction project management consultant; commercial & office buildings, renovation & repair

(P-2499)
TWI- TECHNO WEST INC
1391 S Allec St, Anaheim (92805-6304)
PHONE..................714 635-4070
Fax: 714 635-4078
Marcia Birney, *Chairman*
David Bostwick, *Administration*
Don McCage, *Administration*
Brett Buffington, *Sales Staff*
Rachel Jiminez, *Manager*
EMP: 85
SQ FT: 30,000
SALES (est): 4.1MM **Privately Held**
WEB: www.multipleplantservices.com
SIC: **1721** Commercial painting

(P-2500)
URBAN BROS PAINTING INC
40 Lisbon St, San Rafael (94901-4709)
PHONE..................415 485-1130
Michael James Urban, *President*
Robert S Urban, *Shareholder*
James De Martini, *Vice Pres*
Chris Urban, *Vice Pres*
Martin Flores, *Human Res Mgr*
EMP: 60
SQ FT: 6,000
SALES (est): 5.1MM **Privately Held**
WEB: www.urbanco.com
SIC: **1721** Commercial painting; residential painting

(P-2501)
VERTEX COATINGS INC
1291 W State St, Ontario (91762-4015)
PHONE..................909 923-5795
Russ Phillips, *President*
Stacy Phillips, *Admin Sec*
Jennifer Phillips, *Accounting Mgr*
EMP: 70
SQ FT: 11,000
SALES (est): 6.2MM **Privately Held**
WEB: www.vertexcoatings.com
SIC: **1721** Commercial painting

(P-2502)
WEST COAST INTERIORS INC
Also Called: West Coast Painting
1610 W Linden St, Riverside (92507-6810)
PHONE..................951 778-3592
Fax: 951 786-9702
Mark Herbert, *CEO*
Dan Slavin, *President*
Santos Garcia, *COO*
Milo Way, *General Mgr*
Keith Caneva, *Controller*
EMP: 600
SQ FT: 8,000
SALES (est): 39.6MM **Privately Held**
SIC: **1721** Wallcovering contractors

(P-2503)
WILSON HAMPTON PNTG CONTRS INC
1524 W Mable St, Anaheim (92802-1097)
P.O. Box 9949 (92812-7949)
PHONE..................714 772-5091
Fax: 714 776-6808
Douglas J Hampton, *President*
Alan L Vankirk, *CFO*
Clifford C Hampton, *Vice Pres*
Hallie Scott, *Office Mgr*
Robert D Hampton III, *Admin Sec*
EMP: 60
SQ FT: 44,000
SALES (est): 6.2MM **Privately Held**
WEB: www.wilsonhampton.com
SIC: **1721** **7641** Residential painting; furniture repair & maintenance; office furniture repair & maintenance

(P-2504)
WM B SALEH CO
1364 N Jackson Ave, Fresno (93703-4624)
PHONE..................559 255-2046
Fax: 559 255-2907
Mark Saleh, *President*
Katherine Brusellas, *Corp Secy*
Doyle Fikes, *Vice Pres*
William B Saleh, *Vice Pres*
Connie York, *Admin Asst*
EMP: 75
SQ FT: 6,800
SALES (est): 3.5MM **Privately Held**
SIC: **1721** Commercial painting; industrial painting; commercial wallcovering contractor

---
1731 Electrical Work

(P-2505)
A M ORTEGA CONSTRUCTION INC (PA)
Also Called: Western Rim Pipeline
10125 Channel Rd, Lakeside (92040-1703)
PHONE..................619 390-1988
Fax: 619 390-1941
Archie Maurice Ortega, *President*
Linda Ortega, *Admin Sec*
Renee Creed, *Human Res Dir*
Jose Flores, *Manager*
EMP: 110 EST: 1974
SQ FT: 10,000
SALES (est): 50.6MM **Privately Held**
WEB: www.amortega.com
SIC: **1731** Electrical work

(P-2506)
A M ORTEGA CONSTRUCTION INC
Also Called: A.M. Ortega Construction
224 N Sherman Ave, Corona (92882-1843)
PHONE..................951 360-1352
Archie Ortega, *President*
EMP: 78
SALES (corp-wide): 50.6MM **Privately Held**
SIC: **1731** Electrical work
PA: A. M. Ortega Construction, Inc.
   10125 Channel Rd
   Lakeside CA 92040
   619 390-1988

(P-2507)
A-1 ELECTRIC SERVICE CO INC
4204 Sepulveda Blvd, Culver City (90230-4709)
P.O. Box 6453, Malibu (90264-6453)
PHONE..................310 204-1077
Linda Pieper, *CEO*
Scott Pieper, *Vice Pres*
Eric Cashman, *Technology*
EMP: 50
SQ FT: 5,000
SALES: 13.1MM **Privately Held**
WEB: www.a-1electric.com
SIC: **1731** Electrical work

(P-2508)
AA/ACME LOCKSMITHS INC
1660 Factor Ave, San Leandro (94577-5618)
PHONE..................510 483-6584
Fax: 510 483-8123
Steven Harris, *President*
Steven K Harris, *President*
Eleanor Harris, *Corp Secy*
Anmarie Harris, *Vice Pres*
Domenic Dionisio, *Admin Asst*
EMP: 95
SQ FT: 20,000
SALES (est): 19.8MM **Privately Held**
SIC: **1731** **5999** Fire detection & burglar alarm systems specialization; alarm signal systems

(P-2509)
AAA ELCTRCAL CMMUNICATIONS INC (PA)
Also Called: AAA Property Services
25007 Anza Dr, Valencia (91355-3414)
PHONE..................800 892-4784
Fax: 818 252-9308
Joann Katinos, *CEO*
Brian Higgins, *President*
Lorrain Swanson, *Accounts Mgr*
EMP: 133
SQ FT: 6,000
SALES: 17MM **Privately Held**
SIC: **1731** **1711** **7349** **1721** Electrical work; plumbing, heating, air-conditioning contractors; building maintenance services; commercial painting; commercial & office buildings, renovation & repair

(P-2510)
ACCUNEX INC
Also Called: Accurate Electronics
20700 Lassen St, Chatsworth (91311-4507)
PHONE..................818 882-5858
Farid Jadali, *President*
Roxana Coronado, *Vice Pres*
Karla Carcamo, *Accounts Mgr*
▲ EMP: 50
SQ FT: 25,000
SALES: 6.9MM **Privately Held**
WEB: www.accurate-elec.com
SIC: **1731** Electrical work

1731 - Electrical Work County (P-2511)

(P-2511)
AJ KIRKWOOD & ASSOCIATES INC
2752 Walnut Ave, Tustin (92780-7025)
PHONE.....................714 505-1977
James Klassen, *President*
Aidan Culligan, *Senior VP*
Michelle Kirkwood, *Admin Sec*
Rollie Beaver, *Project Mgr*
Bradley Hanenberg, *Project Mgr*
EMP: 130
SQ FT: 18,000
SALES: 60.4MM **Privately Held**
WEB: www.ajk-a.com
SIC: 1731 7389 8748 Electrical work; design services; communications consulting

(P-2512)
ALASKA EXPERIMENT INC
Also Called: Ricochet Television
3800 Barham Blvd Ste 410, Los Angeles (90068-1042)
PHONE.....................323 904-4680
Kirsti Robson, *President*
EMP: 50
SALES (est): 3.9MM **Privately Held**
SIC: 1731 Cable television installation

(P-2513)
ALBD ELECTRIC AND CABLE
Also Called: A Lighting By Design
2912 E Blue Star St, Anaheim (92806-2509)
PHONE.....................949 440-1216
Chad Lambert, *CEO*
James Black, *President*
EMP: 100
SQ FT: 12,000
SALES: 15MM **Privately Held**
SIC: 1731 3651 General electrical contractor; household audio & video equipment

(P-2514)
ALGONQUIN POWER AND UTILITIES
Also Called: Liberty Energy
933 Eloise Ave, South Lake Tahoe (96150-6470)
PHONE.....................530 543-5288
Fax: 909 390-9949
Ian Robertson, *CEO*
David Bronicheski, *CFO*
Tisha Sanderson, *Accounting Mgr*
Stephen McCrodan, *Manager*
EMP: 400 EST: 2011
SQ FT: 10,000
SALES (est): 20.3MM **Privately Held**
SIC: 1731 Electrical work

(P-2515)
ALL DAY ELECTRIC COMPANY INC
4620 W America Dr B, Fairfield (94534-4186)
PHONE.....................707 748-1036
James Coleman, *Vice Pres*
Monica Lorenzetti, *Manager*
EMP: 50
SQ FT: 300
SALES (est): 4.2MM **Privately Held**
SIC: 1731 Electrical work

(P-2516)
ALL-GUARD ALARM SYSTEMS INC (PA)
Also Called: Grand Central Station
1306 Stealth St, Livermore (94551-9356)
PHONE.....................510 887-7055
Fax: 510 887-7364
Denis Cooke, *President*
Michael Cooke, *Corp Secy*
John P Cooke, *Vice Pres*
Patricia Cooke, *Vice Pres*
Jodie L Osborne, *Controller*
EMP: 59
SQ FT: 12,600
SALES: 10.2MM **Privately Held**
SIC: 1731 7382 Fire detection & burglar alarm systems specialization; burglar alarm maintenance & monitoring

(P-2517)
AMERICAN ELECTRICAL SVCS INC
501 San Benito St Fl 3, Hollister (95023-3903)
PHONE.....................831 638-1737
Ignacio Velazquez, *CEO*
Richard Champion, *President*
▲ **EMP:** 110
SQ FT: 1,700
SALES (est): 9.4MM **Privately Held**
SIC: 1731 Electrical work

(P-2518)
AMERICAN ENGRG CONTRS INC
Also Called: Budget Electric
1204 Holly Dr, Tracy (95376-3509)
PHONE.....................209 229-1591
Fax: 209 832-2387
Larry Walling, *President*
Patricia Walling, *Corp Secy*
Aaron Carlos, *Project Mgr*
Darren Whitney, *Sr Project Mgr*
Brenda Sutton, *Accounts Mgr*
EMP: 180
SQ FT: 4,000
SALES (est): 20.4MM **Privately Held**
WEB: www.budgete.com
SIC: 1731 General electrical contractor

(P-2519)
AMI ELECTRICAL & TELECOM INC
11572 Carnation Cir, Fountain Valley (92708-1801)
PHONE.....................714 531-0872
Nhue David Ngo, *President*
EMP: 70
SQ FT: 6,595
SALES (est): 3.7MM **Privately Held**
SIC: 1731 Communications specialization

(P-2520)
AMS ELECTRIC INC
6905 Sierra Ct, Dublin (94568-2708)
PHONE.....................925 961-1600
William Breyton, *President*
Michael Stellato, *Treasurer*
John Modica, *Vice Pres*
Craig Ayers, *Admin Sec*
Daniel Arenas, *Project Mgr*
EMP: 75
SQ FT: 25,000
SALES (est): 18.5MM **Privately Held**
WEB: www.amselectric.com
SIC: 1731 General electrical contractor

(P-2521)
ANDERSON & HOWARD ELECTRIC INC
Also Called: Anderson Howard
1791 Reynolds Ave, Irvine (92614-5711)
P.O. Box 16309 (92623-6309)
PHONE.....................949 250-4555
Fax: 949 250-1918
Brian E Elliott, *President*
Charles B Howard, *Vice Pres*
Greg Elliott, *General Mgr*
Tom Howard, *Admin Sec*
Brian Busch, *Sr Project Mgr*
EMP: 210
SQ FT: 10,500
SALES (est): 56.7MM **Privately Held**
WEB: www.aandh.com
SIC: 1731 Electrical work

(P-2522)
APOLLO ELECTRIC
330 N Basse Ln, Brea (92821-3906)
PHONE.....................714 256-8414
Fax: 714 671-9972
Leroy H Holt, *CEO*
Gregg L Holt, *Corp Secy*
Brent Holt, *Vice Pres*
Kelly Shay, *Vice Pres*
Quynh Jeong, *Executive*
EMP: 60 EST: 1966
SQ FT: 18,000
SALES (est): 12.4MM **Privately Held**
WEB: www.apolloelect.com
SIC: 1731 General electrical contractor

(P-2523)
ASSI SECURITY (PA)
1370 Reynolds Ave Ste 201, Irvine (92614-5547)
PHONE.....................949 955-0244
Fax: 949 955-0243
William Dominic Vuono, *President*
Tamara Sandoval, *Vice Pres*
Michael Willey, *Vice Pres*
Kevin Gowan, *Prgrmr*
David Bartling, *Project Mgr*
EMP: 67
SQ FT: 10,000
SALES (est): 15.9MM **Privately Held**
WEB: www.assisecurity.com
SIC: 1731 7382 Voice, data & video wiring contractor; fire detection & burglar alarm systems specialization; security systems services; protective devices, security; burglar alarm maintenance & monitoring; confinement surveillance systems maintenance & monitoring

(P-2524)
ATK AUDIOTEK
Also Called: Atk Services
28238 Avenue Crocker, Valencia (91355-1248)
PHONE.....................661 705-3700
Michael Murray Macdonald, *President*
Bill Lincoln, *CFO*
William Lincoln, *CFO*
J Scott Harmala, *Vice Pres*
John M Stewart, *Admin Sec*
EMP: 85
SQ FT: 25,000
SALES (est): 21MM **Privately Held**
WEB: www.atkcorp.com
SIC: 1731 7359 Voice, data & video wiring contractor; sound & lighting equipment rental

(P-2525)
B F C INC
45 Broadway, San Francisco (94111-1403)
PHONE.....................415 495-3085
John M Walsh, *President*
James Toy, *Division Mgr*
Susan Chin, *Office Mgr*
Chelsea Webb, *Admin Asst*
Miles Luquingan, *Network Tech*
EMP: 110
SQ FT: 2,000
SALES (est): 50.2MM **Privately Held**
WEB: www.cbfelectric.com
SIC: 1731 General electrical contractor

(P-2526)
BANISTER ELECTRICAL INC
2532 Verne Roberts Cir, Antioch (94509-7904)
PHONE.....................925 778-7801
Daniel T Pauline, *President*
Shovawn Barrera, *Controller*
EMP: 70
SALES (est): 6.6MM **Privately Held**
SIC: 1731 General electrical contractor

(P-2527)
BARNUM & CELILLO ELECTRIC INC (PA)
135 Main Ave Ste A, Sacramento (95838-2090)
PHONE.....................916 564-9976
Fax: 916 646-0619
Fred Troy Barnum, *CEO*
Paul Celillo, *Vice Pres*
John Aspling, *Project Mgr*
Kirk Ball, *Project Mgr*
Matt Evans, *Project Mgr*
EMP: 91
SQ FT: 3,000
SALES (est): 47.4MM **Privately Held**
WEB: www.barnumcelillo.com
SIC: 1731 General electrical contractor

(P-2528)
BAY ALARM COMPANY (PA)
Also Called: S A S
60 Berry Dr, Pacheco (94553-5601)
P.O. Box 8140, Walnut Creek (94596-8140)
PHONE.....................925 935-1100
Fax: 925 241-5680
Bruce A Westphal, *Ch of Bd*
Roger L Westphal, *CEO*
Graham Westphal, *Co-President*
Matt Westphal, *Co-President*
Shane Clary, *Vice Pres*
▲ **EMP:** 70
SQ FT: 12,000
SALES (est): 160.6MM **Privately Held**
WEB: www.bayalarm.com
SIC: 1731 7382 5063 Fire detection & burglar alarm systems specialization; burglar alarm maintenance & monitoring; fire alarm maintenance & monitoring; electrical apparatus & equipment

(P-2529)
BEAM VACUUMS CALIFORNIA INC
Also Called: Beam "easy Living" Center
422 Henderson St, Grass Valley (95945-7311)
P.O. Box 1803 (95945-1803)
PHONE.....................916 564-3279
Robert Medlyn, *President*
Julie Medlyn, *Planning*
Brian O''brien, *Sales Executive*
EMP: 50
SQ FT: 13,000
SALES (est): 7.8MM **Privately Held**
WEB: www.beameasy.com
SIC: 1731 1799 5722 5731 Environmental system control installation; sound equipment specialization; voice, data & video wiring contractor; closet organizers, installation & design; vacuum cleaners; high fidelity stereo equipment; communication equipment; closet organizers & shelving units

(P-2530)
BERGELECTRIC CORP (PA)
5650 W Centinela Ave, Los Angeles (90045-1501)
PHONE.....................310 337-1377
Fax: 310 337-2662
Thomas R Anderson, *Ch of Bd*
Alan Mashburn, *President*
William Wingrning, *CEO*
William M Wingerning, *Exec VP*
Edward P Billig, *Senior VP*
▲ **EMP:** 250
SQ FT: 14,600
SALES: 507.6MM **Privately Held**
WEB: www.bergelectric.com
SIC: 1731 General electrical contractor

(P-2531)
BERGELECTRIC CORP
650 Opper St, Escondido (92029-1020)
PHONE.....................760 746-1003
Fax: 760 741-0918
Tom Anderson, *Branch Mgr*
George Stivers, *Vice Pres*
Steve Stroder, *General Mgr*
Janet Barnes, *Office Mgr*
Carlene Everhart, *Data Proc Exec*
EMP: 760
SALES (corp-wide): 507.6MM **Privately Held**
WEB: www.bergelectric.com
SIC: 1731 General electrical contractor
PA: Bergelectric Corp.
5650 W Centinela Ave
Los Angeles CA 90045
310 337-1377

(P-2532)
BERGELECTRIC CORP
11333 Sunrise Park Dr, Rancho Cordova (95742-6532)
PHONE.....................916 636-1880
Matt Ordway, *Branch Mgr*
Jessica Oyao, *Office Mgr*
John Bergh, *Sales Staff*
Chris Nelson, *Manager*
Nick Rodriguez, *Supervisor*
EMP: 100
SALES (corp-wide): 507.6MM **Privately Held**
WEB: www.bergelectric.com
SIC: 1731 General electrical contractor
PA: Bergelectric Corp.
5650 W Centinela Ave
Los Angeles CA 90045
310 337-1377

▲ = Import ▼ = Export
◆ = Import/Export

PRODUCTS & SERVICES SECTION
1731 - Electrical Work County (P-2555)

(P-2533)
BERGELECTRIC CORP
1935 Deere Ave, Irvine (92606-4818)
PHONE.................................949 250-7005
Fax: 714 433-7111
Mark Bauer, *Manager*
Randy Drinkward, *Branch Mgr*
Charles Anderson, *Project Mgr*
John Esraelo, *Technology*
Joyce Enderud, *Finance Mgr*
EMP: 95
SALES (corp-wide): 507.6MM **Privately Held**
WEB: www.bergelectric.com
SIC: **1731** General electrical contractor
PA: Bergelectric Corp.
  5650 W Centinela Ave
  Los Angeles CA 90045
  310 337-1377

(P-2534)
BLACK DIAMOND ELECTRIC INC
2595 W 10th St, Antioch (94509-1374)
PHONE.................................925 777-3440
Fax: 925 777-3339
Jason C Pauline, *CEO*
Carey Neely, *Officer*
Tim Pauline, *Project Mgr*
Henry Cifelli, *Accounting Mgr*
Manuel Hernandez, *Manager*
EMP: 100
SQ FT: 9,000
SALES (est): 18.2MM **Privately Held**
SIC: **1731** Electrical work

(P-2535)
BOCKMON & WOODY ELC CO INC
1528 El Pinal Dr, Stockton (95205-2643)
P.O. Box 1018 (95201-1018)
PHONE.................................209 464-2615
Fax: 209 464-2615
Gary E Woody, *President*
Russel Shuman, *CFO*
Greg Bockmon, *Treasurer*
Jeff Bockmon, *Vice Pres*
Wayne Johnson, *Project Mgr*
EMP: 85
SQ FT: 36,000
SALES: 30MM **Privately Held**
WEB: www.bockmonwoody.com
SIC: **1731** General electrical contractor

(P-2536)
BRAUN ELECTRIC COMPANY INC (HQ)
3000 E Belle Ter, Bakersfield (93307-7093)
PHONE.................................661 633-1451
John A Braun, *President*
Kevin B Coghlin, *Vice Pres*
Diana Oei, *Finance*
Joel Rodgers, *Safety Mgr*
Paul Bradford, *Manager*
EMP: 50
SQ FT: 11,000
SALES (est): 34.3MM
SALES (corp-wide): 38.6MM **Privately Held**
WEB: www.braunelec.com
SIC: **1731** General electrical contractor
PA: C&B Holding Co., Inc.
  3000 Belle Terrace
  Bakersfield CA 93304
  661 633-1451

(P-2537)
BRAUN ELECTRIC COMPANY INC
111 Main St, Taft (93268-3519)
PHONE.................................661 763-1531
Fax: 661 765-4869
John Braun, *Manager*
EMP: 140
SALES (corp-wide): 38.6MM **Privately Held**
WEB: www.braunelec.com
SIC: **1731** General electrical contractor
HQ: Braun Electric Company, Inc.
  3000 E Belle Ter
  Bakersfield CA 93307
  661 633-1451

(P-2538)
BRENNAN ELECTRIC INC
460 S Stoddard Ave Ste 3, San Bernardino (92401-2039)
PHONE.................................909 772-2263
Fax: 909 884-6130
Robert Brennan, *President*
Jeff Deputy, *Vice Pres*
EMP: 180
SQ FT: 2,000
SALES (est): 16MM **Privately Held**
SIC: **1731** Electrical work

(P-2539)
BRIGGS ELECTRIC INC (PA)
14381 Franklin Ave, Tustin (92780-7010)
PHONE.................................714 544-2500
Fax: 949 544-4071
Jeff Perry, *President*
Thomas J Perry, *President*
Todd Perry, *CFO*
Penny Coleman, *Accountant*
Lisa Cutts, *Controller*
▲ EMP: 100
SQ FT: 5,500
SALES: 29.4MM **Privately Held**
WEB: www.briggselectric.com
SIC: **1731** Electrical work

(P-2540)
BUDGET ELECTRICAL CONTRS INC
25051 5th St, San Bernardino (92410-5119)
PHONE.................................909 381-2646
Danny E Guy, *CEO*
William Morris Diesel, *President*
Bea Whitehead, *Executive*
Mary McCann, *Project Mgr*
Tommy Woodwaski, *Project Mgr*
EMP: 150
SQ FT: 5,000
SALES (est): 18.4MM **Privately Held**
WEB: www.becelectric.com
SIC: **1731** General electrical contractor

(P-2541)
BUILDING ELCTRONIC CONTRLS INC (PA)
2246 Lindsay Way, Glendora (91740-5398)
PHONE.................................909 305-1600
Richard Taylor, *President*
Shelley Taylor, *Vice Pres*
Karla Steel, *Accounts Mgr*
EMP: 50
SQ FT: 13,000
SALES (est): 11MM **Privately Held**
WEB: www.becinc.net
SIC: **1731** 3699 Electrical work; security control equipment & systems; security devices

(P-2542)
BUTTERFIELD ELECTRIC INC
2101 Freeway Dr Ste A, Woodland (95776-9510)
PHONE.................................530 666-2116
Rick Butterfield, *Branch Mgr*
EMP: 107
SALES (corp-wide): 29MM **Privately Held**
SIC: **1731** Electrical work
PA: Butterfield Electric Inc.
  2101 Freeway Dr Ste A
  Woodland CA 95776
  530 666-2116

(P-2543)
BUTTERFIELD ELECTRIC INC (PA)
2101 Freeway Dr Ste A, Woodland (95776-9510)
P.O. Box 25 (95776-0025)
PHONE.................................530 666-2116
Fax: 530 666-6926
Rick Butterfield, *President*
Rorie Butterfield, *Vice Pres*
Sheila Mullins, *Controller*
EMP: 58
SQ FT: 14,000
SALES (est): 29MM **Privately Held**
WEB: www.butterfieldelectric.com
SIC: **1731** Electrical work

(P-2544)
C & R SYSTEMS INC (PA)
1835 Capital St, Corona (92880-1727)
PHONE.................................951 270-0255
Fax: 760 270-0431
Pam Mosbaugh, *President*
Robert V Cross, *Principal*
Timothy Potts, *Senior Engr*
Linda Van Meter, *Sales Staff*
Robbie Sorensen, *Warehouse Mgr*
EMP: 60
SQ FT: 8,000
SALES (est): 15.9MM **Privately Held**
WEB: www.crsys.net
SIC: **1731** Communications specialization; telephone & telephone equipment installation; safety & security specialization; fire detection & burglar alarm systems specialization

(P-2545)
C H REYNOLDS ELECTRIC INC
Also Called: Ch Reynolds
1281 Wayne Ave, San Jose (95131-3599)
PHONE.................................408 436-9280
Fax: 408 436-9289
Shelly Paiva, *President*
Rick White, *Exec VP*
Charles Reynolds, *Principal*
Vicki Duffley, *Director*
EMP: 130
SQ FT: 25,000
SALES (est): 43.2MM **Privately Held**
WEB: www.chreynolds.com
SIC: **1731** General electrical contractor

(P-2546)
C T AND F INC
7228 Scout Ave, Bell Gardens (90201-4998)
PHONE.................................562 927-2339
Fax: 562 927-3338
Ruby Galland, *CEO*
Todd N Simmons, *Vice Pres*
Kent M Simmons, *Principal*
Judith L Simmons, *Admin Sec*
Ramiro Valdez, *Manager*
EMP: 80
SQ FT: 15,000
SALES (est): 13.2MM **Privately Held**
SIC: **1731** General electrical contractor

(P-2547)
CAL SOUTHERN SOUND IMAGE INC (PA)
2415 Auto Park Way, Escondido (92029-1222)
PHONE.................................760 737-3900
David R Shadoan, *CEO*
Brandon Rinas, *President*
Ralph Wagner, *CFO*
Sharon Phillips, *Executive*
Jesse Adamson, *Business Dir*
EMP: 65
SQ FT: 28,000
SALES (est): 26.3MM **Privately Held**
SIC: **1731** 3651 5064 Communications specialization; speaker systems; electrical appliances, television & radio

(P-2548)
CALENERGY LLC
7030 Gentry Rd, Calipatria (92233-9720)
PHONE.................................402 231-1527
Bill Fehrman, *President*
EMP: 350 EST: 2013
SALES (est): 27.5MM **Privately Held**
SIC: **1731** Electric power systems contractors

(P-2549)
CAROL ELECTRIC COMPANY INC
3822 Cerritos Ave, Los Alamitos (90720-2420)
PHONE.................................562 431-1870
Fax: 562 594-1175
John R Fuqua, *Ch of Bd*
Allen Moffitt, *President*
Brian Moffitt, *Vice Pres*
Kelly Byrne, *Admin Asst*
Jason Shelton, *Project Mgr*
EMP: 90
SQ FT: 10,000
SALES (est): 20.1MM **Privately Held**
WEB: www.carolelectric.com
SIC: **1731** Electrical work

(P-2550)
CHAMPION ELECTRIC INC
3950 Garner Rd, Riverside (92501-1005)
PHONE.................................951 276-9619
Fax: 951 276-1460
Glenn Rowden, *President*
Cynthia D Rowden, *CFO*
Tom Rowden, *Vice Pres*
Brianna Ashley, *Admin Asst*
Mickey Hobbs, *Admin Asst*
EMP: 65
SQ FT: 12,000
SALES: 8MM **Privately Held**
WEB: www.championelec.com
SIC: **1731** General electrical contractor

(P-2551)
CHICO ELECTRIC
36 W Eaton Rd, Chico (95973-0160)
PHONE.................................530 891-1933
Fax: 530 891-6749
Norman Nielsen, *CEO*
Charlene Bellante, *Vice Pres*
Josh Cutler, *Manager*
Frank Vanskike, *Contractor*
EMP: 60
SQ FT: 8,500
SALES: 15MM **Privately Held**
SIC: **1731** General electrical contractor

(P-2552)
CLIMATEC LLC
13715 Stowe Dr, Poway (92064-6836)
PHONE.................................858 391-7000
Fax: 858 625-0119
Eince Scalise, *Branch Mgr*
Laura Papenhagen, *Officer*
EMP: 50
SALES (corp-wide): 268.9MM **Privately Held**
SIC: **1731** Environmental system control installation; energy management controls
HQ: Climatec, Llc
  2851 W Kathleen Rd
  Phoenix AZ 85053
  602 944-3330

(P-2553)
COCKRELL ELECTRIC INC
79553 Country Club Dr B, Bermuda Dunes (92203-1283)
PHONE.................................760 864-6233
Fax: 760 864-6235
John Cockrell, *President*
Jessica Ipina, *CFO*
Michele Cockrell, *Vice Pres*
William Cockrell, *Vice Pres*
Jorge Salas, *Purch Agent*
EMP: 85
SQ FT: 5,000
SALES (est): 8.3MM **Privately Held**
WEB: www.cockrellelectric.com
SIC: **1731** Electrical work

(P-2554)
COLLINS ELECTRICAL COMPANY INC (PA)
3412 Metro Dr, Stockton (95215-9440)
PHONE.................................209 466-3691
Fax: 209 466-3146
Eugene C Gini, *President*
Phil Asborno, *COO*
Gail Wardell, *CFO*
Brian Gini, *Vice Pres*
Craig Gini, *Vice Pres*
EMP: 200
SQ FT: 80,000
SALES (est): 62.5MM **Privately Held**
WEB: www.collinselectric.com
SIC: **1731** Electrical work

(P-2555)
COLLINS ELECTRICAL COMPANY INC
1902 Channel Dr, West Sacramento (95691-3441)
PHONE.................................209 466-3691
Fax: 916 567-1292
Kevin Gini, *Branch Mgr*
Roberto Padilla, *Project Mgr*
Susan Rodriguez, *Human Res Mgr*
Jennifer Hartpence, *Purchasing*

1731 - Electrical Work County (P-2556)

PRODUCTS & SERVICES SECTION

Greg Sutter, *Foreman/Supr*
EMP: 108
SALES (corp-wide): 62.5MM **Privately Held**
WEB: www.collinselectric.com
SIC: 1731 General electrical contractor
PA: Collins Electrical Company, Inc.
3412 Metro Dr
Stockton CA 95215
209 466-3691

(P-2556)
COMCAST CORPORATION
1750 Creekside Oaks Dr # 100, Sacramento (95833-3647)
PHONE..................916 830-6790
Marty Robinson, *Branch Mgr*
Quintan Taylor, *Network Enginr*
Casey Zoller, *Technician*
Adam Horn, *Sales Staff*
Dameon Campbell, *Manager*
EMP: 300
SALES (corp-wide): 74.5B **Publicly Held**
WEB: www.comcast.com
SIC: 1731 Electrical work
PA: Comcast Corporation
1701 Jfk Blvd
Philadelphia PA 19103
215 286-1700

(P-2557)
COMCAST CORPORATION
2093 Salvio St, Concord (94520-2424)
PHONE..................925 271-9794
EMP: 300
SALES (corp-wide): 74.5B **Publicly Held**
WEB: www.comcast.com
SIC: 1731 Communications specialization
PA: Comcast Corporation
1701 Jfk Blvd
Philadelphia PA 19103
215 286-1700

(P-2558)
COMET ELECTRIC INC
21625 Prairie St, Chatsworth (91311-5833)
PHONE..................818 340-0965
Fax: 818 340-4033
Jason Pennington, *CFO*
Keith Berson, *Exec VP*
Steve Goad, *Vice Pres*
Lida Attaran, *Controller*
Amy Tony, *Manager*
EMP: 150
SQ FT: 12,000
SALES (est): 38MM **Privately Held**
WEB: www.cometelectric.com
SIC: 1731 General electrical contractor

(P-2559)
COMMUNCTION WIRG SPCALISTS INC
Also Called: C W S
8909 Complex Dr Ste F, San Diego (92123-1418)
PHONE..................858 278-4545
Fax: 858 278-7709
Eric Templin, *Owner*
Donna Templin, *Shareholder*
Richard Templin, *Vice Pres*
Gregory Reid, *Project Mgr*
Alex Vasquez, *Project Mgr*
EMP: 80
SQ FT: 5,500
SALES: 8.2MM **Privately Held**
WEB: www.cwssandiego.com
SIC: 1731 Telephone & telephone equipment installation; voice, data & video wiring contractor

(P-2560)
COMTEL SYSTEMS TECHNOLOGY
1292 Hammerwood Ave, Sunnyvale (94089-2232)
PHONE..................408 543-5600
Richard Nielsen, *President*
Andrea Nielsen, *Vice Pres*
Patricia Porazynski, *Administration*
Chris Bozzo, *Project Mgr*
Tim Clark, *Project Mgr*
EMP: 70
SQ FT: 10,760
SALES (est): 17.3MM **Privately Held**
WEB: www.comtelsys.com
SIC: 1731 Communications specialization

(P-2561)
CONTRA COSTA ELECTRIC INC (DH)
825 Howe Rd, Martinez (94553-3441)
P.O. Box 2523 (94553-0317)
PHONE..................925 229-4250
Michael Dias, *President*
Dave Galli, *CFO*
Charlie Hadsell, *Vice Pres*
Joey Ramirez, *Vice Pres*
Tom Tatro, *Vice Pres*
EMP: 300
SALES (est): 89.5MM
SALES (corp-wide): 6.7B **Publicly Held**
WEB: www.ccelectric.com
SIC: 1731 Electrical work

(P-2562)
CONTRA COSTA ELECTRIC INC
3208 Landco Dr, Bakersfield (93308-6156)
PHONE..................661 322-4036
Fax: 661 322-4039
Richard Trainer, *Manager*
Larry Wilson, *Purchasing*
Gary Wing, *Manager*
EMP: 104
SALES (corp-wide): 6.7B **Publicly Held**
WEB: www.ccelectric.com
SIC: 1731 Electrical work
HQ: Contra Costa Electric, Inc.
825 Howe Rd
Martinez CA 94553
925 229-4250

(P-2563)
COSCO FIRE PROTECTION INC
7455 Longard Rd, Livermore (94551-8238)
PHONE..................925 455-2751
Fax: 925 455-2761
Phil Raya, *Manager*
EMP: 96
SALES (corp-wide): 400.9MM **Privately Held**
SIC: 1731 3494 8711 7382 General electrical contractor; sprinkler systems, field; engineering services; security systems services; plumbing, heating, air-conditioning contractors
HQ: Cosco Fire Protection, Inc.
29222 Rancho Viejo Rd # 205
San Juan Capistrano CA 92675
714 974-8770

(P-2564)
COVE ELECTRIC INC
77824 Wildcat Dr, Palm Desert (92211-1134)
PHONE..................760 568-9924
Fax: 760 360-7895
Charles Bojkovsky, *President*
Michele Bojkovsky, *Shareholder*
Jeannie Stewart, *CFO*
Steve Tavares, *Vice Pres*
Jack Derman, *Manager*
EMP: 70
SQ FT: 4,500
SALES: 8.7MM **Privately Held**
WEB: www.coveelectric.com
SIC: 1731 Electrical work

(P-2565)
CSI ELECTRICAL CONTRACTORS INC
41769 11th St W Ste B, Palmdale (93551-1418)
PHONE..................661 723-0869
Roland Tamayo, *General Mgr*
Diana Peirano, *Executive*
EMP: 90
SALES (corp-wide): 111.2MM **Privately Held**
SIC: 1731 Electrical work
PA: Csi Electrical Contractors, Inc.
10623 Fulton Wells Ave
Santa Fe Springs CA 90670
562 946-0700

(P-2566)
CSI ELECTRICAL CONTRACTORS INC (PA)
Also Called: C S I
10623 Fulton Wells Ave, Santa Fe Springs (90670-3741)
P.O. Box 2887 (90670-0887)
PHONE..................562 946-0700
Fax: 562 623-1172
Steven M Watts, *President*
Andy Klein, *President*
Paul Pica, *President*
Craig Epperly, *COO*
Gene Acosta, *Vice Pres*
EMP: 150
SALES (est): 111.2MM **Privately Held**
WEB: www.csielectric.com
SIC: 1731 General electrical contractor

(P-2567)
CUPERTINO ELECTRIC INC
350 Lenore Way, Felton (95018-8973)
P.O. Box 1517 (95018-1517)
PHONE..................408 808-8260
EMP: 2029
SALES (corp-wide): 763MM **Privately Held**
SIC: 1731 Electrical work
PA: Cupertino Electric, Inc.
1132 N 7th St
San Jose CA 95112
408 808-8000

(P-2568)
CUPERTINO ELECTRIC INC (PA)
Also Called: Cei
1132 N 7th St, San Jose (95112-4438)
PHONE..................408 808-8000
Fax: 408 275-6987
John Boncher, *President*
Tom Schott, *COO*
Marjorie Goss, *CFO*
Bill Slakey, *CFO*
John Curcio, *Ch Credit Ofcr*
EMP: 400
SQ FT: 90,000
SALES (corp-wide): 763MM **Privately Held**
WEB: www.cei.com
SIC: 1731 General electrical contractor

(P-2569)
CUPERTINO ELECTRIC INC
1740 Cesar Chavez Fl 2, San Francisco (94124-1134)
PHONE..................415 970-3400
Fax: 415 275-8575
Adam Spillane, *Branch Mgr*
Darrell Bender, *Senior VP*
Michele Heppler, *Vice Pres*
BJ Johnson, *Administration*
Bill Diekmann, *Info Tech Dir*
EMP: 55
SALES (corp-wide): 763MM **Privately Held**
WEB: www.cei.com
SIC: 1731 Electrical work
PA: Cupertino Electric, Inc.
1132 N 7th St
San Jose CA 95112
408 808-8000

(P-2570)
D M ELECTRIC INC
336 S Waterman Ave Ste K, San Bernardino (92408-1533)
PHONE..................909 888-8639
Danny Moore, *President*
Michelle Moore, *Corp Secy*
Jacky Jones, *Manager*
EMP: 80
SQ FT: 1,000
SALES (est): 6.2MM **Privately Held**
SIC: 1731 Electrical work

(P-2571)
DAMON ELECTRICAL
7800 Bobbyboyar Ave, West Hills (91304-4418)
PHONE..................818 426-3450
Zekrollah Ali, *Principal*
EMP: 65 **EST:** 2011
SALES (est): 3.1MM **Privately Held**
SIC: 1731 General electrical contractor

(P-2572)
DAN FREITAS ELECTRIC
983 E Levin Ave, Tulare (93274-6525)
PHONE..................559 686-9572
Fax: 559 686-0323
Daniel Freitas, *President*
Jeanette Freitas, *Vice Pres*
Terri Kulzer, *Admin Sec*
EMP: 60
SQ FT: 14,460
SALES (est): 10.7MM **Privately Held**
WEB: www.danfreitaselectric.com
SIC: 1731 Electrical work

(P-2573)
DAWSON ELECTRIC
3775 Pacheco Blvd, Martinez (94553-2130)
P.O. Box 5190, Concord (94524-0190)
PHONE..................925 723-3535
Fax: 925 723-3545
Jim Canaday, *President*
Elbert A Dwson, *Treasurer*
Elbert A Dawson III, *Corp Secy*
William Ose, *Vice Pres*
Terry Estrada, *Project Mgr*
EMP: 60
SQ FT: 2,000
SALES (est): 10.4MM **Privately Held**
WEB: www.dawsonelectric.com
SIC: 1731 General electrical contractor

(P-2574)
DECKER ELC CO INC ELEC CONTRS
147 Beacon St, South San Francisco (94080-6921)
PHONE..................650 635-1390
Fax: 650 635-1732
David Chad, *Vice Pres*
Myra Garces, *Administration*
EMP: 100
SALES (corp-wide): 112.3MM **Privately Held**
WEB: www.deckerelectric.com
SIC: 1731 Electrical work
PA: Decker Electric Co., Inc., Electrical Contractors
1282 Folsom St
San Francisco CA 94103
415 552-1622

(P-2575)
DEPLOYMENT SOLUTIONS LLC
332 Bandini Pl, Vista (92083-5903)
PHONE..................317 281-9682
Jennifer Shaffer, *Partner*
Martin Keith, *Partner*
EMP: 50
SALES (est): 5.4MM **Privately Held**
WEB: www.deploymentsolutions.com
SIC: 1731 Electronic controls installation; communications specialization

(P-2576)
DYNALECTRIC COMPANY
668 Flinn Ave, Moorpark (93021-2077)
PHONE..................805 517-1253
Frank Miller, *Vice Pres*
EMP: 127
SALES (corp-wide): 6.7B **Publicly Held**
SIC: 1731 General electrical contractor
HQ: Dynalectric Company
22930 Shaw Rd Ste 100
Dulles VA 20166
703 288-2866

(P-2577)
DYNALECTRIC COMPANY
9505 Chesapeake Dr, San Diego (92123-6393)
PHONE..................858 712-4700
Fax: 858 712-4701
Daivd Rispolrch, *Manager*
Bob Riel, *Vice Pres*
Claudia Alanis, *Office Mgr*
Casey Cumstay, *Admin Asst*
Eric Liu, *Administration*
EMP: 300
SALES (corp-wide): 6.7B **Publicly Held**
WEB: www.dyna-fl.com
SIC: 1731 General electrical contractor
HQ: Dynalectric Company
22930 Shaw Rd Ste 100
Dulles VA 20166
703 288-2866

(P-2578)
DYNALECTRIC COMPANY
4462 Corporate Center Dr, Los Alamitos (90720-2539)
PHONE..................714 236-2242
Christopher Pesavento, *Branch Mgr*
EMP: 127

PRODUCTS & SERVICES SECTION

1731 - Electrical Work County (P-2601)

SALES (corp-wide): 6.7B **Publicly Held**
WEB: www.dyna-fl.com
SIC: **1731** General electrical contractor
HQ: Dynalectric Company
22930 Shaw Rd Ste 100
Dulles VA 20166
703 288-2866

(P-2579) DYNALECTRIC COMPANY
825 Howe Rd, Martinez (94553-3441)
PHONE.............................415 487-4700
David Raspolich, *Manager*
Renard Anderson, *CFO*
David Stolecki, *Exec VP*
EMP: 150
SALES (corp-wide): 6.7B **Publicly Held**
SIC: **1731** Electrical work
HQ: Dynalectric Company
22930 Shaw Rd Ste 100
Dulles VA 20166
703 288-2866

(P-2580) EDWARD STRALING
Also Called: Quality Electrical Services
2940 Grace Ln Ste C, Costa Mesa (92626-4133)
PHONE.............................760 887-3673
Edward Sterling, *Owner*
EMP: 50
SQ FT: 7,500
SALES (est): 4.1MM **Privately Held**
SIC: **1731** General electrical contractor

(P-2581) EDWARDS TECHNOLOGIES INC
139 Maryland St, El Segundo (90245-4116)
PHONE.............................310 536-7070
Fax: 310 322-1459
Brian Edwards, *President*
Gary Lebous, *Controller*
Aret Mirzkanian, *Controller*
Ravi Shankar, *VP Opers*
▲ EMP: 51
SQ FT: 10,000
SALES (est): 15.8MM **Privately Held**
WEB: www.edwardstechnologies.com
SIC: **1731** Sound equipment specialization

(P-2582) ELCOR ELECTRIC INC
3310 Bassett St, Santa Clara (95054-2702)
PHONE.............................408 986-1320
Fax: 408 986-1324
George Woodley, *General Mgr*
Clint Woodley, *Vice Pres*
Garrett Colton, *Project Engr*
Tammy Manning, *Manager*
EMP: 120
SQ FT: 5,000
SALES (est): 17.4MM **Privately Held**
SIC: **1731** General electrical contractor

(P-2583) ELECTRCAL INSTRUMENTATION INTL
Also Called: E I I
6950 District Blvd, Bakersfield (93313-2012)
P.O. Box 40878 (93384-0878)
PHONE.............................661 836-9466
Gloria Tominaga-Minor, *President*
Craig Coster, *Controller*
Barney J Blanchard, *Director*
Christopher P Minor, *Director*
EMP: 366
SQ FT: 2,000
SALES (est): 22.8MM **Privately Held**
SIC: **1731** General electrical contractor

(P-2584) ELECTRIC SVC & SUP CO PASADENA
Also Called: Essco
2668 E Foothill Blvd, Pasadena (91107-3409)
PHONE.............................626 795-8641
Fax: 626 795-9197
Stanley R Lazarian, *President*
Nancy Rose, *Treasurer*
Iris Lazarian, *Vice Pres*
Susan Lazarian, *Manager*
EMP: 70 EST: 1946

SALES (est): 7.1MM **Privately Held**
WEB: www.esscoelectric.com
SIC: **1731** General electrical contractor

(P-2585) ELECTRIC USA
480 Aldo Ave, Santa Clara (95054-2304)
PHONE.............................800 921-1151
Fax: 408 370-3075
John Lim, *Owner*
EMP: 50
SALES (est): 1.4MM **Privately Held**
SIC: **1731** 1711 General electrical contractor; plumbing contractors

(P-2586) ELECTRICAL & INSTRUMENTATION
Also Called: Eiu of California
6950 District Blvd, Bakersfield (93313-2012)
P.O. Box 40878 (93384-0878)
PHONE.............................661 836-9466
Fax: 661 836-2636
Chris Minor, *President*
Kevin Ortego, *COO*
Barney J Blanchard, *Corp Secy*
Paul Labauve, *Exec VP*
Steve Cosper, *Project Mgr*
EMP: 200
SQ FT: 10,000
SALES (est): 47.9MM **Privately Held**
WEB: www.eiucal.com
SIC: **1731** Electrical work

(P-2587) ELECTRONIC CONTROL SYSTEMS LLC
12575 Kirkham Ct Ste 1, Poway (92064-8844)
PHONE.............................858 513-1911
Dan Coler, *Mng Member*
Seth Schreiner, *Vice Pres*
Peter Trusewicz, *Project Mgr*
Walter Houle, *Accounts Exec*
EMP: 150
SQ FT: 17,000
SALES (est): 35.8MM
SALES (corp-wide): 55MM **Privately Held**
WEB: www.ecscontrols.com
SIC: **1731** 7382 8711 Energy management controls; security systems services; energy conservation engineering
PA: Albireo Energy, Llc
3 Ethel Rd Ste 300
Edison NJ 08817
732 243-4874

(P-2588) ELITE POWER INC
6530 Asher Ln, Sacramento (95828-1832)
PHONE.............................916 739-1580
Fax: 916 739-1581
Walt Zacharias, *President*
Rich Love, *Administration*
Mary Mendence, *Controller*
Keith Diffey, *Foreman/Supr*
Todd May, *Director*
EMP: 54
SQ FT: 15,000
SALES (est): 12.9MM **Privately Held**
WEB: www.elitepower.com
SIC: **1731** General electrical contractor

(P-2589) ENERPATH SERVICES INC
1758 Orange Tree Ln, Redlands (92374-2856)
PHONE.............................909 335-1699
Stephen Guthrie, *President*
Janina Guthrie, *Treasurer*
Jonathan Baty, *Admin Sec*
Isabel Hernandez, *Director*
EMP: 100
SQ FT: 4,500
SALES (est): 18.7MM **Privately Held**
WEB: www.expertlighting.com
SIC: **1731** 8748 Lighting contractor; lighting consultant

(P-2590) EQUAL ACCESS INTERNATIONAL
1212 Market St Ste 200, San Francisco (94102-4817)
PHONE.............................415 561-4884
Fax: 415 561-4885
Ronni Goldfarb, *President*
Lisa Ellis, *COO*
Rebecca Chapman, *Officer*
Rebecca Tuttle, *Officer*
Amandine Weinrob, *Officer*
EMP: 52
SQ FT: 2,459
SALES (est): 7.4MM **Privately Held**
WEB: www.equalaccess.org
SIC: **1731** Communications specialization

(P-2591) FAR WEST ELECTRIC INC
6094 Keswick Ave, Riverside (92506-3747)
PHONE.............................909 684-8661
Fax: 951 684-2360
Joe Ruzzamenti, *President*
Rick Ruzzamanti, *Vice Pres*
Judy Ruzzamanti, *Admin Sec*
EMP: 60
SQ FT: 2,100
SALES (est): 10MM **Privately Held**
SIC: **1731** Electrical work

(P-2592) FEI ENTERPRISES INC
5749 Venice Blvd, Los Angeles (90019-5015)
PHONE.............................323 937-0856
Gabriel Fedida, *CEO*
Veronica Pastor, *Office Mgr*
Esther Fedida, *Financial Exec*
▲ EMP: 50
SQ FT: 3,900
SALES (est): 6.2MM **Privately Held**
WEB: www.feienterprises.com
SIC: **1731** 5063 General electrical contractor; burglar alarm systems

(P-2593) FIRST FIRE SYSTEMS INC (PA)
5947 Burchard Ave, Los Angeles (90034-1701)
PHONE.............................310 559-0900
Fax: 323 965-2700
Juda Roshanzamir, *President*
Robbie Kashani, *Vice Pres*
Ed Klapholz, *Project Mgr*
Robert Sandoval, *Project Mgr*
Abraham Velasco, *Project Mgr*
EMP: 78
SQ FT: 9,400
SALES (est): 21.7MM **Privately Held**
WEB: www.firstfiresystems.com
SIC: **1731** Electrical work; fire detection & burglar alarm systems specialization

(P-2594) FISK ELECTRIC COMPANY
15870 Olden St, Sylmar (91342-1241)
PHONE.............................818 884-1166
Orvil Anthony, *Senior VP*
James Purse, *Purch Mgr*
EMP: 165
SALES (corp-wide): 4.9B **Publicly Held**
SIC: **1731** General electrical contractor
HQ: Fisk Electric Company
10855 Westview Dr
Houston TX 77043
713 868-6111

(P-2595) FLATIRON ELECTRIC GROUP INC
7911 Pine Ave Ste A, Chino (91708-9265)
PHONE.............................714 228-9631
Kurt Welter, *President*
John Diciurcio, *CEO*
Javier Sevilla, *COO*
Lars Leitner, *CFO*
Shawn Bradfield, *Manager*
EMP: 50
SALES (est): 7.9MM
SALES (corp-wide): 506.6MM **Privately Held**
SIC: **1731** General electrical contractor

HQ: Flatiron West, Inc.
1770 La Costa Meadows Dr
San Marcos CA 92078
760 916-9100

(P-2596) FOSHAY ELECTRIC COINC
1555 Laurel Bay Ln, San Diego (92154-7715)
PHONE.............................858 277-7676
Fax: 858 277-2629
Theresa M Faucher, *President*
Michael Beringhaus, *Vice Pres*
Mark Faucher, *Vice Pres*
EMP: 100
SQ FT: 8,000
SALES (est): 15.8MM **Privately Held**
WEB: www.foshayelectric.com
SIC: **1731** General electrical contractor

(P-2597) FRANKE CON J ELECTRIC INC
317 N Grant St, Stockton (95202-2633)
PHONE.............................209 462-0717
Fax: 209 462-2556
Barry Frain, *President*
Diana Frain, *Corp Secy*
Lewis Frain, *Vice Pres*
Larry Woolstrum, *Opers Mgr*
Lori Cass, *Manager*
EMP: 100 EST: 1925
SQ FT: 7,000
SALES (est): 23.5MM **Privately Held**
WEB: www.cjfranke.com
SIC: **1731** Electrical work

(P-2598) GENERAL ELECTRIC COMPANY
428 Ballindine Dr, Vacaville (95688-9236)
PHONE.............................707 469-8346
Gopal Avinash, *Director*
EMP: 51
SALES (corp-wide): 117.3B **Publicly Held**
SIC: **1731** Electrical work
PA: General Electric Company
41 Farnsworth St
Boston MA 02210
617 443-3000

(P-2599) GOULD ELECTRIC INC
12975 Brookprinter Pl # 280, Poway (92064-8895)
PHONE.............................858 486-1727
Russ Thurman, *President*
John Meyers, *Treasurer*
Donn Lowrey, *Vice Pres*
EMP: 125 EST: 1976
SQ FT: 2,400
SALES (est): 37.5MM **Privately Held**
WEB: www.gouldelect.com
SIC: **1731** General electrical contractor

(P-2600) GREATER ALARM COMPANY INC (HQ)
3750 Schaufele Ave # 200, Long Beach (90808-1779)
PHONE.............................949 474-0555
George De Marco, *President*
James De Marco, *Vice Pres*
EMP: 71
SQ FT: 11,500
SALES (est): 7.7MM
SALES (corp-wide): 249.3MM **Privately Held**
SIC: **1731** Safety & security specialization
PA: Interface Security Systems, Llc
3773 Corporate Centre Dr
Earth City MO 63045
314 595-0100

(P-2601) GREGG ELECTRIC INC
608 W Emporia St, Ontario (91762-3709)
PHONE.............................909 983-1794
Fax: 909 983-6912
Randall F Fehlman, *President*
Victoria Mensen, *CFO*
James Fehlman, *Vice Pres*
Michelle Fehlman, *Manager*
EMP: 150 EST: 1961
SQ FT: 15,000

SALES (est): 25.4MM Privately Held
WEB: www.greggelectric.com
SIC: 1731 General electrical contractor

(P-2602)
H & D ELECTRIC
5237 Walnut Ave Ste 100, Sacramento (95841-2694)
P.O. Box 41360 (95841-0360)
PHONE.................................916 332-0794
Fax: 916 332-7554
Mark E Cooper, *President*
EMP: 360
SQ FT: 14,400
SALES (est): 40.6MM Privately Held
WEB: www.hdelectric.com
SIC: 1731 General electrical contractor

(P-2603)
H A BOWEN ELECTRIC INC
2055 Williams St, San Leandro (94577-2305)
P.O. Box 2153 (94577-0329)
PHONE.................................510 483-0500
Fax: 510 483-7210
Herbert A Bowen, *President*
Mike Boehmer, *Manager*
Patrick Boehmer, *Manager*
Nick Mehta, *Manager*
EMP: 60
SQ FT: 9,000
SALES: 16.8MM Privately Held
WEB: www.bowenelectric.com
SIC: 1731 General electrical contractor

(P-2604)
HACKNEY ELECTRIC INC (PA)
23286 Arroyo Vis, Rcho STA Marg (92688-2610)
PHONE.................................949 264-4000
Fax: 949 264-4011
David J Hackney, *President*
Rebecca Hackney, *Vice Pres*
Melissa Jenowski, *Office Mgr*
Debbie Peters, *VP Human Res*
EMP: 55
SQ FT: 6,200
SALES: 13.5MM Privately Held
WEB: www.hackneyelectric.com
SIC: 1731 Electrical work

(P-2605)
HAMILTON AND DILLON ELC INC
1128 Reno Ave, Modesto (95351-1128)
P.O. Box 581890 (95358-0033)
PHONE.................................209 529-6292
Fax: 209 529-6293
Bobby Hamilton, *President*
John Dillon, *Vice Pres*
Barbara Nunes, *Manager*
Doug Dillon, *Supervisor*
EMP: 60
SQ FT: 5,000
SALES (est): 7MM Privately Held
SIC: 1731 Electrical work

(P-2606)
HANOVER BUILDERS INC
141 Duesenberg Dr Ste 6, Westlake Village (91362-3471)
PHONE.................................818 706-2279
Donald Hanover, *President*
EMP: 50
SALES: 2MM Privately Held
WEB: www.hanoverbuildersinc.com
SIC: 1731 General electrical contractor

(P-2607)
HAROLD E NUTTER INC
5934 Rosebud Ln, Sacramento (95841-2914)
PHONE.................................916 334-4343
Norman Nutter, *Manager*
Paul Smith, *Manager*
EMP: 50
SALES (corp-wide): 14MM Privately Held
WEB: www.henutter.com
SIC: 1731 Electrical work
PA: Harold E. Nutter, Inc.
 5930 Rosebud Ln Ste A
 Sacramento CA 95841
 916 334-4343

(P-2608)
HARRIS L WOODS ELEC CONTR
Also Called: Woods Electric Company
9214 Norwalk Blvd, Santa Fe Springs (90670-2924)
P.O. Box 2367 (90670-0367)
PHONE.................................562 945-8751
Fax: 562 698-2261
Sandra Woods, *President*
Ralph L Woods, *Admin Sec*
John Conlon, *Foreman/Supr*
Keith Pengilley, *Superintendent*
EMP: 55
SQ FT: 5,000
SALES (est): 9MM Privately Held
SIC: 1731 General electrical contractor

(P-2609)
HCI SYSTEMS INC (PA)
Also Called: Hcis
1354 S Parkside Pl, Ontario (91761-4555)
PHONE.................................909 628-7773
Hany Dimitry, *President*
Michael Peters, *President*
Daniel Downs, *Vice Pres*
Jeff Kresge, *Vice Pres*
Curtis Vance, *Vice Pres*
EMP: 50 EST: 2008
SQ FT: 12,000
SALES (est): 23MM Privately Held
SIC: 1731 General electrical contractor

(P-2610)
HHS COMMUNICATIONS INC
2042 S Grove Ave, Ontario (91761-5617)
PHONE.................................909 230-5170
Royce S Jaime, *President*
EMP: 60 EST: 2007
SALES (est): 6.8MM Privately Held
SIC: 1731 Fiber optic cable installation

(P-2611)
HIGH-LIGHT ELECTRIC INC
7000 Jurupa Ave, Riverside (92504-1016)
P.O. Box 7339 (92513-7339)
PHONE.................................951 352-9646
Fax: 951 352-2498
Erwin Mendoza, *President*
Iris Leung, *Controller*
Alfredo Limon, *Foreman/Supr*
EMP: 60
SALES: 16.1MM Privately Held
WEB: www.mbe-hlj.com
SIC: 1731 Electrical work

(P-2612)
HILLS FLAT LUMBER CO (PA)
380 Railroad Ave, Grass Valley (95945-5909)
P.O. Box 1630, Colfax (95713-1630)
PHONE.................................530 273-6171
Fax: 530 273-4492
Jeffrey Edward Pardini, *CEO*
Jason Pardini, *Vice Pres*
Kennan Pardini, *Vice Pres*
Sandra Pardini, *Vice Pres*
Edward J Pardini Jr, *Principal*
EMP: 80
SQ FT: 12,000
SALES (est): 26.3MM Privately Held
WEB: www.hillsflatlumber.com
SIC: 1731 5031 5193 5999 Electrical work; doors & windows; nursery stock; plumbing & heating supplies; general merchandise, non-durable; equipment rental & leasing

(P-2613)
HMT ELECTRIC INC
2340 Meyers Ave, Escondido (92029-1008)
PHONE.................................858 458-9771
Brian Hudak, *CEO*
Kevin Dake, *Controller*
Josh Doty, *Purch Agent*
Stefan Southas, *Manager*
EMP: 85
SQ FT: 2,000
SALES (est): 12.9MM Privately Held
SIC: 1731 Electrical work

(P-2614)
HODGES ELECTRIC INC
1239 Hoblitt Ave, Clovis (93612-2807)
PHONE.................................559 298-5533
Fax: 559 298-5639
Roger L Hidy, *President*
Janel M Hidy, *CFO*
Michael Mueller, *Controller*
EMP: 50
SQ FT: 5,000
SALES (est): 5.7MM Privately Held
SIC: 1731 General electrical contractor

(P-2615)
HOT LINE CONSTRUCTION INC
9020 Brentwood Blvd Ste H, Brentwood (94513-4049)
PHONE.................................925 634-9333
Fax: 925 634-4535
Carol Bade, *President*
Kelly G Kutchera, *CFO*
Troy Myers, *Vice Pres*
Cruz Munos, *Office Mgr*
Matt Derosa, *Human Res Dir*
EMP: 425
SQ FT: 4,000
SALES (est): 224.5MM Privately Held
WEB: www.hotlineconstructioninc.com
SIC: 1731 1799 Electric power systems contractors; cable splicing service

(P-2616)
HOWE ELECTRIC CONSTRUCTION INC
4682 E Olive Ave, Fresno (93702-1689)
PHONE.................................559 255-8992
Todd Howe, *President*
Marjorie Montes, *Treasurer*
Ty Howe, *Vice Pres*
Monica Teare, *Admin Sec*
Tee Boon, *Director*
EMP: 140
SALES (est): 14.2MM Privately Held
SIC: 1731 Electrical work

(P-2617)
ICKLER ELECTRIC CORPORATION
12175 Dearborn Pl, Poway (92064-7111)
PHONE.................................858 486-1585
Fax: 858 486-4137
Kurt Ickler, *CEO*
Laurie Ickler, *Vice Pres*
John Metz, *Project Mgr*
Mike Schroeder, *Project Mgr*
Rich Taylor, *Project Mgr*
EMP: 60
SQ FT: 5,435
SALES (est): 10.1MM Privately Held
WEB: www.icklerelectric.com
SIC: 1731 Electrical work

(P-2618)
ICS INTEGRATED COMM SYSTEMS
550 Parrott St Ste 40, San Jose (95112-4125)
PHONE.................................408 491-6000
Fax: 408 998-0100
Aaron Colton, *CEO*
Trevor Hickey, *Technician*
Terry West, *Technician*
Michelle Barajas, *Project Mgr*
Jack Smith, *Project Mgr*
EMP: 65
SQ FT: 18,000
SALES: 16.1MM Privately Held
WEB: www.ceitronics.com
SIC: 1731 Fire detection & burglar alarm systems specialization; access control systems specialization; cable television installation; voice, data & video wiring contractor

(P-2619)
INTERIOR ELECTRIC INCORPORATED
747 N Main St, Orange (92868-1105)
PHONE.................................714 771-9098
Fax: 714 771-3058
Mark Beverly, *President*
Gus Baquerizo, *Vice Pres*
Mark Maskevich, *Vice Pres*
Glen Nielsen, *Vice Pres*
Chad Stewart, *Vice Pres*
EMP: 75
SQ FT: 10,000
SALES (est): 12.1MM Privately Held
WEB: www.interiorelectric.com
SIC: 1731 Electrical work

(P-2620)
IPITEK INC (PA)
2461 Impala Dr, Carlsbad (92010-7227)
P.O. Box 130878 (92013-0878)
PHONE.................................760 438-1010
Fax: 760 438-2412
Michael M Salour, *Ch of Bd*
Carrol Eckmeder, *Security Mgr*
Rich Loveland, *VP Mktg*
Greg Scott, *Manager*
EMP: 50
SQ FT: 40,000
SALES (est): 17.5MM Privately Held
WEB: www.ipitek.com
SIC: 1731 Fiber optic cable installation

(P-2621)
ITRON INC
1111 Broadway Ste 1800, Oakland (94607-4091)
PHONE.................................510 844-2800
Fax: 510 844-2900
Derek Hall, *Manager*
Jennifer Loden, *Business Anlyst*
Leslie Fergison, *Human Resources*
Wendy Lohkamp, *Director*
David Yee, *Director*
EMP: 2000
SALES (corp-wide): 1.9B Publicly Held
WEB: www.siliconenergy.com
SIC: 1731 3571 Energy management controls; electronic computers
PA: Itron, Inc.
 2111 N Molter Rd
 Liberty Lake WA 99019
 509 924-9900

(P-2622)
JAROTH INC
Also Called: Pacific Telemanagement Svcs
2001 Crow Canyon Rd # 200, San Ramon (94583-5368)
PHONE.................................925 553-3650
Thomas R Keane, *CEO*
Michael R Zumbo, *President*
Nancy Rossi, *CFO*
Doug Lubushkin, *General Mgr*
EMP: 130
SALES (est): 35.4MM Privately Held
WEB: www.pts-telecom.com
SIC: 1731 7349 Telephone & telephone equipment installation; telephone booth cleaning & maintenance

(P-2623)
JEEVA CORPORATION
Also Called: Satellite Pros
750 E E St Unit B, Ontario (91764-3821)
PHONE.................................909 238-4073
Orlando Uranga, *CEO*
EMP: 50 EST: 2011
SQ FT: 1,800
SALES: 1.1MM Privately Held
SIC: 1731 Cable television installation

(P-2624)
JENSCO INC
Also Called: J M Electric
400 Griffin St, Salinas (93901-4344)
PHONE.................................831 422-7819
Fax: 831 758-9638
Frederick A Jensen, *President*
Chris Jensen, *CFO*
Jim Shumaker, *Technician*
James Shumaker, *Foreman/Supr*
Linda Taylan, *Manager*
EMP: 50
SQ FT: 8,400
SALES (est): 8.3MM Privately Held
SIC: 1731 General electrical contractor

(P-2625)
JMG SECURITY SYSTEMS INC
17150 Newhope St Ste 109, Fountain Valley (92708-4273)
PHONE.................................714 545-8882
Fax: 714 545-0352
Ken Jacobs, *CEO*
Michael Christensen, *Exec VP*
Gil Ledesma, *Exec VP*
Sue Tjelmeland, *Vice Pres*
Paul Williamson, *Vice Pres*
EMP: 70
SQ FT: 14,000

PRODUCTS & SERVICES SECTION

1731 - Electrical Work County (P-2647)

SALES (est): 17.6MM **Privately Held**
SIC: 1731 5063 Safety & security specialization; burglar alarm systems

(P-2626)
JOE LUNARDI ELECTRIC INC
5334 Sebastopol Rd, Santa Rosa (95407-6423)
P.O. Box 120, Sebastopol (95473-0120)
PHONE.................................707 823-2129
Fax: 707 579-1757
Joseph I Lunardi, *Ch of Bd*
Jolene A Corcoran, *President*
Ronald J Lunardi, *Corp Secy*
Raymond J Lunardi, *Vice Pres*
EMP: 52
SQ FT: 12,000
SALES: 10MM **Privately Held**
WEB: www.lunardielectric.com
SIC: 1731 General electrical contractor

(P-2627)
JOIE DE VIVRE HOSPITALITY LLC
210 E Main St, Los Gatos (95030-6107)
PHONE.................................408 335-1700
EMP: 904
SALES (corp-wide): 231.8MM **Privately Held**
SIC: 1731 Electrical work
PA: Joie De Vivre Hospitality, Llc
530 Bush St Ste 501
San Francisco CA 94108
415 835-0300

(P-2628)
JOINT LABOR MGMT COOP COMMITTE
Also Called: California Lmcc/Ibew-Neca
6300 Village Pkwy Ste 200, Dublin (94568-3002)
PHONE.................................925 828-6352
Bernie Kotlier, *Principal*
Pete Halver, *Division Mgr*
EMP: 99
SALES (est): 7.7MM **Privately Held**
SIC: 1731 Electrical work

(P-2629)
KCS ELECTRIC INC
1585 N Harmony Cir, Anaheim (92807-6003)
P.O. Box 1478, Big Bear Lake (92315-1478)
PHONE.................................623 551-1500
Fax: 714 777-1980
Kenneth C Simonds, *President*
Tracy Collins, *Manager*
EMP: 60
SALES (est): 4.1MM **Privately Held**
WEB: www.kcselectric.com
SIC: 1731 Electrical work

(P-2630)
KDC INC (HQ)
Also Called: Kdc Systems
4462 Corporate Center Dr, Los Alamitos (90720-2539)
PHONE.................................714 828-7000
Fax: 714 484-2385
Johnny Menninga, *President*
William B Davenport, *CFO*
Larry Barcelos, *Executive*
Juan Herrera, *Executive*
Matthew Tamagni, *Executive*
EMP: 140
SQ FT: 57,000
SALES (est): 59.8MM
SALES (corp-wide): 6.7B **Publicly Held**
WEB: www.dyna-la.com
SIC: 1731 1611 3823 General electrical contractor; general contractor, highway & street construction; industrial instrmnts msrmnt display/control process variable
PA: Emcor Group, Inc.
301 Merritt 7 Fl 6
Norwalk CT 06851
203 849-7800

(P-2631)
KERTEL COMMUNICATIONS INC (HQ)
Also Called: Sebastian
7600 N Palm Ave Ste 101, Fresno (93711-5520)
PHONE.................................559 432-5800
Fax: 559 432-5858
William S Barcus, *CEO*
Chrissy Barcus, *Shareholder*
Jack Darrah, *CFO*
Al Baumgarner, *Treasurer*
Ruth Barcus, *Vice Pres*
EMP: 92
SQ FT: 9,436
SALES: 24.8MM
SALES (corp-wide): 51.4MM **Privately Held**
SIC: 1731 Communications specialization
PA: Sebastian Enterprises, Inc.
811 S Madera Ave
Kerman CA 93630
559 846-9311

(P-2632)
KITE ELECTRIC INC
Also Called: K E
2 Thomas, Irvine (92618-2512)
PHONE.................................949 380-7471
Tracy Adams, *President*
EMP: 120
SALES (est): 16.5MM **Privately Held**
SIC: 1731 Electrical work

(P-2633)
KOSITCH ENTERPRISES INC
Also Called: MISSION ELECTRIC COMPANY
5700 Boscell Cmn, Fremont (94538-5111)
PHONE.................................510 657-4460
Fax: 510 657-1160
Jeffrey Kositch, *CEO*
Fawaz Khan, *Project Mgr*
Heather Hartel, *Controller*
Mike Clarke, *Marketing Staff*
Rob Perrill, *Marketing Staff*
EMP: 80
SQ FT: 9,000
SALES: 22MM **Privately Held**
WEB: www.mission-elec.com
SIC: 1731 General electrical contractor

(P-2634)
L TECH NETWORK SERVICES INC
9926 Pioneer Blvd Ste 101, Santa Fe Springs (90670-6248)
PHONE.................................562 222-1121
Fax: 562 222-1533
Robert O Lopez, *President*
Steve Ramirez, *Project Mgr*
David Goldsmith, *Controller*
Steve Romarez, *Purchasing*
Mary Samson, *Mktg Dir*
EMP: 65
SQ FT: 4,060
SALES: 5MM **Privately Held**
WEB: www.ltechnet.com
SIC: 1731 Electrical work

(P-2635)
LAZER ELECTRIC INC
4701 E Hunter Ave, Anaheim (92807-1940)
PHONE.................................714 777-4233
Fax: 714 777-5149
Rodney W Brewer, *President*
David Cameron, *Treasurer*
Richard Southern, *Vice Pres*
EMP: 85
SQ FT: 13,000
SALES: 6MM **Privately Held**
WEB: www.lazerelect.com
SIC: 1731 General electrical contractor

(P-2636)
LEDCOR TECHNICAL SERVICES INC
Also Called: LTS
6405 Mira Mesa Blvd, San Diego (92121-4147)
PHONE.................................858 527-6400
Jimmy Byrd, *CEO*
Chris McLorg, *Vice Pres*
Anselmo Martinez, *Manager*
EMP: 99

SALES (est): 5.6MM **Privately Held**
SIC: 1731 Communications specialization

(P-2637)
LELAND STANFORD JUNIOR UNIV
Also Called: Department of Public Safety
711 Serra St, Stanford (94305-7203)
PHONE.................................650 723-9633
Laura Wilson, *Director*
EMP: 58
SQ FT: 10,000
SALES (corp-wide): 1.9B **Privately Held**
SIC: 1731 8221 Safety & security specialization; university
PA: Leland Stanford Junior University
2575 Sand Hill Rd
Menlo Park CA 94025
650 723-2300

(P-2638)
M & R JOINT VENTURE ELECTRICAL
Also Called: Marrow Meadows
231 Benton Ct, Walnut (91789-5213)
PHONE.................................909 598-7700
Fax: 909 598-3907
Robert E Meadows, *Vice Pres*
Morrow-Meadows Corporation, *Co-Venturer*
John Menicucci, *Project Mgr*
Joe Sandval, *Manager*
EMP: 60
SALES (est): 7.2MM **Privately Held**
SIC: 1731 Electrical work

(P-2639)
MARK III CONSTRUCTION INC
Also Called: Mark III Dvlpers Dsgn/Builders
5101 Florin Perkins Rd, Sacramento (95826-4817)
PHONE.................................916 381-8080
Fax: 916 386-0363
Daniel Carlton, *CEO*
Jennifer O'Brien Cooley, *President*
Michael O'Brien, *Treasurer*
Travis Dales, *Division Mgr*
Mark O'Brien, *Director*
EMP: 75
SQ FT: 11,000
SALES (est): 51.2MM **Privately Held**
SIC: 1731 1542 1711 General electrical contractor; electronic controls installation; commercial & office building, new construction; plumbing contractors; fire sprinkler system installation

(P-2640)
MARK LAND ELECTRIC INC
7876 Deering Ave, Canoga Park (91304-5005)
PHONE.................................818 883-5110
Fax: 818 883-2923
Lloyd Saitman, *CEO*
John Bennet, *CFO*
John Bennett, *CFO*
Stewart Franklin, *Vice Pres*
Jack Mooney, *Vice Pres*
EMP: 74
SQ FT: 10,000
SALES (est): 26.8MM **Privately Held**
WEB: www.landmarkelec.com
SIC: 1731 Electrical work

(P-2641)
MARTICUS ELECTRIC INC
9266 Beatty Dr D, Sacramento (95826-9702)
PHONE.................................916 368-2186
Fax: 916 368-2004
Art Munoz, *President*
Susan Munoz, *Corp Secy*
Melanie Channell, *Admin Asst*
Tim Collins, *Opers Spvr*
Amy Gibson, *Manager*
EMP: 80
SQ FT: 14,000
SALES (est): 7.3MM **Privately Held**
WEB: www.marticus.com
SIC: 1731 General electrical contractor

(P-2642)
MASS ELECTRIC CONSTRUCTION CO
1925 Wright Ave Ste D, La Verne (91750-5847)
PHONE.................................800 933-6322
Rohit Shard, *Branch Mgr*
Fred Hammel, *Branch Mgr*
H Richard Case, *Manager*
Lawrence W Mack, *Agent*
EMP: 100
SALES (corp-wide): 20.9B **Privately Held**
WEB: www.masselec.com
SIC: 1731 General electrical contractor
HQ: Mass. Electric Construction Co.
400 Totten Pond Rd # 400
Waltham MA 02451
781 290-1000

(P-2643)
MAY-HAN ELECTRIC INC
Also Called: M & M Electric
1600 Auburn Blvd, Sacramento (95815-1906)
PHONE.................................916 929-0150
Fax: 916 929-1168
Cecilia J Hanson, *CEO*
Audrey Daugherty, *President*
Connie Gisler, *Corp Secy*
Keith Hoffmann, *VP Opers*
Cecelia Hanson, *Manager*
EMP: 65
SQ FT: 16,000
SALES: 13.3MM **Privately Held**
WEB: www.sacmmelectric.com
SIC: 1731 Electrical work; lighting contractor

(P-2644)
MB HERZOG ELECTRIC INC
15709 Illinois Ave, Paramount (90723-4112)
PHONE.................................562 531-2002
Fax: 562 531-2272
Ryan M Herzog, *CEO*
Michael B Herzog, *Shareholder*
Chuck Fox, *CFO*
Kevin Ryan, *Vice Pres*
Carlie Ryan, *Admin Sec*
EMP: 70
SQ FT: 6,200
SALES (est): 17.6MM **Privately Held**
WEB: www.herzogelectric.com
SIC: 1731 General electrical contractor

(P-2645)
MCH ELECTRIC INC (PA)
7693 Longard Rd, Livermore (94551-8208)
PHONE.................................209 835-9755
James Humphrey, *President*
Christine Morris, *CFO*
EMP: 51 **EST:** 1999
SQ FT: 2,600
SALES (est): 24.4MM **Privately Held**
WEB: www.mchelec.com
SIC: 1731 Electrical work

(P-2646)
MCMILLAN BROS ELECTRIC INC
1950 Cesar Chavez, San Francisco (94124-1132)
PHONE.................................415 826-5100
Fax: 415 826-0142
Patrick J McMillan, *President*
William J Musgrave, *President*
Russell Schmittou, *CFO*
David Auch, *Vice Pres*
Willian J Musgrave, *Vice Pres*
▲ **EMP:** 190 **EST:** 1965
SQ FT: 30,000
SALES (est): 71.6MM **Privately Held**
SIC: 1731 8711 Electrical work; engineering services

(P-2647)
MCMILLAN DATA CMMNICATIONS INC
1950 Cesar Chavez, San Francisco (94124-1132)
PHONE.................................415 826-5100
Mark Mahoney, *Managing Prtnr*
Jim Murray, *Managing Prtnr*
Patrick McMillan, *CEO*
EMP: 55

1731 - Electrical Work County (P-2648)

SALES (est): 1.2MM **Privately Held**
SIC: 1731 Electrical work

(P-2648)
MDE ELECTRIC COMPANY INC
152 Commercial St, Sunnyvale (94086-5201)
PHONE.................................408 738-8600
Fax: 408 738-0385
Marshall Goldman, *President*
Harry Goldman, *Corp Secy*
EMP: 50
SQ FT: 5,000
SALES (est): 8.7MM **Privately Held**
WEB: www.mde-electric.com
SIC: 1731 General electrical contractor

(P-2649)
MEDLEY COMMUNICATIONS INC
255 N Ash St, Escondido (92027-3068)
PHONE.................................760 294-4579
EMP: 82
SALES (corp-wide): 32MM **Privately Held**
WEB: www.medleycom.com
SIC: 1731 8748 Cable television installation; communications consulting
PA: Medley Communications, Inc
  41531 Date St
  Murrieta CA 92562
  951 245-5200

(P-2650)
MEDLEY COMMUNICATIONS INC (PA)
41531 Date St, Murrieta (92562-7086)
PHONE.................................951 245-5200
Darrin Medley, *President*
Rick Hunter, *Vice Pres*
Karen Schuitt, *Finance Mgr*
Allene Villareal, *Manager*
EMP: 175
SALES (est): 32MM **Privately Held**
WEB: www.medleycom.com
SIC: 1731 8748 Cable television installation; communications consulting

(P-2651)
METROPOLITAN ELEC CNSTR INC
2400 3rd St, San Francisco (94107-3111)
PHONE.................................415 642-3000
Fax: 415 550-6615
Mark Friedeberg, *CFO*
Doug Snodgrass, *CFO*
Tiersa Aldridge, *Admin Asst*
Margie Dutto, *Administration*
Mark Pellegrini, *Info Tech Mgr*
EMP: 210 **EST:** 1981
SQ FT: 23,000
SALES: 54.7MM **Privately Held**
WEB: www.metroelectric.com
SIC: 1731 General electrical contractor

(P-2652)
METROPOWER INC
941 Grand Ave, Long Beach (90804-5214)
PHONE.................................562 305-9617
Gary Evan Freenleaf, *Branch Mgr*
EMP: 85
SALES (corp-wide): 128.9MM **Privately Held**
SIC: 1731 Electrical work
HQ: Metropower, Inc.
  798 21st Ave
  Albany GA 31701
  229 432-7345

(P-2653)
MIKE BROWN ELECTRIC CO
561a Mercantile Dr, Cotati (94931-3040)
PHONE.................................707 792-8100
Fax: 707 792-8110
James G Brown, *President*
Tiffany Howe, *Vice Pres*
Susan Allred, *Administration*
Arnold Gonzales, *Project Mgr*
Sean Hartnett, *Warehouse Mgr*
EMP: 65
SQ FT: 14,000
SALES (est): 22.3MM **Privately Held**
WEB: www.mbelectric.com
SIC: 1731 Electrical work

(P-2654)
MJ STAR-LITE INC
Also Called: Star - Lite Electric
9232 Independence Ave, Chatsworth (91311-5931)
PHONE.................................818 717-0834
Fax: 818 717-9376
Michael Rios, *President*
Maria Covarrubias, *Admin Sec*
EMP: 50
SALES: 3MM **Privately Held**
SIC: 1731 Electrical work

(P-2655)
ML ELECTRICWORKS INC
11325 Magnolia Ave, Riverside (92505-3609)
P.O. Box 70962 (92513-0962)
PHONE.................................951 687-5078
Fax: 951 687-2230
Mark S Lowen, *President*
EMP: 67
SQ FT: 2,000
SALES (est): 5.5MM **Privately Held**
WEB: www.mlelectricworks.com
SIC: 1731 Electrical work

(P-2656)
MODESTO INDUSTRIAL ELEC CO INC (PA)
1417 Coldwell Ave, Modesto (95350-5703)
PHONE.................................209 495-1597
Fax: 209 527-4457
David Howell, *CEO*
Laurie Byer, *CFO*
Michelle Howell, *Vice Pres*
Chuck Fleming, *General Mgr*
Tammy Dolberry, *Accounting Mgr*
EMP: 151
SQ FT: 21,000
SALES (est): 62.7MM **Privately Held**
WEB: www.i-e-c.net
SIC: 1731 5063 7694 General electrical contractor; motors, electric; electric motor repair

(P-2657)
MORROW-MEADOWS CORPORATION (PA)
Also Called: Cherry City Electric
231 Benton Ct, City of Industry (91789-5213)
PHONE.................................858 974-3650
Karen V Price, *CEO*
Elizabeth Meadows, *Ch of Bd*
Timothy D Langley, *CFO*
J Robert Meadows, *Chairman*
Bob Atkinson, *Vice Pres*
EMP: 850
SQ FT: 55,000
SALES (est): 323.2MM **Privately Held**
WEB: www.morrow-meadows.com
SIC: 1731 General electrical contractor

(P-2658)
MORROW-MEADOWS CORPORATION
1050 Bing St, San Carlos (94070-5326)
PHONE.................................510 562-1980
Jim Goetz, *Manager*
Robert Meadows, *Exec VP*
Mike Cuthbertson, *Project Mgr*
Lance Slagle, *Director*
EMP: 200
SALES (corp-wide): 323.2MM **Privately Held**
WEB: www.morrow-meadows.com
SIC: 1731 General electrical contractor
PA: Morrow-Meadows Corporation
  231 Benton Ct
  City Of Industry CA 91789
  858 974-3650

(P-2659)
MSL ELECTRIC INC
4938 E La Palma Ave, Anaheim (92807-1912)
PHONE.................................714 693-4837
Warren L Moore, *President*
Sally Moore, *Admin Sec*
Char Delange, *Accountant*
Jim Mosler, *Materials Mgr*
Bret Ballachey, *Foreman/Supr*
EMP: 60
SQ FT: 12,600

SALES (est): 9.9MM **Privately Held**
SIC: 1731 Electrical work

(P-2660)
MURRIETTA CIRCUITS
5000 E Landon Dr, Anaheim (92807-1978)
PHONE.................................714 970-2430
Fax: 714 693-3577
Andrew Murrietta, *CEO*
Albert G Murrietta, *President*
Albert A Murrieta, *COO*
Helen Murrietta, *Treasurer*
Josh Murrietta, *Vice Pres*
EMP: 75
SQ FT: 48,500
SALES (est): 8.2MM **Privately Held**
WEB: www.murrietta.com
SIC: 1731 3672 8711 Closed circuit television installation; printed circuit boards; engineering services

(P-2661)
NATIONAL FAIL SAFE INC
Also Called: National Fail-Safe SEC Systems
6442 Industry Way, Westminster (92683-3600)
PHONE.................................562 493-5447
Fax: 714 892-7313
Al Puskas, *President*
Kathy Puskas, *Vice Pres*
Chris Shimaoka, *Design Engr*
Mike Puskas, *Project Mgr*
Curt Puskas, *Opers Staff*
EMP: 50 **EST:** 1972
SQ FT: 10,000
SALES (est): 8.6MM **Privately Held**
WEB: www.nf-s.com
SIC: 1731 7382 Fire detection & burglar alarm systems specialization; fire alarm maintenance & monitoring

(P-2662)
NAZZARENO ELECTRIC CO INC
1250 E Gene Autry Way, Anaheim (92805-6716)
PHONE.................................714 712-4740
Fax: 714 712-4744
Paul Rick Nazzareno, *President*
Ron Brown, *Vice Pres*
Tim Fyke, *Project Mgr*
Joe Mergelmeyer, *Project Mgr*
EMP: 75
SQ FT: 10,000
SALES (est): 10MM **Privately Held**
SIC: 1731 Electrical work

(P-2663)
NEAL ELECTRIC CORP (HQ)
2790 Business Park Dr, Vista (92081-7860)
P.O. Box 1655, Poway (92074-1655)
PHONE.................................858 513-2525
Fax: 858 442-4097
Daniel Zupp, *President*
Alex Meruelo, *Treasurer*
Luis Armona, *Vice Pres*
Lance Neal, *Vice Pres*
Dennis Ramsey, *Vice Pres*
EMP: 75
SQ FT: 30,000
SALES (est): 60.9MM
SALES (corp-wide): 280.6MM **Privately Held**
WEB: www.whitney.com
SIC: 1731 General electrical contractor
PA: Meruelo Enterprises, Inc.
  9550 Firestone Blvd # 105
  Downey CA 90241
  562 745-2300

(P-2664)
NETRONIX INTEGRATION INC
2170 Paragon Dr, San Jose (95131-1305)
PHONE.................................408 573-1444
Fax: 408 573-1441
Craig E Jarrett, *President*
Steve Piechota, *CFO*
Kris Miles, *Office Admin*
Rigoberto Gomez, *Technician*
David Beale, *Project Mgr*
EMP: 138
SQ FT: 13,500
SALES (est): 30.4MM **Privately Held**
SIC: 1731 General electrical contractor

(P-2665)
NETVERSANT - SILICON VLY INC (PA)
Also Called: Apex Communications
47811 Warm Springs Blvd, Fremont (94539-7400)
PHONE.................................510 771-1200
John Chelstowski, *President*
Dana Fisher, *Sales Executive*
Gregory Kennedy, *Marketing Staff*
Paul Chen, *Director*
EMP: 125
SQ FT: 14,000
SALES (est): 12.2MM **Privately Held**
WEB: www.apexcommunications.com
SIC: 1731 7376 Communications specialization; telephone & telephone equipment installation; computer facilities management

(P-2666)
NEVADA REPUBLIC ELECTRIC N INC
11855 White Rock Rd, Rancho Cordova (95742-6603)
PHONE.................................916 294-0140
Eric Stafford, *President*
Jeff Stafford, *Treasurer*
Hope Weber, *Personnel Exec*
Jerry Stafford, *Director*
Linda Stafford, *Director*
EMP: 140
SQ FT: 14,000
SALES (est): 17.8MM **Privately Held**
WEB: www.republicelectricwest.com
SIC: 1731 Electrical work

(P-2667)
NEW AGE ELECTRIC INC
1085 N 11th St, San Jose (95112-2928)
PHONE.................................408 279-8787
Fax: 408 279-6767
Kurt Rocklage, *President*
Vickie Roberts, *Office Mgr*
Gloria Sauve, *Administration*
Greg Dalton, *Project Mgr*
Alan Pumphrey, *Finance Mgr*
EMP: 60
SQ FT: 8,500
SALES (est): 13.8MM **Privately Held**
SIC: 1731 Electrical work

(P-2668)
NORTH STATE ELEC CONTRS INC
11415 Sunrise Gold Cir # 1, Rancho Cordova (95742-6583)
PHONE.................................916 572-0571
Rodney Bingaman, *President*
Karen French, *Office Mgr*
Jason Alexander, *Project Mgr*
Lori Kirk, *Controller*
EMP: 80
SQ FT: 5,500
SALES (est): 16.5MM **Privately Held**
SIC: 1731 General electrical contractor

(P-2669)
NORTHLAND CONTROL SYSTEMS INC (PA)
44150 S Grimmer Blvd, Fremont (94538-6310)
PHONE.................................510 403-7600
Fax: 510 226-1018
Pierre Trapanese, *CEO*
Jim Conley, *CFO*
Vic Demarzo, *Program Mgr*
Brendan McFall, *Executive Asst*
James Barron, *Info Tech Mgr*
EMP: 86
SALES: 38MM **Privately Held**
WEB: www.northlandcontrols.com
SIC: 1731 7389 Fire detection & burglar alarm systems specialization; automobile recovery service

(P-2670)
NRG POWER INC
3011 S Shannon St, Santa Ana (92704-6320)
PHONE.................................714 424-6484
Fax: 714 424-6477
Than V Nguyen, *President*
John Toan Nguyen, *Vice Pres*
Elaine Diep, *Office Mgr*

PRODUCTS & SERVICES SECTION

1731 - Electrical Work County (P-2694)

Daniel MAI, *Office Mgr*
EMP: 57
SQ FT: 5,700
SALES (est): 6.7MM **Privately Held**
SIC: 1731 Electrical work

(P-2671)
OBRYANT ELECTRIC INC
9314 Eton Ave, Chatsworth (91311-5809)
PHONE 818 407-1986
Cathy O'Bryant, *President*
Steve O'Bryant, *Admin Sec*
EMP: 200 **EST:** 1978
SQ FT: 25,000
SALES (est): 46.8MM **Privately Held**
WEB: www.obryantelectric.com
SIC: 1731 General electrical contractor

(P-2672)
OILFIELD ELECTRIC COMPANY
Also Called: Oilfield Electric & Motor
1801 N Ventura Ave, Ventura (93001-1597)
PHONE 805 648-3131
Fax: 805 648-4806
Alan Dale Fletcher, *CEO*
Jana Fletcher, *President*
Nelson Cooper, *Sales Dir*
EMP: 60 **EST:** 1941
SQ FT: 10,000
SALES (est): 16.8MM **Privately Held**
SIC: 1731 7629 General electrical contractor; electrical repair shops

(P-2673)
ONLINE COMMUNICATIONS INC
3291 Swetzer Rd, Loomis (95650-7607)
PHONE 916 652-7253
Martin P Green, *President*
Christopher Green, *Vice Pres*
EMP: 110
SALES (est): 6.9MM **Privately Held**
SIC: 1731 4813 8748 Fiber optic cable installation; telephone & telephone equipment installation; telephone communication, except radio; telecommunications consultant

(P-2674)
PACIFIC METRO ELECTRIC INC
3150 E Fremont St, Stockton (95205-3918)
P.O. Box 127 (95201-0127)
PHONE 209 939-3222
Fax: 209 939-3225
Glen Rigsbee, *President*
EMP: 60
SALES (est): 11.3MM **Privately Held**
WEB: www.pacificmetroelectric.com
SIC: 1731 Electrical work

(P-2675)
PACIFIC UTLITY INSTLLATION INC
1585 N Harmony Cir, Anaheim (92807-6003)
PHONE 714 970-6430
Fax: 714 970-6287
William B Pfeifer, *CEO*
Daniel Mole, *President*
Bill Pfeifer, *Officer*
Joann Stamp, *Controller*
▲ **EMP:** 65
SALES (est): 18.3MM **Privately Held**
SIC: 1731 1623 General electrical contractor; water, sewer & utility lines

(P-2676)
PAGANINI ELECTRIC CORPORATION
Also Called: Paganini Companies
190 Hubbell St Ste 200, San Francisco (94107-2240)
PHONE 415 575-3900
Fax: 415 575-3920
Kenneth A Paganini, *CEO*
Michael K Paganini, *President*
Steve Donaugh, *Vice Pres*
Benson Lee, *Info Tech Dir*
Ron Baxter, *Project Mgr*
EMP: 115
SQ FT: 20,000
SALES (est): 27.8MM **Privately Held**
WEB: www.pagcos.com
SIC: 1731 General electrical contractor

(P-2677)
PAR ELECTRICAL CONTRACTORS INC
525 Corporate Dr, Escondido (92029-1500)
PHONE 760 291-1192
Fax: 760 471-0321
Jay Taylor, *Vice Pres*
EMP: 58
SALES (corp-wide): 7.5B **Publicly Held**
SIC: 1731 General electrical contractor
HQ: Par Electrical Contractors, Inc.
4770 N Belleview Ave # 300
Kansas City MO 64116
816 474-9340

(P-2678)
PAR ELECTRICAL CONTRACTORS INC
11276 5th St Ste 100, Rancho Cucamonga (91730-0922)
PHONE 909 854-2880
Jim Stapp, *Manager*
EMP: 100
SALES (corp-wide): 7.5B **Publicly Held**
WEB: www.parelectric.com
SIC: 1731 General electrical contractor
HQ: Par Electrical Contractors, Inc.
4770 N Belleview Ave # 300
Kansas City MO 64116
816 474-9340

(P-2679)
PAR ELECTRICAL CONTRACTORS INC
1416 Midway Rd, Vacaville (95688-9437)
PHONE 707 693-1237
Fax: 707 693-1345
Kenny Bruce, *Vice Pres*
EMP: 80
SALES (corp-wide): 7.5B **Publicly Held**
WEB: www.parelectric.com
SIC: 1731 General electrical contractor
HQ: Par Electrical Contractors, Inc.
4770 N Belleview Ave # 300
Kansas City MO 64116
816 474-9340

(P-2680)
PARADISE ELECTRIC INC
697 Greenfield Dr, El Cajon (92021-2983)
PHONE 619 449-4141
Mike Manos, *President*
Jeff Platt, *CFO*
Tom Hamm, *General Mgr*
EMP: 70
SQ FT: 7,000
SALES: 6MM
SALES (corp-wide): 134.6MM **Privately Held**
WEB: www.paradise-electric.com
SIC: 1731 General electrical contractor
HQ: Builders Tradesource Corp
697 Greenfield Dr
El Cajon CA 92021
619 792-1795

(P-2681)
PATRIC COMMUNICATIONS INC (PA)
Also Called: Advanced Electronic Solutions
1488 Pioneer Way Ste 4, El Cajon (92020-1633)
PHONE 619 579-2898
Sean P McDermott, *President*
Colleen Emick, *CFO*
Richard P Apgar, *Vice Pres*
Kathy Alford, *Admin Sec*
EMP: 70
SQ FT: 27,000
SALES (est): 9MM **Privately Held**
WEB: www.aes2.net
SIC: 1731 1751 3699 Fire detection & burglar alarm systems specialization; carpentry work; security devices

(P-2682)
PAVLETICH ELC CMMNICATIONS INC (PA)
6308 Seven Seas Ave, Bakersfield (93308-5132)
PHONE 661 589-9473
John Pavletich, *CEO*
Scott Pavletich, *President*
Richard Darilek, *Bd of Directors*
Ryon Depencier, *VP Admin*

Keith Field, *Manager*
EMP: 89
SQ FT: 15,000 **Privately Held**
WEB: www.pavelectric.com
SIC: 1731 Electrical work; fiber optic cable installation

(P-2683)
PETRELLI ELECTRIC INC
11615 Davenport Rd, Agua Dulce (91390-4690)
P.O. Box 801148, Santa Clarita (91380-1148)
PHONE 661 268-7312
Cindy Petrelli, *CEO*
Bill Murray, *Vice Pres*
Salvatore Petrelli, *Vice Pres*
EMP: 66
SALES (est): 14.5MM **Privately Held**
SIC: 1731 7629 Electrical work; electrical equipment repair, high voltage

(P-2684)
PINNACLE NETWORKING SVCS INC
Also Called: Pinnacle Communication Svcs
730 Fairmont Ave, Glendale (91203-1078)
PHONE 818 241-6009
Fax: 818 241-6880
Avo Amirian, *CEO*
Joe Licursi, *President*
Jose Aguirre, *Executive*
Cerrita Clark, *Administration*
Mark Alfonso, *Technician*
EMP: 75
SQ FT: 10,000
SALES (est): 16.4MM **Privately Held**
SIC: 1731 Communications specialization; general electrical contractor; telephone & telephone equipment installation; computer installation

(P-2685)
PIVOT INTERIORS INC
Pivot Interiors-Receiving Only
3200 Park Center Dr # 100, Costa Mesa (92626-7104)
PHONE 949 988-5400
Ken Baugh, *CEO*
EMP: 60
SALES (corp-wide): 171MM **Privately Held**
WEB: www.pivotinteriors.com
SIC: 1731 Electrical work
PA: Pivot Interiors, Inc.
3355 Scott Blvd Ste 110
Santa Clara CA 95054
408 432-5600

(P-2686)
PMD INDUSTRIES INC
Also Called: Eie Electric
703 Randolph Ave, Costa Mesa (92626-5917)
PHONE 949 222-0999
Fax: 949 222-0536
Phillip M Davis, *President*
Howard C Waters, *CFO*
John Davis, *Vice Pres*
Manolito Ocampo, *Engineer*
Matt Engle, *Manager*
EMP: 50
SQ FT: 2,500
SALES (est): 7.7MM **Privately Held**
WEB: www.eieelectric.com
SIC: 1731 7373 Electrical work; computer integrated systems design

(P-2687)
PONDEROSA ELECTRIC INC
17155 Von Karman Ave # 101, Irvine (92614-0906)
PHONE 949 253-3100
Fax: 949 253-3110
Dale Arnold, *President*
EMP: 60
SQ FT: 2,400
SALES: 4.8MM **Privately Held**
SIC: 1731 General electrical contractor

(P-2688)
PORTERMATT ELECTRIC INC
5431 Production Dr, Huntington Beach (92649-1524)
PHONE 714 596-8788
Fax: 714 596-8718

Tim Matthews, *President*
John F Porter III, *Vice Pres*
Stefanie Janssen, *Admin Asst*
Linzey Koahou, *Manager*
Keith Muraoka, *Manager*
EMP: 90
SQ FT: 5,300
SALES (est): 19.9MM **Privately Held**
SIC: 1731 1799 Electrical work; athletic & recreation facilities construction

(P-2689)
POWER PLUS SOLUTIONS CORP
1210 N Red Gum St, Anaheim (92806-1820)
PHONE 714 507-1881
Steven Bray, *President*
EMP: 50
SALES (est): 4.2MM **Privately Held**
SIC: 1731 Electric power systems contractors

(P-2690)
PROFESSNAL ELEC CNSTR SVCS INC
Also Called: Pecs
9112 Santa Anita Ave, Rancho Cucamonga (91730-6143)
PHONE 909 373-4100
Diane L Casey, *CEO*
Robert W Casey, *CFO*
EMP: 120
SQ FT: 15,000
SALES (est): 38MM **Privately Held**
SIC: 1731 Electric power systems contractors

(P-2691)
PS DEVELOPMENT CORPORATION
21625 Prairie St, Chatsworth (91311-5833)
PHONE 818 340-0965
Adam Saitman, *President*
Jaison Pennington, *CFO*
David Blender, *Agent*
EMP: 100 **EST:** 1976
SQ FT: 5,000
SALES (est): 5.4MM **Privately Held**
SIC: 1731 General electrical contractor

(P-2692)
PYRO-COMM SYSTEMS INC (PA)
15531 Container Ln, Huntington Beach (92649-1530)
PHONE 714 902-8000
Fax: 714 902-8001
Michael Donahue, *President*
Nanci Donahue, *Vice Pres*
Melissa Tadlock, *Admin Asst*
Margarita Hristeva, *Info Tech Mgr*
Alex Guerrero, *Design Engr*
EMP: 150
SQ FT: 10,000
SALES (est): 38.1MM **Privately Held**
WEB: www.pyrocomm.com
SIC: 1731 5063 Safety & security specialization; fire alarm systems

(P-2693)
R & R ELECTRIC
2029 Century Park E A4, Los Angeles (90067-1915)
PHONE 310 785-0288
Fax: 310 785-0621
Ricardo Ramos, *Owner*
Rob Szilagyi, *Project Mgr*
Omar Ramos, *Controller*
Saul Chavarria, *Purch Agent*
John Kevany, *Manager*
EMP: 50
SQ FT: 5,000
SALES (est): 4.2MM **Privately Held**
SIC: 1731 Electrical work

(P-2694)
RADONICH CORP
Also Called: Cal Coast Telecom
886 Faulstich Ct, San Jose (95112-1361)
PHONE 408 275-8888
Fax: 408 275-8895
Rick M Radonich, *CEO*
David S Miguel, *Corp Secy*
William L Radonich Jr, *Vice Pres*

1731 - Electrical Work County (P-2695)

EMP: 50
SQ FT: 5,000
SALES: 18MM Privately Held
WEB: www.calcoasttelecom.com
SIC: 1731 Fiber optic cable installation; voice, data & video wiring contractor

(P-2695)
RANCHO PACIFIC ELECTRIC INC
201 W State St, Ontario (91762-4360)
PHONE 909 476-1022
Fax: 909 391-4369
Steve Robinson, *President*
Dave Robinson, *Corp Secy*
Jennifer Schmidt, *Manager*
EMP: 50
SQ FT: 4,500
SALES (est): 2.8MM Privately Held
SIC: 1731 General electrical contractor

(P-2696)
RAYLEE ELECTRIC
1202 Tarapin Ln, Lincoln (95648-8138)
PHONE 916 408-7556
R George Alvarado, *President*
Raymond George Alvarado, *President*
Cindy Alvarado, *Vice Pres*
EMP: 50
SALES (est): 140.7K Privately Held
SIC: 1731 Electrical work

(P-2697)
RCI ELECTRIC INC
Also Called: Rayco Electric
3144 Fitzgerald Rd, Rancho Cordova (95742-6802)
PHONE 916 858-8000
Fax: 916 858-8008
Raymond Alvarado, *President*
Jimmy Green, *Purch Mgr*
EMP: 99
SALES (est): 16MM Privately Held
WEB: www.raycoelectric.com
SIC: 1731 General electrical contractor

(P-2698)
RDM ELECTRIC CO INC
13867 Redwood Ave, Chino (91710-6010)
PHONE 909 591-0990
Robert McDonnell, *President*
Diane McDonnell, *CFO*
Anthony Gerdes, *Vice Pres*
Robert D McDonnell Jr, *Vice Pres*
Yolanda Connaughton, *Office Admin*
EMP: 75
SALES: 19MM Privately Held
SIC: 1731 General electrical contractor

(P-2699)
RED HAWK FIRE & SEC CA INC
4384 Enterprise Pl, Fremont (94538-6365)
PHONE 510 438-1300
Fax: 510 782-1729
Mack Katal, *President*
EMP: 90
SALES (corp-wide): 220MM Privately Held
SIC: 1731 Fire detection & burglar alarm systems specialization
HQ: Red Hawk Fire & Security (Ca), Inc.
2705 Media Center Dr
Los Angeles CA 90065
818 683-1500

(P-2700)
RED HAWK FIRE & SEC CA INC
1640 N Batavia St, Orange (92867-3509)
PHONE 714 685-8100
Bob Berkery, *Manager*
EMP: 105
SALES (corp-wide): 220MM Privately Held
WEB: www.detectionlogic.com
SIC: 1731 Fire detection & burglar alarm systems specialization
HQ: Red Hawk Fire & Security (Ca), Inc.
2705 Media Center Dr
Los Angeles CA 90065
818 683-1500

(P-2701)
RED HAWK FIRE & SEC CA INC (HQ)
2705 Media Center Dr, Los Angeles (90065-1700)
PHONE 818 683-1500
Fax: 818 745-6820
Sean Flint, *CEO*
Marc Serrio, *CFO*
Mark Clinton, *Info Tech Mgr*
Matthew Troidl, *Controller*
Sara Tapia, *Human Resources*
EMP: 74
SQ FT: 15,500
SALES (est): 22.9MM
SALES (corp-wide): 220MM Privately Held
WEB: www.chubbfs.com
SIC: 1731 Fire detection & burglar alarm systems specialization
PA: Red Hawk Fire & Security, Llc
5100 Town Center Cir # 350
Boca Raton FL 33486
561 672-3737

(P-2702)
RED HAWK FIRE & SEC CA INC
920 S Andreasen Dr # 102, Escondido (92029-1936)
PHONE 760 233-9787
Brad Mattonen, *Branch Mgr*
Miguel Rivera, *Manager*
EMP: 68
SALES (corp-wide): 220MM Privately Held
SIC: 1731 Fire detection & burglar alarm systems specialization
HQ: Red Hawk Fire & Security (Ca), Inc.
2705 Media Center Dr
Los Angeles CA 90065
818 683-1500

(P-2703)
REDWOOD ELECTRIC GROUP INC (PA)
2775 Northwestern Pkwy, Santa Clara (95051-0947)
PHONE 707 451-7348
Fax: 408 369-4963
Victor Castello, *President*
Jeff Tarzwell, *CFO*
Gordon Armstrong, *Vice Pres*
Bruce Kelly, *Vice Pres*
Frank Alvernaz, *Project Mgr*
EMP: 680 EST: 1974
SQ FT: 35,000
SALES (est): 182.1MM Privately Held
SIC: 1731 General electrical contractor

(P-2704)
REPUBLIC ELECTRIC INC
3820 Happy Ln, Sacramento (95827-9721)
PHONE 916 294-0140
Fax: 916 257-0618
Eric Stafford, *Manager*
Hope Weber, *Personnel Exec*
EMP: 100
SALES (corp-wide): 29.9MM Privately Held
SIC: 1731 Electrical work
PA: Republic Electric, Inc.
3985 N Pecos Rd
Las Vegas NV 89115
702 643-2688

(P-2705)
REPUBLIC ELECTRIC WEST INC
3820 Happy Ln, Sacramento (95827-9721)
PHONE 916 294-0140
Eric J Stafford, *President*
Gerald Stafford, *CFO*
Jerry Stafford, *Admin Sec*
Cindy Findley, *CIO*
EMP: 70
SALES (est): 10MM Privately Held
SIC: 1731 Electrical work

(P-2706)
REX MOORE GROUP INC
6001 Outfall Cir, Sacramento (95828-1020)
PHONE 916 372-1300
David Rex Moore, *President*
Doug Cuthbert, *President*
J Brock Littlejohn, *CFO*
James Brock Littlejohn, *CFO*
William C Hubbard, *Exec VP*
EMP: 450
SQ FT: 36,000
SALES (est): 130.2MM Privately Held
WEB: www.rmi-systems.com
SIC: 1731 8711 Electrical work; engineering services

(P-2707)
REX MORE ELEC CONTRS ENGINEERS (PA)
6001 Outfall Cir, Sacramento (95828-1020)
PHONE 916 372-1300
Fax: 916 372-4013
David R Moore, *CEO*
William C Hubbard, *Partner*
James B Littlejohn, *Partner*
Steven R Moore, *Partner*
Jason Blum, *Regional Mgr*
EMP: 350
SQ FT: 36,000
SALES (est): 84.9MM Privately Held
WEB: www.rexmoore.com
SIC: 1731 General electrical contractor

(P-2708)
REX MORE ELEC CONTRS ENGINEERS
5803 E Harvard Ave, Fresno (93727-1366)
P.O. Box 7677 (93747-7677)
PHONE 559 294-1300
Fax: 559 294-1374
John Abele, *Manager*
Daniel Costilla, *Project Engr*
Francisco Hernandez, *Project Engr*
Tristan Hankla, *Sr Project Mgr*
EMP: 70
SALES (corp-wide): 94.4MM Privately Held
SIC: 1731 Electrical work
PA: Rex Moore Electrical Contractors & Engineers, Inc
6001 Outfall Cir
Sacramento CA 95828
916 372-1300

(P-2709)
REX MORE ELEC CONTRS ENGINEERS
6001 Outfall Cir, Sacramento (95828-1020)
PHONE 510 785-1300
Fax: 510 785-1319
Brent Iseman, *Manager*
EMP: 100
SALES (corp-wide): 94.4MM Privately Held
SIC: 1731 Electrical work
PA: Rex Moore Electrical Contractors & Engineers, Inc
6001 Outfall Cir
Sacramento CA 95828
916 372-1300

(P-2710)
RFI ENTERPRISES INC (PA)
Also Called: RFI Communications SEC Systems
360 Turtle Creek Ct, San Jose (95125-1389)
PHONE 408 298-5400
Fax: 408 275-0156
Dee Ann Harn, *President*
Michelle Brooks, *Vice Pres*
Dale Mac McComb, *Vice Pres*
Dale Mc Comb, *Vice Pres*
Brad J Wilson, *Principal*
EMP: 54
SQ FT: 30,000
SALES (est): 68.1MM Privately Held
SIC: 1731 7382 Safety & security specialization; communications specialization; security systems services

(P-2711)
RIS ELECTRICAL CONTRS INC
7330 Sycamore Canyon Blvd # 1, Riverside (92508-2317)
PHONE 951 688-8049
Bob Hayes, *President*
Donna Blankenship, *Office Mgr*
Mike Finnigan, *Project Mgr*
EMP: 50
SQ FT: 1,600
SALES (est): 6.5MM Privately Held
SIC: 1731 General electrical contractor

(P-2712)
RJB ENTERPRISES INC
Also Called: Ultimate Communication Systems
2579 W Woodland Dr, Anaheim (92801-2608)
PHONE 714 484-3101
Robert Bohan, *President*
Donald Ramirez, *Engineer*
William Ramirez, *Opers Mgr*
Don Averill, *Manager*
EMP: 50
SQ FT: 3,500
SALES (est): 7.2MM Privately Held
WEB: www.ucomsys.com
SIC: 1731 Voice, data & video wiring contractor

(P-2713)
RK ELECTRIC INC
42021 Osgood Rd, Fremont (94539-5028)
PHONE 510 580-2850
Lonnie Robinson, *President*
Raul Real, *Vice Pres*
Dale Swanson, *Vice Pres*
Dan Yeggy, *Vice Pres*
Michael Wonderlin, *Info Tech Mgr*
EMP: 130
SQ FT: 11,500
SALES: 27.5MM Privately Held
SIC: 1731 General electrical contractor

(P-2714)
ROCKET EMS INC
2950 Patrick Henry Dr, Santa Clara (95054-1813)
PHONE 408 727-3700
Craig Arcuri, *CEO*
Michael Kottke, *President*
Chris Mak, *CFO*
Peter Chipman, *Vice Pres*
Paul Lyons, *Vice Pres*
EMP: 140
SQ FT: 40,000
SALES (est): 11.5MM Privately Held
SIC: 1731 Electrical work

(P-2715)
ROSENDIN ELECTRIC INC (PA)
880 Mabury Rd, San Jose (95133-1021)
P.O. Box 49070 (95161-9070)
PHONE 408 286-2800
Fax: 408 971-7170
Tom Sorley, *Ch of Bd*
Kyle Louis, *Managing Prtnr*
Larry Beltramo, *President*
Lorne Rundquist, *CFO*
Rich Calia, *Bd of Directors*
EMP: 3000 EST: 1919
SQ FT: 45,000
SALES (est): 1.2B Privately Held
WEB: www.rosendin.com
SIC: 1731 General electrical contractor

(P-2716)
ROSENDIN ELECTRIC INC
2698 Orchard Pkwy, San Jose (95134-2020)
PHONE 408 321-2200
Mary Marshall, *Principal*
Susan Fermil, *Engineer*
Karen Le, *Engineer*
Mao Le, *Engineer*
Bertha Torres, *Engineer*
EMP: 668
SALES (corp-wide): 1.2B Privately Held
SIC: 1731 Electrical work
PA: Rosendin Electric, Inc.
880 Mabury Rd
San Jose CA 95133
408 286-2800

(P-2717)
ROSENDIN ELECTRIC INC
2121 Oakdale Ave, San Francisco (94124-1530)
PHONE 415 495-9300
Fax: 415 495-9303
Rick Shandrew, *Manager*
Michelle Francis, *Admin Asst*
Nicole Gusha, *Admin Asst*
Paul Hauck, *Project Mgr*
Joseph Leoncavallo, *Project Mgr*
EMP: 213

PRODUCTS & SERVICES SECTION
1731 - Electrical Work County (P-2741)

SALES (corp-wide): 1.2B **Privately Held**
WEB: www.rosendin.com
SIC: **1731** General electrical contractor
PA: Rosendin Electric, Inc.
  880 Mabury Rd
  San Jose CA 95133
  408 286-2800

(P-2718)
ROSENDIN ELECTRIC INC
1001 Potrero Ave, San Francisco
(94110-3518)
PHONE.............................415 495-9300
EMP: 668
SALES (corp-wide): 1.2B **Privately Held**
SIC: **1731** General electrical contractor
PA: Rosendin Electric, Inc.
  880 Mabury Rd
  San Jose CA 95133
  408 286-2800

(P-2719)
ROWAN INCORPORATED
Also Called: Rowan Electric
2778 Loker Ave W, Carlsbad (92010-6611)
PHONE.............................760 692-0700
Fax: 760 692-0707
Paul J Rowan, *CEO*
Mark B Rowan, *Vice Pres*
Tom Skibinski, *Superintendent*
EMP: 67
SQ FT: 6,000
SALES (est): 15.4MM **Privately Held**
WEB: www.rowanelectric.com
SIC: **1731** Electrical work

(P-2720)
RYE ELECTRIC INC
3940 Electric Ave, Laguna Hills (92653)
PHONE.............................949 441-0545
Christopher Dale Golden, *CEO*
EMP: 62
SALES (est): 160.7K **Privately Held**
SIC: **1731** Electrical work

(P-2721)
SABAH INTERNATIONAL INC (PA)
5925 Stoneridge Dr, Pleasanton
(94588-2705)
PHONE.............................925 734-5750
Fax: 925 463-1047
Michele Sabah, *CEO*
Richard Cottle, *Vice Pres*
Patricia Ram, *Executive*
Donna Halliday, *General Mgr*
Sheri Learmonth, *Controller*
EMP: 51
SQ FT: 13,000
SALES (est): 17.8MM **Privately Held**
WEB: www.sabah-intl.com
SIC: **1731** **7382** Safety & security specialization; protective devices, security

(P-2722)
SAGE ELECTRIC COMPANY
9144 Owensmouth Ave, Chatsworth
(91311-5851)
PHONE.............................818 718-9080
Fax: 818 718-9083
Greg Stevens, *President*
Ilya Sitnitsky, *President*
Mark Custodero, *Treasurer*
Donald Huff, *Vice Pres*
Brad Pennington, *Admin Sec*
EMP: 75
SQ FT: 3,500
SALES (est): 12.8MM **Privately Held**
SIC: **1731** General electrical contractor

(P-2723)
SAN DIEGO BAY AREA ELC INC
13100 Kirkham Way Ste 205, Poway
(92064-7128)
PHONE.............................858 748-2060
Fax: 858 748-6012
Dennis P Phillips, *President*
Beverly Phillips, *Accounts Mgr*
EMP: 60
SQ FT: 3,500
SALES (est): 5.8MM **Privately Held**
SIC: **1731** Electrical work

(P-2724)
SAN DIEGO GAS & ELECTRIC CO
2300 Harveson Pl, Escondido
(92029-1965)
PHONE.............................760 432-2508
Carl La Peter, *Principal*
EMP: 113
SALES (corp-wide): 10.2B **Publicly Held**
SIC: **1731** Electrical work
HQ: San Diego Gas & Electric Company
  8326 Century Park Ct
  San Diego CA 92123
  619 696-2000

(P-2725)
SANTA CRUZ WESTSIDE ELC INC
Also Called: Sandbar Solar and Electric
2119 Delaware Ave, Santa Cruz
(95060-5706)
PHONE.............................831 469-8888
Scott Laskey, *President*
EMP: 55
SALES (est): 1.4MM **Privately Held**
SIC: **1731** Electrical work

(P-2726)
SATURN ELECTRIC INC
7552 Trade St Ste A, San Diego
(92121-2412)
PHONE.............................858 271-4100
Fax: 858 271-0230
Ron Dudek, *President*
Tim A Dudek, *President*
Thomas J Dudek, *Vice Pres*
Amy Dudek, *Manager*
EMP: 50
SQ FT: 7,000
SALES (est): 6.7MM **Privately Held**
WEB: www.saturnelectric.com
SIC: **1731** Electrical work

(P-2727)
SCHETTER ELECTRIC INC (PA)
471 Bannon St, Sacramento (95811-0296)
P.O. Box 1377 (95812-1377)
PHONE.............................916 446-2521
Fax: 916 446-2621
Frank E Schetter, *President*
Linda Schetter, *Shareholder*
Vince Bernacchi, *Vice Pres*
Keith M Hoffman, *Executive*
Rick Richards, *Exec Dir*
EMP: 90
SQ FT: 7,800
SALES (est): 28.4MM **Privately Held**
WEB: www.schetter.com
SIC: **1731** General electrical contractor

(P-2728)
SEAL ELECTRIC INC
1162 Greenfield Dr, El Cajon (92021-3314)
PHONE.............................619 449-7323
Frank Bongiovanni, *President*
Kathy Bongiovanni, *Network Mgr*
Shelley Walters, *VP Finance*
Marcia Reardon, *Accounting Mgr*
Victor Lopez, *Purchasing*
EMP: 145
SQ FT: 5,000
SALES (est): 30.5MM **Privately Held**
WEB: www.sealelectric.com
SIC: **1731** Electrical work

(P-2729)
SEMANS COMMUNICATIONS (PA)
112 Stonegate Rd, Portola Valley
(94028-7649)
PHONE.............................650 529-9984
Greg Semans, *President*
Roland Valtierra, *Vice Pres*
Steve Semans, *General Mgr*
Bonnie Semans, *Admin Sec*
EMP: 80
SQ FT: 10,000
SALES (est): 6.6MM **Privately Held**
SIC: **1731** Telephone & telephone equipment installation

(P-2730)
SERRANO ELECTRIC INC
1705 Russell Ave, Santa Clara
(95054-2032)
PHONE.............................408 986-1570
Fax: 408 986-1571
Daniel Serrano, *President*
Harry Serrano, *Vice Pres*
Leslie Nakamura, *Admin Sec*
David Haney, *Project Mgr*
Dennis La Plante, *Project Mgr*
EMP: 50
SQ FT: 8,000
SALES (est): 11.9MM **Privately Held**
WEB: www.serranoelectric.com
SIC: **1731** Electrical work

(P-2731)
SERVICE 1ST ELECTRICAL SVCS
1092 N Armando St, Anaheim
(92806-2605)
PHONE.............................714 630-9699
James Graham, *President*
Susie Graham, *Office Mgr*
EMP: 50
SALES (est): 5.2MM **Privately Held**
SIC: **1731** Electrical work

(P-2732)
SFADIA INC
Also Called: Green Energy Innovations
10011 Pioneer Blvd, Santa Fe Springs
(90670-3221)
PHONE.............................323 622-1930
Pilje Park, *President*
Pil Soon Um, *Vice Pres*
Mira Kim, *Accountant*
Nick Guillen, *Manager*
▲ EMP: 86
SQ FT: 8,000
SALES (est): 9.2MM **Privately Held**
SIC: **1731** Energy management controls

(P-2733)
SHORELINE HOLDINGS INC (PA)
2505 Mira Mar Ave, Long Beach
(90815-1759)
PHONE.............................562 498-6444
Fax: 562 498-0282
Robert Yellin, *President*
Linda Yellin, *Treasurer*
Dennis Forel, *Executive*
Nancy Provencher, *Executive*
Jenine McQuaid, *Branch Mgr*
EMP: 105
SQ FT: 15,000
SALES (est): 8.2MM **Privately Held**
SIC: **1731** **8748** Fire detection & burglar alarm systems specialization; business consulting

(P-2734)
SOUTHERN CONTRACTING COMPANY
559 N Twin Oaks Valley Rd, San Marcos
(92069-1798)
P.O. Box 445 (92079-0445)
PHONE.............................760 744-0760
Fax: 760 744-6475
Timothy R McBride, *CEO*
Richard W Mc Bride, *President*
David Eveland, *CFO*
Tim Mc Bride, *Vice Pres*
Jim Filanc, *Info Tech Mgr*
▲ EMP: 125
SQ FT: 8,400
SALES (est): 46.4MM **Privately Held**
WEB: www.southerncontracting.com
SIC: **1731** General electrical contractor

(P-2735)
SOUTHLAND ELECTRIC INC (PA)
4950 Greencraig Ln, San Diego
(92123-1673)
PHONE.............................858 634-5050
Leanne M Peterson, *CEO*
Mark E Peterson, *President*
Allen Ruckle, *Project Mgr*
Tim Kouma, *Purch Agent*
EMP: 78 EST: 1977
SQ FT: 18,000
SALES: 18MM **Privately Held**
SIC: **1731** General electrical contractor

(P-2736)
SPECIALTY CONSTRUCTION INC
645 Clarion Ct, San Luis Obispo
(93401-8177)
PHONE.............................805 543-1706
Fax: 805 543-1712
Rudolph Bachmann, *President*
T McBryde, *CFO*
Chris Teaford, *CFO*
Jeffrey Martin, *Senior VP*
Doug Clay, *Vice Pres*
EMP: 80
SQ FT: 8,000
SALES (est): 29MM **Privately Held**
WEB: www.specialtyconstruction.com
SIC: **1731** Telephone & telephone equipment installation

(P-2737)
SPECTRA I CALIFORNIA
Also Called: Spectra Industrial Electric
21818 S Wilmington Ave # 402, Carson
(90810-1642)
PHONE.............................310 835-0808
Michael J Merrill, *President*
Cliff Krueger, *CFO*
Richard Mangan, *Vice Pres*
Jeff Baldwin, *General Mgr*
Patricia Sandoval, *Finance Mgr*
EMP: 70
SQ FT: 20,000
SALES (est): 6.5MM **Privately Held**
WEB: www.spectrainc.com
SIC: **1731** Access control systems specialization

(P-2738)
SPRIG ELECTRIC CO
65 Oak Grove St, San Francisco
(94107-1018)
PHONE.............................415 947-0138
Michael McAlister, *Branch Mgr*
EMP: 99
SALES (corp-wide): 66.1MM **Privately Held**
SIC: **1731** General electrical contractor
PA: Sprig Electric Co.
  1860 S 10th St
  San Jose CA 95112
  408 298-3134

(P-2739)
SPRIG ELECTRIC CO (PA)
1860 S 10th St, San Jose (95112-4108)
PHONE.............................408 298-3134
Fax: 408 298-2132
Medford Snyder, *CEO*
Brian Vargas, *Technology*
Michael Clifton, *Engineer*
Sheila Margaret, *Controller*
Paula Harvey, *Human Res Dir*
EMP: 151 EST: 1970
SQ FT: 24,100
SALES (est): 66.1MM **Privately Held**
WEB: www.sprigelectric.com
SIC: **1731** General electrical contractor

(P-2740)
SPRINT SPECTRUM LP
3733 W Sunset Blvd, Los Angeles
(90026-1527)
PHONE.............................323 473-5454
EMP: 89
SALES (corp-wide): 78.2B **Publicly Held**
SIC: **1731** Telephone & telephone equipment installation
HQ: Sprint Spectrum L.P.
  6800 Sprint Pkwy
  Overland Park KS 66251
  703 433-4000

(P-2741)
SPRINT SPECTRUM LP
11201 National Blvd, Los Angeles
(90064-3902)
PHONE.............................424 372-2500
EMP: 93
SALES (corp-wide): 78.2B **Publicly Held**
SIC: **1731** Telephone & telephone equipment installation
HQ: Sprint Spectrum L.P.
  6800 Sprint Pkwy
  Overland Park KS 66251
  703 433-4000

1731 - Electrical Work County (P-2742)

(P-2742)
SR BRAY LLC (PA)
Also Called: Power Plus
1210 N Red Gum St, Anaheim
(92806-1820)
PHONE..................714 765-7551
Steven R Bray, *President*
Mike Lang, *COO*
Keith Bjelajac, *CFO*
Brian Bates, *Senior VP*
Randy Kerst, *Vice Pres*
EMP: 50
SQ FT: 60,000
SALES (est): 120.3MM **Privately Held**
SIC: 1731 7359 Standby or emergency power specialization; equipment rental & leasing

(P-2743)
ST DENIS ELECTRIC INC
734 Ralcoa Way, Arroyo Grande
(93420-9620)
PHONE..................805 343-9999
Jeffery S St Denis, *President*
EMP: 50
SALES (est): 453K **Privately Held**
SIC: 1731 Electrical work

(P-2744)
ST FRANCIS ELECTRIC INC
975 Carden St, San Leandro (94577-1102)
P.O. Box 2057 (94577-0317)
PHONE..................510 639-0639
Robert Spinardi, *President*
Krebs Randy, *CFO*
Joseph Medeiros, *Vice Pres*
Guy Smith, *Vice Pres*
Sharon Bassett, *Admin Sec*
EMP: 250 **EST:** 1947
SQ FT: 32,500
SALES: 60MM **Privately Held**
SIC: 1731 General electrical contractor

(P-2745)
ST FRANCIS ELECTRIC LLC
975 Carden St, San Leandro (94577-1102)
P.O. Box 2057 (94577-0317)
PHONE..................510 750-8271
Guy Smith,
EMP: 250
SALES: 30MM **Privately Held**
SIC: 1731 Electrical work

(P-2746)
STADTNER CO INC
Also Called: Sierra Electric Co
3112 Geary Blvd, San Francisco
(94118-3317)
PHONE..................415 752-2850
Fax: 415 752-1102
Rose Stadtner, *President*
David Stadtner, *Vice Pres*
Larry Stadtner, *Vice Pres*
Maria McDowell, *Controller*
EMP: 50
SQ FT: 2,500
SALES (est): 9.3MM **Privately Held**
SIC: 1731 General electrical contractor

(P-2747)
STAR ELECTRIC
517 E Baseline Rd, San Dimas
(91773-1506)
PHONE..................626 422-9227
Norman Vernon Meredith Jr, *Principal*
EMP: 55
SALES (est): 2.4MM **Privately Held**
SIC: 1731 Electrical work

(P-2748)
STC NETCOM INC (PA)
11611 Industry Ave, Fontana (92337-6931)
PHONE..................951 685-8181
Fax: 951 685-1281
Giuseppe Floro, *President*
Mandy Anderson, *Treasurer*
Shawnda Letourneau, *Treasurer*
Jeff Kinne, *General Mgr*
Jeffry Kinne, *Admin Sec*
EMP: 70
SQ FT: 6,000
SALES (est): 13.7MM **Privately Held**
WEB: www.stcnetcom.com
SIC: 1731 Fiber optic cable installation; telephone & telephone equipment installation

(P-2749)
STEINY AND COMPANY INC (PA)
221 N Ardmore Ave, Los Angeles
(90004-4503)
PHONE..................626 962-1055
Fax: 626 337-6899
Susan Steiny, *President*
John O Steiny, *Ch of Bd*
Vincent Mauch, *CFO*
Gayle Kappelman, *Admin Sec*
Cristina Bernal, *Admin Asst*
EMP: 65 **EST:** 1956
SQ FT: 13,000
SALES (est): 91.6MM **Privately Held**
WEB: www.steinyco.com
SIC: 1731 General electrical contractor; safety & security specialization

(P-2750)
STEINY AND COMPANY INC
27 Sheridan St, Vallejo (94590-6911)
P.O. Box 3008 (94590-0673)
PHONE..................707 552-6900
Fax: 707 552-7705
Susan Steiny, *President*
Rick Potter, *Administration*
Hector Avilla, *Applctn Cnslt*
Jim Krause, *Project Mgr*
Jerry Morgan, *Project Mgr*
EMP: 110
SALES (corp-wide): 91.6MM **Privately Held**
SIC: 1731 8711 General electrical contractor; engineering services
PA: Steiny And Company, Inc.
221 N Ardmore Ave
Los Angeles CA 90004
626 962-1055

(P-2751)
STEINY AND COMPANY INC
221 N Ardmore Ave, Los Angeles
(90004-4503)
PHONE..................213 382-2331
Joan Schultz, *Branch Mgr*
EMP: 150
SALES (corp-wide): 91.6MM **Privately Held**
SIC: 1731 General electrical contractor
PA: Steiny And Company, Inc.
221 N Ardmore Ave
Los Angeles CA 90004
626 962-1055

(P-2752)
STOUT & BURG ELECTRIC INC
17256 Red Hill Ave, Irvine (92614-5628)
PHONE..................714 544-5066
Jeff Wilson, *President*
Erika Rodriguez, *Manager*
EMP: 50
SALES (est): 10.4MM **Privately Held**
SIC: 1731 Electrical work

(P-2753)
SUMMIT ELECTRIC INC
2450 Bluebell Dr Ste C, Santa Rosa
(95403-2546)
PHONE..................707 542-4773
Fax: 707 542-1614
Laurence W Dashiell, *President*
Nigel Hartley, *Manager*
EMP: 50
SQ FT: 5,000
SALES (est): 6.4MM **Privately Held**
WEB: www.summit-e.com
SIC: 1731 General electrical contractor

(P-2754)
SUMMIT TECHNOLOGY GROUP INC
Also Called: Summit Electric
2450c Bluebell Dr Ste C, Santa Rosa
(95403-2509)
PHONE..................707 542-4773
Laurence W Dashiell, *President*
EMP: 50
SALES (est): 1.4MM **Privately Held**
SIC: 1731 Voice, data & video wiring contractor

(P-2755)
SUN ELECTRIC LP
2101 S Yale St Ste B, Santa Ana
(92704-4424)
PHONE..................714 210-3744
EMP: 100 **EST:** 2003
SALES (est): 4MM **Privately Held**
SIC: 1731 General electrical contractor

(P-2756)
SUNBELT CONTROLS INC (HQ)
6265 San Fernando Rd, Glendale
(91201-2214)
PHONE..................818 244-6571
Fax: 626 610-2350
Kenneth B Westphal, *CEO*
John Hansen, *President*
Bob Hamill, *Vice Pres*
Josh Reding, *Vice Pres*
Michael Ridout, *Vice Pres*
EMP: 300
SQ FT: 20,000
SALES (est): 12.3MM
SALES (corp-wide): 765MM **Privately Held**
SIC: 1731 Environmental system control installation
PA: Acco Engineered Systems, Inc.
6265 San Fernando Rd
Glendale CA 91201
818 244-6571

(P-2757)
SUNRUN INSTALLATION SVCS INC (HQ)
775 Fiero Ln Ste 200, San Luis Obispo
(93401-7904)
PHONE..................805 528-9705
Helen Wallace, *CEO*
David Termondt, *CFO*
Betsy Wallace, *CFO*
Chris Fennimore, *Business Dir*
Paul Detering, *Principal*
▲ **EMP:** 151
SQ FT: 26,000
SALES (est): 83.5MM
SALES (corp-wide): 304.6MM **Publicly Held**
WEB: www.recsolar.com
SIC: 1731 Electric power systems contractors
PA: Sunrun Inc.
595 Market St Fl 29
San Francisco CA 94105
415 580-6900

(P-2758)
SUNSHINE COMMUNICATIONS INC
350 Cypress Ln Ste D, El Cajon
(92020-1664)
P.O. Box 3509, Apollo Beach FL (33572-1005)
PHONE..................619 448-7600
Robert Straub, *CEO*
Mary Straub, *Manager*
EMP: 235
SALES (est): 18MM **Privately Held**
WEB: www.sunshinecom.com
SIC: 1731 Cable television installation

(P-2759)
SUNWEST ELECTRIC INC
3064 E Miraloma Ave, Anaheim
(92806-1810)
PHONE..................714 630-8700
Fax: 714 630-8740
Brien Pariseau, *President*
Doug Lyvers, *CFO*
Jim Aaron, *Project Mgr*
Valerie Castro, *Project Engr*
Terry Pentoney, *Project Engr*
EMP: 175
SQ FT: 20,000
SALES (est): 36.3MM **Privately Held**
SIC: 1731 Electrical work

(P-2760)
SUPERIOR ELEC MECH & PLBG INC
8613 Helms Ave, Rancho Cucamonga
(91730-4521)
PHONE..................909 357-9400
David A Stone Jr, *CEO*
Walt Schobel, *President*
Pam Metzer, *CFO*
EMP: 291
SQ FT: 50,000
SALES (est): 87.5MM **Privately Held**
SIC: 1731 1711 General electrical contractor; mechanical contractor

(P-2761)
SURGENER ELECTRIC INC
Also Called: McKee Electric
1406 N Chester Ave, Bakersfield
(93308-3525)
PHONE..................661 399-3321
Fax: 661 399-3323
Lester C Surgener II, *CEO*
R L Surgener, *President*
Diane Dansby, *Corp Secy*
Patrick Bell Jr, *Vice Pres*
Jody Johnston, *Info Tech Mgr*
EMP: 85 **EST:** 1947
SQ FT: 5,000
SALES (est): 18.8MM **Privately Held**
SIC: 1731 General electrical contractor

(P-2762)
SWINFORD ELECTRIC INC
Also Called: A & R Electric
1150 E Elm Ave, Fullerton (92831-5024)
PHONE..................714 578-8888
Fax: 714 578-8885
Sharon Swinford, *President*
Michael Swinford, *Corp Secy*
EMP: 50
SQ FT: 5,400
SALES (est): 9.9MM **Privately Held**
SIC: 1731 General electrical contractor

(P-2763)
T BOYER COMPANY
1656 Babcock St, Costa Mesa
(92627-4330)
PHONE..................949 642-2431
Fax: 949 642-6114
Thomas Boyer, *President*
EMP: 50
SQ FT: 1,600
SALES (est): 6.8MM **Privately Held**
SIC: 1731 General electrical contractor

(P-2764)
T MCGEE ELECTRIC INC
2390 S Reservoir St, Pomona
(91766-6410)
P.O. Box 1111, Chino (91708-1111)
PHONE..................909 591-6461
Fax: 909 590-2971
Trent L Mc Gee, *President*
EMP: 100
SALES (est): 10.2MM **Privately Held**
SIC: 1731 General electrical contractor

(P-2765)
T S J ELEC COMMUNICATIONS INC
Also Called: Masters Electric Telcom
7490 Jurupa Ave, Riverside (92504-1030)
PHONE..................951 785-0921
Fax: 951 785-5248
Philip Schaefer, *President*
Lisa Schaefer, *Admin Sec*
EMP: 100
SQ FT: 33,000
SALES (est): 15.2MM **Privately Held**
WEB: www.masterssec.com
SIC: 1731 Electrical work

(P-2766)
TAFT ELECTRIC COMPANY (PA)
1694 Eastman Ave, Ventura (93003-5782)
P.O. Box 3416 (93006-3416)
PHONE..................805 642-0121
Fax: 805 644-6488
Walter E Hartman, *Chairman*
James Marsh, *President*
Carol A Smith, *Admin Sec*
Carol Smith, *Controller*
EMP: 131
SQ FT: 40,000
SALES (est): 67.8MM **Privately Held**
WEB: www.tecelect.com
SIC: 1731 1629 Electrical work; waste water & sewage treatment plant construction

(P-2767)
TAFT ELECTRIC COMPANY
42209 5th St E, Lancaster (93535-5465)
PHONE..................661 729-2581
EMP: 201
SALES (corp-wide): 67.8MM **Privately Held**
SIC: 1731 Electrical work

PRODUCTS & SERVICES SECTION

1731 - Electrical Work County (P-2789)

PA: Taft Electric Company
1694 Eastman Ave
Ventura CA 93003
805 642-0121

(P-2768)
TEL TECH PLUS INC
Also Called: Ttp-US
393 Enterprise St, San Marcos (92078-4374)
PHONE.................760 510-1323
Fax: 760 510-8559
Gregory A Stearns, *President*
Cindy Stearns, *Admin Sec*
EMP: 50
SQ FT: 10,268
SALES (est): 10.9MM **Privately Held**
SIC: 1731 1623 7382 Voice, data & video wiring contractor; telephone & communication line construction; security systems services

(P-2769)
TELECMMNCTONS MGT SLUTIONS INC
Also Called: T M S
570 Division St, Campbell (95008-6906)
PHONE.................408 866-5495
Fax: 408 866-5589
Bruce Jaftok, *President*
Michael Finn, *Vice Pres*
Kelly Cox, *Project Mgr*
Jay Wiles, *Project Mgr*
Andrew Bautista, *Analyst*
EMP: 57
SALES: 11.5MM **Privately Held**
WEB: www.yru.com
SIC: 1731 Voice, data & video wiring contractor

(P-2770)
TELSTAR INSTRUMENTS (PA)
1717 Solano Way Ste 34, Concord (94520-5478)
PHONE.................925 671-2888
Robert S Marston Jr, *CEO*
John Gardiner, *Vice Pres*
Chris Gaffga, *Info Tech Mgr*
June Johnson, *Project Mgr*
Paul Berson, *Engineer*
EMP: 53 **EST:** 1981
SQ FT: 4,000
SALES (est): 14.9MM **Privately Held**
SIC: 1731 7629 Electrical work; electrical repair shops

(P-2771)
TENNYSON ELECTRIC INC
7275 National Dr, Livermore (94550-8869)
PHONE.................925 606-1038
Fax: 925 606-7655
Michael A Tennyson, *CEO*
Cathleen Tennyson, *Treasurer*
Michelle Pham, *Controller*
J Inocencio, *Manager*
EMP: 50
SQ FT: 26,000
SALES (est): 18.2MM **Privately Held**
SIC: 1731 Electrical work

(P-2772)
THOMA ELECTRIC INC
Also Called: Thoma Electric Co
3562 Empleo St Ste C, San Luis Obispo (93401-7367)
P.O. Box 1167 (93406-1167)
PHONE.................805 543-3850
Fax: 805 543-3829
William A Thoma, *President*
Edward C Thoma, *Vice Pres*
Bill Thoma, *Admin Sec*
Sheri Budrow, *Administration*
Steve Arnold, *Project Mgr*
EMP: 55
SQ FT: 7,500
SALES (est): 10.2MM **Privately Held**
WEB: www.thomaelec.com
SIC: 1731 8711 General electrical contractor; electrical or electronic engineering

(P-2773)
TIGER ELECTRIC INC (PA)
650 N Berry St, Brea (92821-3011)
PHONE.................714 529-8061
Fax: 714 529-6757
Stanley Longenecker, *President*
Michael Ditsler, *Vice Pres*
Carol Kupon, *Office Mgr*
Jacqueline Durham, *Office Admin*
Mary D Longenecker, *Admin Sec*
▲ **EMP:** 70
SQ FT: 12,500
SALES (est): 12.6MM **Privately Held**
WEB: www.tigerelectric.com
SIC: 1731 Electrical work

(P-2774)
TIME AND ALARM SYSTEMS (PA)
3828 Wacker Dr, Mira Loma (91752-1147)
PHONE.................951 685-1761
Keith A Senn, *CEO*
Darren Balch, *Admin Asst*
Kristen Lane, *Admin Asst*
Vanessa Wood, *Admin Asst*
Gilbert Contreras, *Comp Tech*
EMP: 57
SQ FT: 12,000
SALES (est): 15.2MM **Privately Held**
WEB: www.timeandalarm.com
SIC: 1731 Fire detection & burglar alarm systems specialization; communications specialization; telephone & telephone equipment installation

(P-2775)
TRI-SIGNAL INTEGRATION INC (PA)
15853 Monte St Ste 101, Sylmar (91342-7671)
PHONE.................818 566-8558
Fax: 818 450-2571
Robert McKibben, *President*
Michael Swisher, *COO*
Dennis Furden, *CFO*
Tom Kommer, *Senior VP*
Rett Hicks, *Vice Pres*
EMP: 100 **EST:** 1998
SQ FT: 16,000
SALES (est): 92.1MM **Privately Held**
WEB: www.tri-signal.com
SIC: 1731 Fire detection & burglar alarm systems specialization

(P-2776)
TRL SYSTEMS INCORPORATED
Also Called: T R L
9531 Milliken Ave, Rancho Cucamonga (91730-6006)
PHONE.................909 390-8392
Fax: 909 390-8397
Lynn Purdy, *Chairman*
Mark L Purdy, *President*
Steve Adams, *Vice Pres*
Patrick Lewis, *Vice Pres*
Jackie Ramsdell, *Pharmacy Dir*
EMP: 100
SQ FT: 14,000
SALES (est): 54.3MM **Privately Held**
SIC: 1731 General electrical contractor

(P-2777)
TUCKER ELECTRIC CORPORATION
Also Called: Tucker Electrical
3365 Chestnut Ln, Santa Rosa Valley (93012-8225)
PHONE.................818 426-7645
Dean Tucker, *CEO*
Ray Marino, *Vice Pres*
EMP: 50
SQ FT: 1,500
SALES: 5.8MM **Privately Held**
SIC: 1731 Electrical work

(P-2778)
TURNUPSEED ELECTRIC SERVICE
1580 S K St, Tulare (93274-6400)
P.O. Box 26 (93275-0026)
PHONE.................559 686-1541
Fax: 559 686-4454
Wallace J Nelson, *President*
Terri Grant, *Corp Secy*
David Turnupseed, *Vice Pres*
Stephen Powell, *Manager*
EMP: 55
SQ FT: 8,000
SALES (est): 8.5MM **Privately Held**
WEB: www.turnupseed.com
SIC: 1731 7694 5063 Electrical work; rewinding stators; electric motor repair; motors, electric

(P-2779)
UNISON ELECTRIC
16652 Gemini Ln, Huntington Beach (92647-4429)
PHONE.................714 375-5915
Lance E Charlesworth, *President*
Kristi Kirkenslager, *Corp Secy*
Gary Charlesworth, *Exec VP*
Steven Ehrlich, *Electrical Engi*
Marie Acosta, *Manager*
EMP: 50
SQ FT: 6,000
SALES (est): 11.2MM **Privately Held**
WEB: www.unisonltd.com
SIC: 1731 Electrical work

(P-2780)
UNITED STATES INFO SYSTEMS INC
7621 Galilee Rd, Roseville (95678-6972)
PHONE.................845 353-9224
EMP: 68
SALES (corp-wide): 115.5MM **Privately Held**
SIC: 1731 Communications specialization
PA: United States Information Systems Inc.
35 W Jefferson Ave
Pearl River NY 10965
845 358-7755

(P-2781)
VALLEY COMMUNICATIONS INC (PA)
6921 Roseville Rd, Sacramento (95842-1660)
PHONE.................916 349-7300
Fax: 916 349-7329
Ken Hurst, *President*
Kate Dewitt, *Vice Pres*
Jeff Frydenlund, *Vice Pres*
Justin Cooper, *Info Tech Dir*
Leann Kress, *Manager*
EMP: 60
SQ FT: 12,000
SALES: 11.8MM **Privately Held**
SIC: 1731 3699 Voice, data & video wiring contractor; closed circuit television installation; security control equipment & systems

(P-2782)
VASKO ELECTRIC INC
4300 Astoria St, Sacramento (95838-3004)
PHONE.................916 568-7700
Fax: 916 568-7713
Darryl A Vasko, *President*
Ron Gracik, *Vice Pres*
EMP: 80
SQ FT: 8,500
SALES (est): 20.9MM **Privately Held**
WEB: www.vasko.com
SIC: 1731 General electrical contractor

(P-2783)
VECTOR RESOURCES INC (PA)
Also Called: Vectorusa
3530 Voyager St, Torrance (90503-1666)
PHONE.................310 436-1000
Fax: 310 436-1060
David Zukerman, *President*
D Zuckerman, *COO*
Matt Recknagel, *Officer*
Robert Messinger, *Exec VP*
John Schuman, *Vice Pres*
EMP: 151
SQ FT: 20,000
SALES (est): 83MM **Privately Held**
SIC: 1731 3651 7373 Communications specialization; computer installation; clock radio & telephone combinations; video camera-audio recorders, household use; systems engineering, computer related; turnkey vendors, computer systems; value-added resellers, computer systems

(P-2784)
VECTOR SECURITY INC
5411 Valley Blvd, Los Angeles (90032-3518)
PHONE.................323 224-6700
John Murphy, *Manager*
David Levine, *Branch Mgr*
EMP: 59
SALES (corp-wide): 741.8MM **Privately Held**
SIC: 1731 7382 Fire detection & burglar alarm systems specialization; burglar alarm maintenance & monitoring
HQ: Vector Security Inc.
2000 Ericsson Dr Ste 250
Warrendale PA 15086
724 741-2200

(P-2785)
VERIZON COMMUNICATIONS INC
176 E Badillo St, Covina (91723-2113)
PHONE.................626 858-1739
Mark Clark, *Director*
EMP: 60
SALES (corp-wide): 131.6B **Publicly Held**
WEB: www.verizon.com
SIC: 1731 4813 Telephone & telephone equipment installation; telephone communication, except radio
PA: Verizon Communications Inc.
1095 Ave Of The Americas
New York NY 10036
212 395-1000

(P-2786)
W BRADLEY ELECTRIC INC
501 Seaport Ct Ste 103a, Redwood City (94063-2776)
PHONE.................650 701-1502
EMP: 125
SALES (corp-wide): 61.4MM **Privately Held**
SIC: 1731
PA: W. Bradley Electric, Inc.
90 Hill Rd
Novato CA 94945
415 898-1400

(P-2787)
W BRADLEY ELECTRIC INC (PA)
90 Hill Rd, Novato (94945-4506)
PHONE.................415 898-1400
Leslie Murphy, *CEO*
Mike Murphy, *COO*
Ralph Greenwood, *CFO*
Bob Bourdet, *Vice Pres*
Kevin Bradley, *Sales Mgr*
EMP: 50
SQ FT: 24,000
SALES (est): 67.6MM **Privately Held**
SIC: 1731 General electrical contractor; communications specialization

(P-2788)
WALKER COMMUNICATIONS INC
521 Railroad Ave, Suisun City (94585-4244)
PHONE.................707 421-1300
Fax: 707 421-1359
Gary Walker, *President*
Donald Walker, *Senior VP*
Linda Spering, *Manager*
EMP: 100
SQ FT: 2,200
SALES (est): 7.2MM **Privately Held**
SIC: 1731 3669 4812 Communications specialization; emergency alarms; radio telephone communication

(P-2789)
WALTON ELECTRIC CORPORATION
755 N Central Ave, Upland (91786-9474)
P.O. Box 1599, Claremont (91711-8599)
PHONE.................909 981-5051
Tanyon D Dunkley, *CEO*
Don R Davis, *Exec VP*
Ron C Stickel, *Vice Pres*
Gary Gladson, *Chief*
Barbara Long, *Manager*
EMP: 60
SQ FT: 10,150
SALES: 7MM **Privately Held**
SIC: 1731 3669 General electrical contractor; fire alarm apparatus, electric

1731 - Electrical Work County (P-2790)

(P-2790)
WB ELECTRIC INC
30611 Road 400, Coarsegold (93614-9437)
PHONE..................408 842-7911
Randy Walker, *CEO*
Susan Walker, *CFO*
EMP: 60
SALES: 11.7MM **Privately Held**
WEB: www.wbelectric.com
SIC: 1731 General electrical contractor

(P-2791)
WECKWORTH CONSTRUCTION CO INC
Also Called: Weckworth Electric Company
3941 Park Dr Ste 20-373, El Dorado Hills (95762-4549)
PHONE..................916 939-6636
Kristen Weckworth, *President*
EMP: 65
SALES (est): 5.9MM **Privately Held**
SIC: 1731 Switchgear & related devices installation

(P-2792)
WEST COAST LTG & ENRGY INC
18550 Minthorn St, Lake Elsinore (92530-2784)
PHONE..................951 296-0680
Johnny Odell Leach, *President*
Thomas Hazen, *CFO*
Tammy Leach, *Corp Secy*
Micah Hazen, *Project Mgr*
Karen Fay, *Manager*
EMP: 90
SQ FT: 2,646
SALES (est): 13.4MM **Privately Held**
WEB: www.es-corp.com
SIC: 1731 Electrical work

(P-2793)
WESTECH SYSTEMS INC
827 Jefferson Ave, Clovis (93612-2260)
PHONE..................559 298-5237
Larry Troglin, *President*
Helder Domingos, *Vice Pres*
Kate Clark, *Accountant*
Shannon Schuotheis, *Manager*
EMP: 60 **EST:** 1997
SQ FT: 10,000
SALES (est): 13.4MM **Privately Held**
SIC: 1731 Electrical work

(P-2794)
WESTERN SUN ENTERPRISES INC
Also Called: Three D Electric
4690 E 2nd St Ste 4, Benicia (94510-1008)
PHONE..................707 748-2542
David Alan Whitt, *President*
Laura Whitt, *Corp Secy*
Nitya Litcler, *Accountant*
EMP: 150
SQ FT: 4,700
SALES (est): 18.4MM **Privately Held**
WEB: www.threedelectric.com
SIC: 1731 Electrical work

(P-2795)
WILD ELECTRIC INCORPORATED
4626 E Olive Ave, Fresno (93702-1660)
PHONE..................559 251-7770
Fax: 559 251-2372
Fred Merlo, *President*
Jan Merlo, *Vice Pres*
EMP: 55
SQ FT: 3,750
SALES: 8MM **Privately Held**
WEB: www.wildelectric.net
SIC: 1731 General electrical contractor

(P-2796)
WOLTCOM INC
Also Called: W C I
2300 Tech Pkwy Ste 8, Hollister (95023)
PHONE..................831 638-4900
Mona K Wolters, *President*
Lisa Scheufler, *Shareholder*
Pat Scheufler, *CFO*
Kimberly A Morgan, *Vice Pres*
Gayle Moore, *Finance Dir*
EMP: 150
SQ FT: 2,250

SALES: 10.3MM **Privately Held**
SIC: 1731 Communications specialization

(P-2797)
WORLDWIND SERVICES LLC
915 Tehachapi Wllw Spgs, Tehachapi (93561-8178)
PHONE..................661 822-4877
Edward Cummings,
Bridget Weiss, *CFO*
Alex Castanon, *Engineer*
Suzannah Cummings,
Ivan Varela, *Director*
EMP: 51
SALES (est): 12.4MM **Privately Held**
SIC: 1731 1389 8742 Electrical work; construction, repair & dismantling services; maintenance management consultant

(P-2798)
WP ELECTRIC COMMUNICATIONS INC
14198 Albers Way, Chino (91710-6938)
PHONE..................909 606-3510
Debra Rooney, *President*
Jim Roche, *Vice Pres*
EMP: 50
SQ FT: 8,100
SALES: 6MM **Privately Held**
SIC: 1731 General electrical contractor

(P-2799)
WPCS INTRNTIONAL-SUISUN CY INC
2208 Srra Madows Dr Ste B, Rocklin (95677)
PHONE..................916 624-1300
EMP: 60
SALES (corp-wide): 24.4MM **Publicly Held**
SIC: 1731
HQ: Wpcs International-Suisun City, Inc.
521 Railroad Ave
Suisun City CA 94585
707 398-3421

(P-2800)
YOUNG ELECTRIC CO
Also Called: Young Communications
195 Erie St, San Francisco (94103-2416)
PHONE..................415 648-3355
Fax: 415 648-8259
James P Young, *President*
Wayne Huie, *President*
Richard Green, *Corp Secy*
Chuck Walters, *Vice Pres*
Young Electric, *CTO*
EMP: 120 **EST:** 1977
SQ FT: 5,000
SALES: 28MM **Privately Held**
WEB: www.youngelec.com
SIC: 1731 General electrical contractor

1741 Masonry & Other Stonework

(P-2801)
3M/PHARMACEUTICALS
19901 Nordhoff St, Northridge (91324-3213)
PHONE..................818 341-1300
Fax: 818 709-3044
Kathy Yamaoka, *Owner*
Gina Riddle, *General Mgr*
Krish RAO, *General Mgr*
Ray Fritz, *QA Dir*
Alejandro REA, *Info Tech Mgr*
▼ **EMP:** 86
SALES (est): 10.3MM **Privately Held**
SIC: 1741 Masonry & other stonework

(P-2802)
B&B INDUSTRIAL SERVICES INC (PA)
14549 Manzanita Dr, Fontana (92335-5378)
PHONE..................909 428-3167
Fax: 909 428-2553
Lyndon Brewer, *President*
Ted Brewer, *Vice Pres*
Tim Brewer, *Admin Sec*
Anthony Deaton, *Warehouse Mgr*

Carey Collier, *Manager*
EMP: 78
SQ FT: 12,000
SALES (est): 31.4MM **Privately Held**
WEB: www.bb-industrial.com
SIC: 1741 Refractory or acid brick masonry

(P-2803)
BARAZANI PAVE STONE INC
14546 Hamlin St Ste 201, Van Nuys (91411-4194)
PHONE..................818 701-6977
Yuval Barazani, *President*
Aviva Barazani, *Vice Pres*
Renee REA, *Accountant*
EMP: 185
SQ FT: 20,000
SALES (est): 9.8MM **Privately Held**
WEB: www.barazani.com
SIC: 1741 1771 1611 Masonry & other stonework; driveway, parking lot & blacktop contractors; surfacing & paving

(P-2804)
BLEDSOE MASONRY INC
Also Called: RMC Transport
4680 Felspar St Ste A, Riverside (92509-3086)
PHONE..................951 360-6140
Fax: 951 360-0132
Dyana Bledsoe, *President*
Robert Bledsoe, *Corp Secy*
Cynthia Lacava, *Accounts Mgr*
EMP: 60
SQ FT: 1,300
SALES: 1MM **Privately Held**
SIC: 1741 Masonry & other stonework

(P-2805)
BOSTON BRICK & STONE INC
2005 Lincoln Ave, Pasadena (91103-1322)
PHONE..................626 269-2622
Fax: 626 797-7848
David Laverdiere, *President*
Karen Laverdiere, *CEO*
Dan Shay, *CEO*
EMP: 50
SALES (est): 6.2MM **Privately Held**
WEB: www.bostonbrick.com
SIC: 1741 Chimney construction & maintenance

(P-2806)
BRAD WATKINS MASONRY INC
10315 Woodley Ave Ste 130, Granada Hills (91344-6953)
P.O. Box 8466, Mission Hills (91346-8466)
PHONE..................818 360-3796
Brad Watkins, *President*
EMP: 70
SALES: 15MM **Privately Held**
SIC: 1741 Masonry & other stonework

(P-2807)
CLEVELAND MARBLE LP
219 E Bristol Ln, Orange (92865-2715)
PHONE..................714 998-3280
Elias N Ghattas, *Partner*
Gale Chrostowski, *Controller*
▲ **EMP:** 50
SALES: 950K **Privately Held**
SIC: 1741 Masonry & other stonework

(P-2808)
CULVER-MELIN ENTERPRISES
Also Called: ServiceMaster
2150 Wardrobe Ave, Merced (95341-6400)
P.O. Box 2192 (95344-0192)
PHONE..................209 726-9182
David Melin, *President*
EMP: 70
SALES (est): 5MM **Privately Held**
SIC: 1741 Building maintenance services

(P-2809)
DESIGN MASONRY INC
20703 Santa Clara St, Canyon Country (91351-2424)
PHONE..................661 252-2784
Scott Floyd, *President*
Randall Carpenter, *Vice Pres*
Marilyn Carpenter, *Executive*
Cecilia Wong, *Controller*
Kim Jones, *Manager*
EMP: 70

SALES (est): 9.1MM **Privately Held**
SIC: 1741 Masonry & other stonework

(P-2810)
DIABLO VALLEY MASONRY INC
6600 Asher Ln, Sacramento (95828-1896)
PHONE..................916 438-0607
Fax: 925 838-4370
Avery Pratt, *President*
Connie Pratt, *Admin Sec*
James Truscott, *Sales Executive*
Jill Marymonte, *Manager*
EMP: 50
SQ FT: 1,200
SALES (est): 9.2MM **Privately Held**
WEB: www.diablovalleymasonry.com
SIC: 1741 Masonry & other stonework

(P-2811)
DJ SCHEFFLER INC (PA)
2500 Pomona Blvd, Pomona (91768-3218)
PHONE..................909 595-2924
Fax: 909 598-8639
Dale J Scheffler, *President*
Mark Nye, *Vice Pres*
Cindy Scheffler, *Manager*
▲ **EMP:** 50
SALES (est): 11.6MM **Privately Held**
WEB: www.djscheffler.com
SIC: 1741 Foundation building

(P-2812)
EKEDAL MASONRY & CONCRETE INC
19600 Fairchild Ste 123, Irvine (92612-2509)
PHONE..................949 720-8011
Dave Ekedal, *Branch Mgr*
EMP: 81
SALES (corp-wide): 20MM **Privately Held**
SIC: 1741 Masonry & other stonework
PA: Ekedal Masonry & Concrete Inc
220 Newport Center Dr # 11
Newport Beach CA 92660
949 729-8082

(P-2813)
ELSTON MASONRY INC
1422 Santa Margarita Dr, Fallbrook (92028-1634)
PHONE..................760 728-3593
Fax: 760 728-1872
Paul Elston, *President*
Carol Elston, *Vice Pres*
EMP: 85
SALES: 10.4MM **Privately Held**
SIC: 1741 Bricklaying

(P-2814)
ENGINEERED SOIL REPAIRS INC
1267 Springbrook Rd, Walnut Creek (94597-3916)
PHONE..................408 297-2150
Steve O'Connor, *President*
Mark Wilhite, *Treasurer*
Morgan Anderson, *Vice Pres*
Bill Gibson, *Vice Pres*
Richard Holsinger, *Engineer*
EMP: 55
SQ FT: 3,000
SALES (est): 8.5MM **Privately Held**
SIC: 1741 1771 Foundation building; foundation & footing contractor

(P-2815)
FRANK S SMITH MASONRY INC
2830 Pomona Blvd, Pomona (91768-3224)
PHONE..................909 468-0525
Fax: 909 468-0531
Frank E Smith, *President*
Kevin J Smith, *CFO*
Brian E Smith, *Vice Pres*
Jennifer Doolittle, *Accountant*
EMP: 100 **EST:** 1938
SQ FT: 54,000
SALES (est): 11.6MM **Privately Held**
WEB: www.fssmi.com
SIC: 1741 Bricklaying; concrete block masonry laying

▲ = Import ▼ = Export
◆ = Import/Export

PRODUCTS & SERVICES SECTION
1741 - Masonry & Other Stonework County (P-2842)

(P-2816)
GBC CONCRETE MASNRY CNSTR INC
561 Birch St, Lake Elsinore (92530-2732)
PHONE.................................951 245-2355
Tom Daniel, *President*
EMP: 170
SQ FT: 8,000
SALES (est): 17.6MM **Privately Held**
WEB: www.gbcconstruction.com
SIC: 1741 1771 Masonry & other stonework; concrete work

(P-2817)
HARDROCK TILE & MARBLE INC
23151 Verdugo Dr Ste 111, Laguna Hills (92653-1340)
PHONE.................................714 282-1766
Fax: 714 282-0501
John Golloian, *President*
EMP: 52
SQ FT: 1,400
SALES (est): 4.9MM **Privately Held**
WEB: www.hardrocktilemarble.com
SIC: 1741 Drain tile installation; marble masonry, exterior construction

(P-2818)
HBA INCORPORATED
421 E Cerritos Ave, Anaheim (92805-6320)
P.O. Box 25861 (92825-5861)
PHONE.................................714 635-8602
Gerald G Pyle, *President*
Joe Alessandrini, *CFO*
Henry Blatnik, *Director*
John Blatnik, *Director*
Kristi Pruter, *Director*
EMP: 100
SALES (est): 13.6MM **Privately Held**
SIC: 1741 Masonry & other stonework

(P-2819)
INDUSTRIAL MASONRY INC
3299 Horse Carri Rd Ste H, Norco (92860)
PHONE.................................951 284-0251
Greg E Wilson, *President*
Guy W Yocom, *CFO*
Dan Ricketts, *Sales Mgr*
EMP: 100
SALES (est): 5MM **Privately Held**
SIC: 1741 Masonry & other stonework

(P-2820)
J GINGER MASONRY LP (PA)
8188 Lincoln Ave Ste 100, Riverside (92504-4329)
PHONE.................................951 688-5050
John L Ginger, *Partner*
Brad Fogg, *President*
Linda Trappen, *Accounts Mgr*
EMP: 265
SALES (est): 58.7MM **Privately Held**
SIC: 1741 Masonry & other stonework

(P-2821)
JAMES FEDOR MASONRY INC
54859 Bodine Dr, Thermal (92274-8911)
P.O. Box 1397, La Quinta (92247-1397)
PHONE.................................760 772-3036
James Fedor, *President*
EMP: 70
SALES: 2MM **Privately Held**
WEB: www.jamesfedormasonryinc.com
SIC: 1741 Masonry & other stonework

(P-2822)
JOHN JACKSON MASONRY
5691 Power Inn Rd Ste B, Sacramento (95824-2361)
PHONE.................................916 381-8021
Fax: 916 381-1202
Jeff Barber, *President*
Cheryl Lincoln, *Corp Secy*
Anne Ekstrom, *Vice Pres*
Donald C Ekstrom, *Vice Pres*
Tom Sneed, *General Mgr*
EMP: 60
SQ FT: 6,200
SALES: 9.9MM **Privately Held**
WEB: www.johnjacksonmasonry.com
SIC: 1741 Masonry & other stonework

(P-2823)
JOHN L GINGER MASONRY INC
8188 Lincoln Ave Ste 100, Riverside (92504-4329)
PHONE.................................951 688-5050
Fax: 951 688-1434
John L Ginger, *President*
Shelley L Rocco, *Agent*
EMP: 100
SQ FT: 8,000
SALES (est): 6.7MM **Privately Held**
WEB: www.gingermasonry.com
SIC: 1741 Masonry & other stonework

(P-2824)
KENNEDY MASONRY INC
Also Called: John Kennedy Masonry
7533 Navigator Cir, Carlsbad (92011-5405)
P.O. Box 130340 (92013-0340)
PHONE.................................760 931-2671
John Kennedy, *President*
Roberta Kennedy, *Vice Pres*
Danielle Mohn, *Marketing Mgr*
EMP: 75
SALES (est): 3.8MM **Privately Held**
SIC: 1741 Masonry & other stonework

(P-2825)
KRETSCHMAR & SMITH INC
6293 Pedley Rd, Riverside (92509-6002)
PHONE.................................951 361-1405
Fax: 951 361-1381
Jimmy Smith, *President*
Donna Bolinger, *Manager*
Andrew Kretschmar, *Manager*
EMP: 50
SQ FT: 2,500
SALES (est): 5.2MM **Privately Held**
SIC: 1741 Masonry & other stonework

(P-2826)
MASONRY CONCEPTS INC
15408 Cornet St, Santa Fe Springs (90670-5534)
PHONE.................................562 802-3700
Fax: 562 802-3776
Ronald O Udall, *President*
Peter Sturdivant, *Corp Secy*
Russell Knight, *Vice Pres*
Dana Kemp, *Mktg Dir*
EMP: 100
SQ FT: 10,000
SALES (est): 9.8MM **Privately Held**
WEB: www.masonry-concepts.com
SIC: 1741 Masonry & other stonework

(P-2827)
MASONRY GROUP NEVADA INC
8188 Lincoln Ave Ste 99, Riverside (92504-4329)
PHONE.................................951 509-5300
Chad Hirschi, *CEO*
EMP: 99
SALES (est): 950K **Privately Held**
SIC: 1741 Masonry & other stonework

(P-2828)
MONTEREY BAY MASONRY INC
333 Phelan Ave, San Jose (95112-4104)
PHONE.................................408 289-8295
Casey Ricks, *President*
EMP: 50
SQ FT: 11,000
SALES (est): 3.9MM **Privately Held**
SIC: 1741 Masonry & other stonework; concrete block masonry laying

(P-2829)
NIBBELINK MASONRY CNSTR CORP
2010 W Avenue K, Lancaster (93536-5229)
PHONE.................................661 948-7859
Fax: 661 942-7258
Troy Nibbelink, *President*
Gerald J Nibbelink, *Vice Pres*
Leann Fenner, *Office Mgr*
EMP: 60 EST: 1976
SQ FT: 2,000
SALES (est): 8.7MM **Privately Held**
SIC: 1741 Masonry & other stonework

(P-2830)
ORANGE COAST MASONRY ACQUISIT
601 N Batavia St, Orange (92868-1220)
P.O. Box 608 (92856-6608)
PHONE.................................714 538-4386
Fax: 714 538-5146
Todd Essenmacher, *President*
Tammy Tuskie, *Controller*
EMP: 100
SQ FT: 10,000
SALES: 16MM **Privately Held**
SIC: 1741 Masonry & other stonework

(P-2831)
PACIFIC SHORES MASONRY
1369 Walker Ln, Corona (92879-1775)
PHONE.................................951 371-8550
Jeff McAninch, *President*
EMP: 50
SALES (est): 5.3MM **Privately Held**
SIC: 1741 Masonry & other stonework

(P-2832)
PENHALL COMPANY (DH)
320 N Crescent Way, Anaheim (92801-6752)
P.O. Box 4609 (92803-4609)
PHONE.................................714 772-6450
Fax: 714 778-8437
Jeff Long, *CEO*
C George Bush, *President*
Lynn Behler, *CFO*
George Bush, *Vice Pres*
Sean Butler, *Vice Pres*
EMP: 100
SALES: 296.6MM
SALES (corp-wide): 2.4B **Privately Held**
SIC: 1741 1795 Foundation & retaining wall construction; demolition, buildings & other structures
HQ: Penhall International Corp.
320 N Crescent Way
Anaheim CA 92801
714 772-6450

(P-2833)
RAYCON CONSTRUCTION INC
1795 E Lemonwood Dr, Santa Paula (93060-9651)
P.O. Box 910 (93061-0910)
PHONE.................................805 525-5256
Paul Reyes, *President*
Robert Reyes, *Treasurer*
Augie Reyes, *Vice Pres*
Chris Urrea, *Admin Sec*
EMP: 50
SQ FT: 6,000
SALES: 8MM **Privately Held**
SIC: 1741 Masonry & other stonework

(P-2834)
SMG STONE COMPANY INC
8460 San Fernando Rd, Sun Valley (91352-3227)
PHONE.................................818 767-0000
Fax: 818 767-2200
Solomon Aryeh, *President*
Maria Arciaga, *Manager*
Massood Assad, *Manager*
▲ **EMP:** 80
SQ FT: 12,000
SALES (est): 9.3MM **Privately Held**
WEB: www.smgstone.com
SIC: 1741 8711 5032 Masonry & other stonework; engineering services; marble building stone

(P-2835)
SPECTRA COMPANY
2510 Supply St, Pomona (91767-2113)
PHONE.................................909 599-0760
Ray Adamyk, *CEO*
Tim Harris Sr, *COO*
Paul Chambers, *Executive*
Cristy Caballero, *Business Dir*
Ann Dresselhaus, *Admin Sec*
▲ **EMP:** 125
SQ FT: 7,000
SALES: 17.6MM **Privately Held**
WEB: www.spectracompany.com
SIC: 1741 1771 1743 1721 Masonry & other stonework; concrete work; terrazzo, tile, marble, mosaic work; painting & paper hanging; carpentry work

(P-2836)
SUPERIOR MASONRY WALLS LTD
300 W Olive St Ste A, Colton (92324-1765)
PHONE.................................909 370-1800
Daniel Lee, *President*
EMP: 75
SALES: 950K **Privately Held**
SIC: 1741 Masonry & other stonework

(P-2837)
SYSTEMS PAVING INC (PA)
1570 Brookhollow Dr, Santa Ana (92705-5438)
PHONE.................................714 957-5776
Fax: 949 263-0452
Larry Green, *CEO*
Douglas Lueck, *President*
Wade Barrack, *Vice Pres*
Steven Leuck, *Vice Pres*
Armando Escalante, *Info Tech Dir*
EMP: 61
SQ FT: 13,000
SALES (est): 40.4MM **Privately Held**
SIC: 1741 Masonry & other stonework

(P-2838)
VILLA PACIFIC CONTRACTORS INC
3505 Cadillac Ave Ste L3, Costa Mesa (92626-1432)
PHONE.................................714 850-1640
Brad Gilbert, *President*
EMP: 50
SALES (est): 4.4MM **Privately Held**
SIC: 1741 Masonry & other stonework

(P-2839)
WILKIE MASONRY INC
4016 Hunter Oaks Ln, Loomis (95650-9280)
P.O. Box 387 (95650-0387)
PHONE.................................916 652-0118
Fax: 916 652-8337
Brian Wilkie, *President*
Brian Wilke, *Vice Pres*
EMP: 50
SQ FT: 700
SALES: 750K **Privately Held**
SIC: 1741 5082 Masonry & other stonework; masonry equipment & supplies

(P-2840)
WILLIAMS & SONS MASONRY INC
8531 Winter Gardens Blvd A, Lakeside (92040-5475)
PHONE.................................619 443-1751
Fax: 619 443-0314
Darwin Todd Williams, *President*
Derrick Williams, *Admin Sec*
Debbie Lewis, *Manager*
EMP: 70
SQ FT: 1,200
SALES (est): 4.5MM **Privately Held**
WEB: www.sons.sdcoxmail.com
SIC: 1741 Masonry & other stonework

(P-2841)
WINEGARDNER MASONRY INC
32147 Dunlap Blvd Ste A, Yucaipa (92399-1757)
PHONE.................................909 795-9711
Fax: 909 795-2676
Carolyn Winegardner, *CEO*
Julie Salazar, *President*
Dean Saavedra, *Project Mgr*
Tammy Bender, *Manager*
Casey Ricks, *Manager*
EMP: 50
SQ FT: 7,500
SALES: 7.5MM **Privately Held**
SIC: 1741 Bricklaying; concrete block masonry laying

(P-2842)
WIRTZ QULTY INSTALLATIONS INC
7932 Armour St, San Diego (92111-3718)
PHONE.................................858 569-3816
Amber Fox, *President*
Ida Wirtz, *Vice Pres*
John Wirtz, *Vice Pres*
Paul Murillo, *Warehouse Mgr*

1742 - Plastering, Drywall, Acoustical & Insulation Work County (P-2843)

PRODUCTS & SERVICES SECTION

Gavin Bangs, *Manager*
EMP: 65
SALES (est): 5.9MM **Privately Held**
SIC: 1742 1741 1752 1743 1799 Masonry & other stonework; floor laying & floor work; wood floor installation & refinishing; terrazzo, tile, marble, mosaic work; cleaning building exteriors

1742 Plastering, Drywall, Acoustical & Insulation Work

(P-2843)
A & A PLASTERING CO INC
3787 W Bullard Ave, Fresno (93711-6536)
PHONE.................................559 439-2500
Fax: 559 432-9732
Ellis Atrat, *President*
Betty Snyder, *Corp Secy*
Frank J Stefanich, *Agent*
EMP: 60
SALES (est): 3.3MM **Privately Held**
SIC: 1742 Plastering, plain or ornamental

(P-2844)
A A GONZALEZ INC
13264 Ralston Ave, Sylmar (91342-7607)
P.O. Box 408, San Fernando (91341-0408)
PHONE.................................818 367-2242
Fax: 818 364-8760
Albert Gonzales, *President*
Aida Lepe, *Treasurer*
EMP: 100
SALES (est): 8MM **Privately Held**
SIC: 1742 Plastering, drywall & insulation

(P-2845)
A COLMENERO PLASTERING INC
1710 W San Madele Ave, Fresno (93711-2929)
PHONE.................................559 435-3606
Fax: 559 435-7886
Augie Colmenero, *President*
Sylvia Robles, *Office Mgr*
EMP: 55
SALES (est): 4MM **Privately Held**
SIC: 1742 Plaster & drywall work

(P-2846)
ADERHOLT SPECIALTY COMPANY INC
1557 Cummins Dr, Modesto (95358-6413)
PHONE.................................209 526-2000
Fax: 209 526-9954
Herbert Aderholt, *Ch of Bd*
Sherry Lynette Aderholt, *CEO*
Helen Aderholt, *Admin Sec*
Carmella Moody, *Teacher*
Tara Gaspar, *Manager*
EMP: 100
SQ FT: 4,000
SALES (est): 10.3MM **Privately Held**
WEB: www.aderholt.com
SIC: 1742 1799 Drywall; plastering, plain or ornamental; fireproofing buildings

(P-2847)
ADVANCED ACOUSTICS
3430 Golden Gate Way, Lafayette (94549-4518)
PHONE.................................925 299-0515
Steve Bossert, *Partner*
Ron Bossert, *Partner*
EMP: 50
SQ FT: 850
SALES (est): 1.9MM **Privately Held**
WEB: www.advancedacoustics.net
SIC: 1742 Acoustical & ceiling work

(P-2848)
ALAN SMITH POOL PLASTERING INC
227 W Carleton Ave, Orange (92867-3607)
PHONE.................................714 628-9494
Stephen Scherer, *President*
Teresa Smith, *CFO*
Alan Smith, *Principal*
Dorthy Gulbro, *Human Resources*
▲ **EMP:** 78
SQ FT: 5,000
SALES (est): 10MM **Privately Held**
WEB: www.alansmithpools.com
SIC: 1742 Plastering, plain or ornamental

(P-2849)
ALERT INSULATION COMPANY INC
15913 Old Valley Blvd A, La Puente (91744-5439)
PHONE.................................626 961-9113
Fax: 626 333-0978
Donald W Kent, *President*
Charles Klinakis, *Vice Pres*
Joe Rodriguez, *General Mgr*
Bruce Abott, *Project Mgr*
EMP: 66
SQ FT: 4,500
SALES (est): 10.9MM **Privately Held**
WEB: www.alertinsulation.net
SIC: 1742 Plastering, drywall & insulation; insulation, buildings

(P-2850)
ALL PRO DRYWALL
22148 Buckeye Pl, Cottonwood (96022-7701)
PHONE.................................530 722-5182
EMP: 50
SALES (est): 3MM **Privately Held**
SIC: 1742

(P-2851)
ALLEN DRYWALL & ASSOCIATES
380 Lang Rd, Burlingame (94010-2003)
PHONE.................................650 579-0664
Fax: 650 344-9261
Richard Allen, *President*
Julie Allen, *Corp Secy*
EMP: 60
SALES (est): 6.2MM **Privately Held**
SIC: 1742 Drywall

(P-2852)
ALLIANCE WALL SYSTEMS INC
4638 Skyway Dr, Marysville (95901)
PHONE.................................530 740-7800
Gregory L Bolin, *President*
Shawn Shingler, *Vice Pres*
Kathy Anderson, *Office Mgr*
EMP: 50
SALES (est): 1.8MM **Privately Held**
SIC: 1742 Plastering, drywall & insulation

(P-2853)
ALMA CONSTRUCTION CO INC
1377 N La Cadena Dr, Colton (92324-2416)
PHONE.................................909 825-1328
Fax: 909 825-8566
Alfredo Fernandez, *President*
Michelle Ransome, *Vice Pres*
EMP: 70
SALES (est): 4.2MM **Privately Held**
SIC: 1742 Plaster & drywall work

(P-2854)
ALTA INTERIORS INC
847 Palmyrita Ave, Riverside (92507-1805)
PHONE.................................951 784-1400
Frank Apeldoorn, *CFO*
▲ **EMP:** 99 **EST:** 2012
SQ FT: 50,000
SALES (est): 4.9MM **Privately Held**
SIC: 1742 Drywall

(P-2855)
ANCCA CORPORATION
Also Called: N-U Enterprise
17401 Armstrong Ave, Irvine (92614-5723)
PHONE.................................949 553-0084
Nicole Hunt, *Corp Secy*
EMP: 99
SALES: 950K **Privately Held**
SIC: 1742 Plastering, drywall & insulation

(P-2856)
ANNING-JOHNSON COMPANY
22955 Kidder St, Hayward (94545-1670)
PHONE.................................510 670-0100
Fax: 510 670-0329
R Todd Fearon, *Vice Pres*
Mike Flanagan, *General Mgr*
Carol Crowder, *Info Tech Mgr*
Rafael Luna, *Project Mgr*
Nadine Lokollo, *Manager*
EMP: 140
SQ FT: 16,000
SALES (corp-wide): 334.2MM **Privately Held**
SIC: 1742 Drywall; acoustical & ceiling work
HQ: Anning-Johnson Company
1959 Anson Dr
Melrose Park IL 60160
708 681-1300

(P-2857)
ANNING-JOHNSON COMPANY
13250 Temple Ave, City of Industry (91746-1583)
PHONE.................................626 369-7131
Fax: 626 336-3673
Larry Domino, *Vice Pres*
Tina Prado, *Vice Pres*
Lance Mills, *Project Mgr*
Andy Widin, *Sales Executive*
Bill Funderburg, *Manager*
EMP: 50
SALES (corp-wide): 334.2MM **Privately Held**
SIC: 1742 1761 1799 Acoustical & ceiling work; roofing, siding & sheet metal work; building site preparation
HQ: Anning-Johnson Company
1959 Anson Dr
Melrose Park IL 60160
708 681-1300

(P-2858)
ANSCHUTZ FILM GROUP
1888 Century Park E # 1400, Los Angeles (90067-1718)
PHONE.................................310 887-1000
EMP: 5002
SALES (est): 4.9MM
SALES (corp-wide): 110.5MM **Privately Held**
SIC: 1742
PA: The Anschutz Corporation
555 17th St Ste 2400
Denver CO 80202
303 298-1000

(P-2859)
AYALA DRYWALL
2600 Alexander St, Oxnard (93033-4728)
PHONE.................................805 487-3392
Abel Ayala, *Owner*
Abe Ayala, *Owner*
EMP: 50
SALES (est): 1.1MM **Privately Held**
SIC: 1742 Drywall

(P-2860)
B S I HOLDINGS INC
100 Clock Tower Pl # 200, Carmel (93923-8774)
PHONE.................................831 622-1840
Richard A Manoogian, *Ch of Bd*
EMP: 2000
SQ FT: 1,400
SALES (est): 44.4MM
SALES (corp-wide): 7.1B **Publicly Held**
WEB: www.bsiholdings.com
SIC: 1742 Insulation, buildings
PA: Masco Corporation
21001 Van Born Rd
Taylor MI 48180
313 274-7400

(P-2861)
BAYSIDE INTERIORS INC (PA)
3220 Darby Cmn, Fremont (94539-5601)
PHONE.................................510 580-3950
Fax: 510 438-9375
Steven A Rivera, *CEO*
Tim Hogan, *President*
Michael Nicholson, *COO*
Jon Braden, *CFO*
Norma Nicholson, *Treasurer*
▲ **EMP:** 144
SQ FT: 20,000
SALES (est): 23.4MM **Privately Held**
WEB: www.baysideinteriors.com
SIC: 1742 Drywall

(P-2862)
BEST INTERIORS INC (PA)
2100 E Via Burton, Anaheim (92806-1219)
PHONE.................................714 490-7999
Fax: 714 490-7990
Dennis Ayres, *President*
Michael Herrig, *CFO*
Dan Jost, *Vice Pres*
Prudencia Rios, *Office Mgr*
Colin Cross, *Project Mgr*
EMP: 150
SQ FT: 20,000
SALES (est): 26.3MM **Privately Held**
WEB: www.bestinteriors.net
SIC: 1742 Drywall

(P-2863)
BOYETT CONSTRUCTION INC (PA)
2404 Tripaldi Way, Hayward (94545-5017)
PHONE.................................510 264-9100
Vernon H Boyett, *President*
James Roberts, *Corp Secy*
Gilbert Murrieta, *Division Mgr*
Cindy Le, *Admin Asst*
Jennifer Romano, *Admin Asst*
EMP: 78
SQ FT: 2,600
SALES (est): 21.8MM **Privately Held**
SIC: 1742 1751 Drywall; acoustical & ceiling work; window & door installation & erection

(P-2864)
BRADY COMPANY/CENTRAL CAL
13540 Blackie Rd, Castroville (95012-3212)
PHONE.................................831 633-3315
Allen D Larson, *President*
Keith Eshelman, *CFO*
Janet Massolo, *Office Mgr*
Gregg Brady, *Admin Sec*
Brannon Riley, *Asst Controller*
EMP: 200
SALES (est): 12.7MM **Privately Held**
SIC: 1742 Plastering, plain or ornamental; insulation, buildings; acoustical & ceiling work; drywall

(P-2865)
BRADY COMPANY/LOS ANGELES INC
1010 N Olive St, Anaheim (92801-2539)
P.O. Box 1780, La Mesa (91944-1780)
PHONE.................................714 533-9850
Fax: 714 533-7113
William Saddler, *CEO*
John Dewey, *CFO*
Bill Saddler, *Vice Pres*
Ron Brady, *Admin Sec*
Diane Love, *Manager*
EMP: 100
SALES (est): 5.5MM **Privately Held**
SIC: 1742 Drywall

(P-2866)
BRADY COMPANY/SAN DIEGO INC
8100 Center St, La Mesa (91942-2925)
P.O. Box 968 (91944-0968)
PHONE.................................619 462-2600
Scott Brady, *CEO*
Sue Blanchard, *Executive*
Larry McClure, *Opers Mgr*
Gerry Geron, *Director*
EMP: 300
SQ FT: 4,000
SALES (est): 22.4MM **Privately Held**
SIC: 1742 1542 Plastering, plain or ornamental; insulation, buildings; acoustical & ceiling work; drywall; commercial & office buildings, renovation & repair

(P-2867)
BRADY SOCAL INCORPORATED
8100 Center St, La Mesa (91942-2925)
PHONE.................................619 462-2600
Ricky Marshall, *President*
Scott Brady, *Senior VP*
Sue Blanchard, *Mktg Coord*
EMP: 99
SALES (est): 8.8MM **Privately Held**
SIC: 1742 1751 Plastering, drywall & insulation; window & door installation & erection

▲ = Import ▼ = Export
◆ = Import/Export

1742 - Plastering, Drywall, Acoustical & Insulation Work County (P-2895)

(P-2868)
C A HOFMANN CONSTRUCTION INC
8923 Laramie Dr, Rancho Cucamonga (91737-1466)
P.O. Box 8463 (91701-0463)
PHONE.................909 484-5888
Clarence A Hofmann, *CEO*
EMP: 50
SALES (est): 3.7MM **Privately Held**
SIC: 1742 1751 7389 Drywall; framing contractor;

(P-2869)
C D R ENTERPRISES INC
42302 8th St E, Lancaster (93535-5440)
P.O. Box 507, Friant (93626-0507)
PHONE.................661 940-0344
Samuel D McDowell, *President*
Randy McDowell, *Vice Pres*
Audrey McDowell, *Admin Sec*
EMP: 70
SALES (est): 2.6MM **Privately Held**
SIC: 1742 Plastering, drywall & insulation

(P-2870)
C R S DRYWALL INC
Also Called: Cr Drywall
135 San Jose Ave, San Jose (95125-1018)
PHONE.................408 998-4360
Fax: 408 998-4363
Carlos Silveria, *President*
Mary Jo, *Office Mgr*
EMP: 80
SQ FT: 4,000
SALES (est): 5.3MM **Privately Held**
SIC: 1742 Drywall

(P-2871)
CALIFORNIA DRYWALL CO (PA)
2290 S 10th St, San Jose (95112-4114)
PHONE.................408 292-7500
Fax: 408 292-4252
Greg Eckstrom, *Vice Pres*
Kent Bowles, *President*
David Garrett, *COO*
Stephen Eckstrom, *Vice Pres*
Liz Pinon, *Admin Asst*
EMP: 119
SQ FT: 15,000
SALES (est): 56.5MM **Privately Held**
WEB: www.caldrywall.com
SIC: 1742 Drywall

(P-2872)
CANYON INSULATION INC
645 E Harrison St Ste 100, Corona (92879-1376)
PHONE.................951 278-9200
Robert Donoghue, *President*
EMP: 70
SALES: 16.5MM **Privately Held**
SIC: 1742 Insulation, buildings

(P-2873)
CAPITAL CITY DRYWALL INC
6525 32nd St Ste B1, North Highlands (95660-3028)
PHONE.................916 331-9200
John Beers, *President*
Andrew Sellers, *Vice Pres*
Amy Peterson, *Manager*
EMP: 100 EST: 2000
SQ FT: 2,500
SALES (est): 10MM **Privately Held**
WEB: www.capitalcitydrywall.com
SIC: 1742 Drywall

(P-2874)
CASTON INC
354 S Allen St, San Bernardino (92408-1508)
PHONE.................909 381-1619
James I Malachowski Jr, *President*
Cindy Hutton, *Manager*
EMP: 100
SALES (est): 11.2MM **Privately Held**
SIC: 1742 Plaster & drywall work

(P-2875)
CEN CAL PLASTERING INC
1256 W Lathrop Rd, Manteca (95336-9671)
PHONE.................209 858-1045
Jeffery F Gann, *President*

Jeffrey F Gann, *President*
EMP: 450
SALES: 17MM **Privately Held**
SIC: 1742 Plastering, drywall & insulation

(P-2876)
CHARLES CULBERSON INC
Also Called: Culberson Drywall
1084 Allen Way, Campbell (95008-4509)
P.O. Box 1954, Chester (96020-1954)
PHONE.................650 335-4730
Fax: 650 335-4736
EMP: 150
SQ FT: 8,000
SALES (est): 7.3MM **Privately Held**
SIC: 1742

(P-2877)
CHURCH & LARSEN INC
16103 Avenida Padilla, Irwindale (91702-3223)
PHONE.................626 303-8741
Fax: 626 303-0027
Raymond W Larsen, *President*
Kenneth R Larsen, *Vice Pres*
Kenneth P Larsen, *Vice Pres*
EMP: 250
SQ FT: 10,800
SALES (est): 20.7MM **Privately Held**
SIC: 1742 Plaster & drywall work

(P-2878)
CLOVIS CUSTOM DRYWALL INC
Also Called: Custom Drywall Service
141 Sunnyside Ave Ste 108, Clovis (93611-0570)
PHONE.................559 297-7073
Fax: 559 297-8600
D Ployungunsri, *President*
Khatiya Hanvongse, *Vice Pres*
EMP: 50
SQ FT: 5,000
SALES (est): 2.7MM **Privately Held**
SIC: 1742 Drywall

(P-2879)
COAST BUILDING PRODUCTS
Also Called: Century-Coast Building Pdts
11 W Lake St, Salinas (93901-2811)
PHONE.................831 757-1089
John Ackerman, *President*
EMP: 50
SALES (est): 3.4MM **Privately Held**
SIC: 1742 Insulation, buildings

(P-2880)
COAST INSULATION CONTRS INC (DH)
Also Called: Coast Building Products
1341 Old Oakland Rd, San Jose (95112-1317)
PHONE.................386 304-2222
Michael Raridon, *President*
EMP: 65
SQ FT: 10,000
SALES (est): 8MM
SALES (corp-wide): 1.6B **Publicly Held**
SIC: 1742 Insulation, buildings
HQ: American National Services, Inc.
13000 Kirkham Way Ste 203
Poway CA 92064
858 486-9155

(P-2881)
CUSTOM DRYWALL INC
1570 Gladding Ct, Milpitas (95035-6898)
PHONE.................408 263-1616
Fax: 408 263-1142
Gene Cox, *President*
Tom Knight, *Project Mgr*
Craig Lammers, *Project Mgr*
EMP: 90
SQ FT: 10,000
SALES (est): 7.5MM **Privately Held**
WEB: www.custom-drywall-inc.com
SIC: 1742 Drywall

(P-2882)
CUTTING EDGE DRYWALL INC
7046 Convoy Ct, San Diego (92111-1017)
PHONE.................858 408-0870
Robert Pearn, *President*
EMP: 50
SQ FT: 4,800

SALES (est): 4MM **Privately Held**
WEB: www.cuttingedgedrywall.net
SIC: 1742 Plastering, drywall and insulation

(P-2883)
DALEYS DRYWALL AND TAPING INC
960 Camden Ave, Campbell (95008-4104)
PHONE.................408 378-9500
Fax: 408 378-8965
Craig Spencer Daley, *President*
Brittni Bailey, *CFO*
Daniel Lutchansky, *CFO*
Chris Daley, *Vice Pres*
Geordie Burdick, *CIO*
EMP: 200
SQ FT: 20,000
SALES (est): 29.9MM **Privately Held**
WEB: www.daleysdrywall.com
SIC: 1742 Drywall

(P-2884)
DEL MAR PLASTERING INC
7085 Jurupa Rd Ut2, Riverside (92509-4118)
PHONE.................951 343-5955
Dale Pratte, *President*
Milton Qualley, *Manager*
EMP: 100
SQ FT: 2,000
SALES (est): 12MM **Privately Held**
SIC: 1742 Plaster & drywall work

(P-2885)
DEMKO DRYWALL & DEMOLITION CO
419 S Marshall Ave, El Cajon (92020-4210)
PHONE.................619 590-0025
Fax: 619 590-0028
Nicholas Demko, *President*
Debra Demko, *Corp Secy*
James Woodford, *Opers Staff*
EMP: 50
SALES (est): 5.5MM **Privately Held**
WEB: www.demkodemolition.com
SIC: 1742 1751 1795 Drywall; framing contractor; wrecking & demolition work

(P-2886)
DH SMITH COMPANY INC
6000 Hellyer Ave Ste 150, San Jose (95138-1031)
P.O. Box 730189 (95173-0189)
PHONE.................408 532-7617
Fax: 408 532-5995
Daniel Smith III, *President*
Cheryl Smith, *Corp Secy*
Steven Smith, *Vice Pres*
EMP: 85
SQ FT: 20,000
SALES (est): 8.8MM **Privately Held**
SIC: 1742 Plastering, plain or ornamental

(P-2887)
DRY CREEK LATH & PLASTER INC
27940 Kennefick Rd, Galt (95632-8290)
P.O. Box 1051 (95632-1051)
PHONE.................209 367-8607
Ron Bohlender, *President*
Roger Fox, *CFO*
EMP: 70
SQ FT: 6,000
SALES (est): 4MM **Privately Held**
SIC: 1742 Plaster & drywall work

(P-2888)
DRYWALL WORKS INC
5900 Warehouse Way, Sacramento (95826-4911)
PHONE.................916 383-6667
Xavier Valdez, *President*
Michael A Rizo, *Treasurer*
Lydia Belo, *Controller*
EMP: 80
SQ FT: 26,000
SALES: 9MM **Privately Held**
SIC: 1742 Drywall

(P-2889)
EA ENVIRONMENTAL CONSTRUCTION
15239 Stagg St, Van Nuys (91405-1003)
PHONE.................818 785-0956
Jeff Aviezer, *President*

Maritza Aviezer, *Vice Pres*
EMP: 50
SQ FT: 1,200
SALES: 24.3MM **Privately Held**
SIC: 1742 Acoustical & ceiling work

(P-2890)
EASTBROOK CONSTRUCTION INC
403 E Arrow Hwy Ste 302, San Dimas (91773-3367)
PHONE.................909 394-4994
Harold W Babcock, *President*
Lee Arthur Ferguson, *Corp Secy*
A Lacy, *Manager*
EMP: 58
SQ FT: 2,800
SALES (est): 2.9MM **Privately Held**
SIC: 1742 Drywall

(P-2891)
EDCO DRYWALL INC
Also Called: Edco Drywall Company
7200 Hazard Ave, Westminster (92683-5027)
PHONE.................714 799-9886
Dave Blunk, *President*
Kris Blanc, *Office Mgr*
Steffany Blunk, *Admin Sec*
EMP: 50
SQ FT: 4,257
SALES (est): 2.7MM **Privately Held**
SIC: 1742 Drywall; acoustical & ceiling work

(P-2892)
ELLJAY ACOUSTICS INC
511 Cameron St, Placentia (92870-6425)
PHONE.................714 961-1173
Ronald B Bishop, *President*
Narda Reyes, *Admin Asst*
Tim Coggins, *Project Mgr*
Matt Paul, *Project Mgr*
EMP: 70
SQ FT: 6,900
SALES (est): 8.4MM **Privately Held**
WEB: www.elljay.com
SIC: 1742 Acoustical & ceiling work

(P-2893)
ENERGETIC PNTG & DRYWALL INC (PA)
Also Called: Energetic Lath & Plaster
2929 Orange Grove Ave, North Highlands (95660-5703)
P.O. Box 191840, Sacramento (95819-7840)
PHONE.................916 488-8455
Edwin G Gerber, *President*
Tom Meler, *General Mgr*
Beth Conley, *Controller*
EMP: 210
SQ FT: 10,000
SALES: 12MM **Privately Held**
SIC: 1742 Drywall

(P-2894)
ERIC STARK INTERIORS INC
2284 Paragon Dr, San Jose (95131-1306)
PHONE.................408 441-6136
Fax: 408 441-6137
Eric Stark, *President*
Dora Stanich, *Admin Asst*
EMP: 100
SQ FT: 10,000
SALES (est): 8.6MM **Privately Held**
WEB: www.ericstarkinteriors.com
SIC: 1742 Drywall

(P-2895)
FARIA DRYWALL INC
8518 Church St Ste 5, Gilroy (95020-4200)
PHONE.................408 847-2058
Fax: 408 847-3349
Jose Faria, *President*
EMP: 50
SQ FT: 5,000
SALES (est): 3.6MM **Privately Held**
SIC: 1742 Drywall

1742 - Plastering, Drywall, Acoustical & Insulation Work County (P-2896)

PRODUCTS & SERVICES SECTION

(P-2896)
FARWEST INSULATION CONTRACTING
Also Called: Pacific Insulation
2741 Yates Ave, Commerce (90040-2623)
PHONE.................................310 634-2800
Fax: 323 728-5489
Linda Chadarria, Manager
Linda Chavarria, Controller
EMP: 50
SALES (corp-wide): 51.7MM Privately Held
SIC: 1742 Insulation, buildings
PA: Farwest Insulation Contracting, Inc
1220 S Sherman St
Anaheim CA 92805
714 520-5600

(P-2897)
FOUNDATION BUILDING MTLS LLC (PA)
Also Called: Great Western Building Mtl
2552 Walnut Ave Ste 160, Tustin (92780-6992)
PHONE.................................714 380-3127
Ruben Mendoza, Mng Member
Pete Welly, COO
Betty Padilla, Accounting Mgr
EMP: 94
SALES (est): 149.7MM Privately Held
SIC: 1742 Plastering, drywall & insulation

(P-2898)
FREDERICK MEISWINKEL INC
850 S Van Ness Ave, San Francisco (94110-1911)
PHONE.................................415 550-0400
Fax: 415 550-0221
Rudy F Meiswinkel, President
Rob Barwick, Controller
EMP: 215
SQ FT: 10,000
SALES (est): 8.1MM Privately Held
WEB: www.frederickmeiswinkel.com
SIC: 1742 1799 Plastering, plain or ornamental; drywall; exterior insulation & finish (EIFS) applicator; fireproofing buildings

(P-2899)
FRESNO CNTY ECONOMIC OPPORTUNT
3120 W Nielsen Ave # 102, Fresno (93706-1139)
PHONE.................................559 485-3733
Fax: 559 485-3737
George Egewa, Manager
George Egawa, Branch Mgr
EMP: 100
SALES (corp-wide): 108.8MM Privately Held
SIC: 1742 Insulation, buildings
PA: Fresno County Economic Opportunities Commission
1920 Mariposa Mall # 300
Fresno CA 93721
559 263-1010

(P-2900)
FRYE CONSTRUCTION INC
18807 Highway 65, Bakersfield (93308-9794)
P.O. Box 21568 (93390-1568)
PHONE.................................661 588-8870
Inez M Frye, CEO
David Frye, President
Betty Criner, Manager
EMP: 60
SQ FT: 7,450
SALES (est): 7.3MM Privately Held
WEB: www.fryeinc.net
SIC: 1742 Drywall; plastering, plain or ornamental

(P-2901)
FUTURE ENERGY CORPORATION
4120 Avenida De La Plata, Oceanside (92056-6001)
PHONE.................................760 477-9700
Jeffrey Adkins, Branch Mgr
EMP: 102
SALES (corp-wide): 33MM Privately Held
SIC: 1742 1521 Acoustical & insulation work; single-family home remodeling, additions & repairs
PA: Future Energy Corporation
8980 Grant Line Rd
Upland CA 91786
800 985-0733

(P-2902)
G BROTHERS CONSTRUCTION INC
7070 Patterson Dr, Garden Grove (92841-1438)
PHONE.................................714 590-3070
Fax: 714 590-3079
Rick Gutierrez, President
Mike Gutierrez, Vice Pres
David Gutierrez, Purch Mgr
EMP: 50
SQ FT: 6,500
SALES (est): 7MM Privately Held
WEB: www.gbrothers.net
SIC: 1742 Drywall

(P-2903)
GIERAHN DRY WALL INC
28490 Westinghouse Pl # 150, Santa Clarita (91355-0955)
PHONE.................................661 257-7900
Henry Carl Gierahn, President
Robin Nixon, Manager
EMP: 50
SQ FT: 1,200
SALES (est): 3.9MM Privately Held
WEB: www.gierahn.com
SIC: 1742 Drywall

(P-2904)
GOLD STAR INSULATION INC
210 N 10th St, Sacramento (95811-0307)
PHONE.................................916 928-1100
Fax: 209 521-9055
Randy Marigold, President
Dean Sager, Principal
EMP: 50
SALES (est): 2.2MM Privately Held
SIC: 1742 Insulation, buildings

(P-2905)
GREYSTONE PLASTERING INC
1716 Stone Ave Ste B, San Jose (95125-1308)
P.O. Box 41457 (95160-1457)
PHONE.................................408 298-5934
Fax: 408 298-6929
Michael Stonehocker, President
EMP: 80
SQ FT: 1,500
SALES (est): 6.7MM Privately Held
SIC: 1742 Plaster & drywall work

(P-2906)
GYPSUM CONTRACTORS INC
23785 El Toro Rd Ste 135, Lake Forest (92630-4762)
PHONE.................................949 340-9100
Aram Fatourehchian, CEO
Aram Fatoure, President
EMP: 50 EST: 2012
SQ FT: 1,000
SALES (est): 2.7MM Privately Held
SIC: 1742 Insulation, buildings

(P-2907)
H B J CORPORATION
Also Called: Superior Pntg Drywall Fnshings
5806 Frontier Way, Carmichael (95608-5137)
PHONE.................................707 333-7066
Fax: 916 481-0364
Harry Boyajian Jr, President
EMP: 80
SQ FT: 2,000
SALES (est): 1.5MM Privately Held
SIC: 1742 Drywall

(P-2908)
HARRISON DRYWALL INC
447 10th St, San Francisco (94103-4303)
P.O. Box 508, Cotati (94931-0508)
PHONE.................................415 821-9584
Fax: 415 821-9523
Jeff Harrison, President
Dan Harrison, Project Mgr
Melanie Rivera, Controller
EMP: 50
SQ FT: 5,000
SALES (est): 7.1MM Privately Held
WEB: www.harrisondrywallinc.com
SIC: 1742 Plastering, plain or ornamental; drywall

(P-2909)
INFINITY DRYWALL CONTG INC
225 S Loara St, Anaheim (92802-1019)
PHONE.................................714 634-2255
Dennis Lafreniere, President
James Darling, Vice Pres
Liza Lafreniere, Vice Pres
Nadia Preciado, Manager
EMP: 60
SALES (est): 7MM Privately Held
SIC: 1742 1751 Plastering, drywall & insulation; framing contractor

(P-2910)
INNOVATIVE DRYWALL SYSTEMS INC
Also Called: Alta Drywall
116 Market Pl, Escondido (92029-1352)
P.O. Box 3268, Ramona (92065-0956)
PHONE.................................760 743-0331
Doug Bellamy, President
April Carlson, Office Mgr
EMP: 80
SQ FT: 3,500
SALES: 4.5MM Privately Held
SIC: 1742 Drywall

(P-2911)
INTERIOR EXPERTS GENERAL BLDRS
4534 Carter Ct, Chino (91710-5060)
PHONE.................................909 203-4922
Adam Lopez, President
Kenny Pham, Office Mgr
EMP: 80
SQ FT: 9,000
SALES (est): 7.9MM Privately Held
WEB: www.expert-email.com
SIC: 1742 Drywall

(P-2912)
INTERWALL DEV SYSTEMS INC
17401 Armstrong Ave, Irvine (92614-5723)
PHONE.................................949 553-9102
Fax: 949 553-9107
William Hunt, President
Cynthia Hunt, Vice Pres
EMP: 75
SQ FT: 2,100
SALES (est): 3.8MM Privately Held
WEB: www.wchuntco.com
SIC: 1742 Drywall

(P-2913)
IVO WALL EXPERTS INC
5359 Sheila St, Commerce (90040-2101)
PHONE.................................323 246-4026
Ildefonso V Osorio, President
Frank Osorio, Vice Pres
Jose A Osorio, Vice Pres
Valentin Osorio, Admin Sec
Gloria Osorio, Manager
EMP: 98
SQ FT: 7,200
SALES (est): 6.3MM Privately Held
SIC: 1742 Plaster & drywall work

(P-2914)
J & J ACOUSTICS INC
2260 De La Cruz Blvd, Santa Clara (95050-3008)
PHONE.................................408 275-9255
Fax: 408 275-9285
James Jean, President
Joseph Jean, Vice Pres
Marge Meide, Admin Sec
Catherine Lawson, Administration
Dan Brown, Project Mgr
EMP: 140 EST: 1975
SALES (est): 15.1MM Privately Held
WEB: www.jjacoustics.com
SIC: 1742 Drywall

(P-2915)
J W LEAVY INC
3100 Dutton Ave Ste 126, Santa Rosa (95407-5773)
P.O. Box 11204 (95406-1204)
PHONE.................................707 579-3805
Sarah Leavy, President
Joe W Leavy, Admin Sec
EMP: 50
SQ FT: 3,000
SALES (est): 2.9MM Privately Held
SIC: 1742 Drywall

(P-2916)
JADE INC
11126 Sepulveda Blvd B, Mission Hills (91345-1130)
PHONE.................................818 365-7137
Fax: 818 361-2059
Steven Arteaga, CEO
Jay Arteaga, President
Cheryl Taylor, Treasurer
Michelle Vojtech, Vice Pres
Gail De Ande, Admin Sec
EMP: 75
SQ FT: 5,000
SALES (est): 8.1MM Privately Held
WEB: www.jade.net
SIC: 1742 Drywall

(P-2917)
JCV INC
1118 W Orangethorpe Ave, Fullerton (92833-4743)
P.O. Box 856 (92836-0856)
PHONE.................................714 871-2007
Mario Valadez, President
Juan Valadez, CEO
EMP: 50
SQ FT: 1,900
SALES (est): 3.4MM Privately Held
SIC: 1742 Drywall

(P-2918)
JOHN JORY CORPORATION (PA)
1894 N Main St, Orange (92865-4117)
PHONE.................................714 279-7901
Fax: 714 279-7902
Kenneth Johnson, CEO
Jack Jory, Admin Sec
EMP: 385
SQ FT: 9,000
SALES (est): 63.3MM Privately Held
WEB: www.johnjorycorp.com
SIC: 1742 Drywall

(P-2919)
KEENAN HOPKINS SUDER & STOWELL (PA)
Also Called: Khs & S Contractors
5109 E La Palma Ave Ste A, Anaheim (92807-2066)
PHONE.................................714 695-3670
Fax: 714 695-3671
David Suder, President
Philip Cherne, COO
Dennis Norman, CFO
Mark Gill, Senior VP
John Platon, Senior VP
▲ EMP: 65
SALES (est): 291.1MM Privately Held
SIC: 1742 1751 1743 1741 Plastering, plain or ornamental; carpentry work; terrazzo, tile, marble, mosaic work; masonry & other stonework; painting & paper hanging

(P-2920)
KENYON CONSTRUCTION INC
4667 N Blythe Ave, Fresno (93722-3908)
PHONE.................................559 277-5645
Jose Valenzuela, Manager
EMP: 56
SQ FT: 9,182
SALES (corp-wide): 157.7MM Privately Held
SIC: 1742 Plastering, drywall & insulation
PA: Kenyon Construction, Inc.
4001 W Indian School Rd
Phoenix AZ 85019
602 484-0080

PRODUCTS & SERVICES SECTION
1742 - Plastering, Drywall, Acoustical & Insulation Work County (P-2946)

(P-2921)
KENYON CONSTRUCTION INC
Also Called: Kenyon Plastering
3223 E St, North Highlands (95660-4606)
P.O. Box 2077 (95660-8077)
PHONE..................................916 514-9502
Fax: 916 349-1801
Carl Schmidt, *Principal*
Karl Schmidt, *General Mgr*
EMP: 200
SALES (corp-wide): 157.7MM **Privately Held**
WEB: www.kenyonconstruction.com
SIC: 1742 Plastering, drywall & insulation
PA: Kenyon Construction, Inc.
4001 W Indian School Rd
Phoenix AZ 85019
602 484-0080

(P-2922)
KURT MEISWINKEL INC
1407 E 3rd Ave, San Mateo (94401-2109)
PHONE..................................650 344-7200
Kurt Meiswinkel, *President*
EMP: 50
SQ FT: 25,000
SALES: 3.3MM **Privately Held**
WEB: www.km.net
SIC: 1742 Plastering, drywall & insulation

(P-2923)
LANCASTER BURNS CNSTR INC
Also Called: L B Construction
8655 Washington Blvd, Roseville (95678-5945)
PHONE..................................916 624-8404
Jordan Edward Burns, *President*
Christine Lancaster, *CFO*
Vance Lancaster, *Vice Pres*
John Jones, *Engineer*
EMP: 150
SQ FT: 43,000
SALES (est): 21.2MM **Privately Held**
SIC: 1742 1751 1791 Drywall; framing contractor; building front installation metal

(P-2924)
LEAVY BROTHERS INCORPORATED
Also Called: Solid Drywall
4117 Elverta Rd Ste 102, Antelope (95843-4734)
PHONE..................................916 773-5636
Joseph W Leavy, *CEO*
Masami Yoshieda, *Corp Secy*
Kevin Leavy, *Vice Pres*
EMP: 54
SALES: 500K **Privately Held**
SIC: 1742 Plastering, drywall & insulation

(P-2925)
MAGNUM DRYWALL INC
42027 Boscell Rd, Fremont (94538-3106)
PHONE..................................510 979-0420
Fax: 510 979-0484
Gary Robinson, *President*
EMP: 72
SQ FT: 3,200
SALES (est): 16.2MM **Privately Held**
WEB: www.magnumdrywall.com
SIC: 1742 Drywall

(P-2926)
MARTIN BROS/MARCOWALL INC (PA)
17104 S Figueroa St, Gardena (90248-3097)
P.O. Box 2089 (90247-0089)
PHONE..................................310 532-5335
Fax: 310 516-1829
Mohammad Chahine, *CEO*
Dave Aguilera, *Vice Pres*
Damon Hoover, *Vice Pres*
Ana Tinajero, *Office Mgr*
Joe Colavita, *Information Mgr*
EMP: 110
SQ FT: 6,000
SALES (est): 25.6MM **Privately Held**
WEB: www.martinbros-marcowall.com
SIC: 1742 Plastering, drywall & insulation

(P-2927)
MARTIN INTEGRATED SYSTEMS
2330 N Pacific St, Orange (92865-2618)
PHONE..................................714 998-9100
Fax: 714 998-1414
Marshall Hovivian, *President*
Anne Reizer, *Corp Secy*
Jeff Anderson, *Project Mgr*
Myron Mathis, *Project Mgr*
Laurie Bonelli, *Manager*
EMP: 55
SQ FT: 5,540
SALES (est): 7MM **Privately Held**
SIC: 1742 Acoustical & ceiling work

(P-2928)
MASTER DESIGN DRYWALL INC
Also Called: Pacific Lath & Plaster
360 S Spruce St, Escondido (92025-4052)
P.O. Box 3058 (92033-3058)
PHONE..................................760 480-9001
Fax: 858 480-0512
Mary Kathawa, *President*
EMP: 140
SALES (est): 8.7MM **Privately Held**
WEB: www.pacificlathandplaster.com
SIC: 1742 Plaster & drywall work

(P-2929)
MASTER DRYWALL INC
6727 Bucktown Ln, Vacaville (95688-9719)
PHONE..................................707 448-8659
Fax: 707 448-3446
Joseph R Mendonca, *President*
Manuela Mendonc, *Vice Pres*
EMP: 125
SALES (est): 7.1MM **Privately Held**
WEB: www.masterdrywall.com
SIC: 1742 Drywall

(P-2930)
MELOS PLST LTHG & DRYWALL
2038 E Jensen Ave, Fresno (93706-5054)
PHONE..................................559 237-0028
Carlos Melo, *President*
Maria Melo, *Vice Pres*
EMP: 100
SQ FT: 5,820
SALES (est): 5.5MM **Privately Held**
SIC: 1742 Plastering, plain or ornamental; plaster & drywall work; drywall

(P-2931)
MGM DRYWALL INC
1165 Peach Ct, San Jose (95116-2814)
PHONE..................................408 292-4085
Miguel Guillen, *President*
Gonzalo Guillen, *Vice Pres*
Sal Madrigal, *Vice Pres*
William Guillen, *Project Engr*
Raul Lopez, *Foreman/Supr*
EMP: 100
SALES (est): 2.6MM **Privately Held**
WEB: www.mgmdrywall.com
SIC: 1742 Drywall

(P-2932)
MICHAEL B MAYOCK INC
Also Called: A Complete Drywall Co
1945 Francisco Blvd E # 31, San Rafael (94901-5525)
PHONE..................................415 456-9306
Fax: 415 456-9375
Michael B Mayock, *President*
Lisa Mayock, *Corp Secy*
EMP: 60
SALES (est): 3.5MM **Privately Held**
SIC: 1742 1751 Drywall; lightweight steel framing (metal stud) installation

(P-2933)
MID VALLEY PLASTERING INC
15300 Mckinley Ave, Lathrop (95330-8782)
PHONE..................................209 858-9766
Fax: 209 858-9756
Jeff Gann, *President*
Kevin Gann, *Corp Secy*
Jeremy Gann, *Vice Pres*
Kathy Beeson, *Manager*
EMP: 400 **EST:** 1998
SQ FT: 5,000
SALES (est): 31.1MM **Privately Held**
WEB: www.midvalleyplastering.com
SIC: 1742 Plastering, plain or ornamental

(P-2934)
MOWERY THOMASON INC
1225 N Red Gum St, Anaheim (92806-1821)
PHONE..................................714 666-1717
Fax: 714 666-1211
Robert J Heimerl, *President*
Toni Heimerl, *Corp Secy*
Todd Heimerl, *Vice Pres*
EMP: 175
SQ FT: 8,000
SALES (est): 16.3MM **Privately Held**
WEB: www.mowerythomason.com
SIC: 1742 Drywall; plastering, plain or ornamental

(P-2935)
NEW WEST PARTITIONS
2550 Sutterville Rd, Sacramento (95820-1020)
PHONE..................................916 456-8365
Kem P Modellas, *CEO*
Mark Modellas, *Admin Sec*
Richard Ishibashi, *Manager*
EMP: 120
SQ FT: 3,000
SALES (est): 9.8MM **Privately Held**
SIC: 1742 Drywall

(P-2936)
NOROGACHI CONSTRUCTION INC/CA
600 Industrial Dr Ste 100, Galt (95632-8164)
PHONE..................................916 236-4201
Anival Guerrero, *CEO*
Laura Guerrero, *Vice Pres*
Gerardo Guerrero, *Office Mgr*
EMP: 100
SALES (est): 9.1MM **Privately Held**
SIC: 1742 1542 Drywall; acoustical & insulation work; acoustical & ceiling work; institutional building construction

(P-2937)
NORTH BAY DRYWALL & PLST INC
715 Southpoint Blvd Ste B, Petaluma (94954-6836)
P.O. Box 750007 (94975-0007)
PHONE..................................707 763-6819
Fax: 707 778-0512
John Levo, *CEO*
Charles R Stephens, *President*
Lee Marc, *Info Tech Mgr*
Karen Thompson, *Manager*
EMP: 110
SQ FT: 81,029
SALES (est): 8.5MM **Privately Held**
WEB: www.northbayco.com
SIC: 1742 Plaster & drywall work

(P-2938)
NORTH COUNTIES DRYWALL INC
20563 Broadway, Sonoma (95476-7590)
P.O. Box 260 (95476-0260)
PHONE..................................707 996-0198
Diane Merlo, *President*
Richard Merlo, *President*
Fred Burbage, *Project Mgr*
Tony Rosales, *Project Mgr*
Melissa Smittcamp, *Accountant*
EMP: 50
SQ FT: 2,000
SALES (est): 7.1MM **Privately Held**
WEB: www.ncdinc.net
SIC: 1742 1542 1521 Drywall; commercial & office building, new construction; new construction, single-family houses

(P-2939)
OHANIANS DRYWALL INC
4655 W Jacquelyn Ave, Fresno (93722-6413)
PHONE..................................559 277-2946
Fax: 559 277-3097
Tom Ohanian, *President*
Kim O Hanian, *Vice Pres*
EMP: 90
SALES (est): 6.1MM **Privately Held**
SIC: 1742 Drywall

(P-2940)
OJ INSULATION LP
5820 Obata Way Unit B, Gilroy (95020-7038)
PHONE..................................408 842-6315
Griff Jenkins, *Branch Mgr*
EMP: 73
SALES (corp-wide): 29.8MM **Privately Held**
SIC: 1742 1751 1741 Insulation, buildings; carpentry work; masonry & other stonework
PA: Oj Insulation, L.P.
600 S Vincent Ave
Azusa CA 91702
626 812-6070

(P-2941)
OJ INSULATION LP
Also Called: Oj Insulation & Fireplaces
2061 Albergrov Ave, Escondido (92029)
PHONE..................................760 839-3200
Tom Berry, *Manager*
Alma Lopez, *Office Mgr*
EMP: 50
SALES (corp-wide): 29.8MM **Privately Held**
WEB: www.ojinc.com
SIC: 1742 Insulation, buildings
PA: Oj Insulation, L.P.
600 S Vincent Ave
Azusa CA 91702
626 812-6070

(P-2942)
OJ INSULATION LP
78 015 Wildcat Dr Ste 105, Palm Desert (92211)
PHONE..................................760 200-4343
Griff Jenkins, *Branch Mgr*
EMP: 73
SALES (corp-wide): 29.8MM **Privately Held**
SIC: 1742 1751 1741 Insulation, buildings; carpentry work; masonry & other stonework
PA: Oj Insulation, L.P.
600 S Vincent Ave
Azusa CA 91702
626 812-6070

(P-2943)
OJ INSULATION LP (PA)
Also Called: Abco Insulation
600 S Vincent Ave, Azusa (91702-5145)
PHONE..................................626 812-6070
Fax: 626 334-8167
Pamela A Henson, *Partner*
Mark Newman, *Division Mgr*
Michelle Skeldon, *Business Mgr*
Charlene Smith, *Human Res Dir*
Jorge Cortez, *Prdtn Mgr*
EMP: 148
SQ FT: 12,000
SALES (est): 29.8MM **Privately Held**
WEB: www.ojinc.com
SIC: 1742 1751 1741 Insulation, buildings; carpentry work; masonry & other stonework

(P-2944)
ORANGE COUNTY PLST CO INC
3191 Arprt Loop Dr Ste B1, Costa Mesa (92626)
PHONE..................................714 957-1971
Fax: 714 957-0958
Robert G Smith, *President*
Rose Schriever, *Controller*
EMP: 128
SALES (est): 12.8MM **Privately Held**
WEB: www.ocplastering.com
SIC: 1742 Plastering, plain or ornamental

(P-2945)
P H B CONTRACTING INC
43180 Sunburst St, Indio (92201-2083)
PHONE..................................760 347-7290
Fax: 760 863-3836
Dave Boggs, *President*
Nicholas Panzarini, *Vice Pres*
Laura Mariscal, *Office Mgr*
EMP: 225
SALES (est): 8.7MM **Privately Held**
SIC: 1742 Plaster & drywall work

(P-2946)
PACE INC
Also Called: Pace Drywall
2301 Arnold Industrial Wa, Concord (94520-5375)
P.O. Box 573 (94522-0573)
PHONE..................................925 602-0900
Fax: 925 602-0905

1742 - Plastering, Drywall, Acoustical & Insulation Work County (P-2947)

PRODUCTS & SERVICES SECTION

Alan D Mauldin, *President*
Patricia Mauldin, *Corp Secy*
Brett Brady, *Manager*
Elizabeth Snedlker, *Manager*
EMP: 80
SQ FT: 17,000
SALES (est): 7.9MM **Privately Held**
WEB: www.pacedrywall.com
SIC: 1742 Drywall

(P-2947)
PACIFIC BUILDING GROUP
13541 Stoney Creek Rd, San Diego (92129-2050)
PHONE.................................858 552-0600
Jim Roherty, *Branch Mgr*
EMP: 107
SALES (corp-wide): 52MM **Privately Held**
SIC: 1742 Acoustical & ceiling work
PA: Pacific Building Group
 9752 Aspen Creek Ct # 100
 San Diego CA 92126
 858 552-0600

(P-2948)
PACIFIC EXTERIORS INC
13911 Enterprise Dr Ste B, Garden Grove (92843-4042)
PHONE.................................714 265-1998
Fax: 714 265-1911
Frank Blasetti, *President*
Christine Blasetti, *CFO*
Mark Blasetti, *Treasurer*
Paul Blasetti, *Project Mgr*
Todd Layman, *Project Mgr*
EMP: 75
SALES (est): 5.6MM **Privately Held**
WEB: www.pacificexteriors.com
SIC: 1742 Plastering, drywall & insulation

(P-2949)
PACIFIC RIM CONTRACTORS INC
1315 E Saint Andrew Pl B, Santa Ana (92705-4919)
PHONE.................................714 641-7380
Fax: 714 641-8502
Jerry Tyner, *President*
Aaron Tyner, *Vice Pres*
Martha Tyner, *Vice Pres*
Tina Feraco, *Manager*
Nichole Dray, *Asst Mgr*
EMP: 65
SQ FT: 3,000
SALES (est): 5.3MM **Privately Held**
WEB: www.pacificrimcontractors.com
SIC: 1742 1721 Drywall; painting & paper hanging

(P-2950)
PACIFIC SYSTEMS INTERIORS INC
1612 W 139th St, Gardena (90249-3003)
PHONE.................................310 436-6820
Jonathan Miasnik, *President*
Steve Yeschenko, *CFO*
Mischeal Orr, *Manager*
EMP: 150
SQ FT: 30,000
SALES: 37.6MM **Privately Held**
SIC: 1742 Plastering, drywall & insulation

(P-2951)
PACIFIC WEST LATH & PLASTER
6853 Mccomber St, Sacramento (95828-2515)
PHONE.................................916 329-9028
Fax: 916 387-5766
Theodore Brown, *CEO*
Greg Brown, *President*
Paul Maples, *Vice Pres*
EMP: 50
SALES (est): 3.8MM **Privately Held**
SIC: 1742 Plaster & drywall work

(P-2952)
PADILLA CONSTRUCTION COMPANY
Also Called: Garris Plastering
1130 W Trenton Ave, Orange (92867-3536)
P.O. Box 2847 (92859-0847)
PHONE.................................714 685-8500
Fax: 714 685-8501

Ralph Padilla Jr, *President*
Mary H Warren, *VP Sales*
EMP: 250
SQ FT: 5,000
SALES (est): 23.6MM **Privately Held**
WEB: www.padillaconstruction.com
SIC: 1742 Plastering, drywall & insulation

(P-2953)
PAUL PIETRZYK
Also Called: Pauls Drywall
1142 Acapulco Ct, Merced (95348-1859)
PHONE.................................209 726-5034
Fax: 209 328-2240
Paul Pietrzyk, *President*
Loree Pietryk, *CFO*
EMP: 50
SALES: 2.5MM **Privately Held**
SIC: 1742 Drywall

(P-2954)
PETROCHEM INSULATION INC
19010 S Alameda St, Compton (90221-6201)
PHONE.................................310 638-6663
Fax: 310 638-6572
Erich Freudenthaler, *Manager*
Mark Huchida, *Sales Executive*
EMP: 200
SALES (corp-wide): 2.5B **Privately Held**
WEB: www.petrocheminc.com
SIC: 1742 3531 Insulation, buildings; construction machinery
HQ: Petrochem Insulation, Inc.
 110 Corporate Pl
 Vallejo CA 94590
 707 644-7455

(P-2955)
PRE CON INDUSTRIES INC
4340 Viewridge Ave Ste B, San Diego (92123-1682)
P.O. Box 5728, Santa Maria (93456-5728)
PHONE.................................805 928-3397
John Amburgey, *President*
Anne Temple, *Principal*
EMP: 99 **EST:** 2008
SALES (est): 3.2MM **Privately Held**
SIC: 1742 Drywall

(P-2956)
PRE CON INDUSTRIES INC
917 W Inyokern Rd Ste C, Ridgecrest (93555-5602)
P.O. Box 5728, Santa Maria (93456-5728)
PHONE.................................760 499-6176
John Amburgey, *President*
Anne Temple, *Manager*
EMP: 99
SALES (est): 2.9MM **Privately Held**
SIC: 1742 Plastering, drywall & insulation

(P-2957)
PREMIER DRYWALL
725 Oak St, Santa Maria (93454-6215)
P.O. Box 57 (93456-0057)
PHONE.................................805 928-3397
Fax: 805 928-0977
John Amburgey, *CEO*
Danny Amburgery, *Principal*
EMP: 99 **EST:** 1990
SALES (est): 4.9MM **Privately Held**
SIC: 1742 Plastering, drywall & insulation

(P-2958)
PREMIUM ROCK DRYWALL INC
31348 Via Colinas Ste 103, Westlake Village (91362-6805)
PHONE.................................818 676-3350
Rick Cook, *President*
Stacy Cook, *Corp Secy*
EMP: 80
SQ FT: 800
SALES: 3MM **Privately Held**
SIC: 1742 Drywall

(P-2959)
PROWALL LATH AND PLASTER
360 S Spruce St, Escondido (92025-4052)
PHONE.................................760 480-9001
Mary Kathawa, *President*
Pam Summerfield, *Admin Sec*
EMP: 99
SALES (est): 6.7MM **Privately Held**
SIC: 1742 Plastering, plain or ornamental

(P-2960)
QUALITY PRODUCTION SVCS INC
3730 Skypark Dr, Torrance (90505-4704)
PHONE.................................310 406-3350
Fax: 310 406-3351
Arshak George Kotoyantz, *President*
Shana Monllor, *Office Mgr*
EMP: 100
SALES (est): 11.8MM **Privately Held**
SIC: 1742 Drywall

(P-2961)
QUALITY WALL SYSTEMS INC
Also Called: Residential Wall Systems
104 S Maple St, Corona (92880-1704)
P.O. Box 2649 (92878-2649)
PHONE.................................951 739-4409
Glenn L Crowther, *President*
EMP: 99
SALES (est): 6.2MM **Privately Held**
SIC: 1742 1721 Drywall; painting & paper hanging

(P-2962)
R A GREENE CORPORATION
1234 Industrial Ave, Escondido (92029-1424)
PHONE.................................760 747-0810
Fax: 760 747-2368
Nancy Greene, *President*
Richard A Greene, *Vice Pres*
EMP: 60
SQ FT: 8,928
SALES (est): 5.1MM **Privately Held**
WEB: www.ragreenecorp.com
SIC: 1742 Plastering, plain or ornamental

(P-2963)
RANGEL DRYWALL INC
1401 S 7th St, Modesto (95351-9401)
P.O. Box 5236 (95352-5236)
PHONE.................................209 525-9490
Fax: 209 525-9485
Reyes F Rangel III, *President*
Al Aries, *Sales Staff*
EMP: 50
SQ FT: 6,000
SALES (est): 4.6MM **Privately Held**
SIC: 1742 Drywall

(P-2964)
REDDING DRYWALL SYSTEMS INC
Also Called: High Performance Wall Systems
3092 Crossroads Dr, Redding (96003-8058)
P.O. Box 494156 (96049-4156)
PHONE.................................530 222-8767
Fax: 530 222-6778
Marvin O'Dell, *President*
Elelin Sutfin, *Office Mgr*
EMP: 50
SQ FT: 3,800
SALES (est): 4.3MM **Privately Held**
WEB: www.drywallsystems.com
SIC: 1742 Drywall

(P-2965)
RENAISSANCE INC
Also Called: Renaissance Total Comfort
2615 W Dudley Ave, Fresno (93728-2410)
P.O. Box 13039 (93794-3039)
PHONE.................................559 320-0048
Fax: 559 444-1840
David J Robinson, *President*
Luell Robinson, *Corp Secy*
EMP: 60
SQ FT: 5,000
SALES (est): 5.5MM **Privately Held**
SIC: 1742 Insulation, buildings

(P-2966)
RFJ CORPORATION
Also Called: Rfj Meiswinkel
930 Innes Ave, San Francisco (94124-2905)
PHONE.................................415 824-6890
Fax: 415 282-7868
Joseph Meiswinkel, *President*
Kristen Meiswinkel, *Office Mgr*
EMP: 60
SQ FT: 15,000

SALES (est): 8.2MM **Privately Held**
WEB: www.rfjmeiswinkel.com
SIC: 1742 Plastering, plain or ornamental; drywall

(P-2967)
RICE DRYWALL INC
919 E 6th St, Santa Ana (92701-4725)
PHONE.................................714 543-5400
Fax: 626 443-3329
John H Laing, *President*
Keith Barakat, *Vice Pres*
Kim Riker, *Admin Sec*
Susan Stone, *Manager*
EMP: 90
SQ FT: 8,000
SALES: 2.3MM **Privately Held**
SIC: 1742 Drywall

(P-2968)
RICHMOND PLASTERING INC
12102 Centralia Rd Ste B, Hawaiian Gardens (90716-1003)
PHONE.................................562 924-4202
Fax: 562 924-6332
Tim Richmond, *President*
Debbie Richmond, *Corp Secy*
Sue Bredesen, *Office Mgr*
Claude Curtis, *Opers Staff*
▲ **EMP:** 50 **EST:** 1979
SQ FT: 1,375
SALES (est): 6.6MM **Privately Held**
WEB: www.richmondplastering.com
SIC: 1742 Plastering, plain or ornamental

(P-2969)
RICK H HITCH PLASTERING INC
Also Called: Venture Lath and Plaster
3306 Orange Grove Ave, North Highlands (95660-5808)
PHONE.................................916 334-3591
Fax: 916 334-3593
Jason Wu, *President*
Loretta Hitch, *Vice Pres*
EMP: 125
SALES (est): 4.5MM **Privately Held**
WEB: www.venturelp.com
SIC: 1742 Plastering, plain or ornamental

(P-2970)
ROYAL WEST DRYWALL INC
2008 2nd St, Norco (92860-2804)
PHONE.................................951 271-4600
Fax: 951 278-8247
Paul Diguiseppe, *CEO*
EMP: 100
SQ FT: 20,473
SALES (est): 9.1MM **Privately Held**
WEB: www.westcoastdrywallinc.com
SIC: 1742 Plastering, drywall & insulation

(P-2971)
RUDY CARRILLO DRYWALL INC
1913 W Magnolia Blvd, Burbank (91506-1727)
PHONE.................................818 841-2011
Rudy Carrillo, *CEO*
Darcy Carrillo, *Vice Pres*
EMP: 80
SQ FT: 2,399
SALES (est): 4.9MM **Privately Held**
SIC: 1742 Drywall

(P-2972)
RUTHERFORD CO INC (PA)
2905 Allesandro St, Los Angeles (90039-3406)
PHONE.................................323 666-5284
Fax: 323 665-0328
Paul Rutherford, *President*
James Rutherford, *Treasurer*
Brad Rutherford, *Vice Pres*
Sheila Rutherford, *Admin Sec*
Maricela Meza, *Manager*
EMP: 100
SQ FT: 15,000
SALES: 19MM **Privately Held**
SIC: 1742 Plastering, plain or ornamental

(P-2973)
S & L SPECIALTY CONTRACTING
4514 Federal Blvd Ste C, San Diego (92102-2517)
PHONE.................................619 264-3771
Jim Leana, *President*

▲ = Import ▼ =Export
◆ =Import/Export

PRODUCTS & SERVICES SECTION
1742 - Plastering, Drywall, Acoustical & Insulation Work County (P-2999)

EMP: 50
SALES (est): 2.2MM Privately Held
SIC: 1742 Acoustical & insulation work

(P-2974)
S A CALI-U ACOUSTICS INC
Also Called: Acoustical Contractor
1111 Rancho Conejo Blvd # 501, Thousand Oaks (91320-1412)
PHONE.................................805 376-9300
Fax: 805 498-8092
Diego Velasquez, *President*
Anna Velasquez, *Vice Pres*
Marta Gedney, *Info Tech Mgr*
Tim Velasquez, *Technology*
EMP: 60
SQ FT: 3,000
SALES: 1.4MM Privately Held
WEB: www.caliusa.net
SIC: 1742 Acoustical & ceiling work; insulation, buildings

(P-2975)
S PATTERSON CONSTRUCTION INC
3335 Pegasus Dr Apt 308, Bakersfield (93308-7031)
P.O. Box 82554 (93380-2554)
PHONE.................................661 391-9939
Fax: 661 393-9989
Shaun Patterson, *CEO*
EMP: 55
SQ FT: 5,000
SALES (est): 4.4MM Privately Held
SIC: 1742 Plaster & drywall work

(P-2976)
SAN MARINO PLASTERING INC
4501 E La Palma Ave # 200, Anaheim (92807-1950)
PHONE.................................714 693-7840
Fax: 714 693-7856
Fred Erdtsieck, *President*
Edward Birn, *CFO*
Edward Buchanan, *CIO*
Satcey West, *Manager*
EMP: 820
SALES (est): 35.3MM Privately Held
WEB: www.smcompanies.com
SIC: 1742 Plastering, drywall & insulation

(P-2977)
SANTA FE PLASTER
620 Alpine Way, Escondido (92029-1204)
PHONE.................................760 747-9950
Eric E Rozema, *President*
Sam Morfin, *Project Mgr*
EMP: 50
SQ FT: 4,800
SALES: 2.5MM Privately Held
SIC: 1742 Plastering, drywall & insulation

(P-2978)
SERVICE LATHING COMPANY
1090 139th Ave, San Leandro (94578-2615)
PHONE.................................510 483-9732
Fax: 510 357-3183
Robert G Brown, *President*
Ernest Schorno, *Treasurer*
Anthony B Varni, *Agent*
EMP: 50
SQ FT: 4,500
SALES (est): 4.5MM Privately Held
SIC: 1742 1751 Plastering, plain or ornamental; framing contractor

(P-2979)
SIERRA LATHING COMPANY INC
1189 Leiske Dr, Rialto (92376-8633)
PHONE.................................909 421-0211
Fax: 909 421-0346
Gary K Waldron, *CEO*
Connie Waldron, *Treasurer*
Diana Lacy, *Manager*
EMP: 200
SQ FT: 10,000
SALES (est): 14MM Privately Held
SIC: 1742 1751 Drywall; framing contractor

(P-2980)
SNEARY CONSTRUCTION INC
1182 Monte Vista Ave # 2, Upland (91786-8204)
PHONE.................................909 982-1833
Fax: 909 982-3596
Montie Sneary, *President*
Nicole Van Gundy, *CFO*
Shawna Sneary, *Vice Pres*
Deborah Herring, *Manager*
EMP: 50
SALES (est): 3.5MM Privately Held
SIC: 1742 Drywall

(P-2981)
SPACETONE ACOUSTICS INC
1051 Serpentine Ln # 300, Pleasanton (94566-8451)
PHONE.................................925 931-0749
Robert A Libby, *President*
Joan Libby, *Vice Pres*
Bret Chandler, *General Mgr*
Katie Chan, *Office Mgr*
Lisafe Henthorn, *Office Mgr*
EMP: 50
SQ FT: 3,500
SALES (est): 8.3MM Privately Held
WEB: www.spacetoneacoustics.com
SIC: 1742 Acoustical & ceiling work

(P-2982)
SPECIALTY TEAM PLASTERING INC
4652 Vintage Ranch Ln, Santa Barbara (93110-2079)
PHONE.................................805 966-3858
Fax: 805 966-0924
Jaime Melgosa, *President*
Robin Melgosa, *Vice Pres*
EMP: 130
SQ FT: 1,000
SALES: 8.2MM Privately Held
SIC: 1742 Plastering, drywall & insulation

(P-2983)
STANDARD DRYWALL INC (HQ)
Also Called: S D I
9902 Channel Rd, Lakeside (92040-3042)
PHONE.................................619 443-7034
Fax: 619 443-7065
Robert E Caya, *Principal*
Blaine Caya, *Vice Pres*
Barbara Berg, *Controller*
Brett Betters, *Human Resources*
Ann Followmen, *Manager*
EMP: 300
SQ FT: 4,500
SALES (est): 133.7MM Privately Held
WEB: www.standarddrywall.net
SIC: 1742 Drywall; acoustical & ceiling work
PA: E M P Interiors Inc
9902 Channel Rd
Lakeside CA 92040
619 443-7034

(P-2984)
STUCCO WORKS INC
5900 Warehouse Way, Sacramento (95826-4911)
PHONE.................................916 383-6699
Fax: 916 383-6668
Kevin Nelson, *President*
Anselmo Padilla, *Vice Pres*
Renee Scriver, *Vice Pres*
Xavier Valdez, *Admin Sec*
EMP: 300
SQ FT: 26,000
SALES (est): 10.8MM Privately Held
SIC: 1742 Stucco work, interior

(P-2985)
SUNSHINE METAL CLAD INC
7201 Edison Hwy, Bakersfield (93307-9011)
PHONE.................................661 366-0575
James R Eudy, *President*
Linda Payne, *CFO*
Mark Given, *Project Mgr*
Bill Lutz, *Project Mgr*
Sandra Eudy, *Director*
▲ EMP: 100
SQ FT: 50,000
SALES (est): 10.5MM Privately Held
WEB: www.smc3000.com
SIC: 1742 Acoustical & insulation work

(P-2986)
TEMECULA VALLEY DRYWALL INC
Also Called: Timberlake Painting
41228 Raintree Ct, Murrieta (92562-7089)
PHONE.................................951 600-1742
Fax: 951 600-2815
Doug A Misemer, *CEO*
Sandy Villella, *Corp Secy*
Lorry Hales, *Vice Pres*
EMP: 75
SQ FT: 8,000
SALES (est): 10.9MM Privately Held
SIC: 1742 1721 Drywall; painting & paper hanging

(P-2987)
THERMO POWER INDUSTRIES
10570 Humbolt St, Los Alamitos (90720-2439)
PHONE.................................562 799-0087
Fax: 562 799-0176
Edward Lydic, *CEO*
John G Carroll, *CFO*
Bunny Mayfield, *Office Mgr*
Nathan Heffran, *Project Mgr*
Lyvonne G Mayfield, *Manager*
EMP: 60
SQ FT: 5,500
SALES (est): 9.3MM Privately Held
WEB: www.thermopowerindustries.com
SIC: 1742 1721 3479 Insulation, buildings; commercial painting; coating, rust preventive

(P-2988)
TOMMY GUN PLASTERING INC
944 4th St, Calimesa (92320-1205)
PHONE.................................909 795-9966
Tommy Lucero, *CEO*
EMP: 60
SQ FT: 1,800
SALES (est): 3.9MM Privately Held
SIC: 1742 Plastering, plain or ornamental

(P-2989)
TONY MARQUEZ POOL PLST INC
14960 Foothill Blvd, Sylmar (91342-1301)
PHONE.................................818 767-5177
Antonio R Marquez, *President*
Tony Marquez, *President*
Georgette Marquez, *CFO*
Melissa Carcia, *Manager*
EMP: 63
SALES (est): 3.4MM Privately Held
SIC: 1742 1799 Plastering, plain or ornamental; swimming pool construction

(P-2990)
TOTAL DRYWALL INC
2867 Sampson Ave, Corona (92879-6126)
PHONE.................................951 279-0044
Fred Vian, *President*
EMP: 50
SALES (est): 4.3MM Privately Held
SIC: 1742 Drywall

(P-2991)
TOWNE CONSTRUCTION INC
12115 Lakeside Ave, Lakeside (92040-1712)
PHONE.................................619 390-4557
Fax: 619 390-4559
Tom Towne, *President*
EMP: 60
SQ FT: 1,700
SALES (est): 6.8MM Privately Held
SIC: 1742 Drywall

(P-2992)
TRI-STAR DRYWALL LP
2479 Burgan Ave, Clovis (93611-4107)
P.O. Box 1081 (93613-1081)
PHONE.................................559 299-9858
Raymond William McGuire, *Partner*
EMP: 80
SALES (est): 3.2MM Privately Held
SIC: 1742 Drywall

(P-2993)
VANTAGE PLASTER & DRYWALL
79607 Country Club Dr, Bermuda Dunes (92203-1207)
PHONE.................................760 345-3622
Jim Morales, *President*
EMP: 85
SALES (est): 2.3MM Privately Held
SIC: 1742 Plastering, drywall & insulation

(P-2994)
VINEYARD PLASTERING INC
10335 Vineyard Dr, Fontana (92337-7458)
PHONE.................................909 357-3701
Ray Hays, *President*
EMP: 50
SALES (est): 3.5MM Privately Held
SIC: 1742 Plastering, drywall & insulation

(P-2995)
W F HAYWARD CO
629 Main St Ste 101, Placerville (95667-5752)
PHONE.................................530 303-3030
Daryll Hayward, *Vice Pres*
EMP: 70
SALES (corp-wide): 4.3MM Privately Held
SIC: 1742 Drywall
PA: W. F. Hayward Co.
1264 W 130th St
Gardena CA 90247
310 532-9501

(P-2996)
WALL SYSTEMS INC
11975 Discovery Ct, Moorpark (93021-7120)
PHONE.................................805 523-9091
Fax: 805 523-8438
Kenyon Lee, *President*
Frank Bass, *Vice Pres*
Darrell Talavera, *Vice Pres*
EMP: 90
SQ FT: 6,200
SALES: 10MM Privately Held
SIC: 1742 Drywall; stucco work, interior

(P-2997)
WALTER N COFFMAN INC
5180 Naranja St, San Diego (92114-3515)
PHONE.................................619 266-2642
Fax: 619 266-2424
Walter Coffman, *President*
Inez Coffman, *Vice Pres*
Mickey Coffman, *General Mgr*
Sherry Williams, *Manager*
EMP: 70
SALES (est): 9MM Privately Held
SIC: 1742 Plastering, plain or ornamental

(P-2998)
WEST COAST DRYWALL & CO INC
1610 W Linden St, Riverside (92507-6810)
PHONE.................................951 778-3592
Mark Herbert, *CEO*
Dan Slavin, *President*
Santos Garcia, *Vice Pres*
Colleen Butler, *Human Resources*
Milo Way, *Opers Staff*
EMP: 400
SQ FT: 18,962
SALES (est): 30.7MM Privately Held
WEB: www.westcoastpainting.com
SIC: 1742 Drywall

(P-2999)
WESTERN BUILDING MATERIALS CO (PA)
4620 E Olive Ave, Fresno (93702-1660)
PHONE.................................559 454-8500
Fax: 559 454-0621
Peter Hastrup, *President*
Jessie Dell, *Info Tech Dir*
Patrick Quigley, *Financial Exec*
Pat Quigley, *Controller*
Jonathan Regalado, *Sales Staff*
EMP: 60
SQ FT: 32,000
SALES: 17MM Privately Held
WEB: www.western-building.com
SIC: 1742 5211 5031 Acoustical & ceiling work; millwork & lumber; veneer

1742 - Plastering, Drywall, Acoustical & Insulation Work County (P-3000) — PRODUCTS & SERVICES SECTION

(P-3000)
WESTERN DRYWALL INC
4981 Salida Blvd, Salida (95368-9420)
P.O. Box 11130, Oakdale (95361-1025)
PHONE..................................209 847-6401
Fax: 209 543-9026
Cecil Shatswell, *President*
John Shatswell, *Vice Pres*
Kevin Shatswell, *Vice Pres*
Jonathan Ceja, *Manager*
EMP: 70
SQ FT: 5,000
SALES: 3MM Privately Held
WEB: www.westerndrywall.com
SIC: 1742 Drywall

(P-3001)
WGG ENTERPRISES INC
Also Called: Pierce Enterprises
11340 Stewart St, El Monte (91731-2747)
PHONE..................................626 442-5493
Fax: 626 442-4515
Weldon G Gainer, *President*
EMP: 150 EST: 1969
SQ FT: 25,000
SALES (est): 11.4MM Privately Held
SIC: 1742 Plastering, plain or ornamental

(P-3002)
WINEGARD ENERGY INC
2885 S Chestnut Ave, Fresno (93725-2211)
PHONE..................................559 441-0243
Fax: 559 441-0377
Wallas Winegard, *Owner*
EMP: 100
SALES (corp-wide): 9.1MM Privately Held
WEB: www.winegardenergy.com
SIC: 1742 Insulation, buildings
PA: Winegard Energy, Inc.
5354 Irwindale Ave Ste B
Irwindale CA 91706
626 722-0595

(P-3003)
WINEGARD ENERGY INC
2159 Zeus Ct, Bakersfield (93308-6866)
PHONE..................................661 393-9467
Fax: 661 328-1546
Jessica Landrum, *Manager*
EMP: 72
SALES (corp-wide): 9.1MM Privately Held
WEB: www.winegardenergy.com
SIC: 1742 Plastering, drywall & insulation
PA: Winegard Energy, Inc.
5354 Irwindale Ave Ste B
Irwindale CA 91706
626 722-0595

1743 Terrazzo, Tile, Marble & Mosaic Work

(P-3004)
AMERICAN TILE BRICK VENEER INC
1389 E 28th St, Signal Hill (90755-1841)
PHONE..................................562 595-9293
Fax: 562 426-8127
Albert Weinstein, *President*
Taghi Nahidi, *CFO*
Andrew Nahidi, *Vice Pres*
Bardia Nahidi, *Vice Pres*
EMP: 50
SQ FT: 3,000
SALES: 6MM Privately Held
SIC: 1743 1741 Tile installation, ceramic; bricklaying

(P-3005)
ARRIAGA USA INC
Also Called: Stoneland
11831 Vose St, North Hollywood (91605-5748)
PHONE..................................818 982-9559
Shalom Rubin, *President*
Elizabeth Pepper, *Human Res Mgr*
Clare Chua, *Assistant*
EMP: 95
SALES (est): 5.1MM Privately Held
SIC: 1743 Tile installation, ceramic

(P-3006)
BREWSTER MARBLE CO INC
13576 Desmond St, Pacoima (91331-2315)
PHONE..................................818 834-2195
Teo Zeolla, *President*
Christina Elias, *Accountant*
▲ EMP: 70
SQ FT: 11,000
SALES (est): 3.6MM Privately Held
WEB: www.brewstermarble.net
SIC: 1743 Marble installation, interior

(P-3007)
CARRARA MARBLE COMPANY AMERICA (PA)
15939 Phoenix Dr, City of Industry (91745-1624)
PHONE..................................626 961-6010
Fax: 626 961-8192
William Cordova, *President*
James Hogan, *Vice Pres*
Carl Weiskopf, *Personnel*
▲ EMP: 70
SQ FT: 30,000
SALES (est): 19.1MM Privately Held
SIC: 1743 5032 1741 Marble installation, interior; ceramic wall & floor tile; masonry & other stonework

(P-3008)
CERAMIC TILE ART INC
11601 Pendleton St, Sun Valley (91352-2502)
PHONE..................................818 767-9088
Itamar Levy, *President*
Bobbie Knet, *Manager*
▲ EMP: 75
SALES (est): 6MM Privately Held
WEB: www.ceramictileart.us
SIC: 1743 Tile installation, ceramic

(P-3009)
COASTAL TILE INC
Also Called: Coastal The
7403 Greenbush Ave, North Hollywood (91605-4006)
PHONE..................................818 988-6134
Fax: 818 988-9691
Ronig Yemini, *President*
Eyal Reguev, *Vice Pres*
▲ EMP: 150
SALES (est): 9.7MM Privately Held
SIC: 1743 Terrazzo, tile, marble, mosaic work

(P-3010)
D & J TILE COMPANY INC
1045 Terminal Way, San Carlos (94070-3226)
PHONE..................................650 632-4000
Fax: 650 632-4006
David Newman, *Principal*
John Reich, *Admin Sec*
▲ EMP: 100
SALES (est): 13.7MM Privately Held
WEB: www.djtile.com
SIC: 1743 Tile installation, ceramic

(P-3011)
DELLA MAGGIORE TILE INC
87 N 30th St, San Jose (95116-1124)
PHONE..................................408 286-3991
Fax: 408 288-2166
Nick D Maggiore, *President*
Julie D Maggiore, *Admin Sec*
Richard D Maggiore, *Admin Sec*
▲ EMP: 80
SQ FT: 20,000
SALES (est): 6.5MM Privately Held
WEB: www.slabshop.com
SIC: 1743 Tile installation, ceramic

(P-3012)
DENNETT TILE & STONE INC
3310 Industrial Dr, Santa Rosa (95403-2056)
PHONE..................................707 541-3700
Fax: 707 586-5396
Rick Dennett, *President*
Bambi Dennett, *Admin Sec*
Sara Terry, *Human Resources*
EMP: 50
SQ FT: 5,500
SALES (est): 5.6MM Privately Held
WEB: www.dennett-tile.com
SIC: 1743 Tile installation, ceramic

(P-3013)
FISCHER TILE AND MARBLE INC
1800 23rd St, Sacramento (95816-7112)
PHONE..................................916 452-1426
Fax: 916 452-9204
Jay H Fischer, *President*
Matt Beauchant, *Manager*
Marty Lin, *Manager*
▲ EMP: 150
SQ FT: 22,000
SALES (est): 17.3MM Privately Held
WEB: www.fischertile.com
SIC: 1743 Tile installation, ceramic; marble installation, interior

(P-3014)
GINO RINALDI INC
Also Called: Rinaldi Tile & Marble
51 Fremont St, Royal Oaks (95076-5213)
PHONE..................................831 761-0195
Fax: 831 761-0197
Gino Rinaldi Sr, *President*
Yvonne Rinaldi, *Corp Secy*
Lee Vega, *Materials Mgr*
Rick Scurich, *Plant Mgr*
Rahelia Ronko, *Accounts Mgr*
▲ EMP: 80
SQ FT: 10,000
SALES (est): 11.4MM Privately Held
WEB: www.rinalditileandmarble.com
SIC: 1743 Tile installation, ceramic

(P-3015)
GMG STONE INC
7988 Stromesa Ct, San Diego (92126-4329)
P.O. Box 722917 (92172-2917)
PHONE..................................619 258-6899
Fax: 619 258-6346
Jean Francois Hope, *President*
Robert Bruce, *Assistant*
EMP: 50
SALES (est): 4MM Privately Held
WEB: www.gmgstone.com
SIC: 1743 Marble installation, interior

(P-3016)
KDI ELEMENTS
79431 Country Club Dr, Bermuda Dunes (92203-1200)
P.O. Box 14150, Palm Desert (92255-4150)
PHONE..................................760 345-9933
Fax: 760 345-9944
Paul Klein, *CEO*
Lew Piper, *CFO*
Lauri Nichols, *Senior VP*
Mike Castro, *Info Tech Dir*
Jeanette Nichols, *Project Mgr*
EMP: 250
SALES (est): 23.4MM Privately Held
WEB: www.kdistoneworks.com
SIC: 1743 5999 1741 Terrazzo, tile, marble, mosaic work; monuments & tombstones; masonry & other stonework

(P-3017)
KELLY MOSES FLOORS
27430 Bostik Ct Ste 101, Temecula (92590-5511)
PHONE..................................951 296-5147
Moses Kelly, *Principal*
EMP: 50
SALES (est): 1.7MM Privately Held
SIC: 1743 Tile installation, ceramic

(P-3018)
MARBLEWEST INC
Also Called: Marbleworks
7421 Vincent Cir, Huntington Beach (92648-1246)
PHONE..................................714 847-6472
Fax: 714 842-9835
Gordon Bair, *President*
Suzanne Bair, *Vice Pres*
▲ EMP: 50
SQ FT: 6,800
SALES (est): 4.1MM Privately Held
WEB: www.marbleworks.org
SIC: 1743 Marble installation, interior

(P-3019)
MATRIX SURFACES INC
5449 E La Palma Ave, Anaheim (92807-2022)
PHONE..................................714 696-5449
Jerry Eugene Jones, *CEO*
Laura J Jones, *Vice Pres*
▲ EMP: 60 EST: 2001
SQ FT: 5,000
SALES (est): 8.2MM Privately Held
WEB: www.matrixtile.com
SIC: 1743 Tile installation, ceramic

(P-3020)
MTHURON INC
Also Called: Elite Tile
1903 Rutan Dr, Livermore (94551-7646)
PHONE..................................925 932-4101
Fax: 925 945-2744
Dennis Hourany, *President*
EMP: 115 EST: 1976
SQ FT: 7,474
SALES (est): 7.8MM Privately Held
WEB: www.elitetileusa.com
SIC: 1743 Marble installation, interior; tile installation, ceramic

(P-3021)
PAUL WILLIAMS TILE CO INC
77570 Springfield Ln K, Palm Desert (92211-0473)
PHONE..................................760 772-7440
Fax: 760 772-7444
Randy Coulter, *President*
Debbie Keley, *Office Mgr*
▲ EMP: 60
SQ FT: 10,000
SALES (est): 4.5MM Privately Held
WEB: www.paulwilliamstile.com
SIC: 1743 Tile installation, ceramic

(P-3022)
PREMIER TILE & MARBLE
15000 S Main St, Gardena (90248-1945)
PHONE..................................310 516-1712
Fax: 310 516-1713
Greg Games, *President*
Lilian Games, *Admin Sec*
Chris Samp, *Manager*
EMP: 55
SALES: 15MM Privately Held
SIC: 1743 5032 Terrazzo, tile, marble, mosaic work; ceramic wall & floor tile

(P-3023)
RICK BERRY INC
Also Called: Cal Custom Tile
1300 Commerce Way, Sanger (93657-8731)
PHONE..................................559 875-1460
Fax: 559 292-6769
Rick Berry, *President*
Michele Berry, *Vice Pres*
Craig Armstrong, *Manager*
Gerson Cruz, *Supervisor*
EMP: 95
SQ FT: 10,000
SALES (est): 10.7MM Privately Held
SIC: 1743 Tile installation, ceramic

(P-3024)
SHERMN-LEHR CSTM TILE WRKS INC
5691 Power Inn Rd Ste A, Sacramento (95824-2361)
PHONE..................................916 386-0417
Fax: 916 386-0239
James P Loehr, *President*
Jane Sherman, *Treasurer*
Eber T Sherman, *Vice Pres*
Joyce Loehr, *Admin Sec*
EMP: 100
SQ FT: 3,400
SALES (est): 12.6MM Privately Held
SIC: 1743 Terrazzo, tile, marble, mosaic work

(P-3025)
SOSA GRANITE & MARBLE INC
Also Called: Sosa Tile Co
7701 Marathon Dr, Livermore (94550-9550)
PHONE..................................925 373-7675
Mario Sosa, *President*
Melissa Sosa, *Accountant*
▲ EMP: 50

▲ = Import ▼ = Export ◆ = Import/Export

PRODUCTS & SERVICES SECTION

1751 - Carpentry Work County (P-3051)

SQ FT: 16,000
SALES (est): 5.7MM **Privately Held**
WEB: www.sosagranite.com
SIC: **1743** Tile installation, ceramic

(P-3026)
TRM CORPORATION (PA)
Also Called: Superior Tile Co
2300 Polvorosa Ave, San Leandro (94577-2218)
P.O. Box 2106, Oakland (94621-0006)
PHONE 510 895-2700
Fax: 510 895-6700
Jerry D Riggs, *Ch of Bd*
Bill Regis, *President*
Tommy A Conner, *CEO*
Jerry T Sue, *CFO*
Bob Herman, *Vice Pres*
EMP: 65 EST: 1975
SQ FT: 12,000
SALES (est): 33.4MM **Privately Held**
SIC: **1743** Tile installation, ceramic; marble installation, interior

(P-3027)
U S PERMA INC
Also Called: California Tile Installers
1696 Rogers Ave, San Jose (95112-1105)
PHONE 408 436-0600
Fax: 408 436-1126
Jack O'Brien, *President*
Randall Sundberg, *Vice Pres*
Donald K O'Brien, *Admin Sec*
Judy White, *Accounts Mgr*
▲ EMP: 50
SQ FT: 9,000
SALES: 7MM **Privately Held**
WEB: www.usperma.com
SIC: **1743** Terrazzo, tile, marble, mosaic work

1751 Carpentry Work

(P-3028)
ALL SEASONS FRAMING CORP
644 N Eckhoff St, Orange (92868-1004)
PHONE 714 634-2324
Fax: 714 634-2325
Dave Karos, *President*
Gerado Rodarte, *Admin Sec*
EMP: 50
SQ FT: 3,600
SALES: 4MM **Privately Held**
WEB: www.allseasonspressed.com
SIC: **1751** Framing contractor

(P-3029)
ALLEN CONSTRUCTION INC
31356 Via Colinas Ste 107, Westlake Village (91362-6799)
PHONE 818 879-5334
Darrel Allen, *President*
Karen Scheneman, *Vice Pres*
Steve Weinshenk, *Agent*
EMP: 50
SALES (est): 3.5MM **Privately Held**
SIC: **1751** Framing contractor

(P-3030)
ALLIED FRAMERS INC
4990 Allison Pkwy, Vacaville (95688-9346)
PHONE 707 452-7050
Fax: 707 452-7055
Jakki Kutz, *President*
Dave Burrell, *Vice Pres*
Mark Johnson, *Vice Pres*
Mile Thomason, *Vice Pres*
Chris Cannon, *Project Mgr*
EMP: 130
SQ FT: 6,000
SALES (est): 12.5MM **Privately Held**
WEB: www.alliedframers.com
SIC: **1751** Framing contractor

(P-3031)
BAY AREA CNSTR FRAMERS INC
1150 W Center St Ste 105, Manteca (95337-4313)
PHONE 925 454-8514
Fax: 925 454-0507
EMP: 175
SQ FT: 6,700
SALES (est): 14MM **Privately Held**
SIC: **1751** 1521

(P-3032)
BMC STOCK HOLDINGS INC
3333 Vaca Valley Pkwy, Vacaville (95688-9421)
PHONE 707 301-4475
EMP: 334
SALES (corp-wide): 1.5B **Publicly Held**
SIC: **1751** Carpentry work
PA: Bmc Stock Holdings, Inc.
980 Hammond Dr Ste 500
Atlanta GA 30328
678 222-1219

(P-3033)
BOB DILLON CONSTRUCTION INC
856 Calle Margarita, Thousand Oaks (91360-4852)
PHONE 805 495-2607
Bob Dillon, *President*
Tracy Dillon, *Admin Sec*
EMP: 150
SALES (est): 6.7MM **Privately Held**
SIC: **1751** Framing contractor

(P-3034)
C W CONSTRUCTION INC
8380 Maple Pl Ste 100, Rancho Cucamonga (91730-7664)
PHONE 909 989-9099
Fax: 909 989-5919
Wayne Carey, *President*
Ashley Young, *Administration*
EMP: 300
SQ FT: 1,150
SALES (est): 18.2MM **Privately Held**
SIC: **1751** Framing contractor

(P-3035)
CHATEAUX FRAMING INC
3701 Georgeann Pl, Ceres (95307-9317)
PHONE 209 537-6799
Steve Durossette, *President*
Derk Durossette, *Treasurer*
Jill Durossette, *Corp Secy*
William Durossette, *Vice Pres*
EMP: 150
SALES: 750K **Privately Held**
SIC: **1751** Framing contractor

(P-3036)
CLOSET WORLD INC
14438 Don Julian Rd, City of Industry (91746-3101)
PHONE 626 855-0846
EMP: 81
SALES (corp-wide): 105MM **Privately Held**
WEB: www.closetworld.net
SIC: **1751** **5211** Cabinet building & installation; closets, interiors & accessories
PA: Closet World, Inc.
3860 Capitol Ave
City Of Industry CA 90601
562 699-9945

(P-3037)
CLOVERLEAF CONSTRUCTION CO
16470 Vineyard Blvd, Morgan Hill (95037-5497)
P.O. Box 1818 (95038-1818)
PHONE 408 776-3122
Fax: 408 776-3130
Billy Absher, *President*
William Merriott, *Vice Pres*
Valerie Haverland, *CTO*
Dick Abernathy, *Purch Mgr*
Christie Persia, *Manager*
EMP: 300
SALES (est): 17.4MM **Privately Held**
WEB: www.cloverleaf-const.com
SIC: **1751** 1521 Framing contractor; single-family housing construction

(P-3038)
COMMERCIAL WOOD PRODUCTS CO
Also Called: Cwp
10019 Yucca Rd, Adelanto (92301-2242)
PHONE 760 246-4530
Fax: 760 246-8226
Craig B Roberts, *President*
Mark Kinnison, *Vice Pres*
EMP: 115 EST: 1946
SQ FT: 107,500
SALES (est): 12.2MM **Privately Held**
WEB: www.commercialwood.com
SIC: **1751** Cabinet building & installation

(P-3039)
COOK CABINETS INC
6428 Capitol Ave, Diamond Springs (95619-9393)
PHONE 530 621-0851
Fax: 530 621-1395
Richard Gularte, *President*
Steve Gularte, *Vice Pres*
Barbara Bell, *Office Mgr*
Steve Schurman, *Project Mgr*
EMP: 65
SQ FT: 35,000
SALES (est): 3.4MM **Privately Held**
SIC: **1751** 5712 5031 2434 Cabinet building & installation; cabinet work, custom; lumber, plywood & millwork; wood kitchen cabinets

(P-3040)
CWP CABINETS INC
10007 Yucca Rd, Adelanto (92301-2242)
PHONE 760 246-4530
Michael Rodriguez, *CEO*
EMP: 115 EST: 2011
SALES (est): 4.9MM **Privately Held**
SIC: **1751** 2434 2541 5712 Cabinet building & installation; wood kitchen cabinets; wood partitions & fixtures; cabinet work, custom

(P-3041)
D F RIOS CONSTRUCTION INC
45847 Warm Springs Blvd, Fremont (94539-6779)
PHONE 510 226-7467
Fax: 510 226-0919
David F Rios, *President*
EMP: 75
SQ FT: 4,000
SALES (est): 4.8MM **Privately Held**
SIC: **1751** Framing contractor

(P-3042)
DAVIS BROTHERS FRAMING INC
8780 Prestige Ct, Rancho Cucamonga (91730-5138)
PHONE 909 944-4899
Fax: 909 944-7952
Randy Davis, *President*
George E Davis, *CEO*
EMP: 200
SALES (est): 10.1MM **Privately Held**
SIC: **1751** Framing contractor

(P-3043)
DAVIS FRAMING INC
8103 Commercial St, La Mesa (91942-2927)
PHONE 619 463-2394
Steve Davis, *President*
EMP: 50
SQ FT: 1,200
SALES (est): 3.9MM **Privately Held**
SIC: **1751** Carpentry work

(P-3044)
DAY STAR FIXTURES
1802 Riverford Rd, Tustin (92780-3950)
PHONE 714 838-4613
Dan Prigmore, *Owner*
EMP: 50
SALES (est): 4MM **Privately Held**
SIC: **1751** Cabinet building & installation

(P-3045)
ELLISON FRAMING INC
Also Called: Ellison Construction-Framing
160 Guthrie Ln Ste 13, Brentwood (94513-4060)
P.O. Box 580 (94513-0580)
PHONE 925 516-9269
Matthew M Ellison, *President*
Ron Kapphahn, *Treasurer*
EMP: 125
SQ FT: 15,000
SALES (est): 9.5MM **Privately Held**
WEB: www.ellisonframing.com
SIC: **1751** Framing contractor

(P-3046)
EMPIRE LEASING INC
Also Called: Alliance Construction
2045 Placentia Ave Ste A, Costa Mesa (92627-6239)
PHONE 949 646-7400
Fax: 949 645-3461
EMP: 75
SALES (est): 3.1MM **Privately Held**
WEB: www.empireleasinginc.com
SIC: **1751** 1795

(P-3047)
EPPINK OF CALIFORNIA INC
11900 Center St, South Gate (90280-7834)
PHONE 562 633-1275
Fax: 562 633-0325
Erik Eppink, *CEO*
Michael Hunter, *Vice Pres*
Corinne Mendoza, *Controller*
▲ EMP: 50
SQ FT: 20,000
SALES (est): 5.2MM **Privately Held**
WEB: www.davisandwells.com
SIC: **1751** Carpentry work

(P-3048)
ERICKSON CONSTRUCTION LP
8350 Industrial Ave, Roseville (95678-6239)
PHONE 916 774-1100
Fax: 916 774-1117
Randall Folts, *President*
Anthony D'Attomo, *CFO*
Luanne Wiltz, *Controller*
EMP: 200
SALES (est): 10.2MM
SALES (corp-wide): 7.1B **Publicly Held**
SIC: **1751** Carpentry work
PA: Masco Corporation
21001 Van Born Rd
Taylor MI 48180
313 274-7400

(P-3049)
ERICKSON FRAMING AZ LLC
8350 Industrial Ave, Roseville (95678-6239)
PHONE 916 774-1100
EMP: 72
SALES (corp-wide): 12.4MM **Privately Held**
SIC: **1751** Framing contractor
PA: Erickson Framing Az Llc
250 N Beck Ave
Chandler AZ 85226
480 627-1100

(P-3050)
GE HOLDINGS INC
Also Called: Cabinet Supply
82545 Showcase Pkwy # 104, Indio (92203-9652)
PHONE 760 343-1299
Fax: 760 262-6486
Guy Evans, *President*
Malia Evans, *Corp Secy*
Mark Croudy, *Vice Pres*
Jana Corbeil, *Office Mgr*
EMP: 510
SQ FT: 40,000
SALES (est): 16.6MM
SALES (corp-wide): 1.6B **Publicly Held**
WEB: www.guyevans.com
SIC: **1751** 5031 Finish & trim carpentry; doors, molding, all materials
HQ: Topbuild Services Group Corp.
260 Jimmy Ann Dr
Daytona Beach FL 32114
386 304-2200

(P-3051)
GRANT CONSTRUCTION INC
7702 Meany Ave Ste 103, Bakersfield (93308-5199)
PHONE 661 588-4586
Grant Fraysier, *President*
Cezar Florin, *CFO*
Leanna Wagner, *Manager*
EMP: 230 EST: 1994
SQ FT: 1,000

1751 - Carpentry Work County (P-3052)

SALES: 31MM Privately Held
WEB: www.gciframing.com
SIC: 1751 1771 Framing contractor; concrete work

(P-3052)
HAKES SASH & DOOR INC
31945 Corydon St, Lake Elsinore (92530-8524)
PHONE.................................951 674-2414
Allen J Hakes, *President*
Christina Rupp, *Office Mgr*
April Robinson, *Manager*
Todd Rohlmeier, *Superintendent*
EMP: 190
SQ FT: 2,000
SALES (est): 23.2MM Privately Held
SIC: 1751 3442 5211 Window & door installation & erection; window & door frames; sash, wood or metal

(P-3053)
HANES & ASSOCIATES INC
43917 Division St, Lancaster (93535-4059)
PHONE.................................661 723-0779
Fax: 661 723-1734
Gregory F Hanes, *President*
Steven Wane, *Vice Pres*
Tammy Chavez, *Executive*
Steven Wayne, *Sales Executive*
Cheryl Archdale, *Accounts Mgr*
EMP: 50
SQ FT: 10,000
SALES (est): 4.9MM Privately Held
WEB: www.hanesandassociatesinc.com
SIC: 1751 1521 1542 1522 Framing contractor; general remodeling, single-family houses; commercial & office building contractors; apartment building construction; industrial buildings & warehouses

(P-3054)
HERITAGE INTERESTS LLC (PA)
4300 Jetway Ct, North Highlands (95660-5702)
P.O. Box 214609, Sacramento (95821-0609)
PHONE.................................916 481-5030
Fax: 916 481-7097
Edward Zuckerman, *President*
Dennis Gardemeyer, *CFO*
Charlie Gardemeyer, *Vice Pres*
EMP: 90
SQ FT: 80,000
SALES (est): 89.5MM Privately Held
SIC: 1751 5031 2431 Cabinet & finish carpentry; finish & trim carpentry; lumber, plywood & millwork; windows & window parts & trim, wood; louver windows, glass, wood frame

(P-3055)
HEWITT AND CANFIELD CNSTR INC
495 E Easy St Ste A, Simi Valley (93065-1845)
PHONE.................................805 522-4426
Ron Hewitt, *President*
Dale Canfield, *Admin Sec*
Liz Weigland, *Manager*
EMP: 80
SQ FT: 10,000
SALES: 13MM Privately Held
WEB: www.rondaleconstruction.com
SIC: 1751 Framing contractor

(P-3056)
JAG FRAMING INC
16741 Los Alimos St, Granada Hills (91344-5052)
PHONE.................................818 822-7110
Jose Antoio Guerra, *President*
EMP: 50 EST. 2008
SALES: 3.9MM Privately Held
SIC: 1751 Framing contractor

(P-3057)
JB FINISH INC
82750 Atlantic St, Indio (92203-9626)
P.O. Box 3093 (92202-3093)
PHONE.................................760 342-6300
Fax: 760 342-6213
John Broyles, *President*
EMP: 56
SQ FT: 12,500
SALES: 31MM Privately Held
WEB: www.gciframing.com
SIC: 1751 1771 Framing contractor; concrete work

(P-3058)
JENCOR DOOR AND TRIM INC
26845 Oak Ave Ste 12, Canyon Country (91351-6645)
PHONE.................................661 251-8161
Jeno Horvath, *President*
EMP: 50
SQ FT: 10,000
SALES (est): 2.8MM Privately Held
SIC: 1751 Finish & trim carpentry

(P-3059)
JOHN BIRDSELL CONSTRUCTION INC
Also Called: J B C
284 W Lester Ave, Clovis (93619-3788)
PHONE.................................559 834-6212
John Birdsell, *CEO*
EMP: 50
SQ FT: 5,000
SALES (est): 4MM Privately Held
WEB: www.jbirdsell.com
SIC: 1751 Finish & trim carpentry

(P-3060)
JONCE THOMAS CONSTRUCTION CO
3390 Seldon Ct, Fremont (94539-5625)
P.O. Box 1856 (94538-0034)
PHONE.................................510 657-7171
Fax: 510 659-9308
Donna Jean Thomas, *President*
Jonce Thomas, *Vice Pres*
Tammy Eliselm, *Agent*
EMP: 50
SQ FT: 10,000
SALES (est): 3.4MM Privately Held
SIC: 1751 Framing contractor

(P-3061)
KRC BUILDERS INCORPORATED
6141 W 4th St, Rio Linda (95673-4011)
PHONE.................................916 417-1200
Fax: 916 992-1579
Gene M Kindy, *CEO*
Jack E Ross, *Admin Sec*
EMP: 80
SALES (est): 3.6MM Privately Held
SIC: 1751 1521 Framing contractor; new construction, single-family houses

(P-3062)
LANE FRAMING SYSTEMS INC
1038 E Bastanchury Rd # 606, Fullerton (92835-2786)
PHONE.................................714 630-7686
Debbie Adams, *President*
EMP: 50
SALES (est): 2MM Privately Held
WEB: www.laneframing.com
SIC: 1751 Framing contractor

(P-3063)
LAURENCE-HOVENIER INC
179 N Maple St, Corona (92880-1760)
PHONE.................................951 736-2990
Fax: 951 736-0973
Ronald Laurence, *President*
Fred Hovenier, *Vice Pres*
Karen Diercksmeier, *Admin Asst*
Jason Laurence, *Safety Mgr*
Steve Waltenberg, *Opers Mgr*
EMP: 190
SQ FT: 6,000
SALES (est): 21.7MM Privately Held
WEB: www.framingcontractor.com
SIC: 1751 Framing contractor

(P-3064)
LEXINGTON SCENERY & PROPS INC
12800 Rangoon St, Arleta (91331-4321)
PHONE.................................818 768-5768
Richard Bencivengo, *CEO*
Frank Benchivengo, *President*
Andy Hanlen, *Vice Pres*
John Wright, *Principal*
Ron Kyhn, *Info Tech Dir*
EMP: 120

SALES (est): 4.9MM Privately Held
SIC: 1751 2542 3993 Finish & trim carpentry; partitions & fixtures, except wood; signs & advertising specialties

(P-3065)
LUCAS AND MERCIER CNSTR INC
29712 Ave De Las Bandera, Rcho STA Marg (92688-2606)
PHONE.................................949 589-4480
Fax: 949 589-8682
Frank E Mercier Jr, *President*
Thomas Lucas, *Treasurer*
Rick Mercier, *Vice Pres*
EMP: 250
SQ FT: 6,500
SALES (est): 6.3MM Privately Held
SIC: 1751 Framing contractor

(P-3066)
MCCARTHY FRAMING CONSTRUCTION
Also Called: McCarthy Construction
15133 Grevillea Ave, Lawndale (90260-2017)
PHONE.................................310 219-3038
Patrick McCarthy, *Owner*
▲ EMP: 100
SALES (est): 7.5MM Privately Held
SIC: 1751 Framing contractor

(P-3067)
NORCAL INC
Also Called: Seeley Brothers
1400 Moonstone, Brea (92821-2801)
PHONE.................................714 224-3949
Philip J Norys, *President*
Michelle Walthers, *Controller*
EMP: 105
SQ FT: 60,000
SALES (est): 4.5MM Privately Held
WEB: www.seeleybros.com
SIC: 1751 Finish & trim carpentry

(P-3068)
OLIVIERI ENTERPRISES LP
Also Called: Olympic Construction
210 Estates Dr Ste 200, Roseville (95678-2300)
P.O. Box 2490, Granite Bay (95746-2490)
PHONE.................................916 791-7857
Fax: 916 791-7852
John Olivieri, *Partner*
Teresa Olivieri, *Partner*
Tracy Bishop, *Manager*
EMP: 200
SQ FT: 2,300
SALES (est): 5.5MM Privately Held
SIC: 1751 Framing contractor

(P-3069)
ON TRAC OVERHEAD DOOR CO INC
1430 Richardson St, San Bernardino (92408-2962)
PHONE.................................909 799-8555
Fax: 909 799-8554
Charles L Colton, *CEO*
Chuck Colton, *President*
Lee Morrison, *CFO*
Terri Colton, *Vice Pres*
Trina Martinez, *Sales Executive*
EMP: 50
SQ FT: 16,600
SALES (est): 5.5MM Privately Held
WEB: www.ontracdoor.com
SIC: 1751 Garage door, installation or erection

(P-3070)
OVERHEAD DOOR CORPORATION
1617 N Orangethorpe Way, Anaheim (92801-1228)
PHONE.................................714 680-0600
Dave Fowler, *Vice Pres*
EMP: 93
SALES (corp-wide): 3.1B Privately Held
SIC: 1751 Garage door, installation or erection
HQ: Overhead Door Corporation
2501 S State Hwy 121 Ste Lewisville TX 75067
469 549-7100

(P-3071)
PRE CON INDUSTRIES INC
Also Called: Premier Drywall
725 Oak St, Santa Maria (93454-6215)
P.O. Box 5728 (93456-5728)
PHONE.................................805 345-3147
John Amburgey, *President*
James Amburgey, *Vice Pres*
Jose Rosas, *Vice Pres*
Anne Temple, *Administration*
Juan Sifuentes, *Project Mgr*
EMP: 85
SQ FT: 3,200
SALES (est): 16.2MM Privately Held
SIC: 1751 1742 Lightweight steel framing (metal stud) installation; drywall

(P-3072)
PRECISION FRAMING INC
1504 Eureka Rd Ste 160, Roseville (95661-3084)
PHONE.................................916 791-7464
Fax: 916 791-3655
William Peterson, *President*
Cindy Arico, *Manager*
EMP: 260
SQ FT: 1,100
SALES (est): 7.4MM Privately Held
SIC: 1751 Framing contractor

(P-3073)
PRIME TECH CABINETS INC
2652 White Rd, Irvine (92614-6248)
PHONE.................................714 558-4837
Fax: 714 250-4901
Hassan Farjamrad, *President*
Bobby Farjamrad, *Treasurer*
Zora Farjamrad, *Vice Pres*
Saeed Atef, *Sales Mgr*
Nina Vazin, *Sales Staff*
EMP: 110
SALES (est): 11.5MM Privately Held
WEB: www.ptcabinets.com
SIC: 1751 Cabinet & finish carpentry

(P-3074)
PRODUCTION FRAMING INC
2000 Opportunity Dr # 140, Roseville (95678-3020)
PHONE.................................916 978-2843
Fax: 916 978-2882
Doyle Headrick, *President*
EMP: 99
SALES (est): 2.8MM Privately Held
SIC: 1751 Carpentry work

(P-3075)
PRODUCTION FRAMING SYSTEMS INC (PA)
2000 Opportunity Dr # 140, Roseville (95678-3020)
PHONE.................................916 978-2888
Steve J Benjamin, *President*
Kerry Palmer, *Vice Pres*
Christie Robinson, *Controller*
Doyle Headrick, *Opers Mgr*
EMP: 150
SALES (est): 13.8MM Privately Held
WEB: www.productionframing.com
SIC: 1751 Framing contractor

(P-3076)
PROTEGE BUILDERS INC
4306 Pinell St, Sacramento (95838-2928)
PHONE.................................916 825-8478
Leah Rivera, *President*
Shelly Hinkle, *Corp Secy*
EMP: 50
SALES (est): 5.3MM Privately Held
WEB: www.protegebuilders.com
SIC: 1751 Framing contractor

(P-3077)
R D S UNLIMITED INC
14372 Olde Highway 80 E, El Cajon (92021-2865)
P.O. Box 21066
PHONE.................................619 443-0221
Fax: 619 443-0448
Ronnie Swaim, *President*
EMP: 50
SQ FT: 3,000
SALES: 3.5MM Privately Held
SIC: 1751 Framing contractor

PRODUCTS & SERVICES SECTION
1751 - Carpentry Work County (P-3103)

(P-3078)
R H FRAMING INCORPORATED
1000 Pajaro St Ste Bb, Salinas (93901-3061)
PHONE..................831 759-8860
Fax: 831 759-8861
Ryan Harrod, *President*
Megan Harrod, *Office Mgr*
EMP: 150
SALES: 5.9MM **Privately Held**
SIC: 1751 Framing contractor

(P-3079)
R T FRAMING CORPORATION
299 W Hillcrest Dr # 212, Thousand Oaks (91360-7838)
PHONE..................805 496-3985
Fax: 805 496-3984
Lorene Fuess, *President*
Raymond Fuess, *Vice Pres*
EMP: 100
SQ FT: 1,000
SALES (est): 5.7MM **Privately Held**
SIC: 1751 Framing contractor

(P-3080)
ROCKY COAST BUILDERS INC
135 Market Pl, Escondido (92029-1353)
PHONE..................760 489-7770
Douglas J Ladderbush, *CEO*
Cris Madsen, *Treasurer*
Amanda Kerins, *Admin Sec*
Heather Rice, *Administration*
EMP: 60
SQ FT: 6,200
SALES: 8.7MM **Privately Held**
SIC: 1751 Framing contractor

(P-3081)
ROY E WHITEHEAD INC
2245 Via Cerro, Riverside (92509-2412)
PHONE..................951 682-1490
Fax: 951 682-1565
David R Whitehead, *CEO*
Chris Bagley, *President*
Dennis W Whitehead, *Treasurer*
Daniel B Gilley, *Vice Pres*
Byron Mitchell, *Vice Pres*
EMP: 75
SQ FT: 36,000
SALES (est): 12.3MM **Privately Held**
WEB: www.royewhitehead.com
SIC: 1751 Cabinet building & installation

(P-3082)
RSI PROFESSIONAL CAB SOLUTIONS
11350 Riverside Dr Frnt, Mira Loma (91752-3703)
PHONE..................909 614-2900
Eric Vanderheyden, *President*
Larry Woodcock, *Executive*
Karen Alcala, *Info Tech Dir*
Alfredo Castro, *Engineer*
Audra Greenberg, *Credit Mgr*
EMP: 250
SALES (est): 29.1MM
SALES (corp-wide): 962.2MM **Privately Held**
SIC: 1751 Cabinet & finish carpentry
PA: Rsi Home Products, Inc.
400 E Orangethorpe Ave
Anaheim CA 92801
714 449-2200

(P-3083)
S I J INC
26035 Jefferson Ave, Murrieta (92562-6983)
PHONE..................951 304-9444
Briana Sather-Layfield, *President*
Joseph Sather, *Treasurer*
Patricia Sather, *Admin Sec*
EMP: 50
SALES: 5.5MM **Privately Held**
WEB: www.sicorp.us
SIC: 1751 Carpentry work

(P-3084)
S W CONSTRUCTION INC
Also Called: Wilson Stephen Construction Co
1145 E Stanford Ct, Anaheim (92805-6822)
PHONE..................714 978-7871
Fax: 714 978-3675
Stephen L Wilson, *President*
EMP: 120
SQ FT: 7,500
SALES (est): 8.6MM **Privately Held**
SIC: 1751 Framing contractor

(P-3085)
SAN-MAR CONSTRUCTION CO INC
4875 E La Palma Ave # 601, Anaheim (92807-1955)
PHONE..................714 693-5400
Fax: 714 693-5401
Sandra Drew, *CEO*
Tamara Kennedy, *Controller*
Sue Moran, *Associate*
EMP: 200
SQ FT: 3,000
SALES (est): 22.9MM **Privately Held**
SIC: 1751 Carpentry work

(P-3086)
SANTA CLARITA VALLEY BLDRS INC
Also Called: Main Frame Construction
24307 Magic Mountain Pkwy # 122, Santa Clarita (91355-3402)
PHONE..................661 295-6722
Fax: 661 799-2601
Mike Spigno, *President*
Cheryl A Spigno, *Shareholder*
EMP: 225
SALES (est): 11MM **Privately Held**
SIC: 1751 7389 Framing contractor; interior design services

(P-3087)
SEELEY BROTHERS
1400 Moonstone, Brea (92821-2801)
PHONE..................714 224-3949
Michael Seeley, *Partner*
Joe Calvillo, *Partner*
Phil Norys, *Partner*
EMP: 175
SQ FT: 62,000
SALES (est): 22.9MM **Privately Held**
SIC: 1751 Finish & trim carpentry

(P-3088)
SHOOK & WALLER CNSTR INC
7677 Bell Rd Ste 101, Windsor (95492-7432)
PHONE..................707 578-3933
Fax: 707 578-4820
Eddie Waller, *President*
Shawn Dolan, *CFO*
Steven Shook, *Corp Secy*
Carla Waller, *Property Mgr*
Candy Wickton, *Manager*
EMP: 350
SQ FT: 8,000
SALES (est): 29.5MM **Privately Held**
WEB: www.shookandwaller.com
SIC: 1751 1521 1542 Framing contractor; new construction, single-family houses; nonresidential construction

(P-3089)
SI INC
Also Called: Sather Installation
26035 Jefferson Ave, Murrieta (92562-6983)
PHONE..................951 304-9444
EMP: 50
SQ FT: 8,000
SALES (est): 4.7MM **Privately Held**
WEB: www.sicorp.us
SIC: 1751

(P-3090)
SIERRA LUMBER CO
Also Called: Sierra Lumber & Decking
1711 Senter Rd, San Jose (95112-2598)
PHONE..................408 286-7071
Fax: 408 279-0108
Roger Burch, *President*
James Moblad, *Vice Pres*
EMP: 125
SQ FT: 22,000
SALES (est): 8.6MM
SALES (corp-wide): 211.3MM **Privately Held**
WEB: www.sierrafence.com
SIC: 1751 5211 Carpentry work; lumber products
PA: Pacific States Industries, Incorporated
10 Madrone Ave
Morgan Hill CA 95037
408 779-7354

(P-3091)
SIERRA WEST CONSTRUCTION INC
24744 Connie Ct, Auburn (95602-8525)
PHONE..................530 268-7614
Richard T Ahrens, *President*
Melinda Ahrens, *Corp Secy*
Terry Lislie, *Manager*
EMP: 50
SALES (est): 4.5MM **Privately Held**
SIC: 1751 Framing contractor

(P-3092)
SILVER STRAND
8945 Fullbright Ave, Chatsworth (91311-6124)
PHONE..................818 701-9707
David Meador, *CEO*
EMP: 50
SQ FT: 7,500
SALES (est): 5.6MM **Privately Held**
WEB: www.silverstrandinc.com
SIC: 1751 Cabinet & finish carpentry

(P-3093)
SR FREEMAN INC
89 Dillon Ave Ste A, Campbell (95008-3067)
PHONE..................408 364-2200
Fax: 408 364-2100
Shone Freeman, *President*
Michael Lewis, *Vice Pres*
Josie Freeman, *Admin Sec*
Shayne Freeman, *Manager*
EMP: 60 **EST:** 1992
SALES (est): 12.3MM **Privately Held**
WEB: www.srfreemaninc.com
SIC: 1751 Framing contractor

(P-3094)
STOCKHAM CONSTRUCTION INC
475 Portal St Ste F, Cotati (94931-3006)
PHONE..................707 664-0945
Boyd L Stockham, *President*
Dani Stockham, *Treasurer*
Shani Cavazos, *Executive*
EMP: 120
SQ FT: 12,000
SALES (est): 17.1MM **Privately Held**
WEB: www.stockhamconstruction.com
SIC: 1751 1742 Lightweight steel framing (metal stud) installation; drywall; acoustical & ceiling work

(P-3095)
SUNDANCE CONSTRUCTION INC
3500 W Lake Center Dr B, Santa Ana (92704-6900)
PHONE..................714 437-0802
Fax: 714 546-7464
Tim Boggess, *President*
Ernie Castro Sr, *CEO*
Mario Munoz, *Vice Pres*
EMP: 200
SALES (est): 7MM **Privately Held**
WEB: www.woodsgrouparch.com
SIC: 1751 Framing contractor

(P-3096)
SURECRAFT SUPPLY INC
2875 Executive Pl, Escondido (92029-1524)
PHONE..................760 737-2120
Fax: 760 737-2125
Richard J Smerud, *President*
Scott Smerud, *CEO*
Paul Smarud, *Vice Pres*
Randy Stoddard, *Vice Pres*
EMP: 145
SQ FT: 33,000
SALES (est): 14.4MM **Privately Held**
SIC: 1751 Carpentry work

(P-3097)
TRUFORM CONSTRUCTION CORP
1041 N Shepard St, Anaheim (92806-2817)
PHONE..................714 630-7447
Dan Ruppe, *President*
EMP: 50
SQ FT: 1,400
SALES (est): 3.9MM **Privately Held**
SIC: 1751 1742 Lightweight steel framing (metal stud) installation; drywall

(P-3098)
TWR ENTERPRISES INC
1661 Railroad St, Corona (92880-2503)
PHONE..................951 279-2000
Fax: 951 279-2799
Thomas W Rhodes, *President*
Deborah Dieter, *Finance*
Debbie Diter, *Controller*
Amy Strommer, *Human Res Dir*
Yesenia Salazar, *Human Res Mgr*
EMP: 200
SQ FT: 20,000
SALES (est): 19.9MM **Privately Held**
SIC: 1751 Framing contractor

(P-3099)
ULTIMATE CONSTRUCTION INC
8811 Alonzo Blvd, Long Beach (90805)
P.O. Box 571117, Tarzana (91357-1117)
PHONE..................562 633-3389
Enrique Vera, *President*
Gloria Vera, *CFO*
EMP: 112
SQ FT: 10,000
SALES (est): 7MM **Privately Held**
SIC: 1751 1522 1541 1521 Carpentry work; residential construction; industrial buildings, new construction; new construction, single-family houses

(P-3100)
WALTERS & WOLF INTERIORS (PA)
41450 Boscell Rd, Fremont (94538-3103)
PHONE..................415 243-9400
Randall Alan Wolf, *CEO*
Michael Wolf, *President*
Jeff Belzer, *CFO*
Annetta Calhoun, *Manager*
Daniel Kaupie, *Manager*
▲ **EMP:** 80
SQ FT: 30,000
SALES (est): 13MM **Privately Held**
SIC: 1751 Carpentry work

(P-3101)
WESLAR INC
28310 Constellation Rd, Valencia (91355-5078)
PHONE..................661 702-1362
Fax: 661 702-1366
Larry Kern, *President*
Wes Toy, *Vice Pres*
EMP: 100
SQ FT: 5,500
SALES (est): 10.1MM **Privately Held**
WEB: www.weslarinc.com
SIC: 1751 Framing contractor

(P-3102)
WIN-DOR INC (PA)
450 Delta Ave, Brea (92821-2935)
PHONE..................714 576-2030
Gary Templin, *CEO*
Wolfgang Wirthgen, *President*
Phil Wirthgen, *Sales Mgr*
Dave May, *Marketing Staff*
Paula Hillebrechc, *Manager*
EMP: 170
SQ FT: 73,000
SALES (est): 20.9MM **Privately Held**
WEB: www.win-dor.com
SIC: 1751 3446 Window & door (prefabricated) installation; guards, made from pipe

(P-3103)
WINDOW FACTORY INC
Also Called: Factory Remodeling
7550 Miramar Rd Ste 220, San Diego (92126-4217)
PHONE..................858 689-9737

1751 - Carpentry Work County (P-3104)

PRODUCTS & SERVICES SECTION

Toll Free:..................................877 -
Fax: 858 689-0804
Dan Dean, *President*
John Jedynak, *Vice Pres*
Mark Wilson, *Vice Pres*
Elena Romero, *Executive*
EMP: 50
SQ FT: 37,000
SALES (est): 4.9MM **Privately Held**
SIC: 1751 Window & door (prefabricated) installation

(P-3104)
X-ACT FINISH & TRIM INC
248 Glider Cir, Corona (92880-2533)
PHONE...........................951 582-9229
Fax: 951 582-9228
Jessie A Moreno, *President*
Maria Loaisiga, *Administration*
EMP: 60
SALES (est): 8.3MM **Privately Held**
SIC: 1751 Finish & trim carpentry

1752 Floor Laying & Other Floor Work, NEC

(P-3105)
ANTHONY TREVINO
Also Called: A&S Floors
938 Adams St Ste A, Benicia (94510-2948)
PHONE...........................707 747-4776
Fax: 707 746-7757
Anthony Trevino, *Owner*
EMP: 52 **EST:** 1993
SALES (est): 3.7MM **Privately Held**
SIC: 1752 Floor laying & floor work

(P-3106)
B T MANCINI CO INC (PA)
Also Called: B.T. Mancini Company
876 S Milpitas Blvd, Milpitas (95035-6311)
P.O. Box 361930 (95036-1930)
PHONE...........................408 942-7900
Brooks T Mancini Jr, *President*
Brooks T Mancini Sr, *Vice Pres*
Tom McGovern, *Vice Pres*
Sheila Rhoads, *Vice Pres*
David B Roddick, *Vice Pres*
▲ **EMP:** 100
SQ FT: 36,000
SALES (est): 69.1MM **Privately Held**
WEB: www.btmancini.com
SIC: 1752 1761 Floor laying & floor work; roofing, siding & sheet metal work; siding contractor

(P-3107)
BIG OAK HARDWOOD FLOOR CO INC
1731 Leslie St, San Mateo (94402-2409)
PHONE...........................650 591-8651
Richard Mack, *President*
Robert Connor, *Treasurer*
Diana Rogers, *Manager*
EMP: 58
SQ FT: 7,500
SALES (est): 4.4MM **Privately Held**
SIC: 1752 Floor laying & floor work

(P-3108)
CAPITAL COMMERCIAL FLRG INC
3709 Bradview Dr Ste 100, Sacramento (95827-9737)
PHONE...........................916 569-1960
Fax: 916 569-1970
Douglas Lawson, *CEO*
Scott Fairley, *CFO*
Diana Lawson, *Admin Sec*
Carlos Cabera, *Data Proc Exec*
Justin Bailey, *Project Mgr*
EMP: 50
SQ FT: 14,000
SALES: 6.9MM **Privately Held**
WEB: www.ccfinc.net
SIC: 1752 Floor laying & floor work

(P-3109)
CREATIVE DESIGN INTERIORS INC (PA)
Also Called: C D I
737 Del Paso Rd, Sacramento (95834-1106)
PHONE...........................916 641-1121
Ronald Lapp, *President*
Kathy Lapp, *Vice Pres*
EMP: 100
SQ FT: 10,000
SALES (est): 36.4MM **Privately Held**
SIC: 1752 Ceramic floor tile installation

(P-3110)
DAVENPORT DEVELOPMENT CORP
Also Called: Classic Hardwood Floors
5160 Mercury Pt Ste D, San Diego (92111-1225)
PHONE...........................858 300-3333
Fax: 858 300-3334
Marc Davenport, *President*
Lisa Davenport, *Admin Sec*
▲ **EMP:** 50
SALES (est): 5.5MM **Privately Held**
SIC: 1752 Wood floor installation & refinishing

(P-3111)
DFS FLOORING INC (PA)
15651 Saticoy St, Van Nuys (91406-3234)
PHONE...........................818 374-5200
Fax: 818 779-1504
Richard Friedman, *CEO*
Greg Keyes, *Vice Pres*
Bel Bitok, *Admin Asst*
Brenda Palomares, *Project Mgr*
Lyle Pedersen, *Project Mgr*
EMP: 65
SQ FT: 19,865
SALES (est): 31.4MM **Privately Held**
WEB: www.dfsflooring.com
SIC: 1752 Floor laying & floor work

(P-3112)
DT FLOORMASTERS INC
Also Called: Floormasters, The
31164 Huntwood Ave, Hayward (94544-7817)
PHONE...........................510 476-1000
Teresa Lau, *CEO*
Don Lau, *General Mgr*
Shanelle Lorenzo, *Accounting Mgr*
Brian Higgins, *VP Opers*
Danny Cruz, *Opers Mgr*
EMP: 70
SQ FT: 1,000
SALES (est): 17.6MM **Privately Held**
SIC: 1752 Floor laying & floor work

(P-3113)
ENVIRON HARDWOOD FLOORS
2827 Mariposa St, San Francisco (94110-1307)
PHONE...........................415 487-0200
Fax: 415 487-0137
Leah Smith, *Principal*
Steve Allenson, *Owner*
EMP: 90 **EST:** 1986
SQ FT: 3,000
SALES: 4MM **Privately Held**
SIC: 1752 Floor laying & floor work

(P-3114)
FLOORGATE INC
3350 N San Fernando Rd, Los Angeles (90065-1417)
PHONE...........................323 478-2000
Al Hembarsoonian, *President*
EMP: 55
SQ FT: 27,400
SALES: 3.2MM **Privately Held**
SIC: 1752 5713 Floor laying & floor work; floor covering stores

(P-3115)
H V WELKER CO INC
Also Called: Welker Bros
970 S Milpitas Blvd, Milpitas (95035-6323)
PHONE...........................408 263-4400
Fax: 408 263-6813
Stuart Welker, *President*
Chuck Gulan, *Shareholder*
Stuart H Welker, *President*
Jack Sanguinitti, *Exec VP*
Vincent A Grana, *Vice Pres*
EMP: 65
SQ FT: 18,375
SALES (est): 33.8MM **Privately Held**
WEB: www.welkers.com
SIC: 1752 Floor laying & floor work

(P-3116)
HOEM & ASSOCIATES INC
951 Linden Ave, South San Francisco (94080-1753)
PHONE...........................650 871-5194
Fax: 650 875-1048
Sean Hogan, *President*
Russ Hoem, *CFO*
Mike Valerio, *Vice Pres*
Al Dalessio, *Executive*
Gabriel Guzman, *Opers Mgr*
EMP: 55
SQ FT: 24,000
SALES (est): 14.9MM **Privately Held**
WEB: www.hoemschurba.com
SIC: 1752 Carpet laying; vinyl floor tile & sheet installation; wood floor installation & refinishing

(P-3117)
HOME CARPET INVESTMENT INC (PA)
Also Called: Americas Finest Carpet Co
730 Design Ct Ste 401, Chula Vista (91911-6160)
PHONE...........................619 262-8040
Fax: 619 827-7213
Carlos Ledesma, *CEO*
Veriónca Mendova, *Office Mgr*
Veronica Mendoza, *Plant Mgr*
Justin Baker, *Sales Associate*
Mary Geerdes, *Agent*
EMP: 81
SQ FT: 2,500
SALES (est): 23.1MM **Privately Held**
WEB: www.americasfinestcarpet.com
SIC: 1752 7217 Carpet laying; carpet & upholstery cleaning; carpet & upholstery cleaning on customer premises; carpet & upholstery cleaning plants

(P-3118)
HY-TECH TILE INC
1355 Palmyrita Ave, Riverside (92507-1601)
P.O. Box 5577 (92517-5577)
PHONE...........................951 788-0550
Fax: 951 788-0551
Michael Postolache, *CEO*
Tom Shoemaker, *President*
Narcis Postolache, *CEO*
Cristina Olteanu, *CFO*
EMP: 110
SQ FT: 12,000
SALES (est): 16.3MM **Privately Held**
WEB: www.hytechtile.com
SIC: 1752 5211 Ceramic floor tile installation; tile, ceramic

(P-3119)
ICS PROFESSIONAL SERVICES INC
7755 Center Ave Fl 11, Huntington Beach (92647-3007)
PHONE...........................714 868-3900
Jessie Croteau, *CEO*
Vance Cook, *Vice Pres*
▲ **EMP:** 123
SALES (est): 7.7MM **Privately Held**
SIC: 1752 Floor laying & floor work

(P-3120)
INTERIOR SPECIALISTS INC (HQ)
1630 Faraday Ave, Carlsbad (92008-7313)
PHONE...........................760 929-6700
Fax: 951 600-1425
Alan Davenport, *President*
Brian Reed, *President*
Lee Singer, *President*
Joe Terrana, *President*
Tom Tidmore, *President*
▲ **EMP:** 75
SALES (est): 371.4MM **Privately Held**
WEB: www.isidc.com
SIC: 1752 1799 Carpet laying; drapery track installation

(P-3121)
INTERIOR SPECIALISTS INC
9300 Hubbard Rd, Auburn (95602-7819)
PHONE...........................530 885-0632
Doug Ederer, *Owner*
EMP: 70
SALES (corp-wide): 371.4MM **Privately Held**
SIC: 1752 Floor laying & floor work
HQ: Interior Specialists, Inc.
1630 Faraday Ave
Carlsbad CA 92008
760 929-6700

(P-3122)
J W FLOOR COVERING INC (PA)
9881 Carroll Centre Rd, San Diego (92126-4554)
PHONE...........................858 536-8565
Fax: 858 530-1670
John S Wallace, *President*
Ashlee Grubaugh, *Opers Staff*
Alan Biswick, *Sales Executive*
Doug Barnett, *Education*
Dean Bednar, *Director*
EMP: 140
SQ FT: 20,500
SALES (est): 49MM **Privately Held**
WEB: www.jwfloors.com
SIC: 1752 Floor laying & floor work

(P-3123)
JJJ FLOOR COVERING INC (PA)
4831 Passons Blvd Ste A, Pico Rivera (90660-2173)
PHONE...........................562 692-9008
Fax: 562 692-5979
Rick Barba, *President*
Maria Gutierrez, *CEO*
Joseph P Miano, *COO*
John Kells, *Project Mgr*
Yolanda Excobar, *Persnl Mgr*
▲ **EMP:** 52
SQ FT: 13,000
SALES (est): 10.7MM **Privately Held**
WEB: www.jjjfloorcovering.com
SIC: 1752 5023 Carpet laying; resilient floor laying; carpets; resilient floor coverings: tile or sheet

(P-3124)
KYA SERVICES LLC
1522 Brookhollow Dr Ste 3, Santa Ana (92705-5412)
PHONE...........................714 659-6476
John Leyds,
Ericka Licon, *Administration*
Derrick B Mendoza,
EMP: 50
SALES (est): 448K **Privately Held**
SIC: 1752 Floor laying & floor work; carpet laying; resilient floor laying

(P-3125)
MAGNESITE SPECIALTIES INC
Also Called: American Deck Systems
8686 Production Ave Ste A, San Diego (92121-2207)
PHONE...........................858 578-4186
Fax: 858 578-0293
Curtis Tyree, *President*
Dwain Stratton, *Shareholder*
Vikki J Tyree, *Corp Secy*
EMP: 50
SQ FT: 2,500
SALES (est): 7.5MM **Privately Held**
WEB: www.magnesitespecialties.com
SIC: 1752 1521 1799 1743 Floor laying & floor work; patio & deck construction & repair; waterproofing; terrazzo, tile, marble, mosaic work

(P-3126)
NATIONAL APARTMENT FLOORING
3205 Ocean Park Blvd # 180, Santa Monica (90405-3233)
PHONE...........................800 773-6904
Richard Berle, *President*
Jackie Lemus, *Director*
EMP: 75
SALES (est): 12.5MM **Privately Held**
SIC: 1752 Access flooring system installation

▲ = Import ▼ =Export
◆ =Import/Export

PRODUCTS & SERVICES SECTION
1761 - Roofing, Siding & Sheet Metal Work County (P-3149)

(P-3127)
NATIONAL CITY FLOOR COVERING
132 W 8th St, National City (91950-1130)
PHONE.................619 477-7000
Chris Hadley, *Manager*
Phyllis Cutler, *President*
Bob Wood, *Vice Pres*
Allan Ziman, *Vice Pres*
Carlos Lopez, *Admin Asst*
EMP: 60
SALES (est): 3.2MM **Privately Held**
SIC: 1752 Floor laying & floor work

(P-3128)
PROGRESSIVE FLOOR COVERING INC
924 S Highland Ave, Fullerton (92832-2903)
PHONE.................714 213-8805
Rita Spinella, *President*
Oanh Pham, *CFO*
Kevin Deehan, *Vice Pres*
Tommy Zivitz, *General Mgr*
Loren Gladstone, *Manager*
EMP: 50
SQ FT: 17,500
SALES: 9.2MM **Privately Held**
WEB: www.progressivefloorcovering.com
SIC: 1752 Floor laying & floor work

(P-3129)
R E CUDDIE CO
1751 Junction Ave, San Jose (95112-1029)
PHONE.................408 998-1250
Fax: 408 998-5040
Thomas Cuddie, *CEO*
Robert Cuddie, *Vice Pres*
Tish Allen, *Admin Sec*
Joanne Brock, *Manager*
EMP: 50
SQ FT: 30,000
SALES (est): 8.9MM **Privately Held**
WEB: www.recuddie.com
SIC: 1752 Floor laying & floor work

(P-3130)
SIGNATURE FLOORING INC
Also Called: Signature Floors
701 N Hariton St, Orange (92868-1313)
PHONE.................714 558-9200
Jeffery Grimsley, *President*
Margaret Anderson, *COO*
Daniel Salazar, *Treasurer*
Michael Gray, *Vice Pres*
Blake Grimsley, *Manager*
EMP: 65
SALES: 14.5MM **Privately Held**
WEB: www.floorsbysignature.com
SIC: 1752 Floor laying & floor work

(P-3131)
SIMAS FLOOR CO INC (PA)
Also Called: Simas Floor Co Design Center
3550 Power Inn Rd, Sacramento (95826-3892)
PHONE.................916 452-4933
Fax: 916 454-2916
Ken Simas, *President*
Mark Simas, *Sr Corp Ofcr*
David G Simas, *Vice Pres*
John U Simas, *Vice Pres*
Chris Simas, *Comms Mgr*
EMP: 180
SQ FT: 10,000
SALES (est): 38.8MM **Privately Held**
SIC: 1752 5713 Floor laying & floor work; floor covering stores

(P-3132)
VINTAGE DESIGN INC (PA)
5 Whatney, Irvine (92618-2806)
PHONE.................714 974-4822
Fax: 714 283-1317
Timothy Patrick Buckley, *CEO*
Keith Buckley, *President*
Matt Munson, *CFO*
Terry Russell, *Vice Pres*
Jennifer Buckley, *Admin Sec*
EMP: 60
SQ FT: 16,000
SALES (est): 33.4MM **Privately Held**
WEB: www.vintagedesigninc.com
SIC: 1752 Carpet laying; vinyl floor tile & sheet installation; asphalt tile installation

(P-3133)
WIRTZ TILE & STONE INC
7932 Armour St, San Diego (92111-3718)
PHONE.................858 569-3816
Fax: 858 569-3821
John David Wirtz, *President*
Ida F Wirtz, *Vice Pres*
Kim Dennis, *Manager*
EMP: 86 **EST:** 1974
SQ FT: 4,600
SALES (est): 7.7MM **Privately Held**
WEB: www.wirtztile.com
SIC: 1752 Floor laying & floor work; ceramic floor tile installation

1761 Roofing, Siding & Sheet Metal Work

(P-3134)
16 3 INC
Also Called: ARC of Southern California
529 Front St, El Cajon (92020-4231)
PHONE.................619 588-2000
John Ogle, *President*
Carolyn Ogle, *Vice Pres*
EMP: 55
SQ FT: 4,400
SALES: 4.3MM **Privately Held**
SIC: 1761 Roofing contractor

(P-3135)
4 SEASONS ROOFING
11 Commerce Ct Ste 1, Chico (95928-7133)
PHONE.................530 865-4998
Fax: 530 895-9201
Terry Taylor, *President*
EMP: 73
SALES (est): 4.5MM **Privately Held**
SIC: 1761 Roofing contractor

(P-3136)
ACETECK ROOFING CO INC
5830 Woodlawn Ave, Los Angeles (90003-1226)
PHONE.................323 231-6060
Jay Kim, *President*
Song Kim, *Treasurer*
EMP: 50
SALES (est): 5MM **Privately Held**
WEB: www.acetekroofing.com
SIC: 1761 Roofing contractor

(P-3137)
AEP SPAN INC
2110 Enterprise Blvd, West Sacramento (95691-3428)
PHONE.................916 372-0933
Al Price, *Manager*
Daine Whatley, *Human Resources*
EMP: 85
SQ FT: 16,000
SALES: 3.6MM
SALES (corp-wide): 6.7B **Privately Held**
WEB: www.ascpacific.com
SIC: 1761 3448 3444 3443 Roofing contractor; prefabricated metal buildings; sheet metalwork; fabricated plate work (boiler shop)
HQ: Asc Profiles Llc
2110 Enterprise Blvd
West Sacramento CA 95691
916 372-6851

(P-3138)
ALL FAB PRCSION SHEETMETAL INC
1015 Timothy Dr, San Jose (95133-1050)
PHONE.................408 279-1099
Fax: 408 297-3803
Son P Ho, *CEO*
Kelly T Ho, *CFO*
Bernard Miller, *Info Tech Dir*
▲ **EMP:** 100
SQ FT: 58,000
SALES (est): 19.6MM **Privately Held**
SIC: 1761 3444 Sheet metalwork; sheet metalwork

(P-3139)
ALLIANCE ROOFING COMPANY INC (PA)
630 Martin Ave, Santa Clara (95050-2914)
PHONE.................800 579-2595
Fax: 408 261-2657
Roderick Miller, *CEO*
Donna Miller, *Admin Sec*
Michael Archer, *Project Mgr*
Luis Gutierrez, *Opers Mgr*
Josh Barthel, *Manager*
EMP: 50
SQ FT: 2,800
SALES (est): 38.1MM **Privately Held**
WEB: www.allianceroofingcal.com
SIC: 1761 1799 Roofing contractor; roof repair; waterproofing

(P-3140)
AZTEC SHEET METAL INC
11222 Woodside Ave N, Santee (92071-4716)
PHONE.................619 937-0005
Fax: 619 448-0179
Dick Buxton, *President*
Tom Buxton, *CFO*
Larry Hendry, *Admin Sec*
Gilbert B Buxton, *Agent*
EMP: 60
SALES (est): 4.1MM **Privately Held**
WEB: www.ltdsheetmetal.com
SIC: 1761 Architectural sheet metal work

(P-3141)
BEST CONTRACTING SERVICES INC
4301 Bettencourt Way, Union City (94587-1519)
PHONE.................510 886-7240
Mohmmad Beigi, *Branch Mgr*
EMP: 75
SALES (corp-wide): 80MM **Privately Held**
SIC: 1761 Roofing contractor
PA: Best Contracting Services, Inc.
19027 S Hamilton Ave
Gardena CA 90248
310 328-6969

(P-3142)
BEST CONTRACTING SERVICES INC (PA)
19027 S Hamilton Ave, Gardena (90248-4408)
PHONE.................310 328-6969
Modjtaba Tabazadeh, *President*
Sean Tabazadeh, *CEO*
Fatemeh Tabazadeh, *Treasurer*
Penni Barnes, *General Mgr*
Sean Taba, *General Mgr*
▲ **EMP:** 400
SQ FT: 57,000
SALES (est): 80MM **Privately Held**
WEB: www.bestcontracting.com
SIC: 1761 Roofing contractor

(P-3143)
BEVEN-HERRON INC
14511 Industry Cir, La Mirada (90638-5865)
P.O. Box 848 (90637-0848)
PHONE.................714 523-5870
Fax: 714 523-5627
J D Herron, *President*
Joseph A Herron, *Chairman*
Rollin Herron, *Vice Pres*
EMP: 120 **EST:** 1959
SQ FT: 26,000
SALES (est): 11.8MM **Privately Held**
WEB: www.bevenherron.com
SIC: 1761 Roofing contractor

(P-3144)
BIGHAM TAYLOR ROOFING CORP
22721 Alice St, Hayward (94541-6401)
PHONE.................510 886-0197
Fax: 510 886-4347
Stephen E Bigham, *CEO*
Laura Jo Bigham, *Corp Secy*
Don Taylor, *Vice Pres*
Bryce Davey, *Project Mgr*
Darby Lampi, *Controller*
EMP: 70 **EST:** 1977
SQ FT: 10,000
SALES (est): 12.4MM **Privately Held**
WEB: www.btroof.com
SIC: 1761 Roofing contractor

(P-3145)
BYERS ENTERPRISES INC
Also Called: Byers Leafguard Gutter Systems
11773 Slow Poke Ln, Grass Valley (95945-8417)
PHONE.................530 272-7777
Fax: 530 272-6957
Raymond W Byers Sr, *CEO*
Danny Accernan, *Cust Mgr*
EMP: 69
SQ FT: 2,400
SALES (est): 8MM **Privately Held**
WEB: www.byersleafguard.com
SIC: 1761 Sheet metalwork

(P-3146)
CANNON FABRICATION INC
Also Called: Canfab
182 Granite St Ste 101, Corona (92879-1288)
PHONE.................951 278-1830
Fax: 909 278-8444
Donald J Prosser, *CEO*
Mary D Prosser, *President*
William Prosser Jr, *Vice Pres*
Scott Bailey, *Engineer*
EMP: 61
SQ FT: 43,000
SALES (est): 10.3MM **Privately Held**
WEB: www.canfab.com
SIC: 1761 Sheet metalwork

(P-3147)
CARMEL ARCHITECTURAL SALES
2300 E Katella Ave # 370, Anaheim (92806-6048)
PHONE.................714 630-7221
Fax: 714 630-0668
David Traino, *CEO*
Quentin Edwards, *CFO*
James M Henry, *Vice Pres*
Patricia Dalton, *Admin Sec*
Bryan Boyce, *CTO*
▲ **EMP:** 60
SQ FT: 10,500
SALES (est): 6.8MM **Privately Held**
WEB: www.carmelsales.com
SIC: 1761 Skylight installation; architectural sheet metal work

(P-3148)
CENTIMARK CORPORATION
Also Called: Centimark Roofing Systems
2380 W Winton Ave, Hayward (94545-1102)
PHONE.................510 614-1140
Anthony Zahteila, *President*
Pete Cannizzaro, *Project Mgr*
EMP: 108
SALES (corp-wide): 605.3MM **Privately Held**
WEB: www.centimark.com
SIC: 1761 1752 6331 Roofing contractor; floor laying & floor work; resilient floor laying; fire, marine & casualty insurance; automobile insurance; workers' compensation insurance
PA: Centimark Corporation
12 Grandview Cir
Canonsburg PA 15317
724 743-7777

(P-3149)
CHALLENGER SHEET METAL INC
9353 Abraham Way Ste A, Santee (92071-5641)
PHONE.................619 596-8040
Fax: 858 233-7816
Joel Quinonez, *CEO*
William Ehmcke, *President*
Robert Basso, *CFO*
Helen G Ehmcke, *Admin Sec*
Chris Salinas, *Manager*
▲ **EMP:** 80
SQ FT: 10,000
SALES (est): 17MM **Privately Held**
WEB: www.challengersm.com
SIC: 1761 Sheet metalwork

1761 - Roofing, Siding & Sheet Metal Work County (P-3150)

PRODUCTS & SERVICES SECTION

(P-3150)
CITADEL ROOFING & SOLAR
4980 Allison Pkwy, Vacaville (95688-9346)
PHONE 707 446-5500
Dieter Folk, *CEO*
EMP: 150
SALES (est): 56.6K **Privately Held**
SIC: 1761 Roofing contractor

(P-3151)
CLAUD TOWNSLEY INC
Also Called: Central Roofing Company
555 W 182nd St, Gardena (90248-3400)
PHONE 310 527-6770
William E Knapp, *President*
Jonathan Townsley, *CEO*
Janet Townsley, *Exec VP*
Marcia Kumashita, *Controller*
EMP: 60
SQ FT: 12,000
SALES (est): 7.7MM **Privately Held**
WEB: www.centralroof.com
SIC: 1761 Roofing contractor

(P-3152)
CMF INC
Also Called: Custom Metal Fabricators
1317 W Grove Ave, Orange (92865-4137)
PHONE 714 637-2409
Fax: 714 637-4017
David Duclett, *CEO*
Vic Maynez, *President*
Darren Sagert, *CFO*
Mark Allen, *Vice Pres*
Jason Antone, *Project Mgr*
EMP: 100
SQ FT: 11,000
SALES: 20.5MM **Privately Held**
SIC: 1761 Siding contractor

(P-3153)
COMMERCIAL INDUS ROOFG CO INC
Also Called: C & I
9239 Olive Dr, Spring Valley (91977-2306)
PHONE 619 465-3737
Fax: 619 465-8578
Barry Turnour, *President*
Deette Key, *Administration*
Barry Turenouer, *Technology*
Ron Albrecht, *Manager*
EMP: 60
SQ FT: 4,500
SALES (est): 11MM **Privately Held**
SIC: 1761 Roof repair; roofing contractor

(P-3154)
COMMERCIAL ROOFING SYSTEMS INC
11735 Goldring Rd, Arcadia (91006-5894)
PHONE 626 359-5354
Fax: 626 359-2659
Glenn Hiller, *President*
EMP: 55 **EST:** 1989
SQ FT: 9,800
SALES (est): 6.3MM **Privately Held**
WEB: www.comroofsys.com
SIC: 1761 Roofing contractor

(P-3155)
COOL ROOFING SYSTEMS INC (PA)
1286 Dupont Ct, Manteca (95336-6003)
PHONE 209 825-0818
Jamie Billman, *President*
Angel Lopez, *CFO*
Daniel Edge, *Vice Pres*
Alan Orton, *Project Mgr*
Thurston Kiang, *Technology*
EMP: 55
SQ FT: 3,000
SALES (est): 17.5MM **Privately Held**
WEB: www.coolroofingsystems.net
SIC: 1761 Roofing contractor

(P-3156)
CROWNER SHEET METAL PDTS INC
14346 Arrow Hwy, Baldwin Park (91706-1335)
PHONE 626 960-4971
Fax: 626 962-0071
Kim M Baier, *CEO*
Dennis Curran, *Vice Pres*
Russell Dunegan, *Admin Sec*
EMP: 50 **EST:** 1945
SQ FT: 9,000
SALES (est): 9.9MM **Privately Held**
WEB: www.crowner.net
SIC: 1761 Sheet metalwork

(P-3157)
CULVER CITY ROOFING COMPANY
5741 W Adams Blvd, Los Angeles (90016-2440)
PHONE 323 930-1311
Fax: 323 930-0729
Brad Coyne, *President*
Paula Coyne, *Vice Pres*
EMP: 60
SQ FT: 13,000
SALES (est): 3.8MM **Privately Held**
WEB: www.culvercityroofing.biz
SIC: 1761 Roofing contractor

(P-3158)
CUSTOM PRODUCT DEV CORP
4603 Las Positas Rd Ste A, Livermore (94551-8845)
PHONE 925 960-0577
Fax: 925 294-8548
Gerald John Ammirato, *President*
Delores Jumper, *Program Mgr*
Nancy Ammirato, *Admin Sec*
Ed Tahvilian, *Info Tech Mgr*
Sean Alsop, *Design Engr*
▲ **EMP:** 55
SQ FT: 33,500
SALES (est): 14.5MM **Privately Held**
WEB: www.cpd-corp.com
SIC: 1761 Sheet metalwork

(P-3159)
D C TAYLOR CO
5060 Forni Dr Ste B, Concord (94520-8579)
PHONE 925 603-1100
James Meyersieck, *Branch Mgr*
Jana Madsen, *Comms Dir*
Rene Boyd, *Sales Executive*
EMP: 50
SALES (corp-wide): 96.9MM **Privately Held**
WEB: www.dctaylorco.com
SIC: 1761 Roofing contractor
PA: D. C. Taylor Co.
312 29th St Ne
Cedar Rapids IA 52402
319 363-2073

(P-3160)
D R I RESIDENTIAL CORPORATION
2081 Bus Ctr Dr Ste 195, Irvine (92612)
PHONE 949 266-1950
Tom Kiley, *President*
Alan Ruben, *CFO*
Patrick Kay, *Vice Pres*
Tom England, *Controller*
▲ **EMP:** 175
SALES (est): 6.4MM
SALES (corp-wide): 52.9MM **Privately Held**
WEB: www.dricompanies.com
SIC: 1761 Roofing contractor
PA: Dri Companies
2081 Bus Ctr Dr Ste 195
Irvine CA 92612
949 266-1900

(P-3161)
D7 ROOFING SERVICES INC
205 23rd St, Sacramento (95816-3067)
PHONE 916 447-2175
Fax: 916 447-2176
Jeffrey Lyn Williamson, *CEO*
James J English Jr, *Vice Pres*
Sandra Robison, *Personnel Exec*
Amy Smith, *Manager*
EMP: 70
SQ FT: 15,000
SALES (est): 10.3MM **Privately Held**
WEB: www.d7roofing.com
SIC: 1761 Roofing, siding & sheet metal work

(P-3162)
DE MELLO ROOFING INC
45 Jordan St, San Rafael (94901-3918)
PHONE 415 456-0741
Fax: 415 456-1273
Richard H Garzoli Jr, *President*
EMP: 55
SQ FT: 500
SALES (est): 5.4MM **Privately Held**
WEB: www.demelloroofing.com
SIC: 1761 Roofing contractor

(P-3163)
DEFCON INC
Also Called: Associated Roofing Contractors
20795 Main St, Carson (90745-1118)
PHONE 310 516-5200
Brian J Eagan, *President*
Jennifer Chacon, *CFO*
EMP: 110
SQ FT: 25,000
SALES (est): 5.1MM **Privately Held**
SIC: 1761 1522 Roofing contractor; residential construction

(P-3164)
DESERT AIR CONDITIONING INC
590 S Williams Rd, Palm Springs (92264-1551)
PHONE 760 323-3383
Fax: 760 323-8983
Jeffrey Shaw, *CEO*
Bruce Shaw, *Vice Pres*
Valerie Botts, *Admin Asst*
Jacqueline Ratliff, *Admin Asst*
EMP: 50
SQ FT: 1,500
SALES (est): 10MM **Privately Held**
WEB: www.desertairconditioning.com
SIC: 1761 1711 Sheet metalwork; warm air heating & air conditioning contractor

(P-3165)
DRI COMPANIES (PA)
2081 Bus Ctr Dr Ste 195, Irvine (92612)
PHONE 949 266-1900
Timothy Michael Davey, *CEO*
Alan Ruben, *CFO*
Brian Flaherty, *Vice Pres*
Tom England, *Controller*
EMP: 50
SALES (est): 52.9MM **Privately Held**
WEB: www.dricompanies.com
SIC: 1761 Roofing contractor

(P-3166)
DUKE PACIFIC INC
13950 Monte Vista Ave, Chino (91710-5535)
P.O. Box 1800 (91708-1800)
PHONE 909 591-0191
Fax: 909 627-2142
Gregory C Severson, *President*
Judith E Braaten, *Corp Secy*
James J Enright IV, *Vice Pres*
Stan Little, *Manager*
EMP: 100 **EST:** 1958
SQ FT: 10,000
SALES (est): 17.3MM **Privately Held**
WEB: www.dukepacific.com
SIC: 1761 Roofing contractor

(P-3167)
DWAYNE NASH INDUSTRIES INC
Also Called: Kodiak Roofing & Waterproofing
8825 Washington Blvd # 100, Roseville (95678-6213)
PHONE 916 253-1900
Fax: 916 253-1901
Dwayne Nash, *CEO*
Richard Palmer, *President*
Erin Anderson, *CFO*
David Pope, *Vice Pres*
Ricky Kendall, *Project Mgr*
▲ **EMP:** 250
SQ FT: 23,617
SALES (est): 64.5MM **Privately Held**
WEB: www.kodiakroofing.com
SIC: 1761 Roofing contractor

(P-3168)
EHMCKE SHEET METAL CORP
840 W 19th St, National City (91950-5406)
P.O. Box 13010, San Diego (92170-3010)
PHONE 619 477-6484
Fax: 619 477-6485
John F Cornell, *CEO*
Dennis Isaacs, *Treasurer*
Dennis Stainbrook, *Admin Sec*
Cecile Walsh, *Administration*
Marilyn Cornell, *Financial Exec*
EMP: 55
SQ FT: 25,000
SALES (est): 12.9MM **Privately Held**
WEB: www.ehmckesheetmetal.com
SIC: 1761 8712 3446 Sheet metalwork; architectural services; architectural metalwork

(P-3169)
ELITE & ASSOCIATES
Also Called: Elite Roofing Company
18605 Parthenia St, Northridge (91324-4028)
PHONE 805 582-0353
Fax: 818 910-1610
Shawn Reeves, *Owner*
EMP: 80
SQ FT: 14,000
SALES (est): 3.4MM **Privately Held**
SIC: 1761 Roofing contractor

(P-3170)
ELLIOTT AND ELLIOTT CO
745 Kevin Ct, Oakland (94621-4039)
PHONE 510 444-7270
Robert A Elliott, *President*
Mark Elliot, *Vice Pres*
Mark C Elliott, *Vice Pres*
EMP: 65
SQ FT: 40,000
SALES (est): 6.1MM **Privately Held**
WEB: www.elliottroofing.com
SIC: 1761 Roofing contractor

(P-3171)
ENTERPRISE ROOFING SERVICE INC
2400 Bates Ave, Concord (94520-1217)
P.O. Box 5130 (94524-0130)
PHONE 925 689-8100
Fax: 925 825-5027
Lawrence T Reardon, *President*
Steven L Reardon, *President*
Aubrey Shehorn, *Treasurer*
Scott Lynd, *Vice Pres*
Lynda She Horn, *Admin Sec*
EMP: 80
SQ FT: 1,200
SALES (est): 16MM **Privately Held**
WEB: www.enterpriseroofing.com
SIC: 1761 Roofing, siding & sheet metal work; roofing contractor

(P-3172)
FIDELITY ROOF COMPANY
1075 40th St, Oakland (94608-3691)
PHONE 510 547-6330
Fax: 510 658-0868
Montague M Upshaw Sr, *Ch of Bd*
Stephen H Cadet, *President*
Kenneth White, *COO*
Montague M Upshaw Jr, *Vice Pres*
Angela Pleece, *Controller*
EMP: 60 **EST:** 1948
SQ FT: 8,000
SALES: 13.8MM **Privately Held**
WEB: www.fidelityroof.com
SIC: 1761 Roofing contractor

(P-3173)
FIRST AVENUE INC
5105 Heintz St, Baldwin Park (91706-1820)
PHONE 626 856-2076
Brett Maurer, *President*
EMP: 60
SALES (est): 4.1MM **Privately Held**
SIC: 1761 Roofing, siding & sheet metal work

(P-3174)
FOUR CS SERVICE INC
1560 H St, Fresno (93721-1616)
PHONE 559 237-3990
Fax: 559 237-3999
Preston Cross, *CEO*
Graydon Cross, *Vice Pres*
Joanne Berryhill, *Controller*
EMP: 80
SQ FT: 22,500
SALES (est): 12.4MM **Privately Held**
WEB: www.sheetmetalco.com
SIC: 1761 Sheet metalwork

PRODUCTS & SERVICES SECTION
1761 - Roofing, Siding & Sheet Metal Work County (P-3199)

(P-3175)
FRESNO ROOFING CO INC
5950 E Olive Ave, Fresno (93727-2710)
P.O. Box 7676 (93747-7676)
PHONE.................................559 255-8377
Fax: 559 255-8378
Scott Logan Raypholtz, *CEO*
Michael Raypholtz, *Corp Secy*
Marti Borba, *Manager*
Edward Duarte, *Manager*
EMP: 60
SQ FT: 23,746
SALES (est): 8.3MM **Privately Held**
SIC: **1761** Roofing contractor; roof repair

(P-3176)
GARCIA ROOFING INC
201 Mount Vernon Ave, Bakersfield (93307-2741)
P.O. Box 70250 (93387-0250)
PHONE.................................661 325-5736
Fax: 661 325-1226
Mike Garcia, *President*
Denise Roberts, *Corp Secy*
Denice Schweer, *Admin Asst*
Debbie Garcia, *Administration*
Marco Garay, *Human Res Mgr*
▲ EMP: 50 EST: 1975
SQ FT: 5,000
SALES (est): 7.1MM **Privately Held**
WEB: www.garciaroofinginc.com
SIC: **1761** Roofing contractor

(P-3177)
GUDGEL ROOFING INC
Also Called: Yancey Roofing
5321 84th St, Sacramento (95826-4803)
PHONE.................................916 387-6900
Fax: 916 387-6904
Janet M Gudgel, *President*
Jason Gudgel, *Vice Ch Bd*
Jason W Gudgel, *Vice Pres*
Catherine Youngblood, *Admin Sec*
Jeff Buschey, *Superintendent*
EMP: 50
SQ FT: 6,000
SALES (est): 10.7MM **Privately Held**
WEB: www.yanceyroofing.com
SIC: **1761** Roofing & gutter work

(P-3178)
HILLCREST SHEET METAL INC
Also Called: Hillcrest AC & Shtmtl
2324 Perseus Ct, Bakersfield (93308-6943)
PHONE.................................661 335-1500
Jim Barker, *President*
David Grijalva, *Project Dir*
Kurt Watson, *Opers Mgr*
EMP: 67 EST: 1952
SQ FT: 14,010
SALES (est): 7MM
SALES (corp-wide): 6.7B **Publicly Held**
WEB: www.emcorgroup.com
SIC: **1761 1711** Sheet metalwork; heating & air conditioning contractors; ventilation & duct work contractor
HQ: Mesa Energy Systems, Inc.
2 Cromwell
Irvine CA 92618
949 460-0460

(P-3179)
HOWARD ROOFING COMPANY INC
245 N Mountain View Ave, Pomona (91767-5629)
PHONE.................................909 622-5598
Fax: 909 623-2927
Larry K Malekow, *President*
Mitch T Caldwell, *Vice Pres*
Ron A Malekow, *Vice Pres*
Maurden Flanigan, *Office Mgr*
EMP: 70
SQ FT: 27,000
SALES (est): 12.4MM **Privately Held**
SIC: **1761** Roofing contractor

(P-3180)
J P WITHEROW ROOFING COMPANY
10176 Riverford Rd, Lakeside (92040-2740)
PHONE.................................619 297-4701
Fax: 619 297-4704
Richard S Witherow, *President*
Charlie Walters, *General Mgr*
Linda Witherow, *Admin Sec*
Jennifer Tapia, *Human Resources*
Laurence L Pillsbury, *Agent*
EMP: 53 EST: 1935
SQ FT: 42,000
SALES (est): 13.6MM **Privately Held**
SIC: **1761** Roofing contractor

(P-3181)
JM ROOFING COMPANY INC
Also Called: Action Roofing
534 E Ortega St, Santa Barbara (93103-3016)
PHONE.................................805 966-3696
Fax: 805 966-6102
John J Martin Jr, *President*
Sharon Fritz, *Corp Secy*
Peggy Martin, *Vice Pres*
Steve Martin, *Vice Pres*
Stuart Kane, *Division Mgr*
EMP: 70
SQ FT: 5,000
SALES (est): 11.4MM **Privately Held**
SIC: **1761** Roofing contractor

(P-3182)
JONES JOHN
Also Called: Excell Sheet Metal
72700 Bel Air Rd, Palm Desert (92260-6003)
PHONE.................................760 275-4168
John Jones, *Owner*
Mimi Jones, *Co-Owner*
EMP: 80
SQ FT: 2,000
SALES (est): 2.8MM **Privately Held**
SIC: **1761** Roofing, siding & sheet metal work

(P-3183)
L I METAL SYSTEMS
9041 Bermudez St, Pico Rivera (90660-4505)
PHONE.................................562 948-5950
Anthony Chiovare, *President*
Peter Bueckert, *Treasurer*
Frank Lemmo, *Vice Pres*
▲ EMP: 50
SQ FT: 12,600
SALES (est): 5.6MM **Privately Held**
SIC: **1761** Gutter & downspout contractor

(P-3184)
LAWSON ROOFING CO INC
1495 Tennessee St, San Francisco (94107-3420)
PHONE.................................415 285-1661
Fax: 415 285-5214
Frank E Lawson Sr, *Ch of Bd*
Frank E Lawson Jr, *President*
Richard J Lawson, *Vice Pres*
Manuel Cotla, *Manager*
David Govorko, *Manager*
EMP: 70
SQ FT: 10,000
SALES (est): 12.7MM **Privately Held**
WEB: www.lawsonroofing.com
SIC: **1761 1799** Roofing contractor; waterproofing

(P-3185)
LBC INC
1881 Duncan St, Simi Valley (93065-3411)
PHONE.................................805 581-1068
Luke Richard Bancroft, *Principal*
EMP: 60
SALES (est): 3MM **Privately Held**
SIC: **1761** Roofing, siding & sheet metal work

(P-3186)
LJC CONSTRUCTION INC
712 W Harding Rd, Turlock (95380-9743)
PHONE.................................209 668-2700
Lon Jones, *President*
Marie Jones, *Executive Asst*
EMP: 55 EST: 2000
SQ FT: 2,719
SALES (est): 3.5MM **Privately Held**
SIC: **1761** Roofing, siding & sheet metal work

(P-3187)
LUCKY INSTALLATIONS
9041 Bermudez St, Pico Rivera (90660-4505)
PHONE.................................562 948-5950
Frank Lemmo, *Owner*
EMP: 50
SALES (est): 1.5MM **Privately Held**
SIC: **1761** Roofing, siding & sheet metal work

(P-3188)
MAJESTIC ROOFING INC
3124 Patton Way, Bakersfield (93308-5716)
PHONE.................................661 588-6120
Francis Giangross, *President*
Laura Skiba, *Human Res Mgr*
Madica Giangrossi, *Accounts Mgr*
EMP: 40
SALES (est): 4.5MM **Privately Held**
SIC: **1761** Roofing, siding & sheet metal work

(P-3189)
MASTER ROOFING SYSTEMS INC
52 S Linden Ave, South San Francisco (94080-6431)
PHONE.................................415 407-4450
Angela Sohn-Lee, *CEO*
Stephen Lee, *Director*
EMP: 60
SALES (est): 272.7K **Privately Held**
SIC: **1761** Roofing, siding & sheet metal work

(P-3190)
MCCORMACK ROOFNG CONSTRCTN & E
1260 N Hancock St Ste 108, Anaheim (92807-1951)
PHONE.................................714 777-4040
James McCormack, *President*
EMP: 60
SALES (est): 5.1MM **Privately Held**
SIC: **1761** Roofing contractor

(P-3191)
MID-PENINSULA ROOFING INC
1326 Marsten Rd, Burlingame (94010-2406)
PHONE.................................650 375-7850
Fax: 650 375-7858
Matthew Greening, *President*
Monique Martinez, *Controller*
EMP: 55
SQ FT: 10,000
SALES (est): 9.4MM **Privately Held**
SIC: **1761** Roofing contractor

(P-3192)
MILAN CORPORATION
Also Called: Marco Roofing
43230 Osgood Rd, Fremont (94539-5607)
P.O. Box 1691 (94538-0169)
PHONE.................................510 656-6400
Fax: 510 656-3021
Michael Edward Creeden, *President*
EMP: 50
SQ FT: 20,000
SALES (est): 6.3MM **Privately Held**
SIC: **1761** Roofing contractor

(P-3193)
MS INDUSTRIAL SHTMTL INC
Also Called: Baghouse and Indus Shtmtl Svcs
1731 Pomona Rd, Corona (92880-6963)
PHONE.................................951 272-6610
Fax: 951 272-1241
Nancy Nicola, *Ch of Bd*
Dan Suffel, *Vice Pres*
Warren Lampkin, *Principal*
Mary Serna, *Technology*
Dennis Fonte, *Controller*
EMP: 130
SQ FT: 35,000
SALES (est): 46MM **Privately Held**
SIC: **1761** Sheet metalwork

(P-3194)
NUSHAKE INC
Also Called: Nushake Roofing
319 S Parallel Ave, Ripon (95366-2910)
PHONE.................................209 239-8616
Fax: 209 239-5815
Douglas Heath, *President*
Elizabeth Heath, *Vice Pres*
Nicole Corral, *Admin Asst*
EMP: 60
SQ FT: 2,800
SALES (est): 7.2MM **Privately Held**
WEB: www.nushake.com
SIC: **1761** Roofing contractor

(P-3195)
OSSCIM INC
Also Called: Royal Roofing Construction Co
172 E Orangethorpe Ave, Placentia (92870-6410)
PHONE.................................714 680-0015
Ronald Ossenberg, *President*
Anna Camarillo, *Exec Sec*
Janine Ossenberg, *Manager*
EMP: 50
SQ FT: 3,000
SALES (est): 3.7MM **Privately Held**
SIC: **1761** Roofing contractor

(P-3196)
PATTON SHEET METAL WORKS INC
Also Called: Patton Air Conditioning
272 N Palm Ave, Fresno (93701-1436)
PHONE.................................559 486-5222
Fax: 559 486-5596
Robert M Patton, *President*
Ellen D Patton, *Corp Secy*
Dawn Kelley, *Admin Asst*
Chris May, *Admin Asst*
Steve Gejeian, *Controller*
EMP: 50
SQ FT: 14,500
SALES (est): 11MM **Privately Held**
WEB: www.pattonac.com
SIC: **1761 1711** Sheet metalwork; warm air heating & air conditioning contractor

(P-3197)
PENNY ROOFING COMPANY
2501 Exposition Blvd, Los Angeles (90018-4299)
P.O. Box 18737 (90018-0737)
PHONE.................................323 731-5424
Fax: 323 733-0820
Lance Mahler, *President*
EMP: 50
SQ FT: 3,000
SALES (est): 3.3MM **Privately Held**
SIC: **1761** Roofing contractor

(P-3198)
PERFORMANCE SHEETS LLC
440 Baldwin Park Blvd, City of Industry (91746-1407)
PHONE.................................626 333-0195
Fax: 626 855-8844
Mike Crosson, *President*
Wes Slaughter, *CTO*
Lisa Magrigal, *Accountant*
Forest Felvey,
Michael Feterik, *Mng Member*
▲ EMP: 125
SALES (est): 13MM
SALES (corp-wide): 8.7B **Privately Held**
SIC: **1761** Sheet metalwork
HQ: Smurfit Kappa North America Llc
13400 Nelson Ave
City Of Industry CA 91746
626 333-6363

(P-3199)
PETERSEN-DEAN INC
Also Called: Petersendean
21616 Golden Triangle Rd # 101, Santa Clarita (91350-3993)
PHONE.................................661 254-3322
Greg O'Donnell, *Manager*
EMP: 100
SALES (corp-wide): 311.5MM **Privately Held**
WEB: www.needaroof.com
SIC: **1761** Roofing contractor
PA: Petersen-Dean, Inc.
39300 Civic Center Dr # 300
Fremont CA 94538
707 469-7470

1761 - Roofing, Siding & Sheet Metal Work County (P-3200)

(P-3200) PETERSEN-DEAN INC
Petersendean
1705 Enterprise Dr, Fairfield (94533-6807)
PHONE..................707 469-7470
Dieter Folk, Senior VP
Jim Petersen, CEO
EMP: 50
SALES (corp-wide): 342.6MM Privately Held
WEB: www.needaroof.com
SIC: 1761 Roofing contractor
PA: Petersen-Dean, Inc.
 39300 Civic Center Dr # 300
 Fremont CA 94538
 707 469-7470

(P-3201) PETERSEN-DEAN INC
Also Called: Petersendean
2210 S Dupont Dr, Anaheim (92806-6104)
PHONE..................714 629-9670
Greg O'Donnell, Manager
EMP: 202
SALES (corp-wide): 311.5MM Privately Held
WEB: www.needaroof.com
SIC: 1761 Roofing contractor
PA: Petersen-Dean, Inc.
 39300 Civic Center Dr # 300
 Fremont CA 94538
 707 469-7470

(P-3202) PETERSEN-DEAN INC
Also Called: Petersendean
39300 Civic Center Dr # 300, Fremont (94538-2337)
PHONE..................510 494-9982
Fax: 510 494-8365
James Petersen, President
Jeica Carvalho, Exec VP
Jason Brinkmann, Senior VP
Robert Dauth, Vice Pres
Eric Owen, VP Finance
EMP: 155
SALES (corp-wide): 342.6MM Privately Held
WEB: www.needaroof.com
SIC: 1761 Roofing contractor
PA: Petersen-Dean, Inc.
 39300 Civic Center Dr # 300
 Fremont CA 94538
 707 469-7470

(P-3203) PETERSEN-DEAN COMMERCIAL INC
Also Called: Petersendean
1705 Enterprise Dr, Fairfield (94533-6807)
PHONE..................707 469-7470
James Petersen, President
David V Beek, COO
Dan Nichols, Senior VP
Steve Crivelli, Vice Pres
Jennifer Faircloth, Sales Staff
EMP: 170
SALES (est): 6.7MM
SALES (corp-wide): 342.6MM Privately Held
WEB: www.needaroof.com
SIC: 1761 1711 Roofing contractor; solar energy contractor
PA: Petersen-Dean, Inc.
 39300 Civic Center Dr # 300
 Fremont CA 94538
 707 469-7470

(P-3204) PLATINUM ROOFING INC
1900 Dobbin Dr, San Jose (95133-1758)
PHONE..................408 280-5028
Fax: 408 280-5775
Bill Shevlin, CEO
Sean Marzola, COO
Darin Darneal, Vice Pres
Brandi Rodriguez, Manager
EMP: 80
SALES (est): 10.8MM Privately Held
SIC: 1761 Roofing contractor

(P-3205) R HAUPT ROOFING CONSTRUCTION
1305 W 132nd St Fl 2, Gardena (90247-1507)
PHONE..................310 515-9709
Fax: 310 769-5813
Robert Haupt, President
Donna Haupt, Principal
EMP: 50
SALES (est): 5MM Privately Held
SIC: 1761 Roofing contractor

(P-3206) R2G ENTERPRISES INC
Also Called: Advanced Fabrication Tech
31154 San Benito St, Hayward (94544-7912)
PHONE..................510 489-6218
Stephen Green, President
Tim Menns, Engineer
EMP: 65
SALES (est): 5MM Privately Held
SIC: 1761 Sheet metalwork

(P-3207) REACH REMOVAL INC
8989 Elder Creek Rd, Sacramento (95829-1032)
P.O. Box 292486 (95829-2486)
PHONE..................916 447-9679
Fax: 916 379-9358
Anthony Cianchetta, President
Lisa Cianchetta, Admin Sec
EMP: 93
SALES: 5.1MM Privately Held
SIC: 1761 Roofing contractor; roof repair; gutter & downspout contractor

(P-3208) RED POINTE ROOFING LP
9542 Topanga Canyon Blvd, Chatsworth (91311-4011)
PHONE..................818 998-3857
EMP: 64
SALES (corp-wide): 18.6MM Privately Held
SIC: 1761 Roof repair
PA: Red Pointe Roofing, Lp
 2106 N Glassell St
 Orange CA 92865
 714 685-0010

(P-3209) REINHARDT ROOFING INC
19258 Donna Ct, Morgan Hill (95037-9319)
P.O. Box 2230 (95038-2230)
PHONE..................510 713-7014
Fax: 510 713-2240
Carole Lowrance, President
Ray Lowrance, Vice Pres
Emily Chin, Office Mgr
EMP: 60
SQ FT: 17,000
SALES (est): 4.3MM Privately Held
WEB: www.reinhardtroofing.net
SIC: 1761 Roofing contractor

(P-3210) ROOFING CONSTRUCTORS INC
Also Called: Western Roofing Service
15002 Wicks Blvd, San Leandro (94577-6600)
PHONE..................415 648-6472
Mark Gene Bledsoe, CEO
Robert Ferrando, CFO
George O'Neill, Senior VP
Ramon Marquez, Vice Pres
John Nolan, Vice Pres
▼ EMP: 150
SQ FT: 3,000
SALES (est): 22.9MM
SALES (corp-wide): 644.2MM Privately Held
WEB: www.westroof.com
SIC: 1761 Roofing contractor
PA: Tecta America Corp.
 9450 Bryn Mawr Ave
 Rosemont IL 60018
 847 581-3888

(P-3211) ROYAL ROOFING & CNSTR CO
1144 N Armando St, Anaheim (92806-2609)
PHONE..................714 764-1100
EMP: 100
SQ FT: 20,000
SALES: 16.4MM Privately Held
SIC: 1761 Roofing contractor

(P-3212) SBB ROOFING INC (PA)
Also Called: Bilt-Well Roofing & Mtl Co
3310 Verdugo Rd, Los Angeles (90065-2845)
P.O. Box 65827 (90065-0827)
PHONE..................323 254-2888
Fax: 323 254-3000
Bruce Radenbaugh, President
Steven Radenbaugh, Vice Pres
Jodi Burks, Executive
Lupe Diaz, Executive
Clint Radenbaugh, Controller
EMP: 180
SQ FT: 5,000
SALES (est): 14.5MM Privately Held
SIC: 1761 Roofing contractor

(P-3213) SONORAN ROOFING INC (PA)
4161 Citrus Ave, Rocklin (95677-4008)
PHONE..................916 624-1080
Fax: 916 624-1143
John Daly, CEO
Jim Pelton, Corp Secy
Monica Dooling, Human Res Dir
EMP: 120
SQ FT: 5,000
SALES (est): 20.6MM Privately Held
SIC: 1761 Roofing contractor

(P-3214) STATE ROOFING SYSTEMS INC
15444 Hesperian Blvd, San Leandro (94578-3959)
PHONE..................510 317-1477
Fax: 510 317-1470
Keith Symons, President
Jack White, Corp Secy
EMP: 100
SQ FT: 6,000
SALES (est): 17.4MM Privately Held
WEB: www.stateroofingsystems.com
SIC: 1761 Roofing contractor

(P-3215) STRAIGHT LINE ROOFING & CNSTR
3811 Dividend Dr Ste A, Shingle Springs (95682-8592)
PHONE..................530 672-9995
Fax: 530 672-9994
John Borba, President
Karen Laizure, Manager
EMP: 50
SALES (est): 7MM Privately Held
WEB: www.straightlineroofing.com
SIC: 1761 Roofing contractor

(P-3216) SYLVESTER ROOFING COMPANY INC
2593 Auto Park Way, Escondido (92029-2088)
PHONE..................760 743-0048
Fax: 760 743-4152
Anthony Zaffuto, CEO
Wesley Sylvester, CFO
Dedie Angelier, Manager
EMP: 50
SQ FT: 1,000
SALES (est): 18.8MM Privately Held
WEB: www.sylvesterroofing.com
SIC: 1761 Roofing contractor

(P-3217) T&C ROOFING INC
Also Called: Town & Country Roofing
2155 Elkins Way Ste H, Brentwood (94513-7365)
PHONE..................925 513-8463
Fax: 925 634-0890
Jeff Tamayo, President
Sara Tamayo, Corp Secy
EMP: 75
SQ FT: 5,000
SALES (est): 12.3MM Privately Held
WEB: www.canawine.com
SIC: 1761 Roofing contractor

(P-3218) TECTA AMERICA SOUTHERN CAL INC (HQ)
1217 E Wakeham Ave, Santa Ana (92705-4145)
PHONE..................714 973-6233
Daniel L Klein, CEO
Javier Sarabia, Foreman/Supr
Debbie Klein, Manager
Frank Downing, Superintendent
EMP: 50 EST: 2002
SALES (est): 9MM
SALES (corp-wide): 644.2MM Privately Held
WEB: www.laveyroofingservices.com
SIC: 1761 Roofing, siding & sheet metal work
PA: Tecta America Corp.
 9450 Bryn Mawr Ave
 Rosemont IL 60018
 847 581-3888

(P-3219) THORSENS INC
Also Called: Thorsens Plumbing & AC
2310 N Walnut Rd, Turlock (95382-8910)
P.O. Box 2310 (95381-2310)
PHONE..................209 524-5296
Craig Vernon Pitau, CEO
Esther Thorsen, Corp Secy
Kathy Kennedy, Office Mgr
Craig Vernon, Agent
EMP: 55
SQ FT: 19,500
SALES (est): 9.4MM Privately Held
WEB: www.thorsensinc.com
SIC: 1761 1711 5722 5075 Sheet metalwork; plumbing contractors; heating & air conditioning contractors; household appliance stores; warm air heating equipment & supplies; sheet metalwork

(P-3220) TINCO SHEET METAL INC
958 N Eastern Ave, Los Angeles (90063-1308)
PHONE..................323 263-0511
Michael Nevarez, CEO
Mike Serrato, President
John Millan, CFO
▲ EMP: 100
SQ FT: 18,000
SALES (est): 21.9MM Privately Held
SIC: 1761 Gutter & downspout contractor

(P-3221) TITAN SHEET METAL INC
180 Vander St, Corona (92880-1719)
PHONE..................951 372-1362
Dale Auslander, President
Linda Sands, Office Mgr
EMP: 150
SALES (est): 8.5MM Privately Held
SIC: 1761 Sheet metalwork

(P-3222) VILLARA CORPORATION
Also Called: Beutler Heating & AC
499 Watt Dr Ste A, Suisun City (94534-1611)
PHONE..................707 863-8222
Fax: 707 863-8226
Rod Schoppe, General Mgr
Vickie Hatfield, Social Dir
EMP: 50
SALES (corp-wide): 183.8MM Privately Held
WEB: www.beutlerhvac.com
SIC: 1761 1711 Sheet metalwork; heating & air conditioning contractors; warm air heating & air conditioning contractor
PA: Villara Corporation
 4700 Lang Ave
 Mcclellan CA 95652
 916 646-2700

(P-3223) WESTERN TEAR-OFF & DISPOSAL
Also Called: Western Waste Services
10920 Grand Ave, Temple City (91780-3551)
P.O. Box 1794, Glendora (91740-1794)
PHONE..................626 443-9984
Fax: 626 443-9987

PRODUCTS & SERVICES SECTION

1771 - Concrete Work County (P-3249)

Michael D Debarry, *President*
EMP: 70
SALES (est): 5.7MM **Privately Held**
SIC: 1761 Roofing contractor

(P-3224)
ZIMMERMAN ROOFING INC
3675 R St, Sacramento (95816-6624)
PHONE 916 454-3667
Fax: 916 455-3784
David Zimmerman, *President*
Allan Donald, *Office Mgr*
EMP: 65
SQ FT: 5,500
SALES: 12MM **Privately Held**
SIC: 1761 Roofing contractor; siding contractor; sheet metalwork

1771 Concrete Work

(P-3225)
ADORNO CONSTRUCTION INC
520 Westchester Dr Ste A, Campbell (95008-5070)
PHONE 408 369-8675
Frank Adorno III, *President*
Frank Adorno Jr, *Treasurer*
Victor M Perez Jr, *Vice Pres*
Monica Barreda, *Office Mgr*
Janet Sanchez, *Admin Sec*
EMP: 52
SQ FT: 1,300
SALES (est): 6MM **Privately Held**
SIC: 1771 Concrete work

(P-3226)
AMERICAN CONCRETE
1125 Linda Vista Dr Ste 1, San Marcos (92078-3819)
PHONE 760 471-9907
Fax: 760 471-0867
Anthony Cannariato, *President*
EMP: 90
SQ FT: 1,500
SALES (est): 5.7MM **Privately Held**
SIC: 1771 Concrete work

(P-3227)
AUS DECKING INC
2999 Promenade St Ste 100, West Sacramento (95691-6418)
P.O. Box 698 (95691-0698)
PHONE 916 373-5320
Eric Meissner, *President*
Patty Rawstron, *Accounting Mgr*
Marcel Meissner, *Sales Staff*
Chantia Sircy, *Manager*
EMP: 57
SQ FT: 56,628
SALES (est): 6.1MM **Privately Held**
SIC: 1771 Concrete work

(P-3228)
B & M CONTRACTORS INC
4473 Cochran St, Simi Valley (93063-3065)
PHONE 805 581-5480
Dave C Moore, *CEO*
Randall Bilsland, *Vice Pres*
Racquel Madred, *Manager*
EMP: 68
SALES (est): 7.8MM **Privately Held**
WEB: www.bandmcontractors.com
SIC: 1771 Concrete work

(P-3229)
BALTAZAR CONSTRUCTION INC
236 E Arrow Hwy, Covina (91722-1817)
PHONE 626 339-8620
Baltazar Jimenez Siqueiros, *CEO*
Bernise Paz, *Office Mgr*
EMP: 50
SALES: 12MM **Privately Held**
SIC: 1771 Blacktop (asphalt) work

(P-3230)
BAYMARR CONSTRUCTORS INC (PA)
6950 Mcdivitt Dr, Bakersfield (93313-2046)
PHONE 661 395-1676
Fax: 661 395-3127
Eric Recktenwald, *CEO*
Jack Whitney, *President*
Pat Howes, *Corp Secy*
EMP: 100
SQ FT: 10,000
SALES (est): 18.5MM **Privately Held**
WEB: www.baymarr.com
SIC: 1771 Concrete work

(P-3231)
BEDROCK COMPANY
2970 Myers St, Riverside (92503-5524)
PHONE 951 273-1931
Glenn E Jackson Jr, *President*
Jackie Oconnell, *Office Mgr*
Carlene Jackson, *Admin Sec*
Andrew Carrillo, *Project Engr*
EMP: 70
SQ FT: 5,000
SALES: 8MM **Privately Held**
SIC: 1771 Concrete work

(P-3232)
BEN F SMITH INC
Also Called: Concrete Construction
8655 Miramar Pl Ste B, San Diego (92121-2567)
PHONE 858 271-4320
Fax: 858 271-4972
Stuart Shelton, *Manager*
Stuart Schouten, *Vice Pres*
Tony Thor, *Financial Exec*
EMP: 120
SALES (corp-wide): 24.3MM **Privately Held**
WEB: www.benfsmithinc.com
SIC: 1771 Concrete work
PA: Ben F. Smith, Inc.
4420 Baldwin Ave
El Monte CA 91731
626 444-2543

(P-3233)
BERKELEY CEMENT INC
1200 6th St, Berkeley (94710-1402)
PHONE 510 525-8175
Fax: 510 527-0782
Ron Fadelli, *CEO*
Andy A Fadelli, *President*
Ronald M Fadelli, *Vice Pres*
Scott Fadelli, *Admin Sec*
EMP: 140
SQ FT: 10,000
SALES (est): 30.4MM **Privately Held**
WEB: www.bciconcrete.com
SIC: 1771 Concrete work

(P-3234)
BITECH-ACE A JOINT VENTURE
7371 Walnut Ave, Buena Park (90620-1759)
PHONE 714 521-1477
Benjamin Kim,
Simon Jeon, *Vice Pres*
EMP: 75
SALES (est): 1.7MM **Privately Held**
SIC: 1771 1522 1611 1623 Concrete work; remodeling, multi-family dwellings; general contractor, highway & street construction; water, sewer & utility lines; renovation, remodeling & repairs: industrial buildings

(P-3235)
BLUE ROSE CONCRETE CONTRS INC
14636 Ceres Ave, Fontana (92335-4204)
PHONE 909 823-6190
Fax: 909 823-6194
James Hernandez, *CEO*
Arthur Carrillo, *President*
Lori Jagusgh, *Manager*
Christina McCown, *Manager*
Teresa Coe, *Accounts Mgr*
EMP: 140
SALES (est): 8MM **Privately Held**
SIC: 1771 Concrete work

(P-3236)
BRONCO CONCRETE INC
3197 E North Ave 101, Fresno (93725-2626)
PHONE 559 323-5005
Frank Jimenez, *President*
Kisha Ray, *Office Mgr*
EMP: 65
SALES (est): 5.7MM **Privately Held**
WEB: www.broncoconcrete.com
SIC: 1771 Concrete work

(P-3237)
CALIFRNIAS GNITE POOL PLST INC
510 Greenville Rd, Livermore (94550-9297)
PHONE 925 960-9500
Fax: 925 606-0961
Manuel Rodriguez, *President*
Jose Arellano, *Vice Pres*
Alvaro Lando, *Vice Pres*
Monroe Rodriguez, *Vice Pres*
Luz Rodriguez, *Accounting Mgr*
EMP: 60
SQ FT: 15,625
SALES (est): 9MM **Privately Held**
SIC: 1771 Gunite contractor

(P-3238)
CALMEX ENGINEERING INC
2764 S Vista Ave, Bloomington (92316-3270)
PHONE 909 546-1311
Fax: 909 686-9011
Robert Stone, *President*
Rosie Lopez, *Director*
EMP: 51
SQ FT: 11,000
SALES (est): 8.5MM **Privately Held**
SIC: 1771 Blacktop (asphalt) work

(P-3239)
CASEY-FOGLI CON CONTRS INC
1970 National Ave, Hayward (94545-1710)
PHONE 510 887-0837
Fax: 510 887-3084
Vincent Ippolito, *CEO*
Glenn Grossman, *CFO*
Dominic Ippolito, *Treasurer*
Thomas Budgick, *Project Mgr*
EMP: 100
SQ FT: 4,000
SALES (est): 11.5MM **Privately Held**
SIC: 1771 Concrete work

(P-3240)
CELL-CRETE CORPORATION
995 Zephyr Ave, Hayward (94544-7917)
PHONE 510 471-7257
Fax: 510 471-6426
Joe Barclay, *Manager*
Scott Taylor, *Engineer*
Eva Bassam, *Sales Staff*
Ephraim Wilson, *Sales Staff*
EMP: 55
SALES (corp-wide): 38.6MM **Privately Held**
SIC: 1771 Flooring contractor
PA: Cell-Crete Corporation
135 Railroad Ave
Monrovia CA 91016
626 357-3500

(P-3241)
CEMENT CUTTING INC
3610 Hancock St Frnt Frnt, San Diego (92110-4335)
PHONE 619 296-9592
Fax: 619 286-4760
Harold O Grafton, *CEO*
Steve Quinn, *Treasurer*
John Gregory Becker, *Vice Pres*
Donald Valadao, *Executive*
Steven Morgan, *Admin Sec*
EMP: 80
SQ FT: 7,000
SALES (est): 16.8MM **Privately Held**
WEB: www.cementcutting.com
SIC: 1771 Concrete work

(P-3242)
CM CONCRETE INC
650 E Easy St, Simi Valley (93065-1808)
PHONE 805 520-8100
Charles Melia, *President*
Joe Melia, *Vice Pres*
Noi Popovich, *Manager*
EMP: 125
SALES (est): 9.8MM **Privately Held**
SIC: 1771 Concrete work

(P-3243)
COAN CONSTRUCTION CO INC
1481 E Grand Ave, Pomona (91766-3806)
PHONE 909 868-6812
Fax: 909 868-7118
Jeffery Coan, *President*
Perry Coan, *Vice Pres*
Sharon Coan, *Admin Sec*
Ryan Granger, *Project Mgr*
John Rich, *Project Mgr*
EMP: 100
SQ FT: 4,300
SALES: 6.2MM **Privately Held**
WEB: www.coanconstruction.com
SIC: 1771 Concrete work

(P-3244)
COASTAL PAVING INCORPORATED
1295 Norman Ave, Santa Clara (95054-2027)
PHONE 408 988-5559
Fax: 408 988-1757
Anna Jarvis, *CEO*
Clifford Heaps, *Treasurer*
Ray Jarvis, *Vice Pres*
Kathy Heaps, *Controller*
Alan Bronner, *Opers Mgr*
EMP: 52
SQ FT: 1,000
SALES (est): 8.9MM **Privately Held**
WEB: www.coastalpaving.com
SIC: 1771 1611 Concrete work; surfacing & paving; concrete construction: roads, highways, sidewalks, etc.; sidewalk construction

(P-3245)
COFFMAN SPECIALTIES INC (PA)
9685 Via Excelencia # 200, San Diego (92126-7500)
PHONE 858 536-3100
Fax: 858 536-3131
Colleen Coffman, *President*
Kevin Coffman, *Vice Pres*
Mel Nutter, *Sr Software Eng*
Pablo Aranalde, *Project Mgr*
Gus Rios, *Project Mgr*
EMP: 151
SQ FT: 6,000
SALES (est): 63.6MM **Privately Held**
WEB: www.coffmanspecialties.com
SIC: 1771 Concrete work

(P-3246)
CONCO PUMPING
13052 Dahlia St, Fontana (92337-6926)
PHONE 909 350-0503
Fax: 909 350-0708
Doug Marquis, *Manager*
EMP: 60
SALES (est): 3.1MM **Privately Held**
SIC: 1771 Concrete pumping

(P-3247)
CONCRETE CONCEPTS INC
2317 Auto Park Way, Escondido (92029-1218)
PHONE 760 737-5470
Fax: 760 737-5477
Chuck Clary, *President*
Christopher Bramwell, *Vice Pres*
EMP: 60
SQ FT: 8,000
SALES (est): 4MM **Privately Held**
SIC: 1771 Concrete work

(P-3248)
CONCRETE IMAGES INTERNATIONAL
17237 Saint Andrews Dr, Poway (92064-1228)
PHONE 858 676-1253
Ernest Hoffman, *CEO*
Edward Stafford, *President*
EMP: 75
SALES (est): 6MM **Privately Held**
SIC: 1771 Concrete work

(P-3249)
CONCRETE NORTH INC
10695 Twin Cities Rd, Galt (95632-8829)
PHONE 209 745-7400
James Grimes, *Owner*
Kim Grimes, *Principal*
Jenny Quigel, *Office Mgr*
Michael Soave, *Project Mgr*
Lisa Rodriguez, *Accounts Mgr*
EMP: 75

1771 - Concrete Work County (P-3250)

(P-3250)
CONDON-JOHNSON & ASSOC INC (PA)
480 Roland Way Ste 200, Oakland (94621-2053)
P.O. Box 12368 (94604-2150)
PHONE.....................510 636-2100
Fax: 510 568-9316
Gerard Jerry Condon, *President*
Jeremy Condon, *Vice Pres*
Siavash Motlagh, *Project Engr*
Katie Condon, *Human Res Dir*
Hayward Baker, *Human Res Mgr*
▲ **EMP:** 50
SQ FT: 12,400
SALES (est): 68MM **Privately Held**
SIC: 1771 Concrete work

(P-3251)
CS CONCRETE SOLUTIONS INC
27758 Snta Margarita Pkwy, Mission Viejo (92691-6709)
PHONE.....................949 285-3122
Curt Stidham, *President*
EMP: 99
SALES (est): 5.6MM **Privately Held**
SIC: 1771 Concrete work

(P-3252)
D AND D CONCRETE CNSTR INC
13795 Blaisdell Pl # 201, Poway (92064-8896)
PHONE.....................619 518-9737
Dereck Leffler, *President*
Edwin Stougton, *Vice Pres*
Diane Leffler, *Admin Sec*
Sheila Clark, *Accountant*
EMP: 60 **EST:** 1989
SQ FT: 2,500
SALES (est): 7.2MM **Privately Held**
SIC: 1771 Concrete work

(P-3253)
DAVID L AMADOR INC
Also Called: Amador Development
762 N Loren Ave, Azusa (91702-2255)
P.O. Box 907 (91702-0907)
PHONE.....................626 334-2011
Fax: 626 969-8406
David Amador, *President*
Debra Amador, *Corp Secy*
EMP: 55
SQ FT: 2,500
SALES (est): 6.1MM **Privately Held**
SIC: 1771 Curb construction

(P-3254)
DE OLIVIERA CONCRETE INC
14111 Soledad Canyon Rd, Santa Clarita (91387-2224)
PHONE.....................661 252-7522
Fax: 661 252-3034
Fred De Oliviera, *President*
Alfred Samora, *Vice Pres*
Darrell Kruse, *Controller*
EMP: 50
SQ FT: 1,000
SALES (est): 3.7MM **Privately Held**
SIC: 1771 Concrete work

(P-3255)
DENNIS BLAZONA CONSTRUCTION
525 Harbor Blvd Ste 10, West Sacramento (95691-2246)
PHONE.....................916 375-8337
Fax: 916 375-8239
J Dennis Balzona, *President*
Patty Garza, *Office Mgr*
Karin Blazona, *Admin Sec*
EMP: 65
SALES (est): 4.5MM **Privately Held**
SIC: 1771 Concrete work

(P-3256)
DEVINCENZI CONCRETE CNSTR
3276 Dutton Ave, Santa Rosa (95407-7866)
P.O. Box 508 (95402-0508)
PHONE.....................707 568-4370
Fax: 707 525-8532
Gary Dahl, *President*
Jean Dahl, *Vice Pres*
EMP: 50
SQ FT: 3,500
SALES: 11.6MM **Privately Held**
SIC: 1771 Curb construction; sidewalk contractor; driveway contractor; parking lot construction

(P-3257)
DIAZ CONSTRUCTION COMPANY INC
9782 Indiana Ave, Riverside (92503-5563)
P.O. Box 70239 (92513-0239)
PHONE.....................951 352-9960
Fax: 951 352-9886
Ramon D Diaz, *President*
Maria Diaz, *Vice Pres*
Jeff Grant, *Vice Pres*
Keith Dobbins, *Branch Mgr*
EMP: 300
SALES (est): 29.6MM **Privately Held**
SIC: 1771 Concrete work

(P-3258)
DISTINCTIVE CONCRETE INC
9320 Chesapeake Dr # 214, San Diego (92123-1021)
PHONE.....................858 277-9707
Steven G Zoumaras, *President*
EMP: 50
SALES (est): 3.6MM **Privately Held**
SIC: 1771 Concrete work

(P-3259)
DOLAN CONCRETE CONSTRUCTION
3045 Alfred St, Santa Clara (95054-3303)
PHONE.....................408 869-3250
Fax: 408 869-3252
Leo A Gutierrez, *President*
Benjamin C Newsom, *Corp Secy*
Robert F Dumesnil Jr, *Vice Pres*
Ramon Velez, *Info Tech Mgr*
EMP: 90
SQ FT: 8,500
SALES (est): 11.4MM **Privately Held**
WEB: www.dolanconcrete.com
SIC: 1771 Concrete work; curb construction; sidewalk contractor

(P-3260)
E & M CONCRETE CONSTRUCTION
2842 Sherwin Ave Ste A, Ventura (93003-7272)
P.O. Box 5600 (93005-0600)
PHONE.....................805 658-2888
Fax: 805 650-9428
Edmundo Mendez, *President*
Mariel Mendez, *Admin Sec*
EMP: 80
SQ FT: 3,478
SALES (est): 8.6MM **Privately Held**
WEB: www.emconcrete.com
SIC: 1771 Concrete work

(P-3261)
EBS CONCRETE INC
1320 E 6th St Ste 100, Corona (92879-1700)
PHONE.....................951 279-6869
Thomas Nanci, *President*
EMP: 50 **EST:** 2000
SQ FT: 3,000
SALES (est): 3.9MM **Privately Held**
SIC: 1771 Concrete work

(P-3262)
EMPIRE DEMOLITION INC
1623 Leeson Ln, Corona (92879-2061)
PHONE.....................909 393-8300
Kris Huff, *CEO*
Collin Cumbee, *CFO*
EMP: 100 **EST:** 1997
SQ FT: 8,000
SALES (est): 10.9MM **Privately Held**
WEB: www.empiredemolition.com
SIC: 1771 Concrete work

(P-3263)
EPIDENDIO CONSTRUCTION INC
11325 Highway 29, Lower Lake (95457-9412)
P.O. Box 452 (95457-0452)
PHONE.....................707 994-5100
Fax: 707 994-7030
Mike Epidendio, *President*
Joan Epidendio, *Corp Secy*
Anthony Epidendio, *Vice Pres*
Donald Epidendio, *Vice Pres*
EMP: 50 **EST:** 1973
SQ FT: 14,000
SALES (est): 5.6MM **Privately Held**
SIC: 1771 Blacktop (asphalt) work

(P-3264)
FORD PLASTERING INC
732 W Grove Ave, Orange (92865-3214)
PHONE.....................714 921-0624
Gary L Ford, *President*
Darrell Ford, *Vice Pres*
EMP: 300
SQ FT: 1,200
SALES (est): 11.3MM **Privately Held**
WEB: www.fordplastering.com
SIC: 1771 1742 Stucco, gunite & grouting contractors; plastering, drywall & insulation

(P-3265)
GINO/GIUSEPPE INC
Also Called: G & G Construction Co
700 Enterprise Ct Ste A, Atwater (95301-9512)
PHONE.....................209 358-0556
Fax: 209 358-0320
Giuspe Castiglione, *CEO*
Giuseppe Castiglione, *CEO*
Gino Graziano, *CFO*
Maria Leon, *Purch Agent*
Bobbi Geoble, *Manager*
EMP: 250
SQ FT: 7,600
SALES (est): 32.3MM **Privately Held**
WEB: www.ggconcrete.com
SIC: 1771 Concrete work

(P-3266)
GOLDEN EMPIRE CONCRETE PDTS
Also Called: Structure Cast
8261 Mccutchen Rd, Bakersfield (93311-9407)
PHONE.....................661 833-4490
Fax: 661 833-4493
Brent Dezember, *CEO*
Anna Dezember, *Admin Sec*
Amy Nakanishi, *Administration*
EMP: 60 **EST:** 2011
SALES: 10MM **Privately Held**
SIC: 1771 Concrete work

(P-3267)
GOLDSMITH CONSTRUCTION CO INC
2683 Lime Ave, Signal Hill (90755-2709)
PHONE.....................562 595-5975
Fax: 562 490-9615
William Goldsmith, *President*
Susan Goldsmith, *Corp Secy*
Kelly Goldsmith, *Vice Pres*
Kelly Mogg, *Office Mgr*
EMP: 50
SQ FT: 6,000
SALES (est): 9.8MM **Privately Held**
SIC: 1771 1629 Concrete work; oil refinery construction

(P-3268)
GONSALVES & SANTUCCI INC (PA)
Also Called: Conco Cement Company
5141 Commercial Cir, Concord (94520-8523)
PHONE.....................925 685-6799
Fax: 925 685-6851
Mathew Gonsalves, *Ch of Bd*
Steven Gonsalves, *President*
Barry Silberman, *CFO*
Holly Bertuccelli, *Vice Pres*
Joseph Santucci, *Vice Pres*
EMP: 50
SQ FT: 35,000
SALES (est): 237MM **Privately Held**
WEB: www.thecoococompanies.com
SIC: 1771 Concrete work

(P-3269)
GRAHAM CONCRETE CNSTR INC
1323 Dayton Ave Ste 103, Clovis (93612-5869)
PHONE.....................559 292-6571
Fax: 559 292-4443
James Graham, *President*
Jason Graham, *Admin Sec*
Heather Bender, *Admin Asst*
Teena Graham, *Manager*
EMP: 75
SQ FT: 10,000
SALES (est): 12MM **Privately Held**
WEB: www.grahamconcrete.com
SIC: 1771 Concrete work

(P-3270)
GREG H CARPENTER CONCRETE INC
955 N Guild Ave, Lodi (95240-0877)
PHONE.....................209 367-4224
Fax: 209 367-4211
Greg Carpenter, *President*
Judy McLacchy, *Office Mgr*
EMP: 50
SALES (est): 6.4MM **Privately Held**
SIC: 1771 Concrete work

(P-3271)
GROUNDWORKS INC
2145 Elkins Way Ste C, Brentwood (94513-7363)
PHONE.....................925 513-0300
Bryan Lucay, *President*
Michele Lucay, *CFO*
Lalo Sanchez, *Opers Mgr*
EMP: 80
SQ FT: 2,500
SALES (est): 6.4MM **Privately Held**
SIC: 1771 1611 1629 Concrete work; grading; drainage system construction

(P-3272)
GUY YOCOM CONSTRUCTION INC (PA)
3299 Horseless Carriage R, Norco (92860-3604)
PHONE.....................951 284-3456
Fax: 951 284-3457
Greg Wilson, *CFO*
Richard Majestic, *Exec VP*
John Hamilton, *Vice Pres*
Dave Kent, *Vice Pres*
Shirley Kowalke, *Admin Sec*
EMP: 95
SQ FT: 41,000
SALES: 33.6MM **Privately Held**
WEB: www.yocominc.com
SIC: 1771 Concrete work

(P-3273)
HB PARKCO CONSTRUCTION INC (PA)
3190 Arprt Loop Dr Ste F, Costa Mesa (92626)
PHONE.....................714 444-1441
Fax: 714 444-1443
Brett D Behrns, *CEO*
W Adrian Hoyle, *President*
Micheal Barry, *CFO*
Joseph Denuse, *Controller*
Lora Wermontese, *Manager*
EMP: 394
SQ FT: 4,000
SALES (est): 36.1MM **Privately Held**
WEB: www.hbparkco.com
SIC: 1771 Parking lot construction

(P-3274)
HOFFMAN CONCRETE COMPANY INC
102 E Grand Blvd, Corona (92879-1364)
PHONE.....................951 372-8333
Dean Hoffman Jr, *President*
EMP: 50
SALES: 5MM **Privately Held**
SIC: 1771 Concrete work

(P-3275)
INLAND CC INC
Also Called: ICC
13820 Slover Ave, Fontana (92337-7037)
PHONE.....................909 355-1318

PRODUCTS & SERVICES SECTION
1771 - Concrete Work County (P-3299)

Marvin Hawkins, *CEO*
Karen Hawkins, *President*
Bill Tibetts, *General Mgr*
EMP: 150
SALES (est): 16.3MM **Privately Held**
SIC: 1771 Concrete work

(P-3276)
INTERNTNAL PVMENT SLUTIONS INC
1209 Van Buren St Ste 3, Thermal (92274-8800)
P.O. Box 10458, San Bernardino (92423-0458)
PHONE.................................909 794-2101
Brent Rieger, *President*
Dennis Rieger, *Treasurer*
Lee Kreinbrook, *Accountant*
Elias Rios, *Controller*
William Fisher, *VP Sls/Mktg*
EMP: 80
SQ FT: 3,000
SALES (est): 5.7MM **Privately Held**
WEB: www.pavement-solutions.com
SIC: 1771 Blacktop (asphalt) work

(P-3277)
INTERSTATE CON PMPG CO INC
11180 Vallejo Ct, French Camp (95231-9783)
PHONE.................................209 983-3092
Fax: 209 983-8655
Andy Paulazzo, *CEO*
Shawn Slate, *Treasurer*
Lisa Hernandez, *Human Res Dir*
Ken Anderson, *Manager*
Myra Nolan, *Manager*
EMP: 52
SALES (est): 9.8MM **Privately Held**
WEB: www.icpumps.com
SIC: 1771 Concrete pumping

(P-3278)
J L S CONCRETE PUMPING INC
2055 N Ventura Ave, Ventura (93001-1308)
PHONE.................................805 643-0766
Jeffrey L Switzer, *President*
Joel Silkett, *President*
Jeffrey Switzer, *Vice Pres*
Dave Cook, *Sales Staff*
Carrie Turner, *Manager*
▲ **EMP:** 75
SQ FT: 10,000
SALES (est): 4.9MM **Privately Held**
WEB: www.jlspumping.com
SIC: 1771 Concrete pumping

(P-3279)
JEZOWSKI & MARKEL CONTRS INC
749 N Poplar St, Orange (92868-1013)
PHONE.................................714 978-2222
Fax: 714 978-2223
Leonard Michael Barth, *President*
Joseph Dean, *Vice Pres*
Dorothy Destefano, *Admin Sec*
Mark Destefano, *Controller*
EMP: 145
SQ FT: 4,500
SALES (est): 27.4MM **Privately Held**
SIC: 1771 Concrete work

(P-3280)
JKB CORPORATION
561 S Walnut St, La Habra (90631-6035)
PHONE.................................562 905-3477
Fax: 562 905-3480
John D Brown, *President*
Kathy Brown, *Vice Pres*
EMP: 50
SQ FT: 4,000
SALES (est): 5.8MM **Privately Held**
SIC: 1771 Concrete work

(P-3281)
JOHN KENNEY CONSTRUCTION INC
619 E Montecito St, Santa Barbara (93103-3217)
P.O. Box 40929 (93140-0929)
PHONE.................................805 884-1579
Fax: 805 884-1581
Jonathan Kenney, *President*
EMP: 52
SQ FT: 5,000

SALES (est): 8.8MM **Privately Held**
SIC: 1771 Concrete work

(P-3282)
JOHNSEN CONSTRUCTION INC
6448 Capitol Ave, Diamond Springs (95619-9393)
PHONE.................................530 642-2123
David W Johnsen, *President*
David W Johnson, *President*
EMP: 70
SQ FT: 300
SALES (est): 5.6MM **Privately Held**
WEB: www.johnsenconstruction.com
SIC: 1771 Concrete work

(P-3283)
JOHNSON WESTERN GUNITE COMPANY (PA)
940 Doolittle Dr, San Leandro (94577-1021)
PHONE.................................510 568-8112
Fax: 510 568-1601
Anthony L Federico, *CEO*
Lawrence J Totten, *President*
Matt Peterson, *Vice Pres*
Alice James, *Admin Sec*
Orville Keller, *Info Tech Mgr*
EMP: 75
SQ FT: 3,000
SALES (est): 12.9MM **Privately Held**
WEB: www.jwgunite.com
SIC: 1771 Gunite contractor

(P-3284)
JOSEPH J ALBANESE INC
851 Martin Ave, Santa Clara (95050-2903)
P.O. Box 667 (95052-0667)
PHONE.................................408 727-5700
Joseph J Albanese, *Principal*
Nick Dalis, *Officer*
Leslie M Cusimano, *Vice Pres*
Stephanie Nguyen, *Executive*
Melissa Delgado, *Office Mgr*
EMP: 700
SALES (est): 158.5MM **Privately Held**
WEB: www.jjalbanese.com
SIC: 1771 Concrete work

(P-3285)
JT WIMSATT CONTG CO INC (PA)
28064 Avenue Stanford B, Valencia (91355-1159)
PHONE.................................661 775-8090
Fax: 661 775-8099
John E Wimsatt III, *President*
Tricia Wimsatt, *Vice Pres*
Maria Dela Cruz, *Director*
EMP: 71
SALES (est): 36.8MM **Privately Held**
WEB: www.jtwimsatt.com
SIC: 1771 Concrete work

(P-3286)
JYG CONCRETE CONSTRUCTION INC
24841 Avenue Tibbitts, Valencia (91355-3405)
PHONE.................................661 607-0337
John Stich, *President*
EMP: 110
SALES (est): 6.7MM **Privately Held**
WEB: www.jygconstruction.com
SIC: 1771 Concrete work

(P-3287)
K A R CONSTRUCTION INC
1306 Brooks St, Ontario (91762-3611)
PHONE.................................909 988-5054
Kurt Rothweiler, *President*
Peggy Rothweiler, *Corp Secy*
Todd Rothweiler, *Vice Pres*
Margaret Rothweiler, *Admin Sec*
Roberta Ingletto, *Broker*
EMP: 60
SQ FT: 2,700
SALES (est): 5.8MM **Privately Held**
WEB: www.karconstruction.com
SIC: 1771 1541 1542 Concrete work; industrial buildings & warehouses; nonresidential construction

(P-3288)
KENYON CONSTRUCTION INC
Also Called: Kenyon Plastream
63 Trevarno Rd D, Livermore (94551-4931)
PHONE.................................925 371-8102
Fax: 925 371-5689
Laura Neil, *Manager*
EMP: 300
SALES (corp-wide): 157.7MM **Privately Held**
WEB: www.kenyonconstruction.com
SIC: 1771 1742 Stucco, gunite & grouting contractors; plastering, plain or ornamental
PA: Kenyon Construction, Inc.
4001 W Indian School Rd
Phoenix AZ 85019
602 484-0080

(P-3289)
LARGO CONCRETE INC
1690 W Foothill Blvd B, Upland (91786-8433)
PHONE.................................909 981-7844
Paul Burkel, *Principal*
EMP: 233
SALES (corp-wide): 93.6MM **Privately Held**
SIC: 1771 Concrete work
PA: Largo Concrete, Inc.
2741 Walnut Ave Ste 110
Tustin CA 92780
714 731-3600

(P-3290)
LARGO CONCRETE INC
891 W Hamilton Ave, Campbell (95008-0402)
PHONE.................................408 874-2500
Ken Long, *Manager*
EMP: 116
SALES (corp-wide): 93.6MM **Privately Held**
SIC: 1771 Concrete work
PA: Largo Concrete, Inc.
2741 Walnut Ave Ste 110
Tustin CA 92780
714 731-3600

(P-3291)
LEONARDS CARPET SERVICE INC
6767 Nancy Ridge Dr, San Diego (92121-2225)
PHONE.................................858 453-9525
Fax: 858 453-1391
Daniel Nagel, *Manager*
EMP: 50
SQ FT: 12,000
SALES (corp-wide): 39.2MM **Privately Held**
WEB: www.lcsdesign.com
SIC: 1771 Flooring contractor
PA: Leonard's Carpet Service, Inc.
1121 N Red Gum St
Anaheim CA 92806
714 630-1930

(P-3292)
LOMBARDO DIAMND CORE DRLG INC
2225 De La Cruz Blvd, Santa Clara (95050-3007)
PHONE.................................408 727-7922
Fax: 408 988-5326
Richard D Long, *President*
Helen T Lombardo, *Treasurer*
Dorothy Long, *Admin Sec*
Michael Dugan, *Manager*
EMP: 58 EST: 1961
SQ FT: 1,300
SALES (est): 12.2MM **Privately Held**
WEB: www.lombardodrilling.com
SIC: 1771 1795 Concrete work; demolition, buildings & other structures

(P-3293)
MARNE CONSTRUCTION INC
749 N Poplar St, Orange (92868-1013)
PHONE.................................714 935-0995
Fax: 714 935-0585
Charles Randolph, *President*
L Michael Barth, *Vice Pres*
Michael Barth, *Vice Pres*
Steven McKeon, *General Mgr*

Maureen Abel, *Manager*
EMP: 80
SQ FT: 10,000
SALES: 12.3MM **Privately Held**
WEB: www.marneconstruction.com
SIC: 1771 Concrete work

(P-3294)
MCGUIRE CONTRACTING INC
16579 Slover Ave, Fontana (92337-7508)
PHONE.................................909 357-1200
David McGuire, *President*
Kathie Vilas, *CEO*
Sandy McGuire, *Admin Sec*
Manny Wilson, *Project Mgr*
EMP: 51
SQ FT: 1,800
SALES (est): 6MM **Privately Held**
WEB: www.mcguirecontracting.com
SIC: 1771 Concrete work

(P-3295)
MELO CONCRETE CONSTRUCTION
5820 Obata Way, Gilroy (95020-7038)
PHONE.................................408 842-3484
Fax: 408 842-3235
Manuel Melo, *President*
Maria Melo, *Vice Pres*
EMP: 80
SALES (est): 8.3MM **Privately Held**
WEB: www.meloconcrete.com
SIC: 1771 Concrete work

(P-3296)
MINEGAR CONTRACTING INC
925 Poinsettia Ave Ste 10, Vista (92081-8452)
PHONE.................................760 598-5001
Michael Dahlquist, *President*
EMP: 50
SALES (est): 5.9MM **Privately Held**
SIC: 1771 Concrete work

(P-3297)
MITCHELL JONES CONCRETE INC
Also Called: Mitchell Concrete
3185 Fitzgerald Rd, Rancho Cordova (95742-6801)
PHONE.................................916 638-6870
Fax: 916 638-6885
Mitchell L Jones, *President*
Peggy Jones, *Vice Pres*
Kim Parigoris, *Opers Staff*
Bob Miller, *Manager*
Larry McDaniel, *Superintendent*
EMP: 175
SQ FT: 7,200
SALES (est): 17.6MM **Privately Held**
WEB: www.mitchellconcrete.com
SIC: 1771 Concrete work

(P-3298)
MORLEY CONSTRUCTION COMPANY (HQ)
3330 Ocean Park Blvd, Santa Monica (90405-3240)
PHONE.................................310 399-1600
Jeff Simonson, *CEO*
Mark Benjamin, *Ch of Bd*
Tod Paris, *CFO*
Bert Lewitt, *Exec VP*
Arun Asher, *Vice Pres*
▲ **EMP:** 80
SQ FT: 20,000
SALES (est): 36.1MM
SALES (corp-wide): 166MM **Privately Held**
WEB: www.morleybuilders.com
SIC: 1771 1522 1542 Concrete work; condominium construction; commercial & office building, new construction
PA: Morley Builders, Inc.
3330 Ocean Park Blvd # 101
Santa Monica CA 90405
310 399-1600

(P-3299)
MORRISON CONCRETE INC
14114 Rosecrans Ave Ste C, Santa Fe Springs (90670-5214)
PHONE.................................562 802-1450
Fax: 562 802-1318
Bradley Morrison, *President*

1771 - Concrete Work County (P-3300)

Tom Curran, *Vice Pres*
Karen Allison, *Manager*
EMP: 50
SALES: 8MM **Privately Held**
SIC: 1771 Concrete work

(P-3300)
NED L WEBSTER CONCRETE CNSTR
8800 Grimes Canyon Rd, Moorpark (93021-9768)
PHONE..................805 529-4900
Ned Webster, *Principal*
Travis Taylor, *Office Mgr*
EMP: 75
SALES (est): 7MM **Privately Held**
SIC: 1771 Concrete work

(P-3301)
NMN CONSTRUCTION INC
1077 Lakeville St, Petaluma (94952-3331)
P.O. Box 110244, Campbell (95011-0244)
PHONE..................707 763-6981
Fax: 408 874-2574
EMP: 100
SALES (est): 4.5MM **Privately Held**
SIC: 1771

(P-3302)
NOAH CONCRETE CORPORATION
5900 Rossi Ln, Gilroy (95020-7013)
PHONE..................408 842-7211
Fax: 408 842-7212
Don Alvarez, *CEO*
Eugene Pacchetti, *Exec Dir*
Jacob Alvarez, *Manager*
Yvonne Chaves, *Manager*
▲ **EMP:** 60
SALES (est): 8.9MM **Privately Held**
SIC: 1771 Concrete work

(P-3303)
NORTH BAY CONSTRUCTION INC
930 Shiloh Rd Bldg 46, Windsor (95492-9679)
PHONE..................707 836-8500
Fax: 707 542-5970
Lohrie Pardue, *President*
Robert Pardue, *Vice Pres*
Sharon Taylor, *Manager*
EMP: 50
SQ FT: 10,000
SALES (est): 6.6MM **Privately Held**
SIC: 1771 Concrete work

(P-3304)
NORTHSTATE PLASTERING INC
2210 Cordelia Rd, Fairfield (94534-1912)
PHONE..................707 207-0950
Buck W Kimbriel Jr, *President*
Francisco Tolento, *Vice Pres*
EMP: 80
SALES (est): 6.7MM **Privately Held**
WEB: www.northstateplastering.com
SIC: 1771 Stucco, gunite & grouting contractors

(P-3305)
ODYSSEY LANDSCAPING CO INC
Also Called: Odyssey Environmental Services
5400 W Highway 12, Lodi (95242-9170)
PHONE..................209 369-6197
Fax: 209 367-0183
Martin Gates, *President*
Steve Mills, *General Mgr*
Matt Lawson, *Project Mgr*
Mark Schultz, *Sales Executive*
EMP: 80
SQ FT: 2,400
SALES (est): 12.8MM **Privately Held**
WEB: www.odysseylandscape.com
SIC: 1771 0781 Concrete work; landscape architects

(P-3306)
PACIFIC CONCRETE SPECIALTIES
101 Business Park Way, Atwater (95301-9483)
PHONE..................209 358-0741
Veryl Esau, *President*
Don Semans, *Vice Pres*
Josie Esau, *Admin Sec*
Chris Esau, *Clerk*
EMP: 75
SQ FT: 3,200
SALES (est): 7.1MM **Privately Held**
WEB: www.pacificconcretespecialties.com
SIC: 1771 Concrete work

(P-3307)
PACIFIC PAVINGSTONE INC
Also Called: Pacific Outdoor Living
8309 Tujunga Ave Unit 201, Sun Valley (91352-3216)
PHONE..................818 244-4000
Terry Morrill, *President*
Trent Morrill, *Vice Pres*
Chad Morrill, *Admin Sec*
Matthew Shepherd, *Controller*
EMP: 115
SALES (est): 11.9MM **Privately Held**
WEB: www.pacificpavingstone.com
SIC: 1771 Driveway contractor

(P-3308)
PACIFIC STHWST STRUCTURES INC
7845 Lemon Grove Way A, Lemon Grove (91945-1880)
PHONE..................619 469-2323
Fax: 619 469-6868
Daniel Fitzgerald, *President*
Victoria Anderson, *Office Mgr*
Meg Travis, *Office Mgr*
Micheal Luedke, *Controller*
Tim Boyd, *Sr Project Mgr*
EMP: 150
SQ FT: 7,500
SALES (est): 14.3MM **Privately Held**
WEB: www.pswsi.com
SIC: 1771 Concrete work

(P-3309)
PACIFIC STRUCTURES INC
953 Mission St Ste 200, San Francisco (94103-2987)
PHONE..................415 367-9399
Ross Edwards, *Ch of Bd*
David E Williams, *President*
Eric Horn, *CFO*
Jason Berry, *General Mgr*
Kim Zabel, *Admin Sec*
EMP: 250
SQ FT: 4,500
SALES: 137.7MM **Privately Held**
SIC: 1771 Concrete work

(P-3310)
PACIFIC STRUCTURES CNSTR INC
101 State Pl Ste E, Escondido (92029-1365)
PHONE..................740 480-4133
Michael Meier, *President*
L Chris Meier, *CFO*
Andrew Meier III, *Vice Pres*
EMP: 50
SQ FT: 2,500
SALES (est): 6.4MM **Privately Held**
SIC: 1771 Concrete work

(P-3311)
PECK & HILLER COMPANY
870 Napa Vally Corp Way Ste A, NAPA (94558)
PHONE..................707 258-8800
Ben Kerr, *Vice Pres*
Tom H O'Connor, *Vice Pres*
Cindy Joy Westerberg, *Controller*
EMP: 100
SQ FT: 8,680
SALES (est): 18.7MM **Privately Held**
WEB: www.peckandhiller.com
SIC: 1771 Concrete work

(P-3312)
PERRY FLOOR SYSTEMS INC
261 Industry Way, Upland (91786-4570)
PHONE..................909 949-1211
Brian Perry, *President*
Angela Perry, *Vice Pres*
Diane Lopez, *Manager*
EMP: 65
SQ FT: 6,000
SALES (est): 5.7MM **Privately Held**
SIC: 1771 Flooring contractor

(P-3313)
PETERSON BROS CONTRUCTION INC
Also Called: Pbc Companies
1560 W Lambert Rd, Brea (92821-2826)
PHONE..................714 278-0488
Elden Peterson, *CEO*
Robert K Peterson, *Ch of Bd*
Patrick Burns, *CFO*
Mike Hoefnagels, *Vice Pres*
Jack Saldate, *Vice Pres*
▲ **EMP:** 600
SQ FT: 24,000
SALES (est): 63MM **Privately Held**
SIC: 1771 3531 1741 Concrete work; pavers; concrete block masonry laying

(P-3314)
POWERHOUSE BUILDING INC
4320 Redwood Hwy Ste 200, San Rafael (94903-2151)
PHONE..................415 446-0188
Fax: 415 446-0189
David Hynes, *President*
Philip Hynes, *Vice Pres*
John Cotten, *Manager*
EMP: 60
SQ FT: 1,200
SALES (est): 5.3MM **Privately Held**
SIC: 1771 1522 Concrete work; residential construction

(P-3315)
PRESTIGE CONCRETE
13507 Midland Rd, Poway (92064-4711)
PHONE..................858 679-2772
Fax: 858 679-8499
Jerry Green, *President*
James Okeefe, *Personnel Exec*
Ed Hernandez, *Sales Mgr*
EMP: 60
SALES (est): 7.2MM **Privately Held**
SIC: 1771 Concrete work

(P-3316)
PRESTIGE GUNITE CALIFORNIA INC
18300 Wood Edge Ln, Riverside (92504-9580)
PHONE..................909 276-9096
Fax: 909 276-2506
Carl Pagel, *President*
William Huchton, *Vice Pres*
EMP: 50
SQ FT: 10,000
SALES (est): 3.2MM **Privately Held**
SIC: 1771 Gunite contractor

(P-3317)
R E MAHER INC
4545 Hess Rd, American Canyon (94503-9727)
PHONE..................707 642-3907
Fax: 707 642-4014
Rod E Maher, *CEO*
Jennifer Luciere, *Controller*
EMP: 95
SQ FT: 1,000
SALES: 22MM **Privately Held**
SIC: 1771 Concrete work

(P-3318)
RESCUE CONCRETE INC
9275 Beatty Dr, Sacramento (95826-9702)
P.O. Box 276812 (95827-6812)
PHONE..................916 852-2400
Fax: 916 852-2401
David Winn, *President*
EMP: 60 EST: 1995
SALES (est): 4.5MM **Privately Held**
WEB: www.rescueconcrete.com
SIC: 1771 Concrete work

(P-3319)
REY CON CONSTRUCTION INC
1795 E Lemonwood Dr, Santa Paula (93060-9651)
P.O. Box 910 (93061-0910)
PHONE..................805 525-8134
Fax: 805 933-2282
Paul Reyes, *President*
Robert Reyes, *Treasurer*
Augie Reyes, *Vice Pres*
Chris Urrea, *Admin Sec*
EMP: 150

SQ FT: 5,000
SALES (est): 16.8MM **Privately Held**
SIC: 1771 1741 1751 Sidewalk contractor; masonry & other stonework; framing contractor

(P-3320)
RJS & ASSOCIATES INC
1675 Sabre St, Hayward (94545-1013)
PHONE..................510 670-9111
Fax: 510 670-1181
Robert J Simmons, *President*
Nita Walker, *Manager*
EMP: 225
SQ FT: 10,000
SALES (est): 31.6MM **Privately Held**
SIC: 1771 1521 Foundation & footing contractor; single-family housing construction

(P-3321)
RMR INC (PA)
2311 S Oakley Ave Ste C, Santa Maria (93455-1131)
P.O. Box 1715 (93456-1715)
PHONE..................805 928-4013
Fax: 805 922-0833
Mario Perea, *President*
Gloria Perea, *Vice Pres*
EMP: 60
SQ FT: 5,000
SALES (est): 5.7MM **Privately Held**
WEB: www.rmrinc.com
SIC: 1771 1389 Concrete work; oil field services

(P-3322)
ROBERT A BOTHMAN INC (PA)
Also Called: B & B Concrete
2690 Scott Blvd, Santa Clara (95050-2511)
PHONE..................408 279-2277
Fax: 408 279-2286
Robert A Bothman, *President*
Saeed Yousuf, *COO*
Andy Bothman, *Vice Pres*
Brian Bothman, *Vice Pres*
James Moore, *Vice Pres*
EMP: 121
SQ FT: 20,000
SALES (est): 43.1MM **Privately Held**
WEB: www.bothman.com
SIC: 1771 0782 Concrete work; landscape contractors

(P-3323)
RON NURSS INC
Also Called: Blueline Construction
11290 Sunrise Park Dr B, Rancho Cordova (95742-6895)
PHONE..................916 631-9761
Fax: 916 631-7104
Ron Nurss, *President*
Darcy Nurss, *Admin Sec*
EMP: 65
SQ FT: 6,400
SALES (est): 5.9MM **Privately Held**
WEB: www.blueline-construction.com
SIC: 1771 Concrete work

(P-3324)
SACRAMENTO PRESTIGE GUNITE INC
8634 Antelope North Rd, Antelope (95843-3930)
PHONE..................916 723-0404
Fax: 916 773-6555
George Wagner, *President*
Eric Schmidt, *General Mgr*
Debbie Castro, *Office Mgr*
Brian Green, *Accountant*
EMP: 60
SQ FT: 1,100
SALES (est): 2.8MM **Privately Held**
WEB: www.sacgunite.com
SIC: 1771 Gunite contractor
HQ: Vcna Prestige Gunite Inc
 8529 Suthpark Cir Ste 320
 Orlando FL 32819
 407 802-3540

(P-3325)
SANTA CLARITA CONCRETE
16164 Sierra Hwy, Santa Clarita (91390-4733)
PHONE..................661 252-2012
Wayne Crawford, *President*
Keith Crawford, *Vice Pres*

PRODUCTS & SERVICES SECTION
1771 - Concrete Work County (P-3351)

Eric Stoh, *Vice Pres*
Eric Stroh, *Vice Pres*
Margarita Figueroa, *Office Mgr*
EMP: 50
SQ FT: 5,000
SALES (est): 10MM **Privately Held**
SIC: 1771 Concrete work

(P-3326)
SANTANA CONCRETE
18241 Slover Ave, Bloomington (92316-2366)
PHONE 909 421-2218
Fax: 909 875-6370
Jesse Santana, *Owner*
EMP: 60
SALES (est): 4.7MM **Privately Held**
SIC: 1771 Concrete work

(P-3327)
SCI INC
18501 Collier Ave B106, Lake Elsinore (92530-2764)
PHONE 951 245-7511
Mark A Dix, *President*
Richard Hallihan, *Controller*
EMP: 53
SALES (est): 8.4MM **Privately Held**
WEB: www.tiltupsbysci.com
SIC: 1771 Concrete work

(P-3328)
SCOTT SILVA CONCRETE INC
11374 Gold Dredge Way, Rancho Cordova (95742-6867)
PHONE 916 859-0593
Scott Silva, *President*
EMP: 100
SALES (est): 3.6MM **Privately Held**
SIC: 1771 Concrete work

(P-3329)
SERVICON SYSTEMS INC
3329 Jack Northrop Ave, Hawthorne (90250-4426)
PHONE 310 970-0700
Julio E Ramirez, *Branch Mgr*
EMP: 1472
SALES (corp-wide): 68.1MM **Privately Held**
SIC: 1771 Flooring contractor
PA: Servicon Systems, Inc.
3965 Landmark St
Culver City CA 90232
310 204-5040

(P-3330)
SIMPLE LUXURIES LLC
1560 N Sycamore Ave, Rialto (92376-3666)
PHONE 310 627-6514
Heather Tiger,
EMP: 50
SALES (est): 1.4MM **Privately Held**
SIC: 1771 7389 8712 Exterior concrete stucco contractor; interior design services; house designer

(P-3331)
SINCLAIR CONCRETE
7205 Church St, Penryn (95663-9411)
PHONE 916 663-0303
Fax: 916 663-1713
Keith Sinclair, *Admin Sec*
Karin Sinclair, *CFO*
EMP: 85
SALES (est): 7.6MM **Privately Held**
SIC: 1771 Foundation & footing contractor

(P-3332)
SOUTH COAST CONCRETE CNSTR
6770 Central Ave Ste B, Riverside (92504-1443)
PHONE 951 351-7777
Fax: 951 351-7783
Monica Perry, *President*
Bob Perry, *CFO*
Pedro Rico, *Vice Pres*
Susana Roddy, *Manager*
EMP: 50
SQ FT: 14,000
SALES (est): 8.7MM **Privately Held**
SIC: 1771 Concrete work

(P-3333)
SOUTHERN BUILDING & CON INC
2303 Weakley St, El Centro (92243-9658)
PHONE 760 337-8932
Fax: 760 337-8014
Hector Salgado, *President*
Randy Akacich, *Accountant*
EMP: 50
SALES (est): 4MM **Privately Held**
SIC: 1771 Curb & sidewalk contractors; foundation & footing contractor

(P-3334)
SOUTHLAND PAVING INC
361 N Hale Ave, Escondido (92029-1798)
PHONE 760 747-6895
Fax: 760 747-1008
Richard Fleck, *CEO*
Anne Fleck, *Corp Secy*
Daniel Devlin, *Vice Pres*
Bob Kennedy, *Vice Pres*
Robert Kennedy, *Vice Pres*
EMP: 75
SQ FT: 35,000
SALES (est): 15.3MM **Privately Held**
WEB: www.southlandpaving.com
SIC: 1771 2951 Blacktop (asphalt) work; asphalt paving mixtures & blocks; asphalt paving blocks (not from refineries)

(P-3335)
SOUTHWEST CONSTRUCTION CO INC
2909 Rainbow Valley Blvd, Fallbrook (92028-8859)
PHONE 760 728-4460
Fax: 760 728-8649
David Simon, *President*
Lorie Simon, *Vice Pres*
Paul Simon, *Admin Sec*
Kenny Clotz, *Human Res Mgr*
EMP: 60
SQ FT: 5,000
SALES (est): 7.9MM **Privately Held**
SIC: 1771 Concrete work

(P-3336)
STEFAN MERLI PLASTERING CO INC (PA)
Also Called: Merli Concrete Pumping
1230 W 130th St, Gardena (90247-1502)
PHONE 310 323-0404
Stefan R Merli, *President*
Adele Merli, *Treasurer*
Gunther Merli, *Admin Sec*
Maria Ryan, *Manager*
EMP: 63
SQ FT: 5,000
SALES (est): 24.8MM **Privately Held**
SIC: 1771 Concrete work

(P-3337)
STEVE DUICH INC
Also Called: H & D Construction
1369 N Magnolia Ave, El Cajon (92020-1619)
P.O. Box 12859 (92022-2859)
PHONE 619 444-6118
Fax: 619 441-8414
Steve Duich, *President*
Joyce Duich, *Vice Pres*
EMP: 50
SQ FT: 3,700
SALES (est): 6.8MM **Privately Held**
SIC: 1771 Concrete work; sidewalk contractor; curb construction

(P-3338)
STRUCTURES WEST INC
300 W Grand Ave Ste 201, Escondido (92025-2617)
PHONE 760 737-2349
Jeff Steele, *President*
Robert Davidson, *CFO*
EMP: 100
SALES (est): 7MM **Privately Held**
SIC: 1771 Concrete work

(P-3339)
SUPERIOR GUNITE (PA)
12306 Van Nuys Blvd, Sylmar (91342-6086)
PHONE 818 896-9199
Fax: 323 896-6699

Anthony L Federico, *President*
Steve Crawford, *Vice Pres*
Gene McKay, *General Mgr*
David Bowers, *Admin Sec*
Mark Patton, *Materials Mgr*
EMP: 145
SQ FT: 5,000
SALES (est): 41.5MM **Privately Held**
WEB: www.shotcrete.com
SIC: 1771 Gunite contractor

(P-3340)
SURE FORMING SYSTEMS INC
10602 Humbolt St, Los Alamitos (90720-2448)
PHONE 562 598-6348
Fax: 562 493-6200
Samuel F Shon, *President*
Wanda L Shon, *Corp Secy*
Conni Bittner, *Manager*
EMP: 50
SQ FT: 6,200
SALES (est): 5.8MM **Privately Held**
SIC: 1771 Concrete work

(P-3341)
TEAM FINISH INC
155 Arovista Cir Ste A, Brea (92821-3842)
PHONE 714 671-9190
Fax: 714 671-9390
Thomas M Stangl, *President*
Mary Stangl, *CFO*
EMP: 80 **EST:** 1996
SQ FT: 1,200
SALES: 12.6MM **Privately Held**
WEB: www.teamvelocity.org
SIC: 1771 Concrete work

(P-3342)
TERRY TUELL CONCRETE INC
287 W Fallbrook Ave # 105, Fresno (93711-5805)
P.O. Box 3933 (93650-3933)
PHONE 559 431-0812
Fax: 559 431-5201
Terry Tuell, *President*
Matthew Tuell, *Treasurer*
Joel Stokes, *Supervisor*
EMP: 90
SQ FT: 3,000
SALES (est): 8.6MM **Privately Held**
SIC: 1771 Concrete work

(P-3343)
UNITED BROTHERS CONCRETE INC
41905 Boardwalk Ste K, Palm Desert (92211-9091)
P.O. Box 756, Thousand Palms (92276-0756)
PHONE 760 346-1013
Lauro Barcenas, *President*
Oscar Barcenas, *Treasurer*
Luis Barcenas, *Vice Pres*
Rachel Stevens, *Controller*
EMP: 150 **EST:** 1999
SQ FT: 2,000
SALES (est): 15.1MM **Privately Held**
SIC: 1771 Concrete work

(P-3344)
URATA & SONS CEMENT INC
3430 Luyung Dr, Rancho Cordova (95742-6871)
PHONE 916 638-5364
Fax: 916 638-4375
Charles Urata, *President*
Darrell Dwyer, *CFO*
Kelly Urata, *Corp Secy*
John P Bell, *President*
Frank M Urata, *Vice Pres*
EMP: 125
SQ FT: 10,000
SALES (est): 38.8MM **Privately Held**
WEB: www.urataconcrete.com
SIC: 1771 Concrete work; foundation & footing contractor; curb construction; driveway contractor

(P-3345)
VALENCIA BROS INC
Also Called: Valencia Brothers Concrete
257 Maple Ave, El Centro (92243-3311)
PHONE 760 353-2168
George Valencia, *President*
Guillermo Valencia, *Vice Pres*

Karla Romero, *Office Mgr*
EMP: 80 **EST:** 2000
SQ FT: 1,700
SALES (est): 4.6MM **Privately Held**
SIC: 1771 Concrete work

(P-3346)
VALENTE CONCRETE
255 Benjamin Dr, Corona (92879-6509)
PHONE 951 279-2221
Fax: 951 279-2221
Matthew R Valente, *President*
Sandra Echerd, *Office Mgr*
EMP: 70
SQ FT: 3,600
SALES (est): 5MM **Privately Held**
WEB: www.valenteconcrete.com
SIC: 1771 Foundation & footing contractor

(P-3347)
VALLEY PACIFIC CONCRETE INC
27580 Tabb Ln, Menifee (92584-9521)
PHONE 951 672-6151
Fax: 951 672-6110
Chris Russo, *President*
Kristi Russo, *Vice Pres*
Pam McElwain, *Controller*
EMP: 110
SQ FT: 1,500
SALES (est): 11MM **Privately Held**
WEB: www.vpconcrete.com
SIC: 1771 Concrete work

(P-3348)
VINCE FUCILLO
Also Called: V C Concrete
3564 Atwater Blvd, Atwater (95301-9501)
P.O. Box 698 (95301-0698)
PHONE 209 358-9175
Fax: 209 357-8414
Vince Fucillo, *Owner*
EMP: 80
SQ FT: 1,920
SALES (est): 5.8MM **Privately Held**
WEB: www.vcconcreteinc.com
SIC: 1771 Concrete work

(P-3349)
WAYNE E SWISHER CEM CONTR INC
2620 E 18th St, Antioch (94509-7229)
PHONE 925 757-3660
Fax: 925 757-3731
Wayne Swisher, *President*
Elma Swisher, *Vice Pres*
EMP: 75
SQ FT: 4,000
SALES (est): 14.5MM **Privately Held**
SIC: 1771 Concrete work

(P-3350)
WESTERN CONCRETE PUMPING INC (PA)
2181 La Mirada Dr, Vista (92081-8830)
PHONE 760 598-7855
Fax: 760 598-5850
Charles D Reed, *President*
Brett Reid, *CFO*
Judy Reid, *Vice Pres*
Hannah Reed, *Office Admin*
Lynda Woodin, *Admin Asst*
EMP: 55
SQ FT: 5,000
SALES (est): 49.2MM **Privately Held**
SIC: 1771 Concrete pumping

(P-3351)
WHITING CONSTRUCTION INC
Also Called: Whiting Concrete Construction
7281 Lone Pine Dr, Rancho Murieta (95683-9715)
P.O. Box 887, Sloughhouse (95683-0887)
PHONE 916 354-2756
Fax: 916 354-2037
Tim Whiting, *President*
Sarah Hallam, *Manager*
EMP: 55
SALES (est): 6MM **Privately Held**
WEB: www.whitingcc.com
SIC: 1771 Concrete work

1771 - Concrete Work County (P-3352)

(P-3352)
Z-BEST CONCRETE INC
2575 Main St, Riverside (92501-2238)
PHONE..................951 774-1870
Fax: 951 774-3117
Roger Crott, *President*
Jerry Faust, *Vice Pres*
Shann Griffin, *Accountant*
EMP: 80
SQ FT: 2,400
SALES (est): 14.1MM **Privately Held**
SIC: 1771 1741 Concrete work; masonry & other stonework

1781 Water Well Drilling

(P-3353)
BEKS ACQUISITION INC
Also Called: Bc2 Environmental
1150 W Trenton Ave, Orange (92867-3536)
PHONE..................714 744-2990
Kurt Samuelson, *President*
Scott Traub, *General Mgr*
EMP: 50
SALES (est): 3.7MM **Privately Held**
SIC: 1781 Water well drilling

(P-3354)
CASCADE DRILLING LP
1333 W 9th St, Upland (91786-5712)
PHONE..................909 946-1605
Kirk McGeee, *Branch Mgr*
EMP: 50
SALES (corp-wide): 762.6MM **Privately Held**
SIC: 1781 Water well drilling
HQ: Cascade Drilling, L.P.
17270 Woodinville Redmond
Woodinville WA 98072
425 527-9700

(P-3355)
GEO GUIDANCE DRILLING SVCS INC
200 Old Yard Dr, Bakersfield (93307-4268)
P.O. Box 42647 (93384-2647)
PHONE..................661 833-9999
Joseph Williams, *CEO*
Charles B Peters, *Treasurer*
Matt Lemke, *Admin Sec*
EMP: 50
SQ FT: 3,000
SALES: 6.4MM **Privately Held**
SIC: 1781 Geothermal drilling

(P-3356)
GREGG DRILLING & TESTING INC
Also Called: Gregg Dilling and Testing
950 Howe Rd, Martinez (94553-3444)
PHONE..................925 313-5800
Fax: 925 313-0302
Chris Christensen, *Branch Mgr*
EMP: 61
SALES (corp-wide): 36.3MM **Privately Held**
WEB: www.greggdrilling.com
SIC: 1781 Water well drilling
PA: Gregg Drilling & Testing, Inc.
2726 Walnut Ave
Signal Hill CA 90755
562 427-6899

(P-3357)
HMS CONSTRUCTION INC (PA)
2885 Scott St, Vista (92081-8547)
PHONE..................760 727-9808
Michael High, *President*
Ian High, *Vice Pres*
Sharon High, *Admin Sec*
Victoria Castellones, *Project Mgr*
Shawn Gunter, *Project Mgr*
EMP: 75
SQ FT: 5,200
SALES (est): 34.3MM **Privately Held**
WEB: www.hmsconstructioninc.com
SIC: 1781 8711 Geothermal drilling; engineering services

(P-3358)
MAGGIORA BROSDRILLING INC (PA)
595 Airport Blvd, Watsonville (95076-2094)
PHONE..................831 724-1338
Fax: 831 724-3228
David T Maggiora, *CEO*
Mark Maggiora, *Treasurer*
Joanne Maggiora, *Vice Pres*
Mike Maggiora, *Admin Sec*
Robert Filippi, *Agent*
EMP: 50
SQ FT: 5,000
SALES (est): 8MM **Privately Held**
SIC: 1781 1711 Water well drilling; plumbing contractors

(P-3359)
PACIFIC BORING INCORPORATED
1985 W Mountain View Ave, Caruthers (93609-9701)
P.O. Box 727 (93609-0727)
PHONE..................559 864-9444
Fax: 559 864-9256
David Cline, *President*
James Gardner, *Vice Pres*
Fred Ferrari, *Admin Sec*
Calastro Terrasas, *Admin Sec*
Cory Bell, *CPA*
EMP: 50
SQ FT: 750
SALES (est): 9.1MM **Privately Held**
WEB: www.pacificboring.com
SIC: 1781 Water well drilling

(P-3360)
ZIM INDUSTRIES INC
Bakersfield Well & Pump Co
7212 Fruitvale Ave, Bakersfield (93308-9529)
PHONE..................661 393-9661
Fax: 661 393-9647
John Zimmerer, *Manager*
Debra Hornback, *Office Mgr*
EMP: 90
SALES (corp-wide): 51.6MM **Privately Held**
SIC: 1781 7699 Water well drilling; pumps & pumping equipment repair
PA: Zim Industries, Inc.
4545 E Lincoln Ave
Fresno CA 93725
559 834-1551

1791 Structural Steel Erection

(P-3361)
ALLIED STEEL CO INC
1027 Palmyrita Ave, Riverside (92507-1701)
PHONE..................951 241-7000
Brian P Chapman, *President*
Nicky Chapman, *Treasurer*
Perry K Chapman, *Vice Pres*
Gary Chapman, *General Mgr*
Jeanette Chapman, *Admin Sec*
EMP: 60
SQ FT: 48,000
SALES (est): 18.9MM **Privately Held**
WEB: www.alliedsteelco.com
SIC: 1791 3441 Structural steel erection; fabricated structural metal

(P-3362)
ANDERSON CHRNESKY STRL STL INC
Also Called: Acss
353 Risco Cir, Beaumont (92223-2676)
PHONE..................951 769-5700
Kevin Charneskey, *Treasurer*
Kevin Charnesky, *President*
EMP: 72
SQ FT: 6,600
SALES (est): 21.6MM **Privately Held**
SIC: 1791 Structural steel erection

(P-3363)
ANVIL STEEL CORPORATION
Also Called: Anvil Iron
134 W 168th St, Gardena (90248-2729)
PHONE..................310 329-5811
Fax: 310 329-2473
Gerry Bustrum, *CEO*
Paul Schifino, *President*
Mike Norton, *Vice Pres*
Marcela Guerrero, *Admin Asst*
Johnatan Garcia, *Purch Agent*
▲ **EMP:** 90
SQ FT: 4,000
SALES (est): 23.7MM **Privately Held**
WEB: www.anvilsteel.com
SIC: 1791 Structural steel erection

(P-3364)
BAJA CONSTRUCTION CO INC (PA)
223 Foster St, Martinez (94553-1029)
P.O. Box 3080 (94553-8080)
PHONE..................925 229-0732
Fax: 925 229-0161
Robert Hayworth, *Chairman*
Laura Daum, *President*
Brandon Morford, *CEO*
Jack Bohr, *COO*
Robert J Hayworth, *Chairman*
EMP: 90
SQ FT: 7,200
SALES (est): 26MM **Privately Held**
SIC: 1791 Structural steel erection

(P-3365)
BAPKO METAL INC
838 N Cypress St, Orange (92867-6608)
PHONE..................714 639-9380
Fax: 714 639-8278
Fred Bagatourian, *President*
Clint Rieber, *CFO*
Heather Wiliams, *Admin Sec*
Michael Bagatourian, *Plant Mgr*
Farhad Azadi, *Director*
EMP: 80 **EST:** 1978
SQ FT: 4,000
SALES (est): 26.6MM **Privately Held**
WEB: www.bapko.com
SIC: 1791 3441 Structural steel erection; fabricated structural metal

(P-3366)
BELLIS STEEL COMPANY INC (PA)
8740 Vanalden Ave, Northridge (91324-3691)
PHONE..................818 886-5601
Fax: 818 993-3018
Theron Arthur Ghrist, *CEO*
Gail R Ghrist, *Vice Pres*
Alan Miley, *General Mgr*
Steve Smith, *Administration*
Anna Longoria, *Controller*
EMP: 52
SQ FT: 2,500
SALES (est): 10MM **Privately Held**
WEB: www.bellissteel.com
SIC: 1791 5051 Concrete reinforcement, placing of; iron & steel (ferrous) products

(P-3367)
BLAZING INDUSTRIAL STEEL INC
9040 Jurupa Rd, Riverside (92509-3106)
PHONE..................951 360-8340
Fax: 951 681-9662
Fernando Herrera, *President*
Roberta Calderon, *Treasurer*
Mike Calderon, *Vice Pres*
Brad McGlothlin, *General Mgr*
Melody Villano, *Manager*
EMP: 110
SQ FT: 100,000
SALES (est): 17.5MM **Privately Held**
SIC: 1791 Structural steel erection

(P-3368)
BONNEVILLE STEEL INC
13654 Live Oak Ln, Irwindale (91706-1317)
PHONE..................866 956-8323
Fax: 626 303-5898
Joe Wigginton, *President*
Kathryn Wigginton, *CFO*
Billie Wigginton, *Corp Secy*
Albert Vanderden, *Vice Pres*
EMP: 100
SQ FT: 6,000
SALES (est): 6.1MM **Privately Held**
SIC: 1791 Structural steel erection

(P-3369)
BRUNTON ENTERPRISES INC
Also Called: Plas-Tal Manufacturing Co
8815 Sorensen Ave, Santa Fe Springs (90670-2636)
PHONE..................562 945-0013
John W Brunton Jr, *President*
Doug Robson, *Treasurer*
Alan Baker, *Vice Pres*
Sean Brunton, *Executive*
Patrick Scott, *Network Mgr*
EMP: 125 **EST:** 1947
SQ FT: 45,000
SALES (est): 36.2MM **Privately Held**
WEB: www.plas-tal.com
SIC: 1791 Structural steel erection

(P-3370)
C M C STEEL FABRICATORS INC
Also Called: Fontana Steel
12451 Arrow Rte, Etiwanda (91739-9601)
P.O. Box 2219, Rancho Cucamonga (91729-2219)
PHONE..................909 899-9993
Fax: 909 899-9799
Deborah Marshall, *Manager*
Mike Marino, *Department Mgr*
Tim Folsom, *Manager*
EMP: 200
SQ FT: 70,348
SALES (corp-wide): 5.9B **Publicly Held**
WEB: www.cmcsg.com
SIC: 1791 3441 3496 Concrete reinforcement, placing of; fabricated structural metal; miscellaneous fabricated wire products
HQ: C M C Steel Fabricators, Inc.
1 Steel Mill Dr
Seguin TX 78155
830 372-8200

(P-3371)
C M C STEEL FABRICATORS INC
Also Called: CMC Rebar Fabricators
2755 S Willow Ave, Bloomington (92316-3260)
PHONE..................909 873-3060
Fax: 909 873-3020
Keith Dixon, *Branch Mgr*
EMP: 75
SQ FT: 45,032
SALES (corp-wide): 5.9B **Publicly Held**
WEB: www.cmcsg.com
SIC: 1791 Iron work, structural
HQ: C M C Steel Fabricators, Inc.
1 Steel Mill Dr
Seguin TX 78155
830 372-8200

(P-3372)
CAL-STATE STEEL CORPORATION
1801 W Compton Blvd, Compton (90220-2758)
P.O. Box 572034, Tarzana (91357-2034)
PHONE..................310 632-2772
Fax: 310 632-0502
Salvador Valenzuelam, *CEO*
Les Furdek, *CFO*
David Olson, *Corp Secy*
Reina Varela, *Office Mgr*
Kate Ji, *Project Mgr*
▲ **EMP:** 150
SQ FT: 10,000
SALES (est): 30.7MM **Privately Held**
WEB: www.calstatesteel.com
SIC: 1791 Structural steel erection; iron work, structural

(P-3373)
CALIFRNIA ERCTORS BAY AREA INC
4500 California Ct, Benicia (94510-1021)
PHONE..................707 746-1990
Fax: 707 746-0752
David W McEuen, *CEO*
Dennis Mc Euen, *Ch of Bd*
Galen Jaeger, *Vice Pres*
EMP: 150
SQ FT: 16,000

PRODUCTS & SERVICES SECTION
1791 - Structural Steel Erection County (P-3399)

SALES (est): 19.3MM **Privately Held**
WEB: www.calerectors.com
SIC: **1791** Structural steel erection; concrete reinforcement, placing of

(P-3374)
CAMPBELL CERTIFIED INC
1629 Ord Way, Oceanside (92056-3599)
PHONE..................................760 842-5226
Fax: 760 722-9000
Mark A Campbell, *CEO*
Mark Anthony Campbell, *CEO*
Lauralee Campbell, *Treasurer*
Jerry Sanders, *Project Engr*
EMP: 50
SQ FT: 45,000
SALES (est): 14.8MM **Privately Held**
WEB: www.campbellwelding.com
SIC: **1791** Building front installation metal

(P-3375)
CB&I INC
250 W 1st St Ste 346, Claremont (91711-4742)
PHONE..................................909 962-6400
Rick Gorder, *Manager*
EMP: 267 **Privately Held**
SIC: **1791** Structural steel erection
HQ: Cb&I Llc
2103 Research Forest Dr
The Woodlands TX 77380
832 513-1000

(P-3376)
CENTRAL REINFORCING CORP
14166 Slover Ave, Fontana (92337-7162)
P.O. Box 4967, San Dimas (91773-8967)
PHONE..................................909 773-0840
Eugene E Gutierrez, *President*
Patricia Cipriano, *CFO*
EMP: 60
SQ FT: 8,000
SALES: 6MM **Privately Held**
SIC: **1791** Concrete reinforcement, placing of

(P-3377)
CMC FONTANA STEEL
12451 Arrow Rte, Rancho Cucamonga (91739-9601)
P.O. Box 2219 (91729-2219)
PHONE..................................909 899-9993
Paul D Ware, *Ch of Bd*
Donald G Ware, *President*
John E Ware, *Corp Secy*
Adam Raines, *Manager*
▲ EMP: 300
SQ FT: 10,000
SALES (est): 20.5MM **Privately Held**
SIC: **1791** Concrete reinforcement, placing of

(P-3378)
CMC REBAR
12451 Arrow Rte, Rancho Cucamonga (91739-9601)
P.O. Box 11117, San Bernardino (92423-1117)
PHONE..................................909 899-9993
Alfredo Bubion, *Owner*
Nancy Koehler, *Info Tech Mgr*
Mike Moreno, *Info Tech Mgr*
▼ EMP: 63
SALES (est): 8.6MM **Privately Held**
SIC: **1791** Structural steel erection

(P-3379)
COAST IRON & STEEL CO
12300 Lakeland Rd, Santa Fe Springs (90670-3869)
P.O. Box 2846 (90670-0846)
PHONE..................................562 946-4421
Fax: 562 946-3508
Greg White, *President*
Cyndi White Cramer, *Shareholder*
Carrie White, *Shareholder*
Jared White, *Shareholder*
Ronald G White, *CEO*
▲ EMP: 50 EST: 1953
SQ FT: 360,000
SALES (est): 12.7MM **Privately Held**
WEB: www.indiainfoline.com
SIC: **1791** 3441 Structural steel erection; fabricated structural metal

(P-3380)
CONCORD IRON WORKS INC
Also Called: C I W
1501 Loveridge Rd Ste 15, Pittsburg (94565-2812)
PHONE..................................925 432-0136
Fax: 925 432-0440
Jill Lee, *President*
Rita Gonsalves, *Corp Secy*
David Maggi, *Vice Pres*
Rosa Cendejas, *Office Mgr*
Mark Ewing, *Project Mgr*
EMP: 50
SQ FT: 65,000
SALES (est): 12.4MM **Privately Held**
WEB: www.concordiron.com
SIC: **1791** Iron work, structural

(P-3381)
DEL REY LATHING INC
10960 Hole Ave, Riverside (92505-2755)
PHONE..................................951 343-1177
Greg Connick, *President*
EMP: 50
SALES (est): 3.4MM **Privately Held**
SIC: **1791** Metal lath & furring

(P-3382)
GONSALVES & SANTUCCI INC
Also Called: Conco Cement Company
5141 Commercial Cir, Concord (94520-8523)
PHONE..................................707 745-5019
Fax: 707 747-1714
Brent Alamillo, *Manager*
Catherine Santucci, *Office Mgr*
EMP: 250
SALES (corp-wide): 237MM **Privately Held**
SIC: **1791** Iron work, structural
PA: Gonsalves & Santucci, Inc.
5141 Commercial Cir
Concord CA 94520
925 685-6799

(P-3383)
INTEGRITY REBAR PLACERS
1345 Nandina Ave, Perris (92571-9402)
PHONE..................................951 696-6843
Fax: 951 304-3161
Kenneth Negrete, *President*
Richard Rabay, *Vice Pres*
EMP: 200
SALES (est): 30.9MM **Privately Held**
SIC: **1791** Structural steel erection

(P-3384)
IWORKS US INC
2501 S Malt Ave, Commerce (90040-3203)
PHONE..................................323 278-8363
Eric Dortch, *CEO*
Gilbert Belmontes, *Design Engr*
Matthew Dehnert, *Director*
▲ EMP: 53
SQ FT: 35,000
SALES (est): 10.1MM **Privately Held**
WEB: www.interironworks.com
SIC: **1791** Iron work, structural

(P-3385)
JS REAL ESTATE PRPTS INC
146 W 168th St, Gardena (90248-2729)
PHONE..................................310 856-6868
Gerry A Bustrum, *CEO*
Paul Schisino, *President*
Scott Bustrum, *Project Mgr*
Lorraine Getup, *Manager*
EMP: 85
SQ FT: 4,000
SALES (est): 7.8MM **Privately Held**
WEB: www.juniorsteel.com
SIC: **1791** Structural steel erection

(P-3386)
KCB TOWERS INC
27260 Meines St, Highland (92346-4223)
P.O. Box 100 (92346-0100)
PHONE..................................909 862-0322
Fax: 909 864-0653
S Lynn Bogh, *CEO*
Sharon Bogh, *Corp Secy*
Miles Bogh, *Vice Pres*
Lynne Behunin, *Office Mgr*
Lonnie Gallaher, *Office Mgr*
EMP: 100
SQ FT: 12,000
SALES (est): 18.1MM **Privately Held**
WEB: www.kcbtowers.com
SIC: **1791** 3441 Structural steel erection; fabricated structural metal

(P-3387)
KERN STEEL FABRICATION INC (PA)
627 Williams St, Bakersfield (93305-5445)
PHONE..................................661 327-9588
Fax: 661 327-5890
Tom Champness, *President*
Gene Panelli, *Vice Pres*
Bruce Alton, *Program Mgr*
Cynthia Olivas, *Executive Asst*
Steven A Heber, *Admin Sec*
EMP: 80
SQ FT: 50,000
SALES (est): 24.3MM **Privately Held**
WEB: www.kernsteel.com
SIC: **1791** 3441 3721 3728 Structural steel erection; fabricated structural metal; aircraft; aircraft parts & equipment; miscellaneous metalwork

(P-3388)
KWAN WO IRONWORKS INC
31628 Hayman St, Hayward (94544-7122)
PHONE..................................415 822-9628
Fax: 415 822-9068
Florence Kong, *President*
Ada Tang, *Office Mgr*
Fay Chu, *Admin Asst*
Owen Kuang, *Purchasing*
Kj Tong, *Sr Project Mgr*
▲ EMP: 120
SQ FT: 32,000
SALES (est): 34.4MM **Privately Held**
SIC: **1791** Iron work, structural

(P-3389)
LA STEEL SERVICES INC
1760 California Ave # 201, Corona (92881-3396)
PHONE..................................951 393-2013
Lee Albright, *President*
Richard Rabay, *Vice Pres*
EMP: 50
SALES (est): 832.6K **Privately Held**
SIC: **1791** Structural steel erection

(P-3390)
LONG SWIMMING POOL STEEL INC
3920 E Coronado St # 205, Anaheim (92807-1647)
PHONE..................................714 524-8172
Fax: 714 632-7757
Larry E Long, *President*
EMP: 50 EST: 1971
SQ FT: 15,000
SALES (est): 5.9MM **Privately Held**
WEB: www.lspsinc.com
SIC: **1791** Concrete reinforcement, placing of

(P-3391)
M BAR C CONSTRUCTION INC
674 Rancheros Dr, San Marcos (92069-3005)
PHONE..................................760 744-4131
Fax: 760 744-4449
Jason Ianni, *CEO*
Erik Krivokopich, *Vice Pres*
Megan McReynolds, *Manager*
EMP: 85
SQ FT: 6,000
SALES (est): 38.8MM **Privately Held**
WEB: www.mbarcconstruction.com
SIC: **1791** 1623 Structural steel erection; electric power line construction

(P-3392)
MECHANICAL INDUSTRIES INC
Also Called: M I I
314 Yampa St, Bakersfield (93307-2722)
PHONE..................................661 634-9477
Fax: 661 634-9460
Jerry L Nordine, *President*
Jerry Miranda, *Vice Pres*
Anna Dowdy, *Office Mgr*
EMP: 50
SQ FT: 43,000
SALES (est): 12.1MM **Privately Held**
SIC: **1791** Structural steel erection

(P-3393)
MID STATE STEEL ERECTION (PA)
1916 Cherokee Rd, Stockton (95205-2721)
PHONE..................................209 464-9497
Fax: 209 464-0538
Jerry Shipman, *President*
Patty Shipman, *Corp Secy*
Glenda Roe, *Technology*
Melissa Scott, *Technology*
EMP: 70
SALES (est): 13MM **Privately Held**
SIC: **1791** Structural steel erection

(P-3394)
PACIFIC REBAR INC
501 S Oaks Ave, Ontario (91762-4020)
PHONE..................................909 984-7199
Fax: 909 984-8386
Tim Herwehe, *President*
Erin Phillip, *Manager*
EMP: 60
SQ FT: 3,000
SALES (est): 7.8MM **Privately Held**
SIC: **1791** Concrete reinforcement, placing of

(P-3395)
PASO ROBLES TANK (PA)
825 26th St, Paso Robles (93446-1242)
P.O. Box 3229 (93447-3229)
PHONE..................................805 227-1641
Fax: 805 238-9654
Shawn P Owens, *CEO*
Robert Caldwell, *Vice Pres*
Waldon Davis, *Vice Pres*
Renee Cook, *Principal*
Carla Jobson, *Admin Asst*
EMP: 63
SALES: 39.1MM **Privately Held**
WEB: www.pasoroblestank.com
SIC: **1791** 3795 Structural steel erection; amphibian tanks, military

(P-3396)
QUALITY REINFORCING INC
13275 Gregg St, Poway (92064-7120)
PHONE..................................858 748-8400
Bryan Miller, *President*
▲ EMP: 85
SQ FT: 5,000
SALES (est): 11.9MM **Privately Held**
WEB: www.qualityreinforcing.com
SIC: **1791** Structural steel erection

(P-3397)
R & B REINFORCING STEEL CORP
13581 5th St, Chino (91710-5166)
PHONE..................................909 591-1726
David McDaniel, *CEO*
Robert Bessette, *President*
Dave McDaniel, *CFO*
Nancy Bessette, *Admin Sec*
EMP: 80
SQ FT: 30,000
SALES: 24MM **Privately Held**
SIC: **1791** Structural steel erection

(P-3398)
REBAR ENGINEERING INC
10706 Painter Ave, Santa Fe Springs (90670-4581)
P.O. Box 3986 (90670-1986)
PHONE..................................562 946-2461
Fax: 562 941-7740
Charles L Krebs, *President*
Jack Garroutte, *Exec VP*
Kevin Krebs, *General Mgr*
Patricia E Krebs, *Admin Sec*
Jim Sarafini, *Manager*
EMP: 250
SQ FT: 6,500
SALES: 45MM **Privately Held**
WEB: www.rebareng.com
SIC: **1791** Concrete reinforcement, placing of

(P-3399)
RIKA CORPORATION
Also Called: Diversified Metal Works
332 W Brenna Ln, Orange (92867-5637)
PHONE..................................949 830-9050
Fax: 714 771-3442
John E Ferguson, *CEO*

1791 - Structural Steel Erection

Justin Ferguson, *Vice Pres*
▲ **EMP:** 100
SQ FT: 8,000
SALES: 15MM **Privately Held**
SIC: 1791 Structural steel erection

(P-3400)
SANTA CLARITA INTERIORS INC
25682 Springbrook Ave # 130, Santa Clarita (91350-2432)
PHONE 661 253-0861
Fax: 661 253-4431
Brian Schienle, *President*
Patty Schienle, *Treasurer*
EMP: 75
SQ FT: 10,000
SALES (est): 5.7MM **Privately Held**
SIC: 1791 1742 Iron work, structural; drywall

(P-3401)
SCHUFF STEEL COMPANY
2324 Navy Dr, Stockton (95206-1161)
PHONE 209 938-0869
Chase Abbott, *Branch Mgr*
EMP: 149
SALES (corp-wide): 1.1B **Publicly Held**
SIC: 1791 3441 Structural steel erection; fabricated structural metal
HQ: Schuff Steel Company
1841 W Buchanan St
Phoenix AZ 85007
602 252-7787

(P-3402)
SCRAPE CERTIFIED WELDING INC
2525 Old Highway 395, Fallbrook (92028-8794)
PHONE 760 728-1308
Jeff D Scrape, *President*
Francis Johnsen, *Office Mgr*
EMP: 91
SALES (est): 14.7MM **Privately Held**
SIC: 1791 Structural steel erection

(P-3403)
SO-CAL STRL STL FBRICATION INC
130 S Spruce Ave, Rialto (92376-9005)
PHONE 909 877-1299
Fax: 909 877-1298
Craig B Yates, *CEO*
Kim Yates, *Vice Pres*
Sally Johnson, *Manager*
EMP: 50
SQ FT: 40,000
SALES (est): 8.5MM **Privately Held**
SIC: 1791 Structural steel erection

(P-3404)
STROCAL INC (PA)
4651 Quail Lakes Dr, Stockton (95207-5258)
P.O. Box 77937 (95267-1237)
PHONE 209 948-4646
Fax: 209 948-4585
David Long, *President*
Doug Muniz, *CFO*
David M Berrens, *Admin Sec*
Darlene Ingersoll, *Human Res Mgr*
Robert Felton, *Manager*
EMP: 255
SQ FT: 6,000
SALES (est): 22.9MM **Privately Held**
WEB: www.strocal.com
SIC: 1791 3441 Structural steel erection; fabricated structural metal

(P-3405)
T L FABRICATIONS LP
2921 E Coronado St, Anaheim (92806-2502)
PHONE 562 802-3980
Ryan Kerrigan, *President*
Michael Hsu, *Vice Pres*
▲ **EMP:** 60
SQ FT: 30,000
SALES (est): 9.8MM **Privately Held**
WEB: www.tlfab.com
SIC: 1791 Structural steel erection

(P-3406)
TAP RAM REINFORCING INC
11658 Excelsior Dr, Norwalk (90650-5826)
PHONE 562 484-0859

Maria G Tapia, *President*
EMP: 80
SALES (est): 553.3K **Privately Held**
SIC: 1791 Smoke stacks, steel: installation & maintenance

(P-3407)
TEXTURE SPECIALTIES INC
295 Mccreary Ave, Hanford (93230-2032)
PHONE 559 904-6047
Robert Tarlton, *President*
Mollie Pusich, *Principal*
EMP: 50
SALES: 950K **Privately Held**
SIC: 1791 1742 Metal lath & furring; plaster & drywall work

1793 Glass & Glazing Work

(P-3408)
CENTER GLASS CO NO 3
7853 El Cajon Blvd, La Mesa (91942-0621)
P.O. Box 1088 (91944-1088)
PHONE 619 469-6181
Jackson R Witte, *Ch of Bd*
Donald Witte, *Shareholder*
Ronald A Leaverton, *President*
David C Lawrenz, *Vice Pres*
EMP: 55 **EST:** 1963
SQ FT: 20,000
SALES: 6MM **Privately Held**
WEB: www.centerglass.com
SIC: 1793 Glass & glazing work

(P-3409)
DIVISION 8 INC
1920 Cordell Ct Ste 105, El Cajon (92020-0900)
PHONE 619 741-7552
Robert Hoyt, *President*
David W Vincent, *CFO*
Debra Hoyt, *Corp Secy*
Stephanie Lindsay, *Vice Pres*
Miguel Rodriguez, *Vice Pres*
EMP: 50
SQ FT: 5,000
SALES: 4MM **Privately Held**
WEB: www.division8inc.com
SIC: 1793 Glass & glazing work

(P-3410)
GIROUX GLASS INC (PA)
850 W Washington Blvd, Los Angeles (90015-3359)
PHONE 213 747-7406
Fax: 213 747-8778
Nataline Lomedico, *CEO*
Anne-Merelie Murrell, *Ch of Bd*
Jerod Allen, *President*
Ralph Deligio, *Project Mgr*
Jesse Ponce, *Project Mgr*
▲ **EMP:** 120 **EST:** 1946
SALES: 25.2MM **Privately Held**
WEB: www.girouxglass.com
SIC: 1793 Glass & glazing work

(P-3411)
HABENICHT & HOWLETT A CORP
25 Patterson St, San Francisco (94124-1328)
PHONE 415 824-7040
Fax: 415 824-3290
Tom Bukard, *CEO*
EMP: 75
SALES (est): 2.7MM **Privately Held**
SIC: 1793 5231 Glass & glazing work; glass

(P-3412)
PERFECTION GLASS INC
554 3rd St, Lake Elsinore (92530-2729)
PHONE 951 674-0240
Fax: 951 674-0841
Richard L Warren, *President*
Dane Warren, *Treasurer*
Chris Bonnet, *Admin Sec*
Cheryll Bonnet, *Controller*
EMP: 50
SQ FT: 4,200
SALES (est): 7.6MM **Privately Held**
SIC: 1793 Glass & glazing work

(P-3413)
PROGRESS GLASS CO INC (PA)
25 Patterson St, San Francisco (94124-1377)
PHONE 415 824-7040
Tom Burkard, *CEO*
Chuck Burkard, *President*
Thomas C Burkard III, *President*
Shirley Wallace, *Treasurer*
Jim Holmberg, *Senior VP*
▲ **EMP:** 105 **EST:** 1956
SQ FT: 16,250
SALES (est): 25.3MM **Privately Held**
WEB: www.progressglass.com
SIC: 1793 Glass & glazing work

(P-3414)
ROYAL GLASS COMPANY INC
3200 De La Cruz Blvd, Santa Clara (95054-2602)
PHONE 408 969-0444
Fax: 408 964-0751
John Maggiore, *CEO*
James Maggiore, *Vice Pres*
Lei Shigezawa, *Accounts Mgr*
EMP: 80
SALES (est): 26.2MM **Privately Held**
SIC: 1793 Glass & glazing work

(P-3415)
SAFECO DOOR & HARDWARE INC
Also Called: Safeco Glass
31054 San Antonio St, Hayward (94544-7904)
PHONE 510 429-4768
Mahboubeh Ahmadi, *President*
Milagors Missaghi, *Treasurer*
Ali Missaghi Akoub, *Vice Pres*
Hamid Ahmadi, *Admin Sec*
Sina Ahmadi, *Controller*
EMP: 65
SQ FT: 13,000
SALES (est): 11.1MM **Privately Held**
SIC: 1793 Glass & glazing work

(P-3416)
TOWER GLASS INC
9570 Pathway St Ste A, Santee (92071-4100)
PHONE 619 596-6199
Fax: 619 596-0325
Evelyn Dee Swaim, *CEO*
Barry Swaim, *CFO*
Jeffrey Swaim, *General Mgr*
Carl Marquette, *Project Mgr*
Kirk Venzor, *Project Mgr*
EMP: 100
SQ FT: 15,000
SALES (est): 28MM **Privately Held**
WEB: www.towerglass.com
SIC: 1793 Glass & glazing work

(P-3417)
WALTERS & WOLF GLASS COMPANY (PA)
Also Called: Walter & Wolf
41450 Boscell Rd, Fremont (94538-3103)
PHONE 510 490-1115
Fax: 408 651-7172
Randall A Wolf, *President*
Jeff Belzer, *CFO*
Nick Kocelj, *Vice Pres*
Ida Divenere, *Admin Asst*
Ray Lagucik, *Admin Asst*
▲ **EMP:** 135 **EST:** 1977
SALES (est): 128.5MM **Privately Held**
WEB: www.waltersandwolf.com
SIC: 1793 Glass & glazing work

(P-3418)
WOODBRIDGE GLASS INC
14321 Myford Rd, Tustin (92780-7022)
PHONE 714 838-4444
Fax: 949 734-1293
Virginia Siciliani, *President*
Jim Siciliani, *Corp Secy*
John Siciliani, *Vice Pres*
Gail Rainsberger, *Executive Asst*
Mike Legault, *Project Mgr*
▲ **EMP:** 205
SQ FT: 8,500

SALES (est): 84.6MM **Privately Held**
WEB: www.woodbridgeglass.com
SIC: 1793 5231 Glass & glazing work; glass, leaded or stained

1794 Excavating & Grading Work

(P-3419)
BAY CITIES PAV & GRADING INC
1450 Civic Ct Bldg B, Concord (94520-5295)
PHONE 925 687-6666
Fax: 925 687-2122
Ben L Rodriguez, *CEO*
Marlo Manqueros, *Vice Pres*
Kim Rodriguez, *Admin Sec*
Steven Caudill, *Human Res Mgr*
EMP: 250
SQ FT: 4,000
SALES (est): 57.5MM **Privately Held**
SIC: 1794 1611 7353 Excavation work; highway & street construction; earth moving equipment, rental or leasing

(P-3420)
CALEX ENGINEERING INC
23651 Pine St, Newhall (91321-3106)
PHONE 661 254-1866
Fax: 661 259-1083
Kenny Seitz, *Partner*
Mike Neilson, *CEO*
Josephine Mape, *Controller*
EMP: 70
SQ FT: 1,800
SALES (est): 15.8MM **Privately Held**
SIC: 1794 Excavation work

(P-3421)
CARONE & COMPANY INC
Also Called: Diablo Valley Rock
5009 Forni Dr Ste A, Concord (94520-8525)
PHONE 925 602-8800
Fax: 925 602-8801
Richard Lloyd Carone, *President*
EMP: 60
SQ FT: 48,000
SALES (est): 12MM **Privately Held**
SIC: 1794 Excavation work

(P-3422)
CHINO GRADING INC
3613 Philadelphia St, Chino (91710-2068)
PHONE 909 364-8667
Norm Gorgone, *President*
Shannon Nunn, *Controller*
EMP: 60
SALES (est): 5.3MM **Privately Held**
SIC: 1794 Excavation & grading, building construction

(P-3423)
COASTAL GRADING AND EXCAVATING
756 Calle Plano, Camarillo (93012-8555)
PHONE 805 445-6433
Thomas Staben Jr, *President*
Carrie Cox, *Office Mgr*
EMP: 50
SALES (est): 4.9MM **Privately Held**
SIC: 1794 Excavation work

(P-3424)
COMMERCIAL SITE IMPRVS INC
192 Poker Flat Rd, Copperopolis (95228-9601)
PHONE 209 785-1920
Ron Batch, *Vice Pres*
EMP: 50
SALES (est): 1.1MM **Privately Held**
SIC: 1794 Excavation & grading, building construction

(P-3425)
CREW INC
19618 S Susana Rd, Compton (90221-5716)
PHONE 310 608-6860
Fax: 310 608-6865
David M Lalonde, *President*
Darrin Lalonde, *Admin Sec*
Andrew Kerr, *Controller*
Warren Duke, *Purch Mgr*

EMP: 60
SQ FT: 5,000
SALES (est): 12.7MM **Privately Held**
WEB: www.crew.net
SIC: 1794 Excavation & grading, building construction

(P-3426)
DAVE SPURR EXCAVATING INC
Also Called: Spurr Co.
935 Riverside Ave Ste 18, Paso Robles (93446-2649)
P.O. Box 1920 (93447-1920)
PHONE 805 238-0834
Fax: 805 467-3683
David Spurr, *President*
Amanda Cross, *Manager*
Missy Tuck, *Manager*
EMP: 50
SQ FT: 1,000
SALES (est): 6.6MM **Privately Held**
SIC: 1794 Excavation & grading, building construction

(P-3427)
ERRECAS INC
12570 Slaughter House, Lakeside (92040)
P.O. Box 640 (92040-0640)
PHONE 619 390-6400
Fax: 619 443-2758
Charles M Erreca, *President*
Charmaine Bridwell, *Shareholder*
Mike Conroy, *CFO*
John East, *Vice Pres*
Scott Erreca, *Vice Pres*
EMP: 100
SQ FT: 48,450
SALES (est): 9.3MM **Privately Held**
WEB: www.errecas.com
SIC: 1794 1771 Excavation & grading, building construction; concrete work

(P-3428)
FJ WILLERT CONTRACTING CO
1869 Nirvana Ave, Chula Vista (91911-6117)
PHONE 619 421-1980
Fax: 619 421-1910
Fred M Willert, *President*
Marie Wales, *Administration*
EMP: 110 **EST:** 1972
SQ FT: 11,748
SALES (est): 33.5MM **Privately Held**
WEB: www.fjwillert.com
SIC: 1794 Excavation & grading, building construction

(P-3429)
GILLIAM & SONS INC
Also Called: Valco Construction
9831 Rosedale Hwy, Bakersfield (93312-2604)
P.O. Box 9955 (93389-1955)
PHONE 661 589-0913
Fax: 661 589-6334
Bill W Gilliam, *CEO*
Scott Gilliam, *Vice Pres*
Ken Spiker, *Human Res Dir*
John Ruiz, *Safety Dir*
EMP: 50
SQ FT: 2,500
SALES (est): 10.8MM **Privately Held**
WEB: www.gilliamandsons.com
SIC: 1794 Excavation work

(P-3430)
GLAZIER STEEL INC
650 Sandoval Way, Hayward (94544-7129)
PHONE 510 471-5300
Fax: 510 471-5301
Craig Glazier, *CEO*
Harold Glazier, *President*
Thomas Glazier, *Vice Pres*
Jeremy Loebs, *Project Mgr*
Rick Liu, *Controller*
EMP: 75
SQ FT: 26,897
SALES (est): 27.4MM **Privately Held**
SIC: 1794 Excavation & grading, building construction

(P-3431)
GUINN CORPORATION
6533 Rosedale Hwy, Bakersfield (93308-5903)
P.O. Box 1339 (93302-1339)
PHONE 661 325-6109
Fax: 661 325-5173
Gary Guinn, *CEO*
Jeff Affonso, *Corp Secy*
Tim Guinn, *Vice Pres*
Adrienne Reitsma, *Controller*
B Krompkamp, *Human Res Mgr*
EMP: 75
SQ FT: 3,600
SALES (est): 18.9MM **Privately Held**
WEB: www.guinnconstruction.com
SIC: 1794 Excavation work; excavation & grading, building construction

(P-3432)
HOWARD CONTRACTING INC
12354 Carson St, Hawaiian Gardens (90716-1604)
PHONE 562 596-2969
Frederick Stanley Howard, *CEO*
Viki R Howard, *Corp Secy*
Stanley L Howard, *Vice Pres*
EMP: 50
SQ FT: 3,500
SALES (est): 10.2MM **Privately Held**
SIC: 1794 Excavation work

(P-3433)
INLAND EROSION CONTROL SVCS
42181 Avenida Alvarado A, Temecula (92590-3429)
P.O. Box 728, Murrieta (92564-0728)
PHONE 951 301-8334
Fax: 951 296-0807
Todd Close, *President*
Carlos Garcia, *Vice Pres*
Leo Rodriguez, *Controller*
EMP: 59
SQ FT: 1,000
SALES (est): 6.8MM **Privately Held**
SIC: 1794 Excavation work

(P-3434)
JEFF CARPENTER INC
1380 W Oleander Ave, Perris (92571-7863)
PHONE 951 657-5115
Fax: 951 657-0615
Jeff Carpenter, *President*
Brenda Unterseher, *Office Mgr*
Kevin Bowls, *Project Mgr*
EMP: 60
SQ FT: 1,300
SALES (est): 10.1MM **Privately Held**
SIC: 1794 Excavation work

(P-3435)
LOVCO CONSTRUCTION INC
1300 E Burnett St, Signal Hill (90755-3512)
P.O. Box 90335, Long Beach (90809-0335)
PHONE 562 595-1601
Fax: 562 988-0094
Terry C Lovingier, *President*
Katie Lovingier, *Treasurer*
Steve Barnett, *Vice Pres*
Matt Lovinger, *Vice Pres*
Mike McGougan, *Vice Pres*
EMP: 125
SQ FT: 2,500
SALES (est): 25.2MM **Privately Held**
WEB: www.lovco.com
SIC: 1794 1771 1611 Excavation work; concrete work; highway & street construction; general contractor, highway & street construction

(P-3436)
LUPTON EXCAVATION INC
8467 Florin Rd, Sacramento (95828-2512)
PHONE 916 387-1104
Fax: 916 387-1153
Kenneth Lupton Jr, *President*
Sheryl Lavoie, *Office Mgr*
EMP: 75
SQ FT: 4,000
SALES (est): 10.8MM **Privately Held**
SIC: 1794 Excavation work

(P-3437)
MEYERS EARTHWORK INC
4150 Fig Tree Ln, Redding (96002-9315)
P.O. Box 493730 (96049-3730)
PHONE 530 365-8858
Jacob Meyers, *President*
Charleen Meyers, *Vice Pres*
▼ **EMP:** 55
SQ FT: 2,000
SALES (est): 8.4MM **Privately Held**
SIC: 1794 Excavation & grading, building construction

(P-3438)
MITCHELL ENGINEERING
1395 Evans Ave, San Francisco (94124-1703)
P.O. Box 880308 (94188-0308)
PHONE 415 227-1040
Michael A Silva, *President*
Curtis F Mitchell, *Vice Pres*
Thelma Welch, *Manager*
▲ **EMP:** 50
SQ FT: 2,000
SALES (est): 9.9MM **Privately Held**
WEB: www.mitchell-engineering.com
SIC: 1794 1623 1622 1629 Excavation & grading, building construction; water main construction; pipeline construction; bridge, tunnel & elevated highway; railroad & subway construction

(P-3439)
MOZINGO CONSTRUCTION INC
751 Wakefield Ct, Oakdale (95361-7761)
PHONE 209 848-0160
Fax: 209 533-2403
Kurtis Mozingo, *CEO*
Doni Mozingo, *President*
Michael Freeman, *Vice Pres*
Philip Gianfortone, *Vice Pres*
Ruth A Brickner, *Executive*
EMP: 50
SALES (est): 11.4MM **Privately Held**
SIC: 1794 Excavation work

(P-3440)
PACIFIC EXCAVATION INC
9796 Kent St, Elk Grove (95624-4823)
PHONE 916 686-2800
Fax: 916 686-2806
Tim Paxin, *President*
Jim Paxin, *Vice Pres*
Priscilla Gaspelum, *Manager*
EMP: 75
SQ FT: 30,000
SALES (est): 10.2MM **Privately Held**
WEB: www.pacexcavation.com
SIC: 1794 Excavation work

(P-3441)
REED THOMAS COMPANY INC
1025 N Santiago St, Santa Ana (92701-3800)
PHONE 714 558-7691
Fax: 714 558-7361
Harvey T Biegle, *President*
Kelly Williams, *CIO*
Samuel Matthews, *Finance*
EMP: 90
SQ FT: 8,800
SALES (est): 14.2MM **Privately Held**
WEB: www.reedthomas.com
SIC: 1794 Excavation & grading, building construction

(P-3442)
STURGEON SON GRADING & PAV INC (PA)
3511 Gilmore Ave, Bakersfield (93308-6205)
P.O. Box 2840 (93303-2840)
PHONE 661 322-4408
John E Powell, *CEO*
Paul Sturgeon, *President*
Oliver Sturgeon, *Principal*
Joseph D'Angelo, *Controller*
Mickey Duggan, *Sales Staff*
EMP: 180 **EST:** 1927
SQ FT: 3,500
SALES (est): 56.7MM **Privately Held**
WEB: www.sturgeonandson.com
SIC: 1794 8711 Excavation work; engineering services

(P-3443)
SUKUT CONSTRUCTION INC (PA)
4010 W Chandler Ave, Santa Ana (92704-5202)
PHONE 714 540-5351
Fax: 714 545-2003
Michael H Crawford, *President*
Paul Kuliev, *CFO*
Myron C Sukut, *Chairman*
Robbie Zwick, *VP Bus Dvlpt*
Janice Reiber, *Executive Asst*
▲ **EMP:** 60
SQ FT: 12,000
SALES (est): 58.3MM **Privately Held**
WEB: www.sukut.com
SIC: 1794 1611 1623 1629 Excavation work; general contractor, highway & street construction; water & sewer line construction; dams, waterways, docks & other marine construction

(P-3444)
TIDWELL EXCAV ACQUISITION INC
1691 Los Angeles Ave, Ventura (93004-3213)
PHONE 805 647-4707
Fax: 805 647-8590
Alex Miruello, *President*
Louis Armona, *Treasurer*
Timothy Wayne Goodwin, *Vice Pres*
Christa Kalli, *Manager*
EMP: 90 **EST:** 1956
SALES (est): 10.7MM
SALES (corp-wide): 280.6MM **Privately Held**
SIC: 1794 Excavation & grading, building construction
PA: Meruelo Enterprises, Inc.
9550 Firestone Blvd # 105
Downey CA 90241
562 745-2300

(P-3445)
TIM PAXINS PACIFIC EXCAVATION
9796 Kent St, Elk Grove (95624-4823)
PHONE 916 686-2800
Tim Paxin, *President*
EMP: 50
SQ FT: 2,500
SALES (est): 5.4MM **Privately Held**
SIC: 1794 Excavation work; excavation & grading, building construction

(P-3446)
VANDER WEERD GENERAL CNSTR
837 Commercial Ave, Tulare (93274-7101)
PHONE 559 688-1099
Fax: 559 688-8784
Ron A Vander Weerd, *President*
Rosalinda Vander Weerd, *Corp Secy*
EMP: 65
SQ FT: 10,000
SALES (est): 4.5MM **Privately Held**
SIC: 1794 Excavation & grading, building construction

1795 Wrecking & Demolition Work

(P-3447)
AMERICAN CONCRETE CUTTING INC
Also Called: American Dmltion/Concrete Cutng
620 N Poinsettia St, Santa Ana (92701-3999)
PHONE 714 547-7181
Fax: 714 547-0584
F Richard Stewart, *President*
John Moore, *Vice Pres*
EMP: 100
SALES (est): 8.3MM **Privately Held**
WEB: www.americandemo.com
SIC: 1795 Wrecking & demolition work; concrete breaking for streets & highways

1795 - Wrecking & Demolition Work County (P-3448)

(P-3448)
AMERICAN WRECKING INC
2459 Lee Ave, South El Monte (91733-1407)
PHONE.................................626 350-8303
Fax: 626 350-8322
Jose Luis Galaviz, *President*
Jay Gonzalez, *COO*
Warne Galaviz, *Vice Pres*
Robert Hall, *Vice Pres*
Luis Galaviz, *Project Mgr*
EMP: 100
SQ FT: 1,000
SALES (est): 19.5MM **Privately Held**
WEB: www.americanwreckinginc.com
SIC: 1795 Demolition, buildings & other structures

(P-3449)
CASPER COMPANY
3825 Bancroft Dr, Spring Valley (91977-2122)
PHONE.................................619 589-6001
Fax: 619 589-7158
Roger Casper, *CEO*
William R Haithcock, *President*
Greg T Casper, *Vice Pres*
Steven Casper, *Vice Pres*
Isabel Ortiz Marocco, *Vice Pres*
EMP: 143
SQ FT: 6,000
SALES (est): 45MM **Privately Held**
SIC: 1795 Concrete breaking for streets & highways

(P-3450)
CLAUSS CONSTRUCTION
8956 Winter Gardens Blvd, Lakeside (92040-4935)
PHONE.................................619 390-4940
Fax: 619 390-4944
Patrick Michael Clauss, *CEO*
William Musbach, *Senior VP*
Josh Clauss, *Vice Pres*
Briana Munoz, *Admin Asst*
Aaron Vincent, *Project Mgr*
EMP: 80
SALES (est): 18.5MM **Privately Held**
WEB: www.claussconstruction.com
SIC: 1795 1629 4959 Wrecking & demolition work; earthmoving contractor; toxic or hazardous waste cleanup

(P-3451)
CLEVELAND WRECKING COMPANY
999 W Town And Country Rd, Orange (92868-4713)
PHONE.................................510 568-2626
Susan Walgenbach, *Manager*
EMP: 100
SALES (corp-wide): 17.9B **Publicly Held**
WEB: www.clevelandwrecking.com
SIC: 1795 Demolition, buildings & other structures
HQ: Cleveland Wrecking Company
999 W Town And Country Rd
Orange CA 92868
626 967-4287

(P-3452)
CLEVELAND WRECKING COMPANY (DH)
Also Called: CWC Acquisition
999 W Town And Country Rd, Orange (92868-4713)
PHONE.................................626 967-4287
Fax: 626 967-1479
James Sheridan, *President*
Andrew Varga, *President*
Steve Fugate, *Vice Pres*
Eshaq Rosie, *Personnel Exec*
Sheree Kaplan, *Director*
EMP: 78
SQ FT: 60,000
SALES (est): 20.8MM **Privately Held**
SALES (corp-wide): 17.9B **Publicly Held**
WEB: www.clevelandwrecking.com
SIC: 1795 1796 1799 Demolition, buildings & other structures; machinery dismantling; asbestos removal & encapsulation
HQ: Urs Group, Inc.
300 S Grand Ave Ste 1100
Los Angeles CA 90071
213 593-8000

(P-3453)
DANNY RYAN PRECISION CONTG INC
1818 N Orangethorpe Park, Anaheim (92801-1140)
PHONE.................................949 642-6664
Fax: 949 642-6664
Danny Ryan, *President*
Janet Dean, *Office Admin*
EMP: 90
SQ FT: 10,000
SALES (est): 19MM **Privately Held**
SIC: 1795 1799 Demolition, buildings & other structures; asbestos removal & encapsulation

(P-3454)
DIRT CHEAP DEMOLITION INC
171 Mace St Ste A4, Chula Vista (91911-5861)
P.O. Box 1186, Bonita (91908-1186)
PHONE.................................619 426-9598
Dan Cannon, *President*
EMP: 50
SALES (est): 3.2MM **Privately Held**
SIC: 1795 Demolition, buildings & other structures

(P-3455)
GD HEIL INC
1031 Segovia Cir, Placentia (92870-7137)
PHONE.................................714 687-9100
Fax: 714 687-9108
James A Langford, *CEO*
Gary Heil, *President*
Steve Mc Clain, *Vice Pres*
Carl Crave, *Branch Mgr*
Laura Heil, *Admin Sec*
EMP: 160
SQ FT: 20,770
SALES (est): 27.4MM **Privately Held**
WEB: www.gdheil.com
SIC: 1795 Demolition, buildings & other structures

(P-3456)
HULK CONSTRUCTION
4352 Lakeview Ave, Yorba Linda (92886-2422)
PHONE.................................714 701-9458
Ronald Short, *President*
EMP: 80
SALES (est): 2.9MM **Privately Held**
SIC: 1795 Dismantling steel oil tanks

(P-3457)
INTERIOR RMOVAL SPECIALIST INC
8990 Atlantic Ave, South Gate (90280-3505)
PHONE.................................323 357-6900
Fax: 323 357-9400
Carlos Herrera, *CEO*
Isabel Herrera, *Vice Pres*
Gary Shelton, *Info Tech Dir*
Chuck Brode, *Project Mgr*
Roy Ludt, *Project Mgr*
EMP: 150
SALES (est): 26.9MM **Privately Held**
WEB: www.irsdemo.com
SIC: 1795 Demolition, buildings & other structures

(P-3458)
KROEKER INC
4627 S Chestnut Ave, Fresno (93725-9238)
PHONE.................................559 237-3764
Fax: 559 268-3366
Joyce Kroeker, *President*
Jeff Kroeker, *Corp Secy*
Ed Kroeker, *Vice Pres*
Rodney Ainsworth, *General Mgr*
John Ramirez, *Office Mgr*
EMP: 120
SQ FT: 9,000
SALES: 25MM **Privately Held**
SIC: 1795 1629 4953 Wrecking & demolition work; land reclamation; earthmoving contractor; recycling, waste materials

(P-3459)
LOS ANGELES ENGINEERING INC
633 N Barranca Ave, Covina (91723-1229)
PHONE.................................626 869-1400
Fax: 626 869-0902
Henry Angus O'Brien, *President*
Kim Zuccaro, *Vice Pres*
Glenn Kovac, *Project Mgr*
John Risch, *Project Mgr*
EMP: 110
SQ FT: 5,000
SALES (est): 24.3MM **Privately Held**
WEB: www.laeng.net
SIC: 1795 1629 1611 8711 Demolition, buildings & other structures; earthmoving contractor; concrete construction: roads, highways, sidewalks, etc.; engineering services; water, sewer & utility lines

(P-3460)
MILLER ENVIRONMENTAL INC
1130 W Trenton Ave, Orange (92867-3536)
PHONE.................................714 385-0099
Fax: 714 385-0011
Gregg Miller, *President*
Rob Schaefer, *Vice Pres*
Heather Cline, *Admin Asst*
Marissa Perales, *Programmer Anys*
Mindy Peek, *Sales Executive*
EMP: 150
SQ FT: 3,000
SALES (est): 38.3MM **Privately Held**
WEB: www.millerenvironmental.com
SIC: 1795 4953 Demolition, buildings & other structures; hazardous waste collection & disposal

(P-3461)
NORTHSTAR CONTG GROUP INC
13320 Cambridge St, Santa Fe Springs (90670-4904)
PHONE.................................714 639-7600
Joe Capania, *General Mgr*
EMP: 145
SALES (corp-wide): 371.8MM **Privately Held**
SIC: 1795 Wrecking & demolition work
HQ: Northstar Contracting Group, Inc.
31500 Hayman St
Hayward CA 94544
510 491-1300

(P-3462)
NORTHSTAR DEM & REMEDIATION LP (DH)
404 N Berry St, Brea (92821-3104)
PHONE.................................714 672-3500
Fax: 714 672-3501
Jose Alonso, *General Mgr*
Subhas Khara, *President*
Duane Kerr, *CFO*
Joseph Delahunty, *Vice Pres*
Trent Michaels, *Vice Pres*
EMP: 215
SQ FT: 19,000
SALES (est): 248.9MM
SALES (corp-wide): 371.8MM **Privately Held**
SIC: 1795 1799 8744 Wrecking & demolition work; decontamination services;
HQ: Northstar Group Services, Inc.
370 7th Ave Ste 1803
New York NY 10001
212 951-3660

(P-3463)
PENHALL COMPANY
Also Called: Penhall San Leandro 153
13750 Catalina St, San Leandro (94577-5502)
PHONE.................................510 357-8810
Fax: 510 357-8817
Scott Hustad, *Manager*
Lisa Ortiz, *Admin Asst*
Valerie Sanchez, *Sales Staff*
Dana Directo, *Manager*
Ed Ferguson, *Manager*
EMP: 60
SALES (corp-wide): 2.4B **Privately Held**
SIC: 1795 Wrecking & demolition work
HQ: Penhall Company
320 N Crescent Way
Anaheim CA 92801
714 772-6450

(P-3464)
PENHALL INTERNATIONAL CORP (HQ)
Also Called: Concrete Demolition
320 N Crescent Way, Anaheim (92801-6752)
P.O. Box 4609 (92803-4609)
PHONE.................................714 772-6450
Jeff Long, *Principal*
C George Bush, *CEO*
Bruce Lux, *CFO*
Erika L Maniace, *Admin Mgr*
Ruby Belew, *Office Mgr*
EMP: 175 **EST:** 1957
SQ FT: 10,000
SALES (est): 296.6MM
SALES (corp-wide): 2.4B **Privately Held**
WEB: www.penhall.com
SIC: 1795 1771 Wrecking & demolition work; concrete work
PA: Centerbridge Partners, L.P.
375 Park Ave Fl 13
New York NY 10152
212 672-5000

(P-3465)
RANDAZZO ENTERPRISES INC
13550 Blackie Rd, Castroville (95012-3200)
PHONE.................................831 633-4420
Fax: 831 633-4588
John Randazzo, *President*
Alice Randazzo, *CFO*
Mark Randazzo, *Vice Pres*
EMP: 61 **EST:** 1965
SQ FT: 13,000
SALES (est): 12.4MM **Privately Held**
WEB: www.randazzoenterprises.com
SIC: 1795 Demolition, buildings & other structures

(P-3466)
SECA EQP REMOVAL & DISMANTLE
Also Called: Seca Eqp Removal & Dismantling
684 Bitritto Ct, Modesto (95356-9272)
PHONE.................................209 543-1600
Maria Carbenas, *President*
EMP: 50
SQ FT: 2,300
SALES (est): 3.1MM **Privately Held**
SIC: 1795 Wrecking & demolition work

(P-3467)
SIERRA RECYCLING & DEM INC
1620 E Brundage Ln Frnt, Bakersfield (93307-2756)
PHONE.................................661 327-7073
Philip Sacco, *President*
Stephen Larsen, *Manager*
Steve Simmons, *Manager*
EMP: 71
SQ FT: 20,000
SALES (est): 9.8MM **Privately Held**
SIC: 1795 Wrecking & demolition work

(P-3468)
SILVERADO CONTRACTORS INC (PA)
2855 Mandela Pkwy Fl 2, Oakland (94608-4011)
PHONE.................................510 658-9960
Joseph M Capriola, *President*
Sue Capriola, *Treasurer*
Peter Knutch, *Vice Pres*
Richard Riggs, *Vice Pres*
Troy Wright, *Project Mgr*
EMP: 65
SALES (est): 18.1MM **Privately Held**
WEB: www.silveradocontractors.com
SIC: 1795 Wrecking & demolition work

(P-3469)
STOMPER CO INC
7799 Enterprise Dr, Newark (94560-3408)
PHONE.................................510 574-0570
Fax: 510 574-0550
Donna R Rehrmann, *President*
George Rehrmann, *Vice Pres*

PRODUCTS & SERVICES SECTION
1799 - Special Trade Contractors, NEC County (P-3491)

EMP: 60
SQ FT: 15,000
SALES (est): 10.9MM Privately Held
WEB: www.stomper.org
SIC: 1795 Concrete breaking for streets & highways

(P-3470)
TWO RIVERS DEMOLITION INC
2620 Mercantile Dr 100, Rancho Cordova (95742-6519)
PHONE.....................916 638-6775
Fax: 916 638-0511
W Roderick Palon, President
Carin Rodriguez, Vice Pres
Adam Barrows, Division Mgr
Mark Davis, Division Mgr
Julie Polisso, Project Mgr
EMP: 55
SALES (est): 11.8MM Privately Held
WEB: www.2riversdemo.com
SIC: 1795 Wrecking & demolition work; concrete breaking for streets & highways; demolition, buildings & other structures

(P-3471)
ULTIMATE REMOVAL INC
Also Called: ULTIMATE DEMO
2168 Pomona Blvd, Pomona (91768-3332)
P.O. Box 1220 (91769-1220)
PHONE.....................909 524-0800
John W Welch, President
Patrick Coleman, CFO
Derek Mireles, Senior VP
Rudy Trujillo, Superintendent
EMP: 124
SQ FT: 9,900
SALES: 9.4MM Privately Held
WEB: www.ultimateremoval.com
SIC: 1795 Demolition, buildings & other structures

(P-3472)
VIKING EQUIPMENT CORP
Also Called: Viking Demolition
540 W Windsor Rd, Glendale (91204-1812)
P.O. Box 251257 (91225-1257)
PHONE.....................818 500-9447
Berger Jostad, President
John Mike Tredick, CFO
Scott Tredick, Corp Secy
EMP: 65
SALES (est): 5.9MM Privately Held
WEB: www.vikingdemo.com
SIC: 1795 1799 5932 Wrecking & demolition work; building mover, including houses; building materials, secondhand

1796 Installation Or Erection Of Bldg Eqpt & Machinery, NEC

(P-3473)
ANDERSON & MARTELLA INC
1200 Mt Diablo Blvd # 400, Walnut Creek (94596-4890)
PHONE.....................925 934-3831
Marc Anderson, President
EMP: 50
SQ FT: 1,000
SALES (est): 5.4MM Privately Held
SIC: 1796 Installing building equipment

(P-3474)
CLASSIC INSTALLS INC
22475 Baxter Rd, Wildomar (92595-9040)
PHONE.....................951 678-9906
Dirk Steffen, CEO
Nicole Steen, Relations
EMP: 70
SALES (est): 10.9MM Privately Held
SIC: 1796 Installing building equipment

(P-3475)
FIBRWRAP CONSTRUCTION LP (HQ)
Also Called: Fibrwrap Construction Services
3940 Ruffin Rd Ste C, San Diego (92123-1844)
PHONE.....................909 390-4363
Heath Carr Fyfe, CEO
Jason Alexander, Partner
Chibby Alloway, Partner
Heath Carr, Partner
Edward Fyfe, Partner
EMP: 71
SQ FT: 9,000
SALES (est): 42.6MM
SALES (corp-wide): 1.3B Publicly Held
WEB: www.fibrwrapconstruction.com
SIC: 1796 Installing building equipment
PA: Aegion Corporation
    17988 Edison Ave
    Chesterfield MO 63005
    636 530-8000

(P-3476)
FOSTER WHEELER ENERGY SVCS INC
9645 Scranton Rd Ste 230, San Diego (92121-1790)
PHONE.....................800 500-1993
Ed Linck, President
Denny Jump, Manager
EMP: 50
SALES (est): 3.2MM
SALES (corp-wide): 6.3B Publicly Held
SIC: 1796 1629 1731 4911 Power generating equipment installation; power plant construction; electric power systems contractors; cogeneration specialization; generation, electric power
HQ: Amec Foster Wheeler North America Corp.
    Perryville Corporate Pk 5
    Hampton NJ 08827
    908 713-2891

(P-3477)
INFINITY METALS INC
2001 Emery Ave, La Habra (90631-5777)
PHONE.....................562 697-8826
Fax: 562 697-8876
Kevin Ufholtz, President
Joellyn Bowker, Accounting Mgr
Chad Blotzer, Sales Staff
EMP: 50
SQ FT: 2,000
SALES (est): 8.9MM Privately Held
SIC: 1796 Installing building equipment

(P-3478)
OTIS ELEVATOR COMPANY
444 Spear St Ste 100, San Francisco (94105-1642)
PHONE.....................415 546-0880
Fax: 415 546-0907
Rob Neill, Branch Mgr
George V Klan, Analyst
Tom Haras, Manager
EMP: 150
SALES (corp-wide): 56.1B Publicly Held
WEB: www.otis.com
SIC: 1796 7699 Installing building equipment; elevator installation & conversion; miscellaneous building item repair services; elevators: inspection, service & repair
HQ: Otis Elevator Company
    10 Farm Springs Rd
    Farmington CT 06032
    860 676-6000

(P-3479)
OTIS ELEVATOR INTL INC
1358 14th St, Oakland (94607-2209)
PHONE.....................510 874-5129
Dennis Fuller, Branch Mgr
EMP: 58
SALES (corp-wide): 56.1B Publicly Held
WEB: www.otis.com
SIC: 1796 7699 Elevator installation & conversion; elevators: inspection, service & repair
HQ: Otis Elevator Company
    10 Farm Springs Rd
    Farmington CT 06032
    860 676-6000

(P-3480)
SUNPRO SOLAR INC
34859 Frederick St # 101, Wildomar (92595-7007)
PHONE.....................951 678-7733
Fax: 951 678-7730
Adam Joshua Evans, President
Shannon Jackson, Admin Asst
Karl Johnstone, Sales Mgr
Jessica Knight, Manager
Danielle Kraack, Manager
EMP: 64
SQ FT: 2,300
SALES (est): 9.6MM Privately Held
WEB: www.sunpro-solar.com
SIC: 1796 Installing building equipment

(P-3481)
TRANSBAY FIRE PROTECTION INC (PA)
2182 Rheem Dr, Pleasanton (94588-2796)
PHONE.....................925 846-9484
Charlie Marlin, President
Julie Schmidt, CFO
Hossein Tabatabai, Vice Pres
William Haley, Design Engr
Randy Ralston, Project Mgr
▲ EMP: 50
SQ FT: 17,000
SALES (est): 12.9MM Privately Held
WEB: www.transbayfire.com
SIC: 1796 7389 Installing building equipment; safety inspection service

(P-3482)
UNITED RIGGERS & ERECTORS INC (PA)
4188 Valley Blvd, Walnut (91789-1446)
P.O. Box 728 (91788-0728)
PHONE.....................909 978-0400
Fax: 562 978-0410
Brian D Kelley, CEO
Thomas J Kruss, COO
Leonard Reese, Vice Pres
Ann McElvain, Administration
Sean Kelley, Project Engr
EMP: 100
SQ FT: 58,000
SALES (est): 10.5MM Privately Held
SIC: 1796 Machinery installation

1799 Special Trade Contractors, NEC

(P-3483)
1ST LIGHT ENERGY INC (PA)
1869 Moffat Blvd, Manteca (95336-8944)
PHONE.....................209 824-5500
Justin Krum, CEO
Gregory E Smith, COO
Gregory Smith, CFO
Gina L Dickman, Administration
Gina Dickman, Administration
EMP: 50
SQ FT: 6,300
SALES (est): 42.2MM Privately Held
SIC: 1799 Hydraulic equipment, installation & service

(P-3484)
AAA RESTORATION INC
29850 2nd St, Lake Elsinore (92532-2420)
PHONE.....................951 471-5828
Kirk Munio, President
Terry Christian, Office Mgr
EMP: 50
SQ FT: 1,400
SALES (est): 3.8MM Privately Held
SIC: 1799 Home/office interiors finishing, furnishing & remodeling

(P-3485)
AJC SANDBLASTING INC
932 Schley Ave, Wilmington (90744-4060)
PHONE.....................562 436-3606
Fax: 562 436-8120
Lisa Charleston, President
Larry Dowling, Corp Secy
Daniel Charleston, Vice Pres
Sherley Danting, Human Res Mgr
Lupe Molina, Manager
EMP: 90
SQ FT: 10,000
SALES (est): 8.3MM Privately Held
SIC: 1799 Sandblasting of building exteriors; epoxy application

(P-3486)
ALCORN FENCE COMPANY (PA)
9901 Glenoaks Blvd, Sun Valley (91352-1089)
P.O. Box 1249 (91353-1249)
PHONE.....................818 983-0650
Fax: 818 768-9719
Greg Erickson, President
Thomas Tack, President
Oscar Mancialla, CFO
Theresa Wells, Treasurer
Oscar Mancilla, Info Tech Mgr
EMP: 60 EST: 1942
SQ FT: 18,000
SALES: 23MM Privately Held
SIC: 1799 Fence construction

(P-3487)
ALL STAR MAINTENANCE INC
12250 El Camino Real # 300, San Diego (92130-3001)
PHONE.....................858 259-0900
Fax: 858 259-9350
John Junge, President
Dean Bailey, Info Tech Dir
EMP: 100
SALES (est): 5.3MM Privately Held
SIC: 1799 Building site preparation

(P-3488)
ALL STARS
Also Called: Sab Pacific
12250 El Camino Real # 300, San Diego (92130-3076)
PHONE.....................858 259-0900
John P Junge, Partner
John Jung, Partner
Lowell Davis, Opers Staff
Thomas Kern, Manager
EMP: 300
SQ FT: 17,000
SALES: 10MM Privately Held
SIC: 1799 Home/office interiors finishing, furnishing & remodeling

(P-3489)
AMERICAN SYNERGY ASBESTOS REMO
Also Called: Synergy Environmental
28436 Satellite St, Hayward (94545-4863)
PHONE.....................510 444-2333
David C Clark, President
EMP: 100
SQ FT: 6,000
SALES (est): 10MM Privately Held
WEB: www.synergyenvironmental.com
SIC: 1799 Asbestos removal & encapsulation

(P-3490)
AMERICAN TECHNOLOGIES INC
Also Called: American Restoration Services
25000 Industrial Blvd, Hayward (94545-2349)
PHONE.....................510 429-5000
Toll Free:.....................888 -
Kyle Picket, Manager
Kevin Payne, Admin Asst
Andy Olsen, Project Mgr
Dave Peterson, Project Mgr
Marvin Guevara, Safety Dir
EMP: 60
SALES (corp-wide): 180.8MM Privately Held
WEB: www.amer-tech.com
SIC: 1799 1521 Asbestos removal & encapsulation; decontamination services; single-family home remodeling, additions & repairs; repairing fire damage, single-family houses
PA: American Technologies Inc.
    210 W Baywood Ave
    Orange CA 92865
    714 283-9990

(P-3491)
ANDRIGHETTO PRODUCE INC
Also Called: Shasta Produce Co
155 Terminal Ct Stalls 15 Stalls, South San Francisco (94083)
P.O. Box 2328 (94083-2328)
PHONE.....................650 588-0930
Fax: 650 588-1657
Steven Andrighetto, CEO
David Andrighetto, Owner
Peter Carcione, President
Steven Hurwitz, Treasurer
Domenic Andrighetto, Vice Pres
EMP: 55
SQ FT: 10,000

1799 - Special Trade Contractors, NEC County (P-3492)

SALES (est): 12MM **Privately Held**
SIC: 1799 5411 Bowling alley installation; supermarkets, chain

(P-3492)
APPLE VALLEY FARMS INC
1828 E Hedges Ave, Fresno (93703-3633)
PHONE..................................559 498-7115
Durbin Breckenridge, *President*
Xue Lee, *Applctn Conslt*
Hilary Hale, *QC Mgr*
Adrinna Nino, *Accounts Mgr*
EMP: 50
SALES (est): 3.8MM **Privately Held**
SIC: 1799 Food service equipment installation

(P-3493)
APW CONSTRUCTION INC
15135 Salt Lake Ave, City of Industry (91746-3316)
PHONE..................................626 855-1720
America Tang, *Branch Mgr*
EMP: 65
SALES (corp-wide): 20.3MM **Privately Held**
SIC: 1799 Fence construction
PA: Apw Construction, Inc.
727 Glendora Ave
La Puente CA 91744
626 820-0812

(P-3494)
AQUA GUNITE INC
5830 S Naylor Rd, Livermore (94551-8308)
PHONE..................................408 271-2782
Jose G Aguayo, *CEO*
Fargio Garcia, *Vice Pres*
Sharon Chapman, *Sales Staff*
Sharon Chatman, *Manager*
EMP: 50
SQ FT: 2,120
SALES (est): 5.5MM **Privately Held**
SIC: 1799 Swimming pool construction

(P-3495)
ASBESTOS INSTANT RESPONSE INC
3517 W Washington Blvd, Los Angeles (90018-1122)
PHONE..................................323 733-0508
Eric Chevasson, *President*
Steven Liedernan, *COO*
Alma Pineda, *Accountant*
EMP: 65
SQ FT: 1,500
SALES (est): 7.4MM **Privately Held**
WEB: www.airinc.ws
SIC: 1799 Asbestos removal & encapsulation

(P-3496)
BARON POOL PLST STHERN CAL INC
495 Industrial Rd, San Bernardino (92408-3715)
PHONE..................................909 792-8891
Fax: 909 796-1073
Craig Bennion, *President*
Lisa Stephens, *Financial Exec*
Lisa Stevens, *Human Res Mgr*
EMP: 55
SQ FT: 5,000
SALES (est): 5.5MM **Privately Held**
WEB: www.baronpool.com
SIC: 1799 Swimming pool construction

(P-3497)
BAY AREA INSTALLATIONS INC (PA)
2481 Verna Ct, San Leandro (94577-4222)
PHONE..................................510 895-8196
Fax: 510 895-8199
Thomas Clark Mohamed, *President*
Herman B Chibnick, *Vice Pres*
Henning Bloech, *Comms Dir*
Alta Clark, *Admin Sec*
Roberta Curtis, *Persnl Mgr*
▲ EMP: 53
SQ FT: 25,000
SALES (est): 7.3MM **Privately Held**
WEB: www.baiinc.com
SIC: 1799 4212 Demountable partition installation; office furniture installation; delivery service, vehicular

(P-3498)
BEACHSIDE REALTORS
4197 Chino Hills Pkwy, Chino Hills (91709-2614)
PHONE..................................909 606-1299
Iris Tonti, *Manager*
EMP: 68
SALES (corp-wide): 10.5MM **Privately Held**
WEB: www.mikelembeck.com
SIC: 1799 5084 7389 7331 Steam cleaning of building exteriors; cleaning equipment, high pressure, sand or steam; packaging & labeling services; mailing service; real estate agents & managers
PA: Beachside Realtors
19671 Beach Blvd Ste 101
Huntington Beach CA 92648
714 969-6100

(P-3499)
BLUEWATER ENVMTL SVCS INC
2075 Williams St, San Leandro (94577-2305)
PHONE..................................510 346-8800
Fax: 510 346-8924
Chris J Kirschenheuter, *CEO*
Maryann Kirschenheuter, *Treasurer*
Clarissa Graape, *Vice Pres*
Todd Kirschenheuter, *Vice Pres*
Jose Garcia, *Accountant*
EMP: 100
SQ FT: 15,000
SALES (est): 14.5MM **Privately Held**
WEB: www.bwserv.com
SIC: 1799 Asbestos removal & encapsulation

(P-3500)
BRAND ENERGY SOLUTIONS LLC
4755 E Commerce Ave, Fresno (93725-2205)
PHONE..................................559 444-1970
Steve Mulen, *General Mgr*
EMP: 60
SALES (corp-wide): 7.8B **Privately Held**
SIC: 1799 Scaffolding construction
HQ: Brand Energy Solutions Llc
1325 Cobb Intl Dr Nw A1
Kennesaw GA 30152
678 285-1408

(P-3501)
BRAND SERVICES LLC
Also Called: Brand Scaffold Service
940 Hensley St, Richmond (94801-2106)
PHONE..................................510 231-9640
Fax: 510 231-9009
Art Cruz, *Branch Mgr*
Migul Ayane, *Manager*
EMP: 52
SALES (corp-wide): 7.8B **Privately Held**
WEB: www.brandscaffold.com
SIC: 1799 Scaffolding construction
HQ: Brand Services, Llc
1325 Cobb Intl Dr Nw A1
Kennesaw GA 30152
678 285-1400

(P-3502)
BRICKLEY CONSTRUCTION CO INC
Also Called: Brickley Environmental
957 Reece St, San Bernardino (92411-2356)
PHONE..................................909 888-2010
Fax: 909 381-3433
James L Brickley, *CEO*
Thomas Brickley, *President*
Annorr Gowdy, *CFO*
Shane Brickley, *Vice Pres*
Becky Romano, *General Mgr*
EMP: 50
SQ FT: 10,000
SALES (est): 6.7MM **Privately Held**
WEB: www.brickleyenv.com
SIC: 1799 4959 Asbestos removal & encapsulation; environmental cleanup services

(P-3503)
BURDICK PAINTING
705 Nuttman St, Santa Clara (95054-2623)
PHONE..................................408 567-1330
Fax: 408 567-1339
John C Cintas, *CEO*
Luanne McNab, *Manager*
EMP: 67
SQ FT: 8,000
SALES (est): 7MM **Privately Held**
SIC: 1799 1721 Paint & wallpaper stripping; coating, caulking & weather, water & fireproofing; coating of concrete structures with plastic; coating of metal structures at construction site; commercial painting

(P-3504)
C E TOLAND & SON
5300 Industrial Way, Benicia (94510-1025)
PHONE..................................707 747-1000
Fax: 707 747-5300
Clyde E Toland Jr, *Ch of Bd*
Blake Toland, *President*
Rey Trias, *Vice Pres*
Jeanette Vaiana, *Executive*
Mike Avaiana, *MIS Dir*
▲ EMP: 120
SQ FT: 90,000
SALES (est): 19.7MM **Privately Held**
WEB: www.cetoland.com
SIC: 1799 Ornamental metal work

(P-3505)
CALIFORNIA ACCESS SCAFFOLD LLC
16525 Avalon Blvd, Carson (90746-1006)
PHONE..................................310 324-3388
Daniel Johnson, *CEO*
Daniel Styles, *CFO*
James Johnson, *Vice Pres*
Kevin Johnson, *Info Tech Mgr*
Travis Crowell, *Project Mgr*
EMP: 56 EST: 2012
SALES (est): 5.2MM **Privately Held**
SIC: 1799 Rigging & scaffolding

(P-3506)
CALIFORNIA CLOSET CO O
5921 Skylab Rd, Huntington Beach (92647-2062)
PHONE..................................714 899-4905
Fax: 714 899-4706
Bill Barton, *President*
Scott Seigel, *President*
Rob Donaldson, *Vice Pres*
Davyd Funk, *Vice Pres*
Leslie Seigel, *Admin Sec*
▲ EMP: 115
SQ FT: 3,200
SALES: 16MM **Privately Held**
SIC: 1799 Closet organizers, installation & design

(P-3507)
CHERNE CONTRACTING CORPORATION
150 Solano Way, Pacheco (94553-1465)
PHONE..................................952 944-4300
EMP: 200
SALES (est): 108K
SALES (corp-wide): 20.9B **Privately Held**
SIC: 1799 Athletic & recreation facilities construction
HQ: Cherne Contracting Corporation
9855 W 78th St Ste 400
Eden Prairie MN 55344
952 944-4300

(P-3508)
CITY OF SANTA CLARA
Also Called: City of Santa Clra Parks Svc
2600 Benton St, Santa Clara (95051-4802)
PHONE..................................408 615-3770
George Friedenbach, *Manager*
EMP: 55 **Privately Held**
SIC: 1799 Parking facility equipment & maintenance
PA: City Of Santa Clara
1500 Warburton Ave
Santa Clara CA 95050
408 615-2200

(P-3509)
COURTNEY INC (PA)
16781 Millikan Ave, Irvine (92606-5009)
PHONE..................................949 222-2050
George Courtney, *CEO*
Mildred Courtney, *Admin Sec*
EMP: 80

SALES (est): 37.3MM **Privately Held**
SIC: 1799 Waterproofing

(P-3510)
CROWN FENCE CO
12118 Bloomfield Ave, Santa Fe Springs (90670-4703)
PHONE..................................562 864-5177
Fax: 562 864-1299
Matt Brock, *COO*
Eric W Fiedler, *Vice Pres*
M Williams, *Managing Dir*
Tony Blankemeyer, *Project Mgr*
Mike Plechot, *Project Mgr*
▲ EMP: 96 EST: 1923
SQ FT: 36,000
SALES (est): 38.5MM **Privately Held**
SIC: 1799 5039 Fence construction; wire fence, gates & accessories

(P-3511)
DAVE GROSS ENTERPRISES INC
Also Called: Adams Pool Specialties
7 Wayne Ct, Sacramento (95829-1300)
PHONE..................................916 388-2000
David William Gross, *CEO*
Michel McDonnell, *Vice Pres*
Barbara Hall, *Controller*
EMP: 65
SQ FT: 25,000
SALES: 7MM **Privately Held**
SIC: 1799 Swimming pool construction

(P-3512)
DEHART INC
Also Called: California Closet Co
7550 Miramar Rd Ste 300, San Diego (92126-4217)
PHONE..................................858 695-0882
Fax: 619 695-0843
Mike Cayheart, *President*
Margaret Kres, *Marketing Staff*
EMP: 72
SQ FT: 5,700
SALES (est): 6.5MM **Privately Held**
WEB: www.dehart.com
SIC: 1799 2541 2521 1751 Closet organizers, installation & design; wood partitions & fixtures; wood office furniture; carpentry work; wood television & radio cabinets

(P-3513)
ENCORE AEROSPACE LLC
1729 Apollo Ct, Seal Beach (90740-5617)
PHONE..................................562 344-1700
Tom McFarland,
David Jorgenson, *Program Mgr*
Robert Fisher, *Design Engr*
Evgueni Gubergrits, *Design Engr*
EMP: 100
SALES (est): 3.8MM **Privately Held**
SIC: 1799 Renovation of aircraft interiors

(P-3514)
EXCEL MDULAR SCAFFOLD LSG CORP
2555 Birch St, Vista (92081-8433)
PHONE..................................760 598-0050
Benjamin Bartlett, *Branch Mgr*
EMP: 1200 **Privately Held**
SIC: 1799 Rigging & scaffolding
PA: Excel Modular Scaffold And Leasing Corporation
720 Washington St Unit 5
Hanover MA 02339

(P-3515)
FARWEST CORROSION CONTROL CO (PA)
12029 Regentview Ave, Downey (90241-5517)
PHONE..................................310 532-9524
Troy Gordon Rankin Jr, *CEO*
Roy Rankin Jr, *President*
Gordon Rankin, *COO*
Marian Rankin, *Treasurer*
Dan McGrew, *Vice Pres*
▲ EMP: 65
SQ FT: 42,000
SALES (est): 52.3MM **Privately Held**
WEB: www.farwst.com
SIC: 1799 Corrosion control installation

PRODUCTS & SERVICES SECTION
1799 - Special Trade Contractors, NEC County (P-3538)

(P-3516)
FENCECORP INC
111 Main St Ste A, Riverside (92501-1058)
PHONE.....................951 686-3170
T Perrry Massie, *CEO*
Dale Marriott, *President*
Gary Hansen, *Vice Pres*
Perry Massie, *Vice Pres*
Robert McPherson, *Vice Pres*
EMP: 170
SQ FT: 5,000
SALES (est): 14.1MM
SALES (corp-wide): 128.6MM **Privately Held**
SIC: 1799 Fence construction
PA: Fenceworks, Inc.
870 Main St
Riverside CA 92501
951 788-5620

(P-3517)
FENCEWORKS INC
Also Called: Golden State Fence
2861 E La Cresta Ave, Anaheim (92806-1817)
PHONE.....................714 238-0091
Fax: 714 238-0096
Steve Anderson, *Principal*
EMP: 75
SALES (corp-wide): 128.6MM **Privately Held**
WEB: www.goldenstatefence.com
SIC: 1799 Fence construction
PA: Fenceworks, Inc.
870 Main St
Riverside CA 92501
951 788-5620

(P-3518)
FENCEWORKS INC (PA)
Also Called: Golden State Fence Co.
870 Main St, Riverside (92501-1016)
PHONE.....................951 788-5620
Fax: 951 788-5649
Jason Ostrander, *CEO*
Mel Kay, *President*
Aaron Garcia, *CFO*
Floyd N Nixon, *Officer*
Dawn Smith, *General Mgr*
▲ **EMP:** 250
SQ FT: 20,000
SALES (est): 128.6MM **Privately Held**
WEB: www.goldenstatefence.com
SIC: 1799 Fence construction

(P-3519)
FENCEWORKS INC
Also Called: Golden State Fence
891 Corporation St, Santa Paula (93060-3005)
PHONE.....................661 265-0082
Fax: 661 265-0179
Pete Schank, *Manager*
EMP: 100
SALES (corp-wide): 128.6MM **Privately Held**
WEB: www.goldenstatefence.com
SIC: 1799 Fence construction
PA: Fenceworks, Inc.
870 Main St
Riverside CA 92501
951 788-5620

(P-3520)
FLIGHT LINE PRODUCTS LLC
28732 Witherspoon Pkwy, Valencia (91355-5425)
PHONE.....................661 775-8366
Fax: 661 775-8367
Eric Jensen, *President*
Sean Herndon, *QC Mgr*
EMP: 276
SQ FT: 86,000
SALES: 21MM
SALES (corp-wide): 490.2MM **Privately Held**
SIC: 1799 2399 Renovation of aircraft interiors; seat belts, automobile & aircraft
PA: Wencor Group, Llc
416 Dividend Dr
Peachtree City GA 30269
678 490-0140

(P-3521)
FLUOR ENTERPRISES INC
1 Fluor Daniel Dr, Aliso Viejo (92698-1000)
PHONE.....................469 398-7000
Scott Snyder, *Manager*
Gregory Amparano, *Vice Pres*
Robert Brown, *Supervisor*
EMP: 52
SALES (corp-wide): 18.1B **Publicly Held**
SIC: 1799 Building site preparation
HQ: Fluor Enterprises, Inc.
6700 Las Colinas Blvd
Irving TX 75039
469 398-7000

(P-3522)
FRESH AIR ENVIRONMENTAL SVCS
10675 Rush St, South El Monte (91733-3439)
PHONE.....................323 913-1965
Fax: 323 269-0636
Kevan Stark, *President*
EMP: 60
SQ FT: 7,000
SALES (est): 4MM **Privately Held**
WEB: www.4freshair.biz
SIC: 1799 Asbestos removal & encapsulation

(P-3523)
GARDNER POOL COMPANY INC (PA)
Also Called: Gardner Pool Plastering
801 Gable Way, El Cajon (92020-1910)
PHONE.....................619 593-8880
Fax: 760 593-8886
Scott McKenna, *President*
Richard McKenna, *Treasurer*
Mike McKenna, *Vice Pres*
Eric Greenley, *Asst Controller*
EMP: 53
SQ FT: 6,000
SALES (est): 15.9MM **Privately Held**
WEB: www.gardnerpoolplastering.com
SIC: 1799 Swimming pool construction

(P-3524)
GETTLER-RYAN INC (PA)
6805 Sierra Ct Ste G, Dublin (94568-2694)
PHONE.....................925 551-7555
Fax: 925 551-7888
Jeffrey M Ryan, *CEO*
Dave Byron, *Vice Pres*
Janice Grant, *Admin Sec*
Michael Chalender, *Admin Asst*
Desiree Walton, *Admin Asst*
EMP: 65
SQ FT: 20,000
SALES (est): 18.4MM **Privately Held**
WEB: www.grinc.com
SIC: 1799 Petroleum storage tanks, pumping & draining; service station equipment installation, maintenance & repair

(P-3525)
GLOBAL ENTERTAINMENT INDS INC
2948 N Ontario St, Burbank (91504-2016)
PHONE.....................818 567-0000
Christopher Hyde, *President*
Teresa Harris, *Manager*
▲ **EMP:** 55
SQ FT: 65,000
SALES (est): 6.3MM **Privately Held**
WEB: www.globalentind.com
SIC: 1799 Prop, set or scenery construction, theatrical

(P-3526)
GREGG DRILLING & TESTING INC (PA)
2726 Walnut Ave, Signal Hill (90755-1832)
PHONE.....................562 427-6899
Fax: 562 427-3314
John M Gregg, *President*
Chris Christensen, *Vice Pres*
Patrick Keating, *Vice Pres*
Brian Savela, *Info Tech Mgr*
Sonja De Keyser Meurs, *Controller*
▲ **EMP:** 71
SQ FT: 17,000
SALES: 36.3MM **Privately Held**
WEB: www.greggdrilling.com
SIC: 1799 1781 Core drilling & cutting; water well drilling

(P-3527)
GUARDIAN ENVIRONMENTAL INC (PA)
4330 Pinell St, Sacramento (95838-2928)
P.O. Box 41258 (95841-0258)
PHONE.....................916 641-5695
Jack James, *President*
Jessica Belding, *Controller*
EMP: 60
SQ FT: 5,000
SALES: 3MM **Privately Held**
WEB: www.guardianenvironmental.net
SIC: 1799 4953 8744 Building site preparation; hazardous waste collection & disposal;

(P-3528)
HAYWARD BAKER INC
1780 E Lemonwood Dr, Santa Paula (93060-9510)
PHONE.....................805 933-1331
Fax: 805 933-1338
Alan Ringen, *Branch Mgr*
Gary Taylor, *Senior VP*
Francis Galartti, *Vice Pres*
Joseph Mann, *Project Mgr*
EMP: 75
SALES (corp-wide): 2.3B **Privately Held**
WEB: www.haywardbaker.com
SIC: 1799 Building site preparation
HQ: Hayward Baker Inc
7550 Teague Rd Ste 300
Hanover MD 21076
410 551-8200

(P-3529)
HEAVENLY CONSTRUCTION INC
Also Called: Heavenly Greens
370 Umbarger Rd Ste A, San Jose (95111-2070)
PHONE.....................408 723-4954
Fax: 408 723-4952
Daniel Theis, *President*
Kristin Pisano,
Brad Borgman, *Director*
EMP: 73
SQ FT: 75,000
SALES (est): 8.1MM **Privately Held**
WEB: www.heavenlygreens.com
SIC: 1799 Artificial turf installation

(P-3530)
HEINAMAN CONTRACT GLAZING INC (PA)
26981 Vista Ter Ste E, Lake Forest (92630-8127)
PHONE.....................949 587-0266
Fax: 949 587-0267
John L Heinaman, *President*
Gaye Howhannesian, *Treasurer*
Angela Heinaman, *Exec VP*
Mark Heinaman, *Vice Pres*
Andrew Swanson, *Project Mgr*
◆ **EMP:** 50
SQ FT: 4,950
SALES (est): 23.5MM **Privately Held**
SIC: 1799 1793 Window treatment installation; glass & glazing work

(P-3531)
HIGH END DEVELOPMENT INC
5600 Imhoff Dr Ste E, Concord (94520-5354)
PHONE.....................925 687-2540
Jim Metzger, *President*
Larry V Harmen, *CFO*
Anthony Froyd, *Admin Sec*
EMP: 60
SALES: 16.4MM **Privately Held**
SIC: 1799 Waterproofing

(P-3532)
HOME IMPROVEMENT COMPANY INC
1585 Creek St, San Marcos (92078-2442)
PHONE.....................760 744-4840
Chet Johnston, *President*
Ron Helmes, *CFO*
Pharrell Worthylake, *Administration*
Rod Johnston, *Manager*
EMP: 50
SALES (est): 5.5MM **Privately Held**
SIC: 1799 1521 1541 Post-disaster renovations; general remodeling, single-family houses; renovation, remodeling & repairs: industrial buildings

(P-3533)
J PEREZ ASSOCIATES INC (PA)
Also Called: J. Perez & Associates
10833 Valley View St # 200, Cypress (90630-5049)
PHONE.....................562 801-5397
Fax: 562 424-7008
Joe Perez, *CEO*
Tony Perez, *Vice Pres*
Jerry Floyd, *Opers Mgr*
EMP: 55
SQ FT: 15,000
SALES (est): 18.4MM **Privately Held**
WEB: www.jperez.com
SIC: 1799 Sign installation & maintenance

(P-3534)
JANUS CORPORATION (PA)
1081 Shary Cir, Concord (94518-2407)
PHONE.....................925 969-9200
Fax: 925 969-9290
Mike Ely, *CEO*
Sean Tavernier, *President*
Pat Kirkland, *CFO*
Tom Kirkland, *Vice Pres*
Craig M Uhle, *Vice Pres*
EMP: 100
SQ FT: 15,000
SALES (est): 43MM **Privately Held**
WEB: www.januscorp.com
SIC: 1799 Decontamination services

(P-3535)
JANUS CORPORATION
2025 Tandem, Norco (92860-3610)
PHONE.....................951 479-0700
Fax: 951 479-0701
Chad Chandler, *Manager*
EMP: 50
SQ FT: 21,780
SALES (corp-wide): 43MM **Privately Held**
WEB: www.januscorp.com
SIC: 1799 Decontamination services
PA: Janus Corporation
1081 Shary Cir
Concord CA 94518
925 969-9200

(P-3536)
JARKA ENTERPRISES INC
1059 Vine St Ste 108, Sacramento (95811-0339)
PHONE.....................916 491-6180
Ken Binsmore, *Branch Mgr*
EMP: 70
SALES (est): 14.2MM **Privately Held**
SIC: 1799 Office furniture installation
PA: Jarka Enterprises, Inc.
675 Brennan St
San Jose CA 95131
408 325-5700

(P-3537)
JEFF KERBER POOL PLST INC
10735 Kadota Ave, Montclair (91763-6005)
PHONE.....................909 465-0677
Jeff Kerber, *President*
Mark Feldstein, *COO*
Lisa Martin, *Executive Asst*
▲ **EMP:** 260
SQ FT: 77,100
SALES (est): 18.3MM **Privately Held**
WEB: www.jeffkerber.com
SIC: 1799 Athletic & recreation facilities construction

(P-3538)
JOES SWEEPING INC
Also Called: Nationwide Environmental Svcs
11914 Front St, Norwalk (90650-2911)
PHONE.....................562 929-4344
Fax: 562 868-5726
Never Samuelian, *President*
Joe Samuelian, *Vice Pres*
Ani Samuelian, *Admin Sec*
EMP: 65

1799 - Special Trade Contractors, NEC County (P-3539)

SQ FT: 10,500
SALES (est): 14MM **Privately Held**
WEB: www.nes-sweeping.com
SIC: **1799** Parking lot maintenance

(P-3539)
JOHNSON FINCH & MCCLURE CNSTR (PA)
Also Called: Jfm
9749 Cactus St, Lakeside (92040-4117)
PHONE.................................619 938-9727
Fax: 619 938-9757
Mark Finch, *CEO*
Scott McClure, *President*
Jim Johnson, *Chairman*
EMP: 180 EST: 1977
SQ FT: 10,000
SALES (est): 28.5MM **Privately Held**
SIC: **1799** **1742** Demountable partition installation; acoustical & ceiling work

(P-3540)
JONES/COVEY GROUP INCORPORATED
Also Called: Jones Covey Group
9595 Lucas Ranch Rd # 100, Rancho Cucamonga (91730-5794)
PHONE.................................888 972-7581
Bret Christopher Covey, *CEO*
Ellen Collins, *Office Mgr*
James Chamberlin, *Controller*
Rick Deathriage, *Opers Staff*
Mark Crum, *Manager*
EMP: 63
SQ FT: 2,400
SALES (est): 19.4MM **Privately Held**
SIC: **1799** Service station equipment installation & maintenance

(P-3541)
KARCHER ENVIRONMENTAL INC (PA)
2300 E Orangewood Ave, Anaheim (92806-6112)
P.O. Box 7385, Orange (92863-7385)
PHONE.................................714 385-1490
Fax: 619 385-1878
Benjamin R Karcher, *President*
Shirley Lawson, *Office Mgr*
Amy Anton, *Agent*
EMP: 50
SQ FT: 26,400
SALES (est): 12.8MM **Privately Held**
WEB: www.karcherenv.com
SIC: **1799** **1742** Asbestos removal & encapsulation; insulation, buildings

(P-3542)
KARCHER ENVIRONMENTAL INC
1718 Fairway Dr, San Leandro (94577-5628)
PHONE.................................510 297-0180
Steve Bramlett, *Manager*
Earl Maijala, *Opers Mgr*
EMP: 70
SALES (corp-wide): 12.8MM **Privately Held**
SIC: **1799** Asbestos removal & encapsulation
PA: Karcher Environmental, Inc.
2300 E Orangewood Ave
Anaheim CA 92806
714 385-1490

(P-3543)
KERBER BROS INC
14006 Gracebee Ave, Norwalk (90650-4506)
PHONE.................................562 921-3447
Fax: 562 802-7702
Skip Hawkins, *President*
EMP: 236
SQ FT: 2,800
SALES (est): 10.8MM **Privately Held**
WEB: www.kerberbrothers.com
SIC: **1799** **1742** Swimming pool construction; plastering, drywall & insulation

(P-3544)
KING SUPPLY COMPANY LLC
6340 Valley View St, Buena Park (90620-1032)
PHONE.................................714 670-8980
Fax: 714 266-6807
EMP: 142
SALES (corp-wide): 129.3MM **Privately Held**
SIC: **1799** Ornamental metal work
PA: King Supply Company, Llc
9611 E R L Thornton Fwy
Dallas TX 75228
214 388-9834

(P-3545)
L&G CABLE CONSTRUCTION
2776 E Miraloma Ave, Anaheim (92806-1701)
PHONE.................................714 630-6174
Fax: 714 630-6274
Lou Gentile, *President*
Joe Winek, *Supervisor*
EMP: 60
SALES (est): 5MM **Privately Held**
SIC: **1799** Cable splicing service

(P-3546)
LAYFIELD USA CORPORATION (DH)
2500 Sweetwater Spgs, Spring Valley (91978-2007)
PHONE.................................619 562-1200
Thomas Rose, *CEO*
Gary Pinkerton, *President*
Robert Remtel, *General Mgr*
Toni Smith, *Admin Asst*
Rick Taylor, *Business Mgr*
▲ EMP: 85
SQ FT: 1,000
SALES (est): 29.6MM
SALES (corp-wide): 1.3MM **Privately Held**
SIC: **1799** Building board-up contractor
HQ: Layfield Group Limited
11131 Hammersmith Gate
Richmond BC V7A 5
604 275-5588

(P-3547)
LITEWAVE US LLC
9107 Wilshire Blvd # 450, Beverly Hills (90210-5531)
PHONE.................................888 399-6710
Mike Steadman,
Dave Mackenzie,
EMP: 50 EST: 2013
SALES (est): 1.3MM **Privately Held**
SIC: **1799** Cable splicing service

(P-3548)
M GAW INC
Also Called: Jet Sets
6910 Farmdale Ave, North Hollywood (91605-6210)
PHONE.................................818 503-7997
Fax: 818 764-6655
Michael Gaw, *President*
Mary Thomas, *Controller*
Jessee Powell, *Manager*
EMP: 90
SQ FT: 15,000
SALES (est): 9.3MM **Privately Held**
SIC: **1799** Prop, set or scenery construction, theatrical

(P-3549)
MALCO MAINTENANCE INC
Also Called: Malco Services
3703 E Melville Way, Anaheim (92806-2122)
PHONE.................................714 630-0194
Fax: 714 630-0195
Duane Malone, *President*
Katie Goldsberry, *Manager*
EMP: 66
SQ FT: 15,000
SALES (est): 6.1MM **Privately Held**
SIC: **1799** Exterior cleaning, including sandblasting; cleaning building exteriors; cleaning new buildings after construction; steam cleaning of building exteriors

(P-3550)
MALCOLM DRILLING COMPANY INC (PA)
92 Natoma St Ste 400, San Francisco (94105-2685)
PHONE.................................415 901-4400
Fax: 415 901-4421
John M Malcolm, *CEO*
Terry Tucker, *President*
Derek Yamashita, *Treasurer*
Chase Chappelle, *Senior VP*
Heinrich Majewski, *Vice Pres*
▲ EMP: 151
SQ FT: 7,500
SALES (est): 745.3MM **Privately Held**
WEB: www.malcolmdrilling.com
SIC: **1799** Building site preparation; boring for building construction

(P-3551)
MARCOR ENVIRONMENTAL-WEST
16027 Carmenita Rd, Cerritos (90703-2208)
PHONE.................................562 921-2733
Matthew Westrup, *Branch Mgr*
EMP: 100
SALES (corp-wide): 32.2MM **Privately Held**
SIC: **1799** Asbestos removal & encapsulation
HQ: Marcor Environmental-West, Inc
8203 Woodside Ct
Parkville MD

(P-3552)
MATRIX ENVIRONMENTAL INC
2330 E Cherry Indl Cir, Long Beach (90805-4417)
PHONE.................................562 236-2704
Fax: 562 236-2727
Jason McKeever, *President*
Adam Lowe, *Manager*
EMP: 60
SQ FT: 9,000
SALES (est): 8MM **Privately Held**
SIC: **1799** Athletic & recreation facilities construction

(P-3553)
MATRIX INDUSTRIES INC
2330 E Cherry Indus Cir, Long Beach (90805-4417)
PHONE.................................562 236-2700
Larry Larkin, *President*
EMP: 260
SQ FT: 10,000
SALES (est): 14.8MM **Privately Held**
SIC: **1799** Asbestos removal & encapsulation

(P-3554)
MEMO SCAFFOLDING INC
12722 Carmenita Rd, Santa Fe Springs (90670-4804)
PHONE.................................562 404-8600
Jose G Santos, *President*
Lynn Hollister, *CFO*
Loudes Garceia, *Manager*
Marcela Macedo, *Manager*
EMP: 100
SQ FT: 9,000
SALES (est): 7.1MM **Privately Held**
WEB: www.memoscaffolding.com
SIC: **1799** Scaffolding construction

(P-3555)
MP AERO LLC
7701 Woodley Ave, Van Nuys (91406-1732)
PHONE.................................818 901-9828
Christine Paschal, *CFO*
Marco Vargas, *VP Opers*
EMP: 85 EST: 2013
SQ FT: 165,000
SALES (est): 11.7MM **Privately Held**
SIC: **1799** Renovation of aircraft interiors

(P-3556)
MUEHLHAN CERTIFED COATINGS INC
2320 Cordelia Rd, Fairfield (94534-1600)
PHONE.................................707 639-4414
Erich Stolz, *CEO*
David Brockman, *COO*
EMP: 150
SQ FT: 18,000
SALES (est): 5.2MM
SALES (corp-wide): 256.7MM **Privately Held**
SIC: **1799** Coating, caulking & weatherwater & fireproofing; coating of metal structures at construction site; coating of concrete structures with plastic

HQ: Muehlhan Surface Protection Inc
2320 Cordelia Rd
Fairfield CA 94534
707 639-4421

(P-3557)
MY OFFICE INC
6060 Nncy Rdge Dr Ste 100, San Diego (92121)
PHONE.................................858 549-6700
Shaun Alger, *CEO*
Ronald D Harrell, *President*
Regina Franco, *Executive Asst*
Michelle Ghani, *Finance Mgr*
▲ EMP: 100
SQ FT: 29,000
SALES (est): 21MM **Privately Held**
WEB: www.4myoffice.com
SIC: **1799** Office furniture installation

(P-3558)
NORTH VALLEY CONSTRUCTION INC
4010 Raymond Rd, Livermore (94551-9776)
P.O. Box 2511 (94551-2511)
PHONE.................................925 373-1246
Fax: 925 373-1108
Charles E Inderbitzen, *President*
Sandra Inderbitzen, *Treasurer*
Sharon Casello, *Officer*
Mario Alvarez, *Project Mgr*
EMP: 70
SQ FT: 1,000
SALES (est): 5MM **Privately Held**
SIC: **1799** Construction site cleanup

(P-3559)
NORTHSTAR CONTG GROUP INC (DH)
Also Called: LVI Facility Services
31500 Hayman St, Hayward (94544-7120)
PHONE.................................510 491-1300
Trip, Turner, *Manager*
Joe Catania, *Co-President*
Michael Kinelski, *Co-President*
Michael Moore, *Co-President*
Paul S Cutrone, *Vice Pres*
EMP: 98
SALES: 56.3MM
SALES (corp-wide): 371.8MM **Privately Held**
SIC: **1799** Asbestos removal & encapsulation
HQ: Northstar Group Services, Inc.
370 7th Ave Ste 1803
New York NY 10001
212 951-3660

(P-3560)
PACIFIC AQUASCAPE INC
17520 Newhope St Ste 120, Fountain Valley (92708-8203)
PHONE.................................714 481-7260
Johan Perslow, *Chairman*
Cory M Severson, *President*
Kevin Curran, *COO*
Richard Boultinghous, *CFO*
Bob Lobo, *Vice Pres*
EMP: 75
SQ FT: 21,000
SALES (est): 17MM **Privately Held**
SIC: **1799** Athletic & recreation facilities construction

(P-3561)
PACIFIC HOME WORKS INC
20725 S Wstn Ave Ste 100, Torrance (90501)
PHONE.................................310 781-3012
Fax: 310 781-3051
Marcus Mac, *President*
Adam Konrad, *Vice Pres*
Charle Pendule, *Manager*
EMP: 195
SQ FT: 7,000
SALES (est): 18.8MM **Privately Held**
SIC: **1799** **1751** Kitchen & bathroom remodeling; window & door installation & erection; window & door (prefabricated) installation

PRODUCTS & SERVICES SECTION
1799 - Special Trade Contractors, NEC County (P-3586)

(P-3562)
PACIFIC LINE CLEAN-UP INC
27601 Forbes Rd Ste 29, Laguna Niguel (92677-1240)
P.O. Box 7765 (92607-7765)
PHONE...............................949 348-0245
Raul Rios, *President*
Fermina Rios, *Vice Pres*
EMP: 120
SQ FT: 1,000
SALES (est): 8.2MM **Privately Held**
SIC: 1799 Cleaning new buildings after construction

(P-3563)
PARC SPECIALTY CONTRACTORS
1400 Vinci Ave, Sacramento (95838-1716)
PHONE...............................916 992-5405
Fax: 916 992-6177
Greg Johnson, *President*
John Kimmel, *Vice Pres*
Paul Lane, *Admin Sec*
Mike Kidd,
Laura Greer, *Manager*
EMP: 85
SQ FT: 10,000
SALES: 6MM **Privately Held**
SIC: 1799 Asbestos removal & encapsulation

(P-3564)
PARKING NETWORK INC
350 S Figueroa St Ste 420, Los Angeles (90071-1203)
PHONE...............................213 613-1500
Fax: 213 613-1502
Frank Zelaya, *CEO*
Rose Zelaya, *President*
Robert Neer, *Senior VP*
Ron Parto, *Vice Pres*
EMP: 120
SQ FT: 2,400
SALES: 4MM **Privately Held**
WEB: www.parkingnetwork.net
SIC: 1799 8748 Parking lot maintenance; business consulting

(P-3565)
PARTITIONS INSTALLATION INC
Also Called: Showcase Installations
13021 Leffingwell Ave, Santa Fe Springs (90670-6341)
PHONE...............................562 207-9868
Rick A Faist Jr, *President*
Brenda Byars, *Office Mgr*
Carlos Mispireta, *Sr Project Mgr*
▲ **EMP:** 60
SQ FT: 60,000
SALES: 4MM **Privately Held**
WEB: www.showcaseinstall.com
SIC: 1799 Demountable partition installation

(P-3566)
PATRICK DEAN BRYAN
Also Called: Affordable Installations
12481 Lttle Deer Creek Ln, Nevada City (95959-8919)
PHONE...............................530 273-5484
Patrick Dean Bryan, *Owner*
Patricia Bryan, *Principal*
EMP: 60
SALES (est): 2.9MM **Privately Held**
SIC: 1799 Office furniture installation

(P-3567)
PBC SOLUTION ONE INC
Also Called: Pacific Building Care
2695 N Fowler Ave Ste 110, Fresno (93727-8655)
PHONE...............................559 348-0019
Troy Coker, *President*
Mike Cruz, *General Mgr*
EMP: 150
SQ FT: 15,000
SALES (est): 6.9MM **Privately Held**
SIC: 1799 Cleaning new buildings after construction

(P-3568)
PCW CONTRACTING SERVICES
981 W 18th St Ste D, Costa Mesa (92627-6343)
PHONE...............................949 548-9969
Fax: 949 548-9711

Greg Beebout, *President*
Stephanie Beebout, *Vice Pres*
Janie Aguilar, *Administration*
Greg Borzilleri, *Mktg Dir*
Gary Grant, *Sales Staff*
EMP: 55
SALES (est): 6.6MM **Privately Held**
WEB: www.pcwservices.com
SIC: 1799 Waterproofing

(P-3569)
PEACE OFFICRS FOR A GRN ENVIRN
21800 Barton Rd Ste 108, Grand Terrace (92313-4438)
PHONE...............................909 798-1122
Patricia Gonzalez, *President*
Allison Nutter, *Human Resources*
EMP: 50
SALES (est): 3.4MM **Privately Held**
SIC: 1799 Appliance installation

(P-3570)
PREMIER POOLS AND SPAS LP (PA)
11250 Pyrites Way, Gold River (95670-4481)
PHONE...............................916 852-0223
Fax: 916 852-0861
Keith H Harbeck, *General Ptnr*
Paul Porter, *General Ptnr*
Ryan Langford, *Finance Mgr*
Ryan Mysser, *Controller*
Mike Strasburg, *Sales Staff*
EMP: 90
SQ FT: 3,500
SALES (est): 22MM **Privately Held**
SIC: 1799 Spa or hot tub installation or construction; swimming pool construction

(P-3571)
PROJECT GO INCORPORATED
801 Vernon St, Roseville (95678-3149)
PHONE...............................916 782-3443
Fax: 916 782-1517
Linda Timbers, *Exec Dir*
EMP: 50
SQ FT: 3,000
SALES: 3.3MM **Privately Held**
SIC: 1799 Waterproofing

(P-3572)
PW STEPHENS ENVMTL INC
4047 Clipper Ct, Fremont (94538-6540)
PHONE...............................510 651-9506
Steve Macfarlane, *Principal*
EMP: 55
SALES (corp-wide): 21.3MM **Privately Held**
SIC: 1799 Athletic & recreation facilities construction
PA: P.W. Stephens Environmental, Inc.
15201 Pipeline Ln Ste B
Huntington Beach CA 92649
714 892-2028

(P-3573)
QUALITY SYSTEMS INSTALLATIONS
Also Called: Q S I
212 Shaw Rd Ste 3, South San Francisco (94080-6613)
PHONE...............................650 875-9000
Fax: 650 375-7081
Jon Chase, *President*
Daniel Castillo, *Vice Pres*
Robert W Lindstrom, *Vice Pres*
Ben Nava, *Vice Pres*
Gani Dowd, *Executive Asst*
EMP: 60
SQ FT: 40,000
SALES (est): 4.2MM **Privately Held**
WEB: www.qsiltd.com
SIC: 1799 Office furniture installation

(P-3574)
RAINBOW WTRPROFING RESTORATION
600 Treat Ave, San Francisco (94110-2016)
PHONE...............................415 641-1578
Christopher Abel, *President*
Rob Browne, *Corp Secy*
Ken Resinger, *Office Mgr*
EMP: 124

SALES: 18MM **Privately Held**
WEB: www.rainbow415.com
SIC: 1799 Waterproofing

(P-3575)
RAYCON ENVIRONMENTAL CNSTR
882 Patriot Dr Ste G, Moorpark (93021-3544)
PHONE...............................805 955-0900
Dennis Ray, *President*
EMP: 50
SALES: 5MM **Privately Held**
WEB: www.rayconenvironmental.com
SIC: 1799 Waterproofing

(P-3576)
RESTEC CONTRACTORS INC
22955 Kidder St, Hayward (94545-1670)
PHONE...............................510 670-0100
John Andrzejewski, *President*
Freeman Boyett, *Treasurer*
R Todd Fearon, *Vice Pres*
David Brueggen, *Asst Sec*
EMP: 100
SALES (est): 10.6MM
SALES (corp-wide): 386.4MM **Privately Held**
WEB: www.restecontractors.com
SIC: 1799 Asbestos removal & encapsulation
HQ: Vertecs Corporation
14700 Ne 95th St Ste 201
Redmond WA
425 885-1990

(P-3577)
REY-CREST ROOFG WATERPROOFING
Also Called: Rey-Crest Roofg Waterproofing
3065 Verdugo Rd, Los Angeles (90065-2014)
PHONE...............................323 257-9329
George Reyes, *President*
Bob Fegley, *COO*
Georgia Reyes, *Corp Secy*
Michael Reyes, *Project Mgr*
Steven Reed, *Agent*
EMP: 80
SQ FT: 10,000
SALES (est): 8.8MM **Privately Held**
WEB: www.reycrest.com
SIC: 1799 1761 Waterproofing; roofing contractor

(P-3578)
SCENIC ROUTE INC
13516 Desmond St, Pacoima (91331-2315)
PHONE...............................818 896-6006
Ulf Henriksson, *President*
Sean Culhane, *Vice Pres*
Micheal Goglia, *Vice Pres*
EMP: 50 **EST:** 1987
SQ FT: 25,000
SALES (est): 7.1MM **Privately Held**
WEB: www.the-scenic-route.com
SIC: 1799 Prop, set or scenery construction, theatrical

(P-3579)
SCHAEFER MARY-JUDITH
Also Called: Schaefer Parking Lot Service
7202 Petterson Ln, Paramount (90723-2022)
PHONE...............................562 634-3164
Fax: 323 630-3706
Mary-Judith Schaefer, *Owner*
Joe Orello, *Sales Staff*
EMP: 55
SALES (est): 3.5MM **Privately Held**
SIC: 1799 Parking lot maintenance

(P-3580)
SELEX INC
930 Shiloh Rd, Windsor (95492-9659)
P.O. Box 1920 (95492-1920)
PHONE...............................707 836-8836
Fax: 707 836-8838
Dave Boettger, *Branch Mgr*
EMP: 51
SALES (corp-wide): 13.6MM **Privately Held**
SIC: 1799 Fence construction

PA: Selex, Inc.
50 Contractors St
Livermore CA 94551
707 836-8836

(P-3581)
SHADE STRUCTURES INC
1085 N Main St Ste C, Orange (92867-5458)
PHONE...............................714 427-6981
John Saunders, *CEO*
Ashley Donde, *Director*
EMP: 349
SALES (corp-wide): 196MM **Privately Held**
SIC: 1799 2394 Building site preparation; canvas & related products; shades, canvas: made from purchased materials
HQ: Shade Structures, Inc.
8505 Chancellor Row
Dallas TX 75247
214 905-9500

(P-3582)
SHORING ENGINEERS
Also Called: Shoring & Excavating
12645 Clark St, Santa Fe Springs (90670-3951)
PHONE...............................562 944-9331
Fax: 562 941-8098
George A Woodley Sr, *Vice Pres*
George A Woodleysr, *President*
Ren Contreras, *Vice Pres*
Rene Contreras, *Vice Pres*
Jason E Weinstein, *Vice Pres*
▲ **EMP:** 60
SALES (est): 13.5MM **Privately Held**
WEB: www.shoringengineers.com
SIC: 1799 8711 Shore cleaning & maintenance; engineering services

(P-3583)
SOUTH COAST FENCING CENTER
3518 W Lake Center Dr C, Santa Ana (92704-6979)
PHONE...............................714 549-2946
Brenden Richard, *President*
EMP: 60
SALES: 135.8K **Privately Held**
WEB: www.southcoastfencing.com
SIC: 1799 Fence construction

(P-3584)
SP PLUS CORPORATION
3470 Wilshire Blvd # 400, Los Angeles (90010-3927)
PHONE...............................213 488-3100
Marjorie Jones, *Branch Mgr*
EMP: 60
SALES (corp-wide): 1.6B **Publicly Held**
SIC: 1799 Parking lot maintenance
PA: Sp Plus Corporation
200 E Randolph St # 7700
Chicago IL 60601
312 274-2000

(P-3585)
SPECIAL SERVICE CONTRS INC
3580 Airport Rd, Paso Robles (93446-9554)
P.O. Box 3121 (93447-3121)
PHONE...............................805 227-1081
Fax: 805 227-0915
Russell Wilson, *President*
Ron Kaggs, *Controller*
EMP: 51
SQ FT: 1,600
SALES (est): 8MM **Privately Held**
WEB: www.sscinfo.com
SIC: 1799 Cable splicing service

(P-3586)
STUMBAUGH & ASSOCIATES INC (PA)
3303 N San Fernando Blvd, Burbank (91504-2531)
PHONE...............................818 240-1627
Fax: 818 956-6684
Jeff Stumbaugh, *President*
Richard Stumbaugh, *Ch of Bd*
Tim Reardon, *Vice Pres*
Dorothy Blanchette, *Executive Asst*
Brian Dempsey, *Director*
EMP: 54

1799 - Special Trade Contractors, NEC County (P-3587)

SALES (est): 11MM **Privately Held**
WEB: www.stumbaugh.net
SIC: **1799** 5046 Demountable partition installation; partitions

(P-3587)
TAILORED LIVING CHOICES LLC
1957 Sierra Ave, NAPA (94558-2840)
PHONE..................707 259-0526
Vicki Robinson, *Mng Member*
Jessica Garrison, *Administration*
Stacy Perez,
EMP: 112
SALES (est): 7.3MM **Privately Held**
SIC: **1799** Home/office interiors finishing, furnishing & remodeling

(P-3588)
TAIT ENVIRONMENTAL SVCS INC (PA)
701 Parkcenter Dr, Santa Ana (92705-3541)
P.O. Box 11118 (92711-1118)
PHONE..................714 560-8200
Thomas F Tait, *CEO*
Richard Tait, *President*
Jason Jones, *Controller*
▲ EMP: 55
SQ FT: 8,900
SALES (est): 16MM **Privately Held**
SIC: **1799** 8748 Gas leakage detection; environmental consultant

(P-3589)
THE TEECOR GROUP INC
Also Called: Key Environmental Services
1450 S Burlington Ave, Los Angeles (90006-5409)
PHONE..................213 632-2350
Kalani Childs, *President*
Rui Saldanha, *CFO*
Eric Youssef, *Vice Pres*
EMP: 60
SQ FT: 5,000
SALES (est): 5MM **Privately Held**
WEB: www.teecor.com
SIC: **1799** Asbestos removal & encapsulation

(P-3590)
TOPBUILD SERVICES GROUP CORP
Also Called: Masco
1341 Old Oakland Rd, San Jose (95112-1317)
PHONE..................408 882-0411
Fax: 408 298-7257
Bob Colla, *Branch Mgr*
Michael Fitzpatrick, *Branch Mgr*
Rick Henson, *Contractor*
EMP: 75
SALES (corp-wide): 1.6B **Publicly Held**
WEB: www.galeind.com
SIC: **1799** Prefabricated fireplace installation
HQ: Topbuild Services Group Corp.
260 Jimmy Ann Dr
Daytona Beach FL 32114
386 304-2200

(P-3591)
TORRES FENCE CO INC
2357 S Orange Ave, Fresno (93725-1021)
P.O. Box 10137 (93745-0137)
PHONE..................559 237-4141
Ralph Torres, *President*
Rebecca Torres, *Corp Secy*
Ralph Torres Jr, *Vice Pres*
Rene J Torres, *Vice Pres*
Mari Salas, *Admin Sec*
▲ EMP: 50
SQ FT: 6,000
SALES (est): 6.3MM **Privately Held**
WEB: www.torresfence.com
SIC: **1799** 3315 3496 Fence construction; chain link fencing; barbed wire, made from purchased wire

(P-3592)
TROYER CONTRACTING COMPANY INC
10122 Freeman Ave, Santa Fe Springs (90670-3408)
PHONE..................562 944-6452

Fax: 562 944-6469
Mark Troyer, *CEO*
Susan Troyer, *Admin Sec*
▲ EMP: 55 EST: 1995
SQ FT: 15,208
SALES (est): 9.5MM **Privately Held**
SIC: **1799** 1761 Waterproofing; roofing contractor

(P-3593)
UNION ENVIRONMENTAL INC
1534 E Edinger Ave Ste 1, Santa Ana (92705-4912)
PHONE..................714 550-0005
Jerome Vitta, *President*
Linda Vitta, *Vice Pres*
Joan Minassalli, *Admin Sec*
EMP: 50
SQ FT: 9,000
SALES (est): 3.2MM **Privately Held**
SIC: **1799** 1795 Asbestos removal & encapsulation; wrecking & demolition work

(P-3594)
UNITED SPECTRUM INC
Also Called: Spectrum Abatement
1910 N Lime St, Orange (92865-4123)
P.O. Box 5747 (92863-5747)
PHONE..................714 283-1010
Fax: 949 771-6404
David Fischer, *President*
EMP: 50
SQ FT: 20,000
SALES (est): 5.3MM **Privately Held**
WEB: www.asbestos-removal.com
SIC: **1799** 1795 Asbestos removal & encapsulation; demolition, buildings & other structures

(P-3595)
VALENTINE CORPORATION
111 Pelican Way, San Rafael (94901-5519)
P.O. Box 9337 (94912-9337)
PHONE..................415 453-3732
Toll Free:..................877 -
Fax: 415 457-5820
Robert O Valentine, *CEO*
Robert Valentine Jr, *President*
Alan Hanley, *CFO*
Madeline Valentine, *Corp Secy*
David Levine, *Vice Pres*
EMP: 50
SQ FT: 3,000
SALES (est): 12.8MM **Privately Held**
SIC: **1799** 8711 1622 Waterproofing; building construction consultant; bridge construction

(P-3596)
VALLEY SUN MECHANICAL CNSTR
4205 Atlas Ct, Bakersfield (93308-4510)
P.O. Box 515, Oxford IN (47971-0515)
PHONE..................661 321-9070
Fax: 661 321-9090
Charles J Richmond, *President*
EMP: 64
SQ FT: 5,200
SALES (est): 4.6MM **Privately Held**
WEB: www.vsmc.com
SIC: **1799** Food service equipment installation; welding on site

(P-3597)
VALLEY WATER PROOFING INC
825 Civic Center Dr Ste 6, Santa Clara (95050-3961)
P.O. Box 20003, San Jose (95160-0003)
PHONE..................408 985-7701
Fax: 408 985-0956
Donna O'Brien, *President*
Michael O'Brien, *Vice Pres*
Kevin Ruffoni, *General Mgr*
Nicole Tabilla, *Project Mgr*
EMP: 80
SQ FT: 1,000
SALES (est): 7.6MM **Privately Held**
WEB: www.valleyh2o.com
SIC: **1799** Waterproofing

(P-3598)
WALTON ENGINEERING INC
3900 Commerce Dr, West Sacramento (95691-2157)
P.O. Box 1025 (95691-1025)
PHONE..................916 372-1888

Fax: 916 373-1172
Michael Walton, *President*
Richard Walton, *Vice Pres*
Larry Schleiger, *Controller*
EMP: 65
SQ FT: 13,000
SALES (est): 13.4MM **Privately Held**
SIC: **1799** 1542 7389 Service station equipment installation, maintenance & repair; service station construction; drafting service, except temporary help

(P-3599)
WASHINGTON ORNA IR WORKS INC (PA)
Also Called: Washington Iron Works
17926 S Broadway, Gardena (90248-3540)
P.O. Box 460 (90247-0846)
PHONE..................310 327-8660
Fax: 310 329-4180
Daniel Welsh, *CEO*
Chris Powell, *CFO*
Tom Pederson, *Corp Secy*
Luke Welsh, *VP Opers*
EMP: 90 EST: 1966
SQ FT: 141,240
SALES (est): 24.6MM **Privately Held**
WEB: www.washingtoniron.com
SIC: **1799** 3446 Ornamental metal work; architectural metalwork

(P-3600)
WAYNE PERRY INC (PA)
8281 Commonwealth Ave, Buena Park (90621-2537)
PHONE..................714 826-0352
Fax: 714 523-7880
Wayne Perry, *President*
Tom Ritchie, *President*
Adam Leiter, *Treasurer*
Daniel McGill, *Vice Pres*
Greg Nicholson, *Vice Pres*
EMP: 185
SQ FT: 4,000
SALES (est): 50.8MM **Privately Held**
WEB: www.wpinc.com
SIC: **1799** 8711 Decontamination services; petroleum storage tank installation, underground; engineering services

(P-3601)
WELL WITHIN SPA
417 Cedar St, Santa Cruz (95060-4304)
PHONE..................831 458-9355
Fax: 831 458-9016
David Levan, *Owner*
Eric Heckert, *Co-Owner*
Cynthia Begin, *Manager*
EMP: 60
SALES: 360K **Privately Held**
WEB: www.wellwithinspa.com
SIC: **1799** 7299 Spa or hot tub installation or construction; massage parlor & steam bath services

(P-3602)
WEST COAST FIRESTOPPING INC
1130 W Trenton Ave, Orange (92867-3536)
PHONE..................714 935-1104
Karl Stoll, *President*
EMP: 80
SALES (est): 6.9MM **Privately Held**
SIC: **1799** Fireproofing buildings

(P-3603)
WESTAR MANUFACTURING INC
Also Called: Fix Shore
13217 Laureldale Ave, Downey (90242-5140)
PHONE..................562 633-0581
Fax: 562 602-2913
Thomas Feldmar, *President*
Al Huggans, *VP Opers*
EMP: 60
SALES (est): 1.4MM
SALES (corp-wide): 64.4MM **Privately Held**
SIC: **1799** 3531 Shoring & underpinning work; construction machinery
PA: Trench Plate Rental Co.
13217 Laureldale Ave
Downey CA 90242
562 602-1642

(P-3604)
WESTERN MAGNESITE INC
11927 Sherman Rd Unit 1, North Hollywood (91605-3717)
PHONE..................818 255-1150
Bernard Fainstein, *Owner*
EMP: 50 EST: 2000
SALES (est): 3.9MM **Privately Held**
WEB: www.westernmagnesite.com
SIC: **1799** Waterproofing

(P-3605)
WLMD (PA)
Also Called: Wellmade Products
1715 Kibby Rd, Merced (95341-9301)
PHONE..................209 723-9120
Fax: 209 723-9131
Mark R Riley, *CEO*
Doug Bartman, *CFO*
Jerry Yon, *Controller*
Tim Smith, *Sales Mgr*
▲ EMP: 127
SQ FT: 120,000
SALES (est): 19.8MM **Privately Held**
WEB: www.wlmd.com
SIC: **1799** 1761 Lightning conductor erection; roofing, siding & sheet metal work

(P-3606)
WOODS MAINTENANCE SERVICES INC
Also Called: Hydro-Pressure Systems
7260 Atoll Ave, North Hollywood (91605-4104)
PHONE..................818 764-2515
Fax: 818 764-2516
Barry Woods, *President*
Diane Woods, *Principal*
Jeff Woods, *General Mgr*
Enrique Lopez, *Project Mgr*
Josh Woods, *Opers Staff*
EMP: 135
SQ FT: 26,000
SALES (est): 15.5MM **Privately Held**
WEB: www.graffiticontrol.com
SIC: **1799** Cleaning building exteriors

4011 Railroads, Line-Hauling Operations

(P-3607)
BNSF RAILWAY COMPANY
Also Called: Burlington Northern
740 Carnegie Dr, San Bernardino (92408-3571)
PHONE..................909 386-4002
Michael Shirelif, *General Mgr*
Terry Easley, *Admin Dir*
Brian Brewer, *Opers Mgr*
David Ayers, *Manager*
Drayton McLane Jr, *Manager*
EMP: 120
SALES (corp-wide): 210.8B **Publicly Held**
WEB: www.billpurdy.com
SIC: **4011** Railroads, line-haul operating
HQ: Bnsf Railway Company
2650 Lou Menk Dr
Fort Worth TX 76131
800 795-2673

(P-3608)
BNSF RAILWAY COMPANY
Also Called: Burlington Northern
200 N Avenue H, Barstow (92311-2553)
PHONE..................760 255-7803
Brandon Mabry, *Superintendent*
EMP: 110
SALES (corp-wide): 210.8B **Publicly Held**
WEB: www.billpurdy.com
SIC: **4011** 4111 4213 4225 Interurban railways; commuter rail passenger operation; trucking, except local; general warehousing; railroad freight agency; railroad property lessors
HQ: Bnsf Railway Company
2650 Lou Menk Dr
Fort Worth TX 76131
800 795-2673

PRODUCTS & SERVICES SECTION

4111 - Local & Suburban Transit County (P-3630)

(P-3609)
BNSF RAILWAY COMPANY
Also Called: Burlington Northern
6300 Sheila St, Commerce (90040-2411)
PHONE....................................323 869-3002
Julian Sanchez, *Superintendent*
EMP: 180
SALES (corp-wide): 210.8B **Publicly Held**
WEB: www.billpurdy.com
SIC: 4011 Railroads, line-haul operating
HQ: Bnsf Railway Company
2650 Lou Menk Dr
Fort Worth TX 76131
800 795-2673

(P-3610)
BNSF RAILWAY COMPANY
Also Called: Burlington Northern
3770 E Washington Blvd, Vernon
(90058-8125)
PHONE....................................323 267-4133
John Hynes, *Principal*
EMP: 200
SALES (corp-wide): 210.8B **Publicly Held**
WEB: www.billpurdy.com
SIC: 4011 Railroads, line-haul operating
HQ: Bnsf Railway Company
2650 Lou Menk Dr
Fort Worth TX 76131
800 795-2673

(P-3611)
CALIFRNIA HIGH SPEED RAIL AUTH
770 L St Ste 800, Sacramento
(95814-3359)
PHONE....................................916 324-1541
Thomas Fellenz, *CEO*
Melissa Dumond, *Plan/Corp Dev D*
Rachel Wall, *Admin Sec*
Kevin Thompson, *Engineer*
Scott Jarvis, *Chief Engr*
EMP: 100
SALES (est): 9.4MM **Privately Held**
SIC: 4011 Railroads, line-haul operating
PA: State Of California
State Capital
Sacramento CA 95814
916 445-2864

(P-3612)
CSX CORPORATION
14863 Clark Ave, Hacienda Heights
(91745-1308)
PHONE....................................626 336-1377
EMP: 149
SALES (corp-wide): 12.6B **Publicly Held**
SIC: 4011
PA: Csx Corporation
500 Water St Fl 15
Jacksonville FL 32202
904 359-3200

(P-3613)
NATIONAL RAILROAD PASS CORP
601 Marina Vista Ave, Martinez
(94553-1132)
PHONE....................................925 335-5180
EMP: 2046 **Publicly Held**
SIC: 4011 4013 Interurban railways; railroad terminals
HQ: National Railroad Passenger Corporation
60 Massachusetts Ave Ne
Washington DC 20002
202 906-3741

(P-3614)
NATIONAL RAILROAD PASS CORP
Also Called: Amtrak
1050 Kettner Blvd Ste 1, San Diego
(92101-3339)
PHONE....................................619 239-9989
Debbi Dewfwood, *Branch Mgr*
EMP: 138 **Publicly Held**
WEB: www.amtrak.com
SIC: 4011 9621 Railroads, line-haul operating; regulation, administration of transportation;
HQ: National Railroad Passenger Corporation
60 Massachusetts Ave Ne
Washington DC 20002
202 906-3741

(P-3615)
RR DONNELLEY & SONS COMPANY
Also Called: Moore Business Forms
1646 N Calif Blvd Ste 510, Walnut Creek
(94596-4171)
PHONE....................................925 951-1320
Wes McCracken, *Branch Mgr*
EMP: 50
SQ FT: 9,000
SALES (corp-wide): 11.2B **Publicly Held**
WEB: www.moore.com
SIC: 4011 5943 Railroads, line-haul operating; office forms & supplies
PA: R.R. Donnelley & Sons Company
35 W Wacker Dr Ste 3650
Chicago IL 60601
312 326-8000

(P-3616)
SAN JOAQUIN VALLEY RAILROAD CO
221 N F St, Exeter (93221-1119)
P.O. Box 937 (93221-0937)
PHONE....................................559 592-1857
Fax: 559 592-1859
Randy Perry, *CEO*
Rex Bergholm, *President*
Richard McGowan, *Chief Mktg Ofcr*
Steve Coomes, *Vice Pres*
Joe Evans, *General Mgr*
EMP: 200
SQ FT: 1,100
SALES (est): 20.3MM
SALES (corp-wide): 1.6B **Publicly Held**
WEB: www.statesrail.com
SIC: 4011 Railroads, line-haul operating
HQ: Railamerica, Inc.
20 West Ave
Darien CT 06820
203 656-1092

(P-3617)
SIERRA ENTERTAINMENT
341 Industrial Way, Woodland
(95776-6012)
PHONE....................................530 666-9646
David Magew, *President*
Robert Pinoli, *Vice Pres*
Torgny Nilsson, *Admin Sec*
EMP: 50
SALES (est): 83.7K
SALES (corp-wide): 335K **Privately Held**
SIC: 4011 Railroads, line-haul operating
PA: Sierra Railroad Company
341 Industrial Way
Woodland CA 95776
530 666-9646

(P-3618)
SOUTHERN PACIFIC TRNSP
1 Market Plz, San Francisco (94105-1101)
PHONE....................................415 541-2589
Lawrence Yarberry, *Principal*
EMP: 60
SALES (est): 5.3MM **Privately Held**
SIC: 4011 Electric railroads

(P-3619)
UNION PACIFIC CORPORATION
9451 Atkinson St Ste 100, Roseville
(95747-9301)
P.O. Box 42 (95747)
PHONE....................................916 789-5311
Mike Evans, *President*
Kim Day, *Executive Asst*
Davy Pavlica, *Manager*
EMP: 503
SALES (corp-wide): 21.8B **Publicly Held**
SIC: 4011 Railroads, line-haul operating
PA: Union Pacific Corporation
1400 Douglas St
Omaha NE 68179
402 544-5000

(P-3620)
UNION PACIFIC RAILROAD COMPANY
999 Paso Robles St, Paso Robles
(93446-2628)
PHONE....................................805 286-5851
Athey Roy, *Branch Mgr*
EMP: 80
SALES (corp-wide): 21.8B **Publicly Held**
SIC: 4011 Railroads, line-haul operating
HQ: Union Pacific Railroad Company Inc
1400 Douglas St
Omaha NE 68179
402 544-5000

(P-3621)
UNION PACIFIC RAILROAD COMPANY
3135 N Weber Ave, Fresno (93705-3655)
PHONE....................................559 443-2244
Randy Esquiza, *Manager*
EMP: 125
SALES (corp-wide): 21.8B **Publicly Held**
WEB: www.uprr.com
SIC: 4011 Railroads, line-haul operating
HQ: Union Pacific Railroad Company Inc
1400 Douglas St
Omaha NE 68179
402 544-5000

(P-3622)
UNION PACIFIC RAILROAD COMPANY
2000 S Sycamore Ave, Bloomington
(92316-2463)
PHONE....................................909 685-2710
EMP: 80
SALES (corp-wide): 21.8B **Publicly Held**
SIC: 4011 Railroads, line-haul operating
HQ: Union Pacific Railroad Company Inc
1400 Douglas St
Omaha NE 68179
402 544-5000

(P-3623)
UNION PACIFIC RAILROAD COMPANY
9391 Atkinson St Ste 100, Roseville
(95747-9605)
PHONE....................................916 789-5930
Jack Huddleston, *Branch Mgr*
Mario Sanchez, *Foreman/Supr*
Patrick McGrath, *Manager*
EMP: 80
SALES (corp-wide): 21.8B **Publicly Held**
SIC: 4011 Railroads, line-haul operating
HQ: Union Pacific Railroad Company Inc
1400 Douglas St
Omaha NE 68179
402 544-5000

(P-3624)
UNION PACIFIC RAILROAD COMPANY
4341 E Washington Blvd, Commerce
(90023-4470)
PHONE....................................213 446-1900
Kiley Freeman, *Business Mgr*
EMP: 80
SALES (corp-wide): 21.8B **Publicly Held**
SIC: 4011 Railroads, line-haul operating
HQ: Union Pacific Railroad Company Inc
1400 Douglas St
Omaha NE 68179
402 544-5000

(P-3625)
UNION PACIFIC RAILROAD COMPANY
10031 Fthlls Blvd Ste 200, Roseville
(95747)
PHONE....................................916 789-6055
Karen Calli, *Manager*
Robert N Belt,
Michael L Johnson,
James C Spaulding,
Ricky Durrant, *Director*
EMP: 120
SALES (corp-wide): 21.8B **Publicly Held**
WEB: www.uprr.com
SIC: 4011 Railroads, line-haul operating

HQ: Union Pacific Railroad Company Inc
1400 Douglas St
Omaha NE 68179
402 544-5000

(P-3626)
UNION PACIFIC RAILROAD COMPANY
224 Curtis Ave, Milpitas (95035-5309)
PHONE....................................510 874-1174
Don Seil, *Manager*
EMP: 50
SALES (corp-wide): 21.8B **Publicly Held**
WEB: www.uprr.com
SIC: 4011 Railroads, line-haul operating
HQ: Union Pacific Railroad Company Inc
1400 Douglas St
Omaha NE 68179
402 544-5000

(P-3627)
UNION PACIFIC RAILROAD COMPANY
Also Called: Southern Pacific Railroad
730 Sumner St, Bakersfield (93305-5251)
PHONE....................................661 321-4604
Fax: 661 321-4608
Bill Gafford, *President*
EMP: 80
SALES (corp-wide): 21.8B **Publicly Held**
WEB: www.uprr.com
SIC: 4011 Railroads, line-haul operating
HQ: Union Pacific Railroad Company Inc
1400 Douglas St
Omaha NE 68179
402 544-5000

4013 Switching & Terminal Svcs

(P-3628)
LOS ANGELES JUNCTION RLWY CO
4433 Exchange Ave, Vernon (90058-2622)
PHONE....................................323 277-2004
Chuck Potempa, *CEO*
Rob Rellyl, *President*
Rm Reilly, *Vice Pres*
Marion Alexander, *General Mgr*
R W Edwards, *General Mgr*
EMP: 50 EST: 1922
SALES (est): 5.3MM
SALES (corp-wide): 210.8B **Publicly Held**
WEB: www.billpurdy.com
SIC: 4013 Switching & terminal services
HQ: Bnsf Railway Company
2650 Lou Menk Dr
Fort Worth TX 76131
800 795-2673

(P-3629)
UNION PACIFIC RAILROAD COMPANY
1300 E Shaw Ave, Fresno (93710-7917)
PHONE....................................559 443-2277
EMP: 76
SALES (corp-wide): 21.8B **Publicly Held**
WEB: www.uprr.com
SIC: 4013 Switching & terminal services
HQ: Union Pacific Railroad Company Inc
1400 Douglas St
Omaha NE 68179
402 544-5000

4111 Local & Suburban Transit

(P-3630)
ACCESS SERVICES
Also Called: Access Paratransit
3449 Santa Anita Ave, El Monte
(91731-2424)
P.O. Box 5728 (91734-1728)
PHONE....................................213 270-6000
Doran J Barnes, *CEO*
F S Jewell, *COO*
Shelly Verrinder, *Exec Dir*
Jess Segovia, *Analyst*
Faye Moseley, *Deputy Dir*
EMP: 80

4111 - Local & Suburban Transit County (P-3631)

SALES: 123.3MM Privately Held
SIC: 4111 Local & suburban transit

(P-3631)
ADVANTAGE GROUND TRNSP CORP
Also Called: Advantage Ground Trnsp
2960 Airway Ave Ste B102, Costa Mesa (92626-6001)
PHONE.................714 557-2465
Fax: 714 557-2328
Vo Van Vu, *President*
Joseph Dullulo, *Vice Pres*
EMP: 80
SQ FT: 3,200
SALES (est): 5MM Privately Held
WEB: www.agtcorp.com
SIC: 4111 Airport limousine, scheduled service

(P-3632)
AIRLINE COACH SERVICE INC (PA)
863 Malcolm Rd, Burlingame (94010-1406)
P.O. Box 250628, San Francisco (94125-0628)
PHONE.................650 697-7733
Fax: 650 697-3389
Gregory Choo, *Ch of Bd*
Klaus Gelinski, *President*
Song Lim, *Vice Pres*
Klaus Gelinsky, *Personnel Exec*
EMP: 50
SQ FT: 7,000
SALES (est): 11.1MM Privately Held
SIC: 4111 Airport transportation services, regular route

(P-3633)
AIRPORT CONNECTION INC
Also Called: Roadrunner Shuttle
240 S Glenn Dr, Camarillo (93010-7940)
PHONE.................805 389-8196
Fax: 805 987-7294
Sumaia Sandlin, *CEO*
Desmond P Sandlin, *Admin Sec*
Nitin Miller, *Info Tech Dir*
Nitin Pai, *Info Tech Dir*
Roschelle Ayon, *Human Res Dir*
EMP: 180
SQ FT: 3,500
SALES (est): 36.2MM Privately Held
WEB: www.rrshuttle.com
SIC: 4111 4119 Airport transportation; airport transportation services, regular route; limousine rental, with driver

(P-3634)
ALAMEDA-CONTRA COSTA TRNST DST (PA)
Also Called: AC Transit
1600 Franklin St, Oakland (94612-2806)
P.O. Box 28507 (94604-8507)
PHONE.................510 891-4777
Fax: 510 891-4818
David J Armijo, *General Mgr*
Lewis Clinton, *CFO*
Dennis Lim, *Bd of Directors*
Kathleen Kelly, *Officer*
Kurt De Stigter, *Executive*
EMP: 250 **EST:** 1956
SQ FT: 100,000
SALES: 68.6MM Privately Held
WEB: www.actransit.org
SIC: 4111 Bus line operations

(P-3635)
ARCADIA TRANSIT INC
Also Called: Super Shuttle
7955 San Fernando Rd, Sun Valley (91352-4614)
PHONE.................818 252-0630
Tim Mardirossian, *President*
Patrick Voskian, *CFO*
Sedik Mardirossian, *Treasurer*
Rozan Mardosian, *Accounting Mgr*
EMP: 50
SQ FT: 25,000
SALES (est): 2.8MM Privately Held
SIC: 4111 Airport transportation services, regular route

(P-3636)
BAY PORTER EX ARPRT SHUTTLE
27 Industrial Way, Brisbane (94005-1001)
PHONE.................415 467-1800
Allen Chow, *President*
Jay Ver, *Admin Sec*
EMP: 85
SQ FT: 7,500
SALES (est): 3.4MM Privately Held
WEB: www.bayporter.com
SIC: 4111 Airport transportation services, regular route

(P-3637)
CALIFORNIA TRANSIT INC
3201 Hooper Ave, Los Angeles (90011-2128)
PHONE.................323 234-8750
Timmy Mardirossian, *President*
Eda Aghajanian, *Treasurer*
Carol Story, *Treasurer*
Petros Keshishian, *Principal*
Christina Pineda, *General Mgr*
EMP: 99 **EST:** 2008
SQ FT: 16,000
SALES (est): 4.5MM Privately Held
SIC: 4111 Local & suburban transit

(P-3638)
CITY OF ARCADIA
240 W Huntington Dr, Arcadia (91007-3401)
PHONE.................626 574-5435
Dominic Lazzaietto, *Principal*
EMP: 300 Privately Held
SIC: 4111 Local & suburban transit
PA: City Of Arcadia
240 W Huntington Dr
Arcadia CA 91007
626 574-5400

(P-3639)
CITY OF GARDENA
Also Called: Gardena Municipal Bus Lines
13999 S Western Ave, Gardena (90249-3005)
PHONE.................310 324-1475
Fax: 310 538-1989
Whitman Ballenger, *Director*
Stephany Santin, *Admin Asst*
Paula Faust, *Deputy Dir*
Jack Gabig, *Director*
EMP: 97 Privately Held
WEB: www.gardenapd.org
SIC: 4111 9621 Bus line operations; regulation, administration of transportation;
PA: City Of Gardena
1700 W 162nd St
Gardena CA 90247
310 217-9500

(P-3640)
CUSA AWC LLC
Also Called: All West Coachlines
7701 Wilbur Way, Sacramento (95828-4929)
PHONE.................916 423-4000
Linda King,
Craig Lentzch,
Jeanine Smith, *Manager*
EMP: 50
SALES (est): 2.1MM Privately Held
SIC: 4111 Bus transportation

(P-3641)
DESTINATION SHUTTLE SVCS LLC
6150 W 96th St, Los Angeles (90045-5218)
PHONE.................310 338-9466
Brian Clark,
Regneil Prasad, *Opers Mgr*
Brian Lott,
Jack Lott,
EMP: 130
SALES (est): 3.9MM Privately Held
SIC: 4111 Local & suburban transit

(P-3642)
DIVERSIFIED TRANSPORTATION LLC
6053 W Century Blvd # 900, Los Angeles (90045-6400)
PHONE.................310 981-9500
Lisa Jasper, *Manager*
EMP: 58 Privately Held
SIC: 4111 4121 Local & suburban transit; taxicabs
HQ: Diversified Transportation Llc
1400 E Mission Blvd
Pomona CA
909 622-1313

(P-3643)
EAST BAY CONNECTION INC
Also Called: East Bay Airport Shuttle
1970 Arnold Industrial Pl, Concord (94520-5318)
PHONE.................925 609-1920
Fax: 925 609-1937
Amid Alefi, *Manager*
EMP: 50
SQ FT: 11,600
SALES (est): 2MM Privately Held
WEB: www.eastbayconnection.net
SIC: 4111 Airport transportation

(P-3644)
EL DORADO COUNTY TRANSIT AUTH
Also Called: Edcta
6565 Commerce Way Ste A, Diamond Springs (95619-9454)
PHONE.................530 642-5383
Fax: 530 622-2877
Mindy Jackson, *Exec Dir*
Bob O'Brien, *Supervisor*
EMP: 74
SQ FT: 174,240
SALES: 1.6MM Privately Held
WEB: www.eldoradotransit.com
SIC: 4111 Local & suburban transit

(P-3645)
FIRST STUDENT INC
550 E C St, Dixon (95620-3634)
PHONE.................707 678-8679
Fax: 707 678-8849
Valerie Salaun, *Branch Mgr*
EMP: 71
SALES (corp-wide): 7.5B Privately Held
SIC: 4111 Local & suburban transit
HQ: First Student, Inc.
600 Vine St Ste 1400
Cincinnati OH 45202
513 241-2200

(P-3646)
FIRST STUDENT INC
Also Called: Community Transit Services
4337 Rowland Ave, El Monte (91731-1119)
PHONE.................626 448-9446
Fax: 626 448-9519
John Desmond, *Branch Mgr*
EMP: 100
SALES (corp-wide): 7.5B Privately Held
WEB: www.leag.com
SIC: 4111 4119 Bus line operations; local passenger transportation
HQ: First Student, Inc.
600 Vine St Ste 1400
Cincinnati OH 45202
513 241-2200

(P-3647)
FIRST STUDENT INC
801 Wilbur Ave, Antioch (94509-7500)
PHONE.................925 754-4878
Dwight Ashburn, *Manager*
Lori Babcock, *Finance*
EMP: 160
SALES (corp-wide): 7.5B Privately Held
WEB: www.leag.com
SIC: 4111 Bus line operations
HQ: First Student, Inc.
600 Vine St Ste 1400
Cincinnati OH 45202
513 241-2200

(P-3648)
FIRST TRANSIT
Also Called: First Group of America
1303 Fairway Dr, Santa Maria (93455-1407)
PHONE.................805 925-5254
Mary McKinley, *Principal*
EMP: 71
SALES (est): 3.4MM Privately Held
SIC: 4111 Local & suburban transit

(P-3649)
FIRST TRANSIT INC
2400 E Dominguez St, Long Beach (90810-1012)
PHONE.................310 515-8270
EMP: 54
SALES (corp-wide): 9.2B Privately Held
SIC: 4111
HQ: First Transit, Inc.
600 Vine St Ste 1400
Cincinnati OH 45202
513 241-2200

(P-3650)
FIRST TRANSIT INC
6616 Lake Isabella Blvd, Lake Isabella (93240-9477)
PHONE.................760 379-1711
Fax: 760 379-1723
Marlene Echeverria, *Principal*
EMP: 54
SALES (corp-wide): 7.5B Privately Held
SIC: 4111 Local & suburban transit
HQ: First Transit, Inc.
600 Vine St Ste 1400
Cincinnati OH 45202
513 241-2200

(P-3651)
FIRST TRANSIT INC
5438 Victor St Ste B, Bakersfield (93308-4053)
PHONE.................661 391-3614
Fax: 661 392-3619
Lora Mallory, *Manager*
EMP: 54
SALES (corp-wide): 7.5B Privately Held
WEB: www.firsttransit.com
SIC: 4111 Local & suburban transit
HQ: First Transit, Inc.
600 Vine St Ste 1400
Cincinnati OH 45202
513 241-2200

(P-3652)
FIRST TRANSIT INC
Also Called: Dispatch Office
407 High St, Oakland (94601-3903)
PHONE.................510 437-8990
Fax: 510 535-9301
Harris, *Branch Mgr*
EMP: 54
SALES (corp-wide): 7.5B Privately Held
WEB: www.firsttransit.com
SIC: 4111 Local & suburban transit
HQ: First Transit, Inc.
600 Vine St Ste 1400
Cincinnati OH 45202
513 241-2200

(P-3653)
FOOTHILL TRANSIT SERVICE CORP (PA)
100 S Vincent Ave Ste 200, West Covina (91790-2944)
PHONE.................626 967-3147
Fax: 626 915-1143
Julie Austin, *CEO*
Doran Barnes, *Exec Dir*
Toran Barns, *Exec Dir*
Sharlane Bailey, *Project Mgr*
Vicente Sauceda, *Project Mgr*
EMP: 55
SQ FT: 9,626
SALES (est): 7.2MM Privately Held
SIC: 4111 Bus line operations

(P-3654)
GOLDEN EMPIRE TRANSIT DISTRICT (PA)
Also Called: Get-A-Lift Handicap Bus Trnsp
1830 Golden State Ave, Bakersfield (93301-1012)
PHONE.................661 869-2438
Fax: 661 324-7849
Steven Woods, *CEO*
Karen King, *President*
Martin Lizer, *Info Tech Mgr*
Jeanie Hill, *Human Res Dir*
Christine Carrillo, *Purch Agent*
EMP: 232
SALES (est): 30.3MM Privately Held
WEB: www.getbus.org
SIC: 4111 Bus line operations

PRODUCTS & SERVICES SECTION

4111 - Local & Suburban Transit County (P-3676)

(P-3655)
IDEAL TRANSIT INC
2301 Troy Ave, South El Monte
(91733-2539)
PHONE..................................626 448-2690
Fax: 626 448-2698
Baldo M Paseta, *President*
EMP: 50
SALES (est): 3.8MM **Privately Held**
SIC: 4111 Local & suburban transit

(P-3656)
LONG BEACH PUBLIC TRNSP CO
1300 Gardenia Ave, Long Beach
(90813-2599)
PHONE..................................562 591-2301
Laurence Jackson, *Branch Mgr*
EMP: 325
SALES (corp-wide): 37MM **Privately Held**
SIC: 4111 Local & suburban transit
PA: Long Beach Public Transportation Co Inc
    1963 E Anaheim St
    Long Beach CA 90813
    562 591-8753

(P-3657)
LONG BEACH PUBLIC TRNSP CO (PA)
Also Called: Long Beach Public Transit
1963 E Anaheim St, Long Beach
(90813-3907)
P.O. Box 731 (90801-0731)
PHONE..................................562 591-8753
Fax: 562 218-1994
Laurence W Jackson, *President*
Robyn Peterson, *COO*
Sarah Miller, *Bd of Directors*
Vince Rouzaud, *Vice Pres*
Laverne David, *Executive*
EMP: 570
SQ FT: 10,000
SALES (est): 37MM **Privately Held**
SIC: 4111 Bus line operations

(P-3658)
LONG BEACH PUBLIC TRNSP CO
1963 E Anaheim St, Long Beach
(90813-3907)
P.O. Box 731 (90801-0731)
PHONE..................................562 591-8753
Larry Jackson, *Manager*
Deborah Ellis, *Director*
EMP: 80
SALES (corp-wide): 37MM **Privately Held**
SIC: 4111 Bus line operations
PA: Long Beach Public Transportation Co Inc
    1963 E Anaheim St
    Long Beach CA 90813
    562 591-8753

(P-3659)
LOS ANGELES COUNTY MTA
9201 Canoga Ave, Chatsworth
(91311-5839)
PHONE..................................213 922-6308
Pat Orr, *Manager*
EMP: 217
SALES (corp-wide): 699.1MM **Privately Held**
WEB: www.mta.net
SIC: 4111 Local & suburban transit
PA: Los Angeles County Metropolitan Transportation Authority
    1 Gateway Plz Fl 25
    Los Angeles CA 90012
    323 466-3876

(P-3660)
LOS ANGELES COUNTY MTA
900 Lyon St, Los Angeles (90012-2913)
PHONE..................................213 922-5887
John Drayton, *Manager*
Michael Chang, *Senior Engr*
EMP: 217
SALES (corp-wide): 699.1MM **Privately Held**
WEB: www.mta.net
SIC: 4111 Local & suburban transit
PA: Los Angeles County Metropolitan Transportation Authority
    1 Gateway Plz Fl 25
    Los Angeles CA 90012
    323 466-3876

(P-3661)
LOS ANGELES COUNTY MTA
1130 E 6th St, Los Angeles (90021-1108)
PHONE..................................213 922-6301
Ron Reedy, *Branch Mgr*
EMP: 150
SALES (corp-wide): 699.1MM **Privately Held**
WEB: www.mta.net
SIC: 4111 8111 Local & suburban transit; legal services
PA: Los Angeles County Metropolitan Transportation Authority
    1 Gateway Plz Fl 25
    Los Angeles CA 90012
    323 466-3876

(P-3662)
LOS ANGELES COUNTY MTA
630 W Avenue 28, Los Angeles
(90065-1502)
PHONE..................................213 922-6203
Cheryl Brown, *Manager*
Richard Famighetti, *Assistant*
EMP: 400
SALES (corp-wide): 699.1MM **Privately Held**
WEB: www.mta.net
SIC: 4111 Bus line operations
PA: Los Angeles County Metropolitan Transportation Authority
    1 Gateway Plz Fl 25
    Los Angeles CA 90012
    323 466-3876

(P-3663)
LOS ANGELES COUNTY MTA
Also Called: Los Angeles Cnty Mtro Trnspt
1 Gateway Plz, Los Angeles (90012-3745)
PHONE..................................213 922-6202
Maria Japardi, *Branch Mgr*
Frank C Roberts, *Vice Chairman*
Richard Brumbaugh, *CFO*
Michael D Antonovich, *Bd of Directors*
Doug Failing, *Bd of Directors*
EMP: 217
SALES (corp-wide): 699.1MM **Privately Held**
WEB: www.mta.net
SIC: 4111 Bus transportation
PA: Los Angeles County Metropolitan Transportation Authority
    1 Gateway Plz Fl 25
    Los Angeles CA 90012
    323 466-3876

(P-3664)
LOS ANGELES COUNTY MTA (PA)
1 Gateway Plz Fl 25, Los Angeles
(90012-3745)
P.O. Box 512296 (90051-0296)
PHONE..................................323 466-3876
Fax: 213 922-6186
Arthur Leahy, *CEO*
Rick Thorpe, *CEO*
Carolyn Flowers, *COO*
Robert Holland, *COO*
Lonnie Mitchell, *COO*
EMP: 900
SALES (est): 699.1MM **Privately Held**
WEB: www.mta.net
SIC: 4111 Bus line operations; subway operation

(P-3665)
LOS ANGELES COUNTY MTA
8800 Santa Monica Blvd, Los Angeles
(90069-4536)
PHONE..................................213 922-6207
Grant Myers, *Manager*
Elizabeth Benett, *CIO*
EMP: 700
SALES (corp-wide): 699.1MM **Privately Held**
WEB: www.mta.net
SIC: 4111 Bus line operations; local railway passenger operation
PA: Los Angeles County Metropolitan Transportation Authority
    1 Gateway Plz Fl 25
    Los Angeles CA 90012
    323 466-3876

(P-3666)
LOS ANGELES COUNTY MTA
11900 Branford St, Sun Valley
(91352-1003)
PHONE..................................213 922-6215
Gary Stivack, *Manager*
EMP: 500
SALES (corp-wide): 699.1MM **Privately Held**
WEB: www.mta.net
SIC: 4111 Local & suburban transit
PA: Los Angeles County Metropolitan Transportation Authority
    1 Gateway Plz Fl 25
    Los Angeles CA 90012
    323 466-3876

(P-3667)
LOS ANGELES COUNTY MTA
720 E 15th St, Los Angeles (90021-2122)
PHONE..................................213 533-1506
Carla Aleman, *Branch Mgr*
EMP: 360
SALES (corp-wide): 699.1MM **Privately Held**
SIC: 4111 Bus line operations
PA: Los Angeles County Metropolitan Transportation Authority
    1 Gateway Plz Fl 25
    Los Angeles CA 90012
    323 466-3876

(P-3668)
LOS ANGELES COUNTY MTA
Also Called: Lacmta
470 Bauchet St, Los Angeles (90012-2907)
PHONE..................................213 922-5012
Jim Montoya, *Branch Mgr*
Michael Singer, *Maintence Staff*
Paul Lewicki, *Manager*
Angel Noriega, *Supervisor*
EMP: 217
SALES (corp-wide): 699.1MM **Privately Held**
WEB: www.mta.net
SIC: 4111 Bus transportation
PA: Los Angeles County Metropolitan Transportation Authority
    1 Gateway Plz Fl 25
    Los Angeles CA 90012
    323 466-3876

(P-3669)
LOS ANGELES COUNTY MTA
Also Called: Division 7
100 Sunset Ave, Venice (90291-2517)
PHONE..................................310 392-8636
John Adams, *Manager*
EMP: 120
SALES (corp-wide): 699.1MM **Privately Held**
WEB: www.mta.net
SIC: 4111 Bus transportation
PA: Los Angeles County Metropolitan Transportation Authority
    1 Gateway Plz Fl 25
    Los Angeles CA 90012
    323 466-3876

(P-3670)
LOS ANGELES COUNTY MTA
Also Called: Office of Inspector General
818 W 7th St Ste 500, Los Angeles
(90017-3463)
PHONE..................................213 244-6783
Arthur Sinai, *Manager*
EMP: 217
SALES (corp-wide): 699.1MM **Privately Held**
WEB: www.mta.net
SIC: 4111 Local & suburban transit
PA: Los Angeles County Metropolitan Transportation Authority
    1 Gateway Plz Fl 25
    Los Angeles CA 90012
    323 466-3876

(P-3671)
LOS ANGELES COUNTY MTA
320 S Santa Fe Ave, Los Angeles
(90013-1812)
P.O. Box 194 (90078-0194)
PHONE..................................213 626-4455
Julian Burke, *CEO*
Mahesh Singh, *Project Mgr*
Russell Bradshaw, *Engineer*
Aida Lagrimas, *Manager*
EMP: 217
SALES (corp-wide): 699.1MM **Privately Held**
WEB: www.mta.net
SIC: 4111 Bus line operations
PA: Los Angeles County Metropolitan Transportation Authority
    1 Gateway Plz Fl 25
    Los Angeles CA 90012
    323 466-3876

(P-3672)
MENDOCINO TRANSIT AUTHORITY
111 Boatyard Dr, Fort Bragg (95437-5709)
P.O. Box 556, Gualala (95445-0556)
PHONE..................................707 462-1422
Sam Kingsley, *Principal*
EMP: 60
SALES (corp-wide): 6.6MM **Privately Held**
WEB: www.4mta.org
SIC: 4111 4131 Bus line operations; intercity & rural bus transportation
PA: Mendocino Transit Authority
    241 Plant Rd
    Ukiah CA 95482
    707 462-3881

(P-3673)
METROPOLITAN TRNSP COMM (PA)
Also Called: M T C
375 Beale St, San Francisco (94105-2066)
PHONE..................................510 817-5700
Fax: 510 464-7848
Steve Hieminger, *Exec Dir*
Brian Mayhew, *CFO*
Jake Mackenzie, *Vice Ch Bd*
Bond Counsel, *Executive*
Steve Heminger, *Exec Dir*
EMP: 115
SQ FT: 21,000
SALES: 305.4MM **Privately Held**
SIC: 4111 Bus line operations

(P-3674)
MOBILITY PLUS TRNSP LLC
4961 Pacheco Blvd, Martinez
(94553-4324)
PHONE..................................925 957-9841
Michael Griffus, *President*
Francis G Homan, *CFO*
Susan Soh, *Accounts Mgr*
EMP: 99
SALES (est): 2.6MM **Privately Held**
WEB: www.tectransinc.com
SIC: 4111 4121 Local & suburban transit; taxicabs
HQ: Keolis Transit America, Inc.
    6053 W Century Blvd # 900
    Los Angeles CA 90045
    310 981-9500

(P-3675)
MONTEBELLO TRANSIT
400 S Taylor Ave, Montebello (90640-5057)
PHONE..................................323 887-4600
Allan Pollock, *Director*
Darren Lew, *Info Tech Dir*
Joe Perino, *Manager*
Manchi Yi, *Manager*
EMP: 250
SALES (est): 3.6MM **Privately Held**
SIC: 4111 Local & suburban transit

(P-3676)
MV TRANSPORTATION INC
13690 Vaughn St, San Fernando
(91340-3017)
PHONE..................................323 666-0856
EMP: 78
SALES (corp-wide): 2.7B **Privately Held**
SIC: 4111 Local & suburban transit

(PA)=Parent Co (HQ)=Headquarters (DH)=Div Headquarters
✪ = New Business established in last 2 years

4111 - Local & Suburban Transit County (P-3677)

PA: Mv Transportation, Inc
5910 N Cntrl Expy # 1145
Dallas TX 75206
707 474-7784

(P-3677)
MV TRANSPORTATION INC
16721 Hale Ave, Irvine (92606-5006)
PHONE..................949 553-1639
Kishelle Holland, *Manager*
EMP: 78
SALES (corp-wide): 2.7B **Privately Held**
SIC: 4111 Local & suburban transit
PA: Mv Transportation, Inc
5910 N Cntrl Expy # 1145
Dallas TX 75206
707 474-7784

(P-3678)
MV TRANSPORTATION INC
1242 Los Angeles St, Glendale (91204-2404)
PHONE..................818 409-3387
Fax: 818 548-5195
Herman Roeper, *Branch Mgr*
Richard Gilmore, *Administration*
EMP: 78
SALES (corp-wide): 2.7B **Privately Held**
SIC: 4111 Local & suburban transit
PA: Mv Transportation, Inc
5910 N Cntrl Expy # 1145
Dallas TX 75206
707 474-7784

(P-3679)
MV TRANSPORTATION INC
1250 S Wilson Way Ste A1, Stockton (95205-7026)
PHONE..................209 547-7879
Fax: 209 547-7880
Nick Harbut, *Branch Mgr*
EMP: 78
SALES (corp-wide): 2.7B **Privately Held**
SIC: 4111 Local & suburban transit
PA: Mv Transportation, Inc
5910 N Cntrl Expy # 1145
Dallas TX 75206
707 474-7784

(P-3680)
MV TRANSPORTATION INC
24 S Sacramento St, Lodi (95240-2150)
PHONE..................209 339-1972
Fax: 209 339-2387
Elizabeth Davidiaz, *Manager*
EMP: 78
SALES (corp-wide): 2.7B **Privately Held**
SIC: 4111 Local & suburban transit
PA: Mv Transportation, Inc
5910 N Cntrl Expy # 1145
Dallas TX 75206
707 474-7784

(P-3681)
MV TRANSPORTATION INC
265 S Rancho Rd, Thousand Oaks (91361-5222)
PHONE..................805 557-7372
Cheryl Seafert, *Branch Mgr*
EMP: 76
SALES (corp-wide): 2.7B **Privately Held**
SIC: 4111 Local & suburban transit
PA: Mv Transportation, Inc
5910 N Cntrl Expy # 1145
Dallas TX 75206
707 474-7784

(P-3682)
MV TRANSPORTATION INC
7231 Rosecrans Ave, Paramount (90723-2501)
PHONE..................562 790-8642
EMP: 78
SALES (corp-wide): 2.7B **Privately Held**
SIC: 4111 Local & suburban transit
PA: Mv Transportation, Inc
5910 N Cntrl Expy # 1145
Dallas TX 75206
707 474-7784

(P-3683)
NORTH COUNTY TRANSIT DISTRICT (PA)
Also Called: Nctd
810 Mission Ave, Oceanside (92054-2825)
PHONE..................760 966-6500
Matt Tucker, *Exec Dir*
Bryant Abel, *Officer*
Jarrett Wade, *Officer*
Suheil Rodriguez, *Executive*
Karen King, *Exec Dir*
EMP: 60
SQ FT: 7,000
SALES (est): 18.3MM **Privately Held**
SIC: 4111 Local & suburban transit; bus transportation; commuter rail passenger operation

(P-3684)
NORWALK TRANSIT SYSTEM
Also Called: City of Norwalk
12650 Imperial Hwy, Norwalk (90650-3137)
PHONE..................562 929-5550
Fax: 562 929-5572
James C Parker, *Director*
Suresh Paul, *Admin Asst*
Al Pierce, *Manager*
Grahan Ridley, *Manager*
Lois Smith, *Manager*
EMP: 99
SALES (est): 4.6MM **Privately Held**
SIC: 4111 Local & suburban transit

(P-3685)
OMNITRANS
4748 Arrow Hwy, Montclair (91763-1208)
PHONE..................909 379-7100
John Steffon, *Branch Mgr*
EMP: 150
SALES (corp-wide): 15.6MM **Privately Held**
SIC: 4111 Bus line operations
PA: Omnitrans
1700 W 5th St
San Bernardino CA 92411
909 379-7100

(P-3686)
ORANGE COUNTY TRNSP AUTH
11790 Cardinal Cir, Garden Grove (92843-3839)
P.O. Box 14184, Orange (92863-1584)
PHONE..................714 560-6282
Arthur Leahy, *CEO*
EMP: 1000
SALES (corp-wide): 607.7MM **Privately Held**
WEB: www.octa.net
SIC: 4111 Bus line operations
PA: Orange County Transportation Authority
550 S Main St
Orange CA 92868
714 636-7433

(P-3687)
ORANGE COUNTY TRNSP AUTH (PA)
Also Called: ORANGE COUNTY TRANSIT DISTRICT
550 S Main St, Orange (92868-4506)
P.O. Box 14184 (92863-1584)
PHONE..................714 636-7433
Fax: 714 560-5795
Darrell Johnson, *CEO*
Jaime Hernandez, *COO*
Michael Hennessey, *Bd of Directors*
Chris Norby, *Bd of Directors*
Jim Kenan, *Exec Dir*
EMP: 350
SQ FT: 77,000
SALES: 607.7MM **Privately Held**
WEB: www.octa.net
SIC: 4111 8711 Bus line operations; construction & civil engineering

(P-3688)
ORANGE COUNTY TRNSP AUTH
Also Called: Octa
600 S Main St Ste 910, Orange (92868-4689)
PHONE..................714 999-1726
Oscar Moreno, *Branch Mgr*
Kirk Avila, *Treasurer*
Veronica Garcia, *Admin Asst*
Mary Toutounchi, *Project Mgr*
Patrick Matarazzo, *Corp Counsel*
EMP: 600
SALES (corp-wide): 607.7MM **Privately Held**
WEB: www.octa.net
SIC: 4111 Bus line operations

PA: Orange County Transportation Authority
550 S Main St
Orange CA 92868
714 636-7433

(P-3689)
OUTREACH & ESCORT INC (PA)
2221 Oakland Rd Ste 200, San Jose (95131-1415)
P.O. Box 640910 (95164-0910)
PHONE..................408 436-2865
Fax: 408 382-0470
Katheryn H Heatley, *President*
William Chawarz, *Vice Pres*
Vinodh Kanchi, *Info Tech Mgr*
EMP: 51
SQ FT: 20,000
SALES: 23.8MM **Privately Held**
WEB: www.outreach1.org
SIC: 4111 Local & suburban transit

(P-3690)
PENINSULA CRRDOR JINT PWERS BD
Also Called: Caltrain
1250 San Carlos Ave, San Carlos (94070-2468)
P.O. Box 3006 (94070-1306)
PHONE..................650 508-6200
Michael J Scanlon, *Exec Dir*
Virginia Harrington, *CEO*
Chuck Harvey, *CEO*
Don Gage, *Bd of Directors*
Jose Cisneros, *Principal*
EMP: 105
SALES: 90.7MM **Privately Held**
SIC: 4111 Local railway passenger operation

(P-3691)
REDDING AERO ENTERPRISES INC
Also Called: Redding Jet Center
3775 Flight Ave Ste 100, Redding (96002-9376)
PHONE..................530 224-2300
Fax: 530 224-2315
Doug Unknown, *President*
Jack Kilpatrick, *President*
Steve Hoppes, *Corp Secy*
Victor Clarke, *Vice Pres*
EMP: 60
SQ FT: 31,000
SALES: 7.2MM **Privately Held**
WEB: www.reddingjet.com
SIC: 4111 4581 Airport transportation services, regular route; aircraft servicing & repairing

(P-3692)
RIVERSIDE TRANSIT AGENCY (PA)
Also Called: R T A
1825 3rd St, Riverside (92507-3484)
P.O. Box 59968 (92517-1968)
PHONE..................951 565-5000
Fax: 951 565-5007
Larry Rubio, *CEO*
Tom Franklinn, *COO*
Craig Fajnor, *CFO*
Rohan Kuruppu, *Plan/Corp Dev D*
Tammi Ford, *Executive Asst*
EMP: 350
SQ FT: 10,400
SALES: 11.2MM **Privately Held**
WEB: www.riversidetransit.com
SIC: 4111 Bus transportation

(P-3693)
ROYAL COACH TOURS (PA)
630 Stockton Ave, San Jose (95126-2433)
PHONE..................408 279-4801
Fax: 408 286-1410
Sandra Allen, *CEO*
Joanne Smith Christian, *Shareholder*
Daniel Smith, *Vice Pres*
Diana Yuan, *Accountant*
Suzan Walker, *Mktg Dir*
EMP: 82
SQ FT: 2,500
SALES: 13MM **Privately Held**
WEB: www.royal-coach.com
SIC: 4111 Bus transportation

(P-3694)
SACRAMENTO REGIONAL TRNST DIST (PA)
1400 29th St, Sacramento (95816-6406)
P.O. Box 2110 (95812-2110)
PHONE..................916 726-2877
Fax: 916 444-2156
Mike Wiley, *CEO*
Brent Bernegger, *Treasurer*
Trisha Perez, *Admin Sec*
Connie Garcia, *Admin Asst*
Gloria Boyce, *Administration*
EMP: 700
SQ FT: 10,000
SALES (est): 96.4MM **Privately Held**
WEB: www.sacrt.com
SIC: 4111 Bus line operations; commuter rail passenger operation

(P-3695)
SAN DIEGO METRO TRNST SYS
1255 Imperial Ave # 1000, San Diego (92101-7490)
PHONE..................619 231-1466
Fax: 619 234-3407
Paul Jadlonski, *CEO*
Stan Abrams, *CEO*
Cliff Telfer, *CFO*
Jeff Stumbo, *Executive*
Vicki Rogers, *Executive Asst*
EMP: 1600
SQ FT: 40,000
SALES (est): 91.1MM **Privately Held**
WEB: www.sdtc.sdmts.com
SIC: 4111 Local & suburban transit

(P-3696)
SAN DIEGO TRANSIT CORPORATION (PA)
100 16th St, San Diego (92101-7694)
PHONE..................619 238-0100
Fax: 619 696-5241
Langley Powell, *President*
Bill Spraul, *COO*
Clifford Telfer, *Exec VP*
Jeff Stumbo, *Vice Pres*
Steve Tomkiel, *Executive Asst*
EMP: 650
SQ FT: 20,000
SALES (est): 49.5MM **Privately Held**
WEB: www.sdcommute.com
SIC: 4111 Commuter bus operation

(P-3697)
SAN DIEGO TRANSIT CORPORATION
100 16th St, San Diego (92101-7694)
PHONE..................619 238-0100
Cliff Telfer, *Branch Mgr*
EMP: 350
SALES (corp-wide): 49.5MM **Privately Held**
WEB: www.sdcommute.com
SIC: 4111 Commuter bus operation
PA: San Diego Transit Corporation
100 16th St
San Diego CA 92101
619 238-0100

(P-3698)
SAN DIEGO TROLLEY INC
1341 Commercial St, San Diego (92113-1021)
PHONE..................619 595-4933
Bill Brown, *Branch Mgr*
EMP: 370
SALES (corp-wide): 28.6MM **Privately Held**
WEB: www.sdrotary.org
SIC: 4111 Trolley operation
PA: San Diego Trolley Inc
1255 Imperial Ave Ste 900
San Diego CA 92101
619 595-4949

(P-3699)
SAN FRANCISCO BAY AREA RAPID
2000 Bart Way, Fremont (94538-1705)
PHONE..................510 441-2278
Fran San, *Principal*
EMP: 262
SALES (corp-wide): 384.8MM **Privately Held**
SIC: 4111 Local & suburban transit

PRODUCTS & SERVICES SECTION
4111 - Local & Suburban Transit County (P-3719)

PA: San Francisco Bay Area Rapid Transit District
300 Lakeside Dr
Oakland CA 94604
510 464-6000

(P-3700) SAN FRANCISCO BAY AREA RAPID
Also Called: 1st Interstate Bank Building
1330 Broadway, Oakland (94612-2503)
PHONE.....................510 464-6000
Thomas Margro, Manager
Tuan Hoang, Senior Engr
William Black, Manager
Christopher Flynn, Manager
Bridget Shaefer, Supervisor
EMP: 50
SALES (corp-wide): 384.8MM Privately Held
SIC: 4111 Local railway passenger operation
PA: San Francisco Bay Area Rapid Transit District
300 Lakeside Dr
Oakland CA 94604
510 464-6000

(P-3701) SAN FRANCISCO BAY AREA RAPID
Also Called: Operations Control Center
800 Madison St, Oakland (94607-4730)
PHONE.....................510 834-1297
Rudy Crespo, Manager
Paula Eubanks-Major, Buyer
EMP: 100
SALES (corp-wide): 384.8MM Privately Held
SIC: 4111 Local railway passenger operation
PA: San Francisco Bay Area Rapid Transit District
300 Lakeside Dr
Oakland CA 94604
510 464-6000

(P-3702) SAN FRANCISCO BAY AREA RAPID
Also Called: Records Center/Storage
300 Lakeside Dr 23, Oakland (94612-3534)
P.O. Box 12688 (94604-2688)
PHONE.....................510 464-6126
Tom Margaro, Branch Mgr
EMP: 103
SALES (corp-wide): 384.8MM Privately Held
SIC: 4111 Local railway passenger operation
PA: San Francisco Bay Area Rapid Transit District
300 Lakeside Dr
Oakland CA 94604
510 464-6000

(P-3703) SAN FRANCISCO BAY AREA RAPID
Also Called: Richmond Repair Shop
1101 13th St, Richmond (94801-2302)
PHONE.....................510 233-6848
Sean Steel, Branch Mgr
Sean Branch, Manager
EMP: 150
SALES (corp-wide): 384.8MM Privately Held
SIC: 4111 Local railway passenger operation
PA: San Francisco Bay Area Rapid Transit District
300 Lakeside Dr
Oakland CA 94604
510 464-6000

(P-3704) SAN FRANCISCO BAY AREA RAPID
699 B St, Hayward (94541-5005)
PHONE.....................510 441-2278
Carole Allen, Branch Mgr
EMP: 262

SALES (corp-wide): 384.8MM Privately Held
SIC: 4111 Local & suburban transit
PA: San Francisco Bay Area Rapid Transit District
300 Lakeside Dr
Oakland CA 94604
510 464-6000

(P-3705) SAN FRANCISCO BAY AREA RAPID (PA)
Also Called: Bart
300 Lakeside Dr, Oakland (94604)
P.O. Box 12688 (94604-2688)
PHONE.....................510 464-6000
Fax: 510 464-7103
Grace Crunican, General Mgr
Scott Schroeder, Treasurer
Contra Costa, Vice Pres
Elaine Kurtz, Department Mgr
Bart Blog, General Mgr
EMP: 400
SQ FT: 150,000
SALES (est): 384.8MM Privately Held
SIC: 4111 Local railway passenger operation

(P-3706) SAN FRANCISCO BAY AREA RAPID
Also Called: Oakland Shops/Annex
101 8th St, Oakland (94607-4707)
PHONE.....................510 286-2893
Richard Leonard, Superintendent
Theresa Stuart, Admin Asst
Brian Witt, Engineer
Verinder Dhesi, Supervisor
EMP: 200
SALES (corp-wide): 384.8MM Privately Held
SIC: 4111 Local railway passenger operation
PA: San Francisco Bay Area Rapid Transit District
300 Lakeside Dr
Oakland CA 94604
510 464-6000

(P-3707) SAN FRANCISCO BAY AREA RAPID
Also Called: Police Department
800 Madison St, Oakland (94607-4730)
P.O. Box 12668 (94604)
PHONE.....................510 464-7000
Fax: 510 869-2414
Kenton Rainey, Chief
Ezra Raptort, Exec Dir
Michael McCormick, Engineer
EMP: 99
SALES (corp-wide): 384.8MM Privately Held
SIC: 4111 Local railway passenger operation
PA: San Francisco Bay Area Rapid Transit District
300 Lakeside Dr
Oakland CA 94604
510 464-6000

(P-3708) SAN FRANCISCO BAY AREA RAPID
Also Called: Madison Square Building
300 Lakeside Dr Fl 17, Oakland (94612-3534)
P.O. Box 12688 (94604-2688)
PHONE.....................510 464-6000
Thomas Margro, Manager
Timothy Moore, Info Tech Mgr
EMP: 103
SALES (corp-wide): 384.8MM Privately Held
SIC: 4111 Local railway passenger operation
PA: San Francisco Bay Area Rapid Transit District
300 Lakeside Dr
Oakland CA 94604
510 464-6000

(P-3709) SAN GABRIEL TRANSIT INC (PA)
Also Called: San Gabriel Valley Cab Co
3650 Rockwell Ave, El Monte (91731-2322)
PHONE.....................626 258-1310
Fax: 626 258-1329
Timmy Mardirossian, President
Eda Aghajanian, Treasurer
Luisa Sun, General Mgr
Sedik Mardirossian, Admin Sec
EMP: 220
SQ FT: 8,000
SALES (est): 22.4MM Privately Held
WEB: www.sgtransit.com
SIC: 4111 Local & suburban transit

(P-3710) SAN JOAQUIN REGIONAL TRNST DST
421 E Weber Ave, Stockton (95202-3024)
P.O. Box 201010 (95201-9010)
PHONE.....................209 948-5566
Donna Demartino, CEO
Gloria Salazar, CFO
Donna Kelsay, General Mgr
Greg Love, Info Tech Dir
Helen Sicsic, Accountant
EMP: 201
SQ FT: 29,100
SALES (est): 13.4MM Privately Held
WEB: www.sanjoaquinrtd.com
SIC: 4111 Bus line operations

(P-3711) SAN MATEO COUNTY TRANSIT DST (PA)
1250 San Carlos Ave, San Carlos (94070-2468)
P.O. Box 3006 (94070-1306)
PHONE.....................650 508-6200
Mike Scanlon, CEO
Jerry Deal, Vice Chairman
Jim Kellner, President
Ch Harvey, COO
Jim Shelton, COO
EMP: 250
SQ FT: 20,000
SALES: 18.8MM Privately Held
WEB: www.samtrans.com
SIC: 4111 Local & suburban transit

(P-3712) SAN MATEO COUNTY TRANSIT DST
Also Called: Sam Trans
301 N Access Rd, South San Francisco (94080-6901)
PHONE.....................650 588-4860
John Gerbo, Branch Mgr
EMP: 300
SQ FT: 2,000
SALES (corp-wide): 18.8MM Privately Held
SIC: 4111 Local & suburban transit
PA: San Mateo County Transit District
1250 San Carlos Ave
San Carlos CA 94070
650 508-6200

(P-3713) SANTA BARBARA METRO TRNST DST (PA)
Also Called: M T D
550 Olive St, Santa Barbara (93101-1610)
PHONE.....................805 963-3364
Fax: 805 962-4794
Gary Gleason, General Mgr
John Britton, Ch of Bd
Richard Weinberg, Exec Dir
Sherry Fisher, General Mgr
Jerry Estrada, Controller
EMP: 69
SQ FT: 8,500
SALES (est): 16.3MM Privately Held
WEB: www.sbmtd.gov
SIC: 4111 Bus line operations

(P-3714) SANTA MONICA CITY OF
Also Called: Santa Monica Municpl Bus Line
1660 7th St, Santa Monica (90401-3324)
PHONE.....................310 451-5444
Stephanie Megriff, Director
Stephanie Negriff, Director

EMP: 300 Privately Held
WEB: www.santamonicapd.org
SIC: 4111 9111 Local & suburban transit; mayors' offices
PA: City Of Santa Monica
1685 Main St
Santa Monica CA 90401
310 458-8281

(P-3715) SFO AIRPORTER INC (PA)
Also Called: Compass Transportation Charter
160 S Linden Ave Ste 300, South San Francisco (94080-6436)
PHONE.....................650 246-2775
Fax: 650 624-0515
Nicholas C Leonoudakis, Ch of Bd
Jeffrey G Leonoudakis, President
Stephan C Leonoudakis, Exec VP
Timothy K Leonoudakis, Vice Pres
Cindy Bryand, Opers Spvr
▼ EMP: 100 EST: 1976
SALES (est): 28.8MM Privately Held
SIC: 4111 4141 4131 Airport transportation; local bus charter service; intercity bus line

(P-3716) SFO AIRPORTER INC
325 5th St, San Francisco (94107-1040)
PHONE.....................415 495-3909
Gordis Esposto, Branch Mgr
EMP: 100
SALES (corp-wide): 28.8MM Privately Held
SIC: 4111 4141 4131 Airport transportation; local bus charter service; intercity bus line
PA: Sfo Airporter, Inc.
160 S Linden Ave Ste 300
South San Francisco CA 94080
650 246-2775

(P-3717) SFO SHUTTLE BUS INC
San Francisco Intl Arprt, San Francisco (94128)
PHONE.....................650 877-0430
Fax: 650 877-1557
Jeffrey Leonoudakis, President
Tim Leonoudakis, Vice Pres
EMP: 197
SQ FT: 20,000
SALES: 7.2MM Privately Held
SIC: 4111 Airport transportation services, regular route

(P-3718) SMS TRANSPORTATION SVCS INC
865 S Figueroa St # 2750, Los Angeles (90017-2627)
PHONE.....................213 489-5367
Fax: 213 489-3761
John Harris, CEO
Delilah Lanoix, President
Jennifer Wiltz, COO
Danielle Wiltz, CFO
Gerri Willis, General Mgr
EMP: 150
SQ FT: 3,000
SALES: 10MM Privately Held
SIC: 4111 Local & suburban transit

(P-3719) SONOMA COUNTY AIRPORT EXPRESS
5807 Old Redwood Hwy, Santa Rosa (95403-1167)
PHONE.....................707 837-8700
Fax: 707 528-2877
Howard Emigh, President
Tony Geraldi, Corp Secy
Janet Emigh, Vice Pres
EMP: 80
SQ FT: 5,500
SALES: 5.5MM Privately Held
WEB: www.airportexpressinc.com
SIC: 4111 4141 Airport transportation services, regular route; local bus charter service

4111 - Local & Suburban Transit County (P-3720) — PRODUCTS & SERVICES SECTION

(P-3720)
SOUTH BAY AIRPORT SHUTTLE
Also Called: East Bay Airport Shuttle
14420 Union Ave, San Jose (95124-2815)
P.O. Box 219, Campbell (95009-0219)
PHONE..................................408 225-4444
Fax: 408 226-4444
Behzad Fatemi, *President*
Donia Fatemi, *Treasurer*
EMP: 95
SQ FT: 2,000
SALES: 15MM Privately Held
WEB: www.southbayairportshuttle.com
SIC: 4111 Airport transportation services, regular route

(P-3721)
SOUTHERN CAL RGIONAL RAIL AUTH (PA)
Also Called: Metrolink
1 Gateway Plz Fl 12, Los Angeles (90012-3747)
P.O. Box 531776 (90053-1776)
PHONE..................................213 452-0200
Fax: 213 452-0425
Michael De Pallo, *CEO*
Gary Lettengarver, *COO*
Sam Joumblat, *CFO*
Pat Kataura, *Vice Pres*
Robert Turnauckas, *Principal*
EMP: 100
SALES (est): 36.5MM Privately Held
WEB: www.metrolinktrains.com
SIC: 4111 Commuter rail passenger operation

(P-3722)
SOUTHLAND TRANSIT INC
44110 Yucca Ave, Lancaster (93534-4421)
PHONE..................................661 726-4225
Fax: 661 726-4495
Len Angel, *Manager*
Bernard Brown, *Project Mgr*
EMP: 100
SALES (corp-wide): 16.1MM Privately Held
SIC: 4111 Local & suburban transit
PA: Southland Transit, Inc.
 3650 Rockwell Ave
 El Monte CA 91731
 626 258-1310

(P-3723)
STORER TRANSPORTATION
1909 S Argonaut St, Stockton (95206-1826)
PHONE..................................209 644-5100
Fax: 209 644-5130
Donald Storer, *Owner*
EMP: 80
SALES (est): 1.8MM Privately Held
WEB: www.storerbus.com
SIC: 4111 Bus transportation

(P-3724)
SUPERSHUTTLE INTERNATIONAL INC
9559 Center Ave Ste F, Rancho Cucamonga (91730-5815)
PHONE..................................909 944-2606
Margaret Nathan, *Principal*
Mark Lundy, *General Mgr*
Shawn Targhibi, *General Mgr*
Jennifer Streeter, *Director*
Adriana Galvan, *Manager*
EMP: 150
SALES (corp-wide): 507.8MM Privately Held
SIC: 4111 Airport transportation
HQ: Supershuttle International, Inc.
 14500 N Northsight Blvd # 329
 Scottsdale AZ 85260
 480 609-3000

(P-3725)
SUPERSHUTTLE INTERNATIONAL INC
Also Called: Supershuttle Sacramento
3100 Northgate Blvd, Sacramento (95833-1349)
PHONE..................................916 648-2500
Fax: 916 648-2505
Igor Avanto, *General Mgr*
EMP: 65
SQ FT: 1,600
SALES (corp-wide): 507.8MM Privately Held
WEB: www.execucar.com
SIC: 4111 Airport transportation services, regular route
HQ: Supershuttle International, Inc.
 14500 N Northsight Blvd # 329
 Scottsdale AZ 85260
 480 609-3000

(P-3726)
SUPERSHUTTLE LOS ANGELES INC
531 Van Ness Ave, Torrance (90501-6233)
PHONE..................................310 222-5500
Fax: 310 222-5535
Gene Hauk, *President*
R Brian Wier, *CEO*
Thomas C Lavoy, *CFO*
EMP: 165
SQ FT: 15,000
SALES: 6MM
SALES (corp-wide): 507.8MM Privately Held
WEB: www.execucar.com
SIC: 4111 Local & suburban transit
HQ: Supershuttle International, Inc.
 14500 N Northsight Blvd # 329
 Scottsdale AZ 85260
 480 609-3000

(P-3727)
SUPERSHUTTLE ORANGE COUNTY
531 Van Ness Ave, Torrance (90501-6233)
PHONE..................................310 222-5500
Steven Allan, *President*
EMP: 300
SQ FT: 12,000
SALES (est): 4.9MM
SALES (corp-wide): 507.8MM Privately Held
WEB: www.execucar.com
SIC: 4111 Airport transportation
HQ: Supershuttle International, Inc.
 14500 N Northsight Blvd # 329
 Scottsdale AZ 85260
 480 609-3000

(P-3728)
THE CENTRAL VALLEY TRNSP AUTH
675 W Manning Ave, Reedley (93654-2427)
PHONE..................................559 305-7037
Mark Garza, *Director*
EMP: 60
SALES (est): 934.9K Privately Held
SIC: 4111 Local & suburban transit

(P-3729)
TRANSITAMERICA SERVICES INC
1 Coaster Way, Camp Pendleton (92055)
P.O. Box 2480, Oceanside (92051-2480)
PHONE..................................760 430-0770
Robert J Smith, *President*
Robert Purgavie, *General Mgr*
Jeans Mark, *Finance*
EMP: 50
SALES (est): 5.4MM Privately Held
SIC: 4111 Local & suburban transit

(P-3730)
TRANSPORTATION CONCEPT INC
Also Called: T C I
1521 Kingsdale Ave, Redondo Beach (90278-3939)
PHONE..................................323 268-2202
Brian Connell, *Office Mgr*
EMP: 70
SALES (est): 2.2MM Privately Held
SIC: 4111 Bus transportation

(P-3731)
TWO HARBORS ENTERPRISES INC
150 Metropole Ave, Avalon (90704)
P.O. Box 5086 (90704-5086)
PHONE..................................310 510-2000
Kathy Thompson, *Vice Pres*
Dave Coiner, *Master*
EMP: 75
SALES (est): 5.2MM Privately Held
SIC: 4111 Bus transportation

(P-3732)
VEOLIA TRANSPORTATION SVCS INC
Also Called: Shuttleport California
1601 Airport Blvd, San Jose (95110-1209)
PHONE..................................408 277-3661
Fax: 408 971-6240
Terry Van Der Ray, *Branch Mgr*
EMP: 142
SALES (corp-wide): 555.3MM Privately Held
WEB: www.sctransit.com
SIC: 4111 Airport transportation
HQ: Veolia Transportation Services, Inc.
 2015 Spring Rd Ste 750
 Oak Brook IL 60523
 630 571-7070

(P-3733)
VEOLIA TRANSPORTATION SVCS INC
17150 Smoketree St, Hesperia (92345-3299)
PHONE..................................760 947-5719
Simon Herrera, *Manager*
EMP: 128
SALES (corp-wide): 507.8MM Privately Held
WEB: www.sctransit.com
SIC: 4111 4141 Local & suburban transit; local bus charter service
HQ: Veolia Transportation Services, Inc.
 2015 Spring Rd Ste 750
 Oak Brook IL 60523
 630 571-7070

(P-3734)
VEOLIA TRANSPORTATION SVCS INC
25663 Avenue Stanford, Valencia (91355-1103)
PHONE..................................661 294-2541
Ken Graska, *Branch Mgr*
EMP: 145
SALES (corp-wide): 555.3MM Privately Held
WEB: www.sctransit.com
SIC: 4111 4141 Local & suburban transit; local bus charter service
HQ: Veolia Transportation Services, Inc.
 2015 Spring Rd Ste 750
 Oak Brook IL 60523
 630 571-7070

(P-3735)
VEOLIA TRANSPORTATION SVCS INC
326 Huss Dr, Chico (95928-8261)
PHONE..................................530 342-6851
Terry L Van Der, *Ch of Bd*
Kent Christian, *General Mgr*
EMP: 128
SALES (corp-wide): 507.8MM Privately Held
WEB: www.sctransit.com
SIC: 4111 Local & suburban transit
HQ: Veolia Transportation Services, Inc.
 2015 Spring Rd Ste 750
 Oak Brook IL 60523
 630 571-7070

(P-3736)
VEOLIA TRANSPORTATION SVCS INC
1362 Rutan Dr Ste 200, Livermore (94551-7318)
PHONE..................................925 455-7500
David Brofee, *Branch Mgr*
EMP: 65
SALES (corp-wide): 555.3MM Privately Held
WEB: www.sctransit.com
SIC: 4111 Local & suburban transit
HQ: Veolia Transportation Services, Inc.
 2015 Spring Rd Ste 750
 Oak Brook IL 60523
 630 571-7070

(P-3737)
VEOLIA TRANSPORTATION SVCS INC
355 W Robles Ave, Santa Rosa (95407-8126)
PHONE..................................707 585-7516
Kent Hinton, *General Mgr*
Terry Vanderaa, *President*
EMP: 104
SALES (corp-wide): 555.3MM Privately Held
WEB: www.sctransit.com
SIC: 4111 Local & suburban transit
HQ: Veolia Transportation Services, Inc.
 2015 Spring Rd Ste 750
 Oak Brook IL 60523
 630 571-7070

4119 Local Passenger Transportation: NEC

(P-3738)
A-PARA TRANSIT CORP
Also Called: Yefllow Shttle Vtrans Sdan Svc
1400 Doolittle Dr, San Leandro (94577-2226)
PHONE..................................510 732-9400
Shiv D Kumar, *President*
Sara Kaur, *Office Mgr*
EMP: 110
SQ FT: 2,200
SALES (est): 5.8MM Privately Held
SIC: 4119 Local passenger transportation

(P-3739)
ALLIED MEDICAL SERVICE OF CAL
2570 Bush St, San Francisco (94115-3002)
PHONE..................................415 931-1400
Josette Mani, *President*
Leif Engman, *President*
Glen Millar, *CFO*
EMP: 50
SQ FT: 6,000
SALES (est): 2.2MM Privately Held
WEB: www.kingamerican.com
SIC: 4119 6411 Ambulance service; insurance agents, brokers & service

(P-3740)
AMATO INDUSTRIES INCORPORATED
Also Called: Gateway Limousine
1550 Gilbreth Rd, Burlingame (94010-1605)
PHONE..................................650 697-2087
Fax: 650 697-7739
Sam A Mato, *CEO*
Joel Amato, *Vice Pres*
Karen Amato, *Vice Pres*
Gerry Jacinto, *Manager*
Tommy Amato, *Accounts Mgr*
EMP: 75
SQ FT: 9,500
SALES (est): 6.3MM Privately Held
WEB: www.gatewaylimousine.com
SIC: 4119 Limousine rental, with driver

(P-3741)
AMERICAN MED
5151 Port Chicago Hwy, Concord (94520-8585)
PHONE..................................925 602-1300
EMP: 106 Publicly Held
SIC: 4119 Local passenger transportation
HQ: American Medical Response, Inc.
 6363 S Fiddlers Green Cir # 1400
 Greenwood Village CO 80111
 303 495-1200

(P-3742)
AMERICAN MED
Also Called: Redlands Division
600 Iowa St, Redlands (92373-8047)
PHONE..................................909 793-7676
James Price, *Director*
EMP: 250 Publicly Held
WEB: www.amr-inc.com
SIC: 4119 Ambulance service
HQ: American Medical Response, Inc.
 6363 S Fiddlers Green Cir # 1400
 Greenwood Village CO 80111
 303 495-1200

PRODUCTS & SERVICES SECTION

4119 - Local Passenger Transportation: NEC County (P-3767)

(P-3743)
AMERICAN MED
Also Called: A M R
5257 Vincent Ave, Irwindale (91706-2042)
PHONE..................626 633-4600
Art McKierman, *Branch Mgr*
Gary Scott, *CTO*
Gary Cevello, *Supervisor*
EMP: 260 **Publicly Held**
SIC: 4119 Ambulance service
HQ: American Medical Response, Inc.
6363 S Fiddlers Green Cir # 1400
Greenwood Village CO 80111
303 495-1200

(P-3744)
AMERICAN MED
1510 Rollins Rd, Burlingame (94010-2306)
PHONE..................650 235-1333
John Odle, *Principal*
EMP: 106 **Publicly Held**
WEB: www.amr-inc.com
SIC: 4119 Ambulance service
HQ: American Medical Response, Inc.
6363 S Fiddlers Green Cir # 1400
Greenwood Village CO 80111
303 495-1200

(P-3745)
AMERICAN MED
1111 Montalvo Way, Palm Springs
(92262-5440)
PHONE..................760 883-5000
Mark Bowen, *Supervisor*
Lynne Liko, *Office Mgr*
EMP: 106 **Publicly Held**
SIC: 4119 Ambulance service
HQ: American Medical Response, Inc.
6363 S Fiddlers Green Cir # 1400
Greenwood Village CO 80111
303 495-1200

(P-3746)
AMERICAN MED
7925 Center Ave, Rancho Cucamonga
(91730-3007)
PHONE..................909 948-1714
Fax: 909 477-5009
Rene Polarossa, *General Mgr*
EMP: 106 **Publicly Held**
WEB: www.amr-inc.com
SIC: 4119 Ambulance service
HQ: American Medical Response, Inc.
6363 S Fiddlers Green Cir # 1400
Greenwood Village CO 80111
303 495-1200

(P-3747)
AMERICAN MED
7575 Southfront Rd, Livermore
(94551-8226)
PHONE..................510 895-7600
Brad Cooper, *CFO*
EMP: 106 **Publicly Held**
SIC: 4119 Ambulance service
HQ: American Medical Response, Inc.
6363 S Fiddlers Green Cir # 1400
Greenwood Village CO 80111
303 495-1200

(P-3748)
AMERICAN MED RESP AMBLNC SVC
Also Called: Sonoma Life Support
930 S A St, Santa Rosa (95404-5439)
PHONE..................707 536-0400
Lori Price, *Director*
EMP: 70 **Publicly Held**
WEB: www.amr-inc.com
SIC: 4119 Ambulance service
HQ: American Medical Response, Inc.
6363 S Fiddlers Green Cir # 1400
Greenwood Village CO 80111
303 495-1200

(P-3749)
AMERICAN MED RSPNSE STHERN CAL
1055 W Avenue J, Lancaster (93534-3328)
PHONE..................661 945-9310
Louis Meyer, *President*
Don Harvey, *COO*
Randel Owen, *CFO*
Todd Zimmerman, *Exec VP*
Tim Dorn, *Vice Pres*

EMP: 2806 **EST:** 2000
SALES (est): 22.3MM **Publicly Held**
SIC: 4119 Ambulance service
HQ: American Medical Response, Inc.
6363 S Fiddlers Green Cir # 1400
Greenwood Village CO 80111
303 495-1200

(P-3750)
AMERICAN MEDICAL RESPONSE
2400 Bisso Ln, Concord (94520-4832)
PHONE..................925 454-6000
Mike Esslinger, *Director*
Don Johnson, *Telecomm Mgr*
Dan Miner, *Network Enginr*
Tony Fernandes, *IT/INT Sup*
Linda Kissling, *Personnel*
EMP: 180 **Publicly Held**
SIC: 4119 Local passenger transportation; ambulance service
HQ: American Medical Response
879 Marlborough Ave
Riverside CA 92507
951 782-5200

(P-3751)
AMERICAN MEDICAL RESPONSE
1041 Fee Dr, Sacramento (95815-3908)
PHONE..................916 563-0600
Doug Petric, *Director*
EMP: 400 **Publicly Held**
SIC: 4119 Ambulance service
HQ: American Medical Response
879 Marlborough Ave
Riverside CA 92507
951 782-5200

(P-3752)
AMERICAN MEDICAL RESPONSE
1300 Illinois St, San Francisco (94107-3107)
PHONE..................415 922-9400
James Salvante, *Manager*
EMP: 75 **Publicly Held**
SIC: 4119 Ambulance service
HQ: American Medical Response
879 Marlborough Ave
Riverside CA 92507
951 782-5200

(P-3753)
AMERICAN MEDICAL RESPONSE
116 Hubbard St, Santa Cruz (95060-2938)
PHONE..................831 423-7030
David Zenker, *Manager*
EMP: 57 **Publicly Held**
SIC: 4119 Ambulance service
HQ: American Medical Response
879 Marlborough Ave
Riverside CA 92507
951 782-5200

(P-3754)
AMERICAN MEDICAL RESPONSE (DH)
879 Marlborough Ave, Riverside (92507-2133)
PHONE..................951 782-5200
Bill Fanger, *President*
Anthony Wong, *Prgrmr*
Louise Lewis, *Manager*
Erik Mandler, *Manager*
Tom McKentee, *Manager*
EMP: 80
SQ FT: 24,000
SALES (est): 40.3MM **Publicly Held**
SIC: 4119 Ambulance service
HQ: American Medical Response, Inc.
6363 S Fiddlers Green Cir # 1400
Greenwood Village CO 80111
303 495-1200

(P-3755)
AMERICAN MEDICAL RESPONSE
1510 Rollins Rd, Burlingame (94010-2306)
PHONE..................650 235-1333
Lily Farmer, *Branch Mgr*
Susan Stapleton, *Supervisor*
EMP: 100 **Publicly Held**
SIC: 4119 Ambulance service

HQ: American Medical Response
879 Marlborough Ave
Riverside CA 92507
951 782-5200

(P-3756)
AMERICAN MEDICAL RESPONSE INC
208 E Devonshire Ave A, Hemet (92543-2985)
PHONE..................951 658-2826
Jack Hanson, *Branch Mgr*
EMP: 113 **Publicly Held**
SIC: 4119 Ambulance service
HQ: American Medical Response, Inc.
6363 S Fiddlers Green Cir # 1400
Greenwood Village CO 80111
303 495-1200

(P-3757)
AMERICAN MEDICAL RESPONSE INC
8808 Balboa Ave Ste 150, San Diego (92123-6502)
PHONE..................858 492-3500
Rich Ahrendt, *Vice Pres*
Randy Owen, *Director*
EMP: 250 **Publicly Held**
WEB: www.amr-inc.com
SIC: 4119 Ambulance service
HQ: American Medical Response, Inc.
6363 S Fiddlers Green Cir # 1400
Greenwood Village CO 80111
303 495-1200

(P-3758)
AMERICAN MEDICAL RESPONSE INC
Mobile Life Support
240 E Highway 246 Ste 300, Buellton (93427-9648)
PHONE..................805 688-6550
John H Eaglesham, *Branch Mgr*
EMP: 125
SQ FT: 2,000 **Publicly Held**
WEB: www.amr-inc.com
SIC: 4119 Ambulance service
HQ: American Medical Response, Inc.
6363 S Fiddlers Green Cir # 1400
Greenwood Village CO 80111
303 495-1200

(P-3759)
AMERICAN MEDICAL RESPONSE INC
1111 Montalvo Way, Palm Springs (92262-5440)
PHONE..................760 322-4134
Keren Heavlin, *Branch Mgr*
Mark Bowen, *Supervisor*
EMP: 85 **Publicly Held**
WEB: www.amr-inc.com
SIC: 4119 Ambulance service
HQ: American Medical Response, Inc.
6363 S Fiddlers Green Cir # 1400
Greenwood Village CO 80111
303 495-1200

(P-3760)
AMERICAN MEDICAL RESPONSE INC
4548 A St, Marina (93933)
PHONE..................831 718-9555
Chris Weinress, *Manager*
Lynne Liko, *Office Mgr*
EMP: 175 **Publicly Held**
WEB: www.amr-inc.com
SIC: 4119 Ambulance service
HQ: American Medical Response, Inc.
6363 S Fiddlers Green Cir # 1400
Greenwood Village CO 80111
303 495-1200

(P-3761)
AMERICAN MEDICAL RESPONSE INC
Also Called: Hemet Valley Ambulance
208 E Devonshire Ave A, Hemet (92543-2985)
PHONE..................951 765-3900
Jack Hansen, *Branch Mgr*
EMP: 106 **Publicly Held**
SIC: 4119 Ambulance service

HQ: American Medical Response, Inc.
6363 S Fiddlers Green Cir # 1400
Greenwood Village CO 80111
303 495-1200

(P-3762)
AMERICAN MEDICAL RESPONSE INC
1870 Hillcrest Rd, Hollister (95023-5204)
PHONE..................831 636-9391
Edward Van Horne, *Branch Mgr*
EMP: 107 **Publicly Held**
SIC: 4119 Ambulance service
HQ: American Medical Response, Inc.
6363 S Fiddlers Green Cir # 1400
Greenwood Village CO 80111
303 495-1200

(P-3763)
AMERICAN MEDICAL RESPONSE INC
13146 Lincoln Way, Auburn (95603-4114)
PHONE..................530 887-9440
Michael Mendenhall, *Manager*
EMP: 50 **Publicly Held**
WEB: www.amr-inc.com
SIC: 4119 Ambulance service
HQ: American Medical Response, Inc.
6363 S Fiddlers Green Cir # 1400
Greenwood Village CO 80111
303 495-1200

(P-3764)
AMERICAN MEDICAL RESPONSE INC
1420 Lander Ave, Turlock (95380-6202)
PHONE..................209 567-4030
Cindy Woolston, *Manager*
EMP: 106 **Publicly Held**
SIC: 4119 Local passenger transportation
HQ: American Medical Response, Inc.
6363 S Fiddlers Green Cir # 1400
Greenwood Village CO 80111
303 495-1200

(P-3765)
AMERICAN MEDICAL RSPNSE AMBLNC
Also Called: AMR
879 Marlborough Ave, Riverside (92507-2133)
PHONE..................303 495-1217
William A Sanger, *CEO*
Don Harvey, *President*
Randel Owen, *Vice Pres*
Lynne Liko, *Office Mgr*
Jim Graves, *Manager*
EMP: 1813
SALES (est): 6.8MM **Publicly Held**
SIC: 4119 Ambulance service
HQ: American Medical Response, Inc.
6363 S Fiddlers Green Cir # 1400
Greenwood Village CO 80111
303 495-1200

(P-3766)
AMERICAN PROF AMBULANCE CORP
16945 Sherman Way, Van Nuys (91406-3614)
P.O. Box 7263 (91409-7263)
PHONE..................818 996-2200
Lyubov Popok, *President*
Alexander Chase, *Director*
EMP: 175
SALES (est): 7.3MM **Privately Held**
SIC: 4119 Ambulance service

(P-3767)
AMERICARE MEDSERVICES INC (PA)
Also Called: Americare Ambulance Service
1059 E Bedmar St, Carson (90746-3601)
PHONE..................310 632-1141
Michael Summers, *President*
Scott Smith, *COO*
Mark Ewing, *Manager*
Steve Gloss, *Manager*
EMP: 140
SQ FT: 10,000
SALES (est): 12.3MM **Privately Held**
WEB: www.americare.org
SIC: 4119 Ambulance service

4119 - Local Passenger Transportation: NEC County (P-3768)

(P-3768)
ATLANTIC EXPRESS TRNSP
Also Called: Atlantic Express of California
2450 Long Beach Blvd, Long Beach (90806-3125)
PHONE..................562 997-6868
Fax: 562 997-1228
Darinda Garnett, *Manager*
EMP: 120
SALES (corp-wide): 252MM **Privately Held**
SIC: 4119 8748 4151 Local passenger transportation; traffic consultant; school buses
HQ: Atlantic Express Transportation Corp
7 North St
Staten Island NY 10302

(P-3769)
BAUERS INTELLIGENT TRNSP INC (PA)
50 Pier, San Francisco (94158-2193)
PHONE..................415 522-1212
Fax: 415 522-1600
Gary Bauer, *CEO*
Dennis Jackson, *COO*
Gary Schwartz, *CFO*
Lon Baylor, *Exec VP*
John Conway, *CTO*
EMP: 250
SQ FT: 125,000
SALES: 48.3MM **Privately Held**
WEB: www.bauersIT.com
SIC: 4119 Local rental transportation

(P-3770)
BAY MEDIC TRANSPORTATION INC
959 Detroit Ave, Concord (94518-2501)
PHONE..................800 689-9511
Fax: 925 280-2860
Nesar Abdiani, *CEO*
Ali Abdani, *President*
EMP: 56
SQ FT: 1,600
SALES (est): 2.3MM **Privately Held**
WEB: www.baymedic.com
SIC: 4119 Ambulance service

(P-3771)
BAYSHORE AMBULANCE INC (PA)
370 Hatch Dr, Foster City (94404-1106)
P.O. Box 4622 (94404-0622)
PHONE..................650 525-9700
Fax: 650 578-1498
William Bockholt, *President*
David Bockholt, *Treasurer*
EMP: 51
SQ FT: 5,000
SALES (est): 6.2MM **Privately Held**
WEB: www.bayshoreambulance.com
SIC: 4119 Ambulance service

(P-3772)
BELLA LIMOUSINES
4502 Melisa Way, San Diego (92117-3545)
PHONE..................619 302-4062
Ilya Kurpchi, *Owner*
EMP: 58
SALES (est): 668.5K **Privately Held**
WEB: www.bellalimousines.com
SIC: 4119 Limousine rental, with driver

(P-3773)
BI-COUNTY AMBULANCE SERVICE
1700 Poole Blvd, Yuba City (95993-2610)
P.O. Box 3130 (95992-3130)
PHONE..................530 674-2780
Kelly W Bumpus, *President*
Tracy Rossnan, *Manager*
EMP: 50
SQ FT: 1,600
SALES (est): 2MM **Privately Held**
WEB: www.bicountyambulance.com
SIC: 4119 Ambulance service

(P-3774)
BLACK TIE TRANSPORTATION LLC
7080 Comm Dr, Pleasanton (94588)
PHONE..................925 847-0747
Fax: 925 847-9247
Bill Wheeler, *Mng Member*
Britney Keele, *Officer*
Larry Dennis, *Opers Mgr*
Sonia Alvarado, *Marketing Staff*
Debbie Moore,
EMP: 130
SQ FT: 18,000
SALES (est): 8.3MM **Privately Held**
WEB: www.blacktietrans.com
SIC: 4119 4724 Limousine rental, with driver; travel agencies

(P-3775)
BLS LMSINE SVC LOS ANGELES INC (PA)
Also Called: B L S Limousine Service
2860 Fletcher Dr, Los Angeles (90039-2452)
PHONE..................323 644-7166
Fax: 323 644-7177
Jay D Okon, *President*
Kevin Hornik, *CFO*
Phyllis Okon, *Corp Secy*
Vincent Aquino, *General Mgr*
William Kain, *Manager*
EMP: 200
SQ FT: 20,000
SALES (est): 22.1MM **Privately Held**
SIC: 4119 Limousine rental, with driver

(P-3776)
BOWERS COMPANIES INC (HQ)
Also Called: Bowers Ambulance Service
3355 E Spring St Ste 301, Long Beach (90806-6826)
PHONE..................562 988-6460
Fax: 562 988-6466
Michael P Dimino, *CEO*
Brian Cates, *President*
Raymond S Iskander, *Vice Pres*
EMP: 83
SQ FT: 32,000
SALES (est): 9.1MM
SALES (corp-wide): 15.6MM **Privately Held**
SIC: 4119 Ambulance service
PA: Rural/Metro Of Northern California, Inc.
550 Sycamore Dr
Milpitas CA 95035
619 726-6495

(P-3777)
BOWERS COMPANIES INC
Also Called: Bowers Ambulance Service
3355 E Spring St Ste 301, Long Beach (90806-6826)
PHONE..................562 988-6460
Fax: 562 591-3681
Daniel Santillan, *Manager*
Carl Sharfe, *Comp Spec*
Michael Diman, *IT/INT Sup*
Diman Michael, *IT/INT Sup*
Ken Bowers, *Engineer*
EMP: 50
SALES (corp-wide): 15.6MM **Privately Held**
SIC: 4119 Ambulance service
HQ: Bowers Companies, Inc.
3355 E Spring St Ste 301
Long Beach CA 90806
562 988-6460

(P-3778)
CALIFORNIA LIMOUSINES
23016 Lake Forest Dr A, Laguna Hills (92653-1324)
PHONE..................949 581-7531
Joseph Magnano, *President*
Frank J Duvall, *Senior VP*
EMP: 55
SQ FT: 5,600
SALES (est): 2.5MM **Privately Held**
SIC: 4119 Local passenger transportation

(P-3779)
CALIFORNIA MED RESPONSE INC
Also Called: Cal-Med Ambulance
12409 Slauson Ave Ste B, Whittier (90606-3834)
PHONE..................562 968-1818
Fax: 562 968-1808
Ronald A Marks, *President*
Linda Marks, *Treasurer*
Tyler Marks, *Officer*
EMP: 70
SALES (est): 2.6MM **Privately Held**
SIC: 4119 Ambulance service

(P-3780)
CAV INC
Also Called: Care A Van Transport
5411 Avenida Encinas # 210, Carlsbad (92008-4409)
PHONE..................760 729-5199
Richard Dripps, *President*
Bob Newkirk, *Director*
Robert Sneedon, *Director*
Margaret Hills, *Manager*
Deana Mason, *Manager*
EMP: 75
SQ FT: 1,200
SALES (est): 4.4MM **Privately Held**
SIC: 4119 Ambulance service

(P-3781)
CITY OF CALEXICO (PA)
608 Heber Ave, Calexico (92231-2840)
PHONE..................760 768-2130
Fax: 760 768-2103
Bill Hodge, *Mayor*
Lilliana Falomir, *Project Mgr*
Eduardo Gutierrez, *Finance Mgr*
Judy Hashem, *Finance*
Victor Carrillo, *Manager*
EMP: 165
SALES (est): 40.4MM **Privately Held**
SIC: 4119 Mayors' offices

(P-3782)
CLS TRNSPRTTION LOS ANGLES LLC (HQ)
Also Called: Empire Cls Worldwide
600 S Allied Way, El Segundo (90245-4727)
PHONE..................310 414-8189
David Singler, *Mng Member*
William Minich, *CFO*
Jamie Thompson, *Human Res Mgr*
Steven Delgado, *Traffic Dir*
Wesley Gipson, *Traffic Dir*
EMP: 150
SALES (est): 18.9MM
SALES (corp-wide): 71.5MM **Privately Held**
WEB: www.clslimo.com
SIC: 4119 Limousine rental, with driver
PA: Gts Holdings, Inc.
225 Meadowlands Pkwy
Secaucus NJ 07094
201 784-1200

(P-3783)
COLS INC
1611 S Melrose Dr 253&278, Vista (92081-5407)
PHONE..................714 720-6100
MO Garkani, *President*
EMP: 150 EST: 2008
SALES: 12MM **Privately Held**
SIC: 4119 Limousine rental, with driver

(P-3784)
CROWN TRANSPORTATION INC
Also Called: Crown Limousine L.A.
12300 W Washington Blvd, Los Angeles (90066-5510)
PHONE..................310 737-0888
David Navon, *President*
EMP: 51
SQ FT: 1,000
SALES (est): 3.7MM **Privately Held**
WEB: www.crownlimola.com
SIC: 4119 Local passenger transportation

(P-3785)
EAST SAN GBRIEL VLY CONSORTIUM
Also Called: La Works
5200 Irwindale Ave # 210, Irwindale (91706-2097)
PHONE..................626 960-3964
Fax: 626 813-2035
Salvador Velasquez, *President*
Kevin Stapleston, *Chairman*
EMP: 60
SQ FT: 28,000
SALES (est): 2.6MM **Privately Held**
SIC: 4119 8331 Local passenger transportation; job training services

(P-3786)
EASTWESTPROTO INC
Also Called: Lifeline Ambulance
1120 S Maple Ave Ste 200, Montebello (90640-6043)
PHONE..................888 535-5728
Genady Gorin, *CEO*
Genia Gorin, *President*
Matthew Sundquist, *Office Mgr*
Maria Keys, *Manager*
Jorge Sazzini, *Manager*
EMP: 120
SQ FT: 10,000
SALES (est): 6.1MM **Privately Held**
SIC: 4119 Ambulance service

(P-3787)
EMERGENCY AMBULANCE SERVICE
3200 E Birch St Ste A, Brea (92821-6287)
PHONE..................714 990-1331
Fax: 714 792-3689
Phillip E Davis, *President*
Scott Pipkin, *CFO*
Jim Karrass, *General Mgr*
Cyrene Poe, *QA Dir*
Terri Davis, *Finance*
EMP: 80
SALES (est): 4.4MM **Privately Held**
WEB: www.emergencyambulance.com
SIC: 4119 Ambulance service

(P-3788)
EMPIRE ENTERPRISES INC
Also Called: Empire Parking
8800 Park St, Bellflower (90706-5529)
PHONE..................562 529-2676
Mike Oliver, *President*
Silvia Llamas, *Manager*
EMP: 145
SQ FT: 1,700
SALES (est): 3.7MM **Privately Held**
SIC: 4119 7521 4725 4142 Local rental transportation; automobile parking; tour operators; bus charter service, except local; local bus charter service

(P-3789)
EXECUTIVE NETWORK ENTPS INC
1224 21st St Apt E, Santa Monica (90404-1390)
PHONE..................310 457-8822
Patricia Stephenson, *Manager*
EMP: 60 **Privately Held**
WEB: www.ezeclimo.com
SIC: 4119 Limousine rental, with driver
PA: Executive Network Enterprises, Inc.
13440 Beach Ave
Marina Del Rey CA 90292

(P-3790)
EXECUTIVE NETWORK ENTPS INC (PA)
Also Called: Malibu Limousine Service
13440 Beach Ave, Marina Del Rey (90292-5624)
PHONE..................310 447-2759
Patricia Stephenson, *President*
Trish Rudd, *CFO*
Stori Stephenson, *Vice Pres*
EMP: 80
SQ FT: 5,000
SALES (est): 22.8MM **Privately Held**
WEB: www.ezeclimo.com
SIC: 4119 Limousine rental, with driver

(P-3791)
FILYN CORPORATION
Also Called: Lynch Ambulance Service
2950 E La Jolla St, Anaheim (92806-1307)
PHONE..................714 632-0225
Walter John Lynch, *CEO*
Nancy Lynch, *CEO*
Eric Somers, *Info Tech Mgr*
Robert Banuelos, *Manager*
EMP: 200
SALES (est): 9.5MM **Privately Held**
WEB: www.lynchambulance.com
SIC: 4119 Ambulance service

PRODUCTS & SERVICES SECTION
4119 - Local Passenger Transportation: NEC County (P-3816)

(P-3792)
FIRST RESPONDER EMS INC
10161 Croydon Way Ste 1, Sacramento (95827-2107)
PHONE.................................916 381-3780
Fax: 916 363-6135
Byron Parsons, *CEO*
Thomas Arjil, *President*
Robert Hall, *General Mgr*
Angela Vanella, *Finance*
Jim Clark, *Opers Staff*
EMP: 114
SALES (est): 3.7MM **Privately Held**
SIC: 4119 Ambulance service

(P-3793)
FIRST RSPONDER EMRGNCY MED SVC
Also Called: Chico Paramedic Rescue
333 Huss Dr Ste 300, Chico (95928-8242)
P.O. Box 24 (95927-0024)
PHONE.................................530 891-4357
Byron Parsons, *President*
Bob Hall, *General Mgr*
Louwayne Parsons, *Admin Sec*
EMP: 106
SALES (est): 3.8MM **Privately Held**
SIC: 4119 4522 Ambulance service; air transportation, nonscheduled

(P-3794)
FIRST STUDENT INC
Also Called: Laidlaw Transit Services
123 N E St Ste 102, Madera (93638-3286)
PHONE.................................559 661-7433
Roberta Collins, *Branch Mgr*
EMP: 126
SALES (corp-wide): 7.5B **Privately Held**
WEB: www.leag.com
SIC: 4119 Local passenger transportation
HQ: First Student, Inc.
600 Vine St Ste 1400
Cincinnati OH 45202
513 241-2200

(P-3795)
FIRSTMED AMBULANCE SVCS INC
8630 Tamarack Ave, Sun Valley (91352-2504)
PHONE.................................800 608-0311
EMP: 62
SALES (est): 26MM **Privately Held**
SIC: 4119

(P-3796)
FRANCISCAN LINES INC
Also Called: San Francisco Sightseeing
41 Pier, San Francisco (94133-1009)
PHONE.................................415 642-9400
Fax: 415 642-1500
Michael Waters, *Vice Pres*
Jim Casey, *General Mgr*
EMP: 130
SQ FT: 50,000
SALES (est): 3.6MM **Privately Held**
WEB: www.graylinesanfrancisco.com
SIC: 4119 Sightseeing bus

(P-3797)
GARY CARDIFF ENTERPRISES INC
Also Called: Cardiff Transportation
75255 Sheryl Ave, Palm Desert (92211-5129)
PHONE.................................760 568-1403
Fax: 760 568-0895
Gary Cardiff, *CEO*
Sharon Cardiff, *Admin Sec*
Cathy Smith, *Human Res Dir*
Rodney Betsargon, *Manager*
Kyle Brooks, *Manager*
EMP: 89
SQ FT: 10,000
SALES (est): 7MM **Privately Held**
WEB: www.cardifflimo.com
SIC: 4119 Local passenger transportation

(P-3798)
GENTLECARE TRANSPORT INC
Also Called: Gcti
3539 Casitas Ave, Los Angeles (90039-1903)
PHONE.................................323 662-8777
Mike Panassian, *CEO*
Eddie Avakian, *CFO*
Robert Camarena, *Manager*
EMP: 75
SQ FT: 8,000
SALES (est): 3.7MM **Privately Held**
SIC: 4119 Ambulance service

(P-3799)
GERBER AMBULANCE COMPANY INC
Also Called: Gerber Ambulance Service
19801 Mariner Ave, Torrance (90503-1651)
P.O. Box 3487 (90510-3487)
PHONE.................................310 542-6464
Fax: 310 542-1152
Robert Gerber, *President*
Rebecca Gerber, *Vice Pres*
EMP: 110
SQ FT: 2,400
SALES (est): 4.2MM **Privately Held**
SIC: 4119 Ambulance service

(P-3800)
GLOBAL PARATRANSIT INC
400 W Compton Blvd, Gardena (90248-1700)
PHONE.................................310 715-7550
Reza Nasrollahy, *President*
Alexander Levertov, *Shareholder*
Sahar Mahmoudian, *Shareholder*
Luis Preciado, *Risk Mgmt Dir*
Lee Habibi, *General Mgr*
EMP: 300 EST: 2000
SQ FT: 17,000
SALES (est): 13.8MM **Privately Held**
SIC: 4119 Local passenger transportation

(P-3801)
GREYBOR MEDICAL TRANSPORTATION
119 Belmont Ave Ste 107, Los Angeles (90026-5708)
P.O. Box 17239, Beverly Hills (90209-3239)
PHONE.................................213 250-4444
Gregory Plotkin, *Ch of Bd*
Boris Shpirt, *President*
EMP: 50
SQ FT: 1,000
SALES (est): 1.1MM **Privately Held**
SIC: 4119 5999 Ambulance service; technical aids for the handicapped

(P-3802)
HALCORE GROUP INC
Leader Industries
10941 Weaver Ave, South El Monte (91733-2752)
PHONE.................................626 575-0880
Gary Hunter, *Manager*
EMP: 100
SALES (corp-wide): 1.5B **Privately Held**
WEB: www.hortonambulance.com
SIC: 4119 Local passenger transportation
HQ: Halcore Group, Inc.
3800 Mcdowell Rd
Grove City OH 43123
614 539-8181

(P-3803)
HALL AMBULANCE SERVICE INC
2001 O St O, Bakersfield (93301-4724)
PHONE.................................661 322-8741
Harvy Hall, *President*
Mary L Kenny, *Agent*
EMP: 55
SALES (corp-wide): 45.3MM **Privately Held**
WEB: www.hallamb.com
SIC: 4119 Ambulance service
PA: Hall Ambulance Service, Inc
1001 21st St
Bakersfield CA 93301
661 322-8741

(P-3804)
HERREN ENTERPRISES INC
Also Called: Doctors Ambulance Services
23091 Terra Dr, Laguna Hills (92653-1320)
PHONE.................................949 951-1666
Fax: 949 951-2891
Bruce W Herren, *President*
Michael Herren, *Vice Pres*
Darcy Vargas, *Superintendent*
EMP: 56
SQ FT: 4,000
SALES (est): 2.2MM **Privately Held**
WEB: www.doctorsambulance.com
SIC: 4119 Ambulance service

(P-3805)
INTEGRATED TRNSP SVCS INC
9740 W Pico Blvd, Los Angeles (90035-4711)
P.O. Box 6960, Beverly Hills (90212-6960)
PHONE.................................310 553-6060
Fax: 310 553-0523
Albert E Sabroff, *President*
Jonna Sabroff, *Vice Pres*
Kay Miyamoto, *Accounting Mgr*
Beverly Jones, *Director*
EMP: 75
SQ FT: 3,000
SALES (est): 5.5MM **Privately Held**
WEB: www.itslimo.com
SIC: 4119 Local passenger transportation; limousine rental, with driver

(P-3806)
JASON PROCTOR TRNSP CO
2375 Dairy Ave, Corcoran (93212-3503)
P.O. Box 623 (93212-0623)
PHONE.................................559 992-1767
Jason Proctor, *Owner*
EMP: 50
SALES (est): 1.2MM **Privately Held**
SIC: 4119 Automobile rental, with driver

(P-3807)
JP MOTORSPORTS INC
11067 Olinda St, Sun Valley (91352-3302)
PHONE.................................818 381-8313
Ovsep Sukunyan, *CEO*
George Sukunyan, *President*
EMP: 54 EST: 2009
SQ FT: 18,000
SALES (est): 2.4MM **Privately Held**
SIC: 4119 Automobile rental, with driver

(P-3808)
K W P H ENTERPRISES
Also Called: American Ambulance
2911 E Tulare St, Fresno (93721-1502)
PHONE.................................559 443-5900
James Kaufman, *President*
Todd R Valeri, *CEO*
Edgar Escobedo, *Business Dir*
Erik Peterson, *Info Tech Dir*
Donna Hankins, *Info Tech Mgr*
EMP: 500
SQ FT: 22,000
SALES (est): 29MM **Privately Held**
WEB: www.americanambulance.com
SIC: 4119 Ambulance service

(P-3809)
KEOLIS TRANSIT AMERICA INC (DH)
6053 W Century Blvd # 900, Los Angeles (90045-6400)
PHONE.................................310 981-9500
Michael Griffus, *President*
Joseph Cardoso, *CFO*
Francis Homan, *CFO*
Kevin Adams, *Exec VP*
Dwight D Brashear, *Exec VP*
EMP: 50
SQ FT: 25,000
SALES (est): 163.8MM **Privately Held**
WEB: www.tectransinc.com
SIC: 4119 7699 Local passenger transportation; customizing services
HQ: Keolis America Inc.
3003 Washington Blvd
Arlington VA 22201
301 251-5612

(P-3810)
KMA EMERGENCY SERVICES INC
Also Called: West Medions
14275 Wicks Blvd, San Leandro (94577-5613)
PHONE.................................510 614-1420
Erik Mandler, *President*
EMP: 100
SALES (est): 2.9MM **Privately Held**
SIC: 4119 Ambulance service

(P-3811)
LA COSTA LIMOUSINE (PA)
2770 Loker Ave W, Carlsbad (92010-6610)
PHONE.................................760 438-4455
Fax: 760 438-4456
Rick Brown, *Partner*
Dale Theriot, *Partner*
Vern Gaston, *Controller*
Frank Stone, *Persnl Dir*
Darren Croasdale, *Director*
EMP: 58
SQ FT: 11,000
SALES (est): 17.2MM **Privately Held**
WEB: www.lacostalimo.com
SIC: 4119 Limousine rental, with driver

(P-3812)
LEADER INDUSTRIES INC
Also Called: Leader Emergency Vehicles
10941 Weaver Ave, South El Monte (91733-2752)
PHONE.................................626 575-0880
Fax: 626 575-0286
Garry Hunter, *President*
Austin Adamson, *Admin Asst*
Bruce Stipe, *Project Mgr*
Patty Thomas, *Accountant*
Boyd Barlett, *Controller*
EMP: 160
SALES (est): 10.4MM **Privately Held**
WEB: www.leader-ambulance.com
SIC: 4119 5046 3711 Local passenger transportation; commercial equipment; motor vehicles & car bodies

(P-3813)
LEGRANDE AFFAIRE INC
651 Aldo Ave, Santa Clara (95054-2208)
PHONE.................................408 988-4884
Fax: 408 988-2116
James Brown, *CEO*
Phil Restivo, *President*
Jennifer Hauck, *CFO*
EMP: 120
SQ FT: 25,000
SALES (est): 3.6MM **Privately Held**
WEB: www.lagrandeaffaire.com
SIC: 4119 4724 Limousine rental, with driver; travel agencies

(P-3814)
LIBERTY AMBULANCE LLC
9441 Washburn Rd, Downey (90242-2912)
PHONE.................................562 741-6230
Kelvin Carlisle,
Daniel Graham, *Vice Pres*
Frank Heyman, *Managing Dir*
Joshua Effle-Hoy, *Opers Spvr*
Zajia Lima, *Manager*
EMP: 68
SALES (est): 2.9MM **Privately Held**
SIC: 4119 Ambulance service

(P-3815)
LYFT INC
185 Berry St Ste 5000, San Francisco (94107-2503)
PHONE.................................415 230-2905
Logan Green, *CEO*
Boris Korsunsky, *President*
John Zimmer, *President*
Olivia Henry, *Trust Officer*
David Estrada, *Vice Pres*
EMP: 200
SALES (est): 38.9MM **Privately Held**
SIC: 4119 Local rental transportation; automobile rental, with driver

(P-3816)
MED-LIFE AMBULANCE SERVICES
4304 Aiger St, Los Angeles (90039-1206)
P.O. Box 4525, Glendale (91222-0525)
PHONE.................................818 242-1785
Shake Seysyan, *CEO*
EMP: 94
SQ FT: 3,000
SALES (est): 3.9MM **Privately Held**
SIC: 4119 Ambulance service

4119 - Local Passenger Transportation: NEC County (P-3817)

(P-3817)
MEDIC AMBULANCE SERVICE INC (PA)
506 Couch St, Vallejo (94590-2408)
P.O. Box 4467 (94590-0446)
PHONE..................................707 644-1761
Fax: 707 644-1784
Rodolfo Manfredi, *President*
Helen Pierson, *CFO*
Marissa Luchini, *Vice Pres*
Gary Crenshaw, *Info Tech Mgr*
Les Carter, *Human Resources*
EMP: 130
SQ FT: 7,000
SALES (est): 16.7MM **Privately Held**
SIC: 4119 Ambulance service

(P-3818)
MEDSTAR LLC
20 Busneca Pk Way Ste 100, Sacramento (95828)
P.O. Box 292007 (95829-2007)
PHONE..................................916 669-0550
Fax: 916 669-0362
Adam C Ruggles,
Alison Lugo, *Opers Mgr*
Adam Ruggles,
Todd J Ruggles,
Todd Ruggles,
EMP: 65
SQ FT: 2,000
SALES (est): 3.6MM **Privately Held**
SIC: 4119 Ambulance service

(P-3819)
MISSION AMBULANCE INC
1055 E 3rd St, Corona (92879-1606)
P.O. Box 3111 (92878-3111)
PHONE..................................951 272-2300
Daniel Gold, *President*
EMP: 81
SALES (est): 4.9MM **Privately Held**
WEB: www.missionambulance.com
SIC: 4119 Ambulance service

(P-3820)
MV TRANSPORTATION INC
1944 Williams St, San Leandro (94577-2304)
PHONE..................................510 351-1603
Jay Jeter, *Branch Mgr*
EMP: 180
SALES (corp-wide): 2.7B **Privately Held**
WEB: www.mvtransit.com
SIC: 4119 Local passenger transportation
PA: Mv Transportation, Inc
5910 N Cntrl Expy # 1145
Dallas TX 75206
707 474-7784

(P-3821)
NAPA AMBULANCE SERVICE INC
Also Called: Piner's NAPA Ambulance Service
1820 Pueblo Ave, NAPA (94558-4751)
PHONE..................................707 224-3123
Gary Piner, *President*
Jeremy Piner, *Vice Pres*
Starr Piner, *Admin Sec*
EMP: 100
SALES (est): 5.3MM **Privately Held**
SIC: 4119 Ambulance service

(P-3822)
NORTH STAR EMERGENCY SVCS INC
Also Called: Norcal Ambulance Services
2537 Willow St, Oakland (94607-1723)
PHONE..................................510 452-3400
David Plaza, *COO*
Barry Sutherland, *CEO*
Makenzie Kelly, *CFO*
Karla Nazareno, *Administration*
Heather Ackad, *Human Resources*
EMP: 52
SALES: 2.1MM **Privately Held**
WEB: www.norcalambulance.com
SIC: 4119 Ambulance service

(P-3823)
OJAI AMBULANCE INC
Also Called: Lifeline Medical Transport
632 E Thompson Blvd, Ventura (93001-2829)
P.O. Box 1089 (93002-1089)
PHONE..................................805 653-9111
Fax: 805 653-0545
Stephen Frank, *President*
Karen Frank, *Vice Pres*
Jaycen Justus,
Wynne Schumacher, *Director*
James Rosolek, *Supervisor*
EMP: 50
SALES: 7MM **Privately Held**
WEB: www.lifelineems.net
SIC: 4119 Ambulance service

(P-3824)
PACIFIC AMBULANCE INC
5550 Oberlin Dr Ste A, San Diego (92121-1738)
PHONE..................................949 470-2355
Donna Bailey, *Owner*
Daniel Santillan, *Comms Mgr*
Theron Neal, *Manager*
EMP: 300
SALES (est): 6.5MM
SALES (corp-wide): 15.6MM **Privately Held**
WEB: www.pacificambulance.com
SIC: 4119 Ambulance service
PA: Rural/Metro Of Northern California, Inc.
550 Sycamore Dr
Milpitas CA 95035
619 726-6495

(P-3825)
PARADISE AMBULANCE SERVICE
Also Called: First Responder
333 Huss Dr, Chico (95928-8242)
PHONE..................................530 879-5520
Byron Parsons, *Owner*
Greg Knopp, *Systs Prg Mgr*
EMP: 70
SALES (est): 1.4MM **Privately Held**
SIC: 4119 Ambulance service

(P-3826)
PARATRANSIT INCORPORATED (PA)
2501 Florin Rd, Sacramento (95822-4467)
P.O. Box 231100 (95823-0401)
PHONE..................................916 429-2009
Fax: 916 429-2409
Linda Jean Deavens, *CEO*
Ninh Dao-Dickinson, *COO*
Christie Scheffer, *COO*
Steve Robinson-Burmester, *CFO*
Scott Leventon, *Treasurer*
EMP: 77
SQ FT: 250,000
SALES: 22.1MM **Privately Held**
SIC: 4119 7539 Local passenger transportation; automotive repair shops

(P-3827)
PARATRANSIT INCORPORATED
3300 Tully Rd, Modesto (95350-0836)
PHONE..................................209 522-2300
Andrea Anderson, *Branch Mgr*
EMP: 143
SALES (corp-wide): 22.1MM **Privately Held**
SIC: 4119 Ambulance service
PA: Paratransit, Incorporated
2501 Florin Rd
Sacramento CA 95822
916 429-2009

(P-3828)
PREMIER MEDICAL TRNSP INC
575 Maple Ct Ste A, Colton (92324-3209)
P.O. Box 690 (92324-0690)
PHONE..................................909 433-3939
Fax: 909 433-3933
Antonio Myrell, *CEO*
Rick Card, *Vice Pres*
Richmond Taylor, *Vice Pres*
Rosemary Dudevoir, *Opers Staff*
Louie Maylad, *Manager*
EMP: 65

SALES (est): 5.4MM **Privately Held**
WEB: www.premiermedicaltransportation.com
SIC: 4119 Local passenger transportation

(P-3829)
PRIORITY ONE MED TRNSPT INC (PA)
9327 Fairway View Pl # 300, Rancho Cucamonga (91730-0968)
PHONE..................................909 948-4400
Michael Parker, *President*
Sao Soun, *Executive*
EMP: 70
SQ FT: 7,000
SALES (est): 12MM **Privately Held**
WEB: www.prioritylink.com
SIC: 4119 Ambulance service

(P-3830)
PRN AMBULANCE LLC
8928 Sepulveda Blvd, North Hills (91343-4306)
PHONE..................................818 810-3600
Mike Sechrist, *CEO*
Avo Avetisyan, *President*
Elena Whorton, *President*
Michael Gorman, *COO*
Kevin Gorman, *CFO*
EMP: 300
SQ FT: 3,000
SALES (est): 14MM
SALES (corp-wide): 39.2MM **Privately Held**
WEB: www.prnambulance.com
SIC: 4119 Ambulance service
PA: Protransport-1, Llc
720 Portal St
Cotati CA 94931
707 975-2386

(P-3831)
PURE LUXURY LIMOUSINE SERVICE
Also Called: Pure Luxury Worldwide Trnsp
4246 Petaluma Blvd N, Petaluma (94952-1240)
P.O. Box 910, Penngrove (94951-0910)
PHONE..................................800 626-5466
Fax: 707 775-2929
Gary L Buffo Jr, *CEO*
Gary Buffo Sr, *General Mgr*
Antoinette Allison, *Business Mgr*
Linda Reinecke, *Business Mgr*
Micah Stoufer, *Traffic Dir*
EMP: 111
SQ FT: 35,000
SALES (est): 9.4MM **Privately Held**
WEB: www.pureluxury.com
SIC: 4119 Limousine rental, with driver

(P-3832)
RENTY LLC
8025 Clairemont Mesa Blvd, San Diego (92111-1634)
PHONE..................................858 560-0066
Fax: 858 560-9799
Shariar Delalat, *Mng Member*
EMP: 50
SQ FT: 45,000
SALES: 5MM **Privately Held**
SIC: 4119 Limousine rental, with driver

(P-3833)
RESTIVO ENTERPRISES
Also Called: Legrande Affaire
2590 Lafayette St, Santa Clara (95050-2602)
PHONE..................................408 988-4884
Phil Restivo, *General Mgr*
EMP: 100
SQ FT: 22,120
SALES (est): 2.4MM **Privately Held**
SIC: 4119 Limousine rental, with driver

(P-3834)
ROYAL AMBULANCE INC
14472 Wicks Blvd, San Leandro (94577-6712)
PHONE..................................510 568-6161
Fax: 510 568-6160
Steve Grau, *President*
Leon Botoshansky, *CFO*
Eve Grau, *Human Res Mgr*
Sean Young, *Opers Mgr*
Hasieb Lemar, *Manager*

EMP: 120
SQ FT: 5,000
SALES (est): 9.4MM **Privately Held**
WEB: www.royalambulance.com
SIC: 4119 Ambulance service

(P-3835)
RURAL/METRO CORPORATION
2364 W Winton Ave, Hayward (94545-1102)
PHONE..................................510 266-0885
Michael Dimino, *Branch Mgr*
EMP: 111 **Publicly Held**
SIC: 4119 Ambulance service
HQ: Rural/Metro Corporation
8465 N Pima Rd
Scottsdale AZ 85258
480 606-3886

(P-3836)
RURAL/METRO CORPORATION
1345 Vander Way, San Jose (95112-2809)
PHONE..................................888 876-0740
Scott Bartos, *Branch Mgr*
EMP: 111 **Publicly Held**
SIC: 4119 Ambulance service
HQ: Rural/Metro Corporation
8465 N Pima Rd
Scottsdale AZ 85258
480 606-3886

(P-3837)
RURAL/METRO SAN DIEGO INC
10405 San Diego Mission R, San Diego (92108-2174)
PHONE..................................619 280-6060
Fax: 619 280-6644
Michael P Dimino, *CEO*
Maureen Oconner, *Manager*
EMP: 99
SALES (est): 3.5MM **Publicly Held**
SIC: 4119 Ambulance service
HQ: Rural/Metro Of California, Inc.
1345 Vander Way
San Jose CA 95112
408 275-6744

(P-3838)
SAN DIEGO MED SVCS ENTP LLC
10405 Sn Diego Mn Rd 20 Ste 201, San Diego (92108)
PHONE..................................619 280-6060
Michael P Dimino,
Rural Metro Corporation,
Kathy Kendrick, *Manager*
Vinny Walgren, *Manager*
EMP: 375
SALES (est): 6.5MM **Privately Held**
SIC: 4119 Ambulance service

(P-3839)
SAN LUIS AMBULANCE SERVICE INC
3546 S Higuera St, San Luis Obispo (93401-7352)
P.O. Box 954 (93406-0954)
PHONE..................................805 543-2626
Fax: 805 546-0885
Frank I Kelton, *President*
Betsy Kelton, *Corp Secy*
Jason Baron, *Info Tech Mgr*
Roxanne Malone, *Human Resources*
Joe Piedalue, *Opers Staff*
EMP: 124
SQ FT: 7,500
SALES: 11.6MM **Privately Held**
WEB: www.sanluisambulance.com
SIC: 4119 Ambulance service

(P-3840)
SANTA BARBARA AIRBUS
750 Technology Dr, Goleta (93117-3839)
PHONE..................................805 964-7759
Fax: 805 683-0307
Eric Onnen, *President*
Kelly Onnen, *Corp Secy*
Mark Klopstein, *Vice Pres*
Kathy Campbell, *Executive Asst*
EMP: 60
SQ FT: 10,000
SALES: 5MM **Privately Held**
WEB: www.sbairbus.com
SIC: 4119 4724 Limousine rental, with driver; travel agencies

PRODUCTS & SERVICES SECTION

4121 - Taxi Cabs County (P-3866)

(P-3841)
SCHAEFER AMBULANCE SERVICE INC (PA)
Also Called: Gold Cross Ambulance
4627 Beverly Blvd, Los Angeles (90004-3101)
P.O. Box 74609 (90004-0609)
PHONE................323 469-1473
Fax: 323 465-1892
James McNeal II, *CEO*
Louella McNeal, *President*
Leslie McNeal, *Treasurer*
Samir Yanni, *Vice Pres*
Marlene McNeal, *Principal*
EMP: 100
SQ FT: 45,000
SALES (est): 44.7MM **Privately Held**
WEB: www.schaeferamb.com
SIC: 4119 Ambulance service

(P-3842)
SCHAEFER AMBULANCE SERVICE INC
Gold Cross Ambulance Service
905 S Imperial Ave, El Centro (92243-3721)
P.O. Box 1834 (92244-1834)
PHONE................760 353-3380
Fax: 760 353-2645
John Goodall, *Branch Mgr*
EMP: 50
SALES (corp-wide): 44.7MM **Privately Held**
WEB: www.schaeferamb.com
SIC: 4119 Ambulance service
PA: Schaefer Ambulance Service, Inc.
 4627 Beverly Blvd
 Los Angeles CA 90004
 323 469-1473

(P-3843)
SCHAEFER AMBULANCE SERVICE INC
Also Called: Cole-Schaefer Ambulance Svc
324 N Towne Ave, Pomona (91767-5648)
PHONE................626 333-4533
Manny Galvez, *Manager*
EMP: 100
SALES (corp-wide): 44.7MM **Privately Held**
WEB: www.schaeferamb.com
SIC: 4119 Ambulance service
PA: Schaefer Ambulance Service, Inc.
 4627 Beverly Blvd
 Los Angeles CA 90004
 323 469-1473

(P-3844)
SECURE TRANSPORTATION COMPANY
12785 Magnolia Ave # 102, Riverside (92503-4686)
PHONE................951 737-7300
EMP: 71
SALES (corp-wide): 48.2MM **Privately Held**
SIC: 4119
PA: Secure Transportation Company, Inc.
 13111 Meyer Rd
 Whittier CA 90802
 562 941-0107

(P-3845)
SECURED SHUTTLE SERVICE INC
20475 Yellow Brick Rd 3a, Walnut (91789-2929)
P.O. Box 525 (91788-0525)
PHONE................909 594-9054
Meged E Farag-Boktor, *President*
EMP: 80
SQ FT: 2,200
SALES (est): 2MM **Privately Held**
WEB: www.shuttle4u.com
SIC: 4119 Local rental transportation

(P-3846)
SOL TRANSPORTATION INC
1555 S Coast Hwy Ste 120, Oceanside (92054-5473)
PHONE................310 800-8069
Arturo Ayala, *President*
EMP: 50 EST: 2007
SALES: 426K **Privately Held**
SIC: 4119 Local passenger transportation

(P-3847)
SPRINGS AMBULANCE SERVICE INC
Also Called: American Medical Response
1111 Montalvo Way, Palm Springs (92262-5440)
PHONE................760 883-5000
Edward Vanhorne, *President*
Timothy Dorn, *CFO*
EMP: 99
SALES (est): 573.2K **Privately Held**
SIC: 4119 Local passenger transportation

(P-3848)
STUDENT TRNSP AMER INC
Also Called: Student Transportation America
1540 S 7th St, San Jose (95112-5929)
PHONE................408 998-8275
Fax: 408 998-8141
Evie Galdraith, *Manager*
John Carey, *President*
Paul Fichner, *Vice Pres*
Cheryl Browinski, *Branch Mgr*
Brian Hemenway, *General Mgr*
EMP: 100
SALES (corp-wide): 2B **Privately Held**
SIC: 4119 4151 Local passenger transportation; school buses
PA: Student Transportation Of America, Inc.
 3349 Hwy 138
 Wall Township NJ 07719
 732 280-4200

(P-3849)
SUNLINE TRANSIT AGENCY
790 Vine Ave, Coachella (92236-1736)
PHONE................760 972-4059
EMP: 119
SALES (corp-wide): 29.1MM **Privately Held**
SIC: 4119 Local passenger transportation
PA: Sunline Transit Agency
 32505 Harry Oliver Trl
 Thousand Palms CA 92276
 760 343-3456

(P-3850)
TRANSDEV SERVICES INC
110 S G St, Perris (92570-2267)
PHONE................951 943-1371
EMP: 171
SALES (corp-wide): 555.3MM **Privately Held**
SIC: 4119 4121 Local passenger transportation; taxicabs
HQ: Transdev Services, Inc.
 720 E Bttrfeld Rd Ste 300
 Lombard IL 60148
 630 571-7070

(P-3851)
TRANSDEV SERVICES INC
5640 Peck Rd, Arcadia (91006-5850)
PHONE................626 357-7912
EMP: 251
SALES (corp-wide): 555.3MM **Privately Held**
SIC: 4119 4121 Local passenger transportation; taxicabs
HQ: Transdev Services, Inc.
 720 E Bttrfeld Rd Ste 300
 Lombard IL 60148
 630 571-7070

(P-3852)
TRIPLE R TRANSPORTATION INC
978 Rd 192, Delano (93215)
P.O. Box 38 (93216-0038)
PHONE................661 725-6494
Fax: 661 725-6474
Joe Rodriguez, *President*
Laura Rodrigez, *Manager*
EMP: 80 EST: 2008
SALES (est): 3.6MM **Privately Held**
SIC: 4119 Local rental transportation

(P-3853)
UNIVERSAL LIMOUSINE & TRNSP CO
9944 Mills Station Rd C, Sacramento (95827-2229)
PHONE................916 361-5466
Marc Sievers, *CEO*
Mike Carlson, *IT/INT Sup*

Christy McElfish, *Manager*
EMP: 70
SQ FT: 10,000
SALES (est): 3MM **Privately Held**
SIC: 4119 Local passenger transportation

(P-3854)
VERIHEALTH INC
200 Montgomery Dr Ste D, Santa Rosa (95404-6634)
P.O. Box 750416, Petaluma (94975-0416)
PHONE................707 303-8000
Fax: 707 581-2609
Gary Tennyson, *President*
Holly Igarashi, *Case Mgmt Dir*
EMP: 125 EST: 2000
SQ FT: 16,000
SALES (est): 3.6MM **Privately Held**
WEB: www.verihealth.com
SIC: 4119 Ambulance service

(P-3855)
VIRGIN FISH INC (PA)
Also Called: Avalon Transportation Co
1000 Corporate Pointe # 150, Culver City (90230-7690)
PHONE................310 391-6161
Fax: 310 391-8017
Jeff Brush, *Principal*
David Dinwiddie, *Vice Pres*
Vicki Tanner, *Controller*
EMP: 150
SQ FT: 3,000
SALES (est): 30.8MM **Privately Held**
WEB: www.avalontrans.com
SIC: 4119 Limousine rental, with driver

(P-3856)
WEST COAST AMBULANCE CORP
Also Called: Wca
6739 S Victoria Ave, Los Angeles (90043-4617)
P.O. Box 8721 (90008-0721)
PHONE................310 435-1862
Olga Binman, *President*
EMP: 135
SALES (est): 3.9MM **Privately Held**
SIC: 4119 Ambulance service

(P-3857)
WESTMED AMBULANCE
14275 Wicks Blvd, San Leandro (94577-5613)
PHONE................510 401-5420
Alan Cress, *Director*
Andrew Thomas, *Admin Mgr*
Wendy Weston, *Finance*
Mike Skillings, *Controller*
Kathy Whelan, *Marketing Staff*
EMP: 88
SALES (est): 3.2MM **Privately Held**
WEB: www.westmedambulance.com
SIC: 4119 Ambulance service

(P-3858)
WESTMED AMBULANCE INC
3872 Las Flores Canyon Rd, Malibu (90265-5264)
PHONE................310 456-3830
EMP: 165
SALES (corp-wide): 34.9MM **Privately Held**
SIC: 4119 Ambulance service
PA: Westmed Ambulance, Inc
 13933 Crenshaw Blvd
 Hawthorne CA 90250
 510 614-1420

(P-3859)
WESTMED AMBULANCE INC
2537 Old San Pasqual Rd, Escondido (92027-4753)
PHONE................310 219-1779
Allen Cress, *Principal*
EMP: 245
SALES (corp-wide): 31.7MM **Privately Held**
SIC: 4119 Ambulance service
PA: Westmed Ambulance, Inc
 13933 Crenshaw Blvd
 Hawthorne CA 90250
 510 614-1420

(P-3860)
WORLDWIDE GROUND TRANSPORTATIO
Also Called: El Paseo Limousine
651 Aldo Ave, Santa Clara (95054-2208)
PHONE................408 727-0000
James Brown, *President*
EMP: 75
SQ FT: 8,900
SALES (est): 3.6MM **Privately Held**
SIC: 4119 4131 Limousine rental, with driver; intercity bus line

4121 Taxi Cabs

(P-3861)
A WHITE AND YELLOW CAB INC
Also Called: A Taxi Cab
2406 S Main St, Santa Ana (92707-3255)
PHONE................714 258-1000
Fax: 949 434-1400
Hossein Nabati, *President*
Lynn Strong, *General Mgr*
EMP: 180
SALES (est): 9.8MM **Privately Held**
SIC: 4121 Taxicabs

(P-3862)
ADMINISTRATIVE SERVICES SD
Also Called: Yellow Radio Service
3473 Kurtz St, San Diego (92110-4430)
PHONE................619 398-2314
Anthony Palmeri, *Principal*
Patrick Wilson, *Marketing Mgr*
Michele Meathe, *Marketing Staff*
Sharon Geraty,
EMP: 50
SALES: 950K **Privately Held**
SIC: 4121 Taxicabs

(P-3863)
CITYWIDE LIMO SERVICES INC
Also Called: Uber
3202 E Foothill Blvd, Pasadena (91107-3109)
PHONE................424 335-9818
Peter Saroyie, *CEO*
Allen Zaroyan, *General Mgr*
EMP: 250
SQ FT: 2,000
SALES (est): 1.9MM **Privately Held**
SIC: 4121 Taxicabs

(P-3864)
LAURELS MEDICAL SERVICES
Also Called: Chariot
5120 Manzanita Ave # 140, Carmichael (95608-0500)
PHONE................408 898-6360
Mir Tariz Riaz, *President*
Sheharyar Mir, *Shareholder*
Shiraz Mir, *Shareholder*
EMP: 51
SALES (est): 2.3MM **Privately Held**
SIC: 4121 7389 Taxicabs;

(P-3865)
LUXOR CABS INC
2230 Jerrold Ave, San Francisco (94124-1012)
PHONE................415 282-4141
Fax: 415 282-1706
John Lazar, *CEO*
William Falcon, *Corp Secy*
Dolores Parlomenko, *Vice Pres*
EMP: 51 EST: 1946
SQ FT: 7,000
SALES (est): 4.4MM **Privately Held**
WEB: www.luxorcab.com
SIC: 4121 7521 Taxicabs; parking lots

(P-3866)
NEESE INC
Also Called: Georges Yellow Taxi Cao Co
588 Roseland Ave, Santa Rosa (95407-6837)
PHONE................707 544-4444
Ray Neese, *President*
EMP: 50
SQ FT: 1,500
SALES: 1.6MM **Privately Held**
SIC: 4121 Taxicabs

4121 - Taxi Cabs County (P-3867)

(P-3867)
SAN GABRIEL TRANSIT INC
Also Called: Southland Transit Co
14913 Ramona Blvd, Baldwin Park
(91706-3421)
PHONE.................................626 430-3650
EMP: 78
SALES (corp-wide): 20.3MM Privately Held
SIC: 4121
PA: San Gabriel Transit, Inc.
3650 Rockwell Ave
El Monte CA 91731
626 258-1310

(P-3868)
SAN GABRIEL TRANSIT INC
7955 San Fernando Rd, Sun Valley
(91352-4614)
PHONE.................................818 771-0374
Debbie Waters, Manager
Eugene OH, Network Tech
Corey Barrett, Opers Mgr
EMP: 75
SALES (corp-wide): 22.4MM Privately Held
WEB: www.sgtransit.com
SIC: 4121 4119 Taxicabs; local passenger transportation
PA: San Gabriel Transit, Inc.
3650 Rockwell Ave
El Monte CA 91731
626 258-1310

(P-3869)
SITOA
6900 Airport Blvd, Sacramento
(95837-1109)
PHONE.................................916 444-0008
Kuldip Dosanjh, Owner
EMP: 98 EST: 2015
SALES (est): 1MM Privately Held
SIC: 4121 Taxicabs

(P-3870)
UNITED INDEPENDENT TAXI CO
900 N Alvarado St, Los Angeles
(90026-3105)
PHONE.................................213 385-2227
Fax: 323 483-7632
Andrey Primushko, President
Mohammad Pourrsegar, Vice Pres
Felix Knyazher, Admin Sec
Kass Schkherdimian, Mktg Dir
EMP: 50 EST: 1977
SALES (est): 1.5MM Privately Held
SIC: 4121 Taxicabs

(P-3871)
WESTERN TRANSIT SYSTEMS INC
13591 Harbor Blvd, Garden Grove
(92843-3818)
PHONE.................................949 515-0188
Fax: 714 535-8828
Michael Griffus, President
Francis G Homan, CFO
Susan Soh, Accounts Mgr
EMP: 65
SQ FT: 6,000
SALES (est): 2.6MM Privately Held
WEB: www.tectransinc.com
SIC: 4121 Taxicabs
HQ: Keolis Transit America, Inc.
6053 W Century Blvd # 900
Los Angeles CA 90045
310 981-9500

(P-3872)
YELLOW A CAB
Also Called: AAA Yellow Cab
5 Aragon Blvd Ste 125, San Mateo
(94402-2363)
PHONE.................................650 344-2060
Paul Dillan, Owner
EMP: 50
SALES (est): 898.2K Privately Held
SIC: 4121 Taxicabs

(P-3873)
YELLOW CAB COMPANY
Also Called: Antioch Cab
100 Willow St, Pacheco (94553-5621)
PHONE.................................925 779-9292
Fax: 925 288-9292
Mustafa Rahimi, Owner
EMP: 50
SALES (est): 1.4MM Privately Held
SIC: 4121 Taxicabs

(P-3874)
YELLOW CAB COMPANY PENNINSULA
Also Called: Yellow Cabs
1330 Memorex Dr, Santa Clara
(95050-2853)
PHONE.................................408 739-1234
Vikramjeet Singh, President
EMP: 150 EST: 1948
SQ FT: 5,000
SALES: 1.2MM Privately Held
WEB: www.yellowcabpeninsula.com
SIC: 4121 Taxicabs

(P-3875)
YELLOW CAB COOPERATIVE INC
Also Called: All Taxi Electronics
1200 Mississippi St, San Francisco
(94107-3490)
PHONE.................................415 333-3333
Richard Wiener, CEO
Harlan Mellegard, Exec VP
Sheldon Miller, Admin Sec
Fee Wong, Accountant
Pam Martinez, Controller
EMP: 90
SQ FT: 150,000
SALES (est): 10.5MM Privately Held
SIC: 4121 Taxicabs

4131 Intercity & Rural Bus Transportation

(P-3876)
CITY OF NAPA
Also Called: Vine Transit
1151 Pearl St, NAPA (94559-2528)
PHONE.................................707 255-7631
Fax: 707 251-1096
Rick Levitt, General Mgr
EMP: 50 Privately Held
WEB: www.naparcd.org
SIC: 4131 9111 Intercity & rural bus transportation; mayors' offices
PA: City Of Napa
955 School St
Napa CA 94559
707 257-9516

(P-3877)
CITY OF SANTA MONICA
Also Called: Santa Monica Big Blue Bus
1660 7th St, Santa Monica (90401-3324)
PHONE.................................310 451-5444
Fax: 310 451-3163
John Catoe, Director
David Carr, Admin Asst
Michael Ferguson, Admin Asst
Peter Dzewaltowski, Planning
Stella Huang, Accountant
EMP: 325
SALES (est): 16.7MM Privately Held
SIC: 4131 Intercity bus line

(P-3878)
EASTERN SIERRA TRANSIT AUTH
703 Airport Rd, Bishop (93514-3603)
P.O. Box 1357 (93515-1357)
PHONE.................................760 872-1901
Brad Koehn, Principal
John Helm, Principal
Jill Batchelder, General Mgr
Susan Rottner, Administration
EMP: 50
SALES (est): 2.2MM Privately Held
SIC: 4131 Intercity & rural bus transportation

(P-3879)
FIRST STUDENT INC
436 Parr Blvd, Richmond (94801-1123)
PHONE.................................510 237-2677
Brian Rutford, Principal
EMP: 79
SALES (corp-wide): 7.5B Privately Held
SIC: 4131 Intercity & rural bus transportation
HQ: First Student, Inc.
600 Vine St Ste 1400
Cincinnati OH 45202
513 241-2200

(P-3880)
FIRST STUDENT INC
Also Called: Laidlaw Education Services
3401 W Castor St, Santa Ana
(92704-3909)
PHONE.................................714 850-7578
Fax: 714 545-1852
Debi Manley, Manager
EMP: 100
SALES (corp-wide): 7.5B Privately Held
WEB: www.leag.com
SIC: 4131 Intercity & rural bus transportation
HQ: First Student, Inc.
600 Vine St Ste 1400
Cincinnati OH 45202
513 241-2200

(P-3881)
LINCOLN SCHOOL BUS TRNSP
6749 Harrisburg Pl, Stockton (95207-3444)
PHONE.................................209 953-8596
Fax: 209 951-9516
George Anzo, Director
Ted Bestolarides, Bd of Directors
Tanisha Sykes, Bd of Directors
Susan Lenz, Vice Pres
Saragon Yousef, Principal
EMP: 65
SALES (est): 1.3MM Privately Held
WEB: www.lusd.net
SIC: 4131 Intercity & rural bus transportation

(P-3882)
MARIN AIRPORTER INC
1455 N Hamilton Pkwy, Novato
(94949-8205)
PHONE.................................415 884-2878
Guy Murta, Branch Mgr
Lawrence Forrest, Project Mgr
EMP: 63
SALES (corp-wide): 6.1MM Privately Held
WEB: www.marinairporter.com
SIC: 4131 Intercity & rural bus transportation
PA: Marin Airporter, Inc
8 Lovell Ave
San Rafael CA 94901
415 256-8830

(P-3883)
MONTEREY-SALINAS TRANSIT CORP
1375 Burton Ave, Salinas (93901-4403)
PHONE.................................831 754-2804
Fax: 831 754-2009
Carl Sedoryk, Branch Mgr
Lance Antecio, Manager
Lance Atencio, Manager
EMP: 140
SALES (corp-wide): 16.1MM Privately Held
SIC: 4131 Intercity & rural bus transportation
PA: Monterey-Salinas Transit Corporation
19 Upper Ragsdale Dr
Monterey CA 93940
831 424-7695

(P-3884)
NIPOMO DIAL A RIDE
179 Cross St, San Luis Obispo
(93401-7597)
PHONE.................................805 929-2881
Catherine Wynn, Manager
EMP: 80
SALES (est): 1MM Privately Held
SIC: 4131 Intercity highway transport, special service

(P-3885)
SANTA CLARA VALLEY TRNSP AUTH
3331 N 1st St, San Jose (95134-1906)
PHONE.................................408 321-5555
Fax: 408 955-9753
Michael Burns, Manager
Grace Salandanan, Officer
Linda Willis, Finance Mgr
Kay L Eveth, Human Resources
Suzanne Gifford, General Counsel
EMP: 500 Privately Held
SIC: 4131 9111 Intercity bus line; county supervisors' & executives' offices
PA: Santa Clara Valley Transportation Authority
3331 N 1st St
San Jose CA 95134
408 321-2300

(P-3886)
SANTA CLARITA CITY OF
Also Called: Bus Company
28250 Constellation Rd, Santa Clarita
(91355-5000)
PHONE.................................661 294-1287
Mike Hynes, Director
EMP: 300 Privately Held
WEB: www.golfsantaclarita.com
SIC: 4131 Intercity & rural bus transportation; mayors' offices
PA: Santa Clarita, City Of
23920 Valencia Blvd # 300
Santa Clarita CA 91355
661 259-2489

(P-3887)
SANTA CRUZ METRO
135 Aviation Way Ste 2, Watsonville
(95076-2046)
PHONE.................................831 426-6080
Lesley White, Manager
Angela Aitken, COO
Isaac Holly, Administration
Cheri Callis, Technician
Harlan Glatt, Director
EMP: 300
SALES (est): 12.5MM Privately Held
SIC: 4131 Intercity & rural bus transportation

(P-3888)
SANTA CRUZ METRO TRNST DST
Also Called: Fleet Maintenance Dept
110 Vernon St Ste B, Santa Cruz
(95060-2130)
PHONE.................................831 469-1954
Tom Stickel, Manager
EMP: 54
SALES (corp-wide): 9.8MM Privately Held
WEB: www.scmtd.com
SIC: 4131 Intercity bus line
PA: Santa Cruz Metropolitan Transit District
110 Vernon St
Santa Cruz CA 95060
831 426-6143

(P-3889)
SUNLINE TRANSIT AGENCY (PA)
Also Called: STA
32505 Harry Oliver Trl, Thousand Palms
(92276-3501)
PHONE.................................760 343-3456
Fax: 760 343-3845
Glenn Miller, Chairman
Greg Pettis, Principal
Caroline Rude, Admin Sec
Michael Jones, Admin Asst
Anita M Petke, Planning
EMP: 160 EST: 1977
SQ FT: 19,006
SALES (est): 29.1MM Privately Held
WEB: www.sunline.org
SIC: 4131 Intercity bus line

4141 Local Bus Charter Svc

(P-3890)
AMADOR STAGE LINES INC
Also Called: Allen Transportation Co
1331 C St, Sacramento (95814-0913)
P.O. Box 15707 (95852-0707)
PHONE.................................916 444-7880
Fax: 916 444-7837
W R Allen, CEO
Alex B Allen, President
William R Allen, Treasurer
R E Allen, Vice Pres
Kay Scott, Administration
EMP: 80
SQ FT: 2,000

PRODUCTS & SERVICES SECTION
4151 - School Buses County (P-3913)

SALES (est): 9.1MM **Privately Held**
SIC: 4141 Local bus charter service

(P-3891)
BUSWEST LLC (HQ)
Also Called: John Deere Authorized Dealer
21107 Chico St, Carson (90745-1648)
PHONE.................................310 984-3900
Jim Bernacchi, *President*
Daryl Trueblood, *General Mgr*
Jim Bernachy, *Administration*
Doug Snyder, *Administration*
David Yuill, *Graphic Designe*
EMP: 60
SALES (est): 8.6MM
SALES (corp-wide): 72.5MM **Privately Held**
SIC: 4141 5082 Local bus charter service; construction & mining machinery
PA: Los Angeles Truck Centers, Llc
2429 Peck Rd
Whittier CA 90601
562 447-1200

(P-3892)
CALIFORNIA CHARTER INC
3333 E 69th St, Long Beach (90805-1809)
PHONE.................................562 634-7969
Fax: 562 634-5818
Scott Keller, *President*
F E Kaiser, *Ch of Bd*
George Marudas, *Vice Pres*
Darlene Cochran, *Controller*
EMP: 150
SALES (est): 3.4MM **Privately Held**
SIC: 4141 4142 Local bus charter service; bus charter service, except local

(P-3893)
EMPIRE TRANSPORTATION
8800 Park St, Bellflower (90706-5529)
PHONE.................................562 529-2676
Miguel Oliver, *CEO*
Bertha Aguirre, *President*
Monica Escorza Oliver, *CFO*
Jaime Acosta, *Controller*
EMP: 425
SQ FT: 25,000
SALES (est): 27.5MM **Privately Held**
SIC: 4141 7521 4111 Local bus charter service; indoor parking services; bus transportation

(P-3894)
MC CLINTOCK ENTERPRISES
Also Called: Goldfield Stage & Co
795 Gable Way, El Cajon (92020-1908)
P.O. Box 13672 (92022-3672)
PHONE.................................619 579-5300
Fax: 619 579-1809
Kevin McClintock, *President*
Dalyce McClintock, *Admin Sec*
Elaine P Placa-Heston, *Sales Mgr*
Elaine Heston, *Manager*
EMP: 60
SQ FT: 1,000
SALES: 6.7MM **Privately Held**
WEB: www.goldfieldstage.com
SIC: 4141 Local bus charter service

(P-3895)
MICHAELS TRNSP SVC INC
140 Yolano Dr, Vallejo (94589-2251)
PHONE.................................707 674-6013
Fax: 707 643-1906
Michael Brown, *President*
Carl Mosebach, *General Mgr*
Keith Judkins, *Recruiter*
EMP: 95
SQ FT: 26,000
SALES (est): 8.4MM **Privately Held**
WEB: www.bustransportation.com
SIC: 4141 7363 8331 4111 Local bus charter service; employee leasing service; job training services; bus transportation; school buses

(P-3896)
STORER TRANSPORTATION SERVICE (PA)
Also Called: Storer Travel Service
3519 Mcdonald Ave, Modesto (95358-9771)
PHONE.................................209 521-8250
Donald Storer, *CEO*
Warren Storer, *CEO*

Jim Hsia, *CFO*
Steven Fernandes, *Sls & Mktg Exec*
EMP: 275
SQ FT: 6,000
SALES (est): 43.5MM **Privately Held**
WEB: www.storercoachways.com
SIC: 4141 4725 4151 Local bus charter service; tours, conducted; travel agencies; school buses; bus charter service, except local

4142 Bus Charter Service, Except Local

(P-3897)
ALL WEST COACHLINES INC
Also Called: A Coach USA Company
7701 Wilbur Way, Sacramento (95828-4994)
PHONE.................................916 423-4000
Dan Eisentrager, *President*
EMP: 65
SALES (est): 2.4MM
SALES (corp-wide): 5.4B **Privately Held**
WEB: www.allwestcoachlines.com
SIC: 4142 Bus charter service, except local
PA: Stagecoach Group Plc
10 Dunkeld Road
Perth PH1 5
173 844-2111

(P-3898)
CITY CHARTER SCHOOL
11625 W Pico Blvd, Los Angeles (90064-2908)
PHONE.................................310 273-2489
EMP: 85
SALES (est): 71.6K **Privately Held**
SIC: 4142 Bus charter service, except local

(P-3899)
CUSA FL LLC
Also Called: Coach Bus Lines
41 Pier, San Francisco (94133-1009)
PHONE.................................415 642-9400
Michael Waters, *President*
Jeffrey Griffin, *Controller*
Ted Horsley, *Controller*
Craig Lentzch, *Manager*
EMP: 150
SALES (est): 4.1MM **Privately Held**
WEB: www.cusa.org
SIC: 4142 Bus charter service, except local

(P-3900)
DORR DISTRIBUTION SYSTEMS
Also Called: Discovery
11020 Commercial Pkwy, Castroville (95012-3210)
PHONE.................................831 633-7111
Fax: 831 633-7113
Richard G Dorr Jr, *President*
Richard G Dorr Sr, *Vice Pres*
Patricia Dorr, *Manager*
EMP: 50
SQ FT: 22,000
SALES (est): 3.6MM **Privately Held**
WEB: www.discoverycharters.com
SIC: 4142 4141 Bus charter service, except local; local bus charter service

(P-3901)
EL PAS-LOS ANGELES LMSNE EX INC
Also Called: Los Angeles Terminal
260 E 6th St, Los Angeles (90014-2117)
PHONE.................................213 623-2323
Fax: 213 689-8417
Marisela Gonzalez, *Branch Mgr*
Ricardo Cepeda, *Manager*
EMP: 50
SQ FT: 5,680
SALES (corp-wide): 21.4MM **Privately Held**
SIC: 4142 Bus charter service, except local
PA: El Paso-Los Angeles Limousine Express, Inc.
720 S Oregon St
El Paso TX 79901
915 778-3337

(P-3902)
FIRST STUDENT INC
2477 Arnold Indus Way, Concord (94520-5327)
PHONE.................................925 676-1976
Mary Walker, *Manager*
Chan Saechao, *Info Tech Mgr*
Katherine Casenaze, *Finance Mgr*
Jay Castro, *Finance*
EMP: 90
SALES (corp-wide): 7.5B **Privately Held**
WEB: www.leag.com
SIC: 4142 Bus charter service, except local
HQ: First Student, Inc.
600 Vine St Ste 1400
Cincinnati OH 45202
513 241-2200

(P-3903)
HOT DOGGER TOURS INC
Also Called: Gold Coast Tours
223 Imperial Hwy Ste 165, Fullerton (92835-1060)
PHONE.................................714 449-6888
Fax: 714 879-4525
John Hartley, *President*
Mark Wilkerson, *Vice Pres*
EMP: 120
SQ FT: 955
SALES (est): 13.1MM **Privately Held**
WEB: www.goldcoasttours.com
SIC: 4142 4725 4141 Bus charter service, except local; tours, conducted; local bus charter service

(P-3904)
MV TRANSPORTATION INC
827 Missouri St Ste 6, Fairfield (94533-6204)
PHONE.................................707 446-5573
Nigel Browne, *Manager*
Richard Ray, *Safety Mgr*
Robin Vanvalkenbugh, *Manager*
EMP: 60
SALES (corp-wide): 2.7B **Privately Held**
WEB: www.mvtransit.com
SIC: 4142 Bus charter service, except local
PA: Mv Transportation, Inc
5910 N Cntrl Expy # 1145
Dallas TX 75206
707 474-7784

(P-3905)
ORANGE BELT STAGES (PA)
Also Called: Orange Belt Adventures
2134 E Mineral King Ave, Visalia (93292-6905)
P.O. Box 949 (93279-0949)
PHONE.................................559 733-4408
Fax: 559 733-0538
Michael Haworth, *President*
Bryan A Haworth Trust, *Shareholder*
Margaret V Haworth Trust, *Shareholder*
Bruce Lynn, *President*
Virginia Gonzalez, *Info Tech Mgr*
EMP: 65
SQ FT: 10,000
SALES (est): 14.4MM **Privately Held**
WEB: www.orangebelt.com
SIC: 4142 4141 Bus charter service, except local; local bus charter service

(P-3906)
STUDENT TRNSP AMER INC
12560 Raymer St, North Hollywood (91605-4305)
PHONE.................................818 982-1663
Pam Layral, *Training Super*
Alvin Aragon, *Supervisor*
EMP: 343
SALES (corp-wide): 2B **Privately Held**
SIC: 4142 Bus charter service, except local
PA: Student Transportation Of America, Inc.
3349 Hwy 138
Wall Township NJ 07719
732 280-4200

(P-3907)
SURERIDE CHARTER INC
Also Called: Sun Diego Charter
522 W 8th St, National City (91950-1004)
PHONE.................................619 336-9200
Fax: 619 336-9212
Richard Illes, *President*
Lorenzo Ortiz, *Executive*
Brian Webber, *Business Dir*

Debbie McLeod, *Sales Dir*
Hector Cuatepotzo, *Parts Mgr*
EMP: 120
SQ FT: 60,000
SALES (est): 10.4MM **Privately Held**
WEB: www.sundiegocharter.com
SIC: 4142 Bus charter service, except local

(P-3908)
THE GRAY-LINE TOURS COMPANY
6541 Hollywood Blvd, Los Angeles (90028-6256)
PHONE.................................323 463-3333
Vahid Sapir, *President*
EMP: 200
SQ FT: 10,000
SALES (est): 6MM **Privately Held**
SIC: 4142 Bus charter service, except local

(P-3909)
TRANSPORTATION CHRTR SVCS INC
1931 N Batavia St, Orange (92865-4107)
PHONE.................................714 396-0346
Fax: 714 637-4377
Terry Fischer, *President*
Kathryn Mayer, *Vice Pres*
Dave Jeffers, *Principal*
Cerissa Riley, *Admin Asst*
Candice Martinez, *Controller*
EMP: 50
SALES: 9.7MM **Privately Held**
WEB: www.tcsbus.com
SIC: 4142 Bus charter service, except local

(P-3910)
VIA ADVENTURES INC (PA)
Also Called: Via Charter Lines
300 Grogan Ave, Merced (95341-6446)
PHONE.................................209 384-1315
Curtis A Riggs, *President*
Gaye Riggs, *Corp Secy*
Denise Demery, *Manager*
EMP: 50
SALES (est): 8.7MM **Privately Held**
WEB: www.via-adventures.com
SIC: 4142 4724 4725 Bus charter service, except local; travel agencies; sightseeing tour companies

4151 School Buses

(P-3911)
ANTELOPE VLY SCHL TRNSP AGCY
670 W Avenue L8, Lancaster (93534-7100)
PHONE.................................661 945-3621
Fax: 661 949-7393
Jene Jansen, *CEO*
Morris Fuselier III, *CEO*
Kathy Phillips, *Info Tech Mgr*
Joanne Downen, *Accountant*
Gary Russell, *Manager*
EMP: 190
SALES: 12.5MM **Privately Held**
WEB: www.avsta.org
SIC: 4151 School buses

(P-3912)
BEAUMONT UNIFIED SCHOOL DST
1001 Cougar Way, Beaumont (92223-5124)
P.O. Box 187 (92223-0187)
PHONE.................................951 845-3010
Fax: 951 769-0649
Robin Dailey, *Director*
EMP: 856
SALES (corp-wide): 586.9K **Privately Held**
SIC: 4151 School buses
PA: Beaumont Unified School District
350 W Brookside Ave
Cherry Valley CA 92223
951 845-1631

(P-3913)
BERKELEY UNIFIED SCHOOL DST
Also Called: Transportation Department
1314 7th St, Berkeley (94710-1465)
PHONE.................................510 644-6182

4151 - School Buses County (P-3914)

PRODUCTS & SERVICES SECTION

Bernadette Cormier, *Manager*
EMP: 50
SALES (corp-wide): 157.2MM **Privately Held**
WEB: www.latms.berkeley.k12.ca.us
SIC: 4151 School buses
PA: Berkeley Unified School District
2020 Bonar St Rm 202
Berkeley CA 94702
510 644-4500

(P-3914)
CARDINAL TRNSP GROUP INC
14800 S Avalon Blvd, Gardena (90248-2012)
PHONE.................................310 769-2400
Roy J Weber, *President*
EMP: 220
SQ FT: 18,000
SALES (est): 7.1MM **Privately Held**
WEB: www.cardinaltransportationltd.com
SIC: 4151 School buses

(P-3915)
CATHOLIC CHRTS CYO ARCHDIOCS
Also Called: CATHOLIC YOUTH ORGANIZATION
699 Serramonte Blvd 210, Daly City (94015-4132)
PHONE.................................650 757-2110
Fax: 650 758-1425
Bill Avalos, *Manager*
EMP: 50
SALES (corp-wide): 39.6MM **Privately Held**
SIC: 4151 School buses; individual & family services
PA: Catholic Charities Cyo Of The Archdiocese Of San Francisco
990 Eddy St
San Francisco CA 94109
415 972-1200

(P-3916)
CERTIFIED TRNSP SVCS INC
1038 N Custer St, Santa Ana (92701-3915)
PHONE.................................714 835-8676
Fax: 714 835-3675
David Gregory, *CEO*
Howard W Faccou, *Agent*
EMP: 70
SQ FT: 3,000
SALES (est): 6.3MM **Privately Held**
WEB: www.ctsbus.com
SIC: 4151 School buses

(P-3917)
COUNTY OF LOS ANGELES
Also Called: Pupil Transportation
9402 Greenleaf Ave, Whittier (90605)
P.O. Box 3497 (90605-0497)
PHONE.................................562 945-2581
Fax: 562 945-6353
Dan Ibarra, *Director*
Dana Williams, *Admin Sec*
Vernon Kinder, *Manager*
EMP: 110 **Privately Held**
WEB: www.co.la.ca.us
SIC: 4151 9621 School buses; regulation, administration of transportation;
PA: County Of Los Angeles
500 W Temple St Ste 375
Los Angeles CA 90012
213 974-1101

(P-3918)
DURHAM SCHOOL SERVICES L P
16627 Avalon Blvd Ste B, Carson (90746-1051)
PHONE.................................310 767-5820
Fax: 310 767-5823
Raphael Balonos, *Manager*
Alma Lawrence, *Human Res Dir*
EMP: 250
SALES (corp-wide): 2.8B **Privately Held**
SIC: 4151 School buses
HQ: Durham School Services, L. P.
4300 Weaver Pkwy Ste 100
Warrenville IL 60555
630 836-0292

(P-3919)
DURHAM SCHOOL SERVICES L P
365 E Avnda De Los Alvare, Thousand Oaks (91360)
PHONE.................................805 495-8338
Fax: 805 495-3665
Terry Walker, *Branch Mgr*
Terry L Walker, *Manager*
EMP: 55
SALES (corp-wide): 2.8B **Privately Held**
SIC: 4151 4142 4141 School buses; bus charter service, except local; local bus charter service
HQ: Durham School Services, L. P.
4300 Weaver Pkwy Ste 100
Warrenville IL 60555
630 836-0292

(P-3920)
DURHAM SCHOOL SERVICES L P
1506 White Oaks Rd, Campbell (95008-6724)
PHONE.................................408 377-6655
EMP: 105
SALES (corp-wide): 2.8B **Privately Held**
SIC: 4151 School buses
HQ: Durham School Services, L. P.
4300 Weaver Pkwy Ste 100
Warrenville IL 60555
630 836-0292

(P-3921)
DURHAM SCHOOL SERVICES L P
27577 Industrial Blvd A, Hayward (94545-4044)
PHONE.................................510 887-6005
Fax: 510 887-6336
Chris Stone, *Principal*
EMP: 190
SQ FT: 1,200
SALES (corp-wide): 2.8B **Privately Held**
SIC: 4151 School buses
HQ: Durham School Services, L. P.
4300 Weaver Pkwy Ste 100
Warrenville IL 60555
630 836-0292

(P-3922)
DURHAM SCHOOL SERVICES L P
10701 E Bennett Rd, Grass Valley (95945-9361)
PHONE.................................530 273-7282
Fax: 530 273-2210
Paula Davidson, *General Mgr*
Brian Shuldberg, *Vice Pres*
Jack Hughes, *Human Resources*
Dan Williams, *Opers Mgr*
Joe Ortiz, *Facilities Mgr*
EMP: 70
SALES (corp-wide): 2.8B **Privately Held**
SIC: 4151 4119 4111 School buses; local passenger transportation; local & suburban transit
HQ: Durham School Services, L. P.
4300 Weaver Pkwy Ste 100
Warrenville IL 60555
630 836-0292

(P-3923)
DURHAM SCHOOL SERVICES L P
5029 Forni Dr, Concord (94520-1224)
PHONE.................................925 686-3391
Fax: 925 689-1540
Joe Cobillas, *Branch Mgr*
EMP: 120
SALES (corp-wide): 2.8B **Privately Held**
SIC: 4151 School buses
HQ: Durham School Services, L. P.
4300 Weaver Pkwy Ste 100
Warrenville IL 60555
630 836-0292

(P-3924)
DURHAM SCHOOL SERVICES L P
2713 River Ave, Rosemead (91770-3303)
PHONE.................................626 573-3769
David Gonzales, *General Mgr*
Larry Durham, *Div Sub Head*
EMP: 150
SALES (corp-wide): 2.8B **Privately Held**
SIC: 4151 School buses
HQ: Durham School Services, L. P.
4300 Weaver Pkwy Ste 100
Warrenville IL 60555
630 836-0292

(P-3925)
ELK GROVE UNIFIED SCHOOL DST
Also Called: Transportation Department
8421 Gerber Rd, Sacramento (95828-3711)
PHONE.................................916 686-7733
Jill Gayaldo, *Branch Mgr*
EMP: 200
SALES (corp-wide): 418.4MM **Privately Held**
SIC: 4151 School buses
PA: Grove Elk Unified School District
9510 Elk Grove Florin Rd
Elk Grove CA 95624
916 686-5085

(P-3926)
FACILITIES OPERATION AND TRNSP
Also Called: Los Banos School District
2657 E Pacheco Blvd, Los Banos (93635-9417)
PHONE.................................209 826-1936
Tom Worthy, *Director*
Edward Kersey, *Manager*
EMP: 100
SALES (est): 2.8MM **Privately Held**
SIC: 4151 School buses

(P-3927)
FIRST STUDENT INC
991 E Poplar Ave, San Mateo (94401-1479)
PHONE.................................650 685-8245
EMP: 83
SALES (corp-wide): 7.5B **Privately Held**
SIC: 4151 School buses
HQ: First Student, Inc.
600 Vine St Ste 1400
Cincinnati OH 45202
513 241-2200

(P-3928)
FIRST STUDENT INC
234 S I St, San Bernardino (92410-2408)
PHONE.................................909 383-1640
Cheryl Seifert, *Manager*
Brian Niemann, *Manager*
EMP: 100
SALES (corp-wide): 7.5B **Privately Held**
WEB: www.leag.com
SIC: 4151 School buses
HQ: First Student, Inc.
600 Vine St Ste 1400
Cincinnati OH 45202
513 241-2200

(P-3929)
FIRST STUDENT INC
Also Called: Laidlaw Educational Services
5006 E Calle San Raphael, Palm Springs (92264-3452)
PHONE.................................760 320-4659
Fax: 760 327-6668
Mike Robertson, *Manager*
John Perkins, *Safety Mgr*
EMP: 75
SALES (corp-wide): 7.5B **Privately Held**
WEB: www.leag.com
SIC: 4151 School buses
HQ: First Student, Inc.
600 Vine St Ste 1400
Cincinnati OH 45202
513 241-2200

(P-3930)
FIRST STUDENT INC
2005 Navy Dr, Stockton (95206-1142)
PHONE.................................209 466-7737
Drigden Summers, *Manager*
EMP: 200
SALES (corp-wide): 7.5B **Privately Held**
WEB: www.leag.com
SIC: 4151 School buses
HQ: First Student, Inc.
600 Vine St Ste 1400
Cincinnati OH 45202
513 241-2200

(P-3931)
FIRST STUDENT INC
Also Called: Laidlaw Education Services
844 E 9th St, San Bernardino (92410-4012)
PHONE.................................909 383-7104
Fax: 909 885-2991
Norm Foisy, *Manager*
Tatia Florence, *Opers Staff*
Norman Fosy, *Manager*
Trina Ritch, *Manager*
EMP: 65
SQ FT: 2,500
SALES (corp-wide): 7.5B **Privately Held**
WEB: www.leag.com
SIC: 4151 School buses
HQ: First Student, Inc.
600 Vine St Ste 1400
Cincinnati OH 45202
513 241-2200

(P-3932)
FIRST STUDENT INC
14800 S Avalon Blvd, Gardena (90248-2012)
PHONE.................................310 715-6122
Mike Sherrill, *Branch Mgr*
EMP: 250
SALES (corp-wide): 7.5B **Privately Held**
WEB: www.leag.com
SIC: 4151 4141 School buses; local bus charter service
HQ: First Student, Inc.
600 Vine St Ste 1400
Cincinnati OH 45202
513 241-2200

(P-3933)
FIRST STUDENT INC
2270 Jerrold Ave, San Francisco (94124-1012)
PHONE.................................415 647-9012
Bob Gonzales, *Manager*
EMP: 285
SALES (corp-wide): 7.5B **Privately Held**
WEB: www.leag.com
SIC: 4151 School buses
HQ: First Student, Inc.
600 Vine St Ste 1400
Cincinnati OH 45202
513 241-2200

(P-3934)
FIRST STUDENT INC
436 Parr Blvd, Richmond (94801-1123)
PHONE.................................510 237-6365
Brian Rudford, *Branch Mgr*
EMP: 100
SQ FT: 6,488
SALES (corp-wide): 7.5B **Privately Held**
WEB: www.firststudentinc.com
SIC: 4151 School buses
HQ: First Student, Inc.
600 Vine St Ste 1400
Cincinnati OH 45202
513 241-2200

(P-3935)
FIRST STUDENT INC
5320 Derry Ave Ste O, Agoura Hills (91301-5029)
PHONE.................................818 707-2082
EMP: 79
SALES (corp-wide): 9.2B **Privately Held**
SIC: 4151
HQ: First Student, Inc.
600 Vine St Ste 1400
Cincinnati OH 45202
513 241-2200

(P-3936)
FIRST STUDENT INC
11233 San Fernando Rd, San Fernando (91340-3409)
PHONE.................................818 896-0333
Fax: 818 686-6448
Sue Wagnon, *Branch Mgr*
EMP: 135
SALES (corp-wide): 7.5B **Privately Held**
WEB: www.leag.com
SIC: 4151 School buses

PRODUCTS & SERVICES SECTION

4173 - Bus Terminal & Svc Facilities County (P-3958)

HQ: First Student, Inc.
600 Vine St Ste 1400
Cincinnati OH 45202
513 241-2200

(P-3937) FIRST TRANSIT INC
411 High St, Oakland (94601-3903)
PHONE.................510 535-9192
Fax: 510 437-8996
Brian Nieman, Branch Mgr
EMP: 100
SALES (corp-wide): 7.5B Privately Held
WEB: www.firsttransit.com
SIC: 4151 School buses
HQ: First Transit, Inc.
600 Vine St Ste 1400
Cincinnati OH 45202
513 241-2200

(P-3938) FRESNO CNTY SUPT SCHOOLS CENT
Also Called: Southwest Transportation Agcy
16644 S Elm Ave, Caruthers (93609-9757)
P.O. Box 785, Riverdale (93656-0785)
PHONE.................559 644-1000
Fax: 559 644-1050
Tony Mendes, Branch Mgr
Lynn Hill, Admin Asst
Yolanda Martinez, Admin Asst
Dennis Wells, Technology
Kathy Devries, Training Super
EMP: 75
SALES (corp-wide): 84.8MM Privately Held
WEB: www.southwestjpa.org
SIC: 4151 School buses
PA: Fresno County Superintendent Of Schools Central Valley
1111 Van Ness Ave
Fresno CA 93721
559 265-3000

(P-3939) IRVINE UNIFIED SCHOOL DISTRICT
Also Called: Maintenance & Trnsp Fcilty
100 Nightmist, Irvine (92618-1710)
PHONE.................949 936-5300
Rose Clegg, Director
Ron Chang, Admin Sec
Steve Garretson, Senior Mgr
EMP: 100
SALES (corp-wide): 145.4MM Privately Held
WEB: www.gvarvas.com
SIC: 4151 7349 School buses; building maintenance services
PA: Irvine Unified School District
5050 Barranca Pkwy
Irvine CA 92604
949 936-5000

(P-3940) LAIDLAW INTERNATIONAL INC
959 Sebastopol Rd, Santa Rosa (95407-6830)
PHONE.................707 545-8064
Fax: 707 545-0337
Robert Kilian, Manager
Aletha Anconetani, Executive
Leland Kinard, Executive
EMP: 200
SQ FT: 12,000
SALES (corp-wide): 7.5B Privately Held
SIC: 4151 4141 School buses; local bus charter service
HQ: Laidlaw International, Inc.
55 Shuman Blvd Ste 400
Naperville IL 60563
214 849-8100

(P-3941) LAIDLAW INTERNATIONAL INC
9055 Hwy 53, Lower Lake (95457)
PHONE.................707 994-3384
EMP: 108
SALES (corp-wide): 7.5B Privately Held
SIC: 4151 School buses
HQ: Laidlaw International, Inc.
55 Shuman Blvd Ste 400
Naperville IL 60563
214 849-8100

(P-3942) LAKE ELSINORE UNIFIED SCHL DST
Also Called: Lake Elsn SC Trans
21641 Bundy Canyon Rd, Wildomar (92595-8778)
PHONE.................951 253-7830
Fax: 951 245-0394
Silvia Schwing, Director
EMP: 100
SALES (corp-wide): 93.4MM Privately Held
WEB: www.leusd.k12.ca.us
SIC: 4151 School buses
PA: Lake Elsinore Unified School District
545 Chaney St
Lake Elsinore CA 92530
951 253-7000

(P-3943) LODI UNIFIED SCHOOL DISTRICT
Also Called: Transportation
820 S Cuff Ave, Lodi (95240)
PHONE.................209 331-7169
Carlos Garcia, Director
EMP: 120
SALES (corp-wide): 297MM Privately Held
WEB: www.lodiusd.net
SIC: 4151 School buses
PA: Lodi Unified School District
1305 E Vine St
Lodi CA 95240
209 331-7000

(P-3944) LONG BEACH UNIFIED SCHOOL DST
Also Called: Transportation Department
2700 Pine Ave, Long Beach (90806-2617)
PHONE.................562 426-6176
Fax: 562 427-6922
Paul Bailey, Director
Susan Perkins, Asst Director
Ed La Freniere, Manager
EMP: 100
SALES (corp-wide): 810.4MM Privately Held
WEB: www.lbusd.k12.ca.us
SIC: 4151 School buses
PA: Long Beach Unified School District
1515 Hughes Way
Long Beach CA 90810
562 997-8000

(P-3945) MERCED TRANSPORTATION COMPANY
300 Grogan Ave, Merced (95341-6446)
PHONE.................209 384-2575
Fax: 209 384-3805
Curtis Riggs, President
Gaye Riggs, CFO
EMP: 100
SQ FT: 8,000
SALES (est): 8MM Privately Held
SIC: 4151 School buses

(P-3946) MONTEBELLO SCHOOL TRANSPORTION
505 S Greenwood Ave, Montebello (90640-5109)
PHONE.................323 887-7900
Fax: 323 720-5462
Kennedy E Benedetta, Principal
Lea Yeng, Admin Sec
Daniel Ibarra, Director
EMP: 55
SALES (est): 1.2MM Privately Held
SIC: 4151 School buses

(P-3947) SANTA BARBARA TRNSP CORP (HQ)
6414 Hollister Ave, Goleta (93117-3145)
PHONE.................805 681-8355
Denis J Hallagher, CEO
Patrick Walker, CFO
Dennis McGurk, Director
EMP: 90
SQ FT: 15,000
SALES (est): 42MM
SALES (corp-wide): 2B Privately Held
WEB: www.sta-ips.com
SIC: 4151 4141 School buses; local bus charter service
PA: Student Transportation Of America, Inc.
3349 Hwy 138
Wall Township NJ 07719
732 280-4200

(P-3948) SANTA BARBARA TRNSP CORP
Also Called: Student Transportation America
1331 Jason Way, Santa Maria (93455-1000)
PHONE.................805 928-0402
Fax: 805 925-4212
Paula Sauvadon, Vice Pres
Sauvadon Paula, Vice Pres
EMP: 75
SALES (corp-wide): 2B Privately Held
WEB: www.sta-ips.com
SIC: 4151 4121 School buses; taxicabs
HQ: Santa Barbara Transportation Corporation
6414 Hollister Ave
Goleta CA 93117
805 681-8355

(P-3949) SAUGUS UNION SCHOOL DISTRICT
Also Called: Transportation Department
26501 Ruether Ave, Santa Clarita (91350-2600)
PHONE.................661 298-3240
Daniel Cuevas, General Mgr
EMP: 68
SALES (corp-wide): 118.6MM Privately Held
WEB: www.saugus.k12.ca.us
SIC: 4151 School buses
PA: Saugus Union School District
24930 Avenue Stanford
Santa Clarita CA 91355
661 294-5300

(P-3950) STUDENT TRNSP AMER INC
2935 Indian Ave, Perris (92571-3205)
PHONE.................951 940-0300
EMP: 73
SALES (corp-wide): 2B Privately Held
SIC: 4151 4142 School buses; bus charter service, except local
PA: Student Transportation Of America, Inc.
3349 Hwy 138
Wall Township NJ 07719
732 280-4200

(P-3951) TEMECULA VLY UNIFIED SCHL DST
40516 Roripaugh Rd, Temecula (92591-4563)
PHONE.................951 695-7110
Thomas Forrest, Branch Mgr
Bill McKinney, Manager
EMP: 234
SALES (corp-wide): 208.5MM Privately Held
SIC: 4151 School buses
PA: Temecula Valley Unified School District
31350 Rancho Vista Rd
Temecula CA 92592
951 676-2661

(P-3952) UKIAH SC TRANSPORTATION
710 Maple Ave, Ukiah (95482-3743)
PHONE.................707 463-5234
Dave Turner, Director
EMP: 55
SALES (est): 988.9K Privately Held
SIC: 4151 School buses

(P-3953) WOODLAND JINT UNIFIED SCHL DST
25 Matmor Rd, Woodland (95776-6008)
PHONE.................530 662-0201
John Houston, Manager
EMP: 50
SALES (corp-wide): 72.4MM Privately Held
WEB: www.leejhs.wjusd.k12.ca.us
SIC: 4151 School buses
PA: Woodland Joint Unified School District
435 6th St
Woodland CA 95695
530 662-0201

4173 Bus Terminal & Svc Facilities

(P-3954) ALAMEDA-CONTRA COSTA TRNST DST
A C Transit
10626 International Blvd, Oakland (94603-3806)
PHONE.................510 577-8816
Glen Andrade, Manager
Elsa Ortiz, Director
EMP: 130
SALES (corp-wide): 68.6MM Privately Held
WEB: www.actransit.org
SIC: 4173 Maintenance facilities for motor vehicle passenger transport
PA: Alameda-Contra Costa Transit District
1600 Franklin St
Oakland CA 94612
510 891-4777

(P-3955) CITY OF LOS ANGELES
Also Called: Port of Los Angeles
500 Pier A Pl, Wilmington (90744-6210)
PHONE.................310 732-3550
Fax: 310 834-8248
Joannie Mukai, Branch Mgr
EMP: 500 Privately Held
WEB: www.lacity.org
SIC: 4173 9621 Maintenance facilities for motor vehicle passenger transport; regulation, administration of transportation;
PA: City Of Los Angeles
200 N Spring St Ste 303
Los Angeles CA 90012
213 978-0600

(P-3956) CITY OF LOS ANGELES
Also Called: General Services
2513 E 24th St, Vernon (90058-1205)
PHONE.................213 485-4981
John Ferris, Superintendent
EMP: 100 Privately Held
WEB: www.lacity.org
SIC: 4173 9621 Maintenance facilities for motor vehicle passenger transport; regulation, administration of transportation;
PA: City Of Los Angeles
200 N Spring St Ste 303
Los Angeles CA 90012
213 978-0600

(P-3957) DURHAM SCHOOL SERVICES LP
2818 W 5th St, Santa Ana (92703-1824)
PHONE.................714 542-8989
Fax: 714 542-1157
Debbie Williams, Manager
EMP: 200
SQ FT: 4,843
SALES (corp-wide): 2.8B Privately Held
SIC: 4173 4151 Maintenance facilities for motor vehicle passenger transport; school buses
HQ: Durham School Services, L. P.
4300 Weaver Pkwy Ste 100
Warrenville IL 60555
630 836-0292

(P-3958) FIRST STUDENT INC
300 S Buena Vista Ave, Corona (92882-1937)
PHONE.................951 736-3234
Jackie Mansperger, Manager
EMP: 101
SALES (corp-wide): 7.5B Privately Held
WEB: www.leag.com
SIC: 4173 4151 Maintenance facilities, buses; school buses

4173 - Bus Terminal & Svc Facilities County (P-3959)

HQ: First Student, Inc.
600 Vine St Ste 1400
Cincinnati OH 45202
513 241-2200

(P-3959)
GREYHOUND LINES INC
1033 Broadway St, Fresno (93721-2535)
PHONE...................559 268-1829
Fax: 559 442-8095
Tom Fries, *Manager*
EMP: 118
SALES (corp-wide): 7.5B **Privately Held**
WEB: www.greyhound.com
SIC: 4173 Bus terminal operation
HQ: Greyhound Lines, Inc.
350 N Saint Paul St # 300
Dallas TX 75201
214 849-8000

(P-3960)
GREYHOUND LINES INC
1716 E 7th St, Los Angeles (90021-1202)
PHONE...................213 629-8400
Fax: 213 489-7849
Mark Jacobson, *Principal*
EMP: 400
SQ FT: 100,000
SALES (corp-wide): 7.5B **Privately Held**
WEB: www.greyhound.com
SIC: 4173 Bus terminal & service facilities
HQ: Greyhound Lines, Inc.
350 N Saint Paul St # 300
Dallas TX 75201
214 849-8000

(P-3961)
LOS ANGELES UNIFIED SCHOOL DST
Also Called: Transportation Branch
2011 N Soto St, Los Angeles (90032-3628)
PHONE...................323 227-4400
Antonio Rodgriquez, *Manager*
Matt Webb, *Supervisor*
EMP: 150
SALES (corp-wide): 4.4B **Privately Held**
WEB: www.lausd.k12.ca.us
SIC: 4173 8211 Bus terminal operation; public elementary & secondary schools
PA: Los Angeles Unified School District
333 S Beaudry Ave Ste 209
Los Angeles CA 90017
213 241-1000

(P-3962)
RELIANT TRAVEL LLC
2000 Mandela Pkwy, Oakland (94607-1629)
P.O. Box 1580, Palo Alto (94302-1580)
PHONE...................847 509-0097
Fax: 510 451-1380
Larry King,
Quentin Gray, *General Mgr*
EMP: 60
SQ FT: 20,000
SALES (est): 3.2MM **Privately Held**
WEB: www.relianttravel.com
SIC: 4173 Bus terminal & service facilities

(P-3963)
SAN MATEO COUNTY TRANSIT DST
Also Called: Sam Trans
501 Pico Blvd, San Carlos (94070-2706)
PHONE...................650 508-6412
Ed Proctor, *Manager*
John Sicarra, *COO*
EMP: 175
SALES (corp-wide): 18.8MM **Privately Held**
SIC: 4173 4111 Maintenance facilities, buses; local & suburban transit
PA: San Mateo County Transit District
1250 San Carlos Ave
San Carlos CA 94070
650 508-6200

4212 Local Trucking Without Storage

(P-3964)
A & D HAULING SERVICES INC
13337 South St, Cerritos (90703-7308)
PHONE...................310 514-8969
Lillian Wang, *Exec Dir*
Andrew Wang, *General Mgr*
Grace Wang, *General Mgr*
EMP: 60
SQ FT: 75,000
SALES (est): 5.8MM **Privately Held**
WEB: www.adhls.net
SIC: 4212 Light haulage & cartage, local

(P-3965)
A A A PACKING AND SHIPPING INC
806 W 47th St, Los Angeles (90037-2910)
PHONE...................626 310-7787
Fax: 626 310-7796
Bruce Nebens, *President*
Frank Hallberg, *COO*
Judy Johnson, *Controller*
EMP: 50
SQ FT: 80,000
SALES (est): 5.9MM **Privately Held**
WEB: www.aaapack.com
SIC: 4212 4213 4783 Local trucking, without storage; trucking, except local; packing goods for shipping

(P-3966)
A G HACIENDA INCORPORATED
32794 Sherwood Ave, Mc Farland (93250-9626)
P.O. Box 367 (93250-0367)
PHONE...................661 792-2418
Xochilht Gonzalez, *President*
EMP: 400
SALES (est): 28.4MM **Privately Held**
SIC: 4212 0761 4214 Local trucking, without storage; farm labor contractors; local trucking with storage

(P-3967)
A J R TRUCKING INC
915 Monterey Rd, Glendale (91206-2518)
PHONE...................562 989-9555
Khachatur Khudikyan, *President*
Jehan Reyes, *Shareholder*
Hakop Khudikyan, *CFO*
Angel Reyes, *Director*
EMP: 84
SQ FT: 12,000
SALES (est): 9.9MM **Privately Held**
SIC: 4212 Mail carriers, contract

(P-3968)
A-1 DELIVERY CO
19805 Business Pkwy, Walnut (91789-2839)
PHONE...................909 444-1220
Joe Romine, *President*
William Turner, *Corp Secy*
Johnny Romine, *Vice Pres*
EMP: 75
SQ FT: 10,000
SALES (est): 11.9MM **Privately Held**
WEB: www.jromine.com
SIC: 4212 Furniture moving, local: without storage

(P-3969)
ACCURATE COURIER SERVICES INC
11022 Santa Monica Blvd # 360, Los Angeles (90025-7513)
P.O. Box 252061 (90025-8939)
PHONE...................310 481-3937
Joseph Yemini, *President*
EMP: 92
SALES (est): 8.6MM **Privately Held**
SIC: 4212 Delivery service, vehicular

(P-3970)
ACCURATE DELIVERY SYSTEMS INC
Also Called: ADS
173 Resource Dr, Bloomington (92316-3540)
P.O. Box 1620, Chino (91708-1620)
PHONE...................951 823-8870
Mahmoud Maraach, *President*
EMP: 55
SQ FT: 10,000
SALES: 8.5MM **Privately Held**
SIC: 4212 Delivery service, vehicular

(P-3971)
ACE RELOCATION SYSTEMS INC
189 W Victoria St, Long Beach (90805-2162)
PHONE...................310 632-2800
Fax: 310 632-9721
Kevin Casey, *Branch Mgr*
Chris Shipp, *General Mgr*
Eric Kronebusch, *Technology*
Dan Reyes, *Opers Staff*
Bob Blanchard, *Sales Staff*
EMP: 50
SALES (corp-wide): 65MM **Privately Held**
WEB: www.acerelocation.com
SIC: 4212 4213 Local trucking, without storage; trucking, except local
PA: Ace Relocation Systems, Inc.
5608 Eastgate Dr
San Diego CA 92121
858 677-5500

(P-3972)
ADVANCED CLEANUP TECH INC
Also Called: Spell Control
4548 Wesley Ln, Bakersfield (93308-9625)
PHONE...................661 392-7765
Fax: 661 392-7762
Henry Garcia, *Branch Mgr*
EMP: 90
SALES (corp-wide): 38.2MM **Privately Held**
WEB: www.actird.com
SIC: 4212 4953 Hazardous waste transport; refuse systems
PA: Advanced Cleanup Technologies, Inc.
20928 S Lamberton Ave
Carson CA 90810
310 763-1423

(P-3973)
ADVANCED ENVIRONMENTAL INC
Also Called: Advanced Resources
13579 Whittram Ave, Fontana (92335-2950)
PHONE...................909 356-9025
Fax: 909 356-5841
Bruce De Menno, *President*
Franklin Hill, *Manager*
Delmar Parker, *Manager*
EMP: 50
SALES (est): 3.6MM
SALES (corp-wide): 136.8MM **Privately Held**
SIC: 4212 8742 Hazardous waste transport; management consulting services
HQ: De Menno-Kerdoon Trading Company
2000 N Alameda St
Compton CA 90222
310 537-7100

(P-3974)
AGRI-MIX TRANSPORT INC
1400 S Union Ave Ste 110, Bakersfield (93307-4179)
P.O. Box 327, Lamont (93241-0327)
PHONE...................661 833-6280
Fax: 661 397-8293
Cesar Juarez, *President*
Gonzalo Juarez, *Treasurer*
Walter Juarez, *Vice Pres*
Orelia Ornelas, *General Mgr*
Ramon Juarez, *Admin Sec*
EMP: 150
SQ FT: 435,600
SALES: 30MM **Privately Held**
SIC: 4212 Local trucking, without storage

(P-3975)
AJR TRUCKING INC
2700 Rose Ave Ste A, Signal Hill (90755-1929)
P.O. Box 10129, Glendale (91209-3129)
PHONE...................562 989-9555
Jack Khudikyan, *Vice Pres*
EMP: 140
SALES (est): 10.5MM **Privately Held**
SIC: 4212 Delivery service, vehicular

(P-3976)
ALL STATE ASSOCIATION INC
11487 San Fernando Rd, San Fernando (91340-3406)
PHONE...................877 425-2558
Alfred Megrabyan, *President*
Steve Avetyan, *CEO*
Armen Karibyan, *COO*
EMP: 250
SALES: 120MM **Privately Held**
SIC: 4212 Local trucking, without storage

(P-3977)
ANDERSNCTTONWOOD DISPOSAL SVCS
Also Called: Waste Managment
3281 State Highway 99w S, Corning (96021-9736)
P.O. Box 496 (96021-0496)
PHONE...................530 824-4700
Fax: 530 824-2699
Bill Manneo, *Manager*
EMP: 51
SALES (corp-wide): 4.4MM **Privately Held**
SIC: 4212 Garbage collection & transport, no disposal
PA: Andersoncottonwood Disposal Services Inc
8592 Commercial Way
Redding CA 96002
530 221-6510

(P-3978)
ASBURY ENVIRONMENTAL SERVICES (PA)
1300 N Santa Fe Ave, Compton (90221-4916)
PHONE...................310 886-3400
Fax: 310 763-5922
Steve Kerdoon, *CEO*
Chris Mahoney, *CFO*
Anne Asbury, *Treasurer*
Bruce De Menno, *Vice Pres*
EMP: 75
SQ FT: 22,000
SALES (est): 67.5MM **Privately Held**
WEB: www.asburyenv.com
SIC: 4212 Local trucking, without storage

(P-3979)
ATCHESONS EXPRESS INC
201 E La Palma Ave, Anaheim (92801-2523)
PHONE...................714 808-9199
Brad Atcheson, *President*
Gail Atcheson, *CFO*
Mark Atcheson, *Vice Pres*
Evelyn Abel, *Sales Staff*
Jeni Bowles, *Manager*
EMP: 50
SQ FT: 10,000
SALES (est): 6.8MM **Privately Held**
WEB: www.atchesonexpress.com
SIC: 4212 4731 Local trucking, without storage; freight transportation arrangement

(P-3980)
B & G DELIVERY SYSTEM INC
2549 Harris Ave, Sacramento (95838-3128)
PHONE...................916 921-4401
Fax: 916 921-4414
Bruce Allgier, *President*
Vicky Allgier, *CFO*
John Margetich, *General Mgr*
Rebecca Allgier, *Admin Sec*
Scott Allgier, *Manager*
EMP: 125
SQ FT: 20,000
SALES (est): 28.6MM **Privately Held**
WEB: www.bgdelivery.com
SIC: 4212 4215 Delivery service, vehicular; courier services, except by air

(P-3981)
BEST OVERNITE EXPRESS INC (PA)
Also Called: Best Overnight Express
406 Live Oak Ave, Irwindale (91706-1314)
P.O. Box 90816, City of Industry (91715-0816)
PHONE...................626 256-6340
Fax: 626 256-0568

PRODUCTS & SERVICES SECTION
4212 - Local Trucking Without Storage County (P-4003)

William K Applebee, *President*
Mike Salcedo, *COO*
Mike White, *CFO*
Mike Saucedo, *Vice Pres*
Monica Conrekas, *General Mgr*
EMP: 100
SQ FT: 25,000
SALES (est): 33.5MM **Privately Held**
SIC: 4212 Local trucking, without storage

(P-3982)
BLUE EAGLE CONTRACTING INC
2059 Nev Cy Hwy Ste 204, Grass Valley (95945)
PHONE.................530 272-0287
Fax: 530 470-0801
Daniel L Rackley, *President*
Marvin L Rackley, *Ch of Bd*
Debbie Lemay, *Officer*
Ray Rackley, *Vice Pres*
Dana Perry, *Manager*
EMP: 53
SQ FT: 700
SALES (est): 7.7MM **Privately Held**
SIC: 4212 Mail carriers, contract

(P-3983)
BOB HUBBARD HORSE TRNSP INC (PA)
3730 S Riverside Ave, Colton (92324-3329)
PHONE.................951 369-3770
Fax: 951 369-0719
Bob Hubbard, *CEO*
Tom Hubbard, *President*
Patricia Hubbard, *Vice Pres*
Kathy Copeland, *CIO*
Sally Wollinzer, *Safety Mgr*
EMP: 50
SQ FT: 9,375
SALES (est): 13.9MM **Privately Held**
WEB: www.bobhubbardhorsetrans.com
SIC: 4212 4213 4789 Animal transport; trucking, except local; cargo loading & unloading services

(P-3984)
BUDS & SON TRUCKING INC
12570 Highway 67, Lakeside (92040-1159)
P.O. Box 1521 (92040-0912)
PHONE.................619 443-4200
Fax: 619 561-3916
Marvin J Struiksma, *President*
Robert Struiksma, *Corp Secy*
John Struiksma, *Vice Pres*
Michael Willingham, *Admin Sec*
Roy Smith, *Engineer*
EMP: 85 **EST:** 1942
SQ FT: 10,800
SALES (est): 6MM **Privately Held**
SIC: 4212 4213 Local trucking, without storage; trucking, except local

(P-3985)
BURNS AND SONS TRUCKING INC
Also Called: Dependable Disposal and Recycl
9210 Olive Dr, Spring Valley (91977-2305)
P.O. Box 1640 (91979-1640)
PHONE.................619 460-5394
Fax: 619 465-2371
Eva N Burns, *CEO*
Jack Burns Sr, *President*
Tom McFarlane, *CFO*
Jim Burns, *Vice Pres*
Wanda Estrada, *Accountant*
EMP: 85
SQ FT: 6,000
SALES (est): 17.7MM **Privately Held**
WEB: www.burnsandsonstrucking.com
SIC: 4212 4214 Local trucking, without storage; local trucking with storage

(P-3986)
BURRTEC WASTE GROUP INC
2340 W Main St, Barstow (92311-3612)
PHONE.................760 256-2730
Fax: 760 256-2770
EMP: 84
SALES (corp-wide): 288.4MM **Privately Held**
SIC: 4212 Garbage collection & transport, no disposal

PA: Burrtec Waste Group, Inc.
9890 Cherry Ave
Fontana CA 92335
909 429-4200

(P-3987)
C & M TRANSFER SAN DIEGO INC
Also Called: C&M Relocation Systems
8787 Olive Ln, Santee (92071-4137)
P.O. Box 1543, El Cajon (92022-1543)
PHONE.................619 562-6111
Mick Mahaffey, *President*
Aron Fleck, *Business Mgr*
Andy Mahaffey, *Opers Staff*
Joyce Persichilli, *Manager*
EMP: 60
SALES (est): 8MM **Privately Held**
WEB: www.cmtransfer.com
SIC: 4212 Moving services

(P-3988)
C P S EXPRESS (HQ)
3401 Etiwanda Ave 711a, Mira Loma (91752-1128)
P.O. Box 248 (91752-0248)
PHONE.................951 685-1041
Fax: 951 685-3944
William Smerber, *CEO*
Kirt Allen, *Corp Secy*
James E Ford, *Vice Pres*
Elly Medrano, *Office Admin*
Jeff Woolsey, *Controller*
EMP: 100
SQ FT: 7,000
SALES (est): 11.6MM
SALES (corp-wide): 38.3MM **Privately Held**
SIC: 4212 4213 4214 Local trucking, without storage; trucking, except local; local trucking with storage
PA: Haddy, J G Sales Co, Inc
3401 Etiwanda Ave
Mira Loma CA 91752
951 681-0666

(P-3989)
CALIFORNIA MATERIALS INC
Also Called: Cmat
3736 S Highway 99, Stockton (95215-8028)
P.O. Box 32314 (95213-2314)
PHONE.................209 472-7422
Earl Rogers, *President*
EMP: 50
SALES (est): 7.1MM **Privately Held**
SIC: 4212 Dump truck haulage

(P-3990)
CALMET INC
7202 Petterson Ln, Paramount (90723-2022)
PHONE.................562 869-0901
Tom Blackman, *President*
Mike Adnoff, *Vice Pres*
Art Kazarian, *Vice Pres*
EMP: 180
SQ FT: 4,000
SALES (est): 9MM **Privately Held**
SIC: 4212 4953 Garbage collection & transport, no disposal; refuse collection & disposal services

(P-3991)
CEMAK TRUCKING INC
3252 E 70th St, Long Beach (90805-1821)
PHONE.................949 253-2800
Kurt Callier, *Branch Mgr*
Randy Caillier, *Vice Pres*
Mike Cook, *Purchasing*
EMP: 51
SALES (corp-wide): 4.3MM **Privately Held**
SIC: 4212 Local trucking, without storage
PA: Cemak Trucking Inc
4621 Teller Ave Ste 130
Newport Beach CA 92660
949 253-2800

(P-3992)
CENTRAL COURIER LLC
1957 Eastman Ave Ste C, Ventura (93003-6491)
PHONE.................805 654-1145
Fax: 805 654-1274
Nkosi Khumalo, *President*

Debbie Senate, *Officer*
Michael Winner, *Manager*
EMP: 55
SQ FT: 3,038
SALES: 3MM **Privately Held**
SIC: 4212 Light haulage & cartage, local

(P-3993)
CENTRAL FREIGHT LINES INC
4575 S Chestnut Ave, Fresno (93725-9211)
PHONE.................559 233-5559
Robert Ibarra, *Manager*
Chuck Salazar, *Vice Pres*
Brandon McKeehan, *Manager*
Will Young, *Manager*
EMP: 53
SQ FT: 5,790
SALES (corp-wide): 1.1B **Privately Held**
WEB: www.centralfreight.com
SIC: 4212 4213 Local trucking, without storage; trucking, except local
HQ: Central Freight Lines, Inc.
5601 W Waco Dr
Waco TX 76710
254 772-2120

(P-3994)
CENTRAL VALLEY CONCRETE INC (PA)
Also Called: Central Valley Trucking
3823 N State Highway 59, Merced (95348-9370)
PHONE.................209 723-8846
Fax: 209 384-2395
Scott Neal, *CEO*
Brad Filburn, *CFO*
Brad Philbren, *Controller*
Chuck Falkenstein, *Opers Mgr*
EMP: 150
SQ FT: 2,000
SALES (est): 30.5MM **Privately Held**
WEB: www.centralvalleyconcrete.com
SIC: 4212 3273 Local trucking, without storage; ready-mixed concrete

(P-3995)
CLAY MIRANDA TRUCKING INC
3220 W Belmont Ave, Fresno (93722-5905)
P.O. Box 11983 (93776-1983)
PHONE.................559 275-6250
Fax: 559 275-6091
Debbie Cooper, *Vice Pres*
Mike Miranda, *President*
EMP: 53
SQ FT: 9,600
SALES (est): 6.1MM **Privately Held**
SIC: 4212 5032 Dump truck haulage; asphalt mixture; gravel; sand, construction; stone, crushed or broken

(P-3996)
CLEM-TRANS INC
213 W Valley Blvd, Rialto (92376-7713)
P.O. Box 3124, San Dimas (91773-7124)
PHONE.................909 877-4450
Fax: 909 877-4504
Glory M Clemons, *President*
Heather Clements, *Office Mgr*
Glory M Brown, *Agent*
EMP: 50 **EST:** 1965
SQ FT: 3,500
SALES (est): 4.3MM **Privately Held**
SIC: 4212 4213 Mail carriers, contract; contract haulers

(P-3997)
COASTAL TRANSPORT CO INC
9950 San Diego Mission Rd F, San Diego (92108-1705)
PHONE.................619 584-1055
Fax: 619 584-0959
Brian Martin, *Manager*
EMP: 52
SALES (corp-wide): 90MM **Privately Held**
SIC: 4212 4213 Liquid haulage, local; liquid petroleum transport, non-local
PA: Coastal Transport Co., Inc.
1603 Ackerman Rd
San Antonio TX 78219
210 661-4287

(P-3998)
COMPLETE LOGISTICS COMPANY
13831 Slover Ave, Fontana (92337-7037)
PHONE.................909 427-9800
Tim Telbsio, *Manager*
Ronald Ryan, *Vice Pres*
Richard Wheeler, *VP Opers*
Steve Madrigal, *Manager*
EMP: 150
SALES (corp-wide): 78MM **Privately Held**
SIC: 4212 Local trucking, without storage
PA: The Complete Logistics Company
1670 Etiwanda Ave Ste A
Ontario CA 91761
909 544-5040

(P-3999)
COORDNTED DLVRY INSTLLTION INC
905 E Katella Ave, Anaheim (92805-6616)
PHONE.................714 501-4040
Fax: 714 372-3208
Flynn A Olsen, *CEO*
Jimmie D Mc Gee, *President*
David Stout, *Executive Asst*
Frank Dieterich, *Personnel Exec*
Paul Brown, *Agent*
EMP: 60
SQ FT: 35,000
SALES (est): 3.8MM **Privately Held**
WEB: www.coordinateddelivery.com
SIC: 4212 Delivery service, vehicular

(P-4000)
CR ENGLAND INC
4131 Etiwanda Ave, Mira Loma (91752-1403)
P.O. Box 3286, Rancho Cucamonga (91729-3286)
PHONE.................909 946-1555
Cory England, *Branch Mgr*
EMP: 100
SALES (corp-wide): 1.4B **Privately Held**
WEB: www.crengland.com
SIC: 4212 4214 Local trucking, without storage; local trucking with storage
PA: C.R. England, Inc.
4701 W 2100 S
Salt Lake City UT 84120
800 421-9004

(P-4001)
DALTON TRUCKING INC (PA)
13560 Whittram Ave, Fontana (92335-2951)
P.O. Box 5025 (92334-5025)
PHONE.................909 823-0663
Fax: 909 823-4628
Terry Klenske, *CEO*
Mathew Klenske, *Vice Pres*
Josh Klenske, *General Mgr*
Eleanor Klenske, *Admin Sec*
Roland Roberts, *CIO*
EMP: 74
SQ FT: 11,000
SALES: 23.9MM **Privately Held**
SIC: 4212 Local trucking, without storage

(P-4002)
DEDICATED FLEET SYSTEMS INC (PA)
1350 Philadelphia St, Pomona (91766-5563)
P.O. Box 2829 (91769-2829)
PHONE.................909 590-8209
Fax: 909 590-3540
Anthony Osterkamp Jr, *Ch of Bd*
Gene Segrist, *Vice Pres*
Shelley Fajardo, *Admin Sec*
EMP: 59 **EST:** 1970
SALES (est): 5.5MM **Privately Held**
WEB: www.dedicatedfleetsystems.com
SIC: 4212 Local trucking, without storage

(P-4003)
DELANCEY STREET FOUNDATION
600 The Embarcadero, San Francisco (94107-2116)
PHONE.................415 512-5110
Fax: 415 512-5119
Mimi Silbert, *Branch Mgr*
EMP: 367

4212 - Local Trucking Without Storage County (P-4004)

SALES (corp-wide): 46.4MM **Privately Held**
SIC: 4212 Local trucking, without storage
PA: Delancey Street Foundation
600 The Embarcadero
San Francisco CA 94107
415 957-9800

(P-4004)
DELIVERY SOLUTIONS INC
650 85th Ave, Oakland (94621-1223)
PHONE..................................925 819-1289
EMP: 68
SALES (corp-wide): 8.3MM **Privately Held**
SIC: 4212 Delivery service, vehicular
PA: Delivery Solutions Inc.
595 Tamarack Ave Ste D
Brea CA 92821
800 335-6557

(P-4005)
DELUXE AUTO CARRIERS INC
Also Called: Excel Auto Transporting Towing
15810 Gale Ave Ste 120, La Puente (91745-1601)
PHONE..................................909 823-1617
Fax: 909 823-1619
Jesus Holguin, *President*
Raul Silva, *Vice Pres*
Russell Schilling, *Director*
EMP: 60
SALES (est): 16.3MM **Privately Held**
SIC: 4212 Local trucking, without storage

(P-4006)
DEMENNO-KERDOON
1300 S Santa Fe Ave, Compton (90221-4916)
PHONE..................................310 898-3848
Steve Kerdoon, *President*
EMP: 500
SALES (est): 19.9MM **Privately Held**
SIC: 4212 Hazardous waste transport

(P-4007)
DEPENDABLE HIGHWAY EXPRESS INC
820 E St, West Sacramento (95605-2309)
PHONE..................................916 374-0782
Micheal Laporte, *Branch Mgr*
Mike La Porte, *Manager*
EMP: 75
SALES (corp-wide): 292.7MM **Privately Held**
WEB: www.godependable.com
SIC: 4212 4213 Local trucking, without storage; trucking, except local
PA: Dependable Highway Express, Inc.
2555 E Olympic Blvd
Los Angeles CA 90023
323 526-2200

(P-4008)
DESMOND MAIL DELIVERY SERVICE
4600 Worth St, Los Angeles (90063-1623)
P.O. Box 4836, Anaheim (92803-4836)
PHONE..................................323 262-1085
Fax: 323 262-6440
John Hoskins, *President*
EMP: 75
SQ FT: 3,000
SALES (est): 2.9MM
SALES (corp-wide): 36.7MM **Privately Held**
WEB: www.norcodelivery.com
SIC: 4212 Mail carriers, contract
PA: Norco Delivery Service, Inc.
851 E Cerritos Ave
Anaheim CA 92805
714 520-8600

(P-4009)
DOUBLE D TRANSPORTATION CO
22991 Clawiter Rd, Hayward (94545-1316)
P.O. Box 2999, Dublin (94568-0999)
PHONE..................................510 783-2335
Fax: 925 828-7407
Kathryn De Silva, *President*
Ernest D Lampkin, *Agent*
EMP: 55
SQ FT: 1,000
SALES (est): 5.7MM **Privately Held**
SIC: 4212 Local trucking, without storage; dump truck haulage

(P-4010)
DOUGLAS L MYOVICH TRUCKING INC
1895 W Jefferson Ave, Fresno (93706-9732)
PHONE..................................559 264-1181
Fax: 559 233-1573
Douglas Myovich, *President*
Cynthia Myovich, *Admin Sec*
EMP: 60
SALES (est): 5.1MM **Privately Held**
SIC: 4212 Liquid haulage, local

(P-4011)
DSC LOGISTICS INC
12350 Philadelphia Ave, Mira Loma (91752-3228)
PHONE..................................909 605-7233
Fax: 909 605-1037
Adrian Potgieter, *Manager*
Mark Diaz, *General Mgr*
Alisha Contreras, *Human Res Mgr*
Chris Boughey, *Opers Mgr*
Rigo Mendoza, *Opers Mgr*
EMP: 56
SALES (corp-wide): 493.3MM **Privately Held**
SIC: 4212 4213 4225 4731 Local trucking, without storage; trucking, except local; general warehousing & storage; freight consolidation
PA: Dsc Logistics, Inc.
1750 S Wolf Rd
Des Plaines IL 60018
847 390-6800

(P-4012)
DTI INC
1628 S Sportsman Dr, Compton (90221-4714)
P.O. Box 1739, Paramount (90723-1739)
PHONE..................................310 635-9002
Fax: 310 635-6376
Gary Cross, *Partner*
Geoff Cross, *Partner*
Emilia Lane, *Fellow*
EMP: 57 EST: 1975
SQ FT: 90,000
SALES (est): 5.4MM **Privately Held**
SIC: 4212 Liquid haulage, local

(P-4013)
EDS WEST LLC
6666 E Washington Blvd, Commerce (90040-1814)
PHONE..................................323 887-7367
Fax: 323 887-0586
Ronnie Moyal, *Partner*
Lisa Casillas, *Manager*
Rick Thomason, *Manager*
▲ EMP: 75
SALES (est): 5.8MM **Privately Held**
SIC: 4212 Local trucking, without storage

(P-4014)
EMPIRE CHAUFFEUR SERVICE LTD
Also Called: Empire Internation
600 S Allied Way, El Segundo (90245-4727)
PHONE..................................310 414-8189
David Seelinger, *President*
Lino Palencia, *Manager*
EMP: 80
SALES (est): 6MM **Privately Held**
SIC: 4212 Local trucking, without storage

(P-4015)
ENCORE TRUCKING INC
650 Aldo Ave, Santa Clara (95054-2207)
P.O. Box 35638, Monte Sereno (95030-0638)
PHONE..................................408 330-7600
Fax: 408 330-7610
Kenneth J Madsen, *President*
Joan Lee Ilse, *Treasurer*
Jay Donny, *Manager*
EMP: 65
SQ FT: 10,000
SALES (est): 4.7MM **Privately Held**
WEB: www.encoretrucking.com
SIC: 4212 Local trucking, without storage

(P-4016)
ESTES EXPRESS LINES INC
14727 Alondra Blvd, La Mirada (90638-5617)
PHONE..................................714 994-3770
Benjamin J Torman, *Branch Mgr*
EMP: 105
SALES (corp-wide): 2.3B **Privately Held**
SIC: 4212 Local trucking, without storage
PA: Estes Express Lines, Inc.
3901 W Broad St
Richmond VA 23230
804 353-1900

(P-4017)
FEDERAL EXPRESS CORPORATION
Also Called: Fedex
1600 63rd St, Emeryville (94608-2033)
PHONE..................................800 463-3339
Mark Morris, *General Mgr*
Rishi Maharaja, *Human Res Mgr*
EMP: 120
SALES (corp-wide): 50.3B **Publicly Held**
WEB: www.federalexpress.com
SIC: 4212 4513 Local trucking, without storage; air courier services
HQ: Federal Express Corporation
3610 Hacks Cross Rd
Memphis TN 38125
901 369-3600

(P-4018)
FEDEX FREIGHT CORPORATION
3255 Victor St, Santa Clara (95054-2318)
PHONE..................................408 988-2111
Mike Lujan, *Manager*
Rico Flores, *Branch Mgr*
Melissa Belardes, *Info Tech Dir*
Larry Wollert, *Info Tech Dir*
Ray Courtney, *MIS Mgr*
EMP: 50
SQ FT: 18,200
SALES (corp-wide): 50.3B **Publicly Held**
SIC: 4212 4213 Local trucking, without storage; trucking, except local
HQ: Fedex Freight Corporation
1715 Aaron Brenner Dr
Memphis TN 38120
901 434-3100

(P-4019)
FOOD EXPRESS INC
5127 Maywood Ave, Maywood (90270-2009)
PHONE..................................323 589-1417
Fax: 323 589-7146
Mike Hess, *Manager*
Michael Rocco, *Mktg Dir*
Bill Baldridge, *Manager*
EMP: 50
SALES (corp-wide): 40.2MM **Privately Held**
WEB: www.foodexp.com
SIC: 4212 5411 4214 Local trucking, without storage; grocery stores; local trucking with storage
PA: Food Express Inc.
521 N 1st Ave
Arcadia CA 91006
626 574-9094

(P-4020)
FRANK GHIGLIONE INC (PA)
Also Called: Rodgers Trucking Co
14327 Washington Ave, San Leandro (94578-3418)
P.O. Box 923 (94577-0445)
PHONE..................................510 483-7000
Fax: 510 483-4918
Frank Ghiglione, *President*
Winifred Ghiglione, *Admin Sec*
Steve Strom, *Personnel*
Nancy Primrose, *Manager*
EMP: 80
SQ FT: 8,000
SALES (est): 11.7MM **Privately Held**
WEB: www.rodgerstrucking.com
SIC: 4212 Local trucking, without storage

(P-4021)
FRANK GHIGLIONE INC
Also Called: Rogers Trucking
2972 Alvarado St Ste H, San Leandro (94577-5732)
PHONE..................................510 483-2063
Frank Ghiglione, *Manager*
EMP: 100
SALES (corp-wide): 11.7MM **Privately Held**
WEB: www.rodgerstrucking.com
SIC: 4212 4214 Local trucking, without storage; local trucking with storage
PA: Frank Ghiglione, Inc.
14327 Washington Ave
San Leandro CA 94578
510 483-7000

(P-4022)
HANKS INC
Also Called: Sun Express
13866 Slover Ave, Fontana (92337-7037)
PHONE..................................909 350-8365
Fax: 909 356-0530
Brian Bachar, *President*
Shirley Bachar, *Vice Pres*
Donna Nava, *Manager*
▲ EMP: 68
SQ FT: 24,000
SALES (est): 12.8MM **Privately Held**
WEB: www.shipsun.com
SIC: 4212 4213 Local trucking, without storage; trucking, except local

(P-4023)
HARTWICK & HAND INC (PA)
Also Called: H & H Truck Terminal
16953 N D St, Victorville (92394-1417)
P.O. Box 1595 (92393-1595)
PHONE..................................760 245-1666
Fax: 760 245-3298
Stacy L Hand, *CEO*
Edward Perreria, *President*
EMP: 73
SQ FT: 8,800
SALES (est): 11.5MM **Privately Held**
SIC: 4212 Local trucking, without storage

(P-4024)
HES TRANSPORTATION SVCS INC
3623 Munster St, Hayward (94545-1646)
P.O. Box 57136 (94545-7136)
PHONE..................................510 783-6100
Jeff Graham, *President*
Joyce C Schaul, *Vice Pres*
EMP: 50
SQ FT: 38,000
SALES (est): 5.9MM **Privately Held**
SIC: 4212 Draying, local: without storage

(P-4025)
HUB GROUP TRUCKING INC
Also Called: Hgt
4221 E Mariposa Rd, Stockton (95215-8139)
PHONE..................................209 943-6975
Ryan Kotaka, *Opers Mgr*
EMP: 77
SALES (corp-wide): 3.5B **Publicly Held**
SIC: 4212 Draying, local: without storage
HQ: Hub Group Trucking, Inc.
2000 Clearwater Dr
Oak Brook IL 60523
630 271-3600

(P-4026)
HUB GROUP TRUCKING INC
Also Called: Hgt
3801 E Guasti Rd, Ontario (91761-1575)
PHONE..................................951 693-9813
EMP: 174
SALES (corp-wide): 3.5B **Publicly Held**
SIC: 4212 Draying, local: without storage
HQ: Hub Group Trucking, Inc.
2000 Clearwater Dr
Oak Brook IL 60523
630 271-3600

(P-4027)
ICE DELIVERY SYSTEMS INC
Also Called: Inner-City Express
6920 Santa Teresa Blvd # 206, San Jose (95119-1344)
PHONE..................................408 640-4625
Michael S Hubert, *President*
Lizette P Hubert, *Principal*
EMP: 130
SQ FT: 30,000

PRODUCTS & SERVICES SECTION

4212 - Local Trucking Without Storage County (P-4050)

SALES (est): 11.7MM **Privately Held**
SIC: 4212 7389 4215 Delivery service, vehicular; courier or messenger service; courier services, except by air

(P-4028)
J D L MOTOR EXPRESS
1250 Delevan Dr, San Diego (92102-2437)
PHONE.................................619 232-6136
John Lenore, *President*
Dorothy Lenore, *Treasurer*
Harold Gursky, *Vice Pres*
EMP: 75
SALES (est): 3.3MM
SALES (corp-wide): 143.9MM **Privately Held**
WEB: www.johnlenore.com
SIC: 4212 4213 Local trucking, without storage; automobiles, transport & delivery
PA: Lenore John & Co
1250 Delevan Dr
San Diego CA 92102
619 232-6146

(P-4029)
JACOBS FARM/DEL CABO INC
144 Holm Rd Spc 42, Watsonville (95076-2428)
PHONE.................................831 460-3500
Fax: 831 460-2646
Paul Rabadan, *Branch Mgr*
EMP: 180
SALES (corp-wide): 77.9MM **Privately Held**
WEB: www.delcabo.com
SIC: 4212 5148 Farm to market haulage, local; fresh fruits & vegetables
PA: Jacobs Farm/Del Cabo, Inc.
2450 Stage Rd
Pescadero CA 94060
650 879-0580

(P-4030)
JIM AARTMAN INC (PA)
Also Called: Jim Aartman Milk Transport
805 S Locust Ave, Ripon (95366-2789)
PHONE.................................209 599-5066
Fax: 209 599-8734
Adrian Aartman, *President*
Kathryn Aartman, *Corp Secy*
James Aartman, *Vice Pres*
Cheryl Arbakel, *Office Mgr*
EMP: 120
SQ FT: 40,000
SALES (est): 13.9MM **Privately Held**
SIC: 4212 Liquid haulage, local

(P-4031)
JOHN AGUILAR & COMPANY INC
Also Called: Vernon Transportation Company
1505 Navy Dr, Stockton (95206-4104)
P.O. Box 31450 (95213-1450)
PHONE.................................209 546-0171
Fax: 209 546-0176
Gregg Wilson, *President*
Tony Ketner, *Vice Pres*
Dave Wilson, *Admin Sec*
Dave Ward, *Info Tech Mgr*
Ernie Accuar, *Opers Mgr*
EMP: 85
SQ FT: 5,600
SALES (est): 20.3MM **Privately Held**
WEB: www.sugartrux.com
SIC: 4212 Liquid haulage, local

(P-4032)
JS HOMEN TRUCKING INC
4224 Turlock Rd, Snelling (95369-9729)
P.O. Box 382 (95369-0382)
PHONE.................................209 723-9559
Joe Homen, *President*
Margaret Homen, *Corp Secy*
EMP: 65
SQ FT: 2,484
SALES (est): 1.8MM **Privately Held**
SIC: 4212 Local trucking, without storage

(P-4033)
KEENEY TRUCK LINES INC
3500 Fruitland Ave, Maywood (90270-2008)
PHONE.................................323 589-3231
Dan Hubbard, *President*
Carol Alsip, *Corp Secy*
Mark Dillow, *Director*

EMP: 50
SALES (est): 8.3MM **Privately Held**
WEB: www.keeneytruck.com
SIC: 4212 4731 Local trucking, without storage; freight transportation arrangement

(P-4034)
KELVIN HILDEBRAND INC
6 Lewis Rd, Royal Oaks (95076-5303)
PHONE.................................831 768-9104
Fax: 831 768-1020
Kelvin Hildebrand, *President*
EMP: 50
SALES (est): 1.1MM **Privately Held**
SIC: 4212 Local trucking, without storage

(P-4035)
KFCO INC
Also Called: Labite
12100 W Washington Blvd, Los Angeles (90066-5502)
PHONE.................................310 441-2483
Kenneth Fischer, *President*
EMP: 117 **EST:** 2014
SQ FT: 300
SALES (est): 2.9MM **Privately Held**
SIC: 4212 5812 Delivery service, vehicular; carry-out only (except pizza) restaurant

(P-4036)
KNIGHT TRANSPORTATION INC
4450 S Blackstone St, Tulare (93274-7405)
PHONE.................................559 685-9838
Mark Rogers, *Principal*
EMP: 102
SQ FT: 24,920
SALES (corp-wide): 1.1B **Publicly Held**
SIC: 4212 4213 Local trucking, without storage; trucking, except local
PA: Knight Transportation, Inc.
20002 N 19th Ave
Phoenix AZ 85027
602 269-2000

(P-4037)
MAD DOG EXPRESS INC (PA)
299 Lawrence Ave, South San Francisco (94080-6818)
P.O. Box 281585, San Francisco (94128-1585)
PHONE.................................650 588-1900
Fax: 650 588-4571
Steve Harth, *President*
John Coleman, *Vice Pres*
▲ **EMP:** 70
SQ FT: 18,500
SALES (est): 3.7MM **Privately Held**
WEB: www.maddogexpress.com
SIC: 4212 Local trucking, without storage

(P-4038)
MATHESON POSTAL SERVICES INC
9785 Goethe Rd, Sacramento (95827-3559)
PHONE.................................916 685-2330
Mark Matheson, *President*
Robert B Matheson, *CEO*
Laurie Johnson, *Corp Secy*
Carole L Matheson, *Exec VP*
Tim Noel, *General Mgr*
EMP: 750
SQ FT: 1,000
SALES (est): 80.5MM
SALES (corp-wide): 347.3MM **Privately Held**
SIC: 4212 Mail carriers, contract
PA: Matheson Trucking, Inc.
9785 Goethe Rd
Sacramento CA 95827
916 685-2330

(P-4039)
MIKE CAMPBELL & ASSOCIATES LTD
Also Called: MCA Logistics-Stockton
2121 Boeing Way, Stockton (95206-4934)
PHONE.................................209 234-7920
Fax: 209 234-7972
Megan Mitchell, *Branch Mgr*
EMP: 251

SALES (corp-wide): 123MM **Privately Held**
SIC: 4212 4225 Local trucking, without storage; general warehousing & storage
PA: Mike Campbell & Associates, Ltd.
13031 Temple Ave
City Of Industry CA 91746
626 369-3981

(P-4040)
MIS INTERNATIONAL INC
370 Crenshaw Blvd E206, Torrance (90503-1729)
PHONE.................................310 320-4546
Ken Ishiyama, *President*
Bobby Ortega, *Vice Pres*
EMP: 180
SALES (est): 10.4MM **Privately Held**
SIC: 4212 4214 7361 4731 Local trucking, without storage; local trucking with storage; labor contractors (employment agency); freight consolidation; trucking, except local

(P-4041)
MISSION TRAIL WSTE SYSTEMS INC
Also Called: Recycle Waste
1060 Richard Ave, Santa Clara (95050-2816)
PHONE.................................408 727-5365
Fax: 408 727-7730
Louie Pellegrini, *President*
William Dobert, *CFO*
Robert Molinaro, *Vice Pres*
Maria Gutierrez, *Executive*
Douglas Button, *Admin Sec*
EMP: 75 **EST:** 1960
SALES (est): 16.3MM **Privately Held**
SIC: 4212 4953 Garbage collection & transport, no disposal; recycling, waste materials

(P-4042)
MORE TRUCK LINES INC
1776 All American Way, Corona (92879-2070)
P.O. Box 2229 (92878-2229)
PHONE.................................951 371-6673
Fax: 951 736-3848
Daniel D Sisemore, *President*
Thomas Toscas, *Corp Secy*
William Villalogos, *Software Dev*
Mark Luer, *Agent*
EMP: 80 **EST:** 1952
SQ FT: 800
SALES (est): 5.8MM **Privately Held**
WEB: www.moretrucklines.com
SIC: 4212 Local trucking, without storage

(P-4043)
NEAL TRUCKING INC
9749 Bellegrave Ave, Riverside (92509-2642)
PHONE.................................951 685-5048
Fax: 951 685-8282
Dianne Neal, *CEO*
Randy Neal, *Principal*
EMP: 65
SQ FT: 1,500
SALES (est): 10.9MM **Privately Held**
SIC: 4212 Local trucking, without storage

(P-4044)
NIPPON EX NEC LGSTICS AMER INC
18615 S Ferris Pl, Rancho Dominguez (90220-6452)
PHONE.................................310 604-6100
Fax: 310 604-6160
Kazuhiko Takahashi, *CEO*
Hidehito Tachikawa, *CEO*
Hideo Tsujioka, *Vice Pres*
Brian Driesse, *Info Tech Dir*
Kuin Legaspi, *Accounting Mgr*
▲ **EMP:** 75
SQ FT: 353,000
SALES (est): 23.9MM
SALES (corp-wide): 24.1B **Privately Held**
WEB: www.necam.com
SIC: 4212 4213 4225 Local trucking, without storage; trucking, except local; general warehousing & storage

HQ: Nec Corporation Of America
3929 W John Carpenter Fwy
Irving TX 75063
214 262-6000

(P-4045)
NR 2 GROUP INC
1561 Chapin Unit C, Baldwin Park (91706)
PHONE.................................626 251-6681
CHI On Wong, *CEO*
EMP: 50
SQ FT: 100,000
SALES: 2.5MM **Privately Held**
SIC: 4212 Local trucking, without storage

(P-4046)
OCEAN BLUE ENVMTL SVCS INC (PA)
925 W Esther St, Long Beach (90813-1423)
PHONE.................................562 624-4120
Fax: 562 624-4127
Maria C Lee, *CEO*
Ron Dare, *President*
Moonho C Lee, *CFO*
Scott Tracy, *Sales Executive*
EMP: 63
SQ FT: 5,000
SALES (est): 13.5MM **Privately Held**
WEB: www.ocean-blue.com
SIC: 4212 8734 Hazardous waste transport; hazardous waste testing

(P-4047)
OLDENKAMP TRUCKING INC (PA)
13535 S Union Ave, Bakersfield (93307-9124)
PHONE.................................661 833-3400
Harold Oldenkamp, *CEO*
Dana Oldenkamp, *CFO*
EMP: 56
SALES (est): 6MM **Privately Held**
SIC: 4212 Local trucking, without storage

(P-4048)
PACIFIC WINE DISTRIBUTORS INC
15751 Tapia St, Irwindale (91706-2177)
PHONE.................................626 471-9997
Fax: 626 471-9959
Gino Pacella, *President*
EMP: 85
SQ FT: 46,546
SALES: 6MM **Privately Held**
SIC: 4212 4225 Local trucking, without storage; general warehousing & storage

(P-4049)
PROPANE TRANSPORT SERVICE INC
903 W Center St Ste 7, Manteca (95337-7315)
PHONE.................................209 823-8005
Fax: 209 239-6090
John Paul, *President*
Treca Killough, *Officer*
Jack Penzes, *Vice Pres*
Jan Peterson, *Vice Pres*
Debbie Wilson, *Manager*
EMP: 170
SALES (est): 8.5MM **Privately Held**
WEB: www.economytransport.com
SIC: 4212 Petroleum haulage, local
PA: Kamps Propane, Inc.
1262 Dupont Ct
Manteca CA 95336

(P-4050)
PSC INDUSTRIAL OUTSOURCING LP
62117 Railroad Ave, San Ardo (93450)
P.O. Box 431 (93450-0431)
PHONE.................................831 627-2595
Paul Dewitt, *Principal*
Elaine Talerico, *Human Res Mgr*
EMP: 55 **Privately Held**
WEB: www.tscnow.com
SIC: 4212 Hazardous waste transport
HQ: Psc Industrial Outsourcing, Lp
5151 San Felipe St # 1100
Houston TX
713 623-8777

4212 - Local Trucking Without Storage County (P-4051)

(P-4051)
PT LOGISTICS INC
144 W Lake Ave Ste B, Watsonville (95076-4554)
P.O. Box 1450 (95077-1450)
PHONE..................................831 728-4535
Rainderpau S Tut, *President*
EMP: 50
SALES (est): 2.2MM **Privately Held**
SIC: 4212 Light haulage & cartage, local

(P-4052)
R M S CAR MOVERS CORP
24632 Maple Ln, Harbor City (90710-4551)
PHONE..................................310 325-2192
Ron Snyder, *CEO*
Carol Snyder, *Vice Pres*
EMP: 50
SALES: 2.5MM **Privately Held**
SIC: 4212 Moving services

(P-4053)
RADFORD ALEXANDER CORPORATION
Also Called: Chemtrans
14700 S Avalon Blvd, Gardena (90248-2010)
PHONE..................................310 523-2555
Reginald Lathan, *CEO*
Nancy Lathan, *Vice Pres*
EMP: 55 **EST:** 1973
SQ FT: 4,000
SALES (est): 9.5MM **Privately Held**
WEB: www.chemtrans.com
SIC: 4212 Local trucking, without storage

(P-4054)
RAIL DELIVERY SERVICES INC
8600 Banana Ave, Fontana (92335-3033)
PHONE..................................909 355-4100
Judi Girard, *Ch of Bd*
Sharon Brooks, *President*
Greg Steffire, *CEO*
Jannet Galgani, *CFO*
Ron Smith, *CFO*
EMP: 68
SQ FT: 50,000
SALES (est): 13MM **Privately Held**
WEB: www.raildelivery.com
SIC: 4212 Moving services

(P-4055)
RHINO READY MIX TRUCKING INC (PA)
3701 Pegasus Dr Ste 126, Bakersfield (93308-6843)
P.O. Box 80297 (93380-0297)
PHONE..................................661 679-3643
Freddy Amaya, *President*
Marco Arambula, *Vice Pres*
Jaime Barragan, *Director*
EMP: 50
SALES (est): 8MM **Privately Held**
SIC: 4212 Local trucking, without storage

(P-4056)
ROLO TRANSPORTATION COMPANY
Also Called: Rolo Logistics
9935 Beverly Blvd, Pico Rivera (90660-1812)
P.O. Box 6845 (90661-6845)
PHONE..................................562 463-1440
Fax: 562 463-1441
D Antonio Roman, *President*
Margarita Roman, *Vice Pres*
EMP: 60
SQ FT: 91,000
SALES (est): 6.3MM **Privately Held**
SIC: 4212 Local trucking, without storage

(P-4057)
RON FAULKNER TRUCKING
24134 Road 208, Lindsay (93247-9646)
PHONE..................................559 684-8536
Fax: 559 684-9297
Ronald Faulkner, *Principal*
EMP: 55 **EST:** 2010
SALES (est): 3.4MM **Privately Held**
SIC: 4212 Local trucking, without storage

(P-4058)
ROY MILLER FREIGHT LINES LLC (PA)
3165 E Coronado St, Anaheim (92806-1915)
P.O. Box 18419 (92817-8419)
PHONE..................................714 632-5511
Fax: 714 632-5522
Danny Miller, *CEO*
Lyle Stone, *Opers Mgr*
Wiley R Miller Jr, *Mng Member*
EMP: 100 **EST:** 1942
SALES (est): 27.1MM **Privately Held**
WEB: www.roymiller.com
SIC: 4212 Local trucking, without storage

(P-4059)
RUAN
830 W Glenwood Ave, Turlock (95380-5751)
PHONE..................................209 634-4928
Bill Hagney, *Manager*
EMP: 85
SALES (corp-wide): 6MM **Privately Held**
SIC: 4212 Local trucking, without storage
PA: Ruan
1354 S Blackstone St
Tulare CA 93274
559 688-0591

(P-4060)
RUSH ENTERPRISES INC
15463 Valley Blvd, Fontana (92335-6347)
P.O. Box 223, Pico Rivera (90660-0223)
PHONE..................................800 776-3647
EMP: 125
SALES (corp-wide): 4.9B **Publicly Held**
SIC: 4212 Local trucking, without storage
PA: Rush Enterprises, Inc.
555 S Ih 35 Ste 500
New Braunfels TX 78130
830 302-5200

(P-4061)
SAM FREITAS TRUCKING INC
2420 E Eight Mile Rd, Stockton (95210-9600)
PHONE..................................209 474-0294
Fax: 209 474-0419
Sam Freitas, *President*
Marie Freitas, *Vice Pres*
EMP: 70
SQ FT: 3,600
SALES (est): 4.7MM **Privately Held**
WEB: www.sfti.us
SIC: 4212 Local trucking, without storage

(P-4062)
SANTA MONICA EXPRESS INC
12424 Wilshire Blvd # 740, Los Angeles (90025-1052)
P.O. Box 7457, Santa Monica (90406-7457)
PHONE..................................310 458-6000
Fax: 310 395-9004
Muhammed Mahmodi, *President*
Afshin Roohani, *Vice Pres*
Edwin Valvez, *Manager*
EMP: 65
SQ FT: 3,500
SALES (est): 5.5MM **Privately Held**
WEB: www.smexpress.com
SIC: 4212 Delivery service, vehicular

(P-4063)
SHIPBYCOM LLC
Also Called: Sb Freight
900 Turnbull Canyon Rd, City of Industry (91745-1404)
PHONE..................................626 271-9800
James Lin, *President*
Wing Lau, *Controller*
EMP: 80
SALES (est): 2MM **Privately Held**
SIC: 4212 Local trucking, without storage

(P-4064)
SHUSTERS TRANSPORTATION INC
750 E Valley St, Willits (95490-9749)
PHONE..................................707 459-4131
Fax: 707 459-1855
Phillip L Shuster, *President*
Marvin Lawrence, *Corp Secy*
Steve Shuster, *Vice Pres*
EMP: 100
SQ FT: 3,000
SALES (est): 7MM **Privately Held**
SIC: 4212 Local trucking, without storage

(P-4065)
SIERRA TRANSPORT INC
12856 Old River Rd, Bakersfield (93311-9707)
PHONE..................................661 836-3166
Roy Lutrel, *President*
Mark Lutrel, *Vice Pres*
Gayle Lutrel, *Admin Sec*
EMP: 53
SALES (est): 5.9MM **Privately Held**
WEB: www.sierratransport.com
SIC: 4212 Local trucking, without storage

(P-4066)
SILVA TRUCKING INC
36 W Mathews Rd, French Camp (95231-9684)
P.O. Box 1449 (95231-1449)
PHONE..................................209 982-1114
Fax: 209 982-5834
David Silva, *President*
Judy Askes, *Manager*
EMP: 50 **EST:** 1943
SALES (est): 8.8MM **Privately Held**
SIC: 4212 Local trucking, without storage

(P-4067)
SO CAL TRUCK MANAGEMENT
Also Called: So-Cal Truck Management
1742 Burgundy Rd, Encinitas (92024-1209)
P.O. Box 9806, Rancho Santa Fe (92067-4806)
PHONE..................................858 759-1964
Edward Hayes, *Owner*
EMP: 75
SQ FT: 2,700
SALES (est): 3MM **Privately Held**
SIC: 4212 4731 Truck rental with drivers; truck transportation brokers

(P-4068)
SOUTHWEST EXPRESS LLC
1720 E Garry Ave Ste 107, Santa Ana (92705-5831)
PHONE..................................949 474-5038
Fax: 949 474-5080
Bill Ruxby,
William Roxby, *Financial Exec*
Ron Lind,
Charles McDonald,
Michael O'Brien,
EMP: 60
SQ FT: 1,000
SALES (est): 1.2MM **Privately Held**
WEB: www.southwestexpress.net
SIC: 4212 4731 Delivery service, vehicular; freight transportation arrangement

(P-4069)
SUGAR TRANSPORT OF THE NW
5463 Cherokee Rd, Stockton (95215-1128)
PHONE..................................209 931-3587
Gary Scannavino, *President*
Leanne Scannavino, *Corp Secy*
Jack Riella, *Vice Pres*
EMP: 100
SQ FT: 1,000
SALES (est): 6.2MM **Privately Held**
SIC: 4212 Farm to market haulage, local

(P-4070)
TALLEY TRANSPORTATION
12325 Road 29, Madera (93638-8401)
P.O. Box 568 (93639-0568)
PHONE..................................559 673-9013
Martin Talley, *CEO*
Kenneth Talley, *Vice Pres*
EMP: 57
SQ FT: 5,500
SALES (est): 7.5MM **Privately Held**
WEB: www.talleytrans.com
SIC: 4212 Local trucking, without storage

(P-4071)
TIMMERMAN STARLITE TRCKG INC
3955 Starlite Dr, Ceres (95307-9733)
P.O. Box 2710 (95307-7710)
PHONE..................................209 538-1706
Molly Craver-Peck, *CEO*
Agnes Timmerman, *Corp Secy*
Geneveve Timmerman, *Vice Pres*
EMP: 65 **EST:** 1976
SALES (est): 15.4MM **Privately Held**
SIC: 4212 Farm to market haulage, local

(P-4072)
TRAIL LINES INC
9415 Sorensen Ave, Santa Fe Springs (90670-2648)
P.O. Box 3567 (90670-1567)
PHONE..................................562 758-6980
Ofer Shitrit, *CEO*
Reuven Spivak, *Vice Pres*
Lisa Trujillo, *Accountant*
Adriana Ortega, *Manager*
EMP: 75
SALES (est): 18.2MM **Privately Held**
SIC: 4212 4789 Local trucking, without storage; pipeline terminal facilities, independently operated

(P-4073)
TRANSPORTATION MANAGEMENT LLC
880 Apollo St Ste 235, El Segundo (90245-4752)
PHONE..................................310 524-1555
Fax: 310 524-1556
Eric Reese,
Chris Carey,
EMP: 50
SQ FT: 14,000
SALES: 5.4MM **Privately Held**
SIC: 4212 4513 Delivery service, vehicular; air courier services

(P-4074)
TRIPLE E TRUCKING
1215 E White Ln, Bakersfield (93307-5061)
PHONE..................................661 834-0071
Fax: 661 366-3386
Mike Ehoff, *Partner*
Jim Ehoff, *Partner*
Loretta Ehoff, *Partner*
EMP: 50
SALES (est): 5.7MM **Privately Held**
SIC: 4212 Local trucking, without storage

(P-4075)
TST INC
Timco
11601 Etiwanda Ave, Fontana (92337-6929)
P.O. Box 1563, Wildomar (92595-1563)
PHONE..................................310 835-0115
Andrew G Stein, *CEO*
EMP: 100
SALES (corp-wide): 81.2MM **Privately Held**
SIC: 4212 Local trucking, without storage
PA: Tst, Inc.
13428 Benson Ave
Chino CA 91710
951 685-2155

(P-4076)
UNION ASPHALT INC
1625 E Donovan Rd, Santa Maria (93454-2500)
PHONE..................................805 922-3551
George Hamill, *President*
Andy Hermreck, *Admin Sec*
EMP: 60
SQ FT: 4,000
SALES (est): 2.6MM **Privately Held**
SIC: 4212 Dump truck haulage

(P-4077)
UNITED PUMPING SERVICE INC
14000 Valley Blvd, City of Industry (91746-2801)
PHONE..................................626 961-9326
Fax: 626 336-7734
Eduardo T Perry Jr, *President*
Eduardo Perry Jr, *Corp Secy*
Daniel C Perry, *Vice Pres*
Margaret Perry, *Vice Pres*

PRODUCTS & SERVICES SECTION

4213 - Trucking, Except Local County (P-4099)

Pamela Heintz, *Sales Staff*
EMP: 95
SQ FT: 25,000
SALES (est): 37.9MM **Privately Held**
WEB: www.unitedpumping.com
SIC: 4212 Local trucking, without storage; hazardous waste transport

(P-4078)
UNIVERSAL MAIL DELIVERY SVC (PA)
Also Called: Universal Custom Courier
501 S Brand Blvd Ste 4, San Fernando (91340-4931)
P.O. Box 60250, Los Angeles (90060-0250)
PHONE 818 997-7531
Fax: 818 780-5926
Bernard Reznick, *CEO*
Barbara Reznick, *Shareholder*
Saddie Reznick, *Shareholder*
EMP: 95
SQ FT: 1,000
SALES (est): 12.5MM **Privately Held**
WEB: www.umds.biz
SIC: 4212 Delivery service, vehicular

(P-4079)
UNIVERSAL MAIL DELIVERY SVC
220 W Victoria St, Compton (90220-6034)
PHONE 310 884-5900
EMP: 68
SALES (corp-wide): 12.5MM **Privately Held**
SIC: 4212 Delivery service, vehicular
PA: Universal Mail Delivery Service
501 S Brand Blvd Ste 4
San Fernando CA 91340
818 997-7531

(P-4080)
USA WASTE OF CALIFORNIA INC
Also Called: Sac Val Waste Disposal
8761 Younger Creek Dr, Sacramento (95828-1023)
PHONE 916 379-2611
Alex Oseguerra, *General Mgr*
Ginger Kaladas, *Credit Staff*
Lee Hicks, *Contract Law*
EMP: 115
SALES (corp-wide): 12.9B **Publicly Held**
SIC: 4212 4953 Garbage collection & transport, no disposal; refuse systems
HQ: Usa Waste Of California, Inc.
11931 Foundation Pl # 200
Gold River CA 95670
916 387-1400

(P-4081)
USA WASTE OF CALIFORNIA INC
Also Called: Carmel Marina
11240 Commercial Pkwy, Castroville (95012-3206)
P.O. Box 1306 (95012-1306)
PHONE 831 384-4860
George Reddom, *President*
Lee Hicks, *Contract Law*
Jesse Tellas, *Manager*
EMP: 120
SALES (est): 6.3MM **Privately Held**
SIC: 4212 Local trucking, without storage

(P-4082)
USA WASTE OF CALIFORNIA INC
Also Called: Stockton Scavengers Assn
1240 Navy Dr, Stockton (95206-1167)
PHONE 209 946-5721
Fax: 209 948-4013
Frank Jarvis, *Branch Mgr*
Earl Defrates, *CFO*
Ginger Kaladas, *Credit Staff*
Lee Hicks, *Contract Law*
Osvaldo Jauregui, *Manager*
EMP: 50
SALES (corp-wide): 12.9B **Publicly Held**
SIC: 4212 Garbage collection & transport, no disposal
HQ: Usa Waste Of California, Inc.
11931 Foundation Pl # 200
Gold River CA 95670
916 387-1400

(P-4083)
USA WASTE OF CALIFORNIA INC
Also Called: Waste Management Nevada County
13083 Grass Valley Ave, Grass Valley (95945-9325)
PHONE 530 274-3090
Art Rassmussen, *Principal*
Ginger Kaladas, *Credit Staff*
Lee Hicks, *Contract Law*
EMP: 50
SQ FT: 8,000
SALES (corp-wide): 12.9B **Publicly Held**
SIC: 4212 8748 4953 Garbage collection & transport, no disposal; business consulting; refuse systems
HQ: Usa Waste Of California, Inc.
11931 Foundation Pl # 200
Gold River CA 95670
916 387-1400

(P-4084)
VALLEY AGGREGATE TRANSPORT INC
753 N George Wash Blvd, Yuba City (95993-9065)
PHONE 530 821-2600
Fax: 530 854-5910
Kevin Cotter, *CEO*
Lori Carrol, *Director*
EMP: 65
SALES (est): 4.2MM **Privately Held**
WEB: www.valleyaggregate.com
SIC: 4212 Local trucking, without storage; trucking, except local

(P-4085)
VALLEY COURIERS INC
1111 W Twn And Cntry Rd # 28, Orange (92868-4667)
PHONE 714 541-0111
Cyrus Ghasseni, *Manager*
EMP: 75
SALES (corp-wide): 13.7MM **Privately Held**
SIC: 4212 Local trucking, without storage
PA: Valley Couriers, Inc
646 N San Fernando Rd
Los Angeles CA 90065
818 591-2212

(P-4086)
VALLEY COURIERS INC (PA)
646 N San Fernando Rd, Los Angeles (90065-1031)
P.O. Box 8036, Calabasas (91372-8036)
PHONE 818 591-2212
Fax: 818 222-5889
Nasrollah Alamdari, *President*
Hassan Alamadari, *Vice Pres*
Asdullah Alamdari, *Vice Pres*
EMP: 65
SQ FT: 8,000
SALES (est): 13.7MM **Privately Held**
SIC: 4212 Delivery service, vehicular

(P-4087)
VAN DYK TANK LINES INC
Also Called: Cool Transport
1800 S Riverside Ave, Colton (92324-3349)
P.O. Box 341, Bloomington (92316-0341)
PHONE 951 682-5000
Fax: 951 682-1882
Ronald Nuckles, *President*
EMP: 50
SALES (est): 6.4MM **Privately Held**
SIC: 4212 4213 Local trucking, without storage; trucking, except local

(P-4088)
VAN KING & STORAGE INC (PA)
Also Called: King Relocation Services
13535 Larwin Cir, Santa Fe Springs (90670-5032)
PHONE 562 921-0555
Fax: 562 407-5092
Steve Komorous, *President*
Edwin Nabal, *CFO*
Keith Hindsley, *Senior VP*
Jj Krukenkamp, *Vice Pres*
Mary O'Donnell, *Vice Pres*
EMP: 74
SQ FT: 60,000
SALES: 16MM **Privately Held**
WEB: www.kingrelocation.com
SIC: 4212 4225 Moving services; general warehousing & storage

(P-4089)
VPL INC
Also Called: Vpl Transport
11199 N Highway 99, Lodi (95240-6810)
PHONE 209 931-2682
Vincent P Loduca Jr, *President*
Betty Loduca, *Corp Secy*
Sandra Glasgow, *Accounts Mgr*
EMP: 100
SQ FT: 10,000
SALES (est): 6.2MM **Privately Held**
SIC: 4212 Local trucking, without storage

(P-4090)
WAITERS ON WHEELS INC (PA)
Also Called: Home Dining Restaurant Guide
5425 Mission St, San Francisco (94112-3739)
P.O. Box 12248 (94112-0248)
PHONE 415 452-6600
Fax: 415 255-9143
Panagiotis Zarikos, *President*
Fernando J Hidalgo, *CFO*
Gus Hidalgo, *Vice Pres*
Angie Zarikos, *Vice Pres*
EMP: 200
SQ FT: 2,000
SALES (est): 15.1MM **Privately Held**
WEB: www.waitersonwheels.com
SIC: 4212 5812 4215 Delivery service, vehicular; eating places; courier services, except by air

(P-4091)
WASTE MANAGEMENT CAL INC
Also Called: Environmental Recovery Svcs
15902 S Main St, Gardena (90248-2551)
PHONE 562 427-7277
Robert Scott, *Branch Mgr*
EMP: 75
SALES (corp-wide): 12.9B **Publicly Held**
SIC: 4212 Hazardous waste transport
HQ: Waste Management Of California, Inc.
9081 Tujunga Ave
Sun Valley CA 91352
877 836-6526

(P-4092)
WASTE MGT COLLECTN & RECYCL
2658 N Main St, Walnut Creek (94597-2729)
PHONE 925 935-8900
Ronald J Proto, *Manager*
Barry Caldwell, *Vice Pres*
Richard Felago, *Vice Pres*
Jeff Harris, *Vice Pres*
Jay Romans, *Vice Pres*
EMP: 170
SALES (corp-wide): 12.9B **Publicly Held**
SIC: 4212 4953 Garbage collection & transport, no disposal; refuse systems
HQ: Waste Management Collection And Recycling Inc
2050 N Glassell St
Orange CA 92865
714 282-0200

(P-4093)
WESTAR TRANSPORT
9220 E South Ave, Selma (93662-9768)
PHONE 559 834-3551
Fax: 559 834-3133
Ronald J Silva, *President*
Marcie Silva, *Admin Sec*
EMP: 53
SQ FT: 3,400
SALES (est): 5.3MM **Privately Held**
WEB: www.westartransport.com
SIC: 4212 Local trucking, without storage

(P-4094)
WESTERN MESSENGER SERVICE INC
75 Columbia Sq, San Francisco (94103-4099)
PHONE 415 487-4229
Fax: 415 864-6238
Dennis Golladay, *President*
Joe McManus, *President*
Raymond Corsetti, *Chief Mktg Ofcr*
Barbara Driscoll, *Office Mgr*
Patty Sokolecki, *Admin Sec*
EMP: 115
SQ FT: 11,000
SALES (est): 10.6MM **Privately Held**
WEB: www.westernmessenger.com
SIC: 4212 Delivery service, vehicular

(P-4095)
XPO CARTAGE INC (DH)
Also Called: Pacer
5800 Sheila St, Commerce (90040-2322)
PHONE 800 837-7584
Daniel W Avramovich, *CEO*
Val T Noel, *President*
John J Hafferty, *Exec VP*
Julie A Krehbiel, *Exec VP*
James E Ward, *Exec VP*
EMP: 60
SQ FT: 16,000
SALES (est): 18.9MM
SALES (corp-wide): 7.6B **Publicly Held**
WEB: www.pacercartage.com
SIC: 4212 Local trucking, without storage
HQ: Xpo Intermodal, Inc.
5165 Emerald Pkwy 300
Dublin OH 43017
614 923-1400

4213 Trucking, Except Local

(P-4096)
A C FREIGHT SYSTEMS INC (PA)
850 Service St, San Jose (95112-1360)
P.O. Box 90816, City of Industry (91715-0816)
PHONE 408 392-8900
Fax: 408 392-8914
Blair Johnson, *President*
Edgar Sogg, *Vice Pres*
Maria Greber, *Manager*
EMP: 85
SQ FT: 20,000
SALES (est): 7.7MM **Privately Held**
SIC: 4213 Trucking, except local

(P-4097)
ABF FREIGHT SYSTEM INC
2135 Otoole Ave, San Jose (95131-1314)
PHONE 408 435-8550
Fax: 408 435-0161
Penny Podio, *Manager*
Aaron Gold, *General Mgr*
James Lewis, *Manager*
EMP: 50
SALES (corp-wide): 2.6B **Publicly Held**
WEB: www.abfs.com
SIC: 4213 Trucking, except local
HQ: Abf Freight System, Inc.
3801 Old Greenwood Rd
Fort Smith AR 72903
479 785-8700

(P-4098)
ABF FREIGHT SYSTEM INC
8001 Telegraph Rd, Pico Rivera (90660-4822)
PHONE 323 773-2580
Kelly Underwood, *Manager*
Phil Smith, *Branch Mgr*
Mavis Buck, *Manager*
EMP: 50
SALES (corp-wide): 2.6B **Publicly Held**
WEB: www.abfs.com
SIC: 4213 Trucking, except local
HQ: Abf Freight System, Inc.
3801 Old Greenwood Rd
Fort Smith AR 72903
479 785-8700

(P-4099)
ABF FREIGHT SYSTEM INC
4575 Tidewater Ave, Oakland (94601-3917)
PHONE 510 533-8575
Fax: 510 533-3020
Josh Eversville, *Manager*
Doug Thiel, *Branch Mgr*
EMP: 70
SQ FT: 10,000

4213 - Trucking, Except Local County (P-4100)

SALES (corp-wide): 2.6B **Publicly Held**
WEB: www.abfs.com
SIC: 4213 Trucking, except local
HQ: Abf Freight System, Inc.
3801 Old Greenwood Rd
Fort Smith AR 72903
479 785-8700

(P-4100)
ABF FREIGHT SYSTEM INC
1601 N Batavia St, Orange (92867-3508)
PHONE.................................714 974-2485
Fax: 714 974-2384
Jerry Wright, *Manager*
EMP: 50
SQ FT: 13,326
SALES (corp-wide): 2.6B **Publicly Held**
WEB: www.abfs.com
SIC: 4213 Trucking, except local
HQ: Abf Freight System, Inc.
3801 Old Greenwood Rd
Fort Smith AR 72903
479 785-8700

(P-4101)
ABF FREIGHT SYSTEM INC
3250 47th Ave, Sacramento (95824-2441)
PHONE.................................916 428-3531
Fax: 916 393-2513
David Fox, *General Mgr*
Jeremy Sands, *General Mgr*
EMP: 65
SALES (corp-wide): 2.6B **Publicly Held**
WEB: www.abfs.com
SIC: 4213 Trucking, except local
HQ: Abf Freight System, Inc.
3801 Old Greenwood Rd
Fort Smith AR 72903
479 785-8700

(P-4102)
ABF FREIGHT SYSTEM INC
10744 Almond Ave, Fontana (92337-7153)
PHONE.................................909 355-9805
Fax: 909 355-9894
Matt Trirta, *Manager*
Jeff Ferber, *Safety Dir*
Jason Apple, *Opers Mgr*
Chris Fair, *Manager*
Gary Gutensohn, *Supervisor*
EMP: 200
SQ FT: 30,248
SALES (corp-wide): 2.6B **Publicly Held**
WEB: www.abfs.com
SIC: 4213 Trucking, except local
HQ: Abf Freight System, Inc.
3801 Old Greenwood Rd
Fort Smith AR 72903
479 785-8700

(P-4103)
ACE RELOCATION SYSTEMS INC (PA)
5608 Eastgate Dr, San Diego (92121-2816)
PHONE.................................858 677-5500
Fax: 858 677-5588
Lawrence R Lammers, *President*
Paul Sanford, *CFO*
Gary Bialowas, *Vice Pres*
Michelle Blake, *Vice Pres*
Carrie Corless, *Vice Pres*
EMP: 69
SQ FT: 48,000
SALES: 65MM **Privately Held**
WEB: www.acerelocation.com
SIC: 4213 Household goods transport

(P-4104)
ADVANCED LOGISTICS MGT INC
Also Called: Advanced Trans Grp
19067 S Reyes Ave, Compton (90221-5813)
PHONE.................................310 638-0715
Rene Edmunds, *President*
Gerald R Edmunds, *Vice Pres*
EMP: 50
SQ FT: 100,000
SALES (est): 8.3MM **Privately Held**
SIC: 4213 Trucking, except local

(P-4105)
AMAR TRANSPORTATION INC (PA)
Also Called: Paul Trucking
144 W Lake Ave Ste C, Watsonville (95076-4554)
P.O. Box 39 (95077-0039)
PHONE.................................831 728-8209
Fax: 831 728-4697
Amarjit S Tut, *President*
Surjit S Tut, *Treasurer*
Paritan S Tut, *Vice Pres*
Ranjit S Tut, *Vice Pres*
Robert Dawkins, *Opers Staff*
EMP: 130
SQ FT: 4,872
SALES (est): 11MM **Privately Held**
SIC: 4213 4212 Trucking, except local; local trucking, without storage

(P-4106)
AMERICAN FREIGHTWAYS LP
10845 Rancho Bernardo Rd # 100, San Diego (92127-2107)
PHONE.................................866 326-5902
Fax: 858 217-3305
Kirk Carmichael, *General Ptnr*
Mark Goodacre, *General Ptnr*
Jon Hyemaster, *Branch Mgr*
Renee Goodacre, *Accountant*
Stephen McMath, *VP Human Res*
EMP: 62
SQ FT: 10,000
SALES (est): 17.7MM **Privately Held**
SIC: 4213 Trucking, except local

(P-4107)
AMERICAN LINEHAUL CORPORATION
12333 S Van Ness Ave, Hawthorne (90250-3320)
PHONE.................................323 418-8900
Daniel Kuric, *General Mgr*
EMP: 98
SALES (corp-wide): 25MM **Privately Held**
SIC: 4213 Trucking, except local
PA: American Linehaul Corporation
9 Mount Bethel Rd Ste 206
Warren NJ 07059
973 589-0101

(P-4108)
AMERICAN WEST
511 Zaca Ln Ste 120, San Luis Obispo (93401)
PHONE.................................805 926-2800
Fax: 805 926-2817
Josh Brown, *CEO*
EMP: 50 EST: 2014
SALES (est): 2.7MM **Privately Held**
SIC: 4213 Heavy hauling

(P-4109)
AMGEN DISTRIBUTION INC
1910 Palomar Oaks Way, Carlsbad (92008-6510)
PHONE.................................760 438-2538
Richard Neil Berry, *President*
EMP: 73
SALES (est): 5.3MM **Privately Held**
SIC: 4213 Trucking, except local

(P-4110)
AMGEN DISTRIBUTION INC
1244 Valley View Rd # 119, Glendale (91202-1752)
PHONE.................................760 989-4424
Richard Berry, *President*
EMP: 73
SQ FT: 3,900
SALES (est): 5.2MM **Privately Held**
SIC: 4213 Trucking, except local

(P-4111)
ARDWIN INC
Also Called: Ardwin Freight
2940 N Hollywood Way, Burbank (91505-1024)
P.O. Box 1609 (91507-1609)
PHONE.................................818 767-7777
Fax: 818 767-8182
Edwin Sahakian, *President*
Richard Breault, *Info Tech Mgr*
Rouben Oshian, *Technology*
Oscar Calderon, *Manager*
Saul Fernandez, *Manager*
EMP: 130
SQ FT: 10,000
SALES (est): 34.5MM **Privately Held**
WEB: www.ardwin.com
SIC: 4213 Trucking, except local

(P-4112)
ASBURY TRANSPORTATION CO
2144 Parker Ln, Bakersfield (93308-6036)
PHONE.................................661 327-2271
Richard Boyer, *President*
Bruce Haupt, *Vice Pres*
Rolando Ramos, *Traffic Dir*
Mike Hinson, *Director*
Jeff Ferguson, *Manager*
EMP: 52
SQ FT: 2,100
SALES (est): 11.4MM **Privately Held**
WEB: www.asburytrans.com
SIC: 4213 Trucking, except local

(P-4113)
ATECH WAREHOUSING & DIST INC (PA)
7 College Ave, Santa Rosa (95401-4702)
P.O. Box 6836 (95406-0836)
PHONE.................................707 526-1910
Fax: 707 526-1924
Jesse E Amaral, *President*
Geri Amaral, *Vice Pres*
Travis Northern, *Opers Staff*
EMP: 60
SQ FT: 35,000
SALES (est): 16.2MM **Privately Held**
WEB: www.atechdist.com
SIC: 4213 Less-than-truckload (LTL) transport

(P-4114)
BERT E JESSUP TRANSPORTATION
641 Old Gilroy St, Gilroy (95020-6233)
PHONE.................................408 848-3390
Fax: 408 848-5943
Leonard Milanowski, *CEO*
Len Milanowski, *CFO*
Robin Jessup, *Admin Sec*
Ken Fry, *Safety Dir*
Leonard Milan, *Agent*
EMP: 85
SQ FT: 10,000
SALES (est): 15.8MM **Privately Held**
WEB: www.jessup.net
SIC: 4213 Trucking, except local

(P-4115)
BETTENDORF ENTERPRISES INC
Also Called: Bettendorf Trucking
20943 Bettendorf Way, Anderson (96007-8721)
PHONE.................................530 365-1937
Fax: 530 365-1957
Mike Tully, *Branch Mgr*
Josh Youngman, *Human Res Mgr*
EMP: 60
SALES (corp-wide): 35.1MM **Privately Held**
WEB: www.bettendorftrucking.com
SIC: 4213 Contract haulers
PA: Bettendorf Enterprises, Inc.
4545 West End Rd
Arcata CA 95521
707 822-0173

(P-4116)
BHANDAL BROS INC
2490 San Juan Rd, Hollister (95023-9107)
P.O. Box 190 (95024-0190)
PHONE.................................831 728-2691
Maninder Singh, *President*
EMP: 50 EST: 2012
SALES (est): 9MM **Privately Held**
SIC: 4213 Trucking, except local

(P-4117)
BHANDAL BROS TRUCKING INC
2490 San Juan Rd, Hollister (95023-9107)
P.O. Box 1900 (95024-1900)
PHONE.................................831 728-2691
Mangal S Bhandal, *President*
Ruthie Evans, *Safety Dir*
Manny Bhandal, *Director*
EMP: 55
SQ FT: 4,000
SALES (est): 14MM **Privately Held**
WEB: www.bhandalbrotherstrucking.com
SIC: 4213 Refrigerated products transport

(P-4118)
BJJ COMPANY LLC (PA)
Also Called: Westland Trailer Mfg
1040 W Kettleman Ln, Lodi (95240-6056)
PHONE.................................209 941-8361
Fax: 209 941-0476
EMP: 70
SQ FT: 4,000
SALES: 12.1MM **Privately Held**
SIC: 4213

(P-4119)
BLUE CHIP MOVING AND STOR INC
Also Called: Blue Chip Mayflower
13525 Crenshaw Blvd, Hawthorne (90250-7811)
PHONE.................................323 463-6888
Fax: 310 978-2287
Dennis Doody, *CEO*
Jack Doody, *Vice Pres*
EMP: 55 EST: 1963
SQ FT: 30,000
SALES (est): 8.9MM **Privately Held**
SIC: 4213 4214 Household goods transport; contract haulers; local trucking with storage

(P-4120)
BUDWAY ENTERPRISES INC (PA)
Also Called: Budway Trucking & Warehousing
13600 Napa St, Fontana (92335-2944)
PHONE.................................909 463-0500
Fax: 909 463-0552
Vincent McLeod, *CEO*
Vincent Mc Leod Jr, *President*
Jim Barbour, *CFO*
Daniel Heykoop, *Exec VP*
Marcy McKenzie, *Vice Pres*
EMP: 55 EST: 1974
SQ FT: 120,000
SALES (est): 20.2MM **Privately Held**
SIC: 4213 Contract haulers

(P-4121)
BUILDING SERVICES MAINT INC
Also Called: BUILDING SERVICES MAINTENANCE,INC.
7677 Oakport St, Oakland (94621-1929)
PHONE.................................510 636-1224
Sam Martinovich, *Branch Mgr*
EMP: 172
SALES (corp-wide): 11.3MM **Privately Held**
SIC: 4213 Heavy hauling
PA: Dave Calhoun And Associates, Llc
2575 Stanwell Dr Ste 100
Concord CA 94520
925 688-1234

(P-4122)
BULK TRANSPORTATION (PA)
415 S Lemon Ave, Walnut (91789-2911)
P.O. Box 390 (91788-0390)
PHONE.................................909 594-2855
Fax: 909 595-9983
Brett Richardson, *President*
Gary K Cross, *President*
George G Cross, *CEO*
Frank Cutter, *Vice Pres*
Jeff Machado, *Vice Pres*
▲ EMP: 60
SQ FT: 3,500
SALES: 38.4MM **Privately Held**
WEB: www.bulk-dti.com
SIC: 4213 4789 Trucking, except local; cargo loading & unloading services

(P-4123)
BUTTON TRANSPORTATION INC
8629 Robben Rd, Dixon (95620-9608)
PHONE.................................707 678-1983
Fax: 707 678-4603
Robert Button, *President*
Anthony Iten, *President*
Barbara Allen, *Controller*

PRODUCTS & SERVICES SECTION

4213 - Trucking, Except Local County (P-4146)

Christopher Reeding, *Controller*
Dan Sartel, *Opers Mgr*
EMP: 175
SQ FT: 5,000
SALES (est): 26.6MM **Privately Held**
SIC: 4213 Trucking, except local; liquid petroleum transport, non-local

(P-4124)
CALIFRNIA INTERMODAL ASSOC INC (PA)
6666 E Washington Blvd, Commerce (90040-1814)
PHONE 323 562-7788
Gabriel Chaul, *CEO*
Alfredo Garcia, *Controller*
Elias Chaul, *Opers Mgr*
EMP: 50
SALES (est): 4.6MM **Privately Held**
WEB: www.ciatrucking.com
SIC: 4213 Trucking, except local

(P-4125)
CERTIFIED FRT LOGISTICS INC (PA)
1344 White Ct, Santa Maria (93458-3732)
P.O. Box 5668 (93456-5668)
PHONE 805 925-9900
Fax: 805 346-7803
James O Nelson, *President*
Scott Cramer, *CFO*
Jon Cramer, *Vice Pres*
Edwin F Nelson Jr, *Vice Pres*
Racel Cota, *Accounting Mgr*
EMP: 120
SQ FT: 40,000
SALES: 38.4MM **Privately Held**
WEB: www.cfl-usa.com
SIC: 4213 Refrigerated products transport

(P-4126)
CHEEMA FREIGHTLINES LLC
223 W 5th St, Ripon (95366-2771)
P.O. Box 2224, Sumner WA (98390-0490)
PHONE 209 599-0777
Harman Sinh,
Simarjit Kaur,
Sam Sinh, *Manager*
EMP: 70
SQ FT: 1,900
SALES: 21.8MM **Privately Held**
SIC: 4213 Trucking, except local

(P-4127)
CHIPMAN CORPORATION
Also Called: Unitd Van Lines Agnt
1555 Zephyr Ave, Hayward (94544-7835)
PHONE 510 748-8787
Fax: 510 748-8729
John Chipman Jr, *Branch Mgr*
Tom Byron, *Business Dir*
Gina Ellis, *Asst Mgr*
EMP: 60
SALES (corp-wide): 24.7MM **Privately Held**
WEB: www.chipmancorp.com
SIC: 4213 4212 Trucking, except local; moving services
PA: Chipman Corporation
1040 Marina Village Pkwy # 100
Alameda CA 94501
510 748-8700

(P-4128)
CONTRACTORS CARGO COMPANY (PA)
Also Called: Contractors Rigging & Erectors
500 S Alameda St, Compton (90221-3801)
P.O. Box 5290 (90224-5290)
PHONE 310 609-1957
Fax: 310 609-1767
Carla Ann Wheeler, *CEO*
Gerald D Wheeler, *President*
Kimberly Dorio, *Corp Secy*
Jean Charles, *Office Mgr*
Jim Cunningham, *Project Mgr*
EMP: 80
SQ FT: 25,000
SALES: 42.3MM **Privately Held**
WEB: www.contractorscargo.com
SIC: 4213 4731 1623 4741 Contract haulers; freight transportation arrangement; water, sewer & utility lines; rental of railroad cars; cargo loading & unloading services; boiler maintenance contractor

(P-4129)
CRST INTERNATIONAL INC
10641 Calabash Ave, Fontana (92337-7011)
PHONE 909 829-1313
EMP: 149
SALES (corp-wide): 2B **Privately Held**
SIC: 4213
PA: Crst International, Inc.
3930 16th Ave Sw
Cedar Rapids IA 52404
319 396-4400

(P-4130)
CUNHA DRAYING INC
1500 Madruga Rd, Lathrop (95330-9779)
PHONE 209 858-1400
Fax: 209 858-1455
Paul Buttini, *President*
Peggy Deforest, *Vice Pres*
Sunny Enos, *Controller*
Paul F Bottini, *Agent*
EMP: 65
SQ FT: 10,000
SALES (est): 10MM **Privately Held**
WEB: www.cunhadraying.com
SIC: 4213 Contract haulers

(P-4131)
D E F EXPRESS CORPORATION
2626 S Railroad Ave, Fresno (93725-1925)
P.O. Box 12427 (93777-2427)
PHONE 559 264-0500
Mike Shuemake, *President*
EMP: 100
SQ FT: 20,000
SALES (est): 7.6MM **Privately Held**
SIC: 4213 Trucking, except local

(P-4132)
DAYLIGHT TRANSPORT LLC (PA)
1501 Hughes Way Ste 200, Long Beach (90810-1879)
P.O. Box 93155 (90809-3155)
PHONE 310 507-8200
Richard S Breen, *CEO*
Jim Mc Carthy, *CFO*
Edward Marsh, *Vice Pres*
Jonathan Jamias, *Administration*
Gary McElligatt, *Info Tech Dir*
EMP: 100 **EST:** 1997
SQ FT: 3,000
SALES (est): 44.6MM **Privately Held**
WEB: www.dylt.com
SIC: 4213 Trucking, except local

(P-4133)
DC TRANSPORT INC
5411 Raley Blvd, Sacramento (95838-1726)
PHONE 916 438-0888
Andrew Romanov, *President*
Sergey Romanov, *Vice Pres*
Evelina R Popovich, *Admin Sec*
EMP: 60
SQ FT: 21,000
SALES (est): 21MM **Privately Held**
WEB: www.dctransport.com
SIC: 4213 Trucking, except local

(P-4134)
DEPENDABLE AUTO SHIPPERS INC
18004 S Broadway, Gardena (90248-3538)
PHONE 310 719-9915
Fax: 310 719-9643
Bob London, *Branch Mgr*
Amanda Jones, *Vice Pres*
Nick Gomez, *General Mgr*
Sara Evans, *Marketing Staff*
Glenda Gideon, *Cust Mgr*
EMP: 156
SALES (corp-wide): 111.3MM **Privately Held**
SIC: 4213 Trucking, except local
PA: Dependable Auto Shippers, Inc.
3020 U S 80 Frontage Rd
Mesquite TX 75149
214 381-0181

(P-4135)
DEPENDABLE HIGHWAY EXPRESS INC
Also Called: Dhe
1351 S Campus Ave, Ontario (91761-4352)
PHONE 909 923-0065
Bob Bianchi, *Branch Mgr*
Bob Massman, *Vice Pres*
EMP: 60
SALES (corp-wide): 292.7MM **Privately Held**
WEB: www.godependable.com
SIC: 4213 Trucking, except local
PA: Dependable Highway Express, Inc.
2555 E Olympic Blvd
Los Angeles CA 90023
323 526-2200

(P-4136)
DEPENDABLE HIGHWAY EXPRESS INC (PA)
2555 E Olympic Blvd, Los Angeles (90023-2605)
P.O. Box 58047 (90058-0047)
PHONE 323 526-2200
Fax: 323 526-2223
Ronald Massman, *President*
Michael Dougan, *CFO*
Bob Massman, *CFO*
Robert Massman, *Vice Pres*
Bill Butler, *Branch Mgr*
EMP: 300
SQ FT: 1,680,000
SALES (est): 292.7MM **Privately Held**
WEB: www.godependable.com
SIC: 4213 4225 Trucking, except local; general warehousing & storage

(P-4137)
DEPENDABLE HIGHWAY EXPRESS INC
Also Called: Dhe
3199 Alvarado St, San Leandro (94577-5709)
PHONE 510 357-2223
Georgia Briggs, *Branch Mgr*
EMP: 82
SALES (corp-wide): 292.7MM **Privately Held**
WEB: www.godependable.com
SIC: 4213 4225 Trucking, except local; general warehousing & storage
PA: Dependable Highway Express, Inc.
2555 E Olympic Blvd
Los Angeles CA 90023
323 526-2200

(P-4138)
DESERT COASTAL TRANSPORT INC (PA)
Also Called: Dct
10686 Banana Ave, Fontana (92337-7002)
PHONE 909 357-3395
Fax: 909 357-0896
Tim Wyant, *President*
Timothy A Wyant, *CEO*
Chuck Wyant, *Admin Sec*
Dale Barke, *Controller*
Paola Gaytan, *Manager*
EMP: 55
SQ FT: 6,000
SALES: 29.2MM **Privately Held**
WEB: www.desertcoastal.com
SIC: 4213 Trucking, except local

(P-4139)
DOT-LINE TRANSPORTATION INC
4366 E 26th St, Vernon (90058-4301)
P.O. Box 8739, Fountain Valley (92728-8739)
PHONE 877 900-7768
Dennis Watson, *President*
Dottie Watson, *Corp Secy*
Robert Brewster, *Controller*
EMP: 55
SALES (est): 5.3MM **Privately Held**
SIC: 4213 Trucking, except local

(P-4140)
DOUBLE EAGLE TRNSP CORP
12135 Scarbrough Ct, Oak Hills (92344-9200)
PHONE 760 956-3770
Fax: 760 956-6362

Gerald E Butcher, *President*
EMP: 140
SQ FT: 10,125
SALES: 16MM **Privately Held**
SIC: 4213 4212 Trucking, except local; local trucking, without storage

(P-4141)
DOUDELL TRUCKING COMPANY (PA)
1505 N 4th St, San Jose (95112-4607)
P.O. Box 5879 (95150-5879)
PHONE 408 263-7300
Fax: 408 263-7524
Armand Kunde, *President*
John Kunde, *CFO*
EMP: 80
SQ FT: 20,000
SALES (est): 9.8MM **Privately Held**
SIC: 4213 4214 4212 Trucking, except local; local trucking with storage; local trucking, without storage

(P-4142)
DSC LOGISTICS INC
1895 Marigold Ave, Redlands (92374-5028)
PHONE 909 363-4354
Greg Hart, *General Ptnr*
EMP: 68
SALES (corp-wide): 355MM **Privately Held**
SIC: 4213 4212 Trucking, except local; local trucking, without storage
PA: Dsc Logistics, Inc.
1750 S Wolf Rd
Des Plaines IL 60018
847 390-6800

(P-4143)
EAGLE SYSTEMS INC
Also Called: Eagle Intermodel Services
395 N Mount Vernon Ave, San Bernardino (92411-2673)
PHONE 909 386-4343
Fax: 909 386-4340
Al Thompson, *Branch Mgr*
EMP: 250 **Privately Held**
WEB: www.eagleis.com
SIC: 4213 Trucking, except local
HQ: Eagle Systems, Inc.
230 Grant Rd Ste A1
East Wenatchee WA 98802
509 884-7575

(P-4144)
EARLY TRANSPORTATION SERVICES
Also Called: Bay Area Garment
30796 San Clemente St, Hayward (94544-7131)
PHONE 510 324-1119
Fax: 510 324-1221
Earl I Ramer Sr, *President*
EMP: 100
SALES (est): 6.3MM **Privately Held**
SIC: 4213 Trucking, except local

(P-4145)
ED ROCHA LIVESTOCK TRNSP INC
Also Called: Rocha Transportation
2400 Nickerson Dr, Modesto (95358-9409)
P.O. Box 40, Ceres (95307-0040)
PHONE 209 538-1302
Fax: 209 538-6302
Henry Dirksen, *President*
Zachary Dirksen, *Treasurer*
Ed Rocha, *Exec Dir*
Linda Hopkins, *Office Mgr*
Corrie M Toste, *Admin Sec*
EMP: 70
SQ FT: 5,500
SALES (est): 12.1MM **Privately Held**
WEB: www.rochatrans.com
SIC: 4213 Trucking, except local

(P-4146)
ERRAMA TRUCKING COMPANY INC
Also Called: Tough2beat Auto Sales
11336 Montgomery Ave, Granada Hills (91344-3841)
PHONE 818 381-3341
Souhayl Errama, *President*

4213 - Trucking, Except Local County (P-4147)

Alejandro Pacheco, *Vice Pres*
Taha Aerrama, *Director*
EMP: 50
SQ FT: 15,000
SALES: 3.1MM **Privately Held**
SIC: 4213 5511 Household goods transport; automobiles, new & used

(P-4147)
ESPARZA ENTERPRISES INC
500 Workman St, Bakersfield (93307-6871)
PHONE.................................661 631-0347
Fax: 661 631-0290
EMP: 1377
SALES (corp-wide): 56.6MM **Privately Held**
SIC: 4213 Trucking, except local
PA: Esparza Enterprises, Inc.
   3851 Fruitvale Ave Ste A
   Bakersfield CA 93308
   661 831-0002

(P-4148)
ESTES EXPRESS LINES INC
10736 Cherry Ave, Fontana (92337-7196)
PHONE.................................909 427-9850
Mark Brown, *Manager*
John Wood, *VP Finance*
Brad Arison, *Sales Mgr*
EMP: 58
SALES (corp-wide): 2.3B **Privately Held**
WEB: www.estes-express.com
SIC: 4213 4212 Less-than-truckload (LTL) transport; local trucking, without storage
PA: Estes Express Lines, Inc.
   3901 W Broad St
   Richmond VA 23230
   804 353-1900

(P-4149)
ESTES EXPRESS LINES INC
13327 Temple Ave, City of Industry (91746-1513)
PHONE.................................626 333-9090
Kieran O'Carroll, *Manager*
Martin Sakamoto, *Accounts Mgr*
EMP: 67
SQ FT: 6,156
SALES (corp-wide): 2.3B **Privately Held**
WEB: www.estes-express.com
SIC: 4213 4212 Less-than-truckload (LTL) transport; local trucking, without storage
PA: Estes Express Lines, Inc.
   3901 W Broad St
   Richmond VA 23230
   804 353-1900

(P-4150)
ESTES EXPRESS LINES INC
1634 S 7th St, San Jose (95112-5931)
PHONE.................................408 286-3894
John Martin, *Branch Mgr*
EMP: 50
SALES (corp-wide): 2.3B **Privately Held**
WEB: www.estes-express.com
SIC: 4213 Contract haulers
PA: Estes Express Lines, Inc.
   3901 W Broad St
   Richmond VA 23230
   804 353-1900

(P-4151)
ESTES EXPRESS LINES INC
1750 Adams Ave, San Leandro (94577-1002)
PHONE.................................510 635-0165
Bill Wardell, *Manager*
Fran Glidewell, *Exec VP*
Bob Allen, *Sales Dir*
Gus Valdez, *Manager*
EMP: 58
SALES (corp-wide): 2.3B **Privately Held**
WEB: www.estes-express.com
SIC: 4213 Contract haulers
PA: Estes Express Lines, Inc.
   3901 W Broad St
   Richmond VA 23230
   804 353-1900

(P-4152)
ESTES EXPRESS LINES INC
9120 San Fernando Rd, Sun Valley (91352-1413)
PHONE.................................818 504-4155
Eric Reyes, *Manager*
Larry Mercado, *Manager*

EMP: 58
SALES (corp-wide): 2.3B **Privately Held**
WEB: www.estes-express.com
SIC: 4213 Trucking, except local
PA: Estes Express Lines, Inc.
   3901 W Broad St
   Richmond VA 23230
   804 353-1900

(P-4153)
ESTES EXPRESS LINES INC
7611 S Airport Way, Stockton (95206-3918)
PHONE.................................209 982-1841
Mark Hancock, *Branch Mgr*
EMP: 58
SALES (corp-wide): 2.3B **Privately Held**
WEB: www.estes-express.com
SIC: 4213 Trucking, except local
PA: Estes Express Lines, Inc.
   3901 W Broad St
   Richmond VA 23230
   804 353-1900

(P-4154)
ESTES EXPRESS LINES INC
1531 Blinn Ave, Wilmington (90744-1601)
PHONE.................................310 549-7306
Rob Clagg, *Manager*
EMP: 58
SALES (corp-wide): 2.3B **Privately Held**
WEB: www.estes-express.com
SIC: 4213 Trucking, except local
PA: Estes Express Lines, Inc.
   3901 W Broad St
   Richmond VA 23230
   804 353-1900

(P-4155)
ESTES EXPRESS LINES INC
14727 Alondra Blvd, La Mirada (90638-5617)
PHONE.................................714 523-1122
William Reid, *President*
John Wood, *CFO*
Pat Martin, *Vice Pres*
Rich Stevens, *Vice Pres*
Greg Atkins, *General Mgr*
EMP: 58
SALES (corp-wide): 2.3B **Privately Held**
WEB: www.estes-express.com
SIC: 4213 Trucking, except local
PA: Estes Express Lines, Inc.
   3901 W Broad St
   Richmond VA 23230
   804 353-1900

(P-4156)
EZE TRUCKING LLC (DH)
2584 N Locust Ave, Rialto (92377-4120)
PHONE.................................909 770-8800
Kirk Jensen, *CEO*
Katie Navarro, *Vice Pres*
Bob York, *Vice Pres*
EMP: 64
SALES (est): 49.5MM
SALES (corp-wide): 95.5MM **Privately Held**
SIC: 4213 Trucking, except local
HQ: Farren International Holdings, Inc.
   519 N Sam Houston Pkwy E
   Houston TX 77060
   832 871-4900

(P-4157)
FAST LANE TRANSPORTATION INC (PA)
Also Called: Fast Lane Container Services
2400 E Pacific Coast Hwy, Wilmington (90744-2921)
PHONE.................................562 435-3000
Fax: 562 432-4399
Patrick L Wilson, *President*
Christine Henry, *Corp Secy*
James Henry, *Exec VP*
Susan Miller, *Human Resources*
▲ **EMP:** 70
SQ FT: 36,000
SALES (est): 10.6MM **Privately Held**
WEB: www.fastlanetrans.com
SIC: 4213 4214 Trailer or container on flat car (TOFC/COFC); local trucking with storage

(P-4158)
FAULKNER TRUCKING INC
3645 S K St, Tulare (93274-7178)
PHONE.................................559 684-9298
Fax: 559 685-9159
Ronald D Faulkner, *President*
Wade Magden, *Safety Dir*
Mike Servillo, *Facilities Mgr*
Lori Utterback, *Accounts Mgr*
EMP: 58
SQ FT: 3,600
SALES (est): 15.9MM **Privately Held**
WEB: www.faulknertrucking.com
SIC: 4213 Contract haulers

(P-4159)
FEDERAL EXPRESS CORPORATION
Also Called: Fedex
3333 S Grand Ave, Los Angeles (90007-4116)
PHONE.................................800 463-3339
Dave Vint, *Branch Mgr*
Deborah Diehl, *Sales Staff*
EMP: 100
SALES (corp-wide): 50.3B **Publicly Held**
WEB: www.federalexpress.com
SIC: 4213 Contract haulers
HQ: Federal Express Corporation
   3610 Hacks Cross Rd
   Memphis TN 38125
   901 369-3600

(P-4160)
FEDEX FREIGHT CORPORATION
4500 Bandini Blvd, Vernon (90058-5409)
PHONE.................................323 269-9800
Matt Lowe, *Sales/Mktg Mgr*
Tore Richardson, *Technology*
Dan Stevens, *Sales Executive*
Juan Gutierrez, *Manager*
EMP: 200
SQ FT: 20,000
SALES (corp-wide): 50.3B **Publicly Held**
WEB: www.watkins.com
SIC: 4213 4231 Contract haulers; trucking terminal facilities
HQ: Fedex Freight Corporation
   1715 Aaron Brenner Dr
   Memphis TN 38120
   901 434-3100

(P-4161)
FEDEX FREIGHT CORPORATION
1379 N Miller St, Anaheim (92806-1412)
PHONE.................................714 996-8720
Brad Housner, *Manager*
Mike Hutton, *General Mgr*
Cruz Mendoza, *Warehouse Mgr*
EMP: 160
SQ FT: 20,802
SALES (corp-wide): 50.3B **Publicly Held**
SIC: 4213 4212 7538 Trucking, except local; delivery service, vehicular; general automotive repair shops
HQ: Fedex Freight Corporation
   1715 Aaron Brenner Dr
   Memphis TN 38120
   901 434-3100

(P-4162)
FEDEX FREIGHT CORPORATION
7250 Cajon Blvd, San Bernardino (92407-1887)
PHONE.................................909 887-3970
EMP: 185
SALES (corp-wide): 50.3B **Publicly Held**
SIC: 4213 7513 Less-than-truckload (LTL) transport; truck leasing, without drivers
HQ: Fedex Freight Corporation
   1715 Aaron Brenner Dr
   Memphis TN 38120
   901 434-3100

(P-4163)
FEDEX FREIGHT CORPORATION
193 Willow St, Bishop (93514-2750)
PHONE.................................760 873-8655
EMP: 53
SALES (corp-wide): 50.3B **Publicly Held**
SIC: 4213 Less-than-truckload (LTL) transport
HQ: Fedex Freight Corporation
   1715 Aaron Brenner Dr
   Memphis TN 38120
   901 434-3100

(P-4164)
FEDEX FREIGHT CORPORATION
2250 Airway Ln, San Diego (92154-6205)
PHONE.................................619 710-0268
Willie Macias, *Branch Mgr*
EMP: 76
SALES (corp-wide): 50.3B **Publicly Held**
SIC: 4213 Trucking, except local
HQ: Fedex Freight Corporation
   1715 Aaron Brenner Dr
   Memphis TN 38120
   901 434-3100

(P-4165)
FEDEX FREIGHT CORPORATION
15200 S Main St, Gardena (90248-1957)
PHONE.................................310 323-5230
Chaug Rios, *Manager*
Robert Painter, *Opers Mgr*
EMP: 280
SALES (corp-wide): 50.3B **Publicly Held**
SIC: 4213 4215 4731 Trucking, except local; courier services, except by air; freight forwarding
HQ: Fedex Freight Corporation
   1715 Aaron Brenner Dr
   Memphis TN 38120
   901 434-3100

(P-4166)
FEDEX FREIGHT CORPORATION
29001 Hopkins St, Hayward (94545-5003)
PHONE.................................510 895-0440
Mike Farrell, *Manager*
EMP: 350
SALES (corp-wide): 50.3B **Publicly Held**
SIC: 4213 4231 4212 4731 Trucking, except local; trucking terminal facilities; local trucking, without storage; freight forwarding; airports, flying fields & services
HQ: Fedex Freight Corporation
   1715 Aaron Brenner Dr
   Memphis TN 38120
   901 434-3100

(P-4167)
FEDEX FREIGHT CORPORATION
11911 Branford St, Sun Valley (91352-1026)
PHONE.................................818 899-1141
Greg Sullivan, *Manager*
Ladd George, *Info Tech Dir*
Matt McAloon, *Technology*
Nanna Lamelas, *Purch Mgr*
Dani Chivi, *Purch Agent*
EMP: 75
SALES (corp-wide): 50.3B **Publicly Held**
SIC: 4213 Less-than-truckload (LTL) transport
HQ: Fedex Freight Corporation
   1715 Aaron Brenner Dr
   Memphis TN 38120
   901 434-3100

(P-4168)
FEDEX FREIGHT CORPORATION
4520 S Highway 99, Stockton (95215-8235)
PHONE.................................209 466-7726
Carlos Gonzales, *Manager*
Adam Urango, *Info Tech Mgr*
Dylan Paxton, *Opers Staff*
EMP: 200
SALES (corp-wide): 50.3B **Publicly Held**
SIC: 4213 Trucking, except local
HQ: Fedex Freight Corporation
   1715 Aaron Brenner Dr
   Memphis TN 38120
   901 434-3100

(P-4169)
FEDEX FREIGHT CORPORATION
56 Fairbanks, Irvine (92618-1602)
PHONE.................................800 706-1687
Mike Sendayhoff, *Manager*
Kathy Valentine, *Risk Mgmt Dir*
Bart Burris, *Manager*
EMP: 76
SALES (corp-wide): 50.3B **Publicly Held**
SIC: 4213 4731 Trucking, except local; freight forwarding
HQ: Fedex Freight Corporation
   1715 Aaron Brenner Dr
   Memphis TN 38120
   901 434-3100

PRODUCTS & SERVICES SECTION

4213 - Trucking, Except Local County (P-4195)

(P-4170)
FEDEX FREIGHT WEST INC
3050 Teagarden St, San Leandro (94577-5721)
PHONE 650 244-9522
EMP: 89
SALES (corp-wide): 47.4B **Publicly Held**
SIC: 4213
HQ: Fedex Freight West, Inc.
6411 Guadalupe Mines Rd
San Jose CA 95120
775 356-7600

(P-4171)
FEDEX FREIGHT WEST INC
4570 S Maple Ave, Fresno (93725-9358)
PHONE 559 266-0732
EMP: 125
SALES (corp-wide): 47.4B **Publicly Held**
SIC: 4213 4231 4214
HQ: Fedex Freight West, Inc.
6411 Guadalupe Mines Rd
San Jose CA 95120
775 356-7600

(P-4172)
FEDEX FREIGHT WEST INC
11153 Mulberry Ave, Fontana (92337-7030)
PHONE 909 357-3555
EMP: 355
SQ FT: 79,735
SALES (corp-wide): 47.4B **Publicly Held**
SIC: 4213 4731 4212
HQ: Fedex Freight West, Inc.
6411 Guadalupe Mines Rd
San Jose CA 95120
775 356-7600

(P-4173)
FEDEX FREIGHT WEST INC
1230 N Mcdowell Blvd, Petaluma (94954-1113)
PHONE 707 778-3191
EMP: 50
SQ FT: 13,920
SALES (corp-wide): 47.4B **Publicly Held**
SIC: 4213
HQ: Fedex Freight West, Inc.
6411 Guadalupe Mines Rd
San Jose CA 95120
775 356-7600

(P-4174)
FEDEX GROUND PACKAGE SYS INC
1497 George Dr Ste G, Redding (96003-1472)
PHONE 530 247-0935
Troy Manns, *Branch Mgr*
EMP: 50
SALES (corp-wide): 50.3B **Publicly Held**
SIC: 4213 Contract haulers
HQ: Fedex Ground Package System, Inc.
1000 Fed Ex Dr
Coraopolis PA 15108
412 269-1000

(P-4175)
FEDEX GROUND PACKAGE SYS INC
590 E Orangethorpe Ave, Anaheim (92801-1021)
PHONE 714 879-0788
Martin Daza, *Manager*
Mike Weiss, *Purch Agent*
EMP: 250
SALES (corp-wide): 50.3B **Publicly Held**
SIC: 4213 4215 Contract haulers; courier services, except by air
HQ: Fedex Ground Package System, Inc.
1000 Fed Ex Dr
Coraopolis PA 15108
412 269-1000

(P-4176)
FEDEX GROUND PACKAGE SYS INC
1 Carousel Ln Unit B, Ukiah (95482-9509)
PHONE 707 485-8638
EMP: 87
SALES (corp-wide): 50.3B **Publicly Held**
SIC: 4213 Contract haulers

HQ: Fedex Ground Package System, Inc.
1000 Fed Ex Dr
Coraopolis PA 15108
412 269-1000

(P-4177)
FEDEX GROUND PACKAGE SYS INC
101 Book Farm Rd, Durham (95938-9521)
PHONE 530 534-5924
EMP: 146
SALES (corp-wide): 50.3B **Publicly Held**
SIC: 4213 Contract haulers
HQ: Fedex Ground Package System, Inc.
1000 Fed Ex Dr
Coraopolis PA 15108
412 269-1000

(P-4178)
FEDEX GROUND PACKAGE SYS INC
375 Airport Rd, Bishop (93514-3614)
PHONE 760 873-3133
EMP: 146
SALES (corp-wide): 50.3B **Publicly Held**
SIC: 4213 Contract haulers
HQ: Fedex Ground Package System, Inc.
1000 Fed Ex Dr
Coraopolis PA 15108
412 269-1000

(P-4179)
FEDEX GROUND PACKAGE SYS INC
500 Caletti Ave, Windsor (95492-6822)
PHONE 707 836-9890
EMP: 146
SALES (corp-wide): 50.3B **Publicly Held**
SIC: 4213 Contract haulers
HQ: Fedex Ground Package System, Inc.
1000 Fed Ex Dr
Coraopolis PA 15108
412 269-1000

(P-4180)
FEDEX GROUND PACKAGE SYS INC
696 E Trimble Rd Ste 10, San Jose (95131-1236)
PHONE 408 943-9960
Steve Brenner, *Principal*
EMP: 300
SALES (corp-wide): 50.3B **Publicly Held**
SIC: 4213 Trucking, except local
HQ: Fedex Ground Package System, Inc.
1000 Fed Ex Dr
Coraopolis PA 15108
412 269-1000

(P-4181)
FEDEX GROUND PACKAGE SYS INC
330 Resource Dr, Bloomington (92316-3528)
PHONE 909 879-7180
Richard Greene, *Manager*
EMP: 800
SALES (corp-wide): 50.3B **Publicly Held**
SIC: 4213 Contract haulers
HQ: Fedex Ground Package System, Inc.
1000 Fed Ex Dr
Coraopolis PA 15108
412 269-1000

(P-4182)
FEDEX GROUND PACKAGE SYS INC
165 Technology Dr, Watsonville (95076-2448)
PHONE 831 786-0751
EMP: 88
SALES (corp-wide): 50.3B **Publicly Held**
SIC: 4213 Contract haulers
HQ: Fedex Ground Package System, Inc.
1000 Fed Ex Dr
Coraopolis PA 15108
412 269-1000

(P-4183)
FEDEX GROUND PACKAGE SYS INC
9175 San Fernando Rd, Sun Valley (91352-1414)
PHONE 818 767-7650

Kevin Dixon, *Manager*
EMP: 90
SALES (corp-wide): 50.3B **Publicly Held**
SIC: 4213 Trucking, except local
HQ: Fedex Ground Package System, Inc.
1000 Fed Ex Dr
Coraopolis PA 15108
412 269-1000

(P-4184)
FLASH TRANSPORT INC
14796 Washington Dr, Fontana (92335-6263)
P.O. Box 4712, Diamond Bar (91765-0712)
PHONE 909 829-1369
William Faulkner, *President*
EMP: 75
SQ FT: 2,000
SALES (est): 5.7MM **Privately Held**
SIC: 4213 4212 Trucking, except local; local trucking, without storage

(P-4185)
FRANK C ALEGRE TRUCKING INC (PA)
5100 W Highway 12, Lodi (95242-9529)
P.O. Box 1508 (95241-1508)
PHONE 209 334-2112
Fax: 209 367-0572
Anthony J Alegre, *President*
Michelle Schultz, *General Mgr*
Lary Lacy, *Purch Agent*
Lonnie Moore, *Safety Dir*
Dan Ruoff, *Foreman/Supr*
EMP: 185
SQ FT: 34,200
SALES (est): 47.7MM **Privately Held**
SIC: 4213 4212 Trucking, except local; dump truck haulage

(P-4186)
FRIENDS GROUP EXPRESS INC
14520 Village Dr Apt 1013, Fontana (92337-2501)
PHONE 909 346-6814
Parmjit Singh Grewal, *Principal*
EMP: 78 EST: 2014
SQ FT: 700
SALES: 194K **Privately Held**
SIC: 4213 4212 Trucking, except local; local trucking, without storage

(P-4187)
FUEL DELIVERY SERVICES INC
4895 S Airport Way, Stockton (95206-3915)
P.O. Box 1369 (95201-1369)
PHONE 209 751-2185
Fax: 209 234-7568
Ronald M Vandepol, *CEO*
David Atwater, *Shareholder*
Mike Boswart, *Shareholder*
Tom V Depol, *Shareholder*
Mike Reed, *Controller*
EMP: 94
SQ FT: 2,000
SALES (est): 16.2MM **Privately Held**
SIC: 4213 Liquid petroleum transport, non-local

(P-4188)
GCU TRUCKING INC
7819 Crane Rd, Oakdale (95361-8114)
P.O. Box 1423 (95361-1423)
PHONE 209 845-2117
Leo Arcos, *CEO*
Rene Arcos, *Manager*
Terry Arcos, *Manager*
Daniel Cox, *Manager*
EMP: 52
SQ FT: 7,000
SALES (est): 8.5MM **Privately Held**
SIC: 4213 5032 Trucking, except local; brick, stone & related material

(P-4189)
GILL TRANSPORT LLC
1051 Pacific Ave, Oxnard (93030-7254)
PHONE 805 240-1979
Steven H Gill, *Mng Member*
David L Gill, *Mng Member*
EMP: 400
SALES (est): 22.2MM **Privately Held**
SIC: 4213 Trucking, except local

(P-4190)
GOLDEN EAGLE MOVING SVCS INC
1450 N Benson Ave, Upland (91786-2165)
PHONE 909 946-7655
Fax: 909 949-8037
Robert Johnson, *President*
Thomas Johnson Jr, *CFO*
Constance Johnson, *Vice Pres*
EMP: 55
SQ FT: 50,000
SALES: 6.2MM **Privately Held**
WEB: www.goldeneaglemoving.com
SIC: 4213 4214 Household goods transport; household goods moving & storage, local

(P-4191)
GREATWIDE LOGISTICS SVCS LLC
Also Called: Greatwide Dedicated Transport
4310 Bandini Blvd, Vernon (90058-4308)
PHONE 323 268-7100
Angela Remling, *Branch Mgr*
EMP: 75
SALES (corp-wide): 2.4B **Privately Held**
SIC: 4213 Trucking, except local
HQ: Greatwide Logistics Services, Llc.
12404 Park Central Dr # 300
Dallas TX 75251
972 228-7389

(P-4192)
GREEN VALLEY TRNSP CORP
30131 Highway 33, Tracy (95304-9319)
P.O. Box 254, Vernalis (95385-0254)
PHONE 209 836-5192
Fax: 209 836-5025
Steve Grove, *CEO*
Nancy J Houghton, *President*
Cathy Gilbert, *Admin Sec*
EMP: 50
SQ FT: 3,800
SALES (est): 10.1MM **Privately Held**
SIC: 4213 4212 Trucking, except local; local trucking, without storage

(P-4193)
H & H TRANSPORTATION LLC
300 El Sobrante Rd, Corona (92879-5757)
P.O. Box 77697 (92877-0123)
PHONE 951 817-2300
Tim Hyde, *President*
Roger Anich, *Accounts Mgr*
EMP: 60
SALES (est): 6.6MM **Privately Held**
SIC: 4213 4212 Trucking, except local; local trucking, without storage

(P-4194)
H F COX INC (PA)
Also Called: Cox Petroleum Transport
118 Cox Transport Way, Bakersfield (93307)
PHONE 661 366-3236
Fax: 661 366-0822
Dainiel L Mairs, *President*
Larry O'Connell, *COO*
Brue McKinnon, *CFO*
Gwen Mairs, *Treasurer*
Bruce McKinnon, *Vice Pres*
EMP: 60
SQ FT: 5,000
SALES: 971K **Privately Held**
WEB: www.coxpetroleum.com
SIC: 4213 4212 Trucking, except local; petroleum haulage, local

(P-4195)
HAWK TRANSPORTATION INC
15238 Arrow Blvd, Fontana (92335-3250)
PHONE 800 709-4295
Manprit K Sandhu, *CEO*
Jagtar Sandhu, *President*
Harry Bhangu, *Opers Mgr*
Flor Marquez, *Manager*
EMP: 60
SQ FT: 1,300
SALES (est): 14.6MM **Privately Held**
WEB: www.hawktrans.com
SIC: 4213 Trucking, except local

4213 - Trucking, Except Local County (P-4196)

PRODUCTS & SERVICES SECTION

(P-4196)
HENDRICKSON TRUCKING INC
7080 Florin Perkins Rd, Sacramento (95828-2609)
P.O. Box 292219 (95829-2219)
PHONE 916 387-9614
Fax: 916 387-5176
William Hendrickson, *CEO*
Ward Hendrickson, *President*
Alban Lang, *CFO*
Steve Farnsworth, *Controller*
Candice Masters, *Safety Dir*
EMP: 280
SQ FT: 5,480
SALES (est): 78MM **Privately Held**
WEB: www.hendricksontrucking.com
SIC: 4213 Trucking, except local

(P-4197)
INDIAN RIVER TRANSPORT CO
5100 Taylor Ct, Turlock (95382-9579)
PHONE 209 664-0456
John J Harned Jr, *Branch Mgr*
EMP: 257
SALES (corp-wide): 107.5MM **Privately Held**
SIC: 4213 Trucking, except local
PA: Indian River Transport Co.
2580 Executive Rd
Winter Haven FL 33884
863 324-2430

(P-4198)
INTERSTATE DISTRIBUTOR CO
10131 Redwood Ave, Fontana (92335-6236)
PHONE 909 349-3400
Matt Enes, *Branch Mgr*
EMP: 50
SALES (corp-wide): 2.2B **Privately Held**
WEB: www.intd.com
SIC: 4213 Trucking, except local
HQ: Interstate Distributor Co.
11707 21st Avenue Ct S
Tacoma WA 98444
253 537-9455

(P-4199)
J B HUNT TRANSPORT INC
11559 Jersey Blvd, Rancho Cucamonga (91730-4924)
PHONE 909 466-5361
EMP: 167
SALES (corp-wide): 6.1B **Publicly Held**
SIC: 4213
HQ: J. B. Hunt Transport, Inc.
615 J B Hunt Corporate Dr
Lowell AR 72745
479 820-0000

(P-4200)
JOE L COELHO INC
18637 E Bradbury Rd, Turlock (95380)
P.O. Box 3640 (95381-3640)
PHONE 209 667-2676
Fax: 209 667-1008
Dominic Coelho, *President*
Mary Kelly, *Admin Sec*
EMP: 50
SQ FT: 3,100
SALES: 5.4MM **Privately Held**
SIC: 4213 5191 Trucking, except local; hay

(P-4201)
K K W TRUCKING INC (PA)
3100 Pomona Blvd, Pomona (91768-3230)
P.O. Box 2960 (91769-2960)
PHONE 909 869-1200
Dennis W Firestone, *CEO*
Steve Benninghoss, *COO*
Lynnette Brown, *CFO*
Susan Dancel, *Office Mgr*
Heather Hess, *Asst Controller*
EMP: 180
SQ FT: 150,000
SALES (est): 76.6MM **Privately Held**
SIC: 4213 4231 4226 4214 Trucking, except local; trucking terminal facilities; special warehousing & storage; local trucking with storage

(P-4202)
KENAN ADVANTAGE GROUP INC
2709 E 37th St, Vernon (90058-1706)
PHONE 323 582-3778
Tom Franz, *Manager*
EMP: 70
SALES (corp-wide): 1.4B **Privately Held**
SIC: 4213 Trucking, except local
PA: The Kenan Advantage Group Inc
4366 Mount Pleasant St Nw
North Canton OH 44720
877 999-2524

(P-4203)
KINGS COUNTY TRUCK LINES (HQ)
754 S Blackstone St, Tulare (93274-5757)
P.O. Box 1016 (93275-1016)
PHONE 559 686-2857
Mark Tisdale, *Vice Pres*
Rosemary Gomes, *Marketing Mgr*
EMP: 162 **EST:** 1940
SQ FT: 45,000
SALES (est): 15.1MM
SALES (corp-wide): 1.9B **Privately Held**
WEB: www.kctl.com
SIC: 4213 Trucking, except local; refrigerated products transport; contract haulers
PA: Ruan Transportation Management Systems, Inc.
666 Grand Ave Ste 3200
Des Moines IA 50309
515 245-2500

(P-4204)
KLX INC
3645 S K St, Tulare (93274-7178)
P.O. Box 4438, Visalia (93278-4438)
PHONE 559 684-1037
Ron Greenberg, *President*
Jeff Peterson, *Corp Secy*
Percy Greenberg, *Director*
EMP: 65
SQ FT: 12,000
SALES (est): 9MM **Privately Held**
WEB: www.klx.net
SIC: 4213 Trucking, except local

(P-4205)
KNIGHT TRANSPORTATION INC
Also Called: Knight Port Services
2960 E Victoria St, Compton (90221-5615)
PHONE 888 549-7802
EMP: 130
SALES (corp-wide): 1.1B **Publicly Held**
SIC: 4213 Trucking, except local
PA: Knight Transportation, Inc.
20002 N 19th Ave
Phoenix AZ 85027
602 269-2000

(P-4206)
L A S TRANSPORTATION INC
Also Called: Produces Dairy
250 E Belmont Ave, Fresno (93701-1405)
PHONE 559 264-6583
Richard Shehady, *President*
Lawrence Shehady, *Chairman*
Reynold Morris, *Administration*
Dewayne Scott, *Purch Agent*
Jim Olsen, *Plant Engr*
EMP: 300
SQ FT: 30,000
SALES (est): 26.6MM **Privately Held**
SIC: 4213 Refrigerated products transport

(P-4207)
L J TRUCKING USA
120 S Anderson St, Los Angeles (90033-3220)
PHONE 323 469-9663
John Stewart, *President*
Carlin Ferro, *Vice Pres*
EMP: 80
SALES (est): 7.5MM **Privately Held**
SIC: 4213 Trucking, except local

(P-4208)
LANDFORCE EXPRESS CORPORATION
17201 N D St, Victorville (92394-1401)
PHONE 760 843-7839
Rajinder Bhangu, *CEO*
Rick Thieme, *Traffic Dir*
EMP: 120
SALES (est): 30.6MM **Privately Held**
SIC: 4213 Trucking, except local

(P-4209)
LANGE TRUCKING INC (PA)
2226 Campbell St, Oakland (94607-1719)
P.O. Box 1557, Pleasanton (94566-0155)
PHONE 510 836-1105
Fax: 510 836-2010
Bill Lange, *President*
Twan Lange, *President*
Bob Lange, *Vice Pres*
Willy Lange, *Principal*
EMP: 74
SALES (est): 25.9MM **Privately Held**
SIC: 4213 Contract haulers

(P-4210)
LAS VEGAS / LA EXPRESS INC (PA)
1000 S Cucamonga Ave, Ontario (91761-3461)
PHONE 909 972-3100
Fax: 909 972-3106
Ronald Cain Jr, *CEO*
Beverly A Adley, *Vice Pres*
Richard Hunt, *Vice Pres*
Michael P Adley, *Admin Sec*
Michael Adley, *Admin Sec*
EMP: 170
SQ FT: 163,000
SALES (est): 53.7MM **Privately Held**
WEB: www.lvla.com
SIC: 4213 Trucking, except local

(P-4211)
LAZTRANS INC
5200 District Blvd, Bakersfield (93313-2330)
P.O. Box 10655 (93389-0655)
PHONE 661 833-3783
Bill Lazzerini Jr, *President*
Mary Huser, *Shareholder*
Maria Pisar, *Shareholder*
Anthony Lazzerini, *Vice Pres*
EMP: 50
SQ FT: 52,000
SALES (est): 5.6MM **Privately Held**
WEB: www.laztrans.com
SIC: 4213 Heavy hauling

(P-4212)
LEMORE TRANSPORTATION INC (PA)
Also Called: Royal Trucking
1420 Royal Industrial Way, Concord (94520-4914)
P.O. Box 6085 (94524-1085)
PHONE 925 689-6444
Fax: 925 689-7668
Barbara Querio, *CEO*
Roy Querio, *President*
Laura Johnson, *Senior VP*
Heidi Becker, *Vice Pres*
Catherine Hern, *Admin Asst*
EMP: 73
SQ FT: 6,000
SALES (est): 8.7MM **Privately Held**
WEB: www.royaltruckingco.com
SIC: 4213 Trucking, except local

(P-4213)
LORETTA LIMA TRNSP CORP
240 S 6th Ave, City of Industry (91746-2915)
P.O. Box 3984 (91744-0984)
PHONE 626 330-5517
Fax: 626 330-6818
Michael Lima, *President*
Cherlyn Converse, *CFO*
Loretta Lima, *Vice Pres*
Cathy Watts, *Accountant*
EMP: 65
SALES (est): 8.5MM **Privately Held**
SIC: 4213 Trucking, except local

(P-4214)
MAJOR TRANSPORTATION SVCS INC
3342 N Weber Ave, Fresno (93722-4909)
PHONE 559 485-5949
Gill Baljinder, *President*
Bhupinde Gill, *Vice Pres*
Joe Garcia, *Principal*
EMP: 50
SALES (est): 7.1MM **Privately Held**
SIC: 4213 Trucking, except local

(P-4215)
MAMMOET WESTERN INC
1419 Potrero Ave, El Monte (91733-3014)
PHONE 626 444-4942
Fax: 626 442-0841
Dennis Davenport, *President*
Brian Saad, *Treasurer*
Donald L Davenport, *Vice Pres*
David H Davenport, *Admin Sec*
Al Cortez, *Personnel Exec*
EMP: 80
SQ FT: 50,000
SALES (est): 5.9MM **Privately Held**
WEB: www.mammoetwestern.com
SIC: 4213 4212 1796 Heavy machinery transport; local trucking, without storage; machine moving & rigging
HQ: Mammoet Holding B.V.
Van Deventerlaan 30 40
Utrecht 3528
102 042-424

(P-4216)
MASHBURN TRNSP SVCS INC
1423 Kern St, Taft (93268-4607)
P.O. Box 66 (93268-8066)
PHONE 661 763-5724
Fax: 661 763-5731
Denise Mashburn, *President*
Michael Mashburn, *Vice Pres*
Dwight Mashburn, *General Mgr*
EMP: 120
SQ FT: 2,000
SALES: 15.1MM **Privately Held**
SIC: 4213 4212 Trucking, except local; local trucking, without storage

(P-4217)
MATHESON FAST FREIGHT INC
9785 Goethe Rd, Sacramento (95827-3559)
PHONE 209 342-0184
Mark Matheson, *Branch Mgr*
Paul Janekay, *Manager*
EMP: 70
SALES (corp-wide): 347.3MM **Privately Held**
SIC: 4213 Less-than-truckload (LTL) transport
HQ: Matheson Fast Freight, Inc.
9780 Dino Dr
Elk Grove CA 95624
916 686-4600

(P-4218)
MATHESON FAST FREIGHT INC (HQ)
9780 Dino Dr, Elk Grove (95624-9477)
PHONE 916 686-4600
Fax: 916 686-6386
Robert B Matheson, *Ch of Bd*
Mark B Matheson, *President*
Laurie Johnson, *Corp Secy*
Carole L Matheson, *Exec VP*
Donald G Brocca, *Vice Pres*
EMP: 70
SQ FT: 7,200
SALES (est): 21.5MM
SALES (corp-wide): 347.3MM **Privately Held**
SIC: 4213 Less-than-truckload (LTL) transport
PA: Matheson Trucking, Inc.
9785 Goethe Rd
Sacramento CA 95827
916 685-2330

(P-4219)
MATHESON TRUCKING INC (PA)
9785 Goethe Rd, Sacramento (95827-3559)
PHONE 916 685-2330
Mark Matheson, *President*
Patricia Kepner, *CEO*
Charles J Mellor, *Officer*
Carole L Matheson, *Exec VP*
Laurie Johnson, *Vice Pres*
EMP: 50
SQ FT: 3,000

4213 - Trucking, Except Local County (P-4242)

SALES (est): 347.3MM **Privately Held**
SIC: 4213 4731 Trucking, except local; less-than-truckload (LTL) transport; freight transportation arrangement

(P-4220)
MCCOLLISTERS TRNSP GROUP INC
Also Called: United Van Lines
10672 Jasmine St, Fontana (92337-8242)
PHONE..................909 428-5700
Fax: 909 428-9100
Chris Ciofreddi, *Branch Mgr*
EMP: 55
SALES (corp-wide): 150.6MM **Privately Held**
SIC: 4213 Trucking, except local
PA: Mccollister's Transportation Group, Inc.
1800 N Route 130
Burlington NJ 08016
609 386-0600

(P-4221)
MEADOWBROOK MEAT COMPANY INC
Also Called: Mbm
1050 Palmyrita Ave, Riverside (92507-1700)
PHONE..................951 686-1200
Fax: 951 686-1295
Kevin O'Grady, *Manager*
Teri Latta, *Executive*
Kevin Ogrady, *District Mgr*
EMP: 250
SALES (corp-wide): 210.8B **Publicly Held**
WEB: www.mbmlc.com
SIC: 4213 5149 5147 5142 Trucking, except local; groceries & related products; meats & meat products; packaged frozen goods; food brokers
HQ: Meadowbrook Meat Company, Inc.
2641 Meadowbrook Rd
Rocky Mount NC 27801
252 985-7200

(P-4222)
MEATHEAD MOVERS
300 Rolling Oaks Dr, Thousand Oaks (91361-1269)
PHONE..................805 496-1416
EMP: 70
SALES (corp-wide): 14.4MM **Privately Held**
SIC: 4213 4212 Household goods transport; moving services
PA: Meathead Movers, Inc.
3600 S Higuera St
San Luis Obispo CA 93401
805 544-6328

(P-4223)
MEATHEAD MOVERS
101 W Canon Perdido St, Santa Maria (93454)
PHONE..................805 349-8000
Aaron Steed, *Branch Mgr*
EMP: 70
SALES (corp-wide): 14.4MM **Privately Held**
SIC: 4213 4789 Household goods transport; cargo loading & unloading services
PA: Meathead Movers, Inc.
3600 S Higuera St
San Luis Obispo CA 93401
805 544-6328

(P-4224)
MEATHEAD MOVERS INC
964 Johnson Ave, San Luis Obispo (93401-3112)
PHONE..................805 541-4285
Aaron B Steed, *President*
Evan Steed, *Vice Pres*
EMP: 70
SALES (corp-wide): 14.4MM **Privately Held**
WEB: www.meatheadmovers.com
SIC: 4213 Household goods transport
PA: Meathead Movers, Inc.
3600 S Higuera St
San Luis Obispo CA 93401
805 544-6328

(P-4225)
MEATHEAD MOVERS INC (PA)
3600 S Higuera St, San Luis Obispo (93401-7306)
PHONE..................805 544-6328
Fax: 805 781-0872
Evan Steed, *COO*
Aaron B Steed, *CEO*
Angela Aleen, *General Mgr*
Angela Allen, *General Mgr*
Cromwell Erin, *Controller*
EMP: 68
SQ FT: 1,700
SALES (corp-wide): 14.4MM **Privately Held**
WEB: www.meatheadmovers.com
SIC: 4213 Household goods transport

(P-4226)
MEATHEAD MOVERS INC
331 Dawson Dr, Camarillo (93012-8093)
PHONE..................805 437-5100
Aaron Steed, *Branch Mgr*
Landon Torgerson, *COO*
Erin Norton, *Opers Mgr*
Megan Betterley, *Sales Associate*
Julien Farasat, *Sales Associate*
EMP: 70
SALES (corp-wide): 14.4MM **Privately Held**
SIC: 4213 4212 Household goods transport; moving services
PA: Meathead Movers, Inc.
3600 S Higuera St
San Luis Obispo CA 93401
805 544-6328

(P-4227)
MEATHEAD MOVERS INC
1524 State St, Santa Barbara (93101-2514)
PHONE..................805 966-6328
EMP: 70
SALES (corp-wide): 14.4MM **Privately Held**
SIC: 4213 4212 Household goods transport; moving services
PA: Meathead Movers, Inc.
3600 S Higuera St
San Luis Obispo CA 93401
805 544-6328

(P-4228)
METROPOLITAN VAN AND STOR INC (PA)
5400 Industrial Way, Benicia (94510-1037)
P.O. Box 829, Martinez (94553-0082)
PHONE..................707 745-1150
Fax: 707 745-2759
Dennis Paulley, *President*
Keith Estes, *Vice Pres*
Donna Reynolds, *Administration*
Art Harvey, *VP Opers*
Denise Meredith, *Opers Mgr*
EMP: 50
SQ FT: 121,400
SALES (est): 7.9MM **Privately Held**
WEB: www.metrovan.com
SIC: 4213 4214 Household goods transport; household goods moving & storage, local

(P-4229)
MIGUELITO MANPOWER INC
Also Called: Smitty Transportation
23295 Buckland Ln, Lake Forest (92630-3702)
PHONE..................323 582-3376
Michael Smith, *President*
EMP: 110
SALES: 8MM **Privately Held**
SIC: 4213 Trucking, except local

(P-4230)
MJ BROTHERS TRUCKING
20969 Road 52, Tulare (93274-9657)
P.O. Box 1946 (93275-1946)
PHONE..................559 686-4413
Fernando Martin, *Partner*
Danny Martin, *Partner*
Ronny Martin, *Partner*
EMP: 50
SALES (est): 3.4MM **Privately Held**
SIC: 4213 0711 Trucking, except local; fertilizer application services

(P-4231)
MOUNTAIN VALLEY EXPRESS CO INC (PA)
6750 Longe St Ste 100, Stockton (95206-4938)
P.O. Box 2569, Manteca (95336-1167)
PHONE..................209 823-2168
Fax: 209 823-0859
James Scott Blevins, *President*
Dick McIntosh, *Vice Pres*
Jackie Torres, *Executive*
Penny Regelman, *Office Mgr*
Ryan V Veen, *Info Tech Mgr*
EMP: 100
SALES (est): 44MM **Privately Held**
WEB: www.mountainvalleyexpress.com
SIC: 4213 Trucking, except local

(P-4232)
MULTIMODAL ESQUER INC
8856 Siempre Viva Rd, San Diego (92154-6272)
PHONE..................619 710-0477
Fax: 619 710-0478
Alfonsa Esquer Sr, *President*
Federico Esquer, *Treasurer*
Jose Esquer, *Admin Sec*
EMP: 56
SQ FT: 2,100
SALES (est): 8.2MM **Privately Held**
WEB: www.fletesesquer.com
SIC: 4213 Trucking, except local

(P-4233)
NATIONAL RETAIL TRNSP INC
355 W Carob St, Compton (90220-5212)
PHONE..................310 605-3777
Manuel Villasenor, *Branch Mgr*
EMP: 100
SALES (corp-wide): 237.3MM **Privately Held**
WEB: www.nrsonline.com
SIC: 4213 Trucking, except local
HQ: National Retail Transportation, Inc.
2820 16th St
North Bergen NJ 07047
201 866-0462

(P-4234)
NEW LEGEND INC
Also Called: Legend Transpotation
1235 Oswald Rd, Yuba City (95991-9719)
PHONE..................530 674-3100
Sunny Samara, *President*
Bobby Samara, *CFO*
Christin Martinez, *Admin Asst*
Wallace Hope, *Chief Acct*
Terri Aguilar, *Accounting Mgr*
EMP: 200
SQ FT: 5,000
SALES (est): 69.9MM **Privately Held**
SIC: 4213 4212 Trucking, except local; local trucking, without storage

(P-4235)
NORTHERN RFRIGERATED TRNSP INC (PA)
2700 W Main St, Turlock (95380-9537)
PHONE..................209 664-3800
Richard Mello, *CEO*
Judi Mello, *Treasurer*
John Doidge, *Vice Pres*
EMP: 120
SQ FT: 25,000
SALES (est): 39.6MM **Privately Held**
WEB: www.northernrefrigerated.com
SIC: 4213 Refrigerated products transport

(P-4236)
NORTHERN RFRIGERATED TRNSP INC
Also Called: Poppy State Express
3261 N Marks Ave, Fresno (93722-4921)
PHONE..................559 241-7350
Fax: 559 241-7352
Richard Nello, *Branch Mgr*
EMP: 61
SALES (corp-wide): 39.6MM **Privately Held**
SIC: 4213 Refrigerated products transport
PA: Northern Refrigerated Transportation, Inc.
2700 W Main St
Turlock CA 95380
209 664-3800

(P-4237)
NY TRANSPORT INC
14998 Washington Dr, Fontana (92335-6268)
PHONE..................909 355-9832
Nazario Y Perez, *President*
Jose Conrado, *Controller*
EMP: 65
SQ FT: 1,000
SALES: 16MM **Privately Held**
SIC: 4213 Trucking, except local

(P-4238)
OAK HARBOR FREIGHT LINES INC
6700 Smith Ave, Newark (94560-4222)
PHONE..................510 608-8841
Toll Free:..................888 -
Fax: 510 791-1436
Dennis Weishaar, *Manager*
EMP: 75
SALES (corp-wide): 217.9MM **Privately Held**
WEB: www.oakh.com
SIC: 4213 Trucking, except local
PA: Oak Harbor Freight Lines, Inc
1339 W Valley Hwy N
Auburn WA 98001
206 246-2600

(P-4239)
OAK HARBOR FREIGHT LINES INC
832 F St, West Sacramento (95605-2314)
PHONE..................916 371-3960
Fax: 916 371-6322
Greg Gommenginger, *Manager*
David Martin, *Safety Mgr*
EMP: 80
SALES (corp-wide): 217.9MM **Privately Held**
WEB: www.oakh.com
SIC: 4213 4212 Trucking, except local; local trucking, without storage
PA: Oak Harbor Freight Lines, Inc
1339 W Valley Hwy N
Auburn WA 98001
206 246-2600

(P-4240)
OLD DOMINION FREIGHT LINE INC
1225 Washington Blvd, Montebello (90640-6013)
PHONE..................323 725-3400
Fax: 323 728-8206
EMP: 200
SQ FT: 4,000
SALES (corp-wide): 2.9B **Publicly Held**
WEB: www.odfl.com
SIC: 4213 4212 Contract haulers; local trucking, without storage
PA: Old Dominion Freight Line Inc
500 Old Dominion Way
Thomasville NC 27360
336 889-5000

(P-4241)
PAN PACIFIC PETROLEUM CO INC
Also Called: Truck Terminal
1850 Coffee Rd, Bakersfield (93308-5746)
PHONE..................661 589-3200
Fax: 661 589-1147
Dave Palmer, *Manager*
EMP: 100
SALES (corp-wide): 499.3K **Privately Held**
SIC: 4213 Liquid petroleum transport, non-local
PA: Pan Pacific Petroleum Company, Inc.
9302 Garfield Ave
South Gate CA 90280
562 928-0100

(P-4242)
PAN PACIFIC PETROLEUM CO INC (PA)
9302 Garfield Ave, South Gate (90280-3805)
P.O. Box 1966 (90280-1966)
PHONE..................562 928-0100
Benard B Roth, *CEO*
Robert Roth, *President*
Bernard B Roth, *CEO*

4213 - Trucking, Except Local County (P-4243)

Dale Snyder, *Exec VP*
Steven Roth, *Vice Pres*
EMP: 100
SQ FT: 600
SALES: 499.3K **Privately Held**
SIC: 4213 5172 Liquid petroleum transport, non-local; petroleum brokers

(P-4243)
PENSKE LOGISTICS LLC
2090 Etiwanda Ave, Ontario (91761-2803)
PHONE 800 529-6531
Fax: 909 390-2707
EMP: 60
SALES (corp-wide): 12.5B **Privately Held**
WEB: www.penskelogistics.com
SIC: 4213 4212 Trucking, except local; furniture moving, local; without storage
HQ: Penske Logistics Llc
Green Hls Rr 10
Reading PA 19603
800 529-6531

(P-4244)
PIEDMONT TRANSFER & STORAGE
1555 S 7th St Ste A, San Jose (95112-5926)
PHONE 408 288-5600
Fax: 408 287-3367
David R Bartels, *President*
EMP: 50
SQ FT: 100,000
SALES (est): 5.2MM **Privately Held**
WEB: www.piedmontmoving.com
SIC: 4213 4214 Household goods transport; local trucking with storage

(P-4245)
POPPY STATE EXPRESS INC (PA)
2700 W Main St, Turlock (95380-9537)
PHONE 209 664-3950
Fax: 209 664-3960
Richard D Mello, *President*
Daniel N Watson, *CFO*
Judy Mello, *Treasurer*
John Doidge, *Vice Pres*
Claudia Doidge, *Admin Sec*
EMP: 52
SQ FT: 30,000
SALES (est): 7MM **Privately Held**
WEB: www.poppystate.com
SIC: 4213 Refrigerated products transport

(P-4246)
PRODUCTION DELIVERY SVCS INC
Also Called: Production Transport
12133 Greenstone Ave, Santa Fe Springs (90670-4728)
PHONE 562 777-0060
James Harkins, *President*
Michelle Harkins, *Corp Secy*
EMP: 55
SALES: 7MM **Privately Held**
SIC: 4213 Trucking, except local

(P-4247)
PYRAMID LOGISTICS SERVICES INC (PA)
14650 Hoover St, Westminster (92683-5346)
PHONE 714 903-2600
Fax: 714 898-9360
Timothy J Winningham, *CEO*
Jeannie Rivera, *Executive*
Michael Connolly, *Principal*
Robert Dissman, *Admin Sec*
Amy Wiedner, *Accounting Mgr*
EMP: 57
SQ FT: 59,000
SALES (est): 14.6MM **Privately Held**
SIC: 4213 4731 4225 Heavy hauling; contract haulers; foreign freight forwarding; general warehousing & storage

(P-4248)
QUALITY CARRIERS INC
Also Called: Montgomery Tank Lines
5042 Cecelia St, South Gate (90280-3511)
PHONE 800 282-2031
Fax: 310 771-3177
George Heinze, *Manager*
Skip Haddock, *Manager*
EMP: 70
SALES (corp-wide): 871.2MM **Privately Held**
WEB: www.qualitycarriers.com
SIC: 4213 Trucking, except local
HQ: Quality Carriers, Inc.
4041 Park Oaks Blvd # 200
Tampa FL 33610
800 282-2031

(P-4249)
REEVE TRUCKING COMPANY INC (PA)
5050 Carpenter Rd, Stockton (95215-8105)
P.O. Box 5126 (95205-0126)
PHONE 209 948-4061
Fax: 209 948-1791
Lori J Reeve, *President*
Pierre Korsmoe, *CFO*
Donald E Reeve, *Vice Pres*
Bob Costanza, *Executive*
Robert Protz, *Principal*
▲ **EMP:** 70
SQ FT: 100,000
SALES (est): 45MM **Privately Held**
WEB: www.reevetrucking.com
SIC: 4213 Trucking, except local; heavy machinery transport

(P-4250)
RELIABLE CARRIERS INC
Also Called: Relibale Carries
9122 Glenoaks Blvd, Sun Valley (91352-2611)
PHONE 818 252-6400
Tom Abraham, *Branch Mgr*
EMP: 50
SALES (corp-wide): 34MM **Privately Held**
SIC: 4213 Automobiles, transport & delivery
PA: Reliable Carriers, Inc.
41555 Koppernick Rd
Canton MI 48187
734 453-6677

(P-4251)
RENN TRANSPORTATION INC
8845 Forest St, Gilroy (95020-3651)
PHONE 408 842-3545
Brad E Renn, *President*
Robert Renn, *Vice Pres*
Patricia Renn, *Admin Sec*
Steven Boyle, *Manager*
EMP: 100
SQ FT: 9,609
SALES (est): 19.8MM **Privately Held**
WEB: www.renntransportation.com
SIC: 4213 Trucking, except local

(P-4252)
RICK STUDER
Also Called: Nordstrom
2610 Wisconsin Ave, South Gate (90280-5598)
P.O. Box 471 (90280-0471)
PHONE 323 357-1720
Rick Studer, *Owner*
EMP: 50
SALES (est): 5.4MM **Privately Held**
SIC: 4213 Trucking, except local

(P-4253)
ROADSTAR TRUCKING INC
30527 San Antonio St, Hayward (94544-7101)
PHONE 510 487-2404
Charles Ramorino, *Chairman*
Robert Ramorino, *President*
Andy Lin, *Vice Pres*
Robert H Jones, *Agent*
EMP: 55
SQ FT: 43,000
SALES (est): 10.9MM **Privately Held**
SIC: 4213 Trucking, except local

(P-4254)
RPM TRANSPORTATION INC (HQ)
1901 Raymer Ave, Fullerton (92833-2512)
PHONE 714 388-3500
Fax: 562 906-0275
Shawn Duke, *President*
Andrew Lewes, *CFO*
Jeff Lyskosko, *Chief Mktg Ofcr*
Linda Dickey, *Human Res Dir*
EMP: 110
SQ FT: 175,000
SALES (est): 27.3MM
SALES (corp-wide): 63.5MM **Privately Held**
SIC: 4213 4225 4214 Trailer or container on flat car (TOFC/COFC); general warehousing; local trucking with storage
PA: Rpm Consolidated Services, Inc.
1901 Raymer Ave
Fullerton CA 92833
714 388-3500

(P-4255)
S & M MOVING SYSTEMS
Also Called: SM International
48551 Warm Springs Blvd, Fremont (94539-7765)
PHONE 510 497-2300
Fax: 510 657-3617
Gerald P Stadler, *President*
John Stadler, *Vice Pres*
Christal Davis, *Accounting Dir*
▲ **EMP:** 60
SQ FT: 38,000
SALES (est): 13.2MM
SALES (corp-wide): 88.6MM **Privately Held**
WEB: www.sandmoving.com
SIC: 4213 4214 Trucking, except local; local trucking with storage
PA: Torrance Van & Storage Company
12128 Burke St
Santa Fe Springs CA 90670
562 567-2100

(P-4256)
SAIA INC
Also Called: Saia S Reno Barbara K
1508 Wyant Way, Sacramento (95864-2642)
PHONE 916 483-8331
EMP: 153
SALES (corp-wide): 1.2B **Publicly Held**
SIC: 4213 Trucking, except local
PA: Saia, Inc.
11465 Johns Creek Pkwy # 400
Johns Creek GA 30097
770 232-5067

(P-4257)
SAIA MOTOR FREIGHT LINE LLC
9119 Elkmont Dr, Elk Grove (95624-9706)
PHONE 916 690-8417
Joe Meyer, *Branch Mgr*
Jeff Volker, *Marketing Staff*
EMP: 50
SALES (corp-wide): 1.2B **Publicly Held**
WEB: www.saia.com
SIC: 4213 Trucking, except local
HQ: Saia Motor Freight Line, Llc
11465 Johns Creek Pkwy # 400
Duluth GA 30097
770 232-5067

(P-4258)
SAIA MOTOR FREIGHT LINE LLC
2550 E 28th St, Vernon (90058-1430)
PHONE 323 277-2880
Gerard Francois, *Branch Mgr*
Tim Luther, *Executive*
EMP: 100
SALES (corp-wide): 1.2B **Publicly Held**
WEB: www.saia.com
SIC: 4213 Trucking, except local
HQ: Saia Motor Freight Line, Llc
11465 Johns Creek Pkwy # 400
Duluth GA 30097
770 232-5067

(P-4259)
SAIA MOTOR FREIGHT LINE INC
1755 Aurora Dr, San Leandro (94577-3103)
PHONE 510 347-6890
Fax: 510 347-6898
John Dentony, *Manager*
EMP: 51
SALES (corp-wide): 1.2B **Publicly Held**
WEB: www.saia.com
SIC: 4213 4212 Trucking, except local; local trucking, without storage
HQ: Saia Motor Freight Line, Llc
11465 Johns Creek Pkwy # 400
Duluth GA 30097
770 232-5067

(P-4260)
SCAN-VINO LLC (PA)
Also Called: Cherokee Freight Lines
5463 Cherokee Rd, Stockton (95215-1128)
PHONE 209 931-3570
Fax: 209 931-3979
Leanne Scannavino, *President*
Jack Riella, *Vice Pres*
EMP: 69 **EST:** 1965
SQ FT: 1,000
SALES (est): 16.7MM **Privately Held**
WEB: www.gocfl.com
SIC: 4213 Trucking, except local

(P-4261)
SCHNEIDER NATIONAL INC
4193 Industrial Pkwy Dr, Lebec (93243-9719)
PHONE 661 858-1031
Mark Griffin, *Branch Mgr*
EMP: 205
SALES (corp-wide): 4.2B **Privately Held**
SIC: 4213 Trucking, except local
PA: Schneider National, Inc.
3101 Packerland Dr
Green Bay WI 54313
920 592-2000

(P-4262)
SCHNEIDER NATIONAL INC
14392 Valley Blvd, Fontana (92335-5240)
PHONE 909 574-2165
Ray Eastwood, *Manager*
Victor Rosas, *Maintence Staff*
EMP: 140
SALES (corp-wide): 4.2B **Privately Held**
SIC: 4213 Trucking, except local
PA: Schneider National, Inc.
3101 Packerland Dr
Green Bay WI 54313
920 592-2000

(P-4263)
SIRVA INC
2010 Crow Canyon Pl, San Ramon (94583-4634)
PHONE 925 824-3109
EMP: 130
SALES (corp-wide): 2.1B **Privately Held**
SIC: 4213 Household goods transport
PA: Sirva, Inc.
1 Parkview Plz
Oakbrook Terrace IL 60181
630 570-3047

(P-4264)
SNOOZIE SHAVINGS INC (HQ)
525 Elk Valley Rd, Crescent City (95531-9460)
PHONE 707 464-6186
Dwayne C Reichlin, *President*
Robert Matthess, *Treasurer*
Jay M Freeman, *Vice Pres*
Randy Brazelton, *Branch Mgr*
Charlie F Compton, *Admin Sec*
EMP: 51
SQ FT: 18,000
SALES (est): 3MM
SALES (corp-wide): 26.4MM **Privately Held**
WEB: www.ssitrucking.com
SIC: 4213 5099 Trucking, except local; shavings, wood; wood & wood by-products
PA: Forest Hambro Products Inc
445 Elk Valley Rd
Crescent City CA 95531
707 464-6131

(P-4265)
SPECIAL DISPATCH CAL INC
8328 Central Ave, Newark (94560-3432)
PHONE 510 713-0300
Keith Donahue, *Manager*
Martin Mantilla, *President*
EMP: 60
SALES (corp-wide): 30.1MM **Privately Held**
SIC: 4213 Trucking, except local

PRODUCTS & SERVICES SECTION

4213 - Trucking, Except Local County (P-4289)

PA: Special Dispatch Of California, Inc.
16330 Phoebe Ave
La Mirada CA 90638
602 296-8860

(P-4266)
STIDHAM TRUCKING INC
321 Payne Ln, Yreka (96097-3442)
P.O. Box 308 (96097-0308)
PHONE.................................530 842-4161
Fax: 530 842-2047
Richard Stidham, *President*
Larry Stidham, *Owner*
Frances Stidham, *Corp Secy*
Bill Branch, *Vice Pres*
Teresa Stidham, *Vice Pres*
EMP: 101
SQ FT: 6,000
SALES (est): 25.3MM **Privately Held**
WEB: www.stidhamtrucking.com
SIC: **4213** 4731 Trucking, except local; freight transportation arrangement

(P-4267)
SUDDATH RELO SYS OF NO CA
2055 S 7th St, San Jose (95112-6141)
PHONE.................................408 288-3030
Gene Kopecky, *President*
Peter Pfeilsticker, *General Mgr*
Dan Lambers, *Controller*
Mark Richards, *Purch Agent*
James C Patterson, *Opers Mgr*
EMP: 51
SALES (est): 9.4MM
SALES (corp-wide): 456.3MM **Privately Held**
SIC: **4213** 4731 4214 Household goods transport; freight forwarding; household goods moving & storage, local
HQ: Suddath Van Lines Inc
815 S Main St Ste 400
Jacksonville FL 32207
904 390-7100

(P-4268)
SULLIVAN MOVING & STORAGE (PA)
Also Called: United Van Lines
5704 Copley Dr, San Diego (92111-7905)
PHONE.................................858 874-2600
Fax: 858 874-2611
Rick Smith, *CEO*
Mark Fischer, *President*
Pat Reid, *CFO*
Mark Keiper, *Vice Pres*
Gary Carlisle, *Opers Staff*
EMP: 50 EST: 1988
SQ FT: 60,000
SALES: 16MM **Privately Held**
WEB: www.sullivanunited.com
SIC: **4213** 4214 Trucking, except local; local trucking with storage

(P-4269)
SUN PACIFIC TRUCKING INC
512 E C St, Wilmington (90744-6618)
PHONE.................................310 830-4528
Fax: 310 830-4590
Vicente Zarate, *President*
◆ EMP: 85 EST: 1995
SQ FT: 100,000
SALES: 8.8MM **Privately Held**
WEB: www.sunpacifictrucking.com
SIC: **4213** Trucking, except local

(P-4270)
SWARD TRUCKING INC
1657 Merritt St, Turlock (95380-4241)
PHONE.................................209 847-4210
Fax: 209 847-3725
Wallace V Sward, *President*
Saundra West, *Treasurer*
Nicholas West, *Vice Pres*
EMP: 65
SQ FT: 1,550
SALES (est): 7.3MM **Privately Held**
WEB: www.swardtrucking.com
SIC: **4213** 4731 Contract haulers; freight transportation arrangement

(P-4271)
SWIFT TRANSPORTATION COMPANY
901 Darcy Pkwy, Lathrop (95330-8764)
PHONE.................................209 858-1630
Fax: 209 858-7041
Kevin Vadnal, *Branch Mgr*
Vivian Navarro, *Financial Exec*
EMP: 100
SALES (corp-wide): 4.2B **Publicly Held**
SIC: **4213** Trucking, except local
PA: Swift Transportation Company
2200 S 75th Ave
Phoenix AZ 85043
602 269-9700

(P-4272)
SWIFT TRANSPORTATION COMPANY
2797 S Orange Ave, Fresno (93725-1919)
PHONE.................................559 441-0340
Mark Peed, *Manager*
EMP: 56
SALES (corp-wide): 4.2B **Publicly Held**
SIC: **4213** Trucking, except local
PA: Swift Transportation Company
2200 S 75th Ave
Phoenix AZ 85043
602 269-9700

(P-4273)
SWIFT TRANSPORTATION COMPANY
11888 Mission Blvd, Mira Loma (91752-1003)
PHONE.................................951 360-0130
Fax: 951 360-0966
Renaldo Gonzales, *Manager*
EMP: 56
SALES (corp-wide): 4.2B **Publicly Held**
SIC: **4213** Trucking, except local
PA: Swift Transportation Company
2200 S 75th Ave
Phoenix AZ 85043
602 269-9700

(P-4274)
SWIFT WORLDWIDE INC (PA)
Also Called: Swift Courier Service
1390 Willow Pass Rd # 420, Concord (94520-5200)
P.O. Box 20992, El Sobrante (94820-0992)
PHONE.................................510 351-7949
Qaiser A Chaudhery, *CEO*
Zia Chaudhery, *President*
Shawn Chaudhery, *Vice Pres*
EMP: 150
SQ FT: 120,000
SALES: 35MM **Privately Held**
SIC: **4213** 4215 Trucking, except local; courier services, except by air

(P-4275)
T & T TRUCKING INC (PA)
11396 N Hwy 99, Lodi (95240-6899)
PHONE.................................800 692-3457
Fax: 209 931-6156
Terry M Tarditi, *President*
John King, *Treasurer*
Jennifer Christy, *Office Mgr*
Mary Lou Tarditi, *Admin Sec*
Jennifer Streeter, *Sls & Mktg Exec*
EMP: 107
SQ FT: 25,000
SALES (est): 21.4MM **Privately Held**
WEB: www.tttrucking.com
SIC: **4213** Trucking, except local

(P-4276)
TIGER LINES LLC (HQ)
927 Black Diamond Way, Lodi (95240-0738)
P.O. Box 1120 (95241-1120)
PHONE.................................209 334-4100
Fax: 209 333-7925
Dennis Altnow, *CEO*
Tim Middleton, *Info Tech Mgr*
Robin Sanborn, *Human Res Dir*
Jason Henry, *Purch Agent*
Donald Altnow, *Mng Member*
EMP: 75 EST: 1935
SQ FT: 20,000
SALES: 35.5MM
SALES (corp-wide): 2.2MM **Privately Held**
SIC: **4213** 4214 4212 Trucking, except local; local trucking with storage; local trucking, without storage
PA: Lts Rentals, Llc
927 Black Diamond Way
Lodi CA 95240
209 334-4100

(P-4277)
TMT INDUSTRIES INC
8978 Haven Ave, Rancho Cucamonga (91730-5401)
PHONE.................................909 770-8514
Antonio Y Martinez, *CEO*
Tony Martinez Sr, *President*
Evelyn Martinez, *Corp Secy*
Tony Martinez Jr, *Vice Pres*
Debie Martinez, *Manager*
EMP: 63
SQ FT: 3,000
SALES (est): 22.7MM **Privately Held**
SIC: **4213** 4212 Trucking, except local; local trucking, without storage

(P-4278)
TONYS EXPRESS INC (PA)
10613 Jasmine St, Fontana (92337-8241)
PHONE.................................909 427-8700
Fax: 909 427-8300
George Raluy, *President*
Lorraine Khair, *Corp Secy*
Tony Raluy, *Exec VP*
Ken Fasola, *Vice Pres*
Anthony Raluy, *Vice Pres*
EMP: 127
SQ FT: 180,000
SALES (est): 24.7MM **Privately Held**
SIC: **4213** 4214 4212 Less-than-truckload (LTL) transport; local trucking with storage; local trucking, without storage

(P-4279)
TOTAL TRNSP LOGISTICS INC
4325 Etiwanda Ave Ste A, Mira Loma (91752-3720)
PHONE.................................951 360-9521
Fax: 951 360-8679
Robert E Hicks, *President*
Michael Doliveira, *CFO*
Mike Stadler, *CFO*
Steve Todare, *Vice Pres*
Loriann Aberle, *Executive*
EMP: 75
SQ FT: 125,000
SALES (est): 21.9MM **Privately Held**
WEB: www.ttllogistics.com
SIC: **4213** Trucking, except local

(P-4280)
TRIPLE-E MACHINERY MOVING INC
3301 Gilman Rd, El Monte (91732-3225)
PHONE.................................626 444-1137
Fax: 626 444-3862
Steve Englebrecht, *CEO*
Joe Englebrecht, *Vice Pres*
Jeff Englebrecht, *General Mgr*
Mike Englebrecht, *General Mgr*
Lori Bennett, *Info Tech Mgr*
EMP: 60
SQ FT: 12,000
SALES (est): 9.3MM **Privately Held**
WEB: www.tripleemachinery.com
SIC: **4213** Heavy machinery transport

(P-4281)
U C L INCORPORATED (PA)
Also Called: United Cargo Logistics
620 S Hacienda Blvd, City of Industry (91745-1126)
PHONE.................................323 232-3469
Fax: 323 235-0515
Byung Y Chang, *CEO*
Chris Chang, *President*
EMP: 100
SQ FT: 16,000
SALES (est): 71.3MM **Privately Held**
WEB: www.uclinc.com
SIC: **4213** Trucking, except local

(P-4282)
U S XPRESS INC
363 Nina Lee Rd, Calexico (92231-9527)
PHONE.................................760 768-6707
EMP: 124
SALES (corp-wide): 1.1B **Privately Held**
SIC: **4213** Trucking, except local
HQ: U. S. Xpress, Inc.
4080 Jenkins Rd
Chattanooga TN 37421
423 510-3000

(P-4283)
UNITED VAN LINES AGENT
1450 N Benson Ave, Upland (91786-2165)
PHONE.................................909 946-7655
Bob Johnson, *President*
Tom Johnson, *COO*
EMP: 50
SALES: 5.3MM **Privately Held**
SIC: **4213** 4731 Household goods transport; freight transportation arrangement

(P-4284)
UPS FREIGHT SERVICES INC
2650 S Willow Ave, Bloomington (92316-3257)
PHONE.................................909 879-7400
Criss Sowers, *Manager*
EMP: 73
SALES (corp-wide): 58.3B **Publicly Held**
SIC: **4213** Trucking, except local
HQ: Ups Freight Services, Inc.
1000 Semmes Ave
Richmond VA 23224
804 231-8000

(P-4285)
UPS GROUND FREIGHT INC
Also Called: Martrac
4587 S Chestnut Ave, Fresno (93725-9211)
PHONE.................................559 445-9010
Fax: 559 445-9014
Steve Sutton, *Manager*
EMP: 56
SALES (corp-wide): 58.3B **Publicly Held**
SIC: **4213** Trucking, except local
HQ: Ups Ground Freight, Inc.
1000 Semmes Ave
Richmond VA 23224
866 372-5619

(P-4286)
UPS GROUND FREIGHT INC
600 Williams St, Bakersfield (93305-5438)
PHONE.................................661 395-9500
Fax: 661 395-9510
EMP: 95
SALES (corp-wide): 58.2B **Publicly Held**
SIC: **4213**
HQ: Ups Ground Freight, Inc.
1000 Semmes Ave
Richmond VA 23224
804 231-8000

(P-4287)
UPS GROUND FREIGHT INC
1444 Lathrop Rd, Lathrop (95330-9771)
PHONE.................................209 858-5095
Fax: 209 858-9154
Bill Rose, *Branch Mgr*
EMP: 98
SALES (corp-wide): 58.3B **Publicly Held**
SIC: **4213** Trucking, except local
HQ: Ups Ground Freight, Inc.
1000 Semmes Ave
Richmond VA 23224
866 372-5619

(P-4288)
UPS GROUND FREIGHT INC
12455 Harvest Dr, Mira Loma (91752-1025)
PHONE.................................951 361-1300
Fax: 951 361-1215
Andre Campbell, *Manager*
EMP: 95
SALES (corp-wide): 58.3B **Publicly Held**
WEB: www.overnite.com
SIC: **4213** Trucking, except local
HQ: Ups Ground Freight, Inc.
1000 Semmes Ave
Richmond VA 23224
866 372-5619

(P-4289)
UPS GROUND FREIGHT INC
7 College Ave, Santa Rosa (95401-4702)
P.O. Box 6836 (95406-0836)
PHONE.................................707 526-1910
Jesse Amarel, *Manager*
EMP: 95
SALES (corp-wide): 58.3B **Publicly Held**
WEB: www.overnite.com
SIC: **4213** Trucking, except local

4213 - Trucking, Except Local County (P-4290)

HQ: Ups Ground Freight, Inc.
1000 Semmes Ave
Richmond VA 23224
866 372-5619

(P-4290)
UPS GROUND FREIGHT INC
925 Morse Ave, Sunnyvale (94089-1601)
PHONE....................................408 400-0595
EMP: 95
SALES (corp-wide): 58.2B **Publicly Held**
SIC: 4213
HQ: Ups Ground Freight, Inc.
1000 Semmes Ave
Richmond VA 23224
804 231-8000

(P-4291)
UPS GROUND FREIGHT INC
20760 Spence Rd, Salinas (93908-9511)
PHONE....................................831 751-0262
Pam Keller, *Branch Mgr*
EMP: 95
SALES (corp-wide): 58.3B **Publicly Held**
WEB: www.overnite.com
SIC: 4213 Trucking, except local
HQ: Ups Ground Freight, Inc.
1000 Semmes Ave
Richmond VA 23224
866 372-5619

(P-4292)
UPS GROUND FREIGHT INC
Also Called: UPS Freight
7754 Paramount Blvd, Pico Rivera (90660-4309)
PHONE....................................562 801-1300
Cliff Sowers, *Branch Mgr*
Fred Meeks, *Executive*
EMP: 95
SALES (corp-wide): 58.3B **Publicly Held**
WEB: www.overnite.com
SIC: 4213 Trucking, except local
HQ: Ups Ground Freight, Inc.
1000 Semmes Ave
Richmond VA 23224
866 372-5619

(P-4293)
UPS GROUND FREIGHT INC
900 E St, West Sacramento (95605-2310)
PHONE....................................916 371-9101
EMP: 60
SALES (corp-wide): 58.2B **Publicly Held**
SIC: 4213
HQ: Ups Ground Freight, Inc.
1000 Semmes Ave
Richmond VA 23224
804 231-8000

(P-4294)
UPS GROUND FREIGHT INC
650 S Acacia Ave, Fullerton (92831-5107)
PHONE....................................866 372-5619
Arthur Morales, *General Mgr*
EMP: 80
SALES (corp-wide): 58.3B **Publicly Held**
WEB: www.overnite.com
SIC: 4213 Automobiles, transport & delivery
HQ: Ups Ground Freight, Inc.
1000 Semmes Ave
Richmond VA 23224
866 372-5619

(P-4295)
USA TRUCK INC
5861 Pine Ave Ste A-2, Chino Hills (91709-6540)
PHONE....................................909 334-1406
EMP: 67
SALES (corp-wide): 507.9MM **Publicly Held**
SIC: 4213 Trucking, except local
PA: Usa Truck, Inc.
3200 Industrial Park Rd
Van Buren AR 72956
479 471-2500

(P-4296)
USF REDDAWAY INC
11937 Regentview Ave, Downey (90241-5515)
PHONE....................................562 923-0648
Sal Leal, *Manager*
EMP: 150

SQ FT: 28,300
SALES (corp-wide): 4.8B **Publicly Held**
SIC: 4213 Trucking, except local
HQ: Usf Reddaway Inc.
7720 Sw Mohawk St Bldg H
Tualatin OR 97062
503 650-1286

(P-4297)
VALLEY BULK INC
17649 Turner Rd, Victorville (92394-8716)
P.O. Box 1100 (92393-1100)
PHONE....................................760 843-0574
Fax: 760 951-7369
Jeff W Golson, *President*
Connie Desterhouse, *Manager*
EMP: 85
SALES (est): 14.2MM **Privately Held**
WEB: www.valleybulk.com
SIC: 4213 Trucking, except local

(P-4298)
VALLEY RELOCATION AND STORAGE (PA)
Also Called: Valley Northamerican
5000 Marsh Dr, Concord (94520-5322)
PHONE....................................925 230-2025
Fax: 925 603-7119
James Robson, *President*
John A Burks, *CEO*
Mark Robson, *General Mgr*
Nick Gabadou, *Accounts Mgr*
EMP: 50
SQ FT: 58,000
SALES (est): 27.3MM **Privately Held**
SIC: 4213 Trucking, except local

(P-4299)
VENTURA TRANSFER COMPANY (PA)
Also Called: Lesbro Company
2418 E 223rd St, Long Beach (90810-1697)
PHONE....................................310 549-1660
Fax: 310 835-9175
Randall Clifford, *CEO*
Brian Oken, *President*
Ian Hart, *CFO*
Galen Clifford, *Vice Pres*
Greg Clifford, *Vice Pres*
▲ **EMP:** 75 **EST:** 1927
SQ FT: 10,000
SALES (est): 17MM **Privately Held**
WEB: www.venturatransfercompany.com
SIC: 4213 4212 4214 Trucking, except local; local trucking, without storage; local trucking with storage

(P-4300)
VIP TRANSPORT INC
2703 Wardlow Rd, Corona (92882-2869)
PHONE....................................951 272-3700
Fax: 909 272-1133
Brittany Johnson, *President*
Laurie Griffiths, *Treasurer*
Laurie Johnson, *Treasurer*
Shea B Russell, *Business Dir*
Brittany Griffiths, *Admin Sec*
♦ **EMP:** 50 **EST:** 1982
SQ FT: 127,000
SALES (est): 10.6MM **Privately Held**
WEB: www.viptransport.com
SIC: 4213 4214 4731 Trucking, except local; local trucking with storage; foreign freight forwarding

(P-4301)
WAGGONERS TRUCKING
801 Mcwane Blvd, Port Hueneme (93043-0001)
PHONE....................................800 999-9097
Fax: 805 271-9569
Rick Salazar, *Manager*
EMP: 60
SALES (corp-wide): 242.1MM **Privately Held**
SIC: 4213 Trucking, except local
PA: The Waggoners Trucking
5220 Midland Rd
Billings MT 59101
406 248-1919

(P-4302)
WERNER ENTERPRISES INC
10251 Calabash Ave, Fontana (92335-5275)
PHONE....................................909 823-5803
John Bidaurri, *Branch Mgr*
John Vidaurri, *Terminal Mgr*
EMP: 50
SQ FT: 1,316
SALES (corp-wide): 2B **Publicly Held**
WEB: www.werner.com
SIC: 4213 4731 Trucking, except local; freight consolidation
PA: Werner Enterprises, Inc
14507 Frontier Rd
Omaha NE 68138
402 895-6640

(P-4303)
WILDWOOD EXPRESS
12416 Swanson Ave, Kingsburg (93631-9516)
P.O. Box 397 (93631-0397)
PHONE....................................559 805-3237
Mark Anthony Woods, *President*
Matthew Woods, *Treasurer*
Sue Woods, *Vice Pres*
EMP: 50
SQ FT: 3,500
SALES (est): 11.1MM **Privately Held**
SIC: 4213 Contract haulers

(P-4304)
WILLIAMS TANK LINES (PA)
1477 Tillie Lewis Dr, Stockton (95206-1130)
PHONE....................................209 944-5613
Fax: 209 944-9230
Michael I Williams, *CEO*
Marlys A Williams, *Admin Sec*
Anna Vorn, *Human Resources*
Geoff Sage, *Traffic Dir*
Eli Vasquez, *Foreman/Supr*
EMP: 90 **EST:** 1978
SQ FT: 15,000
SALES (est): 82.9MM **Privately Held**
SIC: 4213 Liquid petroleum transport, non-local

(P-4305)
WOLFE TRUCKING INC
7131 Valjean Ave, Van Nuys (91406-3917)
PHONE....................................818 376-6960
Fax: 818 376-6970
Jack Wolfe, *President*
Stephen Malley, *Agent*
EMP: 107
SQ FT: 7,200
SALES (est): 14.2MM **Privately Held**
SIC: 4213 Trucking, except local

(P-4306)
WRAGTIME AIR FREIGHT INC (PA)
Also Called: Vision Express/Wrag-Time Trnsp
596 W 135th St, Gardena (90248-1506)
PHONE....................................800 586-9701
Fax: 323 277-1446
Leonard C Emrick, *President*
Nick Brooks, *Admin Sec*
Patrick Diehl, *Credit Mgr*
Jeff Billman, *Marketing Staff*
Dave Thomas, *Manager*
EMP: 68
SQ FT: 200,000
SALES (est): 46.3MM **Privately Held**
SIC: 4213 4731 Trucking, except local; freight forwarding

(P-4307)
XPO ENTERPRISE SERVICES INC
5475 S Airport Way, Stockton (95206-3918)
PHONE....................................209 983-8285
Fax: 209 982-5341
Rudy Romo, *Manager*
Tom Baeton, *Manager*
Jerry Barajas, *Manager*
EMP: 60
SQ FT: 1,000
SALES (corp-wide): 7.6B **Publicly Held**
WEB: www.con-way.com
SIC: 4213 Trucking, except local

HQ: Xpo Enterprise Services, Inc.
2211 Old Earhart Rd # 100
Ann Arbor MI 48105
734 998-4200

(P-4308)
XPO ENTERPRISE SERVICES INC
4965 Convoy St, San Diego (92111-1600)
PHONE....................................858 569-8921
Fax: 858 576-1621
Tim Tuerk, *Manager*
EMP: 50
SQ FT: 20,344
SALES (corp-wide): 7.6B **Publicly Held**
WEB: www.con-way.com
SIC: 4213 Trucking, except local
HQ: Xpo Enterprise Services, Inc.
2211 Old Earhart Rd # 100
Ann Arbor MI 48105
734 998-4200

(P-4309)
XPO ENTERPRISE SERVICES INC
2171 Otoole Ave, San Jose (95131-1314)
PHONE....................................408 435-3876
Fax: 408 435-8580
Jon Sullivan, *Branch Mgr*
Ryan Walker, *Manager*
EMP: 60
SQ FT: 8,834
SALES (corp-wide): 7.6B **Publicly Held**
WEB: www.con-way.com
SIC: 4213 Trucking, except local
HQ: Xpo Enterprise Services, Inc.
2211 Old Earhart Rd # 100
Ann Arbor MI 48105
734 998-4200

(P-4310)
XPO ENTERPRISE SERVICES INC
4195 E Central Ave, Fresno (93725-9026)
PHONE....................................559 485-1164
Bud Whitney, *Principal*
EMP: 62
SQ FT: 39,620
SALES (corp-wide): 7.6B **Publicly Held**
WEB: www.con-way.com
SIC: 4213 Trucking, except local
HQ: Xpo Enterprise Services, Inc.
2211 Old Earhart Rd # 100
Ann Arbor MI 48105
734 998-4200

(P-4311)
XPO ENTERPRISE SERVICES INC
787 Airport Blvd, Salinas (93901-4509)
PHONE....................................831 758-8874
Fax: 831 758-4912
Ted Garcia, *Sales/Mktg Mgr*
EMP: 62
SALES (corp-wide): 7.6B **Publicly Held**
WEB: www.con-way.com
SIC: 4213 Trucking, except local
HQ: Xpo Enterprise Services, Inc.
2211 Old Earhart Rd # 100
Ann Arbor MI 48105
734 998-4200

(P-4312)
XPO ENTERPRISE SERVICES INC
12466 Montague St, Pacoima (91331-2121)
PHONE....................................818 890-2095
Fax: 818 897-2626
Paul Styers, *Manager*
EMP: 200
SQ FT: 20,187
SALES (corp-wide): 7.6B **Publicly Held**
WEB: www.con-way.com
SIC: 4213 4214 Trucking, except local; local trucking with storage
HQ: Xpo Enterprise Services, Inc.
2211 Old Earhart Rd # 100
Ann Arbor MI 48105
734 998-4200

▲ = Import ▼=Export
♦ =Import/Export

PRODUCTS & SERVICES SECTION

4214 - Local Trucking With Storage County (P-4333)

(P-4313)
XPO ENTERPRISE SERVICES INC
2102 N Batavia St, Orange (92865-3104)
PHONE 714 282-7717
Fax: 714 282-7762
Tim Worner, *Manager*
EMP: 100
SALES (corp-wide): 7.6B **Publicly Held**
WEB: www.con-way.com
SIC: 4213 Trucking, except local
HQ: Xpo Enterprise Services, Inc.
2211 Old Earhart Rd # 100
Ann Arbor MI 48105
734 998-4200

(P-4314)
XPO ENTERPRISE SERVICES INC
3516 Kiessig Ave, Sacramento (95823-1036)
PHONE 916 399-8291
Fax: 916 399-8579
Wes Stucki, *Branch Mgr*
Butch Russell, *Branch Mgr*
EMP: 120
SALES (corp-wide): 7.6B **Publicly Held**
WEB: www.con-way.com
SIC: 4213 Trucking, except local
HQ: Xpo Enterprise Services, Inc.
2211 Old Earhart Rd # 100
Ann Arbor MI 48105
734 998-4200

(P-4315)
XPO ENTERPRISE SERVICES INC
20697 Prism Pl, Lake Forest (92630-7803)
PHONE 949 581-9030
Fax: 949 581-9390
Joseph Tickford, *Branch Mgr*
EMP: 60
SQ FT: 13,890
SALES (corp-wide): 7.6B **Publicly Held**
WEB: www.con-way.com
SIC: 4213 Less-than-truckload (LTL) transport
HQ: Xpo Enterprise Services, Inc.
2211 Old Earhart Rd # 100
Ann Arbor MI 48105
734 998-4200

(P-4316)
XPO ENTERPRISE SERVICES INC
1955 E Washington Blvd, Los Angeles (90021-3206)
PHONE 213 744-0664
Fax: 213 744-1069
Todd Liverman, *Branch Mgr*
EMP: 120
SQ FT: 39,842
SALES (corp-wide): 7.6B **Publicly Held**
WEB: www.con-way.com
SIC: 4213 4212 4731 Trucking, except local; local trucking, without storage; freight forwarding
HQ: Xpo Enterprise Services, Inc.
2211 Old Earhart Rd # 100
Ann Arbor MI 48105
734 998-4200

(P-4317)
XPO ENTERPRISE SERVICES INC
Also Called: Con-Way
12555 Mesa Dr, Blythe (92225-3363)
PHONE 760 922-8538
Fax: 760 922-7043
Butch Russell, *Manager*
EMP: 62
SALES (corp-wide): 7.6B **Publicly Held**
WEB: www.con-way.com
SIC: 4213 Trucking, except local
HQ: Xpo Enterprise Services, Inc.
2211 Old Earhart Rd # 100
Ann Arbor MI 48105
734 998-4200

(P-4318)
XPO ENTERPRISE SERVICES INC
Also Called: Con-Way
4095 S Moorland Ave, Santa Rosa (95407-8110)
PHONE 707 584-0211
Fax: 707 584-2378
Rich Gonzales, *Manager*
EMP: 62
SALES (corp-wide): 7.6B **Publicly Held**
WEB: www.con-way.com
SIC: 4213 Trucking, except local
HQ: Xpo Enterprise Services, Inc.
2211 Old Earhart Rd # 100
Ann Arbor MI 48105
734 998-4200

(P-4319)
XPO ENTERPRISE SERVICES INC
Also Called: Con-Way
3810 Hill Rd, Lakeport (95453-7015)
PHONE 916 399-8291
EMP: 120
SALES (corp-wide): 7.6B **Publicly Held**
SIC: 4213
HQ: Xpo Enterprise Services, Inc.
2211 Old Earhart Rd # 100
Ann Arbor MI 48105
734 998-4200

(P-4320)
XPO ENTERPRISE SERVICES INC
2200 Claremont Ct, Hayward (94545-5002)
PHONE 510 785-6920
Fax: 510 782-5732
Terry Smith, *Manager*
Jon Sullivan, *Sales Executive*
Ted Reeves, *Manager*
Tom Wehrell, *Manager*
EMP: 200
SQ FT: 28,704
SALES (corp-wide): 7.6B **Publicly Held**
WEB: www.con-way.com
SIC: 4213 4212 4731 Trucking, except local; local trucking, without storage; freight transportation arrangement
HQ: Xpo Enterprise Services, Inc.
2211 Old Earhart Rd # 100
Ann Arbor MI 48105
734 998-4200

(P-4321)
XPO ENTERPRISE SERVICES INC
13364 Marlay Ave, Fontana (92337-6919)
PHONE 951 685-1244
Fax: 951 685-5717
Mark Logan, *General Mgr*
Jim Lutz, *Director*
EMP: 200
SALES (corp-wide): 7.6B **Publicly Held**
SIC: 4213 Trucking, except local
HQ: Xpo Enterprise Services, Inc.
2211 Old Earhart Rd # 100
Ann Arbor MI 48105
734 998-4200

(P-4322)
XPO ENTERPRISE SERVICES INC
12903 Lakeland Rd, Santa Fe Springs (90670-4516)
PHONE 562 946-8331
Jim Lutze, *Manager*
Les Phillips, *Human Res Dir*
Patrick Touhey, *Manager*
EMP: 200
SALES (corp-wide): 7.6B **Publicly Held**
WEB: www.con-way.com
SIC: 4213 Trucking, except local
HQ: Xpo Enterprise Services, Inc.
2211 Old Earhart Rd # 100
Ann Arbor MI 48105
734 998-4200

(P-4323)
YRC INC
Also Called: Yellow Transportation
25555 Clawiter Rd, Hayward (94545-2740)
PHONE 510 783-7010
Fax: 510 783-3230
Pete Kell, *Manager*

Trevor Schirmer, *Manager*
Trevor Sherman, *Manager*
EMP: 100
SQ FT: 33,872
SALES (corp-wide): 4.8B **Publicly Held**
WEB: www.roadway.com
SIC: 4213 4231 Contract haulers; trucking terminal facilities
HQ: Yrc Inc.
10990 Roe Ave
Overland Park KS 66211
913 696-6100

(P-4324)
YRC INC
Also Called: Yellow Transportation
15400 S Main St, Gardena (90248-2215)
PHONE 310 404-2221
Fax: 310 217-0222
Tony Edmondson, *Manager*
Steven Martinez, *Manager*
Jack Workman, *Manager*
Robert Bilick, *Accounts Exec*
Angela Trevino, *Accounts Exec*
EMP: 200
SQ FT: 56,821
SALES (corp-wide): 4.8B **Publicly Held**
WEB: www.roadway.com
SIC: 4213 Contract haulers
HQ: Yrc Inc.
10990 Roe Ave
Overland Park KS 66211
913 696-6100

(P-4325)
YRC INC
3210 52nd Ave, Sacramento (95823-1024)
PHONE 916 371-4555
Scott Kamman, *Owner*
Denise Hummer, *Admin Sec*
EMP: 99
SALES (corp-wide): 4.8B **Publicly Held**
SIC: 4213 Trucking, except local
HQ: Yrc Inc.
10990 Roe Ave
Overland Park KS 66211
913 696-6100

(P-4326)
YRC WORLDWIDE INC
201 Haskins Way, South San Francisco (94080-6215)
PHONE 650 952-1112
Mike Sighn, *Principal*
Dave Black, *Director*
Mike Singh, *Manager*
EMP: 100
SALES (corp-wide): 4.8B **Publicly Held**
SIC: 4213 Less-than-truckload (LTL) transport
PA: Yrc Worldwide Inc.
10990 Roe Ave
Overland Park KS 66211
913 696-6100

4214 Local Trucking With Storage

(P-4327)
AMERICAN RLCTION LOGISTICS INC
13565 Larwin Cir, Santa Fe Springs (90670-5032)
PHONE 562 229-3600
Fax: 562 229-3679
Lawrence D Whittet, *CEO*
James Hooper, *President*
Robert Lechich, *CFO*
Jim Huckestein, *Executive*
Cindy Muniz, *Info Tech Mgr*
EMP: 95
SQ FT: 120,000
SALES (est): 22.3MM **Privately Held**
WEB: www.american-moving.com
SIC: 4214 4213 4212 Local trucking with storage; trucking, except local; household goods transport; moving services

(P-4328)
AMERICAN WEST WORLDWIDE EX INC (PA)
51 Zaca Ln Ste 120, San Luis Obispo (93401-7353)
PHONE 800 788-4534

Josh Brown, *CEO*
Cathie Brown, *President*
Connie Johansen, *Controller*
EMP: 68
SALES (est): 47.8MM **Privately Held**
SIC: 4214 4213 4225 Local trucking with storage; trucking, except local; general warehousing

(P-4329)
AMS RELOCATION INCORPORATED
Also Called: AMS Bekins Van Lines
1873 Rollins Rd, Burlingame (94010-2209)
PHONE 650 697-3530
Fax: 650 697-7810
Gary P Wolfe, *President*
Bill Evans, *Sales Staff*
Mike Foster, *Manager*
EMP: 55
SQ FT: 45,000
SALES (est): 5.7MM **Privately Held**
SIC: 4214 Local trucking with storage

(P-4330)
BEAR TRUCKING INC
Also Called: Gate City Beverage Bear Trckg
19768 Kendall Dr, San Bernardino (92407-1633)
P.O. Box 9158 (92427-0158)
PHONE 909 799-1616
Fax: 909 799-1618
Leona Aronoff, *President*
EMP: 100
SQ FT: 10,000
SALES (est): 21MM **Privately Held**
SIC: 4214 Local trucking with storage

(P-4331)
BEKINS MOVING SOLUTIONS INC (PA)
Also Called: Bekins Moving & Storage
12610 Shoemaker Ave, Santa Fe Springs (90670-6344)
PHONE 714 736-6100
Fax: 714 768-3346
David Caruso, *President*
Chris Fultz, *Vice Pres*
Doug Nichols, *Opers Mgr*
EMP: 79
SALES (est): 20.5MM **Privately Held**
SIC: 4214 4213 Local trucking with storage; trucking, except local

(P-4332)
BIAGI BROS INC
Also Called: Biagi Brothers Bezzerides Co
650 Stone Rd, Benicia (94510-1140)
PHONE 707 745-8115
Tom Tunt, *Branch Mgr*
Scott Okano, *Data Proc Exec*
EMP: 80
SALES (corp-wide): 106.1MM **Privately Held**
WEB: www.biagibros.com
SIC: 4214 Local trucking with storage
PA: Biagi Bros., Inc.
787 Airpark Rd
Napa CA 94558
707 745-8115

(P-4333)
CALKO TRANSPORT COMPANY INC
Also Called: Redman Container
720 E Watson Center Rd, Carson (90745-4108)
PHONE 310 816-0602
Fax: 310 638-3427
Chong Suh, *President*
Simon Chung, *Vice Pres*
Elena Yi, *Accountant*
Tim Suh, *Manager*
EMP: 58
SQ FT: 24,000
SALES (est): 6.7MM **Privately Held**
WEB: www.calko.com
SIC: 4214 4225 Local trucking with storage; general warehousing

4214 - Local Trucking With Storage County (P-4334)

(P-4334)
CHIPMAN CORPORATION (PA)
Also Called: Caton Moving & Storage
1040 Marina Village Pkwy # 100, Alameda (94501-6478)
PHONE..................510 748-8700
Tom Chipman, *CEO*
John H Chipman, *Chairman*
Greg Dolan, *Senior VP*
Paul Kilian, *Vice Pres*
Debbie Sparks, *Vice Pres*
EMP: 50
SQ FT: 400,000
SALES (est): 24.7MM **Privately Held**
WEB: www.chipmancorp.com
SIC: 4214 4213 4731 Household goods moving & storage, local; household goods transport; foreign freight forwarding

(P-4335)
COMPLETE RELOCATION SVCS INC
7361 Doig Dr, Garden Grove (92841-1806)
PHONE..................714 901-7411
Marc Kranz, *President*
EMP: 99 **EST:** 2007
SALES (est): 4.4MM **Privately Held**
SIC: 4214 Local trucking with storage

(P-4336)
COROVAN CORPORATION (PA)
12302 Kerran St, Poway (92064-6884)
PHONE..................858 762-8100
Richard R Schmitz, *CEO*
Robert J Schmitz, *Ch of Bd*
Thomas A Schmitz, *Admin Sec*
Jim Goff, *Technician*
John Schmitthenner, *Controller*
EMP: 175
SQ FT: 80,000
SALES (est): 78.2MM **Privately Held**
SIC: 4214 Local trucking with storage

(P-4337)
COROVAN MOVING & STORAGE CO (HQ)
12302 Kerran St, Poway (92064-6884)
PHONE..................858 748-1100
Fax: 760 758-1379
Richard R Schmitz, *President*
Jerry P Brothers, *CFO*
Robert J Schmitz, *Co-President*
Curtis Becker, *Executive*
Thomas A Schmitz, *Admin Sec*
EMP: 100
SQ FT: 600,000
SALES (est): 32.6MM
SALES (corp-wide): 70.7MM **Privately Held**
SIC: 4214 4213 Household goods moving & storage, local; household goods transport
PA: Corovan Corporation
  12302 Kerran St
  Poway CA 92064
  858 762-8100

(P-4338)
CRUZ MODULAR INC (PA)
Also Called: Systechs
249 W Baywood Ave Ste B, Orange (92865-2604)
PHONE..................714 283-2890
Fax: 714 283-1744
Linda Galleran, *CEO*
Vince Schlachter, *President*
Paul Bottorff, *Vice Pres*
Malcolm Craycroft, *Vice Pres*
Tim Schulte, *Opers Staff*
EMP: 56
SALES (est): 11.6MM **Privately Held**
WEB: www.systechs.com
SIC: 4214 7641 4226 1799 Furniture moving & storage, local; reupholstery & furniture repair; special warehousing & storage; office furniture installation

(P-4339)
DARRELL L GREEN INC
Also Called: Green Trucking
12652 Avenue 240, Tulare (93274-9531)
PHONE..................559 688-0680
Fax: 559 688-0614
Phyllis Green, *President*
Darrell L Green, *Corp Secy*
EMP: 67 **EST:** 1973
SQ FT: 4,000
SALES: 12MM **Privately Held**
WEB: www.greentrucking.com
SIC: 4214 Local trucking with storage

(P-4340)
DART INTERNATIONAL A CORP (HQ)
Also Called: Dart Entities
1430 S Eastman Ave, Commerce (90023-4006)
P.O. Box 23944, Los Angeles (90023-0944)
PHONE..................323 264-8746
Fax: 323 262-2218
Terence Dedeaux, *CEO*
Paul Martin, *President*
Steve Okamura, *CFO*
William J Smollen, *Corp Secy*
Steve Roskelley, *Exec VP*
EMP: 110
SQ FT: 50,000
SALES (est): 21.4MM
SALES (corp-wide): 98.1MM **Privately Held**
SIC: 4214 Local trucking with storage
PA: Dart Transportation Service, A Corporation
  1430 S Eastman Ave Ste 1
  Commerce CA 90023
  323 981-8205

(P-4341)
DGA SERVICES INC (PA)
Also Called: J I T Transportation
540 E Trimble Rd, San Jose (95131-1221)
P.O. Box 41372 (95160-1372)
PHONE..................408 232-4800
Deborah S Ashley, *CEO*
Gene Ashley, *President*
David Butcher, *Executive*
Ross Williams, *Info Tech Mgr*
Michelle Agellon, *Accounting Mgr*
EMP: 54
SQ FT: 125,000
SALES (est): 14.4MM **Privately Held**
WEB: www.jittransportation.com
SIC: 4214 4213 Local trucking with storage; trucking, except local

(P-4342)
DOUBLE DAY OFFICE SERVICES INC
340 Shaw Rd, South San Francisco (94080-6606)
P.O. Box 591405, San Francisco (94159-1405)
PHONE..................650 872-6600
Fax: 650 872-1692
Cheryl Ringelmann, *President*
Thomas Rodrigues, *General Mgr*
Eric Nelson, *Director*
EMP: 50
SQ FT: 45,000
SALES (est): 4.5MM **Privately Held**
WEB: www.doubleday-corprelo.com
SIC: 4214 7389 Local trucking with storage; relocation service

(P-4343)
DURKEE DRAYAGE COMPANY
3655 Collins Ave, San Pablo (94806-2074)
PHONE..................510 970-7550
Fax: 510 970-7565
Jeffrey J Fenton, *President*
Cathy Lashin, *Vice Pres*
EMP: 80
SQ FT: 80,000
SALES (est): 6.7MM **Privately Held**
WEB: www.durkeedrayage.com
SIC: 4214 Local trucking with storage

(P-4344)
EXCEL MOVING SERVICES
30047 Ahern Ave, Union City (94587-1234)
PHONE..................800 392-3596
Fax: 650 259-9485
Bruce D Owashi, *President*
Vyvyanne S Owashi, *Shareholder*
Robert Friederang, *Vice Pres*
EMP: 60
SQ FT: 23,400
SALES (est): 4.3MM **Privately Held**
SIC: 4214 Household goods moving & storage, local

(P-4345)
EXPRESS TRANSPORT SOLUTIONS
13285 Temple Ave, City of Industry (91746-1519)
PHONE..................626 961-4800
John Vach, *President*
Lilliana Vach, *Admin Sec*
Michael Bennett, *Agent*
David F Nicholson, *Agent*
EMP: 99
SQ FT: 16,000
SALES (est): 9.9MM **Privately Held**
SIC: 4214 4213 Local trucking with storage; trucking, except local

(P-4346)
GANDUGLIA TRUCKING
4737 E Florence Ave, Fresno (93725-1148)
P.O. Box 2568 (93745-2568)
PHONE..................559 251-7101
Fax: 559 251-5479
James Ganduglia, *Manager*
Karla Sutton, *Human Resources*
EMP: 61
SQ FT: 2,000
SALES (est): 5.5MM **Privately Held**
SIC: 4214 Local trucking with storage

(P-4347)
GILBERT SERVICE CORP
Also Called: Gilbert West
6725 Kimball Ave, Chino (91708-9177)
PHONE..................909 393-7575
Ken Gross, *President*
Charlie Sampera, *Senior VP*
Richard Gilbert, *Vice Pres*
Johnny Sheldon, *Natl Sales Mgr*
Richard Kleinberg, *VP Sales*
EMP: 125
SALES (est): 14.7MM **Privately Held**
SIC: 4214 4225 Local trucking with storage; general warehousing

(P-4348)
GSC LOGISTICS INC (PA)
530 Water St Fl 5, Oakland (94607-3532)
PHONE..................510 844-3700
Fax: 510 844-3810
Scott E Taylor, *CEO*
Marc Jensen, *CFO*
Joel Lesser, *CFO*
Norman Robert, *CFO*
Andres Garcia, *Exec VP*
EMP: 64
SQ FT: 8,000
SALES (est): 23.2MM **Privately Held**
SIC: 4214 4225 4213 Local trucking with storage; general warehousing; trucking, except local

(P-4349)
HALBERT BROTHERS INC
17400 Chestnut St, City of Industry (91748-1013)
PHONE..................626 913-1800
Fax: 626 913-6420
John W Miller, *CEO*
James R Miller, *Treasurer*
Rebecca Sierro, *Credit Mgr*
EMP: 60
SQ FT: 110,000
SALES: 5.8MM **Privately Held**
WEB: www.halbertbrothersinc.com
SIC: 4214 1796 Local trucking with storage; machine moving & rigging

(P-4350)
HARRISON NICHOLS CO LTD
501 W Foothill Blvd, Azusa (91702-2345)
PHONE..................626 337-5020
Fax: 626 338-1610
Kenneth Harrison, *CEO*
Randall P Harrison, *President*
EMP: 133
SQ FT: 12,000
SALES (est): 15.6MM **Privately Held**
SIC: 4214 4212 Local trucking with storage; local trucking, without storage

(P-4351)
HIDDEN VALLEY MVG & STOR INC (PA)
1218 Pacific Oaks Pl, Escondido (92029-2900)
PHONE..................602 252-7800
Fax: 760 741-0179
Robert L Berti, *CEO*
David Boeller, *CFO*
Roland Gutierrez, *Finance*
EMP: 100
SQ FT: 55,000
SALES (est): 17.8MM **Privately Held**
SIC: 4214 4213 Local trucking with storage; contract haulers

(P-4352)
JACK JONES TRUCKING INC
1090 E Belmont St, Ontario (91761-4501)
PHONE..................909 456-2500
Fax: 909 456-2520
Valerie Liese, *President*
Erin Craig, *Exec VP*
Robert Liese, *Vice Pres*
Sarah Kerns, *Executive*
Bob Liese, *General Mgr*
EMP: 100
SQ FT: 3,000
SALES (est): 15.7MM **Privately Held**
WEB: www.jjtinc.com
SIC: 4214 Local trucking with storage

(P-4353)
JAMES B BRANCH INC (PA)
Also Called: Gemini Moving Specialists
4367 Clybourn Ave, Toluca Lake (91602-2906)
PHONE..................818 765-3521
Eugene W Luni, *President*
Mark A Luni, *Corp Secy*
Louise W Luni, *Vice Pres*
EMP: 50
SQ FT: 35,000
SALES (est): 5.9MM **Privately Held**
SIC: 4214 Furniture moving & storage, local

(P-4354)
JAVELIN LOGISTICS CORPORATION (PA)
7447 Morton Ave Ste A, Newark (94560-4208)
PHONE..................510 795-7287
Fax: 510 608-3105
Malcolm George Winspear, *CEO*
Jeff Hoover, *Vice Pres*
Kc John, *Finance Dir*
Julie Young, *Finance*
Scott Casto, *Opers Spvr*
EMP: 50
SQ FT: 100,000
SALES (est): 38.4MM **Privately Held**
SIC: 4214 4731 4225 Local trucking with storage; freight transportation arrangement; general warehousing & storage

(P-4355)
KINGDOM EXPRESS INC
18640 Crenshaw Blvd, Torrance (90504-5032)
P.O. Box 622, Newbury Park (91319-0622)
PHONE..................310 258-0900
Fax: 310 258-0910
Larry King, *President*
Brenda King, *Shareholder*
Greg King, *Vice Pres*
Jim Stone, *Vice Pres*
Pat Eberhart, *Manager*
EMP: 65
SQ FT: 40,000
SALES (est): 8.4MM **Privately Held**
WEB: www.kingdomexpress.com
SIC: 4214 Local trucking with storage

(P-4356)
LDI TRANSPORTATION INC
200 Erie St, Pomona (91768-3327)
PHONE..................909 620-7001
Alex Kolesnikov, *President*
EMP: 10
SQ FT: 2,500
SALES: 3.5MM **Privately Held**
SIC: 4214 Local trucking with storage

PRODUCTS & SERVICES SECTION

4214 - Local Trucking With Storage County (P-4377)

(P-4357)
LEGACY TRANSPORTATION SVCS INC (PA)
Also Called: Legacy Global Logistics Svcs
935 Mclaughlin Ave, San Jose (95122-2612)
PHONE.................................408 294-9800
Fax: 408 283-1667
John Migliozzi, *President*
Michael Quinn, *Exec VP*
Laura Deflores, *Senior VP*
Shelly Gipson, *Senior VP*
Rick Wada, *Senior VP*
▲ EMP: 140
SQ FT: 200,000
SALES (est): 50.3MM **Privately Held**
SIC: 4214 4213 Local trucking with storage; trucking, except local

(P-4358)
LEXMAR DISTRIBUTION INC
200 Erie St, Pomona (91768-3327)
PHONE.................................909 620-7001
Fax: 909 620-8001
Alex Kole, *President*
Alex Kolesnikov, *Vice Pres*
Marlin Brover, *General Mgr*
Apollo Reyes, *Information Mgr*
Tony Kolesnikov, *Controller*
EMP: 170
SQ FT: 10,000
SALES (est): 25MM **Privately Held**
WEB: www.lexmardistribution.com
SIC: 4214 Local trucking with storage

(P-4359)
LINEAGE LOGISTICS HOLDINGS LLC
17911 Von Karman Ave # 400, Irvine (92614-6209)
PHONE.................................909 433-3100
Bill Hendricksen, *CEO*
EMP: 800
SALES (corp-wide): 1.5B **Privately Held**
SIC: 4214 4213 4222 Household goods moving & storage, local; household goods transport; warehousing, cold storage or refrigerated
PA: Lineage Logistics Holdings, Llc
17911 Von Karman Ave # 400
Irvine CA 92614
800 678-7271

(P-4360)
LINEAGE LOGISTICS HOLDINGS LLC
Also Called: Inland Cold Storage
2551 S Lilac Ave, Bloomington (92316-3209)
PHONE.................................909 874-1200
Fax: 909 820-4950
Bill Hendricksen, *CEO*
Ken Evans, *Vice Pres*
Merle Lemmen, *Vice Pres*
Paul McEntee, *Vice Pres*
Kenny Stotelmyre, *Vice Pres*
EMP: 800
SALES (corp-wide): 1.5B **Privately Held**
SIC: 4214 4222 Household goods moving & storage, local; warehousing, cold storage or refrigerated
PA: Lineage Logistics Holdings, Llc
17911 Von Karman Ave # 400
Irvine CA 92614
800 678-7271

(P-4361)
MASA TRUCKING CO
231 W 135th St, Los Angeles (90061-1625)
PHONE.................................310 329-1567
Fax: 310 329-1906
Mauro A Arce, *President*
Paula Morales, *Corp Secy*
Bernard Valmores, *General Mgr*
Marcial Mancilla, *Director*
EMP: 50
SQ FT: 40,000
SALES: 9MM **Privately Held**
SIC: 4214 Local trucking with storage

(P-4362)
MICHAEL DUSI TRUCKING INC
3230 Rverside Ave Ste 220, Paso Robles (93446)
P.O. Box 2339 (93447-2339)
PHONE.................................805 237-9499
Michael Dusi, *President*
Matt Dusi, *CFO*
Sharon Lawson, *Manager*
Melinda Wankum, *Manager*
EMP: 68
SALES (est): 17.5MM **Privately Held**
WEB: www.michaeldusitrucking.com
SIC: 4214 Local trucking with storage

(P-4363)
MOVER SERVICES INC
Also Called: ATLAS MOVER SERVICES
721 E Compton Blvd, Rancho Dominguez (90220-1153)
PHONE.................................310 868-5143
Fax: 310 868-5157
John Moses, *President*
Michelle Moses, *Vice Pres*
Chevel Mendoza, *Manager*
EMP: 50
SQ FT: 33,000
SALES: 5.5MM **Privately Held**
WEB: www.msiatlas.com
SIC: 4214 Household goods moving & storage, local

(P-4364)
MOVING SOLUTIONS INC
Also Called: North American Van Lines
376 Martin Ave, Santa Clara (95050-3112)
P.O. Box 360843, Milpitas (95036-0843)
PHONE.................................408 920-0110
Rick S Philpott, *CEO*
Janet Philpott, *Vice Pres*
Pam Welsh, *Vice Pres*
Ralph Andrade, *Project Mgr*
George Meza, *Opers Staff*
EMP: 150
SQ FT: 200,000
SALES (est): 26.3MM **Privately Held**
WEB: www.movingsolutionsinc.com
SIC: 4214 8742 7376 1799 Local trucking with storage; construction project management consultant; computer facilities management; office furniture installation

(P-4365)
NELSON MOVING & STORAGE INC
Also Called: Nelson North American
25742 Atlantic Ocean Dr, Lake Forest (92630-8854)
PHONE.................................949 582-0380
Gust Nelson, *President*
Rosean Maricondo, *Office Mgr*
EMP: 50
SQ FT: 24,000
SALES (est): 4.4MM **Privately Held**
WEB: www.nelsonmoving.com
SIC: 4214 4213 4731 Local trucking with storage; household goods moving & storage, local; household goods transport; freight transportation arrangement

(P-4366)
NOR-CAL MOVING SERVICES (PA)
Also Called: Allied Intl San Franisco
3129 Corporate Pl, Hayward (94545-3915)
PHONE.................................510 371-4942
Fax: 510 357-9678
Peter Mazzetti Jr, *CEO*
Dennis D Goza, *President*
John Mizera, *CFO*
John Mizira, *CFO*
Dave Konecny, *Exec VP*
EMP: 125
SQ FT: 200,000
SALES (est): 16.6MM **Privately Held**
WEB: www.nor-calmoving.com
SIC: 4214 4213 Household goods moving & storage, local; furniture moving & storage, local; household goods transport

(P-4367)
NOR-CAL MOVING SERVICES
560 E Trimble Rd, San Jose (95131-1221)
PHONE.................................408 954-1175
Fax: 408 954-1039
Karen Aparton, *Branch Mgr*
Peter Mazzetti, *General Counsel*
EMP: 100
SALES (corp-wide): 15.8MM **Privately Held**
WEB: www.nor-calmoving.com
SIC: 4214 4213 Household goods & storage, local; trucking, except local
PA: Nor-Cal Moving Services
3129 Corporate Pl
Hayward CA 94545

(P-4368)
OFFICE MOVERS INC
4020 Nelson Ave Ste 200, Concord (94520-8526)
PHONE.................................408 254-5010
Fax: 408 490-5983
James Robinson, *President*
EMP: 50
SALES (est): 2.8MM **Privately Held**
SIC: 4214 Local trucking with storage

(P-4369)
PACIFIC BULK TRNSP CO INC
6250 Caballero Blvd, Buena Park (90620-1124)
PHONE.................................714 521-2399
James N Tausz, *President*
Ronda Tausz, *Treasurer*
James A Banister, *Vice Pres*
Tim Inzana, *Vice Pres*
EMP: 55
SQ FT: 275,000
SALES (est): 6.5MM
SALES (corp-wide): 555.9MM **Privately Held**
WEB: www.arpdsi.com
SIC: 4214 4213 Local trucking with storage; trucking, except local
HQ: A&R Logistics, Inc.
600 N Hurstbourne Pkwy # 110
Louisville KY 40222
815 941-5200

(P-4370)
PACK & CRATE SERVICES INC
238 N Quince St, Escondido (92025-2518)
P.O. Box 2964 (92033-2964)
PHONE.................................760 737-6893
Fax: 760 737-9806
Robert H Shepard, *President*
Rick Farley, *Manager*
Bernadette Fellows, *Manager*
EMP: 50
SQ FT: 35,000
SALES (est): 4.5MM **Privately Held**
SIC: 4214 Local trucking with storage

(P-4371)
PEETERS TRANSPORTATION CO
Also Called: Peeters/Mayflower
451 Eccles Ave, South San Francisco (94080-1902)
P.O. Box 2724 (94083-2724)
PHONE.................................800 356-5877
Fax: 650 872-7912
Robert Peeters, *President*
Frederick D Peeters, *CEO*
Shirley Peeters, *Corp Secy*
Barry Garman, *Officer*
De Loss Wood, *Vice Pres*
EMP: 50 EST: 1915
SALES (est): 4.5MM **Privately Held**
SIC: 4214 Household goods moving & storage, local

(P-4372)
REDDING LUMBER TRANSPORT INC
Also Called: R L T
4301 Eastside Rd, Redding (96001-3801)
P.O. Box 492110 (96049-2110)
PHONE.................................530 241-8193
Fax: 530 241-3530
Albert Shufelberger, *President*
William Weber, *Vice Pres*
Judith Rickey, *Asst Controller*
Jenn Hector, *Human Resources*
EMP: 62
SQ FT: 4,000
SALES (est): 16.6MM **Privately Held**
WEB: www.rlttrucking.com
SIC: 4214 4213 Local trucking with storage; refrigerated products transport

(P-4373)
ROYAL EXPRESS INC (PA)
3545 E Date Ave, Fresno (93725-1933)
PHONE.................................559 272-3500
Kirpal S Shiota, *CEO*
Cory Sparks, *Administration*
Adarsh Chhajed, *Controller*
Phillip Randalls, *Manager*
Tarlochan Singh, *Accounts Mgr*
EMP: 111
SQ FT: 435,600
SALES (est): 22MM **Privately Held**
WEB: www.royalexp.com
SIC: 4214 Local trucking with storage

(P-4374)
SAMUEL J PIAZZA & SON INC (PA)
Also Called: Piazza Trucking
9001 Rayo Ave, South Gate (90280-3606)
PHONE.................................323 357-1999
Fax: 323 357-1990
Michael Piazza, *CEO*
Basil Piazza, *President*
Robert Piazza, *Vice Pres*
William Piazza, *Vice Pres*
Shaun Roblee, *Project Dir*
EMP: 70
SQ FT: 20,000
SALES (est): 20.8MM **Privately Held**
WEB: www.piazzatrucking.com
SIC: 4214 4213 Local trucking with storage; trucking, except local

(P-4375)
SCHICK MOVING & STORAGE CO (PA)
2721 Michelle Dr, Tustin (92780-7018)
P.O. Box 3627 (92781-3627)
PHONE.................................714 731-5500
Fax: 714 669-4245
Gordon C Schick, *President*
Lynn Larson, *CFO*
Lynne M Larson, *Treasurer*
Arthur C Schick Jr, *Vice Pres*
Beverly C Schick, *Vice Pres*
EMP: 100
SQ FT: 113,000
SALES: 7.4MM **Privately Held**
WEB: www.schickusa.com
SIC: 4214 Local trucking with storage

(P-4376)
SOUTH COAST LOGISTICS
Also Called: North American Van Lines
12572 Western Ave, Garden Grove (92841-4013)
PHONE.................................714 894-4744
Fax: 714 894-4727
Craig Schueller, *President*
Pam Nelson, *President*
Corie Johns, *Admin Asst*
Jon Munro, *Opers Staff*
Sanders Howard, *VP Sales*
EMP: 50
SALES (est): 7.8MM **Privately Held**
WEB: www.southcoastlogistics.com
SIC: 4214 Local trucking with storage

(P-4377)
SPECIAL DISPATCH CAL INC (PA)
16330 Phoebe Ave, La Mirada (90638-5612)
P.O. Box 3838, Cerritos (90703-3838)
PHONE.................................602 296-8860
John Edward Dearing, *CEO*
Thomas Dearing, *Vice Pres*
Veronica Belmonte, *Office Mgr*
Ronnie Lewis, *Opers Mgr*
Chuck Moore, *Terminal Mgr*
EMP: 60
SQ FT: 120,000
SALES (est): 30.1MM **Privately Held**
SIC: 4214 4212 Local trucking with storage; delivery service, vehicular

4214 - Local Trucking With Storage County (P-4378)

PRODUCTS & SERVICES SECTION

(P-4378)
SS SKIKOS INCORPORATED
1289 Sebastopol Rd, Santa Rosa (95407-6834)
PHONE...............................707 575-3000
Shad Skikos, *CEO*
Pete Skikos, *President*
Sheryl Poniatowski, *Manager*
EMP: 80
SALES (est): 9.4MM **Privately Held**
SIC: 4214 Local trucking with storage

(P-4379)
STUDENT MOVERS INC
Also Called: College Movers
825 Chalcedony St, San Diego (92109-2560)
PHONE...............................303 296-0600
Steve Linane, *President*
Gloria Linane, *Chairman*
Paul Barsa, *Accounts Mgr*
EMP: 80
SQ FT: 65,000
SALES: 4.5MM **Privately Held**
WEB: www.studentmovers.com
SIC: 4214 Local trucking with storage; furniture moving & storage, local

(P-4380)
THREE WAY INC
Also Called: 3-Way Air Charter
2940 Mead Ave, Santa Clara (95051-0817)
P.O. Box 1806, Fremont (94538-0032)
PHONE...............................408 748-6902
Greg Hogeland, *President*
Ron Hovard, *Vice Pres*
Robert Reed, *Terminal Mgr*
EMP: 250
SALES (est): 18.2MM **Privately Held**
SIC: 4214 4213 4731 Local trucking with storage; trucking, except local; freight transportation arrangement

(P-4381)
TOTAL TRNSP & DIST INC
1551 E Victoria St, Carson (90746-2861)
PHONE...............................310 603-0467
Fax: 310 638-7583
Ruben Dominguez, *President*
Laurie Salazar, *Business Mgr*
Lauri Salazar, *Controller*
EMP: 75
SQ FT: 100,010
SALES: 12.7MM **Privately Held**
SIC: 4214 Local trucking with storage

(P-4382)
TRANSPORT EXPRESS INC
19801 S Santa Fe Ave, Compton (90221-5915)
PHONE...............................310 898-2000
Fax: 310 223-3730
Robert L Stull, *CEO*
Steven Senecal, *President*
William Meroth, *Vice Pres*
Patricia Senecal, *Admin Sec*
EMP: 55
SQ FT: 230,000
SALES (est): 8.6MM **Privately Held**
SIC: 4214 4225 4731 Local trucking with storage; general warehousing; brokers, shipping

(P-4383)
TRANSWEST SAN DIEGO LLC
Also Called: Miramar Truck Center
6066 Miramar Rd, San Diego (92121-2542)
PHONE...............................858 450-0707
Brad Fauvre, *President*
EMP: 500
SALES (est): 19.3MM **Privately Held**
SIC: 4214 Local trucking with storage

(P-4384)
TRIWAYS INC
Also Called: Warehouse and Distribution
11201 Iberia St Ste B, Mira Loma (91752-3280)
P.O. Box 9342, Ontario (91762-9342)
PHONE...............................951 361-4840
Fax: 951 361-3231
Juan M Jauregui, *President*
Fredy R Jimenez, *CFO*
Bob Schwenig, *Vice Pres*
Maria Paez, *Administration*

Jo Anderson, *Human Resources*
EMP: 65
SQ FT: 228,000
SALES (est): 15.4MM **Privately Held**
WEB: www.triways.net
SIC: 4214 Local trucking with storage

(P-4385)
URIBE TRUCKING INC
Also Called: Alex Moving & Storage
605 S East St, Anaheim (92805-4842)
PHONE...............................714 549-8696
Alejandro Uribe, *President*
Christine Uribe, *Corp Secy*
Mike Kachmar, *Manager*
EMP: 130
SQ FT: 60,000
SALES (est): 15.9MM **Privately Held**
SIC: 4214 4731 4225 Local trucking with storage; freight forwarding; warehousing, self-storage

(P-4386)
USA TRANSPORT INC
12191 Violet Rd, Adelanto (92301-2713)
PHONE...............................559 783-3563
Fax: 760 246-5152
Gary Leslie, *President*
Tony Bunker, *Executive*
Lisa Marks, *Manager*
EMP: 50
SQ FT: 5,000
SALES (est): 3.1MM **Privately Held**
SIC: 4214 4213 Local trucking with storage; trucking, except local

(P-4387)
VAN TORRANCE & STORAGE COMPANY (PA)
Also Called: S & M Moving Systems
12128 Burke St, Santa Fe Springs (90670-2678)
PHONE...............................562 567-2100
Fax: 562 693-5690
Steven Todare, *President*
Anthony Locatelli, *COO*
Michael D'Oliveira, *CFO*
Martin Stadler, *Vice Pres*
Dennis Allsopp, *General Mgr*
EMP: 100
SQ FT: 95,000
SALES (est): 88.6MM **Privately Held**
WEB: www.sandmoving.com
SIC: 4214 4213 Local trucking with storage; trucking, except local

(P-4388)
VERNON CENTRAL WAREHOUSE INC
Also Called: Vernon Warehouse Co
2050 E 38th St, Vernon (90058-1615)
P.O. Box 58426 (90058-0426)
PHONE...............................323 234-2200
Joseph E Tack, *CEO*
Joe Tack, *President*
Jim Boltinghouse, *Corp Secy*
Tom Rodd, *Vice Pres*
Steve Shanklin, *Vice Pres*
EMP: 125
SQ FT: 100,000
SALES (est): 24.4MM **Privately Held**
WEB: www.vernonwarehouse.com
SIC: 4214 5149 Local trucking with storage; natural & organic foods

(P-4389)
VIN LUX LLC
80 Technology Ct, NAPA (94558-7519)
PHONE...............................707 265-4100
Thomas Tunt, *President*
EMP: 50
SALES (est): 4.9MM **Privately Held**
SIC: 4214 Local trucking with storage

(P-4390)
W WHY W ENTERPRISES INC
Also Called: Atlas/Eastern Van Lines
2671 Pomona Blvd, Pomona (91768-3221)
PHONE...............................626 969-4292
Fax: 626 334-3096
William Coffman, *President*
Yvonne Coffman, *Vice Pres*
Noel Fernandez, *Accountant*
Robert King, *Bookkeeper*
Ken Freeman, *Human Res Mgr*
EMP: 60

SALES (est): 6.7MM **Privately Held**
SIC: 4214 4213 Local trucking with storage; household goods transport

(P-4391)
WATERS MOVING & STORAGE INC
37 Bridgehead Rd, Martinez (94553-1300)
P.O. Box 1029 (94553-0102)
PHONE...............................925 372-0914
Ken Waters, *CEO*
Paulette Waters, *CFO*
Douglas Fayne, *Marketing Staff*
EMP: 75
SQ FT: 50,000
SALES (est): 6.2MM **Privately Held**
SIC: 4214 Furniture moving & storage, local

(P-4392)
WETZEL & SONS MOVING AND STOR
Also Called: Wetzel Trucking
12400 Osborne St, Pacoima (91331-2002)
PHONE...............................818 890-0992
Fax: 818 890-2102
Donald C Wetzel, *President*
Daniel S Wetzel, *Vice Pres*
Michael Smith, *Info Tech Mgr*
EMP: 70
SQ FT: 146,000
SALES (est): 4.4MM **Privately Held**
WEB: www.wetzelmovingandstorage.com
SIC: 4214 Furniture moving & storage, local; household goods moving & storage, local

(P-4393)
ZIKKO INC
6345 Auburn Blvd Ste C, Citrus Heights (95621-5277)
PHONE...............................916 949-8989
Vladimir Skots, *CEO*
EMP: 200
SALES (est): 144.6K **Privately Held**
SIC: 4214 Local trucking with storage

4215 Courier Svcs, Except Air

(P-4394)
ALL COUNTIES COURIER INC
14811 Myford Rd, Tustin (92780-7227)
PHONE...............................949 224-0900
Fax: 949 703-7012
Patricia Cochran, *President*
Dean Steward, *COO*
Jack Lipczynski, *General Mgr*
Jack Litsenspy, *Controller*
Julie Paulombo, *Human Resources*
EMP: 200
SALES (est): 25.3MM **Privately Held**
SIC: 4215 Courier services, except by air

(P-4395)
CEA-PACK SERVICES INC
Also Called: Cea-Pack Logistics
12607 Hiddencreek Way, Cerritos (90703-2146)
P.O. Box 3777 (90703-3777)
PHONE...............................562 407-0660
Robert Ceja-Simpson, *President*
EMP: 235
SQ FT: 2,730
SALES (est): 16.6MM **Privately Held**
SIC: 4215 Parcel delivery, vehicular

(P-4396)
COMPREMEX LLC
14849 Firestone Blvd, La Mirada (90638-6017)
P.O. Box 778030, Henderson NV (89077-8030)
PHONE...............................714 739-1348
Mike Catapano,
Eric Morlianes, *Info Tech Mgr*
Alesh Vargas, *Project Mgr*
EMP: 200
SQ FT: 8,000
SALES (est): 9.7MM **Privately Held**
SIC: 4215 Courier services, except by air

(P-4397)
DOMA LASZLO
Also Called: Tele Car
4041 Eagle Rock Blvd, Los Angeles (90065-3607)
PHONE...............................323 478-1313
Laszlo Doma, *Owner*
EMP: 80
SQ FT: 3,600
SALES: 3MM **Privately Held**
SIC: 4215 Package delivery, vehicular

(P-4398)
DYNAMEX INC
4790 Frontier Way Ste A, Stockton (95215-9424)
PHONE...............................209 464-7008
EMP: 60
SALES (corp-wide): 3.2B **Privately Held**
SIC: 4215
HQ: Dynamex Inc.
5429 L B Johnson Fwy 90 Ste 900
Dallas TX 75240
214 560-9000

(P-4399)
DYNAMEX OPERATIONS WEST INC
16900 Valley View Ave, La Mirada (90638-5825)
PHONE...............................714 994-1615
Scott Levrage, *Manager*
EMP: 50
SALES (corp-wide): 2.7B **Privately Held**
SIC: 4215 Courier services, except by air
HQ: Dynamex Operations West, Inc
1870 Crown Dr
Dallas TX 75234

(P-4400)
EXECUTIVE EXPRESS INC (PA)
Also Called: Executive Ex Mssngr-Air Curier
2007 Quail St, Newport Beach (92660-2222)
P.O. Box 8382 (92658-8382)
PHONE...............................949 852-0450
Fax: 949 852-8661
James A Myers Jr, *President*
Pat Shoemaker, *Human Res Mgr*
EMP: 65
SQ FT: 3,600
SALES (est): 4MM **Privately Held**
SIC: 4215 Parcel delivery, vehicular

(P-4401)
EXPRESS MESSENGER SYSTEMS INC
5829 Smithway St, Commerce (90040-1605)
PHONE...............................323 725-2100
Kim Kugel, *Branch Mgr*
Stacey King, *Accounts Exec*
EMP: 68
SALES (corp-wide): 706.7MM **Privately Held**
SIC: 4215 Courier services, except by air
PA: Express Messenger Systems, Inc.
2501 S Price Rd Ste 201
Chandler AZ 85286
800 334-5000

(P-4402)
EXPRESS MESSENGER SYSTEMS INC
11085 Olinda St, Sun Valley (91352-3302)
PHONE...............................818 504-9043
Scott Stone, *Controller*
EMP: 63
SALES (corp-wide): 706.7MM **Privately Held**
SIC: 4215 Courier services, except by air
PA: Express Messenger Systems, Inc.
2501 S Price Rd Ste 201
Chandler AZ 85286
800 334-5000

(P-4403)
EXPRESS MESSENGER SYSTEMS INC
1627 Industrial Dr, Stockton (95206-4984)
PHONE...............................209 234-8255
EMP: 68

PRODUCTS & SERVICES SECTION

4215 - Courier Svcs, Except Air County (P-4427)

SALES (corp-wide): 706.7MM **Privately Held**
SIC: **4215** Courier services, except by air
PA: Express Messenger Systems, Inc.
2501 S Price Rd Ste 201
Chandler AZ 85286
800 334-5000

(P-4404)
EXPRESS MESSENGER SYSTEMS INC
Also Called: California Overnight
1240 S Allec St, Anaheim (92805-6301)
PHONE..................................949 235-1400
Fax: 714 517-9111
Dave Denholm, *Manager*
EMP: 70
SALES (corp-wide): 706.7MM **Privately Held**
WEB: www.calover.com
SIC: **4215** 7389 Courier services, except by air; courier or messenger service
PA: Express Messenger Systems, Inc.
2501 S Price Rd Ste 201
Chandler AZ 85286
800 334-5000

(P-4405)
EXPRESS MESSENGER SYSTEMS INC
Also Called: Ontrac
914 W Boone St, Santa Maria (93458-5450)
PHONE..................................800 488-2829
Polo Cabello, *Branch Mgr*
EMP: 70
SALES (corp-wide): 706.7MM **Privately Held**
SIC: **4215** Courier services, except by air
PA: Express Messenger Systems, Inc.
2501 S Price Rd Ste 201
Chandler AZ 85286
800 334-5000

(P-4406)
EXPRESS MESSENGER SYSTEMS INC
Ontrac
11085 Olinda St, Sun Valley (91352-3302)
PHONE..................................818 504-9043
EMP: 98
SALES (corp-wide): 706.7MM **Privately Held**
SIC: **4215** Courier services, except by air
PA: Express Messenger Systems, Inc.
2501 S Price Rd Ste 201
Chandler AZ 85286
800 334-5000

(P-4407)
EXPRESS MESSENGER SYSTEMS INC
Also Called: California Overnight
1635 Main Ave Ste 3, Sacramento (95838-2452)
PHONE..................................916 921-6016
Fax: 916 419-2037
Ian Burton, *Manager*
EMP: 60
SALES (corp-wide): 706.7MM **Privately Held**
WEB: www.calover.com
SIC: **4215** Courier services, except by air
PA: Express Messenger Systems, Inc.
2501 S Price Rd Ste 201
Chandler AZ 85286
800 334-5000

(P-4408)
EXPRESS MESSENGER SYSTEMS INC
Also Called: California Overnight
101 Spear St Ste A1, San Francisco (94105-1557)
PHONE..................................415 495-7300
Fax: 415 495-7420
Amy Totu, *Manager*
EMP: 63
SALES (corp-wide): 706.7MM **Privately Held**
WEB: www.calover.com
SIC: **4215** Courier services, except by air

PA: Express Messenger Systems, Inc.
2501 S Price Rd Ste 201
Chandler AZ 85286
800 334-5000

(P-4409)
FEDERAL EXPRESS CORPORATION
Also Called: Fedex
2660 Research Park Dr, Soquel (95073-2087)
PHONE..................................800 463-3339
David Rugherford, *Manager*
EMP: 56
SALES (corp-wide): 50.3B **Publicly Held**
SIC: **4215** Package delivery, vehicular
HQ: Federal Express Corporation
3610 Hacks Cross Rd
Memphis TN 38125
901 369-3600

(P-4410)
FEDERAL EXPRESS CORPORATION
Also Called: Fedex
1081 Fullerton Rd, City of Industry (91748-1234)
PHONE..................................800 463-3339
Raquel Moreno, *General Mgr*
EMP: 200
SALES (corp-wide): 50.3B **Publicly Held**
WEB: www.federalexpress.com
SIC: **4215** 4513 Package delivery, vehicular; package delivery, private air
HQ: Federal Express Corporation
3610 Hacks Cross Rd
Memphis TN 38125
901 369-3600

(P-4411)
FEDERAL EXPRESS CORPORATION
Also Called: Fedex
710 Dado St, San Jose (95131-1225)
PHONE..................................800 463-3339
Ruben Maines, *Manager*
Josh Lens, *Senior Mgr*
EMP: 150
SALES (corp-wide): 50.3B **Publicly Held**
WEB: www.federalexpress.com
SIC: **4215** 4512 Package delivery, vehicular; air cargo carrier, scheduled
HQ: Federal Express Corporation
3610 Hacks Cross Rd
Memphis TN 38125
901 369-3600

(P-4412)
FEDERAL EXPRESS CORPORATION
Also Called: Fedex
9190 Edes Ave, Oakland (94603-1116)
PHONE..................................510 382-2344
EMP: 300
SALES (corp-wide): 47.4B **Publicly Held**
SIC: **4215** 4513
HQ: Federal Express Corporation
3610 Hacks Cross Rd
Memphis TN 38125
901 369-3600

(P-4413)
FEDEX GROUND PACKAGE SYS INC
10132 Airway Rd, San Diego (92154-7901)
PHONE..................................619 661-1051
EMP: 104
SALES (corp-wide): 50.3B **Publicly Held**
SIC: **4215** Parcel delivery, vehicular
HQ: Fedex Ground Package System, Inc.
1000 Fed Ex Dr
Coraopolis PA 15108
412 269-1000

(P-4414)
FEDEX OFFICE & PRINT SVCS INC
8642 Whittier Blvd, Pico Rivera (90660-2655)
PHONE..................................562 942-1953
EMP: 100
SALES (corp-wide): 47.4B **Publicly Held**
SIC: **4215** 5999 7221 7389

HQ: Fedex Office And Print Services, Inc.
7900 Legacy Dr
Dallas TX 75024
214 550-7000

(P-4415)
FEDEX SMARTPOST INC
5560 Ferguson Dr, Commerce (90022-5140)
PHONE..................................323 888-8879
EMP: 85
SALES (corp-wide): 47.4B **Publicly Held**
SIC: **4215**
HQ: Fedex Smartpost, Inc.
16555 W Rogers Dr
New Berlin WI 53151
262 796-6800

(P-4416)
MEDICAL COURIERS INC
1282 Montgomery Ave, San Bruno (94066-1522)
PHONE..................................650 872-1144
Stephen Reiff, *President*
Richard Reiff, *Vice Pres*
EMP: 60
SQ FT: 5,000
SALES (est): 4.7MM **Privately Held**
SIC: **4215** Courier services, except by air

(P-4417)
MESSENGER EXPRESS (PA)
5435 Cahuenga Blvd Ste C, North Hollywood (91601-2948)
PHONE..................................213 614-0475
Fax: 818 754-1031
Gilbert Kort, *President*
EMP: 143
SALES (est): 8.1MM **Privately Held**
WEB: www.messengerexpress.net
SIC: **4215** 7389 4212 Courier services, except by air; courier or messenger service; delivery service, vehicular

(P-4418)
MESSENGER EXPRESS
10671 Roselle St Ste 200, San Diego (92121-1525)
P.O. Box 12424 (92112-3424)
PHONE..................................858 550-1400
Fax: 858 550-1414
Greg King, *Manager*
EMP: 85
SALES (corp-wide): 8.1MM **Privately Held**
WEB: www.messengerexpress.net
SIC: **4215** Courier services, except by air
PA: Messenger Express
5435 Cahuenga Blvd Ste C
North Hollywood CA 91601
213 614-0475

(P-4419)
PACIFIC COURIERS INC
1706 W Orangethorpe Ave, Fullerton (92833-4538)
PHONE..................................714 278-6100
Fax: 714 992-1026
Nadia Youssef, *CEO*
Rudy Fregoso, *Opers Mgr*
EMP: 275
SQ FT: 30,000
SALES (est): 22.3MM **Privately Held**
WEB: www.pacific-couriers.com
SIC: **4215** 4214 7389 Courier services, except by air; local trucking with storage; courier or messenger service

(P-4420)
PEACH INC
Also Called: Action Messenger Service
1311 N Highland Ave, Los Angeles (90028-7608)
P.O. Box 69673 (90069-0673)
PHONE..................................323 654-2333
Fax: 323 654-8889
Arthur P Ruben, *President*
Brian Nealy, *Opers Mgr*
EMP: 125
SQ FT: 3,500
SALES: 5MM **Privately Held**
WEB: www.actionmessenger.com
SIC: **4215** 7389 Courier services, except by air; courier or messenger service

(P-4421)
PRIORITY DISPATCH SERVICE INC
309 Laurelwood Rd Ste 10, Santa Clara (95054-2313)
PHONE..................................408 400-3860
Walter Strobel, *CEO*
EMP: 60 EST: 2009
SALES: 950K **Privately Held**
SIC: **4215** Courier services, except by air

(P-4422)
SAN DIEGO MESSENGER INC
Also Called: The Messenger Company
4848 Ronson Ct Ste G, San Diego (92111-1809)
PHONE..................................858 514-8866
Fax: 858 514-8687
Richard Villalodos, *President*
Rick Smith, *Vice Pres*
EMP: 50 EST: 2000
SQ FT: 3,000
SALES: 1.3MM **Privately Held**
SIC: **4215** Courier services, except by air

(P-4423)
SUNRISE DELIVERY SERVICE INC
13351 Riverside Dr 672d, Sherman Oaks (91423-2542)
PHONE..................................323 464-5121
Fax: 323 464-0733
Charles R Audia, *President*
Angela Gilliland, *Controller*
EMP: 60
SQ FT: 3,000
SALES (est): 4.5MM **Privately Held**
SIC: **4215** Courier services, except by air

(P-4424)
TELE-CAR COURIERS INC
Also Called: Tele-Car Courier Service
4035 Eagle Rock Blvd, Los Angeles (90065-3607)
PHONE..................................877 910-1313
Shagen Galstanyan, *Principal*
Vic Galtain, *Manager*
EMP: 75
SALES: 2.8MM **Privately Held**
SIC: **4215** Courier services, except by air

(P-4425)
TF COURIER INC
8331 Demetre Ave, Sacramento (95828-0920)
PHONE..................................916 379-0708
Ed Feliciano, *Manager*
Anita Gilbert, *Safety Mgr*
EMP: 60
SALES (corp-wide): 2.7B **Privately Held**
SIC: **4215** Courier services, except by air
HQ: Tf Courier, Inc.
5429 Lyndon B Johnson Fwy
Dallas TX 75240
214 560-9000

(P-4426)
TF COURIER INC
7130 Miramar Rd Ste 400, San Diego (92121-2340)
PHONE..................................858 271-0021
John Mc Loughlin, *Manager*
Bill Dougherty, *Regional Mgr*
Carla Buchanan, *Opers Mgr*
Bart Jackson, *Opers Staff*
Michael Taylor, *Cust Mgr*
EMP: 60
SALES (corp-wide): 2.7B **Privately Held**
SIC: **4215** Courier services, except by air
HQ: Tf Courier, Inc.
5429 Lyndon B Johnson Fwy
Dallas TX 75240
214 560-9000

(P-4427)
TF COURIER INC
2051 Raymer Ave Ste A, Fullerton (92833-2678)
PHONE..................................714 888-1452
Scott Leveridge, *Manager*
James Witmer, *Vice Pres*
EMP: 70
SALES (corp-wide): 2.7B **Privately Held**
SIC: **4215** Courier services, except by air

4215 - Courier Svcs, Except Air County (P-4428)

HQ: Tf Courier, Inc.
5429 Lyndon B Johnson Fwy
Dallas TX 75240
214 560-9000

(P-4428)
TF COURIER INC
21760 Garcia Ln, City of Industry (91789-0940)
PHONE.................214 560-9000
EMP: 60
SALES (corp-wide): 2.7B **Privately Held**
SIC: 4215 Courier services, except by air
HQ: Tf Courier, Inc.
5429 Lyndon B Johnson Fwy
Dallas TX 75240
214 560-9000

(P-4429)
TOP PRIORITY COURIERS INC (PA)
1257 Columbia Ave Ste D1, Riverside (92507-2124)
P.O. Box 20376 (92516-0376)
PHONE.................951 781-1000
Fax: 951 781-5977
Siroos Zakikhani, *President*
Rick Johnson, *Exec VP*
Sammy Nava, *CIO*
EMP: 60
SQ FT: 6,000
SALES (est): 8.9MM **Privately Held**
WEB: www.topprioritycouriers.com
SIC: 4215 Courier services, except by air

(P-4430)
TRICOR AMERICA INC
1465 N Brasher St, Anaheim (92807-2048)
PHONE.................714 701-9880
Fax: 714 701-3691
David Solis, *Branch Mgr*
EMP: 60
SALES (corp-wide): 114.1MM **Privately Held**
WEB: www.tricor.com
SIC: 4215 Parcel delivery, vehicular; package delivery, vehicular
PA: Tricor America, Inc.
717 Airport Blvd
South San Francisco CA 94080
650 877-3650

(P-4431)
TRICOR AMERICA INC
Also Called: Tricor California
1690 Cebrian St, West Sacramento (95691-3802)
PHONE.................916 371-1704
Fax: 916 371-1812
Fred Kamper, *Branch Mgr*
EMP: 125
SALES (corp-wide): 114.1MM **Privately Held**
WEB: www.tricor.com
SIC: 4215 4212 Courier services, except by air; delivery service, vehicular
PA: Tricor America, Inc.
717 Airport Blvd
South San Francisco CA 94080
650 877-3650

(P-4432)
ULTRAEX LLC
2633 Barrington Ct, Hayward (94545-1100)
PHONE.................510 723-3760
William Carlson,
Alfredo Flores,
Ernesto Holbrook,
EMP: 75 EST: 2014
SALES (est): 3MM **Privately Held**
SIC: 4215 4513 4225 Courier services, except by air; air courier services; general warehousing & storage

(P-4433)
ULTRAEX INC
2633 Barrington Ct, Hayward (94545-1100)
PHONE.................800 882-1000
Ernest Holbrook, *President*
William Carlson, *Business Mgr*
Mike Akina, *Controller*
EMP: 100
SQ FT: 10,000

SALES (est): 10.4MM **Privately Held**
WEB: www.ultraex.com
SIC: 4215 4513 4214 Courier services, except by air; package delivery, vehicular; parcel delivery, vehicular; air courier services; local trucking with storage

(P-4434)
UNITED PARCEL SERVICE INC
Also Called: UPS
12745 Arroyo St, Sylmar (91342-5332)
PHONE.................800 742-5877
EMP: 86
SALES (corp-wide): 58.3B **Publicly Held**
SIC: 4215 4513 4522 Package delivery, vehicular; parcel delivery, vehicular; letter delivery, private air; package delivery, private air; parcel delivery, private air; flying charter service
PA: United Parcel Service, Inc.
55 Glenlake Pkwy
Atlanta GA 30328
404 828-6000

(P-4435)
UNITED PARCEL SERVICE INC
Also Called: UPS
657 Forbes Blvd, South San Francisco (94080-2059)
PHONE.................650 737-3737
Timothy Huxtable, *Branch Mgr*
Brian Wasem, *Area Mgr*
EMP: 159
SALES (corp-wide): 58.3B **Publicly Held**
WEB: www.martrac.com
SIC: 4215 Package delivery, vehicular
PA: United Parcel Service, Inc.
55 Glenlake Pkwy
Atlanta GA 30328
404 828-6000

(P-4436)
UNITED PARCEL SERVICE INC OH
Also Called: UPS
650 N Commercial Rd, Palm Springs (92262-6299)
PHONE.................760 325-1762
Doug Nelson, *Manager*
Rick Vanden Bossche, *Business Mgr*
Richard Day, *Manager*
Rick Vandenbossche, *Manager*
EMP: 500
SALES (corp-wide): 58.3B **Publicly Held**
WEB: www.upsscs.com
SIC: 4215 4513 Parcel delivery, vehicular; air courier services
HQ: United Parcel Service, Inc. (Oh)
55 Glenlake Pkwy
Atlanta GA 30328
404 828-6000

(P-4437)
UNITED PARCEL SERVICE INC OH
Also Called: UPS
716 Main St 1, Weaverville (96093)
PHONE.................530 623-3938
EMP: 158
SALES (corp-wide): 58.3B **Publicly Held**
SIC: 4215 Parcel delivery, vehicular
HQ: United Parcel Service, Inc. (Oh)
55 Glenlake Pkwy
Atlanta GA 30328
404 828-6000

(P-4438)
UNITED PARCEL SERVICE INC OH
Also Called: UPS
1601 Atlas Rd, Richmond (94806-1101)
PHONE.................510 262-2338
Jim Kelly, *President*
Sylvia Keller, *Supervisor*
EMP: 152
SALES (corp-wide): 58.3B **Publicly Held**
WEB: www.upsscs.com
SIC: 4215 4513 Parcel delivery, vehicular; air courier services
HQ: United Parcel Service, Inc. (Oh)
55 Glenlake Pkwy
Atlanta GA 30328
404 828-6000

(P-4439)
UNITED PARCEL SERVICE INC OH
Also Called: UPS
2800 W 227th St, Torrance (90505-2912)
PHONE.................800 742-5877
EMP: 80
SALES (corp-wide): 58.3B **Publicly Held**
SIC: 4215 Package delivery, vehicular
HQ: United Parcel Service, Inc. (Oh)
55 Glenlake Pkwy
Atlanta GA 30328
404 828-6000

(P-4440)
UNITED PARCEL SERVICE INC OH
Also Called: UPS
6845 Eastside Rd, Anderson (96007-9406)
PHONE.................530 365-7850
Fax: 530 365-0512
Lauren Lnd, *Manager*
EMP: 100
SALES (corp-wide): 58.3B **Publicly Held**
WEB: www.upsscs.com
SIC: 4215 4213 Parcel delivery, vehicular; trucking, except local
HQ: United Parcel Service, Inc. (Oh)
55 Glenlake Pkwy
Atlanta GA 30328
404 828-6000

(P-4441)
UNITED PARCEL SERVICE INC OH
Also Called: UPS
2915 N Sierra Hwy, Bishop (93514-7633)
PHONE.................760 872-7661
EMP: 158
SALES (corp-wide): 58.3B **Publicly Held**
WEB: www.upsscs.com
SIC: 4215 Parcel delivery, vehicular
HQ: United Parcel Service, Inc. (Oh)
55 Glenlake Pkwy
Atlanta GA 30328
404 828-6000

(P-4442)
UNITED PARCEL SERVICE INC OH
Also Called: UPS
1380 Shore St, West Sacramento (95691-3522)
PHONE.................916 373-4076
Tom Karls, *Manager*
Courtney Bullen, *Supervisor*
David Molvik, *Supervisor*
EMP: 200
SALES (corp-wide): 58.3B **Publicly Held**
WEB: www.upsscs.com
SIC: 4215 Parcel delivery, vehicular
HQ: United Parcel Service, Inc. (Oh)
55 Glenlake Pkwy
Atlanta GA 30328
404 828-6000

(P-4443)
UNITED PARCEL SERVICE INC OH
Also Called: UPS
1400 Hil Mor Dr, Ceres (95307-9292)
PHONE.................800 742-5877
Dave Walker, *Principal*
EMP: 200
SALES (corp-wide): 58.3B **Publicly Held**
WEB: www.upsscs.com
SIC: 4215 Parcel delivery, vehicular
HQ: United Parcel Service, Inc. (Oh)
55 Glenlake Pkwy
Atlanta GA 30328
404 828-6000

(P-4444)
UNITED PARCEL SERVICE INC OH
Also Called: UPS
5000 W Cordelia Rd, Fairfield (94534-1628)
PHONE.................707 864-8200
EMP: 158
SALES (corp-wide): 58.3B **Publicly Held**
SIC: 4215 Parcel delivery, vehicular

HQ: United Parcel Service, Inc. (Oh)
55 Glenlake Pkwy
Atlanta GA 30328
404 828-6000

(P-4445)
UNITED PARCEL SERVICE INC OH
Also Called: UPS
111 Bingham Dr, San Marcos (92069-1401)
PHONE.................760 752-7809
S Feeder, *Division Mgr*
Jay Welch, *Accounts Exec*
EMP: 158
SALES (corp-wide): 58.3B **Publicly Held**
SIC: 4215 Parcel delivery, vehicular
HQ: United Parcel Service, Inc. (Oh)
55 Glenlake Pkwy
Atlanta GA 30328
404 828-6000

(P-4446)
UNITED PARCEL SERVICE INC OH
Also Called: UPS
2531 Napa Valley Corp Dr, NAPA (94558)
PHONE.................707 224-1205
Josh Young, *Principal*
EMP: 158
SALES (corp-wide): 58.3B **Publicly Held**
SIC: 4215 Package delivery, vehicular
HQ: United Parcel Service, Inc. (Oh)
55 Glenlake Pkwy
Atlanta GA 30328
404 828-6000

(P-4447)
UNITED PARCEL SERVICE INC OH
Also Called: UPS
128 Shore St, Sacramento (95829)
PHONE.................916 373-4089
Chris Wagner, *Manager*
EMP: 70
SALES (corp-wide): 58.3B **Publicly Held**
WEB: www.upsscs.com
SIC: 4215 Parcel delivery, vehicular
HQ: United Parcel Service, Inc. (Oh)
55 Glenlake Pkwy
Atlanta GA 30328
404 828-6000

(P-4448)
UNITED PARCEL SERVICE INC OH
Also Called: UPS
17115 S Western Ave, Gardena (90247-5299)
PHONE.................310 217-2646
Randy Hulhelt, *Manager*
Rick Garcia, *General Mgr*
Mike Nakawatase, *Opers Mgr*
Peter Brantley, *Accounts Exec*
EMP: 500
SALES (corp-wide): 58.3B **Publicly Held**
WEB: www.upsscs.com
SIC: 4215 4513 Parcel delivery, vehicular; air courier services
HQ: United Parcel Service, Inc. (Oh)
55 Glenlake Pkwy
Atlanta GA 30328
404 828-6000

(P-4449)
UNITED PARCEL SERVICE INC OH
Also Called: UPS
1532 N Broadway Ave, Stockton (95205-3083)
PHONE.................209 463-1971
Wendy Bostic, *Manager*
EMP: 200
SALES (corp-wide): 58.3B **Publicly Held**
WEB: www.upsscs.com
SIC: 4215 Parcel delivery, vehicular
HQ: United Parcel Service, Inc. (Oh)
55 Glenlake Pkwy
Atlanta GA 30328
404 828-6000

PRODUCTS & SERVICES SECTION
4215 - Courier Svcs, Except Air County (P-4472)

(P-4450)
UNITED PARCEL SERVICE INC
OH
Also Called: UPS
1999 S 7th St, San Jose (95112-6009)
PHONE..............................408 291-2942
Frank Cademarti, *Manager*
Path Smith, *Division Mgr*
Peter Kolotouros, *Director*
EMP: 300
SALES (corp-wide): 58.3B **Publicly Held**
WEB: www.upsscs.com
SIC: **4215** Parcel delivery, vehicular
HQ: United Parcel Service, Inc. (Oh)
55 Glenlake Pkwy
Atlanta GA 30328
404 828-6000

(P-4451)
UNITED PARCEL SERVICE INC
OH
UPS
2222 17th St, San Francisco (94103-5015)
PHONE..............................415 252-4564
Tom Dalto, *Manager*
Steve Dito, *Info Tech Mgr*
Brian K Davis, *Human Res Mgr*
Harry Lustgarten, *Manager*
Linda Simpson, *Manager*
EMP: 152
SALES (corp-wide): 58.3B **Publicly Held**
WEB: www.upsscs.com
SIC: **4215** 4513 Parcel delivery, vehicular; air courier services
HQ: United Parcel Service, Inc. (Oh)
55 Glenlake Pkwy
Atlanta GA 30328
404 828-6000

(P-4452)
UNITED PARCEL SERVICE INC
OH
Also Called: UPS
1012 Sterling St, Vallejo (94591-8686)
PHONE..............................707 252-4560
EMP: 165
SALES (corp-wide): 58.3B **Publicly Held**
WEB: www.upsscs.com
SIC: **4215** Parcel delivery, vehicular
HQ: United Parcel Service, Inc. (Oh)
55 Glenlake Pkwy
Atlanta GA 30328
404 828-6000

(P-4453)
UNITED PARCEL SERVICE INC
OH
Also Called: UPS
22 Brookline, Aliso Viejo (92656-1461)
PHONE..............................949 643-6595
Fax: 949 643-6590
Carolyn Macneil, *Branch Mgr*
Mary Leon, *Human Res Mgr*
EMP: 152
SALES (corp-wide): 58.3B **Publicly Held**
SIC: **4215** Parcel delivery, vehicular
HQ: United Parcel Service, Inc. (Oh)
55 Glenlake Pkwy
Atlanta GA 30328
404 828-6000

(P-4454)
UNITED PARCEL SERVICE INC
OH
Also Called: UPS
10690 Santa Monica Blvd, Los Angeles (90025-4838)
PHONE..............................310 474-0019
EMP: 158
SALES (corp-wide): 58.3B **Publicly Held**
SIC: **4215** Parcel delivery, vehicular
HQ: United Parcel Service, Inc. (Oh)
55 Glenlake Pkwy
Atlanta GA 30328
404 828-6000

(P-4455)
UNITED PARCEL SERVICE INC
OH
Also Called: UPS
6060 Cornerstone Ct W, San Diego (92121-3712)
PHONE..............................858 455-8800
Donald Higginson, *Vice Pres*
Michael Tillery, *Admin Asst*
Jeff Giboney, *Director*
Lavonda Caffman, *Manager*
Denise Foster, *Manager*
EMP: 158
SALES (corp-wide): 58.3B **Publicly Held**
SIC: **4215** Parcel delivery, vehicular
HQ: United Parcel Service, Inc. (Oh)
55 Glenlake Pkwy
Atlanta GA 30328
404 828-6000

(P-4456)
UNITED PARCEL SERVICE INC
OH
Also Called: UPS
16000 Arminta St, Van Nuys (91406-1895)
PHONE..............................404 828-6000
EMP: 158
SALES (corp-wide): 58.3B **Publicly Held**
SIC: **4215** Parcel delivery, vehicular
HQ: United Parcel Service, Inc. (Oh)
55 Glenlake Pkwy
Atlanta GA 30328
404 828-6000

(P-4457)
UNITED PARCEL SERVICE INC
OH
Also Called: UPS
7925 Ronson Rd, San Diego (92111-1997)
PHONE..............................909 279-5111
Jeff Walsingham, *Marketing Mgr*
Claire Meyer, *Supervisor*
Wally Tran, *Supervisor*
EMP: 158
SALES (corp-wide): 58.3B **Publicly Held**
SIC: **4215** Courier services, except by air
HQ: United Parcel Service, Inc. (Oh)
55 Glenlake Pkwy
Atlanta GA 30328
404 828-6000

(P-4458)
UNITED PARCEL SERVICE INC
OH
Also Called: UPS
10609 W Goshen Ave 304, Visalia (93291-9496)
PHONE..............................559 651-0995
EMP: 158
SALES (corp-wide): 58.3B **Publicly Held**
WEB: www.upsscs.com
SIC: **4215** Parcel delivery, vehicular
HQ: United Parcel Service, Inc. (Oh)
55 Glenlake Pkwy
Atlanta GA 30328
404 828-6000

(P-4459)
UNITED PARCEL SERVICE INC
OH
Also Called: UPS
290 W Avenue L, Lancaster (93534-7109)
PHONE..............................800 828-8264
Fax: 661 942-2930
Mark Overmyer, *Marketing Staff*
EMP: 150
SALES (corp-wide): 58.3B **Publicly Held**
WEB: www.upsscs.com
SIC: **4215** Parcel delivery, vehicular
HQ: United Parcel Service, Inc. (Oh)
55 Glenlake Pkwy
Atlanta GA 30328
404 828-6000

(P-4460)
UNITED PARCEL SERVICE INC
OH
Also Called: UPS
13233 Moore St, Cerritos (90703-2276)
PHONE..............................562 404-3236
Fax: 562 404-1560
Gary Mieredos, *Manager*
EMP: 152
SALES (corp-wide): 58.3B **Publicly Held**
WEB: www.upsscs.com
SIC: **4215** Parcel delivery, vehicular
HQ: United Parcel Service, Inc. (Oh)
55 Glenlake Pkwy
Atlanta GA 30328
404 828-6000

(P-4461)
UNITED PARCEL SERVICE INC
OH
Also Called: UPS
259 Cherry St, Ukiah (95482-5804)
PHONE..............................707 468-5481
EMP: 158
SALES (corp-wide): 58.3B **Publicly Held**
WEB: www.upsscs.com
SIC: **4215** Courier services, except by air
HQ: United Parcel Service, Inc. (Oh)
55 Glenlake Pkwy
Atlanta GA 30328
404 828-6000

(P-4462)
UNITED PARCEL SERVICE INC
OH
Also Called: UPS
6 Upper Ragsdale Dr, Monterey (93940-5730)
PHONE..............................831 757-6294
EMP: 158
SALES (corp-wide): 58.3B **Publicly Held**
SIC: **4215** Courier services, except by air
HQ: United Parcel Service, Inc. (Oh)
55 Glenlake Pkwy
Atlanta GA 30328
404 828-6000

(P-4463)
UNITED PARCEL SERVICE INC
OH
Also Called: UPS
17370 Jasmine St, Victorville (92395-5868)
PHONE..............................619 443-3266
EMP: 158
SALES (corp-wide): 58.3B **Publicly Held**
SIC: **4215** Courier services, except by air
HQ: United Parcel Service, Inc. (Oh)
55 Glenlake Pkwy
Atlanta GA 30328
404 828-6000

(P-4464)
UNITED PARCEL SERVICE INC
OH
Also Called: UPS
3601 Sacramento Dr, San Luis Obispo (93401-7115)
PHONE..............................801 973-3400
EMP: 158
SALES (corp-wide): 58.3B **Publicly Held**
SIC: **4215** Parcel delivery, vehicular
HQ: United Parcel Service, Inc. (Oh)
55 Glenlake Pkwy
Atlanta GA 30328
404 828-6000

(P-4465)
UNITED PARCEL SERVICE INC
OH
Also Called: UPS
3860 Cypress Dr, Petaluma (94954-5613)
PHONE..............................650 952-5200
Ivars Cacs, *Accounts Exec*
Richard Catton, *Supervisor*
EMP: 158
SALES (corp-wide): 58.3B **Publicly Held**
SIC: **4215** Parcel delivery, vehicular
HQ: United Parcel Service, Inc. (Oh)
55 Glenlake Pkwy
Atlanta GA 30328
404 828-6000

(P-4466)
UNITED PARCEL SERVICE INC
OH
Also Called: UPS
505 Pine Ave, Goleta (93117-3707)
PHONE..............................805 964-7848
Jason Chang, *Manager*
EMP: 112
SALES (corp-wide): 58.3B **Publicly Held**
WEB: www.upsscs.com
SIC: **4215** Parcel delivery, vehicular
HQ: United Parcel Service, Inc. (Oh)
55 Glenlake Pkwy
Atlanta GA 30328
404 828-6000

(P-4467)
UNITED PARCEL SERVICE INC
OH
Also Called: UPS
309 Cooley Ln, Santa Maria (93455-1218)
PHONE..............................805 922-7851
Michael King, *Manager*
Steve Glenn, *Business Mgr*
EMP: 140
SALES (corp-wide): 58.3B **Publicly Held**
WEB: www.upsscs.com
SIC: **4215** Parcel delivery, vehicular
HQ: United Parcel Service, Inc. (Oh)
55 Glenlake Pkwy
Atlanta GA 30328
404 828-6000

(P-4468)
UNITED PARCEL SERVICE INC
OH
Also Called: UPS
1970 Olivera Rd, Concord (94520-5425)
PHONE..............................925 689-6584
EMP: 158
SALES (corp-wide): 58.3B **Publicly Held**
SIC: **4215** Parcel delivery, vehicular
HQ: United Parcel Service, Inc. (Oh)
55 Glenlake Pkwy
Atlanta GA 30328
404 828-6000

(P-4469)
UNITED PARCEL SERVICE INC
OH
Also Called: UPS
2342 Gun Club Rd, Angels Camp (95222)
PHONE..............................209 736-0878
EMP: 158
SALES (corp-wide): 58.3B **Publicly Held**
SIC: **4215** Parcel delivery, vehicular
HQ: United Parcel Service, Inc. (Oh)
55 Glenlake Pkwy
Atlanta GA 30328
404 828-6000

(P-4470)
UNITED PARCEL SERVICE INC
OH
Also Called: UPS
1501 Rancho Conejo Blvd, Newbury Park (91320-1410)
PHONE..............................805 375-1832
Grant Nissan, *Branch Mgr*
EMP: 200
SALES (corp-wide): 58.3B **Publicly Held**
WEB: www.upsscs.com
SIC: **4215** Parcel delivery, vehicular
HQ: United Parcel Service, Inc. (Oh)
55 Glenlake Pkwy
Atlanta GA 30328
404 828-6000

(P-4471)
UNITED PARCEL SERVICE INC
OH
Also Called: UPS
3000 E Washington Blvd, Los Angeles (90023-4220)
PHONE..............................323 729-6762
Art Nakamoto, *Branch Mgr*
EMP: 800
SALES (corp-wide): 58.3B **Publicly Held**
WEB: www.upsscs.com
SIC: **4215** Parcel delivery, vehicular
HQ: United Parcel Service, Inc. (Oh)
55 Glenlake Pkwy
Atlanta GA 30328
404 828-6000

(P-4472)
UNITED PARCEL SERVICE INC
OH
Also Called: UPS
2300 Boswell Ct, Chula Vista (91914-3520)
PHONE..............................714 491-7000
EMP: 158
SALES (corp-wide): 58.3B **Publicly Held**
SIC: **4215** Parcel delivery, vehicular
HQ: United Parcel Service, Inc. (Oh)
55 Glenlake Pkwy
Atlanta GA 30328
404 828-6000

4215 - Courier Svcs, Except Air County (P-4473)

(P-4473)
UNITED PARCEL SERVICE INC
OH
Also Called: UPS
7401 W Sunnyview Ave, Visalia (93291-9601)
PHONE.....................559 651-7690
Dave Hill, *Manager*
Barbara Hall, *Supervisor*
EMP: 100
SALES (corp-wide): 58.3B **Publicly Held**
WEB: www.upsscs.com
SIC: 4215 7322 Parcel delivery, vehicular; adjustment & collection services
HQ: United Parcel Service, Inc. (Oh)
55 Glenlake Pkwy
Atlanta GA 30328
404 828-6000

(P-4474)
UNITED PARCEL SERVICE INC
OH
Also Called: UPS
251 Sylvania Ave, Santa Cruz (95060-2161)
PHONE.....................831 425-1054
EMP: 158
SALES (corp-wide): 58.3B **Publicly Held**
WEB: www.upsscs.com
SIC: 4215 Courier services, except by air
HQ: United Parcel Service, Inc. (Oh)
55 Glenlake Pkwy
Atlanta GA 30328
404 828-6000

(P-4475)
UNITED PARCEL SERVICE INC
OH
Also Called: UPS
3140 Jurupa St, Ontario (91761-2902)
PHONE.....................909 974-7000
Brenda Hiza, *Branch Mgr*
Ray Morales, *Technology*
Kurt Kuehn, *Sls & Mktg Exec*
Noel Massie, *Manager*
Craig Kennedy, *Supervisor*
EMP: 80
SALES (corp-wide): 58.3B **Publicly Held**
WEB: www.upsscs.com
SIC: 4215 Package delivery, vehicular; parcel delivery, vehicular
HQ: United Parcel Service, Inc. (Oh)
55 Glenlake Pkwy
Atlanta GA 30328
404 828-6000

(P-4476)
UNITED PARCEL SERVICE INC
OH
Also Called: UPS
4500 Norris Canyon Rd, San Ramon (94583-1369)
PHONE.....................800 833-9943
EMP: 164
SALES (corp-wide): 58.3B **Publicly Held**
WEB: www.upsscs.com
SIC: 4215 Courier services, except by air
HQ: United Parcel Service, Inc. (Oh)
55 Glenlake Pkwy
Atlanta GA 30328
404 828-6000

(P-4477)
UNITED PARCEL SERVICE INC
OH
Also Called: UPS
2559 Palma Dr, Ventura (93003-5733)
PHONE.....................805 656-3442
EMP: 158
SALES (corp-wide): 58.3B **Publicly Held**
WEB: www.upsscs.com
SIC: 4215 Courier services, except by air
HQ: United Parcel Service, Inc. (Oh)
55 Glenlake Pkwy
Atlanta GA 30328
404 828-6000

(P-4478)
UNITED PARCEL SERVICE INC
OH
Also Called: UPS
1100 Baldwin Park Blvd, Baldwin Park (91706-5895)
PHONE.....................626 814-6216

Lero Stamply, *Manager*
EMP: 200
SALES (corp-wide): 58.3B **Publicly Held**
WEB: www.upsscs.com
SIC: 4215 4513 Parcel delivery, vehicular; air courier services
HQ: United Parcel Service, Inc. (Oh)
55 Glenlake Pkwy
Atlanta GA 30328
404 828-6000

(P-4479)
UNITED PARCEL SERVICE INC
OH
Also Called: UPS
3930 Kristi Ct, Sacramento (95827-9716)
PHONE.....................916 857-0311
EMP: 152
SALES (corp-wide): 58.3B **Publicly Held**
SIC: 4215 Parcel delivery, vehicular
HQ: United Parcel Service, Inc. (Oh)
55 Glenlake Pkwy
Atlanta GA 30328
404 828-6000

(P-4480)
UPS SUPPLY CHAIN SOLUTIONS
GEN
11991 Landon Dr, Mira Loma (91752-4000)
PHONE.....................951 749-3134
Gary Lawyer, *Branch Mgr*
EMP: 150
SALES (corp-wide): 58.3B **Publicly Held**
SIC: 4215 Parcel delivery, vehicular
HQ: Ups Supply Chain Solutions General Services, Inc.
55 Glenlake Pkwy
Atlanta GA 30328
404 828-6000

4221 Farm Product Warehousing & Storage

(P-4481)
BUTTE-YB-STTER WTR QLTY CLTION
625 Cooper Ave, Yuba City (95991-3864)
P.O. Box 729 (95992-0729)
PHONE.....................530 673-5131
Stephen F Danna, *Chairman*
EMP: 75
SALES: 428.7K **Privately Held**
SIC: 4221 Farm product warehousing & storage

(P-4482)
HONEYVILLE INC
11600 Dayton Dr, Rancho Cucamonga (91730-5525)
PHONE.....................909 980-9500
Fax: 909 980-6503
Ed Hemphill, *Vice Pres*
Jacob Walters, *Human Res Mgr*
John Hadfield, *VP Sales*
Doug Stoker, *Marketing Staff*
Rodney Scott, *Manager*
EMP: 85
SALES (corp-wide): 198.1MM **Privately Held**
WEB: www.honeyvillegrain.com
SIC: 4221 5153 2045 2041 Grain elevator, storage only; grains; prepared flour mixes & doughs; flour & other grain mill products
PA: Honeyville, Inc.
1080 N Main St Ste 101
Brigham City UT 84302
435 494-4193

(P-4483)
PURATOS CORPORATION
Also Called: Puratos Bakery Supply
11167 White Birch Dr, Rancho Cucamonga (91730-3820)
PHONE.....................909 484-1312
Ron Bouter, *General Mgr*
EMP: 100 **Privately Held**
WEB: www.puratos.com
SIC: 4221 2041 Farm product warehousing & storage; flour
HQ: Puratos Corporation
1941 Old Cuthbert Rd
Cherry Hill NJ 08034

(P-4484)
VEG-LAND INC
Also Called: J B J Distributing
1518 E Valencia Dr, Fullerton (92831-4734)
P.O. Box 1287 (92836-8287)
PHONE.....................714 871-6712
Fax: 714 992-0433
James E Matiasevich, *President*
John P Matiasevich, *Corp Secy*
EMP: 50 **EST:** 1976
SQ FT: 70,000
SALES (est): 5.8MM
SALES (corp-wide): 32.1MM **Privately Held**
SIC: 4221 Farm product warehousing & storage
PA: Veg Land Sales Inc
1518 E Valencia Dr
Fullerton CA 92831
714 871-6712

4222 Refrigerated Warehousing & Storage

(P-4485)
AMERICOLD LOGISTICS LLC
950 S Sanborn Rd, Salinas (93901-4530)
P.O. Box 1548 (93902-1548)
PHONE.....................831 424-1537
Pat Zimmerman, *General Mgr*
Michael Black, *Sales Staff*
EMP: 50
SALES (corp-wide): 4.1B **Privately Held**
SIC: 4222 Warehousing, cold storage or refrigerated
HQ: Americold Logistics, Llc
10 Glenlake Pkwy Ste 324
Atlanta GA 30328
678 441-1400

(P-4486)
AMERICOLD LOGISTICS LLC
Also Called: Christian Salvesen
2750 Orbiter St, Brea (92821-6256)
PHONE.....................714 993-3533
Fax: 714 993-0522
Arthur Boehme, *Manager*
Raul Pereyra, *Manager*
EMP: 50
SQ FT: 100,000
SALES (corp-wide): 4.1B **Privately Held**
SIC: 4222 Warehousing, cold storage or refrigerated
HQ: Americold Logistics, Llc
10 Glenlake Pkwy Ste 324
Atlanta GA 30328
678 441-1400

(P-4487)
AMERICOLD LOGISTICS LLC
Also Called: Americold Realty
700 Malaga St, Ontario (91761-8627)
PHONE.....................909 390-4950
Jeff Canfield, *Manager*
Bonne Martin, *Admin Asst*
Jamie Arnold, *HR Admin*
Tom Kelley, *Manager*
EMP: 50
SALES (corp-wide): 4.1B **Privately Held**
WEB: www.americoldlogistics.com
SIC: 4222 Refrigerated warehousing & storage
HQ: Americold Logistics, Llc
10 Glenlake Pkwy Ste 324
Atlanta GA 30328
678 441-1400

(P-4488)
AMERICOLD LOGISTICS LLC
3420 E Vernon Ave, Vernon (90058-1812)
PHONE.....................323 581-0025
Ian McGagh, *Branch Mgr*
Ethan Toste, *Facilities Mgr*
EMP: 78
SALES (corp-wide): 4.1B **Privately Held**
SIC: 4222 Warehousing, cold storage or refrigerated
HQ: Americold Logistics, Llc
10 Glenlake Pkwy Ste 324
Atlanta GA 30328
678 441-1400

(P-4489)
CAL PACKING & STORAGE LP
Also Called: Bravante Produce
1356 S Buttonwillow Ave, Reedley (93654-9333)
PHONE.....................559 638-2929
Fax: 559 638-9292
George Bravante, *Managing Prtnr*
Rodney Aguiar, *CFO*
Ken Collins, *Manager*
EMP: 70
SQ FT: 100,000
SALES (est): 12MM **Privately Held**
SIC: 4222 7389 5148 Warehousing, cold storage or refrigerated; packaging & labeling services; fresh fruits & vegetables

(P-4490)
CENTRAL COAST COOLING
LLC
1107 Merrill St, Salinas (93901-4430)
P.O. Box 1527 (93902-1527)
PHONE.....................831 422-7265
Fax: 831 422-2792
Mike Storm, *President*
Denny Bertlesman, *Vice Pres*
Shelley Urgartte, *Executive*
Ron Burnett, *General Mgr*
Doyle Burnett, *Plant Mgr*
EMP: 90
SQ FT: 30,000
SALES (est): 15MM **Privately Held**
WEB: www.centralcoastcooling.com
SIC: 4222 Warehousing, cold storage or refrigerated

(P-4491)
DELMART COLD STORAGE CO
INC
1401 19th St, Bakersfield (93301-4453)
PHONE.....................661 849-8608
Robert Vignolo, *Principal*
EMP: 85
SALES (corp-wide): 9.8MM **Privately Held**
SIC: 4222 Warehousing, cold storage or refrigerated
PA: Delmart Cold Storage Co Inc
30988 Riverside Ave
Shafter CA 93263
661 746-2148

(P-4492)
DISNEYLAND INTERNATIONAL
INC
1313 S Harbor Blvd, Anaheim (92802-2309)
P.O. Box 3232 (92803-3232)
PHONE.....................714 999-4000
Bill Ross, *Benefits Mgr*
EMP: 150 **Publicly Held**
SIC: 4222 Cheese warehouse
HQ: Disneyland International, Inc.
500 S Buena Vista St
Burbank CA 91521
818 560-1000

(P-4493)
EXEL N AMERCN LOGISTICS
INC
Freeze Point Cold Storage Div
3735 Imperial Way, Stockton (95215-9691)
PHONE.....................209 942-0102
Mike Hernandez, *Manager*
Jon Drake, *Manager*
EMP: 100
SALES (corp-wide): 63.6B **Privately Held**
SIC: 4222 Storage, frozen or refrigerated goods
HQ: Exel North American Logistics, Inc.
570 Players Pkwy
Westerville OH 43081
800 272-1052

(P-4494)
EXEL N AMERCN LOGISTICS
INC
Also Called: Power Logistics
4512 Frontier Way, Stockton (95215-9676)
PHONE.....................209 932-2400
Fax: 209 932-2411
Charles McElwain, *Manager*
Junior Contreras, *Manager*
EMP: 100

PRODUCTS & SERVICES SECTION
4225 - General Warehousing & Storage County (P-4514)

SALES (corp-wide): 63.6B **Privately Held**
SIC: **4222** 5149 Storage, frozen or refrigerated goods; groceries & related products
HQ: Exel North American Logistics, Inc.
570 Players Pkwy
Westerville OH 43081
800 272-1052

(P-4495)
EXETER PACKERS INC
Also Called: Sun Pacific Cold Storage
33374 Lerdo Hwy, Bakersfield (93308-9782)
PHONE..................................661 399-0416
Richard Peters, *Manager*
EMP: 220
SALES (corp-wide): 146.6MM **Privately Held**
SIC: **4222** 0172 Warehousing, cold storage or refrigerated; grapes
PA: Exeter Packers, Inc.
1250 E Myer Ave
Exeter CA 93221
559 592-5168

(P-4496)
KONOIKE-PACIFIC CALIFORNIA INC (HQ)
Also Called: Kpac
1420 Coil Ave, Wilmington (90744-2205)
PHONE..................................310 518-1000
Fax: 310 518-3900
Bob Smola, *President*
Ulises Sam, *CFO*
Jim Filkins, *Vice Pres*
Wayne Lamb, *Vice Pres*
Yutaka Kane Urabe, *Vice Pres*
EMP: 78
SQ FT: 784,080
SALES (est): 27.5MM
SALES (corp-wide): 2.1B **Privately Held**
SIC: **4222** Warehousing, cold storage or refrigerated
PA: Konoike Transport Co.,Ltd.
4-3-9, Fushimimachi, Chuo-Ku
Osaka OSK 541-0
662 274-600

(P-4497)
LINEAGE LOGISTICS LLC (HQ)
17911 Von Karman Ave # 400, Irvine (92614-6209)
PHONE..................................800 678-7271
Bill Hendricksen, *CEO*
Jeremy Breaux, *CFO*
Tim Smith, *Exec VP*
Jason Burnett, *Senior VP*
John Dittrick, *Senior VP*
EMP: 175
SALES (est): 129MM
SALES (corp-wide): 1.5B **Privately Held**
SIC: **4222** Cheese warehouse; warehousing, cold storage or refrigerated
PA: Lineage Logistics Holdings, Llc
17911 Von Karman Ave # 400
Irvine CA 92614
800 678-7271

(P-4498)
LINEAGE LOGISTICS LLC
3251 De Forest Cir Ste C, Mira Loma (91752-3277)
PHONE..................................951 360-7970
Fax: 951 360-1548
Reginald Burke, *General Mgr*
Fuentes Marina, *Personnel Exec*
EMP: 50
SALES (corp-wide): 1.5B **Privately Held**
SIC: **4222** Warehousing, cold storage or refrigerated
HQ: Lineage Logistics, Llc
17911 Von Karman Ave # 400
Irvine CA 92614
800 678-7271

(P-4499)
LINEAGE LOGISTICS HOLDINGS LLC (PA)
17911 Von Karman Ave # 400, Irvine (92614-6209)
PHONE..................................800 678-7271
Greg Lehmkuhl, *President*
Timothy Dayton, *President*
Paul Hendricksen, *President*
Mike McClendon, *President*

Bill Hendricksen, *CEO*
EMP: 94
SALES (est): 1.5B **Privately Held**
SIC: **4222** Warehousing, cold storage or refrigerated

(P-4500)
MIKE CAMPBELL & ASSOCIATES LTD (PA)
Also Called: Mike Campbell Assoc Logistics
13031 Temple Ave, City of Industry (91746-1418)
PHONE..................................626 369-3981
Fax: 626 369-2732
Vickie J Campbell, *CEO*
James Heermans, *President*
Paul Trump, *President*
Andrea Arce, *Administration*
Francine Rivas, *Accounting Mgr*
EMP: 550
SALES (est): 123MM **Privately Held**
SIC: **4222** 4225 4214 4213 Storage, frozen or refrigerated goods; general warehousing & storage; local trucking with storage; trucking, except local

(P-4501)
STANDARD-SOUTHERN CORPORATION
Also Called: Los Angeles Cold Storage Co
400 S Central Ave, Los Angeles (90013-1712)
P.O. Box 54244 (90054-0244)
PHONE..................................213 624-1831
Larry Rauch, *Manager*
EMP: 80
SALES (corp-wide): 30.1MM **Privately Held**
WEB: www.lacold.com
SIC: **4222** Warehousing, cold storage or refrigerated
PA: Standard-Southern Corporation
4635 Suthwest Fwy Ste 910
Houston TX 77027
713 627-1700

(P-4502)
STANDARD-SOUTHERN CORPORATION
Also Called: L.A. Cold Storage
440 S Central Ave, Los Angeles (90013-1712)
PHONE..................................213 624-1831
Fax: 213 625-2041
Larry Rauch, *President*
John Scherer, *Engineer*
Chuck Gunther, *Chief Engr*
Thom Thomas, *Human Res Dir*
Terry Miller, *Warehouse Mgr*
EMP: 130
SALES (corp-wide): 30.1MM **Privately Held**
SIC: **4222** Warehousing, cold storage or refrigerated
PA: Standard-Southern Corporation
4635 Suthwest Fwy Ste 910
Houston TX 77027
713 627-1700

(P-4503)
STANDARD-SOUTHERN CORPORATION
Also Called: Los Angeles Cold Storage
715 E 4th St, Los Angeles (90013-1727)
PHONE..................................213 624-1831
Thom Thomas, *Branch Mgr*
EMP: 90
SALES (corp-wide): 30.1MM **Privately Held**
WEB: www.lacold.com
SIC: **4222** Warehousing, cold storage or refrigerated
PA: Standard-Southern Corporation
4635 Suthwest Fwy Ste 910
Houston TX 77027
713 627-1700

(P-4504)
UNITED STATES COLD STORAGE
Also Called: United States Cold Storage Cal
6501 District Blvd, Bakersfield (93313-2000)
P.O. Box 45001 (93384-5001)
PHONE..................................661 832-2653

Fax: 661 832-5846
Randall Dorrell, *Manager*
EMP: 75
SALES (corp-wide): 10.4B **Privately Held**
WEB: www.uscold.com
SIC: **4222** Refrigerated warehousing & storage
HQ: United States Cold Storage, Inc.
201 Laurel Rd Ste 400
Voorhees NJ 08043
856 354-8181

(P-4505)
UNITED STATES COLD STORAGE
2003 S Cherry Ave, Fresno (93721-3300)
PHONE..................................559 237-6145
Fax: 559 237-7214
John Bodden, *Manager*
EMP: 50
SQ FT: 87,184
SALES (corp-wide): 10.4B **Privately Held**
WEB: www.uscold.com
SIC: **4222** Warehousing, cold storage or refrigerated
HQ: United States Cold Storage, Inc.
201 Laurel Rd Ste 400
Voorhees NJ 08043
856 354-8181

(P-4506)
UNITED STATES COLD STORAGE INC
Also Called: United States Cold Storage CA
33400 Dowe Ave, Union City (94587-2038)
P.O. Box 1106 (94587-1106)
PHONE..................................510 489-8300
Dave Sweillem, *Opers-Prdtn-Mfg*
Dave Sweillem, *General Mgr*
Ricky Clevalle, *Sales Staff*
EMP: 50
SALES (corp-wide): 10.4B **Privately Held**
WEB: www.uscold.com
SIC: **4222** Warehousing, cold storage or refrigerated
HQ: United States Cold Storage, Inc.
201 Laurel Rd Ste 400
Voorhees NJ 08043
856 354-8181

(P-4507)
UNITED STATES COLD STORAGE INC
810 E Continental Ave, Tulare (93274-6816)
PHONE..................................559 686-1110
Fax: 559 686-3827
Brian Ford, *Opers-Prdtn-Mfg*
Chris Harrington, *General Mgr*
Chad Cox, *Opers Mgr*
Miguel Machado, *Supervisor*
EMP: 50
SALES (corp-wide): 10.4B **Privately Held**
WEB: www.uscold.com
SIC: **4222** Warehousing, cold storage or refrigerated
HQ: United States Cold Storage, Inc.
201 Laurel Rd Ste 400
Voorhees NJ 08043
856 354-8181

(P-4508)
UNITED STATES COLD STORAGE INC
1400 N Macarthur Dr Ste A, Tracy (95376-2829)
PHONE..................................209 835-2653
Fax: 209 835-4117
Stanley Moya, *Manager*
Alejandro Ornelas, *Asst Supt*
EMP: 50
SALES (corp-wide): 10.4B **Privately Held**
WEB: www.uscold.com
SIC: **4222** Warehousing, cold storage or refrigerated
HQ: United States Cold Storage, Inc.
201 Laurel Rd Ste 400
Voorhees NJ 08043
856 354-8181

(P-4509)
US GROWERS COLD STORAGE INC (PA)
3141 E 44th St, Vernon (90058-2405)
PHONE..................................323 583-3163

Fax: 323 583-2542
Angelo V Antoci, *Principal*
Sam Perricone, *Admin Sec*
Peter Corselli, *Engineer*
Robert Milton, *Manager*
Ralph Newton, *Manager*
EMP: 141 EST: 1950
SQ FT: 4,000
SALES (est): 30.4MM **Privately Held**
WEB: www.usgrowers.com
SIC: **4222** Warehousing, cold storage or refrigerated

(P-4510)
US GROWERS COLD STORAGE INC
2045 E Vernon Ave, Vernon (90058-1612)
PHONE..................................323 583-3163
Ralph Newton, *Manager*
EMP: 150
SALES (corp-wide): 30.4MM **Privately Held**
WEB: www.usgrowers.com
SIC: **4222** Warehousing, cold storage or refrigerated
PA: U.S. Growers Cold Storage, Inc.
3141 E 44th St
Vernon CA 90058
323 583-3163

(P-4511)
YOSEMITE MEAT COMPANY INC
601 Zeff Rd, Modesto (95351-3942)
P.O. Box 580008 (95358-0001)
PHONE..................................209 524-5117
Fax: 209 522-4836
Johnnie F Lau, *President*
G Ay Lau, *Vice Pres*
EMP: 100
SQ FT: 3,600
SALES (est): 36.1MM **Privately Held**
WEB: www.yosemitemeat.com
SIC: **4222** 5421 5147 5142 Storage, frozen or refrigerated goods; meat markets, including freezer provisioners; meats, fresh; packaged frozen goods

4225 General Warehousing & Storage

(P-4512)
3M COMPANY
5151 E Philadelphia St, Ontario (91761-2801)
P.O. Box 51459 (91761-1049)
PHONE..................................909 974-3004
Richard Campbell, *Manager*
Mark Hodgeson, *Safety Mgr*
EMP: 150
SALES (corp-wide): 30.2B **Publicly Held**
WEB: www.mmm.com
SIC: **4225** General warehousing
PA: 3m Company
3m Center Bldg 22011w02
Saint Paul MN 55144
651 733-1110

(P-4513)
AAR PARTS TRADING INC
Also Called: AAR Defense Systems Logistics
4400 Ruffin Rd, San Diego (92123-1606)
PHONE..................................858 627-6029
Bill Elyea, *Director*
David Lund, *Credit Mgr*
EMP: 60
SALES (est): 1.8MM **Privately Held**
SIC: **4225** General warehousing & storage

(P-4514)
ACT FULFILLMENT INC
3155 Universe Dr, Mira Loma (91752-3252)
PHONE..................................909 930-9083
Fax: 909 930-9683
Randolph Cox, *President*
Lydiann Cox, *CFO*
Janet Gomez, *QA Dir*
Amy Leffler, *Director*
EMP: 220
SALES (est): 26.8MM **Privately Held**
WEB: www.allcartage.com
SIC: **4225** General warehousing & storage; general warehousing; warehousing, self-storage

4225 - General Warehousing & Storage County (P-4515)

PRODUCTS & SERVICES SECTION

(P-4515)
ACTIVISION BLIZZARD INC
4247 S Minnewawa Ave, Fresno (93725-9345)
PHONE..................310 431-4000
Tony Suarez, *Branch Mgr*
Alan Lamonica, *Senior Mgr*
Bob Wilson, *Manager*
EMP: 200
SALES (corp-wide): 4.6B **Publicly Held**
WEB: www.blizzard.com
SIC: 4225 General warehousing & storage
PA: Activision Blizzard, Inc.
3100 Ocean Park Blvd
Santa Monica CA 90405
310 255-2000

(P-4516)
ADIR INTERNATIONAL LLC
4444-46 Ayers Ave, Los Angeles (90023)
PHONE..................213 386-4412
Russell Yeager, *Vice Pres*
EMP: 77
SALES (corp-wide): 484.7MM **Privately Held**
WEB: www.lacuracao.com
SIC: 4225 Warehousing, self-storage
PA: Adir International, Llc
1605 W Olympic Blvd # 405
Los Angeles CA 90015
213 639-2100

(P-4517)
ADVANCED STERLIZATION
13135 Napa St, Fontana (92335-2961)
PHONE..................909 350-6987
EMP: 100 **Privately Held**
SIC: 4225 General warehousing & storage
PA: Advanced Sterlization Products Services Inc.
33 Technology Dr
Irvine CA 92618

(P-4518)
ADVANTAGE MEDIA SERVICES INC
Also Called: AMS Fulfillment
28220 Industry Dr, Valencia (91355-4105)
PHONE..................661 705-7588
John Bevacqua, *Vice Pres*
EMP: 118
SALES (corp-wide): 59.5MM **Privately Held**
SIC: 4225 General warehousing
PA: Advantage Media Services, Inc.
29010 Commerce Center Dr
Valencia CA 91355
661 775-0611

(P-4519)
ALBERTSONS LLC
Also Called: Albertsons Dist Ctr 8760
777 S Harbor Blvd, La Habra (90631-6800)
PHONE..................714 578-4670
Tony Vasquez, *Manager*
EMP: 100
SALES (corp-wide): 58.7B **Privately Held**
SIC: 4225 General warehousing & storage
HQ: Albertson's Llc
250 E Parkcenter Blvd
Boise ID 83706
208 395-6200

(P-4520)
ALBERTSONS LLC
Also Called: Albertsons Brea Dist Ctr
200 N Puente St, Brea (92821-3841)
PHONE..................714 990-8200
Mike Ketcham, *Branch Mgr*
David Moore, *Persnl Mgr*
Kevin Alves, *Opers Staff*
Roy Almond, *Maintence Staff*
EMP: 1000
SALES (corp-wide): 58.7B **Privately Held**
SIC: 4225 General warehousing & storage
HQ: Albertson's Llc
250 E Parkcenter Blvd
Boise ID 83706
208 395-6200

(P-4521)
ALBERTSONS LLC
Also Called: Albertsons Dist Ctr 8795
700 Crocker Dr, Vacaville (95688-8707)
PHONE..................707 446-5922
Kirk Hansen, *Manager*
EMP: 350
SALES (corp-wide): 58.7B **Privately Held**
WEB: www.albertsons.com
SIC: 4225 General warehousing & storage
HQ: Albertson's Llc
250 E Parkcenter Blvd
Boise ID 83706
208 395-6200

(P-4522)
AMERIFREIGHT INC
Also Called: Logistics Team
218 Machlin Ct, Walnut (91789-3026)
PHONE..................909 839-2600
Alan Mao Yang, *President*
Claudia Fong, *CFO*
Joe Dabbs, *Vice Pres*
Tammy Yung, *Accountant*
Robert Chung, *VP Opers*
EMP: 675
SALES (est): 45.9MM **Privately Held**
SIC: 4225 4731 General warehousing; freight transportation arrangement

(P-4523)
APPLIED MATERIALS INC
2821 Scott Blvd Bldg 17, Santa Clara (95050-2549)
P.O. Box 58039 (95052-8039)
PHONE..................408 727-5555
Johnny Singh, *Principal*
Sharon Timoner, *Managing Dir*
Donn Turner, *General Mgr*
Yvonne Tai, *Info Tech Mgr*
Yoke W Mun, *Technology*
EMP: 100
SALES (corp-wide): 9.6B **Publicly Held**
WEB: www.appliedmaterials.com
SIC: 4225 General warehousing & storage
PA: Applied Materials, Inc.
3050 Bowers Ave
Santa Clara CA 95054
408 727-5555

(P-4524)
ARB INC
Also Called: Northern Division
1875 Loveridge Rd, Pittsburg (94565-4110)
P.O. Box 8189 (94565-8189)
PHONE..................925 432-3649
Fax: 925 432-2958
Donnie Brown, *Branch Mgr*
Don Brown, *Vice Pres*
EMP: 50
SALES (corp-wide): 1.9B **Publicly Held**
WEB: www.arbinc.com
SIC: 4225 1623 3444 General warehousing & storage; pipeline construction; sheet metalwork
HQ: Arb, Inc.
26000 Commercentre Dr
Lake Forest CA 92630
949 598-9242

(P-4525)
ARDEN-MAYFAIR INC
Arden Group
6191 Peachtree St, Commerce (90040-4064)
PHONE..................310 638-2842
Fax: 310 631-0950
Jim Baron, *Manager*
Jim Behrens, *Director*
EMP: 50
SALES (corp-wide): 316.3MM **Privately Held**
SIC: 4225 General warehousing
HQ: Arden-Mayfair, Inc.
13833 Freeway Dr
Santa Fe Springs CA 90670
310 638-2842

(P-4526)
BIAGI BROS INC
1200 Green Island Rd, American Canyon (94503-9639)
PHONE..................707 642-4412
EMP: 74
SALES (corp-wide): 106.1MM **Privately Held**
SIC: 4225 General warehousing & storage
PA: Biagi Bros., Inc.
787 Airpark Rd
Napa CA 94558
707 745-8115

(P-4527)
BIAGI BROS INC
Also Called: F & G Biagi Transportation
3655 E Airport Dr, Ontario (91761-1562)
PHONE..................909 390-6910
John Boggus, *Branch Mgr*
Brian Hartman, *Manager*
EMP: 200
SALES (corp-wide): 106.1MM **Privately Held**
WEB: www.biagibros.com
SIC: 4225 General warehousing & storage
PA: Biagi Bros., Inc.
787 Airpark Rd
Napa CA 94558
707 745-8115

(P-4528)
C & B DELIVERY SERVICES
Also Called: Temco
230 Diamond St, Laguna Beach (92651-3610)
PHONE..................909 623-4708
Fax: 909 622-8208
Virginia Templeton, *President*
Roy Burk, *General Mgr*
EMP: 85
SQ FT: 91,000
SALES (est): 9.2MM **Privately Held**
SIC: 4225 General warehousing & storage

(P-4529)
C & S WHOLESALE GROCERS INC
8301 Fruitridge Rd, Sacramento (95826-4806)
PHONE..................916 383-5275
Ric Clark, *General Mgr*
Adam Grocek, *Info Tech Dir*
Gary Boatman, *Manager*
EMP: 285
SALES (corp-wide): 31.1B **Privately Held**
SIC: 4225 General warehousing
PA: C&S Wholesale Grocers, Inc.
7 Corporate Dr
Keene NH 03431
603 354-7000

(P-4530)
CALIFORNIA SUPER MARKET
Also Called: California Mayoreo-Y-Menudeo
363 W 2nd St, Calexico (92231-2114)
PHONE..................760 357-3065
Fax: 760 357-4041
Alex Loo Jr, *Manager*
Rita Guzman, *Bookkeeper*
Carlos Cuevas, *Opers-Prdtn-Mfg*
EMP: 61
SALES (corp-wide): 18.1MM **Privately Held**
SIC: 4225 General warehousing & storage
PA: California Super Market
601 S Imperial Ave
Calexico CA 92231
760 357-6888

(P-4531)
CARROLL SHELBY LICENSING INC
19021 S Figueroa St, Gardena (90248-4510)
PHONE..................310 914-1843
Tracey Smith, *President*
EMP: 72 EST: 2001
SQ FT: 69,247
SALES (est): 3.8MM
SALES (corp-wide): 9.3MM **Privately Held**
SIC: 4225 General warehousing
PA: Shelby Carroll International Inc
19021 S Figueroa St
Gardena CA 90248
310 538-2914

(P-4532)
CASAS INTERNATIONAL BRKG INC (PA)
9355 Airway Rd Ste 4, San Diego (92154-7931)
PHONE..................619 661-6162
Fax: 619 661-6009
Sylvia Casas, *President*
Martha Casas, *Vice Pres*
John Jolliffe, *Vice Pres*
Elizabeth Estrella, *Admin Asst*
Alberto Ortega, *Info Tech Mgr*
EMP: 65
SQ FT: 120,000
SALES (est): 26.1MM **Privately Held**
WEB: www.casasinternational.com
SIC: 4225 4731 General warehousing & storage; customhouse brokers; freight forwarding

(P-4533)
CASCADE LOGISTICS LLC
857 Stonebridge Dr, Tracy (95376-2852)
P.O. Box 1157, Brattleboro VT (05302-1157)
PHONE..................209 832-4205
James Bringham,
Brian Shaver, *Software Engr*
EMP: 51
SALES (est): 2.7MM
SALES (corp-wide): 40.2MM **Privately Held**
WEB: www.es3.com
SIC: 4225 General warehousing & storage
PA: Es3, Llc
6 Optical Ave
Keene NH 03431
603 354-6100

(P-4534)
CAT LOGISTICS INC
Also Called: Caterpillar
5491 E Francis St, Ontario (91761-3604)
PHONE..................909 390-1920
Fax: 909 390-1922
James Ralston, *Manager*
EMP: 69
SALES (corp-wide): 47B **Publicly Held**
SIC: 4225 General warehousing & storage
HQ: C.A.T. Logistics Inc.
500 N Morton Ave
Morton IL 61550
309 675-1000

(P-4535)
CHINO-PACIFIC WAREHOUSE CORP (PA)
Also Called: Pcwc
3601 Jurupa St, Ontario (91761-2905)
PHONE..................909 545-8100
Fax: 909 464-9967
Jim Marcoly, *President*
David Boras, *CFO*
George Ramirez, *Vice Pres*
David Strawn, *Vice Pres*
Marty Jones, *Programmer Anys*
EMP: 66
SQ FT: 975,000
SALES (est): 23.5MM **Privately Held**
WEB: www.pcwc.com
SIC: 4225 General warehousing

(P-4536)
CITY FIBERS INC
2525 E 25th St, Vernon (90058-1210)
PHONE..................323 583-1013
David Jones, *Manager*
EMP: 60
SALES (corp-wide): 33.8MM **Privately Held**
SIC: 4225 General warehousing & storage
PA: City Fibers, Inc.
2500 S Santa Fe Ave
Vernon CA 90058
323 583-1013

(P-4537)
CONCORDE BATTERY CORPORATION
1125 N Azusa Canyon Rd, West Covina (91790-1002)
PHONE..................626 962-4006
Fax: 626 813-1239
Donald Godberg, *Principal*
EMP: 115
SALES (corp-wide): 24.8MM **Privately Held**
WEB: www.concordebattery.com
SIC: 4225 General warehousing & storage
PA: Concorde Battery Corp
2009 W San Bernardino Rd
West Covina CA 91790
626 813-1234

4225 - General Warehousing & Storage County (P-4561)

(P-4538)
CUSTOM GOODS LLC
1035 E Watson Center Rd, Carson
(90745-4203)
PHONE.............................310 241-6700
Fax: 310 522-0095
Tony Gregory,
James Fox, *CFO*
Jim Jackson, *Engineer*
Bill Cathcart,
▲ EMP: 260
SQ FT: 240,000
SALES: 42MM **Privately Held**
WEB: www.custom-goods.com
SIC: 4225 General warehousing

(P-4539)
DAMCO DISTRIBUTION SVCS INC
19801 S Santa Fe Ave, Compton
(90221-5915)
PHONE.............................310 661-4600
Fax: 310 604-3734
Carol Carpenter, *Manager*
EMP: 50
SALES (corp-wide): 38.6B **Privately Held**
SIC: 4225 General warehousing
HQ: Damco Distribution Services Inc.
180 Park Ave Ste 105
Florham Park NJ 07932
973 514-5000

(P-4540)
DEARDENS
9325 Santa Anita Ave, Rancho Cucamonga
(91730-6116)
PHONE.............................909 942-4599
Mayra Rascon, *Manager*
EMP: 50
SALES (corp-wide): 135.4MM **Privately Held**
SIC: 4225 General warehousing & storage
PA: Dearden's
700 S Main St
Los Angeles CA 90014
213 362-9600

(P-4541)
DELANCEY STREET FOUNDATION
1133 S Greenwood Ave, Montebello
(90640-6003)
PHONE.............................323 890-9339
Fax: 323 890-9334
Mimi Silbert, *President*
EMP: 50
SQ FT: 34,990
SALES (corp-wide): 46.4MM **Privately Held**
SIC: 4225 General warehousing
PA: Delancey Street Foundation
600 The Embarcadero
San Francisco CA 94107
415 957-9800

(P-4542)
DEPENDABLE HIGHWAY EXPRESS INC
3012 Alvarado St, San Leandro
(94577-5735)
PHONE.............................510 357-2223
Trevor Schirmer, *Manager*
EMP: 50
SALES (corp-wide): 292.7MM **Privately Held**
SIC: 4225 General warehousing & storage
PA: Dependable Highway Express, Inc.
2555 E Olympic Blvd
Los Angeles CA 90023
323 526-2200

(P-4543)
DISTRIBUTION ALTERNATIVES INC
Also Called: Scholls
17820 Slover Ave, Bloomington
(92316-2333)
PHONE.............................909 673-1000
Fax: 909 673-1316
Mark Chase, *Manager*
Brian Heston, *Warehouse Mgr*
EMP: 109
SALES (corp-wide): 85.3MM **Privately Held**
SIC: 4225 7319 General warehousing & storage; distribution of advertising material or sample services
PA: Distribution Alternatives, Inc.
435 Park Ct
Lino Lakes MN 55014
651 636-9167

(P-4544)
DIVERSIFIED TRANSPORT SYSTEMS
3150 S Willow Ave, Fresno (93725-9349)
P.O. Box 2879 (93745-2879)
PHONE.............................559 268-2760
Fax: 559 268-2753
Michael Gambos, *Owner*
Bill J Nixon, *Agent*
EMP: 50
SALES (est): 2.1MM **Privately Held**
SIC: 4225 General warehousing & storage

(P-4545)
DOMINOS PIZZA LLC
30852 San Antonio St, Hayward
(94544-7108)
PHONE.............................510 489-0333
Don Fontana, *Branch Mgr*
Vicky Fraser, *General Mgr*
EMP: 100
SQ FT: 24,810
SALES (corp-wide): 2.2B **Publicly Held**
WEB: www.dominos.com
SIC: 4225 5812 Pizzeria, chain
HQ: Domino's Pizza Llc
30 Frank Lloyd Wright Dr
Ann Arbor MI 48105
734 930-3030

(P-4546)
DSC LOGISTICS INC
1565 N Macarthur Dr, Tracy (95376-2839)
PHONE.............................209 833-0200
Fax: 209 833-9382
Bob Justice, *Manager*
EMP: 60
SALES (corp-wide): 355MM **Privately Held**
SIC: 4225 General warehousing & storage
PA: Dsc Logistics, Inc.
1750 S Wolf Rd
Des Plaines IL 60018
847 390-6800

(P-4547)
DURA FREIGHT INC
Also Called: Dura Freight Lines
525 S Lemon Ave, Walnut (91789-2912)
PHONE.............................909 444-1025
Fax: 909 595-4317
Clint Schaffer, *Manager*
EMP: 110
SALES (corp-wide): 50MM **Privately Held**
SIC: 4225 General warehousing & storage
PA: Dura Freight, Inc.
20405 Business Pkwy
Walnut CA 91789
909 595-8100

(P-4548)
EPSON AMERICA INC
Also Called: Epson West
1650 Glenn Curtiss St, Carson
(90746-4013)
PHONE.............................562 290-5855
Fax: 562 290-5999
Dan Wolsey, *Branch Mgr*
Motonori Okumura, *Officer*
Alberto Arredondo, *Vice Pres*
Miko Sion, *Vice Pres*
Andrea Zoeckler, *Vice Pres*
EMP: 140
SALES (corp-wide): 9.3B **Privately Held**
WEB: www.presentersonline.com
SIC: 4225 5045 5044 General warehousing & storage; computers, peripherals & software; office equipment
HQ: Epson America Inc
3840 Kilroy Airport Way
Long Beach CA 90806
800 463-7766

(P-4549)
ES3 LLC
Also Called: Cascade Logistics
857 Stonebridge Dr, Tracy (95376-2852)
PHONE.............................209 832-4205
James Bringham, *Manager*
EMP: 50
SALES (corp-wide): 44.3MM **Privately Held**
WEB: www.es3.com
SIC: 4225 General warehousing & storage
PA: Es3, Llc
6 Optical Ave
Keene NH 03431
603 354-6100

(P-4550)
EXEL INC
2391 W Winton Ave, Hayward
(94545-1101)
PHONE.............................510 784-7360
Fax: 510 786-2127
Mario Lombardi, *Branch Mgr*
EMP: 55
SALES (corp-wide): 63.6B **Privately Held**
WEB: www.exel-logistics.com
SIC: 4225 General warehousing & storage
HQ: Exel Inc.
570 Polaris Pkwy
Westerville OH 43082
614 865-8500

(P-4551)
EXEL INC
5576 Ontario Mills Pkwy B, Ontario
(91764-5101)
PHONE.............................623 907-2338
Kraig Foreman, *Branch Mgr*
EMP: 70
SALES (corp-wide): 63.6B **Privately Held**
WEB: www.exel-logistics.com
SIC: 4225 General warehousing & storage
HQ: Exel Inc.
570 Polaris Pkwy
Westerville OH 43082
614 865-8500

(P-4552)
FARO SERVICES INC
Also Called: Faro Logistics
15625 Shoemaker Ave, Norwalk
(90650-6862)
PHONE.............................562 483-7799
Tim Thomas, *Branch Mgr*
Toby Booth, *General Mgr*
EMP: 102
SALES (corp-wide): 103.6MM **Privately Held**
SIC: 4225 General warehousing & storage
PA: Faro Services, Inc.
7070 Pontius Rd
Groveport OH 43125
614 497-1700

(P-4553)
FRITO-LAY NORTH AMERICA INC
1924 E Maple Ave, El Segundo
(90245-3411)
PHONE.............................310 322-5001
Ed Castro, *Branch Mgr*
EMP: 50
SALES (corp-wide): 63B **Publicly Held**
WEB: www.fritolay.com
SIC: 4225 General warehousing & storage
HQ: Frito-Lay North America, Inc.
7701 Legacy Dr
Plano TX 75024

(P-4554)
GENCO DISTRIBUTION SYSTEM INC
1670 Champagne Ave, Ontario
(91761-3612)
PHONE.............................909 605-9210
Larry Schoeneberger, *Manager*
EMP: 50
SALES (corp-wide): 50.3B **Publicly Held**
SIC: 4225 General warehousing & storage
HQ: Genco Distribution System, Inc.
100 Papercraft Park
Pittsburgh PA 15238
412 820-3700

(P-4555)
GENERAL MOTORS LLC
9150 Hermosa Ave, Rancho Cucamonga
(91730-5304)
PHONE.............................800 521-7300
Mark Smith, *Branch Mgr*
EMP: 141
SALES (corp-wide): 152.3B **Publicly Held**
SIC: 4225 General warehousing & storage
HQ: General Motors Llc
300 Renaissance Ctr L1
Detroit MI 48243
313 556-5000

(P-4556)
GENERAL MOTORS LLC
11900 Cabernet Dr Dr1, Fontana
(92337-7707)
PHONE.............................951 361-6302
Mike Simek, *Manager*
EMP: 80
SALES (corp-wide): 152.3B **Publicly Held**
SIC: 4225 General warehousing & storage
HQ: General Motors Llc
300 Renaissance Ctr L1
Detroit MI 48243
313 556-5000

(P-4557)
GENESIS LOGISTICS INC
4013 Whipple Rd, Union City (94587-1521)
PHONE.............................510 476-0790
Scott Mullins, *General Mgr*
Aran Kahn, *Executive*
Melget Gingnes, *Administration*
Christopher Barnard, *Manager*
EMP: 70
SQ FT: 37,000
SALES (est): 6.5MM
SALES (corp-wide): 63.6B **Privately Held**
WEB: www.genesislogistics.net
SIC: 4225 General warehousing & storage
HQ: Dhl Supply Chain
570 Polaris Pkwy Ste 110
Westerville OH 43082
614 865-8500

(P-4558)
GEODIS LOGISTICS LLC
301 W Walnut St, Compton (90220-5219)
PHONE.............................310 604-8185
Robert Sanders, *Branch Mgr*
EMP: 88 **Privately Held**
SIC: 4225 General warehousing & storage
HQ: Geodis Logistics Llc
7101 Executive Center Dr # 333
Brentwood TN 37027
615 401-6400

(P-4559)
GEODIS LOGISTICS LLC
Also Called: Ohl
2301 W San Bernardino Ave, Redlands
(92374-5007)
PHONE.............................909 801-3145
Jim Moynihan, *Branch Mgr*
EMP: 83 **Privately Held**
SIC: 4225 General warehousing & storage
HQ: Geodis Logistics Llc
7101 Executive Center Dr # 333
Brentwood TN 37027
615 401-6400

(P-4560)
GEODIS LOGISTICS LLC
1710 W Base Line Rd, Rialto (92376-3015)
PHONE.............................909 240-6298
EMP: 90 **Privately Held**
SIC: 4225 General warehousing & storage
HQ: Geodis Logistics Llc
7101 Executive Center Dr # 333
Brentwood TN 37027
615 401-6400

(P-4561)
GEODIS LOGISTICS LLC
Also Called: Stila Styles
3285 De Forest Cir, Mira Loma
(91752-3239)
PHONE.............................951 571-2481
Ozburn Hholdin, *Branch Mgr*
EMP: 60 **Privately Held**
SIC: 4225 General warehousing & storage

4225 - General Warehousing & Storage County (P-4562)

PRODUCTS & SERVICES SECTION

HQ: Geodis Logistics Llc
7101 Executive Center Dr # 333
Brentwood TN 37027
615 401-6400

(P-4562)
GEORGE G SHARP INC
1330 30th St, San Diego (92154-3471)
PHONE..................619 575-0511
Rick Herdman, *Principal*
EMP: 119
SALES (corp-wide): 81.6MM **Privately Held**
SIC: 4225 Warehousing, self-storage
PA: George G. Sharp, Inc.
160 Broadway Fl 8
New York NY 10038
212 732-2800

(P-4563)
GOODWIN AMMONIA COMPANY
Also Called: The Goodwin Company
12361 Monarch St, Garden Grove (92841-2908)
PHONE..................714 894-0531
Tom Goodwin, *President*
EMP: 100
SALES (corp-wide): 35.5MM **Privately Held**
SIC: 4225 General warehousing & storage
PA: The Goodwin Ammonia Company
12102 Industry St
Garden Grove CA 92841
714 894-0531

(P-4564)
GRIFOLS BIOLOGICALS INC
2410 Lillyvale Ave, Los Angeles (90032-3514)
PHONE..................323 255-2221
Edward Colton, *CEO*
Willie Zuniga, *Vice Pres*
Alfred Amoo, *Analyst*
Dennis Bartolotta, *Human Res Dir*
Carolyn Siegal, *Director*
EMP: 350
SALES (corp-wide): 464.6MM **Privately Held**
WEB: www.alphather.com
SIC: 4225 8731 3085 2836 General warehousing & storage; commercial physical research; plastics bottles; biological products, except diagnostic
HQ: Grifols Biologicals Inc.
5555 Valley Blvd
Los Angeles CA 90032
323 227-7028

(P-4565)
GRUPE PROPERTIES CO
Also Called: Executive Living Apartments
2944 W Swain Rd, Stockton (95219-3917)
P.O. Box 7576 (95267-0576)
PHONE..................209 956-7885
Michael V Clark, *President*
EMP: 50
SQ FT: 1,000
SALES (est): 2.4MM
SALES (corp-wide): 82.9MM **Privately Held**
WEB: www.grupe.com
SIC: 4225 Warehousing, self-storage
PA: The Grupe Company
3255 W March Ln Ste 400
Stockton CA 95219
209 473-6000

(P-4566)
H RAUVEL INC (PA)
Also Called: Nova Container Freight Station
1710 E Sepulveda Blvd, Carson (90745-6142)
PHONE..................310 604-0060
Fax: 310 525-2145
Hector R Velasco, *President*
Elsa Acaylar, *Human Resources*
Vicky Ruste, *Manager*
EMP: 70
SQ FT: 258,000
SALES (est): 42.2MM **Privately Held**
WEB: www.novafreight.net
SIC: 4225 4731 General warehousing; agents, shipping; brokers, shipping; freight consolidation; railroad freight agency

(P-4567)
HAULAWAY STORAGE CNTRS INC
11292 Western Ave, Stanton (90680-2912)
P.O. Box 125 (90680-0125)
PHONE..................800 826-9040
Clifford Robert Ronnenberg, *CEO*
Daniel Letto, *President*
Joyce Amato, *CFO*
Dwayne Bartel, *General Mgr*
EMP: 705
SALES (est): 5.9MM
SALES (corp-wide): 100MM **Privately Held**
SIC: 4225 General warehousing & storage
PA: Cr&R Incorporated
11292 Western Ave
Stanton CA 90680
714 826-9049

(P-4568)
HAYWARD AREA RECREATION PK DIST
Also Called: Corporate Yard
1099 E St Rear, Hayward (94541-5210)
PHONE..................510 881-6750
Eric Willyerd, *Superintendent*
EMP: 65 **Privately Held**
SIC: 4225 General warehousing & storage
PA: Hayward Area Recreation & Pk.Dist
1099 E St
Hayward CA 94541
510 670-1665

(P-4569)
HOME DEPOT USA INC
Also Called: Home Depot, The
11650 Venture Dr, Mira Loma (91752-3209)
PHONE..................951 361-1235
John Lawson, *Branch Mgr*
EMP: 190
SALES (corp-wide): 88.5B **Publicly Held**
WEB: www.homerentalsdepot.com
SIC: 4225 General warehousing & storage
HQ: Home Depot U.S.A., Inc.
2455 Paces Ferry Rd Se
Atlanta GA 30339
770 433-8211

(P-4570)
HOME DEPOT USA INC
Also Called: Home Depot, The
2181 Monterey Hwy, San Jose (95125-1057)
PHONE..................408 971-4890
Jessica Miller, *President*
EMP: 165
SALES (corp-wide): 88.5B **Publicly Held**
WEB: www.homerentalsdepot.com
SIC: 4225 General warehousing & storage
HQ: Home Depot U.S.A., Inc.
2455 Paces Ferry Rd Se
Atlanta GA 30339
770 433-8211

(P-4571)
HOME DEPOT USA INC
Also Called: Home Depot, The
18300 S Harlan Rd, Lathrop (95330-8765)
PHONE..................209 858-9243
EMP: 72
SALES (corp-wide): 88.5B **Publicly Held**
WEB: www.homerentalsdepot.com
SIC: 4225 General warehousing & storage
HQ: Home Depot U.S.A., Inc.
2455 Paces Ferry Rd Se
Atlanta GA 30339
770 433-8211

(P-4572)
HOME DEPOT USA INC
Also Called: Home Depot, The
1400 E Pescadero Ave, Tracy (95304-8523)
PHONE..................209 835-5133
Gerry Balagtas, *Branch Mgr*
EMP: 72
SALES (corp-wide): 88.5B **Publicly Held**
WEB: www.homerentalsdepot.com
SIC: 4225 General warehousing & storage
HQ: Home Depot U.S.A., Inc.
2455 Paces Ferry Rd Se
Atlanta GA 30339
770 433-8211

(P-4573)
HOUDINI INC
6311 Knott Ave, Buena Park (90620-1021)
PHONE..................714 228-4406
Timothy J Dean, *President*
EMP: 111
SALES (corp-wide): 40.3MM **Privately Held**
WEB: www.houdiniinc.com
SIC: 4225 General warehousing & storage
PA: Houdini, Inc.
4225 N Palm St
Fullerton CA 92835
714 525-0325

(P-4574)
HOWARDS APPLIANCES INC
Also Called: Howards Warehouse & Svc Ctr
5102 Industry Ave, Pico Rivera (90660-2504)
PHONE..................626 288-4010
Rudy Rodriquez, *Branch Mgr*
EMP: 69
SQ FT: 173,100
SALES (corp-wide): 35.2MM **Privately Held**
SIC: 4225 5722 General warehousing; electric household appliances, major
PA: Howard's Appliances, Inc.
901 E Imperial Hwy
La Habra CA 90631
714 871-2700

(P-4575)
HP INC
481 Cottonwood Dr, Milpitas (95035-7404)
PHONE..................650 857-1501
Shengwu Luo, *Branch Mgr*
Karim Walji, *Prgrmr*
EMP: 1001
SALES (corp-wide): 103.3B **Publicly Held**
SIC: 4225 General warehousing & storage
PA: Hp Inc.
1501 Page Mill Rd
Palo Alto CA 94304
650 857-1501

(P-4576)
HSN LLC
13423 Santa Ana Ave, Fontana (92337-8209)
PHONE..................909 349-2600
Robert Goodwin, *Manager*
Bob Goodwin, *General Mgr*
EMP: 120
SALES (corp-wide): 3.6B **Publicly Held**
WEB: www.hsn.com
SIC: 4225 General warehousing & storage
HQ: Hsn, Llc
1 Hsn Dr
Saint Petersburg FL 33729
727 872-1000

(P-4577)
INFONET SERVICES CORPORATION
Also Called: Warehouse
1320 E Franklin Ave, El Segundo (90245-4306)
PHONE..................310 335-2600
Jose A Collazo, *President*
Ghassan Saab, *Treasurer*
Sue Murray, *Human Res Dir*
EMP: 572
SALES (corp-wide): 27.5B **Privately Held**
WEB: www.infonet.com
SIC: 4225 General warehousing & storage
HQ: Infonet Services Corporation
2160 E Grand Ave
El Segundo CA 90245
310 335-2859

(P-4578)
INLAND STAR DIST CTRS INC (PA)
3146 S Chestnut Ave, Fresno (93725-2606)
P.O. Box 2396 (93745-2396)
PHONE..................559 237-2052
Fax: 559 237-8446
Michael K Kelton, *CEO*
Michael O'Donnell, *Senior VP*
Richard Smith, *General Mgr*
Dave Donathan, *Info Tech Mgr*

Kelly Hinton, *Financial Exec*
◆ **EMP:** 60 **EST:** 1985
SQ FT: 550,000
SALES (est): 44.3MM **Privately Held**
WEB: www.inlandstar.com
SIC: 4225 4213 General warehousing & storage; general warehousing; trucking, except local

(P-4579)
J T R COMPANY INC
Also Called: Area Distributing Company
1102 S 3rd St, San Jose (95112-5918)
P.O. Box 8589 (95155-8589)
PHONE..................408 293-3272
Josephine Ryan, *Manager*
EMP: 50
SALES (corp-wide): 81MM **Privately Held**
WEB: www.jtrsport.com
SIC: 4225 General warehousing & storage
PA: J. T. R. Company, Inc.
1102 S 3rd St
San Jose CA 95112
408 975-7733

(P-4580)
JAM INDUSTRIES INC
Also Called: Jam Warehouse
2101 E Via Arado, Compton (90220-6113)
PHONE..................310 254-0300
Mautiscio Enriques, *Manager*
EMP: 80
SALES (corp-wide): 19.4MM **Privately Held**
WEB: www.jamwarehouse.com
SIC: 4225 General warehousing & storage
PA: J.A.M. Industries, Inc.
13605 Cimarron Ave
Gardena CA
310 532-4526

(P-4581)
JC PENNEY CORPORATION INC
Also Called: JC Penney
6800 Valley View St, Buena Park (90620-1162)
PHONE..................714 523-6558
Paul Langone, *Manager*
Rick Jaramillo, *IT/INT Sup*
Gino Osborne, *Controller*
EMP: 200
SALES (corp-wide): 12.6B **Publicly Held**
SIC: 4225 General warehousing
HQ: J.C. Penney Corporation, Inc.
6501 Legacy Dr
Plano TX 75024
972 431-1000

(P-4582)
KMART CORPORATION
5600 E Airport Dr, Ontario (91761-8609)
PHONE..................909 390-4515
Ken Swager, *Manager*
EMP: 400
SALES (corp-wide): 25.1MM **Publicly Held**
WEB: www.kmart.com
SIC: 4225 General warehousing & storage
HQ: Kmart Corporation
3333 Beverly Rd
Hoffman Estates IL 60179
847 286-2500

(P-4583)
KMART CORPORATION
3100 Milliken Ave, Mira Loma (91752-1023)
PHONE..................951 727-3200
Danny Chavarria, *Manager*
EMP: 300
SALES (corp-wide): 25.1MM **Publicly Held**
WEB: www.kmart.com
SIC: 4225 General warehousing & storage
HQ: Kmart Corporation
3333 Beverly Rd
Hoffman Estates IL 60179
847 286-2500

(P-4584)
KUEHNE + NAGEL INC
2660 W Winton Ave, Hayward (94545-1108)
PHONE..................510 785-0555
Arlene Van Meter, *Manager*

▲ = Import ▼ = Export
◆ = Import/Export

PRODUCTS & SERVICES SECTION
4225 - General Warehousing & Storage County (P-4606)

EMP: 57
SALES (corp-wide): 16.6B **Privately Held**
WEB: www.kuehnenagel.com
SIC: 4225 General warehousing
HQ: Kuehne + Nagel Inc.
10 Exchange Pl
Jersey City NJ 07302
201 413-5500

(P-4585)
KUEHNE + NAGEL INC
9425 Nevada St, Redlands (92374-5106)
PHONE..............................909 574-2300
Paul Schmidt, *Branch Mgr*
Paul Schmitt, *Opers Mgr*
EMP: 52
SALES (corp-wide): 16.6B **Privately Held**
WEB: www.kuehnenagel.com
SIC: 4225 General warehousing & storage
HQ: Kuehne + Nagel Inc.
10 Exchange Pl
Jersey City NJ 07302
201 413-5500

(P-4586)
LEMANS CORPORATION
Also Called: Parts Unlimited
11070 Mulberry Ave Ste A, Fontana (92337-7052)
PHONE..............................909 428-2424
Fax: 909 428-2626
John Van Dermeer, *Manager*
EMP: 100
SALES (corp-wide): 809.8MM **Privately Held**
SIC: 4225 5571 5014 5013 General warehousing & storage; motorcycle parts & accessories; automobile tires & tubes; motorcycle parts
PA: Lemans Corporation
3501 Kennedy Rd
Janesville WI 53545
608 758-1111

(P-4587)
LINDA PLACENTIA-YORBA
Also Called: District Warehouse
1301 E Orangethorpe Ave, Placentia (92870-5302)
PHONE..............................714 985-8775
EMP: 69
SALES (corp-wide): 92.3MM **Privately Held**
SIC: 4225 General warehousing
PA: Placentia-Yorba Linda Unified School District
1301 E Orangethorpe Ave
Placentia CA 92870
714 986-7000

(P-4588)
LMD INTGRTED LGISTICS SVCS INC
3136 E Victoria St, Compton (90221-5618)
PHONE..............................310 605-5100
Louis M Diblosi Jr, *CEO*
Marilyn Zakis, *CFO*
Lisa Lapage, *Purch Mgr*
Miguel Estrella, *VP Opers*
Michael Casciola, *Warehouse Mgr*
EMP: 67
SQ FT: 120,000
SALES (est): 28.5MM **Privately Held**
SIC: 4225 General warehousing & storage

(P-4589)
LMS INTELLIBOUND INC
14900 Garfield Ave, Paramount (90723-3415)
PHONE..............................562 602-2217
EMP: 891
SALES (corp-wide): 85.5MM **Privately Held**
SIC: 4225 General warehousing & storage
PA: Lms Intellibound Inc.
6525 The Corners Pkwy
Norcross GA 30092
770 724-0564

(P-4590)
LONG BEACH CMNTY COLLEGE DST
Also Called: Long Beach City College Whse
1855 Walnut Ave, Long Beach (90806-5724)
PHONE..............................562 938-4291
John Peterson, *Branch Mgr*
EMP: 1610
SALES (corp-wide): 389MM **Privately Held**
SIC: 4225 8222 General warehousing & storage; community college
PA: Long Beach Community College District
4901 E Carson St
Long Beach CA 90808
562 938-5020

(P-4591)
LOWES HOME CENTERS LLC
Luce Ave Bldg 512, Stockton (95203)
PHONE..............................209 513-9560
William James, *Principal*
EMP: 236
SALES (corp-wide): 59B **Publicly Held**
SIC: 4225 General warehousing & storage
HQ: Lowe's Home Centers, Llc
1605 Curtis Bridge Rd
Wilkesboro NC 28697
336 658-4000

(P-4592)
LOWES HOME CENTERS LLC
16850 Heacock St, Moreno Valley (92551-9502)
PHONE..............................951 601-2230
EMP: 236
SALES (corp-wide): 59B **Publicly Held**
SIC: 4225 General warehousing & storage
HQ: Lowe's Home Centers, Llc
1605 Curtis Bridge Rd
Wilkesboro NC 28697
336 658-4000

(P-4593)
M BLOCK & SONS INC
26875 Pioneer Ave, Redlands (92374-2026)
PHONE..............................909 335-6684
Ken Oliveira, *Branch Mgr*
EMP: 200
SALES (corp-wide): 206.8MM **Privately Held**
SIC: 4225 General warehousing & storage
PA: M. Block & Sons, Inc.
5020 W 73rd St
Bedford Park IL 60638
708 728-8400

(P-4594)
M&G DURAVENT INC
877 Cotting Ct, Vacaville (95688-9354)
PHONE..............................800 835-4429
Jeff Cowan, *Manager*
Ed Stegall, *Research*
Todd Lampey, *Purch Agent*
Nicki Harris, *Director*
EMP: 375 **Privately Held**
SIC: 4225 3564 3444 General warehousing; blowers & fans; sheet metalwork
HQ: M&G Duravent, Inc.
877 Cotting Ct
Vacaville CA 95688
707 446-1786

(P-4595)
MAGNELL ASSOCIATE INC
Also Called: ABS Computer Technologies
9997 Rose Hills Rd, Whittier (90601-1701)
PHONE..............................626 271-1420
Fax: 562 271-9500
Brian Cheng, *Branch Mgr*
Charlie Chan, *Info Tech Mgr*
EMP: 200
SALES (corp-wide): 2.5B **Privately Held**
SIC: 4225 General warehousing
HQ: Magnell Associate, Inc.
17560 Rowland St
City Of Industry CA 91748
562 695-8823

(P-4596)
MARUCHAN INC
15800 Laguna Canyon Rd, Irvine (92618-3103)
PHONE..............................949 789-2300
Tom Yoshimora, *General Mgr*
EMP: 100
SQ FT: 90,200
SALES (corp-wide): 3.2B **Privately Held**
WEB: www.maruchaninc.com
SIC: 4225 General warehousing & storage
HQ: Maruchan, Inc.
15800 Laguna Canyon Rd
Irvine CA 92618
949 789-2300

(P-4597)
MECHANICS BANK
Also Called: Operations Center
725 Alfred Nobel Dr, Hercules (94547-1897)
PHONE..............................510 741-7545
Fax: 510 741-7532
Tony Chavez, *Manager*
Patricia I Gross, *Treasurer*
Dylan Gano, *Officer*
George Kerr, *Officer*
Gary Staring, *Senior VP*
EMP: 200
SQ FT: 69,184
SALES (corp-wide): 140.9MM **Privately Held**
SIC: 4225 6029 General warehousing; commercial banks
HQ: The Mechanics Bank
1111 Civic Dr Ste 333
Walnut Creek CA 94596
800 797-6324

(P-4598)
MEIKO AMERICA INC
Also Called: American Honda
12300 Riverside Dr, Mira Loma (91752-1006)
PHONE..............................951 360-0281
Fax: 951 360-6423
Mike Sole, *Branch Mgr*
Sergio Cardenas, *Opers Mgr*
EMP: 63
SALES (corp-wide): 517.9MM **Privately Held**
WEB: www.meikoamerica.com
SIC: 4225 General warehousing
HQ: Meiko America, Inc.
19600 Magellan Dr
Torrance CA 90502
310 483-7400

(P-4599)
MERCY HEALTHCARE SACRAMENTO
Regional Distribution Center
11391 Sunrise Gold Cir # 100, Rancho Cordova (95742-7212)
PHONE..............................916 851-3800
Fax: 916 851-3830
Bob Rodda, *Dir Ops-Prd-Mfg*
EMP: 50
SALES (corp-wide): 7.1B **Privately Held**
WEB: www.mercycare.net
SIC: 4225 General warehousing & storage
HQ: Mercy Healthcare Sacramento
3400 Data Dr
Rancho Cordova CA 95670
916 379-2871

(P-4600)
MITSUBISHI WAREHOUSE CAL CORP
3040 E Victoria St, Compton (90221-5617)
PHONE..............................310 886-5500
Fax: 310 604-1552
Soichiro Sam Orihara, *President*
George Steven, *General Mgr*
Joseph Navarro, *Manager*
Gary Shimbashi, *Manager*
Robert Y Nagata, *Agent*
EMP: 100
SQ FT: 750,000
SALES (est): 11.8MM
SALES (corp-wide): 1.7B **Privately Held**
WEB: www.mwc-corp.com
SIC: 4225 General warehousing
PA: Mitsubishi Logistics Corporation
1-19-1, Nihonbashi
Chuo-Ku TKY 103-0
332 786-611

(P-4601)
NATIONAL DISTRIBUTION AGCY INC (HQ)
Also Called: Pacific Coast Warehouse Co
7025 Central Ave, Newark (94560-4201)
PHONE..............................510 487-6226
Sheryl Sadler, *President*
Steve Tyler, *General Mgr*
EMP: 62
SQ FT: 305,000
SALES (est): 6.3MM
SALES (corp-wide): 19.1MM **Privately Held**
SIC: 4225 General warehousing
PA: Public Investment Corporation
528 Arizona Ave Ste 206
Santa Monica CA 90401
310 451-5227

(P-4602)
NAVY EXCHANGE SERVICE COMMAND
4250 Eucalyptus Ave, Chino (91710-9704)
PHONE..............................909 517-2640
Ron Patel, *Manager*
Michael P Good, *Exec VP*
Winston S Lawrence, *General Mgr*
Allenda Jenkins, *Store Mgr*
Susan Langless, *Marketing Mgr*
EMP: 155 **Publicly Held**
WEB: www.navy-nex.com
SIC: 4225 9711 General warehousing & storage; Navy;
HQ: Navy Exchange Service Command
3280 Virginia Beach Blvd
Virginia Beach VA 23452
800 448-3996

(P-4603)
NEIMAN MARCUS GROUP LLC
Also Called: Neiman Marcus W Coast Svc Ctr
2500 Workman Mill Rd, City of Industry (90601-1455)
PHONE..............................562 463-9333
Craig Reynolds,
Matthew Carlin, *Marketing Staff*
Kristen Spaulding, *Editor*
EMP: 70
SALES (corp-wide): 4.9B **Privately Held**
WEB: www.neimanmarcus.com
SIC: 4225 General warehousing & storage
HQ: The Neiman Marcus Group Llc
1618 Main St
Dallas TX 75201
214 741-6911

(P-4604)
NISSAN NORTH AMERICA INC
3939 N Freeway Blvd, Sacramento (95834-1217)
PHONE..............................916 920-4712
Mariano Loria, *General Mgr*
Ronald Kersey, *Opers Mgr*
Kevin Hamlin, *Sales Dir*
David Latterman, *Manager*
EMP: 51
SALES (corp-wide): 104.1B **Privately Held**
WEB: www.nissan-na.com
SIC: 4225 General warehousing
HQ: Nissan North America Inc
1 Nissan Way
Franklin TN 37067
615 725-1000

(P-4605)
NORDSTROM INC
1600 S Milliken Ave, Ontario (91761-2301)
PHONE..............................909 390-1040
Fax: 909 390-1051
Pat Smith, *Manager*
James Edmon, *Manager*
EMP: 300
SALES (corp-wide): 14.4B **Publicly Held**
WEB: www.nordstrom.com
SIC: 4225 4226 General warehousing & storage; special warehousing & storage
PA: Nordstrom, Inc.
1617 6th Ave
Seattle WA 98101
206 628-2111

(P-4606)
NORDSTROM INC
37599 Filbert St, Newark (94560-3537)
PHONE..............................510 794-5440
Fax: 510 795-5817
Dan Allen, *Manager*
EMP: 150
SALES (corp-wide): 14.4B **Publicly Held**
WEB: www.nordstrom.com
SIC: 4225 General warehousing & storage

4225 - General Warehousing & Storage County (P-4607)

PRODUCTS & SERVICES SECTION

PA: Nordstrom, Inc.
1617 6th Ave
Seattle WA 98101
206 628-2111

(P-4607)
NUGGET MARKET INC
Also Called: Nugget Mkts Pharmacy
157 Main St, Woodland (95695-3163)
PHONE.................530 662-5479
Fax: 530 662-0961
Ray Munoz, *Manager*
Brittany Demes, *Human Resources*
Rafael Bautista, *Manager*
EMP: 120
SALES (corp-wide): 263.6MM **Privately Held**
WEB: www.nuggetmarket.com
SIC: **4225** 5411 5912 5461 General warehousing; grocery stores; drug stores & proprietary stores; bakeries
PA: Nugget Market Inc.
168 Court St
Woodland CA 95695
530 669-3300

(P-4608)
OFFICEMAX INCORPORATED
7300 Chapman Ave, Garden Grove (92841-2105)
PHONE.................951 485-9353
Harry Goodman, *Admin Sec*
Lora Labaree, *Business Dir*
Nicole Rasic, *Business Dir*
Ted Walter, *Opers Mgr*
Dawna Herndon, *Sales Mgr*
EMP: 101
SALES (corp-wide): 14.4B **Publicly Held**
SIC: **4225** 5112 5021 General warehousing & storage; stationery & office supplies; furniture
HQ: Officemax Incorporated
6600 N Military Trl
Boca Raton FL 33496
630 438-7800

(P-4609)
PACIFIC CYCLE INC
Also Called: Pacific Cycle P Finished Goods
9282 Pittsburgh Ave, Rancho Cucamonga (91730-5516)
PHONE.................909 481-5613
Rich Jordan, *Branch Mgr*
EMP: 50
SALES (corp-wide): 2.6B **Privately Held**
WEB: www.pacific-cycle.com
SIC: **4225** General warehousing & storage
HQ: Pacific Cycle Inc.
4902 Hammersley Rd
Madison WI 53711
608 268-2468

(P-4610)
PANAMA-BUENA VISTA UN SCHL DST
Also Called: Purchasing & Warehouse
4200 Ashe Rd, Bakersfield (93313-2029)
PHONE.................661 831-7879
Fax: 661 398-2141
Kip Hearron, *Manager*
EMP: 103
SALES (corp-wide): 152.3MM **Privately Held**
SIC: **4225** 7389 General warehousing; purchasing service
PA: Panama-Buena Vista Union School District
4200 Ashe Rd
Bakersfield CA 93313
661 831-8231

(P-4611)
PEPSI-COLA METRO BTLG CO INC
4701 Park Rd, Benicia (94510-1125)
PHONE.................707 746-5404
Fax: 707 746-5214
Neal Sturrock, *Owner*
Deedee Danielski, *Supervisor*
EMP: 125
SQ FT: 5,000
SALES (corp-wide): 63B **Publicly Held**
WEB: www.joy-of-cola.com
SIC: **4225** 5149 General warehousing & storage; groceries & related products

HQ: Pepsi-Cola Metropolitan Bottling Company, Inc.
1111 Westchester Ave
White Plains NY 10604
914 767-6000

(P-4612)
PEPSI-COLA METRO BTLG CO INC
200 River Rd, Modesto (95351-3912)
PHONE.................209 557-5100
Jake Aigen, *Sales/Mktg Mgr*
Scott Agan, *Financial Exec*
Edgar Rosette, *Safety Mgr*
Paul Trisler, *Manager*
EMP: 150
SQ FT: 5,000
SALES (corp-wide): 63B **Publicly Held**
WEB: www.joy-of-cola.com
SIC: **4225** 5962 5149 2086 General warehousing & storage; merchandising machine operators; soft drinks; bottled & canned soft drinks
HQ: Pepsi-Cola Metropolitan Bottling Company, Inc.
1111 Westchester Ave
White Plains NY 10604
914 767-6000

(P-4613)
PERFORMANCE TEAM FRT SYS INC
12816 Shoemaker Ave, Santa Fe Springs (90670-6346)
PHONE.................562 741-1300
Bob Kaplan, *Branch Mgr*
Jason Cleve, *Technology*
EMP: 55
SALES (corp-wide): 435.6MM **Privately Held**
SIC: **4225** 4731 4213 General warehousing & storage; freight transportation arrangement; trucking, except local
PA: Performance Team Freight Sys, Inc.
2240 E Maple Ave
El Segundo CA 90245
562 345-2200

(P-4614)
PERFORMANCE TEAM FRT SYS INC
Also Called: Gale/Triangle
401 Westmont Dr, San Pedro (90731-1011)
PHONE.................310 241-4100
Fax: 310 221-0498
Scott Pearigan, *Manager*
Robin Clark, *Accounts Mgr*
EMP: 120
SALES (corp-wide): 435.6MM **Privately Held**
WEB: www.ptgt.net
SIC: **4225** General warehousing & storage
PA: Performance Team Freight Sys, Inc.
2240 E Maple Ave
El Segundo CA 90245
562 345-2200

(P-4615)
PRECISE DISTRIBUTION INC
12215 Holly St, Riverside (92509-2315)
PHONE.................951 367-1037
Debra Catherine Martinez, *CEO*
Levone Myro, *Vice Pres*
Ricardo Cazessus, *Admin Sec*
Gilbert Cazessus, *Info Tech Mgr*
Diana Kebisuz, *Manager*
EMP: 50
SQ FT: 350,000
SALES (est): 10.4MM **Privately Held**
SIC: **4225** General warehousing & storage

(P-4616)
PS PARTNERS III LTD
701 Western Ave Ste 200, Glendale (91201-2349)
PHONE.................818 244-8080
B Wayne Hughes, *General Ptnr*
EMP: 114
SALES (est): 4.8MM **Privately Held**
SIC: **4225** Miniwarehouse, warehousing

(P-4617)
PUBLIC STORAGE PRPTS IV LTD
701 Western Ave, Glendale (91201-2349)
PHONE.................818 244-8080
Ronald L Havner Jr, *President*
Mark C Good, *COO*
John Reyes, *CFO*
Candace N Krol, *Senior VP*
EMP: 54
SALES: 12.9MM **Privately Held**
SIC: **4225** Warehousing, self-storage

(P-4618)
QUAKER OATS COMPANY
2501 E Orangethorpe Ave, Fullerton (92831-5333)
PHONE.................714 526-8800
EMP: 50
SALES (corp-wide): 66.4B **Publicly Held**
SIC: **4225** 5149
HQ: The Quaker Oats Company
555 W Monroe St Fl 1
Chicago IL 60661
312 821-1000

(P-4619)
RALPHS GROCERY COMPANY
Also Called: Ralphs 00134
211 N Glendale Ave, Glendale (91206-4455)
PHONE.................818 549-0035
Peggy Lizarraga, *Branch Mgr*
Amanda Riggs, *Store Mgr*
EMP: 164
SALES (corp-wide): 109.8B **Publicly Held**
WEB: www.ralphs.com
SIC: **4225** General warehousing & storage
HQ: Ralphs Grocery Company
1100 W Artesia Blvd
Compton CA 90220
310 884-9000

(P-4620)
RALPHS GROCERY COMPANY
Also Called: Ralph S Distribution Center
1500 Eastridge Ave, Riverside (92507-7109)
PHONE.................310 884-9000
Mike Mellas, *Branch Mgr*
EMP: 57
SALES (corp-wide): 109.8B **Publicly Held**
SIC: **4225** General warehousing & storage
HQ: Ralphs Grocery Company
1100 W Artesia Blvd
Compton CA 90220
310 884-9000

(P-4621)
RALPHS GROCERY COMPANY
4841-45 San Fernando W, Los Angeles (90039)
PHONE.................310 637-1101
Larry Cooper, *Vice Pres*
Jim Behrnes, *Admin Director*
Dan Denmark, *Director*
EMP: 700
SQ FT: 275,000
SALES (corp-wide): 109.8B **Publicly Held**
SIC: **4225** General warehousing & storage
HQ: Ralphs Grocery Company
1100 W Artesia Blvd
Compton CA 90220
310 884-9000

(P-4622)
RALPHS GROCERY COMPANY
Also Called: Food 4 Less
13525 Lakewood Blvd, Downey (90242-5229)
PHONE.................562 633-0830
Fax: 562 633-7285
Dave Dopson, *Director*
EMP: 75
SALES (corp-wide): 109.8B **Publicly Held**
WEB: www.ralphs.com
SIC: **4225** 4212 General warehousing & storage; local trucking, without storage
HQ: Ralphs Grocery Company
1100 W Artesia Blvd
Compton CA 90220
310 884-9000

(P-4623)
RALPHS GROCERY COMPANY
Also Called: Ralphs 6
17840 Ventura Blvd, Encino (91316-3615)
PHONE.................818 345-6882
Fax: 818 345-1782
Jim Sanders, *Manager*
Eric Scantland, *Store Mgr*
EMP: 135
SQ FT: 37,059
SALES (corp-wide): 109.8B **Publicly Held**
WEB: www.ralphs.com
SIC: **4225** General warehousing & storage
HQ: Ralphs Grocery Company
1100 W Artesia Blvd
Compton CA 90220
310 884-9000

(P-4624)
RALPHS GROCERY COMPANY
Also Called: Ralphs 00664
1776 S Victoria Ave, Ventura (93003-6592)
PHONE.................805 650-0239
Thomas Williams, *Manager*
EMP: 75
SALES (corp-wide): 109.8B **Publicly Held**
WEB: www.ralphs.com
SIC: **4225** General warehousing & storage
HQ: Ralphs Grocery Company
1100 W Artesia Blvd
Compton CA 90220
310 884-9000

(P-4625)
RALPHS GROCERY COMPANY
Also Called: Ralphs 00173
9200 Lakewood Blvd, Downey (90240-2909)
PHONE.................562 869-2042
Fernando Ortiz, *Manager*
Tom Eshelman, *Director*
Paul Gabaldon, *Manager*
EMP: 62
SALES (corp-wide): 109.8B **Publicly Held**
WEB: www.ralphs.com
SIC: **4225** General warehousing & storage
HQ: Ralphs Grocery Company
1100 W Artesia Blvd
Compton CA 90220
310 884-9000

(P-4626)
RALPHS GROCERY COMPANY
Also Called: Ralphs 96
160 N Lake Ave, Pasadena (91101-1836)
PHONE.................626 793-7480
Chuck Hamman, *Manager*
EMP: 100
SALES (corp-wide): 109.8B **Publicly Held**
WEB: www.ralphs.com
SIC: **4225** General warehousing & storage
HQ: Ralphs Grocery Company
1100 W Artesia Blvd
Compton CA 90220
310 884-9000

(P-4627)
RALPHS GROCERY COMPANY
Also Called: Ralphs 00131
5241 Warner Ave, Huntington Beach (92649-4060)
PHONE.................714 377-0024
Tim Kato, *Manager*
Jim Mirsch, *Manager*
EMP: 120
SQ FT: 33,350
SALES (corp-wide): 109.8B **Publicly Held**
WEB: www.ralphs.com
SIC: **4225** General warehousing & storage
HQ: Ralphs Grocery Company
1100 W Artesia Blvd
Compton CA 90220
310 884-9000

(P-4628)
RAS MANAGEMENT INC (PA)
Also Called: Aaaaa Rent-A-Space
4545 Crow Canyon Pl, Castro Valley (94552-4803)
P.O. Box 20385 (94546-8385)
PHONE.................510 727-1800

PRODUCTS & SERVICES SECTION

4225 - General Warehousing & Storage County (P-4652)

H James Knuppe, *President*
Barbara Knuppe, *Corp Secy*
David O' Brien, *Manager*
Patrick Carew, *Consultant*
Mike Rizzo, *Consultant*
EMP: 50
SQ FT: 6,000
SALES (est): 16MM **Privately Held**
SIC: 4225 Warehousing, self-storage

(P-4629)
REDWOOD VALLEY INDUSTRIAL PARK
8800 West Rd, Redwood Valley (95470)
PHONE.................707 485-8766
Orin Burgess, *President*
EMP: 65
SALES (est): 2.3MM **Privately Held**
SIC: 4225 General warehousing

(P-4630)
ROMANS TRANSPORTATION INC
Also Called: Roman Services
9935 Beverly Blvd, Pico Rivera (90660-1812)
P.O. Box 6845 (90661-6845)
PHONE.................562 463-1433
Fax: 562 463-1436
D Antonio Roman, *Owner*
Elpidia Cruz, *Bookkeeper*
EMP: 54
SQ FT: 91,616
SALES (est): 2.7MM **Privately Held**
SIC: 4225 7319 General warehousing & storage; distribution of advertising material or sample services

(P-4631)
ROMARK LOGISTICS OF CALIFORNIA
13521 Santa Ana Ave Ste A, Fontana (92337-8243)
PHONE.................909 356-5600
Michael O Conner, *President*
Joyce Artega, *Manager*
EMP: 75
SQ FT: 320,000
SALES (est): 4.7MM **Privately Held**
SIC: 4225 General warehousing & storage

(P-4632)
ROMEO & LAYLA WAREHOUSING INC
1041 Mildred St, Ontario (91761-3500)
PHONE.................909 947-9055
Jeff Fischer, *Branch Mgr*
EMP: 100
SALES (corp-wide): 2.5MM **Privately Held**
SIC: 4225 General warehousing & storage
PA: Romeo & Layla Warehousing, Inc.
  1410 Broadway Fl 8
  New York NY
  -

(P-4633)
RPM CONSOLIDATED SERVICES INC (PA)
1901 Raymer Ave, Fullerton (92833-2512)
PHONE.................714 388-3500
Shawn K Duke, *CEO*
Emily James, *COO*
Dan Laporte, *Vice Pres*
Shelly Holeman, *Accountant*
Chris Dupree, *Opers Mgr*
EMP: 100
SQ FT: 15,000
SALES: 63.5MM **Privately Held**
WEB: www.rpmcsi.com
SIC: 4225 4214 General warehousing & storage; local trucking with storage

(P-4634)
SADDLE CREEK CORPORATION
3010 Saddle Creek Rd, San Diego (92120)
PHONE.................619 229-2200
EMP: 70
SALES (corp-wide): 453.2MM **Privately Held**
SIC: 4225 General warehousing
PA: Saddle Creek Corporation
  3010 Saddle Creek Rd
  Lakeland FL 33801
  863 665-0966

(P-4635)
SAFEWAY INC
3415 Boxford Ave, Commerce (90040-3003)
PHONE.................323 889-4240
Ed Boone, *Branch Mgr*
Greg Miller, *Plant Supt*
Rob Wooten, *Maintence Staff*
EMP: 200
SALES (corp-wide): 58.7B **Privately Held**
WEB: www.safeway.com
SIC: 4225 General warehousing & storage
HQ: Safeway Inc.
  5918 Stoneridge Mall Rd
  Pleasanton CA 94588
  925 467-3000

(P-4636)
SAFEWAY INC
16900 W Schulte Rd, Tracy (95377-8985)
PHONE.................209 833-4700
Fax: 209 832-4490
Mike Kindy, *Branch Mgr*
Dewayne Quock, *Manager*
EMP: 350
SALES (corp-wide): 58.7B **Privately Held**
WEB: www.safeway.com
SIC: 4225 General warehousing & storage
HQ: Safeway Inc.
  5918 Stoneridge Mall Rd
  Pleasanton CA 94588
  925 467-3000

(P-4637)
SAFEWAY INC
2935 Ramco St Ste 10, West Sacramento (95691-5999)
PHONE.................916 373-3900
Mary Ely, *Manager*
EMP: 125
SALES (corp-wide): 58.7B **Privately Held**
WEB: www.safeway.com
SIC: 4225 General warehousing & storage
HQ: Safeway Inc.
  5918 Stoneridge Mall Rd
  Pleasanton CA 94588
  925 467-3000

(P-4638)
SCHAFER BROS TRNSF PANO MOVERS (PA)
Also Called: Schafer Logistics
1981 E 213th St, Carson (90810-1202)
PHONE.................310 835-7231
Fax: 310 830-3362
Gary A Schafer, *President*
Richard W Schafer, *Vice Pres*
Nick Bard, *Safety Mgr*
Patricia A McMahon, *Accounts Mgr*
EMP: 55
SQ FT: 402,000
SALES: 10.4MM **Privately Held**
WEB: www.schaferbros.com
SIC: 4225 4214 4213 General warehousing; local trucking with storage; heavy hauling

(P-4639)
SKY CHEFS INC
1845 Rollins Rd, Burlingame (94010-2209)
PHONE.................650 652-7886
Dan Joseph, *Branch Mgr*
EMP: 106
SALES (corp-wide): 34.4B **Privately Held**
SIC: 4225 General warehousing
HQ: Sky Chefs, Inc.
  6191 N State Highway 161 # 100
  Irving TX 75038
  972 793-9000

(P-4640)
SOLUTION ONE INDUSTRIES INC
Ave G St Bldg 934, Fort Irwin (92310)
PHONE.................254 702-7329
Bettie McLaurin, *CEO*
Tyrone McLaurin, *COO*
EMP: 99 **EST:** 2015
SALES (est): 1.5MM **Privately Held**
SIC: 4225 General warehousing

(P-4641)
SPACE SYSTEMS/LORAL LLC
1140 Hamilton Ct, Menlo Park (94025-1425)
PHONE.................650 852-4000
Pat Downey, *Branch Mgr*
EMP: 200
SALES (corp-wide): 1.5B **Privately Held**
SIC: 4225 General warehousing
HQ: Space Systems/Loral, Llc
  3825 Fabian Way
  Palo Alto CA 94303
  650 852-7320

(P-4642)
STATES LOGISTICS SERVICES INC (PA)
5650 Dolly Ave, Buena Park (90621-1872)
PHONE.................714 521-6520
Fax: 714 521-6944
Cathy Monson, *CEO*
Daniel Monson, *President*
Robert Doidge, *Administration*
Lori Beloat, *Accountant*
Veronica Gomez, *Accountant*
EMP: 140
SQ FT: 900,000
SALES (est): 76.9MM **Privately Held**
WEB: www.stateslogistics.com
SIC: 4225 General warehousing & storage

(P-4643)
SYNNEX CORPORATION
Also Called: Ontario-Don
3655 E Philadelphia St, Ontario (91761-2959)
PHONE.................909 923-8900
Edgar Mendez, *Branch Mgr*
EMP: 52
SALES (corp-wide): 13.3B **Publicly Held**
SIC: 4225 General warehousing
PA: Synnex Corporation
  44201 Nobel Dr
  Fremont CA 94538
  510 656-3333

(P-4644)
TACTICAL LGISTIC SOLUTIONS INC
13799 Monte Vista Ave, Chino (91710-5562)
PHONE.................909 464-2813
Abraham Ausch, *Branch Mgr*
EMP: 66
SALES (corp-wide): 11.1MM **Privately Held**
SIC: 4225 General warehousing
PA: Tactical Logistic Solutions Inc.
  1000 Jefferson Ave
  Elizabeth NJ 07201
  201 809-1222

(P-4645)
TANIMURA & ANTLE INC
761 Commercial Ave, Oxnard (93030-7233)
PHONE.................805 483-2358
Sergio Romero, *Manager*
EMP: 100
SALES (corp-wide): 602MM **Privately Held**
WEB: www.taproduce.com
SIC: 4225 Warehousing, self-storage
PA: Tanimura & Antle Fresh Foods, Inc.
  1 Harris Rd
  Salinas CA 93908
  831 455-2950

(P-4646)
UNITED FACILITIES INC
25451 Mountain House Pkwy, Tracy (95377-8903)
PHONE.................209 839-8051
Rich Turner, *Branch Mgr*
EMP: 50
SALES (corp-wide): 56.8MM **Privately Held**
WEB: www.unifac.com
SIC: 4225 General warehousing
PA: United Facilities, Inc.
  603 N Main St
  East Peoria IL 61611
  309 699-7271

(P-4647)
UNITED FACILITIES INC
11618 Mulberry Ave, Fontana (92337-7618)
PHONE.................951 685-7030
Kevin Alderson, *Manager*
EMP: 50
SALES (corp-wide): 56.8MM **Privately Held**
WEB: www.unifac.com
SIC: 4225 General warehousing & storage
PA: United Facilities, Inc.
  603 N Main St
  East Peoria IL 61611
  309 699-7271

(P-4648)
UNIVERSAL PACKG SYSTEMS INC
Also Called: Paklab
14570 Monte Vista Ave, Chino (91710-5743)
PHONE.................909 517-2442
Michael Chung, *Analyst*
Lana Tennant, *Sales Staff*
EMP: 125
SALES (corp-wide): 127MM **Privately Held**
SIC: 4225 General warehousing
PA: Universal Packaging Systems, Inc.
  6080 Jericho Tpke
  Commack NY 11725
  631 543-2277

(P-4649)
UNIVERSAL SELF STORAGE
25980 Barton Rd, Loma Linda (92354-3869)
P.O. Box 8008, Newport Beach (92658-8008)
PHONE.................951 206-5263
Rene Jacober, *Managing Prtnr*
EMP: 50
SALES (est): 2.7MM **Privately Held**
SIC: 4225 Warehousing, self-storage

(P-4650)
UPS SUPPLY CHAIN SOLUTIONS INC
455 Forbes Blvd, South San Francisco (94080-2017)
PHONE.................650 875-8300
Randy Nelson, *Manager*
EMP: 50
SQ FT: 14,000
SALES (corp-wide): 58.3B **Publicly Held**
SIC: 4225 General warehousing & storage
HQ: Ups Supply Chain Solutions, Inc.
  12380 Morris Rd
  Alpharetta GA 30005
  800 742-5727

(P-4651)
UPS SUPPLY CHAIN SOLUTIONS INC
550-3 Accels Ave, South San Francisco (94080)
PHONE.................650 635-2678
Tony Del Rosario, *Branch Mgr*
Dan Brutto, *Vice Pres*
Rocky Romanella, *Vice Pres*
EMP: 120
SALES (corp-wide): 58.3B **Publicly Held**
SIC: 4225 General warehousing & storage
HQ: Ups Supply Chain Solutions, Inc.
  12380 Morris Rd
  Alpharetta GA 30005
  800 742-5727

(P-4652)
UPS SUPPLY CHAIN SOLUTIONS INC
601 Van Neca Ave Ste E, San Francisco (94102)
PHONE.................415 775-6644
Debbie Wong, *Manager*
EMP: 50
SALES (corp-wide): 58.3B **Publicly Held**
SIC: 4225 General warehousing & storage
HQ: Ups Supply Chain Solutions, Inc.
  12380 Morris Rd
  Alpharetta GA 30005
  800 742-5727

4225 - General Warehousing & Storage County (P-4653) PRODUCTS & SERVICES SECTION

(P-4653)
VAN KING & STORAGE INC
Also Called: King Relocation Services
13535 Larwin Cir, Santa Fe Springs (90670-5032)
PHONE.....................562 921-0555
Steve Komorous, *President*
EMP: 50
SALES (corp-wide): 16MM **Privately Held**
WEB: www.kingrelocation.com
SIC: 4225 Warehousing, self-storage
PA: Van King & Storage Inc
   13535 Larwin Cir
   Santa Fe Springs CA 90670
   562 921-0555

(P-4654)
VANGUARD LGISTICS SVCS USA INC
2665 E Del Amo Blvd, Compton (90221-6003)
PHONE.....................310 637-3700
Owen Glenn, *Manager*
Jeantte Bateman, *Info Tech Mgr*
EMP: 100
SALES (corp-wide): 209MM **Privately Held**
SIC: 4225 4731 General warehousing & storage; freight transportation arrangement
HQ: Vanguard Logistics Services (Usa), Inc.
   5000 Airport Plaza Dr
   Long Beach CA 90815
   310 847-3000

(P-4655)
VERIFONE INC
1401 Aviation Blvd, Lincoln (95648-9312)
PHONE.....................916 408-4900
Darrin Richards, *Manager*
EMP: 100
SALES (corp-wide): 2B **Publicly Held**
SIC: 4225 Warehousing, self-storage
HQ: Verifone, Inc.
   88 W Plumeria Dr
   San Jose CA 95134
   408 232-7800

(P-4656)
VITRAN LOGISTICS INC
1000 S Cucamonga Ave, Ontario (91761-3461)
PHONE.....................909 972-3100
Rick Gaetz, *CEO*
Mike Glodziak, *President*
Joanna Pencak, *Admin Sec*
Jody McGuire, *Manager*
EMP: 78 **EST:** 2009
SALES (est): 6.5MM **Privately Held**
SIC: 4225 General warehousing

(P-4657)
VONS COMPANIES INC
Also Called: Vons Meat Distribution Center
4300 N Shirley Ave, El Monte (91731)
PHONE.....................626 350-8405
Dewy Maroney, *Branch Mgr*
EMP: 70
SALES (corp-wide): 58.7B **Privately Held**
SIC: 4225 General warehousing & storage
HQ: The Vons Companies Inc
   5918 Stoneridge Mall Rd
   Pleasanton CA 94588
   626 821-7000

(P-4658)
WAL-MART STORES INC
Also Called: Walmart
13550 Valley Blvd, Fontana (92335-5243)
PHONE.....................909 349-3600
Fax: 909 350-8060
Marcus Lester, *Branch Mgr*
EMP: 477
SALES (corp-wide): 482.1B **Publicly Held**
SIC: 4225 General warehousing & storage
PA: Wal-Mart Stores, Inc.
   702 Sw 8th St
   Bentonville AR 72716
   479 273-4000

(P-4659)
WAL-MART STORES INC
Also Called: Walmart
21101 Johnson Rd, Apple Valley (92307-9357)
PHONE.....................760 961-6300
Scott Kubicek, *Manager*
EMP: 484
SALES (corp-wide): 482.1B **Publicly Held**
SIC: 4225 General warehousing & storage
PA: Wal-Mart Stores, Inc.
   702 Sw 8th St
   Bentonville AR 72716
   479 273-4000

(P-4660)
WAL-MART STORES INC
Also Called: Walmart
10815 Highway 99w, Red Bluff (96080-7747)
PHONE.....................530 529-0916
Fax: 530 529-8404
Darwyn Jones, *Manager*
Brandon Tandy, *General Mgr*
Gordon Rasmussen, *VP Sales*
Mike Baker, *Manager*
Leroy Crye, *Manager*
EMP: 670
SALES (corp-wide): 482.1B **Publicly Held**
WEB: www.walmartstores.com
SIC: 4225 General warehousing & storage
PA: Wal-Mart Stores, Inc.
   702 Sw 8th St
   Bentonville AR 72716
   479 273-4000

(P-4661)
WAL-MART STORES INC
Also Called: Walmart
4250 Hamner Ave, Mira Loma (91752-1019)
PHONE.....................951 681-7256
Fax: 951 360-5032
Bill Day, *Manager*
EMP: 450
SALES (corp-wide): 482.1B **Publicly Held**
WEB: www.walmartstores.com
SIC: 4225 General warehousing & storage
PA: Wal-Mart Stores, Inc.
   702 Sw 8th St
   Bentonville AR 72716
   479 273-4000

(P-4662)
WAL-MART STORES INC
Also Called: Walmart
1300 S F St, Porterville (93257-5969)
PHONE.....................559 783-1109
Fax: 559 783-6004
Kent Delperdang, *Manager*
EMP: 477
SALES (corp-wide): 482.1B **Publicly Held**
WEB: www.walmartstores.com
SIC: 4225 General warehousing & storage
PA: Wal-Mart Stores, Inc.
   702 Sw 8th St
   Bentonville AR 72716
   479 273-4000

(P-4663)
WALGREEN ARIZONA DRUG CO
Walgreens
17500 Perris Blvd, Moreno Valley (92551-9547)
PHONE.....................928 526-1400
Will Duncan, *Manager*
EMP: 110
SALES (corp-wide): 117.3B **Publicly Held**
SIC: 4225 General warehousing & storage
HQ: Walgreen Arizona Drug Co.
   200 Wilmot Rd
   Deerfield IL 60015
   847 940-2500

(P-4664)
WALGREEN CO
Also Called: Walgreens
2370 E Main St, Woodland (95776-9502)
PHONE.....................530 406-7700
Fax: 530 668-7719
John Coman, *Branch Mgr*
Shawna Compton, *Human Res Mgr*
Vince Rogers, *Sales Executive*
EMP: 60
SALES (corp-wide): 117.3B **Publicly Held**
WEB: www.walgreens.com
SIC: 4225 General warehousing & storage
HQ: Walgreen Co.
   200 Wilmot Rd
   Deerfield IL 60015
   847 315-2500

(P-4665)
WALT DISNEY COMPANY
1313 S Harbor Blvd, Anaheim (92802-2309)
PHONE.....................714 781-4532
Fax: 714 502-3938
Paul Margdia, *Manager*
Randy Brooks, *Admin Mgr*
Eric Froberg, *QC Mgr*
Jeff Giacomi, *QC Mgr*
Lisa Miller, *Security Mgr*
EMP: 500 **Publicly Held**
SIC: 4225 7699 General warehousing & storage; engine repair & replacement, non-automotive
PA: The Walt Disney Company
   500 S Buena Vista St
   Burbank CA 91521

(P-4666)
WEBER DISTRIBUTION WAREHOUSES
Also Called: Weber Distribution Cwo
9345 Santa Anita Ave B, Rancho Cucamonga (91730-6126)
PHONE.....................909 481-1600
Fax: 909 481-1612
John Nutt, *Vice Pres*
Herb Ng, *Manager*
EMP: 50
SALES (corp-wide): 112MM **Privately Held**
WEB: www.weberdist.com
SIC: 4225 4214 General warehousing; local trucking with storage
PA: Weber Distribution Warehouses
   13530 Rosecrans Ave
   Santa Fe Springs CA 90670
   562 356-6300

(P-4667)
WEBER DISTRIBUTION WAREHOUSES
Also Called: Weber Logistics
1366 30th St, San Diego (92154-3434)
PHONE.....................619 423-8770
John Nutt, *Manager*
Gary Fisher, *Manager*
Raul Nercado, *Manager*
Richard Timms, *Manager*
EMP: 50
SALES (corp-wide): 112MM **Privately Held**
WEB: www.weberdist.com
SIC: 4225 4214 General warehousing; local trucking with storage
PA: Weber Distribution Warehouses
   13530 Rosecrans Ave
   Santa Fe Springs CA 90670
   562 356-6300

(P-4668)
WEBER DISTRIBUTION WAREHOUSES
15301 Shoemaker Ave, Norwalk (90650-6859)
PHONE.....................562 404-9996
Fax: 562 404-6566
John Nutt, *Vice Pres*
Al Remington, *Sales Staff*
Greg Westover, *Sales Staff*
EMP: 50
SALES (corp-wide): 112MM **Privately Held**
WEB: www.weberdist.com
SIC: 4225 4214 General warehousing; local trucking with storage
PA: Weber Distribution Warehouses
   13530 Rosecrans Ave
   Santa Fe Springs CA 90670
   562 356-6300

(P-4669)
WESTCOAST WAREHOUSING LLC
100 W Manville St, Rancho Dominguez (90220-5612)
PHONE.....................310 537-9958
Jay Patel,
EMP: 50 **EST:** 2002
SQ FT: 61,440
SALES: 6MM **Privately Held**
SIC: 4225 General warehousing & storage

(P-4670)
WESTERN WINE SERVICES INC (PA)
875 Hanna Dr, American Canyon (94503-9606)
PHONE.....................707 645-4300
Michael W Hodes, *President*
Bruce Cohen, *Senior VP*
Marc Cohen, *Vice Pres*
Tad Franzman, *Vice Pres*
EMP: 99
SALES (est): 15MM **Privately Held**
SIC: 4225 General warehousing & storage

(P-4671)
WILSONART LLC
Also Called: Ralph Wilson Plastics
13911 Gannet St, Santa Fe Springs (90670-5326)
P.O. Box 2336 (90670-0336)
PHONE.....................562 921-7426
Fax: 562 921-7849
Carl Stephens, *Manager*
EMP: 58
SQ FT: 72,000
SALES (corp-wide): 7.8B **Privately Held**
WEB: www.wilsonart.com
SIC: 4225 5162 3083 2891 General warehousing & storage; plastics materials & basic shapes; laminated plastics plate & sheet; adhesives & sealants
HQ: Wilsonart Llc
   2501 Wilsonart Dr
   Temple TX 76504
   254 207-7000

(P-4672)
WORLD CLASS DISTRIBUTION INC
2121 Boeing Way, Stockton (95206-4934)
PHONE.....................909 574-4140
Michael Campbell, *Principal*
EMP: 259 **Privately Held**
SIC: 4225 General warehousing & storage
PA: World Class Distribution Inc.
   10288 Calabash Ave
   Fontana CA 92335

(P-4673)
WORLD CLASS DISTRIBUTION INC
800 S Shamrock Ave, Monrovia (91016-6346)
PHONE.....................909 574-4140
Charles Pilliter, *Branch Mgr*
EMP: 311 **Privately Held**
SIC: 4225 General warehousing & storage
PA: World Class Distribution Inc.
   10288 Calabash Ave
   Fontana CA 92335

(P-4674)
WWL VEHICLE SVCS AMERICAS INC
500 E Water St, Wilmington (90744-6517)
PHONE.....................310 835-8806
Fax: 310 518-3034
Martin Richards, *Branch Mgr*
EMP: 163
SALES (corp-wide): 1.9B **Privately Held**
SIC: 4225 5531 7549 General warehousing & storage; automotive accessories; automotive maintenance services
HQ: Wwl Vehicle Services Americas, Inc.
   188 Broadway Ste 1
   Woodcliff Lake NJ 07677
   201 505-5100

PRODUCTS & SERVICES SECTION

4226 - Special Warehousing & Storage, NEC County (P-4697)

(P-4675)
YUSEN LOGISTICS AMERICAS INC
2417 E Carson St Ste 100, Long Beach (90810-1252)
PHONE..................310 518-3008
P Smith, *Branch Mgr*
Donald Meewes, *Vice Pres*
Peter Patenko, *Business Mgr*
Andy Wilson, *Opers Mgr*
Guy Hempel, *Marketing Staff*
EMP: 200
SALES (corp-wide): 19.4B **Privately Held**
SIC: 4225 General warehouse
HQ: Yusen Logistics (Americas) Inc.
300 Lighting Way Ste 600
Secaucus NJ 07094
201 553-3800

4226 Special Warehousing & Storage, NEC

(P-4676)
AZ/CFS WEST INC
Also Called: AZ West
250 W Manville St, Compton (90220-5600)
PHONE..................310 898-2090
Fax: 310 898-1576
Richard Lombardi, *President*
Donald Schmelz, *General Mgr*
Rose Cruz, *Bookkeeper*
EMP: 60
SQ FT: 175,000
SALES (est): 17.7MM
SALES (corp-wide): 48.4MM **Privately Held**
SIC: 4226 Storage of goods at foreign trade zones
PA: Az Container Freight Station, Inc.
2001 Lower Rd
Linden NJ 07036
908 374-2250

(P-4677)
CALIFORNIA CARTAGE COMPANY LLC
2401 E Pacific Coast Hwy, Wilmington (90744-2920)
PHONE..................562 590-8591
Fax: 562 432-7835
Pete Jacpin, *General Mgr*
David Garcia, *General Mgr*
Dawn Espinoza, *Controller*
Freddy Rivera, *Facilities Mgr*
Diana West, *Facilities Mgr*
EMP: 70
SALES (corp-wide): 121.5MM **Privately Held**
SIC: 4226 4225 Storage of goods at foreign trade zones; general warehousing & storage
PA: California Cartage Company, Llc
2931 Redondo Ave
Long Beach CA 90806
562 427-1143

(P-4678)
CAPACITY LLC
19852 Business Pkwy, Walnut (91789-2838)
PHONE..................732 745-7770
Anthony P Ruiz, *Branch Mgr*
EMP: 171
SALES (corp-wide): 81.8MM **Privately Held**
SIC: 4226 Special warehousing & storage
PA: Capacity Llc
1112 Corporate Rd
North Brunswick NJ 08902
732 745-7770

(P-4679)
CEVA LOGISTICS US INC
11290 Cntu Gllano Rnch Rd, Mira Loma (91752-1448)
PHONE..................951 332-3202
Greg Hart, *Branch Mgr*
EMP: 50
SQ FT: 400,000 **Publicly Held**
SIC: 4226 Automobile dead storage
HQ: Ceva Logistics U.S., Inc.
15350 Vickery Dr
Houston TX 77032
281 618-3100

(P-4680)
CONGLOBAL INDUSTRIES LLC
1711 Alameda St, Wilmington (90744-1700)
P.O. Box 1617 (90748-1617)
PHONE..................310 518-2850
Tom Dielman, *Branch Mgr*
EMP: 73 **Privately Held**
WEB: www.cgini.com
SIC: 4226 Special warehousing & storage
HQ: Conglobal Industries, Llc
8200 185th St Ste A
Tinley Park IL 60487
925 543-0977

(P-4681)
CORODATA CORPORATION (PA)
12375 Kerran St, Poway (92064-6801)
PHONE..................858 748-1100
Robert J Schmitz, *President*
Jerry Brothers, *CFO*
Richard R Schmitz, *Principal*
Thomas A Schmitz, *Admin Sec*
Chris Cahill, *Sales Mgr*
EMP: 65
SQ FT: 600,000
SALES (est): 29.4MM **Privately Held**
SIC: 4226 Document & office records storage

(P-4682)
DATASAFE INC (PA)
574 Eccles Ave, South San Francisco (94080-1905)
P.O. Box 7794, San Francisco (94120-7794)
PHONE..................650 875-3800
Fax: 650 873-3808
Robert S Reis, *Ch of Bd*
Thomas S Reis, *CEO*
Ron Kott, *CFO*
Debra Pierce, *Vice Pres*
Ronald P Reis, *Vice Pres*
EMP: 50
SQ FT: 375,000
SALES (est): 8.8MM **Privately Held**
WEB: www.datasafe.com
SIC: 4226 Document & office records storage

(P-4683)
DATASAFE INC
3160 W Bayshore Rd, Palo Alto (94303-4042)
P.O. Box 7794, San Francisco (94120-7794)
PHONE..................650 875-3800
Tom Reis, *CEO*
Jose Moreno, *Executive*
EMP: 50
SALES (corp-wide): 8.8MM **Privately Held**
WEB: www.datasafe.com
SIC: 4226 4225 Document & office records storage; general warehousing & storage
PA: Datasafe, Inc.
574 Eccles Ave
South San Francisco CA 94080
650 875-3800

(P-4684)
DNOW LP
Also Called: Wilson Supply
1111 W Artesia Blvd, Compton (90220-5107)
PHONE..................310 900-3900
Nick Leute, *Branch Mgr*
EMP: 53
SALES (corp-wide): 3B **Publicly Held**
WEB: www.iwilson.com
SIC: 4226 Special warehousing & storage
HQ: Dnow L.P.
7402 N Eldridge Pkwy
Houston TX 77041
281 823-4700

(P-4685)
DOMINOS PIZZA LLC
301 S Rockefeller Ave, Ontario (91761-7865)
PHONE..................909 390-1990
Fax: 909 390-1988
Sal Melgoza, *General Mgr*
Dan Shoemaker, *Engineer*
Madeline Harris, *Human Res Mgr*
EMP: 120
SALES (corp-wide): 2.2B **Publicly Held**
SIC: 4226 4222 Special warehousing & storage; refrigerated warehousing & storage
HQ: Domino's Pizza Llc
30 Frank Lloyd Wright Dr
Ann Arbor MI 48105
734 930-3030

(P-4686)
EXPRESS IMAGING SERVICES INC
1805 W 208th St Ste 202, Torrance (90501-1808)
PHONE..................888 846-8804
Paul Terry, *President*
Kenny Ly, *Vice Pres*
Tan Ly, *CIO*
Anni Ly, *Manager*
EMP: 100
SQ FT: 10,000
SALES: 13MM **Privately Held**
SIC: 4226 Document & office records storage

(P-4687)
IMPERIAL CFS INC
1000 Francisco St, Torrance (90502-1216)
PHONE..................310 768-8188
Tong Hsing Hsu, *CEO*
Kathy Hsu, *CFO*
I-Hsin Chen, *Admin Sec*
Jackie Hsu, *Accounts Mgr*
David Hsu, *Accounts Exec*
EMP: 50
SQ FT: 200,000
SALES (est): 15.8MM **Privately Held**
WEB: www.imperialcfs.com
SIC: 4226 Special warehousing & storage

(P-4688)
IRON MNTIN/PACIFIC REC MGT INC
711 Striker Ave, Sacramento (95834-1115)
P.O. Box 13735 (95853-3735)
PHONE..................916 924-1558
Bill Garcia, *Branch Mgr*
EMP: 52
SALES (corp-wide): 3B **Publicly Held**
SIC: 4226 Document & office records storage
HQ: Iron Mountain/Pacific Records Management, Inc.
1 Federal St
Boston MA 02110
617 357-4455

(P-4689)
IRON MOUNTAIN INCORPORATED
28751 Witherspoon Pkwy, Valencia (91355-5415)
PHONE..................661 775-9008
EMP: 51
SALES (corp-wide): 3B **Publicly Held**
SIC: 4226 Special warehousing & storage
PA: Iron Mountain Incorporated
1 Federal St Fl 7
Boston MA 02110
617 535-4766

(P-4690)
IRON MOUNTAIN INCORPORATED
8595 Milliken Ave Ste 102, Rancho Cucamonga (91730-4942)
PHONE..................909 484-4333
Ron Harrington, *Manager*
Eve Beebe, *Opers Mgr*
EMP: 51
SALES (corp-wide): 3B **Publicly Held**
SIC: 4226 Document & office records storage
PA: Iron Mountain Incorporated
1 Federal St Fl 7
Boston MA 02110
617 535-4766

(P-4691)
IRON MOUNTAIN INCORPORATED
P.O. Box 7877 (92658-7877)
PHONE..................562 345-6900
EMP: 51
SALES (corp-wide): 3B **Publicly Held**
SIC: 4226 Document & office records storage
PA: Iron Mountain Incorporated
1 Federal St Fl 7
Boston MA 02110
617 535-4766

(P-4692)
IRON MOUNTAIN INFO MGT LLC
12958 Midway Pl, Cerritos (90703-2119)
PHONE..................714 526-0916
Richard Melrose, *Manager*
EMP: 60
SALES (corp-wide): 3B **Publicly Held**
SIC: 4226 Special warehousing & storage
HQ: Iron Mountain Information Management, Llc
1 Federal St
Boston MA 02110
617 357-4455

(P-4693)
KINDER MRGAN ENRGY PARTNERS LP
2000 E Sepulveda Blvd, Carson (90810-1937)
P.O. Box 9007, Long Beach (90810-0007)
PHONE..................310 518-7700
Randy Hartle, *Branch Mgr*
EMP: 50
SALES (corp-wide): 14.4B **Publicly Held**
SIC: 4226 Oil & gasoline storage caverns for hire
HQ: Kinder Morgan Energy Partners, L.P.
1001 La St Ste 1000
Houston TX 77002
713 369-9000

(P-4694)
KINDER MRGAN LQDS TRMINALS LLC
950 Tunnel Ave, Brisbane (94005-1100)
PHONE..................415 467-8107
Mike Rounds, *Branch Mgr*
EMP: 62
SALES (corp-wide): 14.4B **Publicly Held**
SIC: 4226 Special warehousing & storage
HQ: Kinder Morgan Liquids Terminals Llc
500 Dallas St Ste 1000
Houston TX 77002
713 369-8758

(P-4695)
KINDER MRGAN LQDS TRMINALS LLC
9950 San Diego Mission Rd, San Diego (92108-1705)
PHONE..................619 283-6511
Craig Bishop, *Branch Mgr*
EMP: 62
SALES (corp-wide): 14.4B **Publicly Held**
SIC: 4226 Special warehousing & storage
HQ: Kinder Morgan Liquids Terminals Llc
500 Dallas St Ste 1000
Houston TX 77002
713 369-8758

(P-4696)
KINDER MRGAN LQDS TRMINALS LLC
2150 Kruse Dr, San Jose (95131-1213)
PHONE..................408 435-7399
Fax: 408 434-0283
Kelly Johnson, *Manager*
EMP: 62
SALES (corp-wide): 14.4B **Publicly Held**
SIC: 4226 Special warehousing & storage
HQ: Kinder Morgan Liquids Terminals Llc
500 Dallas St Ste 1000
Houston TX 77002
713 369-8758

(P-4697)
MACYS INC
6200 Franklin Blvd, Sacramento (95824-3412)
PHONE..................916 373-0333
Craig O'Connor, *Manager*
EMP: 80
SALES (corp-wide): 27B **Publicly Held**
SIC: 4226 4225 Special warehousing & storage; general warehousing & storage

4226 - Special Warehousing & Storage, NEC County (P-4698)

PA: Macy's, Inc.
7 W 7th St
Cincinnati OH 45202
513 579-7000

(P-4698) MIDAS EXPRESS LOS ANGELES INC
11854 Alameda St, Lynwood (90262-4019)
PHONE...............................310 609-0366
Jack Wu, *President*
Jacky Strong, *Shareholder*
EMP: 200
SQ FT: 90,000
SALES (est): 18.6MM **Privately Held**
WEB: www.midasexpress.com
SIC: 4226 4225 4731 Special warehousing & storage; textile warehousing; general warehousing & storage; freight forwarding

(P-4699) PACIFIC CHEMICAL DIST CORP (DH)
6250 Caballero Blvd, Buena Park (90620-1124)
PHONE...............................714 521-7161
Fax: 714 521-7133
James N Tausz, *President*
Rhonda Tausz, *Corp Secy*
James Banister, *Vice Pres*
Joann Rowe, *Manager*
EMP: 100 **EST:** 1978
SQ FT: 144,000
SALES (est): 9.3MM
SALES (corp-wide): 555.9MM **Privately Held**
SIC: 4226 Special warehousing & storage
HQ: A&R Logistics, Inc.
600 N Hurstbourne Pkwy # 110
Louisville KY 40222
815 941-5200

(P-4700) PRIDE INDUSTRIES (PA)
10030 Foothills Blvd, Roseville (95747-7102)
P.O. Box 1200, Rocklin (95677-7200)
PHONE...............................916 788-2100
Fax: 916 788-2552
Michael Ziegler, *CEO*
Mary Flores, *President*
Steve Twitchell, *President*
Peter Berghuis, *COO*
Jeff Dern, *CFO*
EMP: 250
SQ FT: 177,000
SALES: 279.8MM **Privately Held**
WEB: www.prideindustries.com/
SIC: 4226 7349 3679 Special warehousing & storage; building maintenance services; electronic circuits

(P-4701) S N S WEST LLC
10700 Business Dr, Fontana (92337-8232)
PHONE...............................909 350-8118
Fax: 909 350-8139
James Stein,
Dan Lioni,
Jack Carp, *Manager*
EMP: 90
SQ FT: 72,000
SALES: 2.5MM **Privately Held**
SIC: 4226 7389 Textile warehousing; textile folding & packing services

(P-4702) SEES CANDY SHOPS INCORPORATED
Also Called: See's Candies
20600 S Alameda St, Long Beach (90810-1105)
PHONE...............................310 559-4911
Fax: 562 604-1038
Jahnnie Woods, *Manager*
Anna Fajardo, *Executive*
Joe Kanan, *Executive*
Lynette Hernandez, *Manager*
Stephanie Mason, *Manager*
EMP: 150
SALES (corp-wide): 210.8B **Publicly Held**
WEB: www.sees.com
SIC: 4226 Special warehousing & storage

HQ: See's Candy Shops, Incorporated
210 El Camino Real
South San Francisco CA 94080
650 761-2490

(P-4703) STANDARD REGISTER INC
Also Called: Workflowone
5775 Brisa St, Livermore (94550-2513)
PHONE...............................925 449-3700
Randy Dehart, *Branch Mgr*
Sue Brown, *Personnel Exec*
Lesley Murane, *Purchasing*
EMP: 86
SALES (corp-wide): 5.1B **Privately Held**
SIC: 4226 Document & office records storage
HQ: Standard Register, Inc.
600 Albany St
Dayton OH 45417
937 221-1000

(P-4704) TARGET CORPORATION
2050 E Beamer St, Woodland (95776-6213)
PHONE...............................530 666-3705
Fax: 530 668-2357
Dave Sartin, *Manager*
Daryl Finnie, *Purchasing*
Ted Garbey, *Purchasing*
EMP: 400
SALES (corp-wide): 73.7B **Publicly Held**
WEB: www.target.com
SIC: 4226 Special warehousing & storage
PA: Target Corporation
1000 Nicollet Mall
Minneapolis MN 55403
612 304-6073

(P-4705) TARGET CORPORATION
7600 N Blackstone Ave, Fresno (93720-4300)
PHONE...............................559 431-0104
Fax: 559 431-0104
Ralph Watkins, *Manager*
Alice Beck, *Manager*
EMP: 200
SALES (corp-wide): 73.7B **Publicly Held**
WEB: www.target.com
SIC: 4226 Special warehousing & storage
PA: Target Corporation
1000 Nicollet Mall
Minneapolis MN 55403
612 304-6073

(P-4706) UTI INTEGRATED LOGISTICS LLC
Also Called: Corp., R.g Barry
13230 San Bernardino Ave B, Fontana (92335-5266)
PHONE...............................909 427-1939
EMP: 152
SALES (corp-wide): 7.3B **Privately Held**
SIC: 4226 Textile warehousing
HQ: Uti Integrated Logistics, Llc
700 Gervais St Ste 100
Columbia SC 29201
803 771-6785

(P-4707) VINTRUST INC
38 Keyes Ave Ste 200, San Francisco (94129-1769)
PHONE...............................877 846-8787
Barry Waitte, *CEO*
Ozzie Ayscue, *CFO*
Andr De Baubigny, *Chairman*
Edwin O Ayscue, *Treasurer*
EMP: 50
SALES (est): 3.7MM **Privately Held**
WEB: www.vintrust.com
SIC: 4226 Whiskey warehousing

(P-4708) WILLIAMS SERVICE CORPORATION (PA)
Also Called: Williams Data Management
1925 E Vernon Ave Ste 4, Vernon (90058-1632)
PHONE...............................323 234-3453
Fax: 323 233-5451
David C Williams, *CEO*
Douglas C Williams, *Treasurer*

Mark Williams, *Vice Pres*
Lindsay Bosza, *Accounts Mgr*
EMP: 50
SQ FT: 440,000
SALES (est): 6.9MM **Privately Held**
WEB: www.williamsrecords.com
SIC: 4226 4225 Document & office records storage; general warehousing

4231 Terminal & Joint Terminal Maint Facilities

(P-4709) CENTRAL FREIGHT LINES INC
1621 Main Ave, Sacramento (95838-2427)
PHONE...............................800 782-5036
Fax: 916 921-5193
Jack Buckley, *Manager*
EMP: 100
SALES (corp-wide): 1.1B **Privately Held**
WEB: www.centralfreight.com
SIC: 4231 Trucking terminal facilities
HQ: Central Freight Lines, Inc.
5601 W Waco Dr
Waco TX 76710
254 772-2120

(P-4710) FEDEX FREIGHT CORPORATION
310 W Grove Ave, Orange (92865-3206)
PHONE...............................714 637-9346
Jim O'Conner, *Manager*
Juan Gutierrez, *Manager*
EMP: 50
SQ FT: 18,195
SALES (corp-wide): 50.3B **Publicly Held**
WEB: www.watkins.com
SIC: 4231 Trucking terminal facilities
HQ: Fedex Freight Corporation
1715 Aaron Brenner Dr
Memphis TN 38120
901 434-3100

(P-4711) FEDEX FREIGHT CORPORATION
3200 Workman Mill Rd, Whittier (90601-1550)
PHONE...............................800 288-0743
Darrin Van Wagenen, *Manager*
Jinyu Sun, *Info Tech Dir*
Joe Marques, *Sales Staff*
EMP: 500
SQ FT: 38,090
SALES (corp-wide): 50.3B **Publicly Held**
SIC: 4231 4785 4213 Trucking terminal facilities; inspection & fixed facilities; trucking, except local
HQ: Fedex Freight Corporation
1715 Aaron Brenner Dr
Memphis TN 38120
901 434-3100

(P-4712) YRC INC
Also Called: Yrc Freight
17401 Adelanto Rd, Adelanto (92301-2701)
PHONE...............................760 246-0031
EMP: 54
SALES (corp-wide): 4.8B **Publicly Held**
SIC: 4231 Trucking terminal facilities
HQ: Yrc Inc.
10990 Roe Ave
Overland Park KS 66211
913 696-6100

4412 Deep Sea Foreign Transportation Of Freight

(P-4713) APL LOGISTICS LTD
614 Terminal Way, San Pedro (90731-7453)
PHONE...............................310 548-8700
Gale Bull, *Branch Mgr*
EMP: 200
SALES (corp-wide): 3.5B **Privately Held**
WEB: www.apl.com
SIC: 4412 Deep sea foreign transportation of freight

HQ: Apl Logistics, Ltd.
16220 N Scottsdale Rd # 300
Scottsdale AZ 85254
602 586-4800

(P-4714) FOSS MARITIME COMPANY
1316 Canal Blvd, Richmond (94804-3556)
PHONE...............................510 307-4271
Fax: 510 307-7821
Bob Gregory, *Manager*
EMP: 100
SALES (corp-wide): 2.2B **Privately Held**
WEB: www.foss-maritime.com
SIC: 4412 4492 Deep sea foreign transportation of freight; tugboat service
HQ: Foss Maritime Company
1151 Fairview Ave N
Seattle WA 98109
206 281-4001

(P-4715) FOSS MARITIME COMPANY
Also Called: Pacific Southwest
St Pier D, Long Beach (90801)
P.O. Box 1940 (90801-1940)
PHONE...............................562 435-0171
Bob Gregory, *Manager*
Allan Martin, *Manager*
EMP: 200
SALES (corp-wide): 2.2B **Privately Held**
WEB: www.foss-maritime.com
SIC: 4412 4492 Deep sea foreign transportation of freight; towing & tugboat service
HQ: Foss Maritime Company
1151 Fairview Ave N
Seattle WA 98109
206 281-4001

(P-4716) K LINE AMERICA INC
17011 Beach Blvd Ste 1100, Huntington Beach (92647-7402)
PHONE...............................714 861-5000
Michelle Boden, *Manager*
Peter Bennett, *Vice Pres*
Stacey Macwilliams, *Manager*
Melissa Spata, *Manager*
EMP: 50
SALES (corp-wide): 10.6B **Privately Held**
SIC: 4412 4212 Deep sea foreign transportation of freight; local trucking, without storage
HQ: K Line America, Inc.
8730 Stony Point Pkwy # 400
Richmond VA 23235
804 560-3600

(P-4717) PATRIOT CONTRACT SERVICES LLC
Also Called: P C S
1320 Willow Pass Rd # 485, Concord (94520-5232)
PHONE...............................925 296-2000
Jordan Truchan, *CEO*
Judy Collins, *CFO*
Frank Angelacci, *Vice Pres*
EMP: 400
SQ FT: 7,800
SALES (est): 25MM **Privately Held**
SIC: 4412 4424 4449 4481 Deep sea foreign transportation of freight; deep sea domestic transportation of freight; canal & intracoastal freight transportation; deep sea passenger transportation, except ferry; ferries; marine surveyors

4424 Deep Sea Domestic Transportation Of Freight

(P-4718) MATSON NAVIGATION COMPANY INC (HQ)
555 12th St, Oakland (94607-4046)
PHONE...............................510 628-4000
Fax: 510 628-7359
Matthew J Cox, *President*
Joel M Wine, *CFO*
Benedict J Bowler, *Treasurer*

▲ = Import ▼=Export
◆ =Import/Export

PRODUCTS & SERVICES SECTION

4489 - Water Transport Of Passengers, NEC County (P-4736)

Rusty Rolfe, *Exec VP*
Ronald Forest, *Senior VP*
EMP: 200 **EST:** 1882
SQ FT: 105,000
SALES (est): 900.4MM
SALES (corp-wide): 1.8B **Publicly Held**
WEB: www.matson.com
SIC: 4424 4491 4492 Deep sea domestic transportation of freight; marine cargo handling; stevedoring; marine terminals; tugboat service
PA: Matson, Inc.
   1411 Sand Island Pkwy
   Honolulu HI 96819
   808 848-1211

(P-4719)
PASHA STEVEDORING TERMINALS LP
802 S Fries Ave, Wilmington (90744-6415)
PHONE 415 927-6353
Fax: 310 835-1082
Jeff Burgin, *Senior VP*
Jackie Bailey, *Treasurer*
David Vanwaardenburg, *General Mgr*
Braxton Craghill, *Controller*
EMP: 50
SALES (est): 10.6MM
SALES (corp-wide): 313.8MM **Privately Held**
WEB: www.psterminals.com
SIC: 4424 4412 Deep sea domestic transportation of freight; deep sea foreign transportation of freight
PA: The Pasha Group
   4040 Civic Center Dr # 350
   San Rafael CA 94903
   415 927-6400

(P-4720)
POLAR TANKERS INC (DH)
300 Oceangate, Long Beach (90802-6801)
PHONE 562 388-1400
Fax: 562 388-1429
John R Hennon, *President*
George McShea, *Vice Pres*
John L Sullivan, *Vice Pres*
EMP: 75
SALES (est): 25.6MM
SALES (corp-wide): 30.9B **Publicly Held**
WEB: www.polartankers.com
SIC: 4424 4412 Deep sea domestic transportation of freight; deep sea foreign transportation of freight
HQ: Phillips Petroleum Company
   600 N Dairy Ashford Rd
   Houston TX 77079
   281 293-1000

4449 Water Transportation Of Freight, NEC

(P-4721)
DEVINE & SON TRUCKING CO INC (PA)
Also Called: Devine Intermodal
3870 Channel Dr, West Sacramento (95691-3466)
P.O. Box 980160 (95798-0160)
PHONE 559 486-7440
Fax: 916 371-0355
John Frederick Drewes, *CEO*
Richard Coyle, *President*
Tammy Sanders, *Technology*
Karen M Vellutini, *Sales Executive*
Bennie Gamble, *Terminal Mgr*
EMP: 200
SQ FT: 6,000
SALES (est): 30.8MM **Privately Held**
WEB: www.devineintermodal.com
SIC: 4449 4213 Canal & intracoastal freight transportation; trucking, except local

(P-4722)
FINN HOLDING CORPORATION (PA)
Also Called: Platinum Equity
360 N Crescent Dr, Beverly Hills (90210-4874)
PHONE 310 712-1850
Tom Gores, *Ch of Bd*
Mary Ann Sigler, *CFO*
Eva M Kalawski, *Vice Pres*

EMP: 2575
SALES (est): 1.1B **Privately Held**
SIC: 4449 3731 4491 Canal barge operations; barges, building & repairing; marine terminals

(P-4723)
SHIPCO TRANSPORT INC
100 W Victoria St, Long Beach (90805-2147)
PHONE 562 295-2900
Fax: 310 538-0787
Gary Osterbach, *Principal*
Christine Solorzano, *General Mgr*
Bjoernholt Karapetia, *Director*
EMP: 65
SALES (corp-wide): 634.3MM **Privately Held**
SIC: 4449 Transportation (freight) on bays & sounds of the ocean
HQ: Shipco Transport Inc.
   80 Washington St
   Hoboken NJ 07030
   973 457-3300

4481 Deep Sea Transportation Of

(P-4724)
CRYSTAL CRUISES LLC (DH)
11755 Wilshire Blvd # 900, Los Angeles (90025-1506)
PHONE 310 785-9300
Fax: 310 785-0011
Eddie Rodriguez, *President*
Thomas Mazloum, *COO*
Jack Anderson, *Senior VP*
Richard Paulsen, *Technology*
Maxwell Blanchard, *Financial Analy*
◆ **EMP:** 181
SQ FT: 50,000
SALES (est): 59.1MM
SALES (corp-wide): 570.8MM **Privately Held**
WEB: www.crystalcruises.com
SIC: 4481 4724 Deep sea passenger transportation, except ferry; travel agencies
HQ: Genting Hong Kong Limited
   Rm 1501 15/F Ocean Ctr
   Tsim Sha Tsui KLN
   237 820-00

(P-4725)
PRINCESS CRUISE LINES LTD (HQ)
Also Called: Princess Cruises
24305 Town Center Dr, Santa Clarita (91355-1307)
PHONE 661 753-0000
Fax: 661 284-4765
Jan Swartz, *CEO*
Nina Kass, *President*
Dean Brown, *Exec VP*
Mary Horwath, *Exec VP*
David De Merlier, *Vice Pres*
EMP: 2000
SALES (est): 2.4B
SALES (corp-wide): 15.7B **Privately Held**
WEB: www.princess.com
SIC: 4481 4725 7011 Deep sea passenger transportation, except ferry; tour operators; hotels
PA: Carnival Plc
   Carnival House
   Southampton HANTS SO15
   238 065-6653

(P-4726)
PRINCESS CRUISE LINES LTD
Also Called: Princess Cruises
P.O. Box 966 (91380-9066)
PHONE 661 753-2291
Princess Cruise, *Principal*
EMP: 1114
SALES (corp-wide): 15.7B **Privately Held**
SIC: 4481 Deep sea passenger transportation, except ferry
HQ: Princess Cruise Lines, Ltd.
   24305 Town Center Dr
   Santa Clarita CA 91355
   661 753-0000

(P-4727)
PRINCESS CRUISE LINES LTD
24300 Town Center Dr # 100, Valencia (91355-1332)
PHONE 661 753-0000
Kristen Lin, *Buyer*
Mona Ehrenreich, *Corp Counsel*
EMP: 900
SALES (corp-wide): 15.7B **Privately Held**
SIC: 4481 Deep sea passenger transportation, except ferry
HQ: Princess Cruise Lines, Ltd.
   24305 Town Center Dr
   Santa Clarita CA 91355
   661 753-0000

(P-4728)
PRINCESS CRUISE LINES LTD
Also Called: Princess Cruises
24300 Town Center Dr # 100, Valencia (91355-1332)
PHONE 661 753-0000
Fax: 661 753-0124
Peter Ratcliffe, *President*
Karl Wernett, *CFO*
Ron Cearnecki, *Vice Pres*
Ron Czarnecki, *Vice Pres*
T Harris, *Vice Pres*
EMP: 900
SALES (corp-wide): 15.7B **Privately Held**
WEB: www.princess.com
SIC: 4481 4725 Deep sea passenger transportation, except ferry; tour operators
HQ: Princess Cruise Lines, Ltd.
   24305 Town Center Dr
   Santa Clarita CA 91355
   661 753-0000

(P-4729)
PRINCESS CRUISE LINES LTD
24305 Town Center Dr, Valencia (91355-1307)
PHONE 661 753-0000
Alan B Buckelew, *Branch Mgr*
Mona Ehrenreich, *Vice Pres*
Terry Hobson, *Vice Pres*
Tara Konar, *Project Leader*
Jennifer Baharian, *Analyst*
EMP: 900
SALES (corp-wide): 15.7B **Privately Held**
SIC: 4481 7011 4725 Deep sea passenger transportation, except ferry; hotels; tour operators
HQ: Princess Cruise Lines, Ltd.
   24305 Town Center Dr
   Santa Clarita CA 91355
   661 753-0000

4489 Water Transport Of Passengers, NEC

(P-4730)
BAHIA STERNWHEELERS INC
998 W Mission Bay Dr, San Diego (92109-7803)
PHONE 858 539-7720
Fax: 858 539-7726
William L Evans, *Ch of Bd*
Grace Chershore, *President*
Nancy Evans-Kyzer, *Treasurer*
Anne Evans-Quinn, *Vice Pres*
Margaret Evans, *Admin Sec*
EMP: 50
SQ FT: 5,000
SALES (est): 3.4MM **Privately Held**
WEB: www.bahiahotel.com
SIC: 4489 7299 4499 Excursion boat operators; banquet hall facilities; chartering of commercial boats

(P-4731)
BLUE AND GOLD FLEET
Also Called: Pier Restaurant
Marine Terminal Pier 41 St Pier, San Francisco (94133)
PHONE 415 705-8200
Fax: 415 421-1113
Ron Duckhorn, *Owner*
Molly South, *Treasurer*
Robert Moore, *Admin Sec*
Kent McGrath, *Engineer*
Fariba Vassseghi, *Controller*
EMP: 70 **EST:** 1979

SALES (est): 14.7MM
SALES (corp-wide): 40MM **Privately Held**
WEB: www.blueandgoldfleet.com
SIC: 4489 4724 Excursion boat operators; travel agencies
PA: Pier 39 Limited Partnership
   Beach Embarcadero Level 3
   San Francisco CA 94133
   415 705-5500

(P-4732)
CATALINA CHANNEL EXPRESS INC (HQ)
Also Called: Catalina Express Cruises
400 Oceangate Ste 300, Long Beach (90802-4392)
Rural Route 400 Oceangate (90802)
PHONE 310 519-7971
Douglas Bombard, *Ch of Bd*
Greg Bombard, *President*
Lori Bombard, *CFO*
Audrey Bombard, *Treasurer*
Tony Ross, *Vice Pres*
EMP: 200
SQ FT: 20,000
SALES (est): 36.8MM **Privately Held**
WEB: www.catalinaexpress.com
SIC: 4489 Excursion boat operators
PA: Bombard Marine And Resort Management Services Inc
   95 Berth
   San Pedro CA 90731
   310 519-7971

(P-4733)
CATALINA CHANNEL EXPRESS INC
Also Called: Catalina Express
1046 Queens Hwy, Long Beach (90802-6329)
PHONE 562 495-3565
Greg Bombard, *Manager*
Frank Madera, *Director*
EMP: 200
SALES (corp-wide): 36.8MM **Privately Held**
WEB: www.catalinaexpress.com
SIC: 4489 4482 Excursion boat operators; deep sea passenger transportation, except ferry
HQ: Catalina Channel Express, Inc.
   400 Oceangate Ste 300
   Long Beach CA 90802
   310 519-7971

(P-4734)
CATALINA GLASSBOTTOM BOAT INC
1 Cabrillo Mole, Avalon (90704)
PHONE 310 510-2888
Jeff Stickler, *CEO*
Steve Smith, *Vice Pres*
EMP: 65
SALES: 6MM **Privately Held**
SIC: 4489 Sightseeing boats

(P-4735)
GOLDEN GATE SCNIC STMSHIP CORP
Also Called: Red and White Fleet
Shed C Pier 45 St Pier, San Francisco (94133)
PHONE 415 901-5249
Thomas E Escher, *President*
EMP: 50
SALES: 10MM **Privately Held**
SIC: 4489 4482 Sightseeing boats; ferries

(P-4736)
HORNBLOWER YACHTS INC
Also Called: Hornblower Cruises & Events
2825 5th Ave, San Diego (92103-6326)
PHONE 619 686-8700
Jim Unger, *Branch Mgr*
Gretchen Webber, *Info Tech Mgr*
Mandy Brown, *Sales Mgr*
Bill Lovens, *Manager*
EMP: 160
SALES (corp-wide): 101.7MM **Privately Held**
WEB: www.hornbloweryachts.com
SIC: 4489 7299 4499 Excursion boat operators; banquet hall facilities; chartering of commercial boats

4489 - Water Transport Of Passengers, NEC County (P-4737)

PA: Hornblower Yachts, Llc
On The Embarcadero Pier 3 St Pier
San Francisco CA 94111
415 788-8866

(P-4737)
HORNBLOWER YACHTS LLC (PA)
Also Called: Hornblower Cruises & Event
On The Embarcadero Pier 3 St Pier, San Francisco (94111)
PHONE.................415 788-8866
Fax: 415 394-8444
Terry Macrae, CEO
Andreas Sappok, Vice Pres
Annabella Stagner, Vice Pres
Jim Unger, Vice Pres
Kevin Lorton, General Mgr
EMP: 250
SALES (est): 101.7MM Privately Held
WEB: www.hornbloweryachts.com
SIC: 4489 Excursion boat operators

(P-4738)
KERN RIVER ADVENTURES
Also Called: Eagle Rafting
721 W Graaf Ave, Ridgecrest (93555-2412)
P.O. Box 2013, Kernville (93238-2013)
PHONE..................760 376-3648
Loxie Chesney, Owner
EMP: 250
SALES: 5MM Privately Held
WEB: www.eaglerafting.com
SIC: 4489 Excursion boat operators

(P-4739)
SO CAL SHIP SERVICES
971 S Seaside Ave, San Pedro (90731-7331)
PHONE..................310 519-8411
Fax: 310 519-1545
Michael A Lanham, President
Doug Malin, Executive
Mark Wrobel, General Mgr
Toni Banda, Office Mgr
Michelle Camphill, Manager
EMP: 85
SQ FT: 10,000
SALES (est): 14.4MM Privately Held
WEB: www.ship-services.com
SIC: 4489 Water taxis

(P-4740)
STAR & CRESCENT BOAT COMPANY (PA)
Also Called: San Diego Harbor Excursion
1311 1st St, Coronado (92118-1502)
P.O. Box 120751, San Diego (92112-0751)
PHONE..................619 234-4111
Fax: 619 522-6150
Arthur E Engel, CEO
George Palermo, President
David Engel, Vice Pres
Herbert Engel, Vice Pres
William Johnston, Vice Pres
EMP: 50 EST: 1905
SALES (est): 16.3MM Privately Held
WEB: www.sdhe.com
SIC: 4489 4482 5812 5947 Excursion boat operators; sightseeing boats; ferries operating across rivers or within harbors; cafe; gift shop

(P-4741)
USG ENTERPRISES INC
Also Called: Fantasea Yacht Charters
4325 Glencoe Ave, Marina Del Rey (90292-6444)
PHONE..................310 827-2220
Uri S Ginzburg, President
Daniel Ginzburg, President
Stephanie Ginsburg, Vice Pres
Jasmine Lee, General Mgr
Marin Ness, Executive Asst
▲ EMP: 55
SQ FT: 13,000
SALES (est): 7.1MM Privately Held
WEB: www.fantaseayachts.com
SIC: 4489 7299 Excursion boat operators; banquet hall facilities

4491 Marine Cargo Handling

(P-4742)
APM TERMINALS PACIFIC LLC (DH)
2500 Navy Way, San Pedro (90731-7554)
PHONE..................704 571-2768
John Loeprich, Senior VP
John Loepprich, Treasurer
Michael Ahern, General Mgr
Bill Lynch, General Mgr
Mario De La Pena, Opers Mgr
EMP: 104
SQ FT: 33,000
SALES (est): 69.4MM
SALES (corp-wide): 38.6B Privately Held
SIC: 4491 Marine cargo handling
HQ: Apm Terminals North America, Inc.
9300 Arrowpoint Blvd
Charlotte NC 28273
704 571-2768

(P-4743)
AVIATION PORT SERVICES LLC
Also Called: Aviation Port Services LLC
2081 Adams Ave, San Leandro (94577-1007)
PHONE..................510 636-8790
EMP: 73 Privately Held
SIC: 4491 Unloading vessels
PA: Aviation Port Services L.L.C
5814 Graham Ave Ste 205
Sumner WA 98390

(P-4744)
CALIFORNIA UNTD TERMINALS INC
2525 Navy Way, San Pedro (90731-7554)
PHONE..................310 521-5000
Fax: 562 432-6430
Gyou Bong Kim, CEO
John Maddox, President
George Lang, COO
Lang George, Senior VP
Yvonne Robertson, Executive Asst
EMP: 50 EST: 1968
SQ FT: 16,000
SALES: 12.9MM
SALES (corp-wide): 4.8B Privately Held
WEB: www.hmma.com
SIC: 4491 Docks, piers & terminals
HQ: Hyundai Merchant Marine (America), Inc.
222 Las Colinas Blvd W
Irving TX 75039
972 501-1100

(P-4745)
CATALINA CHANNEL EXPRESS INC
Also Called: Catalina Express
320 Golden Shore Lbby, Long Beach (90802-4200)
PHONE..................562 435-8686
Rachel Lane, Branch Mgr
EMP: 125
SALES (corp-wide): 36.8MM Privately Held
WEB: www.catalinaexpress.com
SIC: 4491 Docks, piers & terminals
HQ: Catalina Channel Express, Inc.
400 Oceangate Ste 300
Long Beach CA 90802
310 519-7971

(P-4746)
CITY OF LOS ANGELES
Also Called: Harbor Department
425 S Palos Verdes St, San Pedro (90731-3309)
PHONE..................310 732-7681
Geraldine Knatz, Branch Mgr
Jill Jefferies, Research
EMP: 250 Privately Held
WEB: www.lacity.org
SIC: 4491 9199 Marine cargo handling; general government administration;
PA: City Of Los Angeles
200 N Spring St Ste 303
Los Angeles CA 90012
213 978-0600

(P-4747)
INTERNATIONAL TRNSP SVC (HQ)
Also Called: I T S
1281 Pier G Way, Long Beach (90802-6353)
P.O. Box 22704 (90801-5704)
PHONE..................562 435-7781
Fax: 562 491-0279
Sho Ishitobi, President
Yuji Yamamoto, Corp Secy
John Miller, Exec VP
Masanora Kurose, Vice Pres
Michael Shanks, Vice Pres
EMP: 220
SQ FT: 10,000
SALES (est): 46.1MM
SALES (corp-wide): 10.6B Privately Held
WEB: www.itsasafety.org
SIC: 4491 Marine loading & unloading services
PA: Kawasaki Kisen Kaisha, Ltd.
2-1-1, Uchisaiwaicho
Chiyoda-Ku TKY 100-0
335 955-000

(P-4748)
LEVIN-RICHMOND TERMINAL CORP
402 Wright Ave, Richmond (94804-3532)
PHONE..................510 232-4422
Fax: 510 236-0129
Gary Levin, President
Sylvia San Andres, Admin Asst
Pat O'Driscoll, Opers Mgr
Joel Torres, Opers Staff
Mike McCoy, Sales Staff
EMP: 60
SALES (est): 8.3MM
SALES (corp-wide): 9.6MM Privately Held
WEB: www.levinterminal.com
SIC: 4491 Marine cargo handling
PA: Levin Enterprises Inc
112 Wshington Ave Ste 250
Richmond CA 94801
510 215-1515

(P-4749)
M T C HOLDINGS (DH)
3 Embarcadero Ctr Ste 550, San Francisco (94111-4048)
PHONE..................912 651-4000
Michael Hassing, President
Gail Parris, CFO
Christopher Redlich Jr, Chairman
Catherine Scaturo, IT/INT Sup
Ruth Demore, Purchasing
EMP: 50
SALES (est): 44.4MM
SALES (corp-wide): 58.3B Publicly Held
SIC: 4491 Stevedoring; marine terminals; loading vessels; unloading vessels
HQ: Ports America, Inc.
525 Washington Blvd
Jersey City NJ 07310
732 635-3899

(P-4750)
NAVIS CORPORATION
55 Harrison St, Oakland (94607-3790)
PHONE..................510 267-5000
Rob Dillon, CEO
Leif Chastaine, Vice Pres
Lou Chauvin, Vice Pres
Michael Cho, Vice Pres
Philip Gerskovich, Vice Pres
EMP: 300
SALES (est): 31.5MM Privately Held
SIC: 4491 Marine cargo handling

(P-4751)
OFFSHORE SERVICE VESSELS LLC
Also Called: Alfa Marine Services
757 Emory St Pm565, Imperial Beach (91932-2231)
PHONE..................619 237-1314
Paul Castle, Manager
EMP: 85
SALES (corp-wide): 287.5MM Privately Held
SIC: 4491 Marine cargo handling

PA: Offshore Service Vessels, L.L.C.
16201 E Main St
Cut Off LA 70345
985 601-4444

(P-4752)
PASHA STEVEDORING TERMINALS LP
802 S Fries Ave, Wilmington (90744-6415)
PHONE..................310 233-2006
EMP: 50
SALES (est): 1.6MM Privately Held
SIC: 4491

(P-4753)
PORT DEPT CITY OF OAKLAND (PA)
Also Called: Port of Oakland
530 Water St Fl 3, Oakland (94607-3525)
P.O. Box 2064 (94604-2064)
PHONE..................510 627-1100
Fax: 510 839-1766
Veteran Chris Lytle, Exec Dir
Fred Rickert, CFO
Amel Atienza, Officer
Jerry A Bridges, Exec Dir
Chris Lytle, Exec Dir
EMP: 350
SQ FT: 285,600
SALES (est): 50MM Privately Held
WEB: www.portofoakland.com
SIC: 4491 4581 Marine cargo handling; airport leasing, if operating airport

(P-4754)
PORTS AMERICA INC
1601 Harbor Bay Pkwy # 150, Alameda (94502-3029)
PHONE..................510 749-7400
Michael Hassing, President
Naftali Lyandres, QA Dir
Jimmy Husman, Comp Tech
Ho Lam, Technology
Aleksandr Latman, Med Doctor
EMP: 80
SALES (corp-wide): 58.3B Publicly Held
SIC: 4491 Stevedoring; marine terminals
HQ: Ports America, Inc.
525 Washington Blvd
Jersey City NJ 07310
732 635-3899

(P-4755)
SACRAMENTO-YOLO PORT DISTRICT
Also Called: Port of Sacramento
1110 W Capitol Ave, West Sacramento (95691-2717)
PHONE..................916 371-8000
Fax: 916 372-4802
Mic Linken, Director
John Sulpizio, Exec Dir
Teresa Bledsoe, Manager
EMP: 125
SALES (est): 9.4MM Privately Held
WEB: www.portofsacramento.com
SIC: 4491 Marine terminals

(P-4756)
SAN DIEGO UNIFIED PORT DST
Also Called: San Diego Unified Hbr Police
3380 N Harbor Dr, San Diego (92101-1023)
PHONE..................619 686-6585
Betty Kelepecz, Branch Mgr
Pam Carpenter, Info Tech Mgr
James Hutzelman, Info Tech Mgr
Terri Pocock, Info Tech Mgr
Lon Safko, Info Tech Mgr
EMP: 120
SALES (corp-wide): 149.5MM Privately Held
WEB: www.thebigbay.com
SIC: 4491 Marine cargo handling
PA: San Diego Unified Port District
3165 Pacific Hwy
San Diego CA 92101
619 686-6200

PRODUCTS & SERVICES SECTION

4512 - Air Transportation, Scheduled County (P-4779)

(P-4757)
SAN DIEGO UNIFIED PORT DST (PA)
Also Called: Port of San Diego
3165 Pacific Hwy, San Diego (92101-1128)
P.O. Box 120488 (92112-0488)
PHONE 619 686-6200
Fax: 619 291-0753
John Bolduc, CEO
Robert Deangelis, CFO
Lori Poore, CFO
Georgina Carbajal, Treasurer
Randa Coniglio, Exec VP
EMP: 240 EST: 1962
SQ FT: 120,000
SALES: 149.5MM Privately Held
WEB: www.thebigbay.com
SIC: 4491 Marine cargo handling

(P-4758)
SSA CONTAINERS INC
1521 Pier J Ave, Long Beach (90802-6327)
P.O. Box 24868, Seattle WA (98124-0868)
PHONE 206 623-0304
Knud Stubkjaer, CEO
John Aldaya, CFO
Jaime Neal, Senior VP
Theresa Bicknell, Vice Pres
Kyle Lukins, Admin Sec
EMP: 99
SALES (est): 4.1MM
SALES (corp-wide): 1.1B Privately Held
SIC: 4491 Stevedoring
HQ: Ssa Marine, Inc.
1131 Sw Klickitat Way
Seattle WA 98134
206 623-0304

(P-4759)
SSA MARINE INC
1521 Pier J Ave, Long Beach (90802-6327)
PHONE 562 983-1001
Sal Ferrigno, Manager
Chuck Wallace, Vice Pres
Patty Lopez, Manager
Chen Xuefeng, Manager
EMP: 50
SALES (corp-wide): 1.1B Privately Held
WEB: www.ssamarine.com
SIC: 4491 Stevedoring
HQ: Ssa Marine, Inc.
1131 Sw Klickitat Way
Seattle WA 98134
206 623-0304

(P-4760)
SSA PACIFIC INC
2895 Industrial Blvd # 100, West Sacramento (95691-3804)
P.O. Box 24868, Seattle WA (98124-0868)
PHONE 916 374-1866
Mark Knudsen, President
Theresa Bicknell, Vice Pres
Kyle Lukins, Admin Sec
EMP: 99 EST: 2004
SALES (est): 2.6MM Privately Held
SIC: 4491 Stevedoring

(P-4761)
SSA PACIFIC INC
Outer Harbor Berth 54 55, San Pedro (90731)
PHONE 310 833-9606
Mark Knudsen, President
Kyle Lukins, Corp Secy
Theresa Bicknell, Vice Pres
Chad Pittman, Vice Pres
EMP: 99
SALES (est): 10.2MM Privately Held
SIC: 4491 Stevedoring; marine terminals; waterfront terminal operation

(P-4762)
STOCKTON PORT DISTRICT
Also Called: Port of Stockton
2201 W Washington St # 13, Stockton (95203-2991)
P.O. Box 2089 (95201-2089)
PHONE 209 946-0246
Fax: 209 465-7244
Richard Aschieris, Director
Diana Baker, Finance Dir
Bill Lewicki, Finance
Michelle Bowling, Controller
Jeff Vine, Safety Mgr
EMP: 100

SQ FT: 18,000
SALES: 35.8MM Privately Held
WEB: www.stocktonport.com
SIC: 4491 4225 Waterfront terminal operation; warehousing, self-storage

(P-4763)
TOTAL INTERMODAL SERVICES INC (PA)
2396 E Sepulveda Blvd, Long Beach (90810-1943)
PHONE 562 427-6300
Fax: 562 981-6334
Amador Sanchez Jr, President
Leanne Cordoza, Manager
EMP: 50
SALES (est): 6.1MM Privately Held
WEB: www.totalintermodal.com
SIC: 4491 4213 7534 4731 Marine cargo handling; trucking, except local; tire retreading & repair shops; freight forwarding

(P-4764)
TRAPAC LLC (HQ)
630 W Harry Bridges Blvd, Wilmington (90744-5733)
P.O. Box 1178 (90748-1178)
PHONE 310 513-1572
Yoshiharu Hirakawa, CEO
Scott Axelson, President
K Kurahara, CFO
Robert Owens, Vice Pres
Dave Bendorf, Info Tech Mgr
EMP: 50
SQ FT: 50,000
SALES (est): 15.8MM
SALES (corp-wide): 14.6B Privately Held
WEB: www.trapac.com
SIC: 4491 Waterfront terminal operation
PA: Mitsui O.S.K. Lines, Ltd.
2-1-1, Toranomon
Minato-Ku TKY 105-0
335 877-017

(P-4765)
YUSEN TERMINALS INC (DH)
Also Called: Yti
701 New Dock St, San Pedro (90731-7535)
PHONE 310 548-8000
Patrick Burgoyne, CEO
Betsy Christie, CFO
Olivia Ortega, Planning Mgr
Deborah Schoonover, Executive Asst
Tracy Burdine, VP Opers
EMP: 63
SALES (est): 17.8MM
SALES (corp-wide): 19.4B Privately Held
WEB: www.yti.com
SIC: 4491 Marine terminals

4492 Towing & Tugboat

(P-4766)
CROSS LINK INC
Also Called: Westar Marine Services
Bldg C Pier 50, San Francisco (94158)
P.O. Box 78100 (94107-8100)
PHONE 415 495-3191
Mary C McMillan, CEO
Wendy Heffron-Morrow, Vice Pres
Leilani Emanuel, Accountant
Bill Capasso, Sls & Mktg Exec
EMP: 65
SQ FT: 16,000
SALES (est): 11.5MM Privately Held
SIC: 4492 Marine towing services

(P-4767)
OFFICIAL POLICE GARAGE ASSN OF
67 W Boulder Creek Rd, Simi Valley (93065-7362)
PHONE 805 624-0572
Eric Rose, Exec Dir
EMP: 800
SALES (est): 20MM Privately Held
SIC: 4492 Towing & tugboat service

(P-4768)
PACIFIC MARITIME FREIGHT INC
1512 Pier C St, Long Beach (90813-4043)
PHONE 562 590-8188

Fax: 562 590-8318
EMP: 72
SALES (corp-wide): 15.1MM Privately Held
SIC: 4492 Tugboat service
PA: Pacific Maritime Freight, Inc.
1444 Cesar E Chavez Pkwy
San Diego CA 92113
619 533-7932

(P-4769)
PACIFIC TOWBOAT & SALVAGE CO
Berth 35 Pier D, Long Beach (90802)
PHONE 562 435-0171
Fax: 562 435-1190
Steve Scalzo, President
Kayte Teeple, Manager
EMP: 85
SQ FT: 50,000
SALES (est): 3.8MM
SALES (corp-wide): 2.2B Privately Held
WEB: www.foss-maritime.com
SIC: 4492 Marine towing services
HQ: Foss Maritime Company
1151 Fairview Ave N
Seattle WA 98109
206 281-4001

4493 Marinas

(P-4770)
K N PROPERTIES INC
210 San Mateo Rd, Half Moon Bay (94019-7111)
P.O. Box 158 (94019-0158)
PHONE 650 726-4419
Keith Nerhan, Owner
EMP: 100
SALES (est): 10MM Privately Held
SIC: 4493 Marinas

(P-4771)
OAKLAND MRTIME SPPORT SVCS INC
11 Burma Rd, Oakland (94607-1010)
PHONE 510 868-1005
William Aboudi, President
Nishant Sharma, CFO
EMP: 50
SALES (est): 2.4MM Privately Held
SIC: 4493 Marinas

(P-4772)
SHELTER POINTE LLC
Also Called: Shelter Pointe Hotel & Marina
1551 Shelter Island Dr, San Diego (92106-3102)
PHONE 619 221-8000
Fax: 619 819-8101
Jeff Foster, Mng Member
EMP: 200
SALES (est): 17.8MM
SALES (corp-wide): 154.9MM Privately Held
WEB: www.shelterpointe.com
SIC: 4493 7011 7997 5812 Marinas; resort hotel; country club, membership; American restaurant; drinking places
HQ: Pacifica Hotel Company
1933 Cliff Dr Ste 1
Santa Barbara CA 93109
805 957-0095

(P-4773)
WESTREC MARINA MANAGEMENT INC
Also Called: Tower Park Marina
14900 W Highway 12 Frnt, Lodi (95242-9514)
PHONE 209 369-1041
Jeff Lewis, Manager
EMP: 60
SALES (corp-wide): 27.2MM Privately Held
WEB: www.martinez-marina.com
SIC: 4493 7299 Marinas; banquet hall facilities
HQ: Westrec Marina Management Inc
16633 Ventura Blvd Fl 6
Encino CA 91436
818 907-0400

4499 Water Transportation Svcs, NEC

(P-4774)
C & C BOATS INC
1861 Baja Vista Way, Camarillo (93010-9273)
P.O. Box 2359 (93011-2359)
PHONE 805 445-9456
Tom Croft, President
EMP: 50
SALES (est): 2.2MM Privately Held
SIC: 4499 Chartering of commercial boats

(P-4775)
GLOBAL WORLD GROUP
635 N Twin Oaks Valley Rd # 15, San Marcos (92069-1728)
PHONE 760 744-4800
Bruce Wilkinson, Principal
EMP: 99
SALES: 90K Privately Held
SIC: 4499 Water transportation services

(P-4776)
WESTSTAR MARINE SERVICES INC
50 Pier, San Francisco (94158-2193)
PHONE 415 495-3191
Mary McMillan, President
Wendy Morrow, Vice Pres
Mark Gustin, Safety Mgr
Ken Friman, Director
Dan Deforge, Port Captain
EMP: 160
SALES (est): 9.1MM Privately Held
SIC: 4499 7359 Boat & ship rental & leasing, except pleasure; equipment rental & leasing

4512 Air Transportation, Scheduled

(P-4777)
AEROFLOT RUSSIAN AIRLINES
Also Called: Aeroflot Rssina Internatl Arln
8383 Wilshire Blvd # 648, Beverly Hills (90211-2444)
PHONE 323 272-4861
Olga Alexeva, Manager
Yuriy Gregorev, Manager
EMP: 75 Privately Held
WEB: www.aeroflot.ru
SIC: 4512 Air passenger carrier, scheduled
HQ: Aeroflot, Pao
10 Ul. Arbat
Moscow 11900
495 258-0684

(P-4778)
AEROTRANSPORTE DE CARGE UNION
Also Called: Aerounion
5625 W Imperial Hwy, Los Angeles (90045-6316)
PHONE 310 649-0069
Luis Ramo, Partner
Steven Connolly, Partner
Hannia Velez, Vice Pres
Jing Zhang, Manager
EMP: 400
SALES (est): 25.4MM Privately Held
SIC: 4512 Air cargo carrier, scheduled

(P-4779)
AIR FRANCE (AIR NATIONALE)
San Francisco Intl A, San Francisco (94125)
PHONE 415 877-0179
Percy Bouloux, Branch Mgr
EMP: 51
SALES (corp-wide): 33.3MM Privately Held
WEB: www.airfrance.com
SIC: 4512 Air transportation, scheduled
PA: Air France - Klm
2 Rue Robert Esnault Pelterie
Paris 75007
143 172-098

4512 - Air Transportation, Scheduled County (P-4780)

(P-4780)
AIR NEW ZEALAND LIMITED
222 N Sepulveda Blvd # 900, El Segundo (90245-5670)
PHONE..................................310 648-7000
Fax: 310 648-7017
Roger Poulton, *Vice Pres*
Jennifer Bishop, *Officer*
Diane Stripsky, *Officer*
Eric Bimber, *Vice Pres*
Jean Eiffe, *Vice Pres*
EMP: 100
SALES (corp-wide): 3B **Privately Held**
SIC: **4512** Air transportation, scheduled
PA: Air New Zealand Limited
　　185 Fanshawe Street
　　Auckland, 1010
　　800 737-000

(P-4781)
ALASKA AIRLINES INC
Ontario Intl Arprt, Ontario (91761)
PHONE..................................800 426-0333
John Kelly, *President*
Pam Patty, *Manager*
EMP: 75
SALES (corp-wide): 5.6B **Publicly Held**
WEB: www.alaskaair.com
SIC: **4512** Air transportation, scheduled
HQ: Alaska Airlines, Inc
　　19300 International Blvd
　　Seatac WA 98188
　　206 433-3200

(P-4782)
ALASKA AIRLINES INC
300 World Way, Los Angeles (90045-5856)
PHONE..................................310 342-4401
Linn Sloper, *Manager*
EMP: 150
SALES (corp-wide): 5.6B **Publicly Held**
WEB: www.alaskaair.com
SIC: **4512** Air cargo carrier, scheduled; air passenger carrier, scheduled
HQ: Alaska Airlines, Inc
　　19300 International Blvd
　　Seatac WA 98188
　　206 433-3200

(P-4783)
ALASKA AIRLINES INC
3665 N Harbor Dr Ste 228, San Diego (92101-1039)
PHONE..................................619 238-2042
Fax: 619 543-1318
Danny Flores, *Manager*
EMP: 50
SALES (corp-wide): 5.6B **Publicly Held**
WEB: www.alaskaair.com
SIC: **4512** Air cargo carrier, scheduled; air passenger carrier, scheduled
HQ: Alaska Airlines, Inc
　　19300 International Blvd
　　Seatac WA 98188
　　206 433-3200

(P-4784)
ALASKA AIRLINES INC
1 Airport Dr Ste 24, Oakland (94621-1466)
PHONE..................................510 577-5813
Kathy Denkar, *General Mgr*
EMP: 64
SALES (corp-wide): 5.6B **Publicly Held**
WEB: www.alaskaair.com
SIC: **4512** 4729 Air cargo carrier, scheduled; air passenger carrier, scheduled; airline ticket offices
HQ: Alaska Airlines, Inc
　　19300 International Blvd
　　Seatac WA 98188
　　206 433-3200

(P-4785)
AMERICA WEST AIRLINES INC
3835 N Harbor Dr Ste 128, San Diego (92101-1081)
PHONE..................................619 231-7340
Fax: 619 238-2013
Murray Bauer, *Manager*
Kara L Smith, *Human Res Mgr*
Scott Larocco, *Manager*
EMP: 150
SALES (corp-wide): 40.9B **Publicly Held**
WEB: www.americawest.com
SIC: **4512** Air transportation, scheduled
HQ: America West Airlines, Inc.
　　4000 E Sky Harbor Blvd
　　Phoenix AZ 85034
　　480 693-0800

(P-4786)
AMERICA WEST AIRLINES INC
18601 Airport Way Ste 238, Santa Ana (92707-5204)
PHONE..................................949 852-5471
Fax: 949 252-6189
Paul Berns, *Manager*
Lary Pitts, *Manager*
EMP: 80
SALES (corp-wide): 40.9B **Publicly Held**
WEB: www.americawest.com
SIC: **4512** Air transportation, scheduled
HQ: America West Airlines, Inc.
　　4000 E Sky Harbor Blvd
　　Phoenix AZ 85034
　　480 693-0800

(P-4787)
AMERICAN AIRLINES INC
2077 Airport Blvd Ste 103, San Jose (95110-1219)
PHONE..................................408 291-3800
Fax: 408 291-5841
Lee Sims, *General Mgr*
EMP: 80
SALES (corp-wide): 40.9B **Publicly Held**
WEB: www.aa.com
SIC: **4512** Air passenger carrier, scheduled
HQ: American Airlines, Inc.
　　4333 Amon Carter Blvd
　　Fort Worth TX 76155
　　817 963-1234

(P-4788)
AMERICAN AIRLINES INC
International Airport, San Francisco (94128)
P.O. Box 8277 (94128-8277)
PHONE..................................650 877-6000
Fax: 650 877-6225
Phillip Bock, *Manager*
Anthony Shiao, *Human Res Mgr*
EMP: 450
SQ FT: 4,000
SALES (corp-wide): 40.9B **Publicly Held**
WEB: www.aa.com
SIC: **4512** Air passenger carrier, scheduled
HQ: American Airlines, Inc.
　　4333 Amon Carter Blvd
　　Fort Worth TX 76155
　　817 963-1234

(P-4789)
AMERICAN AIRLINES INC
Also Called: AMR
5950 Avion Dr, Los Angeles (90045-5682)
PHONE..................................310 215-7054
Fax: 310 417-2725
EMP: 228
SALES (corp-wide): 40.9B **Publicly Held**
WEB: www.aa.com
SIC: **4512** Air cargo carrier, scheduled
HQ: American Airlines, Inc.
　　4333 Amon Carter Blvd
　　Fort Worth TX 76155
　　817 963-1234

(P-4790)
AMERICAN AIRLINES INC
Also Called: US Airways
3400 E Tahqtz Cyn Way # 12, Palm Springs (92262-6966)
PHONE..................................760 778-2878
Brandy Lavato, *Principal*
EMP: 55
SALES (corp-wide): 40.9B **Publicly Held**
SIC: **4512** Air passenger carrier, scheduled
HQ: American Airlines, Inc.
　　4333 Amon Carter Blvd
　　Fort Worth TX 76155
　　817 963-1234

(P-4791)
AMERICAN AIRLINES INC
18601 Airport Way Ste 213, Santa Ana (92707-5219)
PHONE..................................949 852-5470
Fax: 949 852-5369
Catherine Connolly, *Branch Mgr*
EMP: 250
SALES (corp-wide): 40.9B **Publicly Held**
WEB: www.aa.com
SIC: **4512** Air transportation, scheduled
HQ: American Airlines, Inc.
　　4333 Amon Carter Blvd
　　Fort Worth TX 76155
　　817 963-1234

(P-4792)
AMERICAN AIRLINES INC
Also Called: US Airways
7183 World Way W, Los Angeles (90045-5824)
PHONE..................................310 646-3013
George Knoblock, *Branch Mgr*
Bill Baggelaar, *Manager*
EMP: 175
SALES (corp-wide): 40.9B **Publicly Held**
WEB: www.usair.com
SIC: **4512** Air transportation, scheduled
HQ: American Airlines, Inc.
　　4333 Amon Carter Blvd
　　Fort Worth TX 76155
　　817 963-1234

(P-4793)
AMERICAN AIRLINES GROUP INC
3543 Carlisle St, Perris (92571-7303)
PHONE..................................310 251-9184
Susie Kimball, *Principal*
EMP: 658
SALES (corp-wide): 40.9B **Publicly Held**
SIC: **4512** Air passenger carrier, scheduled
PA: American Airlines Group Inc.
　　4333 Amon Carter Blvd
　　Fort Worth TX 76155
　　817 963-1234

(P-4794)
AMERIFLIGHT LLC
21889 Skywest Dr, Hayward (94541-7021)
PHONE..................................510 569-6000
EMP: 57
SALES (corp-wide): 183.1MM **Privately Held**
SIC: **4512**
PA: Ameriflight, Llc
　　4700 W Empire Ave
　　Burbank CA 75261
　　818 847-0000

(P-4795)
ASIANA AIRLINES INC
3530 Wilshire Blvd # 1700, Los Angeles (90010-2341)
PHONE..................................213 365-2000
Fax: 213 365-9630
Young Doo Yoon, *CEO*
Chan Bup Park, *President*
Dong N Choi, *Senior VP*
S Kang, *Vice Pres*
Jerry Chuang, *General Mgr*
EMP: 250
SALES (est): 39.4MM **Privately Held**
SIC: **4512** Air cargo carrier, scheduled

(P-4796)
CHINA AIRLINES LTD (HQ)
11201 Aviation Blvd, Los Angeles (90045-6100)
PHONE..................................310 646-4233
Fax: 310 641-3233
Huang Hsiang Sun, *President*
Yu-Kuang Yu, *Human Res Mgr*
David Tang, *Opers Mgr*
Jenny Huang, *Marketing Mgr*
Jeff Hu, *Marketing Staff*
EMP: 145
SALES (est): 34.4MM
SALES (corp-wide): 4.4B **Privately Held**
SIC: **4512** Air transportation, scheduled
PA: China Airlines Ltd.
　　1, Hang Zhan S. Rd.,
　　Taoyuan City TAY 33758
　　339 988-88

(P-4797)
CNC WORLDWIDE INC
5343 W Imperial Hwy # 300, Los Angeles (90045-6241)
PHONE..................................310 670-1222
Fax: 310 670-1556
Henry Kim, *President*
EMP: 100
SALES (est): 9.3MM **Privately Held**
WEB: www.cncworldwide.com
SIC: **4512** Air cargo carrier, scheduled

(P-4798)
DELTA AIR LINES INC
Also Called: Delta Airlines
500 World Way, Los Angeles (90045-5891)
P.O. Box 90676 (90009-0676)
PHONE..................................323 417-7374
Dick Cassella, *Manager*
EMP: 64
SALES (corp-wide): 40.7B **Publicly Held**
WEB: www.delta.com
SIC: **4512** Air transportation, scheduled
PA: Delta Air Lines, Inc.
　　1030 Delta Blvd
　　Atlanta GA 30354
　　404 715-2600

(P-4799)
ENVOY AIR INC
Also Called: AMR Eagle
3707 N Harbor Dr Ste 103, San Diego (92101-1068)
PHONE..................................619 231-5452
Robert Stewart, *Manager*
EMP: 300
SALES (corp-wide): 40.9B **Publicly Held**
WEB: www.americanair.com
SIC: **4512** Air transportation, scheduled
HQ: Envoy Air Inc.
　　4301 Regent Blvd
　　Irving TX 75063
　　972 374-5200

(P-4800)
FEDERAL EXPRESS CORPORATION
Also Called: Fedex
11340 Sherman Way, Sun Valley (91352-4944)
PHONE..................................800 463-3339
Rus Bronson, *Manager*
George Ladd, *Technology*
EMP: 135
SALES (corp-wide): 50.3B **Publicly Held**
WEB: www.federalexpress.com
SIC: **4512** 4513 4215 Air transportation, scheduled; air courier services; courier services, except by air
HQ: Federal Express Corporation
　　3610 Hacks Cross Rd
　　Memphis TN 38125
　　901 369-3600

(P-4801)
FEDERAL EXPRESS CORPORATION
Also Called: Fedex
1500 Nichols Dr, Rocklin (95765-1310)
PHONE..................................800 463-3339
Nick Drikas, *Manager*
EMP: 122
SALES (corp-wide): 50.3B **Publicly Held**
WEB: www.federalexpress.com
SIC: **4512** Air cargo carrier, scheduled
HQ: Federal Express Corporation
　　3610 Hacks Cross Rd
　　Memphis TN 38125
　　901 369-3600

(P-4802)
FEDERAL EXPRESS CORPORATION
Also Called: Fedex
1111 Bird Center Dr, Palm Springs (92262-8000)
PHONE..................................800 463-3339
EMP: 122
SALES (corp-wide): 50.3B **Publicly Held**
WEB: www.federalexpress.com
SIC: **4512** Air cargo carrier, scheduled
HQ: Federal Express Corporation
　　3610 Hacks Cross Rd
　　Memphis TN 38125
　　901 369-3600

(P-4803)
FEDERAL EXPRESS CORPORATION
Also Called: Fedex
2601 Main St Ste 1000, Irvine (92614-4233)
PHONE..................................949 862-4500

PRODUCTS & SERVICES SECTION
4512 - Air Transportation, Scheduled County (P-4826)

EMP: 120
SALES (corp-wide): 47.4B **Publicly Held**
SIC: 4512 4513
HQ: Federal Express Corporation
 3610 Hacks Cross Rd
 Memphis TN 38125
 901 369-3600

(P-4804)
HAWAIIAN AIRLINES INC
200 World Way Ste 9, Los Angeles (90045-5844)
PHONE..................310 417-1677
Lisa Jones, *General Mgr*
EMP: 55
SALES (corp-wide): 2.3B **Publicly Held**
WEB: www.hawaiianair.com
SIC: 4512 Air passenger carrier, scheduled
HQ: Hawaiian Airlines, Inc.
 3375 Koapaka St Ste G350
 Honolulu HI 96819
 808 835-3700

(P-4805)
JET AIRWAYS OF INDIA INC
111 Anza Blvd Ste 300, Burlingame (94010-1917)
PHONE..................650 762-2345
Victoriano P Dungca, *President*
Brinda Bermubez, *Accountant*
Gordana Onica, *Supervisor*
EMP: 70
SALES (est): 4.3MM **Privately Held**
SIC: 4512 Air passenger carrier, scheduled

(P-4806)
JETBLUE AIRWAYS CORPORATION
Also Called: Burbank Bob Hope Airport
2627 N Hollywood Way, Burbank (91505-1062)
PHONE..................718 286-7900
Tom Greer, *Branch Mgr*
Ed Rettberg, *Officer*
Brent Devey, *Supervisor*
Kevin Loiseau, *Supervisor*
Gonzalo Mayo, *Supervisor*
EMP: 77
SALES (corp-wide): 6.4B **Publicly Held**
SIC: 4512 Air passenger carrier, scheduled
PA: Jetblue Airways Corporation
 2701 Queens Plz N
 Long Island City NY 11101
 718 286-7900

(P-4807)
JETBLUE AIRWAYS CORPORATION
130 Alan Shepard Way M, Oakland (94621-4501)
PHONE..................510 381-1369
Pat Rounds, *Human Resources*
EMP: 81
SALES (corp-wide): 6.4B **Publicly Held**
SIC: 4512 Air passenger carrier, scheduled
PA: Jetblue Airways Corporation
 2701 Queens Plz N
 Long Island City NY 11101
 718 286-7900

(P-4808)
JETBLUE AIRWAYS CORPORATION
3835 N Harbor Dr Ste 108, San Diego (92101-1059)
PHONE..................619 725-0807
EMP: 81
SALES (corp-wide): 6.4B **Publicly Held**
SIC: 4512 Air passenger carrier, scheduled
PA: Jetblue Airways Corporation
 2701 Queens Plz N
 Long Island City NY 11101
 718 286-7900

(P-4809)
KOREAN AIR LINES CO LTD
380 World Way Ste S4, Los Angeles (90045-5847)
PHONE..................310 646-4866
Fax: 310 417-5026
Min Choi, *Vice Pres*
Joanna Kim, *Administration*
Ann Park, *Deputy Dir*
EMP: 175
SALES (corp-wide): 9.9B **Privately Held**
WEB: www.laxda.koreanair.com
SIC: 4512 Air transportation, scheduled
PA: Korean Air Lines Co., Ltd.
 260 Haneul-Gil, Gangseo-Gu
 Seoul SEO 07505
 519 705-795

(P-4810)
KOREAN AIRLINES
380 World Way, Los Angeles (90045-5800)
PHONE..................310 417-5294
Tom Bradley, *Manager*
EMP: 175
SALES (corp-wide): 9.9B **Privately Held**
WEB: www.laxda.koreanair.com
SIC: 4512 Air transportation, scheduled
PA: Korean Air Lines Co., Ltd.
 260 Haneul-Gil, Gangseo-Gu
 Seoul SEO 07505
 519 705-795

(P-4811)
KOREAN AIRLINES
800 Airport Blvd Ste 506, Burlingame (94010-1930)
PHONE..................650 375-7123
Won MA, *Principal*
Jennifer Eom, *Marketing Staff*
EMP: 175
SALES (corp-wide): 9.9B **Privately Held**
SIC: 4512 Air passenger carrier, scheduled
PA: Korean Air Lines Co., Ltd.
 260 Haneul-Gil, Gangseo-Gu
 Seoul SEO 07505
 519 705-795

(P-4812)
KOREAN AIRLINES CO LTD
Also Called: Korean Arln Crgo Reservations
6101 W Imperial Hwy, Los Angeles (90045-6305)
PHONE..................310 410-2000
Fax: 310 337-0762
Jinkul Lee, *President*
Jong Myung Park, *Treasurer*
Kim Gon, *Exec VP*
Kim Sik, *Executive*
Lee SOO, *Executive*
EMP: 250
SALES (corp-wide): 9.9B **Privately Held**
WEB: www.laxda.koreanair.com
SIC: 4512 4513 Air transportation, scheduled; package delivery, private air
PA: Korean Air Lines Co., Ltd.
 260 Haneul-Gil, Gangseo-Gu
 Seoul SEO 07505
 519 705-795

(P-4813)
KOREAN AIRLINES CO LTD
1813 Wilshire Blvd # 400, Los Angeles (90057-3600)
PHONE..................213 484-1900
Fax: 213 484-5757
Kyung Kim, *Branch Mgr*
Dong OH, *Officer*
Jong C Kim, *Vice Pres*
Kim J Nam, *Vice Pres*
Jung J Bae, *General Mgr*
EMP: 100
SALES (corp-wide): 9.9B **Privately Held**
WEB: www.laxda.koreanair.com
SIC: 4512 4729 Air transportation, scheduled; airline ticket offices
PA: Korean Air Lines Co., Ltd.
 260 Haneul-Gil, Gangseo-Gu
 Seoul SEO 07505
 519 705-795

(P-4814)
LUFTHNSA CRGO AKTNGESELLSCHAFT
5721 W Imperial Hwy, Los Angeles (90045-6301)
PHONE..................310 242-2590
Veli Polat, *President*
Sabry Buhary, *Manager*
EMP: 150
SALES (est): 7.9MM
SALES (corp-wide): 34.4B **Privately Held**
SIC: 4512 Air passenger carrier, scheduled
HQ: Lufthansa Cargo Ag
 Frankfurt Flughafen
 Frankfurt Am Main 60549
 696 960-

(P-4815)
LUKENBILL ENTERPRISES
Also Called: Sky King
3600 Power Inn Rd Ste H, Sacramento (95826-3826)
PHONE..................916 454-2400
Fax: 916 266-0855
Greg Lukenbill, *Partner*
EMP: 100
SQ FT: 12,000
SALES (est): 7.6MM **Privately Held**
SIC: 4512 6531 Air transportation, scheduled; real estate agents & managers

(P-4816)
PHILIPPINE AIRLINES
11001 Aviation Blvd, Los Angeles (90045-6123)
PHONE..................310 646-1981
CHI Marquec, *Branch Mgr*
EMP: 65 **Privately Held**
WEB: www.pal.com
SIC: 4512 Air passenger carrier, scheduled
HQ: Philippine Airlines, Inc.
 8th Floor Pnb Financial Centre
 Pasay 1300
 277 759-95

(P-4817)
PHILIPPINE AIRLINES INC
447 Sutter St Ste 200, San Francisco (94108-4636)
PHONE..................415 217-3100
Fax: 415 391-3967
Rodolfo Llora, *Branch Mgr*
Manuel Palomo, *Manager*
EMP: 150 **Privately Held**
WEB: www.pal.com
SIC: 4512 8741 4513 Air passenger carrier, scheduled; management services; package delivery, private air
HQ: Philippine Airlines, Inc.
 8th Floor Pnb Financial Centre
 Pasay 1300
 277 759-95

(P-4818)
POLAR AIR CARGO LP
100 Oceangate Fl 15, Long Beach (90802-4347)
PHONE..................310 568-4551
Fax: 562 436-9333
Edwin H Wallace, *Partner*
Polar Air Cargo, *General Ptnr*
Mark West, *Partner*
Jill Muckenthaler, *Controller*
Tony Werner, *VP Mktg*
EMP: 480
SALES (est): 17.7MM
SALES (corp-wide): 1.8B **Publicly Held**
SIC: 4512 Air cargo carrier, scheduled
PA: Atlas Air Worldwide Holdings, Inc.
 2000 Westchester Ave
 Purchase NY 10577
 914 701-8000

(P-4819)
SINGAPORE AIRLINES CARGO PTE
710 Mcdonald Rd, San Francisco (94128)
P.O. Box 280746 (94128-0746)
PHONE..................650 876-7363
Lee Liik Hsin, *CEO*
EMP: 60
SQ FT: 60,000
SALES (est): 6.8MM **Privately Held**
SIC: 4512 Air cargo carrier, scheduled

(P-4820)
SINGAPORE AIRLINES LIMITED
222 N Sepulveda Blvd # 1600, El Segundo (90245-5615)
PHONE..................310 647-1922
Fax: 323 934-4482
Tee Hooi Teoh, *Manager*
Paula Harrall, *Officer*
Victor Lim, *Officer*
Tarulatha Raj, *Officer*
Lilian Tan, *Officer*
EMP: 135 **Privately Held**
WEB: www.singaporeair.com
SIC: 4512 Air cargo carrier, scheduled
HQ: Singapore Airlines Limited
 25 Airline Road
 Singapore 81982
 654 110-85

(P-4821)
SKYWEST AIRLINES INC
32128 Chagall Ct, Winchester (92596-9024)
PHONE..................951 926-9511
EMP: 75
SALES (corp-wide): 3.5B **Publicly Held**
SIC: 4512
HQ: Skywest Airlines, Inc.
 444 S River Rd
 St George UT 84790
 435 634-3000

(P-4822)
SKYWEST AIRLINES INC
26818 Bahama Way, Murrieta (92563-2553)
PHONE..................951 600-9181
EMP: 75
SALES (corp-wide): 3.1B **Publicly Held**
SIC: 4512 7389 Air passenger carrier, scheduled;
HQ: Skywest Airlines, Inc.
 444 S River Rd
 St George UT 84790
 435 634-3000

(P-4823)
SOUTHWEST AIRLINES CO
1 Airport Dr Ste 25, Oakland (94621-1432)
PHONE..................510 563-1000
Teddy Rowell, *Manager*
Robert Alderete, *Manager*
Steve Bernhart, *Manager*
EMP: 75
SALES (corp-wide): 19.8B **Publicly Held**
WEB: www.southwest.com
SIC: 4512 Air passenger carrier, scheduled
PA: Southwest Airlines Co.
 2702 Love Field Dr
 Dallas TX 75235
 214 792-4000

(P-4824)
SOUTHWEST AIRLINES CO
3665 N Harbor Dr Ste 216, San Diego (92101-1038)
PHONE..................619 231-7345
Cheryl Black, *Branch Mgr*
EMP: 255
SQ FT: 11,137
SALES (corp-wide): 19.8B **Publicly Held**
WEB: www.southwest.com
SIC: 4512 Air passenger carrier, scheduled
PA: Southwest Airlines Co.
 2702 Love Field Dr
 Dallas TX 75235
 214 792-4000

(P-4825)
SOUTHWEST AIRLINES CO
100 World Way Ste 328, Los Angeles (90045-5854)
PHONE..................310 665-5700
Fax: 310 670-0723
Chris Johnson, *Sales/Mktg Mgr*
Larry Pitts, *Sales Executive*
EMP: 70
SALES (corp-wide): 19.8B **Publicly Held**
WEB: www.southwest.com
SIC: 4512 4581 Air passenger carrier, scheduled; airports, flying fields & services
PA: Southwest Airlines Co.
 2702 Love Field Dr
 Dallas TX 75235
 214 792-4000

(P-4826)
SOUTHWEST AIRLINES CO
10 Alan Shepard Way, Oakland (94621-4501)
PHONE..................510 563-1234
John Mactherson, *Manager*
John Minor, *Manager*
EMP: 105
SALES (corp-wide): 19.8B **Publicly Held**
WEB: www.southwest.com
SIC: 4512 Air passenger carrier, scheduled
PA: Southwest Airlines Co.
 2702 Love Field Dr
 Dallas TX 75235
 214 792-4000

4512 - Air Transportation, Scheduled County (P-4827)

PRODUCTS & SERVICES SECTION

(P-4827)
UNITED AIRLINES INC
United Airlines Mnt Optnb, San Francisco (94128)
PHONE..................................650 634-4209
Bill Norman, *Vice Pres*
Haosheng Wu, *Engineer*
Paul Wyman, *Senior Engr*
Bess Roces, *Asst Mgr*
EMP: 102
SALES (corp-wide): 37.8B **Publicly Held**
WEB: www.united.com
SIC: **4512** Air transportation, scheduled
HQ: United Airlines, Inc.
233 S Wacker Dr Ste 430
Chicago IL 60606
872 825-4000

(P-4828)
UNITED AIRLINES INC
Also Called: Continental Airlines
1661 Airport Blvd, San Jose (95110-1216)
PHONE..................................408 294-4028
Fax: 408 277-5616
Al Camacho, *Manager*
EMP: 61
SALES (corp-wide): 37.8B **Publicly Held**
SIC: **4512** Air passenger carrier, scheduled
HQ: United Airlines, Inc.
233 S Wacker Dr Ste 430
Chicago IL 60606
872 825-4000

(P-4829)
UNITED AIRLINES INC
2435 Whitman Way, San Bruno (94066-3852)
PHONE..................................650 634-2468
Lon Wildurin, *Manager*
Duane Goldman, *Buyer*
EMP: 101
SALES (corp-wide): 37.8B **Publicly Held**
WEB: www.united.com
SIC: **4512** Air passenger carrier, scheduled
HQ: United Airlines, Inc.
233 S Wacker Dr Ste 430
Chicago IL 60606
872 825-4000

(P-4830)
UNITED AIRLINES INC
6018 Avion Dr, Los Angeles (90045-5679)
PHONE..................................310 342-8086
Don Nelson, *Office Mgr*
EMP: 102
SALES (corp-wide): 37.8B **Publicly Held**
SIC: **4512** Air passenger carrier, scheduled
HQ: United Airlines, Inc.
233 S Wacker Dr Ste 430
Chicago IL 60606
872 825-4000

(P-4831)
UNITED AIRLINES INC
Maintenance Operation Ctr, San Francisco (94128)
PHONE..................................650 634-7800
D K Loo, *Director*
Torya Koger, *Manager*
Patrick Duffy, *Supervisor*
EMP: 60
SALES (corp-wide): 37.8B **Publicly Held**
WEB: www.united.com
SIC: **4512** Air transportation, scheduled
HQ: United Airlines, Inc.
233 S Wacker Dr Ste 430
Chicago IL 60606
872 825-4000

(P-4832)
UNITED AIRLINES INC
700 World Way Ste I, Los Angeles (90045-5846)
PHONE..................................310 646-3107
Barry Batson, *Branch Mgr*
EMP: 102
SALES (corp-wide): 37.8B **Publicly Held**
WEB: www.united.com
SIC: **4512** Air transportation, scheduled
HQ: United Airlines, Inc.
233 S Wacker Dr Ste 430
Chicago IL 60606
872 825-4000

(P-4833)
UNITED AIRLINES INC
3835 N Harbor Dr Ste 115, San Diego (92101-1081)
PHONE..................................619 692-3310
Fax: 619 231-5688
Al Turner, *Manager*
James Baldwin, *Manager*
EMP: 140
SQ FT: 80,705
SALES (corp-wide): 37.8B **Publicly Held**
WEB: www.united.com
SIC: **4512** Air transportation, scheduled
HQ: United Airlines, Inc.
233 S Wacker Dr Ste 430
Chicago IL 60606
872 825-4000

(P-4834)
UNITED AIRLINES INC
Also Called: Continental Airlines
7300 World Way W Rm 144, Los Angeles (90045-5829)
PHONE..................................310 258-3319
Fax: 310 646-4835
Ken Jaminson, *Manager*
Louis Fiallos, *Manager*
EMP: 275
SALES (corp-wide): 37.8B **Publicly Held**
WEB: www.continental.com
SIC: **4512** Air passenger carrier, scheduled
HQ: United Airlines, Inc.
233 S Wacker Dr Ste 430
Chicago IL 60606
872 825-4000

(P-4835)
UNITED AIRLINES INC
San Francisco Intl Arprt, San Francisco (94128)
PHONE..................................650 634-4469
Fax: 650 634-4919
Daniel Cummins, *Manager*
Adam Calmis, *Senior Mgr*
Gil Shaw, *Manager*
EMP: 102
SALES (corp-wide): 37.8B **Publicly Held**
WEB: www.united.com
SIC: **4512** Air passenger carrier, scheduled
HQ: United Airlines, Inc.
233 S Wacker Dr Ste 430
Chicago IL 60606
872 825-4000

(P-4836)
UNITED AIRLINES INC
3400 E Tahquitz Cyn 17, Palm Springs (92262-6920)
PHONE..................................760 778-5690
Fax: 760 778-2846
Peg James, *Manager*
EMP: 57
SALES (corp-wide): 37.8B **Publicly Held**
WEB: www.united.com
SIC: **4512** Air passenger carrier, scheduled
HQ: United Airlines, Inc.
233 S Wacker Dr Ste 430
Chicago IL 60606
872 825-4000

(P-4837)
UNITED AIRLINES INC
545 Mcdonald Rd 68305, San Francisco (94128)
PHONE..................................650 634-2772
DK Loo, *Branch Mgr*
EMP: 101
SALES (corp-wide): 37.8B **Publicly Held**
SIC: **4512** Air transportation, scheduled
HQ: United Airlines, Inc.
233 S Wacker Dr Ste 430
Chicago IL 60606
872 825-4000

(P-4838)
UNITED COURIERS INC (DH)
Also Called: U C I Distribution Plus
3280 E Foothill Blvd, Pasadena (91107-3103)
PHONE..................................213 383-3611
Stephan Cretier, *CEO*
Richard R Irvin, *President*
Robert G Irvin, *Treasurer*
Dennis Love, *Controller*
EMP: 200
SQ FT: 25,000
SALES (est): 27.8MM
SALES (corp-wide): 1.3B **Privately Held**
WEB: www.unitedcouriers.net
SIC: **4512** 4215 4212 7381 Air cargo carrier, scheduled; courier services, except by air; local trucking, without storage; armored car services; freight forwarding
HQ: Ati Systems International, Inc.
2000 Nw Corp Blvd Ste 101
Boca Raton FL 33431
561 939-7000

(P-4839)
VIRGIN AMERICA INC (PA)
555 Airport Blvd Ste 400, Burlingame (94010-2036)
PHONE..................................877 359-8474
C David Cush, *President*
Donald J Carty, *Ch of Bd*
Samuel K Skinner, *Vice Chairman*
Stephen A Forte, *COO*
Peter D Hunt, *CFO*
EMP: 225
SQ FT: 85,674
SALES: 1.5B **Publicly Held**
WEB: www.virginamerica.com
SIC: **4512** Air passenger carrier, scheduled

(P-4840)
WORLDWIDE FLIGHT SERVICES INC
Also Called: Wfs
5758 W Century Blvd, Los Angeles (90045-5613)
P.O. Box 90220 (90009-0220)
PHONE..................................310 342-7830
John OH, *Branch Mgr*
EMP: 120
SALES (corp-wide): 2.2B **Privately Held**
SIC: **4512** Air cargo carrier, scheduled
PA: Worldwide Flight Services, Inc.
1925 W John Carpenter Fwy # 450
Irving TX 75063
972 629-5001

4513 Air Courier Svcs

(P-4841)
CEVA FREIGHT LLC
Also Called: Ceva Ocean Line
19600 S Western Ave, Torrance (90501-1117)
PHONE..................................310 972-5500
Randy Mondello, *Vice Pres*
Claire Glass, *Export Mgr*
EMP: 80 **Publicly Held**
WEB: www.tntlogistics.com
SIC: **4513** Air courier services
HQ: Ceva Freight, Llc
15350 Vickery Dr
Houston TX 77032
281 618-3100

(P-4842)
DHL EXPRESS (USA) INC
401 23rd St, San Francisco (94107-3102)
PHONE..................................415 826-7338
Jeffrey Funk, *Manager*
Marsten Tullius, *Manager*
EMP: 70
SALES (corp-wide): 63.6B **Privately Held**
SIC: **4513** Air courier services
HQ: Dhl Express (Usa), Inc.
1210 S Pine Island Rd
Plantation FL 33324
954 888-7000

(P-4843)
EXPRESS MESSENGER SYSTEMS INC
Also Called: Ontrac
4603 N Brawley Ave # 103, Fresno (93722-3960)
PHONE..................................559 277-4910
Jim Dugan, *Branch Mgr*
Mike Erb, *Manager*
EMP: 56
SALES (corp-wide): 706.7MM **Privately Held**
WEB: www.calover.com
SIC: **4513** Package delivery, private air
PA: Express Messenger Systems, Inc.
2501 S Price Rd Ste 201
Chandler AZ 85286
800 334-5000

(P-4844)
FEDERAL EXPRESS CORPORATION
Also Called: Fedex
3541 Regional Pkwy, Petaluma (94954)
PHONE..................................800 463-3339
EMP: 80
SALES (corp-wide): 47.4B **Publicly Held**
SIC: **4513**
HQ: Federal Express Corporation
3610 Hacks Cross Rd
Memphis TN 38125
901 369-3600

(P-4845)
FEDERAL EXPRESS CORPORATION
Also Called: Fedex
1650 47th St, San Diego (92102-2508)
PHONE..................................800 463-3339
John Staback, *Manager*
EMP: 225
SALES (corp-wide): 50.3B **Publicly Held**
WEB: www.federalexpress.com
SIC: **4513** Air courier services
HQ: Federal Express Corporation
3610 Hacks Cross Rd
Memphis TN 38125
901 369-3600

(P-4846)
FEDERAL EXPRESS CORPORATION
Also Called: Fedex
1330 Fortress St, Chico (95973-9031)
PHONE..................................800 463-3339
EMP: 109
SALES (corp-wide): 50.3B **Publicly Held**
SIC: **4513** Air courier services
HQ: Federal Express Corporation
3610 Hacks Cross Rd
Memphis TN 38125
901 369-3600

(P-4847)
FEDERAL EXPRESS CORPORATION
Also Called: Fedex
1286 Lawrence Station Rd, Sunnyvale (94089-2220)
PHONE..................................800 463-3339
Gail Caldwell, *Branch Mgr*
EMP: 100
SALES (corp-wide): 50.3B **Publicly Held**
WEB: www.federalexpress.com
SIC: **4513** 4215 Letter delivery, private air; package delivery, private air; parcel delivery, private air; courier services, except by air
HQ: Federal Express Corporation
3610 Hacks Cross Rd
Memphis TN 38125
901 369-3600

(P-4848)
FEDERAL EXPRESS CORPORATION
Also Called: Fedex
12600 Prairie Ave, Hawthorne (90250-4685)
PHONE..................................800 463-3339
Ted Strong, *Branch Mgr*
Jessica Brumbly, *Manager*
EMP: 200
SALES (corp-wide): 50.3B **Publicly Held**
WEB: www.federalexpress.com
SIC: **4513** 4215 Air courier services; courier services, except by air
HQ: Federal Express Corporation
3610 Hacks Cross Rd
Memphis TN 38125
901 369-3600

(P-4849)
FEDERAL EXPRESS CORPORATION
Also Called: Fedex
1650 Sunflower Ave, Costa Mesa (92626-1513)
PHONE..................................800 463-3339

PRODUCTS & SERVICES SECTION

4513 - Air Courier Svcs County (P-4871)

Mike Stanley, *Manager*
EMP: 53
SQ FT: 75,000
SALES (corp-wide): 50.3B **Publicly Held**
WEB: www.federalexpress.com
SIC: 4513 Air courier services
HQ: Federal Express Corporation
3610 Hacks Cross Rd
Memphis TN 38125
901 369-3600

(P-4850)
FEDERAL EXPRESS CORPORATION
Also Called: Fedex
1601 Aurora Dr, San Leandro (94577-3101)
PHONE 510 347-2430
EMP: 130
SALES (corp-wide): 47.4B **Publicly Held**
SIC: 4513 4215
HQ: Federal Express Corporation
3610 Hacks Cross Rd
Memphis TN 38125
901 369-3600

(P-4851)
FEDERAL EXPRESS CORPORATION
Also Called: Fedex
1 Lower Ragsdale Dr # 4, Monterey (93940-5757)
PHONE 800 463-3339
Mike Luders, *Manager*
Don Bailey, *General Mgr*
Dave Cox, *General Mgr*
Marce Gatdula, *Facilities Mgr*
EMP: 60
SALES (corp-wide): 50.3B **Publicly Held**
WEB: www.federalexpress.com
SIC: 4513 Package delivery, private air
HQ: Federal Express Corporation
3610 Hacks Cross Rd
Memphis TN 38125
901 369-3600

(P-4852)
FEDERAL EXPRESS CORPORATION
Also Called: Fedex
8455 Pardee Dr, Oakland (94621-1411)
PHONE 800 463-3339
Fax: 510 635-8714
Ron Fraser, *Manager*
EMP: 100
SALES (corp-wide): 50.3B **Publicly Held**
WEB: www.federalexpress.com
SIC: 4513 4215 Letter delivery, private air; package delivery, private air; parcel delivery, private air; courier services, except by air
HQ: Federal Express Corporation
3610 Hacks Cross Rd
Memphis TN 38125
901 369-3600

(P-4853)
FEDERAL EXPRESS CORPORATION
Also Called: Fedex
500 12th St Ste 139, Oakland (94607-4010)
PHONE 510 465-5209
EMP: 107
SALES (corp-wide): 47.4B **Publicly Held**
SIC: 4513
HQ: Federal Express Corporation
3610 Hacks Cross Rd
Memphis TN 38125
901 369-3600

(P-4854)
FEDERAL EXPRESS CORPORATION
Also Called: Fedex
6775 Woodrum Cir, Redding (96002-9386)
PHONE 800 463-3339
Craig McLaughlin, *Manager*
EMP: 150
SALES (corp-wide): 50.3B **Publicly Held**
WEB: www.federalexpress.com
SIC: 4513 4215 Letter delivery, private air; package delivery, private air; parcel delivery, private air; package delivery, vehicular

HQ: Federal Express Corporation
3610 Hacks Cross Rd
Memphis TN 38125
901 369-3600

(P-4855)
FEDERAL EXPRESS CORPORATION
Also Called: Fedex
935 Performance Dr, Stockton (95206-4930)
PHONE 800 463-3339
Val Thomas, *Principal*
EMP: 50
SALES (corp-wide): 50.3B **Publicly Held**
SIC: 4513 Package delivery, private air; letter delivery, private air
HQ: Federal Express Corporation
3610 Hacks Cross Rd
Memphis TN 38125
901 369-3600

(P-4856)
FEDERAL EXPRESS CORPORATION
Also Called: Fedex
9339 Ann St, Santa Fe Springs (90670-2655)
PHONE 800 463-3339
Doug Sander, *Branch Mgr*
EMP: 100
SALES (corp-wide): 50.3B **Publicly Held**
WEB: www.federalexpress.com
SIC: 4513 Package delivery, private air; letter delivery, private air
HQ: Federal Express Corporation
3610 Hacks Cross Rd
Memphis TN 38125
901 369-3600

(P-4857)
FEDERAL EXPRESS CORPORATION
Also Called: Fedex
9510 W Airport Dr, Visalia (93277-9501)
PHONE 800 463-3339
Richard Keeling, *Branch Mgr*
EMP: 150
SALES (corp-wide): 50.3B **Publicly Held**
WEB: www.federalexpress.com
SIC: 4513 Package delivery, private air; letter delivery, private air
HQ: Federal Express Corporation
3610 Hacks Cross Rd
Memphis TN 38125
901 369-3600

(P-4858)
FEDERAL EXPRESS CORPORATION
Also Called: Fedex
2060 S Wineville Ave B, Ontario (91761-3633)
PHONE 909 390-3237
EMP: 60
SALES (corp-wide): 47.4B **Publicly Held**
SIC: 4513
HQ: Federal Express Corporation
3610 Hacks Cross Rd
Memphis TN 38125
901 369-3600

(P-4859)
FEDERAL EXPRESS CORPORATION
Also Called: Fedex
2500 Kimberly Ave, Fullerton (92831-5142)
PHONE 800 463-3339
Kim Cooper, *Branch Mgr*
EMP: 130
SALES (corp-wide): 50.3B **Publicly Held**
WEB: www.federalexpress.com
SIC: 4513 Letter delivery, private air; package delivery, private air; parcel delivery, private air
HQ: Federal Express Corporation
3610 Hacks Cross Rd
Memphis TN 38125
901 369-3600

(P-4860)
FEDERAL EXPRESS CORPORATION
Also Called: Fedex
3150 Paseo Mercado, Oxnard (93036-8918)
PHONE 800 463-3339
Bert Hawkins, *Director*
EMP: 70
SALES (corp-wide): 50.3B **Publicly Held**
WEB: www.federalexpress.com
SIC: 4513 Letter delivery, private air; package delivery, private air; parcel delivery, private air
HQ: Federal Express Corporation
3610 Hacks Cross Rd
Memphis TN 38125
901 369-3600

(P-4861)
FEDERAL EXPRESS CORPORATION
Also Called: Fedex
8950 Cal Center Dr # 370, Sacramento (95826-3262)
PHONE 916 361-5500
EMP: 100
SALES (corp-wide): 47.4B **Publicly Held**
SIC: 4513 4512 4212 4213
HQ: Federal Express Corporation
3610 Hacks Cross Rd
Memphis TN 38125
901 369-3600

(P-4862)
FEDERAL EXPRESS CORPORATION
Also Called: Fedex
1875 Marin St, San Francisco (94124-1139)
PHONE 800 463-3339
EMP: 109
SALES (corp-wide): 50.3B **Publicly Held**
WEB: www.federalexpress.com
SIC: 4513 4512 4522 4213 Air courier services; air transportation, scheduled; air transportation, nonscheduled; trucking, except local
HQ: Federal Express Corporation
3610 Hacks Cross Rd
Memphis TN 38125
901 369-3600

(P-4863)
FEDERAL EXPRESS CORPORATION
Also Called: Fedex
2451 N Palm Dr, Long Beach (90755-4006)
PHONE 800 463-3339
EMP: 150
SALES (corp-wide): 47.4B **Publicly Held**
SIC: 4513
HQ: Federal Express Corporation
3610 Hacks Cross Rd
Memphis TN 38125
901 369-3600

(P-4864)
FEDERAL EXPRESS CORPORATION
Also Called: Fedex
1 World Trade Ctr Ste 191, Long Beach (90831-0191)
PHONE 562 522-4014
EMP: 150
SALES (corp-wide): 45.5B **Publicly Held**
SIC: 4513
HQ: Federal Express Corporation
3610 Hacks Cross Rd
Memphis TN 38125
901 369-3600

(P-4865)
FEDEX GROUND PACKAGE SYS INC
9999 Olson Dr Ste 100, San Diego (92121-2837)
PHONE 800 463-3339
EMP: 107
SALES (corp-wide): 50.3B **Publicly Held**
SIC: 4513 Package delivery, private air
HQ: Fedex Ground Package System, Inc.
1000 Fed Ex Dr
Coraopolis PA 15108
412 269-1000

(P-4866)
GREYHOUND LINES INC
121 S Center St, Stockton (95202-2817)
PHONE 209 466-3568
Fax: 209 466-4913
Jackie Wilson, *Manager*
EMP: 50
SALES (corp-wide): 7.5B **Privately Held**
WEB: www.greyhound.com
SIC: 4513 Package delivery, private air
HQ: Greyhound Lines, Inc.
350 N Saint Paul St # 300
Dallas TX 75201
214 849-8000

(P-4867)
LBC MUNDIAL CORPORATION (HQ)
3563 Inv Blvd Ste 3, Hayward (94545)
PHONE 650 873-0750
Fax: 650 873-3914
Hugo Bonilla, *President*
Carlos Araneta, *Ch of Bd*
Fely Ruiz, *Corp Secy*
Anna Mamaril, *Manager*
EMP: 60
SQ FT: 25,000
SALES (est): 46.6MM **Privately Held**
SIC: 4513 4215 6099 6221 Air courier services; courier services, except by air; foreign currency exchange; commodity contracts brokers, dealers

(P-4868)
MEJICO EXPRESS INC (PA)
Also Called: Grupoex
14849 Firestone Blvd Fl 1, La Mirada (90638-6017)
PHONE 714 690-8300
Jose Leon, *President*
Raul Cancinos, *Opers Mgr*
EMP: 150
SALES (est): 23.3MM **Privately Held**
SIC: 4513 Letter delivery, private air

(P-4869)
MIDNITE AIR CORP
8801 Bellanca Ave, Los Angeles (90045-4705)
PHONE 310 330-2300
Tom Belmont, *Branch Mgr*
EMP: 50
SALES (corp-wide): 4.1B **Privately Held**
SIC: 4513 Air courier services
HQ: Midnite Air Corp.
2132 Michelson Dr
Irvine CA 92612
310 330-2300

(P-4870)
MIDNITE AIR CORP (HQ)
Also Called: MNX
2132 Michelson Dr, Irvine (92612-1304)
PHONE 310 330-2300
Fax: 310 330-2358
Paul Martins, *CEO*
Thomas Belmont, *COO*
Sergio Palad, *CFO*
Steve Stubitz, *Treasurer*
Ed Rochat, *General Mgr*
EMP: 55
SQ FT: 10,000
SALES (est): 96.5MM
SALES (corp-wide): 4.1B **Privately Held**
WEB: www.mnx.com
SIC: 4513 Air courier services
PA: Riverside Partners L.L.C.
45 Rockefeller Plz # 400
New York NY 10111
212 265-6575

(P-4871)
NETWORK GLOBAL LOGISTICS LLC
Also Called: NGL
13479 Valley Blvd, Fontana (92335-5245)
PHONE 888 285-7447
EMP: 139

4513 - Air Courier Svcs

SALES (corp-wide): 192.1MM Privately Held
SIC: 4513 4214 4225 Air courier services; local trucking with storage; general warehousing & storage
PA: Network Global Logistics, Llc
320 Interlocken Pkwy # 100
Broomfield CO 80021
866 938-1870

(P-4872)
TNT USA INC
Also Called: TNT Express Worldwide
8500 Osage Ave, Los Angeles (90045-4421)
PHONE.................................310 242-9700
David Giannelli, *Branch Mgr*
EMP: 70
SALES (corp-wide): 50.3B Publicly Held
WEB: www.tnt.com
SIC: 4513 Air courier services
HQ: Tnt Usa Inc.
68 S Service Rd Ste 340
Melville NY 11747
631 712-6700

(P-4873)
TRICOR AMERICA INC
3149 Diablo Ave, Hayward (94545-2701)
PHONE.................................510 293-3960
Fax: 510 670-9192
Mike Chung, *Branch Mgr*
EMP: 150
SALES (corp-wide): 114.1MM Privately Held
WEB: www.tricor.com
SIC: 4513 4215 Air courier services; courier services, except by air
PA: Tricor America, Inc.
717 Airport Blvd
South San Francisco CA 94080
650 877-3650

(P-4874)
UNITED PARCEL SERVICE INC OH
Also Called: UPS
3333 S Downey Rd, Vernon (90058-4116)
PHONE.................................323 260-8957
Tony Peralta, *Manager*
EMP: 350
SALES (corp-wide): 58.3B Publicly Held
WEB: www.upsscs.com
SIC: 4513 4215 Air courier services; courier services, except by air
HQ: United Parcel Service, Inc. (Oh)
55 Glenlake Pkwy
Atlanta GA 30328
404 828-6000

(P-4875)
UNITED PARCEL SERVICE INC OH
Also Called: UPS
25283 Sherman Rd, Sun City (92585-9352)
PHONE.................................951 928-5221
Sean Nichols, *Branch Mgr*
Fred Calwell, *Manager*
EMP: 208
SALES (corp-wide): 58.3B Publicly Held
SIC: 4513 Parcel delivery, private air
HQ: United Parcel Service, Inc. (Oh)
55 Glenlake Pkwy
Atlanta GA 30328
404 828-6000

(P-4876)
UNITED PARCEL SERVICE INC OH
Also Called: UPS
1724 Wawona St, Manteca (95337-9437)
PHONE.................................209 944-5932
EMP: 208
SALES (corp-wide): 58.3B Publicly Held
WEB: www.upsscs.com
SIC: 4513 Parcel delivery, private air
HQ: United Parcel Service, Inc. (Oh)
55 Glenlake Pkwy
Atlanta GA 30328
404 828-6000

(P-4877)
UNITED PARCEL SERVICE INC OH
Also Called: UPS
Ontario Airport, Ontario (91758)
PHONE.................................909 974-7190
Steve Welsh, *Manager*
EMP: 208
SALES (corp-wide): 58.3B Publicly Held
WEB: www.upsscs.com
SIC: 4513 Parcel delivery, private air
HQ: United Parcel Service, Inc. (Oh)
55 Glenlake Pkwy
Atlanta GA 30328
404 828-6000

(P-4878)
WEST AIR INC
5005 E Andersen Ave, Fresno (93727-1502)
PHONE.................................559 454-7843
Fax: 559 454-7840
Lawrence W Olson, *Ch of Bd*
Timothy Flynn, *Shareholder*
Maurice Gallagher, *Shareholder*
Beth Wood, *President*
Pauline E Wood, *President*
EMP: 70
SQ FT: 10,000
SALES: 7.5MM Privately Held
WEB: www.westair.net
SIC: 4513 Package delivery, private air

4522 Air Transportation, Nonscheduled

(P-4879)
CALIFRNIA SHOCK TRUMA A RESCUE (PA)
Also Called: Calstar
4933 Bailey Loop, McClellan (95652-2516)
PHONE.................................916 921-4000
Fax: 916 921-4099
Lynn Malmstrom, *President*
Tad Henderson, *COO*
Mark Vincenzini, *CFO*
Don Cook, *Managing Dir*
Deanna Bingham, *Admin Asst*
EMP: 63
SQ FT: 44,000
SALES: 48.6MM Privately Held
WEB: www.calstar.org
SIC: 4522 Ambulance services, air

(P-4880)
ELITE AVIATION LLC
7501 Hayvenhurst Pl, Van Nuys (91406-2851)
PHONE.................................818 988-5387
Fax: 818 988-2111
Kacani Shina, *Mng Member*
John Wilkins, *CFO*
Jason Duncan, *VP Human Res*
Shina Kacani, *Director*
Kevin Rothfus, *Director*
EMP: 100
SQ FT: 54,000
SALES (est): 16.4MM Privately Held
WEB: www.eliteaviation.com
SIC: 4522 4581 Flying charter service; aircraft maintenance & repair services

(P-4881)
JETSUITE INC
18952 Macarthur Blvd # 200, Irvine (92612-1401)
PHONE.................................949 892-4300
Alex Wilcox, *CEO*
Keith Rabin, *CFO*
Daryl Wadsworth, *Officer*
Chuck Stumpf, *Senior VP*
Frank Buratti, *Vice Pres*
EMP: 170
SQ FT: 7,641
SALES (est): 39.2MM Privately Held
SIC: 4522 Air transportation, nonscheduled

(P-4882)
JONAIR SERVICES LLC
9800 S Sepulveda Blvd, Los Angeles (90045-5208)
PHONE.................................310 529-5482
David Jones, *CEO*
EMP: 99
SQ FT: 110,000
SALES (est): 2.1MM Privately Held
SIC: 4522 Air transportation, nonscheduled

(P-4883)
LOGISTIC AIR INC
231 Market Pl Ste 203, San Ramon (94583-4743)
PHONE.................................925 465-0400
Vandi Cooyar, *President*
Andy Cooper, *Vice Pres*
EMP: 50
SALES (est): 3.4MM Privately Held
SIC: 4522 Flying charter service

(P-4884)
MAGUIRE AVIATION GROUP LLC
7155 Valjean Ave, Van Nuys (91406-3917)
PHONE.................................818 989-2300
Alec Maguire, *President*
Tom Magglos, *Manager*
EMP: 50
SALES (est): 6.8MM Privately Held
SIC: 4522 Air transportation, nonscheduled

(P-4885)
MERCY AIR TRI-COUNTY LLC
1670 Miro Way, Rialto (92376-8629)
P.O. Box 2532, Fontana (92334-2532)
PHONE.................................909 829-1051
Fax: 909 357-1009
David Dolstein, *Mng Member*
Aaron Todd,
EMP: 250
SQ FT: 11,288
SALES (est): 10.6MM
SALES (corp-wide): 1B Publicly Held
SIC: 4522 4119 7623 7359 Ambulance services, air; local passenger transportation; air conditioning repair; aircraft & industrial truck rental services; helicopters
PA: Air Methods Corporation
7301 S Peoria St
Englewood CO 80112
303 749-1330

(P-4886)
MERLIN GLOBAL SERVICES LLC
380 Stevens Ave Ste 305, Solana Beach (92075-2069)
PHONE.................................904 305-9559
Conner Searcy, *President*
Brian Raduenz, *CEO*
David Scott, *COO*
J Wayne Miller, *Vice Pres*
David Stinnett, *Admin Sec*
EMP: 110
SALES (est): 13.1MM Privately Held
WEB: www.merlinramco.com
SIC: 4522 8711 8731 8748 Air transportation, nonscheduled; engineering services; commercial physical research; test development & evaluation service; educational services

(P-4887)
SUNSET AVIATION LLC (PA)
Also Called: Solairus Aviation
201 1st St Ste 307, Petaluma (94952-4290)
PHONE.................................707 775-2786
Daniel Drohan, *CEO*
John King, *President*
Greg Petersen, *COO*
Mark Dennen, *CFO*
Bob Marinace, *Exec VP*
EMP: 50
SALES (est): 66.2MM Privately Held
SIC: 4522 3721 Air transportation, nonscheduled; aircraft

(P-4888)
SUTTER CENTRAL VLY HOSPITALS
Also Called: Medi-Flight Northern Cal
1700 Coffee Rd, Modesto (95355-2803)
PHONE.................................209 526-4500
Fax: 209 572-7050
Terry Sweeney, *Director*
William Madsen, *Pharmacist*
William Bragdon, *Asst Mgr*
EMP: 50
SALES (corp-wide): 11B Privately Held
WEB: www.memorialmedicalcenter.org
SIC: 4522 Air transportation, nonscheduled
HQ: Sutter Central Valley Hospitals
1700 Coffee Rd
Modesto CA 95355
209 526-4500

(P-4889)
TWC AVIATION LLC
16700 Roscoe Blvd Hngr C, Van Nuys (91406-1102)
PHONE.................................888 923-1001
Fax: 818 441-0117
Andrew Richmond, *CFO*
EMP: 50
SALES (corp-wide): 2.1B Privately Held
WEB: www.twcaviation.com
SIC: 4522 7359 Flying charter service; aircraft rental
HQ: Twc Aviation, Llc
16700c Roscoe Blvd Hngr C
Van Nuys CA 91406
818 441-0100

(P-4890)
TWC AVIATION LLC
1162 Aviation Ave, San Jose (95110-1143)
PHONE.................................408 286-3832
Andrew M Lessman, *Owner*
EMP: 50
SALES (corp-wide): 2.1B Privately Held
SIC: 4522 7699 Air transportation, nonscheduled; aircraft & heavy equipment repair services
HQ: Twc Aviation, Llc
16700c Roscoe Blvd Hngr C
Van Nuys CA 91406
818 441-0100

4581 Airports, Flying Fields & Terminal Svcs

(P-4891)
AEROGROUND INC (DH)
Also Called: Air Cargo Handling Service
270 Lawrence Ave, South San Francisco (94080-6817)
PHONE.................................650 266-6965
Anthony Bonino, *CEO*
Steven Ballard, *Senior VP*
John Peery, *Vice Pres*
▲ **EMP:** 800
SQ FT: 175,000
SALES (est): 66.6MM
SALES (corp-wide): 2.8B Privately Held
SIC: 4581 4213 Air freight handling at airports; trucking, except local

(P-4892)
AIR SERV CORPORATION
601 Gateway Blvd Ste 1145, South San Francisco (94080-7413)
PHONE.................................650 872-5400
Doug Kreuckamp, *Vice Pres*
Mary Alexander, *General Mgr*
Lydia Faitalia, *Human Res Mgr*
EMP: 400
SALES (corp-wide): 4.9B Publicly Held
SIC: 4581 Airports, flying fields & services
HQ: Air Serv Corporation
3399 Peachtree Rd Ne
Atlanta GA 30326
404 926-4200

(P-4893)
AIRCRAFT SERVICE INTERNATIONAL
Ontario Intl Airport, Ontario (91761)
P.O. Box 4178 (91761-1011)
PHONE.................................909 937-3210
John Norman, *Manager*
EMP: 100
SALES (corp-wide): 2.1B Privately Held
WEB: www.asig.com
SIC: 4581 Airport terminal services
HQ: Aircraft Service International, Inc.
201 S Orange Ave Ste 1100
Orlando FL 32801
407 648-7373

PRODUCTS & SERVICES SECTION
4581 - Airports, Flying Fields & Terminal Svcs County (P-4915)

(P-4894)
AIRCRAFT SERVICE INTL INC
Also Called: Asig
1049 S Vineyard Ave, Ontario (91761-8029)
P.O. Box 4178 (91761-1011)
PHONE..................909 937-3998
Fax: 909 937-7158
Debbie Martin, *Manager*
Darrell Mullins, *Manager*
EMP: 63
SALES (corp-wide): 2.2B **Privately Held**
WEB: www.asig.com
SIC: **4581** Airport
HQ: Aircraft Service International, Inc.
201 S Orange Ave Ste 1100
Orlando FL 32801
407 648-7373

(P-4895)
AIRCRAFT SERVICE INTL INC
2161 E Avion Ave, Ontario (91761-8067)
PHONE..................909 937-3210
George Williams, *Manager*
EMP: 50
SALES (corp-wide): 2.2B **Privately Held**
WEB: www.asig.com
SIC: **4581** Airport terminal services
HQ: Aircraft Service International, Inc.
201 S Orange Ave Ste 1100
Orlando FL 32801
407 648-7373

(P-4896)
AIRFLITE INC
3250 Airflite Way, Long Beach (90807-5312)
PHONE..................562 490-6200
Fax: 562 381-5838
Bob Daly, *CEO*
Miles King, *President*
Christopher Reynolds, *Admin Sec*
John Skoglund, *Controller*
Thomas Fleming, *Director*
EMP: 68
SQ FT: 200,000
SALES (est): 180.7K
SALES (corp-wide): 242.7B **Privately Held**
WEB: www.toyotahub.com
SIC: **4581** 4522 Airport terminal services; air transportation, nonscheduled
HQ: Toyota Motor Sales Usa Inc
19001 S Western Ave
Torrance CA 90501
310 468-4000

(P-4897)
AIRPORT COMMISIONS
Also Called: Business of Finance
San Francisco Intl Arprt, San Francisco (94128)
PHONE..................650 821-5000
John L Martin, *Director*
Michelle Dipilla, *Manager*
EMP: 1121
SALES (est): 33.2MM **Privately Held**
SIC: **4581** Airports, flying fields & services
PA: City & County Of San Francisco
1 Dr Carlton B Goodlett P
San Francisco CA 94102
415 554-7500

(P-4898)
ALLIANCE GROUND INTL LLC
6181 W Imperial Hwy, Los Angeles (90045-6305)
PHONE..................310 646-2446
EMP: 73
SALES (corp-wide): 76.6MM **Privately Held**
SIC: **4581** Airfreight loading & unloading services
PA: Alliance Ground International, Llc
6705 S Red Rd Ste 700
South Miami FL 33143
305 740-3252

(P-4899)
ALLIANCE GROUND INTL LLC
648 Rest Field Rd, San Francisco (94128)
PHONE..................650 821-0855
EMP: 73
SALES (corp-wide): 76.6MM **Privately Held**
SIC: **4581** Airfreight loading & unloading services
PA: Alliance Ground International, Llc
6705 S Red Rd Ste 700
South Miami FL 33143
305 740-3252

(P-4900)
AMERICAN AIRLINES INC
Also Called: US Airways
100 World Way Ste D, Los Angeles (90045-5854)
PHONE..................310 646-0093
Mike Cilani, *Branch Mgr*
EMP: 325
SALES (corp-wide): 40.9B **Publicly Held**
WEB: www.usair.com
SIC: **4581** Aircraft servicing & repairing
HQ: American Airlines, Inc.
4333 Amon Carter Blvd
Fort Worth TX 76155
817 963-1234

(P-4901)
AMERICAN AIRLINES INC
3100 Wright Rd, Camarillo (93010-8307)
PHONE..................805 988-0407
Wilma Barkley, *Branch Mgr*
EMP: 75
SALES (corp-wide): 40.9B **Publicly Held**
WEB: www.aa.com
SIC: **4581** Airports, flying fields & services
HQ: American Airlines, Inc.
4333 Amon Carter Blvd
Fort Worth TX 76155
817 963-1234

(P-4902)
ARINWINE ARCFT MAINT SVCS LLC
Also Called: F&E Aircraft Maintenance
1720 E Holly Ave, El Segundo (90245-4404)
PHONE..................310 338-0063
Lisa Arinwine, *COO*
EMP: 63
SQ FT: 10,000
SALES (est): 3.6MM **Privately Held**
SIC: **4581** Aircraft maintenance & repair services; aircraft servicing & repairing

(P-4903)
AVIATION & DEFENSE INC
Also Called: ADI
255 S Leland Norton Way, San Bernardino (92408-0103)
PHONE..................909 382-3487
Daniel M Scanlon, *CEO*
Hector Guerrero, *Ch of Bd*
Mike Scanlon, *President*
Ben Flores, *CFO*
Dan Scanlon, *Vice Pres*
EMP: 180
SQ FT: 180,000
SALES (est): 30.2MM **Privately Held**
SIC: **4581** Aircraft maintenance & repair services

(P-4904)
BOEING COMPANY
Slc 2 Bldg 1628, San Luis Obispo (93401)
P.O. Box 5219, Lompoc (93437-0219)
PHONE..................805 606-6340
Rich Niederhauser, *Manager*
James B Boyle, *Mng Officer*
EMP: 80
SALES (corp-wide): 96.1B **Publicly Held**
SIC: **4581** 3761 3721 Airports & flying fields; guided missiles & space vehicles; aircraft
PA: The Boeing Company
100 N Riverside Plz
Chicago IL 60606
312 544-2000

(P-4905)
CESSNA AIRCRAFT COMPANY
Also Called: Cessna Scrmnto Ctation Svc Ctr
5850 Citation Way, Sacramento (95837-1105)
PHONE..................916 929-5656
Ken Kantola, *Sales/Mktg Mgr*
Jeff Bakker, *Manager*
Roger Searls, *Supervisor*
Lillibelle Balli, *Clerk*
Cindy Nouarhchanh, *Clerk*
EMP: 85
SALES (corp-wide): 13.4B **Publicly Held**
WEB: www.cessna.com
SIC: **4581** Aircraft cleaning & janitorial service
HQ: The Cessna Aircraft Company
1 Cessna Blvd
Wichita KS 67215
316 517-6000

(P-4906)
CITY OF FRESNO
Fresno Yosimite Intl Arprt
5175 E Clinton Way, Fresno (93727-2086)
PHONE..................559 621-4500
EMP: 56 **Privately Held**
SIC: **4581** Airports, flying fields & services
PA: City Of Fresno
2600 Fresno St
Fresno CA 93721
559 621-7001

(P-4907)
CITY OF LONG BEACH
Also Called: Long Beach Airport
4100 E Don Douglas Dr Fl Flr 2, Long Beach (90808)
PHONE..................562 570-2600
Fax: 562 496-4981
Chris Kunze, *Manager*
Claudia Lewis, *Executive*
EMP: 65 **Privately Held**
WEB: www.polb.com
SIC: **4581** 9111 Airport; mayors' offices
PA: City Of Long Beach
333 W Ocean Blvd Fl 10
Long Beach CA 90802
562 570-6450

(P-4908)
CITY OF LOS ANGELES
Also Called: Van Nuys Airport
16461 Sherman Way Ste 210, Van Nuys (91406-3841)
PHONE..................818 908-5950
Fax: 818 908-5963
Selena Birk, *Manager*
Danielle Stewart, *Sales Executive*
EMP: 100 **Privately Held**
WEB: www.lacity.org
SIC: **4581** 9621 6531 Airport; regulation, administration of transportation; ; real estate managers
PA: City Of Los Angeles
200 N Spring St Ste 303
Los Angeles CA 90012
213 978-0600

(P-4909)
CITY OF PALM SPRINGS
3400 E Thqitz Cyn Way Ofc, Palm Springs (92262-6918)
P.O. Box 2743 (92263-2743)
PHONE..................760 318-3800
Thomas Nolan, *Director*
EMP: 58 **Privately Held**
WEB: www.psfire.com
SIC: **4581** Airport
PA: City Of Palm Springs
3200 E Tahquitz Cyn Way
Palm Springs CA 92262
760 322-8362

(P-4910)
CITY OF SAN JOSE
Also Called: Mineta San Jose Intl Arprt
1701 Arprt Blvd Ste B1130, San Jose (95110)
PHONE..................408 392-3600
William Sherry, *Director*
John Aitken, *Director*
Ralph G Tonseth, *Director*
EMP: 310
SQ FT: 30,000 **Privately Held**
WEB: www.csjfinance.org
SIC: **4581** 9199 Airport;
PA: City Of San Jose
200 E Santa Clara St
San Jose CA 95113
408 535-3500

(P-4911)
CLAY LACY AVIATION INC (PA)
Also Called: C L A
7435 Valjean Ave, Van Nuys (91406-2977)
PHONE..................818 989-2900
Fax: 818 904-3450
Clay H Lacy, *Ch of Bd*
Hershel Clay Lacy, *President*
Brad Wright, *CFO*
Scott Cutshall, *Vice Pres*
Andrew Richmond, *Vice Pres*
EMP: 100
SQ FT: 18,000
SALES (est): 48.8MM **Privately Held**
WEB: www.claylacy.com
SIC: **4581** 7335 Airport terminal services; aerial photography, except mapmaking

(P-4912)
COUNTY OF MENDOCINO
Also Called: Department of Transportation
340 Lake Mendocino Dr, Ukiah (95482-9432)
PHONE..................707 463-4363
Fax: 707 463-5474
Howard Dashiell, *Branch Mgr*
Rachel Ingwell, *Info Tech Mgr*
Patty Black, *Manager*
EMP: 96 **Privately Held**
WEB: www.mcdss.org
SIC: **4581** Airport
PA: County Of Mendocino
501 Low Gap Rd Rm 1010
Ukiah CA 95482
707 463-4441

(P-4913)
COUNTY OF ORANGE
Also Called: John Wayne Airport
3160 Airway Ave, Costa Mesa (92626-4608)
PHONE..................949 252-5006
Fax: 949 252-5290
Loan Leblow, *Branch Mgr*
Andreana Pineda, *Info Tech Dir*
Leo Tang, *Project Mgr*
Adam Steckler, *Accounting Mgr*
Julie Henkels, *Buyer*
EMP: 135 **Privately Held**
SIC: **4581** 9621 Airport; aircraft regulating agencies;
PA: County Of Orange
333 W Santa Ana Blvd 3f
Santa Ana CA 92701
714 834-6200

(P-4914)
DSD TRUCKING INC (PA)
8840 Bellanca Ave, Los Angeles (90045-4700)
P.O. Box 15292 (90015-0292)
PHONE..................310 338-1210
Fax: 310 338-0329
Dan Cuevas, *President*
Kalonde Gilbert, *CTO*
Wendy Silva, *Human Res Mgr*
Luis Rodriguez, *Human Resources*
Carlos Guerra, *Facilities Mgr*
EMP: 69
SQ FT: 300,000
SALES (est): 17.7MM **Privately Held**
SIC: **4581** Air freight handling at airports

(P-4915)
DYNAMO AVIATION INC
16760 Schoenborn St, North Hills (91343-6108)
P.O. Box 14040, Van Nuys (91409-4040)
PHONE..................818 785-9561
Masoud S Rabadi, *CEO*
Robin C Scott, *CFO*
Lary Hockens,
Adan Frausto, *Info Tech Mgr*
Anil Krishnamurthy, *Project Mgr*
EMP: 75
SALES (est): 45.9MM **Privately Held**
WEB: www.dynamoaviation.com
SIC: **4581** 3444 3679 5063 Aircraft servicing & repairing; sheet metalwork; harness assemblies for electronic use: wire or cable; storage batteries, industrial

4581 - Airports, Flying Fields & Terminal Svcs County (P-4916)

(P-4916)
ENVOY AIR INC
Also Called: AMR Eagle
3707 N Harbor Dr Ste 124, San Diego (92101-1080)
PHONE.................................619 260-9069
Steve Terry, *Branch Mgr*
EMP: 50
SALES (corp-wide): 40.9B **Publicly Held**
WEB: www.americanair.com
SIC: 4581 Airports, flying fields & services
HQ: Envoy Air Inc.
4301 Regent Blvd
Irving TX 75063
972 374-5200

(P-4917)
F KORBEL & BROS
Korbel Flight Department
4384 Becker Blvd, Santa Rosa (95403-8283)
PHONE.................................707 525-1875
Gary Krambs, *Branch Mgr*
EMP: 129
SALES (corp-wide): 92.7MM **Privately Held**
SIC: 4581 Airport
PA: F. Korbel & Bros.
13250 River Rd
Guerneville CA 95446
707 824-7000

(P-4918)
F&E AIRCRAFT MAINTENANCE (PA)
531 Main St, El Segundo (90245-3060)
PHONE.................................310 338-0063
Everett R Arinwine,
Keiney Mosley, *Manager*
EMP: 50
SALES (est): 24MM **Privately Held**
SIC: 4581 7699 Aircraft servicing & repairing; aircraft & heavy equipment repair services

(P-4919)
GAT AIRLINE GROUND SUPPORT
6701 Lindbergh Dr, Sacramento (95837-1138)
PHONE.................................916 923-2349
EMP: 332
SALES (corp-wide): 126.1MM **Privately Held**
SIC: 4581 Airports, flying fields & services; airfreight loading & unloading services
PA: Gat Airline Ground Support Inc
8400 Airport Blvd
Mobile AL 36608
251 633-3888

(P-4920)
GE AVIATION SYSTEMS LLC
295 N Wolfe Ave Bldg 3810, Edwards Afb (93524-6003)
PHONE.................................661 277-7308
EMP: 193
SALES (corp-wide): 117.3B **Publicly Held**
SIC: 4581 Airports, flying fields & services
HQ: Ge Aviation Systems Llc
1 Neumann Way
Cincinnati OH 45215
513 243-2000

(P-4921)
HUNTLEIGH USA CORPORATION
3707 N Harbor Dr A-110, San Diego (92101-1096)
PHONE.................................619 231-8111
Fax: 619 298-2885
Richard Madison, *Branch Mgr*
EMP: 75
SALES (corp-wide): 174MM **Privately Held**
SIC: 4581 Airports, flying fields & services
HQ: Huntleigh Usa Corporation
545 E John Carpenter Fwy
Irving TX
972 719-9180

(P-4922)
JETT PRO LINE MAINTENANCE INC (PA)
2910 Inland Empire Blvd # 102, Ontario (91764-4896)
P.O. Box 3190 (91761-0919)
PHONE.................................909 944-7035
Sam Nugud, *CEO*
Willie Nugud, *President*
Al Nugud, *CFO*
David Lee, *Vice Pres*
EMP: 60
SQ FT: 1,500
SALES (est): 9.9MM **Privately Held**
SIC: 4581 Aircraft servicing & repairing

(P-4923)
LEADING EDGE AVIATION SERVS
13640 Phantom St, Victorville (92394-7900)
PHONE.................................760 246-1651
Fax: 760 246-4375
Niall Cunningham, *CEO*
EMP: 573
SALES (corp-wide): 65MM **Privately Held**
SIC: 4581 Air freight handling at airports
PA: Leading Edge Aviation Services, Inc.
5251 California Ave # 170
Irvine CA 92617
714 556-0576

(P-4924)
LOCKHEED MARTIN CORPORATION
Also Called: Lockheed Martin Astronautics
Bldg 8401, Lompoc (93437)
P.O. Box 5219 (93437-0219)
PHONE.................................303 971-4631
Tom Heter, *Branch Mgr*
EMP: 83
SALES (corp-wide): 46.1B **Publicly Held**
SIC: 4581 Military flying field
PA: Lockheed Martin Corporation
6801 Rockledge Dr
Bethesda MD 20817
301 897-6000

(P-4925)
LOS ANGELES WORLD AIRPORTS (PA)
6320 W 96th St, Los Angeles (90045-5233)
P.O. Box 92216 (90009-2216)
PHONE.................................310 646-7911
Arif Alikhan, *Director*
Michael Cummings, *Principal*
Larry Genuth, *Analyst*
Steve Manick, *Manager*
EMP: 194 **EST:** 2010
SALES (est): 64.9MM **Privately Held**
SIC: 4581 Airport

(P-4926)
MERCURY AIR CARGO INC (HQ)
Also Called: Mercury World Cargo
6040 Avion Dr Ste 200, Los Angeles (90045-5654)
PHONE.................................310 258-6100
Fax: 310 258-6188
Joseph A Czyzyk, *CEO*
John Peery, *COO*
Lawrence Samuels, *CFO*
Dan K Barnard, *Treasurer*
Clive Langeveldt, *Exec VP*
EMP: 180
SQ FT: 206,000
SALES: 50MM
SALES (corp-wide): 678.1MM **Privately Held**
WEB: www.mercuryaircargo.com
SIC: 4581 4512 4522 Airports, flying fields & services; air cargo carrier, scheduled; air cargo carriers, nonscheduled
PA: Mercury Air Group, Inc.
2780 Skypark Dr Ste 300
Torrance CA 90505
310 602-3770

(P-4927)
PACIFIC AVIATION CORPORATION (PA)
380 World Way Ste S31, Los Angeles (90045-5898)
PHONE.................................310 646-4015
Fax: 310 646-4016
Phil Shah, *President*
Victor Mena, *Corp Secy*
Changhyun Lee, *Human Res Dir*
Acquanetta Willis, *Human Res Dir*
Preethi Cheriyan, *Human Res Mgr*
EMP: 200
SQ FT: 3,500
SALES: 13.8MM **Privately Held**
WEB: www.pacificaviation.com
SIC: 4581 Airport terminal services

(P-4928)
PHASE 3 INC
Also Called: Sierra Aviation
8191 Laughlin Rd, Oakdale (95361-9451)
PHONE.................................209 848-0290
Fax: 209 848-0299
Ken Robinson, *President*
Justin Barnes, *Manager*
EMP: 50
SQ FT: 6,000
SALES (est): 5.6MM **Privately Held**
WEB: www.phase3.com
SIC: 4581 Aircraft cleaning & janitorial service

(P-4929)
PHS / MWA (HQ)
Also Called: Phs/Mwa Aviation Services
42355 Rio Nedo, Temecula (92590-3701)
PHONE.................................950 695-1008
Fax: 951 695-0863
Mary Bale, *CEO*
Bill Voetsch, *President*
Jennifer Blake, *Production*
Craig Bale, *Marketing Staff*
Scott Stanton, *Director*
EMP: 50
SQ FT: 30,000
SALES (est): 32.1MM
SALES (corp-wide): 490.2MM **Privately Held**
WEB: www.phsmwa.com
SIC: 4581 3492 7629 Aircraft servicing & repairing; control valves, aircraft: hydraulic & pneumatic; electrical repair shops
PA: Wencor Group, Llc
416 Dividend Dr
Peachtree City GA 30269
678 490-0140

(P-4930)
PLH AVIATION SERVICES CORP
7251 World Way W, Los Angeles (90045-5826)
PHONE.................................310 417-0124
Fax: 310 417-3928
Lloyd Peddle, *President*
EMP: 65
SALES (est): 6.9MM
SALES (corp-wide): 2.1B **Privately Held**
SIC: 4581 Aircraft servicing & repairing
HQ: Aircraft Service International, Inc.
201 S Orange Ave Ste 1100
Orlando FL 32801
407 648-7373

(P-4931)
PORT DEPT CITY OF OAKLAND
Also Called: Metropilitan Oakland Intl Arprt
1 Airport Dr Ste 45, Oakland (94621-1476)
PHONE.................................510 563-3300
Fax: 510 430-9392
Bill Wade, *Manager*
Matt Davis, *Opers Staff*
EMP: 250
SALES (est): 50MM **Privately Held**
WEB: www.portofoakland.com
SIC: 4581 Airport
PA: Port Department Of The City Of Oakland
530 Water St Fl 3
Oakland CA 94607
510 627-1100

(P-4932)
SAN DEGO CNTY RGNAL ARPRT AUTH (PA)
Also Called: Sdcraa
3225 N Harbor Dr Fl 3, San Diego (92101-1045)
P.O. Box 82776 (92138-2776)
PHONE.................................619 400-2400

Thella F Bowens, *CEO*
Vernon Evans, *President*
Jim Janney, *Bd of Directors*
Maria Quiroz, *Vice Pres*
Keith Wilschetz, *Plan/Corp Dev D*
EMP: 117
SALES (est): 44.1MM **Privately Held**
SIC: 4581 Airports, flying fields & services; air freight handling at airports

(P-4933)
SAN JOSE JET CENTER INC
1250 Aviation Ave Ste 235, San Jose (95110-1119)
PHONE.................................408 297-7552
Fax: 408 280-5701
Dan Ryan, *President*
Harold Deguzman, *CFO*
Jim Blair, *Treasurer*
Jim Rutherford, *Exec VP*
Barry Fernald, *Admin Sec*
EMP: 50
SQ FT: 196,000
SALES (est): 5.4MM **Privately Held**
WEB: www.sjjc.com
SIC: 4581 6531 Aircraft maintenance & repair services; hangars & other aircraft storage facilities; real estate agent, commercial

(P-4934)
SIGNATURE FLIGHT SUPPORT CORP
3050 N Winery Ave, Fresno (93703-1616)
PHONE.................................559 981-2490
Justin Zaklan, *Manager*
EMP: 74
SALES (corp-wide): 2.1B **Privately Held**
SIC: 4581 Aircraft maintenance & repair services
HQ: Signature Flight Support Corporation
201 S Orange Ave Ste 1100
Orlando FL 32801
407 648-7200

(P-4935)
SIGNATURE FLIGHT SUPPORT CORP
1052 N Access Rd, San Francisco (94128-3120)
PHONE.................................650 877-6800
Ken Setser, *Manager*
EMP: 76
SALES (corp-wide): 2.1B **Privately Held**
SIC: 4581 Airports, flying fields & services
HQ: Signature Flight Support Corporation
201 S Orange Ave Ste 1100
Orlando FL 32801
407 648-7200

(P-4936)
SIGNATURE FLIGHT SUPPORT CORP
7240 Hayvenhurst Ave, Van Nuys (91406)
PHONE.................................818 464-9500
Stephen W Lee, *Vice Pres*
EMP: 74
SALES (corp-wide): 2.1B **Privately Held**
SIC: 4581 Airports, flying fields & services
HQ: Signature Flight Support Corporation
201 S Orange Ave Ste 1100
Orlando FL 32801
407 648-7200

(P-4937)
SIGNATURE FLIGHT SUPPORT CORP
3333 E Spring St Ste 205, Long Beach (90806-2446)
PHONE.................................562 997-0700
Eric Hill, *Branch Mgr*
Bonnie Pike, *Manager*
EMP: 74
SALES (corp-wide): 2.1B **Privately Held**
SIC: 4581 Airports, flying fields & services
HQ: Signature Flight Support Corporation
201 S Orange Ave Ste 1100
Orlando FL 32801
407 648-7200

PRODUCTS & SERVICES SECTION

4724 - Travel Agencies County (P-4958)

(P-4938)
SOUTHERN CALIFORNIA AVI LLC
Also Called: S C A
18438 Readiness St, Victorville (92394-7945)
PHONE.................................760 523-5057
Fax: 760 246-1186
Craig Garrick, *CEO*
Laurie Gutzeit, *Bd of Directors*
Diana Fenton, *Program Mgr*
Brian Austin, *General Mgr*
Charlie Alexiev, *Store Mgr*
EMP: 155
SQ FT: 75,000
SALES (est): 40.8MM **Privately Held**
WEB: www.scaviation.com
SIC: 4581 Aircraft servicing & repairing

(P-4939)
STANDARDAERO BUS AVI SVCS LLC
6201 W Imperial Hwy, Los Angeles (90045-6306)
PHONE.................................310 568-3700
Robert Lummus, *General Mgr*
Marc McGowan, *President*
Rusell Ford, *CEO*
Michael Scott, *CFO*
Diane Roseborough, *Admin Sec*
EMP: 80
SALES (corp-wide): 1.7B **Privately Held**
SIC: 4581 Airports, flying fields & services
HQ: Standardaero Business Aviation Services, Llc
6710 N Scottsdale Rd
Scottsdale AZ 85253
480 377-3100

(P-4940)
SWISSPORT CARGO SERVICES LP
Also Called: Cargo Service Center
11001 Aviation Blvd, Los Angeles (90045-6123)
PHONE.................................310 910-9541
Fax: 310 641-6958
Mark Wood, *General Mgr*
EMP: 562
SALES (corp-wide): 679.6MM **Privately Held**
SIC: 4581 Air freight handling at airports
HQ: Swissport Cargo Services, L.P.
23723 Air Frt Ln Bldg 5
Dulles VA 20166
703 742-4300

(P-4941)
SWISSPORT USA INC
Also Called: Employment Intake Training Ctr
7025 W Imperial Hwy, Los Angeles (90045-6313)
PHONE.................................310 345-1986
Jerry Harris, *General Mgr*
EMP: 400
SALES (corp-wide): 679.6MM **Privately Held**
SIC: 4581 Air freight handling at airports
PA: Swissport Usa, Inc.
45025 Aviation Dr Ste 350
Dulles VA 20166
703 742-4300

(P-4942)
SWISSPORT USA INC
San Francisco Intl Arprt, San Francisco (94128)
PHONE.................................650 821-6220
Fax: 650 821-8285
Cecilia Guillen, *Station Mgr*
Pat Carr, *General Mgr*
EMP: 220
SALES (corp-wide): 679.6MM **Privately Held**
WEB: www.swissport-sfo.com
SIC: 4581 Airport terminal services
PA: Swissport Usa, Inc.
45025 Aviation Dr Ste 350
Dulles VA 20166
703 742-4300

(P-4943)
SWISSPORT USA INC
Delta Cargo Bldg 612, San Francisco (94128)
P.O. Box 251650 (94125-1650)
PHONE.................................571 214-7068
Joe Phelan, *Exec VP*
EMP: 216
SALES (corp-wide): 679.6MM **Privately Held**
SIC: 4581 Airports, flying fields & services
PA: Swissport Usa, Inc.
45025 Aviation Dr Ste 350
Dulles VA 20166
703 742-4300

(P-4944)
SWISSPORT USA INC
11001 Aviation Blvd, Los Angeles (90045-6123)
PHONE.................................310 910-9560
Dion Fatafehi, *Manager*
EMP: 453
SALES (corp-wide): 679.6MM **Privately Held**
WEB: www.swissport-sfo.com
SIC: 4581 Airport terminal services
PA: Swissport Usa, Inc.
45025 Aviation Dr Ste 350
Dulles VA 20166
703 742-4300

(P-4945)
THRESHOLD TECHNOLOGIES INC
8352 Kimball Ave Bldg F35, Chino (91708-9267)
PHONE.................................909 606-1666
Fax: 909 606-6451
Mark Dilullo, *CEO*
Lisa Dilullo, *President*
Ivan Dodson, *Mktg Dir*
Jerry Perez, *Director*
EMP: 55
SQ FT: 10,000
SALES (est): 8MM **Privately Held**
WEB: www.flytti.com
SIC: 4581 Aircraft storage at airports; airport hangar rental; aircraft cleaning & janitorial service; aircraft servicing & repairing

(P-4946)
TOTAL AIRPORT SERVICES INC
3537 Branson Dr, San Mateo (94403-2901)
PHONE.................................650 358-0144
Ralph Eichenbaum, *Branch Mgr*
EMP: 65
SALES (corp-wide): 144MM **Privately Held**
SIC: 4581 Airports, flying fields & services
PA: Total Airport Services, Inc.
34406 N 27th Dr Ste 140
Phoenix AZ 85085
623 215-9941

(P-4947)
WORLD SERVICE WEST
Also Called: L A Inflight Service Company
1812 W 135th St, Gardena (90249-2520)
PHONE.................................310 538-7000
Byung Yoon,
Marty Tautrim, *Human Resources*
Rudy Barba, *Opers Staff*
Mall Yoon,
Aida Agoialar, *Manager*
EMP: 170
SQ FT: 13,572
SALES (est): 8MM **Privately Held**
SIC: 4581 Aircraft maintenance & repair services; aircraft cleaning & janitorial service; aircraft servicing & repairing

(P-4948)
WORLDWIDE FLIGHT SERVICES INC
5908 Avion Dr, Los Angeles (90045-5622)
P.O. Box 90220 (90009-0220)
PHONE.................................310 646-7510
Dennis Hudson, *Manager*
Terri Johnson, *Finance Other*
EMP: 250
SALES (corp-wide): 2.2B **Privately Held**
SIC: 4581 Aircraft upholstery repair
PA: Worldwide Flight Services, Inc.
1925 W John Carpenter Fwy # 450
Irving TX 75063
972 629-5001

(P-4949)
XOJET INC (PA)
2000 Sierra Point Pkwy # 200, Brisbane (94005-1846)
PHONE.................................650 594-6300
Fax: 650 636-2525
Bradley Stewart, *CEO*
David N Siegel, *Ch of Bd*
Paul Touw, *Ch of Bd*
Benjamin Murray, *President*
Eilif Serck-Hanssen, *President*
EMP: 54
SALES (est): 48.7MM **Privately Held**
WEB: www.xojet.com
SIC: 4581 Aircraft maintenance & repair services

4613 Refined Petroleum Pipelines

(P-4950)
SFPP LP (DH)
1100 W Town And Country R, Orange (92868-4647)
PHONE.................................714 560-4400
Park Shaper, *General Ptnr*
Richard D Kinder, *General Ptnr*
Don Quinn, *Engineer*
Gary Prim, *Controller*
EMP: 150
SQ FT: 75,000
SALES (est): 27.4MM
SALES (corp-wide): 14.4B **Publicly Held**
SIC: 4613 Gasoline pipelines (common carriers)
HQ: Kinder Morgan Energy Partners, L.P.
1001 La St Ste 1000
Houston TX 77002
713 369-9000

4619 Pipelines, NEC

(P-4951)
KINDER MRGAN ENRGY PARTNERS LP
Also Called: Santa Fe Pacific Pipeline
2319 S Riverside Ave, Bloomington (92316-2931)
PHONE.................................909 873-1553
Fax: 909 877-9036
Ron Moranes, *Manager*
EMP: 50
SALES (corp-wide): 14.4B **Publicly Held**
WEB: www.kindermorgan.com
SIC: 4619 1623 Coal pipeline operation; pipeline construction
HQ: Kinder Morgan Energy Partners, L.P.
1001 La St Ste 1000
Houston TX 77002
713 369-9000

(P-4952)
UNITED STATES PIPE FNDRY LLC
1295 Whipple Rd, Union City (94587-2036)
P.O. Box 707 (94587-0707)
PHONE.................................510 441-5810
Jim Kelly, *General Mgr*
Omar Rajabi, *Engineer*
Ann Kelley, *Purchasing*
Teresa Rednoich, *Purchasing*
Alfredo Gonzales, *Supervisor*
EMP: 115
SALES (est): 401.9K **Privately Held**
SIC: 4619 Coal pipeline operation
HQ: United States Pipe And Foundry Company Llc
2 Chase Corporate Dr # 200
Hoover AL 35244
205 263-8540

4724 Travel Agencies

(P-4953)
ALTOUR INTERNATIONAL INC
Also Called: Altour Travel Master
12100 W Olympic Blvd # 300, Los Angeles (90064-1051)
PHONE.................................310 571-6000
Julie Valentine, *Branch Mgr*
Lee Thomas, *Exec VP*
Elizabeth Rona, *Vice Pres*
Lisi Rona, *Vice Pres*
Paul Yung, *Vice Pres*
EMP: 130
SALES (corp-wide): 50.2MM **Privately Held**
WEB: www.altourtravelmaster.com
SIC: 4724 Travel agencies
PA: Altour International, Inc.
1270 Av Of The Amricas Fl Flr 1
New York NY 10020
212 897-5000

(P-4954)
ALTOUR INTERNATIONAL INC (PA)
12100 W Olympic Blvd # 300, Los Angeles (90064-1051)
PHONE.................................310 571-6000
Fax: 310 571-3157
Alexander Chemla, *President*
Lynn Minard, *COO*
Jeanine Sefton, *Sr Corp Ofcr*
David Sefton, *Senior VP*
Ellen Newman, *Vice Pres*
EMP: 80
SQ FT: 8,000
SALES: 1.6MM **Privately Held**
SIC: 4724 Travel agencies

(P-4955)
AMERICAN EXPRESS TRAVEL
15353 Barranca Pkwy, Irvine (92618-2216)
PHONE.................................949 453-7123
Linda Duffy, *Director*
EMP: 100
SALES (corp-wide): 34.4B **Publicly Held**
WEB: www.astoriasoftware.com
SIC: 4724 Travel agencies
HQ: American Express Travel Related Services Company, Inc.,
200 Vesey St
New York NY 10285
212 640-2000

(P-4956)
AMERICAN TRAVEL SOLUTIONS LLC
Also Called: Amtrav
26707 Agoura Rd Ste 204, Calabasas (91302-3831)
PHONE.................................800 243-2724
EMP: 65
SQ FT: 4,000
SALES (est): 13.4MM **Privately Held**
SIC: 4724 4729

(P-4957)
ATKINSON & MULLEN TRAVEL INC
2025 Gateway Pl, San Jose (95110-1014)
PHONE.................................408 452-0202
A S Mittal, *Branch Mgr*
EMP: 297
SALES (corp-wide): 40.2MM **Privately Held**
WEB: www.aandmtravel.com
SIC: 4724 Travel agencies
PA: Atkinson & Mullen Travel, Inc.
7 Campus Blvd Ste 100
Newtown Square PA 19073
610 359-6500

(P-4958)
B T & T TRAVEL INC
Also Called: Best Tours & Travel
2609 E Mckinley Ave Ste N, Fresno (93703-3028)
PHONE.................................559 237-9410
Fax: 559 237-8814
Nick W Sayah, *President*
Margaret Sayah, *Treasurer*
EMP: 56 EST: 1980

4724 - Travel Agencies County (P-4959)

SQ FT: 4,200
SALES (est): 13.3MM Privately Held
WEB: www.besttoursandtravel.com
SIC: 4724 4725 Travel agencies; tours, conducted

(P-4959) CARIBBEAN SOUTH AMERCN COUNCIL
Also Called: Internationl TV Media Wireless
12 Ambrose Ave, Bay Point (94565-3106)
PHONE.....................925 709-3433
Dalchand Singhbhairo, President
EMP: 50 EST: 1984
SALES (est): 4.6MM Privately Held
SIC: 4724 8748 Travel agencies; telecommunications consultant

(P-4960) CARNIVAL CORPORATION
231 Windsor Way, Long Beach (90802-6350)
PHONE.....................562 901-3232
Hector Patino, Principal
Rajendra Palikala, Analyst
EMP: 5020
SALES (corp-wide): 15.7B Publicly Held
SIC: 4724 Travel agencies
PA: Carnival Corporation
3655 Nw 87th Ave
Doral FL 33178
305 599-2600

(P-4961) GOWAY TRAVEL INC
Also Called: Global Network Travel
400 N Brand Blvd Ste 920, Glendale (91203-2367)
PHONE.....................800 810-3687
Bruce Hodge, CEO
Peter Lacy, CFO
Dale Scott, Business Mgr
Steven Spurlock, Business Mgr
Marilyn Bryson, Opers Mgr
EMP: 95
SQ FT: 1,200
SALES (est): 11MM Privately Held
WEB: www.goway.com
SIC: 4724 Travel agencies

(P-4962) IDEA TRAVEL COMPANY
13145 Byrd Ln Ste 101, Los Altos Hills (94022-3211)
PHONE.....................650 948-0207
Fax: 650 948-8700
Michael Schoendorf, CEO
Ram Bodapati, CTO
Beverly Hoh, Software Dev
EMP: 1100
SALES (est): 86.1MM Privately Held
WEB: www.ideatravel.com
SIC: 4724 Travel agencies

(P-4963) JAPAN AIRLINES CO LTD
300 Continental Blvd # 620, El Segundo (90245-5047)
PHONE.....................310 607-2305
Hiroyuki Hioka, CEO
Noriyuki Aoki, Vice Pres
Hidekazu Fujioka, Vice Pres
Steve Smith, Vice Pres
Carol Anderson, Marketing Staff
EMP: 90
SALES (corp-wide): 11.4B Privately Held
WEB: www.jal.co.jp
SIC: 4724 8741 4581 4512 Travel agencies; management services; airports, flying fields & services; air transportation, scheduled
PA: Japan Airlines Co.,Ltd.
2-4-11, Higashishinagawa
Shinagawa-Ku TKY 140-0
354 603-121

(P-4964) JTB AMERICAS LTD (HQ)
19700 Mariner Ave, Torrance (90503-1648)
PHONE.....................310 303-3750
Tsuneo Irita, President
Shiro Monden
Reiko Matsudo, Account Dir
EMP: 100
SALES (est): 140.2MM
SALES (corp-wide): 1.1B Privately Held
SIC: 4724 Travel agencies
PA: Jtb Corp.
2-3-11, Higashishinagawa
Shinagawa-Ku TKY 140-0
354 792-211

(P-4965) KINTETSU INTL EX USA INC
879 W 190th St Ste 720, Gardena (90248-4205)
PHONE.....................310 525-1650
Shoichi Gonda, President
EMP: 161 EST: 2015
SALES (est): 7MM
SALES (corp-wide): 10.4B Privately Held
SIC: 4724 Travel agencies
HQ: Knt-Ct Holdings Co.,Ltd.
1-7-8, Higashikanda
Chiyoda-Ku TKY 101-0
368 916-800

(P-4966) L B C HOLDINGS U S A CORP (PA)
362 E Grand Ave, South San Francisco (94080-6210)
PHONE.....................650 873-0750
Carlos Araneta, Ch of Bd
Fely Ruiz, Treasurer
EMP: 164
SQ FT: 25,000
SALES (est): 47.2MM Privately Held
SIC: 4724 4513 4412 Travel agencies; air courier services; deep sea foreign transportation of freight

(P-4967) LBF TRAVEL INC
4545 Murphy Canyon Rd # 210, San Diego (92123-4363)
PHONE.....................858 429-7599
Michael H Thomas, CEO
Philip Ferri, CFO
Steve Pello, Exec VP
Peter Harders, Vice Pres
EMP: 300
SALES (est): 57.2MM Privately Held
SIC: 4724 Travel agencies

(P-4968) LOVES TRAVEL STOPS
2000 E Tehachapi Blvd, Tehachapi (93561-9680)
PHONE.....................661 823-1484
EMP: 133
SALES (corp-wide): 4.7B Privately Held
SIC: 4724 Travel agencies
PA: Love's Travel Stops & Country Stores, Inc.
10601 N Pennsylvania Ave
Oklahoma City OK 73120
405 302-6500

(P-4969) NIPPON TRAVEL AGENCY AMER INC
Also Called: Nta America
1025 W 190th St Ste 301, Gardena (90248-4332)
PHONE.....................310 768-1817
Tadashi Wakayama, President
Rintaro Yoshida, Human Res Dir
Natsu Ofhiri, Human Resources
Romeo Dublin, Asst Mgr
Miyuki Holihan, Consultant
EMP: 70 EST: 1999
SQ FT: 8,000
SALES (est): 18.9MM
SALES (corp-wide): 12.4B Privately Held
WEB: www.ntasfb.com
SIC: 4724 Travel agencies
HQ: Nippon Travel Agency Pacific, Inc.
1025 W 190th St Ste 300
Gardena CA 90248
310 768-0017

(P-4970) NIPPON TRAVEL AGENCY PCF INC (DH)
Also Called: Nta Pacific
1025 W 190th St Ste 300, Gardena (90248-4332)
PHONE.....................310 768-0017
Fax: 310 323-4032
Tadashi Wakayama, President
Akio Tsuna, CFO
Yoshiko Hashimoto, Accountant
Yukiko Hamano, Human Res Mgr
Thomas T Liu, Agent
EMP: 80
SQ FT: 20,000
SALES (est): 30.7MM
SALES (corp-wide): 12.4B Privately Held
SIC: 4724 Travel agencies
HQ: Nippon Travel Agency Co., Ltd.
1-19-1, Nihombashi
Chuo-Ku TKY 103-0
368 957-800

(P-4971) PROTRAVEL INTERNATIONAL LLC
9171 Wilshire Blvd # 428, Beverly Hills (90210-5530)
PHONE.....................310 271-9566
Fax: 310 271-9597
Lois Mitchell, Vice Pres
Janet Szabo, Manager
EMP: 58
SALES (corp-wide): 73MM Privately Held
WEB: www.protravelinternational.com
SIC: 4724 Travel agencies
PA: Protravel International Llc
515 Madison Ave Fl 10
New York NY 10022
212 755-4550

(P-4972) REVEL TRAVEL SERVICE INC
Also Called: Revel Travel At Altour
449 S Beverly Dr Ste 101, Beverly Hills (90210-4463)
PHONE.....................310 553-5555
Fax: 310 553-5554
Jack Revel, President
Ken Macconnell, Controller
EMP: 65
SALES (est): 130K
SALES (corp-wide): 1.6MM Privately Held
SIC: 4724 Travel agencies
PA: Altour International Inc.
12100 W Olympic Blvd # 300
Los Angeles CA 90064
310 571-6000

(P-4973) SARA ENTERPRISES INC (HQ)
Also Called: Montrose Travel
2349 Honolulu Ave, Montrose (91020-2512)
PHONE.....................818 553-3200
Fax: 818 248-1923
Joseph McClure, President
Julie McClure, CFO
Andrea McClure, Vice Pres
Rhonda Holguin, General Mgr
Emily Peters, Executive Asst
EMP: 68
SQ FT: 31,700
SALES (est): 20.6MM
SALES (corp-wide): 191.6MM Privately Held
SIC: 4724 Travel agencies
PA: Corporate Travel Management Limited
Level 24
Brisbane QLD 4000
180 066-3622

(P-4974) STELLA TRAVEL SERVICES USA INC
Also Called: Qantas Vctons Nwmans Vacations
6171 W Century Blvd # 160, Los Angeles (90045-5335)
PHONE.....................310 535-1000
Fax: 310 535-1057
Ross Webster, President
Gary Goeldner, CEO
Colin Storrie, CFO
Kavita Ramnani, CIO
Andrew Root, Technology
EMP: 100
SQ FT: 18,000
SALES (est): 27.3MM
SALES (corp-wide): 218.7MM Privately Held
WEB: www.jetaboutfijivacations.com
SIC: 4724 Travel agencies
PA: Helloworld Limited
Level 14
North Sydney NSW 2060
180 019-8455

(P-4975) STUDENT GOVERNMENT ASSOCIAT
Also Called: Associated Students Uc Irvine
D200 Student Center, Irvine (92697-0001)
PHONE.....................949 824-5547
Dennis Hampton, Exec Dir
Amy Schulz, Sr Corp Ofcr
EMP: 155
SQ FT: 6,000
SALES: 4.2MM Privately Held
SIC: 4724 5813 5947 4481 Travel agencies; drinking places; gifts & novelties; deep sea passenger transportation, except ferry; women's accessory & specialty stores

(P-4976) TRAVANA INC
600 Townsend St Fl 5, San Francisco (94103-5696)
PHONE.....................415 919-4140
Jason Chen, CEO
Lei Shi, President
Jonathan Feng, Executive Asst
Mohamed Ulla, Controller
EMP: 70
SQ FT: 11,000
SALES (est): 75MM Privately Held
SIC: 4724 Tourist agency arranging transport, lodging & car rental
HQ: Hna Group (International) Company Limited
26/F Three Pacific Place
Wan Chai HK
319 609-59

(P-4977) TRAVEL STORE
Also Called: Travelstore
4980 Verdugo Way, Camarillo (93012-8632)
PHONE.....................805 987-3425
EMP: 58
SALES (corp-wide): 38.2MM Privately Held
SIC: 4724 Travel agencies
PA: Travel Store
11601 Wilshire Blvd
Los Angeles CA 90025
310 575-5540

(P-4978) TRAVEL STORE
633 S Brea Blvd, Brea (92821-5308)
PHONE.....................714 529-1947
Eva Bailon, Manager
EMP: 58
SALES (est): 4.7MM
SALES (corp-wide): 38.2MM Privately Held
SIC: 4724 Travel agencies
PA: Travel Store
11601 Wilshire Blvd
Los Angeles CA 90025
310 575-5540

(P-4979) TRAVEL STORE (PA)
Also Called: Travelstore
11601 Wilshire Blvd, Los Angeles (90025-0509)
PHONE.....................310 575-5540
Fax: 310 575-5541
Wido Schaefer, President
Osvaldo Ramos, CFO
Dan Ilves, Vice Pres
Joann Finning, Executive
Eva Bailon, General Mgr
EMP: 70
SQ FT: 7,000
SALES (est): 38.2MM Privately Held
WEB: www.travel-store.com
SIC: 4724 Travel agencies

PRODUCTS & SERVICES SECTION

4725 - Tour Operators County (P-5000)

(P-4980)
TRAVEL SYNDICATE
350 S Beverly Dr Ste 170, Beverly Hills (90212-4818)
PHONE..................................818 297-9979
Fax: 818 710-9572
Arline Fiorto, *Partner*
Roger Lipkis, *Partner*
EMP: 60
SQ FT: 9,800
SALES (est): 6.9MM **Privately Held**
WEB: www.travelsyndicate.com
SIC: 4724 Travel agencies

(P-4981)
TRAVELMASTERS INC
Also Called: Goldrush Getaways
8350 Auburn Blvd Ste 200, Citrus Heights (95610-0396)
PHONE..................................916 722-1648
Fax: 916 722-2556
Brian A Carr, *President*
Karen Chavez, *Training Spec*
John Oestreich, *Marketing Staff*
Julie McCullough, *Consultant*
EMP: 50
SALES (est): 7.3MM **Privately Held**
WEB: www.goldrushgetaways.com
SIC: 4724 Travel agencies

(P-4982)
VIKING RIVER CRUISES INC (HQ)
5700 Canoga Ave Ste 200, Woodland Hills (91367-6569)
PHONE..................................818 227-1234
Fax: 818 227-1237
Milton Hugh, *CEO*
Cheri Allen, *Vice Pres*
Pete Levine, *Vice Pres*
Tine Nilsen, *Vice Pres*
Cheri Stratton, *Vice Pres*
EMP: 82
SALES (est): 20MM **Privately Held**
WEB: www.vikingrivercruises.com
SIC: 4724 Travel agencies
PA: Viking River Cruises Ag
Schaferweg 18
Basel BS
616 386-000

4725 Tour Operators

(P-4983)
AAT KINGS TOURS USA INC
801 E Katella Ave Fl 3, Anaheim (92805-6614)
PHONE..................................714 456-0505
Richard Launder, *President*
Bob Housepenny, *Director*
EMP: 75
SALES (est): 7.5MM **Privately Held**
SIC: 4725 Tour operators

(P-4984)
ALCATRAZ CRUISES LLC
Hornb Alcat Landi Pier 33 St Pier, San Francisco (94111)
PHONE..................................415 981-7625
Terry A Macrae,
Michael Badolato, *Admin Asst*
Andrew Autore, *Engineer*
Bobby Martinez, *Purch Mgr*
Maria A Sespene, *Sales Mgr*
EMP: 120
SALES (est): 14.5MM **Privately Held**
SIC: 4725 Arrangement of travel tour packages, wholesale

(P-4985)
AMERICANTOURS INTL LLC (HQ)
6053 W Century Blvd, Los Angeles (90045-6430)
PHONE..................................310 641-9953
Noel Irwin-Hentschel,
Anwar Noorzay, *Controller*
Michael Fitzpatrick,
EMP: 105
SQ FT: 20,000
SALES (est): 27.8MM
SALES (corp-wide): 36.4MM **Privately Held**
SIC: 4725 4724 Tour operators; travel agencies
PA: Americantours International Inc
6053 W Century Blvd Ste 7
Los Angeles CA 90045
310 641-9953

(P-4986)
APPELLATION TOURS INC
Also Called: Beau Wine Tours
21707 8th St E, Sonoma (95476-9781)
PHONE..................................707 938-9390
Thomas Buck, *President*
EMP: 50
SQ FT: 21,000
SALES (est): 7MM **Privately Held**
WEB: www.appellationtours.com
SIC: 4725 4111 4141 Tour operators; airport limousine, scheduled service; local bus charter service

(P-4987)
BACKROADS (PA)
801 Cedar St, Berkeley (94710-1800)
PHONE..................................510 527-1555
Fax: 510 527-1444
Tom Hale, *CEO*
Allison Harbour, *Vice Pres*
Ryon Rosvold, *Executive*
Christian Chumbley, *Regional Mgr*
Michelle Muench, *Regional Mgr*
EMP: 100
SQ FT: 10,000
SALES (est): 47.7MM **Privately Held**
WEB: www.walkingvacation.com
SIC: 4725 4724 Sightseeing tour companies; travel agencies

(P-4988)
BRENDAN TOURS (PA)
Also Called: Brendan Worldwide Vacations
801 E Katella Ave, Anaheim (92805-6614)
PHONE..................................818 428-6000
Fax: 818 772-6492
James J Murphy, *CEO*
Gary J Murphy, *President*
Carl Laury, *CIO*
Nancy Bradach, *Manager*
Trish Noa, *Manager*
EMP: 140
SQ FT: 26,000
SALES (est): 14MM **Privately Held**
SIC: 4725 Arrangement of travel tour packages, wholesale

(P-4989)
CLASSIC CUSTOM VACATIONS INC
5893 Rue Ferrari, San Jose (95138-1857)
PHONE..................................800 221-3949
Timothy Scott Macdonald, *CEO*
Gregge Brockway, *President*
Kathy Shaw, *CFO*
Robert Burja, *Administration*
Phyllis Hikawa, *Administration*
EMP: 250
SQ FT: 31,000
SALES (est): 1MM
SALES (corp-wide): 6.6B **Publicly Held**
WEB: www.classicvacations.com
SIC: 4725 Arrangement of travel tour packages, wholesale
PA: Expedia, Inc.
333 108th Ave Ne
Bellevue WA 98004
425 679-7200

(P-4990)
CLASSIC VACATIONS LLC
Also Called: Classic Custom Vacations
5893 Rue Ferrari, San Jose (95138-1857)
PHONE..................................800 221-3949
Fax: 408 281-0973
David Hu, *President*
Ronald M Letterman, *Vice Chairman*
Concetta Tracy, *COO*
Debbie Lindquist, *CFO*
Susan Anderson, *Vice Pres*
EMP: 149
SALES (est): 16.6MM
SALES (corp-wide): 6.6B **Publicly Held**
WEB: www.expedia.com
SIC: 4725 Arrangement of travel tour packages, wholesale
PA: Expedia, Inc.
333 108th Ave Ne
Bellevue WA 98004
425 679-7200

(P-4991)
COACH USA INC
Also Called: Pacific Cast Sightseeing Tours
2001 S Manchester Ave, Anaheim (92802-3803)
PHONE..................................714 978-8855
Fax: 714 978-2617
Darlene Cochran, *Branch Mgr*
EMP: 200
SALES (corp-wide): 5.4B **Privately Held**
SIC: 4725 Tour operators
HQ: Coach Usa, Inc.
160 S Route 17 N
Paramus NJ 07652

(P-4992)
CONTIKI US HOLDINGS INC
Also Called: Contiki Holidays
801 E Katella Ave Frnt, Anaheim (92805-6614)
PHONE..................................714 935-0808
Fax: 714 935-2556
Frank Marini, *President*
Michael Kidd, *CFO*
Amanda Kelly, *Info Tech Mgr*
Sharon Deng, *Human Res Mgr*
Brianna McCarthy, *Opers Spvr*
EMP: 60
SALES (est): 10.2MM **Privately Held**
SIC: 4725 4724 Tour operators; tourist agency arranging transport, lodging & car rental

(P-4993)
CUSA GCBS LLC
Also Called: Goodall's Charter Bus Company
3888 Beech St, San Diego (92105-5905)
PHONE..................................619 266-7365
Craig Lentzsch, *Mng Member*
Darlene Cochram, *General Mgr*
John Busskohl, *Mng Member*
EMP: 100
SALES (est): 8.1MM **Privately Held**
SIC: 4725 Arrangement of travel tour packages, wholesale; sightseeing tour companies

(P-4994)
LIVERMORE WORLD TRAVEL INC
Also Called: Livermore Travel
1453 1st St Ste A, Livermore (94550-4203)
PHONE..................................925 373-2400
Fax: 925 373-1302
Richard K Corbett, *President*
Pamela Corbett, *Corp Secy*
EMP: 65
SQ FT: 3,200
SALES (est): 4.9MM **Privately Held**
WEB: www.livermoretravel.com
SIC: 4725 4724 Arrangement of travel tour packages, wholesale; tourist agency arranging transport, lodging & car rental

(P-4995)
MARITZCX RESEARCH LLC
20285 S Wstn Ave Ste 101, Torrance (90501)
PHONE..................................310 783-4300
Fax: 310 783-9107
Joe Sarquiz, *Principal*
Ron Steinkamp, *President*
Janice Blevins, *Vice Pres*
Tom Reinhart, *Vice Pres*
Jeannie Voss, *Program Mgr*
EMP: 61
SALES (corp-wide): 1.2B **Privately Held**
SIC: 4725 8748 8732 4899 Arrangement of travel tour packages, wholesale; employee programs administration; market analysis or research; data communication services; advertising consultant
HQ: Maritzcx Research Llc
1355 N Highway Dr
Fenton MO 63026
636 827-4000

(P-4996)
OKABE INTERNATIONAL INC (PA)
Also Called: Pacific Leisure Management
1739 Buchanan St Ste B, San Francisco (94115-3208)
PHONE..................................415 921-0808
Fax: 415 921-9212
Mitsufumi Okabe, *President*
Rumi Okabe, *Corp Secy*
EMP: 50
SQ FT: 3,600
SALES (est): 2.6MM **Privately Held**
SIC: 4725 4833 5941 Tour operators; television broadcasting stations; sporting goods & bicycle shops; tennis goods & equipment; golf goods & equipment

(P-4997)
OLD TOWN TRLLEY TURS SAN DIEGO
Also Called: Historic Tours of America
2115 Kurtz St, San Diego (92110-2016)
PHONE..................................619 298-8687
Chris Belland, *CEO*
Edwin O Swift, *President*
Gerald Mosher, *Vice Pres*
Lorin Stewart, *General Mgr*
Carmen Thulin, *Human Res Mgr*
EMP: 60
SQ FT: 22,000
SALES (est): 10.2MM
SALES (corp-wide): 51.3MM **Privately Held**
WEB: www.conchtourtrain.com
SIC: 4725 Sightseeing tour companies
HQ: Conch Tour Trains Inc
1805 Staples Ave Ste 101
Key West FL 33040
305 294-5161

(P-4998)
PLEASANT HOLIDAYS LLC (HQ)
Also Called: Pleasant Hawaiian Holiday
2404 Townsgate Rd, Westlake Village (91361-2505)
PHONE..................................818 991-3390
Fax: 805 379-3040
Jack E Richards, *CEO*
Dal Dewolf, *Senior VP*
Bruce Rosenberg, *Senior VP*
Todd Castor, *Vice Pres*
Mark Klaschka, *Vice Pres*
EMP: 300
SQ FT: 55,000
SALES (est): 82.8MM
SALES (corp-wide): 4.8B **Privately Held**
WEB: www.pleasantactivities.com
SIC: 4725 Tour operators
PA: Automobile Club Of Southern California
2601 S Figueroa St
Los Angeles CA 90007
213 741-3686

(P-4999)
ROYALTY TOURS
630 Stockton Ave, San Jose (95126-2433)
PHONE..................................408 279-4801
Sandra S Allen, *President*
EMP: 50
SQ FT: 3,000
SALES (est): 4.2MM
SALES (corp-wide): 13MM **Privately Held**
WEB: www.royal-coach.com
SIC: 4725 Arrangement of travel tour packages, wholesale; sightseeing tour companies
PA: Royal Coach Tours
630 Stockton Ave
San Jose CA 95126
408 279-4801

(P-5000)
RYANS EXPRESS TRNSP SVCS INC (PA)
19500 Mariner Ave, Torrance (90503-1644)
PHONE..................................702 795-7021
John Busskohl, *CEO*
George Cohen, *CFO*
Alexander E Hansen, *CFO*

4725 - Tour Operators County (P-5001)

Chris Sanchez, *Vice Pres*
Jessie Alcocer, *General Mgr*
EMP: 80
SQ FT: 20,000
SALES (est): 33.8MM **Privately Held**
SIC: 4725 Tour operators

(P-5001)
SANTA CATALINA ISLAND COMPANY (PA)
Also Called: Scico
150 Metropole Ave, Avalon (90704)
P.O. Box 737 (90704-0737)
PHONE..................310 510-2000
Randall Herrel Sr, *CEO*
Paxson H Offield, *Ch of Bd*
John T Dravinski, *COO*
Ronald C Doutt, *Treasurer*
Lubos Pech, *Vice Pres*
EMP: 82 **EST:** 1959
SALES (est): 31.6MM **Privately Held**
WEB: www.scico.com
SIC: 4725 Sightseeing tour companies

(P-5002)
UNIWORLD RIVER CRUISES INC
Also Called: Uniworld Boutique River Cruise
17323 Ventura Blvd # 300, Encino (91316-3964)
PHONE..................818 382-2322
Fax: 818 382-7829
Guy A Young, *President*
Denise TSO, *VP Admin*
Silva Reyes, *Office Mgr*
Beth Cox, *Business Mgr*
Eve Reid, *Business Mgr*
EMP: 110
SALES (est): 20.7MM **Privately Held**
SIC: 4725 Tour operators
PA: Uniworld River Cruises Sa
Rue Guillaume Kroll 5
Luxembourg
-

(P-5003)
VIP TOURS OF CALIFORNIA INC
9830 Bellanca Ave, Los Angeles (90045-5608)
PHONE..................310 216-7507
Fax: 310 641-1210
Marco Khorasani, *President*
Nicole J Khorasani, *Vice Pres*
Luis Aguiler, *Controller*
EMP: 70
SALES (est): 12.8MM **Privately Held**
WEB: www.viptoursandcharters.com
SIC: 4725 Tour operators

(P-5004)
YOUR MAN TOURS INC (DH)
Also Called: Jet Advertising
100 N Sepulveda Blvd # 1700, El Segundo (90245-5662)
PHONE..................310 649-3820
William Price, *President*
Frank Chanell, *Vice Pres*
James Gallas, *Vice Pres*
Eileen Amagna, *Controller*
EMP: 80
SQ FT: 20,000
SALES (est): 17.5MM
SALES (corp-wide): 22.1B **Privately Held**
WEB: www.ymtvacations.com
SIC: 4725 Tour operators

4729 Passenger Transportation

(P-5005)
AMERICAN AIRLINES INC
7000 World Way W, Los Angeles (90045-7503)
PHONE..................213 935-6045
P A Haney, *Branch Mgr*
EMP: 150
SALES (corp-wide): 40.9B **Publicly Held**
SIC: 4729 Airline ticket offices
HQ: American Airlines, Inc.
4333 Amon Carter Blvd
Fort Worth TX 76155
817 963-1234

(P-5006)
CATHAY PACIFIC AIRWAYS LIMITED
1960 E Grand Ave Ste 540, El Segundo (90245-5092)
PHONE..................310 615-1113
Fax: 310 615-0042
Jake Olver, *Branch Mgr*
Lisa Manning, *Executive*
James Barrington, *Sales Dir*
Timothy Remedios, *Sales Staff*
EMP: 100
SALES (corp-wide): 13.2B **Privately Held**
WEB: www.cathaypacific.com
SIC: 4729 4512 Airline ticket offices; air transportation, scheduled
PA: Cathay Pacific Airways Limited
33/F One Pacific Place
Admiralty HK
274 750-00

(P-5007)
CUSTOM TOURS INC
Also Called: Kushner & Associates
24003 Ventura Blvd 100a, Calabasas (91302-2542)
PHONE..................310 274-8819
Susan Kushner, *CEO*
Jonathon Dekarr, *Program Mgr*
Val Hamann, *Info Tech Mgr*
Daniel Whitehouse, *Bookkeeper*
Leanne Anell, *Director*
EMP: 85
SQ FT: 3,000
SALES (est): 10.1MM **Privately Held**
WEB: www.kushnerdmc.com
SIC: 4729 Carpool/vanpool arrangement

(P-5008)
EL AL ISRAEL AIRLINES LTD
6404 Wilshire Blvd # 1250, Los Angeles (90048-5501)
PHONE..................323 852-1252
Fax: 323 852-9783
Rami Fischer, *Branch Mgr*
EMP: 150
SALES (corp-wide): 2B **Privately Held**
WEB: www.elal.co.il
SIC: 4729 4512 Ticket offices, transportation; air transportation, scheduled
PA: El Al Israel Airlines Ltd

Lod 71285
397 172-59

(P-5009)
FIVE STAR TRANSPORTATION INC
8703 La Tijera Blvd # 102, Los Angeles (90045-3900)
PHONE..................310 348-0820
Fax: 310 348-0822
George Reyes, *President*
Linda Reyes, *Vice Pres*
Demetri Ross, *Exec Dir*
Alvin Dapson, *Marketing Staff*
EMP: 50
SALES (est): 7.4MM **Privately Held**
SIC: 4729 Airline ticket offices

(P-5010)
GAT AIRLINE GROUND SUPPORT
2627 N Hollywood Way, Burbank (91505-1062)
PHONE..................818 847-9127
EMP: 332
SALES (corp-wide): 126.1MM **Privately Held**
SIC: 4729 Airline ticket offices
PA: Gat Airline Ground Support Inc
8400 Airport Blvd
Mobile AL 36608
251 633-3888

(P-5011)
MALAYSIAN AIRLINE SYSTEM
Also Called: Malaysia Airlines
17215 Studebaker Rd # 120, Cerritos (90703-2521)
PHONE..................310 535-9288
Fax: 310 535-9088
Zaiful Hasmi Hashim, *Vice Pres*
Chee Teng, *CFO*
Anneliza Zainal, *Vice Pres*
Jyh Jong, *General Mgr*
Azha Jalil, *Finance Mgr*
EMP: 150 **Privately Held**
WEB: www.malaysiaairlines.com
SIC: 4729 4581 Airline ticket offices; airports, flying fields & services
HQ: Malaysian Airline System Berhad
Ground Floor Malaysian Airport
Subang SLG 47200
378 403-517

(P-5012)
MATRIX AVIATION SERVICES INC
200 World Way Ste 6, Los Angeles (90045-5844)
PHONE..................310 337-3037
Ramez Reno, *CEO*
Borseen Oushana, *CFO*
EMP: 175 **EST:** 2008
SALES (est): 14.6MM **Privately Held**
SIC: 4729 Airline ticket offices

(P-5013)
UNITED AIRLINES INC
6850 Airport Blvd Ste 34, Sacramento (95837-1126)
PHONE..................916 877-3002
Ken Brown, *Manager*
EMP: 150
SALES (corp-wide): 37.8B **Publicly Held**
WEB: www.united.com
SIC: 4729 4512 Airline ticket offices; air transportation, scheduled
HQ: United Airlines, Inc.
233 S Wacker Dr Ste 430
Chicago IL 60606
872 825-4000

4731 Freight Forwarding & Arrangement

(P-5014)
ADVANCED QUALITY LOGISTICS LLC
350 Westmont Dr, San Pedro (90731-1000)
PHONE..................310 221-6651
David Latona, *Mng Member*
Owen Schmidt,
EMP: 220
SQ FT: 767,000
SALES (est): 26.6MM **Privately Held**
SIC: 4731 Domestic freight forwarding

(P-5015)
ADVANTAGE LOGISTICS INC
Also Called: CTS Advantage Logistics
2071 Ringwood Ave Ste D, San Jose (95131-1760)
P.O. Box 612438 (95161-2438)
PHONE..................408 943-6300
Steve L Haney, *President*
Donna Haney, *CFO*
Nick Sartoris, *Terminal Mgr*
EMP: 185
SQ FT: 183,000
SALES (est): 28.7MM **Privately Held**
SIC: 4731 Freight transportation arrangement

(P-5016)
AGILITY HOLDINGS INC (DH)
Also Called: Agility Logistics
240 Commerce, Irvine (92602-1318)
PHONE..................714 617-6300
Essa Al-Saleh, *President*
Dale Aman, *Vice Chairman*
John Iacouzzi, *President*
Jamie Robertson, *President*
Mark Soubry, *CEO*
EMP: 80
SALES (est): 462.5MM **Privately Held**
WEB: www.agilitylogistics.com
SIC: 4731 4213 4214 Domestic freight forwarding; foreign freight forwarding; transportation agents & brokers; household goods transport; heavy machinery transport; household goods moving & storage, local
HQ: Agility Logistics International B.V.
Fokkerweg 300 Gebouw 2a
Oude Meer
205 214-777

(P-5017)
AGILITY LOGISTICS CORP
21906 Arnold Center Rd, Carson (90810-1646)
PHONE..................310 507-6700
Kia Kittscher, *Manager*
Joanna Bradanovic, *Office Mgr*
EMP: 65 **Privately Held**
SIC: 4731 Freight forwarding
HQ: Agility Logistics Corp.
240 Commerce
Irvine CA 92602
714 617-6300

(P-5018)
AGILITY LOGISTICS CORP
111 Anza Blvd Ste 122, Burlingame (94010-1932)
PHONE..................650 645-5800
Ove Anderson, *Manager*
EMP: 54 **Privately Held**
SIC: 4731 Freight forwarding
HQ: Agility Logistics Corp.
240 Commerce
Irvine CA 92602
714 617-6300

(P-5019)
AIR TIGER EXPRESS (USA) INC
17000 Gale Ave, City of Industry (91745-1807)
PHONE..................626 965-8647
Sean Lee, *Manager*
Garry Summers, *Executive*
Matt Tran, *Sales Executive*
Pat Kastner, *Manager*
EMP: 50
SALES (corp-wide): 55.1MM **Privately Held**
WEB: www.airtiger.com
SIC: 4731 Freight forwarding
PA: Air Tiger Express (Usa), Inc.
14909 183rd St Ste 2
Springfield Gardens NY 11413
718 244-1824

(P-5020)
AIR-SEA FORWARDERS INC (PA)
9009 S La Cienega Blvd, Inglewood (90301-4403)
P.O. Box 90637, Los Angeles (90009-0637)
PHONE..................310 216-1616
Fax: 310 216-2625
Todd Hinkley, *CEO*
Paul Talley, *COO*
Edward Kushner, *Manager*
EMP: 60
SQ FT: 42,000
SALES (est): 27MM **Privately Held**
WEB: www.airseainc.com
SIC: 4731 Freight forwarding

(P-5021)
AIT WORLDWIDE LOGISTICS INC
19901 Hamilton Ave Ste D, Torrance (90502-1364)
PHONE..................310 538-4383
Ty Bradford, *Manager*
Sam Cortez, *Manager*
EMP: 100
SALES (corp-wide): 368.2MM **Privately Held**
WEB: www.aitworldwide.com
SIC: 4731 Freight forwarding
PA: Ait Worldwide Logistics, Inc.
701 N Rohlwing Rd
Itasca IL 60143
630 766-0711

(P-5022)
ALG WORLDWIDE LOGISTICS LLC
220 W Victoria St, Rancho Dominguez (90220-6034)
PHONE..................800 932-3383
Bob Reznick, *Manager*
EMP: 50
SALES (corp-wide): 11.7MM **Privately Held**
SIC: 4731 4213 Freight forwarding; trucking, except local

PRODUCTS & SERVICES SECTION
4731 - Freight Forwarding & Arrangement County (P-5046)

PA: Alg Worldwide Logistics, Llc
745 Dillon Dr
Wood Dale IL 60191
630 350-7000

(P-5023)
ALLEN LUND COMPANY INC (PA)
4529 Angeles Crest Hwy, La Canada Flintridge (91011-3247)
P.O. Box 1369, La Canada (91012-5369)
PHONE..................818 790-8412
David Allen Lund, *President*
Steve Doerfler, *CFO*
David F Lund, *Vice Pres*
Edward V Lund, *Vice Pres*
Ken Lund, *Vice Pres*
EMP: 50
SQ FT: 18,000
SALES (est): 476.6MM **Privately Held**
SIC: 4731 Truck transportation brokers

(P-5024)
ALLEN LUND COMPANY LLC (HQ)
4529 Angeles Crest Hwy # 300, La Canada Flintridge (91011-3247)
P.O. Box 1369, La Canada (91012-5369)
PHONE..................818 790-1110
Fax: 818 950-5863
Allen Lund, *Mng Member*
Steve Doerfler, *CFO*
David F Lund, *Vice Pres*
Ed Lund, *Vice Pres*
Edward V Lund, *Vice Pres*
EMP: 70
SQ FT: 16,000
SALES: 457.4MM **Privately Held**
WEB: www.allenlund.com
SIC: 4731 Freight transportation arrangement; truck transportation brokers
PA: Allen Lund Corporation
4529 Angeles Crest Hwy
La Canada Flintridge CA 91011
818 790-8412

(P-5025)
ALLEN LUND COMPANY LLC
1825 S Grant St Ste 320, San Mateo (94402-2660)
PHONE..................650 358-9454
Fax: 650 358-9456
Bob Rose, *Branch Mgr*
EMP: 60 **Privately Held**
SIC: 4731 Truck transportation brokers
HQ: Allen Lund Company, Llc
4529 Angeles Crest Hwy # 300
La Canada Flintridge CA 91011
818 790-1110

(P-5026)
ALLPRO INDUSTRY SOLUTIONS LLC
7850 White Ln, Bakersfield (93309-7698)
PHONE..................661 854-3613
Josh Kimball, *President*
EMP: 50
SALES (est): 3.9MM **Privately Held**
SIC: 4731 4212 3537 3523 Freight transportation arrangement; local trucking, without storage; platforms, stands, tables, pallets & similar equipment; crop storage bins; grain storage bins

(P-5027)
AP EXPRESS LLC
Also Called: A P Express Worldwide
8500 Rex Rd, Pico Rivera (90660-3779)
PHONE..................562 236-2250
Jeffery D Pont, *CEO*
Mario Herrera, *Controller*
EMP: 75
SQ FT: 170,000
SALES (est): 27.9MM **Privately Held**
WEB: www.apexpress.com
SIC: 4731 Freight transportation arrangement

(P-5028)
APEX LOGISTICS INTL INC
17511 S Susana Rd, Compton (90221-5405)
PHONE..................310 665-0288
Minjiang Song, *President*
Kathy Wu, *Manager*

Sandy Chan, *Accounts Mgr*
EMP: 58
SALES (est): 36.8MM **Privately Held**
SIC: 4731 Freight forwarding

(P-5029)
APM TERMINALS PACIFIC LLC
Also Called: Mearsk
2500 Navy Way Pier 400, San Pedro (90731-7554)
PHONE..................310 221-4000
Dan Carnahan, *Administration*
EMP: 50
SALES (corp-wide): 38.6B **Privately Held**
SIC: 4731 Freight transportation arrangement
HQ: Apm Terminals Pacific Llc
2500 Navy Way
San Pedro CA 90731
704 571-2768

(P-5030)
APM TERMINALS PACIFIC LTD
5801 Christie Ave, Emeryville (94608-1964)
PHONE..................510 992-6430
EMP: 350
SALES (corp-wide): 38.6B **Privately Held**
SIC: 4731
HQ: Apm Terminals Pacific Ltd.
9300 Arrowpoint Blvd
Charlotte NC 90731
704 571-2768

(P-5031)
ARMSTRONG LOGISTICS LLC
5655 Union Pacific Ave, Commerce (90022-5136)
PHONE..................323 721-1500
Abraham Paez Jr,
EMP: 56
SQ FT: 101,141
SALES (est): 1.8MM **Privately Held**
SIC: 4731 Agents, shipping

(P-5032)
ATECH LOGISTICS INC
7 College Ave, Santa Rosa (95401-4702)
P.O. Box 6836 (95406-0836)
PHONE..................707 526-1910
Jesse E Amaral, *President*
Geri Amaral, *Vice Pres*
EMP: 130
SQ FT: 35,000
SALES (est): 47MM **Privately Held**
WEB: www.atechlogistics.com
SIC: 4731 Freight transportation arrangement

(P-5033)
BINEX LINE CORP (PA)
19515 S Vermont Ave, Torrance (90502-1121)
PHONE..................310 416-8600
Fax: 310 416-8601
David Paek, *President*
James Yoon, *COO*
Hyun K Cho, *CFO*
Tim Park, *Vice Pres*
Jan Mercado, *General Mgr*
EMP: 50
SQ FT: 8,043
SALES: 94.4MM **Privately Held**
SIC: 4731 4513 Freight transportation arrangement; air courier services

(P-5034)
BLACKROCK LOGISTICS INC
5870 Stoneridge Mall Rd # 208, Pleasanton (94588-3286)
PHONE..................925 523-3878
Larry T James, *Director*
EMP: 50
SALES (est): 17.2MM **Privately Held**
SIC: 4731 Freight forwarding

(P-5035)
BLUE SKY SERVICES INC
Also Called: Blue Freight
5530 Corbin Ave Ste 220, Tarzana (91356-6020)
P.O. Box 571085 (91357-1085)
PHONE..................818 609-8779
Barry Keller, *President*
Brian Friedman, *Regl Sales Mgr*
EMP: 100

SQ FT: 1,500
SALES: 2.8MM **Privately Held**
SIC: 4731 Freight forwarding

(P-5036)
BROKERAGE LGSTICS SLUTIONS INC
Also Called: JD Group
1659 Gailes Blvd, San Diego (92154-8230)
PHONE..................619 671-0276
Fax: 619 671-0277
Jorge Diaz Jr, *President*
Ricardo Rebeil, *Vice Pres*
Alexandra Ramos, *Financial Exec*
Bertha Carrera, *Sales Dir*
◆ **EMP:** 55 **EST:** 2001
SQ FT: 50,000
SALES (est): 18.3MM **Privately Held**
WEB: www.agenciajorgediaz.com
SIC: 4731 Domestic freight forwarding

(P-5037)
C H ROBINSON INTL INC
680 Knox St Ste 210, Torrance (90502-1325)
PHONE..................310 763-6080
John Vestal, *Manager*
EMP: 100
SALES (corp-wide): 13.4B **Publicly Held**
SIC: 4731 Foreign freight forwarding
HQ: C. H. Robinson International, Inc.
14701 Charlson Rd
Eden Prairie MN 55347
952 683-2800

(P-5038)
C-AIR INTERNATIONAL INC
9841 Arprt Blvd Ste 1400, Los Angeles (90045)
PHONE..................310 695-3400
Guss Antico, *President*
EMP: 55
SQ FT: 7,000
SALES (est): 15.5MM **Privately Held**
WEB: www.cairla.com
SIC: 4731 Customhouse brokers; domestic freight forwarding

(P-5039)
CALIFORNIA SIERRA EXPRESS INC
2975 Oates St Ste 30, West Sacramento (95691-6401)
PHONE..................916 375-7070
Jeff Phillips, *Manager*
Kandra Ebster, *Finance Mgr*
John Ball, *Human Res Dir*
Blaine Anderson, *Marketing Mgr*
Mike Kerby, *Manager*
EMP: 97
SALES (corp-wide): 20MM **Privately Held**
WEB: www.calsierraexpress.com
SIC: 4731 4212 Agents, shipping; delivery service, vehicular
PA: California Sierra Express, Inc.
4965 Joule St
Reno NV 89502
775 856-8008

(P-5040)
CARMICHAEL INTERNATIONAL SVC (DH)
Also Called: C I Container Line
533 Glendale Blvd Ste 102, Los Angeles (90026-5097)
PHONE..................213 353-0800
Fax: 213 250-0710
John Salvo, *President*
Vince Salvo, *President*
Jim Ryan, *CFO*
Enrico Salvo, *Senior VP*
Susan Dec, *Branch Mgr*
◆ **EMP:** 100
SQ FT: 19,000
SALES: 24MM
SALES (corp-wide): 3.5B **Privately Held**
WEB: www.carmnet.com
SIC: 4731 Customhouse brokers
HQ: Apl Logistics Americas, Ltd.
16220 N Scottsdale Rd
Scottsdale AZ 85254
602 586-4800

(P-5041)
CASESTACK INC (PA)
3000 Ocean Park Blvd, Santa Monica (90405-3020)
PHONE..................310 473-8885
Daniel A Sanker, *President*
Keith Carvin, *CFO*
Colby Beland, *Vice Pres*
Jim Harder, *Vice Pres*
Adam Wakefield, *Vice Pres*
EMP: 65
SQ FT: 10,000
SALES (est): 66MM **Privately Held**
WEB: www.casestack.com
SIC: 4731 4225 Freight transportation arrangement; general warehousing & storage

(P-5042)
CEVA FREIGHT LLC
Also Called: Ceva Ocean Line
8670 Younger Creek Dr, Sacramento (95828-1043)
PHONE..................916 379-6000
Scott Mann, *Branch Mgr*
EMP: 150 **Publicly Held**
WEB: www.tntlogistics.com
SIC: 4731 Domestic freight forwarding
HQ: Ceva Freight, Llc
15350 Vickery Dr
Houston TX 77032
281 618-3100

(P-5043)
CEVA LOGISTICS LLC
18120 Bishop Ave, Carson (90746-4032)
PHONE..................310 223-6500
Marvin O Schlanger, *Manager*
EMP: 300 **Publicly Held**
SIC: 4731 Domestic freight forwarding; foreign freight forwarding
HQ: Ceva Logistics, Llc
15350 Vickery Dr
Houston TX 77032
281 618-3100

(P-5044)
CFR RINKEN LLC
Also Called: Cfr Line Rinkens International
15501 Texaco Ave, Paramount (90723-3921)
PHONE..................310 223-0474
Maximiliaan Hoes,
Branko Stanojevic, *Accountant*
Gino Bermeo, *Export Mgr*
Jesus Garrido, *Opers Mgr*
Christoph Seitz,
EMP: 51 **EST:** 2012
SALES (est): 24.1MM **Privately Held**
SIC: 4731 Freight forwarding

(P-5045)
CH ROBINSON FREIGHT SVCS LTD
Also Called: Phoenix International
680 Knox St Ste 210, Torrance (90502-1325)
PHONE..................310 515-7755
Fax: 310 515-7788
Pat Nelms, *Branch Mgr*
Amy K Elliott, *Marketing Staff*
Craig S Carter, *Warehouse Mgr*
John Bestal, *Manager*
EMP: 50
SALES (corp-wide): 13.4B **Publicly Held**
SIC: 4731 4225 Freight forwarding; customhouse brokers; general warehousing
HQ: C.H. Robinson Freight Services, Ltd.
1501 N Mittel Blvd Ste A
Wood Dale IL 60191
630 766-4445

(P-5046)
CHINA SHIPG N AMER HOLDG LTD
111 W Ocean Blvd Ste 1700, Long Beach (90802-4694)
PHONE..................562 590-3845
Paul Raneyi, *General Mgr*
EMP: 50 **Privately Held**
SIC: 4731 Freight transportation arrangement

4731 - Freight Forwarding & Arrangement County (P-5047)

PRODUCTS & SERVICES SECTION

HQ: China Shipping (North America) Holding Co., Ltd.
11 Philips Pkwy
Montvale NJ 07645
201 505-6900

(P-5047)
CHINA SHIPG N AMER HOLDG LTD
444 W Ocean Blvd, Long Beach (90802-4518)
PHONE 562 590-0900
Paul Raney, *Principal*
Nancy Wang, *Marketing Staff*
Joy Furtado, *Manager*
EMP: 50 **Privately Held**
SIC: 4731 Freight transportation arrangement
HQ: China Shipping (North America) Holding Co., Ltd.
11 Philips Pkwy
Montvale NJ 07645
201 505-6900

(P-5048)
CITY FASHION EXPRESS INC
Also Called: C F X
2888 E El Presidio St, Carson (90810-1119)
PHONE 310 223-1010
Walter John Malishka, *CEO*
Michel Gary, *COO*
Isabelle Gonzalaz, *Admin Asst*
Gary Michel, *VP Opers*
EMP: 58
SALES (est): 13.8MM **Privately Held**
WEB: www.cityx.com
SIC: 4731 Freight forwarding

(P-5049)
CNS LOGISTICS INC
108 W Walnut St Ste 270, Gardena (90248-3102)
PHONE 562 229-1133
Kevin Kim, *COO*
Jay Lim, *COO*
Jae Lee, *CFO*
Sean Choi, *Finance Mgr*
Jason Hwang, *Opers Mgr*
EMP: 84
SALES (est): 15MM **Privately Held**
SIC: 4731 Freight forwarding

(P-5050)
COMMODITY FORWARDERS INC (PA)
Also Called: C F I
11101 S La Cienega Blvd, Los Angeles (90045-6111)
PHONE 310 348-8855
Fax: 310 348-8879
Alfred P Kuehlewind, *CEO*
Christopher A Connell, *President*
Paul Greg, *CFO*
Tan Nguyen, *Regional Mgr*
Evelyn Menjivar, *Human Res Mgr*
◆ **EMP:** 60
SQ FT: 30,000
SALES (est): 74.4MM **Privately Held**
WEB: www.cfi-lax.com
SIC: 4731 Freight forwarding

(P-5051)
CONTINENTAL AGENCY INC (PA)
1768 W 2nd St, Pomona (91766-1206)
PHONE 909 595-8884
Jimmy Jaing, *CEO*
Beverly Jiang, *President*
EMP: 53
SQ FT: 105,000
SALES: 150.6MM **Privately Held**
WEB: www.continentalagency.com
SIC: 4731 Customhouse brokers

(P-5052)
COSCO AGENCIES (LOS ANGELES) (DH)
588 Harbor Scenic Way, Long Beach (90802-6317)
PHONE 213 689-6700
Jin Guoqiang, *President*
Tom Somma, *Exec VP*
Zhang Xiaolan, *General Mgr*
Yang Yong, *General Mgr*
Howard Finkel, *CIO*
EMP: 56
SQ FT: 11,000
SALES (est): 7.4MM **Privately Held**
SIC: 4731 Agents, shipping
HQ: Cosco Container Lines Americas, Inc.
100 Lighting Way Fl 3
Secaucus NJ 07094
201 422-0500

(P-5053)
CUSTOM COMPANIES INC
13012 Molette St, Santa Fe Springs (90670-5522)
PHONE 310 672-8800
Mark Inman, *Manager*
EMP: 70
SALES (corp-wide): 112.2MM **Privately Held**
SIC: 4731 4214 Transportation agents & brokers; freight forwarding; local trucking with storage
PA: The Custom Companies Inc
317 W Lake St
Northlake IL 60164
708 344-5555

(P-5054)
DEFENDERS TRNSP SVCS INC
Also Called: Sam Kholi Transport
14562 Slover Ave, Fontana (92337-7148)
PHONE 909 854-7000
Christopher T Kato, *CEO*
EMP: 110 **EST:** 2010
SQ FT: 10,000
SALES: 10MM **Privately Held**
SIC: 4731 Agents, shipping

(P-5055)
DELTA AIR LINES INC
Also Called: Delta Airlines
5625 W Imperial Hwy, Los Angeles (90045-6316)
PHONE 310 646-9614
Kelvin Wimbish, *Branch Mgr*
EMP: 72
SALES (corp-wide): 40.7B **Publicly Held**
WEB: www.delta.com
SIC: 4731 4581 4512 Freight forwarding; airports, flying fields & services; air transportation, scheduled
PA: Delta Air Lines, Inc.
1030 Delta Blvd
Atlanta GA 30354
404 715-2600

(P-5056)
DEPENDABLE AIRCARGO EX INC
19201 S Susana Rd, Compton (90221-5710)
PHONE 310 537-2000
Bradley Dechter, *President*
EMP: 150
SALES (est): 16.1MM **Privately Held**
SIC: 4731 Transportation agents & brokers

(P-5057)
DEPENDABLE GLOBAL EXPRESS INC
Also Called: D G X
19201 S Susana Rd, E Rncho Dmngz (90221-5710)
P.O. Box 513370, Los Angeles (90051-3370)
PHONE 310 537-2000
Ronald Massman, *CEO*
Bradley Dechter, *President*
Tim Rice, *CFO*
Jorge Quintana, *Vice Pres*
Dan Dechter, *Technology*
EMP: 150
SALES (est): 40.6MM **Privately Held**
SIC: 4731 Freight forwarding

(P-5058)
DHX-DEPENDABLE HAWAIIAN EX INC (PA)
19201 S Susana Rd, Rancho Dominguez (90220)
PHONE 310 537-2000
Fax: 310 537-1400
Ronald Massman, *Chairman*
Gerard Crisostomo, *President*
Cammie Laster, *President*
Tim Rice, *CFO*
Ralph Merolla, *Vice Pres*
EMP: 150
SQ FT: 106,000
SALES (est): 99.4MM **Privately Held**
SIC: 4731 Freight forwarding

(P-5059)
DISPATCH TRUCKING INC (PA)
14032 Santa Ana Ave, Fontana (92337-7035)
PHONE 909 355-5531
Fax: 909 355-5537
Bruce L Degler, *CEO*
Jalayne Pugmire, *Vice Pres*
EMP: 70 **EST:** 1991
SQ FT: 600
SALES (est): 9.2MM **Privately Held**
WEB: www.dispatchtrans.com
SIC: 4731 Truck transportation brokers

(P-5060)
DSC LOGISTICS INC
5690 Industrial Pkwy, San Bernardino (92407-1885)
PHONE 540 377-2302
EMP: 338
SALES (corp-wide): 355MM **Privately Held**
SIC: 4731 Freight transportation arrangement
PA: Dsc Logistics, Inc.
1750 S Wolf Rd
Des Plaines IL 60018
847 390-6800

(P-5061)
DTM SERVICES INC (PA)
Also Called: Diversified Trnsp Svcs
19829 Hamilton Ave, Torrance (90502-1341)
PHONE 310 521-1200
Fax: 310 521-1212
Marc Meskin, *CEO*
Robbie Thone, *Senior VP*
Michael Doyle, *Vice Pres*
Najat Janbay, *Office Admin*
Tim Tackett, *QA Dir*
EMP: 54
SQ FT: 7,000
SALES (est): 13.9MM **Privately Held**
WEB: www.dtsone.com
SIC: 4731 Truck transportation brokers

(P-5062)
DW MORGAN LLC
4185 Blackhawk Ste 260, Danville (94506)
PHONE 925 460-2700
David W Morgan, *CEO*
EMP: 63 **EST:** 2013
SALES (est): 4.5MM **Privately Held**
SIC: 4731 4212 4789 Domestic freight forwarding; local trucking, without storage; cargo loading & unloading services

(P-5063)
DYNAMIC WORLDWIDE WEST INC
14141 Alondra Blvd, Santa Fe Springs (90670-5804)
PHONE 310 357-2460
EMP: 67
SALES (corp-wide): 19.6MM **Privately Held**
SIC: 4731 Freight consolidation
PA: Dynamic Worldwide West, Inc.
14141 Alondra Blvd
Santa Fe Springs CA 90670
562 407-1000

(P-5064)
ECO FLOW TRANSPORTATION LLC
18735 S Ferris Pl, Rancho Dominguez (90220-6405)
PHONE 310 816-0260
Bill Allen, *President*
EMP: 60
SALES (est): 1.5MM **Privately Held**
SIC: 4731 Freight transportation arrangement

(P-5065)
ELITE ANYWHERE CORP
82585 Showcase Pkwy, Indio (92203-9811)
PHONE 917 860-9247
Robert Sabo, *CEO*
EMP: 70
SQ FT: 50,000
SALES: 2MM **Privately Held**
SIC: 4731 4225 Freight transportation arrangement; general warehousing & storage

(P-5066)
ERIC JONES CUSTOMS BROKERAGE
9841 Arprt Blvd Ste 1400, Los Angeles (90045)
PHONE 310 348-3777
Fax: 310 216-9525
Eric Jones, *Vice Pres*
EMP: 50
SALES (est): 3.3MM **Privately Held**
SIC: 4731 Customhouse brokers

(P-5067)
EXEL INC
Also Called: Msas Cargo International
485 Valley Dr, Brisbane (94005-1209)
PHONE 415 531-0596
Fax: 415 468-8796
Kevin Duson, *General Mgr*
EMP: 125
SALES (corp-wide): 63.6B **Privately Held**
SIC: 4731 Freight forwarding
HQ: Exel Inc.
570 Polaris Pkwy
Westerville OH 43082
614 865-8500

(P-5068)
EXPEDITORS INTL WASH INC
Also Called: Sfo-3 - San Francisco Full Svc
425 Valley Dr, Brisbane (94005-1209)
PHONE 415 657-3600
Fax: 415 657-3990
Kevin Niduaza, *General Mgr*
Rehnish Patel, *Broker*
Lor Melvin, *Manager*
EMP: 50
SALES (corp-wide): 6.6B **Publicly Held**
WEB: www.expd.com
SIC: 4731 Foreign freight forwarding
PA: Expeditors International Of Washington, Inc.
1015 3rd Ave Fl 12
Seattle WA 98104
206 674-3400

(P-5069)
EXPEDITORS INTL WASH INC
578 Eccles Ave, South San Francisco (94080-1905)
PHONE 919 489-7431
Fax: 650 737-0933
Jeff Musser, *Vice Pres*
Jennifer Kiefer, *Financial Exec*
EMP: 131
SALES (corp-wide): 6.6B **Publicly Held**
WEB: www.expd.com
SIC: 4731 Freight forwarding; foreign freight forwarding; domestic freight forwarding
PA: Expeditors International Of Washington, Inc.
1015 3rd Ave Fl 12
Seattle WA 98104
206 674-3400

(P-5070)
EXPEDITORS INTL WASH INC
5757 W Century Blvd, Los Angeles (90045-6401)
PHONE 310 343-6200
EMP: 64
SALES (corp-wide): 6.6B **Publicly Held**
SIC: 4731 Foreign freight forwarding
PA: Expeditors International Of Washington, Inc.
1015 3rd Ave Fl 12
Seattle WA 98104
206 674-3400

(P-5071)
EXPEDITORS INTL WASH INC
5757 W Century Blvd, Los Angeles (90045-6401)
PHONE 310 343-6200
Fax: 310 649-1995
Karl Francisco, *Branch Mgr*
Angelica Sanchez, *Sales Executive*

▲ = Import ▼ = Export
◆ = Import/Export

PRODUCTS & SERVICES SECTION
4731 - Freight Forwarding & Arrangement County (P-5094)

Sara Fielder, *Sales Staff*
Felecia Dufauchard, *Manager*
Pepito Holandez, *Supervisor*
EMP: 125
SALES (corp-wide): 6.6B **Publicly Held**
WEB: www.expd.com
SIC: 4731 Freight forwarding
PA: Expeditors International Of Washington, Inc.
1015 3rd Ave Fl 12
Seattle WA 98104
206 674-3400

(P-5072)
EXPEDITORS INTL WASH INC
1470 Expo Way Ste 110, San Diego (92154)
PHONE 619 710-1900
Fax: 619 710-4956
Trevor Moulton, *Manager*
EMP: 60
SALES (corp-wide): 6.6B **Publicly Held**
WEB: www.expd.com
SIC: 4731 Freight transportation arrangement
PA: Expeditors International Of Washington, Inc.
1015 3rd Ave Fl 12
Seattle WA 98104
206 674-3400

(P-5073)
EXPRESS SYSTEM INTERMODAL INC
2633 Camino Ramon Ste 400, San Ramon (94583-2176)
PHONE 801 302-6625
Peter Leng, *President*
Adam P Chiu, *Admin Sec*
EMP: 150
SALES (est): 20.2MM **Privately Held**
WEB: www.esi-intermodal.com
SIC: 4731 Freight transportation arrangement
HQ: Oocl (Usa) Inc.
10913 S River Front Pkwy # 200
South Jordan UT 84095
801 302-6625

(P-5074)
EXTRA EXPRESS (CERRITOS) INC
3050 Enterprise St, Brea (92821-6214)
P.O. Box 5100, Cerritos (90703-5100)
PHONE 714 985-6000
Kirk Baerwaldt, *President*
Robert Bell, *Vice Pres*
Timm Vu, *Controller*
Tom Webb, *Director*
EMP: 50
SALES (est): 14.5MM
SALES (corp-wide): 16.8MM **Privately Held**
WEB: www.extraexpress.com
SIC: 4731 Freight transportation arrangement
HQ: Dicom West Llc
676 N Michigan Ave # 3700
Chicago IL 60611
312 255-4800

(P-5075)
F R T INTERNATIONAL INC
Also Called: Frontier Logistics Services
2825 Jurupa St, Ontario (91761-2903)
PHONE 909 390-4892
Steven Hall, *Branch Mgr*
EMP: 173
SALES (corp-wide): 23.6MM **Privately Held**
SIC: 4731 Customhouse brokers
PA: F. R. T. International, Inc.
1700 N Alameda St
Compton CA 90222
310 604-8208

(P-5076)
FEDERAL EXPRESS CORPORATION
Also Called: Fedex
2221 W Washington St, San Diego (92110-2037)
PHONE 619 688-9203
Doug Eacros, *Manager*
EMP: 140

SALES (corp-wide): 50.3B **Publicly Held**
WEB: www.federalexpress.com
SIC: 4731 Agents, shipping
HQ: Federal Express Corporation
3610 Hacks Cross Rd
Memphis TN 38125
901 369-3600

(P-5077)
FNS INC (PA)
1545 Francisco St, Torrance (90501-1330)
PHONE 661 615-2300
Fax: 310 667-4829
Bennett B Koo, *CEO*
Iris H Shin, *CFO*
Jason Kwon, *Branch Mgr*
Wook Jin Choi, *Admin Sec*
Erin Hong, *Accounting Mgr*
EMP: 100
SQ FT: 100,000
SALES (est): 122.4MM **Privately Held**
WEB: www.fnsusa.com
SIC: 4731 Freight forwarding

(P-5078)
FNS CUSTOMS BROKERS INC
18301 S Broadwick St, Compton (90220-6442)
PHONE 310 667-4880
Bennett Koo, *CEO*
Wookjin Choi, *CFO*
Judy Choe, *Manager*
Kelvin Jung, *Accounts Mgr*
EMP: 50
SQ FT: 2,000
SALES (est): 8.6MM **Privately Held**
SIC: 4731 Freight transportation arrangement

(P-5079)
FORWARD AIR INC
427 Valley Dr, Brisbane (94005-1209)
PHONE 415 570-6040
Fax: 650 794-9923
Michelle Thompson, *Manager*
EMP: 50
SALES (corp-wide): 959.1MM **Publicly Held**
WEB: www.forwardair.net
SIC: 4731 Freight transportation arrangement
HQ: Forward Air, Inc.
430 Airport Rd
Greeneville TN 37745
423 639-7196

(P-5080)
FRITZ COMPANIES INC (HQ)
Also Called: U P S
550-1 Eccles Ave, San Francisco (94101)
PHONE 650 635-2693
◆ **EMP:** 200
SALES (est): 399.5MM
SALES (corp-wide): 58.3B **Publicly Held**
WEB: www.ups-scs.com
SIC: 4731 Freight transportation arrangement
PA: United Parcel Service, Inc.
55 Glenlake Pkwy
Atlanta GA 30328
404 828-6000

(P-5081)
FURNITURE TRNSP SYSTEMS
3100 Pomona Blvd, Pomona (91768-3230)
P.O. Box 2960 (91769-2960)
PHONE 909 869-1200
Fax: 909 869-1215
Dennis Firestone, *President*
Lynnette Genereux, *Corp Secy*
John Naughton, *Vice Pres*
Scott Pressley, *Accountant*
EMP: 65
SQ FT: 100,000
SALES (est): 12.5MM
SALES (corp-wide): 76.6MM **Privately Held**
SIC: 4731 4212 Freight consolidation; local trucking, without storage
PA: K. K. W. Trucking, Inc.
3100 Pomona Blvd
Pomona CA 91768
909 869-1200

(P-5082)
G KATEN PARTNERS LTD LBLTY CO
Also Called: My Express Freight
9903 Santa Monica Blvd, Beverly Hills (90212-1671)
PHONE 424 354-3241
Gerald Katen,
EMP: 550
SALES (est): 42.1MM **Privately Held**
SIC: 4731 Freight transportation arrangement; freight forwarding; freight consolidation; freight rate information service

(P-5083)
G3 ENTERPRISES INC (PA)
502 E Whitmore Ave, Modesto (95358-9411)
P.O. Box 624 (95353-0624)
PHONE 209 341-7515
Robert Lubeck, *President*
Michael Ellis, *CFO*
John Kalal, *Vice Pres*
John Cunningham, *Executive*
Deborah Creps, *Executive Asst*
EMP: 160 **EST:** 1961
SQ FT: 10,000
SALES (est): 120.6MM **Privately Held**
SIC: 4731 Transportation agents & brokers

(P-5084)
G3 ENTERPRISES INC
G3 Enterprises Mineral Div
1300 Camino Diablo Rd, Byron (94514)
P.O. Box 216 (94514-0216)
PHONE 209 341-3441
EMP: 51
SALES (corp-wide): 120.6MM **Privately Held**
SIC: 4731 Transportation agents & brokers
PA: G3 Enterprises, Inc.
502 E Whitmore Ave
Modesto CA 95358
209 341-7515

(P-5085)
G3 ENTERPRISES INC
G3 Enterprises Closure Div
500 S Santa Rosa Ave, Modesto (95354-3717)
PHONE 209 341-4045
EMP: 101
SALES (corp-wide): 120.6MM **Privately Held**
SIC: 4731 Transportation agents & brokers
PA: G3 Enterprises, Inc.
502 E Whitmore Ave
Modesto CA 95358
209 341-7515

(P-5086)
GELS LOGISTICS INC
20275 Business Pkwy, City of Industry (91789-2950)
PHONE 909 610-2277
Xindi Hu, *CEO*
Ling Wang, *CFO*
Liangna Zhong, *General Mgr*
EMP: 60
SALES (est): 568.7K **Privately Held**
SIC: 4731 Transportation agents & brokers

(P-5087)
GEODIS WILSON USA INC
229 Littlefield Ave Ste 1, South San Francisco (94080-6926)
PHONE 650 692-9850
Jimmy Huang, *Branch Mgr*
EMP: 125 **Privately Held**
SIC: 4731 Freight forwarding
HQ: Geodis Wilson Usa, Inc.
485c Us Highway 1 S # 410
Iselin NJ 08830
732 362-0600

(P-5088)
GLOVIS AMERICA INC (HQ)
17305 Von Karman Ave # 200, Irvine (92614-6674)
PHONE 714 435-2960
Kyung B Kim, *President*
Glenn Clift, *COO*
Greg Ekman, *Human Res Mgr*
Jinyoung Kim, *Manager*
Richard Kim, *Manager*
EMP: 68

SQ FT: 34,700
SALES (est): 36MM
SALES (corp-wide): 10.3B **Privately Held**
WEB: www.glovisusa.com
SIC: 4731 Freight forwarding
PA: Hyundai Glovis Co., Ltd.
301 Teheran-Ro Gangnam-Gu
Seoul SEO 06152
261 919-454

(P-5089)
GOLDEN HOUR DATA SYSTEMS INC
10052 Mesa Ridge Ct # 200, San Diego (92121-2971)
PHONE 858 768-2500
Kevin Hutton, *President*
Bill Dow, *CFO*
Donna Clark, *Vice Pres*
Charles Haczewski, *Vice Pres*
Eric Angle, *Info Tech Mgr*
EMP: 120 **EST:** 1997
SQ FT: 14,000
SALES (est): 31.8MM **Privately Held**
WEB: www.goldenhour.com
SIC: 4731 Transportation agents & brokers

(P-5090)
GONZALEZ BARBA ENTERPRISES
1575 E 46th St, Los Angeles (90011-4315)
PHONE 323 233-7995
Elizabeth Gonzalez, *Principal*
EMP: 50
SALES (est): 3.8MM **Privately Held**
SIC: 4731 Transportation agents & brokers

(P-5091)
GREATWIDE LOGISTICS SVCS LLC
3350 E Cedar St, Ontario (91761-7630)
PHONE 877 379-6394
Vincent Gulisano, *Manager*
EMP: 50
SALES (corp-wide): 2.4B **Privately Held**
SIC: 4731 Truck transportation brokers
HQ: Greatwide Logistics Services, Llc.
12404 Park Central Dr # 300
Dallas TX 75251
972 228-7389

(P-5092)
HANJIN TRANSPORTATION CO LTD
Also Called: Hanjin Global Logistics
1111 E Watson Center Rd C, Carson (90745-4217)
PHONE 310 522-5030
Bryce Dalziel, *President*
J B Park, *Admin Sec*
Chris Chung, *Administration*
EMP: 90
SQ FT: 28,000
SALES (est): 35.5MM **Privately Held**
SIC: 4731 Transportation agents & brokers
PA: Hanjin Corporation Co., Ltd
137 Hongdo-Dong, Tong-Gu
Daejeon
426 254-747

(P-5093)
HANSOL GOLDPOINT LLC
12792 Valley View St # 211, Garden Grove (92845-2510)
PHONE 714 594-5073
Min Ho Inn, *Branch Mgr*
EMP: 84
SALES (corp-wide): 4MM **Privately Held**
SIC: 4731 Freight forwarding
PA: Hansol Goldpoint Llc
2396 E Pacifica Pl # 290
Rancho Dominguez CA 90220
619 710-1728

(P-5094)
HAPAG-LLOYD (AMERICA) LLC
180 Grand Ave Ste 1535, Oakland (94612-3702)
PHONE 510 251-8405
Fax: 415 927-8833
Manfred Braun, *Manager*
EMP: 50
SQ FT: 16,639
SALES (corp-wide): 9.5B **Privately Held**
SIC: 4731 Agents, shipping

4731 - Freight Forwarding & Arrangement County (P-5095)

HQ: Hapag-Lloyd (America) Llc
399 Hoes Ln Ste 101
Piscataway NJ 08854
732 562-1800

(P-5095)
HARBOR FREIGHT TOOLS USA INC
1750 N Imperial Ave, El Centro (92243-1336)
PHONE.............................760 336-0532
EMP: 193
SALES (corp-wide): 2.3B **Privately Held**
SIC: 4731 Transportation agents & brokers
PA: Harbor Freight Tools Usa, Inc.
26541 Agoura Rd
Calabasas CA 91302
818 836-5000

(P-5096)
HARBOR FREIGHT TOOLS USA INC
23314 Valencia Blvd, Valencia (91355-1712)
PHONE.............................661 799-4907
EMP: 193
SALES (corp-wide): 2.3B **Privately Held**
SIC: 4731 Transportation agents & brokers
PA: Harbor Freight Tools Usa, Inc.
26541 Agoura Rd
Calabasas CA 91302
818 836-5000

(P-5097)
HARBOR FREIGHT TOOLS USA INC
40516 Mrreta Hot Sprng Rd, Murrieta (92563-6403)
PHONE.............................951 304-2714
EMP: 77
SALES (corp-wide): 2.3B **Privately Held**
SIC: 4731 Transportation agents & brokers
PA: Harbor Freight Tools Usa, Inc.
26541 Agoura Rd
Calabasas CA 91302
818 836-5000

(P-5098)
HARRY GROUP INC
Also Called: J M K C Express
2839 E El Presidio St, Carson (90810-1120)
PHONE.............................310 631-9646
Tom Villardi, *President*
Georganna Villardi, *Corp Secy*
EMP: 100
SQ FT: 65,000
SALES (est): 13.8MM **Privately Held**
SIC: 4731 Freight transportation arrangement

(P-5099)
HELLMANN WRLDWIDE LGISTICS INC
2270 E 220th St, Long Beach (90810-1638)
PHONE.............................310 847-4600
Fax: 310 847-4685
Jonas Welch, *Branch Mgr*
Markus Fellmann, *General Mgr*
Jacqueline Flores, *Manager*
Steve Kim, *Manager*
Tatiana Grunauer, *Accounts Exec*
EMP: 60
SALES (corp-wide): 3.9B **Privately Held**
SIC: 4731 Freight forwarding
HQ: Hellmann Worldwide Logistics Inc.
10450 Doral Blvd
Doral FL 33178
305 406-4500

(P-5100)
HELLMANN WRLDWIDE LGISTICS INC
2270 E 220th St, Carson (90810-1638)
PHONE.............................310 847-4600
Roger Haeussler, *President*
Julian Riches, *CFO*
Dieter Kasprzyk, *Officer*
Klaus Fuerstaller, *Director*
Ernst Grubenmann, *Director*
EMP: 50
SALES (corp-wide): 3.9B **Privately Held**
WEB: www.hellmann.net
SIC: 4731 Freight forwarding

HQ: Hellmann Worldwide Logistics Inc.
10450 Doral Blvd
Doral FL 33178
305 406-4500

(P-5101)
HIDDEN VALLEY COMPANIES INC
Also Called: Hv
1218 Pacific Oaks Pl, Escondido (92029-2900)
PHONE.............................760 466-7100
Robert L Berti, *CEO*
EMP: 300 **Privately Held**
SIC: 4731 Freight transportation arrangement

(P-5102)
HONOLULU FREIGHT SERVICE (PA)
1400 Date St, Montebello (90640-6323)
PHONE.............................323 887-6777
Fax: 323 887-6769
Michael Biedleman, *President*
Dorene Beidleman, *CFO*
Thomas Biedleman, *Vice Pres*
Patrick Toves, *General Mgr*
Elaine Bradley, *Office Mgr*
EMP: 50 **EST:** 1945
SQ FT: 1,500
SALES (est): 31.3MM **Privately Held**
WEB: www.hfsnet.com
SIC: 4731 Freight forwarding; domestic freight forwarding

(P-5103)
I3PL LLC
Also Called: Logistics Team
218 Machlin Ct, Walnut (91789-3026)
PHONE.............................909 839-2600
Denia Virgen,
EMP: 100
SALES: 25MM **Privately Held**
SIC: 4731 Freight transportation arrangement

(P-5104)
INNOVEL SOLUTIONS INC
Also Called: Sears
521 Stone Rd, Benicia (94510-1113)
PHONE.............................707 748-1940
Dave Aguirre, *Manager*
EMP: 99
SALES (corp-wide): 25.1MM **Publicly Held**
WEB: www.slslogistics.com+%22sears+logistics+servi
SIC: 4731 Agents, shipping
HQ: Innovel Solutions, Inc.
3333 Beverly Rd
Hoffman Estates IL 60179
847 286-2500

(P-5105)
INNOVEL SOLUTIONS INC
Also Called: Sears
1700 Schuster Rd, Delano (93215-9572)
PHONE.............................661 721-5910
Mike Velton, *General Mgr*
Timothy Cargle, *Admin Mgr*
Michael Velten, *General Mgr*
Cornelio Arrellanes, *Manager*
Stephanie Pedraza, *Manager*
EMP: 600
SALES (corp-wide): 25.1MM **Publicly Held**
WEB: www.slslogistics.com+%22sears+logistics+servi
SIC: 4731 Agents, shipping
HQ: Innovel Solutions, Inc.
3333 Beverly Rd
Hoffman Estates IL 60179
847 286-2500

(P-5106)
INNOVEL SOLUTIONS INC
Also Called: Sears
5691 E Philadelphia St # 125, Ontario (91761-2806)
PHONE.............................909 605-1400
Fax: 909 390-2350
Derrick Daniel, *Manager*
EMP: 100

SALES (corp-wide): 25.1MM **Publicly Held**
WEB: www.slslogistics.com+%22sears+logistics+servi
SIC: 4731 Agents, shipping
HQ: Innovel Solutions, Inc.
3333 Beverly Rd
Hoffman Estates IL 60179
847 286-2500

(P-5107)
JS INTERNATIONAL SHIPG CORP (PA)
Also Called: Jsi Shipping
1535 Rollins Rd Ste B, Burlingame (94010-2305)
P.O. Box 4267 (94011-4267)
PHONE.............................650 697-3963
Fax: 650 697-3831
James G Cullen, *CEO*
Yvonne Angelo, *COO*
Scott French, *Vice Pres*
Bobby Solis, *Vice Pres*
Will Waller, *Vice Pres*
EMP: 80
SQ FT: 50,000
SALES (est): 194.7MM **Privately Held**
WEB: www.jsishipping.com
SIC: 4731 Freight forwarding; customhouse brokers

(P-5108)
KLS AIR EXPRESS INC (PA)
Also Called: Freight Solution Providers
2851 Gold Tailings Ct, Rancho Cordova (95670-6189)
PHONE.............................916 373-3353
Lielanie Steers, *CEO*
Kenneth Steers, *President*
Elizabeth Adair, *Exec VP*
Jeff Adams, *Vice Pres*
Ron Steers, *Executive*
EMP: 60
SQ FT: 9,700
SALES (est): 30.1MM **Privately Held**
WEB: www.shipfsp.com
SIC: 4731 Freight transportation arrangement

(P-5109)
KOJENOV ARKADI NILOVICH
5335 Hackberry Ln, Sacramento (95841-3268)
PHONE.............................916 718-1790
Arkadi Kojenov, *Owner*
Tanya Tekun, *Manager*
EMP: 50 **EST:** 1997
SQ FT: 2,000
SALES: 5MM **Privately Held**
SIC: 4731 Freight transportation arrangement

(P-5110)
KSI CORP (PA)
839 Mitten Rd, San Bruno (94066)
P.O. Box 2182, South San Francisco (94083-2182)
PHONE.............................650 952-0815
Fax: 650 952-1024
Carl Bellante, *CEO*
Dennis Siu, *CFO*
Michael Ford, *Senior VP*
Chris Ramos, *Vice Pres*
Albert Foong, *Manager*
EMP: 64
SQ FT: 13,000
SALES (est): 8.9MM **Privately Held**
WEB: www.ksicorp.com
SIC: 4731 8741 Customhouse brokers; management services

(P-5111)
KUEHNE + NAGEL INC
150 W Hill Pl, Brisbane (94005-1216)
PHONE.............................415 656-4100
Fax: 415 467-7414
Matthew Hamilton, *Branch Mgr*
Sean Williams, *Opers Mgr*
Olaf Greifenhagen, *Director*
EMP: 50
SALES (corp-wide): 16.6B **Privately Held**
WEB: www.kuehnenagel.com
SIC: 4731 Freight forwarding

HQ: Kuehne + Nagel Inc.
10 Exchange Pl
Jersey City NJ 07302
201 413-5500

(P-5112)
KW INTERNATIONAL INC
18511 S Broadwick St, Rancho Dominguez (90220-6440)
PHONE.............................310 747-1380
Dj Kim, *Manager*
EMP: 70 **Privately Held**
SIC: 4731 Freight transportation arrangement
PA: Kw International, Inc.
18655 Bishop Ave
Carson CA 90746

(P-5113)
KW INTERNATIONAL INC
18724 S Broadwick St, Rancho Dominguez (90220-6426)
PHONE.............................213 703-6914
Allen Lee, *Branch Mgr*
Chris Shin, *Opers Mgr*
EMP: 349 **Privately Held**
SIC: 4731 4226 8744 Freight transportation arrangement; freight forwarding; special warehousing & storage; facilities support services
PA: Kw International, Inc.
18655 Bishop Ave
Carson CA 90746

(P-5114)
L E COPPERSMITH INC (PA)
Also Called: Coppersmith Global Logistics
525 S Douglas St Ste 100, El Segundo (90245-4828)
P.O. Box 51845 (90245)
PHONE.............................310 607-8000
Fax: 310 607-8001
Jeffrey Craig Coppersmith, *President*
Doug Walkley, *CFO*
Douglas S Walkley, *CFO*
Lew Coppersmith Jr, *Vice Pres*
Lew E Coppersmith II, *Admin Sec*
◆ **EMP:** 80
SQ FT: 40,000
SALES: 20MM **Privately Held**
SIC: 4731 4789 Customhouse brokers; cargo loading & unloading services

(P-5115)
L E COPPERSMITH INC
525 S Douglas St, El Segundo (90245-4826)
PHONE.............................310 607-8000
D Walkley, *Branch Mgr*
EMP: 80
SALES (corp-wide): 58.6MM **Privately Held**
SIC: 4731 Customhouse brokers
PA: L. E. Coppersmith, Inc.
525 S Douglas St Ste 100
El Segundo CA 90245
310 607-8000

(P-5116)
LTL EX INC
11081 Cherry Ave, Fontana (92337-7118)
PHONE.............................951 255-1222
Ivett Vargas, *President*
Manual Vargas, *Admin Sec*
EMP: 60
SQ FT: 10,000
SALES (est): 11.4MM **Privately Held**
SIC: 4731 Freight transportation arrangement

(P-5117)
LUTREL TRUCKING INC
12856 Old River Rd, Bakersfield (93311-9707)
PHONE.............................661 397-9756
Roy G Lutrel, *President*
Gail Lutrel, *Treasurer*
Mark Lutrel, *Vice Pres*
Keith Lutrel, *Manager*
EMP: 65 **EST:** 1973
SALES (est): 11.3MM **Privately Held**
WEB: www.lutreltrucking.com
SIC: 4731 Customs clearance of freight; freight forwarding

PRODUCTS & SERVICES SECTION

4731 - Freight Forwarding & Arrangement County (P-5140)

(P-5118)
MAERSK INC
Also Called: Maersk Line
555 Anton Blvd Ste 300, Costa Mesa (92626-7667)
PHONE....................714 428-5500
Fax: 714 428-5349
Celia Miller, *Branch Mgr*
Eric Sandoval, *Manager*
EMP: 80
SALES (corp-wide): 38.6B Privately Held
WEB: www.maersksealand.com
SIC: 4731 Agents, shipping
HQ: Maersk Inc.
    180 Park Ave Ste 105
    Florham Park NJ 07932
    973 514-5000

(P-5119)
MAINFREIGHT INC (HQ)
1400 Glenn Curtiss St, Carson (90746-4030)
PHONE....................310 900-1974
John Hepworth, *President*
Christopher Coppersmith, *CEO*
John Eshuis, *Vice Pres*
Michelle Merino, *Sales Mgr*
Charles E Brown, *Director*
EMP: 90
SQ FT: 100,000
SALES (est): 282.6MM
SALES (corp-wide): 1.5B Privately Held
WEB: www.mainfreightusa.com
SIC: 4731 Domestic freight forwarding; foreign freight forwarding
PA: Mainfreight Limited
    2 Railway Lane
    Auckland, 1062
    925 955-19

(P-5120)
MAP CARGO GLOBAL LOGISTICS (PA)
2501 Santa Fe Ave, Redondo Beach (90278-1117)
PHONE....................310 297-8300
Marek Adam Panasewicz, *President*
Elvie Castill, *Accounts Mgr*
EMP: 74
SQ FT: 20,000
SALES (est): 28.8MM Privately Held
WEB: www.mapcargo.com
SIC: 4731 2448 Domestic freight forwarding; cargo containers, wood & wood with metal

(P-5121)
MENDOCINO RAILWAY
Also Called: Skunk Train, The
341 Industrial Way, Woodland (95776-6012)
PHONE....................530 666-9646
David Magaw, *President*
Ed Ring, *Treasurer*
Chris Hart, *Vice Pres*
Torgny Nilsson, *Admin Sec*
EMP: 103
SALES (est): 172.5K
SALES (corp-wide): 335K Privately Held
SIC: 4731 4011 Railroad freight agency; railroads, line-haul operating
PA: Sierra Railroad Company
    341 Industrial Way
    Woodland CA 95776
    530 666-9646

(P-5122)
MERIT INTEGRATED LOGISTICS LLC
Also Called: Drop Lot Services
29122 Rancho Viejo Rd # 211, San Juan Capistrano (92675-1039)
PHONE....................949 481-0685
Fariba Amjadi, *Manager*
EMP: 1100 EST: 2013
SALES: 40MM Privately Held
SIC: 4731 Freight transportation arrangement

(P-5123)
MILLENNIUM TRANSPORTATION INC
3164 E La Palma Ave Ste D, Anaheim (92806-2811)
PHONE....................714 956-7882
Reuban Bedi, *President*
EMP: 99
SALES (est): 14.1MM Privately Held
SIC: 4731 Freight transportation arrangement

(P-5124)
MIRAMAR TRANSPORTATION INC
Also Called: Pilot Freight Services
9340 Cabot Dr Ste I, San Diego (92126-4397)
PHONE....................858 693-0071
Richard Evan Fore, *President*
Robert Mirenda, *Vice Pres*
Bob Mirinda, *Vice Pres*
Brian Flower, *District Mgr*
John Petree, *General Mgr*
EMP: 45
SALES (est): 26.1MM Privately Held
SIC: 4731 Freight forwarding

(P-5125)
MOUNTAIN VALLEY EXPRESS CO INC
7701 Rosecrans Ave, Paramount (90723-2534)
P.O. Box 152, Manteca (95336-1122)
PHONE....................562 630-5500
Fax: 562 630-0489
Robert Baker, *Branch Mgr*
Elizabeth Moss, *Sales Staff*
Ray Tellez, *Sales Staff*
EMP: 130
SALES (corp-wide): 44MM Privately Held
WEB: www.mountainvalleyexpress.com
SIC: 4731 4212 Freight transportation arrangement; local trucking, without storage
PA: Mountain Valley Express Co. , Inc.
    6750 Longe St Ste 100
    Stockton CA 95206
    209 823-2168

(P-5126)
NATIONAL AIR CARGO INC
222 N Sepulveda Blvd # 2000, El Segundo (90245-5648)
PHONE....................310 662-4766
Ray Macchlowski, *Manager*
EMP: 80
SALES (corp-wide): 97.8MM Privately Held
SIC: 4731 Freight forwarding
HQ: National Air Cargo Inc
    350 Windward Dr
    Orchard Park NY 14127
    716 631-0011

(P-5127)
NATIONWIDE TRANS INC (PA)
1633 S Campus Ave, Ontario (91761-4335)
P.O. Box 4207 (91761-8907)
PHONE....................909 355-3211
Kong Lee, *President*
EMP: 100
SALES (est): 19.8MM Privately Held
SIC: 4731 Freight transportation arrangement

(P-5128)
NEOVIA LOGISTICS DIST LP
600 Live Oak Ave, Baldwin Park (91706-1344)
PHONE....................626 358-8025
Christy Myer, *Branch Mgr*
EMP: 60
SALES (corp-wide): 139.2MM Privately Held
SIC: 4731 4212 Freight transportation arrangement; local trucking, without storage
HQ: Neovia Logistics Distribution, Lp
    6363 N State Highway # 700
    Irving TX 75038

(P-5129)
NEOVIA LOGISTICS DIST LP
600 Live Oak Ave, Irwindale (91706-1344)
PHONE....................626 359-4500
Hector Legaspi, *Branch Mgr*
EMP: 106
SALES (corp-wide): 139.2MM Privately Held
SIC: 4731 Truck transportation brokers
HQ: Neovia Logistics Distribution, Lp
    6363 N State Highway # 700
    Irving TX 75038

(P-5130)
NIPPON EXPRESS USA INC
970 Francisco St, Torrance (90502-1201)
PHONE....................310 532-6300
Fax: 310 324-5962
Yozo Komiya, *Vice Pres*
EMP: 50
SALES (corp-wide): 16.3B Privately Held
SIC: 4731 4412 4491 Freight transportation arrangement; deep sea foreign transportation of freight; marine cargo handling
HQ: Nippon Express U.S.A., Inc.
    2401 44th Rd Fl 14
    Long Island City NY 11101
    212 758-6100

(P-5131)
NIPPON EXPRESS USA INC
300 Westmont Dr, San Pedro (90731-1000)
PHONE....................310 532-6300
Fax: 310 241-1687
Y Totani, *Manager*
EMP: 62
SALES (corp-wide): 16.3B Privately Held
SIC: 4731 4424 Freight transportation arrangement; deep sea domestic transportation of freight
HQ: Nippon Express U.S.A., Inc.
    2401 44th Rd Fl 14
    Long Island City NY 11101
    212 758-6100

(P-5132)
NIPPON EXPRESS USA INC
2233 E Grand Ave, El Segundo (90245-2837)
PHONE....................310 535-7200
Fax: 310 335-4886
Yozo Komiya, *Manager*
EMP: 56
SALES (corp-wide): 16.3B Privately Held
SIC: 4731 Foreign freight forwarding; domestic freight forwarding; customhouse brokers
HQ: Nippon Express U.S.A., Inc.
    2401 44th Rd Fl 14
    Long Island City NY 11101
    212 758-6100

(P-5133)
NISSIN INTL TRNSPT USA INC (HQ)
1540 W 190th St, Torrance (90501-1121)
PHONE....................310 222-8500
Fax: 310 787-7150
Yasushi Ihara, *CEO*
Masahiro Ugai, *COO*
Mitsugu Matsusaka, *CFO*
Hiro Kawano, *Branch Mgr*
Tak Kono, *Branch Mgr*
EMP: 50
SQ FT: 98,000
SALES (est): 201.4MM
SALES (corp-wide): 1.7B Privately Held
WEB: www.nitusa.com
SIC: 4731 Domestic freight forwarding
PA: Nissin Corporation
    6-81, Onoecho, Naka-Ku
    Yokohama KNG 231-0
    456 716-111

(P-5134)
NNR GLOBAL LOGISTICS USA INC
Also Called: N N R
21023 Main St Ste D, Carson (90745-1246)
PHONE....................310 357-2100
Natomi Yamata, *Branch Mgr*
William Chancy, *Supervisor*
EMP: 110
SQ FT: 23,650
SALES (corp-wide): 3B Privately Held
WEB: www.northportlandwellness.com
SIC: 4731 Foreign freight forwarding

HQ: Nnr Global Logistics Usa Inc.
    450 E Devon Ave Ste 260
    Itasca IL 60143
    630 773-1490

(P-5135)
NRI USA LLC
Also Called: Nri Distribution
13200 S Broadway, Los Angeles (90061-1124)
PHONE....................323 345-6456
Chris Maydaniuk,
EMP: 100
SQ FT: 65,000
SALES (est): 24.6MM
SALES (corp-wide): 197.8K Privately Held
SIC: 4731 Freight transportation arrangement
PA: Nri Distribution Ltd
    450 Derwent Pl
    Delta BC V3M 5
    604 527-7275

(P-5136)
O E C SHIPG LOS ANGELES INC
Also Called: Oec Group
13100 Alondra Blvd # 100, Cerritos (90703-2278)
PHONE....................562 926-7186
Fax: 310 642-1321
Robert Han, *President*
John Su, *President*
Amy Wang, *Manager*
EMP: 50
SALES (est): 28MM Privately Held
SIC: 4731 Freight forwarding

(P-5137)
OCEAN KNIGHT SHIPPING INC
19516 S Susana Rd # 101, Compton (90221-5714)
PHONE....................310 885-3388
Henry Chu, *President*
You Luo, *Analyst*
Wenny Chen, *Accountant*
EMP: 200
SALES: 3.1MM Privately Held
WEB: www.okshipping.com
SIC: 4731 Freight transportation arrangement

(P-5138)
OOCL (USA) INC
2700 Zanker Rd Ste 200, San Jose (95134-2140)
PHONE....................408 576-6543
Fax: 408 576-6556
Karen Heller, *Branch Mgr*
Dorinda Jung, *Business Dir*
Elisabeth Erickson, *General Mgr*
Jim Stewart, *CPA*
Scott Dille, *Marketing Mgr*
EMP: 64 Privately Held
SIC: 4731 Freight transportation arrangement
HQ: Oocl (Usa) Inc.
    10913 S River Front Pkwy # 200
    South Jordan UT 84095
    801 302-6625

(P-5139)
OOCL (USA) INC
111 W Ocean Blvd Ste 1800, Long Beach (90802-7936)
PHONE....................562 499-2600
Fax: 562 435-2650
Chris Favro, *Human Res Mgr*
Michael Toomey, *Opers Staff*
EMP: 56 Privately Held
WEB: www.esi-intermodal.com
SIC: 4731 4729 Agents, shipping; steamship ticket offices
HQ: Oocl (Usa) Inc.
    10913 S River Front Pkwy # 200
    South Jordan UT 84095
    801 302-6625

(P-5140)
OOCL (USA) INC
17777 Center Court Dr N # 500, Cerritos (90703-9320)
PHONE....................562 499-2600
Paul Conolly, *Principal*
Jeannine Susi, *Business Anlyst*
Liana Gardner-Griffie, *Manager*

4731 - Freight Forwarding & Arrangement County (P-5141)

PRODUCTS & SERVICES SECTION

James Lester, *Manager*
EMP: 65 **Privately Held**
WEB: www.esi-intermodal.com
SIC: 4731 Agents, shipping
HQ: Oocl (Usa) Inc.
10913 S River Front Pkwy # 200
South Jordan UT 84095
801 302-6625

(P-5141)
P& JP BROKERAGE LLC
15301 Ventura Blvd Ste P2, Sherman Oaks (91403-5882)
PHONE.................................310 801-9707
Paul Mantea,
EMP: 50
SQ FT: 15,000
SALES (est): 3.9MM **Privately Held**
SIC: 4731 Brokers, shipping

(P-5142)
PACIFIC LOGISTICS CORP (PA)
Also Called: Paclo
7255 Rosemead Blvd, Pico Rivera (90660-4047)
PHONE.................................562 478-4700
Fax: 714 809-0413
Douglas E Hockersmith, *President*
Timothy K Hewey, *COO*
Diane J Hockersmith, *Admin Sec*
Bob Bullock, *Info Tech Dir*
Ryan Heyman, *Technology*
EMP: 208
SQ FT: 206,000
SALES (est): 115.4MM **Privately Held**
WEB: www.pacific-logistics.com
SIC: 4731 Freight transportation arrangement

(P-5143)
PANALPINA INC
401 E Grand Ave, South San Francisco (94080-6208)
P.O. Box 1850 (94083-1850)
PHONE.................................650 873-1390
Fax: 650 634-0488
Tommy Lau, *Branch Mgr*
EMP: 50
SALES (corp-wide): 5.8B **Privately Held**
WEB: www.panalpina.com
SIC: 4731 Freight forwarding
HQ: Panalpina, Inc.
1776 On The Green 67
Morristown NJ 07960
973 683-9000

(P-5144)
PANALPINA INC
19900 S Vermont Ave Ste A, Torrance (90502-1147)
PHONE.................................310 819-4060
Fax: 310 819-4055
Maurice Joseph, *Branch Mgr*
EMP: 60
SALES (corp-wide): 5.8B **Privately Held**
WEB: www.panalpina.com
SIC: 4731 Freight forwarding
HQ: Panalpina, Inc.
1776 On The Green 67
Morristown NJ 07960
973 683-9000

(P-5145)
PARAMOUNT TRNSP SYSTEMS INC (PA)
1350 Grand Ave, San Marcos (92078-2404)
PHONE.................................760 510-7979
Fax: 760 510-7999
Mike Keller, *CEO*
Grace Bishar, *CFO*
Brian Goates, *Vice Pres*
Robert Vespa, *Vice Pres*
Kanahele Keenan, *Executive*
EMP: 50
SQ FT: 32,000
SALES (est): 58.3MM **Privately Held**
WEB: www.pts-ca.com
SIC: 4731 Transportation agents & brokers

(P-5146)
PASHA DISTRIBUTION SVCS LLC
5882 Bolsa Ave Ste 200, Huntington Beach (92649-5702)
PHONE.................................714 889-2460
George W Pasha IV, *Branch Mgr*
EMP: 87 **Privately Held**
SIC: 4731 Freight transportation arrangement
PA: Pasha Distribution Services Llc
320 Brookes Dr Ste 217
Hazelwood MO 63042

(P-5147)
PASHA GROUP (PA)
Also Called: Pasha Freight
4040 Civic Center Dr # 350, San Rafael (94903-4187)
PHONE.................................415 927-6400
Fax: 415 924-5672
George W Pasha III, *Ch of Bd*
James Britton, *CFO*
Glenn Yamaguchi, *CFO*
Steve Hunter, *Treasurer*
David Beckerman, *Senior VP*
EMP: 400 **EST:** 1973
SQ FT: 18,000
SALES (est): 313.8MM **Privately Held**
WEB: www.pashagroup.com
SIC: 4731 Freight transportation arrangement

(P-5148)
PASHA GROUP
19020 S Dminguez Hills Dr, Compton (90220-6404)
PHONE.................................310 735-0952
EMP: 103
SALES (corp-wide): 313.8MM **Privately Held**
SIC: 4731 Freight transportation arrangement
PA: The Pasha Group
4040 Civic Center Dr # 350
San Rafael CA 94903
415 927-6400

(P-5149)
PEGASUS MARITIME INC
535 N Brand Blvd Ste 400, Glendale (91203-3907)
PHONE.................................714 728-8565
Khurram Mahmood, *President*
Moazam Mahmood, *CEO*
Mookie Mahmood, *Exec VP*
Syed M Ali, *Vice Pres*
EMP: 75
SQ FT: 10,000
SALES (est): 12.6MM **Privately Held**
SIC: 4731 Freight transportation arrangement

(P-5150)
PERFORMANCE TEAM FRT SYS INC
1331 Torrance Blvd, Torrance (90501-2351)
PHONE.................................562 345-2200
Craig Kaplan, *CEO*
EMP: 355
SALES (corp-wide): 435.6MM **Privately Held**
SIC: 4731 Customs clearance of freight
PA: Performance Team Freight Sys, Inc.
2240 E Maple Ave
El Segundo CA 90245
562 345-2200

(P-5151)
PERFORMANCE TEAM FRT SYS INC (PA)
2240 E Maple Ave, El Segundo (90245-6507)
PHONE.................................562 345-2200
Fax: 562 741-2500
Craig Kaplan, *CEO*
Cliff Katab, *President*
Thierno Amath Fall, *CFO*
Michael Kaplan, *CFO*
Amath Sall, *CFO*
EMP: 200
SQ FT: 80,000
SALES (est): 435.6MM **Privately Held**
WEB: www.ptgt.net
SIC: 4731 4225 4213 Freight transportation arrangement; general warehousing & storage; trucking, except local

(P-5152)
POINTDIRECT TRANSPORT INC
10858 Almond Ave, Fontana (92337-7103)
PHONE.................................909 371-0837
Adolfo De La Herran, *Owner*
EMP: 100
SALES: 500K **Privately Held**
SIC: 4731 Freight forwarding

(P-5153)
PORT LOGISTICS GROUP INC
15530 Salt Lake Ave, City of Industry (91745-1113)
PHONE.................................626 330-1300
Louis P Gram, *Principal*
Cristina Wilson, *Human Res Mgr*
Noemi Cabanilla, *Warehouse Mgr*
Todd Larson, *Warehouse Mgr*
EMP: 350
SALES (corp-wide): 227MM **Privately Held**
SIC: 4731 4225 Agents, shipping; general warehousing
PA: Port Logistics Group, Inc.
288 S Mayo Ave
Walnut CA 91789
713 439-1010

(P-5154)
PORTS AMERICA GROUP
389 Terminal Way, San Pedro (90731-7430)
PHONE.................................310 241-1742
David Wear, *Branch Mgr*
EMP: 51 **EST:** 2013
SALES (est): 4.7MM **Privately Held**
SIC: 4731 Freight transportation arrangement

(P-5155)
PREMIER MEDICAL TRANSPORT INC
530 N Puente St, Brea (92821-2804)
PHONE.................................888 353-9556
David Johnson, *President*
Greg Valenzuela, *Opers Mgr*
EMP: 90
SALES (est): 18.5MM **Privately Held**
SIC: 4731 Freight transportation arrangement

(P-5156)
PUROLATOR INTERNATIONAL INC
775 W Manville St, Compton (90220-5505)
PHONE.................................650 871-7075
John T Costanzo, *Branch Mgr*
EMP: 59
SALES (corp-wide): 225.9B **Privately Held**
SIC: 4731 Transportation agents & brokers
HQ: Purolator International, Inc.
2 Jericho Plz Ste 204
Jericho NY 11753
888 511-4811

(P-5157)
QUIK PICK EXPRESS LLC
1021 E 233rd St, Carson (90745-6206)
P.O. Box 1129, Lakewood (90714-1129)
PHONE.................................310 763-3000
George Boyle, *CEO*
EMP: 70
SQ FT: 350,000
SALES (est): 24.7MM **Privately Held**
WEB: www.quikpickexpress.com
SIC: 4731 4214 Freight transportation arrangement; local trucking with storage

(P-5158)
R L JONES-SAN DIEGO INC (PA)
1778 Zinetta Rd Ste A, Calexico (92231-9511)
P.O. Box 472 (92232-0472)
PHONE.................................760 357-3177
Fax: 760 357-7028
Russell L Jones, *President*
Earl Roberts, *Vice Pres*
Lucy Topete, *Info Tech Dir*
Baltazar Espinoza, *Info Tech Mgr*
Jarr Baltazar, *Web Dvlpr*
EMP: 100
SALES (est): 34.3MM **Privately Held**
WEB: www.rljones.com
SIC: 4731 4225 Customhouse brokers; freight forwarding; general warehousing & storage

(P-5159)
R L JONES-SAN DIEGO INC
1778 Zinetta Rd Ste A1, Calexico (92231-9510)
PHONE.................................760 357-0140
Russell L Jones, *Branch Mgr*
EMP: 63
SALES (corp-wide): 34.3MM **Privately Held**
SIC: 4731 4225 Customhouse brokers; general warehousing & storage
PA: R. L. Jones-San Diego, Inc.
1778 Zinetta Rd Ste A
Calexico CA 92231
760 357-3177

(P-5160)
RAILEX LLC
2121 S Browning Rd, Delano (93215-9298)
PHONE.................................661 370-4300
Kim Sakata, *Branch Mgr*
EMP: 100
SALES (corp-wide): 67MM **Privately Held**
WEB: www.railex.net
SIC: 4731 Railroad freight agency
PA: Railex, Llc
889 Harrison Ave Fl 4
Riverhead NY 11901
631 369-7000

(P-5161)
RITE WAY ENTERPRISES
7131 Valjean Ave, Van Nuys (91406-3917)
PHONE.................................818 376-6960
Helen Wolfe, *President*
Stephan Malley, *Agent*
EMP: 50
SQ FT: 18,000
SALES (est): 8.8MM **Privately Held**
SIC: 4731 Truck transportation brokers

(P-5162)
RK LOGISTICS GROUP INC
Also Called: Rk Logistics Goup, The
41707 Christy St, Fremont (94538-4195)
P.O. Box 610670, San Jose (95161-0670)
PHONE.................................408 942-8107
Rodney F Kalune, *President*
Michael Powell, *General Mgr*
Deborah Friedemann, *Controller*
Judi Kalune, *Human Res Dir*
Ray Stoutenburg, *Traffic Dir*
EMP: 193
SQ FT: 180,000
SALES (est): 29MM **Privately Held**
WEB: www.rkgllc.com
SIC: 4731 8742 4214 4225 Freight transportation arrangement; transportation consultant; local trucking with storage; general warehousing & storage

(P-5163)
ROADEX AMERICA INC
1515 W 178th St, Gardena (90248-3203)
PHONE.................................310 878-9800
Fax: 310 673-0386
Nicholas Sim, *President*
Russle Loh, *Vice Pres*
Johnny Kwan, *Principal*
Rob Chan, *Human Res Dir*
Derrick Yabe, *Traffic Dir*
▲ **EMP:** 100
SALES (est): 28.4MM **Privately Held**
WEB: www.roadexamerica.com
SIC: 4731 5113 4789 Domestic freight forwarding; industrial & personal service paper; cargo loading & unloading services

(P-5164)
ROCK-IT CARGO USA LLC
120 N Topanga Canyon Blvd, Topanga (90290-3851)
PHONE.................................310 455-1900
Sasha Goodman, *Branch Mgr*
EMP: 60
SALES (corp-wide): 151.6MM **Privately Held**
SIC: 4731 Freight forwarding

▲ = Import ▼ = Export ◆ = Import/Export

PRODUCTS & SERVICES SECTION
4731 - Freight Forwarding & Arrangement County (P-5187)

HQ: Rock-It Cargo Usa Llc
1002 Lititz Pike Ste 238
Lititz PA 17543
215 947-5400

(P-5165)
SCHENKER INC
380 Littlefield Ave, South San Francisco (94080-6103)
PHONE.................................650 745-3000
Fax: 650 742-0669
Tammy Breen, *Manager*
Jerome Tillery, *Sales Staff*
Christopher Lim, *Director*
Karen Chan, *Supervisor*
EMP: 61
SQ FT: 60,000 **Privately Held**
SIC: 4731 Foreign freight forwarding
HQ: Schenker, Inc.
150 Albany Ave
Freeport NY 11520
516 377-3000

(P-5166)
SCHUMACHER CARGO LOGISTICS INC (PA)
Also Called: S C L
550 W 135th St, Gardena (90248-1506)
PHONE.................................310 324-1365
Martin D Baker, *CEO*
Angela Reyna, *Executive Asst*
Bart Goedhard, *Sales Staff*
Ruth Ortiz, *Manager*
EMP: 59
SQ FT: 200,000
SALES (est): 20.3MM **Privately Held**
WEB: www.schumachercargo.com
SIC: 4731 Freight forwarding

(P-5167)
SEA-AIR INTERNATIONAL INC
11222 S La Cienega Blvd # 100, Inglewood (90304-1109)
PHONE.................................310 338-0778
Fax: 310 641-1450
Milton Heid, *President*
Eric Jones, *Vice Pres*
EMP: 52
SALES (est): 4.5MM **Privately Held**
SIC: 4731 Customhouse brokers

(P-5168)
SHO-AIR INTERNATIONAL INC (PA)
5401 Argosy Ave Ste 102, Huntington Beach (92649-1038)
PHONE.................................949 476-9111
Fax: 949 476-0518
James Nicoll, *Ch of Bd*
R Scott Tedro, *President*
Jessica Elende, *CFO*
Jessica Steambridgen, *CFO*
Gregg Thomas, *Vice Pres*
EMP: 50
SQ FT: 18,000
SALES (est): 24.8MM **Privately Held**
WEB: www.shoair.com
SIC: 4731 Freight forwarding

(P-5169)
STARLINK FREIGHT SYS SFO INC (PA)
206 Utah Ave, South San Francisco (94080-6801)
PHONE.................................650 589-2575
Vic Cheung, *President*
Cecilia TSE, *Vice Pres*
EMP: 50
SALES (est): 6.5MM **Privately Held**
SIC: 4731 Freight forwarding

(P-5170)
STATES LOGISTICS SERVICES INC
7221 Cate Dr, Buena Park (90621-1883)
PHONE.................................714 523-1276
Cathy J Monson, *Branch Mgr*
EMP: 200
SALES (corp-wide): 76.9MM **Privately Held**
SIC: 4731 Freight transportation arrangement
PA: States Logistics Services, Inc.
5650 Dolly Ave
Buena Park CA 90621
714 521-6520

(P-5171)
STEVENS GLOBAL LOGISTICS INC (PA)
Also Called: Steven Global Freight Services
3700 Redondo Beach Ave, Redondo Beach (90278-1108)
P.O. Box 729, Lawndale (90260-0729)
PHONE.................................310 216-5645
Thomas J Petrizzio, *CEO*
Gary Hooper, *CFO*
Karl Chambers, *Vice Pres*
Carlos Monarrez, *General Mgr*
Joy Derick, *Manager*
EMP: 95
SQ FT: 48,000
SALES (est): 38.7MM **Privately Held**
WEB: www.stevensglobal.com
SIC: 4731 Freight forwarding

(P-5172)
SURETY WEST LOGISTICS INC
Also Called: Surety West Transportation
980 9th St Fl 16, Sacramento (95814-2736)
PHONE.................................800 761-2551
Barry Henning, *President*
EMP: 77
SALES (est): 2.4MM **Privately Held**
SIC: 4731 Transportation agents & brokers

(P-5173)
TAYLORED SERVICES HOLDINGS LLC
1495 E Locust St, Ontario (91761-4570)
PHONE.................................909 628-5300
Bill Butler, *CEO*
Michael Yusko, *CFO*
Brandon Nakamura, *Administration*
Bina Patel, *Human Res Mgr*
Eric Almaraz, *Human Resources*
EMP: 110 **EST:** 2012
SALES (est): 35.6MM **Privately Held**
SIC: 4731 Agents, shipping

(P-5174)
TRAFFIC TECH INC
910 Hale Pl Ste 100, Chula Vista (91914-3598)
PHONE.................................800 396-2531
Paul Johnson, *President*
EMP: 155
SALES (corp-wide): 102.8MM **Privately Held**
SIC: 4731 Brokers, shipping
HQ: Traffic Tech, Inc.
910 Hale Pl Ste 100
Chula Vista CA 91914
514 343-0044

(P-5175)
TRAFFIC TECH INC (DH)
910 Hale Pl Ste 100, Chula Vista (91914-3598)
PHONE.................................514 343-0044
Fax: 619 200-8635
Brian Arnott, *CEO*
Andrea Martens, *Vice Pres*
Joshua Musen, *Vice Pres*
Tasia Melnichenko, *Admin Asst*
Andrew Hazle, *Broker*
EMP: 300
SQ FT: 3,500
SALES (est): 100.7MM
SALES (corp-wide): 102.8MM **Privately Held**
SIC: 4731 Brokers, shipping; domestic freight forwarding; foreign freight forwarding

(P-5176)
TRANSIT AIR CARGO INC
2204 E 4th St, Santa Ana (92705-3868)
PHONE.................................714 571-0393
Fax: 714 571-0398
Gulnawaz Khodayar, *CEO*
Christy Colton, *Vice Pres*
Michelle Nguyen, *Vice Pres*
Frank Uxa, *Sales Executive*
Rick Caldira, *Sales Mgr*
EMP: 75
SQ FT: 10,000
SALES (est): 35.7MM **Privately Held**
WEB: www.transitair.com
SIC: 4731 Foreign freight forwarding

(P-5177)
TRICOR AMERICA INC
12441 Eucalyptus Ave 7, Hawthorne (90250-4208)
PHONE.................................310 676-0800
Fax: 310 973-1565
W Maria Escobar, *Principal*
Collin Johnson, *Accounts Mgr*
EMP: 100
SALES (corp-wide): 114.1MM **Privately Held**
WEB: www.tricor.com
SIC: 4731 Freight forwarding
PA: Tricor America, Inc.
717 Airport Blvd
South San Francisco CA 94080
650 877-3650

(P-5178)
TRICOR INTERNATIONAL
1320 San Mateo Ave, South San Francisco (94080-6501)
P.O. Box 8100, San Francisco (94128-8100)
PHONE.................................650 877-3678
Fax: 650 737-5718
Chee B Louie, *President*
John Hoard, *Controller*
Peter Shue, *Director*
EMP: 100
SQ FT: 20,000
SALES (est): 11.7MM **Privately Held**
SIC: 4731 4581 4424 Freight forwarding; airports, flying fields & services; deep sea domestic transportation of freight

(P-5179)
TRIPLE PLAY SERVICES INC (PA)
Also Called: Three Way
42505 Christy St, Fremont (94538-3993)
P.O. Box 1806 (94538-0032)
PHONE.................................408 748-3929
Anthony J Bonino, *CEO*
Kevin Scherer, *President*
Philipp Scherer, *CFO*
Stan Aikman, *Vice Pres*
Michael Bonino, *Vice Pres*
EMP: 60
SQ FT: 135,000
SALES (est): 47.7MM **Privately Held**
WEB: www.threeway.com
SIC: 4731 Freight transportation arrangement

(P-5180)
TRITON CONSOLIDATED INDUSTRIES
7710 Kester Ave, Van Nuys (91405-1104)
PHONE.................................323 852-0370
Fax: 323 374-9160
Archalous Garabedian, *President*
Gary Garabedian, *Vice Pres*
Gaby Flores, *Manager*
EMP: 54
SQ FT: 10,680
SALES (est): 3.9MM **Privately Held**
SIC: 4731 Freight consolidation

(P-5181)
TRITON LOGISTICS CORPORATION
706 Steffy Rd, Ramona (92065-3533)
PHONE.................................619 822-8832
Jason Lawrence Foyer, *Principal*
EMP: 70
SALES (corp-wide): 5.4MM **Privately Held**
SIC: 4731 Foreign freight forwarding
PA: Triton Logistics, Corporation
6780 Miramar Rd Ste 200b
San Diego CA 92121
619 822-8832

(P-5182)
TRIUS TRUCKING INC
4692 E Lincoln Ave, Fowler (93625-9685)
P.O. Box 2700, Fresno (93745-2700)
PHONE.................................559 834-4000
Tehal Singh Thandi, *CEO*
J T Thandi, *Manager*
EMP: 87
SQ FT: 3,900
SALES (est): 32.6MM **Privately Held**
SIC: 4731 Freight transportation arrangement

(P-5183)
UNITED STTES INTRMDAL SVCS LLC
Also Called: G3 Enterprises
502 E Whitmore Ave, Modesto (95358-9411)
PHONE.................................209 341-4045
John R Gallo,
Don Frederick, *Controller*
Julie Cascia,
Gregory J Coleman,
EMP: 75
SQ FT: 10,000
SALES (est): 17.7MM **Privately Held**
SIC: 4731 5182 Truck transportation brokers; bottling wines & liquors

(P-5184)
UPS SUPPLY CHAIN SOLUTIONS INC
U P S
19701 Hamilton Ave # 250, Torrance (90502-1316)
PHONE.................................310 404-2719
Homayoun Kandari, *Branch Mgr*
Joe Frank, *Branch Mgr*
Brian Fujishige, *Info Tech Dir*
Mary Argenas, *Persnl Mgr*
Daniel Kuzdzal, *Director*
EMP: 200
SALES (corp-wide): 58.3B **Publicly Held**
SIC: 4731 Freight transportation arrangement
HQ: Ups Supply Chain Solutions, Inc.
12380 Morris Rd
Alpharetta GA 30005
800 742-5727

(P-5185)
UPS WORLDWIDE LOGISTICS INC
3600 W Century Blvd, Inglewood (90303-1139)
PHONE.................................310 673-7661
Tom Bliss, *Branch Mgr*
Tony Polenit, *Executive*
Robert Evans, *Sales Executive*
EMP: 200
SALES (corp-wide): 58.3B **Publicly Held**
SIC: 4731 Freight transportation arrangement
HQ: Ups Worldwide Logistics Inc
12380 Morris Rd
Alpharetta GA 30005
678 746-4100

(P-5186)
USAS EXPRESS INTERNATIONAL
420 Hindry Ave Ste G, Inglewood (90301-2062)
PHONE.................................310 645-2313
Young I Choi, *President*
John Cho, *Export Mgr*
EMP: 56
SALES (est): 8.4MM **Privately Held**
WEB: www.usasexpress.com
SIC: 4731 Freight transportation arrangement

(P-5187)
UTI UNITED STATES INC
573 Forbes Blvd, South San Francisco (94080-2019)
PHONE.................................650 588-9477
Fax: 650 616-1950
Richard English, *Branch Mgr*
Jayson Gispan, *General Mgr*
EMP: 60
SALES (corp-wide): 7.3B **Privately Held**
SIC: 4731 Freight transportation arrangement
HQ: Uti, United States, Inc.
100 Walnut Ave Ste 405
Clark NJ 07066
732 850-8000

4731 - Freight Forwarding & Arrangement County (P-5188)

(P-5188)
VANGUARD LGISTICS SVCS USA INC (HQ)
5000 Airport Plaza Dr, Long Beach (90815-1271)
PHONE.....................310 847-3000
Charles Brennan, *Chairman*
Bruce Ericson, *President*
J Thurso Barendse, *CFO*
Jeff Alinsangan, *Treasurer*
Scott Shellow, *Treasurer*
EMP: 100
SALES (est): 201.6MM
SALES (corp-wide): 232.2MM **Privately Held**
SIC: 4731 Freight consolidation
PA: Naca Holdings, Inc.
   5000 Arprt Plz Dr Ste 200
   Long Beach CA 90815
   650 872-0800

(P-5189)
WESTERN OVERSEAS CORPORATION (PA)
10731 Walker St Ste B, Cypress (90630-4757)
P.O. Box 90099, Long Beach (90809-0099)
PHONE.....................562 985-0616
Fax: 714 986-1345
Michael F Dugan, *President*
Paul Abe, *Vice Pres*
Carlo Deatougia, *Vice Pres*
Barbara Chopin, *Branch Mgr*
Bonnie Englert, *Branch Mgr*
EMP: 50
SQ FT: 40,000
SALES: 11MM **Privately Held**
SIC: 4731 Customhouse brokers; foreign freight forwarding

(P-5190)
WESTRUX INTERNATIONAL INC
2200 E Steel Rd, Colton (92324-4509)
PHONE.....................909 825-5121
Don Kenney, *CFO*
EMP: 60
SALES (corp-wide): 125.9MM **Privately Held**
SIC: 4731 Truck transportation brokers
PA: Westrux International, Inc.
   15555 Valley View Ave
   Santa Fe Springs CA 90670
   562 404-1020

(P-5191)
WSC AMERICA
Also Called: Tradeworld.com
1 World Trade Ctr Ste 800, Long Beach (90831-0800)
PHONE.....................562 367-4212
David Winzo, *CEO*
Paul Faustin, *President*
Chris Wiles, *General Mgr*
EMP: 140
SALES (est): 9.2MM **Privately Held**
SIC: 4731 Freight forwarding

(P-5192)
XPO LOGISTICS SUPPLY CHAIN INC
5200b E Airport Dr, Ontario (91761-8601)
PHONE.....................909 390-9799
Fax: 909 937-6089
Bob Krajewski, *Branch Mgr*
EMP: 156
SALES (corp-wide): 7.6B **Publicly Held**
SIC: 4731 Freight transportation arrangement
HQ: Xpo Logistics Supply Chain, Inc.
   4035 Piedmont Pkwy
   High Point NC 27265
   336 232-4100

(P-5193)
XPO LOGISTICS SUPPLY CHAIN INC
3825 S Willow Ave, Fresno (93725-9025)
PHONE.....................559 408-7951
EMP: 109
SALES (corp-wide): 7.6B **Publicly Held**
SIC: 4731 Freight transportation arrangement

HQ: Xpo Logistics Supply Chain, Inc.
   4035 Piedmont Pkwy
   High Point NC 27265
   336 232-4100

(P-5194)
XPO LOGISTICS SUPPLY CHAIN INC
5200a E Airport Dr, Ontario (91761-8601)
PHONE.....................909 975-6300
Steve Mackintosh, *Branch Mgr*
Matthew Rogers, *Vice Pres*
EMP: 124
SALES (corp-wide): 7.6B **Publicly Held**
SIC: 4731 Freight transportation arrangement
HQ: Xpo Logistics Supply Chain, Inc.
   4035 Piedmont Pkwy
   High Point NC 27265
   336 232-4100

(P-5195)
YANG MING AMERICA CORPORATION
181 W Huntington Dr # 202, Monrovia (91016-8406)
PHONE.....................626 782-9797
Frank Chao, *Branch Mgr*
EMP: 55
SALES (corp-wide): 3.9B **Privately Held**
SIC: 4731 Agents, shipping
HQ: Ming Yang America Corporation
   1085 Raymond Blvd Fl 9
   Newark NJ 07102
   201 222-8899

4783 Packing & Crating Svcs

(P-5196)
ADVANTAGE MEDIA SERVICES INC (PA)
Also Called: AMS Fulfillment
29010 Commerce Center Dr, Valencia (91355-4188)
PHONE.....................661 775-0611
Jay Catlin, *President*
Ken Wiseman, *CEO*
Louise Aldrich, *Principal*
David Catlin, *Director*
EMP: 55
SQ FT: 142,000
SALES (est): 59.5MM **Privately Held**
WEB: www.amsfulfillment.com
SIC: 4783 4731 Packing goods for shipping; agents, shipping; brokers, shipping; domestic freight forwarding; foreign freight forwarding

(P-5197)
CALAVO GROWERS INC
Also Called: Calavo Foods
15765 W Telegraph Rd, Santa Paula (93060-3041)
P.O. Box 751 (93061-0751)
PHONE.....................805 525-5511
Fax: 805 525-1151
George Hatfield, *Plant Mgr*
Gary Gunther, *Engineer*
EMP: 80
SALES (corp-wide): 856.8MM **Publicly Held**
WEB: www.calavo.com
SIC: 4783 Packing goods for shipping
PA: Calavo Growers, Inc.
   1141 Cummings Rd Ste A
   Santa Paula CA 93060
   805 525-1245

(P-5198)
CENTRA FREIGHT SERVICES INC (PA)
279 Lawrence Ave, South San Francisco (94080-6818)
PHONE.....................650 873-8147
Jonathan Wang, *CEO*
Stanley Wang, *President*
Goldine Wang, *Vice Pres*
Winnie Lo, *General Mgr*
Sugio Juwono, *Office Mgr*
EMP: 53 **EST:** 1980
SQ FT: 11,500
SALES (est): 18MM **Privately Held**
SIC: 4731 Containerization of goods for shipping; domestic freight forwarding

(P-5199)
FLEXTRONICS LOGISTICS USA INC
6201 America Center Dr, San Jose (95002-2563)
PHONE.....................408 576-7000
Michael McNamara, *President*
EMP: 1300
SALES (est): 83.4MM
SALES (corp-wide): 24.4B **Privately Held**
SIC: 4783 Packing goods for shipping
HQ: Flextronics International Usa, Inc.
   6201 America Center Dr
   San Jose CA 95002

(P-5200)
GLASS PAK INC
5825 Old School Rd, Pleasanton (94588-9407)
PHONE.....................707 207-0400
Fax: 707 207-0900
Marc Silvani, *President*
Rick Silvani, *Vice Pres*
Dallas Nelson, *General Mgr*
Maria Andrade, *Exec Sec*
EMP: 70
SQ FT: 90,000
SALES (est): 8MM **Privately Held**
WEB: www.glasspak.com
SIC: 4783 Packing & crating

(P-5201)
INTEGRATED PKG & CRATING SVCS
Also Called: Inovative Packaging
38505 Cherry St Ste C, Newark (94560-4700)
PHONE.....................510 494-1622
Ben F Polando, *CEO*
Donna Fernandez, *HR Admin*
EMP: 50
SQ FT: 90,000
SALES (est): 6.6MM **Privately Held**
SIC: 4783 Packing & crating

(P-5202)
L&L FOODS HOLDINGS LLC
333 N Euclid Way, Anaheim (92801-6738)
PHONE.....................714 254-1430
John Pooley, *CEO*
Roger Douglas, *CFO*
Matt Sonneman, *VP Sales*
EMP: 200
SQ FT: 100,000
SALES (est): 63.6MM
SALES (corp-wide): 1.6B **Privately Held**
SIC: 4783 Packing goods for shipping
HQ: Peacock Engineering Company, Llc
   1800 Averill Rd
   Geneva IL 60134
   630 845-9400

(P-5203)
SUNTREAT PKG SHIPG A LTD PRTNR
391 Oxford Ave, Lindsay (93247-2208)
P.O. Box 850 (93247-0850)
PHONE.....................559 562-4991
Fax: 559 562-6814
Dennis A Griffith, *Managing Prtnr*
Dwight J Griffith, *Partner*
▼ **EMP:** 200
SQ FT: 75,000
SALES (est): 31.4MM **Privately Held**
WEB: www.suntreat.net
SIC: 4783 8742 Packing goods for shipping; management consulting services

(P-5204)
TRANS-PAK INCORPORATED
8710 Avenida De La Fuente, San Diego (92154-6243)
PHONE.....................858 292-9094
Jennifer Kay, *Branch Mgr*
Arlene Inch, *CEO*
Lauren Nickerson, *Office Mgr*
EMP: 51

SALES (corp-wide): 84.1MM **Privately Held**
SIC: 4783 2449 3081 3086 Packing & crating; wood containers; packing materials, plastic sheet; packaging & shipping materials, foamed plastic; corrugated & solid fiber boxes; nailed wood boxes & shook
PA: Trans-Pak, Incorporated
   520 Marburg Way
   San Jose CA 95133
   408 254-0500

(P-5205)
UNIFIED AIRCRAFT SERVICES INC (PA)
1571 S Lilac Ave, Bloomington (92316-2141)
P.O. Box 401060, Las Vegas NV (89140-1060)
PHONE.....................909 877-0535
Fax: 909 875-0488
Ben C Warren, *President*
Venida L Warren, *Corp Secy*
Benjamin T Warren, *Vice Pres*
Tom Warren, *Manager*
EMP: 65
SQ FT: 14,500
SALES (est): 17.1MM **Privately Held**
WEB: www.uasnet.com
SIC: 4783 Packing goods for shipping; containerization of goods for shipping

(P-5206)
VENIDA PACKING COMPANY
19823 Avenue 300, Exeter (93221-9771)
P.O. Box 212 (93221-0212)
PHONE.....................559 592-2816
Fax: 559 592-6521
Verne Crookshanks, *CEO*
Michael Murray, *Treasurer*
George Tantua, *Admin Sec*
EMP: 125
SQ FT: 50,000
SALES (est): 18.2MM **Privately Held**
SIC: 4783 Packing goods for shipping

4785 Fixed Facilities, Inspection, Weighing Svcs Transptn

(P-5207)
CALIFORNIA PRIVATE TRNSP CO LP
Also Called: C P T C
180 N Rverview Dr Ste 200, Anaheim (92808)
PHONE.....................714 637-9191
Greg Hulsizer, *General Mgr*
EMP: 75
SQ FT: 5,000
SALES (est): 3.8MM **Privately Held**
SIC: 4785 Toll road operation

(P-5208)
GOLDEN GATE
Also Called: Golden Gate Ferry
101 E Sir Francis Drake, Larkspur (94939-1803)
PHONE.....................415 455-2000
David Clark, *Manager*
EMP: 84
SALES (corp-wide): 15.9MM **Privately Held**
WEB: www.goldengatetransit.org
SIC: 4785 4482 Toll bridge operation; ferries operating across rivers or within harbors
PA: Golden Gate Bridge Highway & Transportation District
   Toll Plz
   San Francisco CA 94129
   415 921-5858

(P-5209)
GOLDEN GATE BRDG HWY & TRANSPO (PA)
Toll Plz, San Francisco (94129)
PHONE.....................415 921-5858
Fax: 415 923-2012
James C Eddie, *President*
Geoff Jarvis, *Vice Pres*

PRODUCTS & SERVICES SECTION

4789 - Transportation Svcs, NEC County (P-5233)

Denis J Mulligan, *General Mgr*
Dennis Mulligan, *General Mgr*
Donnalei Sumner, *General Mgr*
EMP: 250
SQ FT: 20,000
SALES (est): 15.9MM **Privately Held**
WEB: www.goldengatetransit.org
SIC: 4785 4131 4482 4111 Toll bridge operation; interstate bus line; ferries operating across rivers or within harbors; bus transportation

(P-5210)
GOLDEN GATE BRIDGE HIGH
Also Called: Golden Gate Transit
1011 Andersen Dr, San Rafael (94901-5318)
PHONE 415 457-3110
Fax: 415 923-2367
Susan Chiaroni, *Manager*
Aida Caputo, *Officer*
Susan Spencer, *Admin Asst*
D'Ann Moore, *Engineer*
Harvey Pye, *Human Res Dir*
EMP: 535
SQ FT: 50,000
SALES (corp-wide): 15.9MM **Privately Held**
WEB: www.goldengatetransit.org
SIC: 4785 4111 Toll bridge operation; airport transportation services, regular route
PA: Golden Gate Bridge Highway & Transportation District
Toll Plz
San Francisco CA 94129
415 921-5858

4789 Transportation Svcs, NEC

(P-5211)
ALEXANDERS MOBILITY SERVICES
2942 Dow Ave, Tustin (92780-7220)
PHONE 714 731-1658
Mike Shaughnessy, *General Mgr*
Beth Meyers, *CFO*
Karen Kinney, *Controller*
Lizabeth Urdea, *Controller*
Jesse Howe, *Sales Executive*
EMP: 93
SALES (est): 12.3MM **Privately Held**
SIC: 4789 Freight car loading & unloading; cargo loading & unloading services

(P-5212)
AMERIFLEET TRANSPORTATION INC
3044 Elkhorn Blvd Ste J, North Highlands (95660-3025)
PHONE 916 331-2355
Shirley Tyler, *Principal*
EMP: 80
SALES (corp-wide): 146.2MM **Privately Held**
SIC: 4789 Car loading
PA: Amerifleet Transportation Inc
1111 Alderman Dr
Alpharetta GA 30005
770 442-0222

(P-5213)
AMERIFLEET TRANSPORTATION INC
5000 E Spring St Ste 350, Long Beach (90815-5209)
PHONE 562 420-5604
Liane Blanche, *Principal*
EMP: 107
SALES (corp-wide): 146.2MM **Privately Held**
SIC: 4789 Pipeline terminal facilities, independently operated
PA: Amerifleet Transportation Inc
1111 Alderman Dr
Alpharetta GA 30005
770 442-0222

(P-5214)
ANS WORLD SERVICE INC
2751 E Chapman Ave # 204, Fullerton (92831-3752)
P.O. Box 784, Placentia (92871-0784)
PHONE 714 441-2400

Charles S An, *President*
EMP: 100
SQ FT: 600
SALES (est): 3.2MM **Privately Held**
SIC: 4789 4212 Cargo loading & unloading services; local trucking, without storage

(P-5215)
AP EXPRESS INTERNATIONAL LLC
8500 Rex Rd, Pico Rivera (90660-3779)
PHONE 562 236-2250
Jeff Pont, *President*
EMP: 75 **EST:** 1987
SQ FT: 50,000
SALES: 14.5MM **Privately Held**
WEB: www.championtransportation.com
SIC: 4789 Freight car loading & unloading

(P-5216)
COUNTY OF LOS ANGELES
Also Called: Transportation Bureau
441 Bauchet St, Los Angeles (90012-2906)
PHONE 213 974-4561
EMP: 250 **Privately Held**
SIC: 4789 9621
PA: County Of Los Angeles
500 W Temple St Ste 375
Los Angeles CA 90012
213 974-1101

(P-5217)
EASY RIDE TRANSPORTATION
1820 W Carson St Ste 202, Torrance (90501-2885)
PHONE 424 999-8830
Said Dabas, *President*
EMP: 100 **EST:** 2014
SALES (est): 2.4MM **Privately Held**
SIC: 4789 Transportation services

(P-5218)
HARBOR FREIGHT TOOLS USA INC
820 Civic Center Dr, Vista (92084-6153)
PHONE 760 631-0347
Marc Friedman, *Principal*
EMP: 77
SALES (corp-wide): 2.3B **Privately Held**
SIC: 4789 Pipeline terminal facilities, independently operated
PA: Harbor Freight Tools Usa, Inc.
26541 Agoura Rd
Calabasas CA 91302
818 836-5000

(P-5219)
HARBOR FREIGHT TOOLS USA INC
1330 W Olive Ave, Merced (95348-1663)
PHONE 209 386-0829
EMP: 77
SALES (corp-wide): 2.3B **Privately Held**
SIC: 4789 Pipeline terminal facilities, independently operated
PA: Harbor Freight Tools Usa, Inc.
26541 Agoura Rd
Calabasas CA 91302
818 836-5000

(P-5220)
HARBOR FREIGHT TOOLS USA INC
4403 Century Blvd, Pittsburg (94565-7114)
PHONE 925 757-8435
EMP: 77
SALES (corp-wide): 2.3B **Privately Held**
SIC: 4789 Pipeline terminal facilities, independently operated
PA: Harbor Freight Tools Usa, Inc.
26541 Agoura Rd
Calabasas CA 91302
818 836-5000

(P-5221)
HEALTH LINK MEDI VAN
Also Called: Medi-Van Ambulette
6053 W Century Blvd # 900, Los Angeles (90045-6430)
PHONE 310 981-9500
Greg Linsmeier, *General Mgr*
EMP: 100

SALES (est): 6.5MM **Privately Held**
SIC: 4789 Freight car loading & unloading

(P-5222)
HYPERLOOP ONE
2161 Sacramento St, Los Angeles (90021-1721)
PHONE 213 800-3270
Robert W Lloyd, *CEO*
Brogan Bambrogan, *Owner*
Josh Giegel, *Vice Pres*
William Mulholland, *Vice Pres*
Erin Kearns, *Director*
EMP: 200
SALES (est): 9.3MM **Privately Held**
SIC: 4789 Pipeline terminal facilities, independently operated

(P-5223)
INTER-RAIL TRNSPT NSHVILLE LLC
861 Wharf St, Richmond (94804-3557)
PHONE 510 231-2744
Francisco Oliver, *Manager*
EMP: 52
SALES (corp-wide): 32.9MM **Privately Held**
WEB: www.interrail-transport.com
SIC: 4789 Freight car loading & unloading
PA: Inter-Rail Transport Of Nashville, Llc
115 Lawyers Row Ste 3
Centreville MD 21617
410 758-2893

(P-5224)
INTER-RAIL TRNSPT NSHVILLE LLC
3800 Industrial Way, Benicia (94510-1200)
PHONE 707 746-1596
Fax: 707 746-1695
Luis Michel, *Manager*
Armando Diaz, *Director*
Kenneth Black, *Manager*
EMP: 60
SALES (corp-wide): 32.9MM **Privately Held**
WEB: www.interrail-transport.com
SIC: 4789 4213 Freight car loading & unloading; automobiles, transport & delivery
PA: Inter-Rail Transport Of Nashville, Llc
115 Lawyers Row Ste 3
Centreville MD 21617
410 758-2893

(P-5225)
ITS TECHNOLOGIES LOGISTICS LLC
6540 Austin Rd, Stockton (95215-9662)
PHONE 209 460-6023
Dave Carlock, *Branch Mgr*
EMP: 60 **Privately Held**
SIC: 4789 Cargo loading & unloading services
HQ: Its Technologies & Logistics, Llc
8200 185th St Ste A
Tinley Park IL 60487
708 225-2400

(P-5226)
JB HUNT TRANSPORT SVCS INC
Also Called: Jbhunt Transport
1620 5th Ave, San Diego (92101-2703)
PHONE 619 230-0054
EMP: 549
SALES (corp-wide): 6.1B **Publicly Held**
SIC: 4789 Cargo loading & unloading services
PA: J.B. Hunt Transport Services, Inc.
615 Jb Hunt Corp Dr
Lowell AR 72745
479 820-0000

(P-5227)
JET SOURCE INC
2056 Palomar Airport Rd # 103, Carlsbad (92011-4463)
PHONE 760 438-1042
Fax: 818 804-1515
Vivianne B McWilliam, *CEO*
Jay Brentzel, *President*
Ian Ewing, *Vice Pres*
Joey Crawford, *CTO*
Nick Morganti, *Controller*
EMP: 80

SALES (est): 14.1MM **Privately Held**
SIC: 4789 Space flight operations, except government

(P-5228)
KENCO GROUP INC
7875 Hemlock Ave, Fontana (92336-4278)
PHONE 909 356-1635
Zhang Ruimin, *CEO*
EMP: 100
SALES (corp-wide): 1.6B **Privately Held**
SIC: 4789 Pipeline terminal facilities, independently operated
PA: Kenco Group, Inc.
2001 Riverside Dr Ste 3100
Chattanooga TN 37406
423 622-1113

(P-5229)
KENCO GROUP INC
740 Vintage Ave, Ontario (91764-5365)
PHONE 909 483-1199
EMP: 100
SALES (corp-wide): 1.6B **Privately Held**
SIC: 4789 Cargo loading & unloading services
PA: Kenco Group, Inc.
2001 Riverside Dr Ste 3100
Chattanooga TN 37406
423 622-1113

(P-5230)
M V TRANSPORTATION
1375 Britain Ave, Salinas (93901)
PHONE 831 373-1395
Lance Atencio, *Branch Mgr*
EMP: 200
SALES (corp-wide): 18.1MM **Privately Held**
SIC: 4789 Pipeline terminal facilities, independently operated
PA: M V Transportation
16738 Stagg St
Van Nuys CA 91406
818 374-9145

(P-5231)
M V TRANSPORTATION
1612 State St, Barstow (92311-4107)
PHONE 760 255-3330
Fax: 760 255-0006
Tom Conlon, *Manager*
EMP: 200
SALES (corp-wide): 18.1MM **Privately Held**
SIC: 4789 Pipeline terminal facilities, independently operated
PA: M V Transportation
16738 Stagg St
Van Nuys CA 91406
818 374-9145

(P-5232)
PACIFIC COAST CONTAINER INC (PA)
Also Called: PCC Northwest
432 Estudillo Ave Ste 1, San Leandro (94577-4908)
PHONE 510 346-6100
Michael Mc Donnell, *CEO*
Abdel Zaharan, *CFO*
Dina Lau, *Accountant*
Brandon S McDonald, *Assistant VP*
◆ **EMP:** 148
SQ FT: 12,000
SALES (est): 84.7MM **Privately Held**
WEB: www.pccfs.com
SIC: 4789 4225 4222 Cargo loading & unloading services; general warehousing; warehousing, cold storage or refrigerated

(P-5233)
PACIFIC COAST TRNSP SVCS INC
Also Called: Material Transport
7500 San Joaquin St, Sacramento (95820-2141)
PHONE 916 266-5300
Tom Aligaier, *Manager*
EMP: 50
SALES (corp-wide): 926.8MM **Privately Held**
SIC: 4789 Cargo loading & unloading services

4789 - Transportation Svcs, NEC County (P-5234)

PRODUCTS & SERVICES SECTION

HQ: Pacific Coast Transportation Services, Inc.
10600 White Rock Rd Ste 1
Rancho Cordova CA 95670
916 631-6500

(P-5234)
PARSEC INC
4940 Sheila St, Commerce (90040-1112)
PHONE.................................323 268-5011
Fax: 323 307-5771
Jose Huerta, *Manager*
EMP: 600
SALES (corp-wide): 197MM **Privately Held**
WEB: www.parsecinc.com
SIC: **4789** 1629 Cargo loading & unloading services; railroad & subway construction
PA: Parsec Inc.
1100 Gest St
Cincinnati OH 45203
513 621-6111

(P-5235)
PARSEC INC
750 Lamar St, Los Angeles (90031-2515)
PHONE.................................323 276-3116
Tony Madrigar, *Manager*
EMP: 54
SALES (corp-wide): 197MM **Privately Held**
WEB: www.parsecinc.com
SIC: **4789** Cargo loading & unloading services
PA: Parsec Inc.
1100 Gest St
Cincinnati OH 45203
513 621-6111

(P-5236)
PORT LOGISTICS GROUP INC
19801 S Santa Fe Ave, Compton (90221-5915)
PHONE.................................310 669-2551
Timothy Page, *Principal*
Ron Bono, *Traffic Dir*
Michael Johnson, *Opers Mgr*
EMP: 208
SALES (corp-wide): 227MM **Privately Held**
SIC: **4789** Cargo loading & unloading services
PA: Port Logistics Group, Inc.
288 S Mayo Ave
Walnut CA 91789
713 439-1010

(P-5237)
POSTMATES INC (PA)
425 Market St Fl 8, San Francisco (94105-2465)
PHONE.................................800 882-6106
Bastian Lehmann, *CEO*
Holger Luedorf, *Senior VP*
Cezanne Baghdadlian, *Office Mgr*
Annie Wu, *Executive Asst*
Alan Liu, *Software Engr*
EMP: 273
SQ FT: 2,400
SALES (est): 7.7MM **Privately Held**
SIC: **4789** Cargo loading & unloading services

(P-5238)
PROGRESS RAIL SERVICES CORP
Also Called: Progress Van Guard
3909 Cincinnati Ave, Rocklin (95765-1303)
PHONE.................................916 645-6006
Fax: 916 645-6076
Tracey Fangogoria, *CEO*
Dino Lopez, *Administration*
Ken Baker, *Draft/Design*
Doug Hoffman, *Purch Agent*
Lee Kisling, *Director*
EMP: 70
SALES (corp-wide): 47B **Publicly Held**
WEB: www.progressrail.com
SIC: **4789** Railroad maintenance & repair services
HQ: Progress Rail Services Corporation
1600 Progress Dr
Albertville AL 35950
256 593-1260

(P-5239)
RIOLO TRANSPORTATION INC
2725 Jefferson St Ste 2d, Carlsbad (92008-1705)
PHONE.................................760 729-4405
Gail Phipps, *Branch Mgr*
EMP: 162
SALES (corp-wide): 45.3MM **Privately Held**
SIC: **4789** Pipeline terminal facilities, independently operated
PA: Riolo Transportation, Inc.
1425 Simpson St
Kingsburg CA 93631
877 646-4911

(P-5240)
SALSON LOGISTICS INC
1331 Torrance Blvd, Torrance (90501-2351)
PHONE.................................310 328-6906
Fax: 310 328-6897
Brian Howver, *Branch Mgr*
Eric Nowak, *General Mgr*
EMP: 172
SALES (corp-wide): 196MM **Privately Held**
SIC: **4789** Pipeline terminal facilities, independently operated
PA: Salson Logistics, Inc.
888 Doremus Ave
Newark NJ 07114
973 986-0200

(P-5241)
SAN FRANCISCO BAY AREA RAPID
Also Called: Richmond Yard Tower
1101 13th St, Richmond (94801-2302)
PHONE.................................510 233-7444
Steve Brigham, *Branch Mgr*
Sean Steel, *Manager*
EMP: 100
SALES (corp-wide): 384.8MM **Privately Held**
SIC: **4789** Cargo loading & unloading services
PA: San Francisco Bay Area Rapid Transit District
300 Lakeside Dr
Oakland CA 94604
510 464-6000

(P-5242)
SECURE TRANSPORTATION CO INC
9557 Candida St, San Diego (92126-4539)
PHONE.................................858 790-3958
Shawana Walters, *Manager*
EMP: 83
SALES (corp-wide): 45.7MM **Privately Held**
SIC: **4789** Pipeline terminal facilities, independently operated
PA: Secure Transportation Company, Inc.
434 E Broadway
Long Beach CA 90802
562 941-0107

(P-5243)
SIERRA WASTE TRANSPORT INC
6956 Florin Perkins Rd, Sacramento (95828-2607)
PHONE.................................916 386-9937
Sunil Dutt, *CEO*
Farima Mushtaq, *General Mgr*
EMP: 50
SALES: 3.5MM **Privately Held**
SIC: **4789** Cargo loading & unloading services

(P-5244)
SOUTHERN CALIFORNIA CAR TRANSF
11139 Roxboro Rd, San Diego (92131-3655)
PHONE.................................858 586-0006
Mike Magnett, *President*
EMP: 100
SALES (est): 3.6MM **Privately Held**
SIC: **4789** Cargo loading & unloading services

(P-5245)
STORER TRANSPORTATION SERVICE
21429 Centre Pointe Pkwy, Santa Clarita (91350-2684)
PHONE.................................661 288-0400
EMP: 124
SALES (corp-wide): 43.5MM **Privately Held**
SIC: **4789** Pipeline terminal facilities, independently operated
PA: Storer Transportation Service Inc
3519 Mcdonald Ave
Modesto CA 95358
209 521-8250

(P-5246)
TOLL GLOBAL FWDG AMERICAS
780 Nogales St Ste D, City of Industry (91748-1306)
PHONE.................................626 363-8600
Myles O'Brien, *CEO*
Robert Wu, *CFO*
Wayne Takenouchi, *VP Opers*
EMP: 57
SALES (est): 6.7MM **Privately Held**
SIC: **4789** Car loading

(P-5247)
TRANSMONTAIGNE PDT SVCS LLC
Also Called: Morgan Stanley
555 California St # 2100, San Francisco (94104-1503)
PHONE.................................415 576-2000
Fax: 415 576-2090
Susan Clampsey, *Branch Mgr*
Louis Gerhardy, *Vice Pres*
John Marren, *Principal*
Fred Fogg, *Exec Dir*
Gordon Williams, *Exec Dir*
EMP: 300
SALES (corp-wide): 757.5MM **Privately Held**
SIC: **4789** Pipeline terminal facilities, independently operated
HQ: Transmontaigne Product Services Llc
1670 Broadway Ste 3100
Denver CO 80202
303 626-8200

(P-5248)
TW SERVICES INC
2751 E Chapman Ave # 204, Fullerton (92831-3758)
PHONE.................................714 441-2400
Charles An, *President*
Dave Fabela, *COO*
Thomas Hwang, *Controller*
Christian Pita, *Manager*
EMP: 300
SALES (est): 27.4MM **Privately Held**
SIC: **4789** Freight car loading & unloading

(P-5249)
UTI INTEGRATED LOGISTICS LLC
3454 E Miraloma Ave, Anaheim (92806-2101)
PHONE.................................714 630-0110
EMP: 74
SALES (corp-wide): 7.3B **Privately Held**
SIC: **4789** Pipeline terminal facilities, independently operated
HQ: Uti Integrated Logistics, Llc
700 Gervais St Ste 100
Columbia SC 29201
803 771-6785

(P-5250)
VITAL EXPRESS INC
4000 Macarthur Blvd Ste 6, Newport Beach (92660-2558)
PHONE.................................330 777-5450
Fax: 661 775-5400
Steve Janssen, *President*
Dan Boaz, *President*
Lisa Boaz, *CEO*
Tammy Hutten, *Finance*
Chris Fall, *Marketing Staff*
EMP: 50
SQ FT: 10,000

SALES (est): 6.1MM **Privately Held**
SIC: **4789** 4212 Pipeline terminal facilities, independently operated; delivery service, vehicular

(P-5251)
YRC INC
Also Called: Yellow Transportation
1535 E Pescadero Ave, Tracy (95304-8501)
PHONE.................................209 833-1300
Fax: 209 833-1475
Maynard Skarka, *Manager*
Kevin Anderson, *Manager*
Kevin Shoemaker, *Manager*
EMP: 217
SALES (corp-wide): 4.8B **Publicly Held**
WEB: www.roadway.com
SIC: **4789** Cargo loading & unloading services
HQ: Yrc Inc.
10990 Roe Ave
Overland Park KS 66211
913 696-6100

4812 Radiotelephone Communications

(P-5252)
4G WIRELESS INC (PA)
Also Called: Verizon Wireless
8871 Research Dr, Irvine (92618-4236)
PHONE.................................949 748-6100
Fax: 949 748-6107
Mohammad Honarkar, *President*
Morris Delfino, *District Mgr*
Earl Fowler, *Store Mgr*
Siavosh Talakar, *CTO*
CHI Lu, *Accounting Mgr*
EMP: 170
SQ FT: 5,000
SALES (est): 450MM **Privately Held**
SIC: **4812** Cellular telephone services

(P-5253)
AERONAUTICAL RADIO INC
6011 Industrial Way, Livermore (94551-9755)
PHONE.................................925 294-8400
Fax: 925 294-9597
Mike Ostapiej, *Manager*
EMP: 80
SQ FT: 27,781 **Publicly Held**
SIC: **4812** Radio telephone communication
HQ: Aeronautical Radio, Inc.
2551 Riva Rd
Annapolis MD 21401
410 266-4000

(P-5254)
AMTEL LLC
1074 University Ave, Berkeley (94710-2135)
PHONE.................................510 529-3220
EMP: 82
SALES (corp-wide): 34MM **Privately Held**
SIC: **4812** Cellular telephone services
PA: Amtel, Llc
909 Lake Carolyn Pkwy # 1400
Irving TX 75039
972 791-4444

(P-5255)
AT&T CORP
2508 S Grove Ave, Ontario (91761-6253)
PHONE.................................909 930-6508
Lorenzo Mejia, *Branch Mgr*
EMP: 97
SALES (corp-wide): 146.8B **Publicly Held**
SIC: **4812** Radio telephone communication
HQ: At&T Corp.
1 At&T Way
Bedminster NJ 07921
800 403-3302

(P-5256)
AT&T CORP
6833 Pacific Blvd, Huntington Park (90255-4111)
PHONE.................................323 589-7045
Frankie Valenzuela, *Manager*
EMP: 97

PRODUCTS & SERVICES SECTION
4812 - Radiotelephone Communications County (P-5282)

SALES (corp-wide): 146.8B **Publicly Held**
WEB: www.cingular.com
SIC: **4812** Radio telephone communication
HQ: At&T Corp.
   1 At&T Way
   Bedminster NJ 07921
   800 403-3302

(P-5257)
AT&T CORP
6328 Irvine Blvd, Irvine (92620-2102)
PHONE..................................949 559-1457
Linda Fisher, *Owner*
EMP: 97
SALES (corp-wide): 146.8B **Publicly Held**
WEB: www.att.com
SIC: **4812** Radio telephone communication
HQ: At&T Corp.
   1 At&T Way
   Bedminster NJ 07921
   800 403-3302

(P-5258)
AT&T CORP
2333 S Sepulveda Blvd, Los Angeles (90064-1910)
PHONE..................................310 473-3649
Carolyn Wilder, *Manager*
EMP: 97
SALES (corp-wide): 146.8B **Publicly Held**
WEB: www.att.com
SIC: **4812** Radio telephone communication
HQ: At&T Corp.
   1 At&T Way
   Bedminster NJ 07921
   800 403-3302

(P-5259)
AT&T CORP
7060 Market Place Dr, Goleta (93117-5902)
PHONE..................................805 562-0121
Nicole Jurzenski, *Manager*
EMP: 97
SALES (corp-wide): 146.8B **Publicly Held**
WEB: www.cingular.com
SIC: **4812** Radio telephone communication
HQ: At&T Corp.
   1 At&T Way
   Bedminster NJ 07921
   800 403-3302

(P-5260)
AT&T CORP
217 N Lemon St Rm 205, Anaheim (92805-2943)
PHONE..................................714 284-3818
Tim Baumann, *Technical Mgr*
Chris Nguyen, *Technical Mgr*
EMP: 95
SALES (corp-wide): 146.8B **Publicly Held**
SIC: **4812** Cellular telephone services
HQ: At&T Corp.
   1 At&T Way
   Bedminster NJ 07921
   800 403-3302

(P-5261)
AT&T CORP
1100 Pacific Coast Hwy # 5, Hermosa Beach (90254-3951)
PHONE..................................310 303-3888
Dennis Graber, *Branch Mgr*
EMP: 97
SALES (corp-wide): 146.8B **Publicly Held**
WEB: www.cingular.com
SIC: **4812** Radio telephone communication
HQ: At&T Corp.
   1 At&T Way
   Bedminster NJ 07921
   800 403-3302

(P-5262)
AT&T CORP
3750 Morrow Ln, Chico (95928-8865)
PHONE..................................530 891-2025
Bill Rose, *Branch Mgr*
EMP: 96

SALES (corp-wide): 146.8B **Publicly Held**
SIC: **4812** Cellular telephone services
HQ: At&T Corp.
   1 At&T Way
   Bedminster NJ 07921
   800 403-3302

(P-5263)
AT&T CORP
8817 N Cedar Ave, Fresno (93720-1832)
PHONE..................................559 353-3999
Amy Durham, *Branch Mgr*
Theresa Nesroney, *Manager*
EMP: 97
SALES (corp-wide): 146.8B **Publicly Held**
SIC: **4812** Cellular telephone services
HQ: At&T Corp.
   1 At&T Way
   Bedminster NJ 07921
   800 403-3302

(P-5264)
AT&T CORP
2883 Jamacha Rd Ste A-D, El Cajon (92019-4312)
PHONE..................................619 660-0637
EMP: 97
SALES (corp-wide): 146.8B **Publicly Held**
SIC: **4812** Cellular telephone services
HQ: At&T Corp.
   1 At&T Way
   Bedminster NJ 07921
   800 403-3302

(P-5265)
AT&T CORP
835 4th St, San Rafael (94901-3260)
PHONE..................................415 721-1470
Don Klein, *Branch Mgr*
EMP: 97
SALES (corp-wide): 146.8B **Publicly Held**
SIC: **4812** Cellular telephone services
HQ: At&T Corp.
   1 At&T Way
   Bedminster NJ 07921
   800 403-3302

(P-5266)
AT&T CORP
1620 Mendocino Ave, Santa Rosa (95401-4345)
PHONE..................................707 591-9500
Christina French, *Manager*
EMP: 97
SALES (corp-wide): 146.8B **Publicly Held**
WEB: www.att.com
SIC: **4812** Cellular telephone services
HQ: At&T Corp.
   1 At&T Way
   Bedminster NJ 07921
   800 403-3302

(P-5267)
AT&T CORP
1855 41st Ave, Capitola (95010-2511)
PHONE..................................831 465-6771
Amel Dunanes, *Principal*
EMP: 97
SALES (corp-wide): 146.8B **Publicly Held**
SIC: **4812** Cellular telephone services
HQ: At&T Corp.
   1 At&T Way
   Bedminster NJ 07921
   800 403-3302

(P-5268)
AT&T CORP
1263 Simi Town Center Way, Simi Valley (93065-8406)
PHONE..................................805 583-9483
Fax: 805 520-2260
Kim Erwin, *Branch Mgr*
EMP: 97
SALES (corp-wide): 146.8B **Publicly Held**
SIC: **4812** Cellular telephone services
HQ: At&T Corp.
   1 At&T Way
   Bedminster NJ 07921
   800 403-3302

(P-5269)
AT&T CORP
24321 Avend De La Carlt Carlota, Laguna Hills (92653)
PHONE..................................949 581-1600
EMP: 97
SALES (corp-wide): 146.8B **Publicly Held**
WEB: www.att.com
SIC: **4812** Cellular telephone services
HQ: At&T Corp.
   1 At&T Way
   Bedminster NJ 07921
   800 403-3302

(P-5270)
AT&T CORP
1810 E Main St, Woodland (95776-6234)
PHONE..................................530 661-7724
EMP: 97
SALES (corp-wide): 146.8B **Publicly Held**
SIC: **4812** Cellular telephone services
HQ: At&T Corp.
   1 At&T Way
   Bedminster NJ 07921
   800 403-3302

(P-5271)
AT&T CORP
550 River St Ste D, Santa Cruz (95060-2670)
PHONE..................................831 457-8255
Steve Toriumi, *Principal*
EMP: 94
SALES (corp-wide): 146.8B **Publicly Held**
SIC: **4812** Cellular telephone services
HQ: At&T Corp.
   1 At&T Way
   Bedminster NJ 07921
   800 403-3302

(P-5272)
AT&T CORP
7100 Santa Monica Blvd # 125, West Hollywood (90046-5896)
PHONE..................................323 874-7000
EMP: 95
SALES (corp-wide): 146.8B **Publicly Held**
SIC: **4812** Cellular telephone services
HQ: At&T Corp.
   1 At&T Way
   Bedminster NJ 07921
   800 403-3302

(P-5273)
AT&T CORP
134 Sunset Dr, San Ramon (94583-2340)
PHONE..................................925 327-7100
Carolyn Wilder, *Owner*
EMP: 95
SALES (corp-wide): 146.8B **Publicly Held**
SIC: **4812** Cellular telephone services
HQ: At&T Corp.
   1 At&T Way
   Bedminster NJ 07921
   800 403-3302

(P-5274)
AT&T CORP
998 S Robertson Blvd # 103, Los Angeles (90035-1626)
PHONE..................................310 659-7600
Sia Bardi, *Branch Mgr*
EMP: 94
SALES (corp-wide): 146.8B **Publicly Held**
SIC: **4812** Cellular telephone services
HQ: At&T Corp.
   1 At&T Way
   Bedminster NJ 07921
   800 403-3302

(P-5275)
AT&T CORP
2980 Main St, Susanville (96130-4730)
PHONE..................................530 251-0666
Lyle May, *Branch Mgr*
EMP: 97
SALES (corp-wide): 146.8B **Publicly Held**
SIC: **4812** Radio telephone communication

HQ: At&T Corp.
   1 At&T Way
   Bedminster NJ 07921
   800 403-3302

(P-5276)
AT&T CORP
400 Del Monte Ctr, Monterey (93940-6159)
PHONE..................................831 642-0100
Mike Godina, *Branch Mgr*
EMP: 97
SALES (corp-wide): 146.8B **Publicly Held**
WEB: www.att.com
SIC: **4812** Cellular telephone services
HQ: At&T Corp.
   1 At&T Way
   Bedminster NJ 07921
   800 403-3302

(P-5277)
B-PER ELECTRONIC INC
Also Called: My Wireless
1600 N Broadway Ste 810, Santa Ana (92706-3927)
PHONE..................................626 912-0600
Fax: 626 912-3228
Shawn Yeh, *CEO*
EMP: 100
SALES (est): 12.9MM **Privately Held**
SIC: **4812** Cellular telephone services

(P-5278)
BLACK DOT WIRELESS LLC
27271 Las Ramblas Ste 300, Mission Viejo (92691-8042)
PHONE..................................949 502-3800
Marc Anthony, *CEO*
Gary Arnett, *President*
Kimberly Coble, *Executive Asst*
Chris Ngai, *Controller*
Shirellie McFadden, *Personnel Exec*
EMP: 85
SQ FT: 22,000
SALES (est): 13.6MM **Privately Held**
SIC: **4812** Cellular telephone services

(P-5279)
BRAVO TECH INC
Also Called: Bti Wireless
6185 Phyllis Dr Unit D, Cypress (90630-5242)
PHONE..................................714 230-8333
Bailey Zheng, *CEO*
Jianqing He, *Principal*
Jason Lu, *Engineer*
Jean Zhao, *Manager*
▲ EMP: 50
SALES: 19.4MM **Privately Held**
WEB: www.bravotechinc.com
SIC: **4812** **3669** Cellular telephone services; burglar alarm apparatus, electric

(P-5280)
CAL NORTH CELLULAR INC
30 Telco Way, Etna (96027)
PHONE..................................530 467-6128
James Hendricks, *President*
EMP: 50
SALES (est): 959.2K **Privately Held**
SIC: **4812** Cellular telephone services

(P-5281)
CAL-NORTH WIRELESS
1209 Broadway, Eureka (95501-0129)
PHONE..................................707 442-8334
Jimm Lowers, *Owner*
EMP: 80
SALES (est): 1.3MM **Privately Held**
SIC: **4812** **5999** Cellular telephone services; telephone equipment & systems

(P-5282)
CALIFORNIA WIRELESS SOLUTIONS
4095 Evergrn Vlg S 200, Milpitas (95035)
PHONE..................................408 771-1249
Zaid Hamed, *President*
EMP: 80
SALES (est): 8MM **Privately Held**
SIC: **4812** Cellular telephone services

4812 - Radiotelephone Communications County (P-5283)

(P-5283)
CELL SITE MANAGEMENT GROUP LLC
25109 Jefferson Ave, Murrieta (92562-8116)
PHONE..................800 906-9778
Jack W Hawley, *Mng Member*
EMP: 50
SQ FT: 3,000
SALES (est) 3.5MM **Privately Held**
SIC: 4812 Cellular telephone services

(P-5284)
CELLCO PARTNERSHIP
Also Called: Verizon Wireless
1484 E 2nd St, Beaumont (92223-3161)
PHONE..................951 769-0985
Fax: 951 769-9239
EMP: 71
SALES (corp-wide): 131.6B **Publicly Held**
SIC: 4812 4813 Cellular telephone services; telephone communication, except radio
HQ: Cellco Partnership
1 Verizon Way
Basking Ridge NJ 07920
-

(P-5285)
CELLCO PARTNERSHIP
Also Called: Verizon Wireless
26480 Ynez Rd, Temecula (92591-5628)
PHONE..................951 296-3499
Fax: 951 296-9848
Mike Remily, *Branch Mgr*
EMP: 71
SALES (corp-wide): 131.6B **Publicly Held**
SIC: 4812 Cellular telephone services
HQ: Cellco Partnership
1 Verizon Way
Basking Ridge NJ 07920
-

(P-5286)
CELLCO PARTNERSHIP
Also Called: Verizon
24329 Crenshaw Blvd Ste D, Torrance (90505-5338)
PHONE..................310 891-6991
Fax: 310 891-6933
Norma Torqueza, *Manager*
EMP: 71
SALES (corp-wide): 131.6B **Publicly Held**
SIC: 4812 5999 Radio telephone communication; mobile telephones & equipment
HQ: Cellco Partnership
1 Verizon Way
Basking Ridge NJ 07920
-

(P-5287)
CELLCO PARTNERSHIP
Also Called: Verizon
2428 Las Positas Rd, Livermore (94551-8838)
PHONE..................925 245-0494
Fax: 925 245-0470
Gary Larsen, *Manager*
EMP: 71
SALES (corp-wide): 131.6B **Publicly Held**
SIC: 4812 Cellular telephone services
HQ: Cellco Partnership
1 Verizon Way
Basking Ridge NJ 07920
-

(P-5288)
CELLCO PARTNERSHIP
Also Called: Verizon Wireless
1680 Del Monte Ctr, Monterey (93940-6169)
PHONE..................831 644-0858
Fax: 831 644-0864
EMP: 71
SALES (corp-wide): 131.6B **Publicly Held**
SIC: 4812 Cellular telephone services
HQ: Cellco Partnership
1 Verizon Way
Basking Ridge NJ 07920

(P-5289)
CELLCO PARTNERSHIP
Also Called: Verizon Wireless
1500 E Village Way # 2205, Orange (92865-3616)
PHONE..................714 921-5130
Fax: 714 921-5135
EMP: 76
SALES (corp-wide): 131.6B **Publicly Held**
SIC: 4812 Cellular telephone services
HQ: Cellco Partnership
1 Verizon Way
Basking Ridge NJ 07920

(P-5290)
CELLCO PARTNERSHIP
Also Called: Verizon Wireless
6471 Lone Tree Way, Brentwood (94513-5265)
PHONE..................925 626-3480
Fax: 925 626-3486
EMP: 71
SALES (corp-wide): 131.6B **Publicly Held**
SIC: 4812 Cellular telephone services
HQ: Cellco Partnership
1 Verizon Way
Basking Ridge NJ 07920

(P-5291)
CELLCO PARTNERSHIP
Also Called: Verizon Wireless
2851 Canyon Springs Pkwy, Riverside (92507-0935)
PHONE..................951 697-3035
Fax: 951 653-5835
EMP: 76
SALES (corp-wide): 131.6B **Publicly Held**
SIC: 4812 Cellular telephone services
HQ: Cellco Partnership
1 Verizon Way
Basking Ridge NJ 07920
-

(P-5292)
CELLCO PARTNERSHIP
2535 W Hillcrest Dr, Thousand Oaks (91320-2457)
PHONE..................805 376-8917
EMP: 71
SALES (corp-wide): 131.6B **Publicly Held**
SIC: 4812 Cellular telephone services
HQ: Cellco Partnership
1 Verizon Way
Basking Ridge NJ 07920
-

(P-5293)
CELLCO PARTNERSHIP
255 Parkshore Dr, Folsom (95630-4716)
P.O. Box 2167 (95763-2167)
PHONE..................212 395-1000
Brad Keller, *Associate Dir*
Franklin Castberg, *Marketing Staff*
Dave Thatcher, *Marketing Staff*
Chris Rock, *Manager*
Bradley Vance, *Manager*
EMP: 71
SALES (corp-wide): 131.6B **Publicly Held**
SIC: 4812 Cellular telephone services
HQ: Cellco Partnership
1 Verizon Way
Basking Ridge NJ 07920
-

(P-5294)
CELLCO PARTNERSHIP
1101 Los Olivos Ave, Los Osos (93402-3232)
PHONE..................805 596-2300
EMP: 71
SALES (corp-wide): 131.6B **Publicly Held**
SIC: 4812 Cellular telephone services
HQ: Cellco Partnership
1 Verizon Way
Basking Ridge NJ 07920
-

(P-5295)
CELLCO PARTNERSHIP
Also Called: Verizon Wireless
550 S Clovis Ave Ste 105, Fresno (93727-4513)
PHONE..................559 454-0803
Fax: 559 454-1759
Joe Gomez, *Branch Mgr*
EMP: 71
SALES (corp-wide): 131.6B **Publicly Held**
SIC: 4812 Cellular telephone services
HQ: Cellco Partnership
1 Verizon Way
Basking Ridge NJ 07920

(P-5296)
CELLCO PARTNERSHIP
Also Called: Verizon
901 S Coast Dr Ste K120, Costa Mesa (92626-7710)
PHONE..................714 427-0733
Fax: 714 431-0337
David Mendoza, *Manager*
Ohan Filian, *Manager*
EMP: 71
SALES (corp-wide): 131.6B **Publicly Held**
SIC: 4812 5999 Radio telephone communication; telephone equipment & systems
HQ: Cellco Partnership
1 Verizon Way
Basking Ridge NJ 07920

(P-5297)
CELLCO PARTNERSHIP
Also Called: Verizon Wireless
12459 Limonite Ave, Mira Loma (91752-2458)
PHONE..................951 361-1850
Fax: 951 361-1580
EMP: 71
SALES (corp-wide): 131.6B **Publicly Held**
SIC: 4812 Cellular telephone services
HQ: Cellco Partnership
1 Verizon Way
Basking Ridge NJ 07920

(P-5298)
CELLCO PARTNERSHIP
Also Called: Verizon
1900 Douglas Blvd Ste D, Roseville (95661-3823)
PHONE..................916 786-6151
Fax: 916 786-3354
Rapheal Jones, *Branch Mgr*
EMP: 71
SALES (corp-wide): 131.6B **Publicly Held**
SIC: 4812 Cellular telephone services
HQ: Cellco Partnership
1 Verizon Way
Basking Ridge NJ 07920

(P-5299)
CELLCO PARTNERSHIP
Also Called: Verizon
15505 Sand Canyon Ave, Irvine (92618-3114)
PHONE..................949 286-7000
Margaret Holzmann, *Administration*
Luis Cruz, *President*
Larry Bell, *Exec Dir*
Scott Mohr, *Exec Dir*
Jay Tang, *Network Mgr*
EMP: 2000
SALES (corp-wide): 131.6B **Publicly Held**
SIC: 4812 Cellular telephone services
HQ: Cellco Partnership
1 Verizon Way
Basking Ridge NJ 07920

(P-5300)
CELLCO PARTNERSHIP
Also Called: Verizon Wireless
1051 S Green Valley Rd, Watsonville (95076-4164)
PHONE..................831 786-0267
Fax: 831 786-3970

EMP: 71
SALES (corp-wide): 131.6B **Publicly Held**
SIC: 4812 Cellular telephone services
HQ: Cellco Partnership
1 Verizon Way
Basking Ridge NJ 07920

(P-5301)
CELLCO PARTNERSHIP
Also Called: Verizon Wireless
1401 W Imperial Hwy Ste C, La Habra (90631-6996)
PHONE..................562 694-8630
David Mendova, *Principal*
EMP: 71
SALES (corp-wide): 131.6B **Publicly Held**
SIC: 4812 Cellular telephone services
HQ: Cellco Partnership
1 Verizon Way
Basking Ridge NJ 07920

(P-5302)
CELLCO PARTNERSHIP
Also Called: Verizon Wireless
691 S Main St Ste 80, Orange (92868-5619)
PHONE..................714 564-0050
Fax: 714 564-0055
Jorge Prieto, *Manager*
EMP: 71
SALES (corp-wide): 131.6B **Publicly Held**
SIC: 4812 Cellular telephone services
HQ: Cellco Partnership
1 Verizon Way
Basking Ridge NJ 07920

(P-5303)
CELLCO PARTNERSHIP
Also Called: Verizon Wireless
711 Center Dr Ste 6a, San Marcos (92069-3500)
PHONE..................760 738-0088
Fax: 760 738-2007
EMP: 71
SALES (corp-wide): 131.6B **Publicly Held**
SIC: 4812 Cellular telephone services
HQ: Cellco Partnership
1 Verizon Way
Basking Ridge NJ 07920

(P-5304)
CELLCO PARTNERSHIP
Also Called: Verizon
1440 41st Ave Ste B, Capitola (95010-2940)
PHONE..................831 475-3100
Fax: 831 475-3540
Jeff Dehaven, *Manager*
EMP: 71
SALES (corp-wide): 131.6B **Publicly Held**
SIC: 4812 Cellular telephone services
HQ: Cellco Partnership
1 Verizon Way
Basking Ridge NJ 07920

(P-5305)
CELLCO PARTNERSHIP
Also Called: Verizon
2701 Ming Ave Spc 100a, Bakersfield (93304-4451)
PHONE..................661 827-8728
Fax: 661 827-8766
Tricia Brown, *Branch Mgr*
Howard Chapman, *General Mgr*
EMP: 71
SALES (corp-wide): 131.6B **Publicly Held**
SIC: 4812 5999 Cellular telephone services; mobile telephones & equipment
HQ: Cellco Partnership
1 Verizon Way
Basking Ridge NJ 07920

PRODUCTS & SERVICES SECTION

4812 - Radiotelephone Communications County (P-5329)

(P-5306)
CELLCO PARTNERSHIP
Also Called: Verizon
1846 Marron Rd, Carlsbad (92008-1172)
PHONE..............................760 720-8400
Arlene Strametz, *Principal*
EMP: 71
SALES (corp-wide): 131.6B **Publicly Held**
SIC: **4812** 5999 Cellular telephone services; telephone equipment & systems
HQ: Cellco Partnership
1 Verizon Way
Basking Ridge NJ 07920

(P-5307)
CELLCO PARTNERSHIP
Also Called: Verizon
125 Corte Madera Town Ctr, Corte Madera (94925-1209)
PHONE..............................415 924-9084
Fax: 415 945-7932
Lonnie Tuck, *Principal*
EMP: 71
SALES (corp-wide): 131.6B **Publicly Held**
SIC: **4812** Cellular telephone services
HQ: Cellco Partnership
1 Verizon Way
Basking Ridge NJ 07920

(P-5308)
CELLCO PARTNERSHIP
Also Called: Verizon
1571 N Magnolia Ave # 212, El Cajon (92020-1208)
PHONE..............................619 596-7201
Fax: 619 596-7210
Larry Shuller, *Principal*
EMP: 71
SALES (corp-wide): 131.6B **Publicly Held**
SIC: **4812** Cellular telephone services
HQ: Cellco Partnership
1 Verizon Way
Basking Ridge NJ 07920

(P-5309)
CELLCO PARTNERSHIP
Also Called: Verizon
7723 N Blackstone Ave # 102, Fresno (93720-4311)
PHONE..............................559 451-0556
Fax: 559 438-6305
Holly O Brien, *Manager*
Randall Pettyjohn, *Manager*
EMP: 71
SALES (corp-wide): 131.6B **Publicly Held**
SIC: **4812** Cellular telephone services
HQ: Cellco Partnership
1 Verizon Way
Basking Ridge NJ 07920

(P-5310)
CELLCO PARTNERSHIP
Also Called: Verizon
12607 Artesia Blvd, Cerritos (90703-8501)
PHONE..............................562 809-5650
Fax: 562 809-5688
Bill Seager, *Manager*
EMP: 71
SALES (corp-wide): 131.6B **Publicly Held**
SIC: **4812** 5999 Cellular telephone services; mobile telephones & equipment
HQ: Cellco Partnership
1 Verizon Way
Basking Ridge NJ 07920

(P-5311)
CELLCO PARTNERSHIP
Also Called: Verizon
1950 E 20th St Ste 803, Chico (95928-7330)
PHONE..............................530 892-6900
Fax: 530 898-0755
Erik Zuniga, *Branch Mgr*
EMP: 71
SALES (corp-wide): 131.6B **Publicly Held**
SIC: **4812** Cellular telephone services
HQ: Cellco Partnership
1 Verizon Way
Basking Ridge NJ 07920

(P-5312)
CELLCO PARTNERSHIP
Also Called: Verizon
2210 Griffin Way Ste 101, Corona (92879-6532)
PHONE..............................951 549-6400
Fax: 951 898-9247
Kyung OH, *Manager*
EMP: 71
SALES (corp-wide): 131.6B **Publicly Held**
SIC: **4812** 5999 Cellular telephone services; mobile telephones & equipment
HQ: Cellco Partnership
1 Verizon Way
Basking Ridge NJ 07920

(P-5313)
CELLCO PARTNERSHIP
Also Called: Verizon Wireless
39050 Argonaut Way, Fremont (94538-1302)
PHONE..............................510 490-3800
Dolores Joy, *Manager*
EMP: 71
SALES (corp-wide): 131.6B **Publicly Held**
SIC: **4812** Cellular telephone services
HQ: Cellco Partnership
1 Verizon Way
Basking Ridge NJ 07920

(P-5314)
CELLCO PARTNERSHIP
Also Called: Verizon
2500 E Imperial Hwy # 178, Brea (92821-6122)
PHONE..............................714 256-6015
Fax: 714 256-6024
Greg Schuler, *Manager*
EMP: 71
SALES (corp-wide): 131.6B **Publicly Held**
SIC: **4812** Cellular telephone services
HQ: Cellco Partnership
1 Verizon Way
Basking Ridge NJ 07920

(P-5315)
CELLCO PARTNERSHIP
Also Called: Verizon
67 N Broadway Ste A, Chula Vista (91910-1429)
PHONE..............................619 409-4600
EMP: 71
SALES (corp-wide): 131.6B **Publicly Held**
SIC: **4812** Cellular telephone services
HQ: Cellco Partnership
1 Verizon Way
Basking Ridge NJ 07920

(P-5316)
CELLCO PARTNERSHIP
1023 E Colorado St, Glendale (91205-4542)
PHONE..............................818 500-7779
Albrik Mirzakhanyan, *Principal*
EMP: 71
SALES (corp-wide): 131.6B **Publicly Held**
SIC: **4812** Cellular telephone services
HQ: Cellco Partnership
1 Verizon Way
Basking Ridge NJ 07920

(P-5317)
CELLCO PARTNERSHIP
Also Called: Verizon Wireless
980 Camino De La Reina D, San Diego (92108-3290)
PHONE..............................619 209-5818
Fax: 619 209-5819
Amy Berman, *Principal*
Sherri Sanchez, *Manager*
EMP: 71
SALES (corp-wide): 131.6B **Publicly Held**
SIC: **4812** Cellular telephone services
HQ: Cellco Partnership
1 Verizon Way
Basking Ridge NJ 07920

(P-5318)
CELLCO PARTNERSHIP
10525 Vista Sorrento Pkwy # 150, San Diego (92121-2745)
PHONE..............................858 625-7751
Stan Parker, *Manager*
EMP: 71
SALES (corp-wide): 131.6B **Publicly Held**
SIC: **4812** Cellular telephone services
HQ: Cellco Partnership
1 Verizon Way
Basking Ridge NJ 07920

(P-5319)
CELLCO PARTNERSHIP
Also Called: Verizon Wireless
8300 Van Nuys Blvd, Panorama City (91402-3608)
PHONE..............................818 920-4848
Fax: 818 830-1293
EMP: 71
SALES (corp-wide): 131.6B **Publicly Held**
SIC: **4812** Cellular telephone services
HQ: Cellco Partnership
1 Verizon Way
Basking Ridge NJ 07920

(P-5320)
CELLCO PARTNERSHIP
Also Called: Verizon Wireless
488 S Mills Rd, Ventura (93003-3498)
PHONE..............................805 650-0410
Fax: 805 650-9695
EMP: 71
SALES (corp-wide): 131.6B **Publicly Held**
SIC: **4812** Cellular telephone services
HQ: Cellco Partnership
1 Verizon Way
Basking Ridge NJ 07920

(P-5321)
CELLCO PARTNERSHIP
205 Oak Hill Rd, Paso Robles (93446-5438)
PHONE..............................805 237-8200
Maria Navarro, *Manager*
EMP: 71
SALES (corp-wide): 131.6B **Publicly Held**
SIC: **4812** Cellular telephone services
HQ: Cellco Partnership
1 Verizon Way
Basking Ridge NJ 07920

(P-5322)
CELLCO PARTNERSHIP
204 W 12th St Ste 1, Alturas (96101-3200)
PHONE..............................530 233-2100
John Perry, *Branch Mgr*
EMP: 71
SALES (corp-wide): 131.6B **Publicly Held**
SIC: **4812** Cellular telephone services
HQ: Cellco Partnership
1 Verizon Way
Basking Ridge NJ 07920

(P-5323)
CELLCO PARTNERSHIP
Also Called: Verizon Wireless
258 N El Cmino Real Ste A, Encinitas (92024)
PHONE..............................760 642-0430
Fax: 760 642-0436
EMP: 71

(P-5324)
CELLCO PARTNERSHIP
Also Called: Verizon Wireless
2540 Tuscany St, Corona (92881-4649)
PHONE..............................951 898-0980
Fax: 951 898-1451
EMP: 71
SALES (corp-wide): 131.6B **Publicly Held**
SIC: **4812** Cellular telephone services
HQ: Cellco Partnership
1 Verizon Way
Basking Ridge NJ 07920

(P-5325)
CELLCO PARTNERSHIP
Also Called: Verizon Wireless
26445 Bouquet Canyon Rd, Santa Clarita (91350-2396)
PHONE..............................661 296-7585
Fax: 661 296-8969
Yesenia Alapisco, *Branch Mgr*
EMP: 71
SALES (corp-wide): 131.6B **Publicly Held**
SIC: **4812** Cellular telephone services
HQ: Cellco Partnership
1 Verizon Way
Basking Ridge NJ 07920

(P-5326)
CELLCO PARTNERSHIP
125 Cyber Ct, Rocklin (95765-1205)
PHONE..............................916 408-7958
Benji Alicea, *Engineer*
Nno Alo, *Engineer*
Nno-Stephanie Ford, *Engineer*
Nno Goemann, *Engineer*
Nno Hadrych, *Engineer*
EMP: 71
SALES (corp-wide): 131.6B **Publicly Held**
SIC: **4812** Cellular telephone services
HQ: Cellco Partnership
1 Verizon Way
Basking Ridge NJ 07920

(P-5327)
CELLCO PARTNERSHIP
Also Called: Verizon Wireless
1729 N Victory Pl, Burbank (91502-1646)
PHONE..............................818 842-2722
Fax: 818 842-6844
Abe Osman, *Principal*
EMP: 71
SALES (corp-wide): 131.6B **Publicly Held**
SIC: **4812** Cellular telephone services
HQ: Cellco Partnership
1 Verizon Way
Basking Ridge NJ 07920

(P-5328)
CELLCO PARTNERSHIP
Also Called: Verizon Wireless
14510 Baldwn Prk Town Ctr, Baldwin Park (91706-5549)
PHONE..............................626 472-6196
Fax: 626 962-2463
EMP: 76
SALES (corp-wide): 131.6B **Publicly Held**
SIC: **4812** Cellular telephone services
HQ: Cellco Partnership
1 Verizon Way
Basking Ridge NJ 07920

(P-5329)
CELLCO PARTNERSHIP
Also Called: Verizon Wireless
6965 Camino Arroyo Ste 60, Gilroy (95020-7343)
PHONE..............................408 846-5170

4812 - Radiotelephone Communications County (P-5330)

Fax: 408 848-2537
Ignacio Solorio, *Principal*
EMP: 71
SALES (corp-wide): 131.6B **Publicly Held**
SIC: 4812 Cellular telephone services
HQ: Cellco Partnership
  1 Verizon Way
  Basking Ridge NJ 07920

(P-5330)
CELLCO PARTNERSHIP
Also Called: Verizon Wireless
368 S Lake Ave, Pasadena (91101-3508)
PHONE 626 395-0956
Fax: 626 395-0966
EMP: 71
SALES (corp-wide): 131.6B **Publicly Held**
SIC: 4812 Cellular telephone services
HQ: Cellco Partnership
  1 Verizon Way
  Basking Ridge NJ 07920

(P-5331)
CELLCO PARTNERSHIP
Also Called: Verizon Wireless
5051 Auburn Blvd, Sacramento (95841-2661)
PHONE 916 331-6833
Fax: 916 331-6840
Walter Gallo, *Principal*
EMP: 71
SALES (corp-wide): 131.6B **Publicly Held**
SIC: 4812 Cellular telephone services
HQ: Cellco Partnership
  1 Verizon Way
  Basking Ridge NJ 07920

(P-5332)
CELLCO PARTNERSHIP
Also Called: Verizon Wireless
71800 Highway 111 A110, Rancho Mirage (92270-4492)
PHONE 760 568-5542
Fax: 760 568-9585
Hicks Duana, *Principal*
EMP: 71
SALES (corp-wide): 131.6B **Publicly Held**
SIC: 4812 Cellular telephone services
HQ: Cellco Partnership
  1 Verizon Way
  Basking Ridge NJ 07920

(P-5333)
CELLCO PARTNERSHIP
Also Called: Verizon Wireless
172 Ranch Dr, Milpitas (95035-5101)
PHONE 408 263-1960
Fax: 408 263-9032
Paul Gutierrez, *Principal*
EMP: 71
SALES (corp-wide): 131.6B **Publicly Held**
SIC: 4812 Cellular telephone services
HQ: Cellco Partnership
  1 Verizon Way
  Basking Ridge NJ 07920

(P-5334)
CELLCO PARTNERSHIP
Also Called: Verizon Wireless
23718 El Toro Rd Ste A, Lake Forest (92630-8908)
PHONE 949 472-0700
Fax: 949 472-4989
Tracie Kemper, *Branch Mgr*
EMP: 71
SALES (corp-wide): 131.6B **Publicly Held**
SIC: 4812 Cellular telephone services
HQ: Cellco Partnership
  1 Verizon Way
  Basking Ridge NJ 07920

(P-5335)
CELLCO PARTNERSHIP
6600 Topanga Canyon Blvd # 9001, Canoga Park (91303-2609)
PHONE 818 316-0865
Vic Lozano, *Principal*
EMP: 71
SALES (corp-wide): 131.6B **Publicly Held**
SIC: 4812 Cellular telephone services

(P-5336)
CELLCO PARTNERSHIP
Also Called: Verizon Wireless
768 Market St, San Francisco (94102-2514)
PHONE 415 402-0640
Bob Wall, *Principal*
EMP: 71
SALES (corp-wide): 131.6B **Publicly Held**
SIC: 4812 Cellular telephone services
HQ: Cellco Partnership
  1 Verizon Way
  Basking Ridge NJ 07920

(P-5337)
CELLCO PARTNERSHIP
Also Called: Verizon Wireless
3202 W Monte Vista Ave, Turlock (95380-8412)
PHONE 209 668-9579
Fax: 209 668-9586
Irene Alvarez, *Principal*
EMP: 71
SALES (corp-wide): 131.6B **Publicly Held**
SIC: 4812 Cellular telephone services
HQ: Cellco Partnership
  1 Verizon Way
  Basking Ridge NJ 07920

(P-5338)
CELLCO PARTNERSHIP
18012 Bollinger Canyon Rd, San Ramon (94583-1502)
PHONE 925 743-9327
EMP: 74
SALES (corp-wide): 127B **Publicly Held**
SIC: 4812
HQ: Cellco Partnership
  1 Verizon Way
  Basking Ridge NJ 07920

(P-5339)
CELLCO PARTNERSHIP
Also Called: Verizon Wireless
2687 Park Ave, Tustin (92782-2707)
PHONE 714 258-8870
Fax: 714 258-8869
Ernie Lewis, *Associate Dir*
Nima Asgharnia, *Senior Mgr*
Wilson Quecano, *Manager*
EMP: 71
SALES (corp-wide): 131.6B **Publicly Held**
SIC: 4812 Cellular telephone services
HQ: Cellco Partnership
  1 Verizon Way
  Basking Ridge NJ 07920

(P-5340)
CELLCO PARTNERSHIP
Also Called: Verizon Wireless
17237 Ventura Blvd, Encino (91316-4058)
PHONE 818 990-4610
Fax: 818 990-4611
EMP: 71
SALES (corp-wide): 131.6B **Publicly Held**
SIC: 4812 Cellular telephone services
HQ: Cellco Partnership
  1 Verizon Way
  Basking Ridge NJ 07920

(P-5341)
CELLCO PARTNERSHIP
333 Biscayne Dr, San Rafael (94901-1577)
PHONE 415 258-8404
EMP: 71
SALES (corp-wide): 131.6B **Publicly Held**
SIC: 4812 Cellular telephone services
HQ: Cellco Partnership
  1 Verizon Way
  Basking Ridge NJ 07920

(P-5342)
CELLCO PARTNERSHIP
Also Called: Verizon Wireless
3458 Wilshire Blvd, Los Angeles (90010-2204)
PHONE 213 380-2299
Fax: 213 380-3340
Jay Trujillo, *Principal*
EMP: 71
SALES (corp-wide): 131.6B **Publicly Held**
SIC: 4812 Cellular telephone services
HQ: Cellco Partnership
  1 Verizon Way
  Basking Ridge NJ 07920

(P-5343)
CELLCO PARTNERSHIP
Also Called: Verizon Wireless
3635 N Freeway Blvd, Sacramento (95834-2926)
PHONE 916 419-6200
Fax: 916 419-6259
Dennis Strigl, *Principal*
Phil Quezada, *Associate Dir*
EMP: 71
SALES (corp-wide): 131.6B **Publicly Held**
SIC: 4812 Cellular telephone services
HQ: Cellco Partnership
  1 Verizon Way
  Basking Ridge NJ 07920

(P-5344)
CELLCO PARTNERSHIP
11265 Ventura Blvd, Studio City (91604-3136)
PHONE 818 980-4200
EMP: 71
SALES (corp-wide): 131.6B **Publicly Held**
SIC: 4812 Cellular telephone services
HQ: Cellco Partnership
  1 Verizon Way
  Basking Ridge NJ 07920

(P-5345)
CELLCO PARTNERSHIP
1199 Dunsyre Dr, Lafayette (94549-3217)
PHONE 925 472-0487
EMP: 74
SALES (corp-wide): 131.6B **Publicly Held**
SIC: 4812 Cellular telephone services
HQ: Cellco Partnership
  1 Verizon Way
  Basking Ridge NJ 07920

(P-5346)
CELLCO PARTNERSHIP
Also Called: Verizon Wireless
12006 Lakewood Blvd, Downey (90242-2661)
PHONE 562 401-1045
Fax: 562 401-1044
Ronnie Mendoza, *Branch Mgr*
EMP: 71
SALES (corp-wide): 131.6B **Publicly Held**
SIC: 4812 Cellular telephone services
HQ: Cellco Partnership
  1 Verizon Way
  Basking Ridge NJ 07920

(P-5347)
CELLCO PARTNERSHIP
Also Called: Verizon Wireless
12821 Main St, Hesperia (92345-9126)
PHONE 760 662-5914
Fax: 760 662-5472
EMP: 71
SALES (corp-wide): 131.6B **Publicly Held**
SIC: 4812 Cellular telephone services
HQ: Cellco Partnership
  1 Verizon Way
  Basking Ridge NJ 07920

(P-5348)
CELLCO PARTNERSHIP
Also Called: Verizon Wireless
2015 Birch Rd Ste 1805, Chula Vista (91915-2014)
PHONE 619 216-5840
Fax: 619 216-5841
EMP: 71
SALES (corp-wide): 131.6B **Publicly Held**
SIC: 4812 Cellular telephone services
HQ: Cellco Partnership
  1 Verizon Way
  Basking Ridge NJ 07920

(P-5349)
CELLCO PARTNERSHIP
Also Called: Verizon Wireless
3264 Lakeshore Ave, Oakland (94610-2720)
PHONE 510 267-0731
Fax: 510 267-0737
EMP: 71
SALES (corp-wide): 131.6B **Publicly Held**
SIC: 4812 Cellular telephone services
HQ: Cellco Partnership
  1 Verizon Way
  Basking Ridge NJ 07920

(P-5350)
CELLCO PARTNERSHIP
Also Called: Verizon Wireless
1398 Shaw Ave, Clovis (93612-3977)
PHONE 559 325-1420
Fax: 559 325-1240
EMP: 71
SALES (corp-wide): 131.6B **Publicly Held**
SIC: 4812 Cellular telephone services
HQ: Cellco Partnership
  1 Verizon Way
  Basking Ridge NJ 07920

(P-5351)
CELLCO PARTNERSHIP
Also Called: Verizon Wireless
39575 Trade Center Dr, Palmdale (93551-3783)
PHONE 661 274-2112
Fax: 661 274-1312
Andy Taylor, *Principal*
EMP: 71
SALES (corp-wide): 131.6B **Publicly Held**
SIC: 4812 Cellular telephone services
HQ: Cellco Partnership
  1 Verizon Way
  Basking Ridge NJ 07920

(P-5352)
CELLCO PARTNERSHIP
Also Called: Verizon Wireless
16120 Beach Blvd, Huntington Beach (92647-3805)
PHONE 714 847-8799
Fax: 714 847-8760
Thomas Johnson, *Branch Mgr*
EMP: 71
SALES (corp-wide): 131.6B **Publicly Held**
SIC: 4812 Cellular telephone services
HQ: Cellco Partnership
  1 Verizon Way
  Basking Ridge NJ 07920

PRODUCTS & SERVICES SECTION
4812 - Radiotelephone Communications County (P-5376)

(P-5353)
CELLCO PARTNERSHIP
Also Called: Verizon Wireless
100 N La Cienega Blvd # 233, Los Angeles (90048-1938)
PHONE..............................310 659-0775
Fax: 310 659-4690
Tony Chu, *Principal*
EMP: 71
SALES (corp-wide): 131.6B **Publicly Held**
SIC: **4812** Cellular telephone services
HQ: Cellco Partnership
   1 Verizon Way
   Basking Ridge NJ 07920

(P-5354)
CELLCO PARTNERSHIP
Also Called: Verizon
255 Parkshore Dr Bldg B, Folsom (95630-4716)
PHONE..............................916 357-1000
C Lee Cox, *CEO*
Brad Keller, *Associate Dir*
Robert Elmore, *Senior Engr*
Chris Rock, *Manager*
Mic Sedlak, *Manager*
EMP: 400
SALES (corp-wide): 131.6B **Publicly Held**
SIC: **4812** Cellular telephone services
HQ: Cellco Partnership
   1 Verizon Way
   Basking Ridge NJ 07920

(P-5355)
CELLCO PARTNERSHIP
Also Called: Verizon Wireless
3801 Pelandale Ave Ste B3, Modesto (95356-8308)
PHONE..............................209 543-6500
EMP: 76
SALES (corp-wide): 131.6B **Publicly Held**
SIC: **4812** Cellular telephone services
HQ: Cellco Partnership
   1 Verizon Way
   Basking Ridge NJ 07920

(P-5356)
CELLCO PARTNERSHIP
Also Called: Verizon Wireless
3785 Wilshire Blvd, Los Angeles (90010-2889)
PHONE..............................213 738-9771
Fax: 213 738-9756
EMP: 76
SALES (corp-wide): 131.6B **Publicly Held**
SIC: **4812** Cellular telephone services
HQ: Cellco Partnership
   1 Verizon Way
   Basking Ridge NJ 07920

(P-5357)
CELLCO PARTNERSHIP
Also Called: Verizon Wireless
20820 Avalon Blvd, Carson (90746-3300)
PHONE..............................310 329-9325
EMP: 76
SALES (corp-wide): 131.6B **Publicly Held**
SIC: **4812** Cellular telephone services
HQ: Cellco Partnership
   1 Verizon Way
   Basking Ridge NJ 07920

(P-5358)
CELLCO PARTNERSHIP
Also Called: Verizon Wireless
1503 Vine St, Hollywood (90028-7304)
PHONE..............................323 465-0640
Fax: 323 465-0071
EMP: 76
SALES (corp-wide): 131.6B **Publicly Held**
SIC: **4812** Cellular telephone services
HQ: Cellco Partnership
   1 Verizon Way
   Basking Ridge NJ 07920

(P-5359)
CELLCO PARTNERSHIP
Also Called: Verizon Wireless
7100 Santa Monica Blvd, West Hollywood (90046-5896)
PHONE..............................323 603-0369
Fax: 323 850-8135
EMP: 76
SALES (corp-wide): 131.6B **Publicly Held**
SIC: **4812** Cellular telephone services
HQ: Cellco Partnership
   1 Verizon Way
   Basking Ridge NJ 07920

(P-5360)
CELLCO PARTNERSHIP
Also Called: Verizon Wireless
2654 Mission St, San Francisco (94110-3102)
PHONE..............................415 695-8400
Fax: 415 695-8406
EMP: 76
SALES (corp-wide): 131.6B **Publicly Held**
SIC: **4812** Cellular telephone services
HQ: Cellco Partnership
   1 Verizon Way
   Basking Ridge NJ 07920

(P-5361)
CELLCO PARTNERSHIP
Also Called: Verizon Wireless
30935 Courthouse Dr Spc 1, Union City (94587-1716)
PHONE..............................510 324-5740
Fax: 510 324-5746
EMP: 76
SALES (corp-wide): 131.6B **Publicly Held**
SIC: **4812** Cellular telephone services
HQ: Cellco Partnership
   1 Verizon Way
   Basking Ridge NJ 07920

(P-5362)
CELLCO PARTNERSHIP
Also Called: Verizon Wireless
900 Dana Dr Ste 6, Redding (96003-4845)
PHONE..............................530 223-0420
Fax: 530 223-0419
EMP: 76
SALES (corp-wide): 131.6B **Publicly Held**
SIC: **4812** Cellular telephone services
HQ: Cellco Partnership
   1 Verizon Way
   Basking Ridge NJ 07920

(P-5363)
CELLCO PARTNERSHIP
Also Called: Verizon Wireless
24201 Valencia Blvd, Valencia (91355-1861)
PHONE..............................661 286-2399
Fax: 661 286-2365
EMP: 76
SALES (corp-wide): 131.6B **Publicly Held**
SIC: **4812** Cellular telephone services
HQ: Cellco Partnership
   1 Verizon Way
   Basking Ridge NJ 07920

(P-5364)
CELLCO PARTNERSHIP
Also Called: Verizon Wireless
6856 Katella Ave, Cypress (90630-5108)
PHONE..............................714 899-4690
Fax: 714 892-0963
EMP: 76
SALES (corp-wide): 131.6B **Publicly Held**
SIC: **4812** Cellular telephone services
HQ: Cellco Partnership
   1 Verizon Way
   Basking Ridge NJ 07920

(P-5365)
CELLCO PARTNERSHIP
Also Called: Verizon Wireless
880 N Imperial Ave, El Centro (92243-1916)
PHONE..............................760 337-5508
Fax: 760 337-6489
EMP: 76
SALES (corp-wide): 131.6B **Publicly Held**
SIC: **4812** Cellular telephone services
HQ: Cellco Partnership
   1 Verizon Way
   Basking Ridge NJ 07920

(P-5366)
CELLCO PARTNERSHIP
Also Called: Verizon Wireless
1555 Simi Town Center Way, Simi Valley (93065-0518)
PHONE..............................805 955-9035
Fax: 805 955-9036
EMP: 76
SALES (corp-wide): 131.6B **Publicly Held**
SIC: **4812** Cellular telephone services
HQ: Cellco Partnership
   1 Verizon Way
   Basking Ridge NJ 07920

(P-5367)
CELLCO PARTNERSHIP
Also Called: Verizon Wireless
6600 Topanga Canyon Blvd, Canoga Park (91303-2609)
PHONE..............................818 715-9143
Fax: 818 932-7940
EMP: 76
SALES (corp-wide): 131.6B **Publicly Held**
SIC: **4812** Cellular telephone services
HQ: Cellco Partnership
   1 Verizon Way
   Basking Ridge NJ 07920

(P-5368)
CELLCO PARTNERSHIP
Also Called: Verizon Wireless
110 Cooper St Ste A, Santa Cruz (95060-4566)
PHONE..............................831 421-0753
Fax: 831 421-0759
EMP: 76
SALES (corp-wide): 131.6B **Publicly Held**
SIC: **4812** Cellular telephone services
HQ: Cellco Partnership
   1 Verizon Way
   Basking Ridge NJ 07920

(P-5369)
CELLCO PARTNERSHIP
Also Called: Verizon Wireless
500 Inland Ctr 459, San Bernardino (92408-1925)
PHONE..............................909 381-0576
Fax: 909 383-8534
EMP: 76
SALES (corp-wide): 131.6B **Publicly Held**
SIC: **4812** Cellular telephone services
HQ: Cellco Partnership
   1 Verizon Way
   Basking Ridge NJ 07920

(P-5370)
CELLCO PARTNERSHIP
Also Called: Verizon Wireless
6065 Sunrise Blvd, Citrus Heights (95610-6833)
PHONE..............................916 536-0440
Fax: 916 864-0059
EMP: 76
SALES (corp-wide): 131.6B **Publicly Held**
SIC: **4812** Cellular telephone services
HQ: Cellco Partnership
   1 Verizon Way
   Basking Ridge NJ 07920

(P-5371)
CELLCO PARTNERSHIP
Also Called: Verizon
1 Daniel Burnham Ct Bsmt, San Francisco (94109-5474)
PHONE..............................415 351-1700
Minh Luong, *Manager*
EMP: 71
SALES (corp-wide): 131.6B **Publicly Held**
SIC: **4812** **5999** Cellular telephone services; mobile telephones & equipment
HQ: Cellco Partnership
   1 Verizon Way
   Basking Ridge NJ 07920

(P-5372)
CELLCO PARTNERSHIP
Also Called: Verizon
12376 Washington Blvd A, Whittier (90606-3810)
PHONE..............................562 789-0911
Fax: 562 789-1976
Victor Cardenes, *Manager*
EMP: 71
SALES (corp-wide): 131.6B **Publicly Held**
SIC: **4812** Cellular telephone services
HQ: Cellco Partnership
   1 Verizon Way
   Basking Ridge NJ 07920

(P-5373)
CELLCO PARTNERSHIP
Also Called: Verizon Wireless
7061 Clairemont Mesa Blvd, San Diego (92111-1041)
PHONE..............................858 614-0011
Fax: 858 614-0010
EMP: 71
SALES (corp-wide): 131.6B **Publicly Held**
SIC: **4812** Radio telephone communication
HQ: Cellco Partnership
   1 Verizon Way
   Basking Ridge NJ 07920

(P-5374)
CELLCO PARTNERSHIP
Also Called: Verizon Wireless
3825 Grand Ave, Chino (91710-5448)
PHONE..............................909 591-9740
Fax: 909 591-8015
EMP: 71
SALES (corp-wide): 131.6B **Publicly Held**
SIC: **4812** Cellular telephone services
HQ: Cellco Partnership
   1 Verizon Way
   Basking Ridge NJ 07920

(P-5375)
CELLCO PARTNERSHIP
Also Called: Verizon Wireless
1145 Colusa Ave Ste A, Yuba City (95991-3630)
PHONE..............................530 674-8007
Fax: 530 674-9150
Luis Ayala, *Sales Staff*
EMP: 76
SALES (corp-wide): 131.6B **Publicly Held**
SIC: **4812** Cellular telephone services
HQ: Cellco Partnership
   1 Verizon Way
   Basking Ridge NJ 07920

(P-5376)
CELLCO PARTNERSHIP
Also Called: Verizon
27040 Alicia Pkwy Ste E, Laguna Niguel (92677-3408)
PHONE..............................949 831-3955
Fax: 949 831-4660
Lawrence Lee, *Manager*
EMP: 71
SALES (corp-wide): 131.6B **Publicly Held**
SIC: **4812** Cellular telephone services

4812 - Radiotelephone Communications County (P-5377)

HQ: Cellco Partnership
1 Verizon Way
Basking Ridge NJ 07920

(P-5377)
CELLCO PARTNERSHIP
12475 N Mainstreet, Rancho Cucamonga (91739-8603)
PHONE.....................909 899-8910
EMP: 71
SALES (corp-wide): 131.6B Publicly Held
SIC: 4812 Cellular telephone services
HQ: Cellco Partnership
1 Verizon Way
Basking Ridge NJ 07920

(P-5378)
CELLCO PARTNERSHIP
Also Called: Verizon Wireless
2980 State St, Santa Barbara (93105-3445)
PHONE.....................805 569-2525
Fax: 805 569-7601
Kevin Warren, *Principal*
Leah Cartney, *Manager*
EMP: 71
SALES (corp-wide): 131.6B Publicly Held
SIC: 4812 Cellular telephone services
HQ: Cellco Partnership
1 Verizon Way
Basking Ridge NJ 07920

(P-5379)
CELLCO PARTNERSHIP
Also Called: Verizon Wireless
844 4th St, Santa Rosa (95404-4505)
PHONE.....................707 525-5010
Garrett Arends, *Manager*
David Saldivar, *Admin Asst*
David Salberg, *Manager*
EMP: 71
SALES (corp-wide): 131.6B Publicly Held
SIC: 4812 Cellular telephone services
HQ: Cellco Partnership
1 Verizon Way
Basking Ridge NJ 07920

(P-5380)
CELLCO PARTNERSHIP
503 N State College Blvd, Fullerton (92831-3545)
PHONE.....................714 449-0715
EMP: 71
SALES (corp-wide): 131.6B Publicly Held
SIC: 4812 Cellular telephone services
HQ: Cellco Partnership
1 Verizon Way
Basking Ridge NJ 07920

(P-5381)
CELLCO PARTNERSHIP
Also Called: Verizon Wireless
219 University Ave, Palo Alto (94301-1712)
PHONE.....................650 323-6127
Fax: 650 323-6458
Ian Yahya, *Manager*
EMP: 71
SALES (corp-wide): 131.6B Publicly Held
SIC: 4812 5065 5999 Cellular telephone services; telephone & telegraphic equipment; mobile telephones & equipment
HQ: Cellco Partnership
1 Verizon Way
Basking Ridge NJ 07920

(P-5382)
CELLCO PARTNERSHIP
Also Called: Verizon
5221 Martinelli Way, Dublin (94568-7136)
PHONE.....................925 847-0320
Denise Perrmorrse, *Manager*
EMP: 71
SALES (corp-wide): 131.6B Publicly Held
SIC: 4812 Cellular telephone services

HQ: Cellco Partnership
1 Verizon Way
Basking Ridge NJ 07920

(P-5383)
CELLCO PARTNERSHIP
Also Called: Verizon
994 Mill St Ste 100, San Luis Obispo (93401-2777)
PHONE.....................805 549-6260
Robin Okoneski, *Branch Mgr*
Gianna Autry, *Natl Sales Mgr*
EMP: 71
SALES (corp-wide): 131.6B Publicly Held
SIC: 4812 Cellular telephone services
HQ: Cellco Partnership
1 Verizon Way
Basking Ridge NJ 07920

(P-5384)
CELLCO PARTNERSHIP
Also Called: Verizon Wireless
3770 W Mcfadden Ave Ste H, Santa Ana (92704-1395)
PHONE.....................714 775-0600
EMP: 76
SALES (corp-wide): 131.6B Publicly Held
SIC: 4812 Cellular telephone services
HQ: Cellco Partnership
1 Verizon Way
Basking Ridge NJ 07920

(P-5385)
CELLCO PARTNERSHIP
Also Called: Verizon
2792 Walnut Ave, Tustin (92780-7029)
PHONE.....................714 669-3500
Mark Loop, *Branch Mgr*
Mark R Loop, *Technical Staff*
EMP: 71
SALES (corp-wide): 131.6B Publicly Held
SIC: 4812 Radio telephone communication
HQ: Cellco Partnership
1 Verizon Way
Basking Ridge NJ 07920

(P-5386)
CELLCO PARTNERSHIP
Also Called: Verizon Wireless
43458 10th St W Ste C, Lancaster (93534-6417)
PHONE.....................661 726-4762
Fax: 661 726-4587
EMP: 71
SALES (corp-wide): 131.6B Publicly Held
SIC: 4812 Cellular telephone services
HQ: Cellco Partnership
1 Verizon Way
Basking Ridge NJ 07920

(P-5387)
CELLCO PARTNERSHIP
638 Camino De Ls Mrs H140 Ste H, San Clemente (92673)
PHONE.....................949 488-9990
Fax: 949 488-9989
Aj Bezer, *Branch Mgr*
EMP: 71
SALES (corp-wide): 131.6B Publicly Held
SIC: 4812 Cellular telephone services
HQ: Cellco Partnership
1 Verizon Way
Basking Ridge NJ 07920

(P-5388)
CELLCO PARTNERSHIP
Also Called: Verizon Wireless
5438 Whittier Blvd, Commerce (90022-4113)
PHONE.....................323 725-9750
Fax: 323 725-9744
Kristina King, *Branch Mgr*
EMP: 71

SALES (corp-wide): 131.6B Publicly Held
SIC: 4812 Cellular telephone services
HQ: Cellco Partnership
1 Verizon Way
Basking Ridge NJ 07920

(P-5389)
CELLCO PARTNERSHIP
Also Called: Verizon Wireless
8724 Washington Blvd, Pico Rivera (90660-3791)
PHONE.....................562 942-8527
Fax: 562 948-1663
EMP: 71
SALES (corp-wide): 131.6B Publicly Held
SIC: 4812 Cellular telephone services
HQ: Cellco Partnership
1 Verizon Way
Basking Ridge NJ 07920

(P-5390)
CORTEL INC
14621 Arroyo Hondo, San Diego (92127-3641)
PHONE.....................650 703-7217
Michael Jackson, *President*
John Barker, *CFO*
Michael Miller, *Admin Sec*
EMP: 52
SALES (est): 3.6MM Privately Held
SIC: 4812 Cellular telephone services

(P-5391)
CRICKET COMMUNICATIONS LLC (DH)
Also Called: Cricket Wireless
7337 Trade St, San Diego (92121-2423)
PHONE.....................858 882-6000
S Douglas Hutcheson, *CEO*
Nitu Arora, *President*
David Davis, *President*
Glen Flowers, *President*
Annette Jacobs, *President*
EMP: 65
SALES (est): 555.3MM
SALES (corp-wide): 146.8B Publicly Held
WEB: www.cricketcommunications.com
SIC: 4812 Radio telephone communication
HQ: Leap Wireless International, Inc.
7337 Trade St
San Diego CA 92121
858 882-6000

(P-5392)
CRICKET INDIANA PROPERTY CO
10307 Pacific Center Ct, San Diego (92121-4340)
PHONE.....................858 587-2648
EMP: 96
SALES (est): 2.5MM
SALES (corp-wide): 146.8B Publicly Held
WEB: www.leapwireless.com
SIC: 4812 Radio telephone communication
HQ: Leap Wireless International, Inc.
7337 Trade St
San Diego CA 92121
858 882-6000

(P-5393)
DIGITAL COMMUNICATIONS NETWORK (PA)
Also Called: D C N Wireless
6300 Canoga Ave Ste 1625, Woodland Hills (91367-8045)
PHONE.....................818 227-3333
Fax: 818 227-3300
Robert H Mogadam, *President*
Margrit Dorgelo, *Vice Pres*
Della Chue, *Manager*
EMP: 54
SALES (est): 11.3MM Privately Held
WEB: www.digitalcomnet.com
SIC: 4812 5999 Cellular telephone services; telephone & communication equipment

(P-5394)
DOWNTOWN METRO
1030 6th St Ste 16, Coachella (92236-1710)
PHONE.....................760 398-3310
H Yun, *Owner*
EMP: 50
SALES (est): 663.7K Privately Held
SIC: 4812 Cellular telephone services

(P-5395)
DUST NETWORKS INC
32990 Alvrdo Niles Rd # 910, Union City (94587-8103)
PHONE.....................510 400-2900
Fax: 510 489-3799
Joy Weiss, *President*
Eva Chen, *Vice Pres*
Brenda Glaze, *Vice Pres*
Dave Lynch, *Vice Pres*
David Skelton, *Vice Pres*
EMP: 51
SQ FT: 15,000
SALES (est): 4.6MM
SALES (corp-wide): 1.4B Publicly Held
WEB: www.dust-inc.com
SIC: 4812 Cellular telephone services
PA: Linear Technology Corporation
1630 Mccarthy Blvd
Milpitas CA 95035
408 432-1900

(P-5396)
EA MOBILE INC
5510 Lincoln Blvd, Los Angeles (90094-2034)
PHONE.....................310 754-7125
Mitch Lasky, *Ch of Bd*
Scott Lahman, *President*
Craig Gatarz, *COO*
Michael Marchetti, *CFO*
Minard Hamilton, *Exec VP*
EMP: 400
SQ FT: 23,000
SALES (est): 12.9MM
SALES (corp-wide): 4.4B Publicly Held
SIC: 4812 Cellular telephone services
PA: Electronic Arts Inc.
209 Redwood Shores Pkwy
Redwood City CA 94065
650 628-1500

(P-5397)
FRONTIER CALIFORNIA INC
Also Called: Verizon
5195 N Blackstone Ave, Fresno (93710-6701)
PHONE.....................559 224-9222
Fax: 559 224-5049
Randall Petty-John, *Manager*
EMP: 60
SALES (corp-wide): 5.5B Publicly Held
SIC: 4812 Cellular telephone services
HQ: Frontier California Inc.
140 West St
New York NY 10007
212 395-1000

(P-5398)
FUTURE PAGING & CELLULAR INC
2445 Alvin Ave, San Jose (95121-1611)
PHONE.....................408 238-8833
Quang Pak, *Branch Mgr*
EMP: 103
SALES (corp-wide): 13.9MM Privately Held
SIC: 4812 Paging services; cellular telephone services
PA: Future Paging & Cellular Inc
1014 Clement St
San Francisco CA
415 386-7928

(P-5399)
IMOBILE LLC
2613 Naglee Rd, Tracy (95304-7317)
PHONE.....................209 833-6757
EMP: 345 Privately Held
SIC: 4812 Cellular telephone services
PA: Imobile Llc
206 Terminal Dr
Plainview NY 11803

PRODUCTS & SERVICES SECTION
4812 - Radiotelephone Communications County (P-5424)

(P-5400)
MALKA COMMUNICATIONS GROUP
Also Called: Malka Vrs
15736 Hartsook St, Encino (91436-1502)
PHONE..................818 528-6894
Nataly Malka, *Principal*
EMP: 50
SALES: 950K **Privately Held**
SIC: 4812 Radio telephone communication

(P-5401)
MBIT WIRELESS INC
4340 Von Karman Ave # 140, Newport Beach (92660-1201)
PHONE..................949 205-4559
Bhasker Patel, *President*
Mw Sohn, *Vice Pres*
Sithanandam Chandran, *Director*
EMP: 212
SALES (est): 10.2MM **Privately Held**
SIC: 4812 Cellular telephone services

(P-5402)
NEW CINGULAR WIRELESS SVCS INC
Also Called: AT&T Wireless
9830 Norwalk Blvd Ste 100, Santa Fe Springs (90670-2987)
PHONE..................562 941-6422
Yong Kim, *Branch Mgr*
EMP: 100
SALES (corp-wide): 146.8B **Publicly Held**
WEB: www.attws.com
SIC: 4812 Cellular telephone services
HQ: New Cingular Wireless Services, Inc.
7277 164th Ave Ne
Redmond WA 98052
425 827-4500

(P-5403)
NEXTEL COMMUNICATIONS INC
1810 W Slauson Ave Ste G, Los Angeles (90047-1133)
PHONE..................323 290-2400
Fax: 323 290-9325
Ivan Arvizu, *Principal*
EMP: 60
SALES (corp-wide): 78.2B **Publicly Held**
SIC: 4812 Radio telephone communication
HQ: Nextel Communications, Inc.
12502 Sunrise Valley Dr
Reston VA 20191
703 433-4000

(P-5404)
NEXTEL COMMUNICATIONS INC
272 Sun Valley Mall, Concord (94520-5808)
PHONE..................925 682-2355
Sean Fanopulous, *Manager*
EMP: 60
SALES (corp-wide): 78.2B **Publicly Held**
WEB: www.nextel.com
SIC: 4812 5999 Radio telephone communication; mobile telephones & equipment
HQ: Nextel Communications, Inc.
12502 Sunrise Valley Dr
Reston VA 20191
703 433-4000

(P-5405)
NEXTEL COMMUNICATIONS INC
16 Technology Dr, Irvine (92618-2355)
PHONE..................949 727-1400
EMP: 62
SALES (corp-wide): 78.2B **Publicly Held**
SIC: 4812 Radio telephone communication
HQ: Nextel Communications, Inc.
12502 Sunrise Valley Dr
Reston VA 20191
703 433-4000

(P-5406)
OFFICE OF THE LEGISLATIVE COUN
Also Called: Legislative Data Center
1100 J St Fl 7, Sacramento (95814-2826)
PHONE..................916 341-8708
Nancy Pabst, *IT/INT Sup*
Parm Pabla, *Info Tech Mgr*
Elizabeth Espinosa, *Project Mgr*
Shahzad Anwar, *Technology*
Steven Levitt, *Technology*
EMP: 330 **Privately Held**
SIC: 4812 Radio telephone communication
HQ: Office Of The Legislative Counsel
State Capitol Bldg Rm 3021
Sacramento CA 95814
916 341-8000

(P-5407)
SIERRA WIRELESS AMERICA INC
2738 Loker Ave W Ste A, Carlsbad (92010-6629)
PHONE..................760 444-5650
Fax: 760 476-8701
Jason W Cohenour, *CEO*
Jim Kirkpatrick, *Vice Pres*
Bruce Rowe, *Info Tech Mgr*
William Lee, *Finance*
Donna Bevington, *Accounts Mgr*
EMP: 82
SALES (est): 15.5MM
SALES (corp-wide): 607.8MM **Privately Held**
SIC: 4812 Cellular telephone services
PA: Sierra Wireless, Inc.
13811 Wireless Way
Richmond BC V6V 3
604 231-1100

(P-5408)
SLING MEDIA INC (HQ)
1051 E Hillsdale Blvd # 500, Foster City (94404-1640)
PHONE..................650 293-8000
Fax: 650 293-8800
Blake Krikorian, *President*
Mike Dugan, *CEO*
Raghu Tarra, *Senior VP*
Ilya Asnis, *Vice Pres*
Jay Berryhill, *Vice Pres*
▲ **EMP:** 65
SALES (est): 61.3MM
SALES (corp-wide): 3.1B **Publicly Held**
WEB: www.slingmedia.com
SIC: 4812 Radio telephone communication
PA: Echostar Corporation
100 Inverness Ter E
Englewood CO 80112
303 706-4000

(P-5409)
SONIM TECHNOLOGIES INC (PA)
1825 S Grant St Ste 200, San Mateo (94402-2672)
PHONE..................650 378-8100
Fax: 650 378-8109
Terrence Valeski, *Ch of Bd*
Asha Seshagiri, *Vice Chairman*
John Burns, *President*
Bob Plaschke, *CEO*
Richard Long, *CFO*
▲ **EMP:** 57
SALES (est): 25.8MM **Privately Held**
WEB: www.sonimtech.com
SIC: 4812 Cellular telephone services

(P-5410)
SPRINT CORPORATION
6591 Irvine Center Dr # 100, Irvine (92618-2129)
PHONE..................949 748-3353
Fax: 714 368-4501
Mohammed Nasser, *Exec Dir*
EMP: 400
SALES (corp-wide): 78.2B **Publicly Held**
SIC: 4812 Cellular telephone services
HQ: Sprint Corporation
6200 Sprint Pkwy
Overland Park KS 66251
855 848-3280

(P-5411)
STX WIRELESS OPERATIONS LLC
Also Called: Cricket Stx
5887 Copley Dr, San Diego (92111-7906)
PHONE..................858 882-6000
Douglas Hutcheson, *President*
Jerry Elliot, *CFO*
EMP: 4000
SALES (est): 414.8MM **Privately Held**
SIC: 4812 Cellular telephone services

(P-5412)
SYBASE 365 LLC
1 Sybase Dr, Dublin (94568-7986)
PHONE..................925 236-5000
Gino Picasso, *CEO*
Nick Macilveen, *Partner*
Marty Beard, *President*
Joseph Kuhn, *CFO*
William Peters, *Corp Secy*
EMP: 250
SQ FT: 17,500
SALES (est): 17.8MM
SALES (corp-wide): 22.3B **Privately Held**
WEB: www.mobile365.com
SIC: 4812 Cellular telephone services
HQ: Sybase, Inc.
1 Sybase Dr
Dublin CA 94568
925 236-5000

(P-5413)
T-MOBILE USA INC
Also Called: Metropcs-Roseville
1420 E Roseville Pkwy, Roseville (95661-3078)
PHONE..................916 786-3339
EMP: 170
SALES (corp-wide): 74.3B **Publicly Held**
SIC: 4812 4813 Radio telephone communication; telephone communication, except radio; wire telephone
HQ: T-Mobile Usa, Inc.
12920 Se 38th St
Bellevue WA 98006
425 378-4000

(P-5414)
T-MOBILE USA INC
Also Called: Metropcs-Fremont
4095 Mowry Ave, Fremont (94538-1339)
PHONE..................510 797-8290
EMP: 170
SALES (corp-wide): 74.3B **Publicly Held**
SIC: 4812 4813 Cellular telephone services; telephone communication, except radio; wire telephone
HQ: T-Mobile Usa, Inc.
12920 Se 38th St
Bellevue WA 98006
425 378-4000

(P-5415)
T-MOBILE USA INC
Also Called: Metropcs-Modesto
2225 Plaza Pkwy Ste I1b, Modesto (95350-6220)
PHONE..................209 529-0539
EMP: 170
SALES (corp-wide): 74.3B **Publicly Held**
SIC: 4812 4813 Cellular telephone services; telephone communication, except radio; wire telephone
HQ: T-Mobile Usa, Inc.
12920 Se 38th St
Bellevue WA 98006
425 378-4000

(P-5416)
T-MOBILE USA INC
Also Called: Metropcs-Van Ness
900 Van Ness Ave Ste 1, San Francisco (94109-6970)
PHONE..................415 440-5370
EMP: 170
SALES (corp-wide): 74.3B **Publicly Held**
SIC: 4812 4813 Radio telephone communication; telephone communication, except radio; wire telephone
HQ: T-Mobile Usa, Inc.
12920 Se 38th St
Bellevue WA 98006
425 378-4000

(P-5417)
TEAM MOBILE
2008 Mcgaw Ave, Irvine (92614-0911)
PHONE..................949 567-6800
William Buck, *Regional Mgr*
Brett Thompson, *Manager*
EMP: 200
SALES (est): 4.1MM **Privately Held**
WEB: www.teammobile.com
SIC: 4812 Cellular telephone services

(P-5418)
TEXTPLUS INC
Also Called: Gogii
13160 Mindanao Way # 217, Marina Del Rey (90292-6358)
PHONE..................424 272-0296
Nanea Reeves, *President*
Zachary Norman, *President*
Tricia Bertero, *Chief Mktg Ofcr*
Chandra Hill, *Vice Pres*
Cory Radcliff, *Vice Pres*
EMP: 65
SALES (est): 9.1MM **Privately Held**
SIC: 4812 Cellular telephone services

(P-5419)
TIME WARNER CABLE INC
19780 Hawthorne Blvd # 102, Torrance (90503-1537)
PHONE..................714 709-3617
Fax: 310 634-1836
Warner Cable, *Branch Mgr*
EMP: 170
SALES (corp-wide): 9.7MM **Publicly Held**
SIC: 4812 Cellular telephone services
HQ: Spectrum Management Holding Company, Llc
400 Atlantic St
Stamford CT 06901
203 905-7801

(P-5420)
TOTALLYFREEPAGINGCOM INC
10000 Culver Blvd, Culver City (90232-2705)
PHONE..................310 845-8700
Richard White, *Manager*
EMP: 60
SALES (est): 1.6MM **Privately Held**
SIC: 4812 Paging services

(P-5421)
TRELLISWARE TECHNOLOGIES INC
16516 Via Esprillo # 300, San Diego (92127-1728)
PHONE..................858 753-1600
Fax: 858 753-1640
Thomas Carter, *CEO*
Metin Bayram, *Vice Pres*
Jim Morse, *Vice Pres*
Jeff Thomas, *Vice Pres*
Michael Schmitt, *Program Mgr*
EMP: 90
SQ FT: 46,000
SALES (est): 25.5MM **Privately Held**
WEB: www.trellisware.com
SIC: 4812 4813 3663 Radio telephone communication; local & long distance telephone communications; airborne radio communications equipment

(P-5422)
UST DEVELOPMENT INC
Also Called: UST Telecom
2001 Elm Ct, Ontario (91761-7619)
P.O. Box 3790 (91761-0977)
PHONE..................626 205-1123
David William Bell, *CEO*
Monique Santini, *Office Mgr*
EMP: 127
SALES (est): 7.7MM **Privately Held**
SIC: 4812 Radio telephone communication

(P-5423)
VERIZON WIRELESS INC
570 E Betteravia Rd, Santa Maria (93454-8805)
PHONE..................805 928-7433
EMP: 85
SALES (corp-wide): 131.6B **Publicly Held**
SIC: 4812 Cellular telephone services
HQ: Verizon Wireless, Inc.
1 Verizon Way
Basking Ridge NJ 07920
908 559-2000

(P-5424)
VERIZON WIRELESS INC
15 Montebello Way, Los Gatos (95030-6808)
PHONE..................408 354-6374
Joseph Edens, *Branch Mgr*
EMP: 113

4812 - Radiotelephone Communications County (P-5425)

SALES (corp-wide): 131.6B **Publicly Held**
WEB: www.verizonwireless.com
SIC: **4812** Cellular telephone services
HQ: Verizon Wireless, Inc.
 1 Verizon Way
 Basking Ridge NJ 07920
 908 559-2000

(P-5425)
VERIZON WIRELESS INC
78742 Highway 111, La Quinta (92253-2062)
PHONE..........................760 771-5587
Fax: 760 771-3607
Michelle Henson, *Branch Mgr*
Dwight Forest, *Director*
EMP: 64
SALES (corp-wide): 131.6B **Publicly Held**
SIC: **4812** Cellular telephone services
HQ: Verizon Wireless, Inc.
 1 Verizon Way
 Basking Ridge NJ 07920
 908 559-2000

(P-5426)
VERIZON WIRELESS INC
1331 S Lone Hill Ave # 170, Glendora (91740-5338)
PHONE..........................909 592-5211
Fax: 909 592-4991
Vernica Rocha, *Manager*
EMP: 140
SALES (corp-wide): 131.6B **Publicly Held**
SIC: **4812** Cellular telephone services
HQ: Verizon Wireless, Inc.
 1 Verizon Way
 Basking Ridge NJ 07920
 908 559-2000

(P-5427)
VERIZON WIRELESS INC
1586 Gateway Blvd, Fairfield (94533-6901)
PHONE..........................707 399-0866
Fax: 707 399-0897
Sarah Carson, *Principal*
EMP: 82
SALES (corp-wide): 131.6B **Publicly Held**
SIC: **4812** Cellular telephone services
HQ: Verizon Wireless, Inc.
 1 Verizon Way
 Basking Ridge NJ 07920
 908 559-2000

(P-5428)
VERIZON WIRELESS INC
13262 Jamboree Rd, Irvine (92602-2309)
PHONE..........................714 730-7790
Fax: 714 730-7701
Lawrence Lee, *Branch Mgr*
EMP: 133
SALES (corp-wide): 131.6B **Publicly Held**
SIC: **4812** Cellular telephone services
HQ: Verizon Wireless, Inc.
 1 Verizon Way
 Basking Ridge NJ 07920
 908 559-2000

(P-5429)
VERIZON WIRELESS INC
16695 Sierra Lakes Pkwy, Fontana (92336-1258)
PHONE..........................909 355-0725
Fax: 909 355-0727
EMP: 90
SALES (corp-wide): 131.6B **Publicly Held**
SIC: **4812** Cellular telephone services
HQ: Verizon Wireless, Inc.
 1 Verizon Way
 Basking Ridge NJ 07920
 908 559-2000

(P-5430)
VERIZON WIRELESS INC
1208 Galleria Blvd, Roseville (95678-1953)
PHONE..........................916 784-6886
Fax: 916 784-1350
Mike Hennig, *Branch Mgr*
Ryan Tattersfield, *Sales Mgr*
EMP: 95

SALES (corp-wide): 131.6B **Publicly Held**
SIC: **4812** Cellular telephone services
HQ: Verizon Wireless, Inc.
 1 Verizon Way
 Basking Ridge NJ 07920
 908 559-2000

(P-5431)
VERIZON WIRELESS INC
1122 Broadway, Eureka (95501-0128)
PHONE..........................707 442-8334
Fax: 707 442-8548
EMP: 77
SALES (corp-wide): 131.6B **Publicly Held**
SIC: **4812** Cellular telephone services
HQ: Verizon Wireless, Inc.
 1 Verizon Way
 Basking Ridge NJ 07920
 908 559-2000

(P-5432)
VERIZON WIRELESS INC
1460 Stoneridge Mall Rd, Pleasanton (94588-3215)
PHONE..........................925 224-9868
Fax: 925 598-9760
Mary Booker, *Principal*
EMP: 112
SALES (corp-wide): 131.6B **Publicly Held**
SIC: **4812** Cellular telephone services
HQ: Verizon Wireless, Inc.
 1 Verizon Way
 Basking Ridge NJ 07920
 908 559-2000

(P-5433)
VERIZON WIRELESS INC
2350 White Ln, Bakersfield (93304-7284)
PHONE..........................661 836-3141
Fax: 661 836-3168
EMP: 108
SALES (corp-wide): 131.6B **Publicly Held**
SIC: **4812** Cellular telephone services
HQ: Verizon Wireless, Inc.
 1 Verizon Way
 Basking Ridge NJ 07920
 908 559-2000

(P-5434)
VODAFONE AMERICAS INC
2999 Oak Rd Fl 5, Walnut Creek (94597-2066)
PHONE..........................925 210-3812
Tomas Isaksson, *CEO*
EMP: 100
SALES (corp-wide): 59.3B **Privately Held**
SIC: **4812 4813 4899 7389** Radio telephone communication; long distance telephone communications; data communication services; credit card service
HQ: Vodafone Americas Inc.
 1 Buccaneer Ln
 Redwood City CA 94065
 650 832-6600

(P-5435)
VODAFONE AMERICAS INC (HQ)
1 Buccaneer Ln, Redwood City (94065-2832)
PHONE..........................650 832-6600
Mark Hickey, *President*
Julian Horn-Smith, *COO*
Phil Clark, *Treasurer*
Robert Chu, *CTO*
Marco Favre, *IT/INT Sup*
EMP: 85
SALES (est): 62.7MM
SALES (corp-wide): 59.3B **Privately Held**
WEB: www.vodafone-us.com
SIC: **4812 4813 4899 7389** Radio telephone communication; cellular telephone services; paging services; long distance telephone communications; data communication services; credit card service
PA: Vodafone Group Public Limited Company
 Vodafone House
 Newbury BERKS RG14
 163 533-251

(P-5436)
WM WIRELESS INC
6723 N Paramount Blvd, Long Beach (90805-1901)
PHONE..........................562 633-9288
Ferdinand L Aguinaldo, *President*
Rose Sajo, *Manager*
EMP: 50
SALES (est): 6.9MM **Privately Held**
SIC: **4812** Cellular telephone services

4813 Telephone Communications, Except

(P-5437)
11 MAIN INC
527 Flume St, Chico (95928-5608)
PHONE..........................530 892-9191
Jeff Schlicht, *CEO*
Mike Effle, *President*
Ray Kaminski, *Vice Pres*
Christina Liu, *Vice Pres*
Amber Minson, *Vice Pres*
EMP: 105
SALES (est): 23.1MM **Privately Held**
SIC: **4813**
HQ: Alibaba.Com Inc
 400 S El Camino Real # 400
 San Mateo CA 94402
 408 748-1200

(P-5438)
2WIRE INC (DH)
1764 Automation Pkwy, San Jose (95131-1873)
PHONE..........................678 473-2907
Fax: 408 428-9590
Tim O'Loughlin, *CEO*
Pasquale Romano, *President*
Tom Bohan, *Admin Sec*
Ravi Kohli, *CIO*
Chris Bajorek, *CTO*
▲ EMP: 138
SQ FT: 82,000
SALES (est): 131.8MM
SALES (corp-wide): 1MM **Privately Held**
WEB: www.2wire.com
SIC: **4813**

(P-5439)
4G WIRELESS INC
Also Called: Verizon Wreless Authorized Ret
7220 Eastern Ave, Bell (90201-4505)
PHONE..........................562 928-2972
EMP: 55
SALES (corp-wide): 450MM **Privately Held**
SIC: **4813 4812** Telephone communication, except radio; cellular telephone services
PA: 4g Wireless, Inc.
 8871 Research Dr
 Irvine CA 92618
 949 748-6100

(P-5440)
4G WIRELESS INC
Also Called: Verizon Wreless Authorized Ret
4620 Tassajara Rd, Dublin (94568-4607)
PHONE..........................925 307-8990
EMP: 55
SALES (corp-wide): 450MM **Privately Held**
SIC: **4813 4812** Telephone communication, except radio; cellular telephone services
PA: 4g Wireless, Inc.
 8871 Research Dr
 Irvine CA 92618
 949 748-6100

(P-5441)
4G WIRELESS INC
Also Called: Verizon Wreless Authorized Ret
8342 Lincoln Blvd, Los Angeles (90045-2414)
PHONE..........................310 429-9048
EMP: 55
SALES (corp-wide): 450MM **Privately Held**
SIC: **4813 4812** Telephone communication, except radio; cellular telephone services

PA: 4g Wireless, Inc.
 8871 Research Dr
 Irvine CA 92618
 949 748-6100

(P-5442)
4G WIRELESS INC
Also Called: Verizon Wireless Authorized Ret
4925 Eagle Rock Blvd, Los Angeles (90041-1906)
PHONE..........................323 679-9991
EMP: 55
SALES (corp-wide): 450MM **Privately Held**
SIC: **4813 4812** Telephone communication, except radio; cellular telephone services
PA: 4g Wireless, Inc.
 8871 Research Dr
 Irvine CA 92618
 949 748-6100

(P-5443)
4G WIRELESS INC
Also Called: Verizon Wireless Authorized Ret
501 W Felicita Ave # 104, Escondido (92025-5638)
PHONE..........................760 705-7133
EMP: 55
SALES (corp-wide): 450MM **Privately Held**
SIC: **4813 4812** Telephone communication, except radio; cellular telephone services
PA: 4g Wireless, Inc.
 8871 Research Dr
 Irvine CA 92618
 949 748-6100

(P-5444)
4G WIRELESS INC
Also Called: Verizon Wireless Premium Ret
2635 Gateway Rd Ste 103, Carlsbad (92009-1753)
PHONE..........................760 828-2543
Ameen Elashqar, *Branch Mgr*
EMP: 55
SALES (corp-wide): 450MM **Privately Held**
SIC: **4813 4812 4833** Telephone communication, except radio; cellular telephone services; television broadcasting stations
PA: 4g Wireless, Inc.
 8871 Research Dr
 Irvine CA 92618
 949 748-6100

(P-5445)
4G WIRELESS INC
Also Called: Verizon Wreless Authorized Ret
2560 N Perris Blvd Ste G8, Perris (92571-3253)
PHONE..........................951 210-7980
EMP: 55
SALES (corp-wide): 450MM **Privately Held**
SIC: **4813 4812** Telephone communication, except radio; cellular telephone services
PA: 4g Wireless, Inc.
 8871 Research Dr
 Irvine CA 92618
 949 748-6100

(P-5446)
4G WIRELESS INC
Also Called: Verizon Wreless Authorized Ret
407 N Pacific Coast Hwy # 101, Redondo Beach (90277-2872)
PHONE..........................310 376-2299
EMP: 55
SALES (corp-wide): 450MM **Privately Held**
SIC: **4813 4812** Telephone communication, except radio; cellular telephone services
PA: 4g Wireless, Inc.
 8871 Research Dr
 Irvine CA 92618
 949 748-6100

(P-5447)
4G WIRELESS INC
Also Called: Verizon Wreless Authorized Ret
285 E 5th St, Long Beach (90802-2484)
PHONE..........................562 432-7744

PRODUCTS & SERVICES SECTION
4813 - Telephone Communications, Except Radio County (P-5469)

EMP: 55
SALES (corp-wide): 450MM **Privately Held**
SIC: **4813** 4812 Telephone communication, except radio; cellular telephone services
PA: 4g Wireless, Inc.
8871 Research Dr
Irvine CA 92618
949 748-6100

(P-5448)
4G WIRELESS INC
Also Called: Verizon Wreless Authorized Ret
8590 W Sunset Blvd 9.1, West Hollywood (90069-2354)
PHONE..................................310 310-7998
EMP: 55
SALES (corp-wide): 450MM **Privately Held**
SIC: **4813** 4812 Telephone communication, except radio; cellular telephone services
PA: 4g Wireless, Inc.
8871 Research Dr
Irvine CA 92618
949 748-6100

(P-5449)
8X8 INC (PA)
2125 Onel Dr, San Jose (95131-2032)
PHONE..................................408 727-1885
Vikram Verma, *CEO*
Bryan Martin, *Ch of Bd*
Mary Ellen Genovese, *CFO*
Puneet Arora, *Senior VP*
Darren Hakeman, *Senior VP*
EMP: 161
SQ FT: 140,831
SALES: 209.3MM **Publicly Held**
WEB: www.bryanandlisa.com
SIC: **4813** 7372 Telephone communication, except radio; ; prepackaged software

(P-5450)
AAMCOM LLC
800 N Pacific Coast Hwy, Redondo Beach (90277-2148)
PHONE..................................310 318-8100
Fax: 310 318-3379
Steve Diels, *Mng Member*
Lorena Lopez, *COO*
Maria Lona, *QA Dir*
Norma Soto, *Business Mgr*
Elisabeth Diels,
EMP: 50 EST: 2009
SQ FT: 4,000
SALES: 2.6MM **Privately Held**
SIC: **4813** Telephone communication, except radio

(P-5451)
AB CELLULAR HOLDING LLC
Also Called: At & T Wireless Service
1452 Edinger Ave, Tustin (92780-6246)
PHONE..................................562 468-6846
Glen Lurie,
Andy Lee, *Mktg Dir*
EMP: 2100
SALES (est): 263.9MM
SALES (corp-wide): 146.8B **Publicly Held**
WEB: www.cingular.com
SIC: **4813** Local & long distance telephone communications
HQ: At&T Mobility Llc
1025 Lenox Park Blvd Ne
Brookhaven GA 30319
425 580-6014

(P-5452)
ACTELIS NETWORKS INC (PA)
Also Called: Actelis USA
47800 Westinghouse Dr, Fremont (94539-7469)
PHONE..................................510 545-1045
Fax: 510 545-1075
Tuvia Barlev, *CEO*
Stephen Cordial, *COO*
Charles Clawson, *Assoc VP*
Bruce Hammergren, *Vice Pres*
Joe Manuele, *Vice Pres*
EMP: 139

SALES (est): 67.4MM **Privately Held**
WEB: www.actelis.com
SIC: **4813** Telephone communication, except radio

(P-5453)
ADAPTIVE SPECTRUM AND SIGNAL A
333 Twin Dolphin Dr # 300, Redwood City (94065-1401)
PHONE..................................650 264-2667
John M Cioffi, *CEO*
Barry Gray, *Senior VP*
Ardavan Tehrani, *Senior VP*
Amit Kathuria, *Technology*
EMP: 60
SALES (est): 2.9MM
SALES (corp-wide): 2.1MM **Privately Held**
SIC: **4813**
PA: Assia Ela Sl.
Calle Claudio Coello, 24 - Piso 4 A 2
Madrid 28001
917 815-130

(P-5454)
ADICIO INC
5993 Avenida Encinas, Carlsbad (92008-4459)
PHONE..................................760 602-9502
Fax: 760 602-9260
Richard Miller, *President*
Richette Lock, *COO*
Paul Jarrad, *CFO*
Mike Cavallo, *Exec VP*
Tina Carnow, *Vice Pres*
EMP: 90
SQ FT: 15,000
SALES: 15MM **Privately Held**
WEB: www.adicio.com
SIC: **4813**

(P-5455)
AERIS COMMUNICATIONS INC
2350 Mission College Blvd # 600, Santa Clara (95054-1574)
PHONE..................................408 557-1900
Marc Jones, *CEO*
Subu Balakrishnan, *Vice Pres*
Michael Doran, *Vice Pres*
Drew Johnson, *Vice Pres*
Richard Johnson, *Vice Pres*
EMP: 99
SALES (est): 13.1MM **Privately Held**
SIC: **4813** Local & long distance telephone communications

(P-5456)
AIRESPRING INC
Also Called: Global Fibernet
6060 Sepulveda Blvd # 220, Van Nuys (91411-2512)
PHONE..................................818 786-8990
AVI Lonstein, *CEO*
Daniel Lonstein, *COO*
Vigen Arno, *CFO*
Arno Vigen, *CFO*
Ellen Cahill, *Senior VP*
▲ EMP: 100
SQ FT: 12,500
SALES (est): 48.9MM **Privately Held**
SIC: **4813** Telephone communication, except radio

(P-5457)
AMERICAN INTL TELEPHONICS LLC
9601 Wilshire Blvd, Beverly Hills (90210-5213)
PHONE..................................800 600-6151
Michael Framer, *Mng Member*
EMP: 130
SQ FT: 1,500
SALES (est): 4MM **Privately Held**
WEB: www.aitelephone.com
SIC: **4813** Long distance telephone communications

(P-5458)
AMERICAN MESSAGING SVCS LLC
Also Called: Verizon
2181 W Winton Ave, Hayward (94545-1209)
PHONE..................................510 889-2300

Scott Falconer, *Branch Mgr*
Kathy Tamblin, *Sales Staff*
Brian Despeaux, *Accounts Mgr*
EMP: 70
SALES (corp-wide): 467.2MM **Privately Held**
SIC: **4813** Telephone communication, except radio
PA: American Messaging Services, Llc
1720 Lakepointe Dr # 100
Lewisville TX 75057
888 699-9014

(P-5459)
ARRAY NETWORKS INC (PA)
1371 Mccarthy Blvd, Milpitas (95035-7432)
PHONE..................................408 240-8700
Michael Zhao, *President*
Robert Shen, *Ch of Bd*
Sameena Ahmed, *CFO*
Fara Zarrabi, *Vice Pres*
Xiaochong Zhang, *Software Dev*
▲ EMP: 66
SQ FT: 20,000
SALES (est): 22.8MM **Privately Held**
WEB: www.arraynetworks.net
SIC: **4813**

(P-5460)
ASIAINFO-LINKAGE INC
5201 Great America Pkwy # 356, Santa Clara (95054-1127)
PHONE..................................408 970-9788
Steve Zhang, *CEO*
Ying Han, *CFO*
Michael Wu, *CFO*
Yadong Jin, *Exec VP*
Jie LI, *Vice Pres*
EMP: 1500
SALES: 481MM **Privately Held**
SIC: **4813**
HQ: Asiainfo Technologies(China), Inc.
Asiainfo Global R & D Center Headquarters Building, Area East, Y Beijing
108 216-6688

(P-5461)
AT&T CORP
10035 Adams Ave, Huntington Beach (92646-4940)
PHONE..................................714 965-4685
Nora Facenda, *Branch Mgr*
EMP: 69
SALES (corp-wide): 146.8B **Publicly Held**
WEB: www.att.com
SIC: **4813** Telephone communication, except radio
HQ: At&T Corp.
1 At&T Way
Bedminster NJ 07921
800 403-3302

(P-5462)
AT&T CORP
2390 Monument Blvd, Pleasant Hill (94523-3983)
PHONE..................................925 603-9476
Nichol McCroy, *Branch Mgr*
EMP: 69
SALES (corp-wide): 146.8B **Publicly Held**
SIC: **4813** Telephone communication, except radio
HQ: At&T Corp.
1 At&T Way
Bedminster NJ 07921
800 403-3302

(P-5463)
AT&T CORP
2410 Mission St, San Francisco (94110-2415)
PHONE..................................415 970-8520
EMP: 69
SALES (corp-wide): 146.8B **Publicly Held**
SIC: **4813** Telephone communication, except radio
HQ: At&T Corp.
1 At&T Way
Bedminster NJ 07921
800 403-3302

(P-5464)
AT&T CORP
50 Town Center Pkwy, Santee (92071-5806)
PHONE..................................619 448-1798
EMP: 69
SALES (corp-wide): 146.8B **Publicly Held**
WEB: www.sbc.com
SIC: **4813** Local & long distance telephone communications
HQ: At&T Corp.
1 At&T Way
Bedminster NJ 07921
800 403-3302

(P-5465)
AT&T CORP
795 Folsom St, San Francisco (94107-1243)
PHONE..................................415 442-2600
K McNeely, *Principal*
Ellen Gargiulo, *Vice Pres*
Steve Montoya, *Technology*
Bailey Hartmeyer, *Sales Dir*
Cora Dyer, *Sales Associate*
EMP: 575
SALES (corp-wide): 146.8B **Publicly Held**
WEB: www.att.com
SIC: **4813** 4812 Long distance telephone communications; radio telephone communication
HQ: At&T Corp.
1 At&T Way
Bedminster NJ 07921
800 403-3302

(P-5466)
AT&T CORP
2219 Park Ave Ste 8a, Tustin (92782-2701)
PHONE..................................714 258-8290
Russel Martinez, *Branch Mgr*
EMP: 69
SALES (corp-wide): 146.8B **Publicly Held**
WEB: www.sbc.com
SIC: **4813** Local & long distance telephone communications
HQ: At&T Corp.
1 At&T Way
Bedminster NJ 07921
800 403-3302

(P-5467)
AT&T CORP
12379 S Mainstreet, Rancho Cucamonga (91739-8810)
PHONE..................................909 646-9644
EMP: 69
SALES (corp-wide): 146.8B **Publicly Held**
WEB: www.sbc.com
SIC: **4813** Local & long distance telephone communications
HQ: At&T Corp.
1 At&T Way
Bedminster NJ 07921
800 403-3302

(P-5468)
AT&T CORP
5434 Ygnacio Valley Rd, Concord (94521-3887)
PHONE..................................925 673-2120
Alexis King, *Branch Mgr*
EMP: 69
SALES (corp-wide): 146.8B **Publicly Held**
SIC: **4813** Telephone communication, except radio
HQ: At&T Corp.
1 At&T Way
Bedminster NJ 07921
800 403-3302

(P-5469)
AT&T CORP
29273 Central Ave, Lake Elsinore (92532-2254)
PHONE..................................951 253-3304
EMP: 69
SALES (corp-wide): 146.8B **Publicly Held**
SIC: **4813** Telephone communication, except radio

4813 - Telephone Communications, Except Radio County (P-5470)

HQ: At&T Corp.
  1 At&T Way
  Bedminster NJ 07921
  800 403-3302

(P-5470)
AT&T CORP
  810 E Valley Blvd, Alhambra (91801-5200)
  PHONE..................................626 382-0241
  EMP: 69
  SALES (corp-wide): 146.8B Publicly Held
  WEB: www.att.com
  SIC: 4813 Telephone communication, except radio
  HQ: At&T Corp.
    1 At&T Way
    Bedminster NJ 07921
    800 403-3302

(P-5471)
AT&T CORP
  20810 Avalon Blvd, Carson (90746-3316)
  PHONE..................................310 225-3028
  Carolyn Wilder, Manager
  EMP: 69
  SALES (corp-wide): 146.8B Publicly Held
  SIC: 4813 Local & long distance telephone communications
  HQ: At&T Corp.
    1 At&T Way
    Bedminster NJ 07921
    800 403-3302

(P-5472)
AT&T CORP
  83 E Colorado Blvd, Pasadena (91105-1916)
  PHONE..................................626 396-0100
  Fax: 626 396-0101
  Martin Choe, Branch Mgr
  EMP: 69
  SALES (corp-wide): 146.8B Publicly Held
  WEB: www.att.com
  SIC: 4813 Telephone communication, except radio
  HQ: At&T Corp.
    1 At&T Way
    Bedminster NJ 07921
    800 403-3302

(P-5473)
AT&T CORP
  980 N Western Ave Ste H, San Pedro (90732-2451)
  PHONE..................................310 547-0400
  Jack Aiello, Manager
  EMP: 69
  SALES (corp-wide): 146.8B Publicly Held
  WEB: www.att.com
  SIC: 4813 Local & long distance telephone communications
  HQ: At&T Corp.
    1 At&T Way
    Bedminster NJ 07921
    800 403-3302

(P-5474)
AT&T CORP
  26453 Bouquet Canyon Rd, Santa Clarita (91350-2396)
  PHONE..................................661 297-1720
  Carolyn Wilder, Owner
  EMP: 69
  SALES (corp-wide): 146.8B Publicly Held
  WEB: www.att.com
  SIC: 4813 Local & long distance telephone communications
  HQ: At&T Corp.
    1 At&T Way
    Bedminster NJ 07921
    800 403-3302

(P-5475)
AT&T CORP
  24935 Pico Canyon Rd, Stevenson Ranch (91381-1708)
  PHONE..................................661 799-0800
  Chris Lopez, Branch Mgr
  EMP: 69
  SALES (corp-wide): 146.8B Publicly Held
  WEB: www.att.com
  SIC: 4813 Local & long distance telephone communications
  HQ: At&T Corp.
    1 At&T Way
    Bedminster NJ 07921
    800 403-3302

(P-5476)
AT&T CORP
  3977 Chicago Ave, Riverside (92507-5338)
  PHONE..................................951 275-8801
  Gil Leon, Branch Mgr
  EMP: 69
  SALES (corp-wide): 146.8B Publicly Held
  SIC: 4813 Telephone communication, except radio
  HQ: At&T Corp.
    1 At&T Way
    Bedminster NJ 07921
    800 403-3302

(P-5477)
AT&T CORP
  4332 Tweedy Blvd, South Gate (90280-6220)
  PHONE..................................323 568-2006
  Carolyn Wilder, Branch Mgr
  EMP: 69
  SALES (corp-wide): 146.8B Publicly Held
  WEB: www.att.com
  SIC: 4813 Local & long distance telephone communications
  HQ: At&T Corp.
    1 At&T Way
    Bedminster NJ 07921
    800 403-3302

(P-5478)
AT&T CORP
  27762 Antonio Pkwy Ste L3, Ladera Ranch (92694-1141)
  PHONE..................................949 364-4052
  EMP: 69
  SALES (corp-wide): 146.8B Publicly Held
  WEB: www.att.com
  SIC: 4813 Telephone communication, except radio
  HQ: At&T Corp.
    1 At&T Way
    Bedminster NJ 07921
    800 403-3302

(P-5479)
AT&T CORP
  501 S Marengo Ave, Alhambra (91803-1640)
  PHONE..................................626 576-3616
  Gail Bankston-Hill, Compensation Mg
  Maureen Sahyouni, Director
  Christine Wang, Director
  Vincent Maichrowicz, Manager
  EMP: 69
  SALES (corp-wide): 146.8B Publicly Held
  SIC: 4813 Telephone communication, except radio
  HQ: At&T Corp.
    1 At&T Way
    Bedminster NJ 07921
    800 403-3302

(P-5480)
AT&T CORP
  2745 Cloverdale Ave, Concord (94518-2402)
  PHONE..................................925 356-6204
  Hugh Johnston, Branch Mgr
  EMP: 69
  SALES (corp-wide): 146.8B Publicly Held
  SIC: 4813 Telephone communication, except radio
  HQ: At&T Corp.
    1 At&T Way
    Bedminster NJ 07921
    800 403-3302

(P-5481)
AT&T CORP
  151 W Mcknight Way Ste F, Grass Valley (95949-9611)
  PHONE..................................530 274-8255
  Vincent Palori, Branch Mgr
  EMP: 69
  SALES (corp-wide): 146.8B Publicly Held
  SIC: 4813 Telephone communication, except radio
  HQ: At&T Corp.
    1 At&T Way
    Bedminster NJ 07921
    800 403-3302

(P-5482)
AT&T CORP
  1955 E Daily Dr, Camarillo (93010-6300)
  PHONE..................................805 445-6562
  EMP: 82
  SALES (corp-wide): 146.8B Publicly Held
  SIC: 4813 Local & long distance telephone communications
  HQ: At&T Corp.
    1 At&T Way
    Bedminster NJ 07921
    800 403-3302

(P-5483)
AT&T CORP
  1054 Harter Pkwy Ste 9, Yuba City (95993-2653)
  PHONE..................................530 822-2700
  EMP: 69
  SALES (corp-wide): 146.8B Publicly Held
  SIC: 4813 Telephone communication, except radio
  HQ: At&T Corp.
    1 At&T Way
    Bedminster NJ 07921
    800 403-3302

(P-5484)
AT&T CORP
  1821 S San Jacinto Ave G, San Jacinto (92583-5608)
  PHONE..................................951 654-2081
  EMP: 69
  SALES (corp-wide): 146.8B Publicly Held
  WEB: www.att.com
  SIC: 4813 Telephone communication, except radio
  HQ: At&T Corp.
    1 At&T Way
    Bedminster NJ 07921
    800 403-3302

(P-5485)
AT&T CORP
  7860 West Ln, Stockton (95210-3317)
  PHONE..................................209 954-1033
  EMP: 69
  SALES (corp-wide): 146.8B Publicly Held
  SIC: 4813 Telephone communication, except radio
  HQ: At&T Corp.
    1 At&T Way
    Bedminster NJ 07921
    800 403-3302

(P-5486)
AT&T CORP
  133 S Las Posas Rd # 141, San Marcos (92078-2468)
  PHONE..................................760 752-3273
  Ron Manley, Branch Mgr
  EMP: 69
  SALES (corp-wide): 146.8B Publicly Held
  WEB: www.att.com
  SIC: 4813 Telephone communication, except radio
  HQ: At&T Corp.
    1 At&T Way
    Bedminster NJ 07921
    800 403-3302

(P-5487)
AT&T CORP
  624 S Grand Ave Ste 2940, Los Angeles (90017-3872)
  PHONE..................................213 787-0055
  Arnold Larson, Branch Mgr
  EMP: 69
  SALES (corp-wide): 146.8B Publicly Held
  WEB: www.att.com
  SIC: 4813 Telephone communication, except radio
  HQ: At&T Corp.
    1 At&T Way
    Bedminster NJ 07921
    800 403-3302

(P-5488)
AT&T CORP
  1610 W Yosemite Ave Ste 2, Manteca (95337-5189)
  PHONE..................................209 956-8324
  Fax: 209 956-8334
  Brian McCart, Manager
  EMP: 69
  SALES (corp-wide): 146.8B Publicly Held
  WEB: www.att.com
  SIC: 4813 Telephone communication, except radio
  HQ: At&T Corp.
    1 At&T Way
    Bedminster NJ 07921
    800 403-3302

(P-5489)
AT&T CORP
  8225 Mira Mesa Blvd, San Diego (92126-2603)
  PHONE..................................858 693-0815
  Matt Holderness, Branch Mgr
  EMP: 69
  SALES (corp-wide): 146.8B Publicly Held
  WEB: www.att.com
  SIC: 4813 Local & long distance telephone communications
  HQ: At&T Corp.
    1 At&T Way
    Bedminster NJ 07921
    800 403-3302

(P-5490)
AT&T CORP
  6920 Van Nuys Blvd Rm 100, Van Nuys (91405-3986)
  PHONE..................................818 374-6458
  Randy Paquette, Manager
  EMP: 100
  SALES (corp-wide): 146.8B Publicly Held
  WEB: www.swbell.com
  SIC: 4813 Local & long distance telephone communications
  HQ: At&T Corp.
    1 At&T Way
    Bedminster NJ 07921
    800 403-3302

(P-5491)
AT&T CORP
  1121 Jefferson Ave Rm 222, Redwood City (94063-1814)
  PHONE..................................650 780-1005
  EMP: 69
  SALES (corp-wide): 146.8B Publicly Held
  SIC: 4813 Telephone communication, except radio
  HQ: At&T Corp.
    1 At&T Way
    Bedminster NJ 07921
    800 403-3302

(P-5492)
AT&T CORP
  14709 Vanoan St, Van Nuys (91405)
  PHONE..................................818 373-6896
  EMP: 69
  SALES (corp-wide): 146.8B Publicly Held
  SIC: 4813 Telephone communication, except radio

PRODUCTS & SERVICES SECTION
4813 - Telephone Communications, Except Radio County (P-5515)

HQ: At&T Corp.
1 At&T Way
Bedminster NJ 07921
800 403-3302

(P-5493)
AT&T CORP
1546 Saratoga Ave, San Jose
(95129-4961)
PHONE.....................408 871-3870
Ben Hosseini, *Manager*
EMP: 69
SALES (corp-wide): 146.8B **Publicly Held**
SIC: **4813** Telephone communication, except radio
HQ: At&T Corp.
1 At&T Way
Bedminster NJ 07921
800 403-3302

(P-5494)
AT&T CORP
17675 Harvard Ave Ste B, Irvine
(92614-3527)
PHONE.....................949 622-8240
Fax: 949 622-8249
Travis Stanford, *Branch Mgr*
EMP: 69
SALES (corp-wide): 146.8B **Publicly Held**
SIC: **4813** Telephone communication, except radio
HQ: At&T Corp.
1 At&T Way
Bedminster NJ 07921
800 403-3302

(P-5495)
AT&T CORP
6000 Lankershim Blvd, North Hollywood
(91606-4806)
PHONE.....................818 506-9118
EMP: 69
SALES (corp-wide): 146.8B **Publicly Held**
SIC: **4813** Telephone communication, except radio
HQ: At&T Corp.
1 At&T Way
Bedminster NJ 07921
800 403-3302

(P-5496)
AT&T CORP
2600 Camino Ramon, San Ramon
(94583-5000)
PHONE.....................415 394-3000
Marianne Strobel, *Manager*
Angie Wiskocil, *Senior VP*
Herb Patten, *Vice Pres*
Imre Solymosi, *Associate Dir*
Michael Flynn, *Exec Dir*
EMP: 200
SALES (corp-wide): 146.8B **Publicly Held**
WEB: www.swbell.com
SIC: **4813** 7375 Local telephone communications; information retrieval services
HQ: At&T Corp.
1 At&T Way
Bedminster NJ 07921
800 403-3302

(P-5497)
AT&T CORP
18805 Bear Valley Rd, Apple Valley
(92308-2728)
PHONE.....................760 240-3592
EMP: 69
SALES (corp-wide): 146.8B **Publicly Held**
SIC: **4813** 4812 Local & long distance telephone communications; cellular telephone services
HQ: At&T Corp.
1 At&T Way
Bedminster NJ 07921
800 403-3302

(P-5498)
AT&T CORP
6917 El Camino Real, Atascadero
(93422-4227)
PHONE.....................805 461-6400
EMP: 85

SALES (corp-wide): 146.8B **Publicly Held**
SIC: **4813** Local & long distance telephone communications
HQ: At&T Corp.
1 At&T Way
Bedminster NJ 07921
800 403-3302

(P-5499)
AT&T CORP
2400 E Katella Ave, Anaheim (92806-5945)
PHONE.....................714 940-9976
EMP: 107
SALES (corp-wide): 146.8B **Publicly Held**
SIC: **4813** Telephone communication, except radio
HQ: At&T Corp.
1 At&T Way
Bedminster NJ 07921
800 403-3302

(P-5500)
AT&T CORP
2600 Camino Ramon, San Ramon
(94583-5000)
PHONE.....................925 275-8048
Kathleen Randazo, *Manager*
Brian Bower, *Associate Dir*
Bon Pipkin, *Associate Dir*
Lisa Stenberg, *Associate Dir*
Michael Cuckler, *Administration*
EMP: 69
SALES (corp-wide): 146.8B **Publicly Held**
WEB: www.swbell.com
SIC: **4813** Telephone communication, except radio
HQ: At&T Corp.
1 At&T Way
Bedminster NJ 07921
800 403-3302

(P-5501)
AT&T CORP
2600 Camino Ramon 2w856, San Ramon
(94583-5000)
PHONE.....................925 823-5388
Debbie Johnson, *Manager*
John Berringer, *Exec VP*
Mike Meredith, *Exec VP*
Lori Lee, *Executive*
Denise Quackenbush, *Executive*
EMP: 8500
SALES (corp-wide): 146.8B **Publicly Held**
WEB: www.att.com
SIC: **4813** Telephone communication, except radio
HQ: At&T Corp.
1 At&T Way
Bedminster NJ 07921
800 403-3302

(P-5502)
AT&T CORP
4130 S Market Ct, Sacramento
(95834-1222)
PHONE.....................916 830-5000
Welty P Espine, *Manager*
EMP: 400
SALES (corp-wide): 146.8B **Publicly Held**
WEB: www.att.com
SIC: **4813** Local telephone communications
HQ: At&T Corp.
1 At&T Way
Bedminster NJ 07921
800 403-3302

(P-5503)
AT&T CORP
3375 Peach Ave, Clovis (93612-5617)
PHONE.....................559 294-5431
EMP: 69
SALES (corp-wide): 146.8B **Publicly Held**
SIC: **4813** Telephone communication, except radio
HQ: At&T Corp.
1 At&T Way
Bedminster NJ 07921
800 403-3302

(P-5504)
AT&T CORP
I 15 & Razor, Yermo (92398)
P.O. Box 1240 (92398-1240)
PHONE.....................909 381-7378
EMP: 69
SALES (corp-wide): 146.8B **Publicly Held**
WEB: www.att.com
SIC: **4813** Local & long distance telephone communications
HQ: At&T Corp.
1 At&T Way
Bedminster NJ 07921
800 403-3302

(P-5505)
AT&T CORP
455 W 2nd St, San Bernardino
(92401-1525)
PHONE.....................909 381-7729
Fax: 909 381-7829
Ken Fenton, *Manager*
John Bradley, *Manager*
EMP: 69
SALES (corp-wide): 146.8B **Publicly Held**
WEB: www.att.com
SIC: **4813** Telephone communication, except radio
HQ: At&T Corp.
1 At&T Way
Bedminster NJ 07921
800 403-3302

(P-5506)
AT&T CORP
3025 Raymond St, Santa Clara
(95054-3431)
PHONE.....................408 980-2004
EMP: 69
SALES (corp-wide): 146.8B **Publicly Held**
SIC: **4813** Telephone communication, except radio
HQ: At&T Corp.
1 At&T Way
Bedminster NJ 07921
800 403-3302

(P-5507)
AT&T CORP
2105 Macdonald Ave, Richmond
(94801-3310)
PHONE.....................510 965-9714
EMP: 69
SALES (corp-wide): 146.8B **Publicly Held**
WEB: www.att.com
SIC: **4813** Local & long distance telephone communications
HQ: At&T Corp.
1 At&T Way
Bedminster NJ 07921
800 403-3302

(P-5508)
AT&T CORP
8420 Firestone Blvd, Downey
(90241-3844)
PHONE.....................562 923-3032
EMP: 69
SALES (corp-wide): 146.8B **Publicly Held**
WEB: www.att.com
SIC: **4813** Telephone communication, except radio
HQ: At&T Corp.
1 At&T Way
Bedminster NJ 07921
800 403-3302

(P-5509)
AT&T CORP
3175 Spring St, Redwood City
(94063-3928)
PHONE.....................800 222-0300
Steve O'Hara, *Branch Mgr*
EMP: 69
SALES (corp-wide): 146.8B **Publicly Held**
WEB: www.att.com
SIC: **4813** Telephone communication, except radio

HQ: At&T Corp.
1 At&T Way
Bedminster NJ 07921
800 403-3302

(P-5510)
AT&T CORP
625 Ellis St Ste 205, Mountain View
(94043-2223)
PHONE.....................415 276-0039
Ed Trumbull, *Branch Mgr*
EMP: 69
SALES (corp-wide): 146.8B **Publicly Held**
WEB: www.att.com
SIC: **4813** Telephone communication, except radio
HQ: At&T Corp.
1 At&T Way
Bedminster NJ 07921
800 403-3302

(P-5511)
AT&T CORP
700 S Flower St Ste 810, Los Angeles
(90017-4121)
PHONE.....................213 787-0055
Robert Annunziata, *President*
EMP: 80
SALES (corp-wide): 146.8B **Publicly Held**
WEB: www.att.com
SIC: **4813** Telephone communication, except radio
HQ: At&T Corp.
1 At&T Way
Bedminster NJ 07921
800 403-3302

(P-5512)
AT&T CORP
2701 Verne Roberts Cir, Antioch
(94509-7913)
PHONE.....................925 776-1200
EMP: 70
SALES (corp-wide): 146.8B **Publicly Held**
SIC: **4813** Telephone communication, except radio
HQ: At&T Corp.
1 At&T Way
Bedminster NJ 07921
800 403-3302

(P-5513)
AT&T CORP
14500 Roscoe Blvd, Panorama City
(91402-4190)
PHONE.....................818 920-1216
EMP: 69
SALES (corp-wide): 146.8B **Publicly Held**
SIC: **4813** Local & long distance telephone communications
HQ: At&T Corp.
1 At&T Way
Bedminster NJ 07921
800 403-3302

(P-5514)
AT&T CORP
2600 Camino Ramon 4cn100, San Ramon
(94583-5000)
PHONE.....................925 823-9700
Jim Beck, *Vice Pres*
EMP: 5000
SALES (corp-wide): 146.8B **Publicly Held**
SIC: **4813** Telephone communication, except radio
HQ: At&T Corp.
1 At&T Way
Bedminster NJ 07921
800 403-3302

(P-5515)
AT&T SERVICES
Also Called: SBC
2 Circle E Ranch Pl, San Ramon
(94583-9134)
PHONE.....................925 901-9318
William Dyer, *Branch Mgr*
EMP: 170

4813 - Telephone Communications, Except Radio County (P-5516)

SALES (corp-wide): 146.8B **Publicly Held**
WEB: www.dsdllc.com
SIC: **4813** Telephone communication, except radio
HQ: At&T Services, Inc.
208 S Akard St Ste 110
Dallas TX 75202
210 821-4105

(P-5516)
AT&T SERVICES
50101 Office Park Dr, Bakersfield (93304)
PHONE..............................661 327-6030
Janice Bernette, *Manager*
EMP: 300
SALES (corp-wide): 146.8B **Publicly Held**
WEB: www.dsdllc.com
SIC: **4813** 4812 Local telephone communications; radio telephone communication
HQ: At&T Services, Inc.
208 S Akard St Ste 110
Dallas TX 75202
210 821-4105

(P-5517)
AT&T SERVICES
3464 El Camino Ave, Sacramento (95821-6310)
P.O. Box 15038 (95851-0038)
PHONE..............................916 972-2248
Ed Widker, *Manager*
Joseph Michehl, *Cust Mgr*
Jill Sales, *Director*
Bill Jackson, *Manager*
EMP: 187
SALES (corp-wide): 146.8B **Publicly Held**
WEB: www.dsdllc.com
SIC: **4813** Telephone communication, except radio
HQ: At&T Services, Inc.
208 S Akard St Ste 110
Dallas TX 75202
210 821-4105

(P-5518)
AT&T SERVICES
1122 Western St, Fairfield (94533-2459)
PHONE..............................707 428-2512
Carl Alexander, *Branch Mgr*
EMP: 500
SALES (corp-wide): 146.8B **Publicly Held**
WEB: www.dsdllc.com
SIC: **4813** Local telephone communications
HQ: At&T Services, Inc.
208 S Akard St Ste 110
Dallas TX 75202
210 821-4105

(P-5519)
AT&T SERVICES
39 Beta Ct Rm 235, San Ramon (94583-1201)
PHONE..............................925 831-4443
William R Mulgrew, *Principal*
Alex Eseparza, *Finance Mgr*
Mark Almeida, *Director*
Laurel Buck, *Director*
Dennis Penrose, *Director*
EMP: 80
SALES (corp-wide): 146.8B **Publicly Held**
WEB: www.dsdllc.com
SIC: **4813** Telephone communication, except radio
HQ: At&T Services, Inc.
208 S Akard St Ste 110
Dallas TX 75202
210 821-4105

(P-5520)
AT&T SERVICES
2345 Pine St, San Francisco (94115-2714)
PHONE..............................415 774-1957
Robert L Miller, *Branch Mgr*
EMP: 187
SALES (corp-wide): 146.8B **Publicly Held**
WEB: www.dsdllc.com
SIC: **4813** Local telephone communications
HQ: At&T Services, Inc.
208 S Akard St Ste 110
Dallas TX 75202
210 821-4105

(P-5521)
AT&T SERVICES
Also Called: SBC
2727 Oceanside Blvd, Oceanside (92054-4542)
PHONE..............................760 722-7261
Daniel Menendez, *Manager*
EMP: 187
SALES (corp-wide): 146.8B **Publicly Held**
WEB: www.dsdllc.com
SIC: **4813** Local telephone communications
HQ: At&T Services, Inc.
208 S Akard St Ste 110
Dallas TX 75202
210 821-4105

(P-5522)
AT&T SERVICES
Also Called: SBC
3707 Kings Way, Sacramento (95821-6405)
PHONE..............................916 972-2423
Hector Lenaos, *Manager*
Roger Howlett, *Technical Mgr*
Jonathan Yee, *Sr Project Mgr*
Paul Ortega, *Consultant*
EMP: 127
SALES (corp-wide): 146.8B **Publicly Held**
WEB: www.dsdllc.com
SIC: **4813** 4812 Telephone communication, except radio; radio telephone communication
HQ: At&T Services, Inc.
208 S Akard St Ste 110
Dallas TX 75202
210 821-4105

(P-5523)
AT&T SERVICES
1755 Locust St Fl 2, Walnut Creek (94596-4120)
PHONE..............................925 943-4383
Timothy Bayliss, *Manager*
Robert C Wiles, *Manager*
EMP: 500
SALES (corp-wide): 146.8B **Publicly Held**
WEB: www.dsdllc.com
SIC: **4813** Telephone communication, except radio
HQ: At&T Services, Inc.
208 S Akard St Ste 110
Dallas TX 75202
210 821-4105

(P-5524)
AT&T SERVICES
2600 Camino Ramon Rm 1-E, San Ramon (94583-5000)
PHONE..............................415 823-0993
Greg Torretta, *Exec Dir*
Mark Fishler, *Vice Pres*
Philip Ghosh, *Engineer*
Sophia Chang,
EMP: 187
SALES (corp-wide): 146.8B **Publicly Held**
WEB: www.dsdllc.com
SIC: **4813** Local telephone communications
HQ: At&T Services, Inc.
208 S Akard St Ste 110
Dallas TX 75202
210 821-4105

(P-5525)
AT&T SERVICES INC
Also Called: SBC
101 Broadway, San Diego (92101-5001)
PHONE..............................619 515-5100
Daena Mason, *Principal*
EMP: 187
SALES (corp-wide): 146.8B **Publicly Held**
WEB: www.dsdllc.com
SIC: **4813** Telephone communication, except radio

HQ: At&T Services, Inc.
208 S Akard St Ste 110
Dallas TX 75202
210 821-4105

(P-5526)
AT&T SERVICES INC
4300 Ming Ave, Bakersfield (93309-4802)
PHONE..............................661 398-2000
Charles Moe, *Branch Mgr*
Kelecia L Breaux, *Network Enginr*
EMP: 187
SALES (corp-wide): 146.8B **Publicly Held**
WEB: www.dsdllc.com
SIC: **4813** Telephone communication, except radio
HQ: At&T Services, Inc.
208 S Akard St Ste 110
Dallas TX 75202
210 821-4105

(P-5527)
AT&T SERVICES INC
Also Called: SBC
161 Calle Del Oaks, Monterey (93940-5701)
PHONE..............................831 394-2690
Rodney Graves, *Manager*
EMP: 70
SALES (corp-wide): 146.8B **Publicly Held**
WEB: www.dsdllc.com
SIC: **4813** Telephone communication, except radio
HQ: At&T Services, Inc.
208 S Akard St Ste 110
Dallas TX 75202
210 821-4105

(P-5528)
AT&T SERVICES INC
610 Brannan St, San Francisco (94107-1512)
PHONE..............................415 545-9051
EMP: 187
SALES (corp-wide): 146.8B **Publicly Held**
SIC: **4813**
HQ: At&T Services, Inc.
208 S Akard St Ste 110
Dallas TX 75202
210 821-4105

(P-5529)
AT&T SERVICES INC
Also Called: SBC
1548 N Carpenter Rd, Modesto (95351-1110)
P.O. Box 3929 (95352-3929)
PHONE..............................209 578-7161
Ray Wilkins, *President*
Patrick McGovern, *Manager*
EMP: 60
SALES (corp-wide): 146.8B **Publicly Held**
WEB: www.dsdllc.com
SIC: **4813** Telephone communication, except radio
HQ: At&T Services, Inc.
208 S Akard St Ste 110
Dallas TX 75202
210 821-4105

(P-5530)
AT&T SERVICES INC
Also Called: SBC
303 Church St, Jackson (95642-2103)
PHONE..............................209 223-0012
Dan Adam, *Manager*
EMP: 187
SALES (corp-wide): 146.8B **Publicly Held**
WEB: www.dsdllc.com
SIC: **4813** Local telephone communications
HQ: At&T Services, Inc.
208 S Akard St Ste 110
Dallas TX 75202
210 821-4105

(P-5531)
AT&T SERVICES INC
Also Called: S B C
5555 E Olive Ave Ste A315, Fresno (93727-2559)
PHONE..............................559 454-3579
Greg Toeman, *Manager*
David Anania, *Technical Staff*
EMP: 300
SALES (corp-wide): 146.8B **Publicly Held**
WEB: www.dsdllc.com
SIC: **4813** Telephone communication, except radio
HQ: At&T Services, Inc.
208 S Akard St Ste 110
Dallas TX 75202
210 821-4105

(P-5532)
AT&T SERVICES INC
1834 W Victoria Ave, Anaheim (92804-2537)
P.O. Box 3644, Tustin (92781-3644)
PHONE..............................714 259-4441
Glyns Falls, *Manager*
EMP: 187
SALES (corp-wide): 146.8B **Publicly Held**
WEB: www.dsdllc.com
SIC: **4813** Telephone communication, except radio
HQ: At&T Services, Inc.
208 S Akard St Ste 110
Dallas TX 75202
210 821-4105

(P-5533)
AT&T SERVICES INC
Also Called: SBC
908 28th St, Paso Robles (93446-1250)
PHONE..............................805 237-9503
EMP: 187
SALES (corp-wide): 146.8B **Publicly Held**
WEB: www.dsdllc.com
SIC: **4813** Telephone communication, except radio
HQ: At&T Services, Inc.
208 S Akard St Ste 110
Dallas TX 75202
210 821-4105

(P-5534)
AT&T SERVICES INC
Also Called: S B C
787 Munras Ave, Monterey (93940-3128)
PHONE..............................831 649-2029
Carlime Plummer, *General Mgr*
Klyde Aipoalani, *Manager*
EMP: 73
SALES (corp-wide): 146.8B **Publicly Held**
WEB: www.dsdllc.com
SIC: **4813** Local telephone communications
HQ: At&T Services, Inc.
208 S Akard St Ste 110
Dallas TX 75202
210 821-4105

(P-5535)
AT&T SERVICES INC
Also Called: SBC
7337 Trade St Rm 3600, San Diego (92121-2423)
PHONE..............................858 886-2762
Fax: 858 578-2106
John Nelson, *Manager*
Melissa Dahl, *Info Tech Mgr*
Waymon Roberts, *Info Tech Mgr*
Kellie Scroggins, *Info Tech Mgr*
Chris Barnes, *Network Mgr*
EMP: 187
SALES (corp-wide): 146.8B **Publicly Held**
WEB: www.dsdllc.com
SIC: **4813** Telephone communication, except radio
HQ: At&T Services, Inc.
208 S Akard St Ste 110
Dallas TX 75202
210 821-4105

PRODUCTS & SERVICES SECTION
4813 - Telephone Communications, Except Radio County (P-5555)

(P-5536)
AT&T SERVICES INC
Also Called: SBC
200 W Center Street Prome, Anaheim (92805-3960)
PHONE..........................210 886-4922
Heewon Lee, *Exec Dir*
Kathy Passmore, *Executive*
Isaac Torres, *Mktg Dir*
EMP: 187
SALES (corp-wide): 146.8B **Publicly Held**
WEB: www.dsdllc.com
SIC: **4813** Telephone communication, except radio
HQ: At&T Services, Inc.
208 S Akard St Ste 110
Dallas TX 75202
210 821-4105

(P-5537)
AT&T SERVICES INC
Also Called: SBC
360 Pioneer Way, Mountain View (94041-1506)
PHONE..........................650 960-2255
Nancy Cruz, *Manager*
EMP: 170
SALES (corp-wide): 146.8B **Publicly Held**
WEB: www.dsdllc.com
SIC: **4813** Telephone communication, except radio
HQ: At&T Services, Inc.
208 S Akard St Ste 110
Dallas TX 75202
210 821-4105

(P-5538)
AT&T SERVICES INC
Also Called: SBC
1010 Wilshire Blvd, Los Angeles (90017-5662)
PHONE..........................213 975-4089
Cathy Bazieto, *Branch Mgr*
David Molina, *Sales Mgr*
EMP: 800
SALES (corp-wide): 146.8B **Publicly Held**
WEB: www.dsdllc.com
SIC: **4813** 2741 7331 4812 Local & long distance telephone communications; local telephone communications; directories, telephone: publishing only, not printed on site; direct mail advertising services; radio telephone communication
HQ: At&T Services, Inc.
208 S Akard St Ste 110
Dallas TX 75202
210 821-4105

(P-5539)
AT&T SERVICES INC
2600 Camino Ramon 2e750ll, San Ramon (94583-5000)
PHONE..........................925 823-1443
Mark Fishler, *Branch Mgr*
EMP: 3000
SALES (corp-wide): 146.8B **Publicly Held**
WEB: www.dsdllc.com
SIC: **4813** Telephone communication, except radio
HQ: At&T Services, Inc.
208 S Akard St Ste 110
Dallas TX 75202
210 821-4105

(P-5540)
AT&T SERVICES INC
Also Called: SBC Communications
2615 Mercantile Dr, Rancho Cordova (95742-6521)
PHONE..........................916 638-6096
Scott Heiser, *Manager*
Robert Pullen, *Manager*
EMP: 200
SALES (corp-wide): 146.8B **Publicly Held**
WEB: www.dsdllc.com
SIC: **4813** 1542 Telephone communication, except radio; nonresidential construction
HQ: At&T Services, Inc.
208 S Akard St Ste 110
Dallas TX 75202
210 821-4105

(P-5541)
AT&T SERVICES INC
4734 E Carmen Ave, Fresno (93703-4501)
PHONE..........................800 662-6252
Linda Smith, *Principal*
EMP: 50
SALES (corp-wide): 146.8B **Publicly Held**
WEB: www.dsdllc.com
SIC: **4813** Local telephone communications
HQ: At&T Services, Inc.
208 S Akard St Ste 110
Dallas TX 75202
210 821-4105

(P-5542)
AT&T SERVICES INC
3939 E Coronado St, Anaheim (92807-1608)
PHONE..........................714 575-8320
Glenda Hudson, *Principal*
Todd Lillestol, *Manager*
Gary Wise, *Manager*
EMP: 50
SALES (corp-wide): 146.8B **Publicly Held**
WEB: www.dsdllc.com
SIC: **4813** Telephone communication, except radio
HQ: At&T Services, Inc.
208 S Akard St Ste 110
Dallas TX 75202
210 821-4105

(P-5543)
AT&T SERVICES INC
Also Called: SBC West
5101 Office Park Dr # 303, Bakersfield (93309-0615)
PHONE..........................661 398-4650
Dennis Cassidy, *Systems Mgr*
EMP: 101
SALES (corp-wide): 146.8B **Publicly Held**
WEB: www.dsdllc.com
SIC: **4813** 4812 Local telephone communications; radio telephone communication
HQ: At&T Services, Inc.
208 S Akard St Ste 110
Dallas TX 75202
210 821-4105

(P-5544)
AT&T SERVICES INC
Also Called: SBC
2125 Occidental Rd, Santa Rosa (95401-9034)
PHONE..........................707 545-5000
Curtis Cavin, *Manager*
Fred Klingbeil, *Engineer*
Matthew Laws, *Property Mgr*
EMP: 200
SALES (corp-wide): 146.8B **Publicly Held**
WEB: www.dsdllc.com
SIC: **4813** 4812 Local telephone communications; radio telephone communication
HQ: At&T Services, Inc.
208 S Akard St Ste 110
Dallas TX 75202
210 821-4105

(P-5545)
AT&T SERVICES INC
1480 Burlingame Ave, Burlingame (94010-4111)
PHONE..........................650 579-5266
Sally Calvert, *Branch Mgr*
EMP: 187
SALES (corp-wide): 146.8B **Publicly Held**
WEB: www.dsdllc.com
SIC: **4813** Local telephone communications
HQ: At&T Services, Inc.
208 S Akard St Ste 110
Dallas TX 75202
210 821-4105

(P-5546)
AT&T SERVICES INC
Also Called: SBC
1900 S Grand Ave Rm 100, Los Angeles (90007-1436)
PHONE..........................213 741-3111
Al Hernandez, *Branch Mgr*
EMP: 55
SALES (corp-wide): 146.8B **Publicly Held**
WEB: www.dsdllc.com
SIC: **4813** Local telephone communications
HQ: At&T Services, Inc.
208 S Akard St Ste 110
Dallas TX 75202
210 821-4105

(P-5547)
AT&T SERVICES INC
Also Called: SBC
140 New Montgomery St, San Francisco (94105-3705)
PHONE..........................415 394-3000
Ed Mueller, *President*
Michael J Fitzpatrick, *President*
Cheryl Crabtree, *Vice Pres*
Thomas Selhorst, *Vice Pres*
Wes Warnock, *Vice Pres*
EMP: 300
SALES (corp-wide): 146.8B **Publicly Held**
WEB: www.dsdllc.com
SIC: **4813** 2741 Local & long distance telephone communications; directories, telephone: publishing only, not printed on site
HQ: At&T Services, Inc.
208 S Akard St Ste 110
Dallas TX 75202
210 821-4105

(P-5548)
AT&T SERVICES INC
Also Called: SBC
44900 Industrial Dr, Fremont (94538-6435)
PHONE..........................510 791-6605
Bob Alex, *General Mgr*
Maria Ho, *Database Admin*
EMP: 60
SALES (corp-wide): 146.8B **Publicly Held**
WEB: www.dsdllc.com
SIC: **4813** Local telephone communications
HQ: At&T Services, Inc.
208 S Akard St Ste 110
Dallas TX 75202
210 821-4105

(P-5549)
AT&T SERVICES INC
146 S Broadway, Escondido (92025-4239)
PHONE..........................760 489-3519
EMP: 187
SALES (corp-wide): 146.8B **Publicly Held**
WEB: www.dsdllc.com
SIC: **4813** Local telephone communications
HQ: At&T Services, Inc.
208 S Akard St Ste 110
Dallas TX 75202
210 821-4105

(P-5550)
AT&T SERVICES INC
Also Called: SBC
8925 Orangethorpe Ave, Buena Park (90621-3716)
PHONE..........................714 992-3359
Fax: 714 680-3958
Pat Gonzalez, *Systems Analyst*
Mike Matrese, *Systems Analyst*
EMP: 99

SALES (corp-wide): 146.8B **Publicly Held**
WEB: www.dsdllc.com
SIC: **4813** 2741 4822 7331 Local & long distance telephone communications; local telephone communications; voice telephone communications; data telephone communications; directories, telephone: publishing only, not printed on site; telegraph & other communications; electronic mail; direct mail advertising services; radio telephone communication
HQ: At&T Services, Inc.
208 S Akard St Ste 110
Dallas TX 75202
210 821-4105

(P-5551)
AT&T SERVICES INC
Also Called: SBC
1714 Colfax St Ste 300, Concord (94520-2134)
PHONE..........................925 671-1902
Jennifer Sullivan, *Manager*
EMP: 100
SALES (corp-wide): 146.8B **Publicly Held**
WEB: www.dsdllc.com
SIC: **4813** 4812 Local telephone communications; radio telephone communication
HQ: At&T Services, Inc.
208 S Akard St Ste 110
Dallas TX 75202
210 821-4105

(P-5552)
AT&T SERVICES INC
7701 Artesia Blvd, Buena Park (90621-2313)
PHONE..........................510 732-0830
Scott Shelly, *Director*
EMP: 187
SALES (corp-wide): 146.8B **Publicly Held**
WEB: www.dsdllc.com
SIC: **4813** Local & long distance telephone communications
HQ: At&T Services, Inc.
208 S Akard St Ste 110
Dallas TX 75202
210 821-4105

(P-5553)
AT&T SERVICES INC
Also Called: SBC
1821 24th St Rm 122, Sacramento (95816-7208)
PHONE..........................916 453-6267
Steven Solis, *Principal*
EMP: 77
SALES (corp-wide): 146.8B **Publicly Held**
WEB: www.dsdllc.com
SIC: **4813** Local & long distance telephone communications
HQ: At&T Services, Inc.
208 S Akard St Ste 110
Dallas TX 75202
210 821-4105

(P-5554)
AT&T SERVICES INC
Also Called: SBC
1033 Shary Cir Ste A, Concord (94518-2469)
PHONE..........................925 671-1059
EMP: 500
SQ FT: 15,600
SALES (corp-wide): 146.8B **Publicly Held**
WEB: www.dsdllc.com
SIC: **4813** 4812 Local & long distance telephone communications; radio telephone communication
HQ: At&T Services, Inc.
208 S Akard St Ste 110
Dallas TX 75202
210 821-4105

(P-5555)
AT&T SERVICES INC
Also Called: SBC
7650 Convoy Ct Ste 106, San Diego (92111-1104)
PHONE..........................858 495-3907
Pattie St Clair, *Branch Mgr*

4813 - Telephone Communications, Except Radio County (P-5556)

PRODUCTS & SERVICES SECTION

Catherine Robeck, *Manager*
EMP: 500
SALES (corp-wide): 146.8B **Publicly Held**
WEB: www.dsdllc.com
SIC: 4813 4812 Local & long distance telephone communications; local telephone communications; radio telephone communication
HQ: At&T Services, Inc.
208 S Akard St Ste 110
Dallas TX 75202
210 821-4105

(P-5556)
AT&T SERVICES INC
Also Called: SBC
950 W Washington Ave, Escondido (92025-1637)
PHONE..................760 489-3187
George Rivera, *Principal*
EMP: 500
SALES (corp-wide): 146.8B **Publicly Held**
WEB: www.dsdllc.com
SIC: 4813 2741 4822 7331 Local & long distance telephone communications; local telephone communications; voice telephone communications; data telephone communications; directories, telephone: publishing only, not printed on site; telegraph & other communications; electronic mail; direct mail advertising services; radio telephone communication
HQ: At&T Services, Inc.
208 S Akard St Ste 110
Dallas TX 75202
210 821-4105

(P-5557)
AT&T SERVICES INC
SBC
8335 Century Park Ct # 150, San Diego (92123-1560)
PHONE..................858 268-6751
David Nichols, *Manager*
John Stone, *Director*
EMP: 50
SALES (corp-wide): 146.8B **Publicly Held**
WEB: www.dsdllc.com
SIC: 4813 2741 4822 Local & long distance telephone communications; local telephone communications; voice telephone communications; data telephone communications; directories, telephone: publishing only, not printed on site; telegraph & other communications; electronic mail
HQ: At&T Services, Inc.
208 S Akard St Ste 110
Dallas TX 75202
210 821-4105

(P-5558)
AT&T SERVICES INC
1429 N Gower St, Los Angeles (90028-8317)
PHONE..................323 468-6813
Dovon Green, *Branch Mgr*
EMP: 500
SALES (corp-wide): 146.8B **Publicly Held**
WEB: www.dsdllc.com
SIC: 4813 Local telephone communications
HQ: At&T Services, Inc.
208 S Akard St Ste 110
Dallas TX 75202
210 821-4105

(P-5559)
AT&T SERVICES INC
Also Called: SBC
501 S Marengo Ave, Alhambra (91803-1640)
PHONE..................626 308-8582
Ed Mueller, *CEO*
EMP: 500
SALES (corp-wide): 146.8B **Publicly Held**
WEB: www.dsdllc.com
SIC: 4813 4812 Local telephone communications; radio telephone communication
HQ: At&T Services, Inc.
208 S Akard St Ste 110
Dallas TX 75202
210 821-4105

(P-5560)
AT&T SERVICES INC
Also Called: SBC
5285 Doyle Rd Rm 3, San Jose (95129-4230)
PHONE..................408 973-7504
Art Sebantis, *Manager*
EMP: 70
SALES (corp-wide): 146.8B **Publicly Held**
WEB: www.dsdllc.com
SIC: 4813 Telephone communication, except radio
HQ: At&T Services, Inc.
208 S Akard St Ste 110
Dallas TX 75202
210 821-4105

(P-5561)
AT&T SERVICES INC
3900 Channel Dr, West Sacramento (95691-3432)
PHONE..................916 376-2006
Richard Cronan, *Branch Mgr*
Sharon Harrison, *Info Tech Dir*
Will Venlos, *Business Mgr*
EMP: 187
SALES (corp-wide): 146.8B **Publicly Held**
WEB: www.dsdllc.com
SIC: 4813 Telephone communication, except radio
HQ: At&T Services, Inc.
208 S Akard St Ste 110
Dallas TX 75202
210 821-4105

(P-5562)
AUTOMATTIC INC
132 Hawthorne St, San Francisco (94107-1308)
PHONE..................650 388-0901
Toni Schneider, *CEO*
Stuart West, *CFO*
Raanan Bar-Cohen, *Info Tech Mgr*
Joseph Scott, *Engineer*
Drew Hackney, *Human Res Mgr*
EMP: 62
SALES (est): 11.9MM **Privately Held**
SIC: 4813

(P-5563)
AVAYA INC
2989 Flanagan Dr, Simi Valley (93063-5706)
PHONE..................805 581-6119
Marie Laguna, *Manager*
Brandon Parker, *Executive*
EMP: 51
SALES (corp-wide): 4B **Privately Held**
WEB: www.avaya.com
SIC: 4813 Telephone communication, except radio
HQ: Avaya Inc.
4655 Great America Pkwy
Santa Clara CA 95054
908 953-6000

(P-5564)
BAID VIVEK
Also Called: Bizringer.com
2335 Irvine Ave, Newport Beach (92660-3410)
PHONE..................888 550-8553
Vivek Baid, *Owner*
EMP: 75 EST: 2013
SALES (est): 1.7MM **Privately Held**
SIC: 4813 7389 Telephone communication, except radio;

(P-5565)
BROADSPIRE INC
19425 Soled Canyo Rd Ste, Santa Clarita (91351)
PHONE..................213 785-8043
Suresh Srinivasan, *CEO*
Arun Srinivasan, *COO*
Barbara Arnold, *Manager*
EMP: 65 EST: 2000
SALES (est): 6.2MM
SALES (corp-wide): 13.2B **Privately Held**
WEB: www.broadspire.com
SIC: 4813
PA: Platinum Equity, Llc
360 N Crescent Dr Bldg S
Beverly Hills CA 90210
310 712-1850

(P-5566)
CAL CONSOLDATED COMMUNICATIONS
Also Called: Surewest Telephone
211 Lincoln St, Roseville (95678-2614)
PHONE..................916 786-6141
Bob Udell, *CEO*
Kathy Rogers, *Accountant*
Gary Wordelman, *Opers Mgr*
EMP: 78 EST: 1914
SQ FT: 21,500
SALES (est): 10.5MM
SALES (corp-wide): 775.7MM **Publicly Held**
SIC: 4813 Local telephone communications; long distance telephone communications
HQ: Surewest Communications
211 Lincoln St
Roseville CA 95678
916 786-6141

(P-5567)
CALIFRNIA RGIONAL INTRANET INC
Also Called: Carinet
8929 Complex Dr Ste A, San Diego (92123-1454)
PHONE..................858 974-5080
Fax: 858 974-5091
Tim Caulfield, *CEO*
Michael C Robert, *CFO*
Joe McMillen, *Principal*
David Cosley, *Manager*
EMP: 85 EST: 1997
SQ FT: 40,000
SALES (est): 16.8MM **Privately Held**
WEB: www.cari.net
SIC: 4813

(P-5568)
CALLCATCHERS INC
Also Called: Freedom Voice Systems
169 Saxony Rd Ste 212, Encinitas (92024-6781)
PHONE..................800 477-1477
Fax: 760 479-2063
Eric Thomas, *President*
Lorenzo Marando, *Senior Engr*
Candice Malmstrom, *Marketing Staff*
Joey Powers, *Manager*
EMP: 59
SALES (est): 20.9MM **Privately Held**
WEB: www.callcatchers.com
SIC: 4813 Telephone communication, except radio

(P-5569)
CALPOINT
9860 Wilshire Blvd, Beverly Hills (90210-3115)
PHONE..................310 274-6680
Samuel Surloff, *Manager*
EMP: 50
SALES (est): 1.9MM **Privately Held**
WEB: www.calpoint.com
SIC: 4813

(P-5570)
CAMPUS EXPLORER INC
2850 Ocean Park Blvd # 310, Santa Monica (90405-6208)
PHONE..................310 574-2243
Jerry Slavonia, *CEO*
Stephen Caldwell, *Vice Pres*
Eric Hammond, *Vice Pres*
Brian Hartnack, *Vice Pres*
Kara Taylor, *Vice Pres*
EMP: 54
SQ FT: 8,000
SALES (est): 11.3MM **Privately Held**
WEB: www.campusexplorer.com
SIC: 4813

(P-5571)
CASTLE ACCESS INC (PA)
Also Called: Kio Networks
9606 Aero Dr Ste 1900, San Diego (92123-1888)
PHONE..................858 836-0200
Fax: 858 836-0201
Matt Thoene, *CEO*
Michael Vignato, *President*
Mark Hopperton, *CEO*
Mark Barlow, *COO*
Joseph Alfrey, *CFO*
EMP: 60
SQ FT: 3,462
SALES (est): 7.4MM **Privately Held**
WEB: www.castleaccess.com
SIC: 4813 Telephone communication, except radio

(P-5572)
CBS MAXPREPS INC
4080 Plaza Goldorado Cir, Cameron Park (95682-7455)
PHONE..................530 676-6440
Fax: 530 672-8559
Andy Beal, *President*
Deb Finneran, *Office Mgr*
Deborah Finneran, *Office Mgr*
Dan Haynosch Jr, *Web Dvlpr*
Eric Swanson, *Web Dvlpr*
EMP: 50
SQ FT: 9,000
SALES (est): 10.4MM
SALES (corp-wide): 27.1B **Publicly Held**
WEB: www.maxpreps.com
SIC: 4813
HQ: Cbs Corporation
51 W 52nd St Bsmt 1
New York NY 10019
212 975-4321

(P-5573)
CDNETWORKS INC (DH)
1919 S Bascom Ave Ste 600, Campbell (95008-2220)
PHONE..................408 228-3379
Jongchan Kim, *CEO*
John J Kang, *President*
Samuyeol Ko, *President*
Hyoungsuk Kim, *COO*
Chris Lim, *CFO*
EMP: 76
SALES (est): 27.3MM
SALES (corp-wide): 38.1B **Privately Held**
SIC: 4813
HQ: Cdnetworks Co., Ltd.
2/F Yuksam-Dong
Seoul SEO 06239
234 410-400

(P-5574)
CELLCO PARTNERSHIP
Also Called: Verizon Wireless
30098 Haun Rd, Menifee (92584-6818)
PHONE..................951 679-6083
Fax: 951 679-3497
EMP: 170
SALES (corp-wide): 131.6B **Publicly Held**
SIC: 4813 Telephone communication, except radio
HQ: Cellco Partnership
1 Verizon Way
Basking Ridge NJ 07920

(P-5575)
CHANNEL INTELLIGENCE INC (DH)
1600 Amphitheatre Pkwy, Mountain View (94043-1351)
PHONE..................321 939-5600
Doug Alexander, *CEO*
Robert Wight, *Ch of Bd*
Michael Evanoff, *CFO*
Frank Lane, *Officer*
Lanny Tucker, *Senior VP*
EMP: 90
SALES (est): 40.1MM
SALES (corp-wide): 74.9B **Publicly Held**
WEB: www.channelintelligence.com
SIC: 4813 ;;;
HQ: Google Inc.
1600 Amphitheatre Pkwy
Mountain View CA 94043
650 253-0000

PRODUCTS & SERVICES SECTION
4813 - Telephone Communications, Except Radio County (P-5597)

(P-5576)
CISCO WEBEX LLC
Also Called: Cisco Systems
2868 Prospect Park Dr # 500, Rancho Cordova (95670-6067)
PHONE..................................916 861-3135
Fax: 916 636-8099
Min Zhu, *Owner*
Donna Bourland, *Marketing Mgr*
EMP: 50
SALES (corp-wide): 49.2B **Publicly Held**
WEB: www.webex.com
SIC: 4813 7379 8322 ;;;; hotline
HQ: Cisco Webex Llc
   3979 Freedom Cir Ste 100
   Santa Clara CA 95054
   408 435-7000

(P-5577)
CLEAR WORLD COMMUNICATIONS
3100 S Harbor Blvd # 300, Santa Ana (92704-6823)
PHONE..................................714 445-3900
Fax: 714 445-3925
Mike Mancuso, *President*
James Mancuso, *Admin Sec*
John Sorenson, *Info Tech Dir*
Fola Anjorin, *IT/INT Sup*
EMP: 450
SQ FT: 10,000
SALES (est): 29.8MM **Privately Held**
SIC: 4813 Telephone communication, except radio

(P-5578)
CLEARCAPTIONS LLC
595 Menlo Dr, Rocklin (95765-3708)
PHONE..................................866 868-8695
Robert Rae, *President*
Rita Beier Braman, *Vice Pres*
Gordon L Ellis, *Vice Pres*
Blaine Reeve, *CTO*
EMP: 50 **EST:** 2015
SALES (est): 1.9MM
SALES (corp-wide): 247.7MM **Privately Held**
SIC: 4813 ; telephone/video communications
PA: Purple Communications, Inc.
   595 Menlo Dr
   Rocklin CA 95765
   888 600-4780

(P-5579)
CLOVER NETWORK INC
415 N Mathilda Ave, Sunnyvale (94085-4222)
PHONE..................................650 210-7888
Leonard Speiser, *CEO*
John Beatty, *Vice Pres*
Nico Posner, *Vice Pres*
Alex Kuzmin, *QA Dir*
Raj Yeruva, *Engineer*
EMP: 65
SQ FT: 8,200
SALES (est): 9.8MM **Privately Held**
WEB: www.clover.com
SIC: 4813

(P-5580)
COFA MEDIA GROUP LLC
5650 El Camino Real, Carlsbad (92008-7124)
PHONE..................................877 293-2007
Edwin Lap, *CEO*
Damjnan Matejic, *Software Dev*
Sanja Soltic, *Prgrmr*
Ivica Sekulic, *Project Mgr*
Nikola Mitic, *Production*
EMP: 104 **EST:** 2009
SALES (est): 203.7K
SALES (corp-wide): 93.9MM **Privately Held**
SIC: 4813
PA: Geary Lsf Group, Inc.
   332 Pine St Fl 6
   San Francisco CA 94104
   877 616-8226

(P-5581)
CONNEXITY INC (HQ)
Also Called: Shopzilla.com
12200 W Olympic Blvd # 300, Los Angeles (90064-1041)
PHONE..................................310 571-1235
William Glass, *CEO*
Bill Glass, *CEO*
Scott Macon, *COO*
Brad Kates, *CFO*
Bob Michaelian, *Exec VP*
EMP: 203
SALES (est): 125MM
SALES (corp-wide): 915MM **Privately Held**
WEB: www.shopzilla.com
SIC: 4813 7383 ; news syndicates
PA: Symphony Technology Group, L.L.C.
   2475 Hanover St
   Palo Alto CA 94304
   650 935-9500

(P-5582)
COX CALIFORNIA TELCOM LLC
43 Peninsula Ctr, Rllng HLS Est (90274-3583)
PHONE..................................310 377-1800
Fax: 310 544-2546
Paul Fornelli, *Branch Mgr*
Dionne Huskins, *Executive Asst*
Katherine Paezle Harris, *Manager*
Elizabeth Simon, *Manager*
EMP: 85
SALES (corp-wide): 33.6B **Privately Held**
SIC: 4813 Telephone communication, except radio
HQ: Cox California Telcom, L.L.C.
   1400 Lake Hearn Dr Ne
   Brookhaven GA 30319

(P-5583)
COX CALIFORNIA TELCOM LLC
1922 Avenida Del Oro, Oceanside (92056-5803)
PHONE..................................760 966-0447
Jeff Trotter, *Manager*
Dionne Huskins, *Executive Asst*
Katherine Paezle Harris, *Manager*
Elizabeth Simon, *Manager*
EMP: 190
SALES (corp-wide): 33.6B **Privately Held**
SIC: 4813 Telephone communication, except radio
HQ: Cox California Telcom, L.L.C.
   1400 Lake Hearn Dr Ne
   Brookhaven GA 30319

(P-5584)
CREDO MOBILE INC
Also Called: Working Assets Long Distance
101 Market St Ste 700, San Francisco (94105-1533)
P.O. Box 7015 (94120-7015)
PHONE..................................415 369-2000
Fax: 415 371-1048
Michael Hall Kieschnick, *CEO*
Doug Moore, *CFO*
Douglas Moore, *CFO*
Stephen Gunn, *Vice Pres*
Lori Ogden, *Vice Pres*
EMP: 100
SQ FT: 21,000
SALES (est): 22.7MM **Privately Held**
WEB: www.giveforchange.com
SIC: 4813 Long distance telephone communications

(P-5585)
CURATEL LLC
1605 W Olympic Blvd # 600, Los Angeles (90015-3808)
PHONE..................................213 427-7411
Ron Sahar Azarkman, **
Jerry Azarkman, **
EMP: 300
SALES (est): 18.6MM **Privately Held**
WEB: www.curatel.com
SIC: 4813 Telephone communication, except radio

(P-5586)
CURVATURE LLC (HQ)
6500 Hollister Ave # 210, Goleta (93117-3011)
PHONE..................................805 964-9975
Fax: 805 964-9405
Mike Sheldon, *CEO*
Jeff Zanardi, *President*
Andrea Greene, *CFO*
Chuck Sheldon, *Chairman*
Jesse Newton, *Officer*
EMP: 77
SALES (est): 180MM
SALES (corp-wide): 364MM **Privately Held**
SIC: 4813
PA: Nhr Newco Holdings Llc
   6500 Hollister Ave # 210
   Santa Barbara CA 93117
   800 230-6638

(P-5587)
DANGER INC
3101 Park Blvd, Palo Alto (94306-2233)
PHONE..................................650 323-9700
Fax: 650 289-5001
Hank Nothhaft, *Ch of Bd*
Andy Rubin, *President*
Nancy Hilker, *CFO*
Joe Britt, *Senior VP*
Joe F Britt, *Senior VP*
▲ EMP: 135
SALES (est): 10.5MM
SALES (corp-wide): 85.3B **Publicly Held**
WEB: www.danger.com
SIC: 4813 Telephone communication, except radio
PA: Microsoft Corporation
   1 Microsoft Way
   Redmond WA 98052
   425 882-8080

(P-5588)
DAVIS ZIFF PUBLISHING INC
235 2nd St, San Francisco (94105-3124)
PHONE..................................415 551-4800
Kenneth Evans, *Principal*
EMP: 150
SALES (corp-wide): 720.8MM **Publicly Held**
WEB: www.zdnet.com
SIC: 4813
HQ: Davis Ziff Publishing Inc
   28 E 28th St Fl 10
   New York NY 10016
   212 503-3500

(P-5589)
DEVXCOM INC
Also Called: Development Exchange
310 Villa St, Mountain View (94041-1321)
PHONE..................................650 390-6553
James E Fawcette, *President*
Peter Horan, *CEO*
Jim Cook, *COO*
Greg Stern, *Vice Pres*
Randi Brissman, *Sales Staff*
EMP: 50
SALES (est): 1.9MM **Privately Held**
SIC: 4813

(P-5590)
DIGEX INC
2950 Zanker Rd, San Jose (95134-2113)
PHONE..................................408 468-5000
Benjamin Yang, *Principal*
EMP: 50
SALES (corp-wide): 131.6MM **Publicly Held**
WEB: www.digex.com
SIC: 4813
HQ: Digex, Incorporated
   14400 Sweitzer Ln
   Laurel MD 20707
   301 957-1360

(P-5591)
DIGITAL PATH INC
1065 Marauder St, Chico (95973-9039)
PHONE..................................800 676-7284
James A Higgins, *President*
Erica Higgins, *CFO*
Donald Lampe, *General Mgr*
Mark Albertcht, *Controller*
Mark Albrecht, *Controller*
▲ EMP: 50
SALES (est): 18.3MM **Privately Held**
WEB: www.dgitalpath.net
SIC: 4813 5045 ;; computers, peripherals & software

(P-5592)
DIVERSFIED CMMNCTIONS SVCS INC
Also Called: D C S
1260 Pioneer St, Brea (92821-3725)
PHONE..................................562 696-9660
Fax: 562 696-0529
Ken Doll, *President*
Steven Hurley, *Vice Pres*
Bill Shields, *Vice Pres*
Sharon Brezben, *Controller*
Kim Burnham, *Mktg Dir*
▲ EMP: 63
SQ FT: 19,000
SALES (est): 22.3MM **Privately Held**
WEB: www.diversified.net
SIC: 4813 Telephone communications broker

(P-5593)
ECOMPANIES LLC
2120 Colorado Ave Fl 3, Santa Monica (90404-5510)
PHONE..................................310 586-4000
Fax: 310 586-4425
Jake Winebaum, **
Sky Dayton, **
EMP: 50
SALES: 38.2K **Privately Held**
WEB: www.ecompanies.com
SIC: 4813

(P-5594)
EDGEWATER NETWORKS INC
5225 Hellyer Ave Ste 100, San Jose (95138-1021)
PHONE..................................408 351-7200
Fax: 408 727-6430
David G Norman, *CEO*
David A Norman, *Ch of Bd*
Mike Ward, *Senior VP*
Monear Jalal, *Vice Pres*
John Macario, *Vice Pres*
▲ EMP: 75
SALES (est): 22.9MM **Privately Held**
WEB: www.edgewaternetworks.com
SIC: 4813 Telephone/video communications

(P-5595)
ENVIVIO INC (DH)
535 Mission St Fl 27, San Francisco (94105-3224)
PHONE..................................650 243-2700
Fax: 650 243-2750
Julien Signes, *President*
Erik E Miller, *CFO*
David Baranski, *Vice Pres*
Pascal Bernard, *Vice Pres*
Judith Coley, *Vice Pres*
EMP: 77
SALES: 41.5MM
SALES (corp-wide): 28.2B **Privately Held**
WEB: www.envivio.com
SIC: 4813 Telephone/video communications
HQ: Ericsson Ab
   Torshamnsgatan 23
   Kista 164 4
   107 190-000

(P-5596)
EQUINIX INC (PA)
1 Lagoon Dr Ste 400, Redwood City (94065-1564)
PHONE..................................650 598-6000
Stephen Smith, *President*
Greg Adgate, *Partner*
Charles Meyers, *COO*
Keith Taylor, *CFO*
Keith D Taylor, *CFO*
EMP: 220
SALES: 2.7B **Publicly Held**
WEB: www.equinix.com
SIC: 4813 Telephone communication, except radio; data telephone communications

(P-5597)
EVERCOM SYSTEMS INC
Also Called: T-Netix Telecom Svcs
10258 Carey Dr, Grass Valley (95945-4803)
PHONE..................................530 272-8223
Richard Mooers, *Principal*
EMP: 88 **Privately Held**

4813 - Telephone Communications, Except Radio County (P-5598)

WEB: www.gateway-tech.com
SIC: 4813 Telephone communication, except radio
HQ: Evercom Systems, Inc
14651 Dallas Pkwy Ste 600
Dallas TX 75254

(P-5598)
EVERETT BASHAM
Also Called: Labrent.com
3567 Benton St Ste 300, Santa Clara (95051-4404)
PHONE.................................408 261-3000
Everett Basham, Owner
Joe Reid, CFO
EMP: 99
SQ FT: 4,060
SALES (est): 2.2MM Privately Held
SIC: 4813 Telephone communication, except radio

(P-5599)
EVERNOTE CORPORATION (PA)
Also Called: Skitch
305 Walnut St, Redwood City (94063-1731)
PHONE.................................650 216-7700
Phil Libin, CEO
Chris O'Neill, CEO
Linda Kozlowski, COO
Linda Kozlowski, COO
Jeff Shotts, CFO
▲ EMP: 118
SALES (est): 186.4MM Privately Held
SIC: 4813

(P-5600)
EVOLVE MEDIA LLC (PA)
5140 W Goldleaf Cir Fl 3, Los Angeles (90056-1655)
PHONE.................................310 449-1890
Aaron Broder, CEO
Brian Fitzgerald, President
Michael C Dodge, COO
Moises Magana, CFO
Amber Karom, Exec VP
EMP: 67
SALES (est): 27.4MM Privately Held
SIC: 4813 7311 Telephone communication, except radio; advertising agencies

(P-5601)
EXODUS WIRELESS CORP
14352 Chambers Rd, Tustin (92780-6912)
PHONE.................................714 665-6500
Scott S Jang, CEO
EMP: 100
SQ FT: 30,000
SALES: 34.7MM Privately Held
WEB: www.exoduswireless.com
SIC: 4813 7629 Wire telephone; telephone set repair

(P-5602)
EXTREME TELECOM INC
9221 Corbin Ave Ste 260, Northridge (91324-1625)
PHONE.................................818 902-4821
ARI Ramezani, CEO
James Murphy, President
EMP: 113 EST: 1997
SQ FT: 12,000
SALES (est): 6.6MM Privately Held
SIC: 4813

(P-5603)
FREE CONFERENCING CORPORATION
Also Called: Freeconferencecall.com
4300 E Pacific Coast Hwy, Long Beach (90804-2114)
P.O. Box 41069 (90853-1069)
PHONE.................................562 437-1411
David Erickson, CEO
Josh Lowenthal, COO
Scott Southron, CFO
Robert Wise, Exec VP
Jeff Erickson, Vice Pres
EMP: 116
SQ FT: 10,000
SALES: 65MM Privately Held
SIC: 4813 7389 Voice telephone communications;

(P-5604)
FREEDOM COLORADO INFO INC
Also Called: Gazette, The
729 N Grand Ave, Santa Ana (92701-4350)
PHONE.................................719 632-5511
Richard E Mirman, CEO
Steve Pope, Principal
Justin Williams, Exec Dir
Janet Ryan, Executive Asst
EMP: 400
SALES (corp-wide): 3.1B Privately Held
WEB: www.freedom.com
SIC: 4813
HQ: Freedom Communications Inc
625 N Grand Ave
Santa Ana CA 92701
714 796-7000

(P-5605)
FRONTIER CALIFORNIA INC
Also Called: Verizon
83793 Dr Carreon Blvd, Indio (92201-7035)
PHONE.................................760 342-0500
EMP: 64
SALES (corp-wide): 5.5B Publicly Held
SIC: 4813 Local & long distance telephone communications
HQ: Frontier California Inc.
140 West St
New York NY 10007
212 395-1000

(P-5606)
FRONTIER CALIFORNIA INC
Also Called: Verizon
200 W Church St, Santa Maria (93458-5005)
PHONE.................................805 925-0000
Carrie Ramsey, Manager
EMP: 64
SALES (corp-wide): 5.5B Publicly Held
SIC: 4813 Long distance telephone communications
HQ: Frontier California Inc.
140 West St
New York NY 10007
212 395-1000

(P-5607)
FRONTIER CALIFORNIA INC
Also Called: Verizon
135 Cozy Ln, Barstow (92311-2238)
PHONE.................................760 256-3511
Frank Herrera, Branch Mgr
EMP: 55
SALES (corp-wide): 5.5B Publicly Held
SIC: 4813 Telephone communication, except radio
HQ: Frontier California Inc.
140 West St
New York NY 10007
212 395-1000

(P-5608)
FRONTIER CALIFORNIA INC
Also Called: Verizon
510 Park Ave, San Fernando (91340-2527)
PHONE.................................818 365-0542
Gloria Caudill, Branch Mgr
EMP: 150
SALES (corp-wide): 5.5B Publicly Held
SIC: 4813 Telephone communication, except radio
HQ: Frontier California Inc.
140 West St
New York NY 10007
212 395-1000

(P-5609)
FRONTIER CALIFORNIA INC
Also Called: Verizon
525 E Yosemite Ave, Manteca (95336-5806)
P.O. Box 992 (95336-1139)
PHONE.................................209 239-4128
Luanne Weldon, Branch Mgr
EMP: 180
SALES (corp-wide): 5.5B Publicly Held
SIC: 4813 4812 Local telephone communications; radio telephone communication
HQ: Frontier California Inc.
140 West St
New York NY 10007
212 395-1000

(P-5610)
FRONTIER CALIFORNIA INC
Also Called: Verizon
800 N Haven Ave, Ontario (91764-4915)
PHONE.................................951 461-7713
EMP: 64
SALES (corp-wide): 5.5B Publicly Held
SIC: 4813 Telephone communication, except radio
HQ: Frontier California Inc.
140 West St
New York NY 10007
212 395-1000

(P-5611)
FRONTIER CALIFORNIA INC
Also Called: Verizon
1 Wellpoint Way, Westlake Village (91362-3893)
PHONE.................................805 372-6000
Alex Stadler, Principal
George Fu, Engineer
John Dixon,
EMP: 64
SALES (corp-wide): 5.5B Publicly Held
SIC: 4813 Telephone communication, except radio
HQ: Frontier California Inc.
140 West St
New York NY 10007
212 395-1000

(P-5612)
FRONTIER CALIFORNIA INC
Also Called: Verizon
200 W Firebaugh Ave, Exeter (93221-1653)
PHONE.................................559 592-2100
Steve Bryant, Branch Mgr
EMP: 64
SALES (corp-wide): 5.5B Publicly Held
SIC: 4813 Local telephone communications
HQ: Frontier California Inc.
140 West St
New York NY 10007
212 395-1000

(P-5613)
FRONTIIR CORPORATION
1586 Parkview Ave Apt 3, San Jose (95130-1042)
PHONE.................................510 996-2071
Godfrey Tan, CEO
EMP: 250 EST: 2012
SALES: 3MM Privately Held
SIC: 4813 7389 ;

(P-5614)
FUTUREWEI TECHNOLOGIES INC
2330 Central Expy, Santa Clara (95050-2516)
PHONE.................................469 277-5700
EMP: 51 Privately Held
SIC: 4813 Telephone communication, except radio
HQ: Futurewei Technologies, Inc.
5700 Tennyson Pkwy # 500
Plano TX 75024
972 509-5599

(P-5615)
GAIA INTERACTIVE INC
Also Called: Gaia Online
2550 N 1st St Ste 250, San Jose (95131-1019)
PHONE.................................408 573-8800
Gary A Schofield, CEO
Jason Loia, COO
Elaine Kitagawa, CFO
Derek Liu, CTO
Will Park, Marketing Mgr
▲ EMP: 105
SALES (est): 18.5MM Privately Held
SIC: 4813

(P-5616)
GLOBAL DOMAINS INTERNATIONAL
Also Called: Worldsite.ws
701 Palomar Airport Rd # 300, Carlsbad (92011-1027)
PHONE.................................760 602-3000
Fax: 760 602-3099
Michael S Starr, President
Allen Ezier, Vice Pres
Robert Stevens, Vice Pres
Paul Apanowicz, Project Dir
EMP: 50
SQ FT: 5,000
SALES: 14MM Privately Held
WEB: www.globaldomainsinternational.com
SIC: 4813

(P-5617)
GOOGLE FIBER INC
1600 Amphitheatre Pkwy, Mountain View (94043-1351)
PHONE.................................650 253-0000
Milo Medin, Vice Pres
Lance Cotton, Manager
EMP: 75 EST: 2010
SALES (est): 19.3MM
SALES (corp-wide): 74.9B Publicly Held
SIC: 4813
HQ: Google Inc.
1600 Amphitheatre Pkwy
Mountain View CA 94043
650 253-0000

(P-5618)
GOOGLE INC (HQ)
1600 Amphitheatre Pkwy, Mountain View (94043-1351)
PHONE.................................650 253-0000
Sundar Pichai, CEO
Ruth M Porat, CFO
Alex Kwok, Treasurer
Jonathan Cranmer, Bd of Directors
Lauren Desmond, Bd of Directors
▲ EMP: 250 EST: 1998
SQ FT: 4,800,000
SALES (est): 74.9B Publicly Held
WEB: www.google.com
SIC: 4813 7375 ; information retrieval services; data base information retrieval; on-line data base information retrieval
PA: Alphabet Inc.
1600 Amphitheatre Pkwy
Mountain View CA 94043
650 253-0000

(P-5619)
GOOGLE INTERNATIONAL LLC (DH)
1600 Amphitheatre Pkwy, Mountain View (94043-1351)
PHONE.................................650 253-0000
Fax: 650 618-1499
Eric Schmidt, Ch of Bd
Larry Page, CEO
David C Drummond, Senior VP
Stephen M Segari, Software Dev
Chris Hayes, Software Engr
▼ EMP: 54
SALES (est): 429.4MM
SALES (corp-wide): 74.9B Publicly Held
SIC: 4813 7375 ; ; information retrieval services
HQ: Google Inc.
1600 Amphitheatre Pkwy
Mountain View CA 94043
650 253-0000

(P-5620)
GORILLA OFFROAD LIGHTS LLC (HQ)
5140 W Goldleaf Cir Fl 3, Los Angeles (90056-1655)
PHONE.................................310 449-1890
Fax: 310 449-1891
Sean Samuelsen, Mng Member
Bill Foltz, CFO
Frank Simonelli, Senior VP
ARI Lee Bayme, Vice Pres
Jose Inigo, Graphic Designe
EMP: 52
SQ FT: 24,500
SALES (est): 81.6MM Privately Held
WEB: www.gorillanation.com
SIC: 4813
PA: Evolve Media Holdings, Llc
5140 W Goldleaf Cir Fl 3
Los Angeles CA 90056
310 449-1890

PRODUCTS & SERVICES SECTION
4813 - Telephone Communications, Except Radio County (P-5641)

(P-5621)
GRAND CENTRAL COMMUNICATIONS
50 Fremont St Fl 16, San Francisco (94105-2276)
PHONE..............................415 344-3200
Halsey Minor, *Ch of Bd*
Ted Waitt, *Bd of Directors*
Dave Linthicum, *Exec VP*
Stephen B Reade, *Exec VP*
Susan C Dwyer, *Vice Pres*
EMP: 70
SALES (est): 4.7MM **Privately Held**
SIC: 4813 7371 ; ; computer software development & applications

(P-5622)
GT NEXUS INC (DH)
1111 Broadway 5f, Oakland (94607-4139)
PHONE..............................510 808-2222
Fax: 510 808-2220
Sean Feeney, *CEO*
Greg Kefer, *President*
Guy Rey-Herme, *COO*
Allen M Barr, *Co-CFO*
David Adams, *Exec VP*
EMP: 85
SALES (est): 36.2MM
SALES (corp-wide): 2.6B **Privately Held**
WEB: www.gtnexus.com
SIC: 4813 Telephone communication, except radio
HQ: Infor, Inc.
641 Ave Of The Americas # 4
New York NY 10011
646 336-1700

(P-5623)
GTE CORPORATION
994 Mill St, San Luis Obispo (93401-2788)
PHONE..............................805 441-4001
Fax: 805 441-6254
EMP: 143
SALES (corp-wide): 131.6B **Publicly Held**
WEB: www.gte.com
SIC: 4813 Telephone communication, except radio
HQ: Gte Corporation
140 West St
New York NY 10007
212 395-1000

(P-5624)
GTE CORPORATION
Also Called: Verizon
1220 Oak St Ste M, Bakersfield (93301-1072)
PHONE..............................661 328-2226
Fax: 661 328-0622
Mike Minord, *Principal*
Ryan Monnastes, *Site Mgr*
EMP: 50
SALES (corp-wide): 131.6B **Publicly Held**
WEB: www.gte.com
SIC: 4813 Telephone communication, except radio
HQ: Gte Corporation
140 West St
New York NY 10007
212 395-1000

(P-5625)
GTE CORPORATION
2943 Exposition Blvd, Santa Monica (90404-5024)
PHONE..............................310 319-6148
Steve Campanion, *Manager*
EMP: 300
SALES (corp-wide): 131.6B **Publicly Held**
WEB: www.gte.com
SIC: 4813 4812 Local & long distance telephone communications; radio telephone communication
HQ: Gte Corporation
140 West St
New York NY 10007
212 395-1000

(P-5626)
GTT COMMUNICATIONS (MP) INC
555 Anton Blvd Ste 200, Costa Mesa (92626-7811)
PHONE..............................714 327-2000
Fax: 714 327-2001
Steve Schilling, *President*
Pj Marcelo, *Senior Partner*
Paul Marra, *President*
David McMorrow, *Exec VP*
Steve Chisholm, *Senior VP*
EMP: 88
SALES (corp-wide): 369.2MM **Publicly Held**
SIC: 4813
HQ: Gtt Communications (Mp), Inc.
6800 Koll Center Pkwy # 200
Pleasanton CA 94566
925 201-2500

(P-5627)
GTT COMMUNICATIONS (MP) INC (DH)
Also Called: Megapath
6800 Koll Center Pkwy # 200, Pleasanton (94566-7045)
PHONE..............................925 201-2500
Fax: 925 201-2550
Craig Young, *CEO*
Dan Foster, *President*
Mark Senda, *COO*
Paul Milley, *CFO*
Kurt Hoffman, *Co-President*
EMP: 150
SQ FT: 12,000
SALES (est): 162.1MM
SALES (corp-wide): 369.2MM **Publicly Held**
WEB: www.megapath.net
SIC: 4813 7375 ; information retrieval services
HQ: Global Telecom & Technology Americas, Inc.
7900 Tysons One Pl
Mc Lean VA 22102
703 442-5500

(P-5628)
HERE MEDIA INC (PA)
10990 Wilshire Blvd Fl 18, Los Angeles (90024-3927)
PHONE..............................310 943-5858
Fax: 415 834-6502
Paul Colichman, *CEO*
Tony Shyngle, *CFO*
Stephen Jarchow, *Chairman*
Miki Onuma, *Exec Sec*
EMP: 66
SQ FT: 12,000
SALES (est): 30.9MM **Publicly Held**
WEB: www.heremedia.com
SIC: 4813 2721 ; periodicals: publishing only; magazines: publishing only, not printed on site

(P-5629)
HIGHTAIL INC (PA)
1919 S Bascom Ave Ste 600, Campbell (95008-2220)
PHONE..............................408 879-9118
Brad Garlinghouse, *CEO*
Irwin Koon, *President*
Renee Budig, *CFO*
Ned Sizer, *CFO*
Sandra Vaughan, *Chief Mktg Ofcr*
EMP: 100 **EST:** 2005
SQ FT: 20,000
SALES (est): 41.1MM **Privately Held**
WEB: www.yousendit.com
SIC: 4813

(P-5630)
HORNITOS TELEPHONE CO
Also Called: TDS
2896 Bear Vly, Hornitos (95325)
PHONE..............................608 831-1000
David Wittwer, *President*
Mike Gasser, *Principal*
Debbie Meier, *Admin Sec*
EMP: 99
SQ FT: 4,000
SALES: 950K
SALES (corp-wide): 5.1B **Publicly Held**
SIC: 4813 Telephone communication, except radio
HQ: Tds Telecommunications Corporation
525 Junction Rd Ste 1000
Madison WI 53717
608 664-4000

(P-5631)
HOTWIRE INC
655 Montgomery St Ste 600, San Francisco (94111-2627)
PHONE..............................415 645-7350
Dara Khosrowshahi, *CEO*
Nate Parman, *Senior Partner*
Clem Bason, *President*
Taek Kwon, *Vice Pres*
Laura Macdonald, *Associate Dir*
EMP: 175
SALES (est): 55.4MM
SALES (corp-wide): 6.6B **Publicly Held**
WEB: www.hotwire.com
SIC: 4813
PA: Expedia, Inc.
333 108th Ave Ne
Bellevue WA 98004
425 679-7200

(P-5632)
HUAWEI ENTERPRISE USA INC
20400 Stevens Creek Blvd, Cupertino (95014-2217)
PHONE..............................408 394-4295
EMP: 80
SALES (est): 6.4MM **Privately Held**
SIC: 4813
PA: Huawei Investment & Holding Co., Ltd.
Bantian Huawei Base, Longgang District
Shenzhen 51812

(P-5633)
ICALLFIRST
18141 Beach Blvd Ste 290, Huntington Beach (92648-8602)
PHONE..............................808 557-9299
Charlie Waters, *Partner*
EMP: 99
SALES (est): 2.3MM **Privately Held**
SIC: 4813 Telephone communication, except radio

(P-5634)
IFNCOM INC (PA)
Also Called: Tollfreeforwarding.com
9841 Airport Blvd Fl 9, Los Angeles (90045-5421)
PHONE..............................213 452-1505
Travis May, *CEO*
Jason O'Brien, *COO*
Jason Obrien, *COO*
John Carter, *Exec Dir*
Mitch May, *Opers Mgr*
▲ **EMP:** 50 **EST:** 2009
SQ FT: 3,000
SALES: 30MM **Privately Held**
SIC: 4813 Local & long distance telephone communications; voice telephone communications

(P-5635)
IMOBILE LLC
875 W Arrow Hwy, San Dimas (91773-2406)
PHONE..............................909 599-8822
Nahrain Simonov, *Branch Mgr*
EMP: 483 **Privately Held**
SIC: 4813 Local & long distance telephone communications
PA: Imobile Llc
206 Terminal Dr
Plainview NY 11803

(P-5636)
INFONET SERVICES CORPORATION (DH)
Also Called: BT Infonet
2160 E Grand Ave, El Segundo (90245-5024)
PHONE..............................310 335-2859
Fax: 310 335-2679
David Andrew, *CEO*
Jose A Collazo, *President*
Pete Sweers, *COO*
Akbar H Firdosy, *CFO*
John Martinez, *Sr Corp Ofcr*
▲ **EMP:** 600
SQ FT: 150,000
SALES (est): 218.6MM
SALES (corp-wide): 27.5B **Privately Held**
WEB: www.infonet.com
SIC: 4813 7373 7375 Data telephone communications; computer integrated systems design; information retrieval services
HQ: British Telecommunications Public Limited Company
81 Newgate Street
London EC1A
207 356-5985

(P-5637)
INGENIO INC
182 Howard St 826, San Francisco (94105-1611)
PHONE..............................415 248-4000
Fax: 415 248-4100
Warren Heffelfinger, *CEO*
Mark Britto, *CEO*
Joe Defelice, *CFO*
Daiane Shakrei, *Accountant*
Fatima Oukacha, *Human Res Mgr*
EMP: 120
SQ FT: 25,000
SALES (est): 13.7MM
SALES (corp-wide): 146.8B **Publicly Held**
SIC: 4813
PA: At&T Inc.
208 S Akard St
Dallas TX 75202
210 821-4105

(P-5638)
INREACH INTERNET LLC (HQ)
4635 Georgetown Pl, Stockton (95207-6203)
P.O. Box 312, West Enfield ME (04493-0312)
PHONE..............................888 467-3224
Lisa Bickford, *COO*
Mike Culy, *Info Tech Mgr*
EMP: 57
SQ FT: 5,075
SALES (est): 7.3MM
SALES (corp-wide): 17.2MM **Privately Held**
SIC: 4813
PA: Mobilepro Corp.
6100 Oak Tree Blvd # 200
Independence OH 44131
216 986-2745

(P-5639)
INTELPEER CLOUD CMMNCTIONS LLC
177 Bovet Rd Ste 400, San Mateo (94402-3120)
PHONE..............................650 525-9200
Frank Fawzi, *President*
Andre Simone, *CFO*
Phil Bronsdon, *Senior VP*
John Hart, *Senior VP*
Michael Schirmer, *Office Mgr*
EMP: 106
SQ FT: 6,000
SALES (est): 42.3MM **Privately Held**
WEB: www.intelepeer.com
SIC: 4813 Data telephone communications; telephone/video communications

(P-5640)
IPASS INC (PA)
3800 Bridge Pkwy, Redwood City (94065-1171)
PHONE..............................650 232-4100
Gary A Griffiths, *President*
Michael Tedesco, *Ch of Bd*
Darin R Vickery, *CFO*
Patricia R Hume, *Ch Credit Ofcr*
John Alsop, *Officer*
EMP: 78
SQ FT: 48,000
SALES: 62.5MM **Publicly Held**
SIC: 4813 7374 ; ; data processing & preparation

(P-5641)
JAMCRACKER INC
4677 Old Ironsides Dr # 450, Santa Clara (95054-1845)
PHONE..............................408 496-5500
Fax: 408 496-9944

4813 - Telephone Communications, Except Radio County (P-5642)

K B Chandrasekhar, *Ch of Bd*
Todd Johnson, *President*
Harold Chen, *CFO*
Tom Beale, *Vice Pres*
Samir Bodas, *Vice Pres*
EMP: 50
SALES (est): 9.2MM **Privately Held**
WEB: www.jamcracker.com
SIC: 4813 7375 ; information retrieval services

(P-5642)
JIM COUCH
Also Called: Cr Labs
1 Kearny St Ste 1450, San Francisco (94105-5569)
PHONE 415 381-2800
Jim Couch, *Owner*
EMP: 50
SALES (est): 4.4MM **Privately Held**
SIC: 4813 Telephone communication, except radio

(P-5643)
KERMAN TELEPHONE CO
Also Called: Sebastian
811 S Madera Ave, Kerman (93630-1740)
PHONE 559 846-4868
Fax: 559 846-6139
William S Barcus, *President*
Rick Yribarren, *CFO*
Al Baumgarner, *Treasurer*
Rhonda Armstrong, *Vice Pres*
Ruth Barcus, *Vice Pres*
EMP: 52 **EST:** 1911
SQ FT: 36,000
SALES: 12.5MM
SALES (corp-wide): 51.4MM **Privately Held**
WEB: www.kermantel.net
SIC: 4813 Local telephone communications
PA: Sebastian Enterprises, Inc.
811 S Madera Ave
Kerman CA 93630
559 846-9311

(P-5644)
KERMANTELNET INTERNET SERVICE
811 S Madera Ave, Kerman (93630-1740)
PHONE 559 842-2223
Bill Sebastian, *Owner*
EMP: 60
SALES (est): 6.2MM **Privately Held**
WEB: www.kertelweb.com
SIC: 4813

(P-5645)
KOSMIX CORPORATION
444 Castro St Ste 109, Mountain View (94041-2071)
PHONE 605 938-2300
Venky Harinarayan, *CEO*
Travis Adlman, *Vice Pres*
Anand Rajaraman, *Co-Founder*
Vijay Chittoor, *Director*
EMP: 75
SQ FT: 15,000
SALES (est): 4.8MM **Privately Held**
SIC: 4813

(P-5646)
LAUNCH MEDIA INC (HQ)
Also Called: Tourdates.com
25 Taylor St, San Francisco (94102-3916)
PHONE 310 593-6152
Fax: 310 526-4400
David Goldberg, *Ch of Bd*
Robert Roback, *President*
Jeff Mickeal, *CFO*
Briggs Ferguson, *Exec VP*
Heather Crosby, *Vice Pres*
EMP: 120
SQ FT: 21,375
SALES (est): 25.2MM
SALES (corp-wide): 4.9B **Publicly Held**
SIC: 4813
PA: Yahoo Inc.
701 First Ave
Sunnyvale CA 94089
408 349-3300

(P-5647)
LEGACY LONG DISTANCE INTL INC
Also Called: Legacy Inmate Communications
10833 Valley View St # 150, Cypress (90630-5046)
PHONE 800 670-0015
Curtis Brown, *President*
Rafael Quinto, *Vice Pres*
Paul Truong, *CTO*
Essy Nabavian, *Finance Dir*
Duane Cutler, *VP Sales*
EMP: 80
SALES (est): 17.2MM **Privately Held**
WEB: www.golegacy.com
SIC: 4813 Telephone communication, except radio

(P-5648)
LIVEWORLD INC (PA)
4340 Stevens Creek Blvd, San Jose (95129-1147)
PHONE 408 564-6286
Peter H Friedman, *CEO*
David Houston, *CFO*
Chris N Christensen, *Exec VP*
Jenna Woodul, *Exec VP*
Constance Mallon, *Administration*
EMP: 66
SQ FT: 2,500
SALES (est): 21.5MM **Publicly Held**
WEB: www.liveworld.com
SIC: 4813

(P-5649)
LUXAR TECH INC
42840 Christy St Ste 101, Fremont (94538-3154)
PHONE 408 835-2551
Tongqing Wang, *CEO*
Sean Chen, *Manager*
EMP: 130 **EST:** 2014
SQ FT: 4,000
SALES: 16MM **Privately Held**
SIC: 4813 Data telephone communications

(P-5650)
MATOMY USA INC
2900 Gordon Ave, Santa Clara (95051-0718)
PHONE 408 400-2401
Ofer Druker, *Director*
Sagi Niri, *CFO*
David Zerah, *Senior VP*
Dina Rosenthal, *Sales Mgr*
David Lovell, *Director*
EMP: 200
SQ FT: 120
SALES (est): 10.9MM
SALES (corp-wide): 271.2MM **Privately Held**
SIC: 4813
PA: Matomy Media Group Ltd
6 Hanechoshet
Tel Aviv-Jaffa 69710
363 919-90

(P-5651)
MCI COMMUNICATIONS SVCS INC
Also Called: Verizon Business
1957 N Bronson Ave # 106, Los Angeles (90068-5605)
PHONE 323 460-5178
Carlisle Joseph, *Principal*
EMP: 450
SALES (corp-wide): 131.6B **Publicly Held**
SIC: 4813 Telephone communication, except radio
HQ: Mci Communications Services, Inc.
22001 Loudoun County Pkwy
Ashburn VA 20147
703 886-5600

(P-5652)
MCI COMMUNICATIONS SVCS INC
Also Called: Verizon Business
700 S Flower St Ste 1600, Los Angeles (90017-4203)
PHONE 213 625-1005
Ron Garretson, *Manager*
Attila Tota, *Executive*
Marco Berkhout, *Network Enginr*
Kendra Koch, *Project Mgr*
Julie Berkland, *Research*
EMP: 200
SALES (corp-wide): 131.6B **Publicly Held**
WEB: www.mci.com
SIC: 4813 4812 Telephone communication, except radio; radio telephone communication
HQ: Mci Communications Services, Inc.
22001 Loudoun County Pkwy
Ashburn VA 20147
703 886-5600

(P-5653)
MEDIA TEMPLE INC
6060 Center Dr Fl 5, Los Angeles (90045-1596)
PHONE 877 578-4000
Russell P Reeder, *CEO*
Marc Dumont, *Ch of Bd*
Rod Stoddard, *President*
John Carey, *CFO*
Kim Brubeck, *Chief Mktg Ofcr*
EMP: 203
SQ FT: 33,000
SALES (est): 61.5MM
SALES (corp-wide): 503.5MM **Privately Held**
WEB: www.mediatemple.net
SIC: 4813 7371 ; computer software development & applications
HQ: Godaddy.Com, Llc
14455 N Hayden Rd Ste 219
Scottsdale AZ 85260

(P-5654)
MEEBO INC (PA)
1600 Amphitheatre Pkwy, Mountain View (94043-1351)
PHONE 650 253-0000
Seth Sternberg, *President*
Martin Green, *COO*
Natalie Fair, *CFO*
PIP Marquez De La Plata, *Senior VP*
Eric Miraglia, *Vice Pres*
▲ **EMP:** 71
SALES (est): 11.8MM **Privately Held**
WEB: www.meebo.com
SIC: 4813

(P-5655)
MEGAPATH CLOUD COMPANY LLC (PA)
6800 Koll Center Pkwy, Pleasanton (94566-7045)
PHONE 925 201-2500
Donald Craig Young, *CEO*
Paul Milley, *CFO*
Derek Heins, *Vice Pres*
EMP: 59
SALES (est): 288.8MM **Privately Held**
SIC: 4813 Data telephone communications

(P-5656)
MEGAPATH GROUP INC (HQ)
2510 Zanker Rd, San Jose (95131-1127)
PHONE 408 952-6400
Fax: 408 952-7687
D Craig Young, *CEO*
Brett Flinchum, *COO*
Catherine Hemmer, *COO*
Jeffrey Bailey, *CFO*
Justin Spencer, *CFO*
▲ **EMP:** 154 **EST:** 1996
SQ FT: 133,310
SALES (est): 259.1MM
SALES (corp-wide): 288.8MM **Privately Held**
WEB: www.covad.com
SIC: 4813 Voice telephone communications; data telephone communications;
PA: Megapath Cloud Company, Llc
6800 Koll Center Pkwy
Pleasanton CA 94566
925 201-2500

(P-5657)
MEGAPATH GROUP INC
Also Called: Covad Communications
2510 Zanker Rd, San Jose (95131-1127)
PHONE 408 324-1353
Robetr Knowling Jr, *Principal*
Diana Leonard, *Bd of Directors*
Alan C Douglas, *Vice Pres*
William Ferraiuolo, *Vice Pres*
Jake Heinz, *Vice Pres*
EMP: 203
SALES (corp-wide): 288.8MM **Privately Held**
WEB: www.covad.com
SIC: 4813 Data telephone communications
HQ: Megapath Group, Inc.
2510 Zanker Rd
San Jose CA 95131
408 952-6400

(P-5658)
MICROSOFT CORPORATION
1065 La Avenida St, Mountain View (94043-1421)
PHONE 650 964-7200
Susan Peletta, *Executive*
Stephen Shaw, *Program Mgr*
Bryan McDonald, *Info Tech Dir*
Rich Kopel, *Network Enginr*
Jason Chan, *Project Leader*
EMP: 95
SALES (corp-wide): 85.3B **Publicly Held**
SIC: 4813
PA: Microsoft Corporation
1 Microsoft Way
Redmond WA 98052
425 882-8080

(P-5659)
MIS SCIENCES CORP
2550 N Hollywood Way, Burbank (91505-1055)
PHONE 818 847-0213
Fax: 818 847-0214
Lauren Ross, *President*
Jeff Willis, *Exec VP*
Ricky Torre, *General Mgr*
EMP: 125
SQ FT: 7,500
SALES (est): 15.4MM **Privately Held**
WEB: www.missciences.com
SIC: 4813 8748 7376 8742 ; ; systems engineering consultant, ex. computer or professional; computer facilities management; management information systems consultant; custom computer programming services

(P-5660)
MOBITV INC (PA)
6425 Christie Ave Fl 5, Emeryville (94608-1091)
PHONE 510 981-1303
Fax: 510 450-5001
Charlie Nooney, *Ch of Bd*
Paul Scanlan, *President*
Anders Norstr M, *COO*
Anders Norstrom, *COO*
Bill Routt, *COO*
EMP: 100 **EST:** 2000
SQ FT: 3,200
SALES (est): 49.8MM **Privately Held**
WEB: www.mobitv.com
SIC: 4813 4899 ; data communication services

(P-5661)
MPOWER COMMUNICATIONS CORP (DH)
515 S Flower St, Los Angeles (90071-2201)
PHONE 213 213-3000
Rolla P Huff, *Ch of Bd*
Joseph M Wetzel, *President*
S Gregory Clevenger, *CFO*
Tim Medina, *CFO*
Michael J Tschiderer, *Treasurer*
▲ **EMP:** 75
SQ FT: 20,000
SALES (est): 136.9MM
SALES (corp-wide): 494.6MM **Privately Held**
WEB: www.mpowercom.com
SIC: 4813 Telephone communication, except radio
HQ: Telepacific Communications
515 S Flower St Fl 36
Los Angeles CA 90071
213 213-3000

4813 - Telephone Communications, Except Radio County (P-5682)

(P-5662)
MYINTERNETSERVICESCOM LLC
Also Called: Fairfight
1010 E Union St Ste 125, Pasadena (91106-1793)
PHONE.................213 256-0575
Greg Howard, *CEO*
Trenton Hill, *COO*
Michael Reichardt, *CFO*
Tim Cooper, *Officer*
Kevin Hollabaugh, *Vice Pres*
EMP: 100
SQ FT: 2,000
SALES (est): 702.2K **Privately Held**
WEB: www.myinternetservices.com
SIC: 4813

(P-5663)
NAMECHEAP INC
11400 W Olympic Blvd, Los Angeles (90064-1550)
PHONE.................310 259-3259
Richard Kirkendall, *President*
EMP: 70
SQ FT: 500
SALES (est): 9.4MM **Privately Held**
WEB: www.NameCheap.com
SIC: 4813

(P-5664)
NAVISITE LLC
2720 Zanker Rd, San Jose (95134-2116)
PHONE.................408 965-9000
Fax: 408 965-9201
Lorie Tolley, *Branch Mgr*
Mike Davis, *Technology*
Steven Godsey, *Sales Dir*
German Barros, *Cust Mgr*
EMP: 50
SALES (corp-wide): 9.7MM **Publicly Held**
WEB: www.navisite.com
SIC: 4813
HQ: Navisite Llc
400 Minuteman Rd
Andover MA 01810
-

(P-5665)
NETLINE CORPORATION (PA)
750 University Ave # 200, Los Gatos (95032-7697)
PHONE.................408 374-4200
Robert S Alvin, *CEO*
Werner Mansfeld, *President*
Richard Schaefer, *Exec VP*
David Fortino, *Vice Pres*
Jayaram Kalpathy, *Vice Pres*
EMP: 53
SALES (est): 23MM **Privately Held**
WEB: www.netline.com
SIC: 4813

(P-5666)
NETNOW
41 Heritage Village Ln, Campbell (95008-2036)
PHONE.................408 370-0425
Daniel Bryant, *Owner*
Peggy Patwardhan, *Vice Pres*
EMP: 300
SALES: 15MM **Privately Held**
WEB: www.netnow.com
SIC: 4813

(P-5667)
NEW CINGULAR WIRELESS SVCS INC
Also Called: AT&T
P.O. Box 68055
PHONE.................562 924-0000
Hank Bonde, *Branch Mgr*
Laren Whiddon, *CFO*
Bill Prevot, *Info Tech Dir*
Shirlene Miyake, *Analyst*
Greg Farrell, *Marketing Mgr*
EMP: 170
SALES (corp-wide): 146.8B **Publicly Held**
WEB: www.attws.com
SIC: 4813 Local & long distance telephone communications
HQ: New Cingular Wireless Services, Inc.
7277 164th Ave Ne
Redmond WA 98052
425 827-4500

(P-5668)
NEW DREAM NETWORK LLC (PA)
Also Called: Dreamhost.com
135 S State College Blvd, Brea (92821-5823)
PHONE.................626 644-9466
Simon Anderson, *Mng Member*
Patrick Lane, *Vice Pres*
Ahmed Nagy, *Administration*
Dallas Kashuba, *CTO*
John Varner, *Controller*
EMP: 60
SQ FT: 16,380
SALES (est): 60.7MM **Privately Held**
WEB: www.newdream.net
SIC: 4813

(P-5669)
NEW DREAM NETWORK LLC
Also Called: Dreamhost.com
707 Wilshire Blvd # 5050, Los Angeles (90017-3607)
PHONE.................323 375-3842
Art Elivarov, *Manager*
Mike Schroder, *Software Dev*
John Varner, *VP Finance*
Dona Holmberg, *Business Mgr*
Mark Medina, *Director*
EMP: 74
SALES (corp-wide): 60.7MM **Privately Held**
SIC: 4813
PA: New Dream Network, Llc
135 S State College Blvd
Brea CA 92821
626 644-9466

(P-5670)
NEXTPOINT INC (PA)
Also Called: Break Media
8750 Wilshire Blvd 300e, Beverly Hills (90211-2700)
PHONE.................310 360-5904
Keith Richman, *President*
Andrew Doyle, *CFO*
Mitch Rotte, *Senior VP*
Brian Tu, *Senior VP*
David Subar, *CTO*
EMP: 80
SALES (est): 34.6MM **Privately Held**
SIC: 4813

(P-5671)
O1 COMMUNICATIONS INC
4359 Town Center Blvd # 217, El Dorado Hills (95762-7113)
PHONE.................888 444-1111
Fax: 916 554-2180
Bradley Jenkins, *CEO*
Jim Beausoleil, *CFO*
Max Seely, *Senior VP*
Shavinder Singh, *CTO*
Linda Clarke, *Marketing Mgr*
EMP: 89 EST: 1998
SQ FT: 20,000
SALES (est): 29MM **Privately Held**
WEB: www.o1tel.com
SIC: 4813 Data telephone communications

(P-5672)
ODYSSEY TELECORP INC
550 Lytton Ave Fl 2, Palo Alto (94301-1577)
PHONE.................650 470-7550
Sean Doherty, *CEO*
Joe Stockwell, *COO*
Michael Hakimi, *Vice Pres*
EMP: 131
SALES (est): 6.5MM **Privately Held**
WEB: www.odysseytel.com
SIC: 4813 Telephone communication, except radio

(P-5673)
ON24 INC (PA)
201 3rd St Fl 3, San Francisco (94103-3165)
PHONE.................877 202-9599
Sharat Sharan, *President*
Drew Hamer, *CFO*
Joe Hyland, *Chief Mktg Ofcr*
Ken Robinson, *Chief Mktg Ofcr*
Mahesh Kheny, *Vice Pres*
EMP: 142
SQ FT: 27,000
SALES (est): 119.5MM **Privately Held**
WEB: www.on24.com
SIC: 4813

(P-5674)
OOMA INC
1880 Embarcadero Rd, Palo Alto (94303-3308)
PHONE.................650 566-6600
Fax: 650 325-7197
Eric B Stang, *Ch of Bd*
Ravi Narula, *CFO*
Jim Gustke, *Treasurer*
John Summers, *Treasurer*
Tami Bhaumik, *Vice Pres*
▲ EMP: 139
SQ FT: 18,000
SALES: 88.7MM **Privately Held**
WEB: www.ooma.com
SIC: 4813

(P-5675)
OPEX COMMUNICATIONS INC
3777 Long Beach Blvd # 300, Long Beach (90807-3339)
P.O. Box 9270, Uniondale NY (11555-9270)
PHONE.................562 968-5420
Mark Leafstedt, *CEO*
Sean Trepeta, *President*
Daniel Roushia, *COO*
John Wonak, *CFO*
Lucy Sung, *Principal*
EMP: 50 EST: 1998
SQ FT: 14,400
SALES (est): 7.9MM **Privately Held**
WEB: www.opexld.com
SIC: 4813 Local & long distance telephone communications
PA: Premiercom Management Company
6 Jacqueline Ln
Fox River Grove IL

(P-5676)
ORANGE COUNTY INTERNET XCHANGE
2001 E Dyer Rd Ste 102, Santa Ana (92705-5728)
PHONE.................714 450-7109
EMP: 179 EST: 2010
SALES (est): 6.2MM
SALES (corp-wide): 494.6MM **Privately Held**
SIC: 4813 Local & long distance telephone communications
HQ: U.S. Telepacific Corp.
515 S Flower St Fl 47
Los Angeles CA 90071
213 213-3000

(P-5677)
PACIFIC BELL TELEPHONE COMPANY (HQ)
Also Called: Pacbell
430 Bush St Fl 3, San Francisco (94108-3735)
PHONE.................415 542-9000
Fax: 415 362-8628
Kenneth P McNeely, *CEO*
Ray Wilkins Jr, *President*
Paul Suchecki, *Vice Pres*
Lois Jones, *Director*
▲ EMP: 2000
SQ FT: 500,000
SALES (est): 11.3B
SALES (corp-wide): 146.8B **Publicly Held**
WEB: www.pacbell.com
SIC: 4813 2741 4822 Local & long distance telephone communications; local telephone communications; voice telephone communications; data telephone communications; directories; telephone: publishing only, not printed on site; telegraph & other communications; electronic mail
PA: At&T Inc.
208 S Akard St
Dallas TX 75202
210 821-4105

(P-5678)
PACIFIC CENTREX SERVICES INC
Also Called: Pcs1
28001 Dorothy Dr, Agoura Hills (91301-2609)
PHONE.................818 623-2300
M Devin Semler, *President*
Bertha Leung, *Mktg Dir*
Damon Kenney, *Sales Mgr*
EMP: 52
SALES (est): 5.9MM **Privately Held**
WEB: www.pcs1.net
SIC: 4813 5999 Telephone communication, except radio; telephone equipment & systems

(P-5679)
PARETO NETWORKS INC
1183 Bordeaux Dr Ste 22, Sunnyvale (94089-1201)
PHONE.................877 727-8020
Daniel Ryan, *CEO*
Steven Woo, *Vice Pres*
Matthew Young, *Vice Pres*
EMP: 187
SALES (est): 4.9MM
SALES (corp-wide): 151.6MM **Publicly Held**
SIC: 4813
PA: Aerohive Networks, Inc.
1011 Mccarthy Blvd
Milpitas CA 95035
408 510-6100

(P-5680)
PAYCHEX BENEFIT TECH INC
Also Called: Benetrac
2385 Northside Dr Ste 100, San Diego (92108-2716)
PHONE.................800 322-7292
Fax: 619 788-5801
Martin Mucci, *CEO*
B Thomas Golisano, *Ch of Bd*
John B Gibson, *Senior VP*
Jan Hawthorne, *Vice Pres*
Susan Short, *Vice Pres*
EMP: 110
SALES (est): 17.8MM
SALES (corp-wide): 2.9B **Publicly Held**
WEB: www.benetrac.com
SIC: 4813
PA: Paychex, Inc.
911 Panorama Trl S
Rochester NY 14625
585 385-6666

(P-5681)
PAYCYCLE INC
210 Portage Ave, Palo Alto (94306-2242)
P.O. Box 397850, Mountain View (94039-7850)
PHONE.................866 729-2925
Jim Heeger, *CEO*
John Eichhorn, *CFO*
Martin Gates, *CTO*
Bill Gallinger, *QA Dir*
Gail Pruitt, *Accountant*
EMP: 75
SQ FT: 15,000
SALES (est): 5.8MM
SALES (corp-wide): 4.6B **Publicly Held**
WEB: www.paycycle.com
SIC: 4813 8721 ; accounting, auditing & bookkeeping
PA: Intuit Inc.
2700 Coast Ave
Mountain View CA 94043
650 944-6000

(P-5682)
PAYPAL INC (HQ)
2211 N 1st St, San Jose (95131-2021)
PHONE.................877 981-2163
Daniel H Schulman, *President*
Daniel Schulman, *President*
Patrick Dupuis, *CFO*
Jonathan Auerbach, *Senior VP*
James Barrese, *Senior VP*
EMP: 170
SALES (est): 4.1B
SALES (corp-wide): 4.3B **Publicly Held**
WEB: www.paypal.com
SIC: 4813 7374 ; data processing & preparation; data processing service

4813 - Telephone Communications, Except Radio County (P-5683)

PRODUCTS & SERVICES SECTION

PA: Paypal Holdings, Inc.
2211 N 1st St
San Jose CA 95131
408 967-1000

(P-5683)
PC WORLD CORP (PA)
Also Called: Sap, Oracle, Service Provider
2017 Merkley Ave, West Sacramento
(95691-3119)
PHONE..................240 855-8988
Mohammad Naz, *President*
EMP: 250
SALES (est): 9MM **Privately Held**
SIC: 4813

(P-5684)
PEARSON ENGLISH CORPORATION (HQ)
2000 Sierra Point Pkwy # 300, Brisbane
(94005-1845)
PHONE..................650 246-6000
Karine Allouche Salanon, *CEO*
Tom Kahl, *President*
Roger Piskulick, *CFO*
Nicole Brown, *Vice Pres*
Jim Griffin, *Vice Pres*
▲ **EMP:** 105
SQ FT: 46,000
SALES (est): 33.3MM
SALES (corp-wide): 6.7B **Privately Held**
WEB: www.globalenglish.net
SIC: 4813 7375 ; information retrieval services
PA: Pearson Plc
Shell Mex House
London WC2R
207 010-2000

(P-5685)
PLANETOUT INC (HQ)
795 Folsom St Fl 1, San Francisco
(94107-4226)
PHONE..................415 834-6500
Daniel E Steimle, *CEO*
Karen Magee, *CEO*
Derek Barnes, *Vice Pres*
Bob Cohen, *Interim Pres*
Phillip Kleweno, *Exec Dir*
EMP: 50 **EST:** 2000
SQ FT: 56,000
SALES (est): 16.8MM
SALES (corp-wide): 30.9MM **Publicly Held**
WEB: www.planetoutinc.com
SIC: 4813
PA: Here Media Inc.
10990 Wilshire Blvd Fl 18
Los Angeles CA 90024
310 943-5858

(P-5686)
PLIVO INC
Also Called: Plivo US
340 Pine St Ste 503, San Francisco
(94104-3237)
PHONE..................415 758-3659
Venkatesh Balasubramanian, *President*
Michael Lauricella, *Vice Pres*
Michael Ricordeau, *Principal*
EMP: 72
SQ FT: 2,500
SALES: 10MM **Privately Held**
SIC: 4813 Data telephone communications

(P-5687)
PRODEGE LLC (PA)
Also Called: Swagbucks
100 N Sepulveda Blvd Fl 8, El Segundo
(90245-4359)
PHONE..................310 294-9599
Chuck Davis, *CEO*
Adam Portner, *President*
Brad Kates, *CFO*
Ron Leshem, *Chief Mktg Ofcr*
Joe Detuno, *Senior VP*
EMP: 62 **EST:** 2005
SALES (est): 50.8MM **Privately Held**
SIC: 4813 ;

(P-5688)
PUBLIC COMMUNICATIONS SVCS INC
11859 Wilshire Blvd # 600, Los Angeles
(90025-6616)
P.O. Box 2868, Mobile AL (36652-2868)
PHONE..................310 231-1000
Paul Jennings, *CEO*
Tommie Joe, *President*
Dennis Komai, *CFO*
Charles B Freedman, *Treasurer*
Lucien Jervis, *Human Res Dir*
EMP: 150
SQ FT: 15,000
SALES (est): 15.8MM **Privately Held**
WEB: www.pcstelcom.com
SIC: 4813 Local & long distance telephone communications

(P-5689)
QWEST CORPORATION
624 S Grand Ave Ste 315, Los Angeles
(90017-3304)
PHONE..................213 612-0193
Fax: 213 612-0368
Earl Lyon, *Manager*
Daniel Reid, *Program Mgr*
EMP: 59
SALES (corp-wide): 17.9B **Publicly Held**
SIC: 4813 Voice telephone communications
HQ: Qwest Corporation
100 Centurylink Dr
Monroe LA 71203
318 388-9000

(P-5690)
QWEST CORPORATION
1350 Treat Blvd Ste 200, Walnut Creek
(94597-2150)
PHONE..................925 974-4908
Trish Stuber, *Branch Mgr*
Karrie Connors, *Sales Dir*
EMP: 59
SALES (corp-wide): 17.9B **Publicly Held**
SIC: 4813 Telephone communication, except radio
HQ: Qwest Corporation
100 Centurylink Dr
Monroe LA 71203
318 388-9000

(P-5691)
RENTJUICE CORPORATION
225 Bush St Ste 1100, San Francisco
(94104-4250)
PHONE..................415 376-0369
David Vivero, *CEO*
Kunal Shah, *CTO*
EMP: 97
SALES (est): 6.1MM
SALES (corp-wide): 644.6MM **Publicly Held**
SIC: 4813
HQ: Zillow, Inc.
1301 2nd Ave Fl 31
Seattle WA 98101
206 470-7000

(P-5692)
RHYTHMONE LLC (HQ)
1 Market St Ste 1810, San Francisco
(94105-1420)
PHONE..................415 655-1450
Brian Mukherjee, *CEO*
Edward Reginelli, *CFO*
Sudhi Herle,
Frances Smith, *Admin Sec*
Thomas Guyot, *Administration*
EMP: 100
SQ FT: 3,200
SALES (est): 72.2MM
SALES (corp-wide): 166.7MM **Privately Held**
WEB: www.blinkx.com
SIC: 4813 2741 7319 ; ; display advertising service

(P-5693)
RIVIO INC
2500 Augustine Dr Ste 100, Santa Clara
(95054-3020)
PHONE..................408 653-4400
Navin Chaddha, *President*
Pradip Madan, *COO*
James Walker, *Exec VP*

Craig Douchy, *Admin Sec*
EMP: 50
SALES (est): 2.8MM
SALES (corp-wide): 247.5MM **Privately Held**
WEB: www.cpa2biz.com
SIC: 4813
HQ: Cpa.Com
1211 Ave Of The Americas
New York NY 10036
212 596-6230

(P-5694)
RUCKUS WIRELESS INC (HQ)
350 W Java Dr, Sunnyvale (94089-1026)
PHONE..................650 265-4200
Fax: 408 738-2065
Selina Lo, *CEO*
Daniel Rabinovitsj, *COO*
Seamus Hennessy, *CFO*
Ian Whiting, *Ch Credit Ofcr*
Barton Burstein, *Senior VP*
▲ **EMP:** 137
SQ FT: 95,000
SALES (est): 373.3MM **Publicly Held**
WEB: www.ruckuswireless.com
SIC: 4813

(P-5695)
SALESFORCECOM FOUNDATION
The Landmark One St The Landma, San Francisco (94105)
PHONE..................800 667-6389
Marc Benioff, *CEO*
Keith Block, *President*
Suzanne Dibianca, *President*
Rob Acker, *COO*
Kurt Hagen, *CFO*
EMP: 150
SALES (est): 9MM **Privately Held**
SIC: 4813

(P-5696)
SENDMAIL INC (HQ)
892 Ross Dr, Sunnyvale (94089-1443)
PHONE..................510 594-5400
Fax: 510 594-5411
Gary Steele, *CEO*
Sandy Abbott, *CFO*
Paul Auvil, *CFO*
Kimberly Getgem Bargero, *Vice Pres*
Shea Haley, *Vice Pres*
EMP: 75
SQ FT: 30,000
SALES (est): 34MM
SALES (corp-wide): 265.4MM **Publicly Held**
WEB: www.sendmail.com
SIC: 4813 7371 7372 7373 ; computer software development; prepackaged software; computer integrated systems design
PA: Proofpoint, Inc.
892 Ross Dr
Sunnyvale CA 94089
408 517-4710

(P-5697)
SENDME INC
Also Called: Sendmemobile.com
150 Spear St Ste 1400, San Francisco
(94105-1540)
P.O. Box 190878 (94119-0878)
PHONE..................415 978-9504
Russell Klein, *CEO*
John Witchel, *CTO*
John Goddard, *Accountant*
EMP: 60
SQ FT: 8,400
SALES (est): 8.3MM **Privately Held**
SIC: 4813 Data telephone communications

(P-5698)
SIERRA TEL CMMUNICATIONS GROUP
Also Called: Sierra Tel Business Systems
40044 Highway 49 Ste C2, Oakhurst
(93644-8875)
P.O. Box 160 (93644-0160)
PHONE (93644-0160)..................559 683-7777
Fax: 559 683-6983
Mike Cary, *Manager*
John Baker, *Vice Pres*
Lee Lambert, *Vice Pres*
Sandy Brinlee, *Executive*

John Bevins, *Info Tech Mgr*
EMP: 80
SALES (est): 97.7MM **Privately Held**
WEB: www.sierratelephone.com
SIC: 4813 Local telephone communications
PA: Sierra Tel Communications Group
49150 Road 426
Oakhurst CA 93644
559 683-4611

(P-5699)
SIERRA TEL CMMUNICATIONS GROUP (PA)
Also Called: Seirra Telephone
49150 Road 426, Oakhurst (93644-8702)
P.O. Box 219 (93644-0219)
PHONE..................559 683-4611
John H Baker, *CEO*
Harry H Baker, *Ch of Bd*
Lee Lambert, *Admin Asst*
Matt Faulkner, *MIS Staff*
Cindy Huber, *Controller*
EMP: 62
SQ FT: 12,000
SALES (est): 97.7MM **Privately Held**
WEB: www.sierratelephone.com
SIC: 4813 Local telephone communications; long distance telephone communications;

(P-5700)
SIERRA TELEPHONE COMPANY INC
49150 Crane Valley Rd 426, Oakhurst
(93644)
P.O. Box 219 (93644-0219)
PHONE..................559 683-4611
Fax: 559 683-6913
Harry H Baker, *President*
Charlene Klinger, *President*
John H Baker, *Vice Pres*
Heidi D Baker, *Admin Sec*
Judi Thomas, *Info Tech Mgr*
EMP: 190
SALES (est): 43.2MM
SALES (corp-wide): 97.7MM **Privately Held**
WEB: www.stcg.net
SIC: 4813 Local telephone communications; long distance telephone communications
PA: Sierra Tel Communications Group
49150 Road 426
Oakhurst CA 93644
559 683-4611

(P-5701)
SIGMA NETWORKS INC
2191 Zanker Rd, San Jose (95131-2109)
PHONE..................408 876-4002
John K Peters, *President*
Michael A Depatie, *CFO*
Robert Decker, *Vice Pres*
Lonny Orona, *Vice Pres*
Scott Young, *Vice Pres*
EMP: 120
SALES (est): 4.2MM **Privately Held**
SIC: 4813 Local telephone communications

(P-5702)
SKYPE INC
1 Microsoft Way Redmond, Palo Alto
(94304)
PHONE..................650 493-7900
Donald Albert, *President*
Tony Bates, *CEO*
Laura Shesgreen, *Vice Pres*
Shauna Kline, *Controller*
Elisa Steele, *VP Mktg*
▲ **EMP:** 70
SQ FT: 90,698
SALES (est): 16.2MM
SALES (corp-wide): 85.3B **Publicly Held**
SIC: 4813 ;
PA: Microsoft Corporation
1 Microsoft Way
Redmond WA 98052
425 882-8080

(P-5703)
SPIDERCLOUD WIRELESS INC
475 Sycamore Dr, Milpitas (95035-7428)
PHONE..................408 567-9165

▲ = Import ▼=Export
◆ =Import/Export

Michael Gallagher, *CEO*
Thomas Scott, *CFO*
Behrooz Parsay, *Senior VP*
Theresa McCarthy, *Vice Pres*
Ron Pelley, *Vice Pres*
▲ **EMP:** 51
SALES (est): 41.1MM **Privately Held**
SIC: 4813

(P-5704)
SPRINT COMMUNICATIONS CO LP
111 Universal Hollywood Dr, Universal City (91608-1054)
PHONE.................................818 755-7100
Bill Henry, *Manager*
EMP: 50
SALES (corp-wide): 78.2B **Publicly Held**
SIC: 4813 4812 Long distance telephone communications; radio telephone communication
HQ: Sprint Communications Company L.P.
6391 Sprint Pkwy
Overland Park KS 66251
800 829-0965

(P-5705)
SPRINT COMMUNICATIONS CO LP
1505 E Enterprise Dr, San Bernardino (92408-0159)
PHONE.................................909 382-6030
Bill Neece, *Manager*
EMP: 100
SALES (corp-wide): 72.9B **Publicly Held**
SIC: 4813 4812 Long distance telephone communications; radio telephone communication
HQ: Sprint Communications Company L.P.
6391 Sprint Pkwy
Overland Park KS 66251
800 829-0965

(P-5706)
TACHYON INC
9339 Carroll Park Dr # 150, San Diego (92121-3278)
PHONE.................................858 882-8108
Belinda Quindara, *Controller*
Tim Wiegand, *Human Res Mgr*
EMP: 50
SALES (est): 6MM **Privately Held**
SIC: 4813

(P-5707)
TALKMEX CALIFORNIA CORPORATION
1221 W 3rd St, Los Angeles (90017-5181)
PHONE.................................323 479-3279
Paolo Lago, *President*
Christian Smith, *CFO*
Daniel Zauvala, *Director*
EMP: 100 **EST:** 2013
SQ FT: 700
SALES: 6MM **Privately Held**
SIC: 4813 Telephone communications broker

(P-5708)
TELISIMO INTERNATIONAL CORP
2330 Shelter Island Dr 210a, San Diego (92106-3126)
PHONE.................................619 325-1593
Fax: 619 326-0226
Linda G Noda Hobbs, *President*
Jane E Judd, *CFO*
Mark D Wooster, *CFO*
Brian Christie, *Vice Pres*
Dan Hom, *Managing Dir*
EMP: 400
SQ FT: 15,000
SALES (est): 19.6MM **Privately Held**
SIC: 4813 Telephone communication, except radio

(P-5709)
TNCI OPERATING COMPANY LLC (HQ)
114 E Haley St Ste I, Santa Barbara (93101-5323)
PHONE.................................800 800-8400
Laura Thomas, *CEO*
Brian McClintock, *COO*
Michael Masini, *Vice Pres*
Jason Welch, *Vice Pres*
Charlie Sinclair, *Administration*
EMP: 85 **EST:** 2013
SQ FT: 5,000
SALES (est): 32.9MM
SALES (corp-wide): 187MM **Privately Held**
SIC: 4813 Telephone communication, except radio
PA: Garrison Investment Group Lp
1290 Avenue Of The Americ
New York NY 10104
212 372-9500

(P-5710)
TOPICA INC
1 Post St Ste 875, San Francisco (94104-5262)
P.O. Box 34280 (94134-0280)
PHONE.................................415 344-0800
Fax: 415 344-0900
Ariel Poler, *CEO*
Tony Humphries, *Managing Prtnr*
Tag LLP, *Shareholder*
Anna Zornosa, *President*
Paul Luykx, *COO*
EMP: 93
SALES (est): 8.7MM **Privately Held**
WEB: www.topica.com
SIC: 4813 7375   ; information retrieval services

(P-5711)
TRUECAR INC
140 New Montgomery St # 2400, San Francisco (94105-3824)
PHONE.................................415 821-8270
Tim Chen, *Engineer*
EMP: 192
SALES (corp-wide): 259.8MM **Publicly Held**
SIC: 4813
PA: Truecar, Inc.
120 Broadway Ste 200
Santa Monica CA 90401
800 200-2000

(P-5712)
TRUSTE
835 Market St, San Francisco (94103-1903)
PHONE.................................415 520-3490
Chris Babel, *CEO*
Tim Sullivan, *CFO*
Elizabeth Blass, *Vice Pres*
Kevin Mullen, *Business Dir*
Kate Freeman, *Comms Mgr*
EMP: 52
SALES (est): 5.3MM **Privately Held**
SIC: 4813

(P-5713)
US INTERSTATE DISTRG INC
Also Called: Allstate Communications ASC
21621 Nordhoff St, Chatsworth (91311-5825)
PHONE.................................818 678-4592
Russel Leventhal, *President*
Frank Montelione, *Vice Pres*
Steve Casis, *MIS Dir*
EMP: 150
SALES (est): 11.9MM **Privately Held**
SIC: 4813 Telephone communication, except radio

(P-5714)
US TELEPACIFIC CORP (HQ)
Also Called: Telepacific Communications
515 S Flower St Fl 47, Los Angeles (90071-2208)
PHONE.................................213 213-3000
Richard A Jalkut, *President*
David Glickman, *Ch of Bd*
Timothy Medina, *CFO*
Timothy J Medina, *CFO*
Ken Bisnoff, *Senior VP*
◆ **EMP:** 50
SQ FT: 75,000
SALES (est): 356.6MM
SALES (corp-wide): 494.6MM **Privately Held**
WEB: www.telepacific.com
SIC: 4813 Local & long distance telephone communications
PA: U.S. Telepacific Holdings Corp.
515 S Flower St Fl 47
Los Angeles CA 90071
213 213-3000

(P-5715)
VERIZON BUS NETWRK SVCS INC
11080 White Rock Rd # 100, Rancho Cordova (95670-6299)
PHONE.................................916 779-5600
Bert C Roberts, *Branch Mgr*
EMP: 225
SALES (corp-wide): 131.6B **Publicly Held**
WEB: www.gtl.net
SIC: 4813 Telephone communication, except radio
HQ: Verizon Business Network Services Inc.
22001 Loudoun County Pkwy
Ashburn VA 20147
703 729-5615

(P-5716)
VERIZON BUS NETWRK SVCS INC
55 S Market St Ste 1250, San Jose (95113-2387)
PHONE.................................408 975-2244
Rich C Werner, *Principal*
EMP: 119
SALES (corp-wide): 131.6MM **Publicly Held**
WEB: www.gtl.net
SIC: 4813 Long distance telephone communications
HQ: Verizon Business Network Services Inc.
22001 Loudoun County Pkwy
Ashburn VA 20147
703 729-5615

(P-5717)
VERIZON BUS NETWRK SVCS INC
1740 Creekside Oaks 200, Sacramento (95833)
PHONE.................................916 569-5999
Suresh Madala, *Principal*
EMP: 119
SALES (corp-wide): 131.6MM **Publicly Held**
WEB: www.gtl.net
SIC: 4813 Telephone communication, except radio
HQ: Verizon Business Network Services Inc.
22001 Loudoun County Pkwy
Ashburn VA 20147
703 729-5615

(P-5718)
VERIZON BUSINESS GLOBAL LLC
1516 Stillwell Rd Apt F, San Francisco (94129-1054)
PHONE.................................415 606-3621
Scott Smallsreed, *Principal*
EMP: 79
SALES (corp-wide): 131.6B **Publicly Held**
SIC: 4813 Telephone communication, except radio
HQ: Verizon Business Global Llc
22001 Loudoun County Pkwy
Ashburn VA 20147
703 886-5600

(P-5719)
VERIZON BUSINESS GLOBAL LLC
464 Oakmead Pkwy, Sunnyvale (94085-4708)
PHONE.................................408 222-2300
Jim Sturtebant, *Branch Mgr*
EMP: 50
SALES (corp-wide): 131.6B **Publicly Held**
WEB: www.mccmt.com
SIC: 4813 Telephone communication, except radio
HQ: Verizon Business Global Llc
22001 Loudoun County Pkwy
Ashburn VA 20147
703 886-5600

(P-5720)
VERIZON BUSINESS GLOBAL LLC
800 W 6th St Ste 1150, Los Angeles (90017-2714)
PHONE.................................909 466-5633
Fax: 213 489-3712
Mark Levy, *Branch Mgr*
Scott Sullivan, *CFO*
Cynthia Chin, *Executive*
Mickey Clark, *Executive*
Kristi Hager, *Executive*
EMP: 60
SALES (corp-wide): 131.6B **Publicly Held**
WEB: www.mccmt.com
SIC: 4813 Telephone communication, except radio
HQ: Verizon Business Global Llc
22001 Loudoun County Pkwy
Ashburn VA 20147
703 886-5600

(P-5721)
VERIZON COMMUNICATIONS INC
5077 E Lew Davis St, Long Beach (90808-1714)
PHONE.................................562 496-0288
Fax: 562 429-4818
Jerry Milton, *Manager*
Martin Gilmore, *Manager*
EMP: 250
SALES (corp-wide): 131.6B **Publicly Held**
WEB: www.verizon.com
SIC: 4813 4812 Telephone communication, except radio; radio telephone communication
PA: Verizon Communications Inc.
1095 Ave Of The Americas
New York NY 10036
212 395-1000

(P-5722)
VERIZON COMMUNICATIONS INC
16461 Mojave Dr, Victorville (92395-3800)
PHONE.................................760 245-0409
Susan Rowe, *Branch Mgr*
EMP: 113
SALES (corp-wide): 131.6B **Publicly Held**
WEB: www.verizon.com
SIC: 4813 Local telephone communications
PA: Verizon Communications Inc.
1095 Ave Of The Americas
New York NY 10036
212 395-1000

(P-5723)
VERIZON COMMUNICATIONS INC
1417 Howe Ave, Sacramento (95825-3203)
PHONE.................................916 568-0440
Glenn Guzman, *Financial Exec*
EMP: 113
SALES (corp-wide): 131.6B **Publicly Held**
WEB: www.verizon.com
SIC: 4813 Telephone communication, except radio
PA: Verizon Communications Inc.
1095 Ave Of The Americas
New York NY 10036
212 395-1000

(P-5724)
VERIZON COMMUNICATIONS INC
21306 Superior St, Chatsworth (91311-4312)
PHONE.................................818 388-8549
EMP: 113
SALES (corp-wide): 131.6B **Publicly Held**
SIC: 4813 Local & long distance telephone communications

4813 - Telephone Communications, Except Radio County (P-5725)

PA: Verizon Communications Inc.
1095 Ave Of The Americas
New York NY 10036
212 395-1000

(P-5725)
VERIZON SOUTH INC
424 S Patterson Ave, Goleta (93111-2404)
PHONE.................................805 681-8527
Dennis Candini, *Manager*
EMP: 75
SALES (corp-wide): 131.6B **Publicly Held**
SIC: 4813 Local & long distance telephone communications
HQ: Verizon South Inc.
600 Hidden Rdg
Irving TX 75038
972 718-5600

(P-5726)
VIRGIN MOBILE USA INC
Also Called: Helio
10960 Wilshire Blvd Fl 5, Los Angeles (90024-3708)
PHONE.................................310 445-7000
Sky Dayton, *Manager*
Kim Yijoong, *CFO*
Matias Duarte, *Vice Pres*
Inho Shin, *Vice Pres*
Jay Lee, *Info Tech Dir*
EMP: 200
SALES (corp-wide): 72.9B **Publicly Held**
SIC: 4813 Telephone communication, except radio
HQ: Virgin Mobile Usa, Inc.
10 Independence Blvd # 200
Warren NJ 07059
908 607-4000

(P-5727)
VISION TECH SOLUTIONS LLC
222 N Sepulveda Blvd, El Segundo (90245-5648)
PHONE.................................310 656-3100
David M Nachman, *CEO*
Steve Chapin, *CFO*
Kevin Chen, *Info Tech Mgr*
John Vu, *Prgrmr*
Binh Nguyen, *Technology*
EMP: 60
SALES (est): 3.8MM **Privately Held**
SIC: 4813 ;

(P-5728)
VOLCANO COMMUNICATIONS COMPANY (PA)
Also Called: Volcano Telephone Company
20000 State Highway 88, Pine Grove (95665-9512)
P.O. Box 1070 (95665-1070)
PHONE.................................209 296-7502
Sharon J Lundgren, *President*
Earl Bishop, *CFO*
Elizabeth Lundgren, *Treasurer*
John M Lundgren, *Vice Pres*
Delia P Dede Harder, *Admin Sec*
EMP: 100
SQ FT: 19,600
SALES (est): 21.6MM **Privately Held**
WEB: www.volcanovti.com
SIC: 4813 4841 Local telephone communications; cable television services

(P-5729)
VSS MONITORING INC
178 E Tasman Dr, San Jose (95134-1619)
PHONE.................................408 585-6800
Fax: 408 585-6899
Terrence M Breslin, *President*
James McNicholas, *CFO*
Rob Markovich, *Senior VP*
Dave Butler, *Vice Pres*
Andrew R Harding, *Vice Pres*
EMP: 160
SQ FT: 10,000
SALES (est): 51.7MM
SALES (corp-wide): 955.4MM **Publicly Held**
WEB: www.vssmonitoring.com
SIC: 4813
PA: Netscout Systems, Inc.
310 Littleton Rd
Westford MA 01886
978 614-4000

(P-5730)
VTA TELEPHONE INFORMATION
3331 N 1st St, San Jose (95134-1927)
PHONE.................................408 321-7127
Ash Kalra, *Ch of Bd*
Leonardo Griepentrog, *Associate Dir*
Jonn Duesterhaus, *Project Engr*
Manjit Khalsa, *Dir*
Teresa Smith, *Transptn Dir*
EMP: 61
SALES (est): 5.9MM **Privately Held**
SIC: 4813 Local & long distance telephone communications

(P-5731)
WEBPASS INC
267 8th St, San Francisco (94103-3910)
PHONE.................................415 233-4100
Charles Barr, *President*
Blake Drager, *President*
Casey Peacock, *Admin Asst*
Teddy Solano, *Admin Asst*
Brenton Hale, *Info Tech Mgr*
EMP: 100
SQ FT: 8,000
SALES (est): 13.7MM **Privately Held**
SIC: 4813

(P-5732)
WHOLESALE AIR-TIME INC
27515 Enterprise Cir W, Temecula (92590-4864)
PHONE.................................951 693-1880
Greg Michaels, *President*
Kevin Reno, *Vice Pres*
Wendy L Walker, *Admin Sec*
EMP: 50
SQ FT: 9,000
SALES (est): 5.6MM **Privately Held**
SIC: 4813 Local & long distance telephone communications

(P-5733)
WILINE NETWORKS INC (PA)
1164 Triton Dr, Foster City (94404-1240)
PHONE.................................888 494-5463
John McGuire, *CEO*
David Hertgen, *President*
Jaret Grann, *Accounting Mgr*
Sean Quinn, *Human Res Dir*
Spike Traceski, *Human Res Dir*
▲ EMP: 58
SALES (est): 26.3MM **Privately Held**
WEB: www.wiline.com
SIC: 4813

(P-5734)
WINGZ INC
2800 3rd St, San Francisco (94107-3502)
PHONE.................................415 420-2222
Christopher Brandon, *CEO*
Geoff Mathieux, *Exec VP*
EMP: 50
SALES (est): 214.8K **Privately Held**
SIC: 4813

(P-5735)
XO COMMUNICATIONS LLC
1400 Parkmoor Ave, San Jose (95126-3797)
PHONE.................................408 817-2800
Fax: 408 817-2810
EMP: 59
SALES (corp-wide): 1.4B **Privately Held**
SIC: 4813 Local & long distance telephone communications
HQ: Xo Communications, Llc
13865 Sunrise Valley Dr # 400
Herndon VA 20171
703 547-2000

(P-5736)
XSOLLA (USA) INC
15260 Ventura Blvd # 2230, Sherman Oaks (91403-5356)
PHONE.................................818 435-6613
Aleksandr Agapitov, *President*
Alexander Deyna, *CFO*
Anastasia Tihomirova, *CFO*
Ulyana Chernyak, *Chief Mktg Ofcr*
Margarit Karapetian, *Admin Sec*
EMP: 80
SQ FT: 950
SALES (est): 10.8MM **Privately Held**
WEB: www.xsolla.com
SIC: 4813

(P-5737)
YAHOO INC
Also Called: Geocities
3420 Central Expy, Santa Clara (95051-0703)
PHONE.................................408 349-5080
Terry Semel, *Principal*
Patrick Bennett, *President*
Chuck Haas, *President*
P Hanley, *President*
Charlie Hoffman, *Sr Corp Ofcr*
EMP: 200
SALES (corp-wide): 4.9B **Publicly Held**
WEB: www.yahoo.com
SIC: 4813 7375 ; information retrieval services
PA: Yahoo Inc.
701 First Ave
Sunnyvale CA 94089
408 349-3300

(P-5738)
YOUR PRACTICE ONLINE LLC
18662 Macarthur Blvd # 200, Irvine (92612-1200)
PHONE.................................877 388-8569
Prem Lobo, *Mng Member*
Holly Edmonds, *Vice Pres*
EMP: 110
SALES: 1.8MM **Privately Held**
SIC: 4813

(P-5739)
ZOOSK INC
989 Market St Fl 5, San Francisco (94103-1741)
PHONE.................................415 728-9543
Kelly Steckelberg, *CEO*
Behzad Behrouzi, *Vice Pres*
Mike Riccio, *Vice Pres*
Diane Dietz, *Principal*
Aida Lvarez, *Principal*
EMP: 52
SALES (est): 23.9MM **Privately Held**
SIC: 4813 7299 ; dating service

(P-5740)
ZUORA INC (PA)
1051 E Hillsdale Blvd # 600, Foster City (94404-1640)
PHONE.................................650 241-4508
Tien Tzuo, *CEO*
Marc Diouane, *President*
Shawn Price, *President*
Steve Umphreys, *CEO*
Cheng Zou, *CEO*
EMP: 113
SALES (est): 51.8MM **Privately Held**
SIC: 4813

(P-5741)
ZYXEL COMMUNICATIONS INC
1130 N Miller St, Anaheim (92806-2001)
PHONE.................................714 632-0882
Dr Shun-I Chu, *CEO*
Howie Chu, *President*
Steven Joe, *Exec VP*
Jatin Patel, *Engineer*
Lorie Esber, *Accountant*
◆ EMP: 80
SQ FT: 32,000
SALES: 70MM
SALES (corp-wide): 695.4MM **Privately Held**
WEB: www.zyxel.com.tw
SIC: 4813
HQ: Zyxel Communications Corporation
11f, 223, Pei Hsin Rd., Sec. 3,
New Taipei City 23143
227 399-889

4822 Telegraph & Other Message Communications

(P-5742)
CELLCO PARTNERSHIP
Also Called: Verizon Wireless
11134 Rancho Carmel Dr # 101, San Diego (92128-4671)
PHONE.................................858 618-2100
Fax: 858 618-2112
Joann Hartmann, *Branch Mgr*
EMP: 170
SALES (corp-wide): 131.6B **Publicly Held**
SIC: 4822 Electronic mail
HQ: Cellco Partnership
1 Verizon Way
Basking Ridge NJ 07920

(P-5743)
J2 CLOUD SERVICES INC (HQ)
6922 Hollywood Blvd # 500, Los Angeles (90028-6117)
PHONE.................................323 860-9200
Fax: 323 843-9965
Nehemia Zucker, *CEO*
R Scott Turicchi, *President*
Kathleen M Griggs, *CFO*
Allen K Jones, *CFO*
Allen Jones, *CFO*
EMP: 167
SQ FT: 40,000
SALES: 599MM
SALES (corp-wide): 720.8MM **Publicly Held**
WEB: www.efaxcorporate.com
SIC: 4822 Telegraph & other communications
PA: J2 Global, Inc.
6922 Hollywood Blvd # 500
Los Angeles CA 90028
323 860-9200

(P-5744)
J2 GLOBAL INC (PA)
6922 Hollywood Blvd # 500, Los Angeles (90028-6125)
PHONE.................................323 860-9200
Nehemia Zucker, *CEO*
Richard S Ressler, *Ch of Bd*
R Scott Turicchi, *President*
Kevin Feldman, *Vice Pres*
Michael Guadarrama, *Vice Pres*
EMP: 80
SQ FT: 40,000
SALES: 720.8MM **Publicly Held**
SIC: 4822 Telegraph & other communications

4832 Radio Broadcasting Stations

(P-5745)
ABC CABLE NETWORKS GROUP (DH)
500 S Buena Vista St, Burbank (91521-0007)
PHONE.................................818 460-7477
John F Cooke, *President*
Anne M Sweeney, *President*
Patrick Lopker, *Senior VP*
Julie Piepenkotter, *Senior VP*
Adam Bonnett, *Vice Pres*
▲ EMP: 200
SALES (est): 246.5MM **Publicly Held**
WEB: www.breakbar.com
SIC: 4832 4833 Radio broadcasting stations; television broadcasting stations
HQ: Disney Enterprises, Inc.
500 S Buena Vista St
Burbank CA 91521
818 560-1000

(P-5746)
ABC CABLE NETWORKS GROUP
Also Called: Jimmy Kimmel Live
6834 Hollywood Blvd, Los Angeles (90028-6116)
PHONE.................................323 860-5900
Jill Leiderman, *Principal*
EMP: 200 **Publicly Held**
SIC: 4832 4833 Radio broadcasting stations; television broadcasting stations
HQ: Abc Cable Networks Group
500 S Buena Vista St
Burbank CA 91521
818 460-7477

PRODUCTS & SERVICES SECTION

4832 - Radio Broadcasting Stations County (P-5768)

(P-5747)
ABE ENTERCOM HOLDINGS LLC
Also Called: Kbzt Broadcasting
1615 Murray Canyon Rd # 710, San Diego (92108-4314)
PHONE.................................619 291-9797
Fax: 619 543-1353
Bob Boliger, *Vice Pres*
John Mayer, *Vice Pres*
Scott Moorehouse, *Vice Pres*
Fay Von Herzen, *Data Proc Exec*
Erin Kenney, *Info Tech Mgr*
EMP: 75
SALES (corp-wide): 411.3MM **Publicly Held**
WEB: www.jpc.com
SIC: 4832 Radio broadcasting stations
HQ: Abe Entercom Holdings Llc
401 E City Ave Ste 809
Bala Cynwyd PA 19004
404 239-7211

(P-5748)
AMATURO SONOMA MEDIA GROUP LLC
1410 Neotomas Ave Ste 200, Santa Rosa (95405-7533)
PHONE.................................707 543-0126
Michael Williams, *President*
Michaela Young, *Sales Staff*
Danny Wright, *Program Dir*
Jennifer Routh, *Director*
Cathy Slack, *Accounts Mgr*
EMP: 67
SALES: 5.5MM **Privately Held**
SIC: 4832 Radio broadcasting stations

(P-5749)
BIRD STREET MEDIA PROJECT
Also Called: Krbs FM 107.1
2360 Oro Quincy Hwy, Oroville (95966-5226)
P.O. Box 9 (95965-0009)
PHONE.................................530 534-1200
Fax: 530 534-1200
Lee Edwards, *President*
Erv Knorzer, *Treasurer*
Por Yang, *Vice Pres*
Salud Vasquez-Almaguel, *General Mgr*
EMP: 50
SALES (est): 2.9MM **Privately Held**
SIC: 4832 Radio broadcasting stations

(P-5750)
BONNEVILLE INTERNATIONAL CORP
Also Called: Kswb
5900 Wilshire Blvd # 1900, Los Angeles (90036-5020)
PHONE.................................323 634-1800
Peter Durton, *Branch Mgr*
Craig Wilbraham, *Senior VP*
Robert Scorpio, *Vice Pres*
Jacob Lasar, *Info Tech Dir*
Dominique Diprima, *Manager*
EMP: 50
SALES (corp-wide): 2.3B **Privately Held**
SIC: 4832 Radio broadcasting stations
HQ: Bonneville International Corporation
55 N 300 W
Salt Lake City UT 84101
801 575-5555

(P-5751)
BONNEVILLE INTERNATIONAL CORP
Also Called: Koit
201 3rd St Fl 12, San Francisco (94103-3133)
PHONE.................................415 777-0965
Fax: 415 896-0965
Chuck Tweedle, *General Mgr*
Bill Conway, *Vice Pres*
Bill Lueth, *Vice Pres*
Laura Alexander, *Info Tech Mgr*
Shingo Kamada, *Engineer*
EMP: 50
SALES (corp-wide): 2.3B **Privately Held**
SIC: 4832 7313 Radio broadcasting stations; radio advertising representative
HQ: Bonneville International Corporation
55 N 300 W
Salt Lake City UT 84101
801 575-5555

(P-5752)
BROADCAST CO OF AMERICAS LLC (PA)
6160 Cornerstone Ct E, San Diego (92121-3720)
PHONE.................................858 453-0658
Larry Patrick, *CEO*
John T Lynch,
EMP: 50
SALES (est): 10.3MM **Privately Held**
SIC: 4832 Radio broadcasting stations

(P-5753)
CAPITAL PUBLIC RADIO INC
7055 Folsom Blvd, Sacramento (95826-2625)
PHONE.................................916 278-8900
Rick Eytcheson, *President*
Craig McMurray, *Managing Dir*
Marcie Serrano, *Analyst*
Vuctoria Hagele, *Human Res Mgr*
Linda Adkins, *VP Prdtn*
EMP: 50
SQ FT: 19,838
SALES: 11.3MM **Privately Held**
WEB: www.capradio.net
SIC: 4832 Radio broadcasting stations

(P-5754)
CBS BROADCASTING INC
A65 Bettery St, San Francisco (94111)
PHONE.................................415 765-4097
Fax: 415 781-3697
Doug Harvill, *CEO*
Greg Nemitz, *General Mgr*
EMP: 100
SALES (corp-wide): 13.9B **Publicly Held**
WEB: www.cbs4.com
SIC: 4832 Radio broadcasting stations
HQ: Cbs Broadcasting Inc.
51 W 52nd St
New York NY 10019
212 975-4321

(P-5755)
CBS CORPORATION
865 Battery St Fl 2/3, San Francisco (94111-1503)
PHONE.................................415 765-4000
Fax: 415 765-4080
Doug Harvill, *General Mgr*
Ryan Brooks, *Vice Pres*
Amy Poling, *Executive*
Grace Moore, *Admin Mgr*
Greg Nemitz, *Admin Mgr*
EMP: 84
SALES (corp-wide): 13.9B **Publicly Held**
SIC: 4832 Radio broadcasting stations
HQ: Cbs Corporation
51 W 52nd St Bsmt 1
New York NY 10019
212 975-4321

(P-5756)
CBS RADIO
280 Commerce Cir, Sacramento (95815-4212)
PHONE.................................916 923-6800
Fax: 916 927-9696
Micheal Hornetto, *Manager*
Steve Cottingim, *General Mgr*
Jim Balcom, *Chief Engr*
Charese Fruge, *Program Dir*
Breanna Ousley, *Assistant*
EMP: 150
SALES (corp-wide): 13.9B **Publicly Held**
WEB: www.infinityradio.com
SIC: 4832 Radio broadcasting stations
HQ: Cbs Radio Inc.
1271 Ave Of The Amer 44
New York NY 10020
212 314-9200

(P-5757)
CBS RADIO INC
1071 W Shaw Ave, Fresno (93711-3702)
PHONE.................................559 490-0106
El Smith, *Manager*
EMP: 195
SQ FT: 5,938
SALES (corp-wide): 13.9B **Publicly Held**
WEB: www.infinityradio.com
SIC: 4832 Radio broadcasting stations
HQ: Cbs Radio Inc.
1271 Ave Of The Amer 44
New York NY 10020
212 314-9200

(P-5758)
CBS RADIO INC
8033 Linda Vista Rd, San Diego (92111-5108)
PHONE.................................858 560-1037
Fax: 858 571-0326
Peter Schwartz, *Manager*
Marlo Rhodes, *Social Dir*
Jean Arrollado, *CIO*
Ilene Kipnis, *Mktg Dir*
Kevin Becker, *Mktg Coord*
EMP: 70
SQ FT: 8,251
SALES (corp-wide): 13.9B **Publicly Held**
WEB: www.infinityradio.com
SIC: 4832 Radio broadcasting stations
HQ: Cbs Radio Inc.
1271 Ave Of The Amer 44
New York NY 10020
212 314-9200

(P-5759)
CBS RADIO INC
865 Battery St Fl 3, San Francisco (94111-1503)
PHONE.................................415 765-4097
Dan Mason, *Branch Mgr*
Gabriel Haigazian, *Vice Pres*
Howard Wise, *Program Mgr*
Catherine Weldon, *Natl Sales Mgr*
Cindy Clementz, *Accounts Exec*
EMP: 100
SALES (corp-wide): 13.9B **Publicly Held**
SIC: 4832 Radio broadcasting stations
HQ: Cbs Radio Inc.
1271 Ave Of The Amer 44
New York NY 10020
212 314-9200

(P-5760)
CBS RADIO INC
5670 Wilshire Blvd # 200, Los Angeles (90036-5657)
PHONE.................................323 525-0980
Fax: 323 634-9283
Sials Marshall, *Branch Mgr*
Rosemary Hernandez, *Sales Executive*
Pablo Chaparro, *Sales Staff*
Doug Vincent, *Director*
Jonathon Serviss, *Editor*
EMP: 200
SALES (corp-wide): 13.9B **Publicly Held**
SIC: 4832 Radio broadcasting stations
HQ: Cbs Radio Inc.
1271 Ave Of The Amer 44
New York NY 10020
212 314-9200

(P-5761)
CBS RADIO INC
900 E Washington St # 315, Colton (92324-8182)
PHONE.................................909 825-9525
Kevin Murphy, *General Mgr*
Lynn Coleman, *Sales Dir*
Steve Hay, *Sales Mgr*
Jamie Villalobos, *Accounts Exec*
Sara Briseno, *Superintendent*
EMP: 65
SALES (corp-wide): 13.9B **Publicly Held**
WEB: www.infinityradio.com
SIC: 4832 Radio broadcasting stations
HQ: Cbs Radio Inc.
1271 Ave Of The Amer 44
New York NY 10020
212 314-9200

(P-5762)
CBS RADIO INC
5901 Venice Blvd, Los Angeles (90034-1708)
PHONE.................................323 930-1067
Kevin Weatherly, *Manager*
Blake Handler, *IT/INT Sup*
Bob McCormick, *Research*
Trevor Shand, *Producer*
Aissa Juarez, *Mktg Dir*
EMP: 100
SALES (corp-wide): 13.9B **Publicly Held**
WEB: www.infinityradio.com
SIC: 4832 Radio broadcasting stations
HQ: Cbs Radio Inc.
1271 Ave Of The Amer 44
New York NY 10020
212 314-9200

(P-5763)
CBS RADIO INC
5901 Venice Blvd, Los Angeles (90034-1708)
PHONE.................................323 930-7580
Ed Krampf, *Manager*
Rosie Delacruz, *Controller*
Scott Springer, *Sales Mgr*
EMP: 150
SALES (corp-wide): 13.9B **Publicly Held**
WEB: www.infinityradio.com
SIC: 4832 Radio broadcasting stations
HQ: Cbs Radio Inc.
1271 Ave Of The Amer 44
New York NY 10020
212 314-9200

(P-5764)
CITADEL BROADCASTING CORP
Also Called: Kabc 790 Talk Radio
3321 S La Cienega Blvd, Los Angeles (90016-3114)
PHONE.................................310 840-4900
Fax: 310 558-7602
Octavio Gallardo, *Principal*
EMP: 74
SALES (corp-wide): 1.1B **Publicly Held**
SIC: 4832 Radio broadcasting stations
HQ: Citadel Broadcasting Corporation
3280 Peachtree Rd Ne # 2300
Atlanta GA 30305
404 949-0700

(P-5765)
CITADEL BROADCASTING CORP
Also Called: Khop
3136 Boeing Way 125, Stockton (95206-4989)
PHONE.................................209 766-5103
Roy Williams, *General Mgr*
Joanne REA, *Opers Mgr*
Jordan Lowe, *Director*
EMP: 125
SALES (corp-wide): 1.1B **Publicly Held**
WEB: www.citadelradio.com
SIC: 4832 Radio broadcasting stations
HQ: Citadel Broadcasting Corporation
3280 Peachtree Rd Ne # 2300
Atlanta GA 30305
404 949-0700

(P-5766)
EDUCATIONAL MEDIA FOUNDATION (PA)
Also Called: K-Love Radio Network
5700 W Oaks Blvd, Rocklin (95765-3719)
PHONE.................................916 251-1600
Fax: 916 251-1650
Darrell Chambliss, *Ch of Bd*
Richard Jenkins, *President*
Bill Lyons, *President*
Mike Novak, *CEO*
Jon Taylor, *CFO*
EMP: 200
SQ FT: 55,000
SALES: 155.2MM **Privately Held**
SIC: 4832 Radio broadcasting stations

(P-5767)
EMMIS COMMUNICATIONS CORP
790 E Colorado Blvd Fl 9, Pasadena (91101-2193)
PHONE.................................626 484-4440
EMP: 123
SALES (corp-wide): 231.4MM **Publicly Held**
SIC: 4832 Radio broadcasting stations
PA: Emmis Communications Corp
40 Monument Cir Ste 700
Indianapolis IN 46204
317 266-0100

(P-5768)
EMMIS RADIO LLC
Also Called: Kpwr
2600 W Olive Ave Fl 8, Burbank (91505-4553)
PHONE.................................818 525-5000
Val Maki,
Perri Dourian, *Office Mgr*

4832 - Radio Broadcasting Stations County (P-5769)

Janet Brainin, *Sales Staff*
EMP: 170
SQ FT: 11,000
SALES (est): 6.6MM **Privately Held**
WEB: www.kzla.com
SIC: 4832 Radio broadcasting stations

(P-5769)
ENTERCOM COMMUNICATIONS CORP
Also Called: Kseg-FM
5345 Madison Ave, Sacramento (95841-3141)
PHONE 916 766-5000
Fax: 916 334-0822
John Geary, *Manager*
Tom Nakashima, *Executive*
Derrick Dodson, *Info Tech Mgr*
Rick Rapalee, *Engineer*
David Moore, *Opers Mgr*
EMP: 120
SALES (corp-wide): 411.3MM **Publicly Held**
WEB: www.entercom.com
SIC: 4832 7929 Radio broadcasting stations; entertainers & entertainment groups
PA: Entercom Communications Corp.
  401 E City Ave Ste 809
  Bala Cynwyd PA 19004
  610 660-5610

(P-5770)
ENTERCOM COMMUNICATIONS CORP
201 3rd St Fl 12, San Francisco (94103-3133)
PHONE 610 660-5610
Betsy O'Connor, *Branch Mgr*
Lynn Hooper, *Marketing Staff*
Carolyn Shaw, *Marketing Staff*
Jaye Strait, *Marketing Staff*
Jennifer Ishii, *Accounts Mgr*
EMP: 109
SALES (corp-wide): 411.3MM **Publicly Held**
WEB: www.entercom.com
SIC: 4832 Radio broadcasting stations
PA: Entercom Communications Corp.
  401 E City Ave Ste 809
  Bala Cynwyd PA 19004
  610 660-5610

(P-5771)
ENTERCOM COMMUNICATIONS CORP
Also Called: K S S J Radio-101.9 FM City
5345 Madison Ave Ste 100, Sacramento (95841-3141)
PHONE 916 334-7777
John Geary, *Vice Pres*
Rick Rapalee, *Engineer*
Jill Christl, *Purchasing*
EMP: 120
SALES (corp-wide): 411.3MM **Publicly Held**
WEB: www.entercom.com
SIC: 4832 7929 Radio broadcasting stations; entertainers & entertainment groups
PA: Entercom Communications Corp.
  401 E City Ave Ste 809
  Bala Cynwyd PA 19004
  610 660-5610

(P-5772)
ENTRAVSION COMMUNICATIONS CORP
Also Called: Krcx 99 9 FM Tricolor
1436 Auburn Blvd, Sacramento (95815-2745)
PHONE 916 646-4000
Fax: 916 646-3237
Angie Balderas, *Manager*
Pattie Moreno, *Director*
EMP: 50 **Publicly Held**
SIC: 4832 Radio broadcasting stations
PA: Entravision Communications Corporation
  2425 Olympic Blvd Ste 600
  Santa Monica CA 90404

(P-5773)
FAMILY STATIONS INC (PA)
Also Called: Family Radio
1350 S Loop Rd, Alameda (94502-7095)
PHONE 510 568-6200
Fax: 510 430-0893
Harold Camping, *President*
Gary Cook, *CFO*
Sue Espinoza, *Treasurer*
Bill Thornton, *Treasurer*
Mike Wood, *Technology*
EMP: 130 **EST:** 1958
SQ FT: 3,000
SALES (est): 69.8MM **Privately Held**
WEB: www.familyradio.com
SIC: 4832 Radio broadcasting stations

(P-5774)
FAR EAST BROADCASTING CO INC
Also Called: RADIO STATION KFBS
15700 Imperial Hwy, La Mirada (90638-2598)
P.O. Box 1 (90637-0001)
PHONE 562 947-4651
Fax: 562 943-0160
Gregg Harris, *President*
Charles Blake, *CFO*
Peter Anaminyi, *Bd of Directors*
Wayne Shepherd, *Bd of Directors*
Luke Cheng, *Vice Pres*
▲ **EMP:** 52 **EST:** 1945
SQ FT: 20,000
SALES: 11.1MM **Privately Held**
SIC: 4832 Radio broadcasting stations

(P-5775)
FM SEOUL BANG SONG INC
Also Called: Kfox
4525 Wilshire Blvd Fl 3, Los Angeles (90010-3845)
PHONE 323 525-1650
Fax: 323 935-7779
Seong Hwan Jun, *President*
Michele Haisman, *Director*
Gregory Hyde, *Manager*
EMP: 50
SALES (est): 2.6MM
SALES (corp-wide): 63.4MM **Privately Held**
WEB: www.koreatimeshawaii.com
SIC: 4832 Radio broadcasting stations
PA: The Korea Times Los Angeles Inc
  4525 Wilshire Blvd
  Los Angeles CA 90010
  323 692-2000

(P-5776)
FOOTH-DE ANZA COMMUN COLLEG DI
Also Called: Kfjc FM
12345 S El Monte Rd # 6202, Los Altos Hills (94022-4504)
PHONE 650 949-7260
Eric Johnson, *General Mgr*
EMP: 70
SALES (corp-wide): 114.3MM **Privately Held**
WEB: www.fhda.edu
SIC: 4832 Radio broadcasting stations, music format
PA: Foothill-De Anza Community College District Financing Corporation
  12345 S El Monte Rd
  Los Altos Hills CA 94022
  650 949-6100

(P-5777)
HENRY BROADCASTING CO
2277 Jerrold Ave, San Francisco (94124-1011)
PHONE 415 285-1133
Fax: 415 285-3592
C H Buckley, *President*
EMP: 50 **EST:** 1996
SALES (est): 2.1MM
SALES (corp-wide): 13.9B **Publicly Held**
SIC: 4832 Radio broadcasting stations
HQ: Cbs Radio Inc.
  83 Leo M Birmingham Pkwy
  Boston MA 02135
  973 817-5627

(P-5778)
I HEART MEDIA INC
Also Called: Kbos Radio B
83 E Shaw Ave Ste 150, Fresno (93710-7622)
PHONE 559 243-4300
Mark Mays, *President*
Jeff Negrete, *General Mgr*
David Abenojar, *Director*
EMP: 150
SALES (est): 7.9MM **Privately Held**
SIC: 4832 Radio broadcasting stations

(P-5779)
IHEARTCOMMUNICATIONS INC
Also Called: K Y L D
340 Townsend St Fl 4, San Francisco (94107-1633)
PHONE 415 975-5555
Fax: 415 267-0949
Kim Bryant, *Manager*
Joe Bayliss, *Senior VP*
Michael Martin, *Mfg Staff*
Karen Donner, *Sales Executive*
Joe Cariffe, *Sales Staff*
EMP: 300
SALES (corp-wide): 6.2B **Publicly Held**
SIC: 4832 7313 Radio broadcasting stations; radio advertising representative
HQ: Iheartcommunications, Inc.
  200 E Basse Rd
  San Antonio TX 78209
  210 822-2828

(P-5780)
IHEARTCOMMUNICATIONS INC
Also Called: Clear Channel Riverside
2030 Iowa Ave Ste A, Riverside (92507-7412)
PHONE 951 684-1992
Bob Ridzak, *General Mgr*
Thresa Hutchinson, *Office Mgr*
EMP: 61
SALES (corp-wide): 6.2B **Publicly Held**
SIC: 4832 Radio broadcasting stations
HQ: Iheartcommunications, Inc.
  200 E Basse Rd
  San Antonio TX 78209
  210 822-2828

(P-5781)
IHEARTCOMMUNICATIONS INC
Also Called: Kogoam
9660 Gran Rdge Dr Ste 100, San Diego (92123)
PHONE 858 522-5547
Dave Schroeder, *Manager*
Jack Rice, *Social Dir*
EMP: 280
SALES (corp-wide): 6.2B **Publicly Held**
SIC: 4832 Radio broadcasting stations
HQ: Iheartcommunications, Inc.
  200 E Basse Rd
  San Antonio TX 78209
  210 822-2828

(P-5782)
IHEARTCOMMUNICATIONS INC
9660 Gran Rdge Dr Ste 200, San Diego (92123)
PHONE 858 292-2000
Dave Schroeder, *Controller*
Mike Larson, *CTO*
EMP: 61
SALES (corp-wide): 6.2B **Publicly Held**
SIC: 4832 Radio broadcasting stations
HQ: Iheartcommunications, Inc.
  200 E Basse Rd
  San Antonio TX 78209
  210 822-2828

(P-5783)
IHEARTCOMMUNICATIONS INC
1545 River Park Dr # 500, Sacramento (95815-4616)
PHONE 916 929-5325
Sarah McClure, *General Mgr*
EMP: 120
SALES (corp-wide): 6.2B **Publicly Held**
SIC: 4832 Radio broadcasting stations
HQ: Iheartcommunications, Inc.
  200 E Basse Rd
  San Antonio TX 78209
  210 822-2828

(P-5784)
IHEARTCOMMUNICATIONS INC
352 E Avenue K4, Lancaster (93535-4505)
PHONE 661 942-1268
EMP: 61
SALES (corp-wide): 6.2B **Publicly Held**
SIC: 4832
HQ: Iheartcommunications, Inc.
  200 E Basse Rd
  San Antonio TX 78209
  210 822-2828

(P-5785)
IHEARTCOMMUNICATIONS INC
1440 Ethan Way, Sacramento (95825-2225)
PHONE 916 929-5325
EMP: 61
SALES (corp-wide): 6.2B **Publicly Held**
SIC: 4832 Radio broadcasting stations
HQ: Iheartcommunications, Inc.
  200 E Basse Rd
  San Antonio TX 78209
  210 822-2828

(P-5786)
IHEARTCOMMUNICATIONS INC
Also Called: Kgb
5745 Kearny Villa Rd M, San Diego (92123-1153)
PHONE 858 565-6006
Fax: 619 560-8090
Mike Gilckenhaus, *Branch Mgr*
EMP: 200
SALES (corp-wide): 6.2B **Publicly Held**
SIC: 4832 Radio broadcasting stations
HQ: Iheartcommunications, Inc.
  200 E Basse Rd
  San Antonio TX 78209
  210 822-2828

(P-5787)
IHEARTCOMMUNICATIONS INC
Also Called: Krzr 103 7 FM
83 E Shaw Ave Ste 150, Fresno (93710-7622)
PHONE 559 230-4300
Jeff Negrete, *Manager*
EMP: 75
SALES (corp-wide): 6.2B **Publicly Held**
SIC: 4832 Radio broadcasting stations
HQ: Iheartcommunications, Inc.
  200 E Basse Rd
  San Antonio TX 78209
  210 822-2828

(P-5788)
INFINITY BROADCASTING CORP CAL
Also Called: Krth Radio 101 FM
5670 Wilshire Blvd # 200, Los Angeles (90036-5679)
PHONE 323 936-5784
Fax: 323 936-3427
John Sykes, *President*
Maureen Lesourd, *Vice Pres*
Jhani Kaye, *Director*
Bob Malik, *Publisher*
Andy Schmidt, *Publisher*
EMP: 60 **EST:** 2001
SALES (est): 3.5MM
SALES (corp-wide): 13.9B **Publicly Held**
SIC: 4832 Radio broadcasting stations
HQ: Cbs Corporation
  51 W 52nd St Bsmt 1
  New York NY 10019
  212 975-4321

(P-5789)
INNER CITY BROADCASTING CORP
Also Called: 102.9 Kblx-FM Radio
55 Hawthorne St Ste 900, San Francisco (94105-3967)
PHONE 415 284-1029
Fax: 415 764-4909
Harvey Stone, *Manager*
Kimmie Taylor, *Teacher*
Matt Addy, *Assistant*
EMP: 50
SQ FT: 1,000
SALES (corp-wide): 31.6MM **Privately Held**
WEB: www.innercitysc.com
SIC: 4832 Radio broadcasting stations

PRODUCTS & SERVICES SECTION
4832 - Radio Broadcasting Stations County (P-5813)

PA: Inner City Broadcasting Corp
333 7th Ave Rm 1401
New York NY 10001
212 447-1000

(P-5790)
K G O T V NEWS BUREAU
520 3rd St Ste 200, Oakland (94607-3505)
PHONE.....................510 451-4772
Ed Kosowski, *Principal*
EMP: 100
SALES (est): 65.7K
SALES (corp-wide): 1.1B **Publicly Held**
SIC: 4832 Radio broadcasting stations
HQ: San Francisco Radio Assets Llc
750 Battery St Fl 2
San Francisco CA 94111
415 216-1300

(P-5791)
K LOVE (KLQV)
Also Called: K-Love 102
600 W Broadway Ste 2150, San Diego (92101-3389)
PHONE.....................619 235-0600
Peter Moore, *General Mgr*
EMP: 58
SALES (est): 3.7MM **Privately Held**
WEB: www.klove.com
SIC: 4832 Radio broadcasting stations

(P-5792)
KCBS NEWS RADIO 74
865 Battery St, San Francisco (94111-1554)
PHONE.....................415 765-4112
Doug Harvill, *Manager*
Douglas Sterne, *General Mgr*
Patrick Truesdale, *Controller*
Ed Cavagnaro, *Director*
EMP: 90
SALES (est): 4.3MM **Privately Held**
SIC: 4832 Radio broadcasting stations

(P-5793)
KIFM SMOOTH JAZZ 981 INC
1615 Murray Canyon Rd, San Diego (92108-4314)
PHONE.....................619 297-3698
Mike Stafford, *President*
EMP: 110
SQ FT: 12,000
SALES (est): 2.2MM
SALES (corp-wide): 411.3MM **Publicly Held**
SIC: 4832 Radio broadcasting stations
HQ: Abe Entercom Holdings Llc
401 E City Ave Ste 809
Bala Cynwyd PA 19004
404 239-7211

(P-5794)
KION NEWS TALK 1460
903 N Main St, Salinas (93906-3912)
PHONE.....................831 633-1460
Lowry Mayes, *Owner*
EMP: 50
SALES (est): 833.2K **Privately Held**
SIC: 4832 Radio broadcasting stations

(P-5795)
KKZZ 1590
Also Called: Gold Coast Broadcasting
2284 S Victoria Ave 2g, Ventura (93003-6641)
PHONE.....................805 289-1400
Chip Ehrhardt, *Partner*
John Hearne, *Partner*
EMP: 50
SALES (est): 3.2MM **Privately Held**
SIC: 4832 Radio broadcasting stations

(P-5796)
KNAX COUNTRY 98
Also Called: Peak Broadcasting
1071 W Shaw Ave, Fresno (93711-3702)
PHONE.....................559 490-9800
Fax: 559 490-5888
Todd Lowely, *CEO*
Tim Lyons, *CFO*
EMP: 50
SALES (est): 624.6K **Privately Held**
SIC: 4832 Radio broadcasting stations

(P-5797)
KOXR SPANISH RADIO
Also Called: K O X R
200 S A St Ste 400, Oxnard (93030-5723)
PHONE.....................805 487-0444
Fax: 805 487-5804
Alfredo Placencia, *Owner*
Terry Janisch, *General Mgr*
Vicky Orozco, *Sales Mgr*
EMP: 50
SALES (est): 1.5MM **Privately Held**
SIC: 4832 Radio broadcasting stations

(P-5798)
KPWR INC
Also Called: Kpwr Power 106
2600 W Olive Ave Ste 850, Burbank (91505-4568)
PHONE.....................818 953-4200
Fax: 818 848-0961
Jeffrey Smulyan, *CEO*
Doyle Rose, *President*
Jimmy Steal, *President*
Candice Del Villar, *Executive*
Terri Dourian, *Human Res Dir*
EMP: 88
SQ FT: 1,700
SALES (est): 4.2MM
SALES (corp-wide): 231.4MM **Publicly Held**
WEB: www.power106la.com
SIC: 4832 Radio broadcasting stations
PA: Emmis Communications Corp
40 Monument Cir Ste 700
Indianapolis IN 46204
317 266-0100

(P-5799)
KRTY LTD A CAL LTD PARTNR
750 Story Rd, San Jose (95122-2604)
PHONE.....................408 293-8030
Robert S Kieve, *Partner*
EMP: 50
SALES (est): 3.6MM **Privately Held**
WEB: www.krty.com
SIC: 4832 Radio broadcasting stations

(P-5800)
KSCF 1037 FM
Also Called: Planet
8033 Linda Vista Rd, San Diego (92111-5108)
PHONE.....................858 560-1037
Bob Bolinger, *Vice Pres*
Charlie Quinn, *Opers Mgr*
Kiku Boyance, *Mktg Dir*
Kevin Becker, *Mktg Coord*
Ilene Kipnis, *Accounts Mgr*
EMP: 80
SALES (est): 2.8MM **Privately Held**
WEB: www.planetfm.com
SIC: 4832 Radio broadcasting stations

(P-5801)
KUIC INC
Also Called: Kuic-FM
555 Mason St Ste 245, Vacaville (95688-4640)
PHONE.....................707 446-0200
Fax: 707 446-0122
James Levitt, *Ch of Bd*
John F Levitt, *President*
Lori Smith, *Business Mgr*
Ken Hiemke, *Sales Mgr*
EMP: 60
SQ FT: 4,200
SALES (est): 2.3MM
SALES (corp-wide): 30MM **Privately Held**
WEB: www.kuic.com
SIC: 4832 2711 Radio broadcasting stations; newspapers
PA: Coast Radio Company Inc
555 Mason St Ste 245
Vacaville CA 95688
707 446-0200

(P-5802)
L B I HOLDINGS I INC (PA)
1845 W Empire Ave, Burbank (91504-3402)
PHONE.....................818 563-5722
Jose Liberman, *President*
William S Keenan, *CFO*
Lenard Liberman, *Exec VP*
Winter Horton, *Vice Pres*
Eduardo Leon, *Vice Pres*
EMP: 100
SALES (est): 43.1MM **Privately Held**
SIC: 4832 Radio broadcasting stations; ethnic programming

(P-5803)
LA RADIO LLC
3321 S La Cienega Blvd, Los Angeles (90016-3114)
PHONE.....................310 840-4900
Randy L Taylor, *Senior VP*
EMP: 50
SQ FT: 43,313
SALES (est): 2.6MM
SALES (corp-wide): 1.1B **Publicly Held**
WEB: www.kabc.com
SIC: 4832 Radio broadcasting stations
HQ: Citadel Broadcasting Corporation
3280 Peachtree Rd Ne # 2300
Atlanta GA 30305
404 949-0700

(P-5804)
LBI MEDIA INC
1845 W Empire Ave, Burbank (91504-3402)
PHONE.....................818 729-5316
Lloyd Isbell, *Manager*
Michael Sheron, *Senior VP*
Dana Sparber, *Vice Pres*
Jimmy Diaz, *Executive*
Ralph Ortiz, *Executive*
EMP: 408
SALES (est): 217.3K
SALES (corp-wide): 265MM **Privately Held**
SIC: 4832 Radio broadcasting stations
HQ: Lbi Media Holdings, Inc.
1845 W Empire Ave
Burbank CA 91504
818 563-5722

(P-5805)
LELAND STANFORD JUNIOR UNIV
Also Called: Kzsu 90.1 FM
551 Srra Mall Mem Adtrium Memorial Auditorium, Stanford (94305)
P.O. Box 20190 (94309-0190)
PHONE.....................650 725-4868
Mark Lawrence, *Principal*
EMP: 100
SALES (corp-wide): 1.9B **Privately Held**
SIC: 4832 Radio broadcasting stations
PA: Leland Stanford Junior University
2575 Sand Hill Rd
Menlo Park CA 94025
650 723-2300

(P-5806)
LIBERMAN BROADCASTING INC (PA)
1845 W Empire Ave, Burbank (91504-3402)
PHONE.....................818 729-5300
Lenard D Liberman, *CEO*
Jose Liberman, *President*
Frederic T Boyer, *CFO*
Winter Horton, *Vice Pres*
Thuy Le, *Vice Pres*
EMP: 83
SALES (est): 265MM **Privately Held**
SIC: 4832 Radio broadcasting stations

(P-5807)
LOCAL MEDIA OF AMERICA LLC
Also Called: Magic 92.5
6160 Cornerstone Ct E # 150, San Diego (92121-3720)
PHONE.....................858 888-7000
John Lynch, *CEO*
Norman McKee, *CFO*
Jim Votaw, *Sales Executive*
EMP: 100
SALES (est): 6.5MM **Privately Held**
SIC: 4832 Radio broadcasting stations

(P-5808)
LOTUS COMMUNICATIONS CORP (PA)
3301 Barham Blvd Ste 200, Los Angeles (90068-1358)
PHONE.....................323 512-2225
Fax: 323 512-2224
Howard Kalmenson, *President*
William H Shriftman, *Treasurer*
Jim Kalmenson, *Senior VP*
Jerry Roy, *Senior VP*
Jasmin Dorismond, *Vice Pres*
EMP: 60 **EST:** 1959
SQ FT: 25,848
SALES (est): 111.7MM **Privately Held**
WEB: www.lotuscorp.com
SIC: 4832 Radio broadcasting stations

(P-5809)
LOYOLA MARYMOUNT UNIVERSITY
Also Called: Radio Station
1 Lmu Dr Ste 100, Los Angeles (90045-2677)
PHONE.....................310 338-2866
Fax: 310 338-2866
Devin Valdesuso, *Manager*
Jennifer Magnabosco, *Associate Dir*
Cheryl Wawrzaszek, *Admin Asst*
Stephen Nuno, *Research*
Barbara Baltazar, *Human Res Mgr*
EMP: 120
SALES (corp-wide): 349.8MM **Privately Held**
WEB: www.lmu.edu
SIC: 4832 8221 Radio broadcasting stations; university
PA: Loyola Marymount University Inc
1 Lmu Dr Uhall 4900 4900 Uhall
Los Angeles CA 90045
310 568-6688

(P-5810)
MINNEAPOLIS RADIO ASSETS LLC
Also Called: Radio Disney Kdiz AM
3800 W Alameda Ave 17, Burbank (91505-4300)
PHONE.....................612 617-4000
Fax: 612 676-8214
Randy L Taylor, *Senior VP*
EMP: 220
SALES (est): 4.3MM
SALES (corp-wide): 1.1B **Publicly Held**
SIC: 4832 Radio broadcasting stations
HQ: Citadel Broadcasting Corporation
3280 Peachtree Rd Ne # 2300
Atlanta GA 30305
404 949-0700

(P-5811)
NBC UNIVERSAL INC
55 Hawthorne St Ste 1100, San Francisco (94105-3914)
PHONE.....................415 995-6800
Anthony Salvadore, *Manager*
EMP: 176
SALES (corp-wide): 74.5B **Publicly Held**
WEB: www.nbc.com
SIC: 4832 Radio broadcasting stations
HQ: Nbc Universal, Llc
1221 Avenue Of The Americ
New York NY 10020
212 664-4444

(P-5812)
NBCUNIVERSAL MEDIA LLC
Also Called: Universal Pictures Intl
100 Universal City Plz, Universal City (91608-1002)
PHONE.....................818 777-1000
Max Liles, *Branch Mgr*
EMP: 91
SALES (corp-wide): 74.5B **Publicly Held**
SIC: 4832 7812 Radio broadcasting stations; motion picture production & distribution; motion picture production & distribution, television; non-theatrical motion picture production; non-theatrical motion picture production, television
HQ: Nbcuniversal Media, Llc
30 Rockefeller Plz Fl 2
New York NY 10112
212 664-4444

(P-5813)
NEW INSPIRATION BRDCSTG CO INC
4880 Santa Rosa Rd, Camarillo (93012-5190)
PHONE.....................805 987-0400
Edward G Atsinger III, *CEO*

4832 - Radio Broadcasting Stations County (P-5814)

Stuart Epperson, *Ch of Bd*
David Evans, *President*
Evan Masyr, *CFO*
Christopher Henderson, *Vice Pres*
EMP: 1457
SQ FT: 40,000
SALES (est): 39.5MM
SALES (corp-wide): 265.7MM **Publicly Held**
SIC: 4832 2731 Radio broadcasting stations; book publishing
PA: Salem Media Group, Inc.
4880 Santa Rosa Rd
Camarillo CA 93012
818 956-0400

(P-5814)
PACIFIC SPANISH NETWORK INC
296 H St Ste 300, Chula Vista (91910-4753)
PHONE..................................619 427-6323
Jaime Bonilla Valdez, *President*
EMP: 69
SQ FT: 5,000
SALES (est): 2.7MM **Privately Held**
SIC: 4832 Radio broadcasting stations

(P-5815)
PANDORA MEDIA INC
3000 Ocean Park Blvd # 3050, Santa Monica (90405-3020)
PHONE..................................424 653-6803
EMP: 440
SALES (corp-wide): 1.1B **Publicly Held**
SIC: 4832 Radio broadcasting stations
PA: Pandora Media, Inc.
2101 Webster St Ste 1650
Oakland CA 94612
510 451-4100

(P-5816)
POWER 106 RADIO
2600 W Olive Ave Fl 8, Burbank (91505-4553)
PHONE..................................818 953-4200
Pat Thomas, *Manager*
Val Maki, *General Mgr*
Aimee Bittourna, *Director*
Terry McGovern, *Director*
EMP: 90
SALES (est): 3.4MM **Privately Held**
WEB: www.power106radio.com
SIC: 4832 Radio broadcasting stations

(P-5817)
SALEM MEDIA GROUP INC (PA)
4880 Santa Rosa Rd, Camarillo (93012-5190)
PHONE..................................818 956-0400
Fax: 805 384-4520
Edward G Atsinger III, *CEO*
Stuart W Epperson, *Ch of Bd*
David A R Evans, *President*
David P Santrella, *President*
Evan D Masyr, *CFO*
EMP: 115
SQ FT: 40,000
SALES: 265.7MM **Publicly Held**
WEB: www.srnradio.com
SIC: 4832 2731 4813 Radio broadcasting stations; book publishing;

(P-5818)
SALEM MEDIA GROUP INC
Also Called: Krlh-AM 590-AM
701 N Brand Blvd Ste 550, Glendale (91203-1235)
P.O. Box 29023 (91209-9023)
PHONE..................................818 956-5254
Fax: 818 553-1220
Terry Sahy, *Manager*
Jim Tinker, *Prdtn Mgr*
Richard Blythe, *Opers Staff*
Terry Fahy, *Sales Mgr*
Richard Kennedy, *Director*
EMP: 100
SALES (corp-wide): 265.7MM **Publicly Held**
WEB: www.srnradio.com
SIC: 4832 Radio broadcasting stations
PA: Salem Media Group, Inc.
4880 Santa Rosa Rd
Camarillo CA 93012
818 956-0400

(P-5819)
SAN DIEGO STATE UNIV FOUNDATION
Kpbs TV
5200 Campanile Dr, San Diego (92182-1901)
PHONE..................................619 594-1515
Doug Myrland, *General Mgr*
Skot Norton, *Technology*
Kathryn Nelson, *Opers Mgr*
Stefanie Levine, *Producer*
Charlotte Albergetis, *Mktg Dir*
EMP: 100 **Privately Held**
SIC: 4832 4833 8221 9411 Radio broadcasting stations; television broadcasting stations; university; administration of educational programs;
HQ: San Diego State University Foundation
5250 Campanile Dr Mc1947
San Diego CA 92182
619 594-1900

(P-5820)
SAN DIEGO STATE UNIVERSITY
Also Called: K P B S
5200 Campanile Dr, San Diego (92182-1901)
PHONE..................................619 265-6438
Fax: 619 594-3812
Tom Karlo, *Manager*
Elle Masri, *Volunteer Dir*
Tom Fudge, *Social Dir*
Tom Carlo, *General Mgr*
John Johnson, *Engineer*
EMP: 100 **Privately Held**
SIC: 4832 Radio broadcasting stations; educational; news
HQ: San Diego State University
5500 Campanile Dr
San Diego CA 92182
619 594-7985

(P-5821)
SAN FRANCISCO RADIO ASSETS LLC (DH)
Also Called: Kgo 810am
750 Battery St Fl 2, San Francisco (94111-1524)
PHONE..................................415 216-1300
Fax: 415 954-7377
Deidrea Lieberman, *General Mgr*
Jack Swanson, *Administration*
Marnie Tattersal, *Controller*
EMP: 150
SQ FT: 51,000
SALES (est): 48.8MM
SALES (corp-wide): 1.1B **Publicly Held**
SIC: 4832 Radio broadcasting stations

(P-5822)
SPANISH BRDCSTG SYS OF CAL
Also Called: Klax Radio Station
7007 Nw 77th Ave, Los Angeles (90064)
PHONE..................................310 203-0900
Fax: 310 203-8989
Raul Alarcon Sr, *Ch of Bd*
Joseph Garcia, *CFO*
Rafael Navarro, *Managing Dir*
Rosa Ambriz, *Executive Asst*
EMP: 70
SALES: 4.3MM
SALES (corp-wide): 146.9MM **Publicly Held**
SIC: 4832 7313 Radio broadcasting stations; radio advertising representative
HQ: Spanish Broadcasting System Of Greater Miami, Inc.
7007 Nw 77th Ave
Medley FL 33166
305 644-4800

(P-5823)
TOAD 1350
2030 Iowa Ave Ste A, Riverside (92507-7412)
PHONE..................................951 369-1350
Bob Ridzak, *Administration*
EMP: 50
SALES (est): 781.2K **Privately Held**
SIC: 4832 Radio broadcasting stations

(P-5824)
TRIAD BROADCASTING COMPANY (PA)
2511 Garden Rd Ste A104, Monterey (93940-5376)
P.O. Box 7539, Carmel By The Sea (93921-7539)
PHONE..................................831 655-6350
Fax: 831 655-6355
David J Benjamin, *President*
Brian Emkjer, *Senior VP*
Steve Feder, *Vice Pres*
James Traver, *Vice Pres*
Mike Wild, *Vice Pres*
EMP: 140
SALES (est): 31.7MM **Privately Held**
SIC: 4832 Radio broadcasting stations

(P-5825)
TRITON MEDIA GROUP LLC
Also Called: Dial Global Digital
8935 Lindblade St, Culver City (90232-2438)
PHONE..................................661 294-9000
Phil Barry, *Branch Mgr*
Roger Fyee, *Data Proc Dir*
EMP: 75
SALES (corp-wide): 380.6MM **Privately Held**
SIC: 4832 Radio broadcasting stations, music format
PA: Triton Media Group, Llc
15303 Ventura Blvd # 1500
Sherman Oaks CA 91403
323 290-6900

(P-5826)
TURNER BROADCASTING SYSTEM INC
1888 Century Park E # 1200, Los Angeles (90067-1715)
PHONE..................................310 788-6767
Frank Merauto, *Principal*
Denise Chung, *Manager*
Christine Spellman, *Manager*
Soroush Ismaili, *Accounts Exec*
Nadia Zia, *Accounts Exec*
EMP: 70
SALES (corp-wide): 28.1B **Publicly Held**
WEB: www.turner.com
SIC: 4832 Radio broadcasting stations
HQ: Turner Broadcasting System, Inc.
1 Cnn Ctr Nw
Atlanta GA 30303
404 827-1700

(P-5827)
UNIVISION COMMUNICATIONS INC
655 N Central Ave # 2500, Glendale (91203-1422)
PHONE..................................818 484-7399
Thomas McSweeney, *Branch Mgr*
Andres Juarez, *Consultant*
EMP: 140
SALES (corp-wide): 2.5B **Privately Held**
WEB: www.univision.com
SIC: 4832 Radio broadcasting stations
HQ: Univision Communications Inc.
605 3rd Ave Fl 12
New York NY 10158
212 455-5200

(P-5828)
UNIVISION RADIO INC
601 W Univision Plz, Fresno (93704-1092)
PHONE..................................559 430-8500
Angela Navarrete, *Branch Mgr*
Alvaro Martinez, *Production*
James Meyer, *Director*
Joe Chacon, *Editor*
Ana Fuerte, *Accounts Exec*
EMP: 50
SALES (corp-wide): 2.5B **Privately Held**
WEB: www.heftel.com
SIC: 4832 Radio broadcasting stations
HQ: Univision Radio, Inc.
2323 Bryan St Ste 1900
Dallas TX 75201
214 758-2300

(P-5829)
WALT DISNEY COMPANY
Also Called: Kiid
8265 Sierra College Blvd # 21, Roseville (95661-9403)
PHONE..................................916 780-1470
EMP: 53 **Publicly Held**
SIC: 4832
PA: The Walt Disney Company
500 S Buena Vista St
Burbank CA 91521

(P-5830)
WALT DISNEY COMPANY
Also Called: Radio Disney
3800 W Alameda Ave # 1150, Burbank (91505-4300)
PHONE..................................972 448-3143
Karen Pipps, *Principal*
Jennifer Rogers-Doyle, *Vice Pres*
Laura C Bohner, *Executive*
Doina Osborn, *Social Dir*
Kristin Corrigan, *Exec Dir*
EMP: 331 **Publicly Held**
SIC: 4832 Radio broadcasting stations
PA: The Walt Disney Company
500 S Buena Vista St
Burbank CA 91521

4833 Television Broadcasting Stations

(P-5831)
ABC INC
500 Circle Seven Dr, Glendale (91201-2331)
PHONE..................................818 863-7801
Fax: 818 863-7080
Arnold J Kleiner, *Director*
Jeremiah Tachna, *Natl Sales Mgr*
Cari Skillman, *Adv Mgr*
Kenny Plotnik, *Director*
Aditi Roy, *Correspondent*
EMP: 500 **Publicly Held**
WEB: www.abc.com
SIC: 4833 Television broadcasting stations
HQ: Abc, Inc.
77 W 66th St Rm 100
New York NY 10023
212 456-7777

(P-5832)
ABC CABLE NETWORKS GROUP
900 Front St, San Francisco (94111-1427)
PHONE..................................415 954-7911
Lynn Dooley, *Branch Mgr*
Rosendo Pena, *Info Tech Mgr*
EMP: 200 **Publicly Held**
WEB: www.breakbar.com
SIC: 4833 Television broadcasting stations
HQ: Abc Cable Networks Group
500 S Buena Vista St
Burbank CA 91521
818 460-7477

(P-5833)
ACCESS HOLLYWOOD
Also Called: Channel 4-NBC 4 Television
3000 W Alameda Ave, Burbank (91523-0001)
PHONE..................................818 840-4444
Fax: 818 526-7001
Jeff Zaker, *CEO*
Hugl Troncoso, *Producer*
EMP: 170
SALES (est): 7.5MM **Privately Held**
SIC: 4833 Television broadcasting stations

(P-5834)
BAY CITY TELEVISION INC (PA)
8253 Ronson Rd, San Diego (92111-2004)
PHONE..................................858 279-6666
Jose Antonio Baston Patino, *CEO*
Robert Taylor, *President*
Lupe Zavala, *Executive Asst*
Mark Jacobs, *Research*
Stan Murphy, *Credit Mgr*
EMP: 100
SQ FT: 12,000

PRODUCTS & SERVICES SECTION
4833 - Television Broadcasting Stations County (P-5856)

SALES (est): 47.5MM **Privately Held**
SIC: **4833** 7311 Television broadcasting stations; advertising agencies

(P-5835)
BURBANK TELEVISION ENTPS LLC
4000 Warner Blvd, Burbank (91522-0001)
PHONE................818 954-6000
Barry M Meyer, *CEO*
Michael Puopolo, *Administration*
EMP: 200
SALES (est): 4.5MM
SALES (corp-wide): 28.1B **Publicly Held**
SIC: **4833** Television broadcasting stations
HQ: Warner Bros. Entertainment Inc.
  4000 Warner Blvd
  Burbank CA 91522
  818 954-6000

(P-5836)
BUZZTIME INC
2231 Rutherford Rd # 210, Carlsbad (92008-8811)
PHONE................760 476-1976
Dario Santana, *CEO*
Darlene French-Porter, *Controller*
EMP: 120
SALES (est): 5.2MM **Privately Held**
WEB: www.buzztime.com
SIC: **4833** Television broadcasting stations

(P-5837)
CALIFORNIA OREGON BROADCASTING (HQ)
Also Called: Krcr TV
755 Auditorium Dr, Redding (96001-0920)
PHONE................530 243-7777
Fax: 530 243-0217
Sarah Smith, *General Mgr*
Sheri Green, *Info Tech Mgr*
Robin Jordan, *Info Tech Mgr*
Cris Aguilar, *Program Dir*
Teresa Yuan, *Manager*
EMP: 60 EST: 1963
SQ FT: 14,000
SALES (est): 13.2MM
SALES (corp-wide): 29.9MM **Privately Held**
WEB: www.krcrtv.com
SIC: **4833** Television broadcasting stations
PA: Appalachian Broadcasting Corp
  101 Lee St
  Bristol VA
  276 645-1555

(P-5838)
CATAMOUNT BROADCASTING OF CHIC (PA)
Also Called: Khsl TV
3460 Silverbell Rd, Chico (95973-0388)
PHONE................530 893-2424
Fax: 530 894-1033
Raymond Johns, *President*
Evan Santi, *COO*
Alex Marin, *Executive*
Justine Clark, *Sls & Mktg Exec*
Duncan Laing, *Sls & Mktg Exec*
EMP: 104
SQ FT: 18,000
SALES (est): 13.6MM **Privately Held**
WEB: www.knvn.com
SIC: **4833** Television broadcasting stations

(P-5839)
CBS BROADCASTING INC
855 Battery St, San Francisco (94111-1503)
PHONE................415 765-0928
Fax: 415 765-8844
Bruno Cohen, *Manager*
Len Ramirez, *Officer*
Kathie Culleton, *Senior VP*
Jodi Roth, *Senior VP*
Francisco Arias, *Vice Pres*
EMP: 300
SALES (corp-wide): 13.9B **Publicly Held**
WEB: www.cbs4.com
SIC: **4833** Television broadcasting stations
HQ: Cbs Broadcasting Inc.
  51 W 52nd St
  New York NY 10019
  212 975-4321

(P-5840)
CBS BROADCASTING INC
12641 Beatrice St, Los Angeles (90066-7003)
PHONE................310 577-3457
Jim Chory, *Branch Mgr*
EMP: 70
SALES (corp-wide): 13.9B **Publicly Held**
WEB: www.cbs4.com
SIC: **4833** Television broadcasting stations
HQ: Cbs Broadcasting Inc.
  51 W 52nd St
  New York NY 10019
  212 975-4321

(P-5841)
CBS BROADCASTING INC
4200 Radford Ave, Studio City (91604-2189)
PHONE................818 655-2000
Fax: 818 655-2291
Steve Mauldin, *General Mgr*
Michael Lam, *Officer*
Dennis Nieves, *Info Tech Dir*
Eric Kern, *Sales Mgr*
Pat Leong, *Manager*
EMP: 500
SALES (corp-wide): 13.9B **Publicly Held**
WEB: www.cbs4.com
SIC: **4833** Television broadcasting stations
HQ: Cbs Broadcasting Inc.
  51 W 52nd St
  New York NY 10019
  212 975-4321

(P-5842)
CBS CORPORATION
7800 Beverly Blvd, Los Angeles (90036-2112)
PHONE................323 575-2345
Fax: 323 651-1961
Jonathan Anshell, *Branch Mgr*
Rob Gelick, *Senior VP*
Roni Mueller, *Senior VP*
Marc Rayfield, *Senior VP*
Steve King, *Vice Pres*
EMP: 72
SALES (corp-wide): 13.9B **Publicly Held**
SIC: **4833** Television broadcasting stations
HQ: Cbs Corporation
  51 W 52nd St Bsmt 1
  New York NY 10019
  212 975-4321

(P-5843)
CBS CORPORATION
31276 Dunham Way, Thousand Palms (92276-3310)
PHONE................760 343-5700
Mike Stutz, *Office Mgr*
EMP: 64
SALES (corp-wide): 13.9B **Publicly Held**
SIC: **4833** Television broadcasting stations
HQ: Cbs Corporation
  51 W 52nd St Bsmt 1
  New York NY 10019
  212 975-4321

(P-5844)
CBS TELEVISION CITY
7800 Beverly Blvd, Los Angeles (90036-2112)
PHONE................323 651-0255
Fax: 323 651-5900
Sumner M Redstone, *Chairman*
Pete Ely, *Vice Pres*
Dana Kwiatkowski, *Engineer*
Susan Kayl, *Human Res Dir*
Lyn Sereno, *Human Res Mgr*
EMP: 52
SALES (est): 5.3MM **Privately Held**
SIC: **4833** Television broadcasting stations

(P-5845)
CHANNEL 40 INC
Also Called: Ktxl-Fox 40
4655 Fruitridge Rd, Sacramento (95820-5201)
PHONE................916 454-4422
Fax: 916 739-0559
Jerry Del Core, *Vice Pres*
Greg Virtue, *Systems Mgr*
Troy Conhain, *Producer*
Kieran Clarke, *Manager*
EMP: 105
SQ FT: 25,000
SALES (est): 10.5MM
SALES (corp-wide): 2B **Publicly Held**
WEB: www.tribune.com
SIC: **4833** Television translator station
PA: Tribune Media Company
  435 N Michigan Ave Fl 2
  Chicago IL 60611
  212 210-2786

(P-5846)
CHRONICLE BROADCASTING CO
Also Called: Kron-Tv
900 Front St, San Francisco (94111-1427)
PHONE................415 561-8000
Fax: 415 561-8136
Francis A Martin III, *President*
Glen E Pickell, *Treasurer*
Ronald Ingram, *Vice Pres*
Robert M Raymer, *Admin Sec*
EMP: 400
SQ FT: 90,000
SALES (est): 24.1MM
SALES (corp-wide): 419.4MM **Privately Held**
SIC: **4833** Television broadcasting stations
PA: Hearst Communications, Inc.
  901 Mission St
  San Francisco CA 94103
  415 777-1111

(P-5847)
COLLINS AVENUE LLC
5410 Wilshire Blvd # 800, Los Angeles (90036-4267)
PHONE................323 930-6633
Jeff Collins, *President*
Michael Hammond, *Senior VP*
Melanie Moreau, *Senior VP*
John Bradley, *Vice Pres*
Sandi Johnson, *Vice Pres*
EMP: 50
SALES (est): 4.7MM **Privately Held**
SIC: **4833** Television broadcasting stations

(P-5848)
COWLES CALIFORNIA MEDIA CO
Also Called: Kcba Fox TV 35
1550 Moffett St, Salinas (93905-3342)
PHONE................831 422-3500
Fax: 831 422-6448
Paul Daghi, *President*
Karen Orehoski, *Vice Chairman*
Richard E Mitchell, *Treasurer*
James A Andrus, *Vice Pres*
Brent Calvin, *Manager*
EMP: 70
SALES (corp-wide): 3.9MM **Privately Held**
WEB: www.kion46.com
SIC: **4833** Television broadcasting stations
PA: Cowles California Media Company
  1550 Moffett St
  Salinas CA 93905
  831 784-6300

(P-5849)
CROWN MEDIA HOLDINGS INC
Also Called: Hallmark Channel, The
3745 Calle Joaquin, Calabasas (91302-3041)
PHONE................818 755-2400
Henry Schleiff, *President*
Joan Gundlach, *Exec VP*
EMP: 130
SALES (est): 13.6MM **Privately Held**
SIC: **4833** Television broadcasting stations

(P-5850)
CW NETWORK LLC (PA)
Also Called: Cwtv
3300 W Olive Ave Fl 3, Burbank (91505-4640)
PHONE................818 977-2500
John Maatta,
Robert Cosci, *Exec VP*
Russell Myerson, *Exec VP*
Thomas Sherman, *Exec VP*
Robert Tuck, *Exec VP*
EMP: 93
SALES (est): 112.3MM **Privately Held**
WEB: www.cwtv.com
SIC: **4833** Television broadcasting stations

(P-5851)
DESERT TELEVISION LLC
Also Called: U-Dub Productions
73185 Highway 111 Ste D, Palm Desert (92260-3929)
P.O. Box 13917 (92255-3917)
PHONE................760 343-5700
Fax: 760 343-5794
Jacqueline L Houston,
Don Perry, *General Mgr*
Joyce Wheelock, *Business Mgr*
Barry Gorfine, *Sales Dir*
James R Houston,
EMP: 85
SQ FT: 6,500
SALES (est): 5.3MM **Privately Held**
WEB: www.deserttelevision.com
SIC: **4833** Television broadcasting stations

(P-5852)
DISNEY ENTERPRISES INC
3800 W Alameda Ave # 565, Burbank (91505-4300)
PHONE................818 569-7500
Fax: 818 566-1358
Don Reis, *Branch Mgr*
Tricia Wilber, *Senior VP*
Tiffany Iino, *Vice Pres*
Becca Vodnoy, *Exec Dir*
Alice Cline, *Executive Asst*
EMP: 52 **Publicly Held**
SIC: **4833** Television broadcasting stations
HQ: Disney Enterprises, Inc.
  500 S Buena Vista St
  Burbank CA 91521
  818 560-1000

(P-5853)
ENCOMPASS DGTAL MDIA GROUP INC
2901 W Alameda Ave, Burbank (91505-4407)
PHONE................323 344-4500
Brian Stewart, *CFO*
Bill Tillson, *COO*
Scott Baskin, *Exec VP*
Chris Myers, *Exec VP*
Jim Schuster, *Exec VP*
EMP: 91
SALES (est): 9.5MM **Privately Held**
SIC: **4833** Television broadcasting stations

(P-5854)
ENTERTAINMENT & SPORTS TODAY
Also Called: Rakstar Production
2966 Wilshire Blvd Ste C, Los Angeles (90010-1128)
PHONE................213 388-9050
Fax: 213 388-9050
William Sturges, *CEO*
Frank Rakovic, *Vice Pres*
Yolanda Aguas, *CTO*
Martin Altonaga, *Director*
EMP: 100
SALES: 22MM **Privately Held**
SIC: **4833** 7812 Television broadcasting stations; video production

(P-5855)
ENTRAVSION COMMUNICATIONS CORP
Also Called: Univision 67
67 Garden Ct, Monterey (93940-5302)
PHONE................831 333-9736
Aaron Scoby, *Manager*
Eric Gams, *Sales Executive*
Jeanne Harrison, *Manager*
EMP: 50 **Publicly Held**
SIC: **4833** Television broadcasting stations
PA: Entravsion Communications Corporation
  2425 Olympic Blvd Ste 600
  Santa Monica CA 90404

(P-5856)
ENTRAVSION COMMUNICATIONS CORP
Also Called: K S S C - F M
5700 Wilshire Blvd # 250, Los Angeles (90036-3659)
PHONE................323 900-6100
Fax: 323 900-6200
Jeff Liberman, *President*

4833 - Television Broadcasting Stations County (P-5857)

PRODUCTS & SERVICES SECTION

EMP: 100 **Publicly Held**
SIC: **4833** 4832 Television broadcasting stations; radio broadcasting stations
PA: Entravision Communications Corporation
2425 Olympic Blvd Ste 600
Santa Monica CA 90404

(P-5857)
ENTRAVSION COMMUNICATIONS CORP
Also Called: Entravision Radio
1436 Auburn Blvd, Sacramento (95815-2745)
PHONE..................916 648-6029
Larry Lamansky, Manager
EMP: 50 **Publicly Held**
SIC: **4833** 4832 Television broadcasting stations; radio broadcasting stations
PA: Entravision Communications Corporation
2425 Olympic Blvd Ste 600
Santa Monica CA 90404

(P-5858)
ENTRAVSION COMMUNICATIONS CORP (PA)
2425 Olympic Blvd Ste 600, Santa Monica (90404-4030)
PHONE..................310 447-3870
Fax: 310 447-3899
Walter F Ulloa, Ch of Bd
Jeffery A Liberman, COO
Christopher T Young, CFO
Esteban Lopez Blanco, Officer
Mario M Carrera, Risk Mgmt Dir
EMP: 170
SQ FT: 16,000
SALES: 254.1MM **Publicly Held**
SIC: **4833** 4832 Television broadcasting stations; radio broadcasting stations

(P-5859)
ESTRELLA COMMUNICATIONS INC
Also Called: Kvea-Tv-Channel 52
3000 W Alameda Ave, Burbank (91523-0001)
PHONE..................818 260-5700
EMP: 90
SALES (est): 3.7MM
SALES (corp-wide): 68.7B **Publicly Held**
SIC: **4833**
HQ: Telemundo Communications Group, Inc.
2290 W 8th Ave
Hialeah FL 33010
305 884-8200

(P-5860)
EW SCRIPPS COMPANY
Also Called: Kgtv
4600 Air Way, San Diego (92102-2528)
PHONE..................619 237-1010
Fax: 619 262-1302
Derek Dalton, Vice Pres
Ed Quinn, Social Dir
Clayton Brace, General Mgr
Erwin Laquindanum, Info Tech Mgr
Benjamin Hayley, Engineer
EMP: 150
SALES (corp-wide): 715.6MM **Publicly Held**
WEB: www.rtv6radio.com
SIC: **4833** Television broadcasting stations
PA: The E W Scripps Company
312 Walnut St Ste 2800
Cincinnati OH 45202
513 977-3000

(P-5861)
FISHER COMMUNICATIONS INC
Also Called: Kbaktv
1901 Westwind Dr, Bakersfield (93301-3016)
PHONE..................661 327-7955
Teresa Burgess, Manager
Pete Capra, Engineer
Nancy Clarke, Program Dir
Joseph Berenholz, Director
EMP: 85
SALES (corp-wide): 1.9B **Publicly Held**
SIC: **4833** Television broadcasting stations

HQ: Fisher Communications, Inc.
140 4th Ave N Ste 500
Seattle WA 98109
206 404-7000

(P-5862)
FOX INC (DH)
Also Called: Home Entertainment Div
2121 Ave Of The Ste 1100, Los Angeles (90067)
P.O. Box 900, Beverly Hills (90213-0900)
PHONE..................310 369-1000
Fax: 310 369-4407
K Rupert Murdoch, Ch of Bd
Dan Bell, President
Mike Dunn, President
Robert Fusco, President
Jay Itzkowitz, President
▲ EMP: 2000
SQ FT: 25,000
SALES (est): 950.7MM
SALES (corp-wide): 27.3B **Publicly Held**
WEB: www.foxhome.com
SIC: **4833** 7812 Television broadcasting stations; motion picture production & distribution; motion picture production & distribution, television
HQ: 21st Century Fox America, Inc.
1211 Ave Of The Americas
New York NY 10036
212 852-7000

(P-5863)
FOX BROADCASTING COMPANY (DH)
10201 W Pico Blvd, Los Angeles (90064-2606)
P.O. Box 900, Beverly Hills (90213-0900)
PHONE..................310 369-1000
Fax: 310 369-1049
David F Devoe Jr, CEO
Nancy Utley, President
Joe Earley, COO
Del Mayberry, CFO
Tracy Dolgin, Exec VP
EMP: 200
SQ FT: 41,000
SALES (est): 151.2MM
SALES (corp-wide): 27.3B **Publicly Held**
WEB: www.wghp.com
SIC: **4833** Television broadcasting stations
HQ: Fox Entertainment Group, Inc.
2029 Century Park E # 1400
Los Angeles CA 90067
310 369-1000

(P-5864)
FOX TELEVISION STATIONS LLC (DH)
Also Called: K T T V-Fox 11
1999 S Bundy Dr, Los Angeles (90025-5203)
PHONE..................310 584-2000
Fax: 310 584-2217
Jim Burke, President
Roger Ailes, Ch of Bd
Tom Herwitz, President
Dennis Swanson, President
Brian Lewis, Exec VP
▲ EMP: 300
SALES (est): 445.7MM
SALES (corp-wide): 27.3B **Publicly Held**
WEB: www.foxtv.com
SIC: **4833** 7313 Television broadcasting stations; radio, television, publisher representatives
HQ: Fox Entertainment Group, Inc.
2029 Century Park E # 1400
Los Angeles CA 90067
310 369-1000

(P-5865)
FUEL TV
1440 S Sepulveda Blvd, Los Angeles (90025-3458)
PHONE..................310 444-8564
John Stouffer, Director
George Greenberg, Vice Pres
Sara Thompson, Manager
EMP: 75
SALES (est): 5.5MM **Privately Held**
SIC: **4833** Television broadcasting stations

(P-5866)
GULF- CALIFORNIA BROADCAST CO
Also Called: Kesq TV
31276 Dunham Way, Thousand Palms (92276-3310)
PHONE..................760 773-0342
Fax: 760 773-5128
John Kuenuke, President
James Hoetger, CTO
BJ Daup, Info Tech Dir
Mike Roberts, Engineer
Catherine Ferguson, Hum Res Coord
EMP: 116
SALES (est): 9.8MM
SALES (corp-wide): 166.6MM **Privately Held**
WEB: www.kesq.com
SIC: **4833** 7922 Television translator station; theatrical producers & services
PA: News-Press & Gazette Company Inc
825 Edmond St
Saint Joseph MO 64501
816 271-8500

(P-5867)
HEARST COMMUNICATIONS INC
Also Called: Kron-Tv
900 Front St, San Francisco (94111-1427)
P.O. Box 3412 (94109)
PHONE..................415 441-4444
Amy Mc Combs, Principal
Ben Schmid, Manager
EMP: 300
SALES (corp-wide): 419.4MM **Privately Held**
WEB: www.telegram.com
SIC: **4833** Television broadcasting stations
PA: Hearst Communications, Inc.
901 Mission St
San Francisco CA 94103
415 777-1111

(P-5868)
HEARST TELEVISION INC
Also Called: K S B W- T V
238 John St, Salinas (93901-3339)
P.O. Box 81651 (93912)
PHONE..................831 422-8206
Fax: 831 424-3750
Joseph W Heston, President
Brittany Nielsen, Producer
Wendy Hillan, Advt Staff
Ray Cleaveland, Director
Christopher Nolan, Director
EMP: 80
SQ FT: 31,681
SALES (corp-wide): 4.9B **Privately Held**
WEB: www.wbal.com
SIC: **4833** Television broadcasting stations
HQ: Hearst Television, Inc.
300 W 57th St
New York NY 10019
212 887-6800

(P-5869)
HERRING BROADCASTING COMPANY
Also Called: Wealthtv
4757 Morena Blvd, San Diego (92117-3462)
PHONE..................858 270-6900
Robert Herring Sr, President
Terry Wilson, Producer
Heather Hull, Director
EMP: 50
SQ FT: 40,000
SALES (est): 6.3MM **Privately Held**
SIC: **4833** Television broadcasting stations

(P-5870)
HERRING NETWORKS INC
Also Called: Awe
4757 Morena Blvd, San Diego (92117-3462)
PHONE..................858 270-6900
Charles P Herring, President
EMP: 130
SALES (est): 4.6MM **Privately Held**
SIC: **4833** Television broadcasting stations

(P-5871)
HULU LLC (PA)
2500 Broadway Fl 2, Santa Monica (90404-3065)
PHONE..................310 571-4700
Mike Hopkins, CEO
Jason Kilar, CEO
Tiffany Bollin, Vice Pres
Tim Connolly, Vice Pres
Chad Ho, Vice Pres
EMP: 108
SALES (est): 810MM **Privately Held**
WEB: www.hulu.com
SIC: **4833** 4813 Television translator station;

(P-5872)
IHEARTCOMMUNICATIONS INC
Also Called: Channel 47
4880 N 1st St, Fresno (93726-0514)
PHONE..................559 222-4302
Fax: 559 440-0097
Diana Wilkin-Zapata, General Mgr
Don Drilling, Coordinator
EMP: 85
SALES (corp-wide): 6.2B **Publicly Held**
SIC: **4833** Television broadcasting stations
HQ: Iheartcommunications, Inc.
200 E Basse Rd
San Antonio TX 78209
210 822-2828

(P-5873)
IHEARTCOMMUNICATIONS INC
3400 W Olive Ave Ste 550, Burbank (91505-5544)
PHONE..................818 846-0029
Fax: 818 955-8439
Greg Ashlock, Executive
Paul Wall, Program Dir
Kristin Osborn, Publisher
EMP: 81
SALES (corp-wide): 6.2B **Publicly Held**
WEB: www.kget.com
SIC: **4833** Television broadcasting stations
HQ: Iheartcommunications, Inc.
200 E Basse Rd
San Antonio TX 78209
210 822-2828

(P-5874)
INTERNATIONAL MEDIA GROUP INC
1990 S Bundy Dr Ste 850, Los Angeles (90025-5253)
PHONE..................310 478-1818
Peter Mathes, Ch of Bd
Beverly McMillan, Executive Asst
EMP: 80
SQ FT: 17,000
SALES (est): 3.8MM
SALES (corp-wide): 9.3MM **Privately Held**
SIC: **4833** Television broadcasting stations
PA: Asianmedia Group Llc
1990 S Bundy Dr Ste 850
Los Angeles CA 90025
310 478-1818

(P-5875)
ION MEDIA NETWORKS INC
Also Called: Kpxn-TV
2600 W Olive Ave Ste 900, Burbank (91505-4568)
PHONE..................818 953-7193
Tyra Donatto, Branch Mgr
Jorge Delgado, Vice Pres
EMP: 50
SALES (corp-wide): 246.4MM **Privately Held**
SIC: **4833** Television broadcasting stations
PA: Ion Media Networks, Inc.
601 Clearwater Park Rd
West Palm Beach FL 33401
561 659-4122

(P-5876)
JOURNAL BROADCAST GROUP INC
Also Called: Kmir-Tv6
72920 Parkview Dr, Palm Desert (92260-9357)
PHONE..................760 568-3636
Craig E Marrs, President
Gene Steinberg, General Mgr

PRODUCTS & SERVICES SECTION
4833 - Television Broadcasting Stations County (P-5898)

Sandie Ware, *Natl Sales Mgr*
Paul M Posen, *Agent*
EMP: 75
SALES (corp-wide): 677.1MM **Privately Held**
WEB: www.journalbroadcastgroup.com
SIC: 4833 Television broadcasting stations
HQ: Journal Broadcast Group, Inc.
720 E Capitol Dr
Milwaukee WI 53212
414 332-9611

(P-5877)
KAZA AZTECA AMERICA INC
1139 Grand Central Ave, Glendale (91201-2423)
PHONE................................818 241-5400
Eduardo Urdiola, *President*
Alejandra Wachler, *Manager*
EMP: 140
SALES (est): 9.7MM **Privately Held**
SIC: 4833 Television broadcasting stations

(P-5878)
KBAK TV CHANNEL 29 CBS
Also Called: Westwind Communications
1901 Westwind Dr, Bakersfield (93301-3016)
PHONE................................661 327-7955
Fax: 661 327-5603
Wayne Lansche, *Owner*
Gloria Bratton, *Webmaster*
EMP: 80
SALES (est): 1.9MM **Privately Held**
SIC: 4833 Television broadcasting stations

(P-5879)
KCETLINK (PA)
Also Called: Community TV Southern Cal
2900 W Alameda Ave # 600, Burbank (91505-4267)
PHONE................................747 201-5000
Al Jerome, *President*
Richard Cook, *Ch of Bd*
Brittany Piehl, *Associate Dir*
Amanda Martin, *Executive Asst*
Michael Feng, *Analyst*
EMP: 91
SQ FT: 50,000
SALES: 22.7MM **Privately Held**
SIC: 4833 Television broadcasting stations

(P-5880)
KFSN TELEVISION LLC
Also Called: ABC 30
1777 G St, Fresno (93706-1688)
PHONE................................559 442-1170
Dan Adams, *President*
Daniel Simms, *Controller*
EMP: 117
SQ FT: 26,962
SALES (est): 10.6MM **Publicly Held**
SIC: 4833 Television broadcasting stations
HQ: Disney Enterprises, Inc.
500 S Buena Vista St
Burbank CA 91521
818 560-1000

(P-5881)
KFTV
601 W Univision Plz, Fresno (93704-1092)
PHONE................................559 222-2121
Jose Elgorriaga, *General Mgr*
EMP: 85
SALES (est): 1.4MM **Privately Held**
SIC: 4833 Television broadcasting stations

(P-5882)
KGO TELEVISION INC
Also Called: Abc7 Broadcast Center
900 Front St, San Francisco (94111-1413)
PHONE................................415 954-7777
Fax: 415 954-7294
Bill Burton, *President*
Todd Farber, *Vice Pres*
David Rosati, *Vice Pres*
Rick Rubin, *Graphic Designe*
Raymond Lee, *Accounts Exec*
EMP: 230
SQ FT: 153,000
SALES (est): 25.8MM **Publicly Held**
WEB: www.kgoam810.com
SIC: 4833 Television broadcasting stations

HQ: Abc Holding Company Inc.
77 W 66th St Rm 100
New York NY 10023
212 456-7777

(P-5883)
KMPH FOX 26
Also Called: Pappas Telecasting Company
5111 E Mckinley Ave, Fresno (93727-2033)
PHONE................................559 255-2600
Fax: 559 456-1542
Harry Pappas, *Principal*
EMP: 170 **EST:** 1971
SALES (est): 7.6MM
SALES (corp-wide): 1.9B **Publicly Held**
WEB: www.kmph.com
SIC: 4833 Television broadcasting stations
PA: Sinclair Broadcast Group, Inc.
10706 Beaver Dam Rd
Hunt Valley MD 21030
410 568-1500

(P-5884)
KNET TV
5757 Wilshire Blvd # 470, Los Angeles (90036-5810)
PHONE................................323 469-5638
Fax: 323 469-2193
Larry Rogow, *Chairman*
EMP: 50
SALES (est): 855.1K **Privately Held**
SIC: 4833 Television broadcasting stations

(P-5885)
KOCE-TV FOUNDATION
Also Called: PBS SOCAL
3080 Bristol St Ste 400, Costa Mesa (92626-7335)
P.O. Box 25113, Santa Ana (92799-5113)
PHONE................................714 241-4100
Mel Rogers, *CEO*
Susan Truesdale, *VP*
Greg Hyska, *Info Tech Mgr*
EMP: 52
SALES: 15.7MM **Privately Held**
WEB: www.koce.org
SIC: 4833 Television broadcasting stations

(P-5886)
KQED INC (PA)
Also Called: KQED PUBLIC MEDIA
2601 Mariposa St, San Francisco (94110-1426)
P.O. Box 410865 (94141-0865)
PHONE................................415 864-2000
Fax: 415 553-2118
John Boland, *President*
James E Canals, *Vice Chairman*
Donald W Derheim, *COO*
Kevin E Martin, *COO*
Joseph Bruns, *CFO*
EMP: 258 **EST:** 1952
SQ FT: 75,000
SALES: 70MM **Privately Held**
WEB: www.kqed.org
SIC: 4833 4832 Television broadcasting stations; radio broadcasting stations

(P-5887)
KRCA TELEVISION INC
Also Called: Krca Tv-62
1845 W Empire Ave, Burbank (91504-3402)
PHONE................................818 563-5722
Jose Liberman, *President*
Wisdom W Lu, *CFO*
Leonard Liberman, *Exec VP*
Ozzie Mendoza, *Sales Mgr*
EMP: 130
SQ FT: 50,000
SALES (est): 5.4MM
SALES (corp-wide): 265MM **Privately Held**
SIC: 4833 7922 Television broadcasting stations; television program, including commercial producers
PA: Liberman Broadcasting Inc
1845 W Empire Ave
Burbank CA 91504
818 729-5300

(P-5888)
KSWB INC
Also Called: C W 5
7191 Engineer Rd, San Diego (92111-1406)
PHONE................................858 492-9269
Fax: 858 268-0401
Robert J Ramsey, *President*
Pat Mille, *Executive Asst*
Lindsay Nettinga, *Producer*
EMP: 56
SQ FT: 30,000
SALES (est): 6.6MM
SALES (corp-wide): 2B **Publicly Held**
WEB: www.tribune.com
SIC: 4833 Television broadcasting stations
PA: Tribune Media Company
435 N Michigan Ave Fl 2
Chicago IL 60611
212 210-2786

(P-5889)
KTSF CHANNEL 26
100 Valley Dr, Brisbane (94005-1318)
PHONE................................415 467-6397
Lincoln Howell, *CEO*
Yalek Huynh, *Editor*
EMP: 50
SALES (est): 5.6MM
SALES (corp-wide): 13.6MM **Privately Held**
WEB: www.ktsf.com
SIC: 4833 Television broadcasting stations
PA: Lincoln Broadcasting Company, A California Limited Partnership
100 Valley Dr
Brisbane CA 94005
415 508-1056

(P-5890)
KTVU PARTNERSHIP INC
Also Called: Ktvu Television Fox 2
2 Jack London Sq, Oakland (94607-3727)
PHONE................................510 834-1212
Fax: 510 272-9957
Murdock Lachlan, *CEO*
Brian Hastings, *Executive*
Diane Baldwin, *Business Dir*
◆ **EMP:** 230
SALES (est): 26.8MM
SALES (corp-wide): 27.3B **Publicly Held**
SIC: 4833 Television broadcasting stations
HQ: Fox Television Stations, Llc
1999 S Bundy Dr
Los Angeles CA 90025
310 584-2000

(P-5891)
KVIE INC (PA)
Also Called: KVIE CHANNEL 6
2030 W El Camino Ave # 100, Sacramento (95833-1867)
P.O. Box 6 (95812-0006)
PHONE................................916 929-5843
Fax: 916 929-7215
David Lowe, *CEO*
David Hosley, *President*
Julie Saqueton, *CFO*
Sonja Spowart, *CFO*
Mike Cappi, *Info Tech Dir*
EMP: 60
SQ FT: 69,000
SALES: 11.3MM **Privately Held**
WEB: www.capitolweek.com
SIC: 4833 Television broadcasting stations

(P-5892)
KXTV INC
Also Called: K X T V - T V Channel 10
400 Broadway, Stockton (95205)
PHONE................................209 463-8471
Fax: 209 463-8490
Tim Daly, *Principal*
EMP: 160
SALES (corp-wide): 3B **Publicly Held**
WEB: www.news10.net
SIC: 4833 Television broadcasting stations
HQ: Kxtv Inc
400 Broadway
Sacramento CA 95818
916 441-2345

(P-5893)
KXTV INC (HQ)
Also Called: K X T V Channel 10
400 Broadway, Sacramento (95818-2041)
PHONE................................916 441-2345
Fax: 916 321-3275
Risa Omega, *President*
Brad Wantt, *Admin Sec*
Terri Acevedo, *Traffic Mgr*
Elizabeth Bishop, *VP Mktg*
Laverne Blair, *Assistant*
EMP: 155
SQ FT: 29,000
SALES (est): 39.6MM
SALES (corp-wide): 3B **Publicly Held**
WEB: www.news10.net
SIC: 4833 Television broadcasting stations
PA: Tegna Inc.
7950 Jones Branch Dr
Mc Lean VA 22102
703 854-7000

(P-5894)
LIFETIME ENTRMT SVCS LLC
Also Called: Lifetime TV Network
2049 Century Park E # 840, Los Angeles (90067-3101)
PHONE................................310 556-7500
Fax: 310 772-0393
Maryann Harris, *General Mgr*
Dan Suratt, *Exec VP*
Tanya Lopez, *Senior VP*
Carla Cortis, *Vice Pres*
Marianne Goode, *Vice Pres*
EMP: 70
SALES (corp-wide): 693.8MM **Privately Held**
WEB: www.lifetimepress.com
SIC: 4833 5942 Television broadcasting stations; book stores
HQ: Lifetime Entertainment Services, Llc
235 E 45th St
New York NY 10017
212 424-7000

(P-5895)
LINCOLN TELEVISION INC
Also Called: Ktff
100 Valley Dr, Brisbane (94005-1318)
PHONE................................415 468-2626
Lillian Lincoln Howell, *President*
EMP: 60
SQ FT: 20,800
SALES (est): 2.9MM **Privately Held**
SIC: 4833 Television broadcasting stations

(P-5896)
M NETWORK TELEVISION INC
6007 Sepulveda Blvd, Van Nuys (91411-2502)
PHONE................................818 756-5150
Jonathan Murray, *President*
EMP: 50
SALES (est): 805.2K **Privately Held**
SIC: 4833 Television broadcasting stations

(P-5897)
MCKINNON PUBLISHING COMPANY
4575 Viewridge Ave, San Diego (92123-1623)
PHONE................................858 571-5151
Michael McKinnon, *President*
Richard Large, *Chief Engr*
EMP: 600
SALES (est): 14MM
SALES (corp-wide): 50.3MM **Privately Held**
WEB: www.kusi.com
SIC: 4833 Television broadcasting stations
HQ: Mckinnon Broadcasting Company
4575 Viewridge Ave
San Diego CA 92123
858 571-5151

(P-5898)
NBC SUBSIDIARY (KNBC-TV) LLC
100 Universal City Plz, Universal City (91608-1002)
PHONE................................818 684-5746
Steve Carlston, *President*
Fred Weeden, *Info Tech Mgr*
Bambi Tascarella, *Project Mgr*
Jenik Badalian, *Finance*

4833 - Television Broadcasting Stations County (P-5899)

PRODUCTS & SERVICES SECTION

Matt Edwards, *Producer*
EMP: 250
SALES (est): 4.5MM **Privately Held**
SIC: 4833 Television broadcasting stations

(P-5899)
NBC UNIVERSAL INC
3000 W Alameda Ave, Burbank (91523-0002)
PHONE..................818 260-5746
Fax: 818 840-3546
Greg Robinson, *Manager*
Scot Chastain, *Vice Pres*
Mark Fuhrman, *Vice Pres*
Kathy Jacquemin, *Vice Pres*
Stephen Boehm, *VP Info Sys*
EMP: 250
SALES (corp-wide): 74.5B **Publicly Held**
WEB: www.nbc.com
SIC: 4833 Television broadcasting stations
HQ: Nbc Universal, Llc
1221 Avenue Of The Americ
New York NY 10020
212 664-4444

(P-5900)
NBC UNIVERSAL INC
3000 W Alameda Ave Rm 320, Burbank (91523-0002)
PHONE..................818 840-4395
Gene Rek, *Branch Mgr*
EMP: 150
SALES (corp-wide): 74.5B **Publicly Held**
WEB: www.nbc.com
SIC: 4833 Television broadcasting stations
HQ: Nbc Universal, Llc
1221 Avenue Of The Americ
New York NY 10020
212 664-4444

(P-5901)
NEWPORT TELEVISION LLC
Kget-TV
2120 L St, Bakersfield (93301-2331)
PHONE..................661 283-1700
Fax: 661 283-1855
Sandy Dipasquale, *President*
EMP: 90
SALES (corp-wide): 48.9MM **Privately Held**
SIC: 4833 Television translator station
PA: Newport Television Llc
460 Nichols Rd Ste 250
Kansas City MO 64112
816 751-0200

(P-5902)
NEXSTAR BROADCASTING GROUP INC
Also Called: Ksee-TV 24
5035 E Mckinley Ave, Fresno (93727-1964)
PHONE..................559 222-2411
Fax: 559 454-2485
Larry Wills, *Senior VP*
EMP: 125
SALES (corp-wide): 896.3MM **Publicly Held**
SIC: 4833 Television broadcasting stations
PA: Nexstar Broadcasting Group, Inc.
545 E John Carpenter Fwy # 700
Irving TX 75062
972 373-8800

(P-5903)
NTN BUZZTIME INC (PA)
2231 Rutherford Rd # 200, Carlsbad (92008-8811)
PHONE..................760 438-7400
Fax: 760 438-3505
Ram Krishnan, *CEO*
Jeffrey A Berg, *Ch of Bd*
Allen Wolff, *CFO*
Sandra Gurrola, *VP Finance*
▲ **EMP:** 134
SQ FT: 28,000
SALES: 24.5MM **Publicly Held**
WEB: www.ntnwireless.com
SIC: 4833 4841 7372 Television broadcasting stations; direct broadcast satellite services (DBS); prepackaged software

(P-5904)
ODS TECHNOLOGIES LP
Also Called: Television Games Network
6701 Center Dr W Ste 160, Los Angeles (90045-1558)
PHONE..................310 242-9400
Fax: 310 242-9401
David Nathanson, *General Ptnr*
Tracy Beasley, *Vice Pres*
Steve Norry, *IT/INT Sup*
Mark Depping, *Opers Staff*
Stillman Kelly, *Senior Mgr*
EMP: 165
SQ FT: 20,000
SALES (est): 26.1MM **Privately Held**
SIC: 4833 7948 Television broadcasting stations; horses, racing
HQ: Betfair Group Limited
Waterfront
London W6 9H
208 834-8000

(P-5905)
PHOENIX SATELLITE TV US INC
3810 Durbin St, Baldwin Park (91706-6800)
PHONE..................626 388-1188
Fax: 626 388-1119
Xiaoyong Wu, *CEO*
Shing Ping, *CEO*
Glenn Lin, *Finance*
Michael Park, *Finance*
Karin Hsu, *Manager*
▲ **EMP:** 50
SQ FT: 18,000
SALES (est): 7.7MM **Privately Held**
WEB: www.pstv-us.net
SIC: 4833 Television translator station
HQ: Phoenix Satellite Television Holdings Limited
Tai Po Indl Est
Tai Po NT

(P-5906)
REVOLT MEDIA AND TV LLC
1800 N Highland Ave Fl 7, Los Angeles (90028-4522)
PHONE..................323 645-3000
Keith Clinkscales,
EMP: 120
SALES (est): 11MM
SALES (corp-wide): 26.2MM **Privately Held**
SIC: 4833 Television broadcasting stations
PA: Bad Boy Entertainment Holdings, Inc.
1710 Broadway Fl 2
New York NY 10019
212 381-2000

(P-5907)
S F BROADCASTING OF WISCONSIN
2425 Olympic Blvd, Santa Monica (90404-4030)
PHONE..................310 586-2410
EMP: 151
SALES (est): 2.9MM
SALES (corp-wide): 3.2B **Publicly Held**
SIC: 4833
PA: Iac/Interactivecorp
555 W 18th St
New York NY 10011
212 314-7300

(P-5908)
SACRAMENTO TELEVISION STNS INC (DH)
Also Called: Kmax Tv
2713 Kovr Dr, West Sacramento (95605-1600)
PHONE..................916 374-1452
Fax: 916 921-1018
Peter Dunn, *CEO*
Mark Allen, *Social Dir*
Donna Sehablague, *Engineer*
Ken Cobberhad, *Business Mgr*
Charlise Silva, *Credit Staff*
EMP: 152
SQ FT: 40,000
SALES (est): 59.2MM
SALES (corp-wide): 13.9B **Publicly Held**
SIC: 4833 Television broadcasting stations

HQ: Cbs Corporation
51 W 52nd St Bsmt 1
New York NY 10019
212 975-4321

(P-5909)
SAN MATEO COUNTY COMMUNITY
Also Called: Kcsm TV & Radio
1700 W Hillsdale Blvd, San Mateo (94402-3757)
PHONE..................650 574-6586
Fax: 650 524-6975
Marilyn Lawrence, *Manager*
Carolina Avalos, *Office Admin*
Jiaolan Bu, *Technical Staff*
Michele Muller, *Engineer*
Alisa Clancy, *Opers Staff*
EMP: 51
SALES (corp-wide): 57.6MM **Privately Held**
WEB: www.smcccd.cc.ca.us
SIC: 4833 4832 Television broadcasting stations; radio broadcasting stations
PA: San Mateo County Community College District Financing Corporation
3401 Csm Dr
San Mateo CA 94402
650 358-6742

(P-5910)
SITV INC
Also Called: Nuvo Tv
700 N Central Ave Ste 600, Glendale (91203-3438)
PHONE..................323 317-9534
Michael Schwimmer, *CEO*
Abilia Barraza, *Opers Staff*
Edward Mateo, *Facilities Mgr*
Marcus Best, *Director*
EMP: 62
SALES (est): 3.1MM
SALES (corp-wide): 21.1MM **Privately Held**
SIC: 4833 Television broadcasting stations
PA: Fuse Media Inc.
700 N Central Ave Fl 6
Glendale CA 91203
323 256-8900

(P-5911)
SMITH BROADCASTING GROUP INC
Also Called: Keyt Television
730 Miramonte Dr, Santa Barbara (93109-1417)
P.O. Box 729 (93102-0729)
PHONE..................805 882-3933
Fax: 805 882-3934
Michael Granados, *General Mgr*
Gerry Fall, *Manager*
EMP: 85
SALES (corp-wide): 14MM **Privately Held**
SIC: 4833 7313 Television broadcasting stations; television & radio time sales
PA: Smith Broadcasting Group, Inc
2315 Red Rose Way
Santa Barbara CA 93109
805 965-0400

(P-5912)
STATION VENTURE OPERATIONS LP
Also Called: NBC 7/Channel 39
225 Broadway 100-300, San Diego (92101-5005)
PHONE..................619 578-0233
Fax: 619 578-0225
Dick Kelley, *General Mgr*
Greg Dawson, *Vice Pres*
Jackie Bradford, *General Mgr*
Ljupzo Sidanovski, *Finance*
Patricia Casillas, *Traffic Mgr*
EMP: 76 **EST:** 1967
SQ FT: 23,000
SALES (est): 90.6K
SALES (corp-wide): 74.5B **Publicly Held**
WEB: www.nbc.com
SIC: 4833 Television broadcasting stations
HQ: Nbc Universal, Llc
1221 Avenue Of The Americ
New York NY 10020
212 664-4444

(P-5913)
STATIONS GROUP LLC
Also Called: Azteca America
1139 Grand Central Ave, Glendale (91201-2423)
PHONE..................818 247-0400
Manuel Abud, *Principal*
EMP: 65
SALES (est): 1.6MM **Privately Held**
SIC: 4833 Television broadcasting stations
HQ: Azteca International Corporation
1139 Grand Central Ave
Glendale CA 91201
818 247-0400

(P-5914)
TELEMUNDO OF NORTHERN CAL
Also Called: Ksts Channel 48
2450 N 1st St, San Jose (95131-1002)
PHONE..................408 432-6221
Eddy Dominguez, *President*
Alberto Martinez, *Vice Pres*
Kenneth E Elkin Jr, *IT/INT Sup*
Ken Elkin, *Business Mgr*
Cesar Angulo, *Director*
EMP: 80
SQ FT: 16,000
SALES (est): 2.3MM
SALES (corp-wide): 74.5B **Publicly Held**
SIC: 4833 Television broadcasting stations
HQ: Telemundo Communications Group, Inc.
2290 W 8th Ave
Hialeah FL 33010
305 884-8200

(P-5915)
TIME WARNER CABLE ENTPS LLC
5432 W 100 2nd St, Los Angeles (90045)
PHONE..................818 972-0328
Paul Saccone, *General Mgr*
EMP: 69
SALES (corp-wide): 9.7MM **Publicly Held**
SIC: 4833 Television broadcasting stations
HQ: Time Warner Cable Enterprises Llc
60 Columbus Cir Fl 17
New York NY 10023
877 495-9201

(P-5916)
TRINITY BRDCSTG NETWRK INC
Also Called: Ktbo-Tv
2442 Michelle Dr, Tustin (92780-7015)
PHONE..................714 832-2950
Paul F Crouch, *President*
EMP: 150
SALES: 6.3MM
SALES (corp-wide): 141.2MM **Privately Held**
SIC: 4833 Television broadcasting stations
PA: Trinity Christian Center Of Santa Ana, Inc.
2442 Michelle Dr
Tustin CA 92780
714 665-3619

(P-5917)
TRINITY CHRISTIAN CENTER OF SA (PA)
Also Called: Trinity Broadcasting Network
2442 Michelle Dr, Tustin (92780-7015)
P.O. Box A, Santa Ana (92711-2101)
PHONE..................714 665-3619
Fax: 714 665-2191
Paul F Crouch, *President*
John Casoria, *Treasurer*
Margie Tuccillo, *Treasurer*
Norman G Juggert, *Corp Secy*
Colby May, *Bd of Directors*
▲ **EMP:** 200
SQ FT: 20,000
SALES: 141.2MM **Privately Held**
WEB: www.paulcrouch.com
SIC: 4833 7922 Television broadcasting stations; television program, including commercial producers

(P-5918)
TV 36
Also Called: Kicu Tv 36
2102 Commerce Dr, San Jose (95131-1804)
PHONE..................408 953-3636

▲ = Import ▼ = Export
◆ = Import/Export

PRODUCTS & SERVICES SECTION

4841 - Cable & Other Pay TV Svcs County (P-5938)

Tom Raponi, *General Mgr*
Robert Martinez, *Manager*
EMP: 50
SQ FT: 25,000
SALES (est): 2.8MM **Privately Held**
SIC: 4833 Television broadcasting stations

(P-5919)
TWENTIETH CENTURY FOX HOME E (DH)
10201 W Pico Blvd, Los Angeles (90064-2651)
PHONE 310 369-1000
K Rupert Murdoch,
Dean Hallett, *CFO*
Vincent Marcais, *Exec VP*
Joanne Burns, *Senior VP*
Yoni Cohen, *Senior VP*
EMP: 1000
SQ FT: 25,000
SALES (est): 312.3MM
SALES (corp-wide): 27.3B **Publicly Held**
SIC: 4833 Television broadcasting stations
HQ: Twentieth Century Fox Film Corporation
10201 W Pico Blvd
Los Angeles CA 90064
310 369-1000

(P-5920)
UNIVISION COMMUNICATIONS INC
1710 Arden Way, Sacramento (95815-5008)
PHONE 916 927-2041
Fax: 916 614-1904
Diego T Ruiz, *Manager*
Gustavo Ortiz, *Social Dir*
Bob Fitzhugh, *Chief Engr*
Ricardo Sigala, *Human Resources*
Steve Stuck, *Sales Mgr*
EMP: 75
SALES (corp-wide): 2.5B **Privately Held**
WEB: www.univision.com
SIC: 4833 Television broadcasting stations
HQ: Univision Communications Inc.
605 3rd Ave Fl 12
New York NY 10158
212 455-5200

(P-5921)
UNIVISION TELEVISION GROUP INC
601 W Univision Plz, Fresno (93704-1092)
PHONE 559 222-2121
Maria Guttierrez, *Branch Mgr*
Angelica Freitas, *Admin Asst*
Alan Chapman, *Accountant*
Monserrat Gallegoz, *Production*
Vladimir Araya, *Producer*
EMP: 65
SALES (corp-wide): 2.5B **Privately Held**
WEB: www.univison.net
SIC: 4833 Television broadcasting stations
HQ: Univision Television Group, Inc.
500 Frank W Burr Blvd # 20
Teaneck NJ 07666
201 287-4141

(P-5922)
UNIVISION TELEVISION GROUP INC
Also Called: Kdtv
50 Fremont St Fl 41, San Francisco (94105-2240)
PHONE 415 538-8000
Fax: 415 538-8053
Marcela Medina, *Principal*
Sarah Squiers, *Vice Pres*
Mahelda Rodriguez, *Producer*
Jose Tello, *Editor*
EMP: 70
SALES (corp-wide): 2.5B **Privately Held**
WEB: www.univison.net
SIC: 4833 Television broadcasting stations
HQ: Univision Television Group, Inc.
500 Frank W Burr Blvd # 20
Teaneck NJ 07666
201 287-4141

(P-5923)
UNIVISION TELEVISION GROUP INC
5770 Ruffin Rd, San Diego (92123-1013)
PHONE 858 576-1919

Philip Wilkinson, *Manager*
Jesus Mendoza, *Executive*
EMP: 50
SALES (corp-wide): 2.5B **Privately Held**
WEB: www.univison.net
SIC: 4833 Television broadcasting stations
HQ: Univision Television Group, Inc.
500 Frank W Burr Blvd # 20
Teaneck NJ 07666
201 287-4141

(P-5924)
WALT DISNEY COMPANY
532 Paula Ave, Glendale (91201-2328)
PHONE 818 544-5009
Won Lee, *Info Tech Mgr*
Dan McBrearty, *Project Mgr*
Art Lopez, *Technical Staff*
Aric Bellman, *Prdtn Mgr*
Chris Bodden, *Prdtn Mgr*
EMP: 331 **Publicly Held**
SIC: 4833 Television broadcasting stations
PA: The Walt Disney Company
500 S Buena Vista St
Burbank CA 91521

(P-5925)
WALT DISNEY COMPANY
914 N Victory Blvd, Burbank (91502-1632)
PHONE 818 295-3134
EMP: 331 **Publicly Held**
SIC: 4833 4841 7011 7996 Television broadcasting stations; cable television services; resort hotel; amusement parks; motion picture & video production; books; publishing only
PA: The Walt Disney Company
500 S Buena Vista St
Burbank CA 91521

(P-5926)
WALT DISNEY COMPANY
Also Called: Lighting Department
121 E Buena Vista, Burbank (91521-0001)
PHONE 818 560-1268
Anthony Orefice, *Branch Mgr*
Nikki Reed, *Senior VP*
Cyrus Hoomani, *Manager*
Hsin-Yi Lin, *Manager*
Joe Stewart, *Manager*
EMP: 100 **Publicly Held**
SIC: 4833 Television broadcasting stations
PA: The Walt Disney Company
500 S Buena Vista St
Burbank CA 91521

(P-5927)
WALT DISNEY COMPANY
500 S Buena Vista St, Burbank (91521-0007)
PHONE 818 460-6655
EMP: 331 **Publicly Held**
SIC: 4833 4841 7011 7996 Television broadcasting stations; cable television services; resort hotel; amusement parks; motion picture & video production; books; publishing only
PA: The Walt Disney Company
500 S Buena Vista St
Burbank CA 91521

(P-5928)
WALT DISNEY COMPANY
Walt Disney Studios HM Entrmt
500 S Buena Vista St, Burbank (91521-0007)
PHONE 818 560-1000
EMP: 1000 **Publicly Held**
SIC: 4833 Television broadcasting stations
PA: The Walt Disney Company
500 S Buena Vista St
Burbank CA 91521

(P-5929)
WALT DISNEY COMPANY (PA)
500 S Buena Vista St, Burbank (91521-0007)
PHONE 818 560-1000
Fax: 818 560-1035
Robert A Iger, *Ch of Bd*
Paul Candland, *President*

Leslie Ferraro, *President*
Thomas Staggs, *COO*
Christine M McCarthy, *CFO*
◆ **EMP:** 6000
SALES: 52.4B **Publicly Held**
WEB: www.corporate.disney.go.com
SIC: 4833 4841 7011 7996 Television broadcasting stations; cable television services; resort hotel; amusement parks; motion picture & video production; books; publishing only

(P-5930)
WALT DISNEY COMPANY
Also Called: Walt Disney Studios
350 S Buena Vista St, Burbank (91521-0004)
PHONE 818 560-1000
Fax: 818 845-5924
Walter Disney, *Owner*
Eddie Drake, *Vice Pres*
Eric Handler, *Comms Dir*
Ewout Schneider, *Exec Dir*
Felicita Giannavola, *Meeting Planner*
EMP: 331 **Publicly Held**
SIC: 4833 4841 7011 7996 Television broadcasting stations; cable television services; resort hotel; amusement parks
PA: The Walt Disney Company
500 S Buena Vista St
Burbank CA 91521

(P-5931)
YOUNG BRDCSTG OF SAN FRANCISCO
Also Called: Kron-TV
900 Front St, San Francisco (94111-1427)
P.O. Box 3412 (94109)
PHONE 415 441-4444
Deb McDermot, *President*
Henry Tenenbaum, *Info Tech Dir*
Debra Chambers, *Finance Dir*
Angela Fawcett, *Manager*
EMP: 150
SALES (est): 13.4MM
SALES (corp-wide): 312.2MM **Privately Held**
WEB: www.kron-tv.com
SIC: 4833 Television broadcasting stations
PA: Young Broadcasting, Llc
599 Lexington Ave
New York NY 10022
517 372-8282

4841 Cable & Other Pay TV Svcs

(P-5932)
A&E TELEVISION NETWORKS LLC
2049 Century Park E # 800, Los Angeles (90067-3101)
PHONE 310 201-6015
Jenny Barmach, *Branch Mgr*
Ashley Mettille, *Hum Res Coord*
Cishawn Randolph, *Human Resources*
Kristi Alires, *Director*
Steven Goore, *Account Dir*
EMP: 208
SALES (corp-wide): 693.8MM **Privately Held**
SIC: 4841 Cable television services
PA: A&E Television Networks, Llc
235 E 45th St Frnt C
New York NY 10017
212 210-1400

(P-5933)
ABS-CBN INTERNATIONAL (DH)
150 Shoreline Dr, Redwood City (94065-1400)
PHONE 800 527-2820
Fax: 650 508-6001
Eugenio Lopez III, *CEO*
Raffy Lopez, *COO*
Anna K Rodriguez, *CFO*
Olivia De Jesus, *Bd of Directors*
Pia Lopezbanos, *Top Exec*
▲ **EMP:** 140
SQ FT: 12,000

SALES (est): 103.3MM
SALES (corp-wide): 9.2MM **Privately Held**
WEB: www.abs-cbni.com
SIC: 4841 7822 Cable & other pay television services; television & video tape distribution
HQ: Abs-Cbn Interactive, Inc.
9th Floor Eugenio Lopez Jr., Communication Center
Quezon City
241 111-67

(P-5934)
ACCESS CONTROL CENTRES INC
6450 Sequence Dr, San Diego (92121-4376)
PHONE 858 455-1500
Richard C Smith, *President*
EMP: 60
SALES (est): 1.9MM **Privately Held**
WEB: www.gi.com
SIC: 4841 Cable & other pay television services
HQ: Motorola Mobility Llc
222 Merchandise Mart Plz
Chicago IL 60654

(P-5935)
BDR INDUSTRIES INC (PA)
Also Called: R N D Enterprises
820 E Avenue L12, Lancaster (93535-5403)
PHONE 661 940-8554
Fax: 661 940-0388
Scott Riddle, *President*
Edward Donovan, *Vice Pres*
Linda Franklin, *Executive*
▲ **EMP:** 95
SQ FT: 30,000
SALES (est): 21.9MM **Privately Held**
WEB: www.rndcable.com
SIC: 4841 Cable television services

(P-5936)
BRIGHT HOUSE NETWORKS LLC
4450 California Ave Ste A, Bakersfield (93309-1196)
PHONE 661 634-2200
Fax: 661 395-3385
Joseph Schoenstein, *Manager*
Rich Cozzi, *Vice Pres*
Scott Laris, *Vice Pres*
Jason Norton, *Network Enginr*
Alessandro Spagna, *Network Enginr*
EMP: 100
SALES (corp-wide): 9.7MM **Publicly Held**
SIC: 4841 Cable television services
HQ: Bright House Networks, Llc
5823 Widewaters Pkwy # 2
East Syracuse NY 13057
315 438-4100

(P-5937)
C V PRODUCTIONS INC
Also Called: Dish Network
812 N Broadway, Santa Ana (92701-3424)
P.O. Box 1137 (92702-1137)
PHONE 714 352-4446
Fax: 714 245-9480
Carlos Valdez, *President*
Luis Ajuilar, *Vice Pres*
Valdez Carlos, *Vice Pres*
EMP: 60 **EST:** 1998
SALES (est): 4.1MM **Privately Held**
WEB: www.beyondmicro.com
SIC: 4841 Direct broadcast satellite services (DBS)

(P-5938)
CABLE DOCTORS INC
8677 Villa La Jolla Dr, La Jolla (92037-2354)
PHONE 619 595-4650
Morton Carey, *President*
EMP: 78
SALES (est): 1.5MM **Privately Held**
SIC: 4841 Cable television services

4841 - Cable & Other Pay TV Svcs County (P-5939)

(P-5939)
CALIFORNIA BROADCAST CTR LLC
3800 Via Oro Ave, Long Beach (90810-1866)
PHONE..................310 233-2425
Bruce Churchill, *CEO*
Joyce Smith, *Supervisor*
EMP: 200
SALES (est): 10.7MM
SALES (corp-wide): 146.8B **Publicly Held**
SIC: 4841 Cable & other pay television services
HQ: Directv Latin America, Llc
1 Rockefeller Plz
New York NY 10020
212 205-0500

(P-5940)
CHARTER CMMNCTONS OPRATING LLC
12180 Ridgecrest Rd # 102, Victorville (92395-7798)
PHONE..................760 452-8609
Toll Free:......................877 -
Robert Brown, *Branch Mgr*
EMP: 100
SALES (corp-wide): 9.7MM **Publicly Held**
WEB: www.charter.ordercableonline.com
SIC: 4841 Cable & other pay television services
HQ: Charter Communications Operating Llc
12405 Powerscourt Dr
Saint Louis MO 63131
314 965-0555

(P-5941)
CHARTER CMMNCTONS OPRATING LLC
4031 Via Oro Ave, Long Beach (90810-1458)
PHONE..................310 971-4001
Fax: 310 971-4093
Eric Brown, *Vice Pres*
EMP: 300
SALES (corp-wide): 9.7MM **Publicly Held**
WEB: www.charter.ordercableonline.com
SIC: 4841 7371 Cable television services; custom computer programming services
HQ: Charter Communications Operating Llc
12405 Powerscourt Dr
Saint Louis MO 63131
314 965-0555

(P-5942)
CHARTER CMMNCTONS OPRATING LLC
5797 Eastside Rd, Redding (96001-4548)
PHONE..................530 241-7352
Marcie Farmer, *Manager*
EMP: 50
SALES (corp-wide): 9.7MM **Publicly Held**
WEB: www.charter.ordercableonline.com
SIC: 4841 Cable & other pay television services
HQ: Charter Communications Operating Llc
12405 Powerscourt Dr
Saint Louis MO 63131
314 965-0555

(P-5943)
CNN AMERICA INC
6430 W Sunset Blvd # 300, Los Angeles (90028-7901)
PHONE..................323 993-5000
Fax: 323 993-5081
Suzanne Spurgeon, *Principal*
Jason Hochheimer, *Director*
Stella Chan, *Editor*
EMP: 80
SALES (corp-wide): 28.1B **Publicly Held**
SIC: 4841 Cable television services
HQ: Cnn America Inc
190 Marietta St Nw 12s
Atlanta GA 30303
404 827-1700

(P-5944)
COMCA SPORT NET BAY AREA
360 3rd St Fl 2, San Francisco (94107-2154)
PHONE..................415 896-2557
Richard Cotton, *Mng Member*
National Broadcasting, *General Ptnr*
G C Broadc, *Director*
EMP: 150
SALES (est): 9.3MM
SALES (corp-wide): 74.5B **Publicly Held**
WEB: www.ifc.com
SIC: 4841 Cable television services
HQ: Nbcuniversal Media, Llc
30 Rockefeller Plz Fl 2
New York NY 10112
212 664-4444

(P-5945)
COMCAST CALIFORNIA IX INC
1111 Andersen Dr, San Rafael (94901-5394)
PHONE..................215 286-3345
Paul Gibson, *Vice Pres*
Mary Cane, *Legal Staff*
EMP: 99
SALES: 950K **Privately Held**
SIC: 4841 Cable & other pay television services

(P-5946)
COMCAST CBLE CMMUNICATIONS LLC
6320 Arizona Cir, Los Angeles (90045-1202)
PHONE..................310 216-3500
Donna Delaney, *Manager*
Ron Morin, *Manager*
EMP: 50
SALES (corp-wide): 74.5B **Publicly Held**
WEB: www.comcastmediacenter.com
SIC: 4841 Cable television services
HQ: Comcast Cable Communications, Llc
1701 John Fk Blvd
Philadelphia PA 19103
215 665-1700

(P-5947)
COMCAST CBLE CMMUNICATIONS LLC
Also Called: Comcast West Bay Area
1485 Bay Shore Blvd # 125, San Francisco (94124-3002)
PHONE..................415 715-0524
EMP: 101
SALES (corp-wide): 74.5B **Publicly Held**
WEB: www.comcastmediacenter.com
SIC: 4841 Cable television services
HQ: Comcast Cable Communications, Llc
1701 John Fk Blvd
Philadelphia PA 19103
215 665-1700

(P-5948)
COMCAST CBLE CMMUNICATIONS LLC
1031 N Plaza Dr, Visalia (93291-9473)
PHONE..................559 253-4050
Tony Queasada, *Principal*
EMP: 101
SALES (corp-wide): 74.5B **Publicly Held**
SIC: 4841 Cable television services
HQ: Comcast Cable Communications, Llc
1701 John Fk Blvd
Philadelphia PA 19103
215 665-1700

(P-5949)
COMCAST CBLE CMMUNICATIONS LLC
6357 Arizona Cir, Los Angeles (90045-1201)
PHONE..................310 216-3686
Dave Scharrer, *Manager*
EMP: 101
SALES (corp-wide): 74.5B **Publicly Held**
WEB: www.comcastmediacenter.com
SIC: 4841 Cable & other pay television services
HQ: Comcast Cable Communications, Llc
1701 John Fk Blvd
Philadelphia PA 19103
215 665-1700

(P-5950)
COMCAST CORPORATION
2860 Gateway Oaks Dr, Sacramento (95833-3508)
PHONE..................916 459-2964
Bruce W Quick, *Manager*
Jason Campbell, *Finance*
Ann Scott, *Manager*
Danita Adams, *Supervisor*
EMP: 56
SALES (corp-wide): 74.5B **Publicly Held**
SIC: 4841 Cable television services
PA: Comcast Corporation
1701 Jfk Blvd
Philadelphia PA 19103
215 286-1700

(P-5951)
COMCAST CORPORATION
2166 Rheem Dr, Pleasanton (94588-2775)
PHONE..................925 249-2060
Brenda Gisi, *Branch Mgr*
Brad Williamson, *Technician*
Brian B California, *Engineer*
EMP: 57
SALES (corp-wide): 74.5B **Publicly Held**
WEB: www.comcast.com
SIC: 4841 Cable television services
PA: Comcast Corporation
1701 Jfk Blvd
Philadelphia PA 19103
215 286-1700

(P-5952)
COMCAST CORPORATION
860 Stanton Rd, Burlingame (94010-1404)
PHONE..................650 689-5392
Jim Howell, *Accounts Exec*
EMP: 57
SALES (corp-wide): 74.5B **Publicly Held**
SIC: 4841 Cable television services
PA: Comcast Corporation
1701 Jfk Blvd
Philadelphia PA 19103
215 286-1700

(P-5953)
COMCAST CORPORATION
1 La Avanzada St Rm 111, San Francisco (94131-1124)
PHONE..................415 665-5507
Bob Dichappari, *Branch Mgr*
EMP: 57
SALES (corp-wide): 74.5B **Publicly Held**
WEB: www.comcast.com
SIC: 4841 Cable & other pay television services
PA: Comcast Corporation
1701 Jfk Blvd
Philadelphia PA 19103
215 286-1700

(P-5954)
COMCAST CORPORATION
166 Watson Ln, American Canyon (94503-9632)
PHONE..................707 266-7584
EMP: 57
SALES (corp-wide): 74.5B **Publicly Held**
SIC: 4841 Cable & other pay television services
PA: Comcast Corporation
1701 Jfk Blvd
Philadelphia PA 19103
215 286-1700

(P-5955)
COMCAST CORPORATION
Also Called: A Comcast
3801 Pelandale Ave A11, Modesto (95356-8303)
PHONE..................209 222-3656
Luis Gaytan, *Manager*
Anthony Castelli, *Supervisor*
EMP: 56
SALES (corp-wide): 74.5B **Publicly Held**
SIC: 4841 Cable & other pay television services
PA: Comcast Corporation
1701 Jfk Blvd
Philadelphia PA 19103
215 286-1700

(P-5956)
COMCAST CORPORATION
221 2nd St, Sausalito (94965-2429)
PHONE..................415 367-4153
EMP: 55
SALES (corp-wide): 74.5B **Publicly Held**
SIC: 4841 Cable television services
PA: Comcast Corporation
1701 Jfk Blvd
Philadelphia PA 19103
215 286-1700

(P-5957)
COMCAST CORPORATION
23525 Clawiter Rd, Hayward (94545-1328)
PHONE..................510 266-3200
Simon Chung, *Software Engr*
William Olson, *Engineer*
EMP: 57
SALES (corp-wide): 74.5B **Publicly Held**
SIC: 4841 Cable television services
PA: Comcast Corporation
1701 Jfk Blvd
Philadelphia PA 19103
215 286-1700

(P-5958)
COMCAST CORPORATION
1000 Van Ness Ave, San Francisco (94109-6971)
PHONE..................415 255-5644
EMP: 56
SALES (corp-wide): 74.5B **Publicly Held**
SIC: 4841 Cable television services
PA: Comcast Corporation
1701 Jfk Blvd
Philadelphia PA 19103
215 286-1700

(P-5959)
COMCAST CORPORATION
425 Corona Mall, Corona (92879-1419)
PHONE..................951 268-9378
Mark Hooper, *Principal*
EMP: 57
SALES (corp-wide): 74.5B **Publicly Held**
SIC: 4841 Cable & other pay television services
PA: Comcast Corporation
1701 Jfk Blvd
Philadelphia PA 19103
215 286-1700

(P-5960)
COMCAST CORPORATION
Also Called: Comcast Cable
4991 E Mckinley Ave, Fresno (93727-1900)
PHONE..................559 389-7251
EMP: 56
SALES (corp-wide): 74.5B **Publicly Held**
SIC: 4841 Cable television services
PA: Comcast Corporation
1701 Jfk Blvd
Philadelphia PA 19103
215 286-1700

(P-5961)
COMCAST CORPORATION
Also Called: Comcast Cable
1300 W Yosemite Ave, Madera (93637-6320)
PHONE..................559 474-4194
EMP: 56
SALES (corp-wide): 74.5B **Publicly Held**
SIC: 4841 Cable television services
PA: Comcast Corporation
1701 Jfk Blvd
Philadelphia PA 19103
215 286-1700

(P-5962)
COMCAST CORPORATION
Also Called: Comcast Cable
2414 E Acacia Ave, Fresno (93726-0303)
PHONE..................559 718-9917
EMP: 56
SALES (corp-wide): 74.5B **Publicly Held**
SIC: 4841 Cable television services
PA: Comcast Corporation
1701 Jfk Blvd
Philadelphia PA 19103
215 286-1700

(P-5963)
COMCAST CORPORATION
Also Called: Comcast Cable
810 Randolph St, NAPA (94559-2911)
PHONE..................707 266-7012
Timothy J Thorp, *Technician*
EMP: 56
SALES (corp-wide): 74.5B **Publicly Held**
SIC: 4841 Cable television services
PA: Comcast Corporation
1701 Jfk Blvd
Philadelphia PA 19103
215 286-1700

PRODUCTS & SERVICES SECTION

4841 - Cable & Other Pay TV Svcs County (P-5986)

(P-5964)
COMCAST CORPORATION
Also Called: Comcast Cable
415 River St, Santa Cruz (95060-2724)
PHONE..............................831 316-9258
EMP: 56
SALES (corp-wide): 74.5B **Publicly Held**
SIC: 4841 Cable television services
PA: Comcast Corporation
    1701 Jfk Blvd
    Philadelphia PA 19103
    215 286-1700

(P-5965)
COMCAST CORPORATION
Also Called: Comcast Cable
6500 47th St, Sacramento (95823-1273)
PHONE..............................916 520-6813
EMP: 56
SALES (corp-wide): 74.5B **Publicly Held**
SIC: 4841 Cable television services
PA: Comcast Corporation
    1701 Jfk Blvd
    Philadelphia PA 19103
    215 286-1700

(P-5966)
COMCAST CORPORATION
Also Called: Comcast Cable
203 N 27th St, San Jose (95116-1121)
PHONE..............................408 216-2878
EMP: 56
SALES (corp-wide): 74.5B **Publicly Held**
SIC: 4841 Cable television services
PA: Comcast Corporation
    1701 Jfk Blvd
    Philadelphia PA 19103
    215 286-1700

(P-5967)
COMCAST CORPORATION
Also Called: Advertising Department
5462 E Del Amo Blvd 239, Long Beach (90808-1122)
PHONE..............................800 240-3640
EMP: 57
SALES (corp-wide): 74.5B **Publicly Held**
SIC: 4841 4813 7812 7996 Cable television services; subscription television services; telephone communication, except radio; ; ; ; television film production; theme park, amusement
PA: Comcast Corporation
    1701 Jfk Blvd
    Philadelphia PA 19103
    215 286-1700

(P-5968)
COMCAST CORPORATION
550 Garcia Ave, Pittsburg (94565-4901)
PHONE..............................925 432-0500
Dee Trotta, *Principal*
Patrick Earl, *Engineer*
Greg McEntee, *Director*
Lesia Johnson, *Manager*
William Crawford, *Supervisor*
EMP: 81
SALES (corp-wide): 74.5B **Publicly Held**
WEB: www.comcast.com
SIC: 4841 Cable television services
PA: Comcast Corporation
    1701 Jfk Blvd
    Philadelphia PA 19103
    215 286-1700

(P-5969)
COMCAST CORPORATION
1500 Auto Center Dr, Ontario (91761-2243)
PHONE..............................909 390-4777
Kathy Ouilleptte, *General Mgr*
EMP: 57
SALES (corp-wide): 74.5B **Publicly Held**
WEB: www.comcast.com
SIC: 4841 Cable television services
PA: Comcast Corporation
    1701 Jfk Blvd
    Philadelphia PA 19103
    215 286-1700

(P-5970)
COMCAST CORPORATION
6505 Tam O Shanter Dr, Stockton (95210-3349)
PHONE..............................209 955-6521
Eileen Martin, *Manager*
Roberto Gonzalez, *Planning*
Richard Pattee, *Network Enginr*
Nedinette Madarang, *Human Resources*
Donna Perry, *Cust Mgr*
EMP: 57
SALES (corp-wide): 74.5B **Publicly Held**
WEB: www.comcast.com
SIC: 4841 Cable & other pay television services
PA: Comcast Corporation
    1701 Jfk Blvd
    Philadelphia PA 19103
    215 286-1700

(P-5971)
COMCAST CORPORATION
900 N Cahuenga Blvd, Los Angeles (90038-2615)
PHONE..............................323 993-8000
Paula David, *Principal*
Franklyn Athias, *Vice Pres*
Bill Ferry, *Pub Rel Dir*
Judi Alvey, *Marketing Staff*
Bryan Christiansen, *Senior Mgr*
EMP: 57
SALES (corp-wide): 74.5B **Publicly Held**
WEB: www.comcast.com
SIC: 4841 Cable television services
PA: Comcast Corporation
    1701 Jfk Blvd
    Philadelphia PA 19103
    215 286-1700

(P-5972)
COMCAST CORPORATION
2455 Henderson Way, Monterey (93940-5303)
P.O. Box 1711 (93942-1711)
PHONE..............................831 657-6095
Bob Haehnel, *Branch Mgr*
Glenn Alonzo, *Manager*
EMP: 57
SALES (corp-wide): 74.5B **Publicly Held**
WEB: www.comcast.com
SIC: 4841 Cable television services
PA: Comcast Corporation
    1701 Jfk Blvd
    Philadelphia PA 19103
    215 286-1700

(P-5973)
COX COMMUNICATIONS INC
140 Columbia, Aliso Viejo (92656-1495)
PHONE..............................949 716-2020
Michael Hale, *Manager*
EMP: 76
SALES (corp-wide): 33.6B **Privately Held**
SIC: 4841 Cable television services
HQ: Cox Communications, Inc.
    6205 B Pchtree Dunwody Ne
    Atlanta GA 30328
    404 843-5000

(P-5974)
COX COMMUNICATIONS INC
1535 Euclid Ave, San Diego (92105-5426)
PHONE..............................858 715-4500
Deborah Lawrence, *Director*
EMP: 100
SALES (corp-wide): 33.6B **Privately Held**
SIC: 4841 4812 1731 Cable television services; radio telephone communication; electrical work
HQ: Cox Communications, Inc.
    6205 B Pchtree Dunwody Ne
    Atlanta GA 30328
    404 843-5000

(P-5975)
COX COMMUNICATIONS INC
26181 Avenida Aeropuerto, San Juan Capistrano (92675-4821)
PHONE..............................949 240-1212
Leo Brennan, *Branch Mgr*
EMP: 250
SALES (corp-wide): 33.6B **Privately Held**
SIC: 4841 Cable television services
HQ: Cox Communications, Inc.
    6205 B Pchtree Dunwody Ne
    Atlanta GA 30328
    404 843-5000

(P-5976)
COX COMMUNICATIONS INC
6771 Quail Hill Pkwy, Irvine (92603-4233)
PHONE..............................949 546-1000
Leone Duffy, *Owner*
EMP: 76
SALES (corp-wide): 33.6B **Privately Held**
SIC: 4841 Cable & other pay television services
HQ: Cox Communications, Inc.
    6205 B Pchtree Dunwody Ne
    Atlanta GA 30328
    404 843-5000

(P-5977)
COX COMMUNICATIONS INC
27121 Towne Centre Dr # 200, Foothill Ranch (92610-2817)
PHONE..............................949 546-2000
Fax: 949 546-2424
Lee Brennan, *Branch Mgr*
EMP: 100
SALES (corp-wide): 33.6B **Privately Held**
SIC: 4841 Cable television services
HQ: Cox Communications, Inc.
    6205 B Pchtree Dunwody Ne
    Atlanta GA 30328
    404 843-5000

(P-5978)
COX COMMUNICATIONS INC
3303 State St, Santa Barbara (93105-2623)
PHONE..............................805 681-6600
Janice Cass, *Branch Mgr*
Dionne Huskins, *Executive Asst*
Katherine Paezle Harris, *Manager*
Elizabeth Simon, *Manager*
EMP: 85
SALES (corp-wide): 33.6B **Privately Held**
SIC: 4841 Cable & other pay television services
HQ: Cox Communications, Inc.
    6205 B Pchtree Dunwody Ne
    Atlanta GA 30328
    404 843-5000

(P-5979)
COX COMMUNICATIONS CAL LLC
1175 N Cuyamaca St, El Cajon (92020-1805)
PHONE..............................619 562-9820
Randall Phillips, *Manager*
EMP: 380
SALES (corp-wide): 33.6B **Privately Held**
SIC: 4841 Cable television services
HQ: Cox Communications California, Llc
    6205 Pachtree Dunwoody Rd
    Atlanta GA 30328
    404 843-5000

(P-5980)
COX COMMUNICATIONS CAL LLC
581 Telegraph Canyon Rd, Chula Vista (91910-6436)
PHONE..............................619 263-9251
EMP: 380
SQ FT: 3,025
SALES (corp-wide): 33.6B **Privately Held**
SIC: 4841 Cable television services
HQ: Cox Communications California, Llc
    6205 Pachtree Dunwoody Rd
    Atlanta GA 30328
    404 843-5000

(P-5981)
COX COMMUNICATIONS CAL LLC
5159 Federal Blvd, San Diego (92105-5428)
PHONE..............................619 262-1122
Fax: 619 266-5046
James Robbins, *CEO*
Anna Young, *Programmer Anys*
Melissa Walters, *Technology*
Joyce Shinohara, *Human Resources*
EMP: 380
SALES (corp-wide): 33.6B **Privately Held**
SIC: 4841 Cable television services
HQ: Cox Communications California, Llc
    6205 Pachtree Dunwoody Rd
    Atlanta GA 30328
    404 843-5000

(P-5982)
CROWN MEDIA HOLDINGS INC (HQ)
12700 Ventura Blvd # 100, Studio City (91604-2469)
PHONE..............................888 390-7474
William J Abbott, *President*
Kristen Roberts, *President*
Michelle Vicary, *President*
Andrew Rooke, *CFO*
Andrew P Brilliant, *Exec VP*
EMP: 77
SQ FT: 41,423
SALES: 478.7MM
SALES (corp-wide): 7.5B **Privately Held**
SIC: 4841 Cable & other pay television services
PA: Hallmark Cards, Incorporated
    2501 Mcgee St
    Kansas City MO 64108
    816 274-5111

(P-5983)
CROWN MEDIA UNITED STATES LLC (DH)
Also Called: Hallmark Channel
12700 Ventura Blvd # 100, Studio City (91604-2469)
PHONE..............................818 755-2400
Fax: 818 755-2564
David Evans,
Susanne McAvoy, *President*
Andrew Rooke, *CFO*
Ed Georger, *Exec VP*
Charles Stanford, *Exec VP*
EMP: 95
SALES (est): 24.5MM
SALES (corp-wide): 7.5B **Privately Held**
SIC: 4841 Cable & other pay television services
HQ: Crown Media Holdings, Inc.
    12700 Ventura Blvd # 100
    Studio City CA 91604
    888 390-7474

(P-5984)
DIRECTV LLC
1055 E Francis St, Ontario (91761-5633)
PHONE..............................909 509-4790
Don Gillespie, *Branch Mgr*
EMP: 80
SALES (corp-wide): 146.8B **Publicly Held**
SIC: 4841 Direct broadcast satellite services (DBS)
HQ: Directv, Llc
    2260 E Imperial Hwy
    El Segundo CA 90245
    310 964-8384

(P-5985)
DIRECTV CUSTOMER SERVICES INC (DH)
2230 E Imperial Hwy, El Segundo (90245-3504)
PHONE..............................310 964-5000
Michael D White, *Site Mgr*
Alison Pascola, *Vice Pres*
Frank Paonessa, *Purchasing*
EMP: 60
SALES (est): 18.3MM
SALES (corp-wide): 146.8B **Publicly Held**
SIC: 4841 Cable & other pay television services
HQ: Directv, Llc
    2260 E Imperial Hwy
    El Segundo CA 90245
    310 964-8384

(P-5986)
DIRECTV ENTERPRISES LLC
2230 E Imperial Hwy, El Segundo (90245-3504)
PHONE..............................310 535-5000
Fax: 310 964-5000
Michael D White, *Site Mgr*
Eddy W Hartenstein, *Ch of Bd*
Odie C Donald, *President*
R L Myers, *CFO*
Mike Palkovic, *CFO*
EMP: 1500
SQ FT: 75,000

4841 - Cable & Other Pay TV Svcs County (P-5987) — PRODUCTS & SERVICES SECTION

SALES (est): 114.7MM
SALES (corp-wide): 146.8B **Publicly Held**
SIC: 4841 Direct broadcast satellite services (DBS)
HQ: Directv Holdings Llc
2230 E Imperial Hwy
El Segundo CA 90245
310 964-5000

(P-5987)
DIRECTV GROUP INC
340 Commerce Ave, Fairfield (94533)
PHONE..................707 452-7409
EMP: 128
SALES (corp-wide): 31.7B **Publicly Held**
SIC: 4841
HQ: The Directv Group Inc
2260 E Imperial Hwy
El Segundo CA 90245
310 964-5000

(P-5988)
DIRECTV GROUP INC
1129 B St, San Lorenzo (94580)
PHONE..................510 481-1324
EMP: 128
SALES (corp-wide): 31.7B **Publicly Held**
SIC: 4841
HQ: The Directv Group Inc
2260 E Imperial Hwy
El Segundo CA 90245
310 964-5000

(P-5989)
DIRECTV GROUP HOLDINGS LLC (HQ)
2260 E Imperial Hwy, El Segundo (90245-3501)
PHONE..................310 964-5000
Michael White, *President*
Patrick Doyle, *CFO*
Fazal Merchant, *Treasurer*
Joseph Bosch, *Officer*
Paul Guyardo, *Exec VP*
▲ EMP: 170
SALES (est): 19.6B
SALES (corp-wide): 146.8B **Publicly Held**
SIC: 4841 Cable & other pay television services
PA: At&T Inc.
208 S Akard St
Dallas TX 75202
210 821-4105

(P-5990)
DIRECTV GROUP INC (DH)
2260 E Imperial Hwy, El Segundo (90245-3501)
PHONE..................310 964-5000
Michael White, *CEO*
Fred Christensen, *CFO*
Patrick T Doyle, *CFO*
J William Little, *Treasurer*
Romulo Pontual, *Exec VP*
▲ EMP: 128
SALES (est): 4.3B
SALES (corp-wide): 146.8B **Publicly Held**
WEB: www.hughes.com
SIC: 4841 Cable & other pay television services
HQ: Directv Group Holdings, Llc
2260 E Imperial Hwy
El Segundo CA 90245
310 964-5000

(P-5991)
DIRECTV INTERNATIONAL INC (DH)
2230 E Imperial Hwy Fl 10, El Segundo (90245-3504)
PHONE..................310 964-6460
Michael D White, *Site Mgr*
Kevin McGrath, *President*
Celso Azevedo, *Senior VP*
Michael W Palkovic, *Vice Pres*
EMP: 150
SALES (est): 50.2MM
SALES (corp-wide): 146.8B **Publicly Held**
SIC: 4841 Cable & other pay television services

HQ: The Directv Group Inc
2260 E Imperial Hwy
El Segundo CA 90245
310 964-5000

(P-5992)
DISH NETWORK CORPORATION
396 Orange Show Ln, San Bernardino (92408-2012)
PHONE..................909 381-4767
EMP: 52
SALES (corp-wide): 15B **Publicly Held**
SIC: 4841 Direct broadcast satellite services (DBS)
PA: Dish Network Corporation
9601 S Meridian Blvd
Englewood CO 80112
303 723-1000

(P-5993)
DISH NETWORK CORPORATION
1297 N Verdugo Rd, Glendale (91206-1508)
PHONE..................818 334-8740
EMP: 50
SALES (corp-wide): 15B **Publicly Held**
SIC: 4841 Direct broadcast satellite services (DBS)
PA: Dish Network Corporation
9601 S Meridian Blvd
Englewood CO 80112
303 723-1000

(P-5994)
DISH NETWORK CORPORATION
2602 Halladay St, Santa Ana (92705-5601)
PHONE..................714 424-0503
Charles W Ergen, *Principal*
Raul Guidi, *General Mgr*
EMP: 50
SALES (corp-wide): 15B **Publicly Held**
SIC: 4841 Direct broadcast satellite services (DBS)
PA: Dish Network Corporation
9601 S Meridian Blvd
Englewood CO 80112
303 723-1000

(P-5995)
DISH NETWORK CORPORATION
5671 Warehouse Way, Sacramento (95826-4906)
PHONE..................916 381-5084
Jim Spreitcer, *Manager*
Bryan Bonacquisti, *Opers Mgr*
EMP: 50
SALES (corp-wide): 15B **Publicly Held**
WEB: www.dishnetwork.com
SIC: 4841 Direct broadcast satellite services (DBS)
PA: Dish Network Corporation
9601 S Meridian Blvd
Englewood CO 80112
303 723-1000

(P-5996)
DIVA SYSTEMS CORPORATION
800 Saginaw Dr, Redwood City (94063-4740)
PHONE..................650 779-3000
Fax: 650 779-3099
Hendrik A Hanselaar, *President*
Paul Cook, *Ch of Bd*
Robert B Snow, *COO*
William M Scharninghausen, *CFO*
Emily Husstashman, *Treasurer*
EMP: 179
SQ FT: 82,000
SALES: 18.4MM **Privately Held**
SIC: 4841 7829 7822 Cable & other pay television services; motion picture distribution services; motion picture distribution

(P-5997)
EASTERN BROADCASTING AMER CORP
Also Called: B N E U S A
18430 San Jose Ave Ste A, City of Industry (91748-1263)
PHONE..................626 581-8899
Fax: 626 581-8877
May Chiang, *Exec VP*
Cindy Huang, *Executive*
Betty Tsai, *Creative Dir*
Justin Hsieh, *Finance*
Su Kuo, *Manager*

EMP: 80
SQ FT: 300,000
SALES (est): 5.4MM **Privately Held**
SIC: 4841 Cable television services

(P-5998)
ESPN INC
800 W Olympic Blvd, Los Angeles (90015-1360)
PHONE..................212 456-7439
Steven Bornstein, *Ch of Bd*
EMP: 300 **Publicly Held**
SIC: 4841 Cable television services
HQ: Espn, Inc.
Espn Plz
Bristol CT 06010
860 766-2000

(P-5999)
EXPRESS CABLE COMMUNICATION
350 S Maple St Ste L, Corona (92880-6948)
PHONE..................951 272-2029
Fax: 909 272-2028
Sam Kouhkan, *President*
EMP: 60
SALES: 12.1MM **Privately Held**
SIC: 4841 Cable television services

(P-6000)
FOX LATIN AMERICAN CHANNEL LLC
10201 W Pico Blvd, Los Angeles (90064-2606)
PHONE..................305 774-4167
Ruben Arreola, *Exec Dir*
EMP: 500
SALES (est): 12.5MM **Privately Held**
SIC: 4841 Cable television services

(P-6001)
FOX NETWORKS GROUP INC
Also Called: Fox Network Center
10201 W Pico Blvd 101, Los Angeles (90064-2606)
PHONE..................310 369-9369
Fax: 310 369-0468
Rupert Murdoch, *President*
Brian Sullivan, *President*
Jeb Terry, *Vice Pres*
Renee Sherriff, *Executive Asst*
Don Covington, *Info Tech Dir*
EMP: 1385
SALES (est): 31.7MM
SALES (corp-wide): 27.3B **Publicly Held**
SIC: 4841 Direct broadcast satellite services (DBS)
HQ: Fox Entertainment Group, Inc.
2029 Century Park E # 1400
Los Angeles CA 90067
310 369-1000

(P-6002)
FX NETWORKS LLC
10201 W Pico Blvd, Los Angeles (90064-2606)
P.O. Box 900, Beverly Hills (90213-0900)
PHONE..................310 369-1000
Fax: 310 969-4688
John Landgraf, *President*
Stephanie Gibbons, *Partner*
Nick Grad, *Exec VP*
Audrey Steele, *Senior VP*
Matt Cherniss, *Vice Pres*
EMP: 150
SALES (est): 19.7MM
SALES (corp-wide): 27.3B **Publicly Held**
WEB: www.fox.com
SIC: 4841 Cable & other pay television services
HQ: Fox Entertainment Group, Inc.
2029 Century Park E # 1400
Los Angeles CA 90067
310 369-1000

(P-6003)
GAME SHOW NETWORK LLC (DH)
Also Called: G S N
2150 Colorado Ave Ste 100, Santa Monica (90404-5514)
PHONE..................310 255-6800
Fax: 310 255-6810
David Goldhill, *CEO*

Frank Cartwright, *President*
Brent Williams, *CFO*
Andrew Pedersen, *Officer*
Steven Brunell, *Exec VP*
EMP: 147
SALES (est): 85.8MM
SALES (corp-wide): 146.8B **Publicly Held**
WEB: www.gsn.com
SIC: 4841 Cable & other pay television services
HQ: Liberty Entertainment Inc
2230 E Imperial Hwy
El Segundo CA 90245
310 964-5000

(P-6004)
GLOBECAST AMERICA INCORPORATED (HQ)
10525 Washington Blvd, Culver City (90232-3311)
PHONE..................212 373-5140
Michele Gosetti, *CEO*
Lisa Coelho, *CEO*
Batrice De Lagrevol, *Vice Pres*
Elisabeth Mazurie, *Vice Pres*
Sharon Dacosta, *Office Mgr*
▲ EMP: 76
SALES (est): 94.4MM
SALES (corp-wide): 25.3B **Privately Held**
SIC: 4841 Satellite master antenna systems services (SMATV)
PA: Orange
78 Rue Olivier De Serres
Paris Cedex 15 75505
144 442-222

(P-6005)
HEARST COMMUNICATIONS INC
Also Called: Western Communications
2323 Teller Rd, Newbury Park (91320-2219)
PHONE..................805 375-3121
Dave Laroue, *Branch Mgr*
EMP: 500
SALES (corp-wide): 419.4MM **Privately Held**
WEB: www.telegram.com
SIC: 4841 Cable television services
PA: Hearst Communications, Inc.
901 Mission St
San Francisco CA 94103
415 777-1111

(P-6006)
HOME BOX OFFICE INC
2500 Broadway Ste 400, Santa Monica (90404-3176)
PHONE..................310 382-3000
Chris Albrecht, *Manager*
EMP: 95
SALES (corp-wide): 28.1B **Publicly Held**
WEB: www.hbo.com
SIC: 4841 7812 Cable & other pay television services; motion picture & video production
HQ: Home Box Office, Inc.
1100 Avenue Of The Americ
New York NY 10036
212 512-1000

(P-6007)
INTEL MEDIA INC
2200 Mission College Blvd, Santa Clara (95054-1549)
PHONE..................408 765-0063
Erik Huggers, *President*
Doug Klucevek, *Finance Dir*
Brian J Fox, *Counsel*
EMP: 350
SALES: 33.2K
SALES (corp-wide): 55.3B **Publicly Held**
SIC: 4841 Subscription television services
PA: Intel Corporation
2200 Mission College Blvd
Santa Clara CA 95054
408 765-8080

(P-6008)
INTERNATIONAL FMLY ENTRMT INC (DH)
Also Called: Fox Family Channel
3800 W Alameda Ave, Burbank (91505-4300)
PHONE..................818 560-1000

PRODUCTS & SERVICES SECTION

4841 - Cable & Other Pay TV Svcs County (P-6029)

Mel Woods, *President*
Tom Cosgrove, *Senior VP*
Tracey Stuart, *MIS Dir*
EMP: 144
SALES (est): 30.1MM **Publicly Held**
SIC: 4841 7812 7922 7999 Cable television services; television film production; theatrical producers; legitimate live theater producers; television program, including commercial producers; recreation services
HQ: Abc Family Worldwide, Inc.
500 S Buena Vista St
Burbank CA 91521
818 560-1000

(P-6009)
NDS AMERICAS INC (DH)
3500 Hyland Ave, Costa Mesa
(92626-1469)
PHONE 714 434-2100
Abe Peled, *President*
Michael Ick, *Vice Pres*
Edward Landsberg, *Vice Pres*
Peter Lynskey, *Vice Pres*
Dov Rubin, *Vice Pres*
EMP: 90
SALES (est): 47.2MM
SALES (corp-wide): 49.2B **Publicly Held**
WEB: www.ndsuk.com
SIC: 4841 Cable & other pay television services
HQ: Nds Group Limited
One London Road
Staines MIDDX
208 824-1000

(P-6010)
OC COMMUNICATIONS INC
2204 Kausen Dr Ste 100, Elk Grove
(95758-7176)
PHONE 916 686-3700
Forrest C Freeman, *President*
Peter Tataryn, *CFO*
EMP: 650
SQ FT: 7,335
SALES (est): 104.5MM **Privately Held**
WEB: www.occommunications.com
SIC: 4841 Cable & other pay television services

(P-6011)
OWN LLC
Also Called: Oprah Winfrey Network
1041 N Formosa Ave, West Hollywood
(90046-6703)
PHONE 323 602-5500
Fax: 323 602-5680
Oprah Winfrey, *CEO*
Erik Logan, *Co-President*
Sheri Salata, *Co-President*
Maurizio Vitale, *Vice Pres*
Chelsea Hettrick, *Comms Dir*
EMP: 140
SQ FT: 50,000
SALES (est): 21.2MM **Privately Held**
SIC: 4841 Cable & other pay television services; cable television services

(P-6012)
PETES CONNECTION INC
280 N Benson Ave Ste 78, Upland
(91786-5652)
PHONE 909 373-6414
Pete Cavaretta, *President*
Ann Cavaretta, *Vice Pres*
EMP: 80
SQ FT: 2,100
SALES (est): 5.8MM **Privately Held**
SIC: 4841 Cable television services

(P-6013)
PETES CONNECTION INC
407 Ranger Rd, Fallbrook (92028-8482)
P.O. Box 2080 (92088-2080)
PHONE 760 723-1972
Peter Cavaretta, *President*
Ann Cavaretta, *Vice Pres*
EMP: 50
SALES (est): 3.2MM **Privately Held**
SIC: 4841 Direct broadcast satellite services (DBS)

(P-6014)
PHOENIX AMERICAN INCORPORATED (PA)
2401 Kerner Blvd, San Rafael
(94901-5569)
PHONE 415 485-4500
Fax: 415 485-4823
Gus Constantin, *Ch of Bd*
Andrew N Gregson, *CFO*
Gary W Martinez, *Exec VP*
Alfred Armenteros, *Vice Pres*
Muna A Hobaika, *Vice Pres*
EMP: 100
SQ FT: 60,000
SALES (est): 40.9MM **Privately Held**
SIC: 4841 7377 Cable television services; computer rental & leasing

(P-6015)
ROKU INC (PA)
150 Winchester Cir, Los Gatos
(95032-1812)
PHONE 408 556-9040
Anthony Wood, *President*
Steve Louden, *CFO*
Matthew Anderson, *Chief Mktg Ofcr*
Mary E Broganer, *Vice Pres*
Mark Goodwin, *Vice Pres*
▲ **EMP:** 360
SALES (est): 163.1MM **Privately Held**
WEB: www.roku.com
SIC: 4841 Cable & other pay television services

(P-6016)
SKY SCAN SATELITE SYSTEMS
9994 Willowbrook Rd, Riverside
(92509-8827)
PHONE 909 322-1393
Mike Khan, *Owner*
EMP: 68
SALES (est): 1.5MM **Privately Held**
SIC: 4841 Satellite master antenna systems services (SMATV)

(P-6017)
SONIFI SOLUTIONS INC
1065 E Hillsdale Blvd # 228, Foster City
(94404-1614)
PHONE 650 752-1980
Sean Minnit, *Branch Mgr*
EMP: 109
SALES (corp-wide): 87MM **Privately Held**
SIC: 4841 Subscription television services
PA: Sonifi Solutions, Inc.
3900 W Innovation St
Sioux Falls SD 57107
605 988-1000

(P-6018)
SPECTRUM MGT HOLDG CO LLC
Also Called: Time Warner
41551 10th St W, Palmdale (93551-1405)
PHONE 661 947-3130
Phil Marley, *Branch Mgr*
Nancy Monohan, *Marketing Staff*
Janet Spatz, *Manager*
John Wyly, *Manager*
Nancy Monahan, *Supervisor*
EMP: 83
SQ FT: 31,426
SALES (corp-wide): 9.7MM **Publicly Held**
SIC: 4841 Cable television services
HQ: Spectrum Management Holding Company, Llc
400 Atlantic St
Stamford CT 06901
203 905-7801

(P-6019)
SPECTRUM MGT HOLDG CO LLC
Also Called: Time Warner Media Sales
6021 Katella Ave Ste 100, Cypress
(90630-5250)
PHONE 714 657-1040
Rich Ambrose, *Vice Pres*
Teresa Oser, *Research*
David Oster, *Accounts Exec*
EMP: 83
SALES (corp-wide): 9.7MM **Publicly Held**
SIC: 4841 Cable television services

HQ: Spectrum Management Holding Company, Llc
400 Atlantic St
Stamford CT 06901
203 905-7801

(P-6020)
SPECTRUM MGT HOLDG CO LLC
4077 W Stetson Ave, Hemet (92545-9704)
PHONE 951 260-3143
Andre Mora, *Manager*
Christian B Jison, *Technician*
EMP: 83
SALES (corp-wide): 9.7MM **Publicly Held**
SIC: 4841 Cable television services
HQ: Spectrum Management Holding Company, Llc
400 Atlantic St
Stamford CT 06901
203 905-7801

(P-6021)
SPECTRUM MGT HOLDG CO LLC
3550 Wilshire Blvd, Los Angeles
(90010-2401)
PHONE 323 657-0899
EMP: 84
SALES (corp-wide): 9.7MM **Publicly Held**
SIC: 4841 Cable television services
HQ: Spectrum Management Holding Company, Llc
400 Atlantic St
Stamford CT 06901
203 905-7801

(P-6022)
SPECTRUM MGT HOLDG CO LLC
350 Stonewood St, Downey (90241-3909)
PHONE 562 372-4008
EMP: 83
SALES (corp-wide): 9.7MM **Publicly Held**
SIC: 4841 Cable television services
HQ: Spectrum Management Holding Company, Llc
400 Atlantic St
Stamford CT 06901
203 905-7801

(P-6023)
SPECTRUM MGT HOLDG CO LLC
6695 Green Valley Cir, Culver City
(90230-7024)
PHONE 310 417-4260
Rosa Hill, *Branch Mgr*
Romona Henderson, *Manager*
EMP: 86
SALES (corp-wide): 9.7MM **Publicly Held**
SIC: 4841 Cable television services
HQ: Spectrum Management Holding Company, Llc
400 Atlantic St
Stamford CT 06901
203 905-7801

(P-6024)
SPECTRUM MGT HOLDG CO LLC
Also Called: Time Warner
6021 Katella Ave Ste 100, Cypress
(90630-5250)
PHONE 714 657-1060
Tim Young, *Manager*
Angelia McCormick, *Branch Mgr*
Debbie Johnston, *General Mgr*
Derek Benedict, *Sales Staff*
Harlan Johnson, *Sales Staff*
EMP: 120
SALES (corp-wide): 9.7MM **Publicly Held**
SIC: 4841 Cable & other pay television services
HQ: Spectrum Management Holding Company, Llc
400 Atlantic St
Stamford CT 06901
203 905-7801

(P-6025)
SPECTRUM MGT HOLDG CO LLC
Also Called: Time Warner
7441 Chapman Ave, Garden Grove
(92841-2115)
PHONE 714 903-4000
Fax: 714 903-8210
Tad Yo, *Manager*
John Martin, *Exec VP*
Robert Marcus, *Vice Pres*
Judith Whyte, *Technology*
Dale Bowles, *Engineer*
EMP: 83
SALES (corp-wide): 9.7MM **Publicly Held**
SIC: 4841 Cable television services
HQ: Spectrum Management Holding Company, Llc
400 Atlantic St
Stamford CT 06901
203 905-7801

(P-6026)
SPECTRUM MGT HOLDG CO LLC
Time Warner
41725 Cook St, Palm Desert (92211-5100)
PHONE 760 340-2225
Juan Ochoa, *Principal*
David Roblee, *Technical Mgr*
Michael Sagona, *Engineer*
Irma Baca, *Recruiter*
Patti Johnson, *Sls & Mktg Exec*
EMP: 200
SALES (corp-wide): 9.7MM **Publicly Held**
SIC: 4841 Cable & other pay television services
HQ: Spectrum Management Holding Company, Llc
400 Atlantic St
Stamford CT 06901
203 905-7801

(P-6027)
SPECTRUM MGT HOLDG CO LLC
Also Called: Time Warner
3430 E Miraloma Ave, Anaheim
(92806-2101)
PHONE 714 414-1431
Preston Hayslette, *Branch Mgr*
Frank Villegas, *Engineer*
Enrico Diaz, *Regl Sales Mgr*
Kathryn Goff, *Sales Staff*
HP Le, *Sales Staff*
EMP: 83
SALES (corp-wide): 9.7MM **Publicly Held**
SIC: 4841 Cable television services
HQ: Spectrum Management Holding Company, Llc
400 Atlantic St
Stamford CT 06901
203 905-7801

(P-6028)
TIME WARNER CABLE ENTPS LLC
1438 N Gower St, Los Angeles
(90028-8383)
PHONE 323 993-7076
Richard Battaglia, *President*
EMP: 120
SALES (corp-wide): 9.7MM **Publicly Held**
SIC: 4841 Cable television services
HQ: Time Warner Cable Enterprises Llc
60 Columbus Cir Fl 17
New York NY 10023
877 495-9201

(P-6029)
TIME WARNER CABLE ENTPS LLC
550 Continental Blvd # 250, El Segundo
(90245-5063)
P.O. Box 60074, City of Industry (91716-0074)
PHONE 469 665-7735
Debi Picciolo, *Principal*
EMP: 2500
SALES (corp-wide): 9.7MM **Publicly Held**
SIC: 4841 Cable television services
HQ: Time Warner Cable Enterprises Llc
60 Columbus Cir Fl 17
New York NY 10023
877 495-9201

4841 - Cable & Other Pay TV Svcs County (P-6030)   PRODUCTS & SERVICES SECTION

(P-6030)
TIME WARNER CABLE ENTPS LLC
3300 Warner Blvd, Burbank (91505-4632)
PHONE 818 953-3283
Tom Whalley, *Branch Mgr*
EMP: 200
SALES (corp-wide): 9.7MM **Publicly Held**
SIC: 4841 Cable television services
HQ: Time Warner Cable Enterprises Llc
60 Columbus Cir Fl 17
New York NY 10023
877 495-9201

(P-6031)
TIME WARNER CABLE INC
3051 Clairemont Dr, San Diego (92117-6802)
PHONE 619 346-4573
Margie Herrera, *Branch Mgr*
EMP: 76
SALES (corp-wide): 9.7MM **Publicly Held**
SIC: 4841 Cable television services
HQ: Spectrum Management Holding Company, Llc
400 Atlantic St
Stamford CT 06901
203 905-7801

(P-6032)
TIME WARNER CABLE INC
118 N 8th St, Santa Paula (93060-2710)
PHONE 888 892-2253
Warner Cable, *Owner*
EMP: 86
SALES (corp-wide): 9.7MM **Publicly Held**
SIC: 4841 Cable television services
HQ: Spectrum Management Holding Company, Llc
400 Atlantic St
Stamford CT 06901
203 905-7801

(P-6033)
TIME WARNER CABLE INC
2323 Teller Rd, Newbury Park (91320-2219)
PHONE 805 214-1353
David Bultman, *Branch Mgr*
Brian Messina, *Supervisor*
EMP: 83
SALES (corp-wide): 9.7MM **Publicly Held**
SIC: 4841 Cable television services
HQ: Spectrum Management Holding Company, Llc
400 Atlantic St
Stamford CT 06901
203 905-7801

(P-6034)
TIME WARNER CABLE INC
1041 E Route 66, Glendora (91740-6357)
PHONE 626 857-1075
Fax: 626 857-1075
Erwin Tando, *Branch Mgr*
EMP: 86
SALES (corp-wide): 9.7MM **Publicly Held**
SIC: 4841 Cable television services
HQ: Spectrum Management Holding Company, Llc
400 Atlantic St
Stamford CT 06901
203 905-7801

(P-6035)
TIME WARNER CABLE INC
27555 Ynez Rd Ste 203, Temecula (92591-4677)
PHONE 951 587-8660
Fax: 951 695-2316
Doug Walker, *Branch Mgr*
Jill Boyd, *Accounts Exec*
EMP: 83
SALES (corp-wide): 9.7MM **Publicly Held**
SIC: 4841 Cable television services
HQ: Spectrum Management Holding Company, Llc
400 Atlantic St
Stamford CT 06901
203 905-7801

(P-6036)
TIME WARNER CABLE INC
1078 E Hospitality Ln D, San Bernardino (92408-2863)
PHONE 909 918-6972
Kathleen Ouilette, *Branch Mgr*
EMP: 83
SALES (corp-wide): 9.7MM **Publicly Held**
SIC: 4841 Cable television services; subscription television services
HQ: Spectrum Management Holding Company, Llc
400 Atlantic St
Stamford CT 06901
203 905-7801

(P-6037)
TIME WARNER CABLE INC
5120 W Goldleaf Cir, Los Angeles (90056-1292)
PHONE 213 599-7968
EMP: 86
SALES (corp-wide): 9.7MM **Publicly Held**
SIC: 4841 Cable television services
HQ: Spectrum Management Holding Company, Llc
400 Atlantic St
Stamford CT 06901
203 905-7801

(P-6038)
TIME WARNER CABLE INC
17777 Center Court Dr N, Cerritos (90703-9320)
PHONE 562 677-0228
Jayne Guilford, *Mktg Dir*
Steve Klein, *Sales Mgr*
Andy Sahli, *Sales Mgr*
Hector Carmona, *Accounts Exec*
EMP: 84
SALES (corp-wide): 9.7MM **Publicly Held**
SIC: 4841 Cable television services
HQ: Spectrum Management Holding Company, Llc
400 Atlantic St
Stamford CT 06901
203 905-7801

(P-6039)
TIME WARNER CABLE INC
12763 Mitchell Ave, Los Angeles (90066-4717)
PHONE 951 682-6180
EMP: 77
SALES (corp-wide): 9.7MM **Publicly Held**
SIC: 4841 Cable television services
HQ: Spectrum Management Holding Company, Llc
400 Atlantic St
Stamford CT 06901
203 905-7801

(P-6040)
TIME WARNER CABLE INC
10450 Pacific Center Ct, San Diego (92121-4338)
PHONE 858 695-3220
Jim Fellhauer, *President*
David Dalton, *Treasurer*
Pradman Kaul, *Bd of Directors*
Houtan Dehesh, *Vice Pres*
Ron Johnson, *Vice Pres*
EMP: 410
SQ FT: 25,500
SALES (corp-wide): 9.7MM **Publicly Held**
SIC: 4841 Cable television services
HQ: Spectrum Management Holding Company, Llc
400 Atlantic St
Stamford CT 06901
203 905-7801

(P-6041)
TIME WARNER CABLE INC
660 W Acacia Ave, Hemet (92543-4073)
PHONE 951 306-3117
EMP: 84
SALES (corp-wide): 9.7MM **Publicly Held**
SIC: 4841 Cable television services
HQ: Spectrum Management Holding Company, Llc
400 Atlantic St
Stamford CT 06901
203 905-7801

(P-6042)
TIME WARNER CABLE INC
5865 Friars Rd, San Diego (92110-6009)
PHONE 619 684-6106
EMP: 86

(P-6043)
TIME WARNER CABLE INC
Also Called: Adelphia
1565 S Harbor Blvd, Fullerton (92832-3402)
PHONE 714 871-2643
Rick Rivas, *Branch Mgr*
EMP: 84
SALES (corp-wide): 9.7MM **Publicly Held**
SIC: 4841 Cable television services
HQ: Spectrum Management Holding Company, Llc
400 Atlantic St
Stamford CT 06901
203 905-7801

(P-6044)
TIME WARNER CABLE INC
9260 Topanga Canyon Blvd, Chatsworth (91311-5726)
PHONE 818 700-6126
Michael Snider, *Branch Mgr*
Ellen East, *Exec VP*
Sheila Sizemore, *Executive Asst*
Anahita Melancon, *Admin Asst*
Russell Taylor, *Info Tech Dir*
EMP: 86
SALES (corp-wide): 9.7MM **Publicly Held**
SIC: 4841 Cable television services
HQ: Spectrum Management Holding Company, Llc
400 Atlantic St
Stamford CT 06901
203 905-7801

(P-6045)
TIME WARNER CABLE INC
500 Lakewood Center Mall, Lakewood (90712-2407)
PHONE 424 529-6011
EMP: 170
SALES (corp-wide): 9.7MM **Publicly Held**
SIC: 4841 Cable television services
HQ: Spectrum Management Holding Company, Llc
400 Atlantic St
Stamford CT 06901
203 905-7801

(P-6046)
TIME WARNER CABLE INC
15255 Salt Lake Ave, City of Industry (91745-1130)
PHONE 626 705-7482
Kurt Taylor, *Manager*
Jake Weisling, *Engineer*
Yolonda Frando, *Assistant*
EMP: 95
SALES (corp-wide): 9.7MM **Publicly Held**
SIC: 4841 Cable television services
HQ: Spectrum Management Holding Company, Llc
400 Atlantic St
Stamford CT 06901
203 905-7801

(P-6047)
TIME WARNER CABLE INC
1881 W Main St, Barstow (92311-3715)
PHONE 760 256-3526
Fax: 760 256-8046
Chuck Gibson, *Branch Mgr*
EMP: 83
SALES (corp-wide): 9.7MM **Publicly Held**
SIC: 4841 Cable television services
HQ: Spectrum Management Holding Company, Llc
400 Atlantic St
Stamford CT 06901
203 905-7801

(P-6048)
TIME WARNER CABLE INC
900 N Cahuenga Blvd, Los Angeles (90038-2615)
PHONE 323 993-8000
Debbie Piccolio, *Branch Mgr*
EMP: 300
SALES (corp-wide): 9.7MM **Publicly Held**
SIC: 4841 Cable television services
HQ: Spectrum Management Holding Company, Llc
400 Atlantic St
Stamford CT 06901
203 905-7801

(P-6049)
TIME WARNER CABLE INC
550 Continental Blvd # 250, El Segundo (90245-5063)
PHONE 310 647-3000
Debi Picciolo, *Branch Mgr*
Deane Leavenworth, *Vice Pres*
Patricia Romero, *Vice Pres*
Pamela Crawford, *Regional Mgr*
Leticia Valencia, *Executive Asst*
EMP: 83
SALES (corp-wide): 9.7MM **Publicly Held**
SIC: 4841 Cable & other pay television services
HQ: Spectrum Management Holding Company, Llc
400 Atlantic St
Stamford CT 06901
203 905-7801

(P-6050)
TIME WARNER CABLE INC
8949 Ware Ct, San Diego (92121-2222)
PHONE 858 695-3110
Lisa Simon, *Branch Mgr*
Joe Traczek, *Admin Asst*
Betty Fekete, *Auditor*
David Harris, *Marketing Staff*
EMP: 300
SALES (corp-wide): 9.7MM **Publicly Held**
SIC: 4841 Cable television services; subscription television services
HQ: Spectrum Management Holding Company, Llc
400 Atlantic St
Stamford CT 06901
203 905-7801

(P-6051)
TIME WARNER CABLE INC
313 N 8th St, El Centro (92243-2303)
PHONE 760 335-4800
Rosa Delgado, *Branch Mgr*
EMP: 83
SALES (corp-wide): 9.7MM **Publicly Held**
SIC: 4841 Cable television services
HQ: Spectrum Management Holding Company, Llc
400 Atlantic St
Stamford CT 06901
203 905-7801

(P-6052)
TIME WARNER CABLE INC
12625 Frederick St F10, Moreno Valley (92553-5440)
PHONE 951 571-8738
Steve Naber, *Branch Mgr*
EMP: 83
SALES (corp-wide): 9.7MM **Publicly Held**
SIC: 4841 Cable & other pay television services
HQ: Spectrum Management Holding Company, Llc
400 Atlantic St
Stamford CT 06901
203 905-7801

(P-6053)
TIME WARNER INC
2014 W Avenue K, Lancaster (93536-5229)
PHONE 661 344-1546
EMP: 76
SALES (corp-wide): 28.1B **Publicly Held**
SIC: 4841 Cable television services
PA: Time Warner Inc.
1 Time Warner Ctr Bsmt B
New York NY 10019
212 484-8000

(P-6054)
TIME WARNER INC
2650 Tapo Canyon Rd, Simi Valley (93063-2308)
PHONE 805 421-4467
EMP: 76
SALES (corp-wide): 28.1B **Publicly Held**
SIC: 4841 Cable television services

PRODUCTS & SERVICES SECTION

4899 - Communication Svcs, NEC County (P-6077)

PA: Time Warner Inc.
1 Time Warner Ctr Bsmt B
New York NY 10019
212 484-8000

(P-6055)
TVB (USA) INC (DH)
15411 Blackburn Ave, Norwalk
(90650-6844)
PHONE.................................562 345-9871
Fax: 562 802-5096
Philip Tam, *President*
Agnes Tam, *Vice Pres*
Melissa Wang, *Vice Pres*
Vivian Keung, *Sales Dir*
I Lai, *Director*
▲ EMP: 50
SQ FT: 25,000
SALES (est): 8.9MM
SALES (corp-wide): 574.7MM Privately Held
SIC: 4841 Cable television services
HQ: Tvb Holdings (Usa) Inc
15411 Blackburn Ave
Norwalk CA 90650
562 802-8868

(P-6056)
VERIZON BUSINESS GLOBAL LLC
6177 River Crest Dr Ste B, Riverside
(92507-0786)
P.O. Box 635, Jackson MS (39205-0635)
PHONE.................................951 653-4482
Gar Gatia, *Manager*
EMP: 50
SALES (corp-wide): 131.6B Publicly Held
WEB: www.mccmt.com
SIC: 4841 Cable television services
HQ: Verizon Business Global Llc
22001 Loudoun County Pkwy
Ashburn VA 20147
703 886-5600

(P-6057)
VOLCANO VISION INC
Also Called: Volcano Telephone Co.
20000 State Highway 88, Pine Grove
(95665-9512)
P.O. Box 1070 (95665-1070)
PHONE.................................209 296-2288
Toll Free:..................................888 -
Sharon J Lundgren, *President*
John M Lundgren, *Vice Pres*
Deilia P Harder, *Admin Sec*
EMP: 115
SQ FT: 1,000
SALES (est): 2.5MM Privately Held
SIC: 4841 Cable television services

(P-6058)
VUBIQUITY HOLDINGS INC (PA)
15301 Ventura Blvd # 3000, Sherman Oaks
(91403-5837)
PHONE.................................818 526-5000
Fax: 818 526-5106
Darcy Antonellis, *CEO*
Doug Sylvester, *President*
William G Arendt, *CFO*
Diane Smith, *Sr Corp Ofcr*
Brian Matthews, *Chief Mktg Ofcr*
EMP: 185
SALES (est): 300MM Privately Held
SIC: 4841 Cable & other pay television services

4899 Communication Svcs, NEC

(P-6059)
1105 MEDIA INC
4 Venture Ste 150, Irvine (92618-7442)
PHONE.................................949 265-1520
Richard Vitale, *Owner*
Mallory Bundy, *Project Mgr*
EMP: 152
SALES (corp-wide): 147.9MM Privately Held
SIC: 4899 Data communication services
PA: 1105 Media, Inc.
9201 Oakdale Ave Ste 101
Chatsworth CA 91311
818 814-5200

(P-6060)
BELLA TERRA TECHNOLOGIES INC
1600 Amphitheatre Pkwy, Mountain View
(94043-1351)
PHONE.................................650 316-6660
Fax: 650 472-9063
Tom Ingersoll, *CEO*
Dan Berkenstock,
Tobias Nassif, *Senior VP*
John Fenwick, *Vice Pres*
Ollie Guinan, *Vice Pres*
EMP: 54
SALES (est): 7.3MM
SALES (corp-wide): 74.9B Publicly Held
SIC: 4899 Satellite earth stations
HQ: Google Inc.
1600 Amphitheatre Pkwy
Mountain View CA 94043
650 253-0000

(P-6061)
BYTEMOBILE INC (DH)
Also Called: Byte Mobile
2860 De La Cruz Blvd # 200, Santa Clara
(95050-2635)
PHONE.................................408 327-7700
Fax: 408 327-7701
Hatim Tyabji, *CEO*
Ricky Chan, *President*
Adrian Hall, *COO*
Thomas Hubbs, *CFO*
JD Howard, *Vice Pres*
▲ EMP: 68
SQ FT: 30,000
SALES (est): 66.4MM
SALES (corp-wide): 3.2B Publicly Held
SIC: 4899 7361 Communication signal enhancement network system; employment agencies
HQ: Citrix Systems International Gmbh
Rheinweg 9
Schaffhausen SH
526 357-700

(P-6062)
CAMBIUM NETWORKS INC
2010 N 1st St, San Jose (95131-2018)
PHONE.................................847 640-3809
EMP: 149
SALES (corp-wide): 72.1MM Privately Held
SIC: 4899 Data communication services
PA: Cambium Networks, Inc.
3800 Golf Rd Ste 360
Rolling Meadows IL 60008
888 863-5250

(P-6063)
CELLCO PARTNERSHIP
5508 Young St, Bakersfield (93311-9648)
PHONE.................................661 663-9451
EMP: 57
SALES (corp-wide): 131.6B Publicly Held
SIC: 4899 Data communication services
HQ: Cellco Partnership
1 Verizon Way
Basking Ridge NJ 07920

(P-6064)
CELLCO PARTNERSHIP
Also Called: Verizon Wireless
6400 Pacific Blvd, Huntington Park
(90255-4104)
PHONE.................................323 826-9880
Fax: 310 603-0071
Louis Armendariz, *Principal*
EMP: 57
SALES (corp-wide): 131.6B Publicly Held
SIC: 4899 Data communication services
HQ: Cellco Partnership
1 Verizon Way
Basking Ridge NJ 07920

(P-6065)
COMCAST E SAN FERNANDO VLY LP
1111 Andersen Dr, San Rafael
(94901-5394)
PHONE.................................415 233-8328
Paul Gibson, *Partner*

Chris Coffman, *Technician*
Aung Maung, *Technician*
Mary Cane, *Legal Staff*
Sam Hudson, *Director*
EMP: 99
SALES: 950K Privately Held
SIC: 4899 Communication services

(P-6066)
COMMUNICATIONS SUPPLY CORP
6251 Knott Ave, Buena Park (90620-1010)
PHONE.................................714 670-7711
Michael Davis, *General Mgr*
Remy Saguin, *Buyer*
Roland Viola, *Sales Executive*
Howard Fox, *Marketing Mgr*
Miryam Lopez, *Sales Associate*
EMP: 70
SALES (corp-wide): 7.5B Publicly Held
WEB: www.gocsc.com
SIC: 4899 1731 3577 3357 Data communication services; communications specialization; computer peripheral equipment; nonferrous wiredrawing & insulating
HQ: Communications Supply Corp
200 E Lies Rd
Carol Stream IL 60188
630 221-6400

(P-6067)
COX COMMUNICATIONS INC
9180 Manor Dr, La Mesa (91942-3612)
PHONE.................................619 218-2967
EMP: 83
SALES (corp-wide): 33.6B Privately Held
SIC: 4899 Data communication services
HQ: Cox Communications, Inc.
6205 B Pchtree Dunwody Ne
Atlanta GA 30328
404 843-5000

(P-6068)
CUMULUS MEDIA INC
750 Battery St, San Francisco
(94111-1523)
PHONE.................................415 835-8120
EMP: 93
SALES (corp-wide): 1.1B Publicly Held
SIC: 4899 Data communication services
PA: Cumulus Media Inc.
3280 Peachtree Rd Ne Ne2300
Atlanta GA 30305
404 949-0700

(P-6069)
DIGITAL NETWORKS GROUP INC
20382 Hermana Cir, Lake Forest
(92630-8701)
PHONE.................................949 428-6333
Michael Stammire, *President*
Bart Moran, *Vice Pres*
Chris Ursetta, *Vice Pres*
Carl Blum, *Design Engr*
Sandi Pangallo, *Controller*
EMP: 63
SALES (est): 24.4MM Privately Held
WEB: www.digitalnetworksgroup.com
SIC: 4899 Data communication services

(P-6070)
DIMENSION DATA (DH)
27202 Turnberry Ln # 100, Valencia
(91355-1022)
PHONE.................................661 257-1500
Fax: 661 676-3606
Deron Pearson, *CEO*
Waheed Choudhry, *President*
Dan Dougherty, *CFO*
Sabrina Anderson, *Vice Pres*
Dale Hardy, *Vice Pres*
EMP: 100
SALES (est): 240.2MM
SALES (corp-wide): 98.6B Privately Held
WEB: www.nexusis.com
SIC: 4899 Data communication services
HQ: Dimension Data North America, Inc.
1 Penn Plz Ste 1600
New York NY 10119
212 613-1220

(P-6071)
DISCOVERY COMMUNICATIONS INC
10100 Santa Monica Blvd, Los Angeles
(90067-4003)
PHONE.................................310 975-5906
David Zazlov, *CEO*
EMP: 400
SALES (est): 3.5MM Privately Held
SIC: 4899 Data communication services

(P-6072)
EQUINIX (US) ENTERPRISES INC
1 Lagoon Dr Fl 4, Redwood City
(94065-1562)
PHONE.................................650 598-6363
Stephen M Smith, *President*
Donald Campbell, *CFO*
EMP: 99 EST: 2005
SALES (est): 2.7MM
SALES (corp-wide): 2.7B Publicly Held
SIC: 4899 Communication signal enhancement network system
PA: Equinix, Inc.
1 Lagoon Dr Ste 400
Redwood City CA 94065
650 598-6000

(P-6073)
EVERBRIDGE INC
155 N Lake Ave Ste 900, Pasadena
(91101-1849)
PHONE.................................818 230-9700
EMP: 194
SALES (corp-wide): 58.7MM Publicly Held
SIC: 4899 Data communication services
PA: Everbridge, Inc.
25 Corporate Dr Ste 400
Burlington MA 01803
818 230-9700

(P-6074)
FOUR MEDICA INC
13160 Mindanao Way # 280, Marina Del Rey (90292-6358)
PHONE.................................310 348-4100
Fax: 310 348-4104
Oleg Bess, *Principal*
EMP: 91
SALES (est): 11.1MM Privately Held
SIC: 4899 Data communication services

(P-6075)
GOD HELP FILMS INC
8200 Wilshire Blvd # 200, Beverly Hills
(90211-2328)
PHONE.................................323 556-0699
Pure Brisbon, *Principal*
EMP: 80
SALES: 500K Privately Held
SIC: 4899 Communication services

(P-6076)
INTELSAT CORPORATION
Also Called: Intell Set
1600 Forbes Way, Long Beach
(90810-1830)
PHONE.................................310 525-5500
Fax: 310 525-5875
Tom Nassis, *Vice Pres*
EMP: 150 Privately Held
SIC: 4899 Satellite earth stations
HQ: Intelsat Corporation
7900 Tysons One Pl
Mc Lean VA 22102
703 559-6800

(P-6077)
IPS GROUP INC (PA)
5601 Oberlin Dr Ste 100, San Diego
(92121-3747)
PHONE.................................858 404-0607
David W King, *CEO*
Chad Randal, *COO*
Dario Paduano, *CFO*
Amir Sedadi, *Vice Pres*
Ananda Hiler, *Administration*
▲ EMP: 55
SQ FT: 23,000

4899 - Communication Svcs, NEC County (P-6078)

SALES (est): 34.1MM **Privately Held**
WEB: www.ipsgroupinc.com
SIC: **4899** 3824 Communication signal enhancement network system; parking meters

(P-6078)
KBRWYLE TECH SOLUTIONS LLC
Also Called: Honeywell
Vanonbrg Air Frc Bldg 660, Lompoc (93438)
P.O. Box 305 (93438-0305)
PHONE..................................805 734-2982
T A Yancey, *Manager*
EMP: 277
SALES (corp-wide): 5.1B **Publicly Held**
WEB: www.honeywell-tsi.com
SIC: **4899** Missile tracking by telemetry & photography
HQ: Kbrwyle Technology Solutions, Llc
7000 Columbia Gateway Dr # 100
Columbia MD 21046
410 964-7000

(P-6079)
L-3 COMMUNICATIONS CORPORATION
10770 Wtridge Cir Ste 200, San Diego (92121)
PHONE..................................858 623-6513
Michelle Petty, *Branch Mgr*
David Oglesby, *Officer*
Scott Wiley, *Software Engr*
Jonathan Stewart, *Design Engr*
Serjio Gonzalez, *Technology*
EMP: 100
SALES (corp-wide): 10.4B **Publicly Held**
SIC: **4899** Data communication services
HQ: L-3 Communications Corporation
600 3rd Ave
New York NY 10016
212 697-1111

(P-6080)
LEVEL 3 COMMUNICATIONS INC
23965 Connecticut St, Hayward (94545-1610)
PHONE..................................510 887-8920
Vince Richards, *Principal*
EMP: 53
SALES (corp-wide): 8.2B **Publicly Held**
SIC: **4899** Data communication services
PA: Level 3 Communications, Inc.
1025 Eldorado Blvd
Broomfield CO 80021
720 888-1000

(P-6081)
LUXN INC
580 Maude Ct, Sunnyvale (94085-2822)
PHONE..................................408 213-7437
Fax: 408 522-5212
Thomas Alexander, *President*
Lee Zipin, *Ch of Bd*
Agnes Emory, *Vice Pres*
Paul Strudwick, *Vice Pres*
EMP: 53 EST: 1998
SALES (est): 2.1MM
SALES (corp-wide): 142.9MM **Publicly Held**
WEB: www.luxn.com
SIC: **4899** Data communication services
HQ: Sorrento Networks Corporation
7195 Oakport St
Oakland CA 94621
510 577-1400

(P-6082)
MOBILEUM INC (PA)
2880 Lakeside Dr Ste 135, Santa Clara (95054-2830)
PHONE..................................408 844-6600
Bobby Srinivasan, *CEO*
Ori Sasson, *CEO*
Stephen Baker, *CFO*
Neil Laird, *CFO*
Craig Ehrilch, *Bd of Directors*
EMP: 77
SQ FT: 4,000
SALES (est): 105.2MM **Privately Held**
WEB: www.roamware.com
SIC: **4899** 7373 Data communication services; computer systems analysis & design

(P-6083)
NETFORTRIS CORPORATION
455 Market St Ste 620, San Francisco (94105-2449)
PHONE..................................888 469-5100
Grant Evans, *CEO*
EMP: 160
SALES (est): 7.3MM
SALES (corp-wide): 20.5MM **Privately Held**
SIC: **4899** 7379 Data communication services; computer related consulting services
PA: Netfortris Acquisition Co., Inc.
455 Market St Ste 620
San Francisco CA

(P-6084)
NEW CINGULAR WIRELESS SVCS INC
6408 Pacific Blvd, Huntington Park (90255-4104)
PHONE..................................323 588-9348
Jesse Avila, *Manager*
Robert Linnez, *Manager*
EMP: 86
SALES (corp-wide): 146.8B **Publicly Held**
WEB: www.attws.com
SIC: **4899** 4812 Data communication services; cellular telephone services
HQ: New Cingular Wireless Services, Inc.
7277 164th Ave Ne
Redmond WA 98052
425 827-4500

(P-6085)
NPHASE LLC
6195 Lusk Blvd Ste 200, San Diego (92121-3723)
PHONE..................................312 577-1650
Steve Pazol, *Mng Member*
Mark Lama, *CFO*
Pat Kilzer, *Finance*
Steve Altman,
Andrew Gilbert,
EMP: 75
SQ FT: 20,000
SALES (est): 4.3MM **Privately Held**
WEB: www.nphasem2m.com
SIC: **4899** Data communication services

(P-6086)
PAGERDUTY INC
600 Townsend St Ste 200e, San Francisco (94103-5690)
PHONE..................................650 989-2965
Jennifer Tejada, *CEO*
Tim Armandpour, *Vice Pres*
Sophie Kitson, *Vice Pres*
Richard Steinhart, *Vice Pres*
Jonathan Wilkinson, *Vice Pres*
EMP: 58
SALES (est): 11.3MM **Privately Held**
WEB: www.pagerduty.com
SIC: **4899** Data communication services

(P-6087)
PROSOFT TECHNOLOGY INC (PA)
9201 Camino Media Ste 200, Bakersfield (93311-1362)
PHONE..................................661 716-5100
Thomas Crone, *CEO*
Janice Hungerford, *President*
Doug Sharratt, *President*
Ken Roslan, *Vice Pres*
Chris Williams, *Vice Pres*
EMP: 64
SALES (est): 37.3MM **Privately Held**
WEB: www.psft.com
SIC: **4899** Data communication services

(P-6088)
SILVER SPRING NETWORKS INC (PA)
230 W Tasman Dr, San Jose (95134-1714)
PHONE..................................669 770-4000
Fax: 650 363-5240
Michael Bell, *President*
Scott A Lang, *Ch of Bd*
Ayse Ildeniz, *COO*
Kenneth P Gianella, *CFO*
Ambrish Chitnis, *Sr Corp Ofcr*
▲ EMP: 400

SQ FT: 171,100
SALES: 489.5MM **Publicly Held**
WEB: www.silverspringnetworks.com
SIC: **4899** 7372 Communication signal enhancement network system; prepackaged software

(P-6089)
SOUTH BAY RGONAL PUB COMM AUTH
Also Called: S B COMMUNICATIONS
4440 W Broadway, Hawthorne (90250-3802)
PHONE..................................310 973-1802
Fax: 310 978-0892
Ralph Mailloux, *Exec Dir*
Agnes Walker, *Finance Mgr*
Shannon Kauffman, *Opers Mgr*
EMP: 50
SQ FT: 1,632
SALES: 9.6MM **Privately Held**
SIC: **4899** Communication signal enhancement network system

(P-6090)
SPECTRUM COMMUNICATIONS CABLIN
310 S Maple St Ste F, Corona (92880-6946)
P.O. Box 2195, Chino Hills (91709-0074)
PHONE..................................951 371-0549
Fax: 909 273-3114
Sherry Perry Rivera, *CEO*
Angie Hobson, *Admin Sec*
EMP: 130
SQ FT: 14,800
SALES (est): 12.1MM **Privately Held**
WEB: www.spectrumccsi.com
SIC: **4899** 1731 5063 1623 Data communication services; computer installation; wire & cable; water, sewer & utility lines; computer integrated systems design; cable & other pay television services

(P-6091)
SS8 NETWORKS INC (PA)
Also Called: S S 8
750 Tasman Dr, Milpitas (95035-7456)
PHONE..................................408 894-8400
Fax: 408 432-2691
Dennis Haar, *CEO*
Faizel Lakhani, *President*
Kam Wong, *CFO*
Derek Roga, *Vice Pres*
Cemal Dikmen, *Principal*
EMP: 120
SQ FT: 83,000
SALES (est): 69.9MM **Privately Held**
WEB: www.ss8.com
SIC: **4899** Communication signal enhancement network system

(P-6092)
TELECOMMUNICTNS CMMNCTNS SRVCS
Also Called: San Francisco Hq
21 Locust Ave, Mill Valley (94941-2852)
PHONE..................................415 869-9000
Brandon Chaney, *CEO*
Anthony Zabit, *COO*
Hoi Ng, *Credit Staff*
Scott Waldron, *Sales Associate*
Dominick Niboli, *Marketing Staff*
EMP: 50
SALES (corp-wide): 57.2MM **Privately Held**
SIC: **4899** Data communication services
PA: Telecommunications Communications Services, Inc.
800 S Michigan St
Seattle WA 98108
888 469-5100

(P-6093)
TELETRAC INC (HQ)
7391 Lincoln Way, Garden Grove (92841-1428)
PHONE..................................714 897-0877
Fax: 714 891-6784
Tj Chung, *President*
Frank Goodman, *President*
Tim Van Cleve, *COO*
Fred Himburg, *Vice Pres*
Jackson Ku, *Administration*
▲ EMP: 124
SQ FT: 40,000

SALES (est): 217.3MM
SALES (corp-wide): 5B **Publicly Held**
WEB: www.teletrac.net
SIC: **4899** Data communication services
PA: Fortive Corporation
6920 Seaway Blvd
Everett WA 98203
425 446-5000

(P-6094)
TERABURST NETWORKS INC
1289 Anvilwood Ave, Sunnyvale (94089-2204)
PHONE..................................408 400-4100
Ashok Jain, *CEO*
Christopher Weller, *Vice Pres*
EMP: 50
SALES (est): 3.5MM **Privately Held**
WEB: www.teraburst.com
SIC: **4899** Communication signal enhancement network system

(P-6095)
THINKOM SOLUTIONS INC
4881 W 145th St, Hawthorne (90250-6701)
PHONE..................................310 371-5486
Fax: 310 214-1066
Mark Silk, *CEO*
Michael Burke, *President*
Stuart Coppedge, *CFO*
Matthew Turk, *CFO*
William W Milroy, *Principal*
EMP: 65
SQ FT: 74,000
SALES (est): 15.3MM **Privately Held**
WEB: www.thin-kom.com
SIC: **4899** Satellite earth stations; television antenna construction & rental

(P-6096)
TRI-POWER GROUP INC
617 N Mary Ave, Sunnyvale (94085-2907)
PHONE..................................925 583-8200
Seth Buechley, *CEO*
Chip Laughton, *President*
Bryan Kemper, *COO*
Barry Bruce, *CFO*
Mike Wing, *Info Tech Dir*
▲ EMP: 60
SQ FT: 13,000
SALES (est): 7.5MM **Privately Held**
WEB: www.tripowergroup.com
SIC: **4899** Data communication services

(P-6097)
US DEPT OF THE AIR FORCE
Also Called: 95cs/Scxc Comp
35 N Wolfe Ave, Edwards (93524-6701)
PHONE..................................661 277-3030
EMP: 250 **Publicly Held**
WEB: www.af.mil
SIC: **4899** 9711 Communication signal enhancement network system; Air Force;
HQ: United States Department Of The Air Force
1000 Air Force Pentagon
Washington DC 20330
703 545-6700

(P-6098)
VERIZON COMMUNICATIONS INC
9900 Flower St, Bellflower (90706-5411)
PHONE..................................562 804-0354
EMP: 165
SALES (corp-wide): 131.6B **Publicly Held**
WEB: www.verizon.com
SIC: **4899** Data communication services
PA: Verizon Communications Inc.
1095 Ave Of The Americas
New York NY 10036
212 395-1000

(P-6099)
WHATSAPP INC
3561 Homestead Rd 416, Santa Clara (95051-5161)
PHONE..................................650 336-3079
Jan Koum, *CEO*
Tedd Osborne, *Marketing Mgr*
Eleen Chen, *Sales Mgr*
Cristina Trujillo, *Cust Mgr*
EMP: 70

PRODUCTS & SERVICES SECTION

4911 - Electric Svcs County (P-6121)

SALES (est): 4.7MM
SALES (corp-wide): 17.9B **Publicly Held**
SIC: **4899** 5999 Data communication services; mobile telephones & equipment
PA: Facebook, Inc.
  1 Hacker Way Bldg 10
  Menlo Park CA 94025
  650 543-4800

(P-6100)
WIRELESS STORE INC
11290 Point East Dr # 210, Rancho Cordova (95742-6243)
PHONE...................................916 206-3600
Fadi Rashed, *CEO*
EMP: 250 EST: 2005
SQ FT: 5,000
SALES: 60MM **Privately Held**
SIC: **4899** 4812 Data communication services; cellular telephone services

(P-6101)
WOVEN DIGITAL INC (PA)
Also Called: Redwood
10381 Jefferson Blvd, Culver City (90232-3511)
PHONE...................................310 488-8941
Colin Digiaro, *CEO*
Michael Laur, *COO*
Sarah Phelps, *Human Res Dir*
Angelin Okamura, *Director*
Robert Hall, *Manager*
EMP: 90
SQ FT: 12,000
SALES (est): 17.1MM **Privately Held**
SIC: **4899** Data communication services

(P-6102)
WPCS INTERNATIONAL INC (PA)
521 Railroad Ave, Suisun City (94585-4244)
PHONE...................................707 421-1300
Sebastian Giordano, *CEO*
Robert Roller, *President*
David Allen, *CFO*
EMP: 72 EST: 1997
SALES: 14.5MM **Publicly Held**
SIC: **4899** 4813 Data communication services; telephone communication, except radio; ; telephone cable service, land or submarine

4911 Electric Svcs

(P-6103)
AES HUNTINGTON BEACH LLC
21730 Newland St, Huntington Beach (92646-7612)
PHONE...................................714 374-1476
Eric Pendergraft,
Ania Irwin, *Controller*
Mike Livingston, *Controller*
Jason Molina, *Buyer*
Minh Hoang,
EMP: 50 EST: 1997
SALES (est): 37.4MM
SALES (corp-wide): 14.9B **Publicly Held**
WEB: www.aescorp.com
SIC: **4911** Generation, electric power
PA: The Aes Corporation
  4300 Wilson Blvd Ste 1100
  Arlington VA 22203
  703 522-1315

(P-6104)
AES SOUTHLAND LLC
690 N Studebaker Rd, Long Beach (90803-2221)
PHONE...................................562 430-8685
Jeff Evans, *Mng Member*
Linda Edran, *Manager*
EMP: 89 EST: 1998
SALES (est): 30.8MM
SALES (corp-wide): 14.9B **Publicly Held**
WEB: www.aescorp.com
SIC: **4911** Electric services
PA: The Aes Corporation
  4300 Wilson Blvd Ste 1100
  Arlington VA 22203
  703 522-1315

(P-6105)
AL - AMIR GROUP LLC
380 Northlake Dr Apt 28, San Jose (95117-1245)
PHONE...................................408 505-9458
Omar Janin, *President*
Omar Jamil, *President*
Ala Jamil, *Vice Pres*
Howard Eldin, *Admin Sec*
EMP: 65
SQ FT: 1,500
SALES: 10MM **Privately Held**
SIC: **4911** 6792 Distribution, electric power; oil royalty traders

(P-6106)
ALAMEDA BUREAU ELEC IMPRV CORP (PA)
Also Called: Alameda Municpal Power
2000 Grand St, Alameda (94501-1228)
P.O. Box H (94501-0263)
PHONE...................................510 748-3901
Fax: 510 814-5699
Edwin Dankworth, *CEO*
Gregory Hamm, *President*
Peter Holmes, *Vice Pres*
Bob Mackey, *Vice Pres*
Ann McCormick, *Vice Pres*
▲ EMP: 85
SALES (est): 77.7MM **Privately Held**
WEB: www.alamedapt.com
SIC: **4911** 4899 4841 Transmission, electric power; distribution, electric power; communication signal enhancement network system; cable & other pay television services

(P-6107)
ALTAMONT INFRASTRUCTURE CO
6185 Industrial Way, Livermore (94551-9750)
PHONE...................................925 245-5500
Tom Kelly, *Principal*
Green Ridge LLC, *Mng Member*
EMP: 60
SQ FT: 8,000
SALES: 30MM **Privately Held**
SIC: **4911** Generation, electric power

(P-6108)
CALIFRNIA IND SYS OPRATOR CORP (PA)
Also Called: CALIFORNIA ISO
250 Outcropping Way, Folsom (95630-8773)
P.O. Box 639014 (95763-9014)
PHONE...................................916 351-4400
Stephen Berberich, *President*
Bob Foster, *Ch of Bd*
William J Regan, *CFO*
Philip Leiber, *Treasurer*
Philip Leiver, *Treasurer*
EMP: 450
SQ FT: 79,000
SALES: 213.4MM **Privately Held**
WEB: www.caiso.com
SIC: **4911** Distribution, electric power; transmission, electric power

(P-6109)
CATALINA SLAR LSSEE HOLDCO LLC
15445 Innovation Dr, San Diego (92128-3432)
PHONE...................................888 903-6926
Tristan Grimbert, *President*
Robert Miller, *Corp Secy*
Richard Jigarjian, *Vice Pres*
EMP: 82 EST: 2014
SQ FT: 70,000
SALES (est): 7.9MM **Privately Held**
SIC: **4911** Electric services

(P-6110)
CATALINA SOLAR 2 LLC
15445 Innovation Dr, San Diego (92128-3432)
PHONE...................................888 903-6926
Tristan Grimbert, *President*
Ryan Pfaff, *Vice Pres*
Robert Miller, *Admin Sec*
EMP: 826
SQ FT: 70,000

SALES (est): 255.7MM **Privately Held**
SIC: **4911** Electric services

(P-6111)
CATALINA SOLAR LESSEE LLC
11585 Willow Springs Rd, Rosamond (93560)
P.O. Box 504080, San Diego (92150-4080)
PHONE...................................888 903-6926
Tristan Grimbert, *President*
Robert Miller, *Admin Sec*
EMP: 826 EST: 2014
SQ FT: 70,000
SALES (est): 265.9MM
SALES (corp-wide): 769.9MM **Privately Held**
SIC: **4911** Electric services
PA: Edf Renewable Energy, Inc.
  15445 Innovation Dr
  San Diego CA 92128
  858 521-3300

(P-6112)
CITY OF GLENDALE
Also Called: Glendale Water & Power
141 N Glendale Ave Fl 2, Glendale (91206-4975)
PHONE...................................818 548-3300
John Dolan, *Manager*
EMP: 300 **Privately Held**
WEB: www.glendaleca.com
SIC: **4911** Electric services
PA: City Of Glendale
  141 N Glendale Ave Fl 2
  Glendale CA 91206
  818 548-2085

(P-6113)
CITY OF GLENDALE
Also Called: Power Plant
634 Bekins Way, Glendale (91201-3013)
PHONE...................................818 548-3980
Larry Moorehouse, *Superintendent*
EMP: 50 **Privately Held**
WEB: www.glendaleca.com
SIC: **4911** Generation, electric power
PA: City Of Glendale
  141 N Glendale Ave Fl 2
  Glendale CA 91206
  818 548-2085

(P-6114)
CITY OF LOS ANGELES
Also Called: Harbor Generating Station
161 Island Ave, Wilmington (90744-6303)
PHONE...................................310 522-1750
Bradford Chow, *Branch Mgr*
Joel Ackermann, *Supervisor*
Clifford Matias, *Supervisor*
EMP: 8800 **Privately Held**
SIC: **4911** Electric services
PA: City Of Los Angeles
  200 N Spring St Ste 303
  Los Angeles CA 90012
  213 978-0600

(P-6115)
CITY OF LOS ANGELES
Also Called: Water & Power Dept
6550 Van Nuys Blvd, Van Nuys (91401-1426)
PHONE...................................818 902-3000
Margaret Wallace, *Branch Mgr*
EMP: 99 **Privately Held**
WEB: www.lacity.org
SIC: **4911** 9631 Distribution, electric power; regulation, administration of utilities;
PA: City Of Los Angeles
  200 N Spring St Ste 303
  Los Angeles CA 90012
  213 978-0600

(P-6116)
CITY OF SANTA CLARA
Also Called: Silicon Valley Power
1500 Warburton Ave, Santa Clara (95050-3796)
PHONE...................................408 615-2300
Fax: 408 249-0217
John Roukema, *Director*
Regin Pen, *Senior VP*
Debbie Barry, *Division Mgr*
Dan Grebinski, *Administration*
Tony Canter, *Systs Prg Mgr*
EMP: 50 **Privately Held**

SIC: **4911** Electric services
PA: City Of Santa Clara
  1500 Warburton Ave
  Santa Clara CA 95050
  408 615-2200

(P-6117)
CITY OF SANTA CLARA
Also Called: Electric Department
1705 Martin Ave, Santa Clara (95050-2557)
PHONE...................................408 615-2046
Chris Cervelli, *Principal*
EMP: 125
SQ FT: 15,000 **Privately Held**
SIC: **4911**
PA: City Of Santa Clara
  1500 Warburton Ave
  Santa Clara CA 95050
  408 615-2200

(P-6118)
COMBUSTION ASSOCIATES INC
Also Called: Cai
555 Monica Cir, Corona (92880-5447)
PHONE...................................951 272-6999
Fax: 909 272-8066
Mukund Kavia, *President*
Kusum Kavia, *Vice Pres*
Prajesh Kavia, *Admin Sec*
Mark Bernal, *Design Engr*
Kevin Wilson, *Design Engr*
▼ EMP: 50
SQ FT: 40,000
SALES (est): 90.8MM **Privately Held**
WEB: www.cai3.com
SIC: **4911** 3443 ; boiler & boiler shop work

(P-6119)
CONSTELLATION NEWENERGY INC
350 S Grand Ave Ste 3800, Los Angeles (90071-3479)
PHONE...................................213 576-6001
Fax: 213 576-6060
Michael Peevey, *Branch Mgr*
Ron Ryan, *Vice Pres*
Arron Thomas, *Vice Pres*
Gustav Beerel, *VP Finance*
Stephen Kass, *Marketing Mgr*
EMP: 70
SALES (corp-wide): 29.4B **Publicly Held**
SIC: **4911** Electric services
HQ: Constellation Newenergy, Inc.
  100 Constellation Way
  Baltimore MD 21202
  410 783-2800

(P-6120)
COSO OPERATING COMPANY LLC
2 Gill Station Coso Rd, Little Lake (93542)
P.O. Box 1690, Inyokern (93527-1690)
PHONE...................................760 764-1300
Jim Pagano, *CEO*
Joseph Greco, *Senior VP*
Aislinn Smith, *Admin Sec*
Dick Arruda, *Project Mgr*
Richard Arruda, *Manager*
EMP: 90
SALES (est): 83.9MM
SALES (corp-wide): 103.6MM **Privately Held**
SIC: **4911** Generation, electric power
PA: Terra-Gen Power, Llc
  1095 Avenue Of The Americ
  New York NY 10036
  646 829-3900

(P-6121)
COVANTA DELANO INC
Also Called: Delano Energy
31500 Pond Rd, Delano (93215)
P.O. Box 39, Mariposa (95338-0039)
PHONE...................................661 792-3067
Fax: 661 792-3072
Anthony J Orlando, *CEO*
Tony Villarreal, *Controller*
Rick Lloyd, *Buyer*
Tim Myers, *Plant Engr*
John Puskas, *Manager*
▲ EMP: 50

4911 - Electric Svcs County (P-6122)

SALES (est): 21.4MM
SALES (corp-wide): 1.6B Publicly Held
WEB: www.aescorp.com
SIC: 4911 Generation, electric power
PA: Covanta Holding Corporation
 445 South St
 Morristown NJ 07960
 862 345-5000

(P-6122)
CPN WILD HORSE GEOTHERMAL LLC
10350 Socrates Mine Rd, Middletown (95461-9732)
PHONE 707 431-6229
James Kluesner, *Vice Pres*
EMP: 300
SQ FT: 4,000
SALES: 1.8MM
SALES (corp-wide): 6.4B Publicly Held
SIC: 4911 Generation, electric power;
PA: Calpine Corporation
 717 Texas St Ste 1000
 Houston TX 77002
 713 830-2000

(P-6123)
DESERT VIEW POWER INC
2600 Capitol Ave, Sacramento (95816-5927)
P.O. Box 758, Mecca (92254-0758)
PHONE 916 596-2500
Hugh W Smith, *President*
Charles Abbott, *COO*
Robert Tennington, *CFO*
EMP: 54
SQ FT: 5,000
SALES (est): 54.9MM Privately Held
WEB: www.colmac-energy.com
SIC: 4911
PA: American Consumer Industries Inc
 1105 N Market St Ste 1300
 Wilmington DE
 -

(P-6124)
DUKE ENERGY CORPORATION
8001 Irvine Center Dr, Irvine (92618-2938)
PHONE 949 727-7434
EMP: 170
SALES (corp-wide): 23.4B Publicly Held
SIC: 4911 4924
PA: Duke Energy Corporation
 550 S Tryon St
 Charlotte NC 28285
 704 382-3853

(P-6125)
DYNEGY MARKETING & TRADE LLC
Hwy 1 & Dolan Rd, Moss Landing (95039)
P.O. Box 690 (95039-0690)
PHONE 831 633-6700
Sharon Andresen, *IT/INT Sup*
Kent Nelson, *Engineer*
Craig Hill, *Plant Engr*
Mike Minafo, *Maint Spvr*
Ernie Bloecher, *Manager*
EMP: 100
SALES (corp-wide): 1.4B Publicly Held
SIC: 4911 4923 Generation, electric power; gas transmission & distribution
HQ: Dynegy Marketing & Trade, Llc
 601 Travis St Ste 1400
 Houston TX 77002
 713 507-6400

(P-6126)
DYNEGY MOSS LANDING LLC
7301 Highway 1, Moss Landing (95039)
P.O. Box 690 (95039-0690)
PHONE 831 633-6618
Robert C Flexon, *CEO*
Curtis H Davis, *Vice Pres*
David Gillespie, *Vice Pres*
Phillip C Grigsby, *Vice Pres*
C G Harper, *Vice Pres*
EMP: 75
SALES (est): 65.4MM
SALES (corp-wide): 1.4B Publicly Held
WEB: www.dynegy.com
SIC: 4911 Electric services
PA: Dynegy Inc.
 601 Travis St Ste 1400
 Houston TX 77002
 713 507-6400

(P-6127)
EDF MSSCHSTTS SPNSOR MMBER LLC
15445 Innovation Dr, San Diego (92128-3432)
PHONE 888 903-6926
Tristan Grimber, *President*
Kara Vongphakdy, *Treasurer*
Larry Barr, *Exec VP*
Robert Miller, *Exec VP*
Ryan Pfaff, *Exec VP*
EMP: 827 **EST:** 2014
SQ FT: 70,000
SALES (est): 205.1K
SALES (corp-wide): 769.9MM Privately Held
SIC: 4911 Electric services
PA: Edf Renewable Energy, Inc.
 15445 Innovation Dr
 San Diego CA 92128
 858 521-3300

(P-6128)
EDF RENEWABLE ENERGY INC (PA)
15445 Innovation Dr, San Diego (92128-3432)
P.O. Box 504080 (92150-4080)
PHONE 858 521-3300
Tristan Grimbert, *President*
Al Kurzenhauser, *COO*
Jean Roche, *CFO*
Luis Silva, *CFO*
Todd Benett, *Treasurer*
▲ **EMP:** 225
SALES (est): 769.9MM Privately Held
WEB: www.enxco.com
SIC: 4911 Generation, electric power

(P-6129)
EDF RNWABLE ASSET HOLDINGS INC
15445 Innovation Dr, San Diego (92128-3432)
PHONE 888 903-6926
Tristan Grimbert, *President*
Richard Jigarjian, *Vice Pres*
Robert Miller, *Admin Sec*
EMP: 826 **EST:** 2009
SQ FT: 70,000
SALES (est): 288.4MM Privately Held
SIC: 4911 Electric services

(P-6130)
EDISON INTERNATIONAL (PA)
2244 Walnut Grove Ave, Rosemead (91770-3714)
P.O. Box 976 (91770-0976)
PHONE 626 302-2222
Fax: 626 302-2117
Theodore F Craver Jr, *Ch of Bd*
Pedro J Pizarro, *President*
Maria Rigatti, *CFO*
W James Scilacci, *CFO*
Ronald L Litzinger, *Exec VP*
▲ **EMP:** 52
SALES: 11.5B Publicly Held
WEB: www.edisonx.com
SIC: 4911 Electric services; distribution, electric power; generation, electric power; transmission, electric power

(P-6131)
EDISON MSSION MIDWEST HOLDINGS
2244 Walnut Grove Ave, Rosemead (91770-3714)
PHONE 626 302-2222
Guy F Gorney, *President*
Johanna Pyles, *Program Mgr*
Jeffrey Balaban, *Info Tech Mgr*
Efrain Gonzalez, *Info Tech Mgr*
Kenneth Pramana, *Info Tech Mgr*
EMP: 2483
SALES (est): 4.3B
SALES (corp-wide): 11.5B Publicly Held
SIC: 4911 Electric services
HQ: Edison Mission Group Inc.
 2244 Walnut Grove Ave
 Rosemead CA 91770
 626 302-2222

(P-6132)
ENPOWER MANAGEMENT CORP
2420 Camino Ramon Ste 101, San Ramon (94583-4207)
PHONE 925 244-1100
Edward Tomeo, *President*
Alex Sugaoka, *Vice Pres*
Roland Allred, *Controller*
Scott Riddle, *Manager*
EMP: 50
SQ FT: 3,500
SALES (est): 12.1MM
SALES (corp-wide): 66MM Privately Held
WEB: www.enpowercorp.com
SIC: 4911 Generation, electric power; distribution, electric power
PA: Enpower Corp.
 2420 Camino Ramon Ste 101
 San Ramon CA 94583
 925 244-1100

(P-6133)
GENERAL ELECTRIC COMPANY
288 Campus Dr Bldg 14105, Stanford (94305-4109)
PHONE 650 725-0516
Ron Dahlin, *Manager*
EMP: 217
SALES (corp-wide): 117.3B Publicly Held
SIC: 4911 Generation, electric power
PA: General Electric Company
 41 Farnsworth St
 Boston MA 02210
 617 443-3000

(P-6134)
GOLDEN STATE WATER COMPANY
Bear Valley Electric
42020 Garstin Rd, Big Bear Lake (92315)
P.O. Box 1547 (92315-1547)
PHONE 909 866-4678
Fax: 909 866-5056
Roger Kropke, *Manager*
Bob Bradford, *Purch Mgr*
Bob Davison, *Senior Buyer*
Harry Scarborough, *Director*
EMP: 50
SALES (corp-wide): 458.6MM Publicly Held
WEB: www.gswater.com
SIC: 4911 Distribution, electric power
HQ: Golden State Water Company
 630 E Foothill Blvd
 San Dimas CA 91773
 909 394-3600

(P-6135)
GREAT WESTERN WIND ENERGY LLC
15445 Innovation Dr, San Diego (92128-3432)
PHONE 888 903-6926
Tristan Grimbert, *President*
Kara Vongphakdy, *Treasurer*
Ryan Pfaff, *Vice Pres*
Robert Miller, *Admin Sec*
EMP: 99
SALES (est): 1.8MM Privately Held
SIC: 4911

(P-6136)
GREEN RIDGE SERVICES LLC
6185 Industrial Way, Livermore (94551-9750)
PHONE 925 245-5500
Tom Kelly,
Kitty Duer, *Administration*
EMP: 60
SQ FT: 30,000
SALES (est): 23.8MM Privately Held
SIC: 4911 Electric services

(P-6137)
HANERGY HOLDING AMERICA INC
1350 Bayshore Hwy Ste 825, Burlingame (94010-1848)
PHONE 650 288-3722
Yi Wu, *Ch of Bd*
Jeff Zhou, *President*
Richard Gaertner, *COO*
Pyramyth Liu, *COO*
Julie Du, *Admin Mgr*
EMP: 360
SQ FT: 7,000
SALES (est): 280.6MM Privately Held
SIC: 4911 6719 Generation, electric power; investment holding companies, except banks
PA: Hanergy Holding Group Limited
 No.0-A, Anli Road, Chaoyang Dist.
 Beijing
 108 391-4567

(P-6138)
HIGH RIDGE WIND LLC
15445 Innovation Dr, San Diego (92128-3432)
PHONE 888 903-6926
Tristan Grimbert, *President*
Robert Miller, *Corp Secy*
Ryan Pfaff, *Vice Pres*
EMP: 826 **EST:** 2013
SQ FT: 70,000
SALES (est): 258.5MM Privately Held
SIC: 4911 Electric services

(P-6139)
HUDSON RANCH POWER I LLC
409 W Mcdonald St, Calipatria (92233-9701)
P.O. Box 67 (92233-0067)
PHONE 858 509-0150
Eric L Spomer, *Mng Member*
George Donlou, *Treasurer*
Carol A Thimot, *Asst Treas*
David K Watson,
EMP: 55
SALES (est): 52.2MM Privately Held
SIC: 4911 Generation, electric power

(P-6140)
IMPERIAL IRRIGATION DISTRICT (PA)
Also Called: I I D
333 E Barioni Blvd, Imperial (92251-1773)
P.O. Box 937 (92251-0937)
PHONE 800 303-7756
Fax: 760 339-9470
Stephen Benson, *President*
Anthony Sanchez, *President*
Keven Kelly, *CEO*
Ronnie Jones, *Bd of Directors*
Raquel Lopez, *Officer*
▲ **EMP:** 700
SQ FT: 10,000
SALES (est): 995.5MM Privately Held
WEB: www.iidwater.com
SIC: 4911 4971 4931 ; water distribution or supply systems for irrigation; electric & other services combined

(P-6141)
JETMORE WIND LLC
15445 Innovation Dr, San Diego (92128-3432)
PHONE 888 903-6926
Tristan Grimbert, *President*
Ryan Pfaff, *Vice Pres*
Robert Miller, *Admin Sec*
EMP: 826 **EST:** 2013
SQ FT: 70,000
SALES (est): 193.7MM Privately Held
SIC: 4911 Electric services

(P-6142)
KERN RIVER CO GENERATION CO
Sw China Grade Loop, Bakersfield (93308)
PHONE 661 392-2663
Neil Bridges, *Exec Dir*
Gaylord Edward, *Treasurer*
Gordon Thomson, *Exec Dir*
Vickie Bicera, *Accounts Mgr*
EMP: 65
SALES (est): 35.6MM
SALES (corp-wide): 14.6B Publicly Held
SIC: 4911 4961 ; steam supply systems, including geothermal
HQ: Southern Sierra Energy Company
 18101 Von Karman Ave # 330
 Irvine CA 92612
 949 752-5588

▲ = Import ▼ = Export
◆ = Import/Export

PRODUCTS & SERVICES SECTION

4911 - Electric Svcs County (P-6164)

(P-6143)
KJC OPERATING COMPANY
41100 Us Highway 395, Boron
(93516-2109)
PHONE................................760 762-5562
Fax: 760 762-5546
Chris Kelleher, *Chairman*
Janet Doyle, *President*
Scott Frier, *COO*
Tom Upah, *Manager*
EMP: 117
SQ FT: 10,000
SALES (est): 30.2MM **Privately Held**
WEB: www.kjcsolar.com
SIC: **4911** Electric services

(P-6144)
LEEMAH ELECTRONICS INC
Also Called: (415 LOCATION)
1080 Sansome St, San Francisco
(94111-1308)
PHONE................................415 394-1288
Jack Wang, *Manager*
Ben Jones, *Purchasing*
Warren Lam, *Manager*
Rick Pacettie, *Manager*
EMP: 120
SALES (corp-wide): 101.9MM **Privately Held**
SIC: **4911** 3672 3669 3571 Electric services; printed circuit boards; intercommunication systems, electric; electronic computers
HQ: Leemah Electronics, Inc.
155 S Hill Dr
Brisbane CA 94005
415 394-1288

(P-6145)
LIBERTY UTLTIES CLPECO ELC LLC
Also Called: Liberty Energy
933 Eloise Ave, South Lake Tahoe
(96150-6470)
PHONE................................530 543-5288
Ian Robertson, *Mng Member*
Mike Smart, *President*
David Bronicheski,
Stephen McCrodan, *Manager*
EMP: 60
SQ FT: 10,000
SALES (est): 55MM **Privately Held**
SIC: **4911** Distribution, electric power

(P-6146)
LOS ANGELES DEPT WTR & PWR
Also Called: Los Angeles Cy of Dept Wtr Pwr
111 N Hope St 743, Los Angeles
(90012-2607)
P.O. Box 51111 (90051-5700)
PHONE................................213 367-4211
Fax: 213 367-4588
Ronald Nichols, *General Mgr*
Kimberly Ohara, *Admin Asst*
Jackie Staten, *Admin Asst*
Estella Moreno, *Administration*
Walter Ramirez, *Administration*
EMP: 99
SALES (corp-wide): 3.8B **Privately Held**
SIC: **4911** 9511 Electric services; air, water & solid waste management
PA: Los Angeles Department Of Water And Power
111 N Hope St Rm 1063
Los Angeles CA 90012
213 367-4043

(P-6147)
MERCED IRRIGATION DISTRICT (PA)
744 W 20th St, Merced (95340-3601)
P.O. Box 2288 (95344-0288)
PHONE................................209 722-5761
Fax: 209 722-6421
Tim Pellissier, *President*
Andre Urquidez, *Treasurer*
Dave Long, *Vice Pres*
Ted Selb, *General Mgr*
John Sweigard, *General Mgr*
EMP: 50 EST: 1919
SQ FT: 20,000
SALES (est): 103.3MM **Privately Held**
WEB: www.mercedid.org
SIC: **4911** 4971 Electric services; water distribution or supply systems for irrigation

(P-6148)
MILO WIND PROJECT LLC
Also Called: Edf Renewable Energy
15445 Innovation Dr, San Diego
(92128-3432)
PHONE................................888 903-6926
Tristan Grimbert, *President*
Ryan Pfaff, *Vice Pres*
Robert Miller, *Admin Sec*
EMP: 82
SQ FT: 70,000
SALES (est): 6.8MM **Privately Held**
SIC: **4911** Electric services

(P-6149)
MODESTO IRRIGATION DISTRICT
1231 11th St, Modesto (95354-0701)
P.O. Box 4060 (95352-4060)
PHONE................................209 526-7563
Don Durman, *Treasurer*
EMP: 400
SALES (corp-wide): 425MM **Privately Held**
SIC: **4911** 4941 ; water supply
PA: Modesto Irrigation District (Inc)
1231 11th St
Modesto CA 95354
209 526-7337

(P-6150)
MODESTO IRRIGATION DISTRICT (PA)
1231 11th St, Modesto (95354-0701)
P.O. Box 4060 (95352-4060)
PHONE................................209 526-7337
Fax: 209 526-7358
Allen Short, *President*
Angela Cartisano, *Bd of Directors*
Roger Vanhoy, *Bd of Directors*
Scott Vuren, *Risk Mgmt Dir*
Colleen Rangel, *Executive Asst*
EMP: 175
SQ FT: 90,000
SALES: 425MM **Privately Held**
SIC: **4911** 4971 ; water distribution or supply systems for irrigation

(P-6151)
MODESTO IRRIGATION DISTRICT
929 Woodland Ave, Modesto (95351-1553)
P.O. Box 4060 (95352-4060)
PHONE................................209 526-7373
Ellen Short, *General Mgr*
Sandy Rebiero, *Buyer*
Mike McHann, *Supervisor*
EMP: 400
SALES (corp-wide): 425MM **Privately Held**
SIC: **4911** 4971 Electric services; irrigation systems
PA: Modesto Irrigation District (Inc)
1231 11th St
Modesto CA 95354
209 526-7337

(P-6152)
NORTHERN CALIFORNIA POWER AGCY (PA)
Also Called: Ncpa
651 Commerce Dr, Roseville (95678-6411)
PHONE................................916 781-3636
Ute Woodall, *Treasurer*
Karen England, *Bd of Directors*
Diane Morgan, *Bd of Directors*
Rui Dai, *Risk Mgmt Dir*
Vicki Cichocki, *General Mgr*
EMP: 65 EST: 1968
SQ FT: 17,400
SALES (est): 126.1MM **Privately Held**
WEB: www.NCPA.com
SIC: **4911** Transmission, electric power; generation, electric power

(P-6153)
NORTHERN CALIFORNIA POWER AGCY
Also Called: Ncpa- Plant 1
12000 Ridge Rd, Middletown (95461-9585)
P.O. Box 663 (95461-0663)
PHONE................................707 987-2381
Fax: 707 987-4039
Murry Grande, *Opers-Prdtn-Mfg*
Jeff Furst, *Research*
Marty Lebrett, *Opers Mgr*
EMP: 56
SALES (corp-wide): 126.1MM **Privately Held**
SIC: **4911** Electric services
PA: Northern California Power Agency
651 Commerce Dr
Roseville CA 95678
916 781-3636

(P-6154)
NRG CALIFORNIA SOUTH LP
Also Called: Etiwanda Power Plant
8996 Etiwanda Ave, Rancho Cucamonga
(91739-9662)
PHONE................................909 899-7241
Lee Moore, *Branch Mgr*
Gary Ackerman, *Exec Dir*
Vince Munoz, *Analyst*
Mark Greene, *Maintence Staff*
EMP: 55
SALES (corp-wide): 14.6B **Publicly Held**
SIC: **4911** Electric services
HQ: Nrg California South Lp
804 Carnegie Ctr
Princeton NJ 08540

(P-6155)
NRG EL SEGUNDO OPERATIONS INC
301 Vista Del Mar, El Segundo
(90245-3650)
PHONE................................310 615-6344
John Ragan, *President*
Keith Richards, *Controller*
John Gray, *Manager*
Jeff Huhs, *Supervisor*
▲ EMP: 65
SALES (est): 28.6MM
SALES (corp-wide): 14.6B **Publicly Held**
SIC: **4911** Electric services
PA: Nrg Energy, Inc.
804 Carnegie Ctr
Princeton NJ 08540
609 524-4500

(P-6156)
NRG ENERGY INC
455 Golden Gate Ave, San Francisco
(94102-3660)
PHONE................................415 255-8105
EMP: 65
SALES (corp-wide): 14.6B **Publicly Held**
SIC: **4911** Electric services
PA: Nrg Energy, Inc.
804 Carnegie Ctr
Princeton NJ 08540
609 524-4500

(P-6157)
NRG ENERGY INC
3201 Wilbur Ave, Antioch (94509-8546)
PHONE................................913 689-3904
Vanessa Vidal, *Buyer*
EMP: 55
SALES (corp-wide): 14.6B **Publicly Held**
SIC: **4911** Electric services
PA: Nrg Energy, Inc.
804 Carnegie Ctr
Princeton NJ 08540
609 524-4500

(P-6158)
OASIS REPOWER LLC
15445 Innovation Dr, San Diego
(92128-3432)
PHONE................................888 903-6926
Tristan Grimbert, *President*
Robert Miller, *Corp Secy*
Ryan Pfaff, *Vice Pres*
EMP: 826
SQ FT: 70,000
SALES (est): 283.6MM **Privately Held**
SIC: **4911** Electric services

(P-6159)
OLYMPUS POWER LLC
34759 Lencioni Ave, Bakersfield
(93308-9797)
PHONE................................661 393-6885
Todd Witwer, *Manager*
EMP: 147
SALES (corp-wide): 124.8MM **Privately Held**
WEB: www.deltapower.com
SIC: **4911** Generation, electric power
HQ: Olympus Power, Llc
67 E Park Pl Ste 4
Morristown NJ 07960
973 889-9100

(P-6160)
ORMESA LLC
3300 E Evan Hewes Hwy, Holtville
(92250-9429)
P.O. Box 86 (92250-0086)
PHONE................................760 356-3020
Lucien Brunicki,
▲ EMP: 55
SALES (est): 17.4MM **Publicly Held**
WEB: www.ormesa.com
SIC: **4911**
PA: Ormat Technologies, Inc.
6225 Neil Rd
Reno NV 89511

(P-6161)
PACIFIC GAS AND ELECTRIC CO
Also Called: PG&e
425 Beck Ave, Fairfield (94533-6808)
PHONE................................415 973-7000
Fax: 707 427-7855
Dana McKiddin, *Principal*
Rick McMasters, *Engineer*
EMP: 100 **Publicly Held**
WEB: www.pge.com
SIC: **4911** Transmission, electric power
HQ: Pacific Gas And Electric Company
77 Beale St
San Francisco CA 94105
415 973-7000

(P-6162)
PACIFIC GAS AND ELECTRIC CO (HQ)
Also Called: PG&e
77 Beale St, San Francisco (94105-1814)
P.O. Box 770000 (94177-0001)
PHONE................................415 973-7000
Fax: 415 267-7250
Christopher P Johns, *President*
Dinyar B Mistry, *CFO*
David S Thomason, *CFO*
Nickolas Stavropoulos, *Exec VP*
Bryant Tong, *Exec VP*
▲ EMP: 3000
SQ FT: 167,000
SALES: 16.8B **Publicly Held**
WEB: www.pge.com
SIC: **4911** 4924 Generation, electric power; transmission, electric power; distribution, electric power; natural gas distribution

(P-6163)
PACIFIC GAS AND ELECTRIC CO
Also Called: PG&e
885 Embarcadero Dr, West Sacramento
(95605-1503)
PHONE................................916 375-5005
Richard Yamacuchi, *Branch Mgr*
EMP: 130 **Publicly Held**
WEB: www.pge.com
SIC: **4911** Transmission, electric power
HQ: Pacific Gas And Electric Company
77 Beale St
San Francisco CA 94105
415 973-7000

(P-6164)
PACIFIC GAS AND ELECTRIC CO
Also Called: PG&e
530 E St, Marysville (95901-5530)
P.O. Box 671 (95901-0018)
PHONE................................530 742-3251
Dennis Grilione, *Branch Mgr*
EMP: 450 **Publicly Held**
WEB: www.pge.com
SIC: **4911** 4924 Distribution, electric power; natural gas distribution

4911 - Electric Svcs County (P-6165)

HQ: Pacific Gas And Electric Company
77 Beale St
San Francisco CA 94105
415 973-7000

(P-6165)
PACIFIC GAS AND ELECTRIC CO
PG&e
4525 Hollis St, Oakland (94608-2911)
PHONE.....................510 450-5744
G L Fairbanks, *Branch Mgr*
EMP: 90 **Publicly Held**
WEB: www.pge.com
SIC: 4911 Transmission, electric power
HQ: Pacific Gas And Electric Company
77 Beale St
San Francisco CA 94105
415 973-7000

(P-6166)
PACIFIC GAS AND ELECTRIC CO
PG&e
1970 Industrial Way, Belmont (94002)
PHONE.....................650 592-9411
Michele A Silva, *Branch Mgr*
Wendy Bossier, *Supervisor*
EMP: 300 **Publicly Held**
WEB: www.pge.com
SIC: 4911 4923 Electric services; gas transmission & distribution
HQ: Pacific Gas And Electric Company
77 Beale St
San Francisco CA 94105
415 973-7000

(P-6167)
PACIFIC GAS AND ELECTRIC CO
PG&e
111 Stony Cir, Santa Rosa (95401-9599)
PHONE.....................800 756-7243
Gary F Heitz, *Principal*
Maria Siordia, *Marketing Mgr*
Jim Chaaban, *Accounts Mgr*
William Silkett, *Supervisor*
EMP: 240
SQ FT: 100,000 **Publicly Held**
WEB: www.pge.com
SIC: 4911 Transmission, electric power
HQ: Pacific Gas And Electric Company
77 Beale St
San Francisco CA 94105
415 973-7000

(P-6168)
PACIFIC GAS AND ELECTRIC CO
15449 Humbug Rd, Magalia (95954-9000)
PHONE.....................530 892-4519
Mike Malloy, *Branch Mgr*
EMP: 60 **Publicly Held**
WEB: www.pge.com
SIC: 4911 Transmission, electric power
HQ: Pacific Gas And Electric Company
77 Beale St
San Francisco CA 94105
415 973-7000

(P-6169)
PACIFIC GAS AND ELECTRIC CO
Also Called: PG&e
788 Taylorville Rd, Grass Valley (95949-7713)
PHONE.....................530 477-3245
Fax: 530 477-3252
Art Bartolome, *Manager*
Rich Thompson, *Manager*
EMP: 200 **Publicly Held**
WEB: www.pge.com
SIC: 4911 4922 Generation, electric power; natural gas transmission
HQ: Pacific Gas And Electric Company
77 Beale St
San Francisco CA 94105
415 973-7000

(P-6170)
PACIFIC GAS AND ELECTRIC CO
Also Called: PG&e
210 Corona Rd, Petaluma (94954-1319)
PHONE.....................707 765-5118
Tom Reimer, *Manager*
EMP: 50
SQ FT: 168,577 **Publicly Held**
WEB: www.pge.com
SIC: 4911 Electric services

HQ: Pacific Gas And Electric Company
77 Beale St
San Francisco CA 94105
415 973-7000

(P-6171)
PACIFIC GAS AND ELECTRIC CO
650 O St, Fresno (93721-2708)
PHONE.....................559 268-2868
C R Martin, *Branch Mgr*
EMP: 450 **Publicly Held**
WEB: www.pge.com
SIC: 4911 4922 Generation, electric power; natural gas transmission
HQ: Pacific Gas And Electric Company
77 Beale St
San Francisco CA 94105
415 973-7000

(P-6172)
PACIFIC GAS AND ELECTRIC CO
Also Called: PG&e
9 Mi Nw Of Avila Bch, Avila Beach (93424)
P.O. Box 56 (93424-0056)
PHONE.....................805 506-5280
Fax: 805 541-7680
David Oatley, *Branch Mgr*
Karen Brower, *Executive*
Teryl McKnight, *Info Tech Mgr*
John Poole, *Info Tech Mgr*
Arthur Mortorff, *Engineer*
EMP: 1400 **Publicly Held**
WEB: www.pge.com
SIC: 4911 Generation, electric power
HQ: Pacific Gas And Electric Company
77 Beale St
San Francisco CA 94105
415 973-7000

(P-6173)
PACIFIC GAS AND ELECTRIC CO
Also Called: PG&e
3600 Meadow View Dr, Redding (96002-9701)
PHONE.....................530 365-7672
Fax: 530 246-6508
John Duncan, *Manager*
EMP: 109 **Publicly Held**
WEB: www.pge.com
SIC: 4911 Electric services
HQ: Pacific Gas And Electric Company
77 Beale St
San Francisco CA 94105
415 973-7000

(P-6174)
PACIFIC GAS AND ELECTRIC CO
Also Called: PG&e
303 2nd Ave, San Francisco (94118-2413)
PHONE.....................415 973-0778
R A Clarke, *Branch Mgr*
EMP: 65 **Publicly Held**
WEB: www.pge.com
SIC: 4911 Transmission, electric power
HQ: Pacific Gas And Electric Company
77 Beale St
San Francisco CA 94105
415 973-7000

(P-6175)
PACIFIC GAS AND ELECTRIC CO
Also Called: PG&e
4690 Evora Rd, Concord (94520-1004)
PHONE.....................925 676-0948
John Glenn, *Branch Mgr*
EMP: 65 **Publicly Held**
WEB: www.pge.com
SIC: 4911 Transmission, electric power
HQ: Pacific Gas And Electric Company
77 Beale St
San Francisco CA 94105
415 973-7000

(P-6176)
PACIFIC GAS AND ELECTRIC CO
Also Called: PG&e
1850 Gateway Blvd Ste 800, Concord (94520-8473)
PHONE.....................925 674-6305
Kim Lawson, *Branch Mgr*
EMP: 65 **Publicly Held**
WEB: www.pge.com
SIC: 4911 Electric services

HQ: Pacific Gas And Electric Company
77 Beale St
San Francisco CA 94105
415 973-7000

(P-6177)
PACIFIC GAS AND ELECTRIC CO
Also Called: PG&e
1000 King Salmon Ave, Eureka (95503-6859)
PHONE.....................707 444-0700
Roy Willis, *Manager*
Robin Walton, *Sales Associate*
EMP: 100 **Publicly Held**
WEB: www.pge.com
SIC: 4911 Generation, electric power
HQ: Pacific Gas And Electric Company
77 Beale St
San Francisco CA 94105
415 973-7000

(P-6178)
PACIFIC GAS AND ELECTRIC CO
Also Called: PG&e
450 Eastmoor Ave, Daly City (94015-2041)
PHONE.....................650 755-1236
Len Jackson, *Branch Mgr*
EMP: 150 **Publicly Held**
WEB: www.pge.com
SIC: 4911 Transmission, electric power
HQ: Pacific Gas And Electric Company
77 Beale St
San Francisco CA 94105
415 973-7000

(P-6179)
PACIFIC GAS AND ELECTRIC CO
Also Called: PG&e
1524 N Carpenter Rd, Modesto (95351-1110)
PHONE.....................209 576-6636
Sheila Radford, *Branch Mgr*
Kevin Chacon, *Manager*
EMP: 50 **Publicly Held**
WEB: www.pge.com
SIC: 4911 4923 4932 Electric services; gas transmission & distribution; gas & other services combined
HQ: Pacific Gas And Electric Company
77 Beale St
San Francisco CA 94105
415 973-7000

(P-6180)
PACIFIC GAS AND ELECTRIC CO
Also Called: PG&e
3136 Boeing Way, Stockton (95206-4989)
PHONE.....................209 942-1787
Robert Eggert, *Branch Mgr*
Melissa Wikle, *Director*
EMP: 54
SQ FT: 138,000 **Publicly Held**
WEB: www.pge.com
SIC: 4911 4922 Generation, electric power; natural gas transmission
HQ: Pacific Gas And Electric Company
77 Beale St
San Francisco CA 94105
415 973-7000

(P-6181)
PACIFIC GAS AND ELECTRIC CO
Also Called: PG&e
776 S State St Ste 103, Ukiah (95482-5833)
PHONE.....................707 468-3954
Stacy Black, *Branch Mgr*
EMP: 60 **Publicly Held**
WEB: www.pge.com
SIC: 4911 Transmission, electric power
HQ: Pacific Gas And Electric Company
77 Beale St
San Francisco CA 94105
415 973-7000

(P-6182)
PACIFIC GAS AND ELECTRIC CO
Also Called: PG&e
800 Price Canyon Rd, Pismo Beach (93449-2722)
PHONE.....................805 773-6109
Don Boatman, *Branch Mgr*
EMP: 65 **Publicly Held**
WEB: www.pge.com
SIC: 4911

HQ: Pacific Gas And Electric Company
77 Beale St
San Francisco CA 94105
415 973-7000

(P-6183)
PACIFIC GAS AND ELECTRIC CO
Also Called: PG&e
5555 Florin Perkins Rd, Sacramento (95826-4815)
P.O. Box 997300 (95899-7300)
PHONE.....................916 386-5204
Fax: 916 386-5125
Maria Jordan, *Manager*
Kevin McCoy, *Opers Mgr*
Marie Jimenez, *Manager*
EMP: 200 **Publicly Held**
WEB: www.pge.com
SIC: 4911 4923 Distribution, electric power; generation, electric power; transmission, electric power; gas transmission & distribution
HQ: Pacific Gas And Electric Company
77 Beale St
San Francisco CA 94105
415 973-7000

(P-6184)
PACIFIC GAS AND ELECTRIC CO
Also Called: PG&e
2311 Garden Rd, Monterey (93940-5325)
PHONE.....................831 648-3231
Richard Brent, *Branch Mgr*
EMP: 50 **Publicly Held**
WEB: www.pge.com
SIC: 4911 Transmission, electric power
HQ: Pacific Gas And Electric Company
77 Beale St
San Francisco CA 94105
415 973-7000

(P-6185)
PACIFIC GAS AND ELECTRIC CO
Also Called: PG&e
42105 Boyce Rd, Fremont (94538-3110)
PHONE.....................510 770-2025
Gary Commick, *Principal*
Michael Carlson, *Systems Analyst*
Steve Coleman, *Systems Analyst*
EMP: 150 **Publicly Held**
WEB: www.pge.com
SIC: 4911 Transmission, electric power
HQ: Pacific Gas And Electric Company
77 Beale St
San Francisco CA 94105
415 973-7000

(P-6186)
PACIFIC GAS AND ELECTRIC CO
Also Called: PG&e
33755 Old Mill Rd, Auberry (93602-9655)
P.O. Box 425 (93602-0425)
PHONE.....................559 855-6112
John Moore, *General Mgr*
EMP: 50 **Publicly Held**
WEB: www.pge.com
SIC: 4911 ; generation, electric power
HQ: Pacific Gas And Electric Company
77 Beale St
San Francisco CA 94105
415 973-7000

(P-6187)
PACIFIC GAS AND ELECTRIC CO
Also Called: PG&e
3797 1st St, Livermore (94551-4905)
PHONE.....................925 373-2623
Kermit Pol, *Branch Mgr*
EMP: 120 **Publicly Held**
WEB: www.pge.com
SIC: 4911 Transmission, electric power
HQ: Pacific Gas And Electric Company
77 Beale St
San Francisco CA 94105
415 973-7000

(P-6188)
PACIFIC GAS AND ELECTRIC CO
Also Called: PG&e
316 L St, Davis (95616-4231)
PHONE.....................530 757-5803
Gail Sanchez, *Manager*
EMP: 300 **Publicly Held**
WEB: www.pge.com
SIC: 4911 Electric services

PRODUCTS & SERVICES SECTION

4911 - Electric Svcs County (P-6211)

HQ: Pacific Gas And Electric Company
77 Beale St
San Francisco CA 94105
415 973-7000

(P-6189)
PACIFIC GAS AND ELECTRIC CO
Also Called: PG&e
2180 Harrison St, San Francisco (94110-1300)
PHONE..................415 695-3513
Dave Bradley, Branch Mgr
EMP: 300 Publicly Held
WEB: www.pge.com
SIC: 4911 4922 4924 1311 Generation, electric power; transmission, electric power; distribution, electric power; pipelines, natural gas; natural gas distribution; natural gas production; crude petroleum production; land subdividers & developers, residential; land subdividers & developers, commercial; power plant construction
HQ: Pacific Gas And Electric Company
77 Beale St
San Francisco CA 94105
415 973-7000

(P-6190)
PACIFIC GAS AND ELECTRIC CO
Also Called: PG&e
66 Ranch Dr, Milpitas (95035-5103)
PHONE..................408 945-6215
Jeff Klotz, Branch Mgr
EMP: 65 Publicly Held
WEB: www.pge.com
SIC: 4911 Transmission, electric power
HQ: Pacific Gas And Electric Company
77 Beale St
San Francisco CA 94105
415 973-7000

(P-6191)
PACIFIC GAS AND ELECTRIC CO
Also Called: PG&e
28570 Tiger Creek Rd, Pioneer (95666-9646)
PHONE..................209 295-2651
EMP: 65 Publicly Held
WEB: www.pge.com
SIC: 4911 Transmission, electric power
HQ: Pacific Gas And Electric Company
77 Beale St
San Francisco CA 94105
415 973-7000

(P-6192)
PACIFIC GAS AND ELECTRIC CO
Also Called: PG&e
4201 Arrow St, Bakersfield (93308-4938)
PHONE..................661 398-5918
Don Hacks, Manager
EMP: 65 Publicly Held
WEB: www.pge.com
SIC: 4911 Electric services
HQ: Pacific Gas And Electric Company
77 Beale St
San Francisco CA 94105
415 973-7000

(P-6193)
PACIFIC GAS AND ELECTRIC CO
Also Called: PG&e
160 Cow Meadow Pl, Templeton (93465)
PHONE..................805 434-4418
Bob Burroughs, Branch Mgr
EMP: 60 Publicly Held
WEB: www.pge.com
SIC: 4911 Transmission, electric power
HQ: Pacific Gas And Electric Company
77 Beale St
San Francisco CA 94105
415 973-7000

(P-6194)
PACIFIC GAS AND ELECTRIC CO
Also Called: PG&e
245 Market St Ste 104, San Francisco (94105-1708)
PHONE..................415 973-8089
EMP: 65 Publicly Held
SIC: 4911 4924 Electric services; generation, electric power; transmission, electric power; natural gas distribution

HQ: Pacific Gas And Electric Company
77 Beale St
San Francisco CA 94105
415 973-7000

(P-6195)
PATTERN ENERGY GROUP LP (PA)
Bay 3 Pier 1, San Francisco (94111)
PHONE..................415 283-4000
Michael Garland, President
Alan Batkin, Chairman
Christopher Shugart, Senior VP
Dyann S Blaine, Vice Pres
Collie Powell, General Mgr
EMP: 94
SALES (est): 99.2MM Privately Held
SIC: 4911 Transmission, electric power

(P-6196)
PLACER COUNTY WATER AGENCY (PA)
144 Ferguson Rd, Auburn (95603-3231)
P.O. Box 6570 (95604-6570)
PHONE..................530 823-4850
Fax: 530 823-4960
David Breninger, General Mgr
Andy Fecko, Admin Asst
Stephanie Wens, Admin Asst
Greg Young, Admin Asst
Ken Powers, Engineer
EMP: 90
SQ FT: 22,750
SALES: 70MM Privately Held
WEB: www.pcwa.net
SIC: 4911 4941 4971 Electric services; water supply; irrigation systems

(P-6197)
RE BARREN RIDGE 1 LLC
300 California St Fl 7, San Francisco (94104-1415)
PHONE..................415 675-1500
Greg Wilson,
EMP: 130 EST: 2013
SQ FT: 10,000
SALES (est): 19.2MM Privately Held
SIC: 4911

(P-6198)
ROCKLIN POWER INVESTORS LP
Also Called: Rio Bravo Rocklin
3100 Thunder Valley Ct, Lincoln (95648-9579)
PHONE..................916 645-3383
Fax: 916 645-9209
Stephen B Gross, CFO
Brent Yatman, Engineer
Charles Odrechowski, Plant Mgr
EMP: 60
SALES (est): 45.2MM Privately Held
SIC: 4911 Generation, electric power

(P-6199)
ROOSEVELT WIND HOLDINGS LLC
15445 Innovation Dr, San Diego (92128-3432)
PHONE..................888 903-6926
Tristan Grimbert, President
Ryan Pfaff, Vice Pres
Robert Miller, Admin Sec
EMP: 826 EST: 2013
SQ FT: 70,000
SALES (est): 232.7MM Privately Held
SIC: 4911 Electric services; generation, electric power

(P-6200)
SACRAMENTO MUNICPL UTILITY DST (PA)
Also Called: S M U D
6201 S St, Sacramento (95817-1818)
P.O. Box 15830 (95852-0830)
PHONE..................916 452-3211
Fax: 916 732-5601
Arlen Orchard, CEO
James A Tracy, CFO
Jim Tracy, CFO
Noreen Roche, Treasurer
Noreen Roche-Carter, Treasurer
▲ EMP: 710
SQ FT: 118,000

SALES: 1.5B Privately Held
WEB: www.smud.org
SIC: 4911 Electric services

(P-6201)
SACRAMENTO MUNICPL UTILITY DST
6201 S St, Sacramento (95817-1818)
PHONE..................916 452-3211
Carlos Diaz, Branch Mgr
EMP: 1000
SALES (corp-wide): 1.5B Privately Held
SIC: 4911 Electric services
PA: Sacramento Municipal Utility District
6201 S St
Sacramento CA 95817
916 452-3211

(P-6202)
SACRAMENTO MUNICPL UTILITY DST
Also Called: Smud Energy Services
6301 S St, Sacramento (95817)
P.O. Box 15830 (95852-0830)
PHONE..................916 732-5155
Jan Schori, Manager
Yuva R Palaniappan, Admin Asst
Thomas Lyons, Info Tech Mgr
Ann Graef, Project Mgr
Dwight Maccurdy, Project Mgr
EMP: 88
SALES (corp-wide): 1.5B Privately Held
SIC: 4911 Electric services
PA: Sacramento Municipal Utility District
6201 S St
Sacramento CA 95817
916 452-3211

(P-6203)
SACRAMENTO MUNICPL UTILITY DST
Also Called: Supply Change Services
6201 S St, Sacramento (95817-1818)
P.O. Box 15830 (95852-0830)
PHONE..................916 732-5616
Frankie McDermott, Manager
Susan Kooiman, Finance Mgr
EMP: 300
SALES (corp-wide): 1.5B Privately Held
SIC: 4911 ; generation, electric power
PA: Sacramento Municipal Utility District
6201 S St
Sacramento CA 95817
916 452-3211

(P-6204)
SACRAMENTO MUNICPL UTILITY DST
7540 Hwy 50, Pacific House (95726)
P.O. Box 1500, Pollock Pines (95726-1500)
PHONE..................530 644-2013
Fax: 916 732-5108
Gail Higgins, Manager
Brian Gorrell, Supervisor
EMP: 85
SALES (corp-wide): 1.5B Privately Held
SIC: 4911 Electric services
PA: Sacramento Municipal Utility District
6201 S St
Sacramento CA 95817
916 452-3211

(P-6205)
SCE EASTERN HYDRO DIVISION
4000 Bishop Creek Rd, Bishop (93514-7026)
PHONE..................760 873-0767
John Bryson, Principal
Susie Davis, Principal
EMP: 99
SALES (est): 7.5MM Privately Held
SIC: 4911 Electric services

(P-6206)
SEMPRA ENERGY INTERNATIONAL (HQ)
Also Called: Sempra Energy Utilities
101 Ash St, San Diego (92101-3017)
PHONE..................619 696-2000
Luis Eduardo Pawluszek, CEO
Mark A Snell, President
Donald E Felsinger, Chairman
Javade Chaudhri, Exec VP
Vicki Zeiger, Exec VP
EMP: 800

SALES (est): 753.8MM
SALES (corp-wide): 10.2B Publicly Held
SIC: 4911 Electric services
PA: Sempra Energy
488 8th Ave
San Diego CA 92101
619 696-2000

(P-6207)
SILVERADO ENERGY COMPANY
18101 Von Karman Ave, Irvine (92612-1012)
PHONE..................949 752-5588
Thomas McDaniel, Principal
Alan Fohrer, President
EMP: 300
SALES (est): 59.8MM
SALES (corp-wide): 14.6B Publicly Held
SIC: 4911 Generation, electric power
HQ: Edison Mission Energy
3 Macarthur Pl Ste 100
Santa Ana CA 92707
714 513-8000

(P-6208)
SLATE CREEK WIND PROJECT LLC
15445 Innovation Dr, San Diego (92128-3432)
PHONE..................888 903-6926
Tristan Grimbert, President
Kara Vongphakdy, Treasurer
Ryan Pfaff, Vice Pres
Robert Miller, Admin Sec
EMP: 826 EST: 2013
SQ FT: 70,000
SALES (est): 351.8MM Privately Held
SIC: 4911 Electric services

(P-6209)
SMART SYSTEMS TECHNOLOGIES (PA)
9 Goodyear, Irvine (92618-2001)
PHONE..................949 367-9375
Craig Steven Curran, CEO
Peter Scolara, CFO
Melissa Ramos, Office Mgr
Pete Scalera, Financial Exec
EMP: 64
SQ FT: 7,000
SALES (est): 34.8MM Privately Held
WEB: www.smartsystemstechnologies.com
SIC: 4911 Electric services

(P-6210)
SOUTHERN CALIFORNIA EDISON CO (HQ)
2244 Walnut Grove Ave, Rosemead (91770-3714)
P.O. Box 800 (91770-0800)
PHONE..................626 302-1212
Fax: 626 302-4775
Pedro J Pizarro, President
Ashraf T Dajani, COO
John P Finneran, CFO
Ken Pickrahn, CFO
Maria Rigatti, CFO
▲ EMP: 1200
SALES: 11.4B
SALES (corp-wide): 11.5B Publicly Held
WEB: www.sce.com
SIC: 4911 Generation, electric power; transmission, electric power; distribution, electric power
PA: Edison International
2244 Walnut Grove Ave
Rosemead CA 91770
626 302-2222

(P-6211)
SOUTHERN CALIFORNIA EDISON CO
4900 Rivergrade Rd 2b1, Irwindale (91706-1401)
PHONE..................626 543-8081
Peter Quon, Branch Mgr
Mario Ang, CIO
Elizabeth Wallenius, Manager
EMP: 155
SALES (corp-wide): 11.5B Publicly Held
SIC: 4911 Generation, electric power
HQ: Southern California Edison Company
2244 Walnut Grove Ave
Rosemead CA 91770
626 302-1212

4911 - Electric Svcs County (P-6212)

PRODUCTS & SERVICES SECTION

(P-6212)
SOUTHERN CALIFORNIA EDISON CO
Also Called: Northern Hydro
54205 Mt Poplar Ave, Big Creek (93605)
PHONE..................559 893-3611
David Dormire, *Manager*
Ian Robertson, *Project Mgr*
Bryan Troll, *Human Res Mgr*
EMP: 160
SALES (corp-wide): 11.5B **Publicly Held**
SIC: 4911 Electric services
HQ: Southern California Edison Company
2244 Walnut Grove Ave
Rosemead CA 91770
626 302-1212

(P-6213)
SOUTHERN CALIFORNIA EDISON CO
Also Called: Monrovia Service Center
1440 S California Ave, Monrovia (91016-4211)
PHONE..................626 303-8480
Robert Robinson, *Principal*
EMP: 97
SQ FT: 31,603
SALES (corp-wide): 11.5B **Publicly Held**
WEB: www.sce.com
SIC: 4911 Electric services
HQ: Southern California Edison Company
2244 Walnut Grove Ave
Rosemead CA 91770
626 302-1212

(P-6214)
SOUTHERN CALIFORNIA EDISON CO
2425 S Blackstone St, Tulare (93274-6953)
PHONE..................559 685-3742
Don Cordeniz, *Manager*
Robert Juskalian, *Technical Staff*
Steve Ralston, *Foreman/Supr*
Jacob Sertich, *Facilities Mgr*
EMP: 75
SALES (corp-wide): 11.5B **Publicly Held**
WEB: www.sce.com
SIC: 4911 Electric services
HQ: Southern California Edison Company
2244 Walnut Grove Ave
Rosemead CA 91770
626 302-1212

(P-6215)
SOUTHERN CALIFORNIA EDISON CO
4000 Bishop Creek Rd, Bishop (93514-7026)
PHONE..................760 873-0715
Joseph Dier, *Technician*
Dan Golden, *Plant Mgr*
Seth Carr, *Foreman/Supr*
EMP: 155
SALES (corp-wide): 11.5B **Publicly Held**
SIC: 4911 Generation, electric power
HQ: Southern California Edison Company
2244 Walnut Grove Ave
Rosemead CA 91770
626 302-1212

(P-6216)
SOUTHERN CALIFORNIA EDISON CO
14799 Chestnut St, Westminster (92683-5240)
PHONE..................714 934-0838
Frank Salomone, *CEO*
Timothy Lowry, *Business Anlyst*
Aaron Renfro, *Project Mgr*
Jerome Thode, *Project Mgr*
Zeus Xioco, *Engineer*
EMP: 176
SALES (corp-wide): 11.5B **Publicly Held**
SIC: 4911 Generation, electric power
HQ: Southern California Edison Company
2244 Walnut Grove Ave
Rosemead CA 91770
626 302-1212

(P-6217)
SOUTHERN CALIFORNIA EDISON CO
55481 Mt Poplar, Big Creek (93605)
P.O. Box 130 (93605-0130)
PHONE..................559 893-2037
Southern Edison, *Branch Mgr*
EMP: 155
SALES (corp-wide): 11.5B **Publicly Held**
SIC: 4911 Distribution, electric power; transmission, electric power
HQ: Southern California Edison Company
2244 Walnut Grove Ave
Rosemead CA 91770
626 302-1212

(P-6218)
SOUTHERN CALIFORNIA EDISON CO
8380 Klingerman St, Rosemead (91770-3609)
PHONE..................626 302-5101
Arthur Guerra, *Principal*
EMP: 176
SALES (corp-wide): 11.5B **Publicly Held**
SIC: 4911 Generation, electric power
HQ: Southern California Edison Company
2244 Walnut Grove Ave
Rosemead CA 91770
626 302-1212

(P-6219)
SOUTHERN CALIFORNIA EDISON CO
4900 Rivergrade Rd, Baldwin Park (91706-1401)
PHONE..................626 543-6093
Linda Gilleland, *Principal*
Paul Caldarone, *Manager*
EMP: 149
SALES (corp-wide): 11.5B **Publicly Held**
SIC: 4911 Generation, electric power
HQ: Southern California Edison Company
2244 Walnut Grove Ave
Rosemead CA 91770
626 302-1212

(P-6220)
SOUTHERN CALIFORNIA EDISON CO
Also Called: North Orange County Svc Ctr
1851 W Valencia Dr, Fullerton (92833-3215)
PHONE..................714 870-3225
David Kama, *District Mgr*
Kathy Conway, *Treasurer*
Donn W Haefele, *Foreman/Supr*
Sally Williams, *Sls & Mktg Exec*
EMP: 70
SALES (corp-wide): 11.5B **Publicly Held**
WEB: www.sce.com
SIC: 4911 Electric services; distribution, electric power
HQ: Southern California Edison Company
2244 Walnut Grove Ave
Rosemead CA 91770
626 302-1212

(P-6221)
SOUTHERN CALIFORNIA EDISON CO
Also Called: San Onfre Nclear Gnerating Stn
14300 Mesa Rd, San Clemente (92672)
PHONE..................949 368-2881
R W Kreiger, *Vice Pres*
Kellie Otis, *CIO*
John Foulk, *MIS Dir*
Sandy Bostrom, *Info Tech Dir*
Richard Stephenson, *Info Svcs Mgr*
EMP: 1998
SALES (corp-wide): 11.5B **Publicly Held**
SIC: 4911 Generation, electric power
HQ: Southern California Edison Company
2244 Walnut Grove Ave
Rosemead CA 91770
626 302-1212

(P-6222)
SOUTHERN CALIFORNIA EDISON CO
Also Called: Southern Clfrn Edsn - Prvt CHR
2131 Walnut Grove Ave, Rosemead (91770-3769)
PHONE..................626 302-1212
Grant Thomas, *Branch Mgr*
Chris Pahl, *Program Mgr*
Susan Nakashima, *General Mgr*
Doreen Mendoza, *Executive Asst*
Patricia Murillo, *Executive Asst*
EMP: 155
SALES (corp-wide): 11.5B **Publicly Held**
SIC: 4911 Distribution, electric power; generation, electric power; transmission, electric power

(P-6223)
SOUTHERN CALIFORNIA EDISON CO
Also Called: Big Creek Division Office
54205 Mountain Poplar Rd, Big Creek (93605)
P.O. Box 100 (93605-0100)
PHONE..................559 893-3646
Jeff Mc Pheeters, *Manager*
EMP: 100
SALES (corp-wide): 11.5B **Publicly Held**
WEB: www.sce.com
SIC: 4911 4939 Generation, electric power; combination utilities
HQ: Southern California Edison Company
2244 Walnut Grove Ave
Rosemead CA 91770
626 302-1212

(P-6224)
SOUTHERN CALIFORNIA EDISON CO
Also Called: Central Orange County Svc Ctr
1241 S Grand Ave, Santa Ana (92705-4404)
PHONE..................714 973-5481
Percy Haralson, *Principal*
Ernie Solorzano, *District Mgr*
Cindy Leejulien, *Engineer*
Ron Wold, *Engineer*
EMP: 216
SALES (corp-wide): 11.5B **Publicly Held**
WEB: www.sce.com
SIC: 4911 Electric services
HQ: Southern California Edison Company
2244 Walnut Grove Ave
Rosemead CA 91770
626 302-1212

(P-6225)
SOUTHERN CALIFORNIA EDISON CO
Also Called: Thousand Oaks Service Center
3589 Foothill Dr, Thousand Oaks (91361-2475)
PHONE..................818 999-1880
Jerry Willaferd, *Branch Mgr*
EMP: 122
SALES (corp-wide): 11.5B **Publicly Held**
WEB: www.sce.com
SIC: 4911 8741 Electric services; business management
HQ: Southern California Edison Company
2244 Walnut Grove Ave
Rosemead CA 91770
626 302-1212

(P-6226)
SOUTHERN CALIFORNIA EDISON CO
Also Called: Irwindale 6000
6000 N Irwindale Ave A, Irwindale (91702-3200)
PHONE..................626 815-7296
Ray Maese, *Branch Mgr*
Charles Pickering, *Project Mgr*
Jack Shih, *Sr Project Mgr*
Mark Martinez, *Manager*
Richard Rocha, *Accounts Exec*
EMP: 50
SALES (corp-wide): 11.5B **Publicly Held**
WEB: www.sce.com
SIC: 4911 Electric services
HQ: Southern California Edison Company
2244 Walnut Grove Ave
Rosemead CA 91770
626 302-1212

(P-6227)
SOUTHERN CALIFORNIA EDISON CO
265 N East End Ave, Pomona (91767-5803)
PHONE..................909 469-0251
John Risen, *Branch Mgr*
Gary Furukawa, *Network Analyst*
Leah Smith, *Technology*
Javier Garcia, *Technical Staff*
Jorge Araiza, *Engineer*
EMP: 65
SALES (corp-wide): 11.5B **Publicly Held**
WEB: www.sce.com
SIC: 4911 Electric services
HQ: Southern California Edison Company
2244 Walnut Grove Ave
Rosemead CA 91770
626 302-1212

(P-6228)
SOUTHERN CALIFORNIA EDISON CO
Also Called: San Dimas Bushnell Building
1515 Walnut Grove Ave, Rosemead (91770-3710)
PHONE..................714 895-0488
Helen Ronando, *Manager*
Nataliya Smolich, *Business Anlyst*
Greg Buchler, *Project Mgr*
Venus Jenkins, *Project Mgr*
Brad Nelson, *Project Mgr*
EMP: 67
SALES (corp-wide): 11.5B **Publicly Held**
WEB: www.sce.com
SIC: 4911 Electric services
HQ: Southern California Edison Company
2244 Walnut Grove Ave
Rosemead CA 91770
626 302-1212

(P-6229)
SOUTHERN CALIFORNIA EDISON CO
Also Called: Compton Service Center
1924 E Cashdan St, Compton (90220-6403)
PHONE..................310 608-5029
Fax: 310 608-5174
Floyd Rich, *Branch Mgr*
David Ertel, *Treasurer*
Pedro Pizzaro, *Vice Pres*
Fred Francia, *Regional Mgr*
Lorane Luna, *Admin Asst*
EMP: 180
SALES (corp-wide): 11.5B **Publicly Held**
WEB: www.sce.com
SIC: 4911 Electric services
HQ: Southern California Edison Company
2244 Walnut Grove Ave
Rosemead CA 91770
626 302-1212

(P-6230)
SOUTHERN CALIFORNIA EDISON CO
Also Called: Santa Barbara Service Center
103 Love Pl, Goleta (93117-3200)
PHONE..................805 683-5291
Brian Adair, *Manager*
Randy Yanez, *Manager*
EMP: 60
SALES (corp-wide): 11.5B **Publicly Held**
WEB: www.sce.com
SIC: 4911 Electric services
HQ: Southern California Edison Company
2244 Walnut Grove Ave
Rosemead CA 91770
626 302-1212

(P-6231)
SOUTHERN CALIFORNIA EDISON CO
10231 Woodbury Rd Apt B, Garden Grove (92843-3108)
PHONE..................714 636-2166
T Craver, *President*
EMP: 147
SALES (corp-wide): 11.5B **Publicly Held**
WEB: www.sce.com
SIC: 4911 Generation, electric power
HQ: Southern California Edison Company
2244 Walnut Grove Ave
Rosemead CA 91770
626 302-1212

PRODUCTS & SERVICES SECTION

4911 - Electric Svcs County (P-6251)

(P-6232)
SOUTHERN CALIFORNIA EDISON CO
1444 E Mcfadden Ave, Santa Ana (92705-4306)
PHONE 714 973-5574
Rod Thalimer, *Branch Mgr*
Percy Haralson, *Programmer Anys*
Robert Binns, *Project Mgr*
Ilya Glinsky, *Project Mgr*
David Zimmerman, *Project Mgr*
EMP: 116
SALES (corp-wide): 11.5B Publicly Held
WEB: www.sce.com
SIC: 4911 Electric services
HQ: Southern California Edison Company
   2244 Walnut Grove Ave
   Rosemead CA 91770
   626 302-1212

(P-6233)
SOUTHERN CALIFORNIA EDISON CO
Also Called: Southeastern Westminster
7300 Fenwick Ln, Westminster (92683-5238)
PHONE 714 895-0420
Dee Pak Nanda, *Vice Pres*
Catherine Melton, *Program Mgr*
J J Burdick, *Systems Mgr*
Charles Rihbany, *Technology*
Lamar Cunningham, *Technical Staff*
EMP: 320
SALES (corp-wide): 11.5B Publicly Held
WEB: www.sce.com
SIC: 4911 Electric services
HQ: Southern California Edison Company
   2244 Walnut Grove Ave
   Rosemead CA 91770
   626 302-1212

(P-6234)
SOUTHERN CALIFORNIA EDISON CO
Also Called: Saddleback Valley Service Ctr
14155 Bake Pkwy, Irvine (92618-1818)
PHONE 949 587-5416
Robert Torres, *Manager*
Richard Sturrus, *Technical Mgr*
Blake Politte, *Manager*
Edgardo Cruz, *Supervisor*
EMP: 143
SALES (corp-wide): 11.5B Publicly Held
WEB: www.sce.com
SIC: 4911 Electric services
HQ: Southern California Edison Company
   2244 Walnut Grove Ave
   Rosemead CA 91770
   626 302-1212

(P-6235)
SOUTHERN CALIFORNIA EDISON CO
6042a N Irwindale Ave, Irwindale (91702-3207)
PHONE 626 633-3070
Jami McDonald, *Branch Mgr*
Anne Miller-George, *Program Mgr*
Teren Abear, *Project Mgr*
Sean Edwards, *Project Mgr*
Vireak Ly, *Project Mgr*
EMP: 147
SALES (corp-wide): 11.5B Publicly Held
WEB: www.sce.com
SIC: 4911 Generation, electric power
HQ: Southern California Edison Company
   2244 Walnut Grove Ave
   Rosemead CA 91770
   626 302-1212

(P-6236)
SOUTHERN CALIFORNIA EDISON CO
Also Called: Orange Coast Service Center
7333 Bolsa Ave, Westminster (92683-5210)
PHONE 714 895-0163
Fax: 714 895-0188
Jeff Lebow, *Branch Mgr*
Michelle Muramoto, *District Mgr*
Kasey Chapman, *Planning*
Ben Garcia, *Opers Mgr*
Tami Bui, *Manager*
EMP: 133
SALES (corp-wide): 11.5B Publicly Held
WEB: www.sce.com
SIC: 4911 Electric services
HQ: Southern California Edison Company
   2244 Walnut Grove Ave
   Rosemead CA 91770
   626 302-1212

(P-6237)
SOUTHERN CALIFORNIA EDISON CO
13025 Los Angeles St, Irwindale (91706-2241)
PHONE 626 814-4212
Ed Entillon, *Branch Mgr*
EMP: 53
SQ FT: 21,000
SALES (corp-wide): 11.5B Publicly Held
WEB: www.sce.com
SIC: 4911 Electric services
HQ: Southern California Edison Company
   2244 Walnut Grove Ave
   Rosemead CA 91770
   626 302-1212

(P-6238)
SOUTHERN CALIFORNIA EDISON CO
Also Called: Covina Service Center
800 W Cienega Ave, San Dimas (91773-2490)
PHONE 909 592-3757
Gary Martinez, *Branch Mgr*
EMP: 210
SALES (corp-wide): 11.5B Publicly Held
WEB: www.sce.com
SIC: 4911 Electric services
HQ: Southern California Edison Company
   2244 Walnut Grove Ave
   Rosemead CA 91770
   626 302-1212

(P-6239)
SOUTHERN CALIFORNIA EDISON CO
Also Called: Whittier Service Center
9901 Geary Ave, Santa Fe Springs (90670-3251)
PHONE 562 903-3191
Fred Swearingen, *Principal*
Megan Mao, *Project Mgr*
Walter Allen, *Supervisor*
Inkyoo Chang, *Supervisor*
EMP: 60
SALES (corp-wide): 11.5B Publicly Held
WEB: www.sce.com
SIC: 4911 Electric services
HQ: Southern California Edison Company
   2244 Walnut Grove Ave
   Rosemead CA 91770
   626 302-1212

(P-6240)
SOUTHERN CALIFORNIA EDISON CO
Also Called: Western Division Regional Off
125 Elm Ave, Long Beach (90802-4918)
PHONE 562 491-3803
Lorene Miller, *Manager*
Raul Ornelas, *Technical Staff*
Kenneth Chow, *Analyst*
Linda Sagen, *Mfg Staff*
Scott Yoshikawa, *Manager*
EMP: 310
SALES (corp-wide): 11.5B Publicly Held
WEB: www.sce.com
SIC: 4911 Electric services
HQ: Southern California Edison Company
   2244 Walnut Grove Ave
   Rosemead CA 91770
   626 302-1212

(P-6241)
SOUTHERN CALIFORNIA EDISON CO
Also Called: High Desert
12353 Hesperia Rd, Victorville (92395-4797)
PHONE 760 951-3242
Sheila Luna, *Branch Mgr*
Roger Heldoorn, *District Mgr*
Craig Henderson, *Supervisor*
Mikhael Markanson, *Supervisor*
Paul Millan, *Supervisor*
EMP: 200
SALES (corp-wide): 11.5B Publicly Held
WEB: www.sce.com
SIC: 4911 Electric services
HQ: Southern California Edison Company
   2244 Walnut Grove Ave
   Rosemead CA 91770
   626 302-1212

(P-6242)
SOUTHERN CALIFORNIA EDISON CO
Also Called: So CA Edison
1515 Walnut Grove Ave, Rosemead (91770-3710)
PHONE 626 302-0530
Helen Ronando, *Manager*
Patricia Click, *Treasurer*
Arthur Southerland, *Senior VP*
Alfred Cantu, *Technical Staff*
Anthony R Hernandez, *Manager*
EMP: 149
SALES (corp-wide): 11.5B Publicly Held
SIC: 4911 Electric services
HQ: Southern California Edison Company
   2244 Walnut Grove Ave
   Rosemead CA 91770
   626 302-1212

(P-6243)
SPINNING SPUR WIND THREE LLC
15445 Innovation Dr, San Diego (92128-3432)
PHONE 858 521-3319
Tristan Grimbert, *President*
Kara Vongphakdy, *Treasurer*
Larry Barr, *Exec VP*
Robert Miller, *Exec VP*
Ryan Pfaff, *Exec VP*
EMP: 827 EST: 2014
SQ FT: 70,000
SALES (est): 1MM
SALES (corp-wide): 769.9MM Privately Held
SIC: 4911 Electric services
PA: Edf Renewable Energy, Inc.
   15445 Innovation Dr
   San Diego CA 92128
   858 521-3300

(P-6244)
SUN EDISON LLC (HQ)
600 Clipper Dr, Belmont (94002-4119)
PHONE 650 453-5600
Jubran Whalan, *Senior VP*
Michael Demers, *Vice Pres*
Martha Duggan, *Vice Pres*
Scott Fraass, *Vice Pres*
Len Jornlin, *Vice Pres*
◆ EMP: 70
SQ FT: 30,200
SALES (est): 150.5MM
SALES (corp-wide): 2.4B Publicly Held
SIC: 4911 Electric services
PA: Sunedison Inc
   13736 Rverport Dr Ste 180
   Maryland Heights MO 63043
   314 770-7300

(P-6245)
SYCAMORE COGENERATION CO (PA)
1546 China Grade Loop, Bakersfield (93308-9700)
P.O. Box 81438 (93380-1438)
PHONE 661 615-4630
Neal Burgess, *Exec Dir*
Vicky Vbicera, *Accountant*
▲ EMP: 57
SQ FT: 10,000
SALES (est): 41.9MM Privately Held
SIC: 4911 4961 Distribution, electric power; steam supply systems, including geothermal

(P-6246)
TRUCKEE DONNER PUB UTILITY DST
Also Called: TRUCKEE DONNER PUD
11570 Donner Pass Rd, Truckee (96161-4947)
PHONE 530 587-3896
Fax: 530 587-5056
Michael D Holley, *General Mgr*
Robert Meascher, *Treasurer*
Barbara Kayhill, *Admin Sec*
Bob Ellis, *Broker*
EMP: 68
SQ FT: 48,000
SALES: 32.9MM Privately Held
WEB: www.tdpud.org
SIC: 4911 4941 Distribution, electric power; water supply

(P-6247)
TURLOCK IRRIGATION DISTRICT (PA)
Also Called: T | D
333 E Canal Dr, Turlock (95380-3946)
P.O. Box 949 (95381-0949)
PHONE 209 883-8222
Fax: 209 656-2144
Ron Macedo, *President*
Joe Alamo, *Vice Pres*
Alison Bryson, *Vice Pres*
Robert Santos, *Vice Pres*
Kate Schulenberg, *Vice Pres*
EMP: 375
SQ FT: 20,000
SALES (est): 329.7MM Privately Held
WEB: www.tid.org
SIC: 4911 4971 Generation, electric power; distribution, electric power; impounding reservoir, irrigation; water distribution or supply systems for irrigation

(P-6248)
TWIN OAKS POWER LP (HQ)
101 Ash St Hq10b, San Diego (92101-3017)
PHONE 619 696-2034
Mike Niggli, *Managing Dir*
EMP: 100
SALES (est): 53.6MM
SALES (corp-wide): 10.2B Publicly Held
SIC: 4911 4924 Generation, electric power; transmission, electric power; distribution, electric power; natural gas distribution
PA: Sempra Energy
   488 8th Ave
   San Diego CA 92101
   619 696-2000

(P-6249)
TYLER BLUFF WIND PROJECT LLC
15445 Innovation Dr, San Diego (92128-3432)
PHONE 888 903-6926
Tristan Grimbert, *President*
Kara Vongphakdy, *Treasurer*
Larry Barr, *Exec VP*
Robert Miller, *Exec VP*
Ryan Pfaff, *Exec VP*
EMP: 827
SQ FT: 70,000
SALES (est): 85.5MM
SALES (corp-wide): 769.9MM Privately Held
SIC: 4911 Electric services
PA: Edf Renewable Energy, Inc.
   15445 Innovation Dr
   San Diego CA 92128
   858 521-3300

(P-6250)
VEXILLUM INC
Also Called: EZ Electric
10636 Industrial Ave, Roseville (95678-5902)
PHONE 916 218-3815
Fax: 916 218-3801
Scott Zachman, *President*
EMP: 175
SALES (corp-wide): 18.6MM Privately Held
WEB: www.ez-electric.com
SIC: 4911 Electric services
PA: Vexillum, Inc.
   1250 Birchwood Dr
   Sunnyvale CA 94089
   408 541-4245

(P-6251)
WATSON COGENERATION CO INC
22850 Wilmington Ave, Carson (90745-5021)
P.O. Box 6203 (90749-6203)
PHONE 310 816-8100

4911 - Electric Svcs County (P-6252)

PRODUCTS & SERVICES SECTION

Joshua Valdez, *Exec Dir*
Darrin Fost, *Business Mgr*
Shawn Gresham, *Controller*
EMP: 63
SQ FT: 1,000
SALES (est): 46.9MM **Privately Held**
SIC: 4911 Generation, electric power

(P-6252)
WELLHEAD ELECTRIC COMPANY INC
650 Bercut Dr Ste C, Sacramento (95811-0100)
PHONE..................916 447-5171
Fax: 916 447-7602
Harold Dittner, *President*
Colin Clements, *CFO*
Paul Cummins, *Vice Pres*
Tom Tinucci, *Engineer*
EMP: 50
SALES (est): 37.8MM **Privately Held**
SIC: 4911 Electric services

(P-6253)
WHEATLAND WIND PROJECT LLC
15445 Innovation Dr, San Diego (92128-3432)
PHONE..................888 903-6926
Tristan Grimbert, *President*
Robert Miller, *Corp Secy*
Ryan Pfaff, *Vice Pres*
EMP: 826 **EST:** 2013
SQ FT: 70,000
SALES (est): 229.6MM **Privately Held**
SIC: 4911 Electric services

4922 Natural Gas Transmission

(P-6254)
SAN DIEGO GAS & ELECTRIC CO
Also Called: South Bay Power Plant
990 Bay Blvd, Chula Vista (91911-1651)
PHONE..................800 411-7343
Carl Creelman, *Branch Mgr*
EMP: 120
SALES (corp-wide): 10.2B **Publicly Held**
SIC: 4922 4911 Natural gas transmission; generation, electric power
HQ: San Diego Gas & Electric Company
8326 Century Park Ct
San Diego CA 92123
619 696-2000

(P-6255)
SEMPRA US GAS & POWER LLC (HQ)
Also Called: Sempra Natural Gas
488 8th Ave, San Diego (92101-7123)
PHONE..................877 736-7721
Jeff Martin, *President*
Pat Birney, *President*
Mike Gallagher, *President*
Bruce Folkmann, *CFO*
Sharon Cohen, *Vice Pres*
EMP: 60 **EST:** 2011
SALES (est): 53.9MM
SALES (corp-wide): 10.2B **Publicly Held**
SIC: 4922 Natural gas transmission
PA: Sempra Energy
488 8th Ave
San Diego CA 92101
619 696-2000

(P-6256)
SOUTHERN CALIFORNIA GAS CO
8141 Gulana Ave, Venice (90293-7930)
PHONE..................310 823-7945
Fax: 310 578-2610
James Wine, *Manager*
EMP: 67
SALES (corp-wide): 10.2B **Publicly Held**
WEB: www.gasselect.com
SIC: 4922 Natural gas transmission
HQ: Southern California Gas Company
555 W 5th St Fl 31
Los Angeles CA 90013
213 244-1200

(P-6257)
SOUTHERN CALIFORNIA GAS CO
1050 Overland Ct, San Dimas (91773-1704)
PHONE..................909 305-8297
Janet Yee, *Manager*
Tom Souders, *Project Mgr*
EMP: 600
SQ FT: 39,344
SALES (corp-wide): 10.2B **Publicly Held**
WEB: www.gasselect.com
SIC: 4922 Natural gas transmission
HQ: Southern California Gas Company
555 W 5th St Fl 31
Los Angeles CA 90013
213 244-1200

(P-6258)
SOUTHERN CALIFORNIA GAS CO
9400 Oakdale Ave, Chatsworth (91311-6511)
P.O. Box 2300 (91313-2300)
PHONE..................818 701-2592
Cathy Maguire, *Branch Mgr*
Edward Wiegman, *Info Tech Dir*
James Mansdorfer, *Manager*
EMP: 300
SALES (corp-wide): 10.2B **Publicly Held**
WEB: www.gasselect.com
SIC: 4922 4923 Pipelines, natural gas; gas transmission & distribution
HQ: Southern California Gas Company
555 W 5th St Fl 31
Los Angeles CA 90013
213 244-1200

(P-6259)
WILD GOOSE STORAGE INC
2780 W Liberty Rd, Gridley (95948-9335)
P.O. Box 8 (95948-0008)
PHONE..................530 846-7350
Fax: 530 846-7353
David Pope, *President*
Helen McSweeney, *Manager*
EMP: 70
SALES (est): 6.3MM **Privately Held**
SIC: 4922 Storage, natural gas

4923 Natural Gas Transmission & Distribution

(P-6260)
PACIFIC TANK LINES INC
5230 Wilson St Ste A, Riverside (92509-2435)
PHONE..................951 680-1900
Fax: 951 680-1993
Ted Honcharik, *CEO*
Gregory Batten, *President*
Mathew McDonald, *COO*
▲ **EMP:** 76
SALES (est): 21.7MM **Privately Held**
WEB: www.pacifictanklines.com
SIC: 4923 Gas transmission & distribution

(P-6261)
SOUTHERN CALIFORNIA GAS CO
701 S Bullis Rd, Compton (90221-4007)
P.O. Box 9099 (90224-9099)
PHONE..................310 605-7800
Chance Williams, *Manager*
EMP: 54
SALES (corp-wide): 10.2B **Publicly Held**
WEB: www.gasselect.com
SIC: 4923 Gas transmission & distribution
HQ: Southern California Gas Company
555 W 5th St Fl 31
Los Angeles CA 90013
213 244-1200

(P-6262)
SOUTHERN CALIFORNIA GAS CO
1 Liberty, Aliso Viejo (92656-3830)
PHONE..................714 634-7221
Bill Jameson, *Branch Mgr*
Kathy Douglas, *Planning*
EMP: 54
SALES (corp-wide): 10.2B **Publicly Held**
SIC: 4923 Gas transmission & distribution
HQ: Southern California Gas Company
555 W 5th St Fl 31
Los Angeles CA 90013
213 244-1200

(P-6263)
SOUTHERN CALIFORNIA GAS CO
Also Called: Northern Reg. Sub Base
1510 N Chester Ave, Bakersfield (93308-2559)
PHONE..................661 399-4431
James Pina, *Manager*
Dave Korn, *Manager*
EMP: 50
SALES (corp-wide): 10.2B **Publicly Held**
WEB: www.gasselect.com
SIC: 4923 Gas transmission & distribution
HQ: Southern California Gas Company
555 W 5th St Fl 31
Los Angeles CA 90013
213 244-1200

(P-6264)
SOUTHERN CALIFORNIA GAS CO
6738 Bright Ave, Whittier (90601-4306)
PHONE..................562 803-3341
Richard Duran, *Branch Mgr*
EMP: 69
SALES (corp-wide): 10.2B **Publicly Held**
WEB: www.gasselect.com
SIC: 4923 Gas transmission & distribution
HQ: Southern California Gas Company
555 W 5th St Fl 31
Los Angeles CA 90013
213 244-1200

(P-6265)
SOUTHERN CALIFORNIA GAS CO
155 S G St, San Bernardino (92410-3317)
PHONE..................909 335-7941
Al Garcia, *Branch Mgr*
EMP: 117
SALES (corp-wide): 10.2B **Publicly Held**
WEB: www.gasselect.com
SIC: 4923 Gas transmission & distribution
HQ: Southern California Gas Company
555 W 5th St Fl 31
Los Angeles CA 90013
213 244-1200

(P-6266)
SOUTHERN CALIFORNIA GAS CO
1600 Corporate Center Dr, Monterey Park (91754-7626)
P.O. Box C (91756-0001)
PHONE..................213 244-1200
Joe M Rivera, *Regional Mgr*
Terry Fleskes, *Finance*
EMP: 223
SALES (corp-wide): 10.2B **Publicly Held**
WEB: www.gasselect.com
SIC: 4923 Gas transmission & distribution
HQ: Southern California Gas Company
555 W 5th St Fl 31
Los Angeles CA 90013
213 244-1200

(P-6267)
SOUTHERN CALIFORNIA GAS CO
3 Mi S, Newberry Springs (92365)
P.O. Box 9 (92365-0009)
PHONE..................800 427-0018
Fax: 619 257-3341
Lilian Gorman, *VP Human Res*
John Stjohn, *Manager*
EMP: 54
SALES (corp-wide): 10.2B **Publicly Held**
WEB: www.gasselect.com
SIC: 4923 Gas transmission & distribution
HQ: Southern California Gas Company
555 W 5th St Fl 31
Los Angeles CA 90013
213 244-1200

4924 Natural Gas Distribution

(P-6268)
CLEAN ENERGY
4675 Macarthur Ct Ste 800, Newport Beach (92660-1895)
PHONE..................949 437-1000
Andrew Littlefair, *President*
Mitchell Pratt, *COO*
Robert Vreeland, *CFO*
Alan Short, *VP Finance*
Negin Jafari, *Accountant*
EMP: 1000
SALES (est): 354.5MM
SALES (corp-wide): 384.3MM **Publicly Held**
SIC: 4924 Natural gas distribution
PA: Clean Energy Fuels Corp.
4675 Macarthur Ct Ste 800
Newport Beach CA 92660
949 437-1000

(P-6269)
CLEAN ENERGY FUELS CORP (PA)
4675 Macarthur Ct Ste 800, Newport Beach (92660-1895)
PHONE..................949 437-1000
Andrew J Littlefair, *President*
Warren I Mitchell, *Ch of Bd*
Mitchell W Pratt, *COO*
Robert M Vreeland, *CFO*
Tony Kritzer, *Officer*
▲ **EMP:** 170
SQ FT: 68,000
SALES: 384.3MM **Publicly Held**
SIC: 4924 4922 Natural gas distribution; natural gas transmission

(P-6270)
PACIFIC ENERGY FUELS COMPANY
Also Called: PG&e
77 Beale St Ste 100, San Francisco (94105-1814)
PHONE..................415 973-8200
Gordon R Smith, *President*
Ellen Conti, *Analyst*
John Kennedy, *Director*
EMP: 999
SALES (est): 30.2MM **Publicly Held**
WEB: www.pge.com
SIC: 4924 Natural gas distribution
HQ: Pacific Gas And Electric Company
77 Beale St
San Francisco CA 94105
415 973-7000

(P-6271)
PACIFIC GAS AND ELECTRIC CO
Also Called: PG&e
24300 Clawiter Rd, Hayward (94545-2218)
PHONE..................510 784-3253
Tom Webb, *Branch Mgr*
Richard Torres, *Facilities Mgr*
EMP: 409 **Publicly Held**
WEB: www.pge.com
SIC: 4924 4911 Natural gas distribution; distribution, electric power
HQ: Pacific Gas And Electric Company
77 Beale St
San Francisco CA 94105
415 973-7000

(P-6272)
PACIFIC GAS AND ELECTRIC CO
Also Called: PG&e
460 Rio Lindo Ave, Chico (95926-1815)
PHONE..................530 894-4739
Todd Stewart, *Manager*
Galen Hollis, *Engineer*
EMP: 110 **Publicly Held**
WEB: www.pge.com
SIC: 4924 4911 4923 Natural gas distribution; electric services; gas transmission & distribution
HQ: Pacific Gas And Electric Company
77 Beale St
San Francisco CA 94105
415 973-7000

PRODUCTS & SERVICES SECTION

4931 - Electric & Other Svcs Combined County (P-6292)

(P-6273)
SEMPRA ENERGY GLOBAL ENTPS
101 Ash St, San Diego (92101-3017)
PHONE.................................619 696-2000
Mark Snell, *President*
Michael Allman, *CFO*
Randall Peterson, *Ch Credit Ofcr*
Frank Ault, *Senior VP*
Mark Fisher, *Vice Pres*
EMP: 1000
SQ FT: 10,000
SALES (est): 64.9MM
SALES (corp-wide): 10.2B **Publicly Held**
SIC: 4924 4911 Natural gas distribution; generation, electric power
PA: Sempra Energy
 488 8th Ave
 San Diego CA 92101
 619 696-2000

(P-6274)
SOUTHERN CALIFORNIA GAS CO (DH)
Also Called: GAS COMPANY, THE
555 W 5th St Fl 31, Los Angeles (90013-1018)
PHONE.................................213 244-1200
Fax: 213 244-8161
Debra L Reed, *CEO*
Mark A Snell, *President*
Robert M Schlax, *CFO*
Steven D Davis, *Exec VP*
Joseph A Householder, *Exec VP*
EMP: 170 **EST:** 1910
SALES: 3.4B
SALES (corp-wide): 10.2B **Publicly Held**
WEB: www.gasselect.com
SIC: 4924 4922 4932 Natural gas distribution; natural gas transmission; gas & other services combined
HQ: Pacific Enterprises
 101 Ash St
 San Diego CA 92101
 619 696-2020

(P-6275)
SOUTHERN CALIFORNIA GAS CO
Also Called: Regional Office
1981 W Lugonia Ave, Redlands (92374-9796)
P.O. Box 3003 (92373-0306)
PHONE.................................909 335-7802
Fax: 909 335-7990
James Boland, *Manager*
Claudia Dodson, *Supervisor*
Robert E Quiroz, *Supervisor*
Steve York, *Supervisor*
EMP: 383
SALES (corp-wide): 10.2B **Publicly Held**
WEB: www.gasselect.com
SIC: 4924 Natural gas distribution
HQ: Southern California Gas Company
 555 W 5th St Fl 31
 Los Angeles CA 90013
 213 244-1200

(P-6276)
SOUTHERN CALIFORNIA GAS CO
Also Called: Industry Station
920 S Stimson Ave, City of Industry (91745-1640)
PHONE.................................213 244-1200
EMP: 69
SALES (corp-wide): 10.2B **Publicly Held**
SIC: 4924 Natural gas distribution
HQ: Southern California Gas Company
 555 W 5th St Fl 31
 Los Angeles CA 90013
 213 244-1200

(P-6277)
SOUTHERN CALIFORNIA GAS CO
25200 Trumble Rd, Romoland (92585-9664)
PHONE.................................213 244-1200
Rod Paculba, *Planning*
EMP: 69
SALES (corp-wide): 10.2B **Publicly Held**
SIC: 4924 Natural gas distribution

HQ: Southern California Gas Company
 555 W 5th St Fl 31
 Los Angeles CA 90013
 213 244-1200

(P-6278)
SOUTHERN CALIFORNIA GAS CO
333 E Main St Ste J, Alhambra (91801-3914)
PHONE.................................323 881-3587
G H Chavez, *Branch Mgr*
EMP: 72
SALES (corp-wide): 10.2B **Publicly Held**
WEB: www.gasselect.com
SIC: 4924 Natural gas distribution
HQ: Southern California Gas Company
 555 W 5th St Fl 31
 Los Angeles CA 90013
 213 244-1200

(P-6279)
SOUTHERN CALIFORNIA GAS CO
Also Called: Energy Resource Center
9240 Firestone Blvd, Downey (90241-5388)
PHONE.................................562 803-7453
Fax: 562 803-7551
Carlos Ruiz, *Manager*
Brand Darrell, *Assistant*
Sheila Hartley, *Relations*
EMP: 50
SALES (corp-wide): 10.2B **Publicly Held**
WEB: www.gasselect.com
SIC: 4924 Natural gas distribution
HQ: Southern California Gas Company
 555 W 5th St Fl 31
 Los Angeles CA 90013
 213 244-1200

(P-6280)
SOUTHERN CALIFORNIA GAS CO
Also Called: Honor Rancho Station
23130 Valencia Blvd, Valencia (91355-1716)
PHONE.................................800 427-2200
Dan Skope, *Vice Pres*
EMP: 64
SALES (corp-wide): 10.2B **Publicly Held**
WEB: www.gasselect.com
SIC: 4924 Natural gas distribution
HQ: Southern California Gas Company
 555 W 5th St Fl 31
 Los Angeles CA 90013
 213 244-1200

(P-6281)
SOUTHERN CALIFORNIA GAS TOWER (DH)
555 W 5th St Ste 1700, Los Angeles (90013-1083)
PHONE.................................213 244-1200
Ed Guiles, *President*
Margot Kyd, *Vice Pres*
John J Kralik IV,
EMP: 400
SALES (est): 115.7MM
SALES (corp-wide): 10.2B **Publicly Held**
SIC: 4924 Natural gas distribution
HQ: Southern California Gas Company
 555 W 5th St Fl 31
 Los Angeles CA 90013
 213 244-1200

(P-6282)
STEELRIVER INFRASTRUCTURE FUND (HQ)
1 Letterman Dr Ste 500, San Francisco (94129-1496)
PHONE.................................415 848-5448
Chris Kinney, *Partner*
John Anderson, *Partner*
Dennis Mahoney, *Partner*
Brian Carmichael, *Commissioner*
Vittorio Lacagnina, *Director*
EMP: 200
SALES (est): 918.9MM
SALES (corp-wide): 146.3MM **Privately Held**
SIC: 4924 Natural gas distribution

PA: Steelriver Infrastructure Partners Lp
 1 Letterman Dr
 San Francisco CA 94129
 415 512-1515

4925 Gas Production &/Or Distribution

(P-6283)
PRAXAIR DISTRIBUTION INC
19200 Hawthorne Blvd, Torrance (90503-1505)
PHONE.................................310 371-1254
Fred Casey, *Branch Mgr*
Len Kajimoto, *Plant Mgr*
O'Neal Summers, *Plant Mgr*
EMP: 70
SALES (corp-wide): 10.7B **Publicly Held**
SIC: 4925 Gas production and/or distribution
HQ: Praxair Distribution, Inc.
 39 Old Ridgebury Rd
 Danbury CT 06810
 203 837-2000

4931 Electric & Other Svcs Combined

(P-6284)
CITY OF BURBANK
Also Called: Burbank Water & Power
164 W Magnolia Blvd, Burbank (91502-1772)
PHONE.................................818 238-3550
Ronald E Davis, *Branch Mgr*
Fred Lantz, *General Mgr*
Todd Campbell, *Council Mbr*
Dave Golonski, *Council Mbr*
Xavier Baldwin, *Asst Mgr*
EMP: 315 **Privately Held**
SIC: 4931 4941 4911 Electric & other services combined; water supply; mayors' offices; electric services
PA: City Of Burbank
 275 E Olive Ave
 Burbank CA 91502
 818 238-5800

(P-6285)
CITY OF CORONADO
Also Called: Public Services
101 B Ave, Coronado (92118-1510)
PHONE.................................619 522-7380
Fax: 619 435-4479
Scott Huth, *Director*
Cliff Maurer, *Deputy Dir*
Linda Hascup, *Manager*
Diane Shea, *Manager*
EMP: 55 **Privately Held**
WEB: www.coronadoplayhouse.com
SIC: 4931 9111 Electric & other services combined; mayors' offices
PA: City Of Coronado
 1825 Strand Way
 Coronado CA 92118
 619 522-7300

(P-6286)
EDISON MISSION ENERGY (DH)
3 Macarthur Pl Ste 100, Santa Ana (92707-6068)
PHONE.................................714 513-8000
Fax: 949 474-2372
Pedro J Pizarro, *President*
Daryl David, *Senior VP*
Andrew J Hertneky, *Senior VP*
Paul Jacob, *Senior VP*
John C Kennedy, *Senior VP*
▲ **EMP:** 63
SQ FT: 71,000
SALES (est): 2.1B
SALES (corp-wide): 14.6B **Publicly Held**
SIC: 4931 Electric & other services combined

(P-6287)
GWF POWER SYSTEMS LP
225 Lennon Ln Ste 120, Walnut Creek (94598-2492)
PHONE.................................925 933-7000
Fax: 925 938-5117
Duane Nelson, *President*

Cea Gwf, *General Ptnr*
Harbert Gwf, *General Ptnr*
Harbert Cogen, *Ltd Ptnr*
Cea USA, *Ltd Ptnr*
EMP: 118
SQ FT: 10,000
SALES (est): 4.1MM **Privately Held**
SIC: 4931 Electric & other services combined

(P-6288)
IMPERIAL IRRIGATION DISTRICT
2151 W Adams Ave, El Centro (92243-9457)
P.O. Box 937, Imperial (92251-0937)
PHONE.................................760 339-9800
Fax: 760 339-9895
Frank Montoya, *Branch Mgr*
Brian Brady, *General Mgr*
EMP: 75
SALES (corp-wide): 995.5MM **Privately Held**
WEB: www.iidwater.com
SIC: 4931 Electric & other services combined
PA: Imperial Irrigation District
 333 E Barioni Blvd
 Imperial CA 92251
 800 303-7756

(P-6289)
MEKWUS SOLAR ENERGY
20283 Santa Maria Ave # 2103, Castro Valley (94546-5098)
PHONE.................................510 731-4134
De Anna Mekwunye, *Partner*
Elijah Mekwunye, *Partner*
EMP: 99
SQ FT: 1,200
SALES (est): 10.9MM **Privately Held**
SIC: 4931 Electric & other services combined;

(P-6290)
NOBLE AMRCAS ENRGY SLTIONS LLC (HQ)
Also Called: Noble Americas Enrgy Solutions
401 W A St Ste 500, San Diego (92101-7991)
PHONE.................................877 273-6772
James Wood, *President*
Dee Chambless, *Vice Pres*
Alex Fazekas-Paul, *Vice Pres*
Gayle McCutchan, *Vice Pres*
Drake Welch, *Vice Pres*
EMP: 91
SALES (est): 306.8MM **Privately Held**
WEB: www.noblesolutions.com
SIC: 4931 4932 Electric & other services combined; gas & other services combined
PA: Noble Group Limited
 C/O Conyers, Dill & Pearman
 Hamilton
 441 295-1422

(P-6291)
PG&E CORPORATION (PA)
77 Beale St, San Francisco (94105-1814)
P.O. Box 770000 (94177-0001)
PHONE.................................415 973-1000
Fax: 415 267-7262
Anthony F Earley Jr, *Ch of Bd*
Nickolas Stavropoulos, *President*
Geisha J Williams, *President*
Jason P Wells, *CFO*
Loraine M Giammona, *Officer*
▲ **EMP:** 170
SQ FT: 42,000
SALES: 16.8B **Publicly Held**
WEB: www.pgecorp.com
SIC: 4931 4923 Electric & other services combined; gas transmission & distribution

(P-6292)
SAN DIEGO GAS & ELECTRIC CO (DH)
8326 Century Park Ct, San Diego (92123-1530)
PHONE.................................619 696-2000
J Walker Martin, *CEO*
Jessie J Knight Jr, *Ch of Bd*
Steven D Davis, *President*
Robert M Schlax, *CFO*
J Chris Baker, *Officer*
◆ **EMP:** 170

4931 - Electric & Other Svcs Combined

SALES: 4.2B
SALES (corp-wide): 10.2B **Publicly Held**
SIC: **4931** 4911 4924 Electric & other services combined; generation, electric power; transmission, electric power; distribution, electric power; natural gas distribution
HQ: Enova Corporation
　101 Ash St
　San Diego CA 92101
　619 239-7700

(P-6293)
SAN DIEGO GAS & ELECTRIC CO
Also Called: Orange County Service Center
662 Camino De Los Mares, San Clemente (92673-2827)
PHONE....................949 361-8090
James Valentine, *Branch Mgr*
EMP: 50
SALES (corp-wide): 10.2B **Publicly Held**
SIC: **4931** 4911 Electric & other services combined; electric services
HQ: San Diego Gas & Electric Company
　8326 Century Park Ct
　San Diego CA 92123
　619 696-2000

(P-6294)
UNDERGROUND CNSTR CO INC
5145 Industrial Way, Benicia (94510-1042)
PHONE....................707 746-8800
Fax: 707 746-1314
Christopher Ronco, *President*
Jeff Tinsley, *CFO*
George R Bradshaw, *Exec VP*
Lynn Barr, *Vice Pres*
Loren Hudson, *Vice Pres*
EMP: 250 EST: 1936
SQ FT: 32,946
SALES (est): 77.2MM
SALES (corp-wide): 7.5B **Publicly Held**
WEB: www.undergrnd.com
SIC: **4931** 5172 4923 Electric & other services combined; aircraft fueling services; gas transmission & distribution
PA: Quanta Services, Inc.
　2800 Post Oak Blvd # 2600
　Houston TX 77056
　713 629-7600

(P-6295)
VOLT INFORMATION SCIENCES INC
2401 N Glassell St, Orange (92865-2705)
PHONE....................714 921-8000
Fax: 714 921-5410
William Shaw, *Manager*
Cy Hashemi, *Info Tech Dir*
Chris Netz, *Info Tech Mgr*
Joel Rivera, *Web Dvlpr*
Pam Solano, *Data Proc Staff*
EMP: 144
SALES (corp-wide): 1.5B **Publicly Held**
SIC: **4931** 4932 Electric & other services combined; gas & other services combined
PA: Volt Information Sciences Inc
　1133 Ave Of The Americas
　New York NY 10036
　212 704-2400

4932 Gas & Other Svcs Combined

(P-6296)
CITY OF LONG BEACH
City of Long Beach Gas & Oil
2400 E Spring St, Long Beach (90806-2203)
PHONE....................562 570-2000
Fax: 562 570-2114
Christopher J Garner, *Manager*
Robert Siedler, *Facilities*
Peter Hayes, *Manager*
EMP: 204 **Privately Held**
WEB: www.polb.com
SIC: **4932** 9111 4924 Gas & other services combined; mayors' offices; natural gas distribution
PA: City Of Long Beach
　333 W Ocean Blvd Fl 10
　Long Beach CA 90802
　562 570-6450

(P-6297)
FIELDSERVER TECHNOLOGIES
1991 Tarob Ct, Milpitas (95035-6825)
PHONE....................408 262-2299
Fax: 408 262-2269
Gordon Arnold, *Principal*
EMP: 50
SALES (est): 4.3MM
SALES (corp-wide): 20.3MM **Publicly Held**
WEB: www.fieldserver.com
SIC: **4932** Gas & other services combined
PA: Sierra Monitor Corporation
　1991 Tarob Ct
　Milpitas CA 95035
　408 262-6611

(P-6298)
SEMPRA ENERGY (PA)
488 8th Ave, San Diego (92101-7123)
P.O. Box 129400 (92101)
PHONE....................619 696-2000
Fax: 619 696-4611
Debra L Reed, *Ch of Bd*
Justice Urbas, *Vice Chairman*
Mark A Snell, *President*
Joseph A Householder, *CFO*
Tim Ransdell, *Treasurer*
EMP: 1000
SALES: 10.2B **Publicly Held**
WEB: www.sempra.com
SIC: **4932** 4911 5172 4922 Gas & other services combined; electric services; distribution, electric power; generation, electric power; transmission, electric power; petroleum products; natural gas transmission; pipelines, natural gas; storage, natural gas

4939 Combination Utilities, NEC

(P-6299)
AGILE SOURCING PARTNERS INC
2385 Railroad St, Corona (92880-5411)
PHONE....................951 279-4154
Maria Thompson, *President*
Courtney Gaik, *Vice Pres*
Ryan Swindel, *Manager*
EMP: 180
SQ FT: 2,300
SALES: 222.5MM **Privately Held**
SIC: **4939** Combination utilities

(P-6300)
CHESTER PUBLIC UTILITY DST
251 Chester Airport Rd, Chester (96020)
P.O. Box 177 (96020-0177)
PHONE....................530 258-2171
Fax: 530 258-2064
William D Turner, *Manager*
▲EMP: 70
SALES (est): 3.9MM **Privately Held**
SIC: **4939** Combination utilities

(P-6301)
CITY OF CORONA
Also Called: Public Works
400 S Vicentia Ave # 210, Corona (92882-2187)
PHONE....................951 736-2266
Fax: 951 736-2496
Kip D Field, *Manager*
Steve Larson, *Info Tech Dir*
Bill Newman, *Personnel*
EMP: 99 **Privately Held**
WEB: www.coronautilities.com
SIC: **4939** Combination utilities
PA: City Of Corona
　400 S Vicentia Ave
　Corona CA 92882
　951 736-2372

(P-6302)
CITY OF PASADENA
Also Called: Pasadena Water & Power
45 E Glenarm St, Pasadena (91105-3418)
PHONE....................626 405-4409
George Wilson, *Branch Mgr*
Don Howe, *Technical Staff*
EMP: 80 **Privately Held**
WEB: www.cityofpasadena.net
SIC: **4939** Combination utilities

PA: City Of Pasadena
　100 N Garfield Ave
　Pasadena CA 91101
　626 744-4386

(P-6303)
IMPERIAL IRRIGATION DISTRICT
81600 58th Ave, La Quinta (92253-7663)
P.O. Box 1080 (92247-1080)
PHONE....................760 398-5811
Fax: 760 398-5848
Charles Haskin, *General Mgr*
Oscar Jauregui, *Info Tech Mgr*
Mary Perry, *Technician*
Cedric Stephens, *Technology*
Sandra Corella, *Human Res Mgr*
EMP: 150
SALES (corp-wide): 995.5MM **Privately Held**
WEB: www.iidwater.com
SIC: **4939** 4911 Combination utilities; electric services
PA: Imperial Irrigation District
　333 E Barioni Blvd
　Imperial CA 92251
　800 303-7756

(P-6304)
LOS ANGELES DEPT WTR & PWR
Also Called: Scattergood Generation Plant
12700 Vista Del Mar, Playa Del Rey (90293-8502)
PHONE....................310 524-8500
Nazih Batarseh, *Branch Mgr*
EMP: 100
SALES (corp-wide): 3.8B **Privately Held**
SIC: **4939** Combination utilities
PA: Los Angeles Department Of Water And Power
　111 N Hope St Rm 1063
　Los Angeles CA 90012
　213 367-4043

(P-6305)
ORMAT NEVADA INC
947 Dogwood Rd, Heber (92249-9762)
PHONE....................760 353-8200
Celia Velasco, *Admin Mgr*
Marie L Franklin, *Administration*
Omar Vasquez, *IT/INT Sup*
Israel Blumgart, *Program Dir*
Greg Griffith, *Manager*
EMP: 50 **Publicly Held**
SIC: **4939** Combination utilities
HQ: Ormat Nevada, Inc.
　6225 Neil Rd
　Reno NV 89511
　775 356-9029

(P-6306)
SAN DIEGO GAS & ELECTRIC CO
North Coast O & M Center
5016 Carlsbad Blvd, Carlsbad (92008-4303)
PHONE....................760 438-6200
Jim Boland, *Director*
Jim Valentine, *Director*
Tim Yuskin, *Manager*
EMP: 120
SALES (corp-wide): 10.2B **Publicly Held**
SIC: **4939** 4924 4911 Combination utilities; natural gas distribution; electric services
HQ: San Diego Gas & Electric Company
　8326 Century Park Ct
　San Diego CA 92123
　619 696-2000

(P-6307)
SAN DIEGO GAS & ELECTRIC CO
Also Called: Northern Cnstr & Operations
571 Enterprise St, Escondido (92029-1244)
PHONE....................760 432-5885
Victor Gonzales, *Manager*
Ed Caudillo, *QA Dir*
Vicky Serrano, *Opers Mgr*
EMP: 400
SQ FT: 1,660
SALES (corp-wide): 10.2B **Publicly Held**
SIC: **4939** Combination utilities

HQ: San Diego Gas & Electric Company
　8326 Century Park Ct
　San Diego CA 92123
　619 696-2000

(P-6308)
SAN DIEGO GAS & ELECTRIC CO
Project Construction Metro
701 33rd St, San Diego (92102-3341)
PHONE....................619 699-1018
Scott Furgerson, *Manager*
EMP: 200
SALES (corp-wide): 10.2B **Publicly Held**
SIC: **4939** Combination utilities
HQ: San Diego Gas & Electric Company
　8326 Century Park Ct
　San Diego CA 92123
　619 696-2000

4941 Water Sply

(P-6309)
AAB WATER COMPANY INC
Also Called: Yosemite Waters
226 S Avenue 54, Los Angeles (90042-4512)
PHONE....................559 497-2700
Fax: 559 268-1923
Mike Larue, *President*
EMP: 75
SALES: 10K **Privately Held**
SIC: **4941** Water supply

(P-6310)
ALAMEDA COUNTY WATER DISTRICT (PA)
Also Called: Acwd
43885 S Grimmer Blvd, Fremont (94538-6375)
P.O. Box 5110 (94537-5110)
PHONE....................510 668-4200
Fax: 510 770-1793
Walt Wadlow, *General Mgr*
Gina Markou, *Executive Asst*
Todd Christner, *Admin Asst*
Michael Yee, *Administration*
John Musser, *Info Tech Dir*
EMP: 182
SQ FT: 60,000
SALES (est): 150.8MM **Privately Held**
WEB: www.acwd.org
SIC: **4941** Water supply

(P-6311)
AMADOR WATER AGENCY
12800 Ridge Rd, Sutter Creek (95685-9630)
PHONE....................209 223-3018
Fax: 209 257-5281
Jim Abercrombie, *General Mgr*
Terance W Moore, *President*
John P Swift, *Vice Pres*
Gray Thomas, *Vice Pres*
Karen Gish, *General Mgr*
EMP: 52
SQ FT: 2,000
SALES (est): 18.1MM **Privately Held**
WEB: www.amadorwa.com
SIC: **4941** 4952 Water supply; sewerage systems

(P-6312)
AMERICAN WATER WORKS CO INC
4701 Beloit Dr, Sacramento (95838-2434)
P.O. Box 15468 (95851-0468)
PHONE....................916 568-4236
Rob Roscoe, *Engineer*
Darrell Eck, *Research*
Catherine Bowie, *Pub Rel Mgr*
EMP: 80
SALES (corp-wide): 3.1B **Publicly Held**
WEB: www.amwater.com
SIC: **4941** Water supply
PA: American Water Works Company, Inc.
　1025 Laurel Oak Rd
　Voorhees NJ 08043
　856 346-8200

PRODUCTS & SERVICES SECTION

4941 - Water Sply County (P-6333)

(P-6313)
CALAVERAS COUNTY WATER DST
120 Toma Ct, San Andreas (95249)
P.O. Box 846 (95249-9002)
PHONE.................................209 754-3543
Fax: 209 754-1069
Scott Ratterman, *President*
Jeff Davidson, *Vice Pres*
EMP: 66
SQ FT: 5,000
SALES (est): 25.3MM **Privately Held**
WEB: www.ccwd.org
SIC: 4941 Water supply

(P-6314)
CALIFORNIA AMERICAN WATER CO (HQ)
655 W Broadway Ste 1410, San Diego (92101-8491)
PHONE.................................619 409-7703
Kent Turner, *President*
Judith Almond, *COO*
Christopher Buls, *CFO*
Anthony J Cerasuolo, *Vice Pres*
Laura Jordan, *Manager*
EMP: 57
SQ FT: 16,500
SALES (est): 115.4MM
SALES (corp-wide): 3.1B **Publicly Held**
SIC: 4941 Water supply
PA: American Water Works Company, Inc.
1025 Laurel Oak Rd
Voorhees NJ 08043
856 346-8200

(P-6315)
CALIFORNIA AMERICAN WATER CO
511 Forest Lodge Rd 100, Pacific Grove (93950-5040)
P.O. Box 951, Monterey (93942-0951)
PHONE.................................831 373-3051
Fax: 831 375-4367
L D Foy, *Branch Mgr*
EMP: 86
SALES (corp-wide): 3.1B **Publicly Held**
SIC: 4941 Water supply
HQ: California American Water Co.
655 W Broadway Ste 1410
San Diego CA 92101
619 409-7703

(P-6316)
CALIFORNIA AMERICAN WATER CO
880 Kuhn Dr, Chula Vista (91914-3514)
PHONE.................................619 656-2400
Kent Turner, *Controller*
John Barker, *Vice Pres*
Craig Close, *Vice Pres*
EMP: 70
SALES (corp-wide): 3.1B **Publicly Held**
SIC: 4941 Water supply
HQ: California American Water Co.
655 W Broadway Ste 1410
San Diego CA 92101
619 409-7703

(P-6317)
CALIFORNIA AMERICAN WATER CO
4787 Old Redwood Hwy, Santa Rosa (95403-1485)
PHONE.................................707 542-1717
Tony Lindstrom, *Manager*
EMP: 50
SALES (corp-wide): 3.1B **Publicly Held**
SIC: 4941 4953 Water supply; refuse systems
HQ: California American Water Co.
655 W Broadway Ste 1410
San Diego CA 92101
619 409-7703

(P-6318)
CALIFORNIA AMERICAN WATER CO
4701 Beloit Dr, Sacramento (95838-2434)
PHONE.................................916 568-4216
Robert Bloor, *CFO*
Judy Almond, *Finance Mgr*
EMP: 50

SALES (corp-wide): 3.1B **Publicly Held**
SIC: 4941 4953 Water supply; refuse systems
HQ: California American Water Co.
655 W Broadway Ste 1410
San Diego CA 92101
619 409-7703

(P-6319)
CALIFORNIA WATER SERVICE CO (HQ)
1720 N 1st St, San Jose (95112-4598)
PHONE.................................408 367-8200
Fax: 408 367-8430
Martin A Kropelnicki, *CEO*
Michael P Ireland, *President*
Helen Del Grosso, *Vice Pres*
Francis S Ferraro, *Vice Pres*
Robert R Guzzetta, *Vice Pres*
EMP: 160 **EST:** 1926
SQ FT: 43,000
SALES (est): 481.2MM
SALES (corp-wide): 588.3MM **Publicly Held**
SIC: 4941 Water supply
PA: California Water Service Group
1720 N 1st St
San Jose CA 95112
408 367-8200

(P-6320)
CALIFORNIA WATER SERVICE CO
3725 S H St, Bakersfield (93304-6535)
PHONE.................................661 396-2400
Fax: 661 396-2411
Tim Terloar, *Manager*
Tim Traylor, *District Mgr*
Kim Solis, *Office Spvr*
Ron Gibbs, *Maintence Staff*
EMP: 77
SALES (corp-wide): 588.3MM **Publicly Held**
SIC: 4941 Water supply
HQ: California Water Service Company
1720 N 1st St
San Jose CA 95112
408 367-8200

(P-6321)
CALIFORNIA WATER SERVICE CO
1505 E Sonora St, Stockton (95205-6112)
PHONE.................................209 547-7900
Henry Wind, *Manager*
Ross Moilan, *District Mgr*
Mike Camy, *Manager*
EMP: 51
SALES (corp-wide): 588.3MM **Publicly Held**
SIC: 4941 Water supply
HQ: California Water Service Company
1720 N 1st St
San Jose CA 95112
408 367-8200

(P-6322)
CALLEGUAS MUNICIPAL WATER DICT
2100 E Olsen Rd, Thousand Oaks (91360-6800)
PHONE.................................805 526-9323
Fax: 805 522-5730
William R Seaver, *Director*
Gail Pringle, *Treasurer*
Thomas Slosson, *Treasurer*
Alita Inouye, *Office Mgr*
Resources Division, *Software Dev*
EMP: 59
SQ FT: 8,000
SALES (est): 23.7MM **Privately Held**
WEB: www.calleguas.com
SIC: 4941 Water supply

(P-6323)
CARLSBAD MUNICIPAL WATER DST
5950 El Camino Real, Carlsbad (92008-8802)
PHONE.................................760 438-2722
Fax: 760 431-1601
Robert Greaney, *Manager*
Pat Guevara, *Superintendent*
EMP: 50
SQ FT: 12,000

SALES (est): 7.2MM **Privately Held**
SIC: 4941 Water supply
PA: City Of Carlsbad
1635 Faraday Ave
Carlsbad CA 92008
760 602-2490

(P-6324)
CITY OF FRESNO
Also Called: Water Division
1910 E University Ave, Fresno (93703-2927)
PHONE.................................559 621-5300
Lon Martin, *Manager*
Martin McIntyre, *Manager*
Cynthia Fischer, *Supervisor*
EMP: 165 **Privately Held**
WEB: www.fresnocitizencorps.org
SIC: 4941 Water supply
PA: City Of Fresno
2600 Fresno St
Fresno CA 93721
559 621-7001

(P-6325)
CITY OF GLENDALE
Also Called: Public Service Yard
800 Air Way, Glendale (91201-3012)
PHONE.................................818 548-2011
Pat Reily, *Manager*
EMP: 150 **Privately Held**
WEB: www.glendaleca.com
SIC: 4941 Water supply
PA: City Of Glendale
141 N Glendale Ave Fl 2
Glendale CA 91206
818 548-2085

(P-6326)
CITY OF LOMITA
Also Called: Water Department
24300 Narbonne Ave, Lomita (90717-1198)
P.O. Box 1809 (90717-5809)
PHONE.................................310 325-7114
Wendell Johnson, *Manager*
EMP: 50 **Privately Held**
WEB: www.lomita.com
SIC: 4941 9111 Water supply; mayors' offices
PA: City Of Lomita
24300 Narbonne Ave
Lomita CA 90717
310 325-7110

(P-6327)
CITY OF LOMITA
Also Called: Publis Works
24373 Walnut St, Lomita (90717-1259)
PHONE.................................310 325-9830
Fax: 310 325-3627
Vince Demasse, *Manager*
Mike Sansbury, *Manager*
James Shely, *Manager*
EMP: 50
SQ FT: 59,893 **Privately Held**
WEB: www.lomita.com
SIC: 4941 9111 Water supply; mayors' offices
PA: City Of Lomita
24300 Narbonne Ave
Lomita CA 90717
310 325-7110

(P-6328)
CITY OF LONG BEACH
Also Called: Water Emergency Dispatch
1800 E Wardlow Rd, Long Beach (90807-4931)
PHONE.................................562 570-2390
Fax: 562 427-7061
Kevin Wattier, *General Mgr*
Robert Cole, *President*
Deena Long, *Admin Sec*
Isaac Pai, *Engineer*
Paul Fujita, *Financial Exec*
EMP: 100 **Privately Held**
WEB: www.polb.com
SIC: 4941 9511 Water supply; air, water & solid waste management;
PA: City Of Long Beach
333 W Ocean Blvd Fl 10
Long Beach CA 90802
562 570-6450

(P-6329)
CITY OF OXNARD
Also Called: Water Svcs Operations & Repr
251 S Hayes Ave, Oxnard (93030-6058)
PHONE.................................805 385-8136
Fax: 805 385-8137
Anthony Emmert, *Superintendent*
Diego Zabala, *Technician*
David Birch, *Manager*
EMP: 60 **Privately Held**
WEB: www.oxnardtourism.com
SIC: 4941 9111 Water supply; mayors' offices
PA: City Of Oxnard
300 W 3rd St Uppr Fl4
Oxnard CA 93030
805 385-7803

(P-6330)
COACHELLA VALLEY WATER DST (PA)
Also Called: C V Water District
85995 Avenue 52, Coachella (92236-2568)
P.O. Box 1058 (92236-1058)
PHONE.................................760 398-2651
Toll Free:.................................888 -
Fax: 760 398-2071
Steve Robbins, *General Mgr*
Rick Dickhaut, *CFO*
Jim Barrett, *General Mgr*
Robert Cheng, *General Mgr*
Isabel Luna, *Executive Asst*
▲ **EMP:** 225
SALES: 150.2MM **Privately Held**
SIC: 4941 4971 4952 7389 Water supply; water distribution or supply systems for irrigation; sewerage systems; water softener service

(P-6331)
COACHELLA VALLEY WATER DST
75515 Hovley Ln E, Palm Desert (92211-5104)
PHONE.................................760 398-2651
Steve Robins, *Branch Mgr*
EMP: 226
SALES (corp-wide): 150.2MM **Privately Held**
SIC: 4941 4952 4971 Water supply; sewerage systems; water distribution or supply systems for irrigation
PA: Coachella Valley Water District
85995 Avenue 52
Coachella CA 92236
760 398-2651

(P-6332)
COACHELLA VALLEY WATER DST
75 525 Hovley Ln, Palm Desert (92260)
PHONE.................................760 398-2651
Steve Robins, *Branch Mgr*
EMP: 226
SALES (corp-wide): 150.2MM **Privately Held**
SIC: 4941 4952 4971 Water supply; sewerage systems; irrigation systems
PA: Coachella Valley Water District
85995 Avenue 52
Coachella CA 92236
760 398-2651

(P-6333)
CONTRA COSTA WATER DISTRICT (PA)
1331 Concord Ave, Concord (94520-4907)
P.O. Box H20 (94524)
PHONE.................................925 688-8000
Fax: 925 603-8345
Joseph L Campbell, *Principal*
Peter Colby, *Bd of Directors*
Mary Neher, *Bd of Directors*
Leah Orloff, *Bd of Directors*
Chris Dundon, *Vice Pres*
▲ **EMP:** 225
SQ FT: 22,000
SALES: 107.6MM **Privately Held**
WEB: www.ccwater.com
SIC: 4941 Water supply

4941 - Water Sply County (P-6334)

(P-6334)
CONTRA COSTA WATER DISTRICT
Also Called: Randall-Bold Wtr Trtmnt Plant
3760 Neroly Rd, Oakley (94561-2084)
PHONE.................925 625-6534
Fax: 925 625-6505
Walter Bishop, *General Mgr*
Dan Sadler, *Manager*
EMP: 55
SALES (corp-wide): 115.3MM **Privately Held**
WEB: www.ccwater.com
SIC: **4941** Water supply
PA: Contra Costa Water District Inc
1331 Concord Ave
Concord CA 94520
925 688-8000

(P-6335)
COUNTY OF LOS ANGELES
Also Called: Public Works, Dept of
900 S Fremont Ave, Alhambra (91803-1331)
P.O. Box 1460 (91802-2460)
PHONE.................626 458-3126
Dean Efstathiou, *Branch Mgr*
Eric Wickland, *Bd of Directors*
Diane Lee, *CTO*
Keith Lilley, *Info Tech Mgr*
Azam Popalzai, *Info Tech Mgr*
EMP: 300
SQ FT: 10,000 **Privately Held**
WEB: www.co.la.ca.us
SIC: **4941** 9511 4971 Water supply; air, water & solid waste management; ; irrigation systems
PA: County Of Los Angeles
500 W Temple St Ste 375
Los Angeles CA 90012
213 974-1101

(P-6336)
COUNTY OF LOS ANGELES
Also Called: Water & Power Department
6801 E 2nd St, Long Beach (90803-4324)
PHONE.................213 367-3176
Victor Barra, *Director*
EMP: 160 **Privately Held**
WEB: www.co.la.ca.us
SIC: **4941** 9511 9631 4939 Water supply; air, water & solid waste management; regulation, administration of utilities; combination utilities
PA: County Of Los Angeles
500 W Temple St Ste 375
Los Angeles CA 90012
213 974-1101

(P-6337)
COUNTY OF LOS ANGELES
Also Called: Community Facilities Dst No 6
500 W Temple St Ste 525, Los Angeles (90012-3873)
PHONE.................213 974-8301
Dan Haller, *Analyst*
Mayan Nath, *Analyst*
Wendy Watanabe, *Auditor*
Michael Antonovich, *Mayor*
Conny McCormack, *Recorder*
EMP: 172 **Privately Held**
SIC: **4941** Water supply
PA: County Of Los Angeles
500 W Temple St Ste 375
Los Angeles CA 90012
213 974-1101

(P-6338)
COUNTY OF SOLANO
Also Called: Water Supply
810 Vaca Valley Pkwy # 203, Vacaville (95688-8835)
PHONE.................707 451-6090
Fax: 707 451-6099
David Okita, *Manager*
Amanda Ladd, *Administration*
EMP: 100 **Privately Held**
SIC: **4941** 8641 Water supply; civic social & fraternal associations
PA: County Of Solano
675 Texas St Ste 2600
Fairfield CA 94533
707 784-6706

(P-6339)
CUCAMONGA VALLEY WATER DST
10440 Ashford St, Rancho Cucamonga (91730-3057)
P.O. Box 638 (91729-0638)
PHONE.................909 987-2591
Martin Zvirbulis, *CEO*
Diane Schumacher, *Senior Partner*
Kathleen Tiegs, *President*
Braden Yu, *CFO*
Chad Brantley, *Officer*
EMP: 100 EST: 1955
SQ FT: 15,000
SALES: 77.9MM **Privately Held**
WEB: www.ccwdwater.com
SIC: **4941** Water supply

(P-6340)
DESERT WATER AGENCY FING CORP
Also Called: DWA
1200 S Gene Autry Trl, Palm Springs (92264-3533)
P.O. Box 1710 (92263-1710)
PHONE.................760 323-4971
Fax: 760 325-6505
Patricia G Oyga, *CEO*
David K Luker, *General Mgr*
Joseph Stu, *Admin Sec*
Mario Ballesteros, *Info Tech Dir*
Kory Knox, *Info Tech Mgr*
EMP: 72
SQ FT: 38,000
SALES: 30.2MM **Privately Held**
WEB: www.dwa.org
SIC: **4941** Water supply

(P-6341)
DUBLIN SAN RAMON SERVICES DIST
Also Called: DUBLIN SAN RAMON SERVICES DIST.
7399 Johnson Dr, Pleasanton (94588-3862)
PHONE.................925 846-4565
Fax: 925 462-0658
Bert Michalczyk, *General Mgr*
EMP: 100 **Privately Held**
WEB: www.dsrsd.com
SIC: **4941** Water supply
PA: Dublin San Ramon Services District
7051 Dublin Blvd
Dublin CA 94568
925 875-2276

(P-6342)
EAST BAY MUNICIPL UTILTY DISTR
Also Called: Ebmud
3999 Lakeside Dr, Richmond (94806-1964)
PHONE.................866 403-2683
Karl Gillson, *Branch Mgr*
Alexander Coate, *General Mgr*
David Klein, *Controller*
EMP: 110
SALES (corp-wide): 1.4B **Privately Held**
WEB: www.ebmud.com
SIC: **4941** Water supply
PA: East Bay Municipal Utility District, Water System
375 11th St
Oakland CA 94607
866 403-2683

(P-6343)
EAST BAY MUNICIPL UTILTY DISTR (PA)
Also Called: Ebmud
375 11th St, Oakland (94607-4246)
P.O. Box 24055 (94623-1055)
PHONE.................866 403-2683
Alexander Coate, *General Mgr*
Sophia Skoda, *Treasurer*
Andy Katz, *Vice Pres*
Vladimir Besarabov, *Risk Mgmt Dir*
Josh Hallmark, *Admin Sec*
EMP: 629
SQ FT: 264,427
SALES (est): 1.4B **Privately Held**
WEB: www.ebmud.com
SIC: **4941** Water supply

(P-6344)
EAST VALLEY WATER DISTRICT
31111 Greenspot Rd, Highland (92346-4427)
P.O. Box 3427, San Bernardino (92413-3427)
PHONE.................909 889-9501
Fax: 909 889-5732
John Mura, *CEO*
Matt Levesque, *President*
Brian W Tompkins, *CFO*
Kip E Sturgeon, *Vice Pres*
Robert E Martin, *General Mgr*
EMP: 61
SALES: 30.7MM **Privately Held**
WEB: www.eastvalley.org
SIC: **4941** 8734 Water supply; water testing laboratory

(P-6345)
EASTERN MUNICIPAL WATER DST (PA)
2270 Trumble Rd, Perris (92572)
P.O. Box 8300 (92572-8300)
PHONE.................951 928-3777
Paul D Jones II, *CEO*
Charles M Rathbone Jr, *CFO*
Doug Hefley, *Executive*
Roxanne Rountree, *Executive*
Mike Dad, *General Mgr*
▲ EMP: 420
SQ FT: 160,000
SALES: 200.8MM **Privately Held**
SIC: **4941** 4952 Water supply; sewerage systems

(P-6346)
EL DORADO IRRIGATION DISTRICT
2890 Mosquito Rd, Placerville (95667-4700)
PHONE.................530 622-4513
Fax: 530 622-1195
George Osborne, *President*
Karen Cross, *Executive*
Jim Abercrombie, *General Mgr*
Ane Deister, *General Mgr*
Monica Penney, *Admin Sec*
EMP: 300
SQ FT: 27,000
SALES: 55.3MM **Privately Held**
SIC: **4941** 4952 8741 4971 Water supply; sewerage systems; management services; irrigation systems

(P-6347)
EL DORADO WTR & SHOWER SVC INC
5821 Mother Lode Dr, Placerville (95667-8227)
P.O. Box 944 (95667-0944)
PHONE.................530 622-8995
Robert V Williams, *President*
Mellisa Peterson, *Principal*
EMP: 50
SQ FT: 816
SALES: 2MM **Privately Held**
SIC: **4941** Water supply

(P-6348)
ELSINORE VLY MUNICPL WTR DST (PA)
31315 Chaney St, Lake Elsinore (92530-2743)
P.O. Box 3000 (92531-3000)
PHONE.................951 674-3146
Fax: 951 674-9872
Harvey R Ryan, *President*
Andy Morris, *Treasurer*
Phil Williams, *Vice Pres*
Ronald Young, *Vice Pres*
Tammy Ramirez, *General Mgr*
EMP: 65
SQ FT: 4,000
SALES: 67.8MM **Privately Held**
WEB: www.evmwd.com
SIC: **4941** 4971 4952 Water supply; water distribution or supply systems for irrigation; sewerage systems

(P-6349)
FRIANT WATER USERS ASSOCIATION
Also Called: Friant Water Users Authority
854 N Harvard Ave, Lindsay (93247-1715)
PHONE.................559 562-6305
Fax: 559 562-3496
Marvin Huss, *Chairman*
Tom Fousek, *Executive*
Kathy Bennett, *General Mgr*
Kathryn C Santos, *Finance*
Gary Perez, *Opers Spvr*
EMP: 53
SQ FT: 4,000
SALES (est): 6.3MM **Privately Held**
SIC: **4941** Water supply

(P-6350)
GOLDEN STATE WATER COMPANY
1920 W Corporate Way, Anaheim (92801-5373)
PHONE.................714 535-7711
Fax: 714 535-8616
Randall Vogel, *Vice Pres*
Thomas Bunosky, *Vice Pres*
Pat Scomlon, *District Mgr*
Claudia Di-Majo, *Office Admin*
Todd Waltz, *Project Engr*
EMP: 70
SALES (corp-wide): 458.6MM **Publicly Held**
WEB: www.gswater.com
SIC: **4941** 4911 Water supply; distribution, electric power
HQ: Golden State Water Company
630 E Foothill Blvd
San Dimas CA 91773
909 394-3600

(P-6351)
GOLDEN STATE WATER COMPANY (HQ)
630 E Foothill Blvd, San Dimas (91773-1212)
PHONE.................909 394-3600
Robert J Sprowls, *President*
Eva G Tang, *CFO*
Bill Gedney, *Vice Pres*
Denise Kruger, *Vice Pres*
Diane Rentfrow, *Vice Pres*
EMP: 170
SALES: 364.5MM
SALES (corp-wide): 458.6MM **Publicly Held**
WEB: www.gswater.com
SIC: **4941** 4911 Water supply; distribution, electric power
PA: American States Water Company
630 E Foothill Blvd
San Dimas CA 91773
909 394-3600

(P-6352)
GOLDEN STATE WATER COMPANY
Also Called: American State Water Company
630 E Foothill Blvd, San Dimas (91773-1212)
PHONE.................909 394-3600
Floydee Wibks, *CEO*
EMP: 100
SALES (corp-wide): 458.6MM **Publicly Held**
WEB: www.gswater.com
SIC: **4941** Water supply
HQ: Golden State Water Company
630 E Foothill Blvd
San Dimas CA 91773
909 394-3600

(P-6353)
GOLDEN STATE WATER COMPANY
Also Called: Sanitation
600 W Los Angeles Ave, Simi Valley (93065-1642)
PHONE.................805 583-6400
Jim Buell, *Manager*
EMP: 50
SALES (corp-wide): 458.6MM **Publicly Held**
WEB: www.gswater.com
SIC: **4941** Water supply

▲ = Import ▼ = Export
◆ = Import/Export

PRODUCTS & SERVICES SECTION

4941 - Water Sply County (P-6374)

HQ: Golden State Water Company
630 E Foothill Blvd
San Dimas CA 91773
909 394-3600

(P-6354)
HELIX WATER DISTRICT
1233 Vernon Way, El Cajon (92020-1838)
PHONE.................................619 466-0585
Mark Weston, *Branch Mgr*
Rita Mooney, *Admin Asst*
Paul Lafalce, *Supervisor*
EMP: 55
SALES (corp-wide): 74.6MM **Privately Held**
WEB: www.hwd.com
SIC: 4941 Water supply
PA: Helix Water District
7811 University Ave
La Mesa CA 91942
619 466-0585

(P-6355)
INLAND EMPIRE UTILITIES AGENCY
12811 6th St, Rancho Cucamonga (91739-9222)
PHONE.................................909 993-1755
Fax: 909 899-4245
Dan Foley, *Branch Mgr*
EMP: 71
SALES (corp-wide): 264.5MM **Privately Held**
SIC: 4941 Water supply
PA: Inland Empire Utilities Agency A Municipal Water District (Inc)
6075 Kimball Ave
Chino CA 91708
909 993-1600

(P-6356)
INLAND EMPIRE UTILITIES AGENCY (PA)
6075 Kimball Ave, Chino (91708-9174)
P.O. Box 9020, Chino Hills (91709-0902)
PHONE.................................909 993-1600
Terry Catlin, *President*
John Anderson, *President*
Jon Florio, *COO*
Christina Valencia, *CFO*
Ging Cookman, *Corp Secy*
EMP: 92
SQ FT: 60,000
SALES (est): 264.5MM **Privately Held**
SIC: 4941 Water supply

(P-6357)
INLAND EMPIRE UTILITIES AGENCY
9400 Cherry Ave, Fontana (92335-5359)
PHONE.................................909 357-0241
Fax: 909 357-3870
Cameron Langner, *Branch Mgr*
Toby Lee, *Info Tech Mgr*
EMP: 71
SALES (corp-wide): 264.5MM **Privately Held**
SIC: 4941 Water supply
PA: Inland Empire Utilities Agency A Municipal Water District (Inc)
6075 Kimball Ave
Chino CA 91708
909 993-1600

(P-6358)
IRVINE RANCH WATER DISTRICT (PA)
15600 Sand Canyon Ave, Irvine (92618-3102)
P.O. Box 57000 (92619-7000)
PHONE.................................949 453-5300
Fax: 949 453-0128
Paul Jones, *General Mgr*
Robert Jacobson, *Treasurer*
Marg Pulles, *Admin Sec*
Debby Cherney, *Finance Dir*
Leslie Bonkowski, *Director*
EMP: 110
SQ FT: 52,000
SALES: 124.4MM **Privately Held**
SIC: 4941 4952 Water supply; sewerage systems

(P-6359)
IRVINE RANCH WATER DISTRICT
3512 Michelson Dr, Irvine (92612-1757)
P.O. Box 14128 (92623-4128)
PHONE.................................949 453-5300
Carl Ballard, *Director*
EMP: 170
SALES (corp-wide): 124.4MM **Privately Held**
SIC: 4941 4952 Water supply; sewerage systems
PA: Irvine Ranch Water District Inc
15600 Sand Canyon Ave
Irvine CA 92618
949 453-5300

(P-6360)
KERN COUNTY WATER AGENCY
811 Nadine Ln, Bakersfield (93308)
P.O. Box 58 (93302-0058)
PHONE.................................661 634-1512
James M Beck, *District Mgr*
Steve Ruettgers, *Business Mgr*
Don Leonard, *Controller*
Renee Kinzel, *Human Res Mgr*
EMP: 63
SALES (corp-wide): 51MM **Privately Held**
SIC: 4941 Water supply
PA: Kern County Water Agency
3200 Rio Mirada Dr
Bakersfield CA 93308
661 634-1400

(P-6361)
LAKE HEMET MUNICIPAL WTR DST (PA)
26385 Fairview Ave, Hemet (92544-6607)
P.O. Box 5039 (92544-0039)
PHONE.................................951 927-1816
Fax: 951 766-7031
Tom Wagoner, *General Mgr*
EMP: 53
SQ FT: 4,900
SALES (est): 27MM **Privately Held**
WEB: www.lhmwd.org
SIC: 4941 4971 Water supply; water distribution or supply systems for irrigation

(P-6362)
LAS VIRGENES MUNICIPAL WTR DST
4232 Las Virgenes Rd Lbby, Calabasas (91302-3594)
PHONE.................................818 251-2100
Fax: 818 251-2109
Glen Peterson, *President*
Jay Lewitt, *Treasurer*
Lee Renger, *Vice Pres*
John R Mundy, *General Mgr*
Janice Jarmillo, *CIO*
EMP: 125
SQ FT: 10,000
SALES (est): 48.3MM **Privately Held**
WEB: www.lvmwd.com
SIC: 4941 Water supply

(P-6363)
LIBERTY UTILITIES PK WTR CORP (DH)
9750 Washburn Rd, Downey (90241-5625)
PHONE.................................562 923-0711
Fax: 562 861-5902
Greg Sorensen, *President*
Chris Alario, *CFO*
Jeanne Marie Bruno, *Senior VP*
Gary Lynch, *Vice Pres*
Mary Young, *Vice Pres*
EMP: 68
SQ FT: 15,000
SALES (est): 91.7MM
SALES (corp-wide): 772.8MM **Privately Held**
SIC: 4941 Water supply
HQ: Liberty Utilities (Canada) Corp
354 Davis Rd
Oakville ON L6J 2
905 465-4500

(P-6364)
LINDA YORBA WATER DISTRICT (PA)
1717 E Miraloma Ave, Placentia (92870-6785)
P.O. Box 309, Yorba Linda (92885-0309)
PHONE.................................714 701-3000
Fax: 714 777-8304
Ken Vecchiarelli, *General Mgr*
Marc Marcantonio, *General Mgr*
Michael Payne, *General Mgr*
Todd Howard, *Administration*
Rick Hipolito, *Comp Tech*
▲ **EMP:** 69
SQ FT: 7,900
SALES: 29.6MM **Privately Held**
WEB: www.ylwd.com
SIC: 4941 4952 Water supply; sewerage systems

(P-6365)
LOS ANGELES DEPT WTR & PWR
11801 Sheldon St, Sun Valley (91352-1508)
PHONE.................................213 367-1342
Kirk Bergland, *Branch Mgr*
David Kolacinski, *Opers Spvr*
EMP: 2877
SALES (corp-wide): 3.8B **Privately Held**
SIC: 4941 Water supply
PA: Los Angeles Department Of Water And Power
111 N Hope St Rm 1063
Los Angeles CA 90012
213 367-4043

(P-6366)
LOS ANGELES DEPT WTR & PWR
Also Called: Ladwp
201 S Webster St, Independence (93526-1769)
PHONE.................................760 878-2156
Steve Howe, *Supervisor*
EMP: 1439
SALES (corp-wide): 3.8B **Privately Held**
SIC: 4941 Water supply
PA: Los Angeles Department Of Water And Power
111 N Hope St Rm 1063
Los Angeles CA 90012
213 367-4043

(P-6367)
LOS ANGELES DEPT WTR & PWR (PA)
Also Called: Ladwp
111 N Hope St Rm 1063, Los Angeles (90012-2607)
P.O. Box 51111 (90051-5700)
PHONE.................................213 367-4043
Fax: 213 367-1455
Thomas Sayles, *President*
Phil Leiber, *CFO*
Philip Leiver, *CFO*
David H Wiggs Jr, *Officer*
Jeremy Wolfson, *Sr Invest Ofcr*
EMP: 170
SALES (est): 3.8B **Privately Held**
WEB: www.lacity.org
SIC: 4941 4911 Water supply; electric services

(P-6368)
LOS ANGELES DEPT WTR & PWR
1141 W 2nd St Bldg D, Los Angeles (90012-2007)
PHONE.................................213 367-5706
Carol Tharp, *Branch Mgr*
Rafik Alsawalny, *Project Mgr*
Vladimir Kapisarov, *Electrical Engi*
Mike Dario, *Foreman/Supr*
Lani Floresca, *Manager*
EMP: 2877
SALES (corp-wide): 3.8B **Privately Held**
SIC: 4941 Water supply
PA: Los Angeles Department Of Water And Power
111 N Hope St Rm 1063
Los Angeles CA 90012
213 367-4043

(P-6369)
MARIN MUNICIPAL WATER DISTRICT (PA)
220 Nellen Ave, Corte Madera (94925-1169)
PHONE.................................415 945-1455
Fax: 415 927-4953
Krishna Kumar, *General Mgr*
Suzanne Whelan, *Volunteer Dir*
Cynthia Koehler, *Vice Pres*
Libby Pischel, *Executive*
Grabow Larry, *Lab Dir*
EMP: 220
SQ FT: 32,000
SALES: 59.2MM **Privately Held**
SIC: 4941 4971 Water supply; irrigation systems

(P-6370)
MESA CNSLD WTR DST IMPRV CORP (PA)
Also Called: Mesa Water District
1965 Placentia Ave, Costa Mesa (92627-3420)
PHONE.................................949 631-1200
Lee Pearl, *Director*
James R Fisler, *President*
Shawn Dewane, *Vice Pres*
Coleen L Monteleone, *Admin Sec*
Brain Hunt, *Controller*
EMP: 67
SQ FT: 26,000
SALES (est): 37.9MM **Privately Held**
WEB: www.mesawater.org
SIC: 4941 Water supply

(P-6371)
METROPOLITAN WATER DISTRICT
700 N Alameda St Ste 1, Los Angeles (90012-3353)
PHONE.................................213 217-6000
Fax: 213 217-7770
Reynaldo Reed, *Principal*
John W Murray Jr, *Vice Chairman*
Tom Debacker, *Manager*
EMP: 69 **EST:** 2011
SALES (est): 19.5MM **Privately Held**
SIC: 4941 Water supply

(P-6372)
METROPOLITAN WATER DISTRICT
1820 Commercenter Cir, San Bernardino (92408-3430)
PHONE.................................909 890-3776
Ron Gastelum, *Principal*
EMP: 50
SALES (corp-wide): 1.5B **Privately Held**
WEB: www.mwdh2o.com
SIC: 4941 Water supply
PA: The Metropolitan Water District Of Southern California
700 N Alameda St
Los Angeles CA 90012
213 217-6000

(P-6373)
METROPOLITAN WATER DISTRICT
18250 La Sierra Ave, Riverside (92503-6531)
PHONE.................................951 688-5672
Fax: 951 689-3076
Al Ubrun, *Manager*
Allan Schlobohm, *Administration*
EMP: 50
SALES (corp-wide): 1.5B **Privately Held**
WEB: www.mwdh2o.com
SIC: 4941 1711 Water supply; septic system construction
PA: The Metropolitan Water District Of Southern California
700 N Alameda St
Los Angeles CA 90012
213 217-6000

(P-6374)
METROPOLITAN WATER DISTRICT
Also Called: Robert B Diemer Trtmnt Plant
3972 Valley View Ave, Yorba Linda (92886-1828)
PHONE.................................714 528-7231

4941 - Water Sply County (P-6375)

Fax: 714 577-5025
Trudi Loy, *Manager*
EMP: 80
SALES (corp-wide): 1.5B **Privately Held**
WEB: www.mwdh2o.com
SIC: 4941 Water supply
PA: The Metropolitan Water District Of
Southern California
700 N Alameda St
Los Angeles CA 90012
213 217-6000

(P-6375)
METROPOLITAN WATER DISTRICT
Gene Cp, Parker Dam (92267)
P.O. Box 38 (92267-0038)
PHONE..................760 663-4911
Fax: 760 663-3715
Greg Ensminger, *Branch Mgr*
EMP: 150
SALES (corp-wide): 1.5B **Privately Held**
WEB: www.mwdh2o.com
SIC: 4941 Water supply
PA: The Metropolitan Water District Of
Southern California
700 N Alameda St
Los Angeles CA 90012
213 217-6000

(P-6376)
METROPOLITAN WATER DISTRICT
Also Called: Joseph Jensen Filtration Plant
13100 Balboa Blvd, Granada Hills (91344-1199)
PHONE..................818 368-3731
Fax: 818 832-2193
Ezell Culver, *Manager*
EMP: 72
SALES (corp-wide): 1.5B **Privately Held**
WEB: www.mwdh2o.com
SIC: 4941 Water supply
PA: The Metropolitan Water District Of
Southern California
700 N Alameda St
Los Angeles CA 90012
213 217-6000

(P-6377)
METROPOLITAN WATER DISTRICT
Also Called: Metropolitan Water Lavern
700 Moreno Ave, La Verne (91750-3399)
P.O. Box 54153, Los Angeles (90054-0153)
PHONE..................909 593-7474
Fax: 909 392-5210
Wendell Williams, *Branch Mgr*
EMP: 370
SALES (corp-wide): 1.5B **Privately Held**
WEB: www.mwdh2o.com
SIC: 4941 Water supply
PA: The Metropolitan Water District Of
Southern California
700 N Alameda St
Los Angeles CA 90012
213 217-6000

(P-6378)
METROPOLITAN WATER DISTRICT
33752 Newport Rd, Winchester (92596-9475)
PHONE..................951 926-7095
Marty Hundley, *Manager*
EMP: 66
SALES (corp-wide): 1.5B **Privately Held**
WEB: www.mwdh2o.com
SIC: 4941 Water supply
PA: The Metropolitan Water District Of
Southern California
700 N Alameda St
Los Angeles CA 90012
213 217-6000

(P-6379)
METROPOLITAN WATER DISTRICT
550 E Alessandro Blvd, Riverside (92508-2400)
PHONE..................951 780-1511
Richard Green, *Branch Mgr*
Debbie Matteson, *Administration*
Kevin Graff, *Supervisor*
EMP: 75

SALES (corp-wide): 1.5B **Privately Held**
WEB: www.mwdh2o.com
SIC: 4941 Water supply
PA: The Metropolitan Water District Of
Southern California
700 N Alameda St
Los Angeles CA 90012
213 217-6000

(P-6380)
METROPOLITAN WATER DISTRICT
Also Called: Robert Sknner Filtration Plant
33740 Borel Rd, Winchester (92596-9625)
PHONE..................951 926-1501
Fax: 951 926-3531
EMP: 80
SALES (corp-wide): 1.5B **Privately Held**
SIC: 4941
PA: The Metropolitan Water District Of
Southern California
700 N Alameda St
Los Angeles CA 90012
213 217-6000

(P-6381)
MOULTON NIGUEL WATER (PA)
27500 La Paz Rd, Laguna Niguel (92677-3402)
P.O. Box 30203 (92607-0203)
PHONE..................949 831-2500
Fax: 949 831-5651
Richard Fiore, *President*
David Cain, *Treasurer*
John V Foley, *General Mgr*
Joone Lopez, *General Mgr*
Paige Gulck, *Executive Asst*
EMP: 76 **EST:** 1960
SQ FT: 9,000
SALES: 5MM **Privately Held**
WEB: www.mnwd.com
SIC: 4941 4959 Water supply; sanitary services

(P-6382)
NORTH MARIN WATER DISTRICT (PA)
Also Called: NMWD
999 Rush Creek Pl, Novato (94945-7716)
P.O. Box 146 (94948-0146)
PHONE..................415 897-4133
Fax: 415 892-8043
Chris Degabriele, *Principal*
Pablo Ramudo, *Research*
Arthur Cantiller, *Technology*
Drew McIntyre, *Sales Mgr*
Robert Clark, *Facilities Mgr*
EMP: 50
SQ FT: 7,200
SALES: 18MM **Privately Held**
WEB: www.nmwd.com
SIC: 4941 Water supply

(P-6383)
OAKDALE IRRGTION DST FING CORP
1205 E F St, Oakdale (95361-4112)
PHONE..................209 847-0341
Fax: 209 847-3468
Alfred Bairos, *President*
Kathy Cook, *CFO*
Steve Knell, *Exec Dir*
Lori F Presley, *Admin Asst*
Tom Laidlaw, *Manager*
▲ **EMP:** 69 **EST:** 1909
SQ FT: 5,000
SALES: 8.5MM **Privately Held**
WEB: www.oakdaleirrigation.com
SIC: 4941 Water supply

(P-6384)
OLIVENHAIN MUNICIPAL WATER DST
1966 Olivenhain Rd, Encinitas (92024-5676)
PHONE..................760 753-6466
Fax: 760 753-1578
Edmund Sprague, *President*
Joni Lockhart, *Senior Partner*
Mark A Muir, *Treasurer*
Robert F Topolovac, *Vice Pres*
Robert Topolovac, *Vice Pres*
EMP: 79
SQ FT: 11,000

SALES: 50.8MM **Privately Held**
SIC: 4941 4971 Water supply; impounding reservoir, irrigation

(P-6385)
OTAY WATER DISTRICT
2554 Swetwater Sprng Blvd, Spring Valley (91978-2096)
PHONE..................619 670-2222
Gary Croucher, *President*
Jose Lopez, *President*
Joseph R Beachem, *CFO*
Adolfo Segura, *CFO*
Armando Buelna, *Executive*
EMP: 170 **EST:** 1956
SQ FT: 6,000
SALES: 83.8MM **Privately Held**
WEB: www.otaywater.gov
SIC: 4941 1623 Water supply; water, sewer & utility lines

(P-6386)
PADRE DAM MUNICIPAL WATER DST (PA)
9300 Fanita Pkwy, Santee (92071-7906)
P.O. Box 719003 (92072-9003)
PHONE..................619 258-4617
Fax: 619 449-9469
Allen Carlisle, *CEO*
William Pommering, *President*
Doug Wilson, *Treasurer*
August Caires, *Vice Pres*
James Maletic, *Vice Pres*
EMP: 63
SQ FT: 10,000
SALES (est): 86.9MM **Privately Held**
WEB: www.padredam.org
SIC: 4941 4952 7033 Water supply; sewerage systems; campgrounds

(P-6387)
PALMDALE WATER DISTRICT
2029 E Avenue Q, Palmdale (93550-4050)
PHONE..................661 947-4111
Randy D Hill, *CEO*
Leo Thibault, *Treasurer*
Steve Cordova, *Vice Pres*
Andy Rutledge, *Admin Sec*
Dan Henry, *Safety Mgr*
EMP: 93
SALES: 23.3MM **Privately Held**
SIC: 4941 Water supply

(P-6388)
RAINBOW MUNICIPAL WATER DST
3707 Old Highway 395, Fallbrook (92028-9372)
PHONE..................760 728-1178
Fax: 760 728-2575
Dave Seymour, *General Mgr*
Joyce E Tomlinson, *Admin Mgr*
Al Write, *Safety Mgr*
Charles Sneed, *Opers Staff*
Ramon Zuniga, *Superintendent*
EMP: 50
SALES: 22MM **Privately Held**
SIC: 4941 Water supply

(P-6389)
SACRAMENTO COUNTY WATER AGENCY
Also Called: Scwa
827 7th St Ste 301, Sacramento (95814-2406)
PHONE..................916 874-6851
Susan Purdin, *Principal*
William Konigsmark, *Principal*
Keith Devore, *Branch Mgr*
EMP: 99
SALES (est): 6.5MM **Privately Held**
SIC: 4941 Water supply

(P-6390)
SACRAMENTO SUBURBAN WATER DST
3701 Marconi Ave Ste 100, Sacramento (95821-5346)
PHONE..................916 972-7171
Robert Roscoe, *President*
Tom Dickinson, *Officer*
Roy Kimura, *Principal*
Annette Oleary, *Principal*
Jerry Ness, *Personnel*
EMP: 60

SQ FT: 13,500
SALES: 26MM **Privately Held**
SIC: 4941 Water supply

(P-6391)
SACRAMENTO SUBURBAN WATER DST
3701 Marconi Ave Ste 100, Sacramento (95821-5346)
PHONE..................916 972-7171
Robert Rosco, *General Mgr*
Frederick Gayle, *Bd of Directors*
Christine Bosley, *Executive Asst*
Jan Gentry, *Executive Asst*
Matthew Winans, *CIO*
EMP: 52
SALES: 41.8MM **Privately Held**
WEB: www.sswd.org
SIC: 4941 Water supply

(P-6392)
SAN DIEGO COUNTY WATER AUTH (PA)
4677 Overland Ave, San Diego (92123-1233)
PHONE..................858 522-6600
Fax: 858 522-6568
Maureen Stapleton, *General Mgr*
Tina Gonzalez, *COO*
Eric Sandler, *CFO*
Thomas V Wornham, *Chairman*
Gary Croucher, *Bd of Directors*
▲ **EMP:** 96
SQ FT: 26,000
SALES: 588.7MM **Privately Held**
SIC: 4941 Water supply

(P-6393)
SAN DIEGO COUNTY WATER AUTH
610 W 5th Ave, Escondido (92025-4093)
PHONE..................760 480-1991
Fax: 760 480-9867
Al R Gaza, *Manager*
Emmnauel O Nwagb, *Manager*
Al Garza, *Supervisor*
EMP: 70
SALES (corp-wide): 588.7MM **Privately Held**
SIC: 4941 Water supply
PA: San Diego County Water Authority
4677 Overland Ave
San Diego CA 92123
858 522-6600

(P-6394)
SAN GABRIEL VALLEY WATER ASSN
725 N Azusa Ave, Azusa (91702-2528)
PHONE..................626 815-1305
Carol Williams, *Principal*
EMP: 100
SALES: 322.6K **Privately Held**
SIC: 4941 Water supply

(P-6395)
SAN GABRIEL VALLEY WATER CO (PA)
Also Called: Fontana Water Company
11142 Garvey Ave, El Monte (91733-2498)
P.O. Box 6010 (91734-2010)
PHONE..................626 448-6183
Fax: 626 448-5530
R H Nicholson Jr, *Ch of Bd*
Michael L Whitehead, *President*
David Batt, *Treasurer*
Frank A Lo Guidice, *Vice Pres*
June Pallie, *Admin Sec*
EMP: 125 **EST:** 1936
SQ FT: 30,000
SALES (est): 136MM **Privately Held**
WEB: www.fontanawater.com
SIC: 4941 Water supply

(P-6396)
SAN GABRIEL VALLEY WATER CO
8440 Nuevo Ave, Fontana (92335-3824)
P.O. Box 987 (92334-0987)
PHONE..................909 822-2201
Mike McGraw, *Manager*
EMP: 76
SQ FT: 2,727

PRODUCTS & SERVICES SECTION

4952 - Sewerage Systems County (P-6417)

SALES (corp-wide): 136MM **Privately Held**
WEB: www.fontanawater.com
SIC: 4941 Water supply
PA: San Gabriel Valley Water Co.
11142 Garvey Ave
El Monte CA 91733
626 448-6183

(P-6397)
SAN JOSE WATER COMPANY (HQ)
Also Called: S J W
110 W Taylor St, San Jose (95110-2131)
PHONE 408 288-5314
W Richard Roth, *CEO*
Charles Toeniskoetter, *Ch of Bd*
Angela Yip, *CFO*
Andrew F Walters, *Officer*
George J Belhumeur, *Senior VP*
EMP: 140
SQ FT: 5,000
SALES (est): 285.6MM
SALES (corp-wide): 305MM **Publicly Held**
SIC: 4941 Water supply
PA: Sjw Corp.
110 W Taylor St
San Jose CA 95110
408 279-7800

(P-6398)
SAN JOSE WATER COMPANY
1221 S Bascom Ave, San Jose (95128-3514)
PHONE 408 298-0364
Paul Schreiber, *Manager*
Rich Hernandez, *Opers Spvr*
Mark Taormina, *Opers Spvr*
Denia Leal, *Director*
EMP: 180
SALES (corp-wide): 305MM **Publicly Held**
SIC: 4941 Water supply
HQ: San Jose Water Company
110 W Taylor St
San Jose CA 95110
408 288-5314

(P-6399)
SANTA CLARA VALLEY WATER (PA)
Also Called: Santa Clara Valley Water Dst
5750 Almaden Expy, San Jose (95118-3614)
P.O. Box 20670 (95160-0670)
PHONE 408 265-2600
Fax: 408 266-0271
Beau Goldie, *CEO*
Roderick Jefferson, *Bd of Directors*
Michael B Baratz, *Officer*
Debra Osikominu, *Vice Pres*
Meenakshi Ganjoo, *Executive*
▲ **EMP:** 250 **EST:** 1951
SQ FT: 40,780
SALES: 130.5MM **Privately Held**
WEB: www.valleywater.org
SIC: 4941 Water supply

(P-6400)
SANTA CLARA VALLEY WATER
400 More Ave, Los Gatos (95032-1111)
PHONE 408 395-8121
Greg Gibson, *Branch Mgr*
John Boardman, *Controller*
Stan Williams, *Sales Staff*
Jeff Reid, *Associate*
EMP: 70
SALES (corp-wide): 130.5MM **Privately Held**
WEB: www.valleywater.org
SIC: 4941 Water supply
PA: Santa Clara Valley Water District Public Facilities Financing Corporation
5750 Almaden Expy
San Jose CA 95118
408 265-2600

(P-6401)
SANTA MARGARITA WATER DISTRICT (PA)
26111 Antonio Pkwy, Rcho STA Marg (92688-5596)
P.O. Box 7005, Mission Viejo (92690-7005)
PHONE 949 459-6400
Fax: 949 459-6460

Daniel R Ferons, *Manager*
Christine Griffith, *Finance Dir*
Glynis Litvak, *Financial Analy*
Carol Megara, *Finance*
James Leach, *Director*
EMP: 70 **EST:** 1964
SQ FT: 5,600
SALES: 60MM **Privately Held**
WEB: www.smwd.com
SIC: 4941 4952 Water supply; sewerage systems

(P-6402)
SANTA MARGARITA WATER DISTRICT
26101 Antonio Pkwy, Rcho STA Marg (92688-5505)
P.O. Box 7005, Mission Viejo (92690-7005)
PHONE 949 459-6400
Daniel Ferns, *Manager*
Brian Bowers, *MIS Dir*
Ken Wheel, *Finance*
Kristi Varney, *Purch Mgr*
Jorge Bergera, *Facilities Mgr*
EMP: 135
SALES (corp-wide): 60MM **Privately Held**
WEB: www.smwd.com
SIC: 4941 4952 Water supply; sewerage systems
PA: Santa Margarita Water District
26111 Antonio Pkwy
Rcho Sta Marg CA 92688
949 459-6400

(P-6403)
SJW CORP (PA)
110 W Taylor St, San Jose (95110-2131)
PHONE 408 279-7800
W Richard Roth, *Ch of Bd*
D R Drysdale, *President*
Suzy Papazian, *COO*
James P Lynch, *CFO*
Andrew F Walters, *Officer*
EMP: 357
SALES: 305MM **Publicly Held**
WEB: www.sjwater.com
SIC: 4941 6531 Water supply; real estate agent, commercial

(P-6404)
SONOMA COUNTY WATER AGENCY
404 Aviation Blvd Ste 0, Santa Rosa (95403-9019)
P.O. Box 11628 (95406-1628)
PHONE 707 526-5370
Fax: 707 524-3791
Grant Davis, *General Mgr*
Ann Dubay, *Executive*
George Lincoln, *Project Mgr*
James Jasperse, *Enginr/R&D Mgr*
Don Seymour, *Engineer*
EMP: 200 **EST:** 1950
SQ FT: 57,000
SALES: 26.2MM **Privately Held**
SIC: 4941 Water supply

(P-6405)
SWEETWATER AUTHORITY (PA)
505 Garrett Ave, Chula Vista (91910-5584)
P.O. Box 2328 (91912-2328)
PHONE 619 422-8395
Fax: 619 425-7469
Mark Rogers, *Exec Dir*
Margaret C Welsh, *President*
Andrew Reitzel, *Treasurer*
Rich Stevenson, *Treasurer*
Pete Baranov, *Vice Pres*
EMP: 112
SQ FT: 11,000
SALES (est): 48.8K **Privately Held**
SIC: 4941 Water supply

(P-6406)
TUOLUMNE UTILITIES DISTRICT
Also Called: T U D
18885 Nugget Blvd, Sonora (95370-9284)
PHONE 209 532-5536
Fax: 209 536-2489
Pet Kampa, *General Mgr*
John Maciel, *Bd of Directors*
Casey Prunchak, *Bd of Directors*
Kent Johnson, *Vice Pres*
Thomas Scesa, *General Mgr*
EMP: 80

SQ FT: 6,000
SALES (est): 22.2MM **Privately Held**
WEB: www.tuolumneutilities.com
SIC: 4941 4952 Water supply; sewerage systems

(P-6407)
VALLEY CENTER MUNICIPAL
29300 Valley Center Rd, Valley Center (92082-6207)
P.O. Box 67 (92082-0067)
PHONE 760 735-4500
Fax: 760 749-6478
Gary Broomell, *President*
Jere Jarrell, *CFO*
Bill Jeffrey, *CFO*
Robert A Polito, *Vice Pres*
Gary Arant, *General Mgr*
EMP: 69 **EST:** 1954
SQ FT: 40,000
SALES (est): 24.2MM **Privately Held**
SIC: 4941 Water supply

(P-6408)
WALNUT VALLEY WATER DISTRICT
271 Brea Canyon Rd, Walnut (91789-3002)
P.O. Box 508 (91788-0508)
PHONE 909 595-7554
Fax: 909 594-9532
Theodore Ebenkamp, *President*
Shawna Whallon, *Treasurer*
Scarlet Kwong, *Vice Pres*
Edwin Hilder, *Principal*
Michael Holmes, *General Mgr*
EMP: 55
SQ FT: 7,900
SALES (est): 23.5MM **Privately Held**
WEB: www.wvwd.com
SIC: 4941 Water supply

(P-6409)
YUCAIPA VALLEY WATER DISTRICT (PA)
12770 2nd St, Yucaipa (92399-5670)
P.O. Box 730 (92399-0730)
PHONE 909 797-5117
Fax: 909 797-6381
Bruce Granlund, *President*
Joseph Zoba, *General Mgr*
Vicky Elisalda, *Controller*
Jack Nelson, *Manager*
EMP: 56
SQ FT: 2,500
SALES: 21.4MM **Privately Held**
SIC: 4941 Water supply

4952 Sewerage Systems

(P-6410)
CENTRAL CONTRA COSTA SANIT
5019 Imhoff Pl, Martinez (94553-4316)
PHONE 925 228-9500
Fax: 925 676-7211
James Kelly, *General Mgr*
Shari Deutsch, *Risk Mgmt Dir*
Roger Bailey, *General Mgr*
Suzette Crayton, *Executive Asst*
Cindy Granzella, *Admin Asst*
EMP: 99
SALES (est): 36.5MM **Privately Held**
SIC: 4952 Sewerage systems

(P-6411)
ENCINA WASTEWATER AUTHORITY
Also Called: Encina Water Pollution Control
6200 Avenida Encinas, Carlsbad (92011-1009)
PHONE 760 438-3941
Fax: 760 431-7493
Kevinmhardy, *Principal*
Donald Little, *Vice Pres*
Kevin Hardy, *General Mgr*
Paula Clowar, *Executive Asst*
Taylor Mowr, *Admin Asst*
EMP: 52
SQ FT: 30,000
SALES (est): 20.7MM **Privately Held**
WEB: www.encinajpa.com
SIC: 4952 Sewerage systems

(P-6412)
NAPA SANITATION DISTRICT
1515 Soscol Ferry Rd, NAPA (94558-6247)
P.O. Box 2480 (94558-0522)
PHONE 707 254-9231
Fax: 707 258-6048
Tim Healy, *General Mgr*
Michael Abramson, *President*
John Cuevas, *CFO*
Mark Koekenoer, *Lab Dir*
Jeffery Tucker, *General Mgr*
EMP: 50 **EST:** 1945
SQ FT: 3,600
SALES: 21.5MM **Privately Held**
WEB: www.napasanitationdistrict.com
SIC: 4952 Sewerage systems

(P-6413)
OCCIDENTAL CNTY SANITATION DST
404 Aviation Blvd, Santa Rosa (95403-1069)
PHONE 707 547-1900
Grant Davis, *General Mgr*
Lynne Rosselli, *Accounts Mgr*
EMP: 99
SALES: 519K **Privately Held**
SIC: 4952 Sewerage systems

(P-6414)
ORANGE COUNTY SANITATION
22212 Brookhurst St, Huntington Beach (92646-8406)
PHONE 714 962-2411
Blake Anderson, *Manager*
Mark Castillo, *Technology*
Betty Voss, *Purchasing*
EMP: 200
SALES (corp-wide): 304.5MM **Privately Held**
WEB: www.ocsd.com
SIC: 4952 Sewerage systems
PA: Orange County Sanitation District Financing Corporation
10844 Ellis Ave
Fountain Valley CA 92708
714 962-2411

(P-6415)
SACRAMENTO REG CO SANIT DIST
Sacramento Regional Waste
8521 Laguna Station Rd, Elk Grove (95758-9550)
PHONE 916 875-9000
Ruben Robles, *Manager*
Sharon Sargeant, *Corp Comm Staff*
Janet Pellegrini, *Manager*
EMP: 500
SALES (corp-wide): 316.5MM **Privately Held**
SIC: 4952 Sewerage systems
PA: Sacramento Regional County Sanitation District
10060 Goethe Rd
Sacramento CA 95827
916 876-6000

(P-6416)
SILICON VALLEY CLEAN WATER
Also Called: SBSA
1400 Radio Rd, Redwood City (94065-1220)
PHONE 650 591-7121
Fax: 650 591-7122
Ronald W Shepherd, *Principal*
John Hernandez, *Maintence Staff*
Will Swalve, *Director*
Daniel T Child, *Manager*
Don Cottier, *Manager*
EMP: 79
SQ FT: 180,000
SALES: 32.8MM **Privately Held**
WEB: www.sbsa.org
SIC: 4952 Sewerage systems

(P-6417)
SONOMA VLY CNTY SANITATION DST
404 Aviation Blvd, Santa Rosa (95403-1069)
PHONE 707 547-1900
Grant Davis, *General Mgr*
Lynne Rosselli, *Accounting Mgr*
David Rabbitt, *Supervisor*

4952 - Sewerage Systems County (P-6418)

EMP: 200
SALES: 14.1MM Privately Held
SIC: 4952 Sewerage systems

(P-6418)
SOUTH TAHOE PUBLIC UTILITY DST
1275 Meadow Crest Dr, South Lake Tahoe (96150-7401)
PHONE.....................530 544-6474
Fax: 530 541-0614
Richard Solbrig, *General Mgr*
Paul Hughes, *CFO*
Paul Sciuto, *Principal*
Lynn Nolan, *General Mgr*
Susan Rafmussen, *Admin Asst*
EMP: 113
SALES: 24MM Privately Held
WEB: www.stpud.dst.ca.us
SIC: 4952 4941 Sewerage systems; water supply

(P-6419)
TAHOE-TRUCKEE SANITATION AGCY
Also Called: TTSA
13720 Butterfield Dr, Truckee (96161-3316)
PHONE.....................530 587-2525
Fax: 530 587-5840
Marcia Beals, *General Mgr*
Michael Peak, *Vice Pres*
Jay Parker, *General Mgr*
Robert Gray, *Info Tech Mgr*
Kevin Woods, *Technology*
▲ **EMP:** 59 **EST:** 1972
SQ FT: 500,083
SALES: 12.3MM Privately Held
WEB: www.ttsa.net
SIC: 4952 Sewerage systems

(P-6420)
UNION SANITARY DISTRICT
Also Called: Usd
5072 Benson Rd, Union City (94587-2508)
P.O. Box 5050 (94587-8528)
PHONE.....................510 477-7500
Fax: 510 477-7501
Paul Eldredge, *General Mgr*
Maria Scott, *Sr Corp Ofcr*
Audrey Villanueva, *Office Admin*
Todd Jacob, *Admin Asst*
Paulette Roberson, *Admin Asst*
▲ **EMP:** 130
SALES: 49.9MM Privately Held
WEB: www.unionsanitary.com
SIC: 4952 Sewerage systems

4953 Refuse Systems

(P-6421)
AECOM TECHNICAL SERVICES INC (HQ)
300 S Grand Ave Ste 1100, Los Angeles (90071-3173)
PHONE.....................213 593-8000
Fax: 213 593-8604
Michael Burke, *CEO*
William Stead, *Senior VP*
Michael J Durkin, *Vice Pres*
James D Weinbauer, *Vice Pres*
Cathy Hickman, *Administration*
▲ **EMP:** 100 **EST:** 1970
SQ FT: 43,000
SALES (est): 3.4B
SALES (corp-wide): 17.9B Publicly Held
WEB: www.earthtech.com
SIC: 4953 8748 8742 8711 Refuse systems; environmental consultant; industry specialist consultants; engineering services
PA: Aecom
1999 Avenue Of The Stars # 2600
Los Angeles CA 90067
213 593-8000

(P-6422)
AER ELECTRONICS INC (PA)
Also Called: Aerelectronics
42744 Boscell Rd, Fremont (94538-5132)
PHONE.....................510 300-0500
Andre Weiglein, *President*
William Schoening, *CFO*
John Dickenson, *Vice Pres*
Janet Rianda, *Vice Pres*
James Quintal, *Admin Sec*
▲ **EMP:** 55
SQ FT: 75,000
SALES (est): 52.7MM Privately Held
WEB: www.aerworldwide.com
SIC: 4953 5093 Recycling, waste materials; scrap & waste materials

(P-6423)
ALAMEDA COUNTY INDUSTRIES INC
610 Aladdin Ave, San Leandro (94577-4302)
PHONE.....................510 357-7282
Louis Pellegrini, *Exec VP*
Robert Molinaro, *CEO*
Kent Kenney, *CFO*
Mary Vigil, *Human Resources*
Teresa Montgomery, *Pub Rel Mgr*
EMP: 50
SQ FT: 39,648
SALES (est): 9.3MM Privately Held
WEB: www.alamedacountyindustries.com
SIC: 4953 Rubbish collection & disposal

(P-6424)
ALEMEDA COUNTY INDUSTRIES LLC
610 Aladdin Ave, San Leandro (94577-4302)
PHONE.....................510 357-7282
Robert Molinaro,
EMP: 70 **EST:** 1999
SQ FT: 5,400
SALES (est): 5.7MM Privately Held
SIC: 4953 Refuse systems

(P-6425)
APPLIANCE RECYCL CTRS OF AMER
Also Called: Arca Los Angeles
1920 S Acacia Ave, Compton (90220-4945)
PHONE.....................310 223-2800
Fax: 310 763-1722
Edward Cameron, *President*
EMP: 64
SQ FT: 40,000
SALES (est): 8.3MM
SALES (corp-wide): 111.8MM Publicly Held
WEB: www.arcainc.com
SIC: 4953 Recycling, waste materials
PA: Appliance Recycling Centers Of America, Inc.
175 Jackson Ave N Ste 102
Hopkins MN 55343
952 930-9000

(P-6426)
ARAKELIAN ENTERPRISES INC
11121 Pendleton St, Sun Valley (91352-1513)
PHONE.....................818 768-0689
Godjamanian Mego, *Branch Mgr*
EMP: 184
SQ FT: 4,904
SALES (corp-wide): 150MM Privately Held
SIC: 4953 Rubbish collection & disposal
PA: Arakelian Enterprises, Inc.
14048 Valley Blvd
City Of Industry CA 91746
626 336-3636

(P-6427)
ARAKELIAN ENTERPRISES INC
Also Called: Athens Services
15045 Salt Lake Ave, City of Industry (91746-3315)
PHONE.....................626 336-3636
Ron Arakelian Jr, *Owner*
Steven Estrada, *Marketing Staff*
EMP: 92
SALES (corp-wide): 150MM Privately Held
SIC: 4953 Rubbish collection & disposal; street refuse systems
PA: Arakelian Enterprises, Inc.
14048 Valley Blvd
City Of Industry CA 91746
626 336-3636

(P-6428)
ARAKELIAN ENTERPRISES INC
687 Iowa Ave, Riverside (92507-1610)
PHONE.....................951 342-3300
Fax: 909 342-0073
Sal Orozco, *Manager*
Meher Mazmanian, *COO*
Ernie Langley, *Human Res Dir*
Brenda Reuter, *Mktg Dir*
Mary Caraballo, *Manager*
EMP: 323
SALES (corp-wide): 150MM Privately Held
SIC: 4953 Recycling, waste materials; hazardous waste collection & disposal
PA: Arakelian Enterprises, Inc.
14048 Valley Blvd
City Of Industry CA 91746
626 336-3636

(P-6429)
ARAKELIAN ENTERPRISES INC (PA)
Also Called: Athens Services
14048 Valley Blvd, City of Industry (91746-2801)
P.O. Box 60009 (91716-0009)
PHONE.....................626 336-3636
Ron Arakelian Jr, *CEO*
Michael Arakelian, *CEO*
Gary Clifford, *COO*
Kevin Hanifin, *CFO*
Dennis Chiappetta, *Exec VP*
EMP: 170
SQ FT: 10,000
SALES: 150MM Privately Held
WEB: www.athensservices.com
SIC: 4953 Rubbish collection & disposal; street refuse systems

(P-6430)
ARROW DISPOSAL SERVICES INC
14332 Valley Blvd, La Puente (91746-2931)
P.O. Box 2917 (91746-0917)
PHONE.....................626 336-2255
Fax: 626 336-2155
Kirk Tahmizian, *President*
EMP: 50
SQ FT: 40,000
SALES: 10MM Privately Held
SIC: 4953 Refuse collection & disposal services

(P-6431)
ASCON RECYCLE COMPANY
6500 E Avenue T, Littlerock (93543-1722)
PHONE.....................661 533-0154
Chris Giampietro, *Manager*
EMP: 50
SALES (est): 927.5K Privately Held
SIC: 4953 Recycling, waste materials

(P-6432)
ASCON RECYCLING CO
17671 Bear Valley Rd, Hesperia (92345-4902)
PHONE.....................760 948-1538
John Hove, *President*
EMP: 250 **EST:** 2001
SALES (est): 7.3MM Privately Held
SIC: 4953 Refuse systems

(P-6433)
ATHENS DISPOSAL COMPANY INC (PA)
14048 Valley Blvd, La Puente (91746-2801)
P.O. Box 60009, City of Industry (91716-0009)
PHONE.....................626 336-3636
Ron Arakelian Sr, *President*
Ron Arakelian Jr, *Vice Pres*
Greg Huntingthon, *Vice Pres*
Pete Branda, *General Mgr*
Mary Caraballo, *Office Mgr*
EMP: 350
SALES (est): 290.4MM Privately Held
SIC: 4953 Rubbish collection & disposal

(P-6434)
ATLAS DISPOSAL INDUSTRIES LLC
3000 Power Inn Rd, Sacramento (95826-3801)
PHONE.....................916 455-2800
Fax: 916 736-2931
Dave Sikich, *CEO*
Nick Sikich, *COO*
Bob Angell, *Vice Pres*
Steven Bruce, *Vice Pres*
Art Flores, *General Mgr*
EMP: 70
SALES (est): 17MM Privately Held
WEB: www.atlasdisposal.com
SIC: 4953 Refuse collection & disposal services

(P-6435)
AUBURN PLACER DISPOSAL SERVICE
Also Called: Auburn-Placer Recycling Center
12305 Shale Ridge Ln, Auburn (95602-8879)
P.O. Box 6566 (95604-6566)
PHONE.....................530 885-3735
Fax: 530 885-1922
Michael Sangiacomo, *President*
Mark Lomele, *Vice Pres*
Frank Tamayo, *Executive*
EMP: 80
SQ FT: 2,200
SALES (est): 7.9MM
SALES (corp-wide): 1.6B Privately Held
WEB: www.auburnplacer.com
SIC: 4953 Refuse systems
PA: Recology Inc.
50 California St Fl 24
San Francisco CA 94111
415 875-1000

(P-6436)
BAY COUNTIES WASTE SVCS INC
Also Called: Specialty Solid Waste & Recycl
3355 Thomas Rd, Santa Clara (95054-2060)
PHONE.....................408 565-9900
Fax: 408 565-9909
Robert J Molinaro, *CEO*
William Dobert, *CFO*
Douglas Button, *Treasurer*
Jim Telfer, *Exec Dir*
Jerry Nabhan, *Admin Sec*
▲ **EMP:** 80 **EST:** 1930
SQ FT: 2,000
SALES (est): 19.9MM Privately Held
WEB: www.sswr.com
SIC: 4953 Refuse collection & disposal services

(P-6437)
BENZ SANITATION INC (PA)
Also Called: Benz - One Complete Operation
1401 Goodrick Dr, Tehachapi (93561-1532)
P.O. Box 1750 (93581-1750)
PHONE.....................661 822-5273
Fax: 661 822-1947
Paul Benz, *CEO*
Joan Benz, *Corp Secy*
Louis Visco, *Vice Pres*
Harry Morse, *General Mgr*
EMP: 75
SQ FT: 4,500
SALES (est): 69.1MM Privately Held
SIC: 4953 4212 Refuse collection & disposal services; petroleum haulage, local

(P-6438)
BEST WAY DISPOSAL CO INC
Also Called: Advance Disposal Company
17105 Mesa St, Hesperia (92345-5155)
P.O. Box 400997 (92340-0997)
PHONE.....................760 244-9773
Fax: 760 244-1688
Robert Bath, *Ch of Bd*
Sheila Bath, *President*
EMP: 58
SALES (est): 14.1MM Privately Held
WEB: www.advancedisposal.com
SIC: 4953 Rubbish collection & disposal

▲ = Import ▼ = Export
◆ = Import/Export

PRODUCTS & SERVICES SECTION
4953 - Refuse Systems County (P-6459)

(P-6439)
BFI WASTE SERVICES LLC
5501 N Golden State Blvd, Fresno (93722-5021)
PHONE..................559 275-1551
Keith Hester, *General Mgr*
EMP: 70
SALES (corp-wide): 9.1B **Publicly Held**
WEB: www.sunsetwaste.com
SIC: 4953 Refuse systems
HQ: Bfi Waste Services, Llc
18500 N Allied Way # 100
Phoenix AZ 85054
480 627-2700

(P-6440)
BFI WASTE SYSTEMS N AMER INC
Also Called: Site 910
800 Cacique St, Santa Barbara (93103-3622)
P.O. Box 4010 (93140-4010)
PHONE..................805 965-5248
Fax: 805 965-4993
Darryl Reno, *General Mgr*
EMP: 82
SALES (corp-wide): 9.1B **Publicly Held**
WEB: www.mjes.com
SIC: 4953 Garbage: collecting, destroying & processing; street refuse systems
HQ: Bfi Waste Systems Of North America, Inc.
2394 E Camelback Rd
Phoenix AZ 85016
480 627-2700

(P-6441)
BFI WASTE SYSTEMS N AMER INC
Also Called: Republic Services
271 Rianda St, Salinas (93901-3725)
PHONE..................831 775-3850
Doug Kenyon, *Manager*
EMP: 54
SALES (corp-wide): 9.1B **Publicly Held**
WEB: www.mjes.com
SIC: 4953 Refuse collection & disposal services
HQ: Bfi Waste Systems Of North America, Inc.
2394 E Camelback Rd
Phoenix AZ 85016
480 627-2700

(P-6442)
BFI WASTE SYSTEMS N AMER INC
Also Called: Site 916
42600 Boyce Rd, Fremont (94538-3131)
P.O. Box 5013 (94537-5013)
PHONE..................510 657-1350
Fax: 510 657-1263
Fred Penning, *Manager*
Pam Enriquez, *General Mgr*
EMP: 95
SALES (corp-wide): 9.1B **Publicly Held**
WEB: www.mjes.com
SIC: 4953 4212 Refuse systems; local trucking, without storage
HQ: Bfi Waste Systems Of North America, Inc.
2394 E Camelback Rd
Phoenix AZ 85016
480 627-2700

(P-6443)
BISHOP WASTE DISPOSAL INC
100 Snland Reservation Rd, Bishop (93541)
PHONE..................760 872-6561
Fax: 760 872-4636
George Kelley, *President*
Gina Ellis, *Office Mgr*
Jeff Stevens, *Info Tech Mgr*
Tony Pagel, *CPA*
Pat Fenton, *Manager*
EMP: 50
SQ FT: 7,300
SALES (est): 3.4MM **Privately Held**
SIC: 4953 4952 Garbage: collecting, destroying & processing; sewerage systems

(P-6444)
BKK CORPORATION (PA)
2210 S Azusa Ave, West Covina (91792-1510)
PHONE..................626 965-0911
Fax: 626 965-9569
EMP: 57
SALES (est): 22.2MM **Privately Held**
SIC: 4953

(P-6445)
BROWNING-FERRIS INDS CAL INC
Also Called: Site R46
333 Shoreway Rd, San Carlos (94070-2708)
PHONE..................650 637-1411
Fax: 650 637-9496
Chris Valbusa, *Manager*
EMP: 69
SALES (corp-wide): 9.1B **Publicly Held**
WEB: www.sunshinecanyonlandfill.com
SIC: 4953 Recycling, waste materials
HQ: Browning-Ferris Industries Of California, Inc.
9200 Glenoaks Blvd
Sun Valley CA 91352
818 790-5410

(P-6446)
BROWNING-FERRIS INDUSTRIES INC
Also Called: Site R45
1601 Dixon Landing Rd, Milpitas (95035-8100)
PHONE..................408 262-1401
Fax: 408 262-0603
Gil Cheso, *Manager*
EMP: 65
SALES (corp-wide): 9.1B **Publicly Held**
WEB: www.alliedwaste.com
SIC: 4953 Refuse systems
HQ: Browning-Ferris Industries, Inc.
18500 N Allied Way # 100
Phoenix AZ 85054
480 627-2700

(P-6447)
BROWNING-FERRIS INDUSTRIES INC
Solid Waste Division
9200 Glenoaks Blvd, Sun Valley (91352-2613)
PHONE..................818 790-5410
Fax: 818 504-3009
Pat Gavin, *Manager*
Tina Domian, *Safety Mgr*
Steve Tucker, *Sales Mgr*
Greg Loughnane, *Manager*
EMP: 140
SALES (corp-wide): 9.1B **Publicly Held**
SIC: 4953 Rubbish collection & disposal
HQ: Browning-Ferris Industries, Inc.
18500 N Allied Way # 100
Phoenix AZ 85054
480 627-2700

(P-6448)
BURRTEC WASTE INDUSTRIES INC (HQ)
9890 Cherry Ave, Fontana (92335-5298)
PHONE..................909 429-4200
Cole Burr, *President*
Robert Coon, *CFO*
Eric Herbert, *Vice Pres*
Trevor Scrogins, *Vice Pres*
Victor Urena, *Division Mgr*
EMP: 150 EST: 1978
SQ FT: 10,000
SALES (est): 283.4MM
SALES (corp-wide): 288.4MM **Privately Held**
WEB: www.burrtec.com
SIC: 4953 4212 Rubbish collection & disposal; recycling, waste materials; local trucking, without storage
PA: Burrtec Waste Group, Inc.
9890 Cherry Ave
Fontana CA 92335
909 429-4200

(P-6449)
CALIFORNIA MARINE CLEANING INC (PA)
2049 Main St, San Diego (92113-2216)
P.O. Box 13653 (92170-3653)
PHONE..................619 231-8788
Fax: 619 231-6933
Matthew R Carr, *CEO*
Matt Carr, *President*
Hazel Carr, *CFO*
Joe Enjem, *General Mgr*
Rosie Frausto, *Human Res Mgr*
EMP: 110
SQ FT: 10,000
SALES (est): 86.2MM **Privately Held**
WEB: www.calmarineinc.com
SIC: 4953 Hazardous waste collection & disposal

(P-6450)
CALIFORNIA WASTE SERVICES LLC
621 W 152nd St, Gardena (90247-2732)
PHONE..................310 538-5998
Eric Casper, *President*
Oscar Cruel, *Accounting Mgr*
Ricardo Vallejo, *Human Resources*
Giovanni Lopez, *Opers Mgr*
EMP: 120
SQ FT: 20,000
SALES (est): 34MM **Privately Held**
WEB: www.californiawasteservices.com
SIC: 4953 Refuse systems

(P-6451)
CALIFORNIA WASTE SOLUTIONS INC
1820 10th St, Oakland (94607-1450)
PHONE..................408 292-0830
David Duong, *President*
Treva Reid, *Manager*
EMP: 75
SALES (corp-wide): 63.9MM **Privately Held**
WEB: www.calwaste.com
SIC: 4953 Garbage: collecting, destroying & processing
PA: California Waste Solutions Inc.
1005 Timothy Dr
San Jose CA 95133
510 832-8111

(P-6452)
CALIFORNIA WASTE SOLUTIONS INC (PA)
1005 Timothy Dr, San Jose (95133-1043)
PHONE..................510 832-8111
Fax: 408 292-0833
David Duong, *CEO*
Victor Duong, *Vice Pres*
Kristina Duong, *Exec Dir*
Linda Duong, *Admin Sec*
Sherri Ornelas, *Admin Asst*
▼ **EMP:** 75
SQ FT: 120,000
SALES (est): 63.9MM **Privately Held**
WEB: www.calwaste.com
SIC: 4953 Garbage: collecting, destroying & processing

(P-6453)
CALMET INC (PA)
Also Called: Metropolitan Waste Disposal
7202 Petterson Ln, Paramount (90723-2022)
PHONE..................323 721-8120
Fax: 323 721-0647
Thomas K Blackman, *President*
Gary Kazarian, *Treasurer*
William Kalpakoff, *Vice Pres*
Art Kazarian, *Vice Pres*
Kris Kazarian, *Admin Sec*
EMP: 180
SQ FT: 38,000
SALES (est): 40.7MM **Privately Held**
WEB: www.calmet.com
SIC: 4953 4212 Rubbish collection & disposal; recycling, waste materials; local trucking, without storage

(P-6454)
CALMET SERVICES INC
7202 Petterson Ln, Paramount (90723-2022)
PHONE..................562 259-1239
Bill Kalpakoff, *President*
Verlyn N Jensen, *Agent*
EMP: 59
SALES (est): 17MM **Privately Held**
SIC: 4953 Refuse systems

(P-6455)
CARAUSTAR INDUSTRIES INC
Newark Recovery & Recycling
2575 Grand Canal Blvd # 202, Stockton (95207-8260)
PHONE..................209 476-7710
Fax: 209 476-7710
Crawford Carpenter, *Manager*
Ronald Lewis, *MIS Staff*
Sam Franco, *Persnl Mgr*
Eddie Tolentino, *Manager*
EMP: 120
SALES (corp-wide): 1.6B **Privately Held**
SIC: 4953 Recycling, waste materials
PA: Caraustar Industries, Inc.
5000 Astell Pwdr Sprng Rd
Austell GA 30106
770 948-3101

(P-6456)
CASTLE & COOKE INC
10000 Stockdale Hwy # 300, Bakersfield (93311-3604)
P.O. Box 11165 (93389-1165)
PHONE..................661 664-6500
Fax: 661 664-6030
Bruce Freeman, *President*
Edward C Roohan, *Treasurer*
Bruce Davis, *Vice Pres*
Takashi Fujii, *Vice Pres*
Robert W Hibbs, *Vice Pres*
EMP: 50
SALES (est): 11.2MM
SALES (corp-wide): 563.1MM **Privately Held**
WEB: www.sevenoaksrealestate.com
SIC: 4953 Sanitary landfill operation
PA: Castle & Cooke, Inc.
1 Dole Dr
Westlake Village CA 91362

(P-6457)
CHEMICAL WASTE MANAGEMENT INC
35251 Old Skyline Rd, Kettleman City (93239)
P.O. Box 471 (93239-0471)
PHONE..................559 386-9711
Fax: 559 386-6109
Robert Henry, *Manager*
Ginger Kaladas, *Credit Staff*
EMP: 80
SQ FT: 5,000
SALES (corp-wide): 12.9B **Publicly Held**
WEB: www.wastemanagement.com
SIC: 4953 Non-hazardous waste disposal sites
HQ: Chemical Waste Management, Inc.
1001 Fannin St Ste 4000
Houston TX 77002
713 512-6200

(P-6458)
CHINO VALLEY SAWDUST INC
Also Called: Chino Valley Rock
13434 S Ontario Ave, Ontario (91761-7956)
PHONE..................909 947-5983
Fax: 909 923-7208
Brigiette Delaura, *President*
Mary W Hebb, *Treasurer*
EMP: 75
SALES (est): 3.5MM **Privately Held**
SIC: 4953 Recycling, waste materials

(P-6459)
CITY OF INDUSTRY DISPOSAL CO
17445 Railroad St, City of Industry (91748-1026)
PHONE..................626 336-5439
Manuel Perez, *Partner*
EMP: 50
SALES (est): 2.3MM **Privately Held**
SIC: 4953 Refuse systems

4953 - Refuse Systems County (P-6460)

(P-6460)
CITY OF POMONA
Also Called: Pomona City Refuse Collection
636 W Monterey Ave, Pomona (91768-3527)
PHONE..................................909 620-2361
Fax: 909 620-2485
Henry Pepper, *Manager*
EMP: 132 **Privately Held**
SIC: 4953 Refuse collection & disposal services
PA: Pomona, City Of (Inc)
    585 E Holt Ave
    Pomona CA 91767
    909 620-2051

(P-6461)
CITY OF REDLANDS
Also Called: Purchasing Department
35 Cajon St, Redlands (92373-4746)
PHONE..................................909 798-7525
Gary Vendorst, *Manager*
EMP: 50 **Privately Held**
WEB: www.akspl.org
SIC: 4953 Refuse collection & disposal services
PA: City Of Redlands
    35 Cajon St
    Redlands CA 92373
    909 798-7531

(P-6462)
CITY OF TULARE
3981 S K St, Tulare (93274-7189)
PHONE..................................559 684-4200
Kevin Northcraft, *Manager*
Steve Bonville, *Manager*
EMP: 60 **Privately Held**
WEB: www.ci.tulare.ca.us
SIC: 4953 Refuse collection & disposal services
PA: City Of Tulare
    411 E Kern Ave
    Tulare CA 93274
    559 685-2300

(P-6463)
CIVICORPS
6315 San Leandro St, Oakland (94621-3727)
PHONE..................................510 992-7800
Bill Zenoni, *Branch Mgr*
EMP: 181
SALES (corp-wide): 5.9MM **Privately Held**
SIC: 4953 Recycling, waste materials
PA: Civicorps
    101 Myrtle St
    Oakland CA 94607
    510 992-7800

(P-6464)
CLEAN HARBORS ENVMTL SVCS INC
4101 Industrial Way, Benicia (94510-1211)
PHONE..................................707 747-6699
Kevin Carnahan, *President*
EMP: 100
SALES (corp-wide): 3.2B **Publicly Held**
SIC: 4953 Hazardous waste collection & disposal
HQ: Clean Harbors Environmental Services, Inc.
    42 Longwater Dr
    Norwell MA 02061
    781 792-5000

(P-6465)
COAST WASTE MANAGEMENT
5960 El Camino Real, Carlsbad (92008-8802)
P.O. Box 947 (92018-0947)
PHONE..................................760 753-9412
Arie De Jong, *Director*
Conrad B Pawelski, *President*
Margaret Bierd, *Admin Sec*
Lee Hicks, *Project Mgr*
Margaret Brent, *Business Mgr*
EMP: 180
SQ FT: 3,000
SALES (est): 10.5MM **Privately Held**
SIC: 4953 Rubbish collection & disposal

(P-6466)
CONSOLIDATED DISPOSAL SVC LLC
2495 E 68th St, Long Beach (90805-1729)
PHONE..................................562 531-2670
Tom Vogt, *Branch Mgr*
EMP: 60
SALES (corp-wide): 9.1B **Publicly Held**
WEB: www.consolidateddisposalservice.com
SIC: 4953 4212 Waste materials, disposal at sea; garbage collection & transport, no disposal
HQ: Consolidated Disposal Service, L.L.C.
    12949 Telegraph Rd
    Santa Fe Springs CA 90670
    562 347-2100

(P-6467)
CONTAIN-A-WAY INC
Also Called: 20/20 Recycle Centers
25837 Bus Ctr Dr Ste F, Redlands (92374)
PHONE..................................909 796-2860
Keith Harradence, *CEO*
John Ferrari, *Senior VP*
Mike McCray, *General Mgr*
Jackie Brinlee, *Finance Dir*
Beth Milligan, *Controller*
EMP: 450
SQ FT: 30,000
SALES (est): 29.8MM **Privately Held**
WEB: www.nexcycle.com
SIC: 4953 4212 Recycling, waste materials; local trucking, without storage
PA: Nexcycle, Inc.
    5221 N O Connor Blvd # 850
    Irving TX 75039

(P-6468)
CORRIDOR RECYCLING INC
22500 S Alameda St, Long Beach (90810-1905)
PHONE..................................310 835-3849
Gilbert Dodson, *President*
Steve Young, *Vice Pres*
Kennith Ken, *Office Mgr*
Mark Tranckino, *CPA*
Kenneth Kim, *Opers Staff*
▲ **EMP:** 52
SQ FT: 13,594
SALES (est): 10.1MM **Privately Held**
WEB: www.corridorrecycling.com
SIC: 4953 5941 5093 Recycling, waste materials; sporting goods & bicycle shops; metal scrap & waste materials

(P-6469)
COUNTY OF EL DORADO
Also Called: Waste Connections
3940 Hwy 49, Diamond Springs (95619)
PHONE..................................530 626-4141
Sue Farriss, *Manager*
EMP: 93 **Privately Held**
WEB: www.filmtahoe.com
SIC: 4953 Garbage: collecting, destroying & processing
PA: County Of El Dorado
    330 Fair Ln
    Placerville CA 95667
    530 621-5830

(P-6470)
COUNTY OF ORANGE
Also Called: Oc Waste & Recycling
300 N Sunflower Ste 400, Santa Ana (92703)
PHONE..................................714 834-4000
Mike Giancola, *Manager*
Dave Lowry, *Manager*
EMP: 350 **Privately Held**
SIC: 4953 Recycling, waste materials
PA: County Of Orange
    333 W Santa Ana Blvd 3f
    Santa Ana CA 92701
    714 834-6200

(P-6471)
CROWN DISPOSAL COMPANY INC
Also Called: Coastal Rubbish
9189 De Garmo Ave, Sun Valley (91352-2609)
P.O. Box 1063 (91353-1063)
PHONE..................................818 767-0675
Fax: 818 768-3930
Thomas H Fry, *CEO*
John Richardson, *Treasurer*
John Cammarano, *Manager*
EMP: 200
SQ FT: 12,000
SALES (est): 47MM **Privately Held**
WEB: www.crowndisposal.com
SIC: 4953 Rubbish collection & disposal

(P-6472)
DESERT RECYCLING INC
17105 Mesa St, Hesperia (92345-5155)
P.O. Box 400725 (92340-0725)
PHONE..................................760 948-3122
Sheila Bath, *President*
EMP: 50
SALES (est): 2MM **Privately Held**
SIC: 4953 5093 Recycling, waste materials; metal scrap & waste materials

(P-6473)
E J HARRISON & SONS INC
Also Called: Harrison, E J & Sons Recycling
1589 Lirio Ave, Ventura (93004-3227)
PHONE..................................805 647-1414
Ken Keys, *General Mgr*
David Tripp, *Data Proc Staff*
EMP: 175
SALES (corp-wide): 82.4MM **Privately Held**
WEB: www.ejharrison.com
SIC: 4953 2611 Rubbish collection & disposal; pulp mills
PA: E. J. Harrison & Sons, Inc.
    5275 Colt St
    Ventura CA 93003
    805 647-1414

(P-6474)
EARTH TECHNOLOGY CORP USA
1999 Avenue Of Ste 2600, Los Angeles (90067)
PHONE..................................213 593-8000
Michael S Burke, *Ch of Bd*
Bill Webb, *Exec VP*
Paul Bassi, *Vice Pres*
Brian Burgher, *Vice Pres*
Robert Johnston, *Vice Pres*
EMP: 4655
SALES (est): 505.6K
SALES (corp-wide): 17.9B **Publicly Held**
SIC: 4953 8748 8742 8711 Refuse systems; environmental consultant; management consulting services; engineering services
PA: Aecom
    1999 Avenue Of The Stars # 2600
    Los Angeles CA 90067
    213 593-8000

(P-6475)
EAST BAY MUNICIPL UTILTY DISTR
Also Called: Ebmud
2020 Wake Ave, Oakland (94607-5100)
PHONE..................................866 403-2683
Alexander Coate, *General Mgr*
Brian Bellefeuille, *Technical Staff*
David Klein, *Controller*
Jon Bauer, *Manager*
EMP: 120
SALES (corp-wide): 1.4B **Privately Held**
SIC: 4953 9511 ;
PA: East Bay Municipal Utility District, Water System
    375 11th St
    Oakland CA 94607
    866 403-2683

(P-6476)
ECO2 PLASTICS INC
5300 Claus Rd, Riverbank (95367)
P.O. Box 760 (95367-0760)
PHONE..................................209 863-6200
Rodney S Rougelot, *CEO*
Fred Janz, *Vice Pres*
William Whittaker, *Info Tech Dir*
Jennifer Whiton, *Human Res Mgr*
EMP: 150
SALES (est): 12.3MM **Privately Held**
WEB: www.iteceg.com
SIC: 4953 Recycling, waste materials

(P-6477)
ECS REFINING LLC
2222 S Sinclair Ave, Stockton (95215-7551)
PHONE..................................209 774-5000
Jon Rayray, *Accountant*
EMP: 86
SALES (corp-wide): 119MM **Privately Held**
SIC: 4953 3339 Recycling, waste materials; precious metals
PA: Ecs Refining, Llc
    705 Reed St
    Santa Clara CA 95050
    408 988-4386

(P-6478)
EDCO DISPOSAL CORPORATION INC (PA)
Also Called: La Mesa Disposal
2755 California Ave, Signal Hill (90755-3304)
PHONE..................................619 287-7555
Fax: 619 287-5242
Steve South, *CEO*
Edward Burr, *President*
Sandra Burr, *Vice Pres*
Jamie Symons, *Comms Dir*
Don Harris, *Exec Dir*
EMP: 250 **EST:** 1967
SQ FT: 8,000
SALES (est): 457MM **Privately Held**
SIC: 4953 Garbage: collecting, destroying & processing

(P-6479)
EDCO DISPOSAL CORPORATION INC
Also Called: Park Disposal Service
6762 Stanton Ave, Buena Park (90621-3611)
P.O. Box 398 (90621-0398)
PHONE..................................714 522-3577
Efrain Ramirez, *Manager*
Mark Billings, *Marketing Staff*
EMP: 70
SALES (corp-wide): 457MM **Privately Held**
SIC: 4953 Rubbish collection & disposal
PA: Edco Disposal Corporation Inc.
    2755 California Ave
    Signal Hill CA 90755
    619 287-7555

(P-6480)
EDCO WASTE & RECYCL SVCS INC (HQ)
Also Called: Solid Waste Services
224 S Las Posas Rd, San Marcos (92078-2421)
P.O. Box 6907 (92079-6907)
PHONE..................................760 744-2700
Steve South, *CEO*
Edward Burr, *President*
Alan Walsh, *CFO*
Sandra Burr, *Corp Secy*
Jeffrey Ritchie, *Vice Pres*
EMP: 76 **EST:** 1954
SQ FT: 37,000
SALES (est): 140MM
SALES (corp-wide): 457MM **Privately Held**
SIC: 4953 4212 Rubbish collection & disposal; garbage: collecting, destroying & processing; local trucking, without storage
PA: Edco Disposal Corporation Inc.
    2755 California Ave
    Signal Hill CA 90755
    619 287-7555

(P-6481)
ELECTRONIC RECYCLERS INTL INC (PA)
Also Called: Electronic Recyclers America
7815 N Palm Ave Ste 140, Fresno (93711-5531)
PHONE..................................800 884-8466
John S Shegerian, *CEO*
Dann V Angeloff, *President*
Kelly Thomas, *COO*
James Kim, *CFO*
Aaron Blum, *Officer*
▲ **EMP:** 170
SQ FT: 75,000

PRODUCTS & SERVICES SECTION

4953 - Refuse Systems County (P-6503)

SALES (est): 551.9MM **Privately Held**
SIC: **4953** Recycling, waste materials

(P-6482)
EMPIRE DISPOSAL LLC
Also Called: Curran's Disposal
5455 Industrial Pkwy, San Bernardino (92407-1803)
PHONE..................909 797-9125
Fax: 909 880-1969
Cole Burr,
Lou Estrella, *Manager*
EMP: 50 EST: 1995
SALES (est): 2.4MM
SALES (corp-wide): 288.4MM **Privately Held**
SIC: **4953** 4212 Garbage: collecting, destroying & processing; local trucking, without storage
PA: Burrtec Waste Group, Inc.
9890 Cherry Ave
Fontana CA 92335
909 429-4200

(P-6483)
FAIRFIELD-SUISUN SEWER DST
1010 Chadbourne Rd, Fairfield (94534-9700)
PHONE..................707 429-8930
Fax: 707 429-1280
Richard F Luthy Jr, *General Mgr*
Susan Trovencal, *Administration*
Olivia Ruiz, *Accountant*
Ken Miller, *VP Sales*
Greg Baatrup, *Manager*
EMP: 65
SQ FT: 15,000
SALES: 24.6MM **Privately Held**
WEB: www.fssd.com
SIC: **4953** Refuse collection & disposal services

(P-6484)
FILTER RECYCLING SERVICES INC (PA)
180 W Monte Ave, Rialto (92376)
P.O. Box 449, Colton (92324-0449)
PHONE..................909 873-4141
Jon L Bennett Jr, *President*
Jim Arnold, *Treasurer*
Jim Goyich, *Vice Pres*
Dianna Vepeda, *Admin Sec*
▲ EMP: 63
SQ FT: 33,000
SALES (est): 68.6MM **Privately Held**
WEB: www.filterrecycling.com
SIC: **4953** Hazardous waste collection & disposal

(P-6485)
FOOTHILL WASTE RECLAMATION INC
12221 Lopez Canyon Rd, Sylmar (91342-5730)
P.O. Box 923637 (91392-3637)
PHONE..................818 897-5099
Kevork Sarkisian, *President*
Greg Huntington, *CFO*
Dick Sarkisian, *Vice Pres*
EMP: 55
SQ FT: 2,500
SALES (est): 3.3MM **Privately Held**
SIC: **4953** Refuse systems

(P-6486)
GI INDUSTRIES
195 W Los Angeles Ave, Simi Valley (93065-1651)
P.O. Box 940430 (93094-0430)
PHONE..................805 522-2150
Michael Smith, *Senior VP*
Suzann Sues, *Admin Mgr*
Ginger Kaladas, *Credit Staff*
Maria Aram, *Controller*
Lee Hicks, *Contract Law*
EMP: 100
SQ FT: 7,000
SALES: 31.8MM
SALES (corp-wide): 12.9B **Publicly Held**
WEB: www.wm.com
SIC: **4953** 4212 Garbage: collecting, destroying & processing; recycling, waste materials; local trucking, without storage
PA: Waste Management, Inc.
1001 Fannin St Ste 4000
Houston TX 77002
713 512-6200

(P-6487)
GILTON RESOURCE RECOVERY
755 S Yosemite Ave, Oakdale (95361-4039)
PHONE..................209 527-3781
Richard Gilton, *President*
Bob Pritchard, *CFO*
Tedford Gilton, *Vice Pres*
Karen Gilton Hardister, *Vice Pres*
Donna Love, *Vice Pres*
EMP: 55
SALES (est): 6.9MM **Privately Held**
SIC: **4953** Recycling, waste materials

(P-6488)
GILTON SOLID WASTE MGT INC
755 S Yosemite Ave # 106, Oakdale (95361-4991)
PHONE..................209 527-3781
Richard Gilton, *President*
Tedford Gilton, *Vice Pres*
Karen Gilton Hardister, *Vice Pres*
Donna Gilton Love, *Vice Pres*
Robert Pritchard, *Controller*
EMP: 136
SQ FT: 3,000
SALES (est): 36.4MM **Privately Held**
WEB: www.gilton.com
SIC: **4953** Rubbish collection & disposal; recycling, waste materials

(P-6489)
GREENWASTE RECOVERY INC
565 Charles St, San Jose (95112-1402)
PHONE..................408 283-4804
Chris Almeida, *Manager*
EMP: 50
SQ FT: 7,050
SALES (corp-wide): 137.9MM **Privately Held**
SIC: **4953** Garbage: collecting, destroying & processing
PA: Greenwaste Recovery, Inc.
625 Charles St
San Jose CA 95112
408 283-4800

(P-6490)
GREENWASTE RECOVERY INC (PA)
625 Charles St, San Jose (95112-1402)
PHONE..................408 283-4800
Fax: 408 287-3108
Richard Christina, *President*
Frank Weigel, *COO*
Don Dean, *CFO*
Dave Tilton, *CFO*
Jesse Weigel, *Corp Secy*
EMP: 93
SQ FT: 115,000
SALES (est): 137.9MM **Privately Held**
SIC: **4953** Rubbish collection & disposal; waste materials, disposal at sea

(P-6491)
INTERNTIONAL DISPOSAL CORP CAL
Also Called: Site L69
1601 Dixon Landing Rd, Milpitas (95035-8100)
PHONE..................408 945-2802
Bruce Ranck, *President*
Gil Chesco, *General Mgr*
EMP: 75
SQ FT: 1,613
SALES (est): 4.7MM
SALES (corp-wide): 9.1B **Publicly Held**
WEB: www.alliedwaste.com
SIC: **4953** Sanitary landfill operation
HQ: Browning-Ferris Industries, Inc.
18500 N Allied Way # 100
Phoenix AZ 85054
480 627-2700

(P-6492)
ITRENEW INC (PA)
8356 Central Ave, Newark (94560-3432)
PHONE..................510 795-1591
Fax: 408 744-7963
Mostafa Aghamiri, *CEO*
Daniel Niclas, *Vice Pres*
Aidin Aghamiri, *VP Finance*
Ray Sadeghi, *Sales Executive*
Sharmaine Robinson, *Manager*
▲ EMP: 50
SQ FT: 72,000
SALES (est): 33MM **Privately Held**
SIC: **4953** 7378 Recycling, waste materials; computer maintenance & repair

(P-6493)
JULIE COLEMAN ENTERPRISES INC
Also Called: Pacific Rim Recycling
3690 Sprig Dr Ste A, Benicia (94510-1223)
PHONE..................707 746-6067
Fax: 707 745-8273
Steven A Moore, *President*
Aretha Moore, *Vice Pres*
Robin Borroughs, *Controller*
EMP: 55
SQ FT: 10,000
SALES (est): 12.1MM **Privately Held**
WEB: www.pacificrimrecycling.com
SIC: **4953** Recycling, waste materials

(P-6494)
LOONEY BINS INC (PA)
12153 Montague St, Pacoima (91331-2210)
PHONE..................818 485-8200
Myan Spaccarelli, *President*
Jerry Lucera, *CFO*
Phyllis Shukiar, *Admin Sec*
EMP: 70
SQ FT: 1,000
SALES (est): 16.8MM **Privately Held**
WEB: www.looneybins.com
SIC: **4953** Garbage: collecting, destroying & processing

(P-6495)
LOPEZ CANYON LANDFILL
11950 Lopez Canyon Rd, Sylmar (91342-6036)
PHONE..................818 834-5122
Fax: 818 834-5117
James Kurz, *Superintendent*
Paul Blount, *Manager*
Frank Kiesler, *Manager*
EMP: 110
SALES (est): 3MM **Privately Held**
SIC: **4953** Sanitary landfill operation

(P-6496)
M P VACUUM TRUCK SERVICE (PA)
Also Called: M P Environmental Services
3400 Manor St, Bakersfield (93308-1451)
PHONE..................661 393-1151
Fax: 661 393-0508
Dawn Calderwood, *President*
Richard Turner, *Controller*
EMP: 75 EST: 1958
SQ FT: 2,500
SALES (est): 34.9MM **Privately Held**
SIC: **4953** Hazardous waste collection & disposal

(P-6497)
MADERA DISPOSAL SYSTEMS INC (DH)
Also Called: M D S I
21739 Road 19, Chowchilla (93610-8218)
P.O. Box 12227, Fresno (93777-2227)
PHONE..................559 665-3099
Fax: 559 665-3207
Ron Mittelstaedt, *President*
Greg Popovich, *Business Mgr*
EMP: 85
SQ FT: 1,200
SALES (est): 14.2MM
SALES (corp-wide): 2.5B **Publicly Held**
SIC: **4953** 4212 Street refuse systems; local trucking, without storage
HQ: Waste Connections Us, Inc.
1010 Rogers Bridge Rd
Duncan SC 29334
832 801-1436

(P-6498)
MADISON MATERIALS
1035 E 4th St, Santa Ana (92701-4750)
PHONE..................714 664-0159
Judith Ware, *President*
Ben Ware, *Vice Pres*
Jay Ware, *General Mgr*
EMP: 70
SQ FT: 10,400
SALES (est): 9.8MM **Privately Held**
SIC: **4953** Recycling, waste materials

(P-6499)
MAIN STREET FIBERS INC
608 E Main St, Ontario (91761-1711)
P.O. Box 51491 (91761-0091)
PHONE..................909 986-6310
Fax: 909 986-3942
Gregory S Young, *CEO*
Wayne Young, *President*
Ernie Alvarez, *CFO*
Steve Young, *Corp Secy*
Greg Young, *Vice Pres*
EMP: 60
SQ FT: 25,000
SALES: 46MM **Privately Held**
WEB: www.mainstreetfibers.com
SIC: **4953** Recycling, waste materials

(P-6500)
MARBORG INDUSTRIES (PA)
728 E Yanonali St, Santa Barbara (93103-3233)
P.O. Box 4127 (93140-4127)
PHONE..................805 963-1852
Fax: 805 962-0552
Mario Borgatello Jr, *President*
David Borgatello, *Vice Pres*
Alan Coulter, *Risk Mgmt Dir*
Roberto Medina, *Office Mgr*
Dennis Taylor, *Info Tech Mgr*
EMP: 250 EST: 1974
SALES (est): 140.2MM **Privately Held**
WEB: www.marborg.com
SIC: **4953** 7359 7699 4212 Rubbish collection & disposal; portable toilet rental; septic tank cleaning service; local trucking, without storage

(P-6501)
MARIN SANITARY SERVICE (PA)
Also Called: Marin Resource Recovery Center
1050 Andersen Dr, San Rafael (94901-5316)
P.O. Box 10067 (94912-0067)
PHONE..................415 456-2601
Fax: 415 456-7595
Patricia Garbarino, *CEO*
Mardelle Sarkela, *CFO*
Dave Garbarino, *Vice Pres*
John Oranje, *Vice Pres*
Ron Piombo, *Vice Pres*
EMP: 85
SALES (est): 85.5MM **Privately Held**
WEB: www.marinsanitary.com
SIC: **4953** 5099 4212 Garbage: collecting, destroying & processing; recycling, waste materials; wood chips; local trucking, without storage

(P-6502)
MASTER DISPOSAL CO
1980 S Reservoir St, Pomona (91766-5543)
PHONE..................626 444-6789
Fax: 626 444-4648
Dave Samarin, *President*
Bill Nazaroff Sr, *Vice Pres*
Susane Akopias, *General Mgr*
Bill Nazaroff Jr, *Admin Sec*
EMP: 50
SALES (est): 4.1MM **Privately Held**
SIC: **4953** Refuse systems

(P-6503)
MILL VALLEY REFUSE SERVICE INC
112 Front St, San Rafael (94901-4011)
P.O. Box 3557 (94912-3557)
PHONE..................415 457-2287
Dave Biggio, *President*
James Iavarone, *Corp Secy*
Dave Dellazoppa, *Vice Pres*
Mary Euporia, *Admin Sec*
Jennifer Dami, *Finance Mgr*
EMP: 57
SQ FT: 52,000
SALES (est): 12.5MM **Privately Held**
WEB: www.millvalleyrefuse.com
SIC: **4953** Refuse collection & disposal services; recycling, waste materials

4953 - Refuse Systems County (P-6504)

(P-6504)
MODESTO WSTEWATER TRTMNT PLANT
1221 Sutter Ave, Modesto (95351-3603)
PHONE.....................209 577-5300
Fax: 209 525-9311
Dan Wilkowsky, *Director*
EMP: 70
SALES (est): 2.9MM **Privately Held**
SIC: 4953

(P-6505)
MOLECULAR BIOPRODUCTS INC (DH)
9389 Waples St, San Diego (92121-3903)
PHONE.....................858 453-7551
Fax: 858 452-8093
Seth H Hoogasian, *CEO*
Verner Andersen, *Vice Pres*
Gary J Marmontello, *Admin Sec*
Jesse Cohen, *Project Engr*
Chris Le, *Project Engr*
◆ EMP: 110
SQ FT: 45,000
SALES (est): 282.3MM
SALES (corp-wide): 16.9B **Publicly Held**
WEB: www.mbpinc.com
SIC: 4953 Medical waste disposal
HQ: Fisher Scientific International Llc
81 Wyman St
Waltham MA 02451
781 622-1000

(P-6506)
MONTEREY RGIONAL WASTE MGT DST
14201 Del Monte Blvd, Marina (93933)
P.O. Box 1670 (93933-1670)
PHONE.....................831 384-5313
William Merry, *President*
Charles Rees, *CFO*
Leo Laska, *Chairman*
Richard Norton, *Executive*
Richard Petitt, *Plant Mgr*
EMP: 120 EST: 1951
SQ FT: 5,500
SALES (est): 22.7MM **Privately Held**
WEB: www.mrwmd.org
SIC: 4953 4911 4931 Sanitary landfill operation; recycling, waste materials; generation, electric power; electric & other services combined

(P-6507)
MOUNTAIN MINING INCORPORATED
Also Called: Forco Disposal Service
3097 Southgate Ln, Chico (95928-7427)
PHONE.....................530 342-6059
Julie Johnson, *President*
EMP: 50 EST: 1971
SALES (est): 1.9MM **Privately Held**
SIC: 4953 5531 Street refuse systems; refuse collection & disposal services; automotive & home supply stores

(P-6508)
MP ENVIRONMENTAL SERVICES INC (PA)
3400 Manor St, Bakersfield (93308-1451)
P.O. Box 80358 (93380-0358)
PHONE.....................800 458-3036
Dawn Calderwood, *President*
Nardely Hanney, *Admin Asst*
Matt Hoffman, *Project Mgr*
Laren Kaufman, *Project Mgr*
Jesse Soltero, *Project Mgr*
EMP: 117
SQ FT: 8,000
SALES (est): 119.3MM **Privately Held**
WEB: www.mpenviro.com
SIC: 4953 4213 8748 7699 Hazardous waste collection & disposal; radioactive waste materials, disposal; trucking, except local; environmental consultant; tank repair & cleaning services

(P-6509)
NORTECH WASTE LLC
3033 Fiddyment Rd, Roseville (95747-9705)
PHONE.....................916 645-5230
Paul Szura, *Mng Member*
Paul Scura, *General Mgr*
Sally Dipuccio, *Finance Mgr*
Angela Capra, *Human Resources*
Rena Sims, *Marketing Staff*
EMP: 120
SQ FT: 9,000
SALES (est): 32.6MM **Privately Held**
WEB: www.nortechwaste.com
SIC: 4953 3341 3312 3231 Refuse systems; secondary nonferrous metals; blast furnaces & steel mills; products of purchased glass; pulp mills

(P-6510)
NRC ENVIRONMENTAL SERVICES INC
3777 Long Beach Blvd, Long Beach (90807-3325)
PHONE.....................562 432-1304
Todd Roloff, *Branch Mgr*
Justin Peters, *Supervisor*
EMP: 60
SALES (corp-wide): 127.4MM **Privately Held**
WEB: www.nrces.com
SIC: 4953 Hazardous waste collection & disposal
HQ: Nrc Environmental Services, Inc.
1605 Ferry Pt Ste 200
Alameda CA 94501
510 749-1390

(P-6511)
ORANGE COUNTY SANITATION (PA)
10844 Ellis Ave, Fountain Valley (92708-7018)
P.O. Box 8127 (92728-8127)
PHONE.....................714 962-2411
James Herberg, *General Mgr*
Cathy Green, *Vice Chairman*
Clarice Marcin, *Vice Pres*
Randall Mason, *Risk Mgmt Dir*
Nancy Dooley, *Exec Dir*
▲ EMP: 300
SALES: 304.5MM **Privately Held**
WEB: www.ocsd.com
SIC: 4953 Waste materials, disposal at sea

(P-6512)
PALM SPRINGS DISPOSAL SERVICES
4690 E Mesquite Ave, Palm Springs (92264-3510)
P.O. Box 2711 (92263-2711)
PHONE.....................760 327-1351
Fax: 760 327-8041
Frederic Wade, *CEO*
James Cunningham, *President*
Mike Jaycox, *Treasurer*
Ray Wade, *Vice Pres*
Shari Arias, *Executive Asst*
EMP: 82
SQ FT: 2,000
SALES (est): 22MM **Privately Held**
WEB: www.palmspringsdisposal.com
SIC: 4953 Rubbish collection & disposal

(P-6513)
PENAS DISPOSAL INC
Also Called: Pena's Recycling Center
12094 Avenue 408, Cutler (93615-2055)
PHONE.....................559 528-3909
Gabriel Pena, *President*
Arthur Pena, *Vice Pres*
Maria Pena, *Admin Sec*
EMP: 91 EST: 1968
SQ FT: 1,000
SALES (est): 22.4MM **Privately Held**
WEB: www.penasdisposal.com
SIC: 4953 Garbage: collecting, destroying & processing

(P-6514)
PLEASANT HL BYSHORE DSPSAL INC
Also Called: Site 210
441 N Buchanan Cir, Pacheco (94553-5119)
PHONE.....................925 685-4711
J Frederick Snyder, *CEO*
Tim Argenti, *General Mgr*
EMP: 200
SQ FT: 4,000
SALES (est): 14.1MM
SALES (corp-wide): 9.1B **Publicly Held**
WEB: www.pleasanthillbayshoredisposal.com
SIC: 4953 Refuse collection & disposal services
HQ: Allied Waste Industries, Inc.
18500 N Allied Way # 100
Phoenix AZ 85054
480 627-2700

(P-6515)
POTENTIAL INDUSTRIES INC (PA)
922 E E St, Wilmington (90744-6145)
P.O. Box 293 (90748-0293)
PHONE.....................310 807-4466
Fax: 310 513-1361
Anthony J Fan, *President*
Tony Fan, *President*
Henry J Chen, *CEO*
Jessie Chen, *Corp Secy*
Daniel J Domonoske, *Vice Pres*
◆ EMP: 149
SQ FT: 45,000
SALES (est): 166MM **Privately Held**
SIC: 4953 5093 Recycling, waste materials; scrap & waste materials

(P-6516)
PSC INDUSTRIAL OUTSOURCING LP
1661 E 32nd St, Long Beach (90807-5233)
PHONE.....................562 997-6000
Fax: 562 997-6059
Bill Hearley, *Manager*
EMP: 99
SALES (corp-wide): 33.1MM **Privately Held**
SIC: 4953 4959 5093 Hazardous waste collection & disposal; environmental cleanup services; ferrous metal scrap & waste
PA: Psc Industrial Outsourcing, Lp
5151 San Felipe St # 1600
Houston TX 77056
713 623-8777

(P-6517)
RAINBOW DISPOSAL CO INC (HQ)
Also Called: Rainbow Refuse Recycling
17121 Nichols Ln, Huntington Beach (92647-5719)
P.O. Box 1026 (92647-1026)
PHONE.....................714 847-3581
Fax: 714 841-4660
Jerry Moffatt, *CEO*
Stan Tkaczyck, *President*
Jim Brownell, *Vice Pres*
Craig Campbell, *Vice Pres*
Sue Gordon, *Vice Pres*
EMP: 115 EST: 1956
SQ FT: 6,000
SALES (est): 143.9MM
SALES (corp-wide): 9.1B **Publicly Held**
WEB: www.rainbowdisposal.com
SIC: 4953 Garbage: collecting, destroying & processing; recycling, waste materials
PA: Republic Services, Inc.
18500 N Allied Way # 100
Phoenix AZ 85054
480 627-2700

(P-6518)
RAINBOW TRANSFER RECYCLING
17121 Nichols Ln, Huntington Beach (92647-5719)
P.O. Box 1026 (92647-1026)
PHONE.....................714 847-5818
Jim Brownell, *Principal*
Stan Tkaczyk, *President*
Bruce Shuman, *CFO*
EMP: 165
SQ FT: 10,000
SALES (est): 7.6MM
SALES (corp-wide): 9.1B **Publicly Held**
WEB: www.rainbowdisposal.com
SIC: 4953 Rubbish collection & disposal
HQ: Rainbow Disposal Co. Inc.
17121 Nichols Ln
Huntington Beach CA 92647
714 847-3581

(P-6519)
RECOLOGY INC (PA)
50 California St Fl 24, San Francisco (94111-4796)
PHONE.....................415 875-1000
Michael J Sangiacomo, *President*
George P McGrath, *COO*
Mark R Lomele, *CFO*
Mark Lomele, *CFO*
Dennis Wu, *Chairman*
EMP: 60 EST: 1988
SQ FT: 25,000
SALES (est): 1.6B **Privately Held**
WEB: www.norcalwastesystemsofbutte-county.com
SIC: 4953 Garbage: collecting, destroying & processing; recycling, waste materials

(P-6520)
RECOLOGY INC
Tunnel Ave And Beatty Rd, San Francisco (94134)
P.O. Box 7360 (94120-7360)
PHONE.....................415 330-1300
Mike Sangiacomo, *Branch Mgr*
Daniel Negron, *Manager*
EMP: 64
SALES (corp-wide): 1.6B **Privately Held**
WEB: www.norcalwastesystemsofbutte-county.com
SIC: 4953 Refuse systems
PA: Recology Inc.
50 California St Fl 24
San Francisco CA 94111
415 875-1000

(P-6521)
RECOLOGY INC
245 N 1st St, Dixon (95620-3027)
PHONE.....................916 379-3300
EMP: 63
SALES (corp-wide): 1.6B **Privately Held**
SIC: 4953 Garbage: collecting, destroying & processing
PA: Recology Inc.
50 California St Fl 24
San Francisco CA 94111
415 875-1000

(P-6522)
RECOLOGY INC
Also Called: Recology Sustainable Crushing
100 Cargo Way, San Francisco (94124-1734)
PHONE.....................415 970-1582
EMP: 56
SALES (corp-wide): 1.6B **Privately Held**
SIC: 4953 Refuse systems
PA: Recology Inc.
50 California St Fl 24
San Francisco CA 94111
415 875-1000

(P-6523)
RECOLOGY INC
2720 S 5th Ave, Oroville (95965-5826)
P.O. Box 1512 (95965-1512)
PHONE.....................530 533-5868
Joe Matz, *Manager*
EMP: 76
SQ FT: 9,086
SALES (corp-wide): 1.6B **Privately Held**
WEB: www.norcalwastesystemsofbutte-county.com
SIC: 4953 Refuse collection & disposal services
PA: Recology Inc.
50 California St Fl 24
San Francisco CA 94111
415 875-1000

(P-6524)
RECOLOGY INC
Also Called: Sanitary Fill
501 Tunnel Ave, San Francisco (94134-2940)
PHONE.....................415 330-1400
Fax: 415 330-1402
John Legnitto, *Branch Mgr*
Mike Sweeny, *Accounting Mgr*
EMP: 150
SALES (corp-wide): 1.6B **Privately Held**
WEB: www.norcalwastesystemsofbutte-county.com
SIC: 4953 8611 Refuse systems; business associations

PRODUCTS & SERVICES SECTION

4953 - Refuse Systems County (P-6547)

PA: Recology Inc.
50 California St Fl 24
San Francisco CA 94111
415 875-1000

(P-6525)
RECOLOGY LOS ALTOS
Also Called: Recology South Bay
650 Martin Ave, Santa Clara (95050-2914)
PHONE.................650 961-8044
Michael Sangiacomo, *President*
EMP: 89 **EST:** 1923
SALES (est): 5.5MM
SALES (corp-wide): 1.6B **Privately Held**
WEB: www.losaltosgarbage.com
SIC: 4953 Garbage: collecting, destroying & processing; recycling, waste materials
PA: Recology Inc.
50 California St Fl 24
San Francisco CA 94111
415 875-1000

(P-6526)
RECOLOGY LOS ANGELES
Also Called: Recology Inc.
9189 De Garmo Ave, Sun Valley (91352-2609)
PHONE.................415 875-1140
Michael Sangiacomo, *CEO*
Paul Dougherty, *Finance*
Erin Campion, *Corp Comm Staff*
EMP: 400 **EST:** 2006
SALES (est): 19.1MM **Privately Held**
SIC: 4953 Garbage: collecting, destroying & processing

(P-6527)
RECOLOGY SAN FRANCISCO
501 Tunnel Ave, San Francisco (94134-2940)
PHONE.................415 468-1752
Michael Sangiacomo, *President*
Robert Coyle, *COO*
Deborah Munk, *Adv Board Mem*
Mike Crosetti, *General Mgr*
Jennifer Lewis, *Executive Asst*
EMP: 167
SQ FT: 3,800
SALES (est): 23.3MM
SALES (corp-wide): 1.6B **Privately Held**
WEB: www.sfrecyclinganddisposal.com
SIC: 4953 Refuse collection & disposal services
PA: Recology Inc.
50 California St Fl 24
San Francisco CA 94111
415 875-1000

(P-6528)
RECOLOGY SAN MATEO COUNTY
225 Shoreway Rd, San Carlos (94070-2712)
PHONE.................650 595-3900
Michael J Sangiacomo, *CEO*
Paul Dougherty, *Manager*
EMP: 99
SALES: 950K **Privately Held**
SIC: 4953 Garbage: collecting, destroying & processing

(P-6529)
RECOLOGY SOUTH BAY
650 Martin Ave, Santa Clara (95050-2914)
PHONE.................408 725-4020
Selina Dutra, *Principal*
EMP: 99
SALES (est): 4.7MM **Privately Held**
SIC: 4953 Garbage: collecting, destroying & processing

(P-6530)
RECOLOGY SOUTH VALLEY (HQ)
1351 Pacheco Pass Hwy, Gilroy (95020-9579)
PHONE.................408 842-3358
Robert Coyle, *President*
Mike Sanjiacomo, *Vice Pres*
EMP: 65 **EST:** 1949
SQ FT: 6,000
SALES (est): 16.9MM
SALES (corp-wide): 1.6B **Privately Held**
SIC: 4953 Garbage: collecting, destroying & processing; recycling, waste materials; sanitary landfill operation

PA: Recology Inc.
50 California St Fl 24
San Francisco CA 94111
415 875-1000

(P-6531)
RECOLOGY VACAVILLE SOLANO
1 Town Sq Ste 200, Vacaville (95688-3928)
PHONE.................707 448-2945
Michael Sangiacomo, *President*
Scott Pardini, *General Mgr*
Kathy Deffy, *Manager*
EMP: 75
SQ FT: 10,000
SALES (est): 9.2MM
SALES (corp-wide): 1.6B **Privately Held**
WEB: www.norcalwastesystemsofbutte-county.com
SIC: 4953 Garbage: collecting, destroying & processing
PA: Recology Inc.
50 California St Fl 24
San Francisco CA 94111
415 875-1000

(P-6532)
RECOLOGY VALLEJO
Also Called: Vallejo Garbage & Recycling
2021 Broadway St, Vallejo (94589-1701)
PHONE.................707 552-3110
Ed Farewell, *General Mgr*
Lisa Logoteta, *Human Res Dir*
Tom Phillips, *Opers Mgr*
EMP: 115
SQ FT: 40,000
SALES: 16MM
SALES (corp-wide): 1.6B **Privately Held**
WEB: www.vallejogarbage.com
SIC: 4953 Garbage: collecting, destroying & processing
PA: Recology Inc.
50 California St Fl 24
San Francisco CA 94111
415 875-1000

(P-6533)
RECOLOGY YUBA-SUTTER
3001 N Levee Rd, Marysville (95901-3600)
P.O. Box G (95901)
PHONE.................530 743-6933
Michael Sangiacomo, *President*
Robert Coyle, *COO*
Terry Bentley, *Opers Mgr*
EMP: 90
SQ FT: 7,000
SALES (est): 14.2MM
SALES (corp-wide): 1.6B **Privately Held**
WEB: www.ysdi.com
SIC: 4953 4212 Garbage: collecting, destroying & processing; recycling, waste materials; hazardous waste collection & disposal; hazardous waste transport
PA: Recology Inc.
50 California St Fl 24
San Francisco CA 94111
415 875-1000

(P-6534)
RECYCLING INDUSTRIES INC
4741 Watt Ave, North Highlands (95660-5526)
PHONE.................916 452-3961
Fax: 916 452-2717
Scott Kuhnen, *President*
David Kuhnen, *CFO*
Jeff Donlevy, *Business Mgr*
Mike Rexroad, *Maintence Staff*
EMP: 75
SQ FT: 155,000
SALES (est): 18.7MM **Privately Held**
WEB: www.recyclingindustries.com
SIC: 4953 Recycling, waste materials

(P-6535)
REDWOOD EMPIR
3400 Standish Ave, Santa Rosa (95407-8112)
PHONE.................707 586-5533
James Rappo, *President*
EMP: 70
SALES (est): 5MM **Privately Held**
SIC: 4953 Refuse systems

(P-6536)
REPLANET LLC
Also Called: Tomra Recycling Network
9910 6th St, Rancho Cucamonga (91730-5715)
PHONE.................909 980-1203
Ralph Alcantar, *Manager*
EMP: 55
SALES (corp-wide): 708.8MM **Privately Held**
SIC: 4953 8741 5093 Recycling, waste materials; management services; metal scrap & waste materials
HQ: Replanet, Llc
800 N Haven Ave Ste 120
Ontario CA 91764
951 520-1700

(P-6537)
REPUBLIC SERVICES INC
2059 E Steel Rd, Colton (92324-4008)
PHONE.................909 370-3377
Peter Sperenberg, *Manager*
EMP: 50
SQ FT: 3,200
SALES (corp-wide): 9.1B **Publicly Held**
SIC: 4953 Refuse collection & disposal services
PA: Republic Services, Inc.
18500 N Allied Way # 100
Phoenix AZ 85054
480 627-2700

(P-6538)
REPUBLIC SERVICES INC
1449 W Rosecrans Ave, Gardena (90249-2639)
PHONE.................310 527-6980
Lewis Glynn, *Manager*
Pilar Almeida, *Sales Associate*
Glenn Lewis, *Manager*
Jeff Sadler, *Manager*
EMP: 100
SQ FT: 39,755
SALES (corp-wide): 9.1B **Publicly Held**
WEB: www.republicservices.com
SIC: 4953 Medical waste disposal
PA: Republic Services, Inc.
18500 N Allied Way # 100
Phoenix AZ 85054
480 627-2700

(P-6539)
REPUBLIC SERVICES INC
111 S Del Norte Blvd, Oxnard (93030-7915)
PHONE.................805 385-8060
Anthony Bertrand, *Branch Mgr*
EMP: 58
SALES (corp-wide): 9.1B **Publicly Held**
WEB: www.republicservices.com
SIC: 4953 Refuse systems
PA: Republic Services, Inc.
18500 N Allied Way # 100
Phoenix AZ 85054
480 627-2700

(P-6540)
RETRIEV TECHNOLOGIES INC (PA)
Also Called: Lithchem
125 E Commercial St Ste A, Anaheim (92801-1214)
PHONE.................714 738-8516
Steven Kinsbursky, *President*
Joseph A Acker, *President*
Aaron Zisman, *Treasurer*
Terry Adams, *Admin Sec*
Daniel Kinsbursky,
EMP: 55
SALES (est): 48.9MM **Privately Held**
SIC: 4953 3341 2819 Refuse systems; recovery & refining of nonferrous metals; industrial inorganic chemicals

(P-6541)
SA RECYCLING LLC
3489 S Chestnut Ave, Fresno (93725-2610)
PHONE.................559 237-6677
EMP: 64
SALES (corp-wide): 900MM **Privately Held**
SIC: 4953 Recycling, waste materials

PA: Sa Recycling Llc
2411 N Glassell St
Orange CA 92865
714 632-2000

(P-6542)
SA RECYCLING LLC
3055 Commercial St, San Diego (92113-1412)
PHONE.................619 238-6740
Mark Sweetman, *Manager*
EMP: 68
SALES (corp-wide): 900MM **Privately Held**
SIC: 4953 Recycling, waste materials
PA: Sa Recycling Llc
2411 N Glassell St
Orange CA 92865
714 632-2000

(P-6543)
SA RECYCLING LLC
10313 S Alameda St, Los Angeles (90002-3838)
PHONE.................323 564-5601
Carlos Escamilla, *Manager*
EMP: 68
SALES (corp-wide): 900MM **Privately Held**
SIC: 4953 Recycling, waste materials
PA: Sa Recycling Llc
2411 N Glassell St
Orange CA 92865
714 632-2000

(P-6544)
SA RECYCLING LLC
780 E Easy St, Simi Valley (93065-1810)
PHONE.................805 483-0512
EMP: 68
SALES (corp-wide): 900MM **Privately Held**
SIC: 4953 5093 Recycling, waste materials; scrap & waste materials; ferrous metal scrap & waste; nonferrous metals scrap
PA: Sa Recycling Llc
2411 N Glassell St
Orange CA 92865
714 632-2000

(P-6545)
SA RECYCLING LLC
2006 W 5th St, Santa Ana (92703-2806)
PHONE.................714 667-7898
EMP: 68
SALES (corp-wide): 900MM **Privately Held**
SIC: 4953 5093 Recycling, waste materials; scrap & waste materials; ferrous metal scrap & waste; nonferrous metals scrap
PA: Sa Recycling Llc
2411 N Glassell St
Orange CA 92865
714 632-2000

(P-6546)
SA RECYCLING LLC
9754 San Fernando Rd, Sun Valley (91352-1424)
PHONE.................323 875-2520
Steve Rios, *Branch Mgr*
EMP: 68
SALES (corp-wide): 900MM **Privately Held**
SIC: 4953 Recycling, waste materials
PA: Sa Recycling Llc
2411 N Glassell St
Orange CA 92865
714 632-2000

(P-6547)
SA RECYCLING LLC
2525 S K St, Tulare (93274-6875)
PHONE.................559 688-0271
Brandon Dye, *General Mgr*
EMP: 68
SALES (corp-wide): 900MM **Privately Held**
SIC: 4953 Recycling, waste materials
PA: Sa Recycling Llc
2411 N Glassell St
Orange CA 92865
714 632-2000

4953 - Refuse Systems County (P-6548)

(P-6548)
SA RECYCLING LLC
2495 Buena Vista St, Irwindale (91010-3330)
PHONE................................626 359-5815
Carlos Rodriguez, *Manager*
EMP: 68
SALES (corp-wide): 900MM Privately Held
SIC: 4953 5093 Recycling, waste materials; scrap & waste materials; ferrous metal scrap & waste; nonferrous metals scrap
PA: Sa Recycling Llc
2411 N Glassell St
Orange CA 92865
714 632-2000

(P-6549)
SA RECYCLING LLC
1540 S Greenwood Ave, Montebello (90640-6536)
PHONE................................323 723-8327
James Adams, *Branch Mgr*
EMP: 68
SALES (corp-wide): 900MM Privately Held
SIC: 4953 5093 Recycling, waste materials; scrap & waste materials; ferrous metal scrap & waste; nonferrous metals scrap
PA: Sa Recycling Llc
2411 N Glassell St
Orange CA 92865
714 632-2000

(P-6550)
SA RECYCLING LLC
8822 Etiwanda Ave, Rancho Cucamonga (91739-9662)
PHONE................................909 899-1767
Billy Schmiedel, *Manager*
EMP: 68
SALES (corp-wide): 900MM Privately Held
SIC: 4953 Recycling, waste materials
PA: Sa Recycling Llc
2411 N Glassell St
Orange CA 92865
714 632-2000

(P-6551)
SA RECYCLING LLC
2000 E Brundage Ln, Bakersfield (93307-2734)
PHONE................................661 327-3559
Luis Torres, *Manager*
EMP: 65
SALES (corp-wide): 900MM Privately Held
SIC: 4953 Recycling, waste materials
PA: Sa Recycling Llc
2411 N Glassell St
Orange CA 92865
714 632-2000

(P-6552)
SA RECYCLING LLC
12301 Valley Blvd, El Monte (91732-3603)
PHONE................................626 444-9530
Carlos Escamilla, *Branch Mgr*
EMP: 64
SALES (corp-wide): 900MM Privately Held
SIC: 4953 Recycling, waste materials
PA: Sa Recycling Llc
2411 N Glassell St
Orange CA 92865
714 632-2000

(P-6553)
SA RECYCLING LLC
48100 Harrison St, Coachella (92236-1214)
PHONE................................760 391-5591
Ben Wilcox, *Branch Mgr*
EMP: 68
SALES (corp-wide): 900MM Privately Held
SIC: 4953 Recycling, waste materials
PA: Sa Recycling Llc
2411 N Glassell St
Orange CA 92865
714 632-2000

(P-6554)
SA RECYCLING LLC
11614 Eastend Ave, Chino (91710-1557)
PHONE................................909 622-3337
EMP: 68
SALES (corp-wide): 49.7MM Privately Held
SIC: 4953 5093
PA: Sa Recycling Llc
2411 N Glassell St
Orange CA 92865
714 632-2000

(P-6555)
SA RECYCLING LLC
42353 8th St E, Lancaster (93535-5439)
PHONE................................661 723-1383
EMP: 68
SALES (corp-wide): 49.7MM Privately Held
SIC: 4953
PA: Sa Recycling Llc
2411 N Glassell St
Orange CA 92865
714 632-2000

(P-6556)
SA RECYCLING LLC
790 E M St, Colton (92324-3910)
PHONE................................909 825-1662
Alex Arriaga, *Branch Mgr*
EMP: 68
SALES (corp-wide): 900MM Privately Held
SIC: 4953 Recycling, waste materials
PA: Sa Recycling Llc
2411 N Glassell St
Orange CA 92865
714 632-2000

(P-6557)
SA RECYCLING LLC
3202 Main St, San Diego (92113-3719)
PHONE................................714 632-2000
EMP: 68
SALES (corp-wide): 900MM Privately Held
SIC: 4953 Recycling, waste materials
PA: Sa Recycling Llc
2411 N Glassell St
Orange CA 92865
714 632-2000

(P-6558)
SACRAMENTO AREA SEWER DISTRICT (PA)
10060 Goethe Rd, Sacramento (95827-3553)
PHONE................................916 876-6000
Joseph Maestretti, *CFO*
Prabhaker Somavarapu, *Principal*
Lisa Voight, *General Mgr*
Shannon Alley, *Info Tech Mgr*
Glen Iwamura, *Info Tech Mgr*
EMP: 300
SALES (est): 273.1MM Privately Held
SIC: 4953 Rubbish collection & disposal

(P-6559)
SAN DIEGO RECYLING INC
6670 Federal Blvd, Lemon Grove (91945-1312)
PHONE................................619 287-7555
Edward Burr, *President*
EMP: 300
SALES (est): 9.5MM Privately Held
SIC: 4953 Recycling, waste materials

(P-6560)
SANITATION DISTRICT
Also Called: Puente Hills Landfill
2800 Workman Mill Rd, Whittier (90601-1548)
P.O. Box 4998 (90607-4998)
PHONE................................562 699-5204
Grace Han, *Chief*
James Stahl, *General Mgr*
Kimberly Compton, *Admin Sec*
Howard Wolfer, *Technical Staff*
David Baldwin, *Manager*
EMP: 100 Privately Held
SIC: 4953 9511 Sanitary landfill operation;
PA: Sanitation District Of Los Angeles County District 2
1955 Workman Mill Rd
Whittier CA 90601
562 699-7411

(P-6561)
SANITATION DISTRICTS
1955 Workman Mill Rd, Whittier (90601-1415)
P.O. Box 4998 (90607-4998)
PHONE................................562 908-4288
Fax: 562 699-7411
Steve McGuin, *Manager*
CHI-Chung Tang, *Top Exec*
Grace Robinson Chan, *General Mgr*
Debbie Hong, *Admin Sec*
Patricia Johnson, *Admin Asst*
EMP: 1698
SALES: 576MM Privately Held
SIC: 4953 Refuse systems; rubbish collection & disposal

(P-6562)
SCOPE INDUSTRIES (PA)
Also Called: Scope Products
2811 Wilshire Blvd # 410, Santa Monica (90403-4805)
P.O. Box 2211 (90407-2211)
PHONE................................310 458-1574
Fax: 310 451-5371
Meyer Luskin, *Ch of Bd*
David Luskin, *COO*
Eric Iwafuchi, *CFO*
Rida Hamed, *Exec VP*
Gerald Truelove, *Vice Pres*
EMP: 53
SALES: 203.7MM Privately Held
SIC: 4953 Recycling, waste materials

(P-6563)
SOLAG INC
31641 Ortega Hwy, San Juan Capistrano (92675)
PHONE................................949 728-1206
Clifford Ronnenberg, *Ch of Bd*
Patricia Leyes, *Vice Pres*
EMP: 58
SALES (est): 4MM
SALES (corp-wide): 100MM Privately Held
WEB: www.crrincorporated.com
SIC: 4953 4212 Rubbish collection & disposal; local trucking, without storage
PA: Cr&R Incorporated
11292 Western Ave
Stanton CA 90680
714 826-9049

(P-6564)
SOLANO GARBAGE COMPANY INC
2901 Industrial Ct, Fairfield (94533-6500)
P.O. Box B (94533-0601)
PHONE................................707 437-8900
Fax: 707 437-8955
Richard Granzella, *President*
Dennis Varni, *CFO*
Joe Della Zoppa, *Exec VP*
Pina Barbieri, *Admin Sec*
EMP: 55 **EST:** 1978
SQ FT: 2,000
SALES: 11MM Privately Held
WEB: www.solanorecycles.com
SIC: 4953 Garbage: collecting, destroying & processing

(P-6565)
SOUTH TAHOE REFUSE CO
Also Called: Sierra Disposal Service
2140 Ruth Ave, South Lake Tahoe (96150-4357)
PHONE................................530 541-5105
Fax: 530 544-2608
Jeffrey Tillman, *President*
Gloria Lehman, *Treasurer*
John Tillman, *Vice Pres*
Alan Muller, *Exec Dir*
John De Marchini, *Admin Sec*
EMP: 100
SQ FT: 5,000
SALES (est): 20.7MM Privately Held
WEB: www.southtahoerefuse.com
SIC: 4953 Garbage: collecting, destroying & processing

(P-6566)
SUNSET SCAVENGER COMPANY
Also Called: Recology Sunset Scavenger
250 Executive Park Blvd # 2100, San Francisco (94134-3306)
PHONE................................415 330-1300
Fax: 415 330-1372
Archie Humphrey, *COO*
Gary Kirk, *Administration*
Glen Bongi, *Manager*
John Legnitto, *Manager*
Joe Goldstein, *Supervisor*
EMP: 420 **EST:** 1920
SQ FT: 3,800
SALES (est): 43MM
SALES (corp-wide): 1.6B Privately Held
WEB: www.norcalwastesystemsofbuttecounty.com
SIC: 4953 Rubbish collection & disposal
PA: Recology Inc.
50 California St Fl 24
San Francisco CA 94111
415 875-1000

(P-6567)
TALCO PLASTICS INC (PA)
1000 W Rincon St, Corona (92880-9228)
PHONE................................951 531-2000
Fax: 909 531-2059
John L Shedd Sr, *Chairman*
John L Shedd Jr, *President*
William O'Grady, *Vice Pres*
Ron Petty, *Vice Pres*
Bob Shedd, *Vice Pres*
EMP: 85
SQ FT: 110,000
SALES (est): 100.5MM Privately Held
WEB: www.talcoplastics.com
SIC: 4953 2821 Recycling, waste materials; plastics materials & resins

(P-6568)
TEHACHAPI RECYCLING CENTER
416 N Dennison Rd, Tehachapi (93561-1504)
PHONE................................661 822-6421
Paul Benz, *President*
EMP: 80
SALES (est): 3.8MM Privately Held
SIC: 4953 Recycling, waste materials

(P-6569)
TEMARRY RECYCLING INC
476 Tecate Rd, Tecate (91980)
P.O. Box 476 (91980-0476)
PHONE................................619 270-9453
Matt Songer, *CEO*
Teresa Songer, *Vice Pres*
Larry Burton, *Business Dir*
EMP: 63 **EST:** 2004
SALES (est): 4MM Privately Held
SIC: 4953 Recycling, waste materials

(P-6570)
TRACY DLTA SOLID WASTE MGT INC
Also Called: Delta Disposal Service Co
30703 S Macarthur Dr, Tracy (95377-9170)
P.O. Box 274 (95378-0274)
PHONE................................209 835-0601
Fax: 209 835-7729
Michael Repetto, *President*
Carl Repetto, *Vice Pres*
Scott Stortroen, *Info Tech Mgr*
Anna Lovecchio, *CPA*
Susan Hudson, *Controller*
EMP: 61
SQ FT: 1,000
SALES (est): 12.4MM Privately Held
SIC: 4953 Garbage: collecting, destroying & processing; recycling, waste materials

(P-6571)
TRI-CITY ECONOMIC DEV CORP
Also Called: Tri Ced Community Recycling
33377 Western Ave, Union City (94587-2210)
PHONE................................510 429-8030
Fax: 510 429-8031
Richard Valle, *Principal*
Eduaidio Decena, *Accountant*
EMP: 59
SQ FT: 74,055

PRODUCTS & SERVICES SECTION
4953 - Refuse Systems County (P-6591)

SALES (est): 8.9MM **Privately Held**
SIC: **4953** Recycling, waste materials

(P-6572)
UNITED PACIFIC WASTE
4334 San Gbriel Rver Pkwy, Pico Rivera (90660-1837)
P.O. Box 908 (90660-0908)
PHONE..................562 699-7600
Michael Kandilian, *President*
Paul Kachirsky, *COO*
Mike Kandilian, *Exec VP*
Alan Oganesian, *Executive*
Dave Haprov, *General Mgr*
EMP: 70
SQ FT: 3,500
SALES: 12MM **Privately Held**
SIC: **4953** 4213 Refuse collection & disposal services; rubbish collection & disposal; contract haulers

(P-6573)
UNITED SITE SERVICES CAL INC
1 Oak Rd, Benicia (94510-2910)
PHONE..................707 747-2810
Debbi Thornton, *Manager*
EMP: 50
SALES (corp-wide): 5.4MM **Privately Held**
WEB: www.americanclassicsanitation.com
SIC: **4953** 4959 5082 7359 Refuse systems; sanitary services; construction & mining machinery; equipment rental & leasing
PA: United Site Services Of California, Inc.
242 Live Oak Ave
Irwindale CA 91706
626 462-9110

(P-6574)
USA WASTE OF CALIFORNIA INC
Also Called: Waste Management
26951 Road 140, Visalia (93292-9454)
P.O. Box 78251, Phoenix AZ (85062-8251)
PHONE..................559 741-1766
Kurt Nielson, *Manager*
Ginger Kaladas, *Credit Staff*
Tom Patron, *Manager*
EMP: 75
SALES (corp-wide): 12.9B **Publicly Held**
WEB: www.wastebusinessjournal.com
SIC: **4953** Ashes, collection & disposal
HQ: Usa Waste Of California, Inc.
11931 Foundation Pl # 200
Gold River CA 95670
916 387-1400

(P-6575)
USA WASTE OF CALIFORNIA INC
8491 Fruitridge Rd, Sacramento (95826-4807)
PHONE..................916 379-0500
Alex Oseguera, *Manager*
Shawn Guttersen, *Vice Pres*
EMP: 93
SALES (corp-wide): 12.9B **Publicly Held**
SIC: **4953** Refuse collection & disposal services
HQ: Usa Waste Of California, Inc.
11931 Foundation Pl # 200
Gold River CA 95670
916 387-1400

(P-6576)
USA WASTE OF CALIFORNIA INC (HQ)
Also Called: Waste Management
11931 Foundation Pl # 200, Gold River (95670-4540)
PHONE..................916 387-1400
Barry S Skolnick, *CEO*
Mike Witt, *CEO*
Earl E Defrates, *Treasurer*
Ed Aurand, *Ch Credit Ofcr*
Alex Oseguera, *Vice Pres*
EMP: 126
SQ FT: 3,200
SALES (est): 47.7MM
SALES (corp-wide): 12.9B **Publicly Held**
WEB: www.wm.com
SIC: **4953** Refuse collection & disposal services

PA: Waste Management, Inc.
1001 Fannin St Ste 4000
Houston TX 77002
713 512-6200

(P-6577)
USA WASTE OF CALIFORNIA INC
Also Called: Inland Empire Hauling
800 S Temescal St, Corona (92879-2058)
PHONE..................800 423-9986
Lynn Sisco, *Telecom Exec*
Lee Hicks, *Contract Law*
EMP: 100
SALES (corp-wide): 12.9B **Publicly Held**
SIC: **4953** Refuse systems
HQ: Usa Waste Of California, Inc.
11931 Foundation Pl # 200
Gold River CA 95670
916 387-1400

(P-6578)
USA WASTE OF CALIFORNIA INC
Also Called: Waste Management
11240 Commercial Pkwy, Castroville (95012-3206)
P.O. Box 1306 (95012-1306)
PHONE..................831 633-7878
Richard Legett, *Manager*
Ginger Kaladas, *Credit Staff*
Joseph Juntado, *Manager*
EMP: 150
SALES (corp-wide): 12.9B **Publicly Held**
WEB: www.wastebusinessjournal.com
SIC: **4953** Rubbish collection & disposal
HQ: Usa Waste Of California, Inc.
11931 Foundation Pl # 200
Gold River CA 95670
916 387-1400

(P-6579)
USA WASTE OF CALIFORNIA INC
Also Called: Waste Management
13970 Live Oak Ave, Baldwin Park (91706-1321)
PHONE..................626 856-1285
Fax: 626 814-1955
Richard Schackel, *Director*
Ryan Unmack, *Project Mgr*
Lee Hicks, *Contract Law*
EMP: 100
SALES (corp-wide): 12.9B **Publicly Held**
SIC: **4953** Garbage: collecting, destroying & processing
HQ: Usa Waste Of California, Inc.
11931 Foundation Pl # 200
Gold River CA 95670
916 387-1400

(P-6580)
USA WASTE OF CALIFORNIA INC
Also Called: Waste Management
8740 Pueblo Ave Ste B, Atascadero (93422-4605)
PHONE..................805 466-3636
Randi Rebhan, *Branch Mgr*
Lee Hicks, *Contract Law*
Tina Arvin, *Supervisor*
EMP: 100
SALES (corp-wide): 12.9B **Publicly Held**
SIC: **4953** Refuse collection & disposal services
HQ: Usa Waste Of California, Inc.
11931 Foundation Pl # 200
Gold River CA 95670
916 387-1400

(P-6581)
USA WASTE OF CALIFORNIA INC
Also Called: Waste Management
1001 W Bradley Ave, El Cajon (92020-1501)
PHONE..................619 596-5117
Paul Pistono, *Vice Pres*
Lee Hicks, *Contract Law*
EMP: 100
SALES (corp-wide): 12.9B **Publicly Held**
SIC: **4953** Refuse systems

HQ: Usa Waste Of California, Inc.
11931 Foundation Pl # 200
Gold River CA 95670
916 387-1400

(P-6582)
USA WASTE OF CALIFORNIA INC
Also Called: Waste Management
13793 Redwood St, Chino (91710-5506)
PHONE..................909 590-1793
Steve Kanow, *Director*
Lee Hicks, *Contract Law*
EMP: 100
SALES (corp-wide): 12.9B **Publicly Held**
SIC: **4953** Refuse systems
HQ: Usa Waste Of California, Inc.
11931 Foundation Pl # 200
Gold River CA 95670
916 387-1400

(P-6583)
USA WASTE OF CALIFORNIA INC
Also Called: Fresno Hauling
4333 E Jefferson Ave, Fresno (93725-9707)
PHONE..................559 834-9151
Fax: 559 834-3751
Paul Pistono, *Vice Pres*
Lee Hicks, *Contract Law*
Charlie Franklin, *Manager*
Jerry Murphy, *Manager*
EMP: 100
SALES (corp-wide): 12.9B **Publicly Held**
SIC: **4953** Refuse systems
HQ: Usa Waste Of California, Inc.
11931 Foundation Pl # 200
Gold River CA 95670
916 387-1400

(P-6584)
USA WASTE OF CALIFORNIA INC
Also Called: La Metro Hauling
1970 E 213th St, Long Beach (90810-1201)
PHONE..................310 830-7100
Ed King, *Manager*
Maria Diaz, *Human Resources*
Lee Hicks, *Contract Law*
EMP: 100
SALES (corp-wide): 12.9B **Publicly Held**
SIC: **4953** Refuse systems
HQ: Usa Waste Of California, Inc.
11931 Foundation Pl # 200
Gold River CA 95670
916 387-1400

(P-6585)
USA WASTE OF CALIFORNIA INC
Also Called: Compton Hauling
407 E El Segundo Blvd, Compton (90222-2316)
PHONE..................310 763-8500
Hovseb Shadarevian, *Branch Mgr*
Maureen Vardagesyan, *MIS Mgr*
Lee Hicks, *Contract Law*
EMP: 100
SALES (corp-wide): 12.9B **Publicly Held**
SIC: **4953** Refuse systems
HQ: Usa Waste Of California, Inc.
11931 Foundation Pl # 200
Gold River CA 95670
916 387-1400

(P-6586)
USA WASTE OF CALIFORNIA INC
Also Called: Paradise Solid Waste
951 American Way, Paradise (95969-6315)
PHONE..................530 877-2777
Fax: 530 877-6534
Bill Mannel, *General Mgr*
Doug Speicher, *General Mgr*
Ron Law, *Controller*
Lee Hicks, *Contract Law*
EMP: 100
SALES (corp-wide): 12.9B **Publicly Held**
SIC: **4953** Refuse systems
HQ: Usa Waste Of California, Inc.
11931 Foundation Pl # 200
Gold River CA 95670
916 387-1400

(P-6587)
USA WASTE OF CALIFORNIA INC
Also Called: Salinas Disposal Service
1120 Madison Ln, Salinas (93907-1818)
PHONE..................831 754-2500
Jan McCombs, *Branch Mgr*
Lee Hicks, *Contract Law*
Karla Guerrero, *Manager*
EMP: 93
SALES (corp-wide): 12.9B **Publicly Held**
SIC: **4953** Refuse systems
HQ: Usa Waste Of California, Inc.
11931 Foundation Pl # 200
Gold River CA 95670
916 387-1400

(P-6588)
USA WASTE OF CALIFORNIA INC
Also Called: Fresno Hauling
10725 W Goshen Ave, Visalia (93291-9496)
P.O. Box 541065, Los Angeles (90054-1065)
PHONE..................559 834-4070
Kurt Nielson, *Branch Mgr*
Lee Hicks, *Contract Law*
EMP: 100
SALES (corp-wide): 12.9B **Publicly Held**
SIC: **4953** Refuse systems
HQ: Usa Waste Of California, Inc.
11931 Foundation Pl # 200
Gold River CA 95670
916 387-1400

(P-6589)
USA WASTE OF CALIFORNIA INC
Also Called: Santa Clarita Hauling/Blue
25772 Springbrook Ave, Santa Clarita (91350-2563)
PHONE..................661 259-2398
Lee Hicks, *Contract Law*
EMP: 100
SALES (corp-wide): 12.9B **Publicly Held**
SIC: **4953** Refuse systems
HQ: Usa Waste Of California, Inc.
11931 Foundation Pl # 200
Gold River CA 95670
916 387-1400

(P-6590)
USA WASTE OF CALIFORNIA INC
Also Called: Waste Management Orange County
1800 S Grand Ave, Santa Ana (92705-4800)
PHONE..................714 637-3010
Fax: 714 568-6626
Jeremiah Gilliam, *Accounts Mgr*
Kurt Shrum, *Administration*
Bill Higginbotham, *Controller*
Jill Harrison, *Human Res Mgr*
Mark Oliver, *Marketing Staff*
EMP: 74
SALES (corp-wide): 12.9B **Publicly Held**
SIC: **4953** Refuse systems
HQ: Usa Waste Of California, Inc.
11931 Foundation Pl # 200
Gold River CA 95670
916 387-1400

(P-6591)
USA WASTE OF CALIFORNIA INC
Also Called: Salinas Disposal Service
29331 Pacific St, Hayward (94544-6017)
PHONE..................831 384-5000
Paul Pistono, *Branch Mgr*
Lee Hicks, *Contract Law*
EMP: 100
SALES (corp-wide): 12.9B **Publicly Held**
SIC: **4953** Refuse systems
HQ: Usa Waste Of California, Inc.
11931 Foundation Pl # 200
Gold River CA 95670
916 387-1400

4953 - Refuse Systems County (P-6592)

(P-6592)
VALLEY GARBAGE RUBBISH CO INC
Also Called: Healtth Sanitation Services
1850 W Betteravia Rd, Santa Maria (93455-1065)
PHONE..................805 614-1131
Fax: 805 922-4716
Keith Ramsey, *Principal*
Becky Gipson, *Executive*
Ginger Kaladas, *Credit Staff*
Lee Hicks, *Contract Law*
Brenda Linza, *Manager*
EMP: 70
SQ FT: 3,000
SALES (est): 22.3MM
SALES (corp-wide): 12.9B **Publicly Held**
WEB: www.wm.com
SIC: **4953** Rubbish collection & disposal
PA: Waste Management, Inc.
1001 Fannin St Ste 4000
Houston TX 77002
713 512-6200

(P-6593)
VEOLIA ES WASTE-TO-ENERGY INC
Also Called: Montenay Pacific Power
100 Pier S Ave, Long Beach (90802-1039)
PHONE..................562 436-0636
Fax: 562 435-7825
Francois Screve, *Branch Mgr*
EMP: 70
SALES (corp-wide): 143.1MM **Privately Held**
SIC: **4953** Refuse collection & disposal services
PA: Veolia Es Waste-To-Energy, Inc.
1 Penn Plz Ste 4401
New York NY 10119
212 947-5824

(P-6594)
WARE DISPOSAL INC (PA)
1451 Manhattan Ave, Fullerton (92831-5221)
P.O. Box 8089, Newport Beach (92658-8089)
PHONE..................714 834-0234
Fax: 714 836-4697
Judith Helaine Ware, *CEO*
Ben Ware, *Vice Pres*
Jay Ware, *General Mgr*
Jason Rush, *Info Tech Dir*
Timmons Brad, *Sales Mgr*
EMP: 61
SQ FT: 48,900
SALES (est): 82.8MM **Privately Held**
WEB: www.waredisposal.com
SIC: **4953** Refuse systems

(P-6595)
WASTE CONNECTIONS CAL INC
301 Carl Rd, Sunnyvale (94089-1012)
PHONE..................408 752-8530
Todd Storti, *Manager*
EMP: 110
SALES (corp-wide): 106.4MM **Privately Held**
WEB: www.greenteam.com
SIC: **4953** Garbage: collecting, destroying & processing
PA: Waste Connections Of California, Inc.
1333 Oakland Rd
San Jose CA 95112
408 282-4400

(P-6596)
WASTE CONNECTIONS CAL INC (PA)
Also Called: Greenteam of San Jose
1333 Oakland Rd, San Jose (95112-1364)
PHONE..................408 282-4400
Fax: 408 283-8509
Paul Nelson, *Vice Pres*
Ron Mittelstaedt, *CEO*
Michael Harlan, *Exec VP*
Pual Nelson, *Vice Pres*
Greg Popovich, *Business Mgr*
EMP: 150
SQ FT: 6,000
SALES (est): 106.4MM **Privately Held**
WEB: www.greenteam.com
SIC: **4953** Garbage: collecting, destroying & processing

(P-6597)
WASTE MANAGEMENT CAL INC (HQ)
9081 Tujunga Ave, Sun Valley (91352-1516)
PHONE..................877 836-6526
Fax: 818 252-3231
David Steiner, *President*
Keith Schrumpf, *Area Mgr*
Andy Esser, *District Mgr*
Scott Slighting, *District Mgr*
Aaron Oedewaldt, *Project Mgr*
EMP: 230 EST: 1953
SQ FT: 35,000
SALES (est): 383.2MM
SALES (corp-wide): 12.9B **Publicly Held**
SIC: **4953** Garbage: collecting, destroying & processing; recycling, waste materials
PA: Waste Management, Inc.
1001 Fannin St Ste 4000
Houston TX 77002
713 512-6200

(P-6598)
WASTE MANAGEMENT CAL INC
1001 W Bradley Ave, El Cajon (92020-1501)
PHONE..................619 596-5100
Rex Buck, *Principal*
Ginger Kaladas, *Credit Staff*
Carl Scherbaun, *Opers Mgr*
Lee Hicks, *Contract Law*
EMP: 68
SQ FT: 2,000
SALES (corp-wide): 12.9B **Publicly Held**
WEB: www.wastebusinessjournal.com
SIC: **4953** Rubbish collection & disposal
HQ: Waste Management Of California, Inc.
9081 Tujunga Ave
Sun Valley CA 91352
877 836-6526

(P-6599)
WASTE MANAGEMENT CAL INC
1200 W City Ranch Rd, Palmdale (93551-4456)
P.O. Box 4040 (93590-4040)
PHONE..................661 947-7197
Carl McCarthy, *Manager*
Becky Ayala, *Financial Exec*
Ginger Kaladas, *Credit Staff*
Fred Valentino, *Human Res Mgr*
David Nesbitt, *Director*
EMP: 54
SALES (corp-wide): 12.9B **Publicly Held**
WEB: www.wastebusinessjournal.com
SIC: **4953** Rubbish collection & disposal
HQ: Waste Management Of California, Inc.
9081 Tujunga Ave
Sun Valley CA 91352
877 836-6526

(P-6600)
WASTE MANAGEMENT CAL INC
2141 Oceanside Blvd, Oceanside (92054-4405)
PHONE..................760 439-2824
Fax: 760 754-4109
John Lusignan, *Manager*
Walter Dabbs, *Info Tech Mgr*
Kirk Stauffer, *Opers Mgr*
Lee Hicks, *Contract Law*
EMP: 95
SQ FT: 4,500
SALES (corp-wide): 12.9B **Publicly Held**
SIC: **4953** 4212 Garbage: collecting, destroying & processing; local trucking, without storage
HQ: Waste Management Of California, Inc.
9081 Tujunga Ave
Sun Valley CA 91352
877 836-6526

(P-6601)
WASTE MGT COLLECTN & RECYCL
17700 Indian St, Moreno Valley (92551-9511)
PHONE..................951 242-0421
Scott Jenkins, *Manager*
Ginger Kaladas, *Credit Staff*
Julie Barreda, *Sales Executive*
Damon Defrates, *Manager*
EMP: 200

(P-6602)
WASTE MGT COLLECTN & RECYCL
5701 S Eastrn Ave Ste 300, Commerce (90040)
PHONE..................626 960-7551
Fax: 949 419-2629
Rick Decaiva, *Manager*
Ginger Kaladas, *Credit Staff*
Victor Moradian II, *Accountant*
Sylvia Granillo, *Buyer*
Richard Schackel, *Director*
EMP: 245
SALES (corp-wide): 12.9B **Publicly Held**
SIC: **4953** 4212 Rubbish collection & disposal; local trucking, without storage
HQ: Waste Management Collection And Recycling Inc
2050 N Glassell St
Orange CA 92865
714 282-0200

(P-6603)
WASTE MGT COLLECTN & RECYCL (HQ)
2050 N Glassell St, Orange (92865-3306)
PHONE..................714 282-0200
James Teter, *President*
Ray Burke, *Vice Pres*
John J Ray III, *Admin Sec*
Bert Young, *Info Tech Dir*
Ginger Kaladas, *Credit Staff*
EMP: 50
SALES (est): 447.3MM
SALES (corp-wide): 12.9B **Publicly Held**
SIC: **4953** Refuse systems
PA: Waste Management, Inc.
1001 Fannin St Ste 4000
Houston TX 77002
713 512-6200

(P-6604)
WASTE MGT COLLECTN & RECYCL
1340 W Beach St, Watsonville (95076-5122)
P.O. Box 2347 (95077-2347)
PHONE..................831 768-9505
Fax: 831 768-9901
James Moresco, *Branch Mgr*
Rini Van Every, *Info Tech Dir*
Ginger Kaladas, *Credit Staff*
EMP: 93
SALES (corp-wide): 12.9B **Publicly Held**
SIC: **4953** Refuse collection & disposal services
HQ: Waste Management Collection And Recycling Inc
2050 N Glassell St
Orange CA 92865
714 282-0200

(P-6605)
WASTE MGT COLLECTN & RECYCL
219 Pudding Creek Rd, Fort Bragg (95437-8136)
PHONE..................707 462-0210
Kaladas Ginger, *Branch Mgr*
Lee Hicks, *Contract Law*
EMP: 93
SALES (corp-wide): 12.9B **Publicly Held**
SIC: **4953** Refuse systems
HQ: Waste Management Collection And Recycling Inc
2050 N Glassell St
Orange CA 92865
714 282-0200

(P-6606)
WASTE MGT COLLECTN & RECYCL
16122 Construction Cir E, Irvine (92606-4498)
PHONE..................949 451-2600
Fidel Gutierrez, *Branch Mgr*

David Steiner, *CEO*
Joel Robledo, *Project Mgr*
Jose Loaiza, *Maintence Staff*
Lee Hicks, *Contract Law*
EMP: 93
SALES (corp-wide): 12.9B **Publicly Held**
SIC: **4953** Refuse systems; garbage collection & transport, no disposal
HQ: Waste Management Collection And Recycling Inc
2050 N Glassell St
Orange CA 92865
714 282-0200

(P-6607)
WASTE MGT COLLECTN & RECYCL
17700 Indian St, Moreno Valley (92551-9511)
PHONE..................909 242-0421
Lee Hicks, *Contract Law*
EMP: 93
SALES (corp-wide): 12.9B **Publicly Held**
SIC: **4953** Refuse systems
HQ: Waste Management Collection And Recycling Inc
2050 N Glassell St
Orange CA 92865
714 282-0200

(P-6608)
WASTE MGT COLLECTN & RECYCL
450 Orr Springs Rd, Ukiah (95482-3131)
PHONE..................707 462-0210
Lee Hicks, *Branch Mgr*
EMP: 93
SALES (corp-wide): 12.9B **Publicly Held**
SIC: **4953** Refuse systems
HQ: Waste Management Collection And Recycling Inc
2050 N Glassell St
Orange CA 92865
714 282-0200

(P-6609)
WASTE MGT OF ALAMEDA CNTY (HQ)
172 98th Ave, Oakland (94603-1004)
PHONE..................510 613-8710
Fax: 510 613-8754
Barry S Skolnick, *CEO*
Joe Zanardi, *Treasurer*
James C Fish Jr, *Exec VP*
James E Trevathan, *Exec VP*
Mike Howell, *Vice Pres*
EMP: 550
SALES (est): 270.8MM
SALES (corp-wide): 12.9B **Publicly Held**
WEB: www.wastebusinessjournal.com
SIC: **4953** Rubbish collection & disposal
PA: Waste Management, Inc.
1001 Fannin St Ste 4000
Houston TX 77002
713 512-6200

(P-6610)
WASTE MGT OF ALAMEDA CNTY
2615 Davis St, San Leandro (94577-2211)
PHONE..................510 638-2303
Jack Isloa, *Manager*
Cathy Ng, *Financial Analy*
Ginger Kaladas, *Credit Staff*
Minna Yu II, *Accountant*
Devon Ward, *Safety Mgr*
EMP: 100
SALES (corp-wide): 12.9B **Publicly Held**
WEB: www.wastebusinessjournal.com
SIC: **4953** 5093 Dumps, operation of; scrap & waste materials
HQ: Waste Management Of Alameda County, Inc
172 98th Ave
Oakland CA 94603
510 613-8710

(P-6611)
WASTE MGT OF ALAMEDA CNTY
800 S Temescal St, Corona (92879-2058)
PHONE..................909 280-5438
Alex Braicovich, *Manager*
Lynn Sisto, *Administration*
Robert Gisel, *Technical Staff*

PRODUCTS & SERVICES SECTION

4959 - Sanitary Svcs, NEC County (P-6632)

Ginger Kaladas, *Credit Staff*
Sherry Couba, *Controller*
EMP: 150
SALES (corp-wide): 12.9B **Publicly Held**
WEB: www.wastebusinessjournal.com
SIC: 4953 4212 Rubbish collection & disposal; local trucking, without storage
HQ: Waste Management Of Alameda County, Inc
172 98th Ave
Oakland CA 94603
510 613-8710

(P-6612)
WEST COUNTY RESOURCE RECOVERY
101 Pittsburg Ave, Richmond (94801-1201)
PHONE.................510 231-4200
Fax: 510 412-5880
Richard Granzella, *President*
Dennis Varni, *CFO*
Patricia Dilliam, *Accountant*
EMP: 50
SALES: 12.8MM
SALES (corp-wide): 9.1B **Publicly Held**
WEB: www.recyclemore.com
SIC: 4953 Non-hazardous waste disposal sites
HQ: Richmond Sanitary Service, Inc.
3260 Blume Dr Ste 100
Richmond CA 94806
510 262-7100

(P-6613)
WEST VALLEY MRF LLC
Also Called: West Valley M R F
13373 Napa St, Fontana (92335-2930)
PHONE.................909 899-5501
Richard Crockett, *General Mgr*
Kaiser Recycling Corporation,
West Valley Recycling Transf,
Richard Crocket, *Manager*
EMP: 120 **EST:** 1997
SQ FT: 65,000
SALES (est): 7.5MM **Privately Held**
SIC: 4953 4212 Refuse collection & disposal services; recycling, waste materials; local trucking, without storage

(P-6614)
WM HEALTHCARE SOLUTIONS INC
4280 Bandini Blvd, Vernon (90058-4207)
PHONE.................713 328-7350
David Steiner, *President*
Lee Hicks, *Contract Law*
EMP: 99
SALES (est): 4.5MM **Privately Held**
SIC: 4953 Refuse systems

(P-6615)
WM RECYCLE AMERICA LLC
Waste Management
8405 Loch Lomond Dr, Pico Rivera (90660-2508)
PHONE.................562 948-3888
Fax: 562 948-3297
Gary Lane, *Branch Mgr*
Ginger Kaladas, *Credit Staff*
EMP: 90
SALES (corp-wide): 12.9B **Publicly Held**
WEB: www.wm.com
SIC: 4953 Recycling, waste materials
HQ: Wm Recycle America, L.L.C.
1001 Fannin St Ste 4000
Houston TX 77002
713 512-6200

(P-6616)
ZANKER ROAD RESOURCE MGT LTD
Also Called: Zanker Road Landfill
675 Los Esteros Rd, San Jose (95134-1004)
PHONE.................408 457-1189
Scott Beal, *Manager*
Kellie Lopez, *Admin Asst*
Aaron French, *Sales Staff*
EMP: 90
SALES (corp-wide): 69.8MM **Privately Held**
WEB: www.greenwaste.com
SIC: 4953 Rubbish collection & disposal

PA: Zanker Road Resource Management, Ltd.
705 Los Esteros Rd
San Jose CA 95134
408 263-2385

(P-6617)
ZEREP MANAGEMENT CORPORATION
17445 Railroad St, City of Industry (91748-1026)
PHONE.................626 961-6291
Manuel Perez, *President*
Jesse Quintana, *Controller*
Stella Cortez, *Human Resources*
Christopher P Perez, *Agent*
EMP: 100
SQ FT: 4,000
SALES (est): 25.2MM **Privately Held**
SIC: 4953 4212 Refuse systems; local trucking, without storage

---

4959 Sanitary Svcs, NEC

(P-6618)
AMERICAN CHEM & SANI SUP INC
3800 E Miraloma Ave, Anaheim (92806-2108)
P.O. Box 6436 (92816-0436)
PHONE.................714 632-3010
Louis Salazar, *President*
Sylvia Salazar, *Office Mgr*
Monica Luna, *Human Res Dir*
Charlie Salazar, *VP Mktg*
Shirley Gower, *Accounts Mgr*
▲ **EMP:** 69
SQ FT: 19,000
SALES (est): 19.7MM **Privately Held**
SIC: 4959 2899 2842 Sanitary services; chemical preparations; specialty cleaning, polishes & sanitation goods

(P-6619)
AMPCO CONTRACTING INC
1540 S Lewis St, Anaheim (92805-6423)
PHONE.................949 955-2255
Andrew Pennor, *President*
Bill Vitta, *President*
Joe Ha, *Vice Pres*
Trung Joe Q Ha, *Vice Pres*
Michael King, *Vice Pres*
EMP: 220
SALES (est): 144.7MM **Privately Held**
SIC: 4959 1795 1794 Environmental cleanup services; wrecking & demolition work; excavation & grading, building construction

(P-6620)
CITY OF ANTIOCH
Also Called: Dept of Maintenance
1201 W 4th St, Antioch (94509-1005)
P.O. Box 5007 (94531-5007)
PHONE.................925 779-6950
Fax: 925 779-3003
Pat Scott, *Director*
Frank Palmeri, *Administration*
Willie Frashier, *Manager*
Phil Harrington, *Manager*
EMP: 100 **Privately Held**
WEB: www.ci.antioch.ca.us
SIC: 4959 9111 Sanitary services; mayors' offices
PA: City Of Antioch
200 H St
Antioch CA 94509
925 779-7055

(P-6621)
CITY OF CHINO
Also Called: Street Sidewalks St Tree Maint
5050 Schaefer Ave, Chino (91710-5549)
PHONE.................909 591-9843
Fax: 909 628-1444
Ed Nylund, *Principal*
EMP: 66 **Privately Held**
WEB: www.chinopd.org
SIC: 4959 Sweeping service: road, airport, parking lot, etc.
PA: City Of Chino
13220 Central Ave
Chino CA 91710
909 591-9824

(P-6622)
CITY OF LONG BEACH
Also Called: City Long Bch Prkg Enforcement
2929 E Willow St, Long Beach (90806-2303)
PHONE.................562 570-2890
Fax: 562 570-2875
James Kuhl, *Manager*
EMP: 250 **Privately Held**
WEB: www.polb.com
SIC: 4959 Sweeping service: road, airport, parking lot, etc.
PA: City Of Long Beach
333 W Ocean Blvd Fl 10
Long Beach CA 90802
562 570-6450

(P-6623)
CLEANSTREET
1937 W 169th St, Gardena (90247-5253)
PHONE.................310 329-3078
Jere Costello, *CEO*
Claudia Cervantes, *Executive*
Richard Anderson, *General Mgr*
Sharon Grant, *Executive Asst*
Jennie Gamboa, *Admin Sec*
EMP: 137
SQ FT: 15,000
SALES (est): 38.9MM **Privately Held**
WEB: www.cleanstreet.com
SIC: 4959 Sweeping service: road, airport, parking lot, etc.

(P-6624)
COUNTY OF MENDOCINO
Also Called: Transportation Dept
340 Lake Mendocino Dr, Ukiah (95482-9432)
PHONE.................707 463-4363
Howard Dashiell, *Director*
C R Campbell, *Manager*
EMP: 104 **Privately Held**
WEB: www.mcdss.org
SIC: 4959 1611 8741 Road, airport & parking lot maintenance services; highway & street construction; management services
PA: County Of Mendocino
501 Low Gap Rd Rm 1010
Ukiah CA 95482
707 463-4441

(P-6625)
COUNTY OF STANISLAUS
Also Called: Public Works Operations
1716 Morgan Rd, Modesto (95358-5805)
PHONE.................209 525-4130
Dave Nordell, *General Mgr*
Gary Hayward, *Manager*
EMP: 115 **Privately Held**
WEB: www.co.stanislaus.ca.us
SIC: 4959 Road, airport & parking lot maintenance services
PA: County Of Stanislaus
1010 10th St Ste 5100
Modesto CA 95354
209 525-6398

(P-6626)
ECOLOGY CONTROL INDUSTRIES
255 Parr Blvd, Richmond (94801-1119)
PHONE.................510 235-1393
Curtis Lindskog, *Manager*
EMP: 100
SALES (corp-wide): 41.2MM **Privately Held**
SIC: 4959 4953 4212 Environmental cleanup services; hazardous waste collection & disposal; hazardous waste transport
PA: Ecology Control Industries, Inc
20846 Normandie Ave
Torrance CA 90502
310 354-9999

(P-6627)
ENVIRONMENTAL PROTECTION AGCY
Also Called: E P A
1001 I St Ste 19b, Sacramento (95814-2828)
P.O. Box 4010 (95812-4010)
PHONE.................916 324-7572
Joan Denton, *Director*

Deborah L O'Jones, *Manager*
EMP: 55 **Publicly Held**
WEB: www.epa.gov
SIC: 4959 Toxic or hazardous waste cleanup
HQ: Environmental Protection Agency
1200 Pennsylvania Ave Nw
Washington DC 20460
202 272-0167

(P-6628)
GARYS CONSTRUCTION INC
2517 Dos Lomas, Fallbrook (92028-9159)
P.O. Box 189, Bonsall (92003-0189)
PHONE.................760 639-4456
Fax: 760 639-4458
Gary Albery, *President*
Tammy Albery, *Admin Sec*
EMP: 120
SQ FT: 1,200
SALES (est): 10.1MM **Privately Held**
SIC: 4959 1799 0782 Sweeping service: road, airport, parking lot, etc.; construction site cleanup; lawn & garden services

(P-6629)
GEM MOBILE TREATMENT SVCS INC (DH)
1196 E Willow St, Signal Hill (90755-3441)
PHONE.................562 436-2999
Steve Ragiel, *CEO*
Paul Anderson, *COO*
John Beale, *Vice Pres*
Steve Haskin, *Vice Pres*
Brian Baker, *Project Mgr*
◆ **EMP:** 50 **EST:** 1994
SQ FT: 11,912
SALES (est): 28.3MM
SALES (corp-wide): 56MM **Privately Held**
SIC: 4959 Environmental cleanup services
HQ: Gem Mobile Treatment Services, Inc.
2525 Cherry Ave Ste 105
Signal Hill CA 90755
562 595-7075

(P-6630)
JONSET CORPORATION
Also Called: Sunset Property Services
16251 Construction Cir W, Irvine (92606-4412)
PHONE.................949 551-5151
Fax: 949 551-4371
John Howhannesian, *President*
Carmen Howhannesian, *Admin Sec*
EMP: 96
SQ FT: 6,000
SALES (est): 12.8MM **Privately Held**
WEB: www.sunsetpropertyservices.com
SIC: 4959 7349 Sweeping service: road, airport, parking lot, etc.; janitorial service, contract basis

(P-6631)
NATIONAL PARKING CORPORATION
Also Called: National Parking & Valet
2560 Garden Rd Ste 109, Monterey (93940-5395)
PHONE.................831 646-0426
Fax: 831 646-0433
Robert Rosenthal, *Principal*
EMP: 130
SALES (est): 6MM **Privately Held**
SIC: 4959 1799 7521 Road, airport & parking lot maintenance services; parking facility equipment & maintenance; parking garage

(P-6632)
NRC ENVIRONMENTAL SERVICES INC (HQ)
1605 Ferry Pt Ste 200, Alameda (94501-7592)
PHONE.................510 749-1390
Steven Candito, *President*
Neil Challis, *Senior VP*
Mike Reese, *Senior VP*
Todd Roloff, *Senior VP*
Sal Sacco, *Senior VP*
▲ **EMP:** 80
SQ FT: 18,000

4959 - Sanitary Svcs, NEC County (P-6633)

SALES (est): 57.3MM
SALES (corp-wide): 127.4MM **Privately Held**
WEB: www.nrces.com
SIC: 4959 Toxic or hazardous waste cleanup; oil spill cleanup; environmental cleanup services
PA: National Response Corporation
3500 Sunrise Hwy
Great River NY 11739
631 224-9141

(P-6633)
PSC INDUSTRIAL OUTSOURCING LP
1802 Shelton Dr, Hollister (95023-9497)
PHONE..................................831 635-0220
William Fiedler, *Manager*
Jeannie Hubbs, *Opers Mgr*
Ryan Amodeo, *Transptn Dir*
EMP: 60 **Privately Held**
SIC: 4959 Environmental cleanup services
HQ: Psc Industrial Outsourcing, Lp
5151 San Felipe St # 1100
Houston TX
713 623-8777

(P-6634)
PW STEPHENS ENVMTL INC
3478 Investment Blvd, Hayward (94545-3811)
PHONE..................................510 782-9600
Art Ortiz, *Branch Mgr*
EMP: 93
SALES (corp-wide): 21.3MM **Privately Held**
SIC: 4959 Environmental cleanup services
PA: P.W. Stephens Environmental, Inc.
15201 Pipeline Ln Ste B
Huntington Beach CA 92649
714 892-2028

(P-6635)
RHO CHEM LLC (DH)
425 Isis Ave, Inglewood (90301-2076)
PHONE..................................323 776-6234
Fax: 310 645-6379
Ramon Robles, *CEO*
Sandra Chavez, *Manager*
▲ EMP: 50
SALES (est): 26.3MM
SALES (corp-wide): 2.9B **Publicly Held**
SIC: 4959 Sanitary services
HQ: Nortru, Llc
515 Lycaste St
Detroit MI 48214
313 824-5840

(P-6636)
RICHMOND SANITARY SERVICE INC (HQ)
Also Called: Crockett Garbage Service
3260 Blume Dr Ste 100, Richmond (94806-1960)
P.O. Box 4100 (94804-0100)
PHONE..................................510 262-7100
Fax: 510 222-7499
Richard Granzella, *President*
Dennis Varni, *CFO*
Mario Acquilino, *Vice Pres*
Pina Barbiere, *Principal*
Loyd Bonfante, *Principal*
▲ EMP: 200
SALES (est): 96.3MM
SALES (corp-wide): 9.1B **Publicly Held**
SIC: 4959 Sanitary services
PA: Republic Services, Inc.
18500 N Allied Way # 100
Phoenix AZ 85054
480 627-2700

(P-6637)
SACRAMENTO REG CO SANIT DIST (PA)
Also Called: Srcsd
10060 Goethe Rd, Sacramento (95827-3553)
PHONE..................................916 876-6000
Prabhakar Somavarapu, *Director*
Joe Maestretti, *CFO*
Phil Serna, *Principal*
Christoph Dobson, *Planning*
Jeremy Boyce, *Research*
EMP: 200 EST: 1973
SQ FT: 136,000

SALES (est): 316.5MM **Privately Held**
SIC: 4959 Sanitary services

(P-6638)
SACRAMENTO YOLO CNTY MOSQUITO
8631 Bond Rd, Elk Grove (95624-1477)
PHONE..................................916 685-1022
Fax: 916 685-5464
Raul Deanda, *President*
Vern Bruhn, *Vice Pres*
Jennifer Benito, *Executive*
Luz Rodriguez, *Executive*
Paula Macedo, *Lab Dir*
EMP: 51
SALES (est): 9.5MM **Privately Held**
WEB: www.sac-yolomvcd.com
SIC: 4959 Mosquito eradication

(P-6639)
SANITATION DISTRICT
920 S Alameda St, Compton (90221-4807)
PHONE..................................310 638-1161
Fax: 323 699-5422
Samuel Espinoza, *Manager*
Bill Balas, *Manager*
EMP: 100 **Privately Held**
SIC: 4959 9511 1623 Sanitary services; sanitary engineering agency, government; ; water, sewer & utility lines
PA: Sanitation District Of Los Angeles County District 2
1955 Workman Mill Rd
Whittier CA 90601
562 699-7411

(P-6640)
SULLINOVO
2750 Womble Rd Ste 100, San Diego (92106-6114)
PHONE..................................619 260-1432
Steven Sullivan, *Partner*
Scott Blount, *Partner*
Steven Bonde, *Partner*
EMP: 206
SALES (est): 5.1MM **Privately Held**
SIC: 4959 8744 Toxic or hazardous waste cleanup;

4961 Steam & Air Conditioning Sply

(P-6641)
TRI-STATE AG INC
Also Called: Priority Cooling
47375 W Dakota Ave, Firebaugh (93622-9516)
PHONE..................................209 364-6185
James M Hammonds, *President*
Mary H Hicks, *Treasurer*
William E Hammonds, *Vice Pres*
EMP: 82
SALES (est): 5MM **Privately Held**
SIC: 4961 Cooled air supplier

4971 Irrigation Systems

(P-6642)
ARVIN-EDISON WATER STORAGE DST (PA)
20401 E Bear Mtn Blvd, Arvin (93203)
P.O. Box 175 (93203-0175)
PHONE..................................661 854-4573
Fax: 661 854-5213
Howard Frick, *President*
John C Moore, *Corp Secy*
Salvadore Giumarra, *Vice Pres*
Christy Kong, *Accountant*
EMP: 50
SQ FT: 5,000
SALES (est): 17.7MM **Privately Held**
SIC: 4971 Water distribution or supply systems for irrigation

(P-6643)
FRESNO IRRIGATION DISTRICT
2907 S Maple Ave, Fresno (93725-2218)
PHONE..................................559 233-7161
Fax: 559 233-8227
Gary R Serrato, *General Mgr*
Deann Hailey, *CFO*
Julio Padilla, *Engineer*

Laurence Kimura, *Manager*
Robert Mount, *Manager*
EMP: 83
SQ FT: 18,000
SALES (est): 16.4MM **Privately Held**
WEB: www.fresnoirrigation.com
SIC: 4971 Water distribution or supply systems for irrigation

(P-6644)
IMPERIAL IRRIGATION DISTRICT
Also Called: Imperial Irrgtion Dst Wtr Dept
333 E Barioni Blvd, Imperial (92251-1773)
P.O. Box 937 (92251-0937)
PHONE..................................760 339-9220
Robert McCullough, *Branch Mgr*
EMP: 400
SQ FT: 10,000
SALES (corp-wide): 995.5MM **Privately Held**
WEB: www.iidwater.com
SIC: 4971 Water distribution or supply systems for irrigation
PA: Imperial Irrigation District
333 E Barioni Blvd
Imperial CA 92251
800 303-7756

(P-6645)
MERCED IRRIGATION DISTRICT
3321 Franklin Rd, Merced (95348-9345)
PHONE..................................209 722-2719
Fax: 209 722-2512
Jarith Krause, *Manager*
Brian Kelly, *Senior Engr*
EMP: 160
SALES (corp-wide): 103.3MM **Privately Held**
WEB: www.mercedid.org
SIC: 4971 Water distribution or supply systems for irrigation
PA: Merced Irrigation District
744 W 20th St
Merced CA 95340
209 722-5761

(P-6646)
METROPOLITAN WATER DISTRICT
700 N Alameda St Ste 1, Los Angeles (90012-3353)
PHONE..................................213 217-6667
Ronald Gastelum, *CEO*
EMP: 1000
SALES (corp-wide): 1.5B **Privately Held**
WEB: www.mwdh2o.com
SIC: 4971 Water distribution or supply systems for irrigation
PA: The Metropolitan Water District Of Southern California
700 N Alameda St
Los Angeles CA 90012
213 217-6000

(P-6647)
METROPOLITAN WATER DISTRICT
2300 Palos Verdes Dr N, Rllng HLS Est (90274-4222)
PHONE..................................310 832-6106
Dave Rendon, *Manager*
EMP: 2000
SALES (corp-wide): 1.5B **Privately Held**
WEB: www.mwdh2o.com
SIC: 4971 Impounding reservoir, irrigation
PA: The Metropolitan Water District Of Southern California
700 N Alameda St
Los Angeles CA 90012
213 217-6000

(P-6648)
MOTOIR LTD
Also Called: Motorola Irrigation
23272 Mill Creek Dr, Laguna Hills (92652-1641)
PHONE..................................949 552-6552
Eric Schmidt, *COO*
Jimmy Nikitaridis, *Sales Staff*
Jordan Hirschmann, *Director*
EMP: 120
SALES: 28MM **Privately Held**
SIC: 4971 5049 Water distribution or supply systems for irrigation; engineers' equipment & supplies

(P-6649)
NEVADA IRRIGATION DISTRICT (PA)
Also Called: N I D
1036 W Main St, Grass Valley (95945-5424)
PHONE..................................530 273-6185
Fax: 530 222-4102
Remleh Scherzinger, *General Mgr*
John H Drew, *President*
Keane Sommers, *CEO*
Teresita Andrews, *Treasurer*
Marie Owens, *Treasurer*
▲ EMP: 160
SQ FT: 11,050
SALES: 43.2MM **Privately Held**
SIC: 4971 4911 Irrigation systems; generation, electric power

(P-6650)
OAK SPRINGS NURSERY INC
13761 Eldridge Ave, Sylmar (91342-1764)
P.O. Box 922906 (91392-2906)
PHONE..................................818 367-5832
Manuel Cacho, *President*
Fred Siegler, *Contractor*
EMP: 90
SALES (est): 10.3MM **Privately Held**
SIC: 4971 0781 Irrigation systems; landscape services

(P-6651)
PALO VERDE IRRIGATION DISTRICT
180 W 14th Ave, Blythe (92225-2714)
PHONE..................................760 922-3144
Fax: 760 922-8294
Ed Smith, *General Mgr*
Janice Love, *Treasurer*
Kim Bishoff, *General Mgr*
Richard Gilmore, *General Mgr*
Tommy Hamby, *Administration*
EMP: 85 EST: 1923
SQ FT: 8,125
SALES (est): 13.2MM **Privately Held**
WEB: www.pvid.org
SIC: 4971 Irrigation systems

(P-6652)
SAN LUIS DLTA-MENDOTA WTR AUTH
15990 Kelso Rd, Byron (94514-1916)
PHONE..................................209 835-2593
Frances Mizuno, *Principal*
Dan Nelson, *Exec Dir*
Steve Larsen, *General Mgr*
Jim Lenhardt, *Planning*
Jeff Belwood, *Engineer*
EMP: 80
SALES (corp-wide): 31.3MM **Privately Held**
SIC: 4971 8611 Water distribution or supply systems for irrigation; public utility association
PA: San Luis & Delta-Mendota Water Authority
842 6th St
Los Banos CA 93635
209 826-9696

(P-6653)
SOLANO IRRIGATION DISTRICT
810 Vaca Valley Pkwy # 201, Vacaville (95688-8835)
PHONE..................................707 448-6847
Fax: 707 448-7347
Robert Hansen, *President*
Suzanne Butterfield, *Treasurer*
Guido E Colla, *Vice Pres*
Tracey Fortner, *General Mgr*
Cary Keaten, *General Mgr*
EMP: 99
SQ FT: 8,500
SALES (est): 23.2MM **Privately Held**
WEB: www.sidwater.org
SIC: 4971 Irrigation systems

(P-6654)
SOUTH SAN JQUIN IRRIGATION DST
Also Called: Ssjid
11011 E Highway 120, Manteca (95336-9751)
P.O. Box 747, Ripon (95366-0747)
PHONE..................................209 249-4600

PRODUCTS & SERVICES SECTION
5012 - Automobiles & Other Motor Vehicles Wholesale County (P-6673)

Fax: 209 249-4640
Betty Garcia, *Exec Sec*
Walt Luihn, *Officer*
Chris Whittenburg, *Division Mgr*
Robin Giuntoli, *General Mgr*
Jeff Shields, *General Mgr*
EMP: 93
SQ FT: 8,500
SALES: 13.1MM **Privately Held**
WEB: www.ssjid.com
SIC: 4971 Water distribution or supply systems for irrigation

(P-6655)
TURLOCK IRRIGATION DISTRICT
Also Called: T I D
901 N Broadway, Turlock (95380-3012)
P.O. Box 949 (95381-0949)
PHONE..............................209 883-8300
Fax: 209 656-2146
Larry Weis, *Branch Mgr*
Randy Baysinger, *General Mgr*
Casey Hashimoto, *General Mgr*
Kristi Kettgen, *Admin Asst*
Dave Arounsack, *Sr Ntwrk Engine*
EMP: 400
SQ FT: 1,554
SALES (corp-wide): 329.7MM **Privately Held**
WEB: www.tid.com
SIC: 4971 Impounding reservoir, irrigation; water distribution or supply systems for irrigation
PA: Turlock Irrigation District
  333 E Canal Dr
  Turlock CA 95380
  209 883-8222

(P-6656)
VISTA IRRIGATION DISTRICT
Also Called: Vid
1391 Engineer St, Vista (92081-8836)
PHONE..............................760 597-3100
Fax: 760 598-8757
John Amodeo, *General Mgr*
Eldon Boone, *CFO*
Phil Zamora, *Executive*
Roy Coox, *General Mgr*
Sherry Jorgenson, *Executive Asst*
EMP: 99
SQ FT: 2,500
SALES: 46.6MM **Privately Held**
WEB: www.vid-h2o.org
SIC: 4971 Water distribution or supply systems for irrigation

---
5012 Automobiles & Other Motor Vehicles Wholesale

(P-6657)
A-Z BUS SALES INC (PA)
Also Called: John Deere Authorized Dealer
1900 S Riverside Ave, Colton (92324-3344)
PHONE..............................951 781-7188
Fax: 951 781-4905
James Reynolds, *President*
Andy Anderson, *CFO*
Rubi Cody, *Admin Asst*
Rubi Lawson, *Admin Asst*
Barbara Hileman, *Human Resources*
▼ **EMP:** 90
SQ FT: 20,000
SALES: 3.9MM **Privately Held**
WEB: www.a-zbus.com
SIC: 5012 5082 Buses; construction & mining machinery

(P-6658)
ABC BUS INC
1485 Dale Way, Costa Mesa (92626-3918)
PHONE..............................714 444-5888
Dane Cornell, *CEO*
Ryan McElvaney, *Sales Mgr*
EMP: 57
SALES (corp-wide): 194.7MM **Privately Held**
SIC: 5012 4173 Automobiles & other motor vehicles; bus terminal & service facilities
HQ: Abc Bus, Inc.
  1506 30th St Nw
  Faribault MN 55021
  507 334-1871

(P-6659)
ABC BUS INC
3508 Haven Ave, Redwood City (94063-4603)
PHONE..............................650 368-3364
Ken Montalvo, *Manager*
EMP: 57
SALES (corp-wide): 194.7MM **Privately Held**
SIC: 5012 4173 Automobiles & other motor vehicles; bus terminal & service facilities
HQ: Abc Bus, Inc.
  1506 30th St Nw
  Faribault MN 55021
  507 334-1871

(P-6660)
ADESA CORPORATION LLC
Also Called: Adesa Auction
8649 Kiefer Blvd, Sacramento (95826-3907)
PHONE..............................916 388-8899
Fax: 916 388-0838
Jim Sale, *Branch Mgr*
Carol Sewell, *Vice Pres*
Raymond Klingaman, *General Mgr*
Raymond Killingaman, *Info Tech Mgr*
Jennifer Coulter, *Sls & Mktg Exec*
EMP: 115
SALES (corp-wide): 2.6B **Publicly Held**
WEB: www.adesa.com
SIC: 5012 Automobile auction
HQ: Adesa Corporation, Llc
  13085 Hamilton Crossing B
  Carmel IN 46032
  317 249-4550

(P-6661)
ADESA CORPORATION LLC
11625 Nino Way, Mira Loma (91752-1437)
PHONE..............................951 361-9400
Fax: 951 361-0683
Scott Spalder, *Manager*
Stephen Spinola, *Network Enginr*
Lora Rivera, *Human Res Dir*
Elaine Ramirez, *Marketing Staff*
Jeff Hyde, *Manager*
EMP: 50
SALES (corp-wide): 2.6B **Publicly Held**
WEB: www.adesa.com
SIC: 5012 7549 Automobile auction; automotive maintenance services
HQ: Adesa Corporation, Llc
  13085 Hamilton Crossing B
  Carmel IN 46032
  317 249-4550

(P-6662)
ADESA CORPORATION LLC
2175 Cactus Rd, San Diego (92154-8002)
PHONE..............................619 661-5565
Fax: 619 661-5570
Dale McIlroy, *Manager*
Barry Fabricant, *General Mgr*
Jose Hyoro, *Mktg Dir*
Daryl Ravenscraft, *Marketing Staff*
Dale Mc Ilroy, *Manager*
EMP: 120
SALES (corp-wide): 2.6B **Publicly Held**
WEB: www.adesa.com
SIC: 5012 5521 Automobile auction; used car dealers
HQ: Adesa Corporation, Llc
  13085 Hamilton Crossing B
  Carmel IN 46032
  317 249-4550

(P-6663)
AICHINGER INTERNATIONAL INC
5423 Littlebow Rd, Pls Vrds Pnsl (90275-2364)
PHONE..............................310 375-1533
Hans Aichinger, *President*
EMP: 70
SALES (est): 2.9MM **Privately Held**
SIC: 5012 Automobiles

(P-6664)
AMERICAN HONDA MOTOR CO INC (HQ)
1919 Torrance Blvd, Torrance (90501-2722)
P.O. Box 2200 (90509-2200)
PHONE..............................310 783-2000
Fax: 310 781-4270
Takuji Yamada, *CEO*
Takanobu Ito, *President*
Satoshi Aoki, *COO*
Steve Brandon, *COO*
Steve Mortimer, *COO*
◆ **EMP:** 2375 EST: 1959
SALES (est): 13.3B
SALES (corp-wide): 124.7B **Privately Held**
WEB: www.honda.com
SIC: 5012 3732 Automobiles; jet skis
PA: Honda Motor Co., Ltd.
  2-1-1, Minamiaoyama
  Minato-Ku TKY 107-0
  334 231-111

(P-6665)
AQUIRECORPS NORWALK AUTO AUCTN
12405 Rosecrans Ave, Norwalk (90650-5056)
PHONE..............................562 864-7464
Fax: 562 863-2776
Rj Romero, *Ch of Bd*
Lou Rudich, *COO*
Steve Fleurant, *CFO*
Valerie Romero, *Vice Pres*
Chuck Doskow, *Admin Sec*
EMP: 125
SQ FT: 55,000
SALES (est): 26.7MM **Privately Held**
WEB: www.norwalkautoauction.com
SIC: 5012 Automobile auction

(P-6666)
CALIFRNIA AUTO DALERS EXCH LLC
Also Called: Riverside Auto Auction
1320 N Tustin Ave, Anaheim (92807-1619)
PHONE..............................714 996-2400
Fax: 714 985-8344
Tim Van Dam, *General Mgr*
Carlos Quichocho, *Info Tech Dir*
EMP: 400
SALES (est): 65.8MM
SALES (corp-wide): 33.6B **Privately Held**
WEB: www.riversideautoauction.com
SIC: 5012 Automobile auction
HQ: Manheim Investments, Inc.
  6205 Peachtree Dunwoody Rd
  Atlanta GA 30328
  678 645-0000

(P-6667)
COAST COUNTIES TRUCK & EQP CO
Also Called: Coast Counties Peterbilt
260 Doolittle Dr, San Leandro (94577-1014)
PHONE..............................510 568-6933
Fax: 510 562-5564
Jon Wacker, *Branch Mgr*
EMP: 52
SALES (corp-wide): 72.6MM **Privately Held**
WEB: www.coastcounties.com
SIC: 5012 Automobiles & other motor vehicles
PA: Coast Counties Truck & Equipment Company
  1740 N 4th St
  San Jose CA 95112
  408 453-5510

(P-6668)
COX AUTOMOTIVE INC
Also Called: Los Angeles Auto Auction
8001 Garvey Ave, Rosemead (91770-2420)
PHONE..............................626 573-8001
Fax: 626 307-8283
Ed Pullen, *General Mgr*
Ivana Sifuentes, *Human Res Mgr*
EMP: 200
SALES (corp-wide): 33.6B **Privately Held**
WEB: www.manheim.com
SIC: 5012 5521 7389 Automobile auction; used car dealers; auctioneers, fee basis
HQ: Cox Automotive, Inc.
  3003 Summit Blvd Fl 200
  Brookhaven GA 30319
  404 843-5000

(P-6669)
COX AUTOMOTIVE INC
10700 Beech Ave, Fontana (92337-7205)
PHONE..............................404 843-5000
Russ Norrish, *Manager*
Jessica Albright, *Controller*
Glenn Terrell, *Manager*
EMP: 600
SALES (corp-wide): 33.6B **Privately Held**
WEB: www.manheim.com
SIC: 5012 5521 5531 Automobile auction; used car dealers; automotive accessories
HQ: Cox Automotive, Inc.
  3003 Summit Blvd Fl 200
  Brookhaven GA 30319
  404 843-5000

(P-6670)
COX AUTOMOTIVE INC
29900 Auction Ct, Hayward (94544-6914)
PHONE..............................510 786-4500
Tina Novoa, *General Mgr*
Mike Broe, *Vice Pres*
Della Dorn, *Office Mgr*
Nuno Vergas, *Info Tech Dir*
Cynthia Hall, *Financial Analy*
EMP: 500
SQ FT: 150,000
SALES (corp-wide): 33.6B **Privately Held**
WEB: www.manheim.com
SIC: 5012 Automobiles & other motor vehicles
HQ: Cox Automotive, Inc.
  3003 Summit Blvd Fl 200
  Brookhaven GA 30319
  404 843-5000

(P-6671)
COX AUTOMOTIVE INC
Also Called: Manheim Riverside Auto Auction
6446 Fremont St, Riverside (92504-1437)
PHONE..............................951 689-6000
Fax: 951 602-9043
Scott Hurst, *Manager*
Bill Nelson, *Manager*
EMP: 440
SALES (corp-wide): 33.6B **Privately Held**
WEB: www.manheim.com
SIC: 5012 7389 5531 5521 Automobile auction; auctioneers, fee basis; automotive accessories; automobiles, used cars only
HQ: Cox Automotive, Inc.
  3003 Summit Blvd Fl 200
  Brookhaven GA 30319
  404 843-5000

(P-6672)
COX AUTOMOTIVE INC
Also Called: Manheim San Diego
691 Calle Joven, Oceanside (92057)
PHONE..............................760 754-3600
Jill Scott, *Branch Mgr*
EMP: 290
SALES (corp-wide): 33.6B **Privately Held**
WEB: www.manheim.com
SIC: 5012 Automobiles & other motor vehicles
HQ: Cox Automotive, Inc.
  3003 Summit Blvd Fl 200
  Brookhaven GA 30319
  404 843-5000

(P-6673)
DEALIX CORPORATION
720 Bay Rd Ste 200, Redwood City (94063-2480)
PHONE..............................650 599-5500
Lee J Brunz, *CEO*
Samara Jaffe, *Vice Pres*
Hetal Shah, *Sr Software Eng*
Pankaj Goyal, *IT/INT Sup*
Prasad Wagle, *Engineer*
EMP: 135
SQ FT: 31,000

5012 - Automobiles & Other Motor Vehicles Wholesale County (P-6674)

PRODUCTS & SERVICES SECTION

SALES (est): 22.3MM **Publicly Held**
WEB: www.dealix.com
SIC: 5012 Automotive brokers
PA: Autobytel Inc.
18872 Macarthur Blvd # 200
Irvine CA 92612

(P-6674)
E M THARP INC (PA)
Also Called: Golden Peterbilt
15243 Road 192, Porterville (93257-8967)
PHONE 559 782-5800
Morris Tharp, *President*
Morris A Tharp, *President*
Mike Phillips, *Store Mgr*
Billy West, *Store Mgr*
Carol Tharp, *Admin Sec*
EMP: 97
SALES (est): 39.2MM **Privately Held**
SIC: 5012 5013 5511 5531 Trucks, commercial; truck parts & accessories; trucks, tractors & trailers: new & used; truck equipment & parts; recreational vehicle repairs

(P-6675)
FRESNO AUTO DEALERS AUCTION
278 N Marks Ave, Fresno (93706-1136)
PHONE 559 268-8051
Fax: 559 268-9491
Darryl Ceccolil, *President*
Raylene Mackey, *Accounting Mgr*
▼ **EMP:** 107
SQ FT: 15,000
SALES (est): 11MM
SALES (corp-wide): 33.6B **Privately Held**
SIC: 5012 Automobile auction
HQ: Manheim Investments, Inc.
6205 Pachtree Dunwoody Rd
Atlanta GA 30328
678 645-0000

(P-6676)
FRESNO TRUCK CENTER
2727 E Central Ave, Fresno (93725-2425)
P.O. Box 12346 (93777-2346)
PHONE 559 486-4310
Fax: 661 393-3368
Randy Moore, *Manager*
Jay Choi, *Executive*
Michael Belles, *Principal*
Lynn Pieper, *Sales Staff*
Doug Howard, *Director*
EMP: 80
SQ FT: 40,000
SALES (corp-wide): 179.4MM **Privately Held**
WEB: www.fresnotruckcenter.com
SIC: 5012 5511 7538 5531 Truck tractors; trucks, tractors & trailers: new & used; general truck repair; truck equipment & parts; truck tires & tubes
PA: Fresno Truck Center
2727 E Central Ave
Fresno CA 93725
559 486-4310

(P-6677)
FRESNO TRUCK CENTER
Also Called: Delta Truck Center
10182 S Harlan Rd, French Camp (95231-9647)
P.O. Box 20 (95231-0020)
PHONE 209 983-2400
Fax: 209 983-2444
John Gannon, *Manager*
EMP: 125
SALES (corp-wide): 179.4MM **Privately Held**
WEB: www.fresnotruckcenter.com
SIC: 5012 5013 7538 5531 Trucks, commercial; automotive supplies & parts; general automotive repair shops; truck equipment & parts; pickups, new & used; engines & parts, diesel
PA: Fresno Truck Center
2727 E Central Ave
Fresno CA 93725
559 486-4310

(P-6678)
GATEWAY AUTO SALES & LSG INC
Also Called: Gateway Auto Auction Group
3260 E Annadale Ave, Fresno (93725-1903)
PHONE 800 921-4336
Larry B Champagne, *President*
Jim Barrows, *Business Mgr*
EMP: 52
SQ FT: 4,000
SALES (est): 18.7MM **Privately Held**
WEB: www.champagnecars.com
SIC: 5012 Automobile auction

(P-6679)
HAAKER EQUIPMENT COMPANY (PA)
Also Called: TOTAL CLEAN
2070 N White Ave, La Verne (91750-5679)
PHONE 909 542-0800
Edward R Blackman, *CEO*
Randy Blackman, *President*
Edward C Haaker, *CFO*
John Haaker, *CFO*
Michelle Haaker, *Executive*
▼ **EMP:** 60
SQ FT: 50,000
SALES (est): 62.3MM **Privately Held**
SIC: 5012 5087 5999 Ambulances; cleaning & maintenance equipment & supplies; cleaning equipment & supplies

(P-6680)
HIGH ADRENALINE ENTERPRISES
Also Called: Contra Costa Powersports
1150 Concord Ave Ste 100, Concord (94520-5609)
PHONE 925 687-7742
Dave Antonson, *President*
EMP: 80 **EST:** 2009
SALES (est): 12.5MM **Privately Held**
SIC: 5012 Motorcycles

(P-6681)
INLAND KENWORTH (US) INC (HQ)
9730 Cherry Ave, Fontana (92335-5257)
PHONE 909 823-9955
Fax: 909 823-2004
Leigh Parker, *Chairman*
Jim Beidrwieden, *President*
William Currie, *CEO*
Les Ziegler, *CFO*
Mitch Casey, *Credit Mgr*
EMP: 105 **EST:** 1934
SQ FT: 60,000
SALES (est): 130.4MM
SALES (corp-wide): 452.3K **Privately Held**
WEB: www.inland-group.com
SIC: 5012 7538 5013 7513 Trucks, commercial; diesel engine repair: automotive; truck parts & accessories; truck rental & leasing, no drivers
PA: Inland Industries Ltd
2482 Douglas Rd
Burnaby BC V5C 6
604 291-6021

(P-6682)
INLAND KENWORTH (US) INC
500 N Johnson Ave, El Cajon (92020-3118)
PHONE 619 328-1600
EMP: 50
SALES (corp-wide): 452.3K **Privately Held**
SIC: 5012 Trucks, commercial
HQ: Inland Kenworth (Us) Inc.
9730 Cherry Ave
Fontana CA 92335
909 823-9955

(P-6683)
INSURANCE AUTO AUCTIONS INC
7245 Laurel Canyon Blvd # 5, North Hollywood (91605-3718)
PHONE 818 487-2222
Fax: 818 487-2402
Charles Sanders, *Manager*
EMP: 59
SALES (corp-wide): 2.6B **Publicly Held**
SIC: 5012 5531 5093 Automobile auction; automobiles; automotive accessories; automotive wrecking for scrap
HQ: Insurance Auto Auctions, Inc.
2 Westbrook Corporate Ctr # 1000
Westchester IL 60154
708 492-7000

(P-6684)
INTERSTATE TRUCK CENTER LLC (PA)
Also Called: Valley Peterbilt
2110 S Sinclair Ave, Stockton (95215-7556)
PHONE 209 944-5821
David T Morganson, *Mng Member*
Rick Coslett, *CFO*
Don Hoffman, *Info Tech Mgr*
Bill Dugo, *Marketing Staff*
John Barnes, *Sales Staff*
EMP: 100
SQ FT: 22,000
SALES (est): 82.5MM **Privately Held**
WEB: www.itctrucks.com
SIC: 5012 7513 Trucks, commercial; truck rental, without drivers

(P-6685)
JETWORLD INC
Also Called: Jetmore International
2656 Chico Ave, South El Monte (91733-1617)
PHONE 626 448-0150
Fax: 626 448-2816
Leo Lea Young Lee, *President*
Chen Li-Fun Lee, *Corp Secy*
EMP: 110
SQ FT: 5,000
SALES (est): 11.1MM **Privately Held**
WEB: www.jetworld.com
SIC: 5012 5065 5063 5999 Automobiles & other motor vehicles; security control equipment & systems; flashlights; alarm signal systems; automotive supplies & parts

(P-6686)
KAWASAKI MOTORS CORP USA (HQ)
26972 Burbank, Foothill Ranch (92610-2506)
P.O. Box 25252, Santa Ana (92799-5252)
PHONE 949 837-4683
Fax: 949 458-5600
Masatoshi Tsurutani, *President*
Richard N Beattie, *Officer*
Terunori Kitajima, *Executive*
Tom Leimkuhler, *Exec Dir*
Jim Bullard, *District Mgr*
◆ **EMP:** 400 **EST:** 1967
SQ FT: 40,000
SALES (est): 254.4MM
SALES (corp-wide): 13.1B **Privately Held**
SIC: 5012 5013 5084 5091 Motorcycles; motorcycle parts; engines, gasoline; boats, canoes, watercrafts & equipment
PA: Kawasaki Heavy Industries, Ltd.
1-1-3, Higashikawasakicho, Chuo-Ku
Kobe HYO 650-0
783 719-530

(P-6687)
LOS ANGELES TRUCK CENTERS LLC
Also Called: Los Angeles Freightliner
13800 Valley Blvd, Fontana (92335-5216)
PHONE 909 510-4000
Ricardo Flores, *Manager*
Dave Roberts, *Safety Dir*
Manuel Ocampo, *Foreman/Supr*
Robert McConnell, *Sales Associate*
Barbara Boardman, *Sales Staff*
EMP: 200
SALES (corp-wide): 72.5MM **Privately Held**
WEB: www.laflr.com
SIC: 5012 7538 5531 5511 Trucks, commercial; general automotive repair shops; automotive & home supply stores; new & used car dealers
PA: Los Angeles Truck Centers, Llc
2429 Peck Rd
Whittier CA 90601
562 447-1200

(P-6688)
MARATHON INDUSTRIES INC
Also Called: Marathon Truck Bodies
25597 Springbrook Ave, Santa Clarita (91350-2427)
P.O. Box 800279 (91380-0279)
PHONE 661 286-1520
Fax: 661 286-1533
Chad Hess, *President*
Roger K Hess, *Chairman*
Ramon Perez, *Safety Mgr*
Tom Garcia, *VP Sales*
John Baragan, *Sales Staff*
EMP: 145
SQ FT: 75,000
SALES (est): 25MM **Privately Held**
WEB: www.marathontruckbody.com
SIC: 5012 3713 Automobiles & other motor vehicles; truck & bus bodies

(P-6689)
MIRAMAR FORD TRUCK SALES INC
Also Called: NationaLease
6066 Miramar Rd, San Diego (92121-2591)
PHONE 858 450-0707
Fax: 858 450-1182
Michael Buscher, *President*
Michael Maury, *Corp Secy*
Richard Harrigan, *Vice Pres*
Karrie Charest, *Admin Sec*
Justin Brown, *Purch Mgr*
EMP: 74 **EST:** 1982
SQ FT: 22,000
SALES (est): 15.8MM **Privately Held**
WEB: www.miramartruck.com
SIC: 5012 5013 7513 Trucks, commercial; trucks, noncommercial; truck parts & accessories; truck rental & leasing, no drivers

(P-6690)
MOBIS PARTS AMERICA LLC (HQ)
10550 Talbert Ave Fl 4, Fountain Valley (92708-6031)
PHONE 786 515-1101
Yun Dong Park, *Mng Member*
Tae Hwan Chung, -
Beomseo Koo, -
Cathy Ryu, *Manager*
Daniel Tchui, *Associate*
▲ **EMP:** 90
SALES (est): 245.7MM
SALES (corp-wide): 16.7B **Privately Held**
SIC: 5012 Automobiles & other motor vehicles
PA: Hyundai Mobis Co., Ltd.
203 Teheran-Ro, Gangnam-Gu
Seoul SEO 06141
220 185-114

(P-6691)
NISSAN NORTH AMERICA INC
Nissan Division
1683 Sunflower Ave, Costa Mesa (92626-1540)
P.O. Box 5555 (92628-5555)
PHONE 714 433-3700
Fax: 714 433-3746
J E Connelly, *Branch Mgr*
Mike Davin, *Manager*
EMP: 150
SALES (corp-wide): 104.1B **Privately Held**
WEB: www.nissan-na.com
SIC: 5012 Automotive brokers
HQ: Nissan North America Inc
1 Nissan Way
Franklin TN 37067
615 725-1000

(P-6692)
NORMANDIN AUTO BROKERS
900 Cptl Expy Aut Mall, San Jose (95136-1102)
PHONE 408 266-2824
Louis Normandin, *Owner*
EMP: 80
SALES (est): 4.5MM **Privately Held**
SIC: 5012 Automobiles & other motor vehicles

▲ = Import ▼ = Export
◆ = Import/Export

PRODUCTS & SERVICES SECTION

5013 - Motor Vehicle Splys & New Parts Wholesale County (P-6715)

(P-6693)
SHIFT TECHNOLOGIES INC
2500 Market St, San Francisco
(94114-1915)
PHONE..................................415 800-2038
George Arison, *CEO*
I Arison Areshidze, *President*
Joel Washington, *CFO*
Katie Horne, *Principal*
EMP: 60 **EST:** 2013
SQ FT: 1,500
SALES (est): 21MM **Privately Held**
SIC: 5012 5511 Automotive brokers; automobiles, new & used

(P-6694)
SOUTH BAY AUTO AUCTION
13210 S Normandie Ave, Gardena
(90249-2208)
PHONE..................................310 719-2000
Rod Rentfrow, *Manager*
Jeffrey Quinn, *Manager*
EMP: 60
SALES (est): 9.9MM **Privately Held**
SIC: 5012 Automobile auction

(P-6695)
SSMB PACIFIC HOLDING CO INC (PA)
Also Called: Bay Area Kenworth
1755 Adams Ave, San Leandro
(94577-1001)
PHONE..................................510 836-6100
Harry Mamizuka, *President*
Thomas Parodi, *CFO*
Tom Bertolino, *Vice Pres*
Mike Lee, *Vice Pres*
Bruce Nobles, *Vice Pres*
EMP: 55 **EST:** 1942
SQ FT: 35,000
SALES (est): 165MM **Privately Held**
WEB: www.bayareakenworth.com
SIC: 5012 7699 Trucks, commercial; industrial truck repair

(P-6696)
SSMB PACIFIC HOLDING CO INC
20769 Industry Rd, Anderson
(96007-8703)
PHONE..................................530 222-1212
Glenn Reed, *Branch Mgr*
EMP: 52
SALES (corp-wide): 165MM **Privately Held**
SIC: 5012 Trucks, commercial
PA: Ssmb Pacific Holding Co Inc
1755 Adams Ave
San Leandro CA 94577
510 836-6100

(P-6697)
SSMB PACIFIC HOLDING CO INC
Also Called: Sacramento Kenworth
707 Display Way, Sacramento
(95838-3371)
PHONE..................................916 371-3372
Fax: 916 371-4612
Tom Bertolino, *Branch Mgr*
Bob Christensen, *Vice Pres*
EMP: 52
SALES (corp-wide): 165MM **Privately Held**
WEB: www.bayareakenworth.com
SIC: 5012 7538 5531 5511 Automobiles & other motor vehicles; general truck repair; truck equipment & parts; pickups, new & used
PA: Ssmb Pacific Holding Co Inc
1755 Adams Ave
San Leandro CA 94577
510 836-6100

(P-6698)
TRUECAR INC (PA)
120 Broadway Ste 200, Santa Monica
(90401-2385)
PHONE..................................800 200-2000
Chip Perry, *President*
Alice Fluker, *Senior Partner*
Adri Lewis, *Senior Partner*
Chris Shaw, *Senior Partner*
Jason Nierman, *Partner*
EMP: 50
SQ FT: 38,000
SALES: 259.8MM **Publicly Held**
WEB: www.zag.com
SIC: 5012 7299 Automobiles & other motor vehicles; automotive brokers; information services, consumer

(P-6699)
UTILITY TRAILER SALES OF S CA (PA)
15567 Valley Blvd, Fontana (92335-6351)
PHONE..................................909 428-8300
Paul F Bennett, *President*
Raymond Gonzalez, *Managing Dir*
Walter Figueroa, *Administration*
Stephen F Bennet,
Craig M Bennett,
EMP: 100
SALES (est): 38.3MM **Privately Held**
SIC: 5012 5013 5531 5561 Trailers for passenger vehicles; automotive supplies & parts; automobile & truck equipment & parts; travel trailers: automobile, new & used

(P-6700)
WAH HUNG INTL MCHY INC
800 Monterey Pass Rd, Monterey Park
(91754-3609)
PHONE..................................323 263-3513
Raymond Ng, *Manager*
Shirley Luo, *Accountant*
Jack L Schoellerman, *Agent*
EMP: 69
SALES (corp-wide): 33.8MM **Privately Held**
SIC: 5012 5521 Automobiles; automobiles, used cars only
PA: Wah Hung International Machinery, Inc.
1000 E Garvey Ave
Monterey Park CA 91755
626 307-9090

(P-6701)
ZERO MOTORCYCLES INC
380 El Pueblo Rd, Scotts Valley
(95066-4212)
PHONE..................................831 438-3500
Richard Michael Walker, *CEO*
Karl Wharton, *COO*
John Boroska, *CFO*
Curt Sacks, *CFO*
Jay Friedland, *Vice Pres*
▲ **EMP:** 95
SQ FT: 34,000
SALES (est): 82.8MM **Privately Held**
WEB: www.zeromotorcycles.com
SIC: 5012 Motorcycles

5013 Motor Vehicle Splys & New Parts Wholesale

(P-6702)
1-800 RADIATOR & A/C (PA)
Also Called: 1-800-Radiator
4401 Park Rd, Benicia (94510-1124)
PHONE..................................707 747-7400
Fax: 707 747-7401
Mike Rippey, *Ch of Bd*
Joe Rippey, *President*
Niki French, *Business Dir*
Dennis Snyder, *Admin Sec*
Carlo Llanes, *Software Dev*
▲ **EMP:** 100
SALES (est): 70.8MM **Privately Held**
WEB: www.radiater.com
SIC: 5013 Radiators

(P-6703)
ALL STAR AUTOMOTIVE PRODUCTS
4150 Puente Ave, Baldwin Park
(91706-3497)
PHONE..................................626 960-5164
Fax: 626 962-1436
Fritz Ehlers, *President*
▲ **EMP:** 80
SQ FT: 28,000
SALES (est): 8.6MM **Privately Held**
WEB: www.allstarproducts.com
SIC: 5013 3714 3694 Automotive supplies & parts; clutches, motor vehicle; engine electrical equipment

(P-6704)
AMERICAN EAGLE WHEEL CORP (PA)
5780 Soestern Ct, Chino (91710-7020)
P.O. Box 1867 (91708-1867)
PHONE..................................909 590-8828
Fax: 909 590-4137
Ray Elbertse, *President*
Maria Furcolon, *Vice Pres*
Louis Garcia, *Manager*
▲ **EMP:** 300
SQ FT: 49,040
SALES (est): 209.3MM **Privately Held**
WEB: www.americaneaglewheel.com
SIC: 5013 Wheels, motor vehicle

(P-6705)
ANTHONY LAMBE
Also Called: Fashion Wheel
1521 W Nielsen Ave Ste 69, Fresno
(93706-1309)
PHONE..................................559 268-0709
Fax: 559 441-1803
Anthony Lambe, *Manager*
Jack Glos, *Owner*
EMP: 66
SQ FT: 25,000
SALES (est): 4.2MM **Privately Held**
WEB: www.steelband.com
SIC: 5013 Wheels, motor vehicle

(P-6706)
APU INC (PA)
14939 Oxnard St, Van Nuys (91411-2611)
PHONE..................................661 948-2880
Fax: 818 786-8158
John Christy Jr, *President*
EMP: 60
SQ FT: 20,000
SALES (est): 16.6MM **Privately Held**
WEB: www.apu.com
SIC: 5013 5531 Automotive supplies & parts; automotive parts

(P-6707)
APW INTERNATIONAL INC
1073 E Artesia Blvd, Carson (90746-1601)
PHONE..................................310 884-5003
Jae W Chang, *President*
Martha Ibarra, *Accountant*
▲ **EMP:** 140
SALES (est): 12.3MM **Privately Held**
SIC: 5013 Motor vehicle supplies & new parts

(P-6708)
APW KNOX-SEEMAN WAREHOUSE INC (HQ)
1073 E Artesia Blvd, Carson (90746-1601)
PHONE..................................310 604-4373
Fax: 310 604-5088
Tong Y Suhr, *CEO*
Susan Suhr, *Admin Sec*
Charles Yu, *Info Tech Dir*
Jorge Hidalgo, *Purch Agent*
Anabell Maradiaga, *Purch Agent*
▲ **EMP:** 98 **EST:** 1972
SQ FT: 32,000
SALES (est): 64.1MM
SALES (est): 65.6MM **Privately Held**
WEB: www.apwks.com
SIC: 5013 5531 Automotive supplies & parts; automotive parts
PA: Auto Parts Warehouse, Inc.
16941 Keegan Ave
Carson CA 90746
800 913-6119

(P-6709)
AUTO EXPRESSIONS LLC
505 E Euclid Ave, Compton (90222-2811)
PHONE..................................310 639-0666
Lawrence McIsaac, *President*
Blake Barnett, *CFO*
John Fiumefreddo, *Senior VP*
Steve Lazzara, *Senior VP*
▲ **EMP:** 100 **EST:** 2010
SALES (est): 22.4MM
SALES (corp-wide): 101.2MM **Privately Held**
SIC: 5013 Alternators
PA: Kraco Enterprises, Llc
505 E Euclid Ave
Compton CA 90222
310 639-0666

(P-6710)
AUTO PARTS WAREHOUSE INC (PA)
16941 Keegan Ave, Carson (90746-1307)
PHONE..................................800 913-6119
T Young Suhr, *President*
Sleung Ja Suhr, *Vice Pres*
Byung Joon Lee, *Admin Sec*
Charles Yu, *Information Mgr*
Mike Littrell, *Benefits Mgr*
▼ **EMP:** 50
SQ FT: 40,000
SALES (est): 65.6MM **Privately Held**
SIC: 5013 Automotive supplies & parts

(P-6711)
AUTOMOTIVE SUP CO SOUTHERN CAL (PA)
Also Called: Asco
10580 Mulberry Ave, Fontana
(92337-7024)
PHONE..................................909 428-9072
Fax: 909 428-2035
Chai Pong, *President*
Tig Wongthaweesap, *CFO*
▲ **EMP:** 65
SQ FT: 46,900
SALES (est): 19.8MM **Privately Held**
SIC: 5013 Automotive supplies & parts

(P-6712)
B&M RACING & PRFMCE PDTS INC (PA)
Also Called: B & M Racing
100 Stony Point Rd # 125, Santa Rosa
(95401-4117)
PHONE..................................707 544-4761
Fax: 818 700-3097
Brian Applegate, *President*
Steve Potter, *CFO*
Jonathan Miller, *Principal*
Debbie Haskell, *Accountant*
Bob Ritzman, *VP Mktg*
▲ **EMP:** 71 **EST:** 2000
SALES (est): 126.9MM **Privately Held**
WEB: www.bmracing.com
SIC: 5013 Automotive engines & engine parts; automotive supplies & parts

(P-6713)
BBK PERFORMANCE INC
Also Called: Gripp
27440 Bostik Ct, Temecula (92590-3698)
PHONE..................................951 296-1771
Brian Murphy, *President*
Ken Murphy, *Treasurer*
EMP: 75
SQ FT: 40,000
SALES (est): 9.1MM **Privately Held**
WEB: www.bbkperformance.com
SIC: 5013 5531 Automotive supplies & parts; automotive parts

(P-6714)
BIG O TIRES LLC (DH)
742 S Main St, Sebastopol (95472-4275)
PHONE..................................707 829-9864
Lawrence C Day, *Ch of Bd*
John B Adams, *President*
Timothy J Miller, *Treasurer*
Kelly A O'Reilly, *Vice Pres*
Steve Seffens, *Vice Pres*
◆ **EMP:** 80
SQ FT: 116,100
SALES (est): 59.7MM
SALES (corp-wide): 34.2B **Privately Held**
SIC: 5013 5531 5014 8742 Automotive supplies; automotive & home supply stores; automobile tires & tubes; truck tires & tubes; site location consultant; land subdividers & developers, commercial

(P-6715)
BMW OF NORTH AMERICA LLC
2201 Corporate Center Dr, Newbury Park
(91320-1421)
PHONE..................................909 975-7355
Scott Scholmer, *General Mgr*
EMP: 50

5013 - Motor Vehicle Splys & New Parts Wholesale County (P-6716)

PRODUCTS & SERVICES SECTION

SALES (corp-wide): 99B **Privately Held**
WEB: www.detroitbmw.com
SIC: 5013 Automotive supplies & parts
HQ: Bmw Of North America, Llc
300 Chestnut Ridge Rd
Woodcliff Lake NJ 07677
201 307-4000

(P-6716)
BMW OF NORTH AMERICA LLC
5900 Arcturus Ave, Oxnard (93033-9004)
PHONE 805 271-2400
Mark S Frazier, *Branch Mgr*
EMP: 50
SALES (corp-wide): 99B **Privately Held**
WEB: www.detroitbmw.com
SIC: 5013 Automotive supplies & parts
HQ: Bmw Of North America, Llc
300 Chestnut Ridge Rd
Woodcliff Lake NJ 07677
201 307-4000

(P-6717)
BMW OF NORTH AMERICA LLC
Also Called: B M W Of North America
5650 Arcturus Ave, Oxnard (93033-9009)
PHONE 805 271-2400
Fax: 805 271-2425
Salim Murr, *Sales Mgr*
Jan Ehlen, *Manager*
EMP: 100
SALES (corp-wide): 99B **Privately Held**
WEB: www.detroitbmw.com
SIC: 5013 Automotive supplies & parts
HQ: Bmw Of North America, Llc
300 Chestnut Ridge Rd
Woodcliff Lake NJ 07677
201 307-4000

(P-6718)
BRAKE PARTS INC LLC
711 S 3rd St, Chowchilla (93610-3502)
PHONE 559 665-5781
Ray Warner, *Manager*
Ray Padilla, *Human Res Dir*
Phyllis German, *Purchasing*
Justin Hand, *QC Dir*
Mark Holley, *Manager*
EMP: 110
SQ FT: 30,100
SALES (corp-wide): 600MM **Privately Held**
WEB: www.raybestosracing.com
SIC: 5013 Automotive brakes
HQ: Brake Parts Inc Llc
4400 Prime Pkwy
Mchenry IL 60050
815 363-9000

(P-6719)
BST ENTERPRISES INC
Also Called: Saddlemen
17801 S Susana Rd, Compton (90221-5411)
PHONE 310 638-1222
Thomas W Seymour, *CEO*
David Echert, *Treasurer*
John Baricevic, *Vice Pres*
Zulema Cruz, *Office Admin*
Teddi Jordan, *CTO*
▲ EMP: 65
SQ FT: 20,000
SALES (est): 19.4MM **Privately Held**
WEB: www.saddlemen.com
SIC: 5013 3751 Motorcycle parts; motor-cycle accessories

(P-6720)
CAL-STATE AUTO PARTS INC (PA)
Also Called: Auto Pride
1361 N Red Gum St, Anaheim (92806-1318)
PHONE 714 630-5954
Fax: 714 632-8637
Richard J Deblasi, *CEO*
John McMillin, *CFO*
Steven Brooker, *Vice Pres*
Luis Madrigal, *Info Tech Dir*
Douglas Mayes, *Info Tech Mgr*
EMP: 105
SQ FT: 76,000
SALES (est): 76.7MM **Privately Held**
WEB: www.csautoparts.com
SIC: 5013 Automotive supplies & parts

(P-6721)
CLUB ASSIST US LLC
Also Called: Battery Assist
888 W 6th St Ste 300, Los Angeles (90017-2729)
PHONE 213 388-4333
John Tutt, *President*
Stuart Davies, *CEO*
Brett Davies, *Chairman*
Darshan Tarikh, *Vice Pres*
Greg Schroeder, *VP Finance*
▲ EMP: 230
SQ FT: 17,000
SALES (est): 100MM
SALES (corp-wide): 15.1MM **Privately Held**
SIC: 5013 Automotive batteries
PA: Club Assist North America Inc.
3550 Wilshire Blvd # 650
Los Angeles CA 90010
213 388-4333

(P-6722)
COAST DISTRIBUTION SYSTEM INC (DH)
350 Woodview Ave Ste 100, Morgan Hill (95037-8105)
PHONE 408 782-6686
Fax: 408 782-7790
James Musbach, *CEO*
Sandra A Knell, *CFO*
David A Berger, *Exec VP*
Dennis A Castagnola, *Exec VP*
Dennis Castagnola, *Exec VP*
▲ EMP: 77 EST: 1977
SQ FT: 13,700
SALES: 118.8MM
SALES (corp-wide): 7.1B **Publicly Held**
WEB: www.coastdist.com
SIC: 5013 Motor vehicle supplies & new parts; trailer parts & accessories
HQ: Keystone Automotive Operations, Inc.
44 Tunkhannock Ave
Exeter PA 18643
570 655-4514

(P-6723)
CYTON INDUSTRIES INC
Also Called: Cytn
5558 Bill Cody Rd, Hidden Hills (91302-1101)
PHONE 818 999-3398
John Graham, *President*
Dean Graham, *Vice Pres*
EMP: 80
SQ FT: 1,000
SALES (est): 4.7MM **Privately Held**
SIC: 5013 Automotive supplies & parts

(P-6724)
DAE-IL USA INC
Also Called: Custom Crome
7227 W Sunnyview Ave, Visalia (93291-9639)
PHONE 559 651-5170
Fax: 559 651-2529
Robert Russell, *Director*
EMP: 69
SALES (corp-wide): 287.9MM **Privately Held**
SIC: 5013 Motorcycle parts
HQ: Dae-Il Usa, Inc.
155 E Main Ave Ste 150
Morgan Hill CA 95037
408 825-5000

(P-6725)
DENSO PDTS & SVCS AMERICAS INC (DH)
Also Called: Dsca
3900 Via Oro Ave, Long Beach (90810-1868)
PHONE 310 834-6352
Fax: 310 513-8597
Yoshihiko Yamada, *CEO*
Hisashi Matsunobu, *President*
Roy Nakaue, *Exec VP*
Peter Clotz, *Vice Pres*
Fran Labun, *Vice Pres*
◆ EMP: 153
SQ FT: 235,000
SALES (est): 187.5MM
SALES (corp-wide): 38.6B **Privately Held**
WEB: www.densorobots.com
SIC: 5013 7361 5075 3714 Automotive supplies & parts; employment agencies; warm air heating & air conditioning; motor vehicle parts & accessories
HQ: Denso International America, Inc.
24777 Denso Dr
Southfield MI 48033
248 350-7500

(P-6726)
DNA SPECIALTY INC
200 W Artesia Blvd, Compton (90220-5500)
PHONE 310 767-4070
James Choi, *President*
Alex Marquez, *Vice Pres*
Sun Choi, *Admin Sec*
Elizabeth Fernandez, *Accounting Mgr*
Eric Kim, *Purchasing*
▲ EMP: 90
SQ FT: 80,000
SALES (est): 24.4MM **Privately Held**
SIC: 5013 3714 Wheels, motor vehicle; wheels, motor vehicle

(P-6727)
E M ELECTRIC CO
14 Cypress St, San Francisco (94110-3951)
PHONE 415 315-3300
Paul Diaz, *President*
EMP: 70
SALES (est): 3.1MM **Privately Held**
SIC: 5013 Automotive engines & engine parts

(P-6728)
ELLIOTT AUTO SUPPLY CO INC
Also Called: Factory Motor Parts
448 W Katella Ave, Orange (92867-4604)
PHONE 800 278-6394
Fax: 714 490-6161
Mike Cote, *Manager*
EMP: 50
SALES (corp-wide): 424.1MM **Privately Held**
SIC: 5013 5015 Motor vehicle supplies & new parts; automotive parts & supplies, used
PA: Elliott Auto Supply Co., Inc.
1380 Corporate Center Cur
Eagan MN 55121
651 454-4100

(P-6729)
ELLIOTT AUTO SUPPLY CO INC
Factory Motor Parts
1600 E Orangethorpe Ave, Fullerton (92831-5231)
PHONE 310 527-2500
Fax: 310 768-8928
Rich Carol, *Principal*
EMP: 65
SALES (corp-wide): 424.1MM **Privately Held**
SIC: 5013 Motor vehicle supplies & new parts
PA: Elliott Auto Supply Co., Inc.
1380 Corporate Center Cur
Eagan MN 55121
651 454-4100

(P-6730)
FAST PRO INC
Also Called: Fast Undercar
2555 Lafayette St Ste 103, Santa Clara (95050-2644)
PHONE 408 566-0200
Fax: 408 566-0290
Brian Smits, *President*
Rob Matuzek, *Manager*
EMP: 60
SQ FT: 13,000
SALES (est): 15.4MM **Privately Held**
SIC: 5013 Automotive supplies & parts

(P-6731)
FORD MOTOR COMPANY
1269 Phoenix Dr, Manteca (95336-6006)
P.O. Box 1666, Richmond (94802-0666)
PHONE 209 824-6600
Fax: 510 231-4350
William Stewart, *Manager*
Rachel Varias, *Analyst*
George Steggal, *Human Res Dir*
Hank Glieden, *Director*
EMP: 220
SALES (corp-wide): 149.5B **Publicly Held**
WEB: www.ford.com
SIC: 5013 5531 Automotive supplies & parts; automotive parts
PA: Ford Motor Company
1 American Rd
Dearborn MI 48126
313 322-3000

(P-6732)
FOX FACTORY HOLDING CORP
750 Vernon Way Ste 101, El Cajon (92020-1979)
PHONE 619 768-1800
John Marking, *Branch Mgr*
EMP: 1219
SALES (corp-wide): 366.8MM **Publicly Held**
SIC: 5013 Springs, shock absorbers & struts
PA: Fox Factory Holding Corp.
915 Disc Dr
Scotts Valley CA 95066
831 274-6500

(P-6733)
GENUINE PARTS DISTRIBUTORS
Also Called: Tracy Industries
3737 Capitol Ave, City of Industry (90601-1732)
PHONE 562 692-9034
Tim Engball, *CEO*
Erma Tracy, *Vice Pres*
David M Rosenberger, *Admin Sec*
Lisa Schumacher, *Info Tech Dir*
Kim Edwards, *Human Res Mgr*
EMP: 75
SALES (est): 4.2MM
SALES (corp-wide): 27.3MM **Privately Held**
SIC: 5013 Automotive engines & engine parts
PA: Fred Jones Enterprises, L.L.C.
6200 Sw 29th St
Oklahoma City OK 73179
800 927-7845

(P-6734)
GOODRIDGE USA INC (DH)
529 Van Ness Ave, Torrance (90501-1424)
PHONE 310 533-1924
Fax: 310 618-0909
Celso Pierre, *CEO*
Nick Heathershaw, *Vice Pres*
Jamie Ramsden, *Vice Pres*
Michael Klapp, *Project Mgr*
Mark Hansen, *Engineer*
▲ EMP: 55
SQ FT: 15,000
SALES (est): 30.3MM
SALES (corp-wide): 391K **Privately Held**
WEB: www.goodridge.net
SIC: 5013 Automotive supplies & parts
HQ: Goodridge Limited
Dart Building
Exeter EX1 3
139 236-9090

(P-6735)
GREEN HILLS SOFTWARE INC (PA)
30 W Sola St, Santa Barbara (93101-2599)
PHONE 805 965-6044
Fax: 805 965-5163
Daniel O Dowd, *CEO*
Michael W Liacko, *President*
Daniel O'Dowd, *CEO*
Brad Jackson, *COO*
Jeffrey Hazarian, *CFO*
EMP: 105
SALES (est): 91.5MM **Privately Held**
WEB: www.ghs.com
SIC: 5013 Motor vehicle supplies & new parts

(P-6736)
HANSON DISTRIBUTING COMPANY (PA)
975 W 8th St, Azusa (91702-2246)
PHONE 626 224-9800

▲ = Import ▼ = Export
◆ = Import/Export

PRODUCTS & SERVICES SECTION
5013 - Motor Vehicle Splys & New Parts Wholesale County (P-6759)

Fax: 626 579-4053
Daniel L Hanson, *CEO*
Stephen Balman, *President*
Steven A Cox, *COO*
Jake Boggs, *Vice Pres*
Daniel L Hanson II, *Vice Pres*
EMP: 115
SQ FT: 160,000
SALES (est): 52.7MM Privately Held
WEB: www.HansonDistributing.com
SIC: 5013 Automotive supplies & parts

(P-6737)
HANSON DISTRIBUTING COMPANY
975 W 8th St, Azusa (91702-2246)
PHONE..................626 357-5241
Daniel L Hanson, *President*
EMP: 145
SALES (corp-wide): 52.7MM Privately Held
SIC: 5013 Automotive supplies & parts
PA: Hanson Distributing Company
975 W 8th St
Azusa CA 91702
626 224-9800

(P-6738)
HINO MOTORS MFG USA INC
4550 Wineville Ave, Mira Loma (91752-3723)
PHONE..................951 727-0286
Debra Martinas, *Branch Mgr*
EMP: 159
SALES (corp-wide): 242.7B Privately Held
WEB: www.hinointl.com
SIC: 5013 Truck parts & accessories
HQ: Hino Motors Manufacturing U.S.A., Inc.
37777 Interchange Dr
Farmington Hills MI 48335
248 442-9077

(P-6739)
IAP WEST INC
20036 S Via Baron, Rancho Dominguez (90220-6105)
PHONE..................310 667-9720
Michel Berg, *CEO*
Louis L Berg, *President*
Sharon Berg, *Admin Sec*
Tom Urbaniak, *VP Mktg*
S Balasubramaian, *Manager*
◆ EMP: 54
SQ FT: 80,000
SALES (est): 15.8MM Privately Held
SIC: 5013 Automotive engines & engine parts

(P-6740)
INTERAMERICAN MOTOR CORP (HQ)
Also Called: IMC
8901 Canoga Ave, Canoga Park (91304-1512)
P.O. Box 3939, Chatsworth (91313-3939)
PHONE..................818 678-6571
John Mosunic, *CEO*
Hanns Hederer, *Treasurer*
Winfred Baur, *Exec VP*
John Taillon, *Vice Pres*
James Loushin, *Area Mgr*
▲ EMP: 200 EST: 1962
SALES (est): 323MM
SALES (corp-wide): 10.1B Publicly Held
WEB: www.imcparts.com
SIC: 5013 5599 Automotive supplies & parts; dunebuggies
PA: Autozone, Inc.
123 S Main St
Memphis TN 38103
901 495-6500

(P-6741)
INTERSTATE BTRY SAN DIEGO INC
9345 Cabot Dr, San Diego (92126-4310)
PHONE..................858 790-8244
Fax: 858 271-6853
Ron Cummings, *President*
Michael Baker, *General Mgr*
EMP: 50
SQ FT: 20,000
SALES: 21MM Privately Held
WEB: www.battery.com
SIC: 5013 5531 Automotive batteries; batteries, automotive & truck

(P-6742)
JAMM MANAGEMENT LLC
Also Called: Fast Undercar Stockton
2447 Stanford Way, Antioch (94531-8249)
PHONE..................510 437-5200
Fax: 209 469-5055
Jose R Montilla,
Francisco Mendoza,
Richards Bullard, *Manager*
John Cabello, *Manager*
EMP: 50
SQ FT: 4,100
SALES (est): 5.4MM Privately Held
WEB: www.jammentgraphics.net
SIC: 5013 Automotive engines & engine parts

(P-6743)
KAY AUTOMOTIVE DISTRS INC (PA)
14650 Calvert St, Van Nuys (91411-2807)
PHONE..................818 781-6850
Fax: 818 778-1717
Jona Kardish, *President*
Jona Karadish, *President*
Annette Karadish, *Admin Sec*
Annette Kardish, *Admin Sec*
Joe Church, *Manager*
EMP: 50
SALES (est): 23.9MM Privately Held
WEB: www.kayauto.com
SIC: 5013 Automotive supplies & parts

(P-6744)
KNIESELS AUTO COLLISION CENTER
4680 Pacific St, Rocklin (95677-2406)
PHONE..................916 315-8888
Tom Kniesel, *Owner*
Kelli Kinesel, *Office Mgr*
EMP: 50
SALES (est): 2.7MM Privately Held
SIC: 5013 Body repair or paint shop supplies, automotive

(P-6745)
LAX WHEEL REFINISHING INC
1520 Spence St, Los Angeles (90023-3920)
PHONE..................323 269-1484
Fax: 323 269-1871
Jesus Sanchez, *President*
EMP: 60
SALES (est): 4.9MM Privately Held
SIC: 5013 Wheels, motor vehicle

(P-6746)
LEXANI WHEEL CORPORATION
2380 Railroad St Ste 101, Corona (92880-5471)
PHONE..................951 808-4220
Fax: 951 808-4230
Frank Hodges, *CEO*
Michael Kim, *General Mgr*
Carlos Parrott, *Marketing Mgr*
John Wallace, *Sales Mgr*
Crystal Porter, *Supervisor*
▲ EMP: 120
SQ FT: 35,000
SALES (est): 41MM Privately Held
SIC: 5013 Wheels, motor vehicle

(P-6747)
MERIDIAN RACK & PINION INC
6740 Cobra Way Ste 200, San Diego (92121-4102)
PHONE..................858 587-8777
Fax: 858 587-8778
Dara Greaney, *CEO*
Matt Glauber, *President*
Chris Struempler, *CFO*
Joe Donegan, *Technician*
▲ EMP: 130
SQ FT: 55,000
SALES (est): 78.3MM Privately Held
WEB: www.meridianautoparts.com
SIC: 5013 5961 Automotive supplies & parts; mail order house, order taking office only

(P-6748)
METROPOLITAN AUTOMOTIVE WHSE (PA)
Also Called: Auto Value
535 Tennis Court Ln, San Bernardino (92408-1615)
P.O. Box 1529 (92402-1529)
PHONE..................909 885-2886
Fax: 909 885-6374
John Spencer, *CEO*
Cheryl Kauffman, *Shareholder*
Richard Guyett, *COO*
Chuck Siemer, *CFO*
Pat Martin, *Vice Pres*
▼ EMP: 80
SQ FT: 60,000
SALES (est): 549.1MM Privately Held
SIC: 5013 Automotive supplies & parts

(P-6749)
MIKUNI AMERICAN CORPORATION (HQ)
Also Called: M A C
8910 Mikuni Ave, Northridge (91324-3403)
PHONE..................310 676-0522
Fax: 818 993-7387
Satoshi Fujimori, *President*
Hirokazu Masahashi, *CFO*
Masaki Ikuta, *Chairman*
Shigeru Ikuta, *Vice Pres*
Masayuki Uemura, *Executive Asst*
▲ EMP: 64
SQ FT: 50,000
SALES (est): 129.1MM
SALES (corp-wide): 836.4MM Privately Held
WEB: www.mikuni.com
SIC: 5013 5088 Automotive hardware; aircraft engines & engine parts; aircraft parts
PA: Mikuni Corporation
6-13-11, Sotokanda
Chiyoda-Ku TKY 101-0
838 330-392

(P-6750)
MYGRANT GLASS COMPANY INC (PA)
3271 Arden Rd, Hayward (94545-3901)
PHONE..................510 785-4360
Fax: 510 785-1724
Michael Mygrant, *CEO*
Cathy Mygrant, *Treasurer*
Kathy Mygrant, *Corp Secy*
Skip Linely, *Sales Staff*
▲ EMP: 50
SQ FT: 128,222
SALES (est): 217.9MM Privately Held
SIC: 5013 Automobile glass

(P-6751)
PARTS WAREHOUSE DISTRS INC
449 Littlefield Ave, South San Francisco (94080-6106)
PHONE..................650 616-4988
Larry Chew, *President*
Tomo Endo, *Treasurer*
Evans Chew, *Admin Sec*
Ebert Kan, *Opers Mgr*
EMP: 100
SQ FT: 40,000
SALES (est): 37.6MM Privately Held
SIC: 5013 Automotive supplies & parts

(P-6752)
PARTSCHANNEL INC
8905 Rex Rd, Pico Rivera (90660-3799)
PHONE..................562 654-3400
Alex Marquez, *Manager*
EMP: 50
SALES (corp-wide): 7.1B Publicly Held
SIC: 5013 Body repair or paint shop supplies, automotive
HQ: Partschannel, Inc.
4003 Grand Lakes Way # 200
Grand Prairie TX 75050
214 688-0018

(P-6753)
PDQ AUTOMATIC TRANSM PARTS INC
8380 Tiogawoods Dr, Sacramento (95828-5048)
PHONE..................916 870-6543
Fax: 916 681-7710
John G Hicks Jr, *President*
John Hicks Sr, *Treasurer*
Tracy Hicks, *Vice Pres*
Amy Hicks, *Admin Sec*
Jim Tuttle, *Purch Mgr*
▲ EMP: 62
SQ FT: 33,600
SALES (est): 19.7MM Privately Held
WEB: www.pdqparts.com
SIC: 5013 Automotive supplies & parts

(P-6754)
PILOT INC (PA)
Also Called: Pilot Automotive
13000 Temple Ave, City of Industry (91746-1416)
PHONE..................800 237-7560
Calvin S Wang, *CEO*
Juan Macias, *Traffic Mgr*
Anne Hsu, *Manager*
▲ EMP: 55
SQ FT: 407,600
SALES (est): 37.8MM Privately Held
WEB: www.pilotautomotive.com
SIC: 5013 Automotive supplies & parts

(P-6755)
PRESTIGE AUTOTECH CORPORATION
Also Called: Panther Custom Wheels
4975 Edison Ave, Chino (91710-5714)
PHONE..................909 627-6411
Fenton Liffick, *President*
Cathy Hung, *Controller*
▲ EMP: 50
SQ FT: 150,000
SALES (est): 10.3MM Privately Held
WEB: www.akuza.com
SIC: 5013 Wheels, motor vehicle

(P-6756)
QUALITY PLUS AUTO PARTS INC
1333 30th St Ste C, San Diego (92154-3486)
PHONE..................619 424-9991
Fax: 619 424-3031
Roger Yang, *President*
Jeffrey Shong Lowe, *Admin Sec*
Fernando Torres, *Buyer*
EMP: 50
SQ FT: 17,000
SALES (est): 8.5MM Privately Held
WEB: www.qualityplusauto.com
SIC: 5013 5531 Automotive supplies & parts; automotive parts

(P-6757)
RAMCAR BATTERIES INC
2700 Carrier Ave, Commerce (90040-2572)
PHONE..................323 726-1212
Fax: 323 727-6869
Clifford J Crowe, *President*
Carol Sullivan, *Cust Mgr*
Maxine Chinn, *Accounts Mgr*
▲ EMP: 50
SQ FT: 90,000
SALES (est): 17MM Privately Held
SIC: 5013 3691 Automotive batteries; lead acid batteries (storage batteries)

(P-6758)
RECYCLER CORE COMPANY INC
2727 Kansas Ave, Riverside (92507-2638)
PHONE..................951 276-1687
Fax: 949 276-8036
Ken Meier, *President*
Gisela Meier, *Corp Secy*
Robert Palmer, *Vice Pres*
Alan Hart, *General Mgr*
Marius Serban, *Human Resources*
▲ EMP: 100
SQ FT: 280,000
SALES (est): 39.3MM Privately Held
WEB: www.rccauto.com
SIC: 5013 Automotive supplies & parts

(P-6759)
RICHARD HUETTER INC
Also Called: Pacific Parts International
21050 Osborne St, Canoga Park (91304-1744)
PHONE..................818 700-8001

5013 - Motor Vehicle Splys & New Parts Wholesale County (P-6760)

Fax: 818 407-5100
Richard Huetter, CEO
Maria L Huetter, Treasurer
Jason Priest, Info Tech Mgr
▲ EMP: 70
SQ FT: 30,000
SALES (est): 14.2MM Privately Held
SIC: 5013 Automotive supplies & parts

(P-6760)
S F AUTO PARTS WHSE INC
Also Called: Mac Kenzie Warehouse
6000 3rd St, San Francisco (94124-3106)
PHONE................................415 255-0115
Fax: 415 865-1617
Michelle Menendez, President
Michelle Mackenzie Menendez, President
Anna-Maria Mac Kenzie, Treasurer
Eduardo Menendez, Exec VP
Jerry Vigil, Info Tech Mgr
EMP: 56 EST: 1951
SQ FT: 53,000
SALES (est): 24MM Privately Held
WEB: www.mackenziewarehouse.com
SIC: 5013 Automotive supplies & parts

(P-6761)
SCAT ENTERPRISES INC
1400 Kingsdale Ave, Redondo Beach (90278-3983)
PHONE................................310 370-5501
Fax: 310 214-2285
Philip T Lieb, President
Craig Schenasi, CFO
Joshua Garner, Graphic Designe
Trisha Condie, Human Resources
◆ EMP: 65
SQ FT: 42,000
SALES (est): 23.3MM Privately Held
WEB: www.scatenterprises.com
SIC: 5013 3714 Automotive supplies & parts; automotive supplies; motor vehicle parts & accessories

(P-6762)
SERRATO-MCDERMOTT INC
Also Called: Allied Auto Store
43815 S Grimmer Blvd, Fremont (94538-6348)
PHONE................................510 656-6233
Fax: 510 656-6890
Bill Bailey, CEO
Joe McDermant, Personnel Exec
Sue Monic, Manager
EMP: 55
SQ FT: 17,000
SALES (est): 22.5MM Privately Held
SIC: 5013 5531 Automotive supplies & parts; automotive parts

(P-6763)
SILLA AUTOMOTIVE LLC
7336 Laurel Canyon Blvd, North Hollywood (91605-3710)
PHONE................................818 902-0334
EMP: 52
SALES (corp-wide): 66.1MM Privately Held
SIC: 5013 Motor vehicle supplies & new parts
PA: Silla Automotive, Llc
1217 W Artesia Blvd
Compton CA 90220
800 624-1499

(P-6764)
SILLA AUTOMOTIVE LLC (PA)
Also Called: Silla Cooling System
1217 W Artesia Blvd, Compton (90220-5305)
PHONE................................800 624-1499
Tom Y K Hsuen, Mng Member
Wesley Sun, Info Tech Dir
Michael Shin, Purchasing
Annie Chun, Marketing Mgr
Erick Chapa, Sales Mgr
▲ EMP: 100
SALES (corp-wide): 66.1MM Privately Held
WEB: www.sillacooling.com
SIC: 5013 Radiators; exhaust systems (mufflers, tail pipes, etc.)

(P-6765)
SILLA AUTOMOTIVE LLC
1554 Juliesse Ave C-D, Sacramento (95815-1826)
PHONE................................916 929-2646
Fax: 916 929-2607
Irene Soria, Manager
EMP: 52
SALES (corp-wide): 66.1MM Privately Held
SIC: 5013 Motor vehicle supplies & new parts
PA: Silla Automotive, Llc
1217 W Artesia Blvd
Compton CA 90220
800 624-1499

(P-6766)
SILLA AUTOMOTIVE LLC
2833 W Pico Blvd, Los Angeles (90006-3910)
PHONE................................323 733-5027
EMP: 52
SALES (corp-wide): 66.1MM Privately Held
SIC: 5013 Radiators
PA: Silla Automotive, Llc
1217 W Artesia Blvd
Compton CA 90220
800 624-1499

(P-6767)
SILLA AUTOMOTIVE LLC
1616 Industrial Blvd, Chula Vista (91911-3943)
PHONE................................619 424-7752
John Nelson, CEO
EMP: 52
SALES (corp-wide): 66.1MM Privately Held
SIC: 5013 Motor vehicle supplies & new parts
PA: Silla Automotive, Llc
1217 W Artesia Blvd
Compton CA 90220
800 624-1499

(P-6768)
SILLA AUTOMOTIVE LLC
1901 Mineral Ct Ste C, Bakersfield (93308-6819)
PHONE................................661 392-8880
EMP: 52
SALES (corp-wide): 73.4MM Privately Held
SIC: 5013
PA: Silla Automotive, Llc
1217 W Artesia Blvd
Compton CA 90220
310 323-0001

(P-6769)
SILLA AUTOMOTIVE LLC
5199 Brooks St Ste G, Montclair (91763-4809)
PHONE................................909 624-2801
EMP: 52
SALES (corp-wide): 66.1MM Privately Held
SIC: 5013 Radiators
PA: Silla Automotive, Llc
1217 W Artesia Blvd
Compton CA 90220
800 624-1499

(P-6770)
SILLA AUTOMOTIVE LLC
1295 N Emerald Ave Ste H, Modesto (95351-2867)
PHONE................................209 577-5089
Jim Moore, Branch Mgr
EMP: 52
SALES (corp-wide): 66.1MM Privately Held
SIC: 5013 Radiators
PA: Silla Automotive, Llc
1217 W Artesia Blvd
Compton CA 90220
800 624-1499

(P-6771)
SILLA AUTOMOTIVE LLC
2695 S Cherry Ave Ste 118, Fresno (93706-5488)
PHONE................................559 457-0711
Steven Boyd, Branch Mgr
EMP: 52
SALES (corp-wide): 66.1MM Privately Held
SIC: 5013 Motor vehicle supplies & new parts
PA: Silla Automotive, Llc
1217 W Artesia Blvd
Compton CA 90220
800 624-1499

(P-6772)
SPECTRA PREMIUM (USA) CORP
14530 Innovation Dr, Riverside (92518-3012)
PHONE................................951 653-0640
Sergio Zapata, Branch Mgr
EMP: 58
SALES (corp-wide): 97.4MM Privately Held
SIC: 5013 Automotive supplies & parts
HQ: Spectra Premium (Usa) Corp.
3052 N Distribution Way
Greenfield IN 46140
317 891-1700

(P-6773)
SSF IMPORTED AUTO PARTS LLC (PA)
Also Called: S S F
466 Forbes Blvd, South San Francisco (94080-2015)
PHONE................................800 203-9287
Fax: 650 873-7893
Robert Ceballos, Administration
Nancy Sanguinetti, Info Tech Dir
Roger Guedikian, Applctn Conslt
Carol Cotter, Technology
Mark Gunson, Graphic Designe
▲ EMP: 100
SALES (est): 137MM Privately Held
WEB: www.ssfautoparts.com
SIC: 5013 Automotive supplies & parts

(P-6774)
SSF IMPORTED AUTO PARTS LLC
21175 Main St Ste A, Carson (90745-1500)
PHONE................................310 782-8859
Bruce Brown, Manager
Nancy Sanguinetti, Manager
EMP: 60
SALES (corp-wide): 137MM Privately Held
WEB: www.ssfautoparts.com
SIC: 5013 4225 Motor vehicle supplies & new parts; general warehousing & storage
PA: Ssf Imported Auto Parts, Llc
466 Forbes Blvd
South San Francisco CA 94080
800 203-9287

(P-6775)
TAP OPERATING CO LLC
400 W Artesia Blvd, Compton (90220-5501)
PHONE................................310 900-5500
EMP: 1200
SALES (est): 87.2MM Privately Held
SIC: 5013 Truck parts & accessories

(P-6776)
TAP WORLDWIDE LLC (PA)
Also Called: 4 Wheel Parts Performance Ctrs
400 W Artesia Blvd, Compton (90220-5501)
PHONE................................310 900-5500
Greg Adler, President
Rich Botello, COO
Tim Mongi, COO
Mark Lane, CFO
Eric Couts, Comms Dir
◆ EMP: 123
SALES (est): 775.8MM Privately Held
SIC: 5013 Motor vehicle supplies & new parts

(P-6777)
TRANSTAR INDUSTRIES INC
Also Called: Transtar Automotive
15010 Calvert St, Van Nuys (91411-2605)
PHONE................................818 785-2000
Fax: 818 785-4758
David Pianannamore, Manager
Jamie Robles, Mktg Dir
EMP: 50
SALES (corp-wide): 708MM Privately Held
WEB: www.transtarindustries.com
SIC: 5013 Automotive supplies & parts
HQ: Transtar Industries, Inc.
7350 Young Dr
Cleveland OH 44146
440 232-5100

(P-6778)
VETRONIX SALES CORPORATION
Also Called: Vetronix Crpration/Bosch Group
2030 Alameda Padre Serra, Santa Barbara (93103-1716)
PHONE................................805 966-2000
Fax: 805 899-9000
James Zaleski, President
Jane Hahn, Sr Software Eng
Scott McIntyre, CIO
Larry James, Engineer
Tina Gibson, Purch Agent
EMP: 68
SQ FT: 26,000
SALES: 8.9MM
SALES (corp-wide): 9.7MM Privately Held
WEB: www.vetronix.com
SIC: 5013 Testing equipment, electrical: automotive
PA: Bosch Automotive Service Solutions Inc.
2030 Alameda Padre Serra
Santa Barbara CA 93103
805 966-2000

(P-6779)
WAGAN CORPORATION
31088 San Clemente St, Hayward (94544-7811)
PHONE................................800 231-5806
Alex Hsu, CEO
John Hsu, Ch of Bd
Po-Jung Hsu, CEO
Mamie Hsu, CFO
Bryan Kawaye, Engineer
▲ EMP: 50
SQ FT: 30,000
SALES (est): 12.1MM Privately Held
WEB: www.wagan.com
SIC: 5013 Automotive supplies & parts

(P-6780)
WARREN DISTRIBUTING INC (PA)
Also Called: Wdi
8737 Dice Rd, Santa Fe Springs (90670-2513)
PHONE................................562 789-3360
Fax: 562 789-3371
Brian David Weiss, CEO
Warren A Weiss, President
Dave Erlenbach, Vice Pres
North Hollywood, Branch Mgr
Las Vegas, Branch Mgr
▲ EMP: 55
SQ FT: 68,000
SALES (est): 83.9MM Privately Held
WEB: www.warrendist.com
SIC: 5013 Automotive supplies & parts

(P-6781)
WORLDPAC INC (DH)
37137 Hickory St, Newark (94560-3340)
P.O. Box 5022 (94560-5522)
PHONE................................510 742-8900
Fax: 510 742-1993
Bob Cushing, CEO
Roy Geddie, President
Darius Kondaki, President
John Mosunic, CFO
Susan Grass, Exec VP
▲ EMP: 200
SQ FT: 256,000
SALES (est): 910.5MM
SALES (corp-wide): 9.7B Publicly Held
WEB: www.worldpac.com
SIC: 5013 5531 Automotive supplies & parts; automotive parts
HQ: General Parts International, Inc.
2635 E Millbrook Rd Ste B
Raleigh NC 27604
919 573-3000

PRODUCTS & SERVICES SECTION

5021 - Furniture Wholesale County (P-6803)

(P-6782)
WSJ WORLDWIDE INC
16775 E Johnson Dr, City of Industry (91745-2415)
PHONE..................626 961-7380
Wong Tai Wan, *President*
Wilson Wong, *Manager*
▲ EMP: 60
SALES (est): 4.8MM Privately Held
SIC: 5013 Automotive supplies & parts

(P-6783)
YOSHIMURA RESEARCH & DEV AMER
5420 Daniels St Ste A, Chino (91710-9012)
PHONE..................909 628-4722
Fujio Yoshimura, *President*
Suehiro Watanabe, *CFO*
Don Sakakura, *Senior VP*
Don Sakakura, *Agent*
▲ EMP: 100
SQ FT: 12,000
SALES (est): 47.9MM Privately Held
WEB: www.yoshimura-rd.com
SIC: 5013 Motorcycle parts

5014 Tires & Tubes Wholesale

(P-6784)
FALKEN TIRE HOLDINGS INC
Also Called: Falken Tires
8656 Haven Ave, Rancho Cucamonga (91730-9103)
PHONE..................800 723-2553
Fax: 909 466-1169
Richard Smallwood, *President*
Hideo Honda, *President*
Joyce Ho, *Executive Asst*
Luis Cortez, *Auditing Mgr*
Verna V Macias, *Accountant*
▲ EMP: 80
SALES (est): 31.3MM
SALES (corp-wide): 6.8B Privately Held
WEB: www.sri.dunlop.co.jp
SIC: 5014 Tires & tubes; automobile tires & tubes; truck tires & tubes
PA: Sumitomo Rubber Industries, Ltd.
 3-6-9, Wakinohamacho, Chuo-Ku
 Kobe HYO 651-0
 782 653-000

(P-6785)
GITI TIRE (USA) LTD (DH)
10404 6th St, Rancho Cucamonga (91730-5831)
PHONE..................909 527-8800
Enki Tan, *CEO*
Armand Allaire, *Exec VP*
Tom McNamara, *Exec VP*
Enk Tan, *Exec Dir*
Lei Huai Chin, *Managing Dir*
▲ EMP: 55
SALES (est): 79.7MM Privately Held
SIC: 5014 Tires & tubes

(P-6786)
GREENBALL CORP (PA)
Also Called: Towmaster Tire & Wheel
222 S Harbor Blvd Ste 700, Anaheim (92805-3730)
PHONE..................714 782-3060
Chris S H Tsai, *CEO*
Jenny Tsai, *Vice Pres*
Ian Chen, *Accounting Mgr*
Carlos Caban, *Analyst*
Rene Schlegel, *Controller*
▲ EMP: 50
SQ FT: 80,000
SALES (est): 69.8MM Privately Held
WEB: www.greenball.com
SIC: 5014 5013 3999 Tires & tubes; wheels, motor vehicle; atomizers, toiletry

(P-6787)
LAKIN TIRE WEST INCORPORATED (PA)
Also Called: Lakin Tire of Calif
15305 Spring Ave, Santa Fe Springs (90670-5645)
PHONE..................562 802-2752
Fax: 562 802-7584
Robert Lakin, *CEO*
David Lakin, *Vice Pres*
Randolph Roth, *Vice Pres*
Phuc Dinh, *Info Tech Mgr*
David Hui, *MIS Mgr*
▼ EMP: 90
SQ FT: 50,000
SALES (est): 101.9MM Privately Held
WEB: www.lakintire.com
SIC: 5014 5531 Tires, used; automotive & home supply stores

(P-6788)
PARKHOUSE TIRE SERVICE INC
13655 Santa Ana Ave, Fontana (92337-8203)
PHONE..................909 428-1415
Fax: 909 428-0257
Jim Parkhouse, *CEO*
EMP: 142
SALES (corp-wide): 136.7MM Privately Held
SIC: 5014 Automobile tires & tubes
PA: Parkhouse Tire Service, Inc.
 5960 Shull St
 Bell Gardens CA 90201
 562 928-0421

(P-6789)
SEALANT SYSTEMS INTERNATIONAL
Also Called: Ssi
125 Venture Dr Ste 210, San Luis Obispo (93401-9105)
PHONE..................805 489-0490
Chris Auerbach, *President*
EMP: 67
SALES: 6.5MM
SALES (corp-wide): 13.4B Publicly Held
SIC: 5014 Tires & tubes
PA: Illinois Tool Works Inc.
 155 Harlem Ave
 Glenview IL 60025
 847 724-7500

(P-6790)
SUMITOMO RUBBER NORTH AMER INC (HQ)
Also Called: Falken Tire Corporation
8656 Haven Ave, Rancho Cucamonga (91730-9103)
PHONE..................909 466-1116
Richard Smallwood, *CEO*
Peter Buck, *Vice Pres*
Fumikazu Yamashita, *Vice Pres*
Rick Brennan, *Exec Dir*
Monica Fuqua, *Executive Asst*
◆ EMP: 75
SQ FT: 190,000
SALES (est): 98.2MM
SALES (corp-wide): 6.8B Privately Held
WEB: www.falkentire.com
SIC: 5014 Tires & tubes; automobile tires & tubes; truck tires & tubes
PA: Sumitomo Rubber Industries, Ltd.
 3-6-9, Wakinohamacho, Chuo-Ku
 Kobe HYO 651-0
 782 653-000

(P-6791)
TIRE CENTERS LLC
Also Called: Berlin Tire Centers
10516 Commerce Way # 875, Fontana (92337-8236)
PHONE..................909 854-1200
Fax: 909 854-1231
J D Cassa, *General Mgr*
Jessi Martinez, *Manager*
EMP: 150
SQ FT: 83,470
SALES (corp-wide): 606.3MM Privately Held
WEB: www.tirecenters.com
SIC: 5014 7534 Automobile tires & tubes; automotive tires; rebuilding & re-treading tires
HQ: Tire Centers, Llc
 310 Inglesby Pkwy
 Duncan SC 29334
 864 329-2700

(P-6792)
TIRECO INC (PA)
500 W 190th St Ste 100, Gardena (90248-4270)
PHONE..................310 767-7990
Chris Holbert, *President*
John Chen, *CFO*
Brenda Flores, *Admin Asst*
Emerald Kapoor, *Admin Asst*
Shang Wang, *Planning*
▲ EMP: 150
SALES (est): 146MM Privately Held
WEB: www.tireco.com
SIC: 5014 5013 5051 Tires, used; wheels, motor vehicle; tubing, metal

(P-6793)
TOYO TIRE USA CORP
2151 S Vintage Ave, Ontario (91761-2824)
PHONE..................562 431-6502
Steve Morgan, *Manager*
EMP: 50
SALES (corp-wide): 3.3B Privately Held
SIC: 5014 Tires & tubes
HQ: Toyo Tire U.S.A. Corp.
 5665 Plaza Dr Ste 300
 Cypress CA 90630
 714 236-2080

5015 Motor Vehicle Parts, Used Wholesale

(P-6794)
AMERICAN CORPORATION
315 N Doheny Dr, Beverly Hills (90211-1621)
PHONE..................310 274-1800
David Morad, *President*
Eli Yadegar, *Vice Pres*
Farhad Elihu, *Info Tech Mgr*
EMP: 80
SQ FT: 300,000
SALES: 22.5MM Privately Held
SIC: 5015 Automotive supplies, used

(P-6795)
CADNCHEV INC
Also Called: Lakenor Auto Salvage
13603 Foster Rd, Santa Fe Springs (90670-4834)
PHONE..................562 944-6422
Fax: 562 944-4687
Donald Flynn, *Ch of Bd*
Thomas Raterman, *CFO*
Frank Erlain, *Vice Pres*
EMP: 60
SQ FT: 10,000
SALES (est): 9.2MM
SALES (corp-wide): 7.1B Publicly Held
WEB: www.lkqcorp.com
SIC: 5015 5531 Automotive parts & supplies, used; automotive parts
PA: Lkq Corporation
 500 W Madison St Ste 2800
 Chicago IL 60661
 312 621-1950

(P-6796)
ROTOR EXCHANGE
Also Called: Rotex
14010 S Western Ave, Gardena (90249-3078)
PHONE..................310 323-5710
Fax: 310 217-9872
Lou Mucciolo, *President*
Sharon Mucciolo, *Vice Pres*
Daniel Felding, *Agent*
▲ EMP: 100
SQ FT: 14,400
SALES (est): 12.8MM Privately Held
SIC: 5015 3694 3625 Automotive parts & supplies, used; engine electrical equipment; relays & industrial controls

(P-6797)
TEAM TRUCK DISMANTLING INC
Also Called: Hillside Auto Salvage
3760 Pyrite St, Riverside (92509-1103)
PHONE..................951 685-6744
Fax: 951 685-8367
Ted Smith, *President*
Jerry Jaeckles, *Corp Secy*
Tom Hutton, *Vice Pres*
Stacey Ramey, *Administration*
EMP: 70
SQ FT: 1,500
SALES (est): 9.2MM Privately Held
WEB: www.hillsideautosalvage.com
SIC: 5015 Automotive parts & supplies, used

5021 Furniture Wholesale

(P-6798)
ABBYSON LIVING CORP
26500 Agoura Rd 102-875, Calabasas (91302-1952)
PHONE..................805 465-5500
Yavar A Rafieha, *President*
Doddy Rafieha, *COO*
Rodd Rafia, *Vice Pres*
Dana Andrew, *Principal*
Mike Pollard, *Principal*
◆ EMP: 325
SQ FT: 156,000
SALES (est): 49.8MM Privately Held
WEB: www.abbysonliving.com
SIC: 5021 Household furniture

(P-6799)
ABM OFFICE SOLUTIONS INC
9550 Hermosa Ave, Rancho Cucamonga (91730-5810)
PHONE..................909 527-8145
Jorge E Robles, *CEO*
Cecilia Varas, *CFO*
▲ EMP: 62
SALES (est): 27.1MM Privately Held
SIC: 5021 Office furniture

(P-6800)
ACME FURNITURE INDUSTRY INC (PA)
Also Called: Acme Trading
18895 Arenth Ave, City of Industry (91748-1304)
PHONE..................626 964-3456
Fax: 213 964-3940
George Chen, *CEO*
CHI-Chu Chen, *President*
Tomy Chen, *Treasurer*
Marvin Ruben, *Senior VP*
James Chen, *Vice Pres*
▲ EMP: 85
SQ FT: 330,000
SALES (est): 60.4MM Privately Held
SIC: 5021 Furniture

(P-6801)
ADM FURNITURE INC
11680 Wright Rd, Lynwood (90262-3945)
PHONE..................310 762-2800
Alfonso Ayon, *President*
▲ EMP: 55
SALES (est): 8.6MM Privately Held
SIC: 5021 2511 Household furniture; wood household furniture

(P-6802)
ALTON IRVINE INC
Also Called: Millwork Holdings
2052 Alton Pkwy, Irvine (92606-4905)
PHONE..................949 428-4141
Alan True, *CEO*
Dan Tacheny, *President*
Tom Pierce, *Info Tech Dir*
Jesse Greenhalgh, *Opers Mgr*
▲ EMP: 53
SQ FT: 45,000
SALES (est): 24MM Privately Held
WEB: www.trueseating.com
SIC: 5021 Office furniture

(P-6803)
AMINI INNOVATION CORP
Also Called: Aico
8725 Rex Rd, Pico Rivera (90660-6703)
PHONE..................562 222-2500
Fax: 562 222-2525
Michael Amini, *CEO*
Martin Ploy, *Exec VP*
Jeff Santanello, *Vice Pres*
James Fang, *Info Tech Dir*
Hsu Ted, *Info Tech Dir*
◆ EMP: 110
SQ FT: 320,000
SALES (est): 88.8MM Privately Held
WEB: www.amini.com
SIC: 5021 Furniture

(PA)=Parent Co (HQ)=Headquarters (DH)=Div Headquarters
✪ = New Business established in last 2 years

5021 - Furniture Wholesale County (P-6804)

(P-6804)
ASPECTS FURNITURE MFG INC
15830 El Prado Rd Ste A, Chino (91708-9127)
PHONE.....................909 606-5806
Amy Sivixay, *President*
Amy A Sivixay, *Vice Pres*
Jay Sivixay, *Info Tech Mgr*
Lisa Lew, *Controller*
▲ **EMP:** 170
SQ FT: 12,900
SALES (est): 23MM **Privately Held**
WEB: www.aspectsfurniture.com
SIC: 5021 Furniture

(P-6805)
BENCHMASTER FURNITURE LLC
1481 N Hundley St, Anaheim (92806-1323)
PHONE.....................714 414-0240
Gene Trobaugh,
Eugene V Trobaugh, *President*
Emmy Chen, *Vice Pres*
▲ **EMP:** 300
SALES: 122MM **Privately Held**
WEB: www.benchmasterfurniture.com
SIC: 5021 Furniture

(P-6806)
BENETTIS ITALIA INC
18554 S Susana Rd, Compton (90221-5620)
PHONE.....................310 537-8036
Mohammad A Ahmadinia, *CEO*
Sarah Ahmadinia, *CFO*
▲ **EMP:** 56
SQ FT: 120,000
SALES (est): 17.3MM **Privately Held**
SIC: 5021 2426 Furniture; furniture stock & parts, hardwood

(P-6807)
BLUMENTHAL DISTRIBUTING INC (PA)
Also Called: Office Star Products
1901 S Archibald Ave, Ontario (91761-8548)
P.O. Box 3520 (91761-0952)
PHONE.....................909 930-2000
Fax: 909 930-5419
Richard Blumenthal, *President*
Rose Blumenthal, *Shareholder*
Jennifer Blumenthal, *Corp Secy*
Lili Avimi, *Vice Pres*
Josh Blumenthal, *Vice Pres*
◆ **EMP:** 150
SQ FT: 200,000
SALES (est): 60.4MM **Privately Held**
WEB: www.officestar.net
SIC: 5021 2522 Office furniture; chairs, office: padded or plain, except wood

(P-6808)
BOYD FLOTATION INC
7551 Cherry Ave, Fontana (92336-4276)
PHONE.....................909 357-6400
Alfred Mayen, *Manager*
EMP: 73
SALES (corp-wide): 55MM **Privately Held**
WEB: www.boydflotation.com
SIC: 5021 2515 Mattresses; household furniture; mattresses & bedsprings
PA: Boyd Flotation, Inc.
2440 Adie Rd
Maryland Heights MO 63043
314 997-5222

(P-6809)
CALIFORNIA CREATIONS INC
1100 S Vail Ave, Montebello (90640-6021)
PHONE.....................323 722-9832
Cuong Huynh, *President*
Julie Nguyen, *Treasurer*
Kim Huynh, *Vice Pres*
EMP: 50
SQ FT: 20,000
SALES (est): 9.2MM **Privately Held**
WEB: www.calcreations.com
SIC: 5021 Furniture

(P-6810)
CAMBIUM BUSINESS GROUP INC (PA)
Also Called: Fairmont Designs
6950 Noritsu Ave, Buena Park (90620-1311)
PHONE.....................714 670-1171
George Tsai, *Ch of Bd*
Vickie Em, *Managing Prtnr*
Brain Edwards, *President*
David Campbell, *CFO*
Nat Mucha, *Vice Pres*
◆ **EMP:** 120
SQ FT: 200,000
SALES (est): 55.9MM **Privately Held**
WEB: www.fairmontdesigns.com
SIC: 5021 2511 Household furniture; dining room furniture; tables, occasional; beds; wood household furniture

(P-6811)
COA INC (PA)
Also Called: Coaster Company of America
12928 Sandoval St, Santa Fe Springs (90670-4061)
PHONE.....................562 944-7899
Fax: 562 946-2850
Michael Yeh, *CEO*
Matthew Chen, *Vice Pres*
Al Grossman, *Vice Pres*
Lisa KAO, *Vice Pres*
Wesley Jacobsen, *Info Tech Dir*
▲ **EMP:** 200
SQ FT: 210,000
SALES (est): 235.1MM **Privately Held**
WEB: www.coa.net
SIC: 5021 Household furniture; dining room furniture; beds & bedding; shelving

(P-6812)
COMPLETE OFFICE CALIFORNIA INC
12724 Moore St, Cerritos (90703-2121)
PHONE.....................714 880-1222
Fax: 858 435-7085
Edward B Walter, *CEO*
Rick Israel, *Principal*
Amy Ruby, *Controller*
Angelo Delnero, *Sales Mgr*
Michael Remillard, *Director*
EMP: 62
SQ FT: 28,000
SALES (est): 79.3MM **Privately Held**
WEB: www.completeofficeca.com
SIC: 5021 5112 Office furniture; office supplies

(P-6813)
COPPEL CORPORATION
503 Scaroni Ave, Calexico (92231-9791)
PHONE.....................760 357-3707
Fax: 760 357-4480
Hermann Gerzabek, *CEO*
Ruben Coppel, *President*
Enrique Coppel, *CFO*
Alberto A Coppel, *Admin Sec*
Gloria Perez, *Admin Asst*
▲ **EMP:** 80
SQ FT: 70,000
SALES: 335.8MM
SALES (corp-wide): 6.2B **Privately Held**
SIC: 5021 5137 5136 Household furniture; women's & children's clothing; men's & boys' clothing
HQ: Coppel, S.A. De C.V.
Republica Poniente No. 2855
Culiacan SIN. 80105
667 759-4200

(P-6814)
EC GROUP INC (PA)
Also Called: Dennis & Leen
5960 Bowcroft St, Los Angeles (90016-4302)
PHONE.....................310 815-2700
Fax: 310 659-0694
Richard Hallberg, *President*
Daniel Cuevas, *Vice Pres*
Barbara Wiseley, *Admin Sec*
Carla Laurell, *Human Res Mgr*
Laura Krever, *Accounts Mgr*
▲ **EMP:** 80
SQ FT: 18,000
SALES (est): 31MM **Privately Held**
SIC: 5021 Furniture

(P-6815)
FURNITURE AMERICA CAL INC
Also Called: Furniture America California
19635 E Walnut Dr N, City of Industry (91789-2815)
P.O. Box 19223 (91748)
PHONE.....................909 718-7276
George Wells, *CEO*
Rocky Yang, *Vice Pres*
Jennifer Huynh, *Accountant*
Jean Chen, *Accounts Mgr*
◆ **EMP:** 71
SQ FT: 200,000
SALES (est): 40.2MM **Privately Held**
WEB: www.importdirectinc.com
SIC: 5021 Furniture

(P-6816)
GOFORTH & MARTI (PA)
Also Called: G/M Business Interiors
110 W A St Ste 140, San Diego (92101-3702)
PHONE.....................951 684-0870
Stephen L Easley, *President*
Mike Akin, *Vice Pres*
William F Easley, *Vice Pres*
Judi Harvey, *Executive*
Michael Lafond, *Executive*
▲ **EMP:** 90
SQ FT: 38,000
SALES (est): 80.9MM **Privately Held**
WEB: www.gmbi.net
SIC: 5021 Office furniture

(P-6817)
HAWORTH INC
931 Cadillac Ct, Milpitas (95035-3053)
PHONE.....................408 262-6400
Agnes Allen, *Branch Mgr*
EMP: 75
SALES (corp-wide): 1.8B **Privately Held**
WEB: www.haworth-furn.com
SIC: 5021 Office furniture
HQ: Haworth, Inc.
1 Haworth Ctr
Holland MI 49423
616 393-3000

(P-6818)
HOMELEGANCE INC
Also Called: A G A
48200 Fremont Blvd, Fremont (94538-6509)
PHONE.....................510 933-6888
Fax: 510 783-3089
Puhsien C Chao, *CEO*
Rosa Chao, *President*
Hutch Chao, *Vice Pres*
Eileen Ai, *Accountant*
Felix Law, *Accounts Mgr*
◆ **EMP:** 90
SQ FT: 600,000
SALES (est): 34MM **Privately Held**
SIC: 5021 Household furniture

(P-6819)
HUMAN TOUCH LLC
3030 Walnut Ave, Long Beach (90807-5222)
PHONE.....................562 426-8700
Andrew Cohen, *President*
David Wood, *CEO*
Thomas Fragpotto, *CFO*
Rosy Gu, *CFO*
Bruce Maccallum, *CFO*
◆ **EMP:** 80
SQ FT: 98,500
SALES (est): 53.5MM **Privately Held**
SIC: 5021 Chairs

(P-6820)
INSIDE SOURCE INC (PA)
Also Called: Inside Source/Young
985 Industrial Rd Ste 101, San Carlos (94070-4157)
PHONE.....................650 508-9101
Fax: 650 508-9102
David Denny, *President*
Kristen Haren, *COO*
Wendy Boeck, *CFO*
Gary Young, *Senior VP*
Tina Fong, *Vice Pres*
EMP: 75
SQ FT: 50,000
SALES (est): 90.1MM **Privately Held**
WEB: www.insidesource.com
SIC: 5021 Office & public building furniture

(P-6821)
INTEX RECREATION CORP
4001 Via Oro Ave Ste 210, Long Beach (90810-1400)
PHONE.....................310 549-1846
Tien P Zee, *CEO*
Jim Lai, *President*
Bill Smith, *Vice Pres*
Bob Howe, *Asst Treas*
Stan Fowler, *Controller*
◆ **EMP:** 100 **EST:** 1966
SQ FT: 330,000
SALES (est): 23.8MM
SALES (corp-wide): 173.5MM **Privately Held**
WEB: www.intexcorp.com
SIC: 5021 5092 5091 5162 Waterbeds; toys; watersports equipment & supplies; plastics materials & basic shapes
PA: Intex Recreation Corp
4001 Via Oro Ave Ste 210
Long Beach CA 90810
310 549-5400

(P-6822)
JANUS ET CIE (PA)
12310 Greenstone Ave, Santa Fe Springs (90670-4737)
PHONE.....................310 601-2958
Janice K Feldman, *CEO*
Cindy Wolf, *President*
Paul Warren, *COO*
Greg Buscher, *CFO*
Brian Schwartz, *General Mgr*
◆ **EMP:** 110
SQ FT: 154,000
SALES (est): 53.7MM **Privately Held**
WEB: www.janusetcie.com
SIC: 5021 5712 Outdoor & lawn furniture; household furniture; furniture stores

(P-6823)
LIFESTYLE SOLUTIONS INC (PA)
5555 Auto Mall Pkwy, Fremont (94538-5128)
PHONE.....................510 249-9301
Sean Pathiratne, *CEO*
Jeff Averitt, *Administration*
Ana Padgaokar, *VP Sales*
J C Gholston, *Sales Mgr*
Ron Friedenthal, *Sales Staff*
◆ **EMP:** 50
SALES (est): 31.9MM **Privately Held**
WEB: www.elitefurniture.com
SIC: 5021 Beds & bedding

(P-6824)
MCMURRAY STERN INC
15511 Carmenita Rd, Santa Fe Springs (90670-5609)
PHONE.....................562 623-3000
Fax: 562 623-3039
Linda Stern, *CEO*
Matthew Denburg, *COO*
Tom O'Neill, *Vice Pres*
John Fisher, *General Mgr*
Jen Heimbach, *General Mgr*
EMP: 50
SQ FT: 30,000
SALES (est): 45.8MM **Privately Held**
SIC: 5021 4226 Filing units; document & office records storage

(P-6825)
MODANI LOS ANGELES LLC
Also Called: Modani Furniture
8873 W Sunset Blvd, West Hollywood (90069-2107)
PHONE.....................310 652-2323
John Momo, *Manager*
Brittany Bordeaux, *Manager*
John Momo, *Manager*
▲ **EMP:** 50
SALES (est): 6.7MM **Privately Held**
SIC: 5021 Furniture

PRODUCTS & SERVICES SECTION

5023 - Home Furnishings Wholesale County (P-6848)

(P-6826)
NAJARIAN FURNITURE COMPANY INC
Also Called: Italian Concepts
265 N Euclid Ave, Pasadena (91101-1594)
PHONE 626 839-8700
Antranik Najarian, *President*
Mike Najarian, *President*
George Najarian, *Vice Pres*
Michael Lawrence, *VP Sales*
◆ **EMP:** 100
SQ FT: 280,000
SALES: 200MM **Privately Held**
WEB: www.najarianfurniture.com
SIC: 5021 5023 Household furniture; home furnishings

(P-6827)
OMNIA ITALIAN DESIGN INC
4900 Edison Ave, Chino (91710-5713)
PHONE 909 393-4400
Fax: 909 393-4401
Peter Zolferino, *President*
Luie Nastri, *Vice Pres*
Randy Gleckman, *Natl Sales Mgr*
Anita Marcy, *Marketing Staff*
Katherine Skinner, *Marketing Staff*
◆ **EMP:** 200
SQ FT: 110,000
SALES (est): 78.1MM **Privately Held**
SIC: 5021 Household furniture

(P-6828)
ONE WORKPLACE L FERRARI LLC
Also Called: One Workplace L Ferrari
475 Brannan St, San Francisco (94107-5418)
PHONE 415 357-2200
Fax: 415 357-2201
Brian Wilson, *Mng Member*
EMP: 50
SALES (est): 10.5MM
SALES (corp-wide): 186.4MM **Privately Held**
SIC: 5021 Filing units
PA: One Workplace L. Ferrari, Llc
2500 De La Cruz Blvd
Santa Clara CA 95050
669 800-2500

(P-6829)
PALECEK IMPORTS INC (PA)
601 Parr Blvd, Richmond (94801-1316)
PHONE 510 236-7730
Fax: 510 234-7234
Allan Palecek, *President*
Andrew T Palecek, *Vice Pres*
Pat Sexson, *General Mgr*
Charles Reisbol, *Administration*
Audry Last, *Purchasing*
◆ **EMP:** 82
SQ FT: 250,000
SALES (est): 44.4MM **Privately Held**
WEB: www.palecek.com
SIC: 5021 5023 Furniture; home furnishings

(P-6830)
POUNDEX ASSOCIATES CORPORATION (PA)
21490 Baker Pkwy, City of Industry (91789-5239)
PHONE 909 444-5874
Lionel Chen, *President*
Danny Wong, *President*
Lance Yin, *Manager*
Kimberly Flores, *Asst Mgr*
◆ **EMP:** 60
SQ FT: 55,000
SALES (est): 26.4MM **Privately Held**
SIC: 5021 Household furniture; dining room furniture; tables, occasional

(P-6831)
PREMIERE RACK SOLUTIONS INC
4502 Brickell Privado St, Ontario (91761-7827)
PHONE 909 605-6300
Don Sturtz, *CEO*
Mike Rubesa, *Vice Pres*
EMP: 76
SQ FT: 48,790
SALES (est): 35.9MM **Privately Held**
SIC: 5021 Racks

(P-6832)
PRIVILEGE INTERNATIONAL INC
2323 Firestone Blvd, South Gate (90280-2646)
PHONE 323 585-0777
Fax: 323 585-0755
Eddy Sarraf, *President*
Mark Darwish, *Senior VP*
Richard Darwish, *Vice Pres*
Luis Saldana, *Manager*
▲ **EMP:** 75
SQ FT: 350,000
SALES (est): 22.2MM **Privately Held**
WEB: www.privilegeinc.com
SIC: 5021 Furniture

(P-6833)
UNISOURCE SOLUTIONS INC (PA)
8350 Rex Rd, Pico Rivera (90660-3785)
PHONE 562 654-3500
Fax: 562 949-7110
James Kastner, *CEO*
Marc Flax, *President*
Ken Kastner, *President*
Clem Mieto, *CFO*
Clem Nieto, *CFO*
▲ **EMP:** 105
SQ FT: 186,000
SALES (est): 67.6MM **Privately Held**
WEB: www.unisourceit.com
SIC: 5021 Office furniture

(P-6834)
VANGUARD LEGATO A CAL CORP
Also Called: Vanguard Legato
2121 Williams St, San Leandro (94577-3224)
PHONE 510 351-3333
Fax: 510 483-0458
Darlene Patch, *Director*
EMP: 68
SQ FT: 20,000
SALES (est): 9.3MM **Privately Held**
WEB: www.brg.com
SIC: 5021 5112 5023 Furniture; office supplies; home furnishings

(P-6835)
VERSA PRODUCTS INC (PA)
Also Called: Versatables.com
14105 Avalon Blvd, Los Angeles (90061-2637)
PHONE 310 353-7100
Christopher Laudadio, *CEO*
Christopher Stormer, *COO*
Rudy Chacon, *CFO*
Dan Weber, *Vice Pres*
Trig Alonzo, *Executive*
▲ **EMP:** 94 EST: 2000
SQ FT: 35,000
SALES (est): 22MM **Privately Held**
WEB: www.versatables.com
SIC: 5021 2512 Office furniture; couches, sofas & davenports: upholstered on wood frames

(P-6836)
VIRCO INC (HQ)
2027 Harpers Way, Torrance (90501-1524)
PHONE 310 533-0474
Fax: 310 533-1906
Robert Virtue, *CEO*
Robert Dose, *Vice Pres*
Doug Vertue, *Vice Pres*
Sharon Okazaki, *Executive*
Scott Newell, *Info Tech Dir*
▼ **EMP:** 69
SQ FT: 560,000
SALES (est): 102.5MM
SALES (corp-wide): 168.6MM **Publicly Held**
WEB: www.virco.com
SIC: 5021 Furniture
PA: Virco Mfg. Corporation
2027 Harpers Way
Torrance CA 90501
310 533-0474

(P-6837)
WATERHILL LTD
140 N Orange Ave, City of Industry (91744-3431)
PHONE 626 369-6828
Fax: 626 369-2198
Brian Yip, *President*
Carol Yip, *Admin Sec*
Arnold Yip, *Manager*
▲ **EMP:** 50
SQ FT: 125,000
SALES (est): 7.3MM **Privately Held**
WEB: www.waterhill.com
SIC: 5021 Dining room furniture

(P-6838)
WINNERS ONLY INC
1365 Park Center Dr, Vista (92081-8338)
PHONE 760 599-0300
Fax: 760 597-0799
Alex Shu, *Chairman*
Sheue-Wen Lee, *CEO*
Fred Dizon, *CFO*
William Lee, *CIO*
▲ **EMP:** 200
SALES (est): 90.3MM **Privately Held**
WEB: www.winnersonly.com
SIC: 5021 Office furniture; dining room furniture

(P-6839)
WMK OFFICE SAN DIEGO LLC (PA)
Also Called: BKM Officeworks
4780 Estgate Mall Ste 100, San Diego (92121)
PHONE 858 569-4700
William Kuhnert, *CEO*
Jim Skidmore, *COO*
Dillon Mahoney, *General Mgr*
Shelly Miller, *General Mgr*
Adriana Kirkland, *Executive Asst*
EMP: 70
SQ FT: 100,000
SALES (est): 73.5MM **Privately Held**
WEB: www.bkmofficeworks.com
SIC: 5021 Furniture

5023 Home Furnishings Wholesale

(P-6840)
ACME LAUNDRY PRODUCTS INC
Also Called: Hi-TEC Garments
21600 Lassen St, Chatsworth (91311-4121)
PHONE 818 341-0700
Jan Rome, *CEO*
▲ **EMP:** 120
SQ FT: 30,000
SALES (est): 13.1MM **Privately Held**
SIC: 5023 2392 Decorative home furnishings & supplies; bags, laundry: made from purchased materials; sheets, fabric: made from purchased materials; pillowcases: made from purchased materials

(P-6841)
AMERICAN FAUCET COATINGS CORP
3280 Corporate Vw, Vista (92081-8528)
PHONE 760 598-5895
Fax: 760 598-0321
Susan E Butler, *President*
Judy Benson, *Accountant*
◆ **EMP:** 50
SALES (est): 27.3MM **Privately Held**
WEB: www.sigmafaucet.com
SIC: 5023 3432 Home furnishings; plumbing fixture fittings & trim

(P-6842)
AMERICAN TEXTILE MAINT CO
Also Called: Republic Master Chefs Textile
3001 E Anaheim St, Long Beach (90804-3810)
PHONE 562 438-1126
Lawrence Pallan, *Branch Mgr*
EMP: 127
SALES (corp-wide): 30.1MM **Privately Held**
SIC: 5023 Home furnishings
PA: American Textile Maintenance Company
1667 W Washington Blvd
Los Angeles CA 90007
323 731-3132

(P-6843)
ARDMORE HOME DESIGN INC
Also Called: Pigeon & Poodle
4700 Littlejohn St, Baldwin Park (91706-2274)
PHONE 626 939-1177
Chris Dewitt, *CEO*
Oscar Yague, *Vice Pres*
▲ **EMP:** 50
SALES (est): 24.2MM **Privately Held**
SIC: 5023 Decorative home furnishings & supplies

(P-6844)
ATLAS TEXTILE CO INC
6047 Tampa Ave Ste 103, Tarzana (91356-1168)
PHONE 818 881-8862
Ernest Schatz, *CEO*
Benjamin Kaye, *President*
EMP: 70
SQ FT: 130,000
SALES (est): 5.9MM **Privately Held**
SIC: 5023 Linens & towels; bedspreads; sheets, textile; pillowcases

(P-6845)
B R FUNSTEN & CO
Also Called: BR Funsten
105 Lndustrial Park, Manteca (95337)
PHONE 209 825-5375
Fax: 209 825-4916
Rod Tilson, *Branch Mgr*
Nanci Stevenson, *Director*
EMP: 60
SALES (corp-wide): 153.4MM **Privately Held**
WEB: www.brfunsten.com
SIC: 5023 5713 Resilient floor coverings: tile or sheet; floor covering stores
PA: B. R. Funsten & Co.
5200 Watt Ct Ste B
Fairfield CA 94534
209 825-5375

(P-6846)
B R FUNSTEN & CO
Tom Duffy Company Division
5200 Watt Ct Ste B, Fairfield (94534-4209)
PHONE 707 863-8300
Don Jackson, *Manager*
EMP: 100
SALES (corp-wide): 153.4MM **Privately Held**
WEB: www.brfunsten.com
SIC: 5023 Floor coverings
PA: B. R. Funsten & Co.
5200 Watt Ct Ste B
Fairfield CA 94534
209 825-5375

(P-6847)
BEAULIEU GROUP LLC
Also Called: Coronet Carpets
15130 Northam St, La Mirada (90638-5758)
PHONE 714 522-2080
Dan Richard, *Manager*
EMP: 100
SALES (corp-wide): 2.5B **Privately Held**
WEB: www.beaulieugroup.com
SIC: 5023 Carpets
PA: Beaulieu Group, Llc
1502 Coronet Dr
Dalton GA 30720
706 259-4511

(P-6848)
BP INDUSTRIES INCORPORATED
5300 Concours, Ontario (91764-5399)
PHONE 909 481-0227
Fax: 909 481-2775
Dong Koo Kim, *President*
Jim Clark, *Senior VP*
Maria Hon, *Controller*
▲ **EMP:** 57
SQ FT: 140,000

5023 - Home Furnishings Wholesale County (P-6849)

SALES (est): 25.8MM **Privately Held**
WEB: www.bpindustries.com
SIC: 5023 Home furnishings; mirrors & pictures, framed & unframed

(P-6849)
BRADSHAW INTERNATIONAL INC (PA)
9409 Buffalo Ave, Rancho Cucamonga (91730-6012)
PHONE 909 476-3884
Fax: 909 476-3616
Michael Rodrigue, *CEO*
Brett R Bradshaw, *President*
Julie Hayes, *President*
Jerry Vigliotti, *CFO*
Julie Lawson, *Chief Mktg Ofcr*
◆ EMP: 280
SQ FT: 750,000
SALES (est): **400MM** **Privately Held**
WEB: www.goodcook.com
SIC: 5023 Kitchenware

(P-6850)
BREVILLE USA INC
19400 S Western Ave, Torrance (90501-1119)
PHONE 310 755-3000
Damian Baden Court, *CEO*
Simon Schober, *CFO*
Henry H Hsu, *Technical Mgr*
Linda Brown, *Credit Mgr*
Anthony Mayor, *VP Opers*
◆ EMP: 50
SQ FT: 135,000
SALES (est): 34.8MM
SALES (corp-wide): 136.7MM **Privately Held**
SIC: 5023 5064 Home furnishings; appliance parts, household
HQ: Breville Holdings Pty Limited
Se 2 G 170 Bourke Rd
Alexandria NSW 2015
130 013-9798

(P-6851)
BYTHEWAYS MANUFACTURING INC
Also Called: B T W
2080 Enterprise Blvd, West Sacramento (95691-5051)
PHONE 916 453-1212
Fax: 916 455-2284
Mervin Bytheway Jr, *President*
Jann Bytheway, *Corp Secy*
Bryan Clabeaux, *Sales Mgr*
EMP: 300
SALES (est): 18.9MM **Privately Held**
SIC: 5023 Window furnishings
HQ: Hunter Douglas N.V.
Piekstraat 2
Rotterdam 3071
104 869-911

(P-6852)
CALIFORNIA FLORAL IMPORTS INC
Also Called: California Floral and Home
14711 Clark Ave, City of Industry (91745-1307)
P.O. Box 661394, Arcadia (91066-1394)
PHONE 562 696-1039
Fax: 626 937-1089
Duen R Cheng, *President*
Robert Chou, *General Mgr*
▲ EMP: 52
SQ FT: 13,000
SALES (est): 11.3MM **Privately Held**
SIC: 5023 Decorating supplies

(P-6853)
COMPASS HOME INC
1900 Burgundy Pl, Ontario (91761-2317)
PHONE 909 605-9899
Chester Lee, *President*
Christina MA, *Controller*
▲ EMP: 60
SQ FT: 400,000
SALES (est): 5.4MM
SALES (corp-wide): 1.1B **Privately Held**
WEB: www.compasshome.com
SIC: 5023 Home furnishings, wicker, rattan or reed

HQ: Test-Rite Products Corp.
1900 Burgundy Pl
Ontario CA 91761
909 605-9899

(P-6854)
CONRAD IMPORTS INC
540 Barneveld Ave Ste H, San Francisco (94124-1805)
PHONE 415 626-3303
Ruth M Holland, *President*
Timothy Moran, *CFO*
Janice Holland, *Vice Pres*
Ed Fernandez, *Info Tech Dir*
Jason Silvera, *Technology*
EMP: 93 EST: 1956
SALES (est): 28MM **Privately Held**
WEB: www.conradshades.com
SIC: 5023 Window furnishings

(P-6855)
CONTRACTORS FLRG SVC CAL INC
300 E Dyer Rd, Santa Ana (92707-3740)
P.O. Box 15106 (92735-0106)
PHONE 714 556-6100
Joseph J Ott, *President*
Michelle Quiles, *Info Tech Dir*
EMP: 110
SQ FT: 10,000
SALES (est): 9MM **Privately Held**
WEB: www.conflorsvcofca.com
SIC: 5023 Home furnishings; floor coverings

(P-6856)
COOKS WAREHOUSE INC
2504 N Ontario St, Burbank (91504-2512)
PHONE 818 556-2740
Fax: 818 556-2746
Daniel Greene, *CEO*
Eileen Stuart Wright, *President*
Howard Teichman, *VP Mktg*
▲ EMP: 50
SALES (est): 11.9MM **Privately Held**
WEB: www.onlinecookery.com
SIC: 5023 Kitchen tools & utensils

(P-6857)
E & E CO LTD (PA)
Also Called: Jla Home
45875 Northport Loop E, Fremont (94538-6414)
PHONE 510 490-9788
Edmund Jin, *CEO*
Susan Wang, *Vice Pres*
Nancy Hattersley, *Admin Sec*
Jeremy Xu, *Info Tech Mgr*
Jessica Jeng, *Controller*
◆ EMP: 180
SQ FT: 60,000
SALES (est): 219.7MM **Privately Held**
WEB: WWW.ESHEER.COM
SIC: 5023 Sheets, textile

(P-6858)
ELEGANCE WOOD PRODUCTS INC
Also Called: Elegance Exotic Wood Flooring
7351 Mcguire Ave, Fontana (92336-1668)
PHONE 909 484-7676
Jean Tong, *CEO*
Michael Liu, *Accountant*
▲ EMP: 60
SQ FT: 500,000
SALES (est): 12.4MM **Privately Held**
SIC: 5023 Wood flooring

(P-6859)
EV RAY INC
6400 Variel Ave, Woodland Hills (91367-2577)
PHONE 818 346-5381
Fax: 818 610-0621
Lee Brown, *President*
Helen Kim, *Finance Mgr*
Beatrice Gomes, *Manager*
Chris W Halling, *Agent*
EMP: 50
SQ FT: 22,000
SALES (est): 6.8MM **Privately Held**
WEB: www.rayev.com
SIC: 5023 2211 2591 2391 Draperies; draperies & drapery fabrics, cotton; drapery hardware & blinds & shades; curtains & draperies

(P-6860)
EVRIHOLDER PRODUCTS LLC (PA)
1500 S Lewis St, Anaheim (92805-6423)
PHONE 714 490-7878
Fax: 714 502-9958
Ivan Stein, *CEO*
Scott Neamand, *CFO*
Hilton Blieden, *Vice Pres*
Lilia Maldonado, *Human Res Mgr*
Laurelle Widgerow, *Marketing Mgr*
▲ EMP: 50
SQ FT: 45,000
SALES (est): 36.4MM **Privately Held**
SIC: 5023 5085 5087 Kitchenware; bins & containers, storage; cleaning & maintenance equipment & supplies

(P-6861)
FORMATION BRANDS LLC
Also Called: Slant
400 Oyster Point Blvd # 200, South San Francisco (94080-1918)
PHONE 650 238-1009
Alex Finch, *Owner*
Christa Leonard, *CFO*
Leslie Miller, *Director*
▲ EMP: 57 EST: 1998
SQ FT: 8,000
SALES (est): 30.7MM **Privately Held**
WEB: www.formationinc.com
SIC: 5023 Decorative home furnishings & supplies

(P-6862)
GALLEHER CORPORATION (PA)
9303 Greenleaf Ave, Santa Fe Springs (90670-3029)
PHONE 562 944-8885
Fax: 562 941-3929
Jeff Hamar, *CEO*
Derek Hui, *President*
Vicki Dryden, *Bd of Directors*
Rick Coates, *Senior VP*
Todd Hamar, *Senior VP*
▲ EMP: 110 EST: 1937
SQ FT: 100,000
SALES: 175MM **Privately Held**
WEB: www.galleher.com
SIC: 5023 Wood flooring

(P-6863)
GATE FIVE GROUP LLC
Also Called: Roost
200 Gate 5 Rd Ste 116, Sausalito (94965-1456)
PHONE 415 339-9500
Scott Donnellan,
Diane Panelo, *Controller*
Kevin Freswick, *Sales Dir*
Lisa Grundy, *Director*
Dave Covey, *Manager*
◆ EMP: 50
SQ FT: 1,500
SALES (est): 16.2MM **Privately Held**
SIC: 5023 Decorative home furnishings & supplies

(P-6864)
GIBSON OVERSEAS INC
2410 Yates Ave, Commerce (90040-1918)
PHONE 323 832-8900
Fax: 323 832-0900
Sohail Gabbay, *CEO*
Helen Gabbay, *Shareholder*
Darioush Gabbay, *COO*
Soloman Gabbay, *CFO*
Belynda Bridges, *Vice Pres*
◆ EMP: 510
SQ FT: 850,000
SALES: 200.5MM **Privately Held**
WEB: www.gibsonusa.com
SIC: 5023 Glassware; china; kitchen tools & utensils

(P-6865)
GINA B LTD INC
Also Called: Gina B Showroom
1601 W 134th St, Gardena (90249-2013)
PHONE 310 366-7926
Fax: 310 366-7937
Rolf Berschneider, *President*
Gina Berschneider, *Vice Pres*
EMP: 62 EST: 1968

SALES (est): 6.9MM **Privately Held**
SIC: 5023 2599 2542 2273 Home furnishings; factory furniture & fixtures; partitions & fixtures, except wood; carpets & rugs

(P-6866)
GLOBAL ACCENTS INC
19808 Normandie Ave, Torrance (90502-1112)
PHONE 310 639-2600
Danny Partielli, *President*
Girly Oreta, *Accountant*
▲ EMP: 110
SQ FT: 50,000
SALES (est): 13.1MM **Privately Held**
SIC: 5023 Floor coverings; bedspreads

(P-6867)
HORNER-GALLEHER HOLDING CO (PA)
9303 Greenleaf Ave, Santa Fe Springs (90670-3029)
PHONE 562 944-8885
David Goodman, *Post Master*
Michelle Credit, *Analyst*
Jonathan Leon, *Buyer*
EMP: 150
SQ FT: 100,000
SALES (est): 14.9MM **Privately Held**
SIC: 5023 Floor coverings

(P-6868)
INTERNTONAL WIN TREATMENTS INC (PA)
Also Called: Custom Craft Company
12301 Hawkins St, Santa Fe Springs (90670-3366)
PHONE 562 236-2120
Tsong Shih, *President*
Hsawn Shih, *Shareholder*
Tony Chang, *Accountant*
◆ EMP: 100
SQ FT: 30,000
SALES (est): 18.5MM **Privately Held**
SIC: 5023 Venetian blinds

(P-6869)
K T W PRODUCTIONS INC
6303 E Cedarbrooks Rd, Orange (92867-2491)
PHONE 714 685-0428
Fax: 714 685-0498
Lola Wang, *President*
Rex Wang, *Vice Pres*
EMP: 800
SALES (est): 64.7MM **Privately Held**
SIC: 5023 Home furnishings

(P-6870)
KEECO LLC (PA)
30736 Wiegman Rd, Hayward (94544-7819)
PHONE 510 324-8800
Dan J Stengel, *Mng Member*
Grant Wee, *IT/INT Sup*
Greg Wyman, *Marketing Staff*
Martin Berry,
Kristine Igoe,
◆ EMP: 70
SQ FT: 500,000
SALES: 212K **Privately Held**
WEB: www.lkeeco.com
SIC: 5023 Linens & towels; linens, table

(P-6871)
LEDRA BRANDS INC
Also Called: Bruck Lighting
15774 Gateway Cir, Tustin (92780-6469)
PHONE 714 259-9959
Fax: 714 259-9969
Alex Ladjevardi, *President*
Farah Emami, *Financial Exec*
Sylvia Alvarado, *Accounts Mgr*
▲ EMP: 55
SQ FT: 30,000
SALES (est): 28.5MM **Privately Held**
WEB: www.brucklightingsystems.com
SIC: 5023 Lamps: floor, boudoir, desk

(P-6872)
LONGUST DISTRIBUTING INC
1206 N Miller St Unit A, Anaheim (92806-1960)
PHONE 480 820-6244
John Trujillo, *Branch Mgr*

▲ = Import ▼=Export
◆ =Import/Export

PRODUCTS & SERVICES SECTION
5023 - Home Furnishings Wholesale County (P-6895)

Jim Golotko, *Manager*
EMP: 50
SALES (corp-wide): 113MM **Privately Held**
SIC: 5023 Floor coverings; resilient floor coverings: tile or sheet; carpets; wood flooring
PA: Longust Distributing, Inc.
2432 W Birchwood Ave
Mesa AZ 85202
480 820-6244

(P-6873)
MARIAK INDUSTRIES INC
Also Called: Mariak Window Fashion
575 W Manville St, Rancho Dominguez (90220-5509)
PHONE..................310 661-4400
Leo Elinson, *CEO*
Patrice Elinson, *Vice Pres*
Bobby Cua, *Accounting Mgr*
Alma Sy, *Accountant*
▲ **EMP:** 380
SQ FT: 80,000
SALES (est): 189.7MM **Privately Held**
SIC: 5023 2591 Vertical blinds; blinds vertical

(P-6874)
MEYER CORPORATION US
Also Called: Faberware Div
2001 Meyer Way, Fairfield (94533-6802)
PHONE..................707 399-2100
Stuart Levine, *Manager*
EMP: 100 **Privately Held**
WEB: www.meyer.com
SIC: 5023 3469 1541 5046 Kitchenware; cooking ware, except porcelain enamelled; industrial buildings & warehouses; commercial equipment; pressed & blown glass
HQ: Meyer Corporation, U.S.
1 Meyer Plz
Vallejo CA 94590
707 551-2800

(P-6875)
NEXGRILL INDUSTRIES INC
14050 Laurelwood Pl, Chino (91710-5454)
PHONE..................909 598-8799
Sherman Lin, *President*
Hailey Erejo, *Administration*
Annie Kuo, *Financial Exec*
Rachel Ngan, *Human Resources*
Sylvia Salgado, *Cust Mgr*
▲ **EMP:** 100
SQ FT: 50,000
SALES (est): 39.5MM **Privately Held**
WEB: www.nexgrill.com
SIC: 5023 3631 Grills, barbecue; barbecues, grills & braziers (outdoor cooking)

(P-6876)
NORMAN INTERNATIONAL INC
Also Called: Norman Charter
12301 Hawkins St, Santa Fe Springs (90670-3366)
PHONE..................562 946-0420
Ranjan Mada, *CEO*
Ricky Wang, *Info Tech Dir*
James Wang, *Info Tech Mgr*
Erica Ching, *Webmaster*
Sabino Liu, *Human Res Mgr*
◆ **EMP:** 70
SALES (est): 66.1MM **Privately Held**
WEB: www.normanintlusa.com
SIC: 5023 Home furnishings

(P-6877)
OLDE THOMPSON INC
3250 Camino Del Sol, Oxnard (93030-8998)
PHONE..................805 983-0388
Jeffrey M Shumway, *CEO*
Scott Ash, *CFO*
Dale Deberry, *Vice Pres*
Steve Pellnitz, *Engineer*
Doug McKenzie, *Safety Mgr*
◆ **EMP:** 150
SQ FT: 88,000
SALES (est): 81.6MM **Privately Held**
WEB: www.oldethompson.com
SIC: 5023 2631 5149 Kitchenware; container, packaging & boxboard; spices & seasonings

(P-6878)
OMEGA MOULDING WEST LLC
5500 Lindbergh Ln, Bell (90201-6410)
PHONE..................323 261-3510
Bernard Portnoy, *Mng Member*
Ken Brodsky, *CFO*
David Merzin,
Anastasia Portnoy,
◆ **EMP:** 130
SQ FT: 130,000
SALES (est): 18.2MM **Privately Held**
WEB: www.omegamoulding.com
SIC: 5023 Frames & framing, picture & mirror

(P-6879)
PAVIGYM AMERICA CORP
1902 Wright Pl Fl 2, Carlsbad (92008-6583)
PHONE..................858 414-8624
Marcos Requena Penat, *CEO*
Dan Polerecky, *Sales Mgr*
EMP: 100
SALES (est): 12.3MM **Privately Held**
SIC: 5023 Floor coverings

(P-6880)
PEKING HANDICRAFT INC (PA)
1388 San Mateo Ave, South San Francisco (94080-6501)
PHONE..................650 871-3788
Fax: 650 871-3781
Annie Lo, *CEO*
Mike King, *CFO*
Laura Donald, *Vice Pres*
Julie Muller, *Analyst*
Doris Fringeli, *Human Res Dir*
▲ **EMP:** 150
SQ FT: 150,000
SALES (est): 64.3MM **Privately Held**
WEB: www.pkhc.com
SIC: 5023 Linens & towels; bedspreads; sheets, textile; decorative home furnishings & supplies

(P-6881)
POTTERY BARN INC
3200 N Sepulveda Blvd B1, Manhattan Beach (90266-2466)
PHONE..................310 545-1906
Jason Farley, *Branch Mgr*
EMP: 50
SALES (corp-wide): 4.9B **Publicly Held**
WEB: www.potterybarn.com
SIC: 5023 Decorative home furnishings & supplies
HQ: Pottery Barn, Inc.
3250 Van Ness Ave
San Francisco CA 94109
415 421-7900

(P-6882)
POTTERY BARN INC
1822 Redwood Hwy, Corte Madera (94925-1235)
PHONE..................415 924-1391
Fax: 415 924-0448
Mariposa Mackley, *Manager*
EMP: 60
SALES (corp-wide): 4.9B **Publicly Held**
WEB: www.potterybarn.com
SIC: 5023 Decorative home furnishings & supplies
HQ: Pottery Barn, Inc.
3250 Van Ness Ave
San Francisco CA 94109
415 421-7900

(P-6883)
R&S CARPET SERVICES INC
Also Called: R & S Floor Covering
1485 Spruce St Ste C106, Riverside (92507-2445)
PHONE..................909 740-6645
Fax: 909 923-2811
Roy Paswaters, *President*
Steven Birito, *Vice Pres*
Marcos Carrasco, *Vice Pres*
Terry Paswaters, *Manager*
EMP: 61
SQ FT: 9,000
SALES (est): 8.7MM **Privately Held**
SIC: 5023 1752 Carpets; carpet laying

(P-6884)
RONCO INVENTIONS LLC (PA)
21344 Superior St, Chatsworth (91311-4312)
PHONE..................800 486-1806
Ronald Popeil,
Keith Smith, *CFO*
Carlos La De Fuente, *Plant Mgr*
Thomas J Lykos, *Director*
EMP: 150 **EST:** 1989
SALES (est): 17.1MM **Privately Held**
SIC: 5023 5719 3634 3556 Kitchenware; kitchenware; electric housewares & fans; food products machinery

(P-6885)
S R S M INC
Also Called: Vm International
945 E Church St, Riverside (92507-1103)
PHONE..................310 952-9000
Roya Vazin, *CEO*
Moe II Afsari, *Manager*
▲ **EMP:** 120
SQ FT: 110,000
SALES (est): 74MM **Privately Held**
WEB: www.srsm.com
SIC: 5023 2821 Home furnishings; kitchenware; plastics materials & resins

(P-6886)
SIMPLEHUMAN LLC (PA)
19850 Magellan Dr, Torrance (90502-1106)
PHONE..................310 436-2250
Frank Yang, *Mng Member*
Yvonne Bao, *CFO*
Jackson Yang,
Julie Yang,
Sanam Lahijani, *Manager*
◆ **EMP:** 55
SQ FT: 55,000
SALES (est): 35.8MM **Privately Held**
WEB: www.simplehuman.net
SIC: 5023 Home furnishings; kitchenware; linens & towels

(P-6887)
SOTO PROVISION INC
Also Called: Soto Food Service
949 S Meridian Ave, Alhambra (91803-1214)
PHONE..................626 458-4600
Fax: 626 458-4646
Catana Renna, *Admin Sec*
EMP: 70
SQ FT: 35,000
SALES (est): 79.7MM **Privately Held**
WEB: www.sotofoodservice.com
SIC: 5023 5046 Kitchen tools & utensils; kitchenware; commercial cooking & food service equipment

(P-6888)
SUNDAY BAZAAR INC
Also Called: Lunares
495 Barneveld Ave, San Francisco (94124-1501)
PHONE..................415 621-0764
Fax: 415 621-0768
Nimerta Oberoi, *President*
▲ **EMP:** 87
SQ FT: 4,000
SALES (est): 11.2MM **Privately Held**
WEB: www.lunares.com
SIC: 5023 5199 Decorative home furnishings & supplies; gifts & novelties

(P-6889)
SUPERIOR HOME DESIGN INC
Also Called: Discount Hrdwood Flors Mldings
1800 E 50th St, Los Angeles (90058-1941)
PHONE..................213 455-8972
Zahal Mansur, *CEO*
Michal Mansur, *CFO*
Michael Fairley, *Officer*
▲ **EMP:** 65
SQ FT: 50,000
SALES: 22MM **Privately Held**
SIC: 5023 Resilient floor coverings: tile or sheet

(P-6890)
TABLETOPS UNLIMITED INC (PA)
23000 Avalon Blvd, Carson (90745-5017)
PHONE..................310 549-6000
Javad Asgari, *CEO*
Mohsen Asgari, *President*
Hamid Ebrahimi, *CFO*
Daryoush Molayem, *Vice Pres*
Masod Tehrani, *Admin Sec*
◆ **EMP:** 68
SQ FT: 350,000
SALES (est): 42.9MM **Privately Held**
WEB: www.tabletopsunltd.com
SIC: 5023 China; glassware; stainless steel flatware

(P-6891)
TEST-RITE PRODUCTS CORP (DH)
1900 Burgundy Pl, Ontario (91761-2317)
PHONE..................909 605-9899
Fax: 909 605-9968
Chester Lee, *President*
Melvin Shiraki, *Exec VP*
Agnes Shih, *Administration*
Erlin Tangpiti, *Accounting Mgr*
Christina MA, *Controller*
◆ **EMP:** 100
SQ FT: 400,000
SALES: 139MM
SALES (corp-wide): 1.1B **Privately Held**
SIC: 5023 Home furnishings
HQ: Test-Rite International (U.S.) Co., Ltd.
1900 Burgundy Pl
Ontario CA 91761
909 605-9899

(P-6892)
THUNDER GROUP INC (PA)
780 Nogales St Ste C, City of Industry (91748-1380)
PHONE..................626 935-1605
Eddie Liu, *CEO*
Chun Chieh Liu, *President*
Ralph Liu, *Vice Pres*
Henry Lin, *Branch Mgr*
Lin CHI Liu, *Admin Sec*
▲ **EMP:** 50
SQ FT: 340,000
SALES (est): 32.8MM **Privately Held**
SIC: 5023 Kitchenware

(P-6893)
TIFFANY DALE INC (PA)
14765 Firestone Blvd, La Mirada (90638-5918)
PHONE..................714 739-2700
Ye H Chung, *CEO*
Connie Chung, *Admin Sec*
Erwin Perlas, *Manager*
▲ **EMP:** 83
SQ FT: 88,480
SALES (est): 13.2MM **Privately Held**
SIC: 5023 Lamps: floor, boudoir, desk

(P-6894)
TOM RAY INDUSTRIES INC
Also Called: Thefloorstore/Flor Stor
23052 Alcalde Dr Ste B, Laguna Hills (92653-1327)
PHONE..................949 380-8333
Fax: 949 380-7902
Thomas Ray, *President*
EMP: 100
SQ FT: 700,000
SALES (est): 17.2MM **Privately Held**
WEB: www.florstor.com
SIC: 5023 5211 1752 5713 Floor coverings; flooring, wood; wood floor installation & refinishing; floor tile; specialty cleaning & sanitation preparations; interior decorating

(P-6895)
TRANSPAC INC
1050 Piper Dr, Vacaville (95688-8709)
PHONE..................707 452-0600
Dan Desantis, *Ch of Bd*
Laurie Gilner, *CEO*
Brian Karr, *CFO*
Craig Mackley, *CFO*
Emily Wang, *Vice Pres*
◆ **EMP:** 90
SQ FT: 180,000
SALES (est): 68.2MM **Privately Held**
SIC: 5023 Decorative home furnishings & supplies

5023 - Home Furnishings Wholesale County (P-6896)

PRODUCTS & SERVICES SECTION

(P-6896)
TRI - STAR WIN COVERINGS INC
Also Called: Carpet Care By Tri-Star
19555 Prairie St, Northridge (91324-2424)
PHONE..................................818 718-3188
Bernard Warshauer, *CEO*
Deborah Newhouse, *Controller*
Maggie Younany, *Sr Project Mgr*
EMP: 50
SQ FT: 22,000
SALES (est): 27.1MM Privately Held
WEB: www.tsinteriors.com
SIC: 5023 5719 Floor coverings; window furnishings; window furnishings

(P-6897)
TRI-WEST LTD (PA)
12005 Pike St, Santa Fe Springs (90670-6100)
PHONE..................................562 692-9166
Fax: 562 692-5109
Allen Gage, *Partner*
Jim Johnston, *CFO*
Randy Sims, *CFO*
Dan Proctor, *Exec VP*
Bob Taylor, *Executive*
▲ **EMP:** 200 EST: 1981
SQ FT: 300,000
SALES: 182.6MM Privately Held
WEB: www.triwestltd.com
SIC: 5023 Floor coverings; resilient floor coverings: tile or sheet; wood flooring

(P-6898)
UMA ENTERPRISES INC (PA)
350 W Apra St, Compton (90220-5529)
PHONE..................................310 631-1166
Fax: 310 631-2124
Naval Bansal, *CEO*
Avadhesh Agarwal, *President*
Uma Agarwal, *Admin Sec*
Amrick Singh, *Administration*
Kamal Arody, *Opers Mgr*
▲ **EMP:** 120
SQ FT: 460,000
SALES (est): 51.9MM Privately Held
WEB: www.umainc.com
SIC: 5023 Decorative home furnishings & supplies

(P-6899)
UNIQUE CARPETS LTD
7360 Jurupa Ave, Riverside (92504-1025)
PHONE..................................951 352-8125
Bill D Graves, *President*
Robert L Binford, *Exec VP*
Martin Lopez, *Vice Pres*
Jenn Ellison, *Director*
▲ **EMP:** 55
SALES (est): 16.8MM Privately Held
WEB: www.uniquecarpets.com
SIC: 5023 2273 Carpets; carpets & rugs

(P-6900)
UNIVERSAL WOOD MOULDING INC (PA)
Also Called: Universal Framing Products
21139 Centre Pointe Pkwy, Santa Clarita (91350-2994)
PHONE..................................661 362-6262
Jon M Bromberg, *CEO*
AVI Feibenlatt, *Ch of Bd*
Mark Gottlieb, *President*
Karla Torres, *Office Mgr*
Cliff Uy, *Info Tech Dir*
▲ **EMP:** 50
SALES (est): 22.7MM Privately Held
WEB: www.universalframing.com
SIC: 5023 3999 Frames & framing, picture & mirror; atomizers; toiletry; advertising curtains

(P-6901)
VALLEY WHOLESALE SUPPLY CORP (PA)
Also Called: Valley Molding & Frame
10708 Vanowen St, North Hollywood (91605-6401)
PHONE..................................818 769-5656
Charles Aaron, *Ch of Bd*
Michelle Merritt, *Shareholder*
David A Labowitz, *President*
Suzanne Ehrmann, *Vice Pres*
▲ **EMP:** 57
SQ FT: 30,000
SALES (est): 22.1MM Privately Held
WEB: www.valleymoulding.com
SIC: 5023 5031 Frames & framing, picture & mirror; decorating supplies; molding, all materials

(P-6902)
VALYRIA LLC ◆
Also Called: Transpac
1050 Aviator Dr, Vacaville (95688)
PHONE..................................707 452-0600
Laurie Gilner, *President*
Craig Mackley, *Vice Pres*
▲ **EMP:** 60 EST: 2016
SQ FT: 175,000
SALES (est): 5.8MM Privately Held
SIC: 5023 Decorative home furnishings & supplies

(P-6903)
VENUS GROUP INC
Also Called: Venus Textiles
25861 Wright, Foothill Ranch (92610-3504)
PHONE..................................949 609-1299
Fax: 949 455-9499
Kirit D Patel, *CEO*
Chuck Loitz, *Vice Pres*
Rajni D Patel, *Vice Pres*
Gerry Rementer, *VP Sales*
Surendra Jain, *Manager*
▲ **EMP:** 85
SALES (est): 89.4MM Privately Held
WEB: www.venusgroup.com
SIC: 5023 2392 5719 Towels; towels, fabric & nonwoven: made from purchased materials; towels

(P-6904)
W DIAMOND SUPPLY CO (DH)
Also Called: Diamond W Floorcovering
19321 E Walnut Dr N, City of Industry (91748-1436)
PHONE..................................909 859-8939
Fax: 909 859-8939
Louis J Bettitta, *CEO*
Mike Klingele, *President*
Kandi Anderson, *COO*
Daniel Erickson, *CFO*
Lenor Newcommer, *Accountant*
▲ **EMP:** 60
SQ FT: 106,000
SALES (est): 28.6MM
SALES (corp-wide): 35.9MM Privately Held
WEB: www.diamondw.com
SIC: 5023 Floor coverings
HQ: Tarkett, Inc
  16910 Munn Rd
  Chagrin Falls OH 44023
  800 899-8916

5031 Lumber, Plywood & Millwork Wholesale

(P-6905)
ALLIED BUILDING PRODUCTS CORP
Also Called: AMS
1620 S Maple Ave, Montebello (90640-6510)
PHONE..................................323 721-9011
Fax: 323 726-7762
Bill Wick, *Branch Mgr*
Eric Ranson, *Treasurer*
April Rodriguez, *Purch Dir*
George Wilber, *Production*
Oj Dutcher, *Sales Associate*
EMP: 100
SALES (corp-wide): 25.3B Privately Held
WEB: www.a-m-s.com
SIC: 5031 Building materials, exterior
HQ: Allied Building Products Corp.
  15 E Union Ave
  East Rutherford NJ 07073
  201 507-8400

(P-6906)
AMERICAN BUILDING SUPPLY INC (PA)
Also Called: Abs-American Building Supply
8360 Elder Creek Rd, Sacramento (95828-1705)
P.O. Box 293030 (95829-3030)
PHONE..................................916 503-4100
Fax: 916 503-4198
Mark Ballantyne, *President*
Son Winn, *President*
Dave Baker, *Vice Pres*
Jan Leonard, *Vice Pres*
Doug Shorey, *Executive*
▲ **EMP:** 250
SQ FT: 230,000
SALES (est): 324.9MM Privately Held
WEB: www.infinitydoor.com
SIC: 5031 3231 Doors; door frames, all materials; doors, glass: made from purchased glass

(P-6907)
AMERICAN BUILDING SUPPLY INC
1488 Tillie Lewis Dr, Stockton (95206-1131)
PHONE..................................209 941-8852
Randy Neto, *Branch Mgr*
Alan Terry, *Maintence Staff*
EMP: 100
SALES (corp-wide): 324.9MM Privately Held
WEB: www.infinitydoor.com
SIC: 5031 Doors & windows
PA: American Building Supply, Inc.
  8360 Elder Creek Rd
  Sacramento CA 95828
  916 503-4100

(P-6908)
ANFINSON LUMBER SALES INC (PA)
13041 Union Ave, Fontana (92337-6952)
PHONE..................................951 681-4707
Fax: 951 681-3566
Richard Anfinson, *President*
Patricia J Anfinson, *Admin Sec*
Dorothy Farone, *Controller*
Doug Willis, *Sales Mgr*
Gary Mathis, *Manager*
EMP: 60
SQ FT: 48,000
SALES (est): 11.2MM Privately Held
WEB: www.anfinson.com
SIC: 5031 Lumber: rough, dressed & finished

(P-6909)
AWM LLC
8180 Industrial Pkwy, Sacramento (95824-2312)
PHONE..................................916 381-4200
EMP: 61
SALES (corp-wide): 124.9MM Privately Held
SIC: 5031 Lumber: rough, dressed & finished; millwork
PA: Awm, Llc
  1800 Washington Blvd # 140
  Baltimore MD 21230
  916 387-7317

(P-6910)
B B & T MANAGEMENT CORP
Also Called: Blomberg Window
1453 Blair Ave, Sacramento (95822-3410)
P.O. Box 22485 (95822-0485)
PHONE..................................916 428-8060
Fax: 916 422-1967
J Philip Collier, *President*
Ralph S Blomberg, *Vice Pres*
Bill Harris, *Mktg Coord*
EMP: 200
SALES (est): 21.9MM Privately Held
SIC: 5031 Windows

(P-6911)
BUILDING MATERIAL DISTRS INC (PA)
Also Called: B M D
225 Elm Ave, Galt (95632-1558)
P.O. Box 606 (95632-0606)
PHONE..................................209 745-3001
Fax: 209 745-0707
Mike Garrison, *Chairman*
Jeff Gore, *President*
Jim Colson, *CFO*
Steven Ellinwood, *Chairman*
Janice Klassen, *Credit Mgr*
▲ **EMP:** 170
SQ FT: 100,000
SALES (est): 286.9MM Privately Held
WEB: www.bmdusa.com
SIC: 5031 Building materials, exterior; building materials, interior; window frames, all materials; door frames, all materials

(P-6912)
BUILDING MATERIAL DISTRS INC
100 Sinclair St, Perris (92571-3167)
PHONE..................................951 341-0708
Ron Shea, *Branch Mgr*
EMP: 100
SALES (corp-wide): 286.9MM Privately Held
SIC: 5031 Building materials, exterior
PA: Building Material Distributors, Inc.
  225 Elm Ave
  Galt CA 95632
  209 745-3001

(P-6913)
CERTAINTEED GYPSUM INC
27442 Portola Pkwy # 100, El Toro (92610-2823)
PHONE..................................949 282-5300
Jeff Dushack, *Manager*
EMP: 50
SALES (corp-wide): 474.1MM Privately Held
WEB: www.bpb-na.com
SIC: 5031 Wallboard
PA: Certainteed Gypsum, Inc.
  750 E Swedesford Rd
  Wayne PA 19087
  813 286-3900

(P-6914)
CHA-DOR REALTY
Also Called: Meek's
4243 Dominguez Rd, Rocklin (95677-2101)
P.O. Box 1688 (95677-7688)
PHONE..................................916 624-0627
Fax: 916 624-5546
Creig Miller, *Manager*
Heidi Scardina, *Sales Staff*
EMP: 52
SQ FT: 30,842
SALES (corp-wide): 47.3MM Privately Held
SIC: 5031 5211 Lumber, plywood & millwork; lumber & other building materials
PA: Cha-Dor Realty
  1651 Response Rd Ste 200
  Sacramento CA 95815
  916 565-1586

(P-6915)
CHAMPION LUMBER CO
1313 Chicago Ave Ste 100, Riverside (92507-2000)
P.O. Box 55068 (92517-0068)
PHONE..................................951 684-5670
Fax: 951 275-0825
George T Champion, *President*
Joe Audette, *CFO*
Clark Taylor, *Officer*
Mark Boone, *Vice Pres*
Mike Smith, *Sales Associate*
EMP: 100
SQ FT: 20,000
SALES (est): 76.9MM Privately Held
WEB: www.championlumber.net
SIC: 5031 Lumber: rough, dressed & finished

(P-6916)
COLLIER WAREHOUSE INC
Also Called: Cwi
90 Dorman Ave, San Francisco (94124-1807)
PHONE..................................415 920-9720
Fax: 415 920-9727
Paul C Akin, *CEO*
David C Freer, *President*
Douglas Whitsitt, *CFO*
Christy Akin, *Admin Sec*
▼ **EMP:** 50
SQ FT: 8,000
SALES (est): 34.1MM Privately Held
WEB: www.collier-sf.com
SIC: 5031 1751 Windows; doors; skylights, all materials; window & door (prefabricated) installation

PRODUCTS & SERVICES SECTION
5031 - Lumber, Plywood & Millwork Wholesale County (P-6936)

(P-6917)
COLLINS PINE COMPANY
1 Chateau Way, Chester (96020)
PHONE 530 258-2111
Mike Zion, *Branch Mgr*
EMP: 100
SALES (corp-wide): 137.7MM **Privately Held**
WEB: www.collinswood.com
SIC: 5031 Lumber: rough, dressed & finished
PA: Collins Pine Company
 29100 Sw Town Ctr
 Wilsonville OR 97070
 503 227-1219

(P-6918)
COMMERCIAL LBR & PALLET CO INC
135 Long Ln, City of Industry (91746-2633)
PHONE 626 968-0631
Catheline Detrick, *Manager*
EMP: 150
SALES (corp-wide): 87.2MM **Privately Held**
SIC: 5031 Lumber: rough, dressed & finished
PA: Commercial Lumber & Pallet Co., Inc.
 135 Long Ln
 City Of Industry CA 91746
 626 968-0631

(P-6919)
COMPLETE MILLWORK SERVICES INC
405 Aldo Ave, Santa Clara (95054-2302)
PHONE 408 567-9664
EMP: 75
SALES (corp-wide): 94.1MM **Privately Held**
SIC: 5031 Millwork
PA: Complete Millwork Services, Inc.
 4909 Goni Rd Ste A
 Carson City NV 89706
 775 246-0485

(P-6920)
DISCOUNT BUILDERS SUPPLY
1695 Mission St, San Francisco (94103-2432)
PHONE 415 285-2800
Charles Goodman, *President*
Randy Ahlgrim, *Info Tech Mgr*
Mike Heffernan, *Manager*
▲ **EMP:** 69
SQ FT: 40,000
SALES (est): 31MM **Privately Held**
SIC: 5031 5211 Building materials, exterior; lumber & other building materials

(P-6921)
EL & EL WOOD PRODUCTS CORP (PA)
6011 Schaefer Ave, Chino (91710-7043)
PHONE 909 591-0339
Fax: 909 627-5083
Cathy Vidas, *President*
Flavia Silva, *Accounting Mgr*
Al Bhakta, *Sales Associate*
Rick Hegemier, *Sales Associate*
Carl Thompson, *Marketing Staff*
▲ **EMP:** 99 **EST:** 1963
SQ FT: 72,000
SALES (est): 89.5MM **Privately Held**
WEB: www.elandelwoodproducts.com
SIC: 5031 Millwork

(P-6922)
EMPIRE COMPANY LLC
31 Heron Ln, Riverside (92507-1243)
PHONE 951 742-5273
Scott Price, *Branch Mgr*
EMP: 82
SALES (corp-wide): 406MM **Privately Held**
SIC: 5031 Lumber, plywood & millwork
HQ: The Empire Company Llc
 8181 Logistics Dr
 Zeeland MI 49464
 616 772-7272

(P-6923)
FOREST PRODUCTS DISTRS INC
1090 W Waterfront Dr, Eureka (95501-0169)
P.O. Box 8088, Rapid City SD (57709-8088)
PHONE 707 443-7024
Carroll Korb, *President*
Jeff Plooster, *Controller*
EMP: 65
SALES: 950K **Privately Held**
SIC: 5031 Lumber, plywood & millwork

(P-6924)
GOLDEN STATE LUMBER INC
3033 S Airport Way, Stockton (95206-3861)
P.O. Box 31810 (95213-1810)
PHONE 209 234-7700
Fax: 209 234-7900
Ralph Panttaja, *Branch Mgr*
David Clarke, *Vice Pres*
Larry Jynes, *Director*
EMP: 200
SALES (corp-wide): 235MM **Privately Held**
WEB: www.goldenstatelumber.com
SIC: 5031 5211 Lumber, plywood & millwork; lumber & other building materials
PA: Golden State Lumber, Inc.
 855 Lakeville St Ste 200
 Petaluma CA 94952
 707 206-4100

(P-6925)
GROVE LUMBER & BLDG SUPS INC (PA)
1300 S Campus Ave, Ontario (91761-4378)
PHONE 909 947-0277
Fax: 909 947-2944
Raymond G Croll Jr, *President*
Bob Lucarelli, *VP Sales*
Dena Mills, *Accounts Mgr*
EMP: 190 **EST:** 1979
SQ FT: 3,000
SALES (est): 182.7MM **Privately Held**
SIC: 5031 5211 Lumber, plywood & millwork; lumber products

(P-6926)
H - INVESTMENT COMPANY
Also Called: Golden State Flooring
450 B St Ste 1900, San Diego (92101-8005)
PHONE 650 872-0500
Fax: 650 872-0719
Richard Coates, *Manager*
Chris Murphy, *Division Mgr*
Sharee Taylor, *Admin Asst*
Derek Swedberg, *Sales Mgr*
EMP: 80
SALES (corp-wide): 103.2MM **Privately Held**
WEB: www.higlum.com
SIC: 5031 Lumber, plywood & millwork
PA: H - Investment Company
 6999 Southfront Rd
 Livermore CA 94551
 925 245-4300

(P-6927)
HEPPNER HARDWOODS INC
555 W Danlee St, Azusa (91702-2342)
PHONE 626 969-7983
Fax: 626 969-8321
Lorraine Heppner, *President*
Brent Heppner, *COO*
Jack Bogle, *CFO*
Brian Giertz, *Executive Asst*
Christine Byrd, *Credit Mgr*
EMP: 60
SQ FT: 217,800
SALES (est): 35MM **Privately Held**
WEB: www.heppnerhardwoods.com
SIC: 5031 Lumber: rough, dressed & finished

(P-6928)
HERITAGE 1 WINDOW AND BUILDING
4300 Jetway Ct, North Highlands (95660-5702)
P.O. Box 214609, Sacramento (95821-0609)
PHONE 916 481-5030
Charles Gardemeyer, *CEO*
Stephen Beckham, *COO*
Geoff Hughes, *CFO*
John Ballou, *Sales Mgr*
Tyler Randolth, *Manager*
EMP: 171
SQ FT: 80,000
SALES: 24MM
SALES (corp-wide): 89.5MM **Privately Held**
SIC: 5031 Doors & windows
PA: Heritage Interests, Llc
 4300 Jetway Ct
 North Highlands CA 95660
 916 481-5030

(P-6929)
HERITAGE ONE CARPENTRY INC
2107 Forest Ave Ste 100, Chico (95928-7696)
PHONE 530 345-6622
Charles Gardemeyer, *President*
Stephen Beckham, *COO*
Geoffrey Hughes, *CFO*
EMP: 162 **EST:** 2012
SQ FT: 3,000
SALES: 33.9MM
SALES (corp-wide): 89.5MM **Privately Held**
SIC: 5031 1751 Lumber, plywood & millwork; cabinet & finish carpentry
PA: Heritage Interests, Llc
 4300 Jetway Ct
 North Highlands CA 95660
 916 481-5030

(P-6930)
HERITAGE ONE DOOR AND BUILDING
4300 Jetway Ct, North Highlands (95660-5702)
P.O. Box 214609, Sacramento (95821-0609)
PHONE 916 481-5030
Charles Gardemeyer, *Mng Member*
Stephen Beckham, *COO*
John Dutter, *COO*
Geoff Hughes, *CFO*
John Ballou, *Sales Mgr*
EMP: 86
SQ FT: 80,000
SALES: 31.6MM
SALES (corp-wide): 89.5MM **Privately Held**
SIC: 5031 2431 Doors & windows; windows & window parts & trim, wood
PA: Heritage Interests, Llc
 4300 Jetway Ct
 North Highlands CA 95660
 916 481-5030

(P-6931)
HIGHLAND LUMBER SALES INC
300 E Santa Ana St, Anaheim (92805-3953)
PHONE 714 778-2293
Fax: 714 778-2298
Ken Lobue, *President*
Richard Phillips, *President*
Richard J Phillips, *CEO*
Carol Robertson, *Credit Mgr*
Alan Arbiso, *Relg Ldr*
▲ **EMP:** 60
SQ FT: 2,000
SALES (est): 26.7MM **Privately Held**
SIC: 5031 2493 2431 5211 Lumber: rough, dressed & finished; reconstituted wood products; millwork; lumber products

(P-6932)
HUTTIG BUILDING PRODUCTS INC
Also Called: Huttig Sash & Door Co
8120 Pwr Rdge Rd Bldg 100, Sacramento (95826)
PHONE 916 383-3721
Fax: 916 381-2834
Doug Brian, *General Mgr*
EMP: 60
SALES (corp-wide): 659.6MM **Publicly Held**
WEB: www.huttig.com
SIC: 5031 Lumber, plywood & millwork
PA: Huttig Building Products, Inc.
 555 Maryville University
 Saint Louis MO 63141
 314 216-2600

(P-6933)
JAMES HARDIE BUILDING PDTS INC (DH)
Also Called: Jameshardie
26300 La Alameda Ste 400, Mission Viejo (92691-8372)
PHONE 949 348-1800
Fax: 949 367-4997
Louis Gries, *CEO*
Matthew Marsh, *CFO*
Ginger Lester, *Treasurer*
Mark Fisher, *Exec VP*
Ryan Sullivan, *Exec VP*
◆ **EMP:** 200
SQ FT: 10,000
SALES (est): 469.3MM **Privately Held**
SIC: 5031 Building materials, exterior; building materials, interior
HQ: James Hardie Transition Co., Inc.
 26300 La Alameda Ste 400
 Mission Viejo CA 92691
 949 348-1800

(P-6934)
JAMES HARDIE BUILDING PDTS INC
10901 Elm Ave, Fontana (92337-7327)
PHONE 909 355-6500
Bob Mussleman, *Branch Mgr*
Louis Gries, *Vice Pres*
Dave Merkley, *Vice Pres*
Steven Terzian, *Technical Mgr*
Charles Fake, *Engineer*
EMP: 190 **Privately Held**
SIC: 5031 3272 Building materials, exterior; areaways, basement window: concrete
HQ: James Hardie Building Products Inc.
 26300 La Alameda Ste 400
 Mission Viejo CA 92691
 949 348-1800

(P-6935)
JELD-WEN INC
Also Called: Jeld-Wen Windows
2760 Progress St Ste B, Vista (92081-8449)
PHONE 760 597-4201
Clint Honeycutt, *Vice Pres*
Jill Yeaman, *Executive*
Bill Maschmeier, *General Mgr*
Will Elchrick, *Technology*
Pat Dehann, *Plant Mgr*
EMP: 300
SALES (corp-wide): 4.1B **Privately Held**
SIC: 5031 Doors & windows
HQ: Jeld-Wen, Inc.
 440 S Church St Ste 400
 Charlotte NC 28202
 800 535-3936

(P-6936)
MENDOCINO FOREST PDTS CO LLC
Also Called: Sawmill
850 Hollow Tree Rd, Ukiah (95482-3187)
P.O. Box 120 (95482-0120)
PHONE 707 468-1431
Mike Benetti, *Branch Mgr*
Mike Bennetti, *Senior VP*
EMP: 100
SALES (corp-wide): 143.2MM **Privately Held**
SIC: 5031 2421 Lumber, plywood & millwork; sawmills & planing mills, general
PA: Mendocino Forest Products Company Llc
 1360 19th Hole Dr Ste 200
 Calpella CA 95418
 707 620-2961

5031 - Lumber, Plywood & Millwork Wholesale County (P-6937)

(P-6937)
MENDOCINO FOREST PDTS CO LLC
Also Called: Calpella Distribution Center
6375 N State St, Calpella (95418)
P.O. Box 336 (95418-0336)
PHONE 707 485-6800
Mike Benetti, Branch Mgr
EMP: 94
SALES (corp-wide): 143.2MM **Privately Held**
SIC: 5031 2421 Lumber, plywood & millwork; sawmills & planing mills, general
PA: Mendocino Forest Products Company Llc
1360 19th Hole Dr Ste 200
Calpella CA 95418
707 620-2961

(P-6938)
NICHOLS LUMBER & HARDWARE CO
13470 Dalewood St, Baldwin Park (91706-5883)
PHONE 626 960-4802
Fax: 626 962-1067
Judith A Nichols, President
Rick Dean, Vice Pres
Charles Nichols, Admin Sec
Derek Chang, Sales Associate
Jose Jimenez, Sales Associate
EMP: 75
SALES (est): 46.5MM **Privately Held**
SIC: 5031 5251 2421 Lumber: rough, dressed & finished; hardware; sawmills & planing mills, general

(P-6939)
OAKLAND PALLET COMPANY INC
4245 Industrial Way, Benicia (94510-1228)
PHONE 707 746-0100
EMP: 55
SALES (corp-wide): 61.9MM **Privately Held**
SIC: 5031 Molding, all materials
PA: Oakland Pallet Company, Inc.
2500 Grant Ave
San Lorenzo CA 94580
510 278-1291

(P-6940)
OAKLAND PALLET COMPANY INC (PA)
2500 Grant Ave, San Lorenzo (94580-1810)
PHONE 510 278-1291
Jose G Padilla, President
Javier Padilla, Corp Secy
Carlos Padilla, Vice Pres
Cesar Gonzalez, Manager
EMP: 130
SALES (est): 56.3MM **Privately Held**
SIC: 5031 7699 Pallets, wood; pallet repair

(P-6941)
OREGON PCF BLDG PDTS CALIF INC
Also Called: Orepac Building Products
8185 Signal Ct Ste A, Sacramento (95824-2354)
PHONE 916 381-8051
Fax: 916 381-4059
John Dutter, Site Mgr
Sharon James, Sales Mgr
Joe Kircher
Cesar Moreno, Manager
EMP: 87
SALES (corp-wide): 558.1MM **Privately Held**
SIC: 5031 Building materials, exterior; building materials, interior; lumber: rough, dressed & finished; millwork
HQ: Oregon Pacific Building Products (Calif.), Inc.
30170 Sw Ore Pac Ave
Wilsonville OR 97070
503 685-5499

(P-6942)
OREGON PCF BLDG PDTS MAPLE INC
Also Called: Orepac Millwork Products
2401 E Philadelphia St, Ontario (91761-7743)
PHONE 909 627-4043
Fax: 909 923-6587
Douglas Hart, President
Mark Calhoun, Director
Art Nila, Director
Jackie Vega, Receptionist
▲ **EMP:** 125
SALES (est): 30.9MM
SALES (corp-wide): 558.1MM **Privately Held**
SIC: 5031 5032 Lumber, plywood & millwork; brick, stone & related material
PA: Orepac Holding Company
30170 Sw Orepac Ave
Wilsonville OR 97070
503 682-5050

(P-6943)
PACIFIC COAST SUPPLY LLC
Also Called: Anderson Lumber
4290 Roseville Rd, North Highlands (95660-5710)
PHONE 916 481-2220
Fax: 916 481-2651
Chris Lucchetti, Branch Mgr
David Swallow, Manager
EMP: 150
SALES (corp-wide): 926.8MM **Privately Held**
SIC: 5031 5211 Lumber, plywood & millwork; lumber & other building materials
HQ: Pacific Coast Supply, Llc
4290 Roseville Rd
North Highlands CA 95660
916 971-2301

(P-6944)
PACIFIC COAST SUPPLY LLC (HQ)
4290 Roseville Rd, North Highlands (95660-5710)
PHONE 916 971-2301
Fax: 916 974-3992
Curt Gomes, President
Robert Ramos, COO
Lisa Goeppner, CFO
Walter Payne, Bd of Directors
Joe Gower, Vice Pres
EMP: 153
SALES (est): 480.5MM
SALES (corp-wide): 926.8MM **Privately Held**
WEB: www.paccoast.com
SIC: 5031 Lumber, plywood & millwork
PA: Pacific Coast Building Products, Inc.
10600 White Rock Rd # 100
Rancho Cordova CA 95670
916 631-6500

(P-6945)
PACIFIC STATES INDUSTRIES INC
Also Called: Redwood Empire Whl Lbr Pdts
10 Madrone Ave, Morgan Hill (95037-9227)
P.O. Box 1300 (95038-1300)
PHONE 408 779-7354
Cindy Hernandez, Manager
EMP: 60
SALES (corp-wide): 213.4MM **Privately Held**
SIC: 5031 5211 Lumber: rough, dressed & finished; lumber products
PA: Pacific States Industries, Incorporated
10 Madrone Ave
Morgan Hill CA 95037
408 779-7354

(P-6946)
PHILLIPS PLYWOOD CO INC
Also Called: Quality Laminating
13599 Desmond St, Pacoima (91331-2300)
P.O. Box 51396, Los Angeles (90051-5696)
PHONE 818 897-7736
Fax: 818 897-6571
Douglas F Madsen, CEO
Shawn Carlisle, President
Lynne Corwin, VP Finance
Jeanne Wilson, Persnl Dir
Robert Perez, Mktg Dir
EMP: 55 **EST:** 1986
SQ FT: 100,000
SALES (est): 30MM **Privately Held**
WEB: www.phillipsplywood.com
SIC: 5031 Plywood

(P-6947)
PINE TREE LUMBER COMPANY LP (PA)
707 N Andreasen Dr, Escondido (92029-1497)
PHONE 760 745-0411
Fax: 760 745-0325
Jacob Brouwer, Partner
Rosemarie Crouch, Officer
Betty Lipton, Controller
Matt Hallendy, Buyer
Mike Wexler, Director
EMP: 56 **EST:** 1945
SQ FT: 45,000
SALES (est): 43.2MM **Privately Held**
WEB: www.pinetreelumber.com
SIC: 5031 5211 Building materials, interior; building materials, exterior; lumber & other building materials

(P-6948)
PJS LUMBER INC
Also Called: P J'S Construction Supplies
45055 Fremont Blvd, Fremont (94538-6318)
PHONE 510 743-5300
Fax: 510 490-3952
Shane McMillan, CEO
Carlton J McMillan, President
Terry W Protto, CFO
Jeff Veilleux, Vice Pres
Bear McGowan, Purch Agent
EMP: 145
SQ FT: 2,000
SALES (est): 102.3MM **Privately Held**
SIC: 5031 5051 Lumber: rough, dressed & finished; steel

(P-6949)
PLY GEM PACIFIC WINDOWS CORP
235 Radio Rd, Corona (92879-1725)
PHONE 951 272-1300
Randy Dasalla, Branch Mgr
Raymond Sears, Manager
EMP: 100
SALES (corp-wide): 1.8B **Publicly Held**
SIC: 5031 Windows
HQ: Ply Gem Pacific Windows Corporation
2600 Grand Blvd Ste 900
Kansas City MO 64108
816 426-8200

(P-6950)
POTTER ROEMER LLC (PA)
17451 Hurley St, City of Industry (91744-5106)
P.O. Box 3527 (91744-0527)
PHONE 626 855-4890
Fax: 626 937-4777
Jay R Smith, Mng Member
Richard Kilbane, Vice Pres
Kevin Norcross, Vice Pres
Buddy Delaney, General Mgr
Roger Gwynn, Engineer
▲ **EMP:** 66
SQ FT: 110,000
SALES (est): 46.4MM **Privately Held**
WEB: www.potterroemer.com
SIC: 5031 3569 2542 Skylights, all materials; firefighting apparatus & related equipment; partitions & fixtures, except wood

(P-6951)
PROBUILD COMPANY LLC
1262 E Main St, El Cajon (92021-7250)
PHONE 619 440-7711
Tom Iannacone, General Mgr
Kurt Schereaum, Manager
EMP: 50
SALES (corp-wide): 3.5B **Publicly Held**
WEB: www.hopelumber.com
SIC: 5031 5072 Lumber, plywood & millwork; hardware
HQ: Probuild Company Llc
7595 E Technology Way # 500
Denver CO 80237
303 262-8500

(P-6952)
PROBUILD COMPANY LLC
3450 Highland Ave, National City (91950-7420)
PHONE 619 425-6660
Ted Teran, Manager
EMP: 50
SALES (corp-wide): 3.5B **Publicly Held**
WEB: www.hopelumber.com
SIC: 5031 Lumber, plywood & millwork
HQ: Probuild Company Llc
7595 E Technology Way # 500
Denver CO 80237
303 262-8500

(P-6953)
PROBUILD COMPANY LLC
663 Lomas Santa Fe Dr, Solana Beach (92075-1412)
PHONE 858 755-0246
Sergio Paz, Branch Mgr
Theodore Teran, Manager
EMP: 66
SALES (corp-wide): 3.5B **Publicly Held**
WEB: www.hopelumber.com
SIC: 5031 Lumber, plywood & millwork
HQ: Probuild Company Llc
7595 E Technology Way # 500
Denver CO 80237
303 262-8500

(P-6954)
RANCH HOUSE DOORS INC
Also Called: R H D
1527 Pomona Rd, Corona (92880-6959)
PHONE 951 278-2884
Fax: 951 278-2686
Sandra Neal, President
Michael James Neal, CEO
Cristian Neal, CFO
Ralph Tan, Sales Mgr
Tony Neal, Manager
EMP: 70
SQ FT: 33,000
SALES (est): 25.5MM **Privately Held**
WEB: www.ranchhousedoors.com
SIC: 5031 Doors, garage

(P-6955)
REDWOOD PRODUCTS CHINO INC
Also Called: Rancho Wholesale
9301 Remington Ave, Chino (91710-9346)
P.O. Box 2662, Corona (92878-2662)
PHONE 909 923-5656
Jaime Carlos, President
Maricela Rodriguez, Vice Pres
EMP: 60 **EST:** 2000
SALES (est): 24.4MM **Privately Held**
WEB: www.redwoodproductschino.com
SIC: 5031 Lumber: rough, dressed & finished

(P-6956)
RELIABLE WHOLESALE LUMBER INC (PA)
7600 Redondo Cir, Huntington Beach (92648-1303)
P.O. Box 191 (92648-0191)
PHONE 714 848-8222
Fax: 714 843-9831
Jerome M Higman, President
Will Higman, COO
David Higman, CFO
John Wenzel, Info Tech Mgr
Scott Nicols, Purch Agent
EMP: 90
SQ FT: 4,500
SALES (est): 178.8MM **Privately Held**
WEB: www.rwli.net
SIC: 5031 2421 Lumber: rough, dressed & finished; sawmills & planing mills, general

(P-6957)
ROBERTS LUMBER SALES INC
Also Called: Robert's Lumber
2661 S Lilac Ave, Bloomington (92316-3211)
PHONE 909 350-9164
Fax: 909 429-8546
Robert Cantero Jr, CEO
Lori Cantero, Principal
Laurie Kentriel, Manager
EMP: 57 **EST:** 1997

5032 - Brick, Stone & Related Construction Mtrls Wholesale County (P-6978)

SALES (est): 18.3MM **Privately Held**
SIC: 5031 2448 Lumber, plywood & millwork; wood pallets & skids

(P-6958)
ROYAL PLYWOOD COMPANY LLC
6003 88th St Ste 100, Sacramento (95828-1143)
P.O. Box 728, La Mirada (90637-0728)
PHONE...................................916 386-9873
Gabriel N Marshi, *Mng Member*
Scott Burns, *Consultant*
EMP: 78
SALES (corp-wide): 78MM **Privately Held**
SIC: 5031 Plywood
PA: Royal Plywood Company, Llc
   14171 Park Pl
   Cerritos CA 90703
   562 404-2989

(P-6959)
ROYAL PLYWOOD COMPANY LLC (PA)
14171 Park Pl, Cerritos (90703-2463)
P.O. Box 728, La Mirada (90637-0728)
PHONE...................................562 404-2989
Fax: 562 404-6224
Gabriel N Marshi,
Cliff Duernberger, *Vice Pres*
Skip Hem, *Vice Pres*
Brian McMaster, *Info Tech Mgr*
Brian McNaster, *Opers Mgr*
▲ EMP: 78
SQ FT: 120,000
SALES (est): 78MM **Privately Held**
WEB: www.royalplywood.com
SIC: 5031 Building materials, exterior

(P-6960)
SAROYAN LUMBER COMPANY INC (PA)
Also Called: Saroyan Lumber and Moulding Co
6230 S Alameda St, Huntington Park (90255-3503)
PHONE...................................800 624-9309
Fax: 323 589-2028
Richard Saroyan, *President*
Dorothy A Robinson, *Shareholder*
Marylne Nahery, *CFO*
John Saroyan, *Corp Secy*
Robert Lemke, *Vice Pres*
▲ EMP: 72
SQ FT: 144,000
SALES (est): 41MM **Privately Held**
WEB: www.saroyanlumber.com
SIC: 5031 Lumber: rough, dressed & finished; millwork

(P-6961)
SHAPP INTERNATIONAL TRDG INC
Also Called: Shapp Internatioonal
6000 Reseda Blvd, Tarzana (91356-1500)
P.O. Box 893, Woodland Hills (91365-0893)
PHONE...................................818 348-3000
Fax: 818 757-0000
Allan Shapiro, *President*
Louis Justin, *Treasurer*
EMP: 118
SQ FT: 8,000
SALES (est): 36.9MM **Privately Held**
SIC: 5031 5064 5112 5021 Lumber, plywood & millwork; electrical appliances, major; stationery & office supplies; furniture

(P-6962)
SINGLEY ENTERPRISES (PA)
Also Called: Garage Door Specialists
2901 Duluth St, West Sacramento (95691-2205)
P.O. Box 572 (95691-0572)
PHONE...................................916 427-4573
Fax: 916 375-8874
Gary B Singley, *CEO*
Charlene Singley, *Treasurer*
EMP: 50
SQ FT: 14,400
SALES (est): 19.9MM **Privately Held**
SIC: 5031 5211 Doors, garage; garage doors, sale & installation

(P-6963)
STATES DRAWER BOX SPC LLC
1482 N Batavia St, Orange (92867-3505)
PHONE...................................714 744-4247
Fax: 714 744-0650
Cathy Blankenship, *President*
EMP: 60
SALES (est): 16.1MM **Privately Held**
WEB: www.dbsdrawers.com
SIC: 5031 Lumber, plywood & millwork
PA: States Industries, Llc
   29545 E Enid Rd
   Eugene OR 97402

(P-6964)
T M COBB COMPANY
Also Called: Tom Ray
8490 Rovana Cir, Sacramento (95828-2529)
PHONE...................................916 381-7330
Fax: 916 381-5004
Steve Grambush, *Manager*
Tim Morris, *Opers Mgr*
EMP: 70
SQ FT: 40,000
SALES (corp-wide): 98.9MM **Privately Held**
WEB: www.tmcobbco.com
SIC: 5031 5032 2431 Doors; door frames, all materials; masons' materials; millwork
PA: T. M. Cobb Company
   500 Palmyrita Ave
   Riverside CA 92507
   951 248-2400

(P-6965)
TABER COMPANY INC
1442 Ritchey St, Santa Ana (92705-4717)
PHONE...................................714 543-7100
Fax: 714 543-7117
Brian Taber, *President*
Kathy Webster, *Accounting Mgr*
Cindy Smith, *Accountant*
Travis Burgdorf, *VP Opers*
EMP: 65
SQ FT: 11,000
SALES (est): 30.9MM **Privately Held**
WEB: www.taberco.net
SIC: 5031 Building materials, interior

(P-6966)
TRIM TECH INDUSTRIES INC
1724 Ringwood Ave, San Jose (95131-1711)
PHONE...................................408 573-4514
Fax: 408 487-8648
Ellen Medeiros, *President*
Andy Medeiros, *Vice Pres*
Cyndy Thomas, *Purch Mgr*
EMP: 50 EST: 1992
SALES (est): 9.2MM **Privately Held**
SIC: 5031 Doors, combination, screenstorm

(P-6967)
USG INTERIORS LLC
2575 Loomis Rd, Stockton (95205-8045)
PHONE...................................209 466-4636
Fax: 209 466-5328
Sandy Hirzel, *Manager*
John Wesley, *COO*
EMP: 70
SALES (corp-wide): 3.7B **Publicly Held**
SIC: 5031 Lumber, plywood & millwork
HQ: Usg Interiors, Llc
   125 S Franklin St
   Chicago IL 60606
   800 874-4968

(P-6968)
VIRGINIA HARDWOOD COMPANY (PA)
1000 W Foothill Blvd, Azusa (91702-2840)
PHONE...................................626 815-0540
David V Ferrari, *Chairman*
Gary Henzie, *President*
Robin Ezzo, *Corp Secy*
Jeannette Ferrari, *Vice Pres*
Mike Ferrari, *Vice Pres*
▲ EMP: 56 EST: 1946
SQ FT: 60,000
SALES (est): 33.5MM **Privately Held**
WEB: www.virginiahardwood.com
SIC: 5031 Hardboard

(P-6969)
WALNUT INVESTMENT CORP
Also Called: AMS
2940 E White Star Ave, Anaheim (92806-2627)
PHONE...................................714 238-9240
Fax: 714 237-1767
Ruben Mendoza, *CEO*
Max Gondon, *Shareholder*
Tony Reinders, *COO*
John Gorey, *CFO*
Tony Van De Walle, *Branch Mgr*
▲ EMP: 550
SQ FT: 100,000
SALES (est): 80.5MM
SALES (corp-wide): 25.3B **Privately Held**
WEB: www.a-m-s.com
SIC: 5031 5039 5072 Building materials, exterior; ceiling systems & products; hardware
HQ: Allied Building Products Corp.
   15 E Union Ave
   East Rutherford NJ 07073
   201 507-8400

(P-6970)
WEYERHAEUSER COMPANY
Also Called: Marketing Sales & Dist Div
17400 Slover Ave, Fontana (92337-8004)
P.O. Box 487 (92334-0487)
PHONE...................................909 877-6100
Fax: 909 877-3808
Mark Davis, *Branch Mgr*
Donna Veatch, *Administration*
Dick Armstrong, *Planning*
Eric Walz, *Manager*
EMP: 65
SQ FT: 85,000
SALES (corp-wide): 7B **Publicly Held**
SIC: 5031 Lumber, plywood & millwork
PA: Weyerhaeuser Company
   220 Occidental Ave S
   Seattle WA 98104
   253 924-2345

5032 Brick, Stone & Related Construction Mtrls Wholesale

(P-6971)
A TEICHERT & SON INC (HQ)
Also Called: Teichert Construction
3500 American River Dr, Sacramento (95864-5893)
P.O. Box 15002 (95851-0002)
PHONE...................................916 484-3011
Fax: 916 484-6506
Judson T Riggs, *President*
Dana M Davis, *President*
Kenneth A Kayser, *President*
Narendra M Pathipati, *CFO*
Bert Sandman, *Exec VP*
▼ EMP: 153
SALES (est): 715.1MM
SALES (corp-wide): 753.8MM **Privately Held**
SIC: 5032 3273 1611 1442 Brick, stone & related material; ready-mixed concrete; highway & street construction; construction sand & gravel; single-family housing construction
PA: Teichert, Inc.
   3500 American River Dr
   Sacramento CA 95864
   916 484-3011

(P-6972)
ARIZONA TILE LLC
1620 S Lewis St, Anaheim (92805-6436)
PHONE...................................714 978-6403
EMP: 100
SALES (corp-wide): 322.1MM **Privately Held**
SIC: 5032
PA: Arizona Tile, L.L.C.
   8829 S Priest Dr
   Tempe AZ 85284
   480 893-9393

(P-6973)
ATLAS CONSTRUCTION SUPPLY INC (PA)
4640 Brinnell St, San Diego (92111-2302)
PHONE...................................858 277-2100
Fax: 858 277-0585
Brian Quinn, *President*
James E Wright, *Corp Secy*
Tom Vargas, *Exec VP*
Debbie Lopez, *Credit Mgr*
Erin Braly, *Human Res Mgr*
▲ EMP: 75
SQ FT: 30,000
SALES (est): 77.5MM **Privately Held**
WEB: www.atlasform.com
SIC: 5032 Concrete building products

(P-6974)
BEST CHEER STONE INC (PA)
3190 E Miraloma Ave, Anaheim (92806-1906)
PHONE...................................714 399-1588
Yanlin K Xu, *CFO*
Max Rohlsing, *General Mgr*
Vicky Apelo, *Accountant*
Kaiser Tang, *Director*
Judy Chang, *Manager*
▲ EMP: 50
SALES (est): 27MM **Privately Held**
SIC: 5032 3281 Brick, stone & related material; building stone; stone, quarrying & processing of own stone products

(P-6975)
CEMEX CEMENT INC
1201 W Gladstone St, Azusa (91702-5142)
P.O. Box 575 (91702-0575)
PHONE...................................626 969-1747
Steve Hayes, *Manager*
EMP: 200
SALES (corp-wide): 13.3B **Privately Held**
SIC: 5032 3273 3251 1411 Concrete mixtures; ready-mixed concrete; brick & structural clay tile; dimension stone
HQ: Cemex Cement, Inc.
   929 Gessner Rd Ste 1900
   Houston TX 77024
   713 650-6200

(P-6976)
CEMEX CNSTR MTLS PCF LLC
Also Called: Cem - Victorville River Plant
16888 E St, Victorville (92394-2999)
PHONE...................................760 381-7600
Don Kelly, *Manager*
Bob Shidal, *Safety Mgr*
Edgar Mancenido, *Manager*
EMP: 234
SQ FT: 2,684
SALES (corp-wide): 13.3B **Privately Held**
SIC: 5032 Cement
HQ: Cemex Construction Materials Pacific, Llc
   1501 Belvedere Rd
   West Palm Beach FL 33406
   561 833-5555

(P-6977)
CENTRAL VALLEY CONCRETE INC
Also Called: Central Valley Trucking
3371 N Highway 59, Merced (95348-9459)
PHONE...................................209 383-7292
Fax: 209 725-8895
Harold Neal, *Owner*
EMP: 70
SALES (corp-wide): 30.5MM **Privately Held**
WEB: www.centralvalleyconcrete.com
SIC: 5032 5211 4212 Concrete mixtures; lumber & other building materials; local trucking, without storage
PA: Central Valley Concrete Inc.
   3823 N State Highway 59
   Merced CA 95348
   209 723-8846

(P-6978)
CLASSIC TILE & MOSAIC INC (PA)
Also Called: Ctm
14463 S Broadway, Gardena (90248-1807)
PHONE...................................310 538-9605
Fax: 310 324-1285
Vincent Cullinan, *CEO*

5032 - Brick, Stone & Related Construction Mtrls Wholesale County (P-6979)

Bonnie Daland, *Vice Pres*
Ana V Gilliam, *Controller*
▲ **EMP:** 60
SALES (est): 25MM **Privately Held**
WEB: www.classictileandmosaic.com
SIC: 5032 5211 Tile, clay or other ceramic, excluding refractory; tile, ceramic

(P-6979)
CONCRETE TIE INDUSTRIES INC (PA)
130 E Oris St, Compton (90222-2714)
P.O. Box 5406 (90224-5406)
PHONE 310 886-1000
Fax: 310 638-8363
Paul J Schoendienst, *President*
Steve Sim, *Admin Sec*
Steve Sims, *Controller*
Doris Jackson, *Human Res Dir*
EMP: 70
SQ FT: 280,000
SALES (est): 30.9MM **Privately Held**
WEB: www.concretetie.com
SIC: 5032 3452 Concrete & cinder building products; bolts, nuts, rivets & washers

(P-6980)
CTS CEMENT MANUFACTURING CORP
1631 W Lincoln Ave, Anaheim (92801-5502)
PHONE 714 808-1945
Bill McCormick, *President*
EMP: 67
SALES (corp-wide): 37.7MM **Privately Held**
SIC: 5032 Cement
PA: Cts Cement Manufacturing Corporation
11065 Knott Ave Ste A
Cypress CA 90630
714 379-8260

(P-6981)
ELEGANT SURFACES
3640 Amrcn Rver Dr 150, Sacramento (95864)
P.O. Box 705, Byron (94514-0705)
PHONE 209 823-9388
John Polimeno, *CEO*
Dan Thompson, *President*
Kristie Polimeno, *Vice Pres*
Lisa Downing, *Manager*
▲ **EMP:** 100
SQ FT: 48,000
SALES (est): 15.5MM **Privately Held**
WEB: www.elegantsurfaces.com
SIC: 5032 3281 Brick, stone & related material; marble, building: cut & shaped

(P-6982)
EMSER INTERNATIONAL LLC (PA)
Also Called: Emser Tile
8431 Santa Monica Blvd, Los Angeles (90069-4294)
PHONE 323 650-2000
Fax: 323 654-3190
Sam Ghodsian, *Mng Member*
Anne Yon, *Technology*
Barry Dambrowsk, *Credit Staff*
Lori Olena, *Sales Staff*
Ehsan Ghodsian,
▲ **EMP:** 70
SQ FT: 50,000
SALES (est): 164MM **Privately Held**
SIC: 5032 Ceramic wall & floor tile

(P-6983)
FRANK SCIARRINO MARBLE G
7505 Trade St, San Diego (92121-2411)
P.O. Box 600265 (92160-0265)
PHONE 858 695-8030
Fax: 858 695-1494
Frank Sciarrino, *President*
Anna Maria, *Vice Pres*
Anna Sciarrino, *Finance*
Fs Marble, *Manager*
EMP: 80
SQ FT: 20,000
SALES (est): 8.3MM **Privately Held**
WEB: www.fsmarble.com
SIC: 5032 5211 1799 1743 Brick, stone & related material; cabinets, kitchen; counter top installation; tile installation, ceramic

(P-6984)
FST SAND & GRAVEL INC
21780 Temescal Canyon Rd, Corona (92883-5669)
P.O. Box 2798 (92878-2798)
PHONE 951 277-8440
Fax: 951 277-8904
Frank Smith, *President*
Steve Donaldson, *Controller*
Dave Sanchez, *Sales Associate*
William Medina, *Sales Staff*
EMP: 50
SQ FT: 1,078
SALES (est): 32.6MM **Privately Held**
WEB: www.fstsand.com
SIC: 5032 Sand, construction; gravel

(P-6985)
GBI TILE & STONE INC (PA)
Also Called: Quarry Collection
5900 Skylab Rd Ste 150, Huntington Beach (92647-2061)
PHONE 949 567-1880
John Jeffrey Jones, *President*
Marco A Gonzalez, *Vice Pres*
Norma Bonilla, *Admin Asst*
Robert Gabrielson, *VP Opers*
Mel Pasquale, *Marketing Staff*
▲ **EMP:** 50
SALES (est): 22.8MM **Privately Held**
SIC: 5032 Brick, stone & related material

(P-6986)
GOLDEN STATE PLASTERING
7082 N Harrison Ave, Fresno (93650-1008)
P.O. Box 3452 (93650-3452)
PHONE 559 439-3920
Fax: 559 438-7039
Monty Bound, *Supervisor*
EMP: 90
SQ FT: 4,920
SALES (est): 4.5MM **Privately Held**
SIC: 5032 Stucco

(P-6987)
GRANITE ROCK CO
Also Called: A R Wilson Quarry & Asp Plant
End Of Quarry Rd, Aromas (95004)
P.O. Box 699 (95004-0699)
PHONE 831 392-3780
Bruce Woolpert, *President*
Henry Ramirez, *Manager*
Dan Slavin, *Manager*
Carey Wong, *Manager*
EMP: 200
SALES (corp-wide): 1.2B **Privately Held**
WEB: www.graniterock.com
SIC: 5032 Brick, stone & related material
PA: Granite Rock Co.
350 Technology Dr
Watsonville CA 95076
831 768-2000

(P-6988)
HOLLIDAY ROCK CO INC (PA)
1401 N Benson Ave, Upland (91786-2166)
PHONE 909 982-1553
Fax: 909 949-6315
Penny Holliday, *CEO*
Ethel Holliday, *President*
Fredrick N Holliday, *Vice Pres*
John Holliday, *Vice Pres*
Dean Browning, *General Mgr*
EMP: 54
SQ FT: 2,000
SALES (est): 53.7MM **Privately Held**
WEB: www.hollidayrock.com
SIC: 5032 Asphalt mixture; concrete mixtures; stone, crushed or broken; sand, construction

(P-6989)
L & W SUPPLY CORPORATION
Also Called: Calply
7750 Convoy Ct, San Diego (92111-1106)
PHONE 858 627-0811
Fax: 858 627-0828
Donald Smith, *Manager*
EMP: 50
SALES (corp-wide): 3.7B **Publicly Held**
WEB: www.calply.com
SIC: 5032 Drywall materials
HQ: L & W Supply Corporation
550 W Adams St
Chicago IL 60661
312 606-4000

(P-6990)
L & W SUPPLY CORPORATION
Also Called: Calply
31625 Hayman St, Hayward (94544-7121)
PHONE 510 429-8003
K W McKinney, *Manager*
Paulos Tilahun, *Admin Asst*
EMP: 70
SALES (corp-wide): 3.7B **Publicly Held**
WEB: www.calply.com
SIC: 5032 5031 Drywall materials; lumber, plywood & millwork
HQ: L & W Supply Corporation
550 W Adams St
Chicago IL 60661
312 606-4000

(P-6991)
M S INTERNATIONAL INC (PA)
Also Called: MSI
2095 N Batavia St, Orange (92865-3101)
PHONE 714 685-7500
Manahar R Shah, *CEO*
Rajesh Shah, *President*
Chandrika M Shah, *Corp Secy*
Marlene Ramirez, *Officer*
Phillip Caudillo, *Vice Pres*
◆ **EMP:** 300
SQ FT: 500,000
SALES (est): 501.9MM **Privately Held**
WEB: www.msistone.com
SIC: 5032 Brick, stone & related material

(P-6992)
PATRICK INDUSTRIES INC
Also Called: Custom Vinyls
13414 Slover Ave, Fontana (92337-6977)
PHONE 909 350-4440
Fax: 909 350-4875
Vince Fergan, *Branch Mgr*
Chris Gazelle, *General Mgr*
Sue Pennick, *Director*
EMP: 150
SALES (corp-wide): 920.3MM **Publicly Held**
WEB: www.patrickind.com
SIC: 5032 1799 2435 3083 Brick, stone & related material; building site preparation; hardwood veneer & plywood; laminated plastics plate & sheet
PA: Patrick Industries, Inc.
107 W Franklin St
Elkhart IN 46516
574 294-7511

(P-6993)
PLAYMAR INC
2502 Channing Ave, San Jose (95131-1004)
PHONE 408 324-1930
EMP: 70
SALES (est): 1.1MM **Privately Held**
SIC: 5032 Granite building stone

(P-6994)
SYAR INDUSTRIES INC
13666 Healdsburg Ave, Healdsburg (95448-9234)
P.O. Box 325 (95448-0325)
PHONE 707 433-3366
Fax: 707 431-7321
Dick Love, *Manager*
EMP: 65
SALES (corp-wide): 91.1MM **Privately Held**
WEB: www.syar.com
SIC: 5032 Gravel; sand, construction; stone, crushed or broken
PA: Syar Industries, Inc.
2301 Napa Vallejo Hwy
Napa CA 94558
707 252-8711

(P-6995)
THOMPSON BUILDING MTLS INC
6618 Federal Blvd, Lemon Grove (91945-1312)
PHONE 619 287-9410
Fax: 619 287-8423
Kenneth R Thompson, *President*
Tracy Pelchat, *Office Mgr*
Derrek Pritchett, *Site Mgr*
EMP: 50
SQ FT: 15,000

SALES (est): 11MM
SALES (corp-wide): 69.6MM **Privately Held**
SIC: 5032 5211 Plastering materials; lime & plaster
PA: Opal Service, Inc.
282 S Anita Dr
Orange CA 92868
714 935-0900

(P-6996)
UGM CITATAH INC (PA)
Also Called: Ugmc
13220 Cambridge St, Santa Fe Springs (90670-4902)
PHONE 562 921-9549
Viken Dave Yaghjian, *President*
Bruce Feaster, *Exec VP*
Irmen Yaghjian, *Admin Sec*
Siska Eman, *Controller*
Debbie Armstrong, *VP Opers*
▲ **EMP:** 125
SQ FT: 46,000
SALES (est): 28.6MM **Privately Held**
WEB: www.ugmcstone.com
SIC: 5032 1741 1743 Marble building stone; stone masonry; terrazzo, tile, marble, mosaic work

(P-6997)
UNITED MARBLE & GRANITE INC
2163 Martin Ave, Santa Clara (95050-2701)
PHONE 408 347-3300
Manuel De Oliveira, *President*
Manny Deoliveira, *IT/INT Sup*
Peter Poon, *Project Mgr*
Greg Thompkins, *Manager*
▲ **EMP:** 80
SALES (est): 174K **Privately Held**
WEB: www.umgslabs.com
SIC: 5032 Marble building stone

(P-6998)
VALORI SAND & GRAVEL COMPANY (PA)
Also Called: Thompson Building Materials
141 W Taft Ave, Orange (92865-4217)
PHONE 714 637-0104
Fax: 714 637-7575
Kenneth R Thompson, *President*
Bob Sandstrom, *Manager*
▲ **EMP:** 100
SALES (est): 56.7MM **Privately Held**
SIC: 5032 Brick, stone & related material; sand, construction; gravel; stucco

(P-6999)
VALORI SAND & GRAVEL COMPANY
Also Called: Thompson Building Materials
11027 Cherry Ave, Fontana (92337-7118)
P.O. Box 950 (92334-0950)
PHONE 909 350-3000
Tom Rievley, *Branch Mgr*
EMP: 150
SALES (corp-wide): 51.6MM **Privately Held**
SIC: 5032 5211 Brick, stone & related material; cement
PA: Valori Sand & Gravel Company Inc
141 W Taft Ave
Orange CA 92865
714 637-0104

(P-7000)
WALKER & ZANGER INC (PA)
16719 Schoenborn St, North Hills (91343-6115)
PHONE 818 280-8300
Fax: 818 504-2226
Jonathan Zanger, *CEO*
Pat Petrocelli, *COO*
Risa Hannig, *Admin Asst*
Chris Tucker, *Finance*
Behrad Karbassi, *Purchasing*
▼ **EMP:** 60
SQ FT: 30,000
SALES (est): 76.8MM **Privately Held**
SIC: 5032 Marble building stone; ceramic wall & floor tile

5033 - Roofing, Siding & Insulation Mtrls Wholesale County (P-7022)

(P-7001)
WEST COAST SAND AND GRAVEL INC (PA)
Also Called: West Coast Materials
7282 Orangethorpe Ave, Buena Park (90621-3331)
P.O. Box 5067 (90622-5067)
PHONE.................................. 714 522-0282
Fax: 714 522-4524
Daniel C Reyneveld, *CEO*
Marvin J Struiksma, *President*
John Struiksma, *Vice Pres*
Robert Struiksma, *Admin Sec*
Kirk Bowman, *Info Tech Mgr*
EMP: 71
SQ FT: 4,200
SALES (est): 51.8MM **Privately Held**
WEB: www.wcsg.com
SIC: 5032 Sand, construction; gravel

(P-7002)
WESTERN PACIFIC DISTRG LLC
Also Called: Westpac Materials
341 W Meats Ave, Orange (92865-2623)
PHONE.................................. 714 974-6837
Mark Hamilton, *General Mgr*
Leslie Dickson, *Manager*
EMP: 150
SALES (est): 36.6MM **Privately Held**
WEB: www.westernpacificdistributing.com
SIC: 5032 Drywall materials

(P-7003)
WESTPAC MATERIALS LLC
341 W Meats Ave, Orange (92865-2623)
PHONE.................................. 714 974-6837
Fax: 714 637-9033
Mark Hamilton,
Bob Kubinski, *Engineer*
Linda Lovejoy, *Controller*
Eric Cox, *Prdtn Mgr*
Mark M Hamilton, *Manager*
◆ **EMP:** 51
SALES (est): 29.4MM **Privately Held**
WEB: www.westpac.biz
SIC: 5032 Drywall materials

(P-7004)
WESTSIDE BUILDING MTL CORP (PA)
1111 E Howell Ave, Anaheim (92805-6453)
P.O. Box 711 (92815-0711)
PHONE.................................. 714 385-1644
Fax: 714 938-0730
Bill Peckham, *CEO*
Geraldine G Peckham, *President*
Tony Lee, *Vice Pres*
Richard Peckham, *Vice Pres*
Mona Temple, *Executive*
▲ **EMP:** 95
SQ FT: 30,000
SALES (est): 118.2MM **Privately Held**
SIC: 5032 Plastering materials

5033 Roofing, Siding & Insulation Mtrls Wholesale

(P-7005)
ALLIED BUILDING PRODUCTS CORP
111 S Minnie St, Santa Ana (92701-5366)
PHONE.................................. 714 647-9792
Stephen Rhorer, *Manager*
EMP: 50
SALES (corp-wide): 25.3B **Privately Held**
WEB: www.alliedbuilding.com
SIC: 5033 Roofing, asphalt & sheet metal
HQ: Allied Building Products Corp.
 15 E Union Ave
 East Rutherford NJ 07073
 201 507-8400

(P-7006)
ALLIED BUILDING PRODUCTS CORP
4159 Santa Rosa Ave, Santa Rosa (95407-8276)
PHONE.................................. 707 584-7599
Jim Brenton, *Manager*
John Ording, *Asst Mgr*
EMP: 50
SALES (corp-wide): 25.3B **Privately Held**
WEB: www.alliedbuilding.com
SIC: 5033 5211 Roofing, siding & insulation; roofing material
HQ: Allied Building Products Corp.
 15 E Union Ave
 East Rutherford NJ 07073
 201 507-8400

(P-7007)
BEACON ROOFING SUPPLY INC
200 San Jose Ave, San Jose (95125-1008)
PHONE.................................. 408 293-5947
Paul M Isabella, *President*
EMP: 99
SALES (corp-wide): 2.5B **Publicly Held**
SIC: 5033 Roofing, siding & insulation
PA: Beacon Roofing Supply, Inc.
 505 Huntmar Park Dr # 300
 Herndon VA 20170
 571 323-3939

(P-7008)
BEACON SALES ACQUISITION INC
Also Called: Pacific Supply
1201 E Mcfadden Ave, Santa Ana (92705-4101)
PHONE.................................. 714 288-1974
Fax: 714 771-3577
EMP: 110
SALES (corp-wide): 2.5B **Publicly Held**
SIC: 5033 5211 Roofing, asphalt & sheet metal; roofing material
HQ: Beacon Sales Acquisition, Inc.
 50 Webster Ave
 Somerville MA 02143
 877 645-7663

(P-7009)
BURLINGAME INDUSTRIES INC
Also Called: Eagle Roofing Products
4555 Mckinley Ave, Stockton (95206-4008)
PHONE.................................. 209 464-9001
Fax: 209 464-1272
Hersch Beahm, *Manager*
Rich Jones, *CFO*
Sal Mattera, *General Mgr*
David Vallas, *Human Res Mgr*
Bob Carol, *Purch Agent*
EMP: 100
SALES (corp-wide): 79.1MM **Privately Held**
SIC: 5033 Roofing, siding & insulation
PA: Burlingame Industries, Incorporated
 3546 N Riverside Ave
 Rialto CA 92377
 909 355-7000

(P-7010)
CARLISLE CONSTRUCTION MTLS INC
Also Called: Western Insulfoam
5635 Schaefer Ave, Chino (91710-9048)
PHONE.................................. 909 591-7425
Fax: 909 591-8083
Tom Tartaglione, *Manager*
Douglass Cassidy, *VP Opers*
Bart Hardle, *Sales Mgr*
Harry Millard, *Manager*
EMP: 100
SQ FT: 45,464
SALES (corp-wide): 3.5B **Publicly Held**
WEB: www.insulfoam.com
SIC: 5033 3086 Insulation materials; cups & plates, foamed plastic
HQ: Carlisle Construction Materials Incorporated
 1285 Ritner Hwy
 Carlisle PA 17013

(P-7011)
CARLISLE CONSTRUCTION MTLS INC
Also Called: Insulfoam
1155 Business Park Dr, Dixon (95620-4303)
PHONE.................................. 707 678-6900
Fax: 707 678-2962
Rick Canady, *Manager*
Frank Barberio, *Regl Sales Mgr*
Rick Tanaday, *Manager*
EMP: 55
SALES (corp-wide): 3.5B **Publicly Held**
WEB: www.insulfoam.com
SIC: 5033 3086 Insulation materials; plastics foam products
HQ: Carlisle Construction Materials Incorporated
 1285 Ritner Hwy
 Carlisle PA 17013

(P-7012)
EXTERIOR SOLUTIONS INC
25752 Simpson Pl, Calabasas (91302-3154)
PHONE.................................. 310 400-3510
Craig Carson, *CEO*
EMP: 70
SALES (est): 11.2MM **Privately Held**
SIC: 5033 Roofing, siding & insulation

(P-7013)
OWENS CORNING SALES LLC
960 Central Expy, Santa Clara (95050-2665)
PHONE.................................. 408 235-1351
Chris Rukman, *Branch Mgr*
Monte Schenken, *Manager*
EMP: 400
SALES (corp-wide): 5.3B **Publicly Held**
WEB: www.owenscorning.com
SIC: 5033 3296 Fiberglass building materials; mineral wool
HQ: Owens Corning Sales, Llc
 1 Owens Corning Pkwy
 Toledo OH 43659
 419 248-8000

(P-7014)
REVCHEM COMPOSITES INC (PA)
Also Called: Revchem Plastics
2720 S Willow Ave B, Bloomington (92316-3259)
P.O. Box 333 (92316-0333)
PHONE.................................. 909 877-8477
Fax: 909 877-8475
Douglas L Dennis, *CEO*
Gina L Dennis, *Principal*
Marvin Fleck, *General Mgr*
Larry Hall, *Controller*
Russ Tegeler, *Opers Staff*
▲ **EMP:** 66
SALES (est): 33.4MM **Privately Held**
WEB: www.revchem.com
SIC: 5033 Fiberglass building materials

(P-7015)
ROOFING SUPPLY GROUP LLC
14128 Kornblum Ave, Hawthorne (90250-8114)
PHONE.................................. 424 269-7330
EMP: 68
SALES (corp-wide): 2.5B **Publicly Held**
SIC: 5033 Roofing, siding & insulation
HQ: Roofing Supply Group, Llc
 3890 W Northwest Hwy # 400
 Dallas TX 75220
 214 956-5100

(P-7016)
ROOFING WHOLESALE CO INC
8674 Jamacha Rd, Spring Valley (91977-4034)
PHONE.................................. 619 287-7600
Fax: 619 464-4076
Mike Nicholson, *Opers-Prdtn-Mfg*
EMP: 50
SALES (corp-wide): 106.9MM **Privately Held**
WEB: www.rwc.org
SIC: 5033 Roofing, siding & insulation
PA: Roofing Wholesale Co., Inc.
 1918 W Grant St
 Phoenix AZ 85009
 602 258-3794

(P-7017)
ROOFING WHOLESALE CO INC
118 Commercial Rd, San Bernardino (92408-4148)
PHONE.................................. 909 825-8440
Fax: 909 825-6987
Rick Knudsen, *Branch Mgr*
Harold Guerrero, *Executive*
Pat Paszternak, *Manager*
EMP: 50
SALES (corp-wide): 106.9MM **Privately Held**
WEB: www.rwc.org
SIC: 5033 Roofing, asphalt & sheet metal
PA: Roofing Wholesale Co., Inc.
 1918 W Grant St
 Phoenix AZ 85009
 602 258-3794

(P-7018)
SERVICE PARTNERS SUPPLY LLC (DH)
8321 Demetre Ave, Sacramento (95828-0920)
PHONE.................................. 916 379-2290
John Garland, *General Mgr*
Robert Brown, *Credit Mgr*
▲ **EMP:** 59
SALES (est): 43.5MM
SALES (corp-wide): 1.6B **Publicly Held**
SIC: 5033 Insulation materials
HQ: Service Partners, Llc
 1029 Technology Park Dr
 Glen Allen VA 23059
 804 515-7400

(P-7019)
SRS DISTRIBUTION INC
Also Called: Roofline Sup Delivery-Burbank
700 N Victory Blvd, Burbank (91502-1641)
PHONE.................................. 818 840-8851
Ronald R Ross, *Branch Mgr*
EMP: 68
SALES (corp-wide): 1.1B **Privately Held**
SIC: 5033 1761 Roofing & siding materials; roofing, siding & sheet metal work
PA: Srs Distribution Inc
 5900 S Lake Forest Dr # 400
 Mckinney TX 75070
 214 491-4149

(P-7020)
STANDARD INDUSTRIES INC
Also Called: GAF Materials
3301 Navone Rd, Stockton (95215-9312)
PHONE.................................. 209 242-5000
David Kirkham, *Director*
Derek Petcher, *Plant Mgr*
EMP: 50
SQ FT: 30,000
SALES (corp-wide): 2B **Privately Held**
SIC: 5033 Roofing & siding materials
HQ: Standard Industries Inc
 1 Campus Dr
 Parsippany NJ 07054
 973 628-3000

(P-7021)
STANDARD INDUSTRIES INC
Also Called: GAF Materials
6505 S Zerker Rd, Shafter (93263-9614)
PHONE.................................. 661 387-1110
Fax: 661 387-1115
Phil Halpin, *General Mgr*
Ron Miller, *Maintence Staff*
EMP: 100
SALES (corp-wide): 2B **Privately Held**
SIC: 5033 Roofing & siding materials
HQ: Standard Industries Inc
 1 Campus Dr
 Parsippany NJ 07054
 973 628-3000

(P-7022)
TRI-VALLEY SUPPLY INC (PA)
Also Called: Tri Valley Wholesale
1705 Enterprise Dr, Fairfield (94533-6807)
PHONE.................................. 707 469-7470
Fax: 510 494-9057
James P Petersen, *President*
Joe Dean, *Vice Pres*
David Van Beek, *Vice Pres*
▲ **EMP:** 85 **EST:** 1993
SQ FT: 15,000
SALES (est): 48.9MM **Privately Held**
WEB: www.trivalleysupply.com
SIC: 5033 Roofing & siding materials

5039 - Construction Materials, NEC Wholesale County (P-7023)

5039 Construction Materials, NEC Wholesale

(P-7023)
ALLIED BUILDING PRODUCTS CORP
Also Called: AMS
456 Industrial Rd, San Bernardino (92408-3716)
PHONE..................909 796-6926
Fax: 909 799-3815
Paul Lynd, *Manager*
Nancy Wetzel, *Project Mgr*
Josh Bejarano, *Traffic Dir*
Kami Gonzalez, *Sales Associate*
Irene Hernandez, *Asst Mgr*
EMP: 50
SQ FT: 25,000
SALES (corp-wide): 25.3B **Privately Held**
WEB: www.a-m-s.com
SIC: 5039 Ceiling systems & products
HQ: Allied Building Products Corp.
15 E Union Ave
East Rutherford NJ 07073
201 507-8400

(P-7024)
JENSEN ENTERPRISES INC
Also Called: Jensen Precast
5400 Raley Blvd, Sacramento (95838-1700)
PHONE..................916 992-8301
Fax: 916 991-8810
Mark Voiselle, *General Mgr*
David Shacklett, *General Mgr*
Brett Evans, *Project Mgr*
Jack Eastwick, *Human Res Dir*
Jose Lara, *Opers Staff*
EMP: 70
SALES (corp-wide): 157.1MM **Privately Held**
SIC: 5039 5211 Septic tanks; masonry materials & supplies
PA: Jensen Enterprises, Inc.
825 Steneri Way
Sparks NV 89431
775 352-2700

(P-7025)
LA CANTINA DOORS INC
1875 Ord Way, Oceanside (92056-3589)
PHONE..................888 221-0141
Matthew Power, *CEO*
Toby Jones, *Vice Pres*
Benjamin Woo, *Marketing Mgr*
Christian Perry, *Sales Associate*
Maania Hopper, *Corp Comm Staff*
▼ **EMP:** 58
SALES (est): 48.7MM **Privately Held**
WEB: www.lacantinadoors.com
SIC: 5039 Doors, sliding

(P-7026)
MODERN ALLOYS INC
1925 Century Park E # 650, Los Angeles (90067-2752)
PHONE..................714 893-0551
Ronald B Grey, *President*
Scott Metko, *Vice Pres*
John D Rehoreg, *Vice Pres*
Scott R Squires, *Vice Pres*
Joanne Shelton, *Controller*
EMP: 91
SALES (est): 32.2MM **Privately Held**
SIC: 5039 Metal guardrails

(P-7027)
SECURITY CONTRACTOR SVCS INC (PA)
Also Called: S C S
5339 Jackson St, North Highlands (95660-5004)
PHONE..................916 338-4200
Fax: 916 338-1012
Barry J Marrs, *CEO*
Guillermo Sanchez, *Branch Mgr*
Tim Miller, *Data Proc Staff*
Robert Grosshaus, *Accountant*
Angela Beyersdorf, *Human Resources*
EMP: 60 **EST:** 1961
SQ FT: 50,000
SALES (est): 41.8MM **Privately Held**
WEB: www.scsfence.com
SIC: 5039 7359 3315 Wire fence, gates & accessories; equipment rental & leasing; steel wire & related products

5043 Photographic Eqpt & Splys Wholesale

(P-7028)
ADOLPH GASSER INC (PA)
181 2nd St, San Francisco (94105-3808)
PHONE..................415 495-3852
Fax: 415 543-2615
John Gasser, *President*
EMP: 68
SQ FT: 13,840
SALES (est): 27.1MM **Privately Held**
WEB: www.adolphgasser.com
SIC: 5043 5946 7359 5731 Photographic cameras, projectors, equipment & supplies; cameras; photographic supplies; audio-visual equipment & supply rental; video cameras & accessories

(P-7029)
CANON USA INC
15955 Alton Pkwy, Irvine (92618-3731)
PHONE..................949 753-4000
Fax: 949 753-4092
Glen Takahashi, *Manager*
Ian Macfarlane, *President*
Jim Wheeler, *Regional Mgr*
Loc Huynh, *Engineer*
MEI Chiu, *Auditing Mgr*
EMP: 350
SALES (corp-wide): 30.8B **Privately Held**
WEB: www.usa.canon.com
SIC: 5043 5044 5045 8741 Photographic cameras, projectors, equipment & supplies; office equipment; computers; management services
HQ: Canon U.S.A., Inc.
1 Canon Park
Melville NY 11747
516 328-5000

(P-7030)
CHRISTIE DGTAL SYSTEMS USA INC (DH)
10550 Camden Dr, Cypress (90630-4600)
PHONE..................714 527-7056
Fax: 714 503-3375
Jack Kline, *President*
Susie Beiersdorf, *Vice Pres*
Pam Preston, *Vice Pres*
Stuart Macdonald, *Software Dev*
Steve McFadden, *Software Dev*
▲ **EMP:** 153
SQ FT: 85,000
SALES (est): 145.6MM
SALES (corp-wide): 1.5B **Privately Held**
SIC: 5043 Projection apparatus, motion picture & slide
HQ: Christie Digital Systems, Inc.
10550 Camden Dr
Cypress CA 90630
714 527-7056

(P-7031)
DAYMEN US INC
Also Called: Lowepro
1435 N Mcdowell Blvd # 200, Petaluma (94954-6547)
PHONE..................707 827-4053
Fax: 707 575-4389
Jeffrey Michael Colton, *CEO*
Paul Crawley, *CFO*
Rick Olson, *Senior VP*
Robin Riley, *Senior VP*
David Riley, *Vice Pres*
▲ **EMP:** 65
SQ FT: 20,000
SALES (est): 33.3MM **Privately Held**
WEB: www.lowepro.com
SIC: 5043 Photographic equipment & supplies

(P-7032)
FUJIFILM NORTH AMERICA CORP
Also Called: Fuji Photo Film
6200 Phyllis Dr, Cypress (90630-5239)
PHONE..................714 372-4200
Fax: 714 637-3452
Bobby Bruce, *Manager*
Ron Carpenter, *Executive*
George Bouchard, *Business Mgr*
Karen Hebert, *Human Res Dir*
Jean Berrien, *Buyer*
EMP: 150
SALES (corp-wide): 21.2B **Privately Held**
SIC: 5043 Photographic equipment & supplies
HQ: Fujifilm North America Corporation
200 Summit Lake Dr Fl 2
Valhalla NY 10595
914 789-8100

(P-7033)
GELSHMAL ENTERPRISES LLC
Also Called: Imageologist
945 W Hyde Park Blvd, Inglewood (90302-3307)
P.O. Box 4668 (90309-4668)
PHONE..................310 672-9090
Fax: 310 672-3030
David Golshirazi,
Andrew Goggin, *Division Mgr*
Doug Pircher, *General Mgr*
Harry Baltazar, *Human Res Dir*
John Guillen, *Sales Staff*
▲ **EMP:** 50
SALES (est): 11.9MM **Privately Held**
WEB: www.orientalphotousa.com
SIC: 5043 Photographic equipment & supplies

(P-7034)
JK IMAGING LTD
17239 S Main St, Gardena (90248-3129)
PHONE..................310 667-4898
Joe Atick, *CEO*
Shu-Ping Wu, *CFO*
Mike Feng, *Admin Sec*
▲ **EMP:** 100
SQ FT: 6,000
SALES (est): 100MM **Privately Held**
SIC: 5043 Cameras & photographic equipment

(P-7035)
KYOCERA INTERNATIONAL INC (HQ)
8611 Balboa Ave, San Diego (92123-1580)
PHONE..................858 576-2600
John Rigby, *CEO*
Yasuhiro Oishi, *President*
Mark Umemura, *CFO*
Kevin King, *Sr Corp Ofcr*
Blanca Reyes, *Exec VP*
▲ **EMP:** 83
SQ FT: 16,000
SALES (est): 296.4MM
SALES (corp-wide): 12.6B **Publicly Held**
SIC: 5043 Cameras & photographic equipment
PA: Kyocera Corporation
6, Tobadonocho, Takeda, Fushimi-Ku
Kyoto KYO 612-8
756 043-500

(P-7036)
KYOCERA INTERNATIONAL INC
222 N Sepulveda Blvd, El Segundo (90245-5648)
PHONE..................310 647-2805
Fax: 310 955-2801
Steve Clark, *Manager*
Jonathan Hong, *Administration*
Dennis Fan, *Senior Mgr*
EMP: 60
SALES (corp-wide): 12.6B **Publicly Held**
SIC: 5043 Cameras & photographic equipment
HQ: Kyocera International, Inc.
8611 Balboa Ave
San Diego CA 92123
858 576-2600

(P-7037)
NORITSU AMERICA CORPORATION (HQ)
6900 Noritsu Ave, Buena Park (90620-1372)
P.O. Box 5039 (90622-5039)
PHONE..................714 521-9040
Fax: 714 670-2049
Michiro Niikura, *CEO*
Kanichi Nishimoto, *Ch of Bd*
Rick Voutour, *President*
Frank Morrow, *Vice Pres*
Patrik Norrby, *Vice Pres*
▲ **EMP:** 115 **EST:** 1978
SQ FT: 27,500
SALES (est): 100MM
SALES (corp-wide): 369.5MM **Privately Held**
WEB: www.noritsu.com
SIC: 5043 Photographic processing equipment
PA: Noritsu Koki Co., Ltd.
1-10-10, Azabujuban
Minato-Ku TKY 106-0
335 055-053

(P-7038)
WARNER BROTHERS STUDIOS
4000 Warner Blvd, Burbank (91522-0001)
PHONE..................818 954-5000
Fax: 818 954-2657
Gary Credle, *Principal*
Jack Nguyen, *Senior VP*
James Halsey, *CIO*
Edward Romano, *VP Finance*
Carol Cheng, *Assistant*
▲ **EMP:** 70
SALES (est): 19.9MM **Privately Held**
WEB: www.warnerbros.com
SIC: 5043 Motion picture studio & theater equipment

5044 Office Eqpt Wholesale

(P-7039)
ACM TECHNOLOGIES INC (PA)
Also Called: Allstate
2535 Research Dr, Corona (92882-7607)
PHONE..................951 738-9898
Fax: 951 273-2174
Stan Shue Lin, *CEO*
Monica Lin, *Corp Secy*
Christine Lin, *Executive*
Patrick Polycarpe, *Administration*
Alan Xie, *Opers Mgr*
◆ **EMP:** 52
SALES (est): 31.7MM **Privately Held**
WEB: www.acmtech.com
SIC: 5044 Office equipment; photocopy machines

(P-7040)
ALLSTATE IMAGING INC (PA)
21621 Nordhoff St, Chatsworth (91311-5825)
PHONE..................818 678-4550
Alan Jurick, *President*
Russel Leventhal, *CEO*
Richard Shapiro, *CFO*
EMP: 80
SALES (est): 53.2MM **Privately Held**
SIC: 5044 Office equipment

(P-7041)
BANKCARD USA MERCHANT SRVC
5701 Lindero Canyon Rd, Westlake Village (91362-4060)
PHONE..................818 597-7000
Shawn Skelton, *President*
Scott Hardy, *President*
Alan Griefer, *Exec VP*
Mike Trujillo, *Tech/Comp Coord*
Robert Brady, *Engineer*
EMP: 85
SQ FT: 20,000
SALES (est): 16.4MM **Privately Held**
WEB: www.busams.com
SIC: 5044 Check writing, signing & endorsing machines

(P-7042)
BMI IMAGING SYSTEMS INC
749 W Stadium Ln, Sacramento (95834-1100)
PHONE..................916 924-6666
Gary Lefebvre, *Manager*
Jim Modrall, *Vice Pres*
Brad Penfold, *Vice Pres*
Hillary Whitney, *Human Resources*
Tonia Champas, *Marketing Mgr*
EMP: 64

▲ = Import ▼ = Export
◆ = Import/Export

PRODUCTS & SERVICES SECTION
5044 - Office Eqpt Wholesale County (P-7063)

SALES (corp-wide): 9MM **Privately Held**
WEB: www.bmiimaging.com
SIC: 5044 Micrographic equipment
PA: Bmi Imaging Systems, Inc
1115 E Arques Ave
Sunnyvale CA 94085
916 924-6666

(P-7043)
CANON BUS SOLUTIONS-WEST INC
110 W Walnut St, Gardena (90248-3100)
P.O. Box 51075, Los Angeles (90074-1075)
PHONE..................................310 217-3000
Fax: 310 715-7050
Bill Joseph, *President*
Keiko Brockel, *Vice Pres*
Art McGinn, *Vice Pres*
Martin Meidl, *Marketing Mgr*
John Murphy, *Director*
EMP: 450
SQ FT: 100,000
SALES (est): 34.9MM
SALES (corp-wide): 30.8B **Privately Held**
WEB: www.usa.canon.com
SIC: 5044 Office equipment
HQ: Canon U.S.A., Inc.
1 Canon Park
Melville NY 11747
516 328-5000

(P-7044)
CANON SOLUTIONS AMERICA INC
1055 W 7th St Ste 1600, Los Angeles (90017-2535)
PHONE..................................213 629-6733
Kip Tashiro, *Branch Mgr*
EMP: 50
SALES (corp-wide): 30.8B **Privately Held**
SIC: 5044 Copying equipment
HQ: Canon Solutions America, Inc.
1 Canon Park
Melville NY 11747
631 330-5000

(P-7045)
CANON SOLUTIONS AMERICA INC
26901 Agoura Rd Ste 110, Agoura Hills (91301-5108)
PHONE..................................818 871-6700
Fax: 818 871-6750
John Malone, *Branch Mgr*
Kathleen Johnston, *Administration*
EMP: 70
SALES (corp-wide): 30.8B **Privately Held**
SIC: 5044 Office equipment
HQ: Canon Solutions America, Inc.
1 Canon Park
Melville NY 11747
631 330-5000

(P-7046)
CANON SOLUTIONS AMERICA INC
201 California St Ste 100, San Francisco (94111-5003)
PHONE..................................415 743-7300
Fax: 415 635-1405
Kim Haydel, *Branch Mgr*
Ellen Murray, *Executive*
Barbara Telesford, *Exec Dir*
Jeff Le, *Software Dev*
Joone Marigomen, *Network Analyst*
EMP: 51
SALES (corp-wide): 30.8B **Privately Held**
SIC: 5044 Office equipment
HQ: Canon Solutions America, Inc.
1 Canon Park
Melville NY 11747
631 330-5000

(P-7047)
CANON SOLUTIONS AMERICA INC
123 Paularino Ave, Costa Mesa (92626-3311)
PHONE..................................949 753-4200
Mark Hix, *Branch Mgr*
EMP: 80
SALES (corp-wide): 30.8B **Privately Held**
SIC: 5044 Copying equipment

HQ: Canon Solutions America, Inc.
1 Canon Park
Melville NY 11747
631 330-5000

(P-7048)
CANON USA INC
6060 W Sunset Blvd, Los Angeles (90028-6433)
PHONE..................................323 461-1862
EMP: 135
SALES (corp-wide): 30.8B **Privately Held**
SIC: 5044 Photocopy machines
HQ: Canon U.S.A., Inc.
1 Canon Park
Melville NY 11747
516 328-5000

(P-7049)
CANON USA INC
1055 W 7th St Ste 1600, Los Angeles (90017-2535)
PHONE..................................213 629-6700
Fax: 213 629-6717
Kip Tashiro, *Branch Mgr*
EMP: 80
SALES (corp-wide): 30.8B **Privately Held**
WEB: www.usa.canon.com
SIC: 5044 Photocopy machines; typewriters; duplicating machines; calcvlators, electronic
HQ: Canon U.S.A., Inc.
1 Canon Park
Melville NY 11747
516 328-5000

(P-7050)
COAST TO COAST BUS EQP INC (PA)
8 Vanderbilt Ste 200, Irvine (92618-2080)
PHONE..................................949 457-7300
Fax: 949 457-7365
Paul M Faus, *President*
Julie Davis, *Treasurer*
Roland Tolan, *Vice Pres*
Marla Gastelum, *Executive*
Manny Torres, *CIO*
EMP: 52
SQ FT: 20,100
SALES (est): 20.5MM **Privately Held**
WEB: www.ctcbe.com
SIC: 5044 5065 Copying equipment; teletype equipment

(P-7051)
CUSTOM BUSINESS SOLUTIONS INC (PA)
Also Called: Northstar
12 Morgan, Irvine (92618-2003)
PHONE..................................949 380-7674
Fax: 714 774-7644
Art Julian, *CEO*
Colleen Julian, *President*
Michael Block, *CFO*
Tammy Brown, *Vice Pres*
Joseph Castillo, *Vice Pres*
▼ **EMP:** 68
SQ FT: 21,000
SALES (est): 58.6MM **Privately Held**
WEB: www.cbs-posi.com
SIC: 5044 Cash registers

(P-7052)
DUPLO USA CORPORATION (PA)
3050 Daimler St, Santa Ana (92705-5813)
PHONE..................................949 752-8222
Fax: 949 752-7766
Peter Tu, *President*
Jim Peffer, *General Mgr*
Eric Von Schimpf, *Info Tech Dir*
Eric Schimpf, *Data Proc Staff*
Jesse Yuan, *Network Tech*
◆ **EMP:** 80
SQ FT: 30,000
SALES (est): 33MM **Privately Held**
WEB: www.duplousa.com
SIC: 5044 Office equipment; duplicating machines

(P-7053)
IMAGE IV SYSTEMS INC (PA)
512 S Varney St, Burbank (91502-2196)
PHONE..................................323 849-3049
Fax: 323 842-0208
Ronald Warren, *President*
Norma Henkel, *Vice Pres*

HQ: Canon Solutions America, Inc.
1 Canon Park
Melville NY 11747
631 330-5000

Sue Warren, *Vice Pres*
Susan Warren, *Vice Pres*
Kelsey Goodrich, *Regional Mgr*
EMP: 79
SQ FT: 4,000
SALES (est): 21.6MM **Privately Held**
WEB: www.imageiv.com
SIC: 5044 Photocopy machines; copying equipment

(P-7054)
INTEGRUS LLC
Also Called: Advanced Office
1430 Village Way Ste K, Santa Ana (92705-4760)
PHONE..................................714 547-9500
Mike Dixon, *CEO*
Richard Van Dyke, *President*
Tim Wickers, *Vice Pres*
EMP: 100 **EST:** 2011
SQ FT: 14,000
SALES: 18MM **Privately Held**
SIC: 5044 Office equipment

(P-7055)
INTERNATIONAL BUS MCHS CORP
Also Called: IBM
425 Market St, San Francisco (94105-2532)
PHONE..................................415 545-4747
Fax: 415 545-2132
Wirt Cook, *CEO*
Rick Savage, *Senior VP*
Tom Hill, *Vice Pres*
Kramer Reeves, *Executive*
Hunter Medney, *Software Dev*
EMP: 208
SALES (corp-wide): 81.7B **Publicly Held**
WEB: www.ibm.com
SIC: 5044 5045 3571 Office equipment; computers, peripherals & software; electronic computers
PA: International Business Machines Corporation
1 New Orchard Rd Ste 1
Armonk NY 10504
914 499-1900

(P-7056)
INTERNATIONAL BUS MCHS CORP
Also Called: IBM
2077 Gateway Pl, San Jose (95110-1090)
P.O. Box 49015 (95161-9015)
PHONE..................................408 452-4800
Barry Gafner, *Principal*
EMP: 200
SALES (corp-wide): 81.7B **Publicly Held**
WEB: www.ibm.com
SIC: 5044 5045 Office equipment; computers, peripherals & software
PA: International Business Machines Corporation
1 New Orchard Rd Ste 1
Armonk NY 10504
914 499-1900

(P-7057)
INTERNATIONAL LITIGATION SVCS
65 Enterprise, Aliso Viejo (92656-2705)
PHONE..................................888 313-4457
Joseph Thorpe, *CEO*
Ketan Parekh, *COO*
Mark Liekkio, *Senior VP*
EMP: 50
SQ FT: 7,000
SALES (est): 10.3MM **Privately Held**
SIC: 5044 Office equipment

(P-7058)
KONICA MINOLTA BUSINESS SOLUTI
1831 Commercenter W, San Bernardino (92408-3303)
PHONE..................................909 824-2000
Fax: 909 801-5211
Linda F Turner, *Manager*
Joseph Lagreca, *Agent*
EMP: 69
SQ FT: 13,000

SALES (corp-wide): 8.8B **Privately Held**
WEB: www.konicabt.com
SIC: 5044 5065 5943 Photocopy machines; facsimile equipment; office forms & supplies
HQ: Konica Minolta Business Solutions U.S.A., Inc.
100 Williams Dr
Ramsey NJ 07446
201 825-4000

(P-7059)
KYOCERA DCMENT SLTONS AMER INC
Also Called: Kyocera Technology Development
1855 Gateway Blvd Ste 400, Concord (94520-3289)
PHONE..................................925 849-3300
Fax: 925 849-3399
Atsushi Yuki, *Manager*
Zhencai Wang, *Sr Software Eng*
Debashis Panda, *Software Dev*
Junichiro Hamaguchi, *Business Mgr*
EMP: 70
SALES (corp-wide): 12.6B **Publicly Held**
SIC: 5044 Photocopy machines
HQ: Kyocera Document Solutions America, Inc.
225 Sand Rd
Fairfield NJ 07004
973 808-8444

(P-7060)
MICROTEK LAB INC (HQ)
13337 South St, Cerritos (90703-7308)
PHONE..................................310 687-5823
Clark Hsu, *President*
Stewart Chow, *President*
Lisa Lin, *Controller*
▲ **EMP:** 110 **EST:** 1980
SQ FT: 126,000
SALES (est): 26.1MM
SALES (corp-wide): 24.9MM **Privately Held**
WEB: www.microtek.com
SIC: 5044 Copying equipment
PA: Microtek International Inc.
6, Ind. E. 3rd Rd.,
Hsinchu City
357 721-55

(P-7061)
MR COPY INC (DH)
Also Called: Mrc, Smart Tech Solutions
5657 Copley Dr, San Diego (92111-7903)
PHONE..................................858 573-6300
Fax: 858 573-6301
Bob Leone, *President*
Kevin McCarty, *CFO*
EMP: 75
SQ FT: 18,000
SALES (est): 126MM
SALES (corp-wide): 18B **Publicly Held**
SIC: 5044 Office equipment; photocopy machines
HQ: Global Imaging Systems, Inc.
3903 Northdale Blvd 200w
Tampa FL 33624
813 960-5508

(P-7062)
NATIONAL LINK INCORPORATED
2235 Auto Centre Dr, Glendora (91740-6721)
PHONE..................................909 670-1900
Fax: 909 447-7989
Sam Kandah, *President*
Jim Scott, *CFO*
Carol Kandah, *Admin Sec*
Shawn Rahim, *Admin Asst*
Carina Teng, *Controller*
EMP: 50
SQ FT: 5,000
SALES (est): 23MM **Privately Held**
SIC: 5044 7389 7359 Bank automatic teller machines; credit card service; electronic equipment rental, except computers

(P-7063)
PINNACLE DOCUMENT SYSTEMS (PA)
470 Boulder Ct Ste 100, Pleasanton (94566-8315)
PHONE..................................925 417-8400

5044 - Office Eqpt Wholesale County (P-7064)

Toll Free:............................877 -
Fax: 925 417-8404
Todd Court, *Ch of Bd*
Samuel Pulino, *President*
Dan Garon, *Accountant*
EMP: 60 **EST:** 1998
SQ FT: 30,000
SALES (est): 12MM **Privately Held**
WEB: www.pinnacleds.com
SIC: 5044 Office equipment

(P-7064)
RICOH USA INC
333 Bush St Ste 2500, San Francisco (94104-2862)
PHONE..........................415 733-5600
Fax: 415 733-5620
Joan Meyer, *Manager*
Mark Coyle, *Vice Pres*
Arturo Chqrues, *CTO*
Jay Kehne, *CTO*
Steve Wallace, *Info Tech Dir*
EMP: 68
SALES (corp-wide): 18.8B **Privately Held**
WEB: www.ikon.com
SIC: 5044 Office equipment
HQ: Ricoh Usa, Inc.
   70 Valley Stream Pkwy
   Malvern PA 19355
   610 296-8000

(P-7065)
RICOH USA INC
9430 Topanga Canyon Blvd # 100, Chatsworth (91311-5765)
PHONE..........................818 294-8601
Daniel Walsh, *Manager*
EMP: 50
SALES (corp-wide): 18.8B **Privately Held**
SIC: 5044 Office equipment
HQ: Ricoh Usa, Inc.
   70 Valley Stream Pkwy
   Malvern PA 19355
   610 296-8000

(P-7066)
RICOH USA INC
Also Called: Ricoh Business Solutions
17011 Beach Blvd Ste 1000, Huntington Beach (92647-7402)
PHONE..........................714 396-0568
Tracy Wood, *Manager*
Dave Underwood, *Manager*
EMP: 50
SALES (corp-wide): 18.8B **Privately Held**
SIC: 5044 5112 3861 3661 Copying equipment; photocopying supplies; photographic equipment & supplies; telephone & telegraph apparatus
HQ: Ricoh Usa, Inc.
   70 Valley Stream Pkwy
   Malvern PA 19355
   610 296-8000

(P-7067)
RICOH USA INC
6330 Variel Ave, Woodland Hills (91367-2543)
PHONE..........................213 629-1838
Steve Smith, *Exec VP*
EMP: 100
SALES (corp-wide): 18.8B **Privately Held**
WEB: www.ikon.com
SIC: 5044 Photocopy machines
HQ: Ricoh Usa, Inc.
   70 Valley Stream Pkwy
   Malvern PA 19355
   610 296-8000

(P-7068)
RICOH USA INC
Also Called: Nightrider Overnite Copy Svc
333 Bush St Ste 2500, San Francisco (94104-2862)
PHONE..........................415 392-6850
Fax: 415 392-0427
John Wilkinson, *Manager*
EMP: 60
SALES (corp-wide): 18.8B **Privately Held**
WEB: www.ikon.com
SIC: 5044 Office equipment
HQ: Ricoh Usa, Inc.
   70 Valley Stream Pkwy
   Malvern PA 19355
   610 296-8000

(P-7069)
RICOH USA INC
21820 Burbank Blvd # 229, Woodland Hills (91367-6476)
PHONE..........................818 703-0265
David Burton, *Manager*
Bryce Decastro, *Accounts Exec*
Roland Hinds, *Accounts Exec*
EMP: 50
SALES (corp-wide): 18.8B **Privately Held**
SIC: 5044 Copying equipment
HQ: Ricoh Usa, Inc.
   70 Valley Stream Pkwy
   Malvern PA 19355
   610 296-8000

(P-7070)
RICOH USA INC
1320 Willow Pass Rd, Concord (94520-5232)
PHONE..........................925 988-4000
Renee Faxton, *Branch Mgr*
Thomas Gernhardt, *Vice Pres*
Cheryl Franklin, *Admin Asst*
Steven Bottini, *Sales Staff*
Vicki Nicholas, *Director*
EMP: 150
SALES (corp-wide): 18.8B **Privately Held**
WEB: www.ikon.com
SIC: 5044 5065 7629 7359 Photocopy machines; typewriters; facsimile equipment; electronic equipment repair; office machine rental, except computers; stationery stores; computer rental & leasing
HQ: Ricoh Usa, Inc.
   70 Valley Stream Pkwy
   Malvern PA 19355
   610 296-8000

(P-7071)
RICOH USA INC
390 N Wiget Ln, Walnut Creek (94598-2489)
PHONE..........................925 938-2049
Jeniffer Cooke, *Branch Mgr*
Abby Hussein, *Manager*
EMP: 125
SQ FT: 55,000
SALES (corp-wide): 18.8B **Privately Held**
WEB: www.ikon.com
SIC: 5044 Office equipment
HQ: Ricoh Usa, Inc.
   70 Valley Stream Pkwy
   Malvern PA 19355
   610 296-8000

(P-7072)
RICOH USA INC
16715 Von Karman Ave # 100, Irvine (92606-4945)
PHONE..........................949 225-2300
Fax: 949 862-6555
Steve Bastien, *Manager*
Craig Weigman, *Div Sub Head*
George Ampagoomian, *Site Mgr*
Bill Cmela, *Manager*
EMP: 75
SALES (corp-wide): 18.8B **Privately Held**
WEB: www.ikon.com
SIC: 5044 Office equipment
HQ: Ricoh Usa, Inc.
   70 Valley Stream Pkwy
   Malvern PA 19355
   610 296-8000

(P-7073)
TOSHIBA AMER BUS SOLUTIONS INC (DH)
9740 Irvine Blvd, Irvine (92618-1608)
PHONE..........................949 462-6000
Fax: 949 462-2900
Masahiro Yamada, *Ch of Bd*
Mark Mathews, *President*
Hiroyuki Watanabe, *President*
Desmond Allen, *CFO*
Michael Torcaso, *CFO*
◆ **EMP:** 350 **EST:** 1999
SQ FT: 90,000
SALES (est): 1.7B
SALES (corp-wide): 48.4B **Privately Held**
WEB: www.levenstein.com
SIC: 5044 Copying equipment
HQ: Toshiba Tec Corporation
   1-11-1, Osaki
   Shinagawa-Ku TKY 141-0
   368 309-100

(P-7074)
TOSHIBA TEC AMERICA RETAIL INF (DH)
2 Musick, Irvine (92618-1631)
PHONE..........................949 462-2850
Fax: 949 462-2851
H Murata, *President*
Angie Bernard, *Admin Asst*
Jeff Warren, *Controller*
John Wilson, *Purch Mgr*
◆ **EMP:** 50
SALES (est): 8.9MM
SALES (corp-wide): 48.4B **Privately Held**
WEB: www.tecamerica.com
SIC: 5044 5046 Cash registers; scales, except laboratory
HQ: Toshiba Tec Corporation
   1-11-1, Osaki
   Shinagawa-Ku TKY 141-0
   368 309-100

(P-7075)
UNITED MERCHANT SVCS CAL INC
Also Called: Ums Banking
750 Fairmont Ave Ste 201, Glendale (91203-1074)
PHONE..........................818 246-6767
Fax: 818 246-0902
Joyce Gaines, *President*
Lynda Neuman, *CFO*
Jorge Torres, *Treasurer*
Bruce Ferguson, *Exec VP*
Suzanne Haas, *Senior VP*
EMP: 72
SQ FT: 8,580
SALES (est): 34.7MM **Privately Held**
WEB: www.umsbanking.com
SIC: 5044 5065 7629 Office equipment; electronic parts & equipment; electronic equipment repair

(P-7076)
XEROX CORPORATION
560 J St Ste 300, Sacramento (95814-2343)
PHONE..........................916 444-8100
Fax: 916 561-6242
Anne Pitt, *Branch Mgr*
EMP: 65
SALES (corp-wide): 18B **Publicly Held**
WEB: www.xerox.com
SIC: 5044 Photocopy machines
PA: Xerox Corporation
   45 Glover Ave Ste 700
   Norwalk CT 06850
   203 968-3000

(P-7077)
XEROX CORPORATION
1218 S 5th Ave, Monrovia (91016-3805)
PHONE..........................626 294-3754
Theresa Klemme, *Vice Pres*
Walt Miller, *Administration*
Tom Logan, *MIS Dir*
Dennis Barnes, *VP Engrg*
Larry Klein, *Controller*
EMP: 120
SQ FT: 200,000
SALES (corp-wide): 18B **Publicly Held**
WEB: www.xerox.com
SIC: 5044 Copying equipment
PA: Xerox Corporation
   45 Glover Ave Ste 700
   Norwalk CT 06850
   203 968-3000

(P-7078)
XEROX CORPORATION
1851 E 1st St Ste 200, Santa Ana (92705-4072)
PHONE..........................714 565-1100
Fax: 714 565-1294
Hunt Gammel, *District Mgr*
Cheryl Sorenson, *Sales Executive*
April Morgan-Leonetti, *Marketing Staff*
EMP: 400
SALES (corp-wide): 18B **Publicly Held**
WEB: www.xerox.com
SIC: 5044 5045 5065 5112 Photocopy machines; typewriters; computers, peripherals & parts; software; printers, computer; facsimile equipment; computer & photocopying supplies
PA: Xerox Corporation
   45 Glover Ave Ste 700
   Norwalk CT 06850
   203 968-3000

(P-7079)
YOUNG SYSTEMS CORPORATION
Also Called: Nuworld Business Systems
13125 Midway Pl, Cerritos (90703-2232)
PHONE..........................562 921-2256
Fax: 562 741-2156
Young H Lee, *President*
Donald Lee, *Vice Pres*
Claudia Reed, *Executive*
June S Lee, *Admin Sec*
Chris Chang, *Info Tech Dir*
◆ **EMP:** 50
SQ FT: 50,000
SALES (est): 38.4MM **Privately Held**
WEB: www.nuworldinc.com
SIC: 5044 5999 Office equipment; typewriters & business machines

---

5045 Computers & Peripheral Eqpt & Software Wholesale

(P-7080)
ACCEL NORTH AMERICA INC
4633 Old Ironsides Dr # 400, Santa Clara (95054-1846)
PHONE..........................408 514-5199
David Kumar, *CEO*
Philip John, *Officer*
Parameswaran Nair, *Officer*
Goda Kumar, *Vice Pres*
Aju Kuriakose, *Vice Pres*
EMP: 217
SQ FT: 4,000
SALES (est): 21.1MM
SALES (corp-wide): 13.6MM **Privately Held**
WEB: www.accelna.com
SIC: 5045 Computers, peripherals & software
HQ: Accel Transmatic Limited
   Accel House, 3rd Floor,
   Chennai TN
   444 225-2000

(P-7081)
ACROSS SYSTEMS INC
100 N Brand Blvd Ste 100, Glendale (91203-2636)
PHONE..........................877 922-7677
Daniel Nackovski, *President*
Federico Nolasco, *Executive*
Nancy Cardone, *Business Mgr*
EMP: 70
SALES (est): 6.4MM **Privately Held**
SIC: 5045 Computers, peripherals & software

(P-7082)
ADAPTV INC (DH)
2 Waters Park Dr Ste 200, San Mateo (94403-1178)
PHONE..........................650 286-4420
Fax: 650 312-9223
Amir Ashkenazi, *CEO*
Toby Gabriner, *President*
Teg Grenager,
Nir Yeffet, *Exec VP*
Sean Behr, *Senior VP*
EMP: 57
SALES (est): 35.4MM
SALES (corp-wide): 131.6MM **Publicly Held**
SIC: 5045 Computer software
HQ: Aol Inc.
   770 Broadway Fl 4
   New York NY 10003
   212 652-6400

(P-7083)
ADESSO INC
Also Called: ADS Techonlogy
160 Commerce Way, Walnut (91789-2714)
PHONE..........................909 839-2929
Fax: 909 839-2930
Allen Ku, *President*
Don Lee, *Finance Dir*

PRODUCTS & SERVICES SECTION **5045 - Computers & Peripheral Eqpt & Software Wholesale County (P-7102)**

Lily Lu, *Accountant*
Ray Shih, *Sales Staff*
▲ EMP: 200
SQ FT: 31,000
SALES (est): 6.5MM **Privately Held**
WEB: www.adesso.com
SIC: 5045 Computer peripheral equipment

(P-7084)
ADVANCED INDUSTRIAL CMPT INC (PA)
Also Called: Aic Inc USA
21808 Garcia Ln, City of Industry (91789-0941)
PHONE..................909 895-8989
Michael Liang, *Ch of Bd*
Shun Ying Liang, *CEO*
Belle Wang, *CFO*
Sherman Tang, *Vice Pres*
Sophia Tsai, *Program Mgr*
▲ EMP: 57
SQ FT: 65,000
SALES (est): 27.4MM **Privately Held**
WEB: www.aicipc.com
SIC: 5045 Mainframe computers

(P-7085)
ADVANTECH CORPORATION (HQ)
380 Fairview Way, Milpitas (95035-3062)
P.O. Box 45895, San Francisco (94145-0895)
PHONE..................408 519-3800
Fax: 408 519-3899
Ke-Cheng Liu, *CEO*
Chaney Ho, *President*
Yizhong Lin, *COO*
Eric Chen, *Vice Pres*
Kenny Deng, *Vice Pres*
▲ EMP: 70
SQ FT: 100,000
SALES: 340MM
SALES (corp-wide): 1.1B **Privately Held**
SIC: 5045 7379 Computers, peripherals & software; computer hardware requirements analysis
PA: Advantech Co., Ltd.
1, Alley 20, Lane 26, Jui Kuang Rd., Taipei City TAP 11491
227 927-818

(P-7086)
AGILYSYS INC
1900 Powell St Ste 230, Emeryville (94608-1837)
PHONE..................702 759-4879
Christian Fisher, *Manager*
Jeff Gebhardt, *Director*
EMP: 50
SALES (corp-wide): 120.3MM **Publicly Held**
WEB: www.pios.com
SIC: 5045 7371 Computer software; computer software development & applications
PA: Agilysys, Inc.
425 Walnut St Ste 1800
Cincinnati OH 45202
770 810-7800

(P-7087)
AIRMAGNET INC
830 E Arques Ave, Sunnyvale (94085-4519)
PHONE..................408 400-0200
Robert S Lutz, *CEO*
Dean Au, *President*
Miles Wu, *Treasurer*
Rich Mirnoff, *Exec VP*
Greg Yates, *Exec VP*
▲ EMP: 80
SQ FT: 26,000
SALES: 9.3MM
SALES (corp-wide): 5B **Publicly Held**
WEB: www.airmagnet.com
SIC: 5045 Computers, peripherals & software
HQ: Fluke Corporation
6920 Seaway Blvd
Everett WA 98203
425 446-5400

(P-7088)
ALTAMETRICS LLC
3191 Red Hill Ave Ste 100, Costa Mesa (92626-3451)
PHONE..................800 676-1281
Mitesh Gala, *President*
Anand Gala, *CFO*
Ryan Biggs, *Vice Pres*
Timothy Yost, *Vice Pres*
Patrick T Connors, *Executive*
EMP: 140
SQ FT: 6,000
SALES (est): 31.7MM **Privately Held**
WEB: www.altametrics.com
SIC: 5045 Computer software

(P-7089)
AMAX ENGINEERING CORPORATION (PA)
Also Called: Amax Computer
1565 Reliance Way, Fremont (94539-6103)
PHONE..................510 651-8886
Jerry Kc Shih, *CEO*
Azaa Lee, *Vice Pres*
CHI-Lei Ni, *Vice Pres*
Jean Shih, *Vice Pres*
Edward Zheng, *Vice Pres*
▲ EMP: 150
SQ FT: 110,000
SALES (est): 216.5MM **Privately Held**
WEB: www.amaxit.com
SIC: 5045 Computer peripheral equipment; computer software

(P-7090)
AMBERFIN LIMITED
7590 N Glenoaks Blvd # 101, Burbank (91504-1011)
PHONE..................818 768-8948
Jeremy Mh Deaner, *President*
Geoff Bowen, *President*
Simon Adler, *Vice Pres*
Richard Kennedy, *Technical Staff*
EMP: 50
SALES (est): 2.3MM **Privately Held**
SIC: 5045 Computers, peripherals & software

(P-7091)
AMERICAN FUTURE TECH CORP
Also Called: Ibuypower
529 Baldwin Park Blvd, City of Industry (91746-1419)
PHONE..................888 462-3899
Alex Hou, *CEO*
Darren Su, *Vice Pres*
▲ EMP: 120
SQ FT: 25,000
SALES (est): 92MM **Privately Held**
WEB: www.aftcorp.com
SIC: 5045 Computers, peripherals & software

(P-7092)
AOPEN AMERICA INCORPORATED
2150 N 1st St Ste 300, San Jose (95131-2044)
PHONE..................408 586-1200
Dale Tsai, *President*
James Huang, *Vice Pres*
▲ EMP: 70 **EST:** 1997
SQ FT: 50,000
SALES: 13MM
SALES (corp-wide): 48.1MM **Privately Held**
SIC: 5045 Computers, peripherals & software
PA: Aopen Incorporated
5f, 15, Lane 128, Sinhu 1st Rd., Taipei City TAP 11494
277 101-195

(P-7093)
ARBITECH LLC
15330 Barranca Pkwy, Irvine (92618-2215)
PHONE..................949 376-6650
Fax: 949 376-6181
Torin Pavia, *CEO*
Francisco Llaca, *President*
Clarissa Zulick, *COO*
Jimmy Whalen, *Exec VP*
Mark Dunlap, *Vice Pres*
▲ EMP: 74
SQ FT: 40,000
SALES (est): 103MM **Privately Held**
WEB: www.arbitech.com
SIC: 5045 Computer peripheral equipment

(P-7094)
ASI COMPUTER TECHNOLOGIES INC (PA)
Also Called: A S I
48289 Fremont Blvd, Fremont (94538-6510)
PHONE..................510 226-8000
Christine Liang, *CEO*
Marcel Liang, *Ch of Bd*
Brian Clark, *Exec VP*
Rex Chu, *Vice Pres*
Kelvin Smith, *Administration*
▲ EMP: 200
SQ FT: 155,000
SALES (est): 1.5B **Privately Held**
WEB: www.asipartner.com
SIC: 5045 3577 Disk drives; keying equipment; printers, computer; terminals, computer; computer output to microfilm units

(P-7095)
ASUS COMPUTER INTERNATIONAL
800 Corp Way, Fremont (94539)
PHONE..................510 739-3777
Fax: 510 608-4555
Steve Chang, *CEO*
Ivan Hoe, *President*
Raymond Chen, *Vice Pres*
Albert Wang, *Vice Pres*
Markus Wierzoch, *Info Tech Dir*
▲ EMP: 130
SQ FT: 13,000
SALES (est): 191.7MM
SALES (corp-wide): 14.5B **Privately Held**
WEB: www.asus.com
SIC: 5045 3577 Computer peripheral equipment; computer peripheral equipment
PA: Asustek Computer Incorporation
15, Lide Rd.,
Taipei City TAP 11259
228 943-447

(P-7096)
ATEN TECHNOLOGY INC
Also Called: Iogear
15365 Barranca Pkwy, Irvine (92618-2216)
PHONE..................949 428-1111
Kevin Sun-Chung Chen, *President*
Vanessa Chen, *CFO*
Mike Adawiya, *Info Tech Mgr*
Olivia KAO, *Info Tech Mgr*
Yojen Huang, *MIS Mgr*
▲ EMP: 100
SALES (est): 46.3MM
SALES (corp-wide): 150.4MM **Privately Held**
SIC: 5045 3577 Computers & accessories, personal & home entertainment; computer peripheral equipment
PA: Aten International Co., Ltd.
3f, 125, Ta Tung Rd., Sec. 2, New Taipei City 22183
286 926-789

(P-7097)
AVER INFORMATION INC
668 Mission Ct, Fremont (94539-8206)
PHONE..................408 263-3828
Arthur S Pait, *President*
Sinar Pait, *CEO*
Moses Lee, *CFO*
Ted Pepping, *Vice Pres*
Jay Zhu, *Administration*
▲ EMP: 50
SQ FT: 15,000
SALES: 23.6MM
SALES (corp-wide): 49.9MM **Privately Held**
SIC: 5045 7382 5099 Computers, peripherals & software; computers & accessories, personal & home entertainment; security systems services; confinement surveillance systems maintenance & monitoring; video & audio equipment
PA: Aver Information Inc.
8f, 157, Ta An Rd,
New Taipei City 23673
222 698-535

(P-7098)
BACKWEB TECHNOLOGIES INC
2727 Walsh Ave Ste 102, Santa Clara (95051-0956)
PHONE..................408 933-1700
Eli Barkat, *Ch of Bd*
Daniel Platzker, *Vice Pres*
Anand Deshpande, *Director*
EMP: 50
SQ FT: 16,000
SALES (est): 4.1MM
SALES (corp-wide): 4.4MM **Privately Held**
WEB: www.backweb.com
SIC: 5045 Computer software
HQ: Backweb Technologies Ltd.
10 Haamal
Rosh Haayin
390 027-00

(P-7099)
BATTERY-BIZ INC
Also Called: Ebatts.com
1380 Flynn Rd, Camarillo (93012-8016)
PHONE..................805 437-7777
Ophir Marish, *CEO*
Yossi Jakubovits, *CFO*
Dave Derse, *Vice Pres*
Raj Mitra, *Vice Pres*
Jessie Revlin, *Director*
▲ EMP: 63
SQ FT: 5,700
SALES (est): 25.4MM **Privately Held**
WEB: www.batterybiz.net
SIC: 5045 Computers, peripherals & software

(P-7100)
BEAR DATA SOLUTIONS INC
300 Broadway Ste 24, San Francisco (94133-4529)
PHONE..................415 788-1501
Don James, *CEO*
Wilcy Sharer, *Accounts Mgr*
EMP: 52
SALES (corp-wide): 764.7MM **Publicly Held**
WEB: www.bdata.com
SIC: 5045 7373 Computers, peripherals & software; computer integrated systems design
HQ: Bear Data Solutions, Inc.
10050 Crosstown Cir
Eden Prairie MN 55344
925 389-1320

(P-7101)
BENQ AMERICA CORP (HQ)
3200 Park Center Dr # 150, Costa Mesa (92626-1982)
PHONE..................714 559-4900
Fax: 949 255-9600
KY Lee, *Chairman*
Lars Yoder, *President*
Conway Lee, *CEO*
Ellin Lee, *CFO*
Timothy Chin, *Software Engr*
▲ EMP: 65 **EST:** 1997
SALES (est): 37.9MM
SALES (corp-wide): 4.1B **Privately Held**
SIC: 5045 Computer peripheral equipment
PA: Qisda Corporation
157, Shan Ying Rd.,
Taoyuan City TAY 33341
335 988-00

(P-7102)
BIZCOM ELECTRONICS INC (HQ)
1171 Montague Expy, Milpitas (95035-6845)
PHONE..................408 262-7877
Fax: 408 262-3900
Ray Chen, *CEO*
Duan Wang, *President*
Gary Lu, *CFO*
Justin Wang, *Senior VP*
Laurens Shu, *Vice Pres*
▲ EMP: 140
SQ FT: 50,000

5045 - Computers & Peripheral Eqpt & Software Wholesale County (P-7103)   PRODUCTS & SERVICES SECTION

SALES (est): 44.8MM
SALES (corp-wide): 26B Privately Held
WEB: www.bizcom-us.com
SIC: 5045 7629 7378 Computers; telecommunication equipment repair (except telephones); computer maintenance & repair
PA: Compal Electronics, Inc.
    581, Ruiguang Rd.,
    Taipei City TAP 11492
    287 978-588

(P-7103)
BROADWAY TYPEWRITER CO INC
Also Called: AREY JONES EDUCATIONAL SOLUTIO
1055 6th Ave Ste 101, San Diego (92101-5229)
PHONE................................619 645-0253
Michael Scarpella, President
David Scarpella, CFO
Peter Scarpella, Vice Pres
Margaret Scarpella, Admin Sec
EMP: 80 EST: 1968
SQ FT: 23,000
SALES: 111.8MM Privately Held
SIC: 5045 7378 Computers, peripherals & software; computer maintenance & repair

(P-7104)
BUSINESS OBJECTS INC (HQ)
3410 Hillview Ave, Palo Alto (94304-1395)
PHONE................................650 849-4000
Fax: 408 953-6001
John Schwarz, CEO
Vronique D'Adhemar, CFO
Bruno Walmsley, CFO
Xuanloan Ho, Chairman
Jonathan Becker, Chief Mktg Ofcr
▲ EMP: 205
SALES (est): 316.5MM
SALES (corp-wide): 22.3B Privately Held
WEB: www.businessobjects.com
SIC: 5045 Computer software
PA: Sap Se
    Dietmar-Hopp-Allee 16
    Walldorf 69190
    622 774-7474

(P-7105)
C9 EDGE INC
177 Bovet Rd Ste 520, San Mateo (94402-3144)
PHONE................................650 561-7855
Fax: 650 637-1473
Michael Howard, CEO
Stephen Lucas, CFO
David Thompson, Vice Pres
Andy Twigg, CTO
Pooja Joshipura, Controller
EMP: 60
SQ FT: 10,000
SALES (est): 5.5MM Privately Held
SIC: 5045 Computer software

(P-7106)
CACI NSS INC
Also Called: Enganering and Technical Svcs
3201 Airpark Dr Ste 109, Santa Maria (93455-1834)
PHONE................................703 841-7800
Fax: 805 928-0869
Brad Bush, Senior VP
Dawna L Wilson, President
Sharon Tanis, Executive
Sorin Bruchental, Program Mgr
Bob Evans, Program Mgr
EMP: 150
SALES (corp-wide): 3.7B Publicly Held
SIC: 5045 3663 Computers, peripherals & software; radio & TV communications equipment
HQ: Caci Nss, Inc.
    11955 Freedom Dr Fl 2
    Reston VA 20190
    703 434-4000

(P-7107)
CASEWISE SYSTEMS INC (HQ)
9465 Wilshire Blvd # 300, Beverly Hills (90212-2612)
PHONE................................424 284-4101
Alexandre Wentzo, CEO
Michael R Hodes, CFO
Darren Bethke, Sales Staff

EMP: 85
SQ FT: 5,000
SALES: 9.7MM
SALES (corp-wide): 17.1MM Privately Held
WEB: www.casewise.com
SIC: 5045 8742 7372 Computer software; management consulting services; business oriented computer software
PA: Casewise Systems Limited
    25 Grosvenor Street
    London W1K 4
    203 758-7250

(P-7108)
CLARA
169 11th St, San Francisco (94103-2533)
PHONE................................415 342-9740
Gunnar Holmsteinn, CEO
EMP: 85
SALES (est): 460.5K
SALES (corp-wide): 195.7MM Publicly Held
SIC: 5045 Computer software
PA: Jive Software, Inc.
    325 Lytton Ave Ste 200
    Palo Alto CA 94301
    650 319-1920

(P-7109)
COMMERCIAL INDUS DESIGN CO INC
Also Called: C I Design
20372 N Sea Cir, Lake Forest (92630-8806)
PHONE................................949 273-6199
Jeff Wu, CEO
Kae J Lee, President
Cupid Chiu, Systs Prg Mgr
Agnes Huang, Manager
▲ EMP: 60
SALES (est): 12.7MM Privately Held
WEB: www.cidesign.com
SIC: 5045 Computer peripheral equipment

(P-7110)
COMPUCOM SYSTEMS INC
16842 Von Karman Ave # 375, Irvine (92606-4950)
PHONE................................949 222-0949
Fax: 949 222-0962
Fred Ross, Principal
EMP: 50 Privately Held
WEB: www.compucom.com
SIC: 5045 Computers, peripherals & software
HQ: Compucom Systems, Inc.
    8383 Dominion Pkwy
    Plano TX 75024
    972 856-3600

(P-7111)
CONTEC MICROELECTRONICS USA
Also Called: Contec USA
17811 Gillette Ave Fl 1, Irvine (92614-6501)
PHONE................................949 250-4025
Fax: 408 400-9115
▲ EMP: 52
SQ FT: 4,500
SALES: 3.2MM Privately Held
SIC: 5045

(P-7112)
CREATIVE LABS INC (DH)
1901 Mccarthy Blvd, Milpitas (95035-7427)
PHONE................................408 428-6600
Fax: 408 428-6611
Keh Long Ng, CEO
Craig McHugh, President
Richard Qiu, General Mgr
Jeff Stoen, General Mgr
Danielle Dunlap, Executive Asst
▲ EMP: 200
SQ FT: 57,000
SALES (est): 109.8MM
SALES (corp-wide): 99.4MM Privately Held
WEB: www.creativelabs.com
SIC: 5045 5734 3577 Computer peripheral equipment; computer & software stores; computer peripheral equipment

HQ: Creative Holdings, Inc
    1901 Mccarthy Blvd
    Milpitas CA 95035
    408 428-6600

(P-7113)
CYBERCSI INC
3511 Thomas Rd Ste 5, Santa Clara (95054-2039)
PHONE................................408 727-2900
Dave Sanders, CEO
Collette Worrell, Admin Asst
Clifford Siquian, Tech/Comp Coord
Chris Herring, Software Dev
Barbara Slossen, Technical Staff
EMP: 95
SQ FT: 11,000
SALES (est): 53.8MM Privately Held
SIC: 5045 7378 Computers, peripherals & software; computer maintenance & repair

(P-7114)
CYBERPOWER INC
Also Called: Cyberpower PC
730 Baldwin Park Blvd, City of Industry (91746-1503)
PHONE................................626 813-7730
Fax: 626 813-3810
Stanley Kwong Ho, CEO
Eric Cheung, President
Andy Kwok, Business Dir
Nelson Chiu, General Mgr
Eddie Vong, VP Adv
▲ EMP: 91
SQ FT: 30,000
SALES (est): 102MM Privately Held
WEB: www.cyberpowerpc.com
SIC: 5045 Computer peripheral equipment

(P-7115)
CYPHORT INC
5451 Great America Pkwy, Santa Clara (95054-3607)
PHONE................................408 841-4665
Manoj B Leelanivas, CEO
Gord Boyce, Ch Credit Ofcr
Fengmin Gong, Officer
Denise Hayman, Vice Pres
Gururaj Singh, Vice Pres
EMP: 50
SQ FT: 10,000
SALES (est): 14.4MM Privately Held
SIC: 5045 Computer software

(P-7116)
D-LINK SYSTEMS INCORPORATED
Also Called: D - Link
17595 Mount Herrmann St, Fountain Valley (92708-4160)
PHONE................................714 885-6000
Steven Joe, President
Carlos Casassus Fontecilla, President
A J Wang, President
William C Brown, Assoc VP
Daniel Kelley, Exec VP
▲ EMP: 164
SQ FT: 120,000
SALES: 122MM
SALES (corp-wide): 819MM Privately Held
WEB: www.dlink.com
SIC: 5045 3577 Computers; computer peripheral equipment
PA: D-Link Corporation
    289, Sinhu 3rd Rd.,
    Taipei City TAP 11494
    266 000-123

(P-7117)
DATA EXCHANGE CORPORATION (PA)
Also Called: D E X
3600 Via Pescador, Camarillo (93012-5035)
PHONE................................805 388-1711
Fax: 805 389-1726
Sheldon Malchicoff, President
Shawn Howie, CFO
Tony Harris, Chairman
Paul Gettings, Exec VP
Dale Cohen, Vice Pres
▲ EMP: 300
SQ FT: 100,000

SALES (est): 183.5MM Privately Held
SIC: 5045 7378 Computers, peripherals & software; computer & data processing equipment repair/maintenance; computer peripheral equipment repair & maintenance

(P-7118)
DATALLEGRO INC
85 Enterprise Ste 200, Aliso Viejo (92656-2614)
PHONE................................949 680-3000
Stuart Frost, Ch of Bd
Mark Theissen, Vice Pres
EMP: 100
SQ FT: 16,000
SALES (est): 13.5MM
SALES (corp-wide): 85.3B Publicly Held
WEB: www.datallegro.com
SIC: 5045 Computer software
PA: Microsoft Corporation
    1 Microsoft Way
    Redmond WA 98052
    425 882-8080

(P-7119)
DEMAND CHAIN INC
Also Called: Homerun.com
301 Howard St Fl 20, San Francisco (94105-6670)
PHONE................................800 466-3786
Brad Brodigan, CEO
EMP: 152
SALES (est): 13MM
SALES (corp-wide): 84.8MM Privately Held
SIC: 5045 Computer software
PA: Deem, Inc.
    642 Harrison St Fl 2
    San Francisco CA 94107
    415 590-8300

(P-7120)
DIGIQUEST CORP
989 Talcey Ter, Riverside (92506-7517)
PHONE................................951 776-4344
Fax: 951 789-7677
K B Reddy, President
EMP: 50
SALES (est): 3.2MM Privately Held
WEB: www.digiquestindia.com
SIC: 5045 7379 Computer peripheral equipment; computer related consulting services

(P-7121)
DINCO INC (HQ)
27520 Hawthorne Blvd # 1808, Rlng HLS Est (90274-3576)
PHONE................................424 331-1200
Fax: 310 338-4855
Attiazaz Din, President
Kevin Schatzle, CEO
Javed Latif, CFO
Fida Abbas, Officer
Robert A Mercer, Senior VP
▲ EMP: 150
SQ FT: 29,032
SALES (est): 247.1MM
SALES (corp-wide): 3.7MM Privately Held
SIC: 5045 7379 Computers, peripherals & software; computers; computer peripheral equipment; computer related consulting services
PA: Din Global Corp.
    27520 Hawthorne Blvd
    Rlng Hls Est CA 90274
    424 331-1200

(P-7122)
DROBO INC
2540 Mission College Blvd, Santa Clara (95054-1215)
PHONE................................408 454-4200
Mihir H Shah, CEO
Stefan Drege, Partner
Tom Buiocchi, President
James Gardner, COO
Danielle Murcray, CFO
▲ EMP: 80
SQ FT: 15,000
SALES (est): 48.2MM Privately Held
SIC: 5045 Computers, peripherals & software

PRODUCTS & SERVICES SECTION
5045 - Computers & Peripheral Eqpt & Software Wholesale County (P-7142)

(P-7123)
ELITEGROUP CMPT SYSTEMS INC
6851 Mowry Ave, Newark (94560-4925)
PHONE..................510 794-2952
Ray Lin, *CEO*
Lena Ruan, *Corp Secy*
See See Lo, *Principal*
Maggie Liu, *Director*
Eva Poon, *Manager*
EMP: 200
SQ FT: 60,000
SALES (est): 43.6MM
SALES (corp-wide): 28.2MM **Privately Held**
SIC: 5045 Computer peripheral equipment
HQ: Elitegroup Computer Systems Holding Company (Inc)
6851 Mowry Ave
Newark CA 94560
510 794-2954

(P-7124)
EMC CORPORATION
6701 Koll Center Pkwy # 150, Pleasanton (94566-8061)
PHONE..................925 948-9000
Rich Napolitano, *Principal*
EMP: 75
SALES (corp-wide): 72.7B **Publicly Held**
SIC: 5045 Computer software
HQ: Emc Corporation
176 South St
Hopkinton MA 01748
508 435-1000

(P-7125)
EMC CORPORATION
Also Called: Emc2
250 Montgomery St Ste 400, San Francisco (94104-3427)
PHONE..................650 871-1970
Fax: 650 871-1318
Chris Kaddaras, *Manager*
Warren Dodge, *Exec VP*
Steve Hartsook, *Exec VP*
Jeffrey White, *Exec VP*
Greg Antholzner, *Vice Pres*
EMP: 50
SALES (corp-wide): 72.7B **Publicly Held**
WEB: www.emc.com
SIC: 5045 Computers, peripherals & software
HQ: Emc Corporation
176 South St
Hopkinton MA 01748
508 435-1000

(P-7126)
EN POINTE TECHNOLOGIES SLS LLC
1940 E Mariposa Ave, El Segundo (90245-3457)
PHONE..................310 337-5200
Frank Khulusi, *CEO*
Robert Miley, *President*
Brandon Laverne, *CFO*
EMP: 200
SQ FT: 29,032
SALES (est): 12.6MM
SALES (corp-wide): 1.6B **Publicly Held**
SIC: 5045 Computers, peripherals & software; computers
PA: Pcm, Inc.
1940 E Mariposa Ave
El Segundo CA 90245
310 354-5600

(P-7127)
ENVIRONMENTAL SYSTEMS RESEARCH
1600 K St Ste 4c, Sacramento (95814-4022)
PHONE..................916 448-2412
EMP: 76
SALES (corp-wide): 624.2MM **Privately Held**
SIC: 5045 Computer software
PA: Environmental Systems Research Institute, Inc.
380 New York St
Redlands CA 92373
909 793-2853

(P-7128)
EPHESOFT INC
23041avnda D L Crlota 1 Carlota, Laguna Hills (92653)
PHONE..................949 335-5335
Donald Field, *CEO*
Don Field, *CEO*
Ike Kavas, *General Mgr*
Chris Macwilliams, *Sales Executive*
Ian Pope, *VP Sales*
▼ **EMP:** 71
SQ FT: 3,600
SALES: 5.9MM **Privately Held**
SIC: 5045 Computer software

(P-7129)
ESET LLC (HQ)
Also Called: Eset North America
610 W Ash St Ste 1700, San Diego (92101-3373)
PHONE..................619 876-5400
Fax: 619 876-5845
Anton Zajac, *President*
Andrew Lee, *CEO*
Kevin Lam, *CFO*
Vladimir Paulen, *Vice Pres*
Ignacio M Sbampato, *Vice Pres*
EMP: 205
SQ FT: 57,000
SALES: 75.2MM
SALES (corp-wide): 409.2MM **Privately Held**
WEB: www.nod32.com
SIC: 5045 Computer software
PA: Eset, Spol. S R.O.
Einsteinova 24
Bratislava 85101
232 244-111

(P-7130)
EWORKPLACE SOLUTIONS INC
Also Called: Batchmaster Software
23191 La Cadena Dr # 101, Laguna Hills (92653-1429)
PHONE..................949 583-1646
Fax: 949 296-0912
Sahib Dudani, *President*
Maria Figueroa, *Office Mgr*
Suraj Chouhan, *Sr Software Eng*
Amit Goyal, *Sr Software Eng*
Pulkit Dube, *Sr Ntwrk Engine*
EMP: 200
SQ FT: 5,000
SALES (est): 89.6MM **Privately Held**
WEB: www.batchmaster.com
SIC: 5045 Computer software

(P-7131)
F-SECURE INC
1735 Tech Dr Ste 850, San Jose (95110)
PHONE..................408 938-6700
Risto Siilasmaa, *Ch of Bd*
Janne Jarvinen, *President*
Ilkka Starck, *Exec VP*
Sean Obrey, *Vice Pres*
Pirkka Palomaki, *CTO*
EMP: 50
SQ FT: 15,000
SALES (est): 25.3MM
SALES (corp-wide): 158.5MM **Privately Held**
WEB: www.f-secure.com
SIC: 5045 Computers, peripherals & software
PA: F-Secure Oyj
Tammisaarenkatu 7
Helsinki 00510
925 200-700

(P-7132)
FRYS ELECTRONICS INC
3600 N Sepulveda Blvd, Manhattan Beach (90266-3633)
PHONE..................310 364-3797
Fax: 310 364-3718
Joel Byer, *Manager*
EMP: 200
SALES (est): 17.4MM **Privately Held**
WEB: www.frys.com
SIC: 5045 5731 Computers, peripherals & software; radio, television & electronic stores

PA: Fry's Electronics, Inc.
600 E Brokaw Rd
San Jose CA 95112
408 350-1484

(P-7133)
FUJITSU COMPUTER PDTS AMER INC (HQ)
1250 E Arques Ave, Sunnyvale (94085-5401)
PHONE..................408 746-6000
Fax: 408 746-6910
Etsuro Sato, *President*
Victor Kan, *COO*
Motoyasu Matsuzaki, *CFO*
Masamichi Yamamoto, *CFO*
Bruce Graham, *Bd of Directors*
▲ **EMP:** 340
SQ FT: 75,335
SALES (est): 155.3MM
SALES (corp-wide): 40.5B **Privately Held**
WEB: www.fcpa.com
SIC: 5045 Computer peripheral equipment
PA: Fujitsu Limited
1-5-2, Higashishimbashi
Minato-Ku TKY 105-0
362 522-220

(P-7134)
GAMMATECH COMPUTER CORPORATION
48303 Fremont Blvd, Fremont (94538-6580)
PHONE..................510 824-6700
Steven Gau, *President*
Bill Liu, *Sr Corp Ofcr*
Paul Kim, *VP Sales*
Lester Crosbie, *Sales Mgr*
Rowena Gammatech, *Sales Mgr*
▲ **EMP:** 55
SQ FT: 25,000
SALES (est): 24MM **Privately Held**
SIC: 5045 Computers

(P-7135)
GAR ENTERPRISES (PA)
Also Called: K G S Electronics
418 E Live Oak Ave, Arcadia (91006-5619)
PHONE..................626 574-1175
Nathan Sugimoto, *CEO*
Lang Nguyen, *General Mgr*
Corie Soto, *Office Mgr*
Elisa Aldape, *Marketing Mgr*
Kazuo G Sugimoto, *Pastor*
EMP: 70 **EST:** 1960
SQ FT: 17,000
SALES (est): 33.3MM **Privately Held**
WEB: www.kgselectronics.com
SIC: 5045 3728 Anti-static equipment & devices; aircraft assemblies, subassemblies & parts

(P-7136)
GBT INC
Also Called: Giga Bite Technology
17358 Railroad St, City of Industry (91748-1023)
PHONE..................626 854-9333
Fax: 626 854-9339
Eric C Lu, *President*
Henry KAO, *Vice Pres*
James Liao, *Principal*
Janie Lin, *Accountant*
Maggie Lin, *Opers Mgr*
▲ **EMP:** 80
SQ FT: 35,000
SALES (est): 37.8MM
SALES (corp-wide): 1.5B **Privately Held**
WEB: www.giga-byte.com
SIC: 5045 Computers & accessories, personal & home entertainment
PA: Giga-Byte Technology Co., Ltd.
6, Baoqiang Rd.,
New Taipei City 23144
289 124-000

(P-7137)
GENERAL DYNMICS MSSION SYSTEMS
250 S Milpitas Blvd, Milpitas (95035-5420)
PHONE..................954 846-3400
EMP: 208
SALES (corp-wide): 31.4B **Publicly Held**
SIC: 5045 7371 Computers, peripherals & software; custom computer programming services

HQ: General Dynamics Mission Systems, Inc
12450 Fair Lakes Cir # 800
Fairfax VA 22033
703 263-2800

(P-7138)
GENERAL PROCUREMENT INC (PA)
Also Called: Connect Computers
800 E Dyer Rd, Santa Ana (92705-5604)
PHONE..................949 679-7960
Imad Boukai, *President*
Sam Boukai, *Vice Pres*
Janet Carmona, *Business Dir*
Sandy Boukai, *Manager*
▲ **EMP:** 50
SQ FT: 2,800
SALES (est): 150MM **Privately Held**
WEB: www.connect-computers.com
SIC: 5045 Computers, peripherals & software

(P-7139)
GENTEK MEDIA INC
13900 Sycamore Way, Chino (91710-7016)
PHONE..................909 476-3818
Gene Seto, *CEO*
Tressa Padilla, *Manager*
▲ **EMP:** 50
SALES (est): 9.5MM **Privately Held**
WEB: www.gentekmedia.com
SIC: 5045 Computers, peripherals & software

(P-7140)
HITACHI DATA SYSTEMS CORP
15231 Ave Of Science # 100, San Diego (92128-3449)
PHONE..................858 537-3000
Hicham Abdessanad, *Vice Pres*
Tom Zack, *Exec VP*
Peter Hurst, *Vice Pres*
Joachim Rahmfeld, *Vice Pres*
Ivan Colon, *Executive*
EMP: 200
SALES (corp-wide): 85.7B **Privately Held**
WEB: www.hds.com
SIC: 5045 7378 Computers, peripherals & software; computer maintenance & repair
HQ: Hitachi Data Systems Corporation
2845 Lafayette St
Santa Clara CA 95050
408 970-1000

(P-7141)
HITACHI DATA SYSTEMS CORP (DH)
2845 Lafayette St, Santa Clara (95050-2642)
PHONE..................408 970-1000
Fax: 408 982-0779
Jack Domme, *President*
Minoru Kosuge, *Ch of Bd*
Susan Lynch, *CFO*
Miklos Sandorfi, *Officer*
Greg Coplans, *Exec VP*
▼ **EMP:** 450 **EST:** 1979
SQ FT: 250,000
SALES (est): 2.3B
SALES (corp-wide): 85.7B **Privately Held**
WEB: www.hds.com
SIC: 5045 7378 7379 5734 Computers; computer & data processing equipment repair/maintenance; computer related maintenance services; computer & software stores; modems, monitors, terminals & disk drives; computers; general warehousing & storage; mainframe computers
HQ: Hitachi Data Systems Holding Corporation
2845 Lafayette St
Santa Clara CA 95050
408 970-1000

(P-7142)
HORIZON TECHNOLOGY
1 Rancho Cir, Lake Forest (92630-8324)
PHONE..................949 454-4614
Kurt Johnson, *Principal*
EMP: 54
SALES (est): 326.6K **Privately Held**
SIC: 5045 Computers, peripherals & software

5045 - Computers & Peripheral Eqpt & Software Wholesale County (P-7143)

PA: Horizon Technology, Llc
1 Rancho Cir
Lake Forest CA 92630

(P-7143)
I2C INC
1300 Island Dr Ste 105, Redwood City (94065-5170)
PHONE 650 480-5222
Fax: 650 593-5402
Amir Wain, CEO
Charlie Noreen, CFO
Marc Winitz, Chief Mktg Ofcr
Jim Ackerson, Senior VP
Stephan Koukis, Senior VP
EMP: 400 EST: 2000
SQ FT: 7,000
SALES (est): 158.2MM Privately Held
WEB: www.i2cinc.com
SIC: 5045 Computers, peripherals & software

(P-7144)
IMAGESTAT CORPORATION
2950 28th St, Santa Monica (90405-2937)
PHONE 310 392-1100
Fax: 310 392-6250
Robert G Milne III, President
EMP: 120
SQ FT: 8,000
SALES (est): 11.5MM Privately Held
WEB: www.imagestat.com
SIC: 5045 7334 Computers, peripherals & software; photocopying & duplicating services

(P-7145)
INGRAM MICRO INC (PA)
3351 Michelson Dr Ste 100, Irvine (92612-0697)
PHONE 714 566-1000
Fax: 714 566-7733
Alain Monie, CEO
Dale R Laurance, Ch of Bd
Shailendra Gupta, President
William D Humes, CFO
Dorothee Penin, CFO
◆ EMP: 4000 EST: 1979
SALES (est): 43B Publicly Held
WEB: www.ingrammicro.com
SIC: 5045 Computers, peripherals & software; computer peripheral equipment; computers; computer software

(P-7146)
INSIDEVIEW TECHNOLOGIES INC
444 De Haro St Ste 210, San Francisco (94107-2398)
PHONE 415 728-9309
Umberto Milletti, CEO
James Desser, COO
Tracy Eiler, Chief Mktg Ofcr
Brian Kelly, Chief Mktg Ofcr
Rand Schulman, Chief Mktg Ofcr
EMP: 150
SALES (est): 89.3MM Privately Held
SIC: 5045 Computers, peripherals & software

(P-7147)
IQ4BIS SOFTWARE INCORPORATED
Also Called: Halo Business Intelligence
4885 Greencraig Ln 200, San Diego (92123-1664)
PHONE 858 565-4238
Raymond Major, President
Louis-Philippe Lalonde, Partner
Brandon Kirby, President
Steven Hamerslag, CEO
Steve Mills, CTO
EMP: 55
SALES (est): 9.2MM Privately Held
WEB: www.q4bis.com
SIC: 5045 7379 Computers, peripherals & software; computer related consulting services

(P-7148)
IXOS SOFTWARE INC (PA)
8717 Research Dr, Irvine (92618-4217)
PHONE 949 784-8000
Mark Smith, CFO
Steve Gulley, CFO

Evana Raley, Executive Asst
Bob Fiorentino, Info Tech Mgr
Patrick Lehner, Info Tech Mgr
EMP: 100
SQ FT: 30,000
SALES (est): 39.2MM Privately Held
WEB: www.ixos.com
SIC: 5045 Computer software

(P-7149)
JAG SOFTWARE INC
2235 Skyline Dr, Milpitas (95035-6682)
PHONE 408 262-0572
Suresh Kottapalli, President
EMP: 69
SQ FT: 2,400
SALES (est): 7.1MM Privately Held
WEB: www.jagsoftware.com
SIC: 5045 Computer software

(P-7150)
JAGUAR COMPUTER SYSTEMS INC
4135 Indus Way, Riverside (92503-4848)
PHONE 951 273-7950
Joan E Hoanzl, President
George Hoanzl, Vice Pres
Jerry Mahana, CIO
Avelia Perkins, Info Tech Dir
James Bertok, Network Enginr
EMP: 50
SQ FT: 17,000
SALES (est): 9.1MM Privately Held
WEB: www.jaguarcomputersystems.com
SIC: 5045 8742 7378 Computer peripheral equipment; marketing consulting services; computer maintenance & repair

(P-7151)
K-MICRO INC
Also Called: Corpinfo Services
1618 Stanford St Ste A, Santa Monica (90404-4121)
PHONE 310 442-3200
Fax: 310 442-3201
Madjid Sabourian, CEO
Michael Sabourian, President
Ahmad Gramian, Vice Pres
EMP: 96
SQ FT: 25,000
SALES (est): 16.6MM Privately Held
SIC: 5045 7378 7373 7371 Computers & accessories, personal & home entertainment; computer maintenance & repair; computer integrated systems design; custom computer programming services

(P-7152)
KEMEERA INCORPORATED
Also Called: Fathom
315 Jefferson St, Oakland (94607-3537)
PHONE 510 281-9000
Michelle Malia Mihevc, President
Richard Stump, Principal
EMP: 64 EST: 2008
SALES (est): 394.9K Privately Held
SIC: 5045 Printers, computer

(P-7153)
LASERTECH COMPUTER DISTR INC
139 N Sunset Ave, City of Industry (91744-1850)
PHONE 626 435-2800
Tony Ho, President
Annie Ho, Admin Sec
Christine Chiu, Accountant
Kitty Lam, Controller
Vicki Cochems, Manager
▲ EMP: 70
SQ FT: 28,000
SALES (est): 9.1MM Privately Held
WEB: www.ltcom.com
SIC: 5045 5734 Computer peripheral equipment; computer & software stores

(P-7154)
LD PRODUCTS INC
Also Called: 4inkjets.com
3700 Cover St, Long Beach (90808-1782)
PHONE 562 986-6940
Aaron Leon, CEO
Patrick Devane, Senior VP
David Calkins, QA Dir
Eric Chun, QA Dir
Michael Fernandez, Info Tech Mgr

▲ EMP: 150
SQ FT: 25,000
SALES (est): 149.8MM Privately Held
WEB: www.ldproducts.com
SIC: 5045 2621 Printers, computer; stationery, envelope & tablet papers

(P-7155)
LITE-ON SALES AND DIST INC
42000 Christy St, Fremont (94538-3182)
PHONE 510 687-1800
Ren-Wu Gong, President
Chin-Sou Tsai Hong, CFO
Jim Bennett, Regional Mgr
Felix Jann, Info Tech Mgr
Vincent Lin, Info Tech Mgr
▲ EMP: 100
SQ FT: 8,100
SALES (est): 18.8MM
SALES (corp-wide): 6.6B Privately Held
SIC: 5045 Computer peripheral equipment
PA: Lite-On Technology Corporation
22f, 392, Ruey Kuang Rd.,
Taipei City TAP 11492
287 982-888

(P-7156)
LIVESCRIBE INC
1 Twin Dolphin Dr, Redwood City (94065-1027)
PHONE 510 777-0071
Gilles Bouchard, CEO
Ken Cucarola, CFO
Paul Machle, CFO
Brett Halle, Senior VP
Scott Rubin, Senior VP
▲ EMP: 50
SQ FT: 24,000
SALES (est): 41.8MM Privately Held
WEB: www.livescribe.com
SIC: 5045 Computer software

(P-7157)
MAGNELL ASSOCIATE INC (HQ)
Also Called: ABS Computer Technologies
17560 Rowland St, City of Industry (91748-1114)
PHONE 562 695-8823
James Wu, CEO
Craig Hayes, Vice Pres
Albert Whale, Security Dir
Mark Lee, Administration
Elizabeth Rojo, Administration
◆ EMP: 130
SALES (est): 2.1B
SALES (corp-wide): 2.5B Privately Held
SIC: 5045 Computers & accessories, personal & home entertainment
PA: Newegg Inc.
17560 Rowland St
City Of Industry CA 91748
626 271-9700

(P-7158)
MAGNELL ASSOCIATE INC
Also Called: ABS Computer Technologies
18045 Rowland St, City of Industry (91748-1205)
PHONE 626 271-1580
Fax: 626 271-9500
Fred Chang, President
Adell Newby, Shareholder
Shi C Lee, Exec VP
Jim Vaughn, General Mgr
Albert Chong, Database Admin
EMP: 100
SALES (corp-wide): 2.5B Privately Held
SIC: 5045 Computers & accessories, personal & home entertainment
HQ: Magnell Associate, Inc.
17560 Rowland St
City Of Industry CA 91748
562 695-8823

(P-7159)
MARIADB USA INC
350 Bay St Ste 100-319, San Francisco (94133-1966)
PHONE 847 562-9000
Michael Howard, CEO
Juha Aropaltio, Controller
EMP: 100
SALES: 34MM Privately Held
SIC: 5045 Computer software

(P-7160)
MAX GROUP CORPORATION (PA)
17011 Green Dr, City of Industry (91745-1800)
PHONE 626 935-0050
Fax: 626 854-1559
Su-Tzu Tsai, CEO
Chung-Jen Tsai, President
Dennis Salvador, Business Mgr
Chunnan LI, Finance Mgr
Jonathan Min, Sales Dir
EMP: 75
SQ FT: 120,000
SALES (est): 80.6MM Privately Held
WEB: www.maxgroup.com
SIC: 5045 Computer peripheral equipment; disk drives; keying equipment; printers, computer

(P-7161)
MBH ENTERPRISES INC
1430 Franklin St Ste 201, Oakland (94612-3209)
PHONE 510 302-6680
Michael B Hudson, CEO
David Rubin, Exec VP
EMP: 55
SALES (est): 3.7MM Privately Held
SIC: 5045 Computers, peripherals & software

(P-7162)
MEMORY TO GO
10801 National Blvd # 101, Los Angeles (90064-4139)
PHONE 310 446-0111
Isaac Faliz, President
Aldert Johnson, Sales Mgr
EMP: 100
SALES (est): 11.3MM Privately Held
WEB: www.memorytogo.com
SIC: 5045 Computers, peripherals & software

(P-7163)
MICRO-TECHNOLOGY CONCEPTS INC
Also Called: M T C
17837 Rowland St, City of Industry (91748-1122)
PHONE 626 839-6800
Fax: 626 839-6899
Roy Han, President
Richard Shyu, Senior VP
Helena Cheunt, Credit Mgr
Helena Cheung, Accountant
Bobby Chen, Opers Staff
EMP: 85
SQ FT: 42,500
SALES (est): 54.3MM
SALES (corp-wide): 90.7MM Privately Held
WEB: www.mtcusa.com
SIC: 5045 Computer peripheral equipment
PA: Mtc Direct, Inc.
17837 Rowland St
City Of Industry CA 91748
626 839-6800

(P-7164)
MITSUBA CORPORATION
2509 Reata Pl, Diamond Bar (91765-3661)
PHONE 909 374-2631
Jen Jon Chen, President
Monica Chen, Corp Secy
Robin Chang, Purch Agent
Ken Martinez, Advt Staff
Nelson Tsay, Marketing Staff
EMP: 75
SQ FT: 40,000
SALES (est): 6.7MM Privately Held
SIC: 5045 Computer peripheral equipment; computers; computer software

(P-7165)
MSI COMPUTER CORP (HQ)
901 Canada Ct, City of Industry (91748-1136)
PHONE 626 913-0828
Andy Tung, CEO
Connie Chang, CFO
David Wu, Assoc VP
Benjamin Hsu, Director
James Brown, Manager

▲ = Import ▼ = Export
◆ = Import/Export

PRODUCTS & SERVICES SECTION
5045 - Computers & Peripheral Eqpt & Software Wholesale County (P-7186)

◆ **EMP:** 90
SQ FT: 77,500
SALES (est): 21.7MM
SALES (corp-wide): 2.6B Privately Held
WEB: www.msicomputer.com
SIC: 5045 Computer peripheral equipment
PA: Micro-Star International Co., Ltd.
  69, Li Te St.,
  New Taipei City 23584
  232 345-599

(P-7166)
MTC WORLDWIDE CORP
17837 Rowland St, City of Industry (91748-1122)
PHONE..................................626 839-6800
Helena Cheung, Credit Mgr
▲ **EMP:** 79
SQ FT: 42,500
SALES (est): 36.4MM
SALES (corp-wide): 90.7MM Privately Held
WEB: www.mtcdirect.com
SIC: 5045 3577 Computer peripheral equipment; computer peripheral equipment
PA: Mtc Direct, Inc.
  17837 Rowland St
  City Of Industry CA 91748
  626 839-6800

(P-7167)
NEXINFO SOLUTIONS INC
8502 E Chapman Ave # 364, Orange (92869-2461)
PHONE..................................714 368-1452
Arun Cavale, President
Kirtan Shah, Personnel Exec
Paula Andrade, Sales Mgr
EMP: 50
SALES: 5MM Privately Held
SIC: 5045 8742 Computer software; management consulting services

(P-7168)
NHR NEWCO HOLDINGS LLC (PA)
6500 Hollister Ave # 210, Santa Barbara (93117-3011)
PHONE..................................800 230-6638
Mike Sheldon, CEO
Sachi Thompson, COO
Thomas Pickett, CFO
Mark Kelly, Vice Pres
Holger Peters, Vice Pres
◆ **EMP:** 425
SQ FT: 59,000
SALES (est): 364MM Privately Held
WEB: www.networkhardware.com
SIC: 5045 5065 7379 Computers, peripherals & software; telephone equipment; computer related maintenance services

(P-7169)
NUMONYX INC
2235 Iron Point Rd, Folsom (95630-8765)
PHONE..................................916 458-3888
Ed Dollar, CEO
Matthew Tasto, Treasurer
William Cass Wilson, Vice Pres
Gabrielle Thompsom, Admin Sec
Kerri Hester, Controller
EMP: 512
SALES (est): 48.3MM Privately Held
SIC: 5045 Computer software

(P-7170)
ORACLE AMERICA INC
500 Oracle Pkwy, Redwood City (94065-1677)
PHONE..................................800 633-0584
Glenda Sakati, Manager
EMP: 58
SALES (corp-wide): 37B Publicly Held
SIC: 5045 8731 Computer software; computer (hardware) development
HQ: Oracle America, Inc.
  500 Oracle Pkwy
  Redwood City CA 94065
  650 506-7000

(P-7171)
PARASOFT CORPORATION (PA)
101 E Huntington Dr Fl 2, Monrovia (91016-3496)
PHONE..................................626 305-0041
Fax: 626 305-9048
Elzbieta Kolawa, President
Jim Perkins, CFO
Marek Pilch, Vice Pres
Nicole Skipworth, Administration
Stefan Potzel, IT/INT Sup
EMP: 50
SALES (est): 33.8MM Privately Held
WEB: www.foodmagic.com
SIC: 5045 7371 8748 Computers; computer software development; systems engineering consultant, ex. computer or professional

(P-7172)
PEEL TECHNOLOGIES INC
321 Castro St, Mountain View (94041-1205)
PHONE..................................650 204-7977
Thiru Arunachalam, CEO
James Gigliotti, Director
Flora Baik, Manager
Daniel Brown, Manager
Patrick Chen, Manager
EMP: 60 **EST:** 2008
SALES (est): 3.9MM Privately Held
SIC: 5045 Computer software

(P-7173)
PENGUIN COMPUTING INC (PA)
45800 Northport Loop W, Fremont (94538-6413)
PHONE..................................415 954-2800
Tom Coull, CEO
Garth Thompson, President
Lisa Cummins, CFO
Matt Jacobs, Senior VP
Andreas Junge, Senior VP
EMP: 50
SQ FT: 42,050
SALES: 95MM Privately Held
WEB: www.penguincomputing.com
SIC: 5045 7379 Computers, peripherals & software; computer related maintenance services

(P-7174)
PHIHONG USA CORP (HQ)
47800 Fremont Blvd, Fremont (94538-6551)
PHONE..................................510 445-0100
Fax: 510 445-1678
Fei Hung Alex Lin, President
Keith Hapwood, Vice Pres
Jane Zheng, Vice Pres
Russ Hu, Info Tech Mgr
Joe Dasilva, Project Engr
▲ **EMP:** 58
SQ FT: 33,000
SALES: 132MM
SALES (corp-wide): 342.3MM Privately Held
WEB: www.phihong.com
SIC: 5045 3572 Computer peripheral equipment; computer disk & drum drives & components
PA: Phihong Technology Co., Ltd.
  568, Fusing 3rd Rd.,
  Taoyuan City TAY 33383
  332 772-88

(P-7175)
PRIVATE LABEL PC LLC
748 Epperson Dr Ste B, City of Industry (91748-1336)
PHONE..................................626 965-8686
Rachel Luke, Mng Member
Chris Luke, Treasurer
Blake Nagle, Business Mgr
Rick Lee, Sales Staff
Sheri Shen, Accounts Mgr
▲ **EMP:** 120
SALES (est): 71.9MM Privately Held
WEB: www.vistapc.com
SIC: 5045 Computers, peripherals & software

(P-7176)
PROMISE TECHNOLOGY INC
580 Cottonwood Dr, Milpitas (95035-7203)
PHONE..................................408 228-1400
Tung-Hsu Lin, CEO
James Lee, President
Zhaolin Wu, President
Alice Chang, Chief Mktg Ofcr
Jamie Kay, Exec Dir
▲ **EMP:** 80
SQ FT: 40,000
SALES (est): 72.9MM
SALES (corp-wide): 92MM Privately Held
WEB: www.promise.com
SIC: 5045 7379 Computers, peripherals & software; data processing consultant
PA: Promise Technology Inc.
  2f, 30, Industry E. 9th Rd.,
  Paoshan Hsiang HSI 30075
  357 823-95

(P-7177)
QUADRANT COMPONENTS INC
46567 Fremont Blvd, Fremont (94538-6409)
PHONE..................................510 656-9988
Fax: 510 656-2208
Chad Yau, Ch of Bd
Wenli Yau, CFO
Anita Hou, Manager
EMP: 80
SQ FT: 30,000
SALES (est): 13.2MM Privately Held
WEB: www.quadrant.com
SIC: 5045 3679 Computers, peripherals & software; electronic circuits

(P-7178)
QUANTA COMPUTER USA INC (HQ)
45630 Northport Loop E, Fremont (94538-6477)
PHONE..................................510 226-1371
Barry Lam, Chairman
Alan Lam, President
CC Leung, President
Pak Lee Lam, CEO
Joseph Chen, Software Engr
▲ **EMP:** 65
SQ FT: 93,000
SALES (est): 126.3MM
SALES (corp-wide): 31B Privately Held
WEB: www.qfremont.com
SIC: 5045 Computers, peripherals & software
PA: Quanta Computer Inc.
  188, Wen Hwa 2nd Rd.,
  Taoyuan City TAY 33383
  332 723-45

(P-7179)
RFXCEL CORPORATION
12667 Alcosta Blvd # 375, San Ramon (94583-4427)
PHONE..................................925 824-0300
Glenn Abood, CEO
Bob Wigmore, Chairman
Haris Kamal, Vice Pres
Jack Tarkoff, Vice Pres
Eddie Pak, Sales Dir
EMP: 55
SQ FT: 10,000
SALES (est): 13MM Privately Held
WEB: www.rfxcel.com
SIC: 5045 Computers, peripherals & software

(P-7180)
ROLAND DGA CORPORATION (HQ)
15363 Barranca Pkwy, Irvine (92618-2216)
PHONE..................................949 727-2100
Fax: 949 727-2112
David Goward, President
Andrew Oransky, President
Bruce Lauper, CFO
Bob Curtis, Vice Pres
Connie Caigoy, Executive
▲ **EMP:** 105
SQ FT: 53,000
SALES: 119.4MM
SALES (corp-wide): 366.3MM Privately Held
WEB: www.rolanddga.com
SIC: 5045 8741 5084 Computer peripheral equipment; management services; industrial machinery & equipment
PA: Roland Dg Corporation
  1-6-4, Shimmiyakoda, Kita-Ku
  Hamamatsu SZO 431-2
  534 841-200

(P-7181)
RUUHWA DANN AND ASSOCIATES INC
Also Called: Cal Micro
1541 Brooks St, Ontario (91762-3619)
PHONE..................................909 467-4800
Fax: 909 467-4855
Ruuhwa Dann, CEO
Harry Saliba, President
Jess Panopio, Project Mgr
▲ **EMP:** 50
SQ FT: 82,000
SALES (est): 22.9MM Privately Held
SIC: 5045 4953 Computers, peripherals & software; recycling, waste materials

(P-7182)
SALESTAR LLC (PA)
300 Lakeside Dr Fl 11, Oakland (94612-3534)
PHONE..................................510 637-4700
David Joseph-Lacagnina, President
EMP: 60
SQ FT: 11,000
SALES (est): 6.5MM Privately Held
SIC: 5045 7372 Computer software; prepackaged software

(P-7183)
SANYO DENKI AMERICA INC (HQ)
468 Amapola Ave, Torrance (90501-1474)
PHONE..................................310 783-5400
Stan Kato, CEO
William Metzger, Treasurer
Rieko Suzuki, Executive
Eddie Tang, Information Mgr
Takashi Tanaka, Technology
▲ **EMP:** 52
SQ FT: 45,000
SALES (est): 32.6MM
SALES (corp-wide): 686MM Privately Held
WEB: www.sanyo-denki.com
SIC: 5045 7373 Computers & accessories, personal & home entertainment; computer-aided system services
PA: Sanyo Denki Co.,Ltd.
  3-33-1, Minamiotsuka
  Toshima-Ku TKY 170-0
  359 271-020

(P-7184)
SECUREMATICS INC
2540 Gateway Rd, Carlsbad (92009-1742)
PHONE..................................408 970-8566
Juhi Aswani, President
Jon Bennett, General Mgr
Tom Verna, Info Tech Mgr
Roger Lau, Business Anlyst
Deborah McMullen, Buyer
▲ **EMP:** 50
SQ FT: 26,000
SALES (est): 79.2MM Privately Held
WEB: www.securematics.com
SIC: 5045 Computer peripheral equipment

(P-7185)
SEGA OF AMERICA INC
350 Rhode Island St # 400, San Francisco (94103-5188)
PHONE..................................415 701-6000
Mike Hayes, CEO
Masanao Maeda, President
John Cheng, CFO
Naoya Tsurumi, Chairman
Shinobu Toyoda, Exec VP
EMP: 165
SQ FT: 70,000
SALES (est): 143.8MM
SALES (corp-wide): 2.9B Privately Held
SIC: 5045 5092 Computers & accessories, personal & home entertainment; video games
HQ: Sega Of America, Inc.
  6400 Oak Cyn Ste 100
  Irvine CA 92618
  415 806-0169

(P-7186)
SIGMANET INC (HQ)
4290 E Brickell St, Ontario (91761-1524)
PHONE..................................909 230-7500
Fax: 909 937-9125
Ahmed Al Khatib, CEO

5045 - Computers & Peripheral Eqpt & Software Wholesale County (P-7187)

Neil Wada, *President*
Apo Hagopian, *Senior VP*
Paul Edge, *Vice Pres*
Stephen Monteros, *Vice Pres*
EMP: 153
SQ FT: 100,000
SALES (est): 294.2MM
SALES (corp-wide): 654.7MM **Privately Held**
WEB: www.sigmanet.com
SIC: 5045 7373 Computers, peripherals & software; computer integrated systems design
PA: Convergeone Holdings Corp.
3344 Highway 149
Eagan MN 55121
651 994-6800

(P-7187)
SMC NETWORKS INC (HQ)
20 Mason, Irvine (92618-2706)
PHONE.................................949 679-8000
Alex Kim, *CEO*
Inho Kim, *President*
Frank Kuo, *President*
Joseph L Wytanis, *COO*
Lane Ruoff, *CFO*
▲ **EMP:** 80 **EST:** 1971
SQ FT: 22,650
SALES (est): 35.1MM
SALES (corp-wide): 761.2MM **Privately Held**
WEB: www.smc.com
SIC: 5045 Computer peripheral equipment
PA: Accton Technology Corporation
1, Creation 3rd Rd.,
Hsinchu City 30077
357 702-70

(P-7188)
SOLVER INC
10780 Santa Monica Blvd # 370, Los Angeles (90025-4779)
PHONE.................................310 691-5300
Fax: 310 691-5324
Nils Rasmussen, *President*
Corey Barak, *COO*
Johan Magnusson, *Managing Dir*
Hadrian Knotz, *CIO*
Michael Applegate, *CTO*
EMP: 50
SQ FT: 5,000
SALES (est): 10.5MM **Privately Held**
WEB: www.solverusa.com
SIC: 5045 7379 Computer software; computer related consulting services

(P-7189)
SOMANSA TECHNOLOGIES INC
3003 N 1st St 301, San Jose (95134-2004)
PHONE.................................408 297-1234
Suk Won Kwon, *CEO*
Don Lee, *Marketing Staff*
EMP: 60
SALES (est): 950K **Privately Held**
SIC: 5045 Computers, peripherals & software

(P-7190)
SOUTHLAND TECHNOLOGY INC
8053 Vickers St, San Diego (92111-1917)
PHONE.................................858 694-0932
Fax: 858 694-0938
Grace Pedigo, *CEO*
Robert Pedigo, *President*
Daniel Abrams, *Vice Pres*
Ray Fernandez, *Admin Asst*
Lisa Wakefield, *Admin Asst*
EMP: 65
SQ FT: 16,000
SALES (est): 54.6MM **Privately Held**
WEB: www.southlandtechnology.com
SIC: 5045 8748 7373 7379 Computer peripheral equipment; systems engineering consultant, ex. computer or professional; computer integrated systems design; computer related maintenance services; home entertainment computer software

(P-7191)
SPACE AGE METAL PRODUCTS INC
23605 Telo Ave, Torrance (90505-4028)
PHONE.................................310 539-5500
Fax: 310 784-5394
Arnold Klein, *CEO*
Emma Klein, *Corp Secy*
EMP: 200
SQ FT: 20,000
SALES (est): 15.8MM **Privately Held**
SIC: 5045 Computer peripheral equipment

(P-7192)
SPIGIT INC
275 Battery St, San Francisco (94111-3305)
PHONE.................................855 774-4480
Scott Raskin, *CEO*
Jim Walker, *COO*
Mark Tisdel, *CFO*
Mat Fogarty, *Exec VP*
James Gardner, *Exec VP*
EMP: 110
SQ FT: 6,500
SALES (est): 581.9K
SALES (corp-wide): 52.5MM **Privately Held**
SIC: 5045 8741 Computer software; business management
PA: Mindjet Corporation
275 Battery St Ste 1000
San Francisco CA 94111
415 229-4200

(P-7193)
SPINACOM INC
42808 Christy St Ste 201, Fremont (94538-3119)
PHONE.................................510 270-2669
Fax: 510 353-1302
Sanjeev Chawla, *President*
Sunanda Chawla, *Shareholder*
Subhash Verma, *COO*
Simon Westbrook, *CFO*
Uday Choudhury, *Vice Pres*
EMP: 150
SQ FT: 3,200
SALES (est): 9.5MM **Privately Held**
SIC: 5045 Computer software

(P-7194)
SPOTCUES INC
Also Called: Smartcues Inc
1975 W El Cmno Real 301, Mountain View (94040)
PHONE.................................408 435-2700
Jay Pullur, *President*
Vijay Pullur, *President*
K V Prasad, *Vice Pres*
Vivek Lakshman, *Director*
EMP: 700 **EST:** 2001
SALES (est): 6MM **Privately Held**
WEB: www.pramati.com
SIC: 5045 Computer peripheral equipment
PA: Pramati Technologies Private Limited
No-301, Block-1 White House
Hyderabad TS
-

(P-7195)
SQUARE ENIX INC
999 N Sepulveda Blvd Fl 3, El Segundo (90245-2731)
PHONE.................................310 846-0400
Mike Fischer, *President*
Clinton Foy, *COO*
Kenji Hisatsune, *Vice Pres*
Phil Rogers, *Principal*
Stephen Ross, *Principal*
▲ **EMP:** 110
SALES (est): 58MM
SALES (corp-wide): 1.8B **Privately Held**
SIC: 5045 7372 Computer software; publishers' computer software
HQ: Square Enix Of America Holdings, Inc.
999 N Sepulveda Blvd Fl 3
El Segundo CA 90245
-

(P-7196)
SUPER TALENT TECHNOLOGY CORP
2077 N Capitol Ave, San Jose (95132-1009)
PHONE.................................408 957-8733
Abraham MA, *President*
Robbie Chikhani, *Vice Pres*
Jonathan Yu, *General Mgr*
Jin Kim, *Design Engr*
James Lee, *Engineer*

◆ **EMP:** 670
SALES (est): 118.1MM **Privately Held**
WEB: www.superlightwave.com
SIC: 5045 Computers, peripherals & software

(P-7197)
SWANN COMMUNICATIONS USA INC
12636 Clark St, Santa Fe Springs (90670-3950)
PHONE.................................562 777-2551
Keith Oldridge, *President*
Jeffrey Lew, *Chairman*
Guy Pithie, *Vice Pres*
Geoff Wanless, *CTO*
Lee Lachmund, *Controller*
▲ **EMP:** 87
SQ FT: 45,000
SALES (est): 120MM **Privately Held**
WEB: www.swann.com
SIC: 5045 7382 Computers, peripherals & software; security systems services

(P-7198)
SWITCHFLY INC (PA)
601 Montgomery St Fl 17, San Francisco (94111-2621)
PHONE.................................415 541-9100
Daniel Farrar, *CEO*
Jared Wright, *Administration*
James Morton, *Sr Ntwrk Engine*
Graham Blankenbaker, *CTO*
Scott Galloway, *Web Dvlpr*
EMP: 100
SALES (est): 33MM **Privately Held**
SIC: 5045 Computer software

(P-7199)
SYSPRO IMPACT SOFTWARE INC
959 S Coast Dr Ste 100, Costa Mesa (92626-1786)
PHONE.................................714 437-1000
Brian Stein, *CEO*
Joey Benadretti, *President*
Michelle Hughes, *Vice Pres*
Debbie Buttacavoli, *Executive Asst*
Amanda Rascoe, *Admin Asst*
EMP: 200
SALES (est): 107.1MM **Privately Held**
WEB: www.syspro.com
SIC: 5045 7372 7371 Computer software; prepackaged software; custom computer programming services

(P-7200)
TIDEBREAK INC
958 San Leandro Ave # 500, Mountain View (94043-1995)
P.O. Box 855, Palo Alto (94302-0855)
PHONE.................................650 289-9869
Andrew J Milne, *CEO*
Michael Eggers, *Vice Pres*
Brad Johanson, *CTO*
Thomas Mallen, *Sales Dir*
EMP: 80
SALES (est): 6.6MM **Privately Held**
SIC: 5045 Computers, peripherals & software

(P-7201)
TONER SUPPLY USA INC
Also Called: Tsu Corporate Services
8055 Lankershim Blvd # 11, North Hollywood (91605-1628)
PHONE.................................818 504-6540
Fax: 818 504-2605
Omar Bian, *President*
Gus Obregon, *Vice Pres*
Robert Garcia, *Manager*
◆ **EMP:** 50
SQ FT: 120,000
SALES (est): 8.4MM **Privately Held**
SIC: 5045 7378 Computers, peripherals & software; computer peripheral equipment repair & maintenance

(P-7202)
TP-LINK USA CORPORATION
3760 Kilroy Airport Way, Long Beach (90806-2443)
PHONE.................................562 528-7700
Dana Knight, *Marketing Staff*
Ginny Tong,
EMP: 71

SALES (corp-wide): 104.6MM **Privately Held**
SIC: 5045 Computer peripheral equipment
PA: Tp-Link Usa Corporation
975 Overland Ct
San Dimas CA 91773
626 333-0234

(P-7203)
TREND MICRO INCORPORATED
10101 N De Anza Blvd, Cupertino (95014-2264)
PHONE.................................408 257-1500
Anrew Lai, *Branch Mgr*
Charles Cheng, *Research*
Anna Cordero, *Director*
Mark Sinclair, *Director*
Andrea Weston, *Director*
EMP: 78
SALES (corp-wide): 1B **Privately Held**
SIC: 5045 7382 7372 Computer software; security systems services; prepackaged software
HQ: Trend Micro Incorporated
225 E John Carpenter Fwy # 1500
Irving TX 75062
408 257-1500

(P-7204)
TRENDNET INC (PA)
Also Called: Trendnet Company
20675 Manhattan Pl, Torrance (90501-1827)
PHONE.................................310 961-5500
Pei Cheng Huang, *President*
Peggy Huang, *CFO*
Sonny Su, *Info Tech Dir*
Lilian Yao, *Opers Dir*
Amilkar Garcia, *Regl Sales Mgr*
◆ **EMP:** 50
SQ FT: 90,000
SALES (est): 28.4MM **Privately Held**
WEB: www.trendware.com
SIC: 5045 Computer peripheral equipment

(P-7205)
TW SECURITY CORP (DH)
Also Called: Trustwave Corporation
8845 Irvine Center Dr # 101, Irvine (92618-4247)
PHONE.................................949 932-1000
Fax: 949 932-1086
John Vigouroux, *CEO*
Bruce Green, *COO*
Rodney S Miller, *CFO*
William Kilmer, *Chief Mktg Ofcr*
Paul D Myer, *Senior VP*
EMP: 120
SQ FT: 28,000
SALES (est): 53.2MM **Privately Held**
WEB: www.marhsa18e6.com
SIC: 5045 Computer software
HQ: Trustwave Holdings, Inc.
70 W Madison St Ste 1050
Chicago IL 60602
312 750-0950

(P-7206)
TYAN COMPUTER CORPORATION
3288 Laurelview Ct, Fremont (94538-6535)
PHONE.................................510 651-8868
Fax: 510 651-7688
Jhi-Wu Ho, *CEO*
James Sytwu, *Exec VP*
Eric Cho, *Senior VP*
Danny Hsu, *Vice Pres*
George Koivun, *Vice Pres*
▲ **EMP:** 85
SALES (est): 29.2MM
SALES (corp-wide): 1.3B **Privately Held**
WEB: www.tyan.com
SIC: 5045 Computers, peripherals & software
HQ: Mitac Computing Technology Corporation
3f, 1, R&D 2nd Rd., Hsinchu Science Park,
Hsinchu City
357 790-88

▲ = Import ▼=Export
◆ =Import/Export

PRODUCTS & SERVICES SECTION

5046 - Commercial Eqpt, NEC Wholesale County (P-7229)

(P-7207)
UNICAL ENTERPRISES INC
Also Called: Northwestern Bell Telephones
16960 Gale Ave, City of Industry
(91745-1805)
PHONE...................................626 965-5588
Fax: 626 965-0970
Frank Liu, *President*
Rebecca Tsui, *Vice Pres*
▲ **EMP:** 65
SQ FT: 72,000
SALES (est): 9.2MM **Privately Held**
WEB: www.unical-usa.com
SIC: 5045 5065 Terminals, computer; telephone & telegraphic equipment

(P-7208)
VALGENESIS INC
42840 Christy St Ste 102, Fremont
(94538-3154)
PHONE...................................510 445-0505
Fax: 510 991-9901
Siva Samy, *President*
Mike Beaudro, *Manager*
▼ **EMP:** 50
SQ FT: 2,200
SALES (est): 8.4MM **Privately Held**
SIC: 5045 7371 Computer software; computer software development & applications

(P-7209)
VISCIRA LLC
200 Vallejo St, San Francisco (94111-1512)
PHONE...................................415 848-8010
Dave Gulezian, *President*
Marie Urban, *President*
Rick Barker, *COO*
Nat Fast, *Vice Pres*
Shan Jaffar, *Vice Pres*
EMP: 100
SQ FT: 10,000
SALES (est): 32.4MM
SALES (corp-wide): 18.4B **Privately Held**
SIC: 5045 7371 Computer software; computer software development & applications
HQ: Sudler & Hennessey, Llc
   230 Park Ave S
   New York NY 10003
   212 614-4100

(P-7210)
WONDERWARE CORPORATION (HQ)
26561 Rancho Pkwy S, Lake Forest
(92630-8301)
PHONE...................................949 727-3200
Fax: 949 727-3270
Rick Bullotta, *Vice Pres*
Johan Victor, *COO*
Brian Dibenedetto, *Senior VP*
Karen Hamilton, *Senior VP*
Peter Kent, *Senior VP*
EMP: 300
SQ FT: 32,000
SALES (est): 132.7MM **Privately Held**
WEB: www.wonderware.com
SIC: 5045 Computer software

(P-7211)
WORLD WIDE TECHNOLOGY INC
1165 W Walnut St, Compton (90220-5113)
PHONE...................................310 537-8335
Rob Macphee, *Manager*
Andrew Quebman, *Network Enginr*
Sevan Yeghiazarian, *Network Enginr*
Peter Chen, *Project Mgr*
Rob Reeves, *Engineer*
EMP: 50
SALES (corp-wide): 7.4B **Privately Held**
SIC: 5045 5065 Computers, peripherals & software; communication equipment
HQ: World Wide Technology, Inc.
   60 Weldon Pkwy
   Maryland Heights MO 63043
   800 432-7008

(P-7212)
XTRAPLUS CORPORATION
Also Called: Zipzoomfly
39889 Eureka Dr, Newark (94560-4811)
PHONE...................................510 897-1890
Fax: 510 360-9611

MEI F Chan, *President*
Angelica Wang, *Finance Mgr*
▲ **EMP:** 90
SALES (est): 9.6MM **Privately Held**
WEB: www.zipzoomfly.com
SIC: 5045 3577 Computer peripheral equipment; computer peripheral equipment

(P-7213)
XYRATEX TECHNOLOGY LTD
840 Embarcadero Dr Ste 80, West Sacramento (95605-1509)
PHONE...................................916 375-8181
Chris Sharman, *Manager*
Andy Brislen, *Sales Staff*
Al Redjaian, *Manager*
EMP: 50 **Privately Held**
SIC: 5045 7379 3825 Computers, peripherals & software; computer related consulting services; instruments to measure electricity
HQ: Seagate Systems (Uk) Limited
   Langstone Technology Park
   Havant HANTS PO9 1
   239 249-6000

(P-7214)
ZL TECHNOLOGIES INC
860 N Mccarthy Blvd, Milpitas
(95035-5114)
PHONE...................................408 240-8989
Kon Leong, *President*
Kenny Lio, *CFO*
Cindy Trieu, *Admin Asst*
Harikrishna Bodicharla, *Software Engr*
Nagarjun R Gaddam, *Software Engr*
EMP: 65
SQ FT: 1,860
SALES (est): 24.8MM **Privately Held**
WEB: www.zlti.com
SIC: 5045 7371 Computers, peripherals & software; computer software; computer software systems analysis & design, custom

---

5046 Commercial Eqpt, NEC Wholesale

(P-7215)
GDM CONCEPTS
15330 Texaco Ave, Paramount
(90723-3920)
PHONE...................................562 633-0195
Fax: 562 633-1561
George Myers, *President*
David Myers, *Vice Pres*
Sherri Honeycutt, *Manager*
EMP: 50
SQ FT: 28,000
SALES: 4.5MM **Privately Held**
WEB: www.gdmconcepts.com
SIC: 5046 2541 Store fixtures; display fixtures, wood

(P-7216)
GLOBAL EQP SVCS & MFG INC
5215 Hellyer Ave Ste 130, San Jose
(95138-1090)
PHONE...................................408 441-0682
Don Tran, *President*
Marty Mason, *VP Sales*
▲ **EMP:** 105
SALES (est): 39.9MM **Privately Held**
SIC: 5046 Commercial equipment

(P-7217)
HANNAM CHAIN USA INC (PA)
Also Called: Hannam Chain Super 1 Market
2740 W Olympic Blvd, Los Angeles
(90006-2633)
PHONE...................................213 382-2922
Fax: 213 382-2913
Kee W Ha, *CEO*
▲ **EMP:** 105
SQ FT: 22,000
SALES (est): 98.8MM **Privately Held**
SIC: 5046 5411 Restaurant equipment & supplies; supermarkets, independent

(P-7218)
HARPER MECHANICAL CONTRS LLC
1011 Camino Del Rio S, San Diego
(92108-3531)
PHONE...................................619 543-1296
Jeffrey A Harper, *Mng Member*
Ronald D Harper,
EMP: 80
SALES (est): 41.8MM **Privately Held**
SIC: 5046 1611 Commercial equipment; grading

(P-7219)
INTERSTATE ELECTRIC CO INC (PA)
Also Called: IEC
2240 Yates Ave, Commerce (90040-1914)
PHONE...................................323 724-0420
Fax: 323 722-5131
Edward Urlik, *President*
Arnie Binter, *Branch Mgr*
Michael Carlson, *Controller*
Robert Dougherty, *Purch Mgr*
Mike Demitcheli, *Opers Mgr*
▲ **EMP:** 94
SQ FT: 72,000
SALES (est): 78.6MM **Privately Held**
WEB: www.interstateelectric.com
SIC: 5046 Signs, electrical

(P-7220)
JC FOODSERVICE INC (PA)
Also Called: Action Sales
415 S Atlantic Blvd, Monterey Park
(91754-3209)
PHONE...................................626 299-3800
Fax: 626 308-9780
Joel Chang, *President*
Jack Chang, *Vice Pres*
Terence Wong, *Controller*
Robert Yag, *Human Resources*
Domanic Lau, *Sales Associate*
◆ **EMP:** 55
SQ FT: 25,000
SALES (est): 50.2MM **Privately Held**
WEB: www.actionsales.com
SIC: 5046 Restaurant equipment & supplies

(P-7221)
JONES SIGN CO INC
Also Called: Ultrasigns Electrical Advg
9025 Balboa Ave Ste 150, San Diego
(92123-1522)
PHONE...................................858 569-1400
John Mortensen, *President*
Mary Jo Wenzel, *Controller*
EMP: 120
SALES (corp-wide): 60.3MM **Privately Held**
SIC: 5046 Signs, electrical
PA: Jones Sign Co., Inc.
   1711 Scheuring Rd
   De Pere WI 54115
   920 983-6700

(P-7222)
OPTEC DISPLAYS INC
1700 S De Soto Pl Ste A, Ontario
(91761-8060)
PHONE...................................626 369-7188
Shu Hwa Wu, *President*
Wenny Tsay, *General Mgr*
Oded Rotem, *Administration*
Jane Hwee, *Opers Mgr*
Chad Engstrom, *Regl Sales Mgr*
▲ **EMP:** 64
SALES (est): 30.3MM **Privately Held**
WEB: www.optecdisplays.com
SIC: 5046 Signs, electrical

(P-7223)
PBI-BIRKENWALD MARKET EQP INC (PA)
Also Called: P B I
2667 Gundry Ave, Long Beach
(90755-1808)
P.O. Box 6097 (90806-0097)
PHONE...................................562 595-4785
Fax: 562 426-2262
Thomas L Everson, *President*
Kim Everson, *COO*
Jim Ennis, *CFO*
Laurie Stone, *Senior VP*

Erik Everson, *Vice Pres*
▲ **EMP:** 50 **EST:** 1949
SQ FT: 85,000
SALES (est): 27.9MM **Privately Held**
WEB: www.pbimarketing.com
SIC: 5046 Store equipment; scales, except laboratory; shelving, commercial & industrial; cooking equipment, commercial

(P-7224)
RECREATIONAL EQUIPMENT INC
2450 Charleston Rd, Mountain View
(94043-1622)
PHONE...................................650 969-1938
Wes Allen, *Branch Mgr*
EMP: 130
SALES (corp-wide): 2.2B **Privately Held**
SIC: 5046 Commercial equipment
PA: Recreational Equipment, Inc.
   6750 S 228th St
   Kent WA 98032
   253 395-3780

(P-7225)
RECREATIONAL EQUIPMENT INC
1590 Leucadia Blvd, Encinitas
(92024-2371)
PHONE...................................760 479-0128
Brian Angelow, *Manager*
Hung Nguyen, *Financial Exec*
EMP: 130
SALES (corp-wide): 2.2B **Privately Held**
WEB: www.rei.com
SIC: 5046 Commercial equipment
PA: Recreational Equipment, Inc.
   6750 S 228th St
   Kent WA 98032
   253 395-3780

(P-7226)
RECREATIONAL EQUIPMENT INC
Also Called: Rei Rancho Cucamonga
12218 Foothill Blvd, Rancho Cucamonga
(91739-9357)
PHONE...................................909 646-8360
Les Hatton, *Manager*
EMP: 130
SALES (corp-wide): 2.2B **Privately Held**
SIC: 5046 Commercial equipment
PA: Recreational Equipment, Inc.
   6750 S 228th St
   Kent WA 98032
   253 395-3780

(P-7227)
RECREATIONAL EQUIPMENT INC
Also Called: Rei
5757 Pacific Ave Ste A105, Stockton
(95207-5100)
PHONE...................................209 957-9479
EMP: 130
SALES (corp-wide): 2.2B **Privately Held**
WEB: www.rei.com
SIC: 5046 Commercial equipment
PA: Recreational Equipment, Inc.
   6750 S 228th St
   Kent WA 98032
   253 395-3780

(P-7228)
SHOPPER INC
3987 Heritage Oak Ct, Simi Valley
(93063-6711)
PHONE...................................805 527-6700
Bill Bieda, *CEO*
Elliot Bieda, *Vice Pres*
Eta Bieda, *Admin Sec*
Solly Quioan, *Controller*
Jerry Zeldes, *Manager*
◆ **EMP:** 300
SQ FT: 80,000
SALES (est): 76.7MM **Privately Held**
WEB: www.shopperinc.com
SIC: 5046 Store fixtures & display equipment

(P-7229)
SILVESTRI STUDIO INC
8830 Miner St, Los Angeles (90002-1834)
PHONE...................................323 277-0800
Matt Seltrecht, *Principal*

5046 - Commercial Eqpt, NEC Wholesale County (P-7230)

EMP: 52
SALES (corp-wide): 17.9MM **Privately Held**
SIC: **5046** Mannequins
PA: Silvestri Studio, Inc.
8125 Beach St
Los Angeles CA 90001
323 277-4420

(P-7230)
TOM DREHER SALES INC
Beach Cities Wholesalers
2021 W 17th St, Long Beach (90813-1011)
P.O. Box 41386 (90853-1386)
PHONE.................................562 355-4074
Tom Dreher, *President*
EMP: 86
SALES (corp-wide): 1.2MM **Privately Held**
SIC: **5046** 5145 Commercial cooking & food service equipment; popcorn & supplies
PA: Tom Dreher Sales Inc.
2021 W 17th St
Long Beach CA
562 355-4074

5047 Medical, Dental & Hospital Eqpt & Splys Wholesale

(P-7231)
ADVANCED REHABILITATION TECH
7950 Dunbrook Rd, San Diego (92126-4371)
P.O. Box 915, Cardiff By The Sea (92007-0915)
PHONE.................................858 621-5959
Fax: 858 621-5960
Richard M Harris, *President*
Jack Bailey, *Shareholder*
Darrel Blomberg, *Shareholder*
Stan Dunlap, *Vice Pres*
Chet Teklinski, *Vice Pres*
EMP: 57
SQ FT: 12,000
SALES (est): 11.4MM **Privately Held**
SIC: **5047** Medical & hospital equipment

(P-7232)
AFTER MARKET GROUP INC (HQ)
10173 Croydon Way Ste 1, Sacramento (95827-2108)
PHONE.................................916 361-1687
Gerald Blouch, *Ch of Bd*
A Malachi Mixon III, *President*
Joseph Richey II, *Vice Pres*
▲ EMP: 75
SALES (est): 13MM
SALES (corp-wide): 1.1B **Publicly Held**
SIC: **5047** Medical & hospital equipment
PA: Invacare Corporation
1 Invacare Way
Elyria OH 44035
440 329-6000

(P-7233)
AMERICAN MEDICAL TECH INC
17595 Cartwright Rd, Irvine (92614-5847)
PHONE.................................949 553-0359
Jean Signore, *President*
Sarah Holden-Mount, *President*
James Sorenson, *CFO*
Heather Hettrick, *Vice Pres*
Jerry Signore, *Vice Pres*
EMP: 100
SALES (est): 27.4MM **Privately Held**
SIC: **5047** Medical & hospital equipment

(P-7234)
AMPRONIX INC
15 Whatney, Irvine (92618-2808)
PHONE.................................949 273-8000
Fax: 949 273-8021
Nausser Fathollahi, *President*
Aladdin Doroudi, *CFO*
Adrian Cirpean, *Info Tech Mgr*
Sina Rastad, *Research*
Jeffrey Chao, *Purch Dir*
◆ EMP: 78 EST: 1982

SQ FT: 58,000
SALES (est): 61.6MM **Privately Held**
WEB: www.ampronix.com
SIC: **5047** Diagnostic equipment, medical

(P-7235)
ANGIOSCORE INC
5055 Brandin Ct, Fremont (94538-3140)
PHONE.................................510 933-7900
Thomas R Trotter, *President*
Kent W Jones, *Senior VP*
Samuel L Omaleki, *Senior VP*
Jeff Bleam, *Vice Pres*
Jackie Wong, *Controller*
EMP: 140
SQ FT: 44,000
SALES (est): 62.1MM
SALES (corp-wide): 245.9MM **Publicly Held**
SIC: **5047** Medical & hospital equipment
PA: Spectranetics Corporation
9965 Federal Dr Ste 100
Colorado Springs CO 80921
719 633-8333

(P-7236)
APRIA HEALTHCARE LLC
480 Carlton Ct, South San Francisco (94080-2012)
PHONE.................................650 588-9744
Fax: 650 872-7949
Geronimo Jimenez, *Manager*
Roy Stark, *Vice Pres*
Jorge Bermudez, *Branch Mgr*
Mark Diaz, *Branch Mgr*
Denise Davis, *Manager*
EMP: 56
SALES (corp-wide): 2.4B **Privately Held**
WEB: www.apria.com
SIC: **5047** 7352 5999 Hospital equipment & furniture; dental equipment & supplies; medical equipment & supplies; medical apparatus & supplies
HQ: Apria Healthcare Llc
26220 Enterprise Ct
Lake Forest CA 92630
949 616-2606

(P-7237)
APRIA HEALTHCARE LLC (DH)
26220 Enterprise Ct, Lake Forest (92630-8405)
P.O. Box 610 (92609-0610)
PHONE.................................949 616-2606
Daniel J Starck, *CEO*
Matt Gallagher, *President*
Erik Degarceau, *Treasurer*
Ken Common, *Vice Pres*
Heather Patterson, *Vice Pres*
◆ EMP: 400
SALES: 1B
SALES (corp-wide): 2.4B **Privately Held**
WEB: www.apria.com
SIC: **5047** 7352 5999 Hospital equipment & furniture; dental equipment & supplies; medical equipment & supplies; medical apparatus & supplies
HQ: Apria Healthcare Group Inc.
26220 Enterprise Ct
Lake Forest CA 92630
949 639-2000

(P-7238)
APRIA HEALTHCARE LLC
1450 Expo Pkwy, Sacramento (95815-4231)
PHONE.................................530 677-2713
Jim Hay, *Branch Mgr*
Denise Ewing, *Admin Asst*
Linda Donovan, *Sales Executive*
EMP: 192
SALES (corp-wide): 2.4B **Privately Held**
WEB: www.apria.com
SIC: **5047** Hospital equipment & furniture
HQ: Apria Healthcare Llc
26220 Enterprise Ct
Lake Forest CA 92630
949 616-2606

(P-7239)
APRIA HEALTHCARE LLC
2510 Dean Lesher Dr Ste D, Concord (94520-1368)
PHONE.................................925 827-8800

Dencio Chua, *Manager*
Ruth Bindrup, *Manager*
Jerry Heller, *Manager*
EMP: 63
SQ FT: 2,400
SALES (corp-wide): 2.4B **Privately Held**
WEB: www.apria.com
SIC: **5047** 7352 Hospital equipment & furniture; medical equipment rental
HQ: Apria Healthcare Llc
26220 Enterprise Ct
Lake Forest CA 92630
949 616-2606

(P-7240)
BACKPROJECT CORPORATION
170 N Wolfe Rd, Sunnyvale (94086-5211)
PHONE.................................408 730-1111
Steve Hoffman, *President*
◆ EMP: 66
SQ FT: 18,000
SALES (est): 9.4MM **Privately Held**
WEB: www.backproject.com
SIC: **5047** Medical & hospital equipment

(P-7241)
BAXTER HEALTHCARE CORPORATION
Baxter Hospital Supply
4551 E Philadelphia St, Ontario (91761-2316)
PHONE.................................303 222-6837
Fax: 909 988-4732
Richard S Justin, *Principal*
Kent Cruickshank, *Info Tech Dir*
Maureen Monanan, *Sales Staff*
EMP: 150
SALES (corp-wide): 9.9B **Publicly Held**
SIC: **5047** Medical & hospital equipment
HQ: Baxter Healthcare Corporation
1 Baxter Pkwy
Deerfield IL 60015
224 948-2000

(P-7242)
BAXTER HEALTHCARE CORPORATION
700 Vaughn Rd, Dixon (95620-9226)
PHONE.................................503 285-0212
Robert Fretwell, *Branch Mgr*
EMP: 72
SALES (corp-wide): 9.9B **Publicly Held**
SIC: **5047** Medical & hospital equipment
HQ: Baxter Healthcare Corporation
1 Baxter Pkwy
Deerfield IL 60015
224 948-2000

(P-7243)
BECTON DICKINSON AND COMPANY
Also Called: Bdc Distribution Center
2200 W San Bernardino Ave, Redlands (92374-5008)
PHONE.................................909 748-7300
Ricardo Frias, *Branch Mgr*
EMP: 100
SALES (corp-wide): 10.2B **Publicly Held**
SIC: **5047** Medical & hospital equipment
PA: Becton, Dickinson And Company
1 Becton Dr
Franklin Lakes NJ 07417
201 847-6800

(P-7244)
BENCO DENTAL SUPPLY CO
3590 Harbor Gtwy N, Costa Mesa (92626-1425)
PHONE.................................714 424-0977
EMP: 98
SALES (corp-wide): 618.9MM **Privately Held**
SIC: **5047** Dental equipment & supplies
PA: Benco Dental Supply Co.
295 Centerpoint Blvd
Pittston PA 18640
570 602-7781

(P-7245)
BINDING SITE INC
6730 Mesa Ridge Rd, San Diego (92121-2951)
PHONE.................................858 453-9177
Fax: 858 453-9189
Doug Kurth, *President*

Doug Anderson, *Exec VP*
▲ EMP: 80
SQ FT: 23,000
SALES (est): 27.3MM **Privately Held**
WEB: www.thebindingsite.com
SIC: **5047** Diagnostic equipment, medical

(P-7246)
BIOSITE INC
9975 Summers Ridge Rd, San Diego (92121-2997)
PHONE.................................510 683-9063
Yonkin John, *President*
Tom Blaey, *Vice Pres*
Norman Paradis, *Vice Pres*
Robert Walkley, *Executive Asst*
Mahasin Daoud, *Administration*
EMP: 85 EST: 2011
SALES (est): 19.3MM **Privately Held**
SIC: **5047** Medical equipment & supplies

(P-7247)
BRADEN PARTNERS LP A CALIF
7500 District Blvd, Bakersfield (93313-4832)
PHONE.................................661 632-1979
Patrick Sullivan, *Manager*
EMP: 87
SALES (corp-wide): 6.7B **Privately Held**
SIC: **5047** Medical equipment & supplies
HQ: Braden Partners, L.P., A California Limited Partnership
773 San Marin Dr Ste 2230
Novato CA 94945
415 893-1518

(P-7248)
BURBANK DENTAL LABORATORY INC
2101 Floyd St, Burbank (91504-3411)
PHONE.................................818 841-2256
Fax: 818 841-8643
Anatony Sedler, *CEO*
Tony Sedler, *President*
Bob Vartanian, *Exec VP*
David French, *Vice Pres*
Robert Vartanian, *Vice Pres*
▲ EMP: 150
SALES (est): 43.2MM **Privately Held**
SIC: **5047** Dentists' professional supplies

(P-7249)
CAFTA
16625 Gridley Rd Unit 5, Cerritos (90703-1737)
PHONE.................................562 860-9808
Tianfu Guo, *President*
EMP: 108
SQ FT: 500
SALES: 3MM **Privately Held**
WEB: www.cispes.org
SIC: **5047** Medical equipment & supplies

(P-7250)
CAMERON HEALTH INC
905 Calle Amanecer # 300, San Clemente (92673-6277)
PHONE.................................949 940-4000
Fax: 949 366-8829
Kevin Hykes, *President*
Mitch C Hill, *CFO*
Pierre Chauvineau, *Vice Pres*
Ward Dykstra, *Vice Pres*
Bill Rissmann, *Vice Pres*
EMP: 100
SQ FT: 15,000
SALES (est): 38.3MM
SALES (corp-wide): 7.4B **Publicly Held**
WEB: www.cameronhealth.com
SIC: **5047** Medical equipment & supplies
PA: Boston Scientific Corporation
300 Boston Scientific Way
Marlborough MA 01752
508 683-4000

(P-7251)
CARDINAL HEALTH INC
793 Via Lata, Colton (92324-3930)
PHONE.................................909 824-1820
Dennis Kephert, *Manager*
EMP: 74
SALES (corp-wide): 121.5B **Publicly Held**
SIC: **5047** Medical & hospital equipment

▲ = Import ▼=Export
◆ =Import/Export

PRODUCTS & SERVICES SECTION
5047 - Medical, Dental & Hospital Eqpt & Splys Wholesale County (P-7273)

PA: Cardinal Health, Inc.
7000 Cardinal Pl
Dublin OH 43017
614 757-5000

(P-7252)
CARDINAL HEALTH INC
1100 Bird Center Dr, Palm Springs (92262-8000)
PHONE................................951 360-2199
EMP: 52
SALES (corp-wide): 102.5B Publicly Held
SIC: 5047
PA: Cardinal Health, Inc.
7000 Cardinal Pl
Dublin OH 43017
614 757-5000

(P-7253)
CARDINAL HEALTH INC
700 Vaughn Rd, Dixon (95620-9226)
PHONE................................530 406-3600
Dan Evert, Branch Mgr
Bob White, Technical Staff
Elaine Chen, Pharmacist
Romeyn Webb, Supervisor
EMP: 230
SALES (corp-wide): 121.5B Publicly Held
SIC: 5047 Artificial limbs
PA: Cardinal Health, Inc.
7000 Cardinal Pl
Dublin OH 43017
614 757-5000

(P-7254)
CARDINAL HEALTH INC
4551 E Philadelphia St, Ontario (91761-2316)
PHONE................................909 605-0900
Fax: 909 605-0978
Mark Summers, Manager
Scott Wagner, Branch Mgr
Robin Lockwood, Human Res Mgr
Jeremy Fortune, Opers Mgr
Christopher Beard, Manager
EMP: 73
SALES (corp-wide): 121.5B Publicly Held
SIC: 5047 Medical & hospital equipment
PA: Cardinal Health, Inc.
7000 Cardinal Pl
Dublin OH 43017
614 757-5000

(P-7255)
CARDINAL HEALTH 200 LLC
3750 Torrey View Ct, San Diego (92130-2622)
PHONE................................951 686-8900
Michael McMahon, Manager
Kathy Cooney, Vice Pres
Dennis Duell, Vice Pres
Sherry Barnes, Executive Asst
Jeff Gray, Project Mgr
EMP: 210
SQ FT: 28,000
SALES (corp-wide): 121.5B Publicly Held
WEB: www.allegiancehealth.com
SIC: 5047 3845 3672 Medical & hospital equipment; electromedical equipment; printed circuit boards
HQ: Cardinal Health 200, Llc
3651 Birchwood Dr
Waukegan IL 60085

(P-7256)
CAREFUSION SOLUTIONS LLC (DH)
3750 Torrey View Ct, San Diego (92130-2622)
PHONE................................858 617-2100
Keiran Gallahue, CEO
Tom Leonard, President
James Hinrichs, CFO
Don Abbey, Exec VP
Scott Bostick, Senior VP
EMP: 600
SALES (est): 273.1MM
SALES (corp-wide): 10.2B Publicly Held
SIC: 5047 Medical equipment & supplies

HQ: Carefusion Corporation
3750 Torrey View Ct
San Diego CA 92130
858 617-2000

(P-7257)
CHINA YNGXIN PHRMCEUTICALS INC
927 Canada Ct, City of Industry (91748-1136)
PHONE................................626 581-9098
Yongxin Liu, Ch of Bd
Ning Liu, President
Harry Zhang, CFO
EMP: 673
SALES: 47.5MM Privately Held
SIC: 5047 Medical equipment & supplies

(P-7258)
CLARITY MEDICAL SYSTEMS INC
5775 W Las Positas Blvd # 200, Pleasanton (94588-4003)
PHONE................................925 463-7984
Fax: 925 463-7993
Mark Mellin, CEO
Greg Sprehn, President
Rick Mangum, CFO
John P Farugia, Chief Mktg Ofcr
John Farugia, Chief Mktg Ofcr
EMP: 55
SALES: 17MM Privately Held
SIC: 5047 Medical & hospital equipment

(P-7259)
CONSENSUS ORTHOPEDICS INC
1115 Windfield Way # 100, El Dorado Hills (95762-9835)
PHONE................................916 355-7110
Collen Gray, President
Daniel Hayes, Sr Corp Ofcr
Gail V Dalen, Exec VP
Thomas Killian, Exec VP
Jeff Groth, Vice Pres
EMP: 85
SQ FT: 25,000
SALES (est): 38.9MM Privately Held
WEB: www.hayesmed.com
SIC: 5047 Medical & hospital equipment

(P-7260)
CUSTOM MEDICAL PRODUCTS INC
9680 Alto Dr, La Mesa (91941-4446)
PHONE................................619 461-2068
Thomas D Petersen, Principal
EMP: 181
SALES (est): 3.7MM
SALES (corp-wide): 101.7B Publicly Held
WEB: www.custommedical.com
SIC: 5047 Medical equipment & supplies
HQ: Express Scripts, Inc.
1 Express Way
Saint Louis MO 63121
314 996-0900

(P-7261)
DR FRESH LLC (PA)
Also Called: Fresh Merge
6645 Caballero Blvd, Buena Park (90620-1131)
PHONE................................714 690-1573
Fax: 714 690-1572
Ted Yun,
Joel G Killion,
Nikhil Jindal, Manager
◆ EMP: 76 EST: 2012
SQ FT: 55,000
SALES: 110.3MM Privately Held
SIC: 5047 3843 Medical & hospital equipment; dental equipment

(P-7262)
DR FRESH INC
6645 Caballero Blvd, Buena Park (90620-1131)
PHONE................................714 690-1573
Puneet Nanda, Ch of Bd
Sandip Grewal, CFO
Geoff Carroll, Chief Mktg Ofcr
Brett Mice, Vice Pres
Natalie Pineda, Admin Asst
◆ EMP: 83

SQ FT: 55,000
SALES (est): 165.1K
SALES (corp-wide): 5.1MM Privately Held
WEB: www.drfresh.com
SIC: 5047 3843 Medical & hospital equipment; dental equipment
PA: Dr Fresh Assets Limited
B-1/E-24,
New Delhi DEL 11004
114 167-9238

(P-7263)
EDGE SYSTEMS LLC
2277 Redondo Ave, Signal Hill (90755-4017)
PHONE................................562 597-0102
Roger Ignon, CEO
Bill Cohen, President
Peter Rumbellow, Human Res Dir
Greg Stickley, Sales Staff
▲ EMP: 60
SQ FT: 12,000
SALES (est): 35.3MM Privately Held
WEB: www.edgesystem.net
SIC: 5047 Medical equipment & supplies

(P-7264)
FEATHER RIVER HOSPITAL
Also Called: Feather River Hospital HM Oxgn
1295 Bille Rd, Paradise (95969-3443)
PHONE................................530 876-7216
Fax: 530 872-2120
Christine Venard, Branch Mgr
EMP: 123
SQ FT: 2,685
SALES (corp-wide): 207MM Privately Held
SIC: 5047 Medical equipment & supplies; oxygen therapy equipment
PA: Feather River Hospital
5974 Pentz Rd
Paradise CA 95969
530 877-9361

(P-7265)
FISHER & PAYKEL HEALTHCARE INC
15365 Barranca Pkwy, Irvine (92618-2216)
PHONE................................949 453-4000
Fax: 949 453-4001
Justin Callahan, President
Tony Barclay, CFO
Bryan Goudzwaard, Vice Pres
Peter Hernandez, VP Finance
Paul Shearer, Director
▲ EMP: 50
SQ FT: 5,000
SALES (est): 49.6MM
SALES (corp-wide): 498.1MM Privately Held
SIC: 5047 Medical equipment & supplies
PA: Fisher & Paykel Healthcare Corporation Limited
15 Maurice Paykel Place
Auckland, 1061
957 401-00

(P-7266)
GORDIAN MEDICAL INC
Also Called: American Medical Technologies
17595 Cartwright Rd, Irvine (92614-5847)
PHONE................................714 556-0200
Joseph Del Signore, President
David Simon, Vice Pres
EMP: 290
SALES (est): 74.9MM Privately Held
SIC: 5047 Medical equipment & supplies

(P-7267)
HARDY DIAGNOSTICS (PA)
1430 W Mccoy Ln, Santa Maria (93455-1005)
PHONE................................805 346-2766
Fax: 805 346-2760
Jay R Hardy, President
Nathaniel Graessle, CFO
Ralph Hardy, Exec VP
Kathleen Salazar, Executive
Jay Hamrick, QA Dir
◆ EMP: 151
SQ FT: 75,000
SALES (est): 72.4MM Privately Held
WEB: www.hardydiagnostics.com
SIC: 5047 2836 Medical equipment & supplies; agar culture media

(P-7268)
HONEY LAKE HOSPICE INC
60 S Lassen St, Susanville (96130-4363)
P.O. Box 1166 (96130-1166)
PHONE................................530 257-3137
Andria Cuypers, Coordinator
Jacki Stovall, Manager
EMP: 60
SALES (est): 4.2MM Privately Held
SIC: 5047 Medical equipment & supplies

(P-7269)
INNOVATIVE SURGICAL PRODUCTS
2761 Walnut Ave, Tustin (92780-7051)
PHONE................................714 836-4474
Lewis Carpenter, President
Mark Gordon, President
Eduardo Sanchez, Engineer
Roger Francis, Facilities Mgr
EMP: 94
SALES (est): 10.7MM
SALES (corp-wide): 2.8B Privately Held
SIC: 5047 Surgical equipment & supplies
HQ: Specialty Silicone Fabricators, Inc.
2761 Walnut Ave
Tustin CA 92780
805 239-4284

(P-7270)
INVUITY INC
444 De Haro St Ste 100, San Francisco (94107-2350)
PHONE................................415 665-2100
Philip Sawyer, President
Gregory T Lucier, Ch of Bd
James H Mackaness, CFO
Paul D Davison, Vice Pres
Joseph Guido, Vice Pres
EMP: 148
SQ FT: 38,135
SALES: 21MM Privately Held
SIC: 5047 Surgical equipment & supplies

(P-7271)
JB DENTAL SUPPLY CO INC (PA)
17000 Kingsview Ave, Carson (90746-1230)
PHONE................................310 202-8855
Fax: 310 525-3023
Joseph Berman, President
Manny Chada, Vice Pres
Kip Giro, Branch Mgr
Scott Linden, Personnel Exec
Ann Westeroff, Sls & Mktg Exec
EMP: 120 EST: 1973
SQ FT: 26,000
SALES (est): 33MM Privately Held
SIC: 5047 Dental equipment & supplies

(P-7272)
JOERNS LLC (HQ)
19748 Dearborn St, Chatsworth (91311-6509)
PHONE................................800 966-6662
Mark Ludwig, Mng Member
Mark Urbania, CFO
Karen Brown, QA Dir
Joanna Lantieri, Finance
Jim Shiller, Controller
EMP: 150
SQ FT: 28,000
SALES (est): 91.5MM
SALES (corp-wide): 163MM Privately Held
WEB: www.trilinemedical.com
SIC: 5047 Hospital equipment & furniture
PA: Quad-C Jh Holdings Inc.
2430 Whitehall Park Dr
Charlotte NC 28273
800 826-0270

(P-7273)
KLM ORTHOTIC LABORATORIES INC
28280 Alta Vista Ave, Valencia (91355-0958)
PHONE................................661 295-2600
Fax: 661 294-2454
Kirk Marshall, President
Scott Marshall, Corp Secy
Kent Marshall, Vice Pres
Jaime Nicolaides, Financial Exec
EMP: 100

5047 - Medical, Dental & Hospital Eqpt & Splys Wholesale County (P-7274)

SQ FT: 35,000
SALES (est): 27MM **Privately Held**
SIC: **5047** 3842 Medical laboratory equipment; foot appliances, orthopedic

(P-7274)
LUMENIS INC (HQ)
2033 Gateway Pl Ste 200, San Jose (95110-3714)
PHONE..................................408 764-3000
Tzipi Ozer Armon, *CEO*
Harel Beit-On, *Ch of Bd*
Abner Ray, *President*
Mark Hoffman, *COO*
Zivi Nedivisioni, *COO*
▲ EMP: 150
SALES (est): 228.9MM
SALES (corp-wide): 290MM **Privately Held**
SIC: **5047** Therapy equipment
PA: Lumenis Ltd.
   6 Hakidma
   Upper Yokneam 20692
   495 991-00

(P-7275)
MARDX DIAGNOSTICS INC
5919 Farnsworth Ct, Carlsbad (92008-7303)
P.O. Box 1059, Jamestown NY (14702-1059)
PHONE..................................760 929-0500
Fax: 760 929-0124
Ian Woodwards, *CEO*
Arnold Aquilino, *Webmaster*
Nicole Kingfley, *Accounts Mgr*
EMP: 53
SQ FT: 21,500
SALES (est): 9.3MM **Privately Held**
SIC: **5047** Diagnostic equipment, medical
HQ: Trinity Biotech, Inc.
   2823 Girts Rd
   Jamestown NY 14701
   800 325-3424

(P-7276)
MCKESSON CORPORATION
3000 Colby St, Berkeley (94705-2083)
PHONE..................................510 666-0854
Micah Wakamatsu, *Branch Mgr*
EMP: 66
SALES (corp-wide): 190.8B **Publicly Held**
SIC: **5047** Hospital equipment & furniture
PA: Mckesson Corporation
   1 Post St Fl 18
   San Francisco CA 94104
   415 983-8300

(P-7277)
MCKESSON MEDICAL-SURGICAL INC
16043 El Prado Rd, Chino (91708-9144)
PHONE..................................800 767-6339
EMP: 78
SALES (corp-wide): 190.8B **Publicly Held**
SIC: **5047** Medical equipment & supplies
HQ: Mckesson Medical-Surgical Inc.
   9954 Mayland Dr Ste 4000
   Richmond VA 23233
   804 264-7500

(P-7278)
MCKESSON MEDICAL-SURGICAL INC
1525 Rnch Conejo Blvd # 104, Newbury Park (91320-1441)
PHONE..................................805 375-8800
Fax: 805 879-8272
Mike Douglas, *Branch Mgr*
Cheryl Wilson, *Opers Staff*
Barbra Young, *Accounts Mgr*
EMP: 54
SALES (corp-wide): 190.8B **Publicly Held**
WEB: www.gmholdings.com
SIC: **5047** Medical equipment & supplies
HQ: Mckesson Medical-Surgical Inc.
   9954 Mayland Dr Ste 4000
   Richmond VA 23233
   804 264-7500

(P-7279)
MENTOR WORLDWIDE LLC
5425 Hollister Ave, Santa Barbara (93111-3341)
PHONE..................................805 681-6000
Diane Becker, *Manager*
Vaclay Podany, *Program Mgr*
Tony Summy, *CIO*
Sal Penza, *Controller*
Terry Demaria, *Human Res Dir*
EMP: 500
SALES (corp-wide): 70B **Publicly Held**
WEB: www.mentordirect.com
SIC: **5047** Medical & hospital equipment
HQ: Mentor Worldwide Llc
   33 Technology Dr
   Irvine CA 92618
   800 636-8678

(P-7280)
MERRY X-RAY CHEMICAL CORP (PA)
Also Called: M X R
4444 Viewridge Ave A, San Diego (92123-1670)
PHONE..................................858 565-4472
Fax: 858 565-2409
Leo Zuckerman, *Principal*
Ted Sloan, *President*
EMP: 153 **EST**: 1962
SQ FT: 10,000
SALES (est): 309.8MM **Privately Held**
SIC: **5047** X-ray machines & tubes; X-ray film & supplies

(P-7281)
MERRY X-RAY CORPORATION
4444 Viewridge Ave, San Diego (92123-1670)
PHONE..................................858 565-4472
Ted Sloan, *President*
Sandie Christensen, *CFO*
Al Lewein, *Vice Pres*
Roger Chamberlain, *Project Mgr*
Sandy Beith, *VP Finance*
EMP: 500
SALES (est): 114.5MM **Privately Held**
SIC: **5047** Hospital equipment & furniture

(P-7282)
MILTENYI BIOTEC INC (HQ)
2303 Lindbergh St, Auburn (95602-9562)
PHONE..................................530 745-2800
Stefan Miltenyi, *President*
Tara Clark, *General Mgr*
Ira Marks, *General Mgr*
Leonard Pulig, *General Mgr*
Robert Waters, *Technology*
▲ EMP: 74
SQ FT: 20,000
SALES (est): 43.3MM
SALES (corp-wide): 203.8MM **Privately Held**
WEB: www.miltenyibiotec.com
SIC: **5047** 8731 Medical & hospital equipment; biotechnical research, commercial
PA: Miltenyi Biotec Gmbh
   Friedrich-Ebert-Str. 68
   Bergisch Gladbach 51429
   220 483-060

(P-7283)
MORIGON TECHNOLOGIES LLC
Also Called: Medstop Medical
7621 Fulton Ave, North Hollywood (91605-1805)
PHONE..................................818 764-8880
Amaury J Agoncillo, *CEO*
Georgina Villagran, *Office Mgr*
EMP: 50
SQ FT: 8,000
SALES: 2.6MM **Privately Held**
SIC: **5047** Medical & hospital equipment; medical equipment & supplies; medical laboratory equipment

(P-7284)
NDS SURGICAL IMAGING LLC
5750 Hellyer Ave, San Jose (95138-1000)
PHONE..................................408 776-0085
Jeff Zhou, *COO*
Karim Khadr, *President*
Rok Sribar, *President*
Sam Brown, *CFO*
Deborah Young, *CFO*
◆ EMP: 215

SQ FT: 73,000
SALES (est): 88.3MM
SALES (corp-wide): 373.6MM **Publicly Held**
WEB: www.ndssi.com
SIC: **5047** Patient monitoring equipment
PA: Novanta Inc.
   125 Middlesex Tpke
   Bedford MA 01730
   781 266-5700

(P-7285)
NIHON KOHDEN AMERICA INC (HQ)
15353 Barranca Pkwy, Irvine (92618-2216)
PHONE..................................949 580-1555
Fax: 949 580-1550
Fumio Izumida, *CEO*
Eiichi Tanaka, *President*
Wilson Constantine, *COO*
Michael Stone, *Senior VP*
Shinya Hama, *Vice Pres*
▲ EMP: 60
SQ FT: 35,000
SALES (est): 69.9MM
SALES (corp-wide): 1.4B **Privately Held**
WEB: www.nkusa.com
SIC: **5047** Electro-medical equipment
PA: Nihon Kohden Corporation
   1-31-4, Nishiochiai
   Shinjuku-Ku TKY 161-0
   359 968-000

(P-7286)
NOVA ORTHO-MED INC
1470 Beachey Pl, Carson (90746-4002)
PHONE..................................310 352-3600
Sue Chen, *Principal*
Ronald Gaudiano, *Vice Pres*
Annette Aoyama, *General Mgr*
Kris Maloney, *Sales Staff*
Tina Chan, *Manager*
▲ EMP: 50
SQ FT: 5,500
SALES (est): 26.5MM **Privately Held**
WEB: www.novaorthomed.com
SIC: **5047** Medical & hospital equipment

(P-7287)
NUVI GLOBAL
518 W Henderson Ave Apt 9, Porterville (93257-1769)
P.O. Box 2568 (93258-2568)
PHONE..................................559 306-2646
Herlinda Ruelas, *Owner*
EMP: 600
SALES (est): 16.4MM **Privately Held**
SIC: **5047** Incontinent care products & supplies

(P-7288)
OLYMPUS AMERICA INC
Also Called: OLYMPUS AMERICA INC.
23342 Madero, Mission Viejo (92691-2796)
PHONE..................................949 466-3548
EMP: 110
SALES (corp-wide): 6.8B **Privately Held**
SIC: **5047** Medical equipment & supplies; diagnostic equipment, medical
HQ: Olympus America Inc
   3500 Corporate Pkwy
   Center Valley PA 18034
   484 896-5000

(P-7289)
OLYMPUS AMERICA INC
2400 Ringwood Ave, San Jose (95131-1700)
PHONE..................................408 935-5000
Fax: 408 935-5010
Paul Schwartz, *QC Mgr*
Nancy McGirk, *Manager*
Avis Momin, *Associate*
EMP: 400
SALES (corp-wide): 6.8B **Privately Held**
SIC: **5047** Medical equipment & supplies
HQ: Olympus America Inc
   3500 Corporate Pkwy
   Center Valley PA 18034
   484 896-5000

(P-7290)
ORCHID MPS
3233 W Harvard St, Santa Ana (92704-3917)
PHONE..................................714 549-9203

Mark Deischter, *Vice Pres*
EMP: 100
SALES (est): 14MM **Privately Held**
SIC: **5047** Medical equipment & supplies

(P-7291)
OTISMED CORPORATION
1600 Harbor Bay Pkwy # 200, Alameda (94502-3085)
PHONE..................................510 786-3171
Charlie CHI, *President*
Jeann Blondia, *Treasurer*
Ilwhan Park, *Vice Pres*
Dana Mead Jr, *Director*
Leslie Arving, *Manager*
EMP: 63
SALES (est): 11.1MM
SALES (corp-wide): 9.9B **Publicly Held**
SIC: **5047** Medical equipment & supplies
PA: Stryker Corporation
   2825 Airview Blvd
   Portage MI 49002
   269 385-2600

(P-7292)
OWENS & MINOR INC
5125 Ontario Mills Pkwy, Ontario (91764-5103)
PHONE..................................909 944-2100
Fax: 909 468-9770
Tom Kelly, *Branch Mgr*
Olwen Cape, *Vice Pres*
Karen Rodriguez, *Finance*
Brian Stofco, *Purch Agent*
Tim Kachur, *Marketing Staff*
EMP: 57
SALES (corp-wide): 9.7B **Publicly Held**
WEB: www.owens-minor.com
SIC: **5047** Medical & hospital equipment
PA: Owens & Minor, Inc.
   9120 Lockwood Blvd
   Mechanicsville VA 23116
   804 723-7000

(P-7293)
OWENS & MINOR INC
18520 Stanford Rd, Tracy (95377-9708)
PHONE..................................209 833-4600
Jim Bierman, *President*
EMP: 57
SALES (corp-wide): 9.7B **Publicly Held**
SIC: **5047** Medical equipment & supplies
PA: Owens & Minor, Inc.
   9120 Lockwood Blvd
   Mechanicsville VA 23116
   804 723-7000

(P-7294)
PASSPORT TO LEARNING INC
41319 12th St W, Palmdale (93551-1414)
PHONE..................................661 538-9200
Betty Walkes, *Branch Mgr*
EMP: 93
SALES (corp-wide): 1.8MM **Privately Held**
SIC: **5047** Technical aids for the handicapped
PA: Passport To Learning Incorporated
   1241 1/2 West Blvd
   Los Angeles CA 90019
   323 549-9328

(P-7295)
PATTERSON DENTAL SUPPLY INC
Also Called: Patterson Dental 426
185 S Douglas St Ste 100, El Segundo (90245-4673)
PHONE..................................310 426-3100
Fax: 310 757-7542
Ken Sartin, *Manager*
EMP: 75
SALES (corp-wide): 5.3B **Publicly Held**
WEB: www.pattersondentalsupply.com
SIC: **5047** Dental equipment & supplies
HQ: Patterson Dental Supply, Inc.
   1031 Mendota Heights Rd
   Saint Paul MN 55120
   651 686-1600

▲ = Import ▼ = Export
◆ = Import/Export

PRODUCTS & SERVICES SECTION
5047 - Medical, Dental & Hospital Eqpt & Splys Wholesale County (P-7316)

(P-7296)
PATTERSON DENTAL SUPPLY INC
Also Called: Patterson Dental 454
1030 Winding Creek Rd # 150, Roseville (95678-7045)
PHONE.................916 780-5100
Fax: 916 630-5521
James Ryan, *Manager*
EMP: 69
SALES (corp-wide): 4.3B **Publicly Held**
WEB: www.pattersondentalsupply.com
SIC: 5047 Dental equipment & supplies
HQ: Patterson Dental Supply, Inc.
1031 Mendota Heights Rd
Saint Paul MN 55120
651 686-1600

(P-7297)
PATTERSON DENTAL SUPPLY INC
Also Called: Patterson Dental 590
800 Monte Vista Dr, Dinuba (93618-9117)
PHONE.................559 595-1450
Fax: 559 595-1454
Ceasar Lopez, *Manager*
Refugio Rios,
Sean Muniz, *Manager*
EMP: 58
SALES (corp-wide): 4.3B **Publicly Held**
WEB: www.pattersondentalsupply.com
SIC: 5047 Dental equipment & supplies
HQ: Patterson Dental Supply, Inc.
1031 Mendota Heights Rd
Saint Paul MN 55120
651 686-1600

(P-7298)
PATTERSON DENTAL SUPPLY INC
5087 Commercial Cir, Concord (94520-1268)
PHONE.................408 773-0776
Armi Onsori, *Owner*
EMP: 50
SQ FT: 1,200
SALES (est): 3.3MM **Privately Held**
SIC: 5047 Dental equipment & supplies

(P-7299)
PEARSON DENTAL SUPPLIES INC (PA)
Also Called: Pearson Surgical Supply Co
13161 Telfair Ave, Sylmar (91342-3574)
PHONE.................818 362-2600
Fax: 818 733-7747
Keyhan Kashfian, *President*
Nader Kashfian, *Corp Secy*
Parviz Kashfian, *Vice Pres*
Sedi Barati, *Executive*
Mat Dyson, *Analyst*
▲ **EMP:** 105 **EST:** 1983
SQ FT: 88,000
SALES (est): 84.3MM **Privately Held**
WEB: www.pearsondental.com
SIC: 5047 Fast-food restaurant, chain

(P-7300)
PHILIPS MEDICAL SYSTEMS CLEVEL
1 Marconi, Irvine (92618-2520)
PHONE.................949 699-2300
David Carter, *Branch Mgr*
Leverda Wallace, *Surgery Dir*
Dan Ravetto, *Info Tech Mgr*
Brian Stevenson, *Network Enginr*
EMP: 100
SALES (corp-wide): 26B **Privately Held**
SIC: 5047 X-ray machines & tubes; diagnostic equipment, medical; X-ray film & supplies
HQ: Philips Medical Systems (Cleveland), Inc.
595 Miner Rd
Cleveland OH 44143
440 247-2652

(P-7301)
POLESTAR LABS INC
1223 Pacific Oaks Pl # 102, Escondido (92029-2913)
PHONE.................760 480-2600
Fax: 760 735-5268
Michael Dunaway, *CEO*
Charles Chuck Fabijanic, *Senior VP*
Trudy Dunaway, *Admin Sec*
EMP: 70
SALES: 5MM **Privately Held**
SIC: 5047 5999 7699 7363 Medical laboratory equipment; medical apparatus & supplies; laboratory instrument repair; medical help service; management services

(P-7302)
PORTERVILLE SHELTERED WORKSHOP
1853 E Cross Ave, Tulare (93274-7388)
PHONE.................559 684-9168
EMP: 59
SALES (corp-wide): 10.4MM **Privately Held**
SIC: 5047
PA: Porterville Sheltered Workshop
194 W Poplar Ave
Porterville CA 93257
559 784-7187

(P-7303)
PRACTICE WARES INC
Also Called: Practicewares Dental Supply
2377 Gold Meadow Way, Gold River (95670-4405)
PHONE.................916 526-2674
EMP: 50
SALES (corp-wide): 12.5MM **Privately Held**
SIC: 5047
PA: Practice Wares, Inc
3400 E Mcdowell Rd
Phoenix AZ 85008
602 225-9090

(P-7304)
PRI MEDICAL TECHNOLOGIES INC (DH)
Also Called: UHS Surgical Services
10939 Pendleton St, Sun Valley (91352-1522)
PHONE.................818 394-2800
Fax: 818 394-2850
Louis Buther, *President*
William M McKay, *Treasurer*
Lee Pulju, *Treasurer*
Gary Blackford, *Director*
Shally Hua, *Manager*
EMP: 55
SQ FT: 14,500
SALES (est): 18.4MM
SALES (corp-wide): 448.6MM **Privately Held**
SIC: 5047 7352 8741 Instruments, surgical & medical; medical equipment rental; administrative management; financial management for business; personnel management
HQ: Universal Hospital Services, Inc.
6625 W 78th St Ste 300
Minneapolis MN 55439
952 893-3200

(P-7305)
PROFESSIONAL HOSPITAL SUP INC (HQ)
42500 Winchester Rd, Temecula (92590-2570)
PHONE.................951 699-5000
Fax: 951 296-2624
Jenise Luttgens, *CEO*
John Augustine, *CFO*
Doug Hoffee, *Exec VP*
Vincent Long, *Executive*
Phr A Travis, *Admin Asst*
▲ **EMP:** 1200
SQ FT: 300,000
SALES (est): 1.5B
SALES (corp-wide): 5.6B **Privately Held**
WEB: www.phsyes.com
SIC: 5047 Medical & hospital equipment
PA: Medline Industries, Inc.
1 Medline Pl
Mundelein IL 60060
847 949-5500

(P-7306)
PROFESSIONAL HOSPITAL SUP INC
2100 Courage Dr, Fairfield (94533-6719)
PHONE.................707 720-0164
David Hagan, *Manager*
Ali Odwa, *Branch Mgr*
Tricia Alesi, *Business Mgr*
Pam Ricci, *Credit Mgr*
Jenise Luttgens, *Safety Mgr*
EMP: 175
SALES (corp-wide): 5.6B **Privately Held**
WEB: www.phsyes.com
SIC: 5047 Medical & hospital equipment
HQ: Professional Hospital Supply, Inc.
42500 Winchester Rd
Temecula CA 92590
951 699-5000

(P-7307)
PROVIDENCE HEALTH & SERVICES
27875 Smyth Dr Ste 100, Valencia (91355-6064)
PHONE.................661 294-1030
EMP: 69
SALES (corp-wide): 10.1B **Privately Held**
SIC: 5047 Medical equipment & supplies
PA: Providence Health & Services
1801 Lind Ave Sw
Renton WA 98057
425 525-3355

(P-7308)
PSS WORLD MEDICAL INC
1938 W Malvern Ave, Fullerton (92833-2105)
PHONE.................714 459-4000
Fax: 714 459-4095
Andy Wood, *Manager*
EMP: 50
SQ FT: 19,800
SALES (corp-wide): 190.8B **Publicly Held**
WEB: www.pssworldmedical.com
SIC: 5047 Medical equipment & supplies; surgical equipment & supplies
HQ: Pss World Medical, Inc.
4345 Southpoint Blvd # 110
Jacksonville FL 32216
904 332-3000

(P-7309)
PURELIFE LLC
201 Santa Monica Blvd # 400, Santa Monica (90401-2212)
PHONE.................877 777-3303
Rodney Hanoon, *CEO*
▲ **EMP:** 54
SALES (est): 13.1MM **Privately Held**
SIC: 5047 Medical & hospital equipment

(P-7310)
RADIOMETER AMERICA INC (HQ)
250 S Kraemer Blvd, Brea (92821-6232)
PHONE.................800 736-0600
Henrik Brandborg, *President*
Frank T McFaden, *Treasurer*
Jens Knobe, *Vice Pres*
James F Oreilly, *Vice Pres*
Sue Graybeal, *Admin Asst*
▲ **EMP:** 174
SQ FT: 35,000
SALES (est): 50.1MM
SALES (corp-wide): 20.5B **Publicly Held**
WEB: www.radiometeramerica.com
SIC: 5047 Medical equipment & supplies
PA: Danaher Corporation
2200 Penn Ave Nw Ste 800w
Washington DC 20037
202 828-0850

(P-7311)
SAKURA FINETEK USA INC (HQ)
1750 W 214th St, Torrance (90501-2857)
PHONE.................310 972-7800
Fax: 310 972-7888
Takashi Tsuzuki, *Ch of Bd*
Anthony C Marotti, *President*
Kenichi Matsumoto, *Chm Emeritus*
Ichiro Seki, *Executive*
Kam Patel, *Corp Secy*
▲ **EMP:** 109
SQ FT: 68,000
SALES (est): 70.7MM **Privately Held**
WEB: www.sakura-americas.com
SIC: 5047 Medical laboratory equipment; diagnostic equipment, medical
PA: Sakura Global Holding Co., Ltd.
3-1-9, Nihombashihoncho
Chuo-Ku TKY
332 701-666

(P-7312)
SAN JOSE SURGICAL SUPPLY INC (PA)
902 S Bascom Ave, San Jose (95128-3599)
PHONE.................408 293-9033
Fax: 408 293-7808
Dennis J Collins, *President*
Kim Smith, *Purch Dir*
▲ **EMP:** 62
SQ FT: 15,000
SALES (est): 22.7MM **Privately Held**
WEB: www.sjsurgical.com
SIC: 5047 5122 Surgical equipment & supplies; pharmaceuticals

(P-7313)
SHIMADZU PRECISION INSTRS INC
Shimadzu Medical Systems
20101 S Vermont Ave, Torrance (90502-1328)
PHONE.................310 217-8855
Fax: 310 217-0661
Koki Aoyama, *President*
Wendy Decastro, *Admin Asst*
Gordan Bowllen, *CIO*
Tom Kloetbly, *Personnel Exec*
Takeshi Nakanishi, *Director*
EMP: 56
SALES (corp-wide): 2.9B **Privately Held**
WEB: www.spi-inc.com
SIC: 5047 Medical equipment & supplies
HQ: Shimadzu Precision Instruments, Inc.
3645 N Lakewood Blvd
Long Beach CA 90808
562 420-6226

(P-7314)
SIEMENS MED SOLUTIONS USA INC
Ultra Sound Division
685 E Middlefield Rd, Mountain View (94043-4045)
P.O. Box 7393 (94039-7393)
PHONE.................650 694-5747
Franz Wiehler, *CFO*
Jackie Ferreira, *Comms Mgr*
Gayatri James, *Admin Asst*
Bryan Malone, *Web Dvlpr*
John Ruckstuhl, *Engineer*
EMP: 300
SQ FT: 373,000
SALES (corp-wide): 83.5B **Privately Held**
WEB: www.siemensmedical.com
SIC: 5047 Diagnostic equipment, medical
HQ: Siemens Medical Solutions Usa, Inc.
40 Liberty Blvd
Malvern PA 19355
610 219-6300

(P-7315)
SOUND TECHNOLOGIES INC
Also Called: Sound-Eklin
5810 Van Allen Way, Carlsbad (92008-7300)
PHONE.................760 918-9626
Fax: 760 918-9620
Kevin Wilson, *President*
Alex Sluiter, *Executive*
Raquel Dearman, *Admin Asst*
Jon Maynard, *Info Tech Dir*
Susan Healy, *Info Tech Mgr*
▼ **EMP:** 52
SALES (est): 76.5MM
SALES (corp-wide): 2.1B **Publicly Held**
WEB: www.soundvet.com
SIC: 5047 Veterinarians' equipment & supplies
PA: Vca Inc.
12401 W Olympic Blvd
Los Angeles CA 90064
310 571-6500

(P-7316)
TEAM MAKENA LLC (PA)
17461 Derian Ave Ste 200, Irvine (92614-5820)
PHONE.................949 474-1753
John Lasso,

5047 - Medical, Dental & Hospital Eqpt & Splys Wholesale County (P-7317)

Jeff Broadhead, *Finance*
Paul Nguyen, *Opers Mgr*
Jim Schuerger, *Opers Staff*
Richard Dutch, *VP Sales*
EMP: 53
SALES: 14.6MM **Privately Held**
SIC: 5047 Hospital equipment & supplies

(P-7317)
TEAM POST-OP INC (DH)
17256 Red Hill Ave, Irvine (92614-5628)
P.O. Box 650846, Dallas TX (75265-0846)
PHONE..............................949 253-5500
Jeffrey Salamon, *President*
John A Krier, *COO*
Kevin Johnson, *Exec VP*
Lisa Salamon, *Admin Sec*
Peter Jimenez, *Sales Associate*
EMP: 60
SQ FT: 1,400
SALES (est): 16.8MM
SALES (corp-wide): 500.5MM **Privately Held**
SIC: 5047 Orthopedic equipment & supplies
HQ: Hanger Prosthetics & Orthotics, Inc.
10910 Main Dr
Austin TX 78758
512 777-3800

(P-7318)
THERAPAK LLC (HQ)
651 Wharton Dr, Claremont (91711-4819)
PHONE..............................909 267-2000
Fax: 626 357-5911
Todd Gates, *President*
Arbie Harootoonian, *CFO*
Frank Brandauer, *Vice Pres*
Renetta Olguin, *Executive*
Rebecca Gumaer, *Project Mgr*
▲ **EMP:** 70
SQ FT: 24,000
SALES (est): 276.8MM
SALES (corp-wide): 4.3B **Publicly Held**
WEB: www.therapak.com
SIC: 5047 Medical equipment & supplies; diagnostic equipment, medical
PA: Vwr Corporation
100 Matsonford Rd 1-200
Radnor PA 19087
610 386-1700

(P-7319)
TOSHIBA AMER MED SYSTEMS INC (DH)
Also Called: Toshiba Medical Systems
2441 Michelle Dr, Tustin (92780-7047)
P.O. Box 2068 (92781-2068)
PHONE..............................714 730-5000
Fax: 714 730-4022
Shuzo Yamamoto, *CEO*
Carol-Davis Grossman, *Managing Prtnr*
Donald Fowler, *CEO*
John Patterson, *CFO*
Peter N S Annand, *Senior VP*
◆ **EMP:** 300
SQ FT: 135,000
SALES (est): 8.5MM
SALES (corp-wide): 48.4B **Privately Held**
WEB: www.tams.com
SIC: 5047 X-ray machines & tubes; medical equipment & supplies
HQ: Toshiba America Inc
1251 Ave Of Ameri Ste 4100
New York NY 10020
212 596-0600

(P-7320)
TOSOH BIOSCIENCE INC
Also Called: Tosoh USA
6000 Shoreline Ct Ste 101, South San Francisco (94080-7206)
PHONE..............................650 615-4970
Max Yamata, *President*
Don York, *Exec Dir*
Dwight Wright, *Prgrmr*
Gil Kelley, *Accountant*
Walt Evans, *Mfg Spvr*
▼ **EMP:** 75
SQ FT: 13,917
SALES (est): 22.7MM
SALES (corp-wide): 6.4B **Privately Held**
WEB: www.tosohbioscience.com
SIC: 5047 Diagnostic equipment, medical
HQ: Tosoh America, Inc.
3600 Gantz Rd
Grove City OH 43123
614 539-8622

(P-7321)
TRADECOM MED TRANSCRIPTION INC
363 Piercy Rd, San Jose (95138-1403)
PHONE..............................408 225-9200
Samit Shah, *President*
Dhaval Patel, *CFO*
Ram Mankad, *Vice Pres*
Deval Nanavati, *Vice Pres*
Dianna Deguvnan, *Manager*
EMP: 110 **EST:** 1997
SQ FT: 1,500
SALES: 850K **Privately Held**
WEB: www.tradecomusa.com
SIC: 5047 X-ray machines & tubes; diagnostic equipment, medical

(P-7322)
TWIN MED LLC (PA)
11333 Greenstone Ave, Santa Fe Springs (90670-4618)
PHONE..............................323 582-9900
Fax: 323 588-3355
Kerry Weems, *CEO*
David Karner, *CFO*
Steve Rechnitz, *Chairman*
Carlos Gonzales, *Vice Pres*
Werner Nischt, *Vice Pres*
▲ **EMP:** 250
SQ FT: 3,000
SALES (est): 418.2MM **Privately Held**
WEB: www.twinmedinc.com
SIC: 5047 Medical equipment & supplies

(P-7323)
ULTRA SOLUTIONS LLC
1137 E Philadelphia St, Ontario (91761-5611)
PHONE..............................909 628-1778
Sterling Peloso, *CEO*
Tommy Ly, *Vice Pres*
Felix Hoang, *Engineer*
Karen Page, *Accountant*
Tess Trudo, *Controller*
▲ **EMP:** 50
SQ FT: 7,500
SALES (est): 33.5MM **Privately Held**
SIC: 5047 Diagnostic equipment, medical

(P-7324)
VARIAN MEDICAL SYSTEMS INC
660 N Mccarthy Blvd, Milpitas (95035-5113)
PHONE..............................408 321-9400
Fax: 408 321-4429
Viki Sparks, *Branch Mgr*
Claudine H MPH, *Program Mgr*
Keith Krugman, *MIS Mgr*
Richard Nusspickel, *Engineer*
Bob Burke, *Finance Mgr*
EMP: 200
SALES (corp-wide): 3.1B **Publicly Held**
WEB: www.varian.com
SIC: 5047 Medical & hospital equipment
PA: Varian Medical Systems, Inc.
3100 Hansen Way
Palo Alto CA 94304
650 493-4000

(P-7325)
VETERINARY SERVICE INC
935 Palmyrita Ave, Riverside (92507-1819)
PHONE..............................951 328-4900
Fax: 951 328-4971
Colin Anderson, *Branch Mgr*
EMP: 57
SALES (corp-wide): 180.1MM **Privately Held**
WEB: www.vsi.cc
SIC: 5047 5199 5083 Veterinarians' equipment & supplies; pet supplies; poultry equipment
PA: Veterinary Service, Inc.
4100 Bangs Ave
Modesto CA 95356
209 545-5100

(P-7326)
VIDENT
Also Called: Vita North America
22705 Savi Ranch Pkwy # 100, Yorba Linda (92887-4604)
PHONE..............................714 221-6700
Fax: 714 961-6299
Emanuel Rauter, *CEO*
Susie Molina, *Executive Asst*
Keith Le, *Asst Admin*
Lynda Anderegg, *Sales Associate*
Yesenia Martinez, *Marketing Staff*
▲ **EMP:** 70
SQ FT: 43,000
SALES (est): 27.1MM
SALES (corp-wide): 172.7MM **Privately Held**
WEB: www.vident.com
SIC: 5047 Dental equipment & supplies
HQ: Vita - Zahnfabrik H. Rauter Gesellschaft Mit Beschrankter Haftung & Co Kg
Spitalgasse 3
Bad Sackingen 79713
776 156-20

(P-7327)
VOCATIONAL IMPRV PROGRAM INC
Also Called: Vit
1310 Riverview Dr, San Bernardino (92408-2944)
PHONE..............................909 478-7537
EMP: 57
SALES (corp-wide): 10.4MM **Privately Held**
SIC: 5047 Hearing aids
PA: Vocational Improvement Program, Inc.
8675 Boston Pl
Rancho Cucamonga CA 91730
909 483-5924

5048 Ophthalmic Goods Wholesale

(P-7328)
ABB/CON-CISE OPTICAL GROUP LLC
Also Called: Primary Eyecare Network
1750 N Loop Rd Ste 150, Alameda (94502-8013)
PHONE..............................800 852-8089
EMP: 80
SALES (corp-wide): 1.3B **Privately Held**
SIC: 5048 5044
HQ: Abb/Con-Cise Optical Group Llc
12301 Nw 39th St
Coral Springs FL 33065
800 852-8089

(P-7329)
ABB/CON-CISE OPTICAL GROUP LLC
1750 N Loop Rd Ste 150, Alameda (94502-8013)
PHONE..............................800 852-8089
Angel Alvarez, *CEO*
EMP: 80
SALES (corp-wide): 114.2MM **Privately Held**
SIC: 5048 5049 Ophthalmic goods; optical goods
HQ: Abb/Con-Cise Optical Group Llc
12301 Nw 39th St
Coral Springs FL 33065
800 852-8089

(P-7330)
ATLANTIC OPTICAL CO INC
Also Called: Limited Editions
20801 Nordhoff St, Chatsworth (91311-5925)
P.O. Box 3519 (91313-3519)
PHONE..............................818 407-1890
Fax: 818 407-1895
Sheldon H Lehrer, *President*
Chett Lehrer, *Corp Secy*
Keith Lehrer, *Vice Pres*
Charles Shower, *Controller*
Janet Axelrad, *Sls & Mktg Exec*
▲ **EMP:** 80
SQ FT: 40,000
SALES (est): 18.1MM **Privately Held**
SIC: 5048 Frames, ophthalmic

(P-7331)
ESSILOR LABORATORIES AMER INC
Also Called: Bartley Optical
1300 W Optical Dr Ste 400, Irwindale (91702-3284)
PHONE..............................626 969-6181
Fax: 626 969-2179
Robert Babcock, *Manager*
EMP: 70
SALES (corp-wide): 88.1MM **Privately Held**
WEB: www.crizal.com
SIC: 5048 3851 Frames, ophthalmic; lenses, ophthalmic; ophthalmic goods
HQ: Essilor Laboratories Of America, Inc.
13515 N Stemmons Fwy
Dallas TX 75234
972 241-4141

(P-7332)
ITALEE OPTICS INC (PA)
Also Called: Lab Italee
2641 W Olympic Blvd, Los Angeles (90006-2810)
PHONE..............................213 385-8805
Jong Young Kim, *President*
Christopher C Song, *Vice Pres*
Yang Sook Kim, *Admin Sec*
Andy Choi, *Engineer*
▲ **EMP:** 115
SQ FT: 28,000
SALES (est): 25.2MM **Privately Held**
WEB: www.italee.com
SIC: 5048 Frames, ophthalmic

(P-7333)
MARCOLIN USA INC
Also Called: Viva International
6 Janet Way Apt 116, Belvedere Tiburon (94920-2164)
PHONE..............................415 383-6348
Fax: 415 485-0726
Harry Scheer, *Vice Pres*
EMP: 66 **Privately Held**
WEB: www.vivagroup.com
SIC: 5048 5099 Ophthalmic goods; sunglasses
HQ: Marcolin U.S.A., Inc.
3140 Us Highway 22
Branchburg NJ 08876
480 951-7174

(P-7334)
NEOSTYLE EYEWEAR CORPORATION
2651 La Mirada Dr Ste 150, Vista (92081-8435)
PHONE..............................760 305-4004
Fax: 760 296-2281
Helmuth Igel, *President*
Helga Igel, *Corp Secy*
EMP: 70
SQ FT: 17,000
SALES (est): 9.5MM **Privately Held**
WEB: www.neostyle.com
SIC: 5048 Frames, ophthalmic

(P-7335)
NIDEK INCORPORATED
47651 Westinghouse Dr, Fremont (94539-7474)
PHONE..............................510 226-5700
Fax: 510 226-5750
Motoki Ozawa, *CEO*
Hideo Ozawa, *Ch of Bd*
Jun Iwata, *COO*
Sheryl A Nicholls, *Chief Mktg Ofcr*
Kato Ken, *Vice Pres*
▲ **EMP:** 50
SQ FT: 18,700
SALES (est): 23.6MM
SALES (corp-wide): 336.1MM **Privately Held**
SIC: 5048 8011 3845 3841 Optometric equipment & supplies; offices & clinics of medical doctors; electromedical equipment; surgical & medical instruments; electrical equipment & supplies
PA: Nidek Co.,Ltd.
34-14, Maehama, Hiroishicho
Gamagoori AIC 443-0
533 676-611

▲ = Import ▼=Export
◆ =Import/Export

PRODUCTS & SERVICES SECTION

5051 - Metals Service Centers County (P-7356)

(P-7336)
OPTICS EAST INC (PA)
Also Called: Continental Sales Co America
180 Westgate Dr, Watsonville (95076-2469)
P.O. Box 50002 (95077-5002)
PHONE.................................831 763-6931
Francois Glon, *CEO*
Greg Kolmehcher, *Controller*
Maria Luna, *Cust Mgr*
▲ EMP: 130
SQ FT: 30,000
SALES (est): 88.1MM Privately Held
WEB: www.csclabs.com
SIC: **5048** 3851 Frames, ophthalmic; eyeglasses, lenses & frames

(P-7337)
REVOLUTION EYEWEAR INC
Also Called: Innovative Eyewear
997 Flower Glen St, Simi Valley (93065-1926)
P.O. Box 4649, Westlake Village (91359-1649)
PHONE.................................818 989-2020
Fax: 805 909-2900
Gary Martin Zelman, *President*
Jacqueline Zelman, *Exec VP*
Urania Perez, *Office Mgr*
Lisa Sporich, *Marketing Staff*
Patrick Morgigno, *Director*
▲ EMP: 50
SQ FT: 30,000
SALES (est): 12MM Privately Held
WEB: www.revolutioneyewear.com
SIC: **5048** Ophthalmic goods

5049 Professional Eqpt & Splys, NEC Wholesale

(P-7338)
ABC SCHOOL EQUIPMENT INC
Also Called: Platinum Visual Systems
1451 E 6th St, Corona (92879-1715)
PHONE.................................951 817-2200
Fax: 951 817-9900
Gary P Stell Jr, *CEO*
Thomas Mendez, *CFO*
Demiris Reid, *Project Mgr*
Tom Mendez, *Controller*
Raymond Brown, *Purchasing*
EMP: 70
SQ FT: 35,000
SALES (est): 36.7MM Privately Held
WEB: www.abcschoolequipment.com
SIC: **5049** 3861 2531 School supplies; photographic equipment & supplies; public building & related furniture

(P-7339)
BIO-RAD LABORATORIES INC
Bio-RAD U S S D
2000 Alfred Nobel Dr, Hercules (94547-1804)
PHONE.................................510 741-1000
Norman Schwartz, *President*
Russell Frost, *Research*
Cindy Han, *Research*
Xin Heng, *Engineer*
Howard Matt, *Corp Comm Staff*
EMP: 125
SQ FT: 95,850
SALES (corp-wide): 2B Publicly Held
WEB: www.bio-rad.com
SIC: **5049** Scientific & engineering equipment & supplies
PA: Bio-Rad Laboratories, Inc.
1000 Alfred Nobel Dr
Hercules CA 94547
510 724-7000

(P-7340)
CPI INTERNATIONAL (PA)
5580 Skylane Blvd, Santa Rosa (95403-1030)
PHONE.................................707 525-5788
Fax: 707 545-7901
Jarrett L Wendt, *President*
Christopher Woodruff, *Vice Pres*
Willem Govaert, *General Mgr*
Robin Huff, *Finance*
Jeff Wilber, *Controller*
▲ EMP: 50
SQ FT: 20,000
SALES (est): 25.7MM Privately Held
WEB: www.colitag.com
SIC: **5049** 3826 Analytical instruments; analytical instruments

(P-7341)
FACTORY R D
23192 Verdugo Dr, Laguna Hills (92653-1377)
PHONE.................................949 900-3460
Tom Swanecamp, *Owner*
EMP: 60
SALES (est): 6.7MM Privately Held
SIC: **5049** Engineers' equipment & supplies

(P-7342)
FISHER SCIENTIFIC COMPANY LLC
6722 Bickmore Ave, Chino (91708-9101)
PHONE.................................909 393-2100
John Pouk, *Vice Pres*
Cliff Waits, *Vice Pres*
Renard Hoffman, *Opers Mgr*
EMP: 100
SALES (corp-wide): 16.9B Publicly Held
WEB: www.fishersci.com
SIC: **5049** Laboratory equipment, except medical or dental
HQ: Fisher Scientific Company Llc
300 Industry Dr
Pittsburgh PA 15275
412 490-8300

(P-7343)
INTERLAB INC
636 Broadway Ste 322, San Diego (92101-5410)
PHONE.................................619 302-3095
Alexander Vedemin, *President*
Boris Urslts, *Admin Sec*
▼ EMP: 50
SALES: 20MM Privately Held
SIC: **5049** Laboratory equipment, except medical or dental

(P-7344)
LUCKY STRIKE ENTERTAINMENT LLC
6801 Hollywood Blvd # 143, Los Angeles (90028-6138)
PHONE.................................818 933-3752
David Bradley, *General Mgr*
EMP: 87
SALES (corp-wide): 241.6MM Privately Held
SIC: **5049** Optical goods
HQ: Lucky Strike Entertainment, Llc
15260 Ventura Blvd # 1110
Sherman Oaks CA 91403
323 467-7776

(P-7345)
MOLECULAR BIOPRODUCTS INC
2200 S Mcdowell Blvd Ext, Petaluma (94954-5659)
PHONE.................................707 762-6689
Warner Johnson, *Director*
Debbie Reed, *Administration*
Paul Akin, *IT/INT Sup*
Carl Streebel, *Engineer*
Lee Tintle, *Human Res Dir*
EMP: 220
SALES (corp-wide): 16.9B Publicly Held
WEB: www.mbpinc.com
SIC: **5049** Scientific recording equipment
HQ: Molecular Bioproducts, Inc.
9389 Waples St
San Diego CA 92121
858 453-7551

(P-7346)
PHILIPS & LITE-ON DIGITAL (DH)
Also Called: P L D S
42000 Christy St, Fremont (94538-3182)
PHONE.................................510 824-9690
Harlie Pseng, *President*
Charlie Pseng, *President*
Armando Abella, *CFO*
Margo Gerber, *Executive Asst*
Walker Su, *Admin Sec*
▲ EMP: 50
SQ FT: 17,088
SALES: 35MM
SALES (corp-wide): 26B Privately Held
WEB: www.liteonit.com
SIC: **5049** Optical goods
HQ: Philips & Lite-On Digital Solutions Corporation
16f, 392, Ruey Kuang Rd.,
Taipei City TAP
287 982-886

(P-7347)
R C I ENTERPRISES INC
Also Called: R C I Image Systems
3848 Del Amo Blvd Ste 301, Torrance (90503-7711)
PHONE.................................310 370-5900
Richard Corrales, *President*
Lynda Deibner, *Corp Secy*
Lyla Corrales, *Vice Pres*
Vickie Corrales, *Sales Mgr*
EMP: 50
SQ FT: 12,000
SALES (est): 8.6MM Privately Held
SIC: **5049** 7389 Optical goods; microfilm recording & developing service

(P-7348)
REM OPTICAL COMPANY INC
Also Called: REM Eye Wear
10941 La Tuna Canyon Rd, Sun Valley (91352-2012)
PHONE.................................818 504-3950
Michael L Hundert, *CEO*
Steve Horowitz, *President*
Donna Gindy, *COO*
Charlie Khoury, *COO*
Gerry Hundert, *Chairman*
▲ EMP: 100 EST: 1977
SQ FT: 42,000
SALES (est): 67.8MM Privately Held
WEB: www.remeyewear.com
SIC: **5049** Optical goods

(P-7349)
SOCIAL STUDIES SCHOOL SERVICE
Also Called: Writing Company
10200 Jefferson Blvd, Culver City (90232-3524)
P.O. Box 802 (90232-0802)
PHONE.................................310 839-2436
Fax: 310 839-2249
David M Weigner, *CEO*
Irwin Ledin, *President*
Sanford Weiner, *President*
Aaron Willis, *Marketing Mgr*
Jan Meldola, *Accounts Mgr*
▲ EMP: 65 EST: 1967
SALES (est): 31.9MM Privately Held
WEB: www.socialstudies.com
SIC: **5049** School supplies

(P-7350)
THERMO FISHER SCIENTIFIC
Also Called: Thermofinnegan
355 River Oaks Pkwy, San Jose (95134-1908)
P.O. Box 49031 (95161-9031)
PHONE.................................408 894-9835
Ian Jardin, *Branch Mgr*
King Poon, *President*
Kenneth Apicerno, *Vice Pres*
Ian Mylchreest, *Vice Pres*
James Hurst, *Executive Asst*
EMP: 400
SALES (corp-wide): 16.9B Publicly Held
WEB: www.thermo.com
SIC: **5049** Scientific recording equipment
HQ: Thermo Fisher Scientific (Ashville) Llc
28 Schenck Pkwy Ste 400
Asheville NC 28803
828 658-2711

(P-7351)
THERMO FISHER SCIENTIFIC INC
200 Oyster Point Blvd, South San Francisco (94080-1911)
PHONE.................................650 876-1949
Ernest Hardy, *Manager*
EMP: 54
SALES (corp-wide): 16.9B Publicly Held
SIC: **5049** Scientific & engineering equipment & supplies
PA: Thermo Fisher Scientific Inc.
168 3rd Ave
Waltham MA 02451
781 622-1000

(P-7352)
VWR INTERNATIONAL LLC
Also Called: VWR Scientific
6609 Mount Whitney Dr, Buena Park (90620-4237)
PHONE.................................714 220-2615
Jenny Nelson, *Branch Mgr*
Valerie Simonsen, *Marketing Staff*
EMP: 50
SALES (corp-wide): 4.3B Publicly Held
WEB: www.vwrsp.com
SIC: **5049** 5169 Laboratory equipment, except medical or dental; chemicals & allied products
HQ: Vwr International, Llc
100 Matsonford Rd Bldg 1
Radnor PA 19087
610 386-1700

5051 Metals Service Centers

(P-7353)
ACME METALS & STEEL SUPPLY INC
14930 S San Pedro St, Gardena (90248-2036)
PHONE.................................310 329-2263
Fax: 310 329-4429
Jack Golden, *CEO*
Millee Goldberg, *Corp Secy*
Alice Melamed, *Credit Mgr*
Rosie Thomas, *Credit Mgr*
Miguel Valadez, *Purch Mgr*
▲ EMP: 60
SQ FT: 265,000
SALES (est): 93.6MM Privately Held
SIC: **5051** Steel

(P-7354)
ALPERT & ALPERT IRON & MET INC
2350 W 16th St, Long Beach (90813-1044)
PHONE.................................562 624-8833
George Soto, *Branch Mgr*
EMP: 50
SALES (corp-wide): 59.9MM Privately Held
SIC: **5051** Iron & steel (ferrous) products; miscellaneous nonferrous products
PA: Alpert & Alpert Iron & Metal, Inc.
1815 S Soto St
Los Angeles CA 90023
323 265-4040

(P-7355)
AM PRODUCTS INC
1661 Palm St, Santa Ana (92701-5189)
PHONE.................................714 662-4454
Tim Van Mechelen, *President*
Case Van Mechelen, *CEO*
EMP: 50
SALES (est): 6.6MM Privately Held
WEB: www.amproducts.net
SIC: **5051** 5072 Sheets, metal; structural shapes, iron or steel; power tools & accessories

(P-7356)
AMERICAN METALS CORPORATION (HQ)
1499 Parkway Blvd, West Sacramento (95691-5019)
P.O. Box 980100 (95798-0100)
PHONE.................................916 371-7700
Fax: 916 371-2827
Nicole Heater, *CEO*
Dan Nethaway, *General Mgr*
Paula Cooley, *Credit Staff*
John Walls, *Safety Mgr*
John Lindsay, *Warehouse Mgr*
▲ EMP: 105
SALES (est): 122.1MM
SALES (corp-wide): 9.3B Publicly Held
WEB: www.rsac.com
SIC: **5051** Iron or steel flat products; castings, rough: iron or steel; steel; aluminum bars, rods, ingots, sheets, pipes, plates, etc.

5051 - Metals Service Centers County (P-7357) **PRODUCTS & SERVICES SECTION**

PA: Reliance Steel & Aluminum Co.
350 S Grand Ave Ste 5100
Los Angeles CA 90071
213 687-7700

(P-7357)
AOC TECHNOLOGIES INC
5960 Inglewood Dr, Pleasanton (94588-8515)
PHONE.................................925 875-0808
Fax: 925 875-0878
Gordon Gu, *President*
Hanna Rasen, *Accounting Mgr*
▲ EMP: 315
SALES (est): 113.1MM **Privately Held**
WEB: www.aoctech.com
SIC: **5051** 3357 Metal wires, ties, cables & screening; fiber optic cable (insulated)

(P-7358)
ARCHITECTURAL GL & ALUM CO INC (PA)
6400 Brisa St, Livermore (94550-2516)
PHONE.................................925 583-2460
Joseph Brescia, *CEO*
John Buckley, *President*
Mark Tofflemire, *President*
John Okubo, *CFO*
William Coll Jr, *Vice Pres*
▲ EMP: 155 EST: 1970
SQ FT: 33,000
SALES (est): 147.4MM **Privately Held**
SIC: **5051** 1793 1791 3442 Aluminum bars, rods, ingots, sheets, pipes, plates, etc.; glass & glazing work; exterior wall system installation; sash, door or window: metal

(P-7359)
B & B SURPLUS INC (PA)
Also Called: B & B Specialty Metals
7020 Rosedale Hwy, Bakersfield (93308-5842)
PHONE.................................661 589-0381
Fax: 661 589-5508
Donice Boylan, *President*
Michael Georgino, *Vice Pres*
Mike Georgino, *Vice Pres*
John Mahan, *Executive*
Bill Scrivner, *Sales Dir*
▲ EMP: 65
SQ FT: 20,000
SALES (est): 72.6MM **Privately Held**
SIC: **5051** Pipe & tubing, steel; steel

(P-7360)
BAKERSFIELD PIPE AND SUP INC (PA)
Also Called: Imperial Pipe & Supply
3301 Zachary Ave, Shafter (93263-9424)
P.O. Box 639, Bakersfield (93302-0639)
PHONE.................................661 589-9141
Fax: 661 589-3739
D Daniel Byrum, *CEO*
Dan Byrum, *President*
Cary Evans, *CFO*
Ted Armenta, *Exec VP*
Kevin Hashim, *Vice Pres*
◆ EMP: 60
SQ FT: 20,000
SALES (est): 187.8MM **Privately Held**
SIC: **5051** 5085 Pipe & tubing, steel; valves & fittings

(P-7361)
BOBCO METALS LLC
Also Called: Sion & Shamoneil Fmly Partner
2000 S Alameda St, Vernon (90058-1016)
PHONE.................................213 748-5171
Fax: 213 748-7869
Sion Shooshani, *Mng Member*
Fred Shooshani, *Human Res Mgr*
Mavic Templo, *Human Res Mgr*
Oscar Arroyo, *Marketing Staff*
Farid Shooshani,
▲ EMP: 50
SQ FT: 100,000
SALES (est): 38.5MM **Privately Held**
WEB: www.bobcometal.com
SIC: **5051** 5251 5072 Aluminum bars, rods, ingots, sheets, pipes, plates, etc.; steel; copper; hardware; hardware

(P-7362)
BORRMANN METAL CENTER (PA)
110 W Olive Ave, Burbank (91502-1822)
PHONE.................................818 846-7171
Fax: 818 846-9347
Robert Wedeen, *President*
Bob Persson, *President*
Jane Borrmann, *CEO*
William L Todd, *Corp Secy*
Michelle Pitini, *Office Mgr*
▲ EMP: 60 EST: 1946
SQ FT: 75,000
SALES (est): 43MM **Privately Held**
WEB: www.borrmannmetalcenter.com
SIC: **5051** Metals service centers & offices; steel; aluminum bars, rods, ingots, sheets, pipes, plates, etc.

(P-7363)
CALPIPE INDUSTRIES INC
Also Called: Calbond
19440 S Dminguez Hills Dr, Rancho Dominguez (90220-6417)
PHONE.................................562 803-4388
Daniel J Markus, *CEO*
Fred Arjani, *CFO*
Sheri Caine-Markus, *Admin Sec*
Esmeralda Delgadillo, *Manager*
▲ EMP: 75
SQ FT: 60,000
SALES (est): 60MM **Privately Held**
SIC: **5051** 3498 Metals service centers & offices; fabricated pipe & fittings; tube fabricating (contract bending & shaping)

(P-7364)
CLEMENT SUPPORT SERVICES INC
1001 Yosemite Dr, Milpitas (95035-5409)
PHONE.................................408 227-1171
Fax: 408 227-1178
Anthony Clement, *CEO*
John White, *CFO*
Michelle Clement, *Vice Pres*
Mike Golini, *Vice Pres*
Vince Onken, *Finance*
EMP: 54
SQ FT: 36,000
SALES (est): 45.3MM **Privately Held**
WEB: www.clementsupport.com
SIC: **5051** Nonferrous metal sheets, bars, rods, etc.

(P-7365)
COAST ALUM & ARCHITECTURAL INC (PA)
10628 Fulton Wells Ave, Santa Fe Springs (90670-3740)
P.O. Box 2144 (90670-0440)
PHONE.................................562 946-6061
Fax: 562 946-4188
Thomas C Clark, *President*
Bonnie Clark, *Shareholder*
Julio Marrero, *COO*
Adrienne McPherson, *Technical Staff*
Russell Bowman, *Controller*
▲ EMP: 125
SQ FT: 112,000
SALES (est): 186.6MM **Privately Held**
SIC: **5051** Miscellaneous nonferrous products; nonferrous metal sheets, bars, rods, etc.

(P-7366)
DIX METALS INC
14801 Able Ln Ste 101, Huntington Beach (92647-2059)
PHONE.................................714 677-0777
Fax: 714 677-0800
Donald Carr, *Vice Pres*
Bob Dix Jr, *Executive*
Lorraine Michels, *Admin Mgr*
Jon-David Nutter, *General Mgr*
Heather Shaw, *Accountant*
▲ EMP: 59
SQ FT: 111,000
SALES (est): 32.4MM **Privately Held**
WEB: www.dixmetals.com
SIC: **5051** Ferrous metals; metal sheets, bars, rods, etc.

(P-7367)
DOUGLAS STEEL SUPPLY INC (PA)
Also Called: Douglas Steel Supply Co.
5764 Alcoa Ave, Vernon (90058-3727)
PHONE.................................323 587-7676
Fax: 323 587-2982
Douglas Stein, *CEO*
Donal Hecht, *Vice Pres*
Sharon L Baker, *Executive*
Donald Miller, *Executive*
Stephen Norwick, *Info Tech Mgr*
▲ EMP: 80
SQ FT: 100,000
SALES (est): 45MM **Privately Held**
WEB: www.douglassteelsupply.com
SIC: **5051** Steel; sheets, metal

(P-7368)
EARLE M JORGENSEN COMPANY
Also Called: EMJ Hayward
31100 Wiegman Rd, Hayward (94544-7850)
PHONE.................................510 487-2700
Barbara Nemeth, *Branch Mgr*
▲ EMP: 54
SQ FT: 91,982
SALES (corp-wide): 9.3B **Publicly Held**
WEB: www.emjmetals.com
SIC: **5051** Steel
HQ: Earle M. Jorgensen Company
10650 Alameda St
Lynwood CA 90262
323 567-1122

(P-7369)
EARLE M JORGENSEN COMPANY
350 S Grand Ave Ste 5100, Los Angeles (90071-3421)
PHONE.................................323 567-1122
Janice Day, *Manager*
E G Leon Jr, *CFO*
Steve Haupt, *Manager*
Steve Munro, *Manager*
▲ EMP: 54
SALES (corp-wide): 9.3B **Publicly Held**
SIC: **5051** Metals service centers & offices
HQ: Earle M. Jorgensen Company
10650 Alameda St
Lynwood CA 90262
323 567-1122

(P-7370)
FALLON LAND COMPANY INC
Also Called: Southland Steel
4 Corporate Plaza Dr # 210, Newport Beach (92660-7906)
P.O. Box 1755 (92659-0755)
PHONE.................................213 880-1279
Robert Fallon, *President*
▲ EMP: 50
SQ FT: 48,000
SALES (est): 9.9MM **Privately Held**
SIC: **5051** Metals service centers & offices

(P-7371)
FOUNDATION BUILDING MTLS LLC
Also Called: Great Western Building Mtls
1975 3rd St, Riverside (92507-3474)
PHONE.................................951 300-2650
Joe George, *Manager*
▲ EMP: 50
SALES (corp-wide): 149.7MM **Privately Held**
WEB: www.obmsales.com
SIC: **5051** Steel
PA: Foundation Building Materials, Llc
2552 Walnut Ave Ste 160
Tustin CA 92780
714 380-3127

(P-7372)
GEORGE FISCHER LLC (DH)
Also Called: Georg Fischer Piping
9271 Jeronimo Rd, Irvine (92618-1906)
PHONE.................................714 731-8800
Fax: 714 731-4688
James Jackson,
Yves Studer, *COO*
Oshaben Daniel, *Exec VP*
Paul Galvin, *Vice Pres*
Keith Jansen, *Vice Pres*
▲ EMP: 70
SQ FT: 55,000
SALES (est): 100MM
SALES (corp-wide): 3.6B **Privately Held**
WEB: www.us.piping.georgefischer.com
SIC: **5051** 5085 Pipe & tubing, steel; valves & fittings
HQ: George Fischer, Inc.
3401 Aero Jet Ave
El Monte CA 91731
626 571-2770

(P-7373)
HADCO METAL TRADING CO LLC
14088 Borate St, Santa Fe Springs (90670-5335)
PHONE.................................562 404-4040
EMP: 59
SALES (corp-wide): 370.4MM **Privately Held**
SIC: **5051** Aluminum bars, rods, ingots, sheets, pipes, plates, etc.
HQ: Hadco Metal Trading Co., Llc
555 State Rd
Bensalem PA 19020
215 695-2705

(P-7374)
HARTMAN INDUSTRIES
Also Called: Commercial Casting Co
14933 Whittram Ave, Fontana (92335-3186)
PHONE.................................909 428-0114
Fax: 909 428-0157
Brad J Hartman, *CEO*
Brett Hartman, *Vice Pres*
Sean Hartman, *Vice Pres*
Jennifer Munoz, *Office Mgr*
▲ EMP: 20
SQ FT: 73,000
SALES (est): 8MM **Privately Held**
WEB: www.cmeworkholding.com
SIC: **5051** Castings, rough: iron or steel

(P-7375)
HUBBARD IRON DOORS INC
7407 Telegraph Rd, Montebello (90640-6515)
PHONE.................................323 724-6500
Fax: 323 721-8100
Ron Hubbard, *President*
Carlos Gordon, *Executive*
EMP: 50
SQ FT: 20,000
SALES (est): 12MM **Privately Held**
WEB: www.hubbardirondoors.com
SIC: **5051** Iron or steel semifinished products

(P-7376)
JFE SHOJI TRADE AMERICA INC (DH)
301 E Ocean Blvd Ste 1750, Long Beach (90802-4879)
PHONE.................................562 637-3500
Itsuji Araki, *President*
Hitoshi Ino, *Treasurer*
Brion Talley, *Senior VP*
Eric Stone, *Manager*
◆ EMP: 85
SQ FT: 7,500
SALES (est): 243.5MM
SALES (corp-wide): 29.3B **Privately Held**
SIC: **5051** Steel
HQ: Jfe Shoji Trade Corporation
1-9-5, Otemachi
Chiyoda-Ku TKY 100-0
352 035-055

(P-7377)
JIMS SUPPLY CO INC (PA)
3530 Buck Owens Blvd, Bakersfield (93308-4920)
P.O. Box 668 (93302-0668)
PHONE.................................661 324-6514
Fax: 661 324-6566
Doreen M Boylan, *CEO*
Bryan Boylan, *President*
Jennifer Drake, *Corp Secy*
Greg Boylan, *Vice Pres*
Jennice Boylan, *Vice Pres*
▲ EMP: 82
SQ FT: 25,300

PRODUCTS & SERVICES SECTION

5051 - Metals Service Centers County (P-7396)

SALES (est): 80.8MM **Privately Held**
WEB: www.jimssupply.com
SIC: 5051 Steel

(P-7378)
JOSEPH T RYERSON & SON INC
4310 Bandini Blvd, Vernon (90058-4308)
P.O. Box 513817, Los Angeles (90051-1817)
PHONE...................................323 267-6000
Fax: 323 266-3311
Steve Bosway, *Branch Mgr*
Edward J Lehner, *CEO*
Mark Silver, *Admin Sec*
Kurt Balder, *Clerk*
EMP: 80
SALES (corp-wide): 3.1B **Publicly Held**
SIC: 5051 5162 5085 Aluminum bars, rods, ingots, sheets, pipes, plates, etc.; iron & steel (ferrous) products; plastics materials & basic shapes; industrial supplies
HQ: Joseph T. Ryerson & Son, Inc.
227 W Monroe St Fl 27
Chicago IL 60606
312 292-5000

(P-7379)
KELLY PIPE CO LLC (DH)
Also Called: Line Pipe International
11680 Bloomfield Ave, Santa Fe Springs (90670-4608)
P.O. Box 2827 (90670-0827)
PHONE...................................562 868-0456
Fax: 562 863-4695
Eddy Ogawa, *Chairman*
Leonard Gross, *CEO*
Steve Livingston, *CEO*
Leo Mann, *CFO*
Hideki Matsumoto, *CFO*
◆ EMP: 85
SQ FT: 40,000
SALES (est): 242.9MM
SALES (corp-wide): 29.3B **Privately Held**
SIC: 5051 Pipe & tubing, steel
HQ: Shoji Jfe Trade America Inc
301 E Ocean Blvd Ste 1750
Long Beach CA 90802
562 637-3500

(P-7380)
KLOECKNER METALS CORPORATION
Also Called: Gary Steel Division
9804 Norwalk Blvd Ste 8, Santa Fe Springs (90670-2936)
PHONE...................................562 906-2020
Fax: 562 906-2006
Bob Tripp, *Branch Mgr*
Said Armanious, *Sales Mgr*
EMP: 75
SALES (corp-wide): 6.9B **Privately Held**
SIC: 5051 Steel
HQ: Kloeckner Metals Corporation
500 Colonial Center Pkwy # 500
Roswell GA 30076
678 259-8800

(P-7381)
KLOECKNER METALS CORPORATION
9804 Norwalk Blvd, Santa Fe Springs (90670-2936)
PHONE...................................562 906-2020
Marshall Katz, *General Mgr*
EMP: 50
SALES (corp-wide): 6.9B **Privately Held**
WEB: www.macsteelusa.com
SIC: 5051 Steel
HQ: Kloeckner Metals Corporation
500 Colonial Center Pkwy # 500
Roswell GA 30076
678 259-8800

(P-7382)
KLOECKNER METALS CORPORATION
2000 S O St, Tulare (93274-6852)
PHONE...................................559 688-7980
Bob Kyle, *Branch Mgr*
EMP: 52
SALES (corp-wide): 6.9B **Privately Held**
SIC: 5051 Iron & steel (ferrous) products
HQ: Kloeckner Metals Corporation
500 Colonial Center Pkwy # 500
Roswell GA 30076
678 259-8800

(P-7383)
MAXX METALS INC
355 Quarry Rd, San Carlos (94070-6217)
P.O. Box 10963, Pleasanton (94588-0963)
PHONE...................................650 654-1500
Paul A Wallace, *President*
Debra L Wallace, *CFO*
Scott Shaw, *Manager*
EMP: 68
SQ FT: 13,000
SALES (est): 3.6MM **Privately Held**
SIC: 5051 Metals service centers & offices

(P-7384)
MITSUI & CO (USA) INC
Also Called: Mitsui USA
601 S Figueroa St # 2650, Los Angeles (90017-5704)
PHONE...................................213 896-1100
Shozaburo Marayama, *Manager*
EMP: 52
SALES (corp-wide): 40.6B **Privately Held**
WEB: www.mitsui.com
SIC: 5051 5094 Iron & steel (ferrous) products; bullion, precious metals
HQ: Mitsui & Co. (U.S.A.), Inc.
200 Park Ave Fl 35
New York NY 10166
212 878-4000

(P-7385)
MWS PRECISION WIRE INDS INC
Also Called: Mws Wire Industries
31200 Cedar Valley Dr, Westlake Village (91362-4035)
PHONE...................................818 991-8553
Toll Free:..............................888 -
Fax: 818 706-0911
Darrell H Friedman, *President*
Alan Friedman, *President*
Lois J Friedman, *Admin Sec*
Teresa Rodorgoze, *Administration*
Tomm Carlson, *Info Tech Mgr*
EMP: 52
SQ FT: 32,000
SALES (est): 48.1MM **Privately Held**
WEB: www.mwswire.com
SIC: 5051 3351 3357 Copper sheets, plates, bars, rods, pipes, etc.; wire, copper & copper alloy; nonferrous wiredrawing & insulating

(P-7386)
NORMAN INDUSTRIAL MTLS INC (PA)
Also Called: Industrial Metal Supply Co
8300 San Fernando Rd, Sun Valley (91352-3222)
PHONE...................................818 729-3333
Fax: 818 729-3381
Eric Steinhauer, *CEO*
David Pace, *COO*
Cleve Adams, *CFO*
David Berkey, *CFO*
Aaron Brown, *General Mgr*
◆ EMP: 125
SQ FT: 70,000
SALES (est): 179.1MM **Privately Held**
WEB: www.industrialmetalsupply.com
SIC: 5051 3441 3449 Metals service centers & offices; fabricated structural metal; miscellaneous metalwork

(P-7387)
NORMAN INDUSTRIAL MTLS INC
Also Called: Industrial Metal Supply Co Eba
7550 Ronson Rd, San Diego (92111-1500)
PHONE...................................858 277-8200
Fax: 858 277-3865
Wesley Sykes, *Manager*
Melissa Dasilva, *Technology*
Damon Bonaccorso, *Safety Mgr*
Megan Humpal, *Mktg Dir*
EMP: 50
SALES (corp-wide): 179.1MM **Privately Held**
WEB: www.industrialmetalsupply.com
SIC: 5051 5211 Metals service centers & offices; lumber & other building materials
HQ: Kloeckner Metals Corporation
500 Colonial Center Pkwy # 500
Roswell GA 30076
678 259-8800
PA: Norman Industrial Materials, Inc.
8300 San Fernando Rd
Sun Valley CA 91352
818 729-3333

(P-7388)
PDM STEEL SERVICE CENTERS
3500 Bassett St, Santa Clara (95054-2704)
P.O. Box 329 (95052-0329)
PHONE...................................408 988-3000
Fax: 408 988-6966
John Norman, *General Mgr*
Debbie Lamica, *Purchasing*
Mike Murrill, *Purch Agent*
Jesse Farrer, *Marketing Staff*
EMP: 65
SQ FT: 46,080
SALES (corp-wide): 9.3B **Publicly Held**
WEB: www.pdmsteel.com
SIC: 5051 3444 3272 Steel; sheet metalwork; concrete products
HQ: Pdm Steel Service Centers, Inc
3535 E Myrtle St
Stockton CA 95205
209 943-0555

(P-7389)
PDM STEEL SERVICE CENTERS
4005 E Church Ave, Fresno (93725-1415)
P.O. Box 11188 (93772-1188)
PHONE...................................559 442-1410
Fax: 559 442-1409
Mike Hill, *Branch Mgr*
Sharon Flores, *Personnel Exec*
Debbie Lamica, *Purchasing*
Gene Grayson, *Opers Mgr*
Kevin Stiles, *Opers Mgr*
EMP: 50
SALES (corp-wide): 9.3B **Publicly Held**
WEB: www.pdmsteel.com
SIC: 5051 Steel
HQ: Pdm Steel Service Centers, Inc
3535 E Myrtle St
Stockton CA 95205
209 943-0555

(P-7390)
PDM STEEL SERVICE CENTERS (HQ)
Also Called: Specialty Steel Service
3535 E Myrtle St, Stockton (95205-4721)
P.O. Box 310 (95201-0310)
PHONE...................................209 943-0555
Derick Halecky, *President*
Joseph Anderson, *Vice Pres*
Brad Blickle, *Vice Pres*
Randy H Kearns, *Vice Pres*
William Nixon, *Vice Pres*
▲ EMP: 100 EST: 1954
SALES (est): 257.6MM
SALES (corp-wide): 9.3B **Publicly Held**
WEB: www.pdmsteel.com
SIC: 5051 Steel
PA: Reliance Steel & Aluminum Co.
350 S Grand Ave Ste 5100
Los Angeles CA 90071
213 687-7700

(P-7391)
PDM STEEL SERVICE CENTERS
Also Called: Feralloy PDM Steel Service
936 Performance Dr, Stockton (95206-4930)
PHONE...................................209 234-0548
Fax: 209 234-0549
Frances Espinosa, *Branch Mgr*
Sean Mollins, *General Mgr*
Denise Dew, *Finance*
Mark Dehl, *VP Sales*
EMP: 60
SALES (corp-wide): 9.3B **Publicly Held**
WEB: www.feralloy.com
SIC: 5051 Steel
HQ: Pdm Steel Service Centers, Inc
3535 E Myrtle St
Stockton CA 95205
209 943-0555

(P-7392)
PHILLIPS STEEL COMPANY
1368 W Anaheim St, Long Beach (90813-2779)
PHONE...................................562 435-7571
Fax: 562 437-1072
Daryl S Phillips, *President*
Greg Phillips, *Vice Pres*
Paul Phillips, *Principal*
Sandy Phillips, *Principal*
Todd Phillips, *Principal*
▲ EMP: 50
SQ FT: 25,000
SALES (est): 67.7MM **Privately Held**
WEB: www.phillipssteel.com
SIC: 5051 Steel; aluminum bars, rods, ingots, sheets, pipes, plates, etc.; copper

(P-7393)
RELIANCE STEEL & ALUMINUM CO (PA)
350 S Grand Ave Ste 5100, Los Angeles (90071-3421)
PHONE...................................213 687-7700
Fax: 213 687-8792
Gregg J Mollins, *President*
David H Hannah, *Ch of Bd*
James D Hoffman, *COO*
Karla R Lewis, *CFO*
Richard Slater, *Bd of Directors*
◆ EMP: 82 EST: 1939
SALES: 9.3B **Publicly Held**
WEB: www.rsac.com
SIC: 5051 Metals service centers & offices; structural shapes, iron or steel; steel; sheets, metal

(P-7394)
RELIANCE STEEL & ALUMINUM CO
Reliance Metal Center
33201 Western Ave, Union City (94587-2208)
PHONE...................................510 476-4400
Fax: 510 476-4444
Dave Buchanan, *Manager*
Mike Page, *Manager*
EMP: 90
SQ FT: 137,757
SALES (corp-wide): 9.3B **Publicly Held**
WEB: www.rsac.com
SIC: 5051 Metals service centers & offices; aluminum bars, rods, ingots, sheets, pipes, plates, etc.; bars, metal; copper
PA: Reliance Steel & Aluminum Co.
350 S Grand Ave Ste 5100
Los Angeles CA 90071
213 687-7700

(P-7395)
RELIANCE STEEL & ALUMINUM CO
Tube Service
9351 Norwalk Blvd, Santa Fe Springs (90670-2925)
P.O. Box 2728 (90670-0728)
PHONE...................................562 695-0467
Fax: 562 695-4027
Jan Hollar, *Branch Mgr*
Karen Hansen, *Purch Mgr*
Dan Hollar, *Purch Mgr*
John Rede, *Purch Mgr*
John Southward, *Safety Mgr*
EMP: 58
SQ FT: 40,000
SALES (corp-wide): 9.3B **Publicly Held**
WEB: www.rsac.com
SIC: 5051 Metals service centers & offices
PA: Reliance Steel & Aluminum Co.
350 S Grand Ave Ste 5100
Los Angeles CA 90071
213 687-7700

(P-7396)
RELIANCE STEEL & ALUMINUM CO
Bralco Metals
15090 Northam St, La Mirada (90638-5757)
PHONE...................................714 736-4800
Fax: 714 736-4840
Michael Hubbart, *Branch Mgr*
Jo A Hudson, *Office Mgr*
Mayra Guzman, *Credit Staff*
Jesse Gonzalez, *Opers Mgr*
Jim Elmore, *Director*
EMP: 118
SALES (corp-wide): 9.3B **Publicly Held**
WEB: www.rsac.com
SIC: 5051 Metals service centers & offices; ferrous metals

5051 - Metals Service Centers

PA: Reliance Steel & Aluminum Co.
350 S Grand Ave Ste 5100
Los Angeles CA 90071
213 687-7700

(P-7397)
RELIANCE STEEL & ALUMINUM CO
Also Called: Reliance Steel Company
2537 E 27th St, Vernon (90058-1284)
PHONE................323 583-6111
Fax: 323 581-1254
John Becknell, *Branch Mgr*
Wendy Iorg, *Manager*
Glen Ortiz, *Manager*
EMP: 200
SALES (corp-wide): 9.3B **Publicly Held**
WEB: www.rsac.com
SIC: 5051 Metals service centers & offices
PA: Reliance Steel & Aluminum Co.
350 S Grand Ave Ste 5100
Los Angeles CA 90071
213 687-7700

(P-7398)
RELIANCE STEEL & ALUMINUM CO
Metalcenter
12034 Greenstone Ave, Santa Fe Springs (90670-4727)
P.O. Box 2101 (90670-0013)
PHONE................562 777-9672
Fax: 562 944-1346
Robert Thommen, *Branch Mgr*
Al Cawley, *Opers Mgr*
Robert Tommen, *Manager*
EMP: 80
SQ FT: 135,711
SALES (corp-wide): 9.3B **Publicly Held**
WEB: www.rsac.com
SIC: 5051 Metals service centers & offices
PA: Reliance Steel & Aluminum Co.
350 S Grand Ave Ste 5100
Los Angeles CA 90071
213 687-7700

(P-7399)
ROLLED STEEL PRODUCTS CORP (PA)
Also Called: R S P
2187 Garfield Ave, Commerce (90040-1855)
PHONE................323 723-8836
Robert Alperson, *Ch of Bd*
Steven Alperson, *President*
Lonnie Alperson, *CFO*
Dennis Moslenko, *MIS Dir*
Nellie Romanu, *Controller*
EMP: 68
SQ FT: 125,000
SALES (est): 40.9MM **Privately Held**
WEB: www.rolledsteel.com
SIC: 5051 3316 Steel; cold finishing of steel shapes

(P-7400)
SAC INTERNATIONAL STEEL INC (PA)
6130 Avalon Blvd, Los Angeles (90003-1633)
PHONE................323 232-2467
Shaukat A Chohan, *President*
Shaukaj Ali Chohan, *President*
Omar Chohan, *Vice Pres*
Jessica Rodriguez, *Executive Asst*
Mahmooda Chohan, *Admin Sec*
▲ **EMP:** 74
SQ FT: 100,000
SALES (est): 18.5MM **Privately Held**
WEB: www.sacintl.com
SIC: 5051 Sheets, metal

(P-7401)
SAMUEL SON & CO INC
6415 Corvette St, Commerce (90040-1702)
PHONE................323 722-0300
David Olivia, *Branch Mgr*
Arnold Bauerly, *Admin Mgr*
EMP: 50
SQ FT: 10,000
SALES (corp-wide): 2.8B **Privately Held**
SIC: 5051 Ferroalloys; steel

HQ: Samuel Son & Co. Inc.
4334 Walden Ave
Lancaster NY 14086
716 681-4200

(P-7402)
SCHNITZER STEEL INDUSTRIES INC
1101 Embarcadero W, Oakland (94607-2536)
P.O. Box 747 (94604-0747)
PHONE................510 444-3919
Fax: 510 444-3370
Gary Schnitzer, *Vice Pres*
Nick Andrusyshyn, *Vice Pres*
Steve Blackman, *Marketing Staff*
Melisa Cohen, *Manager*
EMP: 100
SALES (corp-wide): 1.9B **Publicly Held**
WEB: www.schn.com
SIC: 5051 Steel
PA: Schnitzer Steel Industries, Inc.
299 Sw Clay St Ste 350
Portland OR 97201
503 224-9900

(P-7403)
SIMPSON STRONG-TIE INTL INC
Simpson Strong-Tie Anchor Syst
5956 W Las Positas Blvd, Pleasanton (94588-8540)
PHONE................925 560-9000
Undetermin BR, *Manager*
EMP: 100
SALES (corp-wide): 794MM **Publicly Held**
SIC: 5051 Forms, concrete construction (steel)
HQ: Simpson Strong-Tie International, Inc.
5956 W Las Positas Blvd
Pleasanton CA 94588

(P-7404)
SPECIALTY STEEL SERVICE CO INC (HQ)
3300 Douglas Blvd Ste 128, Roseville (95661-3897)
PHONE................916 771-4737
Fax: 916 771-8658
▲ **EMP:** 70
SQ FT: 3,000
SALES (est): 24.4MM
SALES (corp-wide): 10.4B **Publicly Held**
WEB: www.specialtysteel.net
SIC: 5051
PA: Reliance Steel & Aluminum Co.
350 S Grand Ave Ste 5100
Los Angeles CA 90071
213 687-7700

(P-7405)
STATE PIPE & SUPPLY INC (DH)
183 S Cedar Ave, Rialto (92376-9011)
PHONE................909 877-9999
Byung Joon Lee, *CEO*
Honggie Kim, *President*
Gary Knoroski, *Vice Pres*
Dean McClelland, *Vice Pres*
Howard W Lee, *Admin Sec*
EMP: 55
SQ FT: 20,000
SALES (est): 46.9MM
SALES (corp-wide): 1.7B **Privately Held**
WEB: www.statepipe.com
SIC: 5051 5085 Pipe & tubing, steel; industrial supplies
HQ: Seah Steel California, Llc
2100 Main St Ste 100
Irvine CA 92614
562 692-0600

(P-7406)
TCI ALUMINUM/NORTH INC
2353 Davis Ave, Hayward (94545-1111)
PHONE................510 786-3750
Fax: 510 786-3302
Jeff Bordalampe, *President*
Jim Clifton, *Vice Pres*
Elaine Dm, *Opers Mgr*
George Lambros, *Opers Mgr*
Michael Bordalampe, *Sales Mgr*
EMP: 60
SQ FT: 60,000

SALES (est): 44.8MM **Privately Held**
WEB: www.tcialuminum.com
SIC: 5051 Aluminum bars, rods, ingots, sheets, pipes, plates, etc.

(P-7407)
TELL STEEL INC
2345 W 17th St, Long Beach (90813-1097)
PHONE................562 435-4826
Fax: 562 437-6894
Greg More, *President*
Virginia Hood, *Treasurer*
Pete V Trigt, *Admin Sec*
Russ Carruth, *MIS Mgr*
Dianne Talbert, *Credit Mgr*
▲ **EMP:** 60
SQ FT: 100,000
SALES (est): 65.2MM
SALES (corp-wide): 68.3MM **Privately Held**
WEB: www.tellsteel.com
SIC: 5051 Steel; aluminum bars, rods, ingots, sheets, pipes, plates, etc.
PA: Tuffli Co Inc
2780 Skypark Dr Ste 460
Torrance CA 90505
310 326-5500

(P-7408)
TOTTEN TUBES INC (PA)
500 W Danlee St, Azusa (91702-2341)
PHONE................626 812-0220
Fax: 626 812-0113
Tracy N Totten, *CEO*
Linda Furse, *CFO*
David Totten, *Chairman*
Jeffrey Totten, *Treasurer*
Laura Morick, *Vice Pres*
EMP: 60
SQ FT: 73,000
SALES (est): 67.7MM **Privately Held**
WEB: www.tottentubes.com
SIC: 5051 Pipe & tubing, steel

(P-7409)
VER SALES INC (PA)
2509 N Naomi St, Burbank (91504-3236)
PHONE................818 567-3000
Fax: 818 567-3018
Gloria Ryan, *CEO*
James J Ryan, *CEO*
Craig Ryan, *Vice Pres*
Patrick Ryan, *Vice Pres*
Paul Ryan, *Vice Pres*
▲ **EMP:** 60
SQ FT: 30,000
SALES (est): 27.3MM **Privately Held**
WEB: www.versales.com
SIC: 5051 5099 3357 Metal wires, ties, cables & screening; safety equipment & supplies; nonferrous wiredrawing & insulating

5052 Coal & Other Minerals & Ores Wholesale

(P-7410)
MORRISON LANDSCAPING INC
Also Called: Earthco
1225 E Wakeham Ave, Santa Ana (92705-4145)
PHONE................714 571-0455
Fax: 714 571-0580
Robert Morrison, *President*
Denise Morrison, *Vice Pres*
Kyle Morrison, *Opers Mgr*
EMP: 50
SALES: 4.4MM **Privately Held**
SIC: 5052 Coal & other minerals & ores

5063 Electrl Apparatus, Eqpt, Wiring Splys Wholesale

(P-7411)
ALLIED ELECTRIC MOTOR SVC INC (PA)
4690 E Jensen Ave, Fresno (93725-1698)
PHONE................559 486-4222
Fax: 559 486-1952
Salvatore Rome, *Ch of Bd*

Gail Mandal, *President*
Joyce Barnes, *Corp Secy*
Henry Mandal, *Senior VP*
Richard Johnson, *Vice Pres*
EMP: 55
SQ FT: 100,000
SALES (est): 33MM **Privately Held**
WEB: www.alliedelectric.net
SIC: 5063 7694 Electrical supplies; electric motor repair

(P-7412)
AMERICAN DE ROSA LAMPARTS LLC (PA)
Also Called: Lighting DOT Com.com
1945 S Tubeway Ave, Commerce (90040-1611)
PHONE................323 728-6300
Fax: 323 728-0300
Eric Allen, *CEO*
Mark Ashton, *CFO*
Judie Quach, *Vice Pres*
Myron Rosenauer, *Credit Mgr*
Lilli Rodriguez, *Human Res Dir*
▲ **EMP:** 68 **EST:** 2007
SQ FT: 7,000
SALES (est): 65.4MM **Privately Held**
SIC: 5063 3364 3229 Lighting fixtures; light bulbs & related supplies; lighting fittings & accessories; brass & bronze diecastings; bulbs for electric lights

(P-7413)
AMERICAN ELECTRIC SUPPLY INC (PA)
361 S Maple St, Corona (92880-6907)
P.O. Box 2710 (92878-2710)
PHONE................951 734-7910
Fax: 951 737-9906
Michael Pratt, *CEO*
Jerry Empson, *Treasurer*
Kevin Klinzing, *Admin Sec*
Tim Pratt, *Info Tech Mgr*
Steve Pratt, *Technology*
▲ **EMP:** 99
SQ FT: 13,086
SALES (est): 112.1MM **Privately Held**
WEB: www.amelect.com
SIC: 5063 Electrical fittings & construction materials; wire & cable; lighting fixtures

(P-7414)
ANIXTER INC
30061 Ahern Ave, Union City (94587-1234)
PHONE................510 477-2400
Fax: 510 489-2250
Willie Rivera, *Principal*
Justin Travaille, *IT/INT Sup*
EMP: 60
SALES (corp-wide): 6.1B **Publicly Held**
SIC: 5063 Wire & cable
HQ: Anixter Inc.
2301 Patriot Blvd
Glenview IL 60026
224 521-8000

(P-7415)
ANIXTER INC
4464 Willow Rd Ste 101, Pleasanton (94588-8593)
PHONE................925 469-8500
Fax: 925 469-8909
Sabrina Vasquez, *Manager*
David Smith, *Engineer*
Shannon Bartz, *Sales Staff*
Joe Malone, *Manager*
Greg Gabbani, *Accounts Mgr*
EMP: 50
SALES (corp-wide): 6.1B **Publicly Held**
SIC: 5063 Electrical apparatus & equipment
HQ: Anixter Inc.
2301 Patriot Blvd
Glenview IL 60026
224 521-8000

(P-7416)
APPLIMOTION INC
5915 Jetton Ln, Loomis (95650-9594)
PHONE................916 652-3118
Fax: 916 652-3171
Robert Mastromattei, *CEO*
Justin Cileo, *Engineer*
Steve Bailey, *Opers Mgr*
EMP: 69
SQ FT: 8,368

PRODUCTS & SERVICES SECTION
5063 - Electrl Apparatus, Eqpt, Wiring Splys Wholesale County (P-7436)

SALES (est): 27.5MM
SALES (corp-wide): 373.6MM **Publicly Held**
WEB: www.applimotion.com
SIC: **5063** 8711 3545 Motors, electric; consulting engineer; precision measuring tools
PA: Novanta Inc.
125 Middlesex Tpke
Bedford MA 01730
781 266-5700

(P-7417)
BARTCO LIGHTING INC
5761 Research Dr, Huntington Beach (92649-1616)
PHONE..................................714 230-3200
Fax: 714 230-3222
Robert Barton, *CEO*
Daniel Barton, *Exec VP*
Dana B McKee, *Exec VP*
Brian Labbe, *Vice Pres*
Jennifer Crane, *Accounting Mgr*
▲ EMP: 70
SALES (est): 40.3MM **Privately Held**
WEB: www.bartcolighting.com
SIC: **5063** Lighting fixtures, commercial & industrial

(P-7418)
BAY CITY EQUIPMENT INDS INC
Also Called: John Deere Authorized Dealer
13625 Danielson St, Poway (92064-6829)
PHONE..................................619 938-8200
Fax: 619 482-8202
Mark Loftin, *CEO*
Rodney Lee, *President*
Charles Loftin, *Corp Secy*
Patricia Alarcon, *Administration*
Terryn Dwyer, *Accountant*
EMP: 100
SQ FT: 20,000
SALES (est): 32.8MM **Privately Held**
WEB: www.bcew.com
SIC: **5063** 5082 Generators; motors, electric; construction & mining machinery

(P-7419)
BML INDUSTRIES INC
Also Called: American International Inds
1040 Avenida Acaso, Camarillo (93012-8712)
PHONE..................................805 388-6800
Fax: 805 388-6833
David Eisenstein, *President*
Tom Kulowski, *Financial Exec*
Kelly Ponticelii, *Manager*
▲ EMP: 65
SQ FT: 50,000
SALES (est): 11.4MM
SALES (corp-wide): 56.7MM **Privately Held**
WEB: www.aius.net
SIC: **5063** Electrical apparatus & equipment
PA: Aamp Of Florida, Inc.
15500 Lightwave Dr # 202
Clearwater FL 33760
727 572-9255

(P-7420)
BRITHINEE ELECTRIC
620 S Rancho Ave, Colton (92324-3296)
PHONE..................................909 825-7971
Fax: 909 825-6312
Wallace P Brithinee, *President*
Donald P Brithinee, *Vice Pres*
Carlos Mazariegos, *Design Engr*
Frank Storck, *Draft/Design*
Russ Kennedy, *Production*
EMP: 57
SALES (est): 37.1MM **Privately Held**
WEB: www.brithinee.com
SIC: **5063** 7694 Motors, electric; electric motor repair

(P-7421)
CABLECONN INDUSTRIES INC
7198 Convoy Ct, San Diego (92111-1019)
PHONE..................................858 571-7111
Fax: 858 571-0309
Lisa Coffman, *President*
Rod Coffman, *Vice Pres*
Roger Newman, *Vice Pres*
Blain Kopp, *Info Tech Dir*
Claudia Nunez, *Accountant*
EMP: 65
SQ FT: 20,000
SALES (est): 6.8MM **Privately Held**
WEB: www.cableconn-sd.com
SIC: **5063** 3678 3643 Building wire & cable; electronic connectors; current-carrying wiring devices

(P-7422)
CAL SOUTHERN ILLUMINATION
1881 Mcgaw Ave, Irvine (92614-5733)
PHONE..................................949 622-3000
Fax: 949 622-3070
Thomas Thompson, *President*
Michael Shearer, *Bd of Directors*
Steve Leszuk, *Vice Pres*
Susanna Hammond, *Admin Asst*
Jacob Hernandez, *Admin Asst*
EMP: 50
SALES (est): 16.2MM **Privately Held**
WEB: www.scilights.com
SIC: **5063** Lighting fixtures

(P-7423)
CARPE DIEM ENTERPRISES INC
665 Calumet Ave, Beaumont (92223-7064)
PHONE..................................866 251-0852
Tony Hata, *President*
Lias Hata, *Vice Pres*
EMP: 50
SQ FT: 7,000
SALES (est): 10MM **Privately Held**
SIC: **5063** 5141 Electrical apparatus & equipment; groceries, general line

(P-7424)
CENTRAL WHL ELEC DISTRS INC
6611 Preston Ave Ste E, Livermore (94551-5108)
P.O. Box 5040, Pleasanton (94566-0901)
PHONE..................................925 245-9310
Fax: 925 242-9292
Klaus Hansen, *President*
James Sullivan, *Corp Secy*
Michael Hansen, *Vice Pres*
Manny Castillo, *Branch Mgr*
Steve Chambers, *Branch Mgr*
EMP: 90
SQ FT: 2,500
SALES (est): 15.1MM **Privately Held**
WEB: www.cwed.com
SIC: **5063** Electrical supplies

(P-7425)
CENTURY LIGHTING AND ELECTRIC
12820 Earhart Ave, Auburn (95602-9027)
P.O. Box 6793 (95604-6793)
PHONE..................................530 823-1004
Fax: 530 823-3369
Keith Estes, *President*
Brent Estes, *Vice Pres*
Traci Estes, *Vice Pres*
Brian Kolitsch, *Division Mgr*
Vickie Streeter, *Accounting Mgr*
EMP: 50
SQ FT: 6,500
SALES (est): 40MM **Privately Held**
WEB: www.centurylighting.com
SIC: **5063** 1731 8748 Light bulbs & related supplies; lighting contractor; energy conservation consultant

(P-7426)
CHESTER C LEHMANN CO INC (PA)
Also Called: Electrical Distributors Co
1135 Auzerais Ave, San Jose (95126-3402)
P.O. Box 26830 (95159-6830)
PHONE..................................408 293-5818
Fax: 408 287-1152
Chester C Lehmann III, *CEO*
Scott Lehmann, *President*
Staci Martinez, *Project Mgr*
Juan Pineda, *Sales Associate*
Don Pluth, *Sales Staff*
▼ EMP: 65
SQ FT: 80,000
SALES (est): 166.9MM **Privately Held**
WEB: www.electdist.com
SIC: **5063** Electrical apparatus & equipment

(P-7427)
CIRCLE W ENTERPRISES INC
Also Called: Wirenetics Co
27737 Avenue Hopkins, Valencia (91355-1223)
PHONE..................................661 257-2400
Howard Weiss, *CEO*
Michael Weiss, *President*
Phyllis G Weiss, *CEO*
Mark Lee, *Vice Pres*
▲ EMP: 50
SQ FT: 65,000
SALES (est): 30.8MM
SALES (corp-wide): 32MM **Privately Held**
WEB: www.wireandcable.com
SIC: **5063** Wire & cable
PA: Whitmor Plastic Wire And Cable Corp.
27737 Avenue Hopkins
Santa Clarita CA 91355
661 257-2400

(P-7428)
COASTAL TRAFFIC SYSTEMS INC
9391 Power Dr, Huntington Beach (92646-7236)
PHONE..................................714 641-3744
Fax: 714 641-2747
Steven Beiber, *President*
Paul Beiber, *Treasurer*
Thomas Matthews, *Vice Pres*
Jeff Hebert, *Controller*
Nick Men, *Sales Associate*
EMP: 58
SALES (est): 8.1MM **Privately Held**
SIC: **5063** Signaling equipment, electrical

(P-7429)
COMMERCIAL LIGHTING INDS INC
Also Called: Cli
81161 Indio Blvd, Indio (92201-1931)
PHONE..................................800 755-0155
Frank Halcovich, *CEO*
Greg Read, *Vice Pres*
Jennifer Johnson, *Manager*
Melinda Mullaney, *Manager*
Martina Sherman, *Manager*
EMP: 74
SQ FT: 81,000
SALES (est): 63.3MM **Privately Held**
WEB: www.commercial-lighting.net
SIC: **5063** Light bulbs & related supplies

(P-7430)
CONSOLIDATED ELEC DISTRS INC
5457 Ruffin Rd, San Diego (92123-1312)
PHONE..................................858 268-1020
Fax: 858 974-6372
Scott Branstetter, *Branch Mgr*
Sam Sean, *Project Mgr*
Blake Dmochowski, *Sales Associate*
Kaity Elliott, *Sales Associate*
John Gruen, *Sales Staff*
EMP: 51
SQ FT: 30,000
SALES (corp-wide): 10B **Privately Held**
SIC: **5063** Electrical supplies
PA: Consolidated Electrical Distributors, Inc.
1920 Westridge Dr
Irving TX 75038
972 582-5300

(P-7431)
CONSOLIDATED ELEC DISTRS INC
Also Called: All-Phase Electric Supply
3020 W Empire Ave, Burbank (91504-3109)
PHONE..................................626 345-0000
Fax: 818 843-3448
Ed Carney, *Branch Mgr*
Robert Feller, *Principal*
Carol Stiekaley, *Principal*
Rick Botts, *Branch Mgr*
EMP: 53
SALES (corp-wide): 10B **Privately Held**
SIC: **5063** Electrical supplies

PA: Consolidated Electrical Distributors, Inc.
1920 Westridge Dr
Irving TX 75038
972 582-5300

(P-7432)
CORDELIA LIGHTING INC
20101 S Santa Fe Ave, Compton (90221-5917)
PHONE..................................310 886-3490
James Keng, *President*
James Madden, *Vice Pres*
Jay Spowart, *Vice Pres*
Li-WEI Wang, *Vice Pres*
Jim Blenchird, *Manager*
▲ EMP: 106
SQ FT: 200,000
SALES (est): 28.2MM **Privately Held**
WEB: www.cordelia.com
SIC: **5063** Lighting fixtures

(P-7433)
COUNTY WHL ELC CO LOS ANGELES
Also Called: C E D
560 N Main St, Orange (92868-1102)
PHONE..................................714 633-3801
Joe Mihelich, *Principal*
Fernando Yazon, *Purchasing*
Dan Caballero, *Sales Mgr*
Mark McMahon, *Sales Staff*
Jose Merino, *Sales Staff*
EMP: 76 EST: 1986
SALES (est): 24.6MM
SALES (corp-wide): 10B **Privately Held**
SIC: **5063** Electrical supplies
PA: Consolidated Electrical Distributors, Inc.
1920 Westridge Dr
Irving TX 75038
972 582-5300

(P-7434)
DAHL-BECK ELECTRIC CO
2775 Goodrick Ave, Richmond (94801-1109)
PHONE..................................510 237-2325
Fax: 510 237-0608
Roger Beck, *CEO*
William R Beck, *President*
James Ross, *Corp Secy*
Gerald Vaio, *Vice Pres*
▲ EMP: 65
SQ FT: 75,000
SALES (est): 30.6MM **Privately Held**
WEB: www.dahl-beck.com
SIC: **5063** 1731 Electrical apparatus & equipment; general electrical contractor

(P-7435)
DIAMOND POWER SYSTEM CORP
13980 Mountain Ave, Chino (91710-9018)
PHONE..................................866 882-8088
Richard Han, *President*
John MA, *Accounts Mgr*
EMP: 50 EST: 2008
SALES (est): 5.7MM **Privately Held**
SIC: **5063** Power transmission equipment, electric

(P-7436)
ELECTRIC MOTOR SHOP
Also Called: Electric Motor & Supply Co.
250 Broadway St, Fresno (93721-3103)
P.O. Box 446 (93709-0446)
PHONE..................................559 233-1153
Fax: 559 233-7967
Dicks Caglia, *President*
Frank S Caglia, *Agent*
EMP: 80
SQ FT: 1,296
SALES (corp-wide): 116.2MM **Privately Held**
WEB: www.electricmotorshop.com
SIC: **5063** Electrical apparatus & equipment
PA: Electric Motor Shop
253 Fulton St
Fresno CA 93721
559 233-1153

5063 - Electrl Apparatus, Eqpt, Wiring Splys Wholesale County (P-7437)

(P-7437)
ELECTRIC SALES UNLIMITED
9023 Norwalk Blvd, Santa Fe Springs (90670-2531)
PHONE..................562 463-8300
Fax: 562 692-1744
John J Defazio Jr, *President*
Jeanette Acosta, *Senior VP*
Chuck Beadle, *Vice Pres*
Teresa Fackiner, *Vice Pres*
Hannah Terflinger, *Project Mgr*
▲ EMP: 50
SQ FT: 75,000
SALES (est): 21.6MM **Privately Held**
WEB: www.esu.com
SIC: 5063 Electrical apparatus & equipment

(P-7438)
ELEMENTAL LED INC
Also Called: Diode Led
1195 Park Ave Ste 211, Emeryville (94608-3655)
PHONE..................877 564-5051
Fax: 415 592-1596
Randall Holleschau, *CEO*
Jeff Johnson, *CFO*
Matthew John, *Exec VP*
Christopher Le Blanc, *Exec VP*
Eric King, *Senior VP*
▲ EMP: 85
SQ FT: 32,000
SALES (est): 15MM
SALES (corp-wide): 4.2MM **Privately Held**
SIC: 5063 5719 Light bulbs & related supplies; lighting, lamps & accessories
PA: Elemental Led, Llc
1195 Park Ave Ste 211
Emeryville CA 94608
877 564-5051

(P-7439)
EMERGENCY TECHNOLOGIES INC
Also Called: American Two-Way
7345 Varna Ave, North Hollywood (91605-4009)
PHONE..................818 765-4421
Fax: 818 765-0618
Christopher Baskin, *CEO*
Dave Sumner, *Software Dev*
EMP: 72
SQ FT: 13,000
SALES (est): 15.7MM **Privately Held**
WEB: www.americantwoway.com
SIC: 5063 Alarm systems

(P-7440)
ERS SEC ALARM SYSTEMS INC
Also Called: Emergency Reporting Systems
4538 Santa Anita Ave, El Monte (91731-1318)
PHONE..................626 579-2525
Fax: 626 579-5225
David Chao, *President*
Kevin Tsao, *Exec VP*
Winnie Siu, *Controller*
EMP: 53
SQ FT: 15,000
SALES (est): 18.8MM **Privately Held**
WEB: www.erssecurity.com
SIC: 5063 1731 Burglar alarm systems; fire detection & burglar alarm systems specialization

(P-7441)
FACILITY SOLUTIONS GROUP INC
801 Richfield Rd, Placentia (92870-6731)
PHONE..................714 993-3966
Jeff Johnson, *District Mgr*
Craig Carlson, *Natl Sales Mgr*
Peter Contois, *Accounts Exec*
EMP: 64
SALES (corp-wide): 1.3B **Privately Held**
WEB: www.americanlight.com
SIC: 5063 1731 Lighting fixtures, commercial & industrial; light bulbs & related supplies; electrical work; lighting contractor
PA: Facility Solutions Group, Inc.
4401 West Gate Blvd # 310
Austin TX 78745
512 440-7985

(P-7442)
GRAYBAR ELECTRIC COMPANY INC
1370 Valley Vista Dr # 100, Diamond Bar (91765-3921)
PHONE..................909 451-4300
Fax: 323 451-4399
Bruce Spencer, *Engr R&D*
Edward Ontiveros, *Administration*
Jeff Rodman, *IT/INT Sup*
Melanie Hull, *Human Res Dir*
Yvette Coronado, *Human Resources*
EMP: 153
SALES (corp-wide): 6.1B **Privately Held**
WEB: www.graybar.com
SIC: 5063 5065 Electrical apparatus & equipment; telephone equipment
PA: Graybar Electric Company, Inc.
34 N Meramec Ave
Saint Louis MO 63105
314 573-9200

(P-7443)
GRAYBAR ELECTRIC COMPANY INC
8606 Miralani Dr, San Diego (92126-4353)
PHONE..................858 549-9017
Chris Ruperto, *Manager*
Mike Carroll, *Branch Mgr*
Duane Spring, *Branch Mgr*
Patrick Donahue, *Cust Mgr*
Paul Arruda, *Manager*
EMP: 80
SQ FT: 42,973
SALES (corp-wide): 6.1B **Privately Held**
WEB: www.graybar.com
SIC: 5063 Electrical supplies
PA: Graybar Electric Company, Inc.
34 N Meramec Ave
Saint Louis MO 63105
314 573-9200

(P-7444)
GRAYBAR ELECTRIC COMPANY INC
3089 Whipple Rd, Union City (94587-1236)
PHONE..................925 557-3000
Fax: 510 259-0123
Eric Ortega, *Branch Mgr*
My-lia Harris, *Executive*
Jim Dunn, *Planning*
Eugene Fassiotto, *Sales Mgr*
David Maxwell, *Manager*
EMP: 74
SQ FT: 117,648
SALES (corp-wide): 6.1B **Privately Held**
WEB: www.graybar.com
SIC: 5063 5065 Electrical apparatus & equipment; telephone equipment
PA: Graybar Electric Company, Inc.
34 N Meramec Ave
Saint Louis MO 63105
314 573-9200

(P-7445)
HONEYWELL INTERNATIONAL INC
1635 N Batavia St, Orange (92867-3508)
PHONE..................714 283-0110
Mary Peterson, *Manager*
Frank Owen, *Manager*
EMP: 50
SALES (corp-wide): 38.5B **Publicly Held**
WEB: www.adilink.com
SIC: 5063 Electrical apparatus & equipment; alarm systems; burglar alarm systems; fire alarm systems
PA: Honeywell International Inc.
115 Tabor Rd
Morris Plains NJ 07950
973 455-2000

(P-7446)
INDEPENDENT ELECTRIC SUP INC (DH)
2001 Marina Blvd, San Leandro (94577-3204)
PHONE..................520 908-7900
Fax: 650 594-0484
Doug Walo, *President*
Greg Adrian, *CFO*
Timothy Birky, *Principal*
Kevin Horn, *Branch Mgr*
Kathy Nikrant, *Admin Asst*
EMP: 153 **EST: 1973**
SALES (est): 601.4MM
SALES (corp-wide): 9.8MM **Privately Held**
WEB: www.iesupply.com
SIC: 5063 Electrical apparatus & equipment; wiring devices; electrical construction materials; cable conduit
HQ: Sonepar Management Us, Inc.
510 Walnut St Ste 400
Philadelphia PA 19106
215 399-5900

(P-7447)
JME INC (PA)
Also Called: T M B
527 Prk Ave San Fernando, San Fernando (91340)
PHONE..................818 899-8813
Fax: 818 899-8813
Colin R Waters, *CEO*
Thomas M Bissett, *President*
Irene Klebanov, *CFO*
Don Phillips, *CFO*
Peter Kirkup, *Vice Pres*
▲ EMP: 80
SQ FT: 34,000
SALES (est): 77.9MM **Privately Held**
WEB: www.tmb.com
SIC: 5063 Lighting fittings & accessories

(P-7448)
JOHN SHANNON MC GEE CO INC
Also Called: McGee Company
8190 Byron Rd, Whittier (90606-2616)
PHONE..................562 789-1777
Fax: 562 789-1770
Glenn Hitomi, *President*
Tracey Miller, *CFO*
Lee Hatcher, *Vice Pres*
Ken Porter, *Vice Pres*
Mark Schlueter, *Vice Pres*
▲ EMP: 50 **EST: 1963**
SQ FT: 74,000
SALES (est): 7.8MM **Privately Held**
WEB: www.mcgeeco.com
SIC: 5063 Electrical apparatus & equipment

(P-7449)
KOFFLER ELEC MECH APPRTS REPAI
527 Whitney St, San Leandro (94577-1113)
PHONE..................510 567-0630
Fax: 510 567-0636
Lari Koffler, *President*
Wayne Kelder, *CFO*
Michael Bucedi, *Treasurer*
Charles H Koffler, *Vice Pres*
Kerry Koffler, *Admin Sec*
▲ EMP: 80
SQ FT: 77,548
SALES (est): 14.6MM **Privately Held**
WEB: www.koffler.com
SIC: 5063 7694 Motors, electric; electric motor repair

(P-7450)
LGE ELECTRICAL SALES INC
7866 Convoy Ct, San Diego (92111-1210)
PHONE..................408 379-8568
Gregory Adrian, *CFO*
EMP: 325
SALES (corp-wide): 9.8MM **Privately Held**
SIC: 5063 Electrical apparatus & equipment
HQ: Lge Electrical Sales, Inc.
4351 Northgate Blvd
Sacramento CA 95825
916 563-2737

(P-7451)
LOS ANGELES RUBBER COMPANY (PA)
Also Called: Mechanical Drives and Belting
2915 E Washington Blvd, Los Angeles (90023-4218)
P.O. Box 23910 (90023-0910)
PHONE..................323 263-4131
Carol A Durst, *CEO*
David Durst, *Vice Pres*
Michael Durst, *Vice Pres*
Wayne Roberts, *Vice Pres*
Pat Reynolds, *Accountant*
▲ EMP: 55
SQ FT: 31,000
SALES (est): 33.2MM **Privately Held**
SIC: 5063 Power transmission equipment, electric

(P-7452)
LUMENS (PA)
Also Called: Lumens Light & Living
2020 L St Ste Ll10, Sacramento (95811-4260)
PHONE..................916 444-5585
Fax: 916 444-5885
Ken Plumlee, *President*
Denise Armstrong, *Officer*
Charles Holdredge, *Officer*
Peter Weight, *Admin Sec*
Brian Del Vecchio, *Sr Software Eng*
◆ EMP: 52
SQ FT: 5,700
SALES (est): 23.4MM **Privately Held**
SIC: 5063 5712 Lighting fixtures; furniture stores

(P-7453)
MAGNETIKA INC (PA)
2041 W 139th St, Gardena (90249-2409)
PHONE..................310 527-8100
Fax: 310 527-8101
Francis Ishida, *President*
Basil P Caloyeras, *CEO*
Ameet Butala, *Exec VP*
Nick Defalco, *General Mgr*
Ieng Liu, *Info Tech Mgr*
EMP: 80
SQ FT: 40,000
SALES (est): 40.8MM **Privately Held**
SIC: 5063 3612 Transformers, electric; power transmission equipment, electric; ballasts for lighting fixtures; power transformers, electric

(P-7454)
MAIN ELECTRIC SUPPLY CO (PA)
3600 W Segerstrom Ave, Santa Ana (92704-6408)
P.O. Box 25750 (92799-5750)
PHONE..................949 833-3052
Fax: 323 753-7750
Scott R Germann, *President*
Paul Vowels, *COO*
Karen Morris, *CFO*
Christine Baeza, *Department Mgr*
Carlos Balencia, *Branch Mgr*
▲ EMP: 69
SQ FT: 35,000
SALES (est): 350.8MM **Privately Held**
WEB: www.mainelectricsupply.com
SIC: 5063 Electrical apparatus & equipment

(P-7455)
MAIN ELECTRIC SUPPLY CO
461 Main St, Riverside (92501-1029)
PHONE..................951 784-2900
John Hyland, *Sales Associate*
Rich Ramirez, *Sales Associate*
EMP: 103
SALES (corp-wide): 350.8MM **Privately Held**
SIC: 5063 Electrical apparatus & equipment
PA: Main Electric Supply Co.
3600 W Segerstrom Ave
Santa Ana CA 92704
949 833-3052

(P-7456)
MINKA LIGHTING INC (PA)
Also Called: Minka Group
1151 Bradford Cir, Corona (92882-7166)
PHONE..................951 735-9220
Marian Tang, *CEO*
Kurt Schulzman, *Principal*
Jason Yu, *Info Tech Dir*
John Tarazona, *Controller*
Alvia Briseno, *Human Res Mgr*
◆ EMP: 70
SQ FT: 350,000
SALES (est): 91.5MM **Privately Held**
WEB: www.minka.com
SIC: 5063 Lighting fixtures

▲ = Import ▼ = Export
◆ = Import/Export

PRODUCTS & SERVICES SECTION
5063 - Electrl Apparatus, Eqpt, Wiring Splys Wholesale County (P-7477)

(P-7457)
MOTIVE ENERGY INC (PA)
125 E Coml St Bldg B, Anaheim (92801)
PHONE.................................714 888-2525
Fax: 714 888-2526
Robert J Istwan, *President*
Shane Maxwell, *VP Finance*
Tony Capolino, *VP Sales*
Pete Lopez, *VP Sales*
Adam Brown, *Sales Engr*
▼ EMP: 80
SQ FT: 35,000
SALES (est): 62MM **Privately Held**
SIC: **5063** Storage batteries, industrial

(P-7458)
MULTIQUIP INC (DH)
18910 Wilmington Ave, Carson (90746-2820)
PHONE.................................310 537-3700
Fax: 323 537-3927
Tom Yasuda, *CEO*
Gary Moskovitz, *President*
Jim Henehan, *CFO*
Bob Graydon, *Senior VP*
Mike Howlett, *Senior VP*
◆ EMP: 300
SQ FT: 190,000
SALES (est): 276MM
SALES (corp-wide): 43.4B **Privately Held**
WEB: www.multiquip.com
SIC: **5063** 5082 3645 Generators; general construction machinery & equipment; garden, patio, walkway & yard lighting fixtures: electric
HQ: Itochu International Inc.
1251 Ave Of The Americas
New York NY 10020
212 818-8000

(P-7459)
NELSON & ASSOCIATES INC
12816 Leffingwell Ave, Santa Fe Springs (90670-6343)
PHONE.................................562 921-4423
Todd James Nelson, *CEO*
Brian Haupt, *Exec VP*
Kurt Nelson, *Principal*
Jennifer Murray, *Regional Mgr*
Elisa Clark, *Office Admin*
▲ EMP: 75
SQ FT: 120,000
SALES (est): 35.7MM **Privately Held**
WEB: www.nelsonreps.com
SIC: **5063** Electrical supplies; telephone & telegraph wire & cable

(P-7460)
NORA LIGHTING INC
6505 Gayhart St, Commerce (90040-2507)
PHONE.................................800 686-6672
Fred Farzan, *CEO*
Jill Farzan, *Exec VP*
Mile Leyva, *Manager*
Amalie Romero, *Accounts Mgr*
▲ EMP: 72
SQ FT: 150,000
SALES (est): 61.4MM **Privately Held**
WEB: www.noralighting.com
SIC: **5063** 3648 5719 Lighting fixtures; lighting fixtures, except electric: residential; lighting fixtures

(P-7461)
ONESOURCE DISTRIBUTORS LLC (DH)
Also Called: San Diego Wholesale Electric
3951 Oceanic Dr, Oceanside (92056-5846)
PHONE.................................760 966-4500
Mike Smith, *President*
Tim Walsh, *CFO*
Leslie McCoy, *General Mgr*
Tim Logan, *Info Tech Mgr*
Adrian Lupola, *Engineer*
▲ EMP: 96
SQ FT: 50,000
SALES (est): 488.5MM
SALES (corp-wide): 9.8MM **Privately Held**
WEB: www.1sourcedist.com
SIC: **5063** 3699 Electrical apparatus & equipment; electrical equipment & supplies

HQ: Sonepar Management Us, Inc.
510 Walnut St Ste 400
Philadelphia PA 19106
215 399-5900

(P-7462)
ONESOURCE DISTRIBUTORS LLC
12101 Western Ave, Garden Grove (92841-2914)
PHONE.................................714 523-1012
Donald Ulery, *Principal*
EMP: 59
SALES (corp-wide): 9.8MM **Privately Held**
WEB: www.1sourcedist.com
SIC: **5063** 5065 Electrical apparatus & equipment; electronic parts & equipment
HQ: Onesource Distributors, Llc
3951 Oceanic Dr
Oceanside CA 92056
760 966-4500

(P-7463)
ORIENTAL MOTOR U S A CORP (HQ)
1001 Knox St, Torrance (90502-1030)
PHONE.................................310 715-3300
Fax: 310 325-5983
Ryan Kanemura, *President*
Greg Johnston, *Exec VP*
Pete Derose, *Vice Pres*
Jake Kitayama, *Principal*
Kulie Fintak, *Admin Sec*
◆ EMP: 60
SQ FT: 31,600
SALES: 56.3MM
SALES (corp-wide): 343MM **Privately Held**
SIC: **5063** Motors, electric
PA: Oriental Motor Co., Ltd.
4-8-1, Higashiueno
Taito-Ku TKY 110-0
367 440-411

(P-7464)
PACIFIC LIGHTING MANUFACTURER
Also Called: Utopia Lighting
2329 E Pacifica Pl, Compton (90220-6210)
PHONE.................................310 327-7711
SOO Goo Hong, *CEO*
David Kim, *President*
Millie Park, *Accounts Mgr*
Nelly Park, *Accounts Mgr*
▲ EMP: 62
SQ FT: 100,000
SALES (est): 12.5MM **Privately Held**
SIC: **5063** Lighting fixtures

(P-7465)
POWER PLUS LLC
1210 N Red Gum St, Anaheim (92806-1820)
PHONE.................................714 507-1881
Steven Bray,
EMP: 70
SALES (est): 9.5MM **Privately Held**
SIC: **5063** Generators

(P-7466)
Q L P INC
2285 Ward Ave, Simi Valley (93065-1863)
PHONE.................................805 579-0440
Fax: 818 579-8822
Andy Sreden, *President*
Tracy Yu, *Admin Asst*
Sandy Sreden, *Purchasing*
Hank Bachman, *VP Sales*
Stephanie Patlan, *Assistant*
▲ EMP: 50
SQ FT: 15,000
SALES (est): 16.9MM **Privately Held**
SIC: **5063** Lighting fixtures

(P-7467)
REGENCY ENTERPRISES INC (PA)
Also Called: Regency Lighting
9261 Jordan Ave, Chatsworth (91311-5739)
PHONE.................................818 901-0255
Fax: 818 721-4191
Ron Regenstreif, *CEO*
Scott Anderson, *President*

Isaac Regenstreif, *President*
Judah Regenstreif, *President*
Mike Goldstone, *COO*
EMP: 272
SALES (est): 150MM **Privately Held**
WEB: www.regencylighting.com
SIC: **5063** Light bulbs & related supplies; lighting fixtures

(P-7468)
ROMACH LLC
2956 Sparrow Dr, Fullerton (92835-2322)
PHONE.................................805 378-1174
Alexander Ghibu, *Executive*
John Pierce,
▲ EMP: 65
SALES (est): 4.3MM **Privately Held**
WEB: www.romach.com
SIC: **5063** Motors, electric

(P-7469)
SAMSUNG
Also Called: Samsung Sns Central Valley Off
2603 Camino Ramon Ste 350, San Ramon (94583-9127)
PHONE.................................925 380-6523
Ricardo Dubon, *Principal*
EMP: 55
SALES (est): 8.9MM **Privately Held**
SIC: **5063** Electrical apparatus & equipment

(P-7470)
SCHNEIDER ELECTRIC USA INC
Also Called: Schneider Electric 600
6160 Stoneridge Mall Rd # 200, Pleasanton (94588-3285)
PHONE.................................925 462-0986
Scott Day, *Manager*
Chris Heckler, *Project Mgr*
Yazhou J Liu, *Technology*
Finn Schenck, *Sales Executive*
Rick McKay, *Sales Mgr*
EMP: 55
SALES (corp-wide): 224.4K **Privately Held**
WEB: www.squared.com
SIC: **5063** Electrical apparatus & equipment
HQ: Schneider Electric Usa, Inc.
800 Federal St
Andover MA 01810
978 975-9600

(P-7471)
SCHNEIDER ELECTRIC USA INC
Also Called: Schneider Electric 650
21680 Gateway Center Dr # 300, Diamond Bar (91765-2453)
PHONE.................................909 612-5400
Scott Forry, *Manager*
Edison Nguyen, *Engineer*
Tuan Tran, *Engineer*
EMP: 51
SALES (corp-wide): 224.4K **Privately Held**
WEB: www.squared.com
SIC: **5063** Electrical apparatus & equipment
HQ: Schneider Electric Usa, Inc.
800 Federal St
Andover MA 01810
978 975-9600

(P-7472)
SELECTA PRODUCTS INC (PA)
Also Called: Selecta Switch
1200 E Tehachapi Blvd, Tehachapi (93561-8129)
P.O. Box 888 (93581-0888)
PHONE.................................661 823-7050
Fax: 661 433-4319
John Kenyon, *President*
Charles Kenyon, *Ch of Bd*
James Kenyon, *President*
Dorothy Kenyon, *Vice Pres*
Charlotte Tathwell, *Vice Pres*
▼ EMP: 60
SQ FT: 20,000
SALES (est): 39MM **Privately Held**
WEB: www.selectaproductsinc.com
SIC: **5063** 5065 Electrical supplies; electronic parts

(P-7473)
SILICONSYSTEMS INC
26840 Aliso Viejo Pkwy # 1, Aliso Viejo (92656-2624)
PHONE.................................949 900-9400
Michael Hajeck, *CEO*
Andrew Talbot, *CFO*
David Merry, *CTO*
Bill Vickers, *Engineer*
Edward Meek, *Opers Staff*
▲ EMP: 85
SALES (est): 13.8MM
SALES (corp-wide): 12.9B **Publicly Held**
WEB: www.siliconsystems.com
SIC: **5063** Electrical apparatus & equipment
PA: Western Digital Corporation
3355 Michelson Dr Ste 100
Irvine CA 92612
949 672-7000

(P-7474)
SIMPLEXGRINNELL LP
1099 Industry Way, El Centro (92243-4622)
PHONE.................................760 336-0109
EMP: 52 **Privately Held**
WEB: www.simplexgrinnell.com
SIC: **5063** 5087 5999 Alarm systems; fire alarm systems; sprinkler systems; fire extinguishers
HQ: Simplexgrinnell Lp
4700 Exchange Ct
Boca Raton FL 33431
561 988-7200

(P-7475)
SMK ELECTRONICS CORP USA (HQ)
Also Called: SMK America Group
1055 Tierra Del Rey, Chula Vista (91910-7875)
PHONE.................................619 216-6400
Paul Evans, *President*
Tom Fukushima, *COO*
Nomura Naufumi, *CFO*
Tetsuya Nakamura, *Chairman*
Naomasa Miyata, *Vice Pres*
▲ EMP: 50
SQ FT: 14,688
SALES (est): 56.6MM
SALES (corp-wide): 659.8MM **Privately Held**
WEB: www.smkusa.com
SIC: **5063** Switches, except electronic
PA: Smk Corporation
6-5-5, Togoshi
Shinagawa-Ku TKY 142-0
337 851-111

(P-7476)
SOLARWORLD AMERICAS LLC (DH)
4650 Adohr Ln, Camarillo (93012-8508)
PHONE.................................503 844-3400
Kevin Kilkelly, *President*
Mukesh Dulani, *Vice Pres*
Raju Yenamandra, *Vice Pres*
Carol Smith, *Program Mgr*
Jeff Garrison, *Electrical Engi*
◆ EMP: 75
SALES (est): 25.1MM
SALES (corp-wide): 820MM **Privately Held**
WEB: www.solarworld-ca.com
SIC: **5063** Electrical apparatus & equipment
HQ: Solarworld Americas Inc.
25300 Nw Evergreen Rd
Hillsboro OR 97124
503 844-3400

(P-7477)
SOUTHWIRE COMPANY LLC
Southwire Master Service Ctr
9199 Cleveland Ave # 100, Rancho Cucamonga (91730-8559)
PHONE.................................909 989-2888
Fax: 909 989-0900
David Jordan, *Branch Mgr*
Santa Benavidez, *Admin Asst*
Jim Bright, *Engineer*
Freddy Hernandez, *Supervisor*
EMP: 60

5063 - Electrl Apparatus, Eqpt, Wiring Splys Wholesale County (P-7478)

SALES (corp-wide): 1.9B **Privately Held**
WEB: www.southwire.com
SIC: 5063 Wire & cable
PA: Southwire Company, Llc
1 Southwire Dr
Carrollton GA 30119
770 832-4242

(P-7478)
TENERGY CORPORATION
Also Called: All-Battery.com
436 Kato Ter, Fremont (94539-8332)
PHONE 510 687-0388
Xiangbing LI, *CEO*
Kevin LI, *Vice Pres*
Laura Rice, *Executive*
Ling Ch Liang, *Admin Sec*
Matthew Morley, *Design Engr*
▲ **EMP:** 90
SALES (est): 53.1MM **Privately Held**
SIC: 5063 3691 Batteries; alkaline cell storage batteries

(P-7479)
TRI-ED DISTRIBUTION INC
855 National Dr Ste 103, Sacramento (95834-1195)
PHONE 916 563-7560
Rich Westphal, *Manager*
William Evans, *Branch Mgr*
Bill Chaney, *Sales Staff*
Jed Lingel, *Accounts Mgr*
EMP: 100 **Privately Held**
SIC: 5063 Electrical apparatus & equipment
HQ: Tri-Ed Distribution Inc.
135 Crossways Park Dr # 101
Woodbury NY 11797
516 941-2800

(P-7480)
USHIO AMERICA INC (HQ)
5440 Cerritos Ave, Cypress (90630-4567)
PHONE 714 236-8600
Fax: 714 229-3180
Shinji Kameda, *President*
Yuichi Asaka, *CFO*
Hideaki Takizawa, *CFO*
Keith Sangiacomo, *General Mgr*
Rez Motamed, *Info Tech Mgr*
◆ **EMP:** 90
SQ FT: 70,000
SALES (est): 96.2MM
SALES (corp-wide): 1.5B **Privately Held**
WEB: www.ushio.com
SIC: 5063 Lighting fixtures, commercial & industrial
PA: Ushio Inc.
1-6-5, Marunouchi
Chiyoda-Ku TKY 100-0
356 571-000

(P-7481)
VITRON ELECTRONIC SERVICES INC
Also Called: Vitron Electronics Mfg & Svcs
1901 Las Plumas Ave, San Jose (95133-1700)
PHONE 408 251-1600
Fax: 408 436-8908
Huan Cong Tran, *CEO*
Lieu Ly, *Vice Pres*
Lieu Tran, *Manager*
▲ **EMP:** 60
SQ FT: 3,500
SALES: 15MM **Privately Held**
WEB: www.vitronmfg.com
SIC: 5063 Switchgear

(P-7482)
WALTERS WHOLESALE ELECTRIC CO (HQ)
2825 Temple Ave, Signal Hill (90755-2212)
PHONE 562 988-3100
John L Walter, *CEO*
Bill Durkee, *President*
Roland Wood, *CFO*
Nancy Nielsen, *Treasurer*
Jan Padilla, *Social Dir*
EMP: 50
SQ FT: 10,000
SALES (est): 530MM
SALES (corp-wide): 10B **Privately Held**
WEB: www.walterswholesale.com
SIC: 5063 3699 1731 Wire & cable; electrical equipment & supplies; lighting contractor
PA: Consolidated Electrical Distributors, Inc.
1920 Westridge Dr
Irving TX 75038
972 582-5300

(P-7483)
WALTERS WHOLESALE ELECTRIC CO
200 N Berry St, Brea (92821-3903)
PHONE 714 784-1900
Fax: 714 784-1710
Ron Byrd, *Branch Mgr*
Tom Pellizzari, *Purchasing*
Jay Melphy, *Sales Staff*
EMP: 140
SALES (corp-wide): 10B **Privately Held**
WEB: www.walterswholesale.com
SIC: 5063 Wire & cable
HQ: Walters Wholesale Electric Co.
2825 Temple Ave
Signal Hill CA 90755
562 988-3100

(P-7484)
WW GRAINGER INC
Also Called: Grainger 732
2261 Ringwood Ave, San Jose (95131-1792)
PHONE 408 432-8200
Fax: 408 432-7315
Alicia Bugos, *Manager*
Diedra Carl, *Sales Executive*
EMP: 120
SQ FT: 38,082
SALES (corp-wide): 9.9B **Publicly Held**
WEB: www.grainger.com
SIC: 5063 5084 5075 5078 Motors, electric; motor controls, starters & relays: electric; power transmission equipment, electric; generators; fans, industrial; pumps & pumping equipment; compressors, except air conditioning; pneumatic tools & equipment; warm air heating equipment & supplies; air conditioning equipment, except room units; refrigeration equipment & supplies; electric tools; power tools & accessories; hand tools
PA: W.W. Grainger, Inc.
100 Grainger Pkwy
Lake Forest IL 60045
847 535-1000

(P-7485)
YAMAHA MOTOR CORPORATION USA
Also Called: Yamaha Marine Division
6555 Katella Ave, Cypress (90630-5101)
PHONE 714 761-7300
Kenji Fujimoto, *Branch Mgr*
EMP: 420
SALES (est): 13.1B **Privately Held**
WEB: www.yamaha-motor.com
SIC: 5063 Electrical apparatus & equipment
HQ: Yamaha Motor Corporation Usa
6555 Katella Ave
Cypress CA 90630
714 761-7300

(P-7486)
ZIPPY USA INC
Also Called: Kpower Sup McRswitch Inverters
1 Morgan, Irvine (92618-1917)
PHONE 949 366-9525
Fax: 949 366-9526
Chin W Chou, *President*
Chin S Tsai, *Treasurer*
Frank Lee, *Admin Mgr*
Emily Chang, *Administration*
Thomas Gomez, *Project Mgr*
◆ **EMP:** 54 **EST:** 1996
SQ FT: 19,000
SALES (est): 10.3MM
SALES (corp-wide): 102MM **Privately Held**
WEB: www.zippyusa.com
SIC: 5063 Motor controls, starters & relays: electric
PA: Zippy Technology Corp.
10f, 50, Min Chuan Rd.
New Taipei City 23141
229 188-512

(P-7487)
ZSPACE INC
490 De Guigne Dr 200, Sunnyvale (94085-3903)
PHONE 408 498-4050
Paul Kellenberger, *CEO*
Joseph Powers, *CFO*
Kevin Morishige, *Vice Pres*
Eric Morse, *Vice Pres*
Ed Sesek, *Vice Pres*
EMP: 100
SALES (est): 52.4MM **Privately Held**
SIC: 5063 Transformers, electric

5064 Electrical Appliances, TV & Radios Wholesale

(P-7488)
ALPINE ELECTRONICS AMERICA INC
2012 Abalone Ave Ste D, Torrance (90501-3726)
PHONE 310 783-7391
EMP: 102
SALES (corp-wide): 2.3B **Privately Held**
SIC: 5064 Radios, motor vehicle
HQ: Alpine Electronics Of America, Inc.
19145 Gramercy Pl
Torrance CA 90501
310 326-8000

(P-7489)
ALPINE ELECTRONICS AMERICA INC (HQ)
19145 Gramercy Pl, Torrance (90501-1162)
P.O. Box 2859 (90509-2859)
PHONE 310 326-8000
Fax: 310 533-0369
Toshinori Kobayashi, *CEO*
Isao Nagasako, *President*
Masanobu Takagi, *CFO*
Jim O'Neill, *Exec VP*
Jim Walter, *Program Mgr*
▲ **EMP:** 200 **EST:** 1978
SQ FT: 120,000
SALES (est): 397.4MM
SALES (corp-wide): 2.3B **Privately Held**
WEB: www.alpine-usa.com
SIC: 5064 3651 3679 Radios, motor vehicle; household audio & video equipment; harness assemblies for electronic use: wire or cable
PA: Alpine Electronics, Inc.
1-1-8, Nishigotanda
Shinagawa-Ku TKY 141-0
334 941-101

(P-7490)
APPLIANCE DISTRIBUTION INC
915 N B St, Sacramento (95811-0334)
PHONE 916 497-0274
Roy Fernandez Jr, *CEO*
Roy Fernandez Sr, *Treasurer*
Miguel Maccias, *Vice Pres*
Danny Fernandez, *General Mgr*
EMP: 107
SQ FT: 20,000
SALES (est): 77.3MM **Privately Held**
SIC: 5064 Appliance parts, household

(P-7491)
AVA ENTERPRISES INC
Also Called: Boss Audio Systems
3451 Lunar Ct, Oxnard (93030-8976)
PHONE 805 988-0192
Fax: 805 988-0319
Soheil Rabbani, *President*
Kam Mobini, *Shareholder*
Jeff Holstrom, *Vice Pres*
Sheila Rabbani, *Vice Pres*
Herman Lopez, *Executive*
◆ **EMP:** 50
SQ FT: 70,000
SALES (est): 28MM **Privately Held**
WEB: www.bossaudio.com
SIC: 5064 Radios, motor vehicle

(P-7492)
CLARION CORPORATION AMERICA (DH)
6200 Gateway Dr, Cypress (90630-4842)
PHONE 310 327-9100
Fax: 310 343-7333
Tsuneo Hayashi, *President*
Tatsuhiko Izumi, *President*
Chris Honma, *Exec VP*
Calvin Nichols, *Senior VP*
Paul Lachner, *Admin Sec*
◆ **EMP:** 77
SQ FT: 53,208
SALES: 470.7MM
SALES (corp-wide): 85.7B **Privately Held**
SIC: 5064 Radios, motor vehicle
HQ: Clarion Co., Ltd.
7-2, Shintoshin, Chuo-Ku
Saitama STM 330-0
486 013-700

(P-7493)
CONCEPT ENTERPRISES INC
338 Turnbull Canyon Rd, City of Industry (91745-1009)
PHONE 626 968-8827
Edward Liu, *CEO*
Calvin Liu, *Exec VP*
Willie Liu, *Vice Pres*
Al Miller, *VP Mktg*
Tony LI, *Manager*
▲ **EMP:** 60 **EST:** 1976
SALES (est): 14.3MM **Privately Held**
SIC: 5064 Electrical entertainment equipment; radios, motor vehicle

(P-7494)
E & S INTERNATIONAL ENTPS INC (PA)
Also Called: Import Direct
7801 Hayvenhurst Ave, Van Nuys (91406-1712)
PHONE 818 702-2207
Fax: 818 702-6344
Ehsan Asherian, *Chairman*
Farshad Asherian, *President*
Phillip Asherian, *CEO*
Mike RAD, *COO*
Mark W Barron, *CFO*
▲ **EMP:** 100
SQ FT: 60,000
SALES (est): 136.1MM **Privately Held**
WEB: www.esintl.com
SIC: 5064 Electrical appliances, television & radio

(P-7495)
ELECTROLUX HOME PRODUCTS INC
701 Malaga St, Ontario (91761-8627)
PHONE 909 605-9448
Jeff Bee Cont, *Branch Mgr*
EMP: 64
SALES (corp-wide): 14.1B **Privately Held**
WEB: www.eureka.com
SIC: 5064 Electric household appliances
HQ: Electrolux Home Products, Inc.
10200 David Taylor Dr
Charlotte NC 28262
980 236-2000

(P-7496)
EPSILON ELECTRONICS INC
Also Called: Power Acoustik Electronics
1550 S Maple Ave, Montebello (90640-6508)
PHONE 323 722-3333
Fax: 323 722-1122
Jack Rochel, *President*
Mossa Rochel, *Vice Pres*
Eli Pngilanan, *Controller*
Gene Norvell, *VP Sales*
Hugo Sapetas, *Mktg Dir*
▲ **EMP:** 79
SQ FT: 69,000
SALES (est): 22.9MM **Privately Held**
WEB: www.poweracoustik.com
SIC: 5064 Electrical entertainment equipment; high fidelity equipment

PRODUCTS & SERVICES SECTION
5065 - Electronic Parts & Eqpt Wholesale County (P-7516)

(P-7497)
F O C ELECTRONICS CORPORATION
Also Called: Crazy Gideons
830 Traction Ave, Los Angeles (90013-1816)
PHONE..................213 625-5775
Fax: 213 625-0101
Gideon Kotzer, *President*
Leonie Kotzer, *Corp Secy*
EMP: 50
SQ FT: 50,000
SALES (est): 6.1MM **Privately Held**
WEB: www.crazygideons.com
SIC: 5064 5731 Electrical entertainment equipment; television sets; video cassette recorders & accessories; radios; radio, television & electronic stores

(P-7498)
FUJITSU TEN CORP OF AMERICA
19600 S Vermont Ave, Torrance (90502-1140)
PHONE..................310 327-2151
Fax: 310 515-6718
Masami Yamamoto, *President*
Ray Windsor, *Vice Pres*
Mitch Kida, *Executive*
R Onishi, *Div Sub Head*
Larry Kutsch, *VP Admin*
EMP: 120
SALES (corp-wide): 40.5B **Privately Held**
SIC: 5064 7539 Radios, motor vehicle; radios; automotive repair shops
HQ: Fujitsu Ten Limited
  1-2-28, Goshodori, Hyogo-Ku
  Kobe HYO 652-0
  786 715-081

(P-7499)
HELMAN GROUP LTD (PA)
1621 Beacon Pl, Oxnard (93033-2452)
PHONE..................805 487-7772
Fax: 805 487-9975
Barry Helman, *Ch of Bd*
Andrew Helman, *President*
Wendi Tidwell, *Purchasing*
▲ **EMP:** 60
SQ FT: 100,000
SALES (est): 9.3MM **Privately Held**
WEB: www.helmangroup.com
SIC: 5064 Electric household appliances

(P-7500)
JVCKENWOOD USA CORPORATION (HQ)
2201 E Dominguez St, Long Beach (90810-1009)
P.O. Box 22745 (90801-5745)
PHONE..................310 639-9000
Fax: 310 604-4487
Kuhiro Aigami, *President*
Kazuhiro Aigami, *President*
Joseph Glassett, *CEO*
Dilip Patki, *CFO*
Michael McConnell, *Treasurer*
▲ **EMP:** 160 **EST:** 1961
SQ FT: 238,000
SALES (est): 119.9MM
SALES (corp-wide): 2.5B **Privately Held**
WEB: www.kenwoodusa.com
SIC: 5064 High fidelity equipment
PA: Jvc Kenwood Corporation
  3-12, Moriyacho, Kanagawa-Ku
  Yokohama KNG 221-0
  454 445-232

(P-7501)
MEMOREX PRODUCTS INC
17777 Center Court Dr N S, Cerritos (90703-9320)
P.O. Box 64742, Saint Paul MN (55164-0742)
PHONE..................562 653-2800
Fax: 562 653-2900
Michael Golacinski, *President*
Allan Yap, *Ch of Bd*
Kevin McDonnell, *CFO*
Randy Finchum, *Vice Pres*
Allen H Gharapetian, *Vice Pres*
▲ **EMP:** 159
SQ FT: 212,000
SALES (est): 29.7MM **Publicly Held**
WEB: www.memorex.com
SIC: 5064 5065 5045 3652 Electrical entertainment equipment; radio & television equipment & parts; computer peripheral equipment; pre-recorded records & tapes; household audio & video equipment
PA: Imation Corp.
  1099 Helmo Ave N Ste 250
  Oakdale MN 55128

(P-7502)
PANASONIC
26160 Enterprise Way, Lake Forest (92630-8403)
PHONE..................949 581-0661
Susan Hall, *President*
Al McGowan, *Business Dir*
Kevin Lin, *Program Mgr*
Michelle Yang, *Program Mgr*
Desiree Lopez, *Admin Asst*
EMP: 137
SALES (est): 21.6MM **Privately Held**
SIC: 5064 Electrical appliances, television & radio

(P-7503)
PANASONIC CORP NORTH AMERICA
Also Called: Panasonic Broadcast TV Systems
3330 Chnga Blvd W Ste 505, Los Angeles (90068-1355)
PHONE..................323 436-3500
Fax: 323 436-3615
Russ Walker, *Manager*
Leslie Cheung, *Info Tech Dir*
Vincent Atwood, *Manager*
James Chan, *Manager*
Stephen Weingarten, *Manager*
EMP: 125
SALES (corp-wide): 64.5B **Privately Held**
WEB: www.panasonic.com
SIC: 5064 Electrical appliances, television & radio
HQ: Panasonic Corporation Of North America
  2 Riverfront Plz Ste 200
  Newark NJ 07102
  201 348-7000

(P-7504)
PANASONIC CORP NORTH AMERICA
2033 Gateway Pl Ste 200, San Jose (95110-3714)
PHONE..................201 348-7000
Shauna Peterson, *Director*
Dan Trautmann, *Human Res Dir*
EMP: 54
SALES (corp-wide): 64.5B **Privately Held**
WEB: www.panasonic.com
SIC: 5064 Electrical appliances, television & radio
HQ: Panasonic Corporation Of North America
  2 Riverfront Plz Ste 200
  Newark NJ 07102
  201 348-7000

(P-7505)
PANASONIC CORP NORTH AMERICA
Panasonic Avc Networks Company
2055 Sanyo Ave, San Diego (92154-6229)
PHONE..................619 661-1134
Akiko Woods, *Executive Asst*
EMP: 54
SALES (corp-wide): 64.5B **Privately Held**
SIC: 5064 Television sets
HQ: Panasonic Corporation Of North America
  2 Riverfront Plz Ste 200
  Newark NJ 07102
  201 348-7000

(P-7506)
PAULS TV LLC (PA)
Also Called: Warehouse
900 Glenneyre St, Laguna Beach (92651-2707)
PHONE..................949 596-8800
Steven Strickland, *Chief Mktg Ofcr*
Kevin R Smith, *General Mgr*
Damian Sotelo, *Store Mgr*
Paula Farias, *QA Dir*
Tish Izquierdo, *Asst Treas*
EMP: 60 **EST:** 2006
SALES (est): 130.6MM **Privately Held**
SIC: 5064 Television sets

(P-7507)
PIONEER ELECTRONICS (USA) INC (DH)
1925 E Dominguez St, Long Beach (90810-1089)
P.O. Box 1720 (90801-1720)
PHONE..................310 952-2000
Fax: 310 952-2199
Satoshi Ohdate, *CEO*
Augusto Cardoso, *President*
Kiyokazu Igarahi, *President*
Kiyokazu Igarashi, *COO*
Naoki Horie, *Treasurer*
▲ **EMP:** 300 **EST:** 1982
SQ FT: 86,485
SALES (est): 168.6MM
SALES (corp-wide): 3.8B **Privately Held**
SIC: 5064 High fidelity equipment
HQ: Pioneer North America, Inc.
  2265 E 220th St
  Long Beach CA 90810
  213 746-6337

(P-7508)
PIONEER ELECTRONICS SERVICE (DH)
1925 E Dominguez St, Long Beach (90810-1089)
P.O. Box 1760 (90801-1760)
PHONE..................213 746-6337
Ronald N Stone, *President*
Ken S Okano, *Corp Secy*
Fabian Fugine, *Vice Pres*
Barry Smith, *Marketing Staff*
Joanes Hsusean, *Manager*
▼ **EMP:** 151
SQ FT: 150,000
SALES (est): 32.6MM
SALES (corp-wide): 3.8B **Privately Held**
SIC: 5064 7629 7622 5065 Electrical appliances, television & radio; electrical repair shops; radio & television repair; electronic parts & equipment; special warehousing & storage
HQ: Pioneer North America, Inc.
  2265 E 220th St
  Long Beach CA 90810
  213 746-6337

(P-7509)
PRODUCTS & SERVICES INC
2600 Michelson Dr # 1700, Irvine (92612-1550)
PHONE..................949 583-1681
Kris Boudreau, *Ch of Bd*
EMP: 54
SQ FT: 18,000
SALES (est): 4.4MM **Privately Held**
SIC: 5064 Electrical appliances, major

(P-7510)
R & B WHOLESALE DISTRS INC (PA)
2350 S Milliken Ave, Ontario (91761-2332)
PHONE..................909 230-5400
Fax: 909 230-5415
Robert O Burggraf, *President*
Sam Snyder, *CFO*
Robert Burggrat, *Treasurer*
Masako Burggraf, *Vice Pres*
Romeo Roque, *Vice Pres*
▲ **EMP:** 50
SQ FT: 72,000
SALES (est): 114.5MM **Privately Held**
WEB: www.rbdist.com
SIC: 5064 Electrical appliances, major; electrical entertainment equipment

(P-7511)
SAMSUNG ELECTRONICS AMER INC
18600 S Broadwick St, Rancho Dominguez (90220-6434)
PHONE..................310 537-7000
K Hilm, *General Mgr*
Kyu Lee, *Vice Pres*
Helmut Meinke, *Vice Pres*
Bob Weis, *Vice Pres*
John Suh, *Info Tech Dir*
EMP: 100
SALES (corp-wide): 118.4B **Privately Held**
WEB: www.samsung.com
SIC: 5064 5065 Electrical appliances, television & radio; communication equipment
HQ: Samsung Electronics America, Inc.
  85 Challenger Rd
  Ridgefield Park NJ 07660
  201 229-4000

(P-7512)
SONY ELECTRONICS INC
Also Called: Sony Logistics
2201 E Carson St, Carson (90810-1227)
PHONE..................310 835-6121
Alan Schwab, *Manager*
Catherine Wozney, *Manager*
EMP: 127
SALES (corp-wide): 69.2B **Privately Held**
SIC: 5064 5065 Electrical appliances, television & radio; electronic parts & equipment
HQ: Sony Electronics Inc.
  16535 Via Esprillo Bldg 1
  San Diego CA 92127
  858 942-2400

(P-7513)
WATER HEATERS ONLY INC
3620 Haven Ave, Redwood City (94063-4640)
PHONE..................650 368-9998
Tom Crabtree, *President*
Bill Lee, *Sales Associate*
Yana Carpenter, *Sales Staff*
Nicolas Ratel, *Sales Staff*
EMP: 90
SALES (est): 8.2MM **Privately Held**
SIC: 5064 5999 1711 Water heaters, electric; plumbing & heating supplies; heating systems repair & maintenance

5065 Electronic Parts & Eqpt Wholesale

(P-7514)
7DAYS INC
3503 Jack Northrop Ave, Hawthorne (90250-4433)
PHONE..................424 255-5872
Chou Hongliang, *President*
EMP: 200
SALES: 50MM **Privately Held**
SIC: 5065 Electronic parts & equipment

(P-7515)
ADVANCED MP TECHNOLOGY INC (PA)
1010 Calle Sombra, San Clemente (92673-6227)
PHONE..................949 492-6589
Fax: 949 492-6480
Jafar Yassai, *CEO*
Homayoun Shorooghi, *President*
Mehdi Taghiei PHD, *CFO*
Kamran Malek, *Vice Pres*
Cathy Knight, *Executive*
▲ **EMP:** 126
SQ FT: 86,000
SALES (est): 143.6MM **Privately Held**
WEB: www.advancedmp.com
SIC: 5065 Electronic parts & equipment

(P-7516)
ALIPHCOM (PA)
99 Rhode Island St Fl 3, San Francisco (94103-5233)
PHONE..................415 230-7600
Alexander Asseily, *Chairman*
Mindy Mount, *President*
Hosain Rahman, *CEO*
Patrick Chiang, *CFO*
Richard Drysdale, *Senior VP*
▲ **EMP:** 138
SQ FT: 20,000
SALES (est): 260.8MM **Privately Held**
WEB: www.aliph.com
SIC: 5065 5999 Sound equipment, electronic; electronic parts & equipment

5065 - Electronic Parts & Eqpt Wholesale County (P-7517)

(P-7517)
ALTURA COMM SOLUTIONS LLC (DH)
1335 S Acacia Ave, Fullerton (92831-5315)
PHONE..................................714 948-8400
Robert Blazek, *CEO*
Tim Henion, *President*
David Key, *CFO*
Valerie Dorian, *Info Tech Dir*
Lee Gray, *Info Tech Dir*
EMP: 55
SQ FT: 25,000
SALES (est): 100MM **Privately Held**
WEB: www.alturacs.com
SIC: 5065 Electronic parts & equipment

(P-7518)
ALVARION INC (HQ)
555 N Mathilda Ave # 210, Sunnyvale (94085-3503)
PHONE..................................650 314-2500
Fax: 650 967-3966
Zvi Slonimsky, *President*
Amir Rosenzweg, *President*
Calvin R Hoagland, *CFO*
Efrat Makov, *CFO*
Batya Marks, *Sr Corp Ofcr*
▲ EMP: 50
SQ FT: 16,000
SALES (est): 8.6MM
SALES (corp-wide): 55.4MM **Privately Held**
WEB: www.alvarion-usa.com
SIC: 5065 Communication equipment
PA: Alvarion Ltd
  Givat Yeshayahu
  364 584-23

(P-7519)
AMERICAN ZETTLER INC (HQ)
75 Columbia, Aliso Viejo (92656-4115)
PHONE..................................949 360-5830
Fax: 949 831-8548
Michael P Morgan, *President*
Rainer Moegling, *CFO*
Edward Edsinga, *Manager*
▲ EMP: 60
SQ FT: 63,000
SALES (est): 24.7MM
SALES (corp-wide): 47.1MM **Privately Held**
WEB: www.azettler.com
SIC: 5065 Communication equipment
PA: Zettler Components, Inc.
  1701 W Sequoia Ave
  Orange CA 92868
  714 939-6699

(P-7520)
AP GLOBAL INC
Also Called: Accessory Power
31352 Via Colinas Ste 101, Westlake Village (91362-6810)
PHONE..................................818 707-3167
Robert Breines, *President*
Pascale Malevez, *Office Mgr*
Gail Breines, *VP Finance*
EMP: 60 EST: 2013
SALES: 35MM **Privately Held**
SIC: 5065 Electronic parts & equipment

(P-7521)
APUMAC LLC
Also Called: Apumac.com
6404 Wilshire Blvd # 106, Los Angeles (90048-5501)
P.O. Box 9461 (90048)
PHONE..................................888 248-7775
Lilyane Bensimon,
EMI Okabe, *Opers Staff*
EMP: 214
SQ FT: 1,500
SALES (est): 22.2MM **Privately Held**
SIC: 5065 Mobile telephone equipment

(P-7522)
ARCONIX/USA INC
Also Called: Arconix USA
880 Avenida Acaso Ste 100, Camarillo (93012-8721)
PHONE..................................805 388-2525
Allen Kay, *President*
Mark G Harris, *Vice Pres*
Cameron Hill, *Vice Pres*
Norman Fontes, *Info Tech Mgr*

Ronnie Tan, *Info Tech Mgr*
EMP: 52 EST: 1948
SALES (est): 7MM
SALES (corp-wide): 446MM **Privately Held**
WEB: www.penn-eng.com
SIC: 5065 Electronic parts & equipment
HQ: Penn Engineering & Manufacturing Corp.
  5190 Old Easton Rd
  Danboro PA 18916
  215 766-8853

(P-7523)
ARROW ELECTRONICS INC
Also Called: Arrow Alliance Group
3000 Bowers Ave, Santa Clara (95051-0942)
PHONE..................................631 847-2918
Glen Moore, *Principal*
Keith Spencer, *Engineer*
Patricia Ellwood, *Manager*
Steven C Forster, *Manager*
EMP: 160
SALES (corp-wide): 23.2B **Publicly Held**
WEB: www.arrow.com
SIC: 5065 Electronic parts
PA: Arrow Electronics, Inc.
  9201 E Dry Creek Rd
  Centennial CO 80112
  303 824-4000

(P-7524)
ARROW ELECTRONICS INC
Also Called: Arrow Bell
20935 Warner Center Ln A, Woodland Hills (91367-6581)
PHONE..................................818 932-1022
Fax: 818 932-1020
Mike Jerworski, *General Mgr*
Sara Drulis, *Marketing Mgr*
Jacqueline Counter, *Marketing Staff*
Travis McKague, *Sales Staff*
Lynn Andrus, *Manager*
EMP: 85
SALES (corp-wide): 23.2B **Publicly Held**
WEB: www.arrow.com
SIC: 5065 Electronic parts
PA: Arrow Electronics, Inc.
  9201 E Dry Creek Rd
  Centennial CO 80112
  303 824-4000

(P-7525)
ASE (US) INC (HQ)
Also Called: Advance Semiconductor Engrg
1255 E Arques Ave, Sunnyvale (94085-4701)
PHONE..................................408 636-9500
Pien Wu, *President*
Kay Cheng, *Technology*
Jay Hung, *Technology*
Jane Yan, *Technology*
Desi Judilla, *VP Sales*
EMP: 63
SQ FT: 21,000
SALES (est): 26.1MM
SALES (corp-wide): 8.7B **Privately Held**
WEB: www.asetechforum.com
SIC: 5065 Electronic parts & equipment
PA: Advanced Semiconductor Engineering, Inc.
  26, Chin 3rd Rd., N. E. P. Z.,
  Kaohsiung City 81170
  736 171-31

(P-7526)
AUDIOBAHN INC
114 S Berry St, Brea (92821-4826)
PHONE..................................714 988-0400
Fax: 562 988-0433
Nasser A Abdo, *President*
Saad Abou Abdo, *COO*
Rosie Fajardo, *Manager*
▲ EMP: 60
SQ FT: 130,000
SALES: 35MM **Privately Held**
SIC: 5065 Electronic parts & equipment

(P-7527)
AVAD LLC (PA)
5805 Sepulvda Blvd # 750, Sherman Oaks (91411-2546)
PHONE..................................818 742-4800
Fax: 818 742-4801
Tom Jacoby, *CEO*

Fred Farrar, *President*
Kurt Kilgast, *CFO*
Bob Rossum, *Sr Corp Ofcr*
Wally Whinna, *Exec VP*
◆ EMP: 150
SALES (est): 444.4MM **Privately Held**
WEB: www.avadnc.com
SIC: 5065 7359 Electronic parts; audio-visual equipment & supply rental

(P-7528)
AVNET INC
Also Called: Avnet USI
220 Commerce Ste 100, Irvine (92602-1346)
PHONE..................................949 789-4100
Tony Coletto, *Branch Mgr*
Liza Polin, *Human Res Dir*
Anthony Coleto, *Manager*
Sandy Rey, *Accounts Mgr*
EMP: 75
SALES (corp-wide): 26.2B **Publicly Held**
WEB: www.avnet.com
SIC: 5065 Electronic parts
PA: Avnet, Inc.
  2211 S 47th St
  Phoenix AZ 85034
  480 643-2000

(P-7529)
AVNET INC
Also Called: Avnet Emg
20951 Burbank Blvd Ste A, Woodland Hills (91367-6696)
PHONE..................................818 594-8310
James Williams, *Manager*
EMP: 60
SALES (corp-wide): 26.2B **Publicly Held**
WEB: www.avnet.com
SIC: 5065 Electronic parts & equipment
PA: Avnet, Inc.
  2211 S 47th St
  Phoenix AZ 85034
  480 643-2000

(P-7530)
AVNET INC
2110 Zanker Rd, San Jose (95131-2111)
PHONE..................................408 501-3925
Dan Weiss, *Director*
Steven McIntosh, *Info Tech Dir*
Duyet Dang, *Technology*
Carrie Weiler, *Human Res Mgr*
Christie Campbell, *Marketing Mgr*
EMP: 86
SALES (corp-wide): 26.2B **Publicly Held**
SIC: 5065 Electronic parts
PA: Avnet, Inc.
  2211 S 47th St
  Phoenix AZ 85034
  480 643-2000

(P-7531)
AVNET INC
15231 Avenue Of Science # 150, San Diego (92128-3450)
PHONE..................................858 385-7500
Mark Gooding, *Branch Mgr*
Nick Henry, *Sales Staff*
Debra Jones, *Sales Staff*
Ali Rahbar, *Sales Staff*
EMP: 400
SALES (corp-wide): 26.2B **Publicly Held**
SIC: 5065 5045 7379 Electronic parts; computers, peripherals & software; computer related consulting services
PA: Avnet, Inc.
  2211 S 47th St
  Phoenix AZ 85034
  480 643-2000

(P-7532)
BAYSAND INC
6910 Santa Teresa Blvd, San Jose (95119-1339)
PHONE..................................408 960-8263
EMP: 63
SALES (corp-wide): 14.4MM **Privately Held**
SIC: 5065 Semiconductor devices
PA: Baysand Inc.
  305 Vineyard Town Ctr # 317
  Morgan Hill CA 95037
  408 314-4741

(P-7533)
BELKIN INTERNATIONAL INC (PA)
Also Called: Belkin Components
12045 Waterfront Dr, Playa Vista (90094-2999)
PHONE..................................310 751-5100
Chester J Pipkin, *President*
George C Platisa, *CFO*
Janice Pipkin, *Corp Secy*
D Thomas Triggs,
Jason Chang, *Administration*
◆ EMP: 450 EST: 1983
SQ FT: 218,000
SALES (est): 613.9MM **Privately Held**
WEB: www.belkin.com
SIC: 5065 5045 Intercommunication equipment, electronic; communication equipment; computers & accessories, personal & home entertainment

(P-7534)
BRIX GROUP INC (PA)
Also Called: Pana-Pacific
838 N Laverne Ave, Fresno (93727)
PHONE..................................559 457-4700
Fax: 408 379-3928
Harrison Brix, *CEO*
Kristina Reed, *President*
John Trenberth, *President*
Dennis Pastirik, *CFO*
A J Olsen, *CIO*
▲ EMP: 80
SQ FT: 35,000
SALES (est): 151.7MM **Privately Held**
WEB: www.brixcom.com
SIC: 5065 5013 Mobile telephone equipment; paging & signaling equipment; motor vehicle supplies & new parts

(P-7535)
BRIX GROUP INC
Also Called: Pana-Pacific OEM Division
80 Van Ness Ave, Fresno (93721-3223)
PHONE..................................559 499-1890
EMP: 80
SQ FT: 49,572
SALES (corp-wide): 153.2MM **Privately Held**
SIC: 5065
PA: The Brix Group Inc
  1400 Dell Ave Ste A
  Campbell CA 93727
  800 726-2333

(P-7536)
BROWNSTONE COMPANIES INC
Also Called: Brownstone Security
2629 Manhattan Beach Blvd # 100, Redondo Beach (90278-1604)
PHONE..................................310 297-3600
Walter Tom Bragg, *President*
Shane Pryor, *Marketing Staff*
EMP: 700
SQ FT: 4,000
SALES (est): 47.2MM **Privately Held**
WEB: www.brownstoneps.com
SIC: 5065 Security control equipment & systems

(P-7537)
BT AMERICAS INC
2160 E Grand Ave, El Segundo (90245-5024)
P.O. Box 696098, San Antonio TX (78269-6098)
PHONE..................................310 335-2600
Fax: 310 335-4507
Boustridge Micheal, *Director*
Marc Patterson, *President*
John Hoffman, *Exec VP*
Daniel Rivera, *Senior VP*
David Buckenheimer, *Vice Pres*
EMP: 100
SALES (corp-wide): 553.9MM **Privately Held**
SIC: 5065 Electronic parts & equipment; video equipment, electronic
PA: Bt Americas Inc.
  8951 Cypress Waters Blvd # 200
  Coppell TX 75019
  877 272-0832

▲ = Import ▼ = Export
◆ = Import/Export

PRODUCTS & SERVICES SECTION

5065 - Electronic Parts & Eqpt Wholesale County (P-7558)

(P-7538)
BT AMERICAS INC
2160 E Grand Ave, El Segundo (90245-5024)
PHONE 646 487-7400
Kristen Verderame, *Manager*
Colin Bell, *Technician*
EMP: 100
SALES (corp-wide): 553.9MM **Privately Held**
WEB: www.b-t.com
SIC: 5065 Electronic parts & equipment
PA: Bt Americas Inc.
8951 Cypress Waters Blvd # 200
Coppell TX 75019
877 272-0832

(P-7539)
BUYERS CONSULTATION SVC INC (PA)
Also Called: B C S
8735 Remmet Ave, Canoga Park (91304-1519)
P.O. Box 8427, Calabasas (91372-8427)
PHONE 818 341-4820
Fax: 818 341-0010
Jo Manhan, *President*
Larry Manhan, *Technology*
Peggy Lee, *Accounting Mgr*
Peter Afiuny, *Marketing Staff*
▲ **EMP:** 75
SQ FT: 40,000
SALES (est): 47.8MM **Privately Held**
SIC: 5065 7389 5093 4953 Electronic parts & equipment; auctioneers, fee basis; metal scrap & waste materials; recycling, waste materials

(P-7540)
C P DOCUMENT TECHNOLOGIES LLC (PA)
Also Called: Copypage
800 W 6th St Ste 1400, Los Angeles (90017-2718)
PHONE 213 617-4040
Fax: 213 439-1068
Zorast Driver,
Jack Ziedman, *CFO*
Dave Drawsord, *Controller*
Michael Dutra, *Opers Staff*
EMP: 70
SQ FT: 8,350
SALES (est): 29.2MM **Privately Held**
WEB: www.copypage.com
SIC: 5065 7334 7374 Electronic parts; photocopying & duplicating services; optical scanning data service

(P-7541)
CALIFORNIA EASTERN LABS INC (PA)
4590 Patrick Henry Dr, Santa Clara (95054-1817)
PHONE 408 919-2500
Fax: 408 988-0279
Jerry A Arden, *Ch of Bd*
Paul A S Minton, *President*
Mark A Sargent, *CFO*
Jeremy Dietz, *Officer*
Kevin Beber, *Vice Pres*
▲ **EMP:** 80
SQ FT: 42,000
SALES (est): 36.9MM **Privately Held**
WEB: www.cel.com
SIC: 5065 Electronic parts

(P-7542)
CAVENDISH KINETICS INC
2960 N 1st St, San Jose (95134-2021)
PHONE 408 240-7370
Paul Dal Santo, *CEO*
Patrick Murray, *CFO*
Richard Knipe, *Vice Pres*
EMP: 50
SALES (est): 1MM **Privately Held**
SIC: 5065 Semiconductor devices

(P-7543)
CBOL CORPORATION
19850 Plummer St, Chatsworth (91311-5652)
PHONE 818 704-8200
Howard Nam, *COO*
Spencer H Kim, *CEO*
Kenneth Cheung, *CFO*
Robert Jondall, *Senior VP*
Jason Koh, *General Mgr*
▲ **EMP:** 131
SQ FT: 69,820
SALES (est): 162MM **Privately Held**
WEB: www.cbolcorp.com
SIC: 5065 5072 5013 5088 Electronic parts & equipment; hardware; staples; motor vehicle supplies & new parts; transportation equipment & supplies; industrial machinery & equipment; plastics materials & basic shapes

(P-7544)
CELESTICA LLC
821 S Rockefeller Ave, Ontario (91761-8119)
PHONE 909 418-6986
James Rodriguez, *Branch Mgr*
EMP: 400
SALES (corp-wide): 4.1B **Privately Held**
SIC: 5065 7629 Electronic parts & equipment; electronic equipment repair
HQ: Celestica Llc
11 Continental Blvd # 103
Merrimack NH 03054
603 657-3001

(P-7545)
CELLULAR PALACE INC
Also Called: Wireless Lines
10435 Santa Monica Blvd F, Los Angeles (90025-6936)
PHONE 310 278-2007
Rahim Bobby Malmed, *President*
Shahram Javidzad, *Officer*
▲ **EMP:** 89
SALES (est): 11.4MM **Privately Held**
SIC: 5065 5064 5999 5731 Telephone & telegraphic equipment; paging & signaling equipment; high fidelity equipment; alarm signal systems; telephone & communication equipment; high fidelity stereo equipment; radios, two-way, citizens' band, weather, short-wave, etc.

(P-7546)
CELLUPHONE LLC
6119 E Washington Blvd, Commerce (90040-2416)
PHONE 323 727-9131
EMP: 135
SALES (est): 9.2MM **Privately Held**
SIC: 5065 5999 Electronic parts & equipment; telephone equipment & systems

(P-7547)
CENZIC INC
655 Campbell Tech Pkwy # 100, Campbell (95008-5088)
PHONE 408 200-0700
John Weinschenk, *President*
Dave Ferguson, *CFO*
Bala Venkat, *Chief Mktg Ofcr*
Glenn Gramling, *Vice Pres*
Ralph Johnston, *Vice Pres*
EMP: 50
SQ FT: 7,600
SALES (est): 20.7MM **Privately Held**
WEB: www.cenzic.com
SIC: 5065 Security control equipment & systems

(P-7548)
CITISITE INC
Also Called: Citisite Co
11400 State Highway 49, Jackson (95642-9469)
PHONE 209 418-7620
James Lapham, *CEO*
Cory Kasinger, *CEO*
Jeremy Edwards, *CFO*
Farid Shouekani, *Bd of Directors*
Joseph Fisher, *Vice Pres*
EMP: 62
SALES (est): 6.8MM **Privately Held**
SIC: 5065 3669 1623 3663 Intercommunication equipment, electronic; highway signals, electric; transmitting tower (telecommunication) construction; radio broadcasting & communications equipment

(P-7549)
CNET TECHNOLOGY CORPORATION (HQ)
26291 Prod Ave Ste 205, Hayward (94545)
PHONE 408 392-9966
Simon J Chang, *President*
Ed Sherman, *Director*
▲ **EMP:** 179
SQ FT: 50,000
SALES (est): 30MM
SALES (corp-wide): 103.8MM **Privately Held**
WEB: www.cnetusa.com
SIC: 5065 3661 3577 Communication equipment; modems, computer; telephone & telegraph apparatus; computer peripheral equipment
PA: Kmc (Kuei Meng) International Inc.
8f-5, 425, Jhong Hua Rd,
Tainan City 71079
630 371-11

(P-7550)
CORNER PRODUCTS COMPANY
Also Called: C P Technologies
1370 Reynolds Ave Ste 100, Irvine (92614-5504)
PHONE 949 255-3982
Michael Hsu, *Partner*
Rick Hsu, *Partner*
Chao-Jen Lin, *Partner*
Christine Chang, *Accountant*
▲ **EMP:** 55
SQ FT: 17,000
SALES (est): 12MM **Privately Held**
SIC: 5065 5045 Telephone equipment; computer peripheral equipment

(P-7551)
D B ROBERTS INC
880 Avenida Acaso Ste 100, Camarillo (93012-8721)
PHONE 805 988-4882
Fax: 805 388-0999
Mark Harris, *Vice Pres*
Patrick Chiasson, *Site Mgr*
EMP: 52
SALES (corp-wide): 96.2MM **Privately Held**
WEB: www.dbroberts.com
SIC: 5065 Electronic parts & equipment
PA: D. B. Roberts, Inc.
30 Upton Dr Ste 3
Wilmington MA 01887
978 988-5777

(P-7552)
DAVID LEVY CO INC
Also Called: Dlc
12753 Moore St, Cerritos (90703-2136)
PHONE 562 404-9998
Fax: 562 404-9698
David Levy, *CEO*
John Latino, *Vice Pres*
Gordon Schaer, *Admin Sec*
Alex Blanco, *Marketing Mgr*
Raul Gomez, *Sales Staff*
▲ **EMP:** 50 **EST:** 1978
SQ FT: 25,000
SALES (est): 17MM **Privately Held**
WEB: www.cybertraklocate.com
SIC: 5065 Electronic parts

(P-7553)
DECISION SCIENCES INTL CORP
12345 First American Way # 100, Poway (92064-6828)
P.O. Box 328, Middleburg VA (20118-0328)
PHONE 858 602-1600
Dwight Johnson, *President*
Brian Gallagher, *President*
Mike Goll, *CFO*
Loann Tu, *Accountant*
Ariana Austin, *Receptionist*
EMP: 60 **EST:** 2007
SALES (est): 26.8MM **Privately Held**
SIC: 5065 Radar detectors

(P-7554)
DELTA AMERICA LTD (HQ)
Also Called: Delta Products
46101 Fremont Blvd, Fremont (94538-6468)
PHONE 510 668-5100
Ming H Huang, *President*
Yao Chou, *Admin Sec*
Charlene Ting, *Manager*
Cheryl Lin, *Accounts Mgr*
TI Wang, *Accounts Mgr*
◆ **EMP:** 130
SALES (est): 122.7MM
SALES (corp-wide): 6.2B **Privately Held**
SIC: 5065 3679 8731 Electronic parts & equipment; switches, stepping; power supplies, all types: static; electronic research
PA: Delta Electronics, Inc.
31-1, Xingbang Rd.,
Taoyuan City TAY 33370
336 263-01

(P-7555)
DELTA PRODUCTS CORPORATION (DH)
46101 Fremont Blvd, Fremont (94538-6468)
PHONE 510 668-5100
Fax: 510 668-0686
Ming H Huang, *President*
Sheryl Chen, *CFO*
Julia Yu, *Bd of Directors*
Andrew Lee, *Vice Pres*
Elson Chang, *Division Mgr*
◆ **EMP:** 100
SALES (est): 122.7MM
SALES (corp-wide): 6.2B **Privately Held**
WEB: www.delta-corp.com
SIC: 5065 5045 8741 5063 Electronic parts & equipment; computer peripheral equipment; management services; electrical apparatus & equipment; computer peripheral equipment
HQ: Delta America Ltd
46101 Fremont Blvd
Fremont CA 94538
510 668-5100

(P-7556)
DIGITALPERSONA INC (HQ)
6607 Kaiser Dr, Fremont (94555-3608)
PHONE 650 474-4000
Fax: 650 298-8313
Richard Agostinelli, *President*
Richard A Agostinelli, *President*
Jerry Cahill, *CFO*
Joseph W Kuhn, *CFO*
Vance Bjorn, *Vice Pres*
▲ **EMP:** 80
SQ FT: 40,000
SALES (est): 27.4MM
SALES (corp-wide): 1B **Privately Held**
WEB: www.digitalpersona.com
SIC: 5065 Security control equipment & systems
PA: Francisco Partners Management, L.P.
1 Letterman Dr Ste 410
San Francisco CA 94129
415 418-2900

(P-7557)
DIVX CORPORATION (HQ)
4790 Estgate Mall Ste 200, San Diego (92121)
PHONE 858 882-0700
Fax: 858 882-0601
Kanaan Jemili PHD, *President*
Trevor Renfield, *CFO*
Melissa Foo, *Mktg Dir*
Solange Jacobs, *Director*
Shawn Cen, *Manager*
EMP: 59
SQ FT: 47,000
SALES (est): 71.2MM
SALES (corp-wide): 94MM **Publicly Held**
SIC: 5065 Video equipment, electronic
PA: Neulion, Inc.
1600 Old Country Rd
Plainview NY 11803
516 622-8300

(P-7558)
ECAMSECURE
Also Called: D & M Communications
436 W Walnut St, Gardena (90248-3137)
PHONE 800 257-5512
Christopher Coffey, *President*
EMP: 50
SALES (est): 10.8MM **Privately Held**
SIC: 5065 Electronic parts & equipment

5065 - Electronic Parts & Eqpt Wholesale County (P-7559)

PRODUCTS & SERVICES SECTION

(P-7559)
EFORCITY CORP - NFM
Also Called: Ascend Distribution
18525 Railroad St, City of Industry
(91748-1316)
PHONE.....................626 442-3168
Fax: 626 401-1553
Michael Wong, *Manager*
Jack Sheng, *CEO*
Alvin Wong, *CFO*
Eugene Wong, *CFO*
Bolan Tuskan, *Info Tech Dir*
▲ EMP: 60
SQ FT: 100,000
SALES (est): 48.4MM **Privately Held**
WEB: www.eforcity.com
SIC: 5065 Telephone equipment

(P-7560)
ELROB INC
Also Called: El-Com Cabletek
12691 Monarch St, Garden Grove
(92841-3918)
PHONE.....................714 230-6100
Fax: 714 230-6110
Elie Vrobel, *CEO*
Arik Vrobel, *President*
Dan Balentine, *Vice Pres*
Kevin Melstrom, *Executive*
Kevin Malstrom, *Info Tech Dir*
▲ EMP: 54 EST: 1960
SQ FT: 38,500
SALES (est): 65.3MM **Privately Held**
WEB: www.elcomcabletek.com
SIC: 5065 3679 3613 3643 Electronic parts & equipment; harness assemblies for electronic use: wire or cable; switchgear & switchboard apparatus; current-carrying wiring devices

(P-7561)
EVER WIN INTERNATIONAL CORP
17579 Railroad St, City of Industry
(91748-1125)
PHONE.....................626 810-8218
Fax: 626 810-6628
Charles Chen, *CEO*
Renee Chen, *Shareholder*
Henry Chen, *President*
Christine Cheng, *CFO*
Mae Hsu, *Exec VP*
▲ EMP: 50
SQ FT: 90,000
SALES (est): 44.3MM **Privately Held**
WEB: www.everwin.com
SIC: 5065 Telephone & telegraphic equipment

(P-7562)
EWING-FOLEY INC (PA)
10061 Bubb Rd Ste 100, Cupertino
(95014-4162)
PHONE.....................408 342-1201
Richard Foley, *Ch of Bd*
Gary Lessing, *President*
Robert Lessing, *Corp Secy*
Rachel Sherwood, *Vice Pres*
Roger Mendoza, *General Mgr*
EMP: 50 EST: 1964
SQ FT: 13,000
SALES (est): 17.6MM **Privately Held**
WEB: www.ewingfoley.com
SIC: 5065 Electronic parts

(P-7563)
EXIS INC
1570 The Alameda Ste 150, San Jose
(95126-2331)
PHONE.....................408 944-4600
Fax: 408 321-3200
Jim Bailey, *President*
Suzie Ferreira, *Manager*
EMP: 50
SQ FT: 22,000
SALES (est): 9.2MM **Privately Held**
WEB: www.exisinc.com
SIC: 5065 Electronic parts & equipment

(P-7564)
EXPRESCOM LLC
Also Called: Exprescom S.A. De C.V.
10145 Via De La Amistad, San Diego
(92154-5216)
PHONE.....................619 271-0531
Monica Bernachi, *Principal*
EMP: 58
SALES (corp-wide): 4.1MM **Privately Held**
SIC: 5065 5064 Radio receiving & transmitting tubes; video camera-audio recorders (camcorders)
PA: Exprescom, Llc
3753 Howard Hughes Pkwy
Las Vegas NV 89169
702 943-1859

(P-7565)
FIBERTRON CORPORATION
6400 Artesia Blvd, Buena Park
(90620-1006)
P.O. Box 5220 (90622-5220)
PHONE.....................714 670-7711
Fax: 714 670-8811
Marlene Spiegel, *President*
Eileen Cohen, *Treasurer*
Clint Wellis, *Vice Pres*
Henry J Cohen, *Finance Other*
▼ EMP: 75
SQ FT: 104,000
SALES (est): 34MM **Privately Held**
SIC: 5065 Communication equipment

(P-7566)
FLIR COMMERCIAL SYSTEMS INC (HQ)
6769 Hollister Ave # 100, Goleta
(93117-5572)
PHONE.....................805 690-6685
Thomas A Surran, *CEO*
William A Sundermeier, *President*
Earl R Lewis, *CEO*
Andrew C Teich, *CEO*
William W Davis, *Senior VP*
▲ EMP: 350
SALES (est): 643.6MM
SALES (corp-wide): 1.5B **Publicly Held**
SIC: 5065 3699 Security control equipment & systems; security devices
PA: Flir Systems, Inc.
27700 Sw Parkway Ave
Wilsonville OR 97070
503 498-3547

(P-7567)
FOREIGN TRADE CORPORATION (PA)
Also Called: Technocel
685 Cochran St Ste 200, Simi Valley
(93065-1921)
PHONE.....................805 823-8400
Fax: 805 823-8424
Ramin Rostami, *CEO*
Martine Wols, *COO*
Trinidad Sanchez, *Regional Mgr*
Isabelle Diep, *Accountant*
Jackie Jacquet, *Regl Sales Mgr*
▲ EMP: 94
SQ FT: 28,431
SALES: 80K **Privately Held**
WEB: www.technocel.com
SIC: 5065 Mobile telephone equipment

(P-7568)
FREESCALE SEMICONDUCTOR INC
2680 Zanker Rd Ste 200, San Jose
(95134-2144)
PHONE.....................408 518-5500
Rob Shane, *Branch Mgr*
EMP: 75
SALES (corp-wide): 6.1B **Privately Held**
SIC: 5065 Electronic parts
HQ: Freescale Semiconductor, Inc.
6501 W William Cannon Dr
Austin TX 78735
512 895-2000

(P-7569)
FRONTIER CALIFORNIA INC
Also Called: Verizon
112 S Lakeview Canyon Rd, Westlake Village (91362-3925)
PHONE.....................805 372-6000
Deb Anders, *President*
EMP: 650
SALES (corp-wide): 5.5B **Publicly Held**
SIC: 5065 4813 4812 Telephone equipment; telephone communication, except radio; radio telephone communication
HQ: Frontier California Inc.
140 West St
New York NY 10007
212 395-1000

(P-7570)
FRYS ELECTRONICS INC
1695 Willow Pass Rd, Concord
(94520-2611)
PHONE.....................925 852-0300
Fax: 925 852-0318
Joe Claire, *Branch Mgr*
EMP: 300
SALES (corp-wide): 17.4MM **Privately Held**
SIC: 5065 Electronic parts & equipment
PA: Fry's Electronics, Inc.
600 E Brokaw Rd
San Jose CA 95112
408 350-1484

(P-7571)
FULL CIRCLE WIRELESS INC
8900 Research Dr, Irvine (92618-4245)
PHONE.....................949 783-7979
Shelton Basham, *CEO*
EMP: 50
SALES (est): 6.4MM **Privately Held**
WEB: www.fullcirclewireless.com
SIC: 5065 Mobile telephone equipment

(P-7572)
FUMAI INDUSTRIAL INC
735 W Duarte Rd, Arcadia (91007-7522)
PHONE.....................626 272-1788
John Whang, *Branch Mgr*
EMP: 75
SALES (corp-wide): 1.4K **Privately Held**
SIC: 5065 Communication equipment
PA: Shanghai Pudong Fumei Industry & Trade Co., Ltd.
Group 1, Xinchun Village, Huanglou, Chuansha Town, Pudong New Di Shanghai
-

(P-7573)
GGEC AMERICA INC
100 Pacifica Ste 200, Irvine (92618-7441)
PHONE.....................714 750-2280
Fax: 714 750-2281
Dave Cox, *President*
Jiaxi Huang, *President*
Kobe Zhang, *Vice Pres*
▲ EMP: 72
SQ FT: 2,700
SALES (est): 12.5MM
SALES (corp-wide): 136.2MM **Privately Held**
WEB: www.gabrielkoneta.com
SIC: 5065 Electronic parts & equipment
PA: Guoguang Electric Company Limited
No.8 Jinghu Road, Xinhua Street, Huadu Reg.
Guangzhou 51080
202 860-9982

(P-7574)
GLOBAL CELLULAR INC
1 Stoneridge Mall Rd, Pleasanton
(94588-3281)
PHONE.....................925 469-9039
EMP: 68
SALES (corp-wide): 132.6MM **Privately Held**
SIC: 5065 4812 Telephone & telegraphic equipment; cellular telephone services
PA: Global Cellular, Inc.
6485 Shiloh Rd Ste B100
Alpharetta GA 30005
678 513-4020

(P-7575)
GLOBALFOUNDRIES AMERICAS INC (DH)
2600 Great America Way, Santa Clara
(95054-1169)
PHONE.....................408 462-3900
Ajit Manocha, *CEO*
Jim Norling, *Ch of Bd*
Barry Waite, *Ch of Bd*
Chia Song Hwee, *COO*
Jeremy Lansford, *COO*
EMP: 80
SQ FT: 45,000
SALES (est): 70.3MM **Privately Held**
WEB: www.charteredsemi.com
SIC: 5065 Semiconductor devices
HQ: Globalfoundries Singapore Pte. Ltd.
60 Woodlands Industrial Park D Street 2
Singapore 73840
636 228-38

(P-7576)
HEILIND ELECTRONICS INC
Also Called: Force Electronics
700 N Plaza Dr, Visalia (93291-9327)
PHONE.....................559 651-0168
Mark Adams, *Manager*
EMP: 55
SALES (corp-wide): 745.5MM **Privately Held**
WEB: www.heilind.com
SIC: 5065 Electronic parts
PA: Heilind Electronics, Inc
58 Jonspin Rd
Wilmington MA 01887
978 658-7000

(P-7577)
HIRSCH ELECTRONICS LLC
1900 Carnegie Ave Ste B, Santa Ana
(92705-5557)
PHONE.....................949 250-8888
John Picc, *Mng Member*
Stephen Healy, *Exec VP*
Randy Lehman, *Regional Mgr*
Brian Culhane, *General Mgr*
Stacey Distefano, *General Mgr*
EMP: 85
SQ FT: 34,600
SALES (est): 16.9MM
SALES (corp-wide): 60.7MM **Publicly Held**
WEB: www.hirschelectronics.com
SIC: 5065 Security control equipment & systems
PA: Identiv, Inc.
2201 Walnut Ave Ste 100
Fremont CA 94538
949 250-8888

(P-7578)
HITACHI HIGH TECH AMER INC
5960 Inglewood Dr Ste 200, Pleasanton
(94588-8515)
PHONE.....................925 218-2800
Bob Gordon, *Manager*
John Giudicessi, *Executive*
Eric Person, *Info Tech Mgr*
Dean Gregson, *Business Anlyst*
Marty McCafferty, *Technology*
EMP: 70
SALES (corp-wide): 85.7B **Privately Held**
WEB: www.hitachi-hhta.com
SIC: 5065 Electronic parts & equipment
HQ: Hitachi High Technologies America, Inc.
10 N Martingale Rd # 500
Schaumburg IL 60173
847 273-4141

(P-7579)
HONEYWELL INTERNATIONAL INC
1349 Moffett Park Dr, Sunnyvale
(94089-1134)
PHONE.....................408 962-2000
Barry Russell, *Manager*
Simon Hermano, *Branch Mgr*
Margarita Rosa, *Administration*
Mike Holmes, *Engineer*
Richard Shuflin, *Engineer*
EMP: 50
SALES (corp-wide): 38.5B **Publicly Held**
WEB: www.honeywell.com
SIC: 5065 3674 Electronic parts & equipment; semiconductors & related devices
PA: Honeywell International Inc.
115 Tabor Rd
Morris Plains NJ 07950
973 455-2000

(P-7580)
HONEYWELL INTERNATIONAL INC
487 Mathew St, Santa Clara (95050-3105)
PHONE.....................408 986-8200
Fax: 408 988-5501
Dave Nash, *Owner*

▲ = Import ▼ = Export
◆ = Import/Export

PRODUCTS & SERVICES SECTION
5065 - Electronic Parts & Eqpt Wholesale County (P-7601)

EMP: 57
SALES (corp-wide): 38.5B **Publicly Held**
SIC: 5065 Security control equipment & systems
PA: Honeywell International Inc.
115 Tabor Rd
Morris Plains NJ 07950
973 455-2000

(P-7581)
HP INC
16399 W Bernardo Dr # 66, San Diego (92127-1801)
PHONE..................858 655-4100
Philip Liebscher, *Branch Mgr*
Seta Demirjian, *Vice Pres*
David Collom, *Software Engr*
Jaime Lara, *Design Engr*
Paul Hunter, *Project Mgr*
EMP: 350
SALES (corp-wide): 103.3B **Publicly Held**
SIC: 5065 Electronic parts & equipment
PA: Hp Inc.
1501 Page Mill Rd
Palo Alto CA 94304
650 857-1501

(P-7582)
HYPERCEL CORPORATION
Also Called: Naztech
28385 Constellation Rd, Valencia (91355-5048)
PHONE..................661 310-1000
David Nazar, *President*
Sam Onda, *Vice Pres*
Martha Gaetner, *Executive*
Tanya Azamian, *Executive Asst*
Martha Gaertner, *Executive Asst*
▲ **EMP:** 50
SQ FT: 16,800
SALES (est): 30.5MM **Privately Held**
WEB: www.hypercel.com
SIC: 5065 Telephone & telegraphic equipment

(P-7583)
I C CLASS COMPONENTS CORP (PA)
Also Called: Classic
23605 Telo Ave, Torrance (90505-4028)
PHONE..................310 539-5500
Jeffrey Klein, *President*
Chris Klein, *COO*
Kris Klein, *COO*
Nasser Shamsian, *CFO*
Emma Klein, *Corp Secy*
▲ **EMP:** 100
SQ FT: 53,000
SALES (est): 88.8MM **Privately Held**
WEB: www.connxx.com
SIC: 5065 Electronic parts & equipment

(P-7584)
IDEC CORPORATION (HQ)
1175 Elko Dr, Sunnyvale (94089-2209)
PHONE..................408 747-0550
Toshiyuki Funaki, *CEO*
Mikio Funaki, *President*
Donald L Scrivner, *CFO*
Sada Ohara, *Vice Pres*
Pete Tarantino, *Vice Pres*
▲ **EMP:** 89
SQ FT: 84,000
SALES (est): 57.4MM
SALES (corp-wide): 371.4MM **Privately Held**
WEB: www.idec.com
SIC: 5065 Electronic parts
PA: Idec Corporation
2-6-64, Nishimiyahara, Yodogawa-Ku
Osaka OSK 532-0
663 982-500

(P-7585)
INDUCTORS INC
Also Called: Central Technologies
140 Technology Dr Ste 500, Irvine (92618-2427)
PHONE..................949 623-2460
Fax: 949 623-1401
Judy Macdonald, *CEO*
Hamad Shah, *Engineer*
Angie Pham, *Marketing Staff*
Albert Valentin, *Sales Staff*
Connie Burlin, *Manager*
▲ **EMP:** 50
SQ FT: 24,600
SALES (est): 22.1MM **Privately Held**
WEB: www.inductor.com
SIC: 5065 Electronic parts & equipment

(P-7586)
INSULECTRO (PA)
20362 Windrow Dr Ste 100, Lake Forest (92630-8140)
PHONE..................949 587-3200
Fax: 949 454-0066
Timothy P Redfern, *CEO*
Patrick Redfern, *President*
Brad Biddle, *CFO*
Jason Marsh, *Vice Pres*
Kevin M Miller, *Vice Pres*
▲ **EMP:** 70
SQ FT: 40,000
SALES (est): 145.8MM **Privately Held**
WEB: www.cac-inc.com
SIC: 5065 Electronic parts

(P-7587)
INTERNTNAL CIRCUITS COMPONENTS
Also Called: Icci
3701 E Miraloma Ave, Anaheim (92806-2123)
PHONE..................714 572-1900
Fax: 714 572-2900
Richard Cheng, *President*
▲ **EMP:** 150
SALES (est): 15.2MM **Privately Held**
WEB: www.icciusa.com
SIC: 5065 3679 5047 3841 Electronic parts; electronic circuits; instruments, surgical & medical; surgical & medical instruments; automotive supplies & parts; printed circuit boards

(P-7588)
ITSON INC
Also Called: Zact Mobile
3 Lagoon Dr Ste 230, Redwood City (94065-5152)
PHONE..................650 517-2780
Gregory G Raleigh, *President*
David Johnson, *COO*
Anna Fieler, *Chief Mktg Ofcr*
Mak Azadi, *Senior VP*
Thierry Chassaing, *Senior VP*
EMP: 65
SQ FT: 8,000
SALES (est): 37.7MM **Privately Held**
SIC: 5065 Mobile telephone equipment

(P-7589)
JIT CORPORATION
Also Called: J I T Supply
1610 Commerce Way, Paso Robles (93446-3645)
P.O. Box 10007, Fullerton (92838-6007)
PHONE..................805 238-5000
Fax: 805 238-5001
Brent Smith, *President*
Sharon Smith, *Corp Secy*
Mark Whittaker, *General Mgr*
Tom Earl, *Engineer*
Eric Willeford, *Materials Mgr*
EMP: 60
SQ FT: 30,000
SALES (est): 50.6MM **Privately Held**
WEB: www.jitmfg.com
SIC: 5065 Electronic parts

(P-7590)
JOHNSON CONTROLS INC
1757 Tapo Canyon Rd # 120, Simi Valley (93063-3390)
PHONE..................805 522-5555
Patrick Young, *Regional Mgr*
Peter R Goodman, *Treasurer*
John P Kennedy, *Director*
Dimitri Dorfman, *Manager*
EMP: 60 **Privately Held**
SIC: 5065 Security control equipment & systems
HQ: Johnson Controls, Inc.
5757 N Green Bay Ave
Milwaukee WI 53209
414 524-1200

(P-7591)
JRI INC
Also Called: J R Industries
31280 La Baya Dr, Westlake Village (91362-4005)
PHONE..................818 706-2424
Fax: 818 707-3347
Kathy Becker, *President*
Gary Becker, *Corp Secy*
Debra Cortez, *Accounts Mgr*
▲ **EMP:** 50
SQ FT: 20,000
SALES (est): 23.8MM **Privately Held**
WEB: www.jri.com
SIC: 5065 Electronic parts & equipment

(P-7592)
KYOCERA INTERNATIONAL INC
3565 Cadillac Ave, Costa Mesa (92626-1401)
PHONE..................714 428-3600
EMP: 50
SALES (corp-wide): 12.6B **Publicly Held**
SIC: 5065 5013 5085 Electronic parts & equipment; connectors, electronic; semiconductor devices; heaters, motor vehicle; industrial tools
HQ: Kyocera International, Inc.
8611 Balboa Ave
San Diego CA 92123
858 576-2600

(P-7593)
LE TECHNOLOGY INC
Also Called: Leeco
3553 N 1st St, San Jose (95134-1803)
PHONE..................310 845-5838
Chaoying Deng, *CEO*
Joshua McGuire, *Vice Pres*
Brian Hui, *General Mgr*
May Guo, *Finance*
EMP: 175
SALES: 583.8K **Privately Held**
SIC: 5065 Television parts & accessories

(P-7594)
LEGACY FRAMES
11220 Wright Rd, Lynwood (90262-3124)
PHONE..................310 537-4210
Angelica Serrano, *CEO*
EMP: 54
SALES: 5MM **Privately Held**
SIC: 5065 Mobile telephone equipment

(P-7595)
LEMO USA INC
635 Park Ct, Rohnert Park (94928-7940)
P.O. Box 2408 (94927-2408)
PHONE..................707 206-3700
Dinshaw Pohwala, *CEO*
Bill Lee, *President*
Win Baerthel, *General Mgr*
Wendy Christiansen, *Executive Asst*
Michael Grieco, *CTO*
EMP: 100
SQ FT: 55,000
SALES (est): 85.8MM **Privately Held**
WEB: www.lemousa.com
SIC: 5065 3678 Connectors, electronic; electronic connectors
HQ: Interlemo Usa Inc
635 Park Ct
Rohnert Park CA 94928
707 578-8811

(P-7596)
LG DISPLAY AMERICA INC
2791 Loker Ave W, Carlsbad (92010-6601)
PHONE..................760 692-0900
Byungdo Park, *Branch Mgr*
Michael Kim, *President*
Jiyung Lee, *Human Res Mgr*
EMP: 50
SALES (corp-wide): 22.6B **Privately Held**
SIC: 5065 Modems, computer
HQ: Lg Display America, Inc.
2540 N 1st St 400
San Jose CA 95131
408 350-0190

(P-7597)
LG DISPLAY AMERICA INC (HQ)
2540 N 1st St Ste 400, San Jose (95131-1016)
PHONE..................408 350-0190
Fax: 408 350-7724
Chris Min, *President*
Davis Lee, *President*
James Jeong, *CFO*
Yong Kee Huang, *Senior VP*
Cheol D Ong Jeong, *Principal*
▲ **EMP:** 70
SQ FT: 1,000
SALES: 64.1MM
SALES (corp-wide): 22.6B **Privately Held**
SIC: 5065 Modems, computer
PA: Lg Display Co., Ltd.
128 Yeoui-Daero, Yeongdeungpo-Gu
Seoul SEO 07336
237 772-481

(P-7598)
LG ELCTRNICS MBILECOMM USA INC (DH)
Also Called: Lg Infocomm U.S.A.
10225 Willow Creek Rd, San Diego (92131-1639)
PHONE..................858 635-5300
Fax: 858 635-5399
Wayne Park, *CEO*
Kyung Joo Hwang, *President*
Jae Dong Han, *Treasurer*
Sarah Knight, *Officer*
Naveen Jain, *Vice Pres*
▲ **EMP:** 100
SQ FT: 67,500
SALES (est): 143.8MM
SALES (corp-wide): 24.8B **Privately Held**
SIC: 5065 3663 Mobile telephone equipment; radio & TV communications equipment
HQ: Lg Electronics U.S.A., Inc.
1000 Sylvan Ave
Englewood Cliffs NJ 07632
201 816-2000

(P-7599)
LINKSYS LLC
12045 Waterfront Dr, Playa Vista (90094-2999)
PHONE..................310 751-5100
EMP: 110
SALES (corp-wide): 613.9MM **Privately Held**
SIC: 5065 Electronic parts & equipment
HQ: Linksys Llc
131 Theory
Irvine CA 92617
949 270-8500

(P-7600)
LINKSYS LLC (HQ)
131 Theory, Irvine (92617-3045)
P.O. Box 91830, Los Angeles (90009-1830)
PHONE..................949 270-8500
Ned Hooper,
J Pocock, *Exec VP*
David Boyd, *Regional Mgr*
Michael Peters, *Regional Mgr*
Andrew Tay, *General Mgr*
▲ **EMP:** 275
SQ FT: 20,000
SALES (est): 613.9MM **Privately Held**
WEB: www.cisco.com
SIC: 5065 Electronic parts & equipment; communication equipment
PA: Belkin International, Inc.
12045 Waterfront Dr
Playa Vista CA 90094
310 751-5100

(P-7601)
LITE-ON INC (HQ)
Also Called: Lite-On U S A
720 S Hillview Dr, Milpitas (95035-5455)
PHONE..................408 946-4873
Fax: 408 941-4597
Sonny Hsuen-Ching Chao, *President*
Jerry Basham, *Vice Pres*
Jing Shao, *Sr Software Eng*
Nancy Chow, *CTO*
Julie Huang, *Accountant*
▲ **EMP:** 50
SQ FT: 25,000
SALES (est): 27MM
SALES (corp-wide): 6.6B **Privately Held**
WEB: www.liteonus.com
SIC: 5065 Electronic parts & equipment; semiconductor devices

5065 - Electronic Parts & Eqpt Wholesale County (P-7602)

PA: Lite-On Technology Corporation
22f, 392, Ruey Kuang Rd.,
Taipei City TAP 11492
287 982-888

(P-7602)
MACRONIX AMERICA INC (HQ)
Also Called: Mxic
680 N Mccarthy Blvd # 200, Milpitas
(95035-5120)
PHONE.................................408 262-8887
Arthur Yang, CEO
John J Wong, President
Dang-Hsing T Yiu, Senior VP
Ful-Long Ni, Vice Pres
Richard Culver, Technical Staff
EMP: 53
SQ FT: 20,000
SALES (est): 19.1MM
SALES (corp-wide): 644MM Privately Held
WEB: www.macronix.com
SIC: 5065 3674 Semiconductor devices; semiconductors & related devices
PA: Macronix International Co., Ltd.
16, Li Hsin Rd.,
Hsinchu City 30078
357 866-88

(P-7603)
METRIC EQUIPMENT SALES INC
Also Called: Microlease
25841 Industrial Blvd # 200, Hayward
(94545-2991)
PHONE.................................510 264-0887
Fax: 510 264-0886
Nigel Brown, CEO
Mike Clark, CEO
Nathan Hurst, CFO
Robert Parker, CFO
Deborah Hart-Hugill, Officer
EMP: 70
SQ FT: 25,000
SALES (est): 88.8MM
SALES (corp-wide): 137.8MM Privately Held
WEB: www.metrictest.com
SIC: 5065 5084 7359 3825 Electronic parts & equipment; measuring & testing equipment, electrical; electronic equipment rental, except computers; instruments to measure electricity
HQ: Microlease Inc.
9221 Globe Center Dr # 105
Morrisville NC 27560
866 520-0200

(P-7604)
MICRO-MECHANICS INC
465 Woodview Ave, Morgan Hill
(95037-2800)
PHONE.................................408 779-2927
Christopher R Borch, President
Michael Maguire, Engineer
Kathleen Edmiston, Finance
Mui Chiew, Prdtn Mgr
Thom Wojno, Mfg Staff
EMP: 50
SQ FT: 42,000
SALES (est): 23.1MM
SALES (corp-wide): 39.2MM Privately Held
WEB: www.micromechanics.com
SIC: 5065 3674 Semiconductor devices; semiconductors & related devices
PA: Micro-Mechanics (Holdings) Ltd.
31 Kaki Bukit Place
Singapore 41620
674 688-00

(P-7605)
MITSUBISHI ELECTRIC US INC (DH)
Also Called: Meus
5900 Katella Ave Ste A, Cypress
(90630-5019)
P.O. Box 6007 (90630-0007)
PHONE.................................714 220-2500
Fax: 714 236-6339
Kiyoshi Furukawa, CEO
Makoto Kono, Treasurer
Perry Pappous, Exec VP
Jared Baker, Vice Pres
Don Lee, Vice Pres
◆ EMP: 120 EST: 2000
SQ FT: 10,400
SALES (est): 641.5MM
SALES (corp-wide): 37.5B Privately Held
WEB: www.diamond-vision.com
SIC: 5065 5045 1796 3534 Electronic parts & equipment; semiconductor devices; computer peripheral equipment; elevator installation & conversion; escalators, passenger & freight
HQ: Mitsubishi Electric Us Holdings, Inc.
5900 Katella Ave Ste A
Cypress CA 90630
714 220-2500

(P-7606)
MITSUBISHI ELECTRIC US INC
7345 Orangewood Ave, Garden Grove
(92841-1411)
PHONE.................................,714 934-5300
EMP: 60
SALES (corp-wide): 36.3B Privately Held
SIC: 5065 5045
HQ: Mitsubishi Electric Us, Inc.
5900 Katella Ave Ste A
Cypress CA 90630
714 220-2500

(P-7607)
MOBILE LINE CMMUNICATIONS CORP
1402 Morgan Cir, Tustin (92780-6423)
PHONE.................................877 247-2544
Dennis Curtis, President
Aida Arguelles, Controller
Lori Jacobucci, Human Res Mgr
Ed Reilly, Opers Staff
Dan Husband, Sales Executive
▲ EMP: 75
SQ FT: 45,000
SALES (est): 34.1MM Privately Held
WEB: www.mobileline.com
SIC: 5065 Telephone & telegraphic equipment; paging & signaling equipment

(P-7608)
MOBILYGEN CORPORATION
160 Rio Robles, San Jose (95134-1813)
PHONE.................................408 601-1000
Joseph Perl, Ch of Bd
Chris Day, President
Anoop Khurana, Vice Pres
Christopher Peters, Vice Pres
Ofer Elazar, General Mgr
EMP: 60
SQ FT: 13,000
SALES (est): 5.1MM
SALES (corp-wide): 2.1B Publicly Held
WEB: www.mobilygen.com
SIC: 5065 Semiconductor devices
PA: Maxim Integrated Products, Inc.
160 Rio Robles
San Jose CA 95134
408 601-1000

(P-7609)
MOSCHIP SEMICONDUCTOR TECH USA
840 N Hillview Dr, Milpitas (95035-4544)
PHONE.................................408 737-7141
Ram K Reddey, CEO
Shiri Kadambi, President
Ashok Kumar, Vice Pres
Dayakar Reddy, Managing Dir
Wendy Irwin, Administration
EMP: 120
SQ FT: 4,000
SALES (est): 19.7MM Privately Held
WEB: www.moschip.com
SIC: 5065 Semiconductor devices

(P-7610)
MOTOROLA MOBILITY LLC
6450 Sequence Dr, San Diego
(92121-4376)
PHONE.................................858 455-1500
Rick Neal, Branch Mgr
Mark Schmidl, Vice Pres
Ernie Tate, Vice Pres
Greg J Kaplanek, Executive
Sharon Hong, Engineer
EMP: 135
SQ FT: 30,000 Privately Held
WEB: www.motorola-labs.com
SIC: 5065 3663 Communication equipment; radio & TV communications equipment

HQ: Motorola Mobility Llc
222 Merchandise Mart Plz
Chicago IL 60654
-

(P-7611)
NALLATECH INC
741 Flynn Rd, Camarillo (93012-8056)
PHONE.................................805 383-8997
Colin Rutherford, Chairman
Allan Cantle, President
William P Miller, CEO
Ed Hennessy, Vice Pres
Paul Houlihan, Regl Sales Mgr
EMP: 64
SALES (est): 30.9MM
SALES (corp-wide): 26.7B Privately Held
WEB: www.nallatech.com
SIC: 5065 Electronic parts & equipment
HQ: Interconnect Systems, Inc.
741 Flynn Rd
Camarillo CA 93012
805 482-2870

(P-7612)
NEST LABS INC (DH)
3400 Hillview Ave, Palo Alto (94304-1346)
PHONE.................................650 331-1127
Tony Fadell, CEO
Matthew Rogers, Owner
Bryan James, Vice Pres
David Cassano, Program Mgr
Sarah Schaukowitch, Admin Asst
◆ EMP: 70
SALES (est): 36.4MM
SALES (corp-wide): 74.9B Publicly Held
SIC: 5065 Electronic parts & equipment
HQ: Google Inc.
1600 Amphitheatre Pkwy
Mountain View CA 94043
650 253-0000

(P-7613)
NEXTIVITY INC
12230 World Trade Dr # 250, San Diego
(92128-3799)
PHONE.................................858 485-9442
Jim Berridge, Vice Pres
Michiel Lotter, Vice Pres
Laurent Gil, Executive
Carol Lee, VP Finance
Tony Pun, Finance Dir
▲ EMP: 70
SALES (est): 63.7MM Privately Held
SIC: 5065 Communication equipment

(P-7614)
NU HORIZONS ELECTRONICS CORP
890 N Mccarthy Blvd, San Jose (95131)
PHONE.................................408 946-4154
EMP: 50
SALES (corp-wide): 23.2B Publicly Held
SIC: 5065
HQ: Nu Horizons Electronics Corp.
70 Maxess Rd
Melville NY 11747
631 396-5000

(P-7615)
NUVOTON TECHNOLOGY CORP AMER
2727 N 1st St, San Jose (95134-2029)
PHONE.................................408 544-1718
Arthur Yu-Cheng Chiao, Chairman
Robert Hsu, President
Mark Hemming, Chief Mktg Ofcr
Stephen Rei-Min Huang, Vice Pres
Bor-Yuan Hwang, Vice Pres
EMP: 60
SALES (est): 30MM
SALES (corp-wide): 1.1B Privately Held
SIC: 5065 Semiconductor devices
HQ: Nuvoton Technology Corporation
4, Creation 3rd Rd.,
Hsinchu City 30077
357 700-66

(P-7616)
ODU-USA INC (HQ)
Also Called: O D U
4010 Adolfo Rd, Camarillo (93012-6793)
PHONE.................................805 484-0540
Fax: 805 445-8631
Michael Savage, CEO
Joseph Cisi, President

Kurt Woelfl, CEO
Scott Bogart, General Mgr
Timothy Paulson, Admin Asst
▲ EMP: 60
SQ FT: 20,000
SALES (est): 44.4MM
SALES (corp-wide): 123.5MM Privately Held
WEB: www.odu-usa.com
SIC: 5065 Connectors, electronic
PA: Odu Gmbh & Co. Kg
Pregelstr. 11
Muhldorf A. Inn 84453
863 161-560

(P-7617)
OPTIMUS VENTURES LLC
2608 Spring St, Redwood City
(94063-3522)
PHONE.................................888 881-5969
Meera Koul, CEO
EMP: 50
SALES (est): 1MM Privately Held
SIC: 5065 Mobile telephone equipment

(P-7618)
ORGANIC AFFINITY LLC
3980 Hopevale Dr, Sherman Oaks
(91403-4414)
PHONE.................................801 870-7433
David Surber, Mng Member
EMP: 65
SALES (est): 2.6MM Privately Held
SIC: 5065 Electronic parts & equipment

(P-7619)
OSRAM OPTO SEMICONDUCTORS INC
1150 Kifer Rd Ste 100, Sunnyvale
(94086-5302)
PHONE.................................408 588-3800
Tom Shottes, Manager
Jim Norris, Info Tech Dir
Ian Cathcart, Manager
EMP: 52
SALES (corp-wide): 2B Privately Held
WEB: www.osram-os.com
SIC: 5065 Semiconductor devices
HQ: Osram Opto Semiconductors Inc.
1150 Kifer Rd Ste 100
Sunnyvale CA 94086
408 588-3800

(P-7620)
OSRAM OPTO SEMICONDUCTORS INC (HQ)
1150 Kifer Rd Ste 100, Sunnyvale
(94086-5302)
PHONE.................................408 588-3800
Fax: 408 738-9120
Thomas Shottes, President
Ron Terry, CFO
Rajeev Thakur, Manager
▲ EMP: 50
SALES (est): 32MM
SALES (corp-wide): 2B Privately Held
WEB: www.osram-os.com
SIC: 5065 Semiconductor devices
PA: Osram Gmbh
Marcel-Breuer-Str. 6
Munchen 80807
896 213-0

(P-7621)
PRISM ELECTRONICS CORP (PA)
900 Lightpost Way 100, Morgan Hill
(95037-2869)
PHONE.................................408 778-7050
John Jules Mauro, CEO
Sofia Fedotova, Admin Sec
Monica Alvarez, Marketing Staff
◆ EMP: 50
SQ FT: 21,373
SALES (est): 12.3MM Privately Held
SIC: 5065 Electronic parts

(P-7622)
QMADIX INC
14350 Arminta St, Panorama City
(91402-6869)
PHONE.................................818 988-4300
Ezra Soumekh, CEO
David Khalepari, CEO
Richard Mertz, COO

PRODUCTS & SERVICES SECTION
5065 - Electronic Parts & Eqpt Wholesale County (P-7641)

Craig Keushgerian, *Vice Pres*
Kim Zimmerman, *Accountant*
▲ **EMP:** 51
SQ FT: 30,000
SALES (est): 19.2MM **Privately Held**
WEB: www.paramountwireless.com
SIC: 5065 Mobile telephone equipment

(P-7623)
QUEST COMPONENTS INC
14711 Clark Ave, City of Industry (91745-1307)
PHONE.................626 333-5858
Dave A Hozen, *CEO*
Andre A Hozen, *Treasurer*
Liz Claridge, *Executive Asst*
Diana Nichols, *Credit Mgr*
Elaine Bowker, *Controller*
▲ **EMP:** 50
SQ FT: 32,000
SALES (est): 31.6MM **Privately Held**
WEB: www.quest-comp.com
SIC: 5065 Electronic parts & equipment

(P-7624)
RAKON AMERICA LLC
7600 Dublin Blvd, Dublin (94568-2909)
PHONE.................847 930-5100
Fax: 847 844-3236
Dean Ransom,
Bruce Irvine, *Exec Dir*
Deb Conn, *Manager*
EMP: 600
SALES (est): 46.4MM
SALES (corp-wide): 97.3MM **Privately Held**
WEB: www.rakon.com
SIC: 5065 Electronic parts & equipment
PA: Rakon Limited
8 Sylvia Park Road
Auckland, 1060
957 355-54

(P-7625)
RAND TECHNOLOGY LLC (PA)
15225 Alton Pkwy Unit 100, Irvine (92618-2351)
PHONE.................949 255-5700
Andrea Klein, *President*
Paul Bockstedt, *President*
Sean Sloan, *CFO*
Sharon Wade, *Purch Mgr*
Matt Gallagher, *Manager*
EMP: 71
SQ FT: 25,000
SALES (est): 74MM **Privately Held**
WEB: www.randtech.com
SIC: 5065 Semiconductor devices

(P-7626)
RAYTHEON COMMAND AND CONTROL
2000 E El Segundo Blvd, El Segundo (90245-4501)
PHONE.................714 446-3232
Ron Levesque, *Branch Mgr*
EMP: 50
SALES (corp-wide): 23.2B **Publicly Held**
SIC: 5065 Electronic parts & equipment
HQ: Raytheon Command And Control Solutions Llc
1801 Hughes Dr
Fullerton CA 92833
714 446-3118

(P-7627)
RENESAS ELECTRONICS AMER INC (DH)
2801 Scott Blvd, Santa Clara (95050-2549)
P.O. Box 58062 (95052-8062)
PHONE.................408 588-6000
Ali Sebt, *CEO*
Hideo Kameda, *Vice Pres*
David Weigand, *Vice Pres*
Mohan Rajasekhar, *Principal*
Mike Stocker, *Regional Mgr*
▲ **EMP:** 300
SQ FT: 200,000
SALES (est): 0
SALES (corp-wide): 642.5MM **Privately Held**
WEB: am.renesas.com
SIC: 5065 8731 5731 5045 Semiconductor devices; electronic research; radio, television & electronic stores; computers, peripherals & software; engineering services
HQ: Renesas Electronics Corporation
3-2-24, Toyosu
Koto-Ku TKY 135-0
367 733-000

(P-7628)
RENESAS TECHNOLOGY AMERICA INC
2801 Scott Blvd, Santa Clara (95050-2549)
PHONE.................408 588-6000
Fax: 408 382-7501
Dan Mahoney, *President*
Phil Thomas, *President*
Tetsuya Tsurumaru, *President*
Jean Labrosse, *CEO*
David Schwartz, *COO*
▲ **EMP:** 176
SALES (est): 122.6MM **Privately Held**
WEB: www.renesas.com
SIC: 5065 Semiconductor devices

(P-7629)
SAGER ELECTRICAL SUPPLY CO INC
Also Called: Sager Electronics
3611 S Harbor Blvd # 205, Santa Ana (92704-6928)
PHONE.................714 962-8666
Fax: 714 593-2450
Brian Flynn, *Manager*
Marilyn Ryder, *Director*
EMP: 155
SALES (corp-wide): 210.8B **Publicly Held**
SIC: 5065 Electronic parts & equipment
HQ: Sager Electrical Supply Company Inc.
19 Leona Dr
Middleboro MA 02346
508 923-6600

(P-7630)
SAMSUNG SEMICONDUCTOR INC (DH)
3655 N 1st St, San Jose (95134-1707)
PHONE.................408 544-4000
Fax: 408 544-4980
Young Chang Bae, *President*
Damian Huh, *CFO*
Tom Quinn, *Senior VP*
Bob Brennan, *Vice Pres*
Chris Byrne, *Vice Pres*
▼ **EMP:** 216
SQ FT: 206,816
SALES (est): 745.7MM
SALES (corp-wide): 118.4B **Privately Held**
SIC: 5065 5045 Semiconductor devices; computers, peripherals & software
HQ: Samsung Electronics America, Inc.
85 Challenger Rd
Ridgefield Park NJ 07660
201 229-4000

(P-7631)
SCREEN SPE USA LLC (DH)
Also Called: Dns Electronics
820 Kifer Rd Ste B, Sunnyvale (94086-5200)
PHONE.................408 523-9140
Tadahiro Suhara, *CEO*
Olivier Vatel, *Vice Chairman*
James Beard, *President*
Scott C Galler, *CFO*
Terry Yanagi, *CFO*
▲ **EMP:** 177
SQ FT: 28,400
SALES (est): 51.1MM
SALES (corp-wide): 2.2B **Privately Held**
WEB: www.dnse.com
SIC: 5065 7629 Electronic parts; electrical repair shops
HQ: Screen North America Holdings, Inc.
5110 Tollview Dr
Rolling Meadows IL 60008
847 870-7400

(P-7632)
SILICON VLY MCRELECTRONICS INC (PA)
Also Called: S V M
2985 Kifer Rd, Santa Clara (95051-0802)
PHONE.................408 844-7100
Fax: 408 844-9470
Patrick Callinan, *President*
Helen Tsai, *Branch Mgr*
Delia Zamudio, *Planning Mgr*
Nathan Barnes, *Administration*
Sharon Kunkel, *Sales Mgr*
▲ **EMP:** 50
SQ FT: 30,000
SALES (est): 23.5MM **Privately Held**
WEB: www.svmi.com
SIC: 5065 Semiconductor devices

(P-7633)
SILICONWARE USA INC (HQ)
1735 Tech Dr Ste 300 Fl 3, San Jose (95110)
PHONE.................408 573-5500
Bough Lin, *Ch of Bd*
Randy Hsiao Yu Lo, *President*
Yi Hsin Lin, *CFO*
Eva Chen, *Vice Pres*
Ching Hsu, *Vice Pres*
EMP: 50 **EST:** 1996
SQ FT: 8,000
SALES: 13.2MM
SALES (corp-wide): 2.5B **Privately Held**
WEB: www.spilca.com
SIC: 5065 Electronic parts & equipment
PA: Siliconware Precision Industries Co., Ltd.
123, Da Fong Rd., Sec. 3,
Taichung City 42749
425 341-525

(P-7634)
SK HYNIX AMERICA INC (HQ)
3101 N 1st St, San Jose (95134-1934)
PHONE.................408 232-8000
Fax: 408 232-8103
Kun Chul Suh, *CEO*
Jae H Park, *President*
Richard H Chin, *Chief Mktg Ofcr*
Halfred Hofherr, *Vice Pres*
David Yoo, *Vice Pres*
▲ **EMP:** 80
SQ FT: 190,000
SALES (est): 460.1MM
SALES (corp-wide): 16.4B **Privately Held**
SIC: 5065 5045 Electronic parts & equipment; semiconductor devices; computer peripheral equipment
PA: Sk Hynix Inc.
2091 Gyeongchung-Daero, Bubal-Eup
Icheon 17336
316 304-114

(P-7635)
SMA SOLAR TECHNOLOGY AMER LLC (HQ)
Also Called: SMA America
6020 W Oaks Blvd, Rocklin (95765-5472)
PHONE.................916 625-0870
Fax: 916 625-0871
Jurgen Krehnke,
Maurice C Kemp, *Officer*
Jurgen Reekers, *Vice Pres*
Scott Crabtree, *General Mgr*
Matthew Trias, *Design Engr*
▲ **EMP:** 106
SQ FT: 25,000
SALES (est): 242.3MM
SALES (corp-wide): 1B **Privately Held**
WEB: www.sma-america.com
SIC: 5065 Electronic parts
PA: Sma Solar Technology Ag
Sonnenallee 1
Niestetal 34266
561 952-20

(P-7636)
SOL REPUBLIC INC
1000 Van Ness Ave, San Francisco (94109-6971)
PHONE.................877 400-0310
Kevin Lee, *CEO*
Scott Hix, *President*
Doug Denney, *Finance*
EMP: 100
SQ FT: 10,000
SALES (est): 41.7MM **Privately Held**
SIC: 5065 5731 Electronic parts & equipment; consumer electronic equipment

(P-7637)
SOLIGENT DISTRIBUTION LLC (HQ)
1500 Valley House Dr # 210, Rohnert Park (94928-4924)
PHONE.................707 992-3100
Fax: 707 473-0727
Jonathan Doochin, *CEO*
Thomas Enzendorfer, *President*
Ulrik Binzer, *COO*
Justin Davidson, *Vice Pres*
Mike Raspolich, *Vice Pres*
EMP: 82 **EST:** 2013
SALES (est): 199MM
SALES (corp-wide): 264.7MM **Privately Held**
SIC: 5065 Electronic parts & equipment
PA: Soligent Holdings Inc.
1500 Valley House Dr
Rohnert Park CA 94928
707 992-3100

(P-7638)
STELLAR MICROELECTRONICS INC
28454 Livingston Ave, Valencia (91355-4172)
PHONE.................661 775-3500
Fax: 661 775-3522
Sudesh Arora, *President*
Stephen Crosier, *Comp Tech*
Ping Gan, *Engineer*
Don Hull, *Engineer*
Dan Marquez, *Engineer*
EMP: 239
SQ FT: 140,000
SALES: 184.3MM
SALES (corp-wide): 1.4B **Privately Held**
WEB: www.stellarmicro.com
SIC: 5065 Semiconductor devices
PA: Natel Engineering Company Inc
9340 Owensmouth Ave
Chatsworth CA 91311
818 734-6523

(P-7639)
STEREN ELECTRONICS INTL LLC (PA)
Also Called: Steren Shop
6920 Carroll Rd Ste 100, San Diego (92121-2211)
PHONE.................800 266-3333
Fax: 619 585-8465
Leon Shteremberg Ttee, *Mng Member*
Ben Norton, *Chief Mktg Ofcr*
Williams McGuckin, *CIO*
Steve Kostek, *Controller*
Angela Donerson, *Human Res Mgr*
▲ **EMP:** 100
SQ FT: 75,000
SALES (est): 57.1MM **Privately Held**
WEB: www.steren.com
SIC: 5065 Connectors, electronic

(P-7640)
STMICROELECTRONICS INC
2755 Great America Way, Santa Clara (95054-1170)
PHONE.................408 452-8585
Ted Daniels, *Sales/Mktg Mgr*
Laney Lee, *Officer*
Georges Penalver, *Exec VP*
Claudio Diazzi, *Vice Pres*
Celine Berthier, *Director*
EMP: 140
SALES (corp-wide): 7.4B **Privately Held**
WEB: www.st.com
SIC: 5065 Semiconductor devices
HQ: Stmicroelectronics, Inc
750 Canyon Dr Ste 300
Coppell TX 75019
972 466-6000

(P-7641)
SUMITOMO ELECTRIC DEVICE INNOV
2355 Zanker Rd, San Jose (95131-1109)
PHONE.................408 232-9500
Mike Nishiguchi, *CEO*
Frank Sanada, *President*
Manabu Yoshimura, *President*

5065 - Electronic Parts & Eqpt Wholesale County (P-7642)

PRODUCTS & SERVICES SECTION

Harry Ishida, *CFO*
John Wyatt, *CFO*
▲ **EMP:** 80
SQ FT: 52,600
SALES (est): 39.2MM
SALES (corp-wide): 25B **Privately Held**
WEB: www.sei-device.com
SIC: 5065 Electronic parts & equipment
PA: Sumitomo Electric Industries, Ltd.
 4-5-33, Kitahama, Chuo-Ku
 Osaka OSK 541-0
 662 204-141

(P-7642)
SUPERIOR COMMUNICATIONS INC (PA)
Also Called: PUREGEAR
5027 Irwindale Ave # 900, Baldwin Park (91706-2187)
PHONE 626 388-2573
Fax: 626 608-9043
Solomon Chen, *Ch of Bd*
Michael Cavanah, *Shareholder*
Jeffrey Banks, *President*
James Chen, *President*
Jannifer Ju, *COO*
▲ **EMP:** 248
SQ FT: 11,000
SALES: 854.6MM **Privately Held**
WEB: www.scp4me.com
SIC: 5065 Communication equipment

(P-7643)
SURVEILLANCE SYSTEMS
Also Called: Ssi
4465 Granite Dr Ste 700, Rocklin (95677-2143)
PHONE 800 508-6981
Michael T Flowers, *CEO*
Jon Ward, *President*
Mark Haney, *Chairman*
Olga Suarez, *Accounting Mgr*
Cris Richardson, *Accountant*
EMP: 50
SQ FT: 15,000
SALES (est): 20MM **Privately Held**
WEB: www.ssicctv.com
SIC: 5065 Video equipment, electronic; security control equipment & systems

(P-7644)
TABULA INC
1100 La Avenida St Ste A, Mountain View (94043-1453)
PHONE 408 986-9140
Fax: 408 986-9146
Dennis Segers, *CEO*
Steven Teig, *President*
Steve Haynes, *Vice Pres*
Mike Staiger, *Vice Pres*
Kent Townley, *Engineer*
EMP: 100
SALES (est): 57.3MM **Privately Held**
WEB: www.tabula.com
SIC: 5065 Semiconductor devices

(P-7645)
TALLEY INC (PA)
Also Called: Talley & Associates
12976 Sandoval St, Santa Fe Springs (90670-4061)
P.O. Box 3123 (90670-0123)
PHONE 562 906-8000
John R Talley, *CEO*
Mark D Talley, *President*
George R Hulbert, *CFO*
Elizabeth J Talley, *Exec VP*
Patrick Slynn, *Vice Pres*
◆ **EMP:** 110
SQ FT: 80,000
SALES (est): 159.1MM **Privately Held**
WEB: www.talleycom.com
SIC: 5065 Communication equipment; amateur radio communications equipment

(P-7646)
TEAC AEROSPACE TECH INC
2727 E Imperial Hwy, Brea (92821-6713)
PHONE 323 837-2700
Farah Hassan, *Principal*
Brian S Gora, *President*
Paul V Cappiello, *Vice Pres*
Sally L Geib, *Vice Pres*
Scott E Kuechle, *Vice Pres*
▲ **EMP:** 110
SQ FT: 25,000
SALES (est): 23MM
SALES (corp-wide): 56.1B **Publicly Held**
WEB: www.teac-aerospace.com
SIC: 5065 Video equipment, electronic
HQ: Goodrich Corporation
 4 Coliseum Ctr 2730 W
 Charlotte NC 28217
 704 423-7000

(P-7647)
TECH SYSTEMS INC
7372 Walnut Ave Ste J, Buena Park (90620-1718)
PHONE 714 523-5404
Raymond Downs, *Manager*
EMP: 120
SALES (corp-wide): 32.1MM **Privately Held**
SIC: 5065 Closed circuit television
PA: Tech Systems, Inc.
 4942 Summer Oak Dr
 Buford GA 30518
 770 495-8700

(P-7648)
TECOM INDUSTRIES INCORPORATED
375 Conejo Ridge Ave, Thousand Oaks (91361-4928)
PHONE 818 341-4010
Fax: 805 267-0181
Arsen Melconian, *CEO*
Martin Cox, *President*
Gene Joles, *President*
Gina Gastelum, *Officer*
Mark Rosenthal, *Program Mgr*
▲ **EMP:** 160
SQ FT: 67,000
SALES (est): 24.9MM
SALES (corp-wide): 4.5B **Privately Held**
WEB: www.tecom-ind.com
SIC: 5065 Electronic parts & equipment
HQ: Trak Microwave Corporation
 4726 Eisenhower Blvd
 Tampa FL 33634
 813 901-7200

(P-7649)
THALES-RAYTHEON SYSTEMS CO LLC (HQ)
1801 Hughes Dr, Fullerton (92833-2200)
P.O. Box 34055 (92834-9455)
PHONE 714 446-3118
Peter W Chiarelli, *President*
Matt Pothecary, *Vice Pres*
Steven Bruce, *Program Mgr*
Robert Musulas, *General Mgr*
Andre Bullock, *Sr Ntwrk Engine*
▲ **EMP:** 700
SALES (est): 334.5MM
SALES (corp-wide): 23.2B **Publicly Held**
SIC: 5065 Security control equipment & systems
PA: Raytheon Company
 870 Winter St
 Waltham MA 02451
 781 522-3000

(P-7650)
U-2 HOME ENTERTAINMENT INC
Also Called: Tai Seng Entertainment
170 S Spruce Ave Ste 200, South San Francisco (94080-4557)
P.O. Box 818, San Bruno (94066-0818)
PHONE 650 871-8118
Bernard SOO, *President*
Bill Kwok, *Accountant*
Jackie Wong, *Controller*
Susan Peng, *Accounts Mgr*
▲ **EMP:** 50
SALES (est): 10.2MM **Privately Held**
SIC: 5065 Tapes, audio & video recording

(P-7651)
UNIFIED TELDATA INC
Also Called: Utdi
126 Neider Ln, Mill Valley (94941-2474)
PHONE 415 888-8940
Toll Free: .... 888 -
Lyhn Haller, *President*
William Bivins, *Vice Pres*
Dave Hutto, *Vice Pres*
Kent Heckaman, *Administration*
EMP: 52
SQ FT: 3,500
SALES (est): 7MM **Privately Held**
WEB: www.utdi.com
SIC: 5065 Telephone equipment; communication equipment; intercommunication equipment, electronic

(P-7652)
US MERCHANT SYSTEMS LLC
48073 Fremont Blvd, Fremont (94538-6541)
PHONE 877 432-8871
Fax: 510 771-2117
Stuart Rosenbaum, *CEO*
Richard L Fenn II, *COO*
Jeff Gardiner, *CFO*
Carolyn Garibay, *Vice Pres*
Matthew Zimmermann, *Comp Tech*
EMP: 52
SALES (est): 23.4MM **Privately Held**
SIC: 5065 Electronic parts & equipment

(P-7653)
VALOR COMMUNICATION INC
18071 Arenth Ave, City of Industry (91748-1223)
PHONE 626 581-8085
Hong Dong, *President*
Peter Cheng, *Info Tech Mgr*
David Caulder, *VP Sales*
Cherry Valor, *Sales Staff*
Martin Peter, *Director*
▼ **EMP:** 60
SQ FT: 150,000
SALES (est): 10.5MM **Privately Held**
WEB: www.2valor.com
SIC: 5065 Mobile telephone equipment
PA: Shenzhen Mopoint Technology Co., Ltd.
 Building 5, Gaofa Sci-Tech. Park, Longjing Rd., Nanshan District
 Shenzhen
 755 888-3596

(P-7654)
VERIZON NEW YORK INC
961 N Milliken Ave # 101, Ontario (91764-5021)
PHONE 909 481-7897
Fax: 909 481-9091
Terry L Lukens, *Principal*
Straight Richard, *Webmaster*
EMP: 100
SALES (corp-wide): 131.6B **Publicly Held**
SIC: 5065 Telephone equipment
HQ: Verizon New York Inc.
 140 West St
 New York NY 10007
 212 395-1000

(P-7655)
VIA TECHNOLOGIES INC
Also Called: Via Embedded Store
940 Mission Ct, Fremont (94539-8202)
PHONE 510 683-3300
Fax: 510 687-4654
Wenchi Chen, *President*
Cher Wang, *CFO*
Tzumu Lin, *Senior VP*
Bihua Gao, *Engineer*
Frank Hsu, *Engineer*
▲ **EMP:** 130
SQ FT: 55,000
SALES (est): 54.8MM **Privately Held**
WEB: www.via.com.tw
SIC: 5065 Electronic parts
PA: Via Usa Inc
 940 Mission Ct
 Fremont CA 94539
 510 683-3300

(P-7656)
WDPT FILM DISTRIBUTION LLC
500 S Buena Vista St, Burbank (91521-0001)
PHONE 818 560-1000
Fax: 818 560-1930
Walt Disney Pictures, *Mng Member*
Dawn Jonasson, *Opers Mgr*
Mark Gilbert, *Manager*
EMP: 176
SALES (est): 94.1MM **Privately Held**
SIC: 5065 Video equipment, electronic

(P-7657)
WENZLAU ENGINEERING INC
2950 E Harcourt St, Compton (90221-5502)
PHONE 310 604-3400
Fax: 626 799-4877
William D Wenzlau Jr, *CEO*
Charles Pastre, *Finance*
▲ **EMP:** 64
SQ FT: 40,000
SALES (est): 53.9MM **Privately Held**
WEB: www.wenzlau.com
SIC: 5065 8711 5511 Electronic parts & equipment; consulting engineer; trucks, tractors & trailers: new & used

(P-7658)
WESTAK INTERNATIONAL SALES INC (HQ)
1116 Elko Dr, Sunnyvale (94089-2207)
PHONE 408 734-8686
Louise Crisham, *President*
Jay Latin, *VP Sales*
EMP: 130
SQ FT: 20,000
SALES (est): 21.4MM
SALES (corp-wide): 64MM **Privately Held**
SIC: 5065 Electronic parts
PA: Westak, Inc
 1116 Elko Dr
 Sunnyvale CA 94089
 408 734-8686

(P-7659)
WINBOND ELECTRONICS CORP AMER (HQ)
2727 N 1st St, San Jose (95134-2029)
PHONE 408 943-6666
Fax: 408 544-1789
Yuan-Mou Su, *Ch of Bd*
Yung Chin, *Treasurer*
Eries Tseng, *Engineer*
Rani Cardinaux, *Human Res Mgr*
Syed Hussain, *Marketing Mgr*
▲ **EMP:** 60
SQ FT: 50,000
SALES (est): 32.8MM
SALES (corp-wide): 1.1B **Privately Held**
WEB: www.winbond-usa.com
SIC: 5065 8731 3674 Electronic parts; commercial physical research; semiconductors & related devices
PA: Winbond Electronics Corp.
 8, Keya 1st Rd.,
 Taichung City 42881
 425 218-168

(P-7660)
WURLDTECH SECURITY TECH LTD ⊙
2623 Camino Ramon, San Ramon (94583-9130)
PHONE 604 669-6674
William Ruh, *CEO*
EMP: 75 EST: 2016
SALES: 26MM **Privately Held**
SIC: 5065 Security control equipment & systems

(P-7661)
XCERRA CORPORATION
Also Called: Western Region
1355 California Cir, Milpitas (95035-3021)
PHONE 408 635-4300
Ken Daub, *Branch Mgr*
Mukesh Mowji, *Vice Pres*
Robert Glenn, *Technology*
Nadim Ahmad, *Marketing Mgr*
Linnea Kline, *Marketing Mgr*
EMP: 200
SALES (corp-wide): 324.2MM **Publicly Held**
WEB: www.ltx.com
SIC: 5065 Electronic parts & equipment
PA: Xcerra Corporation
 825 University Ave
 Norwood MA 02062
 781 461-1000

(P-7662)
YUNEEC USA INC
5555 Ontario Mills Pkwy, Ontario (91764-5102)
PHONE 855 284-8888

▲ = Import ▼ = Export
◆ = Import/Export

PRODUCTS & SERVICES SECTION

5072 - Hardware Wholesale County (P-7683)

Yu Liu, *Accountant*
Ed Bi, *Director*
EMP: 90 **EST:** 2013
SQ FT: 37,000
SALES: 35.3MM **Privately Held**
SIC: 5065 7629 Video equipment, electronic; electrical equipment repair services
PA: Yuneec International Co., Limited
2/F Man Shung Indl Bldg
Kwun Tong KLN
-

(P-7663)
ZETTLER COMPONENTS INC (PA)
1701 W Sequoia Ave, Orange (92868-1015)
PHONE 714 939-6699
Fax: 714 939-9130
Kurt Rexius, *General Mgr*
▲ **EMP:** 250
SQ FT: 27,000
SALES (est): 52.3MM **Privately Held**
WEB: www.zettlercomponents.com
SIC: 5065 3669 5087 Intercommunication equipment, electronic; intercommunication systems, electric; firefighting equipment

(P-7664)
ZMODO TECHNOLOGY CORP LTD
17870 Castleton St # 200, City of Industry (91748-1755)
PHONE 217 903-5673
Kejia Wan, *President*
EMP: 700
SALES (est): 47.5MM **Privately Held**
SIC: 5065 Mobile telephone equipment

5072 Hardware Wholesale

(P-7665)
ACF COMPONENTS & FASTENERS INC
Also Called: A C F
742 Arrow Grand Cir, Covina (91722-2147)
PHONE 949 833-0506
Fax: 626 915-7065
Jill Alvarez, *Manager*
Tanya Moore, *Credit Staff*
Lin Baluyut, *Controller*
Laura Chubb, *Sales Mgr*
Dave Hanson, *Marketing Staff*
EMP: 55
SQ FT: 20,000
SALES (corp-wide): 32.5MM **Privately Held**
WEB: www.acfcom.com
SIC: 5072 5065 5085 Miscellaneous fasteners; electronic parts; fasteners, industrial: nuts, bolts, screws, etc.
PA: Acf Components & Fasteners, Inc.
31012 Huntwood Ave
Hayward CA 94544
510 487-2100

(P-7666)
ADEPT FASTENERS INC (PA)
28709 Industry Dr, Valencia (91355-5414)
PHONE 661 257-6600
Gary Young, *President*
Don List, *Vice Pres*
Elaine Young, *Office Mgr*
Cheryl Odermatt, *Info Tech Mgr*
Michael Gunderson, *Technology*
EMP: 56
SQ FT: 40,000
SALES (est): 118.5MM **Privately Held**
WEB: www.adeptfasteners.com
SIC: 5072 Miscellaneous fasteners

(P-7667)
ALL PRO TOOLS INC
Also Called: Allpro Tools.com
1040 S Mount Vernon Ave G292, Colton (92324-4228)
PHONE 888 425-5776
Lori Kelso, *CEO*
Michael Labita, *President*
EMP: 50 **EST:** 1998
SALES (est): 6.5MM **Privately Held**
SIC: 5072 Hardware

(P-7668)
ALLTRADE TOOLS LLC
1431 W Via Plata St, Long Beach (90810-1460)
PHONE 310 522-9008
Andy Livian, *CEO*
Robert Ellis, *CFO*
Don Hart, *Vice Pres*
Price Cruz, *Administration*
Golden Huang, *Info Tech Dir*
▲ **EMP:** 50
SQ FT: 140,000
SALES (est): 31.3MM **Privately Held**
SIC: 5072 Hand tools

(P-7669)
AMERICAN BOLT & SCREW MFG CORP (PA)
Also Called: ABS HARWARE PURCHASING
14650 Miller Ave Ste 200, Fontana (92336-1694)
P.O. Box 548 (92334-0548)
PHONE 909 390-0522
Fax: 909 390-0545
Jimmie W Hooper, *President*
Gary Mosier, *Vice Pres*
Nancy Vega, *Technology*
Laurie Blood, *Controller*
Ricky Venegas, *HR Admin*
▲ **EMP:** 52 **EST:** 1970
SQ FT: 100,000
SALES (est): 41.2MM **Privately Held**
SIC: 5072 Bolts, nuts & screws

(P-7670)
AMERICAN KAL ENTERPRISES INC (PA)
Also Called: Pro America Premium Tools
4265 Puente Ave, Baldwin Park (91706-3420)
PHONE 626 338-7308
John Toshima, *President*
Mila Bierotte, *Admin Sec*
Lisa Kitagawa, *Agent*
▲ **EMP:** 90
SQ FT: 32,000
SALES (est): 22.7MM **Privately Held**
SIC: 5072 3546 3463 3462 Hand tools; power-driven handtools; nonferrous forgings; iron & steel forgings; hand & edge tools

(P-7671)
AMERIWEST INDUSTRIES INC
Also Called: Tenpo Hardware
2910 S Archibald Ave A, Ontario (91761-7323)
PHONE 909 930-1898
Weidan Wu, *CEO*
Sandy Psai, *Accounts Mgr*
▲ **EMP:** 50 **EST:** 2001
SQ FT: 112,000
SALES (est): 8.8MM **Privately Held**
WEB: www.ameriwestindustries.com
SIC: 5072 Hardware

(P-7672)
ARCONIC GLOBAL FAS & RINGS INC
Also Called: Arconic Fstening Systems Rings
1925 N Macarthur Dr # 200, Tracy (95376-2835)
PHONE 209 839-3005
Rod Alavi, *Director*
EMP: 60
SALES (corp-wide): 22.5B **Publicly Held**
WEB: www.alcoafasteners.com
SIC: 5072 Hardware
HQ: Arconic Global Fasteners & Rings, Inc.
3990a Heritage Oak Ct
Simi Valley CA 93063
310 530-2220

(P-7673)
ARROW TOOLS FAS & SAW INC
7635 Burnet Ave, Van Nuys (91405-1006)
PHONE 818 780-1464
Fax: 818 780-3790
Jeffrey S Silverman, *CEO*
Stewart Epstein, *President*
Susan Epstein, *Corp Secy*
Mike Glazier, *Project Mgr*
EMP: 50
SQ FT: 25,000
SALES (est): 55.6MM **Privately Held**
WEB: www.arrowtools.com
SIC: 5072 Hardware

(P-7674)
AWI ACQUISITION COMPANY (PA)
Also Called: Allied International
13207 Bradley Ave, Sylmar (91342-1204)
PHONE 818 364-2333
Fax: 818 362-9066
Timothy Florian, *Ch of Bd*
Melissa Berninger, *CFO*
Fred Yakimoff, *Officer*
Ross Ormsby, *Natl Sales Mgr*
Nina Da Costa, *Manager*
▲ **EMP:** 66
SQ FT: 106,000
SALES (est): 32.8MM **Privately Held**
WEB: www.alliedtools.com
SIC: 5072 3499 Hardware; hand tools; stabilizing bars (cargo), metal

(P-7675)
B & B SPECIALTIES INC
G S Aerospace Division
4321 E La Palma Ave, Anaheim (92807-1887)
PHONE 714 985-3075
Tom Rutan, *Manager*
Robert Allebaugh, *Vice Pres*
Robert Huke, *Info Tech Dir*
Kerry Johnson, *VP Sls/Mktg*
EMP: 100
SALES (corp-wide): 19.6MM **Privately Held**
WEB: www.bbspecialties.com
SIC: 5072 3429 Miscellaneous fasteners; manufactured hardware (general)
PA: B & B Specialties, Inc.
4321 E La Palma Ave
Anaheim CA 92807
714 985-3000

(P-7676)
BAY STANDARD MANUFACTURING INC (PA)
Also Called: Bsmi
24485 Marsh Creek Rd, Brentwood (94513-4319)
P.O. Box 801 (94513-0801)
PHONE 925 634-1181
Gary W Landgraf, *CEO*
Gregory Iverson, *President*
Karen Landgraf, *Vice Pres*
Tom Landgraf, *Vice Pres*
Leeann Forwell, *Accountant*
◆ **EMP:** 50
SQ FT: 25,000
SALES (est): 26.6MM **Privately Held**
WEB: www.baystandard.com
SIC: 5072 3452 Bolts; bolts, metal

(P-7677)
BRSC INC
12801 Leffingwell Ave, Santa Fe Springs (90670-6339)
PHONE 310 549-9180
Fax: 310 513-6326
John B Porteous, *Principal*
EMP: 200
SALES (corp-wide): 1.5B **Privately Held**
WEB: www.porteousfastener.com
SIC: 5072 Nuts (hardware); bolts; screws; washers (hardware)
HQ: Brsc, Inc.
12801 Leffingwell Ave
Santa Fe Springs CA 90670
310 549-9180

(P-7678)
CAMSTAR INTERNATIONAL INC
939 W 9th St, Upland (91786-4543)
PHONE 909 931-2540
Bingging LI, *President*
Don Gold, *Sales Mgr*
Rene Martinez, *Manager*
Monica Wise, *Manager*
Carrie Yang, *Manager*
▲ **EMP:** 75
SQ FT: 1,500
SALES (est): 12.5MM
SALES (corp-wide): 134.9K **Privately Held**
SIC: 5072 Security devices, locks
PA: Yuxin Technology Company
Dayao Village
Weifang
536 784-8108

(P-7679)
CHARLES MCMURRAY CO (PA)
2520 N Argyle Ave, Fresno (93727-1399)
P.O. Box 569 (93709-0569)
PHONE 559 292-5751
Fax: 559 292-3749
Louis Mc Murray, *President*
Marcia Cirrincione, *Office Mgr*
Cassie Mc Murray, *Admin Sec*
Allison Seasholtz, *Administration*
Garry Smith, *CIO*
▲ **EMP:** 62
SQ FT: 58,000
SALES (est): 55.3MM **Privately Held**
SIC: 5072 Builders' hardware

(P-7680)
CORONA CLIPPER INC
22440 Temescal Canyon Rd # 102, Corona (92883-4200)
PHONE 951 737-6515
Stephen J Erickson, *CEO*
Al Schulten, *CFO*
John Reisveck, *Exec VP*
Phill Rogers, *General Mgr*
Kevin Howe, *Info Tech Dir*
◆ **EMP:** 70
SQ FT: 85,000
SALES (est): 51.5MM
SALES (corp-wide): 2.2MM **Privately Held**
WEB: www.coronaclipper.com
SIC: 5072 3524 Hand tools; lawn & garden equipment
HQ: Bellota Us Corp.
22440 Temescal Canyon Rd
Corona CA 92883
951 737-6515

(P-7681)
CPO COMMERCE LLC
120 W Bellevue Dr Ste 300, Pasadena (91105-2579)
PHONE 626 585-3600
Robert H Tolleson, *President*
Girisha Chandraraj, *COO*
Todd A Shelton, *CFO*
Robert J Kelderhouse, *Treasurer*
Eric A Blanchard, *Senior VP*
▼ **EMP:** 81
SALES (est): 110.1MM
SALES (corp-wide): 5.3B **Publicly Held**
SIC: 5072 Power tools & accessories
HQ: Essendant Co.
1 Parkway North Blvd # 100
Deerfield IL 60015
847 627-7000

(P-7682)
CROWN HARDWARE INC
745 S Coast Highway 101 # 104, Encinitas (92024-4450)
PHONE 760 334-0300
Glenn Maguire, *Branch Mgr*
EMP: 141
SALES (corp-wide): 56.3MM **Privately Held**
SIC: 5072 Hardware
PA: Crown Hardware, Inc.
9045 Adams Ave
Huntington Beach CA 92646
714 962-4160

(P-7683)
EXCELTA CORPORATION (PA)
60 Easy St Ste F, Buellton (93427-9560)
PHONE 805 686-4686
Fax: 805 686-9005
Lynn Bonzer, *President*
Joan Dalseme, *CEO*
Greg Johnson, *Vice Pres*
Janis Papiro, *Admin Sec*
Fletcher Dunlap, *Technical Staff*
EMP: 93
SQ FT: 6,300
SALES (est): 37.5MM **Privately Held**
WEB: www.excelta.com
SIC: 5072 Hand tools

5072 - Hardware Wholesale County (P-7684) — PRODUCTS & SERVICES SECTION

(P-7684)
G K TOOL CORP
Also Called: Kal Tool Co
4265 Puente Ave, Baldwin Park (91706-3420)
PHONE...................626 338-7300
John Toshima, *President*
Robert Mandeville, *Shareholder*
Mila Bierotte, *Admin Sec*
Tosh G Kamei, *Agent*
EMP: 90
SQ FT: 32,000
SALES (est): 8.6MM
SALES (corp-wide): 22.7MM **Privately Held**
SIC: 5072 Hand tools
PA: American Kal Enterprises, Inc.
4265 Puente Ave
Baldwin Park CA 91706
626 338-7308

(P-7685)
HAMPTON PRODUCTS INTL CORP (PA)
50 Icon, Foothill Ranch (92610-3000)
PHONE...................949 472-4256
Fax: 949 472-9657
Hayward K Kelley III, *President*
Richard Tysdal, *COO*
Bob Hansen, *Exec VP*
Gary Landress, *Exec VP*
Mike Kreeger, *Senior VP*
▲ **EMP:** 100
SQ FT: 160,000
SALES (est): 153.7MM **Privately Held**
WEB: www.hamptonproducts.com
SIC: 5072 Hardware

(P-7686)
HD SUPPLY CONSTRUCTION SUPPLY
Also Called: White Cap 24
1995 W Cordelia Rd, Fairfield (94534-1661)
PHONE...................707 863-8282
Marcelus Joanes, *Principal*
EMP: 53
SALES (corp-wide): 7.3B **Publicly Held**
SIC: 5072 Hardware
HQ: Hd Supply Construction Supply, Ltd
3100 Cumberland Blvd Se # 1700
Atlanta GA 30339
770 852-9000

(P-7687)
HD SUPPLY CONSTRUCTION SUPPLY
Also Called: White Cap 35
595 Brennan St, San Jose (95131-1202)
P.O. Box 610640 (95161-0640)
PHONE...................408 428-2000
Fax: 408 428-2001
Larry Holloway, *Manager*
Mark Charon, *Branch Mgr*
Elliot Chung, *Sales Staff*
Aldo Quintana, *Sales Staff*
EMP: 50
SALES (corp-wide): 7.3B **Publicly Held**
SIC: 5072 Hardware
HQ: Hd Supply Construction Supply, Ltd
3100 Cumberland Blvd Se # 1700
Atlanta GA 30339
770 852-9000

(P-7688)
JACKSONS HARDWARE INC
Also Called: Marin Industrial Distributors
62 Woodland Ave, San Rafael (94901-5344)
P.O. Box 10247 (94912-0247)
PHONE...................415 454-3740
Fax: 415 454-6452
Matthew R Olson, *President*
Anna Buss, *Treasurer*
EMP: 61
SQ FT: 50,000
SALES (est): 29.7MM **Privately Held**
WEB: www.jacksonshardware.com
SIC: 5072 5251 Hardware; hardware

(P-7689)
LEIGHT SALES CO INC
1611 S Catalina Ave L45, Redondo Beach (90277-5299)
PHONE...................310 223-1000
Fax: 310 223-1005
Bryan Moskowitz, *CEO*
Helene Moskowitz, *Corp Secy*
Alan Moskowitz, *Principal*
Liz Jiang, *Info Tech Dir*
Steve Phillips, *VP Sales*
▲ **EMP:** 75
SQ FT: 60,000
SALES (est): 56.6MM **Privately Held**
WEB: www.leightsales.com
SIC: 5072 Hardware; hand tools

(P-7690)
LIBERTY HARDWARE MFG CORP
5555 Jurupa St, Ontario (91761-3606)
PHONE...................909 605-2300
Kevin Buckner, *Branch Mgr*
EMP: 51
SALES (corp-wide): 7.1B **Publicly Held**
WEB: www.libertyhardware.com
SIC: 5072 Hardware
HQ: Liberty Hardware Mfg. Corp.
140 Business Park Dr
Winston Salem NC 27107
336 769-4077

(P-7691)
LONG-LOK FASTENERS CORPORATION
20501 Belshaw Ave, Carson (90746-3505)
PHONE...................310 667-4200
Robert M Bennett, *CEO*
Christopher Watson, *General Mgr*
EMP: 50
SALES (est): 5.8MM **Privately Held**
SIC: 5072 Miscellaneous fasteners

(P-7692)
LOUIS WURTH AND COMPANY (DH)
895 Columbia St, Brea (92821-2917)
P.O. Box 2253 (92822-2253)
PHONE...................714 529-1771
Fax: 714 990-6184
Vito Mancini, *President*
Tom Mauss, *President*
Ed McGraw, *CFO*
Bob Shine, *Vice Pres*
Jeff Debozy, *Mfg Dir*
◆ **EMP:** 90
SQ FT: 116,000
SALES (est): 117MM
SALES (corp-wide): 11.8B **Privately Held**
WEB: www.louisandcompany.com
SIC: 5072 5198 Furniture hardware; stain
HQ: Wurth Group Of North America Inc.
93 Grant St
Ramsey NJ 07446
201 818-8877

(P-7693)
MAKITA USA INC (HQ)
14930 Northam St, La Mirada (90638-5753)
PHONE...................714 522-8088
Fax: 714 522-8133
Hiroshi Tsujimura, *CEO*
Richzrd Chapman, *Senior VP*
Rich Chapman, *Vice Pres*
Eunice Han, *Vice Pres*
Ron Schachter, *Vice Pres*
▲ **EMP:** 160
SQ FT: 130,000
SALES (est): 344.8MM
SALES (corp-wide): 3.6B **Privately Held**
WEB: www.makita.com
SIC: 5072 Power handtools
PA: Makita Corporation
3-11-8, Sumiyoshicho
Anjo AIC 446-0
566 981-711

(P-7694)
MILSPEC INDUSTRIES INC (DH)
5825 Greenwood Ave, Commerce (90040-3846)
P.O. Box 60887, Los Angeles (90060-3846)
PHONE...................213 680-9690
Fax: 323 725-6437
David Lifschitz, *CEO*
Galen Ho'o, *President*
Saleem Baakza, *Vice Pres*
Anthony Batista, *Vice Pres*
Carl Tom, *VP Mktg*
▲ **EMP:** 70
SALES (est): 19.2MM
SALES (corp-wide): 76.1MM **Privately Held**
WEB: www.milspecind.com
SIC: 5072 5085 Hardware; industrial supplies
HQ: Gehr Industries, Inc.
7400 E Slauson Ave
Commerce CA 90040
323 728-5558

(P-7695)
PRIME-LINE PRODUCTS COMPANY (PA)
Also Called: Slide Go
26950 San Bernardino Ave, Redlands (92374-5022)
PHONE...................909 887-8118
Fax: 909 880-8968
Ronald F Turk, *President*
Rick Papworth, *CFO*
David Richards, *CFO*
Howard Kaufman, *Senior VP*
Bryan Aernan, *Vice Pres*
◆ **EMP:** 325
SQ FT: 100,000
SALES (est): 110.8MM **Privately Held**
WEB: www.prime-line-products.com
SIC: 5072 Hardware

(P-7696)
SEREC ENTERTAINMENT LLC
1671 N Rocky Rd, Upland (91784-2500)
PHONE...................626 893-0600
Steven A Ferraiuolo,
EMP: 50
SALES (est): 4.4MM **Privately Held**
SIC: 5072 7389 Hardware;

(P-7697)
SHAMROCK SUPPLY COMPANY INC (PA)
Also Called: Shamrock Companies, The
3366 E La Palma Ave, Anaheim (92806-2814)
PHONE...................714 575-1800
Fax: 714 575-1801
John J O'Connor, *Ch of Bd*
Michael O'Connor, *President*
Juan Ossa, *Info Tech Dir*
Fanny McShane, *Info Tech Mgr*
Luz Mejia, *Business Mgr*
▲ **EMP:** 52
SQ FT: 45,000
SALES (est): 75.1MM **Privately Held**
WEB: www.shamrocksupply.com
SIC: 5072 5084 3842 Hand tools; industrial machinery & equipment; personal safety equipment

(P-7698)
SNAP-ON INCORPORATED
Also Called: Snap-On Tools
19220 San Jose Ave, City of Industry (91748-1417)
PHONE...................626 965-0668
Michael King, *Branch Mgr*
Martin Ellen, *CFO*
Dwayne Thompson, *CTO*
Patricia Garcia, *Sales Mgr*
Vivian W Lee, *Director*
EMP: 95
SALES (corp-wide): 3.3B **Publicly Held**
WEB: www.snapon.com
SIC: 5072 Hand tools
PA: Snap-On Incorporated
2801 80th St
Kenosha WI 53143
262 656-5200

(P-7699)
SOFFIETTI CO
236 W Orange Show, San Bernardino (92408)
PHONE...................909 907-2277
Kedry Sagizli, *CEO*
EMP: 65 **EST:** 2009
SQ FT: 2,700
SALES (est): 200K **Privately Held**
SIC: 5072 5084 5511 Hardware; industrial machinery & equipment; new & used car dealers

(P-7700)
SUNKIST ENTERPRISES
1308 Rollins Rd, Burlingame (94010-2410)
PHONE...................650 347-3900
Ali Husain, *Owner*
EMP: 75
SQ FT: 6,000
SALES (est): 6.3MM **Privately Held**
WEB: www.sunkistenterprises.com
SIC: 5072 5031 Hardware; lumber, plywood & millwork

(P-7701)
TOMARCO CONTRACTOR SPC INC (PA)
Also Called: Tomarco Fastening Systems
14848 Northam St, La Mirada (90638-5747)
PHONE...................714 523-1771
William Thompson, *CEO*
Keith Watkins, *President*
Nick Ciminello, *Regional Mgr*
Jon Gregg, *Regional Mgr*
Larry Hook, *Regional Mgr*
▲ **EMP:** 60
SQ FT: 33,000
SALES (est): 88.1MM **Privately Held**
WEB: www.tomarco.com
SIC: 5072 Hand tools; power handtools; builders' hardware

(P-7702)
VENTURE PACIFIC TOOLS INC
17152 Daimler St, Irvine (92614-5509)
PHONE...................949 475-5505
Daniel Congellieri, *President*
▲ **EMP:** 61
SALES (est): 8.8MM **Privately Held**
SIC: 5072 Power tools & accessories

(P-7703)
VIAWORLD ADVANCED PRODUCTS
1002 S De Anza Blvd Ste 4, San Jose (95129-2778)
PHONE...................408 597-7051
John Xingqiang Wu, *President*
EMP: 56
SALES (est): 5MM **Privately Held**
WEB: www.viaworld.com
SIC: 5072 Power tools & accessories

(P-7704)
WILDENRADT-MCMURRAY INC
Also Called: Macmurray Pacific
568 7th St, San Francisco (94103-4710)
PHONE...................510 835-5500
Fax: 415 552-5840
Theodore Wildenradt, *President*
Eric Wildenradt, *CEO*
Vernelle Wildenradt, *Corp Secy*
▲ **EMP:** 70
SQ FT: 25,000
SALES (est): 31.5MM **Privately Held**
WEB: www.macmurraypacific.com
SIC: 5072 Builders' hardware

5074 Plumbing & Heating Splys Wholesale

(P-7705)
BRITA PRODUCTS COMPANY
1221 Broadway Ste 290, Oakland (94612-1838)
P.O. Box 24305 (94623-1305)
PHONE...................510 271-7000
Greg Frank, *President*
EMP: 85
SALES (est): 33.2MM
SALES (corp-wide): 5.7B **Publicly Held**
WEB: www.brita.com
SIC: 5074 Water purification equipment
PA: The Clorox Company
1221 Broadway Ste 1300
Oakland CA 94612
510 271-7000

(P-7706)
BUILDCOM INC
Also Called: Faucetdirect.com
402 Otterson Dr Ste 100, Chico (95928-8247)
PHONE...................800 375-3403

▲ = Import ▼ = Export
◆ = Import/Export

PRODUCTS & SERVICES SECTION
5074 - Plumbing & Heating Splys Wholesale County (P-7725)

Christian B Friedland, *CEO*
Danielle Porto Mohn, *Chief Mktg Ofcr*
Ryan Brewer, *Vice Pres*
Lindsay Fee, *Vice Pres*
Julie Gardner, *Vice Pres*
▼ **EMP:** 380
SQ FT: 22,100
SALES (est): 221.8MM
SALES (corp-wide): 20.8B **Privately Held**
WEB: www.improvementdirect.com
SIC: 5074 5999 Plumbing fittings & supplies; plumbing & heating supplies
PA: Wolseley Plc
The Wolseley Center
Leamington Spa CV31
192 670-5000

(P-7707)
CAL-STEAM SUPPLY
777 Mariposa St, San Francisco (94107-2586)
PHONE..................415 861-3071
Stew Corbin, *Manager*
Pamela Frese, *General Mgr*
EMP: 75
SALES (corp-wide): 20.8B **Privately Held**
SIC: 5074 Plumbing fittings & supplies
HQ: Cal-Steam Supply
1595 Crocker Ave
Hayward CA 94544
510 512-7700

(P-7708)
ELMCO/DUDDY INC (HQ)
15070 Proctor Ave, City of Industry (91746-3305)
P.O. Box 3787 (91744-0787)
PHONE..................626 333-9942
Fax: 626 855-4811
Donald E Morris, *CEO*
Thomas Duddy, *President*
Ron Stewart, *Vice Pres*
Jessica Wnuk, *Executive*
Willie Worthan, *General Mgr*
EMP: 50
SQ FT: 49,650
SALES (est): 12.7MM
SALES (corp-wide): 19.1MM **Privately Held**
WEB: www.elmcoduddy.com
SIC: 5074 1711 Sanitary ware, metal; plumbing, heating, air-conditioning contractors
PA: Elmco Sales Inc.
15070 Proctor Ave
City Of Industry CA 91746
626 855-4831

(P-7709)
EPS CORPORATE HOLDINGS INC
1235 S Lewis St, Anaheim (92805-6429)
PHONE..................714 635-3131
Fax: 714 635-3040
Greg Boiko, *Manager*
Kyle Mercer, *Sales Executive*
EMP: 60
SALES (corp-wide): 395.5MM **Privately Held**
SIC: 5074 1711 Plumbing & hydronic heating supplies; plumbing contractors
HQ: Eps Corporate Holdings, Inc.
3100 Donald Douglas
Santa Monica CA 90405
310 204-7238

(P-7710)
EVERSOFT INC (PA)
Also Called: Eversoft Products
707 W 16th St, Long Beach (90813-1410)
PHONE..................562 495-7766
Scott Burrows, *President*
Bruce Burrows, *Vice Pres*
Mathew Burrows, *Controller*
Jason Smith, *Director*
Billie Palmer, *Manager*
EMP: 52
SQ FT: 12,585
SALES (est): 19.8MM **Privately Held**
WEB: www.eversoftwater.net
SIC: 5074 Water purification equipment

(P-7711)
EZ-FLO INTERNATIONAL INC (PA)
2750 E Mission Blvd, Ontario (91761-2909)
PHONE..................909 947-5256
Paul Wilson, *President*
Saleem A Lahlouh, *President*
Emmanuel Lahlouh, *CFO*
Huda Lahlouh, *Admin Sec*
WEI Bowsky, *MIS Dir*
◆ **EMP:** 80
SQ FT: 70,000
SALES (est): 53.4MM **Privately Held**
WEB: www.ez-flo.net
SIC: 5074 Plumbing & hydronic heating supplies

(P-7712)
FERGUSON ENTERPRISES INC
Also Called: Lincoln Products
18825 San Jose Ave, City of Industry (91748-1326)
PHONE..................626 965-0724
Michael Aucoin, *Branch Mgr*
Dee Thorne, *Human Res Mgr*
Brad Blakeley, *Opers Mgr*
Mike Karanovich, *Opers Mgr*
Kevin Taylor, *Manager*
EMP: 80
SALES (corp-wide): 20.8B **Privately Held**
WEB: www.ferguson.com
SIC: 5074 Plumbing & hydronic heating supplies
HQ: Ferguson Enterprises, Inc.
12500 Jefferson Ave
Newport News VA 23602
757 874-7795

(P-7713)
FERGUSON ENTERPRISES INC
704 N Laverne Ave, Fresno (93727-6850)
PHONE..................559 253-2900
Greg Lourente, *Branch Mgr*
Melanie Dean, *Executive*
Greg Lourence, *General Mgr*
EMP: 50
SALES (corp-wide): 20.8B **Privately Held**
SIC: 5074 Plumbing & hydronic heating supplies
HQ: Ferguson Enterprises, Inc.
12500 Jefferson Ave
Newport News VA 23602
757 874-7795

(P-7714)
FERGUSON ENTERPRISES INC
9750 S Town Ave, Pomona (91766)
PHONE..................909 364-8700
Fax: 909 364-8776
Brian Hohn, *Manager*
EMP: 115
SALES (corp-wide): 20.8B **Privately Held**
WEB: www.ferguson.com
SIC: 5074 Plumbing & hydronic heating supplies
HQ: Ferguson Enterprises, Inc.
12500 Jefferson Ave
Newport News VA 23602
757 874-7795

(P-7715)
FERGUSON ENTERPRISES INC
Also Called: Ferguson 667
3280 Market St, San Diego (92102-3334)
PHONE..................619 515-0300
Louie Armstrong, *Branch Mgr*
Elizabeth Perez, *Branch Mgr*
Maricel Duque, *Human Res Dir*
Lisa Butterfield, *Human Resources*
Veronica Crawford, *Marketing Mgr*
EMP: 70
SQ FT: 45,000
SALES (corp-wide): 20.8B **Privately Held**
WEB: www.ferguson.com
SIC: 5074 Plumbing & hydronic heating supplies
HQ: Ferguson Enterprises, Inc.
12500 Jefferson Ave
Newport News VA 23602
757 874-7795

(P-7716)
FERGUSON ENTERPRISES INC
Also Called: Ferguson 601
7651 Woodman Ave, Van Nuys (91402-6536)
PHONE..................818 786-9720
Fred Raviol, *Branch Mgr*
Jeff Van Wagesen, *Vice Pres*
Gary Bennetts, *General Mgr*
Ann Hise, *Human Res Dir*
Jon Balano, *Opers Mgr*
EMP: 50
SALES (corp-wide): 20.8B **Privately Held**
WEB: www.ferguson.com
SIC: 5074 Plumbing & hydronic heating supplies
HQ: Ferguson Enterprises, Inc.
12500 Jefferson Ave
Newport News VA 23602
757 874-7795

(P-7717)
FERGUSON ENTERPRISES INC
Also Called: Ferguson 679
807 Eden St, Salinas (93901-4567)
PHONE..................831 373-5578
Victor Hernandez, *Manager*
Dennis Garcia, *Sales Executive*
Lee Chacon, *Sales Associate*
EMP: 60
SALES (corp-wide): 20.8B **Privately Held**
WEB: www.ferguson.com
SIC: 5074 Plumbing & hydronic heating supplies
HQ: Ferguson Enterprises, Inc.
12500 Jefferson Ave
Newport News VA 23602
757 874-7795

(P-7718)
FERGUSON ENTERPRISES INC
Also Called: Ferguson 677
11552 Monarch St, Garden Grove (92841-1815)
PHONE..................714 893-1936
Matthew Moore, *Manager*
Tom Raleigh, *General Mgr*
Dan Poppen, *Manager*
EMP: 250
SALES (corp-wide): 20.8B **Privately Held**
WEB: www.ferguson.com
SIC: 5074 Plumbing fittings & supplies
HQ: Ferguson Enterprises, Inc.
12500 Jefferson Ave
Newport News VA 23602
757 874-7795

(P-7719)
FERGUSON FIRE FABRICATION INC (DH)
Also Called: Pacific Fire Safety
2750 S Towne Ave, Pomona (91766-6205)
PHONE..................909 517-3085
Fax: 909 517-3980
Leo J Klien, *President*
Leo J Klien, *President*
Bethany Shaw, *Controller*
Ted Nelson, *Opers Mgr*
Melanie Fitzgearld, *Sales Executive*
▲ **EMP:** 100
SQ FT: 120,000
SALES (est): 148.3MM
SALES (corp-wide): 20.8B **Privately Held**
WEB: www.sierracraft.com
SIC: 5074 5099 Plumbing fittings & supplies; safety equipment & supplies; fire extinguishers
HQ: Ferguson Enterprises, Inc.
12500 Jefferson Ave
Newport News VA 23602
757 874-7795

(P-7720)
GCO INC (PA)
27750 Industrial Blvd, Hayward (94545-4043)
PHONE..................510 786-3333
Fax: 510 782-7905
Michael H Groeniger, *Ch of Bd*
Beverly J Groeniger, *Treasurer*
Richard Alexander, *Exec VP*
Richard Old, *Vice Pres*
James Wunsche, *Vice Pres*
EMP: 50
SQ FT: 15,000
SALES (est): 132.1MM **Privately Held**
WEB: www.groeniger.com
SIC: 5074 5087 Pipe & boiler covering; pipes & fittings, plastic; plumbing & heating valves; firefighting equipment; sprinkler systems

(P-7721)
GE IONICS INC
Also Called: Apollo Div Ionics Ultrapure
5900 Silvercreek Vly Rd, San Jose (95138-1083)
PHONE..................408 360-5900
Fax: 408 360-5950
Tim Addleman, *Manager*
EMP: 80
SALES (corp-wide): 117.3B **Publicly Held**
WEB: www.ionics.com
SIC: 5074 Plumbing & hydronic heating supplies
HQ: Ge Ionics, Inc.
3 Burlington Woods Dr # 200
Burlington MA 01803
781 359-7000

(P-7722)
HARRINGTON INDUSTRIAL PLAS LLC (HQ)
14480 Yorba Ave, Chino (91710-5766)
P.O. Box 5128 (91708-5128)
PHONE..................909 597-8641
Fax: 909 597-9826
James W Swanson, *Mng Member*
Patrick Foose, *President*
James Swanson, *President*
Jay Rooney, *CFO*
Jim Reid, *Vice Pres*
▼ **EMP:** 85
SQ FT: 50,000
SALES: 210MM
SALES (corp-wide): 1.1MM **Privately Held**
WEB: www.harringtonplastics.com
SIC: 5074 Pipes & fittings, plastic; plumbing & heating valves
PA: Aliaxis Sa
Avenue De Tervueren 270
Bruxelles 1150
277 550-50

(P-7723)
LARSEN SUPPLY CO (PA)
Also Called: Lasco
12055 Slauson Ave, Santa Fe Springs (90670-2601)
P.O. Box 4388 (90670-1400)
PHONE..................562 698-0731
Fax: 562 696-4063
Richard Larsen, *Ch of Bd*
Ruth Larsen, *Shareholder*
Rella Bodinus, *Vice Pres*
Sandy Soto, *Executive*
Kevin Piersol, *Branch Mgr*
▲ **EMP:** 100
SQ FT: 60,000
SALES (est): 39.6MM **Privately Held**
WEB: www.lasco.net
SIC: 5074 5075 Plumbing & hydronic heating supplies; warm air heating & air conditioning

(P-7724)
MERIDIAN HOLDINGS
2580 El Camino Real, Atascadero (93422-1916)
PHONE..................805 539-2752
Jason Devries, *President*
EMP: 55
SALES (est): 17.9MM **Privately Held**
SIC: 5074 Plumbing & hydronic heating supplies

(P-7725)
MMA RENEWABLE VENTURES LLC
44 Montgomery St Ste 2200, San Francisco (94104-4709)
PHONE..................415 229-8817
Matthew Cheney,
Steve Holman, *General Counsel*
EMP: 100

5074 - Plumbing & Heating Splys Wholesale County (P-7726)

SALES (est): 50.4MM
SALES (corp-wide): 29.7MM **Publicly Held**
WEB: www.munimae.com
SIC: 5074 Heating equipment & panels, solar
PA: Mma Capital Management, Llc
3600 Odonnell St Ste 600
Baltimore MD 21224
443 263-2900

(P-7726)
OATEY SUPPLY CHAIN SVCS INC
6600 Smith Ave, Newark (94560-4220)
PHONE..................510 797-4677
Armando Romo, *Manager*
EMP: 50
SALES (corp-wide): 141.4MM **Privately Held**
SIC: 5074 Plumbing & hydronic heating supplies
PA: Oatey Supply Chain Services, Inc.
4700 W 160th St
Cleveland OH 44135
216 267-7100

(P-7727)
PACE SUPPLY CORP (PA)
6000 State Farm Dr # 200, Rohnert Park (94928-2226)
P.O. Box 6407 (94927-6407)
PHONE..................707 303-0320
Ted M Green, *President*
Kelly Hubley, *Vice Pres*
Albert Bacci, *Admin Sec*
Gene Gorman, *Info Tech Dir*
Lynette Sisemore, *Accounting Mgr*
EMP: 80
SQ FT: 10,000
SALES (est): 206.7MM **Privately Held**
WEB: www.pacesupply.com
SIC: 5074 Plumbing & hydronic heating supplies

(P-7728)
PURCELL-MURRAY COMPANY INC (PA)
185 Park Ln, Brisbane (94005-1311)
PHONE..................415 468-6620
Fax: 415 468-0667
Timothy J Murray, *President*
Laurence D Purcell, *Vice Pres*
Brigitte Polianos, *Admin Asst*
Mildred Sierra, *Administration*
Matt Murray, *Info Tech Dir*
▲ EMP: 67
SQ FT: 40,000
SALES (est): 67.2MM **Privately Held**
SIC: 5074 5064 5078 Plumbing fittings & supplies; electrical appliances, major; refrigeration equipment & supplies

(P-7729)
PURONICS WATER SYSTEMS INC
5775 Las Positas Rd, Livermore (94551-7819)
PHONE..................925 456-7000
Scott Batiste, *CEO*
Mark H Cosmez II, *CFO*
Arnie D Harmon, *VP Sales*
◆ EMP: 60
SQ FT: 25,000
SALES (est): 16.1MM **Privately Held**
WEB: www.ionicsfidelity.com
SIC: 5074 Water purification equipment

(P-7730)
RYAN HERCO PRODUCTS CORP (PA)
Also Called: Ryan Herco Flow Solutions
3010 N San Fernando Blvd, Burbank (91504-2524)
P.O. Box 588 (91503-0588)
PHONE..................818 841-1141
Fax: 818 973-2600
Stewart Howley, *CEO*
Carrie Blankenheim, *CFO*
Terry Obrien, *Exec VP*
Randy Beckwith, *Vice Pres*
Randall Finchum, *Vice Pres*
◆ EMP: 60 EST: 1948
SQ FT: 48,000

SALES (est): 230.5MM **Privately Held**
WEB: www.ryanherco.com
SIC: 5074 5162 Pipes & fittings, plastic; plastics materials & basic shapes

(P-7731)
SNAPNRACK INC
775 Fiero Ln Ste 200, San Luis Obispo (93401-7904)
PHONE..................877 732-2860
Chris Oestreich, *Principal*
Greg McPheeters, *Design Engr*
Cody Norman, *Engineer*
Danny Ryan, *Engineer*
Lyn Cowgill, *Opers Mgr*
EMP: 964
SALES (est): 505.8K
SALES (corp-wide): 304.6MM **Publicly Held**
SIC: 5074 Heating equipment & panels, solar
HQ: Sunrun South Llc
595 Market St Fl 29
San Francisco CA 94105
415 580-6900

(P-7732)
SOUTH WEST SUN SOLAR INC
5871 Westminster Blvd C, Westminster (92683-3580)
PHONE..................714 582-3909
Mimi Ngo, *President*
EMP: 50
SALES (est): 5.9MM **Privately Held**
SIC: 5074 Heating equipment & panels, solar

5075 Heating & Air Conditioning Eqpt & Splys Wholesale

(P-7733)
AIR TREATMENT CORPORATION (PA)
640 N Puente St, Brea (92821-2830)
PHONE..................909 869-7975
Fax: 909 595-6874
Mark Hartman, *President*
Deborah Hudson, *CFO*
Greg Blackfelner, *Vice Pres*
Craig Domagala, *Vice Pres*
Tim Thomas, *Vice Pres*
▲ EMP: 65
SQ FT: 12,238
SALES (est): 92.6MM **Privately Held**
SIC: 5075 Electrical heating equipment; air conditioning equipment, except room units

(P-7734)
ALLIED REFRIGERATION INC ✪
3650 Holdrege Ave, Los Angeles (90016-4304)
PHONE..................310 202-2220
Robert Nichols, *President*
Chinnavy Lyman, *CFO*
EMP: 99 EST: 2016
SALES (est): 2.2MM **Privately Held**
SIC: 5075 Warm air heating & air conditioning

(P-7735)
CALIFORNIA HYDRONICS CORP (PA)
Also Called: Columbia Hydronics Co.
2293 Tripaldi Way, Hayward (94545-5024)
P.O. Box 5049 (94540-5049)
PHONE..................510 293-1993
Fax: 510 293-3080
David Attard, *President*
John Arthur, *CFO*
Kevin McCloud, *Treasurer*
James A Attard, *Vice Pres*
Jeff Flowers, *Associate Dir*
EMP: 50
SQ FT: 50,000
SALES (est): 68.1MM **Privately Held**
WEB: www.calhydro.com
SIC: 5075 3585 Warm air heating & air conditioning; refrigeration & heating equipment

(P-7736)
EDWARD B WARD & COMPANY INC (DH)
Also Called: Ward, E B
99 S Hill Dr Ste B, Brisbane (94005-1282)
PHONE..................415 330-6600
James Lazor, *President*
John Ward, *Ch of Bd*
Robert McDonough, *CEO*
Edward B Ward, *COO*
Paul Caputi, *Vice Pres*
▲ EMP: 50
SQ FT: 45,000
SALES (est): 16.7MM
SALES (corp-wide): 56.1B **Publicly Held**
WEB: www.valair.com
SIC: 5075 Air conditioning equipment, except room units
HQ: Carrier Corporation
17900 Bee Line Hwy
Jupiter FL 33478
561 796-2000

(P-7737)
EL CAJON PLUMBING & HTG SUP CO
1655 N Magnolia Ave, El Cajon (92020-1297)
PHONE..................619 449-7300
Morton B Hirshman, *CEO*
Naomi Hirshman, *Vice Pres*
Shelly Olsher, *Principal*
Kathy Esposito, *Director*
Susie Perez, *Manager*
EMP: 50
SQ FT: 13,000
SALES (est): 13.9MM **Privately Held**
WEB: www.elcajonplumbing.com
SIC: 5075 5074 Dust collecting equipment; plumbing & hydronic heating supplies

(P-7738)
FLORENCE FILTER CORPORATION
530 W Manville St, Compton (90220-5587)
PHONE..................310 637-1137
Fax: 310 631-4323
Adrian M Anhood, *CEO*
Erika A Anhood, *President*
Floriana A Anhood, *CEO*
William Anhood, *General Mgr*
Jillian Aguilar, *Controller*
▲ EMP: 60
SQ FT: 55,000
SALES (est): 21.2MM **Privately Held**
WEB: www.florencefilter.com
SIC: 5075 3564 5211 Air filters; filters, air: furnaces, air conditioning equipment, etc.; lumber & other building materials

(P-7739)
HALDEMAN INC
2937 Tanager Ave, Commerce (90040-2761)
PHONE..................323 726-7011
Fax: 323 726-1644
Albert Thomas Haldeman, *CEO*
Tom Haldeman, *President*
Sue Haldeman, *Treasurer*
Janet Hoffman, *Admin Sec*
EMP: 55
SQ FT: 45,000
SALES (est): 23.3MM **Privately Held**
WEB: www.haldemaninc.com
SIC: 5075 Warm air heating & air conditioning

(P-7740)
HKF INC (PA)
Also Called: Therm Pacific
5983 Smithway St, Commerce (90040-1607)
PHONE..................323 225-1318
Fax: 323 721-7383
James P Hartfield, *President*
Donald Evans, *Accountant*
▲ EMP: 57
SALES (est): 92MM **Privately Held**
SIC: 5075 3873 5064 3567 Warm air heating & air conditioning; watches, clocks, watchcases & parts; electrical appliances, television & radio; industrial furnaces & ovens; current-carrying wiring devices

(P-7741)
HONEYWELL INTERNATIONAL INC
514 S Lyon St, Santa Ana (92701-6362)
PHONE..................714 796-7500
Fax: 714 796-7555
Emily McCue, *Manager*
Donald Sylvester, *Sr Corp Ofcr*
EMP: 115
SALES (corp-wide): 38.5B **Publicly Held**
WEB: www.honeywell.com
SIC: 5075 8748 7382 Warm air heating & air conditioning; business consulting; security systems services
PA: Honeywell International Inc.
115 Tabor Rd
Morris Plains NJ 07950
973 455-2000

(P-7742)
LENNOX INDUSTRIES INC
1790 Iowa Ave, Riverside (92507-2474)
PHONE..................951 241-8966
EMP: 140
SALES (corp-wide): 3.4B **Publicly Held**
SIC: 5075 Warm air heating & air conditioning
HQ: Lennox Industries Inc.
2100 Lake Park Blvd
Richardson TX 75080
972 497-5000

(P-7743)
LENNOX INDUSTRIES INC
19801 Nordhoff Pl Ste 109, Chatsworth (91311-6612)
PHONE..................818 739-1616
EMP: 140
SALES (corp-wide): 3.4B **Publicly Held**
SIC: 5075 Warm air heating & air conditioning
HQ: Lennox Industries Inc.
2100 Lake Park Blvd
Richardson TX 75080
972 497-5000

(P-7744)
NORITZ AMERICA CORPORATION (HQ)
11160 Grace Ave, Fountain Valley (92708-5436)
PHONE..................714 433-2905
Fax: 714 241-1514
Hisashi Uryu, *CEO*
Toshiyuki Otaki, *CEO*
Luis Barba, *Engineer*
Reginald Gholston, *Engineer*
Carlos Morales, *VP Sales*
▲ EMP: 56
SALES (est): 40.7MM
SALES (corp-wide): 1.7B **Privately Held**
SIC: 5075 Warm air heating equipment & supplies
PA: Noritz Corporation
93, Edomachi, Chuo-Ku
Kobe HYO 650-0
783 913-361

(P-7745)
NORMAN S WRIGHT MECH EQP CORP (PA)
99 S Hill Dr Ste A, Brisbane (94005-1282)
PHONE..................415 467-7600
Richard F Leao, *President*
Robert L Beyer, *Exec VP*
Salvatore M Giglio, *Exec VP*
Heather Hodges, *Personnel Assit*
Steve Dobberstein, *Director*
EMP: 62
SQ FT: 50,000
SALES (est): 169MM **Privately Held**
WEB: www.norman-wright.com
SIC: 5075 Warm air heating equipment & supplies; air conditioning & ventilation equipment & supplies

(P-7746)
SIERRA PCF HM & COMFORT INC
Also Called: Sierra Pacific Htg & Air-Solar
2550 Mercantile Dr Ste D, Rancho Cordova (95742-8202)
PHONE..................916 638-0543
Jason Hanson, *President*
Mike Loer, *Vice Pres*

PRODUCTS & SERVICES SECTION
5082 - Construction & Mining Mach & Eqpt Wholesale County (P-7768)

Luis Quintanilla, *Branch Mgr*
Amanda Johnson, *Manager*
Lynne Lockwood, *Manager*
EMP: 75
SALES (est): 59.5MM **Privately Held**
WEB: www.sierrapacifichome.com
SIC: 5075 5074 Warm air heating & air conditioning; heating equipment & panels, solar

(P-7747)
SLAKEY BROTHERS INC
1480 Nicora Ave, San Jose (95133-1639)
PHONE 408 494-0460
Fax: 408 298-3464
Tom Trapani, *Sales/Mktg Mgr*
Diane Blythe, *Financial Exec*
Tom Trapini, *Manager*
EMP: 50
SALES (corp-wide): 148MM **Privately Held**
WEB: www.slakey.com
SIC: 5075 Warm air heating & air conditioning; warm air heating equipment & supplies
PA: Slakey Brothers, Inc.
2215 Kausen Dr Ste 1
Elk Grove CA 95758
916 478-2000

(P-7748)
TRANE US INC
4145 Delmar Ave Ste 2, Rocklin (95677-4041)
PHONE 916 577-1100
Tyler Clemmer, *Manager*
Mark Cresitello, *Admin Sec*
EMP: 90 **Privately Held**
SIC: 5075 Air conditioning & ventilation equipment & supplies
HQ: Trane U.S. Inc.
1 Centennial Ave Ste 101
Piscataway NJ 08854
732 652-7100

(P-7749)
TUCKER DISTRIBUTORS
Also Called: Tucker Sheet Metal Distr
5380 E Hunter Ave, Anaheim (92807-2053)
PHONE 714 970-5742
Tom Tucker, *Partner*
Sue Tucker, *Partner*
EMP: 50
SQ FT: 16,000
SALES: 12.6MM **Privately Held**
SIC: 5075 5051 5084 Ventilating equipment & supplies; tin & tin base metals, shapes, forms, etc.; metalworking machinery

(P-7750)
ULTRAVIOLET DEVICES INC
26145 Technology Dr, Valencia (91355-1138)
PHONE 661 295-8140
Peter Veloz, *CEO*
David Veloz, *Shareholder*
Richard Hayes, *Vice Pres*
Lev Rotkop, *Vice Pres*
David Witham, *Vice Pres*
◆ **EMP:** 53
SQ FT: 45,000
SALES (est): 43.2MM **Privately Held**
WEB: www.uvdi.com
SIC: 5075 5074 Air filters; water purification equipment

(P-7751)
YAMAS CONTROLS GROUP INC (PA)
5030 Hillsdale Cir # 102, El Dorado Hills (95762-5754)
PHONE 916 357-6000
Charles Van Sheet, *President*
Ken Stoves, *Executive*
Jerie Coker, *Executive Asst*
EMP: 50
SQ FT: 14,000
SALES (est): 36.1MM **Privately Held**
SIC: 5075 1711 Fans, heating & ventilation equipment; warm air heating & air conditioning contractor

---

5078 Refrigeration Eqpt & Splys Wholesale

(P-7752)
ALLIED BEVERAGE LLC
13235 Golden State Rd, Sylmar (91342-1129)
PHONE 818 493-6400
Mark Smith, *CEO*
Kimberly Clift, *CFO*
EMP: 500
SALES (est): 27.3MM **Privately Held**
SIC: 5078 Beverage coolers

(P-7753)
BAKER DISTRIBUTING COMPANY LLC
241 Market Pl, Escondido (92029-1301)
P.O. Box 848459, Dallas TX (75284-8459)
PHONE 760 708-4201
EMP: 99
SQ FT: 12,000
SALES (corp-wide): 4.1B **Publicly Held**
SIC: 5078 Refrigeration equipment & supplies
HQ: Baker Distributing Company Llc
14610 Breakers Dr Ste 100
Jacksonville FL 32258
904 407-4500

(P-7754)
COMMERCIAL RFRGN SPCIALIST INC
Also Called: CRS
3480 Arden Rd, Hayward (94545-3906)
PHONE 510 784-8990
Fax: 510 656-3179
Mike Coldren, *CEO*
Alan Ray Bradshaw, *Owner*
George Carr, *President*
Kira Schneider, *Admin Asst*
Diane Domeier, *Controller*
EMP: 50
SQ FT: 7,500
SALES (est): 57MM **Privately Held**
WEB: www.crsref.com
SIC: 5078 Refrigerators, commercial (reach-in & walk-in)

(P-7755)
MAYEKAWA USA INC
Also Called: Mayekawa Manufacturing Company
19475 Gramercy Pl, Torrance (90501-1134)
PHONE 310 618-3170
Yuki Inoue, *Manager*
EMP: 60 **Privately Held**
SIC: 5078 Refrigeration equipment & supplies
HQ: Mayekawa U.S.A., Inc.
1850 Jarvis Ave
Elk Grove Village IL 60007
773 516-5070

(P-7756)
OMNITEAM INC
9300 Hall Rd, Downey (90241-5309)
PHONE 562 923-9660
Kans Haasis Jr, *CEO*
Robert Davis, *Vice Pres*
Don Hyatt Sr, *Vice Pres*
Dick Hendershot, *Finance*
Alfredo Garcia, *Manager*
EMP: 125
SQ FT: 100,000
SALES (est): 68.4MM **Privately Held**
WEB: www.omniteam.com
SIC: 5078 Refrigeration equipment & supplies

(P-7757)
PEPSI-COLA METRO BTLG CO INC
6659 Sycamore Canyon Blvd, Riverside (92507-0733)
PHONE 951 697-3200
Jerry Sime, *Manager*
Nathan Parker, *Maintence Staff*
Jon Hess, *Director*
Mike Poole, *Director*
Fred Jochums, *Manager*
EMP: 500

SALES (corp-wide): 63B **Publicly Held**
WEB: www.joy-of-cola.com
SIC: 5078 2086 5149 Refrigerated beverage dispensers; bottled & canned soft drinks; soft drinks
HQ: Pepsi-Cola Metropolitan Bottling Company, Inc.
1111 Westchester Ave
White Plains NY 10604
914 767-6000

(P-7758)
REFRIGERATION HDWR SUP CORP
9021 Norris Ave, Sun Valley (91352-2618)
PHONE 818 768-3636
Fax: 818 767-4651
Pamela Sylvester, *Branch Mgr*
Pamela Sylvestre, *Sales Executive*
EMP: 50
SALES (corp-wide): 26.6MM **Privately Held**
SIC: 5078 5722 3585 7699 Refrigeration equipment & supplies; household appliance stores; refrigeration & heating equipment; restaurant equipment repair
PA: Refrigeration Hardware Supply Corporation
632 Foresight Cir
Grand Junction CO 81505
970 241-2800

(P-7759)
SOURCE REFRIGERATION
800 E Orangethorpe Ave, Anaheim (92801-1123)
PHONE 714 578-2300
Fax: 714 578-4088
Brad Howard, *Principal*
John Skelton, *Vice Pres*
EMP: 51
SALES (est): 22.1MM **Privately Held**
SIC: 5078 Refrigeration equipment & supplies

(P-7760)
STELLAR GROUP INCORPORATED
1035 Reno Ave, Modesto (95351-1165)
PHONE 209 549-0899
Fax: 209 549-1837
Christine Clark, *Branch Mgr*
Rod Lewis, *Vice Pres*
Mark Turner, *Sales Staff*
Dan McDonough, *Manager*
Ray Roffignol, *Manager*
EMP: 52
SALES (corp-wide): 336.1MM **Privately Held**
SIC: 5078 Refrigeration equipment & supplies
HQ: Stellar Group, Incorporated
2900 Hartley Rd
Jacksonville FL 32257
904 260-2044

(P-7761)
UNITED REFRIGERATION INC
3573a Hayden Ave, Culver City (90232-2412)
PHONE 310 204-2500
EMP: 99
SQ FT: 2,000
SALES (corp-wide): 50MM **Privately Held**
SIC: 5078 Refrigeration equipment & supplies
PA: United Refrigeration, Inc.
11401 Roosevelt Blvd
Philadelphia PA 19154
215 698-9100

5082 Construction & Mining Mach & Eqpt Wholesale

(P-7762)
BIG CITY ACCESS INC (PA)
3131 52nd Ave, West Sacramento (95691)
PHONE 916 428-4090
Fax: 916 428-4078
Linda McCurdy, *CEO*

Barbara Roberts, *President*
Michael McCurdy, *CFO*
EMP: 77
SALES (est): 17.4MM **Privately Held**
SIC: 5082 Scaffolding

(P-7763)
BRAND SERVICES INC
Also Called: Brand Services of California
535 Watt Dr, Fairfield (94534-1790)
PHONE 707 603-3400
Fax: 707 558-1810
Paul Wood, *President*
Pricilla Sherfy, *Executive*
John Monter, *Plant Mgr*
Cliff Malta, *Sales Mgr*
Gary Joules, *Manager*
EMP: 50
SALES (est): 20.7MM **Privately Held**
SIC: 5082 Scaffolding

(P-7764)
CALIFORNIA CONTRS SUPS INC
7729 Burnet Ave, Van Nuys (91405-1008)
PHONE 818 785-8823
Fax: 818 780-3180
David Rogal, *CEO*
Phil Kaufmann, *President*
Al Lester, *Corp Secy*
John Boss, *Manager*
EMP: 55
SQ FT: 16,000
SALES (est): 16MM **Privately Held**
SIC: 5082 General construction machinery & equipment

(P-7765)
CAMERON WEST COAST INC
Also Called: Cameron Surface Systems
4316 Yeager Way, Bakersfield (93313)
PHONE 661 837-4980
Fax: 661 837-8073
Reg Walker, *Controller*
▲ **EMP:** 90 **EST:** 1992
SQ FT: 48,000
SALES (est): 71.4MM **Privately Held**
SIC: 5082 1389 7353 Oil field equipment; oil field services; oil field equipment, rental or leasing
HQ: Cameron International Corporation
4646 W Sam Houston Pkwy N
Houston TX 77041
713 513-3300

(P-7766)
CASE DEALER HOLDING CO LLC
1751 Bell Ave, Sacramento (95838-2862)
PHONE 916 649-0096
Trevor Ward, *Mng Member*
Douglas Wiles, *Manager*
EMP: 150
SALES (est): 15.4MM
SALES (corp-wide): 26.3B **Privately Held**
SIC: 5082 General construction machinery & equipment
HQ: Cnh Industrial America Llc
700 St St
Racine WI 53404
262 636-6011

(P-7767)
CNH INDUSTRIAL AMERICA LLC
1919 Williams St, San Leandro (94577-2303)
PHONE 510 351-2015
Norma Smith, *Manager*
EMP: 50
SALES (corp-wide): 26.3B **Privately Held**
SIC: 5082 General construction machinery & equipment
HQ: Cnh Industrial America Llc
700 St St
Racine WI 53404
262 636-6011

(P-7768)
EMPIRE SOUTHWEST LLC
Also Called: Caterpillar Authorized Dealer
3393 Us Highway 86, Imperial (92251-9527)
PHONE 760 545-6200
Diane Madrigal, *Manager*
EMP: 300

5082 - Construction & Mining Mach & Eqpt Wholesale County (P-7769)

SALES (corp-wide): 881.9MM **Privately Held**
WEB: www.empire-cat.com
SIC: **5082** Construction & mining machinery
PA: Empire Southwest, Llc
1725 S Country Club Dr
Mesa AZ 85210
480 633-4000

(P-7769) FLUOR ENTERPRISES INC
3 Polaris Way, Aliso Viejo (92656-5338)
PHONE................................949 349-2000
Ronald Albright, *Branch Mgr*
James Byrd, *Project Mgr*
Don Lees, *Engineer*
Jody Warren, *Engineer*
Clyde Joseph, *Director*
EMP: 200
SALES (corp-wide): 18.1B **Publicly Held**
SIC: **5082** Construction & mining machinery
HQ: Fluor Enterprises, Inc.
6700 Las Colinas Blvd
Irving TX 75039
469 398-7000

(P-7770) HAWTHORNE MACHINERY CO
Also Called: Caterpillar Authorized Dealer
8050 Othello Ave, San Diego (92111-3714)
PHONE................................858 974-6800
Bob Price, *Manager*
David Ness, *Exec VP*
Patrick Burton, *Sales Staff*
Jim Gilchrist, *Sales Staff*
EMP: 100
SALES (corp-wide): 175.7MM **Privately Held**
SIC: **5082** Construction & mining machinery
PA: Hawthorne Machinery Co.
16945 Camino San Bernardo
San Diego CA 92127
858 674-7000

(P-7771) HERCA TELECOMM SERVICES INC
Also Called: Herca Construction Services
18610 Beck St, Perris (92570-9185)
PHONE................................951 940-5941
Hector R Castellon, *President*
Tracy Hertel, *CFO*
Raul Castellon, *Opers Staff*
Alfonso Castellon, *Director*
Alfredo Castellon, *Director*
EMP: 56
SQ FT: 67,900
SALES: 16.2MM **Privately Held**
WEB: www.hercatelecomm.com
SIC: **5082** 1623 1731 3663 General construction machinery & equipment; communication line & transmission tower construction; general electrical contractor; antennas, transmitting & communications

(P-7772) HOLT OF CALIFORNIA (HQ)
Also Called: Holt CA
7310 Pacific Ave, Pleasant Grove (95668-9708)
P.O. Box 100001 (95668)
PHONE................................916 991-8200
Victor Wykoff Jr, *Ch of Bd*
Kenneth Monroe, *President*
Daniel Johns, *CFO*
Gordon Beatie, *Vice Ch Bd*
Ronald Monroe, *Exec VP*
▲ EMP: 155
SQ FT: 160,000
SALES (est): 465.7MM **Privately Held**
WEB: www.holtcausedparts.com
SIC: **5082** 5084 5083 7359 Construction & mining machinery; tractors, construction; materials handling machinery; agricultural machinery; equipment rental & leasing
PA: Hoc Holdings, Inc.
7310 Pacific Ave
Pleasant Grove CA 95668
916 921-8950

(P-7773) HOLT OF CALIFORNIA
Also Called: Caterpillar Authorized Dealer
3850 Channel Dr, West Sacramento (95691-3466)
PHONE................................916 373-4100
Toll Free:................................888 -
Fax: 916 373-4116
Carry Roulet, *Manager*
Bob Wolfe, *Vice Pres*
Dave Harris, *Sales Engr*
Dave Dobberteen, *Accounts Mgr*
EMP: 150
SALES (corp-wide): 465.7MM **Privately Held**
WEB: www.holtcausedparts.com
SIC: **5082** 5083 5084 General construction machinery & equipment; agricultural machinery & equipment; materials handling machinery
HQ: Holt Of California
7310 Pacific Ave
Pleasant Grove CA 95668
916 991-8200

(P-7774) HOLT OF CALIFORNIA
1234 W Charter Way, Stockton (95206-1109)
PHONE................................209 462-3660
Fax: 209 463-4444
Ken Monroe, *Owner*
Sean Vasko, *Sales Staff*
EMP: 108
SALES (corp-wide): 465.7MM **Privately Held**
SIC: **5082** Construction & mining machinery; tractors, construction
HQ: Holt Of California
7310 Pacific Ave
Pleasant Grove CA 95668
916 991-8200

(P-7775) HUB CONSTRUCTION SPC INC
1856 S Bon View Ave, Ontario (91761-5501)
PHONE................................909 947-4669
Fax: 909 947-5586
Tim Robuck, *Manager*
EMP: 50
SALES (corp-wide): 48.4MM **Privately Held**
SIC: **5082** 3444 Concrete processing equipment; concrete forms, sheet metal
PA: Hub Construction Specialties, Inc.
379 S I St
San Bernardino CA 92410
909 235-4100

(P-7776) J M EQUIPMENT COMPANY INC
3751 E Calwa Ave, Fresno (93725-2002)
P.O. Box 2400 (93745-2400)
PHONE................................559 233-0187
Fax: 559 233-6954
Scott Anderson, *Manager*
Rod Kiser, *Materials Mgr*
Mike Koop, *Manager*
EMP: 50
SQ FT: 900
SALES (corp-wide): 34.9MM **Privately Held**
WEB: www.jmequipment.com
SIC: **5082** 7353 5084 5021 Construction & mining machinery; heavy construction equipment rental; materials handling machinery; lockers
PA: J. M. Equipment Company, Inc.
321 Spreckels Ave
Manteca CA 95336
209 522-3271

(P-7777) JOHNSON MACHINERY CO (PA)
Also Called: Caterpillar Authorized Dealer
800 E La Cadena Dr, Riverside (92507-8715)
P.O. Box 351 (92502-0351)
PHONE................................951 686-4560
Fax: 951 683-7739
William Johnson Jr, *President*
Jerry Welch, *COO*
Stephen Hatch, *CFO*
Kevin Kelly, *Exec VP*
Matt Merickel, *Exec VP*
◆ EMP: 175 EST: 1940
SQ FT: 70,000
SALES (est): 219.7MM **Privately Held**
WEB: www.johnson-machinery.com
SIC: **5082** General construction machinery & equipment

(P-7778) NAUMANN/HOBBS MTL HDLG CORP II
Also Called: Hawthorne Lift Systems
86998 Avenue 52, Coachella (92236-2710)
PHONE................................866 266-2244
Charles Crew, *Vice Pres*
EMP: 105
SALES (corp-wide): 90MM **Privately Held**
SIC: **5082** 5084 General construction machinery & equipment; industrial machinery & equipment
PA: Naumann/Hobbs Material Handling Corporation Ii, Inc.
4335 E Wood St
Phoenix AZ 85040
602 437-1331

(P-7779) PAPE MACHINERY INC
Also Called: John Deere Authorized Dealer
2850 El Centro Rd, Sacramento (95833-9602)
P.O. Box 15017 (95851-0017)
PHONE................................916 922-7181
Josh Juenger, *Branch Mgr*
Jordan Pape, *CEO*
Terri Tuckey, *Executive*
Reid Findley, *Business Mgr*
Mike Pilat, *Sales Mgr*
EMP: 82
SALES (corp-wide): 738.4MM **Privately Held**
WEB: www.papemh.com
SIC: **5082** General construction machinery & equipment
HQ: Pape' Machinery, Inc.
355 Goodpasture Island Rd
Eugene OR 97401
541 683-5073

(P-7780) QUINN COMPANY
13275 Golden State Rd, Sylmar (91342-1129)
PHONE................................818 767-7171
EMP: 61
SALES (corp-wide): 514.9MM **Privately Held**
SIC: **5082** General construction machinery & equipment
HQ: Quinn Company
10006 Rose Hills Rd
City Of Industry CA 90601
562 463-4000

(P-7781) QUINN COMPANY
Also Called: Caterpillar Authorized Dealer
2200 Pegasus Dr, Bakersfield (93308-6801)
PHONE................................661 393-5800
Fax: 661 393-5072
Steve Eucce, *Branch Mgr*
Bob Rayford, *Executive*
Brian Tanaka, *Analyst*
Jason Lee, *Sales Staff*
Nick Tafolla, *Sales Staff*
EMP: 62
SALES (corp-wide): 514.9MM **Privately Held**
WEB: www.quinngroup.net
SIC: **5082** 5083 5084 7353 General construction machinery & equipment; farm & garden machinery; industrial machinery & equipment; heavy construction equipment rental
HQ: Quinn Company
10006 Rose Hills Rd
City Of Industry CA 90601
562 463-4000

(P-7782) QUINN COMPANY
Also Called: Caterpillar Authorized Dealer
801 Del Norte Blvd, Oxnard (93030-8966)
PHONE................................805 485-2171
Jay Ervine, *Branch Mgr*

Angie Casillas, *HR Admin*
Ana Ortega, *Manager*
Mike Reinhart, *Manager*
EMP: 62
SALES (corp-wide): 514.9MM **Privately Held**
WEB: www.quinngroup.net
SIC: **5082** 5083 5084 7353 General construction machinery & equipment; farm & garden machinery; industrial machinery & equipment; heavy construction equipment rental
HQ: Quinn Company
10006 Rose Hills Rd
City Of Industry CA 90601
562 463-4000

(P-7783) QUINN COMPANY
Also Called: Caterpillar Authorized Dealer
1655 Carlotti Dr, Santa Maria (93454-1503)
PHONE................................805 925-8611
Fax: 805 925-1909
Dan Hunt, *Manager*
Jim Niboli, *Manager*
EMP: 62
SALES (corp-wide): 514.9MM **Privately Held**
WEB: www.quinngroup.net
SIC: **5082** 5083 5084 7353 General construction machinery & equipment; farm & garden machinery; industrial machinery & equipment; heavy construction equipment rental
HQ: Quinn Company
10006 Rose Hills Rd
City Of Industry CA 90601
562 463-4000

(P-7784) QUINN GROUP INC
Also Called: Caterpillar Authorized Dealer
1300 Abbott St, Salinas (93901-4507)
PHONE................................831 758-8461
Kelly Francis, *Store Mgr*
Jesse Sandoval, *Manager*
EMP: 1000
SALES (corp-wide): 514.9MM **Privately Held**
WEB: www.quinnengines.com
SIC: **5082** Construction & mining machinery
PA: Quinn Group, Inc.
10006 Rose Hills Rd
City Of Industry CA 90601
562 463-4000

(P-7785) QUINN SHEPHERD MACHINERY
Also Called: Caterpillar Authorized Dealer
10006 Rose Hills Rd, City of Industry (90601-1702)
P.O. Box 226789, Los Angeles (90022-6789)
PHONE................................562 463-6000
Blake Quinn, *President*
Chris Erving, *Manager*
Jonathan Monroe, *Manager*
▲ EMP: 287
SQ FT: 163,000
SALES (est): 114MM
SALES (corp-wide): 514.9MM **Privately Held**
SIC: **5082** 5084 General construction machinery & equipment; excavating machinery & equipment; mining machinery & equipment, except petroleum; industrial machinery & equipment
PA: Quinn Group, Inc.
10006 Rose Hills Rd
City Of Industry CA 90601
562 463-4000

(P-7786) RDO CONSTRUCTION EQUIPMENT CO
Also Called: John Deere Authorized Dealer
20 Iowa Ave, Riverside (92507-1028)
PHONE................................951 778-3700
Fax: 951 778-3746
Greg Burgman, *General Mgr*
Sally Ceja, *Human Res Mgr*
Cindy Baird, *Parts Mgr*
EMP: 50

▲ = Import ▼ = Export
◆ = Import/Export

PRODUCTS & SERVICES SECTION

5083 - Farm & Garden Mach & Eqpt Wholesale County (P-7808)

SALES (corp-wide): 1.9B **Privately Held**
SIC: 5082 General construction machinery & equipment
HQ: Rdo Construction Equipment Co.
 2000 Industrial Dr
 Bismarck ND 58501
 701 223-5798

(P-7787)
RDO VERMEER LLC
Also Called: Vermeer Pacific
3980 Research Dr, Sacramento (95838-3257)
PHONE..................916 643-0999
Fax: 916 643-0998
Christi Offutt,
Nadine Kruk, *Finance*
Nalson Anderson, *Manager*
EMP: 99
SALES (est): 8.4MM **Privately Held**
SIC: 5082 Contractors' materials

(P-7788)
SAFWAY SERVICES LP
1660 Gilbreth Rd, Burlingame (94010-1408)
PHONE..................650 652-9255
Fax: 650 652-9255
EMP: 50
SALES (corp-wide): 1.7B **Privately Held**
SIC: 5082
HQ: Safway Services, L.P.
 N19w24200 Riverwood Dr # 200
 Waukesha WI 53188
 262 523-6500

(P-7789)
SAFWAY SERVICES LP
4072b Teal Ct, Benicia (94510-1238)
PHONE..................707 745-2000
Fax: 707 745-2012
Sully Cittadino, *Manager*
EMP: 50
SALES (corp-wide): 1.6B **Privately Held**
WEB: www.safway.com
SIC: 5082 Scaffolding
HQ: Safway Services, L.P.
 N19w24200 Riverwood Dr # 200
 Waukesha WI 53188
 262 523-6500

(P-7790)
SONSRAY MACHINERY LLC
10062 Live Oak Ave, Fontana (92335-6225)
PHONE..................909 355-1075
Allen Gernier,
Myke Robbins, *General Mgr*
Don Brannies, *Manager*
EMP: 99 EST: 2012
SALES (est): 11.9MM **Privately Held**
SIC: 5531 General construction machinery & equipment; graders, road (construction machinery); bulldozers (construction machinery)

(P-7791)
SOUND-CRETE CONTRACTING
530 Opper St Ste A, Escondido (92029-1034)
PHONE..................760 291-1240
Louis Fisher, *President*
Terry Russo, *Vice Pres*
Jim Dorsey, *Manager*
EMP: 65
SALES (est): 6.3MM **Privately Held**
SIC: 5082 General construction machinery & equipment

(P-7792)
SOUTHWEST GENERAL CONTRS INC
912 S Andreasen Dr # 101, Escondido (92029-1900)
PHONE..................760 480-8747
Fax: 760 480-8782
Dane Crown, *President*
EMP: 50
SQ FT: 4,500
SALES (est): 10.4MM **Privately Held**
SIC: 5082 General construction machinery & equipment

(P-7793)
TOM MALLOY CORPORATION (PA)
Also Called: Trench Shoring Company
636 E Rosecrans Ave, Los Angeles (90059-3507)
PHONE..................310 327-5554
Fax: 310 323-9648
Thomas E Malloy, *CEO*
Kevin Malloy, *President*
Art Boquiren, *CFO*
Bridgett Baril, *Vice Pres*
Dave Medbery, *Branch Mgr*
▲ EMP: 50 EST: 1973
SALES (est): 44.6MM **Privately Held**
SIC: 5082 7353 Construction & mining machinery; heavy construction equipment rental

(P-7794)
TURNER CONSTRUCTION COMPANY
1900 S State College Blvd # 200, Anaheim (92806-6197)
PHONE..................714 940-9000
Fax: 714 486-9857
Bernie Morrissey, *Vice Pres*
Sara Miller, *Assistant*
EMP: 300
SALES (corp-wide): 506.6MM **Privately Held**
WEB: www.tcco.com
SIC: 5082 General construction machinery & equipment
HQ: Turner Construction Company Inc
 375 Hudson St Fl 6
 New York NY 10014
 212 229-6000

(P-7795)
U S ARMY CORPS OF ENGINEERS
915 Wilshire Blvd Ste 930, Los Angeles (90017-3489)
PHONE..................213 452-3403
EMP: 600 **Publicly Held**
SIC: 5082 Dredges & draglines, except ships
HQ: U S Army Corps Of Engineers
 441 G Street Nw
 Washington DC 20314
 804 435-9362

(P-7796)
WEATHERFORD INTERNATIONAL LLC
Also Called: Coroc
21728 Rosedale Hwy, Bakersfield (93314-9787)
PHONE..................661 587-6930
Fax: 661 587-2456
Mark Sarcen, *Branch Mgr*
Steve Wolpe, *District Mgr*
EMP: 60 **Privately Held**
WEB: www.weatherford.com
SIC: 5082 Oil field equipment
HQ: Weatherford International, Llc
 2000 Saint James Pl
 Houston TX 77056
 713 693-4000

(P-7797)
WHITE CAP CONSTRUCTION SUPPLY
1815 Ritchey St, Santa Ana (92705-5127)
PHONE..................949 794-5300
Jack Karg, *Principal*
Bob Bullock, *President*
Ian Heller, *Vice Pres*
Kevin Burns, *Branch Mgr*
Thomas Klevecz, *Branch Mgr*
EMP: 1326
SALES (est): 17MM
SALES (corp-wide): 7.3B **Publicly Held**
SIC: 5082 Construction & mining machinery
HQ: White Cap Construction Supply, Inc.
 3100 Cumberland Blvd Se # 1700
 Atlanta GA 30339
 404 879-7740

5083 Farm & Garden Mach & Eqpt Wholesale

(P-7798)
ALSCO - GEYER IRRIGATION INC
700 5th St, Arbuckle (95912-9550)
P.O. Box 111 (95912-0111)
PHONE..................530 476-2253
Charles Geyer, *President*
Marjoria Martinez, *Admin Sec*
Connie Semon, *Clerk*
EMP: 90
SQ FT: 3,000
SALES (est): 71.7MM **Privately Held**
WEB: www.alscogeyer.com
SIC: 5083 Irrigation equipment

(P-7799)
ATI MACHINERY INC
Also Called: NAPA West
21436 S Lassen Ave, Five Points (93624)
P.O. Box 445 (93624-0445)
PHONE..................559 884-2471
Toll Free:..................888 -
Fax: 559 884-2675
Leo A Marihart, *Ch of Bd*
Mark Moorhead, *President*
EMP: 50
SQ FT: 22,000
SALES (est): 19.2MM **Privately Held**
WEB: www.atimachinery.com
SIC: 5083 7699 7359 Farm equipment parts & supplies; farm machinery repair; equipment rental & leasing

(P-7800)
BOND MANUFACTURING CO INC
1700 W 4th St, Antioch (94509-1008)
PHONE..................925 252-1135
Daryl Merritt, *CEO*
Ronald Merritt, *CEO*
Tom Schloessmann, *CFO*
Tom Schooessmann, *CFO*
Doug Scheer, *Vice Pres*
◆ EMP: 50
SQ FT: 250,000
SALES: 114.5MM **Privately Held**
WEB: www.bondmfg.com
SIC: 5083 3272 Lawn & garden machinery & equipment; garden machinery & equipment; fireplaces, concrete

(P-7801)
EURODRIP USA INC
1850 W Almond Ave, Madera (93637-5214)
PHONE..................559 674-2670
Rowland Wilkinson, *CEO*
Yvonne Marin, *Accountant*
Conchita Lopez, *Human Res Mgr*
Matthew Anthony, *Accounts Mgr*
▲ EMP: 80
SQ FT: 33,180
SALES: 76MM **Privately Held**
WEB: www.eurodripusa.com
SIC: 5083 3084 Irrigation equipment; plastics pipe
HQ: Eurodrip S.A.
 36 Kifissias Ave
 Maroussi 15125
 216 600-2800

(P-7802)
GREEN ACRES NURSERY & SUP LLC
604 Sutter St, Folsom (95630-2575)
PHONE..................916 782-2273
Mark Gill,
▲ EMP: 90
SALES (est): 47.6MM **Privately Held**
SIC: 5083 5261 Irrigation equipment; nursery stock, seeds & bulbs

(P-7803)
KRC EQUIPMENT LLC
700 N Twin Oaks Valley Rd, San Marcos (92069-1714)
P.O. Box 729 (92079-0729)
PHONE..................760 744-1036
Gerald Sebby, *President*
Cathy Sebby,
EMP: 58

SALES (est): 5.2MM **Privately Held**
SIC: 5083 Landscaping equipment

(P-7804)
KUBOTA TRACTOR CORPORATION (DH)
3401 Del Amo Blvd, Torrance (90503-1636)
PHONE..................310 370-3370
Fax: 310 370-2370
Yuichi Kitao, *President*
Masto Yoshikawa, *President*
Kosuke Ota, *Treasurer*
Shingo Banada, *Vice Pres*
Susan Holmes, *Principal*
◆ EMP: 250
SQ FT: 85,000
SALES (est): 422.6MM
SALES (corp-wide): 10.1B **Privately Held**
WEB: www.kubota.com
SIC: 5083 3531 3799 Tractors, agricultural; farm equipment parts & supplies; construction machinery; recreational vehicles
HQ: Kubota U.S.A. Inc.
 3401 Del Amo Blvd
 Torrance CA 90503
 310 370-3370

(P-7805)
NETAFIM IRRIGATION INC (HQ)
5470 E Home Ave, Fresno (93727-2107)
PHONE..................559 453-6800
Fax: 559 442-6803
Igal Aisenberg, *President*
Yossi Ingber, *President*
Lauri Hanover, *CFO*
AVI Schweitzer, *Vice Pres*
Eduardo Currea, *Executive*
▲ EMP: 110 EST: 1965
SQ FT: 100,000
SALES (est): 77MM
SALES (corp-wide): 715.9MM **Privately Held**
WEB: www.netafimusa.com
SIC: 5083 3523 Irrigation equipment; irrigation equipment, self-propelled
PA: Netafim Ltd
 10 Hashalom Rd.
 Tel Aviv-Jaffa
 864 740-00

(P-7806)
QUINN GROUP INC
Also Called: Caterpillar Authorized Dealer
801 Del Norte Blvd, Oxnard (93030-8966)
PHONE..................805 485-2171
Jim Barr, *Manager*
Jonathan Monroe, *Asst Controller*
EMP: 80
SQ FT: 5,000
SALES (corp-wide): 514.9MM **Privately Held**
WEB: www.catpower.com
SIC: 5083 5082 5084 Agricultural machinery & equipment; construction & mining machinery; industrial machinery & equipment
PA: Quinn Group, Inc.
 10006 Rose Hills Rd
 City Of Industry CA 90601
 562 463-4000

(P-7807)
QUINN GROUP INC
2200 Pegasus Dr, Bakersfield (93308-6801)
PHONE..................661 393-5800
Mike Ford, *Branch Mgr*
Robin Camp, *Marketing Staff*
EMP: 110
SALES (corp-wide): 514.9MM **Privately Held**
WEB: www.catpower.com
SIC: 5083 5084 7359 Tractors, agricultural; tractors, industrial; industrial truck rental
PA: Quinn Group, Inc.
 10006 Rose Hills Rd
 City Of Industry CA 90601
 562 463-4000

(P-7808)
RM ESOP INC
1051 S Rose Ave, Oxnard (93030-5180)
PHONE..................805 483-5331
Richard Meyers, *Manager*

5083 - Farm & Garden Mach & Eqpt Wholesale

EMP: 50
SALES (corp-wide): 1.6B **Privately Held**
WEB: www.rmp.com
SIC: 5083 Lawn & garden machinery & equipment
HQ: Rm Esop Inc.
340 El Camino Real S
Salinas CA 93901
831 789-8300

(P-7809)
S A CAMP COMPANIES (PA)
17876 Zerker Rd, Bakersfield (93308-9221)
PHONE 661 399-4451
James S Camp, *President*
D M Hart, *Vice Pres*
EMP: 50
SQ FT: 10,000
SALES: 19.8MM **Privately Held**
WEB: www.sacamp.net
SIC: 5083 0191 6552 Agricultural machinery; general farms, primarily crop; subdividers & developers

(P-7810)
SEABOARD PRODUCE DISTRS INC
Also Called: Del Norte Distribution
710 Del Norte Blvd, Oxnard (93030-8963)
PHONE 805 981-8001
J Woodford Hansen, *President*
Heather Wise, *Controller*
Cody Oxford, *Opers Mgr*
Jim Sullivan, *Manager*
Julio Segoviano, *Supervisor*
EMP: 64
SALES (corp-wide): 25.5MM **Privately Held**
SIC: 5083 Irrigation equipment
PA: Seaboard Produce Distributors, Inc.
601 Mountain View Ave
Oxnard CA 93030
805 486-4773

(P-7811)
THOMASON TRACTOR CO CALIFORNIA
Also Called: John Deere Authorized Dealer
985 12th St, Firebaugh (93622)
P.O. Box 97 (93622-0097)
PHONE 559 659-2039
Fax: 559 659-3267
Audrey Thomason, *President*
Rodney Thomason, *Vice Pres*
Cesar Marin, *Office Mgr*
Bobbi Thomason, *Manager*
Don York Jr, *Manager*
EMP: 50 **EST:** 1967
SQ FT: 33,000
SALES (est): 34.7MM **Privately Held**
WEB: www.thomasontractor.com
SIC: 5083 Farm & garden machinery; agricultural machinery & equipment; farm equipment parts & supplies; tractors, agricultural

(P-7812)
TURF STAR INC
Also Called: Turfstar
79253 Country Club Dr, Bermuda Dunes (92203-1229)
PHONE 760 772-3575
Fax: 760 345-4297
Leonard Gregory, *President*
EMP: 100
SALES (corp-wide): 48.6MM **Privately Held**
WEB: www.turfstar.com
SIC: 5083 Garden machinery & equipment; lawn machinery & equipment; irrigation equipment
PA: Turf Star, Inc.
2438 Radley Ct
Hayward CA 94545
800 585-8001

(P-7813)
TURLOCK DAIRY & RFRGN INC
Also Called: T D R
1819 S Walnut Rd, Turlock (95380-9219)
P.O. Box 1530 (95381-1530)
PHONE 209 667-6455
Fax: 209 667-6484
Mathew Anthony Bruno, *CEO*
Tony Bruno, *President*
John Fish, *Human Res Mgr*
Larry Hardy, *Human Resources*
EMP: 100
SQ FT: 10,000
SALES (est): 95.9MM **Privately Held**
WEB: www.turlockdairy.com
SIC: 5083 7699 1542 Dairy machinery & equipment; industrial equipment services; nonresidential construction

(P-7814)
VUCOVICH INC (PA)
Also Called: John Deere Authorized Dealer
4288 S Bagley Ave, Fresno (93725-9014)
P.O. Box 2513 (93745-2513)
PHONE 559 486-8020
Fax: 559 266-9753
Marsha Vucovich, *President*
Bill Kidd, *General Mgr*
Doris Adams, *Controller*
Brad Wood, *Sales Mgr*
Gary Carstens, *Marketing Staff*
EMP: 60
SQ FT: 42,800
SALES: 50MM **Privately Held**
WEB: www.fresnoequipment.com
SIC: 5083 Agricultural machinery & equipment

(P-7815)
YAMAHA MOTOR CORPORATION USA
6555 Katella Ave, Cypress (90630-5101)
PHONE 714 236-9754
Kelly Jim, *Manager*
EMP: 500
SALES (corp-wide): 13.1B **Privately Held**
WEB: www.yamaha-motor.com
SIC: 5083 Lawn machinery & equipment
HQ: Yamaha Motor Corporation Usa
6555 Katella Ave
Cypress CA 90630
714 761-7300

5084 Industrial Mach & Eqpt Wholesale

(P-7816)
A MEISSNERS HHLD & INDUS SVC
2417 Cormorant Way, Sacramento (95815-2714)
PHONE 916 920-2121
Jim Meissners, *Owner*
Levi Couchot, *Info Tech Mgr*
EMP: 57
SALES (est): 2.8MM **Privately Held**
SIC: 5084 Sewing machines, industrial

(P-7817)
AIRGAS USA LLC
441 Hobson St, San Jose (95110-2016)
PHONE 408 998-6380
Al Shull, *Manager*
Max Hooper, *President*
Peter McCausland, *CEO*
Iqbal Kaur, *Accountant*
EMP: 65
SQ FT: 7,200
SALES (corp-wide): 189.3MM **Privately Held**
SIC: 5084 5169 Welding machinery & equipment; industrial gases
HQ: Airgas Usa Llc
259 N Radnor Chester Rd # 100
Radnor PA 19087
610 687-5253

(P-7818)
ALLTEK COMPANY U S A INC
18281 Gothard St Ste 102, Huntington Beach (92648-1205)
PHONE 714 375-9785
Fax: 714 375-9961
Weishui W Zhang, *President*
Joline Yin, *Vice Pres*
Linda Zhu, *Vice Pres*
EMP: 50
SQ FT: 2,000
SALES (est): 18MM **Privately Held**
WEB: www.alltekusa.com
SIC: 5084 5065 Industrial machinery & equipment; semiconductor devices

(P-7819)
AMADA AMERICA INC (HQ)
7025 Firestone Blvd, Buena Park (90621-1869)
PHONE 714 739-2111
Fax: 714 670-8020
Mike Guarin, *CEO*
KOA Nakata, *CFO*
Pablo Cervantes, *Senior VP*
Stephen Keating, *Executive*
Charles Wittig, *Exec Dir*
▲ **EMP:** 75
SQ FT: 103,000
SALES: 243MM
SALES (corp-wide): 2.6B **Privately Held**
SIC: 5084 6159 Metalworking machinery; metalworking tools (such as drills, taps, dies, files); machinery & equipment finance leasing
PA: Amada Holdings Co., Ltd.
200, Ishida
Isehara KNG 259-1
463 961-111

(P-7820)
ANHEUSER-BUSCH LLC
3101 Busch Dr, Fairfield (94534-9726)
PHONE 707 429-7595
Fax: 707 429-7519
Kevin Finger, *Manager*
Corry Smith, *Area Mgr*
James Wilson, *Area Mgr*
Jack Russell, *Division Mgr*
Emily Hubert, *General Mgr*
EMP: 450
SALES (corp-wide): 1B **Privately Held**
WEB: www.hispanicbud.com
SIC: 5084 Brewery products manufacturing machinery, commercial
HQ: Anheuser-Busch, Llc
1 Busch Pl
Saint Louis MO 63118
314 632-6777

(P-7821)
B C RENTALS INC
Also Called: Bc Traffic Specialists
638 W Southern Ave, Orange (92865-3219)
PHONE 714 974-1190
Robert Carson, *President*
Jensen Carson, *General Mgr*
Sally Carson, *Admin Sec*
Christine Enriquez, *Project Mgr*
Maria Gomez, *Accountant*
▲ **EMP:** 75
SQ FT: 3,000
SALES: 15MM **Privately Held**
SIC: 5084 5999 7359 Safety equipment; safety supplies & equipment; equipment rental & leasing

(P-7822)
BAY ADVANCED TECHNOLOGIES LLC
Also Called: Bay Advanced Tech 0045
8100 Central Ave, Newark (94560-3449)
PHONE 510 857-0900
Mike Stimson, *Branch Mgr*
EMP: 88
SALES (corp-wide): 2.5B **Publicly Held**
SIC: 5084 Pneumatic tools & equipment
HQ: Bay Advanced Technologies, Llc
8100 Central Ave
Newark CA 94560
510 857-0900

(P-7823)
BEJAC CORPORATION (PA)
569 S Van Buren St, Placentia (92870-6613)
PHONE 714 528-6224
Fax: 714 528-2309
Ron Barlet, *President*
Kim Grimes, *CFO*
Kim Smith-Grime, *CFO*
Peggy Barlet, *Corp Secy*
Roger Rivet, *Opers Staff*
▼ **EMP:** 66
SQ FT: 2,000
SALES (est): 52.2MM **Privately Held**
WEB: www.bejac.com
SIC: 5084 7353 Industrial machinery & equipment; heavy construction equipment rental

(P-7824)
BEST LABEL COMPANY INC (PA)
Also Called: Imperial Marking Systems
13260 Moore St, Cerritos (90703-2252)
PHONE 562 926-1452
Fax: 562 404-2076
Ernest Wong, *President*
Timothy Koontz, *CFO*
Donald Ingle, *Admin Sec*
Julie Liu, *Accounting Mgr*
Bonnie Sykes, *Human Res Mgr*
EMP: 120
SQ FT: 60,000
SALES (est): 58.1MM **Privately Held**
WEB: www.bestlabel.com
SIC: 5084 2759 Industrial machinery & equipment; commercial printing

(P-7825)
BIG JOE CALIFORNIA NORTH INC (PA)
Also Called: Big Joe Handling Systems
25932 Eden Landing Rd, Hayward (94545-3816)
PHONE 510 785-6900
Boyd J Kiefus, *CEO*
Rod D Kiefus, *CFO*
Nash Bernardo, *Marketing Mgr*
EMP: 110
SQ FT: 52,000
SALES (est): 40MM **Privately Held**
SIC: 5084 5999 7359 8331 Lift trucks & parts; business machines & equipment; equipment rental & leasing; job training services

(P-7826)
BLAKE H BROWN INC (DH)
Also Called: John Tillman Company
1300 W Artesia Blvd, Compton (90220-5307)
P.O. Box 6257 (90224-6257)
PHONE 310 764-0110
Fax: 310 764-0104
Blake H Brown, *CEO*
▲ **EMP:** 100
SQ FT: 25,000
SALES (est): 65.4MM
SALES (corp-wide): 9.7B **Privately Held**
WEB: www.jtillman.com
SIC: 5084 3842 3548 Safety equipment; personal safety equipment; welding apparatus
HQ: Bunzl Distribution Midcentral, Inc.
11434 Moog Dr
Saint Louis MO 63146
314 569-2800

(P-7827)
BORETECH RESRCE RECOVRY ENGINE
Also Called: Boretech Rsource Recovery Engrg
1820 Industrial Dr, Stockton (95206-4975)
PHONE 209 373-2588
Jo Hua Lee, *President*
Alice KAO, *Vice Pres*
▲ **EMP:** 50
SQ FT: 68,000
SALES: 24MM **Privately Held**
SIC: 5084 2611 Recycling machinery & equipment; pulp manufactured from waste or recycled paper

(P-7828)
BUCKLES-SMITH ELECTRIC COMPANY (PA)
801 Savaker Ave, San Jose (95126-3712)
PHONE 408 280-7777
Fax: 408 280-0720
Art Cook, *CEO*
Matt Peterson, *Treasurer*
Pat Berry, *Vice Pres*
Roger Stanger, *Vice Pres*
Ron Zimmerman, *Admin Sec*
EMP: 55
SALES (est): 90.9MM **Privately Held**
WEB: www.geindustrial.com
SIC: 5084 5063 Industrial machinery & equipment; electrical supplies

PRODUCTS & SERVICES SECTION

5084 - Industrial Mach & Eqpt Wholesale County (P-7848)

(P-7829)
CAL-LIFT INC
13027 Crossroads Pkwy S, La Puente (91746-3406)
PHONE.................................562 566-1400
Fax: 323 869-4048
Mark T Maechling, *CEO*
Michelle L Suire, *Vice Pres*
Robert Bey, *VP Sales*
EMP: 55
SQ FT: 40,000
SALES (est): 35.1MM **Privately Held**
SIC: 5084 7699 7359 Materials handling machinery; industrial equipment services; industrial machinery & equipment repair; equipment rental & leasing

(P-7830)
CANON SOLUTIONS AMERICA INC
Also Called: Ona
15975 Alton Pkwy, Irvine (92618-3731)
PHONE.................................800 333-6395
Fax: 714 824-4090
Richard Adinolsi, *Branch Mgr*
Dorianne Montalvo, *Director*
EMP: 60
SALES (corp-wide): 30.8B **Privately Held**
WEB: www.dgs.oceusa.com
SIC: 5084 5044 Printing trades machinery, equipment & supplies; copying equipment
HQ: Canon Solutions America, Inc.
   1 Canon Park
   Melville NY 11747
   631 330-5000

(P-7831)
CAPITAL ASSET EXCH & TRDG LLC
Also Called: Cae Online
870 E Charleston Rd # 210, Palo Alto (94303-4673)
PHONE.................................650 326-3313
Fax: 650 326-0130
Ryan Jacob, *Mng Member*
Jeff Robbins, *President*
Bryan Burke, *Associate Dir*
Boyd Grubbs, *Associate Dir*
Elizabeth Lauffenburger, *Office Admin*
▲ **EMP:** 75
SQ FT: 10,000
SALES: 75MM **Privately Held**
WEB: www.caeonline.com
SIC: 5084 Industrial machinery & equipment

(P-7832)
CDS MOVING EQUIPMENT INC (PA)
375 W Manville St, Rancho Dominguez (90220-5617)
PHONE.................................310 631-1100
Allen J Sidor, *President*
Hector Buendia, *President*
Margo Castillo, *Office Mgr*
Vickie Costello, *Accounting Mgr*
Lou Morales, *Purch Dir*
▲ **EMP:** 80
SQ FT: 100,000
SALES (est): 67.5MM **Privately Held**
WEB: www.cds-usa.com
SIC: 5084 Industrial machinery & equipment

(P-7833)
CHARLES E THOMAS COMPANY INC (PA)
Also Called: C E T
13701 Alma Ave, Gardena (90249-2523)
PHONE.................................310 323-6730
Fax: 310 323-4433
Jerry Thomas, *President*
Brian Hurley, *Vice Pres*
Ann Thomas, *Vice Pres*
Greg Thomas, *Vice Pres*
Mike Hurley, *Manager*
▼ **EMP:** 60
SQ FT: 15,000
SALES (est): 50.7MM **Privately Held**
WEB: www.cethomas.net
SIC: 5084 1542 7699 Industrial machinery & equipment; service station construction; service station equipment repair

(P-7834)
CLARKLIFT LOS ANGELES INC
8314 Slauson Ave, Pico Rivera (90660-4323)
PHONE.................................562 949-1006
Fax: 562 949-5984
Homan C Moore, *CEO*
Tim Cleary, *President*
Homan C Moore, *CEO*
Tom Labrador, *Vice Pres*
EMP: 160
SALES (est): 13.6MM **Privately Held**
SIC: 5084 Conveyor systems; cranes, industrial; lift trucks & parts

(P-7835)
CLARKLIFT-WEST INC
Also Called: Team Power Forklift
4750 Illinois Ave, Fair Oaks (95628-6313)
PHONE.................................916 381-5674
Joe Hensler, *President*
Pete Thomas, *Vice Pres*
Dean Walker, *Vice Pres*
Vickie Vaulk, *Executive*
▲ **EMP:** 121
SQ FT: 50,000
SALES (est): 20.1MM **Privately Held**
WEB: www.teampowerforklift.com
SIC: 5084 7699 7359 Lift trucks & parts; materials handling machinery; industrial truck repair; industrial machinery & equipment repair; industrial truck rental

(P-7836)
CUMMINS PACIFIC LLC
14775 Wicks Blvd, San Leandro (94577-6717)
PHONE.................................510 351-6101
Mark Yragui, *President*
EMP: 300
SALES (corp-wide): 19.1B **Publicly Held**
SIC: 5084 7629 5063 3519 Engines & parts, diesel; electrical repair shops; electrical apparatus & equipment; internal combustion engines
HQ: Cummins Pacific, Llc
   1939 Deere Ave
   Irvine CA 92606
   949 253-6000

(P-7837)
CUSTOM BILT HOLDINGS LLC
15133 Sierra Bonita Ln, Chino (91710-8904)
PHONE.................................909 664-1587
James Dworkin, *CFO*
Jodie White, *Office Mgr*
Cassondra Goolie, *Admin Asst*
Cindy Williams, *Human Resources*
Lance Dowden, *Director*
EMP: 90
SALES (corp-wide): 50.9MM **Privately Held**
SIC: 5084 1761 Metalworking machinery; roofing contractor
PA: Custom Bilt Holdings, Llc
   3001 Skyway Cir N Ste 160
   Irving TX 75038
   214 699-4882

(P-7838)
E & M ELECTRIC AND MCHY INC (PA)
Also Called: E&M
126 Mill St, Healdsburg (95448-4438)
PHONE.................................707 433-5578
Fax: 707 431-2558
Steven Edgar Deas, *CEO*
Stephen Scholey, *General Mgr*
Scott Townsend, *High Tech Mgr*
Judith L Deas, *Business Mgr*
Rebecca Pulley, *Accountant*
◆ **EMP:** 50
SQ FT: 25,000
SALES (est): 62.1MM **Privately Held**
WEB: www.enm.com
SIC: 5084 5999 5063 7694 Instruments & control equipment; motors, electric; motors, electric; electric motor repair

(P-7839)
EAST BAY CLARKLIFT INC
4646 E Jensen Ave, Fresno (93725-1603)
P.O. Box 2808 (93745-2808)
PHONE.................................559 268-6621
Kerry Perez, *General Mgr*
EMP: 73
SALES (corp-wide): 27.5MM **Privately Held**
SIC: 5084 7359 7699 Materials handling machinery; equipment rental & leasing; industrial equipment services
PA: East Bay Clarklift, Inc.
   4701 Oakport St
   Oakland CA 94601
   510 534-6566

(P-7840)
EDWARDS FRANK CO (HQ)
1565 Adrian Rd, Burlingame (94010-2107)
PHONE.................................801 736-8000
Fax: 801 736-8051
Bruce W Hart, *President*
Robert F Edwards Jr, *Treasurer*
Rick Harman, *Manager*
EMP: 55 EST: 1916
SQ FT: 68,000
SALES (est): 55.1MM
SALES (corp-wide): 91.5MM **Privately Held**
SIC: 5084 5013 5072 5063 Engines, gasoline; automotive supplies & parts; hardware; electrical apparatus & equipment
PA: Frank Edwards Company, Inc.
   1565 Adrian Rd
   Burlingame CA 94010
   650 692-2347

(P-7841)
ELLISON MACHINERY CO (DH)
Also Called: Ellison Technologies
9912 Pioneer Blvd, Santa Fe Springs (90670-3257)
PHONE.................................562 949-8311
Fax: 562 942-8084
W J Ellison, *President*
Donald Bendix, *Corp Secy*
Leonard C Atkins, *Vice Pres*
Klaus Rindt, *Vice Pres*
Michael Davis, *Controller*
EMP: 75
SQ FT: 45,000
SALES (est): 117MM
SALES (corp-wide): 40.6B **Privately Held**
WEB: www.ellisontechnologies.com
SIC: 5084 Metalworking machinery
HQ: Ellison Technologies, Inc.
   9912 Pioneer Blvd
   Santa Fe Springs CA 90670
   562 949-8311

(P-7842)
ESYS ENERGY CONTROL COMPANY
4520 Stine Rd Ste 7, Bakersfield (93313-2372)
PHONE.................................661 833-1902
Fax: 661 833-4008
Fabio Russoniello, *President*
Tim Guenther, *Webmaster*
David Bopp, *Engineer*
Casey Lessley, *Engineer*
EMP: 60
SQ FT: 12,000
SALES (est): 47MM **Privately Held**
WEB: www.esys-tecc.com
SIC: 5084 1731 Controlling instruments & accessories; electronic controls installation

(P-7843)
FARM PUMP & IRRIGATION CO INC (PA)
Also Called: F P I
535 N Shafter Ave, Shafter (93263-1900)
P.O. Box 1477 (93263-1477)
PHONE.................................661 589-6901
Fax: 661 746-1510
John Gargan, *CEO*
Kathy Gargan, *Corp Secy*
Amy Gargan, *Manager*
EMP: 60
SQ FT: 4,000
SALES (est): 20.8MM **Privately Held**
WEB: www.fpi-co.com
SIC: 5084 5083 Pumps & pumping equipment; irrigation equipment

(P-7844)
FLOWSERVE CORPORATION
2300 E Vernon Ave Stop 76, Vernon (90058-1609)
PHONE.................................323 584-1890
Rick Soldo, *Branch Mgr*
Bernard Rethore, *Chairman*
Richard Testwuide, *Div Sub Head*
Howard Wynn, *Div Sub Head*
Angela Ooley, *Admin Asst*
EMP: 342
SALES (corp-wide): 4.5B **Publicly Held**
SIC: 5084 Industrial machinery & equipment
PA: Flowserve Corporation
   5215 N Oconnor Blvd Connor
   Irving TX 75039
   972 443-6500

(P-7845)
FUELING AND SERVICE TECH INC
Also Called: Fastech
7050 Village Dr Ste D, Buena Park (90621-2281)
PHONE.................................714 523-0194
M Dan McGill, *CEO*
Phillip Heinz, *CFO*
Christine Awbrey, *General Mgr*
David Reed, *Controller*
Jonathan Carmona, *Purchasing*
EMP: 75
SQ FT: 15,000
SALES (est): 76.7MM **Privately Held**
SIC: 5084 Industrial machinery & equipment; petroleum industry machinery; drilling bits; drilling equipment, excluding bits

(P-7846)
GLOBAL GROUND AUTOMATION INC
1051 E Hillsdale Blvd, Foster City (94404-1640)
PHONE.................................201 293-4900
EMP: 51
SALES (est): 1.5MM
SALES (corp-wide): 84.8MM **Privately Held**
SIC: 5084 Industrial machinery & equipment
PA: Deem, Inc.
   642 Harrison St Fl 2
   San Francisco CA 94107
   415 590-8300

(P-7847)
HARBOR DIESEL AND EQP INC
Also Called: John Deere Authorized Dealer
537 W Anaheim St, Long Beach (90813-2895)
P.O. Box 21399 (90801-4399)
PHONE.................................562 591-5665
Fax: 562 591-2941
James V Zupanovich, *Ch of Bd*
Mike Zupanovich, *President*
Thomas E Weersing, *Vice Pres*
Brett Roa, *Opers Mgr*
▲ **EMP:** 51
SALES: 26.7MM **Privately Held**
WEB: www.harbordiesel.com
SIC: 5084 5531 7538 Engines & parts, diesel; truck equipment & parts; diesel engine repair: automotive

(P-7848)
HITACHI AMERICA LTD
1000 Marina Blvd Ste 500, Brisbane (94005-1853)
PHONE.................................650 827-6240
Fax: 650 244-7416
Takashi Kawamura, *Chairman*
Alexander Okun, *Admin Asst*
Marjorie Scarborough, *Network Mgr*
James Gonzales, *Network Tech*
Eduardo Garza, *Senior Engr*
EMP: 56
SALES (corp-wide): 85.7B **Privately Held**
SIC: 5084 Industrial machinery & equipment
HQ: Hitachi America Ltd
   50 Prospect Ave
   Tarrytown NY 10591
   914 332-5800

5084 - Industrial Mach & Eqpt Wholesale County (P-7849)

(P-7849)
HOLT OF CALIFORNIA
526 10th St, Modesto (95354-3504)
PHONE....................................209 623-1149
EMP: 83
SALES (corp-wide): 465.7MM Privately Held
SIC: 5084 Materials handling machinery
HQ: Holt Of California
7310 Pacific Ave
Pleasant Grove CA 95668
916 991-8200

(P-7850)
INDUSTRIAL PARTS DEPOT LLC (HQ)
Also Called: Ipd
23231 Normandie Ave, Torrance (90501-5096)
PHONE....................................310 530-1900
Fax: 310 530-6162
Russell Kneipp, President
Richard Grishaber, COO
Marshall Berliner, CFO
Clarke Ashton, CTO
Clark Ashton, Info Tech Dir
▲ EMP: 70
SQ FT: 40,000
SALES (est): 45.2MM
SALES (corp-wide): 74.4MM Privately Held
WEB: www.ipdparts.com
SIC: 5084 3519 Engines & parts, diesel; parts & accessories, internal combustion engines
PA: Storm Industries, Inc.
23223 Normandie Ave
Torrance CA 90501
310 534-5232

(P-7851)
INOXPA USA INC
3721 Santa Rosa Ave B4, Santa Rosa (95407-8240)
PHONE....................................707 585-3900
Candi Granes Campasol, President
Keith Van Note, General Mgr
Mark Sottana, Sales Mgr
Keith Vannote, Sales Mgr
▲ EMP: 300
SQ FT: 1,600
SALES (est): 29.8MM Privately Held
SIC: 5084 Pumps & pumping equipment

(P-7852)
INTERNATIONAL THERMOPRODUCTS
11015 Mission Park Ct, Santee (92071-5601)
PHONE....................................619 562-7001
Fax: 619 562-0074
Randall Newcomb, Owner
Eric Ulrich, Vice Pres
Grace McKeon, Office Mgr
Long Doan, Engineer
Robert Golembieski, Sales Executive
EMP: 50
SALES (est): 3.7MM Privately Held
SIC: 5084 3567 Heat exchange equipment, industrial; electrical furnaces, ovens & heating devices, exc. induction

(P-7853)
JA AUTOMATION & CONTROL LLC
6965 Cmino Mqladora Ste H, San Diego (92154)
PHONE....................................619 661-2591
Jose A Fernandez, Mng Member
Cristabell Marin, Agent
EMP: 50
SALES (est): 6.4MM Privately Held
SIC: 5084 Industrial machinery & equipment

(P-7854)
KENTMASTER MFG CO INC (PA)
1801 S Mountain Ave, Monrovia (91016-4270)
PHONE....................................626 359-8888
Fax: 626 303-5151
Ralph Karubian, CEO
Laurence Karubian, Info Tech Dir
▲ EMP: 50 EST: 1948
SQ FT: 50,000
SALES (est): 30MM Privately Held
WEB: www.kentmaster.com
SIC: 5084 Pneumatic tools & equipment

(P-7855)
LINDSAY TRANSPORTATION
Also Called: Lindsay Trnsp Solutions
180 River Rd, Rio Vista (94571-1208)
PHONE....................................707 374-6800
Bill Cooley, President
Kristel Flores,
EMP: 250
SALES (est): 33.8MM
SALES (corp-wide): 516.4MM Publicly Held
SIC: 5084 Safety equipment
HQ: Lindsay Transportation Solutions, Inc.
180 River Rd
Rio Vista CA 94571
707 374-6800

(P-7856)
LMC WEST INC
5300 Claus Rd, Riverbank (95367)
P.O. Box 325 (95367-0325)
PHONE....................................209 869-0144
Fax: 209 869-0258
EMP: 50
SQ FT: 50,000
SALES (est): 10.3MM
SALES (corp-wide): 2.3B Publicly Held
SIC: 5084
PA: Donaldson Company, Inc.
1400 W 94th St
Minneapolis MN 55431
952 887-3131

(P-7857)
LUFKIN INDUSTRIES LLC
31127 Coberly Rd, Shafter (93263-9702)
PHONE....................................661 746-0030
Fax: 661 327-0690
Mel Trubey, Sales/Mktg Mgr
EMP: 85
SALES (corp-wide): 117.3B Publicly Held
WEB: www.lufkin.com
SIC: 5084 Industrial machinery & equipment
HQ: Lufkin Industries, Llc
601 S Raguet St
Lufkin TX 75904
936 634-2211

(P-7858)
MACHINING TIME SAVERS INC
Also Called: Haas Factory Outlet
1338 S State College Pkwy, Anaheim (92806-5241)
PHONE....................................714 635-7373
Fax: 714 635-3268
Donald Martin, President
EMP: 53
SQ FT: 10,000
SALES (est): 25.1MM Privately Held
WEB: www.mtscnc.com
SIC: 5084 7699 Machine tools & accessories; metalworking machinery; industrial machinery & equipment repair

(P-7859)
MASON-WEST INC
3910 Chapman St Ste D, San Diego (92110-5644)
PHONE....................................619 226-8253
Fax: 619 226-8054
Joe Hastings, Manager
John Mastropolo, Sales Dir
EMP: 50
SALES (corp-wide): 19.6MM Privately Held
SIC: 5084 Controlling instruments & accessories
PA: Mason-West, Inc.
1601 E Miraloma Ave
Placentia CA 92870
714 630-0701

(P-7860)
MATERIAL HANDLING SUPPLY INC (HQ)
12900 Firestone Blvd, Santa Fe Springs (90670-5405)
PHONE....................................562 921-7715
Fax: 562 921-7615
Alexander Stephen Lynn, CEO
Donn C Lynn Jr, Ch of Bd
John Hanson, Corp Secy
Steve Birdsall, Info Tech Dir
Douglas Thorne, Director
EMP: 80 EST: 1962
SQ FT: 85,000
SALES (est): 33.8MM Privately Held
SIC: 5084 7629 5046 Food industry machinery; engines & transportation equipment; materials handling machinery; electrical repair shops; commercial equipment
PA: Envicor
12900 Firestone Blvd
Santa Fe Springs CA 90670
562 921-7715

(P-7861)
MAXON LIFT CORPORATION
11921 Slauson Ave, Santa Fe Springs (90670-2221)
PHONE....................................562 464-0099
Casey Lugash, President
Lawerence Lugash, Exec VP
Brenda Leung, Vice Pres
Bill Moore, Vice Pres
John Teng, Vice Pres
▲ EMP: 110
SQ FT: 30,000
SALES (est): 221.8MM Privately Held
WEB: www.maxonlift.com
SIC: 5084 3537 3534 Lift trucks & parts; industrial trucks & tractors; elevators & moving stairways

(P-7862)
MCCAIN INC (PA)
2365 Oak Ridge Way, Vista (92081-8348)
PHONE....................................760 727-8100
Fax: 760 727-8264
Jeffrey L McCain, CEO
Christine Jersey, COO
Steven Anderson, Administration
Stacy Taylor, Administration
Scott Tolstad, Administration
▲ EMP: 250
SQ FT: 6,700
SALES (est): 89MM Privately Held
WEB: www.mccaintraffic.com
SIC: 5084 3444 3669 Industrial machinery & equipment; sheet metalwork; traffic signals, electric

(P-7863)
MCKINLEY EQUIPMENT CORPORATION (PA)
17611 Armstrong Ave, Irvine (92614-5760)
PHONE....................................800 770-6094
Fax: 949 250-7301
W Michael Mc Kinley, President
Kevin Rusin, CFO
William White Mc Kinley, Vice Pres
William W Mc Kinley, Vice Pres
Mark McKinley, General Mgr
▲ EMP: 50
SQ FT: 12,000
SALES (est): 41.1MM Privately Held
WEB: www.mckinleyequipment.com
SIC: 5084 Materials handling machinery

(P-7864)
MIGHTY ENTERPRISES INC
Also Called: Mighty USA
19706 Normandie Ave, Torrance (90502-1111)
PHONE....................................310 516-7478
Peter Th Tsai, President
Daniel Huang, Vice Pres
Gloria Zuniga, Admin Sec
Emerito Tito, Administration
Ron Dumas, Technology
▲ EMP: 55
SQ FT: 18,000
SALES (est): 35.7MM Privately Held
SIC: 5084 Industrial machinery & equipment

(P-7865)
NAGRA USA INC
485 Clyde Ave, Mountain View (94043-2245)
PHONE....................................310 335-5225
Yves Pitton, Branch Mgr
Henry Fang, Engineer
EMP: 50
SALES (corp-wide): 946.1MM Privately Held
SIC: 5084 Safety equipment
HQ: Nagra Usa, Inc.
841 Apollo St Ste 300
El Segundo CA 90245
310 335-5225

(P-7866)
NAGRA USA INC (HQ)
841 Apollo St Ste 300, El Segundo (90245-4769)
PHONE....................................310 335-5225
Virginio Trevisan, President
Mark Beariault, Admin Sec
Steven Dimitrijevich, Finance Mgr
Subash Krishnankutty, Director
EMP: 85
SQ FT: 1,100
SALES (est): 60.6MM
SALES (corp-wide): 946.1MM Privately Held
WEB: www.nagra.com
SIC: 5084 Safety equipment
PA: Kudelski S.A.
Route De Geneve 22-24
Cheseaux-Sur-Lausanne VD 1033
217 320-311

(P-7867)
NAN FANG DIST GROUP INC
2100 Williams St, San Leandro (94577-3225)
PHONE....................................510 297-5382
Ze Pan, CEO
Zhen Poon, Vice Pres
▲ EMP: 100
SALES (est): 35.8MM Privately Held
SIC: 5084 Engines & parts, diesel

(P-7868)
NAUMANN/HOBBS MATERIAL
Also Called: Hawthorne Lift Systems
8575 Cherry Ave, Fontana (92335-3029)
PHONE....................................909 427-0125
Ed Gen, Manager
EMP: 105
SALES (corp-wide): 90MM Privately Held
SIC: 5084 Materials handling machinery
PA: Naumann/Hobbs Material Handling Corporation Ii, Inc.
4335 E Wood St
Phoenix AZ 85040
602 437-1331

(P-7869)
NAUMANN/HOBBS MATERIAL
Also Called: Hawthorne Lift Systems
1600 E Mission Rd, San Marcos (92069-4564)
PHONE....................................858 207-2800
Fax: 858 207-2837
Jim Ventors, Branch Mgr
Jim Venters, Branch Mgr
David Davis, Opers Mgr
Sal Randazzo, Foreman/Supr
Larry Szilagyi, Sales Mgr
EMP: 105
SALES (corp-wide): 90MM Privately Held
SIC: 5084 Materials handling machinery
PA: Naumann/Hobbs Material Handling Corporation Ii, Inc.
4335 E Wood St
Phoenix AZ 85040
602 437-1331

(P-7870)
NIKON PRECISION INC (DH)
1399 Shoreway Rd, Belmont (94002-4107)
PHONE....................................650 508-4674
Fax: 650 508-4600
Toyohiro Takamine, CEO
Takao Naito, President
Tom Novak, Senior VP
David Mahan, Comp Lab Dir
Clarence Ademu-John, Project Mgr
▲ EMP: 250
SQ FT: 30,000
SALES (est): 176.3MM
SALES (corp-wide): 7B Privately Held
WEB: www.nikonprecision.com
SIC: 5084 5065 Industrial machinery & equipment; electronic parts & equipment

PRODUCTS & SERVICES SECTION
5084 - Industrial Mach & Eqpt Wholesale County (P-7890)

(P-7871)
ONEIL DATA SYSTEMS LLC
12655 Beatrice St, Los Angeles (90066-7300)
P.O. Box 9148, Marina Del Rey (90295-1548)
PHONE..................310 448-6400
William J O'Neil,
James Lucanish, *General Mgr*
Patrick Akkarach, *Administration*
Gene Freeman, *Prgrmr*
Joseph Munoz, *Prgrmr*
▲ **EMP:** 150
SALES (est): 77.7MM
SALES (corp-wide): 287.7MM **Privately Held**
SIC: 5084 Fans, industrial
HQ: O'neil Data Systems, Inc.
12655 Beatrice St
Los Angeles CA 90066
310 448-6400

(P-7872)
ONLINE ENERGY LLC
Also Called: Online Energy Uv Systems
20885 Redwood Rd Unit 405, Castro Valley (94546-5915)
PHONE..................510 583-0091
Craig Blair, *Mng Member*
EMP: 50
SALES (est): 12MM **Privately Held**
SIC: 5084 8711 Industrial machinery & equipment; consulting engineer

(P-7873)
OTIS ELEVATOR COMPANY
2701 Media Center Dr # 2, Los Angeles (90065-1700)
PHONE..................323 342-4500
Marcus Burten, *Manager*
EMP: 50
SALES (corp-wide): 56.1B **Publicly Held**
WEB: www.otis.com
SIC: 5084 Elevators
HQ: Otis Elevator Company
10 Farm Springs Rd
Farmington CT 06032
860 676-6000

(P-7874)
PAPE MATERIAL HANDLING INC
Also Called: Bobcat West
47132 Kato Rd, Fremont (94538-7333)
PHONE..................510 651-8200
Fax: 510 659-4106
Ken Mader, *Branch Mgr*
Chris Wetle, *President*
Jordan Pape, *CEO*
Reid Findley, *Business Mgr*
EMP: 80
SQ FT: 37,536
SALES (corp-wide): 738.4MM **Privately Held**
SIC: 5084 8743 7359 5082 Industrial machinery & equipment; sales promotion; stores & yards equipment rental; contractors' materials
HQ: Pape' Material Handling, Inc.
355 Goodpasture Island Rd
Eugene OR 97401
541 683-5073

(P-7875)
PARSONS AIRGAS INC
Also Called: G S Parsons Co.
9010 Clairemont Mesa Blvd, San Diego (92123-1208)
PHONE..................858 278-2050
Fax: 858 268-0613
Ronald Savage, *President*
Glenn Skirvin, *Treasurer*
Andrew W Cichocki, *Vice Pres*
Jeffrey P Cornwell, *Vice Pres*
Todd R Craun, *Admin Sec*
EMP: 165
SQ FT: 50,000
SALES: 54.9MM
SALES (corp-wide): 189.3MM **Privately Held**
SIC: 5084 5047 4924 7359 Industrial machinery & equipment; medical equipment & supplies; natural gas distribution; equipment rental & leasing

HQ: Airgas, Inc.
259 N Radnor Chester Rd
Radnor PA 19087
610 687-5253

(P-7876)
PRAXAIR INC
2677 Signal Pkwy, Long Beach (90755-2260)
PHONE..................562 427-0099
Fax: 562 427-3566
Mike Alives, *Manager*
Roy Beattie, *VP Sales*
Dwayne Harder, *Manager*
Mark Pizzato, *Manager*
EMP: 60
SALES (corp-wide): 10.7B **Publicly Held**
SIC: 5084 Welding machinery & equipment
PA: Praxair, Inc.
39 Old Ridgebury Rd
Danbury CT 06810
203 837-2000

(P-7877)
PROGAUGE TECHNOLOGIES INC
2331 Cepheus Ct, Bakersfield (93308-6944)
P.O. Box 1312 (93302-1312)
PHONE..................661 392-9600
Donald C Nelson, *CEO*
Danny B Henderson, *Admin Sec*
EMP: 50
SQ FT: 9,000
SALES (est): 16MM **Privately Held**
SIC: 5084 Industrial machinery & equipment

(P-7878)
QUINN COMPANY
Also Called: Caterpillar Authorized Dealer
3500 Shepherd Dr, City of Industry (90601-4700)
P.O. Box 227044, Los Angeles (90022-7044)
PHONE..................562 463-4000
Fax: 562 699-7971
Blake Quinn, *CEO*
Paul Lucini, *Exec VP*
Bob Allen, *Vice Pres*
David Covell, *Info Tech Mgr*
Jonathan Monroe, *Controller*
▼ **EMP:** 126
SALES: 57.4MM
SALES (corp-wide): 514.9MM **Privately Held**
WEB: www.catpower.com
SIC: 5084 5999 3621 3519 Engines & parts, diesel; engine & motor equipment & supplies; motors & generators; internal combustion engines; heavy construction equipment rental
PA: Quinn Group, Inc.
10006 Rose Hills Rd
City Of Industry CA 90601
562 463-4000

(P-7879)
QUINN LIFT INC
Also Called: Caterpillar Authorized Dealer
1300 Abbott St, Salinas (93901-4507)
P.O. Box 1908 (93902-1908)
PHONE..................831 758-4086
Fax: 831 758-4107
Mike Gularte, *Manager*
EMP: 68
SALES (corp-wide): 514.9MM **Privately Held**
WEB: www.altalift.net
SIC: 5084 Industrial machinery & equipment
HQ: Quinn Lift, Inc.
10273 S Golden State Blvd
Selma CA 93662

(P-7880)
R F MACDONALD CO (PA)
25920 Eden Landing Rd, Hayward (94545-3816)
PHONE..................510 784-0110
Fax: 510 784-1004
Michael D Macdonald, *Co-President*
James T Macdonald, *President*
Mike Ricci, *COO*
Chris Sentner, *Vice Pres*

Robert Sygiel, *Vice Pres*
EMP: 55
SQ FT: 25,000
SALES (est): 114.5MM **Privately Held**
SIC: 5084 7699 5074 Pumps & pumping equipment; industrial machinery & equipment repair; boilers, power (industrial)

(P-7881)
RAYMOND HANDLING SOLUTIONS INC (DH)
9939 Norwalk Blvd, Santa Fe Springs (90670-3321)
P.O. Box 3683 (90670-1683)
PHONE..................562 944-8067
Fax: 562 946-1462
James Wilcox, *CEO*
Dale Adams, *CFO*
Chris Bausley, *Business Dir*
Shelley Allec, *Credit Mgr*
Leroy Wood, *Analyst*
EMP: 104
SQ FT: 5,000
SALES (est): 125.9MM
SALES (corp-wide): 19B **Privately Held**
WEB: www.raymondhandlingsolutions.com
SIC: 5084 7699 7359 Industrial machinery & equipment; industrial machinery & equipment repair; industrial truck rental
HQ: Raymond Sales Corporation
22 S Canal St
Greene NY 13778
607 656-2311

(P-7882)
RAYMOND HANDLING SOLUTIONS INC
1945 Burgundy Pl, Ontario (91761-2317)
PHONE..................909 930-9399
Fax: 909 605-0985
James Wilcox, *President*
EMP: 83
SALES (corp-wide): 18.2B **Privately Held**
SIC: 5084 Industrial machinery & equipment
HQ: Raymond Handling Solutions, Inc.
9939 Norwalk Blvd
Santa Fe Springs CA 90670
562 944-8067

(P-7883)
RJMS CORPORATION (PA)
Also Called: Toyota Material Hdlg Nthrn Cal
31010 San Antonio St, Hayward (94544-7904)
PHONE..................510 675-0500
Fax: 510 675-0400
Richard Andres, *CEO*
Mark Andres, *Vice Pres*
Stephen Andres, *Vice Pres*
Timo Soeganda, *Admin Asst*
Chuck Obryan, *Controller*
▲ **EMP:** 100
SQ FT: 45,000
SALES (est): 120MM **Privately Held**
WEB: www.tmhnc.com
SIC: 5084 5085 7699 Materials handling machinery; industrial supplies; industrial machinery & equipment repair

(P-7884)
RKI INSTRUMENTS INC (PA)
Also Called: R K I
33248 Central Ave, Union City (94587-2010)
PHONE..................510 441-5656
Robert Pellissier, *President*
Bob Pellissier, *President*
Shirley Trujillo, *COO*
Conchita Navidad, *CFO*
Sandra Gallagher, *Vice Pres*
▲ **EMP:** 55
SQ FT: 10,000
SALES (est): 29.2MM **Privately Held**
WEB: www.rkiinstruments.com
SIC: 5084 3823 Industrial machinery & equipment; on-stream gas/liquid analysis instruments, industrial

(P-7885)
SCHINDLER ELEVATOR CORPORATION
2000 Avenue Of The Stars, Los Angeles (90067-4700)
PHONE..................310 785-9775
EMP: 88

SALES (corp-wide): 9.3B **Privately Held**
SIC: 5084 Elevators
HQ: Schindler Elevator Corporation
20 Whippany Rd
Morristown NJ 07960
973 397-6500

(P-7886)
SIEMENS INDUSTRY INC
25821 Industrial Blvd # 300, Hayward (94545-2919)
PHONE..................510 783-6000
John P Nichols, *Manager*
Mike Campbell, *Project Mgr*
Carolyn Lorenz, *Sales Staff*
EMP: 150
SALES (corp-wide): 83.5B **Privately Held**
WEB: www.sibt.com
SIC: 5084 Instruments & control equipment
HQ: Siemens Industry, Inc.
1000 Deerfield Pkwy
Buffalo Grove IL 60089
847 215-1000

(P-7887)
SIEMENS INDUSTRY INC
9835 Carroll Ctre Rd 10 Ste 100, San Diego (92126)
PHONE..................858 693-8711
Majd Khleis, *Manager*
Alla Artamonov, *Info Tech Mgr*
Jon Wright, *Engineer*
Nancy Lane, *Financial Analy*
Dietsch Michael, *Sales Executive*
EMP: 75
SQ FT: 3,300
SALES (corp-wide): 83.5B **Privately Held**
WEB: www.sibt.com
SIC: 5084 1711 3822 3825 Pneumatic tools & equipment; mechanical contractor; auto controls regulating residntl & coml environmt & applncs; instruments to measure electricity; industrial instrmnts msrmnt display/control process variable
HQ: Siemens Industry, Inc.
1000 Deerfield Pkwy
Buffalo Grove IL 60089
847 215-1000

(P-7888)
SMC CORPORATION OF AMERICA
2841 Junction Ave Ste 110, San Jose (95134-1921)
PHONE..................408 943-9600
Joe Hanna, *Manager*
Christopher Denny, *Business Anlyst*
Jason Cristobal, *Sales Mgr*
Kathryn Prater, *Sales Mgr*
Shigeki Nowatari, *Sales Staff*
EMP: 50
SALES (corp-wide): 4B **Privately Held**
WEB: www.smcusa.com
SIC: 5084 Pneumatic tools & equipment
HQ: Smc Corporation Of America
10100 Smc Blvd
Noblesville IN 46060

(P-7889)
SOUTHERN CALIFORNIA MTL HDLG
Also Called: Southern Calif Mtl Hdlg Co
19755 Bahama St, Northridge (91324-3304)
PHONE..................805 650-6000
Toni Edgar, *Manager*
EMP: 65
SALES (corp-wide): 2B **Privately Held**
WEB: www.scmh.com
SIC: 5084 Materials handling machinery
HQ: Southern California Material Handling Inc
12393 Slauson Ave
Whittier CA 90606
562 949-1006

(P-7890)
SOUTHERN CALIFORNIA MTL HDLG
8124 Deering Ave, Canoga Park (91304-5013)
PHONE..................818 349-1220
S Handling, *Branch Mgr*
EMP: 61

5084 - Industrial Mach & Eqpt Wholesale County (P-7891)

SALES (corp-wide): 2B Privately Held
SIC: 5084 Conveyor systems
HQ: Southern California Material Handling Inc
12393 Slauson Ave
Whittier CA 90606
562 949-1006

(P-7891)
SOUTHERN CALIFORNIA MTL HDLG (DH)
Also Called: Scmh
12393 Slauson Ave, Whittier (90606-2824)
P.O. Box 80770, San Marino (91118-8770)
PHONE..................................562 949-1006
Tim Cleary, *President*
Mike Wolfe, *COO*
Gary Ortiz, *Exec VP*
Jermaine Ratcliffe, *Admin Asst*
Eric Dobbins, *CIO*
▲ EMP: 140
SALES (est): 70.8MM
SALES (corp-wide): 2B Privately Held
WEB: www.scmh.com
SIC: 5084 Conveyor systems
HQ: Mitsubishi Caterpillar Forklift America, Inc
2121 W Sam Houston Pkwy N
Houston TX 77043
713 365-1000

(P-7892)
SOUTHWEST MATERIAL HDLG INC (PA)
Also Called: Southwest Toyota Lift
3725 Nobel Ct, Mira Loma (91752-3267)
P.O. Box 1070 (91752-8070)
PHONE..................................951 727-0477
Fax: 951 727-0407
Kirt Little, *CEO*
Joseph G Little, *President*
Joe Quinto, *Finance Dir*
Barry Westenhaver, *Manager*
▲ EMP: 115
SQ FT: 10,000
SALES (est): 39.5MM Privately Held
SIC: 5084 7389 7699 7359 Lift trucks & parts; design, commercial & industrial; industrial machinery & equipment repair; equipment rental & leasing; building site preparation

(P-7893)
SUPERIOR MACHINING MFG CO INC
322 Oak Pl, Brea (92821-4135)
PHONE..................................714 529-6000
Hussein Suheimat, *CEO*
EMP: 100 EST: 2015
SALES (est): 8.4MM Privately Held
SIC: 5084 Industrial machinery & equipment

(P-7894)
SURFACE PUMPS INC (PA)
3301 Unicorn Rd, Bakersfield (93308-6852)
P.O. Box 5757 (93388-5757)
PHONE..................................661 393-1545
Steven J Durrett, *President*
Marty Rushing, *Corp Secy*
David Cook, *Vice Pres*
EMP: 51
SQ FT: 14,000
SALES (est): 63.3MM Privately Held
SIC: 5084 7699 8711 3519 Pumps & pumping equipment; pumps & pumping equipment repair; engineering services; parts & accessories; internal combustion engines

(P-7895)
SYCONEX CORPORATION
3200 Wilshire Blvd # 601, Los Angeles (90010-1333)
PHONE..................................213 386-7383
John Bou, *President*
Eui Sup Han, *President*
Kum Soon Lee, *Chairman*
EMP: 50
SALES (est): 4.7MM Privately Held
WEB: www.syconex.com
SIC: 5084 Industrial machinery & equipment

(P-7896)
THYSSENKRUPP ELEVATOR CORP
14400 Catalina St, San Leandro (94577-5516)
PHONE..................................510 476-1900
Ed Persico, *Manager*
EMP: 100
SALES (corp-wide): 47.2B Privately Held
WEB: www.thyssenkruppelevator.com
SIC: 5084 1796 3534 Elevators; elevator installation & conversion; elevators & moving stairways
HQ: Thyssenkrupp Elevator Corporation
11605 Haynes Bridge Rd # 650
Alpharetta GA 30009
678 319-3240

(P-7897)
THYSSENKRUPP ELEVATOR CORP
30984 Santana St, Hayward (94544-7058)
PHONE..................................510 476-1900
Homer Guerra, *Principal*
David Campbell, *Branch Mgr*
EMP: 50
SALES (corp-wide): 47.2B Privately Held
SIC: 5084 Elevators
HQ: Thyssenkrupp Elevator Corporation
11605 Haynes Bridge Rd # 650
Alpharetta GA 30009
678 319-3240

(P-7898)
UNICO MECHANICAL CORP
1209 Polk St, Benicia (94510-2906)
P.O. Box 847 (94510-0847)
PHONE..................................707 745-4540
Fax: 707 745-9973
Michael Potter, *President*
Randy Potter, *President*
Michael Guthrie, *CFO*
Denida Romero, *Controller*
Gordon Potter, *Manager*
▲ EMP: 80
SQ FT: 80,000
SALES (est): 68.4MM Privately Held
WEB: www.unicomechanical.com
SIC: 5084 7699 Industrial machinery & equipment; industrial machinery & equipment repair

(P-7899)
UTILITY TRLR SLS OF CENTL CAL
2680 S East Ave, Fresno (93706-5400)
P.O. Box 11845 (93775-1845)
PHONE..................................559 237-2001
Fax: 559 266-7445
Michael Sutherland, *Manager*
Phyllis Neely, *Office Mgr*
Robert H Tardiff, *Agent*
EMP: 50
SALES (corp-wide): 35.5MM Privately Held
WEB: www.utilitycc.com
SIC: 5084 Trailers, industrial
PA: Utility Trailer Sales Of Central California, Inc
2680 S East Ave
Lathrop CA 95330
209 444-8800

(P-7900)
VALIN CORPORATION (PA)
1941 Ringwood Ave, San Jose (95131-1721)
PHONE..................................408 730-9850
Fax: 408 730-1363
Joseph C Nettemeyer, *President*
Timothy Tritch, *President*
John Pregenzer, *COO*
David Hefler, *CFO*
Ray Herrera, *Vice Pres*
◆ EMP: 96
SQ FT: 66,850
SALES (est): 2.2MM Privately Held
WEB: www.valinonline.com
SIC: 5084 Materials handling machinery; processing & packaging equipment

(P-7901)
VALLEY POWER SYSTEMS INC
Also Called: Valley Detriot Diesel
4000 Rosedale Hwy, Bakersfield (93308-6131)
PHONE..................................661 325-9001
Fax: 661 323-2986
Ken Relyea, *Branch Mgr*
EMP: 50
SALES (corp-wide): 193.8MM Privately Held
WEB: www.valleypowersystems.com
SIC: 5084 Industrial machinery & equipment
PA: Valley Power Systems, Inc.
425 S Hacienda Blvd
City Of Industry CA 91745
626 333-1243

(P-7902)
VERITIV OPERATING COMPANY
Also Called: International Paper
7337 Las Positas Rd, Livermore (94551-5110)
PHONE..................................925 245-6075
EMP: 151
SALES (corp-wide): 8.7B Publicly Held
SIC: 5084 Processing & packaging equipment; printing trades machinery, equipment & supplies
HQ: Veritiv Operating Company
1000 Abernathy Rd
Atlanta GA 30328
770 391-8200

(P-7903)
VOLK ENTERPRISES INC
618 S Kilroy Rd, Turlock (95380-9531)
PHONE..................................209 632-3826
Anthony Volks, *Manager*
Amy Sward, *Accountant*
EMP: 60
SALES (corp-wide): 41.2MM Privately Held
SIC: 5084 3089 Machine tools & metalworking machinery; plastic processing
PA: Volk Enterprises, Inc.
1335 Ridgeland Pkwy # 120
Alpharetta GA 30004
770 663-5400

(P-7904)
WASSER FILTRATION INC
Also Called: Force Measurement Systems
1215 N Fee Ana St, Anaheim (92807-1804)
PHONE..................................714 525-0630
Greg Stewart, *Vice Pres*
EMP: 70
SALES (corp-wide): 16.2MM Privately Held
WEB: www.pacpress.com
SIC: 5084 Industrial machinery & equipment
PA: Wasser Filtration, Inc.
1215 N Fee Ana St
Anaheim CA 92807
714 982-5600

(P-7905)
WESTAIR GASES & EQUIPMENT INC
2300 Haffley Ave, National City (91950-6419)
PHONE..................................619 474-0079
Pat Dalton, *Branch Mgr*
Dave Hosted, *Director*
EMP: 60
SALES (corp-wide): 139.6MM Privately Held
WEB: www.westairgases.com
SIC: 5084 Petroleum industry machinery
PA: Westair Gases & Equipment, Inc.
2506 Market St
San Diego CA 92102
866 937-8247

(P-7906)
WESTAIR GASES & EQUIPMENT INC (PA)
Also Called: San Diego Welders Supply
2506 Market St, San Diego (92102-3010)
P.O. Box 131902 (92170-1902)
PHONE..................................866 937-8247
Fax: 619 239-0529
Andrew J Castiglione, *CEO*
Steve Castiglione, *President*
Tim Van Linge, *CFO*
Sue Castiglione, *Corp Secy*
Mike Fuette, *Vice Pres*
EMP: 50
SQ FT: 10,000
SALES (est): 139.6MM Privately Held
WEB: www.westairgases.com
SIC: 5084 Industrial machinery & equipment; welding machinery & equipment

(P-7907)
YALE/CHASE EQP & SVCS INC (PA)
2615 Pellissier Pl, City of Industry (90601-1508)
P.O. Box 1231 Industry, La Puente (91749)
PHONE..................................562 463-8000
Fax: 562 463-8093
Roger Ketelsleger, *President*
James Douglas Graven, *CFO*
Teresa Abando, *Officer*
Michael Ketelsleger, *Vice Pres*
Jana Ketelsleger, *Admin Mgr*
▲ EMP: 116
SQ FT: 33,000
SALES (est): 94.9MM Privately Held
WEB: www.yalechase.com
SIC: 5084 7699 7359 Lift trucks & parts; industrial machinery & equipment repair; industrial truck rental

(P-7908)
YAMAZEN INC
23700 Via Del Rio Ste C, Yorba Linda (92887-2746)
PHONE..................................800 882-8558
▲ EMP: 52
SALES (est): 3.7MM Privately Held
SIC: 5084 Industrial machinery & equipment

(P-7909)
ZEMARC CORPORATION (PA)
6431 Flotilla St, Commerce (90040-1597)
PHONE..................................323 721-5598
Fax: 323 722-2220
Viren Patel, *CEO*
Dave Manzi, *President*
Abdul Zeke Zahid, *Founder*
Irma K Zahid, *Vice Pres*
Carlos Aguirre, *Regional Mgr*
EMP: 50
SQ FT: 50,000
SALES (est): 34.1MM Privately Held
SIC: 5084 Hydraulic systems equipment & supplies; pneumatic tools & equipment

5085 Industrial Splys Wholesale

(P-7910)
ACHEM INDUSTRY AMERICA INC (PA)
13226 Alondra Blvd, Cerritos (90703-2237)
PHONE..................................562 802-0998
Joseph Lin, *CEO*
Shin Pai Kuei, *President*
Benedict Chen, *Controller*
Bob Kuminski, *Natl Sales Mgr*
Elvira Rodriguez, *Regl Sales Mgr*
▲ EMP: 50
SQ FT: 48,000
SALES (est): 31.9MM Privately Held
WEB: www.achem.com
SIC: 5085 Industrial supplies

(P-7911)
ADCO CONTAINER COMPANY
9959 Canoga Ave, Chatsworth (91311-3090)
PHONE..................................818 998-2565
Fax: 818 998-3648
EMP: 50
SQ FT: 24,000
SALES (est): 12.2MM Privately Held
WEB: www.adcocontainer.com
SIC: 5085 7236

▲ = Import ▼ = Export
◆ = Import/Export

PRODUCTS & SERVICES SECTION
5085 - Industrial Splys Wholesale County (P-7933)

(P-7912)
ALLIED HIGH TECH PRODUCTS INC
2376 E Pacifica Pl, Rancho Dominguez (90220-6214)
P.O. Box 4608, Compton (90224-4608)
PHONE..................................310 635-2466
Fax: 310 762-6808
Robert C Smith, *Ch of Bd*
Clayton A Smith, *President*
Shirley A Smith, *Corp Secy*
Eddie Padilla, *General Mgr*
Sandra Chavez, *Purch Mgr*
▲ EMP: 70
SQ FT: 34,000
SALES (est): 64.7MM **Privately Held**
WEB: www.alliedhightech.com
SIC: **5085** Abrasives

(P-7913)
AMERICAN INDUSTRIAL SUPPLY
9817 Variel Ave, Chatsworth (91311-4317)
PHONE..................................818 841-7788
Robert Nadler, *President*
Thelma Nadler, *Corp Secy*
Brian Stark, *Office Mgr*
Hamie Fonth, *Manager*
EMP: 53
SQ FT: 15,000
SALES (est): 13MM **Privately Held**
SIC: **5085** Industrial supplies

(P-7914)
ARC FASTENER SUPPLY & MFG
Also Called: A R C Fastener Supply
2104 Wembley Ln, Corona (92881-7441)
PHONE..................................909 481-8171
Fax: 909 481-7750
Joseph Myers, *President*
Christie Rockwood, *Controller*
▲ EMP: 78
SQ FT: 70,000
SALES (est): 13.4MM **Privately Held**
WEB: www.arcfasteners.com
SIC: **5085** **5072** Fasteners, industrial: nuts, bolts, screws, etc.; hardware

(P-7915)
ARCONIC GLOBAL FAS & RINGS INC
Also Called: Arconic Fstening Systems Rings
135 N Unruh Ave, City of Industry (91744-4427)
PHONE..................................626 968-3831
Hatty Ao, *Director*
Tom Adland, *Vice Pres*
Jeff Daedler, *Executive*
Ed Park, *Purchasing*
Gregory Emanuelson, *Safety Mgr*
EMP: 350
SQ FT: 58,400
SALES (corp-wide): 22.5B **Publicly Held**
WEB: www.alcoafasteners.com
SIC: **5085** Fasteners & fastening equipment
HQ: Arconic Global Fasteners & Rings, Inc.
3990a Heritage Oak Ct
Simi Valley CA 93063
310 530-2220

(P-7916)
ARCONIC GLOBAL FAS & RINGS INC
Also Called: Arconic Fstening Systems Rings
3000 Lomita Blvd, Torrance (90505-5103)
PHONE..................................310 784-0700
Kenneth Paine, *Manager*
EMP: 60
SALES (corp-wide): 22.5B **Publicly Held**
WEB: www.alcoafasteners.com
SIC: **5085** Industrial supplies
HQ: Arconic Global Fasteners & Rings, Inc.
3990a Heritage Oak Ct
Simi Valley CA 93063
310 530-2220

(P-7917)
ARCONIC GLOBAL FAS & RINGS INC
Also Called: Arconic Fastening Systems
3014 Lomita Blvd, Torrance (90505-5103)
PHONE..................................310 530-2220
Oliver Jarraolt, *President*
Phil Lee, *Manager*
EMP: 500
SALES (corp-wide): 22.5B **Publicly Held**
WEB: www.alcoafasteners.com
SIC: **5085** Industrial supplies
HQ: Arconic Global Fasteners & Rings, Inc.
3990a Heritage Oak Ct
Simi Valley CA 93063
310 530-2220

(P-7918)
ARCONIC GLOBAL FAS & RINGS INC (HQ)
Also Called: Alcoa Global Fasteners, Inc.
3990a Heritage Oak Ct, Simi Valley (93063-6715)
PHONE..................................310 530-2220
Fax: 310 784-6612
Olivier Jarrault, *President*
Craig Brown, *Vice Pres*
Tammy Castillo, *CTO*
Andy Guttierrez, *CTO*
Randy Paulson, *Info Tech Dir*
▲ EMP: 120
SQ FT: 37,000
SALES (est): 1.2B
SALES (corp-wide): 22.5B **Publicly Held**
WEB: www.alcoafasteners.com
SIC: **5085** **5072** **5065** Fasteners & fastening equipment; hardware; electronic parts & equipment
PA: Alcoa Inc.
390 Park Ave Fl 12
New York NY 10022
212 836-2674

(P-7919)
ARCONIC GLOBAL FAS & RINGS INC
Also Called: Arconic Fstening Systems Rings
800 S State College Blvd, Fullerton (92831-5334)
PHONE..................................714 871-1550
Craig Brown, *Manager*
David A Werner, *Admin Sec*
Cynthia Franco, *Human Res Mgr*
Quyen Nguyen, *Purch Mgr*
Bart Preston, *Opers Staff*
EMP: 100
SQ FT: 153,604
SALES (corp-wide): 22.5B **Publicly Held**
WEB: www.alcoafasteners.com
SIC: **5085** Fasteners & fastening equipment
HQ: Arconic Global Fasteners & Rings, Inc.
3990a Heritage Oak Ct
Simi Valley CA 93063
310 530-2220

(P-7920)
ARCONIC GLOBAL FAS & RINGS INC
Also Called: Arconic Fstening Systems Rings
3000 Lomita Blvd, Torrance (90505-5103)
PHONE..................................310 530-2220
William Hart, *Director*
EMP: 50
SALES (corp-wide): 22.5B **Publicly Held**
SIC: **5085** Industrial supplies
HQ: Arconic Global Fasteners & Rings, Inc.
3990a Heritage Oak Ct
Simi Valley CA 93063
310 530-2220

(P-7921)
ARCONIC GLOBAL FAS & RINGS INC
Also Called: Arconic Fastening Systems
3018 Lomita Blvd, Torrance (90505-5103)
PHONE..................................310 530-2220
Melanie Brooks, *Branch Mgr*
Doug Pyle, *Marketing Mgr*
EMP: 1000
SALES (corp-wide): 22.5B **Publicly Held**
WEB: www.alcoafasteners.com
SIC: **5085** Fasteners & fastening equipment
HQ: Arconic Global Fasteners & Rings, Inc.
3990a Heritage Oak Ct
Simi Valley CA 93063
310 530-2220

(P-7922)
ARIES FILTERWORKS
8722 Burton Way 40, West Hollywood (90048-3854)
PHONE..................................323 262-1600
Jeffrey Gottlieb, *President*
▲ EMP: 50
SQ FT: 20,000
SALES (est): 3.7MM **Privately Held**
SIC: **5085** Filters, industrial

(P-7923)
ASKEW INDUSTRIAL CORPORATION (PA)
13071 Arctic Cir, Santa Fe Springs (90670-5505)
PHONE..................................323 727-7772
Fax: 323 727-9567
Turan Kahraman, *President*
Eric Wallerstein, *Analyst*
Jerry Klerr, *Manager*
Jeremy Linderman, *Accounts Mgr*
▲ EMP: 50
SQ FT: 33,000
SALES (est): 24MM **Privately Held**
WEB: www.askewindustrial.com
SIC: **5085** Fasteners, industrial: nuts, bolts, screws, etc.

(P-7924)
BAY STANDARD INC
24485 Marsh Creek Rd, Brentwood (94513-4319)
P.O. Box 801 (94513-0801)
PHONE..................................925 634-1181
Fax: 925 634-1925
Gary W Landgraf, *President*
Karen Landgraf, *Corp Secy*
Tom Landgraf, *Vice Pres*
▲ EMP: 100
SALES (est): 13MM **Privately Held**
SIC: **5085** **3965** Fasteners & fastening equipment; fasteners

(P-7925)
BEARING ENGINEERS INC (PA)
Also Called: Motion Solutions
27 Argonaut, Aliso Viejo (92656-1423)
PHONE..................................949 586-7442
Fax: 949 586-7786
Harold Lee Katz, *President*
Harold Lee Lee, *CEO*
Henry Kim, *Vice Pres*
Wallis Logan, *Vice Pres*
Mary Brooking, *Technology*
▲ EMP: 57
SQ FT: 22,000
SALES (est): 32MM **Privately Held**
WEB: www.bearingengineers.com
SIC: **5085** Bearings

(P-7926)
BELL PIPE & SUPPLY CO
215 E Ball Rd, Anaheim (92805-6394)
P.O. Box 151 (92815-0151)
PHONE..................................714 772-3200
Fax: 714 956-8900
Franklin M Bell III, *CEO*
Kristin C Bell, *Corp Secy*
Jim Kearns, *Warehouse Mgr*
Fred Oconnell, *Accounts Exec*
▲ EMP: 50 EST: 1956
SQ FT: 35,000
SALES (est): 72.1MM **Privately Held**
WEB: www.bellpipe.com
SIC: **5085** Industrial supplies

(P-7927)
BOSSARD NORTH AMERICA INC
2000 Chabot Ct, Tracy (95304-8841)
PHONE..................................562 906-2003
Brent Wright, *Branch Mgr*
EMP: 68 **Privately Held**
SIC: **5085** Fasteners, industrial: nuts, bolts, screws, etc.; tools
HQ: Bossard North America, Inc.
6521 Production Dr
Cedar Falls IA 50613
319 268-3700

(P-7928)
CENTRAL PURCHASING LLC (PA)
Also Called: Harbor Freight Tools
3491 Mission Oaks Blvd, Camarillo (93012-5034)
P.O. Box 6010 (93011-6010)
PHONE..................................805 388-1000
Fax: 805 445-4900
Eric L Smidt, *CEO*
Robert Rene, *COO*
Patty Sinner, *Treasurer*
Bruce Godfray, *Vice Pres*
Christopher Gurtcheff, *Vice Pres*
◆ EMP: 500
SQ FT: 277,000
SALES (est): 1.9B **Privately Held**
WEB: www.harborfreight.com
SIC: **5085** **5961** **5251** Tools; tools & hardware, mail order; tools

(P-7929)
CRANE CO
3201 Walnut Ave, Long Beach (90755-5225)
PHONE..................................562 426-2531
Kevin McKown, *Manager*
EMP: 110
SALES (corp-wide): 2.7B **Publicly Held**
WEB: www.craneco.com
SIC: **5085** Valves & fittings
PA: Crane Co.
100 1st Stamford Pl # 300
Stamford CT 06902
203 363-7300

(P-7930)
DAILY SAW SERVICE
4481 Firestone Blvd, South Gate (90280-3397)
PHONE..................................323 564-1791
Greg R Daily, *CEO*
Chase Rief, *Executive*
Linda Jones, *Manager*
▲ EMP: 50
SQ FT: 65,000
SALES (est): 26.4MM **Privately Held**
SIC: **5085** **7699** **3546** Knives, industrial; industrial machinery & equipment repair; saws & sawing equipment

(P-7931)
DHV INDUSTRIES INC
3451 Pegasus Dr, Bakersfield (93308-6827)
PHONE..................................661 392-8948
Fax: 661 392-8947
Tingchun Huang, *President*
Jessica Lackey, *Marketing Staff*
Sonny Simmons, *Director*
Rena Reiss, *Manager*
◆ EMP: 52
SQ FT: 180,000
SALES (est): 16.5MM **Privately Held**
WEB: www.dhvindustries.com
SIC: **5085** **3491** Valves & fittings; industrial valves

(P-7932)
G W MAINTENANCE INC (PA)
Also Called: Petroquip
1101 E 6th St, Santa Ana (92701-4912)
PHONE..................................714 541-2211
Kami Keshmiri, *President*
Barry F Branin, *Ch of Bd*
Vivian Branin, *Treasurer*
EMP: 59
SQ FT: 24,000
SALES (est): 7.4MM **Privately Held**
WEB: www.gwmaintenance.com
SIC: **5085** **5084** Valves & fittings; gas equipment, parts & supplies; instruments & control equipment; hoists; pumps & pumping equipment

(P-7933)
GENERAL TOOL INC
Also Called: Gt Diamond
2025 Alton Pkwy, Irvine (92606-4904)
PHONE..................................949 261-2322
Jae Woo Kim, *CEO*
In Kim, *Vice Pres*
Jay Kim, *Admin Sec*
David Hwang, *Technology*
Julie Dang, *Human Res Mgr*
▲ EMP: 90

5085 - Industrial Splys Wholesale County (P-7934)

PRODUCTS & SERVICES SECTION

SQ FT: 40,000
SALES (est): 26.8MM Privately Held
WEB: www.gtdiamond.com
SIC: 5085 Diamonds, industrial: natural, crude

(P-7934)
GRISWOLD INDUSTRIES
Also Called: Griswald Industries
24100 Water Ave, Perris (92570-6738)
PHONE................................951 657-1718
Fax: 951 657-8540
Fred Zimmer, Manager
Jennifer Lusha, Manager
EMP: 55
SQ FT: 25,000
SALES (corp-wide): 98.6MM Privately Held
SIC: 5085 3494 Valves & fittings; valves & pipe fittings
PA: Griswold Industries
    1701 Placentia Ave
    Costa Mesa CA 92627
    949 722-4800

(P-7935)
IDG USA LLC
Also Called: Idg California
6842 Walker St, La Palma (90623-1054)
PHONE................................714 994-6960
Fax: 714 952-3025
Chris Pratt, Manager
Phil Jaskoviak, Sales Mgr
EMP: 60
SALES (corp-wide): 9.8MM Privately Held
WEB: www.idgventures.com
SIC: 5085 5251 Tools; tools
HQ: Idg Usa, Llc
    2100 The Oaks Pkwy
    Belmont NC 28012
    704 398-5600

(P-7936)
INDUSTRIAL CONTAINER SERVICES
Also Called: Ics-CA North
749 Galleria Blvd, Roseville (95678-1331)
PHONE................................916 781-2775
Fax: 916 781-2776
Charles Veniez, CEO
Leigh Thomas, Controller
Amanda Cesar, Purchasing
Gerald Butler,
Alain G Magnan,
EMP: 52
SQ FT: 10,000
SALES (est): 19.2MM
SALES (corp-wide): 2.2B Privately Held
WEB: www.capitaldrum.com
SIC: 5085 2655 Commercial containers; fiber cans, drums & similar products
HQ: Industrial Container Services Llc
    2400 Maitland Center Pkwy
    Maitland FL 32751
    800 273-3786

(P-7937)
KAMAN INDUSTRIAL TECH CORP
910 S Wanamaker Ave, Ontario (91761-8151)
PHONE................................909 390-7919
Fax: 909 390-7931
Tom Serafin, Branch Mgr
Ron Henderson, Sales Executive
Mick Horne, Manager
EMP: 50
SALES (corp-wide): 1.7B Publicly Held
SIC: 5085 Industrial supplies
HQ: Kaman Industrial Technologies Corporation
    1 Vision Way
    Bloomfield CT 06002
    860 687-5000

(P-7938)
LEWIS-GOETZ AND COMPANY INC
Also Called: Valley Rubber & Gasket
10182 Croydon Way, Sacramento (95827-2102)
PHONE................................916 366-9340
Debbie Herbers, Technology
Brian Vigil, Mktg Dir
Todd Brenneman, Regl Sales Mgr
EMP: 98 Privately Held
SIC: 5085 3052 3053 Hose, belting & packing; gaskets & seals; gaskets, packing & sealing devices; rubber & plastics hose & beltings
HQ: Lewis-Goetz And Company, Inc.
    650 Washington Rd Ste 500
    Pittsburgh PA 15228
    800 937-9070

(P-7939)
LINEAR INDUSTRIES LTD (PA)
1850 Enterprise Way, Monrovia (91016-4271)
PHONE................................626 303-1130
Fax: 626 303-2035
Anthony Dell Angelica, President
Jean Cade, CFO
Savonia Angelica, Vice Pres
Perry Priestley, Vice Pres
Steve Gaglio, Engineer
▲ EMP: 61
SQ FT: 45,000
SALES (est): 26.6MM Privately Held
WEB: www.linearindustries.com
SIC: 5085 3625 5065 5072 Bearings; positioning controls, electric; electronic parts; hardware; power transmission equipment; machine tool accessories

(P-7940)
MILLENNIA STAINLESS INC
10016 Romandel Ave, Santa Fe Springs (90670-3424)
PHONE................................562 946-3545
Ching-PO LI, CEO
Charlie Wang, Executive
Lisa Chen, Accounting Mgr
▲ EMP: 75
SQ FT: 10,500
SALES (est): 29.1MM
SALES (corp-wide): 444.4MM Privately Held
SIC: 5085 5065 5051 Industrial supplies; coils, electronic; steel
PA: Chain Chon Industrial Co., Ltd.
    178, Ta Guan Rd.,
    Taoyuan City TAY 33753
    338 569-85

(P-7941)
MITSUBISHI MATERIALS USA CORP (HQ)
11250 Slater Ave, Fountain Valley (92708-5421)
PHONE................................714 352-6100
Fax: 714 668-1320
Motoharu Yamamoto, CEO
Niro Odani, Corp Secy
Dan Muldowney, Vice Pres
Michael Pace, Executive
Nick Allen, District Mgr
◆ EMP: 50
SQ FT: 55,000
SALES (est): 73.5MM
SALES (corp-wide): 12.1B Privately Held
SIC: 5085 5084 Industrial tools; machine tools & accessories
PA: Mitsubishi Materials Corporation
    1-3-2, Otemachi
    Chiyoda-Ku TKY 100-0
    352 525-200

(P-7942)
MT SUPPLY INC
Also Called: Machine Tools Supply
3505 Cadillac Ave Ste K2, Costa Mesa (92626-1432)
PHONE................................714 434-4748
George H Ponce Jr, CEO
David Herman, Treasurer
Joseph Custer, Principal
Steve Gurley, Principal
Steve Pixley, Principal
EMP: 163
SALES (est): 185.8MM
SALES (corp-wide): 3B Publicly Held
SIC: 5085 5084 Industrial supplies; materials handling machinery
HQ: Dnow L.P.
    7402 N Eldridge Pkwy
    Houston TX 77041
    281 823-4700

(P-7943)
NMC GROUP INC
Also Called: Nylon Molding Corporation
2755 Thompson Creek Rd, Pomona (91767-1861)
PHONE................................909 451-2290
Fax: 909 593-8309
Douglas P Stephen, CEO
Mitch Iverson, President
Jim Sweeney, President
Ichard Brad Lawrence, CEO
Barbara Stephen, Corp Secy
▲ EMP: 64
SQ FT: 40,000
SALES (est): 42MM
SALES (corp-wide): 3.8B Publicly Held
WEB: www.nmcgroup.com
SIC: 5085 3089 Fasteners & fastening equipment; injection molding of plastics
HQ: Kirkhill-Ta Co.
    300 E Cypress St
    Brea CA 92821
    714 529-4901

(P-7944)
PACIFIC COAST DRUM COMPANY
Also Called: Gene's Cooperage
2200 Rosemead Blvd 2204, El Monte (91733-1520)
P.O. Box 3593 (91733-0593)
PHONE................................626 443-3096
Darryl Bartolotti, President
Gene Bartolotti, Ch of Bd
John Byrnes, Corp Secy
Gino Bartolotti, Vice Pres
Donald S Burris, Agent
EMP: 80 EST: 1961
SQ FT: 50,000
SALES (est): 11.5MM Privately Held
SIC: 5085 Drums, new or reconditioned

(P-7945)
PACIFIC ECHO INC
23540 Telo Ave, Torrance (90505-4098)
PHONE................................310 539-1822
Fax: 310 539-5826
Yasuo Ogami, CEO
Chuck Tsutsumi, Controller
Rie Dukes, Manager
▲ EMP: 90
SQ FT: 110,000
SALES (est): 39MM
SALES (corp-wide): 1.9MM Privately Held
WEB: www.pacificecho.com
SIC: 5085 Hose, belting & packing
HQ: Kakuichi Co.,Ltd.
    1415, Midoricho, Tsuruga
    Nagano NAG 380-0
    262 346-111

(P-7946)
PRH PRO INC
13089 Peyton Dr Ste C362, Chino Hills (91709-6018)
PHONE................................714 510-7226
Wayman Bill Peng, President
EMP: 161
SQ FT: 2,000
SALES: 100MM Privately Held
SIC: 5085 Cooperage stock

(P-7947)
PRINTING TECHNOLOGY INC
Also Called: Pti
21001 Nordhoff St, Chatsworth (91311-5911)
PHONE................................818 576-9220
Peter De Salay, President
Julian Desalay, Vice Pres
Tim Purugganan, Vice Pres
Angie Bhasim, Manager
▲ EMP: 160
SQ FT: 89,000
SALES (est): 41.3MM Privately Held
WEB: www.ptiimaging.com
SIC: 5085 5084 5111 Ink, printers'; printing trades machinery, equipment & supplies; printing paper

(P-7948)
PROGRESSIVE TRNSP SVCS INC
19500 S Alameda St, Compton (90221-6204)
PHONE................................510 268-3776
Edgar Tafolla, Branch Mgr
EMP: 56
SALES (corp-wide): 13.8MM Privately Held
SIC: 5085 Commercial containers
PA: Progressive Transportation Services, Inc.
    1360 W Pacific Coast Hwy
    Long Beach CA 90810
    310 684-2100

(P-7949)
ROPE PARTNER INC
125 Mcpherson St Ste B, Santa Cruz (95060-5883)
PHONE................................831 460-9448
Eric Stanfield, President
Alan David, CFO
Chris Bley, Founder
Wayne Marci, Admin Asst
Eric Ruderman, Technician
EMP: 65
SQ FT: 1,900
SALES: 950K Privately Held
WEB: www.ropepartner.com
SIC: 5085 Rope, cord & thread

(P-7950)
RUTLAND TOOL & SUPPLY CO (HQ)
Also Called: MSC Metalworking
2225 Workman Mill Rd, City of Industry (90601-1437)
PHONE................................562 566-5000
Fax: 562 566-5001
Thomas J Neri, CEO
Andrew Verey, President
Neil E Jenkins, Admin Sec
Mark Palmer, Administration
Fernando Saucedo, Info Tech Mgr
▲ EMP: 140
SALES (est): 28.6MM Publicly Held
SIC: 5085 5251 Industrial supplies; tools

(P-7951)
S & S TOOL & SUPPLY INC (PA)
Also Called: S and S Supplies and Solutions
2700 Maxwell Way, Fairfield (94534-9708)
P.O. Box 1111, Martinez (94553-0111)
PHONE................................925 335-4000
Fax: 925 229-0811
Tracy M Tomkovicz, CEO
Steven Tomkovicz, President
Tanya Powell, CFO
Phil Jones, Info Tech Mgr
Derick Teng, Info Tech Mgr
▲ EMP: 100
SQ FT: 90,000
SALES: 134.5MM Privately Held
WEB: www.sns-tool.com
SIC: 5085 7699 5072 7359 Industrial supplies; industrial equipment services; tool repair services; hand tools; power handtools; equipment rental & leasing; tool rental

(P-7952)
SEGUIN MREAU NAPA COPERAGE INC
Also Called: Fine Northern Oak
151 Camino Dorado, NAPA (94558-6213)
PHONE................................707 252-3408
Thomas J Martin, President
▲ EMP: 57
SQ FT: 40,000
SALES (est): 17.2MM
SALES (corp-wide): 21.8MM Privately Held
SIC: 5085 2449 Barrels, new or reconditioned; barrels, wood: coopered
PA: Seguin Moreau Holdings Inc
    151 Camino Dorado
    Napa CA 94558
    707 252-3408

(P-7953)
SO CAL SANDBAGS INC
12620 Bosley Ln, Corona (92883-6358)
PHONE................................951 277-3404

PRODUCTS & SERVICES SECTION
5087 - Service Establishment Eqpt & Splys Wholesale County (P-7974)

Fax: 951 277-3420
Peter Rasinski, *President*
Dennis Feidner, *General Mgr*
Wanda Chavez, *Controller*
Lynn Hamblin, *Manager*
EMP: 100
SALES (est): 51MM Privately Held
WEB: www.socalsandbags.com
SIC: 5085 5999 Industrial supplies; safety supplies & equipment

(P-7954)
SOLAR LINK INTERNATIONAL INC
4652 E Brickell St Ste A, Ontario (91761-1593)
PHONE..................909 605-7789
Fax: 909 605-7789
Johnny Tsai, *Vice Pres*
Linda Sebky, *Accountant*
▲ EMP: 218 EST: 1998
SALES (est): 72.7MM Privately Held
SIC: 5085 Industrial supplies

(P-7955)
STEVEN ENGINEERING INC
230 Ryan Way, South San Francisco (94080-6370)
PHONE..................650 588-9200
Fax: 650 588-9300
Bonnie Walter, *CEO*
Ken Walter, *President*
Bryan J Woifgram, *Exec VP*
Bryan J Woifgram, *Exec VP*
Rachel Garza, *Admin Asst*
▲ EMP: 93
SQ FT: 66,000
SALES (est): 557.1MM Privately Held
WEB: www.stevenengineering.com
SIC: 5085 Industrial supplies

(P-7956)
SUNNYVALE FLUID SYS TECH INC
Also Called: Swagelok Northern California
3393 W Warren Ave, Fremont (94538-6424)
P.O. Box 14470 (94539-1170)
PHONE..................510 933-2500
Vita Kuhfahl, *Credit Mgr*
Ian Lahaye, *Controller*
Alan Barker, *Purchasing*
Mark Petures, *Accounts Mgr*
EMP: 50
SQ FT: 14,000
SALES (est): 24.9MM Privately Held
WEB: www.sunnyvale.swagelok.com
SIC: 5085 Valves & fittings

(P-7957)
TCT CIRCUIT SUPPLY INC
1200 N Van Buren St Ste A, Anaheim (92807-1638)
PHONE..................714 644-9700
Ian Hemmings, *President*
Kathy Chen, *Principal*
Amie Chien Chien, *Principal*
EMP: 55
SALES (est): 1.2MM Privately Held
SIC: 5085 Tools

(P-7958)
VICTORY FOAM INC (PA)
3 Holland, Irvine (92618-2506)
PHONE..................949 474-0690
Frank M Comerford, *CEO*
Helen Comerford, *Corp Secy*
Myles Comerford, *Vice Pres*
Angel Alvarado, *Manager*
Susan Thompson, *Accounts Mgr*
▲ EMP: 60
SQ FT: 53,000
SALES (est): 39.8MM Privately Held
WEB: www.victoryfoam.com
SIC: 5085 Packing, industrial

(P-7959)
WEST-SPEC PARTNERS
20525 Nordhoff St Ste 42, Chatsworth (91311-6135)
PHONE..................818 725-7000
Fax: 818 725-7014
Dave Kukanek, *Partner*
Tanya Esch, *Sales Mgr*
EMP: 50

SALES (est): 4.8MM Privately Held
WEB: www.vertexdistribution.com
SIC: 5085 Fasteners & fastening equipment

5087 Service Establishment Eqpt & Splys Wholesale

(P-7960)
ANIXTER INC
4775 Viewridge Ave, San Diego (92123-1641)
PHONE..................858 505-1950
Fax: 858 495-0081
Marshall Merrifield, *Branch Mgr*
Monica Belisle, *Social Dir*
Conley Wilds, *Purch Agent*
Thomas Fitton, *Sales Associate*
Vicki Griffith, *Marketing Staff*
EMP: 76
SALES (corp-wide): 6.1B Publicly Held
WEB: www.clarksecurity.com
SIC: 5087 Locksmith equipment & supplies
HQ: Anixter Inc.
  2301 Patriot Blvd
  Glenview IL 60026
  224 521-8000

(P-7961)
ANIXTER INTERNATIONAL INC
7140 Opportunity Rd, San Diego (92111-2202)
PHONE..................858 571-6571
Fax: 619 571-6281
Tina O'Donnell, *Manager*
Frank Ribbe, *Purch Agent*
Thanh Nguyen, *Sales Staff*
Anique Mautner, *Corp Comm Staff*
Nang Nguyen, *Manager*
EMP: 50
SALES (corp-wide): 6.1B Publicly Held
WEB: www.clarksecurity.com
SIC: 5087 Locksmith equipment & supplies
PA: Anixter International Inc.
  2301 Patriot Blvd
  Glenview IL 60026
  224 521-8000

(P-7962)
ANIXTER INTERNATIONAL INC
4775 Viewridge Ave, San Diego (92123-1641)
PHONE..................858 974-6714
Bruce Kammer, *Manager*
Nick Bruno, *Branch Mgr*
Sandi Thomas, *Info Tech Mgr*
Bryan Kruming, *Engineer*
Tina Donnell, *Manager*
EMP: 76
SALES (corp-wide): 6.1B Publicly Held
WEB: www.clarksecurity.com
SIC: 5087 Locksmith equipment & supplies
PA: Anixter International Inc.
  2301 Patriot Blvd
  Glenview IL 60026
  224 521-8000

(P-7963)
ARROW USA
1105 Highland Ct, Beaumont (92223-7091)
PHONE..................951 845-6144
Sam Chang, *President*
Zuhair Klenzi, *President*
Wen Zhang, *Treasurer*
S Kalanzeh, *Vice Pres*
Susan Chen, *Director*
EMP: 75
SQ FT: 3,000
SALES: 500MM Privately Held
SIC: 5087 Beauty salon & barber shop equipment & supplies

(P-7964)
BEAUTITUDES BEAUTY SUPPLY LLC
7850 White Ln Ste E, Bakersfield (93309-7699)
PHONE..................800 830-6076
Jaime Hecht, *President*
EMP: 51 EST: 2015
SQ FT: 1,500

SALES (est): 2.8MM Privately Held
SIC: 5087 Beauty salon & barber shop equipment & supplies

(P-7965)
CHIRO INC (PA)
Also Called: Mr Clean Maintenance Systems
2260 S Vista Ave, Bloomington (92316-2908)
P.O. Box 31, Colton (92324-0031)
PHONE..................909 879-1160
Fax: 909 879-1155
Arthur Rose, *President*
Kanda Lesperance, *Vice Pres*
Timothy Russell, *Vice Pres*
Ben Zdeb, *Info Tech Dir*
Denise Peters, *Human Res Dir*
EMP: 69
SQ FT: 10,000
SALES (est): 87.5MM Privately Held
WEB: www.mrcleansystems.com
SIC: 5087 7349 5169 Cleaning & maintenance equipment & supplies; cleaning service, industrial or commercial; chemicals & allied products

(P-7966)
CSE HOLDINGS INC (DH)
650 Brennan St, San Jose (95131-1204)
PHONE..................408 436-1907
Fax: 408 954-9595
Gary Fredkin, *President*
Marvin Wenger, *COO*
Randall Kippert, *General Mgr*
Bill Leung, *Controller*
Tim Chism, *Regl Sales Mgr*
▲ EMP: 100
SQ FT: 64,000
SALES (est): 195.2MM
SALES (corp-wide): 88.5B Publicly Held
WEB: www.cleansource.com
SIC: 5087 5084 7699 5113 Janitors' supplies; cleaning equipment, high pressure, sand or steam; industrial machinery & equipment repair; industrial & personal service paper; packaging materials; office supplies
HQ: Interline Brands, Inc.
  701 San Marco Blvd
  Jacksonville FL 32207
  904 421-1400

(P-7967)
HUNTER INDUSTRIES INCORPORATED (PA)
1940 Diamond St, San Marcos (92078-5190)
PHONE..................800 383-4747
Fax: 760 591-3451
Gregory Hunter, *President*
Kari Pelters, *Treasurer*
Torrie Magee, *Executive Asst*
Tonijo Parra, *Executive Asst*
Jeff Winckler, *Administration*
◆ EMP: 153
SQ FT: 450,000
SALES (est): 672.3MM Privately Held
WEB: www.hunterindustries.com
SIC: 5087 3084 Sprinkler systems; plastics pipe

(P-7968)
HYDRO TEK SYSTEMS INC
2353 Almond Ave, Redlands (92374-2035)
PHONE..................909 799-9222
Fax: 909 799-9888
John S Koen, *President*
Andrea S Koen, *Admin Sec*
Judi Barkman, *Accounting Mgr*
▲ EMP: 63
SQ FT: 45,000
SALES: 14MM
SALES (corp-wide): 2.3B Privately Held
WEB: www.hydroteksystems.com
SIC: 5087 3589 5084 Service establishment equipment; commercial cleaning equipment; industrial machinery & equipment
HQ: Nilfisk A/S
  Kornmarksvej 1
  BrOndby 2605
  432 381-00

(P-7969)
JWDANGELO COMPANY INC
601 S Harbor Blvd, La Habra (90631-6187)
P.O. Box 3744 (90632-3744)
PHONE..................562 690-1000
Fax: 562 690-3700
John W D Angelo, *CEO*
Cathy Lite, *Senior VP*
Shannon Smith, *Admin Asst*
Rodney Gifford, *Info Tech Mgr*
Julie Stegelvik, *Credit Mgr*
EMP: 50
SQ FT: 35,000
SALES (est): 17.3MM Privately Held
WEB: www.jwdangelo.com
SIC: 5087 Firefighting equipment

(P-7970)
LN CURTIS AND SONS (PA)
1800 Peralta St, Oakland (94607-1609)
P.O. Box 60000, San Francisco (94160-0001)
PHONE..................510 839-5111
Fax: 510 655-1975
Paul F Curtis, *CFO*
John Viboch, *Treasurer*
Nick Lawrence, *Officer*
Jeff Curtis, *Vice Pres*
Tim Henderson, *Vice Pres*
▲ EMP: 65
SQ FT: 25,000
SALES (est): 64.4MM Privately Held
SIC: 5087 5099 Firefighting equipment; safety equipment & supplies

(P-7971)
NAIL EMPORIUM
Also Called: Nail Emporium Beauty Supply
1221 N Lakeview Ave, Anaheim (92807-1830)
PHONE..................714 779-9889
Fax: 714 779-9971
James George, *Owner*
Dave Kellenberger, *General Mgr*
EMP: 50
SQ FT: 41,000
SALES (est): 2.7MM Privately Held
SIC: 5087 5122 Beauty parlor equipment & supplies; cosmetics, perfumes & hair products

(P-7972)
NIKKEN GLOBAL INC (HQ)
2 Corporate Park Ste 100, Irvine (92606-5103)
PHONE..................949 789-2000
Tom Toshizo Watanabe, *Ch of Bd*
Kendall Cho, *President*
David Balzer, *Vice Pres*
Ruth Ann Bellino, *Accountant*
▲ EMP: 155
SQ FT: 213,000
SALES (est): 39.9MM
SALES (corp-wide): 99.9MM Privately Held
SIC: 5087 5023 5013 5122 Stress reducing equipment, electric; bedspreads; seat covers; vitamins & minerals; long distance telephone communications
PA: Nikken International, Inc.
  2 Corporate Park Ste 100
  Irvine CA 92606
  949 789-2000

(P-7973)
NO MORE DIRT INC
1699 Valencia St, San Francisco (94110-5012)
PHONE..................415 821-6757
Nicholas D Mettler, *President*
Edith Cuares, *Human Res Mgr*
Matt Christopher, *Sales Associate*
EMP: 150
SALES (est): 15.7MM Privately Held
SIC: 5087 Carpet installation equipment

(P-7974)
O P I PRODUCTS INC (DH)
13034 Saticoy St, North Hollywood (91605-3510)
PHONE..................818 759-8688
Fax: 818 759-5770
Jules Kaufman, *CEO*
John Heffner, *President*
Eric Schwartz, *COO*
William Halfacre, *Exec VP*

5087 - Service Establishment Eqpt & Splys Wholesale County (P-7975)

Susan Weiss-Fischmann, *Exec VP*
◆ **EMP:** 500
SQ FT: 250,000
SALES (est): 320MM **Publicly Held**
SIC: 5087 2844 Beauty parlor equipment & supplies; toilet preparations

(P-7975)
PAGE FRONT CATERING
Also Called: Pacific Dining Food Svc MGT
34793 Ardentech Ct, Fremont (94555-3657)
P.O. Box 32761, San Jose (95152-2761)
PHONE...........................408 406-8487
Richard McMahon, *Owner*
EMP: 57
SALES (est): 4.6MM **Privately Held**
SIC: 5087 5812 7389 Vending machines & supplies; caterers; coffee service

(P-7976)
PURCHASING 411 INC
Also Called: Socal Janitoral
12670 Paxton St, Pacoima (91331-1127)
PHONE...........................818 717-9980
EMP: 61
SQ FT: 55,000
SALES (corp-wide): 10.1MM **Privately Held**
SIC: 5087 Janitors' supplies
PA: Purchasing 411 Inc.
16192 Coastal Hwy
Lewes DE 19958
302 360-8464

(P-7977)
PUREBEAUTY INC
Also Called: Pure Beauty-A Freeman Company
32920 Alvarado Niles Rd # 220, Union City (94587-8102)
PHONE...........................510 477-7950
Jeno Reynoso, *General Mgr*
EMP: 50
SALES (corp-wide): 49MM **Privately Held**
WEB: www.embarcaderoshop.com
SIC: 5087 Beauty parlor equipment & supplies
HQ: Purebeauty, Inc.
10610 E 26th Cir N
Wichita KS 67226
888 232-8891

(P-7978)
PWS INC (HQ)
12020 Garfield Ave, South Gate (90280-7823)
PHONE...........................323 721-8832
Fax: 323 721-6148
Morton E Pollack, *Chairman*
Brad Pollack, *President*
Eric Steinberg, *CEO*
Victoria Vela, *Vice Pres*
Galen Buckley, *Info Tech Dir*
▲ **EMP:** 51
SQ FT: 50,000
SALES (est): 71.1MM
SALES (corp-wide): 71.5MM **Privately Held**
WEB: www.pwslaundry.com
SIC: 5087 Laundry equipment & supplies
PA: Pws Investments, Inc.
12020 Garfield Ave
South Gate CA 90280
323 490-1900

(P-7979)
PWS HOLDINGS LLC
6500 Flotilla St, Commerce (90040-1714)
PHONE...........................323 721-8832
Morton Pollack, *Mng Member*
Galen Buckley, *Info Tech Mgr*
Eric Steinberg,
EMP: 125
SALES (est): 10.4MM **Privately Held**
WEB: www.pwsholdings.com
SIC: 5087 Laundry equipment & supplies

(P-7980)
RASHMAN CORPORATION
Also Called: UNIFORM ACCESSORIES
8600 Wilbur Ave, Northridge (91324-4338)
PHONE...........................818 993-3030
Fax: 818 993-4151
Richard Rashman, *CEO*

Roger Rashman, *Vice Pres*
Helen Chien, *VP Finance*
Sharon Gaglio, *Credit Mgr*
Lisa Dizon, *Manager*
▲ **EMP:** 65 **EST:** 1969
SQ FT: 50,000
SALES (est): 17.6MM **Privately Held**
WEB: www.neve.com
SIC: 5087 Service establishment equipment

(P-7981)
SPILO WORLDWIDE INC
2950 E Vernon Ave, Vernon (90058-1829)
PHONE...........................213 687-8600
Fax: 213 620-1295
Ann Spilo, *CEO*
Marc Spilo, *President*
Rhonda Hicks, *Human Res Dir*
▲ **EMP:** 100
SQ FT: 24,000
SALES (est): 33MM **Privately Held**
SIC: 5087 Beauty parlor equipment & supplies; barber shop equipment & supplies

(P-7982)
STAR NAIL PRODUCTS INC
29120 Avenue Paine, Valencia (91355-5402)
PHONE...........................661 257-7827
Fax: 661 257-5856
Tony Cuccio, *CEO*
Roberta Cuccio, *COO*
▲ **EMP:** 70
SALES (est): 12.5MM **Privately Held**
SIC: 5087 Beauty parlor equipment & supplies

(P-7983)
SWEIS INC (PA)
23760 Hawthorne Blvd, Torrance (90505-5906)
PHONE...........................310 375-0558
Fax: 310 375-9398
Karl Sweis, *President*
Glen Pacek, *Exec VP*
Theresa Sweis, *Vice Pres*
Caprise Hewes, *Office Mgr*
Susan Andriacchi, *Accountant*
EMP: 70
SQ FT: 4,200
SALES (est): 34.5MM **Privately Held**
WEB: www.sweisinc.com
SIC: 5087 2844 Beauty parlor equipment & supplies; hair preparations, including shampoos

(P-7984)
UNITED FABRICARE SUPPLY INC (PA)
1237 W Walnut St, Compton (90220-5009)
P.O. Box 1796, Los Angeles (90001-0796)
PHONE...........................310 886-3790
Fax: 310 537-7096
Steve S Hong, *CEO*
Hae S Hong, *Corp Secy*
Mike Fahar, *Exec VP*
Kirby Schnebly, *Exec VP*
W David Weimer, *Exec VP*
▲ **EMP:** 75
SQ FT: 50,000
SALES (est): 48.3MM **Privately Held**
WEB: www.unitedfabricaresupply.com
SIC: 5087 Laundry & dry cleaning equipment & supplies

(P-7985)
VEND CATERING SUPPLY INC
14455 Industry Cir, La Mirada (90638-5812)
PHONE...........................562 483-7337
Steven Shapiro, *President*
Nayan Gandhi, *CFO*
Brian Nyhus, *Merchandise Mgr*
EMP: 53
SQ FT: 40,000
SALES (est): 32.1MM **Privately Held**
WEB: www.vendcatering.com
SIC: 5087 Vending machines & supplies

(P-7986)
W W GRAINGER INC
4700 Hamner Ave, Mira Loma (91752-1018)
PHONE...........................951 727-2300
Brian Williams, *Opers-Prdtn-Mfg*

EMP: 220
SQ FT: 20,000
SALES (corp-wide): 9.9B **Publicly Held**
WEB: www.grainger.com
SIC: 5087 Janitors' supplies
PA: W.W. Grainger, Inc.
100 Grainger Pkwy
Lake Forest IL 60045
847 535-1000

(P-7987)
WAXIES ENTERPRISES INC
901 N Canyon Pkwy, Livermore (94551)
PHONE...........................925 454-2900
Fax: 925 454-2911
John Bielenberg, *General Mgr*
Suzanne Garcia, *Human Res Dir*
Matt Lacivita, *Opers Mgr*
Cindy Lacasse, *Sales Mgr*
Tiffany McLaughlin, *Consultant*
EMP: 50
SALES (corp-wide): 220.1MM **Privately Held**
WEB: www.waxie.com
SIC: 5087 Janitors' supplies
PA: Waxie's Enterprises, Inc.
9353 Waxie Way
San Diego CA 92123
858 292-8111

(P-7988)
WEST COAST BEAUTY SUPPLY CO (HQ)
5001 Industrial Way, Benicia (94510-1033)
PHONE...........................707 748-4800
Fax: 707 748-4593
Bruce A Record, *CEO*
Wayne Clark, *Ch of Bd*
Pete Record, *President*
Jim Nordstrom, *COO*
Keiven Bauer, *Treasurer*
▲ **EMP:** 250
SQ FT: 221,000
SALES (est): 135.3MM
SALES (corp-wide): 3.8B **Publicly Held**
SIC: 5087 3069 Beauty parlor equipment & supplies; capes, vulcanized rubber or rubberized fabric; brushes, rubber
PA: Sally Beauty Holdings, Inc.
3001 Colorado Blvd
Denton TX 76210
940 898-7500

(P-7989)
WESTERN STATE DESIGN INC (PA)
2331 Tripaldi Way, Hayward (94545-5022)
PHONE...........................510 786-9271
Fax: 510 783-9748
Dennis Mack, *President*
Todd Hyrn, *CFO*
Tom Marks, *Vice Pres*
Richard Huber, *Info Tech Mgr*
Marianne Lenci, *Controller*
EMP: 70
SQ FT: 9,350
SALES (est): 27.4MM **Privately Held**
WEB: www.westernstatedesign.com
SIC: 5087 Laundry equipment & supplies

(P-7990)
WORLDWIDE INTGRTED RSURCES INC
7171 Telegraph Rd, Montebello (90640-6511)
PHONE...........................323 838-8938
Fred Morad, *President*
Sina Salamat, *CFO*
Susan Morad, *Admin Sec*
Todd M Carlson, *VP Sales*
Ana Marquez, *Manager*
▲ **EMP:** 60
SQ FT: 20,000
SALES (est): 6.6MM **Privately Held**
WEB: www.wwir.com
SIC: 5087 Cleaning & maintenance equipment & supplies

5088 Transportation Eqpt & Splys, Except Motor Vehicles Wholesale

(P-7991)
AERO PRECISION INDUSTRIES LLC
201 Lindbergh Ave, Livermore (94551-7667)
PHONE...........................925 579-5327
Fax: 925 455-9901
Francis Cowle, *President*
Richard Archer, *CFO*
Joseph Massucco, *Senior VP*
Angel Flores, *Vice Pres*
Ryann Ness, *Office Admin*
EMP: 106
SQ FT: 45,000
SALES: 126.7MM
SALES (corp-wide): 362.8MM **Privately Held**
WEB: www.apiinc.net
SIC: 5088 Aircraft & space vehicle supplies & parts
PA: Greenwich Aerogroup, Inc.
475 Steamboat Rd Fl 2
Greenwich CT 06830
203 618-4861

(P-7992)
ALIGN AEROSPACE LLC (DH)
21123 Nordhoff St, Chatsworth (91311-5816)
PHONE...........................818 727-7800
Fax: 818 773-5493
Ian Cohen,
Paul Burmeister, *CFO*
Mike McDonald, *Senior VP*
Patti Bader, *Program Mgr*
Dan Fitch, *General Mgr*
EMP: 103
SQ FT: 73,000
SALES (est): 296.6MM **Privately Held**
SIC: 5088 Aircraft & space vehicle supplies & parts

(P-7993)
ANSETT ARCFT SPARES & SVCS INC (PA)
Also Called: Ansett Aircraft Spares & Svcs
12675 Encinitas Ave, Sylmar (91342-3635)
P.O. Box Dept La, Pasadena (91185-0001)
PHONE...........................818 362-1100
Gregory Quinlan, *President*
Brad Barton, *CFO*
John Boyce, *CFO*
Luis Mora, *Vice Pres*
▲ **EMP:** 60
SQ FT: 50,000
SALES (est): 34.7MM **Privately Held**
WEB: www.ansettspares.com
SIC: 5088 Aircraft & parts

(P-7994)
APICAL INDUSTRIES INC
Also Called: Dart Aerospace
3030 Enterprise Ct Ste A, Vista (92081-8358)
PHONE...........................760 724-5300
Fax: 760 758-9612
Michael O'Reilly, *CEO*
Daniela Delarosa, *Office Mgr*
Lisa Mansfield, *Project Mgr*
Alexander Quan, *Project Engr*
Steve Montgomery, *Engineer*
EMP: 85
SQ FT: 30,000
SALES (est): 63.5MM **Privately Held**
WEB: www.apicalindustries.com
SIC: 5088 3728 Helicopter parts; aircraft landing assemblies & brakes

(P-7995)
BOEING SATELLITE SYSTEMS
2000 E El Segundo Blvd, El Segundo (90245-4501)
PHONE...........................310 662-9000
Randy Brinkley, *Principal*
Kurt Kaemerle, *Purchasing*
Alvin Lee, *Purchasing*
David McNeil, *Manager*
EMP: 115

▲ = Import ▼ = Export
◆ = Import/Export

PRODUCTS & SERVICES SECTION
5091 - Sporting & Recreational Goods & Splys Wholesale County (P-8015)

SALES (corp-wide): 96.1B **Publicly Held**
SIC: **5088** 4899 Aircraft & space vehicle supplies & parts; satellite earth stations
HQ: Boeing Satellite Systems International, Inc.
2260 E Imperial Hwy
El Segundo CA 90245
310 364-4000

(P-7996)
KIRKHILL AIRCRAFT PARTS CO (PA)
Also Called: Kapco Global
3120 Enterprise St, Brea (92821-6236)
PHONE 714 223-5400
Andrew Todhunter, *President*
John Valentine, *President*
Ron Basbas, *Vice Pres*
Lynann Collins, *Vice Pres*
Pete Curti, *Vice Pres*
EMP: 175
SQ FT: 177,000
SALES (est): 227.4MM **Privately Held**
WEB: www.kapcovaltec.com
SIC: **5088** 3728 Aircraft & parts; aircraft parts & equipment

(P-7997)
KIRKHILL AIRCRAFT PARTS CO
3101 Enterprise St, Brea (92821-6237)
PHONE 714 223-5400
EMP: 67
SALES (corp-wide): 227.4MM **Privately Held**
SIC: **5088** Aircraft & parts
PA: Kirkhill Aircraft Parts Co.
3120 Enterprise St
Brea CA 92821
714 223-5400

(P-7998)
KLX INC
1351 Charles Willard St, Carson (90746-4023)
PHONE 310 604-0228
Chris Caudana, *Branch Mgr*
Sherry Hancock, *Sales Dir*
EMP: 246
SALES (corp-wide): 1.7B **Publicly Held**
SIC: **5088** Aircraft equipment & supplies
PA: Klx Inc.
1300 Corporate Center Way # 200
Wellington FL 33414
561 383-5100

(P-7999)
LJ WALCH CO INC
6600 Preston Ave, Livermore (94551-5132)
P.O. Box 2798 (94551-2798)
PHONE 925 449-9252
Fax: 925 294-1780
Ronald W Luty, *CEO*
Tony Ippolito, *President*
Mark Nelson, *Senior VP*
Tom Walch, *Vice Pres*
Deloris Dutra, *Office Mgr*
▲ **EMP**: 60
SQ FT: 38,500
SALES (est): 29.4MM **Privately Held**
WEB: www.ljwalch.com
SIC: **5088** 7629 Aircraft & parts; aircraft electrical equipment repair

(P-8000)
LOGISTICAL SUPPORT LLC
Also Called: RTC Aerospace
20409 Prairie St, Chatsworth (91311-6029)
PHONE 818 341-3344
Joseph Lucan,
Jerry Hill, *Vice Pres*
Pat Welbourn, *Administration*
EMP: 120
SQ FT: 14,600
SALES (est): 8.8MM
SALES (corp-wide): 26.9MM **Privately Held**
WEB: www.logisticalsupport.com
SIC: **5088** Aircraft & parts
PA: Rtc Aerospace Llc
7215 45th Street Ct E
Fife WA 98424
918 407-0291

(P-8001)
ONTIC ENGINEERING AND MFG INC
20400 Plummer St, Chatsworth (91311-5372)
P.O. Box 2424 (91313-2424)
PHONE 818 678-6555
Fax: 818 678-6618
Peg Billson, *President*
Gareth Hall, *Managing Dir*
Maria Avalos, *Admin Asst*
Stacy Kern, *Admin Asst*
Marissa Murphy, *Admin Asst*
EMP: 170
SQ FT: 54,000
SALES (est): 183.3MM
SALES (corp-wide): 2.1B **Privately Held**
SIC: **5088** 3728 3812 Aircraft equipment & supplies; aircraft parts & equipment; search & navigation equipment
PA: Bba Aviation Plc
105 Wigmore Street
London W1U 1
207 514-3999

(P-8002)
PACIFIC CONTOURS CORPORATION (PA)
5340 E Hunter Ave, Anaheim (92807-2053)
PHONE 714 693-1260
Fax: 714 693-1252
Michael Rapacz, *CEO*
Jon Stannard, *COO*
Brian Patterson, *CFO*
Sury Shoney, *Vice Pres*
Frank Stump, *Program Mgr*
EMP: 95
SQ FT: 18,000
SALES: 25.4MM **Privately Held**
WEB: www.pacificcontours.com
SIC: **5088** 3728 Aircraft & parts; aircraft assemblies, subassemblies & parts

(P-8003)
ROTORCRAFT SUPPORT INC
16425 Hart St, Van Nuys (91406-4640)
PHONE 818 997-8060
Fax: 818 997-1513
Phillip G Difiore, *President*
Teri Neville, *Vice Pres*
Matt Roach, *Admin Asst*
Jason Thompson, *Asst Director*
▲ **EMP**: 54
SQ FT: 10,000
SALES (est): 28MM **Privately Held**
SIC: **5088** Aircraft & parts

(P-8004)
SAN DIEGO UNIFIED PORT DST
Also Called: Cruise Ship Terminal
1140 N Harbor Dr Ste 147, San Diego (92101-0902)
PHONE 619 683-8966
Rita Smith Pomatto, *Principal*
EMP: 114
SALES (corp-wide): 149.5MM **Privately Held**
SIC: **5088** Ships
PA: San Diego Unified Port District
3165 Pacific Hwy
San Diego CA 92101
619 686-6200

(P-8005)
SHIMADZU PRECISION INSTRS INC (DH)
Also Called: Shimadzu Medical Systems Div
3645 N Lakewood Blvd, Long Beach (90808-1797)
PHONE 562 420-6226
Fax: 310 517-9180
Yutaka Nakamura, *CEO*
Koki Aoyama, *President*
Atsushi Nishizaki, *President*
Akira Watanabe, *President*
Patrick Fromal, *Regional Mgr*
▲ **EMP**: 52
SQ FT: 60,000
SALES (est): 169MM
SALES (corp-wide): 2.9B **Privately Held**
WEB: www.spi-inc.com
SIC: **5088** 5047 5084 Aircraft equipment & supplies; medical equipment & supplies; industrial machinery & equipment
HQ: Shimadzu America, Inc.
7102 Riverwood Dr
Columbia MD 21046
410 381-1227

(P-8006)
STRECH PLASTICS INC
900 John St Ste J, Banning (92220-6204)
PHONE 951 922-2224
Fax: 909 922-2228
James Strech, *President*
Shon Carey, *Opers Mgr*
Ray Strech, *Production*
Barbara Davis, *Manager*
▲ **EMP**: 50
SQ FT: 52,000
SALES (est): 23MM **Privately Held**
WEB: www.strechplastics.com
SIC: **5088** 3949 Golf carts; sporting & athletic goods

(P-8007)
TPS AVIATION INC (PA)
1515 Crocker Ave, Hayward (94544-7038)
PHONE 510 475-1010
Fax: 510 475-8817
George Sozaburo Kujiraoka, *CEO*
J K Milanes, *Treasurer*
Piera Diganci, *Executive*
Grace Kitagawa, *General Mgr*
G S Kitagawa, *Admin Sec*
EMP: 100
SQ FT: 58,700
SALES (est): 69.9MM **Privately Held**
WEB: www.tpsaviation.com
SIC: **5088** 5065 Aircraft & space vehicle supplies & parts; aircraft engines & engine parts; aircraft equipment & supplies; guided missiles & space vehicles; electronic parts

(P-8008)
UNICAL AVIATION INC (PA)
680 S Lemon Ave, City of Industry (91789-2934)
PHONE 626 813-1901
Han Tan, *President*
Fred Goetschel, *President*
Mercy Tan, *CFO*
Mercy Tjiptorahardjo, *Treasurer*
Florence Sy, *Exec VP*
▲ **EMP**: 190
SQ FT: 480,000
SALES (est): 206.8MM **Privately Held**
WEB: www.unical.com
SIC: **5088** Aircraft & parts

(P-8009)
WESCO AIRCRAFT HARDWARE CORP (HQ)
24911 Avenue Stanford, Valencia (91355-1281)
PHONE 661 775-7200
Fax: 661 295-0515
Dave Castagnola, *CEO*
Alex Murray, *COO*
Gregory A Hann, *CFO*
George Heff, *CFO*
Richard Weller, *CFO*
▲ **EMP**: 370 **EST**: 1953
SALES: 1.5B
SALES (corp-wide): 1.5B **Publicly Held**
SIC: **5088** Aircraft & parts
PA: Wesco Aircraft Holdings, Inc.
24911 Avenue Stanford
Valencia CA 91355
661 775-7200

(P-8010)
WILLIAM F KELLOGG CORPORATION
Also Called: Airmotive Carburetor Co
475 W Riverside Dr 479dr, Burbank (91506-3256)
PHONE 818 845-7455
Elaine Hubbell, *CEO*
Dennis Wright, *President*
EMP: 100 **EST**: 1947
SQ FT: 7,400
SALES: 2MM **Privately Held**
SIC: **5088** 7699 Aircraft engines & engine parts; engine repair & replacement, non-automotive

(P-8011)
YAMAHA MOTOR CORPORATION USA (HQ)
6555 Katella Ave, Cypress (90630-5101)
PHONE 714 761-7300
Fax: 714 761-7302
Toshi Kato, *CEO*
Phil Dyskow, *President*
Richard Hinsz, *COO*
Takuwy Watanabe, *Corp Secy*
Dean Burnett, *Vice Pres*
◆ **EMP**: 400
SQ FT: 200,000
SALES (est): 1.2B
SALES (corp-wide): 13.1B **Privately Held**
WEB: www.yamaha-motor.com
SIC: **5088** 5013 5091 5012 Marine crafts & supplies; golf carts; motor vehicle supplies & new parts; boats, canoes, watercrafts & equipment; motorcycles; snowmobiles; motor scooters; recreation vehicles, all-terrain
PA: Yamaha Motor Co., Ltd.
2500, Shingai
Iwata SZO 438-0
538 321-103

5091 Sporting & Recreational Goods & Splys Wholesale

(P-8012)
BAUER HOCKEY INC
Also Called: Easton Hockey
7855 Haskell Ave Ste 200, Van Nuys (91406-1935)
PHONE 818 782-6445
Bernard McDonell, *Ch of Bd*
EMP: 423 **Privately Held**
SIC: **5091** Sporting & recreation goods
HQ: Bauer Hockey, Inc.
100 Domain Dr Ste 1
Exeter NH 03833
603 430-2111

(P-8013)
CALLAWAY GOLF BALL OPRTONS INC
2180 Rutherford Rd, Carlsbad (92008-7328)
PHONE 760 931-1771
Chip Brewer, *CEO*
Moira Garcia, *Executive Asst*
EMP: 1700 **EST**: 2003
SALES (est): 525K
SALES (corp-wide): 843.7MM **Publicly Held**
SIC: **5091** Golf equipment
PA: Callaway Golf Company
2180 Rutherford Rd
Carlsbad CA 92008
760 931-1771

(P-8014)
CHEM QUIP INC
Also Called: White House Sales
2551 Land Ave, Sacramento (95815-2363)
PHONE 916 923-5091
Fax: 530 241-6743
Don Aston, *CEO*
Greg Durkee, *President*
Steve Hubbard, *CFO*
Brain Long, *Admin Sec*
Sarah Bastiani, *Purchasing*
EMP: 62
SQ FT: 20,000
SALES: 24MM **Privately Held**
WEB: www.chemquip.com
SIC: **5091** 5169 Swimming pools, equipment & supplies; chlorine

(P-8015)
DAIWA CORPORATION
Also Called: Daiwa Golf Company Division
11137 Warland Dr, Cypress (90630-5034)
P.O. Box 6600 (90630-0066)
PHONE 562 375-6800
Tomoaki Komatsu, *CEO*
Tad Suzuki, *President*
William Steiner, *Vice Pres*
Gene Taniguchi, *Vice Pres*
Cynthia Young, *Vice Pres*

5091 - Sporting & Recreational Goods & Splys Wholesale County (P-8016)

◆ EMP: 58
SALES (est): 21.7MM
SALES (corp-wide): 675.3MM Privately Held
WEB: www.daiwa.com
SIC: 5091 3949 Fishing tackle; golf equipment
PA: Globeride, Inc.
3-14-16, Maesawa
Higashi Kurume TKY 203-0
424 752-111

(P-8016)
EASTON HOCKEY INC (DH)
Also Called: Eastern Sports
7855 Haskell Ave Ste 200, Van Nuys (91406-1935)
PHONE.................................818 782-6445
Fax: 818 782-0930
Mary George, CEO
Anthony Palma, President
Mark Tripp, CFO
Duke Stump, Senior VP
Mike Zlaket, Vice Pres
◆ EMP: 500
SQ FT: 30,000
SALES (est): 247.2MM
SALES (corp-wide): 820.9MM Privately Held
WEB: www.eastonbike.com
SIC: 5091 Sporting & recreation goods
HQ: Brg Sports, Inc.
5550 Scotts Valley Dr
Scotts Valley CA 95066
831 461-7500

(P-8017)
EVIKECOM INC
2801 W Mission Rd, Alhambra (91803-1223)
PHONE.................................626 286-0360
Fax: 626 285-8622
Evike Change, CEO
Julie Chang, COO
Clifford Tjing, Mktg Dir
Cargan Lu, Marketing Staff
George Melahn, Marketing Staff
▲ EMP: 70
SALES (est): 27.9MM Privately Held
SIC: 5091 5941 Sporting & recreation goods; sporting goods & bicycle shops

(P-8018)
FESTIVAL FUN PARKS LLC
Also Called: Raging Waters San Dimas 703
111 Raging Waters Dr, San Dimas (91773-3928)
PHONE.................................909 802-2200
Robert Zues, General Mgr
EMP: 700
SALES (corp-wide): 145.2MM Privately Held
SIC: 5091 Water slides (recreation park)
PA: Festival Fun Parks, Llc
4590 Macarthur Blvd # 400
Newport Beach CA 92660
949 261-0404

(P-8019)
GENERAL POOL & SPA SUPPLY INC (PA)
11285 Sunco Dr, Rancho Cordova (95742-6517)
PHONE.................................916 853-2401
Fax: 916 853-2407
Philip Gelhaus, President
Patty Gelhaus, Corp Secy
Mark Yomogida, Vice Pres
▼ EMP: 55
SQ FT: 25,000
SALES (est): 27.4MM Privately Held
WEB: www.gpspool.com
SIC: 5091 Swimming pools, equipment & supplies; spa equipment & supplies

(P-8020)
GIANT BICYCLE INC (DH)
3587 Old Conejo Rd, Newbury Park (91320-2122)
PHONE.................................805 267-4600
Dave Karneboge, Vice Pres
Coree Chen, Info Tech Dir
Anmin LI, Accounting Mgr
Kathy Fliesher, Accountant
Russ Okawa, Marketing Mgr
▲ EMP: 55

SQ FT: 75,000
SALES (est): 37.2MM
SALES (corp-wide): 1.8B Privately Held
SIC: 5091 Bicycles
HQ: Gaiwin B.V.
Pascallaan 66
Lelystad 8218
320 296-296

(P-8021)
INTEX RECREATION CORP (PA)
4001 Via Oro Ave Ste 210, Long Beach (90810-1400)
PHONE.................................310 549-5400
Fax: 310 513-6905
Tien P Zee, President
Tom Lindahl, Executive
Wayne Farmer, Information Mgr
Joseph Garcia, Network Tech
Kevin Wong, Accounting Mgr
◆ EMP: 66
SQ FT: 80,000
SALES (est): 173.5MM Privately Held
WEB: www.intexcorp.net
SIC: 5091 5092 5021 3081 Watersports equipment & supplies; toys; waterbeds; vinyl film & sheet; polyethylene film

(P-8022)
MANDUKA LLC (HQ)
2121 Park Pl Ste 250, El Segundo (90245-4705)
PHONE.................................310 426-1495
Sky Meltzer, CEO
Beau Swenson, CFO
Jill Krishnamurthy, VP Finance
Andrew Chen, Accountant
Stephen Suzuki, Accountant
▲ EMP: 50
SALES: 32.2MM
SALES (corp-wide): 55.5MM Privately Held
SIC: 5091 5941 5699 Sporting & recreation goods; specialty sport supplies; golf, tennis & ski shops; sports apparel
PA: Valor Equity Partner Holdings, Llc
875 N Michigan Ave # 3214
Chicago IL 60611
312 683-1900

(P-8023)
NATIONAL LIQUIDATORS
2715 W Coast Hwy, Newport Beach (92663-4723)
PHONE.................................949 631-6715
Robert G Tony, Director
Robert Tony, President
Matthew Amata, Vice Pres
Michael A Whiteman, Info Tech Mgr
Michael Bacchocchi, VP Finance
EMP: 50
SALES (est): 3.3MM Privately Held
WEB: www.yachtauctions.com
SIC: 5091 Boats, canoes, watercrafts & equipment

(P-8024)
NEW CENTURY SCIENCE & TECH
18031 Cortney Ct, City of Industry (91748-1203)
PHONE.................................626 581-5500
Carson Cheng, President
Diana Avala, Accountant
EMP: 60
SALES: 5MM Privately Held
SIC: 5091 Sporting & recreation goods

(P-8025)
POOLMASTER INC
770 Del Paso Rd, Sacramento (95834-1117)
P.O. Box 340308 (95834-0308)
PHONE.................................916 567-9800
Fax: 818 567-9880
Leon H Tager, President
Carol Tager, Corp Secy
Nora Davis, Vice Pres
Darrell Perry, Graphic Designe
Scheri Adams, Human Res Dir
◆ EMP: 55
SQ FT: 100,000
SALES (est): 28.8MM Privately Held
WEB: www.poolmaster.com
SIC: 5091 3944 Sporting & recreation goods; games, toys & children's vehicles

(P-8026)
RAX INC
12220 Parkway Centre Dr, Poway (92064-6867)
PHONE.................................858 715-2500
Les Edelstein, President
Neville Berman, Vice Pres
EMP: 50
SALES (est): 3.9MM
SALES (corp-wide): 22.2MM Privately Held
WEB: www.rax.com
SIC: 5091 Sporting & recreation goods
PA: Moteng, Inc.
12220 Parkway Centre Dr
Poway CA 92064
858 715-2500

(P-8027)
RAZOR USA LLC (PA)
12723 166th St, Cerritos (90703-2102)
P.O. Box 3610 (90703-3610)
PHONE.................................562 345-6000
Fax: 562 345-6087
Carlton Calvin, Mng Member
Ryan McLean, COO
Larry Rosolowski, CFO
Carlton Calyin, Bd of Directors
Francine Aldana, Vice Pres
◆ EMP: 60
SQ FT: 50,000
SALES (est): 37.5MM Privately Held
WEB: www.razor.com
SIC: 5091 Sporting & recreation goods

(P-8028)
REC CENTER
501 Stanyan St, San Francisco (94117-1898)
PHONE.................................415 831-6818
Elizabeth Goldstein, Director
Joaquin Avelino, Officer
Eugene Hsin, Officer
Andriy Volynets, Officer
Patricia Walsh, Admin Sec
EMP: 129 EST: 2011
SALES (est): 7.2MM Privately Held
SIC: 5091 Water slides (recreation park)

(P-8029)
SHIMANO AMERICAN CORPORATION (HQ)
1 Holland, Irvine (92618-2597)
PHONE.................................949 951-5003
Fax: 949 768-0920
David Pfeiffer, President
Jim Lafrance, Exec VP
Koichi Shimazu, Senior VP
Robert Bakker, Area Mgr
Robert Milne, Area Mgr
▲ EMP: 150
SQ FT: 122,000
SALES (est): 95.6MM
SALES (corp-wide): 3B Privately Held
SIC: 5091 Bicycle parts & accessories; fishing equipment & supplies
PA: Shimano Inc.
3-77, Oimatsucho, Sakai-Ku
Sakai OSK 590-0
722 233-210

(P-8030)
SPORT CHALET LLC
7541 Woodman Pl, Van Nuys (91405-1545)
PHONE.................................818 781-4000
Benjamin Bass, Branch Mgr
Mike Wendell, General Mgr
Dave Knecht, Buyer
Edd Desbrow, Director
EMP: 65
SALES (corp-wide): 1.9B Privately Held
WEB: www.sportchalet.com
SIC: 5091 Sporting & recreation goods
HQ: Sport Chalet Llc
160 Corporate Ct
Meriden CT 06450
818 790-2717

(P-8031)
SPORTS BASEMENT
1590 Bryant St, San Francisco (94103-4808)
PHONE.................................408 732-0300
Eric Prosnitz, Partner
Eden Slezin, General Mgr

Dave Rumsfeld, Mktg Dir
EMP: 99
SALES (est): 9.6MM Privately Held
SIC: 5091 Sporting & recreation goods

(P-8032)
TROY LEE DESIGNS (PA)
155 E Rincon St, Corona (92879-1328)
PHONE.................................951 371-5219
Troy Michael Lee, President
Ricardo Gonzalez, Vice Pres
Maki Ushiroyama, Creative Dir
Bill Keefe, General Mgr
Barbie McGee, Financial Exec
▲ EMP: 79
SQ FT: 6,000
SALES (est): 20MM Privately Held
WEB: www.troyleedesigns.com
SIC: 5091 7336 Sporting & recreation goods; graphic arts & related design

(P-8033)
TUM YETO INC
Also Called: Foundation Super Skateboard
2001 Commercial St, San Diego (92113-1109)
PHONE.................................619 232-7523
Fax: 619 232-9666
Tod Swank, CEO
Tara Lewis, Controller
Jessica Nuttaoo, Bookkeeper
▲ EMP: 50
SQ FT: 29,000
SALES (est): 10.3MM Privately Held
WEB: www.tumyeto.com
SIC: 5091 5137 Sporting & recreation goods; sportswear, women's & children's

(P-8034)
WARRIOR CUSTOM GOLF INC (PA)
Also Called: Warrior Golf
15 Mason, Irvine (92618-2707)
PHONE.................................949 699-2499
Brendan M Flaherty, CEO
Aaron Mun, President
John Fitzmartin, Vice Pres
Pete Wheelahan, Vice Pres
Lora Vanessen, Admin Sec
▲ EMP: 180
SQ FT: 20,000
SALES (est): 56.5MM Privately Held
WEB: www.warriorcustomgolf.com
SIC: 5091 5941 Golf equipment; sporting goods & bicycle shops

5092 Toys & Hobby Goods & Splys Wholesale

(P-8035)
A L S INDUSTRIES INC (PA)
1942 Artesia Blvd, Torrance (90504-3599)
PHONE.................................310 532-9262
Fax: 310 329-0982
Richard D Smith, President
David Albert, Vice Pres
Misti Hayes, Executive
▲ EMP: 50 EST: 1970
SQ FT: 70,000
SALES (est): 11.4MM Privately Held
SIC: 5092 Video games

(P-8036)
AURORA WORLD INC
8820 Mercury Ln, Pico Rivera (90660-6706)
PHONE.................................562 205-1222
Fax: 562 948-1661
Heui-Yul Noh, CEO
Michael Kessler, Chief Mktg Ofcr
Kee Sun Hong, Exec VP
Irene Cho, Admin Asst
Kelly Lee, Admin Asst
◆ EMP: 110
SQ FT: 100,000
SALES: 72.3MM
SALES (corp-wide): 77.5MM Privately Held
WEB: www.auroragift.com
SIC: 5092 Toys
PA: Aurora World Corporation
624 Teheran-Ro, Gangnam-Gu
Seoul SEO 06175
234 204-114

PRODUCTS & SERVICES SECTION

5093 - Scrap & Waste Materials Wholesale County (P-8058)

(P-8037)
AZUBU NORTH AMERICA INC
15303 Ventura Blvd # 220, Sherman Oaks (91403-3110)
PHONE..................................310 759-9529
Ian Sharpe, *CEO*
Jason Katz, *COO*
Abe Gottesman, *Vice Pres*
Andrew Greaves, *Vice Pres*
EMP: 50
SALES (est): 9.3MM **Privately Held**
SIC: 5092 5734 Video games; software, computer games

(P-8038)
BANDAI NAMCO ENTRMT AMER INC
Also Called: Ndga
2051 Mission College Blvd, Santa Clara (95054-1519)
PHONE..................................408 235-2000
Kenji Hisatsune, *CEO*
Masaaki Tsuji, *President*
Hide Irie, *COO*
Shuji Nakata, *CFO*
Eric Hartness, *Vice Pres*
▲ **EMP:** 200
SQ FT: 51,118
SALES (est): 182.5MM
SALES (corp-wide): 4.9B **Privately Held**
WEB: www.namcobandaigames.com
SIC: 5092 Video games
HQ: Bandai Namco Holdings Usa Inc.
2120 Park Pl Ste 120
El Segundo CA 90245

(P-8039)
BLUE BOX OPCO LLC (PA)
Also Called: Infantino
4920 Carroll Canyon Rd # 200, San Diego (92121-3735)
PHONE..................................800 840-4916
Alex Chan, *CEO*
Alicia Barone, *Executive*
Gail Smith, *VP Mktg*
EMP: 52 EST: 2014
SALES (est): 25.3MM **Privately Held**
SIC: 5092 Toys & hobby goods & supplies

(P-8040)
CAPCOM ENTERTAINMENT INC
Also Called: Capcom U.S.a
185 Berry St Ste 1200, San Francisco (94107-1794)
PHONE..................................650 350-6500
Kazuhiro Abe, *CEO*
Hiroshi Tobisawa, *President*
Mark Beaumont, *COO*
Haruhiro Tsujimoto, *COO*
Germaine Gioia, *Senior VP*
▲ **EMP:** 80
SALES (est): 31MM
SALES (corp-wide): 658.2MM **Privately Held**
SIC: 5092 Video games
HQ: Capcom U.S.A. Inc
185 Berry St Ste 1200
San Francisco CA 94107
650 350-6500

(P-8041)
CAPCOM U S A INC (HQ)
185 Berry St Ste 1200, San Francisco (94107-1794)
PHONE..................................650 350-6500
Fax: 408 774-3996
Koko Ishikawa, *President*
Hirohisa Tachibana, *Vice Pres*
Mari Andrews, *Executive Asst*
Jason Jones, *CTO*
Elizabeth Chiu, *Graphic Designe*
▲ **EMP:** 180
SALES (est): 55.7MM
SALES (corp-wide): 658.2MM **Privately Held**
SIC: 5092 7993 7372 Video games; arcades; prepackaged software
PA: Capcom Co., Ltd.
3-1-3, Uchihiranomachi, Chuo-Ku
Osaka OSK 540-0
669 203-600

(P-8042)
DELTA CREATIVE INC
2690 Pellissier Pl, City of Industry (90601-1507)
PHONE..................................800 423-4135
Fax: 562 695-4227
William B George, *President*
Martina Mueller, *CEO*
Alexander Ritchie, *Vice Pres*
Sven Maushake, *CTO*
▲ **EMP:** 105
SQ FT: 112,000
SALES (est): 14.6MM
SALES (corp-wide): 10B **Privately Held**
WEB: www.deltacreative.com
SIC: 5092 5198 Arts & crafts equipment & supplies; paints
HQ: Diethelm Keller Brands Ag
Muhlebachstrasse 20
ZUrich ZH 8008

(P-8043)
DREAMGEAR LLC
20001 S Western Ave, Torrance (90501-1306)
PHONE..................................310 222-5522
Fax: 310 222-5577
Yahya Ahdout, *CEO*
Bre Holley, *Senior VP*
Mark Prince, *Business Dir*
Juliet Tablerion, *Administration*
Daniel Ahdout, *Research*
◆ **EMP:** 70
SQ FT: 60,000
SALES (est): 35.9MM **Privately Held**
WEB: www.dreamgear.com
SIC: 5092 Video games

(P-8044)
HOBBY SHACK (PA)
Also Called: Global Hobby Distributors
18480 Bandilier Cir, Fountain Valley (92708-7011)
PHONE..................................714 964-0827
Paul Bender, *CEO*
Kevin Jacobs, *Shareholder*
Matt Fales, *President*
Gary Bender, *CFO*
Sally Bender, *Corp Secy*
▲ **EMP:** 50
SQ FT: 50,000
SALES (est): 40.3MM **Privately Held**
WEB: www.globalhobby.com
SIC: 5092 Toys & hobby goods & supplies

(P-8045)
INTERNATIONAL TOY INC
17682 Cowan, Irvine (92614-1608)
PHONE..................................949 333-3777
Steve Asher, *President*
EMP: 50
SQ FT: 2,500
SALES (est): 19.4MM **Privately Held**
SIC: 5092 Toys & hobby goods & supplies

(P-8046)
JAKKS SALES CORPORATION
2951 28th St Ste 51, Santa Monica (90405-2961)
PHONE..................................424 268-9444
Jack Friedman, *Ch of Bd*
Stephen Berman, *President*
Joel Bennett, *CFO*
EMP: 50
SALES (est): 4.8MM **Publicly Held**
SIC: 5092 Toys
PA: Jakks Pacific, Inc.
2951 28th St Ste 51
Santa Monica CA 90405

(P-8047)
KELLYTOY WORLDWIDE INC
4811 S Alameda St, Vernon (90058-2805)
PHONE..................................323 923-1300
Fax: 323 584-9566
Jonathan Kelly, *President*
Hannie Kelly, *Vice Pres*
Ben Kim, *Purch Mgr*
John Pablo, *Sales Staff*
▲ **EMP:** 70
SALES (est): 8.8MM
SALES (corp-wide): 33.7MM **Privately Held**
SIC: 5092 Toys

PA: Kellytoy (Usa), Inc.
4811 S Alameda St
Vernon CA 90058
323 923-1300

(P-8048)
KIXEYE INC (PA)
333 Bush St Fl 19, San Francisco (94104-2860)
PHONE..................................415 956-3413
Will Harbin, *CEO*
John Getze, *Vice Pres*
Neil Shepherd, *Vice Pres*
Katie Obrien, *Executive Asst*
Kaci Weirich, *Admin Asst*
EMP: 53
SALES (est): 36.1MM **Privately Held**
SIC: 5092 Video games

(P-8049)
MATTEL TOY COMPANY
333 Continental Blvd, El Segundo (90245-5032)
PHONE..................................310 252-2357
Robert Eckert, *CEO*
Bruce L Stein, *COO*
Brett M Hyder, *Engineer*
▼ **EMP:** 1900
SALES (est): 221.8MM
SALES (corp-wide): 5.7B **Publicly Held**
SIC: 5092 Toys & games
PA: Mattel, Inc.
333 Continental Blvd
El Segundo CA 90245
310 252-2000

(P-8050)
MGA ENTERTAINMENT INC (PA)
16300 Roscoe Blvd Ste 150, Van Nuys (91406-1257)
PHONE..................................818 894-2525
Isaac Larian, *President*
Ninette Pembleton, *Vice Pres*
David Roman, *Sr Software Eng*
Kevin Sandieson, *Draft/Design*
Robert Montesdeoca, *Analyst*
◆ **EMP:** 300
SQ FT: 50,000
SALES (est): 435.6MM **Privately Held**
WEB: www.mgae.com
SIC: 5092 Toys & games

(P-8051)
PERFORMANCE DESIGNED PDTS LLC (HQ)
2300 W Empire Ave # 600, Burbank (91504-3399)
PHONE..................................323 234-9911
Fax: 323 325-9555
Chris Richards,
Kathryn Browne, *President*
Storm Orion, *President*
Kevin Johnson, *CFO*
Dave Muscatel, *CFO*
▲ **EMP:** 64
SQ FT: 18,000
SALES (est): 202.8MM
SALES (corp-wide): 4.2B **Privately Held**
WEB: www.pelicanacc.com
SIC: 5092 Toys & games; video games
PA: Patriarch Partners, Llc
1 Broadway Fl 5
New York NY 10004
212 825-0550

(P-8052)
RADICA ENTERPRISES LTD
Also Called: Radica USA
333 Continental Blvd, El Segundo (90245-5032)
PHONE..................................310 252-2000
Patrick Feely, *CEO*
David Lau, *Controller*
Gary Jones, *Director*
◆ **EMP:** 57
SQ FT: 24,000
SALES (est): 3.7MM
SALES (corp-wide): 5.7B **Publicly Held**
SIC: 5092 Toy novelties & amusements
HQ: Radica Games Limited
C/O Appleby Spurling Hunter
Hamilton
441 292-8666

(P-8053)
SOLUTIONS 2 GO LLC
111 Theory Ste 250, Irvine (92617-3041)
PHONE..................................949 825-7700
Nima Taghavi, *Mng Member*
Wayne Yodzio, *President*
Michael Maas,
▲ **EMP:** 56
SQ FT: 14,000
SALES: 300MM **Privately Held**
SIC: 5092 Toys & hobby goods & supplies

(P-8054)
SONY INTRCTVE ENTRMT AMER LLC
Also Called: 989 Studios
10075 Barnes Canyon Rd, San Diego (92121-2723)
PHONE..................................858 824-5501
Shu Yoshida, *Vice Pres*
Charles Connoy, *Info Tech Dir*
Rick Rossiter, *Info Tech Mgr*
Ryan Patterson, *Network Enginr*
Catherine Wozney, *Manager*
EMP: 165
SALES (corp-wide): 69.2B **Privately Held**
SIC: 5092 Toys & hobby goods & supplies
HQ: Sony Interactive Entertainment America Llc
2207 Bridgepointe Pkwy
Foster City CA 94404
650 655-8000

(P-8055)
SONY INTRCTVE ENTRMT AMER LLC (DH)
2207 Bridgepointe Pkwy, Foster City (94404-5060)
P.O. Box 5888, San Mateo (94402-5888)
PHONE..................................650 655-8000
Fax: 650 655-8001
Shawn Layden, *Mng Member*
Peter Dille, *Senior VP*
Andrew J House, *Senior VP*
Guy W Longworth, *Senior VP*
Philip Rosenberg, *Vice Pres*
▲ **EMP:** 600
SQ FT: 300,000
SALES (est): 2.3B
SALES (corp-wide): 69.2B **Privately Held**
WEB: www.scea.sony.com
SIC: 5092 Video games
HQ: Sony Corporation Of America
25 Madison Ave Fl 27
New York NY 10010
212 833-8000

(P-8056)
STK INTERNATIONAL INC
6160 Peach Tree St, Compton (90220)
PHONE..................................310 720-1277
Stuart Kole, *President*
◆ **EMP:** 70
SQ FT: 120,000
SALES: 12MM **Privately Held**
WEB: www.stkinternational.com
SIC: 5092 5072 5023 Toys; hand tools; power tools & accessories; home furnishings; kitchenware

---

5093 Scrap & Waste Materials Wholesale

(P-8057)
AADLEN BROTHERS AUTO WRECKING (PA)
11590 Tuxford St, Sun Valley (91352-3112)
PHONE..................................323 875-1400
Fax: 818 767-4376
Sam Adlen, *President*
Samuel Lewinstein, *Corp Secy*
Jorge E Trujillo, *Opers Mgr*
Mitchel J Ezer, *Agent*
EMP: 79
SALES (est): 17.7MM **Privately Held**
WEB: www.aadlenbros.com
SIC: 5093 Metal scrap & waste materials

(P-8058)
ALCO IRON & METAL CO (PA)
2140 Davis St, San Leandro (94577-1062)
PHONE..................................510 562-1107
Fax: 510 562-1354

5093 - Scrap & Waste Materials Wholesale County (P-8059)

Kem Kantor, *President*
Michael Bercovich, *COO*
Keith Kantor, *Vice Pres*
Kevin Kantor, *Vice Pres*
Tony Nam, *Vice Pres*
▼ **EMP:** 100
SQ FT: 35,000
SALES (est): 70.7MM **Privately Held**
SIC: 5093 5051 Metal scrap & waste materials; steel

(P-8059)
AMERICA CHUNG NAM (GROUP) (PA)
1163 Fairway Dr, City of Industry (91789-2846)
PHONE..................................909 839-8383
Peter Wang, *CEO*
Kevin Zhao, *CFO*
John Wong, *Vice Pres*
Ming Chung Liu, *Principal*
Laura Hu, *Opers Mgr*
▼ **EMP:** 125
SQ FT: 30,000
SALES (est): 182.8MM **Privately Held**
WEB: www.acni.net
SIC: 5093 Waste paper

(P-8060)
AMERICA CHUNG NAM LLC (HQ)
Also Called: A C N
1163 Fairway Dr Fl 3, City of Industry (91789-2851)
PHONE..................................909 839-8383
Fax: 909 869-6310
Teresa Cheung, *CEO*
Sam Liu, *COO*
Kevin Zhao, *CFO*
Ming Liu, *Vice Pres*
Scott Taylor, *Vice Pres*
▼ **EMP:** 135
SALES (est): 150MM
SALES (corp-wide): 182.8MM **Privately Held**
SIC: 5093 Waste paper
PA: America Chung Nam (Group) Holdings Llc
1163 Fairway Dr
City Of Industry CA 91789
909 839-8383

(P-8061)
AMERICAN METAL & IRON INC
2377 Tulip Rd, San Jose (95128-1141)
P.O. Box 610 (95106-0610)
PHONE..................................408 452-0777
Howard Misle, *President*
Debra L Ginestra, *Principal*
John Velasquez, *Accounting Mgr*
◆ **EMP:** 55
SQ FT: 10,000
SALES (est): 5.8MM **Privately Held**
WEB: www.amerimetals.com
SIC: 5093 Metal scrap & waste materials

(P-8062)
ANGELUS WESTERN PPR FIBERS INC
2474 Porter St, Los Angeles (90021-2511)
PHONE..................................213 623-9221
Fax: 213 623-3435
Greg Rouchon, *President*
Steve Young, *Treasurer*
Tom Rouchon, *Vice Pres*
David Jones, *Admin Sec*
Rimma Markarian, *Manager*
EMP: 51 **EST:** 1977
SQ FT: 10,000
SALES (est): 25MM **Privately Held**
SIC: 5093 Waste paper

(P-8063)
B & B PLASTICS RECYCLERS INC (PA)
3040 N Locust Ave, Rialto (92377-3706)
PHONE..................................909 829-3606
Baltasar Mejia, *President*
Bacilio Mejia, *Vice Pres*
Sophia Cresto, *Accountant*
Maria Carreon, *Opers Mgr*
Ann Vallejo, *Manager*
EMP: 82
SQ FT: 100,000
SALES (est): 155.3MM **Privately Held**
SIC: 5093 2673 Scrap & waste materials; bags: plastic, laminated & coated

(P-8064)
BAJA METAL SHREDDER LLC
402 W Broadway Ste 1120, San Diego (92101-8513)
PHONE..................................847 622-9898
Lawrence S Nora, *President*
Lisa Fiorenza, *CFO*
EMP: 54
SALES (est): 5.2MM **Privately Held**
WEB: www.bajametals.com
SIC: 5093 Ferrous metal scrap & waste; nonferrous metals scrap

(P-8065)
BESTWAY RECYCLING COMPANY INC (PA)
2268 Firestone Blvd, Los Angeles (90002-1546)
P.O. Box 109, South Gate (90280-0109)
PHONE..................................323 588-8157
Fax: 323 588-8436
Edward Young Kim, *President*
David Cho, *CFO*
Nam Sook Kim, *Corp Secy*
Chris Charuwat, *Administration*
Dong Kim, *Opers Mgr*
▼ **EMP:** 52 **EST:** 1963
SQ FT: 165,000
SALES (est): 20.3MM **Privately Held**
SIC: 5093 Waste paper; nonferrous metals scrap; bottles, waste; plastics scrap

(P-8066)
CASS INC (PA)
2730 Peralta St, Oakland (94607-1707)
P.O. Box 24222 (94623-1222)
PHONE..................................510 893-6476
Fax: 510 893-2012
Edward B Kangeter IV, *CEO*
Chal Sulprizio, *President*
Carmen Zeng, *CFO*
Chris Blake, *Executive*
Anne Lee, *Admin Asst*
◆ **EMP:** 60
SQ FT: 20,000
SALES (est): 48MM **Privately Held**
SIC: 5093 Nonferrous metals scrap

(P-8067)
CEDARWOOD-YOUNG COMPANY (PA)
Also Called: Allan Company
14620 Joanbridge St, Baldwin Park (91706-1750)
PHONE..................................626 962-4047
Jason Young, *President*
Michael Ochniak, *CFO*
Stephen Young, *Chairman*
Francisco Del Rincon, *Vice Pres*
Don Rogers, *Vice Pres*
▼ **EMP:** 60
SQ FT: 4,350
SALES (est): 297.7MM **Privately Held**
WEB: www.allancompany.com
SIC: 5093 Waste paper

(P-8068)
CEDARWOOD-YOUNG COMPANY
Also Called: Allan Company
14618 Arrow Hwy, Baldwin Park (91706-1733)
PHONE..................................626 962-4047
Fax: 626 962-7611
Ernesto Lopez, *Branch Mgr*
Francisco Ricon, *Vice Pres*
David Romberg, *Vice Pres*
Jason Young, *Vice Pres*
Liz Barnard, *Manager*
EMP: 55
SQ FT: 10,664
SALES (corp-wide): 338.2MM **Privately Held**
WEB: www.allancompany.com
SIC: 5093 2611 Scrap & waste materials; pulp mills
PA: Cedarwood-Young Company
14620 Joanbridge St
Baldwin Park CA 91706
626 962-4047

(P-8069)
CITY FIBERS INC (PA)
2500 S Santa Fe Ave, Vernon (90058-1116)
P.O. Box 58646, Los Angeles (90058-0646)
PHONE..................................323 583-1013
Fax: 323 583-8424
David T Jones, *President*
Kipp Jones, *Vice Pres*
Scott Jones, *Info Tech Mgr*
Vanessa Acosta, *Purchasing*
Maria Quiane, *Asst Mgr*
EMP: 60
SQ FT: 55,000
SALES (est): 33.8MM **Privately Held**
SIC: 5093 4953 Waste paper & cloth materials; recycling, waste materials

(P-8070)
GEORGIA-PACIFIC LLC
15500 Valley View Ave, La Mirada (90638-5230)
PHONE..................................562 926-8888
Jeff McCranie, *Manager*
Kelley Hill, *Human Res Mgr*
Vanessa Martinez, *Human Res Mgr*
John Taylor, *Plant Mgr*
Scott Benson, *Manager*
EMP: 81
SALES (corp-wide): 26.7B **Privately Held**
SIC: 5093 Waste paper
HQ: Georgia-Pacific Llc
133 Peachtree St Ne # 4810
Atlanta GA 30303
404 652-4000

(P-8071)
GLOBAL PET INC
145 Malbert St, Perris (92570-8624)
PHONE..................................951 657-5466
Nadim Salim Bahou, *President*
Carl Bettis, *Vice Pres*
Patti Gilmour, *Vice Pres*
Paul Bahou, *VP Sales*
▲ **EMP:** 100
SQ FT: 55,000
SALES (est): 48.7MM **Privately Held**
WEB: www.globalpet.com
SIC: 5093 4953 Plastics scrap; recycling, waste materials

(P-8072)
GREENPATH RECOVERY WEST INC
Also Called: Greenpath Recovery Recycl Svcs
330 W Citrus St Ste 250, Colton (92324-1422)
PHONE..................................909 954-0686
Joe Castro, *President*
Jeffrey Racoosin, *VP Opers*
Rebecca Somerville, *Opers Staff*
Vicky Garcia, *Manager*
Steve Chavez, *Consultant*
EMP: 60
SQ FT: 90,000
SALES (est): 38.4MM **Privately Held**
SIC: 5093 3089 2821 Scrap & waste materials; plastic processing; injection molding of plastics; plastics materials & resins; molding compounds, plastics

(P-8073)
IMS RECYCLING SERVICES INC (PA)
2697 Main St, San Diego (92113-3612)
P.O. Box 13666 (92170-3666)
PHONE..................................619 231-2521
Fax: 619 238-1429
Robert M Davis, *CEO*
Teddy Davis, *CFO*
Theodora Davis Inman, *CFO*
Ruth Davis, *Chairman*
Deborah Odle, *Vice Pres*
▼ **EMP:** 70
SQ FT: 25,000
SALES (est): 56.4MM **Privately Held**
WEB: www.imsrecyclingservices.com
SIC: 5093 Ferrous metal scrap & waste

(P-8074)
JACK ENGLE & CO (PA)
8440 S Alameda St, Los Angeles (90001-4112)
P.O. Box 1705 (90001-0705)
PHONE..................................323 589-8111
Fax: 323 589-9189
Alan M Engle, *CEO*
Jack Engle, *CEO*
Andrew Hyde, *Vice Pres*
Julius Miller, *General Mgr*
Karina Moreno, *Office Mgr*
▼ **EMP:** 55 **EST:** 1965
SQ FT: 25,000
SALES (est): 43.4MM **Privately Held**
WEB: www.jackengleco.com
SIC: 5093 Metal scrap & waste materials

(P-8075)
KINSBURSKY BROS SUPPLY INC (PA)
Also Called: K B I
125 E Commercial St Ste A, Anaheim (92801-1214)
PHONE..................................714 738-8516
Fax: 714 441-0857
Steven Kinsbursky, *President*
Sidney Kinsbursky, *Shareholder*
Aaron Zisman, *CFO*
Scott Kinsbursky, *Vice Pres*
Todd Coy, *Admin Sec*
▲ **EMP:** 75
SQ FT: 35,000
SALES (est): 50.7MM **Privately Held**
WEB: www.kinsbursky.com
SIC: 5093 Metal scrap & waste materials

(P-8076)
MIDNIGHT AUTO RECYCLING LLC
434 E 6th St, San Bernardino (92410-4507)
P.O. Box 24003 (92406-0503)
PHONE..................................909 884-5308
Ted Smith, *Administration*
EMP: 50 **EST:** 1998
SALES (est): 6.3MM **Privately Held**
SIC: 5093 Automotive wrecking for scrap

(P-8077)
NEW NGC INC
Also Called: Gold Bond Building Products
1040 Canal Blvd, Richmond (94804-3550)
PHONE..................................510 234-6745
Fax: 510 236-3041
John Phillips, *Principal*
EMP: 50
SALES (corp-wide): 562.5MM **Privately Held**
WEB: www.natgyp.com
SIC: 5093 3275 Scrap & waste materials; gypsum products
HQ: New Ngc, Inc.
2001 Rexford Rd
Charlotte NC 28211
704 365-7300

(P-8078)
PAVEMENT RECYCLING SYSTEMS INC (PA)
Also Called: Prsi
10240 San Sevaine Way, Jurupa Valley (91752-1100)
PHONE..................................951 682-1091
Fax: 951 682-1094
Richard W Gove, *President*
Charles T Harmon, *Ch of Bd*
Stephen Concannon, *President*
Nathan Beyler, *CFO*
Bernard Hale, *Treasurer*
▲ **EMP:** 125
SALES (est): 129.7MM **Privately Held**
SIC: 5093 1611 Scrap & waste materials; surfacing & paving; concrete construction: roads, highways, sidewalks, etc.; resurfacing contractor

(P-8079)
PICK PULL AUTO DISMANTLING INC (HQ)
Also Called: Auto Parts Group
10850 Gold Center Dr # 325, Rancho Cordova (95670-6177)
PHONE..................................916 689-2000
Thomas Klauer, *President*

PRODUCTS & SERVICES SECTION
5094 - Jewelry, Watches, Precious Stones Wholesale County (P-8100)

Maun Tom, *CFO*
Gill Smith, *Admin Sec*
Tiffany Le, *Accounting Mgr*
Alice M Labonte, *Human Resources*
EMP: 50
SQ FT: 9,000
SALES (est): 366.5MM
SALES (corp-wide): 1.9B **Publicly Held**
WEB: www.picknpull.com
SIC: 5093 Automotive wrecking for scrap
PA: Schnitzer Steel Industries, Inc.
   299 Sw Clay St Ste 350
   Portland OR 97201
   503 224-9900

(P-8080)
PICK-A-PART AUTO WRECKING
9445 Cambridge St, Cypress (90630-2705)
PHONE..................559 485-3071
Fax: 559 268-4396
Christopher L McElroy, *CEO*
EMP: 70
SQ FT: 1,200
SALES (est): 18.8MM
SALES (corp-wide): 7.1B **Publicly Held**
WEB: www.pickapart.com
SIC: 5093 5531 5015 Automotive wrecking for scrap; automotive parts; automotive parts & supplies, used
HQ: Pick-Your-Part Auto Wrecking
   1235 S Beach Blvd
   Anaheim CA 92804
   714 385-1200

(P-8081)
RIVERSIDE SCRAP IR & MET CORP (PA)
Also Called: Redlands Recycling
2993 6th St, Riverside (92507-4131)
P.O. Box 5288 (92517-5288)
PHONE..................951 686-2120
Samuel Frankel, *Ch of Bd*
Daniel Jay Frankel, *President*
Raj Gandhi, *Exec VP*
Muriel K Frankel, *Vice Pres*
Geraldo Morano, *Manager*
EMP: 50
SQ FT: 22,275
SALES (est): 15.1MM **Privately Held**
SIC: 5093 Nonferrous metals scrap; waste paper; bottles, waste; plastics scrap

(P-8082)
SA RECYCLING LLC (PA)
2411 N Glassell St, Orange (92865-2705)
PHONE..................714 632-2000
George Adams, *Mng Member*
Patty Dimanni, *Exec VP*
Sandie Moyers, *Regional Mgr*
Debra Noriega, *Regional Mgr*
Moises Figueroa, *General Mgr*
◆ **EMP:** 120
SQ FT: 40,000
SALES (est): 900MM **Privately Held**
SIC: 5093 Scrap & waste materials; ferrous metal scrap & waste; nonferrous metals scrap

(P-8083)
SELF SERVE AUTO DISMANTLERS (PA)
Also Called: Adams Steel
3200 E Frontera St, Anaheim (92806-2822)
P.O. Box 6258 (92816-0258)
PHONE..................714 630-8901
Fax: 714 630-5836
George Adams Jr, *President*
Wendy Adams, *CFO*
Mike Adams, *Vice Pres*
Thomas Knippel, *Vice Pres*
Jed Holley, *General Mgr*
▼ **EMP:** 120
SQ FT: 41,000
SALES (est): 41.4MM **Privately Held**
WEB: www.remedyenvironmental.com
SIC: 5093 Automotive wrecking for scrap

(P-8084)
SIERRA INTERNATIONAL MCHY LLC
1620 E Brundage Ln Frnt, Bakersfield (93307-2756)
P.O. Box 1340 (93302-1340)
PHONE..................661 327-7073
Fax: 661 322-8759
Phillip Sacco, *Mng Member*

Kathy Majusiak, *Office Mgr*
Lisa Lewis, *Accountant*
Deanna Perkins, *Human Resources*
Deanna Kampmeinert, *HR Admin*
▲ **EMP:** 65
SQ FT: 15,000
SALES (est): 56.7MM **Privately Held**
SIC: 5093 5084 Nonferrous metals scrap; ferrous metal scrap & waste; industrial machinery & equipment

(P-8085)
SIMS GROUP USA CORPORATION
Also Called: Sims/LMC Recyclers
1900 Monterey Hwy, San Jose (95112-6100)
PHONE..................408 494-4242
Fax: 408 494-4279
Tom Sorci, *Manager*
EMP: 100
SALES (corp-wide): 3.4B **Privately Held**
SIC: 5093 4953 3231 Ferrous metal scrap & waste; refuse systems; products of purchased glass
HQ: Sims Group Usa Corporation
   600 S 4th St
   Richmond CA 94804
   510 412-5300

(P-8086)
SIMS GROUP USA CORPORATION (DH)
Also Called: Simsmetal America
600 S 4th St, Richmond (94804-3504)
PHONE..................510 412-5300
Galdino Claro, *CEO*
Marie Burk, *President*
Bob Kelman, *President*
Myles Partridge, *CFO*
Jimmie Buckland, *Exec VP*
◆ **EMP:** 100
SQ FT: 4,000
SALES (est): 161.1MM
SALES (corp-wide): 3.4B **Privately Held**
SIC: 5093 4953 Ferrous metal scrap & waste; nonferrous metals scrap; recycling, waste materials
HQ: Sims Group Usa Holdings Corp
   16 W 22nd St Fl 10
   New York NY 10010
   212 604-0710

(P-8087)
SIMS GROUP USA CORPORATION
Simsmtals America-Richmond Div
600 S 4th St, Richmond (94804-3504)
PHONE..................510 236-0606
Jimmie Buckland, *Vice Pres*
EMP: 75
SALES (corp-wide): 3.4B **Privately Held**
SIC: 5093 Ferrous metal scrap & waste
HQ: Sims Group Usa Corporation
   600 S 4th St
   Richmond CA 94804
   510 412-5300

(P-8088)
SOLARIS PAPER INC
13415 Carmenita Rd, Santa Fe Springs (90670-4906)
PHONE..................562 376-9717
Andre Soetjahja, *President*
Mike Murphy, *President*
Corey Rodriguez, *Vice Pres*
Peggy Litwin, *District Mgr*
Lisa Pollinger, *District Mgr*
▲ **EMP:** 231
SQ FT: 200,000
SALES (est): 179.5MM **Privately Held**
SIC: 5093 Waste paper

(P-8089)
SOS METALS INC (DH)
201 E Gardena Blvd, Gardena (90248-2813)
PHONE..................310 217-8848
Fax: 310 217-8088
Kenneth Buck, *CEO*
Patsy Siu, *Vice Pres*
Todd Bell, *Financial Exec*
Niloo Matsuda, *Accountant*
Undine Schwarz, *Controller*
◆ **EMP:** 165
SQ FT: 115,000

SALES (est): 103.1MM
SALES (corp-wide): 210.8B **Publicly Held**
WEB: www.sosmetals.com
SIC: 5093 5051 Ferrous metal scrap & waste; ferroalloys
HQ: Precision Castparts Corp.
   4650 Sw Mcdam Ave Ste 300
   Portland OR 97239
   503 946-4800

(P-8090)
STANDARD IRON & METALS CO
4525 San Leandro St, Oakland (94601-4449)
PHONE..................510 535-0222
Fax: 510 535-1697
Lloyd Weinstein, *Corp Secy*
Marium Villanueva, *Controller*
Ted Loney, *Sales Executive*
Lisa Love, *Manager*
EMP: 50
SQ FT: 20,000
SALES (est): 25MM **Privately Held**
WEB: www.standardiron.net
SIC: 5093 Ferrous metal scrap & waste; nonferrous metals scrap

(P-8091)
STAR SCRAP METAL COMPANY INC
1509 S Bluff Rd, Montebello (90640-6601)
PHONE..................562 921-5045
Fax: 714 670-6764
Rose Starow Stein, *President*
Allen Stein, *Vice Pres*
▼ **EMP:** 70
SQ FT: 600
SALES (est): 30.2MM **Privately Held**
SIC: 5093 Ferrous metal scrap & waste

(P-8092)
SUTTA COMPANY INCORPORATED (PA)
1221 3rd St, Oakland (94607-1805)
PHONE..................510 873-8777
Fax: 510 873-8788
Stephen Sutta, *President*
Lenae Coran, *CFO*
Xu Yang, *Technology*
Lenae Corcoran, *Controller*
Joe Casalini, *Human Res Mgr*
◆ **EMP:** 50
SQ FT: 10,000
SALES (est): 20.7MM **Privately Held**
SIC: 5093 Waste paper

(P-8093)
TST INC
Tandem Division
11601 Etiwanda Ave, Fontana (92337-6929)
PHONE..................909 590-1098
Andrew G Stein, *CEO*
EMP: 75
SALES (corp-wide): 81.2MM **Privately Held**
SIC: 5093 Metal scrap & waste materials
PA: Tst, Inc.
   13428 Benson Ave
   Chino CA 91710
   951 685-2155

5094 Jewelry, Watches, Precious Stones Wholesale

(P-8094)
BASK JEWELRY INC
2607 S Main St, Soquel (95073-2409)
PHONE..................831 479-8849
Fax: 831 476-4531
Steve Battlelle, *President*
▼ **EMP:** 100
SQ FT: 2,400
SALES (est): 9.9MM **Privately Held**
WEB: www.bask.com
SIC: 5094 Jewelry & precious stones

(P-8095)
BJS RESTAURANTS INC
3401 Dale Rd Ste 840, Modesto (95356-0549)
PHONE..................209 526-8850
Brandon Mynear, *Principal*
EMP: 1728
SALES (corp-wide): 919.6MM **Publicly Held**
SIC: 5094 Jewelry
PA: Bj's Restaurants, Inc.
   7755 Center Ave Ste 300
   Huntington Beach CA 92647
   714 500-2400

(P-8096)
BUNGALOW 16 ENTERTAINMENT LLC
8113 Melrose Ave, Los Angeles (90046-7011)
PHONE..................310 226-7870
Pascal Mouawad, *Accountant*
Ruby Conda, *Accountant*
Kate Fisher, *Prdt Dvlpt Mgr*
Nathan Monoshavich, *Director*
▲ **EMP:** 50
SQ FT: 2,000
SALES (est): 4.2MM **Privately Held**
SIC: 5094 Clocks, watches & parts

(P-8097)
CPI LUXURY GROUP
Also Called: China Pearl
10220 Norris Ave, Pacoima (91331-2217)
PHONE..................818 249-9888
Fax: 818 249-4777
Harold Jabarian, *CEO*
Kevork Hasbanian, *Vice Pres*
▲ **EMP:** 54
SQ FT: 15,000
SALES (est): 23MM **Privately Held**
WEB: www.chinapearl-usa.com
SIC: 5094 Pearls

(P-8098)
CW WELDING SERVICE INC
761 Majors Ct, Bakersfield (93308-9436)
PHONE..................661 399-5422
Ellis Firatt, *Branch Mgr*
Rocky Marquez, *General Mgr*
EMP: 51 **Privately Held**
SIC: 5094 5051 1761 Precious stones & metals; metals service centers & offices; sheet metalwork
PA: C.W. Welding Service, Inc.
   1735 Santa Fe Ave
   Long Beach CA 90813

(P-8099)
EMMI INC
Also Called: Emmi Universal Fine Jeweller
631 S Olive St Ste 302, Los Angeles (90014-3656)
PHONE..................213 622-7234
Edward Zohrabian, *President*
Isabel Zohrabian, *Treasurer*
▲ **EMP:** 60
SQ FT: 20,000
SALES (est): 12.2MM **Privately Held**
SIC: 5094 Jewelry & precious stones

(P-8100)
NIXON INC (PA)
Also Called: Nixon Watches
701 S Coast Highway 101, Encinitas (92024-4441)
PHONE..................760 944-0900
Fax: 760 944-9376
Nicholas Stowe, *CEO*
Andrus Laats, *President*
Chad Dinenna, *Admin Sec*
Laura Pertl, *Business Mgr*
Gary Morton, *Controller*
▲ **EMP:** 120
SQ FT: 3,000
SALES (est): 72.7MM **Privately Held**
WEB: www.nixonnow.com
SIC: 5094 5611 5136 Watches & parts; clothing accessories: men's & boys'; leather & sheep lined clothing, men's & boys'

5094 - Jewelry, Watches, Precious Stones Wholesale County (P-8101)

PRODUCTS & SERVICES SECTION

(P-8101)
SWEDA COMPANY LLC
17411 E Valley Blvd, City of Industry (91744-5159)
PHONE...................626 357-9999
Jim Hagan, *CEO*
Kellie Claudio, *Vice Pres*
Scott Pearson, *Vice Pres*
Wendy Lin, *Graphic Designe*
Steven Smith, *Controller*
▲ **EMP:** 200
SQ FT: 350,000
SALES (est): 147.7MM **Privately Held**
WEB: www.sweda.com
SIC: 5094 5044 Watches & parts; clocks; calcvlators, electronic

(P-8102)
TACORI ENTERPRISES
1736 Gardena Ave, Glendale (91204-2907)
PHONE...................818 863-1536
Fax: 818 863-1520
Haig Tacorian, *CEO*
Alred Margousian, *CFO*
Gilda Tacorian, *Vice Pres*
Alfred Margousian, *Accountant*
Lydia Andonian, *Controller*
▲ **EMP:** 58
SQ FT: 16,000
SALES (est): 20.7MM **Privately Held**
WEB: www.tacori.com
SIC: 5094 5944 Jewelry; jewelry, precious stones & precious metals

(P-8103)
TOUCAN INC (PA)
Also Called: Tomas Jewelry
1275 8th St, Arcata (95521-5770)
P.O. Box 4808 (95518-4808)
PHONE...................707 822-6662
Fax: 707 822-8618
Thomas S Perrett, *President*
Chris Albright, *Vice Pres*
Karen Lu, *Manager*
▲ **EMP:** 80
SQ FT: 25,000
SALES (est): 24MM **Privately Held**
WEB: www.tomasjewelry.com
SIC: 5094 Jewelry; precious metals

5099 Durable Goods: NEC Wholesale

(P-8104)
ALPHA SYSTEMS FIRE PROTECTION
7356 Fulton Ave, North Hollywood (91605-4113)
PHONE...................323 227-0700
Fax: 323 882-4984
Jerry Pivnik, *President*
Jill Pivnik, *Principal*
EMP: 50
SQ FT: 2,776
SALES: 5MM **Privately Held**
SIC: 5099 Fire extinguishers

(P-8105)
ARTISAN PICTURES INC
Also Called: Live International
2700 Colorado Ave Fl 2, Santa Monica (90404-5502)
PHONE...................310 449-9200
Jon Feltheimer, *CEO*
Anthony J Scotti, *Ch of Bd*
Steve Beeks, *President*
Amir Malin, *President*
Ronald B Cushey, *CFO*
EMP: 150
SALES (est): 26.3MM
SALES (corp-wide): 2.4B **Privately Held**
SIC: 5099 Video cassettes, accessories & supplies
HQ: Lions Gate Entertainment Inc.
2700 Colorado Ave Ste 200
Santa Monica CA 90404
310 449-9200

(P-8106)
BRETHREN INC
Also Called: Fire Safety First
1170 E Fruit St, Santa Ana (92701-4205)
PHONE...................714 836-4800
Fax: 714 836-4120
Al Saia, *CEO*
Mike Saia, *Vice Pres*
Tara Russo, *Executive Asst*
Peggy Saia, *Admin Sec*
Debbie Mathews, *Info Tech Mgr*
EMP: 50
SQ FT: 4,000
SALES (est): 18.2MM **Privately Held**
WEB: www.firesafetyfirst.com
SIC: 5099 7389 Fire extinguishers; fire extinguisher servicing

(P-8107)
BURGETT INCORPORATED
Also Called: Piano Disc
4111a N Freeway Blvd, Sacramento (95834-1209)
PHONE...................916 567-9999
Fax: 916 567-1941
Gary Burgett, *CEO*
Stephanie Johnston, *President*
Kirk Burgett, *Vice Pres*
Adam Burgett, *Webmaster*
Jack Viegas, *Design Engr*
▲ **EMP:** 70
SQ FT: 48,000
SALES (est): 16MM **Privately Held**
WEB: www.pianodisc.com
SIC: 5099 3429 3931 3651 Pianos; piano hardware; musical instruments; household audio & video equipment

(P-8108)
CELLMARK INC (DH)
Also Called: United International
22 Pelican Way, San Rafael (94901-5545)
PHONE...................415 927-1700
Fax: 415 927-2859
Fredrik Anderson, *CEO*
Michael J Cussen, *CFO*
Mitra Farr, *CFO*
Susan Blanchard, *Vice Pres*
Kevin Daley, *Vice Pres*
◆ **EMP:** 65
SQ FT: 13,000
SALES (est): 108.3MM
SALES (corp-wide): 2.5B **Privately Held**
SIC: 5099 5093 5111 Pulpwood; waste paper; fine paper
HQ: Cellmark Ab
Lilla Bommen 3c
Goteborg 411 0
311 003-00

(P-8109)
D J AMERICAN SUPPLY INC
Also Called: American Dj Group of Companies
6122 S Eastern Ave, Commerce (90040-3402)
PHONE...................323 582-2650
Fax: 323 725-6100
Charles Davies, *President*
Alfred Gonzales, *President*
Toby Velazquez, *President*
Javier Aguilar, *Officer*
Scott Davis, *General Mgr*
◆ **EMP:** 126
SQ FT: 100,000
SALES (est): 71.5MM **Privately Held**
SIC: 5099 5719 5999 Firearms & ammunition, except sporting; lighting fixtures; theatrical equipment & supplies

(P-8110)
DAMAO LUGGAGE INTL INC
Also Called: Chariot Travelware
1909 S Vineyard Ave, Ontario (91761-7747)
PHONE...................909 923-6531
Moon Woo, *President*
Wendy Fan, *CFO*
Abby Kee, *Director*
Jian Kee, *Director*
Wilson Xu, *Director*
▲ **EMP:** 3014
SQ FT: 60,000
SALES (est): 161.4MM **Privately Held**
SIC: 5099 3161 Luggage; luggage

(P-8111)
DAW INDUSTRIES INC
6610 Nncy Rdge Dr Ste 100, San Diego (92121)
PHONE...................858 622-4955
Fax: 858 457-5088
Hugo Belzidsky, *President*
Stuart Marquette, *Vice Pres*
Lisa Miller, *Graphic Designe*
Nick Burrow, *Human Res Mgr*
Craig Johnson, *Sales Mgr*
▲ **EMP:** 50
SALES (est): 8.9MM **Privately Held**
WEB: www.daw-usa.com
SIC: 5099 Safety equipment & supplies; fire extinguishers

(P-8112)
DENNIS FOLAND INC
Also Called: Logo Expressions
1500 S Hellman Ave, Ontario (91761-7634)
PHONE...................909 930-9900
Fax: 909 293-6977
Dennis Foland, *CEO*
Beverly Foland, *Corp Secy*
Ervin Millanes, *Prdtn Mgr*
Hasha Zangana, *Marketing Mgr*
Jackie Hartwig, *Director*
▲ **EMP:** 100
SQ FT: 140,000
SALES (est): 51.2MM **Privately Held**
SIC: 5099 3944 Souvenirs; games, toys & children's vehicles

(P-8113)
EVENTS BIO SERVICES INC
9661 Telstar Ave, El Monte (91731-3003)
PHONE...................626 350-4490
Tom Seratti, *Manager*
EMP: 120
SALES (corp-wide): 2.5MM **Privately Held**
SIC: 5099 5045 Safety equipment & supplies; computers, peripherals & software
PA: Events Bio Services Inc
1440 E Missouri Ave # 211
Phoenix AZ
602 274-1083

(P-8114)
FOX LUGGAGE INC
5353 E Slauson Ave, Commerce (90040-2916)
PHONE...................323 588-1688
Fax: 323 233-5888
Wayne Wang, *CEO*
Sherrishan H Lee, *President*
Naige Tazos, *Manager*
▲ **EMP:** 65
SQ FT: 80,000
SALES (est): 13MM **Privately Held**
WEB: www.foxluggage.com
SIC: 5099 Luggage

(P-8115)
GENIUS PRODUCTS INC
3301 Expo Blvd Ste 100, Santa Monica (90404)
PHONE...................310 453-1222
Trevor Drinkwater, *President*
Stephen K Bannon, *Ch of Bd*
Edward J Byrnes, *CFO*
Christine Martinez, *Exec VP*
Bill Osmondson, *Finance*
▲ **EMP:** 222
SQ FT: 40,520
SALES (est): 99.3K **Privately Held**
SIC: 5099 3652 7819

(P-8116)
GLOBAL STAINLESS SUPPLY
17006 S Figueroa St, Gardena (90248-3019)
PHONE...................310 525-1865
Art Shelton, *President*
Michelle Brunlehler, *Exec Sec*
Steve Martinez, *Manager*
▲ **EMP:** 300
SALES (est): 21.9MM **Privately Held**
SIC: 5099 Firearms & ammunition, except sporting

(P-8117)
GOLDEN WEST CUSTOM WD SHUTTERS
20561 Pascal Way, Lake Forest (92630-8119)
PHONE...................949 951-0600
Fax: 949 595-0363
EMP: 50
SALES (est): 3.4MM **Privately Held**
SIC: 5099

(P-8118)
GUTHY-RENKER LLC (PA)
Also Called: Proactiv
3340 Ocean Park Blvd # 3055, Santa Monica (90405-3268)
P.O. Box 13670, Palm Desert (92255-3670)
PHONE...................760 773-9022
Fax: 760 773-3849
Greg Renker, *President*
Dirk Bunt, *Exec VP*
Kevin Knee, *Exec VP*
Karen Barner, *Senior VP*
Jeff Engler, *Vice Pres*
▲ **EMP:** 60
SQ FT: 15,000
SALES (est): 325.8MM **Privately Held**
WEB: www.sheercover.com
SIC: 5099 7812 5999 7389 Tapes & cassettes, prerecorded; commercials, television: tape or film; cosmetics; telemarketing services

(P-8119)
GUTHY-RENKER LLC
Also Called: Guthy-Renker Direct
3340 Ocean Park Blvd Fl 2, Santa Monica (90405-3248)
PHONE...................310 581-6250
Fax: 310 581-3232
Bill Guthy, *President*
Jay Sung, *Chief Mktg Ofcr*
Kimber Maderazzo, *Senior VP*
Betty Devere, *Vice Pres*
Charlie Jones, *Vice Pres*
EMP: 80
SALES (corp-wide): 325.8MM **Privately Held**
WEB: www.sheercover.com
SIC: 5099 7812 5999 Tapes & cassettes, prerecorded; commercials, television: tape or film; cosmetics
PA: Guthy-Renker Llc
3340 Ocean Park Blvd # 3055
Santa Monica CA 90405
760 773-9022

(P-8120)
H AND H DRUG STORES INC
Also Called: Western Drug Medical Supply
4692 E Waterloo Rd, Stockton (95215-2309)
PHONE...................209 931-5200
Haig J Youredjian, *Principal*
EMP: 67
SALES (corp-wide): 34.7MM **Privately Held**
SIC: 5099 Brass goods
PA: H And H Drug Stores, Inc.
3604 San Fernando Rd
Glendale CA 91204
818 956-6691

(P-8121)
ICU EYEWEAR INC
Also Called: Cable Car Eyewear
1900 Shelton Dr, Hollister (95023-9498)
PHONE...................510 848-4700
Rick Allen, *Manager*
Jeff Linden, *Senior VP*
Harry Cameau, *Director*
Rick Czenernek, *Manager*
EMP: 60
SALES (corp-wide): 23.4MM **Privately Held**
SIC: 5099 Sunglasses
PA: Icu Eyewear Inc
1440 4th St Ste A
Berkeley CA 94710
831 637-9300

(P-8122)
JORGENSEN & SONS INC (PA)
Also Called: Jorgensen & Co
2691 S East Ave, Fresno (93706-5409)
PHONE...................559 268-6241
Fax: 559 268-5239
Darrell Hefley, *CEO*
Donald Jorgensen, *Ch of Bd*
Leon Young, *President*
Jim Rushing, *Treasurer*
Al V Jorgensen, *Vice Ch Bd*
EMP: 55
SQ FT: 6,000

▲ = Import ▼ = Export
◆ = Import/Export

PRODUCTS & SERVICES SECTION
5099 - Durable Goods: NEC Wholesale County (P-8144)

SALES (est): 46.5MM **Privately Held**
SIC: 5099 1731 Safety equipment & supplies; fire detection & burglar alarm systems specialization

(P-8123)
KAWAI AMERICA CORPORATION (HQ)
2055 E University Dr, Compton (90220-6411)
P.O. Box 9045, Rancho Dominguez (90224-9045)
PHONE.................................310 631-1771
Fax: 310 223-2272
Hirotaka Kawai, *President*
Naoki Mori, *President*
Kent Smith, *Branch Mgr*
Yoshiro Kataoka, *Admin Sec*
Andrew Spuur, *Telecomm Mgr*
◆ EMP: 50
SQ FT: 73,000
SALES (est): 25MM
SALES (corp-wide): 591.8MM **Privately Held**
SIC: 5099 Musical instruments; pianos
PA: Kawai Musical Instruments Manufacturing Co., Ltd.
200, Terajimacho, Naka-Ku
Hamamatsu SZO 430-0
534 571-213

(P-8124)
MAKKUNIS INC
Also Called: Simora Trading
2808 Oregon Ct Ste L10, Torrance (90503-2668)
PHONE.................................310 328-1999
Mohanraj Makkuni, *President*
EMP: 70
SALES (est): 4MM **Privately Held**
SIC: 5099 Sunglasses

(P-8125)
MENDOCINO FOREST PDTS CO LLC
6500 Durable Mill Rd, Calpella (95418)
PHONE.................................707 620-2961
Jon Roi, *Branch Mgr*
EMP: 186
SALES (corp-wide): 143.2MM **Privately Held**
SIC: 5099 Wood & wood by-products
PA: Mendocino Forest Products Company Llc
1360 19th Hole Dr Ste 200
Calpella CA 95418
707 620-2961

(P-8126)
MONOPRICE INC
Also Called: Monoprice.com
11701 6th St, Rancho Cucamonga (91730-6030)
PHONE.................................909 989-6887
Fax: 909 989-0078
Jong Lee, *President*
Ajay Kumar, *CEO*
Julie Hong, *Vice Pres*
Jeovahna Vazquez, *Vice Pres*
Larry Chong, *Executive*
◆ EMP: 160
SQ FT: 30,000
SALES (est): 24.4MM **Publicly Held**
SIC: 5099 Video & audio equipment
PA: Blucora, Inc.
10900 Ne 8th St Ste 800
Bellevue WA 98004
-

(P-8127)
MONSTER INC (PA)
Also Called: Monster Products
455 Valley Dr, Brisbane (94005-1209)
PHONE.................................415 840-2000
Fax: 415 468-0311
Noel Lee, *CEO*
Nora Considine, *COO*
Leo Lin, *CFO*
Irene Baron, *Vice Pres*
Kirti Hansji, *Vice Pres*
◆ EMP: 330
SQ FT: 50,000
SALES (est): 274.2MM **Privately Held**
WEB: www.monstercable.com
SIC: 5099 4841 3679 Video & audio equipment; cable & other pay television services; headphones, radio

(P-8128)
MSC CHATSWORTH
9324 Corbin Ave, Northridge (91324-2405)
PHONE.................................818 718-7696
Wendy Araiza, *Principal*
EMP: 89
SALES (est): 11.5MM **Privately Held**
SIC: 5099 Durable goods

(P-8129)
NATIONAL DISTRIBUTION SERVICES
340 N Grant Ave, Corona (92882-1828)
PHONE.................................951 739-2400
Gregor Gekghyan, *President*
EMP: 58
SALES (est): 28.7MM **Privately Held**
SIC: 5099 Firearms & ammunition, except sporting

(P-8130)
NEW CENTURY MEDIA CORP
2727 Pellissier Pl, City of Industry (90601-1510)
PHONE.................................562 695-1000
Fax: 323 908-9007
Carson Yu, *President*
Andy Forman, *Vice Pres*
Jennifer Yu, *Vice Pres*
▲ EMP: 50
SQ FT: 21,000
SALES (est): 19.7MM **Privately Held**
WEB: www.newcenturymediausa.com
SIC: 5099 Video cassettes, accessories & supplies

(P-8131)
OLIVET INTERNATIONAL INC (PA)
11015 Hopkins St, Mira Loma (91752-3248)
PHONE.................................951 681-8888
David Yu, *CEO*
Lydia Hsu, *President*
Julia Yip, *Office Admin*
Pei Te Lin, *Admin Sec*
Peter Lin, *Admin Sec*
▲ EMP: 89
SQ FT: 456,000
SALES (est): 145.3MM **Privately Held**
WEB: www.olivetintl.com
SIC: 5099 Luggage

(P-8132)
ORCHARD SUPPLY COMPANY LLC
1375 Blossom Hill Rd # 24, San Jose (95118-3806)
PHONE.................................408 269-1550
Michael Nagy, *Branch Mgr*
EMP: 70
SALES (corp-wide): 59B **Publicly Held**
SIC: 5099 Firearms & ammunition, except sporting
HQ: Orchard Supply Company, Llc
6450 Via Del Oro
San Jose CA 95119
408 281-3500

(P-8133)
PRAJIN 1 STOP DISTRIBUTORS INC (PA)
Also Called: Prajin Discount Distributors
5701 Pacific Blvd 5711, Huntington Park (90255-2615)
PHONE.................................323 395-5302
Antonio Prajin, *President*
Maria Gina Prajin, *Shareholder*
George Prajin, *Corp Secy*
Anthony Prajin Jr, *Vice Pres*
Peter Prajin, *General Mgr*
EMP: 50
SQ FT: 1,000
SALES (est): 14.8MM **Privately Held**
WEB: www.prajin1stop.com
SIC: 5099 5735 Compact discs; compact discs

(P-8134)
QUEST GROUP (PA)
Also Called: Audioquest
2621 White Rd, Irvine (92614-6247)
PHONE.................................949 585-0111
Fax: 949 585-0444
William E Low, *CEO*
Mike McConnell, *CFO*
Stephen Baker, *Senior VP*
Steve Silberman, *Vice Pres*
Carmen Wilcox, *Office Mgr*
▲ EMP: 67
SQ FT: 45,000
SALES (est): 22.6MM **Privately Held**
WEB: www.audioquest.com
SIC: 5099 Video & audio equipment

(P-8135)
ROLAND CORPORATION US (HQ)
5100 S Eastern Ave, Los Angeles (90040-2938)
P.O. Box 910921 (90091-0921)
PHONE.................................323 890-3700
Fax: 323 890-3701
Christopher Bristol, *CEO*
Fumie Wolff, *President*
Thai Ngo, *CFO*
Dennis M Houlihan, *Vice Pres*
Mark S Malbon, *Vice Pres*
◆ EMP: 165
SQ FT: 50,000
SALES (est): 114MM
SALES (corp-wide): 258.8MM **Privately Held**
SIC: 5099 5045 3931 Musical instruments; computer peripheral equipment; organs, all types: pipe, reed, hand, electronic, etc.
PA: Roland Corporation
2036-1, Nakagawa, Hosoecho, Kita-Ku
Hamamatsu SZO 431-1
535 230-230

(P-8136)
ROSEN ELECTRONICS LLC
Also Called: Rosen Electronics, L.P.
1120 California Ave, Corona (92881-3324)
PHONE.................................951 898-9808
Fax: 951 898-9658
W Thomas Clements, *President*
Charles Lister, *CFO*
Hollie Ellis, *Exec Sec*
Kathy Callihan, *Consultant*
▲ EMP: 75
SQ FT: 48,000
SALES (est): 23.2MM
SALES (corp-wide): 56.7MM **Privately Held**
WEB: www.rosenentertainment.com
SIC: 5099 3679 Video & audio equipment; liquid crystal displays (LCD)
PA: Aamp Of Florida, Inc.
15500 Lightwave Dr # 202
Clearwater FL 33760
727 572-9255

(P-8137)
RWP TRANSFER INC
Also Called: Recycled Wood Products
1313 E Phillips Blvd, Pomona (91766-5431)
PHONE.................................909 868-6882
Fax: 909 868-0595
Chris Kiralla, *President*
EMP: 50
SQ FT: 1,100
SALES (est): 15.5MM **Privately Held**
SIC: 5099 5083 Wood & wood by-products; landscaping equipment

(P-8138)
SAN DIMAS LUGGAGE COMPANY
2095 S Archibald Ave, Ontario (91761-8579)
PHONE.................................909 510-8820
Laurent Kabbabe, *Controller*
Vovoama Castro, *Human Res Mgr*
EMP: 60 EST: 1977
SALES (est): 10.6MM **Privately Held**
SIC: 5099 Luggage

(P-8139)
SCOPE SEVEN LLC
2201 Park Pl Ste 100, El Segundo (90245-4909)
PHONE.................................310 220-3939
Gordon Doran, *Mng Member*
Lee Morgan, *CTO*
Scott Cernetic, *Info Tech Dir*
Mary Unrein, *Accountant*
Kim Gulino, *Manager*
EMP: 62
SALES (est): 7.1MM **Privately Held**
SIC: 5099 Compact discs

(P-8140)
SMARTDRIVE SYSTEMS INC
9450 Carroll Park Dr, San Diego (92121-5201)
PHONE.................................866 933-9930
Fax: 858 638-1757
Steve Mitgang, *CEO*
Jason Palmer, *President*
Kenneth Colby, *Senior VP*
Michael J Baker, *Vice Pres*
Michael Baker, *Vice Pres*
▲ EMP: 362
SQ FT: 18,000
SALES (est): 162.1MM **Privately Held**
WEB: www.smartdrive.net
SIC: 5099 Safety equipment & supplies

(P-8141)
SONY MUSIC ENTERTAINMENT INC
Also Called: Sony Publishers
9830 Wilshire Blvd, Beverly Hills (90212-1804)
PHONE.................................310 272-2555
Stephanie Yu, *Vice Pres*
Peter Anton, *MIS Mgr*
Chris Cuningham, *MIS Mgr*
Marjorie Gayle, *Human Res Dir*
Diane Thompson, *Manager*
EMP: 250
SALES (corp-wide): 69.2B **Privately Held**
WEB: www.sonymusic.com
SIC: 5099 Phonograph records
HQ: Sony Music Entertainment, Inc.
25 Madison Ave Fl 19
New York NY 10010
212 833-8500

(P-8142)
SUN COAST MERCHANDISE CORP
6315 Bandini Blvd, Commerce (90040-3115)
PHONE.................................323 720-9700
Fax: 323 720-1988
Kumar C Bhavnani, *President*
Walter Rubin, *Officer*
Dilip Bhavnani, *Vice Pres*
Vidya Bhavnani, *Admin Sec*
Vinay Arora, *CIO*
◆ EMP: 250
SQ FT: 120,000
SALES (est): 109.1MM **Privately Held**
SIC: 5099 Brass goods

(P-8143)
TRAVELERS CLUB LUGGAGE INC
5911 Fresca Dr Ste B, La Palma (90623-1056)
PHONE.................................714 523-8808
Fax: 714 523-0188
Peter D Yu, *CEO*
Linh Nguyen, *Graphic Designe*
Steve Park, *Manager*
William Sy, *Manager*
Ginny Lee, *Accounts Mgr*
◆ EMP: 54
SQ FT: 120,000
SALES (est): 17.9MM **Privately Held**
WEB: www.travelersclub.com
SIC: 5099 Luggage

(P-8144)
TREEFROG DEVELOPMENTS INC
Also Called: Lifeproof
15110 Ave Of Science, San Diego (92128-3440)
PHONE.................................619 324-7755
Gary Rayner, *CEO*

5099 - Durable Goods: NEC Wholesale County (P-8145)

Kevin Morse, *CFO*
Tim Van Linge, *CFO*
Fredrik Torstensson, *Exec VP*
Dan Koziol, *Vice Pres*
▲ **EMP:** 75
SQ FT: 20,000
SALES (est): 44.2MM
SALES (corp-wide): 347.5MM **Privately Held**
SIC: 5099 Cases, carrying
PA: Otter Products, Llc
 209 S Meldrum St
 Fort Collins CO 80521
 970 493-8446

(P-8145)
TRENDSETTAH USA INC
25950 Acero Ste 210, Mission Viejo (92691-7962)
PHONE 888 775-4881
Akrum Alrahib, *CEO*
Sal Kureh, *CFO*
Ramzy Rahib, *Treasurer*
Carlos Hernandez, *Vice Pres*
Mousa Rahib, *Admin Sec*
▼ **EMP:** 63
SQ FT: 40,000
SALES (est): 19.1MM **Privately Held**
SIC: 5099 Novelties, durable

(P-8146)
TUMI INC
333 Santana Row Apt 230, San Jose (95128-2007)
PHONE 408 244-6512
Laurence Franklin, *President*
EMP: 70 **Privately Held**
SIC: 5099 Luggage
HQ: Tumi, Inc.
 1001 Durham Ave Ste 1b
 South Plainfield NJ 07080
 908 756-4400

(P-8147)
WEST COAST SHIP SUPPLY
Also Called: Wrist Ship Supply
2835 E Ana St, Compton (90221-5601)
PHONE 562 435-5245
Jubi Hillery, *President*
Andrew Licht, *General Mgr*
Bryan Harder, *Director*
Josh Roman, *Manager*
▲ **EMP:** 56
SALES: 28MM **Privately Held**
SIC: 5099 Ammunition, except sporting

(P-8148)
WESTERN NEVADA SUPPLY CO
10990 Industrial Way A, Truckee (96161-0257)
PHONE 530 582-5009
Fax: 530 582-5799
EMP: 237
SALES (corp-wide): 298.4MM **Privately Held**
SIC: 5099 Brass goods
PA: Western Nevada Supply Co.
 950 S Rock Blvd
 Sparks NV 89431
 775 359-5800

(P-8149)
YALEY ENTERPRISES INC
7664 Avianca Dr, Redding (96002-9703)
PHONE 530 365-5252
Fax: 530 365-6483
Patricia J Yaley, *CEO*
Thomas O'Rourke, *Corp Secy*
Thomas J Yaley, *Vice Pres*
Barbara Sletner, *Manager*
EMP: 50
SQ FT: 30,000
SALES (est): 11MM **Privately Held**
SIC: 5099 3544 Brass goods; special dies, tools, jigs & fixtures

(P-8150)
YAMAHA CORPORATION OF AMERICA (HQ)
Also Called: Yamaha Music Corporation U S A
6600 Orangethorpe Ave, Buena Park (90620-1396)
P.O. Box 6600 (90622-6600)
PHONE 714 522-9011
Fax: 714 522-9301

Hitoshi Fukutome, *CEO*
Paul Calvin, *President*
Karl Bruhn, *CFO*
R Shimanuki, *Treasurer*
Takashi Yabusaki, *Treasurer*
◆ **EMP:** 300
SALES (est): 342.2MM
SALES (corp-wide): 3.7B **Privately Held**
WEB: www.yamaha.com
SIC: 5099 5065 5091 3931 Musical instruments; pianos; sound equipment, electronic; sporting & recreation goods; golf equipment; musical instruments
PA: Yamaha Corporation
 10-1, Nakazawacho, Naka-Ku
 Hamamatsu SZO 430-0
 534 602-071

5111 Printing & Writing Paper Wholesale

(P-8151)
BLOWER-DEMPSAY CORPORATION (PA)
Also Called: Pak West Paper & Packaging
4042 W Garry Ave, Santa Ana (92704-6300)
PHONE 714 481-3800
Fax: 714 557-1392
James F Blower, *President*
Serge Poirier, *CFO*
Linda B Dempsay, *Admin Sec*
▲ **EMP:** 217
SQ FT: 190,000
SALES (est): 176.6MM **Privately Held**
SIC: 5111 Printing & writing paper

(P-8152)
DOT LEASING COMPANY
2424 Mcgaw Ave, Irvine (92614-5834)
PHONE 949 474-1100
Bruce Carson, *Managing Prtnr*
William Clark, *Partner*
Charles Massingill, *Partner*
Eric Pepys, *Partner*
EMP: 151
SQ FT: 40,000
SALES (est): 9.5MM **Privately Held**
SIC: 5111 Printing & writing paper

(P-8153)
KELLY PAPER COMPANY (HQ)
288 Brea Canyon Rd, Walnut (91789-3087)
PHONE 909 859-8200
Fax: 909 859-8903
Janice Gottesman, *President*
Rod Schaar, *District Mgr*
Patrick Linares, *Store Mgr*
Kim Antonio, *Office Admin*
Arthur Guerrero, *Data Proc Exec*
▲ **EMP:** 50 **EST:** 1936
SALES (est): 276.3MM
SALES (corp-wide): 2B **Privately Held**
WEB: www.kellypaper.com
SIC: 5111 5943 Printing paper; office forms & supplies
PA: Central National Gottesman Inc.
 3 Manhattanville Rd # 301
 Purchase NY 10577
 914 696-9000

(P-8154)
RR DONNELLEY & SONS COMPANY
Also Called: R R Donnelley Coml Press Plant
955 Gateway Center Way, San Diego (92102-4542)
PHONE 619 527-4600
Jim Rosenberg, *Manager*
Kathy Baldwin, *Administration*
EMP: 150
SALES (corp-wide): 11.2B **Publicly Held**
WEB: www.rrdonnelley.com
SIC: 5111 Printing & writing paper
PA: R.R. Donnelley & Sons Company
 35 W Wacker Dr Ste 3650
 Chicago IL 60601
 312 326-8000

(P-8155)
SPICERS PAPER INC (HQ)
12310 Slauson Ave, Santa Fe Springs (90670-2629)
PHONE 562 698-1199
Fax: 562 693-8339
Janice L Gottesman, *CEO*
Rick Anderson, *Vice Pres*
Mike Snyder, *Regional Mgr*
Jody Kadokawa, *General Mgr*
Nicole M Gonzalez, *Human Resources*
◆ **EMP:** 180
SQ FT: 365,000
SALES (est): 530.4MM
SALES (corp-wide): 2B **Privately Held**
WEB: www.spicers.com
SIC: 5111 Fine paper; printing paper; writing paper
PA: Central National Gottesman Inc.
 3 Manhattanville Rd # 301
 Purchase NY 10577
 914 696-9000

(P-8156)
VERITIV OPERATING COMPANY
International Paper
345 Schwerin St, San Francisco (94134-3246)
PHONE 415 586-9160
Jim Teahan, *Manager*
Shirley Watters, *Finance Mgr*
Carol Curbishley, *Personnel*
Paul Augustini, *Sales Mgr*
EMP: 63
SALES (corp-wide): 8.7B **Publicly Held**
WEB: www.internationalpaper.com
SIC: 5111 Printing & writing paper
HQ: Veritiv Operating Company
 1000 Abernathy Rd
 Atlanta GA 30328
 770 391-8200

5112 Stationery & Office Splys Wholesale

(P-8157)
5 DAY BUSINESS FORMS MFG INC
2921 E La Cresta Ave, Anaheim (92806-1873)
PHONE 714 632-8674
Richard E Streza, *Branch Mgr*
Wendy Schul, *Human Res Mgr*
Scott Kirschner, *Purch Agent*
Pamela Bumer, *Sales Staff*
Donna Goede, *Sales Staff*
EMP: 62
SALES (corp-wide): 12MM **Privately Held**
SIC: 5112 Business forms
PA: 5 Day Business Forms Mfg., Inc.
 2910 E La Cresta Ave
 Anaheim CA 92806
 213 623-3577

(P-8158)
A YAFA PEN COMPANY
21306 Gault St, Canoga Park (91303-2123)
PHONE 818 704-8888
Fax: 818 704-8112
Yair Greenberg, *CEO*
Niv Avidan, *Vice Pres*
Anita Sebetic, *General Mgr*
Sneh Sharma, *Accounting Mgr*
Ross Cameron, *Natl Sales Mgr*
▲ **EMP:** 50
SQ FT: 25,000
SALES (est): 14.3MM **Privately Held**
WEB: www.aldodomani.com
SIC: 5112 5199 Office supplies; advertising specialties

(P-8159)
ALL PHASE BUSINESS SUPPLIES
1920 E Gladwick St, Compton (90220-6201)
PHONE 310 631-1900
Fax: 310 631-4488
Jeffrey Kraus, *President*
EMP: 50
SQ FT: 10,000

SALES (est): 4.5MM **Privately Held**
SIC: 5112 5943 Office supplies; office forms & supplies

(P-8160)
BANGKIT (USA) INC
Also Called: Bazic Product
10511 Valley Blvd, El Monte (91731-2403)
PHONE 626 672-0888
Fax: 323 583-6878
Handy Hioe, *CEO*
Anita Handojo, *Vice Pres*
Hideki Kawai, *Sales Executive*
Lisa Hioe, *Manager*
Nurhayati Johan, *Assistant VP*
◆ **EMP:** 50
SQ FT: 40,000
SALES (est): 31MM **Privately Held**
SIC: 5112 Stationery & office supplies

(P-8161)
CALCEDAR EXPORT INC
400 S Fresno St, Stockton (95203-3007)
P.O. Box 528 (95201-0528)
PHONE 209 944-5800
Phillip Berolzheimer, *President*
Michael Berolzheimer, *Vice Pres*
EMP: 201
SALES (est): 9.2MM
SALES (corp-wide): 95.5MM **Privately Held**
SIC: 5112 Pens &/or pencils
PA: Duraflame, Inc.
 2894 Monte Diablo Ave
 Stockton CA 95203
 209 461-6600

(P-8162)
CARTRIDGE FAMILY INC
Also Called: Cartridge Family Ink
1940 Union St Ste 29, Oakland (94607-2352)
PHONE 510 658-0400
Nate Laskin, *CEO*
Nate Lafkin, *Manager*
EMP: 148
SQ FT: 2,750
SALES (est): 15.6MM **Privately Held**
WEB: www.cartridgefamily.com
SIC: 5112 5065 5044 7389 Laserjet supplies; facsimile equipment; copying equipment; printers' services: folding, collating

(P-8163)
DESTINE ONE WHOLESALE INC
1660 Kendall Dr Apt 24, San Bernardino (92407-2835)
PHONE 951 202-3545
Lynn Lindberg, *President*
EMP: 103
SQ FT: 15,000
SALES: 412K **Privately Held**
SIC: 5112 Stationery & office supplies

(P-8164)
DIETRICH POST CO INC
945 Bryant St, San Francisco (94103-4523)
PHONE 510 596-0080
Dan Bruich, *President*
EMP: 50
SALES (est): 4.6MM **Privately Held**
SIC: 5112 Office supplies

(P-8165)
ENNIS INC
28401 Matthews Rd, Sun City (92585-9655)
P.O. Box 20005 (92586-9501)
PHONE 951 928-1125
Ken Turner, *Principal*
EMP: 50
SALES (corp-wide): 568.9MM **Publicly Held**
WEB: www.ennis.com
SIC: 5112 Business forms
PA: Ennis, Inc.
 2441 Presidential Pkwy
 Midlothian TX 76065
 972 775-9801

▲ = Import ▼ = Export
◆ = Import/Export

PRODUCTS & SERVICES SECTION

5113 - Indl & Personal Svc Paper Wholesale County (P-8185)

(P-8166)
ESSENDANT CO
Also Called: United Stationers
918 S Stimson Ave, City of Industry (91745-1640)
PHONE 626 961-0011
Fax: 626 333-9579
Terry Deines, *Manager*
Mike Meyden, *Executive*
Bill Sutter, *MIS Dir*
Karen Kissell, *Human Res Mgr*
Helen Brewer, *Mktg Dir*
EMP: 230
SALES (corp-wide): 5.3B **Publicly Held**
WEB: www.ussco.com
SIC: 5112 5044 5021 5943 Stationery & office supplies; office equipment; furniture; office forms & supplies
HQ: Essendant Co.
1 Parkway North Blvd # 100
Deerfield IL 60015
847 627-7000

(P-8167)
ESSENDANT CO
5440 Stationers Way, Sacramento (95842-1900)
PHONE 916 344-6707
Fax: 916 924-6639
Greg Birdsall, *Branch Mgr*
Cindy Wright, *Human Res Mgr*
Sheryl Weber, *Safety Mgr*
Tom Berce, *Sales Mgr*
Bill Gamalski, *Senior Mgr*
EMP: 200
SALES (corp-wide): 5.3B **Publicly Held**
WEB: www.ussco.com
SIC: 5112 Stationery & office supplies
HQ: Essendant Co.
1 Parkway North Blvd # 100
Deerfield IL 60015
847 627-7000

(P-8168)
GIVE SOMETHING BACK INC (PA)
Also Called: Give Something Back Off Sups
7730 Pardee Ln Ste A, Oakland (94621-1555)
PHONE 510 635-5500
Toll Free: .... 888 -
Fax: 510 635-4677
Sean Marx, *CEO*
Mike Hannigan, *President*
Verna Carter, *Info Tech Mgr*
Chris Emmons, *Controller*
Deanna Ali, *Human Res Mgr*
▲ EMP: 58
SQ FT: 19,800
SALES (est): 108.8MM **Privately Held**
WEB: www.givesomethingback.com
SIC: 5112 Stationery & office supplies

(P-8169)
IMAGING TECHNOLOGIES GROUP LLC
Also Called: Itd Print Solutions
5220 Pacific Concourse Dr, Los Angeles (90045-6277)
PHONE 310 638-2500
Benjamin Alexander,
Allan Crowe, *Controller*
◆ EMP: 50 EST: 1980
SQ FT: 7,000
SALES (est): 13.3MM **Privately Held**
WEB: www.rhinotek.com
SIC: 5112 Computer & photocopying supplies

(P-8170)
JOHN A MAIDA ENTERPRISES
Also Called: Maida Specialties Co
P.O. Box 6144 (95150-6144)
PHONE 408 254-3100
Neil Callahan, *President*
Sandra Callahan, *Vice Pres*
EMP: 50 EST: 1968
SQ FT: 17,000
SALES (est): 7.8MM **Privately Held**
SIC: 5112 5199 5099 Greeting cards; party favors, balloons, hats, etc.; sunglasses

(P-8171)
NAT SIM CORP
Also Called: U S Office & Industry Supply
7405 Woodley Ave, Van Nuys (91406-2924)
P.O. Box 10540, Canoga Park (91309-1540)
PHONE 818 705-3131
Fax: 818 705-8686
Yzes Yallouz, *President*
EMP: 53
SQ FT: 3,000
SALES (est): 6.3MM **Privately Held**
SIC: 5112 5085 Office supplies; industrial tools

(P-8172)
OFFICE DEPOT INC
4720 Northgate Blvd, Sacramento (95834-1101)
PHONE 916 927-0171
Dennise Moran, *Principal*
Bryan Ludwig, *Purchasing*
Sue McNerney, *Purchasing*
Lisa Crapo, *Manager*
Dan Treat, *Manager*
EMP: 100
SALES (corp-wide): 14.4B **Publicly Held**
WEB: www.officedepot.com
SIC: 5112 5044 5045 Stationery & office supplies; office supplies; office equipment; computers, peripherals & software; computers
PA: Office Depot, Inc.
6600 N Military Trl
Boca Raton FL 33496
561 438-4800

(P-8173)
PENTEL OF AMERICA LTD (HQ)
2715 Columbia St, Torrance (90503-3861)
PHONE 310 320-3831
Fax: 310 533-0697
Joe Koumi, *President*
Chotaro Koumi, *President*
John Goss, *CFO*
Atsumi Nakayama, *CFO*
Ken Okbayshi, *CFO*
▲ EMP: 74 EST: 1966
SQ FT: 46,000
SALES: 283K
SALES (corp-wide): 204.3MM **Privately Held**
WEB: www.pentel.com
SIC: 5112 3951 5199 3952 Pens &/or pencils; pens & mechanical pencils; artists' materials; artists' materials, except pencils & leads
PA: Pentel Co., Ltd.
7-2, Nihonbashikoamicho
Chuo-Ku TKY 103-0
336 673-333

(P-8174)
PENTEL OF AMERICA LTD
4000 E Airport Dr Ste C, Ontario (91761-1592)
PHONE 909 975-2200
Steve Mukai, *Manager*
Michael Storie, *Manager*
Belinda Sumner, *Manager*
EMP: 50
SALES (corp-wide): 204.3MM **Privately Held**
SIC: 5112 Pens &/or pencils
HQ: Pentel Of America, Ltd.
2715 Columbia St
Torrance CA 90503
310 320-3831

(P-8175)
PRO DOCUMENT SOLUTIONS INC
90 W Poplar Ave, Porterville (93257-5326)
PHONE 559 719-1281
Fax: 559 719-1282
Linda Keith, *Branch Mgr*
EMP: 51
SALES (corp-wide): 29.5MM **Privately Held**
WEB: www.prodocumentsolutions.com
SIC: 5112 Business forms
PA: Pro Document Solutions, Inc.
1760 Commerce Way
Paso Robles CA 93446
805 238-6680

(P-8176)
PUNCH STUDIO LLC (PA)
6025 W Slauson Ave, Culver City (90230-6507)
P.O. Box 3663 (90231-3663)
PHONE 310 390-9900
Todd Kirshner, *Mng Member*
Barbara Berwick, *Vice Pres*
Andy Nguyen, *Administration*
Marvin Franklin, *Info Tech Mgr*
Paula Myers, *Production*
◆ EMP: 230
SQ FT: 50,000
SALES: 55MM **Privately Held**
WEB: www.punchstudio.com
SIC: 5112 Greeting cards

(P-8177)
R R DONNELLEY & SONS COMPANY
Also Called: Moore Document Solutions
5000 Executive Pkwy Ste 2, San Ramon (94583-4210)
PHONE 925 901-5300
Dave Kapanka, *Manager*
Jaime Kapanka, *Principal*
Mike Fagan, *General Mgr*
Dolly Bryan, *Marketing Staff*
EMP: 70
SALES (corp-wide): 11.2B **Publicly Held**
WEB: www.rrdonnelley.com
SIC: 5112 Business forms
PA: R.R. Donnelley & Sons Company
35 W Wacker Dr Ste 3650
Chicago IL 60601
312 326-8000

(P-8178)
RR DONNELLEY & SONS COMPANY
Also Called: Moore Business Forms
40610 County Center Dr, Temecula (92591-6017)
PHONE 951 296-2890
Fax: 951 676-9490
Rick Budge, *Manager*
Lisa Garrett, *Manager*
EMP: 100
SALES (corp-wide): 11.2B **Publicly Held**
WEB: www.moore.com
SIC: 5112 2761 2752 Business forms; manifold business forms; color lithography
PA: R.R. Donnelley & Sons Company
35 W Wacker Dr Ste 3650
Chicago IL 60601
312 326-8000

(P-8179)
S P RICHARDS COMPANY
2190 Hanson Way, Woodland (95776-6230)
PHONE 916 564-5891
Sam Carter, *Manager*
Harry Torres, *Branch Mgr*
EMP: 60
SALES (corp-wide): 15.2B **Publicly Held**
WEB: www.sprichards.com
SIC: 5112 5021 Office supplies; office furniture
HQ: S. P. Richards Company
6300 Highlands Pkwy Se
Smyrna GA 30082
770 434-4571

(P-8180)
S P RICHARDS COMPANY
Also Called: S.p Richards
10235 San Sevaine Way # 120, Mira Loma (91752-1153)
PHONE 951 681-3114
Fax: 951 681-6702
Jay Brooks, *Branch Mgr*
Jeremy Murphy, *Plant Mgr*
EMP: 100
SALES (corp-wide): 15.2B **Publicly Held**
WEB: www.sprichards.com
SIC: 5112 5021 Stationery & office supplies; office furniture
HQ: S. P. Richards Company
6300 Highlands Pkwy Se
Smyrna GA 30082
770 434-4571

(P-8181)
SAFEGUARD BUSINESS SYSTEMS INC
414 N A St, Oxnard (93030-4904)
PHONE 805 486-9769
Greg Cook, *Branch Mgr*
EMP: 110
SALES (corp-wide): 1.7B **Publicly Held**
WEB: www.gosafeguard.com
SIC: 5112 Business forms
HQ: Safeguard Business Systems, Inc.
8585 N Stemmons Fwy
Dallas TX 75247
214 640-3916

(P-8182)
UNITED RIBBON COMPANY INC
Also Called: United Imaging
21201 Oxnard St, Woodland Hills (91367-5015)
PHONE 818 716-1515
Fax: 818 716-1584
Michael Cohen, *President*
Yigal Avrahamy, *Vice Pres*
EMP: 85
SQ FT: 22,000
SALES (est): 63.1MM **Privately Held**
WEB: www.unitedimaging.com
SIC: 5112 5044 5943 5021 Stationery & office supplies; computer & photocopying supplies; office equipment; office forms & supplies; office & public building furniture; office equipment & accessory customizing

(P-8183)
VIKING OFFICE PRODUCTS INC (HQ)
3366 E Willow St, Signal Hill (90755-2311)
PHONE 562 490-1000
M Bruce Nelson, *President*
Ronald W Weissman, *Senior VP*
Mark R Brown, *Vice Pres*
James Mandelbaum, *Info Tech Mgr*
Mike Montalbano, *Director*
▲ EMP: 292
SQ FT: 187,000
SALES (est): 1.3B
SALES (corp-wide): 14.4B **Publicly Held**
SIC: 5112 5021 5045 5087 Stationery & office supplies; business forms; stationery; office furniture; computers, peripherals & software; janitors' supplies; photographic equipment & supplies; catalog & mail-order houses
PA: Office Depot, Inc.
6600 N Military Trl
Boca Raton FL 33496
561 438-4800

5113 Indl & Personal Svc Paper Wholesale

(P-8184)
AMERICAN PAPER & PLASTICS INC
Also Called: American Paper & Provisions
550 S 7th Ave, City of Industry (91746-3120)
PHONE 626 444-0000
Fax: 626 444-1000
Daniel Emrani, *CEO*
Myra Zamora, *Executive*
Anthony Paventi, *Business Dir*
Chris Tellez, *Adv Board Mem*
Angel Hernandez, *Executive Asst*
EMP: 119
SQ FT: 300,000
SALES (est): 160.6MM **Privately Held**
WEB: www.appinc.com
SIC: 5113 Industrial & personal service paper

(P-8185)
ANDWIN CORPORATION (PA)
Also Called: Andwin Scientific
6636 Variel Ave, Woodland Hills (91303-2808)
P.O. Box 689 (91365-0689)
PHONE 818 999-2828
Fax: 818 227-0838
Natalie Sarraf, *CEO*
Abner Levy, *President*
Ryan Smith, *General Mgr*

5113 - Indl & Personal Svc Paper Wholesale County (P-8186)

PRODUCTS & SERVICES SECTION

Milana Legeza, *Accountant*
Sandy Rosenblum, *Purch Dir*
▲ **EMP:** 110
SQ FT: 45,000
SALES (est): 103.2MM **Privately Held**
WEB: www.andwin.com
SIC: 5113 3842 5199 5087 Industrial & personal service paper; surgical appliances & supplies; packaging materials; janitors' supplies; hospital equipment & furniture; in vitro & in vivo diagnostic substances

(P-8186)
BUNZL USA INC
Also Called: Papercraft Los Angeles
15959 Piuma Ave, Cerritos (90703-1526)
PHONE 314 997-5959
Jeff McElroy, *Principal*
Jeff Burnett, *General Mgr*
Ty Murphy, *Manager*
Annette Discala, *Agent*
EMP: 66
SALES (corp-wide): 9.7B **Privately Held**
SIC: 5113 Industrial & personal service paper
HQ: Bunzl Usa, Inc.
1 Cityplace Dr Ste 200
Saint Louis MO 63141
314 997-5959

(P-8187)
CALIFORNIA SUPPLY INC (PA)
491 E Compton Blvd, Gardena (90248-2078)
P.O. Box 3906 (90247-7598)
PHONE 310 532-2500
Fax: 310 327-1849
Mark Weinstein, *CEO*
Art Gaford, *CFO*
Michael Rosson, *Exec VP*
Art Gafford, *Controller*
Dan Bartlett, *Purch Dir*
▲ **EMP:** 69 **EST:** 1975
SQ FT: 75,000
SALES (est): 70.4MM **Privately Held**
WEB: www.calsupply.com
SIC: 5113 5087 Industrial & personal service paper; janitors' supplies

(P-8188)
CALPINE CONTAINERS INC
42779 Road 80, Dinuba (93618-9342)
PHONE 559 591-6555
Fax: 559 591-5196
Roger Bell, *Branch Mgr*
Angie Pruett, *Sales Staff*
EMP: 100
SQ FT: 35,780
SALES (corp-wide): 169.7MM **Privately Held**
WEB: www.calpineinc.com
SIC: 5113 5085 2441 2448 Corrugated & solid fiber boxes; boxes, paperboard & disposable plastic; box shooks; boxes, crates, etc., other than paper; boxes, wood; pallets, wood; corrugated & solid fiber boxes
PA: Calpine Containers, Inc.
6425 N Palm Ave Ste 104
Fresno CA 93704
559 519-7199

(P-8189)
ELKAY PLASTICS CO INC (PA)
6000 Sheila St, Commerce (90040-2405)
P.O. Box 910968, Los Angeles (90091-0931)
PHONE 323 722-7073
Fax: 323 869-3911
Louis Chertkow, *President*
Geoffrey Pankau, *CFO*
Vickie Gosnell, *Info Tech Mgr*
Vicki Gosnell, *MIS Mgr*
Noopur Vyas, *Programmer Anys*
▲ **EMP:** 100
SQ FT: 175,000
SALES (est): 103.8MM **Privately Held**
WEB: www.elkayplastics.com
SIC: 5113 Bags, paper & disposable plastic

(P-8190)
ERNEST PACKAGING SOLUTIONS INC (PA)
Also Called: Ernest Paper
5777 Smithway St, Commerce (90040-1507)
PHONE 800 233-7788
Fax: 323 837-1534
Charles Wilson, *Ch of Bd*
Timothy Wilson, *President*
Terry Rodriguez, *Accountant*
David Belinoviz, *Controller*
Dina Pacheco, *Recruiter*
▲ **EMP:** 130
SQ FT: 300,000
SALES (est): 282.5MM **Privately Held**
WEB: www.ipdpkg.com
SIC: 5113 5199 7389 Industrial & personal service paper; shipping supplies; packaging materials; cosmetic kits, assembling & packaging

(P-8191)
FRICK PAPER COMPANY
Also Called: Paper Mart Indus & Ret Packg
2164 N Batavia St, Orange (92865-3104)
PHONE 323 726-8200
John Frick, *Partner*
Thomas Frick, *Partner*
Margaret Hicks, *Vice Pres*
Calvin Lim, *Admin Asst*
Richard Main, *QA Dir*
◆ **EMP:** 106
SQ FT: 210,000
SALES (est): 64MM **Privately Held**
WEB: www.papermart.com
SIC: 5113 Industrial & personal service paper

(P-8192)
GAHVEJIAN ENTERPRISES INC
Also Called: Mid Valley Packaging & Sup Co
2004 S Temperance Ave, Fowler (93625-9759)
P.O. Box 96 (93625-0096)
PHONE 559 834-5956
Fax: 559 834-1922
Carrie L Gahvejian, *President*
John Gahvejian, *President*
Lorrie Gahvejian, *Corp Secy*
Erik Creede, *Principal*
Tom Hudson, *Controller*
▲ **EMP:** 50
SQ FT: 150,000
SALES (est): 53.3MM **Privately Held**
SIC: 5113 Bags, paper & disposable plastic; boxes, paperboard & disposable plastic; folding paperboard boxes

(P-8193)
GEORGIA-PACIFIC LLC
Also Called: Reliable Container
9206 Santa Fe Springs Rd, Santa Fe Springs (90670-2618)
PHONE 562 861-6226
EMP: 275
SALES (corp-wide): 26.7B **Privately Held**
SIC: 5113 2653 Corrugated & solid fiber boxes; bags, paper & disposable plastic; boxes, corrugated: made from purchased materials; display items, corrugated: made from purchased materials
HQ: Georgia-Pacific Llc
133 Peachtree St Ne # 4810
Atlanta GA 30303
404 652-4000

(P-8194)
GREENLEAF PAPER PRODUCTS
Also Called: Moor Products
26431 Crown Valley Pkwy # 150, Mission Viejo (92691-7201)
PHONE 949 348-0048
Greg Mosby, *President*
EMP: 60
SALES (est): 167.8K **Privately Held**
SIC: 5113 Industrial & personal service paper

(P-8195)
JUSTMAN PACKAGING & DISPLAY
5819 Telegraph Rd, Commerce (90040-1515)
PHONE 323 728-8888
Fax: 323 727-7777
Morley Justman, *President*
Barbara Cabaret, *CFO*
Russell Justman, *Vice Pres*
Veronica Martinez, *Assistant*
▲ **EMP:** 70
SQ FT: 125,000
SALES (est): 71MM **Privately Held**
WEB: www.justman.com
SIC: 5113 5046 Corrugated & solid fiber boxes; display equipment, except refrigerated

(P-8196)
KAPSTONE CONTAINER CORPORATION
8511 Blaine St, Oakland (94621-1213)
PHONE 510 569-2616
Robert Perez, *General Mgr*
EMP: 70
SALES (est): 852.4K **Privately Held**
SIC: 5113 Boxes & containers

(P-8197)
MAXCO SUPPLY INC
8419 Di Giorgio Rd, Lamont (93241-2547)
PHONE 559 646-6700
Steve Grote, *Principal*
EMP: 83
SALES (corp-wide): 162.3MM **Privately Held**
SIC: 5113 Bags, paper & disposable plastic
PA: Maxco Supply, Inc.
605 S Zediker Ave
Parlier CA 93648
559 646-8449

(P-8198)
MICHAEL MADDEN CO INC
Also Called: Paper Company, The
2815 Warner Ave, Irvine (92606-4443)
P.O. Box 17807 (92623-7807)
PHONE 800 834-6248
Michael L Madden, *President*
Julie Scheibe, *CFO*
Jody Madden, *Vice Pres*
Julie K Scheide, *Vice Pres*
Kiley Ness, *Comp Spec*
◆ **EMP:** 70
SQ FT: 75,000
SALES (est): 68.2MM **Privately Held**
SIC: 5113 Industrial & personal service paper

(P-8199)
NEWAY PACKAGING CORP (PA)
1973 E Via Arado, Rancho Dominguez (90220-6102)
PHONE 602 454-9000
Fax: 619 898-3430
Russell E Freebury, *President*
Susan McCarthy, *COO*
Sarah D Giles-Bell, *Vice Pres*
Susan Freebury, *Branch Mgr*
Carole Freebury, *Controller*
▲ **EMP:** 60
SQ FT: 36,000
SALES (est): 94.1MM **Privately Held**
WEB: www.newaypackaging.com
SIC: 5113 5084 Shipping supplies; packaging machinery & equipment

(P-8200)
OAK PAPER PRODUCTS CO INC (PA)
Also Called: Oak Distribution
3686 E Olympic Blvd, Los Angeles (90023-3146)
P.O. Box 23965 (90023-0965)
PHONE 323 268-0507
Fax: 323 262-8517
Max Weissberg, *President*
Richard Seff, *Ch of Bd*
David Weissberg, *CEO*
David Karr, *COO*
Bernie Singer, *CFO*
▲ **EMP:** 174
SQ FT: 250,000
SALES (est): 143.4MM **Privately Held**
WEB: www.oakdistribution.com
SIC: 5113 5199 5087 2653 Shipping supplies; packaging materials; janitors' supplies; corrugated & solid fiber boxes

(P-8201)
OASIS BRANDS INC
6700 Artesia Blvd, Buena Park (90620-1014)
PHONE 540 658-2830
Lee Shuchun, *Director*
Winnie Tung, *Marketing Staff*
▲ **EMP:** 75
SALES: 156MM **Privately Held**
SIC: 5113 Napkins, paper

(P-8202)
ORORA NORTH AMERICA
Also Called: Mpp Brea Div 6079
3200 Enterprise St, Brea (92821-6238)
PHONE 714 984-2300
Carol Hortick, *Manager*
Jim Valdez, *Manager*
EMP: 84
SALES (corp-wide): 2.8B **Privately Held**
SIC: 5113 2653 Paper & products, wrapping or coarse; boxes, corrugated: made from purchased materials
HQ: Orora Packaging Solutions
6600 Valley View St
Buena Park CA 90620
714 562-6000

(P-8203)
ORORA NORTH AMERICA
Also Called: Mpp San Diego Div 6064
664 N Twin Oaks Valley Rd, San Marcos (92069-1712)
PHONE 760 510-7170
Scott Romagnoli, *Manager*
Brian Reynolds, *Division Mgr*
Amy Brown, *Human Res Dir*
Jennie Gutierrez, *Purchasing*
Geraldine Saalfeld, *Purchasing*
EMP: 63
SALES (corp-wide): 2.8B **Privately Held**
SIC: 5113 2653 Paper & products, wrapping or coarse; boxes, corrugated: made from purchased materials
HQ: Orora Packaging Solutions
6600 Valley View St
Buena Park CA 90620
714 562-6000

(P-8204)
ORORA NORTH AMERICA
Mpp Union City Div 6062
33463 Western Ave, Union City (94587-3201)
P.O. Box 60000, San Francisco (94160-0001)
PHONE 510 487-1211
Fax: 510 487-0348
Nafiz Korustan, *Manager*
Steven Redd, *COO*
Darrell Chapman, *Production*
Carm Stones, *Production*
EMP: 95
SALES (corp-wide): 2.8B **Privately Held**
SIC: 5113 2653 Paper & products, wrapping or coarse; boxes, corrugated: made from purchased materials
HQ: Orora Packaging Solutions
6600 Valley View St
Buena Park CA 90620
714 562-6000

(P-8205)
ORORA NORTH AMERICA
Also Called: Landsberg Los Angeles Div 1001
1640 S Greenwood Ave, Montebello (90640-6538)
PHONE 323 832-2000
Fax: 323 722-4071
Jed Wockenfuss, *Manager*
David Conley, *CFO*
Roger Merritt, *Social Dir*
David Graney, *Finance*
Lynette Goodrich, *Human Res Mgr*
EMP: 168
SALES (corp-wide): 2.8B **Privately Held**
SIC: 5113 2653 Paper & products, wrapping or coarse; boxes, corrugated: made from purchased materials
HQ: Orora Packaging Solutions
6600 Valley View St
Buena Park CA 90620
714 562-6000

PRODUCTS & SERVICES SECTION
5113 - Indl & Personal Svc Paper Wholesale County (P-8223)

(P-8206)
ORORA NORTH AMERICA
Mpp Los Angeles Div 6060
3201 W Mission Rd, Alhambra
(91803-1113)
PHONE....................626 284-9524
Fax: 626 300-1272
Marc Fenster, *Manager*
David Bake, *Controller*
Lissette Perez, *Human Res Dir*
Maria Portillo, *Purch Agent*
EMP: 140
SALES (corp-wide): 2.8B **Privately Held**
SIC: 5113 2653 Paper & products, wrapping or coarse; boxes, corrugated: made from purchased materials
HQ: Orora Packaging Solutions
6600 Valley View St
Buena Park CA 90620
714 562-6000

(P-8207)
ORORA NORTH AMERICA
Also Called: Mpp Fullerton Div 6061
1901 E Rosslynn Ave, Fullerton
(92831-5141)
PHONE....................714 278-6000
Fax: 714 278-6003
Carol Hortick, *Branch Mgr*
Ron Casto, *Plant Mgr*
Bob Deshazo, *VP Sales*
Paul Ladin, *Sales Mgr*
Andy Barrientos, *Accounts Mgr*
EMP: 101
SALES (corp-wide): 2.8B **Privately Held**
SIC: 5113 2653 Paper & products, wrapping or coarse; boxes, corrugated: made from purchased materials
HQ: Orora Packaging Solutions
6600 Valley View St
Buena Park CA 90620
714 562-6000

(P-8208)
ORORA NORTH AMERICA
Also Called: Landsberg San Diego Div 1007
664 N Twin Oaks Valley Rd, San Marcos
(92069-1712)
PHONE....................760 510-7000
Brian Reynolds, *Branch Mgr*
Scott Magnoli, *Manager*
EMP: 62
SQ FT: 5,000
SALES (corp-wide): 2.8B **Privately Held**
SIC: 5113 2653 Paper & products, wrapping or coarse; boxes, corrugated: made from purchased materials
HQ: Orora Packaging Solutions
6600 Valley View St
Buena Park CA 90620
714 562-6000

(P-8209)
ORORA NORTH AMERICA
Also Called: Corru Kraft Fullerton Div 5068
1911 E Rosslynn Ave, Fullerton
(92831-5141)
PHONE....................714 773-0124
Ron Crawford, *Manager*
Jim Wilczek, *Vice Pres*
EMP: 85
SALES (corp-wide): 2.8B **Privately Held**
SIC: 5113 2653 Paper & products, wrapping or coarse; boxes, corrugated: made from purchased materials
HQ: Orora Packaging Solutions
6600 Valley View St
Buena Park CA 90620
714 562-6000

(P-8210)
ORORA NORTH AMERICA
Also Called: Corru Kraft Buena Pk Div 5058
6200 Caballero Blvd, Buena Park
(90620-1124)
PHONE....................714 562-6002
Fax: 714 562-2034
Jim Wilczek, *Vice Pres*
Riley Jerry, *Controller*
Jerry Riley, *Controller*
Jim Mers, *Opers Mgr*
Ron Crawford, *Plant Mgr*
EMP: 149
SALES (corp-wide): 2.8B **Privately Held**
SIC: 5113 2653 Paper & products, wrapping or coarse; boxes, corrugated: made from purchased materials
HQ: Orora Packaging Solutions
6600 Valley View St
Buena Park CA 90620
714 562-6000

(P-8211)
ORORA PACKAGING SOLUTIONS (HQ)
Also Called: Landsberg Orora
6600 Valley View St, Buena Park
(90620-1145)
PHONE....................714 562-6000
Bernardino Salvatore, *President*
Bernardino Salvatorre, *President*
David Conley, *CFO*
Michael Hodges, *Vice Pres*
Ray Huelskamp, *Vice Pres*
▲ **EMP:** 100 **EST:** 1951
SQ FT: 300,000
SALES (est): 2.1B
SALES (corp-wide): 2.8B **Privately Held**
WEB: www.amcor.com
SIC: 5113 2653 Paper & products, wrapping or coarse; sanitary food containers; boxes, corrugated: made from purchased materials
PA: Orora Limited
109 Burwood Rd
Hawthorn VIC 3122
398 117-111

(P-8212)
P & R PAPER SUPPLY CO INC (PA)
1898 E Colton Ave, Redlands
(92374-9798)
P.O. Box 590 (92373-0201)
PHONE....................909 389-1811
Fax: 909 794-1237
Mark S Maiberger, *CEO*
Joe Maiberger, *CFO*
Luke Maiberger, *Vice Pres*
Ann Mills, *Admin Sec*
Cathy Becker, *Controller*
▼ **EMP:** 76
SQ FT: 75,000
SALES (est): 122.4MM **Privately Held**
WEB: www.prpaper.com
SIC: 5113 5169 5149 5072 Industrial & personal service paper; chemicals & allied products; groceries & related products; hardware; commercial equipment

(P-8213)
PACKAGING INNOVATORS CORP
6650 National Dr, Livermore (94550-8802)
P.O. Box 1110 (94551-1110)
PHONE....................925 371-2000
Fax: 925 371-2001
William E Mazzocco, *CEO*
Alindo Cardelli, *Shareholder*
Beverly J Flynt, *Corp Secy*
John Hart, *Vice Pres*
Mark Andrew Mazzocco, *Vice Pres*
▲ **EMP:** 90
SQ FT: 114,000
SALES (est): 90.3MM **Privately Held**
WEB: www.callpic.com
SIC: 5113 2653 3993 Shipping supplies; corrugated & solid fiber boxes; display items, solid fiber: made from purchased materials; signs & advertising specialties

(P-8214)
ROYAL PAPER CORP (PA)
10232 Palm Dr, Santa Fe Springs
(90670-3368)
PHONE....................562 903-9030
Fax: 562 903-0229
Michael Rashtchi, *CEO*
George ABI-Aad, *President*
Marianne ABI-Aad, *Exec VP*
Johnathan Soon, *Vice Pres*
Kayn Solpanpour, *Sales Mgr*
▲ **EMP:** 60
SQ FT: 65,000
SALES (est): 70MM **Privately Held**
WEB: www.royal-paper.com
SIC: 5113 5087 Containers, paper & disposable plastic; paper & products, wrapping or coarse; cleaning & maintenance equipment & supplies

(P-8215)
SCHURMAN FINE PAPERS (PA)
Also Called: Papyrus
500 Chadbourne Rd, Fairfield
(94534-9656)
P.O. Box 6030 (94533-0690)
PHONE....................707 425-8006
Fax: 707 428-0641
Dominique Schurman, *CEO*
Marcel Schurman, *Chairman*
Christian Carlsson, *Vice Pres*
Laura Courtney, *Vice Pres*
Diana Ruhl, *Vice Pres*
▲ **EMP:** 100
SQ FT: 110,000
SALES (est): 1.2B **Privately Held**
SIC: 5113 2679 2771 5947 Industrial & personal service paper; paper & products, wrapping or coarse; gift wrap & novelties, paper; greeting cards; gift, novelty & souvenir shop; greeting cards

(P-8216)
SCHWARZ PAPER COMPANY LLC
8449 Milliken Ave Ste 102, Rancho Cucamonga (91730-5540)
PHONE....................909 476-2457
Sandy Kittrell, *General Mgr*
EMP: 87
SALES (corp-wide): 9.7B **Privately Held**
SIC: 5113 Industrial & personal service paper
HQ: Schwarz Paper Company, Llc
8338 Austin Ave
Morton Grove IL 60053
847 966-2550

(P-8217)
ULINE INC
2950 Jurupa St, Ontario (91761-2936)
PHONE....................909 605-7090
Toll Free:....................877 -
Fax: 949 605-7096
Israel Baluja, *Manager*
Pat Shea, *General Mgr*
Kathy Peterson, *Admin Asst*
Raymond Miller, *Manager*
Ed Keegan, *Clerk*
EMP: 57
SALES (corp-wide): 3.3B **Privately Held**
WEB: www.uline.com
SIC: 5113 5199 Shipping supplies; packaging materials
PA: Uline, Inc.
12575 Uline Dr
Pleasant Prairie WI 53158
262 612-4200

(P-8218)
UNISOURCE PACKAGING INC
4225 Hacienda Dr Ste A, Pleasanton (94588-2720)
P.O. Box 8803 (94588)
PHONE....................925 227-6000
Fax: 925 227-6084
Allan Dragone, *CEO*
Brenda Mask, *Administration*
Carl Franco, *CIO*
Julie Witz, *QC Mgr*
John Ducote, *Director*
▲ **EMP:** 112
SALES (est): 31.4MM
SALES (corp-wide): 8.7B **Publicly Held**
WEB: www.unisourcelink.com
SIC: 5113 Industrial & personal service paper; shipping supplies; boxes & containers
HQ: Veritiv Operating Company
1000 Abernathy Rd
Atlanta GA 30328
770 391-8200

(P-8219)
VERITIV OPERATING COMPANY
Northern California Mkt Area
2325 S Cedar Ave, Fresno (93725-1007)
P.O. Box 11368 (93773-1368)
PHONE....................559 268-0467
Fax: 559 233-9136
Dave Rhodes, *Branch Mgr*
Robin Rodriguez, *Human Res Dir*
Haig Haikasian, *Opers Staff*
John Oliveira, *VP Sales*
EMP: 90
SALES (corp-wide): 8.7B **Publicly Held**
WEB: www.unisourcelink.com
SIC: 5113 Industrial & personal service paper
HQ: Veritiv Operating Company
1000 Abernathy Rd
Atlanta GA 30328
770 391-8200

(P-8220)
VERITIV OPERATING COMPANY
Also Called: International Paper
15005 Northam St, La Mirada
(90638-5759)
PHONE....................714 690-4000
Fax: 714 690-4027
Dale Alby, *Manager*
Bob Quick, *Mill Mgr*
EMP: 100
SALES (corp-wide): 8.7B **Publicly Held**
WEB: www.internationalpaper.com
SIC: 5113 5111 Industrial & personal service paper; printing & writing paper
HQ: Veritiv Operating Company
1000 Abernathy Rd
Atlanta GA 30328
770 391-8200

(P-8221)
VERITIV OPERATING COMPANY
Also Called: Southern California Mkt Area
13217 S Figueroa St, Los Angeles
(90061-1139)
PHONE....................310 527-3000
Fax: 310 538-1023
Chris Hendrix, *Manager*
Naomi Dallob, *Admin Sec*
Diana Lawson, *Purch Agent*
Clint Smith, *Opers Mgr*
Ken Vuylsteke, *Opers Mgr*
EMP: 200
SQ FT: 13,000
SALES (corp-wide): 8.7B **Publicly Held**
WEB: www.unisourcelink.com
SIC: 5113 Industrial & personal service paper
HQ: Veritiv Operating Company
1000 Abernathy Rd
Atlanta GA 30328
770 391-8200

(P-8222)
VERITIV OPERATING COMPANY
Also Called: Southern California Mkt Area
2600 Commerce Way, Commerce
(90040-1413)
P.O. Box 910907, Los Angeles (90091-0907)
PHONE....................323 725-3700
Fax: 323 720-6754
Garryl Lasayette, *Manager*
Marc Edwards, *Sales Associate*
Kevin Kunda, *Sales Associate*
EMP: 200
SALES (corp-wide): 8.7B **Publicly Held**
WEB: www.unisourcelink.com
SIC: 5113 Industrial & personal service paper
HQ: Veritiv Operating Company
1000 Abernathy Rd
Atlanta GA 30328
770 391-8200

(P-8223)
VERITIV OPERATING COMPANY
Also Called: Unisource Maint Sup Systems
20 Centerpointe Dr # 130, La Palma
(90623-2505)
PHONE....................714 690-6600
Fax: 714 690-6660
Jim Speights, *Manager*
Roger Carmody, *Facilities Mgr*
EMP: 300
SALES (corp-wide): 8.7B **Publicly Held**
WEB: www.unisourcelink.com
SIC: 5113 Industrial & personal service paper
HQ: Veritiv Operating Company
1000 Abernathy Rd
Atlanta GA 30328
770 391-8200

5113 - Indl & Personal Svc Paper Wholesale County (P-8224)

(P-8224)
VITCO DISTRIBUTORS INC
Also Called: Vitco Food Service
10660 Mulberry Ave, Fontana
(92337-7025)
PHONE..................909 355-1300
Fax: 909 923-3391
Kostas Vitakis, *President*
Emmanuel Vitakis, *Treasurer*
EMP: 60
SQ FT: 20,000
SALES (est): 73.5MM **Privately Held**
SIC: 5113 Disposable plates, cups, napkins & eating utensils

5122 Drugs, Drug Proprietaries & Sundries Wholesale

(P-8225)
ACCESS BIOLOGICALS LLC
995 Park Center Dr, Vista (92081-8312)
PHONE..................760 597-9749
Barry Plost, *Mng Member*
Mark Ferreira, *Exec VP*
Kathleen Nelson, *Asst Controller*
Suzanne Nell, *Accountant*
Christopher Hunsucker, *VP Opers*
EMP: 71
SQ FT: 1,000
SALES (est): 34MM **Privately Held**
SIC: 5122 2836 Biologicals & allied products; biological products, except diagnostic

(P-8226)
ALIX TECHNOLOGIES INC
2929 E White Star Ave, Anaheim
(92806-2628)
PHONE..................714 630-6000
David Holmes, *President*
Andrea Bauer, *Treasurer*
Terri Kyser, *Controller*
EMP: 230
SALES (est): 23.9MM
SALES (corp-wide): 122.5MM **Privately Held**
SIC: 5122 Medicinals & botanicals
PA: Pharmachem Laboratories, Inc.
265 Harrison Tpke
Kearny NJ 07032
201 246-1000

(P-8227)
ALLERGAN SALES LLC (DH)
2525 Dupont Dr 14th, Irvine (92612-1599)
P.O. Box 19534 (92623-9534)
PHONE..................714 246-4500
David E I Pyott, *Ch of Bd*
Raymond H Diradoorian, *Exec VP*
Scott D Sherman, *Exec VP*
Scott M Whitcup, *Exec VP*
Julian S Gangolli, *Vice Pres*
EMP: 600
SQ FT: 10,000
SALES (est): 720.3MM **Privately Held**
WEB: www.myallerganbenefits.com
SIC: 5122 Pharmaceuticals
HQ: Allergan, Inc.
400 Interpace Pkwy
Parsippany NJ 07054
862 261-7000

(P-8228)
AMERICAN INTERNATIONAL INDS (PA)
2220 Gaspar Ave, Commerce
(90040-1516)
PHONE..................323 728-2999
Zvi Ryzman, *Partner*
Jennifer Paulson, *Senior VP*
Mark Moesta, *Vice Pres*
David Treho, *Credit Mgr*
Judy Pfleger, *Mktg Dir*
◆ **EMP:** 122
SQ FT: 224,000
SALES (est): 480.2MM **Privately Held**
SIC: 5122 2844 Cosmetics; toilet preparations

(P-8229)
AMERISOURCEBERGEN CORPORATION
Also Called: Valencia Division
24903 Avenue Kearny, Valencia
(91355-1252)
PHONE..................661 257-6400
Ron Green, *Manager*
Nate Tischler, *Regional Mgr*
Dan Cauffiel, *Data Proc Staff*
Rose Todd, *Human Res Dir*
Mike Quick, *VP Sales*
EMP: 150
SALES (corp-wide): 135.9B **Publicly Held**
WEB: www.amerisourcebergen.net
SIC: 5122 Drugs & drug proprietaries
PA: Amerisourcebergen Corporation
1300 Morris Dr Ste 100
Chesterbrook PA 19087
610 727-7000

(P-8230)
AMERISOURCEBERGEN CORPORATION
500 N State College Blvd # 900, Orange
(92868-1604)
P.O. Box 5915 (92863-5915)
PHONE..................714 385-4000
Fax: 213 385-1442
John McAlpine, *Branch Mgr*
Jeff Denton, *Director*
Greg Goldberg, *Director*
John Trippe, *Director*
EMP: 122
SALES (corp-wide): 135.9B **Publicly Held**
SIC: 5122 Drugs, proprietaries & sundries; pharmaceuticals; cosmetics; toiletries
PA: Amerisourcebergen Corporation
1300 Morris Dr Ste 100
Chesterbrook PA 19087
610 727-7000

(P-8231)
AMERISOURCEBERGEN CORPORATION
215 Deininger Cir, Corona (92880-1707)
PHONE..................951 493-2339
EMP: 122
SALES (corp-wide): 135.9B **Publicly Held**
SIC: 5122 Drugs, proprietaries & sundries
PA: Amerisourcebergen Corporation
1300 Morris Dr Ste 100
Chesterbrook PA 19087
610 727-7000

(P-8232)
AMERISOURCEBERGEN CORPORATION
Also Called: Sacramento GF Div
1325 Striker Ave, Sacramento
(95834-1164)
PHONE..................916 830-4500
Bruce Bennett, *Branch Mgr*
Pat Johnson, *Administration*
Randy Howery, *Research*
John Jessee, *Manager*
Michelle Tillman, *Supervisor*
EMP: 102
SALES (corp-wide): 135.9B **Publicly Held**
WEB: www.amerisourcebergen.net
SIC: 5122 Drugs, proprietaries & sundries
PA: Amerisourcebergen Corporation
1300 Morris Dr Ste 100
Chesterbrook PA 19087
610 727-7000

(P-8233)
AMERISOURCEBERGEN CORPORATION
Also Called: Corona Division
1851 California Ave, Corona (92881-6477)
PHONE..................951 371-2000
Joe Cheney, *Manager*
Jerilynn King, *Sales Staff*
John Stavich, *Manager*
Ida Canete, *Supervisor*
Patty Galippo, *Clerk*
EMP: 200

SALES (corp-wide): 135.9B **Publicly Held**
WEB: www.amerisourcebergen.net
SIC: 5122 Drugs & drug proprietaries
PA: Amerisourcebergen Corporation
1300 Morris Dr Ste 100
Chesterbrook PA 19087
610 727-7000

(P-8234)
AVID BIOSERVICES INC
14282 Franklin Ave, Tustin (92780-7009)
PHONE..................714 508-6100
Steve King, *CEO*
Paul Lytle, *CFO*
John L Quick, *Top Exec*
Christopher Eso, *Vice Pres*
Pete Gagnon, *Vice Pres*
EMP: 100
SALES (est): 15.7MM
SALES (corp-wide): 44.6MM **Publicly Held**
WEB: www.avidbioservices.com
SIC: 5122 Pharmaceuticals
PA: Peregrine Pharmaceuticals Inc
14282 Franklin Ave
Tustin CA 92780
714 508-6000

(P-8235)
BAXTER HEALTHCARE CORPORATION
1 Baxter Way Ste 100, Westlake Village
(91362-3813)
PHONE..................805 372-3000
Fax: 805 372-3002
John Bacich, *President*
Barry Deutsch, *President*
Johan Sande, *Vice Pres*
Andi Green, *Executive*
Tina Vazquez, *Executive Asst*
EMP: 1000
SALES (corp-wide): 9.9B **Publicly Held**
SIC: 5122 2834 2836 5047 Drugs, proprietaries & sundries; solutions, pharmaceutical; biological products, except diagnostic; medical equipment & supplies
HQ: Baxter Healthcare Corporation
1 Baxter Pkwy
Deerfield IL 60015
224 948-2000

(P-8236)
BEAUTY 21 COSMETICS INC
Also Called: L A Girl
2021 S Archibald Ave, Ontario
(91761-8535)
PHONE..................909 945-2220
Fax: 909 945-2262
Lan Jack Yu, *CEO*
Mahon Yu, *Vice Pres*
Charles Yu, *Analyst*
David Trinh, *VP Opers*
Jessica Talancon, *Mktg Dir*
▲ **EMP:** 105
SQ FT: 250,000
SALES (est): 92.2MM **Privately Held**
WEB: www.lagirlusa.com
SIC: 5122 2844 Cosmetics, perfumes & hair products; toilet preparations

(P-8237)
BERGEN BRUNSWIG DRUG COMPANY
4000 W Metropolitan Dr # 200, Orange
(92868-3503)
PHONE..................714 385-4000
Fax: 714 385-8840
Brent Martini, *President*
John H Mc Alpine, *CFO*
Doug Batezel,
EMP: 2845
SALES (est): 179.7MM **Privately Held**
SIC: 5122 Drugs, proprietaries & sundries; pharmaceuticals; cosmetics; toiletries

(P-8238)
BRIDGE MEDICAL INC
120 S Sierra Ave, Solana Beach
(92075-1811)
PHONE..................858 350-0100
Fax: 858 350-0115
Denean Rivera, *President*
Kevin S Smyth, *CIO*
Brenda Kraft, *VP Finance*
William J Lapoint Jr, *Director*

EMP: 90
SALES (est): 10.9MM
SALES (corp-wide): 135.9B **Publicly Held**
WEB: www.amerisourcebergen.net
SIC: 5122 Drugs, proprietaries & sundries
PA: Amerisourcebergen Corporation
1300 Morris Dr Ste 100
Chesterbrook PA 19087
610 727-7000

(P-8239)
BRIGHT PHARMACEUTICAL SERVICES
4570 Van Nuys Blvd, Sherman Oaks
(91403-2913)
PHONE..................818 981-9100
Alison Macpherson, *President*
Kadam Freeman, *Managing Prtnr*
Meredith McDonald, *Manager*
Aperna Mital, *Consultant*
EMP: 55
SQ FT: 2,500
SALES (est): 10.6MM **Privately Held**
WEB: www.brightps.com
SIC: 5122 Pharmaceuticals

(P-8240)
BRYANT RANCH PREPACK
1919 N Victory Pl, Burbank (91504-3425)
PHONE..................818 764-7225
Fax: 818 277-7552
Sanjay Anand, *President*
Geoffrey Hichborn, *Chief Engr*
Fred Ganjian, *Sales Dir*
EMP: 50
SALES (est): 20.7MM **Privately Held**
SIC: 5122 Pharmaceuticals

(P-8241)
CALIFORNIA SUNCARE INC
Also Called: California Tan
12777 W Jefferson Blvd, Los Angeles
(90066-7048)
PHONE..................310 578-4400
Fax: 310 824-0082
Duncan Robins, *CEO*
Sandy Kagan, *CFO*
Stephanie Snyder, *CFO*
Jenett Nelson, *Controller*
EMP: 77
SALES (est): 9.8MM **Privately Held**
WEB: www.californiatan.com
SIC: 5122 5199 Cosmetics, perfumes & hair products; pet supplies

(P-8242)
CARDINAL HEALTH INC
3238 Dwight Rd, Elk Grove (95758-6439)
PHONE..................916 372-9880
Trey Almonza, *Manager*
Dan Brechbill, *Technician*
Craig Sitze, *Analyst*
EMP: 200
SALES (corp-wide): 121.5B **Publicly Held**
SIC: 5122 Pharmaceuticals
PA: Cardinal Health, Inc.
7000 Cardinal Pl
Dublin OH 43017
614 757-5000

(P-8243)
CARDINAL HEALTH INC
1007 Canal Blvd, Richmond (94804-3549)
PHONE..................510 232-2030
Alan Kim, *Branch Mgr*
Sung Choi, *Pharmacy Dir*
Robert Kwan, *Pharmacist*
EMP: 74
SALES (corp-wide): 121.5B **Publicly Held**
SIC: 5122 Drugs, proprietaries & sundries
PA: Cardinal Health, Inc.
7000 Cardinal Pl
Dublin OH 43017
614 757-5000

(P-8244)
CARDINAL HEALTH INC
7330 N Palm Ave Ste 104, Fresno
(93711-5768)
PHONE..................559 448-0788
Fax: 559 448-0794
Mark Stassen, *Branch Mgr*
Laurel Bejeckian, *Vice Pres*

5122 - Drugs, Drug Proprietaries & Sundries Wholesale County (P-8265)

Garey Nishimura, *Pharmacy Dir*
Arnold Castro, *Pharmacist*
Martin Jeffries, *Associate*
EMP: 74
SALES (corp-wide): 121.5B **Publicly Held**
SIC: 5122 Drugs, proprietaries & sundries
PA: Cardinal Health, Inc.
  7000 Cardinal Pl
  Dublin OH 43017
  614 757-5000

(P-8245)
CARDINAL HEALTH INC
1935 Pine St, Redding (96001-1921)
PHONE.................................530 225-8735
Kurt Dunphy, *Branch Mgr*
Quy Nguyen, *Manager*
EMP: 74
SALES (corp-wide): 121.5B **Publicly Held**
SIC: 5122 Drugs, proprietaries & sundries
PA: Cardinal Health, Inc.
  7000 Cardinal Pl
  Dublin OH 43017
  614 757-5000

(P-8246)
CARDINAL HEALTH INC
3238 Dwight Rd, West Sacramento (95605)
PHONE.................................916 372-9880
Jim Satonaro, *Vice Pres*
EMP: 230
SALES (corp-wide): 121.5B **Publicly Held**
SIC: 5122 8731 Drugs, proprietaries & sundries; commercial physical research
PA: Cardinal Health, Inc.
  7000 Cardinal Pl
  Dublin OH 43017
  614 757-5000

(P-8247)
CARDINAL HEALTH INC
Also Called: Whitmire Distribution
27680 Avenue Mentry, Valencia (91355-1200)
PHONE.................................661 295-6100
Fax: 661 294-8218
Stewert Levin, *Manager*
Kathy Biggs, *Finance*
John Sanders, *Analyst*
Chris Gong, *Manager*
EMP: 120
SALES (corp-wide): 121.5B **Publicly Held**
SIC: 5122 Drugs, proprietaries & sundries
PA: Cardinal Health, Inc.
  7000 Cardinal Pl
  Dublin OH 43017
  614 757-5000

(P-8248)
CC WELLNESS LLC (HQ)
Also Called: United Consortium
29000 Hancock Pkwy, Valencia (91355-1007)
PHONE.................................661 295-1700
Marek Jan Olszewski, *CEO*
Joe Walls, *COO*
Craig May, *General Mgr*
Grace Riley, *Bookkeeper*
EMP: 55
SQ FT: 38,000
SALES: 15MM **Privately Held**
SIC: 5122 Pharmaceuticals
PA: Cc Wellness Acquisition Llc
  29000 Hancock Pkwy
  Valencia CA 91355
  661 295-1700

(P-8249)
CELGENE CORPORATION
Also Called: Celgene Signal Research
10300 Campus Point Dr # 100, San Diego (92121-1504)
PHONE.................................858 677-0034
Alan Lewis, *Branch Mgr*
Jacqueline Lamay, *Controller*
Afshin Mahmoude, *Manager*
EMP: 134
SALES (corp-wide): 9.2B **Publicly Held**
WEB: www.celgene.com
SIC: 5122 Pharmaceuticals

PA: Celgene Corporation
  86 Morris Ave
  Summit NJ 07901
  908 673-9000

(P-8250)
CENTRAL REFILL PHARMACEUTICALS
Also Called: Central Retail Pharmaceuticals
9521 Dalen St, Downey (90242-4847)
PHONE.................................562 401-4214
Benjamin Chu, *Owner*
Randall Nakahiro, *Research*
Cathy Holiday, *Assistant*
EMP: 100
SALES (est): 5.6MM **Privately Held**
SIC: 5122 Pharmaceuticals

(P-8251)
COUNTY OF LOS ANGELES
Also Called: Health Services, Dept of
1000 W Crson St Bsmnt 404 Basement, Torrance (90502)
PHONE.................................310 222-2357
Wes Kamikawa, *Director*
Connie Chittick, *Executive*
Maria Garibay, *Persnl Dir*
David Lakin, *Purch Agent*
Marcia E Cornford, *Pathologist*
EMP: 95 **Privately Held**
WEB: www.co.la.ca.us
SIC: 5122 9431 Pharmaceuticals; administration of public health programs;
PA: County Of Los Angeles
  500 W Temple St Ste 375
  Los Angeles CA 90012
  213 974-1101

(P-8252)
DAKO NORTH AMERICA INC (HQ)
6392 Via Real, Carpinteria (93013-2921)
PHONE.................................805 566-6655
Fax: 805 566-1344
Marie OH Huber, *President*
Robert Cantrell, *CFO*
Charles Bischof, *Vice Pres*
Pam Redmond, *Vice Pres*
Peter Staben, *Program Mgr*
▲ **EMP:** 225
SQ FT: 38,000
SALES (est): 120.3MM
SALES (corp-wide): 4B **Publicly Held**
WEB: www.dako.com
SIC: 5122 3841 Biologicals & allied products; diagnostic apparatus, medical
PA: Agilent Technologies, Inc.
  5301 Stevens Creek Blvd
  Santa Clara CA 95051
  408 345-8886

(P-8253)
FFF ENTERPRISES INC (PA)
41093 County Center Dr, Temecula (92591-6025)
PHONE.................................951 296-2500
Fax: 951 296-2553
Patrick M Schmidt, *CEO*
Greg Neier, *President*
Chris Ground, *COO*
Kieth Sinclair, *COO*
Brad Cooper, *CFO*
EMP: 150
SQ FT: 80,000
SALES (est): 159.7MM **Privately Held**
WEB: www.fffenterprises.com
SIC: 5122 5047 Pharmaceuticals; medical equipment & supplies

(P-8254)
GALE LINA INC
230 S 9th Ave, City of Industry (91746-3309)
PHONE.................................909 595-8898
John Chen, *CEO*
Lina Chen, *CFO*
EMP: 100 **EST:** 1991
SALES (est): 51.7MM **Privately Held**
SIC: 5122 Cosmetics

(P-8255)
GLAMOUR INDUSTRIES CO
2220 Gaspar Ave, Commerce (90040-1516)
PHONE.................................323 728-2999
Zvi Ryzman, *President*

Theresa Cooper, *Exec VP*
Betty Ryzman, *Admin Sec*
EMP: 300
SQ FT: 224,000
SALES (est): 49.3MM **Privately Held**
SIC: 5122 Cosmetics

(P-8256)
GLAXOSMITHKLINE CONSUMER
2020 E Vine Ave, Fresno (93706-5458)
PHONE.................................559 650-1550
Mark Bullard, *Branch Mgr*
Johanna Guntner, *Director*
EMP: 99
SALES (corp-wide): 36B **Privately Held**
SIC: 5122 Drugs, proprietaries & sundries
HQ: Glaxosmithkline Consumer Healthcare, L.P.
  184 Libery Corner Rd
  Warren NJ 07059
  251 591-4188

(P-8257)
GLAXOSMITHKLINE LLC
3366 N Torrey Pines Ct, La Jolla (92037-1025)
PHONE.................................858 260-5900
EMP: 50
SALES (corp-wide): 36B **Privately Held**
SIC: 5122 2834 Toothbrushes, except electric; pharmaceutical preparations
HQ: Glaxosmithkline Llc
  5 Crescent Dr
  Philadelphia PA 19112
  215 751-4000

(P-8258)
GOLDEN N-LIFE DIAMITE INTL INC (PA)
3500 Gateway Blvd, Fremont (94538-6584)
PHONE.................................510 651-0405
Fax: 510 657-7563
Roget Uys, *CEO*
George Casale, *President*
Kevin Fox, *COO*
Daniel L Lewis, *COO*
Jarm William, *CFO*
▲ **EMP:** 80
SQ FT: 66,000
SALES (est): 30.4MM **Privately Held**
WEB: www.us.gnld.com
SIC: 5122 Cosmetics, perfumes & hair products

(P-8259)
GRIFOLS SHARED SVCS N AMER INC (HQ)
2410 Lillyvale Ave, Los Angeles (90032-3514)
PHONE.................................323 225-2221
Fax: 323 227-7616
Gregory Rich, *CEO*
Max Debrouwer, *CFO*
Raul Alvarez, *Senior VP*
David Bell, *Vice Pres*
Dave Dew, *Vice Pres*
▲ **EMP:** 153
SALES (est): 4.2B
SALES (corp-wide): 464.6MM **Privately Held**
WEB: www.grifolsusa.com
SIC: 5122 2834 Drugs, proprietaries & sundries; druggists' preparations (pharmaceuticals)
PA: Grifols Sa
  Calle Jesus I Maria 6
  Barcelona 08022
  935 710-196

(P-8260)
H D SMITH LLC
1370 E Victoria St, Carson (90746-7501)
P.O. Box 6231 (90749-6231)
PHONE.................................310 641-1885
Bob Schwartz, *Manager*
Rick D Rio, *Controller*
EMP: 100
SALES (corp-wide): 2B **Privately Held**
WEB: www.hdsmith.com
SIC: 5122 5047 Drugs & drug proprietaries; medical & hospital equipment
PA: H. D. Smith, Llc
  3063 Fiat Ave
  Springfield IL 62703
  866 232-1222

(P-8261)
HATCHBEAUTY PRODUCTS LLC (PA)
10951 W Pico Blvd Ste 300, Los Angeles (90064-2182)
P.O. Box 641415 (90064-6415)
PHONE.................................310 396-7070
Ben Bennett, *Managing Prtnr*
Benjamin Bennett, *Partner*
Tracy Holland, *Managing Prtnr*
Erika Beckles, *Office Mgr*
Pamela Silva, *Asst Mgr*
EMP: 83 **EST:** 2010
SALES (est): 120MM **Privately Held**
SIC: 5122 Cosmetics, perfumes & hair products

(P-8262)
HERBALIFE INTL AMER INC (DH)
800 W Olympic Blvd # 406, Los Angeles (90015-1360)
PHONE.................................310 410-9600
Fax: 310 216-5169
Michael O Johnson, *CEO*
Des Walsh, *President*
Rich Goudis, *COO*
John De Simone, *CFO*
Richard Yamashita, *Treasurer*
▲ **EMP:** 500
SQ FT: 115,000
SALES (est): 1.2B **Privately Held**
WEB: www.herbalifefamily.com
SIC: 5122 Vitamins & minerals
HQ: Herbalife Ltd, Inc.
  800 W Olympic Blvd # 406
  Los Angeles CA 90015
  310 410-9600

(P-8263)
HOYU AMERICA CO
Also Called: Samy Co
6265 Phyllis Dr, Cypress (90630-5240)
PHONE.................................714 230-3000
Yoshihiro Sasaki, *President*
Minoru Tsuda, *Senior VP*
Teresa Diaz, *Accountant*
Steve Koch, *Senior Buyer*
Kevin Griffin, *Opers Mgr*
EMP: 58
SALES: 35MM
SALES (corp-wide): 257.2K **Privately Held**
SIC: 5122 5999 Cosmetics, perfumes & hair products; hair care products
HQ: Hoyu Co.,Ltd.
  1-501, Tokugawa, Higashi-Ku
  Nagoya AIC 461-0
  529 359-556

(P-8264)
INTAKE INITIATIVES INC
Also Called: Lash-San Francisco Office
999 Bayhill Dr Ste 200, San Bruno (94066-3052)
PHONE.................................800 788-9637
Tracy Foster, *Principal*
Peyton Howell, *President*
Karri Reynosa, *Finance*
EMP: 110
SQ FT: 8,500
SALES: 6.1MM
SALES (corp-wide): 135.9B **Publicly Held**
WEB: www.amerisourcebergen.net
SIC: 5122 Drugs, proprietaries & sundries
PA: Amerisourcebergen Corporation
  1300 Morris Dr Ste 100
  Chesterbrook PA 19087
  610 727-7000

(P-8265)
IRWIN NATURALS
5310 Beethoven St, Los Angeles (90066-7015)
PHONE.................................310 306-3636
Klee Irwin, *President*
Mark Green, *CFO*
Mike Berg, *Exec VP*
Jeffrey Sugawara, *Senior VP*
Rebecca Pearman, *Vice Pres*
EMP: 80
SQ FT: 52,000
SALES (est): 53.8MM **Privately Held**
SIC: 5122 Vitamins & minerals

5122 - Drugs, Drug Proprietaries & Sundries Wholesale County (P-8266)

(P-8266)
JAN MARINI SKIN RESEARCH INC
5883 Rue Ferrari Ste 175, San Jose (95138-1863)
PHONE..............................408 620-3600
Fax: 408 362-0140
Jan Marini, *CEO*
Robert James, *CFO*
John Connors, *Exec VP*
Katie Petroff, *Admin Sec*
Patricia Bankston, *Admin Asst*
▲ **EMP:** 80
SQ FT: 5,000
SALES (est): 64.4MM **Privately Held**
WEB: www.janmarini.com
SIC: 5122 Drugs, proprietaries & sundries

(P-8267)
JARROW FORMULAS INC (PA)
1824 S Robertson Blvd, Los Angeles (90035-4317)
PHONE..............................310 204-6936
Fax: 310 204-2520
Ben Khowong, *CEO*
Jarrow L Rogovin, *President*
Clayton Dubose, *Treasurer*
Peilin Guo, *Exec VP*
Michael Jacobs, *Vice Pres*
◆ **EMP:** 80
SQ FT: 37,000
SALES (est): 89.9MM **Privately Held**
SIC: 5122 Vitamins & minerals

(P-8268)
JESSICA COSMETICS INTL INC
Also Called: Jessica's Cosmetics
13209 Saticoy St, North Hollywood (91605-3405)
PHONE..............................818 759-1050
Fax: 818 739-1282
Jessica Vartoughian, *President*
Peter Sarkissian, *Marketing Staff*
Valentin Safta, *Senior Mgr*
Valerie Celia, *Director*
▲ **EMP:** 60 **EST:** 1968
SALES (est): 24MM **Privately Held**
SIC: 5122 7231 Cosmetics; beauty shops

(P-8269)
JORDANA COSMETICS CORPORATION
2035 E 49th St, Vernon (90058-2801)
P.O. Box 58668, Los Angeles (90058-0668)
PHONE..............................323 585-4859
Fax: 323 589-0283
Laurie Minc, *President*
Ralph Bijou, *Principal*
Jenny Ponce, *Info Tech Dir*
Robert Wallner, *VP Sales*
Ericka Molina, *Manager*
◆ **EMP:** 65
SQ FT: 30,000
SALES (est): 41.6MM **Privately Held**
WEB: www.jordanacosmetics.com
SIC: 5122 Cosmetics

(P-8270)
KABAFUSION LLC
17777 Center Court Dr N # 550, Cerritos (90703-9320)
PHONE..............................562 863-0555
Dr Sohail Masood,
Aslam Masood,
Mona Masood,
Michael Rigas,
EMP: 80
SQ FT: 4,000
SALES (est): 40MM **Privately Held**
SIC: 5122 8059 Pharmaceuticals; convalescent home

(P-8271)
KATE SOMERVILLE HOLDINGS LLC
144 S Beverly Dr Ste 500, Beverly Hills (90212-3023)
PHONE..............................323 655-4170
Kate Somerville, *Mng Member*
EMP: 100 **EST:** 2007
SALES (est): 15.2MM **Privately Held**
SIC: 5122 Toiletries; cosmetics; perfumes

(P-8272)
KATE SOMERVILLE SKINCARE LLC (HQ)
144 S Beverly Dr Ste 500, Beverly Hills (90212-3023)
PHONE..............................323 655-7546
Kate Somerville, *Mng Member*
Shellie Gainer, *Vice Pres*
Jeff Hansen,
Laura Shaff,
Michelle Taylor,
▲ **EMP:** 51
SALES (est): 46.5MM
SALES (corp-wide): 57.2B **Privately Held**
SIC: 5122 Toiletries; cosmetics; perfumes
PA: Unilever Plc
100 Victoria Embankment
London EC4Y
207 822-5252

(P-8273)
KINSALE HOLDINGS INC
Also Called: Validant
475 Sansome St Ste 700, San Francisco (94111-3129)
PHONE..............................415 400-2600
Brian Healy, *CEO*
Michael Beatrice, *President*
Helm Siegel, *Vice Pres*
Erick Carleton, *Administration*
Richard Stonehouse, *QA Dir*
EMP: 250
SQ FT: 10,000
SALES (est): 129.3MM **Privately Held**
SIC: 5122 Pharmaceuticals

(P-8274)
LOREAL USA INC
1848 4th St, Berkeley (94710-1911)
PHONE..............................510 548-0130
Doug Vangoerkan, *Manager*
EMP: 227
SALES (corp-wide): 3.1B **Privately Held**
SIC: 5122 Cosmetics, perfumes & hair products
HQ: L'oreal Usa, Inc.
10 Hudson Yards
New York NY 10001
212 818-1500

(P-8275)
M P O INC (DH)
3760 Kilroy Airport Way # 5, Long Beach (90806-2443)
PHONE..............................562 628-1007
Al Hummel, *President*
Preston Romm, *CFO*
David Goldstein, *Exec VP*
Nasim Glaubitz, *Vice Pres*
James Hartman, *Vice Pres*
EMP: 80
SQ FT: 16,000
SALES (est): 27.5MM
SALES (corp-wide): 10.4B **Privately Held**
WEB: www.obagi.com
SIC: 5122 Cosmetics
HQ: Obagi Medical Products, Inc.
50 Technology Dr
Irvine CA 92618
562 628-1007

(P-8276)
MARKWINS BEAUTY PRODUCTS INC
22067 Ferrero, City of Industry (91789-5214)
PHONE..............................909 595-8898
Eric Chen, *President*
Shawn Haynes, *Senior VP*
James Koeppl, *Senior VP*
Angelina Pilnedo, *Admin Asst*
Julie Hsu, *Controller*
◆ **EMP:** 66
SQ FT: 200,000
SALES (est): 47MM
SALES (corp-wide): 296.4MM **Privately Held**
WEB: www.markwins.com
SIC: 5122 Cosmetics
PA: Markwins International Corp
22067 Ferrero
Walnut CA 91789
909 595-8898

(P-8277)
MCKESSON CORPORATION
395 Oyster Point Blvd # 500, South San Francisco (94080-1928)
PHONE..............................650 952-8400
Erin Crum, *Principal*
Rajan Jena, *Director*
Dan Lodder, *Director*
Ethan H Wilcox, *Manager*
EMP: 66
SALES (corp-wide): 190.8B **Publicly Held**
SIC: 5122 Drugs, proprietaries & sundries
PA: Mckesson Corporation
1 Post St Fl 18
San Francisco CA 94104
415 983-8300

(P-8278)
MCKESSON CORPORATION
6969 Brockton Ave Ste B, Riverside (92506-3813)
PHONE..............................951 686-3575
Robert Bourne, *Branch Mgr*
Marissa Tamayo, *Human Resources*
Tami Jones, *Opers Staff*
EMP: 65
SALES (corp-wide): 190.8B **Publicly Held**
WEB: www.imckesson.com
SIC: 5122 5047 5199 7372 Pharmaceuticals; proprietary (patent) medicines; toiletries; druggists' sundries; medical equipment & supplies; first aid supplies; general merchandise, non-durable; prepackaged software
PA: Mckesson Corporation
1 Post St Fl 18
San Francisco CA 94104
415 983-8300

(P-8279)
MCKESSON CORPORATION
Also Called: McKesson Drug
9501 Norwalk Blvd, Santa Fe Springs (90670-2929)
P.O. Box 2116 (90670-0116)
PHONE..............................562 463-2100
Fax: 562 463-2124
Todd Kleinow, *Manager*
Matt Verhalen, *Facilities Mgr*
Mike Wetch, *Manager*
EMP: 120
SALES (corp-wide): 190.8B **Publicly Held**
WEB: www.imckesson.com
SIC: 5122 Drugs & drug proprietaries
PA: Mckesson Corporation
1 Post St Fl 18
San Francisco CA 94104
415 983-8300

(P-8280)
MCKESSON CORPORATION
Also Called: McKesson Drug
3775 Seaport Blvd, West Sacramento (95691-3558)
P.O. Box 15858, Sacramento (95852-0858)
PHONE..............................916 372-3655
Fax: 916 371-4611
Larry Honley, *Sales/Mktg Mgr*
Patrick Smith, *Sls & Mktg Exec*
Lori White, *Manager*
EMP: 150
SALES (corp-wide): 190.8B **Publicly Held**
WEB: www.imckesson.com
SIC: 5122 Drugs & drug proprietaries
PA: Mckesson Corporation
1 Post St Fl 18
San Francisco CA 94104
415 983-8300

(P-8281)
MCKESSON CORPORATION (PA)
1 Post St Fl 18, San Francisco (94104-5284)
PHONE..............................415 983-8300
Fax: 415 983-7073
John H Hammergren, *Ch of Bd*
Patrick J Blake, *President*
Paul C Julian, *President*
James A Beer, *CFO*
Lori A Schechter, *Ch Credit Ofcr*
◆ **EMP:** 755
SALES: 190.8B **Publicly Held**
WEB: www.imckesson.com
SIC: 5122 5047 5199 7372 Drugs, proprietaries & sundries; pharmaceuticals; proprietary (patent) medicines; druggists' sundries; medical equipment & supplies; first aid supplies; general merchandise, non-durable; prepackaged software

(P-8282)
MERLE NORMAN COSMETICS INC
15180 Bledsoe St, Sylmar (91342-2797)
PHONE..............................818 362-3235
Kim Frappe, *Manager*
Rick Dela La, *Vice Pres*
Armin Lohbrunner, *Controller*
Rose Flores, *Persnl Mgr*
EMP: 150
SALES (corp-wide): 74.1MM **Privately Held**
WEB: www.merlenorman.com
SIC: 5122 Cosmetics, perfumes & hair products
PA: Merle Norman Cosmetics, Inc.
9130 Bellanca Ave
Los Angeles CA 90045
310 641-3000

(P-8283)
METAGENICS INC (DH)
25 Enterprise Ste 200, Aliso Viejo (92656-2709)
PHONE..............................949 366-0818
Fax: 949 366-2859
Brent Eck, *President*
Jean M Bellin, *President*
Dave Tuit, *CFO*
John Troup, *Officer*
John Babish, *Exec VP*
◆ **EMP:** 150
SQ FT: 88,000
SALES (est): 216.5MM
SALES (corp-wide): 9.4B **Privately Held**
WEB: www.ethicalnutrients.com
SIC: 5122 Vitamins & minerals; medicinals & botanicals
HQ: Alticor Inc.
7575 Fulton St E
Ada MI 49355
616 787-1000

(P-8284)
METAGENICS INC
100 Avenida Lapata, Sacramento (94203-0001)
PHONE..............................800 692-9400
Carol Perkovich, *Manager*
EMP: 100
SALES (corp-wide): 9.4B **Privately Held**
WEB: www.ethicalnutrients.com
SIC: 5122 5047 Vitamins & minerals; physician equipment & supplies
HQ: Metagenics, Inc.
25 Enterprise Ste 200
Aliso Viejo CA 92656
949 366-0818

(P-8285)
N QIAGEN AMERCN HOLDINGS INC (HQ)
27220 Turnberry Ln # 200, Valencia (91355-1018)
PHONE..............................661 702-3000
Fax: 661 295-7652
Peer Schatz, *President*
Amy Hoffer, *Product Mgr*
Melissa Van Dorn, *Marketing Staff*
David Dortch, *Senior Mgr*
Kim Budelier, *Manager*
EMP: 250
SALES (est): 217.8MM
SALES (corp-wide): 1.2B **Privately Held**
SIC: 5122 Biologicals & allied products
PA: Qiagen N.V.
Hulsterweg 82
Venlo 5912
773 556-600

(P-8286)
NATROL LLC (DH)
21411 Prairie St, Chatsworth (91311-5829)
PHONE..............................818 739-6000
Fax: 818 739-6001
Mesrop Khoudagoulian, *Mng Member*
Jeff Perea, *CFO*

PRODUCTS & SERVICES SECTION

5131 - Piece Goods, Notions & Dry Goods Wholesale County (P-8308)

Ivan Milenkovic, *Administration*
Mirrella Jolicoeur, *Info Tech Dir*
Michael Berinde, *Info Tech Mgr*
EMP: 128 **EST:** 2015
SALES: 110MM
SALES (corp-wide): 1.3B **Privately Held**
SIC: 5122 2099 Drugs, proprietaries & sundries; food preparations
HQ: Aurobindo Pharma U.S.A., Inc.
6 Wheeling Rd
Dayton NJ 08810
732 839-9400

(P-8287)
OMNICARE INC
20967 Cabot Blvd, Hayward (94545-1155)
PHONE.................510 293-9663
EMP: 99
SALES (corp-wide): 153.2B **Publicly Held**
SIC: 5122 Pharmaceuticals
HQ: Omnicare, Inc.
900 Omnicare Ctr
Cincinnati OH 45202
513 719-2600

(P-8288)
PACIFIC PHARMA INC
18600 Von Karman Ave, Irvine (92612-1513)
PHONE.................714 246-4600
EMP: 2000
SALES (est): 108.7MM **Privately Held**
SIC: 5122
HQ: Allergan, Inc.
400 Interpace Pkwy
Parsippany NJ 07054
862 261-7000

(P-8289)
PACIRA PHARMACEUTICALS INC
Also Called: Research & Dev & Mfg Site
10578 Science Center Dr, San Diego (92121-1143)
PHONE.................858 625-2424
EMP: 384
SALES (corp-wide): 249MM **Publicly Held**
SIC: 5122 Pharmaceuticals
PA: Pacira Pharmaceuticals, Inc.
5 Sylvan Way Ste 300
Parsippany NJ 07054
973 254-3560

(P-8290)
PAUL MITCHELL JOHN SYSTEMS (PA)
20705 Centre Pointe Pkwy, Santa Clarita (91350-2967)
P.O. Box 10597, Beverly Hills (90213-3597)
PHONE.................661 298-0400
John Paul Dejoria, *CEO*
Luke Jacobellis, *COO*
Rick Battaglini, *CFO*
Rick Battalini, *CFO*
Julia Provost, *Senior VP*
◆ **EMP:** 80
SQ FT: 90,000
SALES (est): 158.4MM **Privately Held**
SIC: 5122 Hair preparations

(P-8291)
ROBINSON PHARMA INC
1683 Sunflower Ave # 103, Costa Mesa (92626-1540)
PHONE.................714 241-0235
EMP: 108
SALES (corp-wide): 106MM **Privately Held**
SIC: 5122 Pharmaceuticals
PA: Robinson Pharma, Inc.
3330 S Harbor Blvd
Santa Ana CA 92704
714 241-0235

(P-8292)
RUGBY LABORATORIES INC (DH)
311 Bonnie Cir, Corona (92880-2882)
PHONE.................951 270-1400
David C Hsia PHD, *President*
Michael E Boser, *CFO*
Michel J Feldman, *Officer*

Frederick Wilkinson, *Vice Pres*
David A Buchen, *Admin Sec*
EMP: 90
SALES (est): 25.7MM
SALES (corp-wide): 121.5B **Publicly Held**
WEB: www.watsonpharm.com
SIC: 5122 2834 Pharmaceuticals; pharmaceutical preparations
HQ: The Harvard Drug Group L L C
17177 N Laurel Park Dr
Livonia MI 48152
734 525-8700

(P-8293)
SGII INC
Also Called: Senegence International
9211 Irvine Blvd, Irvine (92618-1645)
PHONE.................949 521-6161
Joni Rogers Kante, *CEO*
Michael Moad, *President*
Ben Kante, *COO*
▲ **EMP:** 50
SQ FT: 8,000
SALES (est): 15.6MM **Privately Held**
WEB: www.senegence.com
SIC: 5122 Cosmetics; vitamins & minerals

(P-8294)
SHAKLEE CORPORATION
1992 Alpine Way, Hayward (94545-1702)
PHONE.................510 887-5000
Fax: 510 887-8583
Debora Busse, *Branch Mgr*
Valerie Lacey, *Admin Asst*
Barrington Henry, *Software Dev*
Nebin Andersen, *VP Finance*
Bernadine Bailey, *Purch Dir*
EMP: 60
SALES (corp-wide): 119.1MM **Privately Held**
WEB: www.shaklee.net
SIC: 5122 Vitamins & minerals
PA: Shaklee Corporation
4747 Willow Rd
Pleasanton CA 94588
925 924-2000

(P-8295)
SIGNAL PHARMACEUTICALS LLC
10300 Campus Point Dr # 100, San Diego (92121-1504)
PHONE.................858 795-4700
Fax: 858 552-8775
Alan J Lewis PHD, *President*
John Walker, *Chairman*
R Michael Gendreau, *Chief Mktg Ofcr*
Shripad Bhagwat, *Vice Pres*
Douglas E Richards, *Vice Pres*
EMP: 134
SQ FT: 78,202
SALES (est): 40.9MM
SALES (corp-wide): 9.2B **Publicly Held**
SIC: 5122 Pharmaceuticals
PA: Celgene Corporation
86 Morris Ave
Summit NJ 07901
908 673-9000

(P-8296)
STAR NAIL PRODUCTS INC
Also Called: Star Nail International
29120 Avenue Paine, Valencia (91355-5402)
PHONE.................661 257-3376
Tony Cuccio, *CEO*
Anthony Cuccio, *President*
Roberta Cuccio, *Vice Pres*
Patricia Fruend, *Vice Pres*
Elaine Watson, *Vice Pres*
▲ **EMP:** 55
SQ FT: 14,000
SALES (est): 28.2MM **Privately Held**
WEB: www.allseasonnails.com
SIC: 5122 2844 7231 Cosmetics; toilet preparations; beauty shops

(P-8297)
SUPERBALIFE INTERNATIONAL LLC
Also Called: Prostavar Rx
1171 S Robertson Blvd # 525, Los Angeles (90035-1403)
PHONE.................310 553-7400
Fred Buckley, *President*

Corrine Buckley, *Mng Member*
EMP: 62
SALES (est): 22MM **Privately Held**
SIC: 5122 Vitamins & minerals

(P-8298)
TEVA PHARMACEUTICALS USA INC
19 Hughes, Irvine (92618-1902)
PHONE.................949 457-2828
Allan Oberman, *CEO*
Linda Frigger, *Associate Dir*
Manjula Ghosh, *Associate Dir*
Robert Paulson, *Associate Dir*
Ishaq Bajwa, *Principal*
EMP: 77 **EST:** 1985
SALES (est): 32.1MM **Privately Held**
SIC: 5122 Pharmaceuticals

(P-8299)
UNITE EUROTHERAPY INC
1255 Keystone Way Ste 106, Vista (92081-8310)
PHONE.................760 585-1800
Andrew Dale, *President*
Diane Barry, *Sales Staff*
Brandy Cooper, *Sales Staff*
Lindsey Darnell, *Mktg Coord*
Andrew Lievrouw, *Warehouse Mgr*
▲ **EMP:** 66
SALES (est): 14.1MM **Privately Held**
SIC: 5122 Hair preparations

(P-8300)
UNITED EXCHANGE CORP
17211 Valley View Ave, Cerritos (90703-2414)
PHONE.................562 977-4500
Eugene W Choi, *CEO*
Carol J Choi, *President*
Sean Akutagawa, *Technology*
Tom Blaylock, *Sales Dir*
Jocelyn Jocson, *Marketing Mgr*
◆ **EMP:** 50
SQ FT: 100,000
SALES (est): 43.8MM **Privately Held**
WEB: www.ueccorp.com
SIC: 5122 Drugs, proprietaries & sundries

(P-8301)
UNITED SAMPLES INC
Also Called: Dongyu USI
2590 Main St, Irvine (92614-6227)
PHONE.................949 251-1768
Hao Zhuang, *President*
Rick Bravo, *Sales Staff*
William Fang, *Accounts Exec*
Robert Lavender, *Accounts Exec*
▲ **EMP:** 300
SALES (est): 54.4MM **Privately Held**
SIC: 5122 5169 Vitamins & minerals; food additives & preservatives

(P-8302)
VALLEY OF SUN COSMETICS LLC
Also Called: Valley of The Sun Labs
535 Patrice Pl, Gardena (90248-4232)
PHONE.................310 327-9062
Jimmy Ajmal,
Ajmal Shehzad,
Bill Lopez, *Manager*
Morain Lorena, *Manager*
◆ **EMP:** 156
SQ FT: 10,000
SALES (est): 47.5MM **Privately Held**
WEB: www.cosmeticusa.com
SIC: 5122 Cosmetics

(P-8303)
VALLEY WHOLESALE DRUG CO LLC
1401 W Fremont St, Stockton (95203-2627)
P.O. Box 2065 (95201-2065)
PHONE.................209 466-0131
Fax: 209 465-4056
Dale Smith, *CEO*
Dan Matteoli, *Vice Pres*
Angelo Grande, *Principal*
Tim Shoneff, *Buyer*
Bobby Jones, *Sales Mgr*
EMP: 75 **EST:** 1948
SQ FT: 10,000

SALES (est): 110MM
SALES (corp-wide): 2B **Privately Held**
SIC: 5122 Drugs & drug proprietaries; cosmetics; druggists' sundries
PA: H. D. Smith, Llc
3063 Fiat Ave
Springfield IL 62703
866 232-1222

(P-8304)
VETERINARY PHARMACEUTICALS INC
13159 13th Rd W, Hanford (93230-9666)
PHONE.................559 582-6800
Harold Des Jardins, *CEO*
Alice Desjardins, *Vice Pres*
Alice Des Jardins, *Vice Pres*
Narilyn Bracy, *General Mgr*
Marilyn K Bracy, *Director*
▲ **EMP:** 52
SALES (est): 17.2MM **Privately Held**
SIC: 5122 Pharmaceuticals

(P-8305)
VIVA LIFE SCIENCE INC
350 Paularino Ave, Costa Mesa (92626-4616)
PHONE.................949 645-6100
Fax: 949 645-1044
David Fan, *President*
Ning Hong, *Research*
Millie Hardi, *Purch Mgr*
Nasim Moradai, *Mktg Dir*
Jorge Lopez, *Manager*
EMP: 100
SQ FT: 60,000
SALES (est): 14.6MM **Privately Held**
SIC: 5122 2833 Vitamins & minerals; cosmetics; medicinals & botanicals

(P-8306)
WAKUNAGA OF AMERICA CO LTD (HQ)
Also Called: Kyolic
23501 Madero, Mission Viejo (92691-2744)
PHONE.................949 855-2776
Fax: 949 458-2764
Kazuhiko Nomura, *CEO*
Kenro Nakamura, *President*
Hiyoshi Sakai, *Vice Pres*
Kathy Comstock, *Admin Asst*
Nick Nishira, *Controller*
◆ **EMP:** 64
SQ FT: 36,000
SALES: 30.4MM
SALES (corp-wide): 70.6MM **Privately Held**
WEB: www.kyolic.com
SIC: 5122 Drugs & drug proprietaries
PA: Wakunaga Pharmaceutical Co., Ltd.
4-5-36, Miyahara, Yodogawa-Ku
Osaka OSK 532-0
663 503-555

(P-8307)
WITHROW PHRM & HLTH SPC LAB
2235 Via Puerta Unit A, Laguna Woods (92637-8114)
PHONE.................323 721-4281
Sergio Quinones, *President*
Maria Gray, *Human Res Mgr*
EMP: 100 **EST:** 1928
SALES (est): 9.9MM **Privately Held**
WEB: www.withrow-pharm.com
SIC: 5122 7231 Pharmaceuticals; beauty shops

5131 Piece Goods, Notions & Dry Goods Wholesale

(P-8308)
ADERANS HAIR GOODS INC
9135 Independence Ave, Chatsworth (91311-5903)
PHONE.................818 428-1626
Nobuo Nemoto, *President*
Lisa Median, *Accounting Mgr*
▲ **EMP:** 54
SALES (est): 6.3MM **Privately Held**
SIC: 5131 5999 Hair accessories; hair care products

(PA)=Parent Co (HQ)=Headquarters (DH)=Div Headquarters
✪ = New Business established in last 2 years

2017 Directory of California Wholesalers and Services Companies

5131 - Piece Goods, Notions & Dry Goods Wholesale County (P-8309)

(P-8309)
CHARMING TRIM & PACKAGING
28 Brookside Ct, Novato (94947-3847)
PHONE..............................415 302-7021
Richard Ringeisen, *President*
Barry Chan, *Exec Dir*
EMP: 1000
SALES (est): 59.5MM **Privately Held**
SIC: 5131 3111 Trimmings, apparel; garment leather

(P-8310)
DAZIAN LLC
Also Called: Dazian's
10671 Lorne St, Sun Valley (91352-4642)
PHONE..............................818 287-3800
Fax: 818 287-3810
Chris Diaz, *Branch Mgr*
Steven Weiss, *Sales Dir*
EMP: 60
SALES (corp-wide): 91MM **Privately Held**
WEB: www.dazian.com
SIC: 5131 Piece goods & notions
PA: Dazian, Llc
18 Central Blvd
South Hackensack NJ 07606
877 232-9426

(P-8311)
DESIGN COLLECTION INC
Also Called: Global Garments
2209 S Santa Fe Ave, Los Angeles (90058-1109)
PHONE..............................323 277-9200
Fax: 323 277-1717
Simon Barlava, *President*
Sohail Hussain, *CFO*
Sohaila Hussaini, *CFO*
Morris Barlava, *Vice Pres*
Jane Ellison, *Vice Pres*
▲ **EMP:** 60
SQ FT: 67,000
SALES (est): 27.3MM **Privately Held**
WEB: www.designcollection.com
SIC: 5131 5023 Trimmings, apparel; sheets, textile

(P-8312)
FABRIC BARN
3123 E Anaheim St, Long Beach (90804-3862)
PHONE..............................562 494-3450
Fax: 562 597-2043
Jay Keegan, *Partner*
Linda Hanna, *Partner*
Betsy Greenstein, *Human Res Dir*
▲ **EMP:** 230
SQ FT: 8,000
SALES (est): 25.4MM **Privately Held**
SIC: 5131 5092 Lace fabrics; ribbons; toys & hobby goods & supplies

(P-8313)
INNOVO AZTECA APPAREL INC
5901 S Eastern Ave 104, Commerce (90040-4003)
PHONE..............................323 837-3700
Fax: 323 837-3790
Marc Crossman, *President*
Hamish Sandhu, *CFO*
Maria Pletiaosic, *Manager*
Gina Urzua, *Manager*
▲ **EMP:** 80
SALES (est): 11.5MM
SALES (corp-wide): 250.6MM **Publicly Held**
WEB: www.innovogroup.com
SIC: 5131 Trimmings, apparel
PA: Differential Brands Group Inc.
1231 S Gerhart Ave
Commerce CA 90022
323 890-1800

(P-8314)
J ROBERT SCOTT INC (PA)
500 N Oak St, Inglewood (90302-2942)
PHONE..............................310 659-4910
Fax: 310 659-4494
Andrew Frumovitz, *CEO*
Sally Lewis, *President*
Nancy Preller, *Admin Sec*
Carol Weiss, *Marketing Staff*
June Triolo, *Manager*
▲ **EMP:** 120 **EST:** 1972
SQ FT: 110,000
SALES (est): 57.3MM **Privately Held**
WEB: www.jrobertscott.com
SIC: 5131 2512 2511 Textiles, woven; upholstered household furniture; wood household furniture

(P-8315)
L & R DISTRIBUTORS INC
9292 9th St, Rancho Cucamonga (91730-4407)
PHONE..............................909 980-3807
EMP: 275
SALES (corp-wide): 1.4B **Privately Held**
SIC: 5131 Notions
PA: L. & R. Distributors, Inc.
9301 Avenue D
Brooklyn NY 11236
718 272-2100

(P-8316)
LAFAYETTE TEXTILE INDS LLC
2051 E 55th St, Vernon (90058-3441)
PHONE..............................323 264-2212
Ali Reza Zahedi, *CEO*
Ali Dehbahani, *COO*
Moshan Dibaei, *CFO*
Carol Ueng, *Accounting Mgr*
Ali Behbahani, *Manager*
▲ **EMP:** 85
SQ FT: 68,000
SALES (est): 21.9MM **Privately Held**
WEB: www.lafayettetextiles.com
SIC: 5131 Piece goods & notions

(P-8317)
M M FAB INC
Also Called: South Seas Imports
2300 E Gladwick St, Compton (90220-6208)
PHONE..............................310 763-3800
Richard Friedman, *President*
Dave Powell, *Systs Prg Mgr*
Albert Mass, *VP Finance*
▲ **EMP:** 85
SQ FT: 110,000
SALES (est): 26.4MM **Privately Held**
SIC: 5131 Piece goods & other fabrics

(P-8318)
MERIDIAN TEXTILES INC (PA)
6415 Canning St, Commerce (90040-3121)
PHONE..............................323 869-5700
Fax: 323 277-7730
Howard Deutchman, *President*
▲ **EMP:** 74
SQ FT: 36,000
SALES (est): 39.8MM **Privately Held**
WEB: www.markfabrics.com
SIC: 5131 Textile converters

(P-8319)
MODERN BUTTON COMPANY OF CAL
3957 S Hill St, Los Angeles (90037-1313)
PHONE..............................213 747-7431
Fax: 213 747-2307
Alan Failo, *President*
Virginia Acosta, *Vice Pres*
EMP: 50
SQ FT: 4,400
SALES (est): 4.8MM **Privately Held**
SIC: 5131 Buttons

(P-8320)
MORGAN FABRICS CORPORATION (PA)
Also Called: Michael Jon Designs
4265 Exchange Ave, Vernon (90058-2604)
P.O. Box 58523, Los Angeles (90058-0523)
PHONE..............................323 583-9981
Fax: 323 588-0614
Arnold Gittelson, *Chairman*
Michael Gittelson, *President*
Sam Yung, *CFO*
Robert Gittelson, *Vice Pres*
Jon Pelzer, *Vice Pres*
▲ **EMP:** 60
SQ FT: 50,000
SALES (est): 62MM **Privately Held**
WEB: www.morganfabrics.com
SIC: 5131 Piece goods & notions; upholstery fabrics, woven

(P-8321)
PINDLER & PINDLER INC (PA)
Also Called: Wholesale Fabrics
11910 Poindexter Ave, Moorpark (93021-1748)
P.O. Box 8007 (93020-8007)
PHONE..............................805 531-9090
Fax: 805 532-2020
Curt R Pindler, *President*
S L Crawford Jr, *Exec VP*
Barbara Bick, *Admin Sec*
Bill Crawford, *Info Tech Mgr*
Tina Butler, *Technology*
▲ **EMP:** 95 **EST:** 1939
SQ FT: 75,000
SALES (est): 131.5MM **Privately Held**
WEB: www.pindler.com
SIC: 5131 Drapery material, woven; upholstery fabrics, woven

(P-8322)
RADIX TEXTILE INC
819 Towne Ave, Los Angeles (90021-1812)
PHONE..............................213 623-6006
Arad Shemirani, *CEO*
EMP: 99 **EST:** 2007
SQ FT: 6,000
SALES (est): 5MM **Privately Held**
SIC: 5131 2211 Piece goods & other fabrics; broadwoven fabric mills, cotton

(P-8323)
ROBERT KAUFMAN CO INC
135 W 132nd St, Los Angeles (90061-1682)
P.O. Box 59266 (90059-0266)
PHONE..............................310 538-3482
Eric Thompson, *Manager*
EMP: 50
SALES (corp-wide): 61.4MM **Privately Held**
WEB: www.robertkaufman.com
SIC: 5131 Piece goods & other fabrics
PA: Robert Kaufman Co., Inc.
129 W 132nd St
Los Angeles CA 90061
310 538-3482

(P-8324)
SAM JUNG USA INC
Also Called: S & J
843 E 31st St, Los Angeles (90011-2006)
PHONE..............................323 231-0811
Joung Ha Lee, *President*
◆ **EMP:** 60
SQ FT: 50,000
SALES (est): 8.6MM **Privately Held**
SIC: 5131 Piece goods & notions

(P-8325)
SEXY HAIR CONCEPTS
9232 Eton Ave, Chatsworth (91311-5807)
PHONE..............................800 848-3383
Carl Heinzsch, *President*
EMP: 100
SALES (est): 12.4MM **Privately Held**
SIC: 5131 Hair accessories

(P-8326)
SHASON INC (PA)
Also Called: Dream River
4940 Triggs St Ste B, Commerce (90022-4805)
PHONE..............................323 269-6666
Barok Shahery, *President*
Henry Shahery, *Vice Pres*
Sevada Nazzarian, *CIO*
Alicia Andoy, *Accountant*
Vic Japson, *Manager*
▲ **EMP:** 52
SQ FT: 120,000
SALES (est): 18.5MM **Privately Held**
WEB: www.shasoninc.com
SIC: 5131 Textiles, woven

(P-8327)
SOFTLINE HOME FASHIONS INC
13122 S Normandie Ave, Gardena (90249-2128)
PHONE..............................310 630-4848
Fax: 310 630-4858
Jason Carr, *President*
Rodney Carr, *Shareholder*
Karmina Hernandez, *CFO*
Nohemi Ramirez, *Prdtn Mgr*
Gene Ober, *Natl Sales Mgr*
▲ **EMP:** 85
SQ FT: 15,000
SALES (est): 38.1MM **Privately Held**
WEB: www.softlineonline.com
SIC: 5131 2391 Piece goods & other fabrics; curtains & draperies

(P-8328)
SPECIALTY TEXTILE SERVICES LLC
1333 30th St Ste A, San Diego (92154-3484)
PHONE..............................619 476-8750
Fax: 619 476-8775
Mark Wilstine, *Manager*
EMP: 69 **Privately Held**
SIC: 5131 Textiles, woven
PA: Specialty Textile Services Llc
737 W Buchanan St
Phoenix AZ 85007

(P-8329)
UNITED FABRICS INTL INC
1723 S Central Ave, Los Angeles (90021-3030)
PHONE..............................213 749-8200
Fax: 213 749-8300
Shahariar S Simantob, *President*
Ramin Simantob, *Vice Pres*
Angie Nazari, *Credit Mgr*
▲ **EMP:** 51
SQ FT: 35,000
SALES (est): 19.4MM **Privately Held**
WEB: www.unitedfabric.com
SIC: 5131 5949 Piece goods & other fabrics; fabric stores piece goods

(P-8330)
ZABIN INDUSTRIES INC (PA)
3957 S Hill St Ste A, Los Angeles (90037-1343)
P.O. Box 15218 (90015-0218)
PHONE..............................213 749-1215
Fax: 213 747-6162
Alan Faiola, *President*
Virginia Acosta, *Vice Pres*
Yung Lui, *MIS Dir*
David Frank, *Opers Staff*
▲ **EMP:** 70
SQ FT: 43,000
SALES (est): 25.6MM **Privately Held**
WEB: www.zabin.com
SIC: 5131 Zippers; textile converters; buttons; net goods

5136 Men's & Boys' Clothing & Furnishings Wholesale

(P-8331)
ALPHA SHIRT COMPANY
14061 Borate St, Santa Fe Springs (90670-5336)
PHONE..............................562 802-9919
Daniel Prasard, *Manager*
Melinda Roush, *Manager*
EMP: 100
SALES (corp-wide): 2B **Privately Held**
SIC: 5136 5137 5699 Sportswear, men's & boys'; sportswear, women's & children's; T-shirts, custom printed
HQ: Alpha Shirt Company
6 Neshaminy Interplex Dr # 6
Feasterville Trevose PA 19053
215 291-0300

(P-8332)
APPAREL CONCEPTS INTL INC
Also Called: Clh Group, The
4804 Laurel Canyon Blvd # 59, Valley Village (91607-3717)
PHONE..............................626 233-9198
John Vorzimer, *President*
Jocelyn Woo, *Director*
▲ **EMP:** 1560
SQ FT: 6,000
SALES (est): 73.9MM **Privately Held**
SIC: 5136 Men's & boys' clothing

5136 - Men's & Boys' Clothing & Furnishings Wholesale County (P-8353)

(P-8333)
ARTWEAR INC
13621 S Main St, Los Angeles (90061-2163)
PHONE................310 217-1393
Ora Ketpongsuda, *President*
Paul Ketpongsuda, *Vice Pres*
Janchay Bhongjan, *Controller*
▲ EMP: 50
SQ FT: 48,000
SALES (est): 12.4MM **Privately Held**
WEB: www.lesliejordan.com
SIC: 5136 5137 2396 2331 Shirts, men's & boys'; women's & children's sportswear & swimsuits; automotive & apparel trimmings; women's & misses' blouses & shirts; men's & boys' furnishings; finishing plants, cotton

(P-8334)
BLACK BOX INC
371 2nd St Ste 1, Encinitas (92024-3524)
PHONE................760 804-3300
Fax: 760 804-9933
Jamie Thomas, *President*
Rob Dotson, *Sales Executive*
▲ EMP: 100
SQ FT: 22,000
SALES (est): 24.1MM **Privately Held**
WEB: www.mysteryskateboards.com
SIC: 5136 5137 Men's & boys' clothing; women's & children's clothing

(P-8335)
BRAD RAMBO & ASSOCIATES INC (PA)
Also Called: Independent Trading Company
1341 Calle Avanzado, San Clemente (92673-6351)
PHONE................949 366-9911
Brad Rambo, *President*
Brandon Rambo, *Principal*
Wendy Rambo, *Admin Sec*
Dena Marques, *Info Tech Dir*
Jennifer Francisco, *Controller*
▲ EMP: 55
SQ FT: 20,500
SALES (est): 25.7MM **Privately Held**
WEB: www.independenttradingco.com
SIC: 5136 Shirts, men's & boys'

(P-8336)
BRODER BROS CO
3443 E Central Ave, Fresno (93725-2542)
PHONE................559 233-9900
Keith Hamilton, *Manager*
Vicky May, *Executive*
EMP: 59
SALES (corp-wide): 2B **Privately Held**
WEB: www.broderbros.com
SIC: 5136 5137 Sportswear, men's & boys'; sportswear, women's & children's
PA: Broder Bros., Co.
   6 Neshaminy Interplex Dr
   Trevose PA 19053
   215 291-0300

(P-8337)
COLOSSEUM ATHLETICS CORP
2400 S Wilmington Ave, Compton (90220-5403)
PHONE................310 667-8341
Fax: 310 667-8351
Stuart Whang, *President*
Sean Lee, *CFO*
John Testa, *Vice Pres*
Mike Cho, *Administration*
Chanho Park, *Administration*
▲ EMP: 85
SQ FT: 64,227
SALES (est): 54.9MM **Privately Held**
SIC: 5136 5137 Sportswear, men's & boys'; sportswear, women's & children's

(P-8338)
DORFMAN-PACIFIC CO (PA)
Also Called: Dorfman Pacific
2615 Boeing Way, Stockton (95206-3984)
P.O. Box 213005 (95213-9005)
PHONE................209 982-1400
Fax: 209 982-1596
Douglas Highsmith, *CEO*
Debra Highsmith, *Admin Sec*
Mark Dulle, *CIO*
Bakul Patel, *VP Finance*
◆ EMP: 140
SQ FT: 278,000
SALES (est): 83.5MM **Privately Held**
WEB: www.dorfman-pacific.com
SIC: 5136 5137 Caps, men's & boys'; hats, men's & boys'; men's & boys' outerwear; caps & gowns; hats: women's, children's & infants'; women's & children's outerwear

(P-8339)
EISENBERG INTERNATIONAL CORP (PA)
9128 Jordan Ave, Chatsworth (91311-5707)
PHONE................818 365-8161
Fax: 818 365-7510
Joel Eisenberg, *President*
Lynn Eisenberg, *Corp Secy*
Richard Eisenberg, *Vice Pres*
▲ EMP: 55
SQ FT: 36,000
SALES (est): 16.4MM **Privately Held**
WEB: www.eisenbergintl.com
SIC: 5136 Coats, men's & boys'; sportswear, men's & boys'; suits, men's & boys'; trousers, men's & boys'

(P-8340)
FAM LLC
Also Called: Fam Brands
5553 Ste B Bandini Blvd, Bell (90201)
PHONE................323 888-7755
Frank Zarabi, *Mng Member*
Carrie Henley, *President*
Christopher Teo, *Controller*
Rich Campanelli,
Rich Lyons,
▲ EMP: 75
SQ FT: 75,000
SALES (est): 27.6MM **Privately Held**
WEB: www.fambrands.com
SIC: 5136 5137 Sportswear, men's & boys'; women's & children's sportswear & swimsuits

(P-8341)
FORIA INTERNATIONAL INC (PA)
18689 Arenth Ave, City of Industry (91748-1302)
PHONE................626 912-8836
Fax: 626 964-9933
Teddy Mang, *CEO*
Danny K Wang, *President*
Joe Wang, *Vice Pres*
Timothy Wu, *Vice Pres*
Joan Shannon, *Sales Mgr*
▲ EMP: 78
SQ FT: 120,000
SALES (est): 20.5MM **Privately Held**
WEB: www.foria.com
SIC: 5136 Men's & boys' clothing

(P-8342)
FOX HEAD INC (PA)
Also Called: Fox Racing
16752 Armstrong Ave, Irvine (92606-4912)
PHONE................408 776-8633
Fax: 408 852-6913
Peter Fox, *Chairman*
Pete Fox, *President*
Paul E Harrington, *CEO*
Stephanie Baptiste, *COO*
Geoffrey T Fox, *Vice Pres*
◆ EMP: 153 EST: 1974
SALES (est): 313.3MM **Privately Held**
WEB: www.foxbmx.com
SIC: 5136 5137 5961 Sportswear, men's & boys'; sportswear, women's & children's; mail order house

(P-8343)
GONZALES ENTERPRISES INC
Also Called: Aztlan Graphics
495 Ryan Ave, Chico (95973-8846)
PHONE................530 343-8725
Fax: 530 343-8426
Daniel Gonzales, *CEO*
Randy Cook, *President*
Dawn Gonzales, *Treasurer*
BJ Larossa, *Vice Pres*
Alyssa Beltramo, *Executive*
▲ EMP: 174
SQ FT: 26,000
SALES (est): 140.3MM **Privately Held**
WEB: www.5sun.com
SIC: 5136 Shirts, men's & boys'

(P-8344)
H & C HEADWEAR INC (PA)
Also Called: King's Caps
17145 Margay Ave, Carson (90746-1209)
PHONE................310 324-5263
Fax: 310 324-8763
Shun On Ngan, *CEO*
John Lee, *President*
Mitch Mann, *Vice Pres*
Chuck Schoonover, *Executive*
Ken Feldman, *Principal*
▲ EMP: 58
SQ FT: 143,000
SALES (est): 41.9MM **Privately Held**
SIC: 5136 6794 Caps, men's & boys'; copyright buying & licensing

(P-8345)
HELMET HOUSE INC (PA)
Also Called: Tour Master
26855 Malibu Hills Rd, Calabasas Hills (91301-5100)
PHONE................800 421-7247
Fax: 818 880-4550
Robert M Miller, *CEO*
Randy Hutchings, *CFO*
Philip Bellomy, *Vice Pres*
Dennis Yohman, *Vice Pres*
Eli Whitney, *Social Dir*
▲ EMP: 76
SQ FT: 80,000
SALES (est): 73.6MM **Privately Held**
WEB: www.helmethouse.com
SIC: 5136 3949 Men's & boys' clothing; helmets, athletic

(P-8346)
HOUSTON SALEM INC
Also Called: Chaser
217 E 157th St, Gardena (90248-2510)
PHONE................310 719-7004
Fax: 310 719-9894
Stephen Martin Kayne, *CEO*
Ramsey Salem, *COO*
Laura Temenez, *Accountant*
Jackie Sique Molina, *Controller*
▲ EMP: 50
SQ FT: 70,000
SALES (est): 26.7MM **Privately Held**
WEB: www.bhcompany.com
SIC: 5136 5137 Men's & boys' clothing; women's & children's clothing

(P-8347)
HYBRID PROMOTIONS LLC (PA)
Also Called: Hybrid Apparel
10711 Walker St, Cypress (90630-4750)
PHONE................714 952-3866
Jarrod Dogan, *CEO*
David Lederman, *COO*
Michael Disabato, *Vice Pres*
Elmer Madlangbayan, *Info Tech Mgr*
Samantha Mayer, *Analyst*
◆ EMP: 122
SQ FT: 100,000
SALES (est): 544.5MM **Privately Held**
WEB: www.hybridtees.com
SIC: 5136 5137 5611 Men's & boys' clothing; women's & children's clothing; men's & boys' clothing stores

(P-8348)
KELLWOOD COMPANY LLC
Also Called: Xoxo
1307 E Temple Ave, City of Industry (91746)
PHONE................626 934-4133
Arthur K Gordon, *Branch Mgr*
EMP: 120
SALES (corp-wide): 18.3B **Privately Held**
WEB: www.kellwoodco.com
SIC: 5136 5137 Men's & boys' clothing; women's & children's clothing
HQ: Kellwood Company, Llc
   600 Kellwood Pkwy Ste 200
   Chesterfield MO 63017
   314 576-3100

(P-8349)
LANDMARK PROTECTION INC
675 N 1st St Ste 620, San Jose (95112-5145)
PHONE................408 293-6300
Daniel Miranda, *President*
Eva Miranda, *Manager*
EMP: 300
SQ FT: 6,000
SALES: 10MM **Privately Held**
WEB: www.landmarkprotection.com
SIC: 5136 5099 7381 Uniforms, men's & boys'; safety equipment & supplies; guard services; security guard service

(P-8350)
LIFTED RESEARCH GROUP INC (PA)
Also Called: L R G
7 Holland, Irvine (92618-2506)
P.O. Box 4743, Laguna Beach (92652-4743)
PHONE................949 581-1144
Fax: 949 581-0077
Robert D Wright, *President*
Mike Schillmoeller, *Vice Pres*
Zach Wright, *Vice Pres*
Kevin Delaney, *Marketing Mgr*
Paul Hauke, *Sales Mgr*
◆ EMP: 57
SQ FT: 1,400
SALES (est): 109.6MM **Privately Held**
WEB: www.liftedresearchgroup.com
SIC: 5136 Men's & boys' clothing

(P-8351)
LIQUIDITY SERVICES INC
Str
741 E Ball Rd Ste 200, Anaheim (92805-5952)
PHONE................714 738-6446
Carl Jones, *Branch Mgr*
Susan Parham, *Treasurer*
Catrina Louis, *Executive Asst*
Theresa Hardin, *Information Mgr*
Jimmy Nguyen, *Webmaster*
EMP: 100 **Publicly Held**
WEB: www.liquidation.com
SIC: 5136 5137 5139 5611 Men's & boys' clothing; women's & children's clothing; footwear; men's & boys' clothing stores; radio, television & electronic stores; salvaging of damaged merchandise, service only
PA: Liquidity Services, Inc.
   1920 L St Nw Fl 6
   Washington DC 20036

(P-8352)
M & S TRADING INC
Also Called: 7 Diamonds Clothing
15778 Gateway Cir, Tustin (92780-6469)
PHONE................714 241-7190
Fax: 714 241-7199
Sami Khalil, *CEO*
Shawn Stolfus, *Manager*
▲ EMP: 71
SQ FT: 36,000
SALES (est): 15.8MM **Privately Held**
WEB: www.7diamonds.com
SIC: 5136 5137 Men's & boys' clothing; women's & children's clothing

(P-8353)
MOUNTAIN GEAR CORPORATION
Also Called: Tri-Mountain
4889 4th St, Irwindale (91706-2194)
PHONE................626 851-2488
Daniel Tsai, *CEO*
Jennifer Tsai, *Vice Pres*
Rosie Tsai, *Vice Pres*
Olga Duran, *CTO*
Niem Thai, *Info Tech Mgr*
▲ EMP: 125
SQ FT: 300,000
SALES (est): 66.3MM **Privately Held**
WEB: www.trimountain.com
SIC: 5136 Men's & boys' sportswear & work clothing

5136 - Men's & Boys' Clothing & Furnishings Wholesale County (P-8354)

(P-8354)
NORTH BAY DISTRIBUTION INC
2029 E Monte Vista Ave, Vacaville (95688-3100)
PHONE..................707 450-1219
Lee Perry, *Branch Mgr*
EMP: 70
SQ FT: 250,000
SALES (corp-wide): 40MM **Privately Held**
SIC: 5136 Men's & boys' clothing
PA: North Bay Distribution, Inc.
2050 Cessna Dr
Vacaville CA 95688
707 452-9984

(P-8355)
NORTH BAY DISTRIBUTION INC (PA)
2050 Cessna Dr, Vacaville (95688-8712)
PHONE..................707 452-9984
Fax: 707 452-8506
Lee Perry, *President*
Riza Suma, *Exec VP*
Dane Ruud, *IT/INT Sup*
Ray George, *Technology*
Jerry Aduna, *VP Finance*
EMP: 100
SQ FT: 220,000
SALES: 40MM **Privately Held**
WEB: www.northbaydistribution.net
SIC: 5136 Men's & boys' clothing

(P-8356)
OTTO INTERNATIONAL INC (PA)
Also Called: Otto Cap
3550 Jurupa St Ste A, Ontario (91761-2946)
PHONE..................909 937-1998
Razgo Lee, *President*
Frank Jou, *CFO*
Danny Yuen, *Controller*
Adilene Andaya, *Associate*
◆ **EMP:** 50
SQ FT: 136,000
SALES (est): 41.4MM **Privately Held**
WEB: www.ottocap.com
SIC: 5136 Caps, men's & boys'

(P-8357)
PRANA LIVING LLC
3209 Lionshead Ave, Carlsbad (92010-4710)
PHONE..................866 915-6457
Scott Kerslake, *CEO*
Larry Callette, *CFO*
Nancy Dynan, *Vice Pres*
Arnould T'Kint, *Vice Pres*
Jessica Mahoney, *Vice Pres*
▲ **EMP:** 90
SALES (est): 105.1MM
SALES (corp-wide): 2.3B **Publicly Held**
SIC: 5136 5137 Men's & boys' clothing; women's & children's clothing
PA: Columbia Sportswear Company
14375 Nw Science Park Dr
Portland OR 97229
503 985-4000

(P-8358)
QUIKSILVER INC
15202 Graham St, Huntington Beach (92649-1109)
PHONE..................714 893-5187
Brian Ivanhoe, *Branch Mgr*
EMP: 60
SALES (corp-wide): 1.3B **Privately Held**
WEB: www.quiksilverusa.com
SIC: 5136 Men's & boys' clothing
PA: Quiksilver, Inc.
5600 Argosy Ave Ste 100
Huntington Beach CA 92649
714 889-2200

(P-8359)
RICK SOLOMON ENTERPRISES INC (PA)
Also Called: Axis
8460 Higuera St, Culver City (90232-2520)
P.O. Box 266, Los Angeles (90078-0266)
PHONE..................310 280-3700
Fax: 310 280-3805
Richard Solomon, *President*
Barbara Baskin, *CFO*
Loren Krok, *Vice Pres*
Richard Crouse, *Sales Staff*
Sharon Feuer, *Manager*
▲ **EMP:** 64
SQ FT: 14,058
SALES (est): 11.5MM **Privately Held**
WEB: www.axisclothing.com
SIC: 5136 Sportswear, men's & boys'

(P-8360)
SOEX WEST USA LLC
Also Called: Soex Group
3294 E 26th St, Vernon (90058-8008)
PHONE..................323 264-8300
Roubik Aftandilians,
Anne Guevara, *Controller*
Nursis Ohanian,
◆ **EMP:** 300
SQ FT: 120,000
SALES (est): 102MM **Privately Held**
WEB: www.soexgroup.com
SIC: 5136 Men's & boys' clothing

(P-8361)
T M P INC
Also Called: Pro TEC Manufacturing
21051 Osborne St, Canoga Park (91304-1744)
PHONE..................818 718-1222
Humberto Carlos, *CEO*
Jane Alonso, *Administration*
Alicia Subillaga, *Manager*
▲ **EMP:** 100
SQ FT: 16,000
SALES (est): 19.1MM **Privately Held**
SIC: 5136 5137 2329 Uniforms, men's & boys'; uniforms, women's & children's; knickers, dress (separate): men's & boys'

(P-8362)
TOPWIN CORPORATION (PA)
Also Called: People's Place
1808 Abalone Ave, Torrance (90501-3703)
PHONE..................310 325-2255
Fax: 310 325-1877
Tomokazu Yoshimura, *CEO*
Yoko Naka, *General Mgr*
Hiroshi Ogi, *CIO*
Hitomi Yamamoto, *Director*
◆ **EMP:** 60
SQ FT: 22,000
SALES: 32.6MM **Privately Held**
WEB: www.topwin.com
SIC: 5136 5137 5611 5621 Men's & boys' clothing; women's & children's clothing; men's & boys' clothing stores; women's clothing stores; mannequins

(P-8363)
TRUE RELIGION SALES LLC
1888 Rosecrans Ave # 1000, Manhattan Beach (90266-3795)
PHONE..................323 266-3072
John Ermatinger, *President*
Eric Bauer, *CFO*
Ilene Eskenazi,
Gaurav Krishan,
EMP: 350
SALES (est): 63.6MM **Privately Held**
SIC: 5136 5137 Work clothing, men's & boys'; women's & children's dresses, suits, skirts & blouses

(P-8364)
TWO STAR DOG INC
Also Called: T S D
1370 10th St, Berkeley (94710-1510)
PHONE..................510 525-1100
Fax: 510 525-8602
Steven Boutrous, *President*
Allan Boutrous, *Vice Pres*
Attas Boutrous, *Vice Pres*
Stella Boutrous Carakasi, *Vice Pres*
Karen Bomagat, *Manager*
▲ **EMP:** 50
SQ FT: 25,000
SALES (est): 15.9MM **Privately Held**
SIC: 5136 5137 5611 5621 Men's & boys' sportswear & work clothing; women's & children's sportswear & swimsuits; clothing, sportswear, men's & boys'; women's sportswear

(P-8365)
VOLCOM LLC
1725 Monrovia Ave, Costa Mesa (92627-4401)
PHONE..................949 646-2175
Richard R Woolcott, *Branch Mgr*
Ryan Immegart, *Exec VP*
Ed Shaver, *Vice Pres*
Desiree Swanson, *Vice Pres*
Susan Bugg, *Regional Mgr*
EMP: 200
SALES (corp-wide): 10.7MM **Privately Held**
SIC: 5136 Men's & boys' clothing
HQ: Volcom, Llc
1740 Monrovia Ave
Costa Mesa CA 92627
949 646-2175

(P-8366)
WOR INTERNATIONAL INC
Also Called: Nick and MO
15612 1st St, Irwindale (91706-6220)
P.O. Box 1631, Walnut (91788-1631)
PHONE..................626 812-8888
Hsu WEI Wang, *President*
Roger Liang, *Vice Pres*
Cathy Wong, *Manager*
▼ **EMP:** 50
SQ FT: 30,000
SALES (est): 13.2MM **Privately Held**
WEB: www.worusa.com
SIC: 5136 Men's & boys' clothing

5137 Women's, Children's & Infants Clothing Wholesale

(P-8367)
BCBG MAX AZRIA GROUP LLC
2865 Fruitland Ave Ste F, Vernon (90058-3609)
PHONE..................213 624-2224
Jlelati Aziz, *CTO*
Aziz Jlelati, *CIO*
Bob Oleesky, *CTO*
Alison Mc Mahon, *Human Res Dir*
Julie Combs, *Payroll Mgr*
EMP: 50
SALES (corp-wide): 1.9B **Privately Held**
WEB: www.bcbg.com
SIC: 5137 Women's & children's clothing
PA: Bcbg Max Azria Group, Llc
2761 Fruitland Ave
Vernon CA 90058
323 589-2224

(P-8368)
BCBG MAX AZRIA GROUP LLC
2761 Fruitland Ave, Vernon (90058-3607)
PHONE..................323 589-2224
EMP: 69 EST: 2014
SALES (est): 1.1MM
SALES (corp-wide): 1.5B **Privately Held**
SIC: 5137 5621 2335
PA: Guggenheim Partners, Llc
330 Madison Ave Rm 201
New York NY 10017
212 739-0700

(P-8369)
BCBG MAX AZRIA GROUP LLC (PA)
2761 Fruitland Ave, Vernon (90058-3607)
P.O. Box 58345, Los Angeles (90058-0345)
PHONE..................323 589-2224
Fax: 213 277-5454
Max Azria, *CEO*
Daniell Duclon, *CFO*
Brian Fleming, *CFO*
Lubov Azria, *Ch Credit Ofcr*
Donna Franco, *Exec VP*
◆ **EMP:** 525
SQ FT: 500,000
SALES (est): 1.9B **Privately Held**
WEB: www.bcbg.com
SIC: 5137 5621 2335 Women's & children's clothing; women's clothing stores; women's, juniors' & misses' dresses

(P-8370)
BLUE PLANET INTERNATIONAL INC
Also Called: Boom-Boom Jeans
1526 E Washington Blvd, Los Angeles (90021-3122)
PHONE..................213 742-9999
Fax: 213 741-0168
Simon Parsakar, *President*
Ezra Parsakar, *Vice Pres*
Shawn Kay, *Mktg Dir*
▲ **EMP:** 50
SQ FT: 30,000
SALES: 50MM **Privately Held**
WEB: www.boomboomjeans.com
SIC: 5137 5136 Sportswear, women's & children's; sportswear, men's & boys'

(P-8371)
BLUPRINT CLOTHING CORP
5600 Bandini Blvd, Bell (90201-6407)
PHONE..................323 780-4347
Ju Hyun Kim, *CEO*
Peter Kim, *President*
Michelle Lee, *CFO*
▲ **EMP:** 100
SQ FT: 16,000
SALES (est): 52.1MM **Privately Held**
SIC: 5137 Women's & children's clothing

(P-8372)
CALIFORNIA RAIN COMPANY INC
1213 E 14th St A, Los Angeles (90021-2215)
PHONE..................213 624-1771
Fax: 213 627-5703
Jack Jhy C Jang, *President*
Georgia Chang, *Principal*
Mike Cheng, *Info Tech Mgr*
Jensen Jun, *Info Tech Mgr*
Christina Lin, *Accountant*
▲ **EMP:** 90
SQ FT: 8,600
SALES (est): 35.2MM **Privately Held**
WEB: www.californiarainla.com
SIC: 5137 5136 5699 Sportswear, women's & children's; sportswear, men's & boys'; customized clothing & apparel

(P-8373)
CECICO INC
Also Called: Cecico Town
1016 Towne Ave Unit 110, Los Angeles (90021-2078)
PHONE..................323 269-7000
Kelly Kyung Lie Ahn, *Principal*
▲ **EMP:** 55
SALES (est): 8.7MM **Privately Held**
SIC: 5137 2339 Women's & children's clothing; women's & misses' accessories

(P-8374)
CHILDRENS BTQ AT STEVENS HOPE
Also Called: Childrens Botique, The
10730 Fthill Blvd Ste 170, Rancho Cucamonga (91730)
PHONE..................909 256-0100
Tony Campbell, *Owner*
EMP: 50
SALES (est): 2.2MM **Privately Held**
SIC: 5137 3949 8699 Women's & children's clothing; sporting & athletic goods; charitable organization

(P-8375)
CLAUDIA RICHARD INC
4871 S Santa Fe Ave, Vernon (90058-2103)
PHONE..................323 264-3915
Benjamin Boston, *President*
Ram Kundani, *Vice Pres*
◆ **EMP:** 59
SALES (est): 15.9MM **Privately Held**
SIC: 5137 Women's & children's clothing

(P-8376)
COMAK TRADING INC A CAL CORP
2550 S Soto St, Vernon (90058-8013)
PHONE..................323 261-3404
EMP: 100
SALES (est): 12.6MM **Privately Held**
SIC: 5137 5136 5139

PRODUCTS & SERVICES SECTION
5137 - Women's, Children's & Infants Clothing Wholesale County (P-8401)

(P-8377)
DELTA GALIL USA INC
Also Called: Loomworks Apparel
16912 Von Karman Ave, Irvine
(92606-4923)
PHONE 949 296-0380
EMP: 54
SALES (corp-wide): 1.1B **Privately Held**
SIC: 5137 Women's & children's clothing;
women's & children's lingerie & undergarments
HQ: Delta Galil Usa Inc.
1 Harmon Plz Fl 5
Secaucus NJ 07094
201 392-9098

(P-8378)
DUTCH LLC
Also Called: Joie
5300 S Santa Fe Ave, Vernon
(90058-3520)
PHONE 323 277-3900
Serge Azria, *Branch Mgr*
Cristiana Janssen, *Business Mgr*
EMP: 50
SALES (corp-wide): 259.5MM **Privately Held**
SIC: 5137 Women's & children's clothing
HQ: Dutch, Llc
5301 S Santa Fe Ave
Vernon CA 90058
323 277-3900

(P-8379)
DUTCH LLC (HQ)
Also Called: Joie
5301 S Santa Fe Ave, Vernon
(90058-3519)
PHONE 323 277-3900
Serge K Azria, *Mng Member*
Morgan Dreyer, *Executive Asst*
Plaire Nissen, *Executive Asst*
Harriet Cappucio, *Controller*
Florence Azria,
▲ EMP: 85
SQ FT: 40,000
SALES (est): 251.5MM
SALES (corp-wide): 259.5MM **Privately Held**
SIC: 5137 Women's & children's clothing
PA: T.A. Associates
200 Clarendon St Ste 5600
Boston MA 02116
617 574-6700

(P-8380)
EDGEMINE INC
Also Called: Mine Fashion
1801 E 50th St, Los Angeles (90058-1940)
PHONE 323 267-8222
Kevin Chang Kang, *CEO*
Chang Kang, *President*
▲ EMP: 120 EST: 1992
SQ FT: 45,000
SALES (est): 1MM **Privately Held**
SIC: 5137 Women's & children's clothing

(P-8381)
EIGHTY ONE ENTERPRISE INC
9401 Whitmore St, El Monte (91731-2821)
PHONE 626 371-1980
May Sayphraraj, *President*
Darren Sayphraraj, *Treasurer*
◆ EMP: 50 EST: 2012
SQ FT: 60,000
SALES: 18MM **Privately Held**
SIC: 5137 Lingerie

(P-8382)
ESP GROUP LTD
2397 Bateman Ave, Duarte (91010-3313)
PHONE 626 301-0280
Yan Wang, *CEO*
David Ouyang, *President*
William Yue, *CFO*
◆ EMP: 68
SQ FT: 150,000
SALES (est): 28.8MM **Privately Held**
SIC: 5137 Women's & children's clothing

(P-8383)
FACTORY 2-U IMPORT EXPORT INC
Also Called: Oren's Replay
13034 Delano St, Van Nuys (91401-3209)
PHONE 323 587-9900

Liat Madar, *CEO*
Oless Jimenez, *General Mgr*
EMP: 60
SALES (est): 2.1MM **Privately Held**
WEB: www.youimport.com
SIC: 5137 5136 Women's & children's clothing; men's & boys' clothing

(P-8384)
FOREVER 21 RETAIL INC
3880 N Mission Rd, Los Angeles
(90031-3187)
PHONE 323 343-9368
Do Won Chang, *CEO*
Ann Cadier Kim, *CFO*
Jong Sung Kim, *Senior VP*
Lawrence Mayer, *Senior VP*
Jin S Chang, *Admin Sec*
EMP: 71
SALES (est): 59.7MM
SALES (corp-wide): 5.2B **Privately Held**
WEB: www.forever21.com
SIC: 5137 Women's & children's clothing; women's & children's accessories
PA: Forever 21, Inc.
3880 N Mission Rd
Los Angeles CA 90031
213 741-5100

(P-8385)
GURU DENIM INC (DH)
Also Called: True Religion Brand Jeans
1888 Rosecrans Ave # 1000, Manhattan Beach (90266-3712)
PHONE 323 266-3072
John Ermatinger, *CEO*
Eric Bauer, *CFO*
Marcello Bottoli, *Bd of Directors*
Brett Vick, *Store Mgr*
Dan Klink, *Controller*
▲ EMP: 150
SQ FT: 19,300
SALES (est): 335.8MM
SALES (corp-wide): 1.8B **Privately Held**
WEB: www.gurudenim.com
SIC: 5137 5611 Women's & children's clothing; clothing accessories; men's & boys'
HQ: True Religion Apparel, Inc.
1888 Rosecrans Ave # 1000
Manhattan Beach CA 90266
323 266-3072

(P-8386)
HARVEYS INDUSTRIES INC
Also Called: Original Seatbeltbag, The
1918 E Glenwood Pl, Santa Ana
(92705-5108)
PHONE 714 277-4700
Dana Harvey, *CEO*
Melanie Harvey, *Admin Sec*
Cheryl Lindberg, *Associate*
▲ EMP: 55
SQ FT: 12,000
SALES (est): 27.2MM **Privately Held**
WEB: www.harveysboutique.com
SIC: 5137 5632 Handbags; women's accessory & specialty stores

(P-8387)
HIBSHMAN TRADING CORPORATION
Also Called: Mattress Liqidation
9843 6th St Ste 103, Rancho Cucamonga
(91730-5741)
PHONE 909 581-1800
Fax: 909 581-1839
Erik D Hibshman, *President*
EMP: 60
SQ FT: 65,000
SALES: 7.5MM **Privately Held**
SIC: 5137 5136 5021 Women's & children's clothing; men's & boys' clothing; mattresses

(P-8388)
JEAN MART INC
6700 Avalon Blvd, Los Angeles
(90003-1920)
PHONE 323 752-7775
Fax: 323 752-8575
Helen C Yi, *President*
▲ EMP: 100
SQ FT: 5,000

SALES (est): 50.8MM **Privately Held**
SIC: 5137 7389 Women's & children's clothing; sewing contractor

(P-8389)
KASH APPAREL LLC
1929 Hooper Ave, Los Angeles
(90011-1332)
PHONE 213 747-8885
Stephanie Kleinjan, *Mng Member*
Adir Haroni,
▲ EMP: 68
SQ FT: 10,000
SALES: 20.8MM **Privately Held**
SIC: 5137 Women's & children's accessories

(P-8390)
KBL GROUP INTERNATIONAL LTD
Also Called: Kbl International
9142 9150 Norwalk Blvd, Santa Fe Springs
(90670)
PHONE 562 699-9995
Thomas Ko, *Branch Mgr*
EMP: 50
SALES (corp-wide): 57MM **Privately Held**
WEB: www.crystalk.com
SIC: 5137 Sportswear, women's & children's
PA: Kbl Group International Ltd.
1407 Broadway Rm 610
New York NY 10018
212 391-1551

(P-8391)
KELLWOOD COMPANY LLC
Also Called: Xoxo
13085 Temple Ave, City of Industry
(91746-1418)
PHONE 626 934-4155
Sherri Akers, *Branch Mgr*
EMP: 150
SALES (corp-wide): 18.3B **Privately Held**
SIC: 5137 Women's & children's clothing
HQ: Kellwood Company, Llc
600 Kellwood Pkwy Ste 200
Chesterfield MO 63017
314 576-3100

(P-8392)
KOI DESIGN LLC
1757 Stanford St, Santa Monica
(90404-4115)
PHONE 310 828-0055
Kathy Takamoto Peterson, *President*
Debbie Anderson, *Exec VP*
Jeremy Husk, *Exec VP*
▲ EMP: 60
SALES (est): 25.7MM **Privately Held**
SIC: 5137 Uniforms, women's & children's

(P-8393)
KOLONAKI (PA)
Also Called: Georgiou
1216 Broadway Plz, Walnut Creek
(94596-5129)
PHONE 415 554-8000
▲ EMP: 50 EST: 1974
SQ FT: 16,000
SALES (est): 50.5MM **Privately Held**
SIC: 5137 5621 2339

(P-8394)
LDLA CLOTHING LLC
Also Called: Living Doll
1515 E 15th St, Los Angeles (90021-2711)
PHONE 323 312-2805
Amy Powers, *Owner*
Richard Swartz, *CFO*
EMP: 60
SALES: 50MM **Privately Held**
SIC: 5137 Women's & children's clothing

(P-8395)
LEIGH JERRY CALIFORNIA INC (PA)
Also Called: Jerry Leigh Entertainment AP
7860 Nelson Rd, Van Nuys (91402-6044)
PHONE 818 909-6200
Fax: 818 909-7855
Andrew Leigh, *CEO*
Jeff Silver, *CFO*
Jonathan Hirsh, *Exec VP*
Samira Jammal, *Vice Pres*

Pam Bennett, *Executive Asst*
▲ EMP: 131 EST: 1977
SQ FT: 40,000
SALES (est): 372.8MM **Privately Held**
SIC: 5137 Women's & children's clothing

(P-8396)
LING-SU CHINN INC
1653 12th St, Santa Monica (90404-3709)
PHONE 310 396-1102
Ling Su Chinn, *Principal*
James Williams, *CEO*
EMP: 65
SQ FT: 6,000
SALES (est): 12.1MM **Privately Held**
SIC: 5137 5621 Women's & children's clothing; women's clothing stores

(P-8397)
MAD DOGG ATHLETICS INC (PA)
Also Called: Spinning
2111 Narcissus Ct, Venice (90291-4818)
PHONE 310 823-7008
Fax: 310 823-7278
John R Baudhuin, *President*
Aerin Shaw, *COO*
Jonathan Goldberg, *Admin Sec*
Vania Ballo, *CTO*
Michele McDonnell, *Prdtn Mgr*
◆ EMP: 108
SALES (est): 49.2MM **Privately Held**
WEB: www.spinning.com
SIC: 5137 5122 7812 Sportswear, women's & children's; vitamins & minerals; video tape production

(P-8398)
MALIBU DESIGN GROUP
Also Called: Ocean Dream
5445 Jillson St, Commerce (90040-2117)
PHONE 323 271-1700
Fax: 323 271-1701
Tai Chung, *CEO*
Henry Fan, *President*
Ben Quan, *CFO*
Boram Kim, *Production*
◆ EMP: 53
SALES (est): 32.3MM **Privately Held**
SIC: 5137 Swimsuits: women's, children's & infants'

(P-8399)
MARIKA GROUP INC
Also Called: Shiva-Shakthi
8960 Carroll Way, San Diego (92121-2429)
PHONE 858 537-5300
Donald Schumacher, *Vice Pres*
Scott Kalman, *President*
Lew Corpuz, *Vice Pres*
Lu Corpug, *Controller*
Chris Teo, *Personnel Exec*
▲ EMP: 60
SQ FT: 60,000
SALES (est): 10.3MM **Privately Held**
SIC: 5137 2339 Sportswear, women's & children's; women's & misses' outerwear

(P-8400)
MEL BERNIE AND COMPANY INC
Edgar Berebi A Div 1928 Jwly
3000 W Empire Ave, Burbank
(91504-3109)
PHONE 818 841-1928
Mel Bernie, *Branch Mgr*
EMP: 150
SALES (corp-wide): 61.2MM **Privately Held**
WEB: www.1928.com
SIC: 5137 Women's & children's accessories
PA: Mel Bernie And Company, Inc.
3000 W Empire Ave
Burbank CA 91504
818 841-1928

(P-8401)
MIAS FASHION MFG CO INC
Also Called: California Basic
12623 Cisneros Ln, Santa Fe Springs
(90670-3373)
PHONE 562 906-1060
Peter D Anh, *President*
Brian Song, *CFO*
David Yim, *Accounting Mgr*

5137 - Women's, Children's & Infants Clothing Wholesale County (P-8402)

Brandon Kim, *Accounts Mgr*
◆ **EMP:** 252
SALES: 160.7MM **Privately Held**
WEB: www.mfmcoinc.com
SIC: 5137 Women's & children's clothing

(P-8402)
MIKEN SALES INC (PA)
Also Called: Miken Clothing
7230 Oxford Way, Commerce (90040-3643)
PHONE 323 266-2560
Fax: 323 266-2580
Michael Bobbitt, *CEO*
Kenny Landy, *Vice Pres*
Jonathan Namm, *VP Opers*
Michelle Minott, *Director*
Kathryn Higa, *Manager*
◆ **EMP:** 53
SQ FT: 23,000
SALES (est): 31.5MM **Privately Held**
SIC: 5137 Women's & children's clothing

(P-8403)
MOLA INC
2957 E 46th St, Vernon (90058-2423)
PHONE 323 582-0088
▲ **EMP:** 150
SALES (est): 45.2MM **Privately Held**
SIC: 5137

(P-8404)
MYSTIC INC (PA)
2444 Porter St, Los Angeles (90021-2511)
PHONE 213 746-8538
Haejin Han, *President*
Hae Han, *CEO*
Daniel Priano, *COO*
▲ **EMP:** 55
SQ FT: 45,000
SALES: 15.3MM **Privately Held**
SIC: 5137 2339 Women's & children's clothing; athletic clothing: women's, misses' & juniors'

(P-8405)
NEWPORT APPAREL CORPORATION (PA)
Also Called: I N G
1215 W Walnut St, Compton (90220-5009)
PHONE 310 605-1900
Fax: 310 488-1441
James Kim, *President*
Kimberly Kim, *Treasurer*
Susie Ahn, *General Mgr*
Yong Chung, *General Mgr*
Esther Kim, *Info Tech Mgr*
▲ **EMP:** 62
SQ FT: 38,500
SALES (est): 34.9MM **Privately Held**
WEB: www.newporting.com
SIC: 5137 Sportswear, women's & children's

(P-8406)
NYGARD INC
Also Called: Tan Jay-Nygard Outlet Store
14401 S San Pedro St, Gardena (90248-2026)
PHONE 310 776-8900
Fax: 310 538-0468
Murray Batte, *President*
Ernie Cavez, *Executive*
Katrina Cortez, *Manager*
EMP: 63
SALES (corp-wide): 86.6K **Privately Held**
SIC: 5137 Women's & children's clothing
HQ: Nygard Inc.
1435 Broadway
New York NY 10018
646 520-2000

(P-8407)
ONE 3 TWO INC
Also Called: Obey Clothing
17353 Derian Ave, Irvine (92614-5801)
PHONE 949 596-8400
Regan Don Juncal, *CEO*
Don Junkal, *President*
Steve Melgren, *CFO*
Chris Broder, *Vice Pres*
Steve Ternosky, *Marketing Mgr*
◆ **EMP:** 106 **EST:** 2000
SALES (est): 57.1MM **Privately Held**
WEB: www.obey.com
SIC: 5137 Women's & children's clothing

(P-8408)
PARAGON TEXTILES INC
Also Called: Samiyatex
13003 S Figueroa St, Los Angeles (90061-1136)
PHONE 310 323-7500
Fax: 310 323-7600
Murtaza Haji, *President*
Farhana Haji, *Treasurer*
▼ **EMP:** 75
SQ FT: 42,500
SALES (est): 29.9MM **Privately Held**
WEB: www.samiyatex.com
SIC: 5137 Women's & children's clothing

(P-8409)
PIEGE CO (PA)
Also Called: Felina Lingerie
20120 Plummer St, Chatsworth (91311-5448)
PHONE 818 727-9100
Fax: 818 727-0132
Kambiz Zarabi, *President*
Morad Zarabi, *Ch of Bd*
Mia Agahan, *CFO*
Jack Allame, *CFO*
Michael Zarabi, *Exec VP*
▲ **EMP:** 95
SQ FT: 48,000
SALES (est): 81MM **Privately Held**
WEB: www.felinausa.com
SIC: 5137 Lingerie

(P-8410)
ROBIN K
4731 Fruitland Ave, Vernon (90058-2721)
PHONE 323 235-5152
EMP: 60 **EST:** 2010
SALES (est): 7.9MM **Privately Held**
SIC: 5137 5611 Apparel belts, women's & children's; blouses; sportswear, women's & children's; nightwear: women's, children's & infants'; clothing accessories: men's & boys'; clothing, men's & boys': everyday, except suits & sportswear; suits, men's; tie shops

(P-8411)
SEVEN LICENSING COMPANY LLC
Also Called: Seven7 Brands
801 S Figueroa St # 2500, Los Angeles (90017-5504)
PHONE 323 881-0308
Jacqueline Rose Guez, *Mng Member*
Gerald Guez,
▲ **EMP:** 80
SQ FT: 10,000
SALES (est): 18.2MM
SALES (corp-wide): 87.6MM **Privately Held**
SIC: 5137 Women's & children's accessories
PA: Sunrise Brands, Llc
801 S Figueroa St # 2500
Los Angeles CA 90017
323 780-8250

(P-8412)
SEYMOUR GALE & ASSOCIATES
4501 Cedros Ave Unit 118, Sherman Oaks (91403-2839)
PHONE 213 622-5361
Fax: 213 622-5363
Seymour Gale, *Owner*
EMP: 50
SQ FT: 1,500
SALES (est): 12.1MM **Privately Held**
SIC: 5137 Women's & children's clothing

(P-8413)
TARRANT APPAREL GROUP
Also Called: Fashion Resources
801 S Figueroa St # 2500, Los Angeles (90017-5504)
PHONE 323 780-8250
Gerard Guez, *Ch of Bd*
Peter Akaradian, *CFO*
Todd Kay, *Vice Ch Bd*
Dorothy Parker, *Author*
Lauren Hashima, *Assistant*
▲ **EMP:** 250
SALES (est): 68.6MM
SALES (corp-wide): 87.6MM **Privately Held**
SIC: 5137 Women's & children's clothing

PA: Sunrise Brands, Llc
801 S Figueroa St # 2500
Los Angeles CA 90017
323 780-8250

(P-8414)
TOPSON DOWNS CALIFORNIA INC (PA)
3840 Watseka Ave, Culver City (90232-2633)
PHONE 310 558-0300
John Poyer, *President*
Kristopher Scott, *CFO*
Joe Wirht, *Admin Sec*
Alex Perez, *Info Tech Mgr*
Robert L Handler,
▲ **EMP:** 250
SQ FT: 42,000
SALES (est): 351.6MM **Privately Held**
WEB: www.topsondowns.com
SIC: 5137 Women's & children's clothing

(P-8415)
TYR SPORT INC
Also Called: T Y R
1790 Apollo Ct, Seal Beach (90740-5617)
P.O. Box 1930, Huntington Beach (92647-1930)
PHONE 562 430-1380
Fax: 714 677-0522
Steve Furniss, *President*
Christina Reiser, *Administration*
David Melendez, *Info Tech Mgr*
Cy Bledman, *Graphic Designe*
Wadi Talhami, *Graphic Designe*
◆ **EMP:** 60
SQ FT: 80,000
SALES (est): 39.6MM
SALES (corp-wide): 45.5MM **Privately Held**
WEB: www.tyr.com
SIC: 5137 5136 5091 2329 Sportswear, women's & children's; swimsuits: women's, children's & infants'; women's & children's accessories; beachwear, men's & boys'; sporting & recreation goods; bathing suits & swimwear: men's & boys'; basketball uniforms: men's, youths' & boys'
PA: Swimwear Anywhere, Inc.
85 Sherwood Ave
Farmingdale NY 11735
631 420-1400

(P-8416)
WILDCAT RETRO BRANDS LLC
Also Called: Original Retro Brands
2701 Carrier Ave, Commerce (90040-2502)
PHONE 213 572-0431
Marc Herman, *Mng Member*
EMP: 50
SQ FT: 15,000
SALES (est): 12MM **Privately Held**
SIC: 5137 5136 Sportswear, women's & children's; sportswear, men's & boys'

(P-8417)
XENOS FASHION INC
Also Called: Belinda
1616 E 14th St, Los Angeles (90021-2309)
PHONE 323 585-0088
Ho Lee, *President*
Joanne Kang, *Manager*
EMP: 55
SQ FT: 5,000
SALES (est): 12.1MM **Privately Held**
SIC: 5137 2331 Women's & children's clothing; women's & misses' blouses & shirts

(P-8418)
YOUNG BAE FASHIONS INC
4811 Hampton St, Vernon (90058-2135)
PHONE 323 583-8684
Fax: 323 583-9618
Young Bae, *President*
Chung Bae, *Admin Sec*
▲ **EMP:** 75 **EST:** 1976
SQ FT: 40,000
SALES: 12MM **Privately Held**
SIC: 5137 Women's & children's clothing

5139 Footwear Wholesale

(P-8419)
ACI INTERNATIONAL (PA)
844 Moraga Dr, Los Angeles (90049-1632)
PHONE 310 889-3400
Steve Jackson, *CEO*
Dan Young, *President*
David Mankowitz, *CFO*
Muriel Jackson, *Treasurer*
Scott Coble, *Exec VP*
▲ **EMP:** 100
SQ FT: 40,000
SALES (est): 47.9MM **Privately Held**
WEB: www.aciint.com
SIC: 5139 Shoes; slippers, house

(P-8420)
ASICS AMERICA CORPORATION (HQ)
Also Called: Asics Tiger
80 Technology Dr, Irvine (92618-2301)
PHONE 949 453-8888
Fax: 949 453-0292
Kevin Wulff, *CEO*
Seiho Gohashi, *Ch of Bd*
Richard Bourne, *President*
Andrew Richard, *Vice Pres*
Anthony Mancao, *Info Tech Dir*
◆ **EMP:** 109 **EST:** 1973
SQ FT: 45,000
SALES: 199.3MM
SALES (corp-wide): 3.4B **Privately Held**
WEB: www.onitsukatiger.com
SIC: 5139 5136 5137 2369 Footwear, athletic; sportswear, men's & boys'; men's & boys' furnishings; sportswear, women's & children's; women's & children's accessories; girls' & children's outerwear; women's & misses' outerwear; men's & boys' furnishings
PA: Asics Corporation
7-1-1, Minatojimanakamachi, Chuo-Ku
Kobe HYO 650-0
783 032-231

(P-8421)
BIRKENSTOCK USA LP (DH)
8171 Redwood Blvd, Novato (94945-1403)
PHONE 415 884-3200
Stephan Birkenstock, *Partner*
Bernd Hillen, *Partner*
Andrea Tiller, *CFO*
Beth Futter, *Vice Pres*
Aaron A Herskowitz, *Info Tech Dir*
▲ **EMP:** 54
SQ FT: 15,000
SALES (est): 26.8MM **Privately Held**
WEB: www.birkenstockusa.com
SIC: 5139 Footwear

(P-8422)
BUFFALO DISTRIBUTION
Also Called: Keen Account
1624 Pacific St, Union City (94587-2028)
PHONE 510 475-9810
Fax: 510 475-9815
Lee Perry, *President*
▲ **EMP:** 50
SALES (est): 6.9MM **Privately Held**
WEB: www.buffalodistribution.com
SIC: 5139 Footwear

(P-8423)
CELS ENTERPRISES INC (PA)
Also Called: Chinese Laundry Shoes
3485 S La Cienega Blvd A, Los Angeles (90016-4497)
PHONE 310 838-0280
Robert Goldman, *CEO*
Derek Bordeaux, *Vice Pres*
Miryan Nogueira, *Vice Pres*
Ellen Schiff, *Vice Pres*
Carol Goldman, *General Mgr*
◆ **EMP:** 62 **EST:** 1971
SQ FT: 72,000
SALES (est): 48.9MM **Privately Held**
WEB: www.chineselaundry.com
SIC: 5139 Shoes

▲ = Import ▼ = Export
◆ = Import/Export

PRODUCTS & SERVICES SECTION

5141 - Groceries, General Line Wholesale County (P-8448)

(P-8424)
CHAMBERS BELT COMPANY
5840 El Camino Real Ste 1, Carlsbad (92008-8851)
PHONE..................760 602-9688
Scott Sporrer, *CEO*
EMP: 99
SALES: 950K **Privately Held**
SIC: 5139 Footwear

(P-8425)
CHINESE LAUNDRY INC
Also Called: Chinese Laundry Shoes
3485 S La Cienega Blvd, Los Angeles (90016-4497)
PHONE..................310 945-3299
Robert Goldman, *President*
Christine Sung, *Vice Pres*
Mark Northrop, *CTO*
Alan Raport, *VP Sales*
Patty Maldonado, *Manager*
EMP: 50
SQ FT: 72,000
SALES (est): 20MM **Privately Held**
SIC: 5139

(P-8426)
CONVERSE INC
838 Market St, San Francisco (94102-3001)
PHONE..................415 433-1174
EMP: 95
SALES (corp-wide): 32.3B **Publicly Held**
SIC: 5139 Footwear
HQ: Converse Inc.
1 Love Joy Wharf
Boston MA 02114
978 983-3300

(P-8427)
CONVERSE INC
2150 E Montclair Plaza Ln, Montclair (91763-1535)
PHONE..................909 625-6655
EMP: 90
SALES (corp-wide): 32.3B **Publicly Held**
SIC: 5139 Footwear, athletic
HQ: Converse Inc.
1 Love Joy Wharf
Boston MA 02114
978 983-3300

(P-8428)
CONVERSE INC
1437-39 3rd St Promenade, Santa Monica (90401)
PHONE..................310 451-0314
EMP: 89
SALES (corp-wide): 32.3B **Publicly Held**
SIC: 5139 5661 Footwear, athletic; footwear, athletic
HQ: Converse Inc.
1 Love Joy Wharf
Boston MA 02114
978 983-3300

(P-8429)
CONVERSE INC
Also Called: Distrirution Center
4450 E Lowell St, Ontario (91761-2220)
PHONE..................909 974-5695
Fax: 909 937-1385
Samone Carrollin, *Manager*
Samone Carroll, *Business Mgr*
Suzette Heggem, *Site Mgr*
EMP: 90
SALES (corp-wide): 32.3B **Publicly Held**
SIC: 5139 Footwear
HQ: Converse Inc.
1 Love Joy Wharf
Boston MA 02114
978 983-3300

(P-8430)
DECKERS OUTDOOR CORPORATION
1451 3rd Street Promenade, Santa Monica (90401-2321)
PHONE..................310 395-1120
EMP: 108
SALES (corp-wide): 1.8B **Publicly Held**
SIC: 5139 Footwear
PA: Deckers Outdoor Corporation
250 Coromar Dr
Goleta CA 93117
805 967-7611

(P-8431)
DVS SHOE CO INC (PA)
Also Called: Matix Clothing Company
1008 Brioso Dr, Costa Mesa (92627-4501)
PHONE..................310 715-8300
Kevin Dunlap, *President*
Mark Feig, *Senior VP*
Brian Dunlap, *Vice Pres*
Mike Dunlap, *Vice Pres*
Marco Feller, *Corp Comm Staff*
▲ EMP: 80
SALES (est): 28.2MM **Privately Held**
SIC: 5139 5699 Shoes; sports apparel

(P-8432)
E M S TRADING INC
Also Called: Michael-Antonio Studio
5161 Richton St, Montclair (91763-1310)
PHONE..................909 581-7800
Michael C Su, *CEO*
Ruby Su, *CFO*
Alice Su, *Vice Pres*
Jack Su, *Admin Sec*
Lucia Alvarado, *Human Res Mgr*
▲ EMP: 50
SQ FT: 150,000
SALES (est): 14MM **Privately Held**
SIC: 5139 Shoes

(P-8433)
EAST LION CORPORATION
Also Called: Qupid Shoe
318 Brea Canyon Rd, Walnut (91789-3093)
PHONE..................626 912-1818
Fax: 626 935-5858
Ben Yi Kuo, *CEO*
Julie Kuo, *Vice Pres*
Hanson Zhao, *Info Tech Mgr*
Julia Cho, *CPA*
David L Smith, *Sales Mgr*
◆ EMP: 50
SQ FT: 62,000
SALES (est): 29.5MM **Privately Held**
WEB: www.eastlioncorp.com
SIC: 5139 Shoes

(P-8434)
EBUYS INC
Also Called: Shoe Metro
8960 Carroll Way Ste 100, San Diego (92121-2429)
PHONE..................858 547-7545
David Tam Duong, *CEO*
Phuoc Huynh, *Vice Pres*
Will Huynh, *Vice Pres*
Kris Windlinx, *Info Tech Dir*
Jaime Glaze, *Human Res Mgr*
EMP: 50
SQ FT: 8,700
SALES (est): 62.3MM **Privately Held**
WEB: www.shoemetro.com
SIC: 5139 Shoes

(P-8435)
FORTUNE DYNAMIC INC
21923 Ferrero, City of Industry (91789-5210)
PHONE..................909 979-9318
Fax: 909 979-8308
Carol Lee, *President*
James Lee, *Vice Pres*
Joan Lee, *Controller*
Angel Shen, *Sales Staff*
San Weng, *Assistant*
◆ EMP: 90
SQ FT: 150,000
SALES (est): 46.9MM **Privately Held**
WEB: www.fortunedynamic.com
SIC: 5139 Shoes

(P-8436)
HI-TEC SPORTS USA INC (DH)
Also Called: Magnum USA
4801 Stoddard Rd, Modesto (95356-9318)
PHONE..................209 545-1111
Fax: 209 545-2543
Simon Bonham, *CEO*
Ed Van Wezel, *CEO*
William Berta, *CFO*
Frank Van Wezel, *Chairman*
Brad Gebhard, *Principal*
▲ EMP: 57 EST: 1978
SQ FT: 120,000

SALES (est): 28.6MM **Privately Held**
WEB: www.magnumboots.com
SIC: 5139 Footwear, athletic; boots
HQ: Hi-Tec Sports Public Limited Company
Aviation Way
Southend-On-Sea SS2 6
170 254-1741

(P-8437)
J P ORIGINAL CORP (PA)
Also Called: Doll House Footwear
19101 E Walnut Dr N, City of Industry (91748-1429)
PHONE..................626 839-4300
Fax: 909 839-4784
C H Hsueh, *Ch of Bd*
Si-Tuo Hsu, *President*
Christen Ho, *Human Resources*
Nina Hsu, *Purch Mgr*
Grace Chung, *Manager*
◆ EMP: 55
SQ FT: 67,000
SALES (est): 33.4MM **Privately Held**
WEB: www.jpo.com
SIC: 5139 Shoes

(P-8438)
KOMMONWEALTH INC
Also Called: Creative Recreation
6420 Wilshire Blvd, Los Angeles (90048-5502)
PHONE..................310 278-7328
Robert Nand, *CEO*
Joe Foerster, *Accountant*
▲ EMP: 50
SALES (est): 14.4MM **Privately Held**
SIC: 5139 Shoes

(P-8439)
L & L LOGIC AND LOGISTICS LP
6 Hamilton Landing # 250, Novato (94949-8264)
PHONE..................707 795-2475
Stephan Birkenstock, *Partner*
Steven Angel, *Office Mgr*
Meagan Miller, *Credit Mgr*
Bob Esebio, *Accountant*
▲ EMP: 50
SALES (est): 4.3MM **Privately Held**
WEB: www.ll-logistics.com
SIC: 5139 Footwear

(P-8440)
NIKEWOMAN
447 Great Mall Dr, Milpitas (95035-8041)
PHONE..................408 942-6457
Jason Cablag, *Manager*
EMP: 50
SALES (est): 1.9MM **Privately Held**
SIC: 5139 Shoes

(P-8441)
OSATA ENTERPRISES INC
Also Called: Globe Shoes
225 S Aviation Blvd, El Segundo (90245-4604)
PHONE..................310 297-1550
Matthew Hill, *Principal*
Gary Valentine, *Principal*
Audrey Lee, *Admin Sec*
Dora Mester, *Financial Exec*
▲ EMP: 100 EST: 1997
SQ FT: 30,000
SALES (est): 35.9MM **Privately Held**
WEB: www.globeshoes.com
SIC: 5139 Shoes

(P-8442)
PRIMA ROYALE ENTERPRISES LTD
Also Called: Prima Royale
150 S Los Robles Ave # 100, Pasadena (91101-2456)
PHONE..................626 960-8388
Ing Nan Yu, *CEO*
Harry K T Chow, *President*
Judy Chow, *Treasurer*
Bobby Bruce Levy, *Vice Pres*
Peter Hayden, *Program Mgr*
▲ EMP: 55
SQ FT: 55,000
SALES (est): 9.1MM **Privately Held**
WEB: www.primaroyale.com
SIC: 5139 3143 Shoes; men's footwear, except athletic

(P-8443)
PRIMITIVE SHOES INC
Also Called: Primitive Skate
9223 Eton Ave, Chatsworth (91311-5808)
PHONE..................818 639-3690
Andrew Netkin, *CEO*
▲ EMP: 60
SALES: 12MM **Privately Held**
SIC: 5139 5661 Footwear; shoes; shoe stores

(P-8444)
REALLY LIKEABLE PEOPLE INC
2251 Las Palmas Dr, Carlsbad (92011-1527)
PHONE..................760 431-5577
Jon W Humphrey, *President*
Diana Crawford, *CFO*
Amy Arroyo, *Human Res Dir*
EMP: 50
SQ FT: 15,000
SALES (est): 12.4MM **Privately Held**
SIC: 5139 Footwear

(P-8445)
ROCKLAND INTL TRADING INC
Also Called: Rockland Footware
760 E Francis St Ste T, Ontario (91761-5550)
PHONE..................909 923-8061
Rockland Dale, *President*
Jennifer WEI, *CFO*
▲ EMP: 60
SALES (est): 5.7MM **Privately Held**
SIC: 5139 Shoes

(P-8446)
SOUTH CONE INC
Also Called: Reef
5935 Darwin Ct, Carlsbad (92008-7302)
PHONE..................760 431-2300
Jeffrey Moore, *President*
Dave Gatto, *President*
Lee Hieb, *CFO*
Jose Abraham, *Info Tech Dir*
Lance Siefken, *Accountant*
▼ EMP: 120
SQ FT: 37,583
SALES (est): 55.9MM
SALES (corp-wide): 12.3B **Publicly Held**
WEB: www.vfc.com
SIC: 5139 3144 3143 Footwear; shoes; women's footwear, except athletic; men's footwear, except athletic
PA: V.F. Corporation
105 Corporate Center Blvd
Greensboro NC 27408
336 424-6000

5141 Groceries, General Line Wholesale

(P-8447)
ACOSTA INC
Acosta Sales & Marketing
5735 W Las Positas Blvd # 300, Pleasanton (94588-4002)
P.O. Box 9039 (94566-9039)
PHONE..................925 600-3500
Fax: 925 485-6775
Tony Mello, *Director*
Fred Farelly, *Vice Pres*
Robert Gifford, *Vice Pres*
Maureen Eneberg, *Marketing Staff*
Tracy Atamian, *Manager*
EMP: 85
SQ FT: 10,000
SALES (corp-wide): 7.4B **Privately Held**
WEB: www.acosta.com
SIC: 5141 Food brokers
PA: Acosta Inc.
6600 Corporate Ctr Pkwy
Jacksonville FL 32216
904 332-7986

(P-8448)
ADVANTAGE SALES & MARKETING
5064 Franklin Dr, Pleasanton (94588-3354)
P.O. Box 9135 (94566-9135)
PHONE..................925 463-5600
Fax: 925 463-5601
Clyde Le Baron, *President*
Steve Derking, *Exec VP*

5141 - Groceries, General Line Wholesale County (P-8449)

Dave Gonzalez, *Business Mgr*
Betty Topping, *Sales Executive*
David Rostrapper, *Sales Mgr*
EMP: 250
SQ FT: 27,000
SALES (est): 26.8MM **Privately Held**
SIC: 5141 5142 5122 Food brokers; packaged frozen goods; druggists' sundries

(P-8449)
ADVANTAGE SALES & MKTG INC
200 N Sepulveda Blvd # 1000, El Segundo (90245-5606)
PHONE 310 321-6869
S D Dorfman, *Branch Mgr*
EMP: 123
SALES (corp-wide): 13.3B **Privately Held**
SIC: 5141 Food brokers
PA: Advantage Sales & Marketing Inc.
18100 Von Karman Ave # 900
Irvine CA 92612
949 797-2900

(P-8450)
ADVANTAGE SALES & MKTG INC (PA)
Also Called: Advantage Solutions
18100 Von Karman Ave # 900, Irvine (92612-7195)
PHONE 949 797-2900
Fax: 949 797-9112
Sonny King, *Chairman*
Tanya Domier, *CEO*
Mike Salzberg, *COO*
Brian Stevens, *COO*
Andy Colombini, *CFO*
▲ **EMP:** 250
SQ FT: 48,000
SALES (est): 13.3B **Privately Held**
WEB: www.asmnet.com
SIC: 5141 Food brokers

(P-8451)
ADVANTAGE SALES & MKTG LLC
6700 Koll Center Pkwy # 300, Pleasanton (94566-7060)
PHONE 925 463-5600
Barry Johnson, *President*
EMP: 72
SALES (corp-wide): 13.3B **Privately Held**
SIC: 5141 5142 Groceries, general line; packaged frozen goods
HQ: Advantage Sales & Marketing Llc
18100 Von Karman Ave # 900
Irvine CA 92612
949 797-2900

(P-8452)
ADVANTAGE SALES & MKTG LLC (HQ)
Also Called: Advantage Solutions
18100 Von Karman Ave # 900, Irvine (92612-7195)
PHONE 949 797-2900
Sonny King, *Chairman*
Tanya Domier, *CEO*
Mark Meyer, *COO*
Brian Stevens, *COO*
Brian G Stevens, *CFO*
EMP: 250
SALES (est): 4.4B
SALES (corp-wide): 13.3B **Privately Held**
SIC: 5141 8732 Food brokers; commercial nonphysical research
PA: Advantage Sales & Marketing Inc.
18100 Von Karman Ave # 900
Irvine CA 92612
949 797-2900

(P-8453)
ADVANTAGE WAYPOINT LLC
235 Baker St E, Costa Mesa (92626-4504)
PHONE 717 424-4973
Angelica Harris, *Admin Mgr*
Brad Etherton, *Division Mgr*
Kristopher Bloom, *General Mgr*
Clay Folloder, *General Mgr*
Kathaleen Larch, *Sales Staff*
EMP: 81
SALES (corp-wide): 200MM **Privately Held**
SIC: 5141 Food brokers

PA: Advantage Waypoint Llc
13521 Prestige Pl
Tampa FL 33635
813 358-5900

(P-8454)
ADVANTAGE-CROWN SLS & MKTG LLC (DH)
1400 S Douglass Rd # 200, Anaheim (92806-6904)
P.O. Box 66010 (92816-6010)
PHONE 714 780-3000
Fax: 714 926-0526
Sonny King, *CEO*
Bob Vesley, *CFO*
Aj Stukenborg, *General Mgr*
Charles Choi, *Info Tech Dir*
Scott Stroh, *Technology*
▲ **EMP:** 1100
SALES (est): 285MM
SALES (corp-wide): 13.3B **Privately Held**
SIC: 5141 Food brokers
HQ: Advantage Sales & Marketing Llc
18100 Von Karman Ave # 900
Irvine CA 92612
949 797-2900

(P-8455)
AMERICAN ACE INTERNATIONAL CO
Also Called: American Ace Intl Trdg Co
313 Newquist Pl Ste A, City of Industry (91745-1091)
PHONE 626 937-6116
Jimmy S T Young, *Vice Pres*
Walter Kang Young, *President*
EMP: 55
SALES (est): 7.4MM **Privately Held**
SIC: 5141 5012 5064 Groceries, general line; automobiles; television sets; video cassette recorders & accessories

(P-8456)
AMK FOODSERVICES INC
Also Called: Kaney Foods
830 Capitolio Way, San Luis Obispo (93401-7122)
P.O. Box 1188 (93406-1188)
PHONE 805 544-7600
Fax: 805 544-4893
John P Kaney, *CEO*
John Tiedmann, *Purch Mgr*
Jack Senecal, *Opers Mgr*
Rich Mullinix, *Marketing Staff*
Dottie Kaney, *Manager*
EMP: 130
SQ FT: 35,000
SALES (est): 36.5MM **Privately Held**
SIC: 5141 Food brokers

(P-8457)
ANSAR GALLERY
2505 El Camino Rd, Tustin (92782)
PHONE 949 220-0000
Hussein Saadat, *President*
Amir Zeinali, *Accountant*
EMP: 200 **EST:** 2013
SQ FT: 120,000
SALES (est): 110.6MM **Privately Held**
SIC: 5141 Groceries, general line
PA: Ansar Mall
P.O. Box 38880
Sharjah
653 133-39

(P-8458)
BAY BROKERAGE INC
17 Woodleaf Ave, Redwood City (94061-1823)
PHONE 650 413-1721
Fax: 650 595-2287
Richard Hoadley, *President*
Darlene Carrera, *COO*
Bill Winger, *COO*
Kevin Pope, *CFO*
P Santy, *CFO*
EMP: 50
SQ FT: 8,000
SALES (est): 10MM **Privately Held**
WEB: www.baybrokerage.com
SIC: 5141 Food brokers

(P-8459)
BERNARD PERRIN SUPOWITZ INC
Also Called: Fergadis Enterprises
5496 Lindbergh Ln, Bell (90201-6409)
PHONE 323 981-2800
Steve Supowitz, *President*
Peter Missaghi, *Info Tech Mgr*
Sarah Hung, *Accountant*
Steven Arroyo, *VP Sales*
Lora Oyama, *Marketing Staff*
EMP: 50
SQ FT: 175,000
SALES (est): 98.2MM **Privately Held**
WEB: www.fergadis.com
SIC: 5141 Groceries, general line

(P-8460)
BI-RITE RESTAURANT SUP CO INC
Also Called: BI-RITE FOODSERVICE DISTRIBUTO
123 S Hill Dr, Brisbane (94005-1203)
PHONE 415 656-0187
Fax: 415 656-0755
William Barulich, *CEO*
Zachary Barulich, *CFO*
Stephen Barulich, *Vice Pres*
Michael Pendergast, *Vice Pres*
Kelly Pattison, *Administration*
◆ **EMP:** 300
SQ FT: 220,000
SALES: 321.6MM **Privately Held**
WEB: www.biritefoodservice.com
SIC: 5141 5147 5148 5023 Groceries, general line; meats & meat products; fresh fruits & vegetables; kitchenware; linens, table; towels; commercial equipment

(P-8461)
C&S WHOLESALE GROCERS INC
2797 S Orange Ave, Fresno (93725-1919)
P.O. Box 11097 (93771-1097)
PHONE 559 442-4700
Randy Wood, *Branch Mgr*
Michael Papaleo, *COO*
Patrick Kennedy, *Executive*
Albert Barone, *Administration*
Nathan Newman, *Project Mgr*
EMP: 475
SALES (corp-wide): 31.1B **Privately Held**
SIC: 5141 Groceries, general line
PA: C&S Wholesale Grocers, Inc.
7 Corporate Dr
Keene NH 03431
603 354-7000

(P-8462)
CANTON FOOD CO INC
750 S Alameda St, Los Angeles (90021-1624)
PHONE 213 688-7707
Fax: 213 688-1121
Shiu Lit Kwan, *CEO*
Cho W Kwan, *President*
Shui Lit Kwan, *CEO*
Wai Kam Kwan, *Vice Pres*
Nancy Phu, *Admin Asst*
▲ **EMP:** 106
SQ FT: 96,000
SALES (est): 101.2MM **Privately Held**
WEB: www.cantonfoodco.com
SIC: 5141 5146 5411 5421 Groceries, general line; seafoods; grocery stores; seafood markets; groceries & related products; refrigerated warehousing & storage

(P-8463)
CERENZIA FOODS INC
8585 White Oak Ave, Rancho Cucamonga (91730-5146)
P.O. Box 3719 (91729-3719)
PHONE 909 989-4000
Joseph F Annunziato, *CEO*
Anthony Annunziato, *President*
Jon Murphy, *General Mgr*
Laura Deyoung, *Controller*
Erik Zamora, *Buyer*
EMP: 60
SQ FT: 75,000

SALES (est): 78.1MM **Privately Held**
WEB: www.cerenziafoods.com
SIC: 5141 Food brokers

(P-8464)
CHEFS WAREHOUSE WESTCOAST LLC (HQ)
16633 Gale Ave, City of Industry (91745-1802)
PHONE 626 465-4200
Chris Pappas, *President*
Tom Burghardt, *Finance*
Ken Clark, *Mng Member*
John Pappas, *Mng Member*
Jonathan Steckler, *Manager*
▲ **EMP:** 59
SALES (est): 54.5MM
SALES (corp-wide): 1B **Publicly Held**
WEB: www.chefswarehouse.com
SIC: 5141 Food brokers
PA: The Chefs' Warehouse Inc
100 E Ridge Rd
Ridgefield CT 06877
203 894-1345

(P-8465)
CO-SALES COMPANY
7133 Koll Center Pkwy, Pleasanton (94566-3300)
PHONE 925 327-7322
Kathy Jean McOmber, *Administration*
EMP: 59
SALES (corp-wide): 65.4MM **Privately Held**
SIC: 5141 Food brokers
PA: Co-Sales Company
2700 N 3rd St Ste 1000
Phoenix AZ 85004
602 254-5555

(P-8466)
COASTAL PACIFIC FD DISTRS INC (PA)
1015 Performance Dr, Stockton (95206-4925)
P.O. Box 30910 (95213-0910)
PHONE 909 947-2066
Fax: 209 983-8009
Terrence Wood, *CEO*
Jeff King, *COO*
Monica Bertkey, *CFO*
Matthew Payne, *CFO*
John Payne, *Treasurer*
▼ **EMP:** 220
SQ FT: 500,000
SALES: 1.2B **Privately Held**
WEB: www.cpfd.com
SIC: 5141 4225 7519 4222 Groceries, general line; general warehousing & storage; trailer rental; refrigerated warehousing & storage

(P-8467)
COASTAL PACIFIC FD DISTRS INC
Also Called: Coastal Pacific Foods
1520 E Mission Blvd Ste B, Ontario (91761-2124)
PHONE 909 947-2066
Fax: 909 947-3606
David Jared, *President*
Pete Hawks, *Plant Mgr*
EMP: 150
SALES (corp-wide): 1.2B **Privately Held**
WEB: www.cpfd.com
SIC: 5141 Groceries, general line
PA: Coastal Pacific Food Distributors, Inc.
1015 Performance Dr
Stockton CA 95206
909 947-2066

(P-8468)
CONCORD FOODS INC (PA)
4601 E Guasti Rd, Ontario (91761-8105)
PHONE 909 975-2000
Fax: 909 975-2007
Nick J Sciortino Jr, *President*
Roy Sciortino, *CFO*
John Sciortino, *Vice Pres*
Sigrid Michaelson, *Controller*
Deborah Stinson, *Manager*
EMP: 81
SQ FT: 67,000
SALES (est): 124.2MM **Privately Held**
WEB: www.concordfoodsinc.com
SIC: 5141 Groceries, general line

▲ = Import ▼ = Export
◆ = Import/Export

5141 - Groceries, General Line Wholesale County (P-8490)

(P-8469)
CORE-MARK INTERNATIONAL INC (HQ)
395 Oyster Point Blvd # 415, South San Francisco (94080-1955)
PHONE.................................650 589-9445
Fax: 650 872-3658
Thomas Perkins, *CEO*
Eric Rolheiser, *President*
Tom Barry, *CFO*
Stacy Loretz, *CFO*
Stacy Loretz-Congdon, *CFO*
EMP: 100
SQ FT: 26,000
SALES (est): 3.4B
SALES (corp-wide): 11B **Publicly Held**
WEB: www.core-mark.com
SIC: 5141 5194 Groceries, general line; cigarettes
PA: Core-Mark Holding Company, Inc.
395 Oyster Point Blvd # 415
South San Francisco CA 94080
650 589-9445

(P-8470)
CROSSMARK INC
2401 E Katella Ave # 625, Anaheim (92806-5939)
PHONE.................................714 464-6318
Leclerc Michele, *Manager*
EMP: 57
SALES (corp-wide): 3.1B **Privately Held**
SIC: 5141 Groceries, general line
PA: Crossmark, Inc.
5100 Legacy Dr
Plano TX 75024
469 814-1000

(P-8471)
CROSSMARK INCORPORATED
Also Called: Crossmark Sales & Marketing
3875 Hopyard Rd Ste 250, Pleasanton (94588-2784)
PHONE.................................925 463-3555
Fax: 925 460-8581
Jeff Nanna, *Director*
David S Charles, *Vice Pres*
Brenda Grant, *Marketing Staff*
EMP: 300
SALES (corp-wide): 3.1B **Privately Held**
WEB: www.crossmark.com
SIC: 5141 Food brokers
PA: Crossmark, Inc.
5100 Legacy Dr
Plano TX 75024
469 814-1000

(P-8472)
D&A ENTERPRISES INC
34943 Newark Blvd, Newark (94560-1215)
PHONE.................................510 445-1600
Afit Vyas, *President*
EMP: 300
SALES (est): 29.6MM **Privately Held**
SIC: 5141 Food brokers

(P-8473)
DEL MONACO SPECIALTY FOODS INC
18675 Madrone Pkwy # 150, Morgan Hill (95037-2868)
PHONE.................................408 500-4100
Ernestine Del Monaco, *Ch of Bd*
Vic Del Monaco, *CEO*
Tony Del Monaco, *Vice Pres*
Alva Cheing, *Info Tech Mgr*
Mike D Monaco, *Human Res Mgr*
EMP: 88
SQ FT: 18,000
SALES (est): 25.7MM
SALES (corp-wide): 105MM **Privately Held**
WEB: www.delmonacofoods.com
SIC: 5141 Groceries, general line
PA: Kettle Cuisine, Llc
330 Lynnway Ste 405
Lynn MA 01901
617 409-1100

(P-8474)
DOT FOODS INC
2200 Nickerson Dr, Modesto (95358-9489)
PHONE.................................209 581-9090
Fax: 209 581-9082
EMP: 134
SALES (corp-wide): 5.4B **Privately Held**
SIC: 5141
PA: Dot Foods, Inc.
1 Dot Way
Mount Sterling IL 62353
217 773-4411

(P-8475)
DPI SPECIALTY FOODS WEST INC (DH)
601 S Rockefeller Ave, Ontario (91761-7871)
PHONE.................................909 975-1019
John Jordan, *CEO*
James De Keyser, *President*
Donna Robbins, *President*
Francis Haren, *COO*
Conor Crowley, *CFO*
▲ EMP: 91
SQ FT: 250,000
SALES (est): 662.5MM **Privately Held**
WEB: www.dpi-west.com
SIC: 5141 Groceries, general line
HQ: Dpi Specialty Foods, Inc
601 S Rockefeller Ave
Ontario CA 91761
909 390-0892

(P-8476)
E G AYERS DISTRIBUTING INC
5819 S Broadway St, Eureka (95503-6906)
PHONE.................................707 445-2077
Fax: 707 445-5719
Paul A Ayers, *CEO*
Phillip Ayers, *Corp Secy*
Pat Gillmore, *Transptn Dir*
EMP: 50
SQ FT: 15,000
SALES (est): 28MM **Privately Held**
WEB: www.ayersdistributing.com
SIC: 5141 5149 Groceries, general line; beverages, except coffee & tea

(P-8477)
EXANDAL CORPORATION
Also Called: Colorexa
17620 Sherman Way Ste 207, Van Nuys (91406-3527)
PHONE.................................818 705-9497
Carlos Alvaro, *President*
Andrea Alvaro, *Director*
Kathleen Francois, *Manager*
Kirk McDowell, *Manager*
▲ EMP: 150
SALES (est): 25.6MM **Privately Held**
WEB: www.exandal.com
SIC: 5141 Food brokers
PA: Exandal S.A.
Av. Los Alamos Mz. I Lt. 8
Lima LM 22
-

(P-8478)
FOOD SALES WEST INC (PA)
235 Baker St E, Costa Mesa (92626-4521)
P.O. Box 19738, Irvine (92623-9738)
PHONE.................................714 966-2900
Fax: 714 966-0165
David Lyons, *CEO*
Carl Scharffenberger, *President*
Mary Ellen Scharffenberger, *Corp Secy*
Michael Berkson, *Vice Pres*
Robert Watkins, *Vice Pres*
EMP: 60
SQ FT: 12,000
SALES (est): 25.9MM **Privately Held**
WEB: www.foodsaleswest.com
SIC: 5141 Food brokers

(P-8479)
FOOTHILL PACKING INC
2255 S Broadway, Santa Maria (93454-7871)
PHONE.................................805 925-7900
EMP: 489
SALES (corp-wide): 36.1MM **Privately Held**
SIC: 5141 Groceries, general line
PA: Foothill Packing, Inc.
1582 Moffett St
Salinas CA 93905
831 784-1453

(P-8480)
FORTUNE AVENUE FOODS INC
2117 Pointe Ave, Ontario (91761-8529)
PHONE.................................909 930-5989
Daniel C Yang, *CEO*
Fula Yang, *Vice Pres*
▲ EMP: 55
SQ FT: 27,000
SALES (est): 19.2MM **Privately Held**
WEB: www.fortuneavenuefoods.com
SIC: 5141 Groceries, general line

(P-8481)
GOLDBERG AND SOLOVY FOODS INC
Also Called: G and S Foods
5925 Alcoa Ave, Vernon (90058-3955)
PHONE.................................323 581-6161
Fax: 323 583-8629
Paul Paget, *CEO*
Earl Goldberg, *President*
Matt Breenan, *QA Dir*
Essy Fisher, *Accounting Mgr*
Deanne Ito, *Purch Mgr*
EMP: 285
SQ FT: 70,000
SALES (est): 186.5MM
SALES (corp-wide): 50.3B **Publicly Held**
WEB: www.gsfoods.com
SIC: 5141 5149 5046 5169 Groceries, general line; groceries & related products; restaurant equipment & supplies; chemicals & allied products
PA: Sysco Corporation
1390 Enclave Pkwy
Houston TX 77077
281 584-1390

(P-8482)
GOURMET FOODS INC (PA)
2910 E Harcourt St, Compton (90221-5502)
PHONE.................................310 632-3300
Fax: 310 632-0303
Heinz Naef, *President*
Neil Levine, *Managing Prtnr*
Gary David, *CFO*
Ursina Naef, *Corp Secy*
Marcel Lagnaz, *Vice Pres*
▲ EMP: 102
SQ FT: 35,000
SALES (est): 101.9MM **Privately Held**
WEB: www.gourmetfoodsinc.com
SIC: 5141 5812 2099 Food brokers; eating places; food preparations

(P-8483)
GRAND SUPERCENTER INC
8550 Chetle Ave Ste B, Whittier (90606-2662)
PHONE.................................562 318-3451
EMP: 70
SALES (est): 10.8MM **Privately Held**
SIC: 5141 Groceries, general line
HQ: Grand Supercenter Inc.
300 Chubb Ave
Lyndhurst NJ 07071
201 507-9900

(P-8484)
GROCERS SPECIALTY COMPANY (HQ)
Also Called: G S C Ball
5200 Sheila St, Commerce (90040-3906)
P.O. Box 513396, Los Angeles (90051-1396)
PHONE.................................323 264-5200
Fax: 323 264-8572
Joe Falvey, *President*
Rich Martin, *CFO*
Christine Neal, *Treasurer*
Bob Ling, *Admin Sec*
Veronica Campos, *Administration*
▲ EMP: 50 EST: 1981
SQ FT: 106,000
SALES (est): 93.8MM
SALES (corp-wide): 4B **Privately Held**
SIC: 5141 Groceries, general line
PA: Unified Grocers, Inc.
5200 Sheila St
Commerce CA 90040
323 264-5200

(P-8485)
HOMEGROWN NATURAL FOODS INC
Also Called: Consorzio
1610 5th St, Berkeley (94710-1715)
PHONE.................................510 558-7500
John Foraker, *President*
Dale Payton-Engle, *CFO*
T W Illiams, *Vice Pres*
Ed Presson, *Vice Pres*
Michael Hinrichsen, *Info Tech Mgr*
EMP: 75
SQ FT: 10,000
SALES (est): 13.9MM
SALES (corp-wide): 16.5B **Publicly Held**
SIC: 5141 5149 Groceries, general line; natural & organic foods
HQ: Annie's, Inc.
1610 5th St
Berkeley CA 94710
510 558-7500

(P-8486)
HOUWELING NURSERIES OXNARD INC
Also Called: Houweling's Tomatoes
645 Laguna Rd, Camarillo (93012-8523)
PHONE.................................805 488-8832
Fax: 805 271-5107
Casey Houweling, *President*
Christopher Brocklesby, *CFO*
Jacqueline Rodriguez, *Opers Mgr*
William Wilber, *VP Sales*
Monica Houweling, *Sales Staff*
▲ EMP: 450
SALES (est): 221.8MM **Privately Held**
WEB: www.houwelings.com
SIC: 5141 Groceries, general line

(P-8487)
HUG COMPANY
Also Called: Gourmet Foods
2557 Barrington Ct, Hayward (94545-1174)
PHONE.................................510 887-0340
Fax: 510 887-0690
Uwe Henze, *President*
EMP: 90
SALES (est): 22.8MM
SALES (corp-wide): 101.9MM **Privately Held**
SIC: 5141 Food brokers
PA: Gourmet Foods, Inc.
2910 E Harcourt St
Compton CA 90221
310 632-3300

(P-8488)
IMPOSSIBLE FOODS INC
525 Chesapeake Dr, Redwood City (94063-4724)
PHONE.................................650 461-4385
Patrick Brown, *CEO*
Nick Halla, *Finance Dir*
EMP: 60
SALES (est): 47.2MM **Privately Held**
SIC: 5141 Food brokers

(P-8489)
JETRO CASH AND CARRY ENTPS LLC
Also Called: Restaurant Depot
1275 Vine St, Sacramento (95811-0427)
PHONE.................................916 492-2305
MI Thao, *Controller*
Steven Taranto, *Manager*
EMP: 95 **Privately Held**
SIC: 5141 5046 Groceries, general line; restaurant equipment & supplies
HQ: Jetro Cash And Carry Enterprises, Llc
1524 132nd St
College Point NY 11356
718 939-6400

(P-8490)
LAX-C INC
1100 N Main St, Los Angeles (90012-1832)
PHONE.................................323 343-9000
Fax: 323 441-9988
Suprata Bovornsivamon, *President*
▲ EMP: 50
SALES (est): 24.9MM **Privately Held**
WEB: www.lax-c.com
SIC: 5141 Groceries, general line

5141 - Groceries, General Line Wholesale County (P-8491)

(P-8491)
LEE BROS FOODSERVICES INC (PA)
Also Called: Lee Industrial Catering
660 E Gish Rd, San Jose (95112-2707)
PHONE..................408 275-0700
Fax: 408 297-1309
Chieu Van Le, *CEO*
Huong Le, *Vice Pres*
Jimmy Lee, *Vice Pres*
David Hui, *MIS Dir*
Vivian Tran, *Purchasing*
▲ **EMP:** 100
SQ FT: 15,000
SALES (est): 94.7MM **Privately Held**
SIC: 5141 5142 Groceries, general line; packaged frozen goods

(P-8492)
LIVA DISTRIBUTORS INC (HQ)
3173 Iris Ave, San Diego (92173-1234)
PHONE..................619 423-9997
Fax: 619 423-9998
Amanda Limon, *President*
Beddy Gonzalez, *Bookkeeper*
EMP: 60
SALES (est): 18.5MM
SALES (corp-wide): 40.4MM **Privately Held**
WEB: www.livadistributors.com
SIC: 5141 5147 Groceries, general line; meats & meat products
PA: Distribuidora El Florido, S.A. De C.V.
Blvd. Insurgentes No. 8904
Tijuana B.C. 22590
664 383-6700

(P-8493)
MARKET SMART INC
6900 Koll Center Pkwy # 406, Pleasanton (94566-3148)
PHONE..................925 846-6237
Bill Oconnel, *President*
Linda Grassi, *Accounts Exec*
EMP: 59
SALES (est): 3.5MM **Privately Held**
WEB: www.marketsmart.com
SIC: 5141 Groceries, general line

(P-8494)
MARQUEZ BROTHERS ENTPS INC
15480 Valley Blvd, City of Industry (91746-3325)
PHONE..................626 330-3310
Gustavo Marquez, *President*
Dave Villanueva, *CFO*
Jaime Marquez, *Vice Pres*
Juan Marquez, *Vice Pres*
Mario Amecquita, *Credit Mgr*
◆ **EMP:** 200
SQ FT: 200,000
SALES (est): 88.3MM **Privately Held**
SIC: 5141 Groceries, general line

(P-8495)
MARQUEZ BROTHERS INTL INC
Also Called: El Mexicano
1328 W Colegrove Ave, Montebello (90640-5051)
PHONE..................323 722-8103
Fax: 323 722-1938
Sal Alcaraz, *Manager*
Laura Iniguez, *Financial Exec*
Joseph Cannarozzi, *Director*
EMP: 58
SALES (corp-wide): 208.6MM **Privately Held**
WEB: www.elmexicano.net
SIC: 5141 Groceries, general line
PA: Marquez Brothers International, Inc.
5801 Rue Ferrari
San Jose CA 95138
408 960-2700

(P-8496)
MARQUEZ BROTHERS INTL INC
Also Called: Cheese Plant
179 S 11th Ave, Hanford (93230-5056)
PHONE..................559 584-8000
Jaun Marquez, *Vice Pres*
Gloria Green, *Executive*
Anthony Blunt, *Maintence Staff*
Kulwinder Bath, *Director*
Dani Vela, *Director*
EMP: 152
SALES (corp-wide): 208.6MM **Privately Held**
WEB: www.elmexicano.net
SIC: 5141 2022 Groceries, general line; natural cheese
PA: Marquez Brothers International, Inc.
5801 Rue Ferrari
San Jose CA 95138
408 960-2700

(P-8497)
MARTIN-BROWER COMPANY LLC
4704 Fite Ct, Stockton (95215-8308)
P.O. Box 547, Sheridan OR (97378-0547)
PHONE..................209 466-2980
Mark Peterson, *Principal*
EMP: 138 **Privately Held**
SIC: 5141 Groceries, general line
HQ: The Martin-Brower Company L L C
6250 N River Rd Ste 9000
Rosemont IL 60018
847 227-6500

(P-8498)
MCLANE COMPANY INC
800 E Pescadero Ave, Tracy (95304-9799)
PHONE..................209 221-7500
Bruce Bravo, *Manager*
Dan Ball, *General Mgr*
EMP: 217
SALES (corp-wide): 210.8B **Publicly Held**
SIC: 5141 Groceries, general line
HQ: Mclane Company, Inc.
4747 Mclane Pkwy
Temple TX 76504
254 771-7500

(P-8499)
MCLANE/PACIFIC INC
3876 E Childs Ave, Merced (95341-9520)
P.O. Box 2107 (95344-0107)
PHONE..................209 725-2500
Fax: 209 725-2564
William G Rosier, *CEO*
Mike Youngblood, *President*
Kevin Koch, *Treasurer*
Jim Kent, *Exec VP*
Neal Mayes, *Finance*
▲ **EMP:** 498
SQ FT: 220,000
SALES (est): 214.7MM
SALES (corp-wide): 210.8B **Publicly Held**
WEB: www.mclaneco.com
SIC: 5141 Groceries, general line
HQ: Mclane Company, Inc.
4747 Mclane Pkwy
Temple TX 76504
254 771-7500

(P-8500)
MCLANE/SOUTHERN CALIFORNIA INC
4472 Georgia Blvd, San Bernardino (92407-1854)
PHONE..................909 887-7500
Fax: 909 887-3158
David Leach, *President*
Grady Rosier, *President*
William G Rosier, *CEO*
Kevin Koch, *CFO*
Jim Kent, *Exec VP*
◆ **EMP:** 398
SQ FT: 293,000
SALES (est): 189.3MM
SALES (corp-wide): 210.8B **Publicly Held**
WEB: www.mclaneco.com
SIC: 5141 Groceries, general line
HQ: Mclane Company, Inc.
4747 Mclane Pkwy
Temple TX 76504
254 771-7500

(P-8501)
MERCADO LATINO INC (PA)
245 Baldwin Park Blvd, City of Industry (91746-1404)
P.O. Box 6168, El Monte (91734-6168)
PHONE..................626 333-6862
Fax: 626 333-5088
Graciliano Rodriguez, *President*
George Rodriguez, *CFO*
Richard Rodriguez, *Senior VP*
Angelita Rodriguez, *Admin Sec*
▲ **EMP:** 100 **EST:** 1963
SQ FT: 105,000
SALES (est): 255.5MM **Privately Held**
WEB: www.mercadolatinoinc.com
SIC: 5141 5148 Groceries, general line; fresh fruits & vegetables

(P-8502)
MERCADO LATINO INC
33430 Western Ave, Union City (94587-3202)
PHONE..................510 475-5500
Fax: 510 475-5500
Robert Rodriguez, *Principal*
EMP: 50
SALES (corp-wide): 255.5MM **Privately Held**
WEB: www.mercadolatinoinc.com
SIC: 5141 Food brokers
PA: Mercado Latino, Inc.
245 Baldwin Park Blvd
City Of Industry CA 91746
626 333-6862

(P-8503)
MISHIMA FOODS USA INC (PA)
2340 Plaza Del Amo # 105, Torrance (90501-3445)
PHONE..................310 787-1533
Fax: 310 787-1651
Yutaka Mishima, *President*
Tsukasa Hatsukade, *Vice Pres*
▲ **EMP:** 76
SALES (est): 22.8MM **Privately Held**
SIC: 5141 Groceries, general line

(P-8504)
NAFTA DISTRIBUTORS
5120 Santa Ana St, Ontario (91761-8632)
PHONE..................909 605-7515
Fax: 909 937-2016
Samuel Madikians, *CEO*
Bashar Hallak, *Vice Pres*
Anna Noyola, *Manager*
EMP: 50
SQ FT: 12,000
SALES (est): 40.5MM **Privately Held**
WEB: www.naftadist.com
SIC: 5141 Groceries, general line

(P-8505)
NASSER COMPANY INC (PA)
Also Called: Nasser Company of Arizona
22720 Savi Ranch Pkwy, Yorba Linda (92887-4614)
PHONE..................714 279-2100
Fax: 714 921-4592
Burhan Nasser, *President*
Bill Arink, *President*
Bruce Nye, *CFO*
Ken Darienzo, *Chairman*
Mary Beth Nasser, *Corp Secy*
EMP: 60
SQ FT: 17,445
SALES (est): 128.9MM **Privately Held**
SIC: 5141 Food brokers

(P-8506)
NONGSHIM AMERICA INC (HQ)
12155 6th St, Rancho Cucamonga (91730-6115)
PHONE..................909 481-3698
Fax: 909 484-5722
Dong Y Shin, *CEO*
Chris Gepford, *Principal*
John Seo, *Info Tech Mgr*
Ava Taussig, *Research*
Maru Kim, *Engineer*
◆ **EMP:** 250
SALES (est): 245.4MM
SALES (corp-wide): 1.6B **Privately Held**
WEB: www.nongshim.us
SIC: 5141 2098 Groceries, general line; noodles (e.g. egg, plain & water), dry
PA: Nongshim Co., Ltd.
Sindaebang-Dong
Seoul SEO 07057
282 071-14

(P-8507)
OAKHURST INDUSTRIES INC
Also Called: Freund Baking Co
3265 Investment Blvd, Hayward (94545-3806)
PHONE..................510 265-2400
Fax: 510 265-2444
Jim Freund, *Principal*
Donna Stapp, *Office Mgr*
Phil Suniga, *Sales Executive*
B Albrecht, *Manager*
Tim Albrecht, *Manager*
EMP: 80
SQ FT: 67,896
SALES (corp-wide): 148MM **Privately Held**
WEB: www.oakhurstproperties.com
SIC: 5141 2051 Groceries, general line; bread, cake & related products
PA: Oakhurst Industries, Inc.
2050 S Tubeway Ave
Commerce CA 90040
323 724-3000

(P-8508)
PALO ALTO EGG AND FOOD SVC CO
Also Called: Palo Alto Food Company
6691 Clark Ave, Newark (94560-3925)
P.O. Box 327 (94560-0327)
PHONE..................510 456-2420
Eric Jensen, *CEO*
Paul Jensen, *Vice Pres*
Jenny Murray, *Manager*
Nancy Urizar, *Manager*
EMP: 50
SQ FT: 15,000
SALES: 18.9MM **Privately Held**
WEB: www.paloaltoegg.com
SIC: 5141 Groceries, general line

(P-8509)
PERFORMANCE FOOD GROUP INC
Also Called: Performnce Foodservice Ledyard
1047 17th Ave, Santa Cruz (95062-3033)
PHONE..................831 462-4400
Richard Fontana, *Sr Corp Ofcr*
Debby Haskin, *Personnel Exec*
Dave Whiting, *VP Sales*
EMP: 101
SALES (corp-wide): 16.1B **Publicly Held**
SIC: 5141 5046 5087 Groceries, general line; restaurant equipment & supplies; janitors' supplies
HQ: Performance Food Group, Inc.
12500 West Creek Pkwy
Richmond VA 23238
804 484-7700

(P-8510)
PITCO FOODS
1670 Overland Ct, West Sacramento (95691-3490)
PHONE..................916 372-7772
Farzam Hariri, *Manager*
JB Buckley, *Manager*
EMP: 65 **Privately Held**
WEB: www.pitcofoods.com
SIC: 5141 Groceries, general line
PA: Pitco Foods
567 Cinnabar St
San Jose CA 95110

(P-8511)
PIVEG INC
10455 Sorrento Valley Rd # 101, San Diego (92121-1621)
PHONE..................858 436-3070
Roberto L Espinoza, *CEO*
Ryan Mangan, *Sales Staff*
Stephanie Sanders, *Sales Staff*
EMP: 220 **EST:** 2004
SALES: 57.3MM **Privately Held**
SIC: 5141 Food brokers

(P-8512)
RELIANCE INTERMODAL INC
1919 Martin Luther King Ste A, Stockton (95210)
P.O. Box 31238 (95213-1238)
PHONE..................209 946-0200
Lakhbir S Deol, *CEO*

▲ = Import ▼ = Export
◆ = Import/Export

PRODUCTS & SERVICES SECTION
5141 - Groceries, General Line Wholesale County (P-8534)

EMP: 65
SALES: 9.7MM **Privately Held**
SIC: 5141 Groceries, general line

(P-8513)
RESTAURANT DEPOT
10850 Spencer St, Fountain Valley (92708-7009)
PHONE.................714 378-3535
Fax: 714 378-3528
Stanley Fleishman, *President*
Richard Kirshner, *Vice Pres*
Samuel Rubanenko, *Vice Pres*
Andy Rosen, *Executive Asst*
Glen Fleishman, *Controller*
EMP: 50
SQ FT: 42,000
SALES (est): 9.5MM **Privately Held**
SIC: 5141 Groceries, general line

(P-8514)
RIO VISTA VENTURES LLC (PA)
Also Called: Giumarra Companies
15651 Old Milky Way, Escondido (92027-7104)
P.O. Box 861449, Los Angeles (90086-1449)
PHONE.................760 480-8502
Don Corsaro, *Chairman*
Timothy Riley, *President*
Eric Navarro, *Accountant*
Anthony Stallings, *Controller*
Aaron Bedoy, *Manager*
▲ **EMP:** 50
SALES (est): 91.1MM **Privately Held**
SIC: 5141 Food brokers

(P-8515)
RIO VISTA VENTURES LLC
Also Called: Giumarra Company, The
3646 Avenue 416, Reedley (93654-9111)
PHONE.................559 897-6730
Donald Corsaro, *President*
EMP: 50
SALES (corp-wide): 91.1MM **Privately Held**
SIC: 5141 Food brokers
PA: Rio Vista Ventures Llc
15651 Old Milky Way
Escondido CA 92027
760 480-8502

(P-8516)
RUDOLPH FOODS COMPANY INC
Also Called: Rudolph Foods West
145 Hillcrest Ave, San Bernardino (92408-2117)
PHONE.................909 383-7463
Fax: 909 388-2202
Jim Rudolph, *President*
EMP: 75
SALES (corp-wide): 131.4MM **Privately Held**
SIC: 5141 2099 2013 Groceries, general line; food preparations; sausages & other prepared meats
PA: Rudolph Foods Company, Inc.
6575 Bellefontaine Rd
Lima OH 45804
909 383-7463

(P-8517)
SALADINOS INC (PA)
3325 W Figarden Dr, Fresno (93711-3909)
P.O. Box 12266 (93777-2266)
PHONE.................559 271-3700
Fax: 559 271-3701
Craig A Saladino, *CEO*
Owen Escola, *President*
Patrick Peters, *COO*
Mark Schuh, *CFO*
Don Saladino, *Chairman*
EMP: 113
SQ FT: 40,000
SALES (est): 422.7MM **Privately Held**
WEB: www.saladinos.com
SIC: 5141 2099 Groceries, general line; food preparations

(P-8518)
SHOEI FOODS USA INC
1900 Feather River Blvd, Olivehurst (95961-9627)
PHONE.................530 742-7866
Don Soetaert, *CEO*

Sumio Kawanabe, *President*
Tall Matsushima, *President*
Paul Jones, *CFO*
▲ **EMP:** 100
SQ FT: 68,000
SALES (est): 89.8MM
SALES (corp-wide): 888MM **Privately Held**
SIC: 5141 Food brokers
PA: Shoei Foods Corporation
5-7, Akihabara
Taito-Ku TKY 110-0
332 531-211

(P-8519)
SMART & FINAL HOLDINGS LLC
10205 Constellation Blvd, Los Angeles (90067-6201)
PHONE.................310 843-1900
George Golleher,
EMP: 5910
SALES (est): 162.3MM **Privately Held**
SIC: 5141 5411 Groceries, general line; grocery stores

(P-8520)
SOUTHWEST TRADERS INCORPORATED
4747 Frontier Way, Stockton (95215-9671)
PHONE.................209 462-1607
Fax: 209 428-5874
EMP: 91
SALES (corp-wide): 492.3MM **Privately Held**
SIC: 5141 Food brokers
PA: Southwest Traders Incorporated
27565 Diaz Rd
Temecula CA 92590
951 699-7800

(P-8521)
SOUTHWEST TRADERS INCORPORATED (PA)
Also Called: Swt Stockton
27565 Diaz Rd, Temecula (92590-3411)
PHONE.................951 699-7800
Fax: 951 699-5717
Ken Smith, *CEO*
Lynne Bredemeier, *CFO*
Mike Bredemeier, *Vice Pres*
Karen Smith, *Vice Pres*
Angela Bergeron, *Risk Mgmt Dir*
▲ **EMP:** 180
SQ FT: 130,000
SALES (est): 492.3MM **Privately Held**
SIC: 5141 Food brokers

(P-8522)
SPROUTS FARMERS MARKET INC
24235 Magic Mountain Pkwy, Valencia (91355-3401)
PHONE.................661 414-1109
Doug Sanders, *Branch Mgr*
EMP: 215
SALES (corp-wide): 3.5B **Publicly Held**
SIC: 5141 Groceries, general line
PA: Sprouts Farmers Market, Inc.
5455 E High St Ste 111
Phoenix AZ 85054
480 814-8016

(P-8523)
SPROUTS FARMERS MARKET INC
1295 S State St, Hemet (92543-7976)
PHONE.................951 766-6746
Tommy Reingrover, *Principal*
EMP: 215
SALES (corp-wide): 3.5B **Publicly Held**
SIC: 5141 Groceries, general line
PA: Sprouts Farmers Market, Inc.
5455 E High St Ste 111
Phoenix AZ 85054
480 814-8016

(P-8524)
SPROUTS FARMERS MARKET INC
1751 Westwood Blvd, Los Angeles (90024-5607)
PHONE.................310 500-1192
EMP: 215
SALES (corp-wide): 3.5B **Publicly Held**
SIC: 5141 Groceries, general line

PA: Sprouts Farmers Market, Inc.
5455 E High St Ste 111
Phoenix AZ 85054
480 814-8016

(P-8525)
SPROUTS FARMERS MARKET INC
659 Lomas Santa Fe Dr, Solana Beach (92075-1412)
PHONE.................858 350-7900
Tammy Arosemena, *Manager*
EMP: 215
SALES (corp-wide): 3.5B **Publicly Held**
SIC: 5141 Groceries, general line
PA: Sprouts Farmers Market, Inc.
5455 E High St Ste 111
Phoenix AZ 85054
480 814-8016

(P-8526)
SPROUTS FARMERS MARKET INC
17482 Yorba Linda Blvd, Yorba Linda (92886-3823)
PHONE.................714 572-3535
Jason Loomis, *Manager*
EMP: 172
SALES (corp-wide): 3.5B **Publicly Held**
SIC: 5141 Groceries, general line
PA: Sprouts Farmers Market, Inc.
5455 E High St Ste 111
Phoenix AZ 85054
480 814-8016

(P-8527)
SPROUTS FARMERS MARKET INC
3030 Harbor Blvd Ste D, Costa Mesa (92626-2562)
PHONE.................714 751-6399
Mike Emmans, *Manager*
EMP: 172
SALES (corp-wide): 3.5B **Publicly Held**
SIC: 5141 Groceries, general line
PA: Sprouts Farmers Market, Inc.
5455 E High St Ste 111
Phoenix AZ 85054
480 814-8016

(P-8528)
SUNFOODS LLC (HQ)
Also Called: Hinode
1620 E Kentucky Ave, Woodland (95776-6110)
P.O. Box 8729 (95776-8729)
PHONE.................530 661-0578
Matt Alonso, *CEO*
Clyde Uchida, *Plant Mgr*
Jacqueline Hartshorn,
John Koury,
Lionel Meador, *Manager*
◆ **EMP:** 70
SQ FT: 1,600
SALES: 22MM
SALES (corp-wide): 951.3MM **Privately Held**
SIC: 5141 Groceries, general line
PA: Ricegrowers Limited
L 24 Mlc Centre 19 Martin Pl
Sydney NSW 2000
180 025-5999

(P-8529)
SYGMA NETWORK INC
3741 Gold River Ln, Stockton (95215-9669)
PHONE.................209 932-5300
Fax: 209 932-5363
John Rivers, *Manager*
Don Thornburg, *Executive*
Jeff Castle, *Mktg Dir*
Cheryl Roland, *Manager*
EMP: 125
SALES (corp-wide): 50.3B **Publicly Held**
WEB: www.sygmanetwork.com
SIC: 5141 Groceries, general line
HQ: The Sygma Network Inc
5550 Blazer Pkwy Ste 300
Dublin OH 43017
614 734-2500

(P-8530)
SYSCO CENTRAL CALIFORNIA INC
136 Mariposa Rd, Modesto (95354-4122)
P.O. Box 729 (95353-0729)
PHONE.................209 527-7700
Fax: 209 522-4655
Elizabeth Aspray, *President*
Robin Kawashima, *CFO*
Mark Kimmel, *Vice Pres*
Pamela Cullors, *Executive*
Tom Bishop, *Info Tech Mgr*
▲ **EMP:** 312
SQ FT: 177,000
SALES (corp-wide): 50.3B **Publicly Held**
SIC: 5141 5142 5046 5148 Groceries, general line; meat, frozen: packaged; vegetables, frozen; restaurant equipment & supplies; fruits, fresh; vegetables, fresh
PA: Sysco Corporation
1390 Enclave Pkwy
Houston TX 77077
281 584-1390

(P-8531)
SYSCO LOS ANGELES INC
20701 Currier Rd, Walnut (91789-2904)
PHONE.................909 595-9595
Fax: 909 598-6383
Daniel S Haag, *CEO*
Sal Adelberg, *Exec VP*
Saul Adelsberg, *Exec VP*
John KAO, *Senior VP*
Mary Brumbaugh, *Vice Pres*
◆ **EMP:** 1000
SALES (est): 221.8MM
SALES (corp-wide): 50.3B **Publicly Held**
WEB: www.syscola.com
SIC: 5141 5084 Groceries, general line; food industry machinery
PA: Sysco Corporation
1390 Enclave Pkwy
Houston TX 77077
281 584-1390

(P-8532)
SYSCO RIVERSIDE INC
15750 Meridian Pkwy, Riverside (92518-3001)
PHONE.................951 601-5300
Saul Adelsberg, *CEO*
Raul Flores, *Marketing Staff*
Randy Guyer, *Accounts Exec*
EMP: 375
SALES (corp-wide): 50.3B **Publicly Held**
SIC: 5141 5142 5143 5144 Groceries, general line; packaged frozen goods; dairy products, except dried or canned; poultry & poultry products; confectionery; fish & seafoods
PA: Sysco Corporation
1390 Enclave Pkwy
Houston TX 77077
281 584-1390

(P-8533)
SYSCO SACRAMENTO INC
7062 Pacific Ave, Pleasant Grove (95668-9731)
P.O. Box 138007, Sacramento (95813-8007)
PHONE.................916 275-2714
Fax: 916 569-7001
Jackie L Ward, *Ch of Bd*
Bill Delaney, *President*
Delmer Schnuelle, *President*
Tom Bene, *Exec VP*
Delmar Schnelly, *Exec VP*
▼ **EMP:** 393 **EST:** 2000
SQ FT: 350,000
SALES (est): 221.8MM
SALES (corp-wide): 50.3B **Publicly Held**
WEB: www.sac.sysco.com
SIC: 5141 5142 Groceries, general line; packaged frozen goods
PA: Sysco Corporation
1390 Enclave Pkwy
Houston TX 77077
281 584-1390

(P-8534)
SYSCO SAN DIEGO INC
12180 Kirkham Rd, Poway (92064-6879)
PHONE.................858 513-7300
Kevin Mangan, *CEO*
Howard Poole, *President*

5141 - Groceries, General Line Wholesale County (P-8535)

Debbie Morey, *Vice Pres*
Debra Morey, *Vice Pres*
Jeff Orton, *Info Tech Mgr*
◆ **EMP:** 370
SQ FT: 250,000
SALES (est): 221.8MM
SALES (corp-wide): 50.3B **Publicly Held**
SIC: 5141 5142 5147 5148 Groceries, general line; packaged frozen goods; meats & meat products; fresh fruits & vegetables; food industry machinery
PA: Sysco Corporation
1390 Enclave Pkwy
Houston TX 77077
281 584-1390

(P-8535)
SYSCO SAN FRANCISCO INC (HQ)
5900 Stewart Ave, Fremont (94538-3134)
P.O. Box 697 (94537-0697)
PHONE 510 226-3000
Fax: 510 226-3085
James Ehlers, *President*
Bruce Luong, *Vice Pres*
Randy Timmer, *Vice Pres*
Mark Jones, *MIS Dir*
David Wong, *Systems Mgr*
▼ **EMP:** 596 **EST:** 1939
SQ FT: 470,000
SALES (est): 483.1MM
SALES (corp-wide): 50.3B **Publicly Held**
WEB: www.syscosf.com
SIC: 5141 5147 5142 Groceries, general line; meats, fresh; packaged frozen goods
PA: Sysco Corporation
1390 Enclave Pkwy
Houston TX 77077
281 584-1390

(P-8536)
SYSCO SAN FRANCISCO INC
1622 Moffett St, Salinas (93905-3353)
PHONE 831 771-5000
Tom Wason, *Vice Pres*
Ken Muller, *Business Dir*
Michael Hartsaw, *Business Mgr*
King Jenks, *Sls & Mktg Exec*
Mike Hansen, *Manager*
EMP: 205
SALES (corp-wide): 50.3B **Publicly Held**
WEB: www.syscosf.com
SIC: 5141 Groceries, general line
HQ: Sysco San Francisco, Inc.
5900 Stewart Ave
Fremont CA 94538
510 226-3000

(P-8537)
SYSCO VENTURA INC
3100 Sturgis Rd, Oxnard (93030-7276)
PHONE 805 205-7000
Fax: 805 205-7012
Jerry L Barash, *President*
Manny Fernandez, *Ch of Bd*
Bill Delaney, *President*
William Mastrosimone, *CFO*
Brian Beach, *Vice Pres*
EMP: 300
SQ FT: 370,000
SALES (est): 212.4MM
SALES (corp-wide): 50.3B **Publicly Held**
SIC: 5141 Food brokers
PA: Sysco Corporation
1390 Enclave Pkwy
Houston TX 77077
281 584-1390

(P-8538)
TAPIA ENTERPRISES INC (PA)
Also Called: Tapia Brothers Co
6067 District Blvd, Maywood (90270-3560)
PHONE 323 560-7415
Fax: 323 560-8924
Raul Tapia, *CEO*
Francisco Tapia, *Treasurer*
Ramon Tapia, *Admin Sec*
Yolanda Tapia, *Sales Staff*
Ana Geraldo, *Accounts Mgr*
▲ **EMP:** 95
SQ FT: 40,000
SALES (est): 269MM **Privately Held**
WEB: www.tapiabrothers.com
SIC: 5141 Groceries, general line

(P-8539)
U TURN SEVEN CORPORATION
1802 N Vermont Ave, Los Angeles (90027-4213)
PHONE 323 662-1587
Rafik Mgaieth, *Principal*
EMP: 140 **EST:** 2007
SALES: 3.1MM **Privately Held**
SIC: 5141 Food brokers

(P-8540)
UNIFIED GROCERS INC (PA)
5200 Sheila St, Commerce (90040-3906)
P.O. Box 60753, Los Angeles (90060-0753)
PHONE 323 264-5200
Fax: 323 262-0218
Robert M Ling Jr, *President*
Randy Delgado, *President*
Richard J Martin, *CFO*
Christine Neal, *Treasurer*
Leon G Bergmann, *Senior VP*
◆ **EMP:** 550 **EST:** 1922
SQ FT: 358,934
SALES: 4B **Privately Held**
SIC: 5141 6331 Groceries, general line; fire, marine & casualty insurance; workers' compensation insurance

(P-8541)
UNIFIED GROCERS INC
U W G Sthern Cal Sls Purch Div
3626 11th Ave, Los Angeles (90018-3601)
PHONE 323 373-1339
John Bedrosian, *President*
Everet Dingwell, *Exec VP*
Don Grose, *Senior VP*
Gary Herman, *Vice Pres*
Cathy Arminio, *Telecomm Dir*
EMP: 120
SALES (corp-wide): 4B **Privately Held**
SIC: 5141 Groceries, general line
PA: Unified Grocers, Inc.
5200 Sheila St
Commerce CA 90040
323 264-5200

(P-8542)
UNIFIED GROCERS INC
Also Called: U W G Northern California Div
1990 Piccoli Rd, Stockton (95215-2324)
PHONE 209 931-1990
Fax: 209 931-6385
Glenn King, *Administration*
EMP: 238
SALES (corp-wide): 4B **Privately Held**
SIC: 5141 5149 4222 Groceries, general line; groceries & related products; refrigerated warehousing & storage
PA: Unified Grocers, Inc.
5200 Sheila St
Commerce CA 90040
323 264-5200

(P-8543)
UNIFIED GROCERS INC
Also Called: Market Centre
455 N Canyons Pkwy, Livermore (94551-7681)
PHONE 323 264-5200
Joe Falvey, *Exec VP*
EMP: 100 **EST:** 2015
SALES (est): 2.3MM
SALES (corp-wide): 4B **Privately Held**
SIC: 5141 Groceries, general line
PA: Unified Grocers, Inc.
5200 Sheila St
Commerce CA 90040
323 264-5200

(P-8544)
UNION SUPPLY GROUP INC (PA)
Also Called: Union Supply Company
2301 E Pacifica Pl, Rancho Dominguez (90220-6210)
P.O. Box 7006 (90224-7006)
PHONE 310 603-8899
Tom Thomas, *CEO*
Guy Steele, *COO*
Scott Schaldenbrand, *CFO*
Lyndel Hay, *Exec VP*
Dave Cardona, *Vice Pres*
▲ **EMP:** 115
SQ FT: 24,000

SALES: 117.3MM **Privately Held**
SIC: 5141 5139 5136 Groceries, general line; footwear; men's & boys' clothing

(P-8545)
US FOODS INC
1283 Sherborn St Ste 102, Corona (92879-5003)
PHONE 951 256-2400
Kamran Arghavani, *Programmer Anys*
Patrick Oates, *Buyer*
Evan Cheatwood, *Sales Mgr*
Steve Ostergren, *Sales Mgr*
Sabina Cortez, *Sales Staff*
EMP: 155
SALES (corp-wide): 23.1B **Publicly Held**
SIC: 5141 Groceries, general line
HQ: Us Foods, Inc.
9399 W Higgins Rd Ste 500
Rosemont IL 60018
847 720-8000

(P-8546)
US FOODS INC
300 Lawrence Dr Frnt, Livermore (94551-5139)
PHONE 925 606-3525
Phil Collins, *Branch Mgr*
Debbie Oberg, *Credit Staff*
Angela Moiner, *Controller*
Cathey Quiggle, *Human Res Mgr*
Rocio Adelantado, *Human Resources*
EMP: 500
SALES (corp-wide): 23.1B **Publicly Held**
WEB: www.usfoodservice.com
SIC: 5141 Food brokers
HQ: Us Foods, Inc.
9399 W Higgins Rd Ste 500
Rosemont IL 60018
847 720-8000

(P-8547)
US FOODS INC
15155 Northam St, La Mirada (90638-5754)
P.O. Box 29283, Phoenix AZ (85038-9283)
PHONE 714 670-3500
David Patterson, *Branch Mgr*
John Ocarroll, *President*
Owen Schiano, *President*
Charlie Dagostino, *Vice Pres*
Andy Hetzel, *Vice Pres*
EMP: 172
SALES (corp-wide): 23.1B **Publicly Held**
WEB: www.usfoodservice.com
SIC: 5141 5046 3556 2099 Groceries, general line; commercial equipment; food products machinery; food preparations; restaurant equipment repair
HQ: Us Foods, Inc.
9399 W Higgins Rd Ste 500
Rosemont IL 60018
847 720-8000

(P-8548)
US FOODS INC
Also Called: U S Foods
15155 Northam St, La Mirada (90638-5754)
PHONE 714 670-3500
Gene McHugh, *General Mgr*
EMP: 50
SALES (corp-wide): 23.1B **Publicly Held**
WEB: www.usfoodservice.com
SIC: 5141 5142 Groceries, general line; packaged frozen goods
HQ: Us Foods, Inc.
9399 W Higgins Rd Ste 500
Rosemont IL 60018
847 720-8000

(P-8549)
US FOODS INTERNATIONAL LLC
500 W 140th St Fl 2, Gardena (90248-1510)
PHONE 310 515-2189
Gary Place, *Mng Member*
Chris Lee,
Brian Yoo,
Erick Yoo,
Byung H Yoo, *Director*
▲ **EMP:** 100
SALES (est): 20.3MM **Privately Held**
SIC: 5141 Food brokers

(P-8550)
USFI INC
110 W Walnut St 221, Gardena (90248-3100)
PHONE 310 768-1937
Fax: 310 768-1956
Gary Place, *President*
Bong Baek, *CFO*
William Baek, *CFO*
Steven Choi, *Vice Pres*
Gabby Arreola, *Administration*
▲ **EMP:** 75
SQ FT: 4,000
SALES (est): 58.7MM **Privately Held**
WEB: www.usfifoods.com
SIC: 5141 5149 Food brokers; groceries & related products

(P-8551)
VIELE & SONS INC
Also Called: Viele & Sons Instnl Groc
1820 E Valencia Dr, Fullerton (92831-4847)
PHONE 714 446-1686
Fax: 714 447-3920
Anthony J Viele, *President*
Jim Viele, *Shareholder*
Nancy Montez Viele, *Shareholder*
Joseph Viele, *Treasurer*
Anthony Viele Jr, *Vice Pres*
EMP: 90
SQ FT: 95,000
SALES (est): 123.4MM **Privately Held**
WEB: www.vieleandsons.com
SIC: 5141 Groceries, general line

5142 Packaged Frozen Foods Wholesale

(P-8552)
CALBEE NORTH AMERICA LLC
2600 Maxwell Way, Fairfield (94534-1915)
PHONE 707 427-2500
Gene Jensen, *Branch Mgr*
Jina Pierce, *Admin Asst*
Lynn Applegate, *Natl Sales Mgr*
Fumie Mihaly, *Director*
Ryan Hill, *Manager*
EMP: 50
SALES (corp-wide): 130MM **Privately Held**
SIC: 5142 5145 2038 Packaged frozen goods; snack foods; snacks, including onion rings, cheese sticks, etc.
PA: Calbee North America, Llc
72600 Lewis & Clark Dr
Boardman OR 97818
541 481-6550

(P-8553)
GOLD STAR FOODS INC
3781 E Airport Dr, Ontario (91761-1558)
PHONE 909 843-9600
Fax: 323 846-1997
George Thorsen, *CEO*
Leonard Amato, *President*
Cindy Yvanez, *COO*
Greg Johnson, *CFO*
Larry Noble, *Senior VP*
▲ **EMP:** 210
SQ FT: 38,000
SALES (est): 221.8MM **Privately Held**
WEB: www.goldstarfoods.com
SIC: 5142 Packaged frozen goods

(P-8554)
INTERSTATE MEAT & PROVISION
Also Called: Sterling Pacific Meat Company
6114 Scott Way, Commerce (90040-3518)
PHONE 323 838-9400
Jim Asher, *CEO*
Diana Wise, *Human Res Mgr*
▲ **EMP:** 100
SQ FT: 25,038
SALES (est): 95.5MM **Privately Held**
SIC: 5142 5147 Packaged frozen goods; meat brokers

(P-8555)
J AND J WALL BAKING CO INC
8806 Fruitridge Rd, Sacramento (95826-9708)
PHONE 916 381-1410
Fax: 916 381-6008

PRODUCTS & SERVICES SECTION
5142 - Packaged Frozen Foods Wholesale County (P-8575)

John Wall, *CEO*
EMP: 55
SQ FT: 50,000
SALES (est): 16.2MM **Privately Held**
SIC: 5142 Bakery products, frozen

(P-8556)
J GOODMAN & ASSOCIATES
14544 Central Ave, Chino (91710-9508)
PHONE...............310 828-5040
Fax: 310 582-1243
John F Goodman, *President*
Michelle Alva, *Vice Pres*
Gary Bunn, *Vice Pres*
Tom Rohde, *Sales Associate*
Dottie Henderson, *Sales Staff*
EMP: 56 **EST:** 1981
SQ FT: 2,700
SALES (est): 15.7MM
SALES (corp-wide): 28.4MM **Privately Held**
WEB: www.jgoodman.net
SIC: 5142 5141 Packaged frozen goods; food brokers
PA: The Core Group Inc
14544 Central Ave Ste 42
Chino CA 91710
909 438-2626

(P-8557)
JESSIE LORD BAKERY LLC
21100 S Western Ave, Torrance (90501-1705)
PHONE...............310 328-7738
Fax: 310 328-2608
Stephen Y S Lee, *President*
John Freschi, *Vice Pres*
Grace Wang, *Controller*
Mary Hicks, *Human Resources*
Hratch Doctorian, *Purch Mgr*
▲ **EMP:** 50
SQ FT: 130,000
SALES (est): 58.7MM **Privately Held**
SIC: 5142 Fruit pies, frozen

(P-8558)
JETRO CASH AND CARRY ENTPS LLC
1265 N Kraemer Blvd, Anaheim (92806-1921)
PHONE...............714 666-8211
Stanley Fleishman,
Marco Fosado, *Buyer*
EMP: 130 **Privately Held**
SIC: 5142 5046 5181 5147 Packaged frozen goods; restaurant equipment & supplies; beer & other fermented malt liquors; meats, fresh; grocery stores
HQ: Jetro Cash And Carry Enterprises, Llc
1524 132nd St
College Point NY 11356
718 939-6400

(P-8559)
L & T MEAT CO
3050 E 11th St, Los Angeles (90023-3606)
PHONE...............323 262-2815
Fax: 323 262-0867
Chak Por Tea, *President*
Bobby Lu, *Vice Pres*
EMP: 80
SQ FT: 20,000
SALES (est): 33.2MM **Privately Held**
WEB: www.ltmeat.com
SIC: 5142 Frozen fish, meat & poultry

(P-8560)
MARIE CLLENDER WHOLESALERS INC
170 E Rincon St, Corona (92879-1327)
PHONE...............951 737-6760
Phillip Ratner, *President*
Gerald Tanaka, *Senior VP*
Nick Saba, *Vice Pres*
Kurt Schweickhart, *Vice Pres*
Cecy Ruiz, *Accountant*
EMP: 65
SQ FT: 28,000
SALES (est): 20.3MM
SALES (corp-wide): 5.7B **Privately Held**
WEB: www.castleharlan.com
SIC: 5142 Bakery products, frozen
HQ: Castle Harlan Partners Iii Lp
150 E 58th St Fl 38
New York NY 10155
212 644-8600

(P-8561)
MEADOWBROOK MEAT COMPANY INC
Also Called: M B M
5675 Sunol Blvd, Pleasanton (94566-7765)
PHONE...............252 985-7200
Al Monceaux, *Manager*
Layton Pearce, *General Mgr*
Jim Mallon, *Transptn Dir*
Lorena Lapegg, *Director*
Patrick Milligan, *Supervisor*
EMP: 65
SALES (corp-wide): 210.8B **Publicly Held**
WEB: www.mbmlc.com
SIC: 5142 Packaged frozen goods
HQ: Meadowbrook Meat Company, Inc.
2641 Meadowbrook Rd
Rocky Mount NC 27801
252 985-7200

(P-8562)
PACIFIC FRESH SEA FOOD COMPANY (HQ)
Also Called: Pacific Seafood Sacramento
1420 National Dr, Sacramento (95834-1967)
PHONE...............916 419-5500
Frank Dominic Dulcich, *President*
Tim Horgan, *COO*
Joe Cincotta, *General Mgr*
Chuck Holman, *Sales Mgr*
◆ **EMP:** 178
SQ FT: 50,000
SALES (est): 64.7MM
SALES (corp-wide): 476MM **Privately Held**
SIC: 5142 5146 Fish, frozen: packaged; fish, fresh
PA: Dulcich, Inc.
16797 Se 130th Ave
Clackamas OR 97015
503 226-2200

(P-8563)
PRODUCERS DAIRY FOODS INC (PA)
250 E Belmont Ave, Fresno (93701-1405)
PHONE...............559 264-6583
Fax: 559 264-0906
Lawrence A Shehadey, *Ch of Bd*
Richard Shehadey, *CEO*
Scott Shehadey, *Vice Pres*
Donna Garner, *Executive Asst*
Paul Garoogian, *VP Finance*
▲ **EMP:** 200
SALES (est): 259.8MM **Privately Held**
WEB: www.producersdairy.com
SIC: 5142 5143 Fruit juices, frozen; dairy products, except dried or canned

(P-8564)
RESTAURANT DEPOT LLC
180 N San Gabriel Blvd, Pasadena (91107-3426)
PHONE...............626 744-0204
Fax: 626 744-0264
Dan Mihal, *Manager*
William Chapman, *Info Tech Dir*
Mike Leber, *Info Tech Dir*
Charlie Romero, *Manager*
Tony Vasquez, *Manager*
EMP: 150 **Privately Held**
WEB: www.jrdtuning.com
SIC: 5142 5141 5194 5181 Packaged frozen goods; groceries, general line; tobacco & tobacco products; beer & other fermented malt liquors; meats, fresh
HQ: Restaurant Depot, Llc
1524 132nd St
College Point NY 11356

(P-8565)
RESTAURANT DEPOT LLC
400 High St, Oakland (94601-3904)
PHONE...............510 628-0600
John Derosa, *Branch Mgr*
Martha Romo, *Manager*
Gerry Oto, *Asst Mgr*
EMP: 150 **Privately Held**
WEB: www.jrdtuning.com
SIC: 5142 5147 5141 5181 Packaged frozen goods; meats, fresh; groceries, general line; beer & other fermented malt liquors; tobacco & tobacco products
HQ: Restaurant Depot, Llc
1524 132nd St
College Point NY 11356

(P-8566)
RESTAURANT DEPOT LLC
10850 Spencer St, Fountain Valley (92708-7009)
PHONE...............714 378-3535
Alan Cummins, *Manager*
EMP: 150 **Privately Held**
WEB: www.jrdtuning.com
SIC: 5142 5194 5147 5181 Packaged frozen goods; tobacco & tobacco products; meats, fresh; beer & other fermented malt liquors; groceries, general line
HQ: Restaurant Depot, Llc
1524 132nd St
College Point NY 11356

(P-8567)
RESTAURANT DEPOT LLC
2300 E 68th St, Long Beach (90805-1728)
PHONE...............562 634-6771
Adrian Padilla, *Branch Mgr*
EMP: 92 **Privately Held**
WEB: www.jrdtuning.com
SIC: 5142 5147 5141 5181 Packaged frozen goods; meats, fresh; groceries, general line; beer & other fermented malt liquors; tobacco & tobacco products
HQ: Restaurant Depot, Llc
1524 132nd St
College Point NY 11356

(P-8568)
RESTAURANT DEPOT LLC
520 Brennan St, San Jose (95131-1201)
PHONE...............408 344-0107
Fax: 408 432-1512
Ron McGill, *Branch Mgr*
EMP: 150 **Privately Held**
WEB: www.jrdtuning.com
SIC: 5142 5147 5141 5181 Packaged frozen goods; meats, fresh; groceries, general line; beer & other fermented malt liquors; tobacco & tobacco products
HQ: Restaurant Depot, Llc
1524 132nd St
College Point NY 11356

(P-8569)
S J S LINK INTERNATIONAL INC (PA)
468 N Camden Dr Ste 311, Beverly Hills (90210-4507)
PHONE...............310 860-7666
Shiraz Mamedov, *CEO*
Olga Sedova, *CFO*
Alex Zimmer, *Treasurer*
Anna Hebber, *Sales Mgr*
▼ **EMP:** 50
SALES (est): 11.7MM **Privately Held**
WEB: www.sjsusa.com
SIC: 5142 Frozen fish, meat & poultry

(P-8570)
SJ DISTRIBUTORS INC (PA)
625 Vista Way, Milpitas (95035-5433)
P.O. Box 1202, Santa Clara (95052-1202)
PHONE...............888 988-2328
Scot Chun Ho Suen, *CEO*
Jerry Yeung, *CFO*
Jojo Ng, *Accounting Mgr*
Jenny Ling, *Accountant*
EMP: 50
SQ FT: 44,000
SALES: 102.1MM **Privately Held**
SIC: 5142 5148 5149 Meat, frozen: packaged; fresh fruits & vegetables; canned goods: fruit, vegetables, seafood, meats, etc.

(P-8571)
SUPERIOR FOODS INC
Also Called: Superior Foods Companies, The
275 Westgate Dr, Watsonville (95076-2470)
PHONE...............831 728-3691
David E Moore, *Ch of Bd*
Mateo Lettunich, *President*
R Neil Happee, *CEO*
Neil Happee, *COO*
H Monroe Howser III, *CFO*
◆ **EMP:** 100
SQ FT: 10,782
SALES (est): 147.3MM **Privately Held**
SIC: 5142 Fruits, frozen; vegetables, frozen; fruit juices, frozen

(P-8572)
VPS COMPANIES INC (PA)
310 Walker St, Watsonville (95076-4525)
P.O. Box 118 (95077-0118)
PHONE...............831 724-7551
Jack Randle, *Ch of Bd*
Ed Fong, *President*
Byron Johnson, *President*
Ronald Marker, *CFO*
Fred J Haas, *Corp Secy*
▲ **EMP:** 50
SQ FT: 10,000
SALES (est): 299.6MM **Privately Held**
WEB: www.us-foods.com
SIC: 5142 0723 4731 Fruits, frozen; vegetables, frozen; crop preparation services for market; freight transportation arrangement

(P-8573)
VPS COMPANIES INC
Also Called: Central Cold Storage
13526 Blackie Rd, Castroville (95012-3212)
P.O. Box 610 (95012-0610)
PHONE...............831 633-4011
Jonathon Thorton, *President*
Toni Ferreira, *Human Res Mgr*
EMP: 50
SALES (corp-wide): 299.6MM **Privately Held**
WEB: www.us-foods.com
SIC: 5142 Fruits, frozen
PA: The Vps Companies Inc
310 Walker St
Watsonville CA 95076
831 724-7551

(P-8574)
WEI-CHUAN USA INC (PA)
6655 Garfield Ave, Bell Gardens (90201-1807)
PHONE...............323 587-2101
Fax: 323 927-0780
Steve Lin, *President*
William Huang, *Treasurer*
Robert Huang, *Principal*
Benny Chang, *Admin Sec*
Jih Chung, *CTO*
▲ **EMP:** 120
SQ FT: 38,000
SALES (est): 121.4MM **Privately Held**
SIC: 5142 2038 Packaged frozen goods; dinners, frozen & packaged; ethnic foods, frozen

(P-8575)
WEST PICO FOODS INC
5201 S Downey Rd, Vernon (90058-3703)
P.O. Box 58107 (90058-0107)
PHONE...............323 586-9050
Fax: 323 586-2008
Elias Naghi, *President*
James Ong, *CFO*
Don Lubitz, *Treasurer*
Steve Kubota, *Purchasing*
Josie Gallegos, *Mktg Coord*
▲ **EMP:** 125
SQ FT: 42,000
SALES (est): 104.6MM **Privately Held**
WEB: www.westpicofoods.com
SIC: 5142 5144 Packaged frozen goods; poultry: live, dressed or frozen (unpackaged)

5143 Dairy Prdts, Except Dried Or Canned Wholesale

(P-8576)
ALTA-DENA CERTIFIED DAIRY LLC
4656 Cardin St, San Diego (92111-1419)
PHONE.................................858 292-6930
Frank Reimhard, *General Mgr*
Matt Carroll, *Manager*
EMP: 75 **Publicly Held**
WEB: www.altadenadairy.com
SIC: 5143 Dairy depot
HQ: Alta-Dena Certified Dairy, Llc
17637 E Valley Blvd
City Of Industry CA 91744
626 964-6401

(P-8577)
ARYA ICE CREAM DISTRG CO INC
914 E 31st St, Los Angeles (90011-2502)
P.O. Box 456, Harbor City (90710-0456)
PHONE.................................323 234-2994
Fax: 323 234-2995
Ali Pakravan, *CEO*
Mansour Azizian, *Shareholder*
Farhad Karamati, *Shareholder*
Mansour Sahabi, *Shareholder*
Hossein Sahabi, *Vice Pres*
▲ EMP: 60
SQ FT: 46,000
SALES (est): 70.2MM **Privately Held**
WEB: www.aryaicecream.com
SIC: 5143 Ice cream & ices

(P-8578)
BERKELEY FARMS LLC (HQ)
25500 Clawiter Rd, Hayward (94545-2739)
P.O. Box 4616 (94540-4616)
PHONE.................................510 265-8600
Fax: 510 265-8748
Derek Allbee,
Sharon Cornelius, *Executive Asst*
Jim Butler, *Chief Engr*
▲ EMP: 300
SQ FT: 220,000
SALES (est): 553MM **Publicly Held**
WEB: www.berkeleyfarms.com
SIC: 5143 2026 0241 Dairy products, except dried or canned; butter; cheese; ice cream & ices; fluid milk; dairy farms

(P-8579)
CACIQUE DISTRIBUTORS US
14923 Proctor Ave, La Puente (91746-3206)
P.O. Box 91270, City of Industry (91715-1270)
PHONE.................................626 961-3399
Fax: 626 369-8083
Francoise Mattice, *CEO*
Gilbert L De Cardenas, *President*
Christiann Arapostathis, *Admin Asst*
Carlos Wong, *Opers Mgr*
Tirso Iglesias, *Sales Executive*
EMP: 240
SALES (est): 175.1MM **Privately Held**
SIC: 5143 Dairy products, except dried or canned

(P-8580)
CENTRAL VALLEY CHEESE INC
115 S Kilroy Rd, Turlock (95380-9531)
PHONE.................................209 664-1080
Fax: 209 664-1001
Antranik Baghdassarian, *CEO*
Jolena Torres, *Administration*
EMP: 70
SALES (est): 62.5MM **Privately Held**
WEB: www.karouncheese.com
SIC: 5143 Cheese
PA: Karoun Dairies, Inc.
13023 Arroyo St
San Fernando CA 91340
818 767-7000

(P-8581)
CHALLENGE DAIRY PRODUCTS INC
5741 Smithway St, Commerce (90040-1507)
PHONE.................................323 724-3130
Dan Bollinger, *Branch Mgr*
EMP: 50
SALES (corp-wide): 271.5MM **Privately Held**
WEB: www.challengedairy.com
SIC: 5143 2023 2021 Dairy depot; dry, condensed, evaporated dairy products; creamery butter
HQ: Challenge Dairy Products, Inc
11875 Dublin Blvd B230
Dublin CA 94568
925 828-6160

(P-8582)
CHALLENGE DAIRY PRODUCTS INC (HQ)
6701 Donlon Way, Dublin (94568-2850)
P.O. Box 2369 (94568-0706)
PHONE.................................925 828-6160
Fax: 925 551-7591
Irvin Holmes, *President*
Jason Morris, *President*
Stanford Alan Maag, *CFO*
Tom Ditto, *Vice Pres*
David Treiber, *Vice Pres*
▼ EMP: 57
SQ FT: 8,500
SALES (est): 205.7MM
SALES (corp-wide): 271.5MM **Privately Held**
WEB: www.challengedairy.com
SIC: 5143 5149 Butter; milk, canned or dried
PA: California Dairies, Inc.
2000 N Plaza Dr
Visalia CA 93291
559 625-2200

(P-8583)
DEAN SOCAL LLC
Also Called: Swiss Dairy
17637 E Valley Blvd, City of Industry (91744-5731)
PHONE.................................951 734-3950
Fax: 951 734-3786
Nick Van Hoogmoed, *Mng Member*
Gregg L Engles, *Ch of Bd*
Steve James, *President*
Cletus Beshears, *Vice Pres*
John Maddon, *Vice Pres*
EMP: 140
SQ FT: 25,000
SALES (est): 37.7MM **Publicly Held**
WEB: www.deanfoods.com
SIC: 5143 Dairy products, except dried or canned
PA: Dean Foods Company
2711 N Haskell Ave
Dallas TX 75204

(P-8584)
DREYERS GRAND ICE CREAM HOLD (DH)
5929 College Ave, Oakland (94618-1325)
PHONE.................................510 652-8187
Michael T Mitchell, *CEO*
Steve Barbour, *CFO*
Tony Sarsam, *Exec VP*
Suzanne Saltzman, *Principal*
Madelyn Van Der Bokke, *CTO*
◆ EMP: 230
SQ FT: 64,000
SALES (est): 655.9MM
SALES (corp-wide): 88.3B **Privately Held**
SIC: 5143 5451 2024 Frozen dairy desserts; ice cream & ices; ice cream (packaged); ice cream & frozen desserts; ice cream, packaged: molded, on sticks, etc.; ice cream, bulk; yogurt desserts, frozen
HQ: Nestle Prepared Foods Company
5750 Harper Rd
Solon OH 44139
440 248-3600

(P-8585)
FOSTER DAIRY FARMS
3440 Enterprise Ave, Hayward (94545-3219)
PHONE.................................510 783-1270
Fax: 510 888-5688
Ann Bartlett, *Manager*
Jon Swadley, *Mktg Dir*
EMP: 50
SALES (corp-wide): 433.7MM **Privately Held**
SIC: 5143 Dairy products, except dried or canned
PA: Foster Dairy Farms
529 Kansas Ave
Modesto CA 95351
209 576-3400

(P-8586)
KLM MANAGEMENT COMPANY
Also Called: Amcom Food Service
14120 Valley Blvd, City of Industry (91746-2802)
PHONE.................................626 330-3479
Ted Degroot, *President*
Kurt Degroot, *Vice Pres*
Curtis Degroot, *Admin Sec*
Karl Kordik, *Manager*
▼ EMP: 70
SQ FT: 91,000
SALES (est): 50.4MM **Privately Held**
SIC: 5143 Dairy products, except dried or canned

(P-8587)
LOS ALTOS FOOD PRODUCTS INC
450 Baldwin Park Blvd, City of Industry (91746-1407)
PHONE.................................626 330-6555
Fax: 626 330-6755
Raul Andrade, *President*
Corin Andrade, *CFO*
Alin Andrade, *Vice Pres*
Gloria Andrade, *Vice Pres*
Patricia Valera, *Admin Asst*
EMP: 105
SQ FT: 38,000
SALES (est): 139.9MM **Privately Held**
WEB: www.losaltosfoods.com
SIC: 5143 Cheese

(P-8588)
MENCHIES GROUP INC
17555 Ventura Blvd # 200, Encino (91316-3890)
PHONE.................................818 708-0316
Fax: 818 708-0117
Amit Kleinberger, *CEO*
Robert Penney, *COO*
Yotom Regev, *Vice Pres*
Vera Antonyan, *Executive Asst*
Susan Kraus, *Marketing Staff*
▲ EMP: 78
SALES (est): 41.3MM **Privately Held**
SIC: 5143 Yogurt

(P-8589)
NESTLE DREYERS ICE CREAM CO
Also Called: Dreyer's Grand Ice Cream
351 Cheryl Ln, Walnut (91789-3003)
PHONE.................................909 595-0677
Fax: 909 444-2301
Mike Stamper, *Manager*
Desiree Garcia, *Human Res Mgr*
Rick Pinto, *Safety Mgr*
Dave Solorzano, *Manager*
EMP: 175
SALES (corp-wide): 88.3B **Privately Held**
WEB: www.dreyersinc.com
SIC: 5143 2024 4222 Dairy products, except dried or canned; ice cream & frozen desserts; refrigerated warehousing & storage
HQ: Nestle Dreyer's Ice Cream Company
5929 College Ave
Oakland CA 94618
510 594-9466

(P-8590)
NESTLE ICE CREAM COMPANY
7301 District Blvd, Bakersfield (93313-2042)
PHONE.................................661 398-3500

Fax: 661 398-3524
James L Dintaman, *CEO*
Paul Stanberry, *Branch Mgr*
Casey Hefner, *Engineer*
Fred Evarts, *Controller*
Brian Reedy, *Maintence Staff*
▲ EMP: 1920
SALES (est): 221.8MM
SALES (corp-wide): 88.3B **Privately Held**
WEB: www.haagendazsrewards.com
SIC: 5143 5451 Ice cream & ices; ice cream (packaged)
HQ: Dreyer's Grand Ice Cream Holdings, Inc.
5929 College Ave
Oakland CA 94618
510 652-8187

(P-8591)
PACIFIC CHEESE CO INC (PA)
21090 Cabot Blvd, Hayward (94545-1110)
P.O. Box 56598 (94545-6598)
PHONE.................................510 784-8800
Fax: 510 784-1053
Stephen B Gaddis, *President*
Tony Ricker, *COO*
Dale Tate, *CFO*
June M Gaddis, *Corp Secy*
Jeff Richmond, *Vice Pres*
◆ EMP: 153
SQ FT: 107,000
SALES: 800MM **Privately Held**
WEB: www.pacific-cheese.com
SIC: 5143 Cheese

(P-8592)
SPRING HILL JERSEY CHEESE INC
Also Called: Petaluma Creamery
621 Western Ave, Petaluma (94952-2646)
PHONE.................................707 762-3446
Larry K Peter, *President*
Laurie Zerga, *Director*
Michelle Grube, *Manager*
EMP: 100
SQ FT: 151,000
SALES: 41.1MM **Privately Held**
SIC: 5143 Cheese

(P-8593)
SSI-TURLOCK DAIRY DIVISION
Also Called: Sunnyside Farms
2600 Spengler Way, Turlock (95380-8591)
PHONE.................................209 668-2100
Tracy Nicholl, *CFO*
Tracy Twomey, *CFO*
Jared Bjarnason, *Controller*
Todd Hager, *Sales Dir*
Yancy Hopper, *Director*
▲ EMP: 195
SQ FT: 120,000
SALES (est): 188.1MM **Privately Held**
SIC: 5143 2024 5144 2022 Dairy products, except dried or canned; ice cream & ice milk; eggs; cheese, natural & processed

(P-8594)
SVD INC
Also Called: Sun Valley Dairy
8088 San Fernando Rd, Sun Valley (91352-4001)
PHONE.................................818 504-1775
Fax: 818 504-1770
Jack Galadjian, *CEO*
ARA Kozanian, *President*
Doug Campbell, *General Mgr*
▲ EMP: 55
SQ FT: 40,000
SALES (est): 53.5MM **Privately Held**
WEB: www.voskos.com
SIC: 5143 Yogurt

(P-8595)
UNIFIED GROCERS INC
Also Called: U W G Southern California Div
457 E Martin Luther King, Los Angeles (90011-5650)
PHONE.................................323 232-6124
Fax: 323 232-7381
Maurice Ochua, *Branch Mgr*
Norm Bowers, *Sales Staff*
EMP: 74

5145 - Confectionery Wholesale County (P-8616)

SALES (corp-wide): 4B **Privately Held**
SIC: **5143** 8742 2051 Dairy products, except dried or canned; marketing consulting services; bread, cake & related products
PA: Unified Grocers, Inc.
5200 Sheila St
Commerce CA 90040
323 264-5200

5144 Poultry & Poultry Prdts Wholesale

(P-8596)
FOSTER ENTERPRISES
13610 S Archibald Ave, Ontario (91761-7930)
PHONE...................909 947-6207
Stan Foster, *President*
Ashley Shonacy, *Administration*
EMP: 56
SALES (est): 35.7MM **Privately Held**
SIC: **5144** Eggs

(P-8597)
FOSTER POULTRY FARMS
Also Called: Foster Farms
1333 Swan St, Livingston (95334-1559)
P.O. Box 457 (95334-0457)
PHONE...................209 394-7901
Fax: 209 394-6902
Brent Allen, *Branch Mgr*
Sue Watson, *Admin Asst*
Deedee Ormonde, *Purch Mgr*
Kevin Bricker, *Transptn Dir*
Mick Corey, *Manager*
EMP: 125
SALES (corp-wide): 4.3B **Privately Held**
WEB: www.fosterfarms.com
SIC: **5144** Poultry: live, dressed or frozen (unpackaged)
PA: Foster Poultry Farms
1000 Davis St
Livingston CA 95334
209 394-6914

(P-8598)
INTERSTATE FOODS
310 S Long Beach Blvd, Compton (90221-3448)
PHONE...................323 264-4024
Fax: 323 622-1749
Carlos Velasco, *CEO*
Rudy Perez, *Manager*
EMP: 145 EST: 2000
SQ FT: 13,000
SALES (est): 32MM **Privately Held**
SIC: **5144** Poultry products

(P-8599)
LEHAR SALES CO
150 Chestnut St, Oakland (94607-2511)
P.O. Box 24211 (94623-1211)
PHONE...................510 465-3255
Fax: 510 238-1758
Harold J De Luca, *CEO*
Rick Charles, *President*
Hariette Young, *Treasurer*
Tarry Winfrey, *Vice Pres*
Claire Venturini, *Admin Sec*
EMP: 55
SQ FT: 35,000
SALES (est): 8.5MM
SALES (corp-wide): 54MM **Privately Held**
WEB: www.pacagri.com
SIC: **5144** Poultry: live, dressed or frozen (unpackaged); poultry products
PA: Pacific Agri-Products, Inc.
477 Forbes Blvd
South San Francisco CA 94080
650 873-0440

(P-8600)
LUBERSKI INC
Also Called: Hidden Villa Ranch
1811 Mountain Ave, Norco (92860-2863)
PHONE...................951 271-3866
Fax: 951 654-9793
Tim Luberski, *Branch Mgr*
EMP: 70

SALES (corp-wide): 260MM **Privately Held**
WEB: www.calsunshine.com
SIC: **5144** Eggs
PA: Luberski, Inc.
310 N Harbor Blvd Ste 205
Fullerton CA 92832
714 680-3447

(P-8601)
NEW STOCKTON POULTRY INC
302 S San Joaquin St, Stockton (95203-3536)
P.O. Box 2129 (95201-2129)
PHONE...................209 466-1952
Fax: 209 466-6143
William P K Chan, *CEO*
John Luu, *President*
Ming Luu, *Vice Pres*
Minh Luu, *General Mgr*
▲ EMP: 50
SALES (est): 9.1MM **Privately Held**
SIC: **5144** 5499 2015 5421 Poultry: live, dressed or frozen (unpackaged); eggs & poultry; poultry, processed: fresh; meat & fish markets

(P-8602)
NULAID FOODS INC (PA)
200 W 5th St, Ripon (95366-2793)
PHONE...................209 599-2121
Fax: 209 599-5220
David K Crockett, *President*
Scott Hennecke, *CFO*
Kari Bohannan, *Cust Mgr*
Dustin Barnett, *Manager*
Jamie Looper, *Manager*
EMP: 80
SQ FT: 5,000
SALES (est): 43.6MM **Privately Held**
WEB: www.nulaid.com
SIC: **5144** 2047 2015 2023 Eggs; eggs: cleaning, oil treating, packing & grading; dog food; egg processing; cream substitutes

(P-8603)
RACE STREET FOODS INC (PA)
Also Called: Race Street Fish & Poultry
1130 Olinder Ct, San Jose (95122-2619)
P.O. Box 28385 (95159-8385)
PHONE...................408 294-6161
Fax: 408 294-2080
Gino Barsanti, *Chairman*
Paride Riparbelli, *President*
Michael Barsanti, *Corp Secy*
Dan Barsanti, *Vice Pres*
Gabe Morrison, *Vice Pres*
EMP: 80
SQ FT: 63,000
SALES (est): 29.8MM **Privately Held**
WEB: www.racestreetfoods.com
SIC: **5144** 5146 5147 5142 Poultry & poultry products; fish & seafoods; meats & meat products; packaged frozen goods; frozen fish, meat & poultry

(P-8604)
RANDALL FOODS INC
Also Called: California Classics
2905 E 50th St Bldg 12, Vernon (90058-2919)
PHONE...................323 587-2383
Ron Totin, *Vice Pres*
EMP: 175
SALES (corp-wide): 198.1MM **Privately Held**
WEB: www.randallfoods.com
SIC: **5144** 5147 Poultry & poultry products; meats & meat products
PA: Randall Foods, Inc.
2905 E 50th St
Vernon CA 90058
323 261-6565

(P-8605)
ROGERS POULTRY CO (PA)
2020 E 67th St, Los Angeles (90001-2169)
PHONE...................323 585-0802
Fax: 323 588-3396
George V Saffarrans, *CEO*
John C Butler, *COO*
Ken Hayashi, *CFO*
Wen Hai Hong, *Exec VP*
Ralph Schemel, *Administration*
EMP: 100

SQ FT: 15,000
SALES: 54.2MM **Privately Held**
WEB: www.rogerspoultry.com
SIC: **5144** Poultry products

(P-8606)
SQUAB PRODUCERS CALIF INC
409 Primo Way, Modesto (95358-5721)
PHONE...................209 537-4744
Fax: 209 537-2037
Robert Shipley, *President*
Lynn Severns, *Controller*
EMP: 55
SQ FT: 11,000
SALES (est): 6.9MM **Privately Held**
WEB: www.squab.com
SIC: **5144** 2015 Poultry: live, dressed or frozen (unpackaged); poultry slaughtering & processing

(P-8607)
SUNRISE FARMS LLC
395 Liberty Rd, Petaluma (94952-8104)
PHONE...................707 778-6450
James Carlson,
Larry Johnson,
Al Nissen,
Arnold Riebli,
Richard Weber,
▲ EMP: 65 EST: 1966
SQ FT: 10,000
SALES (est): 15.8MM **Privately Held**
SIC: **5144** 2015 Eggs: cleaning, oil treating, packing & grading; poultry slaughtering & processing

5145 Confectionery Wholesale

(P-8608)
A & R WHOLESALE DISTRS INC
1765 W Penhall Way, Anaheim (92801-6728)
PHONE...................714 777-7742
Martin R Alsobrooks, *CEO*
Ron Paz, *President*
Jeff Curieo, *General Mgr*
EMP: 60
SALES (est): 56.6MM **Privately Held**
SIC: **5145** Snack foods

(P-8609)
B B G MANAGEMENT GROUP (PA)
Also Called: Granlund Candies
12164 California St, Yucaipa (92399-4333)
PHONE...................909 797-9581
Fax: 909 790-2383
R Scott Burkle, *President*
Margie Rogan, *Vice Pres*
Sandy Smith, *Manager*
EMP: 50
SQ FT: 10,000
SALES (est): 14MM **Privately Held**
SIC: **5145** 2064 Candy; candy & other confectionery products

(P-8610)
ENERGY CLUB INC
12950 Pierce St, Pacoima (91331-2526)
PHONE...................818 834-8222
Fax: 818 834-8218
Tim Snee, *CEO*
Miron Aviv, *President*
Bill Finkler, *Purch Mgr*
Bryan Cogley, *Opers Staff*
Koby Kalfus, *Sales Mgr*
▲ EMP: 80
SALES (est): 40.9MM **Privately Held**
WEB: www.energyclub.com
SIC: **5145** 2099 Confectionery; food preparations
PA: Shackleton Equity Partners Llc
4119 Guardian St
Simi Valley CA 93063
310 733-5658

(P-8611)
FRITO-LAY NORTH AMERICA INC
14600 Proctor Ave, City of Industry (91746-3249)
PHONE...................626 855-1300
Marty McFadden, *Principal*

EMP: 400
SQ FT: 54,844
SALES (corp-wide): 63B **Publicly Held**
WEB: www.fritolay.com
SIC: **5145** Potato chips
HQ: Frito-Lay North America, Inc.
7701 Legacy Dr
Plano TX 75024

(P-8612)
FRITO-LAY NORTH AMERICA INC
3630 N Hazel Ave, Fresno (93722-4594)
PHONE...................559 226-8153
Fax: 559 226-8836
Cregg Jerri, *Branch Mgr*
Jason Smith, *Senior Mgr*
EMP: 150
SALES (corp-wide): 63B **Publicly Held**
WEB: www.fritolay.com
SIC: **5145** 5149 2096 Snack foods; groceries & related products; potato chips & similar snacks
HQ: Frito-Lay North America, Inc.
7701 Legacy Dr
Plano TX 75024

(P-8613)
FRITO-LAY NORTH AMERICA INC
151 W Hill Pl, Brisbane (94005-1221)
PHONE...................415 467-1860
Fax: 415 467-7746
Luis Andrade, *Manager*
EMP: 85
SALES (corp-wide): 63B **Publicly Held**
WEB: www.fritolay.com
SIC: **5145** 5149 Confectionery; groceries & related products
HQ: Frito-Lay North America, Inc.
7701 Legacy Dr
Plano TX 75024

(P-8614)
FRITO-LAY NORTH AMERICA INC
3810 Seaport Blvd, West Sacramento (95691-3449)
PHONE...................916 372-5400
Fax: 916 372-5808
Troy Shea, *Manager*
Tyler Adams, *Office Mgr*
EMP: 150
SALES (corp-wide): 63B **Publicly Held**
WEB: www.fritolay.com
SIC: **5145** 5149 Snack foods; groceries & related products
HQ: Frito-Lay North America, Inc.
7701 Legacy Dr
Plano TX 75024

(P-8615)
FRITO-LAY NORTH AMERICA INC
6320 District Blvd, Bakersfield (93313-2142)
PHONE...................661 835-0347
Fax: 661 835-5839
Tim King, *Manager*
Bryan Jankans, *Manager*
EMP: 50
SQ FT: 18,000
SALES (corp-wide): 63B **Publicly Held**
WEB: www.fritolay.com
SIC: **5145** 5149 Snack foods; groceries & related products
HQ: Frito-Lay North America, Inc.
7701 Legacy Dr
Plano TX 75024

(P-8616)
FRITO-LAY NORTH AMERICA INC
751 W Avenue L8, Lancaster (93534-7103)
PHONE...................661 951-1399
Fax: 661 951-1472
Glenn Kliewer, *General Mgr*
EMP: 65

5145 - Confectionery Wholesale County (P-8617)   **PRODUCTS & SERVICES SECTION**

SALES (corp-wide): 63B **Publicly Held**
WEB: www.fritolay.com
SIC: 5145 Snack foods
HQ: Frito-Lay North America, Inc.
    7701 Legacy Dr
    Plano TX 75024

(P-8617)
FRITO-LAY NORTH AMERICA INC
1450 S Loop Rd, Alameda (94502-2702)
PHONE 510 769-5000
Fax: 510 769-5055
Steve Pahara, *Principal*
EMP: 62
SALES (corp-wide): 63B **Publicly Held**
WEB: www.fritolay.com
SIC: 5145 Snack foods
HQ: Frito-Lay North America, Inc.
    7701 Legacy Dr
    Plano TX 75024

(P-8618)
FRITO-LAY NORTH AMERICA INC
1390 Vantage Ct, Vista (92081-8524)
PHONE 760 727-6022
Fax: 760 727-1295
Fred Schmidt, *Manager*
Carl Pinkard, *Manager*
EMP: 100
SQ FT: 19,836
SALES (corp-wide): 63B **Publicly Held**
WEB: www.fritolay.com
SIC: 5145 5149 Snack foods; groceries & related products
HQ: Frito-Lay North America, Inc.
    7701 Legacy Dr
    Plano TX 75024

(P-8619)
FRITO-LAY NORTH AMERICA INC
26962 Vista Ter, El Toro (92630-8123)
PHONE 949 586-4644
Fax: 949 586-5344
Tyrone Suruta, *Manager*
EMP: 75
SQ FT: 14,356
SALES (corp-wide): 63B **Publicly Held**
WEB: www.fritolay.com
SIC: 5145 Snack foods
HQ: Frito-Lay North America, Inc.
    7701 Legacy Dr
    Plano TX 75024

(P-8620)
FRITO-LAY NORTH AMERICA INC
8316 W Elowin Ct, Visalia (93291-9262)
PHONE 559 651-1334
Fax: 559 651-2603
Jim Johnson, *Manager*
Dave Clark, *Manager*
EMP: 70
SQ FT: 19,800
SALES (corp-wide): 63B **Publicly Held**
WEB: www.fritolay.com
SIC: 5145 Snack foods
HQ: Frito-Lay North America, Inc.
    7701 Legacy Dr
    Plano TX 75024

(P-8621)
GICO MANAGEMENT
23073 S Frederick Rd, Ripon (95366-9616)
PHONE 209 599-7131
Steve Gikas, *Owner*
Barbara Bain, *Bookkeeper*
▲ EMP: 75
SQ FT: 100,000
SALES (est): 20.3MM **Privately Held**
SIC: 5145 Confectionery

(P-8622)
INNER CIRCLE ENTERTAINMENT
Also Called: Ruby Sky
420 Mason St, San Francisco (94102-1706)
P.O. Box 35520, Monte Sereno (95030-0520)
PHONE 415 693-0777
Fax: 415 693-0373
George Karpaty, *President*
Frank Finelli, *Principal*
Shawn Mercado, *Opers Mgr*
Matt Whitlock, *Director*
EMP: 60
SQ FT: 17,500
SALES (est): 15.4MM **Privately Held**
SIC: 5145 Snack foods

(P-8623)
MORRIS NATIONAL INC (HQ)
Also Called: McGreever and Danlee Very
760 N Mckeever Ave, Azusa (91702-2349)
PHONE 626 385-2000
Fax: 626 969-8670
Gerry Morris Zubatoff, *CEO*
Gerald Morris, *President*
David Pistole, *CFO*
Al Herpt, *Vice Pres*
Alejandra Jaytan, *Executive*
◆ EMP: 56
SQ FT: 125,000
SALES (est): 175.8MM
SALES (corp-wide): 62.8MM **Privately Held**
WEB: www.morrisnational.com
SIC: 5145 5149 Confectionery; chocolate
PA: Morris National Inc
    100 Jacob Keffer Pky
    Concord ON L4K 4
    905 879-7777

(P-8624)
PEPSICO INC
4416 Azusa Canyon Rd, Baldwin Park (91706-2740)
PHONE 626 338-5531
Kip Zaughan, *Manager*
Shane Jay, *Admin Asst*
Curt Fast, *Manager*
EMP: 200
SALES (corp-wide): 63B **Publicly Held**
WEB: www.pepsico.com
SIC: 5145 2086 Confectionery; carbonated beverages, nonalcoholic: bottled & canned
PA: Pepsico, Inc.
    700 Anderson Hill Rd
    Purchase NY 10577
    914 253-2000

(P-8625)
R W GARCIA CO INC (PA)
521 Parrott St, San Jose (95112-4121)
P.O. Box 8290 (95155-8290)
PHONE 408 275-1597
Robert W Garcia, *President*
Margaret Garcia, *Vice Pres*
Janette Rosales, *Office Mgr*
Stacey Thomson, *Accountant*
Jerry Orlando, *Plant Mgr*
◆ EMP: 50
SQ FT: 30,000
SALES (est): 80.4MM **Privately Held**
WEB: www.rwgarcia.com
SIC: 5145 2096 2099 Snack foods; tortilla chips; food preparations

---
5146 Fish & Seafood Wholesale

(P-8626)
ANTHONYS FISH GROTTO
Also Called: Ghio Seafood Products
5575 Lake Park Way # 211, La Mesa (91942-1664)
PHONE 619 713-1853
Fax: 619 298-1212
Anthony A Ghio, *Partner*
Cottardo Ghio, *Partner*
Adele Weber, *Partner*
Dan Shehan, *Controller*
Rosario Gonzsslez, *Human Res Mgr*
EMP: 60 EST: 1946
SQ FT: 11,000
SALES (est): 5.2MM **Privately Held**
SIC: 5146 5141 Fish & seafoods; groceries, general line

(P-8627)
ANTONELLI & SONS FISH & PLTY
119 S Linden Ave, South San Francisco (94080-6410)
PHONE 650 952-7413
Fax: 650 952-2258
EMP: 65
SQ FT: 11,000
SALES (est): 30.5MM **Privately Held**
SIC: 5146 5148 5421 5431

(P-8628)
ATLANTA SEAFOODS LLC
Also Called: Sea Catch Seafoods
1301 S Sunkist St, Anaheim (92806-5614)
PHONE 626 626-4900
Wayne Berman, *Mng Member*
▲ EMP: 65 EST: 1999
SQ FT: 48,000
SALES (est): 35.6MM **Privately Held**
SIC: 5146 Fish & seafoods

(P-8629)
BLUE RIVER SEAFOOD INC
Also Called: Joe Pucci & Sons Seafoods
25447 Industrial Blvd, Hayward (94545-2931)
PHONE 510 300-6800
Fax: 510 300-6805
Chris Lam, *President*
Philip Malik, *CIO*
Myrla Best, *Controller*
▲ EMP: 50
SQ FT: 53,000
SALES (est): 30.5MM **Privately Held**
SIC: 5146 2092 Fish, fresh; fish, frozen, unpackaged; fresh or frozen packaged fish

(P-8630)
CAL SOUTHERN SEAFOOD INC
125 Salinas Rd Ste 5b, Royal Oaks (95076-6706)
P.O. Box 939, Los Olivos (93441-0939)
PHONE 805 698-8262
Pete J Guglielmo, *President*
Mike Salcedo, *Principal*
EMP: 100 EST: 2012
SALES (est): 27.5MM **Privately Held**
SIC: 5146 2092 Seafoods; seafoods, frozen: prepared

(P-8631)
CALIFORNIA SHELLFISH CO INC
Point St George Fisheries
1280 Columbus Ave 300r, San Francisco (94133-1302)
P.O. Box 1386, Santa Rosa (95402-1386)
PHONE 707 542-9490
EMP: 350
SALES (corp-wide): 117.1MM **Privately Held**
SIC: 5146 Fish, fresh; fish, frozen, unpackaged
PA: California Shellfish Company, Inc.
    818 E Broadway C
    San Gabriel CA 91776
    415 923-7400

(P-8632)
DEL MAR SEAFOODS INC
1449 Spinnaker Dr, Ventura (93001-4355)
PHONE 805 850-0421
EMP: 185
SALES (corp-wide): 38.7MM **Privately Held**
SIC: 5146 Seafoods
PA: Del Mar Seafoods, Inc.
    331 Ford St
    Watsonville CA 95076
    831 763-3000

(P-8633)
H & N FOODS INTERNATIONAL INC (HQ)
Also Called: H & N Fish Company
5580 S Alameda St, Vernon (90058-3426)
P.O. Box 58626, Los Angeles (90058-0626)
PHONE 323 586-9300
Hua Thanh Ngo, *President*
Bobby Ngo, *Vice Pres*
Christine Ngo, *Vice Pres*
Dat Trieu, *Vice Pres*
Kathy Lam, *Credit Mgr*
▲ EMP: 125
SQ FT: 45,000
SALES (est): 83.2MM
SALES (corp-wide): 103MM **Privately Held**
SIC: 5146 Fish, fresh; fish, frozen, unpackaged
PA: H & N Group, Inc.
    5580 S Alameda St
    Vernon CA 90058
    323 586-9388

(P-8634)
IMP FOODS INC
1650 Delta Ct, Hayward (94544-7043)
PHONE 510 429-4600
Fax: 510 341-9798
Masamitsu Furuta, *President*
Glen Sakata, *Vice Pres*
Shigenori Yenagiaswa, *Manager*
▲ EMP: 60
SQ FT: 48,000
SALES (est): 10.7MM **Privately Held**
SIC: 5146 Fish, frozen, unpackaged; fish, fresh

(P-8635)
INTERNATIONAL MARINE PDTS INC (HQ)
Also Called: Imp
500 E 7th St, Los Angeles (90014-2410)
PHONE 213 680-0190
Fax: 213 680-0190
James Ho, *CEO*
Yoshihiro Momose, *President*
Meei Wong, *Accounting Mgr*
Taka Kawanami, *Personnel Assit*
Johni Kusayamagi, *Sales Mgr*
▲ EMP: 50
SQ FT: 10,000
SALES (est): 43MM
SALES (corp-wide): 47.5MM **Privately Held**
WEB: www.intmarine.com
SIC: 5146 Fish, fresh; fish, frozen, unpackaged
PA: Eiwa International, Inc.
    500 E 7th St
    Los Angeles CA 90014
    213 893-6123

(P-8636)
KINGS SEAFOOD COMPANY LLC
Also Called: NGS Fish House
12427 N Mainstreet, Rancho Cucamonga (91739-8887)
PHONE 909 803-1280
Fax: 909 803-1288
Bunny Bennett, *Manager*
EMP: 100
SALES (corp-wide): 81MM **Privately Held**
SIC: 5146 Seafoods
PA: King's Seafood Company, Llc
    3185 Airway Ave Ste J
    Costa Mesa CA 92626
    310 451-4595

(P-8637)
KINGS SEAFOOD COMPANY LLC
7691 Edinger Ave, Huntington Beach (92647-3604)
PHONE 714 793-1177
Malia Cappuccio, *Branch Mgr*
EMP: 100
SALES (corp-wide): 81MM **Privately Held**
SIC: 5146 Seafoods
PA: King's Seafood Company, Llc
    3185 Airway Ave Ste J
    Costa Mesa CA 92626
    310 451-4595

(P-8638)
KINGS SEAFOOD COMPANY LLC
1521 W Katella Ave, Orange (92867-3410)
PHONE 714 771-6655
Fred Belez, *Branch Mgr*

▲ = Import ▼ = Export
◆ = Import/Export

PRODUCTS & SERVICES SECTION
5146 - Fish & Seafood Wholesale County (P-8660)

EMP: 100
SALES (corp-wide): 81MM **Privately Held**
SIC: 5146 Seafoods
PA: King's Seafood Company, Llc
 3185 Airway Ave Ste J
 Costa Mesa CA 92626
 310 451-4595

(P-8639)
LUSAMERICA FOODS INC (PA)
16480 Railroad Ave, Morgan Hill (95037-5210)
PHONE....................408 294-6622
Fax: 408 778-4859
Fernando Luis Frederico, *CEO*
Anna Frederico, *Vice Pres*
Paula Silva, *MIS Dir*
Julie Rodriguez, *Human Res Mgr*
John Silva, *Buyer*
▲ EMP: 77
SQ FT: 40,000
SALES (est): 128.8MM **Privately Held**
WEB: www.lusamericafish.com
SIC: 5146 5142 Fish, fresh; fish, frozen, unpackaged; packaged frozen goods

(P-8640)
OCEAN GROUP INC (PA)
Also Called: Ocean Fresh Fish Seafood Mktg
1100 S Santa Fe Ave, Los Angeles (90021-1743)
PHONE....................213 622-3677
Fax: 213 622-3437
Young Won Kim, *President*
Hyojin Ahn, *CFO*
Tae S Kim, *Admin Sec*
Kurt Kim, *Human Resources*
▲ EMP: 60
SQ FT: 20,000
SALES: 40MM **Privately Held**
SIC: 5146 Fish & seafoods

(P-8641)
OCEAN QUEEN 87 INC
4511 Everett Ave, Vernon (90058-2621)
PHONE....................323 585-1200
Yuho Nagata, *President*
EMP: 50
SQ FT: 3,700
SALES (est): 13.2MM **Privately Held**
SIC: 5146 Fish & seafoods

(P-8642)
ORE-CAL CORP (PA)
Also Called: Harvest of The Sea
634 Crocker St, Los Angeles (90021-1002)
PHONE....................213 623-8493
Fax: 213 228-6557
William L Shinbane, *CEO*
Mark Shinbane, *President*
Sandra Shinbane, *Corp Secy*
Connie Delasuente, *Executive*
David Rovner, *Info Tech Dir*
▲ EMP: 55
SQ FT: 80,000
SALES (est): 35.6MM **Privately Held**
SIC: 5146 5142 Fish & seafoods; frozen fish, meat & poultry

(P-8643)
ORIENT FISHERIES INC
Also Called: Ofi Markesa International
1912 E Vernon Ave Ste 110, Vernon (90058-1611)
PHONE....................323 588-4185
Fax: 323 231-0088
Ming Shin Kou, *President*
David L Prince,
▲ EMP: 52
SQ FT: 3,000
SALES (est): 9.7MM **Privately Held**
SIC: 5146 Seafoods

(P-8644)
PACIFIC AMERICAN FISH CO INC (PA)
Also Called: Pafco
5525 S Santa Fe Ave, Vernon (90058-3523)
PHONE....................323 319-1551
Fax: 323 319-1517
Peter Huh, *CEO*
Paul Huh, *Exec VP*
Rick Corl, *Engineer*
Chuck Huh, *Controller*

Robert Stevenson, *Controller*
◆ EMP: 150
SQ FT: 100,000
SALES (est): 225MM **Privately Held**
WEB: www.pafco.net
SIC: 5146 2091 Fish, fresh; fish, frozen, unpackaged; seafoods; fish, filleted (boneless)

(P-8645)
PACIFIC CHOICE SEAFOOD COMPANY
1 Commercial St, Eureka (95501-0241)
PHONE....................707 442-2981
Fax: 707 442-2985
Rick Harris, *Manager*
EMP: 300
SALES (corp-wide): 476MM **Privately Held**
SIC: 5146 Fish & seafoods
HQ: Pacific Choice Seafood Company
 3220 Sw 1st Ave
 Portland OR 97239
 503 226-2200

(P-8646)
PACIFIC SEA FOOD CO INC
Also Called: Jakes Crawfish & Seafood
1420 National Dr, Sacramento (95834-1967)
PHONE....................916 419-5500
Barb Pacella, *Branch Mgr*
Mark Bowen, *General Mgr*
Kara Aakre, *Controller*
Mark Gordon, *Sales Mgr*
Marty Martinez, *Sales Mgr*
EMP: 100
SALES (corp-wide): 476MM **Privately Held**
WEB: www.pacificseafoodco.com
SIC: 5146 5142 5143 Fish, fresh; fish, frozen, unpackaged; seafoods; fish, frozen: packaged; meat, frozen: packaged; poultry, frozen: packaged; cheese
HQ: Pacific Sea Food Co. Inc.
 16797 Se 130th Ave
 Clackamas OR 97015
 503 905-4500

(P-8647)
PACIFIC SEA FOOD CO INC
Also Called: Pacific Fresh Seafood Company
605 Flint Ave, Wilmington (90744-6110)
PHONE....................310 835-4343
Fax: 310 549-9884
James Lanter, *General Mgr*
Larz Malony, *Sales Mgr*
Jolene Dimaggio, *Manager*
EMP: 50
SALES (corp-wide): 476MM **Privately Held**
WEB: www.pacificseafoodco.com
SIC: 5146 Fish & seafoods
HQ: Pacific Sea Food Co. Inc.
 16797 Se 130th Ave
 Clackamas OR 97015
 503 905-4500

(P-8648)
PLD ENTERPRISES INC
Also Called: Superior Seafood Co
440 Stanford Ave, Los Angeles (90013-2121)
PHONE....................213 626-4444
Chip Mezin, *General Mgr*
Rosa Mauro, *Accountant*
EMP: 61 **Privately Held**
SIC: 5146 Fish & seafoods
PA: P.L.D. Enterprises, Inc.
 1621 W 25th St Ste 228
 San Pedro CA 90732

(P-8649)
PROSPECT ENTERPRISES INC (PA)
Also Called: American Fish and Seafood
625 Kohler St, Los Angeles (90021-1023)
PHONE....................213 599-5700
Fax: 213 489-3891
Ernest Y Doizaki, *Ch of Bd*
Jack King, *President*
Paula Eberhardt, *CFO*
Mark Paone, *Vice Pres*
Shawn Sisler, *Info Tech Mgr*
▲ EMP: 160

SQ FT: 20,000
SALES (est): 329MM **Privately Held**
WEB: www.americanfish.com
SIC: 5146 2092 Fish, fresh; fish, frozen, unpackaged; seafoods; fresh or frozen packaged fish

(P-8650)
RED CHAMBER CO (PA)
1912 E Vernon Ave, Vernon (90058-1611)
PHONE....................323 234-9000
Fax: 323 231-8888
Ming Bin Kou, *Principal*
Shan Chun Kou, *Ch of Bd*
Shu Chin Kou, *Ch of Bd*
Eddy Tjong, *Info Tech Mgr*
Sharon Chao, *Controller*
◆ EMP: 81
SQ FT: 15,000
SALES (est): 278.1MM **Privately Held**
WEB: www.redchamber.com
SIC: 5146 4222 Seafoods; warehousing, cold storage or refrigerated

(P-8651)
SANTA MONICA SEAFOOD COMPANY
1000 Wilshire Blvd, Santa Monica (90401-1907)
PHONE....................310 393-5244
Fax: 310 451-3434
Vince Cigiliano, *Director*
Christopher Wade, *Site Mgr*
EMP: 252
SALES (corp-wide): 101.4MM **Privately Held**
SIC: 5146 Seafoods
PA: Santa Monica Seafood Company
 18531 S Broadwick St
 Rancho Dominguez CA 90220
 310 886-7900

(P-8652)
SEA WIN INC
526 Stanford Ave, Los Angeles (90013-2123)
PHONE....................213 688-2899
Fax: 213 688-0006
Nam T Tran, *CEO*
Hubart Tran, *General Mgr*
Frances Tran, *Admin Sec*
Jannie Ho, *Controller*
Stanley Yim, *Controller*
▲ EMP: 50
SQ FT: 29,000
SALES (est): 27.5MM **Privately Held**
SIC: 5146 Fish, fresh; fish, frozen, unpackaged

(P-8653)
SLADE GORTON & CO INC
1 Centerpointe Dr Ste 311, La Palma (90623-2512)
PHONE....................714 676-4200
EMP: 66 **Privately Held**
SIC: 5146
HQ: Gorton Slade & Co Inc
 225 Southampton St
 Boston MA 02118
 617 442-5800

(P-8654)
SM UNI INC
8307 Elsmore Dr, Rosemead (91770-4021)
PHONE....................213 626-2557
Fax: 213 626-2124
Shigeru Matsushita, *President*
Darlene Matsushita, *Vice Pres*
EMP: 50
SQ FT: 8,000
SALES (est): 7.1MM **Privately Held**
WEB: www.smuni.com
SIC: 5146 Seafoods

(P-8655)
SOUTHWIND FOODS LLC (PA)
Also Called: Great Amercn Seafood Import Co
20644 S Fordyce Ave, Carson (90810-1018)
P.O. Box 86021, Los Angeles (90086-0021)
PHONE....................323 262-8222
Buddy Galletti, *President*
Sam Galletti, *President*
Don Sutherland, *CFO*
Paul Galletti, *Vice Pres*

Sal Perri, *Vice Pres*
▲ EMP: 100
SQ FT: 80,000
SALES (est): 232.1MM **Privately Held**
SIC: 5146 5147 Fish & seafoods; meats & meat products

(P-8656)
STAGNARO BROTHERS SEAFOOD INC
320 Washington St, Santa Cruz (95060-4929)
PHONE....................831 423-1188
Fax: 831 423-1238
Giovanni Stagnaro, *Ch of Bd*
Robert Tara, *President*
Virginia Stagnaro, *Treasurer*
Ernest M Stagnaro, *Vice Ch Bd*
Robert Mc Pherson, *Vice Pres*
EMP: 73
SQ FT: 12,000
SALES (est): 19.7MM **Privately Held**
WEB: www.stagnarobros.com
SIC: 5146 5812 5421 Seafoods; seafood restaurants; seafood markets

(P-8657)
STAR FISHERIES
Also Called: Seaport Fish Company
841 Watson Ave, Wilmington (90744-3732)
PHONE....................310 549-4992
Fax: 310 549-4389
Anthony Di Maggio, *President*
EMP: 55
SALES (corp-wide): 67.1MM **Privately Held**
SIC: 5146 Fish & seafoods
PA: Star Fisheries
 2206 Signal Pl
 San Pedro CA 90731
 310 832-8395

(P-8658)
TRADEWIND SEAFOOD INC
1505 Mountain View Ave, Oxnard (93030-5107)
PHONE....................805 483-8555
Fax: 805 486-7167
Mack Demachi, *President*
Hiromi Demachi, *Vice Pres*
Fujio Matsui, *Office Mgr*
EMP: 50
SQ FT: 5,000
SALES (est): 9.3MM **Privately Held**
SIC: 5146

(P-8659)
TRI-MARINE FISH COMPANY LLC
220 Cannery St, San Pedro (90731-7308)
PHONE....................310 547-1144
Fax: 310 547-1166
Vince Torre, *Mng Member*
◆ EMP: 75
SQ FT: 30,000
SALES (est): 27.3MM **Privately Held**
SIC: 5146 Seafoods

(P-8660)
TRI-UNION SEAFOODS LLC (DH)
Also Called: Chicken of Sea International
9330 Scranton Rd Ste 500, San Diego (92121-7706)
P.O. Box 85568 (92186-5568)
PHONE....................858 558-9662
Fax: 858 597-4566
Shue Wing Chan, *President*
Jim Davit, *COO*
John Debeer, *COO*
David E Roszmann, *COO*
Jim Cox, *Senior VP*
▲ EMP: 69
SQ FT: 24,000
SALES (est): 82.2MM **Privately Held**
SIC: 5146 2091 Fish & seafoods; tuna fish: packaged in cans, jars, etc.; salmon: packaged in cans, jars, etc.
HQ: Thai Union International, Inc.
 9330 Scranton Rd Ste 500
 San Diego CA 92121
 858 558-9662

(PA)=Parent Co (HQ)=Headquarters (DH)=Div Headquarters
✪ = New Business established in last 2 years

5146 - Fish & Seafood Wholesale County (P-8661)

(P-8661)
TRUE WRLD FODS LOS ANGELES LLC
4200 S Alameda St, Vernon (90058-1602)
PHONE...................323 846-3300
Fax: 323 232-0365
Toshiaki Kishimoto, *Vice Pres*
Simon Zhang, *General Mgr*
Mike Yamane, *Purch Dir*
Steve Pierce, *Sales Mgr*
Ryoki Yabuuchi, *Sales Mgr*
▲ **EMP:** 55
SQ FT: 55,000
SALES (est): 26.5MM
SALES (corp-wide): 509.8MM **Privately Held**
SIC: 5146 Fish, frozen, unpackaged; fish, fresh
HQ: True World Foods New York Llc
32-34 Papetti Plz
Elizabeth NJ 07206
908 351-9090

(P-8662)
TRUE WRLD FODS SAN FRNCSCO LLC
1815 Williams St, San Leandro (94577-2301)
PHONE...................510 352-8140
Fax: 510 352-7488
Shinryo Shimada, *Mng Member*
Troy Doerschel, *Office Mgr*
Momoyo Miller, *Controller*
Makoto Kikuchi,
David Miller,
◆ **EMP:** 62
SQ FT: 27,000
SALES (est): 20.6MM
SALES (corp-wide): 509.8MM **Privately Held**
SIC: 5146 Fish & seafoods
HQ: True World Holdings Llc
24 Link Dr
Rockleigh NJ 07647
201 750-0024

(P-8663)
US INVESTMNT CMRCE FISHERIES
11067 Petal Ave, Fountain Valley (92708-1727)
P.O. Box 10474, Westminster (92685-0474)
PHONE...................714 823-5209
Jimmy Nguyen, *Exec VP*
EMP: 99
SALES: 950K **Privately Held**
SIC: 5146 Fish & seafoods

5147 Meats & Meat Prdts Wholesale

(P-8664)
BICARA LTD (PA)
1611 S Catalina Ave, Redondo Beach (90277-5255)
PHONE...................310 316-6222
William Jeffrey Hughes, *CEO*
William D Hughes, *President*
Gene Matsuda, *CFO*
Eugene Matsuda, *Vice Pres*
Raymond Rosenthal, *Vice Pres*
◆ **EMP:** 270
SQ FT: 105,000
SALES (est): 96.6MM **Privately Held**
WEB: www.bicara.net
SIC: 5147 5146 5141 Meats & meat products; seafoods; groceries, general line

(P-8665)
BRIDGFORD MARKETING COMPANY (DH)
1308 N Patt St, Anaheim (92801-2551)
P.O. Box 3773 (92803-3773)
PHONE...................714 526-5533
Allan L Bridgford, *Chairman*
John Simmons, *President*
Ray Lancey, *CFO*
William L Bridgford, *Chairman*
Debra Morris, *Manager*
EMP: 89
SQ FT: 100,000
SALES (est): 62MM
SALES (corp-wide): 133.8MM **Publicly Held**
SIC: 5147 5149 Meats & meat products; bakery products
HQ: Bridgford Foods Corporation
1308 N Patt St
Anaheim CA 92801
714 526-5533

(P-8666)
CRAIG AND HAMILTON MEAT CO
1420 National Dr, Sacramento (95834-1967)
P.O. Box 8423, Stockton (95208-0423)
PHONE...................916 419-5500
Fax: 209 464-8135
Pat Craig, *Ch of Bd*
James Good, *Treasurer*
John Craig, *Vice Pres*
Steve Maiben, *Controller*
Dennis Barone, *Sls & Mktg Exec*
EMP: 65
SQ FT: 18,000
SALES (est): 9.1MM **Privately Held**
SIC: 5147 5142 5148 Meats, fresh; meat, frozen: packaged; vegetables, fresh

(P-8667)
DANIELS WESTERN MT PACKERS INC
5217 Industry Ave, Pico Rivera (90660-2505)
PHONE...................562 948-2254
Fax: 562 948-2048
Alfred Santos, *CEO*
Denise Verdugo, *Purchasing*
Richard Hayes, *Agent*
EMP: 80
SQ FT: 12,000
SALES (est): 45.6MM **Privately Held**
WEB: www.danielswesternmeatpackers.com
SIC: 5147 Meats, fresh

(P-8668)
GOLDEN WEST TRADING INC
Also Called: Royal Poultry
4401 S Downey Rd, Vernon (90058-2518)
P.O. Box 58161 (90058-0161)
PHONE...................323 581-3663
Fax: 323 973-4083
Erik Litmanovich, *CEO*
Levi Litmanovich, *Ch of Bd*
Tony Cimolino, *President*
Josh Solovy, *President*
Zack Levenson, *Senior VP*
▲ **EMP:** 180
SQ FT: 40,000
SALES (est): 218.1MM **Privately Held**
WEB: www.gwtinc.com
SIC: 5147 5142 Meats & meat products; meat, frozen: packaged

(P-8669)
HARVEST MEAT COMPANY INC (HQ)
Also Called: Harvest Food Distributors
1022 Bay Marina Dr # 106, National City (91950-6327)
PHONE...................619 477-0185
Fax: 619 477-7090
John J Leavy, *CEO*
Kevin Leavy, *President*
Eric Doan, *CFO*
Dennis Leavy, *Vice Pres*
Dennis Kevin, *Principal*
◆ **EMP:** 80
SQ FT: 60,000
SALES (est): 252.1MM
SALES (corp-wide): 349.5MM **Privately Held**
WEB: www.harvestmeat.com
SIC: 5147 Meats & meat products
PA: Sand Dollar Holdings, Inc.
1022 Bay Marina Dr # 106
National City CA 91950
619 477-0185

(P-8670)
HEARTLAND MEAT COMPANY INC
3461 Main St, Chula Vista (91911-5828)
PHONE...................619 407-3668
Fax: 619 407-3678
Joseph E Stidman, *CEO*
Stephanie Stidman, *Corp Secy*
James Methey, *Vice Pres*
Brandon Marvin, *General Mgr*
Ranae West, *Accountant*
EMP: 70
SQ FT: 49,000
SALES (est): 42.2MM **Privately Held**
WEB: www.heartlandmeat.com
SIC: 5147 2013 Meats & meat products; sausages & other prepared meats

(P-8671)
HILLSHIRE BRANDS COMPANY
Also Called: Sara Lee
2411 Baumann Ave, San Lorenzo (94580-1801)
PHONE...................510 276-1300
Alfred Yu, *Branch Mgr*
Sean Reid, *President*
Kurt Andrews, *Executive*
Ladonna Barthelemy, *Executive*
Cindy Bloomer, *Executive*
EMP: 400
SQ FT: 20,000
SALES (corp-wide): 41.3B **Publicly Held**
SIC: 5147 Meats & meat products
HQ: The Hillshire Brands Company
400 S Jefferson St Fl 1
Chicago IL 60607
312 614-6000

(P-8672)
HOLIDAY MEAT & PROVISION CORP
405 Centinela Ave, Inglewood (90302-3294)
PHONE...................310 674-0541
Fax: 310 674-8501
Nat Rocker, *President*
David Rocker, *General Mgr*
Pat Bryant, *Office Mgr*
Sue Rocker, *Admin Sec*
Cynda Howard, *Bookkeeper*
EMP: 200
SQ FT: 14,000
SALES: 60MM **Privately Held**
SIC: 5147 5144 5146 Meats, fresh; poultry products; seafoods

(P-8673)
JENSEN MEAT COMPANY INC
2550 Britannia Blvd # 101, San Diego (92154-7408)
PHONE...................619 754-6450
Fax: 760 727-8598
Abel Olivera, *CEO*
Jeff Hamann, *Co-Owner*
Sam Acuna, *CFO*
Edmundo Garcia, *Prdtn Mgr*
EMP: 95
SQ FT: 25,000
SALES (est): 122.3MM **Privately Held**
SIC: 5147 Meats & meat products

(P-8674)
JETRO CASH AND CARRY ENTPS LLC
Also Called: Restaurant Depot
2045 Evans Ave, San Francisco (94124-1022)
PHONE...................415 920-2888
Bob Britton, *Branch Mgr*
EMP: 100 **Privately Held**
WEB: www.jetro.com
SIC: 5147 5141 5142 5181 Meats, fresh; groceries, general line; packaged frozen goods; beer & other fermented malt liquors; tobacco & tobacco products
HQ: Jetro Cash And Carry Enterprises, Llc
1524 132nd St
College Point NY 11356
718 939-6400

(P-8675)
MACSEI INDUSTRIES CORPORATION
1784 E Vernon Ave, Vernon (90058-1526)
PHONE...................323 233-7864
Seiichi Shibata, *President*
◆ **EMP:** 52
SQ FT: 8,913
SALES (est): 7.9MM **Privately Held**
SIC: 5147 Meat brokers

(P-8676)
MEADOWBROOK MEAT COMPANY INC
3051 N Church St, Rancho Cucamonga (91730)
PHONE...................909 484-6100
EMP: 153
SALES (corp-wide): 210.8B **Publicly Held**
SIC: 5147 5113 5149 5142 Lard; cardboard & products; breakfast cereals; bakery products, frozen
HQ: Meadowbrook Meat Company, Inc.
2641 Meadowbrook Rd
Rocky Mount NC 27801
252 985-7200

(P-8677)
MPCI HOLDINGS INC (PA)
Also Called: Monterrey The Natural Choice
7850 Waterville Rd, San Diego (92154-8219)
P.O. Box 81046 (92138-1046)
PHONE...................619 294-2222
Fax: 619 294-2220
Thomas Luke Abbott, *President*
Colleen Goodloe, *Vice Pres*
▲ **EMP:** 99 **EST:** 1972
SQ FT: 25,000
SALES (est): 178.2MM **Privately Held**
WEB: www.monprov.com
SIC: 5147 5143 5148 5113 Meats, fresh; cheese; fresh fruits & vegetables; disposable plates, cups, napkins & eating utensils; boxes & containers

(P-8678)
PNC INC
Also Called: Seaport Meat Company
2533 Folex Way, Spring Valley (91978-2038)
P.O. Box 1159 (91979-1159)
PHONE...................619 713-2278
Fax: 619 713-2285
Nancy Camarda, *CEO*
Pete Camarda, *Admin Sec*
Diana Herron, *Accountant*
Rod Pratte, *Plant Mgr*
Alex Limon, *Manager*
EMP: 51
SQ FT: 17,995
SALES: 23MM **Privately Held**
SIC: 5147 Meats, fresh

(P-8679)
R W ZANT CO (PA)
1470 E 4th St, Los Angeles (90033-4288)
PHONE...................323 980-5457
Fax: 323 266-1611
Robert W Zant, *President*
William Zant, *Principal*
Mary Zant, *Admin Sec*
Ibrahim El-Helou, *Info Tech Dir*
Lupe Rincon, *HR Admin*
▲ **EMP:** 90 **EST:** 1950
SQ FT: 42,000
SALES: 301MM **Privately Held**
SIC: 5147 5146 5144 4222 Meats & meat products; fish & seafoods; poultry & poultry products; cheese warehouse

(P-8680)
RANCHO FOODS INC
2528 E 37th St, Vernon (90058-1725)
P.O. Box 58504, Los Angeles (90058-0504)
PHONE...................323 585-0503
Fax: 323 585-3848
Annette Mac Donald, *President*
John Mac Donald, *Vice Pres*
Frank Celano, *General Mgr*
Martin Vigil, *Credit Mgr*
Andrew Abriel, *Opers Mgr*
EMP: 100 **EST:** 1972
SQ FT: 26,000

▲ = Import ▼ = Export
◆ = Import/Export

PRODUCTS & SERVICES SECTION

5148 - Fresh Fruits & Vegetables Wholesale County (P-8703)

SALES (est): 111.5MM Privately Held
WEB: www.ranchofoods.com
SIC: 5147 2013 Meats & meat products; sausages & other prepared meats

(P-8681)
RICHMOND WHOLESALE MEAT CO
Also Called: Richmond Peak Quality
2920 Regatta Blvd, Richmond (94804-4528)
PHONE...................510 233-5111
Fax: 510 233-5116
Richard Doellstedt, *President*
Alan Bell, *CFO*
Laura Steinebach, *CFO*
Carl Doellstedt, *Vice Pres*
Paul Guess, *Vice Pres*
◆ EMP: 85 EST: 1959
SQ FT: 100,000
SALES: 100MM Privately Held
WEB: www.rwm.biz
SIC: 5147 Meats & meat products

(P-8682)
RITE-WAY MEAT PACKERS INC
5151 Alcoa Ave, Vernon (90058-3715)
PHONE...................323 826-2144
Fax: 323 826-2150
Irwin Miller, *President*
Carol Miller, *Corp Secy*
▲ EMP: 69
SQ FT: 64,000
SALES (est): 36MM Privately Held
SIC: 5147 Meats, fresh

(P-8683)
RONGCHENG TRADING LLC
Also Called: Always Best
19319 Arenth Ave, City of Industry (91748-1401)
PHONE...................626 338-1090
MEI Lan Liang, *Mng Member*
Linda Lin, *Buyer*
Xiao Mou Zhang, *Mng Member*
Yi Tuan Zhang, *Mng Member*
Angie Lee, *Accounts Mgr*
▲ EMP: 50
SQ FT: 80,000
SALES (est): 52.8MM Privately Held
SIC: 5147 Meats & meat products

(P-8684)
SAND DOLLAR HOLDINGS INC (PA)
1022 Bay Marina Dr # 106, National City (91950-6398)
PHONE...................619 477-0185
John Leavy, *President*
Eric Doan, *CFO*
Kevin Leavy, *Vice Pres*
Mike Pepin, *Sales Executive*
▲ EMP: 80
SALES: 349.5MM Privately Held
SIC: 5147 Meats & meat products

(P-8685)
SWH MIMIS CAFE LLC
17231 17th St, Tustin (92780-1926)
PHONE...................714 544-5522
Fax: 714 544-8505
Bill Nobles, *Manager*
Matthew Kimble, *VP Human Res*
Nikia Bowen, *Manager*
EMP: 69 Privately Held
WEB: www.mimiscafe.com
SIC: 5147 Meats & meat products
HQ: Swh Mimi's Cafe, Llc
   12201 Merit Dr Ste 900
   Dallas TX 75251
   866 926-6636

(P-8686)
SYSCO NEWPORT MEAT COMPANY
16691 Hale Ave, Irvine (92606-5025)
PHONE...................949 399-4200
Fax: 949 474-8383
Timothy K Hussman, *CEO*
Denise Van Voorhis, *CFO*
Jerry Sagona, *Exec VP*
Michael Drury, *Vice Pres*
Chuck McDaniel, *Vice Pres*
EMP: 227 EST: 1976
SQ FT: 92,000

SALES (est): 167.6MM
SALES (corp-wide): 50.3B Publicly Held
WEB: www.newportmeat.com
SIC: 5147 5142 Meats, fresh; packaged frozen goods
PA: Sysco Corporation
   1390 Enclave Pkwy
   Houston TX 77077
   281 584-1390

(P-8687)
THREE SONS INC
Also Called: American Companies
5201 Industry Ave, Pico Rivera (90660-2505)
P.O. Box 6 (90660-0006)
PHONE...................562 801-4100
Fax: 562 801-4125
Michael Shannon Day, *CEO*
David Day, *Shareholder*
Mariellen Day, *Shareholder*
Michael Day, *Shareholder*
John Brenan, *Vice Pres*
▲ EMP: 87
SQ FT: 40,000
SALES (est): 52.3MM Privately Held
WEB: www.threesons.com
SIC: 5147 2013 2011 Meats, cured or smoked; meats, fresh; sausages & other prepared meats; meat packing plants

(P-8688)
TONYS FINE FOODS (HQ)
3575 Reed Ave, West Sacramento (95605-1628)
P.O. Box 1501, Broderick (95605-0698)
PHONE...................916 374-4000
Scott Berger, *CEO*
Karl Berger, *President*
Felipe Pineda, *COO*
Steve Dietz, *Vice Pres*
Gary Vorce, *Risk Mgmt Dir*
▲ EMP: 390
SQ FT: 143,000
SALES (est): 695.8MM Publicly Held
WEB: www.tonysfinefoods.com
SIC: 5147 5143 5149 Meats, cured or smoked; cheese; groceries & related products

(P-8689)
WAYNE PROVISION CO INC (PA)
Also Called: Premier Meat Company
5030 Gifford Ave, Vernon (90058-2726)
P.O. Box 58183, Los Angeles (90058-0183)
PHONE...................323 277-5888
Naftali Greenberg, *CEO*
Terry Hanks, *Shareholder*
Eldad Hadar, *Vice Pres*
Richard Orosco, *Controller*
▼ EMP: 64
SQ FT: 7,822
SALES (est): 52.6MM Privately Held
WEB: www.premiermeats.com
SIC: 5147 5144 Meats, fresh; poultry & poultry products

(P-8690)
WEBERS QUALITY MEATS INC
Also Called: Butcher's Brand
990 Carden St, San Leandro (94577-1164)
PHONE...................510 635-9892
Fax: 510 635-9964
Stefan Weber, *President*
Linda Weber, *Corp Secy*
EMP: 60
SQ FT: 10,000
SALES (est): 31.4MM Privately Held
WEB: www.webersqualitymeats.com
SIC: 5147 5142 Meats, fresh; meat, frozen: packaged

(P-8691)
WEST COAST PRIME MEATS LLC
344 Cliffwood Park St, Brea (92821-4103)
PHONE...................714 255-8560
William H Hustedt, *Mng Member*
Nathan Bennett, *Vice Pres*
Karla Coughlin, *Administration*
Samuel Rachal, *QA Dir*
Jamie Carrol, *Info Tech Mgr*
EMP: 120
SALES (est): 88.7MM Privately Held
SIC: 5147 Meats & meat products

5148 Fresh Fruits & Vegetables Wholesale

(P-8692)
ABP LIQUIDATING CORP
299 Lawrence Ave, South San Francisco (94080-6818)
PHONE...................650 871-7689
Fax: 650 583-6544
Brett Besser, *CEO*
Ardynne Besser, *Principal*
Paula Amaya, *Buyer*
Oscar Martin, *Sales Dir*
Peter Caraher, *Manager*
EMP: 50 EST: 1971
SQ FT: 11,000
SALES (est): 12.2MM Privately Held
WEB: www.abproduce.com
SIC: 5148 5144 Fruits, fresh; vegetables, fresh; eggs

(P-8693)
ADVANTAGE PRODUCE INC
1511 Bay St, Los Angeles (90021-1634)
P.O. Box 86388 (90086-0388)
PHONE...................213 627-2777
Fax: 213 627-9301
Steven A Beck, *President*
Don Beck, *Vice Pres*
Mark Bloom, *Controller*
EMP: 50
SQ FT: 27,000
SALES (est): 40MM Privately Held
SIC: 5148 Fruits; vegetables

(P-8694)
AMS - EXOTIC LLC
720 S Alameda St, Los Angeles (90021-1616)
PHONE...................213 612-5888
Fax: 213 612-5889
Sinera Chau-Pech, *Mng Member*
David O'Connor, *CFO*
Scott Lehmann, *Sales Dir*
Thierry Delappe,
Martin Seymour,
◆ EMP: 55
SQ FT: 14,000
SALES: 20MM Privately Held
WEB: www.ams-exotic.com
SIC: 5148 Fresh fruits & vegetables

(P-8695)
ANDREW AND WILLIAMSON SALES CO (PA)
Also Called: Andrew Williamson Fresh Prod
9940 Marconi Dr, San Diego (92154-7270)
PHONE...................619 661-6000
Fax: 619 661-6007
Fred M Williamson, *CEO*
Ira Gershow, *CFO*
Gershow Ira, *CFO*
John King, *Vice Pres*
Robert Rendon, *Vice Pres*
▲ EMP: 60
SQ FT: 20,000
SALES (est): 75.1MM Privately Held
WEB: www.andrew-williamson.com
SIC: 5148 Fruits; vegetables

(P-8696)
BETTER LIFE PRODUCE INC
Also Called: Better Life Organic Produce
2020 E 7th Pl, Los Angeles (90021-1702)
P.O. Box 2841, Fullerton (92837-0841)
PHONE...................213 623-0640
Fax: 213 623-0641
German Ruiz, *President*
William McCoy, *CFO*
Dawn McCoy, *Admin Sec*
Lewis Deer, *Manager*
EMP: 50
SQ FT: 22,500
SALES (est): 23.8MM Privately Held
SIC: 5148 Fresh fruits & vegetables

(P-8697)
BONTADELLI INC
2611 Mission St, Santa Cruz (95060-5702)
P.O. Box 879 (95061-0879)
PHONE...................831 423-8572
Ernest J Bontadelli, *President*
Steven Bontadelli, *Vice Pres*
EMP: 60

SALES (est): 10.4MM Privately Held
SIC: 5148 Vegetables, fresh

(P-8698)
CAL FRESCO LLC
6850 Artesia Blvd, Buena Park (90620-1015)
PHONE...................714 690-7700
Fax: 714 690-7718
Fernando Vargas, *President*
Rick Calder, *CFO*
Kris Lopez, *Controller*
David Campbell, *Sales Staff*
Greg Hess, *Sales Staff*
▼ EMP: 70
SQ FT: 75,000
SALES (est): 42.5MM Privately Held
WEB: www.calfresco.com
SIC: 5148 Fresh fruits & vegetables

(P-8699)
CALAVO GROWERS INC (PA)
1141 Cummings Rd Ste A, Santa Paula (93060-9118)
PHONE...................805 525-1245
Fax: 805 921-3232
Lecil E Cole, *Ch of Bd*
Kenneth J Catchot, *President*
Arthur Bruno, *CFO*
B John Lindeman, *CFO*
Alan C Ahmer, *Vice Pres*
◆ EMP: 153 EST: 1924
SALES: 856.8MM Publicly Held
WEB: www.calavo.com
SIC: 5148 5142 5149 Fruits, fresh; fruits, frozen; groceries & related products

(P-8700)
CALAVO GROWERS INC
28410 Vincent Moraga Dr, Temecula (92590-3654)
PHONE...................951 676-7331
Fax: 951 676-7368
Gerry Watts, *Vice Pres*
Art Bruno, *Vice Pres*
Paco Orozco, *Manager*
EMP: 50
SALES (corp-wide): 856.8MM Publicly Held
WEB: www.calavo.com
SIC: 5148 5142 Fruits, fresh; frozen vegetables & fruit products
PA: Calavo Growers, Inc.
   1141 Cummings Rd Ste A
   Santa Paula CA 93060
   805 525-1245

(P-8701)
CALIFORNIA FRUIT EXCHANGE LLC (PA)
Also Called: Golden State Fruit
6011 E Pine St, Lodi (95240-0815)
P.O. Box 1264 (95241-1264)
PHONE...................209 365-2340
Paul Marchand, *Managing Prtnr*
Joan Johnson, *Sales Staff*
▲ EMP: 150
SQ FT: 47,200
SALES: 15MM Privately Held
SIC: 5148 Fruits

(P-8702)
CALIFORNIA PRODUCE WHOLSALERS
6818 Watcher St, Commerce (90040-3715)
PHONE...................562 776-5770
Fax: 562 928-3090
Alex Pappas, *CEO*
Harry Pappas, *Treasurer*
EMP: 50
SQ FT: 18,000
SALES (est): 37MM Privately Held
SIC: 5148 Fruits, fresh; vegetables, fresh

(P-8703)
CAPURRO MARKETING LLC
Also Called: Capurro Farms
2250 Highway 1, Moss Landing (95039-9631)
P.O. Box 450 (95039-0450)
PHONE...................831 728-1767
Fax: 831 728-4807
Frank L Capurro,
Mike Manfre, *Bd of Directors*
Bill Bertone, *MIS Dir*
Steve Timsak, *Sales Mgr*

5148 - Fresh Fruits & Vegetables Wholesale County (P-8704)

Kristofer Capurro,
EMP: 60 **EST:** 2000
SQ FT: 70,000
SALES (est): 21.2MM **Privately Held**
WEB: www.capurromkt.com
SIC: 5148 Fresh fruits & vegetables; vegetables; vegetables, fresh

(P-8704)
CHARLIES ENTERPRISES
Also Called: OK Produce
1888 S East Ave, Fresno (93721-3231)
P.O. Box 12838 (93779-2838)
PHONE 559 445-8600
Fax: 559 445-8627
Matty Matoian, *President*
Angel Burnett, *Partner*
Chris Castro, *General Mgr*
Alex Blaszak, *Project Mgr*
Jennifer Wright, *Project Mgr*
EMP: 200
SQ FT: 70,000
SALES (est): 183MM **Privately Held**
WEB: www.okproduce.com
SIC: 5148 Fruits, fresh; vegetables, fresh

(P-8705)
CHICO PRODUCE INC (PA)
Also Called: Pro Pacific Fresh
70 Pepsi Way, Durham (95938-9798)
P.O. Box 1069 (95938-1069)
PHONE 530 893-0596
Fax: 530 893-0255
Terry Richardson, *CEO*
Bruce Parks, *Ch of Bd*
Dave Deuel, *Technology*
Angela Garcia, *Finance Mgr*
Steve Marsh, *Safety Dir*
▼ **EMP:** 141
SQ FT: 70,000
SALES: 60MM **Privately Held**
WEB: www.propacificfresh.com
SIC: 5148 5149 Fresh fruits & vegetables; dried or canned foods

(P-8706)
CHIQUITA BRANDS INTL INC
746 Market Ct, Los Angeles (90021-1103)
PHONE 213 488-0925
Jay Jebbia, *President*
EMP: 60
SALES (corp-wide): 274.9K **Privately Held**
WEB: www.chiquita.com
SIC: 5148 Fresh fruits & vegetables
HQ: Chiquita Brands International, Inc.
2051 Se 35th St
Fort Lauderdale FL 33316
954 453-1201

(P-8707)
COAST CITRUS DISTRIBUTORS (PA)
7597 Bristow Ct, San Diego (92154-7419)
P.O. Box 530369 (92153-0369)
PHONE 619 661-7950
Fax: 619 661-7965
James M Alvarez, *Ch of Bd*
Nick Alvarez, *COO*
Margarita Alvarez, *Vice Ch Bd*
Stanley Alvarez, *Vice Pres*
Mica Simpson, *Vice Pres*
◆ **EMP:** 130
SQ FT: 80,000
SALES: 311.5MM **Privately Held**
WEB: www.coastcitrus.com
SIC: 5148 Fresh fruits & vegetables

(P-8708)
COAST CITRUS DISTRIBUTORS
Also Called: Olympic Frt & Vegatable Distr
1601 E Olympic Blvd, Los Angeles (90021-1936)
PHONE 213 955-3444
Tom Hall, *Vice Pres*
Jimmy Alverez, *Vice Pres*
EMP: 150
SALES (corp-wide): 311.5MM **Privately Held**
WEB: www.coastcitrus.com
SIC: 5148 Fruits, fresh
PA: Coast Citrus Distributors
7597 Bristow Ct
San Diego CA 92154
619 661-7950

(P-8709)
COAST CITRUS DISTRIBUTORS
Also Called: Coast Tropical
131 Terminal Ct 13, South San Francisco (94080-6526)
P.O. Box 2884 (94083-2884)
PHONE 650 588-0707
Patrick Graham, *Manager*
EMP: 50
SALES (corp-wide): 311.5MM **Privately Held**
WEB: www.coastcitrus.com
SIC: 5148 Fruits
PA: Coast Citrus Distributors
7597 Bristow Ct
San Diego CA 92154
619 661-7950

(P-8710)
COAST PRODUCE COMPANY (PA)
1791 Bay St, Los Angeles (90021-1655)
P.O. Box 86468 (90086-0468)
PHONE 213 955-4900
Fax: 213 895-6838
Mike Ito, *CEO*
Rick Uyeno, *CFO*
John K Dunn, *Principal*
James Chan, *Human Res Mgr*
Joanna Thorpe, *Manager*
EMP: 165
SQ FT: 80,000
SALES (est): 76.9MM **Privately Held**
WEB: www.coastpro.com
SIC: 5148 Fresh fruits & vegetables

(P-8711)
D & D WHOLESALE DISTRS INC
777 Baldwin Park Blvd, City of Industry (91746-1504)
PHONE 626 333-2111
Joe Dupree, *President*
Pamela Dupree, *Corp Secy*
Jean D Dupre, *Vice Pres*
John Fracasso, *Accounting Mgr*
EMP: 90
SQ FT: 20,000
SALES (est): 59.4MM **Privately Held**
SIC: 5148 5143 Fresh fruits & vegetables; dairy products, except dried or canned

(P-8712)
DAVALAN SALES INC
Also Called: Davalan Fresh
1601 E Olympic Blvd # 325, Los Angeles (90021-1957)
PHONE 213 623-2500
Fax: 323 780-2698
Alan Frick, *President*
Dave Bouton, *CEO*
Kathy Evan, *Manager*
▲ **EMP:** 200
SQ FT: 15,000
SALES (est): 119MM **Privately Held**
SIC: 5148 Fruits; vegetables

(P-8713)
DAYLIGHT FOODS INC
660 Vista Way, Milpitas (95035-5456)
PHONE 408 284-7300
Chris Vlahopouliotis, *President*
Paul Jennings, *Vice Pres*
Clara Ayala, *Controller*
▲ **EMP:** 120
SQ FT: 20,000
SALES: 49.5MM **Privately Held**
SIC: 5148 Fruits, fresh; vegetables, fresh

(P-8714)
DEARDORFF-JACKSON CO
Also Called: Deardorff Family Farm
400 Lombard St, Oxnard (93030-5100)
P.O. Box 1188 (93032-1188)
PHONE 805 487-7801
Fax: 805 483-1286
Tom Deardorff Jr, *President*
Scott Deardorff, *Admin Sec*
Juana Gonzalez, *Persnl Dir*
Richard Martinez, *Manager*
Geremy Olsen, *Manager*
EMP: 50 **EST:** 1954
SQ FT: 115,000
SALES (est): 47.5MM **Privately Held**
WEB: www.deardorffjackson.com
SIC: 5148 Fresh fruits & vegetables

(P-8715)
DELANO FARMS COMPANY
10025 Reed Rd, Delano (93215-9562)
PHONE 661 721-1485
Fax: 661 721-7892
Joe Campbell, *Manager*
Eric Damato, *Info Tech Mgr*
Alvaro Avila, *Human Resources*
Isabel Candela, *Human Resources*
Ryan Perkins, *Sales Staff*
EMP: 59
SALES (corp-wide): 12.6MM **Privately Held**
SIC: 5148 Fruits
HQ: Delano Farms Company
111 Market St Ne Ste 360
Olympia WA 98501
360 533-2410

(P-8716)
DIMARE FRESH
4050 Pell Cir, Sacramento (95838-2527)
P.O. Box 340188 (95834-0188)
PHONE 916 921-6302
Jerry Just, *General Mgr*
Trevor Webb, *Buyer*
John Jarin, *Manager*
EMP: 300
SALES (est): 64.4MM **Privately Held**
SIC: 5148 Fresh fruits & vegetables

(P-8717)
DOLE FRESH FRUIT COMPANY (DH)
1 Dole Dr, Westlake Village (91362-7300)
P.O. Box 5700, Thousand Oaks (91359-5700)
PHONE 818 874-4000
Johan Linden, *President*
Johan L Malmqvist, *Treasurer*
Ronald D Bouchard, *Vice Pres*
David Bright, *Vice Pres*
Todd Camel, *Vice Pres*
▲ **EMP:** 460
SQ FT: 57,000
SALES (est): 948.8MM
SALES (corp-wide): 10B **Privately Held**
SIC: 5148 Fruits, fresh; banana ripening
HQ: Dole Food Company, Inc.
1 Dole Dr
Westlake Village CA 91362
818 874-4000

(P-8718)
DRISCOLL STRAWBERRY ASSOC INC (PA)
345 Westridge Dr, Watsonville (95076-4169)
P.O. Box 50045 (95077-5045)
PHONE 831 424-0506
Fax: 831 761-1090
Miles Reiter, *CEO*
Joseph Miles Reiter, *Ch of Bd*
Sean Martin, *CFO*
Soren Bjorn, *Senior VP*
Kevin Murphy, *Senior VP*
◆ **EMP:** 60
SQ FT: 19,932
SALES: 511.5MM **Privately Held**
WEB: www.driscolls.com
SIC: 5148 5431 Fruits, fresh; fruit & vegetable markets

(P-8719)
DRISCOLL STRAWBERRY ASSOC INC
1750 San Juan Rd, Aromas (95004-9027)
P.O. Box 50045, Watsonville (95077-5045)
PHONE 831 763-5100
Rick Reyes, *Branch Mgr*
Luis Guerrero, *Manager*
EMP: 50
SALES (corp-wide): 511.5MM **Privately Held**
WEB: www.driscolls.com
SIC: 5148 Fresh fruits & vegetables
PA: Driscoll Strawberry Associates, Inc.
345 Westridge Dr
Watsonville CA 95076
831 424-0506

(P-8720)
DYNASTY FARMS INC (PA)
11900 Big Tujunga Cyn Rd, Tujunga (91042-1129)
P.O. Box 3737, Salinas (93912-3737)
PHONE 831 755-1398
Fax: 831 755-1397
Thomas G Russell, *President*
Mark Salih, *Shareholder*
David L Johnson, *Admin Sec*
Candy Haynie, *Marketing Staff*
Margaret Gerba, *Mktg Coord*
EMP: 96
SALES: 363.2MM **Privately Held**
SIC: 5148 Fresh fruits & vegetables

(P-8721)
ECO FARMS SALES INC (PA)
28790 Las Haciendas St, Temecula (92590-2614)
PHONE 951 694-3013
Steve Taft, *President*
Norman Traner, *Corp Secy*
▲ **EMP:** 50
SQ FT: 20,000
SALES (est): 34.5MM **Privately Held**
SIC: 5148 Fresh fruits & vegetables

(P-8722)
EVOLUTION FRESH INC (HQ)
Also Called: Evolution Juice
11655 Jersey Blvd, Rancho Cucamonga (91730-4903)
PHONE 909 478-0895
Chris Bruzzo, *CEO*
James Rosenberg, *Ch of Bd*
Ricki Reves, *CFO*
John Reed, *Admin Sec*
Mark Satterfield, *Research*
▲ **EMP:** 74
SQ FT: 70,000
SALES: 424.9MM
SALES (corp-wide): 19.1B **Publicly Held**
SIC: 5148 Fruits, fresh; vegetables, fresh
PA: Starbucks Corporation
2401 Utah Ave S
Seattle WA 98134
206 447-1575

(P-8723)
FAMILY TREE PRODUCE INC
5510 E La Palma Ave, Anaheim (92807-2108)
PHONE 714 693-5688
Fax: 714 695-2950
Fidel Guzman, *President*
Christy Guzman, *Corp Secy*
Frank Guzman, *Controller*
EMP: 115
SQ FT: 33,000
SALES: 38.4MM **Privately Held**
WEB: www.ftproduce.com
SIC: 5148 Fruits, fresh; potatoes, fresh; vegetables, fresh

(P-8724)
FIELD FRESH FARMS LLC
320 Industrial Rd, Watsonville (95076-5116)
P.O. Box 2731 (95077-2731)
PHONE 831 722-1422
Anthony Casnacci,
Paul Betancourt, *Controller*
Cary Lee, *Opers Staff*
Teddy Rico, *Opers Staff*
Fernando Ramirez, *Sales Mgr*
EMP: 80
SQ FT: 66,000
SALES (est): 26.4MM **Privately Held**
SIC: 5148 Vegetables, fresh

(P-8725)
FRESHKO PRODUCE SERVICES INC
2155 E Muscat Ave, Fresno (93725-2326)
P.O. Box 11097 (93771-1097)
PHONE 559 497-7000
Manny Robles, *Principal*
Randall Shepherd, *Principal*
Thai Her, *Network Analyst*
Joe Austin, *Controller*
Ryan Hansen, *Opers Mgr*
EMP: 142
SQ FT: 47,000

▲ = Import ▼=Export
◆ =Import/Export

PRODUCTS & SERVICES SECTION
5148 - Fresh Fruits & Vegetables Wholesale County (P-8747)

SALES (est): 42.6MM
SALES (corp-wide): 31.1B **Privately Held**
WEB: www.freshkoproduce.com
SIC: 5148 5499 Fresh fruits & vegetables; juices, fruit or vegetable
PA: C&S Wholesale Grocers, Inc.
  7 Corporate Dr
  Keene NH 03431
  603 354-7000

(P-8726)
FRESHPOINT INC
30336 Whipple Rd, Union City (94587-1525)
PHONE.................510 476-5900
Robert Gordon, *Branch Mgr*
EMP: 135
SALES (corp-wide): 50.3B **Publicly Held**
SIC: 5148 Fresh fruits & vegetables
HQ: Freshpoint, Inc.
  1390 Enclave Pkwy
  Houston TX 77077
  -

(P-8727)
FRESHPOINT INC
Also Called: Freshpoint Las Vegas
155 N Orange Ave, City of Industry (91744-3432)
PHONE.................626 855-1400
Terry Owen, *President*
Greg Bird, *MIS Dir*
Bob Goldyn, *Human Res Mgr*
Margrit Mayer, *Human Res Mgr*
David Cruz, *Director*
EMP: 136
SALES (corp-wide): 50.3B **Publicly Held**
SIC: 5148 Fresh fruits & vegetables
HQ: Freshpoint, Inc.
  1390 Enclave Pkwy
  Houston TX 77077
  -

(P-8728)
FRESHPOINT CENTRAL CALIFORNIA
5900 N Golden State Blvd, Turlock (95382-9671)
PHONE.................209 216-0200
Brian M Sturgeon, *President*
Jeffrey A Sacchini, *CEO*
Jimmie Almanza, *Purch Agent*
Tim Bettincourt, *Manager*
Bob McKelvey, *Associate*
EMP: 150
SQ FT: 54,000
SALES (est): 73.1MM
SALES (corp-wide): 50.3B **Publicly Held**
WEB: www.piranhaproduce.com
SIC: 5148 Fresh fruits & vegetables
HQ: Freshpoint, Inc.
  1390 Enclave Pkwy
  Houston TX 77077
  -

(P-8729)
FRESHPOINT SOUTHERN CAL INC
Also Called: Freshpoint Southern California
155 N Orange Ave, City of Industry (91744-3432)
PHONE.................626 855-1400
Verne L Lusby Jr, *CEO*
Jeff Ronk, *Exec VP*
Jon Greco, *Vice Pres*
Barbara Euler, *Controller*
Joel Barker, *Director*
EMP: 208
SQ FT: 97,000
SALES (est): 150.7MM
SALES (corp-wide): 50.3B **Publicly Held**
WEB: www.theproducehunter.com
SIC: 5148 5142 Fruits, fresh; vegetables, fresh; packaged frozen goods
PA: Sysco Corporation
  1390 Enclave Pkwy
  Houston TX 77077
  281 584-1390

(P-8730)
FRIEDAS INC
4465 Corporate Center Dr, Los Alamitos (90720-2561)
PHONE.................714 733-7655
Fax: 714 816-0277
Karen Caplan, *CEO*
Jackie Caplan Wiggins, *Vice Pres*
Ann Hawkins, *Executive*
Tom Kieran, *Controller*
Brittany Laukat, *Personnel Assit*
▲ EMP: 80
SQ FT: 81,306
SALES (est): 77MM **Privately Held**
WEB: www.friedas.com
SIC: 5148 Vegetables, fresh; fruits, fresh

(P-8731)
FRUIT GUYS
4465 Corporate Center Dr, Los Alamitos (90720-2540)
PHONE.................714 826-2993
Nicole Joseph, *General Mgr*
EMP: 60 EST: 2014
SALES (est): 3.7MM **Privately Held**
SIC: 5148 Fruits

(P-8732)
GALLI PRODUCE COMPANY
1650 Old Bayshore Hwy, San Jose (95112-4304)
P.O. Box 612620 (95161-2620)
PHONE.................408 436-6100
Fax: 408 436-6119
Gerald Pieracci, *President*
Kristin Killin, *Corp Secy*
Jeff Pieracci, *Vice Pres*
Dennis Tinucci, *Vice Pres*
Joseph Vanni, *Vice Pres*
EMP: 60
SQ FT: 10,000
SALES (est): 22.3MM **Privately Held**
WEB: www.galliproduce.com
SIC: 5148 5142 Fruits, fresh; vegetables, fresh; fruits, frozen; vegetables, frozen

(P-8733)
GENERAL PROD A CAL LTD PARTNR (PA)
1330 N B St, Sacramento (95811-0605)
P.O. Box 308 (95812-0308)
PHONE.................916 441-6431
Fax: 916 441-0640
Tom Chan, *CEO*
Dan Chan, *President*
Willard Harrison, *Vice Pres*
Don Weersing, *Vice Pres*
Sheryl Weichert, *Vice Pres*
◆ EMP: 200 EST: 1933
SQ FT: 110,000
SALES (est): 101.3MM **Privately Held**
WEB: www.generalproduce.com
SIC: 5148 Fruits, fresh; vegetables, fresh

(P-8734)
GIUMARRA BROS FRUIT CO INC (PA)
Also Called: Giumarra International Berry
1601 E Olympic Blvd # 408, Los Angeles (90021-1943)
P.O. Box 861449 (90086-1449)
PHONE.................213 627-2900
Fax: 213 628-4878
Donald Corsaro, *CEO*
John Corsaro, *President*
John Giumarra Jr, *Treasurer*
T I Riley, *Vice Pres*
Erik Navarro, *Accountant*
▲ EMP: 74
SQ FT: 8,000
SALES (est): 59.8MM **Privately Held**
WEB: www.giumarra.com
SIC: 5148 Fresh fruits & vegetables

(P-8735)
GREEN FARMS INC
Also Called: Worldwide Produce
7666 Formula Pl Ste B, San Diego (92121-2443)
PHONE.................858 831-7701
Abbas Ghulam, *Branch Mgr*
EMP: 188 **Privately Held**
SIC: 5148 Fresh fruits & vegetables
PA: Green Farms, Inc.
  1661 Mcgarry St
  Los Angeles CA 90021

(P-8736)
GREEN FARMS INC (PA)
Also Called: Worldwide Produce
1661 Mcgarry St, Los Angeles (90021-3116)
P.O. Box 54399 (90054-0399)
PHONE.................213 747-4411
Fax: 213 741-1777
Stuart Weisfeld, *CEO*
Ron Warenkiewicz, *Officer*
Jason Park, *General Mgr*
Laura Ramos, *General Mgr*
Anthony Galvez, *Marketing Staff*
▲ EMP: 90
SQ FT: 33,000
SALES (est): 230.9MM **Privately Held**
WEB: www.worldwideproduce.com
SIC: 5148 Vegetables

(P-8737)
GREEN THUMB PRODUCE
2648 W Ramsey St, Banning (92220-3716)
P.O. Box 1357 (92220-0010)
PHONE.................951 849-4711
Fax: 951 849-8240
Lonnie Saverino, *President*
David Saverino, *Sales Staff*
EMP: 250
SALES (est): 93.4MM **Privately Held**
SIC: 5148 Fresh fruits & vegetables

(P-8738)
GRIMMWAY ENTERPRISES INC
Also Called: Cal-Organic Farms
12000 Main St, Lamont (93241-2836)
PHONE.................661 845-3758
Fax: 661 845-1414
Roodzant Steve, *General Mgr*
Rhonda Perez, *Admin Asst*
Maria Quiroz, *Purchasing*
Joanne Ford, *Sales Staff*
EMP: 378
SALES (corp-wide): 1.8B **Privately Held**
SIC: 5148 Vegetables, fresh
PA: Grimmway Enterprises, Inc.
  14141 Di Giorgio Rd
  Arvin CA 93203
  661 854-6250

(P-8739)
GROWERS EXPRESS LLC (PA)
150 Mn St Ste 210, Salinas (93901)
P.O. Box 948 (93902-0948)
PHONE.................831 757-9951
Fax: 831 757-9951
David L Gill, *Mng Member*
Kathleen McInnis, *CFO*
Pablo Avila, *Applctn Conslt*
Woody Johnson, *Sales Executive*
Ronald T Harney,
▼ EMP: 90
SQ FT: 10,000
SALES (est): 49.6MM **Privately Held**
SIC: 5148 Vegetables

(P-8740)
HARVEST SENSATIONS LLC (PA)
3030 E Washington Blvd, Los Angeles (90023-4220)
PHONE.................213 895-6968
Chris Coffman, *Mng Member*
Charles Gilbert, *Ch of Bd*
Bob Kiehnle, *CFO*
Alex Torres, *Controller*
Erika Flores, *QC Mgr*
▲ EMP: 50
SALES (est): 75MM **Privately Held**
SIC: 5148 Fresh fruits & vegetables

(P-8741)
J HELLMAN PRODUCE INC
1601 E Olympic Blvd # 200, Los Angeles (90021-1941)
PHONE.................213 627-1093
Fax: 213 243-9280
Chuck Johnson, *President*
Breccia Hellman, *Shareholder*
Tracy Hellman, *Corp Secy*
Justin Layton, *Sales Staff*
Susan Steinberg, *Manager*
EMP: 55
SQ FT: 21,000
SALES (est): 19.3MM **Privately Held**
SIC: 5148 Vegetables; potatoes, fresh; vegetables, fresh; fruits, fresh

(P-8742)
JACK H CALDWELL & SONS INC
Also Called: Choice Pak Products
4035 E 52nd St, Maywood (90270-2205)
PHONE.................323 589-4008
Harry Caldwell, *President*
Duke Caldwell, *Vice Pres*
Morie Thomas, *General Mgr*
EMP: 60
SQ FT: 5,000
SALES (est): 39.7MM **Privately Held**
SIC: 5148 Vegetables, fresh

(P-8743)
KINGSBURG APPLE PACKERS INC
Also Called: Kingsburg Orchards
10363 Davis Ave, Kingsburg (93631-9539)
P.O. Box 38 (93631-0038)
PHONE.................559 897-5132
George H Jackson, *President*
Colleen Jackson, *Treasurer*
Becky Stark, *Controller*
Chad Allred, *Purchasing*
◆ EMP: 450
SQ FT: 10,000
SALES (est): 137.3MM **Privately Held**
SIC: 5148 Fruits, fresh

(P-8744)
LA SPECIALTY PRODUCE CO (PA)
Also Called: San Fransisco Speciality Prod
13527 Orden Dr, Santa Fe Springs (90670-6338)
P.O. Box 2293 (90670-0293)
PHONE.................562 741-2200
Fax: 562 749-2907
Michael Glick, *President*
Kathleen Glick, *Vice Pres*
Joycee Del Toro, *Executive*
Hector Lopez, *Controller*
Alanna Martinez, *Human Resources*
EMP: 375
SQ FT: 188,000
SALES (est): 382.2MM **Privately Held**
WEB: www.laspecialtyproduce.com
SIC: 5148 Fresh fruits & vegetables

(P-8745)
LEGACY FARMS LLC
6625 Caballero Blvd, Buena Park (90620-1131)
PHONE.................714 736-1800
Fax: 714 736-1801
Nick Cancellieri,
Rick Baxter, *Principal*
Vince Mendoza, *Principal*
Ron Shimizu, *Principal*
Wally Sinner, *Principal*
▲ EMP: 120
SQ FT: 95,000
SALES (est): 96.4MM **Privately Held**
SIC: 5148 Fresh fruits & vegetables

(P-8746)
LIBERTY PACKING COMPANY LLC (PA)
Also Called: Morning Star Company The
724 Main St, Woodland (95695-3491)
PHONE.................209 826-7100
Chris Rufer, *Exec Dir*
Kim Higgs, *Exec Dir*
Charles Cummings, *Controller*
Dmitry Istomon, *Controller*
Lou Maffei, *Controller*
▲ EMP: 104
SALES (est): 131.8MM **Privately Held**
SIC: 5148 Vegetables

(P-8747)
LJ DISTRIBUTORS INC
Also Called: Team Tomato
12840 Leyva St, Norwalk (90650-6852)
P.O. Box 610, Bellflower (90707-0610)
PHONE.................562 229-7660
Fax: 562 229-7680
Lute Miyazaki, *President*
Marlene Castro, *Vice Pres*
◆ EMP: 54
SQ FT: 115,000
SALES (est): 13.1MM **Privately Held**
WEB: www.teamtomato.com
SIC: 5148 Fruits; vegetables

5148 - Fresh Fruits & Vegetables Wholesale County (P-8748)

(P-8748)
LOEWY ENTERPRISES
Also Called: Sunrise Produce Company
500 Burning Tree Rd, Fullerton (92833-1400)
PHONE..................323 726-3838
Fax: 323 582-5222
Paul Carone, President
Martha Torres, Accounting Mgr
Al Avila, Controller
Carolee Reed, Human Resources
Jim Proulx, VP Opers
EMP: 90
SQ FT: 41,000
SALES (est): 69.5MM Privately Held
SIC: 5148 Fresh fruits & vegetables

(P-8749)
M & R CO
Also Called: M&R
33 E Tokay St, Lodi (95240-4149)
PHONE..................209 941-2631
Donald Reynolds, Principal
EMP: 65
SALES: 60MM Privately Held
SIC: 5148 Fresh fruits & vegetables

(P-8750)
MAUI FRESH INTERNATIONAL LLC
1601 E Olympic Blvd # 509, Los Angeles (90021-1944)
P.O. Box 21448 (90021-0448)
PHONE..................213 688-0880
Fax: 213 688-9768
Fransico Clouthier,
Francisco Clouthier, Chief Mktg Ofcr
Suzi Arentz, Office Mgr
EMP: 65
SALES (est): 36.5MM Privately Held
SIC: 5148 Fresh fruits & vegetables
PA: San Rafael Distributing, Inc
  1270 N Indus Pk Ave Ste C
  Nogales AZ 85621
  520 281-0566

(P-8751)
MISSION PRODUCE INC
3803 Dufau Rd, Oxnard (93033-8296)
P.O. Box 5267 (93031-5267)
PHONE..................805 981-3650
Fax: 805 488-6196
Steven J Barnard, President
Megan Stevens, Personnel Exec
Michal Wadsworth, QC Mgr
Ron Araiza, Sales Mgr
EMP: 75
SALES (corp-wide): 168.6MM Privately Held
WEB: www.missionpro.com
SIC: 5148 Fresh fruits & vegetables
PA: Mission Produce, Inc.
  2500 E Vineyard Ave # 300
  Oxnard CA 93036
  805 981-3650

(P-8752)
MONSANTO COMPANY
37437 State Highway 16, Woodland (95695-9353)
PHONE..................530 669-6224
Rusty Myer, Branch Mgr
Rebeca Benitez, Research
Francine Dickie, Research
John Uhlig, Manager
Jonathan Ashcraft, Supervisor
EMP: 300
SALES (corp-wide): 13.5B Publicly Held
SIC: 5148 Vegetables
PA: Monsanto Company
  800 N Lindbergh Blvd
  Saint Louis MO 63167
  314 694-1000

(P-8753)
MOONLIGHT PACKING CORPORATION (PA)
Also Called: Moonlight Companies
17719 E Huntsman Ave, Reedley (93654-9205)
P.O. Box 846 (93654-0846)
PHONE..................559 638-7799
Fax: 559 638-7199
Russell Tavlan, President
Ty Tavlan, CFO
Jared Riley, CTO
EMP: 185
SQ FT: 80,000
SALES (est): 539.7MM Privately Held
WEB: www.moonlightcompanies.com
SIC: 5148 4783 Fruits, fresh; packing & crating

(P-8754)
NATURES PRODUCE COMPANY
3305 Bandini Blvd, Vernon (90058-4130)
P.O. Box 58366 (90058-0366)
PHONE..................323 235-4343
Fax: 323 235-8388
Rick Polisky, CEO
Beth Polisky, Controller
▲ EMP: 80
SQ FT: 35,000
SALES (est): 53.8MM Privately Held
WEB: www.naturesproducecompany.com
SIC: 5148 Fresh fruits & vegetables

(P-8755)
NOR-CAL PRODUCE INC
2995 Oates St, West Sacramento (95691-5902)
P.O. Box 980188 (95798-0188)
PHONE..................916 373-0830
Fax: 916 373-0320
Todd Achondo, CEO
Linda Achondo, Vice Pres
EMP: 130
SQ FT: 85,000
SALES (est): 74.1MM Publicly Held
WEB: www.nor-calproduce.com
SIC: 5148 Fruits, fresh
PA: United Natural Foods, Inc.
  313 Iron Horse Way
  Providence RI 02908

(P-8756)
NUNES COMPANY INC (PA)
Also Called: Foxy
925 Johnson Ave, Salinas (93901-4327)
P.O. Box 673 (93902-0673)
PHONE..................831 751-7510
Fax: 831 424-4190
Tom P Nunes Jr, CEO
Mike Chimera, CFO
Mike Scarr, CFO
Enos Barera, Treasurer
Mark Crossgrove, Vice Pres
▼ EMP: 50 EST: 1976
SALES (est): 38.5MM Privately Held
WEB: www.foxy.com
SIC: 5148 Vegetables

(P-8757)
OAKVILLE PRODUCE PARTNERS LLC
Also Called: Greenleaf
453 Valley Dr, Brisbane (94005-1209)
PHONE..................415 647-2991
William F Wilkinson, Mng Member
Frank Ballentine, President
Peter Napolitano, CFO
Mark Natividad, Finance Dir
Ted Cavagnaro, Sales Mgr
EMP: 150
SQ FT: 32,000
SALES (est): 110.5MM Privately Held
WEB: www.greenleafsf.com
SIC: 5148 5451 Fruits, fresh; vegetables, fresh; dairy products stores

(P-8758)
OLAM SPICES & VEGETABLES INC
1350 Pacheco Pass Hwy, Gilroy (95020-9559)
PHONE..................408 846-3200
Lester Karen, Director
Elaine Lustre, Admin Asst
Ann Padilla, Engineer
Toni Rivera, Human Res Dir
David Iniguez, Plant Engr
◆ EMP: 82 EST: 2010
SALES (est): 66.9MM Privately Held
SIC: 5148 Vegetables

(P-8759)
ORGANICGIRL LLC
900 Work St, Salinas (93901-4386)
P.O. Box 5999 (93915-5999)
PHONE..................831 758-7800

Mark Drever,
Don Barnett, CFO
Ken Schoenthal, Controller
Jim Gallagher,
Steve Taylor,
EMP: 650
SQ FT: 125,000
SALES (est): 5.1MM Privately Held
SIC: 5148 Fresh fruits & vegetables

(P-8760)
PACIFIC COAST PRODUCE INC
950 Mountain View Ave # 1, Oxnard (93030-6201)
PHONE..................805 240-3385
Fax: 805 483-9546
Carlos Marez, CEO
Uvence Cortez, Treasurer
Maribelle Cortez, Vice Pres
Susana Marez, Manager
EMP: 50
SQ FT: 16,000
SALES (est): 30.2MM Privately Held
WEB: www.pacificcoastproduce.com
SIC: 5148 5149 5812 5142 Fresh fruits & vegetables; canned goods: fruit, vegetables, seafood, meats, etc.; contract food services; frozen fish, meat & poultry; frozen dairy desserts

(P-8761)
PACIFIC INTL VGETABLE MKTG INC (PA)
Also Called: PACIFIC INTERNATIONAL MARKETIN
740 Airport Blvd, Salinas (93901-4510)
P.O. Box 3737 (93912-3737)
PHONE..................831 422-3745
Fax: 831 424-3045
Thomas G Russell, President
Mike Michaelson, CFO
Dave Johnson, Vice Pres
Robert Negrin, General Mgr
Steven Tripp, Admin Sec
▲ EMP: 55
SQ FT: 1,800
SALES: 35.1MM Privately Held
WEB: www.purepacificorganic.com
SIC: 5148 Fresh fruits & vegetables

(P-8762)
PACIFIC TRELLIS FRUIT LLC (PA)
5108 E Clinton Way # 108, Fresno (93727-2043)
PHONE..................559 255-5437
Linda Chen,
Josh Leichter, General Mgr
Patricia Medina, Controller
Jose Rodriguez, Controller
Patty Denson, Marketing Staff
▲ EMP: 130
SQ FT: 3,600
SALES (est): 220.8MM Privately Held
WEB: www.pacifictrellisfruit.com
SIC: 5148 Fruits

(P-8763)
PRIMETIME INTERNATIONAL INC
86705 Avenue 54 Ste A, Coachella (92236-3814)
PHONE..................760 399-4166
Carl Sam Maggio,
Chuck Hodges, Principal
Mark Nickerson, Principal
Jim Detty, Credit Mgr
▲ EMP: 95
SALES: 200MM
SALES (corp-wide): 123.9MM Privately Held
WEB: www.primetimeproduce.com
SIC: 5148 4783 Vegetables, fresh; packing goods for shipping
PA: Sun And Sands Enterprises, Llc
  86705 Avenue 54 Ste A
  Coachella CA 92236
  760 399-4278

(P-8764)
PRO ACT LLC
40 Ragsdale Dr Ste 200, Monterey (93940-5774)
PHONE..................831 655-4250
Fax: 831 655-4251
Max Yeater, CEO

Steve Grinstead, CEO
Bob Kiehnle, CFO
Allen Hardison, Vice Pres
Kelly Jacob, Vice Pres
▲ EMP: 80
SALES (est): 50.4MM Privately Held
WEB: www.proactusa.com
SIC: 5148 Vegetables

(P-8765)
PRODUCE COMPANY
Also Called: Finest Produce
16809 Bellflower Blvd # 32, Bellflower (90706-5901)
PHONE..................310 508-7760
Edward L Puppo, President
Steven Morris, Vice Pres
EMP: 130
SQ FT: 2,000
SALES: 5.5MM Privately Held
SIC: 5148 Fresh fruits & vegetables

(P-8766)
PRODUCE EXCHANGE INCORPORATED (HQ)
7407 Southfront Rd, Livermore (94551-8224)
PHONE..................925 454-8700
Fax: 925 454-8711
Samuel E Jones Jr, President
Kyle Hickey, CFO
Carrie Barnes, Administration
Marlene Hokanson, Marketing Staff
Frank D Maggiore, Sales Staff
▲ EMP: 65
SQ FT: 10,000
SALES (est): 105.9MM
SALES (corp-wide): 156.3MM Privately Held
WEB: www.tpemail.com
SIC: 5148 Fruits; vegetables
PA: Lipman-Texas, Llc
  315 New Market Rd E
  Immokalee FL 34142
  239 657-4421

(P-8767)
PROFESSIONAL PRODUCE
2570 E 25th St, Los Angeles (90058-1211)
P.O. Box 58308 (90058-0308)
PHONE..................323 277-1550
Fax: 323 582-6826
Ted Kaplan, CEO
Maribel Reyes, CFO
Enrique Morales, Administration
Myrna Mallari, Finance Mgr
Ben Tolentino, Accountant
◆ EMP: 99
SQ FT: 5,000
SALES (est): 76.8MM Privately Held
WEB: www.profproduce.com
SIC: 5148 Fresh fruits & vegetables

(P-8768)
PROGRESSIVE PRODUCE LCC (HQ)
Also Called: Progressive Marketing Group
5790 Peachtree St, Commerce (90040-4000)
PHONE..................323 890-8100
Fax: 323 890-8113
James K Leimkuhler, President
Jack Gyben, Vice Pres
Victor Rodarte, Vice Pres
Donald Hessel, General Mgr
Juanita Benavidez, Admin Asst
▲ EMP: 104
SQ FT: 106,000
SALES (est): 77.7MM
SALES (corp-wide): 3B Privately Held
WEB: www.progressiveproduce.com
SIC: 5148 4213 7389 Fruits, fresh; vegetables, fresh; refrigerated products transport; packaging & labeling services
PA: Total Produce Public Limited Company
  Charles Mccann Building
  Dundalk
  429 335-451

(P-8769)
RIVER RANCH FRESH FOODS LLC (HQ)
911 Blanco Cir Ste B, Salinas (93901-4449)
PHONE..................831 758-1390
Fax: 831 758-1390

▲ = Import ▼ = Export
◆ = Import/Export

PRODUCTS & SERVICES SECTION

5148 - Fresh Fruits & Vegetables Wholesale County (P-8791)

Bruce Knobeloch, *CEO*
John Bowman, *President*
Tom Welch, *CFO*
Debbie Anderson, *Admin Mgr*
Tony Gray, *Controller*
▲ **EMP:** 450
SALES (est): 167.2MM
SALES (corp-wide): 3B **Privately Held**
WEB: www.rrff.com
SIC: 5148 Vegetables, fresh
PA: Taylor Fresh Foods, Inc
150 Main St Ste 400
Salinas CA 93901
831 676-9023

(P-8770)
SAMBAZON INC (PA)
1160 Calle Cordillera, San Clemente (92673-6238)
PHONE.............................877 726-2296
Fax: 949 498-8619
Ryan Black, *CEO*
Corwin Karaffa, *COO*
Bruce Peasland, *CFO*
Renee K Junge, *Senior VP*
Jeremy Black, *Vice Pres*
◆ **EMP:** 60
SQ FT: 10,000
SALES (est): 43.3MM **Privately Held**
WEB: www.sambazon.com
SIC: 5148 5499 Fruits; juices, fruit or vegetable

(P-8771)
SAN VINCENTE LABOR LLC
1140 Abbott St Ste C, Salinas (93901-4503)
P.O. Box 2357 (93902-2357)
PHONE.............................831 755-0955
Sam McKinsey,
Ron Harney,
Ron Jones, *Accounts Mgr*
EMP: 200
SQ FT: 4,000
SALES (est): 16.3MM **Privately Held**
SIC: 5148 7361 Vegetables; labor contractors (employment agency)

(P-8772)
SEASON PRODUCE CO INC
1601 E Olympic Blvd # 315, Los Angeles (90021-1942)
PHONE.............................213 689-0008
Fax: 213 629-2491
Patrick R Horwath, *President*
Daniel Horwath, *Vice Pres*
Timothy R Horwath, *Vice Pres*
Robert Gamble, *Controller*
Pat Carnevali, *Manager*
EMP: 342
SQ FT: 20,000
SALES: 71MM
SALES (corp-wide): 71.5MM **Privately Held**
WEB: www.s-hpacking.com
SIC: 5148 Fresh fruits & vegetables
PA: S & H Packing & Sales Co., Inc.
2590 Harriet St
Vernon CA 90058
323 581-7172

(P-8773)
SEQUOIA ENTERPRISES INC
Also Called: Sequoia Orange
150 W Pine St, Exeter (93221-1613)
PHONE.............................559 592-9455
James Wilson, *CEO*
Marvin L Wilson, *President*
Linda Pescosolido, *Vice Pres*
Pat Atherton, *Manager*
Jan Lee, *Manager*
▼ **EMP:** 70 **EST:** 1975
SQ FT: 5,100
SALES (est): 16.6MM **Privately Held**
SIC: 5148 Fruits, fresh

(P-8774)
SGF PRODUCE HOLDING CORP
701 W Kimberly Ave # 210, Placentia (92870-6342)
PHONE.............................714 630-2170
Ed Haft, *CEO*
Joe McCarthy, *CFO*
EMP: 360

SALES (est): 69.4MM **Privately Held**
SIC: 5148 2037 0191 Fruits; frozen fruits & vegetables; general farms, primarily crop

(P-8775)
SHAPIRO-GILMAN-SHANDLER CO (PA)
Also Called: S G S Produce
739 Decatur St, Los Angeles (90021-1649)
PHONE.............................213 593-1200
Fax: 213 593-1210
Carol C Shandler, *President*
Muriel Shandler, *Vice Pres*
Morris Shander, *Principal*
Hermie Ondrade, *Controller*
▲ **EMP:** 100
SQ FT: 50,000
SALES (est): 40.9MM **Privately Held**
WEB: www.sgsproduce.com
SIC: 5148 Fruits; vegetables

(P-8776)
SOUTHERN FRESH PROD PROVS INC
11954 Washington Blvd, Whittier (90606-2608)
PHONE.............................562 236-2784
Daniel Meza, *President*
Daniel Silverman, *CFO*
Naomi Silverman, *Treasurer*
Sanford Deutsch, *Vice Pres*
Tracey Goldstein, *Admin Sec*
EMP: 65
SALES (est): 35.7MM **Privately Held**
SIC: 5148 Fresh fruits & vegetables

(P-8777)
SOUTHERN FRESH PRODUCE INC
11954 Washington Blvd, Whittier (90606-2608)
PHONE.............................562 236-2784
Daniel G Meza, *President*
Yanira Corral, *Vice Pres*
EMP: 180
SQ FT: 55,000
SALES: 27MM **Privately Held**
SIC: 5148 Fresh fruits & vegetables

(P-8778)
STELLAR DISTRIBUTING INC
21801 Avenue 16, Madera (93637-8608)
PHONE.............................559 664-8400
Paul Catania Jr, *President*
Nick Cappelluti, *Sales Staff*
Brian Lapin, *Sales Staff*
Michael Simmons, *Sales Staff*
Bob Farnam, *Manager*
◆ **EMP:** 350
SALES: 21.7MM
SALES (corp-wide): 5.8MM **Privately Held**
WEB: www.stellardistributing.com
SIC: 5148 5141 Vegetables, fresh; fruits, fresh; food brokers
PA: M. L. Catania Company Limited
575 Orwell St Suite 3
Mississauga ON L5A 2
416 236-9394

(P-8779)
SUN PACIFIC MARKETING COOP INC
Also Called: Sun Pacific Farming
31452 Old River Rd, Bakersfield (93311-9621)
PHONE.............................661 847-1015
Bob Dipiazza, *Branch Mgr*
EMP: 1053
SALES (corp-wide): 538.5MM **Privately Held**
SIC: 5148 Fresh fruits & vegetables
PA: Sun Pacific Marketing Cooperative, Inc.
1095 E Green St
Pasadena CA 91106
213 612-9557

(P-8780)
SUNKIST GROWERS INC (PA)
27770 N Entertainment Dr # 120, Valencia (91355-1093)
PHONE.............................818 986-4800
Fax: 818 379-7141
Russell Hanlin II, *President*

Jim Padden, *COO*
Richard G French, *CFO*
Michael Wootton, *Senior VP*
Russell L Hanlin II, *Vice Pres*
◆ **223 EST:** 1893
SQ FT: 50,000
SALES: 1.1B **Privately Held**
WEB: www.sunkist.com
SIC: 5148 2033 2037 2899 Fruits, fresh; fruit juices: packaged in cans, jars, etc.; fruit juice concentrates, frozen; lemon oil (edible); orange oil; grapefruit oil; copyright buying & licensing; display equipment, except refrigerated

(P-8781)
SUNRISE GROWERS INC (HQ)
Also Called: Sunrise Growers-Frozsun Foods
701 W Kimberly Ave # 210, Placentia (92870-6354)
PHONE.............................714 630-2170
Fax: 714 630-0920
Edward Haft, *President*
Joe McCarthy, *CFO*
Christine Herrera, *Vice Pres*
Erwin Hettervik, *Vice Pres*
Dave Yvanovich, *Vice Pres*
◆ **EMP:** 300
SALES (est): 372MM
SALES (corp-wide): 1.2B **Privately Held**
WEB: www.frozsun.com
SIC: 5148 2037 Fruits; frozen fruits & vegetables
PA: Sunopta Inc
2233 Argentia Rd Suite 401
Mississauga ON L5N 2
905 821-9669

(P-8782)
UMINA BROS INC (PA)
1601 E Olympic Blvd # 403, Los Angeles (90021-1943)
P.O. Box 861146 (90086-1146)
PHONE.............................213 622-9206
Fax: 213 622-0708
Richard Flamminio, *President*
Victor Grosso, *CFO*
Mark Golden, *Vice Pres*
Matt Beltran, *General Mgr*
Janice Quon, *Credit Mgr*
◆ **EMP:** 82
SQ FT: 24,800
SALES (est): 47.7MM **Privately Held**
SIC: 5148 Fresh fruits & vegetables

(P-8783)
V & L PRODUCE INC
Also Called: General Produce
2550 E 25th St, Vernon (90058-1211)
PHONE.............................323 589-3125
Fax: 323 589-8730
Victor Mendoza, *President*
Claudia Lopez, *Manager*
▲ **EMP:** 140
SQ FT: 12,000
SALES (est): 66.6MM **Privately Held**
SIC: 5148 Fresh fruits & vegetables

(P-8784)
VEG-FRESH FARMS LLC
1400 W Rincon St, Corona (92880-9205)
PHONE.............................800 422-5535
Fax: 714 446-8700
Lawrence Cancellieri Jr, *Manager*
Mark Resnikoff, *Systems Staff*
Bob Whitney, *Controller*
EMP: 220
SQ FT: 94,000
SALES (est): 180.1MM **Privately Held**
WEB: www.vegfresh.com
SIC: 5148 Vegetables; fruits

(P-8785)
VEGIWORKS INC
2101 Jerrold Ave, San Francisco (94124-1009)
PHONE.............................415 643-8686
Fax: 415 643-5640
Shing Ho, *CFO*
Calvin Leong, *Vice Pres*
Phillip Woo, *Admin Sec*
Phoebe Tu, *Sales Staff*
EMP: 65
SQ FT: 16,000

SALES (est): 25.5MM **Privately Held**
WEB: www.vegiworks.com
SIC: 5148 Fresh fruits & vegetables

(P-8786)
VERITABLE VEGETABLE INC
1100 Cesar Chavez, San Francisco (94121-1214)
PHONE.............................415 641-3500
Fax: 415 641-3505
Maryjane Evans, *President*
Gerilyn Botting, *CFO*
Shira Tannor, *Officer*
Mary J Evans, *General Mgr*
Ruth Lalputan, *Administration*
EMP: 57
SQ FT: 8,000
SALES (est): 43.2MM **Privately Held**
WEB: www.veritablevegetable.com
SIC: 5148 Fruits; vegetables

(P-8787)
WATSONVILLE COAST PRODUCE INC
275 Kearney Ext Frnt, Watsonville (95076-4463)
P.O. Box 490 (95077-0490)
PHONE.............................831 722-3851
Fax: 831 722-5112
Gary L Manfre, *CEO*
Douglas Peterson, *Treasurer*
John Burkett, *President*
Frank L Capurro, *Vice Pres*
Sergio Gomez, *Human Res Mgr*
EMP: 105
SQ FT: 40,000
SALES: 31MM **Privately Held**
SIC: 5148 Fresh fruits & vegetables

(P-8788)
WEST CENTRAL PRODUCE INC
12840 Leyva St, Norwalk (90650-6852)
PHONE.............................213 629-3600
Fax: 213 629-3700
Michael Dodo, *President*
Jamie Purcell, *CFO*
Espi Demara, *Manager*
▲ **EMP:** 300
SQ FT: 34,000
SALES: 123MM **Privately Held**
WEB: www.westcentralproduce.com
SIC: 5148 Fresh fruits & vegetables

(P-8789)
WHOLE LEAF CO LLC
375 W Market St, Salinas (93901-1423)
P.O. Box 2447 (93902-2447)
PHONE.............................831 755-2057
Roger Mills,
EMP: 100
SALES (est): 22.1MM **Privately Held**
SIC: 5148 Fresh fruits & vegetables

(P-8790)
WIEMAR DISTRIBUTORS INC
Also Called: M & M Distributors
1953 S Alameda St, Los Angeles (90058-1013)
PHONE.............................213 747-7036
Fax: 213 746-5292
Marco Moreno, *President*
Rosa Moreno, *Vice Pres*
Margreta Orduno, *Controller*
▲ **EMP:** 65
SQ FT: 31,000
SALES: 34.6MM **Privately Held**
WEB: www.mmdistributors.org
SIC: 5148 Fresh fruits & vegetables

(P-8791)
WILLIAM BRAMMER
Also Called: Be Wise Ranch
9018 Artesian Rd, San Diego (92127-2128)
PHONE.............................858 756-3088
William Brammer, *Owner*
Bill Brammer, *Telecomm Mgr*
Marsanne Brammer, *Human Res Dir*
Fay Wang, *Human Res Dir*
EMP: 115
SALES (est): 13.7MM **Privately Held**
WEB: www.bewiseranch.com
SIC: 5148 0161 Fresh fruits & vegetables; vegetables & melons

5148 - Fresh Fruits & Vegetables Wholesale County (P-8792)

(P-8792)
WORLD VARIETY PRODUCE INC
Also Called: Melissa's Produce
5325 S Soto St, Vernon (90058-3624)
P.O. Box 514599, Los Angeles (90051-2599)
PHONE..................323 588-0151
Fax: 323 584-7285
Anna Raya, *Principal*
Joe V Hernandez, *President*
Sharon Hernandez, *Treasurer*
Lizette Moya, *Admin Asst*
Kelly Rowe, *CTO*
▲ EMP: 325
SQ FT: 244,000
SALES (est): 221.8MM **Privately Held**
SIC: 5148 Fresh fruits & vegetables

5149 Groceries & Related Prdts, NEC Wholesale

(P-8793)
ALHAMBRA/SIERRA SPRINGS
485 Vista Way, Milpitas (95035-5405)
PHONE..................408 727-0677
K Dillion Schickli, *Principal*
EMP: 99
SALES: 950K **Privately Held**
SIC: 5149 Groceries & related products

(P-8794)
ALLIED FOOD DISTRIBUTORS INC
1225 California Ave, Pittsburg (94565-4112)
P.O. Box 1510, Los Altos (94023-1510)
PHONE..................925 432-1625
Fax: 925 432-9860
James G Scharetg, *President*
Jeffrey Scharetg, *Vice Pres*
Ann Stewart, *Admin Mgr*
Sally Siino, *Finance Mgr*
Sally Vegas, *Finance Mgr*
▲ EMP: 60 EST: 1973
SQ FT: 80,000
SALES (est): 5MM **Privately Held**
SIC: 5149 Canned goods: fruit, vegetables, seafood, meats, etc.

(P-8795)
ANNIES HOMEGROWN INC
1610 5th St, Berkeley (94710-1715)
PHONE..................510 558-7500
John Foraker, *CEO*
Stephen Palmer, *Admin Sec*
David Tran, *VP Sales*
Jocy Upton, *VP Sales*
Fadrhonc Keely, *Corp Comm Staff*
▼ EMP: 75
SQ FT: 10,000
SALES (est): 27.3MM
SALES (corp-wide): 16.5B **Publicly Held**
SIC: 5149 Natural & organic foods
HQ: Annie's, Inc.
1610 5th St
Berkeley CA 94710
510 558-7500

(P-8796)
APP WHOLESALE LLC
3686 E Olympic Blvd, Los Angeles (90023-3146)
PHONE..................323 980-8315
David Weissberg,
Hy Behar, *Marketing Staff*
Phil Castro, *Marketing Staff*
Craig Sanquist, *Sales Staff*
David Behar, *Manager*
EMP: 500 EST: 2013
SQ FT: 220,000
SALES (est): 164.1MM **Privately Held**
SIC: 5149 Specialty food items

(P-8797)
ARTISAN BAKERS
21684 8th St E Ste 400, Sonoma (95476-2816)
PHONE..................707 939-1765
Fax: 707 939-0431
Bill Dozier, *CEO*
Craig Ponsford, *President*
Elizabeth Ponsford, *Treasurer*
Sharon Ponsford, *Vice Pres*
Don Helton, *General Mgr*
EMP: 60
SQ FT: 4,400
SALES (est): 28.7MM **Privately Held**
WEB: www.artisanbakers.com
SIC: 5149 5461 Bakery products; bakeries

(P-8798)
ARYZTA LLC
Also Called: Fresh Start Bakeries
1220 S Baker Ave, Ontario (91761-7739)
P.O. Box 1283, Alhambra (91802-1283)
PHONE..................909 472-3500
Rob Crawford, *General Mgr*
Gary Rosenblum, *Engineer*
Judy Henderson, *Sales Dir*
EMP: 197
SALES (corp-wide): 4.2B **Privately Held**
WEB: www.fsbglobal.net
SIC: 5149 Bakery products
HQ: Aryzta Llc
6080 Center Dr Ste 900
Los Angeles CA 90045
310 417-4700

(P-8799)
ARYZTA LLC
Also Called: Otis Spunkmeyer
14490 Catalina St, San Leandro (94577-5516)
PHONE..................214 630-8292
Dan Thomas, *Manager*
EMP: 75
SQ FT: 49,280
SALES (corp-wide): 4.2B **Privately Held**
WEB: www.spunkmeyer.com
SIC: 5149 4225 Bakery products; general warehousing & storage
HQ: Aryzta Llc
6080 Center Dr Ste 900
Los Angeles CA 90045
310 417-4700

(P-8800)
ARYZTA LLC
Also Called: Otis Spunkmeyer
14490 Catalina St, San Leandro (94577-5516)
PHONE..................704 357-0369
Pete Wimmerstedt, *Manager*
Tony Hilario, *Manager*
EMP: 60
SALES (corp-wide): 4.2B **Privately Held**
WEB: www.spunkmeyer.com
SIC: 5149 Bakery products
HQ: Aryzta Llc
6080 Center Dr Ste 900
Los Angeles CA 90045
310 417-4700

(P-8801)
ARYZTA LLC
Also Called: Fresh Start Bakeries
920 Shaw Rd, Stockton (95215-4014)
PHONE..................209 462-3601
Fax: 209 462-3618
Dan Bailey, *Mng Officer*
Johnathan Slater, *Chief Engr*
Melissa Eldredge, *Controller*
EMP: 50
SALES (corp-wide): 4.2B **Privately Held**
WEB: www.fsbglobal.net
SIC: 5149 2051 Bakery products; bread, cake & related products
HQ: Aryzta Llc
6080 Center Dr Ste 900
Los Angeles CA 90045
310 417-4700

(P-8802)
ASHBURY MARKET INC
Also Called: Raison D'Etre Bakery
179 Starlite St, South San Francisco (94080-6313)
PHONE..................650 952-8889
Arnold E Wong, *President*
Richard Wong, *CEO*
Mary Wong, *CFO*
Yumi Parkinson, *Human Res Mgr*
EMP: 80
SQ FT: 10,000
SALES (est): 21.2MM **Privately Held**
SIC: 5149 Bakery products

(P-8803)
BAKED IN SUN
Also Called: House of Tudor
2560 Progress St, Vista (92081-8465)
PHONE..................760 591-9045
Fax: 760 591-9005
Rachel Shein, *CEO*
Steve Pilarski, *President*
Vicky Cruse, *Executive*
Steve Pilaski, *Info Tech Mgr*
Keith Long, *Research*
EMP: 60
SQ FT: 12,000
SALES (est): 18MM **Privately Held**
WEB: www.bakedinthesun.com
SIC: 5149 Bakery products

(P-8804)
BAKERY EX SOUTHERN CAL LLC
1910 W Malvern Ave, Fullerton (92833-2105)
PHONE..................714 446-9470
Charles Burman,
Ronald Currie, *General Mgr*
Sue Remember, *Manager*
EMP: 100
SQ FT: 28,000
SALES (est): 33.9MM **Privately Held**
SIC: 5149 Crackers, cookies & bakery products

(P-8805)
BASTANCHURY WATERS COMPANY INC (PA)
Also Called: Yosemite Waters
2 Sterling, Irvine (92618-2516)
PHONE..................909 824-2430
Fax: 909 824-3240
Charles Soderstrom, *President*
Dolores Soderstrom, *Corp Secy*
Maya Soderstrom, *Vice Pres*
Michelle Dumalski, *Manager*
EMP: 80
SQ FT: 15,000
SALES (est): 24.1MM **Privately Held**
SIC: 5149 5078 Mineral or spring water bottling; drinking water coolers, mechanical

(P-8806)
BAY BREAD LLC
Also Called: La Boulange
2325 Pine St, San Francisco (94115-2714)
P.O. Box 34507, Seattle WA (98124-1507)
PHONE..................415 440-0356
Fax: 650 866-4716
Pascal Rigo, *Mng Member*
Fred Estrada,
Lori Goodman,
Nancy Kershner, *Manager*
Pascal Ringo, *Manager*
EMP: 70
SALES (est): 16.3MM
SALES (corp-wide): 19.1B **Publicly Held**
SIC: 5149 Breading mixes
PA: Starbucks Corporation
2401 Utah Ave S
Seattle WA 98134
206 447-1575

(P-8807)
BCI COCA-COLA BTLG LOS ANGELES
12925 Bradley Ave, Sylmar (91342-3830)
PHONE..................818 362-4307
Fax: 818 362-7170
Larry Campbell, *Branch Mgr*
Robert Macias, *Branch Mgr*
EMP: 75
SALES (corp-wide): 44.2B **Publicly Held**
SIC: 5149 4225 2086 Soft drinks; general warehousing; bottled & canned soft drinks
HQ: Bci Coca-Cola Bottling Company Of Los Angeles
1334 S Central Ave
Los Angeles CA 90021
213 746-5555

(P-8808)
BIMBO BAKERIES USA INC
Also Called: Oroweat Foods
1220 Howell St, Anaheim (92805)
PHONE..................714 634-8068
Mike Prichard, *General Mgr*
EMP: 60
SALES (corp-wide): 13B **Privately Held**
WEB: www.englishmuffin.com
SIC: 5149 Bakery products
HQ: Bimbo Bakeries Usa, Inc
255 Business Center Dr # 200
Horsham PA 19044
215 347-5500

(P-8809)
BOBOLI INTERNATIONAL LLC (PA)
1718 Boeing Way Ste 100, Stockton (95206-4995)
PHONE..................209 473-3507
Fax: 209 473-0492
Gregory Helland,
Jeffrey Gross, *CFO*
Sheena Delgado, *Accountant*
Julie Pena, *Purchasing*
Angela Rosenquist, *VP Sales*
▲ EMP: 64
SALES (est): 25MM **Privately Held**
WEB: www.boboli-intl.com
SIC: 5149 Sauces; crackers, cookies & bakery products

(P-8810)
BUENA VISTA FOOD PRODUCTS INC
823 W 8th St, Azusa (91702-2247)
PHONE..................626 815-8859
Laura Trujillo, *President*
Corrie Oekawa, *Controller*
Jill Meyers, *Sales Dir*
Peter Woods, *Director*
Silvia Madrid, *Manager*
EMP: 115
SALES (est): 58.6MM **Privately Held**
WEB: www.dvfoods.com
SIC: 5149 Bakery products
HQ: Sterling Foods, Llc
1075 Arion Pkwy
San Antonio TX 78216
210 490-0607

(P-8811)
CALIFORNIA BAKING COMPANY
Also Called: California Bread Co.
681 Anita St, Chula Vista (91911-4663)
PHONE..................619 591-8289
Abraham Levy, *President*
EMP: 300
SALES (est): 25.8MM **Privately Held**
SIC: 5149 2051 Crackers, cookies & bakery products; sponge goods, bakery: except frozen

(P-8812)
CAMPANILE II LP
Also Called: Campanile Restaurant
17001 Ventura Blvd, Encino (91316-4128)
PHONE..................323 939-6813
Fax: 323 938-5840
Lawrence E Silverton, *Partner*
Anthony Cocoran, *CFO*
Rosario Madera, *Human Resources*
EMP: 280
SALES (est): 14.3MM **Privately Held**
SIC: 5149 5812 Bakery products; American restaurant

(P-8813)
CAPITAL BRANDS LLC
11601 Wilshire Blvd Fl 23, Los Angeles (90025-1759)
P.O. Box 4564, Pacoima (91333-4564)
PHONE..................310 996-7200
Leonard Sands, *Mng Member*
Nick Sternberg, *COO*
Mark Suzumoto, *Officer*
Ford Baertlein, *Analyst*
Kelvin Leung, *Analyst*
EMP: 100
SALES (est): 67.7MM **Privately Held**
SIC: 5149 Groceries & related products

(P-8814)
CHOOLJIAN BROS PACKING CO INC
3192 S Indianola Ave, Sanger (93657-9716)
P.O. Box 395 (93657-0395)
PHONE..................559 875-5501
Fax: 559 875-6618

PRODUCTS & SERVICES SECTION
5149 - Groceries & Related Prdts, NEC Wholesale County (P-8838)

Michael Chuoolgin, *CEO*
Sandra Barr, *Vice Pres*
Nicholas Boghosian, *Vice Pres*
Darrell Smith, *Controller*
Bennie Steele, *Controller*
◆ **EMP:** 50
SQ FT: 1,800
SALES (est): 21.9MM **Privately Held**
SIC: 5149 Dried or canned foods

(P-8815)
CMA BAKING CO
28230 Constellation Rd, Santa Clarita (91355-5038)
PHONE.................661 775-0854
Cavin Burgess, *Owner*
Kevin Burgess, *Owner*
EMP: 60
SQ FT: 25,000
SALES (est): 2.8MM **Privately Held**
SIC: 5149 Bakery products

(P-8816)
COLUSA PRODUCE CORPORATION
1954 Progress Rd, Meridian (95957-9643)
PHONE.................530 696-0121
Fax: 530 696-0119
Jim Wallace, *President*
Barbara Overton, *Office Mgr*
◆ **EMP:** 78
SQ FT: 5,000
SALES (est): 16.7MM **Privately Held**
SIC: 5149 5159 5148 Spices & seasonings; broomcorn; fresh fruits & vegetables

(P-8817)
COMPLETE FOOD SERVICE INC
3815 Wabash Dr, Mira Loma (91752-1143)
PHONE.................951 685-8490
Fax: 951 681-7821
Keith Kahn, *President*
Mitchell Kahn, *Vice Pres*
Mark Kahn, *Admin Sec*
EMP: 90
SQ FT: 40,000
SALES (est): 15.9MM **Privately Held**
SIC: 5149 5722 Groceries & related products; sewing machines

(P-8818)
COMPLETELY FRESH FOODS INC
4401 S Downey Rd, Vernon (90058-2518)
P.O. Box 58667, Los Angeles (90058-0667)
PHONE.................323 722-9136
Josh Solovy, *President*
Eric Litmanovich, *Vice Pres*
Levi Litmanovich, *Vice Pres*
Simon Toh, *Controller*
EMP: 200
SQ FT: 15,000
SALES (est): 75.9MM **Privately Held**
SIC: 5149 5046 Specialty food items; commercial cooking & food service equipment

(P-8819)
CORE NUTRITION LLC
630 Clinton Pl, Beverly Hills (90210-1917)
PHONE.................310 424-5077
Lance Collins, *Mng Member*
Christina Kim, *Accountant*
Fred Pinczuk,
EMP: 50
SALES (est): 7.1MM **Privately Held**
SIC: 5149 Mineral or spring water bottling

(P-8820)
CORE NUTRITION LLC
1222 E Grand Ave Ste 102, El Segundo (90245-4219)
PHONE.................310 640-0500
EMP: 50 **EST:** 2014
SALES (est): 4MM **Privately Held**
SIC: 5149 2834

(P-8821)
CORE-MARK INTERNATIONAL INC
200 Coremark Ct, Bakersfield (93307-8402)
P.O. Box 70458 (93387-0458)
PHONE.................661 366-2673
Caral Parker, *President*

EMP: 107
SALES (corp-wide): 11B **Publicly Held**
WEB: www.core-mark.com
SIC: 5149 Groceries & related products
HQ: Core-Mark International, Inc.
395 Oyster Point Blvd # 415
South San Francisco CA 94080
650 589-9445

(P-8822)
CORE-MARK INTERNATIONAL INC
2311 E 48th St, Vernon (90058-2007)
PHONE.................323 583-6531
Fax: 323 589-1828
Julian Puentes, *Branch Mgr*
Kimberly D Banzon, *Human Res Mgr*
Ernie Barney, *Manager*
EMP: 150
SALES (corp-wide): 11B **Publicly Held**
WEB: www.core-mark.com
SIC: 5149 5194 5145 Groceries & related products; tobacco & tobacco products; confectionery
HQ: Core-Mark International, Inc.
395 Oyster Point Blvd # 415
South San Francisco CA 94080
650 589-9445

(P-8823)
CORE-MARK INTERNATIONAL INC
3030 Mulvany Pl, West Sacramento (95691-5745)
PHONE.................916 927-0795
Fax: 916 927-3985
EMP: 150
SQ FT: 25,000
SALES (corp-wide): 10.2B **Publicly Held**
SIC: 5149 5194 5141
HQ: Core-Mark International, Inc.
395 Oyster Point Blvd # 415
South San Francisco CA 94080
650 589-9445

(P-8824)
CORE-MARK INTERNATIONAL INC
31300 Medallion Dr, Hayward (94544-7902)
PHONE.................510 487-3000
Fax: 510 487-3257
Bob Norton, *Manager*
Tom Bayless, *Manager*
EMP: 150
SALES (corp-wide): 11B **Publicly Held**
WEB: www.core-mark.com
SIC: 5149 5194 5145 5141 Groceries & related products; tobacco & tobacco products; confectionery; groceries, general line
HQ: Core-Mark International, Inc.
395 Oyster Point Blvd # 415
South San Francisco CA 94080
650 589-9445

(P-8825)
CORNER BAKERY STORE
1040 W Imperial Hwy Ste A, La Habra (90631-0608)
PHONE.................714 459-1420
Jim Vinz, *CEO*
EMP: 50
SALES (est): 2MM **Privately Held**
SIC: 5149 Bakery products

(P-8826)
CREATIVE ENERGY FOODS INC
9957 Medford Ave Ste 4, Oakland (94603-2360)
PHONE.................510 638-8668
Richard C Dwinell, *CEO*
George Jewell, *President*
Jacker Wong, *CFO*
Wesley Felton, *Principal*
Sue Yim, *Accountant*
▲ **EMP:** 95
SQ FT: 105,000
SALES (est): 59.2MM **Privately Held**
WEB: www.energybar.com
SIC: 5149 2026 Health foods; dips, sour cream based

(P-8827)
CULINARY HISPANIC FOODS INC
Also Called: Productos Chata
805 Bow St, Chula Vista (91914)
PHONE.................619 955-6101
Jorge Aguilar, *CEO*
Carlos Machado, *Principal*
▲ **EMP:** 1458
SQ FT: 4,000
SALES: 1MM **Privately Held**
SIC: 5149 Canned goods: fruit, vegetables, seafood, meats, etc.

(P-8828)
DS SERVICES OF AMERICA INC
Also Called: Alhambra
2217 Revere Ave, San Francisco (94124-1925)
PHONE.................415 282-1060
Phil Holden, *Manager*
Al Wong, *Director*
EMP: 50
SQ FT: 1,662
SALES (corp-wide): 2.9B **Privately Held**
WEB: www.suntorywatergroup.com
SIC: 5149 Water, distilled
HQ: Ds Services Of America, Inc.
2300 Windy Ridge Pkwy Se 500n
Atlanta GA 30339
770 933-1400

(P-8829)
DS SERVICES OF AMERICA INC
Also Called: Sparkletts
7817 Haskell Ave, Van Nuys (91406-1908)
PHONE.................818 787-9397
Frank Lubich, *Branch Mgr*
EMP: 70
SQ FT: 5,805
SALES (corp-wide): 2.9B **Privately Held**
WEB: www.suntorywatergroup.com
SIC: 5149 7389 Water, distilled; coffee service
HQ: Ds Services Of America, Inc.
2300 Windy Ridge Pkwy Se 500n
Atlanta GA 30339
770 933-1400

(P-8830)
DS SERVICES OF AMERICA INC
Also Called: Sparkletts
4548 Azusa Canyon Rd, Irwindale (91706-2742)
PHONE.................626 472-7201
Linda Gonzales, *Manager*
Frank Guercio, *Opers Mgr*
EMP: 200
SQ FT: 67,508
SALES (corp-wide): 2.9B **Privately Held**
WEB: www.suntorywatergroup.com
SIC: 5149 5963 Water, distilled; direct selling establishments
HQ: Ds Services Of America, Inc.
2300 Windy Ridge Pkwy Se 500n
Atlanta GA 30339
770 933-1400

(P-8831)
EARLS ORGANIC
Also Called: Earl's Organic Produce
2101 Jerrold Ave Ste 100, San Francisco (94124-1009)
PHONE.................415 824-7419
Fax: 415 824-7819
Earl Herrick, *Principal*
Fannie Alexander, *Human Res Mgr*
Patrick Stewart, *Sales Mgr*
Mike Stewart, *Sales Associate*
Christal Biddle, *Manager*
▲ **EMP:** 78
SALES: 50MM **Privately Held**
SIC: 5149 Natural & organic foods

(P-8832)
EL GUAPO SPICES INC (PA)
Also Called: El Guapo Spices and Herbs Pkg
6200 E Slauson Ave, Commerce (90040-3012)
PHONE.................213 312-1300
Dan Terrazas, *President*
EMP: 100
SALES (est): 11.8MM **Privately Held**
SIC: 5149 Spices & seasonings

(P-8833)
ENERGIZED DISTRIBUTION LLC
8435 Eastern Ave, Bell Gardens (90201-6116)
PHONE.................562 319-0232
Patrick J Drnec, *Mng Member*
William Juarez, *General Mgr*
Colleen Sleeper, *Finance Dir*
Joe Johnson, *Sales Mgr*
▲ **EMP:** 156
SQ FT: 48,000
SALES (est): 7.9MM **Privately Held**
SIC: 5149 Groceries & related products

(P-8834)
FALCON TRADING COMPANY (PA)
Also Called: Sunridge Farms
423 Salinas Rd, Royal Oaks (95076-5232)
PHONE.................831 786-7000
Fax: 831 763-6900
Morty Cohen, *CEO*
Rebecca Cohen, *Vice Pres*
Maria Marsilio, *Executive*
Darshan Siegman, *Executive*
Ron Giannini, *General Mgr*
▲ **EMP:** 150
SQ FT: 24,500
SALES (est): 169MM **Privately Held**
WEB: www.sunridgefarms.com
SIC: 5149 Natural & organic foods

(P-8835)
FAMOUS RAMONA WATER INC
250 Aqua Ln, Ramona (92065-2024)
P.O. Box 1195 (92065-0860)
PHONE.................760 789-0174
Fax: 760 789-1066
Julian C Filer, *CEO*
Joe Bruni, *President*
Mark Filer, *Vice Pres*
Debbie Bruni, *Admin Sec*
EMP: 50
SQ FT: 48,000
SALES (est): 14.2MM **Privately Held**
WEB: www.famousramonawater.com
SIC: 5149 5085 Mineral or spring water bottling; commercial containers

(P-8836)
FIJI WATER COMPANY LLC (HQ)
11444 W Olympic Blvd # 250, Los Angeles (90064-1534)
PHONE.................310 966-5700
Fax: 310 312-2828
Stewart A Resnick, *Ch of Bd*
Kim Katzenberger, *CFO*
William Foltz, *Senior VP*
Richard Krawiec, *Vice Pres*
Rich Chmilarski, *Executive*
◆ **EMP:** 50
SQ FT: 12,000
SALES (est): 29.4MM
SALES (corp-wide): 61.3MM **Privately Held**
WEB: www.fijiwater.com
SIC: 5149 Mineral or spring water bottling
PA: Roll Properties International, Inc.
11444 W Olympic Blvd # 10
Los Angeles CA 90064
310 966-5700

(P-8837)
FRESH GRILL LLC
111 E Garry Ave, Santa Ana (92707-4201)
PHONE.................714 444-2126
Jeff Heavirland, *Mng Member*
Phil Abreo, *Sales Dir*
▲ **EMP:** 200
SQ FT: 27,000
SALES (est): 80.7MM **Privately Held**
WEB: www.freshgrillfoods.com
SIC: 5149 8742 Specialty food items; food & beverage consultant

(P-8838)
FRESHOLOGY INC
10950 Sherman Way Ste 140, Burbank (91505-1077)
PHONE.................818 847-1888
Todd Demann, *Principal*
Trevor Smith, *CFO*
Rana Mansour, *Vice Pres*
Paul Pichler, *CTO*
Dana Giammaria, *Consultant*
▲ **EMP:** 71

5149 - Groceries & Related Prdts, NEC Wholesale County (P-8839) **PRODUCTS & SERVICES SECTION**

SQ FT: 15,500
SALES (est): 19.3MM **Privately Held**
WEB: www.freshology.com/
SIC: 5149 Diet foods

(P-8839)
FUJI FOOD PRODUCTS INC
8660 Miramar Rd Ste N, San Diego (92126-4362)
PHONE.....................619 268-3118
Kenny Sung, *Branch Mgr*
EMP: 125
SALES (corp-wide): 184.7MM **Privately Held**
WEB: www.fujifood.com
SIC: 5149 Groceries & related products
PA: Fuji Food Products, Inc.
  14420 Bloomfield Ave
  Santa Fe Springs CA 90670
  562 404-2590

(P-8840)
GANO EXCEL (USA) INC
4828 4th St, Irwindale (91706-2191)
P.O. Box 9275, Glendale (91226-0275)
PHONE.....................626 338-8081
Chin Iakooi, *CEO*
Ruben Cardenas, *President*
Bernard Chua, *President*
Soon Seng Leow, *President*
Chang Ching Lew, *Treasurer*
▲ EMP: 67
SQ FT: 3,216
SALES: 18MM **Privately Held**
SIC: 5149 Coffee, green or roasted; coffee & tea

(P-8841)
GIANNAS BAKING COMPANY
11165 Commercial Pkwy, Castroville (95012-3207)
PHONE.....................831 633-3700
Peter Uli, *President*
EMP: 54
SALES (est): 10.4MM **Privately Held**
WEB: www.giannas.com
SIC: 5149 Bakery products

(P-8842)
GLOBAL BAKERIES INC
13336 Paxton St, Pacoima (91331-2339)
PHONE.....................818 896-0525
Fax: 818 896-3237
Albert Boyajian, *President*
▲ EMP: 60
SQ FT: 44,000
SALES (est): 19.7MM **Privately Held**
WEB: www.globalbakeriesinc.com
SIC: 5149 Bakery products

(P-8843)
GOGLANIAN BAKERIES INC (HQ)
3401 W Segerstrom Ave, Santa Ana (92704-6404)
PHONE.....................714 549-1524
Fax: 714 444-3800
William G Gisel, *CEO*
Albert Altro, *CFO*
William Goodlet, *Chief Engr*
Norma Fernandez, *Controller*
Cindy Williams, *Human Res Dir*
◆ EMP: 300
SQ FT: 71,500
SALES (est): 502.4MM
SALES (corp-wide): 3.5B **Privately Held**
WEB: www.goglanian.com
SIC: 5149 Bakery products
PA: Rich Products Corporation
  1 Robert Rich Way
  Buffalo NY 14213
  716 878-8422

(P-8844)
GOLD COAST INGREDIENTS INC
2429 Yates Ave, Commerce (90040-1917)
PHONE.....................323 724-8935
Fax: 323 724-9354
Clarence H Brasher, *CEO*
James A Sgro, *President*
Laurie Goddard, *Vice Pres*
Karyna Flood, *Research*
Nancy Boehm, *Human Res Mgr*
▲ EMP: 53
SQ FT: 50,000

SALES (est): 37MM **Privately Held**
WEB: www.goldcoastinc.com
SIC: 5149 2087 Baking supplies; flavourings & fragrances; flavoring extracts & syrups

(P-8845)
GOLD RUSH COFFEE
3864 Lighthouse Rd, Petrolia (95558)
P.O. Box 58 (95558-0058)
PHONE.....................707 629-3460
Fax: 707 629-3595
Karen Paff, *Owner*
EMP: 50
SALES: 1.5MM **Privately Held**
SIC: 5149 2095 5499 Coffee, green or roasted; coffee roasting (except by wholesale grocers); coffee

(P-8846)
GOLDA & I CHOCOLATIERS INC
23052 Alicia Pkwy Ste H, Mission Viejo (92692-1661)
PHONE.....................949 660-9581
Fax: 949 660-0161
Golda Imbernino, *President*
Mary Anne Osier, *Owner*
EMP: 55
SQ FT: 3,000
SALES (est): 6.5MM **Privately Held**
WEB: www.crowncityconfections.com
SIC: 5149 Chocolate

(P-8847)
GOLDEN CRUST BAKERIES INC
25170 Anza Dr, Santa Clarita (91355-3415)
PHONE.....................661 294-9750
Fax: 661 294-9752
Albert F Mawad, *CEO*
EMP: 52
SALES (est): 6.4MM **Privately Held**
SIC: 5149 Bakery products

(P-8848)
GOURMET INDIA FOOD COMPANY LLC
12220 Rivera Rd Ste A, Whittier (90606-6206)
PHONE.....................562 698-9763
Fax: 562 698-1894
Sam Jeevan,
Saleem Hai,
▲ EMP: 75
SALES (est): 14.2MM **Privately Held**
SIC: 5149 Bakery products

(P-8849)
GOURMETS FRESH PASTA
950 N Fair Oaks Ave, Pasadena (91103-3009)
PHONE.....................626 798-0841
Fax: 626 798-3591
Michael A Yagjian, *President*
William J Cullinane Jr, *Vice Pres*
William Coulvane, *Admin Mgr*
Peggy Flores, *Human Res Mgr*
Bill Cullinane, *Safety Mgr*
▲ EMP: 65
SQ FT: 30,000
SALES (est): 20.6MM **Privately Held**
WEB: www.gourmetpasta.com
SIC: 5149 5812 Pasta & rice; eating places

(P-8850)
HARRIS FREEMAN & CO INC (PA)
Also Called: Harris Tea Company
3110 E Miraloma Ave, Anaheim (92806-1906)
PHONE.....................714 765-1190
Fax: 714 765-1199
Anil J Shah, *CEO*
Kevin Shah, *President*
Meena Shah, *Treasurer*
Edith Espitia, *Administration*
Phoung Nguyen, *Controller*
◆ EMP: 500
SQ FT: 58,000
SALES (est): 272.7MM **Privately Held**
SIC: 5149 2099 Coffee & tea; spices, including grinding

(P-8851)
HEALTH VALLEY FOODS INC
16007 Cmino De La Cantera, Irwindale (91702)
PHONE.....................626 334-3241
Fax: 626 334-0220
Irwin Simon, *President*
▲ EMP: 300
SALES (est): 18.2MM
SALES (corp-wide): 2.6B **Publicly Held**
WEB: www.hain-celestial.com
SIC: 5149 Health foods; natural & organic foods
PA: The Hain Celestial Group Inc
  1111 Marcus Ave Ste 100
  New Hyde Park NY 11042
  516 587-5000

(P-8852)
HILLSHIRE BRANDS COMPANY
Also Called: Superior Coffee & Foods
10715 Springdale Ave # 5, Santa Fe Springs (90670-3858)
PHONE.....................562 903-9260
Fax: 562 903-9266
Kevin Mc Klavende, *Branch Mgr*
EMP: 50
SALES (corp-wide): 41.3B **Publicly Held**
SIC: 5149 Coffee & tea
HQ: The Hillshire Brands Company
  400 S Jefferson St Fl 1
  Chicago IL 60607
  312 614-6000

(P-8853)
HORIZON BEVERAGE COMPANY LP
8380 Pardee Dr, Oakland (94621-1481)
P.O. Box 6639 (94603-0639)
PHONE.....................510 465-2212
Fax: 510 835-5956
Gary Shinn,
Mike Thomas, *President*
Paul Wong, *CFO*
James Tsiumis, *Senior VP*
Sam Cappione, *General Mgr*
▲ EMP: 94
SALES (est): 26.8MM **Privately Held**
SIC: 5149 Groceries & related products

(P-8854)
INTERBAKE FOODS LLC
Also Called: Norse Dairy Systems
1910 W Temple St, Los Angeles (90026-4929)
P.O. Box 26338 (90026-0338)
PHONE.....................213 484-8161
Randy Obrien, *Branch Mgr*
Jack Frysvtak, *Plant Mgr*
EMP: 60
SALES (corp-wide): 35.2B **Privately Held**
WEB: www.interbake.com
SIC: 5149 Bakery products
HQ: Interbake Foods Llc
  3951 Westerre Pkwy # 200
  Henrico VA 23233
  804 755-7107

(P-8855)
INTERNATIONAL DELICACIES
2100 Atlas Rd Ste F, Richmond (94806-1100)
PHONE.....................510 669-2444
Fax: 510 669-2446
Hossein Banejad, *CEO*
Ruth Banejad, *CFO*
Dean Wilkinson, *Vice Pres*
Abu Taghizadeh, *VP Sales*
▲ EMP: 50
SQ FT: 45,000
SALES: 60MM **Privately Held**
WEB: www.internationaldelicacies.net
SIC: 5149 Pasta & rice; cookies; fruits, dried; cooking oils

(P-8856)
IONICS ALTRPURE WTR CRPARATION
Also Called: Apollo Cpr
7777 Industry Ave, Pico Rivera (90660-4303)
PHONE.....................562 948-2188
Winston Mar, *Vice Pres*
Michael Wilbanks, *Vice Pres*
Michael Dimick, *Branch Mgr*

Linwood Dawley, *Plant Mgr*
Prentice Hall, *Agent*
EMP: 95
SQ FT: 12,000
SALES (est): 7.4MM **Privately Held**
SIC: 5149 5999 Mineral or spring water bottling; water purification equipment

(P-8857)
ITALFOODS INC
205 Shaw Rd, South San Francisco (94080-6605)
P.O. Box 2563 (94083-2563)
PHONE.....................650 873-2640
Fax: 650 871-9437
Walter J Guerra, *CEO*
Georgette Guerra, *Corp Secy*
Aldo Guazzelli, *Chief Mktg Ofcr*
Donald Raphael, *General Mgr*
Dan Ginn, *Human Res Mgr*
▲ EMP: 80 EST: 1978
SQ FT: 114,000
SALES (est): 39.9MM **Privately Held**
WEB: www.italfoods.com
SIC: 5149 Specialty food items

(P-8858)
J & D MEAT COMPANY
Also Called: JD Food
4586 E Commerce Ave, Fresno (93725-2203)
P.O. Box 12051 (93776-2051)
PHONE.....................559 445-1123
Fax: 559 445-1044
Mark K Ford, *President*
Robert Maxey, *Vice Pres*
Ken Ford, *Principal*
Jim Maxey, *Principal*
Steven Maxey, *Admin Sec*
EMP: 72
SQ FT: 51,000
SALES (est): 80.1MM **Privately Held**
WEB: www.jdfoodservice.com
SIC: 5149 5147 5148 5143 Groceries & related products; meats & meat products; fresh fruits & vegetables; dairy products, except dried or canned; packaged frozen goods

(P-8859)
JACMAR DDC LLC
Also Called: Jacmar Food Service Dist
3057 Promenade St, West Sacramento (95691-5941)
PHONE.....................916 372-9795
Fax: 916 372-1765
James A Dalpozzo, *Mng Member*
Orlando Andrade, *General Mgr*
Darlene Rigney, *Purch Mgr*
David Reid,
Sarah Hodge, *Accounts Mgr*
EMP: 55
SQ FT: 100,000
SALES (est): 24.7MM
SALES (corp-wide): 699.3MM **Privately Held**
WEB: www.jacmar.com
SIC: 5149 Natural & organic foods
PA: The Jacmar Companies
  300 Baldwin Park Blvd
  City Of Industry CA 91746
  800 834-8806

(P-8860)
JAGPREET ENTERPRISES INC
Also Called: Quick-N-Ezee Indian Foods
25823 Clawiter Rd, Hayward (94545-3217)
PHONE.....................510 336-8376
Fax: 510 782-5500
Sukhjeet K Singh, *CEO*
Surinder Singh, *President*
Sanjog Sikand, *Marketing Staff*
Bandana Chimni, *Director*
Dalbir Singh, *Director*
▲ EMP: 150
SQ FT: 30,000
SALES (est): 69.7MM **Privately Held**
WEB: www.sukhis.com
SIC: 5149 Groceries & related products

▲ = Import ▼=Export
◆ =Import/Export

5149 - Groceries & Related Prdts, NEC Wholesale County (P-8884)

(P-8861)
JFC INTERNATIONAL INC (HQ)
7101 E Slauson Ave, Commerce (90040-3622)
P.O. Box 875349, Los Angeles (90087-0449)
PHONE....................323 721-6100
Yoshiyuki Ishigaki, *CEO*
Hiroyuki Enomoto, *President*
Masanori Takenaka, *Vice Pres*
Masashi Inoue, *Financial Exec*
Van Vuong, *Accountant*
◆ **EMP:** 203 **EST:** 1958
SALES (est): 322.9MM
SALES (corp-wide): 3.4B **Privately Held**
WEB: www.jfc.com
SIC: 5149 Specialty food items
PA: Kikkoman Corporation
2-1-1, Nishishimbashi
Minato-Ku TKY 105-0
355 215-131

(P-8862)
JOHNS DOG FOOD DISTRIBUTING
Also Called: John's Pet Products
1633 Monterey Hwy, San Jose (95112-6111)
PHONE....................408 275-1943
Johnannes G Rademakers, *Owner*
Lori Allander, *Vice Pres*
EMP: 60 **EST:** 1970
SQ FT: 7,000
SALES (est): 3MM **Privately Held**
SIC: 5149 5999 Pet foods; pet supplies

(P-8863)
K T LUCKY CO INC
10925 Schmidt Rd, El Monte (91733-2707)
PHONE....................626 579-7272
Fax: 626 579-1515
Hang Huynh, *President*
▲ **EMP:** 70
SQ FT: 12,000
SALES (est): 11.9MM **Privately Held**
SIC: 5149 Macaroni; rice, polished

(P-8864)
KDK MANAGEMENT INC
15215 Keswick St, Van Nuys (91405-1014)
PHONE....................818 786-1700
David Kay, *President*
EMP: 70
SALES (est): 8MM **Privately Held**
SIC: 5149 Bakery products

(P-8865)
KEHE DISTRIBUTORS LLC
6 Pointe Dr Ste 300, Brea (92821-6323)
PHONE....................714 255-4600
Brandon Barnholt, *President*
EMP: 360
SALES (corp-wide): 3.4B **Privately Held**
SIC: 5149 Health foods
PA: Kehe Distributors, Llc
1245 E Diehl Rd Ste 200
Naperville IL 60563
630 343-0000

(P-8866)
KELLOGG SALES COMPANY
300 Harding Blvd Ste 215, Roseville (95678-2474)
PHONE....................916 787-0414
Shawn Snyder, *Principal*
EMP: 50
SALES (corp-wide): 13.5B **Publicly Held**
WEB: www.kellogg.com
SIC: 5149 Breakfast cereals
HQ: Kellogg Sales Company
1 Kellogg Sq
Battle Creek MI 49017
269 961-2000

(P-8867)
KEVALA INTERNATIONAL LLC
5349 Zambrano St, Commerce (90040-3037)
P.O. Box 6902 Alissa St, Rowlett TX (75089)
PHONE....................210 767-3324
Gerardo Rodriguez, *Opers Staff*
Carlos Rodriguez,
▲ **EMP:** 50
SALES (est): 4.2MM **Privately Held**
SIC: 5149 5169 Honey; oil additives

(P-8868)
KRADJIAN IMPORTING COMPANY INC (PA)
5018 San Fernando Rd, Glendale (91204-1114)
PHONE....................818 502-1313
Fax: 818 502-0546
Raffi Kradjian, *President*
Viken Kradjian, *Vice Pres*
Ram Sethuram, *Controller*
◆ **EMP:** 59
SQ FT: 50,000
SALES (est): 52.2MM **Privately Held**
SIC: 5149 Groceries & related products

(P-8869)
KRAFT HEINZ FOODS COMPANY
5000 Hopyard Rd Ste 235, Pleasanton (94588-3314)
PHONE....................925 469-0057
Fax: 925 469-0537
Carroll Wine, *Branch Mgr*
EMP: 50
SALES (corp-wide): 210.8B **Publicly Held**
SIC: 5149 Groceries & related products
HQ: Heinz Kraft Foods Company
1 Ppg Pl Ste 3200
Pittsburgh PA 15222
412 456-5700

(P-8870)
KRAFT HEINZ FOODS COMPANY
1055 E North Ave, Fresno (93725-1914)
PHONE....................559 499-5300
Tony Lacerva, *General Mgr*
EMP: 50
SALES (corp-wide): 210.8B **Publicly Held**
WEB: www.kraftfoods.com
SIC: 5149 Groceries & related products
HQ: Heinz Kraft Foods Company
1 Ppg Pl Ste 3200
Pittsburgh PA 15222
412 456-5700

(P-8871)
KRONOS FOODS CORP
Also Called: Rain Creek Baking
2401 W Almond Ave, Madera (93637-4807)
PHONE....................559 674-4445
Michael Austin, *CEO*
EMP: 75
SALES (corp-wide): 104.9MM **Privately Held**
SIC: 5149 Bakery products
PA: Kronos Foods Corp.
1 Kronos
Glendale Heights IL 60139
773 847-2250

(P-8872)
LA FLOR DE MEXICO INC (PA)
Also Called: La Flor De Mexico Bakery
5121 Commerce Dr, Baldwin Park (91706-1451)
PHONE....................626 334-0716
Fax: 626 334-1796
Michael Esquivel, *President*
Irene Esquivel, *Vice Pres*
Susan Kay, *QA Dir*
Ray Joya, *Director*
EMP: 52
SQ FT: 14,500
SALES (est): 28.4MM **Privately Held**
SIC: 5149 5461 5411 5812 Bakery products; bakeries; pastries; grocery stores, independent; Mexican restaurant

(P-8873)
LA PROVENCE INC
Also Called: La Provence Bakery
1370 W San Marcos Blvd # 130, San Marcos (92078-1601)
PHONE....................760 736-3299
Fax: 760 736-3296
Philip Dardaine, *CEO*
Julie Welard, *CFO*
Karen Dardaine, *Corp Secy*
Thierry Bouchereau, *Vice Pres*
Lynn Heller, *Controller*
EMP: 60
SQ FT: 6,000
SALES (est): 15.8MM **Privately Held**
SIC: 5149 Bakery products

(P-8874)
LA TORTILLA FACTORY INC (PA)
3300 Westwind Blvd, Santa Rosa (95403-8273)
PHONE....................707 586-4000
Samuel Carlos Tamayo, *CEO*
Carlos G Tamayo, *President*
Carlos Tamayo, *President*
Dave Davis, *COO*
David Trogdon, *CFO*
EMP: 280 **EST:** 1977
SALES (est): 151.9MM **Privately Held**
WEB: www.latortillafactory.com
SIC: 5149 2051 Specialty food items; bakery products; bread, cake & related products

(P-8875)
LENORE JOHN & CO (PA)
1250 Delevan Dr, San Diego (92102-2437)
PHONE....................619 232-6136
Fax: 619 232-8004
John G Lenore, *CEO*
Jamie Lenore, *President*
Julio R Hernandez, *Administration*
Doris Anthony, *Human Res Dir*
Gary Stalians, *Manager*
▲ **EMP:** 120
SQ FT: 50,000
SALES (est): 143.9MM **Privately Held**
WEB: www.johnlenore.com
SIC: 5149 5182 5181 Soft drinks; mineral or spring water bottling; wine; liquor; beer & other fermented malt liquors

(P-8876)
MHH HOLDINGS INC
5653 Alton Pkwy, Irvine (92618-4058)
PHONE....................949 651-9903
Fax: 949 651-9912
Cynthia Espere, *Branch Mgr*
EMP: 103
SALES (corp-wide): 74.3MM **Privately Held**
SIC: 5149 Tea
PA: Mhh Holdings, Inc.
4580 Calle Alto
Camarillo CA 93012
805 484-7924

(P-8877)
MHH HOLDINGS INC
415 S Lake Ave Ste 108, Pasadena (91101-5047)
PHONE....................626 744-9370
Fax: 626 744-9348
Xiomara Bellido, *Principal*
EMP: 68
SALES (corp-wide): 74.3MM **Privately Held**
SIC: 5149 Tea
PA: Mhh Holdings, Inc.
4580 Calle Alto
Camarillo CA 93012
805 484-7924

(P-8878)
MIGHTY LEAF TEA
100 Smith Ranch Rd # 120, San Rafael (94903-1979)
PHONE....................415 491-2650
Shiela Stanziale, *Principal*
Jill Portman, *President*
Bliss Dake, *Vice Pres*
Joane Filler-Varty, *Vice Pres*
Brian Jenkins, *Mktg Coord*
▲ **EMP:** 65
SQ FT: 5,000
SALES (est): 42.5MM
SALES (corp-wide): 2.1B **Privately Held**
WEB: www.mightyleaf.com
SIC: 5149 5499 Tea; tea
HQ: Peet's Coffee & Tea, Llc
1400 Park Ave
Emeryville CA 94608
510 594-2100

(P-8879)
MONDELEZ GLOBAL LLC
Also Called: Nabisco
5815 Clark St, Ontario (91761-3676)
PHONE....................909 605-0140
Fax: 909 605-0199
Botie Magee, *Branch Mgr*
EMP: 70
SALES (corp-wide): 29.6B **Publicly Held**
WEB: www.kraftfoods.com
SIC: 5149 2099 2052 Crackers, cookies & bakery products; food preparations; cookies & crackers
HQ: Mondelez Global Llc
3 Parkway N Ste 300
Deerfield IL 60015
847 943-4000

(P-8880)
MONSTER ENERGY COMPANY (DH)
1 Monster Way, Corona (92879-7101)
PHONE....................951 739-6200
Fax: 951 739-6210
Rodney C Sacks, *CEO*
Hilton H Scholsberg, *Vice Ch Bd*
Gareth Bowen, *Senior VP*
Steve Edgar, *Vice Pres*
Ron Kane, *Vice Pres*
▼ **EMP:** 153
SQ FT: 300,000
SALES (est): 1B
SALES (corp-wide): 2.7B **Publicly Held**
WEB: www.hansens.com
SIC: 5149 Juices; soft drinks
HQ: Monster Beverage 1990 Corporation
1 Monster Way
Corona CA 92879
951 739-6200

(P-8881)
MUTUAL TRADING CO INC (PA)
Also Called: M T C
431 Crocker St, Los Angeles (90013-2180)
PHONE....................213 626-9458
Fax: 213 626-5130
Kosei Yamamoto, *CEO*
Noritoshi Kanai, *President*
Seicho Fujikawa, *Vice Pres*
Kotaro Hoshizaki, *Principal*
Keita Scarola, *Info Tech Dir*
◆ **EMP:** 105
SQ FT: 100,000
SALES (est): 86.1MM **Privately Held**
WEB: www.lamtc.com
SIC: 5149 5141 5023 Groceries & related products; groceries, general line; home furnishings

(P-8882)
NAKED INFUSIONS LLC
23679 Calabasas Rd 305, Calabasas (91302-1502)
P.O. Box 23679 Cala (91302)
PHONE....................818 239-9058
Selene Kepila, *CEO*
EMP: 75 **EST:** 2013
SQ FT: 3,600
SALES: 1.1MM **Privately Held**
SIC: 5149 Organic & diet foods; specialty food items

(P-8883)
NATURES BEST DISTRIBUTION LLC
6 Pointe Dr Ste 300, Brea (92821-6323)
P.O. Box 2248 (92822-2248)
PHONE....................714 255-4600
Fax: 714 441-2330
James Beck, *CEO*
Monique Alonzo, *Administration*
Hai Pham, *Graphic Designe*
Maritza Corrales, *Human Resources*
Andrew Kim, *Purchasing*
EMP: 126 **EST:** 2014
SALES (est): 161.7MM
SALES (corp-wide): 3.4B **Privately Held**
SIC: 5149 Health foods
PA: Kehe Distributors, Llc
1245 E Diehl Rd Ste 200
Naperville IL 60563
630 343-0000

(P-8884)
NAVITAS LLC
Also Called: Navitas Naturals
15 Pamaron Way, Novato (94949-6231)
PHONE....................415 883-8116
Zachary Adelman, *Mng Member*
▲ **EMP:** 50
SALES (est): 20.8MM **Privately Held**
WEB: www.navitasnaturals.com
SIC: 5149 Health foods

5149 - Groceries & Related Prdts, NEC Wholesale County (P-8885)

PRODUCTS & SERVICES SECTION

(P-8885)
NESTLE WATERS NORTH AMER INC
Also Called: Arrowhead Water
619 N Main St, Orange (92868-1103)
PHONE.................................714 532-6220
Fax: 714 639-9471
Dan Miller, *Sales/Mktg Mgr*
EMP: 135
SQ FT: 16,312
SALES (corp-wide): 88.3B **Privately Held**
WEB: www.zephyronline.com
SIC: 5149 5499 5963 5078 Water, distilled; water; distilled mineral or spring; bottled water delivery; refrigeration equipment & supplies; plumbing & hydronic heating supplies
HQ: Nestle Waters North America Inc.
900 Long Ridge Rd Bldg 2
Stamford CT 06902
203 531-4100

(P-8886)
NESTLE WATERS NORTH AMER INC
Also Called: Arrowhead Mountain Spring Wtr
4250 Baldwin Ave, El Monte (91731-1102)
PHONE.................................626 443-3236
Jeff Kuriel, *Manager*
EMP: 100
SQ FT: 15,720
SALES (corp-wide): 88.3B **Privately Held**
WEB: www.zephyronline.com
SIC: 5149 Mineral or spring water bottling
HQ: Nestle Waters North America Inc.
900 Long Ridge Rd Bldg 2
Stamford CT 06902
203 531-4100

(P-8887)
NESTLE WATERS NORTH AMER INC
Also Called: Arrowhead Mountain Spring Wtr
1544 E Washington Blvd, Los Angeles (90021-3130)
PHONE.................................213 763-1380
Manuel Chaidez, *Manager*
EMP: 100
SALES (corp-wide): 88.3B **Privately Held**
WEB: www.zephyronline.com
SIC: 5149 Water, distilled
HQ: Nestle Waters North America Inc.
900 Long Ridge Rd Bldg 2
Stamford CT 06902
203 531-4100

(P-8888)
NESTLE WATERS NORTH AMER INC
7480 Las Positas Rd, Livermore (94551-5115)
PHONE.................................925 294-7720
Bill Klink, *Branch Mgr*
EMP: 60
SALES (corp-wide): 88.3B **Privately Held**
WEB: www.zephyronline.com
SIC: 5149 Mineral or spring water bottling
HQ: Nestle Waters North America Inc.
900 Long Ridge Rd Bldg 2
Stamford CT 06902
203 531-4100

(P-8889)
NESTLE WATERS NORTH AMER INC
Also Called: Arrowhead Mountain Spring Wtr
3230 E Imperial Hwy # 100, Brea (92821-6735)
PHONE.................................714 792-2100
Fax: 714 792-0711
Ed Forrest, *Manager*
David Martinez, *General Mgr*
David Nowell, *Opers Mgr*
EMP: 100
SQ FT: 90,000
SALES (corp-wide): 88.3B **Privately Held**
WEB: www.zephyronline.com
SIC: 5149 Mineral or spring water bottling
HQ: Nestle Waters North America Inc.
900 Long Ridge Rd Bldg 2
Stamford CT 06902
203 531-4100

(P-8890)
NEUROBRANDS LLC
Also Called: Neuro Drinks
2550 N Hollywood Way # 100, Burbank (91505-5015)
PHONE.................................310 393-6444
Diana Jenkins, *CEO*
Calvin Larsen, *Info Tech Dir*
Joe Martin, *Accounting Mgr*
Ron Leblanc, *Regl Sales Mgr*
Sean White, *Regl Sales Mgr*
▲ **EMP:** 125
SALES (est): 65.3MM **Privately Held**
SIC: 5149 Soft drinks

(P-8891)
NEW DESSERTS INC
Also Called: Just Desserts
5000 Fulton Dr, Fairfield (94534-1677)
PHONE.................................415 780-6860
Fax: 510 567-2901
Michael Mendes, *CEO*
Leilani Muller, *CFO*
Terry Watson, *Vice Pres*
Marc Cabi, *Technology*
Leighton Mue, *VP Finance*
EMP: 93
SQ FT: 73,500
SALES (est): 61.5MM **Privately Held**
SIC: 5149 2024 Bakery products; ice cream & frozen desserts

(P-8892)
NGS GROUP INC
4152 W Washington Blvd, Los Angeles (90018-1054)
PHONE.................................323 735-1700
Steven Ngu, *President*
Jenny Neo, *Office Mgr*
Stephanie Ngy, *Admin Asst*
EMP: 54
SQ FT: 1,500
SALES (est): 6.6MM **Privately Held**
WEB: www.pacificfrenchbakery.com
SIC: 5149 Bakery products

(P-8893)
NICOLA INTERNATIONAL INC
11119 Dora St, Sun Valley (91352-3339)
PHONE.................................818 767-1133
Nicola Khachatoorian, *President*
Adik Khachatoorian, *Corp Secy*
Alice Toomanian, *Exec VP*
▲ **EMP:** 125
SQ FT: 150,000
SALES (est): 10.7MM **Privately Held**
WEB: www.nicolainternational.com
SIC: 5149 5148 Cooking oils & shortenings; vegetables

(P-8894)
NOWHER PARTNERS LLC
Also Called: Erewhon Natural Foods Market
26767 Agoura Rd Ste A, Calabasas (91302-1992)
PHONE.................................818 857-3366
Victor Grenner, *Branch Mgr*
EMP: 100
SALES (corp-wide): 17.8MM **Privately Held**
SIC: 5149 Natural & organic foods
PA: Nowher Partners Llc
7600 Beverly Blvd
Los Angeles CA 90036
818 857-3366

(P-8895)
ORWICK FRESH FOODS INC
7940 Cherry Ave Ste 203, Fontana (92336-4021)
PHONE.................................909 985-5604
Richard V Orwick, *President*
EMP: 50 **EST:** 2000
SALES (est): 9.3MM **Privately Held**
SIC: 5149 Groceries & related products

(P-8896)
PACIFIC FOODS & DIST INC
3431 W Carriage Dr, Santa Ana (92704-6411)
PHONE.................................714 547-0787
James H Loftus Jr, *President*
Janet Baker, *Controller*
Michael Robledo, *Opers Mgr*
Dave Pellegrini, *VP Sls/Mktg*
EMP: 100
SALES (est): 35.2MM **Privately Held**
WEB: www.pacificfoodsdistribution.com
SIC: 5149 Bakery products

(P-8897)
PASADENA BAKING CO
70 W Pal Meto Ave, Pasadena (91105)
PHONE.................................626 796-5093
Fax: 626 796-0081
Armen Shirvanvian, *Partner*
Akis Markoutsis, *Partner*
Gonzalo Wieler, *Sales Mgr*
EMP: 50
SQ FT: 10,000
SALES (est): 7.9MM **Privately Held**
WEB: www.pasadenabaking.com
SIC: 5149 Bakery products

(P-8898)
PASTA SHOP (PA)
Also Called: Market Hall Foods
5655 College Ave Ste 201, Oakland (94618-1583)
PHONE.................................510 250-6005
Fax: 510 601-8251
Sara Wilson, *Managing Prtnr*
Anthony Wilson, *Partner*
Peter Wilson, *Partner*
Nel Da Silva, *Executive*
Gustavo Houghton, *Controller*
▲ **EMP:** 80
SQ FT: 4,500
SALES (est): 63.8MM **Privately Held**
WEB: www.rockridgemarkethall.com
SIC: 5149 5411 5812 5431 Pasta & rice; delicatessens; caterers; fruit & vegetable markets

(P-8899)
PEPSI-COLA METRO BTLG CO INC
3029 Coffey Ln, Santa Rosa (95403-2513)
PHONE.................................707 535-4560
Fax: 707 535-4561
Brad Pighin, *General Mgr*
Rick Dardis, *Manager*
EMP: 80
SQ FT: 32,000
SALES (corp-wide): 63B **Publicly Held**
WEB: www.joy-of-cola.com
SIC: 5149 4225 2086 Soft drinks; general warehousing & storage; bottled & canned soft drinks
HQ: Pepsi-Cola Metropolitan Bottling Company, Inc.
1111 Westchester Ave
White Plains NY 10604
914 767-6000

(P-8900)
PEPSI-COLA METRO BTLG CO INC
6659 Sycamore Canyon Blvd, Riverside (92507-0733)
PHONE.................................909 885-0741
Eli Bernard, *Manager*
EMP: 300
SALES (corp-wide): 63B **Publicly Held**
SIC: 5149 Soft drinks
HQ: Pepsi-Cola Metropolitan Bottling Company, Inc.
1111 Westchester Ave
White Plains NY 10604
914 767-6000

(P-8901)
PEPSI-COLA METRO BTLG CO INC
4416 Azusa Canyon Rd, Baldwin Park (91706-2797)
PHONE.................................626 338-5531
Terry Dana, *Manager*
EMP: 200
SQ FT: 65,113
SALES (corp-wide): 63B **Publicly Held**
WEB: www.joy-of-cola.com
SIC: 5149 Soft drinks
HQ: Pepsi-Cola Metropolitan Bottling Company, Inc.
1111 Westchester Ave
White Plains NY 10604
914 767-6000

(P-8902)
PEPSI-COLA METRO BTLG CO INC
1200 Arroyo St, San Fernando (91340-1545)
PHONE.................................818 898-3829
Fax: 818 838-1250
Bob Simpson, *Branch Mgr*
Rachel Spiegel, *Human Res Mgr*
EMP: 207
SALES (corp-wide): 63B **Publicly Held**
WEB: www.joy-of-cola.com
SIC: 5149 2086 Soft drinks; bottled & canned soft drinks
HQ: Pepsi-Cola Metropolitan Bottling Company, Inc.
1111 Westchester Ave
White Plains NY 10604
914 767-6000

(P-8903)
PEPSI-COLA METRO BTLG CO INC
200 Jennings St, San Francisco (94124-1723)
PHONE.................................415 206-7400
Dan Atkins, *Branch Mgr*
EMP: 95
SALES (corp-wide): 63B **Publicly Held**
WEB: www.joy-of-cola.com
SIC: 5149 5142 Soft drinks; packaged frozen goods
HQ: Pepsi-Cola Metropolitan Bottling Company, Inc.
1111 Westchester Ave
White Plains NY 10604
914 767-6000

(P-8904)
PERFECT BAR LLC
Also Called: Perfect Foods
5360 Eastgate Mall Ste A, San Diego (92121-2812)
PHONE.................................866 628-8548
Bill Keith, *CEO*
Leigh Keith, *Vice Pres*
Graham Hawkes, *Controller*
Steve Calderone, *VP Opers*
EMP: 95
SQ FT: 16,000
SALES (est): 43.2MM **Privately Held**
SIC: 5149 Health foods

(P-8905)
PERFORMANCE FOOD GROUP INC
Vistar Southern California
3790 Jurupa St, Ontario (91761-2921)
PHONE.................................909 673-1780
EMP: 106
SALES (corp-wide): 16.1B **Publicly Held**
WEB: www.mfdg.com
SIC: 5149 5145 Groceries & related products; confectionery
HQ: Performance Food Group, Inc.
12500 West Creek Pkwy
Richmond VA 23238
804 484-7700

(P-8906)
PERFORMANCE FOOD GROUP INC
16639 Gale Ave, City of Industry (91745-1802)
PHONE.................................714 535-2111
Fax: 714 781-8220
Ron Johnson, *Manager*
EMP: 127
SALES (corp-wide): 16.1B **Publicly Held**
WEB: www.mfdg.com
SIC: 5149 5142 Pizza supplies; packaged frozen goods
HQ: Performance Food Group, Inc.
12500 West Creek Pkwy
Richmond VA 23238
804 484-7700

(P-8907)
PHILLIPS PET FOOD AND SUPPLIES (PA)
3885 Seaport Blvd Ste 10, West Sacramento (95691-3527)
PHONE.................................916 373-7300
Cedric Damby, *Mng Member*
Rusty Haley, *Treasurer*

▲ = Import ▼ = Export
◆ = Import/Export

Kelli Wall, *Marketing Mgr*
David Mellish, *Mng Member*
Mary Levine, *Manager*
EMP: 75
SALES: 200MM **Privately Held**
SIC: 5149 Pet foods

(P-8908)
POMWONDERFUL LLC (DH)
4805 Centennial Ste 100, Bakersfield (93301)
PHONE 310 966-5800
Richard Cottrell, *CEO*
Matt Tupper, *President*
Mark Norris, *CFO*
Paul Coletta, *Chief Mktg Ofcr*
Malcolm Knight, *Vice Pres*
◆ **EMP:** 153
SALES (est): 847.5MM
SALES (corp-wide): 2.1B **Privately Held**
WEB: www.pomwonderful.com
SIC: 5149 5148 5085 Beverage concentrates; juices; tea; fruits, fresh; plastic bottles
HQ: Pom Wonderful Holdings Llc
11444 W Olympic Blvd # 210
Los Angeles CA 90064
310 966-5800

(P-8909)
POSH BAGEL INC (PA)
445 Nelo St, Santa Clara (95054-2145)
PHONE 408 980-8451
Fax: 408 980-9378
Jeff Ottoveggio, *President*
Sergio Donoso, *Vice Pres*
EMP: 75
SQ FT: 15,000
SALES (est): 38.3MM **Privately Held**
WEB: www.theposhbagel.com
SIC: 5149 Bakery products

(P-8910)
POSH BAKERY INC
445 Nelo St, Santa Clara (95054-2145)
PHONE 408 980-8451
Cherly Lee, *President*
▼ **EMP:** 120 **EST:** 2008
SALES (est): 30.7MM **Privately Held**
SIC: 5149 Bakery products

(P-8911)
PRESTIGE SALES II LLC
1038 E Bastanchury Rd, Fullerton (92835-2786)
PHONE 714 632-8020
Greg Zail, *Mng Member*
Bernie Barrad,
Rosemary Palacios, *Manager*
▲ **EMP:** 75
SQ FT: 27,000
SALES (est): 4.9MM **Privately Held**
WEB: www.psana.com
SIC: 5149 5181 Soft drinks; beer & ale

(P-8912)
RED BULL DISTRIBUTION CO INC (HQ)
Also Called: Redbull Distribution Co Colo
1740 Stewart St, Santa Monica (90404-4022)
PHONE 916 515-3501
Selin Chidiak, *CEO*
Dave Meeks, *General Mgr*
Glynn Rowell, *General Mgr*
Peter Kwon, *Admin Sec*
Michelle Allender, *Finance*
EMP: 57
SALES (est): 104.6MM
SALES (corp-wide): 3.3B **Privately Held**
SIC: 5149 Beverage concentrates
PA: Red Bull Gmbh
Am Brunnen 1
Fuschl Am See 5330
662 658-20

(P-8913)
ROCKVIEW DAIRIES INC (PA)
Also Called: Motive Nation
7011 Stewart And Gray Rd, Downey (90241-4347)
P.O. Box 668 (90241-0668)
PHONE 562 927-5511
Fax: 562 231-1715
Egbert De Groot, *CEO*
Valarie Cooke, *President*
Edgar Del Rio, *CFO*
Joe Valadez, *CFO*
Mark McGrath, *Executive*
◆ **EMP:** 123
SALES (est): 249.3MM **Privately Held**
WEB: www.rockviewfarms.com
SIC: 5149 5143 2026 Dried or canned foods; milk; fluid milk

(P-8914)
ROMA FOOD ENTERPRISES INC
Also Called: Roma of Northern California
6211 Las Positas Rd, Livermore (94551-5101)
PHONE 800 233-6211
EMP: 90
SALES (corp-wide): 15.2B **Publicly Held**
SIC: 5149 5141
HQ: Roma Food Enterprises, Inc.
1 Roma Blvd
Piscataway NJ 08854
732 463-7662

(P-8915)
ROYAL CROWN ENTERPRISES INC (PA)
780 Epperson Dr, City of Industry (91748-1336)
PHONE 626 854-8080
Fax: 626 854-8090
Juergen Lotter, *President*
Christiane Lotter, *Vice Pres*
◆ **EMP:** 100
SQ FT: 60,000
SALES (est): 28.5MM **Privately Held**
SIC: 5149 5141 Canned goods: fruit, vegetables, seafood, meats, etc.; groceries, general line

(P-8916)
ROYAL RIDGE FRT COLD STOR LLC
790 San Rmon Blvd Ste 200, Danville (94526)
PHONE 925 600-0224
EMP: 54
SALES (corp-wide): 34.8MM **Privately Held**
SIC: 5149 5499 Fruits, dried; dried fruit
PA: Royal Ridge Fruit & Cold Storage, Llc
13215 Road F Sw
Royal City WA 99357
509 346-2890

(P-8917)
SADIE ROSE BAKING CO
8926 Ware Ct, San Diego (92121-2222)
PHONE 858 831-0290
Jennifer Ann Curran, *CEO*
Michael Lipman, *President*
Naomi Couse, *Sales Dir*
Therese Wootton, *Regl Sales Mgr*
▲ **EMP:** 70
SQ FT: 23,000
SALES (est): 26.1MM **Privately Held**
SIC: 5149 Bakery products

(P-8918)
SAN FRANCISCO HERB NATURAL FD (PA)
Also Called: San Francisco Herb Tea & Spice
47444 Kato Rd, Fremont (94538-7319)
PHONE 510 770-1215
Fax: 510 770-9021
Kristi Kay Meltzer, *CEO*
Barry L Meltzer, *President*
Rosemary Hagman, *Vice Pres*
Thomas P Kurz, *Director*
Arthur J Swenka, *Director*
◆ **EMP:** 70 **EST:** 1969
SALES (est): 37.1MM **Privately Held**
WEB: www.herbspicetea.com
SIC: 5149 2833 2099 Tea; spices & seasonings; medicinals & botanicals; food preparations

(P-8919)
SEMIFREDDIS INC (PA)
Also Called: Semifreddi's Bakery
1980 N Loop Rd, Alameda (94502-3540)
PHONE 510 596-9930
Thomas Frainier, *President*
Michael Rose, *Admin Sec*
Ken Simmons, *Manager*
EMP: 110
SQ FT: 36,000
SALES (est): 44.3MM **Privately Held**
WEB: www.semifreddis.com
SIC: 5149 5461 Bakery products; bakeries

(P-8920)
SETTON PSTCHIO TERRA BELLA INC (HQ)
9370 Road 234, Terra Bella (93270-9226)
P.O. Box 11089 (93270-1089)
PHONE 559 535-6050
Joshua Setton, *President*
Morris Setton, *Vice Pres*
Nicolo Lapietra, *General Mgr*
Carl Scruton, *QC Mgr*
EMP: 61
SQ FT: 133,000
SALES (est): 63.9MM **Privately Held**
SIC: 5149 5145 0173 2068 Fruits, dried; nuts, salted or roasted; pistachio grove; salted & roasted nuts & seeds
PA: Setton's International Foods, Inc.
85 Austin Blvd
Commack NY 11725
631 543-8090

(P-8921)
SIMONS WHOLESALE BAKERY INC
1901 Ritchey St, Santa Ana (92705-5129)
PHONE 714 259-0855
Fax: 714 259-0858
Simon Meyerowitz, *President*
Marie Ritter, *Office Mgr*
EMP: 50
SQ FT: 3,700
SALES (est): 8MM **Privately Held**
SIC: 5149 Bakery products

(P-8922)
SOOFER CO INC
Also Called: Sadaf Foods
2828 S Alameda St, Vernon (90058-1347)
PHONE 323 234-6666
Fax: 323 234-2447
Dariush Soofer, *CEO*
Jamshid Soofer, *President*
George Melikian, *COO*
Behrooz David Soofer, *COO*
Ramon Sentimental, *Principal*
▲ **EMP:** 75
SQ FT: 70,000
SALES (est): 61.4MM **Privately Held**
WEB: www.sadaf.com
SIC: 5149 Groceries & related products; spices & seasonings; tea; rice, polished

(P-8923)
STARWEST BOTANICALS INC (PA)
161 Main Ave Ste A, Sacramento (95838-2080)
PHONE 916 638-8100
Fax: 916 638-8293
Van Joerger, *President*
Mark Wendley, *Controller*
Burt Dillon, *Plant Mgr*
Steven Riccardelli, *VP Sls/Mktg*
Melissa Waters, *Mktg Dir*
▲ **EMP:** 95 **EST:** 1975
SQ FT: 68,400
SALES (est): 49.7MM **Privately Held**
WEB: www.starwestherb.com
SIC: 5149 Tea; spices & seasonings

(P-8924)
SUJA LIFE LLC
Also Called: Suja Juice
8380 Camino Santa Fe, San Diego (92121-2657)
PHONE 855 879-7852
Jeffrey Church, *CEO*
James Brennan, *President*
David Schneider, *Asst Controller*
Heather Baker, *Opers Mgr*
EMP: 205
SALES (est): 148.9MM **Privately Held**
SIC: 5149 Fruit peel

(P-8925)
SUN CHLORELLA USA CORP
3305 Kashiwa St, Torrance (90505-4022)
PHONE 310 891-0600
Fax: 310 891-0621
Futoshi Nakayama, *CEO*
Yoshihito Nishimaki, *President*
Rose Straub, *COO*
Ellen Kubijanto, *CFO*
Penny Copeland, *Office Mgr*
▲ **EMP:** 54
SQ FT: 20,000
SALES (est): 14.6MM **Privately Held**
WEB: www.sunchlorellausa.com
SIC: 5149 Health foods
PA: Sun Chlorella Corp.
369, Osakacho, Karasumadori-Gojosagaru, Shimogyo-Ku
Kyoto KYO 600-8
752 883-000

(P-8926)
SUN TEN LABS LIQUIDATION CO
9250 Jeronimo Rd, Irvine (92618-1905)
PHONE 949 587-0509
Fax: 949 587-0502
Charleson C Hsu, *CEO*
Daniel Hsu, *Vice Pres*
Qingfu Hu, *Vice Pres*
Kyle Tate, *Info Tech Mgr*
Jack Yang, *VP Sales*
▲ **EMP:** 60
SALES (est): 14.2MM **Privately Held**
WEB: www.sunten.com
SIC: 5149 2834 2833 Spices & seasonings; pharmaceutical preparations; medicinals & botanicals

(P-8927)
SUN-MAID GROWERS CALIFORNIA (PA)
13525 S Bethel Ave, Kingsburg (93631-9232)
PHONE 559 897-6235
Fax: 559 626-4631
Barry F Kriebel, *President*
Braden Bender, *CFO*
Richard Paumen, *Senior VP*
Kayhan Hazrati, *Vice Pres*
Tomo Naito, *Vice Pres*
◆ **EMP:** 750
SALES (est): 384MM **Privately Held**
SIC: 5149 Groceries & related products

(P-8928)
SUN-MAID GROWERS CALIFORNIA
Also Called: Sun Maid Growers
15628 E Nebraska Ave, Kingsburg (93631-9714)
PHONE 559 897-8900
EMP: 273
SALES (corp-wide): 384MM **Privately Held**
SIC: 5149 Groceries & related products
PA: Sun-Maid Growers Of California
13525 S Bethel Ave
Kingsburg CA 93631
559 897-6235

(P-8929)
SUNFOOD CORPORATION
Also Called: Sunfood Superfoods
1830 Gillespie Way # 101, El Cajon (92020-0922)
PHONE 619 596-7979
Robert Deupree, *CEO*
Deion Stromenger, *CFO*
David Wartell, *Financial Exec*
Aaron Howard, *Business Mgr*
Chad McClintock, *Opers Staff*
▲ **EMP:** 54
SALES (est): 26.8MM **Privately Held**
SIC: 5149 Natural & organic foods

(P-8930)
SUPER STORE INDUSTRIES
Ssi
16888 Mckinley Ave, Lathrop (95330-9705)
P.O. Box 549 (95330-0549)
PHONE 209 858-2010
Fax: 209 858-2671
Tom Hughes, *Branch Mgr*
Sarah Goreham, *QA Dir*
Rod Reiswig, *Info Tech Dir*
Russ Davis, *Info Tech Mgr*
Kelly Durrer, *Safety Mgr*
EMP: 774

5149 - Groceries & Related Prdts, NEC Wholesale County (P-8931)

SALES (corp-wide): 155.7MM **Privately Held**
SIC: **5149** 5141 Groceries & related products; groceries, general line
PA: Super Store Industries
2800 W March Ln Ste 210
Stockton CA 95219
209 473-8100

(P-8931)
SURVIVALCAVE INC
10620 Treena St Ste 230, San Diego (92131-1140)
PHONE..................800 719-7650
J R Fisher, *President*
EMP: 50 EST: 2010
SALES (est): 7.8MM **Privately Held**
SIC: **5149** Canned goods: fruit, vegetables, seafood, meats, etc.

(P-8932)
SYGMA NETWORK INC
46905 47th St W, Lancaster (93536-8527)
PHONE..................661 723-0405
Mike Wren, *Branch Mgr*
Karla Bullock, *Human Res Mgr*
EMP: 200
SALES (corp-wide): 50.3B **Publicly Held**
WEB: www.sygmanetwork.com
SIC: **5149** Groceries & related products
HQ: The Sygma Network Inc
5550 Blazer Pkwy Ste 300
Dublin OH 43017
614 734-2500

(P-8933)
TADIN INC
Also Called: Tadin Herb & Tea Co.
3345 E Slauson Ave, Vernon (90058-3914)
PHONE..................213 406-8880
Jose M Gonzalez, *President*
Sandra Gonzales, *Treasurer*
Jim Sanchez, *Controller*
Laura Alvarez-Parra, *Marketing Staff*
Laura A Parra, *Marketing Staff*
▲ EMP: 95
SQ FT: 40,000
SALES (est): 17.4MM **Privately Held**
SIC: **5149** Tea

(P-8934)
TAMA TRADING COMPANY
1920 E 20th St, Vernon (90058-1076)
PHONE..................213 748-8262
Fax: 213 746-8012
William A Sauro, *CEO*
Sandra Sauro, *Corp Secy*
Vicki M Alster, *Controller*
◆ EMP: 61
SQ FT: 60,000
SALES (est): 30.2MM **Privately Held**
SIC: **5149** 5143 5147 5145 Groceries & related products; seasonings, sauces & extracts; pasta & rice; cheese; meats & meat products; candy

(P-8935)
TANAKA FARMS
5380 University Dr, Irvine (92612-2944)
PHONE..................949 653-2100
Glenn Tannaka, *Owner*
Kenny Tanaka, *Manager*
EMP: 60 EST: 1975
SALES (est): 5.1MM **Privately Held**
WEB: www.tanakafarms.com
SIC: **5149** Groceries & related products

(P-8936)
TAWA SERVICES INC (PA)
6281 Regio Ave Fl 2, Buena Park (90620-1023)
PHONE..................714 521-8899
Jonson Chen, *CEO*
Young You, *CEO*
▼ EMP: 220
SALES (est): 197MM **Privately Held**
SIC: **5149** 5411 Groceries & related products; grocery stores

(P-8937)
TOMATOES EXTRAORDINAIRE INC
Also Called: Specialty Produce
1929 Hancock St Ste 150, San Diego (92110-2062)
P.O. Box 82066 (92138-2066)
PHONE..................619 295-3172
Fax: 619 295-9541
Robert Harrington, *President*
Richard Harrington, *Vice Pres*
Cathy Lin, *Controller*
EMP: 150
SQ FT: 26,000
SALES (est): 88.4MM **Privately Held**
SIC: **5149** Specialty food items

(P-8938)
TOO GOOD GOURMET INC
2380 Grant Ave, San Lorenzo (94580-1806)
PHONE..................510 317-8150
Amie G Watson, *CEO*
Jennifer Finley, *President*
Joe Waldrep, *Business Dir*
Alyssa Albatana, *Graphic Designe*
Douglas Cooper, *QC Mgr*
▲ EMP: 100
SQ FT: 50,000
SALES: 6.6MM **Privately Held**
WEB: www.toogoodgourmet.com
SIC: **5149** 5461 2052 Cookies; crackers, cookies & bakery products; cookies; cookies

(P-8939)
TOOT SWEETS LTD (PA)
Also Called: Toot Sweets Fine Desserts
1277 Gilman St, Berkeley (94706-2351)
PHONE..................510 526-0610
Fax: 510 524-3975
Marcy Wheeler, *President*
Robert Kelso, *Admin Sec*
EMP: 50 EST: 1974
SQ FT: 2,000
SALES (est): 12.2MM **Privately Held**
SIC: **5149** Bakery products

(P-8940)
TRAINA DRIED FRUIT INC
Also Called: Traina Foods
337 1/2 Lemon Ave, Patterson (95363-9634)
P.O. Box 157 (95363-0157)
PHONE..................209 892-5472
Fax: 209 892-6231
Willy Traina, *CEO*
Joseph Traina, *CFO*
Justin A Traina, *Vice Pres*
Josephine Traina, *Admin Sec*
Amy Thorpe, *Project Mgr*
▲ EMP: 240
SQ FT: 5,000
SALES (est): 12.9MM **Privately Held**
WEB: www.trainadriedfruit.com
SIC: **5149** Fruits, dried

(P-8941)
TRINITY FRESH DISTRIBUTION LLC
8200 Berry Ave Ste 140, Sacramento (95828-1612)
PHONE..................916 714-7368
Paul Abess,
Karen Joungkeit, *Office Mgr*
EMP: 70
SALES (est): 19.3MM **Privately Held**
SIC: **5149** Dairy products, dried or canned

(P-8942)
UNIFIED FOOD INGREDIENTS INC
145 Vallecitos De Oro # 208, San Marcos (92069-1454)
PHONE..................760 744-7225
Fax: 760 744-7215
George Lin, *President*
Dan Stouder, *Vice Pres*
Vincent Lin, *Principal*
Melissa Coetzee, *Office Mgr*
▲ EMP: 70
SQ FT: 6,000
SALES (est): 1.1MM **Privately Held**
SIC: **5149** Dried or canned foods; fruits, dried

(P-8943)
UNITED NATURAL FOODS INC
2450 17th Ave Ste 250, Santa Cruz (95062-1987)
PHONE..................831 462-5870
Melody Meyer, *Branch Mgr*
Carol R Stephenson, *Human Resources*
EMP: 133 **Publicly Held**
SIC: **5149** 5122 5142 Organic & diet foods; health foods; natural & organic foods; cosmetics, perfumes & hair products; vitamins & minerals; packaged frozen goods
PA: United Natural Foods, Inc.
313 Iron Horse Way
Providence RI 02908

(P-8944)
UNITED NATURAL FOODS INC
Also Called: Unfi
1101 Sunset Blvd, Rocklin (95765-3786)
PHONE..................916 625-4100
Steven L Spinner, *CEO*
Jessica Clancy, *Buyer*
EMP: 96 EST: 1994
SALES (est): 44.9MM **Privately Held**
SIC: **5149** 5122 5142 Organic & diet foods; cosmetics, perfumes & hair products; packaged frozen goods

(P-8945)
UNITED NATURAL FOODS WEST INC (HQ)
Also Called: Unfi
1101 Sunset Blvd, Rocklin (95765-3786)
PHONE..................401 528-8634
Kurt M Luttecke, *CEO*
Michael S Funk, *Ch of Bd*
Steven L Spinner, *President*
Eric A Dorne, *Senior VP*
Sean F Griffin, *Vice Pres*
▲ EMP: 385 EST: 1996
SQ FT: 150,000
SALES (est): 764.2MM **Publicly Held**
WEB: www.mpwnw.com
SIC: **5149** 5141 Groceries & related products; groceries, general line

(P-8946)
US FOODS INC
US Foods Corona
1283 Sherborn St Ste 102, Corona (92879-5003)
PHONE..................800 888-3147
Graylon Macfall, *Division Pres*
EMP: 250
SALES (corp-wide): 23.1B **Publicly Held**
SIC: **5149** Dried or canned foods
HQ: Us Foods, Inc.
9399 W Higgins Rd Ste 500
Rosemont IL 60018
847 720-8000

(P-8947)
US FOODS INC
1283 Sherborn St Ste 102, Corona (92879-5003)
PHONE..................951 582-8500
Fax: 951 582-8925
Patrick Waller, *Manager*
Kelly Anderson, *Administration*
Paul Andrzejczyk, *Marketing Staff*
EMP: 150
SALES (corp-wide): 23.1B **Publicly Held**
WEB: www.usfoodservice.com
SIC: **5149** Groceries & related products
HQ: Us Foods, Inc.
9399 W Higgins Rd Ste 500
Rosemont IL 60018
847 720-8000

(P-8948)
US FOODS INC
Also Called: Mesa Cold Strg 4145
700 S Raymond Ave, Fullerton (92831-5233)
PHONE..................714 449-9990
Ed Libel, *Branch Mgr*
Mickell Potts, *General Mgr*
EMP: 161
SALES (corp-wide): 23.1B **Publicly Held**
SIC: **5149** Dried or canned foods
HQ: Us Foods, Inc.
9399 W Higgins Rd Ste 500
Rosemont IL 60018
847 720-8000

(P-8949)
US FOODS INC
Also Called: Sierra Pacific 4117
4300 Finch Rd, Modesto (95357-4102)
PHONE..................209 572-2882
Joy Perez, *Project Mgr*
Michelle Vanartsdalen, *Accountant*
EMP: 159
SALES (corp-wide): 23.1B **Publicly Held**
SIC: **5149** Dried or canned foods
HQ: Us Foods, Inc.
9399 W Higgins Rd Ste 500
Rosemont IL 60018
847 720-8000

(P-8950)
US FOODS INC
Also Called: Csi Cold Storage 4150
1415 N Raymond Ave, Anaheim (92801-1111)
PHONE..................714 449-2880
EMP: 159
SALES (corp-wide): 23.1B **Publicly Held**
SIC: **5149** Dried or canned foods
HQ: Us Foods, Inc.
9399 W Higgins Rd Ste 500
Rosemont IL 60018
847 720-8000

(P-8951)
US FOODS INC
Also Called: USF-La Mirada 4150
15155 Northam St, La Mirada (90638-5754)
PHONE..................714 670-3500
David Patterson, *Branch Mgr*
Lori Delaney, *Marketing Mgr*
EMP: 159
SALES (corp-wide): 23.1B **Publicly Held**
SIC: **5149** Dried or canned foods
HQ: Us Foods, Inc.
9399 W Higgins Rd Ste 500
Rosemont IL 60018
847 720-8000

(P-8952)
US FOODS INC
Also Called: San Diego CLD Stg 4140
1240 W 28th St, National City (91950-6319)
PHONE..................619 474-6525
EMP: 159
SALES (corp-wide): 23.1B **Publicly Held**
SIC: **5149** Dried or canned foods
HQ: Us Foods, Inc.
9399 W Higgins Rd Ste 500
Rosemont IL 60018
847 720-8000

(P-8953)
US FOODS INC
Also Called: USF Import FWD Wh 4150
1283 Sherborn St Ste 102, Corona (92879-5003)
PHONE..................951 256-2400
Pietro Satriano, *Branch Mgr*
EMP: 159
SALES (corp-wide): 23.1B **Publicly Held**
SIC: **5149** Dried or canned foods
HQ: Us Foods, Inc.
9399 W Higgins Rd Ste 500
Rosemont IL 60018
847 720-8000

(P-8954)
VISTA VERDE FARMS
11251 Melcher Rd, Delano (93215-9310)
PHONE..................661 720-9733
Santos Montmayor, *Owner*
EMP: 50
SALES (est): 2.7MM **Privately Held**
SIC: **5149** Groceries & related products

(P-8955)
WALONG MARKETING INC (PA)
Also Called: Foods and Produce
6281 Regio Ave Fl 1, Buena Park (90620-1023)
PHONE..................714 670-8899
Fax: 714 670-6668
Chang Hua K Chen, *CEO*

PRODUCTS & SERVICES SECTION 5169 - Chemicals & Allied Prdts, NEC Wholesale County (P-8974)

Roger Chen, *Ch of Bd*
Pauline Chen, *President*
Sharon Teal, *Accountant*
Teddy Huang, *Marketing Mgr*
◆ **EMP:** 100
SALES (est): 80.4MM **Privately Held**
SIC: 5149 5411 Groceries & related products; grocery stores

(P-8956)
WISMETTAC ASIAN FOODS INC (DH)
Also Called: Wismettac Fresh Fish
13409 Orden Dr, Santa Fe Springs (90670-6336)
PHONE.................562 802-1900
Fax: 562 229-1720
Takayuki Kanai, *CEO*
Tom Kawaguchi, *CFO*
Toshiyoki Nishikawa, *Vice Pres*
Shoichi Kaku, *Branch Mgr*
Hiroshi Kikumori, *Branch Mgr*
◆ **EMP:** 200
SQ FT: 225,000
SALES (est): 535.3MM
SALES (corp-wide): 2.6MM **Privately Held**
WEB: www.nishimototrading.com
SIC: 5149 Groceries & related products
HQ: Nishimoto Company Limited.
    3-10-5, Nihonbashi
    Chuo-Ku TKY 103-0
    368 702-015

(P-8957)
YAMAMOTO OF ORIENT INC (HQ)
Also Called: Yamamotoyama of America
122 Voyager St, Pomona (91768-3252)
PHONE.................909 594-7356
Kahei Yamamoto, *Ch of Bd*
Hisayuki Nakagawa, *President*
Kazumi Ikeda, *Treasurer*
Kaichiro Yamamoto, *Admin Sec*
Ken Imamura, *Finance*
▲ **EMP:** 130 **EST:** 1975
SQ FT: 60,000
SALES (est): 60.7MM
SALES (corp-wide): 63.5MM **Privately Held**
WEB: www.yamamotoyama.com
SIC: 5149 6512 5812 Tea; shopping center, property operation only; eating places
PA: Yamamotoyama Co., Ltd.
    1-2-5, Kyobashi
    Chuo-Ku TKY 104-0
    332 713-261

(P-8958)
YOGIBOTANICALS
Also Called: Bhai Group Co
1616 Preuss Rd, Los Angeles (90035-4212)
PHONE.................310 275-9891
Ranbir Singh Bhai, *Owner*
EMP: 99
SALES (est): 3.4MM **Privately Held**
SIC: 5149 Natural & organic foods

5153 Grain & Field Beans Wholesale

(P-8959)
A L GILBERT COMPANY
Also Called: Berry Seed & Feed
4431 Jessup Rd, Keyes (95328)
P.O. Box 459 (95328-0459)
PHONE.................209 537-0766
Edwin Gallagher, *Branch Mgr*
EMP: 60
SALES (corp-wide): 124.1MM **Privately Held**
SIC: 5153 Grains
PA: A. L. Gilbert Company
    304 N Yosemite Ave
    Oakdale CA 95361
    209 847-1211

(P-8960)
CALIFORNIA CEREAL PRODUCTS INC (PA)
1267 14th St, Oakland (94607-2246)
PHONE.................510 452-4500
Fax: 510 452-4545

Robert Sterling Savely, *CEO*
Mark Graham, *President*
Richard O'Connor, *Accountant*
Carolyn Savely, *Personnel Exec*
Phil Gunter, *Opers Mgr*
◆ **EMP:** 69
SQ FT: 120,000
SALES (est): 69.3MM **Privately Held**
SIC: 5153 Grain & field beans

(P-8961)
PACIFIC GRAIN & FOODS LLC (PA)
Also Called: Pacific Grain and Foods
4067 W Shaw Ave Ste 116, Fresno (93722-6214)
P.O. Box 3928, Pinedale (93650-3928)
PHONE.................559 276-2580
Fax: 559 276-2936
Lee Perkins, *President*
Elizabeth Sturges, *QA Dir*
Rose Avila, *Accountant*
Jose Alvarado, *Sales Mgr*
Karen Perkins,
◆ **EMP:** 74
SQ FT: 172,000
SALES (est): 30MM **Privately Held**
WEB: www.pacificgrainfoods.com
SIC: 5153 7389 5149 Grain & field beans; packaging & labeling services; spices & seasonings

5154 Livestock Wholesale

(P-8962)
SHASTA LIVESTOCK AUCTION YARD
3917 Main St, Cottonwood (96022)
P.O. Box 558 (96022-0558)
PHONE.................530 347-3793
Fax: 530 347-3786
Ellington Peek, *President*
Beatrice Peek, *Vice Pres*
EMP: 60
SQ FT: 15,000
SALES (est): 9.3MM **Privately Held**
SIC: 5154 Auctioning livestock

5159 Farm-Prdt Raw Mtrls, NEC Wholesale

(P-8963)
ALTRIA GROUP DISTRIBUTION CO
300 N Lake Ave Ste 1100, Pasadena (91101-4123)
PHONE.................804 274-2000
Craig A Johnson, *President*
EMP: 104
SALES (corp-wide): 25.4B **Publicly Held**
SIC: 5159 Tobacco distributors & products
HQ: Altria Group Distribution Company
    6601 W Broad St
    Richmond VA 23230
    804 274-2000

(P-8964)
CALCOT LTD (PA)
Also Called: American Cotton Coop Assn
1900 E Brundage Ln, Bakersfield (93307-2789)
P.O. Box 259 (93302-0259)
PHONE.................661 327-5961
Fax: 661 861-9870
Jarral T Neeper, *CEO*
Roxanne F Wang, *CFO*
Miguel Mory, *Treasurer*
David L Hand, *Vice Pres*
Ellen Patrick, *Accountant*
▼ **EMP:** 70
SQ FT: 20,000
SALES (est): 172.6MM **Privately Held**
WEB: www.calcot.com
SIC: 5159 Cotton, raw

(P-8965)
SELECT HARVEST USA LLC
Also Called: Spycher Brothers
14827 W Harding Rd, Turlock (95380-9012)
PHONE.................209 668-2471
Robert L Nunes, *Mng Member*

Shelly Broumas, *CFO*
Juan-Carlos Veraza, *Officer*
Carol Baldwin, *Human Res Mgr*
Dinesh Bajaj, *Sales Dir*
◆ **EMP:** 124 **EST:** 2008
SQ FT: 100,000
SALES (est): 200MM **Privately Held**
SIC: 5159 0173 Nuts & nut by-products; almond grove

(P-8966)
SOUTH VALLEY ALMOND CO LLC
Also Called: South Valley Farms
15443 Beech Ave, Wasco (93280-7604)
PHONE.................661 391-9000
Fax: 661 391-9012
Paul C Genho, *Mng Member*
Mike Vanorman, *Accountant*
Daryl Wilkendorf,
Merrill Dibble, *Mng Member*
◆ **EMP:** 200
SQ FT: 4,000
SALES (est): 63MM **Privately Held**
SIC: 5159 Nuts & nut by-products

5162 Plastics Materials & Basic Shapes Wholesale

(P-8967)
CIRRUS ENTERPRISES LLC
Also Called: E.V. Roberts
18027 Bishop Ave, Carson (90746-4019)
PHONE.................310 204-6159
Fax: 310 202-7247
Ron Cloud, *CEO*
Donna Knapp, *Executive Asst*
Niki Townsend, *HR Admin*
Teresa Braden, *Opers Mgr*
Tracey H Cloud,
EMP: 52
SQ FT: 26,000
SALES (est): 37.6MM **Privately Held**
WEB: www.evroberts.com
SIC: 5162 2821 2891 Plastics products; epoxy resins; adhesives & sealants

(P-8968)
CONSOLIDATED PLASTICS CORP (PA)
Also Called: Paragon Plastics Co Div
14954 La Palma Dr, Chino (91710-9695)
PHONE.................909 393-8222
Fax: 909 393-2552
Jean Bouris, *President*
Gloria Jean Bouris, *CEO*
Darrell Defazio, *Purchasing*
Billy Corn, *Sales Mgr*
Cesar Nunez, *Manager*
EMP: 50
SQ FT: 45,000
SALES (est): 21.7MM **Privately Held**
WEB: www.planetplastics.com
SIC: 5162 3599 Plastics sheets & rods; machine shop, jobbing & repair

(P-8969)
DONGALEN ENTERPRISES INC (PA)
Also Called: Interstate Plastics
330 Commerce Cir, Sacramento (95815-4213)
P.O. Box 130027 (95853-0027)
PHONE.................916 422-3110
Fax: 916 422-1608
Mark Courtright, *President*
Cole Klokkevold, *CFO*
Rich Brandone, *Controller*
Judy Allen, *Human Res Mgr*
Ben Hardesty, *Sales Staff*
▲ **EMP:** 50
SQ FT: 33,000
SALES (est): 113.3MM **Privately Held**
WEB: www.interstateplastics.com
SIC: 5162 Plastics products

5169 Chemicals & Allied Prdts, NEC Wholesale

(P-8970)
AIRGAS INC
653 N Market St, Redding (96003-3609)
PHONE.................530 241-1544
Fax: 530 241-1568
John Sabo, *Branch Mgr*
EMP: 281
SALES (corp-wide): 189.3MM **Privately Held**
SIC: 5169 Chemicals & allied products
HQ: Airgas, Inc.
    259 N Radnor Chester Rd
    Radnor PA 19087
    610 687-5253

(P-8971)
AIRGAS INC
9010 Clairemont Mesa Blvd, San Diego (92123-1208)
PHONE.................858 279-8200
Leigh Hart, *Branch Mgr*
Samuel Jasso, *Branch Mgr*
Dan Bloch, *Manager*
Virgil Lewis, *Manager*
Marco Lopez, *Manager*
EMP: 110
SALES (corp-wide): 189.3MM **Privately Held**
WEB: www.airgas.com
SIC: 5169 Industrial gases
HQ: Airgas, Inc.
    259 N Radnor Chester Rd
    Radnor PA 19087
    610 687-5253

(P-8972)
AIRGAS SAFETY INC
2355 Workman Mill Rd, City of Industry (90601-1459)
PHONE.................562 699-5239
Olaya Rivera, *Principal*
EMP: 80
SALES (corp-wide): 189.3MM **Privately Held**
WEB: www.airgassafety.com
SIC: 5169 Gases, compressed & liquefied
HQ: Airgas Safety, Inc.
    2501 Green Ln
    Levittown PA 19057

(P-8973)
AIRGAS USA LLC- WEST DIVISION
3737 Worsham Ave, Long Beach (90808-1774)
PHONE.................562 497-1991
Doug Jones, *President*
Joseph Valenzuela, *Vice Chairman*
Terry Cherry, *CFO*
Brian Wolf, *CFO*
Anne Marten, *Info Tech Mgr*
◆ **EMP:** 936
SQ FT: 9,000
SALES (est): 1.3MM
SALES (corp-wide): 189.3MM **Privately Held**
WEB: www.airgaswest.com
SIC: 5169 5085 2813 5084 Industrial gases; industrial supplies; industrial gases; welding machinery & equipment
HQ: Airgas Usa Llc
    259 N Radnor Chester Rd # 100
    Radnor PA 19087
    610 687-5253

(P-8974)
AIRGAS USA LLC
9010 Clairemont Mesa Blvd, San Diego (92123-1208)
P.O. Box 6030, Lakewood (90714-6030)
PHONE.................858 279-8200
Pat Muller, *Vice Pres*
EMP: 110
SALES (corp-wide): 189.3MM **Privately Held**
WEB: www.airgaswest.com
SIC: 5169 5084 5047 5046 Industrial gases; industrial machinery & equipment; medical & hospital equipment; commercial equipment

5169 - Chemicals & Allied Prdts, NEC Wholesale County (P-8975)

PRODUCTS & SERVICES SECTION

HQ: Airgas Usa Llc
259 N Radnor Chester Rd # 100
Radnor PA 19087
610 687-5253

(P-8975)
AIRGAS USA LLC
11711 S Alameda St, Los Angeles (90059-2130)
PHONE 323 568-2244
Fax: 323 564-6394
Dennis Beukelmau, *Branch Mgr*
Peter McCausland, *General Mgr*
EMP: 58
SALES (corp-wide): 189.3MM **Privately Held**
WEB: www.airgaswest.com
SIC: 5169 Industrial gases
HQ: Airgas Usa Llc
259 N Radnor Chester Rd # 100
Radnor PA 19087
610 687-5253

(P-8976)
AIRGAS USA LLC
3737 Worsham Ave, Long Beach (90808-1774)
PHONE 562 497-1991
John P Skulavik, *Branch Mgr*
EMP: 936
SALES (corp-wide): 189.3MM **Privately Held**
SIC: 5169 5085 2813 5084 Industrial gases; industrial supplies; industrial gases; welding machinery & equipment
HQ: Airgas Usa Llc
259 N Radnor Chester Rd # 100
Radnor PA 19087
610 687-5253

(P-8977)
AQUA-SERV ENGINEERS INC (HQ)
13560 Colombard Ct, Fontana (92337-7702)
PHONE 951 681-9696
Fax: 951 681-9698
Earl L Harper, *CEO*
Garland Rachels, *President*
James Ashby, *Treasurer*
Buck Long, *Senior VP*
Tony Carter, *Vice Pres*
EMP: 56 EST: 1958
SQ FT: 63,000
SALES (est): 32.4MM
SALES (corp-wide): 40.5MM **Privately Held**
WEB: www.aqua-serv.com
SIC: 5169 Chemicals & allied products
PA: Harpure Enterprises, Inc.
13560 Colombard Ct
Fontana CA 92337
951 681-9697

(P-8978)
ASHLAND INC
Also Called: Ashland Performance Materials
20915 S Wilmington Ave, Carson (90810-1039)
PHONE 310 223-3505
Randy Weld, *Manager*
EMP: 90
SALES (corp-wide): 5.3B **Publicly Held**
WEB: www.ashland.com
SIC: 5169 Alkalines & chlorine
PA: Ashland Llc
50 E Rivercenter Blvd # 1600
Covington KY 41011
859 815-3333

(P-8979)
ASHLAND INC
Also Called: Ashland Distribution
6608 E 26th St, Commerce (90040-3216)
P.O. Box 22118, Los Angeles (90022-0118)
PHONE 323 767-1300
Fax: 323 720-1196
Reid Mork, *Branch Mgr*
EMP: 60
SQ FT: 45,845
SALES (corp-wide): 5.3B **Publicly Held**
WEB: www.ashland.com
SIC: 5169 Alkalines & chlorine
PA: Ashland Llc
50 E Rivercenter Blvd # 1600
Covington KY 41011
859 815-3333

(P-8980)
BACHEM AMERICAS INC
1271 Avenida Chelsea, Vista (92081-8315)
PHONE 760 597-8820
EMP: 86 **Privately Held**
SIC: 5169 2836 Chemicals & allied products; biological products, except diagnostic
HQ: Bachem Americas, Inc.
3132 Kashiwa St
Torrance CA 90505
310 784-4440

(P-8981)
BRENNTAG PACIFIC INC (DH)
10747 Patterson Pl, Santa Fe Springs (90670-4043)
PHONE 562 903-9626
Fax: 562 906-5287
William A Fidler, *CEO*
Steven Pozzi, *President*
H Edward Boyadjian, *CFO*
Eric Bratton, *Finance Dir*
Julia Tu, *Controller*
▲ EMP: 100
SALES (est): 553MM
SALES (corp-wide): 11.1B **Privately Held**
SIC: 5169 Chemicals, industrial & heavy
HQ: Brenntag North America, Inc.
5083 Pottsville Pike
Reading PA 19605
610 926-6100

(P-8982)
CHEMICAL DEPENDENCY RECOVERY
2829 Watt Ave Ste 150, Sacramento (95821-6245)
PHONE 916 482-1132
Melissa Rose, *Director*
EMP: 50
SALES (est): 2.3MM **Privately Held**
SIC: 5169 Chemicals & allied products

(P-8983)
CJ AMERICA INC (HQ)
Also Called: C J Foods
3530 Wilshire Blvd # 1220, Los Angeles (90010-2341)
PHONE 213 738-1400
Fax: 213 380-5433
Jin Won Kim, *President*
Han Jong Kim, *CFO*
Justin Cho, *General Mgr*
Robbin Jin, *Administration*
Rebecca Cho, *Analyst*
◆ EMP: 118
SQ FT: 6,000
SALES (est): 76.1MM
SALES (corp-wide): 3.9B **Privately Held**
SIC: 5169 5149 1541 3556 Chemicals & allied products; food additives & preservatives; groceries & related products; food products manufacturing or packing plant construction; food products machinery
PA: Cj Cheiljedang Corp.
Cj Jeiljedang Center
Seoul SEO 04560
272 681-14

(P-8984)
CNS INDUSTRIES INC
Also Called: Superco Specialty Products
25041 Anza Dr, Valencia (91355-3414)
PHONE 661 775-8877
Steve Cina, *CEO*
Jeanne M Sher, *President*
Douglas Jones, *Vice Pres*
Robert Smith, *Vice Pres*
Claudia Guzman, *Principal*
EMP: 50
SQ FT: 8,000
SALES (est): 19.8MM **Privately Held**
WEB: www.supercoproducts.com
SIC: 5169 Chemicals, industrial & heavy

(P-8985)
CZECH COMMERCE LTD
3063 Larkin Rd, Pebble Beach (93953-2910)
PHONE 831 649-4633

Jaroslav Stepanek, *President*
Scott Conner, *Vice Pres*
EMP: 53
SQ FT: 450
SALES: 2MM **Privately Held**
SIC: 5169 5031 Alcohols; building materials, exterior

(P-8986)
DESERT STAR CO
23119 Drayton St, Saugus (91350-2547)
PHONE 661 259-5848
Mary Flynn, *Vice Pres*
Ludy Gent, *Purchasing*
Mark S Wilson, *Agent*
EMP: 50
SALES (est): 2.3MM **Privately Held**
WEB: www.desertstar.net
SIC: 5169 Chemicals & allied products

(P-8987)
E T HORN COMPANY (PA)
16050 Canary Ave, La Mirada (90638-5585)
P.O. Box 1238 (90637-1238)
PHONE 714 523-8050
Fax: 714 670-6851
Gene Alley, *Ch of Bd*
Bob Ahn, *President*
Jeff Martin, *President*
Kevin Salerno, *President*
Mike Zarkades, *President*
▲ EMP: 70 EST: 1961
SQ FT: 1,200
SALES: 290MM **Privately Held**
SIC: 5169 Industrial chemicals

(P-8988)
ENVIRO TECH CHEMICAL SVCS INC (PA)
500 Winmoore Way, Modesto (95358-5750)
PHONE 209 581-9576
Michael S Harvey, *President*
John Pray, *CFO*
Michael B Archibald, *Vice Pres*
Sindy Heby, *Executive*
Fernanda Carver, *Executive Asst*
◆ EMP: 100
SQ FT: 136,551
SALES: 37.3MM **Privately Held**
WEB: www.amcor.com.au
SIC: 5169 Chemicals & allied products

(P-8989)
HERBALIFE LTD INC
990 W 190th St Ste 650, Torrance (90502-1075)
PHONE 310 410-9600
Jaideep Bedi, *Branch Mgr*
John Desimone, *CFO*
Stephen Pateyjohns, *Admin Asst*
Jameese Smith, *Info Tech Dir*
Reem Elomeri, *Info Tech Mgr*
EMP: 500 **Privately Held**
WEB: www.herbalife.com
SIC: 5169 Chemicals & allied products
HQ: Herbalife Ltd, Inc.
800 W Olympic Blvd # 406
Los Angeles CA 90015
310 410-9600

(P-8990)
HILL BROTHERS CHEMICAL COMPANY (PA)
1675 N Main St, Orange (92867-3499)
PHONE 714 998-8800
Fax: 714 998-6310
Ronald R Hill, *President*
Thomas F James, *CFO*
Kathryn J Waters, *Corp Secy*
Shane Burkhart, *Officer*
Matthew Thorne, *Exec VP*
▲ EMP: 153
SALES (est): 123.2MM **Privately Held**
WEB: www.durafiber.com
SIC: 5169 2819 Acids; calcium chloride & hypochlorite; magnesium compounds or salts, inorganic

(P-8991)
K R ANDERSON INC (PA)
Also Called: Krayden
18330 Sutter Blvd, Morgan Hill (95037-2841)
PHONE 408 825-1800

Fax: 408 778-2802
Dennis Wagner, *CEO*
Jim Caviglia, *Treasurer*
Martha Kavanaugh, *Human Res Mgr*
Samantha Wagner, *Purch Agent*
Donn Edlund, *Sales Engr*
▲ EMP: 60
SQ FT: 60,000
SALES (est): 47MM **Privately Held**
WEB: www.andfab.com
SIC: 5169 Chemicals & allied products; synthetic resins, rubber & plastic materials; adhesives, chemical

(P-8992)
LABORATORY SPECIALTY GASES
Also Called: Westair Gas and Equipment
2506 Market St, San Diego (92102-3010)
PHONE 619 234-6060
Steve Castiglione, *President*
Joe Barney, *Director*
EMP: 110
SALES (est): 11.7MM **Privately Held**
SIC: 5169 Gases, compressed & liquefied

(P-8993)
MCP INDUSTRIES INC
Also Called: Purosil Division
10039 Norwalk Blvd, Santa Fe Springs (90670-3323)
P.O. Box 2467, Corona (92878-2467)
PHONE 562 944-5511
Fax: 951 944-7711
Surrender Marwaha, *Manager*
Dan Rodriguez, *Engineer*
EMP: 100
SALES (corp-wide): 123.8MM **Privately Held**
WEB: www.missionrubber.com
SIC: 5169 Silicon lubricants
PA: Mcp Industries, Inc.
708 S Temescal St Ste 101
Corona CA 92879
951 736-1881

(P-8994)
MOC PRODUCTS COMPANY INC (PA)
Also Called: Auto Edge Solutions
12306 Montague St, Pacoima (91331-2279)
PHONE 818 794-3500
Fax: 818 896-3760
Mark Waco, *CEO*
Nadelin Waco, *Corp Secy*
Louis Towry, *Vice Pres*
Dave Waco, *Vice Pres*
Annabella Ordonez, *Admin Asst*
▼ EMP: 75
SQ FT: 100,000
SALES (est): 177.4MM **Privately Held**
WEB: www.mocproducts.com
SIC: 5169 7549 Chemicals & allied products; automotive maintenance services

(P-8995)
MUTUAL PROPANE INC
17117 S Broadway, Gardena (90248-3191)
PHONE 310 515-0553
Melvin A Moore, *President*
Mark Medina, *Prgrmr*
Martha Waialae, *Controller*
John Davoust, *Sales Executive*
EMP: 50
SALES (est): 3.7MM
SALES (corp-wide): 20MM **Privately Held**
WEB: www.mutualpropane.com
SIC: 5169 Industrial gases
PA: Mutual Liquid Gas And Equipment Company, Inc.
17117 S Broadway
Gardena CA 90248
310 515-0553

(P-8996)
NALCO COMPANY LLC
1320 Arnold Dr Ste 246, Martinez (94553-6537)
PHONE 925 957-9720
Bob Smith, *District Mgr*
Dorothy Holland, *Admin Sec*
EMP: 100

▲ = Import ▼ = Export ◆ = Import/Export

PRODUCTS & SERVICES SECTION
5172 - Petroleum & Petroleum Prdts Wholesale County (P-9018)

SALES (corp-wide): 13.5B Publicly Held
WEB: www.nalco.com
SIC: 5169 Chemicals & allied products
HQ: Nalco Company Llc
1601 W Diehl Rd
Naperville IL 60563
630 305-1000

(P-8997)
PRAXAIR INC
2300 E Pacific Coast Hwy, Wilmington (90744-2919)
P.O. Box 1309 (90748-1309)
PHONE..................................562 983-2100
Fax: 562 983-2102
Ted Mayberry, Branch Mgr
James Sawyer, CFO
EMP: 96
SALES (corp-wide): 10.7B Publicly Held
SIC: 5169 2813 Industrial gases; industrial gases
PA: Praxair, Inc.
39 Old Ridgebury Rd
Danbury CT 06810
203 837-2000

(P-8998)
PROCTER & GAMBLE DISTRG LLC
1992 Rockefeller Dr, Ceres (95307-7274)
PHONE..................................209 538-3987
Michael Wheatley, Branch Mgr
EMP: 273
SALES (corp-wide): 65.3B Publicly Held
SIC: 5169 Detergents
HQ: Procter & Gamble Distributing Llc
1 Procter And Gamble Plz
Cincinnati OH 45202
513 983-1100

(P-8999)
PROCTER & GAMBLE DISTRG LLC
2400 Camino Ramon Ste 300, San Ramon (94583-4351)
PHONE..................................925 867-4900
Virginia Cavlin, Manager
Rosa Dediego, Manager
EMP: 273
SALES (corp-wide): 65.3B Publicly Held
SIC: 5169 5122 5149 5113 Detergents; laundry soap chips & powder; drugs, proprietaries & sundries; groceries & related products; coffee, green or roasted; napkins, paper; towels, paper; dishes, disposable plastic & paper; diapers; service establishment equipment
HQ: Procter & Gamble Distributing Llc
1 Procter And Gamble Plz
Cincinnati OH 45202
513 983-1100

(P-9000)
UNITED PETROCHEMICALS INC
3000 W Macarthur Blvd # 300, Santa Ana (92704-7930)
PHONE..................................949 629-8736
Lynne Vanderwall, CEO
Zach Smith, Vice Pres
EMP: 75
SQ FT: 25,000
SALES (est): 1.9MM Privately Held
SIC: 5169 Industrial chemicals

(P-9001)
UNIVAR USA INC
2600 Garfield Ave, Commerce (90040-2608)
P.O. Box 512062 (90040)
PHONE..................................323 727-7005
Fax: 323 837-7144
Gary Cramer, Branch Mgr
Brian Faust, Executive
Tim Deal, General Mgr
Dan Polyack, Admin Asst
Darren Wong, Planning
EMP: 175
SALES (corp-wide): 8.9B Publicly Held
SIC: 5169 Chemicals & allied products
HQ: Univar Usa Inc.
17411 Ne Union Hill Rd
Redmond WA 98052
331 777-6000

(P-9002)
UNIVAR USA INC
2256 Junction Ave, San Jose (95131-1216)
PHONE..................................408 435-8649
Dan Manners, Branch Mgr
Shawn Lilley, Vice Pres
Brian Faust, General Mgr
Kristin Kistler, Admin Asst
Corbitt Mike, Admin Asst
EMP: 80
SALES (corp-wide): 8.9B Publicly Held
SIC: 5169 5191 Chemicals & allied products; farm supplies
HQ: Univar Usa Inc.
17411 Ne Union Hill Rd
Redmond WA 98052
331 777-6000

(P-9003)
VALEANT BIOMEDICALS INC (DH)
1 Enterprise, Aliso Viejo (92656-2606)
PHONE..................................949 461-6000
Tim Tyson, President
Barry Bailey, CFO
Linda Dunford, Project Mgr
Trung Thai, Technology
Brigitte Carriere, Human Res Dir
EMP: 100
SQ FT: 55,000
SALES (est): 61.6MM
SALES (corp-wide): 10.4B Privately Held
SIC: 5169 5047 2835 3826 Chemicals & allied products; medical equipment & supplies; in vitro & in vivo diagnostic substances; blood derivative diagnostic agents; analytical instruments; liquid testing apparatus; biotechnical research, commercial
HQ: Valeant Pharmaceuticals International Corporation
400 Somerset Corp Blvd
Bridgewater NJ 08807
908 927-1400

5171 Petroleum Bulk Stations & Terminals

(P-9004)
BP WEST COAST PRODUCTS LLC
Also Called: BP Products W Coast Refinery
1801 E Sepulveda Blvd, Carson (90745-6121)
PHONE..................................310 549-6204
George Nicolaides, Plant Mgr
Karen Eadon, Manager
EMP: 250
SALES (corp-wide): 222.8B Privately Held
SIC: 5171 Petroleum bulk stations & terminals
HQ: Bp West Coast Products Llc
4519 Grandview Rd
Blaine WA 98230
310 549-6204

(P-9005)
C L BRYANT INC
7401 Del Cielo Way, Modesto (95356-8874)
PHONE..................................209 566-5000
Toll Free:..............................877 -
Charles L Bryant Jr, President
Diana Reyes, Credit Mgr
Monique Casara, Human Res Dir
EMP: 159
SQ FT: 16,164
SALES (est): 32.4MM Privately Held
SIC: 5171 5541 Petroleum bulk stations; filling stations, gasoline

(P-9006)
FLYERS ENERGY LLC
11211 G Ave, Hesperia (92345-5134)
PHONE..................................760 949-3356
Rick Teske, Branch Mgr
EMP: 65
SALES (corp-wide): 135.2MM Privately Held
SIC: 5171 Petroleum bulk stations

PA: Flyers Energy, Llc
2360 Lindbergh St
Auburn CA 95602
530 885-0401

(P-9007)
GENERAL PETROLEUM CORPORATION
237 E Whitmore Ave, Modesto (95358-9411)
PHONE..................................209 537-1056
EMP: 70
SALES (corp-wide): 1.1B Privately Held
SIC: 5171
HQ: General Petroleum Corporation
19501 S Santa Fe Ave
Compton CA 90221
562 983-7300

(P-9008)
RAMOS OIL CO INC (PA)
1515 S River Rd, West Sacramento (95691-2882)
P.O. Box 401 (95691-0401)
PHONE..................................916 371-2570
Fax: 916 371-0635
Kent Ramos, President
Kyle Ramos, President
William Ramos, President
John Bailey, CFO
Jan Bard, CFO
EMP: 100
SQ FT: 3,200
SALES (est): 132.5MM Privately Held
WEB: www.ramosoil.com
SIC: 5171 5172 Petroleum bulk stations; lubricating oils & greases

(P-9009)
SOUTHERN COUNTIES OIL CO (PA)
Also Called: SC Fuels
1800 W Katella Ave # 400, Orange (92867-3449)
P.O. Box 4159 (92863-4159)
PHONE..................................714 744-7140
Fax: 714 744-7161
Frank P Greinke, CEO
Steve Greinke, President
David Larimer, COO
Mimi Taylor, CFO
Mimi S Taylor, CFO
EMP: 95
SALES (est): 1B Privately Held
SIC: 5171 5541 5172 Petroleum bulk stations; gasoline service stations; petroleum products

(P-9010)
WESTERN ENERGETIX LLC
Also Called: Berry-Hinckley
2360 Lindbergh St, Auburn (95602-9562)
PHONE..................................530 885-0401
Rick Teske, General Mgr
Dove Bangs, Director
EMP: 140
SALES (est): 53.1MM Privately Held
SIC: 5171 Petroleum bulk stations & terminals

5172 Petroleum & Petroleum Prdts Wholesale

(P-9011)
ALL-POINTS PETROLEUM LLC
640 Noyes Ct, Benicia (94510-1229)
P.O. Box 278 (94510-0278)
PHONE..................................707 745-1116
Ronald Myska,
Michelle Myska, Manager
EMP: 61
SQ FT: 4,000
SALES (est): 50.4MM Privately Held
WEB: www.allpointspetroleum.com
SIC: 5172 Petroleum products

(P-9012)
AMERIGAS PROPANE LP
11030 White Rock Rd # 100, Rancho Cordova (95670-6011)
PHONE..................................916 852-7400
Fax: 916 631-3180
Don Owens, Principal
Linda L Thomas-Leak, MIS Staff

EMP: 100
SALES (corp-wide): 2.8B Publicly Held
SIC: 5172 7374 Gases, liquefied petroleum (propane); data processing & preparation
HQ: Amerigas Propane, L.P.
460 N Gulph Rd Ste 100
King Of Prussia PA 19406
610 337-7000

(P-9013)
BAY AREA/DIABLO PETROLEUM CO (HQ)
1340 Arnold Dr Ste 231, Martinez (94553-4189)
P.O. Box 4450, San Francisco (94144-0001)
PHONE..................................925 228-2222
Dennis M O'Keefe, CEO
Patrick O'Keefe, Vice Pres
Rick Leroux, General Mgr
Michael Bowcut, Finance
EMP: 125
SQ FT: 6,000
SALES (est): 69.5MM
SALES (corp-wide): 110.8MM Privately Held
SIC: 5172 Petroleum products; gasoline; diesel fuel; lubricating oils & greases
PA: Golden Gate Petroleum Co.
1340 Arnold Dr Ste 231
Martinez CA 94553
925 335-3700

(P-9014)
BAY AREA/DIABLO PETROLEUM CO
1800 Sutter St, Concord (94520-2563)
P.O. Box 44550, San Francisco (94144-0001)
PHONE..................................925 228-2222
Russell Mederios, Manager
EMP: 130
SALES (corp-wide): 110.8MM Privately Held
SIC: 5172 Gases, liquefied petroleum (propane)
HQ: Bay Area/Diablo Petroleum, Co.
1340 Arnold Dr Ste 231
Martinez CA 94553
925 228-2222

(P-9015)
DASSELS PETROLEUM INC
340 El Camino Real S, Salinas (93901-4553)
PHONE..................................831 636-5100
Graham Mackie, Branch Mgr
EMP: 50
SALES (corp-wide): 40.8MM Privately Held
WEB: www.dassels.com
SIC: 5172 Gases, liquefied petroleum (propane)
PA: Dassel's Petroleum, Inc.
31 Wright Rd
Hollister CA 95023
831 636-5100

(P-9016)
DOWNS FUEL TRANSPORT INC
1296 Magnolia Ave, Corona (92879-2027)
PHONE..................................951 256-8286
Michael J Downs, President
EMP: 50
SALES (est): 13.3MM Privately Held
SIC: 5172 Engine fuels & oils

(P-9017)
EFUEL LLC
Also Called: Easy Fuel
1346 E Taylor St, San Jose (95133-1040)
PHONE..................................408 280-5235
Donald Harper, CEO
EMP: 80
SQ FT: 5,000
SALES (est): 65MM Privately Held
SIC: 5172 Petroleum products

(P-9018)
EMPIRE OIL CO
2756 S Riverside Ave, Bloomington (92316-3500)
PHONE..................................909 877-0226
Fax: 909 877-0732
Richard Alden Sr, CEO

5172 - Petroleum & Petroleum Prdts Wholesale County (P-9019)

Richard Scott Alden Jr, *President*
Donald Welker, *CFO*
Tim Josse, *Sales Mgr*
EMP: 52
SQ FT: 2,300
SALES (est): 15.7MM **Privately Held**
WEB: www.empireoil.com
SIC: 5172 Diesel fuel; lubricating oils & greases

(P-9019)
FLYERS ENERGY LLC
4200 Buck Owens Blvd, Bakersfield (93308-4935)
PHONE 661 321-9961
Henry Medina, *President*
EMP: 320
SALES (corp-wide): 135.2MM **Privately Held**
SIC: 5172 Engine fuels & oils
PA: Flyers Energy, Llc
 2360 Lindbergh St
 Auburn CA 95602
 530 885-0401

(P-9020)
FLYERS ENERGY LLC
571 W Slover Ave, Bloomington (92316-2454)
PHONE 909 877-2441
EMP: 118
SALES (corp-wide): 135.2MM **Privately Held**
SIC: 5172 Engine fuels & oils
PA: Flyers Energy, Llc
 2360 Lindbergh St
 Auburn CA 95602
 530 885-0401

(P-9021)
FLYERS ENERGY LLC
444 Yolanda Ave Ste A, Santa Rosa (95404-8090)
PHONE 707 546-0766
EMP: 70
SALES (corp-wide): 135.2MM **Privately Held**
SIC: 5172 3569 Petroleum products; lubricating oils & greases; lubrication equipment, industrial
PA: Flyers Energy, Llc
 2360 Lindbergh St
 Auburn CA 95602
 530 885-0401

(P-9022)
GENERAL PETROLEUM CORPORATION (DH)
Also Called: G P Resources
19501 S Santa Fe Ave, Compton (90221-5913)
PHONE 562 983-7300
Fax: 310 637-9231
James A Halsam III, *CEO*
Michael Ruehring, *President*
Scott Smith, *CFO*
Charles McDaniels, *Senior VP*
Sean Kha, *Vice Pres*
▲ **EMP:** 150
SQ FT: 5,000
SALES (est): 87.6MM
SALES (corp-wide): 1B **Privately Held**
SIC: 5172 Petroleum products
HQ: Pecos, Inc.
 19501 S Santa Fe Ave
 Compton CA 90221
 310 356-2300

(P-9023)
INTERSTATE FUEL SYSTEMS INC
8221 Alpine Ave, Sacramento (95826-4708)
PHONE 916 457-6572
Terrance Andrews, *President*
Laurene Andrews, *Treasurer*
Dan Dalio, *Admin Sec*
David Delehant, *Agent*
EMP: 100
SQ FT: 20,000
SALES (est): 20.5MM **Privately Held**
SIC: 5172 Fuel oil

(P-9024)
IPC (USA) INC (HQ)
4 Hutton Cntre Dr Ste 700, Santa Ana (92707)
PHONE 949 648-5600
Hiroki Okinaga, *CEO*
Keiji Shigeoka, *Ch of Bd*
James Takeuchi, *CFO*
Randy Jones, *Vice Pres*
Paul Smith, *Vice Pres*
EMP: 65
SQ FT: 9,450
SALES (est): 302.2MM
SALES (corp-wide): 43.4B **Privately Held**
WEB: www.usipc.com
SIC: 5172 Aircraft fueling services; diesel fuel; gasoline
PA: Itochu Corporation
 2-5-1, Kitaaoyama
 Minato-Ku TKY 107-0
 334 972-121

(P-9025)
KAISERAIR INC (PA)
8735 Earhart Rd, Oakland (94621-4547)
P.O. Box 2626 (94614-0626)
PHONE 510 569-9622
Fax: 310 569-5890
Ronald J Guerra, *President*
Sandy Waters, *President*
Jim Strickland, *CFO*
Rob Guerra, *Senior VP*
Glenn Barrett, *Vice Pres*
EMP: 148
SQ FT: 970,000
SALES (est): 33MM **Privately Held**
WEB: www.kaiserair.com
SIC: 5172 4522 7359 4581 Aircraft fueling services; air transportation, nonscheduled; aircraft rental; aircraft maintenance & repair services

(P-9026)
M O DION & SONS INC (PA)
1543 W 16th St, Long Beach (90813-1210)
PHONE 714 540-5535
Toll Free: .... 888 -
Fax: 562 432-7969
Pat Cullen, *CEO*
Matt Cullen, *President*
Patrick B Cullen, *CEO*
Bill Frank, *CFO*
Brian Busby, *General Mgr*
EMP: 60 EST: 1930
SQ FT: 85,000
SALES (est): 143.5MM **Privately Held**
WEB: www.dionandsons.com
SIC: 5172 Gasoline; diesel fuel; lubricating oils & greases

(P-9027)
SWISSPORT FUELING INC
1 Edward White Way, Oakland (94621-4553)
P.O. Box 6366 (94603-0366)
PHONE 510 562-1701
Ken Carlson, *Manager*
Patrick Chan, *Finance Mgr*
EMP: 72
SALES (corp-wide): 202.3MM **Privately Held**
SIC: 5172 4925 Aircraft fueling services; gas production and/or distribution
PA: Swissport Fueling Inc.
 45025 Aviation Dr Ste 350
 Dulles VA 20166
 703 742-4338

(P-9028)
TOWER ENERGY GROUP (PA)
1983 W 190th St Ste 100, Torrance (90504-6240)
PHONE 310 538-8000
Fax: 310 538-8013
John Rogers, *Principal*
John Hendrick, *Senior VP*
Tom Haug, *Vice Pres*
Twanna Rogers, *Vice Pres*
Nick Battaglia, *General Mgr*
EMP: 153
SQ FT: 22,702
SALES (est): 395.3MM **Privately Held**
SIC: 5172 Gasoline

(P-9029)
UNITED EL SEGUNDO INC (PA)
Also Called: United Oil
17311 S Main St, Gardena (90248-3131)
PHONE 310 323-3992
Fax: 310 323-3483
Ronald Appel, *President*
Jeff Appel, *Corp Secy*
Ken Strong, *General Mgr*
Stan Hecht, *Info Tech Mgr*
Vera Carey, *Software Engr*
EMP: 60
SQ FT: 3,500
SALES (est): 120.6MM **Privately Held**
WEB: www.unitedoil.net
SIC: 5172 6531 Gasoline; real estate leasing & rentals

(P-9030)
VALLEY PACIFIC PETRO SVCS INC
9521 Enos Ln, Bakersfield (93314-8007)
PHONE 661 746-7737
Fax: 661 746-7741
Kat Bowen, *Branch Mgr*
EMP: 113
SALES (corp-wide): 173.2MM **Privately Held**
SIC: 5172 Petroleum products
PA: Valley Pacific Petroleum Services, Inc.
 152 Frank West Cir # 100
 Stockton CA 95206
 209 948-9412

(P-9031)
VAN DE POL ENTERPRISES INC (PA)
4895 S Airport Way, Stockton (95206-3915)
P.O. Box 1107 (95201-1107)
PHONE 209 944-9115
Fax: 209 466-1910
Lee Atwater, *Ch of Bd*
Paul Gosal, *Owner*
Ted Wysoki, *Owner*
Ronald Van De Pol, *President*
Scott Macewan, *CFO*
EMP: 75
SQ FT: 10,000
SALES (est): 139MM **Privately Held**
SIC: 5172 Petroleum products

(P-9032)
VAN DE POL ENTERPRISES INC
3081 E Hamilton Ave, Fresno (93721-3211)
PHONE 559 860-4100
Ron Van De Pol, *Branch Mgr*
EMP: 53
SALES (corp-wide): 139MM **Privately Held**
SIC: 5172 4925 Petroleum products; gas production and/or distribution
PA: Van De Pol Enterprises, Inc.
 4895 S Airport Way
 Stockton CA 95206
 209 944-9115

(P-9033)
VISCOUNT PETROLEUM LLC
Also Called: Vicount Group
3699 Wilshire Blvd # 880, Los Angeles (90010-2718)
PHONE 213 382-1058
Fax: 323 382-2538
Jimmy E Okoki, *President*
Loni Williams, *Vice Chairman*
Mike Davis, *Info Tech Mgr*
EMP: 50
SALES (est): 6.7MM **Privately Held**
SIC: 5172 Crude oil

(P-9034)
WARREN E&P INC
Also Called: Warren E & P
400 Oceangate Ste 200, Long Beach (90802-4306)
PHONE 562 590-0909
James A Watt, *CEO*
Philip A Epstein, *CEO*
Norman Swanton, *CEO*
Michael Jordan, *Project Mgr*
EMP: 62
SQ FT: 7,000
SALES (est): 1.1MM
SALES (corp-wide): 88.3MM **Publicly Held**
SIC: 5172 Gasoline
PA: Warren Resources, Inc.
 1331 17th St Ste 720
 Denver CO 80202
 720 403-8125

(P-9035)
WHOLESALE FUELS INC
2200 E Brundage Ln, Bakersfield (93307-3066)
P.O. Box 82277 (93380-2277)
PHONE 661 327-4900
Fax: 661 327-9405
Charles McCan, *President*
Brian Bucassa, *CFO*
Tom Jamieson, *Corp Secy*
Jeff Shultz, *General Mgr*
EMP: 63
SQ FT: 5,000
SALES: 111.3MM **Privately Held**
WEB: www.wholesalefuels.com
SIC: 5172 Petroleum products

5181 Beer & Ale Wholesale

(P-9036)
ACE BEVERAGE CO
550 S Mission Rd, Los Angeles (90033-4234)
P.O. Box 33256 (90033-0256)
PHONE 323 266-6238
Dan Holland, *Principal*
EMP: 100
SALES (corp-wide): 409.2MM **Privately Held**
SIC: 5181 Beer & ale
HQ: Ace Beverage Co.
 401 S Anderson St
 Los Angeles CA 90033
 323 264-6001

(P-9037)
ADVANCE BEVERAGE CO INC
5200 District Blvd, Bakersfield (93313-2330)
P.O. Box 9517 (93389-9517)
PHONE 661 833-3783
Fax: 661 833-0279
William K Lazzerini Sr, *Ch of Bd*
William K Lazzerini Jr, *President*
Anthony Lazzerini, *Vice Pres*
Tom Maples, *Sales Executive*
Cathy George, *Manager*
▲ **EMP:** 90
SQ FT: 93,000
SALES (est): 49.6MM **Privately Held**
WEB: www.advancebeverage.com
SIC: 5181 5182 Beer & other fermented malt liquors; wine

(P-9038)
ALLIED BEVERAGES INCORPORATED (PA)
Also Called: Best-Way Distributing Co
13235 Golden State Rd, Sylmar (91342-1129)
PHONE 818 493-6400
Fax: 818 362-7180
Kevin Williams, *CEO*
Erin S Gabler, *CFO*
William L Larson, *Vice Pres*
Fran Fimvres, *Executive Asst*
Earl J Whitehead, *Admin Sec*
▲ **EMP:** 295
SQ FT: 240,000
SALES (est): 231MM **Privately Held**
WEB: www.alliedbeverages.com
SIC: 5181 Beer & other fermented malt liquors

(P-9039)
ANHEUSER-BUSCH LLC
1400 Marlborough Ave, Riverside (92507-2097)
PHONE 951 782-3935
Fax: 951 782-3957
Yo Sanchez, *Manager*
Bruce Larson, *President*
Diego Genera, *Opers Mgr*
Mark Harshman, *Sales Executive*
Killam Johnson, *Manager*

PRODUCTS & SERVICES SECTION

5181 - Beer & Ale Wholesale County (P-9060)

EMP: 150
SQ FT: 100,000
SALES (corp-wide): 1B **Privately Held**
WEB: www.hispanicbud.com
SIC: 5181 Beer & other fermented malt liquors
HQ: Anheuser-Busch, Llc
1 Busch Pl
Saint Louis MO 63118
314 632-6777

(P-9040) ANHEUSER-BUSCH LLC
20499 S Reeves Ave, Carson (90810-1011)
PHONE 310 761-4600
Fax: 310 900-2290
Damian Bonnenfant, *Manager*
J Bearss, *Manager*
Al Gee, *Manager*
EMP: 115
SALES (corp-wide): 1B **Privately Held**
WEB: www.hispanicbud.com
SIC: 5181 Beer & ale
HQ: Anheuser-Busch, Llc
1 Busch Pl
Saint Louis MO 63118
314 632-6777

(P-9041) ANHEUSER-BUSCH LLC
18952 Macarthur Blvd, Irvine (92612-1432)
PHONE 949 263-9270
Patrick Waters, *Branch Mgr*
EMP: 111
SALES (corp-wide): 1B **Privately Held**
WEB: www.hispanicbud.com
SIC: 5181 Beer & ale
HQ: Anheuser-Busch, Llc
1 Busch Pl
Saint Louis MO 63118
314 632-6777

(P-9042) BAY AREA DISTRIBUTING CO INC
1061 Factory St, Richmond (94801-2161)
PHONE 510 232-8554
Fax: 510 232-5017
Kenneth G Sodo, *President*
Jackie Defabio, *Office Admin*
Marian Freeman, *Admin Asst*
Michael Bosnich, *VP Sales*
Chris Baker, *Marketing Staff*
▲ **EMP:** 50 **EST:** 1973
SQ FT: 22,000
SALES (est): 16.3MM **Privately Held**
SIC: 5181 5149 Beer & other fermented malt liquors; mineral or spring water bottling; soft drinks

(P-9043) BEAUCHAMP DISTRIBUTING COMPANY
1911 S Santa Fe Ave, Compton (90221-5306)
PHONE 310 639-5320
Fax: 310 537-8641
Patrick L Beauchamp, *President*
Peter J Gumpert, *CFO*
Mary S Beauchamp, *Corp Secy*
Stacee L Beauchamp, *Vice Pres*
▲ **EMP:** 100
SQ FT: 100,000
SALES (est): 62.5MM **Privately Held**
SIC: 5181 5149 Beer & other fermented malt liquors; groceries & related products

(P-9044) BOTTOMLEY DISTRIBUTING CO INC
755 Yosemite Dr, Milpitas (95035-5463)
PHONE 408 945-0660
Fax: 408 262-6992
Donald A Bottomley, *President*
Michael Santos, *Sales Mgr*
Donald Botlanley, *Agent*
▲ **EMP:** 90
SQ FT: 96,000
SALES (est): 19.7MM **Privately Held**
SIC: 5181 Beer & other fermented malt liquors

(P-9045) CAPITAL BEVERAGE COMPANY (PA)
2500 Del Monte St, West Sacramento (95691-3835)
P.O. Box 914 (95691-0914)
PHONE 916 371-8164
Kenneth M Adamson, *President*
Charles Moulton, *CFO*
Coleen Adamson, *Manager*
Don Hamlett, *Manager*
◆ **EMP:** 110
SQ FT: 130,000
SALES (est): 27.2MM **Privately Held**
SIC: 5181 5182 5149 Beer & other fermented malt liquors; wine coolers, alcoholic; juices; mineral or spring water bottling

(P-9046) CENTRAL COAST DISTRIBUTING LLC
815 S Blosser Rd, Santa Maria (93458-4915)
PHONE 805 922-2108
Michael Larrabee,
Gary Rudolph, *Controller*
Rey Haubruge, *Manager*
Bryan Rounds, *Manager*
▲ **EMP:** 90
SQ FT: 51,651
SALES (est): 40.9MM **Privately Held**
SIC: 5181 Beer & other fermented malt liquors

(P-9047) CLASSIC DISTRG & BEV GROUP INC
120 Puente Ave, City of Industry (91746-2301)
PHONE 626 330-8231
Fax: 626 934-3712
Joseph Sanchez III, *CEO*
Victor Fiss, *President*
John Thomas, *CFO*
Lyar Bontigao, *Finance*
John Morales, *Human Resources*
▲ **EMP:** 261
SQ FT: 102,000
SALES (est): 138.9MM **Privately Held**
WEB: www.classicdist.com
SIC: 5181 Beer & other fermented malt liquors

(P-9048) COUCH DISTRIBUTING COMPANY INC
104 Lee Rd, Watsonville (95076-9448)
P.O. Box 50004 (95077-5004)
PHONE 831 724-0649
Fax: 831 724-4293
George W Couch III, *CEO*
Geoffrey A Couch, *Vice Pres*
Louie Pieracci, *Vice Pres*
Michael Star, *Info Tech Mgr*
Daric Holdaway, *Controller*
▲ **EMP:** 160
SQ FT: 72,000
SALES (est): 68.3MM **Privately Held**
WEB: www.couchdistributing.com
SIC: 5181 Beer & other fermented malt liquors

(P-9049) CREST BEVERAGE COMPANY INC
3840 Via De La Valle, Del Mar (92014-4268)
P.O. Box 9160, Rancho Santa Fe (92067-4160)
PHONE 858 452-2300
Steven S Sourapas Sr, *President*
Francisco Fragozo, *District Mgr*
Jeff Christensen, *Manager*
Christina Graten, *Manager*
▲ **EMP:** 170
SQ FT: 160,000
SALES (est): 52.2MM **Privately Held**
WEB: www.crestbeverage.com
SIC: 5181 5182 5149 Beer & ale; wine; groceries & related products

(P-9050) DBI BEVERAGE INC
4140 Brew Master Dr, Ceres (95307-7583)
PHONE 209 524-2477
Jeffrey D Skinner, *Branch Mgr*
EMP: 75
SALES (corp-wide): 206.7MM **Privately Held**
SIC: 5181 Beer & other fermented malt liquors
PA: Dbi Beverage Inc.
2 Ingram Blvd
La Vergne TN 37089
615 793-2337

(P-9051) DBI BEVERAGE SAN FRANCISCO
245 S Spruce Ave Ste 100, South San Francisco (94080-4597)
PHONE 415 643-9900
David Ingram, *Ch of Bd*
Bob Stahl, *Co-President*
Rick Guida, *General Mgr*
Willy Robyanto, *Accountant*
Steven Leesha, *Mktg Dir*
▲ **EMP:** 250
SALES (est): 33MM
SALES (corp-wide): 206.7MM **Privately Held**
WEB: www.goldenbrands.com
SIC: 5181 5149 Beer & other fermented malt liquors; soft drinks; mineral or spring water bottling
PA: Dbi Beverage Inc.
2 Ingram Blvd
La Vergne TN 37089
615 793-2337

(P-9052) DBI BEVERAGE SAN JOAQUIN
Also Called: San Joaquin Beverage
4547 Frontier Way, Stockton (95215-9675)
PHONE 209 948-9400
David Yoder, *President*
Donnie Daniel, *President*
David Ingram, *Chairman*
John Janosko, *Vice Pres*
Kim Paulk, *Vice Pres*
▲ **EMP:** 80
SQ FT: 8,000
SALES (est): 25MM **Privately Held**
SIC: 5181 Beer & other fermented malt liquors

(P-9053) DELTA BRANDS INC
3700 Finch Rd, Modesto (95357-4152)
PHONE 209 522-9044
Fax: 209 523-2149
Donald J Stewart Sr, *Ch of Bd*
Robert Stewart, *President*
Betty Stewart, *Corp Secy*
Donald J Stewart Jr, *Vice Pres*
Dave Dodson, *Executive*
EMP: 67
SQ FT: 62,000
SALES (est): 12.3MM **Privately Held**
SIC: 5181 Beer & other fermented malt liquors

(P-9054) DONAGHY SALES INC
2363 S Cedar Ave, Fresno (93725-1078)
Rural Route 2363 S Cedar (93725)
PHONE 559 486-0901
Fax: 559 266-8015
Edward Donaghy, *CEO*
Janis Donaghy, *Admin Sec*
▲ **EMP:** 150
SQ FT: 75,000
SALES (est): 102.1MM **Privately Held**
SIC: 5181 Beer & other fermented malt liquors

(P-9055) ELYXIR DISTRIBUTING LLC
270 W Riverside Dr, Watsonville (95076-5106)
PHONE 831 761-6400
Fax: 831 761-6404
Paul C Ely III,
Pau Ely, *COO*
Kym Dewitt, *CFO*
Brian Mullaly, *Info Tech Mgr*
Nick Tennessy, *Technician*

EMP: 103
SQ FT: 35,000
SALES (est): 53.3MM **Privately Held**
WEB: www.elyxir.com
SIC: 5181 5149 Beer & ale; beverages, except coffee & tea

(P-9056) FOOTHILL DISTRIBUTING CO INC
1530 Beltline Rd, Redding (96003-1408)
P.O. Box 492800 (96049-2800)
PHONE 530 243-3932
Fax: 530 243-5936
Lance Goble, *President*
Lynn Goble, *Corp Secy*
Mike Bolton, *Vice Pres*
Gary Burks, *Vice Pres*
Joe Pereira, *Vice Pres*
▲ **EMP:** 101
SQ FT: 33,000
SALES (est): 39MM **Privately Held**
WEB: www.foothilldistributing.com
SIC: 5181 5182 Beer & other fermented malt liquors; wine

(P-9057) FRESNO BEVERAGE COMPANY INC
Also Called: Valley Wide Beverage Company
4010 E Hardy Ave, Fresno (93725-2331)
PHONE 559 650-1500
Fax: 559 650-1515
Louis J Amendola, *CEO*
Dan Boitano, *Vice Pres*
Todd Howerton, *Vice Pres*
Carole Gonzales, *Executive*
Brian Kennedy, *VP Admin*
▲ **EMP:** 180
SQ FT: 140,000
SALES (est): 102.6MM **Privately Held**
WEB: www.valleywidebeverage.com
SIC: 5181 Beer & other fermented malt liquors

(P-9058) GATE CITY BEVERAGE DISTRS (PA)
2505 Steele Rd, San Bernardino (92408-3913)
PHONE 909 799-0281
Fax: 909 796-7968
Leona Aronoff, *President*
Barry Aronoff, *CFO*
John Rushing, *Controller*
Greg Raco, *Plant Mgr*
Ed Williams, *Plant Mgr*
▲ **EMP:** 294 **EST:** 1940
SQ FT: 280,000
SALES (est): 65.8MM **Privately Held**
WEB: www.gcbev.com
SIC: 5181 5149 5145 Beer & other fermented malt liquors; soft drinks; mineral or spring water bottling; confectionery

(P-9059) GATE CITY BEVERAGE DISTRS
82309 Market St, Indio (92201-2251)
PHONE 760 775-5483
Barry J Aronoff, *Owner*
EMP: 294
SQ FT: 10,000
SALES (corp-wide): 65.8MM **Privately Held**
WEB: www.gcbev.com
SIC: 5181 5149 Beer & other fermented malt liquors; water, distilled
PA: Gate City Beverage Distributors
2505 Steele Rd
San Bernardino CA 92408
909 799-0281

(P-9060) HARALAMBOS BEVERAGE COMPANY
26717 Palmetto Ave, Redlands (92374-1513)
PHONE 909 307-1777
Gary Leavitt, *Branch Mgr*
EMP: 151
SALES (corp-wide): 262.6MM **Privately Held**
WEB: www.haralambos.com
SIC: 5181 Beer & other fermented malt liquors

5181 - Beer & Ale Wholesale County (P-9061)

PA: Haralambos Beverage Company.
2300 Pellissier Pl
City Of Industry CA 90601
562 347-4300

(P-9061)
HARALAMBOS BEVERAGE COMPANY (PA)
2300 Pellissier Pl, City of Industry (90601-1500)
P.O. Box 6005, El Monte (91734-2005)
PHONE.................................562 347-4300
Fax: 562 463-7840
H T Haralambos, *CEO*
Anthony Haralambos, *President*
Denise Conot, *CFO*
Thomas Haralambos, *Vice Pres*
Ford Poland, *Regional Mgr*
▲ **EMP:** 149
SQ FT: 270,000
SALES (est): 262.6MM **Privately Held**
WEB: www.haralambos.com
SIC: 5181 5149 Beer & other fermented malt liquors; beverages, except coffee & tea

(P-9062)
HARBOR DISTRIBUTING LLC (HQ)
5901 Bolsa Ave, Huntington Beach (92647-2053)
PHONE.................................714 933-2400
Fax: 714 935-0186
David K Reyes,
Paola Alvarez, *VP Human Res*
Cantu Richard, *Inv Control Mgr*
Tim McGuire,
Chris Reyes,
▲ **EMP:** 200
SQ FT: 150,000
SALES (est): 124.7MM **Privately Held**
SIC: 5181 Beer & other fermented malt liquors

(P-9063)
HARBOR DISTRIBUTING LLC
Also Called: Harbor Distributing Co
16407 S Main St, Gardena (90248-2823)
PHONE.................................310 538-5483
Fax: 310 538-0306
David Reyes, *Branch Mgr*
Tim McGuire, *Controller*
Radine Anthony, *Supervisor*
◆ **EMP:** 300 **Privately Held**
SIC: 5181 Beer & ale
HQ: Harbor Distributing, Llc
5901 Bolsa Ave
Huntington Beach CA 92647
714 933-2400

(P-9064)
HORIZON BEVERAGE COMPANY
8380 Pardee Dr, Oakland (94621-1481)
P.O. Box 6639 (94603-0639)
PHONE.................................510 465-2212
Ces Butner, *Partner*
Denny Suzuki, *Partner*
EMP: 80
SQ FT: 20,000
SALES (est): 7.1MM **Privately Held**
SIC: 5181 Beer & other fermented malt liquors

(P-9065)
JETRO CASH AND CARRY ENTPS LLC
5333 W Jefferson Blvd, Los Angeles (90016-3713)
PHONE.................................323 964-1200
Enrique Gallard, *Principal*
Edwin Lugo, *Info Tech Mgr*
EMP: 100 **Privately Held**
WEB: www.jetro.com
SIC: 5181 5142 5194 5147 Beer & other fermented malt liquors; packaged frozen goods; tobacco & tobacco products; meats, fresh; groceries, general line
HQ: Jetro Cash And Carry Enterprises, Llc
1524 132nd St
College Point NY 11356
718 939-6400

(P-9066)
JORDANOS INC (PA)
Also Called: Jordano's Food Service
550 S Patterson Ave, Santa Barbara (93111-2498)
P.O. Box 6803 (93160-6803)
PHONE.................................805 964-0611
Fax: 805 964-9528
Peter Jordano, *CEO*
Michael F Sieckowski, *CFO*
Jeffrey S Jordano, *Exec VP*
Nancy Parker, *Info Tech Mgr*
Steven Coonis, *MIS Staff*
▲ **EMP:** 250
SQ FT: 80,000
SALES (est): 441.7MM **Privately Held**
WEB: www.jordanos.com
SIC: 5181 5182 5149 5141 Beer & other fermented malt liquors; wine; soft drinks; groceries, general line; packaged frozen goods; fresh fruits & vegetables

(P-9067)
LARRABEE BROTHRS DISTRIBTNG CO
815 S Blosser Rd, Santa Maria (93458-4915)
P.O. Box 1850 (93456-1850)
PHONE.................................805 922-2108
Fax: 805 925-9214
Michael Larrabee, *President*
Margaret Larrabee, *Vice Pres*
EMP: 100
SQ FT: 51,651
SALES (est): 11.2MM **Privately Held**
SIC: 5181 Beer & other fermented malt liquors

(P-9068)
LE VECKE CORPORATION (PA)
Also Called: Le Vecke Group
10810 Inland Ave, Mira Loma (91752-3235)
PHONE.................................951 681-8600
Fax: 951 681-8666
Joseph Neil Levecke, *CEO*
Neil Levecke, *President*
Steve Vento, *Vice Pres*
Phil Deconinck, *General Mgr*
Maggie Weaver, *Human Resources*
◆ **EMP:** 62
SALES (est): 58.8MM **Privately Held**
WEB: www.levecke.com
SIC: 5181 Beer & other fermented malt liquors

(P-9069)
LIQUID INVESTMENTS INC (PA)
3840 Via De La Valle # 300, Del Mar (92014-4268)
PHONE.................................858 509-8510
Fax: 858 509-8511
Ron L Fowler, *CEO*
Mark Herculson, *Exec VP*
Terry L Harris, *VP Finance*
▲ **EMP:** 170 **EST:** 1981
SQ FT: 190,000
SALES (est): 167.5MM **Privately Held**
WEB: www.lqdinv.com
SIC: 5181 5145 5182 Beer & other fermented malt liquors; fountain supplies; wine

(P-9070)
MARKSTEIN BEV CO SACRAMENTO
Also Called: Markstein Beverage Company
60 Main Ave, Sacramento (95838-2034)
P.O. Box 15379 (95851-0379)
PHONE.................................916 920-3911
Fax: 916 920-0335
Hayden Markstein, *CEO*
Richard Markstein, *Ch of Bd*
Steve Markstein, *President*
Markstein Hayden, *Exec VP*
John C Ricksen, *Admin Sec*
▲ **EMP:** 150
SALES (est): 120.6MM **Privately Held**
WEB: www.marksteinbev.com
SIC: 5181 5149 Beer & ale; soft drinks; mineral or spring water bottling

(P-9071)
MARKSTEIN BEVERAGE CO
505 S Pacific St, San Marcos (92078-4049)
P.O. Box 6902 (92079-6902)
PHONE.................................760 744-9100
Fax: 760 744-0082
Kenneth W Markstein, *CEO*
Steven Markstein, *Vice Pres*
Herman Huppert, *Info Tech Dir*
Tom Sarrette, *VP Sls/Mktg*
▲ **EMP:** 120
SQ FT: 118,000
SALES (est): 68MM **Privately Held**
WEB: www.abwholesaler.com
SIC: 5181 Beer & other fermented malt liquors

(P-9072)
MATAGRANO INC
440 Forbes Blvd, South San Francisco (94080-2015)
P.O. Box 2588 (94083-2588)
PHONE.................................650 829-4829
Fax: 650 952-9421
Louis Matagrano, *President*
Trevor Bartlett, *CFO*
William Hill, *CFO*
Tom Haas, *Vice Pres*
Frank Matagrano Jr, *Vice Pres*
▲ **EMP:** 175
SQ FT: 100,000
SALES (est): 123.9MM **Privately Held**
WEB: www.matagrano.com
SIC: 5181 5149 Beer & other fermented malt liquors; mineral or spring water bottling; juices

(P-9073)
ME FOX & COMPANY INC
128 Component Dr, San Jose (95131-1180)
PHONE.................................408 435-8510
Fax: 408 435-8738
Michael E Fox Sr, *Ch of Bd*
Terence Fox, *President*
Mark Spoden, *COO*
Doug Webenbauer, *CFO*
Catherine Fox, *Treasurer*
▲ **EMP:** 100
SQ FT: 126,000
SALES: 75.4MM **Privately Held**
SIC: 5181 5149 Beer & other fermented malt liquors; soft drinks; mineral or spring water bottling; juices

(P-9074)
MESA DISTRIBUTING CO INC (HQ)
3840 Via De La Valle # 300, Del Mar (92014-4268)
PHONE.................................858 452-2300
Ronald L Fowler, *Ch of Bd*
Ron L Fowler, *Ch of Bd*
Jack F Studebaker, *Admin Sec*
Sue Lyerly, *Controller*
EMP: 225
SQ FT: 190,000
SALES (est): 25.1MM
SALES (corp-wide): 167.5MM **Privately Held**
WEB: www.mesadistributing.com
SIC: 5181 0182 5182 Beer & other fermented malt liquors; vegetable crops grown under cover; wine & distilled beverages
PA: Liquid Investments, Inc.
3840 Via De La Valle # 300
Del Mar CA 92014
858 509-8510

(P-9075)
MISSION BEVERAGE CO (HQ)
550 S Mission Rd, Los Angeles (90033-4256)
P.O. Box 33256 (90033-0256)
PHONE.................................323 266-6238
Fax: 323 266-6559
John E Anderson Sr, *Ch of Bd*
Don Holland, *President*
Therese D Curtis, *Corp Secy*
Roberto Maltez, *Administration*
▲ **EMP:** 210

SALES (est): 73MM
SALES (corp-wide): 409.2MM **Privately Held**
SIC: 5181 5149 Beer & other fermented malt liquors; soft drinks
PA: Topa Equities, Ltd.
1800 Ave Of The Ste 1400
Los Angeles CA 90067
310 203-9199

(P-9076)
MORRIS DISTRIBUTING INC
3800a Lakeville Hwy, Petaluma (94954-5673)
P.O. Box 5699 (94955-5699)
PHONE.................................707 769-7294
Fax: 707 769-7293
Ronald L Morris, *CEO*
Joe Netter, *Corp Secy*
Julia Turner, *Accountant*
Rick Dardis, *Sales Staff*
Ray McClintock, *Sales Staff*
▲ **EMP:** 80
SQ FT: 13,500
SALES (est): 23.3MM **Privately Held**
SIC: 5181 5149 Beer & other fermented malt liquors; mineral or spring water bottling; juices

(P-9077)
NOR-CAL BEVERAGE CO INC (PA)
2150 Stone Blvd, West Sacramento (95691-4049)
PHONE.................................916 372-0600
Fax: 916 374-2600
Shannon Deary-Bell, *President*
Donald Deary, *Ch of Bd*
Grant Deary, *President*
Tim Deary, *President*
Mike Montroni, *CFO*
▼ **EMP:** 280
SQ FT: 152,000
SALES (est): 245.3MM **Privately Held**
SIC: 5181 2086 Beer & ale; soft drinks: packaged in cans, bottles, etc.; fruit drinks (less than 100% juice): packaged in cans, etc.

(P-9078)
RESTAURANT DEPOT LLC
1265 N Kraemer Blvd, Anaheim (92806-1921)
PHONE.................................714 666-9205
Ralph Vasquez, *Manager*
Clive Gavshon, *Branch Mgr*
Tony Barbi, *Manager*
EMP: 150 **Privately Held**
WEB: www.jrdtuning.com
SIC: 5181 5141 5194 5142 Beer & other fermented malt liquors; groceries, general line; tobacco & tobacco products; packaged frozen goods; meats, fresh
HQ: Restaurant Depot, Llc
1524 132nd St
College Point NY 11356
-

(P-9079)
RESTAURANT DEPOT LLC
19901 Hamilton Ave Ste A, Torrance (90502-1367)
PHONE.................................310 516-7400
Fax: 310 527-3150
Sue Greene, *Branch Mgr*
EMP: 60 **Privately Held**
WEB: www.jrdtuning.com
SIC: 5181 5141 5194 5142 Beer & other fermented malt liquors; groceries, general line; tobacco & tobacco products; packaged frozen goods; meats, fresh
HQ: Restaurant Depot, Llc
1524 132nd St
College Point NY 11356
-

(P-9080)
RESTAURANT DEPOT LLC
2045 Evans Ave, San Francisco (94124-1022)
PHONE.................................415 920-2888
Fax: 415 920-2889
Samuel Cortez, *Branch Mgr*
Sue Greene, *Finance Mgr*
EMP: 150 **Privately Held**
WEB: www.jrdtuning.com

PRODUCTS & SERVICES SECTION
5182 - Wine & Distilled Alcoholic Beverages Wholesale County (P-9101)

SIC: **5181** 5141 5194 5142 Beer & other fermented malt liquors; groceries, general line; tobacco & tobacco products; packaged frozen goods; meats, fresh
HQ: Restaurant Depot, Llc
1524 132nd St
College Point NY 11356

(P-9081)
RESTAURANT DEPOT LLC
5333 W Jefferson Blvd, Los Angeles (90016-3713)
PHONE..................................323 964-1220
Fax: 323 964-1211
Enrique Gallard, *Manager*
Robarto Bolero, *Manager*
EMP: 150 Privately Held
WEB: www.jrdtuning.com
SIC: **5181** 5194 5147 5142 Beer & other fermented malt liquors; tobacco & tobacco products; meats, fresh; packaged frozen goods; groceries, general line
HQ: Restaurant Depot, Llc
1524 132nd St
College Point NY 11356

(P-9082)
RESTAURANT DEPOT LLC
15853 Strathern St, Van Nuys (91406-1310)
PHONE..................................818 376-7687
Dan Mihal, *Manager*
EMP: 150 Privately Held
WEB: www.jrdtuning.com
SIC: **5181** 5147 5141 5142 Beer & other fermented malt liquors; meats, fresh; groceries, general line; packaged frozen goods; tobacco & tobacco products
HQ: Restaurant Depot, Llc
1524 132nd St
College Point NY 11356

(P-9083)
SACCANI DISTRIBUTING COMPANY
2600 5th St, Sacramento (95818-2899)
P.O. Box 1764 (95812-1764)
PHONE..................................916 441-0213
Fax: 916 441-0806
Gary Saccani, *President*
Steven Fishman, *Corp Secy*
Roland Saccani, *Vice Pres*
Bill Earley, *Marketing Mgr*
Anthony Sapeta, *Sales Mgr*
▲ EMP: 90
SQ FT: 40,000
SALES (est): 37.9MM Privately Held
SIC: **5181** 5149 Beer & other fermented malt liquors; soft drinks

(P-9084)
SAN JOAQUIN BEVERAGE INC
3121 W March Ln Ste 100, Stockton (95219-2367)
P.O. Box 32164 (95213-2164)
PHONE..................................209 320-2400
Fax: 209 948-0946
James Plunkett, *President*
David Yoder, *Treasurer*
John Janosko, *Vice Pres*
Laurie Carter, *Accounting Mgr*
Johnathan Chandler, *Human Res Mgr*
EMP: 61
SALES (est): 11.6MM Privately Held
SIC: **5181** 5182 Beer & other fermented malt liquors; wine

(P-9085)
SEQUOIA BEVERAGE
2122 N Plaza Dr, Visalia (93291-9358)
P.O. Box 5025 (93278-5025)
PHONE..................................559 651-2444
Fax: 559 651-3356
Dan Bueno, *Partner*
Rose Bueno, *Partner*
Joan Carpenter, *Partner*
Laurie Zuniga, *Administration*
Bill Diller, *Finance*
EMP: 101
SQ FT: 100,000
SALES: 77.2MM Privately Held
WEB: www.sequoia-beverage.com
SIC: **5181** Beer & other fermented malt liquors

(P-9086)
STRAUB DISTRIBUTING CO LTD (PA)
4633 E La Palma Ave, Anaheim (92807-1909)
PHONE..................................714 779-4000
Michael L Cooper, *General Ptnr*
Robert K Adams, *Partner*
Don Beightol, *Partner*
Lynn Gallagher, *Officer*
John Durazo, *Vice Pres*
▲ EMP: 150
SQ FT: 32,000
SALES (est): 142.2MM Privately Held
WEB: www.sdcoc.net
SIC: **5181** Beer & other fermented malt liquors

(P-9087)
T F LOUDERBACK INC (PA)
Also Called: Bay Area Beverage
700 National Ct, Richmond (94804-2008)
PHONE..................................510 965-6120
Fax: 510 965-6323
Tj Louderback, *President*
Thomas F Louderback, *President*
Ciaran Byrne, *CFO*
Tom Echaniz, *CFO*
David Hendrickson, *CFO*
▲ EMP: 102
SQ FT: 65,000
SALES (est): 98.1MM Privately Held
WEB: www.bayareabev.com
SIC: **5181** 5149 2037 2033 Beer & other fermented malt liquors; beverages, except coffee & tea; juices; frozen fruits & vegetables; canned fruits & specialties

(P-9088)
TRIANGLE DISTRIBUTING CO (PA)
Also Called: Heimark Distributing
12065 Pike St, Santa Fe Springs (90670-2964)
PHONE..................................562 699-3424
Fax: 562 699-2318
Donald Heimark, *Ch of Bd*
Peter H Heimark, *President*
Mike Crow, *Corp Secy*
Greg Scanlon, *Office Mgr*
Tom Snyder, *Manager*
▲ EMP: 170
SQ FT: 150,000
SALES (est): 86.8MM Privately Held
WEB: www.triangle-dist.com
SIC: **5181** Beer & other fermented malt liquors

(P-9089)
TRIANGLE DISTRIBUTING CO
Also Called: Hallmark Distributing
82851 Avenue 45, Indio (92201-2379)
P.O. Box 3108 (92202-3108)
PHONE..................................760 347-4052
Bill Shiner, *General Mgr*
James B Fleming, *President*
EMP: 55
SALES (corp-wide): 86.8MM Privately Held
WEB: www.triangle-dist.com
SIC: **5181** Beer & other fermented malt liquors
PA: Triangle Distributing Co.
12065 Pike St
Santa Fe Springs CA 90670
562 699-3424

5182 Wine & Distilled Alcoholic Beverages Wholesale

(P-9090)
BARREL TEN QUARTER CIRCLE INC
33 Harlow Ct, NAPA (94558-7520)
P.O. Box 3400 (94558-0551)
PHONE..................................707 265-4000
Fred T Franzia, *CEO*
John G Franzia Jr, *Co-President*
Joseph S Franzia, *Co-President*
Daniel Leonard, *Vice Pres*
Suzette Killingsworth, *Purch Agent*
EMP: 300
SALES (est): 64.8MM
SALES (corp-wide): 165.9MM Privately Held
SIC: **5182** Bottling wines & liquors
PA: Bronco Wine Company
6342 Bystrum Rd
Ceres CA 95307
209 538-3131

(P-9091)
BAY AREA BEVERAGE CO
700 National Ct, Richmond (94804-2008)
PHONE..................................510 965-6120
Tj Louderback, *President*
Ciaran Byrne, *CFO*
Larry Green, *Vice Pres*
Philip Choi, *Purchasing*
EMP: 205
SALES (est): 67.7MM Privately Held
SIC: **5182** Wine & distilled beverages

(P-9092)
BEN MYERSON CANDY CO INC (PA)
Also Called: Wine Warehouse
6550 E Washington Blvd, Commerce (90040-1822)
P.O. Box 910900, Los Angeles (90091-0900)
PHONE..................................323 724-1700
Fax: 213 688-7571
James P Myerson, *President*
Linda Perez, *President*
Robert Myerson, *Treasurer*
James Myerson, *Corp Secy*
Trevor Thiret, *Senior VP*
◆ EMP: 350
SQ FT: 135,000
SALES (est): 286.9MM Privately Held
SIC: **5182** 5023 Wine; glassware

(P-9093)
BEN MYERSON CANDY CO INC
Also Called: Wine Warehouse
3463 Collins Ave, Richmond (94806-2000)
P.O. Box 45616, San Francisco (94145-0616)
PHONE..................................510 236-2233
Fax: 510 236-4152
Michael Cimino, *Manager*
Keith Smith, *VP Finance*
Coons Matthew, *Natl Sales Mgr*
Bernie Ryan, *Sales Dir*
Liz Ortiz, *Asst Mgr*
EMP: 95
SQ FT: 2,000
SALES (corp-wide): 286.9MM Privately Held
SIC: **5182** 5181 Liquor; neutral spirits; beer & ale
PA: Ben Myerson Candy Co., Inc.
6550 E Washington Blvd
Commerce CA 90040
323 724-1700

(P-9094)
DBI BEVERAGE SACRAMENTO (HQ)
3500 Carlin Dr, West Sacramento (95691-5872)
PHONE..................................916 373-5700
Jeff Skinner, *CEO*
John J Janosko, *Vice Pres*
Bob Beviacqua, *District Mgr*
Tom Grace, *District Mgr*
Rick Ross, *District Mgr*
▲ EMP: 75 EST: 2007
SQ FT: 200,000
SALES (est): 87.1MM
SALES (corp-wide): 206.7MM Privately Held
SIC: **5182** 5149 Wine & distilled beverages; beverages, except coffee & tea
PA: Dbi Beverage Inc.
2 Ingram Blvd
La Vergne TN 37089
615 793-2337

(P-9095)
DIAGEO NORTH AMERICA INC
21468 8th St E, Sonoma (95476-9767)
PHONE..................................707 939-6200
Fax: 707 935-1389
Claudia Schubert, *Branch Mgr*
Eric Holthouse, *Vice Pres*
Carol Ham, *Technical Staff*
Pamela Thompson, *Human Res Dir*
Milton Feng, *Manager*
EMP: 65
SALES (corp-wide): 16.6B Privately Held
SIC: **5182** Wine
HQ: Diageo North America Inc.
801 Main Ave
Norwalk CT 06851
203 229-2100

(P-9096)
DIAGEO NORTH AMERICA INC
30 Journey, Aliso Viejo (92656-3317)
PHONE..................................949 421-3974
Chris Turbeville, *Branch Mgr*
EMP: 69
SALES (corp-wide): 16.6B Privately Held
SIC: **5182** Wine
HQ: Diageo North America Inc.
801 Main Ave
Norwalk CT 06851
203 229-2100

(P-9097)
DRINKS HOLDINGS LLC (PA)
Also Called: Afternoon Delight
11175 Santa Monica Blvd # 400, Los Angeles (90025-3363)
PHONE..................................310 441-8400
Zac Brandenberg, *Mng Member*
EMP: 92 EST: 2014
SALES (est): 12MM Privately Held
SIC: **5182** Wine

(P-9098)
E & J GALLO WINERY
2650 Commerce Way, Commerce (90040-1413)
PHONE..................................323 720-6400
Bob Gillespie, *Opers Mgr*
Scott Triou, *Executive*
John Sanchez, *General Mgr*
EMP: 300
SALES (corp-wide): 1.9B Privately Held
WEB: www.gallo.com
SIC: **5182** Wine
PA: E. & J. Gallo Winery
600 Yosemite Blvd
Modesto CA 95354
209 341-3111

(P-9099)
EPIC VENTURES INC (PA)
Also Called: Epic Wines
200 Concourse Blvd, Santa Rosa (95403-8210)
PHONE..................................831 219-9100
Fax: 831 689-9082
William Patrick Foley, *CEO*
Scott Edwards, *President*
Robert W Prough, *CEO*
Andrea Mondragon, *COO*
Lorrie Harries, *CFO*
▲ EMP: 4
SQ FT: 4,000
SALES (est): 29.6MM Privately Held
WEB: www.epicventures.com
SIC: **5182** Wine

(P-9100)
FOLIO WINE COMPANY LLC
1285 Dealy Ln, NAPA (94559-9706)
PHONE..................................707 256-2757
Rick Choate, *Branch Mgr*
EMP: 65
SALES (corp-wide): 25.2MM Privately Held
SIC: **5182** Wine
PA: Folio Wine Company, Llc
550 Gateway Dr Ste 220
Napa CA 94558
707 254-9885

(P-9101)
FRANK-LIN DISTILLERS PDTS LTD (PA)
2455 Huntington Dr, Fairfield (94533-9734)
PHONE..................................408 259-8900

5182 - Wine & Distilled Alcoholic Beverages Wholesale County (P-9102)

PRODUCTS & SERVICES SECTION

Fax: 408 258-9527
Frank J Maestri, *President*
Anthony Demaria, *CFO*
Anthony Demorea, *CFO*
Mark S Pechusick, *Exec VP*
Lindley Maestri, *Vice Pres*
▲ **EMP:** 110 **EST:** 1966
SQ FT: 54,216
SALES (est): 116.3MM **Privately Held**
SIC: 5182 2085 Wine; distilled & blended liquors

(P-9102)
FREIXENET USA INC
Also Called: Gloria Ferrer
23555 Arnold Dr, Sonoma (95476-9285)
P.O. Box 1949 (95476-1949)
PHONE 707 996-7256
Jose Maria Ferrer, *President*
Eva Bertran, *Exec VP*
Kristen Hamilton, *Controller*
Efrain Saavedra, *Natl Sales Mgr*
David Brown, *VP Mktg*
▲ **EMP:** 54
SQ FT: 4,000
SALES (est): 31.4MM
SALES (corp-wide): 186.6MM **Privately Held**
WEB: www.freixenetusa.com
SIC: 5182 Wine
PA: Freixenet Sa
Plaza Joan Sala 2
Sant Sadurni D Anoia 08770
938 917-000

(P-9103)
GALLO SALES COMPANY INC (DH)
30825 Wiegman Rd, Hayward (94544-7893)
P.O. Box 1266, Union City (94587-6266)
PHONE 510 476-5000
Fax: 510 476-5455
Joseph E Gallo, *President*
Barbara Wilson, *Credit Mgr*
EMP: 225
SQ FT: 59,000
SALES (est): 42.1MM
SALES (corp-wide): 4.1B **Privately Held**
SIC: 5182 Wine
HQ: Gallo Glass Company
605 S Santa Cruz Ave
Modesto CA 95354
209 341-3710

(P-9104)
GUARACHI WINE PARTNERS INC
Also Called: Tgic Wine Imp & Wholesaler
22837 Ventura Blvd # 300, Woodland Hills (91364-1224)
PHONE 818 225-5100
Alex Guarachi, *Principal*
Joseph Granados, *Vice Pres*
Ray Stoughton, *Vice Pres*
Trisha Curry, *Executive Asst*
Jeffery Levine, *Controller*
▲ **EMP:** 80
SQ FT: 5,000
SALES (est): 50.8MM **Privately Held**
WEB: www.tgicimporters.com
SIC: 5182 Wine

(P-9105)
HALL WINES LLC
401 Saint Helena Hwy S, Saint Helena (94574-2200)
P.O. Box 25, Rutherford (94573-0025)
PHONE 707 967-2626
Fax: 707 967-2634
Mike Reynolds, *President*
Whitney Jacobson, *Vice Pres*
Damon Ainsworth, *Asst Controller*
Steve Meade, *Accountant*
Kathleen Fidler, *Controller*
▲ **EMP:** 50
SQ FT: 20,000
SALES (est): 28MM **Privately Held**
SIC: 5182 0172 Wine; grapes

(P-9106)
HENRY WINE GROUP LLC (HQ)
Also Called: Henry Wine Group of C.A., The
4301 Industrial Way, Benicia (94510-1227)
PHONE 707 745-8500
Fax: 707 745-4217

Ed Hogan, *President*
Kent Fitzgerald, *President*
Don Jennings, *COO*
Stephanie O'Brien, *CFO*
Chris Choate, *Vice Pres*
▲ **EMP:** 297
SALES (est): 74.4MM
SALES (corp-wide): 567.5MM **Privately Held**
SIC: 5182 Wine
PA: The Winebow Group Llc
4800 Cox Rd Ste 300
Glen Allen VA 23060
804 752-3670

(P-9107)
JACKSON FAMILY WINES INC
Regal Wine Company, The
1190 Kittyhawk Blvd Ste A, Santa Rosa (95403-1013)
PHONE 415 819-0301
John Grant, *Branch Mgr*
Mike Bartlett, *VP Opers*
EMP: 150
SQ FT: 20,746
SALES (corp-wide): 342.1MM **Privately Held**
WEB: www.cambriawines.com
SIC: 5182 Wine
PA: Jackson Family Wines, Inc.
421 And 425 Aviation Blvd
Santa Rosa CA 95403
707 544-4000

(P-9108)
MAGAVE TEQUILA INC
6 Park Pl, Belvedere Tiburon (94920-1048)
PHONE 415 515-3536
Michael Patane, *CEO*
▲ **EMP:** 50
SALES (est): 16.8MM **Privately Held**
SIC: 5182 Wine & distilled beverages

(P-9109)
SILVER OAK WINE CELLARS LP
1183 Dunaweal Ln, Calistoga (94515-9799)
PHONE 707 857-3562
David Duncang, *General Mgr*
Daniel Baron, *Exec VP*
EMP: 50
SQ FT: 13,997
SALES (est): 10.5MM **Privately Held**
SIC: 5182 2084 0172 Wine; wines, brandy & brandy spirits; grapes
PA: Silver Oak Wine Cellars, L.P.
915 Oakville Cross Rd
Oakville CA 94562
707 942-7022

(P-9110)
SOUTHERN WINE & SPIRITS AMRCA
723 Palmyrita Ave, Riverside (92507-1811)
PHONE 951 274-2420
Ivan Rouse, *Manager*
EMP: 100
SALES (corp-wide): 5B **Privately Held**
WEB: www.southernwine.com
SIC: 5182 Wine & distilled beverages
PA: Southern Glazer's Wine And Spirits, Llc
1600 Nw 163rd St
Miami FL 33169
305 625-4171

(P-9111)
SOUTHERN WINE & SPIRITS AMRCA
10730 Scripps Ranch Blvd, San Diego (92131-1003)
PHONE 858 537-3912
Fax: 858 537-3932
Craig Fontaine, *Manager*
EMP: 110
SALES (corp-wide): 5B **Privately Held**
WEB: www.southernwine.com
SIC: 5182 Bottling wines & liquors
PA: Southern Glazer's Wine And Spirits, Llc
1600 Nw 163rd St
Miami FL 33169
305 625-4171

(P-9112)
SOUTHERN WINE & SPIRITS AMRCA
2320 Kruse Dr, San Jose (95131-1231)
PHONE 408 750-3540
Julie Long, *Branch Mgr*
EMP: 75
SALES (corp-wide): 5B **Privately Held**
WEB: www.southernwine.com
SIC: 5182 Bottling wines & liquors
PA: Southern Glazer's Wine And Spirits, Llc
1600 Nw 163rd St
Miami FL 33169
305 625-4171

(P-9113)
SOUTHERN WINE & SPIRITS AMRCA
17101 Valley View Ave, Cerritos (90703-2413)
PHONE 562 926-2000
Fax: 562 404-2624
Steve Slader, *Branch Mgr*
Frank Levy, *Info Tech Dir*
Amy Willard, *Training Dir*
Andre Surma, *Purchasing*
Steve Slater, *Sales Mgr*
EMP: 500
SALES (corp-wide): 5B **Privately Held**
WEB: www.southernwine.com
SIC: 5182 5181 Wine; liquor; beer & ale
PA: Southern Glazer's Wine And Spirits, Llc
1600 Nw 163rd St
Miami FL 33169
305 625-4171

(P-9114)
VINO FARMS LLC
1377 E Lodi Ave, Lodi (95240-0840)
PHONE 209 334-6975
James Ledbetter,
Janet Kniss, *Controller*
John Ledbetter,
EMP: 700
SQ FT: 5,000
SALES (est): 123MM **Privately Held**
SIC: 5182 Wine

(P-9115)
VINWOOD CELLARS INC
18700 Geyserville Ave, Geyserville (95441-9526)
P.O. Box 1341, Healdsburg (95448-1341)
PHONE 707 857-4011
Fax: 707 857-3813
Alan Hemphill, *President*
Rene Dautel, *Treasurer*
Pete Downs, *Vice Pres*
Mark Toepke, *Vice Pres*
Mark Castleland, *General Mgr*
EMP: 50
SALES (est): 8MM **Privately Held**
SIC: 5182 2084 Wine & distilled beverages; wines

(P-9116)
WINIARSKI MANAGEMENT INC
5766 Silverado Trl, NAPA (94558-9413)
PHONE 707 944-2020
Warren P Winiarski, *President*
EMP: 100
SALES (est): 9.9MM **Privately Held**
SIC: 5182 0172 Wine; grapes

(P-9117)
YOUNGS HOLDINGS INC (PA)
14402 Franklin Ave, Tustin (92780-7013)
PHONE 714 368-4615
Vernon O Underwood Jr, *President*
Paul Vert, *President*
Janet Smith, *Exec VP*
Marry Doidge, *Vice Pres*
Kyle Knower, *Vice Pres*
EMP: 100
SALES (est): 1.1B **Privately Held**
SIC: 5182 Wine; neutral spirits

(P-9118)
YOUNGS MARKET COMPANY LLC (HQ)
14402 Franklin Ave, Tustin (92780-7013)
PHONE 714 368-4615
Chris Underwood, *CEO*
Dennis Hamann, *CFO*
Kevin Manion, *CFO*

Vern Underwood, *Chairman*
Philana Bouvier, *Exec VP*
◆ **EMP:** 350
SQ FT: 250,000
SALES (est): 972.7MM
SALES (corp-wide): 1.1B **Privately Held**
SIC: 5182 Wine; neutral spirits
PA: Young's Holdings, Inc.
14402 Franklin Ave
Tustin CA 92780
714 368-4615

(P-9119)
YOUNGS MARKET COMPANY LLC
850 Jarvis Dr, Morgan Hill (95037-2846)
PHONE 408 782-3121
Ken Feroli, *Manager*
Sunita Rout, *Programmer Anys*
John Benz, *Marketing Staff*
Chris Church, *Marketing Staff*
Jack Iverson, *Marketing Staff*
EMP: 100
SALES (corp-wide): 1.1B **Privately Held**
SIC: 5182 Liquor
HQ: Young's Market Company, Llc
14402 Franklin Ave
Tustin CA 92780
714 368-4615

(P-9120)
YOUNGS MARKET COMPANY LLC
5100 Franklin Dr, Pleasanton (94588-3355)
PHONE 510 475-2200
Fax: 510 475-2263
Chris Nicks, *Manager*
Megan Harter, *Technology*
Tammy Hall, *Human Res Mgr*
Regan Martinez, *Human Res Mgr*
Lloyd Sgamba, *Sales Staff*
EMP: 400
SQ FT: 20,000
SALES (corp-wide): 1.1B **Privately Held**
SIC: 5182 Wine; liquor
HQ: Young's Market Company, Llc
14402 Franklin Ave
Tustin CA 92780
714 368-4615

(P-9121)
YOUNGS MARKET COMPANY LLC
Also Called: Wine Dept
500 S Central Ave, Los Angeles (90013-1715)
PHONE 213 629-3929
Fax: 213 612-1239
Mark Sneed, *Branch Mgr*
Nick Claitman, *Vice Pres*
Tanya M Griffith, *Vice Pres*
Larry Di, *Program Mgr*
Rachel Tanham, *Office Mgr*
EMP: 450
SALES (corp-wide): 1.1B **Privately Held**
SIC: 5182 Wine & distilled beverages
HQ: Young's Market Company, Llc
14402 Franklin Ave
Tustin CA 92780
714 368-4615

(P-9122)
YOUNGS MARKET COMPANY LLC
256 Sutton Pl Ste 106, Santa Rosa (95407-8163)
PHONE 707 584-5170
Fax: 707 544-6858
Mark Delbenny, *Manager*
Mike Quick, *Sales Staff*
EMP: 65
SALES (corp-wide): 1.1B **Privately Held**
SIC: 5182 Liquor
HQ: Young's Market Company, Llc
14402 Franklin Ave
Tustin CA 92780
714 368-4615

(P-9123)
YOUNGS MARKET COMPANY LLC
3620 Industrial Blvd # 10, West Sacramento (95691-6518)
PHONE 916 617-4402
Jim Morris, *Branch Mgr*

PRODUCTS & SERVICES SECTION

5191 - Farm Splys Wholesale County (P-9144)

Hector Albizo, *Accounts Exec*
EMP: 50
SALES (corp-wide): 1.1B **Privately Held**
SIC: 5182 Liquor; wine
HQ: Young's Market Company, Llc
14402 Franklin Ave
Tustin CA 92780
714 368-4615

5191 Farm Splys Wholesale

(P-9124)
AHERN AGRIBUSINESS INC
Also Called: Ahern International
9465 Customhouse Plz G, San Diego (92154-7632)
PHONE 619 661-9450
Fax: 619 661-9453
Kevin Ahern, *President*
Martin Pulido, *CFO*
Rochel Maldanado, *Corp Secy*
Carolina Ferreria, *Admin Asst*
Jorge Siordia, *Technology*
◆ **EMP:** 63
SQ FT: 7,000
SALES (est): 31.7MM **Privately Held**
WEB: www.ahernseeds.com
SIC: 5191 Seeds: field, garden & flower

(P-9125)
ASSOCIATED FEED & SUPPLY CO (PA)
Also Called: Farwest Trading
5213 W Main St, Turlock (95380-9413)
P.O. Box 2367 (95381-2367)
PHONE 209 667-2708
Fax: 209 667-0409
Matt Swanson, *President*
Jim Hyer, *Exec VP*
Kurt Hertlein, *Vice Pres*
Brian Boyd, *Warehouse Mgr*
Stan Fail, *Manager*
▲ **EMP:** 121
SQ FT: 1,800
SALES (est): 121.9MM **Privately Held**
SIC: 5191 Animal feeds

(P-9126)
BIG F COMPANY INC
3130 Skyway Dr Ste 405, Santa Maria (93455-1801)
PHONE 805 928-2333
Francisco Contreras, *Principal*
Alicia Contreras, *Vice Pres*
Elosia Placencia, *Manager*
EMP: 54
SQ FT: 1,100
SALES (est): 1MM **Privately Held**
SIC: 5191 Straw

(P-9127)
BORDER VALLEY TRADING LTD
604 Mead Rd, Brawley (92227-9748)
P.O. Box 62 (92227-0062)
PHONE 760 344-6700
Lucien Bronicki, *Manager*
EMP: 56
SALES (corp-wide): 44MM **Privately Held**
SIC: 5191 Hay
PA: Border Valley Trading, Ltd.
14503 W Harding Rd
Turlock CA 95380
209 669-6000

(P-9128)
BRITZ FERTILIZERS INC
35836 W Bullard Ave, Firebaugh (93622-9714)
P.O. Box 725 (93622-0725)
PHONE 559 659-2033
Fax: 559 659-2338
John Valov, *General Mgr*
EMP: 50
SALES (corp-wide): 408.2MM **Privately Held**
WEB: www.britzinc.com
SIC: 5191 5261 2879 Chemicals, agricultural; fertilizer & fertilizer materials; fertilizer; soil conditioners
HQ: Britz Fertilizers Inc.
3265 W Figarden Dr
Fresno CA 93711
559 448-8000

(P-9129)
BRITZ FERTILIZERS INC
Also Called: Bsgs Five Points
21817 S Frsno Coalinga Rd, Five Points (93624)
PHONE 559 884-2421
Fax: 559 884-2295
Ken Walls, *Manager*
Scott Soth, *Plant Mgr*
EMP: 100
SALES (corp-wide): 408.2MM **Privately Held**
WEB: www.britzinc.com
SIC: 5191 Chemicals, agricultural; fertilizer & fertilizer materials
HQ: Britz Fertilizers Inc.
3265 W Figarden Dr
Fresno CA 93711
559 448-8000

(P-9130)
BUTTONWILLOW WAREHOUSE CO INC (HQ)
125 Front St, Buttonwillow (93206)
P.O. Box 98 (93206-0098)
PHONE 661 764-5234
Fax: 661 764-5236
Donald Houchin, *President*
Brad Crowder, *COO*
Scott Stanley, *CFO*
Wallace Houchin, *Vice Pres*
Rob Poznoff, *Opers Mgr*
EMP: 75
SALES (est): 100.1MM
SALES (corp-wide): 100.7MM **Privately Held**
SIC: 5191 Fertilizer & fertilizer materials
PA: Tech Agricultural, Inc.
125 Front St
Buttonwillow CA 93206
661 323-1001

(P-9131)
CROP PRODUCTION SERVICES INC
305 Larsen Rd, Imperial (92251-9757)
P.O. Box 698 (92251-0698)
PHONE 760 355-1133
Shane Brady, *Manager*
EMP: 59
SALES (corp-wide): 2.4B **Privately Held**
WEB: www.cropproductionservices.com
SIC: 5191 Fertilizer & fertilizer materials; chemicals, agricultural; herbicides; insecticides
HQ: Crop Production Services, Inc.
3005 Rocky Mountain Ave
Loveland CO 80538
970 685-3300

(P-9132)
CROP PRODUCTION SERVICES INC
1335 W Main St, Santa Maria (93458-4903)
P.O. Box 669 (93456-0669)
PHONE 805 922-5848
Joe Wickham, *Manager*
Gene Berban, *Agent*
EMP: 80
SQ FT: 32,165
SALES (corp-wide): 2.4B **Privately Held**
WEB: www.cropproductionservices.com
SIC: 5191 Fertilizer & fertilizer materials; chemicals, agricultural; herbicides; insecticides
HQ: Crop Production Services, Inc.
3005 Rocky Mountain Ave
Loveland CO 80538
970 685-3300

(P-9133)
CROP PRODUCTION SERVICES INC
21929 S Lassen, Five Points (93624)
P.O. Box 338 (93624-0338)
PHONE 559 884-6010
Scott Desmond, *Manager*
EMP: 50
SQ FT: 5,670
SALES (corp-wide): 2.4B **Privately Held**
WEB: www.cropproductionservices.com
SIC: 5191 Fertilizer & fertilizer materials; chemicals, agricultural; herbicides; insecticides

HQ: Crop Production Services, Inc.
3005 Rocky Mountain Ave
Loveland CO 80538
970 685-3300

(P-9134)
CROP PRODUCTION SERVICES INC
1143 Terven Ave, Salinas (93901-4522)
P.O. Box 657 (93902-0657)
PHONE 831 757-5391
John Patinl, *Manager*
Lon Lanini, *Executive*
EMP: 60
SALES (corp-wide): 2.4B **Privately Held**
WEB: www.cropproductionservices.com
SIC: 5191 Fertilizer & fertilizer materials; chemicals, agricultural; herbicides; insecticides
HQ: Crop Production Services, Inc.
3005 Rocky Mountain Ave
Loveland CO 80538
970 685-3300

(P-9135)
DENIOS ROSEVILLE FARMERS
2013 Opportunity Dr, Roseville (95678-3023)
PHONE 916 782-2704
Fax: 916 786-7858
Jeff Ronten, *CEO*
Ken Denio, *President*
Marilee Denio, *Corp Secy*
Alani Bauer, *Manager*
EMP: 120
SQ FT: 18,212
SALES (est): 32.8MM **Privately Held**
WEB: www.denios.org
SIC: 5191 Farm supplies

(P-9136)
E B STONE & SON INC
Also Called: Greenall
6111 Lambie Rd, Suisun City (94585-9789)
P.O. Box 550 (94585-0550)
PHONE 707 249-4699
Fax: 707 429-8960
Bradford G Crandall, *CEO*
Bradford Crandall Jr, *President*
Lynne Crandall, *Admin Sec*
Russell Hassell, *VP Opers*
Tom Jones, *Sales Staff*
EMP: 65
SQ FT: 79,000
SALES (est): 44.8MM **Privately Held**
WEB: www.ebstone.org
SIC: 5191 2873 2874 2875 Farm supplies; garden supplies; nitrogenous fertilizers; phosphatic fertilizers; fertilizers, mixing only; hand & edge tools

(P-9137)
FOSTER POULTRY FARMS
4107 Ave 360, Traver (93673)
PHONE 559 457-6509
Larry Ficken, *Plant Mgr*
EMP: 1447
SALES (corp-wide): 4.3B **Privately Held**
SIC: 5191 Farm supplies
PA: Foster Poultry Farms
1000 Davis St
Livingston CA 95334
209 394-6914

(P-9138)
L & L NURSERY SUPPLY INC (PA)
Also Called: Unigro
5350 G St, San Bernardino (92407)
PHONE 909 591-0461
Fax: 909 591-3280
Lloyd Swindell, *Ch of Bd*
Harvey Luth, *President*
Tom Medhurst, *President*
Mike Fuson, *Vice Pres*
Damian Mendoza, *General Mgr*
▲ **EMP:** 150 **EST:** 1953
SQ FT: 107,000
SALES (est): 204.9MM **Privately Held**
WEB: www.llnurserysupply.com
SIC: 5191 2875 2449 5193 Insecticides; fertilizer & fertilizer materials; soil, potting & planting; potting soil, mixed; wood containers; flowers & florists' supplies

(P-9139)
L A HEARNE COMPANY (PA)
512 Metz Rd, King City (93930-2503)
PHONE 831 385-5441
Fax: 831 382-4412
Francis Giudici, *President*
Dennis Hearne, *Ch of Bd*
Frank Hearne, *Vice Pres*
Mike Hearne, *Vice Pres*
Tim Hearne, *Vice Pres*
▲ **EMP:** 70 **EST:** 1938
SQ FT: 220,000
SALES (est): 94MM **Privately Held**
WEB: www.hearneco.com
SIC: 5191 0723 5699 4214 Fertilizers & agricultural chemicals; bean cleaning services; grain drying services; seed cleaning; western apparel; local trucking with storage; livestock feeds; lawn & garden supplies

(P-9140)
L J T FLOWERS INC
Also Called: Skyline Flwr Growers Shippers
4279 E Hueneme Rd, Oxnard (93033-8204)
PHONE 805 488-0879
Fax: 805 488-0181
Joe Goldberg, *President*
Tom Goldberg, *Vice Pres*
Katrina Carrasco, *Marketing Staff*
Delilah Chavez, *Supervisor*
EMP: 105
SQ FT: 8,000
SALES (est): 27.1MM **Privately Held**
WEB: www.skylineflowers.com
SIC: 5191 0181 Flower & field bulbs; flowers grown in field nurseries

(P-9141)
LA PALMA FARMS INC
3130 Skyway Dr Ste 405, Santa Maria (93455-1801)
PHONE 805 928-2333
Jose Alfredo Contreras, *President*
Eloisa Placencia, *Manager*
EMP: 60
SALES (est): 1MM **Privately Held**
SIC: 5191 Straw

(P-9142)
LANTING HAY DEALER INC
9032 Merrill Ave, Ontario (91762-7234)
P.O. Box 747, Chino (91708-0747)
PHONE 909 563-5601
Fax: 909 930-5616
Ronald J Lanting, *President*
Lorraine Lanting, *Corp Secy*
Bradley M Lanting, *Vice Pres*
Curtis J Lanting, *Vice Pres*
Ronald P Lanting, *Vice Pres*
EMP: 75
SQ FT: 40,000
SALES (est): 23.3MM **Privately Held**
SIC: 5191 Hay

(P-9143)
MANN LAKE LTD
500 Santa Anita Dr, Woodland (95776-6117)
PHONE 530 662-4061
Fax: 530 662-2808
Eric Foster, *Branch Mgr*
Barbara Lafond, *Info Tech Mgr*
Gabriel Wheeler, *Graphic Designe*
Katie Doyle, *Sales Staff*
Troy Martinson, *Sales Staff*
EMP: 50
SALES (corp-wide): 10.6MM **Privately Held**
SIC: 5191 5149 Beekeeping supplies (non-durable); sugar, refined
PA: Mann Lake, Ltd.
501 1st St S
Hackensack MN 56452
218 675-6688

(P-9144)
MILHOUS FEED
24077 State Highway 49, Nevada City (95959-8519)
PHONE 530 292-3242
Fax: 530 292-3242
Oliver Milhous, *Partner*
Franklin Milhous, *Partner*
Richard Milhous, *Partner*

5191 - Farm Splys Wholesale County (P-9145)

EMP: 150
SQ FT: 1,280
SALES: 1.5MM Privately Held
SIC: 5191 Feed

(P-9145)
NASCO HEALTHCARE INC
Nasco - Modesto
4825 Stoddard Rd, Modesto (95356-9318)
PHONE..................209 545-1600
Thomas Swafford, Opers-Prdtn-Mfg
John Wellman, President
Allan Souza, Vice Pres
Richard Farrester, Project Mgr
Jim Pofahl, Controller
EMP: 75
SQ FT: 68,125
SALES (corp-wide): 802.3MM Publicly Held
WEB: www.aristotlecorp.net
SIC: 5191 5961 Farm supplies; educational supplies & equipment, mail order
HQ: Nasco Healthcare Inc.
901 Janesville Ave
Fort Atkinson WI 53538
920 568-5600

(P-9146)
NEWCO DISTRIBUTORS INC
9060 Rochester Ave, Rancho Cucamonga (91730-5522)
P.O. Box 1449 (91729-1449)
PHONE..................909 291-2240
Fax: 909 291-2242
Randall Barb, CEO
Kellie Clark, CFO
Sarah Watkins, Vice Pres
Jennifer Monteon, Purch Mgr
Scott O'Brien, Marketing Staff
EMP: 60
SQ FT: 60,000
SALES (est): 63.5MM Privately Held
WEB: www.newcodistributors.com
SIC: 5191 5149 Animal feeds; pet foods

(P-9147)
PLANTERS HAY INC
1295 E St 78, Brawley (92227-2119)
PHONE..................760 344-0620
Stephen Benson, CEO
EMP: 52
SALES (est): 12.8MM Privately Held
SIC: 5191 7389 Hay; styling of fashions, apparel, furniture, textiles, etc.

(P-9148)
RENTOKIL NORTH AMERICA INC
Also Called: Target Specialty Products
15415 Marquardt Ave, Santa Fe Springs (90670-5711)
PHONE..................562 802-2238
Fax: 562 802-1786
Bonnie Fallon, Manager
Patricia Cassidy, Office Admin
Sue Smith, Purch Agent
George Covely, Sales Mgr
Andrew L Cain, Marketing Staff
EMP: 100
SALES (corp-wide): 2.6B Privately Held
SIC: 5191 Chemicals, agricultural
HQ: Rentokil North America, Inc.
1125 Berkshire Blvd # 150
Wyomissing PA 19610
610 372-9700

(P-9149)
SAKATA SEED AMERICA INC (HQ)
18095 Serene Dr, Morgan Hill (95037-2833)
P.O. Box 880 (95038-0880)
PHONE..................408 778-7758
Fax: 408 778-7751
David Armstrong, CEO
Koichi Matsunaga, Vice Pres
Kathy Cron, Social Dir
Hiro Hashimoto, Finance Mgr
Tye Anderson, Opers Mgr
▲ EMP: 90
SQ FT: 48,000
SALES (est): 91.9MM
SALES (corp-wide): 585MM Privately Held
WEB: www.sakata.com
SIC: 5191 Seeds: field, garden & flower

PA: Sakata Seed Corporation
2-7-1, Nakamachidai, Tsuzuki-Ku
Yokohama KNG 224-0
459 458-800

(P-9150)
SEEDS OF CHANGE INC
Also Called: Sustainable Agriculture
2555 S Dominguez Hills Dr, Rancho Dominguez (90220-6402)
P.O. Box 4908 (90224-4908)
PHONE..................310 764-7700
Will Righeimer, CEO
Sharkeith Taylor, Finance
◆ EMP: 120
SQ FT: 25,411
SALES (est): 58.3MM
SALES (corp-wide): 5.1B Privately Held
SIC: 5191 0723 Farm supplies; crop preparation services for market
HQ: Mars Food Us, Llc
2001 E Cashdan St Ste 201
Rancho Dominguez CA 90220
310 933-0670

(P-9151)
SEMINIS VEGETABLE SEEDS INC (HQ)
2700 Camino Del Sol, Oxnard (93030-7967)
PHONE..................855 733-3834
Michael J Frank, CEO
Kerry Preete, President
Sergio Becerra, Analyst
Alison Browne, Human Res Mgr
Jim Gomm, Manager
◆ EMP: 600 EST: 1962
SQ FT: 370,000
SALES (est): 556MM
SALES (corp-wide): 13.5B Publicly Held
WEB: www.bruinsma.com
SIC: 5191 0723 Seeds: field, garden & flower; crop preparation services for market
PA: Monsanto Company
800 N Lindbergh Blvd
Saint Louis MO 63167
314 694-1000

(P-9152)
SEMINIS VEGETABLE SEEDS INC
Also Called: Monsanto
37437 State Highway 16, Woodland (95695-9353)
PHONE..................530 669-6903
Seminis Vegetable Seeds, Owner
John Uhlig, Manager
EMP: 50
SALES (corp-wide): 13.5B Publicly Held
WEB: www.bruinsma.com
SIC: 5191 Seeds: field, garden & flower
HQ: Seminis Vegetable Seeds, Inc.
2700 Camino Del Sol
Oxnard CA 93030
855 733-3834

(P-9153)
STANISLAUS FARM SUPPLY COMPANY (PA)
Also Called: Westlink
624 E Service Rd, Modesto (95358-9451)
PHONE..................860 678-5160
Fax: 209 541-3191
Anselmo Bettencourt, CEO
Espiri Ixta, CFO
Espiridion Ixta, CFO
Stuart Bradley, Vice Ch Bd
Ray Sousa, Administration
EMP: 61
SQ FT: 4,000
SALES (est): 91.4MM Privately Held
SIC: 5191 Fertilizer & fertilizer materials; insecticides; seeds: field, garden & flower

(P-9154)
SYNGENTA SEEDS INC
5653 Monterey Frontage Rd, Gilroy (95020-9588)
PHONE..................408 847-4242
Ed Merrell, Branch Mgr
Mark Tappen, Manager
EMP: 50
SALES (corp-wide): 13.4B Privately Held
SIC: 5191 Seeds: field, garden & flower

HQ: Syngenta Seeds, Inc.
11055 Wayzata Blvd
Minnetonka MN 55305
612 656-8600

(P-9155)
WESTERN MILLING LLC (HQ)
Also Called: O.H. Kruse Grain and Milling
31120 West St, Goshen (93227)
P.O. Box 1029 (93227-1029)
PHONE..................559 302-1000
Kevin Kruse, Mng Member
Jeremy Wilhelm, President
Bob Berczynski, COO
Mark La Bounty, COO
Phil Shanon, CFO
◆ EMP: 243
SALES (est): 571.8MM Privately Held
WEB: www.westernmilling.com
SIC: 5191 Animal feeds
PA: Kruse Investment Company, Inc.
31120 W St
Goshen CA 93227
559 302-1000

(P-9156)
WILBUR-ELLIS COMPANY LLC
12550 S Colorado Ave, Helm (93627)
P.O. Box 125 (93627-0125)
PHONE..................559 866-5667
Tim Doss, General Mgr
EMP: 60
SALES (corp-wide): 1.5B Privately Held
WEB: www.wilbur-ellis.com
SIC: 5191 Fertilizer & fertilizer materials
HQ: Wilbur-Ellis Company Llc
345 California St Fl 27
San Francisco CA 94104
415 772-4000

(P-9157)
WILBUR-ELLIS COMPANY LLC (HQ)
345 California St Fl 27, San Francisco (94104-2644)
PHONE..................415 772-4000
John P Thacher, Ch of Bd
Daniel R Vradenburg, President
Michael J Hunter, CFO
Alison J Amonette, Treasurer
Steven J Dietze, Vice Pres
EMP: 2278
SALES (est): 97MM
SALES (corp-wide): 1.5B Privately Held
SIC: 5191 0711 Farm supplies; fertilizer & fertilizer materials; insecticides; fertilizer application services
PA: Wilbur-Ellis Holdings Ii, Inc
345 California St Fl 27
San Francisco CA 94104
415 772-4000

(P-9158)
WILBUR-ELLIS COMPANY LLC
Also Called: Weco - Us.ca. El Centro
45 W Danenberg Rd, El Centro (92243)
PHONE..................760 352-2847
Fax: 760 352-2921
Dan Wray, Manager
Eric Lee, Manager
EMP: 58
SALES (corp-wide): 1.5B Privately Held
WEB: www.wilbur-ellis.com
SIC: 5191 Feed
HQ: Wilbur-Ellis Company Llc
345 California St Fl 27
San Francisco CA 94104
415 772-4000

(P-9159)
WILBUR-ELLIS COMPANY LLC
1427 Abbott St, Salinas (93901-4506)
PHONE..................831 422-6473
D Sites, COO
EMP: 63
SALES (corp-wide): 1.5B Privately Held
SIC: 5191 Chemicals, agricultural
HQ: Wilbur-Ellis Company Llc
345 California St Fl 27
San Francisco CA 94104
415 772-4000

5192 Books, Periodicals & Newspapers Wholesale

(P-9160)
ANDERSON NEWS LLC
15172 Goldenwest Cir, Westminster (92683-5222)
P.O. Box 8401 (92684-8401)
PHONE..................714 892-7766
Fax: 714 894-6542
Dave Schultz, Branch Mgr
EMP: 74
SALES (corp-wide): 219MM Privately Held
WEB: www.kadsi.com
SIC: 5192 Magazines
PA: Anderson News, Llc
265 Brookview Town Ste
Knoxville TN 37919
865 584-9765

(P-9161)
BAKER & TAYLOR LLC
10350 Barnes Canyon Rd # 100, San Diego (92121-2708)
PHONE..................858 457-2500
James Leidich, Director
Edward Leonard, CFO
Curtis Smith, Exec VP
Betsy Klein, Info Tech Dir
Jennifer Thornton, Manager
EMP: 187
SALES (corp-wide): 5.6B Privately Held
WEB: www.accupackinc.com
SIC: 5192 5099 5199 5045 Books; tapes & cassettes, prerecorded; video cassettes, accessories & supplies; calendars; computer software; book stores; audio tapes, prerecorded; video tapes, prerecorded
HQ: Baker & Taylor, Llc
2550 W Tyvola Rd Ste 300
Charlotte NC 28217
704 998-3100

(P-9162)
CONTRA COSTA NEWSPAPERS INC
1650 Cavallo Rd, Antioch (94509-1928)
PHONE..................925 757-2525
Fax: 925 778-7829
Debbie Mathias, Manager
George Riggs, Loan Officer
EMP: 50
SQ FT: 24,534
SALES (corp-wide): 3.9B Privately Held
WEB: www.contracostatimes.com
SIC: 5192 Newspapers
HQ: Contra Costa Newspapers, Inc.
175 Lennon Ln Ste 100
Walnut Creek CA 94598
925 935-2525

(P-9163)
EBSCO INDUSTRIES INC
898 N Sepulveda Blvd # 800, El Segundo (90245-2709)
PHONE..................310 322-5000
Fax: 310 322-2558
Dave Kerin, Branch Mgr
EMP: 55
SALES (corp-wide): 2.1B Privately Held
WEB: www.ebscoind.com
SIC: 5192 Magazines
PA: Ebsco Industries, Inc.
5724 Highway 280 E
Birmingham AL 35242
205 991-6600

(P-9164)
EL AVISO MAGAZINE
4850 Gage Ave, Bell (90201-1409)
P.O. Box 127, Huntington Park (90255-0127)
PHONE..................323 586-9199
Fax: 323 589-9395
Jose Zepeda, CEO
Madai Garanillo, Administration
Jose Ruiz, Editor
EMP: 300
SALES (est): 33.4MM Privately Held
SIC: 5192 Magazines

PRODUCTS & SERVICES SECTION
5193 - Flowers, Nursery Stock & Florists' Splys Wholesale County (P-9186)

(P-9165)
HAY HOUSE INC (PA)
2776 Loker Ave W, Carlsbad (92010-6611)
P.O. Box 5100 (92018-5100)
PHONE..................760 431-7695
Louise L Hay, *Ch of Bd*
Reid Tracy, *President*
Mary Lillibridge, *Accountant*
Jennifer Simmons, *Relations*
▲ EMP: 62
SQ FT: 20,000
SALES (est): 67.8MM **Privately Held**
WEB: www.hayhouse.com
SIC: **5192** 5099 5942 5735 Books; tapes & cassettes, prerecorded; book stores; audio tapes, prerecorded

(P-9166)
INGRAM PUBLISHER SERVICES INC
1700 4th St, Berkeley (94710-1711)
PHONE..................510 528-1444
Richard C Freese, *President*
Lawrence Susskind, *Associate Dir*
Milton Ezrati, *Investment Ofcr*
Vanessa Navarrete, *Marketing Staff*
James Faubion, *Professor*
EMP: 67
SALES (corp-wide): 3.3B **Privately Held**
SIC: **5192** Books, periodicals & newspapers
HQ: Ingram Publisher Services Inc.
    1 Ingram Blvd
    La Vergne TN 37086
    615 213-5000

(P-9167)
LOS ANGELES MAGAZINE INC
5900 Wilshire Blvd Fl 10, Los Angeles (90036-5024)
PHONE..................323 801-0100
Fax: 323 801-0105
Jeffrey Smulyam, *CEO*
Richards J Miller, *Vice Pres*
Jennifer Sotelo, *Vice Pres*
Eileen Rosaly, *General Mgr*
Eugne Supnet, *Business Mgr*
EMP: 55
SALES (est): 16.5MM
SALES (corp-wide): 231.4MM **Publicly Held**
WEB: www.emmis.com
SIC: **5192** Magazines
PA: Emmis Communications Corp
    40 Monument Cir Ste 700
    Indianapolis IN 46204
    317 266-0100

(P-9168)
MADER NEWS INC
913 Ruberta Ave, Glendale (91201-2346)
PHONE..................818 551-5000
Fax: 818 240-7284
Avan Mader, *President*
Rafael Sotomayor, *Opers Mgr*
Mary Mader, *Director*
EMP: 100
SQ FT: 2,400
SALES (est): 29MM **Privately Held**
SIC: **5192** Newspapers

(P-9169)
NEWSWAYS SERVICES INC
Also Called: Newsways Distributors
1324 Cypress Ave, Los Angeles (90065-1220)
PHONE..................323 258-6000
John Dorman, *President*
Danica Arunson, *Buyer*
Jesse Yeomans, *Manager*
▲ EMP: 135
SQ FT: 8,500
SALES (est): 58MM **Privately Held**
SIC: **5192** Magazines

(P-9170)
PUBLISHERS GROUP INCORPORATED (DH)
Also Called: Publishers Group West
1700 4th St, Berkeley (94710-1711)
PHONE..................510 528-1444
Fax: 510 528-3444
Richard Freese, *President*
Chris McKenney, *COO*
Mark Ouimet, *Exec VP*

Paul Rooney, *Senior VP*
Kevin Votel, *VP Mktg*
▲ EMP: 230
SQ FT: 63,000
SALES (est): 42.2MM
SALES (corp-wide): 229.8MM **Privately Held**
SIC: **5192** Books
HQ: Perseus Distribution, Inc.
    210 American Dr
    Jackson TN 38301
    731 988-4440

(P-9171)
SCHOLASTIC BOOK FAIRS INC
2890 E White Star Ave, Anaheim (92806-2632)
PHONE..................714 237-1100
Jim Wind, *Branch Mgr*
John Sims, *Senior VP*
Michelle Dorsi, *Admin Asst*
Ian Judd, *Planning*
Sarah Gardner, *QA Dir*
EMP: 75
SALES (corp-wide): 1.6B **Publicly Held**
WEB: www.scholasticbookfairs.com
SIC: **5192** Books, periodicals & newspapers
HQ: Scholastic Book Fairs, Inc.
    1080 Greenwood Blvd
    Lake Mary FL 32746
    407 829-7300

(P-9172)
SCHOLASTIC BOOK FAIRS INC
42001 Christy St, Fremont (94538-3163)
PHONE..................510 771-1700
Caesey Ryan, *Branch Mgr*
Kelley Baker, *Sales Staff*
Michelle McCarroll, *Sales Staff*
EMP: 100
SALES (corp-wide): 1.6B **Publicly Held**
WEB: www.scholasticbookfairs.com
SIC: **5192** Books
HQ: Scholastic Book Fairs, Inc.
    1080 Greenwood Blvd
    Lake Mary FL 32746
    407 829-7300

(P-9173)
TEN ENTHUSIAST NETWORK LLC (HQ)
831 S Douglas St Ste 100, El Segundo (90245-4956)
PHONE..................310 531-9900
Scott P Dickey, *CEO*
Peter H Englehart, *Ch of Bd*
Chris Argentieri, *President*
Bill Sutman, *CFO*
Jonathan Anastas, *Chief Mktg Ofcr*
EMP: 230
SALES (est): 174.6MM
SALES (corp-wide): 1.3B **Privately Held**
WEB: www.sourceinterlink.com
SIC: **5192** Books, periodicals & newspapers
PA: Source Interlink Companies, Inc.
    27200 Riverview Center Bl
    Bonita Springs FL 34134
    866 276-5584

(P-9174)
TEN THE ENTHUSIAST NETWORK LLC
1821 E Dyer Rd Ste 150, Santa Ana (92705-5730)
PHONE..................714 709-9021
Jose Marquez, *Principal*
EMP: 210
SALES (corp-wide): 1.3B **Privately Held**
SIC: **5192** Books, periodicals & newspapers
HQ: Ten The Enthusiast Network, Llc
    831 S Douglas St Ste 100
    El Segundo CA 90245
    310 531-9900

(P-9175)
WHITE DIGITAL MEDIA INC
Also Called: Wdm Group
5901 Priestly Dr Ste 300, Carlsbad (92008-8825)
PHONE..................760 827-7800
Brian Smith, *CEO*
Glen White, *President*
Andy Turner, *COO*

Matthew P Melucci, *Officer*
Kiron Chavda, *Managing Dir*
EMP: 150
SALES (est): 52.6MM **Privately Held**
SIC: **5192** Magazines

5193 Flowers, Nursery Stock & Florists' Splys Wholesale

(P-9176)
ALTMAN SPECIALTY PLANTS INC (PA)
Also Called: Altman Plants
3742 Blue Bird Canyon Rd, Vista (92084-7432)
PHONE..................760 744-8191
Ken Altman, *CEO*
Phyliss Schmedake, *CFO*
Deena Altman, *Vice Pres*
Rod Baine, *Info Tech Mgr*
Deborah Assman, *Business Anlyst*
▲ EMP: 800
SQ FT: 4,000
SALES (est): 590.1MM **Privately Held**
WEB: www.altmanplants.com
SIC: **5193** 3999 Nursery stock; atomizers, toiletry

(P-9177)
ARMSTRONG GARDEN CENTERS IN C
1492 Wilshire Rd, Fallbrook (92028-8934)
PHONE..................760 414-1490
Fax: 760 414-1361
James Russell, *General Mgr*
Jorg Aylya, *General Mgr*
▲ EMP: 50
SALES (est): 3.1MM **Privately Held**
WEB: www.armstronggrowers.com
SIC: **5193** Flowers & nursery stock

(P-9178)
B & B NURSERIES INC
Also Called: Landscape Center
9505 Cleveland Ave, Riverside (92503-6241)
P.O. Box 7399 (92513-7399)
PHONE..................951 352-8383
Fax: 951 352-3655
Mark Barrett, *CEO*
EMP: 109
SQ FT: 2,100
SALES (est): 16.7MM **Privately Held**
SIC: **5193** 0781 Flowers & nursery stock; landscape counseling services

(P-9179)
BRAND FLOWER FARMS INC (PA)
Also Called: Farmers W Flowers & Bouquets
5300 Foothill Rd, Carpinteria (93013-3017)
P.O. Box 600 (93014-0600)
PHONE..................805 684-5531
Wilja Happ, *CEO*
Maximino Santillon, *President*
Monica Preciado, *CFO*
Will Stewart, *Vice Pres*
Tom Lemus, *Opers Mgr*
▲ EMP: 64
SQ FT: 500,000
SALES (est): 54.3MM **Privately Held**
WEB: www.brandflowers.com
SIC: **5193** Flowers, fresh

(P-9180)
BUSHNELL GARDENS
Also Called: Bushnell's Landscape Creations
5255 Douglas Blvd, Granite Bay (95746-6204)
PHONE..................916 791-4199
Fax: 916 791-6060
David Bushnell, *Owner*
Kim Miller, *Office Mgr*
Shelby Bushnell, *Buyer*
Dhetchai Allison, *Manager*
Rich Swanson, *Manager*
EMP: 80
SQ FT: 1,040

SALES (est): 6.7MM **Privately Held**
SIC: **5193** 0781 0782 5261 Nursery stock; landscape architects; lawn & garden services; landscape contractors; nurseries

(P-9181)
CAL COLOR GROWERS LLC
330 Peebles Ave, Morgan Hill (95037-2712)
P.O. Box 550 (95038-0550)
PHONE..................408 778-0835
Fax: 408 778-9627
David Vincent, *Mng Member*
Michelle Vincnet,
▲ EMP: 73
SQ FT: 478,000
SALES (est): 6.6MM **Privately Held**
SIC: **5193** Nursery stock

(P-9182)
CALIFORNIA PAJAROSA FLORAL
133 Hughes Rd, Watsonville (95076-9458)
P.O. Box 684 (95077-0684)
PHONE..................831 722-6374
John Furman, *President*
Alan Mitchell, *Vice Pres*
Jaime Comilang, *Manager*
EMP: 50
SQ FT: 10,000
SALES (est): 4.9MM **Privately Held**
WEB: www.pajarosa.com
SIC: **5193** Flowers, fresh

(P-9183)
CLEARWATER NURSERY INC
887 Mesa Rd, Nipomo (93444-9325)
P.O. Box 1170 (93444-1170)
PHONE..................805 929-3241
Fax: 805 929-5421
Mahmood Jafroodi, *President*
John E Djafroodi, *Corp Secy*
Syd Ewens, *Controller*
Mella Griffin, *Manager*
Arianne Spittler, *Accounts Exec*
▲ EMP: 50
SQ FT: 1,500,000
SALES (est): 13.9MM **Privately Held**
SIC: **5193** Nursery stock

(P-9184)
COLOR SPOT NURSERIES INC
321 W Sepulveda Blvd, Carson (90745-6313)
PHONE..................310 549-7470
Fax: 310 549-7312
Dixon Suzuki, *Manager*
Joshua Vukelich, *VP Sales*
EMP: 98
SALES (corp-wide): 5.4B **Privately Held**
WEB: www.colorspot.com
SIC: **5193** Nursery stock
HQ: Color Spot Nurseries, Inc.
    27368 Via Ste 201
    Temecula CA 92590

(P-9185)
COREY NURSERY CO INC (PA)
1650 Monte Vista Ave, Claremont (91711-2999)
P.O. Box 609 (91711-0609)
PHONE..................909 621-6886
Fax: 909 621-6889
Jeffrey E Corey, *CEO*
Brian Corey, *Shareholder*
Ken Corey, *Shareholder*
Gene Corey, *Ch of Bd*
Eugene K Corey, *President*
▲ EMP: 60 EST: 1978
SQ FT: 170,000
SALES (est): 38.3MM **Privately Held**
WEB: www.coreynursery.com
SIC: **5193** Nursery stock

(P-9186)
COUNTRY FLORAL SUPPLY INC (PA)
Also Called: Country Furnishings
3802 Weatherly Cir, Westlake Village (91361-3821)
PHONE..................805 520-8026
Fax: 805 520-1961
Mark Reese, *President*
Debbie Reese, *Vice Pres*

5193 - Flowers, Nursery Stock & Florists' Splys Wholesale County (P-9187)

Zerlene Ratzlafs, *Asst Mgr*
▲ EMP: 80
SQ FT: 60,000
SALES (est): 59.9MM **Privately Held**
WEB: www.countryfloralsupply.com
SIC: 5193 5999 Artificial flowers; artificial flowers

(P-9187)
DELTA FLORAL DISTRIBUTORS INC
6810 West Blvd, Los Angeles (90043-4668)
P.O. Box 431802 (90043-8802)
PHONE.................323 751-8116
Fax: 323 751-5873
Archie Defterios, *President*
Foti Defterios, *Corp Secy*
Heidi Hansen, *Controller*
▲ EMP: 200
SQ FT: 30,000
SALES (est): 31.8MM **Privately Held**
SIC: 5193 Flowers & nursery stock

(P-9188)
FISHERS NURSERY
24081 S Austin Rd, Ripon (95366-9646)
P.O. Box 657 (95366-0657)
PHONE.................209 599-3412
Fax: 209 599-6955
Jerry Fisher, *President*
Mary Fisher, *Corp Secy*
Jochele Depaw, *Admin Sec*
Michael Fisher, *Manager*
▲ EMP: 75 EST: 1968
SQ FT: 450,000
SALES (est): 7.2MM **Privately Held**
WEB: www.fishersnursery.com
SIC: 5193 Nursery stock

(P-9189)
G M FLORAL COMPANY
Also Called: G M Floral Supply
740 Maple Ave, Los Angeles (90014-2261)
PHONE.................213 489-7055
Fax: 213 489-7055
Mas Yoshida, *Principal*
Mark Mukai, *Controller*
EMP: 50
SALES (corp-wide): 11.3MM **Privately Held**
WEB: www.gmfloral.com
SIC: 5193 Florists' supplies
PA: G M Floral Company
531 E Evelyn Ave
Mountain View CA 94041
650 903-5020

(P-9190)
GREEN THUMB INTERNATIONAL INC
21812 Sherman Way, Canoga Park (91303-1940)
PHONE.................818 340-6400
Del Berquist, *Principal*
Harold D Bergquist, *Agent*
Lisa Hansen, *Agent*
EMP: 100
SALES (corp-wide): 55MM **Privately Held**
WEB: www.greenthumbinternational.com
SIC: 5193 5261 0782 0181 Nursery stock; nurseries & garden centers; lawn & garden services; ornamental nursery products
PA: Green Thumb International Inc
7105 Jordan Ave
Canoga Park CA 91303
818 340-6400

(P-9191)
GROLINK PLANT COMPANY INC (PA)
4107 W Gonzales Rd, Oxnard (93036-7783)
P.O. Box 5506 (93031-5506)
PHONE.................805 984-7958
Anthony Vollering, *CEO*
Harry Van Wingerden, *Shareholder*
Jerry Van Wingerden, *Corp Secy*
Art Gordijin, *Principal*
Ton Vallering, *Principal*
▲ EMP: 149
SQ FT: 400,000
SALES (est): 59.1MM **Privately Held**
WEB: www.grolink.com
SIC: 5193 0181 Flowers & florists' supplies; ornamental nursery products

(P-9192)
HEADSTART NURSERY INC (PA)
4860 Monterey Rd, Gilroy (95020-9511)
PHONE.................408 842-3030
Fax: 408 842-3224
Steven H Costa, *President*
Don Christopher, *Vice Pres*
Randy Costa, *Vice Pres*
Doug Iten, *General Mgr*
Chris Peck, *General Mgr*
▲ EMP: 85
SQ FT: 3,000
SALES (est): 64.2MM **Privately Held**
WEB: www.headstartnursery.com
SIC: 5193 5261 Plants, potted; nursery stock; nurseries & garden centers

(P-9193)
HINES HORTICULTURE INC
2500 Rainbow Valley Blvd, Fallbrook (92028-9778)
PHONE.................760 723-1500
Jessee Westrup, *Manager*
Jesse Astrup, *General Mgr*
William C Rowe, *Agent*
EMP: 300
SALES (corp-wide): 1.8B **Privately Held**
WEB: www.hineshorticulture.com
SIC: 5193 0181 Flowers & nursery stock; ornamental nursery products
PA: Hines Horticulture, Inc.
12621 Jeffrey Rd
Irvine CA 92620
949 559-4444

(P-9194)
HINES NURSERIES LLC
22941 Mill Creek Dr, Laguna Hills (92653-1215)
PHONE.................602 254-2831
Phil Wayne, *Manager*
Lenore Goldberg, *Regional Mgr*
EMP: 100
SALES (corp-wide): 14.6MM **Privately Held**
WEB: www.hineshort.com
SIC: 5193 Flowers & florists' supplies
PA: Hines Nurseries Llc
1700 E Putnam Ave Ste 401
Old Greenwich CT
-

(P-9195)
HOLLAND FLOWER MARKET INC (PA)
755 Wall St Ste 7g, Los Angeles (90014-2315)
PHONE.................213 627-9900
Fax: 213 627-9950
Jaap Haverkate, *President*
Steve Yuge, *Treasurer*
Magdalena Mercer, *Accountant*
EMP: 51
SQ FT: 11,000
SALES (est): 23.6MM **Privately Held**
SIC: 5193 Flowers, fresh

(P-9196)
KENDAL FLORAL SUPPLY LLC (PA)
Also Called: Kendal North Bouquet Co
1960 Kellogg Ave, Carlsbad (92008-6581)
PHONE.................760 431-4910
Fax: 760 431-4922
Kenneth X Baca, *President*
Cheri Mendelsohn, *Accountant*
▲ EMP: 80
SALES (est): 74.1MM **Privately Held**
WEB: www.kendalfloral.com
SIC: 5193 Flowers, fresh

(P-9197)
LOMA VISTA NURSERY
Also Called: Loma Vista Nursery 2
18272 Bastanchury Rd, Yorba Linda (92886-2447)
PHONE.................714 779-5583
Fax: 714 779-7259
Norman Van Ginkel, *President*
EMP: 57

SALES (est): 4.2MM **Privately Held**
SIC: 5193 5261 Nursery stock; nursery stock, seeds & bulbs

(P-9198)
MAYESH WHOLESALE FLORIST INC (PA)
5401 W 104th St, Los Angeles (90045-6011)
PHONE.................310 342-0980
Fax: 310 348-4933
Patrick Dahlson, *CEO*
Cindie Boer, *COO*
Ben Powell, *COO*
Todd Smith, *Branch Mgr*
Isabelle Buckley, *General Mgr*
▲ EMP: 50
SQ FT: 20,000
SALES (est): 74.8MM **Privately Held**
WEB: www.mayeshwholesale.com
SIC: 5193 5992 Flowers, fresh; florists

(P-9199)
MB LANDSCAPING & NURSERY INC
20300 Figueroa St, Carson (90745-1005)
PHONE.................310 965-1923
Federico Martinez, *President*
Maria Martinez, *Corp Secy*
EMP: 57
SALES (est): 7.8MM **Privately Held**
SIC: 5193 Nursery stock

(P-9200)
MELLANO & CO (PA)
Also Called: Mellano Enterprises
766 Wall St, Los Angeles (90014-2316)
P.O. Box 100, San Luis Rey (92068-0100)
PHONE.................213 622-0796
Fax: 213 622-4942
John Mellano, *President*
Michael Matthew Mellano, *President*
Battista Castellano, *Corp Secy*
Michelle Castellano, *Vice Pres*
Bob Mellano, *Vice Pres*
EMP: 75
SALES (est): 113.4MM **Privately Held**
WEB: www.mellano.com
SIC: 5193 Flowers & florists' supplies

(P-9201)
MELLANO & CO
Also Called: Melano Enterprises
734 Wilshire Rd, Oceanside (92057-2111)
P.O. Box 100, San Luis Rey (92068-0100)
PHONE.................760 433-9550
Fax: 760 433-6721
Harry M Mellano, *Owner*
James Moniz, *Info Tech Mgr*
Kathleen Noack, *Personnel Exec*
Ken Taniguchi, *Foreman/Supr*
Joe Flynn, *Sales Associate*
EMP: 170
SALES (corp-wide): 113.4MM **Privately Held**
WEB: www.mellano.com
SIC: 5193 Flowers, fresh
PA: Mellano & Co.
766 Wall St
Los Angeles CA 90014
213 622-0796

(P-9202)
MONTEREY BAY BOUQUET ACQUISIT
481 San Andreas Rd, Watsonville (95076-9524)
P.O. Box 1778 (95077-1778)
PHONE.................831 786-2700
Phil Buran, *Mng Member*
Elva Patterson, *Human Res Mgr*
EMP: 170
SALES (est): 10.4MM **Privately Held**
SIC: 5193 Flowers & florists' supplies

(P-9203)
NAKASE BROTHERS WHOLESALE NURS (PA)
9441 Krepp Dr, Huntington Beach (92646-2799)
PHONE.................949 855-4388
Fax: 949 855-0948
Shigeo Gary Nakase, *Principal*
Noreen Nakase, *Accountant*
Joanne Shurlock, *Sales Mgr*

David Boos, *Sales Associate*
Les Dubose, *Marketing Staff*
▲ EMP: 100
SALES (est): 79MM **Privately Held**
WEB: www.nakasebros.com
SIC: 5193 Nursery stock

(P-9204)
NAKASE BROTHERS WHOLESALE NURS
20621 Lake Forest Dr, Lake Forest (92630-7743)
PHONE.................949 855-4388
Joann Shurlock, *Manager*
EMP: 200
SALES (corp-wide): 79MM **Privately Held**
WEB: www.nakasebros.com
SIC: 5193 Nursery stock
PA: Nakase Brothers Wholesale Nursery
9441 Krepp Dr
Huntington Beach CA 92646
949 855-4388

(P-9205)
NORMANS NURSERY INC (PA)
8665 Duarte Rd, San Gabriel (91775-1139)
PHONE.................626 285-9795
Fax: 626 286-0311
Charles Norman, *President*
Caroline Norman, *Treasurer*
Nancy Webb, *Vice Pres*
▼ EMP: 50
SQ FT: 4,000
SALES (est): 177.8MM **Privately Held**
WEB: www.nngrower.com
SIC: 5193 0181 Nursery stock; nursery stock, growing of

(P-9206)
NORMANS NURSERY INC
6250 N Escalon Bellota Rd, Linden (95236-9428)
PHONE.................209 887-2033
Fax: 209 887-2815
Barbara Hayes, *Manager*
EMP: 200
SALES (corp-wide): 177.8MM **Privately Held**
WEB: www.nngrower.com
SIC: 5193 0181 Nursery stock; nursery stock, growing of
PA: Norman's Nursery, Inc.
8665 Duarte Rd
San Gabriel CA 91775
626 285-9795

(P-9207)
PAJARO VALLEY GREENHOUSES (PA)
90 Hecker Pass Rd, Watsonville (95076-9776)
Po Box 69
PHONE.................831 722-2773
Fax: 831 722-0124
Arne Thirup, *President*
Doris Thirup, *Treasurer*
Karen Thirup-Sambrailo, *Vice Pres*
Sandy Garcia, *Dir Ops-Prd-Mfg*
EMP: 100
SQ FT: 3,000
SALES (est): 37.4MM **Privately Held**
SIC: 5193 Flowers, fresh

(P-9208)
PARDEE TREE NURSERY
30970 Via Puerta Del Sol, Oceanside (92057)
P.O. Box 240, Bonsall (92003-0240)
PHONE.................760 630-5400
Fax: 760 630-4952
Lauren Davis, *President*
Ann Salazar, *Credit Mgr*
Marianne Lacey, *Bookkeeper*
Ray Davis, *Sales Staff*
Zach Davis, *Sales Staff*
EMP: 75
SALES (est): 14.9MM **Privately Held**
WEB: www.pardeetree.com
SIC: 5193 Nursery stock

(P-9209)
PLANT SCIENCES INC
234 Juniper Knoll Rd, Macdoel (96058)
P.O. Box 269 (96058-0269)
PHONE.................530 398-4042

Fax: 530 398-4045
Tom Alvin, *Manager*
EMP: 50
SALES (corp-wide): 143.7MM **Privately Held**
WEB: www.plantsciences.com
SIC: 5193 Nursery stock
PA: Plant Sciences, Inc.
  342 Green Valley Rd
  Watsonville CA 95076
  831 728-3323

(P-9210)
PONTO NURSERY INC
2545 Ramona Dr, Vista (92084-1632)
P.O. Box 536 (92085-0536)
PHONE.................................760 724-6003
Fax: 760 724-1974
William Ponto, *President*
Judy Ponto, *Corp Secy*
EMP: 70
SQ FT: 2,000
SALES: 3.5MM **Privately Held**
SIC: 5193 Nursery stock

(P-9211)
RIVERSIDE NURSERY & LDSCP INC
5215 N Golden State Blvd, Fresno (93722-5018)
PHONE.................................559 275-1891
Fax: 559 275-3927
Mitchel Hutcheson, *President*
Anglea Hutcheson, *Vice Pres*
James Hutcheson, *Vice Pres*
James Hutcheson, *Admin Sec*
EMP: 60
SQ FT: 4,000
SALES (est): 6.1MM **Privately Held**
WEB: www.riversidelandscape.com
SIC: 5193 0781 Nursery stock; landscape architects

(P-9212)
SILK BOTANICA INC
304 Shaw Rd, South San Francisco (94080-6606)
PHONE.................................415 594-0888
Allen Tong, *President*
Nancy Tong, *Vice Pres*
Dede Seward, *Sales Staff*
▲ **EMP:** 60
SQ FT: 36,000
SALES (est): 4.1MM **Privately Held**
WEB: www.silkbo.com
SIC: 5193 Flowers & florists' supplies

(P-9213)
SONOMA GRAPEVINES INC (PA)
1919 Dennis Ln, Santa Rosa (95403-1520)
P.O. Box 279, Wasco (93280-0279)
PHONE.................................707 542-5521
Fax: 707 542-4801
Richard Kunde, *President*
Saralee McClelland Kunde, *Corp Secy*
EMP: 78 **EST:** 1972
SQ FT: 100,000
SALES (est): 13.9MM **Privately Held**
WEB: www.saraleesvineyard.com
SIC: 5193 Nursery stock

(P-9214)
SUNCREST NURSERIES INC
400 Casserly Rd, Watsonville (95076-9700)
PHONE.................................831 728-2595
Fax: 831 728-3146
Stan Iversen, *President*
Michael Craib, *Marketing Staff*
EMP: 55
SQ FT: 1,000
SALES (est): 6.2MM **Privately Held**
WEB: www.suncrestnurseries.com
SIC: 5193 Nursery stock

(P-9215)
SUNNYSLOPE TREE FARM INC
Also Called: Sunnyslope Trees
4025 E La Palma Ave # 203, Anaheim (92807-1734)
PHONE.................................714 532-1440
Fax: 714 632-6660
Todd Flammer, *President*
Jack W Flammer Sr, *Ch of Bd*
Melanie Labbe, *Controller*
EMP: 100
SQ FT: 1,000
SALES (est): 15.8MM **Privately Held**
WEB: www.sunnyslope.net
SIC: 5193 Nursery stock

(P-9216)
SUNSHINE FLORAL INC
4595 Foothill Rd, Carpinteria (93013-3096)
PHONE.................................805 684-1177
Fax: 805 684-4695
Henry Vanwingerden, *President*
Anthony Vollering, *Vice Pres*
▲ **EMP:** 70
SALES (est): 4.8MM **Privately Held**
SIC: 5193 Flowers & florists' supplies

(P-9217)
SUNSHINE FLORAL LLC
1070 S Rice Ave Ste 1, Oxnard (93033-2110)
PHONE.................................805 982-8822
Fax: 805 982-8877
Anthony Vollering, *Mng Member*
Liz Sanchez, *Administration*
Adri Durieux, *Prdtn Mgr*
Henry Van Wingerden, *Mng Member*
Ton Vollering, *Mng Member*
▲ **EMP:** 60 **EST:** 1985
SQ FT: 10,000
SALES (est): 5.6MM **Privately Held**
WEB: www.sunshinefloral.com
SIC: 5193 Flowers & florists' supplies

(P-9218)
SUPER GARDEN CENTERS INC
Also Called: Green Thumb Nursery
7659 Topanga Canyon Blvd, Canoga Park (91304-5535)
P.O. Box 111 (91305-0111)
PHONE.................................818 348-9266
Nancy Bergquist, *Manager*
EMP: 50
SALES (corp-wide): 28.6MM **Privately Held**
SIC: 5193 5261 Nursery stock; fertilizer; nursery stock, seeds & bulbs
PA: Super Garden Centers, Inc.
  21812 Sherman Way
  Canoga Park CA 91303
  818 340-6400

(P-9219)
T - Y NURSERY INC
15335 Highway 76, Pauma Valley (92061-9583)
P.O. Box 424 (92061-0424)
PHONE.................................760 742-2151
Fax: 760 742-3762
Alfonso Ramos, *Manager*
EMP: 200
SALES (corp-wide): 1.1MM **Privately Held**
SIC: 5193 5261 Plants, potted; nurseries
PA: T - Y Nursery, Inc.
  5221 Arvada St
  Torrance CA 90503
  310 370-2561

(P-9220)
TELAFLORA LLC
11444 W Olympic Blvd Fl 4, Los Angeles (90064-1546)
PHONE.................................310 231-9199
Stewart Resnick,
Lynda Resnick,
Matt Matsuno, *Manager*
EMP: 450
SALES (est): 29.3MM **Privately Held**
SIC: 5193 Flowers & florists' supplies

(P-9221)
TORO NURSERY INC
17585 Crenshaw Blvd, Torrance (90504-3403)
PHONE.................................310 715-1982
Fax: 310 715-1987
Salvador Sanchez, *President*
Antonio Gomez, *Vice Pres*
EMP: 60
SALES (est): 4.6MM **Privately Held**
SIC: 5193 Nursery stock

(P-9222)
UNITED FLORAL EXCHANGE INC
Also Called: Cal Americas Wholesale Florist
2834 La Mirada Dr Ste B, Vista (92081-8440)
PHONE.................................760 597-1940
Fax: 760 597-1960
Jim Dionne, *President*
Thayis Dionne, *Vice Pres*
Pennie Mobley, *Financial Exec*
Martha Haswell, *Controller*
Steve Dionne, *Sales Mgr*
EMP: 75
SQ FT: 30,000
SALES (est): 4MM **Privately Held**
WEB: www.calamericas.com
SIC: 5193 Flowers, fresh

(P-9223)
USA BOUQUET LLC
2834 La Mirada Dr Ste B, Vista (92081-8440)
PHONE.................................800 878-9909
Edgar Lozano,
EMP: 88
SALES (corp-wide): 254.3MM **Privately Held**
SIC: 5193 Flowers, fresh
HQ: Usa Bouquet Llc
  1500 Nw 95th Ave
  Doral FL 33172
  786 437-6500

(P-9224)
VALLEY FLOWERS INC
3920 Via Real, Carpinteria (93013-1266)
P.O. Box 1279 (93014-1279)
PHONE.................................805 684-6651
Walter Vanwingerden, *President*
John Vanwingerden, *Vice Pres*
▲ **EMP:** 60
SALES (est): 3.8MM **Privately Held**
WEB: www.valleyflowers.com
SIC: 5193 Flowers & nursery stock

(P-9225)
VILLAGE NURSERIES WHL LLC (PA)
1589 N Main St, Orange (92867-3439)
PHONE.................................714 279-3100
David House, *Mng Member*
Terri Cooke, *Executive*
Julia Buenafe, *Human Resources*
Mark Marriott, *Opers Mgr*
Wayne Johnson,
EMP: 50
SQ FT: 12,321
SALES (est): 171.1MM **Privately Held**
SIC: 5193 Nursery stock

(P-9226)
VILLAGE NURSERIES WHL LLC
6901 Bradshaw Rd, Sacramento (95829-9303)
PHONE.................................916 993-2292
Steve Sawyer, *Branch Mgr*
EMP: 275
SALES (corp-wide): 171.1MM **Privately Held**
SIC: 5193 Flowers & florists' supplies
PA: Village Nurseries Wholesale, Llc
  1589 N Main St
  Orange CA 92867
  714 279-3100

(P-9227)
VILLAGE NURSERIES WHL LLC
20099 Santa Rosa Mine Rd, Perris (92570-7774)
PHONE.................................951 657-3940
Joseph Jensen, *Branch Mgr*
EMP: 275
SALES (corp-wide): 171.1MM **Privately Held**
SIC: 5193 Nursery stock
PA: Village Nurseries Wholesale, Llc
  1589 N Main St
  Orange CA 92867
  714 279-3100

(P-9228)
WESTERN STAR NURSERIES LLC
9394 Robson Rd, Galt (95632-8841)
P.O. Box 725 (95632-0725)
PHONE.................................209 744-2552
Fax: 209 744-2562
Robert Painter,
Sally B Painter,
EMP: 50
SALES (est): 1.7MM **Privately Held**
SIC: 5193 Flowers & nursery stock

(P-9229)
WESTLAND ORCHIDS INC
Also Called: Westland Floral
1400 Cravens Ln, Carpinteria (93013-3166)
PHONE.................................805 684-1436
David Van Wingerden, *CEO*
Ellie Ramirez, *Human Resources*
Heather Schulenberg, *Marketing Staff*
Kelly Gomez, *Sales Staff*
EMP: 50 **EST:** 2013
SALES (est): 11.8MM **Privately Held**
SIC: 5193 Flowers & florists' supplies

(P-9230)
WINWARD INTERNATIONAL (PA)
Also Called: Winward Silks
31033 Huntwood Ave, Hayward (94544-7007)
PHONE.................................510 487-8686
Fax: 510 886-6888
Patrick Tai, *President*
Garrison Tai, *President*
▲ **EMP:** 60
SQ FT: 10,000
SALES (est): 44.2MM **Privately Held**
SIC: 5193 5023 Artificial flowers; decorative home furnishings & supplies

---
5194 Tobacco & Tobacco Prdts Wholesale

(P-9231)
ALTRIA GROUP DISTRIBUTION CO
300 N Lake Ave Ste 1100, Pasadena (91101-4123)
PHONE.................................626 792-2900
Craig A Johnson, *President*
Nancy Kline, *Sales Staff*
EMP: 70
SALES (corp-wide): 25.4B **Publicly Held**
WEB: www.philipmorrisusa.com
SIC: 5194 Cigarettes
HQ: Altria Group Distribution Company
  6601 W Broad St
  Richmond VA 23230
  804 274-2000

(P-9232)
CORE-MARK INTERNATIONAL INC
8333 Edison Hwy, Bakersfield (93307-9173)
PHONE.................................661 366-2673
Fax: 661 366-5178
Caral Parker, *Principal*
Veronica Forcillo, *Purch Mgr*
EMP: 121
SALES (corp-wide): 11B **Publicly Held**
SIC: 5194 Tobacco & tobacco products
HQ: Core-Mark International, Inc.
  395 Oyster Point Blvd # 415
  South San Francisco CA 94080
  650 589-9445

(P-9233)
CORE-MARK MIDCONTINENT INC (DH)
Also Called: Core-Mark International
395 Oyster Point Blvd # 415, South San Francisco (94080-1932)
PHONE.................................650 589-9445
J M Walsh, *CEO*
Thomas Perkins, *President*
Gregory P Antholzner, *Corp Secy*
Stacy Loretz Congdon, *Vice Pres*
Sarah Agustin, *Human Res Mgr*
EMP: 153

5194 - Tobacco & Tobacco Prdts Wholesale County (P-9234)

SALES (est): 263.5MM
SALES (corp-wide): 11B **Publicly Held**
SIC: 5194 5141 Tobacco & tobacco products; groceries, general line
HQ: Core-Mark International, Inc.
395 Oyster Point Blvd # 415
South San Francisco CA 94080
650 589-9445

(P-9234)
KRETEK INTERNATIONAL INC (PA)
5449 Endeavour Ct, Moorpark (93021-1712)
PHONE.....................805 531-8888
Fax: 805 531-9006
Hugh R Cassar, *CEO*
Sean Cassar, *COO*
Keith Roose, *COO*
Donald Gormley, *CFO*
Lynn K Cassar, *Corp Secy*
◆ EMP: 90
SQ FT: 80,000
SALES (est): 81.3MM **Privately Held**
WEB: www.kretek.com
SIC: 5194 Cigarettes; smoking tobacco; cigars

(P-9235)
PACIFIC GROSERVICE INC
Also Called: Pitco Foods
567 Cinnabar St, San Jose (95110-2306)
PHONE.....................408 727-4826
Pericles Navab, *Ch of Bd*
Azadeh Hariri, *Shareholder*
Frank Hariri, *Shareholder*
Esmael Maboudi, *Shareholder*
Parviz Maboudi, *Shareholder*
▲ EMP: 360
SQ FT: 85,000
SALES (est): 221.8MM **Privately Held**
SIC: 5194 5149 5141 5113 Tobacco & tobacco products; candy; groceries, general line; industrial & personal service paper; service establishment equipment

(P-9236)
TREPCO IMPORTS & DIST LTD
Trepco West
1626 Frontage Rd, Chula Vista (91911-3936)
PHONE.....................619 690-7999
Wiam Paulus, *Branch Mgr*
Raad Audo, *Purch Mgr*
EMP: 50
SALES (corp-wide): 57.7MM **Privately Held**
SIC: 5194 5141 Tobacco & tobacco products; groceries, general line
PA: Trepco Imports & Distribution, Ltd.
1201 E Lincoln Ave
Madison Heights MI 48071
248 546-3661

5198 Paints, Varnishes & Splys Wholesale

(P-9237)
BERG LACQUER CO (PA)
Also Called: Ellis Paint
3150 E Pico Blvd, Los Angeles (90023-3632)
PHONE.....................323 261-8114
Fax: 323 246-4278
Sandra Berg, *President*
Robert O Berg, *Ch of Bd*
Donna Berg, *Treasurer*
Kate Graber, *Admin Mgr*
Debbie Hoover, *Personnel Exec*
▲ EMP: 65
SQ FT: 85,000
SALES (est): 59.9MM **Privately Held**
WEB: www.ellispaint.com
SIC: 5198 2851 Paints, varnishes & supplies; paints & paint additives

(P-9238)
PAINT SUNDRIES SOLUTIONS INC
2930 N San Fernando Blvd, Burbank (91504-2522)
PHONE.....................818 843-2382
Manuel Deavila, *Branch Mgr*
EMP: 63

SALES (corp-wide): 180.1MM **Privately Held**
SIC: 5198 Paints, varnishes & supplies
PA: Paint Sundries Solutions, Inc.
930 7th Ave
Kirkland WA 98033
425 827-9200

(P-9239)
SHILPARK PAINT CORPORATION (PA)
Also Called: Shilpark Paint Automotive
1640 S Vermont Ave, Los Angeles (90006-4522)
PHONE.....................323 732-7093
Fax: 323 732-3712
Shil Kyoung Park, *CEO*
Mina Park, *Treasurer*
EMP: 53
SALES (est): 10.6MM **Privately Held**
SIC: 5198 5231 5013 Paints, varnishes & supplies; paint & painting supplies; body repair or paint shop supplies, automotive

(P-9240)
TCP GLOBAL CORPORATION (PA)
Also Called: Autobody Depot
6695 Rasha St, San Diego (92121-2240)
PHONE.....................858 909-2110
Dean A Faucett, *President*
Dean Faucett, *President*
Rick Faucett, *Vice Pres*
Todd Faucett, *Vice Pres*
Josie Sinclair, *Executive*
◆ EMP: 55
SQ FT: 38,000
SALES (est): 127.2MM **Privately Held**
SIC: 5198 5231 Paints; paint

5199 Nondurable Goods, NEC Wholesale

(P-9241)
ABAD FOAM INC
6560 Caballero Blvd, Buena Park (90620-1130)
PHONE.....................714 994-2223
Fax: 714 523-3626
Abad Chavez, *President*
Cesar Chavez, *Vice Pres*
Carol Burke, *Controller*
Chris Wertz, *Director*
Jerry White, *Manager*
▲ EMP: 50
SALES (est): 20.4MM **Privately Held**
WEB: www.abadfoam.com
SIC: 5199 Foam rubber

(P-9242)
AJM PACKAGING CORPORATION
1160 Vernon Way, El Cajon (92020-1837)
PHONE.....................619 448-4007
Joe Marcelynas, *Principal*
Juan Franco, *Manager*
EMP: 134
SALES (corp-wide): 358.6MM **Privately Held**
SIC: 5199 Packaging materials
PA: A.J.M. Packaging Corporation
E-4111 Andover Rd
Bloomfield Hills MI 48302
248 901-0040

(P-9243)
ALLAQUARIA LLC
Also Called: Quality Marine
5420 W 104th St, Los Angeles (90045-6012)
P.O. Box 2439 (90051-0439)
PHONE.....................310 645-1107
Fax: 310 670-8837
G Christopher Bverner, *Mng Member*
Wazirah Yamin, *VP Human Res*
Bob Pascal, *Sales Mgr*
Mary L Buerner,
Adam Mangino, *Director*
▲ EMP: 60
SQ FT: 45,000
SALES (est): 21.6MM **Privately Held**
SIC: 5199 Tropical fish

(P-9244)
AMD TRADING COMPANY INC
1021 Stockton St, San Francisco (94108-1109)
PHONE.....................415 391-0601
Amanda Ho, *Principal*
▲ EMP: 142 EST: 2008
SALES (est): 11.7MM **Privately Held**
SIC: 5199 Nondurable goods

(P-9245)
ATA RETAIL SERVICES LLC (PA)
7133 Koll Center Pkwy # 100, Pleasanton (94566-3300)
PHONE.....................925 621-4700
Fax: 510 401-5302
Sumner Bennett, *CEO*
Ty Bennett, *President*
Elena Bennett, *Vice Pres*
Harold Benedict, *Accounting Mgr*
Sara Russell, *Accounting Mgr*
▲ EMP: 75
SALES (est): 418.8MM **Privately Held**
WEB: www.ataretail.com
SIC: 5199 General merchandise, nondurable

(P-9246)
BERKLEY INTERNATIONAL LLC
2725 E El Presidio St, Carson (90810-1118)
PHONE.....................310 900-1771
Jeff Berkley, *President*
Eric Berkley, *Vice Pres*
Anthony Russo, *Vice Pres*
Carol Tan, *Technician*
Karen Fuchs, *Director*
▲ EMP: 65
SQ FT: 55,000
SALES (est): 16MM **Privately Held**
SIC: 5199 Packaging materials

(P-9247)
BRANDERSCOM INC (PA)
2551 Casey Ave, Mountain View (94043-1138)
PHONE.....................650 292-2752
Fax: 650 292-2773
Gerald McLaughlin, *President*
Jerry McLaughlin, *Mktg Dir*
Marielle Rodriguez, *Sales Mgr*
Sheena Baltazar, *Sales Staff*
Becky Staup, *Cust Mgr*
◆ EMP: 88 EST: 1999
SQ FT: 19,170
SALES (est): 82.1MM **Privately Held**
WEB: www.branders.com
SIC: 5199 Advertising specialties

(P-9248)
BRANDVIA ALLIANCE INC
2159 Bering Dr, San Jose (95131-2014)
PHONE.....................408 955-0500
Fax: 408 955-0506
James David Childers, *President*
Cindy Kahl, *Corp Secy*
Laura Banyai, *Officer*
Sarah McMahon, *Officer*
Ian McLearon, *Exec VP*
▲ EMP: 100
SQ FT: 21,000
SALES (est): 69.2MM **Privately Held**
SIC: 5199 Advertising specialties

(P-9249)
BUBBLA INC
7931 Deering Ave, Canoga Park (91304-5008)
PHONE.....................818 884-2000
Andrew Cooper, *President*
EMP: 50
SQ FT: 23,500
SALES (est): 4.9MM **Privately Held**
WEB: www.bubbla.com
SIC: 5199 Packaging materials

(P-9250)
CALICO BRANDS
Also Called: Scripto
2055 S Haven Ave, Ontario (91761-0736)
PHONE.....................909 930-5000
Felix M Hon, *CEO*
Mark Deasy, *Vice Pres*
Rick Tensho, *Human Res Mgr*
Fung Moon, *Purch Dir*
Samuel Kamamaru, *VP Opers*

▲ EMP: 50
SQ FT: 125,000
SALES: 12.1MM **Privately Held**
SIC: 5199 Lighters, cigarette & cigar

(P-9251)
CELMOL INC
Also Called: Mark Roberts
1611 E Saint Andrew Pl, Santa Ana (92705-4932)
PHONE.....................714 259-1000
Mark Rees, *President*
Robert White, *Accounting Mgr*
▲ EMP: 60
SQ FT: 36,000
SALES (est): 10.8MM **Privately Held**
WEB: www.xmas-magic.com
SIC: 5199 5193 Christmas novelties; gifts & novelties; flowers, fresh

(P-9252)
CENTRAL GARDEN & PET COMPANY
9235 Activity Rd, San Diego (92126-4440)
PHONE.....................858 695-0743
EMP: 59
SALES (corp-wide): 1.6B **Publicly Held**
WEB: www.centralgardenandpet.com
SIC: 5199 2048 Pet supplies; prepared feeds
PA: Central Garden & Pet Company
1340 Treat Blvd Ste 600
Walnut Creek CA 94597
925 948-4000

(P-9253)
CENTRAL GARDEN & PET COMPANY
13227 Orden Dr, Santa Fe Springs (90670-6332)
PHONE.....................562 926-5252
Fax: 562 404-6182
Scott Rath, *Manager*
Joseph Lee, *Vice Pres*
Chelma Berrcero, *Human Resources*
Michelle Almquist, *Marketing Staff*
Jeff May, *Manager*
EMP: 115
SQ FT: 70,000
SALES (corp-wide): 1.6B **Publicly Held**
WEB: www.centralgardenandpet.com
SIC: 5199 Pet supplies
PA: Central Garden & Pet Company
1340 Treat Blvd Ste 600
Walnut Creek CA 94597
925 948-4000

(P-9254)
CINTAS CORPORATION NO 2
4320 E Miraloma Ave, Anaheim (92807-1886)
PHONE.....................714 288-8400
Robert Sklar, *Branch Mgr*
Karen Carnahan, *Treasurer*
Kyle Dudderar, *Genrl Mgr*
Walter Somoza, *Warehouse Mgr*
Becky Doffing, *Manager*
EMP: 88
SALES (corp-wide): 4.9B **Publicly Held**
WEB: www.cintas-corp.com
SIC: 5199 First aid supplies
HQ: Cintas Corporation No. 2
6800 Cintas Blvd
Mason OH 45040

(P-9255)
CLASSIC SOFT TRIM INC
3201 Diablo Ave, Hayward (94545-2701)
PHONE.....................510 782-4911
Fax: 510 782-3943
Steve Robinson, *Manager*
EMP: 75
SALES (corp-wide): 144.2MM **Privately Held**
WEB: www.cstdi.com
SIC: 5199 Automobile fabrics
PA: Classic Soft Trim, Inc.
4516 Seton Center Pkwy # 135
Austin TX 78759
512 873-7770

▲ = Import ▼ = Export
◆ = Import/Export

PRODUCTS & SERVICES SECTION
5199 - Nondurable Goods, NEC Wholesale County (P-9279)

(P-9256)
CORE-MARK INTERRELATED (DH)
Also Called: Allied Merchandising Industry
311 Reed Cir, Corona (92879-1349)
PHONE 951 272-4790
Fax: 909 272-3595
Thomas Perkins, *CEO*
Mike Dunn, *President*
J Michael Walsh, *CEO*
Laura Castro, *Office Mgr*
Gerald Buldoc, *CIO*
EMP: 58
SQ FT: 70,000
SALES (est): 154MM
SALES (corp-wide): 11B **Publicly Held**
SIC: 5199 5122 5087 General merchandise, non-durable; druggists' sundries; service establishment equipment
HQ: Core-Mark International, Inc.
395 Oyster Point Blvd # 415
South San Francisco CA 94080
650 589-9445

(P-9257)
COSTCO WHOLESALE CORPORATION
16505 Sierra Lakes Pkwy, Fontana (92336-1256)
PHONE 909 823-8270
EMP: 196
SALES (corp-wide): 116.2B **Publicly Held**
SIC: 5199
PA: Costco Wholesale Corporation
999 Lake Dr Ste 200
Issaquah WA 98027
425 313-8100

(P-9258)
DEJUNO CORPORATION
1800 S Milliken Ave, Ontario (91761-2340)
PHONE 909 230-6744
Yuanzhe Gao, *President*
Fei Hong, *Vice Pres*
EMP: 59
SQ FT: 30,000
SALES: 2MM **Privately Held**
SIC: 5199 Leather goods, except footwear, gloves, luggage, belting

(P-9259)
DOLPHIN HKG LTD (PA)
Also Called: Dolphin International
1125 W Hillcrest Blvd, Inglewood (90301-2021)
P.O. Box 91081, Los Angeles (90009-1081)
PHONE 310 215-3356
Fax: 310 337-1393
Steven Lundblad, *President*
Helen Lundblad, *Vice Pres*
▲ **EMP:** 70
SQ FT: 12,000
SALES (est): 45.9MM **Privately Held**
WEB: www.dolphin-int.com
SIC: 5199 Tropical fish

(P-9260)
ECOLOGIC BRANDS INC
550 Carnegie St, Manteca (95337-6141)
PHONE 209 239-3600
Stephen Elledge, *Manager*
EMP: 50 **Privately Held**
SIC: 5199 Packaging materials
PA: Eco.Logic Brands Inc.
550 Carnegie St
Manteca CA 95337
-

(P-9261)
ERLANGER DISTRIBUTION CTR INC
Also Called: Erlanger Sales
797 Palmyrita Ave, Riverside (92507-1811)
PHONE 951 784-5147
Fax: 951 784-4893
David Erlanger, *CEO*
Claude M Erlanger, *President*
Doris Erlanger, *Vice Pres*
Steve Erlanger, *Vice Pres*
Maria Calvillo, *Sales Mgr*
▲ **EMP:** 50
SQ FT: 160,000
SALES (est): 8.2MM **Privately Held**
WEB: www.erlangerdc.com
SIC: 5199 5192 5099 5137 Leather goods, except footwear, gloves, luggage, belting; books; luggage; handbags

(P-9262)
EXOTIC IMPORTS INTL INC
32011 Isle Vis, Laguna Niguel (92677-5413)
P.O. Box 6489 (92607-6489)
PHONE 949 306-8816
Vilai Kirchhoff, *CEO*
EMP: 50
SALES (est): 3.4MM **Privately Held**
SIC: 5199 Nondurable goods

(P-9263)
FIGI ACQUISITION COMPANY LLC
3636 Gateway Center Ave, San Diego (92102-4524)
PHONE 800 678-3444
Woody Laforge,
Greg Bell, *Info Tech Mgr*
Terri Dirkse, *Controller*
EMP: 200
SQ FT: 216,000
SALES (est): 10.2MM **Privately Held**
SIC: 5199 Gifts & novelties

(P-9264)
FOAM DISTRIBUTORS INCORPORATED
Also Called: Foam Fabrication For Packaging
31009 San Antonio St, Hayward (94544-7903)
PHONE 510 441-8377
Fax: 510 475-1079
Stephanie Wright, *Chairman*
Steve M Doyle, *CEO*
David Brown, *CTO*
Brian Doyle, *Plant Supt*
Jim Doyle, *Sales Mgr*
EMP: 75
SQ FT: 72,000
SALES: 12.1MM **Privately Held**
WEB: www.foamdist.com
SIC: 5199 Packaging materials

(P-9265)
FRANK GUSTAFSON
Also Called: A-One Greeting Card Service
1240 Logan Ave Ste N, Costa Mesa (92626-4019)
PHONE 714 438-1590
Fax: 714 438-1591
Frank Gustafson, *Owner*
▲ **EMP:** 55 **EST:** 1989
SQ FT: 1,600
SALES: 2.7MM **Privately Held**
SIC: 5199 Cards, plastic: unprinted

(P-9266)
FREE STREAM MEDIA CORP
Also Called: Samba TV
301 Brannan St Fl 6, San Francisco (94107-3816)
PHONE 415 889-6404
Ashwin Navin, *CEO*
Joseph Baribeau, *Vice Pres*
Dave Harrison, *CTO*
EMP: 145
SQ FT: 11,000
SALES: 35.9MM **Privately Held**
SIC: 5199 Advertising specialties

(P-9267)
GEORGE P JOHNSON COMPANY
999 Skyway Rd Ste 300, San Carlos (94070-2722)
PHONE 650 226-0600
Fax: 650 226-0601
Chris Meyer, *CEO*
Arsey Miller, *Senior VP*
Pamela Bittner, *Social Dir*
Sheila Martin, *Social Dir*
Melissa Stevenson, *Program Mgr*
EMP: 120
SALES (corp-wide): 235.5MM **Privately Held**
SIC: 5199 8742 Advertising specialties; marketing consulting services
HQ: George P Johnson Company
3600 Giddings Rd
Auburn Hills MI 48326
248 475-2500

(P-9268)
GRAHAM PACKAGING COMPANY LP
4500 Finch Rd, Modesto (95357-4145)
PHONE 209 572-5187
Tom Sponder, *Branch Mgr*
Teresa Medina, *Human Resources*
EMP: 168 **Privately Held**
SIC: 5199 Packaging materials
HQ: Graham Packaging Company, L.P.
700 Indian Springs Dr # 100
Lancaster PA 17601
717 849-8500

(P-9269)
GRHT INC
Also Called: Foam Co, The
14818 Raymer St, Van Nuys (91405-1219)
PHONE 323 873-6393
Fax: 323 780-0891
Gil Rosky, *President*
Hossein Tehrani, *Vice Pres*
Pradeep Gupta, *Manager*
EMP: 60
SQ FT: 11,000
SALES (est): 10.5MM **Privately Held**
SIC: 5199 Foam rubber

(P-9270)
HAY KUHN INC
1880 Jeffrey Rd, El Centro (92243-9532)
P.O. Box 338 (92244-0338)
PHONE 760 353-0124
Fax: 760 337-8458
Felipe Irigoyen, *President*
Jim Ohland, *General Mgr*
Terry Allegranza, *Controller*
Kristi Blair, *Controller*
◆ **EMP:** 50
SQ FT: 1,500
SALES (est): 15.2MM **Privately Held**
SIC: 5199 4789 Packaging materials; car loading

(P-9271)
IMPORT COLLECTION (PA)
Also Called: Tic
7885 Nelson Rd, Panorama City (91402-6045)
PHONE 818 782-3060
Fax: 818 904-0584
David Mehdyzadeh, *CEO*
Sina Mehdyzadeh, *Corp Secy*
Sammy Mehdizadeh, *Vice Pres*
Hermine Abkarin, *Manager*
◆ **EMP:** 65
SQ FT: 160,000
SALES (est): 30.1MM **Privately Held**
WEB: www.importcollection.com
SIC: 5199 5023 Gifts & novelties; decorative home furnishings & supplies

(P-9272)
INTERNTIONAL PET SUPS DIST INC
10850 Via Frontera, San Diego (92127-1705)
PHONE 858 453-7845
James Myers, *CEO*
◆ **EMP:** 100
SQ FT: 70,000
SALES (est): 17.6MM
SALES (corp-wide): 317.9K **Privately Held**
WEB: www.petco.com
SIC: 5199 Pet supplies
HQ: Petco Animal Supplies, Inc.
10850 Via Frontera
San Diego CA 92127
858 453-7845

(P-9273)
KATZKIN LEATHER INC (PA)
6868 W Acco St, Montebello (90640-5441)
PHONE 323 725-1243
Brook Mayberry, *President*
Jim Roberson, *President*
Angel Hernandez, *Project Mgr*
Miles Hubbard, *Mktg Dir*
Dara Ward, *Marketing Mgr*
▲ **EMP:** 200
SQ FT: 50,000
SALES (est): 102.1MM **Privately Held**
WEB: www.katzkin.com
SIC: 5199 2531 Leather & cut stock; seats, automobile

(P-9274)
KOLE IMPORTS
Also Called: Basket Basics
24600 Main St, Carson (90745-6332)
PHONE 310 834-0004
Fax: 310 834-0005
Robert Kole, *CEO*
Dan Kole, *Vice Pres*
Andy Kole, *VP Bus Dvlpt*
Leah Hulce, *Executive Asst*
Ty Yolac, *Manager*
▲ **EMP:** 84
SQ FT: 150,000
SALES (est): 41.6MM **Privately Held**
WEB: www.koleimports.com
SIC: 5199 Gifts & novelties

(P-9275)
LEE-MAR AQUARIUM & PET SUPS
Also Called: Lee Mar Aquarium & Pet Sups
2459 Dogwood Way, Vista (92081-8421)
PHONE 760 727-1300
Fax: 760 727-4280
Terran R Boyd, *President*
Jeff Boyd, *VP Sales*
▲ **EMP:** 100
SQ FT: 67,000
SALES (est): 23.4MM **Privately Held**
WEB: www.leemarpet.com
SIC: 5199 3999 Pet supplies; pet supplies

(P-9276)
LIFESTREET CORPORATION
Also Called: Lifestreet Media
981 Industrial Rd Ste F, San Carlos (94070-4150)
PHONE 650 508-2220
Mitchell Wiesman, *CEO*
Patrick McNenny, *CFO*
Vicki Price, *Manager*
EMP: 75 **EST:** 2008
SALES (est): 19.7MM **Privately Held**
SIC: 5199 Advertising specialties

(P-9277)
LIVE NATION MERCHANDISE INC (HQ)
Also Called: Signatures Sni
450 Mission St Ste 300, San Francisco (94105-2518)
PHONE 415 247-7400
Michael Rapino, *President*
Django Bayless, *Officer*
Rick Fish, *Vice Pres*
Christina Mikhail, *Executive Asst*
Mac Scott, *Info Tech Mgr*
▲ **EMP:** 50
SQ FT: 27,000
SALES (est): 61.2MM
SALES (corp-wide): 7.2B **Publicly Held**
WEB: www.signaturesnet.com
SIC: 5199 Advertising specialties
PA: Live Nation Entertainment, Inc.
9348 Civic Center Dr Lbby
Beverly Hills CA 90210
310 867-7000

(P-9278)
LOGOMARK INC
1201 Bell Ave, Tustin (92780-6420)
PHONE 714 675-6100
Fax: 714 675-6111
Trevor Gnesin, *President*
Brian P Padian, *Senior VP*
Vernon Eintracht, *CTO*
Felora Sajjadi, *Credit Mgr*
Margarita Arcinienga, *Human Res Dir*
▲ **EMP:** 250
SQ FT: 200,000
SALES (est): 164.7MM **Privately Held**
WEB: www.logomark.com
SIC: 5199 Advertising specialties

(P-9279)
MAX LEATHER
8533 Washington Blvd, Culver City (90232-7462)
PHONE 310 841-6990
Fax: 310 841-6992

5199 - Nondurable Goods, NEC Wholesale County (P-9280)

Max Khansefid, *President*
EMP: 50
SALES (est): 8.2MM **Privately Held**
WEB: www.maxleatherinc.com
SIC: 5199 Leather, leather goods & furs

(P-9280)
MCEVOY OF MARIN LLC
Also Called: McEvoy Ranch
5935 Red Hill Rd, Petaluma (94952-9437)
P.O. Box 341 (94953-0341)
PHONE 707 778-2307
Fax: 707 778-0128
Nion McEvoy,
Nan Tucker McEvoy,
▲ **EMP:** 100
SALES (est): 23.6MM **Privately Held**
SIC: 5199 Oils, animal or vegetable

(P-9281)
MICHAELS STORES INC
Also Called: Warehouse
3501 W Avenue H, Lancaster (93536-8341)
PHONE 661 951-3500
Fax: 661 951-3532
John Vilotta, *General Mgr*
Lawanna Wheatly, *Recruiter*
EMP: 200
SALES (corp-wide): 4.9B **Publicly Held**
WEB: www.michaels.com
SIC: 5199 4225 5945 Art goods; general warehousing & storage; hobby, toy & game shops
HQ: Michaels Stores, Inc.
8000 Bent Branch Dr
Irving TX 75063
972 409-1300

(P-9282)
MIDWAY INTERNATIONAL INC
13131 166th St, Cerritos (90703-2202)
PHONE 562 802-0800
Fax: 562 921-6682
Ha Suk Chung, *President*
Jason Park, *Finance Other*
◆ **EMP:** 50
SQ FT: 32,700
SALES (est): 16.7MM **Privately Held**
SIC: 5199 Wigs

(P-9283)
NW PACKAGING LLC (PA)
1201 E Lexington Ave, Pomona (91766-5520)
PHONE 909 706-3627
Benson Jahnke, *Marketing Staff*
EMP: 100
SALES (est): 34MM **Privately Held**
SIC: 5199 Packaging materials

(P-9284)
P2F HOLDINGS
Also Called: Milen
1760 Apollo Ct, Seal Beach (90740-5617)
PHONE 562 296-1055
Sandra Piontak, *President*
Leonard Piontak, *CEO*
Jim Kleban, *CFO*
Delynn Lane, *CFO*
Michael Freede, *Chairman*
▲ **EMP:** 75
SQ FT: 64,000
SALES (est): 2.4MM **Privately Held**
WEB: www.p2fholdings.com
SIC: 5199 General merchandise, non-durable

(P-9285)
PACIFIC EASTERN INTL PDTS
Also Called: Pacific Eastern Intl Pdts I
12551 Barrett Ln, Santa Ana (92705-1368)
PHONE 714 538-3434
Thomas Osbourne, *President*
Teri Osbourne, *Admin Sec*
EMP: 90
SALES (est): 4.3MM **Privately Held**
SIC: 5199 General merchandise, non-durable

(P-9286)
PACIFIC METRO LLC (PA)
Also Called: Thomas Kinkade Company, The
235 Pine St Ste 1150, San Francisco (94104-2748)
PHONE 408 201-5000
Eric H Halvorson, *President*
Steve Paszkiewicz, *President*
Herbert D Montgomery, *CFO*
Anthony D Thomopoulos, *Chairman*
Daniel Byrne, *Exec VP*
▲ **EMP:** 350
SQ FT: 400,000
SALES (est): 80.9MM **Privately Held**
SIC: 5199 Art goods

(P-9287)
PACIFIC ROYAL GROUP
5500 Stewart Ave Ste 113, Fremont (94538-3100)
P.O. Box 3457 (94539-0381)
PHONE 510 200-2993
Ronald Ng, *Director*
Kamme Lai, *Vice Pres*
EMP: 120 **EST:** 2013
SQ FT: 1,700
SALES: 5.6MM **Privately Held**
SIC: 5199 Variety store merchandise

(P-9288)
PACIFIC WESTERN SALES
2980 Enterprise St Ste A, Brea (92821-6283)
PHONE 714 572-6730
Fax: 714 572-6747
Lyndsey William Tidwell, *President*
Lorraine Clements, *Treasurer*
Kazem Rezvan, *Vice Pres*
Jane Ho, *Human Res Dir*
Marty Kelly, *VP Sales*
▲ **EMP:** 56
SQ FT: 49,000
SALES: 16MM **Privately Held**
WEB: www.pacificwesternsales.com
SIC: 5199 7336 Packaging materials; package design

(P-9289)
PACKAGING MANUFACTURING INC
9295 Siempre Viva Rd C, San Diego (92154-7648)
PHONE 619 498-9199
Bruce McFarland, *CEO*
EMP: 150 **EST:** 2009
SALES (est): 17.7MM **Privately Held**
SIC: 5199 Packaging materials

(P-9290)
PD LIQUIDATION INC
Also Called: Pipe Dream Products
21350 Lassen St, Chatsworth (91311-4254)
PHONE 818 772-0100
Fax: 818 885-0800
David Feldman, *CEO*
Robert Feldman, *President*
Brian Flowers, *CFO*
Ruben Deitz, *Vice Pres*
Ana Ortiz, *Admin Asst*
◆ **EMP:** 150
SALES (est): 56.7MM
SALES (corp-wide): 57.1MM **Privately Held**
WEB: www.pipedreamproducts.com
SIC: 5199 Gifts & novelties
PA: Diamond Products, Llc
21350 Lassen St
Chatsworth CA 91311
818 772-0100

(P-9291)
PENTAIR TECHNICAL PRODUCTS
7328 Trade St, San Diego (92121-3435)
PHONE 858 740-2400
Chris Lower, *Branch Mgr*
EMP: 120 **Privately Held**
SIC: 5199 Packaging materials
HQ: Pentair Technical Products Inc
170 Commerce Dr
Warwick RI 02886
401 732-3770

(P-9292)
PET PARTNERS INC (PA)
Also Called: North American Pet Products
450 N Sheridan St, Corona (92880-2020)
PHONE 951 279-9888
Keith Bonner, *CEO*
Ronald Bonner, *President*
Yvonne Thulemeyer, *Treasurer*
Gloria Bonner, *Admin Sec*
Eileen Howard, *Sales Staff*
▲ **EMP:** 170
SQ FT: 120,000
SALES (est): 188.5MM **Privately Held**
SIC: 5199 Pet supplies

(P-9293)
POLYVORE INC
701 First Ave, Sunnyvale (94089-1019)
PHONE 650 968-1195
Jessica Lee, *CEO*
Laura Chambers, *Exec VP*
Melanie Jones, *Office Mgr*
Michael Friedman, *Sr Software Eng*
Pasha Sadri, *CTO*
EMP: 60
SALES (est): 6.5MM
SALES (corp-wide): 4.9B **Publicly Held**
SIC: 5199 Advertising specialties
PA: Yahoo Inc.
701 First Ave
Sunnyvale CA 94089
408 349-3300

(P-9294)
PRO SPECIALTIES GROUP INC
4863 Shawline St Ste D, San Diego (92111-1435)
PHONE 858 541-1100
Fax: 858 268-5801
Chao Hsien Lin, *CEO*
Shu-Hwa Lee, *CEO*
Sin Ghim, *COO*
Thomas Barry, *CFO*
Mike Lin, *Exec VP*
▲ **EMP:** 70
SQ FT: 23,000
SALES (est): 35MM **Privately Held**
WEB: www.psginc.com
SIC: 5199 Advertising specialties

(P-9295)
QUAKER PET GROUP INC
160 Mitchell Blvd, San Rafael (94903-2044)
PHONE 415 721-7400
Kevin Fick, *CEO*
Mike Trott, *CFO*
Aaron Lamstein, *Director*
◆ **EMP:** 100
SQ FT: 11,000
SALES (est): 67MM **Privately Held**
SIC: 5199 Pet supplies
HQ: Worldwise, Inc.
6 Hamilton Landing # 150
Novato CA 94949
415 721-7400

(P-9296)
QUETICO LLC
5521 Schaefer Ave, Chino (91710-9070)
PHONE 909 628-6200
Fax: 909 628-8340
Thomas Fenchel, *Mng Member*
Nick Agakanian, *Vice Pres*
David Brudnicki, *Vice Pres*
Antonio Lopez, *Branch Mgr*
Alan Mazursky, *Financial Exec*
▲ **EMP:** 185
SQ FT: 278,500
SALES (est): 130.6MM **Privately Held**
WEB: www.quetico.net
SIC: 5199 7389 General merchandise, non-durable; packaging & labeling services

(P-9297)
R M B PACKAGING CO INC
9667 Canoga Ave, Chatsworth (91311-4115)
PHONE 818 998-0658
Paul Thomas, *CEO*
Cleto Prudente, *Administration*
EMP: 50
SALES (est): 6MM **Privately Held**
SIC: 5199 Packaging materials

(P-9298)
REDBARN PET PRODUCTS INC
Also Called: Redbarn Premium Pet Products
3229 E Spring St Ste 310, Long Beach (90806-2478)
PHONE 562 495-7315
Fax: 562 495-7318
Jeff Baikie, *CEO*
Howard Bloxam, *President*
Patrick Serna, *Exec VP*
Joe Martinez, *Principal*
Ador Delcanto, *Controller*
▼ **EMP:** 160
SQ FT: 50,000
SALES (est): 91.4MM **Privately Held**
WEB: www.redbarninc.com
SIC: 5199 2047 Pet supplies; dog & cat food

(P-9299)
RM ESOP INC
340 El Camino Real S # 36, Salinas (93901-4553)
PHONE 831 783-3140
Steve Carroll, *Manager*
Joe Cabotage, *Plant Mgr*
John Mann, *Opers Staff*
Bill Hanson, *Manager*
EMP: 100
SALES (corp-wide): 1.6B **Privately Held**
WEB: www.rmp.com
SIC: 5199 Packaging materials
HQ: Rm Esop Inc.
340 El Camino Real S
Salinas CA 93901
831 789-8300

(P-9300)
ROCKY PACKAGING SOLUTIONS INC
13980 Mountain Ave, Chino (91710-9018)
PHONE 909 591-3331
Fangguo Liu, *CEO*
Simon Ueng, *Accounts Mgr*
EMP: 50
SQ FT: 100,000
SALES (est): 20MM **Privately Held**
SIC: 5199 Packaging materials

(P-9301)
SAXCO INTERNATIONAL LLC
Also Called: Demptos Glass
1855 Gateway Blvd Ste 400, Concord (94520-3289)
PHONE 707 422-9999
Fax: 707 422-1242
Keith L Sachs, *Chairman*
Katherine Ford, *Accounting Dir*
Todd Brennanb, *Finance Mgr*
Keith Wong, *Controller*
▲ **EMP:** 150
SQ FT: 80,000
SALES (est): 61MM **Privately Held**
WEB: www.demtos.com
SIC: 5199 Packaging materials

(P-9302)
SHIMS BARGAIN INC (PA)
Also Called: J C SALES
2600 S Soto St, Vernon (90058-8015)
PHONE 323 881-0099
Fax: 323 881-6797
K Kenneth Suh, *President*
BJ Chang, *CFO*
James Shim, *Chairman*
Joshua Lee, *Programmer Anys*
Joseph Shin, *Controller*
◆ **EMP:** 100
SQ FT: 420,000
SALES: 182.8MM **Privately Held**
SIC: 5199 General merchandise, non-durable

(P-9303)
SMART LIVING COMPANY (PA)
Also Called: S M C
4100 Guardian St, Simi Valley (93063-6717)
PHONE 805 578-5500
Fax: 805 998-2635
Mark Schelbert, *CEO*
Scott Palladino, *CFO*
Joe Wu, *Sr Corp Ofcr*
Ron Hein, *Exec Dir*
Pamela Onby, *Executive Asst*
▲ **EMP:** 50 **EST:** 1955
SALES (est): 122.7MM **Privately Held**
WEB: www.onlinesmc.com
SIC: 5199 Gifts & novelties

▲ = Import ▼ = Export
◆ = Import/Export

PRODUCTS & SERVICES SECTION

6021 - National Commercial Banks County (P-9325)

(P-9304)
SMITH PACKING INC
680 S Simas Rd, Santa Maria (93455-9700)
P.O. Box 1338 (93456-1338)
PHONE..................805 343-0329
Alvaro Quesada, *Principal*
EMP: 130
SALES (corp-wide): 1MM **Privately Held**
SIC: 5199 Packaging materials
PA: Smith Packing, Inc.
111 W Chapel St
Santa Maria CA 93458
805 348-1818

(P-9305)
SONORA TRADE COMPANY INC
2127 Olympic Pkwy, Chula Vista (91915-1359)
PHONE..................619 878-5848
Hanna Shayota, *CEO*
▲ EMP: 55
SALES (est): 8.6MM **Privately Held**
SIC: 5199 Art goods & supplies

(P-9306)
TARGUS INTERNATIONAL LLC (PA)
1211 N Miller St, Anaheim (92806-1933)
PHONE..................714 765-5555
Fax: 714 765-5599
Mikel Williams, *CEO*
Bill Oppenlander, *President*
Victor C Streufert, *CFO*
Theresa Hope-Reese, *Senior VP*
Robert Shortt, *Senior VP*
◆ EMP: 175
SQ FT: 200,656
SALES: 400MM **Privately Held**
WEB: www.targus.com
SIC: 5199 Bags, baskets & cases

(P-9307)
US FOODS INC
1201 Park Center Dr, Vista (92081-8313)
PHONE..................760 599-6200
Gary Graig, *Branch Mgr*
Adrianne Silveria, *Executive*
Dena Abdallah, *Risk Mgmt Dir*
Anthony Paventi, *Business Dir*
Lolly Martinez, *Admin Asst*
EMP: 375
SALES (corp-wide): 23.1B **Publicly Held**
WEB: www.usfoodservice.com
SIC: 5199 5147 5144 5142 General merchandise, non-durable; meats & meat products; poultry & poultry products; packaged frozen goods; groceries, general line
HQ: Us Foods, Inc.
9399 W Higgins Rd Ste 500
Rosemont IL 60018
847 720-8000

(P-9308)
VEGETABLE GROWERS SUPPLY CO (PA)
Also Called: V G S
1360 Merrill St, Salinas (93901-4432)
P.O. Box 757 (93902-0757)
PHONE..................831 759-4600
Fax: 831 424-3401
Ron Huff, *CEO*
William J Locke III, *President*
Lisa Erling, *CFO*
Bill Locke, *Opers Mgr*
Melissa Stoffel, *Sales Staff*
▲ EMP: 50
SQ FT: 38,000
SALES (est): 114MM **Privately Held**
WEB: www.veggrow.com
SIC: 5199 2449 Packaging materials; rectangular boxes & crates, wood

(P-9309)
VIA TRADING CORPORATION
2520 Industry Way, Lynwood (90262-4015)
PHONE..................877 202-3616
Jacques Stambouli, *CEO*
Alain Stambouli, *President*
Alex Antypas, *COO*
Jose Ramon, *Admin Asst*
Andrew George, *Info Tech Mgr*
◆ EMP: 57
SQ FT: 240,000
SALES: 39.3MM **Privately Held**
WEB: www.viatrading.com
SIC: 5199 General merchandise, non-durable

(P-9310)
VIPSTORE USA CO
13674 Star Ruby Ave, Corona (92880-5557)
PHONE..................626 934-7880
Hongjie Yang, *President*
Edward King, *Manager*
EMP: 400
SALES: 12MM **Privately Held**
SIC: 5199 General merchandise, non-durable

(P-9311)
WARREN AUTO DE MEXICO LLC
517 S Cedros Ave, Solana Beach (92075-1922)
PHONE..................858 794-7947
Ian Higgins, *COO*
EMP: 100
SALES (est): 1.3MM **Privately Held**
SIC: 5199 General merchandise, non-durable

(P-9312)
WEBB SUNRISE INC
3320 Kemper St Ste 201, San Diego (92110-4905)
PHONE..................619 220-7050
Lawrence R Webb Sr, *President*
Joji Mangubat, *Vice Pres*
Donna Webb, *Vice Pres*
EMP: 50
SQ FT: 10,000
SALES (est): 4.6MM **Privately Held**
SIC: 5199 Advertising specialties

(P-9313)
WILCO IMPORTS INC
1811 Adrian Rd, Burlingame (94010-2105)
P.O. Box 1703 (94011-1703)
PHONE..................650 204-7800
Raymond King, *President*
Diana King, *Vice Pres*
Kevin Chang, *Controller*
Patty Chan, *Legal Staff*
▲ EMP: 90
SQ FT: 150,000
SALES (est): 16MM **Privately Held**
WEB: www.wilcoimports.com
SIC: 5199 5023 5193 Baskets; gifts & novelties; home furnishings, wicker, rattan or reed; flowers & florists' supplies

(P-9314)
WONDERTREATS INC
2200 Lapham Dr, Modesto (95354-3911)
PHONE..................209 521-8951
Fax: 209 521-8881
Jocelyn Yu Hall, *CEO*
Greg Hall, *President*
Steve Klapak, *Sales Executive*
Victor Baez, *Director*
▲ EMP: 315
SQ FT: 230,000
SALES (est): 150.9MM **Privately Held**
SIC: 5199 5947 Gift baskets; gift baskets

6011 Federal Reserve Banks

(P-9315)
FEDERAL RSRVE BNK SAN FRNCISCO (HQ)
101 Market St, San Francisco (94105-1530)
P.O. Box 7702 (94120-7702)
PHONE..................415 974-2000
Fax: 415 393-1920
John C Williams, *President*
Patricia E Yarrington, *Ch of Bd*
John F Moore, *COO*
Bradley J Wiskirchen, *Chairman*
Ching Lee, *Sr Corp Ofcr*
EMP: 1397
SQ FT: 471,543
SALES (est): 472MM
SALES (corp-wide): 5.3B **Privately Held**
SIC: 6011 Federal reserve banks
PA: Board Of Governors Of The Federal Reserve System
20th St Cnstitution Ave Nw
Washington DC 20551
202 452-3000

(P-9316)
FEDERAL RSRVE BNK SAN FRNCISCO
Also Called: Los Angeles Branch
950 S Grand Ave, Los Angeles (90015-4202)
P.O. Box 512077 (90051-0077)
PHONE..................213 683-2300
Fax: 213 683-2499
Mark Mullinix, *Manager*
Clifford Croxall, *Human Resources*
Paul Starson, *Plant Engr*
Andres Curtolo, *Senior Mgr*
Anthony Dazzo, *Director*
EMP: 640
SALES (corp-wide): 5.3B **Privately Held**
SIC: 6011 Federal reserve branches
HQ: Federal Reserve Bank Of San Francisco
101 Market St
San Francisco CA 94105
415 974-2000

6021 National Commercial Banks

(P-9317)
BANC OF CALIFORNIA INC
1403 N Tustin Ave, Santa Ana (92705-8691)
PHONE..................714 569-0451
Cameron Scheuplein, *Business Anlyst*
Chris Esser, *Project Mgr*
Aaron Young, *Technology*
Michael Evans, *Loan Officer*
Jim McGill, *Loan Officer*
EMP: 940
SALES (corp-wide): 486.5MM **Publicly Held**
SIC: 6021 National commercial banks
PA: Banc Of California, Inc.
18500 Von Karman Ave # 1100
Irvine CA 92612
855 361-2262

(P-9318)
BANC OF CALIFORNIA INC
Also Called: Wilmington Branch
125 E Anaheim St Unit A, Wilmington (90744-4590)
PHONE..................310 835-9826
Jorge Padilla, *Branch Mgr*
EMP: 564
SALES (corp-wide): 486.5MM **Publicly Held**
SIC: 6021 National commercial banks
PA: Banc Of California, Inc.
18500 Von Karman Ave # 1100
Irvine CA 92612
855 361-2262

(P-9319)
BANC OF CALIFORNIA INC (PA)
18500 Von Karman Ave # 1100, Irvine (92612-0546)
P.O. Box 61452 (92602-6048)
PHONE..................855 361-2262
Fax: 619 691-1350
Steven A Sugarman, *Ch of Bd*
Timothy Sedabres, *Shareholder*
Aida Rodriguez, *President*
James J McKinney, *CFO*
Subir Prasad, *Officer*
EMP: 99
SALES: 486.5MM **Publicly Held**
SIC: 6021 National commercial banks

(P-9320)
BANK AMERICA NATIONAL ASSN
5292 N Palm Ave, Fresno (93704-2209)
PHONE..................559 445-7731
Fax: 559 453-0213
Kim Garcia, *Manager*
Frank Bravo, *Vice Pres*
EMP: 80
SALES (corp-wide): 93B **Publicly Held**
WEB: www.bofa.com
SIC: 6021 National commercial banks
HQ: Bank Of America, National Association
101 S Tryon St
Charlotte NC 28280
704 386-5681

(P-9321)
BANK AMERICA NATIONAL ASSN
1525 Market St, San Francisco (94103-1289)
PHONE..................800 432-1000
Fax: 415 953-4802
John Watson, *Branch Mgr*
Duane Miller, *Senior VP*
EMP: 50
SALES (corp-wide): 93B **Publicly Held**
WEB: www.bofa.com
SIC: 6021 National commercial banks
HQ: Bank Of America, National Association
101 S Tryon St
Charlotte NC 28280
704 386-5681

(P-9322)
BANK AMERICA NATIONAL ASSN
345 Montgomery St, San Francisco (94104-1898)
P.O. Box 37000 (94137-0001)
PHONE..................415 913-5891
Fax: 925 675-4978
Thomas Sidon, *Sales/Mktg Mgr*
Christine Garvey, *Div Sub Head*
Liam McGee, *Div Sub Head*
H Anton Tucher, *Managing Dir*
Kim Bosil, *Manager*
EMP: 120
SALES (corp-wide): 93B **Publicly Held**
WEB: www.bofa.com
SIC: 6021 National commercial banks
HQ: Bank Of America, National Association
101 S Tryon St
Charlotte NC 28280
704 386-5681

(P-9323)
BANK AMERICA NATIONAL ASSN
400 Broadway St, Chico (95928-5323)
P.O. Box 1289 (95927-1289)
PHONE..................530 891-7019
Mark Francis, *Manager*
EMP: 60
SQ FT: 15,763
SALES (corp-wide): 93B **Publicly Held**
WEB: www.bofa.com
SIC: 6021 National commercial banks
HQ: Bank Of America, National Association
101 S Tryon St
Charlotte NC 28280
704 386-5681

(P-9324)
BANK AMERICA NATIONAL ASSN
345 N Brand Blvd, Glendale (91203-2368)
PHONE..................800 432-1000
Fax: 818 502-8810
Don Nodell, *Manager*
Fung Low, *Branch Mgr*
Lucia Jarakian, *Office Mgr*
EMP: 60
SALES (corp-wide): 93B **Publicly Held**
WEB: www.bofa.com
SIC: 6021 National commercial banks
HQ: Bank Of America, National Association
101 S Tryon St
Charlotte NC 28280
704 386-5681

(P-9325)
BANK AMERICA NATIONAL ASSN
6351 E Spring St, Long Beach (90808-4021)
P.O. Box 409 (90801-0409)
PHONE..................562 624-4330
Fax: 562 624-4321
Jennifer Davis, *Branch Mgr*
Betsy Melendez, *Manager*
Ruben Pacheco, *Manager*
EMP: 50

6021 - National Commercial Banks County (P-9326)

SALES (corp-wide): 93B **Publicly Held**
WEB: www.bofa.com
SIC: 6021 National commercial banks
HQ: Bank Of America, National Association
101 S Tryon St
Charlotte NC 28280
704 386-5681

(P-9326)
BANK AMERICA NATIONAL ASSN
120 S Brand Blvd, San Fernando (91340-3377)
PHONE.................818 898-3033
Janice Musgrove, Branch Mgr
EMP: 60
SALES (corp-wide): 93B **Publicly Held**
WEB: www.bofa.com
SIC: 6021 National commercial banks
HQ: Bank Of America, National Association
101 S Tryon St
Charlotte NC 28280
704 386-5681

(P-9327)
BANK AMERICA NATIONAL ASSN
212 E Main St, Visalia (93291-6356)
P.O. Box 551 (93279-0551)
PHONE.................800 432-1000
Gordon Young, President
Wesley Imoto, Vice Pres
Brandy Jacks, Branch Mgr
Bobbie Roth, Customer Svc Re
EMP: 50
SALES (corp-wide): 93B **Publicly Held**
WEB: www.bofa.com
SIC: 6021 National commercial banks
HQ: Bank Of America, National Association
101 S Tryon St
Charlotte NC 28280
704 386-5681

(P-9328)
BANK AMERICA NATIONAL ASSN
550 S Hill St Ste 101, Los Angeles (90013-2403)
PHONE.................310 384-4562
Fax: 213 228-2499
Stacy Young, Manager
Jack Arrington, Vice Pres
Joyce Runyon, Manager
EMP: 65
SALES (corp-wide): 93B **Publicly Held**
WEB: www.bofa.com
SIC: 6021 National commercial banks
HQ: Bank Of America, National Association
101 S Tryon St
Charlotte NC 28280
704 386-5681

(P-9329)
BANK AMERICA NATIONAL ASSN
13220 Harbor Blvd, Garden Grove (92843-1737)
P.O. Box 758 (92842-0758)
PHONE.................714 973-8495
Fax: 714 839-8528
Rita Castro, Branch Mgr
Linda Ropp, Cust Mgr
Martha Albert, Manager
EMP: 50
SALES (corp-wide): 93B **Publicly Held**
WEB: www.bofa.com
SIC: 6021 National commercial banks
HQ: Bank Of America, National Association
101 S Tryon St
Charlotte NC 28280
704 386-5681

(P-9330)
BANK AMERICA NATIONAL ASSN
1687 E Florida Ave, Hemet (92544-8646)
P.O. Box 1406 (92546-1406)
PHONE.................951 929-8614
John Borah, Branch Mgr
EMP: 50
SALES (corp-wide): 93B **Publicly Held**
WEB: www.bofa.com
SIC: 6021 National commercial banks
HQ: Bank Of America, National Association
101 S Tryon St
Charlotte NC 28280
704 386-5681

(P-9331)
BANK AMERICA NATIONAL ASSN
1450 W Redondo Beach Blvd, Gardena (90247-3399)
PHONE.................800 432-1000
Fax: 310 217-2943
Rosa Caldera, Branch Mgr
EMP: 75
SALES (corp-wide): 93B **Publicly Held**
WEB: www.bofa.com
SIC: 6021 National commercial banks
HQ: Bank Of America, National Association
101 S Tryon St
Charlotte NC 28280
704 386-5681

(P-9332)
BANK AMERICA NATIONAL ASSN
4100 Chino Hills Pkwy, Chino Hills (91709-2611)
P.O. Box 727, Chino (91708-0727)
PHONE.................909 393-3002
Fax: 909 393-3005
Kathleen Mossbarger, Branch Mgr
Glenn Lucke, Branch Mgr
Arnie Gonzales, Manager
Roger Sanchez, Manager
EMP: 99
SALES (corp-wide): 93B **Publicly Held**
WEB: www.bofa.com
SIC: 6021 National commercial banks
HQ: Bank Of America, National Association
101 S Tryon St
Charlotte NC 28280
704 386-5681

(P-9333)
BANK AMERICA NATIONAL ASSN
5901 Canoga Ave, Woodland Hills (91367-5010)
PHONE.................818 577-2000
Fax: 818 704-2100
Albert Welch, Sales/Mktg Mgr
EMP: 60
SALES (corp-wide): 93B **Publicly Held**
WEB: www.bofa.com
SIC: 6021 National commercial banks
HQ: Bank Of America, National Association
101 S Tryon St
Charlotte NC 28280
704 386-5681

(P-9334)
BANK AMERICA NATIONAL ASSN
27489 Ynez Rd, Temecula (92591-4612)
PHONE.................951 676-4114
Theresa Fukuda, Branch Mgr
EMP: 53
SALES (corp-wide): 93B **Publicly Held**
WEB: www.bofa.com
SIC: 6021 National commercial banks
HQ: Bank Of America, National Association
101 S Tryon St
Charlotte NC 28280
704 386-5681

(P-9335)
BANK LEUMI USA
Also Called: Bank Leumi Le
555 W 5th St Fl 33, Los Angeles (90013-1050)
PHONE.................323 966-4700
Toll Free:.................877
Fax: 323 655-8680
Abraham Maoz, Exec VP
Alex Menache, Treasurer
Melanie L Krinsky, Vice Pres
Mandie S Rush, Vice Pres
Pina Letavish, Asst Treas
EMP: 61 **Privately Held**
SIC: 6021 National commercial banks
HQ: Bank Leumi Usa
579 5th Ave Frnt A
New York NY 10017
917 542-2343

(P-9336)
BANK OF HOPE (HQ)
3731 Wilshire Blvd # 400, Los Angeles (90010-2830)
PHONE.................213 639-1700
Fax: 213 487-2727
Kevin S Kim, CEO
Min J Kim, President
Scott Yoon-Suk Whang, Vice Ch Bd
Jason Kim, Exec VP
Mark Lee, Exec VP
▲ EMP: 108
SALES (est): 88.1MM
SALES (corp-wide): 357.3MM **Publicly Held**
WEB: www.narabank.com
SIC: 6021 National commercial banks
PA: Hope Bancorp, Inc.
3731 Wilshire Blvd
Los Angeles CA 90010
213 639-1700

(P-9337)
BANK OF SIERRA
Also Called: Bank of Sierra
500 Marsh St, San Luis Obispo (93401-3955)
PHONE.................805 541-0400
Kevin McPhaill, Branch Mgr
EMP: 60
SALES (corp-wide): 80.4MM **Publicly Held**
SIC: 6021 National commercial banks
HQ: Bank Of The Sierra
90 N Main St
Porterville CA 93257
559 782-4300

(P-9338)
BANNER BANK
9340 E Stockton Blvd, Elk Grove (95624-1456)
PHONE.................916 685-6546
Scott A Kisting, CEO
EMP: 60 **Publicly Held**
WEB: www.premierwestbank.com
SIC: 6021 6029 National commercial banks; commercial banks
HQ: Banner Bank
10 S 1st Ave
Walla Walla WA 99362
800 272-9933

(P-9339)
BANNER BANK
1350 Rosecrans St, San Diego (92106-2636)
PHONE.................619 243-7900
Michael R Peters, Branch Mgr
EMP: 50 **Publicly Held**
SIC: 6021 National commercial banks
HQ: Banner Bank
10 S 1st Ave
Walla Walla WA 99362
800 272-9933

(P-9340)
CANADIAN IMPERIAL BANK
620 Newport Center Dr, Newport Beach (92660-6420)
PHONE.................949 759-4718
Robert Ctvrtlik, Principal
EMP: 78
SALES (corp-wide): 10.4B **Privately Held**
WEB: www.cibc.com
SIC: 6021 National commercial banks
PA: Canadian Imperial Bank Of Commerce
199 Bay St Commerce Crt W
Toronto ON M5L 1
416 980-2211

(P-9341)
CARPENTER FUND MANAGER GP LLC
5 Park Plz Ste 950, Irvine (92614-8527)
PHONE.................949 261-8888
Edward J Carpenter,
Curt Christianssen, Exec VP
Arthur Hidalgo, Exec VP
Robert Sjogren, Senior VP
Maryam Hamzeh, Vice Pres
EMP: 188
SALES (est): 16.6MM **Privately Held**
SIC: 6021 National commercial banks

(P-9342)
CIT BANK NA
11310 National Blvd, Los Angeles (90064-3727)
PHONE.................310 477-0546
Delmy Martinez, Branch Mgr
EMP: 63
SALES (corp-wide): 3.8B **Publicly Held**
SIC: 6021 National commercial banks
HQ: Cit Bank, N.A.
888 E Walnut St
Pasadena CA 91101
626 535-4300

(P-9343)
CIT BANK NA
23072 Alicia Pkwy, Mission Viejo (92692-1636)
PHONE.................949 598-9621
Daniel Martin, Manager
EMP: 63
SALES (corp-wide): 3.8B **Publicly Held**
SIC: 6021 National commercial banks
HQ: Cit Bank, N.A.
888 E Walnut St
Pasadena CA 91101
626 535-4300

(P-9344)
CIT BANK NA (HQ)
888 E Walnut St, Pasadena (91101-1895)
P.O. Box 7056 (91109-7056)
PHONE.................626 535-4300
Joseph Otting, Principal
Ellen R Alemany, Ch of Bd
James P Broom, President
James L Hudak, President
C Jeffrey Knittel, President
EMP: 74
SALES: 876.3MM
SALES (corp-wide): 3.8B **Publicly Held**
WEB: www.loanworks.com
SIC: 6021 National commercial banks
PA: Cit Group Inc.
11 W 42nd St Fl 7
New York NY 10036
212 461-5200

(P-9345)
CIT BANK NA
199 E Thousand Oaks Blvd, Thousand Oaks (91360-5710)
PHONE.................805 379-5520
Tracey Sirkus, Branch Mgr
EMP: 56
SALES (corp-wide): 3.8B **Publicly Held**
SIC: 6021 National commercial banks
HQ: Cit Bank, N.A.
888 E Walnut St
Pasadena CA 91101
626 535-4300

(P-9346)
CIT BANK NATIONAL ASSOCIATION
20505 Devonshire St, Chatsworth (91311-3208)
PHONE.................818 885-9065
Phyllis Barber, Branch Mgr
Wendell Grayson, Marketing Staff
EMP: 56
SALES (corp-wide): 3.8B **Publicly Held**
SIC: 6021 National commercial banks
HQ: Cit Bank, N.A.
888 E Walnut St
Pasadena CA 91101
626 535-4300

(P-9347)
CIT BANK NATIONAL ASSOCIATION
900 Huntington Dr, San Marino (91108-1825)
PHONE.................323 767-1180
Fax: 626 382-0255
Terri Ruiz, Branch Mgr
EMP: 65
SALES (corp-wide): 3.8B **Publicly Held**
SIC: 6021 National commercial banks
HQ: Cit Bank, N.A.
888 E Walnut St
Pasadena CA 91101
626 535-4300

PRODUCTS & SERVICES SECTION

6021 - National Commercial Banks County (P-9372)

(P-9348)
CIT BANK NATIONAL ASSOCIATION
78010 Main St, La Quinta (92253-3408)
PHONE.................................760 771-3498
Robert Kehrberg, *Branch Mgr*
EMP: 65
SALES (corp-wide): 3.8B Publicly Held
SIC: 6021 National commercial banks
HQ: Cit Bank, N.A.
  888 E Walnut St
  Pasadena CA 91101
  626 535-4300

(P-9349)
CIT BANK NATIONAL ASSOCIATION
1570 Rosecrans Ave, Manhattan Beach (90266-3718)
PHONE.................................310 727-5660
EMP: 63
SALES (corp-wide): 3.8B Publicly Held
SIC: 6021 National commercial banks
HQ: Cit Bank, N.A.
  888 E Walnut St
  Pasadena CA 91101
  626 535-4300

(P-9350)
CIT BANK NATIONAL ASSOCIATION
220 N Hacienda Blvd, City of Industry (91744-4403)
PHONE.................................626 435-2260
Blanca Deanda, *Manager*
Moses Ortega, *Manager*
EMP: 64
SALES (corp-wide): 3.8B Publicly Held
SIC: 6021 National commercial banks
HQ: Cit Bank, N.A.
  888 E Walnut St
  Pasadena CA 91101
  626 535-4300

(P-9351)
CIT BANK NATIONAL ASSOCIATION
3410 Grand Ave Ste A, Chino Hills (91709-1473)
PHONE.................................909 631-2560
Jennifer Ferguson, *Branch Mgr*
EMP: 63
SALES (corp-wide): 3.8B Publicly Held
SIC: 6021 National commercial banks
HQ: Cit Bank, N.A.
  888 E Walnut St
  Pasadena CA 91101
  626 535-4300

(P-9352)
CIT BANK NATIONAL ASSOCIATION
2920 N Beverly Glen Cir, Los Angeles (90077-1724)
PHONE.................................310 475-4594
Fax: 310 470-7054
Diane Thomas, *Principal*
EMP: 56
SALES (corp-wide): 3.8B Publicly Held
SIC: 6021 National commercial banks
HQ: Cit Bank, N.A.
  888 E Walnut St
  Pasadena CA 91101
  626 535-4300

(P-9353)
CIT BANK NATIONAL ASSOCIATION
1100 Pacific Coast Hwy, Hermosa Beach (90254-3951)
PHONE.................................310 372-8473
Fax: 310 372-7534
Hiran Sumanadasa, *Branch Mgr*
EMP: 56
SALES (corp-wide): 3.8B Publicly Held
SIC: 6021 National commercial banks
HQ: Cit Bank, N.A.
  888 E Walnut St
  Pasadena CA 91101
  626 535-4300

(P-9354)
CIT BANK NATIONAL ASSOCIATION
1111 N Brand Blvd Ste A, Glendale (91202-3072)
PHONE.................................818 502-8400
George Lazar, *Principal*
EMP: 59
SALES (corp-wide): 3.8B Publicly Held
SIC: 6021 National commercial banks
HQ: Cit Bank, N.A.
  888 E Walnut St
  Pasadena CA 91101
  626 535-4300

(P-9355)
CIT BANK NATIONAL ASSOCIATION
401 Wilshire Blvd, Santa Monica (90401-1416)
PHONE.................................310 394-1640
EMP: 63
SALES (corp-wide): 3.8B Publicly Held
SIC: 6021 National commercial banks
HQ: Cit Bank, N.A.
  888 E Walnut St
  Pasadena CA 91101
  626 535-4300

(P-9356)
CIT BANK NATIONAL ASSOCIATION
11611 San Vicente Blvd, Los Angeles (90049-5106)
PHONE.................................310 826-2741
EMP: 64
SALES (corp-wide): 3.8B Publicly Held
SIC: 6021 National commercial banks
HQ: Cit Bank, N.A.
  888 E Walnut St
  Pasadena CA 91101
  626 535-4300

(P-9357)
CIT BANK NATIONAL ASSOCIATION
1750 Ocean Park Blvd, Santa Monica (90405-4938)
PHONE.................................310 452-3802
Art Bikidjian, *Branch Mgr*
EMP: 65
SALES (corp-wide): 3.8B Publicly Held
SIC: 6021 National commercial banks
HQ: Cit Bank, N.A.
  888 E Walnut St
  Pasadena CA 91101
  626 535-4300

(P-9358)
CIT BANK NATIONAL ASSOCIATION
5573 Sepulveda Blvd, Culver City (90230-5513)
PHONE.................................310 390-7745
Millie Davis, *Vice Pres*
EMP: 63
SALES (corp-wide): 3.8B Publicly Held
SIC: 6021 National commercial banks
HQ: Cit Bank, N.A.
  888 E Walnut St
  Pasadena CA 91101
  626 535-4300

(P-9359)
CIT BANK NATIONAL ASSOCIATION
2827 Main St, Santa Monica (90405-4009)
PHONE.................................310 399-9262
Kyle Ranker, *Branch Mgr*
EMP: 63
SALES (corp-wide): 3.8B Publicly Held
SIC: 6021 National commercial banks
HQ: Cit Bank, N.A.
  888 E Walnut St
  Pasadena CA 91101
  626 535-4300

(P-9360)
CIT BANK NATIONAL ASSOCIATION
1727 E Daily Dr, Camarillo (93010-6202)
PHONE.................................805 465-1053
Susan Anderson, *Manager*
EMP: 64
SALES (corp-wide): 3.8B Publicly Held
SIC: 6021 National commercial banks
HQ: Cit Bank, N.A.
  888 E Walnut St
  Pasadena CA 91101
  626 535-4300

(P-9361)
CIT BANK NATIONAL ASSOCIATION
1001 N San Fernando Blvd, Burbank (91504-4303)
PHONE.................................818 525-3760
EMP: 64
SALES (corp-wide): 3.8B Publicly Held
SIC: 6021 National commercial banks
HQ: Cit Bank, N.A.
  888 E Walnut St
  Pasadena CA 91101
  626 535-4300

(P-9362)
CIT BANK NATIONAL ASSOCIATION
25624 Alicia Pkwy, Laguna Hills (92653-5309)
PHONE.................................949 454-4100
David Matl, *Branch Mgr*
EMP: 63
SALES (corp-wide): 3.8B Publicly Held
SIC: 6021 National commercial banks
HQ: Cit Bank, N.A.
  888 E Walnut St
  Pasadena CA 91101
  626 535-4300

(P-9363)
CIT BANK NATIONAL ASSOCIATION
28311 Marguerite Pkwy B, Mission Viejo (92692-3700)
PHONE.................................949 347-7014
Dagmar Richter, *Branch Mgr*
Charity McCarthy, *Regional Mgr*
EMP: 63
SALES (corp-wide): 3.8B Publicly Held
SIC: 6021 National commercial banks
HQ: Cit Bank, N.A.
  888 E Walnut St
  Pasadena CA 91101
  626 535-4300

(P-9364)
CIT BANK NATIONAL ASSOCIATION
17050 Ventura Blvd # 100, Encino (91316-4143)
PHONE.................................818 817-5320
Noel Youcefi, *Branch Mgr*
EMP: 63
SALES (corp-wide): 3.8B Publicly Held
SIC: 6021 National commercial banks
HQ: Cit Bank, N.A.
  888 E Walnut St
  Pasadena CA 91101
  626 535-4300

(P-9365)
CIT BANK NATIONAL ASSOCIATION
10784 Jefferson Blvd, Culver City (90230-4933)
PHONE.................................310 559-7222
Peter Smith, *Branch Mgr*
EMP: 63
SALES (corp-wide): 3.8B Publicly Held
SIC: 6021 National commercial banks
HQ: Cit Bank, N.A.
  888 E Walnut St
  Pasadena CA 91101
  626 535-4300

(P-9366)
CIT BANK NATIONAL ASSOCIATION
3500 E 7th St, Long Beach (90804-5137)
PHONE.................................562 433-0972
Fax: 562 431-4697
Nicole Graves, *Branch Mgr*
EMP: 65
SALES (corp-wide): 3.8B Publicly Held
SIC: 6021 National commercial banks
HQ: Cit Bank, N.A.
  888 E Walnut St
  Pasadena CA 91101
  626 535-4300

(P-9367)
CIT BANK NATIONAL ASSOCIATION
3835 E Thusand Oaks Blvd, Westlake Village (91362)
PHONE.................................805 496-4034
EMP: 65
SALES (corp-wide): 3.8B Publicly Held
SIC: 6021 National commercial banks
HQ: Cit Bank, N.A.
  888 E Walnut St
  Pasadena CA 91101
  626 535-4300

(P-9368)
CIT BANK NATIONAL ASSOCIATION
13405 Washington Blvd, Marina Del Rey (90292-5658)
PHONE.................................310 577-6142
Chris Young, *Branch Mgr*
EMP: 56
SALES (corp-wide): 3.8B Publicly Held
SIC: 6021 National commercial banks
HQ: Cit Bank, N.A.
  888 E Walnut St
  Pasadena CA 91101
  626 535-4300

(P-9369)
CIT BANK NATIONAL ASSOCIATION
12401 Wilshire Blvd, Los Angeles (90025-1085)
PHONE.................................310 820-9650
Leonard Rampulla, *Branch Mgr*
EMP: 56
SALES (corp-wide): 3.8B Publicly Held
SIC: 6021 National commercial banks
HQ: Cit Bank, N.A.
  888 E Walnut St
  Pasadena CA 91101
  626 535-4300

(P-9370)
CIT BANK NATIONAL ASSOCIATION
1630 Montana Ave, Santa Monica (90403-1808)
PHONE.................................310 829-4477
Euzene Brink, *Manager*
Rory Bliss, *Site Mgr*
EMP: 56
SALES (corp-wide): 3.8B Publicly Held
SIC: 6021 National commercial banks
HQ: Cit Bank, N.A.
  888 E Walnut St
  Pasadena CA 91101
  626 535-4300

(P-9371)
CIT BANK NATIONAL ASSOCIATION
3700 E Coast Hwy, Corona Del Mar (92625-2520)
PHONE.................................949 675-2890
Rodney Holder, *Branch Mgr*
EMP: 56
SALES (corp-wide): 3.8B Publicly Held
SIC: 6021 National commercial banks
HQ: Cit Bank, N.A.
  888 E Walnut St
  Pasadena CA 91101
  626 535-4300

(P-9372)
CIT BANK NATIONAL ASSOCIATION
5701 S Eastrn Ave Ste 108, Commerce (90040)
PHONE.................................323 838-6881
Jonathan Silva, *Branch Mgr*
EMP: 56
SALES (corp-wide): 3.8B Publicly Held
SIC: 6021 National commercial banks
HQ: Cit Bank, N.A.
  888 E Walnut St
  Pasadena CA 91101
  626 535-4300

6021 - National Commercial Banks County (P-9373)

PRODUCTS & SERVICES SECTION

(P-9373)
CIT BANK NATIONAL ASSOCIATION
30019 Hawthorne Blvd, Rancho Palos Verdes (90275-5434)
PHONE..............................310 265-1656
Miguel Gonzalez, *Branch Mgr*
Maria Zalamea, *Branch Mgr*
EMP: 56
SALES (corp-wide): 3.8B **Publicly Held**
SIC: 6021 National commercial banks
HQ: Cit Bank, N.A.
  888 E Walnut St
  Pasadena CA 91101
  626 535-4300

(P-9374)
CITIBANK NATIONAL ASSOCIATION
Also Called: Sf-Potrero Hill
150 Pennsylvania Ave, San Francisco (94107-2525)
PHONE..............................415 431-6940
EMP: 211
SALES (corp-wide): 88.2B **Publicly Held**
SIC: 6021 National commercial banks
HQ: Citibank, National Association
  701 E 60th St N
  Sioux Falls SD 57104
  605 331-2626

(P-9375)
CITIBANK NATIONAL ASSOCIATION
Also Called: Otay Lakes Road Branch
2240 Otay Lakes Rd 304-3, Chula Vista (91915-1003)
PHONE..............................619 870-0609
EMP: 211
SALES (corp-wide): 88.2B **Publicly Held**
SIC: 6021 National commercial banks
HQ: Citibank, National Association
  701 E 60th St N
  Sioux Falls SD 57104
  605 331-2626

(P-9376)
CITIBANK N A
3967 E Thousand Oaks Blvd, Westlake Village (91362-3628)
PHONE..............................805 497-7361
EMP: 132
SALES (corp-wide): 88.2B **Publicly Held**
SIC: 6021 National commercial banks
HQ: Citibank Na
  399 Park Ave Bsmt 1
  New York NY 10022
  212 559-1000

(P-9377)
CITIBANK N A
3580 Tyler St, Riverside (92503-4133)
PHONE..............................800 627-3999
Dawn Latshaw, *Branch Mgr*
EMP: 132
SALES (corp-wide): 88.2B **Publicly Held**
SIC: 6021 National commercial banks
HQ: Citibank Na
  399 Park Ave Bsmt 1
  New York NY 10022
  212 559-1000

(P-9378)
CITIGROUP INC
325 E Hillcrest Dr, Thousand Oaks (91360-5828)
PHONE..............................805 557-0930
Jay Abeywardena, *Vice Pres*
EMP: 65
SALES (corp-wide): 88.2B **Publicly Held**
SIC: 6021 National commercial banks
PA: Citigroup Inc.
  399 Park Ave
  New York NY 10022
  212 559-1000

(P-9379)
CITIGROUP INC
300 E State St, Redlands (92373-5235)
PHONE..............................909 335-0547
EMP: 65
SALES (corp-wide): 88.2B **Publicly Held**
SIC: 6021 National commercial banks

(P-9380)
CITIGROUP INC
787 W 5th St, Los Angeles (90071-2003)
PHONE..............................818 638-5714
Michael Kwan, *Executive*
Mary Brower, *Senior VP*
Joseph Kren, *Senior VP*
Andrea Rossato, *Senior VP*
Jacqueline Smith, *Vice Pres*
EMP: 65
SALES (corp-wide): 88.2B **Publicly Held**
SIC: 6021 National commercial banks
PA: Citigroup Inc.
  399 Park Ave
  New York NY 10022
  212 559-1000

(P-9381)
CITIGROUP INC
3996 Barranca Pkwy # 130, Irvine (92606-8239)
PHONE..............................949 726-5124
EMP: 65
SALES (corp-wide): 90.7B **Publicly Held**
SIC: 6021
PA: Citigroup Inc.
  399 Park Ave
  New York NY 10022
  212 559-1000

(P-9382)
CITIGROUP INC
352 H St, Chula Vista (91910-5511)
PHONE..............................619 498-3158
Gustavo Bidart, *Branch Mgr*
EMP: 65
SALES (corp-wide): 88.2B **Publicly Held**
SIC: 6021 National commercial banks
PA: Citigroup Inc.
  399 Park Ave
  New York NY 10022
  212 559-1000

(P-9383)
CITIZEN POTAWATOMI NATION
31150 Road 180, Visalia (93292-9585)
PHONE..............................559 635-1039
John Barrett, *Branch Mgr*
EMP: 53
SALES (corp-wide): 63.1MM **Privately Held**
SIC: 6021 National commercial banks
PA: Citizen Potawatomi Nation
  1601 Gordon Cooper Dr
  Shawnee OK 74801
  405 275-3121

(P-9384)
CITIZENS BUSINESS BANK
4100 W Alameda Ave # 101, Burbank (91505-4153)
PHONE..............................818 843-0707
Fax: 323 843-7870
Edward J Mylett Jr, *Senior VP*
Jim Hoffamann, *Executive*
EMP: 52
SALES (corp-wide): 289.3MM **Publicly Held**
WEB: www.cbbank.com
SIC: 6021 National commercial banks
HQ: Citizens Business Bank
  701 N Haven Ave Ste 350
  Ontario CA 91764
  909 980-4030

(P-9385)
CITY NATIONAL BANK (DH)
555 S Flower St Ste 2500, Los Angeles (90071-2326)
PHONE..............................310 888-6000
Fax: 310 888-6286
Russell Goldsmith, *Ch of Bd*
Gina Calipes, *President*
Christopher J Warmuth, *President*
John Zhang, *President*
Christopher J Carey, *CFO*
EMP: 300 **EST:** 1968
SQ FT: 80,000

SALES: 1.1B
SALES (corp-wide): 31.1B **Privately Held**
SIC: 6021 6022 National commercial banks; state commercial banks
HQ: Rbc Usa Holdco Corporation
  3 World Financial Ctr
  New York NY 10281
  212 858-7200

(P-9386)
CITY NATIONAL BANK
Also Called: C N B Commercial Banking Ctr
3484 Central Ave, Riverside (92506-2156)
PHONE..............................951 276-8800
Fax: 951 276-8864
Bruce Wachtel, *Manager*
Fisher David, *Vice Pres*
Carlie P Polston, *Loan Officer*
EMP: 50
SALES (corp-wide): 31.1B **Privately Held**
SIC: 6021 National commercial banks
HQ: City National Bank
  555 S Flower St Ste 2500
  Los Angeles CA 90071
  310 888-6000

(P-9387)
CITY NATIONAL BANK
Also Called: City National Investments
225 Broadway Ste 500, San Diego (92101-5029)
PHONE..............................619 645-6100
Fax: 619 645-6150
Michael Nunlee, *Manager*
Randall R Reed, *Senior VP*
Craig Murray, *MIS Mgr*
Tom McNair, *Manager*
EMP: 100
SALES (corp-wide): 31.1B **Privately Held**
SIC: 6021 National commercial banks
HQ: City National Bank
  555 S Flower St Ste 2500
  Los Angeles CA 90071
  310 888-6000

(P-9388)
CITY NATIONAL BANK
Also Called: Residential Mortgage Ctr 39
2100 Park Pl Ste 150, El Segundo (90245-4912)
PHONE..............................310 297-6606
J W Lewis, *Senior VP*
EMP: 145
SALES (corp-wide): 31.1B **Privately Held**
SIC: 6021 National commercial banks
HQ: City National Bank
  555 S Flower St Fl 18
  Los Angeles CA 90071
  310 888-6000

(P-9389)
COMERICA BANK
1442 N Main St, Walnut Creek (94596-4605)
PHONE..............................925 941-1900
Fax: 925 988-0356
Christophere Coutelier, *Manager*
James Bryski, *Manager*
EMP: 67
SALES (corp-wide): 2.8B **Publicly Held**
SIC: 6021 National commercial banks
HQ: Comerica Bank
  1717 Main St Ste 2100
  Dallas TX 75201
  214 462-4000

(P-9390)
COMPASS BANCSHARES INC
Also Called: Compass Bank
195 W Ontario Ave, Corona (92882-5276)
PHONE..............................951 279-7071
Fax: 951 372-2960
Eileen Blaga, *Branch Mgr*
EMP: 364 **Privately Held**
SIC: 6021 National commercial banks
HQ: Compass Bancshares, Inc.
  15 20th St S Ste 100
  Birmingham AL 35233
  205 297-1986

(P-9391)
COMPASS BANCSHARES INC
Also Called: Compass Bank
27851 Bradley Rd Ste 125, Sun City (92586-2282)
PHONE..............................951 672-4829

EMP: 337 **Privately Held**
SIC: 6021 National commercial banks
HQ: Compass Bancshares, Inc.
  15 20th St S Ste 100
  Birmingham AL 35233
  205 297-1986

(P-9392)
COMPASS BANCSHARES INC
Also Called: Compass Bank
201 N Main St, Manteca (95336-4632)
PHONE..............................209 239-1381
Fax: 209 239-8295
Grace Henderson, *Branch Mgr*
EMP: 364 **Privately Held**
WEB: www.guarantybank.com
SIC: 6021 National commercial banks
HQ: Compass Bancshares, Inc.
  15 20th St S Ste 100
  Birmingham AL 35233
  205 297-1986

(P-9393)
COMPASS BANCSHARES INC
Also Called: Compass Bank
2427 W Hammer Ln, Stockton (95209-2367)
PHONE..............................209 473-6925
Gabriel Riley, *Branch Mgr*
EMP: 364 **Privately Held**
WEB: www.guarantybank.com
SIC: 6021 National commercial banks
HQ: Compass Bancshares, Inc.
  15 20th St S Ste 100
  Birmingham AL 35233
  205 297-1986

(P-9394)
COMPASS BANCSHARES INC
Also Called: Compass Bank
2562 Pacific Ave, Stockton (95204-4438)
PHONE..............................209 939-3288
Brian Stemen, *Branch Mgr*
Trisha Hayes, *Branch Mgr*
EMP: 364 **Privately Held**
WEB: www.guarantybank.com
SIC: 6021 National commercial banks
HQ: Compass Bancshares, Inc.
  15 20th St S Ste 100
  Birmingham AL 35233
  205 297-1986

(P-9395)
DEUTSCHE BANK TR CO AMERICAS
2000 Av Stars N Powers, Los Angeles (90067)
PHONE..............................213 620-8200
EMP: 87
SALES (corp-wide): 8.8B **Privately Held**
WEB: www.db.com
SIC: 6021 6211 National commercial banks; security brokers & dealers
HQ: Deutsche Bank Trust Company Americas
  60 Wall St Bsmt 1
  New York NY 10005
  212 250-2500

(P-9396)
EXCHANGE BANK
Also Called: Exchange Bank/Loan Service Ctr
440 Aviation Blvd, Santa Rosa (95403-1069)
P.O. Box 760 (95402-0760)
PHONE..............................707 524-3399
Judy Polosuk, *Manager*
EMP: 110
SQ FT: 30,584
SALES (corp-wide): 38.2MM **Privately Held**
WEB: www.exchangebank.com
SIC: 6021 National commercial banks
HQ: Exchange Bank
  440 Aviation Blvd
  Santa Rosa CA 95403
  707 524-3000

(P-9397)
FAR EAST NATIONAL BANK (DH)
977 N Broadway Ste 306, Los Angeles (90012-1786)
P.O. Box Po Box 54198 (90099-0001)
PHONE..............................213 687-1300
Fax: 213 680-2215
Paul C Lo, *Ch of Bd*

Jonathan David, *President*
Christina Ching, *CFO*
Pauline KAO, *Officer*
William Sit, *Officer*
▲ **EMP:** 124
SALES: 46.2MM
SALES (corp-wide): 1.2B **Privately Held**
WEB: www.fareastnationalbank.com
SIC: 6021 8741 National commercial banks; management services
HQ: Sinopac Bancorp
977 N Broadway Ste 500
Los Angeles CA 90012
213 687-1300

(P-9398)
FIRST NATIONAL BANK
401 W A St Ste 200, San Diego (92101-7917)
P.O. Box 85625 (92186-5625)
PHONE.................................760 602-5518
Daniel R Mathis, *President*
EMP: 240 **EST:** 1996
SALES (est): 21.4MM
SALES (corp-wide): 62.5MM **Privately Held**
SIC: 6021 National commercial banks
PA: First National Bank
401 W A St Ste 200
San Diego CA 92101
619 233-5588

(P-9399)
FIRSTFED FINANCIAL CORP
6320 Canoga Ave, Woodland Hills (91367-2526)
PHONE.................................562 618-0573
Fax: 310 319-5899
James Giraldin, *President*
Brian Argrett, *Ch of Bd*
James P Giraldin, *President*
Shannon Millard, *President*
Babette E Heimbuch, *CEO*
EMP: 603
SALES: 439MM **Privately Held**
SIC: 6021 National commercial banks

(P-9400)
MERCHANTS BANK CALIFORNIA N A
1 Civic Plaza Dr Ste 100, Carson (90745-7958)
P.O. Box 4486 (90749-4486)
PHONE.................................310 549-4350
Joyce Yamasaki, *CEO*
Susan Cabano, *COO*
Luana Lopez, *COO*
Jen Chu, *CFO*
Daniel K Roberts, *Principal*
EMP: 75
SQ FT: 5,551
SALES: 12.5MM **Privately Held**
WEB: www.merchantsbankca.com
SIC: 6021 National commercial banks

(P-9401)
MUFG UNION BANK NA (DH)
400 California St, San Francisco (94104-1302)
PHONE.................................212 782-6800
Fax: 415 445-0425
Norimichi Kanari, *President*
Kyota Omori, *Ch of Bd*
Mark W Midkiff, *Vice Chairman*
Timothy H Wennes, *Vice Chairman*
Philip B Flynn, *COO*
EMP: 1000 **EST:** 1864
SALES: 4.3B
SALES (corp-wide): 47.4B **Privately Held**
SIC: 6021 National commercial banks
HQ: Mufg Americas Holdings Corporation
1251 Ave Of The Americas
New York NY 10020
212 782-5911

(P-9402)
MUFG UNION BANK NA
Also Called: U B C 102
120 S San Pedro St, Los Angeles (90012-5300)
P.O. Box 3248 (90051-1248)
PHONE.................................213 972-5500
Yoshio Morita, *Branch Mgr*
Cynthia Rios, *Adv Dir*
Frankie Yim, *Assistant VP*
EMP: 50
SQ FT: 60,299
SALES (corp-wide): 47.4B **Privately Held**
SIC: 6021 National commercial banks
HQ: Mufg Union Bank, N.A
400 California St
San Francisco CA 94104
212 782-6800

(P-9403)
MUFG UNION BANK NA
20 E Carrillo St, Santa Barbara (93101-2707)
PHONE.................................805 969-5091
Fax: 805 564-6439
Steve Mihalic, *Vice Pres*
Bill Klinksi, *Treasurer*
April Montoya, *Officer*
Mary Pierson, *Officer*
Todd McGinley, *Trust Officer*
EMP: 75
SALES (corp-wide): 47.4B **Privately Held**
WEB: www.pacificcapitalbank.com
SIC: 6021 6022 National commercial banks; state commercial banks
HQ: Mufg Union Bank, N.A
400 California St
San Francisco CA 94104
212 782-6800

(P-9404)
MUFG UNION BANK NA
Also Called: U B C 200
9460 Wilshire Blvd # 200, Beverly Hills (90212-2732)
P.O. Box 1268 (90213-1268)
PHONE.................................310 550-6522
Fax: 310 550-6511
G Denton Folkes, *Branch Mgr*
EMP: 80
SALES (corp-wide): 47.4B **Privately Held**
SIC: 6021 National commercial banks
HQ: Mufg Union Bank, N.A
400 California St
San Francisco CA 94104
212 782-6800

(P-9405)
MUFG UNION BANK NA
Also Called: U B C 309
900 S Main St, Los Angeles (90015-1730)
P.O. Box 2278 (90051-0278)
PHONE.................................213 312-4500
Fax: 213 622-3570
Michael Padula, *Sales/Mktg Mgr*
Andrew Macmullen, *Vice Pres*
Alan Previde, *Project Mgr*
Kien Lieu, *Manager*
EMP: 82
SALES (corp-wide): 47.4B **Privately Held**
SIC: 6021 National commercial banks
HQ: Mufg Union Bank, N.A
400 California St
San Francisco CA 94104
212 782-6800

(P-9406)
MUFG UNION BANK NA
Also Called: U B C 1
530 B St Ste 2400, San Diego (92101-4491)
PHONE.................................619 230-4666
Fax: 619 230-4315
Ralph C Allen, *Branch Mgr*
Suzuko Burton, *Officer*
Marguerite Boutelle, *Senior VP*
Mary Curran, *Senior VP*
Mark Schmidt, *Senior VP*
EMP: 62
SALES (corp-wide): 47.4B **Privately Held**
SIC: 6021 National commercial banks
HQ: Mufg Union Bank, N.A
400 California St
San Francisco CA 94104
212 782-6800

(P-9407)
MUFG UNION BANK NA
Also Called: U B C 103
15800 S Western Ave, Gardena (90247-3704)
PHONE.................................310 354-4700
Fax: 310 354-4719
Takeo Kittaka, *Branch Mgr*
EMP: 50
SALES (corp-wide): 47.4B **Privately Held**
SIC: 6021 National commercial banks
HQ: Mufg Union Bank, N.A
400 California St
San Francisco CA 94104
212 782-6800

(P-9408)
MUFG UNION BANK NA
23620 Lyons Ave Fl 2, Santa Clarita (91321-2513)
PHONE.................................661 799-8529
Fax: 661 287-6374
John Reardon, *President*
Janet Ages, *Technology*
Ekram Thomas, *Manager*
EMP: 92
SALES (corp-wide): 47.4B **Privately Held**
SIC: 6021 National commercial banks
HQ: Mufg Union Bank, N.A
400 California St
San Francisco CA 94104
212 782-6800

(P-9409)
MUFG UNION BANK NA
Also Called: North Main Branch
1890 N Main St, Salinas (93906-2045)
PHONE.................................831 449-7251
Alma Saldana, *Manager*
Ruth Humber, *Manager*
EMP: 50
SALES (corp-wide): 47.4B **Privately Held**
SIC: 6021 National commercial banks
HQ: Mufg Union Bank, N.A
400 California St
San Francisco CA 94104
212 782-6800

(P-9410)
MUFG UNION BANK NA
460 Hegenberger Rd Fl 3, Oakland (94621-1423)
PHONE.................................510 891-2495
Fax: 510 632-0288
Steve Nicholson, *Business Anlyst*
Charlie Donner, *Business Anlyst*
EMP: 100
SALES (corp-wide): 47.4B **Privately Held**
SIC: 6021 National commercial banks
HQ: Mufg Union Bank, N.A
400 California St
San Francisco CA 94104
212 782-6800

(P-9411)
MUFG UNION BANK NA
Also Called: First Bank of San Luis Obispo
995 Higuera St, San Luis Obispo (93401-3601)
PHONE.................................805 541-6100
Fax: 805 544-2217
Ken Long, *Branch Mgr*
Ann M Wood, *Assoc VP*
Joyce Clinton, *Exec VP*
Cindy Hall, *Vice Pres*
Sarah Rice, *Personnel Assit*
EMP: 70
SALES (corp-wide): 47.4B **Privately Held**
WEB: www.pacificcapitalbank.com
SIC: 6021 6163 6022 National commercial banks; loan brokers; state commercial banks
HQ: Mufg Union Bank, N.A
400 California St
San Francisco CA 94104
212 782-6800

(P-9412)
MUFG UNION BANK NA
Also Called: San Benito Bank
300 Tres Pinos Rd, Hollister (95023-5578)
P.O. Box 180 (95024-0180)
PHONE.................................831 638-3350
Fax: 831 638-3267
Linda Madden, *Branch Mgr*
Delbert Doty, *Vice Pres*
Gerard Buan, *Personnel Exec*
Janet Brians, *Director*
EMP: 68
SALES (corp-wide): 47.4B **Privately Held**
WEB: www.pacificcapitalbank.com
SIC: 6021 6022 National commercial banks; state commercial banks
HQ: Mufg Union Bank, N.A
400 California St
San Francisco CA 94104
212 782-6800

(P-9413)
MUFG UNION BANK NA
Also Called: Union Bank Data Processing Ctr
9885 Towne Centre Dr, San Diego (92121-1975)
PHONE.................................619 533-7612
Randy Wolf, *Assoc VP*
Michael Daly, *Vice Pres*
Ben Reeve, *Vice Pres*
James Floyd, *Architect*
EMP: 80
SALES (corp-wide): 47.4B **Privately Held**
SIC: 6021 National commercial banks
HQ: Mufg Union Bank, N.A
400 California St
San Francisco CA 94104
212 782-6800

(P-9414)
PACIFIC WESTERN BANK
900 Canterbury Pl Ste 300, Escondido (92025-3846)
PHONE.................................760 432-1350
Bruce Mills, *CFO*
Luanne Bailey, *Admin Asst*
Michael Perdue,
Mike Perdue,
EMP: 108
SALES (corp-wide): 968.2MM **Publicly Held**
WEB: www.pacificwesternbank.com
SIC: 6021 National commercial banks
HQ: Pacific Western Bank
456 Santa Monica Blvd
Santa Monica CA 90401
310 458-1521

(P-9415)
PACIFIC WESTERN BANK
11150 W Olympic Blvd # 100, Los Angeles (90064-1817)
PHONE.................................310 996-9100
Fax: 310 996-9157
Chris Bower, *Manager*
EMP: 50
SALES (corp-wide): 968.2MM **Publicly Held**
WEB: www.pacificwesternbank.com
SIC: 6021 National commercial banks
HQ: Pacific Western Bank
456 Santa Monica Blvd
Santa Monica CA 90401
310 458-1521

(P-9416)
PACIFIC WESTERN BANK
5900 La Place Ct Ste 200, Carlsbad (92008-8832)
PHONE.................................760 918-2469
Suzanne Brennan, *Manager*
AVI Demirdjian, *Senior VP*
EMP: 52
SALES (corp-wide): 968.2MM **Publicly Held**
WEB: www.pacificwesternbank.com
SIC: 6021 National commercial banks
HQ: Pacific Western Bank
456 Santa Monica Blvd
Santa Monica CA 90401
310 458-1521

(P-9417)
PACIFIC WESTERN BANK
12481 High Bluff Dr # 350, San Diego (92130-3585)
PHONE.................................858 436-3500
Richard Casey, *Branch Mgr*
Ken Ledeit, *Senior VP*
Lafe Vittitoe, *Vice Pres*
EMP: 53
SALES (corp-wide): 968.2MM **Publicly Held**
SIC: 6021 National commercial banks
HQ: Pacific Western Bank
456 Santa Monica Blvd
Santa Monica CA 90401
310 458-1521

(P-9418)
PACIFIC WESTERN BANK
900 Cantebury Pl Ste 300, Escondido (92025)
PHONE.................................760 432-1100
Michael Perdue, *Branch Mgr*
Gerry Veal, *Exec VP*
Juan Alonzo, *Vice Pres*

6021 - National Commercial Banks County (P-9419)

Jonathan Harvey, *Vice Pres*
Bonnie Ramirez, *Vice Pres*
EMP: 80
SALES (corp-wide): 968.2MM **Publicly Held**
WEB: www.pacificwesternbank.com
SIC: 6021 National commercial banks
HQ: Pacific Western Bank
456 Santa Monica Blvd
Santa Monica CA 90401
310 458-1521

(P-9419)
PNC REALTY INVESTORS INC
2 N Lake Ave Ste 440, Pasadena (91101-4197)
PHONE 626 432-4500
Thomas Soltz, *Branch Mgr*
EMP: 60
SALES (corp-wide): 16.2B **Publicly Held**
WEB: www.pncfunds.com
SIC: 6021 National trust companies with deposits, commercial
HQ: Pnc Bank, National Association
249 5th Ave Ste 1200
Pittsburgh PA 15222
412 762-2000

(P-9420)
PNC REALTY INVESTORS INC
465 N Halstead St Ste 160, Pasadena (91107-6018)
PHONE 626 351-2211
Fax: 626 351-7470
Dennis Hayashi, *Manager*
Robert Butler, *Manager*
EMP: 76
SALES (corp-wide): 16.2B **Publicly Held**
WEB: www.pncfunds.com
SIC: 6021 National trust companies with deposits, commercial
HQ: Pnc Realty Investors, Inc.
249 5th Ave Ste 1200
Pittsburgh PA 15222
412 762-2000

(P-9421)
PORREY PINES BANK INC
Also Called: Western Alliance Bank
1951 Webster St, Oakland (94612-2909)
PHONE 510 899-7500
Larry Fountain, *Manager*
Wynne Kong, *Vice Pres*
Kiran Rai, *Vice Pres*
Williams Dianne, *Opers Mgr*
Dianne Williams, *Manager*
EMP: 380
SALES (est): 25.8MM
SALES (corp-wide): 554.9MM **Publicly Held**
WEB: www.altaalliancebank.com
SIC: 6021 National commercial banks
PA: Western Alliance Bancorporation
1 E Wshington St Ste 1400
Phoenix AZ 85004
602 389-3500

(P-9422)
SILICON VALLEY BANK
3005 Jasmine Dr, Pleasanton (94588)
PHONE 408 654-7730
EMP: 80
SALES (corp-wide): 1.4B **Publicly Held**
SIC: 6021 National commercial banks
HQ: Silicon Valley Bank
3003 Tasman Dr
Santa Clara CA 95054
408 654-7400

(P-9423)
SILICON VALLEY BANK
15260 Ventura Blvd # 1800, Sherman Oaks (91403-5350)
PHONE 818 382-2600
Fax: 818 783-7984
Mark Turk, *Branch Mgr*
Adam Graham, *Vice Pres*
EMP: 80
SALES (corp-wide): 1.4B **Publicly Held**
SIC: 6021 National commercial banks
HQ: Silicon Valley Bank
3003 Tasman Dr
Santa Clara CA 95054
408 654-7400

(P-9424)
SIX RIVERS NATIONAL BANK (HQ)
402 F St, Eureka (95501-1008)
PHONE 707 443-8400
Fax: 707 443-3631
H Russell Harris, *President*
Becky Del Grande, *Vice Pres*
EMP: 51
SALES: 46.3MM
SALES (corp-wide): 206.7MM **Publicly Held**
SIC: 6021 National commercial banks
PA: Trico Bancshares
63 Constitution Dr
Chico CA 95973
530 898-0300

(P-9425)
TFC HOLDING COMPANY
18605 Gale Ave Ste 238, City of Industry (91748-1361)
PHONE 626 363-9708
Stephen H Liu, *President*
Peter Lam, *Loan Officer*
EMP: 58
SALES (est): 165.4K **Privately Held**
WEB: www.acs-tucson.com
SIC: 6021

(P-9426)
UMPQUA BANK
Also Called: Encino Branch
16501 Ventura Blvd, Encino (91436-2007)
PHONE 818 385-1362
EMP: 62
SALES (corp-wide): 1.2B **Publicly Held**
SIC: 6021 National commercial banks
HQ: Umpqua Bank
445 Se Main St
Roseburg OR 97470
541 440-3961

(P-9427)
US BANK NATIONAL ASSOCIATION
Also Called: US Bank
1420 Kettner Blvd Ste 101, San Diego (92101-2639)
PHONE 619 744-2140
Murray L Galinson, *Branch Mgr*
Gordon Boerner, *Officer*
Connie M Reckling, *Vice Pres*
Donald Wolf, *Data Proc Staff*
Murray L Gainson, *Technology*
EMP: 100
SALES (corp-wide): 21.4B **Publicly Held**
SIC: 6021 National commercial banks
HQ: U.S. Bank National Association
425 Walnut St Fl 1
Cincinnati OH 45202
513 632-4234

(P-9428)
WACHOVIA A DIVISION WELLS F
420 Montgomery St, San Francisco (94104-1207)
PHONE 415 571-2832
John G Stumpf, *Principal*
Eric Irwin, *Officer*
Sharon Murphy, *Senior VP*
Karl Pfeil, *Senior VP*
Peter Stephenson, *Senior VP*
EMP: 790
SALES (est): 354.4MM **Privately Held**
SIC: 6021 National commercial banks

(P-9429)
WELLS FARGO & COMPANY (PA)
420 Montgomery St Frnt, San Francisco (94104-1205)
PHONE 866 249-3302
Fax: 415 788-4150
John G Stumpf, *Ch of Bd*
Rachel Arana, *President*
Mercedes Armendariz, *President*
Amy Birnbaum, *President*
Frances Brady, *President*
▲ **EMP:** 280 **EST:** 1929
SALES: 90B **Publicly Held**
SIC: 6021 6022 6162 6141 National commercial banks; state commercial banks; mortgage bankers; consumer finance companies; data processing service

(P-9430)
WELLS FARGO BANK NATIONAL ASSN
10225 Riverside Dr, Toluca Lake (91602-2501)
PHONE 818 766-7172
Fax: 818 762-2971
Marita Kesheshyn, *Manager*
EMP: 50
SALES (corp-wide): 90B **Publicly Held**
WEB: www.wellsfargo.com
SIC: 6021 National commercial banks
HQ: Wells Fargo Bank, National Association
464 California St
San Francisco CA 94104
415 396-7392

(P-9431)
WELLS FARGO BANK NATIONAL ASSN (DH)
464 California St, San Francisco (94104-1204)
PHONE 415 396-7392
John G Stumpf, *CEO*
Daniel Brown, *President*
Les Biller, *COO*
Howard Atkins, *CFO*
Terri Dial, *Vice Ch Bd*
EMP: 6000 **EST:** 2004
SQ FT: 750,000
SALES (est): 18.1B
SALES (corp-wide): 90B **Publicly Held**
WEB: www.wellsfargo.com
SIC: 6021 National trust companies with deposits, commercial
HQ: Wfc Holdings, Corp
420 Montgomery St
San Francisco CA 94104
415 396-7392

(P-9432)
WELLS FARGO BANK NATIONAL ASSN
120 Kearny St Ste 1750, San Francisco (94108-4814)
PHONE 415 396-6267
Jean Arcos, *Manager*
Jay Bal, *Vice Pres*
Remo Sele, *Branch Mgr*
Doyle Westbrook, *Financial Exec*
Vince Greene, *Manager*
EMP: 50
SALES (corp-wide): 90B **Publicly Held**
WEB: www.wellsfargo.com
SIC: 6021 National commercial banks
HQ: Wells Fargo Bank, National Association
464 California St
San Francisco CA 94104
415 396-7392

(P-9433)
WELLS FARGO BANK NATIONAL ASSN
1 Montgomery St Ste 200, San Francisco (94104-4517)
P.O. Box 63005 (94163-0001)
PHONE 415 396-6161
Bob Besozzi, *Manager*
Sean Flannery, *Senior VP*
Wilma Ryan, *Senior VP*
Patrick Briggs, *Branch Mgr*
EMP: 60
SQ FT: 4,000
SALES (corp-wide): 90B **Publicly Held**
WEB: www.wellsfargo.com
SIC: 6021 National commercial banks
HQ: Wells Fargo Bank, National Association
464 California St
San Francisco CA 94104
415 396-7392

(P-9434)
WELLS FARGO BANK NATIONAL ASSN
1120 K St, Modesto (95354-2398)
PHONE 209 578-6810
Fax: 209 526-8163
Robert Moules, *Manager*
Edward Moore, *Manager*
EMP: 59
SALES (corp-wide): 90B **Publicly Held**
WEB: www.wellsfargo.com
SIC: 6021 National commercial banks
HQ: Wells Fargo Bank, National Association
464 California St
San Francisco CA 94104
415 396-7392

(P-9435)
WELLS FARGO BANK NATIONAL ASSN
2170 Tully Rd, San Jose (95122-1345)
PHONE 408 998-3714
Fax: 408 223-8302
Crystal Nguyen, *Manager*
Amy Kuoyang, *Branch Mgr*
Martin Salkowski, *Manager*
EMP: 50
SALES (corp-wide): 90B **Publicly Held**
WEB: www.wellsfargo.com
SIC: 6021 National commercial banks
HQ: Wells Fargo Bank, National Association
464 California St
San Francisco CA 94104
415 396-7392

(P-9436)
WELLS FARGO BANK NATIONAL ASSN
4365 Executive Dr Fl 18, San Diego (92121-2194)
PHONE 858 622-6958
James Cimino, *Manager*
Sinan Battah, *Loan Officer*
Jack Peluso, *Sales Executive*
Kevin Hughes, *Manager*
Joseph Lobe, *Manager*
EMP: 75
SALES (corp-wide): 90B **Publicly Held**
WEB: www.wellsfargo.com
SIC: 6021 National commercial banks
HQ: Wells Fargo Bank, National Association
464 California St
San Francisco CA 94104
415 396-7392

(P-9437)
WELLS FARGO BANK NATIONAL ASSN
4475 Executive Dr Ste 100, San Diego (92121-3076)
PHONE 858 646-0550
Windy Harris, *Manager*
Jennifer Kay, *Admin Sec*
Martha Philips, *Manager*
EMP: 120
SALES (corp-wide): 90B **Publicly Held**
WEB: www.wellsfargo.com
SIC: 6021 National commercial banks
HQ: Wells Fargo Bank, National Association
464 California St
San Francisco CA 94104
415 396-7392

(P-9438)
WELLS FARGO BANK NATIONAL ASSN
901 Main St, NAPA (94559-3044)
PHONE 707 259-5552
Patty Belt, *Manager*
EMP: 70
SALES (corp-wide): 90B **Publicly Held**
WEB: www.wellsfargo.com
SIC: 6021 National commercial banks
HQ: Wells Fargo Bank, National Association
464 California St
San Francisco CA 94104
415 396-7392

PRODUCTS & SERVICES SECTION
6021 - National Commercial Banks County (P-9458)

(P-9439)
WELLS FARGO BANK NATIONAL ASSN
Merchant Paymnt A0347-023
1200 Montego, Walnut Creek (94598-2876)
PHONE 925 746-3718
Tim Healy, *Manager*
Scott Cameron, *President*
Rex Engstrand, *President*
Mark Allen, *Vice Pres*
Brian Hennigan, *Area Mgr*
EMP: 60
SQ FT: 57,192
SALES (corp-wide): 90B **Publicly Held**
WEB: www.wellsfargo.com
SIC: 6021 National commercial banks
HQ: Wells Fargo Bank, National Association
464 California St
San Francisco CA 94104
415 396-7392

(P-9440)
WELLS FARGO BANK NATIONAL ASSN
Also Called: Trade Services E2002-031
9000 Flair Dr Fl 3, El Monte (91731-2826)
PHONE 626 312-3006
Fax: 626 280-3844
Marilyn Benoit, *Manager*
EMP: 500
SALES (corp-wide): 90B **Publicly Held**
WEB: www.wellsfargo.com
SIC: 6021 National commercial banks
HQ: Wells Fargo Bank, National Association
464 California St
San Francisco CA 94104
415 396-7392

(P-9441)
WELLS FARGO BANK NATIONAL ASSN
7714 Girard Ave, La Jolla (92037-4483)
PHONE 858 454-0362
Fax: 858 456-9776
Ladd Graham, *Manager*
Gavin Ballinger, *Site Mgr*
Edward Proudfoot, *Manager*
Chafic Rouhana, *Manager*
EMP: 525
SALES (corp-wide): 90B **Publicly Held**
WEB: www.wellsfargo.com
SIC: 6021 National commercial banks
HQ: Wells Fargo Bank, National Association
464 California St
San Francisco CA 94104
415 396-7392

(P-9442)
WELLS FARGO BANK NATIONAL ASSN
Also Called: Roseville Foothils and Jct
5007 Foothills Blvd, Roseville (95747-6503)
PHONE 916 724-2982
Susan Adams, *Branch Mgr*
EMP: 85
SALES (corp-wide): 90B **Publicly Held**
SIC: 6021 National commercial banks
HQ: Wells Fargo Bank, National Association
464 California St
San Francisco CA 94104
415 396-7392

(P-9443)
WELLS FARGO BANK NATIONAL ASSN
60 W Hamilton Ave, Campbell (95008-0505)
PHONE 408 378-8155
Fax: 408 370-2675
Titi Vu, *Manager*
EMP: 50
SALES (corp-wide): 90B **Publicly Held**
WEB: www.wellsfargo.com
SIC: 6021 National commercial banks
HQ: Wells Fargo Bank, National Association
464 California St
San Francisco CA 94104
415 396-7392

(P-9444)
WELLS FARGO BANK NATIONAL ASSN
350 W Colorado Blvd # 100, Pasadena (91105-1892)
PHONE 626 685-9900
Fax: 626 844-9087
Gary Harrigian, *Principal*
Robert Kricena, *Branch Mgr*
EMP: 50
SALES (corp-wide): 90B **Publicly Held**
WEB: www.wellsfargo.com
SIC: 6021 National commercial banks
HQ: Wells Fargo Bank, National Association
464 California St
San Francisco CA 94104
415 396-7392

(P-9445)
WELLS FARGO BANK NATIONAL ASSN
100 Spear St Ste 100, San Francisco (94105-1578)
PHONE 415 777-9497
Fax: 415 777-9584
Praneet Chahal, *Principal*
Joshua Drake, *Store Mgr*
EMP: 319
SALES (corp-wide): 90B **Publicly Held**
SIC: 6021 National commercial banks
HQ: Wells Fargo Bank, National Association
464 California St
San Francisco CA 94104
415 396-7392

(P-9446)
WELLS FARGO BANK NATIONAL ASSN
1620 E Roseville Pkwy, Roseville (95661-3995)
PHONE 916 774-2249
Kathie Gedney, *Manager*
Bill Allen, *Assoc VP*
Richard Siegel, *Vice Pres*
Kelly Garfield, *Info Tech Mgr*
Dennis A McKey, *Info Tech Mgr*
EMP: 300
SALES (corp-wide): 90B **Publicly Held**
WEB: www.wellsfargo.com
SIC: 6021 National commercial banks
HQ: Wells Fargo Bank, National Association
464 California St
San Francisco CA 94104
415 396-7392

(P-9447)
WELLS FARGO BANK NATIONAL ASSN
3440 Flair Dr, El Monte (91731-2883)
PHONE 626 573-1338
Lori Morgan, *Principal*
Rick Fisher, *Project Mgr*
Carl Herr, *VP Mktg*
EMP: 250
SALES (corp-wide): 90B **Publicly Held**
WEB: www.wellsfargo.com
SIC: 6021 National commercial banks
HQ: Wells Fargo Bank, National Association
464 California St
San Francisco CA 94104
415 396-7392

(P-9448)
WELLS FARGO BANK NATIONAL ASSN
28350 S Western Ave, Rancho Palos Verdes (90275-1499)
PHONE 310 831-0632
Fax: 310 831-5347
Sandy Walia, *Branch Mgr*
Jose Zeledon, *Manager*
EMP: 60
SALES (corp-wide): 90B **Publicly Held**
WEB: www.wellsfargo.com
SIC: 6021 National commercial banks
HQ: Wells Fargo Bank, National Association
464 California St
San Francisco CA 94104
415 396-7392

(P-9449)
WELLS FARGO BANK NATIONAL ASSN
17945 Chatsworth St, Granada Hills (91344-5606)
PHONE 818 673-1857
Fax: 818 887-5184
Rafeek Raheem, *Manager*
EMP: 100
SALES (corp-wide): 90B **Publicly Held**
WEB: www.wellsfargo.com
SIC: 6021 National commercial banks
HQ: Wells Fargo Bank, National Association
464 California St
San Francisco CA 94104
415 396-7392

(P-9450)
WELLS FARGO BANK NATIONAL ASSN
5798 Stoneridge Mall Rd, Pleasanton (94588-2862)
PHONE 925 463-1983
Richard Thornton, *Branch Mgr*
EMP: 84
SALES (corp-wide): 90B **Publicly Held**
SIC: 6021 National commercial banks
HQ: Wells Fargo Bank, National Association
464 California St
San Francisco CA 94104
415 396-7392

(P-9451)
WELLS FARGO BANK NATIONAL ASSN
2301 Watt Ave, Sacramento (95825-0666)
PHONE 916 440-4570
Fax: 916 481-8931
Scott Caddow, *Manager*
EMP: 50
SALES (corp-wide): 90B **Publicly Held**
WEB: www.wellsfargo.com
SIC: 6021 National commercial banks
HQ: Wells Fargo Bank, National Association
464 California St
San Francisco CA 94104
415 396-7392

(P-9452)
WELLS FARGO BANK NATIONAL ASSN
Also Called: San Lorenzo 0119
16000 Hesperian Blvd, San Lorenzo (94580-2450)
PHONE 510 276-0875
Fax: 510 317-0957
Jan Miller, *Branch Mgr*
Joann Broyant, *Opers Mgr*
Janet Pefley, *Manager*
EMP: 50
SALES (corp-wide): 90B **Publicly Held**
WEB: www.wellsfargo.com
SIC: 6021 National commercial banks
HQ: Wells Fargo Bank, National Association
464 California St
San Francisco CA 94104
415 396-7392

(P-9453)
WELLS FARGO BANK NATIONAL ASSN
39265 Paseo Padre Pkwy, Fremont (94538-1611)
PHONE 510 792-3512
Fax: 510 791-7531
George Sezidarias, *Manager*
EMP: 59
SALES (corp-wide): 90B **Publicly Held**
WEB: www.wellsfargo.com
SIC: 6021 National commercial banks
HQ: Wells Fargo Bank, National Association
464 California St
San Francisco CA 94104
415 396-7392

(P-9454)
WELLS FARGO BANK NATIONAL ASSN
950 Southland Dr, Hayward (94545-1544)
P.O. Box 3367 (94540-3367)
PHONE 510 266-0595
Fax: 510 785-3329
Kay Maloy, *Manager*
Anthony Perez, *Office Mgr*
EMP: 55
SALES (corp-wide): 90B **Publicly Held**
WEB: www.wellsfargo.com
SIC: 6021 National commercial banks
HQ: Wells Fargo Bank, National Association
464 California St
San Francisco CA 94104
415 396-7392

(P-9455)
WELLS FARGO BANK NATIONAL ASSN
665 Marsh St, San Luis Obispo (93401-3930)
PHONE 805 541-0143
Fax: 805 541-4212
Mark Corella, *Branch Mgr*
EMP: 84
SALES (corp-wide): 90B **Publicly Held**
WEB: www.wellsfargo.com
SIC: 6021 National commercial banks
HQ: Wells Fargo Bank, National Association
464 California St
San Francisco CA 94104
415 396-7392

(P-9456)
WELLS FARGO BANK NATIONAL ASSN
420 Montgomery St Fl 6, San Francisco (94104-1207)
PHONE 415 394-4021
Paul Rettig, *Manager*
Shirley Griffin, *Exec VP*
Rick Waldoni, *Programmer Anys*
EMP: 1000
SALES (corp-wide): 90B **Publicly Held**
WEB: www.wellsfargo.com
SIC: 6021 National commercial banks
HQ: Wells Fargo Bank, National Association
464 California St
San Francisco CA 94104
415 396-7392

(P-9457)
WELLS FARGO BANK NATIONAL ASSN
455 Market, Fremont (94536)
PHONE 415 222-6834
Wyman Yuu, *Manager*
EMP: 250
SALES (corp-wide): 90B **Publicly Held**
WEB: www.wellsfargo.com
SIC: 6021 National commercial banks
HQ: Wells Fargo Bank, National Association
464 California St
San Francisco CA 94104
415 396-7392

(P-9458)
WELLS FARGO BANK NATIONAL ASSN
420 Montgomery St, San Francisco (94104-1298)
PHONE 415 222-1360
John Fleling, *Branch Mgr*
William P Hayes, *Incorporator*
Nancy Diao, *CFO*
Stephen Ellis, *CFO*
Craig R Lamp, *Treasurer*
EMP: 250
SALES (corp-wide): 90B **Publicly Held**
WEB: www.wellsfargo.com
SIC: 6021 National commercial banks
HQ: Wells Fargo Bank, National Association
464 California St
San Francisco CA 94104
415 396-7392

6021 - National Commercial Banks County (P-9459) — PRODUCTS & SERVICES SECTION

(P-9459)
WELLS FARGO BANK NATIONAL ASSN
2220 Mountain Blvd # 160, Oakland (94611-2950)
P.O. Box 1559 (94604-1559)
PHONE 510 530-3095
Fax: 510 531-0579
Ellen Thomas, *Manager*
Connie Adachi, *Project Mgr*
EMP: 65
SALES (corp-wide): 90B **Publicly Held**
WEB: www.wellsfargo.com
SIC: 6021 National commercial banks
HQ: Wells Fargo Bank, National Association
464 California St
San Francisco CA 94104
415 396-7392

(P-9460)
WELLS FARGO BANK NATIONAL ASSN
18712 Gridley Rd, Cerritos (90703-5410)
PHONE 562 924-1616
Fax: 562 809-2104
Susan De Lazzer, *Sales/Mktg Mgr*
Susan Delazzer, *Manager*
Ha Nguyen, *Manager*
EMP: 50
SALES (corp-wide): 90B **Publicly Held**
WEB: www.wellsfargo.com
SIC: 6021 National commercial banks
HQ: Wells Fargo Bank, National Association
464 California St
San Francisco CA 94104
415 396-7392

(P-9461)
WELLS FARGO BANK NATIONAL ASSN
3440 Walnut Ave Fl 3, Fremont (94538-2210)
PHONE 510 745-5025
Yung Lew, *Division Mgr*
Kirk Cardinotti, *Vice Pres*
EMP: 300
SALES (corp-wide): 90B **Publicly Held**
WEB: www.wellsfargo.com
SIC: 6021 National commercial banks
HQ: Wells Fargo Bank, National Association
464 California St
San Francisco CA 94104
415 396-7392

(P-9462)
WELLS FARGO BANK NATIONAL ASSN
Wells Fargo Investments
433 N Camden Dr Ste 1200, Beverly Hills (90210-4426)
P.O. Box 20160, Long Beach (90801-3160)
PHONE 310 285-5817
Fax: 310 247-0435
Steve Mann, *Manager*
EMP: 200
SALES (corp-wide): 90B **Publicly Held**
WEB: www.wellsfargo.com
SIC: 6021 National commercial banks
HQ: Wells Fargo Bank, National Association
464 California St
San Francisco CA 94104
415 396-7392

(P-9463)
WELLS FARGO BANK NATIONAL ASSN
2525 N Main St Ste 100, Santa Ana (92705-6603)
PHONE 714 571-2200
Lou Casa, *Manager*
EMP: 50
SALES (corp-wide): 90B **Publicly Held**
WEB: www.wellsfargo.com
SIC: 6021 National commercial banks
HQ: Wells Fargo Bank, National Association
464 California St
San Francisco CA 94104
415 396-7392

(P-9464)
WFC HOLDINGS CORP (HQ)
420 Montgomery St, San Francisco (94104-1207)
PHONE 415 396-7392
Richard M Kovacevich, *Ch of Bd*
Erich Sontag, *Vice Pres*
Sandra Duszak, *Info Tech Mgr*
Jonathan Morrow, *Info Tech Mgr*
Duane Menges, *Manager*
EMP: 200 EST: 1998
SQ FT: 750,000
SALES (est): 20.5B
SALES (corp-wide): 90B **Publicly Held**
SIC: 6021 National commercial banks
PA: Wells Fargo & Company
420 Montgomery St Frnt
San Francisco CA 94104
866 249-3302

(P-9465)
ZB NATIONAL ASSOCIATION
California Bank & Trust
11622 El Camino Real, San Diego (92130-2049)
PHONE 858 793-7400
EMP: 50
SALES (corp-wide): 2.2B **Publicly Held**
SIC: 6021 National commercial banks
HQ: Zb, National Association
1 S Main St
Salt Lake City UT 84133
801 974-8800

(P-9466)
ZB NATIONAL ASSOCIATION
Also Called: California Bank & Trust
100 Crprate Pinte Ste 250, Culver City (90230)
PHONE 310 258-9300
Jeff Watts, *Branch Mgr*
Wayne Ward, *Senior VP*
Beto Martinez, *Vice Pres*
EMP: 149
SALES (corp-wide): 2.2B **Publicly Held**
WEB: www.calbt.com
SIC: 6021 National commercial banks
HQ: Zb, National Association
1 S Main St
Salt Lake City UT 84133
801 974-8800

6022 State Commercial Banks

(P-9467)
1ST CENTURY BANCSHARES INC
1875 Century Park E # 1400, Los Angeles (90067-2572)
PHONE 310 270-9500
Fax: 310 270-9599
EMP: 71
SALES: 24.3MM **Privately Held**
SIC: 6022

(P-9468)
BANAMEX USA (DH)
2029 Century Park E Fl 42, Los Angeles (90067-2901)
P.O. Box 30886 (90030-0886)
PHONE 310 203-3400
Fax: 310 203-3799
Manuel Sanchez Lugo, *Ch of Bd*
Rebecca Macieira-Kaufmann, *CEO*
Roger Johnston, *Ch Credit Ofcr*
Gabriel De La Peza, *Exec VP*
Theodore Michaels, *Exec VP*
EMP: 200
SALES: 33.7MM
SALES (corp-wide): 88.2B **Publicly Held**
WEB: www.ccbusa.com
SIC: 6022 State commercial banks
HQ: Banamex Usa Bancorp
2029 Century Park E Fl 42
Los Angeles CA 90067
310 203-3440

(P-9469)
BANAMEX USA
2029 Century Park E # 4200, Los Angeles (90067-2901)
PHONE 800 222-1234
EMP: 116
SALES: 88.2B **Publicly Held**
SIC: 6022 State commercial banks
HQ: Banamex Usa
2029 Century Park E Fl 42
Los Angeles CA 90067
310 203-3400

(P-9470)
BANC CALIFORNIA NATIONAL ASSN
10100 Santa Monica Blvd, Los Angeles (90067-4003)
PHONE 310 286-0710
Richard Smith, *President*
EMP: 50
SALES (corp-wide): 486.5MM **Publicly Held**
SIC: 6022 State commercial banks
HQ: Banc Of California, National Association
18500 Von Karman Ave
Irvine CA 92612
877 770-2262

(P-9471)
BANK OF MARIN
Also Called: Northgate Branch
4460 Redwood Hwy Ste 1, San Rafael (94903-1952)
PHONE 415 472-2265
Fax: 415 472-8166
Janet Hayward, *Manager*
Todd Zwiaska, *Credit Staff*
Kelly Duenas, *Assistant VP*
EMP: 78
SALES (corp-wide): 78.6MM **Publicly Held**
WEB: www.bankofmarin.com
SIC: 6022 State commercial banks
HQ: Bank Of Marin
504 Redwood Blvd Ste 100
Novato CA 94947
415 763-4520

(P-9472)
BANK OF MARIN BANCORP (PA)
504 Redwood Blvd Fl 1, Novato (94947-6923)
P.O. Box 2039 (94948-2039)
PHONE 415 763-4520
Russell A Colombo, *President*
Brian Sobel, *Ch of Bd*
Tani Girton, *CFO*
Elizabeth Reizman, *Ch Credit Ofcr*
Debbie Campas, *Officer*
EMP: 103
SALES: 78.6MM **Publicly Held**
SIC: 6022 State commercial banks

(P-9473)
BANK OF ORIENT (HQ)
100 Pine St Ste 600, San Francisco (94111-5108)
P.O. Box 2489 (94126-2489)
PHONE 415 338-0668
Fax: 415 338-0619
Ernest L Go, *Ch of Bd*
Michael R Delucchi, *COO*
Carl Andersen, *CFO*
Mark K McDonald, *Exec VP*
John Ng, *Exec VP*
EMP: 65
SQ FT: 20,000
SALES: 18.2MM
SALES (corp-wide): 39.8MM **Privately Held**
SIC: 6022 State commercial banks
PA: Orient Bancorporation
100 Pine St Ste 600
San Francisco CA 94111
415 567-1554

(P-9474)
BANK OF SIERRA (HQ)
90 N Main St, Porterville (93257-3712)
P.O. Box 1930 (93258-1930)
PHONE 559 782-4300
Fax: 559 782-4313
Morris Tharp, *Ch of Bd*
Stephen Ermigarat, *President*
Dustin Oliver, *President*
Kenneth R Taylor, *CFO*
Albert L Berra, *Bd of Directors*
EMP: 105
SQ FT: 37,000
SALES: 71.9MM
SALES (corp-wide): 80.4MM **Publicly Held**
WEB: www.bankofthesierra.com
SIC: 6022 State commercial banks
PA: Sierra Bancorp
86 N Main St
Porterville CA 93257
559 782-4900

(P-9475)
BANK OF STOCKTON (HQ)
301 E Miner Ave, Stockton (95202-2501)
P.O. Box 1110 (95201-3003)
PHONE 209 929-1600
Robert M Eberhardt, *President*
Douglass M Eberhardt, *President*
John Morrison, *President*
Thomas H Shaffer, *COO*
Madeline Hall, *Bd of Directors*
EMP: 180
SQ FT: 15,000
SALES: 94.2MM
SALES (corp-wide): 81MM **Privately Held**
WEB: www.netbos.com
SIC: 6022 State commercial banks

(P-9476)
BANK OF THE WEST (HQ)
180 Montgomery St # 1400, San Francisco (94104-4297)
PHONE 415 765-4800
Fax: 408 374-1242
J Michael Shepherd, *CEO*
Randy Arnold, *Partner*
Nicole Auyang, *President*
Stephanie Beggs, *President*
Teresa Casselberry, *President*
▲ EMP: 1000
SQ FT: 30,000
SALES: 2.5B **Publicly Held**
SIC: 6022 State commercial banks
PA: Bnp Paribas
16 Boulevard Des Italiens
Paris Cedex 09 75450
140 144-546

(P-9477)
BBCN BANK
550 S Western Ave, Los Angeles (90020-4208)
PHONE 213 389-5550
EMP: 50
SALES (corp-wide): 357.3MM **Publicly Held**
SIC: 6022 State commercial banks
HQ: Bank Of Hope
3731 Wilshire Blvd # 400
Los Angeles CA 90010
213 639-1700

(P-9478)
CALIFORNIA UNITED BANK (HQ)
818 W 7th St Ste 220, Los Angeles (90017-3449)
PHONE 213 430-7000
Fax: 818 257-7701
David Rainer, *President*
Anne A Williams, *COO*
Robert Denin, *CFO*
Karen A Schoenbaum, *CFO*
Christine Kordik, *Officer*
EMP: 78
SALES: 62.7MM
SALES (corp-wide): 101.8MM **Publicly Held**
WEB: www.californiaunitedbank.com
SIC: 6022 State commercial banks
PA: Cu Bancorp
15821 Ventura Blvd # 100
Encino CA 91436
818 257-7700

(P-9479)
CATHAY BANK (HQ)
9650 Flair Dr, El Monte (91731-3005)
P.O. Box 80426 (91731)
PHONE 626 279-3698
Dunson K Cheng, *Ch of Bd*
Heng W Chen, *CFO*
Steven Chen, *Officer*
Rose Chow, *Officer*
Corey Jenrich, *Officer*
EMP: 125

▲ = Import ▼ = Export
◆ = Import/Export

PRODUCTS & SERVICES SECTION

6022 - State Commercial Banks County (P-9499)

SALES: 456.2MM
SALES (corp-wide): 486.3MM **Publicly Held**
WEB: www.newasiabk.com
SIC: 6022 State commercial banks
PA: Cathay General Bancorp
777 N Broadway
Los Angeles CA 90012
213 625-4700

(P-9480)
CATHAY BANK
800 W 6th St Ste 200, Los Angeles (90017-2705)
PHONE.................213 896-0098
Fax: 213 972-4263
Wilson Tang, *Manager*
Kai Cheng, *Assistant VP*
EMP: 100
SALES (corp-wide): 486.3MM **Publicly Held**
WEB: www.newasiabk.com
SIC: 6022 6082 State commercial banks; foreign trade & international banking institutions
HQ: Cathay Bank
9650 Flair Dr
El Monte CA 91731
626 279-3698

(P-9481)
CATHAY GENERAL BANCORP
1139 W Huntington Dr, Arcadia (91007-6316)
PHONE.................626 574-9530
MEI X Guo, *Principal*
Bob Romero, *Senior VP*
EMP: 260
SALES (corp-wide): 486.3MM **Publicly Held**
SIC: 6022 State commercial banks
PA: Cathay General Bancorp
777 N Broadway
Los Angeles CA 90012
213 625-4700

(P-9482)
CENTRAL VALLEY CMNTY BANCORP (PA)
7100 N Fincl Dr Ste 101, Fresno (93720)
PHONE.................559 298-1775
James M Ford, *President*
Daniel J Doyle, *Ch of Bd*
David A Kinross, *CFO*
Patrick J Carman, *Ch Credit Ofcr*
Lydia Shaw, *Senior VP*
EMP: 231 EST: 2000
SALES: 51.2MM **Publicly Held**
WEB: www.cvcb.com
SIC: 6022 State commercial banks

(P-9483)
CENTRAL VALLEY COMMUNITY BANK
120 N Floral St, Visalia (93291-6202)
PHONE.................559 625-8733
EMP: 75
SALES (corp-wide): 51.2MM **Publicly Held**
SIC: 6022 State commercial banks
HQ: Central Valley Community Bank
600 Pollasky Ave
Clovis CA 93612
559 323-3384

(P-9484)
CITIZENS BUSINESS BANK (HQ)
701 N Haven Ave Ste 350, Ontario (91764-4920)
P.O. Box 51000 (91761-1087)
PHONE.................909 980-4030
Toll Free:.................877 -
Fax: 909 481-2102
Christopher D Myers, *President*
D Linn Wiley, *Ch of Bd*
Edward J Biebrich Jr, *CFO*
Richard Thomas, *CFO*
George A Borba Jr, *Vice Ch Bd*
▲ **EMP:** 150
SQ FT: 23,000
SALES: 290.3MM
SALES (corp-wide): 289.3MM **Publicly Held**
WEB: www.cbbank.com
SIC: 6022 State commercial banks
PA: Cvb Financial Corp.
701 N Haven Ave Ste 350
Ontario CA 91764
909 980-4030

(P-9485)
CITIZENS BUSINESS BANK
1401 Dove St Ste 100, Newport Beach (92660-2425)
PHONE.................949 440-5200
Christopher D Myers, *President*
Kathy Elam, *Vice Pres*
EMP: 90
SALES (corp-wide): 289.3MM **Publicly Held**
SIC: 6022 State commercial banks
HQ: Citizens Business Bank
701 N Haven Ave Ste 350
Ontario CA 91764
909 980-4030

(P-9486)
CITIZENS BUSINESS BANK
Also Called: Downtown Business Fincl Ctr
1230 17th St, Bakersfield (93301-4609)
PHONE.................661 281-0300
Bart Hill, *Branch Mgr*
Michelle Wolf, *Analyst*
Valerie Prince, *Manager*
EMP: 98
SALES (corp-wide): 289.3MM **Publicly Held**
SIC: 6022 State trust companies accepting deposits, commercial
HQ: Citizens Business Bank
701 N Haven Ave Ste 350
Ontario CA 91764
909 980-4030

(P-9487)
COMMUNITY BANK (PA)
460 Serra Madre Villa Ave, Pasadena (91107-2967)
PHONE.................626 577-1700
David R Misch, *CEO*
Alan Johnson, *Ch of Bd*
Marshall V Laitsch, *Ch of Bd*
Alan Buckle, *President*
Jeanna Threadgill, *President*
▲ **EMP:** 50 EST: 1945
SQ FT: 75,000
SALES: 136.4MM **Privately Held**
WEB: www.communitybank-ca.com
SIC: 6022 6029 State commercial banks; commercial banks

(P-9488)
COMMUNITY BANK
255 E Rincon St Ste 312, Corona (92879-1369)
PHONE.................951 808-8940
Russell Moore, *Manager*
James McKinnon, *Exec VP*
Edda Bernal, *Senior VP*
Marco Arcadia, *Vice Pres*
Brent Breedlove, *Vice Pres*
EMP: 50
SALES (corp-wide): 136.4MM **Privately Held**
WEB: www.communitybank-ca.com
SIC: 6022 State commercial banks
PA: Community Bank
460 Serra Madre Villa Ave
Pasadena CA 91107
626 577-1700

(P-9489)
EAST WEST BANK (HQ)
135 N Ls Rbls Ave 100, Pasadena (91101)
PHONE.................626 768-6000
Fax: 626 564-1129
Dominic Ng, *Ch of Bd*
John Lee, *Vice Chairman*
Donald S Chow, *President*
Julia S Gouw, *President*
Thomas J Tolda, *CFO*
◆ **EMP:** 300
SQ FT: 18,000
SALES: 1.1B
SALES (corp-wide): 1.2B **Publicly Held**
WEB: www.eastwest.com
SIC: 6022 State commercial banks
PA: East West Bancorp, Inc.
135 N Los Robles Ave Fl 7
Pasadena CA 91101
626 768-6000

(P-9490)
EAST WEST BANK
555 Montgomery St Bsmt, San Francisco (94111-2516)
PHONE.................415 391-8912
Fax: 415 391-8916
Michael Kay, *Branch Mgr*
Kelvin Chan, *Senior VP*
Keith Kishiyama, *Senior VP*
Warren Chiu, *Vice Pres*
Bronia Leung, *Vice Pres*
EMP: 200
SALES (corp-wide): 1.2B **Publicly Held**
WEB: www.ibankunited.com
SIC: 6022 State commercial banks
HQ: East West Bank
135 N Ls Rbls Ave 100
Pasadena CA 91101
626 768-6000

(P-9491)
EXCHANGE BANK
2 E Washington St, Petaluma (94952-3197)
PHONE.................707 762-5555
Fax: 707 769-1770
Rick Mossy, *Branch Mgr*
Ron Malnati, *Vice Pres*
Rick Mossi, *Executive*
John Meiscahn, *Branch Mgr*
EMP: 53
SALES (corp-wide): 38.2MM **Privately Held**
WEB: www.exchangebank.com
SIC: 6022 State commercial banks
HQ: Exchange Bank
440 Aviation Blvd
Santa Rosa CA 95403
707 524-3000

(P-9492)
FARMERS MERCHANTS BNK LONG BCH (HQ)
Also Called: F&M Bank
302 Pine Ave, Long Beach (90802-2326)
P.O. Box 1370 (90801-1370)
PHONE.................562 437-0011
W Henry Walker, *CEO*
Jacki Granger, *President*
Lissette Najarro, *President*
Kenneth G Walker, *President*
Melissa Lanfre, *COO*
EMP: 130 EST: 1907
SQ FT: 150,000
SALES: 211.5MM
SALES (corp-wide): 30.6MM **Privately Held**
WEB: www.fmb.com
SIC: 6022 6029 State trust companies accepting deposits, commercial; commercial banks

(P-9493)
FARMERS MERCHANTS BNK LONG BCH
1695 Adolfo Lopez Dr, Seal Beach (90740-5620)
PHONE.................562 430-4724
Leon Aiossa, *Manager*
Ken Nagel, *Info Tech Mgr*
EMP: 150
SALES (corp-wide): 30.6MM **Privately Held**
WEB: www.fmb.com
SIC: 6022 6029 State commercial banks; commercial banks
HQ: Farmers & Merchants Bank Of Long Beach
302 Pine Ave
Long Beach CA 90802
562 437-0011

(P-9494)
FARMERS MRCHANTS BNK CENTL CAL
8799 Elk Grove Blvd, Elk Grove (95624-1742)
PHONE.................916 394-3200
Patti Ruiz, *Manager*
Steven Green, *Manager*
EMP: 214
SALES (corp-wide): 104.6MM **Publicly Held**
WEB: www.fmbonline.com
SIC: 6022 6021 State commercial banks; national commercial banks
HQ: Farmers & Merchants Bank Of Central California
121 W Pine St
Lodi CA 95240
209 367-2300

(P-9495)
FIRST CHOICE BANK (PA)
17785 Center Court Dr N # 750, Cerritos (90703-9310)
PHONE.................562 345-9092
Fax: 562 926-8640
Robert Franko, *Principal*
Peter Lin, *CFO*
Homer Chan, *Bd of Directors*
Yvonne Chen, *Exec VP*
Gene May, *Exec VP*
EMP: 90
SQ FT: 6,000
SALES: 36.4MM **Privately Held**
WEB: www.firstchoicebankca.com
SIC: 6022 State commercial banks

(P-9496)
FIRST NORTHERN BANK OF DIXON (HQ)
Also Called: First Northern Community
195 N 1st St, Dixon (95620-3025)
P.O. Box 547 (95620-0547)
PHONE.................707 678-4422
Fax: 707 678-9734
Owen J Onsum, *President*
Jeremiah Z Smith, *COO*
Louise A Walker, *CFO*
Joe T Danelson, *Ch Credit Ofcr*
T Joe Danelson, *Ch Credit Ofcr*
EMP: 59 EST: 1910
SQ FT: 14,000
SALES: 38.2MM
SALES (corp-wide): 40.7MM **Publicly Held**
SIC: 6022 State commercial banks
PA: First Northern Community Bancorp
195 N 1st St
Dixon CA 95620
707 678-3041

(P-9497)
FIRST REGIONAL BANCORP
1801 Century Park E # 800, Los Angeles (90067-2302)
PHONE.................310 552-1776
H Anthony Gartshore, *President*
Gary M Horgan, *Ch of Bd*
Dexter Kodama, *CFO*
Elizabeth Thompson, *CFO*
Lawrence J Sherman, *Vice Ch Bd*
EMP: 288
SQ FT: 19,734
SALES (est): 54MM **Privately Held**
WEB: www.firstregional.com
SIC: 6022 State commercial banks

(P-9498)
FIRST REPUBLIC BANK (PA)
111 Pine St Ste Bsmt, San Francisco (94111-5628)
PHONE.................415 392-1400
Fax: 415 392-1413
Thomas J Barrack Jr, *CEO*
Katherine August-Dewilde, *Vice Chairman*
Kelly Johnston, *President*
Jason C Bender, *COO*
Mike Selfridge, *COO*
EMP: 332
SQ FT: 60,000
SALES: 1.7B **Publicly Held**
WEB: www.firstrepublic.com
SIC: 6022 6282 6162 State commercial banks; investment advice; mortgage bankers

(P-9499)
FREMONT BANK (HQ)
39150 Fremont Blvd, Fremont (94538-1313)
P.O. Box 5101 (94537-5101)
PHONE.................510 505-5226
Fax: 510 795-5715
Morris Hyman, *Ch of Bd*
Chris Chenoweth, *President*

Keith Fujita, *President*
Andy Mastorakis, *President*
Bradford L Anderson, *CEO*
EMP: 250
SQ FT: 20,000
SALES: 158.8MM
SALES (corp-wide): 151.8MM **Privately Held**
WEB: www.fremontbank.com
SIC: 6022 State commercial banks
PA: Fremont Bancorporation
  39150 Fremont Blvd
  Fremont CA 94538
  510 792-2300

(P-9500)
HANMI BANK (HQ)
3660 Wilshire Blvd Ph A, Los Angeles (90010-2387)
PHONE.............................213 382-2200
Fax: 213 382-5345
Joon H Lee, *Ch of Bd*
Susan Kim, *President*
Chong Guk Kum, *President*
Mohammad Tariq, *President*
Bonita I Lee, *COO*
▲ **EMP:** 95 **EST:** 1981
SQ FT: 35,000
SALES: 162.8MM
SALES (corp-wide): 211.8MM **Publicly Held**
WEB: www.hanmi.com
SIC: 6022 State commercial banks
PA: Hanmi Financial Corporation
  3660 Wilshire Blvd Penths Ste A
  Los Angeles CA 90010
  213 382-2200

(P-9501)
HERITAGE BANK OF COMMERCE (HQ)
Also Called: Heritage Bank of Commerce
150 Almaden Blvd Lbby, San Jose (95113-2010)
PHONE.............................408 947-6900
Fax: 408 947-6910
Walter Kaczmarek, *CEO*
Richard Conniff, *COO*
Keith Wilton, *COO*
Lawrence D McGovern, *CFO*
Michael Ong, *Ch Credit Ofcr*
EMP: 120
SQ FT: 36,000
SALES: 66.9MM
SALES (corp-wide): 87.7MM **Publicly Held**
WEB: www.heritagebankofcommerce.com
SIC: 6022 State commercial banks
PA: Heritage Commerce Corp
  150 Almaden Blvd Lbby
  San Jose CA 95113
  408 947-6900

(P-9502)
HOMESTREET BANK
650 S Grand Ave Ste 105, Glendora (91740-4177)
P.O. Box 6107, Covina (91722-5107)
PHONE.............................626 339-9663
Dustin Luton, *CEO*
EMP: 95
SALES (corp-wide): 446.3MM **Publicly Held**
SIC: 6022 State commercial banks
HQ: Homestreet Bank
  601 Union St Ste 2000
  Seattle WA 98101
  206 623-3050

(P-9503)
INTERNTNAL CH OF FRSQARE GOSPL
4 Crow Canyon Ct, San Ramon (94583-1967)
PHONE.............................925 964-9044
Roger Cone, *Branch Mgr*
EMP: 157
SALES (corp-wide): 206.2MM **Privately Held**
SIC: 6022 State commercial banks
PA: International Church Of The Foursquare Gospel
  1910 W Sunset Blvd # 200
  Los Angeles CA 90026
  213 989-4234

(P-9504)
ISRAEL DISCOUNT BANK NEW YORK
Also Called: Downtown Los Angeles Branch
888 S Figueroa St Ste 550, Los Angeles (90017-5306)
PHONE.............................213 861-6440
Leon Recanati, *Principal*
EMP: 177
SALES (corp-wide): 1.8B **Privately Held**
SIC: 6022 State commercial banks
HQ: Israel Discount Bank Of New York
  511 5th Ave
  New York NY 10017
  212 551-8500

(P-9505)
LOS ROBLES BANK
33 W Thousand Oaks Blvd, Thousand Oaks (91360-4416)
P.O. Box 1438 (91358-0438)
PHONE.............................805 373-6763
Fax: 805 379-2857
Robert B Hamilton, *President*
John G Putnam, *Exec VP*
John Podlesni, *Vice Pres*
Janet Depackh, *Mfg Staff*
EMP: 52
SQ FT: 11,000
SALES (est): 5.4MM
SALES (corp-wide): 47.4B **Privately Held**
SIC: 6022 State commercial banks
HQ: Mufg Americas Holdings Corporation
  1251 Ave Of The Americas
  New York NY 10020
  212 782-5911

(P-9506)
MANUFACTURERS BANK (DH)
515 S Figueroa St Ste 400, Los Angeles (90071-3323)
P.O. Box 556000 (90055-1000)
PHONE.............................213 489-6200
Fax: 213 489-6254
Mitsugu Serizawa, *CEO*
Koichi Miyata, *President*
Naresh Sheth, *President*
Sylvia Martinez, *Officer*
Adrian Danescu, *Exec VP*
EMP: 164
SQ FT: 69,206
SALES: 71.1MM
SALES (corp-wide): 40.8B **Privately Held**
WEB: www.manubank.com
SIC: 6022 State trust companies accepting deposits, commercial
HQ: Sumitomo Mitsui Banking Corporation
  1-1-2, Marunouchi
  Chiyoda-Ku TKY 100-0
  332 821-111

(P-9507)
MECHANICS BANK (DH)
Also Called: Mechanics Bank Atm
1111 Civic Dr Ste 333, Walnut Creek (94596-3894)
PHONE.............................800 797-6324
Fax: 510 262-7236
Carl Webb, *Ch of Bd*
Paula Allen, *President*
Diane Marieiro, *President*
Nicholas Mellon, *President*
Arlene Mulchaey, *President*
EMP: 110 **EST:** 1905
SQ FT: 77,000
SALES: 140.9MM **Privately Held**
SIC: 6022 State commercial banks
HQ: Eb Acquisition Company Llc
  200 Crescent Ct
  Dallas TX 75201
  214 871-5151

(P-9508)
MECHANICS BANK
18400 Von Karman Ave, Irvine (92612-1514)
PHONE.............................949 270-9700
EMP: 270
SALES (corp-wide): 140.9MM **Privately Held**
SIC: 6022 State commercial banks
HQ: The Mechanics Bank
  1111 Civic Dr Ste 333
  Walnut Creek CA 94596
  800 797-6324

(P-9509)
MIZUHO CORPORATE BANK CAL (DH)
350 S Grand Ave Ste 1500, Los Angeles (90071-3471)
PHONE.............................213 612-2848
Fax: 213 612-2875
Takuo Yoshida, *Ch of Bd*
Hiroko Tatebe, *Treasurer*
Elizabeth Whalen, *Assoc VP*
Munetoshi Matsumoto, *Exec VP*
Esther Wilson, *Senior VP*
EMP: 75
SALES (est): 10.9MM
SALES (corp-wide): 26.7B **Privately Held**
SIC: 6022 State commercial banks
HQ: Mizuho Bank, Ltd.
  1-5-5, Otemachi
  Chiyoda-Ku TKY 100-0
  332 141-111

(P-9510)
ONEUNITED BANK
Also Called: Family Savings Bank
3683 Crenshaw Blvd, Los Angeles (90016-4890)
PHONE.............................323 295-3381
Fax: 323 293-7746
Kevin Cohee, *Ch of Bd*
Nila Johnson, *Admin Asst*
EMP: 72
SALES (corp-wide): 27MM **Privately Held**
SIC: 6022 State commercial banks
PA: Oneunited Bank
  100 Franklin St Ste 600
  Boston MA 02110
  617 457-4400

(P-9511)
ONEUNITED BANK
3910 W Martin Luther King, Los Angeles (90008-1714)
PHONE.............................323 290-4848
Carlton Jenkins, *Manager*
Lanet Roberson, *Branch Mgr*
Tamara Ashford, *Office Mgr*
EMP: 90
SALES (corp-wide): 27MM **Privately Held**
SIC: 6022 6021 State commercial banks; national commercial banks
PA: Oneunited Bank
  100 Franklin St Ste 600
  Boston MA 02110
  617 457-4400

(P-9512)
OPUS BANK
2100 Foothill Blvd Ste B, La Verne (91750-2905)
PHONE.............................909 599-0871
John Giambi, *Branch Mgr*
Jennifer Flood, *Manager*
EMP: 55
SALES (corp-wide): 191.7MM **Publicly Held**
SIC: 6022 State trust companies accepting deposits, commercial
PA: Opus Bank
  19900 Macarthur Blvd # 1200
  Irvine CA 92612
  949 250-9800

(P-9513)
PACIFIC COAST BANKERS BANK
1676 N Calif Blvd Ste 300, Walnut Creek (94596-4185)
PHONE.............................415 399-1900
Steve Brown, *President*
Nino Petroni, *COO*
Eric Davis, *Senior VP*
Omar Halwani, *Vice Pres*
Paul Noord, *Vice Pres*
EMP: 60
SALES: 21.1MM
SALES (corp-wide): 21.1MM **Privately Held**
SIC: 6022 State commercial banks
PA: Pacific Coast Bankers' Bancshares
  1676 N Calif Blvd Ste 300
  Walnut Creek CA 94596
  415 399-1900

(P-9514)
PACIFIC MERCANTILE BANK (HQ)
Also Called: Pmbc
949 S Coast Dr Ste 300, Costa Mesa (92626-7733)
PHONE.............................714 438-2500
Steven Buster, *President*
Neil B Kornswiet, *President*
Thomas M Vertin, *President*
Robert E Sjogren, *COO*
Nancy A Gray, *CFO*
EMP: 50
SALES: 42.1MM
SALES (corp-wide): 41.4MM **Publicly Held**
SIC: 6022 6712 State commercial banks; bank holding companies
PA: Pacific Mercantile Bancorp
  949 S Coast Dr Ste 300
  Costa Mesa CA 92626
  714 438-2500

(P-9515)
PACIFIC WESTERN BANK
9955 Mission Gorge Rd, Santee (92071-3841)
PHONE.............................619 562-6400
Bruce Ives, *Manager*
Allan A Farias, *Agent*
EMP: 60
SALES (corp-wide): 968.2MM **Publicly Held**
WEB: www.pacificwesternbank.com
SIC: 6022 State commercial banks
HQ: Pacific Western Bank
  456 Santa Monica Blvd
  Santa Monica CA 90401
  310 458-1521

(P-9516)
PREMIER COMMERCIAL BANCORP
2400 E Katella Ave # 125, Anaheim (92806-5920)
PHONE.............................714 978-2400
Kenneth J Cosgrove, *Ch of Bd*
Ashokkumar Patel, *President*
Viktor R Uehlinger, *CFO*
Stephen W Pihl, *Exec VP*
Brent Walters, *Vice Pres*
EMP: 64
SALES: 22.3MM **Privately Held**
SIC: 6022 State commercial banks

(P-9517)
PROVIDNT SVNGS BANK CHRTBLE FN
Also Called: Provident Bank
3756 Central Ave, Riverside (92506-2421)
PHONE.............................951 686-6060
Craig Blunden, *Ch of Bd*
Robert G Schrader, *COO*
Donavon P Ternes, *CFO*
Donald L Blanchard, *Senior VP*
Lilian Brunner, *Senior VP*
EMP: 100
SALES: 45.5K **Privately Held**
SIC: 6022 State commercial banks

(P-9518)
RABOBANK NATIONAL ASSOCIATION
301 Main St, Salinas (93901-2700)
PHONE.............................831 422-6642
Ida Chan, *Principal*
Lana Adame, *Vice Pres*
Roger Aikin, *Vice Pres*
Chris Raj, *Vice Pres*
Phillip Sullivan, *Vice Pres*
EMP: 125
SALES (corp-wide): 13.9B **Privately Held**
WEB: www.community-bnk.com
SIC: 6022 6163 6029 State commercial banks; loan brokers; commercial banks
HQ: Rabobank, National Association
  915 Highland Pointe Dr
  Roseville CA 95678
  760 352-5000

PRODUCTS & SERVICES SECTION

6022 - State Commercial Banks County (P-9539)

(P-9519)
RCB CORPORATION (PA)
Also Called: River City Bank
2485 Natomas Park Dr # 100, Sacramento (95833-2937)
P.O. Box 15247 (95851-0247)
PHONE 916 567-2600
Fax: 916 567-2784
Stephen Fleming, *President*
Shawn Devlin, *Ch of Bd*
Anker Christensen, *CFO*
Jon Kelly, *Founder*
Jason Hartmann, *Vice Pres*
EMP: 80
SQ FT: 34,000
SALES (est): 44.7MM **Privately Held**
SIC: 6022 State commercial banks

(P-9520)
RIVER CITY BANK (HQ)
2485 Natomas Park Dr # 100, Sacramento (95833-2975)
P.O. Box 15247 (95851-0247)
PHONE 916 567-2600
Fax: 916 567-2780
Stephen A Fleming, *President*
Jay Murray, *President*
Anker Christensen, *CFO*
Michael Lablanc, *Officer*
Pat McHone, *Exec VP*
EMP: 80
SQ FT: 15,000
SALES: 43.6MM
SALES (corp-wide): 44.7MM **Privately Held**
WEB: www.rcbank.com
SIC: 6022 State commercial banks
PA: Rcb Corporation
2485 Natomas Park Dr # 100
Sacramento CA 95833
916 567-2600

(P-9521)
SAEHAN BANK (PA)
3200 Wilshire Blvd # 700, Los Angeles (90010-1313)
PHONE 213 368-7700
Dong IL Kim, *President*
Dong IL Kim, *President*
▲ EMP: 50
SQ FT: 12,000
SALES (est): 21.8MM **Privately Held**
SIC: 6022 State commercial banks

(P-9522)
SAN DIEGO PRIVATE BANK
801 Orange Ave Ste 101, Coronado (92118-2663)
PHONE 619 437-1000
Fax: 619 437-1070
Richard Rico, *Branch Mgr*
Philip Chapman, *Exec VP*
Ellen Jeffries, *Vice Pres*
EMP: 60
SALES (corp-wide): 16.3MM **Privately Held**
SIC: 6022 State commercial banks
PA: San Diego Private Bank
110 W A St Ste 1000
San Diego CA

(P-9523)
SAVINGS BANK MENDOCINO COUNTY (PA)
Also Called: Sbmc
200 N School St, Ukiah (95482-4811)
P.O. Box 3600 (95482-3600)
PHONE 707 462-6613
Fax: 707 462-1269
Charles B Mannon, *Ch of Bd*
Dan Gill, *President*
Scott Yandell, *President*
Bruce Little, *CFO*
Guy Dana, *Ch Credit Ofcr*
EMP: 130 EST: 1903
SALES: 35.3MM **Privately Held**
WEB: www.savingsbank.com
SIC: 6022 State commercial banks

(P-9524)
SCOTT VALLEY BANK (HQ)
2544 Westside Rd, Yreka (96097-9129)
P.O. Box 69 (96097-0069)
PHONE 530 623-2732
Timothy S Avery, *President*
Daniel Northway, *CFO*
Chris Morin, *Exec VP*
John Sparks, *Vice Pres*
Daniel Taylor, *Vice Pres*
EMP: 58
SALES: 22.1MM
SALES (corp-wide): 14.5MM **Privately Held**
WEB: www.scottvalleybank.com
SIC: 6022 State commercial banks
PA: Learner Financial Corporation
590 Ygnacio Valley Rd # 210
Walnut Creek CA 94596
925 934-1601

(P-9525)
STANDARD CHARTERED BANK
601 S Figueroa St # 2775, Los Angeles (90017-5877)
PHONE 626 639-8000
Jim Mc Cabe, *CEO*
Mike Hague, *Branch Mgr*
EMP: 225
SALES (corp-wide): 20.9B **Privately Held**
SIC: 6022 6282 6029 State commercial banks; investment advisory service; commercial banks
HQ: Standard Chartered Bank
1 Basinghall Avenue
London EC2V
207 885-8888

(P-9526)
SUMITOMO MITSUI TR BNK USA INC
601 S Figueroa St # 1800, Los Angeles (90017-5704)
PHONE 213 955-0800
Fax: 213 623-6832
Toshishikiko Ogata, *Principal*
Mark A Tito, *Vice Pres*
Richard Fujii, *Agent*
EMP: 60
SALES (corp-wide): 10.1B **Privately Held**
WEB: www.sumitomobank.co.jp
SIC: 6022 State commercial banks
HQ: Sumitomo Mitsui Trust Bank (U.S.A.), Inc.
111 River St
Hoboken NJ 07030
201 595-8900

(P-9527)
SUNWEST BANK (DH)
2050 Main St Fl 3, Irvine (92614-8255)
P.O. Box 1028, Tustin (92781-1028)
PHONE 714 730-4441
Fax: 714 731-8641
Glenn Gray, *President*
Chris Walsh, *President*
Jason Raefski, *CFO*
Brian Constable, *Officer*
Debra Kupp, *Officer*
EMP: 60
SQ FT: 30,000
SALES: 46.9MM
SALES (corp-wide): 56MM **Privately Held**
SIC: 6022 State commercial banks

(P-9528)
SVB FINANCIAL GROUP (PA)
3003 Tasman Dr, Santa Clara (95054-1191)
PHONE 408 654-7400
Greg W Becker, *President*
Roger F Dunbar, *Ch of Bd*
Harry Kellogg Jr, *Vice Chairman*
Philip C Cox, *President*
John Dossantos, *President*
EMP: 109
SQ FT: 213,625
SALES: 1.4B **Publicly Held**
SIC: 6022 State commercial banks

(P-9529)
TCW GROUP INC (HQ)
Also Called: Trust Company of The West
865 S Figueroa St # 2100, Los Angeles (90017-2543)
PHONE 213 244-0000
Fax: 213 244-0755
Marc I Stern, *CEO*
David B Lippman, *President*
Richard Villa, *CFO*
Meredith S Jackson, *Exec VP*
David Asarnow, *Senior VP*
EMP: 450
SALES (est): 317.6MM
SALES (corp-wide): 3B **Publicly Held**
SIC: 6022 6282 6211 State trust companies accepting deposits, commercial; investment advisory service; security brokers & dealers
PA: The Carlyle Group L P
1001 Pennsylvania Ave Nw 220s
Washington DC 20004
202 729-5626

(P-9530)
TORREY PINES BANK (HQ)
12220 El Camino Real # 200, San Diego (92130-2091)
PHONE 858 523-4600
Fax: 858 755-0875
EMP: 103
SALES (est): 19.1MM
SALES (corp-wide): 554.9MM **Publicly Held**
WEB: www.torreypinesbank.com
SIC: 6022
PA: Western Alliance Bancorporation
1 E Wshington St Ste 1400
Phoenix AZ 85004
602 389-3500

(P-9531)
UMPQUA BANK
7777 Alvarado Rd Ste 515, La Mesa (91942-8306)
PHONE 619 668-5159
Tweed Marie Anne, *Manager*
EMP: 81
SALES (corp-wide): 1.2B **Publicly Held**
SIC: 6022 State commercial banks
HQ: Umpqua Bank
445 Se Main St
Roseburg OR 97470
541 440-3961

(P-9532)
UNION BANK FOUNDATION (DH)
Also Called: Union Bank Cal Foundation
445 S Figueroa St Ste 710, Los Angeles (90071-1615)
PHONE 213 236-4013
Fax: 213 236-5717
Masashi Oka, *President*
John F Harrigan, *Ch of Bd*
W H Wofford, *Exec VP*
Hitesh Mehta, *Senior VP*
David Anderson, *Vice Pres*
EMP: 600
SALES (est): 272.1MM
SALES (corp-wide): 47.4B **Privately Held**
SIC: 6022 State commercial banks
HQ: Mufg Union Bank, N.A
400 California St
San Francisco CA 94104
212 782-6800

(P-9533)
UNION BANK OF CALIFORNIA
445 S Figueroa St Ste 710, Los Angeles (90071-1615)
PHONE 213 236-6444
Fax: 213 236-5717
John Harrigan, *Principal*
Jesus Serrano, *President*
Jose Dizon, *Officer*
Richard Faulkner, *Officer*
Gerald Ford, *Officer*
EMP: 2517
SALES (est): 399.2MM
SALES (corp-wide): 47.4B **Privately Held**
WEB: www.uboc.com
SIC: 6022 State commercial banks
HQ: Mufg Americas Holdings Corporation
1251 Ave Of The Americas
New York NY 10020
212 782-5911

(P-9534)
VIB CORP
1498 W Main St, El Centro (92243-2819)
PHONE 760 352-5000
Dennis L Kern, *President*
Bruce Baccus, *Exec VP*
William Henle, *Exec VP*
Martin E Plourd, *Exec VP*
Jack Stewart Grady, *Senior VP*
EMP: 1705
SQ FT: 20,000
SALES: 136MM
SALES (corp-wide): 13.9B **Privately Held**
WEB: www.vibank.com
SIC: 6022 State commercial banks
HQ: Utrecht - America Holdings, Inc
245 Park Ave Fl 36
New York NY 10167
212 916-7800

(P-9535)
WELLS FARGO BANK LTD
333 S Grand Ave Ste 500, Los Angeles (90071-1569)
PHONE 213 253-6227
Randy Reyes, *Branch Mgr*
John Brownlee, *Info Tech Mgr*
Tony Place, *Info Tech Mgr*
Courtney Cassidy, *Consultant*
Robert Pace, *Consultant*
EMP: 85
SALES: 518.7MM
SALES (corp-wide): 90B **Publicly Held**
SIC: 6022 State commercial banks
HQ: Wfc Holdings, Corp
420 Montgomery St
San Francisco CA 94104
415 396-7392

(P-9536)
WESTAMERICA BANK
15342 Lakeshore Dr, Clearlake (95422-9761)
PHONE 707 995-4140
Julie Hopkins, *Branch Mgr*
EMP: 50
SALES (corp-wide): 184.4MM **Publicly Held**
SIC: 6022 State commercial banks
HQ: West America Bank
1108 5th Ave
San Rafael CA 94901
707 863-6113

(P-9537)
WESTERN ALLIANCE BANK
Bridge Capital Finance Group
55 Almaden Blvd Ste 200, San Jose (95113-1619)
PHONE 408 423-8500
Lee Shodiss, *Vice Pres*
EMP: 70
SALES (corp-wide): 554.9MM **Publicly Held**
SIC: 6022 8742 State commercial banks; management consulting services
HQ: Western Alliance Bank
1 E Wshington St Ste 1400
Phoenix AZ

(P-9538)
WESTERN ALLIANCE BANK
455 Market St Ste 1050, San Francisco (94105-5409)
PHONE 415 230-4834
Fax: 415 230-4374
Bella Betsayad, *Vice Pres*
EMP: 70
SALES (corp-wide): 554.9MM **Publicly Held**
SIC: 6022 State commercial banks
HQ: Western Alliance Bank
1 E Wshington St Ste 1400
Phoenix AZ

(P-9539)
WESTERN ALLIANCE BANK
Also Called: Bridge Bank
55 Almaden Blvd Ste 200, San Jose (95113-1619)
PHONE 408 423-8500
Fax: 408 995-0355
James H Lundy, *CEO*
EMP: 70
SALES (corp-wide): 554.9MM **Publicly Held**
SIC: 6022 8742 State commercial banks; management consulting services
HQ: Western Alliance Bank
1 E Wshington St Ste 1400
Phoenix AZ

6022 - State Commercial Banks County (P-9540)

(P-9540) WESTERN ALLIANCE BANK
3035 Prospect Park Dr # 100, Rancho Cordova (95670-6042)
PHONE...............................916 851-6800
Fax: 916 861-0093
Jim Harris, *Manager*
EMP: 70
SALES (corp-wide): 554.9MM **Publicly Held**
WEB: www.bridgebanksv.com
SIC: **6022** 6029 State commercial banks; commercial banks
HQ: Western Alliance Bank
1 E Wshington St Ste 1400
Phoenix AZ

(P-9541) WESTERN ALLIANCE BANK
1655 The Alameda, San Jose (95126-2203)
PHONE...............................408 282-1670
EMP: 70
SALES (corp-wide): 554.9MM **Publicly Held**
WEB: www.bridgebanksv.com
SIC: **6022** 6029 State commercial banks; commercial banks
HQ: Western Alliance Bank
1 E Wshington St Ste 1400
Phoenix AZ

(P-9542) WESTERN ALLIANCE BANK
55 Almaden Blvd Ste 100, San Jose (95113-1609)
PHONE...............................408 423-8500
Daineal Myers, *Branch Mgr*
Linda Michaels, *Vice Pres*
Michael Moore, *Vice Pres*
Fergal O'Boyle, *Vice Pres*
Owen Brown,
EMP: 70
SALES (corp-wide): 554.9MM **Publicly Held**
WEB: www.bridgebanksv.com
SIC: **6022** 6021 State commercial banks; national commercial banks
HQ: Western Alliance Bank
1 E Wshington St Ste 1400
Phoenix AZ

(P-9543) WESTERN ALLIANCE BANK
7545 Irvine Center Dr # 200, Irvine (92618-2932)
PHONE...............................949 222-0855
EMP: 70
SALES (corp-wide): 554.9MM **Publicly Held**
SIC: **6022** State commercial banks
HQ: Western Alliance Bank
1 E Wshington St Ste 1400
Phoenix AZ

6029 Commercial Banks,

(P-9544) BANK OF TKY-MITSUBISHI UFJ LTD
777 S Figueroa St Ste 600, Los Angeles (90017-5806)
PHONE...............................213 488-3700
Fax: 213 488-3875
EMP: 100
SALES (corp-wide): 47.4B **Privately Held**
SIC: **6029** Commercial banks
HQ: The Bank Of Tokyo-Mitsubishi Ufj Ltd
1251 Ave Of The Americas
New York NY 10020

(P-9545) BORREGO SPRINGS BANK
7777 Alvarado Rd Ste 515, La Mesa (91942-8306)
PHONE...............................619 668-5159
Fax: 619 403-5191
William P Ruhlman II, *CEO*
Frank V Riolo, *President*
Scott Yankton, *COO*
Michelle Whelehan, *CFO*
Julie Smart, *Senior VP*
EMP: 81
SALES: 15.5MM **Privately Held**
WEB: www.bsb.net
SIC: **6029** Commercial banks
PA: Viejas Tribal Council
5005 Willows Rd Ste 229
Alpine CA 91901

(P-9546) CALIFORNIA FIRST NATIONAL BANK
Also Called: University Lease
28 Executive Park Ste 200, Irvine (92614-4741)
P.O. Box 2509, Santa Ana (92707-0509)
PHONE...............................949 255-0500
S Leslie Jewett, *President*
Glen T Tsuma, *Vice Chairman*
Tom Wiedecker, *COO*
Yvonne Cattell, *CFO*
Steve Chaya, *Exec VP*
EMP: 80
SQ FT: 36,000
SALES: 23.8MM
SALES (corp-wide): 32.5MM **Publicly Held**
WEB: www.calfirstbancorp.com
SIC: **6029** Commercial banks
PA: California First National Bancorp
28 Executive Park
Irvine CA 92614
949 255-0500

(P-9547) COMMERCIAL FINANCE & L
8445 Camino Sta Ste 202, San Diego (92121)
P.O. Box 2562, Del Mar (92014-1862)
PHONE...............................858 866-8525
Fax: 949 861-9400
Vadim Garry Lyulkin, *President*
Dean G Lyulkin, *Principal*
William S Stern, *Principal*
EMP: 65
SQ FT: 10,000
SALES (est): 25.5MM **Privately Held**
WEB: www.bankofcardiff.com
SIC: **6029** Commercial banks

(P-9548) FIRST REPUBLIC BANK
101 Pine St, San Francisco (94111-5629)
PHONE...............................415 392-1400
James Herbert, *President*
Darla Sledge, *Administration*
EMP: 800
SALES (corp-wide): 1.7B **Publicly Held**
SIC: **6029** 6162 Commercial banks; mortgage bankers
PA: First Republic Bank
111 Pine St Ste Bsmt
San Francisco CA 94111
415 392-1400

(P-9549) FIRST REPUBLIC BANK
44 Montgomery St Ste 110, San Francisco (94104-4600)
PHONE...............................415 392-1400
Fax: 415 392-7888
Monica Brazil, *Manager*
EMP: 127
SALES (corp-wide): 1.7B **Publicly Held**
WEB: www.firstrepublic.com
SIC: **6029** 6022 6021 Commercial banks; state commercial banks; national commercial banks
PA: First Republic Bank
111 Pine St Ste Bsmt
San Francisco CA 94111
415 392-1400

(P-9550) FIRST REPUBLIC BANK
2550 Sand Hill Rd Ste 100, Menlo Park (94025-7095)
PHONE...............................650 233-8880
Gayle Nickel, *Branch Mgr*
Samir Kaji, *Officer*
EMP: 127
SALES (corp-wide): 1.7B **Publicly Held**
SIC: **6029** 6021 Commercial banks; national commercial banks
PA: First Republic Bank
111 Pine St Ste Bsmt
San Francisco CA 94111
415 392-1400

(P-9551) FIRST REPUBLIC BANK
Also Called: Los Angeles Branch
901 W 7th St, Los Angeles (90017-5522)
PHONE...............................213 239-8883
Fax: 213 239-8882
Sev Araradian, *Branch Mgr*
EMP: 127
SALES (corp-wide): 1.7B **Publicly Held**
SIC: **6029** Commercial banks
PA: First Republic Bank
111 Pine St Ste Bsmt
San Francisco CA 94111
415 392-1400

(P-9552) FIRST REPUBLIC BANK
224 Brookwood Rd, Orinda (94563-3015)
PHONE...............................925 254-8993
Dina Zapanta, *Branch Mgr*
EMP: 127
SALES (corp-wide): 1.7B **Publicly Held**
SIC: **6029** Commercial banks
PA: First Republic Bank
111 Pine St Ste Bsmt
San Francisco CA 94111
415 392-1400

(P-9553) FIRST REPUBLIC BANK
1888 Century Park E # 200, Los Angeles (90067-1706)
PHONE...............................310 712-1888
Fax: 310 203-8177
Simon Clark, *Principal*
John Cummings, *Officer*
Mark Sear, *Director*
Robert Skinner, *Director*
EMP: 65
SALES (corp-wide): 1.7B **Publicly Held**
SIC: **6029** 6162 6141 Commercial banks; mortgage bankers; financing: automobiles, furniture, etc., not a deposit bank
PA: First Republic Bank
111 Pine St Ste Bsmt
San Francisco CA 94111
415 392-1400

(P-9554) PACIFIC CITY BANK
13140 Yale Ave, Irvine (92620-2661)
PHONE...............................714 263-1800
Haeyoung Cho, *Owner*
EMP: 53
SALES (corp-wide): 49.4MM **Privately Held**
SIC: **6029** 6021 Commercial banks; national commercial banks
PA: Pacific City Bank
3701 Wilshire Blvd # 100
Los Angeles CA 90010
626 363-6730

(P-9555) PV ACQUISITION BANK
255 E Rver Pk Cir Ste 180, Fresno (93720)
PHONE...............................559 438-2002
Mike McGowan, *Branch Mgr*
EMP: 102
SALES (corp-wide): 10.7MM **Privately Held**
SIC: **6029** Commercial banks
PA: Pv Acquisition Bank
255 E River Park Cir
Fresno CA 93720
559 438-2002

(P-9556) REDDING BANK OF COMMERCE (HQ)
1951 Churn Creek Rd, Redding (96002-0246)
PHONE...............................530 224-7355
Fax: 530 224-3337
Randall S Eslick, *President*
Linda J Miles, *CFO*
Patrick J Moty, *Ch Credit Ofcr*
Toni Thurber, *Officer*
David Gonzales, *Senior VP*
EMP: 80
SQ FT: 10,000
SALES: 40.5MM
SALES (corp-wide): 41.9MM **Publicly Held**
WEB: www.rosevillebankofcommerce.com
SIC: **6029** Commercial banks
PA: Bank Of Commerce Holdings
1901 Churn Creek Rd
Redding CA 96002
530 722-3939

(P-9557) SCHOOLSFIRST FEDERAL CREDIT UN
15442 Newport Ave, Tustin (92780-6473)
PHONE...............................714 258-4000
Jim Phillips, *Senior VP*
Shaelin Martinez, *Vice Pres*
Robert Osterholt, *Vice Pres*
Julia Simonella, *Executive Asst*
Scott Brownrigg, *Information Mgr*
EMP: 304
SALES (corp-wide): 316.9MM **Privately Held**
SIC: **6029** Commercial banks
PA: Schoolsfirst Federal Credit Union
2115 N Broadway
Santa Ana CA 92706
714 258-4000

(P-9558) SEACOAST COMMERCE BANK (PA)
11939 Rancho Bernardo Rd # 200, San Diego (92128-2075)
PHONE...............................858 432-7000
Fax: 619 476-7770
Richard M Sanborn, *CEO*
Allan W Arendsee, *Ch of Bd*
David H Bartram, *COO*
Thomas Cheek, *Officer*
Joseph Brodsky, *Senior VP*
EMP: 60
SALES: 27.8MM **Privately Held**
WEB: www.seacoastcommercebank.com
SIC: **6029** Commercial banks

(P-9559) SIERRA BANCORP
7029 N Ingram Ave Ste 101, Fresno (93650-1091)
PHONE...............................559 449-8145
Fax: 559 436-0824
Frank Oliver, *Principal*
EMP: 77
SALES (corp-wide): 80.4MM **Publicly Held**
SIC: **6029** Commercial banks
PA: Sierra Bancorp
86 N Main St
Porterville CA 93257
559 782-4900

(P-9560) SILICON VALLEY BANK
58 Commercial St, Sunnyvale (94085)
PHONE...............................415 610-4855
EMP: 75
SALES (corp-wide): 1.4B **Publicly Held**
SIC: **6029** Commercial banks
HQ: Silicon Valley Bank
3003 Tasman Dr
Santa Clara CA 95054
408 654-7400

(P-9561) SILICON VALLEY BANK (HQ)
3003 Tasman Dr, Santa Clara (95054-1191)
PHONE...............................408 654-7400
Fax: 408 496-2420
Kenneth P Wilcox, *CEO*
Michael Dreyer, *COO*
Judy Lee, *CFO*
Cecilia Shea, *CFO*
Jay Mc Neil, *Sr Corp Ofcr*
EMP: 592
SQ FT: 100,000
SALES: 1.1B
SALES (corp-wide): 1.4B **Publicly Held**
WEB: www.svbsecurities.com
SIC: **6029** Commercial banks

PRODUCTS & SERVICES SECTION

6035 - Federal Savings Institutions County (P-9582)

PA: Svb Financial Group
3003 Tasman Dr
Santa Clara CA 95054
408 654-7400

6035 Federal Savings Institutions

(P-9562)
TRI COUNTIES BANK (HQ)
63 Constitution Dr, Chico (95973-4937)
PHONE..................530 898-0300
Fax: 530 898-0310
Richard P Smith, *President*
Alex A Vereschagin Jr, *Ch of Bd*
Robert Steveson, *COO*
Thomas Reddish, *CFO*
Dan Padden, *Treasurer*
EMP: 75
SALES: 155.6MM
SALES (corp-wide): 206.7MM **Publicly Held**
WEB: www.tricountiesbank.com
SIC: **6029** 6163 Commercial banks; loan brokers
PA: Trico Bancshares
63 Constitution Dr
Chico CA 95973
530 898-0300

(P-9563)
TRI COUNTIES BANK
305 Railroad Ave Ste 1, Nevada City (95959-2854)
PHONE..................530 478-6001
Eileen Counts, *Opers Mgr*
EMP: 91
SALES (corp-wide): 206.7MM **Publicly Held**
SIC: **6029** Commercial banks
HQ: Tri Counties Bank
63 Constitution Dr
Chico CA 95973
530 898-0300

(P-9564)
UMPQUA BANK
4040 Macarthur Blvd # 100, Newport Beach (92660-2556)
PHONE..................949 474-1020
Heidi B Stanley, *Ch of Bd*
EMP: 72
SALES (corp-wide): 1.2B **Publicly Held**
SIC: **6029** Commercial banks
HQ: Umpqua Bank
445 Se Main St
Roseburg OR 97470
541 440-3961

(P-9565)
WELLS FARGO & COMPANY
Wells Fargo Commercial Banking
420 Montgomery St Ste 600, San Francisco (94104-1216)
PHONE..................801 246-1774
EMP: 110
SALES (corp-wide): 90B **Publicly Held**
SIC: **6029** Commercial banks
PA: Wells Fargo & Company
420 Montgomery St Frnt
San Francisco CA 94104
866 249-3302

(P-9566)
WESTAMERICA BANCORPORATION
4550 Mangels Blvd, Suisun City (94534-4083)
P.O. Box 1260 (94585-1260)
PHONE..................707 863-6029
Dennis Hansen, *Branch Mgr*
Robert Hwang, *Vice Pres*
William Delgado, *Info Tech Dir*
Phil Ladiero, *Network Analyst*
Beckie Weber, *Opers Spvr*
EMP: 225
SALES (corp-wide): 184.4MM **Publicly Held**
SIC: **6029** Commercial banks
PA: Westamerica Bancorporation
1108 5th Ave
San Rafael CA 94901
707 863-6000

(P-9567)
BANC CALIFORNIA NATIONAL ASSN (HQ)
Also Called: BANC HOME LOANS
18500 Von Karman Ave, Irvine (92612-0504)
P.O. Box 61452 (92602-6048)
PHONE..................877 770-2262
Robert Franko, *President*
Sean Casey, *Principal*
EMP: 69
SALES: 472.9MM
SALES (corp-wide): 486.5MM **Publicly Held**
SIC: **6035** Federal savings banks
PA: Banc Of California, Inc.
18500 Von Karman Ave # 1100
Irvine CA 92612
855 361-2262

(P-9568)
BANNER BANK
1750 Howe Ave Ste 100, Sacramento (95825-3356)
PHONE..................916 648-2100
William Martin, *Branch Mgr*
EMP: 70 **Publicly Held**
SIC: **6035** Federal savings banks
HQ: Banner Bank
10 S 1st Ave
Walla Walla WA 99362
800 272-9933

(P-9569)
CITIBANK N A
1 Sansome St Fl 28, San Francisco (94104-4435)
PHONE..................415 627-6000
Vicki Grunski, *Finance Mgr*
Craig Roche, *MIS Staff*
Jeffrey Steinberg, *MIS Staff*
EMP: 180
SALES (corp-wide): 88.2B **Publicly Held**
WEB: www.citibank.com
SIC: **6035** Federal savings & loan associations
HQ: Citibank Na
399 Park Ave Bsmt 1
New York NY 10022
212 559-1000

(P-9570)
EL DORADO SAVINGS BANK (PA)
4040 El Dorado Rd, Placerville (95667-8238)
P.O. Box 1208 (95667-1208)
PHONE (530) 622-1492
Fax: 530 622-1492
Thomas Meuser, *Ch of Bd*
George Cook Jr, *President*
Anne Wilson, *President*
William H Blucher, *CFO*
William Buechler, *CFO*
EMP: 55
SQ FT: 37,779
SALES: 53.6MM **Privately Held**
WEB: www.eldoradosavingsbank.com
SIC: **6035** Federal savings & loan associations

(P-9571)
JPMORGAN CHASE & CO
400 E Main St Fl 2, Stockton (95202-3002)
PHONE..................209 460-2888
Robert T Barnum, *Manager*
EMP: 950
SALES (corp-wide): 101B **Publicly Held**
SIC: **6035** 6211 Federal savings banks; security brokers & dealers
PA: Jpmorgan Chase & Co.
270 Park Ave Fl 38
New York NY 10017
212 270-6000

(P-9572)
JPMORGAN CHASE BANK NAT ASSN
5095 Business Center Dr, Fairfield (94534-1631)
PHONE..................707 864-4700
Elana Thomas, *Manager*
EMP: 150
SALES (corp-wide): 101B **Publicly Held**
SIC: **6035** Savings institutions, federally chartered
HQ: Jpmorgan Chase Bank, National Association
1111 Polaris Pkwy
Columbus OH 43240
614 436-3055

(P-9573)
JPMORGAN CHASE BANK NAT ASSN
860 E Colorado Blvd, Pasadena (91101-2107)
PHONE..................626 795-5177
Vickie Davinski, *Branch Mgr*
EMP: 60
SQ FT: 74,640
SALES (corp-wide): 101B **Publicly Held**
SIC: **6035** Federal savings banks
HQ: Jpmorgan Chase Bank, National Association
1111 Polaris Pkwy
Columbus OH 43240
614 436-3055

(P-9574)
JPMORGAN CHASE BANK NAT ASSN
Also Called: Washington Mutual
12051 Ventura Blvd, Studio City (91604-2609)
PHONE..................818 763-7343
Fax: 818 769-4607
Manny Abebi, *Branch Mgr*
EMP: 50
SALES (corp-wide): 101B **Publicly Held**
SIC: **6035** Federal savings banks
HQ: Jpmorgan Chase Bank, National Association
1111 Polaris Pkwy
Columbus OH 43240
614 436-3055

(P-9575)
JPMORGAN CHASE BANK NAT ASSN
100 S Vincent Ave Fl 1, West Covina (91790-2902)
PHONE..................626 919-3129
Larry Gomez, *Branch Mgr*
Jackie Breceda, *Manager*
EMP: 89
SALES (corp-wide): 101B **Publicly Held**
SIC: **6035** Federal savings banks
HQ: Jpmorgan Chase Bank, National Association
1111 Polaris Pkwy
Columbus OH 43240
614 436-3055

(P-9576)
JPMORGAN CHASE BANK NAT ASSN
Also Called: Financial Division
1100 Palm Ave, Imperial Beach (91932-1619)
PHONE..................619 424-8197
Roger Debock, *Principal*
Felicia Bomediano, *Site Mgr*
EMP: 50
SALES (corp-wide): 101B **Publicly Held**
SIC: **6035** Federal savings banks
HQ: Jpmorgan Chase Bank, National Association
1111 Polaris Pkwy
Columbus OH 43240
614 436-3055

(P-9577)
ONEWEST BANK NA
3500 E 7th St, Long Beach (90804-5137)
PHONE..................562 433-0971
Fax: 562 433-0975
EMP: 56

SALES (corp-wide): 876.3MM **Privately Held**
SIC: **6035**
HQ: Onewest Bank N.A.
888 E Walnut St
Pasadena CA 91101
626 535-4300

(P-9578)
OPUS BANK
200 W Commonwealth Ave, Fullerton (92832-1811)
PHONE..................714 578-7500
Stephen H Gordon, *Branch Mgr*
EMP: 110
SALES (corp-wide): 191.7MM **Publicly Held**
SIC: **6035** Savings institutions, federally chartered
PA: Opus Bank
19900 Macarthur Blvd # 1200
Irvine CA 92612
949 250-9800

(P-9579)
PACIFIC STATE BANCORP
1899 W March Ln, Stockton (95207-6402)
PHONE..................209 870-3214
Rick D Simas, *President*
Justin R Garner, *CFO*
Joanne Roberts, *CFO*
Gary A Stewart, *Ch Credit Ofcr*
Larry Hernandez, *Officer*
EMP: 89
SALES (est): 385.4K **Privately Held**
WEB: www.pacificstatebank.com
SIC: **6035**

(P-9580)
PACIFIC WESTERN BANK
Also Called: Los Padres Bank
610 Alamo Pintado Rd, Solvang (93463-2202)
PHONE..................805 688-6644
Fax: 805 688-4959
Craig Cerny, *President*
Nicole Painter, *Director*
Gussie Hampson, *Manager*
Sean McEnaney, *Manager*
EMP: 189
SALES (corp-wide): 968.2MM **Publicly Held**
SIC: **6035** Federal savings banks
HQ: Pacific Western Bank
456 Santa Monica Blvd
Santa Monica CA 90401
310 458-1521

(P-9581)
PROVIDENT SAVINGS BANK (HQ)
Also Called: Provident Bank
3756 Central Ave, Riverside (92506-2469)
P.O. Box 59998 (92517-1998)
PHONE..................951 782-6177
Fax: 951 782-6126
Craig G Blunden, *Ch of Bd*
Donavon Ternes, *President*
Lee Sunarto, *Treasurer*
David S Weiant,
Candice Rabe, *Officer*
EMP: 69
SALES: 73.1MM **Publicly Held**
WEB: www.myprovident.com
SIC: **6035** Federal savings & loan associations

(P-9582)
PROVIDENT SAVINGS BANK
Also Called: Provident Bank
6674 Brockton Ave, Riverside (92506-3020)
PHONE..................951 686-6060
Fax: 951 782-6123
Pam Cuthbertson, *Manager*
Darrell Rainwater, *Administration*
EMP: 100 **Publicly Held**
SIC: **6035** Federal savings & loan associations
HQ: Provident Savings Bank
3756 Central Ave
Riverside CA 92506
951 782-6177

6035 - Federal Savings Institutions County (P-9583)

(P-9583)
UNIVERSAL BANK (PA)
3455 S Nogales St Fl 2, West Covina (91792-5106)
PHONE.....................626 854-2818
Fax: 626 854-2838
Frank Chang, *President*
Dwayne Matsuda, *President*
Sarita Ezrol, *Vice Pres*
Edgar Gatchlian, *Vice Pres*
Guy Krikorian, *Vice Pres*
EMP: 53
SQ FT: 28,223
SALES: 12.2MM **Privately Held**
WEB: www.universalbank.com
SIC: 6035 Federal savings banks

6036 Savings Institutions, Except Federal

(P-9584)
EAST WEST BANK
228 W Garvey Ave, Monterey Park (91754-1603)
PHONE.....................626 280-1688
John Lee, *Branch Mgr*
Joe Yuan, *Vice Pres*
EMP: 61
SALES (corp-wide): 1.2B **Publicly Held**
WEB: www.eastwest.com
SIC: 6036 Savings & loan associations, not federally chartered
HQ: East West Bank
   135 N Ls Rbls Ave 100
   Pasadena CA 91101
   626 768-6000

(P-9585)
EXCHANGE BANK (HQ)
Also Called: Eb
440 Aviation Blvd, Santa Rosa (95403-1069)
P.O. Box 403 (95402-0403)
PHONE.....................707 524-3000
Fax: 707 524-3065
Gary T Hartwick, *CEO*
C William Reinking, *Ch of Bd*
Linda Burille, *President*
Jane Daniel, *President*
Pam Maslak, *President*
EMP: 135
SQ FT: 50,000
SALES: 87.3MM
SALES (corp-wide): 38.2MM **Privately Held**
WEB: www.exchangebank.com
SIC: 6036 8741 6022 State savings banks, not federally chartered; management services; state commercial banks

(P-9586)
LUTHER BURBANK SAVINGS CORP (HQ)
500 3rd St, Santa Rosa (95401-6321)
P.O. Box 1783 (95402-1783)
PHONE.....................707 578-9216
Fax: 707 526-7844
John Biggs, *President*
Tom Batson, *Senior Partner*
Victor S Trione, *Ch of Bd*
David Thomas, *Officer*
Susan Allison, *Exec VP*
EMP: 50
SQ FT: 11,000
SALES: 134.9MM **Privately Held**
WEB: www.lutherburbanksavings.com
SIC: 6036 6035 Savings & loan associations, not federally chartered; federal savings & loan associations
PA: Luther Burbank Corporation
   520 3rd St Fl 4
   Santa Rosa CA 95401
   707 523-9898

6061 Federal Credit Unions

(P-9587)
ALTAONE FEDERAL CREDIT UNION (PA)
Also Called: ALTA ONE FCU
701 S China Lake Blvd, Ridgecrest (93555-5027)
P.O. Box 1209 (93556-1209)
PHONE.....................760 371-7000
Fax: 760 614-2304
Robert M Boland, *President*
George M Haslam, *CFO*
Corinna Korpi, *Branch Mgr*
Linda Fisher, *Office Mgr*
Kirsten Ortiz, *Finance Dir*
EMP: 114
SQ FT: 33,000
SALES: 25.8MM **Privately Held**
WEB: www.altaone.net
SIC: 6061 Federal credit unions

(P-9588)
AMERICAN FIRST CREDIT UNION (PA)
700 N Harbor Blvd, La Habra (90631-4000)
PHONE.....................562 691-1112
Fax: 562 691-1021
Jon Shigematsu, *CFO*
Brian Thompson,
EMP: 96
SQ FT: 10,000
SALES: 15.1MM **Privately Held**
SIC: 6061 Federal credit unions

(P-9589)
ARROWHEAD CENTRAL CREDIT UNION (PA)
550 E Hospitality Ln # 200, San Bernardino (92408-4205)
P.O. Box 735 (92402-0735)
PHONE.....................866 212-4333
Fax: 909 338-7263
Darin Woinarowicz, *CEO*
Raymond Mesler, *CFO*
Marie A Alonzo, *Chairman*
Doug Hallen, *Treasurer*
Susan Conjurski, *Exec VP*
EMP: 301
SQ FT: 40,000
SALES: 28.8MM **Privately Held**
SIC: 6061 Federal credit unions

(P-9590)
BAY FEDERAL CREDIT UNION (PA)
3333 Clares St, Capitola (95010-2564)
PHONE.....................831 479-6000
Fax: 831 423-1054
Dennis Osmer, *Chairman*
H Duane Smith, *Vice Chairman*
Rick Weiss, *CFO*
Michael Leung, *Treasurer*
Diane Lipska, *Vice Pres*
EMP: 70
SALES: 26MM **Privately Held**
WEB: www.bayfed.com
SIC: 6061 Federal credit unions

(P-9591)
COAST CENTRAL CREDIT UNION (PA)
2650 Harrison Ave, Eureka (95501-3223)
PHONE.....................707 445-8801
Fax: 707 442-2532
Dean Christensen, *President*
Tom Noonan, *Treasurer*
Philip Petro, *Officer*
Ed Christians, *Vice Pres*
Ches Meierding, *Vice Pres*
EMP: 65 EST: 1932
SQ FT: 17,000
SALES: 29.5MM **Privately Held**
WEB: www.coastccu.org
SIC: 6061 Federal credit unions

(P-9592)
CREDIT UNION SOUTHERN CAL (PA)
8028 Greenleaf Ave, Whittier (90602-2109)
P.O. Box 200 (90608-0200)
PHONE.....................562 698-8326
Fax: 562 331-6423

Dave Gunderson, *President*
Ed Fost, *COO*
Peter Putnam, *CFO*
Jim Holden, *Assoc VP*
Cathey Jones, *Assoc VP*
EMP: 59
SQ FT: 12,000
SALES: 31.4MM **Privately Held**
WEB: www.cusocal.com
SIC: 6061 Federal credit unions

(P-9593)
CREDIT UNION SOUTHERN CAL
8101 E Kaiser Blvd # 300, Anaheim (92808-2261)
PHONE.....................714 671-2700
Dave Gunderson, *CEO*
John Cristopolous, *Exec VP*
EMP: 116
SALES (corp-wide): 31.4MM **Privately Held**
WEB: www.cusocal.com
SIC: 6061 Federal credit unions
PA: Credit Union Of Southern California
   8028 Greenleaf Ave
   Whittier CA 90602
   562 698-8326

(P-9594)
F & A FEDERAL CREDIT UNION
2625 Corporate Pl, Monterey Park (91754-7645)
P.O. Box 30831, Los Angeles (90030-0831)
PHONE.....................323 268-1226
Fax: 323 268-1608
Richard Andrews, *President*
Rene McLean, *Officer*
Janet Wong, *Officer*
Michael Harden, *Vice Pres*
Gail Yarbrough, *Vice Pres*
EMP: 70
SQ FT: 43,000
SALES: 36.4MM **Privately Held**
WEB: www.fafcu.net
SIC: 6061 Federal credit unions

(P-9595)
FARMERS INSURANCE FED CRED UNI (PA)
4601 Wilshire Blvd # 110, Los Angeles (90010-3880)
P.O. Box 36911 (90036-0911)
PHONE.....................323 209-6000
Fax: 323 930-3467
Mark Herter, *CEO*
Laszlo Haredy, *Chairman*
Micah Bouloy, *Officer*
Laura Campbell, *Exec VP*
Roy Smith, *Senior VP*
EMP: 70
SQ FT: 12,000
SALES: 34.1MM **Privately Held**
WEB: www.figfederalcu.com
SIC: 6061 Federal credit unions

(P-9596)
FINANCIAL PARTNERS CREDIT UN (PA)
7800 Imperial Hwy, Downey (90242-3457)
P.O. Box 7005 (90241-7005)
PHONE.....................562 904-3000
Fax: 562 904-4285
John Crites, *Ch of Bd*
Nader Moghaddam, *President*
Don Plog, *Treasurer*
Pam Ellens, *Officer*
Jorge Gonzalez, *Officer*
EMP: 73
SQ FT: 32,000
SALES: 33.6MM **Privately Held**
WEB: www.fpcu.org
SIC: 6061 Federal credit unions

(P-9597)
FIRST CITY CREDIT UNION (PA)
717 W Temple St Ste 400, Los Angeles (90012-2632)
P.O. Box 86008 (90086-0008)
PHONE.....................213 482-3477
Fax: 213 246-0860
James D Likens, *Ch of Bd*
Steve Punch, *CEO*
Terry O'Steen, *COO*
Richard Reese, *CFO*
Robert Ciulik, *Treasurer*
EMP: 50

SQ FT: 24,896
SALES: 19.9MM **Privately Held**
SIC: 6061 Federal credit unions

(P-9598)
FIRST ENTERTAINMENT CREDIT UN (PA)
6735 Forest Lawn Dr # 100, Los Angeles (90068-1055)
P.O. Box 100 (90078-0100)
PHONE.....................323 851-3673
Charles A Bruen, *President*
Lucy Wander-Perna, *Ch of Bd*
Lisa Landt, *CFO*
Irwin Jacobson, *Treasurer*
Dennis Tange, *Admin Sec*
EMP: 80 EST: 1998
SQ FT: 57,000
SALES: 33.3MM **Privately Held**
SIC: 6061 Federal credit unions

(P-9599)
FIRST FINANCIAL CREDIT UNION (PA)
1600 W Cameron Ave, West Covina (91790-2714)
P.O. Box 90 (91793-0090)
PHONE.....................626 814-4611
Fax: 626 337-3588
Dietmar Hsuech, *President*
Dietmar Huesch, *CFO*
Sandra Sarabia, *Vice Pres*
Suyen Campos, *Executive*
Sherryl Espanto, *Executive Asst*
EMP: 180
SQ FT: 35,000
SALES: 19.4MM **Privately Held**
SIC: 6061 Federal credit unions

(P-9600)
FIRST TECHNOLOGY FEDERAL CR UN (PA)
1335 Terra Bella Ave, Mountain View (94043-1835)
PHONE.....................855 855-8805
Greg A Mitchell, *President*
Scott Jenner, *President*
Hank Sigmon, *CFO*
Monique Little,
Brooke Vanvleet, *Exec VP*
EMP: 72
SALES: 336.3MM **Privately Held**
WEB: www.1sttech.com
SIC: 6061 Federal credit unions

(P-9601)
FIRST TECHNOLOGY FEDERAL CR UN
1011 Sunset Blvd Ste 210, Rocklin (95765-3782)
PHONE.....................855 855-8805
Greg A Mitchell, *CEO*
Naveen Jain, *Director*
Noel Magana, *Manager*
EMP: 211
SALES (corp-wide): 290.5MM **Privately Held**
SIC: 6061 Federal credit unions
PA: First Technology Federal Credit Union
   1335 Terra Bella Ave
   Mountain View CA 94043
   855 855-8805

(P-9602)
FRESNO COUNTY FEDERAL CR UN (PA)
2580 W Shaw Ln Frnt, Fresno (93711-2776)
P.O. Box 8027 (93747-8027)
PHONE.....................559 252-5000
Fax: 559 252-5397
Karen B Cobb, *Ch of Bd*
Sanja Kovacevic, *Vice Chairman*
Jeff Bassill, *COO*
Karen Cobb, *CFO*
Doug Papagni, *Chairman*
EMP: 50
SQ FT: 12,000
SALES: 23.6MM **Privately Held**
WEB: www.fresnocfcu.org
SIC: 6061 Federal credit unions

PRODUCTS & SERVICES SECTION

6061 - Federal Credit Unions County (P-9625)

(P-9603)
GOLDEN 1 CREDIT UNION
1282 Stabler Ln Ste 640, Yuba City (95993-2625)
PHONE..............................877 465-3361
Choni Weigman, *Manager*
EMP: 273
SALES (corp-wide): 255.5MM **Privately Held**
SIC: 6061 Federal credit unions
PA: Golden 1 Credit Union
8945 Cal Center Dr
Sacramento CA 95826
916 732-2900

(P-9604)
HERITAGE COMMUNITY CREDIT UN (PA)
10399 Old Placerville Rd, Sacramento (95827-2506)
P.O. Box 790, Rancho Cordova (95741-0790)
PHONE..............................916 364-1700
Judy Flores, *CEO*
Celeste Martinez, *COO*
Mathew Harms, *CFO*
Brandon Ivie, *CFO*
Allan F Wisnicky, *Treasurer*
EMP: 50
SALES: 5.7MM **Privately Held**
SIC: 6061 Federal credit unions

(P-9605)
HERITAGE COMMUNITY CREDIT UN
10399 Old Clasaville Rd, Rancho Cordova (95670)
PHONE..............................916 364-1700
Steve Pogemiller, *Branch Mgr*
Diane Walton, *Executive*
EMP: 50
SALES (corp-wide): 5.7MM **Privately Held**
SIC: 6061 Federal credit unions
PA: Heritage Community Credit Union
10399 Old Placerville Rd
Sacramento CA 95827
916 364-1700

(P-9606)
KERN FEDERAL CREDIT UNION
1717 Truxtun Ave, Bakersfield (93301-5102)
PHONE..............................661 327-9461
Fax: 661 327-2646
Brandon Ivie, *CEO*
Brenda O'Doherty, *President*
Shirley Sanchez, *Officer*
Linda Crosby, *Vice Pres*
George Fuentes, *Loan Officer*
EMP: 65
SQ FT: 17,000
SALES: 7.5MM **Privately Held**
WEB: www.kernfcu.org
SIC: 6061 6163 Federal credit unions; loan brokers

(P-9607)
KERN SCHOOLS FEDERAL CREDIT UN (PA)
Also Called: Ksfcu
9500 Ming Ave, Bakersfield (93311-1364)
P.O. Box 9506 (93389-9506)
PHONE..............................661 833-7900
Fax: 661 833-7989
Stephen P Renock IV, *President*
Neil Marshall, *CFO*
Scott Begin, *Bd of Directors*
Penny Fulton, *Senior VP*
Erin Hodson, *Branch Mgr*
EMP: 60
SQ FT: 18,000
SALES: 38.3MM **Privately Held**
WEB: www.ksfcu.com
SIC: 6061 Federal credit unions

(P-9608)
KINECTA FEDERAL CREDIT UNION (PA)
1440 Rosecrans Ave, Manhattan Beach (90266-3702)
PHONE..............................310 643-5400
Fax: 310 643-8350
Keith Sultemeier, *CEO*
Randall G Dotemoto, *President*

Douglas C Wicks, *President*
Steve Lumm, *CEO*
Joseph E Whitaker, *COO*
EMP: 250
SQ FT: 80,000
SALES: 131MM **Privately Held**
SIC: 6061 Federal credit unions

(P-9609)
LOGIX FEDERAL CREDIT UNION
10324 Mason Ave, Chatsworth (91311-3305)
PHONE..............................818 709-3896
EMP: 66
SALES (corp-wide): 143.6MM **Privately Held**
SIC: 6061 Federal credit unions
PA: Logix Federal Credit Union
2340 N Hollywood Way
Burbank CA 91505
888 718-5328

(P-9610)
LOGIX FEDERAL CREDIT UNION (PA)
2340 N Hollywood Way, Burbank (91505-1124)
P.O. Box 10249 (91510-0249)
PHONE..............................888 718-5328
Fax: 818 563-2927
David Styler, *President*
Dave Styler, *COO*
Ana Fonseca, *CFO*
Sean Brown, *Officer*
Jesse Burk, *Officer*
EMP: 210
SQ FT: 75,000
SALES: 143.6MM **Privately Held**
SIC: 6061 Federal credit unions

(P-9611)
LOS ANGELES FEDERAL CREDIT UN (PA)
300 S Glendale Ave # 100, Glendale (91205-1752)
PHONE..............................818 242-8640
Fax: 818 242-5724
John T DEA, *CEO*
Richard Lie, *CFO*
Anthony Cuevas, *Senior VP*
Leta Cook, *Vice Pres*
Art Sookazian, *Vice Pres*
EMP: 100
SQ FT: 40,000
SALES: 26.3MM **Privately Held**
SIC: 6061 Federal credit unions

(P-9612)
MERCED SCHOOL EMPLOYEES F C U (PA)
Also Called: MSEFCU
1021 Olivewood Dr, Merced (95348-1218)
P.O. Box 1349 (95341-1349)
PHONE..............................209 383-5550
Fax: 209 383-2308
Nancy Deavours, *President*
Lori Smith, *Vice Pres*
Katherine Reid, *CIO*
EMP: 52 **EST:** 1954
SQ FT: 16,500
SALES: 11.2MM **Privately Held**
WEB: www.mercedschoolcu.org
SIC: 6061 Federal credit unions

(P-9613)
MERIWEST CREDIT UNION (PA)
5615 Chesbro Ave Ste 100, San Jose (95123-3057)
P.O. Box 530953 (95153-5353)
PHONE..............................408 363-3200
Toll Free:..............................877 -
Julie A Kirsch, *CEO*
Steven G Johnson, *CEO*
Christopher Owen, *CEO*
Brian Hennessey, *CFO*
Hudson Lee, *CFO*
EMP: 130
SQ FT: 61,000
SALES: 32.8MM **Privately Held**
WEB: www.meriwest.com
SIC: 6061 Federal credit unions

(P-9614)
MISSION FEDERAL SERVICES LLC (PA)
5785 Oberlin Dr Ste 333, San Diego (92121-3752)
P.O. Box 919023 (92191-9023)
PHONE..............................800 500-6328
Fax: 858 524-2891
Debra Schwartz, *CEO*
Rose Hartley, *COO*
Peter Sainato, *CFO*
Gary M Devan, *Senior VP*
Richard Hartley, *Senior VP*
EMP: 150
SQ FT: 55,000
SALES: 74MM **Privately Held**
WEB: www.missionfcu.com
SIC: 6061 Federal credit unions

(P-9615)
MOCSE FEDERAL CREDIT UNION
3600 Coffee Rd, Modesto (95355-1164)
PHONE..............................209 572-3600
Fax: 209 572-1714
Tracey Kerr, *President*
Charlie Rodgers, *CEO*
Justin Garcia, *Technical Staff*
Kathryn Dougherty, *Hum Res Coord*
Donna David, *Marketing Mgr*
EMP: 82
SQ FT: 20,000
SALES: 5.5MM **Privately Held**
WEB: www.mocse.org
SIC: 6061 6062 Federal credit unions; state credit unions

(P-9616)
NAVY FEDERAL CREDIT UNION
2040 Harbison Dr, Vacaville (95687-3906)
PHONE..............................888 842-6328
Patsy Vanouwerkerk, *Branch Mgr*
EMP: 122
SALES (corp-wide): 3.6B **Privately Held**
SIC: 6061 Federal credit unions
PA: Navy Federal Credit Union
820 Follin Ln Se
Vienna VA 22180
703 255-8000

(P-9617)
NORTHROP GRUMMAN FEDERAL CR UN (PA)
879 W 190th St Ste 800, Gardena (90248-4205)
PHONE..............................310 808-4000
Fax: 310 808-9697
Stanley R Swenson Jr, *President*
Kathi Harper, *Chairman*
Rochelle Hazzard, *Officer*
Georgetta A Wolff, *Vice Pres*
Pam Kings, *Executive Asst*
EMP: 60
SALES: 28.6MM **Privately Held**
SIC: 6061 Federal credit unions

(P-9618)
OPERATING ENGNEERS LOCAL UN 3
798 N 1st St B, San Jose (95112-6302)
PHONE..............................408 995-5095
Fax: 408 995-5093
Carol Adelan, *Branch Mgr*
EMP: 73
SQ FT: 5,698
SALES (corp-wide): 19.7MM **Privately Held**
SIC: 6061 Federal credit unions
PA: Operating Engineers Local Union 3
250 N Canyons Pkwy
Livermore CA 94551
925 454-4000

(P-9619)
PACIFIC MARINE CREDIT UNION (PA)
1278 Rocky Point Dr, Oceanside (92056-5867)
PHONE..............................760 430-7511
David L Davis, *CEO*
P R Hoffman, *COO*
Michelle Denton, *CFO*
Carrie Foster, *CFO*
Nancy Harvey, *Officer*
EMP: 107

SQ FT: 22,000
SALES: 20.8MM **Privately Held**
WEB: www.pmcu.com
SIC: 6061 Federal credit unions

(P-9620)
PATELCO CREDIT UNION
310 Hartz Ave, Danville (94526-3308)
PHONE..............................925 785-9487
EMP: 85
SALES (corp-wide): 128.6MM **Privately Held**
SIC: 6061 Federal credit unions
PA: Patelco Credit Union
5050 Hopyard Rd
Pleasanton CA 94588
800 358-8228

(P-9621)
PATELCO CREDIT UNION (PA)
5050 Hopyard Rd, Pleasanton (94588-3353)
P.O. Box 8020 (94588-8601)
PHONE..............................800 358-8228
Fax: 415 442-7193
Erin Mendez, *CEO*
Sue Gruber, *CFO*
Kenn D Darling, *Ch Credit Ofcr*
Alison Jones, *Senior VP*
Martin Doyle, *Vice Pres*
EMP: 250
SQ FT: 36,000
SALES: 128.6MM **Privately Held**
WEB: www.patelco.org
SIC: 6061 Federal credit unions

(P-9622)
SAG- AFTRA FEDERAL
134 N Kenwood St, Burbank (91505-4201)
P.O. Box 11419 (91510-1419)
PHONE..............................818 562-3400
Fax: 818 937-9135
Randy Kahn, *Chairman*
Sid Henderson, *President*
Roger Runyan, *CEO*
Jose Rodriguez, *CFO*
Phillip Weiss, *Vice Pres*
EMP: 52
SQ FT: 5,500
SALES: 5.2MM **Privately Held**
SIC: 6061 Federal credit unions

(P-9623)
SANTA CLARA CNTY FDERAL CR UN (PA)
1641 N 1st St Ste 245, San Jose (95112-4519)
PHONE..............................408 282-0700
Fax: 408 287-8687
Mike Delmonico, *CEO*
Angela Hughes, *Business Dir*
EMP: 55 **EST:** 1950
SQ FT: 42,000
SALES: 19.5MM **Privately Held**
SIC: 6061 Federal credit unions

(P-9624)
SCE FEDERAL CREDIT UNION (PA)
Also Called: SCE FCU
12701 Schabarum Ave, Baldwin Park (91706-6807)
P.O. Box 8017, El Monte (91734-2317)
PHONE..............................626 960-6888
Dennis Huber, *CEO*
George Poitou, *COO*
Daniel Rader, *CFO*
Linda Renaud, *Info Tech Dir*
Mike N Gardner, *IT/INT Sup*
EMP: 90 **EST:** 1952
SQ FT: 30,000
SALES: 23.4MM **Privately Held**
WEB: www.scefcu.org
SIC: 6061 Federal credit unions

(P-9625)
SCHOOLSFIRST FEDERAL CREDIT UN (PA)
2115 N Broadway, Santa Ana (92706-2613)
P.O. Box 11547 (92711-1547)
PHONE..............................714 258-4000
Bill Cheney, *President*
Kary Bemoll, *Vice Chairman*
Francisco Nebot, *CFO*

6061 - Federal Credit Unions County (P-9626)

Martha Monzon, *Exec VP*
Emilio Arenas, *Vice Pres*
EMP: 270
SALES: 316.9MM **Privately Held**
SIC: 6061 Federal credit unions

(P-9626)
SESLOC FEDERAL CREDIT UNION (PA)
11491 Los Osos Valley Rd, San Luis Obispo (93405-6428)
P.O. Box 5360 (93403-5360)
PHONE.................805 543-1816
Fax: 805 546-9622
Bertha Foxford, *President*
Shaun Edrington, *Officer*
Andy Bechinsky, *Senior VP*
Kelli Fite, *Senior VP*
Micki Myall, *Vice Pres*
EMP: 77
SQ FT: 19,700
SALES: 17.1MM **Privately Held**
WEB: www.sesloc.com
SIC: 6061 Federal credit unions

(P-9627)
SKYONE FEDERAL CREDIT UNION (PA)
14600 Aviation Blvd, Hawthorne (90250-6656)
P.O. Box 5003 (90251-5003)
PHONE.................310 491-7500
Eileen C Rivera, *CEO*
Chris Evans, *CFO*
Douglas Murphy, *Treasurer*
Armando Gonzalez, *Vice Pres*
Lourdes Ruano, *Vice Pres*
EMP: 58
SQ FT: 40,000
SALES: 14.4MM **Privately Held**
SIC: 6061 Federal credit unions

(P-9628)
SPECTRUM CREDIT UNION
500 12th St Ste 200, Oakland (94607-4084)
PHONE.................510 251-6000
Jim Mooney, *CEO*
EMP: 200
SALES (est): 10.4MM **Privately Held**
SIC: 6061 Federal credit unions

(P-9629)
STANFORD FEDERAL CREDIT UNION (PA)
Also Called: Sfcu
1860 Embarcadero Rd # 200, Palo Alto (94303-3320)
P.O. Box 10690 (94303-0843)
PHONE.................650 725-1000
Jane S Duperrault, *Ch of Bd*
Tana Hutchison, *Treasurer*
Brian Thornton, *Vice Pres*
Jerry L Jobe, *Admin Sec*
Albert Finn, *HR Admin*
EMP: 61
SALES: 51.9MM **Privately Held**
SIC: 6061 Federal credit unions

(P-9630)
STAR ONE CREDIT UNION (PA)
1306 Bordeaux Dr, Sunnyvale (94089-1005)
P.O. Box 3643 (94088-3643)
PHONE.................408 543-5202
Fax: 408 543-5203
Rick Heldebrant, *President*
Dan Abihider, *Vice Chairman*
Bonnie Kramer, *COO*
Scott Dunlap, *CFO*
Brian Ross, *Treasurer*
EMP: 107
SQ FT: 25,000
SALES: 165.6MM **Privately Held**
SIC: 6061 Federal credit unions

(P-9631)
TELESIS COMMUNITY CREDIT UNION (PA)
9301 Winnetka Ave, Chatsworth (91311-6069)
PHONE.................818 885-1226
Grace Mayo, *President*
Jean Faenza, *Exec VP*
Marnie Holt, *Technology*

Teddie McKay, *Marketing Staff*
EMP: 90
SQ FT: 17,000
SALES: 14.9MM **Privately Held**
SIC: 6061 6163 Federal credit unions; loan brokers

(P-9632)
TRAVIS CREDIT UNION
1300 E Covell Blvd, Davis (95616-1300)
PHONE.................707 449-4000
EMP: 500
SALES (corp-wide): 87.8MM **Privately Held**
SIC: 6061 6062 Federal credit unions; state credit unions
PA: Travis Credit Union
1 Travis Way
Vacaville CA 95687
707 449-4000

(P-9633)
TRAVIS CREDIT UNION
1796 Tuolumne St, Vallejo (94589-2619)
PHONE.................800 877-8328
EMP: 500
SALES (corp-wide): 87.8MM **Privately Held**
SIC: 6061 6022 6021 6029 Federal credit unions; state commercial banks; national commercial banks; commercial banks
PA: Travis Credit Union
1 Travis Way
Vacaville CA 95687
707 449-4000

(P-9634)
TRAVIS CREDIT UNION
1257 Willow Pass Rd, Concord (94520-5218)
PHONE.................800 877-8328
Travis Credit, *Owner*
EMP: 500
SALES (corp-wide): 87.8MM **Privately Held**
SIC: 6061 6062 Federal credit unions; state credit unions
PA: Travis Credit Union
1 Travis Way
Vacaville CA 95687
707 449-4000

(P-9635)
TRAVIS CREDIT UNION
3263 Claremont Way, NAPA (94558-3313)
PHONE.................800 877-8328
Marlene Myers, *Branch Mgr*
EMP: 500
SALES (corp-wide): 87.8MM **Privately Held**
SIC: 6061 6022 6029 Federal credit unions; state commercial banks; commercial banks
PA: Travis Credit Union
1 Travis Way
Vacaville CA 95687
707 449-4000

(P-9636)
TRAVIS CREDIT UNION (PA)
1 Travis Way, Vacaville (95687-3276)
P.O. Box 2069 (95696-2069)
PHONE.................707 449-4000
Fax: 707 449-1817
Patsy Vanouwerkerk, *CEO*
Stacey Meyers, *Branch Mgr*
Steve Vlach, *Branch Mgr*
Patty Altaffer, *Admin Asst*
Steven Straubel, *Admin Asst*
EMP: 300
SQ FT: 12,000
SALES: 87.8MM **Privately Held**
SIC: 6061 Federal credit unions

(P-9637)
TRAVIS CREDIT UNION
1515 K St, Sacramento (95814-4051)
PHONE.................916 443-1446
Richard Schnabel, *Accountant*
EMP: 500
SALES (corp-wide): 87.8MM **Privately Held**
SIC: 6061 Federal credit unions

PA: Travis Credit Union
1 Travis Way
Vacaville CA 95687
707 449-4000

(P-9638)
TRAVIS CREDIT UNION
1194 W Olive Ave, Merced (95348-1952)
PHONE.................209 723-0732
Fax: 209 723-7509
Patsy Vanouwerkerk, *CEO*
EMP: 500
SALES (corp-wide): 87.8MM **Privately Held**
SIC: 6061 Federal credit unions
PA: Travis Credit Union
1 Travis Way
Vacaville CA 95687
707 449-4000

(P-9639)
TRAVIS CREDIT UNION
5819 Lone Tree Way Ste A, Antioch (94531-8602)
PHONE.................925 777-0573
Helen Raoufian, *Branch Mgr*
EMP: 500
SALES (corp-wide): 87.8MM **Privately Held**
SIC: 6061 6062 Federal credit unions; state credit unions
PA: Travis Credit Union
1 Travis Way
Vacaville CA 95687
707 449-4000

(P-9640)
TRAVIS CREDIT UNION
11 Cernon St, Vacaville (95688-2803)
PHONE.................707 449-4000
Fax: 707 449-9566
Phil Christiansen, *Manager*
Marianne Walker, *Office Mgr*
Cathy Dovi, *Administration*
EMP: 500
SALES (corp-wide): 87.8MM **Privately Held**
SIC: 6061 Federal credit unions
PA: Travis Credit Union
1 Travis Way
Vacaville CA 95687
707 449-4000

(P-9641)
TRAVIS CREDIT UNION
2570 N Texas St, Fairfield (94533-1606)
PHONE.................707 449-4000
Fax: 707 425-5361
Gloria Niccoli, *Manager*
John Anderson, *Manager*
EMP: 500
SALES (corp-wide): 87.8MM **Privately Held**
SIC: 6061 Federal credit unions
PA: Travis Credit Union
1 Travis Way
Vacaville CA 95687
707 449-4000

(P-9642)
TRAVIS CREDIT UNION
1372 E Main St, Woodland (95776-3551)
PHONE.................800 877-8328
Jason Braga, *Manager*
EMP: 500
SALES (corp-wide): 87.8MM **Privately Held**
SIC: 6061 6022 6021 6029 Federal credit unions; state commercial banks; national commercial banks; commercial banks
PA: Travis Credit Union
1 Travis Way
Vacaville CA 95687
707 449-4000

(P-9643)
TRAVIS CREDIT UNION
2020 Harbison Dr, Vacaville (95687-3910)
PHONE.................707 449-4000
Fax: 707 451-5197
Cathy Redman, *Branch Mgr*
Craig Beaudry, *Assoc VP*
David Purcell, *Vice Pres*
Prasad More, *Exec Dir*
Brent Leuschen, *Branch Mgr*

EMP: 500
SALES (corp-wide): 87.8MM **Privately Held**
SIC: 6061 Federal credit unions
PA: Travis Credit Union
1 Travis Way
Vacaville CA 95687
707 449-4000

(P-9644)
TUCOEMAS FEDERAL CREDIT UNION
2300 W Whitendale Ave, Visalia (93277-6131)
P.O. Box 5011 (93278-5011)
PHONE.................559 429-7094
Fax: 559 737-5934
John McHarry, *Manager*
Mark Amaral, *Technology*
Debra Davenport, *Marketing Mgr*
Jackie Benson, *Manager*
EMP: 54
SQ FT: 19,413
SALES (corp-wide): 6MM **Privately Held**
SIC: 6061 Federal credit unions
PA: Tucoemas Federal Credit Union
5222 W Cypress Ave
Visalia CA 93277
559 737-5900

(P-9645)
UNIFY FINANCIAL FEDERAL CR UN (PA)
1899 Western Way Ste 100, Torrance (90501-1146)
P.O. Box 10018, Manhattan Beach (90267-7518)
PHONE.................310 536-5000
Gordon M Howe, *Principal*
Gordon Howe, *COO*
Scott Johnson, *Vice Pres*
Jonathan Oliver, *Vice Pres*
Stephen Kewley, *Branch Mgr*
EMP: 80 **EST:** 1958
SALES: 83.2MM **Privately Held**
WEB: www.western.org
SIC: 6061 Federal credit unions

(P-9646)
UNITED SVCS AMER FEDERAL CR UN (PA)
Also Called: USA Federal Credit Union
9999 Willow Creek Rd, San Diego (92131-1117)
P.O. Box 26339 (92196-0339)
PHONE.................858 831-8100
Martin Cassell, *President*
Jim Bedinger, *Vice Pres*
Ron Davis, *Vice Pres*
Cathi Gonzales, *Branch Mgr*
Doug Stocker, *Project Mgr*
EMP: 90
SQ FT: 42,000
SALES (est): 38.8MM **Privately Held**
WEB: www.usafed.org
SIC: 6061 Federal credit unions

(P-9647)
USC CREDIT UNION
1025 W 34th St, Los Angeles (90089-0093)
P.O. Box 2718 (90051-0718)
PHONE.................213 821-7100
Fax: 213 740-8763
Gary J Perez, *President*
Ralph Ramirez, *COO*
Christine Schwarz, *Vice Pres*
Debra Castro, *Finance*
Lucia Mirich, *Finance*
EMP: 56
SQ FT: 4,000
SALES: 11.2MM **Privately Held**
SIC: 6061 Federal credit unions

(P-9648)
XCEED FINANCIAL CREDIT UNION (PA)
888 N Nash St, El Segundo (90245-2826)
PHONE.................800 932-8222
Teresa Freeborn, *President*
Vincent Dudziak, *Officer*
Beth Castelo, *Vice Pres*
Courtnay Lynch, *Vice Pres*
Kelly Karshner, *District Mgr*
EMP: 96
SQ FT: 30,000

PRODUCTS & SERVICES SECTION
6062 - State Credit Unions County (P-9669)

SALES: 30.9MM **Privately Held**
WEB: www.xfcu.org
SIC: **6061** Federal credit unions

6062 State Credit Unions

(P-9649)
1ST UNITED SERVICES CREDIT UN (PA)
5901 Gibraltar Dr, Pleasanton (94588-2718)
P.O. Box 11746 (94588-1746)
PHONE..................800 649-0193
Fax: 925 463-1290
Victor Quint, *President*
Shirley Sifuentes, *COO*
Victoria Pipkin, *CFO*
Steve Stone,
Anne Kenny, *Senior VP*
EMP: 60
SQ FT: 20,000
SALES: 25.7MM **Privately Held**
SIC: **6062** State credit unions, not federally chartered

(P-9650)
ALLIANCE CREDIT UNION (PA)
3315 Almaden Expy Ste 55, San Jose (95118-1557)
P.O. Box 18460 (95158-8460)
PHONE..................408 445-3386
Fax: 408 445-9327
Eileen M Lewis, *President*
Brian Dorcy, *CFO*
Tracy Patel, *Treasurer*
Ram Misra, *Bd of Directors*
Bruce Fox, *Vice Pres*
EMP: 73
SQ FT: 40,000
SALES: 11.8MM **Privately Held**
SIC: **6062** State credit unions

(P-9651)
ALTURA CREDIT UNION (PA)
2847 Campus Pkwy, Riverside (92507-0906)
PHONE..................888 883-7228
Toll Free:......................888 -
Mark Hawkins, *President*
Erik Grier, *President*
Diana Wilcox, *CFO*
Keith Downs, *Treasurer*
Stephany Redmond, *Treasurer*
EMP: 59
SQ FT: 60,000
SALES: 28.7MM **Privately Held**
SIC: **6062** State credit unions

(P-9652)
AMERICAS CHRISTIAN CREDIT UN (PA)
Also Called: ACCU
2100 E Route 66 Ste 100, Glendora (91740-4623)
P.O. Box 5100 (91740-0808)
PHONE..................626 208-5400
Fax: 626 208-5563
Mendell Thompson, *President*
Naomi Paris, *Officer*
Nicolette Harms, *Senior VP*
Terri Snyder, *Senior VP*
Linda Hartounian, *Pharmacy Dir*
EMP: 61 EST: 1958
SQ FT: 22,000
SALES: 12.8MM **Privately Held**
SIC: **6062** State credit unions, not federally chartered

(P-9653)
BAY AREA CREDIT SERVICE LLC
10562 Caminito Flores, San Diego (92126-2804)
PHONE..................858 653-3824
Roy Reese, *Principal*
EMP: 450
SALES (corp-wide): 27MM **Privately Held**
WEB: www.bayareacredit.com
SIC: **6062** State credit unions
PA: Bay Area Credit Service, Llc
    1901 W 10th St
    Antioch CA 94509
    408 392-4425

(P-9654)
CALIFORNIA COAST CREDIT UNION (PA)
9201 Spectrum Center Blvd # 300, San Diego (92123-1407)
P.O. Box 502080 (92150-2080)
PHONE..................858 495-1600
Fax: 619 426-8761
Marla Shepard, *CEO*
Ruth Peshkoff, *Ch of Bd*
Robert Michaels, *Vice Ch Bd*
Carol Walker, *Senior VP*
Charles Wallace, *Vice Pres*
EMP: 74
SALES: 54.6MM **Privately Held**
WEB: www.calcoastcu.org
SIC: **6062** **6163** State credit unions, not federally chartered; loan brokers

(P-9655)
CALIFORNIA COAST CREDIT UNION
5890 Pcf Ctr Blvd Frnt, San Diego (92121)
PHONE..................858 495-1600
Alan Carithers, *Branch Mgr*
EMP: 145
SALES (corp-wide): 54.6MM **Privately Held**
SIC: **6062** State credit unions
PA: California Coast Credit Union
    9201 Spectrum Center Blvd # 300
    San Diego CA 92123
    858 495-1600

(P-9656)
CALIFORNIA COAST CREDIT UNION
8131 Allison Ave, La Mesa (91942-5523)
P.O. Box 502080, San Diego (92150-2080)
PHONE..................858 495-1600
Gail Lillie, *Branch Mgr*
Janette Costello, *General Mgr*
EMP: 55
SALES (corp-wide): 54.6MM **Privately Held**
WEB: www.calcoastcu.org
SIC: **6062** State credit unions
PA: California Coast Credit Union
    9201 Spectrum Center Blvd # 300
    San Diego CA 92123
    858 495-1600

(P-9657)
CALIFORNIA CREDIT UNION (PA)
701 N Brand Blvd Ste 100, Glendale (91203-4231)
P.O. Box 29100 (91209-9100)
PHONE..................818 291-6700
Robert Alm, *Ch of Bd*
Jason Pugh, *President*
Ronald L McDaniel, *CEO*
Mark Lovewell, *CFO*
Teresa Harvey, *Sr Corp Ofcr*
EMP: 120
SALES: 47.1MM **Privately Held**
WEB: www.californiacu.org
SIC: **6062** **6061** State credit unions, not federally chartered; federal credit unions

(P-9658)
CALTECH EMPLYEES FEDERAL CR UN
Also Called: CALTECH EFCU
528 Foothill Blvd, La Canada Flintridge (91011-3506)
P.O. Box 11001 (91012-6001)
PHONE..................818 952-4444
Richard Harris, *Principal*
Stephen L Proia, *Ch of Bd*
Richard L Harris, *President*
John Meeker, *CFO*
Willis Chapman, *Vice Ch Bd*
EMP: 64
SALES: 32.3MM **Privately Held**
WEB: www.caltech.edu
SIC: **6062** State credit unions

(P-9659)
CHRISTIAN COMMUNITY CREDIT UN (PA)
255 N Lone Hill Ave, San Dimas (91773-2308)
P.O. Box 3012, Covina (91722-9012)
PHONE..................626 915-7551
John T Walling, *President*
Jeremy Brown, *Officer*
David Estridge, *Exec VP*
Scott J Reitsma, *Senior VP*
Scott Reitsma, *Senior VP*
EMP: 70
SQ FT: 24,000
SALES: 30.1MM **Privately Held**
WEB: www.christiancommunitycu.com
SIC: **6062** State credit unions, not federally chartered

(P-9660)
COASTHILLS CREDIT UNION (PA)
Also Called: CSCU
3880 Constellation Rd, Lompoc (93436-1404)
P.O. Box 200 (93438-0200)
PHONE..................805 733-7600
Jeff York, *President*
Sandra Pickles, *Officer*
John Ruckman, *Officer*
Bruce Altheide, *Vice Pres*
Marty Chatham, *Vice Pres*
EMP: 80
SQ FT: 30,000
SALES: 34.6MM **Privately Held**
WEB: www.coasthillsfederalcreditunion.com
SIC: **6062** State credit unions

(P-9661)
COMMONWEALTH CENTRAL CREDIT UN (PA)
5890 Silver Creek Vly Rd, San Jose (95138-1027)
P.O. Box 641690 (95164-1690)
PHONE..................408 531-3100
Fax: 408 531-3200
Craig Weber, *CEO*
Michael F Filice Jr, *Vice Chairman*
Harold Deguzman, *Senior VP*
Debbie Urban, *Loan Officer*
EMP: 69
SQ FT: 36,432
SALES: 13.9MM **Privately Held**
WEB: www.commonwealthccu.org
SIC: **6062** State credit unions, not federally chartered

(P-9662)
EDUCATIONAL EMPLOYEES CR UN (PA)
2222 W Shaw Ave, Fresno (93711-3419)
PHONE..................559 437-7700
Fax: 559 241-7343
Barbara Thomas, *Chairman*
Elizabeth Dooley, *President*
Rick Browning, *Treasurer*
Julie Mattern, *Exec VP*
Denda Matthews, *Exec VP*
EMP: 110
SQ FT: 44,000
SALES: 70.8MM **Privately Held**
SIC: **6062** State credit unions, not federally chartered

(P-9663)
EDUCATIONAL EMPLOYEES CR UN
1460 W 7th St, Hanford (93230-4938)
PHONE..................559 587-4460
Dianne Mitchell, *Owner*
EMP: 50
SALES (corp-wide): 70.8MM **Privately Held**
SIC: **6062** **6061** State credit unions, not federally chartered; federal credit unions
PA: Educational Employees Credit Union
    2222 W Shaw Ave
    Fresno CA 93711
    559 437-7700

(P-9664)
EDUCATIONAL EMPLOYEES CR UN
3488 W Shaw Ave, Fresno (93711-3216)
P.O. Box 5242 (93755-5242)
PHONE..................559 896-0222
Bruce L Barnett, *President*
Eric Hovda, *Director*
Rochelle Martin, *Director*
Carlos Romero, *Supervisor*
EMP: 80
SQ FT: 17,939
SALES (corp-wide): 70.8MM **Privately Held**
SIC: **6062** State credit unions
PA: Educational Employees Credit Union
    2222 W Shaw Ave
    Fresno CA 93711
    559 437-7700

(P-9665)
EDUCATIONAL EMPLOYEES CR UN
127 W El Portal Dr Ste A, Merced (95348-2854)
PHONE..................209 726-7421
Leslie Nazario, *Manager*
EMP: 50
SALES (corp-wide): 70.8MM **Privately Held**
SIC: **6062** State credit unions
PA: Educational Employees Credit Union
    2222 W Shaw Ave
    Fresno CA 93711
    559 437-7700

(P-9666)
EL MONTE COMMUNITY CREDIT UN
11718 Ramona Blvd, El Monte (91732-2310)
PHONE..................626 444-0501
Fax: 626 444-6961
Evamarie Reta, *President*
EMP: 87
SQ FT: 3,405
SALES: 917.4K **Privately Held**
WEB: www.emcecu.org
SIC: **6062** State credit unions

(P-9667)
EVANGELICAL CHRISTIAN CR UN
955 W Imperial Hwy, Brea (92821-3812)
PHONE..................714 671-5700
Mark G Holbrook, *Branch Mgr*
Dennis Park, *Info Tech Mgr*
EMP: 157
SALES (corp-wide): 37.2MM **Privately Held**
SIC: **6062** **6061** State credit unions, not federally chartered; federal credit unions
PA: Evangelical Christian Credit Union
    955 W Imperial Hwy # 100
    Brea CA 92821
    714 671-5700

(P-9668)
EVANGELICAL CHRISTIAN CR UN (PA)
Also Called: ECCU
955 W Imperial Hwy # 100, Brea (92821-3812)
P.O. Box 2400 (92822-2400)
PHONE..................714 671-5700
Abel Pomar, *CEO*
Mike Boblit, *Officer*
Joseph Graham, *Officer*
Robert Nolin, *Exec VP*
Susan Rushing, *Senior VP*
EMP: 101
SQ FT: 125,000
SALES: 37.2MM **Privately Held**
WEB: www.ministrypartners.net
SIC: **6062** State credit unions, not federally chartered

(P-9669)
GOLDEN 1 CREDIT UNION (PA)
8945 Cal Center Dr, Sacramento (95826-3239)
P.O. Box 15966 (95852-0966)
PHONE..................916 732-2900
Teresa Halleck, *President*
Richard Alfaro, *Officer*

6062 - State Credit Unions County (P-9670)

Adrianne Pitts, *Officer*
Tom Genessy, *Senior VP*
James Deas, *Vice Pres*
EMP: 400
SQ FT: 100,000
SALES: 255.5MM **Privately Held**
WEB: www.goldenone.com
SIC: 6062 State credit unions, not federally chartered

(P-9670)
KEYPOINT CREDIT UNION (PA)
2805 Bowers Ave Ste 105, Santa Clara (95051-0972)
PHONE 408 731-4100
T Bradford Canfield, *CEO*
Timothy M Kramer, *President*
John Herrick, *CFO*
Doug Schrock, *Vice Pres*
John Mulkerin, *CTO*
EMP: 123
SQ FT: 60,715
SALES: 33.7MM **Privately Held**
WEB: www.keypointcu.com
SIC: 6062 State credit unions

(P-9671)
KEYPOINT CREDIT UNION
2805 Bowers Ave Ste 105, Santa Clara (95051-0972)
PHONE 408 562-7011
Doug Schrock, *Branch Mgr*
EMP: 113
SALES (corp-wide): 33.7MM **Privately Held**
WEB: www.keypointcu.com
SIC: 6062 6061 State credit unions; federal credit unions
PA: Keypoint Credit Union
    2805 Bowers Ave Ste 105
    Santa Clara CA 95051
    408 731-4100

(P-9672)
LOS ANGELES POLICE CREDIT UN (PA)
Also Called: L A P F C U
16150 Sherman Way, Van Nuys (91406-3938)
P.O. Box 10188 (91410-0188)
PHONE 818 787-6520
Fax: 818 786-9508
Tyler E Izen, *Ch of Bd*
G Michael Padgett, *President*
Michael G Padgett, *CFO*
Warren D Spayth, *Treasurer*
Norma Feder-Dong, *Vice Pres*
EMP: 100
SQ FT: 30,000
SALES: 28.1MM **Privately Held**
WEB: www.lapfcu.org
SIC: 6062 6061 State credit unions; federal credit unions

(P-9673)
MONTEREY CREDIT UNION (PA)
501 E Franklin St, Monterey (93940-3077)
P.O. Box 3288 (93942-3288)
PHONE 831 647-1000
David Laredo, *Chairman*
J Stewart Fuller, *CEO*
Penprase Jim, *CFO*
Bibi Lamere, *Officer*
Leanne Moreno, *Officer*
EMP: 55
SQ FT: 10,000
SALES: 9.3MM **Privately Held**
SIC: 6062 State credit unions

(P-9674)
NORTH ISLAND FINANCIAL CR UN (PA)
Also Called: North Island Credit Union
5898 Copley Dr Ste 100, San Diego (92111-7917)
P.O. Box 85833 (92186-5833)
PHONE 619 656-6525
Fax: 619 656-4051
Steve Oconnell, *CEO*
Rebecca Collier, *Ch of Bd*
Michael Scogin, *President*
Dennis Doucette, *Treasurer*
Bill Vidano, *Exec VP*
EMP: 210
SQ FT: 85,000
SALES: 33.3MM **Privately Held**
SIC: 6062 State credit unions

(P-9675)
NUVISION FINCL FEDERAL CR UN (PA)
7812 Edinger Ave Ste 100, Huntington Beach (92647-3727)
P.O. Box 1220 (92647-1220)
PHONE 714 375-8000
Fax: 714 375-8101
Roger Ballard, *CEO*
John Afdem, *CFO*
Robert Geraci, *Treasurer*
Teri Rapp, *Ch Credit Ofcr*
Chris Clausen, *Vice Pres*
EMP: 137
SALES: 47.7MM **Privately Held**
WEB: www.nuvision.coop
SIC: 6062 State credit unions, not federally chartered

(P-9676)
ORANGE COUNTYS CREDIT UNION (PA)
1721 E Saint Andrew Pl, Santa Ana (92705-4934)
P.O. Box 11777 (92711-1777)
PHONE 714 755-5900
Fax: 714 221-2638
Shruti S Miyashiro, *President*
Dan Dillon, *Chairman*
Laura Thompson, *Senior VP*
Susan Huss, *Vice Pres*
Monica Lopez, *Vice Pres*
EMP: 157
SALES: 37.2MM **Privately Held**
SIC: 6062 State credit unions

(P-9677)
PACIFIC SERVICE CREDIT UNION (PA)
3000 Clayton Rd, Concord (94519-2731)
P.O. Box 8191, Walnut Creek (94596-8191)
PHONE 888 858-6878
Fax: 925 296-6209
Stephen R Punch, *CEO*
Jenna Lampson, *COO*
Lawrence Labonte, *CFO*
David Sena, *Chairman*
Vicki Turano, *Treasurer*
EMP: 76
SQ FT: 23,689
SALES: 25.1MM **Privately Held**
SIC: 6062 State credit unions, not federally chartered

(P-9678)
PREMIER AMERICA CREDIT UNION (PA)
19867 Prairie St Lbby, Chatsworth (91311-6504)
P.O. Box 2178 (91313-2178)
PHONE 818 772-4000
Fax: 818 772-4117
John M Merlo, *President*
Brad Cunningham, *CFO*
Catherine Frieze, *CFO*
James Anderson, *Chairman*
Jim Andersen, *Treasurer*
EMP: 135
SQ FT: 80,000
SALES: 61.4MM **Privately Held**
WEB: www.premier.org
SIC: 6062 6163 State credit unions; loan brokers

(P-9679)
PROVIDENT CREDIT UNION (PA)
303 Twin Dolphin Dr # 303, Redwood City (94065-1419)
P.O. Box 8007 (94063-0907)
PHONE 650 508-0300
Fax: 650 508-0310
Maurice Schmid, *Chairman*
Ludelle Morrow, *President*
Wayne Bunker, *CEO*
Scott Powers, *COO*
Jim Miller, *CFO*
EMP: 130
SQ FT: 150,000
SALES: 51.9MM **Privately Held**
SIC: 6062 State credit unions, not federally chartered

(P-9680)
SACRAMENTO CREDIT UNION (PA)
800 H St Ste 100, Sacramento (95814-2686)
P.O. Box 2351 (95812-2351)
PHONE 916 444-6070
Toll Free: .... 888 -
Fax: 916 446-1872
Bhavnesh Makin, *CEO*
James Batson, *CFO*
Blake Cairney, *Vice Pres*
Traci Nagasawa, *Vice Pres*
Jim Hrundas, *General Mgr*
EMP: 64
SQ FT: 39,138
SALES: 15MM **Privately Held**
WEB: www.sactocu.org
SIC: 6062 6163 State credit unions; loan brokers

(P-9681)
SAFE CREDIT UNION (PA)
2295 Iron Point Rd # 100, Folsom (95630-8767)
PHONE 916 979-7233
Fax: 916 482-0343
Henry Wirz, *CEO*
James Allen, *President*
David Pope, *President*
Sharon Whiteley, *Ch Credit Ofcr*
Jayne Anderson, *Officer*
EMP: 160
SQ FT: 57,000
SALES: 103.3MM **Privately Held**
SIC: 6062 State credit unions

(P-9682)
SAFE CREDIT UNION
2295 Iron Point Rd # 100, Folsom (95630-8767)
PHONE 916 979-7233
Kristina Bruegenan, *Supervisor*
EMP: 160
SALES (corp-wide): 103.3MM **Privately Held**
SIC: 6062 6163 7389 6141 State credit unions; loan agents; credit card service; automobile loans, including insurance
PA: Safe Credit Union
    2295 Iron Point Rd # 100
    Folsom CA 95630
    916 979-7233

(P-9683)
SAN DIEGO COUNTY CREDIT UNION (PA)
6545 Sequence Dr, San Diego (92121-4363)
PHONE 858 453-2112
Fax: 858 453-6390
Irene Oberbauer, *President*
Theresa Halleck, *President*
Robert Marchand, *CFO*
Patrick Cosgrove, *Exec VP*
Heather Moshier, *Exec VP*
EMP: 239
SQ FT: 50,000
SALES: 183.4MM **Privately Held**
WEB: www.sdccu.net
SIC: 6062 State credit unions

(P-9684)
SAN DIEGO METROPOLITAN CR UN (PA)
9212 Balboa Ave, San Diego (92123-1514)
P.O. Box 719099 (92171-9099)
PHONE 619 297-4835
Fax: 619 297-6361
Stuart Camblin, *President*
Michelle Villa, *Vice Chairman*
Gloria Liberti, *Vice Pres*
Rebecca Ramos-Arzola, *Vice Pres*
Linda Rossi, *Vice Pres*
EMP: 58
SQ FT: 20,000
SALES: 10.1MM **Privately Held**
WEB: www.sdmcu.com
SIC: 6062 State credit unions, not federally chartered

(P-9685)
SAN FRANCISCO FEDERAL CR UN (PA)
770 Golden Gate Ave Fl 1, San Francisco (94102-3194)
PHONE 415 775-5377
Fax: 415 775-0715
William Wolverton, *CEO*
Steve Ho, *COO*
Jude A Gogan, *Vice Pres*
Mark Michaels, *Vice Pres*
Karen Introcaso, *Branch Mgr*
EMP: 70
SQ FT: 35,500
SALES: 27.4MM **Privately Held**
WEB: www.sffederalcu.org
SIC: 6062 State credit unions, not federally chartered

(P-9686)
SAN MATEO CREDIT UNION (PA)
350 Convention Way # 300, Redwood City (94063-1436)
P.O. Box 910 (94064-0910)
PHONE 650 363-1725
Fax: 650 364-1703
Berry Jolette, *President*
Magda Gonzalez, *Ch of Bd*
Motley Snuth, *Treasurer*
Flora Adkins, *Officer*
Valerie Alsip, *Vice Pres*
EMP: 55
SQ FT: 18,300
SALES: 27.6MM **Privately Held**
SIC: 6062 State credit unions, not federally chartered

(P-9687)
SAN MATEO CREDIT UNION
1515 S El Camino Real # 100, San Mateo (94402-3099)
PHONE 650 363-1725
Fax: 650 367-7423
Preston Monroe, *Principal*
Monica Smith, *Manager*
EMP: 212
SALES (est): 7MM
SALES (corp-wide): 27.6MM **Privately Held**
SIC: 6062 State credit unions
PA: San Mateo Credit Union
    350 Convention Way # 300
    Redwood City CA 94063
    650 363-1725

(P-9688)
SCHOOLS FINANCIAL CREDIT UNION (PA)
1485 Response Rd Ste 126, Sacramento (95815-5261)
P.O. Box 526001 (95852-6001)
PHONE 916 569-5400
Fax: 916 422-0334
James P Jordan III, *President*
Tim Marriott, *CFO*
David Menker, *Vice Pres*
Wanda Barnard, *Branch Mgr*
Rosheda Castille, *Admin Asst*
EMP: 150
SQ FT: 56,000
SALES: 41.9MM **Privately Held**
SIC: 6062 State credit unions

(P-9689)
SIERRA CENTRAL CREDIT UNION (PA)
1351 Harter Pkwy, Yuba City (95993-2604)
PHONE 530 671-3009
Fax: 530 671-3404
John Cassidy, *CEO*
Julie J Kim, *Officer*
Ron Sweeney, *Exec VP*
Pam Sweeney, *Vice Pres*
Jerry Templado, *Technology*
EMP: 90
SQ FT: 8,000
SALES: 26.2MM **Privately Held**
WEB: www.sierracentral.com
SIC: 6062 State credit unions, not federally chartered

6099 - Functions Related To Deposit Banking, NEC County (P-9708)

(P-9690)
SOUTHLAND CREDIT UNION (PA)
10701 Los Alamitos Blvd, Los Alamitos (90720-2353)
P.O. Box 7022, Downey (90241-7022)
PHONE 562 862-6831
Fax: 562 596-9776
Ferris R Foster, *CEO*
Tom Lent, *CFO*
Debie Richards, *Executive Asst*
Jose Loera, *Network Enginr*
Jason Howard, *Analyst*
EMP: 60
SALES: 19.9MM **Privately Held**
WEB: www.southlandcreditunion.com
SIC: 6062 State credit unions

(P-9691)
SOUTHLAND CREDIT UNION
8545 Florence Ave, Downey (90240-4014)
PHONE 562 862-6831
Fax: 562 862-6521
Kathy Vitale, *Manager*
Sharyl Kasarskis, *Vice Pres*
Patrick Bilyk, *Branch Mgr*
EMP: 55
SALES (corp-wide): 19.9MM **Privately Held**
WEB: www.southlandcreditunion.com
SIC: 6062 6141 State credit unions; personal credit institutions
PA: Southland Credit Union
10701 Los Alamitos Blvd
Los Alamitos CA 90720
562 862-6831

(P-9692)
TECHNOLOGY CREDIT UNION
1562 S Bascom Ave, San Jose (95125-6108)
PHONE 408 467-2382
Steve Donahue, *Branch Mgr*
EMP: 74
SALES (corp-wide): 53.2MM **Privately Held**
SIC: 6062 6061 State credit unions; federal credit unions
PA: Technology Credit Union
2010 N 1st St Ste 200
San Jose CA 95131
408 451-9111

(P-9693)
TECHNOLOGY CREDIT UNION
43848 Pcf Commons Blvd, Fremont (94538-3804)
PHONE 408 467-2385
Steven Fisher, *Owner*
Debra Bowman, *Senior VP*
Bea Carrillo, *Vice Pres*
Franca Cozzitorto, *Vice Pres*
Jason Parsons, *Vice Pres*
EMP: 74
SALES (corp-wide): 53.2MM **Privately Held**
SIC: 6062 State credit unions
PA: Technology Credit Union
2010 N 1st St Ste 200
San Jose CA 95131
408 451-9111

(P-9694)
TECHNOLOGY CREDIT UNION (PA)
2010 N 1st St Ste 200, San Jose (95131-2024)
P.O. Box 1409 (95109-1409)
PHONE 408 451-9111
Fax: 408 451-9412
Kenneth Burns, *President*
Barbara B Kamm, *CEO*
Joe Anzalone, *Officer*
Al Cadman, *Officer*
Steven Fisher, *Officer*
EMP: 133
SQ FT: 23,000
SALES: 53.2MM **Privately Held**
SIC: 6062 State credit unions

(P-9695)
TECHNOLOGY CREDIT UNION
490 S California Ave, Palo Alto (94306-1900)
PHONE 650 326-6445
Robert Hayes, *Branch Mgr*
EMP: 74
SALES (corp-wide): 53.2MM **Privately Held**
SIC: 6062 State credit unions
PA: Technology Credit Union
2010 N 1st St Ste 200
San Jose CA 95131
408 451-9111

(P-9696)
UNCLE CREDIT UNION (PA)
2100 Las Positas Ct, Livermore (94551-7301)
PHONE 925 447-5001
Fax: 925 455-7153
Harold Roundtree, *CEO*
Jim Ott, *President*
Wendy Zanotelli, *COO*
Gina Bloomfield, *CFO*
Otis Nostrand, *Chairman*
EMP: 58
SQ FT: 17,000
SALES: 9.1MM **Privately Held**
WEB: www.unclecu.com
SIC: 6062 State credit unions, not federally chartered

(P-9697)
UNIVERSITY CREDIT UNION
1500 S Sepulveda Blvd, Los Angeles (90025-3312)
PHONE 310 477-6628
Charles Bumbarger, *President*
Gary Kuleck, *Bd of Directors*
Jerry Mann, *Bd of Directors*
Wendy Kollwitz, *Officer*
Patrick Aragon, *Vice Pres*
EMP: 104
SALES: 12.2MM **Privately Held**
SIC: 6062 State credit unions

(P-9698)
VENTURA COUNTY CREDIT UNION (PA)
6026 Telephone Rd, Ventura (93003-5399)
P.O. Box 6920 (93006-6920)
PHONE 805 477-4000
Fax: 805 339-4226
Joseph Schroeder, *President*
Linda Sim, *CFO*
Gavin Bradley, *Senior VP*
Linda Rossi, *Senior VP*
Jackie Benoun, *Vice Pres*
EMP: 84
SQ FT: 22,500
SALES: 36.8MM **Privately Held**
SIC: 6062 State credit unions, not federally chartered

(P-9699)
WESCOM CENTRAL CREDIT UNION (PA)
123 S Marengo Ave, Pasadena (91101-2428)
P.O. Box 7058 (91109-7058)
PHONE 888 493-7266
Toll Free: .... 888 -
Darren Williams, *CEO*
Jane Wood, *COO*
Mark Thorpe, *CFO*
Richard M Johnson, *Treasurer*
Bryan Tinoco, *Officer*
EMP: 425
SQ FT: 90,000
SALES: 98.4MM **Privately Held**
WEB: www.wescom.org
SIC: 6062 State credit unions, not federally chartered

6081 Foreign Banks, Branches & Agencies

(P-9700)
HONG KONG & SHANGHAI BANKING
Also Called: Hong Kong Bank
770 Wilshire Blvd Ste 800, Los Angeles (90017-3719)
PHONE 213 626-2460
EMP: 60
SALES (corp-wide): 79.8B **Privately Held**
SIC: 6081
HQ: Hongkong And Shanghai Banking Corporation Limited, The
Hsbc Main Bldg
Central District HK
282 211-11

6082 Foreign Trade & Intl Banks

(P-9701)
BNP PARIBAS ASSET MGT INC
1 Front St Fl 23, San Francisco (94111-5331)
PHONE 415 772-1300
Fax: 415 301-3390
Francois Denis, *Principal*
Xavier Pujos, *COO*
William J La Herran, *Vice Pres*
EMP: 66 **Publicly Held**
WEB: www.bnpparibas.com
SIC: 6082 Foreign trade & international banking institutions
HQ: Bnp Paribas Asset Management, Inc.
200 Park Ave Rm 4520
New York NY 10166
212 681-3000

6091 Nondeposit Trust Facilities

(P-9702)
CATHAY BANK
General Bank Credit ADM Dept
4128 Temple City Blvd, Rosemead (91770-1550)
P.O. Box 3302, Los Angeles (90078-3302)
PHONE 626 452-1582
Fax: 626 454-4860
Domenic Massei, *Manager*
Claire Liaw, *Officer*
Olha Holland, *Senior VP*
Lois Chiang, *Vice Pres*
Craig Lock, *Vice Pres*
EMP: 120
SALES (corp-wide): 486.3MM **Publicly Held**
WEB: www.newasiabk.com
SIC: 6091 Nondeposit trust facilities
HQ: Cathay Bank
9650 Flair Dr
El Monte CA 91731
626 279-3698

(P-9703)
FRANKLIN TEMPLETON INSTNL LLC (HQ)
1 Franklin Pkwy, San Mateo (94403-1906)
PHONE 650 312-2000
Crawford Cargon, *President*
Jennifer Johnson, *COO*
Bradley Radin, *Exec VP*
Bradley Hanson, *Senior VP*
Michael Materasso, *Senior VP*
EMP: 55
SALES (est): 26.5MM
SALES (corp-wide): 7.9B **Publicly Held**
WEB: www.frk.com
SIC: 6091 Nondeposit trust facilities
PA: Franklin Resources, Inc.
1 Franklin Pkwy
San Mateo CA 94403
650 312-2000

(P-9704)
SUNAMERICA INC (HQ)
1 Sun America Ctr Fl 38, Los Angeles (90067-6101)
PHONE 310 772-6000
Eli Broad, *Chairman*
Rodney Haviland, *President*
Jay S Wintrob, *CEO*
Howard Heitner, *COO*
James R Belardi, *Exec VP*
EMP: 1000 **EST:** 1957
SQ FT: 95,845
SALES (est): 2.3B
SALES (corp-wide): 58.3B **Publicly Held**
SIC: 6091 6311 6211 6282 Nondeposit trust facilities; life insurance carriers; mutual funds, selling by independent salesperson; brokers, security; dealers, security; manager of mutual funds, contract or fee basis; pension & retirement plan consultants; pension, health & welfare funds
PA: American International Group, Inc.
175 Water St Rm 1800
New York NY 10038
212 770-7000

6099 Functions Related To Deposit Banking, NEC

(P-9705)
ACCURATE SERVICES INC
Also Called: Accurate Express
3429 Glendale Blvd, Los Angeles (90039-1814)
PHONE 323 906-1000
Fax: 323 906-9633
Ester Fishman, *CEO*
EMP: 107
SQ FT: 2,475
SALES (est): 14.4MM **Privately Held**
SIC: 6099 Check clearing services

(P-9706)
ACE CASH EXPRESS INC
6302 Van Buren Blvd, Riverside (92503-2051)
PHONE 951 509-3506
Michael Mc Knight, *Branch Mgr*
EMP: 105
SALES (corp-wide): 2.1B **Privately Held**
WEB: www.acecashexpress.com
SIC: 6099 Check clearing services
HQ: Ace Cash Express, Inc.
1231 Greenway Dr Ste 600
Irving TX 75038
972 550-5000

(P-9707)
ASCENDANTFX CAPITAL USA INC
3478 Buskirk Ave Ste 1000, Pleasant Hill (94523-4378)
PHONE 201 633-4667
Jason Mugford, *President*
Greg Allen, *Treasurer*
Bernard Beck, *Ch Credit Ofcr*
Dan Caputo, *Vice Pres*
Nabeel Siddiqui, *Principal*
EMP: 57
SALES (est): 10.1MM
SALES (corp-wide): 42.2MM **Privately Held**
SIC: 6099 Foreign currency exchange
PA: Ascendantfx Capital Inc
200 Bay St N Suite 1625
Toronto ON M5J 2
416 943-0123

(P-9708)
ASSOCIATED FOREIGN EXCH INC (HQ)
Also Called: Afex
21045 Califa St, Woodland Hills (91367-5104)
PHONE 888 307-2339
Fax: 818 386-2709
Jan Vlietstra, *CEO*
Irving Barr, *Ch of Bd*
Fred Kunik, *President*
Richard Verasamy, *CFO*
Marcello Castillo, *Chief Mktg Ofcr*
EMP: 57
SALES (est): 23.3MM
SALES (corp-wide): 58MM **Privately Held**
WEB: www.afex.com
SIC: 6099 Foreign currency exchange
PA: Associated Foreign Exchange Holdings, Inc.
21045 Califa St
Woodland Hills CA 91367
818 386-2702

6099 - Functions Related To Deposit Banking, NEC County (P-9709) — **PRODUCTS & SERVICES SECTION**

(P-9709)
ASSOCTED FGN EXCH HOLDINGS INC (PA)
21045 Califa St, Woodland Hills (91367-5104)
PHONE..................818 386-2702
Irving Barr, *Chairman*
Fred Kunik, *President*
Jan Vliestra, *CEO*
EMP: 89
SALES: 58MM **Privately Held**
SIC: 6099 Foreign currency exchange

(P-9710)
BLACKHAWK NETWORK INC (HQ)
6220 Stoneridge Mall Rd, Pleasanton (94588-3260)
PHONE..................925 226-9990
Talbott Roche, *President*
Kim Allen, *President*
Mike Gionfriddo, *President*
Ben King, *President*
Tom Neale, *President*
EMP: 625 EST: 2005
SALES (est): 1B
SALES (corp-wide): 1.8B **Publicly Held**
SIC: 6099 Electronic funds transfer network, including switching
PA: Blackhawk Network Holdings, Inc.
6220 Stoneridge Mall Rd
Pleasanton CA 94588
925 226-9990

(P-9711)
BLACKHAWK NETWORK HOLDINGS INC (PA)
6220 Stoneridge Mall Rd, Pleasanton (94588-3260)
PHONE..................925 226-9990
Fax: 925 226-9083
Talbott Roche, *President*
William Y Tauscher, *Ch of Bd*
Jerry N Ulrich, *Officer*
Christopher C Crum, *Senior VP*
Sachin Dhawan, *Senior VP*
EMP: 500
SQ FT: 149,000
SALES: 1.8B **Publicly Held**
WEB: www.safeway.com
SIC: 6099 Electronic funds transfer network, including switching

(P-9712)
BSERV INC (PA)
Also Called: Bankserv
333 Bush St Fl 26, San Francisco (94104-2846)
PHONE..................415 277-9900
Reuven Ben Menachem, *CEO*
Edward Ho, *President*
Bryan Schreiber, *Treasurer*
Mierzwa Dennis, *Vice Pres*
Randy Gutierrez, *Vice Pres*
EMP: 60
SQ FT: 14,000
SALES (est): 57.1MM **Privately Held**
WEB: www.bankserv.com
SIC: 6099 Electronic funds transfer network, including switching

(P-9713)
CONTINENTAL CURRENCY SVCS INC (HQ)
Also Called: Continental Ex Money Order Co
1108 E 17th St, Santa Ana (92701-2600)
PHONE..................714 569-0300
Irving Barr, *Ch of Bd*
Fred Kunik, *President*
EMP: 50
SQ FT: 10,000
SALES (est): 10.5MM
SALES (corp-wide): 193.4MM **Privately Held**
SIC: 6099 Check cashing agencies
PA: Continental Currency Services, Inc.
1108 E 17th St
Santa Ana CA 92701
714 569-0300

(P-9714)
CONTINENTAL CURRENCY SVCS INC (PA)
Also Called: Cash It Here
1108 E 17th St, Santa Ana (92701-2600)
P.O. Box 10970 (92711-0970)
PHONE..................714 569-0300
Fax: 714 569-0882
Fred Kunik, *President*
Irving Barr, *Ch of Bd*
David Wilder, *COO*
William J Nolan, *CFO*
Helen Cho, *Officer*
EMP: 80 EST: 1977
SQ FT: 12,500
SALES (est): 193.4MM **Privately Held**
SIC: 6099 Check cashing agencies; electronic funds transfer network, including switching; money order issuance

(P-9715)
CU COOPERATIVE SYSTEMS INC (PA)
Also Called: Co-Op Network
9692 Haven Ave, Rancho Cucamonga (91730-5891)
PHONE..................909 948-2500
Fax: 909 948-2642
Stanley Hollen, *CEO*
Tom Sargent, *Ch of Bd*
Kari Wilfong, *CFO*
John Bommarito, *Treasurer*
Lisa Schlehuber, *Bd of Directors*
EMP: 285
SALES: 208.4MM **Privately Held**
SIC: 6099 Automated teller machine (ATM) network; electronic funds transfer network, including switching

(P-9716)
DEBISYS INC (PA)
Also Called: Emida Technologies
27442 Portola Pkwy # 150, Foothill Ranch (92610-2860)
PHONE..................949 699-1401
Fax: 949 699-1420
Dennis Andrews, *CEO*
Jim Wodach, *CFO*
Sandie Gomez, *Bd of Directors*
Rich Lull, *Vice Pres*
Patrick Neill, *Vice Pres*
EMP: 80
SQ FT: 10,000
SALES (est): 60.8MM **Privately Held**
WEB: www.emida.net
SIC: 6099 Automated teller machine (ATM) network

(P-9717)
EDC SERVICE CORPORATION (DEL)
415 N Vineyard Ave # 205, Ontario (91764-5493)
PHONE..................909 390-4747
Fax: 909 390-1170
Stephen Bezuidenhout, *President*
Wendy Bezuidenhout, *Vice Pres*
Arthur Belmont, *Exec Dir*
Tim Bauer, *Manager*
Jim Collins, *Manager*
EMP: 60
SQ FT: 8,500
SALES (est): 5.6MM **Privately Held**
SIC: 6099 Automated clearinghouses

(P-9718)
G P M M MONEY CENTERS INC
Also Called: Dollar Smart
1460 Doris Ave, Oxnard (93030-8771)
P.O. Box 6963 (93031-6963)
PHONE..................619 288-7607
Fax: 805 487-5823
Greg Palmer, *President*
Ryan Romero, *Business Mgr*
EMP: 50
SALES (est): 6.2MM **Privately Held**
SIC: 6099 Check cashing agencies

(P-9719)
GRANITE ESCROW SERVICES
439 N Canon Dr Ste 220, Beverly Hills (90210-3933)
PHONE..................310 288-0110
Sue Nichols, *Branch Mgr*
EMP: 56
SALES (corp-wide): 10MM **Privately Held**
SIC: 6099 Escrow institutions other than real estate
PA: Granite Escrow Services
450 Nwport Ctr Dr Ste 600
Newport Beach CA 92660
949 720-0110

(P-9720)
KINECTA ALTERNATIVE FIN (PA)
Also Called: Nix Check Cashing Service
1440 Rosecrans Ave, Manhattan Beach (90266-3702)
PHONE..................310 538-2242
Thomas E Nix Jr, *President*
Darlene Gavin, *Vice Pres*
EMP: 60
SQ FT: 28,000
SALES: 27.8MM **Privately Held**
WEB: www.nixcheckcashing.com
SIC: 6099 Check cashing agencies

(P-9721)
LENLYN LIMITED WHICH WILL DO B (DH)
6151 W Century Blvd, Los Angeles (90045-5307)
P.O. Box 92192 (90009-2192)
PHONE..................310 417-3432
Bharat Shah, *CEO*
Aleta Lindsay, *Vice Pres*
Bharat Shas, *Vice Pres*
Mark Garrett, *Technology*
EMP: 75
SQ FT: 1,000
SALES (est): 13.3MM
SALES (corp-wide): 1.4B **Privately Held**
WEB: www.iceplc.com
SIC: 6099 Foreign currency exchange
HQ: Lenlyn Limited
Kiosk 13c 381 - 383
London W1C 2
207 499-8853

(P-9722)
MANIFLO MONEY EXCHANGE INC (PA)
1442 Highland Ave, National City (91950-4624)
PHONE..................619 434-7200
Fax: 619 434-7221
Florino Agpaoa, *President*
Ferdinand Agpaoa, *President*
Rodel Agpaoa, *Vice Pres*
EMP: 50
SQ FT: 1,500
SALES (est): 7.6MM **Privately Held**
WEB: www.maniflo.com
SIC: 6099 Electronic funds transfer network, including switching

(P-9723)
TASQ TECHNOLOGY INC
8875 Washington Blvd A, Roseville (95678-6214)
PHONE..................916 632-7600
Dan Mandel, *Branch Mgr*
Margaret Anderson, *Credit Staff*
Jim Macchiusi, *VP Opers*
EMP: 325
SALES (corp-wide): 11.4B **Publicly Held**
SIC: 6099 Electronic funds transfer network, including switching
HQ: Tasq Technology, Inc.
1169 Canton Rd
Marietta GA 30066
770 218-4000

(P-9724)
TIGER FINANCIAL MANAGEMENT LLC
11000 Lower Azusa Rd, El Monte (91731-1440)
PHONE..................626 448-2400
Larry Klaahsen, *Branch Mgr*
EMP: 51
SALES (corp-wide): 62.1MM **Privately Held**
SIC: 6099 Check cashing agencies
PA: Curo Management Llc
3527 N Ridge Rd
Wichita KS 67205
316 722-3801

(P-9725)
XOOM CORPORATION (DH)
425 Market St Fl 12, San Francisco (94105-5404)
PHONE..................415 777-4800
John Kunze, *President*
Ryno Blignaut, *CFO*
Christopher G Ferro, *Ch Credit Ofcr*
Julian King, *Senior VP*
Christopher Ferro, *Vice Pres*
EMP: 83
SQ FT: 35,552
SALES: 159MM
SALES (corp-wide): 4.3B **Publicly Held**
SIC: 6099 Electronic funds transfer network, including switching
HQ: Paypal, Inc.
2211 N 1st St
San Jose CA 95131
877 981-2163

6111 Federal Credit Agencies

(P-9726)
AGAMERICA FCB (PA)
3636 American River Dr # 100, Sacramento (95864-5952)
PHONE..................651 282-8800
Fax: 916 485-6029
James D Kirk, *President*
David B Newlin, *CFO*
Roger J Cramer, *Ch Credit Ofcr*
Gregory J Buehne, *Senior VP*
Chris Doherty, *Vice Pres*
EMP: 85
SALES (est): 788.2K **Privately Held**
SIC: 6111 6163 Federal & federally sponsored credit agencies; loan brokers

(P-9727)
DEUTSCHE BANK NATIONAL TR CO (DH)
2000 Avenue Of The Stars, Los Angeles (90067-4700)
PHONE..................213 620-8200
Michael Demma, *Administration*
EMP: 61
SALES (est): 23.1MM
SALES (corp-wide): 8.8B **Privately Held**
SIC: 6111 National Consumer Cooperative Bank
HQ: Deutsche Bank Trust Company Americas
60 Wall St Bsmt 1
New York NY 10005
212 250-2500

(P-9728)
DEUTSCHE BANK NATIONAL TR CO
1761 E Saint Andrew Pl, Santa Ana (92705-4934)
PHONE..................714 247-6000
Gary Vaughn, *Manager*
Paulina Rodriguez, *Manager*
EMP: 50
SALES (corp-wide): 8.8B **Privately Held**
SIC: 6111 6733 Banks for cooperatives; trusts
HQ: Deutsche Bank National Trust Co
2000 Avenue Of The Stars
Los Angeles CA 90067
213 620-8200

(P-9729)
EDUCATIONAL FUNDING CO LLC
11452 El Camino Real # 110, San Diego (92130-2080)
PHONE..................858 350-1313
Patricia Alexander, *President*
EMP: 79
SALES (est): 7.8MM **Privately Held**
SIC: 6111 Student Loan Marketing Association

(P-9730)
FEDERAL HM LN BNK SAN FRNCISCO (PA)
600 California St, San Francisco (94108-2704)
PHONE..................415 616-1000

PRODUCTS & SERVICES SECTION

6141 - Personal Credit Institutions County (P-9751)

John F Luikart, *Ch of Bd*
Larry Feigenbaum, *President*
Dean Schultz, *President*
Lisa B Macmillen, *COO*
Kenneth C Miller, *CFO*
▲ **EMP:** 77 EST: 1932
SQ FT: 108,147
SALES: 1.2B Privately Held
WEB: www.fhlbsf.com
SIC: 6111 Federal & federally sponsored credit agencies

(P-9731)
FRESNO-MADERA FEDERAL LAND
305 N I St, Madera (93637-3062)
P.O. Box 13069, Fresno (93794-3069)
PHONE...............................559 674-2437
Fax: 559 673-8414
Rob Kratz, *Manager*
EMP: 58
SALES (corp-wide): 9.6MM Privately Held
SIC: 6111 Federal Land Banks
PA: Fresno-Madera Federal Land Bank Association
4635 W Spruce Ave
Fresno CA 93722
559 277-7000

(P-9732)
LAW SCHOOL FINANCIAL INC
Also Called: Law School Loans
175 S Lake Ave Unit 200, Pasadena (91101-2629)
PHONE...............................626 243-1800
Harrison A Barnes, *President*
Dennis Geselowitz, *CFO*
EMP: 190
SQ FT: 25,000
SALES (est): 16.4MM Privately Held
WEB: www.lawschoolloans.com
SIC: 6111 Student Loan Marketing Association

(P-9733)
LBS FINANCIAL CREDIT UNION
1401 Quail St Ste 130, Newport Beach (92660-2772)
PHONE...............................714 893-5111
Laurie Skinner, *Manager*
EMP: 82
SALES (corp-wide): 45.8MM Privately Held
SIC: 6111 6036 Federal & federally sponsored credit agencies; savings & loan associations, not federally chartered
PA: Lbs Financial Credit Union
5505 Garden Grove Blvd # 500
Westminster CA 92683
714 893-5111

(P-9734)
LBS FINANCIAL CREDIT UNION (PA)
5505 Garden Grove Blvd # 500, Westminster (92683-1894)
P.O. Box 4860, Long Beach (90804-0860)
PHONE...............................714 893-5111
Fax: 562 496-1380
Jeffrey A Napper, *President*
Gene Allen, *Ch of Bd*
Dug Woog, *Treasurer*
Charles Thomas, *Officer*
Sean Hardeman, *Senior VP*
EMP: 120
SQ FT: 63,000
SALES: 45.8MM Privately Held
SIC: 6111 6163 6061 Federal & federally sponsored credit agencies; loan brokers; federal credit unions

(P-9735)
YOSEMITE FARM CREDIT ACA (PA)
806 W Monte Vista Ave, Turlock (95382-7242)
P.O. Box 3278 (95381-3278)
PHONE...............................209 667-2366
Leonard Van Eldern, *President*
Tracy Sparks, *CFO*
Robert Fuller, *Vice Pres*
Brian Lemons, *Vice Pres*
Galen Miyamoto, *Vice Pres*
EMP: 60
SQ FT: 9,000

SALES: 88.5MM Privately Held
WEB: www.yosemitefarmcredit.com
SIC: 6111 Federal Land Banks

6141 Personal Credit Institutions

(P-9736)
AMERICAN FINANCIAL NETWORK INC
10 Pointe Dr Ste 330, Brea (92821-7620)
PHONE...............................909 606-3905
John B Sherman, *CEO*
John R Sherman, *President*
EMP: 900 EST: 2001
SALES (est): 315.4MM Privately Held
SIC: 6141 Personal credit institutions

(P-9737)
AMERICAN HONDA FINANCE CORP (DH)
Also Called: Honda Financial Services
20800 Madrona Ave, Torrance (90503-4915)
P.O. Box 2295 (90509-2295)
PHONE...............................310 972-2239
Narutoshi Wakiyama, *CEO*
Hideo Tamaka, *President*
John Weisickle, *CFO*
Shinji Kubaru, *Treasurer*
Mikio Yoshimi, *Treasurer*
EMP: 200
SQ FT: 50,288
SALES: 2B
SALES (corp-wide): 124.7B Privately Held
WEB: www.americanhondafinancecorporation.com
SIC: 6141 Financing: automobiles, furniture, etc., not a deposit bank; automobile & consumer finance companies
HQ: American Honda Motor Co., Inc.
1919 Torrance Blvd
Torrance CA 90501
310 783-2000

(P-9738)
AMERICAN HONDA FINANCE CORP
10801 Walker St Ste 140, Cypress (90630-5042)
PHONE...............................714 816-8110
Stephen Cato, *Manager*
EMP: 72
SALES (corp-wide): 124.7B Privately Held
SIC: 6141 Financing: automobiles, furniture, etc., not a deposit bank; automobile & consumer finance companies
HQ: American Honda Finance Corporation
20800 Madrona Ave
Torrance CA 90503
310 972-2239

(P-9739)
AMERICAN UNION FINCL SVCS INC
210 S Orange Grove Blvd # 1, Pasadena (91105-1705)
PHONE...............................714 619-2520
David Villarreal, *Chairman*
EMP: 150
SALES (est): 11.4MM Privately Held
SIC: 6141 Consumer finance companies

(P-9740)
BALBOA CAPITAL CORPORATION (PA)
575 Anton Blvd Fl 12, Costa Mesa (92626-7169)
PHONE...............................949 756-0800
Fax: 949 399-3110
Patrick Byrne, *CEO*
Phil Silva, *President*
Robert Rasmussen, *COO*
Paul Knapp, *Business Dir*
Michael Curtis, *Managing Dir*
EMP: 200
SQ FT: 24,000
SALES (est): 129.6MM Privately Held
WEB: www.balboacapital.com
SIC: 6141 Automobile & consumer finance companies

(P-9741)
BOFI FEDERAL BANK (HQ)
4350 La Jolla Village Dr # 140, San Diego (92122-1244)
PHONE...............................858 350-6200
Greg Garrabants, *CEO*
Andrew Micheletti, *CFO*
Eduardo Urdapilleta, *Chief Mktg Ofcr*
Bill Baluka, *Officer*
Angie Sussner, *Officer*
EMP: 75
SQ FT: 7,000
SALES: 233.2MM
SALES (corp-wide): 384MM Publicly Held
WEB: www.bankofinternet.com
SIC: 6141 6163 Financing: automobiles, furniture, etc., not a deposit bank; loan brokers
PA: Bofi Holding, Inc.
4350 La Jolla Village Dr
San Diego CA 92122
858 350-6200

(P-9742)
CASHCALL INC
1 City Blvd W Ste 102, Orange (92868-3621)
P.O. Box 66007, Anaheim (92816-6007)
PHONE...............................949 752-4600
John Paul Reddam, *CEO*
Ethan Taub, *Chief Mktg Ofcr*
Thomas Morgan, *Vice Pres*
Pmp Nelson, *Project Mgr*
Laura Perches, *Human Res Dir*
EMP: 1400
SALES (est): 399.2MM Privately Held
WEB: www.cashcall.com
SIC: 6141 Personal finance licensed loan companies, small

(P-9743)
COMMERCE WEST INSURANCE CO
6130 Stoneridge Mall Rd # 400, Pleasanton (94588-3279)
P.O. Box 8006 (94588-8606)
PHONE...............................925 730-6400
Fax: 925 734-1789
Jerald Fels, *President*
Michael Vrban, *CFO*
Albert Harris, *Vice Pres*
Ellen Shiromizu, *Supervisor*
EMP: 60
SQ FT: 23,000
SALES: 83MM
SALES (corp-wide): 72.6K Privately Held
WEB: www.commercewest.net
SIC: 6141 Automobile & consumer finance companies
HQ: The Commerce Insurance Company
211 Main St
Webster MA 01570
508 943-9000

(P-9744)
CONSUMER PORTFOLIO SVCS INC
19500 Jamboree Rd, Irvine (92612-2401)
PHONE...............................949 788-5695
Charles E Bradley Jr, *Manager*
Laurie Straten, *Vice Pres*
Kevin Bowland, *Controller*
Dottie Warren, *Human Res Dir*
Chad Lopes, *Marketing Mgr*
EMP: 227
SALES (corp-wide): 363.6MM Publicly Held
WEB: www.consumerportfolio.com
SIC: 6141 Personal credit institutions
PA: Consumer Portfolio Services, Inc.
3800 Howard Hughes Pkwy
Las Vegas NV 89169
949 753-6800

(P-9745)
CREDIT SOLUTIONS CORP
13520 Evening Creek Dr N # 500, San Diego (92128-8110)
PHONE...............................858 650-0812
Michael A Joplin, *CEO*
Raecelle Joplin, *President*
Stephen Vocal, *Technology*
Melanie Quintana, *Human Res Mgr*
EMP: 110
SQ FT: 15,397

SALES (est): 20.4MM Privately Held
WEB: www.creditsolutionscorp.com
SIC: 6141 Financing: automobiles, furniture, etc., not a deposit bank

(P-9746)
FEDERAL HM LN BNK SAN FRNCISCO
11050 White Rock Rd, Rancho Cordova (95670-6386)
PHONE...............................916 851-6900
Lawrence Parks, *Branch Mgr*
EMP: 182
SALES (corp-wide): 1.2B Privately Held
SIC: 6141 6021 Personal credit institutions; national commercial banks
PA: Federal Home Loan Bank Of San Francisco
600 California St
San Francisco CA 94108
415 616-1000

(P-9747)
FIRSTPLUS BANK (PA)
Also Called: First Plus Bank
1732 Reynolds Ave, Irvine (92614-5712)
PHONE...............................949 851-7101
Mike Mc Guire, *President*
Barry K Williams, *Treasurer*
Gus Mendoza, *Vice Pres*
EMP: 50 EST: 1980
SALES (est): 18.3MM Privately Held
SIC: 6141 Industrial loan banks & companies, not a deposit bank

(P-9748)
FLURISH INC
Also Called: Lendup
225 Bush St Ste 1100, San Francisco (94104-4250)
PHONE...............................855 253-6387
Sasha Orloff, *CEO*
Tammy Eichelkeraz, *Office Mgr*
Jacob Rosenberg, *Admin Sec*
Nicholas Hill, *Accountant*
EMP: 80 EST: 2011
SQ FT: 18,500
SALES: 12MM Privately Held
SIC: 6141 Consumer finance companies

(P-9749)
FUNDING CIRCLE USA INC
Also Called: Endurance Lending Network
747 Front St Fl 4, San Francisco (94111-1922)
PHONE...............................855 385-5356
Fax: 415 875-4501
Sam Hodges, *Director*
Jerome Le Luel, *Officer*
Rohit Sharma, *Vice Pres*
Renee Nichols, *Office Mgr*
Calley Wiener, *Office Mgr*
EMP: 55 EST: 2014
SALES (est): 48.9MM
SALES (corp-wide): 18.8MM Privately Held
SIC: 6141 Licensed loan companies, small
PA: Funding Circle Ltd
71 Queen Victoria Street
London

(P-9750)
GREEN DOT CORPORATION (PA)
3465 E Foothill Blvd # 100, Pasadena (91107-6072)
P.O. Box 1187, Monrovia (91017-1187)
PHONE...............................626 765-2000
Steven W Streit, *Ch of Bd*
Lewis B Goodwin, *President*
Kuan Archer, *COO*
Mark L Shifke, *CFO*
Mark Shifke, *Senior VP*
EMP: 141 EST: 1999
SQ FT: 140,000
SALES: 694.7MM Publicly Held
WEB: www.greendotcorp.com
SIC: 6141 7389 Personal credit institutions; credit card service

(P-9751)
HSBC FINANCE CORPORATION
1420 El Paseo De Saratoga, San Jose (95130-1633)
PHONE...............................408 796-3600

6141 - Personal Credit Institutions County (P-9752)

Cindy Shen, *Loan Officer*
EMP: 142
SALES (corp-wide): 89B **Privately Held**
SIC: 6141 Consumer finance companies
HQ: Hsbc Finance Corporation
1421 W Shure Dr Ste 100
Arlington Heights IL 60004
224 880-7000

(P-9752)
HSBC FINANCE CORPORATION
931 Corporate Center Dr, Pomona
(91768-2642)
PHONE 909 623-3355
Mark Marks, *Principal*
EMP: 800
SALES (corp-wide): 89B **Privately Held**
WEB: www.household.com
SIC: 6141 7389 6351 6159 Consumer finance companies; credit card service; credit & other financial responsibility insurance; machinery & equipment finance leasing; mortgage bankers; life insurance carriers
HQ: Hsbc Finance Corporation
1421 W Shure Dr Ste 100
Arlington Heights IL 60004
224 880-7000

(P-9753)
HSBC FINANCE CORPORATION
725 N Broadway, Los Angeles
(90012-2819)
PHONE 213 628-8167
Clarence Ho, *Branch Mgr*
EMP: 142
SALES (corp-wide): 89B **Privately Held**
SIC: 6141 Consumer finance companies
HQ: Hsbc Finance Corporation
1421 W Shure Dr Ste 100
Arlington Heights IL 60004
224 880-7000

(P-9754)
HYUNDAI CAPITAL AMERICA (DH)
Also Called: Hyundai Finance
3161 Michelson Dr # 1900, Irvine
(92612-4418)
PHONE 714 965-3000
Sam Sanghyuk Suh, *CEO*
Sukjoon Won, *President*
Jwa Jin Cho, *CEO*
Daniel Kwon, *COO*
Minsok Randy Park, *CFO*
EMP: 87
SQ FT: 60,000
SALES (est): 135.4MM
SALES (corp-wide): 38.9B **Privately Held**
SIC: 6141 Automobile loans, including insurance
HQ: Hyundai Motor America
10550 Talbert Ave
Fountain Valley CA 92708
714 965-3000

(P-9755)
JMAC LENDING INC
16782 Von Karman Ave # 12, Irvine
(92606-2417)
PHONE 949 390-2688
MAI Christina Pham, *President*
Michael Truong, *Bd of Directors*
Travis Pham, *Exec VP*
Al Crisanty, *Vice Pres*
John Pham, *Admin Sec*
EMP: 60
SALES (est): 24MM **Privately Held**
WEB: www.jmaclending.com
SIC: 6141 Financing: automobiles, furniture, etc., not a deposit bank

(P-9756)
LOBEL FINANCIAL CORPORATION (PA)
1150 N Magnolia Ave, Anaheim
(92801-2605)
P.O. Box 3000 (92803-3000)
PHONE 714 995-3333
Harvey Lobel, *CEO*
Gary Lobel, *Corp Secy*
David Lobel, *Vice Pres*
Murray Lobel, *Vice Pres*
Eric Wetzel, *Branch Mgr*
EMP: 63 **EST:** 1979
SQ FT: 11,000
SALES (est): 27.8MM **Privately Held**
SIC: 6141 Automobile loans, including insurance

(P-9757)
MITSUBISHI MOTORS CR AMER INC (DH)
6400 Katella Ave, Cypress (90630-5208)
P.O. Box 6014 (90630-0014)
PHONE 714 799-4730
Dan Booth, *President*
Hideyuki Kitamura, *Treasurer*
Charles Tredway, *Exec VP*
Don Wright, *General Mgr*
Ellen Gleberman, *Admin Sec*
EMP: 394
SQ FT: 32,256
SALES (est): 38.8MM
SALES (corp-wide): 19.3B **Privately Held**
WEB: www.acvl.com
SIC: 6141 6159 Automobile loans, including insurance; truck finance leasing; finance leasing, vehicles: except automobiles & trucks
HQ: Mitsubishi Motors North America, Inc.
6400 Katella Ave
Cypress CA 90630
714 799-4730

(P-9758)
MONTEREY FINANCIAL SVCS INC (PA)
4095 Avenida De La Plata, Oceanside
(92056-5802)
P.O. Box 5199 (92052-5199)
PHONE 760 639-3500
Fax: 760 639-3501
Robert Steinke, *President*
Dicks Kussick, *CFO*
Mike Gray, *Exec VP*
Chris Hughes, *Exec VP*
Kathi Steinke, *Vice Pres*
EMP: 110
SQ FT: 27,000
SALES (est): 12.9MM **Privately Held**
WEB: www.montereyfinancial.com
SIC: 6141 8721 7322 8742 Consumer finance companies; billing & bookkeeping service; collection agency, except real estate; financial consultant

(P-9759)
NATIONAL PLANNING CORPORATION
100 N Sepulveda Blvd # 1800, El Segundo
(90245-5612)
PHONE 800 881-7174
Fax: 310 899-7969
John C Johnson, *President*
Ethan Grodofsky, *Managing Prtnr*
Anthony Palmieri, *Managing Prtnr*
Jeffrey Stern, *Managing Prtnr*
Maura Collins, *CFO*
EMP: 150
SALES (est): 40.8MM **Privately Held**
SIC: 6141 Automobile & consumer finance companies

(P-9760)
NORTH AMERICAN ACCEPTANCE CORP
Also Called: An Open Check
3191 Red Hill Ave Ste 100, Costa Mesa
(92626-3451)
PHONE 714 868-3195
Fax: 714 850-7400
Marco J Rasic, *CEO*
Ryan Marek, *President*
Mary Clancey Rasic, *Vice Pres*
Angelina Basen, *Admin Asst*
EMP: 123
SQ FT: 24,000
SALES (est): 16MM **Privately Held**
WEB: www.naacceptance.com
SIC: 6141 6719 Automobile & consumer finance companies; personal holding companies, except banks

(P-9761)
PAYOFF INC
3200 Park Center Dr # 800, Costa Mesa
(92626-1979)
PHONE 949 430-0630
Scott Saunders, *CEO*
John Phamvan, *President*

Lenny Moon, *CFO*
Carey Ransom, *Chief Mktg Ofcr*
Ibrahim Dusi, *Risk Mgmt Dir*
EMP: 53
SQ FT: 19,500
SALES (est): 19.9MM **Privately Held**
SIC: 6141 Personal credit institutions

(P-9762)
REDWOOD CREDIT UNION
1129 S Cloverdale Blvd A, Cloverdale
(95425-4482)
PHONE 800 479-7928
EMP: 129
SALES (corp-wide): 112.6MM **Privately Held**
SIC: 6141 Personal credit institutions
PA: Redwood Credit Union
3033 Cleveland Ave # 100
Santa Rosa CA 95403
707 545-4000

(P-9763)
REDWOOD CREDIT UNION (PA)
3033 Cleveland Ave # 100, Santa Rosa
(95403-2126)
P.O. Box 6104 (95406-0104)
PHONE 707 545-4000
Fax: 707 544-4965
Brett Martinez, *President*
John Pavelka, *Officer*
Luci Young, *Officer*
Ron Felder, *Senior VP*
Tony Hildesheim, *Senior VP*
EMP: 190
SQ FT: 20,000
SALES: 112.6MM **Privately Held**
WEB: www.redwoodcu.org
SIC: 6141 Personal credit institutions

(P-9764)
STEARNS LENDING LLC
44875 Deep Canyon Rd, Palm Desert
(92260-3757)
PHONE 760 776-5555
EMP: 90
SALES (corp-wide): 308.5MM **Privately Held**
SIC: 6141 Personal credit institutions
PA: Stearns Lending, Llc
555 Anton Blvd Ste 300
Costa Mesa CA 92626
714 513-7777

(P-9765)
TOYOTA MOTOR CREDIT CORP
4000 Executive Pkwy # 525, San Ramon
(94583-4339)
PHONE 925 830-8200
Fax: 925 830-1549
Jim Guerra, *Branch Mgr*
Angie Perez, *Admin Asst*
Grace Rabara, *Administration*
EMP: 60
SALES (corp-wide): 242.7B **Privately Held**
WEB: www.toyota.com
SIC: 6141 Consumer finance companies
HQ: Toyota Motor Credit Corporation
19001 S Western Ave
Torrance CA 90501
310 468-1310

(P-9766)
WELLS FARGO DEALER SVCS INC (DH)
23 Pasteur, Irvine (92618-3816)
P.O. Box 25341, Santa Ana (92799-5341)
PHONE 949 727-1002
Thomas A Wolfe, *President*
J Keith Palmer, *Treasurer*
Ronald Terry, *Ch Credit Ofcr*
Robert Galea, *Chief Mktg Ofcr*
Dawn M Martin, *Exec VP*
EMP: 350
SALES (est): 129.3MM
SALES (corp-wide): 90B **Publicly Held**
SIC: 6141 Consumer finance companies
HQ: Wells Fargo Bank, National Association
464 California St
San Francisco CA 94104
415 396-7392

(P-9767)
WILSHIRE CONSUMER CREDIT
Also Called: 1800-R-Ado
4751 Wilshire Blvd, Los Angeles
(90010-3827)
P.O. Box 76809 (90076-0809)
PHONE 323 692-8585
Ian Anderson, *President*
EMP: 50
SALES (est): 4.2MM **Privately Held**
SIC: 6141 Automobile & consumer finance companies

6153 Credit Institutions, Short-Term Business

(P-9768)
AFFIRM INC
Also Called: Affirm Identity
225 Bush St Ste 1600, San Francisco
(94104-4213)
PHONE 415 984-0490
Max Levchin, *CEO*
Rob Pfeifer, *Owner*
Huey Lin, *COO*
Carl Gish, *Chief Mktg Ofcr*
EMP: 200 **EST:** 2012
SALES (est): 18.3MM **Privately Held**
SIC: 6153 Working capital financing

(P-9769)
AMERICAN EXPRESS TRAVEL
1851 E 1st St Ste 600, Santa Ana
(92705-4049)
PHONE 714 547-7116
Rob Rasmussen, *Manager*
Stephen P Norman, *Corp Secy*
Kevin P McDonnell, *Exec VP*
Bradley S Alexander, *Vice Pres*
Linda Fulton, *Human Res Dir*
EMP: 80
SALES (corp-wide): 34.4B **Publicly Held**
WEB: www.astoriasoftware.com
SIC: 6153 Short-term business credit
HQ: American Express Travel Related Services Company, Inc.,
200 Vesey St
New York NY 10285
212 640-2000

(P-9770)
AMERICAN MERCHANT CENTER INC
6819 Sepulveda Blvd # 311, Van Nuys
(91405-4463)
PHONE 818 947-1700
Victor Olechno, *President*
EMP: 70 **EST:** 1987
SQ FT: 5,000
SALES (est): 7.9MM **Privately Held**
WEB: www.americanmerchant.com
SIC: 6153 Credit card services, central agency collection

(P-9771)
BANK AMERICA NATIONAL ASSN
450 American St, Simi Valley (93065-6285)
PHONE 805 520-5100
Danette Samilton, *Senior VP*
Carlos Rivera, *Vice Pres*
Samantha Endicott, *Assistant VP*
EMP: 100
SALES (corp-wide): 93B **Publicly Held**
SIC: 6153 Working capital financing
HQ: Bank Of America, National Association
101 S Tryon St
Charlotte NC 28280
704 386-5681

(P-9772)
BANKAMERICA FINANCIAL INC
Also Called: Bank of America
315 Montgomery St, San Francisco
(94104-1856)
PHONE 415 622-3521
James A Dern, *President*
Lewis W Teel, *Ch of Bd*
Marty Stein, *Vice Chairman*
Michael K Riley, *Treasurer*
John Carson, *Senior VP*
EMP: 1700

PRODUCTS & SERVICES SECTION
6159 - Credit Institutions, Misc Business County (P-9794)

SALES (est): 294.6K
SALES (corp-wide): 93B **Publicly Held**
SIC: 6153 6141 6282 Factors of commercial paper; consumer finance companies; investment advisory service
PA: Bank Of America Corporation
100 N Tryon St Ste 220
Charlotte NC 28202
704 386-5681

(P-9773)
BIC REAL ESTATE DEV CORP
8800 Stockdale Hwy # 100, Bakersfield (93311-1012)
PHONE 661 847-9691
Daniel Nase, *President*
Margarita Nase, *COO*
Dario Montes De Oca, *Manager*
EMP: 504
SQ FT: 10,000
SALES: 20MM **Privately Held**
SIC: 6153 6799 Buying of installment notes; real estate investors, except property operators; investment clubs

(P-9774)
BLUEVINE
401 Warren St Ste 300, Redwood City (94063-1578)
PHONE 888 452-7805
Eyal Lifihitz, *President*
Gerad Hanono, *Opers Mgr*
EMP: 70
SALES (est): 298.4K **Privately Held**
SIC: 6153 Working capital financing

(P-9775)
BROKER SOLUTIONS INC
233 Milford Dr, Corona Del Mar (92625-3118)
PHONE 800 450-2010
EMP: 306
SALES (corp-wide): 107.4MM **Privately Held**
SIC: 6153 Working capital financing
PA: Broker Solutions, Inc.
14511 Myford Rd
Tustin CA 92780
800 450-2010

(P-9776)
BROKER SOLUTIONS INC
Also Called: New American Funding
662 Encinitas Blvd, Encinitas (92024-6788)
PHONE 760 633-0102
EMP: 102
SALES (corp-wide): 107.4MM **Privately Held**
SIC: 6153 Working capital financing
PA: Broker Solutions, Inc.
14511 Myford Rd
Tustin CA 92780
800 450-2010

(P-9777)
CBS BROADCASTING INC
1888 Century Park E # 1900, Los Angeles (90067-1702)
PHONE 310 284-6835
Anita Matthis, *Principal*
EMP: 169
SALES (corp-wide): 13.9B **Publicly Held**
WEB: www.cbs4.com
SIC: 6153 Short-term business credit
HQ: Cbs Broadcasting Inc.
51 W 52nd St
New York NY 10019
212 975-4321

(P-9778)
COGENT FINANCIAL GROUP
5199 E Pacific Coast Hwy, Long Beach (90804-3309)
PHONE 562 985-1388
Theodore Schlegel, *CEO*
EMP: 60
SQ FT: 6,500
SALES (est): 6.6MM **Privately Held**
WEB: www.cogentfinancialgroup.com
SIC: 6153 Purchasers of accounts receivable & commercial paper

(P-9779)
CONRAD ACCEPTANCE CORPORATION
Also Called: Conrad Credit
476 W Vermont Ave, Escondido (92025-6529)
PHONE 760 735-5000
Keith Richenbacher, *President*
William Huss, *CFO*
John Page, *Vice Pres*
Bob Pranik, *Admin Sec*
Sharon Starkey, *Accounting Mgr*
EMP: 50
SQ FT: 6,000
SALES (est): 5.2MM
SALES (corp-wide): 11.9MM **Privately Held**
SIC: 6153 Purchasers of accounts receivable & commercial paper
PA: Conrad Corporation
476 W Vermont Ave
Escondido CA 92025
800 826-6723

(P-9780)
DEALSTRUCK INC
2223 Avenida De Ln Playa, La Jolla (92037)
PHONE 858 218-6703
EMP: 62
SALES (corp-wide): 30.7MM **Privately Held**
SIC: 6153 Working capital financing
PA: Dealstruck, Inc.
1901 Camin Vida Roble Ste
Carlsbad CA 92008
855 610-5626

(P-9781)
EAST LOS ANGELES COMMUNITY UN (PA)
Also Called: Telacu
5400 E Olympic Blvd, Commerce (90022-5147)
PHONE 323 721-1655
Fax: 323 724-3372
David C Lizarraga, *Ch of Bd*
Paul Samuel, *CFO*
Michael D Lizarraga, *Exec VP*
Jay Bell, *Senior VP*
Jerry Barham, *Vice Pres*
EMP: 50
SQ FT: 60,000
SALES: 17.7MM **Privately Held**
WEB: www.telacu.com
SIC: 6153 8322 6512 6514 Short-term business credit; multi-service center; non-residential building operators; dwelling operators, except apartments

(P-9782)
ENCORE CAPITAL GROUP INC (PA)
3111 Camino Del Rio N # 103, San Diego (92108-5720)
PHONE 877 445-4581
Kenneth A Vecchione, *President*
Willem Mesdag, *Ch of Bd*
Jonathan Clark, *CFO*
Ashish Masih, *Exec VP*
Gregory L Call, *Senior VP*
EMP: 148 **EST:** 1998
SQ FT: 118,000
SALES: 1.1B **Publicly Held**
WEB: www.encorecapitalgroup.com
SIC: 6153 Short-term business credit; purchasers of accounts receivable & commercial paper

(P-9783)
GENERAL ELECTRIC CAPITAL CORP
3100 Zinfandel Dr Ste 255, Rancho Cordova (95670-6391)
PHONE 916 286-8020
Fax: 916 286-8050
EMP: 119
SALES (corp-wide): 117.3B **Publicly Held**
SIC: 6153 Short-term business credit
HQ: General Electric Capital Corporation
901 Main Ave
Norwalk CT 06851
203 840-6300

(P-9784)
HSBC BUSINESS CREDIT (USA)
Also Called: Hsbc Bank USA NA
660 S Figueroa St # 1030, Los Angeles (90017-3442)
PHONE 213 553-8089
Fax: 213 312-3630
Celia Anderson-Hayes, *Manager*
Andrew Ratzky, *Loan Officer*
EMP: 85
SQ FT: 4,000
SALES (corp-wide): 89B **Privately Held**
SIC: 6153 Short-term business credit
HQ: Hsbc Business Credit (Usa) Inc
452 5th Ave Fl 4
New York NY 10018
800 511-1918

(P-9785)
LENDINGCLUB CORPORATION (PA)
71 Stevenson St Ste 300, San Francisco (94105-2985)
PHONE 415 632-5600
Fax: 650 482-5228
Scott Sanborn, *President*
Kolya Klimenko, *President*
Sameer Gulati, *COO*
Carrie Dolan, *CFO*
Sandeep Bhandari, *Ch Credit Ofcr*
EMP: 88
SQ FT: 169,000
SALES: 979.6MM **Publicly Held**
SIC: 6153 Working capital financing

(P-9786)
MIDLAND CREDIT MANAGEMENT INC
3111 Camino Del Rio N, San Diego (92108-5720)
P.O. Box 939069 (92193-9069)
PHONE 877 240-2377
Kenneth A Vecchione, *CEO*
Carl Gregory, *President*
Olivier Baudoux, *Senior VP*
Robin Pruitt, *Senior VP*
Manu Rikhye, *Senior VP*
EMP: 1800
SALES (est): 367.9MM
SALES (corp-wide): 1.1B **Publicly Held**
WEB: www.encorecapitalgroup.com
SIC: 6153 Short-term business credit
PA: Encore Capital Group, Inc.
3111 Camino Del Rio N # 103
San Diego CA 92108
877 445-4581

(P-9787)
N A CITIBANK
Citicorp
1 Sansome St Fl 28, San Francisco (94104-4435)
PHONE 415 627-6000
Dorris D Mendoza, *Manager*
Morris Lazefsky, *Assoc VP*
Kevin Nater, *Vice Pres*
Aurum Spiegel, *Vice Pres*
John Wetzler, *Vice Pres*
EMP: 100
SALES (corp-wide): 88.2B **Publicly Held**
SIC: 6153 6159 6082 Short-term business credit; loan institutions, general & industrial; foreign trade & international banking institutions
HQ: Citibank Na
399 Park Ave Bsmt 1
New York NY 10022
212 559-1000

(P-9788)
NATIONS CAPITAL GROUP LLC
Also Called: Nations Surgery Center
5353 Balboa Blvd Ste 300, Encino (91316-2863)
PHONE 818 793-2050
Fax: 818 793-2059
Carolene Morreale, *Manager*
EMP: 50
SALES (corp-wide): 5.1MM **Privately Held**
SIC: 6153 Working capital financing
PA: Nations Capital Group, Llc
5370 S Durango Dr
Las Vegas NV

(P-9789)
SEQUOIA RESIDENTIAL FUNDING
1 Belvedere Pl Ste 330, Mill Valley (94941-2493)
PHONE 415 389-7373
George Bull, *CEO*
EMP: 90
SALES: 13.3MM **Privately Held**
SIC: 6153 7389 Working capital financing; financial services

(P-9790)
WELLS FARGO COML DIST FIN LLC
3100 Zinfandel Dr Ste 255, Rancho Cordova (95670-6391)
PHONE 916 636-2020
EMP: 94
SALES (corp-wide): 90B **Publicly Held**
SIC: 6153 Mercantile financing
HQ: Wells Fargo Commercial Distribution Finance, Llc
5595 Trillium Blvd
Hoffman Estates IL 60192
847 747-6800

6159 Credit Institutions, Misc Business

(P-9791)
ALLIANCE FUNDING GROUP
Also Called: Alliance Capital Markets
3745 W Chapman Ave # 200, Orange (92868-1656)
PHONE 714 940-0653
Fax: 714 704-1448
Brijesh Ashok Patel, *President*
Shawn M Donohue, *Vice Pres*
Vishal V Masani, *Vice Pres*
Mike McNeil, *Training Spec*
Barry Abelsohn, *Natl Sales Mgr*
EMP: 80 **EST:** 1998
SQ FT: 25,000
SALES (est): 393.2MM **Privately Held**
WEB: www.alliancefunds.com
SIC: 6159 Machinery & equipment finance leasing

(P-9792)
ALLY FINANCIAL INC
Also Called: General Motors
2530 Arnold Dr Ste 300, Martinez (94553-4359)
PHONE 925 370-7200
Jim Kucharski, *Branch Mgr*
EMP: 88
SALES (corp-wide): 9.5B **Publicly Held**
WEB: www.gmacfs.com
SIC: 6159 7515 Automobile finance leasing; passenger car leasing
PA: Ally Financial Inc.
200 Renaissance Ctr
Detroit MI 48243
866 710-4623

(P-9793)
AMERICAN AGCREDIT FLCA (PA)
400 Aviation Blvd Ste 100, Santa Rosa (95403-1181)
P.O. Box 1120 (95402-1120)
PHONE 707 545-1200
Ron Carli, *CEO*
Byron Enix, *President*
Bruce Richardson, *COO*
Christopher Call, *CFO*
John Caldwell, *Bd of Directors*
EMP: 91
SQ FT: 26,000
SALES (est): 105.5MM **Privately Held**
WEB: www.agloan.com
SIC: 6159 Agricultural credit institutions

(P-9794)
ATEL CAPITAL GROUP (PA)
Also Called: Leasing Equipment
600 Montgomery St Fl 9, San Francisco (94111-2711)
PHONE 415 989-8800
Dean L Cash, *CEO*
Paritosh K Choksi, *CFO*
Ken Fosina, *Exec VP*

6159 - Credit Institutions, Misc Business County (P-9795)

Russell H Wilder, *Exec VP*
Thomas P Monroe, *Senior VP*
EMP: 80
SALES (est): 35.4MM **Privately Held**
SIC: 6159 Machinery & equipment finance leasing

(P-9795)
BABCOCK & BROWN LATIN AMERICA
2 Harrison St Fl 6, San Francisco (94105-1671)
PHONE..................................415 512-1515
James Babcock, *President*
Camron Peters, *Vice Pres*
Peter Metzner, *Principal*
Mike Garland, *VP Finance*
Francoise Elhag, *Human Res Mgr*
EMP: 85
SALES (est): 8.1MM
SALES (corp-wide): 508.5MM **Privately Held**
SIC: 6159 Loan institutions, general & industrial
HQ: Bbam Llc
  50 California St Fl 14
  San Francisco CA 94111
  415 512-1515

(P-9796)
BANC AMERICA LSG & CAPITL LLC (DH)
555 California St Fl 4, San Francisco (94104-1506)
PHONE..................................415 765-7349
Ronald H Chamides, *CEO*
William Badgio, *Vice Pres*
Kenneth Chesley, *Vice Pres*
Douglas Ducray, *Vice Pres*
William Osmun, *Vice Pres*
EMP: 150
SALES (est): 7.2MM
SALES (corp-wide): 93B **Publicly Held**
SIC: 6159 Machinery & equipment finance leasing
HQ: Bank Of America, National Association
  101 S Tryon St
  Charlotte NC 28280
  704 386-5681

(P-9797)
CAPNET FINANCIAL SERVICES INC (PA)
Also Called: Capital Network Funding Svcs
11901 Santa Monica Blvd, Los Angeles (90025-2767)
PHONE..................................818 859-8377
John Armstron, *CEO*
Blake Johnson, *President*
Michael Kromnick, *CFO*
Armita Dalal, *Controller*
EMP: 90
SQ FT: 23,000
SALES (est): 12MM **Privately Held**
WEB: www.capnetusa.com
SIC: 6159 Equipment & vehicle finance leasing companies

(P-9798)
COLATERAL LENDER INC
Also Called: Loanmart
9640 Santa Monica Blvd, Beverly Hills (90210-4402)
PHONE..................................310 659-4353
Tal Smargal, *President*
EMP: 70 **EST:** 2001
SALES (est): 6.6MM **Privately Held**
SIC: 6159 Miscellaneous business credit

(P-9799)
GENERAL ELECTRIC CAPITAL CORP
2995 Red Hill Ave Ste 100, Costa Mesa (92626-5984)
PHONE..................................714 434-4111
Teri Lo, *Manager*
EMP: 147
SALES (corp-wide): 117.3B **Publicly Held**
WEB: www.gecapital.com
SIC: 6159 Equipment & vehicle finance leasing companies; machinery & equipment finance leasing
HQ: General Electric Capital Corporation
  901 Main Ave
  Norwalk CT 06851
  203 840-6300

(P-9800)
GENERAL ELECTRIC CAPITAL CORP
17911 Von Karman Ave, Irvine (92614-6209)
PHONE..................................949 838-3043
Mark Dawejko, *Branch Mgr*
EMP: 159
SALES (corp-wide): 117.3B **Publicly Held**
WEB: www.gecapital.com
SIC: 6159 Equipment & vehicle finance leasing companies
HQ: General Electric Capital Corporation
  901 Main Ave
  Norwalk CT 06851
  203 840-6300

(P-9801)
INTERLINK
Also Called: Interlink Company The
10940 Wilshire Blvd, Los Angeles (90024-3915)
PHONE..................................310 734-1499
Shezad Rokerya, *Director*
Dr Charles Kohlhaas, *Vice Chairman*
Jason P Caramanis, *Exec VP*
EMP: 103
SQ FT: 4,000
SALES (est): 6.7MM **Privately Held**
SIC: 6159 8742 Intermediate investment banks; banking & finance consultant

(P-9802)
NATIONWIDE FUNDING LLC
5520 Trabuco Rd Ste 100, Irvine (92620-5705)
PHONE..................................949 679-3600
Fax: 949 679-3601
Evan Lang, *Mng Member*
Dan Summers, *COO*
Robert Knudson, *Executive*
Josh Splinter,
EMP: 50
SQ FT: 12,000
SALES (est): 9.6MM **Privately Held**
SIC: 6159 7359 Machinery & equipment finance leasing; equipment rental & leasing

(P-9803)
PACIFIC CAPITAL COMPANIES LLC
11620 Wilshire Blvd, Los Angeles (90025-1706)
PHONE..................................800 583-3015
Charles Anderson, *Managing Prtnr*
EMP: 150
SQ FT: 10,000
SALES (est): 17.8MM **Privately Held**
SIC: 6159 Automobile finance leasing

(P-9804)
TOYOTA MOTOR SALES USA INC (DH)
Also Called: Scion
19001 S Western Ave, Torrance (90501-1106)
PHONE..................................310 468-4000
Yoshimi Inaba, *Chairman*
Kazuo Ohara, *President*
Patrick Moore, *COO*
Tracey Doi, *CFO*
Tracey C Doi, *CFO*
EMP: 500
SQ FT: 387,000
SALES: 23.6MM
SALES (corp-wide): 242.7B **Privately Held**
WEB: www.toyotahub.com
SIC: 6159 5012 3711 Automobile finance leasing; commercial vehicles; motor vehicles & car bodies

(P-9805)
TOYOTA MOTOR SALES USA INC
19340 Van Ness Ave, Torrance (90501-1103)
PHONE..................................310 468-7626
EMP: 285

SALES (corp-wide): 242.7B **Privately Held**
SIC: 6159 Automobile finance leasing
HQ: Toyota Motor Sales Usa Inc
  19001 S Western Ave
  Torrance CA 90501
  310 468-4000

(P-9806)
TRINITY CAPITAL CORPORATION (DH)
475 Sansome St Fl 19, San Francisco (94111-3112)
PHONE..................................415 956-5174
Fax: 415 956-5187
Don J McGrath, *CEO*
Christopher Kelly, *President*
Jerry Newell, *President*
Gregory Weston, *Officer*
Sandra McKenzie, *Finance Mgr*
EMP: 74
SQ FT: 19,232
SALES (est): 43.3MM **Publicly Held**
WEB: www.trinitycapital.com
SIC: 6159 8741 Machinery & equipment finance leasing; management services
HQ: Bank Of The West
  180 Montgomery St # 1400
  San Francisco CA 94104
  415 765-4800

(P-9807)
WELLS FARGO CAPITAL FIN LLC (DH)
2450 Colo Ave Ste 3000w, Santa Monica (90404)
PHONE..................................310 453-7300
Peter E Schwab,
Kevin Coyle, *Ch Credit Ofcr*
Christopher Macdonald, *Senior VP*
David Meier, *Vice Pres*
Steve Scott, *Vice Pres*
EMP: 53
SALES (est): 31.2MM
SALES (corp-wide): 90B **Publicly Held**
WEB: www.wellsfargo.com
SIC: 6159 Loan institutions, general & industrial
HQ: Wells Fargo Bank, National Association
  464 California St
  San Francisco CA 94104
  415 396-7392

(P-9808)
WESTLAKE SERVICES LLC
Also Called: Westlake Financial Services
4751 Wilshire Blvd # 100, Los Angeles (90010-3847)
P.O. Box 76809 (90076-0809)
PHONE..................................323 692-8800
Don Hankey, *Ch of Bd*
Ian Anderson, *President*
James Vagim, *President*
Paul Kerwin, *CFO*
Kent Hagan, *Vice Pres*
EMP: 160
SQ FT: 22,000
SALES (est): 61.6MM **Privately Held**
WEB: www.westlakefinancial.com
SIC: 6159 6141 Automobile finance leasing; personal credit institutions

6162 Mortgage Bankers & Loan Correspondents

(P-9809)
A D BILICH INC
Also Called: Preferred Financial
11 Crow Canyon Ct Ste 100, San Ramon (94583-1981)
PHONE..................................925 820-5557
Fax: 925 820-1141
Tim Barnes, *President*
Anthony D Bilich, *Owner*
Angela Bilich, *Admin Sec*
Amy Sarubbi, *Opers Staff*
Robert Schmitz, *VP Sales*
EMP: 50
SQ FT: 4,000
SALES (est): 8.7MM **Privately Held**
WEB: www.preferredfinancial.com
SIC: 6162 Mortgage bankers & correspondents

(P-9810)
AGIRE MORTGAGE CORPORATION
2125 E Katella Ave # 350, Anaheim (92806-6072)
PHONE..................................714 564-5821
Robin Auerbach, *President*
EMP: 50
SALES (est): 5.7MM **Privately Held**
SIC: 6162 Mortgage bankers & correspondents

(P-9811)
AMERICAN FINANCIAL NETWORK INC
333 S Juniper St 102, Escondido (92025-4924)
PHONE..................................760 291-1059
EMP: 222
SALES (corp-wide): 82MM **Privately Held**
SIC: 6162 Mortgage bankers & correspondents
PA: American Financial Network, Inc.
  3110 Chino Ave Ste 290
  Chino CA 91710
  909 606-3905

(P-9812)
AMERICAN FINANCIAL NETWORK INC (PA)
Also Called: Gateway Home Realty
3110 Chino Ave Ste 290, Chino (91710)
PHONE..................................909 606-3905
Fax: 909 393-1732
John B Sherman, *President*
John R Sherman, *Vice Pres*
Gloria Connelly, *Branch Mgr*
Joe Morgan, *Loan Officer*
Jon Gwin, *General Counsel*
EMP: 200
SQ FT: 800
SALES: 82MM **Privately Held**
SIC: 6162 Mortgage bankers & correspondents

(P-9813)
AMERICAN INTERBANC MRTG LLC
4 Park Plz Ste 650, Irvine (92614-2522)
PHONE..................................714 957-9430
Fax: 949 957-9433
Jiangping JP He,
Blair Kenny, *COO*
Mike Dannelley, *Director*
EMP: 50 **EST:** 1998
SALES (est): 6.5MM
SALES (corp-wide): 9.5MM **Privately Held**
WEB: www.eloans4u.com
SIC: 6162 6163 Mortgage bankers & correspondents; loan brokers
PA: Seashine Financial Llc
  4 Park Plz Ste 650
  Irvine CA 92614
  949 383-5070

(P-9814)
AMERICAN INTERNET MORTGAGE INC
Also Called: Aimloan.com, A Direct Lender
4121 Camino Del Rio S, San Diego (92108-4103)
PHONE..................................619 610-9900
Vincent J Kasperick, *President*
Antero D Iturriria, *Vice Pres*
Jill Lantz, *Opers Mgr*
EMP: 106 **EST:** 1998
SQ FT: 4,500
SALES: 63.6MM **Privately Held**
SIC: 6162 Mortgage bankers & correspondents

(P-9815)
AMERICAN PACIFIC MORTGAGE CORP (PA)
Also Called: Big Valley Mortgage
3000 Lava Ridge Ct # 200, Roseville (95661-2800)
PHONE..................................916 960-1325
Fax: 916 791-1686
Kurt Reisig, *CEO*
Bill Lowman, *President*
David Mack, *COO*

PRODUCTS & SERVICES SECTION
6162 - Mortgage Bankers & Loan Correspondents County (P-9836)

Ralph Hints, *CFO*
Tom Allen, *Treasurer*
EMP: 120
SQ FT: 35,000
SALES (est): 274.9MM **Privately Held**
WEB: www.apmmortgage.com
SIC: 6162 Mortgage bankers & correspondents

(P-9816)
AMERICAN TRANSPORT INC
Also Called: Bankers Diversified Mortgage
3080 S Harbor Blvd, Santa Ana (92704-6431)
P.O. Box 25810 (92799-5810)
PHONE 714 567-8000
Fax: 714 850-3377
David Hahnfeld, *President*
Diane G Hahnfeld, *Corp Secy*
David N Hartman, *Vice Pres*
EMP: 60
SQ FT: 32,000
SALES (est): 4.9MM **Privately Held**
WEB: www.bankersdiversified.com
SIC: 6162 Mortgage brokers, using own money

(P-9817)
AMERICASH
3080 Bristol St Ste 300, Costa Mesa (92626-3059)
PHONE 714 994-7554
Paul Giangrande, *CEO*
Eric Harrington, *Vice Pres*
Michael Martin, *Vice Pres*
Janene Winberry, *Human Resources*
EMP: 50
SALES (est): 12.5MM **Privately Held**
WEB: www.americashloans.com
SIC: 6162 Mortgage bankers

(P-9818)
AMERIPATH MORTGAGE CORPORATION
6410 Oak Cyn Ste 200, Irvine (92618-5215)
PHONE 949 753-9211
Fax: 949 265-3600
Paul B Akers, *President*
Kirk L Redding, *CEO*
Jo Beth Montoya, *Vice Pres*
James Shea, *Info Tech Dir*
EMP: 112
SQ FT: 22,286
SALES (est): 9.3MM **Privately Held**
WEB: www.amclend.com
SIC: 6162 Mortgage bankers

(P-9819)
ARCS COMMERCIAL MORTGAGE CO LP (DH)
26901 Agoura Rd Ste 200, Calabasas (91301-5109)
PHONE 818 676-3274
Fax: 818 880-3333
Timothy White, *CEO*
Lillian Aceituno, *Vice Pres*
Paul Anderson, *Vice Pres*
Kelly Pagett, *Vice Pres*
Don Lydiksen, *Info Tech Mgr*
EMP: 110
SQ FT: 15,000
SALES (est): 27.9MM
SALES (corp-wide): 16.2B **Publicly Held**
SIC: 6162 Mortgage bankers
HQ: Pnc Bank, National Association
249 5th Ave Ste 1200
Pittsburgh PA 15222
412 762-2000

(P-9820)
BAY EQUITY LLC (PA)
Also Called: Bay Equity Home Loans
28 Liberty Ship Way # 2800, Sausalito (94965-3320)
PHONE 415 632-5150
Casey McGovern, *President*
Sue Potter, *COO*
Cindy Smith, *Officer*
Bob Altendorf, *Vice Pres*
Tom McGovern, *Branch Mgr*
EMP: 51
SQ FT: 6,000
SALES (est): 34MM **Privately Held**
SIC: 6162 Mortgage bankers & correspondents

(P-9821)
BEAR STEARNS COMPANIES LLC
Also Called: Bear Stern Residential Mrtg
1833 Alton Pkwy, Irvine (92606-4902)
PHONE 949 856-8300
Troy Gotscahall, *Branch Mgr*
EMP: 780
SALES (corp-wide): 101B **Publicly Held**
WEB: www.bearstearns.com
SIC: 6162 Mortgage bankers
HQ: Bear Stearns Companies Llc
383 Madison Ave
New York NY 10179
212 272-2000

(P-9822)
BERKSHIRE MORTGAGE FIN CORP
Also Called: Vauche Bank Berkshire Mortgage
7575 Irvine Center Dr # 200, Irvine (92618-2987)
PHONE 949 754-6300
Jeff Day, *Manager*
Peter Donovan, *Sr Corp Ofcr*
Stephen Ryan, *General Counsel*
EMP: 80
SALES (corp-wide): 8.8B **Privately Held**
SIC: 6162 Mortgage bankers
HQ: Berkshire Mortgage Finance Corporation
1 North Beacon St Fl 14
Allston MA 02134
617 523-0066

(P-9823)
CALIBER HOME LOANS INC
3700 Hilborn Rd Ste 700, Fairfield (94534-7997)
PHONE 707 432-1000
Sanjiv Das, *Principal*
EMP: 300
SALES (corp-wide): 677.5MM **Privately Held**
SIC: 6162 Mortgage bankers & correspondents
PA: Caliber Home Loans, Inc.
3701 Regent Blvd
Irving TX 75063
800 401-6587

(P-9824)
CALIFORNIA EMPIRE BANCORP INC
10681 Fthill Blvd Ste 200, Rancho Cucamonga (91730)
PHONE 909 484-7988
Lester Hills, *President*
Ken Emminger, *Vice Pres*
Diane Frieze, *Accounting Mgr*
Aaron Kane, *Accounting Mgr*
Celesta McGee, *Accounting Mgr*
EMP: 50
SQ FT: 5,000
SALES (est): 3.5MM **Privately Held**
SIC: 6162 Mortgage bankers & correspondents

(P-9825)
CAMBRIDGE HOME LOANS INC FN
201 Lomas Santa Fe Dr # 340, Solana Beach (92075-1284)
PHONE 858 481-2929
Fax: 858 481-1919
Merrill Moses, *President*
Paul Ivers, *COO*
Khurram Iftikhar, *Info Tech Dir*
Darrel Winbush, *Info Tech Dir*
EMP: 55
SALES (est): 4.9MM **Privately Held**
WEB: www.cambridgeloans.com
SIC: 6162 Mortgage bankers

(P-9826)
CAPITAL PLUS FINANCIAL CORP
909 W Laurel St Ste 250, San Diego (92101-1224)
PHONE 619 744-1900
Frank Sharpe, *President*
Doug Lipar, *Vice Pres*
Evelyn Cervantes, *Office Mgr*
EMP: 50
SQ FT: 5,000
SALES (est): 5.2MM **Privately Held**
SIC: 6162 Mortgage brokers, using own money

(P-9827)
CBRE INC
225 W Santa Clara St # 1050, San Jose (95113-1748)
PHONE 408 453-7400
Mark Schmidt, *Manager*
Sharon Hasegawa, *Vice Pres*
Daniel Schmidt, *Research*
Elizabeth Davis, *Sales Associate*
EMP: 100
SALES (corp-wide): 10.8B **Publicly Held**
SIC: 6162 Mortgage bankers
HQ: Cbre, Inc.
400 S Hope St Ste 25
Los Angeles CA 90071
310 477-5876

(P-9828)
CENTURY FINANCE INCORPORATED
Also Called: Villagecraft Quality Furn
2461 Santa Monica Blvd, Santa Monica (90404-2138)
PHONE 310 281-3081
RC Zarate, *President*
Franceisca Zarate, *CFO*
Ezzio Delpino, *Corp Secy*
Sam Mannino, *General Mgr*
EMP: 56
SALES (est): 4.5MM **Privately Held**
SIC: 6162 2514 Mortgage bankers & correspondents; metal household furniture

(P-9829)
CHAPEL FUNDING CORPORATION
26521 Rancho Pkwy S, Lake Forest (92630-8329)
PHONE 949 580-1800
Nina Mitchel, *President*
Hope Margarit, *Vice Pres*
Eric Spiak, *Vice Pres*
Scott Tiger, *Engineer*
Brad Eilert, *Credit Staff*
EMP: 165
SALES (est): 11.3MM **Privately Held**
WEB: www.chapelfunding.com
SIC: 6162 Mortgage bankers & correspondents

(P-9830)
CHASE HOME FINANCE
Also Called: Chase Manhattan
2633 Camino Ramon Ste 300, San Ramon (94583-2570)
PHONE 925 277-3700
Joann Fabiano, *Manager*
EMP: 50
SALES (corp-wide): 101B **Publicly Held**
WEB: www.chasehomeequity.com
SIC: 6162 Mortgage bankers
HQ: Chase Home Finance
480 Washington Blvd Fl 12
Jersey City NJ 07310
732 205-0600

(P-9831)
CITIGROUP INC
840 N Eckhoff St Ste 140, Orange (92868-1054)
PHONE 714 938-0748
Michael B Zeller, *Branch Mgr*
EMP: 100
SALES (corp-wide): 88.2B **Publicly Held**
WEB: www.citigroup.com
SIC: 6162 6163 Mortgage bankers & correspondents; loan brokers
PA: Citigroup Inc.
399 Park Ave
New York NY 10022
212 559-1000

(P-9832)
COUNTRYWIDE CAPITAL MKTS LLC (DH)
4500 Park Granada, Calabasas (91302-1613)
PHONE 818 225-3000
Fax: 818 225-4032
Angelo R Mozilo, *Ch of Bd*
Stanfard L Kurland, *CFO*
Ron Kripalani, *Director*
EMP: 182
SALES (est): 51.3MM
SALES (corp-wide): 93B **Publicly Held**
SIC: 6162 Mortgage brokers, using own money
HQ: Countrywide Financial Corporation
4500 Park Granada
Calabasas CA 91302
818 225-3000

(P-9833)
COUNTRYWIDE FINANCIAL CORP (HQ)
4500 Park Granada, Calabasas (91302-1613)
P.O. Box 7137, Pasadena (91109-7137)
PHONE 818 225-3000
Fax: 818 225-4051
Angelo R Mozilo, *Ch of Bd*
David Sambol, *President*
Jack W Schakett, *COO*
Eric P Sieracki, *CFO*
Christian Ingerslev, *Exec VP*
EMP: 1100
SQ FT: 225,000
SALES (est): 6.4B
SALES (corp-wide): 93B **Publicly Held**
WEB: www.countrywide.com
SIC: 6162 6211 6361 6411 Mortgage bankers; brokers, security; dealers, security; title insurance; life insurance agents; loan brokers; real estate investors, except property operators
PA: Bank Of America Corporation
100 N Tryon St Ste 220
Charlotte NC 28202
704 386-5681

(P-9834)
COUNTRYWIDE HOME LOANS INC (DH)
225 W Hillcrest Dr, Thousand Oaks (91360-7883)
PHONE 818 225-3000
Fax: 818 225-4070
Michael Schloessmann, *Ch of Bd*
Angelo R Mozilo, *Ch of Bd*
David Sambol, *President*
Carlos M Garcia, *COO*
Thomas K McLaughlin, *CFO*
EMP: 700 **EST:** 1969
SQ FT: 220,000
SALES (est): 543.6MM
SALES (corp-wide): 93B **Publicly Held**
WEB: www.mycountrywide.com
SIC: 6162 Mortgage bankers
HQ: Countrywide Financial Corporation
4500 Park Granada
Calabasas CA 91302
818 225-3000

(P-9835)
COUNTRYWIDE HOME LOANS INC
801 N Brand Blvd Ste 750, Glendale (91203-3218)
PHONE 818 550-8700
Fax: 818 550-5887
Lynda Martinlawley, *Manager*
EMP: 150
SALES (corp-wide): 93B **Publicly Held**
WEB: www.mycountrywide.com
SIC: 6162 Mortgage bankers
HQ: Countrywide Home Loans, Inc.
225 W Hillcrest Dr
Thousand Oaks CA 91360
818 225-3000

(P-9836)
CRESTLINE FUNDING CORPORATION
18851 Pardeen Ave, San Diego (92108)
PHONE 949 863-8600
Fax: 619 624-2501
Scott M Brown, *President*
Brad Helman, *CFO*
Larry Work, *VP Human Res*
Brian Kidd, *Accounts Exec*
EMP: 50
SQ FT: 18,500

6162 - Mortgage Bankers & Loan Correspondents County (P-9837)

SALES (est): 10.6MM **Privately Held**
WEB: www.crestlinewholesale.com
SIC: **6162** Mortgage bankers & correspondents

(P-9837)
DUXFORD FINANCIAL INC
Also Called: William Lyon Fin Services
4490 Von Karman Ave, Newport Beach (92660-2008)
PHONE..................949 471-2010
William Lyon, *Ch of Bd*
Maureen Singer, *Executive*
Heather Hinks, *Executive Asst*
Marie Howard, *Loan*
Shandra Smock, *Manager*
EMP: 50
SALES (est): 5MM
SALES (corp-wide): 37.2MM **Privately Held**
WEB: www.duxford.com
SIC: **6162** Mortgage bankers & correspondents
PA: Lyon Management Group, Inc.
  4901 Birch St Frnt
  Newport Beach CA 92660
  949 252-9101

(P-9838)
EC CLOSING CORP
Also Called: Cal Western Foreclosure Svcs
525 E Main St, El Cajon (92020-4007)
P.O. Box 22004 (92022-9004)
PHONE..................800 546-1531
Fax: 619 590-9299
Gerald R Moss, *President*
Margaret Pedilla, *President*
Avis Thomas, *Vice Pres*
Wendy Perry, *Sales Mgr*
Lorrie Womack, *Sales Mgr*
EMP: 80
SQ FT: 20,000
SALES (est): 23.4MM
SALES (corp-wide): 120.1MM **Privately Held**
WEB: www.cwrc.com
SIC: **6162** Loan correspondents
PA: Prommis Solutions, Llc
  400 Northridge Rd
  Atlanta GA 30350
  800 275-7171

(P-9839)
EXECUTIVE FINANCIAL HM LN CORP
Also Called: Executive Home Loan
12501 Chandler Blvd, Valley Village (91607-1941)
PHONE..................818 285-5626
Fax: 818 285-5660
Michael Nikravesh, *President*
Ron Fattal, *Vice Pres*
EMP: 50
SALES (est): 4.4MM **Privately Held**
SIC: **6162** Mortgage bankers & correspondents

(P-9840)
FINANCE AMERICA LLC (HQ)
1901 Main St Ste 150, Irvine (92614-0516)
PHONE..................949 440-1000
Brian Libman,
Leigh Harris, *Officer*
Antoinette Espinoza, *Administration*
Jeff Hurley, *MIS Dir*
Dean Caley, *Mortgage*
EMP: 230
SQ FT: 60,000
SALES (est): 185.9MM
SALES (corp-wide): 28.1MM **Privately Held**
WEB: www.closeasap.com
SIC: **6162** 6163 Mortgage bankers; loan brokers
PA: Lehman Brothers Holdings Inc.
  1271 Ave Of The Americas
  New York NY 10020
  646 285-9000

(P-9841)
FIRST CALIFORNIA MRTG CO II
1435 N Mcdowell Blvd # 300, Petaluma (94954-6548)
PHONE..................415 209-0910
Dennis M Hart, *Ch of Bd*
Christopher Hart, *President*

David Heier, *CFO*
Ralph Hints, *CFO*
Alice Carmack, *Senior VP*
EMP: 100
SALES (est): 19.4MM **Privately Held**
WEB: www.firstcal.net
SIC: **6162** Mortgage bankers & correspondents

(P-9842)
FREEDOM MORTGAGE CORPORATION
5900 La Place Ct Ste 107, Carlsbad (92008-8832)
PHONE..................760 692-3977
Stanley Middleman, *President*
EMP: 120
SALES (corp-wide): 965.8MM **Privately Held**
SIC: **6162** Loan correspondents
PA: Freedom Mortgage Corporation
  907 Pleasant Valley Ave # 3
  Mount Laurel NJ 08054
  866 759-8624

(P-9843)
FULL SPECTRUM LENDING INC (DH)
35 N Lake Ave Fl 3, Pasadena (91101-4192)
PHONE..................626 584-2220
Greg Lumsden, *Ch of Bd*
Paul Abbamonto, *President*
Thomas Boone, *COO*
Michelle Manzi, *Vice Pres*
Sandor E Samuels, *Admin Sec*
EMP: 83 EST: 1996
SALES (est): 49.5MM
SALES (corp-wide): 93B **Publicly Held**
WEB: www.fullspectrumlending.com
SIC: **6162** 6163 Mortgage bankers & correspondents; loan brokers
HQ: Countrywide Financial Corporation
  4500 Park Granada
  Calabasas CA 91302
  818 225-3000

(P-9844)
GENPACT MORTGAGE SERVICES INC
Also Called: Moneyline Lending Services
15420 Laguna Canyon Rd, Irvine (92618-2119)
PHONE..................949 417-5131
Evan Gentry, *President*
Brett Fish, *President*
Richard Belliston, *CFO*
Chandan Goel, *Treasurer*
Bradley J Barber, *Exec VP*
EMP: 85 EST: 1996
SQ FT: 17,000
SALES (est): 18.4MM **Privately Held**
SIC: **6162** 6163 Mortgage brokers, using own money; loan brokers
PA: Genpact Limited
  C/O : Appleby
  Hamilton
  441 295-2244

(P-9845)
GEORGE ELKINS MRTG BNKG CO LP (DH)
12100 Wilshire Blvd, Los Angeles (90025-7120)
PHONE..................310 979-5749
Jeff Hudson, *Partner*
Brian Eisner, *Vice Pres*
Kelley Griner, *Vice Pres*
Bryan Gortikov, *Associate Dir*
Greg Proniloff, *Associate Dir*
EMP: 60 EST: 1920
SQ FT: 13,000
SALES (est): 78.2K
SALES (corp-wide): 29.7MM **Publicly Held**
SIC: **6162** 6531 6411 Mortgage bankers; real estate agents & managers; insurance agents, brokers & service
HQ: Mma Realty Capital, Llc
  621 E Pratt St Ste 300
  Baltimore MD 21202
  443 263-2900

(P-9846)
GOAL FINANCIAL LLC
401 W A St Ste 1300, San Diego (92101-7906)
PHONE..................858 731-9000
Fax: 858 452-6648
Ryan Katz,
Eley Cruz, *Sales Mgr*
Kim Nguyen, *Marketing Staff*
Dave Bowen, *Director*
Carolyn Dvergsten, *Manager*
EMP: 250
SALES (est): 26.6MM **Privately Held**
WEB: www.goalfinancial.net
SIC: **6162** Loan correspondents

(P-9847)
GOLDEN EMPIRE MORTGAGE
664 Shoppers Ln Ste A, Covina (91723-3536)
PHONE..................626 967-3236
Fax: 626 967-4156
Joe Ewens, *Branch Mgr*
Yvette Sunga, *Mktg Dir*
Hank Greenberg, *Manager*
EMP: 74
SALES (corp-wide): 76.2MM **Privately Held**
SIC: **6162** Mortgage bankers & correspondents
PA: Golden Empire Mortgage
  1200 Discovery Dr Ste 300
  Bakersfield CA 93309
  661 328-1600

(P-9848)
GOLDEN EMPIRE MORTGAGE (PA)
1200 Discovery Dr Ste 300, Bakersfield (93309-7036)
PHONE..................661 328-1600
Fax: 661 328-9521
John Copeland, *Manager*
David Chesney, *CFO*
Rick Roper, *Exec VP*
Alex Lopez, *Branch Mgr*
Tim Silva, *General Mgr*
EMP: 80
SALES (est): 76.2MM **Privately Held**
SIC: **6162** Mortgage bankers

(P-9849)
GOLDEN EMPIRE MORTGAGE INC (PA)
2130 Chester Ave, Bakersfield (93301-4471)
PHONE..................661 328-1600
Fax: 661 328-1659
Howard Kootstra, *CEO*
Rebecca Wegman, *Exec VP*
John Thomas, *Vice Pres*
Alex Lopez, *Branch Mgr*
Stephanie Harrison, *Human Res Dir*
EMP: 100
SQ FT: 25,000
SALES (est): 44.5MM **Privately Held**
WEB: www.gemcorp.com
SIC: **6162** Mortgage bankers & correspondents

(P-9850)
GUARANTEED RATE INC
4180 La Jolla Village Dr # 315, La Jolla (92037-1472)
PHONE..................760 310-6008
Trent Annicharico, *Branch Mgr*
EMP: 129
SALES (corp-wide): 888.2MM **Privately Held**
SIC: **6162** Mortgage bankers & correspondents
PA: Guaranteed Rate, Inc.
  3940 N Ravenswood Ave
  Chicago IL 60613
  866 934-7283

(P-9851)
GUARANTEED RATE INC
31285 Temecula Pkwy, Temecula (92592-6828)
PHONE..................949 430-0809
Brian Decker, *Branch Mgr*
EMP: 95

SALES (corp-wide): 888.2MM **Privately Held**
SIC: **6162** Mortgage bankers & correspondents
PA: Guaranteed Rate, Inc.
  3940 N Ravenswood Ave
  Chicago IL 60613
  866 934-7283

(P-9852)
GUILD MORTGAGE COMPANY (PA)
Also Called: Comstock Mortgage
5898 Copley Dr Fl 4, San Diego (92111-7916)
P.O. Box 85304 (92186-5304)
PHONE..................800 283-8823
Fax: 858 492-5807
Mary Ann McGarry, *President*
Margie Orwig, *President*
Terry Schmidt, *CFO*
Terry L Schmidt, *CFO*
Mike Rish, *Chief Mktg Ofcr*
EMP: 200
SQ FT: 35,000
SALES (est): 428.4MM **Privately Held**
SIC: **6162** 6733 Mortgage bankers; trusts, except educational, religious, charity: management

(P-9853)
HCL FINANCE INC (PA)
Also Called: Home Community Lending
2560 Mission College Blvd, Santa Clara (95054-1217)
PHONE..................408 845-9035
Fax: 408 845-9036
Hong Cheng, *President*
Nancy Cheng, *Vice Pres*
EMP: 56
SQ FT: 9,000
SALES (est): 11MM **Privately Held**
WEB: www.hclfinance.com
SIC: **6162** Mortgage bankers & correspondents

(P-9854)
HFF INC
1999 Avenue Of The Stars # 1200, Los Angeles (90067-4630)
PHONE..................310 407-2100
Brad Black, *Executive*
Andrew Hornblower, *Analyst*
Scott Brown, *Associate*
EMP: 86
SALES (corp-wide): 501.9MM **Publicly Held**
SIC: **6162** Mortgage bankers & correspondents
PA: Hff, Inc.
  301 Grant St Ste 1100
  Pittsburgh PA 15219
  412 281-8714

(P-9855)
HFF INC
18300 Von Karman Ave # 900, Irvine (92612-1054)
PHONE..................949 253-8800
Donald Curtis, *Branch Mgr*
EMP: 68
SALES (corp-wide): 501.9MM **Publicly Held**
SIC: **6162** Mortgage bankers & correspondents
PA: Hff, Inc.
  301 Grant St Ste 1100
  Pittsburgh PA 15219
  412 281-8714

(P-9856)
HOME CAPITAL GROUP
948 N Grand Ave, Covina (91724-2045)
PHONE..................626 331-4213
Raymond Mark Gonzales, *Partner*
Rick Starr, *Partner*
EMP: 68
SALES (est): 4MM **Privately Held**
SIC: **6162** Loan correspondents

(P-9857)
HOMEQ SERVICING CORPORATION (DH)
4837 Watt Ave, North Highlands (95660-5108)
PHONE..................916 339-6192

PRODUCTS & SERVICES SECTION
6162 - Mortgage Bankers & Loan Correspondents County (P-9882)

Arthur Lyon, *President*
Keith G Becher, *COO*
John A Hollstien, *Treasurer*
Mark K Metz, *Admin Sec*
EMP: 1000
SALES (est): 88.2MM
SALES (corp-wide): 1.7B **Publicly Held**
WEB: www.homeq.com
SIC: 6162 6163 6111 6159 Mortgage bankers; agents, farm or business loan; Student Loan Marketing Association; automobile finance leasing
HQ: Ocwen Loan Servicing, Llc
1661 Worthington Rd # 100
West Palm Beach FL 33409
561 682-8000

(P-9858)
HSBC FINANCE CORPORATION
21801 Ventura Bouelvard, Woodland Hills (91364)
PHONE.................................818 999-9175
EMP: 303
SALES (corp-wide): 89B **Privately Held**
WEB: www.household.com
SIC: 6162 Mortgage bankers
HQ: Hsbc Finance Corporation
1421 W Shure Dr Ste 100
Arlington Heights IL 60004
224 880-7000

(P-9859)
IMPAC MORTGAGE CORP
19500 Jamboree Rd, Irvine (92612-2401)
PHONE.................................949 475-3600
Joseph R Tomkinson, *President*
EMP: 298
SALES (est): 85.9MM **Publicly Held**
SIC: 6162 Mortgage bankers & correspondents
PA: Impac Mortgage Holdings, Inc.
19500 Jamboree Rd
Irvine CA 92612
-

(P-9860)
INTEGRITY MRTG SOLUTIONS INC
2321 Rosecrans Ave # 4210, El Segundo (90245-4903)
PHONE.................................310 643-8700
Fax: 310 643-8708
Alan E Wright, *President*
Eric Wade, *Director*
EMP: 50
SQ FT: 2,000
SALES: 2MM **Privately Held**
WEB: www.integritymortgagesolutions.com
SIC: 6162 Bond & mortgage companies

(P-9861)
INTERNATIONAL HOME MORTGAGE
13601 Whittier Blvd # 411, Whittier (90605-1984)
PHONE.................................562 945-7753
Fax: 562 945-5339
Rick Arciniega, *Manager*
EMP: 75
SALES (est): 6.1MM **Privately Held**
SIC: 6162 Mortgage bankers & correspondents

(P-9862)
INVESTORS MORTGAGE ASSET RECOV
Also Called: Imarc
23282 Mill Creek Dr # 370, Laguna Hills (92653-1658)
PHONE.................................657 859-6200
Robert Simpson, *President*
Linda Swaniger, *Executive*
Lynn B Riordan, *Sales Mgr*
EMP: 97
SALES (est): 15.7MM **Privately Held**
WEB: www.mortgagefraud.com
SIC: 6162 Mortgage bankers & correspondents

(P-9863)
ISERVE RESIDENTIAL LENDING LLC
15015 Ave Of Science # 250, San Diego (92128-3436)
PHONE.................................858 486-4169

Doug Wilson, *Director*
Brent Nyitray, *Director*
Michael Wilson, *Director*
Mary Hendrickson, *Manager*
EMP: 100
SALES (est): 25.9MM **Privately Held**
SIC: 6162 Bond & mortgage companies

(P-9864)
JMJ FINANCIAL GROUP (PA)
26800 Aliso Viejo Pkwy # 200, Aliso Viejo (92656-2625)
PHONE.................................949 340-6336
Virgil Kyle, *President*
Thomas Kish, *COO*
Ryan Robertson, *CFO*
Ryan Gale, *Loan Officer*
James Howorth, *Loan Officer*
EMP: 50
SALES: 500MM **Privately Held**
SIC: 6162 Mortgage bankers

(P-9865)
JUST MORTGAGE INC
8577 Haven Ave Ste 306, Rancho Cucamonga (91730-4850)
PHONE.................................562 908-5000
Eun H Choi, *CEO*
Sang H Jeung, *President*
Bryan Choi, *Vice Pres*
EMP: 118
SQ FT: 49,750
SALES (est): 15.9MM **Privately Held**
SIC: 6162 Mortgage bankers & correspondents

(P-9866)
LAKE COUNTY HOME LOANS
Also Called: Selzer Home Loans
350 E Gobbi St, Ukiah (95482-5511)
PHONE.................................707 462-4000
Fax: 707 462-4600
Richard Selzer, *Owner*
Elisa Moilanen, *Admin Sec*
Charles W Elmer, *Manager*
EMP: 50
SALES (est): 4.1MM **Privately Held**
SIC: 6162 Mortgage bankers & correspondents

(P-9867)
LAND HOME FINANCIAL SVCS INC (PA)
1355 Willow Way Ste 250, Concord (94520-8113)
PHONE.................................925 676-7038
Fax: 925 676-0843
Bradley Harold Waite, *CEO*
J Ben Absalom, *Managing Prtnr*
Angela Warren, *President*
Chris Wittrig, *President*
David Waite, *CFO*
EMP: 50
SQ FT: 6,000
SALES (est): 12MM **Privately Held**
SIC: 6162 Loan correspondents

(P-9868)
LENOX FINANCIAL MORTGAGE CORP
Also Called: Weslend Financial
200 Sandpointe Ave # 800, Santa Ana (92707-5783)
PHONE.................................949 428-5100
Wesley C Hoaglund, *CEO*
Carlito Dizon, *Info Tech Dir*
Paul Hampton, *Senior Mgr*
EMP: 105
SALES (est): 42.5MM **Privately Held**
SIC: 6162 Mortgage bankers & correspondents

(P-9869)
LEON CHIEN CORP
Also Called: RE Max 2000 Realty
17843 Colima Rd, City of Industry (91748-1729)
PHONE.................................626 964-8302
Kuan Sung, *CEO*
Shu Cheng, *Real Est Agnt*
EMP: 80
SALES (est): 8.5MM **Privately Held**
SIC: 6162 Mortgage bankers & correspondents

(P-9870)
LOANDEPOTCOM LLC (PA)
26642 Towne Centre Dr, Foothill Ranch (92610-2808)
PHONE.................................949 474-1322
Anthony Hsieh, *CEO*
David Norris, *President*
Jon Frojen, *CFO*
Diana Harvey, *Officer*
Peter Macdonald, *Exec VP*
EMP: 963
SALES (est): 664.8MM **Privately Held**
WEB: www.loandepot.com
SIC: 6162 Mortgage bankers

(P-9871)
LONG BEACH INVESTMENT GROUP
Also Called: Dream Home & Investments Rlty
2041 Pacific Coast Hwy, Lomita (90717-2685)
PHONE.................................562 595-7277
Henry Salazar, *President*
Jenny Gowers, *Manager*
EMP: 50
SQ FT: 6,000
SALES: 2.7MM **Privately Held**
SIC: 6162 Mortgage bankers & correspondents

(P-9872)
MARK 1 MORTGAGE CORPORATION
19147 Bloomsville Ave, Cerritos (90703)
PHONE.................................562 924-6173
Mark Prether, *Branch Mgr*
EMP: 50
SALES (corp-wide): 15.3MM **Privately Held**
SIC: 6162 Mortgage bankers & correspondents
PA: Mark 1 Mortgage Corporation
1428 E Chapman Ave
Orange CA 92866
714 752-5700

(P-9873)
METRO HOME LOAN INC
Also Called: Metro City
15301 Ventura Blvd D300, Sherman Oaks (91403-3102)
PHONE.................................818 461-9840
Paul Whiley, *Vice Pres*
EMP: 99
SALES (est): 5.5MM **Privately Held**
SIC: 6162 Mortgage bankers & correspondents

(P-9874)
MORTGAGE CAPITAL PARTNERS INC
12400 Wilshire Blvd # 900, Los Angeles (90025-1030)
PHONE.................................310 295-2900
Carolyn W Chang, *President*
EMP: 80 **EST:** 2008
SALES (est): 11.7MM **Privately Held**
SIC: 6162 Mortgage bankers & correspondents

(P-9875)
MOUNTAIN WEST FINANCIAL INC (PA)
Also Called: Mortgage Works Financial
1209 Nevada St Ste 200, Redlands (92374-4581)
PHONE.................................909 793-1500
Gary H Martell Jr, *President*
Michael W Douglas, *CFO*
Karen Hirsch, *Admin Asst*
EMP: 391
SQ FT: 4,729
SALES (est): 62.8MM **Privately Held**
WEB: www.mwfinc.com
SIC: 6162 Mortgage bankers & correspondents

(P-9876)
NETWORK CAPITAL FUNDING CORP (PA)
5 Park Plz Ste 800, Irvine (92614-8501)
PHONE.................................949 442-0060
Tri Nguyen, *President*
EMP: 345

SQ FT: 67,000
SALES (est): 45.1MM **Privately Held**
SIC: 6162 Mortgage bankers

(P-9877)
OCMBC INC
Also Called: Ocmban
19000 Macarthur Blvd # 200, Irvine (92612-1420)
PHONE.................................714 479-0999
Rabi H Aziz, *CEO*
Madelina L Colon, *President*
Hector Chaidez, *Division Mgr*
Bernie Cavallucci, *Sales Mgr*
Dale Martin, *General Counsel*
EMP: 70 **EST:** 2001
SQ FT: 12,500
SALES (est): 10.7MM **Privately Held**
WEB: www.helpufinance.com
SIC: 6162 Mortgage bankers

(P-9878)
OPTIMA MORTGAGE CORPORATION
2081 Bus Ctr Dr Ste 230, Irvine (92612)
PHONE.................................714 389-4650
Mansour Sadeghi, *President*
Shiva Sadeghi, *Treasurer*
EMP: 55
SQ FT: 14,000
SALES: 5.1MM **Privately Held**
WEB: www.60minuteloan.com
SIC: 6162 Mortgage bankers

(P-9879)
OWNIT MORTGAGE SOLUTIONS INC
Also Called: Security Pacific Home Loans
4360 Park Terrace Dr # 100, Westlake Village (91361-5696)
PHONE.................................513 872-6922
Bill Dallas, *President*
Bruce Dickinson, *COO*
John Duhadway, *CFO*
John Du Hadway, *Vice Pres*
John C Becker, *Admin Sec*
EMP: 500
SQ FT: 47,857
SALES (est): 35.7MM **Privately Held**
SIC: 6162 6163 Mortgage bankers & correspondents; loan brokers

(P-9880)
PACIFICA HOME LOANS INC
7505 Irvine Center Dr, Irvine (92618-2991)
PHONE.................................949 417-1063
Craig W Tobin, *President*
Craig Tobin, *President*
Chris Roman, *Marketing Staff*
EMP: 50
SQ FT: 9,000
SALES (est): 3.5MM **Privately Held**
SIC: 6162 Mortgage bankers

(P-9881)
PARAMOUNT EQUITY MORTGAGE LLC
10888 White Rock Rd, Rancho Cordova (95670-6044)
PHONE.................................916 290-9999
Hayes Barnard, *President*
EMP: 200
SALES (corp-wide): 87.3MM **Privately Held**
SIC: 6162 Mortgage bankers & correspondents
PA: Paramount Equity Mortgage, Llc
8781 Sierra College Blvd
Roseville CA 95661
916 290-9999

(P-9882)
PARAMOUNT EQUITY MORTGAGE LLC
22 Executive Park Ste 100, Irvine (92614-2700)
PHONE.................................916 290-9999
Hayes Barnard, *President*
EMP: 150
SALES (corp-wide): 87.3MM **Privately Held**
SIC: 6162 Mortgage bankers & correspondents; mortgage bankers

6162 - Mortgage Bankers & Loan Correspondents County (P-9883)

PA: Paramount Equity Mortgage, Llc
8781 Sierra College Blvd
Roseville CA 95661
916 290-9999

(P-9883)
PARAMOUNT EQUITY MORTGAGE LLC
4200 Douglas Blvd, Granite Bay (95746-5902)
PHONE..................916 290-9999
Hayes Barnard, *President*
EMP: 100
SALES (corp-wide): 87.3MM **Privately Held**
SIC: 6162 Mortgage bankers & correspondents
PA: Paramount Equity Mortgage, Llc
8781 Sierra College Blvd
Roseville CA 95661
916 290-9999

(P-9884)
PENNYMAC FINANCIAL SVCS INC
6101 Condor Dr, Moorpark (93021-2602)
PHONE..................818 224-7442
Stanford L Kurland, *Ch of Bd*
David A Spector, *President*
Anne D McCallion, *CFO*
David M Walker, *Ch Credit Ofcr*
Andrew S Chang, *Officer*
EMP: 1370
SQ FT: 142,000
SALES: 731.2MM **Privately Held**
SIC: 6162 6282 Mortgage bankers & correspondents; investment advice

(P-9885)
PEOPLES CHOICE HOME (PA)
7515 Irvine Center Dr, Irvine (92618-2930)
PHONE..................949 494-6167
Neil B Kornswiet, *CEO*
EMP: 55
SQ FT: 20,000
SALES (est): 16.9MM **Privately Held**
SIC: 6162 Mortgage companies, urban

(P-9886)
PLAZA HOME MORTGAGE INC (PA)
4820 Eastgate Mall # 100, San Diego (92121-1993)
PHONE..................858 346-1200
Fax: 858 346-1201
Kevin Parra, *President*
James Cutri, *Exec VP*
Michael Fontaine, *Exec VP*
Julie Manson, *Senior VP*
Michael Modell, *Senior VP*
EMP: 50
SQ FT: 1,000
SALES (est): 130.7MM **Privately Held**
WEB: www.plazahomemortgages.com
SIC: 6162 Mortgage bankers & correspondents

(P-9887)
PRIVATE NAT MRTG ACCPTANCE LLC (PA)
Also Called: Pennymac
6101 Condor Dr, Agoura Hills (91301)
PHONE..................818 224-7401
Jeff Grogin, *Principal*
Steve Bailey, *Security Dir*
David Galen, *Director*
EMP: 800
SALES (est): 132.5MM **Privately Held**
SIC: 6162 Mortgage bankers & correspondents

(P-9888)
PROVIDENT FUNDING ASSOC LP (PA)
851 Traeger Ave Ste 100, San Bruno (94066-3091)
P.O. Box 5914, Santa Rosa (95402-5914)
PHONE..................650 652-1300
Fax: 650 652-1348
Doug Pica, *General Ptnr*
Michelle Blake, *Partner*
Craig Pica, *Partner*
Ralph Pica, *Partner*
Lori Pica, *COO*
EMP: 50

SALES (est): 73.4MM **Privately Held**
SIC: 6162 Mortgage bankers

(P-9889)
PROVIDENT MRTG CPITL ASSOC INC
Also Called: P M C A
1633 Bayshore Hwy Ste 155, Burlingame (94010-1515)
PHONE..................650 652-1300
Craig Pica, *Ch of Bd*
Mark Lefanowicz, *CFO*
Michelle Blake, *Admin Sec*
John Kubiak, *CIO*
EMP: 600
SALES (est): 18.4MM **Privately Held**
SIC: 6162 Mortgage bankers

(P-9890)
PROVIDENT SAVINGS BANK
Also Called: Profed Mortgage
10370 Commerce Center Dr # 200, Rancho Cucamonga (91730-5806)
PHONE..................909 484-6286
Fax: 909 980-7248
Debbie Baker, *General Mgr*
Kenneth Courtney, *Manager*
Susie Alexander, *Accounts Exec*
EMP: 50 **Publicly Held**
SIC: 6162 Mortgage bankers & correspondents
HQ: Provident Savings Bank
3756 Central Ave
Riverside CA 92506
951 782-6177

(P-9891)
QUALITY HOME LOANS
Also Called: Clear Credit Capital
27001 Agoura Rd Ste 200, Agoura Hills (91301-5357)
PHONE..................818 206-6600
Patrick Weaver, *President*
John T Gaiser, *President*
Randy Miller, *CFO*
Christopher Powell, *Vice Pres*
EMP: 220
SQ FT: 47,500
SALES: 18MM **Privately Held**
WEB: www.qualityhomeloans.com
SIC: 6162 Mortgage bankers & correspondents

(P-9892)
RATE IS LOW
Also Called: Ideal Home Sales
3744 Mt Diablo Blvd # 205, Lafayette (94549-3694)
PHONE..................925 299-9364
Fax: 925 283-4520
Ray Newby, *Manager*
EMP: 50 **EST:** 1999
SALES (est): 3.1MM **Privately Held**
WEB: www.rateislow.com
SIC: 6162 Mortgage bankers & correspondents

(P-9893)
RPM MORTGAGE INC (PA)
3240 Stone Valley Rd W, Alamo (94507-1555)
PHONE..................925 295-9300
Fax: 925 944-9883
Erwin R Hirt, *President*
Tracey Hirt, *President*
Rob Hirt, *CEO*
Cindy Ertman, *Exec VP*
Donny Isaak, *Exec VP*
EMP: 66
SALES (est): 89.1MM **Privately Held**
SIC: 6162 Mortgage bankers & correspondents

(P-9894)
RPM MORTGAGE INC
1777 Botelho Dr Ste 200, Walnut Creek (94596-5085)
PHONE..................925 627-7100
Fax: 925 226-1955
Lance Lemoine, *Branch Mgr*
EMP: 57
SALES (corp-wide): 89.1MM **Privately Held**
SIC: 6162 Mortgage bankers & correspondents

PA: Rpm Mortgage, Inc.
3240 Stone Valley Rd W
Alamo CA 94507
925 295-9300

(P-9895)
SEA BREEZE FINANCIAL SERVICES (PA)
Also Called: Sea Breeze Mortgage Services
18191 Von Karman Ave # 150, Irvine (92612-7104)
P.O. Box 19079, Anaheim (92817-9079)
PHONE..................949 223-9700
Fax: 949 223-9790
Leonard Hamilton, *President*
Curtis Green, *Executive*
EMP: 50
SQ FT: 50,000
SALES (est): 9.2MM **Privately Held**
SIC: 6162 Mortgage bankers & correspondents

(P-9896)
SECURITY NAT MSTR HOLDG CO LLC (PA)
323 5th St, Eureka (95501-0305)
P.O. Box 1028 (95502-1028)
PHONE..................707 442-2818
Fax: 707 442-1608
Robin P Arkley II, *CEO*
John Piland, *CFO*
Brandon Bailey, *Executive*
Jeanette Nusbuam, *Human Resources*
EMP: 140
SQ FT: 15,000
SALES (est): 37.1MM **Privately Held**
SIC: 6162 Mortgage bankers & correspondents

(P-9897)
SIERRA PACIFIC MORTGAGE CO INC
104 Traffic Way, Arroyo Grande (93420-3450)
PHONE..................805 489-6060
EMP: 88
SALES (corp-wide): 137.6MM **Privately Held**
SIC: 6162 Mortgage bankers & correspondents
PA: Sierra Pacific Mortgage Company, Inc.
1180 Iron Point Rd # 200
Folsom CA 95630
916 932-1700

(P-9898)
SIERRA PACIFIC MORTGAGE CO INC (PA)
1180 Iron Point Rd # 200, Folsom (95630-8325)
PHONE..................916 932-1700
James Coffrini, *President*
Gary Clark, *COO*
Lorae Oliver, *Officer*
Chuck Iverson, *Vice Pres*
Janet Lewis, *Vice Pres*
EMP: 580
SALES (est): 137.6MM **Privately Held**
WEB: www.premiumlending.com
SIC: 6162 Mortgage bankers

(P-9899)
STEARNS LENDING LLC (PA)
555 Anton Blvd Ste 300, Costa Mesa (92626-7667)
PHONE..................714 513-7777
Fax: 714 513-7222
Brian S Hale, *CEO*
Katherine Le, *President*
James Hecht, *COO*
Gary B Fabian, *CFO*
Tom Hunt, *Exec VP*
EMP: 350
SALES (est): 308.5MM **Privately Held**
WEB: www.stearns.com
SIC: 6162 Mortgage bankers & correspondents

(P-9900)
SUMMIT FUNDING INC (PA)
2241 Harvard St Ste 200, Sacramento (95815-3332)
PHONE..................916 571-3000
Todd Scrima, *President*
Tarica Hoswell, *Partner*

Roger Martin, *Branch Mgr*
Morsa Aziz, *Loan Officer*
Karen Bartholomew, *Loan Officer*
EMP: 50
SALES (est): 41.3MM **Privately Held**
WEB: www.summitfunding.com
SIC: 6162 Mortgage brokers, using own money

(P-9901)
TELACU INDUSTRIES INC (HQ)
5400 E Olympic Blvd # 300, Commerce (90022-5147)
PHONE..................323 721-1655
David Lizarraga, *CEO*
Michael D Lizarraga, *President*
Paul Samuel, *CFO*
Michelle Cuevas, *Administration*
Gabriella Barbarena, *Finance Spvr*
EMP: 50
SQ FT: 17,000
SALES: 195.4K
SALES (corp-wide): 17.7MM **Privately Held**
SIC: 6162 6552 Mortgage bankers & correspondents; loan correspondents; subdividers & developers
PA: East Los Angeles Community Union Inc
5400 E Olympic Blvd
Commerce CA 90022
323 721-1655

(P-9902)
US BANK NATIONAL ASSOCIATION
Also Called: US Bank
10021 Bloomfield St, Los Alamitos (90720-2207)
PHONE..................562 795-7520
Catherine Marker, *Office Mgr*
EMP: 50
SALES (corp-wide): 21.4B **Publicly Held**
SIC: 6162 Mortgage bankers
HQ: U.S. Bank National Association
425 Walnut St Fl 1
Cincinnati OH 45202
513 632-4234

(P-9903)
US CREDIT BANCORP INC
851 20th St, Santa Monica (90403-2002)
P.O. Box 1727 (90406-1727)
PHONE..................310 829-2112
Michel Rone, *President*
M Matsumote, *Corp Secy*
EMP: 85
SQ FT: 6,500
SALES: 45MM **Privately Held**
SIC: 6162 6799 Mortgage bankers; real estate investors, except property operators

(P-9904)
WALKER & DUNLOP INC
2603 Main St Ste 200, Irvine (92614-4246)
PHONE..................949 660-1999
Sheila Pasha, *Officer*
Michael Murphy, *Underwriter*
EMP: 115 **Publicly Held**
SIC: 6162 6531 6282 6141 Mortgage bankers; real estate agent, commercial; investment advice; financing: automobiles, furniture, etc., not a deposit bank
PA: Walker & Dunlop, Inc.
7501 Wisconsin Ave 1200e
Bethesda MD 20814

(P-9905)
WELLS FARGO HOME MORTGAGE INC
1350 Montego, Walnut Creek (94598-2822)
PHONE..................925 288-7100
Fax: 925 288-7944
Lousia Homes, *Manager*
Lynnea Craig-Dunn, *Area Mgr*
Gabriel Mascardo, *Info Tech Mgr*
Laurie O'Callaghan, *Loan Officer*
EMP: 200
SALES (corp-wide): 90B **Publicly Held**
WEB: www.wfhm.com
SIC: 6162 6163 Mortgage bankers & correspondents; loan brokers

PRODUCTS & SERVICES SECTION

6163 - Loan Brokers County (P-9928)

HQ: Wells Fargo Home Mortgage Inc
1 Home Campus
Des Moines IA 50328
515 324-3707

(P-9906)
WELLS FARGO HOME MORTGAGE INC
3010 Lava Ridge Ct # 150, Roseville (95661-3075)
PHONE 916 782-2221
Scott Nutter, *Manager*
EMP: 50
SALES (corp-wide): 90B **Publicly Held**
WEB: www.wfhm.com
SIC: 6162 Mortgage bankers & correspondents
HQ: Wells Fargo Home Mortgage Inc
1 Home Campus
Des Moines IA 50328
515 324-3707

(P-9907)
WELLS FARGO HOME MORTGAGE INC
5540 Fermi Ct Fl 2002, Carlsbad (92008-7325)
PHONE 760 603-7000
Fax: 760 603-7089
Kathleen Vauthan, *Vice Pres*
Liz Wilson, *Officer*
Daniel Friedman, *Technical Staff*
EMP: 400
SALES (corp-wide): 90B **Publicly Held**
WEB: www.wfhm.com
SIC: 6162 Mortgage bankers
HQ: Wells Fargo Home Mortgage Inc
1 Home Campus
Des Moines IA 50328
515 324-3707

(P-9908)
WOODSIDE GROUP INC
Also Called: Hillsborough
3509 Coffee Rd Ste D10, Modesto (95355-1358)
PHONE 209 579-2030
Mike Golkin, *Manager*
EMP: 50
SALES (corp-wide): 119.1MM **Privately Held**
SIC: 6162 Mortgage bankers & correspondents
PA: Woodside Group, Inc.
460 W 50 N Ste 200
Salt Lake City UT 84101
801 299-6700

6163 Loan Brokers

(P-9909)
ACA FINANCIAL GUARANTY CORP
7189 N Figueroa St, Los Angeles (90042-1279)
PHONE 323 255-3583
Robert Snyder, *President*
Steven Joeseph Berkowitz, *CEO*
Allen Overton, *CFO*
Allen Beckel, *Officer*
Brian Foore, *Vice Pres*
EMP: 75
SQ FT: 6,500
SALES (est): 3.9MM **Privately Held**
SIC: 6163 Loan brokers

(P-9910)
ACCESS TO LOANS FOR LEARNING
6701 Center Dr W Ste 500, Los Angeles (90045-1547)
PHONE 310 979-4700
Fax: 310 979-4714
Chris Chapman, *President*
Rick Patton, *Accountant*
Nicol Harris, *Assistant*
EMP: 50
SALES: 61.8MM **Privately Held**
WEB: www.allstudentloan.org
SIC: 6163 Mortgage brokers arranging for loans, using money of others

(P-9911)
AFFILIATED FUNDING CORPORATION
Also Called: Inhouselender.com
5 Hutton Centre Dr # 1100, Santa Ana (92707-8714)
PHONE 714 619-3100
Fax: 714 619-3202
Alfred Hanna, *President*
Alex Khader, *Vice Pres*
Mary Nguyen, *Loan Officer*
Medhad Kirollos, *Accounting Mgr*
Mark Halloran, *Marketing Staff*
EMP: 70
SALES (est): 9.1MM **Privately Held**
WEB: www.inhouselender.com
SIC: 6163 Mortgage brokers arranging for loans, using money of others

(P-9912)
AMERICAN FUNDING
Also Called: American Realty
5369 Camden Ave Ste 240, San Jose (95124-5809)
PHONE 408 269-4238
Fax: 408 583-0719
Ali Haider, *CEO*
Lorena Castedena, *Administration*
EMP: 60
SALES (est): 4.8MM **Privately Held**
WEB: www.americanfunding.com
SIC: 6163 6531 Mortgage brokers arranging for loans, using money of others; real estate agents & managers

(P-9913)
AMERICAN LIBERTY CAPITAL CORP
Also Called: American Liberty Funding
19000 Macarthur Blvd # 400, Irvine (92612-1438)
P.O. Box 10059, Newport Beach (92658-0059)
PHONE 949 623-0288
Christopher Chase, *President*
Mike R Chase, *Shareholder*
Chris Bull, *Corp Secy*
EMP: 105
SALES (est): 7.1MM **Privately Held**
SIC: 6163 Mortgage brokers arranging for loans, using money of others

(P-9914)
AMERICAS HOME LOANS INC
131 Stony Cir Ste 500a, Santa Rosa (95401-9520)
PHONE 707 577-7464
Edward Keech, *President*
Mary E Schmidt, *Accounts Exec*
EMP: 50
SALES (est): 3.6MM **Privately Held**
WEB: www.amhloans.com
SIC: 6163 Loan brokers

(P-9915)
AMERIQUEST CAPITAL CORPORATION (PA)
1100 W Twn Cntry Rd R, Orange (92868-4600)
PHONE 714 564-0600
Aseem Mital, *President*
Steve Goldberg, *Executive*
Pam Allison, *Executive Asst*
Jay Burton, *Manager*
EMP: 400
SQ FT: 85,000
SALES (est): 511.9MM **Privately Held**
SIC: 6163 Mortgage brokers arranging for loans, using money of others

(P-9916)
BRIDGER COMMERCIAL FUNDING LLC
249 Boas Dr, Santa Rosa (95409-3612)
PHONE 707 953-7475
Fax: 415 331-3390
Robert Schonefeld,
Gregory S Aunder, *CFO*
Sharol Collins, *Senior VP*
Lindsay Felix, *Accountant*
Christie Young, *Marketing Mgr*
EMP: 50
SQ FT: 8,000
SALES (est): 7.4MM **Privately Held**
SIC: 6163 Loan brokers

(P-9917)
CINTIVA FINANCIAL CORPORATION
10145 Pacific Hts 800, San Diego (92121-4242)
PHONE 858 526-0955
Richard A Myers, *President*
Niket Kulkarni, *Vice Pres*
Don Sarver, *Vice Pres*
EMP: 60
SQ FT: 12,500
SALES (est): 5.5MM **Privately Held**
WEB: www.cintiva.com
SIC: 6163 Mortgage brokers arranging for loans, using money of others

(P-9918)
CMG MORTGAGE INC (PA)
3160 Crow Canyon Rd # 400, San Ramon (94583-1382)
PHONE 619 554-1327
Fax: 925 866-2002
Christopher M George, *CEO*
Tom Meyer, *President*
Todd L Hempstead, *Senior VP*
Denise Tragale, *Vice Pres*
Mike Seeley, *Branch Mgr*
EMP: 349
SQ FT: 5,500
SALES (est): 74.8MM **Privately Held**
WEB: www.pacificguarantee.com
SIC: 6163 Mortgage brokers arranging for loans, using money of others

(P-9919)
E&S FINANCIAL GROUP INC
Also Called: Capital Mortgage Services
4253 Transport St, Ventura (93003-5659)
PHONE 805 644-1621
Jordan Eller, *President*
EMP: 70
SQ FT: 11,200
SALES (est): 2MM **Privately Held**
SIC: 6163 Loan brokers

(P-9920)
E-LOAN INC (DH)
6230 Stoneridge Mall Rd, Pleasanton (94588-3260)
PHONE 925 847-6200
Fax: 925 847-0831
Mark E Lefanowicz, *President*
Cameron King, *Senior VP*
David Drow, *Vice Pres*
Geoff Halverson, *Vice Pres*
Brunilda Santos, *Admin Sec*
EMP: 850
SQ FT: 118,000
SALES (est): 59.5MM
SALES (corp-wide): 2.1B **Publicly Held**
WEB: www.e-loan.com
SIC: 6163 6162 Mortgage brokers arranging for loans, using money of others; mortgage bankers & correspondents
HQ: Popular Finance Inc
326 Salud St El El Senorial Cond
Ponce PR 00716
787 844-2760

(P-9921)
EMERY FINANCIAL INC (PA)
Also Called: Wjbradley Mortgage Capital
620 Nwport Ctr Dr Ste 800, Newport Beach (92660)
PHONE 949 219-0640
Fax: 949 729-9212
Bradford Sarvak, *President*
Ty Kern, *COO*
Jay Anderson, *Officer*
Kent Kopen, *Officer*
Peggy Suber, *Officer*
EMP: 60
SQ FT: 7,000
SALES (est): 16.8MM **Privately Held**
WEB: www.emeryfinancial.com
SIC: 6163 Mortgage brokers arranging for loans, using money of others

(P-9922)
ESNA CORPORATION
44300 Lowtree Ave Ste 100, Lancaster (93534-4166)
PHONE 661 206-6010
Duane Faust, *President*
EMP: 50
SALES (est): 2.5MM **Privately Held**
SIC: 6163 Mortgage brokers arranging for loans, using money of others

(P-9923)
FIDELITY CAPITAL MORTGAGE BRKS
6380 Wilshire Blvd # 1200, Los Angeles (90048-5003)
PHONE 323 315-1700
Mayer Dallal, *President*
George Zioni, *CEO*
Ben Zioni, *Vice Pres*
Yaniv Zioni, *Vice Pres*
EMP: 50
SQ FT: 900
SALES (est): 3.3MM **Privately Held**
SIC: 6163 Mortgage brokers arranging for loans, using money of others

(P-9924)
FINANCIAL GROUP OF AMERICA
468 N Camden Dr Ste 2, Beverly Hills (90210-4507)
PHONE 310 860-5160
John Safyurtlu, *Branch Mgr*
EMP: 97
SALES (corp-wide): 4.2MM **Privately Held**
WEB: www.financialgroupofamerica.com
SIC: 6163 Mortgage brokers arranging for loans, using money of others
PA: Financial Group Of America
18340 Ventura Blvd # 219
Tarzana CA
818 501-7300

(P-9925)
FIRST AMRCN MRTG SOLUTIONS LLC (HQ)
30005 Ladyface Ct, Agoura Hills (91301-2583)
PHONE 800 333-4510
Fax: 818 871-1941
Jeff Moyer, *President*
Constance Wilson, *Exec VP*
Paul Harris, *Senior VP*
David G Kittle, *Senior VP*
Brett Waterman, *Senior VP*
EMP: 60
SQ FT: 12,000
SALES (est): 93.5MM **Publicly Held**
WEB: www.sysdome.com
SIC: 6163 Mortgage brokers arranging for loans, using money of others

(P-9926)
FIRST NATIONWIDE MORTGAGE CORP
18440 Bermuda St, Northridge (91326-3102)
PHONE 818 209-3134
EMP: 133
SALES (corp-wide): 88.2B **Publicly Held**
SIC: 6163 6162 Mortgage brokers arranging for loans, using money of others; mortgage bankers & correspondents
HQ: First Nationwide Mortgage Corporation
5280 Corporate Dr
Frederick MD 21703
301 791-8108

(P-9927)
GUARANTEE MORTGAGE CORPORATION
300 Tamal Plz Ste 250, Corte Madera (94925-1170)
PHONE 415 925-8080
Ryan Madden, *Branch Mgr*
EMP: 50
SALES (corp-wide): 25.7MM **Privately Held**
SIC: 6163 Mortgage brokers arranging for loans, using money of others
PA: Guarantee Mortgage Corporation
300 Tamal Plz Ste 250
Corte Madera CA 94925
415 925-8080

(P-9928)
GUILD MORTGAGE COMPANY
3626 Fair Oaks Blvd, Sacramento (95864-7200)
PHONE 916 486-6257

6163 - Loan Brokers County (P-9929)

PRODUCTS & SERVICES SECTION

Mary Ann McGarry, *Branch Mgr*
EMP: 50
SALES (corp-wide): 428.4MM **Privately Held**
SIC: 6163 Mortgage brokers arranging for loans, using money of others
PA: Guild Mortgage Company
5898 Copley Dr Fl 4
San Diego CA 92111
800 283-8823

(P-9929) INTERNATIONAL MRTG CORP ASSN
1037 Park View Dr Ste 200, Covina (91724-3764)
PHONE.............................626 339-9094
EMP: 60
SQ FT: 12,000
SALES (est): 4.1MM **Privately Held**
SIC: 6163 Mortgage brokers arranging for loans, using money of others

(P-9930) IZT MORTGAGE INC (PA)
Also Called: Ameritech Mortgage
3011 Citrus Cir Ste 202, Walnut Creek (94598-2631)
P.O. Box 492239, Los Angeles (90049-8239)
PHONE.............................925 946-1858
Fax: 760 423-0301
Zoran Trajanovich, *CEO*
Irina Trajanovich, *President*
Sanford Yester, *Vice Pres*
Donnie Featherstone, *Manager*
Leslie Rainey, *Manager*
EMP: 50
SQ FT: 12,000
SALES (est): 9.9MM **Privately Held**
SIC: 6163 Mortgage brokers arranging for loans, using money of others

(P-9931) J & P FINANCIAL INC (PA)
Also Called: Realty Executives
330 W Felicita Ave Ste E1, Escondido (92025-6534)
PHONE.............................760 738-9000
Joe W Cobb Jr, *President*
Paula Cobb, *Vice Pres*
Sabine Alberti, *Broker*
Lijun Zhou, *Broker*
Jim Daugherty, *Real Est Agnt*
EMP: 50
SQ FT: 5,370
SALES (est): 10MM **Privately Held**
SIC: 6163 Mortgage brokers arranging for loans, using money of others

(P-9932) KINGS PAWNSHOP
Also Called: Kings Jewelry and Loan
800 S Vermont Ave, Los Angeles (90005-1521)
PHONE.............................213 383-5555
Fax: 213 383-4462
Sam Shocket, *President*
Marco Barraz, *General Mgr*
EMP: 52
SQ FT: 11,000
SALES (est): 7.4MM **Privately Held**
WEB: www.kingspawn.com
SIC: 6163 5944 Loan brokers; jewelry stores

(P-9933) LIBERTY AMERICAN MORTGAGE CORP (PA)
193 Blue Ravine Rd # 240, Folsom (95630-4756)
PHONE.............................916 780-3000
Frank A Sousa, *President*
William Templeton, *Ch of Bd*
Dan Martinelli, *COO*
Jennifer Robinson, *CFO*
Patrick White, *Chairman*
EMP: 92
SQ FT: 18,000
SALES (est): 8.7MM **Privately Held**
WEB: www.libam.com
SIC: 6163 6162 Mortgage brokers arranging for loans, using money of others; mortgage bankers

(P-9934) LOANGENIECOM INC
Also Called: Approvalfinder.com
25 Technology Dr Ste B100, Irvine (92618-2381)
PHONE.............................949 788-6161
Peter Homer, *President*
Jim Creamer, *Ch of Bd*
David N Kenneally, *CFO*
Ryan Piwonka, *Vice Pres*
Linda Rounds, *Human Res Mgr*
EMP: 60 **EST:** 1998
SQ FT: 17,000
SALES (est): 2.3MM **Privately Held**
SIC: 6163 Loan brokers

(P-9935) M & A MORTGAGE INC
1600 N Broadway Ste 1020, Santa Ana (92706-3930)
PHONE.............................714 560-1970
Maria Avalos, *President*
Martin Alvarado, *CFO*
EMP: 75
SALES (est): 25MM **Privately Held**
SIC: 6163 Mortgage brokers arranging for loans, using money of others

(P-9936) MARK 1 MORTGAGE CORPORATION (PA)
1428 E Chapman Ave, Orange (92866-2229)
PHONE.............................714 752-5700
Mark D Prather, *President*
EMP: 50
SQ FT: 8,000
SALES (est): 15.3MM **Privately Held**
SIC: 6163 Mortgage brokers arranging for loans, using money of others

(P-9937) MISSION HILLS MORTGAGE CORP (HQ)
Also Called: Mission Hills Mortgage Bankers
18500 Von Karman Ave # 1100, Irvine (92612-0546)
PHONE.............................714 972-3832
Fax: 714 542-0996
Jay Ledbetter, *President*
Melinda Davis, *CFO*
Marsha Boniti, *Vice Pres*
Tim Cooper, *Site Mgr*
Markus Czirban, *Site Mgr*
EMP: 140
SQ FT: 27,000
SALES (est): 36.1MM
SALES (corp-wide): 132.4MM **Privately Held**
WEB: www.mhmc.com
SIC: 6163 Mortgage brokers arranging for loans, using money of others
PA: Tarbell Financial Corporation
1403 N Tustin Ave Ste 380
Santa Ana CA 92705
714 972-0988

(P-9938) MORTGAGE CAPITAL ASSOC INC
11150 W Olympic Blvd # 1160, Los Angeles (90064-1826)
PHONE.............................310 477-6877
Fax: 310 477-9035
Jay Steren, *CEO*
Colleen Mackay, *Executive*
Mark MA, *Controller*
Bradley Ross, *Agent*
EMP: 54
SALES (est): 7.7MM **Privately Held**
WEB: www.100percentloan.com
SIC: 6163 Mortgage brokers arranging for loans, using money of others

(P-9939) MORTGAGE CORP AMERICA INC
Also Called: Mortgage Corp of America
2315 Kuehner Dr Ste 115, Simi Valley (93063-3960)
PHONE.............................805 582-2220
Fax: 805 915-2444
Bradley A Rice, *President*
Deena Monette, *Manager*
Christopher Bunce, *Real Est Agnt*
EMP: 60
SQ FT: 16,000
SALES (est): 5.1MM **Privately Held**
WEB: www.mcastar.com
SIC: 6163 Mortgage brokers arranging for loans, using money of others

(P-9940) MRP REAL ESTATE SERVICES INC
Also Called: Mortgage & Realty Prof Svc
925 Fort Stockton Dr, San Diego (92103-1817)
PHONE.............................858 362-6005
Miguel Patterson, *President*
Chrstopher Scelfo, *Vice Pres*
EMP: 50
SQ FT: 2,000
SALES (est): 3.1MM **Privately Held**
WEB: www.mrpservicesinc.com
SIC: 6163 Mortgage brokers arranging for loans, using money of others

(P-9941) NATIONAL CREDIT INDUSTRIES INC
Also Called: Century 21
1100 Via Verde, San Dimas (91773-4401)
PHONE.............................626 967-4355
Oscar Rodriguez, *President*
Ashley Alvarez, *Admin Sec*
Mireya Ruiz, *Admin Sec*
Lucy Hollingsworth, *Sales Mgr*
Elizabeth Rodriguez, *Manager*
EMP: 90
SALES (est): 1.5MM **Privately Held**
SIC: 6163 Mortgage brokers arranging for loans, using money of others

(P-9942) NEWWEST MORTGAGE COMPANY
Also Called: Newwest Funding
8255 Firestone Blvd # 101, Downey (90241-4800)
PHONE.............................562 861-8393
Fax: 562 861-8386
David Samak, *President*
Kendra Samak, *Treasurer*
EMP: 60
SQ FT: 5,000
SALES (est): 5.6MM **Privately Held**
SIC: 6163 Mortgage brokers arranging for loans, using money of others

(P-9943) PENNYMAC CORP
27001 Agoura Rd, Agoura Hills (91301-5339)
PHONE.............................818 878-8416
Stanford L Kurland, *President*
EMP: 1793
SALES (est): 44.4MM
SALES (corp-wide): 373.4MM **Privately Held**
SIC: 6163 Loan brokers
PA: Pennymac Mortgage Investment Trust
6101 Condor Dr
Moorpark CA 93021
818 224-7442

(P-9944) PINNACLE FUNDING GROUP INC
2092 Omega Rd Ste H, San Ramon (94583-1230)
PHONE.............................925 552-5302
Fax: 925 552-7826
William Howard Paul III, *President*
John Greenwood, *Administration*
John Julson, *Administration*
EMP: 50
SQ FT: 5,000
SALES (est): 3.2MM **Privately Held**
SIC: 6163 Mortgage brokers arranging for loans, using money of others

(P-9945) PROSPECT MORTGAGE LLC (PA)
15301 Ventura Blvd D300, Sherman Oaks (91403-3102)
PHONE.............................818 981-0606
Michael J Williams, *Ch of Bd*
Ron Bergum, *Managing Prtnr*
Richard D Powers, *President*
Amy Brandt, *COO*
Sandra E Bell, *CFO*
EMP: 600 **EST:** 1999
SQ FT: 120,000
SALES (est): 743MM **Privately Held**
SIC: 6163 Mortgage brokers arranging for loans, using money of others

(P-9946) PROSPER MARKETPLACE INC (PA)
221 Main St Fl 3, San Francisco (94105-1911)
PHONE.............................415 593-5400
Fax: 415 362-7233
Aaron Vermut, *CEO*
Ronald Suber, *President*
Joshua M Tonderys, *COO*
David Kimball, *CFO*
Xiaopei Lee, *CFO*
EMP: 74
SALES: 204.2MM **Privately Held**
SIC: 6163 Loan brokers

(P-9947) REALTY ALLIANCE INC
Also Called: Loan Depot Group
20812 Ventura Blvd # 101, Woodland Hills (91364-2335)
PHONE.............................818 610-0080
Fax: 818 610-0067
Tulsi Bhatia, *President*
Anoop Bhatia, *Administration*
EMP: 70
SALES (est): 4.6MM **Privately Held**
SIC: 6163 6411 Mortgage brokers arranging for loans, using money of others; insurance agents, brokers & service

(P-9948) RESMAE FINANCIAL CORPORATION
3350 E Birch St Ste 102, Brea (92821-6266)
PHONE.............................714 577-4577
Edward Resendez, *President*
M Jack Mayesh, *Chairman*
Paul J Abbamonto, *President*
Paul Abbamonto, *Exec VP*
Jon Frojen, *Exec VP*
EMP: 225
SQ FT: 35,000
SALES (est): 14.1MM **Privately Held**
SIC: 6163 Mortgage brokers arranging for loans, using money of others

(P-9949) SAFE CREDIT UNION
Also Called: Financial Transaction
9055 Woodcreek Oaks Blvd # 150, Roseville (95747-5159)
PHONE.............................916 979-7233
Serna Yong, *Branch Mgr*
Staci Blasquez, *General Mgr*
EMP: 50
SALES (corp-wide): 103.3MM **Privately Held**
SIC: 6163 Loan brokers
PA: Safe Credit Union
2295 Iron Point Rd # 100
Folsom CA 95630
916 979-7233

(P-9950) SAND CANYON CORPORATION (HQ)
7595 Irvine Center Dr # 100, Irvine (92618-2958)
P.O. Box 57080 (92619-7080)
PHONE.............................949 727-9425
Robert Dubrish, *President*
Dale M Sugimoto, *CEO*
Steve Nadon, *COO*
William O'Neill, *CFO*
Nancy Rotriguez, *Administration*
EMP: 100
SQ FT: 140,000
SALES: 180.7MM
SALES (corp-wide): 3B **Publicly Held**
WEB: www.oomc.com
SIC: 6163 6162 Loan brokers; mortgage bankers & correspondents

PRODUCTS & SERVICES SECTION

6211 - Security Brokers & Dealers County (P-9972)

PA: H&R Block, Inc.
1 H&R Block Way
Kansas City MO 64105
816 854-3000

(P-9951)
SIMONICH CORPORATION (HQ)
Also Called: Bank of Commerce Mortgage
3130 Crow Canyon Pl # 300, San Ramon
(94583-1386)
PHONE.....................925 830-1500
Scott Simonich, *President*
Michael Beinke, *Regional Mgr*
Zackry Cooper, *Loan Officer*
Brian Schwartz, *Loan Officer*
Scott Stewart, *Loan Officer*
EMP: 60
SQ FT: 1,400
SALES (est): 774.6K
SALES (corp-wide): 41.9MM **Publicly Held**
SIC: **6163** Mortgage brokers arranging for loans, using money of others
PA: Bank Of Commerce Holdings
1901 Churn Creek Rd
Redding CA 96002
530 722-3939

(P-9952)
SOCIAL FINANCE INC
1 Letterman Dr, San Francisco
(94129-1494)
PHONE.....................415 697-2078
Mike Cagney, *CEO*
Joanne Bradford, *COO*
Nino Fanlo, *CFO*
Nathan Hieter, *Controller*
Sonja McIntosh, *VP Opers*
EMP: 65
SALES (est): 9MM **Privately Held**
SIC: **6163** Loan brokers

(P-9953)
STEARNS LENDING LLC
317 Soquel Ave, Santa Cruz (95062-2305)
PHONE.....................831 471-1977
EMP: 90
SALES (corp-wide): 308.5MM **Privately Held**
SIC: **6163** Loan brokers
PA: Stearns Lending, Llc
555 Anton Blvd Ste 300
Costa Mesa CA 92626
714 513-7777

(P-9954)
STEARNS LENDING LLC
1601 E Orangewood Ave, Anaheim
(92805-6810)
PHONE.....................657 999-4915
EMP: 60
SALES (corp-wide): 308.5MM **Privately Held**
SIC: **6163** Loan brokers
PA: Stearns Lending, Llc
555 Anton Blvd Ste 300
Costa Mesa CA 92626
714 513-7777

(P-9955)
TARBELL FINANCIAL CORPORATION (PA)
1403 N Tustin Ave Ste 380, Santa Ana
(92705-8691)
PHONE.....................714 972-0988
Donald Tarbell, *CEO*
Tina Jimov, *President*
Jin Lee, *COO*
Ronald Tarbell, *CFO*
Elizabeth Tarbell, *Admin Sec*
EMP: 100
SQ FT: 60,000
SALES (est): 132.4MM **Privately Held**
SIC: **6163 6531 6099** Mortgage brokers arranging for loans, using money of others; real estate brokers & agents; escrow institutions other than real estate

---

6211 Security Brokers & Dealers

(P-9956)
ABM JANITORIAL SERVICES INC
Also Called: ABM Securities
3580 Wilshire Blvd # 1130, Los Angeles
(90010-2501)
PHONE.....................213 384-0600
EMP: 1500
SALES (corp-wide): 4.9B **Publicly Held**
SIC: **6211** Security brokers & dealers
HQ: Abm Janitorial Services, Inc.
1111 Fannin St Ste 1500
Houston TX 77002
713 654-8924

(P-9957)
ADVENT SECURITIES INVESTMENTS (PA)
Also Called: Olympic Security
9631 Alondra Blvd Ste 202, Bellflower
(90706-3674)
PHONE.....................562 920-5467
Fax: 562 920-5468
Cynthia Jocson, *President*
Eric Sera, *Treasurer*
Victor Cantero, *Purchasing*
EMP: 50
SQ FT: 5,000
SALES (est): 32.4MM **Privately Held**
SIC: **6211 5699** Security brokers & dealers; uniforms

(P-9958)
ANALYTIC US MARKET NEUTRAL OFF
555 W 5th St Fl 50, Los Angeles
(90013-1066)
PHONE.....................213 688-3015
Harindra Desilva, *President*
Gregory McMurran, *Director*
Elliott Hahn, *Agent*
EMP: 70
SALES (est): 6.9MM **Privately Held**
SIC: **6211** Investment firm, general brokerage

(P-9959)
ASSETMARK CAPITAL CORP
Also Called: Asset Marketing Investment Svc
2300 Contra Costa Blvd # 600, Pleasant Hill (94523-3979)
PHONE.....................925 521-1040
Ronald D Cordes, *President*
Lourdes Madariaga, *Treasurer*
Carrie E Hansn, *Officer*
Chris Villas-Chernak, *Senior VP*
Thomas Atkins, *Vice Pres*
EMP: 75
SALES (est): 8.5MM **Privately Held**
SIC: **6211** Security brokers & dealers

(P-9960)
ATRIUM CAPITAL CORP
3000 Sand Hill Rd 2-130, Menlo Park
(94025-7142)
PHONE.....................650 233-7878
Fax: 650 233-6944
Russell B Pyne, *Managing Dir*
Andy Baumbusch, *Principal*
Judy Hyrne, *Office Mgr*
Kelly Macmillan, *Mktg Dir*
EMP: 1505
SALES (est): 117.3MM **Privately Held**
WEB: www.atriumcapital.com
SIC: **6211** Investment firm, general brokerage

(P-9961)
B B & K FUND SERVICES INC
950 Tower Ln Ste 1900, Foster City
(94404-2131)
PHONE.....................650 571-5800
Thomas Bailard, *CEO*
Leon W Vigdorchik, *Senior VP*
Steven R Hibshman, *Opers Staff*
EMP: 50
SALES (est): 2.7MM
SALES (corp-wide): 10.3MM **Privately Held**
WEB: www.bailard.com
SIC: **6211** Security brokers & dealers
HQ: Bailard, Inc.
950 Tower Ln Ste 1900
Foster City CA 94404
650 571-5800

(P-9962)
BABCOCK & BROWN HOLDINGS INC (HQ)
1 Pier Ste 3, San Francisco (94111-2028)
PHONE.....................415 512-1515
James V Babcock, *Chairman*
David Timson, *Human Res Mgr*
Michael Garland, *Mng Member*
EMP: 200
SALES (est): 125.8MM
SALES (corp-wide): 508.5MM **Privately Held**
SIC: **6211** Investment bankers

(P-9963)
BARCLAYS CAPITAL INC
155 Linfield Dr, Menlo Park (94025-3741)
PHONE.....................650 289-6000
Stu Francis, *Branch Mgr*
Jonathan Piazza, *Director*
EMP: 70
SALES (corp-wide): 48.8B **Privately Held**
WEB: www.lehmanbrothers.com
SIC: **6211** Brokers, security
HQ: Barclays Capital Inc.
745 7th Ave
New York NY 10019
212 526-7000

(P-9964)
BARCLAYS CAPITAL INC
Also Called: Lehman Brothers
10250 Santa Monica Blvd # 24, Los Angeles (90067-6501)
PHONE.....................310 481-4100
Fax: 310 481-4132
Barclay Perry, *Branch Mgr*
Barbara Lloyd, *Exec VP*
Navid Moshtaghi, *Exec VP*
Michael Hartmeier, *Managing Dir*
Sonya Del Crognale, *Financial Exec*
EMP: 60
SALES (corp-wide): 48.8B **Privately Held**
WEB: www.lehmanbrothers.com
SIC: **6211** Security brokers & dealers
HQ: Barclays Capital Inc.
745 7th Ave
New York NY 10019
212 526-7000

(P-9965)
BBAM US LP
Also Called: Bbam Arcft Holdings 139 Labuan
50 California St Fl 14, San Francisco
(94111-4683)
PHONE.....................415 267-1600
Steve Vissis, *CEO*
EMP: 194
SALES (est): 22.4MM
SALES (corp-wide): 508.5MM **Privately Held**
SIC: **6211** Investment bankers
HQ: Bbam Llc
50 California St Fl 14
San Francisco CA 94111
415 512-1515

(P-9966)
BROADREACH CAPITL PARTNERS LLC (PA)
248 Homer Ave, Palo Alto (94301-2722)
PHONE.....................650 331-2500
Fax: 650 331-2529
John A Foster, *Director*
Eli Khari,
Philip Flip F Maritz, *Director*
Craig G Vought, *Director*
EMP: 60
SALES (est): 407.4MM **Privately Held**
WEB: www.broadreachcp.com
SIC: **6211** Investment firm, general brokerage

(P-9967)
BTIG LLC (PA)
Also Called: Baypoint Trading
600 Montgomery St Fl 6, San Francisco
(94111-2708)
PHONE.....................415 248-2200
Scott Kovalik,
Brian Endres, *CFO*
Austin Hamilton, *Officer*
Greer Beauregard, *Vice Pres*
Kevin McDonald, *Vice Pres*
EMP: 77
SALES (est): 129.4MM **Privately Held**
SIC: **6211** Security brokers & dealers; security brokers & dealers; investment firm, general brokerage

(P-9968)
CANYON PARTNERS INCORPORATED (PA)
2000 Ave Of The Sts Fl 11, Los Angeles
(90067)
PHONE.....................310 272-1000
Fax: 310 272-1001
Joshua S Friedman, *CEO*
Mitchell R Julis, *CEO*
John Simpson, *COO*
John Plaga, *CFO*
Doug Anderson, *Officer*
EMP: 68
SQ FT: 5,500
SALES (est): 31.1MM **Privately Held**
WEB: www.cjuf.com
SIC: **6211** Investment firm, general brokerage

(P-9969)
CASEY SECURITIES INC (PA)
301 Pine St, San Francisco (94104-3301)
PHONE.....................415 544-5030
Fax: 415 421-5628
Richard Casey, *Ch of Bd*
George Gasparini, *President*
Kathleen Gallagher, *Vice Pres*
Scott Nelson, *Vice Pres*
Kevin Casey, *Administration*
EMP: 67 EST: 1976
SQ FT: 800
SALES (est): 6.7MM **Privately Held**
SIC: **6211** Brokers, security; stock brokers & dealers

(P-9970)
CHARLES SCHWAB CORPORATION (PA)
211 Main St Fl 17, San Francisco
(94105-1901)
PHONE.....................415 667-7000
Fax: 415 974-0617
Walter W Bettinger II, *President*
Charles R Schwab, *Ch of Bd*
Joseph R Martinetto, *CFO*
Barbara Glass-Quintana, *Bd of Directors*
Steven H Anderson, *Exec VP*
EMP: 191 EST: 1986
SQ FT: 772,000
SALES: 6.3B **Publicly Held**
WEB: www.schwab.com
SIC: **6211 6091 6282 7389** Brokers, security; investment bankers; investment firm, general brokerage; nondeposit trust facilities; investment advice; investment advisory service; financial services

(P-9971)
CHARLES SCHWAB CORPORATION
12481 High Bluff Dr # 100, San Diego
(92130-3583)
PHONE.....................858 523-2454
Greg Matthews, *Branch Mgr*
EMP: 50
SALES (corp-wide): 6.3B **Publicly Held**
WEB: www.schwab.com
SIC: **6211** Security brokers & dealers
PA: The Charles Schwab Corporation
211 Main St Fl 17
San Francisco CA 94105
415 667-7000

(P-9972)
CHINA JAPAN GLOBAL INC (PA)
1684 Decoto Rd, Union City (94587-3544)
PHONE.....................510 441-2993
Ye Fong, *CFO*

6211 - Security Brokers & Dealers County (P-9973)

Jonathan Williams, *Treasurer*
Ye Lee, *Manager*
EMP: 200
SALES (est): 52.6MM **Privately Held**
SIC: 6211 Security brokers & dealers

(P-9973)
CITIGROUP GLOBAL MARKETS INC
Also Called: Smith Barney
444 S Flower St Fl 35, Los Angeles (90071-2980)
P.O. Box 30367 (90030-0367)
PHONE 213 486-8811
Fax: 213 486-8857
Bruce Brereton, *Branch Mgr*
Talonna Moore, *Officer*
Sandra Andrade, *Assoc VP*
Gregory Laetsch, *Div Sub Head*
EMP: 180
SALES (corp-wide): 88.2B **Publicly Held**
WEB: www.salomonsmithbarney.com
SIC: 6211 Stock brokers & dealers
HQ: Citigroup Global Markets Inc.
388 Greenwich St Fl 18
New York NY 10013
212 816-6000

(P-9974)
CITIGROUP GLOBAL MARKETS INC
9665 Wilshire Blvd # 600, Beverly Hills (90212-2340)
PHONE 310 285-6500
Don Davis, *Manager*
Steven M Van Brunt, *Vice Pres*
EMP: 80
SALES (corp-wide): 88.2B **Publicly Held**
WEB: www.salomonsmithbarney.com
SIC: 6211 Stock brokers & dealers
HQ: Citigroup Global Markets Inc.
388 Greenwich St Fl 18
New York NY 10013
212 816-6000

(P-9975)
CITIGROUP GLOBAL MARKETS INC
Also Called: Salomon Smith Barney
2381 Rosecrans Ave # 115, El Segundo (90245-4920)
PHONE 310 727-9533
Fax: 310 297-3701
Russ Bortonaro, *Branch Mgr*
John Matson, *Manager*
EMP: 56
SALES (corp-wide): 88.2B **Publicly Held**
WEB: www.salomonsmithbarney.com
SIC: 6211 Security brokers & dealers
HQ: Citigroup Global Markets Inc.
388 Greenwich St Fl 18
New York NY 10013
212 816-6000

(P-9976)
CITIGROUP GLOBAL MARKETS INC
Also Called: Salomon Smith Barney
155 Cadillac Dr Fl 1, Sacramento (95825-5403)
PHONE 916 567-2056
Mike Dellisant, *Manager*
EMP: 50
SALES (corp-wide): 88.2B **Publicly Held**
WEB: www.salomonsmithbarney.com
SIC: 6211 Security brokers & dealers
HQ: Citigroup Global Markets Inc.
388 Greenwich St Fl 18
New York NY 10013
212 816-6000

(P-9977)
CITIGROUP GLOBAL MARKETS INC
4350 La Jolla Village Dr, San Diego (92122-1243)
PHONE 858 597-7777
Joe Capano, *Manager*
Brad T Shaw, *Vice Pres*
Jeff Anderson, *Finance Mgr*
Christopher Myers, *Manager*
Darren A Pfefferman, *Consultant*
EMP: 71

SALES (corp-wide): 88.2B **Publicly Held**
WEB: www.salomonsmithbarney.com
SIC: 6211 Security brokers & dealers; stock brokers & dealers
HQ: Citigroup Global Markets Inc.
388 Greenwich St Fl 18
New York NY 10013
212 816-6000

(P-9978)
CITIGROUP GLOBAL MARKETS INC
Also Called: Smith Barney
21250 Hawthorne Blvd # 650, Torrance (90503-5506)
P.O. Box 2805 (90509-2805)
PHONE 310 540-9511
Fax: 310 543-0223
David Calomese, *Manager*
Yoshihiro Kuroki, *CPA*
Arthur Fu, *Opers Staff*
Evan Hunter, *Opers Staff*
Edward Kawahara, *Opers Staff*
EMP: 50
SALES (corp-wide): 88.2B **Publicly Held**
WEB: www.salomonsmithbarney.com
SIC: 6211 Security brokers & dealers; stock brokers & dealers
HQ: Citigroup Global Markets Inc.
388 Greenwich St Fl 18
New York NY 10013
212 816-6000

(P-9979)
CITIGROUP GLOBAL MARKETS INC
Also Called: Smith Barney
1901 Main St Ste 800, Irvine (92614-0515)
PHONE 949 955-7500
Fax: 949 833-3542
John Konop, *General Mgr*
Gary Olson, *Manager*
EMP: 85
SALES (corp-wide): 88.2B **Publicly Held**
WEB: www.salomonsmithbarney.com
SIC: 6211 6221 Investment firm, general brokerage; commodity contracts brokers, dealers
HQ: Citigroup Global Markets Inc.
388 Greenwich St Fl 18
New York NY 10013
212 816-6000

(P-9980)
CITIGROUP GLOBAL MARKETS INC
Also Called: Smith Barney
1225 Prospect St, La Jolla (92037-3687)
P.O. Box 1944 (92038-1944)
PHONE 858 456-4900
Fax: 858 459-3164
Erik Kivmkrugh, *Office Mgr*
Joe Ulloa, *Manager*
EMP: 72
SALES (corp-wide): 88.2B **Publicly Held**
WEB: www.salomonsmithbarney.com
SIC: 6211 Security brokers & dealers; stock brokers & dealers
HQ: Citigroup Global Markets Inc.
388 Greenwich St Fl 18
New York NY 10013
212 816-6000

(P-9981)
CITIGROUP GLOBAL MARKETS INC
Also Called: Salomon Smith Barney
5250 N Palm Ave Ste 321, Fresno (93704-2213)
PHONE 559 438-2542
Jeff Branch, *Sales/Mktg Mgr*
Chu Pau, *Manager*
Ellen Scheidt, *Manager*
EMP: 50
SALES (corp-wide): 88.2B **Publicly Held**
WEB: www.salomonsmithbarney.com
SIC: 6211 8742 Security brokers & dealers; stock brokers & dealers; financial consultant
HQ: Citigroup Global Markets Inc.
388 Greenwich St Fl 18
New York NY 10013
212 816-6000

(P-9982)
CITIGROUP GLOBAL MARKETS INC
Also Called: Smith Barney
609 Deep Valley Dr # 400, Rllng HLS Est (90274-3629)
P.O. Box 2809, Pls Vrds Pnsl (90274-8809)
PHONE 310 544-3600
Paul Tanzmen, *Manager*
Al Wacsh, *Consultant*
Eric Nichols, *Representative*
EMP: 65
SALES (corp-wide): 88.2B **Publicly Held**
WEB: www.salomonsmithbarney.com
SIC: 6211 Stock brokers & dealers
HQ: Citigroup Global Markets Inc.
388 Greenwich St Fl 18
New York NY 10013
212 816-6000

(P-9983)
CITIGROUP GLOBAL MARKETS INC
456 W Foothill Blvd, Claremont (91711-2711)
PHONE 909 625-0781
Tony Battaglia, *Manager*
EMP: 60
SALES (corp-wide): 88.2B **Publicly Held**
WEB: www.salomonsmithbarney.com
SIC: 6211 Stock brokers & dealers
HQ: Citigroup Global Markets Inc.
388 Greenwich St Fl 18
New York NY 10013
212 816-6000

(P-9984)
CITIGROUP GLOBAL MARKETS INC
Also Called: Smith Barneys
2775 Sand Hill Rd Ste 120, Menlo Park (94025-7085)
PHONE 650 926-7600
Fax: 650 926-7650
Guy Dietrich, *Principal*
Jennifer Davis, *Manager*
Shouchan Lee, *Agent*
EMP: 103
SALES (corp-wide): 88.2B **Publicly Held**
WEB: www.salomonsmithbarney.com
SIC: 6211 Security brokers & dealers
HQ: Citigroup Global Markets Inc.
388 Greenwich St Fl 18
New York NY 10013
212 816-6000

(P-9985)
CITIGROUP INC
1 Sansome St Fl 27, San Francisco (94104-4426)
PHONE 415 617-8524
Chuck Prince, *President*
EMP: 60
SALES (corp-wide): 88.2B **Publicly Held**
WEB: www.citigroup.com
SIC: 6211 Investment bankers
PA: Citigroup Inc.
399 Park Ave
New York NY 10022
212 559-1000

(P-9986)
CITIMORTGAGE INC
6160 Stoneridge Mall Rd # 150, Pleasanton (94588-3285)
PHONE 925 730-3800
Ernie Guzman, *Manager*
EMP: 50
SALES (corp-wide): 88.2B **Publicly Held**
SIC: 6211 Investment firm, general brokerage
HQ: Citimortgage, Inc.
1000 Technology Dr
O Fallon MO 63368
636 261-2484

(P-9987)
COUNTRYWIDE SECURITIES CORP
4500 Park Granada, Calabasas (91302-1613)
P.O. Box 7137, Pasadena (91109-7137)
PHONE 818 225-3000
Fax: 818 225-4015
Angelo Mozilo, *Ch of Bd*

Ranjit Kripalani, *President*
Michael Sorensen, *Sales Staff*
EMP: 275 **EST:** 1981
SALES (est): 48.2MM
SALES (corp-wide): 93B **Publicly Held**
SIC: 6211 Security brokers & dealers
HQ: Countrywide Capital Markets, Llc
4500 Park Granada
Calabasas CA 91302
818 225-3000

(P-9988)
CREDIT SSSE SECURITIES USA LLC
10880 Wilshire Blvd, Los Angeles (90024-4101)
PHONE 213 253-2600
Reza Zafari, *Principal*
Jill Darling, *Manager*
EMP: 75
SALES (corp-wide): 23.1B **Privately Held**
SIC: 6211 Investment bankers
HQ: Credit Suisse Securities (Usa) Llc
11 Madison Ave Bsmt 1b
New York NY 10010
212 325-2000

(P-9989)
CREDIT SUISSE (USA) INC
650 California St Fl 31, San Francisco (94108-2612)
PHONE 415 249-2100
Fax: 415 249-2174
Carey Timbrell, *Manager*
David Luwisch, *Managing Dir*
EMP: 100
SALES (corp-wide): 23.1B **Privately Held**
SIC: 6211 Security brokers & dealers
HQ: Credit Suisse (Usa), Inc.
11 Madison Ave Frnt 1
New York NY 10010
212 325-2000

(P-9990)
CREDIT SUISSE (USA) INC
650 California St Fl 28, San Francisco (94108-2609)
PHONE 415 678-3940
Susan Winegar, *Manager*
EMP: 50
SALES (corp-wide): 23.1B **Privately Held**
SIC: 6211 Security brokers & dealers
HQ: Credit Suisse (Usa), Inc.
11 Madison Ave Frnt 1
New York NY 10010
212 325-2000

(P-9991)
DA DAVIDSON & CO
Also Called: Crowell, Weedon & Co.
624 S Grand Ave, Los Angeles (90017-3335)
PHONE 213 620-1850
Fax: 213 680-3450
Robert Gore, *General Ptnr*
Robert Hassan, *Senior VP*
Neil Papiano, *Executive*
Robert Hartley, *Info Tech Dir*
Ted Ward, *Manager*
EMP: 310
SALES (corp-wide): 435MM **Privately Held**
SIC: 6211 Stock brokers & dealers
HQ: D.A. Davidson & Co.
8 3rd St N
Great Falls MT 59401
406 727-4200

(P-9992)
DEUTSCHE BANK TR CO AMERICAS
101 California St # 4500, San Francisco (94111-5802)
PHONE 415 617-4200
Fax: 415 658-5005
Edmond Hon, *Vice Pres*
Jeff Taylor, *Info Tech Mgr*
EMP: 130
SQ FT: 3,600
SALES (corp-wide): 8.8B **Privately Held**
WEB: www.db.com
SIC: 6211 Investment bankers

HQ: Deutsche Bank Trust Company Americas
60 Wall St Bsmt 1
New York NY 10005
212 250-2500

(P-9993)
EMBASSADOR PRIVATE SECURITIES
1341 Evans Ave, San Francisco (94124-1705)
PHONE..................................415 822-8811
Rj Hongisto, *Director*
Rj Hingisto, *Director*
David Culot, *Manager*
EMP: 55
SQ FT: 4,500
SALES (est): 4.7MM **Privately Held**
SIC: 6211

(P-9994)
EMMETT A LARKIN COMPANY INC (PA)
22 Battery St Ste 806, San Francisco (94111-5522)
PHONE..................................415 986-2332
Gordon F Hing, *President*
George Montez, *CFO*
Mel Petersen, *Exec VP*
Victor Hermann, *Senior VP*
Norma Miranda, *Admin Sec*
EMP: 84 **EST:** 1959
SQ FT: 10,000
SALES (est): 12.4MM **Privately Held**
WEB: www.internettrading.com
SIC: 6211 8742 6282 Stock brokers & dealers; management consulting services; investment advice

(P-9995)
EXMART INTERNATIONAL TRDG CORP
2923 Saturn St Ste H, Brea (92821-6260)
PHONE..................................714 993-1139
Alex L Benedicto, *CEO*
EMP: 51
SALES (est): 61.7MM **Privately Held**
WEB: www.exmart-international.com
SIC: 6211 Traders, security

(P-9996)
FAIRWAY INDEPENDENT MRTG CORP
555 1st St Ste 102, Benicia (94510-3280)
PHONE..................................707 361-5342
EMP: 82 **Privately Held**
SIC: 6211 Mortgages, buying & selling
PA: Fairway Independent Mortgage Corporation
4801 S Biltmore Ln
Madison WI 53718
-

(P-9997)
FAIRWAY INDEPENDENT MRTG CORP
43385 Business Park Dr, Temecula (92590-3688)
PHONE..................................951 676-0527
EMP: 55 **Privately Held**
SIC: 6211 Mortgages, buying & selling
PA: Fairway Independent Mortgage Corporation
4801 S Biltmore Ln
Madison WI 53718
-

(P-9998)
FAS HOLDINGS INC
655 W Broadway Fl 11, San Diego (92101-8487)
PHONE..................................619 702-9600
Adam Antoniades, *President*
Greg Kirk, *Manager*
EMP: 116
SALES (est): 11.6MM
SALES (corp-wide): 130MM **Privately Held**
SIC: 6211 Security brokers & dealers
PA: Advanced Equities Financial Corp.
200 S Wacker Dr Ste 3200
Chicago IL 60606
312 377-5300

(P-9999)
FIRST ALLIED FACILITIES CORP
655 W Broadway Ste 1100, San Diego (92101-8487)
PHONE..................................619 702-9600
Adam Antoniades, *President*
David Dallal, *CFO*
Shannon Condra, *Vice Pres*
Giacomo Licari, *Branch Mgr*
Robert Moses, *Admin Sec*
EMP: 80
SALES (est): 9.3MM **Privately Held**
SIC: 6211 Dealers, security

(P-10000)
FIRST ALLIED SECURITIES INC (PA)
655 W Broadway Fl 11, San Diego (92101-8487)
P.O. Box 85549 (92186-5549)
PHONE..................................619 702-9600
Fax: 619 239-0143
Adam Antoniades, *CEO*
Kevin Keefe, *President*
Tiy O'Neal, *COO*
David Dallal, *CFO*
Gregg S Glaser, *CFO*
EMP: 75
SALES (est): 102.3MM **Privately Held**
SIC: 6211 Security brokers & dealers

(P-10001)
FITZGERALD CANTOR L P
1925 Century Park E # 700, Los Angeles (90067-2718)
PHONE..................................310 282-6500
Fax: 310 282-6531
Bill Wright, *Manager*
Kadija Reeves, *Vice Pres*
Edward Weber, *Vice Pres*
Gary Wang, *Managing Dir*
Chris Larsen, *Sales Staff*
EMP: 100
SALES (corp-wide): 648.7MM **Privately Held**
SIC: 6211 Brokers, security
PA: Fitzgerald Cantor L P
499 Park Ave
New York NY 10022
212 938-5000

(P-10002)
FOREX CAPITAL MARKETS LLC
201 Mission St Ste 290, San Francisco (94105-1859)
PHONE..................................415 343-4874
Chris Pelton, *Branch Mgr*
Sean Meierdiercks, *Administration*
EMP: 89
SALES (corp-wide): 129.1MM **Privately Held**
SIC: 6211 Brokers, security
PA: Forex Capital Markets L.L.C.
55 Water St Fl 50
New York NY 10041
646 355-0839

(P-10003)
FRANKLIN TMPLETON INV SVCS LLC (DH)
Also Called: Franklin Templeton Investment
3344 Quality Dr, Rancho Cordova (95670-7361)
P.O. Box 2258 (95741-2258)
PHONE..................................916 463-1500
Greg Johnson, *President*
Charles B Johnson, *Ch of Bd*
Basil Fox, *President*
Robert Smith, *Senior VP*
Scott Gormley, *Manager*
EMP: 1200
SQ FT: 40,000
SALES (est): 553.9MM
SALES (corp-wide): 7.9B **Publicly Held**
SIC: 6211 6282 Traders, security; investment advisory service
HQ: Templeton Worldwide, Inc.
500 E Broward Blvd # 900
Fort Lauderdale FL 33394
954 527-7500

(P-10004)
FREMONT MUTUAL FUNDS INC
333 Market St Ste 2600, San Francisco (94105-2127)
PHONE..................................800 548-4539
Fax: 925 284-8177
David L Redo, *CEO*
Michael Kosich, *President*
Vincent P Kuhn, *Exec VP*
Albert Kirschbaum, *Senior VP*
Peter Landini, *Senior VP*
EMP: 55
SQ FT: 19,000
SALES (est): 4.8MM **Privately Held**
SIC: 6211 Mutual funds, selling by independent salesperson

(P-10005)
GENSTAR CAPITAL LP
4 Embarcadero Ctr # 1500, San Francisco (94111-4106)
PHONE..................................415 834-2350
Jean-Pierre L Conte, *Partner*
Richard F Hoskins, *Partner*
Richard D Paterson, *Partner*
EMP: 560
SALES (est): 28.1MM **Privately Held**
SIC: 6211 Security brokers & dealers

(P-10006)
GOLDMAN SACHS & CO
Also Called: Goldman Sachs
555 California St # 4500, San Francisco (94104-1675)
PHONE..................................415 393-7500
Fax: 415 249-7389
Eff Martin, *Partner*
Guy Muzio, *Partner*
Peter Cimmet, *Exec VP*
David Countryman, *Exec VP*
Elissa Deutch, *Vice Pres*
EMP: 200
SALES (corp-wide): 39.2B **Publicly Held**
WEB: www.gs.com
SIC: 6211 6282 Investment bankers; investment advice
HQ: Goldman, Sachs & Co.
200 West St Bldg 200
New York NY 10282
212 346-5440

(P-10007)
GOLDMAN SACHS & CO
Also Called: Goldman Sachs
2121 Avenue Stars 2600, Los Angeles (90067)
PHONE..................................310 407-5700
Fax: 310 407-5812
John Mallory, *Branch Mgr*
Matt Babrick, *Vice Pres*
Joan M Dickason, *Vice Pres*
Darell Krasnoff, *Vice Pres*
Charles F Adams, *Managing Dir*
EMP: 120
SALES (corp-wide): 39.2B **Publicly Held**
WEB: www.gs.com
SIC: 6211 Investment bankers
HQ: Goldman, Sachs & Co.
200 West St Bldg 200
New York NY 10282
212 346-5440

(P-10008)
GORES GROUP LLC (PA)
9800 Wilshire Blvd, Beverly Hills (90212-1804)
PHONE..................................310 209-3010
Fax: 310 209-3310
Alec Gores, *CEO*
Eva Lee, *Vice Chairman*
Joseph Page, *COO*
Catherine Scanlon, *CFO*
Kurt Hans, *Senior VP*
EMP: 60
SALES (est): 6.8B **Privately Held**
SIC: 6211 Investment firm, general brokerage

(P-10009)
GREEN EQUITY INVESTORS III L P
11111 Santa Monica Blvd # 2000, Los Angeles (90025-3333)
PHONE..................................310 954-0444
Jonathan D Sokoloff, *Partner*
Leonald G LP, *General Ptnr*

Jessica Ann, *Admin Sec*
Lilly Chang, *Controller*
EMP: 1115
SQ FT: 15,000
SALES (est): 38.5MM **Privately Held**
SIC: 6211 Investment bankers

(P-10010)
GREENHILL & CO INC
10250 Constellation Blvd # 1620, Los Angeles (90067-6238)
PHONE..................................310 432-4400
James Stewart, *Branch Mgr*
EMP: 50
SALES (corp-wide): 261.5MM **Publicly Held**
SIC: 6211 Investment bankers
PA: Greenhill & Co., Inc.
300 Park Ave Fl 23
New York NY 10022
212 389-1500

(P-10011)
HILLTOP SECURITIES INC
8350 Wilshire Blvd, Beverly Hills (90211-2327)
PHONE..................................800 765-2200
Peter Cappos, *Branch Mgr*
EMP: 50
SALES (corp-wide): 1.7B **Publicly Held**
SIC: 6211 Securities flotation companies
HQ: Hilltop Securities Inc.
1201 Elm St Ste 3500
Dallas TX 75270
214 859-1800

(P-10012)
HOULIHAN LOKEY INC (PA)
10250 Constellation Blvd # 5, Los Angeles (90067-6200)
PHONE..................................310 553-8871
Scott L Beiser, *CEO*
Irwin N Gold, *Ch of Bd*
Scott J Adelson, *President*
David A Preiser, *President*
J Lindsey Alley, *CFO*
EMP: 300
SALES: 693.7MM **Publicly Held**
WEB: www.hlhz.com
SIC: 6211 6282 Security brokers & dealers; investment bankers; investment advice

(P-10013)
HYUNDAI ABS FUNDING LLC
3161 Michelson Dr, Irvine (92612-4400)
PHONE..................................949 732-2697
EMP: 102
SALES (est): 6.4MM
SALES (corp-wide): 38.9B **Privately Held**
SIC: 6211 Security brokers & dealers
HQ: Hyundai Capital America
3161 Michelson Dr # 1900
Irvine CA 92612
714 965-3000

(P-10014)
IMPERIAL CAPITAL GROUP LLC (PA)
2000 Ave Of The, Los Angeles (90067)
PHONE..................................310 246-3700
Randall Wooster,
Saro Bos, *Senior VP*
Desmond Chopping, *Senior VP*
Denny Miyazaki-Ross, *Vice Pres*
Jason Reese,
EMP: 70
SQ FT: 14,909
SALES (est): 14.1MM **Privately Held**
SIC: 6211 Stock brokers & dealers

(P-10015)
IMPERIAL CAPITAL LLC (PA)
2000 Avenue Of The Stars 900s, Los Angeles (90067-4716)
PHONE..................................310 246-3700
Randall Wooster, *CEO*
Tom Corcoran, *President*
Randall E Wooster, *CEO*
Kurt Hoffman, *COO*
Mark Martis, *COO*
EMP: 85
SALES (est): 30.9MM **Privately Held**
SIC: 6211 Investment bankers

6211 - Security Brokers & Dealers County (P-10016)

(P-10016)
INTERQUANTUM LLC
22120 Clarendon St # 160, Woodland Hills (91367-6315)
PHONE...................................818 455-4434
Lauren Raisen,
Anthony Raissen, *Sales Staff*
Anthony Raisen,
Robert B Yallen,
Sydney Yallen,
EMP: 50
SALES: 800K **Privately Held**
SIC: 6211 7311 Security brokers & dealers; advertising agencies

(P-10017)
INVESTMENT TECH GROUP INC
400 Crprate Pinte Ste 855, Culver City (90230)
PHONE...................................310 216-6777
EMP: 150
SALES (corp-wide): 634.8MM **Publicly Held**
SIC: 6211 7371
PA: Investment Technology Group, Inc.
 1 Liberty Plz
 New York NY 10006
 212 588-4000

(P-10018)
JEFFERIES LLC
11100 Santa Monica Blvd # 12, Los Angeles (90025-3387)
PHONE...................................310 445-1199
Chris Kanoff, *Branch Mgr*
EMP: 60
SALES (corp-wide): 11.6B **Publicly Held**
SIC: 6211 Brokers, security; dealers, security
HQ: Jefferies Llc
 520 Madison Ave Fl 10
 New York NY 10022
 212 284-2300

(P-10019)
JMP SECURITIES LLC (DH)
600 Montgomery St # 1100, San Francisco (94111-2713)
PHONE...................................415 835-8900
Fax: 415 263-1337
Joseph Jolson, *Mng Member*
Carter D Mack, *President*
Raymond Jackson, *CFO*
Ryan Abbe, *Vice Pres*
Jason Butler, *Vice Pres*
EMP: 55
SALES (est): 60.2MM
SALES (corp-wide): 206.3MM **Publicly Held**
SIC: 6211 Security brokers & dealers
HQ: Jmp Group Inc.
 600 Montgomery St # 1100
 San Francisco CA 94111
 415 835-8900

(P-10020)
JP MORGAN SECURITIES LLC
660 Nwport Ctr Dr Ste 750, Newport Beach (92660)
PHONE...................................949 467-3900
Robert Martensen, *Manager*
EMP: 86
SALES (corp-wide): 101B **Publicly Held**
SIC: 6211 Security brokers & dealers
HQ: J.P. Morgan Securities Llc
 383 Madison Ave Fl 9
 New York NY 10179
 212 272-2000

(P-10021)
JP MORGAN SECURITIES LLC
Also Called: Bear Stearns
14061 Mercado Dr, Del Mar (92014-2949)
PHONE...................................310 201-2693
EMP: 85
SALES (corp-wide): 106.2B **Publicly Held**
SIC: 6211
HQ: J.P. Morgan Securities Llc
 383 Madison Ave Fl 9
 New York NY 10179
 212 272-2000

(P-10022)
K A ASSOCIATES INC
1800 Avenue Of The Stars # 200, Los Angeles (90067-4204)
PHONE...................................310 556-2721
Richard Kayne, *CEO*
David Shladovsky, *Admin Sec*
EMP: 116
SALES: 1.3MM **Privately Held**
SIC: 6211 Security brokers & dealers

(P-10023)
LEAR CAPITAL INC
1990 S Bundy Dr Ste 600, Los Angeles (90025-5256)
PHONE...................................310 571-0190
Fax: 310 656-3280
Kevin Demerit, *President*
Scott Robinson, *CFO*
Tim Senstock, *Executive*
Sandeep D'Souza, *Applctn Conslt*
Michael Fousse, *Portfolio Mgr*
EMP: 72
SQ FT: 4,500
SALES (est): 400MM **Privately Held*
WEB: www.goldcentral.com
SIC: 6211 Mineral, oil & gas leasing & royalty dealers

(P-10024)
LEERINK PARTNERS LLC
255 California St Fl 12, San Francisco (94111-4923)
PHONE...................................800 778-1164
Jeffrey Leerink, *CEO*
EMP: 60 **Privately Held**
SIC: 6211 Brokers, security; investment bankers
PA: Leerink Partners Llc
 1 Federal St Fl 37
 Boston MA 02110

(P-10025)
LERETA LLC (PA)
1123 Park View Dr, Covina (91724-3748)
PHONE...................................626 543-1765
Fax: 626 915-2875
John Walsh, *CEO*
Brett Bennett, *President*
Glenn McCarthy, *President*
Daniel Telles, *President*
James V Micali, *COO*
EMP: 350
SQ FT: 40,000
SALES (est): 336.2MM **Privately Held**
SIC: 6211 6541 6361 Tax certificate dealers; title search companies; real estate title insurance

(P-10026)
LPL HOLDINGS INC (HQ)
4707 Executive Dr, San Diego (92121-3091)
PHONE...................................858 450-9606
Mark Casady, *CEO*
Stephen Molinelli, *Senior Partner*
Robert Comfort, *Exec VP*
Melanie Hardin, *Exec VP*
Jason Borgmann, *Vice Pres*
EMP: 83
SALES (est): 693.2MM
SALES (corp-wide): 4.2B **Publicly Held**
WEB: www.lpl.com
SIC: 6211 Brokers, security; dealers, security
PA: Lpl Financial Holdings Inc.
 75 State St Ste 2401
 Boston MA 02109
 617 423-3644

(P-10027)
M L STERN & CO LLC (DH)
8350 Wilshire Blvd Fl 1, Beverly Hills (90211-2324)
PHONE...................................323 658-4400
Fax: 323 658-2232
Milford L Stern,
Miles Benickes, *Exec VP*
Greg Flack, *Senior VP*
Don Lewis, *Senior VP*
Stacy Stern, *Senior VP*
EMP: 117
SQ FT: 8,100

SALES (est): 47.6MM
SALES (corp-wide): 1.7B **Publicly Held**
SIC: 6211 Brokers, security
HQ: Hilltop Securities Holdings Llc
 200 Crescent Ct Ste 1330
 Dallas TX 75201
 214 855-2177

(P-10028)
MERCER GLOBAL SECURITIES LLC
1801 E Cabrillo Blvd A, Santa Barbara (93108-2897)
PHONE...................................805 565-1681
Gene Dongieux Jr, *Mng Member*
Deb Atwater, *CFO*
Deborah Atwaterrobles, *Admin Sec*
Howard Rochestie,
Glen Wysel,
EMP: 77 **EST:** 1995
SALES (est): 7.4MM **Privately Held**
SIC: 6211 Security brokers & dealers

(P-10029)
MERLIN SECURITIES LLC
45 Fremont St Ste 3000, San Francisco (94105-2256)
PHONE...................................415 848-0269
Stephan P Vermut,
Robert Garrett, *Senior Partner*
John Hiestand, *CFO*
Denise Genovese, *Mktg Dir*
Regina O'Neill,
EMP: 65
SALES (est): 9MM
SALES (corp-wide): 90B **Publicly Held**
SIC: 6211 Security brokers & dealers
HQ: Everen Capital Corporation
 301 S College St
 Charlotte NC 28202
 704 374-6565

(P-10030)
MERRILL LYNCH PIERCE FENNER
333 Middlefield Rd, Menlo Park (94025-3552)
PHONE...................................650 473-7888
Fax: 650 473-7800
EMP: 75
SALES (corp-wide): 95.1B **Publicly Held**
SIC: 6211
HQ: Merrill Lynch, Pierce, Fenner & Smith Incorporated
 111 8th Ave
 New York NY 10011
 800 637-7455

(P-10031)
MERRILL LYNCH PIERCE FENNER
16830 Ventura Blvd # 601, Encino (91436-1707)
PHONE...................................818 528-7809
Paul Pepperman, *Manager*
Zelma Reyes, *Director*
Craig Felten, *Advisor*
EMP: 57
SALES (corp-wide): 93B **Publicly Held**
WEB: www.merlyn.com
SIC: 6211 8742 Security brokers & dealers; financial consultant
HQ: Merrill Lynch, Pierce, Fenner & Smith Incorporated
 111 8th Ave
 New York NY 10011
 800 637-7455

(P-10032)
MERRILL LYNCH PIERCE FENNER
9560 Wilshire Blvd Fl 3, Beverly Hills (90212-2430)
PHONE...................................310 858-1500
Fax: 310 276-1186
Brad Dykes, *Branch Mgr*
Norman Saiger, *Vice Pres*
Nathan Crair, *Managing Dir*
Susan Castruita, *Business Mgr*
Raymond Saldonis, *Financial Analy*
EMP: 50
SALES (corp-wide): 93B **Publicly Held**
WEB: www.merlyn.com
SIC: 6211 6282 Security brokers & dealers; investment advisory service

HQ: Merrill Lynch, Pierce, Fenner & Smith Incorporated
 111 8th Ave
 New York NY 10011
 800 637-7455

(P-10033)
MERRILL LYNCH PIERCE FENNER
3075b Hansen Way, Palo Alto (94304-1000)
PHONE...................................650 842-2440
Fax: 650 849-2101
Huert Chang, *Branch Mgr*
Steve Strandberg, *Info Tech Dir*
Bhavin Merchant, *Technology*
John Fortson, *Director*
Maurice Murphy, *Director*
EMP: 75
SALES (corp-wide): 93B **Publicly Held**
WEB: www.merlyn.com
SIC: 6211 Security brokers & dealers
HQ: Merrill Lynch, Pierce, Fenner & Smith Incorporated
 111 8th Ave
 New York NY 10011
 800 637-7455

(P-10034)
MERRILL LYNCH PIERCE FENNER
730 Patricia Dr, San Luis Obispo (93405-1036)
PHONE...................................661 802-0764
Martin B Epperson, *Principal*
EMP: 50
SALES (corp-wide): 93B **Publicly Held**
SIC: 6211 Brokers, security
HQ: Merrill Lynch, Pierce, Fenner & Smith Incorporated
 111 8th Ave
 New York NY 10011
 800 637-7455

(P-10035)
MERRILL LYNCH PIERCE FENNER
520 Newport Center Dr, Newport Beach (92660-7020)
PHONE...................................949 467-3760
David Gunta, *Branch Mgr*
Ken Yonkers, *Vice Pres*
John Acierno, *Advisor*
Frank Buchholz, *Advisor*
Edwin Yoon, *Advisor*
EMP: 240
SALES (corp-wide): 93B **Publicly Held**
SIC: 6211 Security brokers & dealers
HQ: Merrill Lynch, Pierce, Fenner & Smith Incorporated
 111 8th Ave
 New York NY 10011
 800 637-7455

(P-10036)
MERRILL LYNCH PIERCE FENNER
300 E Esplanade Dr, Oxnard (93036-1238)
PHONE...................................800 964-5182
James Hardy, *Branch Mgr*
M Cuevas, *Advisor*
John Kearney, *Advisor*
EMP: 240
SALES (corp-wide): 93B **Publicly Held**
SIC: 6211 Security brokers & dealers
HQ: Merrill Lynch, Pierce, Fenner & Smith Incorporated
 111 8th Ave
 New York NY 10011
 800 637-7455

(P-10037)
MERRILL LYNCH PIERCE FENNER
333 Middlefield Rd # 202, Menlo Park (94025-3552)
PHONE...................................650 473-7888
Deborah Germenis, *Branch Mgr*
Denise Chiu, *Director*
Hilary Giles, *Manager*
Cory Goligoski, *Manager*
Hilary Jones, *Manager*
EMP: 240
SALES (corp-wide): 93B **Publicly Held**
SIC: 6211 Security brokers & dealers

PRODUCTS & SERVICES SECTION
6211 - Security Brokers & Dealers County (P-10057)

HQ: Merrill Lynch, Pierce, Fenner & Smith
Incorporated
111 8th Ave
New York NY 10011
800 637-7455

(P-10038)
MERRILL LYNCH PIERCE FENNER
701 B St Ste 2350, San Diego (92101-8125)
PHONE.................................619 699-3700
Fax: 619 699-3982
Quinton Ellis, *Branch Mgr*
Mark Kobayashi, *Vice Pres*
Mark Albers, *Exec Dir*
Lawrence Brashears, *Manager*
Edythe De Marco, *Manager*
EMP: 150
SALES (corp-wide): 93B **Publicly Held**
WEB: www.merlyn.com
SIC: **6211** 8742 Security brokers & dealers; financial consultant
HQ: Merrill Lynch, Pierce, Fenner & Smith
Incorporated
111 8th Ave
New York NY 10011
800 637-7455

(P-10039)
MERRILL LYNCH PIERCE FENNER
555 California St Fl 9, San Francisco (94104-1512)
PHONE.................................415 955-3700
Fax: 415 391-2032
Jim Dullanty, *Branch Mgr*
Joseph Garcia, *Exec VP*
Marie Benedetti, *Senior VP*
Larry Fraejak, *Vice Pres*
John Kerrigan, *Vice Pres*
EMP: 150
SALES (corp-wide): 93B **Publicly Held**
WEB: www.merlyn.com
SIC: **6211** 6282 Security brokers & dealers; investment advice
HQ: Merrill Lynch, Pierce, Fenner & Smith
Incorporated
111 8th Ave
New York NY 10011
800 637-7455

(P-10040)
MERRILL LYNCH PIERCE FENNER
2049 Century Park E # 1100, Los Angeles (90067-3101)
PHONE.................................310 407-3900
Michael Rogers, *Branch Mgr*
Lance Polverini, *Analyst*
EMP: 120
SALES (corp-wide): 93B **Publicly Held**
WEB: www.merlyn.com
SIC: **6211** Security brokers & dealers
HQ: Merrill Lynch, Pierce, Fenner & Smith
Incorporated
111 8th Ave
New York NY 10011
800 637-7455

(P-10041)
MERRILL LYNCH PIERCE FENNER
50 W San Fernando St 16, San Jose (95113-2429)
PHONE.................................408 283-3000
Fax: 408 283-3190
Patricia Williams, *Manager*
Richard Johnson, *Admin Mgr*
James E Hays, *Manager*
Lois Eckmann, *Advisor*
Peter Verbica, *Advisor*
EMP: 50
SALES (corp-wide): 93B **Publicly Held**
WEB: www.merlyn.com
SIC: **6211** 6282 Security brokers & dealers; investment advice
HQ: Merrill Lynch, Pierce, Fenner & Smith
Incorporated
111 8th Ave
New York NY 10011
800 637-7455

(P-10042)
MERRILL LYNCH PIERCE FENNER
1331 N Calif Blvd Ste 400, Walnut Creek (94596-4561)
PHONE.................................925 945-4800
Fax: 925 935-3643
Michael Dunn, *Branch Mgr*
Len Nathan, *Vice Pres*
Richard Saldek, *Div Sub Head*
Geraldine Madore, *Broker*
Tim Carlson, *Advisor*
EMP: 85
SALES (corp-wide): 93B **Publicly Held**
WEB: www.merlyn.com
SIC: **6211** 8742 Security brokers & dealers; financial consultant
HQ: Merrill Lynch, Pierce, Fenner & Smith
Incorporated
111 8th Ave
New York NY 10011
800 637-7455

(P-10043)
MERRILL LYNCH PIERCE FENNER
101 California St Fl 24, San Francisco (94111-5898)
PHONE.................................415 274-7000
Fax: 415 274-6191
Jim Delancey, *Manager*
Douglas Howe, *Vice Pres*
George Johnson, *Vice Pres*
Christine Koh-Wong, *Vice Pres*
Jon Dayton, *Managing Dir*
EMP: 50
SALES (corp-wide): 93B **Publicly Held**
WEB: www.merlyn.com
SIC: **6211** 6282 Stock brokers & dealers; investment advice
HQ: Merrill Lynch, Pierce, Fenner & Smith
Incorporated
111 8th Ave
New York NY 10011
800 637-7455

(P-10044)
MERRILL LYNCH PIERCE FENNER
16912 Via De Santa Fe, Rancho Santa Fe (92091-4606)
PHONE.................................858 381-8112
Robert Schulze, *Manager*
Paul Sanit, *Advisor*
EMP: 50
SALES (corp-wide): 93B **Publicly Held**
WEB: www.merlyn.com
SIC: **6211** Security brokers & dealers
HQ: Merrill Lynch, Pierce, Fenner & Smith
Incorporated
111 8th Ave
New York NY 10011
800 637-7455

(P-10045)
MERRILL LYNCH PIERCE FENNER
100 Spectrum Center Dr # 1100, Irvine (92618-4962)
P.O. Box 2550, Laguna Hills (92654-2550)
PHONE.................................949 859-2900
Fax: 949 380-7936
Pete Henvika, *Sales/Mktg Mgr*
Clay Baxter, *VP Mktg*
Michael Flood, *Manager*
Andrew Binkerd, *Advisor*
Ryan Lee, *Advisor*
EMP: 90
SALES (corp-wide): 93B **Publicly Held**
WEB: www.merlyn.com
SIC: **6211** Security brokers & dealers
HQ: Merrill Lynch, Pierce, Fenner & Smith
Incorporated
111 8th Ave
New York NY 10011
800 637-7455

(P-10046)
MERRILL LYNCH PIERCE FENNER
7825 Fay Ave Ste 300, La Jolla (92037-4255)
PHONE.................................858 456-3600
Paul Sullivan, *Manager*
Peter Huffman, *Broker*

Neal Walton, *Manager*
Gary Wardein, *Manager*
Robert Wilcsek, *Manager*
EMP: 60
SALES (corp-wide): 93B **Publicly Held**
WEB: www.merlyn.com
SIC: **6211** Security brokers & dealers
HQ: Merrill Lynch, Pierce, Fenner & Smith
Incorporated
111 8th Ave
New York NY 10011
800 637-7455

(P-10047)
MIZUHO SECURITIES USA INC
3 Embarcadero Ctr # 1620, San Francisco (94111-4049)
PHONE.................................415 268-5500
EMP: 53
SALES (corp-wide): 26.7B **Privately Held**
SIC: **6211** Security brokers & dealers
HQ: Mizuho Securities Usa Inc.
320 Park Ave Fl 12
New York NY 10022
212 282-3000

(P-10048)
MORGAN STANLEY
55 S Lake Ave Ste 800, Pasadena (91101-2677)
PHONE.................................626 405-9313
Alan Whitman, *Branch Mgr*
Kamran Hedjasi, *Agent*
Anny Shen, *Agent*
EMP: 60
SALES (corp-wide): 37.9B **Publicly Held**
SIC: **6211** Stock brokers & dealers
PA: Morgan Stanley
1585 Broadway
New York NY 10036
212 761-4000

(P-10049)
MORGAN STANLEY
4350 La Jolla Village Dr # 1000, San Diego (92122-1247)
PHONE.................................858 597-7777
Joe McDoval, *General Mgr*
Constance Maples, *Branch Mgr*
Kenneth Blattenbauer, *Manager*
EMP: 50
SALES (corp-wide): 37.9B **Publicly Held**
SIC: **6211** Security brokers & dealers
PA: Morgan Stanley
1585 Broadway
New York NY 10036
212 761-4000

(P-10050)
MORGAN STANLEY
1901 Main St Ste 700, Irvine (92614-0514)
PHONE.................................949 809-1200
Fax: 949 756-8908
Jeff Gilbert, *Manager*
Stanley Bannon, *Manager*
EMP: 65
SALES (corp-wide): 37.9B **Publicly Held**
SIC: **6211** Security brokers & dealers
PA: Morgan Stanley
1585 Broadway
New York NY 10036
212 761-4000

(P-10051)
MORGAN STANLEY & CO LLC
407 Capitol Mall Ste 1900, Sacramento (95814-4402)
PHONE.................................916 444-8041
Henry Auwinger, *Branch Mgr*
Jeffrey C Won, *Senior VP*
Rodger Smith, *Branch Mgr*
Gracie Imhoff, *Manager*
EMP: 50
SALES (corp-wide): 37.9B **Publicly Held**
WEB: www.msvp.com
SIC: **6211** Stock brokers & dealers
HQ: Morgan Stanley & Co. Llc
1585 Broadway
New York NY 10036
212 761-4000

(P-10052)
MORGAN STANLEY & CO LLC
5250 N Palm Ave Ste 321, Fresno (93704-2213)
PHONE.................................559 431-5900

Gregory Conner, *Manager*
Jeff W Branch, *Senior VP*
Marlyn Milloy, *Manager*
Chu Pau, *Manager*
EMP: 50
SALES (corp-wide): 37.9B **Publicly Held**
WEB: www.msvp.com
SIC: **6211** Security brokers & dealers
HQ: Morgan Stanley & Co. Llc
1585 Broadway
New York NY 10036
212 761-4000

(P-10053)
MORGAN STANLEY & CO LLC
2677 N Main St Fl 10, Santa Ana (92705-6633)
P.O. Box 11998 (92711-1998)
PHONE.................................714 836-5181
Mark Albers, *Branch Mgr*
John Muirhead, *Executive*
Jose Bohon, *Div Sub Head*
EMP: 60
SALES (corp-wide): 37.9B **Publicly Held**
WEB: www.msvp.com
SIC: **6211** Stock brokers & dealers
HQ: Morgan Stanley & Co. Llc
1585 Broadway
New York NY 10036
212 761-4000

(P-10054)
MORGAN STANLEY & CO LLC
101 W Broadway Ste 1800, San Diego (92101-8298)
PHONE.................................619 236-1331
Eddie Dyer, *Branch Mgr*
James Fitzpatrick, *Opers Mgr*
Michael Rhodes, *Manager*
EMP: 80
SQ FT: 13,000
SALES (corp-wide): 37.9B **Publicly Held**
WEB: www.msvp.com
SIC: **6211** Investment bankers
HQ: Morgan Stanley & Co. Llc
1585 Broadway
New York NY 10036
212 761-4000

(P-10055)
MORGAN STANLEY & CO LLC
9100 Ming Ave Ste 205, Bakersfield (93311-1329)
PHONE.................................661 663-8100
Tom Woodward, *Manager*
EMP: 53
SALES (corp-wide): 37.9B **Publicly Held**
WEB: www.msvp.com
SIC: **6211** Brokers, security
HQ: Morgan Stanley & Co. Llc
1585 Broadway
New York NY 10036
212 761-4000

(P-10056)
MORGAN STANLEY & CO LLC
1999 Harrison St Ste 2200, Oakland (94612-3559)
PHONE.................................510 839-8080
Renee Arst, *Manager*
EMP: 60
SALES (corp-wide): 37.9B **Publicly Held**
WEB: www.msvp.com
SIC: **6211** Security brokers & dealers
HQ: Morgan Stanley & Co. Llc
1585 Broadway
New York NY 10036
212 761-4000

(P-10057)
MORGAN STANLEY & CO LLC
216 Lorton Ave, Burlingame (94010-4204)
PHONE.................................650 340-6550
Jane Kelly, *Principal*
Cindy Cook, *Opers Mgr*
EMP: 75
SALES (corp-wide): 37.9B **Publicly Held**
WEB: www.msvp.com
SIC: **6211** Security brokers & dealers
HQ: Morgan Stanley & Co. Llc
1585 Broadway
New York NY 10036
212 761-4000

6211 - Security Brokers & Dealers County (P-10058)

(P-10058)
MORGAN STANLEY & CO LLC
225 W Santa Clara St # 900, San Jose (95113-1746)
PHONE.............................408 947-2200
William Svoboda, *Branch Mgr*
Wendi Eckdridt, *Manager*
EMP: 60
SALES (corp-wide): 37.9B **Publicly Held**
WEB: www.msvp.com
SIC: 6211 Brokers, security
HQ: Morgan Stanley & Co. Llc
1585 Broadway
New York NY 10036
212 761-4000

(P-10059)
MORGAN STANLEY & CO LLC
335 N Maple Dr Ste 150, Beverly Hills (90210-5197)
PHONE.............................310 285-4800
Margaret Black, *Manager*
Arman Markayan, *CTO*
Elaine Francisco, *Personnel*
Lisa Behar, *Opers Mgr*
EMP: 160
SALES (corp-wide): 37.9B **Publicly Held**
WEB: www.msvp.com
SIC: 6211 Security brokers & dealers
HQ: Morgan Stanley & Co. Llc
1585 Broadway
New York NY 10036
212 761-4000

(P-10060)
MORGAN STANLEY & CO LLC
1453 3rd St Ste 200, Santa Monica (90401-3451)
P.O. Box 2310 (90407-2310)
PHONE.............................310 319-5200
Thomas Padden, *Manager*
EMP: 65
SALES (corp-wide): 37.9B **Publicly Held**
WEB: www.msvp.com
SIC: 6211 Security brokers & dealers
HQ: Morgan Stanley & Co. Llc
1585 Broadway
New York NY 10036
212 761-4000

(P-10061)
MORGAN STANLEY & CO LLC
101 California St Fl 3, San Francisco (94111-5890)
PHONE.............................415 693-6000
Renee Arst, *Manager*
Mitch Sauberman, *Senior VP*
Kenny Blattenbauer, *Vice Pres*
Bhavin Shukla, *Vice Pres*
Michael Abbenante, *Agent*
EMP: 300
SALES (corp-wide): 37.9B **Publicly Held**
WEB: www.msvp.com
SIC: 6211 Brokers, security
HQ: Morgan Stanley & Co. Llc
1585 Broadway
New York NY 10036
212 761-4000

(P-10062)
MORTGAGE X L
3130 Crow Canyon Pl # 325, San Ramon (94583-1346)
PHONE.............................925 830-8951
David Syme, *President*
EMP: 50
SALES (est): 3.7MM **Privately Held**
SIC: 6211 Mortgages, buying & selling

(P-10063)
MYERS CAPITAL PARTNERS LLC
450 S Marengo Ave, Pasadena (91101-3113)
PHONE.............................626 568-1398
Fax: 626 568-3352
William E Myers Jr,
Kit McCoullogh,
EMP: 50
SQ FT: 1,000
SALES (est): 9.8MM **Privately Held**
WEB: www.myerscapitalpartners.com
SIC: 6211 Investment firm, general brokerage

(P-10064)
NETWORK AFFILIATES INC
600 Montgomery St, San Francisco (94111-2702)
PHONE.............................415 291-2914
EMP: 61
SALES (corp-wide): 14.5MM **Privately Held**
SIC: 6211 Security brokers & dealers
PA: Network Affiliates, Inc.
940 Wadsworth Blvd # 300
Lakewood CO 80214
303 232-1100

(P-10065)
NOMURA SECURITIES INTL INC
425 California St # 2600, San Francisco (94104-2211)
PHONE.............................415 445-3831
John Denning, *Branch Mgr*
EMP: 340
SALES (corp-wide): 14.7B **Privately Held**
SIC: 6211 Dealers, security
HQ: Nomura Securities International, Inc.
Worldwide Plaza 309 W 49t
New York NY 10019
212 667-9000

(P-10066)
NORTHWESTERN MUTL FINCL NETWRK (PA)
4225 Executive Sq, La Jolla (92037-9122)
PHONE.............................619 234-3111
Garrett J Bleakley, *Owner*
Jodi Harrell, *Opers Staff*
EMP: 100
SALES (est): 15.6MM **Privately Held**
SIC: 6211 6411 Insurance agents, brokers & service

(P-10067)
PACIFIC GROWTH EQUITIES LLC
1 Bush St Ste 1700, San Francisco (94104-4423)
PHONE.............................415 274-6800
Fax: 415 274-6866
Thomas J Dietz, *CEO*
John C Coleman Jr, *Vice Chairman*
Jack Thrift, *CFO*
Kurtis Fechtmeyer, *Principal*
Brian Alger, *Managing Dir*
EMP: 85
SQ FT: 34,000
SALES: 44MM **Privately Held**
WEB: www.pacgrow.com
SIC: 6211 Security brokers & dealers; investment bankers

(P-10068)
PARKSIDE LENDING LLC
1130 Howard St, San Francisco (94103-3914)
PHONE.............................415 771-3700
Alan Sagatelyan,
Hanford Chiu, *CFO*
Patty Gong, *Exec VP*
James Lamparter, *Exec VP*
Linda Jacopetti, *Senior VP*
EMP: 60
SQ FT: 5,097
SALES (est): 94MM **Privately Held**
WEB: www.parksidelending.com
SIC: 6211 Mortgages, buying & selling

(P-10069)
PLAZA HOME MORTGAGE INC
2001 Gateway Pl Ste 650w, San Jose (95110-1075)
PHONE.............................408 573-7880
Fax: 408 573-7980
EMP: 91
SALES (corp-wide): 130.7MM **Privately Held**
SIC: 6211 6162 Mortgages, buying & selling; loan correspondents
PA: Plaza Home Mortgage, Inc.
4820 Eastgate Mall # 100
San Diego CA 92121
858 346-1200

(P-10070)
PLAZA HOME MORTGAGE INC
420 Exchange Ste 200, Irvine (92602-1319)
PHONE.............................714 508-6406
Fax: 714 832-8299
EMP: 91
SALES (corp-wide): 130.7MM **Privately Held**
SIC: 6211 6162 Mortgages, buying & selling; loan correspondents
PA: Plaza Home Mortgage, Inc.
4820 Eastgate Mall # 100
San Diego CA 92121
858 346-1200

(P-10071)
PROMMIS SOLUTIONS LLC
525 E Main St, El Cajon (92020-4007)
PHONE.............................619 590-9200
Jenifer Victor, *Branch Mgr*
EMP: 300
SALES (corp-wide): 123.9MM **Privately Held**
SIC: 6211 Investment firm, general brokerage
PA: Prommis Solutions, Llc
400 Northridge Rd
Atlanta GA 30350
800 275-7171

(P-10072)
RBC WEALTH MANAGEMENT
9665 Wilshire Blvd Fl 4, Beverly Hills (90212-2311)
PHONE.............................310 273-7600
Elliot Katz, *Branch Mgr*
Brett Bartman, *Senior VP*
George Otto, *Advisor*
Alan Pochter, *Advisor*
EMP: 50
SALES (corp-wide): 31.1B **Privately Held**
WEB: www.hough.com
SIC: 6211 Investment bankers
HQ: Rbc Wealth Management
60 S 6th St Ste 700
Minneapolis MN 55402
612 371-7750

(P-10073)
RCM CAPITAL MANAGEMENT LLC (DH)
555 Mission St Ste 1700, San Francisco (94105-0937)
PHONE.............................415 954-5400
Udo Frank, *Ch of Bd*
David Hollis, *Portfolio Mgr*
Jing Zhou, *Portfolio Mgr*
Iain Clayton, *Analyst*
Robert Galvin, *Director*
EMP: 340 EST: 1970
SALES (est): 55.1MM **Privately Held**
SIC: 6211 6282 Investment firm, general brokerage; investment counselors
HQ: Allianz Asset Management Ag
Seidlstr. 24-24a
Munchen 80335
891 220-70

(P-10074)
REYES HOLDINGS LLC
Also Called: Crest Beverage
8870 Liquid Ct, San Diego (92121-2234)
PHONE.............................858 452-2300
Steve Souratas, *President*
EMP: 300 **Privately Held**
SIC: 6211 Distributors, security
PA: Reyes Holdings, L.L.C.
6250 N River Rd Ste 9000
Rosemont IL 60018
-

(P-10075)
ROTH CAPITAL PARTNERS LLC (PA)
888 San Clemente Dr # 400, Newport Beach (92660-6369)
PHONE.............................800 678-9147
Byron Roth, *CEO*
Donald Straszheim, *Vice Chairman*
John Chambers, *Vice Ch Bd*
Jonathan Alyn, *Vice Pres*
Warren Dunnavant II, *Vice Pres*
EMP: 100
SQ FT: 52,000

SALES (est): 68.8MM **Privately Held**
WEB:
SIC: 6211 Investment bankers; brokers, security

(P-10076)
SHAMROCK PLUS INC
Also Called: Shamrock Center
4444 W Lakeside Dr Lbby, Burbank (91505-4069)
PHONE.............................818 845-4444
Stanley Gold, *President*
Peter Rivera, *Director*
EMP: 50
SQ FT: 12,000
SALES (est): 3.4MM
SALES (corp-wide): 16.3MM **Privately Held**
SIC: 6211 Brokers, security; investment bankers; investment certificate sales
HQ: Shamrock Holdings Of California, Inc.
4444 W Lakeside Dr Lbby
Burbank CA 91505
818 845-4444

(P-10077)
STANDARD PACIFIC CAPITAL LLC
101 California St Fl 36, San Francisco (94111-5831)
PHONE.............................415 352-7100
Fax: 415 352-7117
Andrew Midler, *Managing Prtnr*
Molly Lynch, *General Mgr*
John Beall, *IT/INT Sup*
Amman Fenster, *IT/INT Sup*
Kelly Kennard, *Research*
EMP: 50
SQ FT: 9,000
SALES (est): 13.4MM **Privately Held**
SIC: 6211 Security brokers & dealers; investment firm, general brokerage

(P-10078)
STOCKCROSS FINANCIAL SERVICES (PA)
9464 Wilshire Blvd, Beverly Hills (90212-2707)
PHONE.............................800 225-6196
Andrew Reich, *CEO*
Edmond Dantes, *Exec VP*
Greg Schebece, *Exec VP*
David A Bender, *Senior VP*
Rodney Carrasquillo, *Senior VP*
EMP: 50
SQ FT: 8,000
SALES (est): 39.9MM **Privately Held**
WEB: www.stockcross.com
SIC: 6211 Brokers, security; dealers, security

(P-10079)
STONE & YOUNGBERG LLC (PA)
1 Ferry Plz, San Francisco (94111-4212)
PHONE.............................415 445-2300
Fax: 415 397-9592
Kenneth E Williams, *President*
Mitchell H Gage, *CFO*
Paul Whitaker, *CFO*
B Craig Hutson, *Senior VP*
Kevin R Montoya, *Senior VP*
EMP: 130
SQ FT: 19,034
SALES (est): 46.8MM **Privately Held**
WEB: www.syllc.com
SIC: 6211 6282 Bond dealers & brokers; investment advice

(P-10080)
TANIMURA BROTHERS
81 Hitchcock Rd, Salinas (93908-9449)
PHONE.............................831 424-0841
Fax: 831 455-0225
Tom Tanimura, *Partner*
George Tanimura, *Partner*
John Tanimura, *Partner*
Juan Yebra, *Manager*
EMP: 70 EST: 1948
SALES (est): 9.9MM **Privately Held**
SIC: 6211 Investment firm, general brokerage

PRODUCTS & SERVICES SECTION

6211 - Security Brokers & Dealers County (P-10101)

(P-10081)
TCW FUNDS MANAGEMENT INC
865 S Figueroa St # 2100, Los Angeles (90017-2588)
PHONE 213 244-0000
Thomas Larkin, *Ch of Bd*
Marc I Stern, *President*
William E Sonnebron, *CFO*
Ernest O Ellison, *Officer*
Alvin R Albe Jr, *Exec VP*
EMP: 550
SALES (est): 36.7MM
SALES (corp-wide): 3B **Publicly Held**
SIC: 6211 Security brokers & dealers
HQ: The Tcw Group Inc
865 S Figueroa St # 2100
Los Angeles CA 90017
213 244-0000

(P-10082)
THOMAS WEISEL PARTNERS LLC (DH)
1 Montgomery St Ste 3700, San Francisco (94104-5537)
PHONE 415 364-2500
Fax: 415 364-2695
Thomas Weisel,
Richard Spalding, *General Ptnr*
Janet Barnes, *Vice Pres*
Tracy Beaver, *Vice Pres*
Michael Carr, *Vice Pres*
EMP: 300
SALES (est): 62.9MM
SALES (corp-wide): 2.3B **Publicly Held**
WEB: www.tweisel.com
SIC: 6211 Investment bankers
HQ: Thomas Weisel Partners Group Inc.
1 Montgomery St
San Francisco CA 94104
415 364-2500

(P-10083)
TRANSAMERICA SECURITIES SALES
1150 S Olive St Ste T25, Los Angeles (90015-2214)
PHONE 213 741-7702
Sandy Brown, *President*
Dan S Trivers, *Principal*
EMP: 75
SALES (est): 5.8MM **Privately Held**
SIC: 6211 Security brokers & dealers

(P-10084)
TRANSMERICA FINCL ADVISORS INC
1150 S Olive St Ste T250, Los Angeles (90015-2211)
PHONE 213 741-7702
Sandy Brown, *Branch Mgr*
Karen Perry, *COO*
EMP: 121 **Privately Held**
SIC: 6211 6282 Investment firm, general brokerage; manager of mutual funds, contract or fee basis
HQ: Transamerica Financial Advisors, Inc.
570 Carillon Pkwy
Saint Petersburg FL 33716
727 557-2754

(P-10085)
TRUST COMPANY OF WEST (DH)
865 S Figueroa St # 1800, Los Angeles (90017-2543)
PHONE 213 244-0000
Fax: 213 244-0570
David Lippman, *President*
Robert A Day, *Ch of Bd*
Bill Sonneborn, *CFO*
Richard M Villa, *CFO*
Ernest O Ellison, *Vice Ch Bd*
EMP: 514
SQ FT: 160,000
SALES (est): 111.3MM
SALES (corp-wide): 3B **Publicly Held**
WEB: www.tcw.com
SIC: 6211 Bond dealers & brokers
HQ: The Tcw Group Inc
865 S Figueroa St # 2100
Los Angeles CA 90017
213 244-0000

(P-10086)
UBS FINANCIAL SERVICES INC
777 S Figueroa St # 5100, Los Angeles (90017-5800)
P.O. Box 90051 (90009-0051)
PHONE 213 972-1511
Wes Jennison, *Manager*
Lisa Donahue, *Vice Pres*
EMP: 200
SALES (corp-wide): 30.4B **Privately Held**
SIC: 6211 Brokers, security
HQ: Ubs Financial Services Inc.
1285 Ave Of The Americas
New York NY 10019
212 713-2000

(P-10087)
UBS FINANCIAL SERVICES INC
131 S Rodeo Dr Ste 200, Beverly Hills (90212-2428)
PHONE 310 274-8441
Randall Grossblatt, *Manager*
Joseph Schirripa, *Senior VP*
Gregory Webster, *Senior VP*
Scott Trout, *Vice Pres*
Peter Weintraub, *Vice Pres*
EMP: 100
SALES (corp-wide): 30.4B **Privately Held**
SIC: 6211 Bond dealers & brokers; brokers, security; stock brokers & dealers
HQ: Ubs Financial Services Inc.
1285 Ave Of The Americas
New York NY 10019
212 713-2000

(P-10088)
UBS FINANCIAL SERVICES INC
555 California St # 4650, San Francisco (94104-1789)
PHONE 415 954-6700
Loren Neumann, *Branch Mgr*
Michael Fitzgerald, *Senior VP*
Alexander Taft, *Vice Pres*
Robert Vallercorse, *Vice Pres*
Michael Williams, *Branch Mgr*
EMP: 175
SALES (corp-wide): 30.4B **Privately Held**
SIC: 6211 Stock brokers & dealers
HQ: Ubs Financial Services Inc.
1285 Ave Of The Americas
New York NY 10019
212 713-2000

(P-10089)
UBS FINANCIAL SERVICES INC
3030 Old Ranch Pkwy # 300, Seal Beach (90740-8807)
PHONE 562 495-5500
John W Orr, *Manager*
Ford Howell, *IT/INT Sup*
Kevin B Ou, *Advisor*
EMP: 60
SALES (corp-wide): 30.4B **Privately Held**
SIC: 6211 Security brokers & dealers
HQ: Ubs Financial Services Inc.
1285 Ave Of The Americas
New York NY 10019
212 713-2000

(P-10090)
UBS FINANCIAL SERVICES INC
888 San Clemente Dr # 300, Newport Beach (92660-6366)
PHONE 949 760-5308
Don Dalis, *Branch Mgr*
Michael Hammett, *Advisor*
Greg Zappas, *Advisor*
EMP: 175
SALES (corp-wide): 28.9B **Privately Held**
SIC: 6211 Stock brokers & dealers
HQ: Ubs Financial Services Inc.
1285 Ave Of The Americas
New York NY 10019
212 713-2000

(P-10091)
UBS FINANCIAL SERVICES INC
555 California St # 4650, San Francisco (94104-1789)
PHONE 415 398-6400
Tony Tarrab, *Manager*
David Dicioccio, *Managing Dir*
Allen Brady, *Manager*
Paolo Seiferle, *Manager*
EMP: 100

SALES (corp-wide): 30.4B **Privately Held**
SIC: 6211 Investment bankers; brokers, security
HQ: Ubs Financial Services Inc.
1285 Ave Of The Americas
New York NY 10019
212 713-2000

(P-10092)
UBS FINANCIAL SERVICES INC
200 S Los Robles Ave # 600, Pasadena (91101-4600)
PHONE 626 449-1501
Donald Gorsch, *Manager*
Mark Armstrong, *Senior VP*
Michael Naples, *Advisor*
EMP: 50
SALES (corp-wide): 28.9B **Privately Held**
SIC: 6211 Stock brokers & dealers
HQ: Ubs Financial Services Inc.
1285 Ave Of The Americas
New York NY 10019
212 713-2000

(P-10093)
UBS FINANCIAL SERVICES INC
555 California St # 4650, San Francisco (94104-1789)
PHONE 415 398-6400
Mark Zalinski, *Manager*
EMP: 60
SALES (corp-wide): 28.9B **Privately Held**
SIC: 6211 Security brokers & dealers
HQ: Ubs Financial Services Inc.
1285 Ave Of The Americas
New York NY 10019
212 713-2000

(P-10094)
UBS FINANCIAL SERVICES INC
2029 Century Park E # 3000, Los Angeles (90067-3016)
PHONE 310 556-0746
Richard Lavoice, *Branch Mgr*
Elizabeth Knutson, *Vice Pres*
Christopher Shelburne, *Branch Mgr*
EMP: 150
SALES (corp-wide): 28.9B **Privately Held**
SIC: 6211 Security brokers & dealers
HQ: Ubs Financial Services Inc.
1285 Ave Of The Americas
New York NY 10019
212 713-2000

(P-10095)
UBS SECURITIES LLC
555 California St # 4650, San Francisco (94104-1789)
PHONE 415 352-5650
Kirt Engle, *Branch Mgr*
Bing Presnell, *Senior VP*
John Huwiler, *Exec Dir*
James Feuille, *Rsch/Dvlpt Dir*
EMP: 65
SALES (corp-wide): 30.4B **Privately Held**
SIC: 6211 Brokers, security; dealers, security
HQ: Ubs Securities Llc
677 Washington Blvd
Stamford CT 06901
203 719-3000

(P-10096)
W R HAMBRECHT CO INC (PA)
Bay 3 Pier 1, San Francisco (94111)
PHONE 415 551-8600
William R Hambrecht, *Ch of Bd*
Jonathan Fayman, *CFO*
Clay Corbus, *Co-CEO*
Matt Quen, *CIO*
Gordon Palumbo, *Technology*
EMP: 60 **EST:** 1998
SQ FT: 25,000
SALES (est): 21.2MM **Privately Held**
WEB: www.wrhambrecht.com
SIC: 6211 Investment bankers

(P-10097)
WADDELL & REED INC
695 Town Center Dr # 200, Costa Mesa (92626-7128)
PHONE 714 437-7510
Daralee Barbera, *Director*
Michael Strohm, *Senior VP*
Al Gumb, *District Mgr*
Jerry Walton, *Finance Mgr*

Daralee Barbera, *Mktg Dir*
EMP: 65
SALES (corp-wide): 1.5B **Publicly Held**
SIC: 6211 8742 Security brokers & dealers; financial consultant
HQ: Waddell & Reed, Inc.
6300 Lamar Ave
Shawnee Mission KS 66202
913 236-2000

(P-10098)
WEDBUSH SECURITIES INC (HQ)
1000 Wilshire Blvd # 900, Los Angeles (90017-2457)
P.O. Box 30014 (90030-0014)
PHONE 213 688-8000
Fax: 213 688-6629
Edward W Wedbush, *President*
Alex Brackman, *President*
Ron Yeager, *President*
Peter Allman-Ward, *CFO*
Thomas Ringer, *Chairman*
EMP: 300 **EST:** 1955
SQ FT: 100,000
SALES (est): 351MM
SALES (corp-wide): 361.5MM **Privately Held**
WEB: www.einvestmentbank.com
SIC: 6211 Brokers, security; stock brokers & dealers; bond dealers & brokers
PA: Wedbush Inc.,
1000 Wilshire Blvd # 900
Los Angeles CA 90017
213 688-8080

(P-10099)
WELLS FARGO ADVISORS LLC
555 California St # 2300, San Francisco (94104-1598)
PHONE 415 291-1200
Fax: 415 288-4343
Kevin Kitchin, *Manager*
Donald Bagley, *Senior VP*
Harry Gong, *Vice Pres*
Derek Holtzinger, *Vice Pres*
Bob Behray, *Managing Dir*
EMP: 115
SALES (corp-wide): 90B **Publicly Held**
WEB: www.wachoviasec.com
SIC: 6211 6282 Stock brokers & dealers; investment advice
HQ: Wells Fargo Advisors, Llc
1 N Jefferson Ave
Saint Louis MO 63103
314 955-3000

(P-10100)
WELLS FARGO ADVISORS LLC
3020 Old Ranch Pkwy # 190, Seal Beach (90740-2761)
PHONE 562 594-1220
David Altshuler, *Manager*
Marco Cisneros, *Senior VP*
Richard Jackson, *Senior VP*
Christopher Vanhorn, *Senior VP*
David Boyer, *Vice Pres*
EMP: 50
SALES (corp-wide): 90B **Publicly Held**
WEB: www.wachoviasec.com
SIC: 6211 Stock brokers & dealers
HQ: Wells Fargo Advisors, Llc
1 N Jefferson Ave
Saint Louis MO 63103
314 955-3000

(P-10101)
WELLS FARGO ADVISORS LLC
Also Called: Bateman Eichler Hill Richards
5820 Canoga Ave Ste 100, Woodland Hills (91367-6517)
PHONE 818 226-2222
Jeff Bouchard, *Manager*
Neil Scheinbart, *Assoc VP*
Salim Kimiagar, *Senior VP*
Richard Stevens, *Senior VP*
Thomas A Eisenstadt, *Vice Pres*
EMP: 60
SALES (corp-wide): 90B **Publicly Held**
WEB: www.wachoviasec.com
SIC: 6211 Stock brokers & dealers
HQ: Wells Fargo Advisors, Llc
1 N Jefferson Ave
Saint Louis MO 63103
314 955-3000

6211 - Security Brokers & Dealers County (P-10102)

PRODUCTS & SERVICES SECTION

(P-10102)
WELLS FARGO SECURITIES LLC
600 California St Fl 17, San Francisco (94108-2723)
PHONE.............................415 645-0800
Fax: 415 645-0888
Timothy J Sloan, *Manager*
John Baumgartner, *Vice Pres*
Dan Goggins, *Managing Dir*
John Jinishian, *Managing Dir*
George Huang, *Analyst*
EMP: 90
SALES (corp-wide): 90B **Publicly Held**
WEB: www.wellsfargosecurities.com
SIC: **6211** Investment bankers
HQ: Wells Fargo Securities, Llc
   301 S Tryon St
   Charlotte NC 28282
   312 920-9177

(P-10103)
WILLIAM ONEIL & CO INC
12655 Beatrice St, Los Angeles (90066-7302)
PHONE.............................310 448-6800
Willaim J Oneil, *CEO*
Don Drake, *CFO*
EMP: 250
SQ FT: 5,000
SALES (est): 36.7MM **Privately Held**
SIC: **6211 6282** Brokers, security; investment advisory service

6221 Commodity Contracts Brokers & Dealers

(P-10104)
APEX BULK COMMODITIES INC
14080 Slover Ave, Fontana (92337-7039)
PHONE.............................909 854-9991
Steve Gale, *Branch Mgr*
EMP: 102
SALES (corp-wide): 59.4MM **Privately Held**
SIC: **6221** Commodity contracts brokers, dealers
PA: Apex Bulk Commodities, Inc.
   12531 Violet Rd Ste A
   Adelanto CA 92301
   760 246-6077

(P-10105)
GLOBAL FUTURES EXCH & TRDG CO
19300 Ventura Blvd, Tarzana (91356-3029)
PHONE.............................818 996-0401
Kathy Hakimian, *President*
Jeff Peltz, *Technical Staff*
Francis Marcale, *Manager*
EMP: 80
SALES (est): 16.7MM **Privately Held**
WEB: www.gfetc.com
SIC: **6221** Commodity contracts brokers, dealers

(P-10106)
MERRILL LYNCH PIERCE FENNER
145 S State College Blvd # 300, Brea (92821-5844)
PHONE.............................714 257-4400
Fax: 714 990-8137
Robert Max, *Manager*
Haseong Joo, *Vice Pres*
Stephanie Sheeks, *Director*
Michael Oleary, *Manager*
Chuen-Huey L Chen, *Agent*
EMP: 69
SALES (corp-wide): 93B **Publicly Held**
WEB: www.merlyn.com
SIC: **6221** Commodity brokers, contracts; commodity dealers, contracts
HQ: Merrill Lynch, Pierce, Fenner & Smith Incorporated
   111 8th Ave
   New York NY 10011
   800 637-7455

(P-10107)
MERRILL LYNCH PIERCE FENNER
1111 Broadway Ste 2200, Oakland (94607-4045)
PHONE.............................510 208-3800
Fax: 510 465-8542
Tracy Murphy, *Branch Mgr*
Steve Bearden, *Exec Dir*
Jeremy Niederstadt, *Manager*
Angela F Berry, *Advisor*
Sharon Hamann, *Agent*
EMP: 100
SALES (corp-wide): 93B **Publicly Held**
WEB: www.merlyn.com
SIC: **6221 8742 6282** Commodity brokers, contracts; commodity dealers, contracts; management consulting services; investment advice
HQ: Merrill Lynch, Pierce, Fenner & Smith Incorporated
   111 8th Ave
   New York NY 10011
   800 637-7455

(P-10108)
MERRILL LYNCH PIERCE FENNER
800 E Colo Blvd Ste 400, Pasadena (91101)
PHONE.............................626 844-8500
Fax: 626 304-0411
Mark Mixon, *Manager*
Heidi Leu, *Manager*
Eric Callow, *Advisor*
Lawrence De Santis, *Advisor*
Anthony Gendal, *Advisor*
EMP: 80
SALES (corp-wide): 93B **Publicly Held**
WEB: www.merlyn.com
SIC: **6221** Commodity brokers, contracts; commodity dealers, contracts
HQ: Merrill Lynch, Pierce, Fenner & Smith Incorporated
   111 8th Ave
   New York NY 10011
   800 637-7455

6231 Security & Commodity Exchanges

(P-10109)
INTERCONTINENTAL EXCHANGE INC (HQ)
Also Called: Ice
1415 Moonstone, Brea (92821-2832)
PHONE.............................770 857-4700
Jeffrey C Sprecher, *Ch of Bd*
Ben Jackson, *President*
Bruce Tupper, *President*
Brad Vannan, *President*
Charles A Vice, *President*
EMP: 383
SQ FT: 92,171
SALES: 3B
SALES (corp-wide): 4.6B **Publicly Held**
WEB: www.theice.com
SIC: **6231** Security & commodity exchanges
PA: Intercontinental Exchange, Inc.
   5660 New Northside Dr # 300
   Atlanta GA 30328
   770 857-4700

6282 Investment Advice

(P-10110)
6TH & ISLAND INVESTMENTS
454 6th Ave, San Diego (92101-7008)
PHONE.............................619 236-0624
J Chua, *Principal*
EMP: 85
SALES (est): 6.1MM **Privately Held**
SIC: **6282** Investment advisory service

(P-10111)
ALLIANCEBERNSTEIN LP
1999 Ave Of The Sts 215 Ste 2150, Los Angeles (90067)
PHONE.............................310 286-6000
Fax: 310 286-6053
Alan D Croll, *Branch Mgr*
Stuart Katz, *Vice Pres*
Maryann Best, *Managing Dir*
Daniel Eagan, *Managing Dir*
Carl Ports, *Director*
EMP: 60
SALES (corp-wide): 2.9B **Publicly Held**
WEB: www.bernstein.com
SIC: **6282** Investment research
HQ: Alliancebernstein L.P.
   1345 Ave Of The Americas
   New York NY 10105
   212 969-1000

(P-10112)
ALLIANZ GLOBL INVESTORS US LLC
Also Called: Allianz Life
555 Mission St Ste 1700, San Francisco (94105-0937)
PHONE.............................415 954-5400
Walter White, *CEO*
EMP: 267
SALES (est): 27.2MM **Privately Held**
SIC: **6282** Investment advisory service

(P-10113)
ALLIANZ GLOBL INVSTORS AMER LP
Also Called: Timco
680 New Port Dr Ste 250, Newport Beach (92660)
PHONE.............................949 219-2200
David Flattun, *Manager*
Brent Holden, *Manager*
EMP: 200 **Privately Held**
WEB: www.allianzinvestors.com
SIC: **6282** Investment advisory service; manager of mutual funds, contract or fee basis
HQ: Allianz Global Investors Of America, Lp
   680 Nwport Ctr Dr Ste 250
   Newport Beach CA 92660
   949 219-2200

(P-10114)
ALLIANZ GLOBL INVSTORS AMER LP (HQ)
Also Called: Foreign Prnt Is Alanz AG Mnchn
680 Nwport Ctr Dr Ste 250, Newport Beach (92660)
PHONE.............................949 219-2200
Fax: 949 219-3949
Brian Gaffney, *President*
David Flattun, *Partner*
Greg Goldstein, *COO*
John Maneyy, *CFO*
Steve Buck, *Senior VP*
EMP: 100
SQ FT: 20,000
SALES (est): 519MM **Privately Held**
WEB: www.allianzinvestors.com
SIC: **6282** Investment advisory service; manager of mutual funds, contract or fee basis
PA: Allianz Se
   Konigistr. 28
   Munchen 80802
   893 800-0

(P-10115)
AMERICAN ADVISORS GROUP (PA)
3800 W Chapman Ave Fl 3, Orange (92868-1638)
PHONE.............................866 948-0003
Reza Jahangiri, *President*
Matt Engel, *CFO*
Martin Lenoir, *Chief Mktg Ofcr*
Paul Fiore, *Exec VP*
Kevin Blakeney, *Senior VP*
EMP: 50
SQ FT: 4,500
SALES (est): 26.1MM **Privately Held**
SIC: **6282** Futures advisory service; investment advisory service

(P-10116)
AMERICAN CENTURY INV MGT INC
Also Called: American Century Investments
1665 Charleston Rd, Mountain View (94043-1211)
PHONE.............................650 965-8300
Randy Merk, *Branch Mgr*
Alejandro Aguilar, *Vice Pres*
Brad Bode, *Vice Pres*
Denise Latchford, *Vice Pres*
Darrell Lee, *Vice Pres*
EMP: 200
SALES (corp-wide): 887.7MM **Privately Held**
SIC: **6282** Investment advice
HQ: American Century Investment Management, Inc.
   4500 Main St
   Kansas City MO 64111
   816 531-5575

(P-10117)
AMERICAN FINANCIAL NETWORK INC
8505 Florence Ave, Downey (90240-4014)
PHONE.............................562 861-1414
Alejandro Ascencio, *Branch Mgr*
EMP: 296
SALES (corp-wide): 82MM **Privately Held**
SIC: **6282** Investment advice
PA: American Financial Network, Inc.
   3110 Chino Ave Ste 290
   Chino CA 91710
   909 606-3905

(P-10118)
ARES MANAGEMENT LP (PA)
2000 Avenue Of The Stars, Los Angeles (90067-4700)
PHONE.............................310 201-4100
Antony P Ressler, *Ch of Bd*
Ares M LLC, *General Ptnr*
Michael J Arougheti, *President*
Paul Colatrella, *Managing Dir*
EMP: 56
SALES: 814.4MM **Publicly Held**
SIC: **6282** Investment advice

(P-10119)
ASSETMARK INC (DH)
1655 Grant St, Concord (94520-2445)
PHONE.............................925 521-1040
Fax: 925 521-1050
Ron Cordes, *Ch of Bd*
Charles Goldman, *President*
Jason Thomas, *CEO*
Myra Rothfeld, *Chief Mktg Ofcr*
Jerry Chafkin, *Ch Invest Ofcr*
EMP: 50
SQ FT: 15,000
SALES (est): 38.3MM
SALES (corp-wide): 12.5MM **Privately Held**
WEB: www.genworthwealth.com
SIC: **6282** Manager of mutual funds, contract or fee basis

(P-10120)
AXA ADVISORS LLC
3435 Wilshire Blvd # 2500, Los Angeles (90010-2011)
PHONE.............................213 251-1600
Yong Parks, *Manager*
Young Won, *Vice Pres*
Jenny Jung, *Info Tech Mgr*
Sarah Yi, *Manager*
EMP: 90
SALES (corp-wide): 2.9B **Publicly Held**
WEB: www.axacs.com
SIC: **6282** Investment advisory service
HQ: Axa Advisors, Llc
   1290 Ave Of Amrcs Fl Cncl
   New York NY 10104
   212 554-1234

(P-10121)
AYCO COMPANY LP
17885 Von Karman Ave # 300, Irvine (92614-5225)
PHONE.............................949 955-1544
Emmett Clancy, *Manager*
Kenneth Willetts, *Executive*
Krystle St Claire, *Personnel Assit*
Hilda Parada, *Sales Executive*
EMP: 150
SALES (corp-wide): 39.2B **Publicly Held**
WEB: www.ayco.com
SIC: **6282 8742** Investment counselors; financial consultant
HQ: The Ayco Company L P
   321 Broadway
   Saratoga Springs NY 12866
   518 886-4000

▲ = Import ▼ = Export
◆ = Import/Export

PRODUCTS & SERVICES SECTION

6282 - Investment Advice County (P-10142)

(P-10122)
BLACKROCK GLOBAL INVESTORS
400 Howard St, San Francisco (94105-2618)
PHONE..............................415 670-2000
Patricia Dunn, *CEO*
Sapna Sardana, *Vice Pres*
Kota Shivaranjan, *Vice Pres*
Blake Grossman, *Principal*
Carter Lyons, *Principal*
EMP: 1100
SQ FT: 65,000
SALES (est): 144.7MM
SALES (corp-wide): 11.4B **Publicly Held**
SIC: 6282 Investment advisory service
PA: Blackrock, Inc.
   55 E 52nd St Fl 11
   New York NY 10055
   212 810-5300

(P-10123)
BLX GROUP LLC
777 S Figueroa St # 3200, Los Angeles (90017-5800)
PHONE..............................213 612-2400
EMP: 60 **EST:** 2010
SQ FT: 13,000
SALES (est): 6.3MM **Privately Held**
SIC: 6282

(P-10124)
BRANDES INV PARTNERS INC (PA)
11988 El Cmino Real Ste 6, San Diego (92130)
P.O. Box 919048 (92191-9048)
PHONE..............................858 755-0239
Charles H Brandes, *Ch of Bd*
Christopher Garrett, *Partner*
Brent V Woods, *CEO*
Jeffrey A Busby, *Exec Dir*
Glenn R Carlson, *Exec Dir*
EMP: 126
SQ FT: 27,000
SALES (est): 89.4MM **Privately Held**
WEB: www.brandes.com
SIC: 6282 Investment counselors

(P-10125)
CALIBER CAPITAL GROUP LLC
5900 Katella Ave Ste A101, Cypress (90630-5019)
PHONE..............................714 507-1998
David Kim,
Kevin Foxin, *Opers Staff*
EMP: 2214
SALES (est): 92.3MM **Privately Held**
SIC: 6282 8111 Investment advice; legal services

(P-10126)
CALLAN ASSOCIATES INC (PA)
600 Montgomery St Ste 800, San Francisco (94111-2739)
PHONE..............................415 974-5060
Fax: 415 974-5944
Ronald D Peyton, *CEO*
Robert Callan, *Managing Prtnr*
Gregory C Allen, *President*
Ronald Peyton, *CEO*
James Callahan, *Exec VP*
EMP: 120 **EST:** 1973
SQ FT: 43,000
SALES (est): 47.9MM **Privately Held**
WEB: www.callan.com
SIC: 6282 8742 Investment advice; banking & finance consultant

(P-10127)
CAPITAL GROUP COMPANIES INC
11100 Santa Monica Blvd # 1500, Los Angeles (90025-3384)
PHONE..............................310 996-6238
David Fisher, *Ch of Bd*
Leonard Kim, *Managing Prtnr*
David Barclay, *Senior VP*
Gerald Dumanoir, *Vice Pres*
Sheldon Eng, *Network Analyst*
EMP: 260

SALES (corp-wide): 2.5B **Privately Held**
WEB: www.capgroup.org
SIC: 6282 6722 Manager of mutual funds, contract or fee basis; management investment, open-end
PA: The Capital Group Companies Inc
   333 S Hope St Fl 55
   Los Angeles CA 90071
   213 486-9200

(P-10128)
CAPITAL GROUP COMPANIES INC (PA)
Also Called: Capital Group, The
333 S Hope St Fl 55, Los Angeles (90071-3061)
PHONE..............................213 486-9200
Fax: 213 486-9035
Philip De Toledo, *CEO*
Larry P Clemmensen, *President*
Jacob Gerber, *President*
Cindi Grossinger, *President*
Kevin Hogan, *President*
EMP: 800
SQ FT: 106,000
SALES (est): 2.5B **Privately Held**
WEB: www.capgroup.org
SIC: 6282 6091 6722 8741 Investment advice; nondeposit trust facilities; mutual fund sales, on own account; management services

(P-10129)
CAPITAL GROUP COMPANIES INC
1 Market Plz Ste 1800, San Francisco (94105-1018)
PHONE..............................213 486-1698
Chris Buchbinder, *Branch Mgr*
Stephanie Orr, *President*
Ellen Haynes, *Assoc VP*
Erin Covington, *Senior VP*
James Kang, *Senior VP*
EMP: 413
SALES (corp-wide): 2.5B **Privately Held**
WEB: www.capgroup.org
SIC: 6282 6722 Manager of mutual funds, contract or fee basis; management investment, open-end
PA: The Capital Group Companies Inc
   333 S Hope St Fl 55
   Los Angeles CA 90071
   213 486-9200

(P-10130)
CAPITAL GROUP COMPANIES INC
Also Called: Capital Group, The
6455 Irvine Center Dr, Irvine (92618-4518)
PHONE..............................949 975-5000
Tim Weiss, *President*
Terry Chan, *Info Tech Mgr*
Jim Reis, *Programmer Anys*
Celia Chang, *Analyst*
EMP: 478
SALES (corp-wide): 2.5B **Privately Held**
WEB: www.capgroup.org
SIC: 6282 6091 6722 8741 Investment advice; nondeposit trust facilities; management investment, open-end; management services
PA: The Capital Group Companies Inc
   333 S Hope St Fl 55
   Los Angeles CA 90071
   213 486-9200

(P-10131)
CAPITAL RESEARCH AND MGT CO (HQ)
333 S Hope St Fl 55, Los Angeles (90071-3061)
PHONE..............................213 486-9200
R Michael Shanahan, *Ch of Bd*
James F Rothenberg, *Ch of Bd*
Wally Stern, *Vice Chairman*
Timothy Armour, *President*
Larry C Lemmonsen, *Treasurer*
EMP: 500
SALES (est): 310.7MM
SALES (corp-wide): 2.5B **Privately Held**
SIC: 6282 Investment research; manager of mutual funds, contract or fee basis

PA: The Capital Group Companies Inc
   333 S Hope St Fl 55
   Los Angeles CA 90071
   213 486-9200

(P-10132)
CAPITAL RESEARCH AND MGT CO
6455 Irvine Center Dr, Irvine (92618-4518)
P.O. Box 2205, Brea (92822-2205)
PHONE..............................949 975-5000
Damien Jordan, *Branch Mgr*
Eric Anderson, *Technology*
Christine Mueller, *Facilities Mgr*
John Phelan, *Director*
Tim Weiss, *Director*
EMP: 75
SALES (corp-wide): 2.5B **Privately Held**
SIC: 6282 6211 6726 6722 Investment research; manager of mutual funds, contract or fee basis; underwriters, security; investment offices; management investment, open-end
HQ: Capital Research And Management Company
   333 S Hope St Fl 55
   Los Angeles CA 90071
   213 486-9200

(P-10133)
CHURCHILL MGT GROUP CORP
5900 Wilshire Blvd # 400, Los Angeles (90036-5003)
PHONE..............................877 937-7110
Fax: 323 937-0408
Fred A Fern, *President*
David TSE, *Exec VP*
Ryan Murphy, *Senior VP*
Matthew Arber, *Vice Pres*
Terrie Bray, *Vice Pres*
EMP: 50
SALES (est): 13.7MM **Privately Held**
WEB: www.churchillmanagement.com
SIC: 6282 Investment counselors

(P-10134)
CITCO FUND SVCS SAN FRANCISCO
560 Mission St Fl 26, San Francisco (94105-2993)
PHONE..............................415 228-0390
William Keunen, *President*
Jay Peller, *CFO*
Scott Gross, *Senior VP*
Chris Mokos, *Senior VP*
Mike Sessa, *Senior VP*
EMP: 95
SALES (est): 20.8MM **Privately Held**
SIC: 6282 Manager of mutual funds, contract or fee basis

(P-10135)
CUSO FINANCIAL SERVICES LP
10150 Meanley Dr Fl 1, San Diego (92131-3008)
P.O. Box 85744 (92186-5744)
PHONE..............................800 686-4724
Valorie Seyfert, *Managing Prtnr*
Amelia Beattie, *Partner*
Loraine Wiser, *Partner*
Janine Holmes, *COO*
Daniel J Kilroy, *CFO*
EMP: 95 **EST:** 1996
SQ FT: 13,000
SALES (est): 6.7MM **Privately Held**
SIC: 6282 Investment advice

(P-10136)
DEUTSCHE INV MGT AMERICAS INC
101 California St # 2400, San Francisco (94111-5898)
PHONE..............................415 648-9408
Victor L Hymes, *Director*
EMP: 50
SALES (corp-wide): 8.8B **Privately Held**
SIC: 6282 Investment advisory service
HQ: Deutsche Investment Management Americas Inc.
   345 Park Ave Lowr L-1
   New York NY 10154
   800 349-4281

(P-10137)
ETRADE FINANCIAL CORPORATION
4748 Touchstone Ter, Fremont (94555-2603)
PHONE..............................650 331-6435
Raju Karra, *Principal*
EMP: 63
SALES (corp-wide): 1.4B **Publicly Held**
SIC: 6282 Investment advice
PA: E Trade Financial Corporation
   1271 Ave Of The Americas
   New York NY 10020
   646 521-4300

(P-10138)
FDX ADVISORS INC
Also Called: Foliodynamix
2399 Gateway Oaks Dr # 200, Sacramento (95833-4251)
PHONE..............................916 920-5293
Joseph Mrak, *President*
Jospeh Mrak, *President*
Mark Herman, *CFO*
Jonelle Stenson, *Senior VP*
EMP: 54
SALES (est): 4.9MM **Privately Held**
SIC: 6282 Investment advice

(P-10139)
FIRST AMERICAN FINANCIAL CORP
1150 Coast Village Rd, Santa Barbara (93108-2740)
PHONE..............................805 969-6883
Pat White, *Manager*
EMP: 293 **Publicly Held**
SIC: 6282 Investment advice
PA: First American Financial Corporation
   1 First American Way
   Santa Ana CA 92707

(P-10140)
FIRST AMERICAN TRUST COMPANY (HQ)
5 First American Way, Santa Ana (92707-5913)
P.O. Box 267 (92702-0267)
PHONE..............................714 560-7856
Toll Free:..............................877 -
Thomas M Kelley, *CEO*
Kelly Dudley, *COO*
Teri Pierce, *CFO*
Eric R McMullen, *Officer*
Darliene Evans, *Trust Officer*
EMP: 54
SQ FT: 34,625
SALES: 56.3MM **Publicly Held**
SIC: 6282 Investment advisory service

(P-10141)
FMR LLC
1995 University Ave, Berkeley (94704-1058)
PHONE..............................800 225-6447
EMP: 103
SALES (corp-wide): 25.3B **Privately Held**
SIC: 6282 Investment advisory service
PA: Fmr Llc
   245 Summer St
   Boston MA 02210
   617 563-7000

(P-10142)
FMR LLC
1220 Rsville Pkwy Ste 100, Roseville (95678)
PHONE..............................916 784-3649
Dave Taylor, *Principal*
Doug Juday, *Vice Pres*
EMP: 103
SALES (corp-wide): 25.3B **Privately Held**
SIC: 6282 Investment advisory service
PA: Fmr Llc
   245 Summer St
   Boston MA 02210
   617 563-7000

6282 - Investment Advice County (P-10143)

PRODUCTS & SERVICES SECTION

(P-10143)
FORWARD MANAGEMENT LLC
Also Called: Webster Investment Management
101 California St Fl 16, San Francisco (94111-6100)
P.O. Box 1345, Denver CO (80201-1345)
PHONE....................................415 869-6300
John Blaisdell, *CEO*
Jeffrey P Cusack, *President*
John McGowan, *Sr Corp Ofcr*
Robert S Naka, *Senior VP*
Jim Odonnell,
EMP: 100
SQ FT: 22,000
SALES (est): 13MM
SALES (corp-wide): 37.9MM **Privately Held**
WEB: www.sierraclubfund.com
SIC: 6282 Investment advisory service
PA: Salient Partners, L.P.
  4265 San Felipe St Fl 8
  Houston TX 77027
  713 993-4675

(P-10144)
FRANKLIN ADVISERS INC
1 Franklin Pkwy, San Mateo (94403-1906)
PHONE....................................650 312-2000
Charles B Johnson, *Ch of Bd*
Canyon Chan, *Manager*
Ken Domingues, *Manager*
EMP: 1700
SQ FT: 120,000
SALES (est): 154MM
SALES (corp-wide): 7.9B **Publicly Held**
WEB: www.frk.com
SIC: 6282 Investment advice
PA: Franklin Resources, Inc.
  1 Franklin Pkwy
  San Mateo CA 94403
  650 312-2000

(P-10145)
FRANKLIN TEMPLETON SVCS LLC
1 Franklin Pkwy, San Mateo (94403-1906)
PHONE....................................650 312-3000
Martin L Flanagan, *President*
Charles B Johnson, *Ch of Bd*
EMP: 2500
SALES (est): 209.7MM
SALES (corp-wide): 7.9B **Publicly Held**
WEB: www.frk.com
SIC: 6282 Investment advice
PA: Franklin Resources, Inc.
  1 Franklin Pkwy
  San Mateo CA 94403
  650 312-2000

(P-10146)
FRANKLIN TMPLETON INV SVCS LLC
3366 Quality Dr, Rancho Cordova (95670-7363)
PHONE....................................650 312-2000
Bavel Fox, *Branch Mgr*
Michelle Trolli, *Vice Pres*
Scott Lee, *Managing Dir*
Subarno Bose, *Programmer Anys*
Jorge Jenkins, *Business Anlyst*
EMP: 103
SALES (corp-wide): 7.9B **Publicly Held**
SIC: 6282 Investment advisory service
HQ: Franklin Templeton Investor Services, Llc
  3344 Quality Dr
  Rancho Cordova CA 95670
  916 463-1500

(P-10147)
FRANKLIN TMPLETON INV SVCS LLC
5130 Hacienda Dr Fl 4, Dublin (94568-7598)
PHONE....................................925 875-2619
Priscilla Voyer, *Manager*
EMP: 200
SALES (corp-wide): 7.9B **Publicly Held**
SIC: 6282 Investment advisory service
HQ: Franklin Templeton Investor Services, Llc
  3344 Quality Dr
  Rancho Cordova CA 95670
  916 463-1500

(P-10148)
FREMONT GROUP LLC (PA)
199 Fremont St Ste 2500, San Francisco (94105-6636)
PHONE....................................415 284-8880
Fax: 415 284-8191
Deborah L Duncans, *Mng Member*
Claude Zinngrabe, *Managing Prtnr*
David Covin, *COO*
D W Aronson, *Treasurer*
Stuart Blackie, *Vice Pres*
EMP: 61
SQ FT: 50,000
SALES (est): 38.8MM **Privately Held**
SIC: 6282 Investment advice

(P-10149)
FUND SERVICES ADVISORS INC
777 S Figueroa St # 3200, Los Angeles (90017-5800)
PHONE....................................213 612-2196
Mark Creger, *President*
Lester Wood, *Manager*
EMP: 50
SQ FT: 2,000
SALES (est): 3.6MM **Privately Held**
WEB: www.bondlogistix.com
SIC: 6282 Investment advisory service

(P-10150)
H & Q ASIA PACIFIC LTD
Also Called: Asia Pacific Management
228 Hamilton Ave Fl 3, Palo Alto (94301-2583)
PHONE....................................650 838-8088
Fax: 650 838-8801
Ta-Lin Hsu, *Chairman*
Sean C Warren, *COO*
Hambrecht Quist Group, *Principal*
Chong Sup Park, *Managing Dir*
EMP: 94
SALES (est): 13.4MM **Privately Held**
WEB: www.hqap.com
SIC: 6282 Investment advice

(P-10151)
HEARTHSTONE INC
24151 Ventura Blvd, Calabasas (91302-1449)
PHONE....................................818 385-0005
Fax: 818 385-0310
James Pugash, *CEO*
John Hannum, *Exec VP*
Anthony Botte, *Senior VP*
Susan Bui, *Finance Mgr*
Mark Porath, *Manager*
EMP: 70
SALES (est): 11.6MM **Privately Held**
WEB: www.hearthadvisors.com
SIC: 6282 Investment advice

(P-10152)
HIGHMARK CAPITAL MANAGEMENT
350 California St Fl 22, San Francisco (94104-1435)
PHONE....................................800 582-4734
Earle Malm, *President*
Noel Casale, *Senior VP*
Jonathan Fayman, *Senior VP*
Kevin Rogers, *Senior VP*
Christian Anderson, *Vice Pres*
EMP: 93
SALES (est): 15.4MM
SALES (corp-wide): 47.4B **Privately Held**
SIC: 6282 Investment advice
HQ: Mufg Union Bank, N.A
  400 California St
  San Francisco CA 94104
  212 782-6800

(P-10153)
HLM VENTURE PARTNERS II LP
201 Mission St Ste 2240, San Francisco (94105-1839)
PHONE....................................415 814-6110
Vincent J Fabiani, *Branch Mgr*
EMP: 75
SALES (corp-wide): 0 **Privately Held**
SIC: 6282 Investment advisory service
PA: Hlm Venture Partners Ii, L.P.
  222 Berkeley St Fl 20
  Boston MA 02116
  617 266-0030

(P-10154)
JONES LANG LSALLE AMERICAS INC
2211 Michelson Dr, Irvine (92612-1384)
PHONE....................................949 296-3600
James Jasionowski, *Owner*
EMP: 161
SALES (corp-wide): 5.9B **Publicly Held**
SIC: 6282 Investment advice
HQ: Jones Lang Lasalle Americas, Inc.
  200 E Randolph St # 4300
  Chicago IL 60601
  312 782-5800

(P-10155)
KAGAN CAPITAL MANAGEMENT INC
Also Called: Paul Kagan Associates
126 Clock Tower Pl, Carmel (93923-8791)
PHONE....................................831 624-1536
Paul Kagan, *President*
Norman Glaser, *Vice Pres*
EMP: 85
SQ FT: 18,000
SALES (est): 7.1MM **Privately Held**
SIC: 6282 Investment advisory service

(P-10156)
KAYNE ANDRSON CPITL ADVSORS LP
1800 Avenue Of The Stars 2nd, Los Angeles (90067-4201)
PHONE....................................800 231-7414
Richard Kayne, *Chairman*
Edward Cerny, *Managing Prtnr*
Ralph Walter, *Vice Chairman*
Robert Sinnott, *CEO*
Judy Ridder, *Officer*
EMP: 300
SALES (est): 3MM **Privately Held**
SIC: 6282 Investment advice

(P-10157)
KOLL INVESTMENT MANAGEMENT
Also Called: K/B Realty Advisors
620 Newport Center Dr # 1300, Newport Beach (92660-8013)
PHONE....................................949 833-3030
Peter M Bren, *CEO*
Donald M Koll, *Ch of Bd*
Robert A Feren, *President*
Charles G Schriever, *President*
Lori Klasner, *CFO*
EMP: 65
SALES (est): 13.5MM
SALES (corp-wide): 10.8B **Publicly Held**
WEB: www.cbrichardellis.com
SIC: 6282 Investment counselors
PA: Cbre Group, Inc.
  400 S Hope St Ste 25
  Los Angeles CA 90071
  213 613-3333

(P-10158)
KRAVITZ INVESTMENT SVCS INC
16030 Ventura Blvd # 200, Encino (91436-2731)
PHONE....................................818 995-6100
Daniel Kravitz, *President*
Carlos Tariche, *Consultant*
EMP: 100
SALES (est): 16.4MM **Privately Held**
SIC: 6282 Investment advice

(P-10159)
LORING WARD ADVISOR SERVICES
10 Almaden Blvd Ste 1500, San Jose (95113-2272)
PHONE....................................408 260-3109
Alf Steele, *President*
Ronald Reynolds, *COO*
Meir Statman, *CFO*
Chris Stanley, *Officer*
Steve Atkinson, *Exec VP*
EMP: 60
SQ FT: 21,000
SALES (est): 12.1MM **Privately Held**
SIC: 6282 Investment advisory service

(P-10160)
LPL FINANCIAL HOLDINGS INC
8055 W Manchester Ave # 350, Playa Del Rey (90293-7960)
PHONE....................................310 823-4999
Bernard Jongewaard, *Advisor*
Mark Jongewaard, *Advisor*
EMP: 331
SALES (corp-wide): 4.2B **Publicly Held**
SIC: 6282 Investment advice
PA: Lpl Financial Holdings Inc.
  75 State St Ste 2401
  Boston MA 02109
  617 423-3644

(P-10161)
MARLIN EQUITY PARTNERS LLC (PA)
338 Pier Ave, Hermosa Beach (90254-3617)
PHONE....................................310 364-0100
Fax: 310 364-0110
David McGovern, *Mng Member*
John McCurry, *Exec VP*
Andrew Lawson, *Vice Pres*
Nathan Pingelton, *Vice Pres*
Robb Warwick, *Executive*
EMP: 80
SQ FT: 16,000
SALES (est): 2.6B **Privately Held**
WEB: www.marlinequity.com
SIC: 6282 Investment advisory service

(P-10162)
MELLON CAPITAL MANAGEMENT CORP (HQ)
50 Fremont St Ste 3900, San Francisco (94105-2240)
PHONE....................................415 905-5448
Fax: 415 267-1293
Gabriela Parcella, *CEO*
Charles J Jacklin, *President*
Gregory Lee, *President*
David Manuel, *CFO*
Joanne S Huber, *Treasurer*
EMP: 80
SALES (est): 81.5MM **Privately Held**
SIC: 6282 Investment advice

(P-10163)
MERCER ADVISORS INC (PA)
1801 E Cabrillo Blvd, Santa Barbara (93108-2897)
PHONE....................................805 565-1681
Fax: 805 565-1964
David H Barton, *President*
Christopher Weill, *COO*
Deb Atwater, *CFO*
Scott Kvancz, *Ch Credit Ofcr*
Ralph Ujano,
EMP: 60
SQ FT: 13,510
SALES (est): 53.1MM **Privately Held**
WEB: www.mgadvisors.com
SIC: 6282 8742 Investment advisory service; financial consultant

(P-10164)
MERRILL LYNCH PIERCE FENNER
16830 Ventura Blvd # 601, Encino (91436-1707)
PHONE....................................818 528-7800
Fax: 818 528-7851
Hugh Arian, *Manager*
Andrea Abeger, *Advisor*
EMP: 55
SALES (corp-wide): 93B **Publicly Held**
WEB: www.ml.com
SIC: 6282 Investment counselors
HQ: Merrill Lynch, Pierce, Fenner & Smith Incorporated
  111 8th Ave
  New York NY 10011
  800 637-7455

(P-10165)
MORGAN STANLEY
800 Nwport Ctr Dr Ste 500, Newport Beach (92660)
P.O. Box 2000 (92658-8936)
PHONE....................................949 760-2440
Mark Zielinski, *Branch Mgr*
EMP: 60

PRODUCTS & SERVICES SECTION

6282 - Investment Advice County (P-10186)

SALES (corp-wide): 37.9B **Publicly Held**
SIC: **6282** 6211 Investment advice; security brokers & dealers
PA: Morgan Stanley
1585 Broadway
New York NY 10036
212 761-4000

(P-10166)
NEWLAND REAL ESTATE GROUP LLC (HQ)
4790 Eastgate Mall # 150, San Diego (92121-2061)
PHONE................................858 455-7503
Fax: 619 455-5368
Robert B McLeod, *President*
Darlynn Burke, *Treasurer*
Teri Slavik-Tsuyuki, *Chief Mktg Ofcr*
James Delhamer, *Vice Pres*
Douglas L Hageman, *Vice Pres*
EMP: 54
SQ FT: 12,000
SALES (est): 75.6MM **Privately Held**
SIC: **6282** 6552 Investment advice; subdividers & developers

(P-10167)
OAKTREE CAPITAL MANAGEMENT LP (HQ)
333 S Grand Ave Ste 2800, Los Angeles (90071-1530)
PHONE................................213 830-6300
Fax: 213 830-6293
Bruce Karsh, *President*
J B Forth, *Partner*
Larry Gilson, *Partner*
Larry W Keele, *Partner*
D R Masson, *Partner*
EMP: 120
SALES (est): 237.4MM
SALES (corp-wide): 201.9MM **Publicly Held**
WEB: www.oaktreecapital.com
SIC: **6282** 6722 6211 Investment advisory service; management investment, open-end; security brokers & dealers
PA: Oaktree Capital Group, Llc
333 S Grand Ave Ste 2800
Los Angeles CA 90071
213 830-6300

(P-10168)
PACIFIC INVESTMENT MGT CO LLC (DH)
Also Called: Pimco
650 Nwport Ctr Dr Ste 100, Newport Beach (92660)
P.O. Box 6430 (92658-6430)
PHONE................................949 720-6000
Fax: 949 720-1376
Douglas M Hodge, *CEO*
Jay Jacobs, *President*
Douglas Hodge, *CEO*
Bob Fitzgerald, *CFO*
John Lane, *CFO*
EMP: 240
SQ FT: 25,000
SALES (est): 445.5MM **Privately Held**
SIC: **6282** Investment advice
HQ: Allianz Global Investors Of America, Lp
680 Nwport Ctr Dr Ste 250
Newport Beach CA 92660
949 219-2200

(P-10169)
PACIFIC UNION FINANCIAL LLC
Also Called: Clearvision Funding
3 Macarthur Pl Ste 500, Santa Ana (92707-6069)
PHONE................................714 918-0799
Jon Maddox, *Branch Mgr*
EMP: 125
SALES (corp-wide): 278.1MM **Privately Held**
SIC: **6282** Investment advice
PA: Pacific Union Financial, Llc
8900 Freport Pkwy Ste 150
Irving TX 75063
800 809-0421

(P-10170)
PAYDEN AND RYGEL (PA)
333 S Grand Ave Ste 3200, Los Angeles (90071-1552)
PHONE................................213 625-1900
Fax: 213 625-1943
Joan Payden, *CEO*
Greg Morrison, *President*
Brian Matthews, *CFO*
Joyce Thurman, *CFO*
Brad Hersh, *Treasurer*
EMP: 140
SQ FT: 58,000
SALES (est): 59.3MM **Privately Held**
WEB: www.payden.com
SIC: **6282** 6211 Investment counselors; security brokers & dealers

(P-10171)
PERFORMANT TECHNOLOGIES INC
333 N Canyons Pkwy # 100, Livermore (94551-9478)
PHONE................................925 960-4800
Lisa Im, *President*
Jon Shaver, *Vice Pres*
Bruce Calvin, *Admin Sec*
Asghar Zaidi, *Technology*
Jayana Patel, *Accountant*
EMP: 350
SALES (est): 43.1MM **Privately Held**
SIC: **6282** Investment advice

(P-10172)
PLAN MEMBER FINANCIAL CORP
Also Called: Planmember Services
6187 Carpinteria Ave, Carpinteria (93013-2805)
PHONE................................805 684-1199
Jon Ziehl, *CEO*
Terry Janeway, *COO*
Bill Kemble, *CFO*
Tom Nugent, *Ch Invest Ofcr*
Mike Kulesza, *Vice Pres*
EMP: 100
SQ FT: 6,000
SALES (est): 37.8MM **Privately Held**
WEB: www.planmemberfinancialcorporation.com
SIC: **6282** Investment counselors

(P-10173)
PLATINUM HOME MORTGAGE CORP
3031 W March Ln Ste 239, Stockton (95219-6504)
PHONE................................209 955-2200
Colleen Stewart, *Owner*
Chris Sciortino, *Senior VP*
Anabel Carr, *Loan Officer*
Janie Rocha, *Loan Officer*
Trace McKay, *Broker*
EMP: 51
SALES (corp-wide): 66.1MM **Privately Held**
SIC: **6282** Investment advice
PA: Platinum Home Mortgage Corporation
2200 Hicks Rd Ste 101
Rolling Meadows IL 60008
847 797-9500

(P-10174)
PREMIERE FINANCIAL
Also Called: Premiere Properties
6498 Willow Pl, Carlsbad (92011-4212)
PHONE................................760 518-5034
Richard Luichi, *Owner*
EMP: 100 EST: 2013
SALES: 400K **Privately Held**
SIC: **6282** 8742 Investment advice; financial consultant

(P-10175)
PRESIDIO WEALTH MANAGEMENT LLC
101 California St # 1200, San Francisco (94111-5802)
PHONE................................415 449-2500
Brodie Cobb, *Managing Prtnr*
Michael Russo, *Managing Prtnr*
Jeff Zlot, *Principal*
EMP: 50
SQ FT: 2,500
SALES (est): 4.7MM **Privately Held**
WEB: www.snciInvestment.com
SIC: **6282** Investment advice

(P-10176)
QUADION LLC
Also Called: Mar-Kell Seal
17651 Armstrong Ave, Irvine (92614-5727)
PHONE................................714 546-0994
EMP: 1100 EST: 1945
SQ FT: 30,000
SALES (est): 110.7MM
SALES (corp-wide): 91.2B **Publicly Held**
SIC: **6282**
HQ: Norwest Venture Capital Management, Inc.
80 S 8th St Ste 3600
Minneapolis MN 55402
612 215-1600

(P-10177)
R S INVESTMENTS LLC
1 Bush St Fl 9, San Francisco (94104-4468)
PHONE................................415 591-2700
G Randy Hecht, *Mng Member*
Peter Carlson, *President*
Matthew Fessler, *President*
Joe Geary, *President*
Douglas Keagle, *President*
EMP: 100
SALES (est): 31.5MM
SALES (corp-wide): 33.7MM **Privately Held**
WEB: www.rsinvestments.com
SIC: **6282** Investment advisory service
PA: Rs Investment Management, L.P.
1 Bush St Ste 900
San Francisco CA 94104
415 591-2700

(P-10178)
RCM CAPITAL MANAGEMENT LLC
555 Mission St Ste 1700, San Francisco (94105-0937)
PHONE................................415 364-2327
Fax: 415 954-1778
Udo Frank, *CEO*
Daniel Blake, *Vice Pres*
Michael Konstantinov, *CIO*
Scott Migliori, *CIO*
Herold Rohweder, *CIO*
EMP: 150 **Privately Held**
SIC: **6282** Investment advice
HQ: Rcm Capital Management Llc
555 Mission St Ste 1700
San Francisco CA 94105
415 954-5400

(P-10179)
RELATIONAL INVESTORS LLC
12400 High Bluff Dr # 600, San Diego (92130-3077)
PHONE................................858 704-3333
Fax: 858 704-3344
David Batchelder, *Mng Member*
Lisa Cain, *CFO*
Talar Parunyan, *Accountant*
Sharon Wall, *Human Resources*
Christina Martinez, *Marketing Mgr*
EMP: 52
SALES (est): 23.3MM **Privately Held**
SIC: **6282** Investment advisory service

(P-10180)
RESEARCH AFFILIATES CAPITAL LP
620 Nwport Ctr Ste 900, Newport Beach (92660)
PHONE................................949 325-8700
Rob Arnott, *CEO*
Katrina F Sherrerd, *COO*
Jason Hsu, *CIO*
Stephen Lee, *Portfolio Mgr*
David Hennessy, *Sales Executive*
EMP: 82
SALES (est): 9.9MM **Privately Held**
SIC: **6282** Investment advice; futures advisory service; investment research

(P-10181)
RESEARCH AFFILIATES LLC
620 Nwport Ctr Ste 900, Newport Beach (92660)
PHONE................................949 325-8700
Rob Arnott, *CEO*
Katrina Sherrerd, *COO*
Joseph Hattesohl, *CFO*

Jeff Wilson, *Senior VP*
Tzee Chow, *Vice Pres*
EMP: 80
SALES (est): 20.7MM **Privately Held**
WEB: www.researchaffiliates.com
SIC: **6282** Investment counselors

(P-10182)
RNC CAPITAL MANAGEMENT LLC
Also Called: Rnc Genter Capital Management
11601 Wilshire Blvd Ph, Los Angeles (90025-1770)
PHONE................................310 477-6543
Fax: 310 479-2901
Dan Genter,
Manny Gutierrez, *CFO*
Stephan M Bradasich, *Senior VP*
James C Doan, *Vice Pres*
Cameron Lavey, *Vice Pres*
EMP: 65
SQ FT: 20,000
SALES (est): 19.3MM **Privately Held**
WEB: www.rncgenter.com
SIC: **6282** Investment counselors

(P-10183)
S&P GLOBAL INC
1566 Moffett St, Salinas (93905-3342)
PHONE................................831 393-6044
David Taggard, *President*
EMP: 149
SALES (corp-wide): 5.3B **Publicly Held**
WEB: www.mcgraw-hill.com
SIC: **6282** Investment advisory service
PA: S&P Global Inc.
55 Water St Ste Conc2
New York NY 10041
212 438-1000

(P-10184)
SB GROUP US INC
1 Circle Star Way Fl 1, San Carlos (94070-6235)
PHONE................................650 562-8110
Nikesh Arora, *CEO*
Grace Qiu, *Administration*
EMP: 59 EST: 2014
SALES (est): 1.8MM **Privately Held**
SIC: **6282** Investment advisory service

(P-10185)
SCM ADVISORS LLC
909 Montgomery St Fl 5, San Francisco (94133-4653)
PHONE................................415 486-6500
Gretchen Lash,
Andre Guilloton, *Technology*
Maggie Parros, *Opers Staff*
Gayle Seneca,
Philip Stapleton,
EMP: 53
SALES (est): 11.2MM
SALES (corp-wide): 214.6MM **Privately Held**
WEB: www.scmadv.com
SIC: **6282** Investment advisory service
PA: Virtus Partners, Inc.
100 Pearl St Fl 9
Hartford CT 06103
860 403-5000

(P-10186)
STANDARD POORS FINCL SVCS LLC
1 California St Fl 31, San Francisco (94111-5432)
PHONE................................415 371-5000
Fax: 415 371-5090
Steve Zimmerman, *Manager*
EMP: 50
SALES (corp-wide): 5.3B **Publicly Held**
WEB: www.mcgraw-hill.com
SIC: **6282** Investment advisory service
HQ: Standard & Poor's Financial Services Llc
55 Water St Fl 49
New York NY 10041
212 438-2000

6282 - Investment Advice County (P-10187)

(P-10187)
STEELPOINT CAPITAL PARTNERS LP
437 S Highway 101 Ste 212, Solana Beach (92075-2220)
PHONE..................858 764-8700
James A Caccavo, *General Ptnr*
Adam Dell, *General Ptnr*
Scott Tierney, *General Ptnr*
Jim Sullivan, *Partner*
Timothy Broadhead, *CFO*
EMP: 80
SALES (est): 10.7MM
SALES (corp-wide): 39.1MM **Privately Held**
SIC: 6282 Investment advice
PA: Moore Capital Management, Lp
  11 Times Sq Ste 36
  New York NY 10036
  212 782-7000

(P-10188)
TCW ABSOLUTE RETURN CREDIT LLC
865 S Figueroa St # 2100, Los Angeles (90017-2543)
PHONE..................213 244-0000
Richard Clotfelter, *CEO*
EMP: 248
SALES (est): 10.2MM
SALES (corp-wide): 3B **Publicly Held**
SIC: 6282 Investment advice
HQ: Tcw Asset Management Company
  865 S Figueroa St # 1800
  Los Angeles CA 90017
  213 244-0000

(P-10189)
TRANSAMERICA CBO I INC
600 Montgomery St Fl 16, San Francisco (94111-2718)
PHONE..................415 983-4000
EMP: 64
SALES (est): 2.2MM **Privately Held**
SIC: 6282
HQ: Transamerica Corporation
  4333 Edgewood Rd Ne
  Cedar Rapids IA 52499
  319 398-8511

(P-10190)
UNITED CPITL FNCL ADVISERS LLC
620 Nwport Ctr Dr Ste 500, Newport Beach (92660)
PHONE..................949 999-8500
Joe Duran, *CEO*
Gary Roth, *CFO*
Matt Brinker, *Senior VP*
Rob Brown, *Senior VP*
Gail Graham, *Principal*
EMP: 86 **EST:** 2009
SALES (est): 15.6MM **Privately Held**
SIC: 6282 8742 Investment advice; financial consultant

(P-10191)
VIKING ASSET MANAGEMENT LLC
505 Sansome St Ste 1275, San Francisco (94111-3177)
PHONE..................415 981-5300
Peter Bence, *Partner*
Merrick Okamoto, *Mng Member*
EMP: 1501
SALES (est): 55.6MM **Privately Held**
SIC: 6282 Investment advice

(P-10192)
WENTWORTH HAUSER & VIOLICH INC
301 Battery St Fl 4, San Francisco (94111-3237)
PHONE..................415 981-6911
Fax: 415 288-6103
Steve Rhone, *CEO*
Judith Stevens, *President*
Earl Bell, *CFO*
David Hall, *Sr Corp Ofcr*
King Hall, *Sr Corp Ofcr*
EMP: 78 **EST:** 1937
SQ FT: 14,000
SALES (est): 23MM **Privately Held**
WEB: www.lntyee.com
SIC: 6282 Investment advisory service

PA: Laird Norton Investment Management, Inc.
  801 2nd Ave Ste 1300
  Seattle WA 98104

(P-10193)
WESTERN ASSET MANAGEMENT CO (HQ)
385 E Colorado Blvd # 250, Pasadena (91101-1929)
PHONE..................626 844-9265
James W Hirschmann III, *CEO*
Travis M Carr, *COO*
Andrea Mack, *Ch Invest Ofcr*
Andrew Kang, *Officer*
Vivian Lin, *Officer*
EMP: 50
SQ FT: 55,000
SALES (est): 161.1MM
SALES (corp-wide): 2.6B **Publicly Held**
SIC: 6282 Investment advisory service
PA: Legg Mason Inc
  100 International Dr
  Baltimore MD 21202
  410 539-0000

(P-10194)
WETHERBY ASSET MANAGEMENT
580 California St Fl 8, San Francisco (94104-1029)
PHONE..................415 399-9159
Fax: 415 399-9330
Debra L Wetherby, *President*
Chris Hauswirth, *COO*
Allan Jacobi, *CFO*
Jack Olson, *Officer*
Steve Janowsky, *Principal*
EMP: 55
SALES (est): 17.3MM **Privately Held**
WEB: www.wetherby.com
SIC: 6282 Investment advisory service

6289 Security & Commodity Svcs, NEC

(P-10195)
AMERICAN FUNDS SERVICE COMPANY
Also Called: Emerging Markets Growth Fund
6455 Irvine Center Dr, Irvine (92618-4518)
P.O. Box 6007, Indianapolis IN (46206-6007)
PHONE..................949 975-5000
Josie Cortez, *Branch Mgr*
EMP: 50
SALES (corp-wide): 2.5B **Privately Held**
WEB: www.cganywhere.net
SIC: 6289 6282 Security transfer agents; investment advice
HQ: American Funds Service Company
  6455 Irvine Center Dr
  Irvine CA 92618
  949 975-5000

(P-10196)
INTERACTIVE DATA CORPORATION
E Signal
3955 Point Eden Way, Hayward (94545-3720)
P.O. Box 5028 (94540-5028)
PHONE..................510 266-6000
Chuck Thompson, *President*
Scott Johnson, *Vice Pres*
Aggie Halley, *Human Res Mgr*
Paul Famular, *VP Sales*
Joe Bangkot, *Marketing Staff*
EMP: 150
SALES (corp-wide): 4.6B **Publicly Held**
WEB: www.interactivedata.com
SIC: 6289 Stock quotation service
HQ: Interactive Data Corporation
  32 Crosby Dr
  Bedford MA 01730
  781 687-8500

(P-10197)
SERVICE PRO SECURITY INC
342 Acacia St, Fairfield (94533-3766)
PHONE..................707 746-6532
Robert Edwards, *CEO*

Betty Edwards, *CFO*
Charlotte Gear, *Manager*
EMP: 95
SQ FT: 2,500
SALES (est): 8.6MM **Privately Held**
WEB: www.serviceprosecurity.com
SIC: 6289 Security custodians

(P-10198)
STRATEGIC SECURITY SERVICES
Also Called: Strategic Secuirty Services
48521 Warm Springs Blvd # 302, Fremont (94539-7792)
PHONE..................510 623-2355
Fax: 510 623-2353
Larry Reid, *Manager*
EMP: 190
SALES (corp-wide): 133.1MM **Publicly Held**
WEB: www.strategicsecurity.net
SIC: 6289 Protective committees
HQ: Strategic Security Services, Inc
  3152 University Ave
  San Diego CA
  619 283-3976

(P-10199)
WOODSPUR FARMING LLC
52 200 Industrial Way, Coachella (92236)
PHONE..................760 398-9464
EMP: 84
SALES (corp-wide): 24.9MM **Privately Held**
SIC: 6289 0179 Financial reporting; date orchard
PA: Woodspur Farming Llc
  52200 Industrial Way
  Coachella CA 92236
  323 936-9303

6311 Life Insurance Carriers

(P-10200)
ASSOCIATED INDEMNITY CORP
1465 N Mcdowell Blvd # 100, Petaluma (94954-6516)
PHONE..................415 899-2000
D Andrew Torrance, *Chairman*
Jill E Paterson, *CFO*
Kevin Walker, *CFO*
Linda E Wright, *Treasurer*
Cynthia L Pevehouse, *Senior VP*
EMP: 2498
SQ FT: 240,000
SALES: 48.9MM **Privately Held**
WEB: www.firemansfund.com
SIC: 6311 6321 6331 6351 Life insurance carriers; accident insurance carriers; health insurance carriers; fire, marine & casualty insurance & carriers; surety insurance
HQ: Fireman's Fund Insurance Company
  777 San Marin Dr Ste 2160
  Novato CA 94945
  415 899-2000

(P-10201)
AXA ADVISORS LLC
701 B St Ste 1500, San Diego (92101-8170)
PHONE..................619 239-0018
Patrick Mead, *Exec VP*
Dennis Bavin, *Advisor*
George Chammas, *Advisor*
Stanley Ginsberg, *Advisor*
Jeffrey L Ipscomb, *Advisor*
EMP: 80
SALES (corp-wide): 2.9B **Publicly Held**
WEB: www.axacs.com
SIC: 6311 6321 6411 6282 Life insurance carriers; health insurance carriers; accident insurance carriers; insurance agents, brokers & service; investment advice
HQ: Axa Advisors, Llc
  1290 Ave Of Amrcs Fl Cnc1
  New York NY 10104
  212 554-1234

(P-10202)
BEST LIFE AND HEALTH INSUR CO
17701 Mitchell N, Irvine (92614-6028)
P.O. Box 19721 (92623-9721)
PHONE..................949 253-4080
Fax: 949 222-1004
Donald R Lawrenz, *Ch of Bd*
Alfred Stoefell, *Shareholder*
Paula Knox, *CFO*
Ferdie Pascua, *Administration*
Helen Schuster, *Administration*
EMP: 60
SQ FT: 22,000
SALES (est): 36.6MM **Privately Held**
SIC: 6311 6324 Life insurance carriers; hospital & medical service plans
PA: Pension Administrators Inc
  17701 Mitchell N
  Irvine CA 92614
  949 253-4080

(P-10203)
BUILDERS & TRADESMENS INSUR
6610 Sierra College Blvd, Rocklin (95677-4306)
PHONE..................916 772-9200
EMP: 61
SALES (est): 34.8MM **Privately Held**
WEB: www.btisonline.com
SIC: 6311 Life insurance

(P-10204)
CENTURY-NATIONAL INSURANCE CO (HQ)
16650 Sherman Way, Van Nuys (91406-3782)
PHONE..................818 760-0880
Fax: 818 509-1526
Weldon Wilson, *CEO*
Judy Osborn, *CFO*
Judith Osborn, *Treasurer*
Cheryl Guttenberg, *Vice Pres*
Marie Balicki, *Admin Sec*
EMP: 260
SQ FT: 41,000
SALES: 136.9MM **Publicly Held**
SIC: 6311 Life insurance carriers

(P-10205)
EQUITABLE VARIABLE LF INSUR CO
701 B St Ste 1500, San Diego (92101-8170)
PHONE..................619 239-0018
Jamie Smith, *Manager*
EMP: 65
SALES (est): 7.5MM **Privately Held**
SIC: 6311 Life insurance

(P-10206)
FARMERS GROUP INC
Also Called: Farmers Insurance
700 S Flower St Ste 2800, Los Angeles (90017-4215)
PHONE..................213 615-2500
Agie Lerner, *Manager*
Dina Baladad, *Legal Staff*
EMP: 60
SALES (corp-wide): 62B **Privately Held**
WEB: www.farmers.com
SIC: 6311 6799 Life insurance carriers; real estate investors, except property operators
HQ: Farmers Group, Inc.
  6301 Owensmouth Ave
  Woodland Hills CA 91367
  323 932-3200

(P-10207)
FARMERS GROUP INC
Also Called: Farmers Insurance
11555 Dublin Canyon Rd, Pleasanton (94588-2815)
PHONE..................925 847-3100
Fax: 925 847-3337
Steve Dix, *Manager*
Catherine Jones, *Director*
Bruce Gordon, *Manager*
John McCarthy, *Manager*
EMP: 400
SALES (corp-wide): 62B **Privately Held**
WEB: www.farmers.com
SIC: 6311 Life insurance

PRODUCTS & SERVICES SECTION

6311 - Life Insurance Carriers County (P-10226)

HQ: Farmers Group, Inc.
6301 Owensmouth Ave
Woodland Hills CA 91367
323 932-3200

(P-10208)
FARMERS INSURANCE EXCHANGE (PA)
6301 Owensmouth Ave # 300, Woodland Hills (91367-2268)
PHONE..................................323 932-3200
Jeff Pailey, *CEO*
Reed Whitlock, *President*
Ron Myhan, *CFO*
Mike Cok, *Vice Pres*
Mike Pessetti, *Vice Pres*
EMP: 3000
SQ FT: 210,000
SALES (est): 6.3B **Privately Held**
SIC: **6311** Life insurance

(P-10209)
GOLDEN STATE MUTL LF INSUR CO (PA)
1999 W Adams Blvd, Los Angeles (90018-3500)
P.O. Box 26894, San Francisco (94126-6894)
PHONE..................................713 526-4361
Fax: 323 733-7511
Larkin Teasley, *President*
Artemis Wimstaff, *Admin Sec*
Arlinda Mangerin, *Controller*
John Harrington, *Opers Mgr*
EMP: 100 EST: 1925
SQ FT: 57,000
SALES (est): 42.1MM **Privately Held**
SIC: **6311** Mutual association life insurance; life insurance carriers; life reinsurance

(P-10210)
JACKSON NATIONAL LIFE INSUR CO
401 Wilshire Blvd # 1200, Santa Monica (90401-1416)
PHONE..................................310 899-7900
Fax: 310 899-7945
Clifford Jack, *President*
Kendall Best, *Vice Pres*
Mary Dreffein, *Vice Pres*
Luis Gomez, *Vice Pres*
Kathleen Smith, *Vice Pres*
EMP: 65
SALES (corp-wide): 53.5B **Privately Held**
WEB: www.jnl.com
SIC: **6311** Life insurance carriers; fraternal protective associations; benevolent insurance associations
HQ: Jackson National Life Insurance Co Inc
1 Corporate Way
Lansing MI 48951
517 381-5500

(P-10211)
JOHN ALDEN LIFE INSURANCE CO
20950 Warner Center Ln A, Woodland Hills (91367-6560)
PHONE..................................818 595-7600
Thomas Christenson, *Branch Mgr*
EMP: 65
SALES (corp-wide): 10.3B **Publicly Held**
WEB: www.jalden.com
SIC: **6311** Life insurance
HQ: John Alden Life Insurance Company
501 W Michigan St
Milwaukee WI 53203
414 271-3011

(P-10212)
MASSACHUSETTS MUTL LF INSUR CO
Also Called: Massmutual
8383 Wilshire Blvd # 600, Beverly Hills (90211-2425)
PHONE..................................323 951-0131
Grant D Fraser, *Branch Mgr*
Kathleen Adams, *Financial Analy*
David Streit, *Director*
EMP: 60
SALES (corp-wide): 23.3B **Privately Held**
WEB: www.massmutual.com
SIC: **6311** Life insurance

PA: Massachusetts Mutual Life Insurance Company
1295 State St
Springfield MA 01111
413 788-8411

(P-10213)
NEW YORK LIFE INSURANCE CO
191 Sand Creek Rd Ste 200, Brentwood (94513-2220)
PHONE..................................925 809-7020
Fax: 925 809-7099
Dan Torres, *Branch Mgr*
David J Jagoda, *Opers Mgr*
Rich Englis, *Manager*
George C Garrison, *Agent*
Daniel Torres, *Agent*
EMP: 93
SALES (corp-wide): 12.3B **Privately Held**
SIC: **6311** Life insurance
PA: New York Life Insurance Company
51 Madison Ave Bsmt 1b
New York NY 10010
212 576-7000

(P-10214)
NEW YORK LIFE INSURANCE CO
3757 State St Ste 310, Santa Barbara (93105-3133)
PHONE..................................805 898-7625
Fax: 805 563-2105
Mona Vargas, *Branch Mgr*
EMP: 58
SALES (corp-wide): 12.3B **Privately Held**
WEB: www.newyorklife.com
SIC: **6311** Life insurance carriers
PA: New York Life Insurance Company
51 Madison Ave Bsmt 1b
New York NY 10010
212 576-7000

(P-10215)
NEW YORK LIFE INSURANCE CO
801 N Brand Blvd Ste 1400, Glendale (91203-3274)
PHONE..................................818 662-7500
Fax: 626 795-6712
Tigran Basmadkian, *Managing Prtnr*
Marina Balasanian, *Office Admin*
Rob Arensberg, *Advisor*
Roxana Braganza, *Advisor*
Calvin Chan, *Advisor*
EMP: 58
SALES (corp-wide): 12.3B **Privately Held**
WEB: www.newyorklife.com
SIC: **6311** Life insurance
PA: New York Life Insurance Company
51 Madison Ave Bsmt 1b
New York NY 10010
212 576-7000

(P-10216)
NEW YORK LIFE INSURANCE CO
4204 Riverwalk Pkwy # 200, Riverside (92505-3394)
PHONE..................................951 354-2094
Fax: 909 884-0566
Tim Crumbaker, *Branch Mgr*
EMP: 75
SALES (corp-wide): 12.3B **Privately Held**
WEB: www.newyorklife.com
SIC: **6311** Life insurance
PA: New York Life Insurance Company
51 Madison Ave Bsmt 1b
New York NY 10010
212 576-7000

(P-10217)
NEW YORK LIFE INSURANCE CO
2633 Camino Ramon Ste 525, San Ramon (94583-2174)
PHONE..................................415 999-9576
John Walker, *Manager*
EMP: 57
SALES (corp-wide): 12.3B **Privately Held**
WEB: www.newyorklife.com
SIC: **6311** Life insurance

PA: New York Life Insurance Company
51 Madison Ave Bsmt 1b
New York NY 10010
212 576-7000

(P-10218)
PACIFIC LIFE & ANNUITY COMPANY
700 Newport Center Dr, Newport Beach (92660-6307)
P.O. Box 9000 (92658-9030)
PHONE..................................949 219-3011
Fax: 949 219-5378
James Morris, *President*
David Chang, *President*
Kenneth Fisher, *President*
Frank Boynton, *COO*
Khanh T Tran, *CFO*
EMP: 650
SQ FT: 125,000
SALES (est): 248.1MM
SALES (corp-wide): 8.6B **Privately Held**
SIC: **6311** **6411** Life insurance; insurance agents, brokers & service
HQ: Pacific Life Insurance Company
700 Newport Center Dr
Newport Beach CA 92660
949 219-3011

(P-10219)
PRINCIPAL FINANCIAL GROUP INC
2590 N 1st St Ste 350, San Jose (95131-1054)
PHONE..................................408 273-7500
Fax: 408 437-7205
Ross Borzin, *Manager*
EMP: 80
SALES (corp-wide): 11.9B **Publicly Held**
SIC: **6311** Life insurance
PA: Principal Financial Group, Inc.
711 High St
Des Moines IA 50392
515 247-5111

(P-10220)
PRINCIPAL FINANCIAL GROUP INC
500 N Brand Blvd Ste 1800, Glendale (91203-3305)
PHONE..................................818 243-7141
Fax: 818 548-5914
Jim Rhodes, *Branch Mgr*
Jennifer T Love, *Agent*
EMP: 80
SALES (corp-wide): 11.9B **Publicly Held**
SIC: **6311** Life insurance
PA: Principal Financial Group, Inc.
711 High St
Des Moines IA 50392
515 247-5111

(P-10221)
PRINCIPAL FINANCIAL GROUP INC
1350 E Spruce Ave Ste 100, Fresno (93720-3373)
PHONE..................................559 261-2000
Fax: 559 261-0501
William E Griffith, *Manager*
Michelle Ramirez, *Mktg Coord*
Geoffrey T Barry, *Agent*
Jennifer D Williams, *Agent*
EMP: 80
SALES (corp-wide): 11.9B **Publicly Held**
SIC: **6311** Life insurance
PA: Principal Financial Group, Inc.
711 High St
Des Moines IA 50392
515 247-5111

(P-10222)
SUNAMERICA ANNUITY LF ASRN CO (DH)
1 Sun America Ctr, Los Angeles (90067-6100)
PHONE..................................310 772-6000
Jay Wintrob, *CEO*
Keith Honig, *Managing Prtnr*
Janna Greer, *President*
David J Dietz, *CFO*
N Scott Gillis, *CFO*
EMP: 53

SALES: 2.6B
SALES (corp-wide): 58.3B **Publicly Held**
SIC: **6311** Life insurance funds, savings bank
HQ: Sunamerica Life Insurance Company
1 Sun America Ctr Fl 36
Los Angeles CA 90067
310 772-6000

(P-10223)
SWISS RE AMERICA HOLDING CORP
Also Called: GE
27412 Carino Cir, Mission Viejo (92692-5042)
PHONE..................................858 485-5018
Deborah Boyce, *Branch Mgr*
EMP: 50
SALES (corp-wide): 29.8B **Privately Held**
SIC: **6311** Life reinsurance
HQ: Swiss Re America Holding Corporation
5200 Metcalf Ave
Overland Park KS 66202

(P-10224)
TRANSAMERICA FINANCE CORP
1731 W Medical Center Dr, Anaheim (92801-1837)
PHONE..................................714 778-5100
Jim Karsch, *Manager*
EMP: 65 **Privately Held**
SIC: **6311** **6512** Life insurance; commercial & industrial building operation
HQ: Transamerica Finance Corporation
600 Montgomery St Fl 16
San Francisco CA 94111
415 983-4000

(P-10225)
TRANSMRICA OCCIDENTAL LF INSUR (DH)
1150 S Olive St Fl 23, Los Angeles (90015-2477)
P.O. Box 2101 (90078-2101)
PHONE..................................213 742-2111
Fax: 213 742-5280
Ronald Wagley, *President*
Christopher Castro, *President*
Joseph Gilmour, *CFO*
Laura Scully, *Senior VP*
Julie Quinlan, *Vice Pres*
EMP: 2000 EST: 1906
SQ FT: 1,577,000
SALES (est): 3.3B **Privately Held**
WEB: www.transamerica.com
SIC: **6311** **6371** **6321** **6324** Life insurance carriers; life reinsurance; pension funds; health insurance carriers; accident insurance carriers; reinsurance carriers, accident & health; group hospitalization plans; investors
HQ: Transamerica Service Company, Inc.
1150 S Olive St
Los Angeles CA 90015
213 742-2111

(P-10226)
TRUCK UNDERWRITERS ASSOCIATION
Farmers Insurance
6303 Owensmouth Ave Fl 1, Woodland Hills (91367-2200)
PHONE..................................323 932-3200
Fax: 805 583-7056
Jane Franklin, *Vice Pres*
Gene Maxson, *Technology*
Carla Kimzey, *Finance Mgr*
Jim Harwood, *VP Sales*
Heather Leszczynski, *Sr Associate*
EMP: 900
SQ FT: 275,000
SALES (corp-wide): 62B **Privately Held**
SIC: **6311** **6331** **6321** Life insurance; fire, marine & casualty insurance; accident & health insurance
HQ: Truck Underwriters Association
4680 Wilshire Blvd
Los Angeles CA 90010
323 932-3200

6311 - Life Insurance Carriers County (P-10227)

(P-10227)
ULTRALINK LLC
535 Anton Blvd Ste 200, Costa Mesa (92626-7680)
PHONE.................714 427-5500
Fax: 714 427-5599
Tony Ton, *Owner*
Vince Sheeran, *CEO*
Jack Baumann, *COO*
Dan Lieber, *Chairman*
Jeff Graves, *Vice Ch Bd*
EMP: 120
SALES (est): 31.4MM Privately Held
SIC: 6311 Life insurance carriers

(P-10228)
WILLIS INSURANCE SVCS CAL INC
4250 Executive Sq Ste 250, La Jolla (92037-9104)
PHONE.................858 678-2000
Fax: 858 678-2100
Jack Yelverton, *Branch Mgr*
Lila Smith, *Manager*
Dolores Winfield, *Accounts Mgr*
EMP: 50 Privately Held
SIC: 6311 Life insurance
HQ: Willis Insurance Services Of California, Inc.
525 Market St Ste 3400
San Francisco CA 94105
415 955-0100

(P-10229)
ZENITH INSURANCE COMPANY
4460 Rosewood Dr, Pleasanton (94588-3050)
PHONE.................925 460-0600
Fax: 925 463-0940
Jon Lindsay, *Manager*
Rajiv Mehrotra, *Exec VP*
Steve Bagby, *Sls & Mktg Exec*
Fred Martinez, *Marketing Staff*
Rulla Hernandez, *Manager*
EMP: 90
SALES (corp-wide): 9.5B Privately Held
SIC: 6311 6321 6324 6331 Life insurance; accident & health insurance; hospital & medical service plans; fire, marine & casualty insurance
HQ: Zenith Insurance Company
21255 Califa St
Woodland Hills CA 91367
818 713-1000

6321 Accident & Health Insurance

(P-10230)
21ST CENTURY LF & HLTH CO INC (PA)
Also Called: Lifecare Assurance Company
21600 Oxnard St Ste 1500, Woodland Hills (91367-4972)
P.O. Box 4243 (91365-4243)
PHONE.................818 887-4436
Fax: 818 887-4595
James M Glickman, *President*
Alan S Hughes, *CEO*
Daniel J Di Sipio, *CFO*
Julianne M Sorice, *CFO*
Pete Diffley, *Senior VP*
EMP: 91
SQ FT: 50,000
SALES (est): 380.9MM Privately Held
WEB: www.lifecareassurance.com
SIC: 6321 Accident & health insurance

(P-10231)
AGENT FRANCHISE LLC
9518 9th St Ste C2, Rancho Cucamonga (91730-4568)
PHONE.................949 930-5025
David Jackson,
EMP: 101
SQ FT: 14,980
SALES (est): 26.2MM Privately Held
SIC: 6321 Accident & health insurance

(P-10232)
ANTHEM INC
2100 Corporate Center Dr, Newbury Park (91320-1431)
PHONE.................805 557-6655
Marilyn McCullough, *Vice Pres*
Adrian Lara, *Business Anlyst*
Ella Anastasiu, *Project Dir*
Bernard Carreon, *Analyst*
Jan Clermont, *Marketing Mgr*
EMP: 104
SALES (corp-wide): 79.1B Publicly Held
SIC: 6321 Health insurance carriers
PA: Anthem, Inc.
120 Monument Cir Ste 200
Indianapolis IN 46204
317 488-6000

(P-10233)
AON BENFIELD FAC INC
199 Fremont St Fl 15, San Francisco (94105-2299)
PHONE.................415 486-6900
Fax: 415 486-7016
Matt Davis, *Manager*
Jochen Frey, *CTO*
Aaron Best, *Web Dvlpr*
EMP: 200
SALES (corp-wide): 11.6B Privately Held
SIC: 6321 6311 Reinsurance carriers, accident & health; life insurance
HQ: Aon Benfield Fac Inc.
200 E Randolph St Fl 15
Chicago IL 60601
312 381-5300

(P-10234)
ARTA WESTERN MEDICAL GROUP
1665 Scenic Ave Ste 100, Costa Mesa (92626-1443)
PHONE.................949 260-6575
Baruch Fogel MD, *President*
Karen Richmond, *Vice Pres*
EMP: 150
SALES: 15MM Privately Held
SIC: 6321 Health insurance carriers

(P-10235)
AUTO CLUB ENTERPRISES (PA)
3333 Fairview Rd Msa451, Costa Mesa (92626-1610)
P.O. Box 25001, Santa Ana (92799-5001)
PHONE.................714 850-5111
Robert T Bouttier, *CEO*
Thomas Mc Kernon, *President*
John F Boyle, *Treasurer*
Neiman Sharon, *Senior VP*
Avery Brown, *Vice Pres*
EMP: 1200
SQ FT: 700,000
SALES (est): 4.2B Privately Held
WEB: www.aaa-newmexico.com
SIC: 6321 Accident & health insurance

(P-10236)
AUTO CLUB ENTERPRISES
1950 Century Park E, Los Angeles (90067-1705)
PHONE.................310 914-8500
Fax: 310 312-1856
Bob Szhwab, *Manager*
EMP: 500
SALES (corp-wide): 4.2B Privately Held
WEB: www.aaa-newmexico.com
SIC: 6321 Accident & health insurance
PA: Auto Club Enterprises
3333 Fairview Rd Msa451
Costa Mesa CA 92626
714 850-5111

(P-10237)
B C LIFE & HEALTH INSURANCE CO
21555 Oxnard St, Woodland Hills (91367-4943)
PHONE.................818 703-2345
David Helwig, *President*
Kenneth C Zurek, *CFO*
R D Kretschmer, *Vice Pres*
Nicholas L Becker, *Principal*
Michael C Higgins, *General Mgr*
EMP: 66

SALES (est): 18.7MM Privately Held
SIC: 6321 Indemnity plans health insurance, except medical service

(P-10238)
CAREMORE MEDICAL GROUP
12900 Park Plz Ste 150, Lakewood (90805)
PHONE.................562 622-2900
John Short, *Director*
Josie Rivera, *Manager*
EMP: 300 EST: 2011
SALES (est): 56.4MM
SALES (corp-wide): 79.1B Publicly Held
SIC: 6321 Health insurance carriers
PA: Anthem, Inc.
120 Monument Cir Ste 200
Indianapolis IN 46204
317 488-6000

(P-10239)
E D D 2100
Also Called: Disability Insurance
3127 Transworld Dr # 150, Stockton (95206-4988)
PHONE.................209 941-6501
Judy Cruz, *Office Mgr*
EMP: 92 EST: 1940
SALES (est): 18.7MM Privately Held
SIC: 6321 Disability health insurance

(P-10240)
HEALTHPOCKET INC
444 Castro St Ste 710, Mountain View (94041-2080)
PHONE.................800 984-8015
Bruce Telkamp, *CEO*
Sheldon Wang, *President*
EMP: 90
SALES (est): 29MM
SALES (corp-wide): 104.7MM Publicly Held
SIC: 6321 Health insurance carriers
PA: Health Insurance Innovations, Inc.
15438 N Florida Ave # 201
Tampa FL 33613
877 376-5831

(P-10241)
INLAND EMPIRE HEALTH PLAN (PA)
Also Called: Iehp
10801 6th St Ste 120, Rancho Cucamonga (91730-5987)
P.O. Box 1400 (91729-1400)
PHONE.................909 890-2000
Fax: 909 890-2002
Brad Gilbert, *CEO*
Phillip W Branstetter, *COO*
Chet Uma, *CFO*
Bob Buster, *Chairman*
Terry Terr, *Info Tech Dir*
EMP: 850
SQ FT: 72,000
SALES (est): 1B Privately Held
WEB: www.iehp.org
SIC: 6321 6324 Accident & health insurance; health maintenance organization (HMO), insurance only

(P-10242)
JOINT LABOR MGT RETIREMENT TR
Also Called: Atpa
1640 S Loop Rd, Alameda (94502-7089)
PHONE.................503 454-3800
Peter Harrling, *Principal*
Tony Scelza, *Manager*
EMP: 50
SALES (est): 39.1MM Privately Held
SIC: 6321 Accident & health insurance

(P-10243)
KINGS VIEW WORK EXPERIENCE CTR
703 I St, Los Banos (93635-4308)
PHONE.................209 826-8118
Fax: 209 826-8913
David Toliver, *Administration*
Irma Torrez, *Manager*
EMP: 50
SALES (est): 5.3MM Privately Held
SIC: 6321 7641 Disability health insurance; furniture repair & maintenance

(P-10244)
LIFECARE ASSURANCE COMPANY
21600 Oxnard St Fl 16, Woodland Hills (91367-4976)
Po Box 4243
PHONE.................818 887-4436
James Glickman, *President*
Alan S Hughes, *COO*
Daniel J Disipio, *CFO*
Peter Diffley, *Vice Pres*
Gwen D Franklin, *Vice Pres*
EMP: 246
SQ FT: 35,000
SALES: 380.9MM Privately Held
WEB: www.lifecareassurance.com
SIC: 6321 6411 6311 Accident & health insurance; insurance agents, brokers & service; life insurance
PA: 21st Century Life And Health Company, Inc.
21600 Oxnard St Ste 1500
Woodland Hills CA 91367
818 887-4436

(P-10245)
MD CARE INC
Also Called: MD Care Healthplan
1640 E Hill St, Signal Hill (90755-3612)
P.O. Box 14165, Lexington KY (40512-4165)
PHONE.................562 344-3400
Long Dang, *President*
EMP: 75 EST: 2004
SALES (est): 23MM
SALES (corp-wide): 54.2B Publicly Held
SIC: 6321 Health insurance carriers
PA: Humana Inc.
500 W Main St Ste 300
Louisville KY 40202
502 580-1000

(P-10246)
MOLINA HEALTHCARE OF CALIFORNI
200 Oceangate Ste 100, Long Beach (90802-4317)
PHONE.................562 435-3666
Richard Chambers, *CEO*
Dr J Mario Molina, *President*
Terry Bayer, *COO*
Dr James Howatt, *Officer*
EMP: 2800
SALES (est): 329.7MM
SALES (corp-wide): 14.1B Publicly Held
SIC: 6321 8011 Health insurance carriers; clinic, operated by physicians
PA: Molina Healthcare, Inc.
200 Oceangate Ste 100
Long Beach CA 90802
562 435-3666

(P-10247)
SAN FRANCISCO REINSURANCE CO
1465 N Mcdowell Blvd, Petaluma (94954-6516)
PHONE.................415 899-2000
Fax: 415 899-4696
Joe Beneducci, *President*
Jerry Lowe, *MIS Staff*
Mike Hammond, *Manager*
Viji Vickie, *Manager*
EMP: 70
SQ FT: 240,000
SALES: 248.9MM Privately Held
WEB: www.firemansfund.com
SIC: 6321 Reinsurance carriers, accident & health
HQ: Fireman's Fund Insurance Company
777 San Marin Dr Ste 2160
Novato CA 94945
415 899-2000

(P-10248)
SANTA BARBARA SAN LUIS OBISPO
Also Called: Cencal Health
4050 Calle Real, Santa Barbara (93110-3413)
PHONE.................800 421-2560
Robert Freeman, *CEO*
Paul Jaconette, *COO*
Kashina Bishop, *CFO*
Paula Michal, *Executive Asst*

PRODUCTS & SERVICES SECTION
6324 - Hospital & Medical Svc Plans Carriers County (P-10267)

Betsy Redfield, *Human Res Dir*
EMP: 140
SALES (est): 72MM **Privately Held**
SIC: 6321 Accident & health insurance

(P-10249)
STATE COMPENSATION INSUR FUND
2901 N Ventura Rd Ste 100, Oxnard (93036-1126)
PHONE.............................888 782-8338
Fax: 805 988-5201
Martin Goldman, *Manager*
Pamela Ainslie, *Financial Exec*
Frank Floyd, *Manager*
Helen Christensen, *Assistant*
Jeanette Collet, *Assistant*
EMP: 400
SALES (corp-wide): 1.6B **Privately Held**
WEB: www.scif.com
SIC: 6321 9651 Disability health insurance; insurance commission, government;
PA: State Compensation Insurance Fund Inc
333 Bush St Fl 8
San Francisco CA 94104
888 782-8338

(P-10250)
WESTERN HEALTH ADVANTAGE
2349 Gateway Oaks Dr # 100, Sacramento (95833-4244)
PHONE.............................916 567-1950
Fax: 916 563-3182
Garry Maisel, *President*
Andrea Richardson, *CFO*
Rita Ruecker, *Treasurer*
Rebecca Downing, *Officer*
Heidi Zibull, *Executive*
EMP: 100
SQ FT: 25,000
SALES (est): 77MM **Privately Held**
WEB: www.westernhealth.com
SIC: 6321 Health insurance carriers

6324 Hospital & Medical Svc Plans Carriers

(P-10251)
AETNA HEALTH CALIFORNIA INC
1 Embarcadero Ctr Ste 300, San Francisco (94111-3618)
PHONE.............................415 645-8200
Fax: 415 645-8278
Sue Hallett, *Branch Mgr*
Joan Njoku-Obi, *Mktg Coord*
Dee D'Agostino, *Director*
Glenn Bair, *Manager*
Dan Delucia, *Manager*
EMP: 80 **Publicly Held**
SIC: 6324 Health maintenance organization (HMO), insurance only
HQ: Aetna Health Of California, Inc.
2409 Camino Ramon
San Ramon CA 94583
925 543-9000

(P-10252)
AETNA HEALTH CALIFORNIA INC
727 Pueblo Pl, Chula Vista (91914-2426)
PHONE.............................619 656-3104
EMP: 51
SALES (corp-wide): 36.6B **Publicly Held**
SIC: 6324
HQ: Aetna Health Of California, Inc.
2409 Camino Ramon
San Ramon CA 94583
925 543-9000

(P-10253)
AETNA HEALTH CALIFORNIA INC (DH)
2409 Camino Ramon, San Ramon (94583-4285)
PHONE.............................925 543-9000
Fax: 925 543-9010
John Brian Ternan, *CEO*
Vicki Chubb, *Program Mgr*
Curtis Terry, *Regional Mgr*
Brenda Wichrowski, *Executive Asst*

Kirby Addison, *Admin Asst*
EMP: 198
SALES (est): 343.2MM **Publicly Held**
SIC: 6324 Health maintenance organization (HMO), insurance only
HQ: Aetna Health Management, Inc.
151 Farmington Ave
Hartford CT 06156
860 273-0123

(P-10254)
ALAMEDA ALLIANCE FOR HEALTH
1240 S Loop Rd, Alameda (94502-7084)
PHONE.............................510 747-4555
Fax: 510 747-4507
Ingrid Lamirault, *CEO*
Matthew Woodruff, *COO*
Robert Larue, *CFO*
Kelvin Quan, *CFO*
Lily Boris, *Chief Mktg Ofcr*
EMP: 135
SQ FT: 50,000
SALES (est): 143.4MM **Privately Held**
WEB: www.alamedaalliance.com
SIC: 6324 Health maintenance organization (HMO), insurance only

(P-10255)
ALIGNMENT HEALTH PLAN
Also Called: Citizens Choice Health Plan
1100 W Town & Country, Orange (92868-4600)
PHONE.............................323 728-7232
Chuck Weber, *President*
Elizabeth Tejada, *COO*
Charlotte Leblanc,
Augi Oyola, *Info Tech Mgr*
Mayra Merrick, *Marketing Staff*
EMP: 90
SALES (est): 62MM **Privately Held**
WEB: www.mycchp.com
SIC: 6324 Hospital & medical service plans; health maintenance organization (HMO), insurance only
PA: Alignment Healthcare, Llc
1100 W Town And Country R
Orange CA 92868
949 679-0009

(P-10256)
ANTHEM INSURANCE COMPANIES INC
9655 Granite Ridge Dr, San Diego (92123-2674)
PHONE.............................858 571-8136
Cheryl Noncarrow, *Manager*
Matthew Carmen, *CFO*
Gene Housholter, *Exec VP*
Laurie Beer, *Vice Pres*
Becky Behlendors, *Vice Pres*
EMP: 81
SALES (corp-wide): 79.1B **Publicly Held**
WEB: www.anthem-inc.com
SIC: 6324 Group hospitalization plans
HQ: Anthem Insurance Companies, Inc.
120 Monument Cir Ste 200
Indianapolis IN 46204
317 488-6000

(P-10257)
ANTHEM INSURANCE COMPANIES INC
1 Wellpoint Way, Westlake Village (91362-3893)
PHONE.............................805 557-6655
Michael Lohnberg, *Branch Mgr*
Gene Householter, *Vice Pres*
Peter Juhn, *Vice Pres*
Ivan Kamil, *Vice Pres*
Alan Katz, *Vice Pres*
EMP: 81
SALES (corp-wide): 79.1B **Publicly Held**
WEB: www.anthem-inc.com
SIC: 6324 Group hospitalization plans
HQ: Anthem Insurance Companies, Inc.
120 Monument Cir Ste 200
Indianapolis IN 46204
317 488-6000

(P-10258)
ANTHEM INSURANCE COMPANIES INC
5653 Camino Ruiz Ste A, Camarillo (93012)
PHONE.............................805 557-6655
Les Wilson, *Branch Mgr*
EMP: 81
SALES (corp-wide): 79.1B **Publicly Held**
WEB: www.anthem-inc.com
SIC: 6324 Group hospitalization plans
HQ: Anthem Insurance Companies, Inc.
120 Monument Cir Ste 200
Indianapolis IN 46204
317 488-6000

(P-10259)
BLUE CROSS & BLUE SHIELD MICH
6300 Wilshire Blvd # 970, Los Angeles (90048-5204)
PHONE.............................323 782-3046
Fax: 323 782-3129
Kenneth August, *Branch Mgr*
Timothy A Mc Caslin, *Manager*
EMP: 203
SALES (corp-wide): 12.4B **Privately Held**
SIC: 6324 Hospital & medical service plans
PA: Blue Cross And Blue Shield Of Michigan
600 E Lafayette Blvd
Detroit MI 48226
313 225-9000

(P-10260)
BLUE CROSS OF CALIFORNIA (DH)
4553 La Tienda Rd, Westlake Village (91362-3800)
PHONE.............................805 557-6050
Mark Morgan, *President*
Kenneth C Zurek, *CFO*
Ivan Jeffrey, *Vice Pres*
Josh Valdez, *Vice Pres*
Thomas C Geiser, *Admin Sec*
EMP: 128
SQ FT: 427,104
SALES (est): 168.6MM
SALES (corp-wide): 79.1B **Publicly Held**
SIC: 6324 Health maintenance organization (HMO), insurance only; insurance agents, brokers & service
HQ: Wellpoint California Services, Inc.
4553 La Tienda Rd
Westlake Village CA 91362
805 557-6655

(P-10261)
CALIFORNIA PHYSICIANS SERVICE
2020 17th St, Bakersfield (93301-4252)
PHONE.............................661 631-2277
Ricard Maiatico, *Owner*
EMP: 126
SALES (corp-wide): 9.9B **Privately Held**
WEB: www.blueshieldcafoundation.org
SIC: 6324 6321 Hospital & medical service plans; accident & health insurance
PA: California Physicians' Service
50 Beale St Bsmt 2
San Francisco CA 94105
415 229-5000

(P-10262)
CALIFORNIA PHYSICIANS SERVICE
Also Called: Blue Sheild of California
2066 Camel Ln Apt 24, Walnut Creek (94596-5955)
PHONE.............................925 927-7419
John Durst, *Branch Mgr*
Craig Nelson, *Vice Pres*
EMP: 232
SALES (corp-wide): 9.9B **Privately Held**
WEB: www.blueshieldcafoundation.org
SIC: 6324 Hospital & medical service plans
PA: California Physicians' Service
50 Beale St Bsmt 2
San Francisco CA 94105
415 229-5000

(P-10263)
CALIFORNIA PHYSICIANS SERVICE (PA)
Also Called: Blue Shield of California
50 Beale St Bsmt 2, San Francisco (94105-1819)
P.O. Box 272540, Chico (95927-2540)
PHONE.............................415 229-5000
Bruce Bodoken, *Ch of Bd*
Paul Markovich, *President*
Karen Vigil, *CEO*
Heidi Field, *CFO*
Heidi Kunz, *CFO*
EMP: 900 **EST:** 1939
SQ FT: 120,000
SALES (est): 9.9B **Privately Held**
WEB: www.blueshieldcafoundation.org
SIC: 6324 Hospital & medical service plans

(P-10264)
CALIFORNIA PHYSICIANS SERVICE
4700 Bechelli Ln, Redding (96002-3506)
PHONE.............................530 351-6115
EMP: 158
SALES (corp-wide): 9.9B **Privately Held**
SIC: 6324 Hospital & medical service plans
PA: California Physicians' Service
50 Beale St Bsmt 2
San Francisco CA 94105
415 229-5000

(P-10265)
CALIFORNIA PHYSICIANS SERVICE
Also Called: Blue Shield of California
4203 Town Center Blvd, El Dorado Hills (95762-7100)
P.O. Box 7168, San Francisco (94120-7168)
PHONE.............................916 350-7800
Eric Lam, *Director*
Cathy Campbell, *Vice Pres*
Amit Khanna, *Program Mgr*
Morgan Templar, *Program Mgr*
Carla Hoffman, *Admin Asst*
EMP: 260
SALES (corp-wide): 9.9B **Privately Held**
WEB: www.blueshieldcafoundation.org
SIC: 6324 6321 Hospital & medical service plans; accident & health insurance
PA: California Physicians' Service
50 Beale St Bsmt 2
San Francisco CA 94105
415 229-5000

(P-10266)
CALIFORNIA PHYSICIANS SERVICE
Also Called: Blue Shield of California
100 N Sepulveda Blvd # 2000, El Segundo (90245-4359)
PHONE.............................310 744-2668
Aubrey Chernick, *Branch Mgr*
Paul Heredia, *Human Res Dir*
EMP: 126
SALES (corp-wide): 9.9B **Privately Held**
WEB: www.blueshieldcafoundation.org
SIC: 6324 Hospital & medical service plans
PA: California Physicians' Service
50 Beale St Bsmt 2
San Francisco CA 94105
415 229-5000

(P-10267)
CALIFORNIA PHYSICIANS SERVICE
Also Called: Blue Shield of California
6300 Canoga Ave Ste A, Woodland Hills (91367-8000)
PHONE.............................818 598-8000
Fax: 818 628-5126
John Headberg, *Branch Mgr*
Bonnie Kipper, *Admin Asst*
Pamela Klugman, *Info Tech Mgr*
Lisa Klieger, *Training Spec*
David A Battin, *Med Doctor*
EMP: 400
SALES (corp-wide): 9.9B **Privately Held**
WEB: www.blueshieldcafoundation.org
SIC: 6324 Hospital & medical service plans
PA: California Physicians' Service
50 Beale St Bsmt 2
San Francisco CA 94105
415 229-5000

6324 - Hospital & Medical Svc Plans Carriers County (P-10268)

(P-10268) CENTENE CORPORATION
550 Main St, Placerville (95667-5643)
PHONE................530 626-5773
EMP: 99
SALES (corp-wide): 22.7B Publicly Held
SIC: 6324 Hospital & medical service plans
PA: Centene Corporation
   7700 Forsyth Blvd Ste 800
   Saint Louis MO 63105
   314 725-4477

(P-10269) CENTER FOR ELDERS INDEPENDENCE
Also Called: C E I
510 17th St Ste 400, Oakland (94612-1570)
PHONE................510 433-1150
Fax: 510 452-8836
Peter Szutu, President
Alicia English, Vice Pres
Brendan Thomas, Vice Pres
Mohammed Moharram, Info Tech Mgr
Ping Isengberg, Controller
EMP: 225 EST: 1981
SALES: 55.2MM Privately Held
WEB: www.cei.elders.org
SIC: 6324 Hospital & medical service plans

(P-10270) CHOC HEALTH ALLIANCE
1120 W La Veta Ave # 450, Orange (92868-4224)
PHONE................714 565-5100
Fax: 714 565-5170
Roger Austin, CEO
Misty Huerta, Executive
Javier Sanchez, Manager
EMP: 65
SALES (est): 24.7MM Publicly Held
WEB: www.chochealthalliance.com
SIC: 6324 Hospital & medical service plans
HQ: Anderson Schaller Inc
   4500 E Cotton Center Blvd
   Phoenix AZ 85040
   602 659-1123

(P-10271) CIGNA HEALTHCARE CAL INC
1 Front St Ste 700, San Francisco (94111-5395)
PHONE................415 374-2500
William Burke, Branch Mgr
Michael Player, Accounts Mgr
EMP: 226
SALES (corp-wide): 37.8B Publicly Held
SIC: 6324 Health maintenance organization (HMO), insurance only
HQ: Cigna Healthcare Of California, Inc.
   400 N Brand Blvd Ste 400
   Glendale CA 91203
   818 500-6262

(P-10272) CIGNA HEALTHCARE CAL INC (DH)
400 N Brand Blvd Ste 400, Glendale (91203-2357)
P.O. Box 188045, Chattanooga TN (37422-8045)
PHONE................818 500-6262
Fax: 818 500-6367
Leroy Volberding, President
Barry Ford, Vice Pres
Sandy Mayer, Vice Pres
Eugene Rapisardi, Vice Pres
Nancy Ho, Pharmacy Dir
EMP: 400
SQ FT: 110,000
SALES (est): 228.9MM
SALES (corp-wide): 37.8B Publicly Held
SIC: 6324 Health maintenance organization (HMO), insurance only
HQ: Healthsource, Inc.
   2 College Park Dr
   Hooksett NH 03106
   603 268-7000

(P-10273) CIGNA HEALTHCARE CAL INC
2801 Townsgate Rd Ste 121, Thousand Oaks (91361-3029)
PHONE................805 230-8300
Paul Von Dorpe, Director
EMP: 233
SALES (corp-wide): 37.8B Publicly Held
SIC: 6324 Group hospitalization plans
HQ: Cigna Healthcare Of California, Inc.
   400 N Brand Blvd Ste 400
   Glendale CA 91203
   818 500-6262

(P-10274) CIGNA HEALTHCARE CAL INC
5300 W Tulare Ave Ste 100, Visalia (93277-3700)
PHONE................559 738-2000
Rich Keena, Vice Pres
David Jaqcobson, Vice Pres
Valorie Cukr, Info Tech Mgr
Raemee Anderson, Cust Mgr
Angela Smith, Supervisor
EMP: 500
SALES (corp-wide): 37.8B Publicly Held
SIC: 6324 Health maintenance organization (HMO), insurance only
HQ: Cigna Healthcare Of California, Inc.
   400 N Brand Blvd Ste 400
   Glendale CA 91203
   818 500-6262

(P-10275) COUNTY OF LOS ANGELES
Also Called: Community Health Plan
1000 S Fremont Ave Unit 4, Alhambra (91803-8859)
PHONE................626 299-5300
Dave Beck, Director
Steve Lee, Pharmacy Dir
Duane Asao, Pharmacist
EMP: 140 Privately Held
WEB: www.co.la.ca.us
SIC: 6324 9431 Hospital & medical service plans; mental health agency administration, government
PA: County Of Los Angeles
   500 W Temple St Ste 375
   Los Angeles CA 90012
   213 974-1101

(P-10276) DELTA DENTAL OF CALIFORNIA
1450 Frazee Rd Ste 200, San Diego (92108-4341)
PHONE................619 683-2549
Fax: 619 458-1828
Delta California, Branch Mgr
EMP: 259
SALES (corp-wide): 5.3B Privately Held
SIC: 6324 Dental insurance
PA: Delta Dental Of California
   100 1st St Fl 4
   San Francisco CA 94105
   415 972-8300

(P-10277) DELTA DENTAL OF CALIFORNIA (PA)
100 1st St Fl 4, San Francisco (94105-2657)
PHONE................415 972-8300
Fax: 415 972-8466
Gary D Radine, President
Sandy Trent, Volunteer Dir
Nilesh Patel, COO
Mike Castro, CFO
Michael G Hankinson, Officer
EMP: 487 EST: 1955
SQ FT: 241,000
SALES: 5.3B Privately Held
WEB: www.deltadentalca.com
SIC: 6324 Dental insurance

(P-10278) DELTA DENTAL OF CALIFORNIA
Also Called: Delta Dental Plan
11155 International Dr, Sacramento (95826)
PHONE................916 853-7373
Tony Barth, Branch Mgr
Robert Brown, Network Enginr
Randy Alcantar, Business Anlyst
Stephen Douglas, Business Anlyst
Sara Esparza, Research
EMP: 1000
SALES (corp-wide): 5.3B Privately Held
WEB: www.deltadentalca.com
SIC: 6324 Dental insurance
PA: Delta Dental Of California
   100 1st St Fl 4
   San Francisco CA 94105
   415 972-8300

(P-10279) HEALDSBURG DIST HOSP REHAB SVC
1540 Healdsburg Ave, Healdsburg (95448-3253)
PHONE................707 433-9150
Fax: 707 473-4408
Stacy Smithson, Manager
EMP: 100
SALES (est): 20.1MM Privately Held
WEB: www.healdsburghospital.com
SIC: 6324 Hospital & medical service plans

(P-10280) HEALTH NET INC
Also Called: Health Net of California
21271 Burbank Blvd Fl 2-5, Woodland Hills (91367-6672)
P.O. Box 9103, Van Nuys (91409-9103)
PHONE................818 676-5603
Barry Averill, Branch Mgr
Patricia Clarey, COO
Dave Meadows, Vice Pres
Lori Scott, Vice Pres
Gina Stassi, Vice Pres
EMP: 91
SALES (corp-wide): 22.7B Publicly Held
SIC: 6324 Hospital & medical service plans
HQ: Health Net Of California, Inc.
   21281 Burbank Blvd Fl 4
   Woodland Hills CA 91367
   818 676-6775

(P-10281) HEALTH NET INC (HQ)
21650 Oxnard St Fl 25, Woodland Hills (91367-7829)
PHONE................818 676-6000
Fax: 818 676-8591
Jay M Gellert, President
Thomas F Carrato, President
Steven H Nelson, President
James E Woys, COO
Kevin Low, Treasurer
EMP: 250
SQ FT: 115,488
SALES: 16.2B
SALES (corp-wide): 22.7B Publicly Held
WEB: www.healthnet.com
SIC: 6324 6311 Hospital & medical service plans; life insurance carriers
PA: Centene Corporation
   7700 Forsyth Blvd Ste 800
   Saint Louis MO 63105
   314 725-4477

(P-10282) HEALTH NET INC
101 N Brand Blvd Ste 1500, Glendale (91203-2659)
PHONE................818 543-9037
Kevin J Walker, Manager
Lissette Mendoza, Manager
EMP: 128
SALES (corp-wide): 22.7B Publicly Held
SIC: 6324 Hospital & medical service plans
HQ: Health Net Of California, Inc.
   21281 Burbank Blvd Fl 4
   Woodland Hills CA 91367
   818 676-6775

(P-10283) HEALTH NET INC
155 Grand Ave Lbby, Oakland (94612-3718)
PHONE................510 465-9600
Fax: 510 869-3189
Eric Johnson, Manager
David Anderson, Vice Pres
Sheri Hancock, Manager
Susan Sall, Manager
EMP: 450
SALES (corp-wide): 22.7B Publicly Held
SIC: 6324 6321 Hospital & medical service plans; accident & health insurance
HQ: Health Net Of California, Inc.
   21281 Burbank Blvd Fl 4
   Woodland Hills CA 91367
   818 676-6775

(P-10284) HEALTH NET INC
Also Called: Fhpa
12033 Foundation Pl, Gold River (95670-4502)
PHONE................916 935-3520
Jeffery Slynn, Vice Pres
Karin D Mayhew, Senior VP
Curtis B Westen, Admin Sec
Scott Burg, Admin Asst
Susan Glaudel, Admin Asst
EMP: 300
SALES (corp-wide): 22.7B Publicly Held
SIC: 6324 Hospital & medical service plans
HQ: Health Net Of California, Inc.
   21281 Burbank Blvd Fl 4
   Woodland Hills CA 91367
   818 676-6775

(P-10285) HEALTH NET CALIFORNIA INC
11971 Foundation Pl, Gold River (95670-4502)
PHONE................916 935-1600
Michelle Birksteresur, Manager
James E Woys, COO
Cheryl Davis, Admin Asst
Shanie Lamonica, Admin Asst
John J Padlo II, Administration
EMP: 58
SALES (corp-wide): 22.7B Publicly Held
SIC: 6324 Hospital & medical service plans
HQ: Health Net Of California, Inc.
   21281 Burbank Blvd Fl 4
   Woodland Hills CA 91367
   818 676-6775

(P-10286) HEALTH NET CALIFORNIA INC (DH)
21281 Burbank Blvd Fl 4, Woodland Hills (91367-7073)
P.O. Box 9103, Van Nuys (91409-9103)
PHONE................818 676-6775
Fax: 818 593-8981
Jay Gellert, Ch of Bd
Owen Block, CFO
Patricia Clarey, Ch Credit Ofcr
Bruce Willison, Bd of Directors
Joseph Capezza, Exec VP
EMP: 167
SQ FT: 150,000
SALES (est): 1B
SALES (corp-wide): 22.7B Publicly Held
SIC: 6324 8062 6311 6321 Hospital & medical service plans; general medical & surgical hospitals; life insurance carriers; disability health insurance; accident & health insurance carriers; workers' compensation insurance; drug stores & proprietary stores
HQ: Health Net, Inc.
   21650 Oxnard St Fl 25
   Woodland Hills CA 91367
   818 676-6000

(P-10287) HEALTH NET COMMUNITY SOLUTIONS
21650 Oxnard St Fl 25, Woodland Hills (91367-7829)
PHONE................818 676-6000
EMP: 69
SALES (est): 2.8MM
SALES (corp-wide): 22.7B Publicly Held
SIC: 6324 Hospital & medical service plans
HQ: Health Net, Inc.
   21650 Oxnard St Fl 25
   Woodland Hills CA 91367
   818 676-6000

(P-10288) HEALTH NET FEDERAL SVCS LLC (DH)
2025 Aerojet Rd, Rancho Cordova (95742-6418)
P.O. Box 2890 (95741-2890)
PHONE................916 935-5000
Fax: 916 353-5760
Thomas F Carrato, President
Jay L Siverstein, Chief Mktg Ofcr
Hariharan Sundararajan, Program Mgr
Thomas Carrato, CTO
Jeffrey Thomas, Technology
EMP: 700

PRODUCTS & SERVICES SECTION
6324 - Hospital & Medical Svc Plans Carriers County (P-10310)

SQ FT: 100,000
SALES (est): 636.7MM
SALES (corp-wide): 22.7B **Publicly Held**
SIC: 6324 Hospital & medical service plans
HQ: Health Net Of California, Inc.
21281 Burbank Blvd Fl 4
Woodland Hills CA 91367
818 676-6775

(P-10289)
HEALTH NET LIFE INSURANCE CO
21281 Burbank Blvd, Woodland Hills (91367-7073)
PHONE..................800 865-6288
James Edwin Woys, *Principal*
Franklin Nmr, *Admin Sec*
Steven Sickle, *Admin Sec*
EMP: 343
SALES (est): 54.7MM
SALES (corp-wide): 22.7B **Publicly Held**
WEB: www.healthnet.com
SIC: 6324 Hospital & medical service plans
HQ: Health Net, Inc.
21650 Oxnard St Fl 25
Woodland Hills CA 91367
818 676-6000

(P-10290)
HEALTH PLAN OF SAN JOAQUIN
7751 S Manthey Rd, French Camp (95231-9802)
PHONE..................209 942-6300
Amy Shinn, *CEO*
Nancy Raymond, *Officer*
Kathy Parker, *Executive*
Cathleen Sanchez, *Executive Asst*
Cheron Vail, *CIO*
EMP: 120
SALES (est): 105MM **Privately Held**
SIC: 6324 Health maintenance organization (HMO), insurance only

(P-10291)
INLAND EMPIRE HEALTH PLAN
805 W 2nd St Ste C, San Bernardino (92410-3255)
P.O. Box 1800, Rancho Cucamonga (91729-1800)
PHONE..................866 228-4347
EMP: 428 **Privately Held**
SIC: 6324 8742 Health maintenance organization (HMO), insurance only; hospital & health services consultant
PA: Inland Empire Health Plan
10801 6th St Ste 120
Rancho Cucamonga CA 91730

(P-10292)
INTER-VALLEY HEALTH PLAN INC
300 S Park Ave Ste 300, Pomona (91766-1546)
P.O. Box 6002 (91769-6002)
PHONE..................909 623-6333
Fax: 909 622-2907
Ronald Bolding, *CEO*
Michael Nelson, *CFO*
Don McCain, *Admin Sec*
Dorothy Demandante, *Info Tech Mgr*
Tan Lee, *Software Dev*
EMP: 70
SQ FT: 54,700
SALES: 238.6MM **Privately Held**
WEB: www.ivhp.com
SIC: 6324 8011 Hospital & medical service plans; offices & clinics of medical doctors

(P-10293)
KAISER FOUNDATION HOSPITALS
Also Called: Kaiser Foundation Health Plan
30116 Eigenbrodt Way, Union City (94587-1225)
PHONE..................510 675-5777
Colleen McKeown, *Manager*
Thomas S Hanenburg, *Senior VP*
EMP: 99
SALES (corp-wide): 27.8B **Privately Held**
SIC: 6324 Hospital & medical service plans
HQ: Kaiser Foundation Hospitals Inc
1 Kaiser Plz
Oakland CA 94612
510 271-6611

(P-10294)
KAISER FOUNDATION HOSPITALS
Also Called: Kaiser Foundation Health Plan
2350 Geary Blvd Fl 2, San Francisco (94115-3305)
PHONE..................415 833-2616
Gordon K Leung, *Cardiovascular*
Elizabeth A Andrews, *Med Doctor*
Charity Hill, *Med Doctor*
Gizela M Laskowska, *Med Doctor*
Todd A Levine, *Med Doctor*
EMP: 85
SALES (corp-wide): 27.8B **Privately Held**
SIC: 6324 Hospital & medical service plans
HQ: Kaiser Foundation Hospitals Inc
1 Kaiser Plz
Oakland CA 94612
510 271-6611

(P-10295)
KAISER FOUNDATION HOSPITALS
Also Called: Kaiser Foundation Health Plan
393 E Walnut St, Pasadena (91188-0002)
PHONE..................626 405-5000
Fax: 323 783-1187
David Lamm, *Branch Mgr*
William Gillepsie, *COO*
Dick Tettingill, *Exec Dir*
Chuck Ives, *Prgrmr*
Phillip Lee, *Prgrmr*
EMP: 50
SALES (corp-wide): 27.8B **Privately Held**
WEB: www.kaiser.com
SIC: 6324 Hospital & medical service plans
HQ: Kaiser Foundation Hospitals Inc
1 Kaiser Plz
Oakland CA 94612
510 271-6611

(P-10296)
KAISER FOUNDATION HOSPITALS
Also Called: Kaiser Foundation Health Plan
1761 Broadway St Ste 210, Vallejo (94589-2227)
PHONE..................707 645-2720
Fax: 707 645-2115
Cynthia Chandler, *Director*
Schieree Harmon, *Admin Mgr*
Patricia Ljutic, *QA Dir*
Arlene L Brown, *Psychiatry*
George E Wakerlin, *Med Doctor*
EMP: 75
SALES (corp-wide): 27.8B **Privately Held**
WEB: www.kaiser.com
SIC: 6324 Hospital & medical service plans
HQ: Kaiser Foundation Hospitals Inc
1 Kaiser Plz
Oakland CA 94612
510 271-6611

(P-10297)
KAISER FOUNDATION HOSPITALS
Also Called: Kaiser Foundation Health Plan
1550 W Manchester Ave, Los Angeles (90047-5424)
PHONE..................800 954-8000
EMP: 85
SALES (corp-wide): 27.8B **Privately Held**
SIC: 6324 Hospital & medical service plans
HQ: Kaiser Foundation Hospitals Inc
1 Kaiser Plz
Oakland CA 94612
510 271-6611

(P-10298)
KAISER FOUNDATION HOSPITALS
Also Called: Kaiser Foundation Health Plan
19000 Homestead Rd, Cupertino (95014-0712)
PHONE..................408 366-4247
Theresa Gilliland, *Branch Mgr*
Renee Fahs, *Psychologist*
EMP: 85
SALES (corp-wide): 27.8B **Privately Held**
SIC: 6324 Hospital & medical service plans
HQ: Kaiser Foundation Hospitals Inc
1 Kaiser Plz
Oakland CA 94612
510 271-6611

(P-10299)
KAISER FOUNDATION HOSPITALS
Also Called: Kaiser Foundation Health Plan
255 W Macarthur Blvd, Oakland (94611-5641)
PHONE..................510 752-7864
Albert Carver, *Branch Mgr*
EMP: 85
SALES (corp-wide): 27.8B **Privately Held**
SIC: 6324 Hospital & medical service plans
HQ: Kaiser Foundation Hospitals Inc
1 Kaiser Plz
Oakland CA 94612
510 271-6611

(P-10300)
KAISER FOUNDATION HOSPITALS
Also Called: Kaiser Foundation Health Plan
4785 N 1st St, Fresno (93726-0513)
PHONE..................559 448-4555
EMP: 85
SALES (corp-wide): 27.8B **Privately Held**
SIC: 6324 Hospital & medical service plans
HQ: Kaiser Foundation Hospitals Inc
1 Kaiser Plz
Oakland CA 94612
510 271-6611

(P-10301)
KAISER FOUNDATION HOSPITALS
Also Called: Kaiser Foundation Health Plan
10305 Promenade Pkwy, Elk Grove (95757-9400)
PHONE..................916 544-6000
EMP: 85
SALES (corp-wide): 27.8B **Privately Held**
SIC: 6324 Hospital & medical service plans
HQ: Kaiser Foundation Hospitals Inc
1 Kaiser Plz
Oakland CA 94612
510 271-6611

(P-10302)
KAISER FOUNDATION HOSPITALS
Also Called: Kaiser Foundation Health Plan
14011 Park Ave, Victorville (92392-2413)
PHONE..................888 750-0036
EMP: 85
SALES (corp-wide): 27.8B **Privately Held**
SIC: 6324 Hospital & medical service plans
HQ: Kaiser Foundation Hospitals Inc
1 Kaiser Plz
Oakland CA 94612
510 271-6611

(P-10303)
KAISER FOUNDATION HOSPITALS
Also Called: Kaiser Foundation Health Plan
17140 Bernardo Center Dr, San Diego (92128-2093)
PHONE..................619 528-5000
Fax: 858 674-2322
David Kvancz, *Branch Mgr*
EMP: 85
SALES (corp-wide): 27.8B **Privately Held**
SIC: 6324 Hospital & medical service plans
HQ: Kaiser Foundation Hospitals Inc
1 Kaiser Plz
Oakland CA 94612
510 271-6611

(P-10304)
KAISER FOUNDATION HOSPITALS
Also Called: Kaiser Foundation Health Plan
5893 Copley Dr, San Diego (92111-7906)
PHONE..................619 528-5000
Roberto A Cueva, *Med Doctor*
Bruce L Edens, *Med Doctor*
EMP: 85
SALES (corp-wide): 27.8B **Privately Held**
SIC: 6324 Hospital & medical service plans

(P-10305)
KAISER FOUNDATION HOSPITALS
Also Called: Kaiser Foundation Health Plan
27303 Sleepy Hollow Ave S, Hayward (94545-4203)
PHONE..................510 454-1000
EMP: 85
SALES (corp-wide): 15.7B **Privately Held**
SIC: 6324
HQ: Kaiser Foundation Hospitals Inc
1 Kaiser Plz
Oakland CA 94612
510 271-6611

(P-10306)
KAISER FOUNDATION HOSPITALS
Also Called: Kaiser Foundation Health Plan
8001 Ventura Canyon Ave, Panorama City (91402-6312)
PHONE..................818 375-2028
Teresa Park, *Branch Mgr*
EMP: 85
SALES (corp-wide): 27.8B **Privately Held**
SIC: 6324 Hospital & medical service plans
HQ: Kaiser Foundation Hospitals Inc
1 Kaiser Plz
Oakland CA 94612
510 271-6611

(P-10307)
KAISER FOUNDATION HOSPITALS
Also Called: Kaiser Foundation Health Plan
27309 Madison Ave, Temecula (92590-5685)
PHONE..................866 984-7483
Vu H Tinh, *Family Practiti*
EMP: 85
SALES (corp-wide): 27.8B **Privately Held**
SIC: 6324 Hospital & medical service plans
HQ: Kaiser Foundation Hospitals Inc
1 Kaiser Plz
Oakland CA 94612
510 271-6611

(P-10308)
KAISER FOUNDATION HOSPITALS
Also Called: Kaiser Foundation Health Plan
11001 Sepulveda Blvd, Mission Hills (91345-1413)
PHONE..................888 778-5000
EMP: 85
SALES (corp-wide): 19.1B **Privately Held**
SIC: 6324
PA: Kaiser Foundation Hospitals Inc
1 Kaiser Plz Ste 2600
Oakland CA 94612
510 271-5800

(P-10309)
KAISER FOUNDATION HOSPITALS
Also Called: Kaiser Foundation Health Plan
Maquina, Mission Viejo (92691)
PHONE..................888 988-2800
EMP: 85
SALES (corp-wide): 27.8B **Privately Held**
SIC: 6324 Hospital & medical service plans
HQ: Kaiser Foundation Hospitals Inc
1 Kaiser Plz
Oakland CA 94612
510 271-6611

(P-10310)
KAISER FOUNDATION HOSPITALS
Also Called: Kaiser Foundation Health Plan
5620 Mesmer Ave, Los Angeles (90230-6315)
PHONE..................800 954-8000
EMP: 85
SALES (corp-wide): 27.8B **Privately Held**
SIC: 6324 Hospital & medical service plans
HQ: Kaiser Foundation Hospitals Inc
1 Kaiser Plz
Oakland CA 94612
510 271-6611

6324 - Hospital & Medical Svc Plans Carriers County (P-10311)

(P-10311) KAISER FOUNDATION HOSPITALS
Also Called: Kaiser Foundation Health Plan
820 Las Gallinas Ave, San Rafael (94903-3410)
PHONE.....................415 444-3522
Bob Johnson, Branch Mgr
Wendy A Eberhardt, Psychiatry
Richard A Glass, Psychiatry
Carmen P Irizarry, Psychiatry
Peter P Chinnici, Social Worker
EMP: 100
SALES (corp-wide): 27.8B Privately Held
WEB: www.kaiser.com
SIC: 6324 Hospital & medical service plans
HQ: Kaiser Foundation Hospitals Inc
    1 Kaiser Plz
    Oakland CA 94612
    510 271-6611

(P-10312) KAISER FOUNDATION HOSPITALS
Also Called: Kaiser Foundation Health Plan
1011 S East St Fl 1, Anaheim (92805-5749)
PHONE.....................714 284-6634
Ruth Ann Ferreria, Manager
EMP: 100
SQ FT: 63,920
SALES (corp-wide): 27.8B Privately Held
WEB: www.kaiser.com
SIC: 6324 Hospital & medical service plans
HQ: Kaiser Foundation Hospitals Inc
    1 Kaiser Plz
    Oakland CA 94612
    510 271-6611

(P-10313) KAISER FOUNDATION HOSPITALS
Also Called: Vaxaville Medical Offices
1 Quality Dr, Vacaville (95688-9494)
PHONE.....................707 624-4000
Fax: 707 453-2953
Murty Savitala, Principal
Catherine Sabherwal, Officer
Max Villalobos, Senior VP
Mike Meneni, Administration
Gale Moore, CIO
EMP: 50
SALES (corp-wide): 27.8B Privately Held
WEB: www.kaiserpermanente.org
SIC: 6324 Hospital & medical service plans
HQ: Kaiser Foundation Hospitals Inc
    1 Kaiser Plz
    Oakland CA 94612
    510 271-6611

(P-10314) KAISER FOUNDATION HOSPITALS
Also Called: Kaiser Foundation Health Plan
25 N Via Monte, Walnut Creek (94598-2510)
PHONE.....................925 926-3000
Fax: 925 926-3686
Phil Newbold, Principal
Jack Meyer, Vice Pres
Bill Tomko, Vice Pres
Charra Jones, Admin Asst
Richard Muir, Admin Asst
EMP: 70
SQ FT: 79,360
SALES (corp-wide): 27.8B Privately Held
WEB: www.kaiser.com
SIC: 6324 Hospital & medical service plans
HQ: Kaiser Foundation Hospitals Inc
    1 Kaiser Plz
    Oakland CA 94612
    510 271-6611

(P-10315) KAISER FOUNDATION HOSPITALS
Also Called: Kaiser Foundation Health Plan
2071 Herndon Ave, Clovis (93611-6101)
PHONE.....................559 324-5100
Angela H Kuo, Med Doctor
Toussaint Streat, Family Practiti
Robert C Gamble, Internal Med
Jill M Ason, OB/GYN
Brian Guthrie, Pediatrics
EMP: 99
SQ FT: 67,465
SALES (corp-wide): 27.8B Privately Held
WEB: www.kaiser.com
SIC: 6324 Hospital & medical service plans
HQ: Kaiser Foundation Hospitals Inc
    1 Kaiser Plz
    Oakland CA 94612
    510 271-6611

(P-10316) KAISER FOUNDATION HOSPITALS
Also Called: Kaiser Foundation Health Plan
21263 Erwin St, Woodland Hills (91367-3715)
PHONE.....................888 515-3500
EMP: 99
SALES (corp-wide): 27.8B Privately Held
WEB: www.kaiser.com
SIC: 6324 Hospital & medical service plans
HQ: Kaiser Foundation Hospitals Inc
    1 Kaiser Plz
    Oakland CA 94612
    510 271-6611

(P-10317) KAISER FOUNDATION HOSPITALS
Also Called: Kaiser Foundation Health Plan
1001 Riverside Ave, Roseville (95678-5134)
PHONE.....................916 784-4050
Don Vu, Principal
EMP: 99
SQ FT: 102,150
SALES (corp-wide): 27.8B Privately Held
WEB: www.kaiser.com
SIC: 6324 Hospital & medical service plans
HQ: Kaiser Foundation Hospitals Inc
    1 Kaiser Plz
    Oakland CA 94612
    510 271-6611

(P-10318) KAISER FOUNDATION HOSPITALS
Also Called: Kaiser Foundation Health Plan
40595 Westlake Dr, Oakhurst (93644-9024)
PHONE.....................559 658-8388
CHI Ly, Principal
EMP: 99
SALES (corp-wide): 27.8B Privately Held
WEB: www.kaiser.com
SIC: 6324 Hospital & medical service plans
HQ: Kaiser Foundation Hospitals Inc
    1 Kaiser Plz
    Oakland CA 94612
    510 271-6611

(P-10319) KAISER FOUNDATION HOSPITALS
Also Called: Kaiser Foundation Health Plan
2295 S Vineyard Ave, Ontario (91761-7925)
PHONE.....................888 750-0036
Arlene Freeman, Manager
David Anderson, Surgeon
EMP: 99
SALES (corp-wide): 27.8B Privately Held
WEB: www.kaiser.com
SIC: 6324 Hospital & medical service plans
HQ: Kaiser Foundation Hospitals Inc
    1 Kaiser Plz
    Oakland CA 94612
    510 271-6611

(P-10320) KAISER FOUNDATION HOSPITALS
Also Called: Kaiser Foundation Health Plan
888 S Hill Rd, Ventura (93003-8400)
PHONE.....................888 515-3500
Michael Steinbaum, Manager
Terry Braus, Manager
EMP: 99
SALES (corp-wide): 27.8B Privately Held
WEB: www.kaiser.com
SIC: 6324 Hospital & medical service plans
HQ: Kaiser Foundation Hospitals Inc
    1 Kaiser Plz
    Oakland CA 94612
    510 271-6611

(P-10321) KAISER FOUNDATION HOSPITALS
Also Called: Kaiser Foundation Health Plan
3401 S Harbor Blvd, Santa Ana (92704-7933)
PHONE.....................888 988-2800
Linh Kamikawa, Pharmacy Dir
Connie L Yao, Pediatrics
Tram Luong, Pharmacist
EMP: 99
SALES (corp-wide): 27.8B Privately Held
WEB: www.kaiser.com
SIC: 6324 Hospital & medical service plans
HQ: Kaiser Foundation Hospitals Inc
    1 Kaiser Plz
    Oakland CA 94612
    510 271-6611

(P-10322) KAISER FOUNDATION HOSPITALS
Also Called: Kaiser Foundation Health Plan
1717 Date Pike, San Bernardino (92404)
PHONE.....................888 750-0036
Jim Morrison, Manager
EMP: 99
SQ FT: 18,253
SALES (corp-wide): 27.8B Privately Held
WEB: www.kaiser.com
SIC: 6324 Hospital & medical service plans
HQ: Kaiser Foundation Hospitals Inc
    1 Kaiser Plz
    Oakland CA 94612
    510 271-6611

(P-10323) KAISER FOUNDATION HOSPITALS
Also Called: Kaiser Foundation Health Plan
11911 Central Ave, Chino (91710-1906)
PHONE.....................888 750-0036
Ken Lee, Principal
EMP: 99
SALES (corp-wide): 27.8B Privately Held
WEB: www.kaiser.com
SIC: 6324 Hospital & medical service plans
HQ: Kaiser Foundation Hospitals Inc
    1 Kaiser Plz
    Oakland CA 94612
    510 271-6611

(P-10324) KAISER FOUNDATION HOSPITALS
Also Called: Kaiser Foundation Health Plan
395 Hickey Blvd, Daly City (94015-2770)
PHONE.....................650 301-5860
Arthur Chin, Principal
Ivy Fisher, Med Doctor
EMP: 99
SALES (corp-wide): 27.8B Privately Held
WEB: www.kaiser.com
SIC: 6324 Hospital & medical service plans
HQ: Kaiser Foundation Hospitals Inc
    1 Kaiser Plz
    Oakland CA 94612
    510 271-6611

(P-10325) KAISER FOUNDATION HOSPITALS
Also Called: Kaiser Foundation Health Plan
3553 Whipple Rd, Union City (94587-1507)
PHONE.....................510 675-2170
Mani Kammula, Principal
EMP: 99
SALES (corp-wide): 27.8B Privately Held
WEB: www.kaiser.com
SIC: 6324 Hospital & medical service plans
HQ: Kaiser Foundation Hospitals Inc
    1 Kaiser Plz
    Oakland CA 94612
    510 271-6611

(P-10326) KAISER FOUNDATION HOSPITALS
Also Called: Kaiser Foundation Health Plan
901 El Camino Real, San Bruno (94066-3009)
PHONE.....................650 742-2100
Allen Wu, Principal
Allen Lew, Manager
EMP: 99
SALES (corp-wide): 27.8B Privately Held
WEB: www.kaiser.com
SIC: 6324 Hospital & medical service plans
HQ: Kaiser Foundation Hospitals Inc
    1 Kaiser Plz
    Oakland CA 94612
    510 271-6611

(P-10327) KAISER FOUNDATION HOSPITALS
Also Called: Kaiser Foundation Health Plan
3554 Round Barn Blvd, Santa Rosa (95403-0929)
PHONE.....................707 571-3835
Jay Kelley, Manager
EMP: 99
SALES (corp-wide): 27.8B Privately Held
WEB: www.kaiser.com
SIC: 6324 Hospital & medical service plans
HQ: Kaiser Foundation Hospitals Inc
    1 Kaiser Plz
    Oakland CA 94612
    510 271-6611

(P-10328) KAISER FOUNDATION HOSPITALS
Also Called: Kaiser Foundation Health Plan
3925 Old Redwood Hwy, Santa Rosa (95403-1719)
PHONE.....................707 393-4033
Clay Wheeler, Principal
Nicole Black-Pierce, Nurse Practr
EMP: 99
SALES (corp-wide): 27.8B Privately Held
WEB: www.kaiser.com
SIC: 6324 Hospital & medical service plans
HQ: Kaiser Foundation Hospitals Inc
    1 Kaiser Plz
    Oakland CA 94612
    510 271-6611

(P-10329) KAISER FOUNDATION HOSPITALS
Also Called: Kaiser Foundation Health Plan
1320 Standiford Ave, Modesto (95350-0726)
PHONE.....................855 268-4096
Anita Vohra, Principal
EMP: 99
SALES (corp-wide): 27.8B Privately Held
WEB: www.kaiser.com
SIC: 6324 Hospital & medical service plans
HQ: Kaiser Foundation Hospitals Inc
    1 Kaiser Plz
    Oakland CA 94612
    510 271-6611

(P-10330) KAISER FOUNDATION HOSPITALS
Also Called: Kaiser Foundation Health Plan
5900 State Farm Dr # 100, Rohnert Park (94928-2149)
PHONE.....................707 206-3000
Noel Smith, Branch Mgr
EMP: 85
SALES (corp-wide): 27.8B Privately Held
WEB: www.kaiser.com
SIC: 6324 Hospital & medical service plans
HQ: Kaiser Foundation Hospitals Inc
    1 Kaiser Plz
    Oakland CA 94612
    510 271-6611

(P-10331) KAISER FOUNDATION HOSPITALS
Also Called: Kaiser Foundation Health Plan
2417 Central Ave, Alameda (94501-4515)
PHONE.....................510 752-1190
Michael Gorin, Branch Mgr
Angela L Chan, Med Doctor
EMP: 99
SALES (corp-wide): 27.8B Privately Held
WEB: www.kaiser.com
SIC: 6324 Hospital & medical service plans
HQ: Kaiser Foundation Hospitals Inc
    1 Kaiser Plz
    Oakland CA 94612
    510 271-6611

6324 - Hospital & Medical Svc Plans Carriers County (P-10351)

(P-10332)
KAISER FOUNDATION HOSPITALS
Also Called: Kaiser Foundation Health Plan
969 Broadway, Oakland (94607-4017)
PHONE..................................510 251-0121
Mary Sage, *Branch Mgr*
Hannah J Kusterer, *Psychologist*
Nicola J Longmuir, *Psychiatry*
Marilyn A Ancel, *Med Doctor*
Sarah S Christensen,
EMP: 99
SALES (corp-wide): 27.8B **Privately Held**
WEB: www.kaiser.com
SIC: 6324 Hospital & medical service plans
HQ: Kaiser Foundation Hospitals Inc
1 Kaiser Plz
Oakland CA 94612
510 271-6611

(P-10333)
KAISER FOUNDATION HOSPITALS
Also Called: Kaiser Foundation Health Plan
9333 Rosecrans Ave, Bellflower (90706-2141)
PHONE..................................562 461-3084
Arlene M Dolorico MD, *Manager*
EMP: 99
SALES (corp-wide): 27.8B **Privately Held**
WEB: www.kaiser.com
SIC: 6324 Hospital & medical service plans
HQ: Kaiser Foundation Hospitals Inc
1 Kaiser Plz
Oakland CA 94612
510 271-6611

(P-10334)
KAISER FOUNDATION HOSPITALS
Also Called: Kaiser Foundation Health Plan
2651 Highland Ave, Selma (93662-3392)
PHONE..................................559 898-6000
Hong-Hanh Ton-Nu, *Principal*
Lorraine Lopez, *Med Doctor*
Laurie Berthold, *Nurse Practr*
EMP: 99
SQ FT: 37,081
SALES (corp-wide): 27.8B **Privately Held**
WEB: www.kaiser.com
SIC: 6324 Hospital & medical service plans
HQ: Kaiser Foundation Hospitals Inc
1 Kaiser Plz
Oakland CA 94612
510 271-6611

(P-10335)
KAISER FOUNDATION HOSPITALS
Also Called: Kaiser Foundation Health Plan
4201 W Chapman Ave, Orange (92868-1505)
PHONE..................................714 748-7622
Doug Gustason, *Branch Mgr*
Annie Chao, *Pharmacist*
EMP: 99
SALES (corp-wide): 27.8B **Privately Held**
WEB: www.kaiser.com
SIC: 6324 Hospital & medical service plans
HQ: Kaiser Foundation Hospitals Inc
1 Kaiser Plz
Oakland CA 94612
510 271-6611

(P-10336)
KAISER FOUNDATION HOSPITALS
Also Called: Kaiser Foundation Health Plan
1717 E Vista Chino Ste B2, Palm Springs (92262-3569)
PHONE..................................866 370-1942
Ed McMahon, *Principal*
EMP: 99
SALES (corp-wide): 27.8B **Privately Held**
WEB: www.kaiser.com
SIC: 6324 Hospital & medical service plans
HQ: Kaiser Foundation Hospitals Inc
1 Kaiser Plz
Oakland CA 94612
510 271-6611

(P-10337)
KAISER FOUNDATION HOSPITALS
Also Called: Kaiser Foundation Health Plan
20790 Madrona Ave, Torrance (90503-3777)
PHONE..................................800 780-1230
Shirley Oka, *Principal*
EMP: 99
SALES (corp-wide): 27.8B **Privately Held**
WEB: www.kaiser.com
SIC: 6324 Hospital & medical service plans
HQ: Kaiser Foundation Hospitals Inc
1 Kaiser Plz
Oakland CA 94612
510 271-6611

(P-10338)
KAISER FOUNDATION HOSPITALS
Also Called: Kaiser Foundation Health Plan
3900 Alamo St, Simi Valley (93063-2111)
PHONE..................................888 515-3500
Nami Kim, *Principal*
Cheri Wechsler, *Office Mgr*
EMP: 99
SALES (corp-wide): 27.8B **Privately Held**
WEB: www.kaiser.com
SIC: 6324 Hospital & medical service plans
HQ: Kaiser Foundation Hospitals Inc
1 Kaiser Plz
Oakland CA 94612
510 271-6611

(P-10339)
KAISER FOUNDATION HOSPITALS
Also Called: Kaiser Foundation Health Plan
30400 Camino Capistrano, San Juan Capistrano (92675-1300)
PHONE..................................888 988-2800
Patrick Roth, *Branch Mgr*
EMP: 99
SALES (corp-wide): 27.8B **Privately Held**
WEB: www.kaiser.com
SIC: 6324 Hospital & medical service plans
HQ: Kaiser Foundation Hospitals Inc
1 Kaiser Plz
Oakland CA 94612
510 271-6611

(P-10340)
KAISER FOUNDATION HOSPITALS
Also Called: Kaiser Foundation Health Plan
9961 Sierra Ave, Fontana (92335-6720)
P.O. Box None (92335)
PHONE..................................909 427-3910
Gerald Mc Call, *Branch Mgr*
Gerald M Call, *Branch Mgr*
James Low, *Research*
Assad Moheimani, *Research*
Rod Winegarner, *Finance Mgr*
EMP: 99
SALES (corp-wide): 27.8B **Privately Held**
WEB: www.kaiser.com
SIC: 6324 Hospital & medical service plans
HQ: Kaiser Foundation Hospitals Inc
1 Kaiser Plz
Oakland CA 94612
510 271-6611

(P-10341)
KAISER FOUNDATION HOSPITALS
Also Called: Kaiser Foundation Health Plan
12200 Bellflower Blvd, Downey (90242-2804)
PHONE..................................562 622-4190
Jim Harrington, *Branch Mgr*
Jacqueline Block, *Administration*
Stanley M Fried, *Geriatrics*
EMP: 99
SALES (corp-wide): 27.8B **Privately Held**
WEB: www.kaiser.com
SIC: 6324 Hospital & medical service plans
HQ: Kaiser Foundation Hospitals Inc
1 Kaiser Plz
Oakland CA 94612
510 271-6611

(P-10342)
KAISER FOUNDATION HOSPITALS
Also Called: CVS
5259 Mission Oaks Blvd, Camarillo (93012-5422)
PHONE..................................805 482-0707
Brian Weiss, *Manager*
EMP: 99
SALES (corp-wide): 27.8B **Privately Held**
WEB: www.kaiser.com
SIC: 6324 Hospital & medical service plans
HQ: Kaiser Foundation Hospitals Inc
1 Kaiser Plz
Oakland CA 94612
510 271-6611

(P-10343)
KAISER FOUNDATION HOSPITALS
Also Called: Kaiser Foundation Health Plan
42575 Washington St, Palm Desert (92211-8850)
PHONE..................................760 360-1475
EMP: 99
SALES (corp-wide): 27.8B **Privately Held**
WEB: www.kaiser.com
SIC: 6324 Hospital & medical service plans
HQ: Kaiser Foundation Hospitals Inc
1 Kaiser Plz
Oakland CA 94612
510 271-6611

(P-10344)
KAISER FOUNDATION HOSPITALS
Also Called: Kaiser Foundation Health Plan
2417 Naglee Rd, Tracy (95304-7324)
PHONE..................................209 832-6339
EMP: 84
SALES (corp-wide): 27.8B **Privately Held**
WEB: www.kaiser.com
SIC: 6324 Hospital & medical service plans
HQ: Kaiser Foundation Hospitals Inc
1 Kaiser Plz
Oakland CA 94612
510 271-6611

(P-10345)
KAISER FOUNDATION HOSPITALS
Also Called: Kaiser Foundation Health Plan
365 E Hillcrest Dr, Thousand Oaks (91360-5820)
PHONE..................................888 515-3500
Fax: 805 374-7419
Beverly Torres, *Branch Mgr*
EMP: 72
SALES (corp-wide): 27.8B **Privately Held**
WEB: www.kaiser.com
SIC: 6324 Hospital & medical service plans
HQ: Kaiser Foundation Hospitals Inc
1 Kaiser Plz
Oakland CA 94612
510 271-6611

(P-10346)
KAISER FOUNDATION HOSPITALS
Also Called: Kaiser Foundation Health Plan
5755 Cottle Rd, San Jose (95123-3640)
PHONE..................................408 972-3376
Fax: 408 972-3242
Donald D Mordecai, *Branch Mgr*
Jeffrey C Liu, *Ophthalmology*
Dianna Martin, *Manager*
EMP: 99
SALES (corp-wide): 27.8B **Privately Held**
WEB: www.kaiser.com
SIC: 6324 8062 8011 6321 Hospital & medical service plans; health maintenance organization (HMO), insurance only; dental insurance; group hospitalization plans; general medical & surgical hospitals; offices & clinics of medical doctors; accident & health insurance
HQ: Kaiser Foundation Hospitals Inc
1 Kaiser Plz
Oakland CA 94612
510 271-6611

(P-10347)
KAISER FOUNDATION HOSPITALS
Also Called: Kaiser Foundation Health Plan
1840 Sierra Gardens Dr, Roseville (95661-2912)
PHONE..................................916 784-4190
Karen Riglick, *Principal*
EMP: 99
SALES (corp-wide): 27.8B **Privately Held**
WEB: www.kaiser.com
SIC: 6324 Hospital & medical service plans
HQ: Kaiser Foundation Hospitals Inc
1 Kaiser Plz
Oakland CA 94612
510 271-6611

(P-10348)
KAISER FOUNDATION HOSPITALS
Also Called: Kaiser Foundation Health Plan
1625 I St, Modesto (95354-1121)
P.O. Box 577680 (95357-7680)
PHONE..................................209 557-1000
Fax: 209 557-1080
Larry Stump, *Director*
Christina Hill, *Sales Associate*
Ranjit Shenoy, *Internal Med*
Erik L Kenyon, *Podiatrist*
EMP: 60
SALES (corp-wide): 27.8B **Privately Held**
WEB: www.kaiser.com
SIC: 6324 Health maintenance organization (HMO), insurance only
HQ: Kaiser Foundation Hospitals Inc
1 Kaiser Plz
Oakland CA 94612
510 271-6611

(P-10349)
KAISER FOUNDATION HOSPITALS
Also Called: Kaiser Foundation Health Plan
200 N Lewis St Fl 1, Orange (92868-1538)
PHONE..................................888 988-2800
Harriet Brown, *Director*
Vasant Keny, *Admin Asst*
Mark Janssen, *Pathologist*
Hrag M Marganian, *Pathologist*
Asma S Quddusi, *Pathologist*
EMP: 60
SALES (corp-wide): 27.8B **Privately Held**
WEB: www.kaiser.com
SIC: 6324 8011 Hospital & medical service plans; clinic, operated by physicians
HQ: Kaiser Foundation Hospitals Inc
1 Kaiser Plz
Oakland CA 94612
510 271-6611

(P-10350)
KAISER FOUNDATION HOSPITALS
Also Called: Kaiser Foundation Health Plan
801 Traeger Ave Ste 217, San Bruno (94066-3048)
PHONE..................................650 742-2000
Rosemary Rogers, *Manager*
Deborah Lobo, *Dermatology*
EMP: 99
SALES (corp-wide): 27.8B **Privately Held**
WEB: www.kaiser.com
SIC: 6324 Hospital & medical service plans
HQ: Kaiser Foundation Hospitals Inc
1 Kaiser Plz
Oakland CA 94612
510 271-6611

(P-10351)
KAISER FUNDATION HLTH PLAN INC (PA)
1 Kaiser Plz, Oakland (94612-3610)
PHONE..................................510 271-5800
Fax: 510 271-6493
Bernard J Tyson, *Ch of Bd*
John Rego, *Ch Radiology*
Gregory A Adams, *President*
Kathy Lancaster, *CFO*
Patrick Courneya, *Chief Mktg Ofcr*
EMP: 450 **EST:** 1955
SQ FT: 90,000

6324 - Hospital & Medical Svc Plans Carriers County (P-10352)

SALES (est): 27.8B Privately Held
WEB: www.kaiser.com
SIC: 6324 Hospital & medical service plans; health maintenance organization (HMO), insurance only; dental insurance; group hospitalization plans

(P-10352)
KAISER FUNDATION HLTH PLAN INC
3801 Howe St, Oakland (94611-5312)
PHONE 510 752-7644
David Kvancz, Vice Pres
EMP: 85
SALES (corp-wide): 27.8B Privately Held
SIC: 6324 Hospital & medical service plans
PA: Kaiser Foundation Health Plan, Inc.
  1 Kaiser Plz
  Oakland CA 94612
  510 271-5800

(P-10353)
KAISER FUNDATION HLTH PLAN INC
4460 Hacienda Dr, Pleasanton (94588-2761)
PHONE 510 271-5800
Linsey Dicks, Manager
Manish Vipani, Vice Pres
Sudha Sharma, Exec Dir
Tara Vaishnav, Exec Dir
Michael Won, Program Mgr
EMP: 100
SALES (corp-wide): 27.8B Privately Held
WEB: www.kaiser.com
SIC: 6324 Hospital & medical service plans
PA: Kaiser Foundation Health Plan, Inc.
  1 Kaiser Plz
  Oakland CA 94612
  510 271-5800

(P-10354)
KAISER FUNDATION HLTH PLAN INC
1950 Franklin St Fl 3, Oakland (94612-5190)
PHONE 510 987-2255
Jean Nudellman, Manager
EMP: 70
SALES (corp-wide): 27.8B Privately Held
WEB: www.kaiser.com
SIC: 6324 Hospital & medical service plans
PA: Kaiser Foundation Health Plan, Inc.
  1 Kaiser Plz
  Oakland CA 94612
  510 271-5800

(P-10355)
LIBERTY DENTAL PLAN CAL INC
340 Commerce Ste 100, Irvine (92602-1358)
PHONE 949 223-0007
Fax: 714 223-0011
Amir Hossein Neshat, President
Maja Kapic, CFO
Eric Kim, Info Tech Dir
Gina Baker, Recruiter
Sam Green, Sr Associate
EMP: 300
SALES (est): 216.2MM Privately Held
SIC: 6324 Dental insurance

(P-10356)
LOCAL INITIATIVE HEALTH AUTHOR
Also Called: L A Care Health Plan
1055 W 7th St Fl 11, Los Angeles (90017-2751)
PHONE 213 694-1250
Fax: 213 694-1250
Howard A Kahn, CEO
John Wallace, COO
Tim Reilly, CFO
Andrea Van Hook, Bd of Directors
Gertrude Carter, Chief Mktg Ofcr
EMP: 900
SALES (est): 329.7MM Privately Held
SIC: 6324 Hospital & medical service plans

(P-10357)
MANAGED HEALTH NETWORK
7755 Center Ave Ste 700, Huntington Beach (92647-9126)
PHONE 714 934-5519
Carol McLean, Branch Mgr

Dewitt Whitehurst, Manager
EMP: 580
SALES (corp-wide): 22.7B Publicly Held
SIC: 6324 Hospital & medical service plans
HQ: Managed Health Network
  2370 Kerner Blvd
  San Rafael CA 94901
  415 460-8168

(P-10358)
MANAGED HEALTH NETWORK (DH)
2370 Kerner Blvd, San Rafael (94901-5546)
P.O. Box 10207 (94912-0207)
PHONE 415 460-8168
Fax: 415 472-8183
Jeffrey Bairstow, CEO
Jerry Coil, President
Steven Sell, President
Linda Brisbane, COO
Jonathan Wormhoudt, COO
EMP: 500
SQ FT: 97,314
SALES (est): 246.3MM
SALES (corp-wide): 22.7B Publicly Held
SIC: 6324 8099 8093 8011 Hospital & medical service plans; health maintenance organization (HMO), insurance only; medical services organization; specialty outpatient clinics; offices & clinics of medical doctors
HQ: Health Net, Inc.
  21650 Oxnard St Fl 25
  Woodland Hills CA 91367
  818 676-6000

(P-10359)
MANAGED HEALTH NETWORK
2370 Kerner Blvd, San Rafael (94901-5546)
P.O. Box 10207 (94912-0207)
PHONE 510 620-6143
John Crocker, Branch Mgr
EMP: 1100
SALES (corp-wide): 22.7B Publicly Held
SIC: 6324 Hospital & medical service plans
HQ: Managed Health Network
  2370 Kerner Blvd
  San Rafael CA 94901
  415 460-8168

(P-10360)
MHN SERVICES
2370 Kerner Blvd, San Rafael (94901-5546)
PHONE 415 460-8300
Juanell Hefner, President
Ian Shaffer, Chief Mktg Ofcr
John Crocker, Contract Law
Cynthia Hower, Accounts Mgr
EMP: 40
SALES: 87MM
SALES (corp-wide): 22.7B Publicly Held
SIC: 6324 8011 8742 8322 Hospital & medical service plans; health maintenance organization; management consulting services; social service center
HQ: Health Net, Inc.
  21650 Oxnard St Fl 25
  Woodland Hills CA 91367
  818 676-6000

(P-10361)
ON LOK SENIOR HEALTH SERVICES (PA)
Also Called: On Lok Lifeways
1333 Bush St, San Francisco (94109-5691)
PHONE 415 292-8888
Fax: 415 292-8745
Robert Edmondson, CEO
Grace Li, COO
Sue Wong, CFO
Kelvin Quan, Officer
Eileen Kunz, Director
EMP: 570
SQ FT: 40,000
SALES: 110.2MM Privately Held
SIC: 6324 8082 Health maintenance organization (HMO), insurance only; home health care services

(P-10362)
ON LOK SENIOR HEALTH SERVICES
Also Called: On Lok Life Ways
159 Washington Blvd, Fremont (94539-5209)
PHONE 510 249-2700
Fax: 510 249-0255
Janice Fujii, Manager
Sandra Aguayo, Human Res Mgr
EMP: 50
SALES (corp-wide): 103.5MM Privately Held
SIC: 6324 8082 Health maintenance organization (HMO), insurance only; home health care services
PA: On Lok Senior Health Services
  1333 Bush St
  San Francisco CA 94109
  415 292-8888

(P-10363)
OPTUMRX INC
Also Called: Prescription Solutions
2858 Loker Ave E Ste 100, Carlsbad (92010-6673)
P.O. Box 509075, San Diego (92150-9075)
PHONE 760 804-2399
Sean O'Rourke, Manager
Paul Miller, Officer
Claudia Galambos, Executive
EMP: 400
SALES (corp-wide): 157.1B Publicly Held
SIC: 6324 Hospital & medical service plans
HQ: Optumrx, Inc.
  2300 Main St
  Irvine CA 92614
  714 825-3600

(P-10364)
OPTUMRX INC (DH)
Also Called: Prescription Solutions
2300 Main St, Irvine (92614-6223)
P.O. Box 509075, San Diego (92150-9075)
PHONE 714 825-3600
Fax: 714 226-3653
Mark Thierer, CEO
Timothy Wicks, President
Jeff Park, COO
Jeffrey Grosklags, CFO
Vince Condino, Vice Pres
EMP: 300
SALES (est): 21.6B
SALES (corp-wide): 157.1B Publicly Held
SIC: 6324 6321 Hospital & medical service plans; accident & health insurance
HQ: United Healthcare Services Inc.
  9700 Health Care Ln
  Minnetonka MN 55343
  952 936-1300

(P-10365)
PACIFICARE DENTAL
3110 W Lake Center Dr, Santa Ana (92704-6917)
P.O. Box 25187 (92799-5187)
PHONE 661 631-8613
Jerry Vaccaro, President
Chris Boles, CFO
John W Halley, Vice Pres
John Whalley, Vice Pres
Laurie Oleary, Pharmacy Dir
EMP: 195
SQ FT: 5,000
SALES: 71.3MM
SALES (corp-wide): 157.1B Publicly Held
SIC: 6324 Dental insurance
HQ: Pacificare Health Plan Administrators, Inc.
  3120 W Lake Center Dr
  Santa Ana CA 92704
  714 825-5200

(P-10366)
PACIFICARE HEALTH PLAN ADMIN (DH)
3120 W Lake Center Dr, Santa Ana (92704-6917)
P.O. Box 25186 (92799-5186)
PHONE 714 825-5200
Fax: 714 825-5045
David Reed, Ch of Bd
Kenneth L Watkins, CFO

Kenneth Watkins, CFO
Coy F Baugh, Treasurer
James A Frey, Senior VP
EMP: 400 EST: 1975
SQ FT: 220,000
SALES: 12.2B
SALES (corp-wide): 157.1B Publicly Held
SIC: 6324 Group hospitalization plans

(P-10367)
PACIFICARE HEALTH SYSTEMS LLC (HQ)
5995 Plaza Dr, Cypress (90630-5028)
PHONE 714 952-1121
Fax: 714 236-5803
Howard Phanstiel, CEO
David Erickson, Shareholder
C W Wood, Bd of Directors
Coy Baugh, Exec VP
Sue Berkel, Exec VP
EMP: 550
SQ FT: 104,000
SALES (corp-wide): 157.1B Publicly Held
WEB: www.pacificare.com
SIC: 6324 Hospital & medical service plans
PA: Unitedhealth Group Incorporated
  9900 Bren Rd E Ste 300w
  Minnetonka MN 55343
  952 936-1300

(P-10368)
PACIFICDENTAL BENEFITS INC (PA)
2300 Clayton Rd Ste 1000, Concord (94520-2168)
PHONE 925 363-6000
Fax: 925 363-6098
John Gaebel, President
Randy Breacher, CFO
Nilesh Patel, Vice Pres
Sandy Leaver, Business Anlyst
John Malork, Business Anlyst
EMP: 90
SQ FT: 18,530
SALES (est): 40.9MM Privately Held
SIC: 6324 6321 Dental insurance; accident & health insurance

(P-10369)
PARTNERSHIP HEALTH PLAN CAL
4665 Business Center Dr, Fairfield (94534-1675)
PHONE 707 863-4100
Jack Horn, CEO
Lynn Scuri, Shareholder
Liz Gibboney, COO
Gary Erickson, CFO
Neal Cronin, Technology
EMP: 290
SQ FT: 75,000
SALES (est): 228.2MM Privately Held
SIC: 6324 Hospital & medical service plans

(P-10370)
PHYSICIAN ASSOC SAN GABRIEL
199 S Los Robles Ave, Pasadena (91101-2452)
PHONE 626 817-8300
Fax: 626 817-8596
Barton Wald MD, President
Theresa David, COO
Nakia Roberts, Executive Asst
Ken Trinh, Administration
Meredith Brooks, Finance Mgr
EMP: 210
SALES (est): 65.1MM Privately Held
WEB: www.physicianassoc.com
SIC: 6324 Health maintenance organization (HMO), insurance only

(P-10371)
PRIVATE MEDICAL-CARE INC
12898 Towne Center Dr, Cerritos (90703-8546)
PHONE 562 924-8311
Robert Elliott, President
Patrick Steele, CIO
Anthony S Barth, Agent
EMP: 154

PRODUCTS & SERVICES SECTION
6331 - Fire, Marine & Casualty Insurance County (P-10393)

SALES (est): 55.4MM
SALES (corp-wide): 5.3B **Privately Held**
WEB: www.deltadentalca.org
SIC: 6324 Dental insurance
PA: Delta Dental Of California
100 1st St Fl 4
San Francisco CA 94105
415 972-8300

(P-10372)
REW INC
973 Higuera St Ste A, San Luis Obispo (93401-3614)
PHONE 805 541-1308
Robert Wacker, *CEO*
EMP: 63
SALES: 950K **Privately Held**
SIC: 6324 Hospital & medical service plans

(P-10373)
SAFEGUARD HEALTH ENTERPRISES (HQ)
95 Enterprise Ste 100, Aliso Viejo (92656-2605)
PHONE 949 425-4300
Fax: 949 425-4586
Steven J Baileys DDS, *Ch of Bd*
James E Buncher, *President*
Stephen J Baker, *COO*
Dennis L Gates, *CFO*
Ronald I Brendzel, *Senior VP*
EMP: 355
SQ FT: 68,000
SALES (est): 89.4MM
SALES (corp-wide): 69.9B **Publicly Held**
SIC: 6324 Dental insurance
PA: Metlife, Inc.
200 Park Ave Fl 1200
New York NY 10166
212 578-9500

(P-10374)
SCAN HEALTH PLAN (PA)
3800 Kilroy Airport Way # 100, Long Beach (90806-6818)
PHONE 562 989-5100
Ryan Trimble, *Chairman*
Dave Schmidt, *President*
Chris Wing, *CEO*
Bill Roth, *COO*
Jeff Spurrier, *COO*
EMP: 146
SALES: 2B **Privately Held**
SIC: 6324 Hospital & medical service plans

(P-10375)
SCAN HEALTH PLAN
500 N Central Ave Ste 350, Glendale (91203-3926)
PHONE 818 550-4900
Sherry Stanislaw, *Senior VP*
Dennis Eder, *Executive*
Diane Scott, *Marketing Staff*
EMP: 133
SALES (corp-wide): 2B **Privately Held**
SIC: 6324 Health maintenance organization (HMO), insurance only
PA: Scan Health Plan
3800 Kilroy Airport Way # 100
Long Beach CA 90806
562 989-5100

(P-10376)
SCAN HEALTH PLAN
6633 Telephone Rd Ste 100, Ventura (93003-5569)
PHONE 805 658-0365
Fax: 805 658-8623
Dave Smith, *Manager*
Patricia McDonald, *Planning*
EMP: 133
SALES (corp-wide): 2B **Privately Held**
SIC: 6324 Health maintenance organization (HMO), insurance only
PA: Scan Health Plan
3800 Kilroy Airport Way # 100
Long Beach CA 90806
562 989-5100

(P-10377)
SECOND OPINION MED GRP INC
2876 Sycamore Dr Ste 305, Simi Valley (93065-1550)
PHONE 805 496-4315
Rajeswari Ananda, *Principal*
Punita Khanna, *Vice Pres*

EMP: 99
SQ FT: 1,500
SALES (est): 13.9MM **Privately Held**
SIC: 6324 Hospital & medical service plans

(P-10378)
SENIOR CARE (PA)
Also Called: Scan Health Plan
3800 Kilroy Airport Way, Long Beach (90806-2494)
P.O. Box 22616 (90801-5616)
PHONE 562 989-5100
Fax: 562 989-5200
David Schmidt, *CEO*
Susan Cameron, *COO*
Dennis Eder, *CFO*
William Rice, *CFO*
Rebecca M Learner, *Officer*
▲ **EMP:** 650
SQ FT: 119,219
SALES (est): 302.8MM **Privately Held**
WEB: www.scanhealthplan.com
SIC: 6324 Hospital & medical service plans

(P-10379)
SENIOR CARE
Also Called: Independence At Home Iah
2501 Cherry Ave Ste 380, Long Beach (90755-2050)
PHONE 562 492-9878
Kit Donaldson, *Branch Mgr*
Denise Likar, *Exec Dir*
Christopher Kelly, *Information Mgr*
EMP: 55
SALES (corp-wide): 302.8MM **Privately Held**
WEB: www.scanhealthplan.com
SIC: 6324 Hospital & medical service plans
PA: Senior Care Action Network Foundation
3800 Kilroy Airport Way
Long Beach CA 90806
562 989-5100

(P-10380)
SHARP HEALTH PLAN
8520 Tech Way Ste 200, San Diego (92123-1450)
PHONE 858 499-8300
Kathlyn Mead, *President*
Leslie Pels-Beck, *COO*
Rita Datko, *CFO*
Janet Hoy, *Vice Pres*
Lori Stone, *Vice Pres*
EMP: 98
SALES: 322.6MM **Privately Held**
SIC: 6324 Health maintenance organization (HMO), insurance only

(P-10381)
SOUTHERN CAL PRMNNTE MED GROUP
Also Called: Kaiser Foundation Health Plan
5855 Copley Dr Ste 250, San Diego (92111-7908)
PHONE 858 974-1000
Tom Cooper, *Manager*
Travis Van Ness, *Admin Asst*
Jim Adams, *Info Tech Dir*
Anthony Perez, *Telecomm Mgr*
Tom Hauck, *Database Admin*
EMP: 75
SQ FT: 89,984
SALES (corp-wide): 3.2B **Privately Held**
WEB: www.kaiser.com
SIC: 6324 Hospital & medical service plans
PA: Southern California Permanente Medical Group
393 Walnut Dr
Pasadena CA 91107
626 405-5704

(P-10382)
SOUTHERN CAL PRMNNTE MED GROUP (PA)
Also Called: Kaiser Permanente
393 Walnut Dr, Pasadena (91107-4922)
PHONE 626 405-5704
Irwin Goldstein, *CEO*
Sherry Lovely, *Admin Asst*
Peter J Pellerito, *Administration*
Aileen Nokes, *Meeting Planner*
Norman Jue, *Comp Spec*
EMP: 60
SQ FT: 600,000
SALES (est): 3.2B **Privately Held**

(P-10383)
SUPERIOR VISION SERVICES INC (PA)
11101 White Rock Rd # 150, Rancho Cordova (95670-6996)
PHONE 916 859-6218
Fax: 916 852-2277
Kirk Rothrock, *CEO*
Brian Silverberg, *CFO*
Kimberley Hess, *Senior VP*
Stephanie Lucas, *Senior VP*
Audrey Weinstein, *Senior VP*
EMP: 54
SQ FT: 12,000
SALES (est): 46.3MM **Privately Held**
WEB: www.superiorvision.com
SIC: 6324 Hospital & medical service plans

(P-10384)
UHC OF CALIFORNIA (DH)
Also Called: Pacificare of California
5995 Plaza Dr, Cypress (90630-5028)
PHONE 714 952-1121
Fax: 714 226-2477
Brad A Bowlus, *Principal*
Michael Montevideo, *Treasurer*
Terry Hartshorn, *Managing Dir*
Dominic Ng, *Managing Dir*
Lisa Espinosa, *Branch Mgr*
EMP: 800
SALES (est): 317.6MM
SALES (corp-wide): 157.1B **Publicly Held**
WEB: www.rxsol.com
SIC: 6324 8732 Health maintenance organization (HMO), insurance only; commercial nonphysical research

(P-10385)
UNITED BEHAVIORAL HEALTH
Also Called: Pacificare
2300 Clayton Rd Ste 1000, Concord (94520-2168)
PHONE 925 246-1343
Fax: 925 602-1626
Fred Dodson, *Branch Mgr*
Marty Sing, *Branch Mgr*
EMP: 150
SALES (corp-wide): 157.1B **Publicly Held**
WEB: www.unitedbehavioralhealth.com
SIC: 6324 Hospital & medical service plans
HQ: United Behavioral Health
425 Market St Fl 18
San Francisco CA 94105
415 547-1403

(P-10386)
UNITEDHEALTH GROUP INC
Also Called: Pacificare Health Systems
7891 Moonmist Cir, Huntington Beach (92648-5434)
PHONE 714 969-9050
Andrew Hall, *Branch Mgr*
EMP: 300
SALES (corp-wide): 157.1B **Publicly Held**
WEB: www.unitedhealthgroup.com
SIC: 6324 Hospital & medical service plans
PA: Unitedhealth Group Incorporated
9900 Bren Rd E Ste 300w
Minnetonka MN 55343
952 936-1300

(P-10387)
UNITEDHEALTH GROUP INC
Also Called: Pacificare Health Systems
5701 Katella Ave, Cypress (90630-5006)
PHONE 952 936-1300
Mike Wallace, *Branch Mgr*
Ferial Bahreman, *Senior VP*
Tim Yee, *Vice Pres*
Edlyn James, *Admin Asst*
Suzanne Thompson, *Admin Asst*
EMP: 100
SALES (corp-wide): 157.1B **Publicly Held**
WEB: www.unitedhealthgroup.com
SIC: 6324 Hospital & medical service plans
PA: Unitedhealth Group Incorporated
9900 Bren Rd E Ste 300w
Minnetonka MN 55343
952 936-1300

(P-10388)
UNITEDHEALTH GROUP INC
2080 E 20th St, Chico (95928-7702)
PHONE 530 879-8251
Erica Lajoie, *Admin Asst*
Mark Franks, *Manager*
EMP: 270
SALES (corp-wide): 157.1B **Publicly Held**
SIC: 6324 Hospital & medical service plans
PA: Unitedhealth Group Incorporated
9900 Bren Rd E Ste 300w
Minnetonka MN 55343
952 936-1300

(P-10389)
VICTOR VLY HOSP ACQISITION INC
Also Called: VICTOR VALLEY GLOBAL MEDICAL C
15248 Eleventh St, Victorville (92395-3704)
PHONE 760 245-8691
Suzanne Richards, *CEO*
David Lennon, *Admin Asst*
Mieke Sherwood, *Facilities Asst*
Hasana Aziz, *Director*
EMP: 55
SALES: 73MM **Privately Held**
SIC: 6324 Hospital & medical service plans

(P-10390)
VISION SERVICE PLAN (PA)
Also Called: C V S Optical Lab Div
3333 Quality Dr, Rancho Cordova (95670-9757)
P.O. Box 997100, Sacramento (95899-7100)
PHONE 916 851-5000
Fax: 916 851-4850
James Robinson Lynch, *CEO*
Laura Costa, *COO*
Donald J Ball Jr, *CFO*
Gary Brooks, *Senior VP*
Gary Norman Brooks, *Vice Pres*
EMP: 1600
SQ FT: 300,000
SALES (est): 4.9B **Privately Held**
WEB: www.vsp.com
SIC: 6324 5048 Hospital & medical service plans; ophthalmic goods

(P-10391)
VSP HOLDING COMPANY INC
3333 Quality Dr, Rancho Cordova (95670-7985)
PHONE 916 851-5000
James Robinson Lynch, *CEO*
EMP: 58
SALES (est): 25.2MM **Privately Held**
SIC: 6324 Hospital & medical service plans

(P-10392)
WEST DERMATOLOGY MED MGT INC
101 E RdInds Blvd Ste 212, Redlands (92373)
P.O. Box 19098, Irvine (92623-9098)
PHONE 909 793-3000
J Robert West, *President*
Carmen Burgueno, *Office Mgr*
Matthew J Smith, *Physician Asst*
Donna O'Donell, *Manager*
EMP: 140
SALES (est): 36.7MM **Privately Held**
SIC: 6324 Hospital & medical service plans

6331 Fire, Marine & Casualty Insurance

(P-10393)
AAA NORTHERN CAL NEV & UTAH
1900 Powell St Ste 1200, Emeryville (94608-1814)
PHONE 510 596-3669
Paul Gaffney, *President*
Siobhan McFeeney, *CFO*
Lakshmi Tal, *Admin Sec*
Mike Cordova, *Controller*
Linette Alexander, *Exec Sec*
EMP: 400

6331 - Fire, Marine & Casualty Insurance County (P-10394)

SALES (est): 254.2MM **Privately Held**
SIC: **6331** 8699 Automobile insurance; automobile owners' association

(P-10394)
AAA TRAVEL
1650 S Delaware St, San Mateo (94402-2623)
PHONE..................................650 572-5600
Monica Iskander, *Manager*
EMP: 50
SALES (est): 3.8MM **Privately Held**
SIC: **6331** Automobile insurance

(P-10395)
ALLIANZ GLOBL RISKS US INSUR (DH)
2350 W Empire Ave, Burbank (91504-3350)
P.O. Box 7780 (91510-7780)
PHONE..................................818 260-7500
Hugh Burgess, *CEO*
William Welbourn, *COO*
Randy Renn, *CFO*
Jon Downey, *Senior VP*
Edwin Van Zijll, *Vice Pres*
EMP: 175
SQ FT: 20,000
SALES (est): 415.7MM **Privately Held**
SIC: **6331** Property damage insurance; fire, marine & casualty insurance & carriers; workers' compensation insurance
HQ: Fireman's Fund Insurance Company
777 San Marin Dr Ste 2160
Novato CA 94945
415 899-2000

(P-10396)
ALLIANZ UNDERWRITERS INSUR CO
Also Called: Allianz Globl Corp & Specialty
2350 W Empire Ave, Burbank (91504-3350)
PHONE..................................818 260-7500
Fax: 818 260-7207
Paul Yun, *Vice Pres*
Ruth-Ann Dudik, *Vice Pres*
John E Dewitt, *Executive*
Dina Tayeh, *Executive Asst*
Perry Canning, *Technology*
EMP: 86
SALES (est): 54MM **Privately Held**
WEB: www.azoa.com
SIC: **6331** Fire, marine & casualty insurance
HQ: Allianz Of America, Inc.
55 Greens Farms Rd Ste 1
Westport CT 06880
203 221-8500

(P-10397)
ALLSTATE INSURANCE COMPANY
21950 Copley Dr Ste 130, Diamond Bar (91765-4461)
PHONE..................................909 612-5504
Thomas J Wilson, *Ch of Bd*
EMP: 1005
SALES (corp-wide): 35.6B **Publicly Held**
SIC: **6331** 6351 Fire, marine & casualty insurance: stock; automobile insurance; property damage insurance; mortgage guarantee insurance
HQ: Allstate Insurance Company
2775 Sanders Rd
Northbrook IL 60062
847 402-5000

(P-10398)
AMERICAN AUTOMOBILE
Also Called: Csaa Insurance AAA
1500 Farmers Ln, Santa Rosa (95405-7526)
P.O. Box 2906 (95405-0906)
PHONE..................................707 566-4000
Fax: 707 573-9221
Al Holcomb, *Branch Mgr*
Celia Carsner, *Sales Staff*
EMP: 125
SALES (corp-wide): 1.1B **Privately Held**
WEB: www.californiastateautomobileassociation.c
SIC: **6331** 4724 6311 Automobile insurance; tourist agency arranging transport, lodging & car rental; life insurance

PA: American Automobile Association Of Northern California, Nevada & Utah
1900 Powell St Ste 1200
Emeryville CA 94608
800 922-8228

(P-10399)
AMERICAN HOME ASSURANCE CO
777 S Figueroa St Ste 300, Los Angeles (90017-5801)
PHONE..................................213 689-3500
Lynn Schwertner, *Branch Mgr*
Chris Jacques, *Finance Dir*
EMP: 300
SALES (corp-wide): 58.3B **Publicly Held**
WEB: www.americanhomeassuranceco.com
SIC: **6331** 7371 Fire, marine & casualty insurance; custom computer programming services
HQ: American Home Assurance Co Inc
70 Pine St Fl 1
New York NY 10005
212 770-7000

(P-10400)
AMERICAN INSURANCE COMPANY INC
1465 N Mcdowell Blvd, Petaluma (94954-6516)
PHONE..................................415 899-2000
Mike Larocco, *President*
Susan Etchell, *Asst Treas*
EMP: 4400
SALES (est): 329.7MM **Privately Held**
SIC: **6331** Fire, marine & casualty insurance
PA: Allianz Se
Koniginstr. 28
Munchen 80802
893 800-0

(P-10401)
AMICA MUTUAL INSURANCE COMPANY
3200 Park Center Dr # 650, Costa Mesa (92626-7163)
PHONE..................................877 972-6422
Fax: 562 444-3166
Robert Mc Girr, *Principal*
EMP: 60
SALES (corp-wide): 1.6B **Privately Held**
WEB: www.amica.com
SIC: **6331** Fire, marine & casualty insurance: mutual
PA: Amica Mutual Insurance Company
100 Amica Way
Lincoln RI 02865
800 992-6422

(P-10402)
ARROWHEAD GEN INSUR AGCY INC (DH)
701 B St Ste 2100, San Diego (92101-8197)
PHONE..................................619 881-8600
Chris L Walker, *CEO*
Peter C Arrowsmith, *General Ptnr*
Steve Boyd, *President*
Wendy Castelo, *President*
Robert T Kingsley, *President*
EMP: 240
SQ FT: 74,000
SALES (est): 186MM
SALES (corp-wide): 1.6B **Publicly Held**
SIC: **6331** 6411 Automobile insurance; insurance agents, brokers & service
HQ: Arrowhead Management Company
701 B St Ste 2100
San Diego CA 92101
800 669-1889

(P-10403)
CA STE ATOM ASSOC INTR-INS BUR
Also Called: Via Magazine
150 Van Ness Ave, San Francisco (94102-5208)
PHONE..................................415 565-2012
Fax: 415 565-4516
Kent Evans, *Branch Mgr*
Paula Downey, *CFO*
Ingrid Lamar, *Senior VP*
Brooke Smith, *Info Tech Dir*

Carey Powell, *Engineer*
EMP: 2000
SALES (corp-wide): 1.1B **Privately Held**
WEB: www.viamagazine.com
SIC: **6331** 2721 Automobile insurance; property damage insurance; magazines: publishing & printing
HQ: California State Automobile Association Inter-Insurance Bureau
1276 S California Blvd
Walnut Creek CA 94596
925 287-7600

(P-10404)
CA STE ATOM ASSOC INTR-INS BUR
Also Called: AAA
1650 S Delaware St, San Mateo (94402-2623)
PHONE..................................650 572-5600
Fax: 650 572-5692
Rita Timewell, *Manager*
Sunil Parekh, *Agent*
Kathy Lemon, *Consultant*
EMP: 100
SALES (corp-wide): 1.1B **Privately Held**
WEB: www.viamagazine.com
SIC: **6331** 6411 Automobile insurance; property & casualty insurance agent
HQ: California State Automobile Association Inter-Insurance Bureau
1276 S California Blvd
Walnut Creek CA 94596
925 287-7600

(P-10405)
CALIFORNIA AUTOMOBILE INSUR CO
Also Called: Cai Company
555 W Imperial Hwy, Brea (92821-4802)
P.O. Box 1150 (92822-1150)
PHONE..................................714 232-8669
George Joseph, *President*
Leo Lam, *CFO*
Diaddezio Franco, *Technology*
EMP: 800
SQ FT: 80,000
SALES (est): 526.9MM
SALES (corp-wide): 3B **Publicly Held**
WEB: www.californiaautomobileinsurance-company.com
SIC: **6331** Automobile insurance
PA: Mercury General Corporation
4484 Wilshire Blvd
Los Angeles CA 90010
323 937-1060

(P-10406)
CALIFORNIA CAPITAL INSUR CO (PA)
Also Called: Capital Insurance Group
2300 Garden Rd, Monterey (93940-5326)
P.O. Box 3110 (93942-3110)
PHONE..................................831 233-5500
L Arnold Chatterton, *President*
Andrew Doll, *COO*
Davis Tyndall, *CFO*
Walter Benett, *Vice Pres*
John Halberstadt, *Vice Pres*
EMP: 142
SQ FT: 50,000
SALES (est): 200.7MM **Privately Held**
SIC: **6331** Fire, marine & casualty insurance & carriers; automobile insurance

(P-10407)
CALIFORNIA CASUALTY MGT CO (PA)
Also Called: California Casualty
1900 Almeda De Las Pulgas, San Mateo (94403-1298)
PHONE..................................650 574-4000
Carl B Brown, *Ch of Bd*
Joseph L Volponi, *President*
Michael Ray, *CFO*
James R Englese, *Senior VP*
Mike McCormick, *Vice Pres*
EMP: 135
SALES: 127.5MM **Privately Held**
SIC: **6331** 8741 Reciprocal interinsurance exchanges: fire, marine, casualty; management services

(P-10408)
CALIFORNIA STATE AUTOMOBILE (HQ)
Also Called: Triple A
1276 S California Blvd, Walnut Creek (94596-5123)
P.O. Box 22221, Oakland (94623-2221)
PHONE..................................925 287-7600
James R Pouliot, *CEO*
Paula Downey, *President*
Murat Erdem, *Vice Pres*
John Richmond, *Vice Pres*
Leeann Bethel, *Executive Asst*
EMP: 1600
SQ FT: 400,000
SALES (est): 1B
SALES (corp-wide): 1.1B **Privately Held**
WEB: www.viamagazine.com
SIC: **6331** Automobile insurance
PA: American Automobile Association Of Northern California, Nevada & Utah
1900 Powell St Ste 1200
Emeryville CA 94608
800 922-8228

(P-10409)
CALIFORNIA STATE AUTOMOBILE
Also Called: Triple A Insurance
908 Pleasant Grove Blvd, Roseville (95678-6126)
PHONE..................................916 472-2701
Richard Purvis, *Principal*
Helmer Dara, *Sales Staff*
Bradley Miller, *Sales Staff*
EMP: 50
SALES (corp-wide): 1.1B **Privately Held**
WEB: www.viamagazine.com
SIC: **6331** Automobile insurance
HQ: California State Automobile Association Inter-Insurance Bureau
1276 S California Blvd
Walnut Creek CA 94596
925 287-7600

(P-10410)
CALIFRNIA CSLTY INDEMNITY EXCH (PA)
1900 Almeda De Las Pulgas, San Mateo (94403-1222)
PHONE..................................650 574-4000
Thomas R Brown, *Chairman*
Mike Ray, *CFO*
Mark Kvamme, *Bd of Directors*
Julie Schillings, *Assoc VP*
Thomas Weatherford, *Exec VP*
EMP: 130 EST: 1914
SQ FT: 90,000
SALES: 169MM **Privately Held**
SIC: **6331** Workers' compensation insurance; automobile insurance; property damage insurance; fire, marine & casualty insurance & carriers

(P-10411)
COMMERCIAL CARRIERS INSUR AGCY
12641 166th St, Cerritos (90703-2135)
PHONE..................................562 404-4900
Charles J Escalante, *President*
Henry H Escalante, *Ch of Bd*
Tim Hanst, *COO*
Shannon S Walker, *Treasurer*
Helen M Escalante, *Admin Sec*
EMP: 220 EST: 1979
SQ FT: 16,000
SALES (est): 89MM
SALES (corp-wide): 12.4B **Privately Held**
WEB: www.cciainsurance.com
SIC: **6331** Fire, marine & casualty insurance
HQ: Meadowbrook, Inc.
26255 American Dr
Southfield MI 48034
248 358-1100

(P-10412)
COMPWEST INSURANCE COMPANY
3 Hutton Cntre Dr Ste 550, Santa Ana (92707)
PHONE..................................714 641-9500
Ron Field, *Branch Mgr*
EMP: 67

PRODUCTS & SERVICES SECTION

6331 - Fire, Marine & Casualty Insurance County (P-10431)

SALES (corp-wide): 54MM **Privately Held**
SIC: 6331 Reciprocal interinsurance exchanges: fire, marine, casualty
PA: Compwest Insurance Company Inc
250 Montgomery St Ste 900
San Francisco CA 94104
415 593-5100

(P-10413)
FACTORY MUTUAL INSURANCE CO
Also Called: FM Global
1333 N Calif Blvd Ste 200, Walnut Creek (94596-4559)
PHONE..................925 934-2200
Andrew Scanlon, *Branch Mgr*
Monique Modelo, *Admin Mgr*
Leslie Warren, *Admin Asst*
Damion McGee, *Technology*
Malcolm Doiron, *Engineer*
EMP: 109
SALES (corp-wide): 4B **Privately Held**
SIC: 6331 6411 Fire, marine & casualty insurance; insurance agents, brokers & service
PA: Factory Mutual Insurance Co
270 Central Ave
Johnston RI 02919
401 275-3000

(P-10414)
FACTORY MUTUAL INSURANCE CO
Also Called: FM Global
6320 Canoga Ave Ste 1100, Woodland Hills (91367-2578)
P.O. Box 9270, Van Nuys (91409-9270)
PHONE..................818 227-2200
Neal Bear, *Vice Pres*
David Thoman, *Vice Pres*
Boris Gutman, *Engineer*
John Labanieh, *Engineer*
Antonio Braga, *Sales Staff*
EMP: 100
SALES (corp-wide): 4B **Privately Held**
SIC: 6331 Fire, marine & casualty insurance
PA: Factory Mutual Insurance Co
270 Central Ave
Johnston RI 02919
401 275-3000

(P-10415)
FARMERS GROUP INC (HQ)
Also Called: Farmers Insurance
6301 Owensmouth Ave, Woodland Hills (91367-2216)
P.O. Box 2450, Grand Rapids MI (49501-2450)
PHONE..................323 932-3200
Fax: 323 937-8914
Jeff Dailey, *CEO*
Steve Boshoven, *President*
Tony Desantis, *President*
Mhayse Samalya, *President*
Scott Lindquist, *CFO*
EMP: 2100 **EST:** 1927
SALES (est): 11.1B
SALES (corp-wide): 62B **Privately Held**
WEB: www.farmers.com
SIC: 6331 Automobile insurance; reciprocal interinsurance exchanges: fire, marine, casualty
PA: Zurich Insurance Group Ag
Zurich Versicherungs-Gesellschaft Ag
ZUrich ZH 8002
446 252-525

(P-10416)
FIREMANS FUND INSURANCE CO (HQ)
777 San Marin Dr Ste 2160, Novato (94945-1352)
PHONE..................415 899-2000
Fax: 415 899-2036
Gary Bhojwani, *Ch of Bd*
Antonio Derossi, *COO*
Bruce Petersen, *COO*
Kevin Walker, *CFO*
Robyn Hahn, *Chief Mktg Ofcr*
▲ **EMP:** 2242 **EST:** 1864
SQ FT: 240,000
SALES (est): 8.8B **Privately Held**
WEB: www.firemansfund.com
SIC: 6331 6351 6321 Fire, marine & casualty insurance & carriers; property damage insurance; fire, marine & casualty insurance: stock; workers' compensation insurance; surety insurance; credit & other financial responsibility insurance; liability insurance; reinsurance carriers, accident & health
PA: Allianz Se
Koniginstr. 28
Munchen 80802
893 800-0

(P-10417)
FIREMANS FUND INSURANCE CO
7555 N Palm Ave Ste 108, Fresno (93711-3361)
PHONE..................559 435-5050
Fax: 559 436-2238
Mark Tindle, *Branch Mgr*
EMP: 50 **Privately Held**
WEB: www.firemansfund.com
SIC: 6331 Property damage insurance
HQ: Fireman's Fund Insurance Company
777 San Marin Dr Ste 2160
Novato CA 94945
415 899-2000

(P-10418)
FIREMANS FUND INSURANCE CO
3100 Zinfandel Dr Ste 240, Rancho Cordova (95670-6064)
PHONE..................916 852-4500
Fax: 916 852-4672
Elaine Braddock, *Branch Mgr*
EMP: 180 **Privately Held**
WEB: www.firemansfund.com
SIC: 6331 6351 6311 Property damage insurance; automobile insurance; surety insurance; life insurance
HQ: Fireman's Fund Insurance Company
777 San Marin Dr Ste 2160
Novato CA 94945
415 899-2000

(P-10419)
FIREMANS FUND INSURANCE CO
9275 Sky Park Ct Ste 450, San Diego (92123-4314)
P.O. Box 85920 (92186-5920)
PHONE..................858 492-3019
Kelly Rauch, *Principal*
Scott Carroll, *Program Dir*
Ken Burke, *Manager*
Ron Jones, *Manager*
EMP: 131 **Privately Held**
WEB: www.firemansfund.com
SIC: 6331 Property damage insurance
HQ: Fireman's Fund Insurance Company
777 San Marin Dr Ste 2160
Novato CA 94945
415 899-2000

(P-10420)
FIREMANS FUND INSURANCE CO
3100 Zinfandel Dr Ste 240, Rancho Cordova (95670-6064)
PHONE..................949 255-1981
Steve Sampson, *Manager*
EMP: 90 **Privately Held**
WEB: www.firemansfund.com
SIC: 6331 Property damage insurance
HQ: Fireman's Fund Insurance Company
777 San Marin Dr Ste 2160
Novato CA 94945
415 899-2000

(P-10421)
FIREMANS FUND INSURANCE CO
2350 W Empire Ave Ste 200, Burbank (91504-3350)
PHONE..................818 953-6533
Karmyn Downs, *Manager*
EMP: 206 **Privately Held**
WEB: www.firemansfund.com
SIC: 6331 Property damage insurance
HQ: Fireman's Fund Insurance Company
777 San Marin Dr Ste 2160
Novato CA 94945
415 899-2000

(P-10422)
FRANK GATES SERVICE COMPANY
2400 E Katella Ave # 650, Anaheim (92806-5974)
PHONE..................800 994-4611
Fax: 714 978-1651
Gary Graham, *Manager*
Nancy Neely, *Accountant*
EMP: 60
SALES (corp-wide): 4.3B **Privately Held**
WEB: www.fgsc.com
SIC: 6331 Workers' compensation insurance
HQ: The Frank Gates Service Company
5000 Bradenton Ave # 100
Dublin OH 43017
614 793-8000

(P-10423)
GLENN E PORTER
3955 Coffee Rd, Bakersfield (93308-5024)
PHONE..................661 615-1500
Glenn E Porter, *Principal*
EMP: 50
SALES (est): 4.6MM **Privately Held**
SIC: 6331 Property damage insurance

(P-10424)
GOLDEN EAGLE INSURANCE CORP (DH)
525 B St Ste 1300, San Diego (92101-4421)
P.O. Box 85826 (92186-5826)
PHONE..................619 744-6000
Fax: 619 744-6300
J Paul Condrin III, *CEO*
Frank J Kotarba, *President*
Robert Kennedy, *Treasurer*
Shannon Griepsma, *Vice Pres*
Dennis Levesque, *Vice Pres*
EMP: 250 **EST:** 1997
SALES (est): 132.7MM
SALES (corp-wide): 37.6B **Privately Held**
SIC: 6331 Fire, marine & casualty insurance; property damage insurance
HQ: Liberty Mutual Insurance Company
175 Berkeley St
Boston MA 02116
617 357-9500

(P-10425)
GREAT AMERICAN INSURANCE CO
5750 Wilshire Blvd 360, Los Angeles (90036-3697)
PHONE..................323 937-8600
Bob Nagaishi, *Branch Mgr*
EMP: 100
SALES (corp-wide): 6.1B **Publicly Held**
SIC: 6331 Fire, marine & casualty insurance
HQ: Great American Insurance Company
301 E 4th St Ste 2800
Cincinnati OH 45202
513 369-5000

(P-10426)
GREAT AMERICAN INSURANCE CO
725 S Figueroa St # 3400, Los Angeles (90017-5434)
PHONE..................213 430-4300
Thom Smith, *Division Pres*
Rocio Garcia, *Division Mgr*
Mike Ducheny, *Info Tech Mgr*
Vicki Green, *Analyst*
Dave Levine, *Corp Counsel*
EMP: 142
SALES (corp-wide): 6.1B **Publicly Held**
SIC: 6331 Fire, marine & casualty insurance
HQ: Great American Insurance Company
301 E 4th St Ste 2800
Cincinnati OH 45202
513 369-5000

(P-10427)
HARTFORD CASUALTY INSURANCE CO
595 Market St Ste 500, San Francisco (94105-3483)
PHONE..................415 836-4800
William Reynolds, *Manager*
Patricia Pfeifer, *Manager*
EMP: 600
SALES (corp-wide): 18.3B **Publicly Held**
SIC: 6331 Fire, marine & casualty insurance: mutual; property damage insurance
HQ: Hartford Casualty Insurance Company
690 Asylum Ave
Hartford CT 06155
860 547-5000

(P-10428)
HERITAGE INDEMNITY COMPANY
23 Pasteur, Irvine (92618-3816)
PHONE..................303 987-5500
Adam Pope, *President*
EMP: 80
SALES (est): 5.2MM **Privately Held**
SIC: 6331 Automobile insurance

(P-10429)
ICW GROUP HOLDINGS INC (PA)
11455 El Camino Real, San Diego (92130-2088)
P.O. Box 85563 (92186-5563)
PHONE..................858 350-2400
Fax: 858 350-2699
Kevin M Prior, *CEO*
Ernest Rady, *Ch of Bd*
Sariborz Rostamian, *Treasurer*
John Gustafson, *Vice Pres*
James Senior, *Vice Pres*
EMP: 91
SQ FT: 160,000
SALES (est): 473.2MM **Privately Held**
SIC: 6331 6411 Fire, marine & casualty insurance & carriers; insurance brokers

(P-10430)
INSURANCE COMPANY OF WEST (HQ)
Also Called: I C W
15025 Innovation Dr, San Diego (92128-3455)
P.O. Box 85563 (92186-5563)
PHONE..................858 350-2400
Kevin Prior, *President*
Ernest Rady, *Ch of Bd*
Stacey McAdam, *President*
H Michael Freet, *Treasurer*
Michael H Freet, *Treasurer*
EMP: 146
SQ FT: 150,000
SALES (est): 335.1MM
SALES (corp-wide): 473.2MM **Privately Held**
SIC: 6331 Fire, marine & casualty insurance; property damage insurance
PA: Icw Group Holdings, Inc.
11455 El Camino Real
San Diego CA 92130
858 350-2400

(P-10431)
KRAMER-WILSON COMPANY INC (PA)
Also Called: Century National
6345 Balboa Blvd Ste 190, Encino (91316-1515)
P.O. Box 3999, North Hollywood (91609-0599)
PHONE..................818 760-0880
Fax: 818 519-1526
Weldon Wilson, *CEO*
Kevin Wilson, *President*
Daniel Sherrin, *CFO*
Mary Ann Wagner, *Admin Sec*
Judy Osbourn, *Financial Exec*
EMP: 240
SQ FT: 41,000
SALES (est): 233.8MM **Privately Held**
WEB: www.cnico.com
SIC: 6331 Fire, marine & casualty insurance & carriers

6331 - Fire, Marine & Casualty Insurance County (P-10432)

(P-10432)
LIBERTY MUTUAL INSURANCE CO
222 N Sepulveda Blvd # 2300, El Segundo (90245-5648)
PHONE..................................310 316-9428
Lynnean Chisom, *Branch Mgr*
Josh Scott, *Agent*
EMP: 110
SALES (corp-wide): 37.6B **Privately Held**
SIC: 6331 Fire, marine & casualty insurance
HQ: Liberty Mutual Insurance Company
175 Berkeley St
Boston MA 02116
617 357-9500

(P-10433)
LIBERTY MUTUAL INSURANCE CO
101 Mission St Ste 740, San Francisco (94105-1737)
PHONE..................................415 957-1175
Fax: 415 957-1167
Gary Countryman, *Ch of Bd*
Andrew Padova, *Regl Sales Mgr*
EMP: 150
SALES (corp-wide): 37.6B **Privately Held**
WEB: www.libertymutual.com
SIC: 6331 Fire, marine & casualty insurance
HQ: Liberty Mutual Insurance Company
175 Berkeley St
Boston MA 02116
617 357-9500

(P-10434)
LIBERTY MUTUAL INSURANCE CO
13405 Folsom Blvd Ste 200, Folsom (95630-4738)
PHONE..................................916 294-9518
Fax: 916 294-9851
Charles Frazier, *Principal*
EMP: 107
SALES (corp-wide): 37.6B **Privately Held**
SIC: 6331 Fire, marine & casualty insurance
HQ: Liberty Mutual Insurance Company
175 Berkeley St
Boston MA 02116
617 357-9500

(P-10435)
LIBERTY MUTUAL INSURANCE CO
3633 Inland Empire Blvd # 500, Ontario (91764-4946)
P.O. Box 51486 (91761-0086)
PHONE..................................909 476-6688
Candi Peterson, *Sales/Mktg Mgr*
Andrew Jones, *Sales Mgr*
Don Leary, *Manager*
Caitlin Malone, *Agent*
EMP: 100
SALES (corp-wide): 37.6B **Privately Held**
WEB: www.libertymutual.com
SIC: 6331 6311 Fire, marine & casualty insurance; life insurance carriers
HQ: Liberty Mutual Insurance Company
175 Berkeley St
Boston MA 02116
617 357-9500

(P-10436)
LIBERTY MUTUAL INSURANCE CO
790 The City Dr S Ste 200, Orange (92868-4941)
P.O. Box 11020 (92856-8120)
PHONE..................................714 937-1400
Fax: 714 634-1670
Linda Vanauran, *Manager*
Kimberly Kolach, *Executive*
Virginia Bennett, *Human Resources*
Steve White, *Manager*
Jim Zurawski, *Manager*
EMP: 200
SALES (corp-wide): 37.6B **Privately Held**
WEB: www.libertymutual.com
SIC: 6331 6311 Fire, marine & casualty insurance; life insurance

HQ: Liberty Mutual Insurance Company
175 Berkeley St
Boston MA 02116
617 357-9500

(P-10437)
LIBERTY MUTUAL INSURANCE CO
7600 N Palm Ave Ste 202, Fresno (93711-5520)
PHONE..................................559 435-2144
Chris Gennock, *Manager*
Phyllis Scharnick, *HR Admin*
Sharon Foster, *Opers Staff*
EMP: 200
SALES (corp-wide): 37.6B **Privately Held**
WEB: www.libertymutual.com
SIC: 6331 Fire, marine & casualty insurance
HQ: Liberty Mutual Insurance Company
175 Berkeley St
Boston MA 02116
617 357-9500

(P-10438)
LIBERTY MUTUAL INSURANCE CO
1750 Howe Ave Ste 450, Sacramento (95825-3368)
PHONE..................................916 564-1792
Natalie Dougherty, *Manager*
John Rusk, *Sales Staff*
Bryan Armstrong, *Agent*
Erin Burns, *Agent*
EMP: 340
SALES (corp-wide): 38.5B **Privately Held**
WEB: www.libertymutual.com
SIC: 6331 Fire, marine & casualty insurance
HQ: Liberty Mutual Insurance Company
175 Berkeley St
Boston MA 02116
617 357-9500

(P-10439)
MERCURY CASUALTY COMPANY (HQ)
Also Called: M C C
555 W Imperial Hwy, Brea (92821-4802)
P.O. Box 54600, Los Angeles (90054-0600)
PHONE..................................323 937-1060
Fax: 661 291-6494
Gabriel Tirador, *CEO*
George Joseph, *CEO*
Gus Tepper, *Exec VP*
David Yeager, *Controller*
EMP: 600
SALES (est): 2.9B
SALES (corp-wide): 3B **Publicly Held**
SIC: 6331 6351 Automobile insurance; warranty insurance, home
PA: Mercury General Corporation
4484 Wilshire Blvd
Los Angeles CA 90010
323 937-1060

(P-10440)
MERCURY GENERAL CORPORATION (PA)
4484 Wilshire Blvd, Los Angeles (90010-3710)
P.O. Box 36662 (90036-0662)
PHONE..................................323 937-1060
Fax: 323 857-7116
Gabriel Tirador, *President*
George Joseph, *Ch of Bd*
Theodore R Stalick, *CFO*
Christopher Graves, *Ch Invest Ofcr*
Robert Houlihan, *Officer*
EMP: 133
SQ FT: 41,000
SALES: 3B **Publicly Held**
WEB: www.mercuryinsurance.com
SIC: 6331 6411 Automobile insurance; property damage insurance; fire, marine & casualty insurance & carriers; insurance agents, brokers & service

(P-10441)
MERCURY INSURANCE COMPANY
555 W Imperial Hwy, Brea (92821-4839)
P.O. Box 1150 (92822-1150)
PHONE..................................714 671-6700
Fax: 714 255-5037
Gave Tirador, *President*
Kevin Cao, *Admin Asst*
Harish Kotian, *Technology*
Min Choi, *Sales Dir*
William Hildreth, *Director*
EMP: 89
SALES (corp-wide): 3B **Publicly Held**
WEB: www.coveryourhome.com
SIC: 6331 6411 Fire, marine & casualty insurance; insurance agents, brokers & service
HQ: Mercury Insurance Company
4484 Wilshire Blvd
Los Angeles CA 90010
323 937-1060

(P-10442)
MERCURY INSURANCE COMPANY
Also Called: Mercury Insurance Group
104 Woodmere Rd, Folsom (95630-4705)
PHONE..................................916 353-4859
Beverly Ramm, *Vice Pres*
EMP: 89
SALES (corp-wide): 3B **Publicly Held**
WEB: www.coveryourhome.com
SIC: 6331 6411 Fire, marine & casualty insurance; insurance claim processing, except medical
HQ: Mercury Insurance Company
4484 Wilshire Blvd
Los Angeles CA 90010
323 937-1060

(P-10443)
MERCURY INSURANCE COMPANY
Also Called: Mercury Insurance Broker
1433 Santa Monica Blvd, Santa Monica (90404-1709)
PHONE..................................310 451-4943
Ken Donaldson, *Owner*
EMP: 89
SALES (corp-wide): 3B **Publicly Held**
WEB: www.coveryourhome.com
SIC: 6331 6411 Fire, marine & casualty insurance; insurance agents, brokers & service
HQ: Mercury Insurance Company
4484 Wilshire Blvd
Los Angeles CA 90010
323 937-1060

(P-10444)
MERCURY INSURANCE COMPANY
1700 Greenbriar Ln, Brea (92821-5971)
PHONE..................................714 255-5000
Fax: 714 255-5096
Ken Kitzmiller, *Branch Mgr*
EMP: 96
SALES (corp-wide): 3B **Publicly Held**
SIC: 6331 Fire, marine & casualty insurance
HQ: Mercury Insurance Company
4484 Wilshire Blvd
Los Angeles CA 90010
323 937-1060

(P-10445)
MERCURY INSURANCE COMPANY (HQ)
4484 Wilshire Blvd, Los Angeles (90010-3710)
P.O. Box 54600 (90054-0600)
PHONE..................................323 937-1060
Fax: 323 857-4936
Gabe Tirador, *CEO*
Ted Stalick, *CFO*
George Joseph, *Chairman*
Allan Lubitz, *Senior VP*
Hossein Abby, *Vice Pres*
EMP: 160
SQ FT: 40,809
SALES (est): 3B
SALES (corp-wide): 3B **Publicly Held**
WEB: www.coveryourhome.com
SIC: 6331 Fire, marine & casualty insurance
PA: Mercury General Corporation
4484 Wilshire Blvd
Los Angeles CA 90010
323 937-1060

(P-10446)
MERCURY INSURANCE COMPANY
9635 Gran Rdge Dr Ste 200, San Diego (92123)
P.O. Box 82167 (92138-2167)
PHONE..................................858 694-4100
Randy Petro, *Manager*
EMP: 100
SALES (corp-wide): 3B **Publicly Held**
WEB: www.coveryourhome.com
SIC: 6331 6399 Fire, marine & casualty insurance; warranty insurance, automobile
HQ: Mercury Insurance Company
4484 Wilshire Blvd
Los Angeles CA 90010
323 937-1060

(P-10447)
MERCURY INSURANCE COMPANY
27200 Tourney Rd Ste 400, Valencia (91355-4997)
PHONE..................................661 291-6470
David Levy, *Manager*
Bill Davison, *Recruiter*
Robert Oglesby, *Marketing Staff*
EMP: 89
SALES (corp-wide): 3B **Publicly Held**
SIC: 6331 Fire, marine & casualty insurance
HQ: Mercury Insurance Company
4484 Wilshire Blvd
Los Angeles CA 90010
323 937-1060

(P-10448)
MERCURY INSURANCE SERVICES LLC
4484 Wilshire Blvd, Los Angeles (90010-3710)
PHONE..................................323 937-1060
Gabriel Tirador, *CEO*
David Yeager, *Controller*
Amee Otero, *Purch Mgr*
EMP: 4000
SALES: 2.7B
SALES (corp-wide): 3B **Publicly Held**
SIC: 6331 Fire, marine & casualty insurance; property damage insurance
HQ: Mercury Casualty Company
555 W Imperial Hwy
Brea CA 92821
323 937-1060

(P-10449)
METROMILE INC (PA)
690 Folsom St Ste 200, San Francisco (94107-1397)
PHONE..................................888 244-1702
Dan Preston, *CEO*
Joe Selsavage, *CFO*
Jose Mercado, *CTO*
EMP: 80
SALES (est): 76.6MM **Privately Held**
SIC: 6331 Automobile insurance

(P-10450)
MID CENTURY INSURANCE COMPANY
4680 Wilshire Blvd, Los Angeles (90010-3807)
P.O. Box 2478 (90051-0478)
PHONE..................................323 932-7116
Fax: 323 857-5989
Ron Coble, *Senior VP*
Bob Woudstra, *President*
Lyda Mizmoto, *Administration*
EMP: 250 **EST:** 1953
SQ FT: 210,000
SALES (est): 68.1MM
SALES (corp-wide): 6.3B **Privately Held**
SIC: 6331 6351 Automobile insurance; fidelity insurance
PA: Farmers Insurance Exchange
6301 Owensmouth Ave # 300
Woodland Hills CA 91367
323 932-3200

PRODUCTS & SERVICES SECTION
6331 - Fire, Marine & Casualty Insurance County (P-10467)

(P-10451)
NATIONAL GENERAL INSURANCE CO
Also Called: GMAC Insurance
3633 Inland Empire Blvd # 700, Ontario (91764-4922)
PHONE.................909 944-8085
Fax: 909 945-3040
Steven Wright, *Manager*
EMP: 86
SALES (corp-wide): 9.5B **Publicly Held**
SIC: **6331** Fire, marine & casualty insurance
HQ: National General Insurance Company
5757 Phantom Dr Ste 200
Hazelwood MO 63042
314 493-8000

(P-10452)
PACIFIC COMPENSATION INSUR CO
1 Baxter Way Ste 170, Westlake Village (91362-3819)
P.O. Box 5034, Thousand Oaks (91359-5034)
PHONE.................818 575-8500
Janet D Frank, *Ch of Bd*
Kris Mathis, *Senior VP*
Joe Cardenas, *Vice Pres*
Scot Corrigan, *Vice Pres*
Mark Webb, *Vice Pres*
EMP: 150
SALES (est): 106MM
SALES (corp-wide): 5B **Publicly Held**
WEB: www.edicwc.com
SIC: **6331** Workers' compensation insurance
HQ: Pacific Compensation Corporation
30301 Agoura Rd Ste 100
Agoura Hills CA 91301
818 575-8500

(P-10453)
REPUBLIC INDEMNITY CO AMER
100 Pine St Ste 1400, San Francisco (94111-5116)
P.O. Box 7878 (94120-7878)
PHONE.................415 981-3200
Fax: 415 954-1178
Darryl Yim, *Vice Pres*
Steven Ginn, *Vice Pres*
Leroy Huff, *Vice Pres*
Alexandre Levin, *Info Tech Dir*
Toshit Antani, *Engineer*
EMP: 100
SALES (corp-wide): 6.1B **Publicly Held**
SIC: **6331** Workers' compensation insurance
HQ: Republic Indemnity Company Of America
15821 Ventura Blvd # 370
Encino CA 91436
818 990-9860

(P-10454)
REPUBLIC INDEMNITY CO AMER (DH)
15821 Ventura Blvd # 370, Encino (91436-2936)
P.O. Box 20036 (91416-0036)
PHONE.................818 990-9860
Fax: 818 986-6559
Dwayne Marioni, *CEO*
Marion Chappel, *Senior VP*
Sheila Euper, *Admin Sec*
Debbie Billart, *CTO*
Stuart Haddock, *Sr Sys Analyst*
EMP: 129
SQ FT: 70,000
SALES: 790.2MM
SALES (corp-wide): 6.1B **Publicly Held**
SIC: **6331** Workers' compensation insurance
HQ: Pennsylvania Company Inc
1 E 4th St
Cincinnati OH 45202
513 579-2121

(P-10455)
REPUBLIC INDEMNITY COMPANY CAL
Also Called: RICA
15821 Ventura Blvd # 370, Encino (91436-2936)
P.O. Box 20036 (91416-0036)
PHONE.................818 990-9860
Dwayne T Marioni, *President*
Shila Euper, *Admin Sec*
EMP: 127
SALES (est): 6.9MM
SALES (corp-wide): 6.1B **Publicly Held**
SIC: **6331** Fire, marine & casualty insurance
HQ: Republic Indemnity Company Of America
15821 Ventura Blvd # 370
Encino CA 91436
818 990-9860

(P-10456)
RESIDENCE MUTUAL INSURANCE CO
2172 Dupont Dr Ste 220, Irvine (92612-1359)
P.O. Box 6019, Agoura Hills (91376-6019)
PHONE.................949 724-9402
Joe Crail, *President*
Michael Hardy, *CFO*
Juliana Eramela, *Administration*
Paul Calvet, *Info Tech Mgr*
Carmen Estrada, *Manager*
EMP: 65
SQ FT: 35,000
SALES: 27.1MM **Privately Held**
SIC: **6331** Property damage insurance

(P-10457)
RICHARD J MENDOZA INC
501 2nd St Ste 330, San Francisco (94107-4131)
PHONE.................415 644-0180
Jeff Pallesen, *President*
Todd George, *COO*
EMP: 95 EST: 2001
SALES (est): 14.9MM
SALES (corp-wide): 154.6MM **Publicly Held**
SIC: **6331** Fire, marine & casualty insurance
PA: Nv5 Global, Inc.
200 S Park Rd Ste 350
Hollywood FL 33021
954 495-2112

(P-10458)
ROYAL SPECIALTY UNDWRT INC
Also Called: Rsui Group
15303 Ventura Blvd # 500, Sherman Oaks (91403-3110)
PHONE.................818 922-6700
Fax: 818 922-6699
Christine Chinen, *Administration*
Nancy Murphy, *Vice Pres*
Melanie Stevenson, *Vice Pres*
Ron Cholaj, *Controller*
Mike Wayman, *Assistant VP*
EMP: 75
SALES (corp-wide): 5B **Publicly Held**
SIC: **6331** 6411 Fire, marine & casualty insurance; insurance agents, brokers & service
HQ: Royal Specialty Underwriting, Inc.
945 E Paces Ferry Rd Ne # 189
Atlanta GA 30326
404 231-2366

(P-10459)
SEQUOIA INSURANCE COMPANY (HQ)
31 Upper Ragsdale Dr, Monterey (93940-5771)
P.O. Box 1510 (93942-1510)
PHONE.................831 655-9612
Fax: 831 657-4509
Thomas G Moylan, *President*
Lezlee Beckstead, *Sr Software Eng*
EMP: 60

SALES (est): 48MM
SALES (corp-wide): 4.6B **Publicly Held**
WEB: www.sequoiains.com
SIC: **6331** Fire, marine & casualty insurance & carriers; property damage insurance
PA: Amtrust Financial Services, Inc.
59 Maiden Ln Fl 43
New York NY 10038
212 220-7120

(P-10460)
STATE COMPENSATION INSUR FUND (PA)
Also Called: State Fund
333 Bush St Fl 8, San Francisco (94104-2845)
P.O. Box 8192, Pleasanton (94588-8792)
PHONE.................888 782-8338
Fax: 415 565-3127
Vernon Steiner, *President*
Judy Girdenis, *COO*
Beatriz Sanchez, *COO*
Peter Guastamachio, *CFO*
Peter A Guastamachio, *CFO*
EMP: 75
SQ FT: 80,000
SALES: 1.6B **Privately Held**
WEB: www.scif.com
SIC: **6331** Workers' compensation insurance

(P-10461)
STATE COMPENSATION INSUR FUND
Also Called: Santa Ana District Office
1750 E 4th St Fl 3, Santa Ana (92705-3929)
PHONE.................714 565-5000
Fax: 714 565-5918
Liz Glidden, *Manager*
Katarina Holstein, *Executive*
Jerry Mullin, *District Mgr*
Mark Winsberg, *Sr Consultant*
Dina Camiolo, *Manager*
EMP: 270
SALES (corp-wide): 1.6B **Privately Held**
WEB: www.scif.com
SIC: **6331** 9651 Workers' compensation insurance; insurance commission, government;
PA: State Compensation Insurance Fund Inc
333 Bush St Fl 8
San Francisco CA 94104
888 782-8338

(P-10462)
STATE COMPENSATION INSUR FUND
Also Called: Bakersfield District Office
9801 Camino Media Ste 101, Bakersfield (93311-1312)
P.O. Box 21810 (93390-1810)
PHONE.................661 664-4000
Fax: 661 664-4101
Robert Kean, *Manager*
Mike La Deaux, *Executive*
Andy Jimenez, *District Mgr*
Karel Davis, *Supervisor*
EMP: 190
SALES (corp-wide): 1.6B **Privately Held**
WEB: www.scif.com
SIC: **6331** 9651 Workers' compensation insurance; insurance commission, government;
PA: State Compensation Insurance Fund Inc
333 Bush St Fl 8
San Francisco CA 94104
888 782-8338

(P-10463)
STATE COMPENSATION INSUR FUND
Also Called: Oakland District Office
2955 Peralta Oaks Ct, Oakland (94605-5319)
PHONE.................510 577-3000
Fax: 510 565-2667
Gary Dunlop, *Branch Mgr*
EMP: 200

SALES (corp-wide): 1.6B **Privately Held**
WEB: www.scif.com
SIC: **6331** 9651 6321 Workers' compensation insurance; insurance commission, government; ; accident & health insurance
PA: State Compensation Insurance Fund Inc
333 Bush St Fl 8
San Francisco CA 94104
888 782-8338

(P-10464)
STATE COMPENSATION INSUR FUND
Also Called: San Jose District Office
333 W San Carlos St # 950, San Jose (95110-2734)
PHONE.................888 782-8338
Fax: 408 363-7866
Jerry Madden, *Manager*
Cassie L Ortega, *Office Mgr*
Dory Clark, *Administration*
John Valenzuela, *Administration*
EMP: 210
SALES (corp-wide): 1.6B **Privately Held**
WEB: www.scif.com
SIC: **6331** 9651 Workers' compensation insurance; insurance commission, government;
PA: State Compensation Insurance Fund Inc
333 Bush St Fl 8
San Francisco CA 94104
888 782-8338

(P-10465)
STATE COMPENSATION INSUR FUND
Also Called: Redding District Office
364 Knollcrest Dr, Redding (96002-0175)
P.O. Box 496049 (96049-6049)
PHONE.................888 782-8338
Fax: 530 223-7044
Michael Labeaux, *Manager*
David Olsen, *Analyst*
Dorothy Stewart, *Analyst*
Cynthia Martin, *Corp Counsel*
EMP: 170
SALES (corp-wide): 1.6B **Privately Held**
WEB: www.scif.com
SIC: **6331** 9651 Workers' compensation insurance; regulation, miscellaneous commercial sectors;
PA: State Compensation Insurance Fund Inc
333 Bush St Fl 8
San Francisco CA 94104
888 782-8338

(P-10466)
STATE COMPENSATION INSUR FUND
Also Called: San Diego District Office
10105 Pacific Hgts Blvd, San Diego (92121-4249)
PHONE.................888 782-8338
Fax: 858 552-7110
Lisa Middleton, *Manager*
Laurie Razo, *Supervisor*
EMP: 350
SALES (corp-wide): 1.6B **Privately Held**
WEB: www.scif.com
SIC: **6331** 9651 Workers' compensation insurance; insurance commission, government;
PA: State Compensation Insurance Fund Inc
333 Bush St Fl 8
San Francisco CA 94104
888 782-8338

(P-10467)
STATE COMPENSATION INSUR FUND
Also Called: Fresno District Office
10 E Rver Pk Pl E Ste 110, Fresno (93720)
PHONE.................559 433-2700
Fax: 559 433-2651
John Putnam, *District Mgr*
Stephen A Ray, *Manager*
Monica Segura, *Underwriter*
EMP: 270

6331 - Fire, Marine & Casualty Insurance County (P-10468)

PRODUCTS & SERVICES SECTION

SALES (corp-wide): 1.6B **Privately Held**
WEB: www.scif.com
SIC: **6331** 9651 Workers' compensation insurance; insurance commission, government;
PA: State Compensation Insurance Fund Inc
333 Bush St Fl 8
San Francisco CA 94104
888 782-8338

(P-10468)
STATE COMPENSATION INSUR FUND
Also Called: State Fund Office
655 N Central Ave Ste 200, Glendale (91203-1424)
P.O. Box 92503, Los Angeles (90009-2503)
PHONE.................................213 576-7335
Linda Hoban, *Manager*
Margaret Chu, *Assistant*
EMP: 185
SALES (corp-wide): 1.6B **Privately Held**
WEB: www.scif.com
SIC: **6331** 9651 Workers' compensation insurance; insurance commission, government;
PA: State Compensation Insurance Fund Inc
333 Bush St Fl 8
San Francisco CA 94104
888 782-8338

(P-10469)
STATE COMPENSATION INSUR FUND
Also Called: Stockton District Office
3247 W March Ln Ste 110, Stockton (95219-2363)
PHONE.................................888 782-8338
Fax: 209 476-2750
Tom Clark, *Manager*
Karen Ratto, *Regional Mgr*
Belinda Walker, *Manager*
EMP: 200
SALES (corp-wide): 1.6B **Privately Held**
WEB: www.scif.com
SIC: **6331** 9651 6411 Workers' compensation insurance; insurance commission, government; ; insurance agents, brokers & service
PA: State Compensation Insurance Fund Inc
333 Bush St Fl 8
San Francisco CA 94104
888 782-8338

(P-10470)
STATE COMPENSATION INSUR FUND
655 N Central Ave Ste 200, Glendale (91203-1424)
P.O. Box 92503, Los Angeles (90009-2503)
PHONE.................................323 266-5551
EMP: 185
SALES (corp-wide): 1.6B **Privately Held**
WEB: www.scif.com
SIC: **6331** 9651 Workers' compensation insurance; insurance commission, government
PA: State Compensation Insurance Fund Inc
333 Bush St Fl 8
San Francisco CA 94104
888 782-8338

(P-10471)
STATE COMPENSATION INSUR FUND
Also Called: Sacramento District Office
2275 Gateway Oaks Dr, Sacramento (95833-3224)
PHONE.................................916 924-5100
Gary Dunlap, *Manager*
Mike Ladeaux, *Manager*
Lari Nario, *Manager*
EMP: 325
SALES (corp-wide): 1.6B **Privately Held**
WEB: www.scif.com
SIC: **6331** 9651 Workers' compensation insurance; insurance commission, government;

PA: State Compensation Insurance Fund Inc
333 Bush St Fl 8
San Francisco CA 94104
888 782-8338

(P-10472)
STATE COMPENSATION INSUR FUND
Also Called: Los Angeles District Office
655 N Central Ave Ste 200, Glendale (91203-1424)
P.O. Box 65005, Fresno (93650-5005)
PHONE.................................888 782-8338
Fax: 818 291-7300
Linda Hoban, *Manager*
Michael Banks, *Manager*
Katarina Holstein, *Manager*
Yvette Montano-Anda, *Manager*
EMP: 185
SALES (corp-wide): 1.6B **Privately Held**
WEB: www.scif.com
SIC: **6331** 9651 6321 Workers' compensation insurance; insurance commission, government; ; accident & health insurance
PA: State Compensation Insurance Fund Inc
333 Bush St Fl 8
San Francisco CA 94104
888 782-8338

(P-10473)
STATE COMPENSATION INSUR FUND
Also Called: Eureka District Office
800 W Harris St Ste 37, Eureka (95503-3929)
PHONE.................................707 443-9721
Fax: 707 443-0644
Steve Mackey, *Branch Mgr*
EMP: 55
SALES (corp-wide): 1.6B **Privately Held**
WEB: www.scif.com
SIC: **6331** 9651 Workers' compensation insurance; insurance commission, government;
PA: State Compensation Insurance Fund Inc
333 Bush St Fl 8
San Francisco CA 94104
888 782-8338

(P-10474)
STATE COMPENSATION INSUR FUND
Also Called: Riverside District Office
6301 Day St, Riverside (92507-0902)
PHONE.................................888 782-8338
Fax: 951 653-1597
Barbara Katzka, *Manager*
Jamie Towner-Joyce, *Network Mgr*
Gil D Santos, *Chief Engr*
Laurie Coughenour, *Manager*
Maria Castaneda, *Supervisor*
EMP: 250
SALES (corp-wide): 1.6B **Privately Held**
WEB: www.scif.com
SIC: **6331** 9651 Workers' compensation insurance; insurance commission, government;
PA: State Compensation Insurance Fund Inc
333 Bush St Fl 8
San Francisco CA 94104
888 782-8338

(P-10475)
STATE COMPENSATION INSUR FUND
5880 Owens Dr, Pleasanton (94588-3900)
PHONE.................................925 523-5000
Patricia Smith, *Manager*
Joan Quintanilla, *Regional Mgr*
Jayakrishnan Nair, *Project Leader*
Krishna Vaidya, *Database Admin*
Florangel Bahrami, *Auditor*
EMP: 185
SALES (corp-wide): 1.6B **Privately Held**
WEB: www.scif.com
SIC: **6331** 9441 Workers' compensation insurance; administration of social & manpower programs;

PA: State Compensation Insurance Fund Inc
333 Bush St Fl 8
San Francisco CA 94104
888 782-8338

(P-10476)
STATE COMPENSATION INSUR FUND
5890 Owens Dr, Pleasanton (94588-3900)
PHONE.................................888 782-8338
Alicia Reyes, *Principal*
Teresa E Eng, *Manager*
EMP: 185
SALES (corp-wide): 1.6B **Privately Held**
SIC: **6331** Fire, marine & casualty insurance
PA: State Compensation Insurance Fund Inc
333 Bush St Fl 8
San Francisco CA 94104
888 782-8338

(P-10477)
STATE COMPENSATION INSUR FUND
Also Called: Los Angles Dst Off Policy Svcs
900 Corporate Center Dr, Monterey Park (91754-7618)
P.O. Box 65005, Fresno (93650-5005)
PHONE.................................323 266-5000
Fax: 323 574-2674
Joe Codron, *Officer*
Richard Whiting, *Info Tech Mgr*
Jerri Shaul, *Broker*
Jose Altamirano, *Opers Mgr*
Nick Cuevas, *Marketing Staff*
EMP: 150
SALES (corp-wide): 1.6B **Privately Held**
WEB: www.scif.com
SIC: **6331** 9651 Workers' compensation insurance; insurance commission, government;
PA: State Compensation Insurance Fund Inc
333 Bush St Fl 8
San Francisco CA 94104
888 782-8338

(P-10478)
TRISTAR INSURANCE GROUP INC (PA)
Also Called: Tristart Risk Management
100 Oceangate Ste 700, Long Beach (90802-4368)
PHONE.................................562 495-6600
Thomas J Veale, *President*
Denise J Cotter, *CFO*
Joseph McLaughlin, *Senior VP*
Mary Ann Lubeskie, *Vice Pres*
Richard D Thibault, *Vice Pres*
EMP: 700
SQ FT: 9,000
SALES (est): 401.3MM **Privately Held**
SIC: **6331** 8741 Workers' compensation insurance; management services

(P-10479)
UNITED SERVICES AUTO ASSN
2178 Vista Way Ste E5, Oceanside (92054-5678)
PHONE.................................760 757-1340
EMP: 1082
SALES (corp-wide): 24.3B **Privately Held**
SIC: **6331** Property damage insurance
PA: United Services Automobile Association
9800 Fredericksburg Rd
San Antonio TX 78288
210 498-2211

(P-10480)
WAWANESA GENERAL INSURANCE CO
Also Called: Wawanesa General Insurance
9050 Friars Rd Ste 200, San Diego (92108-5800)
P.O. Box 82867 (92138-2867)
PHONE.................................619 285-6020
Fax: 619 285-1544
Jeff Goy, *CEO*
Larry Smith, *CFO*
David Fitzgibbons, *Admin Sec*
David Johnson, *Info Tech Mgr*
Richard Foote, *Programmer Anys*
EMP: 500

SALES (est): 322.6MM
SALES (corp-wide): 2.6B **Privately Held**
SIC: **6331** Automobile insurance; property damage insurance
PA: Wawanesa Mutual Insurance Company, The
191 Broadway Suite 100
Winnipeg MB R3C 3
204 985-3811

(P-10481)
WESTERN GENERAL HOLDING CO (PA)
5230 Las Virgenes Rd # 100, Calabasas (91302-3448)
PHONE.................................818 880-9070
Robert M Ehrlich, *Ch of Bd*
Daniel Mallut, *President*
Marlene Kushner, *Admin Sec*
John Albanese, *Controller*
Mark Goldsmith, *VP Opers*
EMP: 240 EST: 1999
SQ FT: 51,000
SALES (est): 124.6MM **Privately Held**
SIC: **6331** Fire, marine & casualty insurance

(P-10482)
WESTERN GENERAL INSURANCE CO
5230 Las Virgenes Rd, Calabasas (91302-3448)
PHONE.................................818 880-9070
Fax: 818 880-0682
Robert M Ehrlich, *Ch of Bd*
John Albanese, *CFO*
Daniel Mallut, *Exec VP*
Marleen Kushner, *Admin Sec*
EMP: 165
SQ FT: 51,000
SALES (est): 83.2MM
SALES (corp-wide): 124.6MM **Privately Held**
SIC: **6331** Automobile insurance
PA: Western General Holding Co
5230 Las Virgenes Rd # 100
Calabasas CA 91302
818 880-9070

(P-10483)
WORKERS COMPENSATION (PA)
Also Called: WCIRB
1221 Broadway Ste 900, Oakland (94612-1995)
PHONE.................................415 777-0777
Fax: 415 227-0468
William Mudge, *President*
David Bellusci, *Senior VP*
Brenda Keys, *Senior VP*
Timothy Benjamin, *Vice Pres*
Ward Brooks, *Vice Pres*
EMP: 160
SQ FT: 31,000
SALES: 40.6MM **Privately Held**
SIC: **6331** Workers' compensation insurance

(P-10484)
WORKMENS AUTO INSURANCE CO
714 W Olympic Blvd # 800, Los Angeles (90015-1440)
PHONE.................................213 742-8700
Fax: 213 747-4699
Jeanette Shammas, *Ch of Bd*
Nicholas J Lannotti, *President*
Denise M Tyson, *President*
Shaukat Badani, *Vice Pres*
Carol Unger, *Admin Asst*
EMP: 100
SALES (est): 67.3MM **Privately Held**
SIC: **6331** Fire, marine & casualty insurance

(P-10485)
ZENITH INSURANCE COMPANY (DH)
Also Called: Zenith A Fairfax Company, The
21255 Califa St, Woodland Hills (91367-5021)
P.O. Box 9055, Van Nuys (91409-9055)
PHONE.................................818 713-1000
Fax: 818 592-0265
Stanley R Zax, *Ch of Bd*
Todd Cicero, *President*

PRODUCTS & SERVICES SECTION

6361 - Title Insurance County (P-10507)

Tara Flores, *President*
Jack D Miller, *President*
Kari Van Gundy, *CFO*
EMP: 400 **EST:** 1950
SQ FT: 120,000
SALES (est): 1.2B
SALES (corp-wide): 9.5B **Privately Held**
SIC: 6331 Workers' compensation insurance; automobile insurance; agricultural insurance; property damage insurance
HQ: Zenith National Insurance Corp.
21255 Califa St
Woodland Hills CA 91367
818 713-1000

(P-10486)
ZENITH INSURANCE COMPANY
7676 Hazard Center Dr # 1200, San Diego (92108-4517)
PHONE 619 299-6252
Fax: 619 278-3100
Brian Anderson, *Manager*
Dawne Pitts, *Marketing Mgr*
EMP: 53
SALES (corp-wide): 9.5B **Privately Held**
SIC: 6331 6211 Workers' compensation insurance; underwriters, security
HQ: Zenith Insurance Company
21255 Califa St
Woodland Hills CA 91367
818 713-1000

(P-10487)
ZURICH AMERICAN INSURANCE CO
777 S Figueroa St Ste 400, Los Angeles (90017-5802)
PHONE 213 270-0600
Andre Douglas, *Manager*
Stephen Penwright, *Manager*
EMP: 53
SALES (corp-wide): 62B **Privately Held**
SIC: 6331 Fire, marine & casualty insurance
HQ: Zurich American Insurance Company
1299 Zurich Way
Schaumburg IL 60173
800 987-3373

6351 Surety Insurance Carriers

(P-10488)
AIA HOLDINGS INC (PA)
Also Called: Associated Bond
26560 Agoura Rd Ste 100, Calabasas (91302-2015)
PHONE 818 222-4999
Fax: 818 449-7100
Brian N Nairin, *President*
Robert Kersnick, *COO*
Mark Francis, *CFO*
Mark Prygocki, *Treasurer*
Eric Granof, *Chief Mktg Ofcr*
EMP: 51
SQ FT: 8,000
SALES (est): 23.3MM **Privately Held**
WEB: www.aiasurety.com
SIC: 6351 Fidelity or surety bonding

(P-10489)
ARCH MORTGAGE INSURANCE CO
Pmi Plaza 3003 Oak Rd, Walnut Creek (94597)
PHONE 800 909-4264
David Gansberg, *President*
Chris Hovey, *COO*
Tom Jeter, *CFO*
Andy Cameron, *Exec VP*
Richard Izen, *Exec VP*
EMP: 60
SALES (est): 53.4MM **Privately Held**
SIC: 6351 Mortgage guarantee insurance
PA: Arch Capital Group Ltd
Waterloo House, Ground Floor
Penbroke
441 278-9245

(P-10490)
CAP-MPT (PA)
333 S Hope St Fl 8, Los Angeles (90071-3001)
PHONE 213 473-8600
Fax: 213 473-8774
Jim Weidner, *CEO*
Michael Wormley MD, *Ch of Bd*
John Donaldson, *CFO*
Nancy Brusegaard Johnson, *Senior VP*
Thomas Andre, *Vice Pres*
EMP: 140
SALES (est): 202.7MM **Privately Held**
SIC: 6351 Liability insurance

(P-10491)
DEVELOPERS SURETY INDEMNITY CO (DH)
Also Called: Insco Dico Group , The
17771 Cowan Ste 100, Irvine (92614-6044)
P.O. Box 19725 (92623-9725)
PHONE 949 263-3300
Walter Crowell, *President*
Harry C Crowell, *Ch of Bd*
Sam Zaza, *CFO*
David Rhodes, *Exec VP*
Dan Vincenti, *Vice Pres*
EMP: 70
SQ FT: 25,000
SALES (est): 42.5MM
SALES (corp-wide): 4.6B **Publicly Held**
SIC: 6351 Fidelity or surety bonding
HQ: Insco Insurance Services, Inc.
17771 Cowan Ste 100
Irvine CA 92614
949 797-9243

(P-10492)
DOCTORS COMPANY INSURANCE SVCS
185 Greenwood Rd, NAPA (94558-7540)
P.O. Box 2900 (94558-0900)
PHONE 707 226-0100
Manuel F Puebla, *Ch of Bd*
Jack Meyer, *President*
EMP: 300
SALES (est): 74.2MM
SALES (corp-wide): 473.1MM **Privately Held**
WEB: www.residentialsavingsmortgage.com
SIC: 6351 6331 Liability insurance; fire, marine & casualty insurance
PA: The Doctors' Company An Interinsurance Exchange
185 Greenwood Rd
Napa CA 94558
707 226-0100

(P-10493)
FIDELITY NAT HM WARRANTY CO
1850 Gateway Blvd Ste 400, Concord (94520-8446)
PHONE 925 356-0194
Bill Jensen, *Manager*
Vanessa Rice, *Sales Executive*
Audra Woods, *Assistant VP*
EMP: 150
SALES (corp-wide): 9.1B **Publicly Held**
WEB: www.fnhw.com
SIC: 6351 Warranty insurance, home
HQ: Fidelity National Home Warranty Company
2950 Buskirk Ave Ste 201
Walnut Creek CA

(P-10494)
INDEMNITY COMPANY CALIFORNIA (DH)
17771 Cowan Ste 100, Irvine (92614-6044)
P.O. Box 19725 (92623-9725)
PHONE 949 263-3300
Harry C Crowell, *Chairman*
Fern Haberman, *CFO*
Sam Zaza, *CFO*
Walter A Crowell, *Admin Sec*
Rahat Faghfoor, *Manager*
EMP: 71
SQ FT: 50,000
SALES (est): 9.8MM
SALES (corp-wide): 4.6B **Publicly Held**
SIC: 6351 Fidelity or surety bonding
HQ: Insco Insurance Services, Inc.
17771 Cowan Ste 100
Irvine CA 92614
949 797-9243

(P-10495)
NATIONAL SURETY CORPORATION
1465 N Mcdowell Blvd # 100, Petaluma (94954-6516)
PHONE 415 899-2000
Lori D Fouche, *CEO*
EMP: 1000
SALES (est): 151.3MM **Privately Held**
SIC: 6351 Surety insurance
HQ: Fireman's Fund Insurance Company
777 San Marin Dr Ste 2160
Novato CA 94945
415 899-2000

(P-10496)
NMI HOLDINGS INC
2100 Powell St Fl 12th, Emeryville (94608-1894)
PHONE 855 530-6642
Bradley M Shuster, *Ch of Bd*
John M Sherwood Jr, *President*
Glenn Farrell, *CFO*
Patrick L Mathis, *Exec VP*
Claudia J Merkle, *Exec VP*
EMP: 243
SQ FT: 47,000
SALES (est): 53.6MM **Privately Held**
SIC: 6351 Mortgage guarantee insurance

(P-10497)
XL SPECIALTY INSURANCE CORP
1340 Treat Blvd, Walnut Creek (94597-2101)
P.O. Box 8098 (94596-8098)
PHONE 925 942-6142
Jim Bily, *Assistant VP*
EMP: 70 **Privately Held**
SIC: 6351 Surety insurance
HQ: Xl Specialty Insurance Company
10 N Martingale Rd # 200
Schaumburg IL 60173
847 517-2990

6361 Title Insurance

(P-10498)
CALIFORNIA TITLE CO NTHRN CAL
1955 Hunts Ln Ste 102, San Bernardino (92408-3344)
PHONE 909 825-8800
Jim Sollami, *Manager*
EMP: 103
SALES (corp-wide): 160.8MM **Privately Held**
WEB: www.octitle.com
SIC: 6361 Title insurance
HQ: California Title Company Of Northern California
640 N Tustin Ave Ste 106
Santa Ana CA 92705
714 558-2836

(P-10499)
CALIFORNIA TITLE COMPANY
2365 Northside Dr Ste 250, San Diego (92108-2719)
PHONE 619 516-5227
Fax: 619 465-0958
Jim Waterman, *President*
Chuck Bishop, *Officer*
David Skarman, *Director*
Brian Poole, *Accounts Exec*
EMP: 65
SALES (corp-wide): 17.4MM **Privately Held**
SIC: 6361 Title insurance
PA: California Title Company
28202 Cabot Rd Ste 625
Laguna Niguel CA 92677
949 582-8709

(P-10500)
CHICAGO TITLE AND TRUST CO
535 N Brnd Blvrd Fl 3, Glendale (91203)
PHONE 818 548-0222
Fax: 818 550-3270
Mike Bossard, *Principal*
EMP: 50
SALES (corp-wide): 9.1B **Publicly Held**
SIC: 6361 Title insurance
HQ: Chicago Title And Trust Company
10 S La Salle St Ste 3100
Chicago IL 60603
312 223-2000

(P-10501)
CHICAGO TITLE COMPANY
701 B St Ste 1120, San Diego (92101-8103)
PHONE 619 230-6340
Madeline Lovejoy, *Principal*
Joe Goodman, *Principal*
Madeline G M. Lovejoy, *Principal*
EMP: 107 **EST:** 1984
SQ FT: 2,650
SALES (est): 25.4MM **Privately Held**
SIC: 6361 Title insurance

(P-10502)
CHICAGO TITLE COMPANY
725 S Figueroa St Ste 200, Los Angeles (90017-5403)
PHONE 213 488-4375
Maria Leal, *Supervisor*
Madeline Lovejoy, *Assistant VP*
EMP: 70
SALES (est): 22.3MM **Privately Held**
SIC: 6361 Title insurance

(P-10503)
CHICAGO TITLE COMPANY
7330 N Palm Ave Ste 101, Fresno (93711-5768)
PHONE 559 451-3700
Mark Barsotti, *Vice Pres*
EMP: 60
SQ FT: 10,000
SALES (est): 2.8MM **Privately Held**
SIC: 6361 Title insurance

(P-10504)
CHICAGO TITLE COMPANY
120 N Floral St, Visalia (93291-6202)
P.O. Box 1191 (93279-1191)
PHONE 559 733-3814
Scott Collins, *President*
EMP: 64
SALES (corp-wide): 9.1B **Publicly Held**
SIC: 6361 Title insurance
HQ: Chicago Title Insurance Company
4050 Calle Real
Santa Barbara CA 93110
805 565-6900

(P-10505)
CHICAGO TITLE INSURANCE CO
105 Lake Forest Way, Folsom (95630-4708)
PHONE 916 985-0300
Fax: 916 353-2380
Steve Siqueiros, *Manager*
EMP: 50
SALES (corp-wide): 9.1B **Publicly Held**
SIC: 6361 Title insurance
HQ: Chicago Title Insurance Company
4050 Calle Real
Santa Barbara CA 93110
805 565-6900

(P-10506)
CHICAGO TITLE INSURANCE CO
500 E Esplanade Dr # 102, Oxnard (93036-2110)
PHONE 805 656-1300
Fax: 805 658-2017
Mike Hollins, *Manager*
Mike Hollands, *General Mgr*
EMP: 60
SALES (corp-wide): 9.1B **Publicly Held**
SIC: 6361 Title insurance
HQ: Chicago Title Insurance Company
4050 Calle Real
Santa Barbara CA 93110
805 565-6900

(P-10507)
CHICAGO TITLE INSURANCE CO
316 W Mission Ave Ste 110, Escondido (92025-1731)
PHONE 760 546-1000
Jo A Lockard, *Branch Mgr*
EMP: 60
SALES (corp-wide): 9.1B **Publicly Held**
SIC: 6361 Title insurance

6361 - Title Insurance County (P-10508)

HQ: Chicago Title Insurance Company
4050 Calle Real
Santa Barbara CA 93110
805 565-6900

(P-10508)
CHICAGO TITLE INSURANCE CO
516 Gibson Dr Ste 200, Roseville (95678-5792)
PHONE..................................916 783-7195
Patty Harris, *Vice Pres*
Joanne Tessler, *Marketing Staff*
EMP: 293
SALES (corp-wide): 9.1B **Publicly Held**
SIC: 6361 Title insurance
HQ: Chicago Title Insurance Company
601 Riverside Ave
Jacksonville FL 32204

(P-10509)
CHICAGO TITLE INSURANCE CO (HQ)
4050 Calle Real, Santa Barbara (93110-3413)
PHONE..................................805 565-6900
Fax: 805 696-9578
Raymond R Quirk, *CEO*
William Halvorsen Jr, *President*
A Larry Sisk, *Treasurer*
Peter G Leemputte, *Vice Pres*
Andrea Hyatt, *Accounts Exec*
EMP: 150
SQ FT: 44,637
SALES (est): 400.7MM
SALES (corp-wide): 9.1B **Publicly Held**
SIC: 6361 Title insurance; real estate title insurance
PA: Fidelity National Financial, Inc.
601 Riverside Ave Fl 4
Jacksonville FL 32204
904 854-8100

(P-10510)
COMMONWEALTH LAND TITLE CO
6 Executive Cir Ste 100, Irvine (92614-6732)
PHONE..................................949 460-4500
Carl Brown, *CEO*
EMP: 100
SALES (corp-wide): 9.1B **Publicly Held**
WEB: www.laurabarnetthomes.com
SIC: 6361 Title insurance
HQ: Commonwealth Land Title Insurance Company
201 Cncourse Blvd Ste 200
Glen Allen VA 23059
904 854-8100

(P-10511)
CORINTHIAN TITLE COMPANY INC
5030 Camino De La Siesta, San Diego (92108-3116)
PHONE..................................619 299-4800
Robert Romano, *Co-CEO*
Michael Godwin, *COO*
Larry Vinti, *CFO*
Michelle Elkins, *Marketing Staff*
Chris Keach, *Marketing Staff*
EMP: 70
SQ FT: 6,000
SALES (est): 11MM **Privately Held**
SIC: 6361 Title insurance

(P-10512)
EQUITY TITLE COMPANY (DH)
425 W Broadway Ste 300, Glendale (91204-1219)
PHONE..................................818 291-4400
Fax: 818 547-9606
Jim Cossell, *President*
Kathy Yeko, *President*
Michael Valeri, *Officer*
Dindo De, *Vice Pres*
Corinne Holzman, *Vice Pres*
EMP: 80
SALES (est): 60.2MM
SALES (corp-wide): 5.7B **Publicly Held**
SIC: 6361 Title insurance
HQ: Title Resource Group Llc
3001 Leadenhall Rd
Mount Laurel NJ 08054
856 914-8500

(P-10513)
FEDELITY NATIONAL TITLE CO ORG
5000 Van Nuys Blvd 500, Sherman Oaks (91403-1793)
PHONE..................................818 758-6849
Richard Stine, *Principal*
EMP: 99 **EST:** 2010
SALES (est): 15.7MM **Privately Held**
SIC: 6361 Title insurance

(P-10514)
FIDELITY NAT TITLE INSUR CO (HQ)
3220 El Camino Real, Irvine (92602-1377)
PHONE..................................949 622-4600
Raymond R Quirk, *CEO*
William P Foley II, *Ch of Bd*
Frank Willey, *President*
Pat Stone, *COO*
Peter Sadowski, *Exec VP*
EMP: 150 **EST:** 1913
SALES (est): 189.1MM
SALES (corp-wide): 9.1B **Publicly Held**
WEB: www.fntic.com
SIC: 6361 8741 6541 6531 Real estate title insurance; management services; title abstract offices; escrow agent, real estate
PA: Fidelity National Financial, Inc.
601 Riverside Ave Fl 4
Jacksonville FL 32204
904 854-8100

(P-10515)
FIDELITY NATIONAL TITLE CO
42544 10th St W Ste E, Lancaster (93534-7079)
PHONE..................................818 881-7800
Cynthia L Fried, *President*
Madeline Barewald, *Assistant VP*
EMP: 50 **EST:** 1977
SALES (est): 14.7MM **Privately Held**
SIC: 6361 Real estate title insurance

(P-10516)
FIRST AMERICAN FINANCIAL CORP
Also Called: United General Title Insurance
231 E Alessandro Blvd, Riverside (92508-5084)
PHONE..................................909 376-4247
Thomas McCloud, *Branch Mgr*
EMP: 293 **Publicly Held**
SIC: 6361 Title insurance
PA: First American Financial Corporation
1 First American Way
Santa Ana CA 92707

(P-10517)
FIRST AMERICAN FINANCIAL CORP (PA)
1 First American Way, Santa Ana (92707-5913)
PHONE..................................714 250-3000
Fax: 714 800-4878
Dennis J Gilmore, *CEO*
Parker S Kennedy, *Ch of Bd*
George Livermore, *President*
Kathy Vian, *President*
Robert Lawson, *COO*
EMP: 137
SQ FT: 490,000
SALES: 5.1B **Publicly Held**
SIC: 6361 6351 Title insurance; surety insurance

(P-10518)
FIRST AMERICAN MORTGAGE SVCS
3 First American Way, Santa Ana (92707-5913)
PHONE..................................714 250-4210
Fax: 714 250-4665
Wes Mee, *President*
Jeanie Matten, *Senior VP*
Diana Vazquez, *Senior VP*
Matt Miller, *Vice Pres*
Robert Lay, *Senior Mgr*
EMP: 350
SALES (est): 134.2MM **Privately Held**
SIC: 6361 Title insurance

(P-10519)
FIRST AMERICAN TITLE COMPANY (HQ)
1 First American Way, Santa Ana (92707-5913)
PHONE..................................505 881-3300
Fax: 818 242-0196
Robert Schott, *President*
Ted Bigornia, *Officer*
Kimberly Delpolito, *Officer*
Tracy Eidler, *Officer*
Mila Wright, *Officer*
EMP: 230
SQ FT: 98,000
SALES (est): 291MM **Publicly Held**
WEB: www.fatcola.com
SIC: 6361 Real estate title insurance

(P-10520)
FIRST AMERICAN TITLE INSUR CO (HQ)
1 First American Way, Santa Ana (92707-5913)
P.O. Box 267 (92702-0267)
PHONE..................................800 854-3643
Fax: 714 836-1841
Dennis J Gilmore, *CEO*
Kurt Pfotenhauer, *Vice Chairman*
Kevin Wall, *President*
Curt Caspersen, *COO*
Curt G Johnson, *Vice Ch Bd*
EMP: 146
SALES (est): 2.5B **Publicly Held**
WEB: www.fatc.com
SIC: 6361 Title insurance

(P-10521)
FIRST AMERICAN TITLE INSUR CO
411 Ivy St, San Diego (92101-2108)
PHONE..................................619 238-1776
Fax: 619 231-4696
Steve Mustin, *Manager*
Ed Reitz, *Real Est Agnt*
EMP: 160
SQ FT: 14,911 **Publicly Held**
WEB: www.fatc.com
SIC: 6361 6541 6531 Title insurance; title abstract offices; real estate agents & managers
HQ: First American Title Insurance Company
1 First American Way
Santa Ana CA 92707
800 854-3643

(P-10522)
FIRST AMERICAN TITLE INSUR CO
1855 W Rdlands Blvd 100, Redlands (92373)
PHONE..................................909 889-0311
Dan Williams, *Manager*
Loraine Meek, *Exec VP*
Doris Coonrod, *Persnl Mgr*
Joann Kordyak, *Persnl Mgr*
Jeff Bright, *Manager*
EMP: 140 **Publicly Held**
WEB: www.fatc.com
SIC: 6361 6541 Title insurance; title abstract offices
HQ: First American Title Insurance Company
1 First American Way
Santa Ana CA 92707
800 854-3643

(P-10523)
FIRST AMERICAN TITLE INSUR CO
899 Pacific St, San Luis Obispo (93401-3635)
P.O. Box 1147 (93406-1147)
PHONE..................................805 543-8900
Fax: 805 543-5524
Kevin Irot, *Director*
Baker Herane, *Branch Mgr*
Maryann Gevas, *VP Finance*
EMP: 50 **Publicly Held**
WEB: www.fatc.com
SIC: 6361 Title insurance

HQ: First American Title Insurance Company
1 First American Way
Santa Ana CA 92707
800 854-3643

(P-10524)
FIRST AMERICAN TITLE INSUR CO
Also Called: First American Casualty Insur
9 First American Way, Santa Ana (92707-5913)
PHONE..................................714 800-3000
Fax: 714 835-4813
Raymond Rai, *Branch Mgr*
Darliene Evans, *Senior VP*
Bill Hodges, *Vice Pres*
Scott Kaye, *Vice Pres*
Roger Moore, *Vice Pres*
EMP: 180 **Publicly Held**
WEB: www.fatc.com
SIC: 6361 Title insurance
HQ: First American Title Insurance Company
1 First American Way
Santa Ana CA 92707
800 854-3643

(P-10525)
FIRST AMERICAN TITLE INSUR CO
330 Soquel Ave, Santa Cruz (95062-2300)
PHONE..................................831 426-6500
Fax: 831 426-7312
Tim Guest, *Manager*
Timothy Lloyd, *Engineer*
Dimitruk Barbara, *Marketing Staff*
Jon Gross, *Manager*
Wendy Peterson, *Manager*
EMP: 60 **Publicly Held**
WEB: www.fatc.com
SIC: 6361 Title insurance
HQ: First American Title Insurance Company
1 First American Way
Santa Ana CA 92707
800 854-3643

(P-10526)
FIRST AMERICAN TITLE INSUR CO
Also Called: First Amercn Lenders Advantage
1855 Gateway Blvd Ste 700, Concord (94520-8455)
PHONE..................................925 798-2800
Fax: 925 927-2130
Tom Schlesinger, *Manager*
EMP: 70 **Publicly Held**
WEB: www.fatc.com
SIC: 6361 6541 Title insurance; title & trust companies
HQ: First American Title Insurance Company
1 First American Way
Santa Ana CA 92707
800 854-3643

(P-10527)
FIRST AMERICAN TITLE INSUR CO
First American Mortgage Svcs
3 First American Way, Santa Ana (92707-5913)
PHONE..................................714 250-4000
Pat McLaughlin, *Branch Mgr*
Mike Williams, *President*
Robert Camerota, *COO*
Mike Doting, *Software Dev*
EMP: 534 **Publicly Held**
SIC: 6361 6541 6531 Title insurance; title abstract offices; real estate agents & managers
HQ: First American Title Insurance Company
1 First American Way
Santa Ana CA 92707
800 854-3643

(P-10528)
FIRST AMRCN CASH ADVNCE SC LLC
Also Called: First American Title Insurance
777 S Figueroa St Ste 400, Los Angeles (90017-5802)
PHONE..................................213 271-1700

PRODUCTS & SERVICES SECTION
6371 - Pension, Health & Welfare Funds County (P-10546)

Fax: 213 271-1701
Nori Strong, *General Mgr*
Anthony Rivera, *Officer*
Gloria Neri, *VP Sales*
Melissa M Perez, *VP Sales*
Lawrence Schmidt, *VP Sales*
EMP: 52 **Privately Held**
SIC: 6361 Title insurance
HQ: First American Cash Advance Of South Carolina, Llc
1603 N Longstreet St
Kingstree SC

(P-10529)
LAWYERS TITLE COMPANY
4542 Ruffner St Ste 200, San Diego (92111-2239)
PHONE..................858 650-3900
Fax: 858 268-7884
John Wall, *Branch Mgr*
EMP: 80
SQ FT: 1,800
SALES (corp-wide): 9.1B **Publicly Held**
SIC: 6361 Title insurance
HQ: Lawyers Title Company
7530 N Glenoaks Blvd
Burbank CA 91504
818 767-0425

(P-10530)
LAWYERS TITLE COMPANY (HQ)
7530 N Glenoaks Blvd, Burbank (91504-1052)
PHONE..................818 767-0425
Fax: 818 468-6564
Edward Zerwekh, *CEO*
Edward Beierle, *Senior VP*
Steve Bauer, *Vice Pres*
William Star, *Vice Pres*
Katie Smith, *Branch Mgr*
EMP: 50
SQ FT: 20,000
SALES (est): 131.2MM
SALES (corp-wide): 9.1B **Publicly Held**
SIC: 6361 6531 Real estate title insurance; escrow agent, real estate
PA: Fidelity National Financial, Inc.
601 Riverside Ave Fl 4
Jacksonville FL 32204
904 854-8100

(P-10531)
LAWYERS TITLE INSURANCE CORP
18551 Von Karman Ave # 100, Irvine (92612-1552)
PHONE..................949 223-5575
Dan Williams, *Branch Mgr*
Laura Vincent, *Manager*
EMP: 70
SALES (corp-wide): 9.1B **Publicly Held**
WEB: www.diamondtitleco.com
SIC: 6361 6541 Title insurance; title & trust companies
HQ: Lawyers Title Insurance Corporation
601 Riverside Ave
Jacksonville FL 32204
888 866-3684

(P-10532)
NORTH AMERICAN TITLE CO INC
Also Called: N A T C
6612 Owens Dr 100, Pleasanton (94588-3334)
PHONE..................925 399-3000
Fax: 925 399-3026
Jim White, *Manager*
Dia Demmon, *Sales Executive*
EMP: 60
SQ FT: 32,000
SALES (corp-wide): 9.4B **Publicly Held**
WEB: www.natic.com
SIC: 6361 Title insurance
HQ: North American Title Company, Inc.
1855 Gateway Blvd Ste 600
Concord CA 94520
925 935-5199

(P-10533)
OLD REPUBLIC TITLE COMPANY
101 N Brand Blvd Ste 1400, Glendale (91203-2691)
PHONE..................818 240-1936
Fax: 818 246-4056
Merv Morris, *President*
Rudy Cortez, *Officer*
Michael Demers, *Officer*
Laurel Leftwich, *Officer*
Chris Ritter, *Officer*
EMP: 657 **EST:** 1967
SQ FT: 25,000
SALES (est): 321.9MM
SALES (corp-wide): 5.2B **Publicly Held**
WEB: www.oldrepublictitle.com
SIC: 6361 Title insurance
HQ: Old Republic Title Holding Company, Inc.
275 Battery St Ste 1500
San Francisco CA 94111
415 421-3500

(P-10534)
OLD REPUBLIC TITLE COMPANY
584 S Main St, Salinas (93901-3347)
PHONE..................831 757-8051
Ron Peterson, *President*
Amber Dinh, *HR Admin*
EMP: 50
SALES (corp-wide): 5.2B **Publicly Held**
WEB: www.ortc.com
SIC: 6361 Title insurance
HQ: Old Republic Title Company
275 Battery St Ste 1500
San Francisco CA 94111
415 421-3500

(P-10535)
STEWART TITLE CALIFORNIA INC (DH)
525 N Brand Blvd Ste 100, Glendale (91203-3992)
PHONE..................818 291-9145
Fax: 818 241-9857
Steve Vivanco, *President*
Gregg Unrath, *Treasurer*
Steven Rosansky, *Division Pres*
Kathie Walker, *Officer*
Brian Glaze, *Vice Pres*
EMP: 140
SQ FT: 44,000
SALES (est): 218.1MM
SALES (corp-wide): 2B **Publicly Held**
WEB: www.stewarttitleco.com
SIC: 6361 Guarantee of titles
HQ: Stewart Title Company
1980 Post Oak Blvd Ste 80
Houston TX 77056
713 625-8100

(P-10536)
TICOR TITLE COMPANY CALIFORNIA
4210 Riverwalk Pkwy # 200, Riverside (92505-3313)
PHONE..................951 509-0211
Fax: 951 509-4979
Anthony Andre, *Branch Mgr*
Joyce Sanchez, *Admin Asst*
Kenji Kikuchi, *Manager*
Ray Patchett, *Accounts Exec*
EMP: 50
SALES (corp-wide): 9.1B **Publicly Held**
SIC: 6361 Title insurance
HQ: Ticor Title Company Of California
1500 Quail St Ste 300
Newport Beach CA 92660
714 289-7100

(P-10537)
TICOR TITLE INSURANCE COMPANY (DH)
131 N El Molino Ave, Pasadena (91101-1873)
PHONE..................616 302-3121
John Rau, *Ch of Bd*
Gust Totlis, *CFO*
Peter Leemputte, *Treasurer*
Paul T Sands Jr, *Exec VP*
Bryan Willis, *Vice Pres*
EMP: 146
SQ FT: 44,637
SALES (est): 209MM
SALES (corp-wide): 9.1B **Publicly Held**
WEB: www.ticortitleindy.com
SIC: 6361 Real estate title insurance
HQ: Chicago Title And Trust Company
10 S La Salle St Ste 3100
Chicago IL 60603
312 223-2000

(P-10538)
WFG NATIONAL TITLE INSUR CO (PA)
Also Called: Alliance Title
700 N Brand Blvd Ste 1100, Glendale (91203-1208)
PHONE..................818 476-4000
Fax: 818 500-3982
Jeffrey Fox, *CEO*
Roberto Olivera, *President*
James Lokay, *CFO*
Art Cheyne, *Exec VP*
Rhio H Weir, *Exec VP*
EMP: 75
SQ FT: 15,000
SALES (est): 128.2MM **Privately Held**
WEB: www.investorstitle.com
SIC: 6361 Title insurance

6371 Pension, Health & Welfare Funds

(P-10539)
ALAMEDA COUNTY EMPLOYEES RETIR
Also Called: Acera
475 14th St Ste 1000, Oakland (94612-1916)
PHONE..................510 628-3000
Fax: 510 268-9574
Charles Conrad, *General Mgr*
Catherine Walker, *CEO*
George Dewey, *Bd of Directors*
Elizabeth Rogers, *Bd of Directors*
David Safer, *Bd of Directors*
EMP: 70
SALES (est): 53.6MM **Privately Held**
WEB: www.acera.org
SIC: 6371 Pension funds

(P-10540)
ASSOCTED THIRD PTY ADMNSTRTORS
2831 Camino Del Rio S, San Diego (92108-3802)
PHONE..................619 358-8140
EMP: 200
SALES (corp-wide): 482.8MM **Privately Held**
SIC: 6371 Union welfare, benefit & health funds
PA: Associated Third Party Administrators Inc
222 N Sepulveda Blvd # 2000
El Segundo CA 90245

(P-10541)
ASSOCTED THIRD PTY ADMNSTRTORS
642 Harrison St, San Francisco (94107-1388)
PHONE..................415 777-3707
June Devereaux, *Manager*
EMP: 200
SALES (corp-wide): 482.8MM **Privately Held**
SIC: 6371 Union welfare, benefit & health funds
PA: Associated Third Party Administrators Inc
222 N Sepulveda Blvd # 2000
El Segundo CA 90245

(P-10542)
CAL SOUTHERN UNITED FOOD
Also Called: U F C Pension Trust Fund
6425 Katella Ave, Cypress (90630-5246)
P.O. Box 6010 (90630-0010)
PHONE..................714 220-2297
P Thompson, *Administration*
Carolyn Petrilli, *VP Finance*
William Smith, *Analyst*
EMP: 240
SQ FT: 36,000
SALES (est): 112.9MM **Privately Held**
WEB: www.scufcwfunds.com
SIC: 6371 Pension funds

(P-10543)
CALIFOR STATE TEACH RETIRE SYS (DH)
Also Called: Cal Strs
100 Waterfront Pl, West Sacramento (95605-2807)
P.O. Box 15275, Sacramento (95851-0275)
PHONE..................800 228-5453
Fax: 916 229-3704
James D Mosman, *CEO*
Jen Thompson, *President*
Christopher Ailman, *Ch Invest Ofcr*
Ricardo Duran, *Officer*
Charles Haase, *Officer*
EMP: 146
SQ FT: 100,000
SALES (est): 948.6MM **Privately Held**
WEB: www.calstrs.com
SIC: 6371 9441 Pension, health & welfare funds; administration of social & manpower programs;
HQ: California Government Operations Agency
915 Capitol Mall Ste 200
Sacramento CA 95814
916 651-9011

(P-10544)
CALIFORNIA GOVRNMNT OPR AGNCY
Also Called: Califrnia Tchers Rtirement Sys
7667 Folsom Blvd Fl 3, Sacramento (95826-2618)
PHONE..................800 228-5453
James D Mosman, *Director*
Ray Lewis, *Technology*
Calvin Wu, *Technology*
Phil Larrieu, *Investment Ofcr*
Cynthia Steiger, *Director*
EMP: 535 **Privately Held**
SIC: 6371 Pension, health & welfare funds
HQ: California Government Operations Agency
915 Capitol Mall Ste 200
Sacramento CA 95814
916 651-9011

(P-10545)
CALIFORNIA PUBLIC EMPLYEES RET
Also Called: Calpers Investment Office
400 P St Ste 1204, Sacramento (95814-5346)
PHONE..................916 795-3000
Fax: 916 326-3344
Fred Buenrostro, *Manager*
Lisa Watson, *Officer*
Catherine Enfield, *Admin Asst*
Simmi Bajwa, *Technology*
Angela Lyons, *Investment Ofcr*
EMP: 150 **Privately Held**
WEB: www.calpers.net
SIC: 6371 9441 Pension funds; administration of social & manpower programs;
HQ: California Public Employees' Retirement System
400 Q St
Sacramento CA 95811

(P-10546)
CALIFORNIA PUBLIC EMPLYEES RET (DH)
400 Q St, Sacramento (95811-6201)
P.O. Box 942706 (94229-2706)
PHONE..................916 795-3000
Anne Stausboll, *CEO*
Rob Feckner, *President*
Mike Claybar, *Officer*
Ronald E Gene Reich, *Officer*
Kathie Vaughn, *Officer*
EMP: 1600
SALES (est): 2.3B **Privately Held**
WEB: www.calpers.net
SIC: 6371 9441 Pension funds; administration of social & manpower programs;
HQ: California Government Operations Agency
915 Capitol Mall Ste 200
Sacramento CA 95814
916 651-9011

6371 - Pension, Health & Welfare Funds County (P-10547)

(P-10547)
CHELBAY SCHULER & CHELBAY (PA)
Also Called: United Administrative Services
6800 Santa Teresa Blvd # 100, San Jose (95119-1239)
P.O. Box 5057 (95150-5057)
PHONE.................................408 288-4400
Fax: 408 286-3926
Robert J Bradley, *President*
David Andresen, *Corp Secy*
Sharon Crist, *Vice Pres*
Debbie Hill, *Vice Pres*
Sandy Stephenson, *Vice Pres*
EMP: 100
SQ FT: 35,000
SALES (est): 46.6MM **Privately Held**
WEB: www.chelbayins.com
SIC: 6371 Pension funds

(P-10548)
CITY OF LOS ANGELES
Also Called: Fire and Police Pension Dept
360 E 2nd St Ste 400, Los Angeles (90012-4244)
PHONE.................................213 978-4551
Michael Perez, *Branch Mgr*
EMP: 112 **Privately Held**
WEB: www.lacity.org
SIC: 6371 9441 Pensions; administration of social & manpower programs;
PA: City Of Los Angeles
    200 N Spring St Ste 303
    Los Angeles CA 90012
    213 978-0600

(P-10549)
COUNTY OF LOS ANGELES
Also Called: Public Social Services
27233 Camp Plenty Rd, Canyon Country (91351-2634)
PHONE.................................661 298-3406
Fax: 661 250-2964
Hilda Ochoa, *Manager*
EMP: 60 **Privately Held**
WEB: www.co.la.ca.us
SIC: 6371 Union welfare, benefit & health funds
PA: County Of Los Angeles
    500 W Temple St Ste 375
    Los Angeles CA 90012
    213 974-1101

(P-10550)
COUNTY OF SHASTA
Also Called: Shasta County Calworks
1400 California St, Redding (96001-1004)
PHONE.................................530 225-5000
Linda Parks, *Manager*
EMP: 90 **Privately Held**
WEB: www.rsdnmp.org
SIC: 6371 8748 Union welfare, benefit & health funds; employee programs administration
PA: County Of Shasta
    1450 Court St Ste 308a
    Redding CA 96001
    530 225-5561

(P-10551)
EAST BAY MUNICIPL UTILTY DISTR
Also Called: Ebmud
375 11th St, Oakland (94607-4246)
PHONE.................................510 287-0760
Fax: 510 287-0293
Alexander Coate, *General Mgr*
Elizabeth Grassetti, *Senior VP*
David Klein, *Controller*
EMP: 83
SALES (corp-wide): 1.4B **Privately Held**
SIC: 6371 Pensions
PA: East Bay Municipal Utility District, Water System
    375 11th St
    Oakland CA 94607
    866 403-2683

(P-10552)
EMPLOYEE BENEFITS SECURITY ADM
Also Called: Los Angeles Regional Office
1055 E Colo Blvd Ste 200, Pasadena (91106)
PHONE.................................626 229-1000
EMP: 55 **Publicly Held**
SIC: 6371
HQ: Employee Benefits Security Administration
    200 Constitution Ave Nw
    Washington DC 20210
    202 219-8233

(P-10553)
LABORERS FUNDS ADMINISTRATIVE (PA)
Also Called: Laborers Trust Funds Nthrn Cal
220 Campus Ln, Fairfield (94534-1498)
PHONE.................................707 864-2800
Edward Smith, *Admin Sec*
Anabel Llanos, *Admin Mgr*
Bill Eisley, *Info Tech Dir*
Ken Ridell, *Info Tech Mgr*
Leo Ferrer, *Purch Dir*
EMP: 100
SQ FT: 43,000
SALES (est): 43.2MM **Privately Held**
SIC: 6371 Union welfare, benefit & health funds

(P-10554)
LIPMAN INSUR ADMNISTRATORS INC (PA)
39420 Liberty St Ste 260, Fremont (94538-2297)
P.O. Box 5820 (94537-5820)
PHONE.................................510 796-4676
Fax: 510 795-0680
Frederic J Lipman, *President*
Janet Sylvester, *CFO*
Margaret Epstein, *Admin Sec*
Miriam Rivera, *Admin Asst*
Noah Hart, *Info Tech Dir*
EMP: 60
SQ FT: 14,000
SALES (est): 39MM **Privately Held**
SIC: 6371 Union welfare, benefit & health funds

(P-10555)
LOS ANGELES CNTY EMP RETIREMNT (PA)
Also Called: LACERA
300 N Lake Ave Ste 720, Pasadena (91101-5674)
P.O. Box 7060 (91109-7060)
PHONE.................................626 564-6000
Fax: 626 564-6130
Gregg Rademather, *CEO*
John Barger, *Vice Chairman*
David Green, *Vice Chairman*
Bonnie Nolley, *Bd of Directors*
Ana Chang, *Vice Pres*
EMP: 200
SQ FT: 85,000
SALES: 3.9B **Privately Held**
SIC: 6371 Pension funds

(P-10556)
MOTION PCTURE HLTH WLFARE FUND
11365 Ventura Blvd # 300, Studio City (91604-3148)
P.O. Box 1999 (91614-0999)
PHONE.................................818 769-0007
Fax: 818 769-1793
Thomas Zimmerman, *Exec Dir*
Theodre Friesen, *CFO*
Harley Blankenship, *MIS Staff*
Long Voong, *Technology*
Linda Cannady, *Human Res Mgr*
EMP: 215
SQ FT: 27,715
SALES (est): 20.9MM **Privately Held**
SIC: 6371 Union welfare, benefit & health funds

(P-10557)
MOTION PICTURE INDUSTRY PLANS
11365 Ventura Blvd # 300, Studio City (91604-3148)
PHONE.................................818 769-0007
David Wescoe, *CEO*
Chuck Killian, *CFO*
Ronald Kutak, *Bd of Directors*
Thomas Zimmerman, *Executive*
Marc Schwartz, *Comms Mgr*
EMP: 150
SQ FT: 12,500
SALES (est): 93.8MM **Privately Held**
SIC: 6371 Pension, health & welfare funds

(P-10558)
NORCO FIRE DEPARTMENT
3902 Hillside Ave, Norco (92860-1515)
PHONE.................................951 737-8097
Ron Larson, *President*
EMP: 700
SALES (est): 184.3K **Privately Held**
SIC: 6371 Union funds

(P-10559)
PRODUCER -WRITERS GUILD
2900 W Alameda Ave # 1100, Burbank (91505-4267)
PHONE.................................818 846-1015
Fax: 818 566-4416
Jim Hedges, *Administration*
Alan Weidlich, *CIO*
Stephen Balman, *Info Tech Dir*
Bob Chen, *Network Mgr*
Mary Sullivan, *Human Res Mgr*
EMP: 70
SQ FT: 30,000
SALES (est): 46.6MM **Privately Held**
WEB: www.wgaplans.org
SIC: 6371 Pensions

(P-10560)
PUBLIC EMPLOYEES RETIREMENT
Also Called: Calpers
400 Q St, Sacramento (95811-6201)
PHONE.................................916 795-3400
Russell Fong, *Branch Mgr*
Liana Bailey, *IT/INT Sup*
EMP: 331 **Privately Held**
SIC: 6371 9441 Pension funds; administration of social & manpower programs;
HQ: California Public Employees' Retirement System
    400 Q St
    Sacramento CA 95811

(P-10561)
PUBLIC EMPLOYEES RETIREMENT
400 P St 3260, Sacramento (95814-5345)
P.O. Box 942718 (94229-2718)
PHONE.................................916 326-3065
James E Burton, *Manager*
Dana Bromby, *Meeting Planner*
EMP: 64 **Privately Held**
WEB: www.calpers.net
SIC: 6371 9441 Pension funds; administration of social & manpower programs;
HQ: California Public Employees' Retirement System
    400 Q St
    Sacramento CA 95811

(P-10562)
SAG-AFTRA
Also Called: Screen Actors Guild-Producers
3601 W Olive Ave Fl 2, Burbank (91505-4662)
P.O. Box 7830 (91510-7830)
PHONE.................................818 954-9400
Margaret Olson, *Senior Mgr*
Michelle Bennett, *Director*
EMP: 121
SALES (corp-wide): 58.9MM **Privately Held**
SIC: 6371 6411 Pensions; pension & retirement plan consultants
PA: Sag-Aftra
    5757 Wilshire Blvd Fl 7
    Los Angeles CA 90036
    415 391-7510

(P-10563)
UNITED ADMINISTRATIVE SERVICES
6800 Santa Teresa Blvd # 100, San Jose (95119-1239)
PHONE.................................408 288-4400
David Andresen, *President*
Sharon Crist, *Vice Pres*
EMP: 107
SQ FT: 35,000
SALES (est): 11.7MM
SALES (corp-wide): 46.6MM **Privately Held**
WEB: www.eebenefitplans.com
SIC: 6371 Pension funds; union welfare, benefit & health funds
PA: Chelbay, Schuler & Chelbay
    6800 Santa Teresa Blvd # 100
    San Jose CA 95119
    408 288-4400

(P-10564)
WOODMONT REALTY ADVISORS INC
1050 Ralston Ave, Belmont (94002-2240)
PHONE.................................650 592-3960
Ronald V Granville, *CEO*
Howard Friedman, *President*
Caryn Kali, *CFO*
EMP: 70
SQ FT: 10,000
SALES (est): 15.5MM
SALES (corp-wide): 20.8MM **Privately Held**
WEB: www.wres.com
SIC: 6371 Pension funds
PA: Woodmont Real Estate Services, L.P.
    1050 Ralston Ave
    Belmont CA 94002
    650 592-3960

6399 Insurance Carriers, NEC

(P-10565)
AMERICAN CONTRS INDEMNITY CO (HQ)
Also Called: HCC Surety Group
601 S Figueroa St # 1600, Los Angeles (90017-5721)
PHONE.................................213 330-1309
Fax: 310 649-2452
Adam S Pessin, *President*
Jon Schneider, *Senior VP*
Michael Budnitsky, *Vice Pres*
Jeannie J Lee, *Vice Pres*
Kio Lo, *Vice Pres*
EMP: 150
SALES: 160MM
SALES (corp-wide): 2.6B **Privately Held**
WEB: www.hccsurety.com
SIC: 6399 Bank deposit insurance
PA: Hcc Insurance Holdings, Inc.
    13403 Northwest Fwy
    Houston TX 77040
    713 690-7300

(P-10566)
CALIFRNIA INSUR GUARANTEE ASSN
Also Called: C I G A
101 N Brand Blvd Ste 600, Glendale (91203-2653)
P.O. Box 29066 (91209-9066)
PHONE.................................818 844-4300
Lawrence E Mulryan, *Director*
Wayne Wilson, *Exec Dir*
Richard Herd, *Finance Dir*
Carole Lovato, *Asst Controller*
Richard Hurd, *Finance*
EMP: 110 EST: 1969
SALES (est): 79MM **Privately Held**
WEB: www.caiga.org
SIC: 6399 Health insurance for pets

(P-10567)
FEDERAL DEPOSIT INSURANCE CORP
1333 S Mayflower Ave # 450, Monrovia (91016-4066)
PHONE.................................626 359-7152
Donald Powell, *Manager*
EMP: 123
SALES (corp-wide): 9.3B **Privately Held**
WEB: www.fdic.gov
SIC: 6399 9311 Federal Deposit Insurance Corporation (FDIC); finance, taxation & monetary policy;
PA: Federal Deposit Insurance Corporation
    550 17th St Nw
    Washington DC 20429
    877 275-3342

PRODUCTS & SERVICES SECTION

6411 - Insurance Agents, Brokers & Svc County (P-10586)

(P-10568)
FEDERAL DEPOSIT INSURANCE CORP
Also Called: FDIC-San Frncisco Regional Off
25 Jessie St Ste 2300, San Francisco (94105-2780)
PHONE..............................415 546-0160
Fax: 415 808-7946
Catherine Olsen, *Officer*
Pat Sloan, *Vice Pres*
George Masa, *Principal*
Martin Briseno, *Admin Asst*
Pat Karnes, *Sales Executive*
EMP: 150
SQ FT: 127,215
SALES (corp-wide): 9.3B **Privately Held**
WEB: www.fdic.gov
SIC: **6399** 9311 Federal Deposit Insurance Corporation (FDIC); finance, taxation & monetary policy
PA: Federal Deposit Insurance Corporation
550 17th St Nw
Washington DC 20429
877 275-3342

(P-10569)
FEDERAL DEPOSIT INSURANCE CORP
Also Called: FDIC
5150 W Goldleaf Cir # 405, Los Angeles (90056-1662)
PHONE..............................323 545-9260
EMP: 123
SALES (corp-wide): 6.3B **Privately Held**
WEB: www.fdic.gov
SIC: **6399** 9311 Federal Deposit Insurance Corporation (FDIC);
PA: Federal Deposit Insurance Corporation
550 17th St Nw
Washington DC 20429
877 275-3342

(P-10570)
FEDERAL DEPOSIT INSURANCE CORP
Also Called: F D I C
1532 Eureka Rd Ste 102, Roseville (95661-3054)
PHONE..............................916 789-8580
Andrea Davis, *Manager*
EMP: 123
SALES (corp-wide): 6.3B **Privately Held**
WEB: www.fdic.gov
SIC: **6399** 9311 Federal Deposit Insurance Corporation (FDIC); finance, taxation & monetary policy
PA: Federal Deposit Insurance Corporation
550 17th St Nw
Washington DC 20429
877 275-3342

(P-10571)
KANOPY INSURANCE CENTER LLC
545 N Mountain Ave # 205, Upland (91786-5055)
PHONE..............................877 513-2434
Ryan McClintock, *CEO*
EMP: 140 **EST**: 2013
SQ FT: 1,700
SALES: 650K **Privately Held**
SIC: **6399** 6311 6351 Warranty insurance, automobile; life insurance; warranty insurance, home

(P-10572)
LISI INC
2677 N Main St Ste 350, Santa Ana (92705-6750)
PHONE..............................714 460-5153
Philip Lebherz, *Branch Mgr*
Jody Quinteros, *Executive Asst*
Mona Mehta, *Info Tech Dir*
Kathleen Platz, *Broker*
Rita Wagner, *Broker*
EMP: 75
SALES (corp-wide): 132.4MM **Privately Held**
SIC: **6399** Deposit insurance
PA: Lisi, Inc.
1600 W Hillsdale Blvd # 100
San Mateo CA 94402
650 348-4131

(P-10573)
TOPA INSURANCE COMPANY (HQ)
1800 Ave Of Stars # 1200, Los Angeles (90067-4200)
PHONE..............................310 201-0451
Fax: 310 286-7495
John E Anderson, *Ch of Bd*
Noshirwan Marfatia, *President*
Dan Sherrin, *CFO*
Harry W Degner, *Vice Ch Bd*
William Leone, *Senior VP*
EMP: 79
SALES (est): 49.8MM
SALES (corp-wide): 409.2MM **Privately Held**
WEB: www.mcnabbins.com
SIC: **6399** Warranty insurance, product; except automobile
PA: Topa Equities, Ltd.
1800 Ave Of The Ste 1400
Los Angeles CA 90067
310 203-9199

6411 Insurance Agents, Brokers & Svc

(P-10574)
1-800-4-INSURE INSURANCE SVCS
Also Called: Low Cost Insurance
9310 Reseda Blvd, Northridge (91324-2926)
PHONE..............................818 701-3733
Fax: 818 701-3730
Amy Kong, *President*
Raul Hong, *Administration*
EMP: 138
SQ FT: 8,000
SALES (est): 17.9MM **Privately Held**
SIC: **6411** Insurance agents, brokers & service

(P-10575)
21ST CENTURY INSURANCE COMPANY (DH)
6301 Owensmouth Ave, Woodland Hills (91367-2216)
PHONE..............................877 310-5687
Fax: 818 704-2961
Glenn A Pfeil, *CEO*
Bruce W Marlo, *Vice Chairman*
William Loucks, *COO*
Douglas K Howell, *CFO*
Ed Combs, *Exec VP*
EMP: 1800
SQ FT: 412,000
SALES (est): 1.1B
SALES (corp-wide): 62B **Privately Held**
SIC: **6411** Insurance agents, brokers & service; fire insurance underwriters' laboratories
HQ: 21st Century North America Insurance Company
3 Beaver Valley Rd
Wilmington DE 19803
877 310-5687

(P-10576)
21ST CENTURY INSURANCE COMPANY
9325 Sky Park Ct Ste 100, San Diego (92123-4380)
PHONE..............................858 637-9070
Nolan Richardson, *Branch Mgr*
EMP: 70
SALES (corp-wide): 62B **Privately Held**
SIC: **6411** Insurance agents, brokers & service
HQ: 21st Century Insurance Company
6301 Owensmouth Ave
Woodland Hills CA 91367
877 310-5687

(P-10577)
AB HEALTH INC
9340 Santa Anita Ave # 100, Rancho Cucamonga (91730-6149)
PHONE..............................949 464-4300
David Jackson, *CEO*
EMP: 50

SALES (est): 7.2MM **Privately Held**
SIC: **6411** Insurance agents, brokers & service

(P-10578)
ABD INSURANCE & FINCL SVCS INC (PA)
3 Waters Park Dr Ste 100, San Mateo (94403-1162)
PHONE..............................650 488-8565
Brian M Hetherington, *CEO*
Kurt De Grosz, *President*
Michael F McCloskey, *CFO*
Darren D Brown, *Exec VP*
Stephen Leveroni, *Exec VP*
EMP: 81 **EST**: 2009
SQ FT: 14,000
SALES (est): 94MM **Privately Held**
SIC: **6411** Insurance agents, brokers & service

(P-10579)
ACE FINANCIAL SERVICES INC
Also Called: Ace Property & Casualty
39300 Civic Center Dr # 290, Fremont (94538-2338)
PHONE..............................510 790-4600
Angela Argiros, *Principal*
Alyx Kunz, *Manager*
EMP: 70
SALES (corp-wide): 17.2B **Privately Held**
WEB: www.ace-ina.com
SIC: **6411** 6331 Insurance agents, brokers & service; fire, marine & casualty insurance
HQ: Chubb Insurance Company
11133 Ave Of The Americas
New York NY 10019
212 642-7800

(P-10580)
ACE USA
39300 Civic Center Dr # 290, Fremont (94538-2337)
PHONE..............................510 790-4695
Mike Wood, *Manager*
Alyx Kunz, *Manager*
EMP: 65
SALES (est): 3.8MM
SALES (corp-wide): 17.2B **Privately Held**
SIC: **6411** Insurance agents, brokers & service
HQ: Ace Usa, Inc.
436 Walnut St
Philadelphia PA 19106
215 923-5352

(P-10581)
ACE USA INC
455 Market St Ste 500, San Francisco (94105-2455)
PHONE..............................415 547-4400
Fax: 415 547-4491
Steve Meyers, *Branch Mgr*
Shannon Newman, *Human Res Dir*
Janice Engle, *Facilities Mgr*
Kathleen Melucci, *Counsel*
Russell Crooks, *Assistant VP*
EMP: 68
SALES (corp-wide): 17.2B **Privately Held**
WEB: www.ace.bm
SIC: **6411** Insurance agents, brokers & service
HQ: Ace Usa, Inc.
436 Walnut St
Philadelphia PA 19106
215 923-5352

(P-10582)
ACE USA INC
9200 Oakdale Ave, Chatsworth (91311-6500)
P.O. Box 3500, Woodland Hills (91365-3500)
PHONE..............................818 428-3600
James Perry, *Branch Mgr*
Sharon Barela, *Opers Mgr*
Monique Holzman, *Manager*
EMP: 150
SALES (corp-wide): 17.2B **Privately Held**
WEB: www.ace.bm
SIC: **6411** Insurance agents, brokers & service; patrol services, insurance

HQ: Ace Usa, Inc.
436 Walnut St
Philadelphia PA 19106
215 923-5352

(P-10583)
ACE USA INC
Also Called: Inamar
3131 Camino Del Rio N, San Diego (92108-5701)
PHONE..............................619 563-2400
Fax: 619 563-2420
Linda Andres, *Manager*
Susan Winters, *Underwriter*
EMP: 212
SALES (corp-wide): 17.2B **Privately Held**
WEB: www.ace.bm
SIC: **6411** Insurance agents, brokers & service
HQ: Ace Usa, Inc.
436 Walnut St
Philadelphia PA 19106
215 923-5352

(P-10584)
AIG DIRECT INSURANCE SVCS INC
9640 Gran Rdge Dr Ste 200, San Diego (92123)
PHONE..............................858 309-3000
Fax: 858 309-3003
Ron Harris, *CEO*
Robert F Herbert Jr, *Treasurer*
Laura Huffman, *Exec VP*
Richard Gravette, *Vice Pres*
Patty Karstein, *Vice Pres*
EMP: 275
SQ FT: 24,000
SALES (est): 108.7MM
SALES (corp-wide): 58.3B **Publicly Held**
WEB: www.matrixdirect.com
SIC: **6411** Insurance agents, brokers & service
HQ: American General Life Insurance Company
2727 Allen Pkwy Ste A
Houston TX 77019
713 522-1111

(P-10585)
ALL MOTORISTS INSURANCE AGENCY
Also Called: W G Warranty and Insur Svcs
5230 Las Virgenes Rd # 100, Calabasas (91302-3448)
PHONE..............................818 880-9070
Robert M Ehrlich, *President*
Patsy Brents, *Treasurer*
Daniel Mallut, *Exec VP*
Marleen F Kushner, *Admin Sec*
Mark Goldsmith, *VP Opers*
EMP: 250
SQ FT: 51,000
SALES (est): 41.3MM
SALES (corp-wide): 124.6MM **Privately Held**
WEB: www.westerngeneral.com
SIC: **6411** Insurance agents, brokers & service
PA: Western General Holding Co
5230 Las Virgenes Rd # 100
Calabasas CA 91302
818 880-9070

(P-10586)
ALLIANT INSURANCE SERVICES INC (PA)
1301 Dove St Ste 200, Newport Beach (92660-2436)
P.O. Box 6450 (92658-6450)
PHONE..............................949 756-0271
Thomas Corbett, *Ch of Bd*
Peter Worth, *Vice Chairman*
Carol Russell, *President*
Lisa Thornton, *President*
Greg Zimmer, *President*
EMP: 170
SQ FT: 45,000
SALES (est): 1B **Privately Held**
WEB: www.alliantinsurance.com
SIC: **6411** 8748 Insurance agents & brokers; business consulting

6411 - Insurance Agents, Brokers & Svc County (P-10587)

(P-10587)
ALLIANT INSURANCE SERVICES INC
701 B St Ste 600, San Diego (92101-8156)
PHONE......619 238-1828
Joyce Finizio, *Manager*
Katherine Chung, *Bd of Directors*
David Durham, *Vice Pres*
Anne Lewis, *Vice Pres*
Scott Lihme, *Vice Pres*
EMP: 100
SALES (corp-wide): 1B **Privately Held**
SIC: 6411 Insurance agents
PA: Alliant Insurance Services, Inc.
1301 Dove St Ste 200
Newport Beach CA 92660
949 756-0271

(P-10588)
ALLIED INFORMATION & SERVICES
7750 Pardee Ln Ste 200, Oakland (94621-1493)
PHONE......510 769-9648
Patrick Ho, *President*
Ophelia Ho, *Vice Pres*
EMP: 55
SQ FT: 10,000
SALES: 3MM **Privately Held**
WEB: www.alliedinformation.com
SIC: 6411 Medical insurance claim processing, contract or fee basis

(P-10589)
ALLSTATE RESEARCH AND PLG CTR
4200 Bohannon Dr Ste 200, Menlo Park (94025-1019)
PHONE......650 833-6200
Peggy Brinkmann, *Director*
Wendy Abbott, *Research*
Aldora Lee, *Research*
Joel Winter, *Research Analys*
Polly Ziegler, *Associate*
EMP: 90
SALES (est): 10.6MM **Privately Held**
SIC: 6411 Insurance agents, brokers & service

(P-10590)
AMERICAN AUTOMOBILE
Also Called: Csaa Travel Agency
3055 Oak Rd, Walnut Creek (94597-2098)
PHONE......925 279-2300
John Wu, *Principal*
Liz White, *Programmer Anys*
EMP: 67
SALES (corp-wide): 1.1B **Privately Held**
WEB: www.californiastateautomobileassociation.c
SIC: 6411 7549 Insurance agents, brokers & service; inspection & diagnostic service, automotive
PA: American Automobile Association Of Northern California, Nevada & Utah
1900 Powell St Ste 1200
Emeryville CA 94608
800 922-8228

(P-10591)
AMERICAN FIDELITY ASSURANCE CO
Also Called: Educational Services Division
3200 Inland Empire Blvd # 260, Ontario (91764-5513)
PHONE......909 941-1775
Fax: 909 941-2213
Suzanne Stokes, *Branch Mgr*
EMP: 99
SALES (corp-wide): 1B **Privately Held**
WEB: www.afadvantage.com
SIC: 6411 Insurance agents, brokers & service
HQ: American Fidelity Assurance Company
9000 Cameron Pkwy
Oklahoma City OK 73114
405 523-2000

(P-10592)
AMERICAN FIDELITY ASSURANCE CO
3649 W Beechwood Ave # 103, Fresno (93711-0693)
PHONE......559 230-2107
Amanda Dillon, *Branch Mgr*
EMP: 99
SALES (corp-wide): 1B **Privately Held**
SIC: 6411 Insurance agents
HQ: American Fidelity Assurance Company
9000 Cameron Pkwy
Oklahoma City OK 73114
405 523-2000

(P-10593)
AMERICAN GEN LF ACCIDENT INSUR
Also Called: American International Group
2650 Camino DI Rio N 20 Ste 205, San Diego (92108)
P.O. Box 881509 (92168-1509)
PHONE......619 299-5213
Fax: 619 299-5214
Jeff Comunale, *General Mgr*
Dolores Malabad, *Agent*
EMP: 60
SALES (corp-wide): 58.3B **Publicly Held**
WEB: www.agfg.com
SIC: 6411 Insurance agents, brokers & service
HQ: American General Life & Accident Insurance Co
2000 American General Way
Brentwood TN 37027
800 265-5054

(P-10594)
AMERICAN GEN LF INSUR CO DEL
Also Called: AIG
121 Spear St Fl 5, San Francisco (94105-1572)
PHONE......415 836-2700
Fax: 415 836-3149
Gordon Knight, *President*
Rene McGillicuddy, *Technical Mgr*
Linda Jiao, *Tech/Comp Coord*
Mark P Foletti, *Production*
Janine Lynn, *Marketing Mgr*
EMP: 300
SALES (corp-wide): 58.3B **Publicly Held**
WEB: www.aiglifeinsurancecompany.com
SIC: 6411 Insurance agents, brokers & service
HQ: American General Life Insurance Company Of Delaware
2727 Allen Pkwy Ste A
Houston TX 77019
713 522-1111

(P-10595)
AMERICAN GENERAL LIFE INSUR
455 Hickey Blvd Ste 500, Daly City (94015-2631)
PHONE......650 994-6679
Fax: 650 994-6682
Yuriy Kushnir, *Sales Staff*
Roger Relph, *Administration*
EMP: 80
SALES (corp-wide): 58.3B **Publicly Held**
WEB: www.dejonghfinancial.com
SIC: 6411 6311 Insurance agents, brokers & service; life insurance
HQ: American General Life Insurance
1 Franklin Sq
Springfield IL 62703
217 528-2011

(P-10596)
AMERICAN INTL GROUP INC
Also Called: Sun America
777 S Figueroa St # 1800, Los Angeles (90017-5800)
PHONE......213 689-3500
Fax: 213 689-3595
Vincent Masucci, *President*
Yolanda Razo, *Underwriter*
Melanie Taylor, *Underwriter*
EMP: 300
SALES (corp-wide): 58.3B **Publicly Held**
SIC: 6411 7389 Insurance agents, brokers & service; financial services
PA: American International Group, Inc.
175 Water St Rm 1800
New York NY 10038
212 770-7000

(P-10597)
AMERICAN INTL GROUP INC
Also Called: AIG Private Client Group
9350 Waxie Way Ste 300, San Diego (92123-1052)
PHONE......619 682-4058
Fax: 619 688-0615
Jack Devlin, *Manager*
Brad McGowan, *Finance Mgr*
EMP: 150
SALES (corp-wide): 58.3B **Publicly Held**
WEB: www.aiglifeinsurancecompany.com
SIC: 6411 Insurance agents, brokers & service
PA: American International Group, Inc.
175 Water St Rm 1800
New York NY 10038
212 770-7000

(P-10598)
AMERICAN SPECIALTY HEALTH INC (PA)
10221 Wateridge Cir # 201, San Diego (92121-2702)
PHONE......858 754-2000
George Devries III, *CEO*
Joy Kleinmaier, *President*
Robert White, *President*
William Comer, *CFO*
William Komer Jr, *Treasurer*
EMP: 146
SALES (est): 919.9MM **Privately Held**
SIC: 6411 Insurance information & consulting services

(P-10599)
AMERICAN TEAM MANAGERS INC
Also Called: Atm Insurance
1030 N Armando St, Anaheim (92806-2605)
PHONE......714 414-1200
Fax: 714 414-1290
Christopher Charles Micheals, *CEO*
Eric Magee, *President*
Marty T Martino, *Exec VP*
Bryan Benson, *Vice Pres*
Victor Silva, *Executive*
EMP: 50
SQ FT: 22,400
SALES (est): 13.5MM **Privately Held**
WEB: www.atminsurance.com
SIC: 6411 Insurance agents, brokers & service

(P-10600)
AMERICAS FLOOD SERVICES INC
3350 Country Club Dr # 201, Cameron Park (95682-8657)
P.O. Box 909 (95682-0909)
PHONE......916 636-9460
John F Gibson, *President*
Steven Straub, *Vice Pres*
EMP: 100
SQ FT: 5,000
SALES (est): 14.7MM
SALES (corp-wide): 172.5MM **Privately Held**
SIC: 6411 6331 Insurance agents, brokers & service; fire, marine & casualty insurance
PA: The Bruce Seibels Group Inc
1501 Lady St
Columbia SC 29201
803 748-2000

(P-10601)
AMWINS INSURANCE BRKG CAL LLC (HQ)
21550 Oxnard St Ste 1100, Woodland Hills (91367-7106)
PHONE......818 772-1774
Michael Steven Decarlo,
George Maggay, *President*
John Owen, *Vice Pres*
Janette Jirel, *Admin Dir*
Karren Kelly, *Branch Mgr*
EMP: 60 **EST:** 1981
SQ FT: 16,000
SALES (est): 24.7MM
SALES (corp-wide): 629.9MM **Privately Held**
SIC: 6411 Insurance brokers
PA: Amwins Group, Inc.
4725 Piedmont Row Dr # 600
Charlotte NC 28210
704 749-2700

(P-10602)
ANCHOR GENERAL INSURANCE AGCY
10256 Meanley Dr, San Diego (92131-3009)
P.O. Box 509020 (92150-9020)
PHONE......858 527-3600
Abdulla Badani, *President*
Shaukat Badani, *Senior VP*
Michael Mitchell, *VP Sls/Mktg*
Gladys Anchor, *Marketing Staff*
David McMath, *Marketing Staff*
EMP: 203
SALES (est): 57MM **Privately Held**
SIC: 6411 Insurance agents, brokers & service

(P-10603)
ANDREINI & COMPANY (PA)
220 W 20th Ave, San Mateo (94403-1339)
PHONE......650 573-1111
Fax: 650 378-4361
Michael J Colzani, *CEO*
Craig Oden, *Managing Prtnr*
Jeff Tebow, *Managing Prtnr*
John Andreini, *President*
Dan Centoni, *COO*
EMP: 95
SQ FT: 30,000
SALES (est): 100.9MM **Privately Held**
WEB: www.andreini.com
SIC: 6411 Insurance brokers

(P-10604)
ANKA BEHAVIORAL HEALTH INC
Also Called: Phoenix Home Lf Mutl Insur Co
2100 S State, Hemet (92543)
P.O. Box 3868 (92546-3868)
PHONE......951 929-2744
Don Cox, *Administration*
EMP: 115
SALES (corp-wide): 41.6MM **Privately Held**
SIC: 6411 8051 Property & casualty insurance agent; mental retardation hospital
PA: Anka Behavioral Health, Incorporated
1850 Gateway Blvd Ste 900
Concord CA 94520
925 825-4700

(P-10605)
AON CONSULTING INC
5260 N Palm Ave Ste 400, Fresno (93704-2217)
PHONE......559 449-7200
Fax: 559 449-0512
Marty Lee, *Manager*
Wendy Rose, *Project Mgr*
EMP: 75
SALES (corp-wide): 11.6B **Privately Held**
WEB: www.radford.com
SIC: 6411 Insurance brokers
HQ: Aon Consulting, Inc.
315 W 3rd St
Little Rock AR 72201
501 374-9300

(P-10606)
AON CONSULTING INC
707 Wilshire Blvd # 2500, Los Angeles (90017-3534)
PHONE......818 506-4300
Fax: 213 627-6155
Richard Schumacher, *Manager*
Sylvia Possehl, *Executive Asst*
John Evans, *Manager*
EMP: 60
SQ FT: 18,000
SALES (corp-wide): 11.6B **Privately Held**
WEB: www.radford.com
SIC: 6411 7361 Insurance brokers; employment agencies
HQ: Aon Consulting, Inc.
315 W 3rd St
Little Rock AR 72201
501 374-9300

PRODUCTS & SERVICES SECTION
6411 - Insurance Agents, Brokers & Svc County (P-10629)

(P-10607)
AON CONSULTING INC
3461 Fair Oaks Blvd, Sacramento (95864-5702)
PHONE...................................800 558-0655
Kelly McMillan, *Branch Mgr*
EMP: 61
SALES (corp-wide): 11.6B **Privately Held**
SIC: 6411 Insurance brokers
HQ: Aon Consulting, Inc.
315 W 3rd St
Little Rock AR 72201
501 374-9300

(P-10608)
AON CONSULTING INC
707 Wilshire Blvd # 2500, Los Angeles (90017-3534)
PHONE...................................213 630-2900
Janice Lun, *VP Finance*
Sandy Peters, *Executive*
Stephanie Tucker, *Manager*
Anne Cassidy, *Assistant VP*
EMP: 61
SALES (corp-wide): 11.6B **Privately Held**
SIC: 6411 Insurance brokers
HQ: Aon Consulting, Inc.
315 W 3rd St
Little Rock AR 72201
501 374-9300

(P-10609)
AON CONSULTING INC
16969 Von Karman Ave, Irvine (92606-4948)
PHONE...................................562 345-4600
EMP: 68
SALES (corp-wide): 11.6B **Privately Held**
SIC: 6411 Insurance brokers
HQ: Aon Consulting, Inc.
315 W 3rd St
Little Rock AR 72201
501 374-9300

(P-10610)
AON CONSULTING INC
1600 Iowa Ave Ste 100, Riverside (92507-7424)
PHONE...................................562 345-4900
EMP: 61
SALES (corp-wide): 11.6B **Privately Held**
SIC: 6411 Insurance brokers
HQ: Aon Consulting, Inc.
315 W 3rd St
Little Rock AR 72201
501 374-9300

(P-10611)
AON CONSULTING INC
21900 Burbank Blvd # 101, Woodland Hills (91367-6469)
PHONE...................................562 345-4700
EMP: 61
SALES (corp-wide): 11.6B **Privately Held**
SIC: 6411 Insurance brokers
HQ: Aon Consulting, Inc.
315 W 3rd St
Little Rock AR 72201
501 374-9300

(P-10612)
AON CONSULTING INC
851 Van Ness Ave Fl 2, San Francisco (94109-7876)
PHONE...................................800 283-1667
EMP: 61
SALES (corp-wide): 11.6B **Privately Held**
SIC: 6411 Insurance brokers
HQ: Aon Consulting, Inc.
315 W 3rd St
Little Rock AR 72201
501 374-9300

(P-10613)
AON CONSULTING INC
160 Via Verde Ste 200, San Dimas (91773-5121)
PHONE...................................800 815-1823
EMP: 61
SALES (corp-wide): 11.6B **Privately Held**
SIC: 6411 Insurance brokers
HQ: Aon Consulting, Inc.
315 W 3rd St
Little Rock AR 72201
501 374-9300

(P-10614)
AON CONSULTING INC
199 Fremont St Fl 11, San Francisco (94105-2291)
PHONE...................................415 486-6226
Matt Davis, *Manager*
EMP: 250
SALES (corp-wide): 11.6B **Privately Held**
SIC: 6411 Insurance brokers
HQ: Aon Consulting, Inc.
315 W 3rd St
Little Rock AR 72201
501 374-9300

(P-10615)
AON CONSULTING INC
307 Main St Ste 340, Salinas (93901-2760)
PHONE...................................408 288-8000
Geoffrey Green, *Branch Mgr*
EMP: 68
SALES (corp-wide): 11.6B **Privately Held**
SIC: 6411 Insurance brokers
HQ: Aon Consulting, Inc.
315 W 3rd St
Little Rock AR 72201
501 374-9300

(P-10616)
AON CONSULTING INC
5000 E Spring St Ste 100, Long Beach (90815-5217)
PHONE...................................562 496-2888
EMP: 68
SALES (corp-wide): 11.6B **Privately Held**
SIC: 6411 Insurance brokers
HQ: Aon Consulting, Inc.
315 W 3rd St
Little Rock AR 72201
501 374-9300

(P-10617)
AON CONSULTING INC
255 S Lake Ave Ste 900, Pasadena (91101-3001)
PHONE...................................626 683-5200
Joan Miles, *CEO*
EMP: 68
SALES (corp-wide): 11.6B **Privately Held**
SIC: 6411 Insurance brokers
HQ: Aon Consulting, Inc.
315 W 3rd St
Little Rock AR 72201
501 374-9300

(P-10618)
AON CONSULTING & INSUR SVCS
199 Fremont St Fl 14, San Francisco (94105-2253)
PHONE...................................415 486-7500
Fax: 415 486-7026
Judy Vukovich, *Senior VP*
Niranjan Samant, *Senior VP*
Daniel D Klauss, *Vice Pres*
Gassia Gujral, *Project Mgr*
Brent Rieth, *VP Accounting*
EMP: 85
SALES (est): 25.9MM
SALES (corp-wide): 11.6B **Privately Held**
WEB: www.radford.com
SIC: 6411 8742 Insurance brokers; medical insurance claim processing, contract or fee basis; management consulting services
HQ: Aon Consulting, Inc.
315 W 3rd St
Little Rock AR 72201
501 374-9300

(P-10619)
APFELD & NEAL INSURANCE SVCS
11022 Winners Cir Ste 100, Los Alamitos (90720-2869)
PHONE...................................714 821-7041
Jay Apfeld, *Partner*
Gary Neal, *Partner*
EMP: 50
SQ FT: 7,000
SALES (est): 4.4MM **Privately Held**
SIC: 6411 Insurance agents

(P-10620)
APPLIED UNDERWRITERS INC
950 Tower Ln Ste 1400, Foster City (94404-2128)
P.O. Box 281900, San Francisco (94128-1900)
PHONE...................................415 656-5000
Fax: 415 656-2335
Ellen Gardiner, *Vice Pres*
Clay Cox, *Exec VP*
Steve Menzy, *Vice Pres*
Justin Smith, *Vice Pres*
Joan Klucarich, *Investment Ofcr*
EMP: 50
SALES (corp-wide): 210.8B **Publicly Held**
WEB: www.appliedw.com
SIC: 6411 Insurance agents, brokers & service
HQ: Applied Underwriters, Inc.
10805 Old Mill Rd
Omaha NE 68154
402 342-4900

(P-10621)
ARROWHEAD MANAGEMENT COMPANY (DH)
701 B St Ste 2100, San Diego (92101-8197)
PHONE...................................800 669-1889
Patrick Kilkenny, *Ch of Bd*
Marianne Harmon, *Corp Secy*
Sergio Castro, *QA Dir*
Linh Nguyen, *QA Dir*
Mike Darnaud, *Software Engr*
EMP: 71
SALES (est): 249.2MM
SALES (corp-wide): 1.6B **Publicly Held**
WEB: www.arrowheadgrp.com
SIC: 6411 8741 Insurance agents, brokers & service; administrative management

(P-10622)
ARROYO INSURANCE SERVICES INC (PA)
440 E Huntington Dr # 100, Arcadia (91006-3750)
P.O. Box 661840 (91066-1840)
PHONE...................................626 799-9532
Robert J Knauf, *President*
Richard Beedle, *Corp Secy*
James Armitage, *Vice Pres*
Jim Simands, *Vice Pres*
Barbara Pickett, *Accounts Mgr*
EMP: 52
SQ FT: 3,500
SALES (est): 47.9MM **Privately Held**
SIC: 6411 Insurance agents & brokers

(P-10623)
ARTHUR J GALLAGHER & CO
Also Called: Gallagher Bassett
18201 Von Karman Ave # 200, Irvine (92612-1069)
PHONE...................................949 349-9800
Yvonne Norte, *Manager*
EMP: 50
SALES (corp-wide): 5.3B **Publicly Held**
SIC: 6411 Insurance agents, brokers & service
PA: Arthur J. Gallagher & Co.
2 Pierce Pl
Itasca IL 60143
630 773-3800

(P-10624)
ARTHUR J GALLAGHER & CO
Also Called: Kemper Insurance
505 N Brand Blvd Ste 600, Glendale (91203-3944)
PHONE...................................818 539-2300
Fax: 818 539-2301
Scott Firestone, *Branch Mgr*
Alexandra S Glickman, *Vice Chairman*
Martha Bane, *President*
Jayne S Mazziotti, *President*
Linda Pierce, *President*
EMP: 200
SALES (corp-wide): 5.3B **Publicly Held**
WEB: www.ajg.com
SIC: 6411 Insurance agents, brokers & service
PA: Arthur J. Gallagher & Co.
2 Pierce Pl
Itasca IL 60143
630 773-3800

(P-10625)
ARTHUR J GALLAGHER & CO
Also Called: Gallagher Construction Svcs
1 Market Spear Tower, San Francisco (94105)
PHONE...................................415 546-9300
Douglas B Bowring, *President*
Joel Kornreich, *President*
James F Buckley III, *Senior VP*
Jeff Lane, *Vice Pres*
Sharon Mitchell, *Executive Asst*
EMP: 200
SQ FT: 20,000
SALES (corp-wide): 5.3B **Publicly Held**
WEB: www.ajg.com
SIC: 6411 Insurance agents, brokers & service
PA: Arthur J. Gallagher & Co.
2 Pierce Pl
Itasca IL 60143
630 773-3800

(P-10626)
ARTHUR J GALLAGHER & CO
7910 N Ingram Ave Ste 201, Fresno (93711-5828)
PHONE...................................559 436-0833
Mahlon Buck, *Manager*
Mike Gong, *President*
Chris Cravin, *Info Tech Dir*
EMP: 55
SALES (corp-wide): 5.3B **Publicly Held**
WEB: www.ajg.com
SIC: 6411 Insurance agents, brokers & service
PA: Arthur J. Gallagher & Co.
2 Pierce Pl
Itasca IL 60143
630 773-3800

(P-10627)
ARTHUR J GALLAGHER & CO
Also Called: Kemper Insurance
3697 Mt Diablo Blvd # 300, Lafayette (94549-3747)
PHONE...................................925 299-1112
Douglas Bowring, *Branch Mgr*
Robert Perry, *CFO*
Rich Davis, *Senior VP*
Wally Brown, *Systems Admin*
Scott McGill, *Systems Admin*
EMP: 50
SALES (corp-wide): 5.3B **Publicly Held**
WEB: www.ajg.com
SIC: 6411 Insurance agents, brokers & service
PA: Arthur J. Gallagher & Co.
2 Pierce Pl
Itasca IL 60143
630 773-3800

(P-10628)
ASCENSION INSURANCE INC
7673 N Ingram Ave Ste 103, Fresno (93711-5854)
PHONE...................................661 321-3290
James Ingraham, *Branch Mgr*
EMP: 144
SALES (corp-wide): 91.3MM **Privately Held**
SIC: 6411 Insurance agents, brokers & service
PA: Ascension Insurance, Inc
1277 Treat Blvd Ste 400
Walnut Creek CA 94597
800 404-4969

(P-10629)
ASCENSION INSURANCE INC
12121 Wilshire Blvd # 1001, Los Angeles (90025-1164)
PHONE...................................800 537-1777
Jim McNiel, *Branch Mgr*
EMP: 144
SALES (corp-wide): 91.3MM **Privately Held**
SIC: 6411 Insurance agents, brokers & service
PA: Ascension Insurance, Inc
1277 Treat Blvd Ste 400
Walnut Creek CA 94597
800 404-4969

6411 - Insurance Agents, Brokers & Svc County (P-10630)

(P-10630)
ASSOCIATED PENSION CONS INC (PA)
2035 Forest Ave, Chico (95928-7620)
P.O. Box 1282 (95927-1282)
PHONE..................530 343-4233
Matt Blofsky, *President*
Marc Roberts, *Treasurer*
Linda Madsen, *Vice Pres*
John Olsen, *VP Opers*
Maureen Martinez, *Sr Consultant*
EMP: 51
SQ FT: 20,000
SALES: 6.6MM **Privately Held**
SIC: 6411 Pension & retirement plan consultants

(P-10631)
ASSURANT INC
2677 N Main St Ste 600, Santa Ana (92705-6629)
PHONE..................714 571-3900
Eric Juarez, *Branch Mgr*
Cindy Eastman, *Accounts Exec*
EMP: 300
SALES (corp-wide): 10.3B **Publicly Held**
WEB: www.us.fortis.com
SIC: 6411 Insurance information & consulting services
PA: Assurant, Inc.
28 Liberty St Fl 41
New York NY 10005
212 859-7000

(P-10632)
ATHENS INSURANCE SERVICE INC
Also Called: Athens Administrators
2552 Stanwell Dr Ste 100, Concord (94520-4851)
P.O. Box 4029 (94524-4029)
PHONE..................925 826-1000
Fax: 925 609-5317
James C Jenkins, *Ch of Bd*
James R Jenkins, *President*
Jodi Ellington, *CFO*
Mikhail Zubovich, *Technology*
Randi Cross, *Receptionist*
EMP: 250
SALES (est): 46.9MM **Privately Held**
SIC: 6411 Insurance claim adjusters, not employed by insurance company

(P-10633)
ATLAS GENERAL INSUR SVCS LLC
4365 Executive Dr Ste 400, San Diego (92121-2136)
PHONE..................858 529-6700
William Trzos, *President*
Greg Mosher, *President*
Jonathan Hooven, *Vice Pres*
Anna Rosenwasser, *Admin Asst*
Trzos David, *Info Tech Dir*
EMP: 153
SALES: 27MM **Privately Held**
SIC: 6411 Insurance agents, brokers & service

(P-10634)
AUTO INSUR SPCIALISTS-LONG BCH
Also Called: A I S-Auto Insur Specialists
5000 E Spring St Ste 100, Long Beach (90815-5217)
PHONE..................562 496-2888
James F Caird, *President*
EMP: 60
SALES (est): 6.8MM
SALES (corp-wide): 11.6B **Privately Held**
SIC: 6411 6331 Insurance agents, brokers & service; fire, marine & casualty insurance
HQ: Aon Financial Services Group, Inc.
999 N Sepulveda Blvd
El Segundo CA 90245
800 859-6511

(P-10635)
AUTOMOBILE CLUB SOUTHERN CAL (PA)
Also Called: A A A Automobile Club So Cal
2601 S Figueroa St, Los Angeles (90007-3294)
P.O. Box 25001, Santa Ana (92799-5001)
PHONE..................213 741-3686
Zoo Babies, *President*
Willis B Wood, *Vice Chairman*
Peter R McDonald, *Senior VP*
Phil Bybee, *Vice Pres*
Brian Deephouse, *Vice Pres*
EMP: 150
SQ FT: 425,000
SALES (est): 4.8B **Privately Held**
SIC: 6411 8699 Insurance agents; automobile owners' association

(P-10636)
AUTOMOBILE CLUB SOUTHERN CAL
3333 Fairview Rd, Costa Mesa (92626-1698)
PHONE..................714 885-1343
Becky Martinez, *Branch Mgr*
Derek B Lipscome, *Corp Counsel*
Michael Spore, *Manager*
EMP: 200
SALES (corp-wide): 4.8B **Privately Held**
SIC: 6411 Insurance agents, brokers & service
PA: Automobile Club Of Southern California
2601 S Figueroa St
Los Angeles CA 90007
213 741-3686

(P-10637)
AUTOMOBILE CLUB SOUTHERN CAL
2488 Foothill Blvd Ste A, La Verne (91750-3062)
PHONE..................909 392-1444
Bob Barron, *Manager*
EMP: 108
SALES (corp-wide): 4.8B **Privately Held**
SIC: 6411 Insurance agents, brokers & service
PA: Automobile Club Of Southern California
2601 S Figueroa St
Los Angeles CA 90007
213 741-3686

(P-10638)
AUTOMOBILE CLUB SOUTHERN CAL
19201 Bear Valley Rd C, Apple Valley (92308-2704)
PHONE..................760 247-4110
EMP: 108
SALES (corp-wide): 4.8B **Privately Held**
SIC: 6411 Insurance agents, brokers & service
PA: Automobile Club Of Southern California
2601 S Figueroa St
Los Angeles CA 90007
213 741-3686

(P-10639)
AUTOMOBILE CLUB SOUTHERN CAL
10540 Fthill Blvd Ste 100, Rancho Cucamonga (91730)
PHONE..................909 980-0233
Alice Holguin, *Branch Mgr*
Grace Curtis, *Office Mgr*
Arbella Madden, *Administration*
EMP: 108
SALES (corp-wide): 4.8B **Privately Held**
SIC: 6411 Insurance agents, brokers & service
PA: Automobile Club Of Southern California
2601 S Figueroa St
Los Angeles CA 90007
213 741-3686

(P-10640)
AUTOMOBILE CLUB SOUTHERN CAL
2666 Del Mar Heights Rd, Del Mar (92014-3100)
PHONE..................858 481-7181
Fax: 858 792-5737
Tom McKernan, *Manager*
EMP: 108
SALES (corp-wide): 4.8B **Privately Held**
SIC: 6411 Insurance agents, brokers & service
PA: Automobile Club Of Southern California
2601 S Figueroa St
Los Angeles CA 90007
213 741-3686

(P-10641)
AXA EQUITABLE LIFE INSUR CO
Also Called: Equitable Life Assurance
3777 La Jolla Village Dr, San Diego (92122-1080)
PHONE..................858 552-1234
Alen Farwell, *Manager*
EMP: 70
SALES (corp-wide): 2.9B **Publicly Held**
WEB: www.equitable.com
SIC: 6411 Insurance agents, brokers & service
HQ: Axa Equitable Life Insurance Company
1290 Avenue Of The Americ
New York NY 10104
212 554-1234

(P-10642)
BARNEY & BARNEY INC (DH)
Also Called: Loss and Risk Advisors
9171 Twne Cntre Dr 500, San Diego (92122)
P.O. Box 85638 (92186-5638)
PHONE..................800 321-4696
Fax: 858 452-7530
Paul Hering, *CEO*
Hal Dunning, *President*
Steven Berk, *CFO*
Christine Schindewolf, *Bd of Directors*
Peter Epstine, *Vice Pres*
EMP: 113 **EST:** 1970
SALES (est): 286.6MM
SALES (corp-wide): 12.8B **Publicly Held**
WEB: www.barneyandbarney.com
SIC: 6411 Property & casualty insurance agent; life insurance agents
HQ: Marsh & Mclennan Agency Llc
360 Hamilton Ave Ste 930
White Plains NY 10601
914 397-1600

(P-10643)
BARRY MCPHERSON INC
1932 E Deere Ave Ste 240, Santa Ana (92705-5716)
PHONE..................425 343-5000
Kenneth B McPherson, *President*
EMP: 240
SALES (est): 26.3MM **Privately Held**
SIC: 6411 Insurance agents, brokers & service

(P-10644)
BENEFICIAL ADMINISTRATION CO
Also Called: Best Plans
17701 Mitchell N, Irvine (92614-6028)
PHONE..................949 756-1000
Fax: 949 724-1603
Jim Voegtlin, *President*
John Van Der Schraaf, *Treasurer*
Daniel Frey, *VP Admin*
Diana Abeta, *Admin Sec*
Irene Maciel, *Manager*
EMP: 80
SQ FT: 30,000
SALES (est): 9.6MM **Privately Held**
WEB: www.beneficialadmin.com
SIC: 6411 8741 Insurance agents, brokers & service; management services

(P-10645)
BENEFIT & RISK MANAGEMENT SVCS
80 Iron Point Cir Ste 200, Folsom (95630-8593)
P.O. Box 2140 (95763-2140)
PHONE..................916 467-1200
Matthew Allen Schafer, *CEO*
Scott Reid, *President*
Monica Burns, *Vice Pres*
Luke Schafer, *Vice Pres*
Paul Schafer, *Vice Pres*
EMP: 130
SQ FT: 15,000
SALES (est): 31.9MM **Privately Held**
WEB: www.brms-online.com
SIC: 6411 Insurance information & consulting services

(P-10646)
BENETECH INC
4420 Auburn Blvd Fl 2, Sacramento (95841-4146)
P.O. Box 348570 (95834-8570)
PHONE..................916 484-6811
Fax: 916 488-1743
Kelly Roberts, *Manager*
Janet Chapman, *Manager*
EMP: 50
SALES (corp-wide): 16.6MM **Privately Held**
SIC: 6411 Pension & retirement plan consultants
PA: Benetech, Inc
3947 Lennane Dr Ste 250
Sacramento CA 95834
916 484-6811

(P-10647)
BERKSHIRE HATHAWAY HOMESTATES
2020 Camino Del Rio N, San Diego (92108-1541)
PHONE..................619 686-8424
Michael Millwood, *Manager*
Luis Feldstein, *Director*
EMP: 70
SALES (corp-wide): 210.8B **Publicly Held**
WEB: www.acpac.com
SIC: 6411 Insurance claim processing, except medical
HQ: Berkshire Hathaway Homestates
50 California St Fl 14
San Francisco CA 94111

(P-10648)
BICKMORE AND ASSOCIATES INC (DH)
Also Called: Bickmore Risk Svcs Consulting
1750 Creekside Oaks Dr # 200, Sacramento (95833-3648)
PHONE..................916 244-1100
Fax: 916 244-1199
Greg L Trout, *CEO*
John Alltop, *President*
L Robert Kramer, *President*
Jeffrey C Grubbs, *COO*
David A Tweedy, *Risk Mgmt Dir*
EMP: 70
SQ FT: 25,500
SALES (est): 66.1MM
SALES (corp-wide): 4.3B **Privately Held**
WEB: www.brsrisk.com
SIC: 6411 Insurance agents, brokers & service
HQ: York Risk Services Group, Inc.
1 Upper Pond Bldg F
Parsippany NJ 07054
973 404-1200

(P-10649)
BROOKDALE SENIOR LIVING INC
20801 Devonshire St, Chatsworth (91311-3216)
PHONE..................818 718-1547
EMP: 79
SALES (corp-wide): 4.9B **Publicly Held**
SIC: 6411 Pension & retirement plan consultants
PA: Brookdale Senior Living
111 Westwood Pl Ste 400
Brentwood TN 37027
615 221-2250

(P-10650)
BROWN & BROWN INC
1025 Chapala St, Santa Barbara (93101-3245)
P.O. Box 61010 (93160-1010)
PHONE..................805 965-0071
Fax: 805 690-3200
Susan Rodriguez, *Manager*
EMP: 50
SALES (corp-wide): 1.6B **Publicly Held**
WEB: www.brown-n-brown.com
SIC: 6411 Insurance agents, brokers & service

PRODUCTS & SERVICES SECTION
6411 - Insurance Agents, Brokers & Svc County (P-10672)

PA: Brown & Brown, Inc.
220 S Ridgewood Ave # 180
Daytona Beach FL 32114
386 252-9601

(P-10651)
BUILDERS & TRADESMENS
6610 Sierra College Blvd, Rocklin
(95677-4306)
PHONE.................................916 772-9200
Fax: 916 772-9292
Norbert Hohlbein, *President*
Jeff Erickson, *Vice Pres*
Lisa Erickson, *Vice Pres*
Jeff Hohlbein, *Vice Pres*
Paul Hohlbein, *Vice Pres*
EMP: 75
SQ FT: 15,000
SALES (est): 77.4MM **Privately Held**
WEB: www.btisinc.com
SIC: 6411 Insurance agents, brokers & service; fire insurance underwriters' laboratories

(P-10652)
C M A ALLIANCE
Also Called: Cornerstone Marketing Alliance
16542 Ventura Blvd # 210, Encino
(91436-2005)
PHONE.................................818 981-0800
Fax: 818 981-0835
Steve Pato, *Owner*
EMP: 50 **EST:** 2001
SALES (est): 3.7MM **Privately Held**
WEB: www.cma-la.com
SIC: 6411 Insurance agents, brokers & service

(P-10653)
CA STE ATOM ASSOC INTR-INS BUR
Also Called: AAA
900 Miramonte Ave, Mountain View
(94040-2457)
P.O. Box 391840 (94039-1840)
PHONE.................................650 623-3200
Jerry Hall, *Branch Mgr*
Tracy Traylor, *Securities*
Henry Wong, *Sales Staff*
Cheryl Turner, *Manager*
Andrea Cortez, *Agent*
EMP: 60
SQ FT: 15,414
SALES (corp-wide): 1.1B **Privately Held**
WEB: www.viamagazine.com
SIC: 6411 Insurance claim processing, except medical
HQ: California State Automobile Association Inter-Insurance Bureau
1276 S California Blvd
Walnut Creek CA 94596
925 287-7600

(P-10654)
CABRILLO GEN INSUR AGCY INC
7071 Convoy Ct Ste 201, San Diego
(92111-1023)
P.O. Box 17425 (92177-7425)
PHONE.................................858 244-0550
Fax: 858 244-0551
Robert Jester, *President*
Micheal McNitt, *Vice Pres*
Doug Jester, *Sales Mgr*
EMP: 88
SALES (est): 12MM **Privately Held**
SIC: 6411 Insurance agents, brokers & service

(P-10655)
CAESAR AND SEIDER INSUR SVCS (PA)
Also Called: Talbot Insurance & Fincl Svcs
40 E Alamar Ave Ste 4, Santa Barbara
(93105-3400)
P.O. Box 3310 (93130-3310)
PHONE.................................805 682-2571
Fax: 805 682-1056
Thomas Caesar, *President*
Ray Seider, *Vice Pres*
Carla Miller, *Accountant*
EMP: 52 **EST:** 1954
SQ FT: 2,400
SALES (est): 8.4MM **Privately Held**
SIC: 6411 Insurance brokers

(P-10656)
CALIFORNIA CLINICAL TRIALS
3828 Delmas Ter 2, Culver City
(90232-2713)
PHONE.................................310 945-1780
Shiovitz, *President*
EMP: 200
SALES (est): 20.2MM **Privately Held**
SIC: 6411 8731 Research services, insurance; commercial physical research

(P-10657)
CALIFORNIA FAIR PLAN ASSN
3435 Wilshire Blvd # 1200, Los Angeles
(90010-1911)
PHONE.................................213 487-0111
Fax: 213 487-6699
Stuart M Wilkinson, *President*
Tessa Thomas, *Info Tech Mgr*
Cesar Flores, *Director*
EMP: 80
SALES (est): 14.3MM **Privately Held**
WEB: www.cfpnet.com
SIC: 6411 Insurance agents, brokers & service

(P-10658)
CALIFORNIA HEALTHCARE
Also Called: C.H.M.B.
700 La Terraza Blvd # 200, Escondido
(92025-3868)
PHONE.................................760 520-1333
Bob Svendsen, *CEO*
Janet Boos, *President*
Vicki Brown, *Vice Pres*
Donna Forster, *Vice Pres*
James Trewin, *Vice Pres*
EMP: 135
SQ FT: 16,000
SALES (est): 55.8MM **Privately Held**
WEB: www.chmb.com
SIC: 6411 Medical insurance claim processing, contract or fee basis

(P-10659)
CALIFRNIA PHYSCN REIMBURSEMENT
1321 Butte St, Redding (96001-1064)
PHONE.................................530 241-0473
Fax: 530 241-5377
Jane Rehberg, *President*
EMP: 73
SALES (est): 11.3MM **Privately Held**
WEB: www.cprbilling.com
SIC: 6411 Medical insurance claim processing, contract or fee basis

(P-10660)
CAMICO MUTUAL INSURANCE CO (PA)
1800 Gateway Dr Ste 300, San Mateo
(94404-4072)
PHONE.................................650 378-6874
Ricardo R Rosario, *President*
Robert P Evans, *Ch of Bd*
Jay H Stewart, *CFO*
Rachel Ehrlich, *Officer*
Judith Frederiksen, *Vice Pres*
EMP: 80
SQ FT: 22,000
SALES: 32.4MM **Privately Held**
SIC: 6411 Professional standards services, insurance

(P-10661)
CAPARIO INC
1901 E Alton Ave Ste 100, Santa Ana
(92705-5849)
PHONE.................................949 553-1974
Jim Riley, *CEO*
Ken Hall, *Vice Pres*
Fernando Azouth, *Sr Software Eng*
Ruslan Kostin, *Sr Software Eng*
Raj Vaidyanathan, *Sr Software Eng*
EMP: 130
SALES (est): 150K
SALES (corp-wide): 1.4B **Privately Held**
SIC: 6411 Medical insurance claim processing, contract or fee basis
HQ: Medifax-Edi, Llc
26 Century Blvd
Nashville TN 37214
615 932-3226

(P-10662)
CAPAX MANAGEMENT AND SERVICES
Also Called: Osborne Organization, The
1150 9th St Ste 1400, Modesto
(95354-0840)
P.O. Box 3231 (95353-3231)
PHONE.................................209 526-3110
Fax: 209 529-0230
Joel Geddes, *President*
Sharon Lagier, *Human Res Mgr*
EMP: 70
SQ FT: 14,800
SALES (est): 9MM
SALES (corp-wide): 20.4MM **Privately Held**
SIC: 6411 Pension & retirement plan consultants
PA: Capax Management & Insurance Services
1150 9th St Ste 1400
Modesto CA 95354
209 526-3110

(P-10663)
CARLTON SENIOR LIVING INC
380 Branham Ln Ofc Ofc, San Jose
(95136-4302)
PHONE.................................408 972-1400
Mandi Farrell, *Director*
EMP: 55
SALES (corp-wide): 31.1MM **Privately Held**
SIC: 6411 Pension & retirement plan consultants
PA: Senior Carlton Living Inc
4005 Port Chicago Hwy
Concord CA 94520
925 338-2434

(P-10664)
CARNEGIE AGENCY INC
2101 Corp Cntr Dr Ste 150, Newbury Park
(91320-1436)
PHONE.................................805 445-1470
John Smith, *President*
Chuck Smith, *Vice Pres*
EMP: 50
SQ FT: 40,000
SALES (est): 8.7MM **Privately Held**
WEB: www.cgia.com
SIC: 6411 Insurance agents, brokers & service

(P-10665)
CARTEL MARKETING INC
Also Called: Insure Express Insurance Svc
5230 Las Virgenes Rd # 250, Calabasas
(91302-3448)
PHONE.................................818 483-1130
Fax: 818 817-8513
Robert M Humphreys, *Ch of Bd*
Jack Edelstein, *President*
William Russell, *CFO*
Sean Willis, *Vice Pres*
Jon Danley, *Comms Dir*
EMP: 102
SQ FT: 14,000
SALES (est): 21.6MM
SALES (corp-wide): 14.5MM **Privately Held**
WEB: www.cartel.net
SIC: 6411 Insurance agents & brokers
HQ: Expresslink, Inc.
16501 Ventura Blvd # 300
Encino CA 91436
818 788-5555

(P-10666)
CENTURY 21 A BETTER SVC RLTY
5831 Firestone Blvd Ste J, South Gate
(90280-3718)
PHONE.................................562 806-1000
Fax: 323 806-0167
David Sarinana, *President*
Blanca Sarinana, *Vice Pres*
Jesse Gayoso, *Technology*
Alfredo Rosas, *Real Est Agnt*
EMP: 97
SQ FT: 4,000
SALES (est): 16.7MM **Privately Held**
WEB: www.c21abetterservice.com
SIC: 6411 6531 Insurance agents, brokers & service; real estate agents & managers

(P-10667)
CHARLES M KAMIYA AND SONS INC
Also Called: Kamiya, Kenneth M Insurance
373 Van Ness Ave Ste 200, Torrance
(90501-6239)
PHONE.................................310 781-2066
Fax: 310 781-9411
Kenneth Kamiya, *President*
Edward Kamiya, *Vice Pres*
▲ **EMP:** 54
SALES (est): 7.2MM **Privately Held**
WEB: www.kamiyainsurance.com
SIC: 6411 Insurance agents & brokers

(P-10668)
CHARTER OAK INVESTMENTS INC
Also Called: Chater Oak Real Estate Co
5571 Stacy Ct, Livermore (94550-8125)
PHONE.................................925 447-1753
Raymond Bump, *President*
EMP: 75
SALES (est): 9.1MM **Privately Held**
SIC: 6411 5812 Insurance agents, brokers & service; American restaurant

(P-10669)
CHOIC ADMINI INSUR SERVI
Also Called: California Choice
721 S Parker St Ste 200, Orange
(92868-4772)
PHONE.................................714 542-4200
Fax: 714 542-4244
Ron Goldstein, *President*
Kevin J Counihan, *President*
Tamra Reise, *Senior VP*
Brenda Scott, *Senior VP*
Raymond D Godeke, *Vice Pres*
EMP: 500
SALES (est): 115.7MM **Privately Held**
WEB: www.wordup.com
SIC: 6411 Insurance agents, brokers & service

(P-10670)
CIBA INSURANCE SVCS CAL INC (PA)
655 N Central Ave # 2100, Glendale
(91203-1422)
PHONE.................................818 638-8525
Michael Marino, *President*
Wayne Swanson, *Vice Pres*
Amy Lochmoeller, *Executive Asst*
Lisa Raczek, *Marketing Staff*
EMP: 50
SALES (est): 67.2MM **Privately Held**
WEB: www.cibaservices.com
SIC: 6411 Insurance agents, brokers & service

(P-10671)
CLAIMS MANAGEMENT INC
1101 Crksde Rdge Dr 100, Roseville
(95678)
P.O. Box 619079 (95661-9079)
PHONE.................................916 631-1250
Kathy Peterson, *President*
Robb Miller, *Sales Mgr*
Jada Fredrick, *Manager*
Tina Hudnall, *Manager*
EMP: 130
SQ FT: 23,000
SALES (est): 21.2MM **Privately Held**
WEB: www.claimsmanagement.com
SIC: 6411 Insurance claim adjusters, not employed by insurance company

(P-10672)
CNA FINANCIAL CORPORATION
Also Called: CNA Insurance
1800 E Imperial Hwy # 200, Brea
(92821-6062)
P.O. Box 6500 (92822-6500)
PHONE.................................714 255-2200
Fax: 714 255-2366
John C Magee III, *Branch Mgr*
Joe Barbala, *Sales Staff*
EMP: 200
SALES (corp-wide): 13.4B **Publicly Held**
SIC: 6411 6331 Insurance agents, brokers & service; fire, marine & casualty insurance

6411 - Insurance Agents, Brokers & Svc County (P-10673)

HQ: Cna Financial Corporation
333 S Wabash Ave Ste 300
Chicago IL 60604
312 822-5000

(P-10673)
CNA SURETY CORPORATION
1455 Frazee Rd Ste 801, San Diego (92108-4309)
PHONE..............................619 682-3550
Ron Fawcett, *Manager*
Jennifer Purdon, *Research Analys*
EMP: 71
SALES (corp-wide): 13.4B **Publicly Held**
SIC: 6411 Insurance agents, brokers & service
HQ: Cna Surety Corporation
333 S Wabash Ave Ste 41s
Chicago IL 60604
312 822-5000

(P-10674)
COASTAL SELECT INSURANCE CO
4820 Busineca Ctr Dr 20 Ste 200, Fairfield (94534)
PHONE..............................707 863-3700
Fax: 707 863-9349
Kevin Nish, *President*
Karen Padovese, *COO*
Sheri Harter, *Admin Sec*
Frank Lazarone, *Info Tech Mgr*
Lori Gomez, *Opers Staff*
EMP: 50
SALES (est): 5.2MM
SALES (corp-wide): 17.8MM **Privately Held**
WEB: www.pacificselectproperty.com
SIC: 6411 Insurance agents, brokers & service
PA: Geovera Holdings, Inc.
4820 Busineca Ctr Dr 20 Ste 200
Fairfield CA 94534
707 863-3700

(P-10675)
COLDWELL BANKER
580 El Camino Real, San Carlos (94070-2412)
PHONE..............................650 596-5400
EMP: 80 **EST:** 2011
SALES (est): 5.7MM **Privately Held**
SIC: 6411

(P-10676)
COMBINED MANAGEMENT SVCS INC
1500 W West Covina Pkwy # 100, West Covina (91790-2729)
PHONE..............................626 856-2263
Ziad Dabuni MD, *President*
Christine Rodriguez, *Purch Mgr*
EMP: 150
SALES (est): 18.7MM **Privately Held**
WEB: www.combinedmanagementservices.com
SIC: 6411 Insurance agents, brokers & service

(P-10677)
CONEXIS BNEFT ADMNISTRATORS LP (HQ)
721 S Parker St Ste 300, Orange (92868-4732)
PHONE..............................714 835-5006
Michael Close, *President*
Brad Inghram, *Vice Pres*
Christine Marshall, *Project Mgr*
Chris McGowan, *Controller*
John Ball, *Director*
EMP: 120
SQ FT: 57,000
SALES (est): 259.9MM
SALES (corp-wide): 357.5MM **Privately Held**
SIC: 6411 Insurance information & consulting services
PA: Word & Brown, Insurance Administrators, Inc.
721 S Parker St Ste 300
Orange CA 92868
714 835-5006

(P-10678)
CONFIE SEGUROS INC (HQ)
Also Called: Freeway Insurance
7711 Center Ave Ste 200, Huntington Beach (92647-9124)
PHONE..............................714 252-2500
Joseph Waked, *CEO*
Mordy Rothberg, *President*
Robert Bondi, *COO*
Valeria Rico, *COO*
Robert Trebing, *CFO*
EMP: 146
SALES (est): 1B
SALES (corp-wide): 1B **Privately Held**
SIC: 6411 Insurance brokers
PA: Confie Seguros Holding Co.
7711 Center Ave Ste 200
Huntington Beach CA 92647
714 252-2649

(P-10679)
CONTINUING LF COMMUNITIES LLC (PA)
Also Called: La Costa Glen
1940 Levante St, Carlsbad (92009-5174)
PHONE..............................760 704-1000
Richard Aschenbrenner, *CEO*
E Justin Wilson III, *CEO*
Justin Wilson III, *COO*
Warren E Spieker Jr, *Chairman*
Darolyn Jorgensen, *Exec Dir*
EMP: 100
SALES (est): 159.5MM **Privately Held**
SIC: 6411 Employment agencies

(P-10680)
CORVEL CORPORATION
10750 4th St Ste 100, Rancho Cucamonga (91730-0980)
PHONE..............................909 257-3700
Lorie Gonzalez, *Branch Mgr*
Bryan Piattoni, *Regl Sales Mgr*
Dianne Neal,
Scotty Benton, *Manager*
Richard Yamin, *Manager*
EMP: 151
SALES (corp-wide): 503.5MM **Publicly Held**
WEB: www.corvel.com
SIC: 6411 Insurance agents, brokers & service
PA: Corvel Corporation
2010 Main St Ste 600
Irvine CA 92614
949 851-1473

(P-10681)
CORVEL ENTERPRISE COMP INC
2010 Main St Ste 600, Irvine (92614-7272)
PHONE..............................949 851-1473
Daniel J Starck, *CEO*
EMP: 99
SALES (est): 950K **Privately Held**
SIC: 6411 Insurance agents, brokers & service

(P-10682)
CREST FINANCIAL CORPORATION (DH)
12641 166th St, Cerritos (90703-2101)
P.O. Box 3190 (90703-3190)
PHONE..............................562 733-6500
Susan Scurti, *President*
Shannon S Walker, *CFO*
Michael Costello, *Senior VP*
Walter E Erker, *Vice Pres*
Chanda Carling, *Human Res Mgr*
EMP: 62
SQ FT: 15,000
SALES (est): 33.2MM
SALES (corp-wide): 12.4B **Privately Held**
SIC: 6411 7311 Insurance agents, brokers & service; insurance information & consulting services; insurance adjusters; insurance agents & brokers; advertising agencies
HQ: Meadowbrook Insurance Group, Inc.
26255 American Dr
Southfield MI 48034
248 358-1100

(P-10683)
CSAA INSURANCE EXCHANGE (PA)
3055 Oak Rd, Walnut Creek (94597-2098)
P.O. Box 23392, Oakland (94623-0392)
PHONE..............................800 922-8228
Paula Downey, *President*
Greg Meyer, *COO*
Marie Andel, *Officer*
Michael Zukerman, *Officer*
Stephen O'Connor, *CIO*
EMP: 131
SALES (est): 3.8B **Privately Held**
SIC: 6411 Insurance agents, brokers & service

(P-10684)
CSAC EXCESS INSURANCE AUTH
75 Iron Point Cir Ste 200, Folsom (95630-8813)
PHONE..............................916 850-7300
Michael Fleming, *CEO*
Mary Castruccio, *Vice Chairman*
Dan Calabrese, *Ch Invest Ofcr*
Ken Caldwell, *Exec VP*
Thomas Bryson, *Senior VP*
EMP: 60
SQ FT: 13,613
SALES (est): 7.9MM **Privately Held**
WEB: www.csac-eia.org
SIC: 6411 Insurance agents, brokers & service

(P-10685)
CUSTOMZED SVCS ADMNSTRTORS INC
Also Called: Global Care Travel
4181 Ruffin Rd Ste 150, San Diego (92123-1876)
P.O. Box 939057 (92193-9057)
PHONE..............................858 810-2000
Fax: 858 810-2428
Guillaume Deybach, *CEO*
Lara Brower, *Office Mgr*
Suping Liu, *Database Admin*
Mike Grady, *Controller*
Huong Le, *Agent*
EMP: 140
SQ FT: 11,000
SALES (est): 56.1MM
SALES (corp-wide): 60MM **Privately Held**
WEB: www.csatravelprotection.com
SIC: 6411 Insurance agents
PA: Enhancement Products Specialists Inc
5454 Ruffin Rd
San Diego CA

(P-10686)
DEALEY RENTON AND ASSOCIATES
530 Water St Fl 7th, Oakland (94607-3547)
PHONE..............................510 465-3090
Morgan West, *Principal*
EMP: 55
SALES (est): 1.6MM **Privately Held**
SIC: 6411 Insurance brokers

(P-10687)
DEL AMO INSURANCE SERVICES
910 Lomita Blvd Ste E, Harbor City (90710-2200)
P.O. Box 910 (90710-0910)
PHONE..............................310 534-3444
David Blunt, *President*
EMP: 60
SALES (est): 8.8MM **Privately Held**
SIC: 6411 Insurance agents, brokers & service

(P-10688)
DENTISTS INSURANCE COMPANY (HQ)
Also Called: Tdic
1201 K St Ste 1600, Sacramento (95814-3925)
P.O. Box 1582 (95812-1582)
PHONE..............................916 443-4567
Fax: 916 443-4468
Mark Soeth, *President*
Robert Spinelli, *CFO*
Carolyn Unger, *Vice Pres*
Peter Dubois, *Exec Dir*
Kevin Roach, *VP Finance*
EMP: 118 **EST:** 1979
SQ FT: 12,000
SALES (est): 21.2MM
SALES (corp-wide): 21.4MM **Privately Held**
WEB: www.thedentists.com
SIC: 6411 Insurance agents, brokers & service
PA: California Dental Association Inc
1201 K St Fl 14
Sacramento CA 95814
916 443-0505

(P-10689)
DER MNUEL INSUR FINCL SVCS INC
548 W Cromwell Ave # 101, Fresno (93711-5714)
P.O. Box 28906 (93729-8906)
PHONE..............................559 447-4600
M Der Manouel Jr, *Post Master*
Michael Der Manouel Sr, *Ch of Bd*
Michael Der Manouel Jr, *President*
Chuck Der, *COO*
Kevin Nist, *Treasurer*
EMP: 71
SQ FT: 7,000
SALES (est): 21.6MM **Privately Held**
WEB: www.pcsis.com
SIC: 6411 Insurance agents, brokers & service; insurance agents; insurance brokers; life insurance agents

(P-10690)
DIBUDUO DFENDIS INSUR BRKS LLC (PA)
6873 N West Ave, Fresno (93711-4308)
P.O. Box 5479 (93755-5479)
PHONE..............................559 432-0222
Fax: 559 431-7941
Matt Defendis, *Partner*
Mike De Fendis, *Partner*
Tony Canizales, *Vice Pres*
Steve Ellsworth, *Vice Pres*
Ron Lamm, *Vice Pres*
EMP: 93
SQ FT: 22,000
SALES (est): 102.4MM **Privately Held**
WEB: www.dibu.com
SIC: 6411 Insurance agents

(P-10691)
DMA CLAIMS INC (PA)
Also Called: Dma Claims Services
330 N Brand Blvd Ste 230, Glendale (91203-2380)
P.O. Box 26004 (91222-6004)
PHONE..............................323 342-6800
Thomas J Reitze, *President*
Charles Ohl, *Officer*
Brad Balentine, *Branch Mgr*
Richard Catarineau, *CTO*
Lois Hart, *Manager*
EMP: 59
SQ FT: 20,000
SALES (est): 182.4MM **Privately Held**
WEB: www.davidmorse.com
SIC: 6411 Insurance adjusters

(P-10692)
DMA CLAIMS INC
Also Called: David Morse & Assoc.
330 N Brand Blvd Ste 230, Glendale (91203-2380)
PHONE..............................323 342-6800
Dan Mara, *Branch Mgr*
EMP: 126
SALES (corp-wide): 182.4MM **Privately Held**
SIC: 6411 Insurance agents, brokers & service
PA: Dma Claims, Inc.
330 N Brand Blvd Ste 230
Glendale CA 91203
323 342-6800

(P-10693)
DOCTORS MANAGEMENT COMPANY (HQ)
185 Greenwood Rd, NAPA (94558-6270)
P.O. Box 2900 (94558-0900)
PHONE..............................707 226-0100
Fax: 707 226-0198

PRODUCTS & SERVICES SECTION
6411 - Insurance Agents, Brokers & Svc County (P-10714)

Richard E Anderson, *CEO*
Eugene M Bullis, *CFO*
Kenneth R Chrisman, *Exec VP*
Bruce Crile, *Exec VP*
William J Gallagher, *Senior VP*
EMP: 200
SQ FT: 72,000
SALES (est): 301.6MM
SALES (corp-wide): 473.1MM **Privately Held**
SIC: 6411 Insurance information & consulting services; insurance claim processing, except medical
PA: The Doctors' Company An Interinsurance Exchange
185 Greenwood Rd
Napa CA 94558
707 226-0100

(P-10694)
EASTWOOD INSURANCE SERVICES (PA)
155 N Riverview Dr, Anaheim (92808-1225)
P.O. Box 182405, Columbus OH (43218-2405)
PHONE 800 468-5377
Fax: 714 685-8372
EMP: 124
SQ FT: 6,000
SALES (est): 49.9MM **Privately Held**
SIC: 6411

(P-10695)
EDGEWOOD PARTNERS INSUR CTR
8050 N Palm Ave Ste 110, Fresno (93711-5510)
PHONE 559 451-3189
Patrick McCaleb, *Branch Mgr*
EMP: 51 **Privately Held**
SIC: 6411 Insurance brokers
PA: Edgewood Partners Insurance Center
135 Main St 21f
San Francisco CA 94105
-

(P-10696)
EDGEWOOD PARTNERS INSUR CTR
135 Main St Fl 21, San Francisco (94105-8115)
PHONE 415 356-3900
Joe Vineis, *Branch Mgr*
Tiffany Wright, *Manager*
EMP: 105 **Privately Held**
SIC: 6411 8742 Insurance brokers; property & casualty insurance agent; management consulting services
PA: Edgewood Partners Insurance Center
135 Main St 21f
San Francisco CA 94105
-

(P-10697)
EDGEWOOD PARTNERS INSUR CTR (PA)
Also Called: Epic
135 Main St 21f, San Francisco (94105-1812)
P.O. Box 5900, San Mateo (94402-5900)
PHONE 415 356-3900
Dan Francis, *CEO*
John Hahn, *President*
Stephen Adkins, *COO*
Peter Garvey, *COO*
Karman Chan, *CFO*
EMP: 65
SQ FT: 18,897
SALES (est): 377.7MM **Privately Held**
WEB: www.edgewoodins.com
SIC: 6411 Insurance brokers

(P-10698)
EHEALTH INC (PA)
440 E Middlefield Rd, Mountain View (94043-4006)
PHONE 650 584-2700
Fax: 650 961-2110
Scott Flanders, *CEO*
Ellen Tauscher, *Ch of Bd*
William T Shaughnessy, *President*
Stuart M Huizinga, *CFO*
Robert S Hurley, *Exec VP*
EMP: 81

SQ FT: 36,012
SALES: 189.5MM **Publicly Held**
WEB: www.ehealthinsurance.com
SIC: 6411 Insurance agents, brokers & service; insurance agents & brokers; insurance information & consulting services

(P-10699)
EHEALTHINSURANCE SERVICES INC (HQ)
440 E Middlefield Rd, Mountain View (94043-4006)
PHONE 650 584-2700
Stuart Huizinga, *CFO*
Bill Shaughnessy, *President*
Fahlman Robert, *COO*
Mary J Relja, *Exec VP*
Bruce Telkamp, *Exec VP*
EMP: 100
SQ FT: 20,000
SALES (est): 65.4MM
SALES (corp-wide): 189.5MM **Publicly Held**
WEB: www.anysure.com
SIC: 6411 Insurance agents, brokers & service
PA: Ehealth, Inc.
440 E Middlefield Rd
Mountain View CA 94043
650 584-2700

(P-10700)
ENDURANCE SPECIALTY INSURANCE
725 S Figueroa St # 2100, Los Angeles (90017-5524)
PHONE 213 270-7700
Bin Wolfe, *President*
Beth Berthelsen, *Executive*
EMP: 60
SALES (est): 9.3MM **Privately Held**
WEB: www.enhinsurance.com
SIC: 6411 Insurance agents, brokers & service
HQ: Endurance U.S. Holdings Corp.
750 3rd Ave
New York NY 10017
212 471-2800

(P-10701)
ESIS INC
Also Called: Esis Health Safety and Envmtl
7700 Irvine Center Dr # 900, Irvine (92618-3051)
PHONE 949 242-6950
Steve Rochhi, *Principal*
EMP: 75
SALES (corp-wide): 17.2B **Privately Held**
SIC: 6411 Insurance agents, brokers & service
HQ: Esis, Inc.
436 Walnut St
Philadelphia PA 19106
215 640-1000

(P-10702)
ESURANCE INC (HQ)
Also Called: PNC
650 Davis St, San Francisco (94111-1981)
PHONE 415 875-4500
Gary C Tolman, *CEO*
Jonathan Adkisson, *CFO*
Alan Gellman, *Chief Mktg Ofcr*
Eric Brandt, *Officer*
Wayne Sharrah, *Officer*
EMP: 140
SQ FT: 10,000
SALES (est): 492.5MM
SALES (corp-wide): 35.6B **Publicly Held**
SIC: 6411 Insurance agents, brokers & service
PA: The Allstate Corporation
2775 Sanders Rd
Northbrook IL 60062
847 402-5000

(P-10703)
EVIDERA ARCHIMEDES INC
450 Sansome St Ste 650, San Francisco (94111-3380)
PHONE 415 490-0400
Fax: 415 490-0399
Jon Williams, *President*
Lynn Okamoto, *Senior VP*
Josh Adler, *Vice Pres*
Tuan Dinh, *Vice Pres*

Denis Getsios, *Vice Pres*
EMP: 60
SALES (est): 16MM
SALES (corp-wide): 1.9B **Privately Held**
WEB: www.archimedesmodel.com
SIC: 6411 Insurance information & consulting services
HQ: Evidera, Inc.
7101 Wscnsin Ave Ste 1400
Bethesda MD 20814

(P-10704)
FARMERS GROUP INC
Also Called: Farmers Insurance
13950 Ramona Ave, Chino (91710-5427)
PHONE 909 839-2020
Mike Dyer, *Branch Mgr*
EMP: 82
SALES (corp-wide): 62B **Privately Held**
WEB: www.farmers.com
SIC: 6411 4226 4225 Insurance agents, brokers & service; special warehousing & storage; general warehousing & storage
HQ: Farmers Group, Inc.
6301 Owensmouth Ave
Woodland Hills CA 91367
323 932-3200

(P-10705)
FARMERS GROUP INC
Also Called: Farmers Insurance
429 Llewellyn Ave, Campbell (95008-1948)
PHONE 408 557-1100
William Garrity, *Manager*
EMP: 50
SALES (corp-wide): 62B **Privately Held**
WEB: www.farmers.com
SIC: 6411 Insurance agents, brokers & service
HQ: Farmers Group, Inc.
6301 Owensmouth Ave
Woodland Hills CA 91367
323 932-3200

(P-10706)
FARMERS GROUP INC
Also Called: Farmers Insurance
550 S Hill St Ste 1309, Los Angeles (90013-2292)
PHONE 818 249-3000
Leo Denlea Jr, *President*
EMP: 88
SALES (corp-wide): 62B **Privately Held**
WEB: www.farmers.com
SIC: 6411 Insurance agents, brokers & service
HQ: Farmers Group, Inc.
6301 Owensmouth Ave
Woodland Hills CA 91367
323 932-3200

(P-10707)
FARMERS GROUP INC
Also Called: Farmers Insurance
6518 Antelope Rd, Citrus Heights (95621-1077)
PHONE 916 727-4600
Bruce Bailey, *Manager*
Jana Gatling, *Director*
Bill McAdam, *Manager*
EMP: 75
SALES (corp-wide): 62B **Privately Held**
WEB: www.farmers.com
SIC: 6411 Insurance agents, brokers & service
HQ: Farmers Group, Inc.
6301 Owensmouth Ave
Woodland Hills CA 91367
323 932-3200

(P-10708)
FARMERS GROUP INC
Also Called: Farmers Insurance
6303 Owensmouth Ave, Woodland Hills (91367-2264)
PHONE 888 327-6335
Elias Ruiz, *Manager*
Joe Wintering, *Manager*
EMP: 90
SALES (corp-wide): 62B **Privately Held**
WEB: www.farmers.com
SIC: 6411 6331 Insurance agents, brokers & service; fire, marine & casualty insurance

HQ: Farmers Group, Inc.
6301 Owensmouth Ave
Woodland Hills CA 91367
323 932-3200

(P-10709)
FARMERS GROUP INC
Also Called: Farmers Insurance
6303 Owensmouth Ave Fl 1, Woodland Hills (91367-2200)
PHONE 805 583-7400
EMP: 900
SALES (corp-wide): 74.2B **Privately Held**
SIC: 6411
HQ: Farmers Group, Inc.
6301 Owensmouth Ave
Woodland Hills CA 91367
323 932-3200

(P-10710)
FARMERS INSURANCE
1801 Orange Tree Ln # 200, Redlands (92374-4587)
PHONE 909 801-3300
Sean Sisco, *Manager*
EMP: 62
SALES (est): 2.6MM **Privately Held**
SIC: 6411 Insurance agents, brokers & service

(P-10711)
FARMERS INSURANCE EXCHANGE
7365 Carnelian St Ste 206, Rancho Cucamonga (91730-1157)
PHONE 909 758-7060
EMP: 729
SALES (corp-wide): 6.3B **Privately Held**
SIC: 6411 Insurance agents, brokers & service
PA: Farmers Insurance Exchange
6301 Owensmouth Ave # 300
Woodland Hills CA 91367
323 932-3200

(P-10712)
FARMERS INSURANCE EXCHANGE
5280 Carroll Canyon Rd # 230, San Diego (92121-1784)
PHONE 858 677-1100
Al Lopez, *Manager*
EMP: 100
SQ FT: 28,800
SALES (corp-wide): 6.3B **Privately Held**
SIC: 6411 Insurance agents, brokers & service
PA: Farmers Insurance Exchange
6301 Owensmouth Ave # 300
Woodland Hills CA 91367
323 932-3200

(P-10713)
FARMERS INSURANCE EXCHANGE
411 E Pine St Ste A, Exeter (93221-1800)
PHONE 559 594-4149
Fax: 559 594-4554
Sammy Harrell, *Branch Mgr*
EMP: 326
SALES (corp-wide): 6.3B **Privately Held**
SIC: 6411 Insurance agents, brokers & service
PA: Farmers Insurance Exchange
6301 Owensmouth Ave # 300
Woodland Hills CA 91367
323 932-3200

(P-10714)
FARMERS INSURANCE GROUP (DH)
6301 Owensmouth Ave, Los Angeles (90010)
P.O. Box 149044, Austin TX (78714-9044)
PHONE 888 327-6335
Fax: 323 930-3438
Jim Snikeris, *Exec Dir*
Verginia Lam, *President*
Russina Sgoureva, *President*
Erik J Snikeris, *President*
Ronald G Myhan, *Treasurer*
EMP: 575 **EST:** 1967

6411 - Insurance Agents, Brokers & Svc County (P-10715)

SALES (est): 357.6MM
SALES (corp-wide): 62B **Privately Held**
SIC: 6411 Insurance agents, brokers & service
HQ: Farmers Group, Inc.
6301 Owensmouth Ave
Woodland Hills CA 91367
323 932-3200

(P-10715)
FARMERS SERVICES LLC
4680 Wilshire Blvd, Los Angeles (90010-3807)
PHONE................323 932-3200
Randy Farmer, *Principal*
EMP: 2809
SALES (est): 210.1K
SALES (corp-wide): 62B **Privately Held**
SIC: 6411 Insurance agents, brokers & service
HQ: Farmers Group, Inc.
6301 Owensmouth Ave
Woodland Hills CA 91367
323 932-3200

(P-10716)
FEDERAL INSURANCE COMPANY
Also Called: Chubb
275 Battery St Fl 12, San Francisco (94111-3373)
PHONE................415 273-6300
Cliston Thomas, *Manager*
Frank Rockett, *Executive*
Tyler Bausom, *Underwriter*
EMP: 100
SALES (corp-wide): 17.2B **Privately Held**
WEB: www.federalinsurancecompany.com
SIC: 6411 Insurance agents, brokers & service
HQ: Federal Insurance Company
15 Mountainview Rd
Warren NJ 07059
908 903-2000

(P-10717)
FIDELITY NATIONAL FINCL INC
1300 Dove St Ste 310, Newport Beach (92660-2417)
PHONE................949 622-5000
Fax: 949 477-6814
Rob Vavrock, *Branch Mgr*
Janette Delap, *Officer*
Bobbie Purdy, *Officer*
Jeff Gross, *Vice Pres*
Ginger McCully, *Vice Pres*
EMP: 80
SALES (corp-wide): 9.1B **Publicly Held**
SIC: 6411 Insurance agents, brokers & service
PA: Fidelity National Financial, Inc.
601 Riverside Ave Fl 4
Jacksonville FL 32204
904 854-8100

(P-10718)
FIDELITY NATIONAL TITLE CO CAL
8801 Folsom Blvd Ste 210, Sacramento (95826-3249)
PHONE................916 646-9993
Fax: 916 386-1311
Maria Nickel, *Manager*
EMP: 60
SALES (corp-wide): 9.1B **Publicly Held**
WEB: www.fntic.com
SIC: 6411 Insurance agents, brokers & service
HQ: Fidelity National Title Insurance Company
3220 El Camino Real
Irvine CA 92602
949 622-4600

(P-10719)
FINANCIAL PACIFIC INSUR AGCY
3850 Atherton Rd, Rocklin (95765-3700)
P.O. Box 292220, Sacramento (95829-2220)
PHONE................916 630-5000
Andrew Speaker, *President*
Artur A Terner CPA, *CFO*
EMP: 109
SQ FT: 25,000

SALES (est): 8MM **Publicly Held**
WEB: www.fpicnline.com
SIC: 6411 Property & casualty insurance agent
HQ: Mercer Insurance Group, Inc.
10 N Hwy 31
Pennington NJ 08534
609 737-0426

(P-10720)
FINANCIAL PACIFIC INSURANCE CO
3850 Atherton Rd, Rocklin (95765-3700)
P.O. Box 292220 (95765)
PHONE................916 630-5000
Robert C Goodell, *Principal*
Connor Bickell, *Advisor*
Warren Jinnie, *Advisor*
EMP: 78
SALES (est): 144.6K **Publicly Held**
SIC: 6411 Insurance agents, brokers & service
HQ: Financial Pacific Insurance Group, Inc.
3880 Atherton Rd
Rocklin CA 95765
916 630-5000

(P-10721)
FIRE INSURANCE EXCHANGE (PA)
4680 Wilshire Blvd, Los Angeles (90010-3807)
PHONE................323 932-3200
Martin Feinstein, *President*
John Harrington, *President*
Ron Myhan, *Treasurer*
Doren Hohl, *Admin Sec*
EMP: 2300
SALES: 1B **Privately Held**
SIC: 6411 Insurance agents, brokers & service

(P-10722)
FREEWAY INSURANCE (PA)
Also Called: South Coast Auto Insurance
10801 Walker St Ste 250, Cypress (90630-5044)
P.O. Box 669 (90630-0669)
PHONE................714 252-2500
Fax: 714 226-9900
Elias Assaf, *President*
Norm Hudson, *COO*
John Klaeb, *Vice Pres*
Dian Striccland, *Executive Asst*
Janet Castrejon, *Human Res Mgr*
EMP: 120
SQ FT: 20,000
SALES (est): 95.5MM **Privately Held**
WEB: www.seguroahora.com
SIC: 6411 Insurance agents

(P-10723)
G C H INSURANCE GROUP
Also Called: Capax, Giddings, Corby & Hynes
1150 9th St Ste 1400, Modesto (95354-0840)
P.O. Box 3231 (95353-3231)
PHONE................209 526-3110
Fax: 209 559-3096
Joel Geddes Jr, *CEO*
Joel Gebdes, *Meeting Planner*
EMP: 50
SALES (est): 6.4MM **Privately Held**
SIC: 6411 Insurance agents, brokers & service

(P-10724)
G J SULLIVAN CO INC
800 W 6th St Ste 1800, Los Angeles (90017-2701)
PHONE................213 626-1000
Fax: 213 622-5921
Gerald J Sullivan, *President*
John McCann, *COO*
Ryer Pickren, *Exec VP*
Rafi Koshkerian, *Vice Pres*
Jerald Lob, *Vice Pres*
EMP: 60
SALES (est): 19.5MM
SALES (corp-wide): 172.2MM **Privately Held**
WEB: www.gjs.com
SIC: 6411 Insurance brokers

HQ: Gerald J. Sullivan & Associates, Inc. Insurance Brokers
800 W 6th St Ste 1800
Los Angeles CA
213 626-1000

(P-10725)
GEICO CORPORATION
2195 Monterey Hwy Ste 20, San Jose (95125-1069)
PHONE................408 286-4342
Fax: 408 286-6397
Brent Folk, *Branch Mgr*
EMP: 200
SALES (corp-wide): 210.8B **Publicly Held**
WEB: www.geico.com
SIC: 6411 Insurance agents, brokers & service
HQ: Geico Corporation
1 Geico Plz
Washington DC 20076
301 986-3000

(P-10726)
GEICO CORPORATION
2340 Monument Blvd Ste A, Pleasant Hill (94523-3971)
PHONE................415 330-9999
EMP: 200
SALES (corp-wide): 210.8B **Publicly Held**
SIC: 6411 Insurance agents, brokers & service
HQ: Geico Corporation
1 Geico Plz
Washington DC 20076
301 986-3000

(P-10727)
GEICO CORPORATION
2033 Arden Way Ste C, Sacramento (95825-2210)
PHONE................707 448-7172
Fax: 916 929-4907
Vincent Harris, *Branch Mgr*
EMP: 147
SALES (corp-wide): 210.8B **Publicly Held**
SIC: 6411 Insurance agents, brokers & service
HQ: Geico Corporation
1 Geico Plz
Washington DC 20076
301 986-3000

(P-10728)
GEICO GENERAL INSURANCE CO
14111 Danielson St, Poway (92064-6886)
PHONE................858 848-8200
Elizabeth Shew, *Principal*
Alex S Gomez, *Facilities Mgr*
Margi Rogers, *Assistant VP*
EMP: 378
SALES (corp-wide): 210.8B **Publicly Held**
SIC: 6411 Insurance agents, brokers & service
HQ: Geico General Insurance Company
1 Geico Plz
Washington DC 20076
301 986-3000

(P-10729)
GEOVERA SPECIALTY INSURANCE CO
1455 Oliver Rd, Fairfield (94534-3472)
PHONE................707 863-3700
Karen Padovese, *President*
Bruce Allen, *Incorporator*
Kevin Nish, *President*
Thomas Hanzel, *Treasurer*
Frank Albertson, *Vice Pres*
EMP: 60
SALES (est): 8.3MM
SALES (corp-wide): 19.8MM **Privately Held**
WEB: www.homeinsurer.com
SIC: 6411 Insurance brokers
PA: Geovera Holdings, Inc.
4820 Busineca Ctr Dr 20 Ste 200
Fairfield CA 94534
707 863-3700

(P-10730)
GGIS INSURANCE SERVICES INC
Also Called: Guardian General Insur Svcs
600 N Brand Blvd Ste 300, Glendale (91203-4207)
PHONE................818 553-2110
EMP: 135
SALES (est): 12.7MM **Privately Held**
WEB: www.guardiangeneral.com
SIC: 6411

(P-10731)
GOOD DEAL INSURANCE SERVICES
2140 S Hacienda Blvd A, Hacienda Heights (91745-7200)
PHONE................626 275-6795
Chung Hwei Chang, *President*
Tracy Lee, *Manager*
EMP: 70 EST: 2012
SQ FT: 4,000
SALES (est): 6.6MM **Privately Held**
SIC: 6411 Insurance agents, brokers & service

(P-10732)
GROSSLIGHT INSURANCE INC
Also Called: Kemper Insurance
1333 Westwood Blvd # 200, Los Angeles (90024-4949)
P.O. Box 24946 (90024-0946)
PHONE................310 473-9611
Fax: 310 312-4993
Gilbert F Grosslight, *CEO*
Steven Schiewe, *President*
Colleen Malfitano, *Human Res Dir*
Joan Schiewe, *Sales Executive*
Joanne Blentzas, *VP Mktg*
EMP: 60
SQ FT: 15,000
SALES (est): 18.2MM **Privately Held**
WEB: www.grosslight.com
SIC: 6411 Insurance agents, brokers & service

(P-10733)
GS LEVINE INSURANCE SVCS INC
10505 Sorrento Valley Rd # 200, San Diego (92121-1618)
PHONE................858 481-8692
Gary S Levine, *CEO*
Ross Afsahi, *President*
Dick Avakian, *COO*
Judy King, *Vice Pres*
Anjie Massie, *Personnel Exec*
EMP: 62
SQ FT: 17,000
SALES (est): 16.1MM
SALES (corp-wide): 5.3B **Publicly Held**
WEB: www.gslevineins.com
SIC: 6411 Insurance agents & brokers
PA: Arthur J. Gallagher & Co.
2 Pierce Pl
Itasca IL 60143
630 773-3800

(P-10734)
HAMILTON BRWART INSUR AGCY LLC
1282 W Arrow Hwy, Upland (91786-5040)
P.O. Box 1949 (91785-1949)
PHONE................909 920-3250
Hamilton Brewart,
Derek Brewart,
Derak R Brewart, *Manager*
EMP: 67
SQ FT: 12,000
SALES (est): 12.3MM **Privately Held**
WEB: www.hamiltonbrewart.com
SIC: 6411 Insurance agents; insurance brokers

(P-10735)
HARTFORD FIRE INSURANCE CO
12009 Foundation Pl # 100, Gold River (95670-4534)
P.O. Box 15277, Sacramento (95851-0277)
PHONE................916 294-1000
Fax: 916 294-1000
John Buckalew, *Manager*
Robert Hughes, *President*
Kevin Harneteaux, *Vice Pres*

PRODUCTS & SERVICES SECTION

6411 - Insurance Agents, Brokers & Svc County (P-10755)

EMP: 300
SALES (corp-wide): 18.3B Publicly Held
WEB:
www.hartfordinvestmentscanada.com
SIC: 6411 Insurance agents, brokers & service
HQ: Hartford Fire Insurance Company (Inc)
1 Hartford Plz
Hartford CT 06115
860 547-5000

(P-10736)
HARTFORD FIRE INSURANCE CO
777 S Figueroa St Ste 700, Los Angeles (90017-5861)
PHONE.................................213 452-5179
Rich Long, *Sales Staff*
Eric Waller, *Director*
Gary Mathewson, *Manager*
Kerri Weinstock, *Accounts Exec*
EMP: 212
SALES (corp-wide): 18.3B Publicly Held
WEB:
www.hartfordinvestmentscanada.com
SIC: 6411 Insurance agents, brokers & service
HQ: Hartford Fire Insurance Company (Inc)
1 Hartford Plz
Hartford CT 06115
860 547-5000

(P-10737)
HEALTH COMP ADMINISTRATORS (PA)
621 Santa Fe Ave, Fresno (93721-2724)
P.O. Box 45018 (93718-5018)
PHONE.................................559 499-2450
Fax: 559 499-2464
Phillip Musson, *President*
Don Soper, *President*
Mike Bouskos, *Vice Pres*
Kelly Ferreira, *VP Admin*
Scott Olds, *Info Tech Mgr*
EMP: 165
SALES (est): 58.9MM Privately Held
SIC: 6411 Medical insurance claim processing, contract or fee basis

(P-10738)
HEALTHCOMP
Also Called: Healthcomp Administrators
621 Santa Fe Ave, Fresno (93721-2724)
P.O. Box 45018 (93718-5018)
PHONE.................................559 499-2450
Phillip Musson, *CEO*
Michael Bouskos, *CFO*
Monique Bouskos, *Vice Pres*
Kelly Ferreira, *Vice Pres*
Charles Johnson, *Vice Pres*
EMP: 260
SQ FT: 50,000
SALES (est): 60.1MM Privately Held
WEB: www.healthcomp.com
SIC: 6411 Medical insurance claim processing, contract or fee basis

(P-10739)
HEALTHSMART MANAGEMENT SERVICE
10855 Bus Ctr Dr Ste C, Cypress (90630)
P.O. Box 6300 (90630-0063)
PHONE.................................714 947-8600
Carol Houchins, *President*
Jeff Vedrani, *Administration*
Susan Dullack, *Director*
Berenice Botello, *Manager*
Marcus Yoon, *Manager*
EMP: 90
SALES (est): 16.4MM Privately Held
WEB: www.healthsmartmso.com
SIC: 6411 8741 8721 Medical insurance claim processing, contract or fee basis; hospital management; business management; billing & bookkeeping service

(P-10740)
HEFFERNAN INSURANCE BROKERS
Also Called: Heffernan Group
180 Howard St Ste 200, San Francisco (94105-1663)
PHONE.................................415 398-7733
Fax: 415 778-0301
Steve Williams, *Manager*
Janice Berthold, *Senior VP*
Marc Paletta, *Vice Pres*
Adam Booth, *Sales Staff*
Robin Lorenzini, *Sales Staff*
EMP: 50
SALES (corp-wide): 223.7MM Privately Held
WEB: www.heffgroup.com
SIC: 6411 Insurance agents, brokers & service
PA: Heffernan Insurance Brokers
1350 Carlback Ave
Walnut Creek CA 94596
925 934-8500

(P-10741)
HUB INTRNTIONAL INSUR SVCS INC
3636 American River Dr # 200, Sacramento (95864-5952)
PHONE.................................916 974-7800
EMP: 90
SALES (corp-wide): 2.4B Privately Held
SIC: 6411 Insurance agents; insurance brokers
HQ: Hub International Insurance Services Inc.
3390 University Ave # 300
Riverside CA 92501
951 788-8500

(P-10742)
HUB INTRNTIONAL INSUR SVCS INC
40 E Alamar Ave, Santa Barbara (93105-3469)
PHONE.................................805 682-2571
Darren Tesars, *Manager*
Beth Mitchell, *Broker*
Betty Briggs, *Accounts Exec*
Casey Tadlock, *Accounts Exec*
EMP: 52
SALES (corp-wide): 2.4B Privately Held
SIC: 6411 Insurance agents, brokers & service
HQ: Hub International Insurance Services Inc.
3390 University Ave # 300
Riverside CA 92501
951 788-8500

(P-10743)
INSCO INSURANCE SERVICES INC (HQ)
Also Called: Developers Surety Indemnity Co
17771 Cowan Ste 100, Irvine (92614-6044)
P.O. Box 19725 (92623-9725)
PHONE.................................949 797-9243
Harry Crowell, *Ch of Bd*
Sam Tobis, *Vice Pres*
Steve Murray, *Regional Mgr*
Dave Paloma, *Regional Mgr*
Emil Askew, *Branch Mgr*
EMP: 70
SQ FT: 50,000
SALES (est): 52.3MM
SALES (corp-wide): 4.6B Publicly Held
WEB: www.inscodico.com
SIC: 6411 6351 Property & casualty insurance agent; surety insurance bonding; liability insurance
PA: Amtrust Financial Services, Inc.
59 Maiden Ln Fl 43
New York NY 10038
212 220-7120

(P-10744)
INSURANCE SERVICES AMERCN LLC
300 E Esplanade Dr # 2100, Oxnard (93036-1238)
PHONE.................................805 981-2220
Stanley Braun,
Nancy Braun,
Myrtle Solomon,
EMP: 70
SALES (est): 4.6MM Privately Held
SIC: 6411 Insurance agents & brokers

(P-10745)
INTEGRO USA INC
115 N El Molino Ave, Pasadena (91101-1804)
PHONE.................................626 795-9000
Steve Titus, *General Mgr*
EMP: 50
SALES (corp-wide): 365.8MM Privately Held
SIC: 6411 Insurance agents
HQ: Integro Usa Inc.
1 State St Fl 9
New York NY 10004
212 295-8000

(P-10746)
INTERCARE HOLDINGS INSUR SVCS
Also Called: Ihi
3010 Lava Ridge Ct # 110, Roseville (95661-3063)
P.O. Box 579 (95661-0579)
PHONE.................................916 677-2500
George McLeary, *CEO*
Anges Hoeberling, *Exec VP*
Richard R Rothman, *Exec VP*
Lance Witt, *Exec VP*
Alan Avriett, *Vice Pres*
EMP: 263
SALES (est): 23.7MM Privately Held
SIC: 6411 Insurance adjusters

(P-10747)
INTERNTNAL PRNSRANCE ASSOC LLC
504 Redwood Blvd Ste 240e, Novato (94947-6925)
PHONE.................................415 223-5548
Fax: 415 382-0676
David M Hofele, *Mng Member*
EMP: 50 EST: 2010
SALES (est): 8.2MM Privately Held
SIC: 6411 Insurance brokers

(P-10748)
INTERWEST INSURANCE SVCS INC (PA)
Also Called: Kemper Insurance
3636 American River Dr # 2, Sacramento (95864-5952)
P.O. Box 255188 (95865-5188)
PHONE.................................916 488-3100
Fax: 916 488-3492
Tom Williams, *Chairman*
Thomas Williams, *President*
Keith Schuler, *CEO*
Nancy Luttenbacher, *COO*
Donald Pollard, *CFO*
EMP: 173
SQ FT: 20,000
SALES (est): 183.5MM Privately Held
WEB: www.infosourcecafe.com
SIC: 6411 Insurance brokers

(P-10749)
INTERWEST INSURANCE SVCS INC
Also Called: Lindo Hanna & Abbott
1357 E Lassen Ave Ste 100, Chico (95973-7824)
P.O. Box 8110 (95927-8110)
PHONE.................................530 895-1010
Fax: 530 895-1313
Keith Shuler, *CEO*
Kerry Forwalter, *Assoc VP*
John Hopkins, *Vice Pres*
Ken McKay, *Vice Pres*
Mike McStocker, *Vice Pres*
EMP: 70
SALES (corp-wide): 183.5MM Privately Held
WEB: www.infosourcecafe.com
SIC: 6411 Insurance agents, brokers & service
PA: Interwest Insurance Services, Inc.
3636 American River Dr # 2
Sacramento CA 95864
916 488-3100

(P-10750)
INVESMART INC
55 Almaden Blvd Ste 800, San Jose (95113-1612)
PHONE.................................408 961-2800
Fax: 408 271-2100
Kent Buckles, *CEO*
Michael Rogers, *Vice Pres*
Sarah Farrant, *Executive Asst*
Bryn Graziano, *Education*
EMP: 55 EST: 1993
SALES (est): 5.4MM
SALES (corp-wide): 2.9B Privately Held
WEB: www.stancorpfinancial.com
SIC: 6411 Pension & retirement plan consultants
PA: Stancorp Financial Group, Inc.
1100 Sw 6th Ave
Portland OR 97204
971 321-7000

(P-10751)
JAMES C JENKINS INSUR SVC INC
Also Called: Athens Insurance
1390 Willow Pass Rd # 800, Concord (94520-7924)
P.O. Box 696 (94522-0796)
PHONE.................................925 798-3334
John Hahn, *CEO*
James C Jenkins, *President*
Jodi Ellington, *CFO*
Jason Del Grande, *Vice Pres*
Fredi Foye-Helms, *Vice Pres*
EMP: 125 EST: 1977
SQ FT: 30,000
SALES (est): 53.9MM Privately Held
SIC: 6411 Insurance agents, brokers & service; insurance brokers
PA: Edgewood Partners Insurance Center
135 Main St 21f
San Francisco CA 94105

(P-10752)
JAMES G PARKER INSURANCE ASSOC (PA)
Also Called: Bacome Insurance Agency
1753 E Fir Ave, Fresno (93720-3840)
P.O. Box 3947 (93650-3947)
PHONE.................................559 222-7722
Fax: 559 222-1724
James G Parker, *President*
Janice W Parker, *Treasurer*
Leroy Berrett, *Vice Pres*
Jon Parker, *Vice Pres*
Gerald Thompson, *Vice Pres*
EMP: 70
SQ FT: 13,000
SALES (est): 110.4MM Privately Held
SIC: 6411 Insurance agents

(P-10753)
JANET HILTON
Also Called: Allstate
990 W 190th St Ste 300, Torrance (90502-4461)
PHONE.................................310 851-7200
Janet Hilton, *Principal*
EMP: 100
SALES (est): 5.5MM Privately Held
SIC: 6411 Insurance agents, brokers & service

(P-10754)
KAERCHER CAMPBELL ASSOCIATE IN
600 Corporate Pointe # 1010, Culver City (90230-7600)
PHONE.................................310 556-1900
David Putman, *Ch of Bd*
Rod Austria, *President*
Allan Kaercher, *President*
Penni Campbell, *CEO*
Robert G Sattler, *Senior VP*
EMP: 119
SALES (est): 23.3MM Privately Held
SIC: 6411 Insurance agents, brokers & service

(P-10755)
KEENAN & ASSOCIATES
1791 Broadway St Ste 200, Redwood City (94063-2487)
P.O. Box 2707, Torrance (90509-2707)
PHONE.................................650 306-0616
Fax: 650 306-0620
Jessica Blakiston, *Manager*
EMP: 55
SALES (corp-wide): 732.5MM Privately Held
SIC: 6411 Insurance claim adjusters, not employed by insurance company
PA: Keenan & Associates
2355 Crenshaw Blvd # 200
Torrance CA 90501
310 212-3344

6411 - Insurance Agents, Brokers & Svc County (P-10756)

(P-10756)
KEENAN & ASSOCIATES (PA)
2355 Crenshaw Blvd # 200, Torrance (90501-3395)
P.O. Box 4328 (90510-4328)
PHONE...............................310 212-3344
Fax: 310 328-6793
John Keenan, *Ch of Bd*
Sean Smith, *CEO*
Davis Seres, *COO*
Dave Dewenter, *Exec VP*
Henry Loubet, *Senior VP*
EMP: 339
SQ FT: 80,000
SALES (est): 732.5MM Privately Held
WEB: www.keenanhealthcare.com
SIC: 6411 Insurance brokers

(P-10757)
KEENAN & ASSOCIATES
626 H St, Eureka (95501-1026)
PHONE...............................707 268-1616
Fax: 707 268-8963
Kay Byrnes, *Manager*
EMP: 55
SALES (corp-wide): 732.5MM Privately Held
SIC: 6411 Insurance information & consulting services
PA: Keenan & Associates
2355 Crenshaw Blvd # 200
Torrance CA 90501
310 212-3344

(P-10758)
KEENAN & ASSOCIATES
2868 Prospect Park Dr # 600, Rancho Cordova (95670-6066)
PHONE...............................916 858-2981
Fax: 916 859-7166
Nancy Conner, *Manager*
EMP: 70
SALES (corp-wide): 732.5MM Privately Held
WEB: www.keenanhealthcare.com
SIC: 6411 Insurance agents, brokers & service
PA: Keenan & Associates
2355 Crenshaw Blvd # 200
Torrance CA 90501
310 212-3344

(P-10759)
KEENAN & ASSOCIATES
3550 Vine St Ste 200, Riverside (92507-4175)
P.O. Box 79991 (92513-1991)
PHONE...............................951 788-0330
Karleen Smartiss, *Manager*
Michael Pfeiffer, *Administration*
Josie Thompson, *Manager*
EMP: 65
SALES (corp-wide): 732.5MM Privately Held
WEB: www.keenanhealthcare.com
SIC: 6411 6371 Insurance brokers; pension, health & welfare funds
PA: Keenan & Associates
2355 Crenshaw Blvd # 200
Torrance CA 90501
310 212-3344

(P-10760)
KEENAN & ASSOCIATES
1740 Tech Dr Ste 300, San Jose (95110)
PHONE...............................408 441-0754
Fax: 408 371-1796
Mickey Armstrong, *Manager*
EMP: 50
SALES (corp-wide): 732.5MM Privately Held
WEB: www.keenanhealthcare.com
SIC: 6411 Insurance brokers
PA: Keenan & Associates
2355 Crenshaw Blvd # 200
Torrance CA 90501
310 212-3344

(P-10761)
KEENAN & ASSOCIATES
901 Calle Amanecer # 200, San Clemente (92673-4211)
PHONE...............................949 940-1760
Fax: 949 369-0324
Steve Gedestad, *Principal*
Paul Kaump, *Assoc VP*
EMP: 55
SALES (corp-wide): 732.5MM Privately Held
WEB: www.keenanhealthcare.com
SIC: 6411 Insurance brokers
PA: Keenan & Associates
2355 Crenshaw Blvd # 200
Torrance CA 90501
310 212-3344

(P-10762)
KERN MEMBER INSURANCE SERVICES
Also Called: Kern Federal Credit Union
1717 Truxtun Ave, Bakersfield (93301-5102)
PHONE...............................661 327-9461
Fax: 661 589-8833
Deann Straub, *President*
Neil Marshall, *CFO*
Linda Crosby, *Vice Pres*
Gloria Scales, *Vice Pres*
Susan Jones, *Principal*
EMP: 50
SALES (est): 7.1MM Privately Held
WEB: www.kernfederalcreditunion.com
SIC: 6411 Insurance agents, brokers & service

(P-10763)
L W ROTH INSURANCE AGENCY
Also Called: National Association For Self
6060 Sunrise Vista Dr # 1180, Citrus Heights (95610-7061)
PHONE...............................916 721-6273
Fax: 916 721-7973
L W Roth, *Owner*
EMP: 100
SALES (est): 8.8MM Privately Held
SIC: 6411 Insurance agents, brokers & service

(P-10764)
LISI INC (PA)
1600 W Hillsdale Blvd # 100, San Mateo (94402-3770)
PHONE...............................650 348-4131
Fax: 650 348-0968
Philip Lebherz, *Ch of Bd*
Becky Patel, *CEO*
Tamara Henderson, *Vice Pres*
Ken Doyle, *Exec Dir*
Hadley Weiler, *Exec Dir*
EMP: 60
SQ FT: 18,000
SALES (est): 132.4MM Privately Held
WEB: www.lisibroker.com
SIC: 6411 Insurance agents

(P-10765)
LOCKTON COMPANIES LLC-PACIFIC
Also Called: Lockton Insurance Brokers
2 Embarcadero Ctr # 1700, San Francisco (94111-3823)
PHONE...............................415 568-4000
Fax: 415 992-4000
Rick Ortiz, *Consultant*
EMP: 87
SALES (corp-wide): 1.3B Privately Held
SIC: 6411 Insurance brokers
HQ: Lockton Companies, Llc-Pacific Series
725 S Figueroa St Fl 35
Los Angeles CA 90017
213 689-0500

(P-10766)
LOCKTON COMPANIES LLC-PACIFIC (HQ)
Also Called: Lockton Insurance Brokers
725 S Figueroa St Fl 35, Los Angeles (90017-5435)
PHONE...............................213 689-0500
Leonard Fodemski, *COO*
Philip Hurrle, *Partner*
Timothy J Noonan, *President*
Gary Petrosino, *COO*
Leonard G Fodemski, *CFO*
EMP: 294
SQ FT: 72,300
SALES (est): 244.6MM
SALES (corp-wide): 1.3B Privately Held
SIC: 6411 Insurance brokers
PA: Lockton, Inc.
444 W 47th St Ste 900
Kansas City MO 64112
816 960-9000

(P-10767)
LOCKTON COMPANIES LLC-PACIFIC
Also Called: Lockton Insurance Brokers
4275 Executive Sq Ste 600, San Diego (92121)
PHONE...............................858 587-3100
Fax: 858 909-3100
Grace Bennett, *Project Mgr*
Pamela Vorman, *Marketing Mgr*
Leilani Judah, *Accounts Mgr*
Brenda Zarouri, *Accounts Exec*
EMP: 117
SALES (corp-wide): 1.3B Privately Held
SIC: 6411 Insurance agents, brokers & service
HQ: Lockton Companies, Llc-Pacific Series
725 S Figueroa St Fl 35
Los Angeles CA 90017
213 689-0500

(P-10768)
MANAGED CARE SYSTEMS KERN CNTY
Also Called: MCS
5251 Office Park Dr # 405, Bakersfield (93309-0404)
PHONE...............................661 716-7100
Bob Severs, *CEO*
EMP: 80
SALES (est): 8.2MM Privately Held
SIC: 6411 7363 Medical insurance claim processing, contract or fee basis; medical help service

(P-10769)
MARKEL CORP
Also Called: Associated Intl Insur Co
21600 Oxnard St Ste 900, Woodland Hills (91367-7834)
PHONE...............................818 595-0600
Anthony Markel, *President*
Alan Kirshner, *Ch of Bd*
Steven Markel, *Vice Ch Bd*
Mollie Stone, *Vice Pres*
Robert Vlazer, *Vice Pres*
EMP: 281
SQ FT: 32,000
SALES (est): 25.7MM
SALES (corp-wide): 5.3B Publicly Held
SIC: 6411 Insurance agents, brokers & service
HQ: Markel North America, Inc
4521 Highwoods Pkwy
Glen Allen VA 23060
804 747-0136

(P-10770)
MARKEL WEST INC
21600 Oxnard St Ste 400, Woodland Hills (91367-4800)
PHONE...............................818 595-0600
Fax: 818 316-0380
Anthony Markel, *President*
EMP: 50
SALES (est): 6.4MM
SALES (corp-wide): 5.3B Publicly Held
WEB: www.markelcorp.com
SIC: 6411 Insurance agents, brokers & service
PA: Markel Corporation
4521 Highwoods Pkwy
Glen Allen VA 23060
804 747-0136

(P-10771)
MAROEVICH OSHEA & COGHLAN
Also Called: M O C Insurance Services
44 Montgomery St Ste 1700, San Francisco (94104-4704)
PHONE...............................415 957-0600
Van Maroevich, *CEO*
Gerald Clifford, *CFO*
Jerry Clifford, *CFO*
Peter Brown, *Senior VP*
Steve Elkins, *Senior VP*
EMP: 60
SQ FT: 10,000
SALES (est): 19.6MM Privately Held
WEB: www.mocins.com
SIC: 6411 Insurance brokers

(P-10772)
MARSH & MCLENNAN AGENCY LLC
101 Enterprise Ste 330, Aliso Viejo (92656-2609)
PHONE...............................949 544-8460
Joe Tapias, *Branch Mgr*
Amy Fisher, *Opers Staff*
David Whalley, *Manager*
Jennifer Reyes, *Consultant*
EMP: 86
SALES (corp-wide): 12.8B Publicly Held
WEB: www.barneyandbarney.com
SIC: 6411 Insurance brokers; life insurance agents
HQ: Marsh & Mclennan Agency Llc
360 Hamilton Ave Ste 930
White Plains NY 10601
914 397-1600

(P-10773)
MARSH & MCLENNAN AGENCY LLC
Steuart Towe 1market, San Francisco (94105)
PHONE...............................415 243-4160
Paul Hering, *CEO*
Rich Foley, *Manager*
Cora Silva, *Manager*
EMP: 86
SALES (corp-wide): 12.8B Publicly Held
SIC: 6411 Insurance brokers; life insurance agents
HQ: Marsh & Mclennan Agency Llc
360 Hamilton Ave Ste 930
White Plains NY 10601
914 397-1600

(P-10774)
MARSH & MCLENNAN AGENCY LLC
1340 Treat Blvd Ste 250, Walnut Creek (94597-2144)
PHONE...............................510 273-8888
David Eslick, *Branch Mgr*
EMP: 86
SALES (corp-wide): 12.8B Publicly Held
SIC: 6411 Insurance brokers; life insurance agents
HQ: Marsh & Mclennan Agency Llc
360 Hamilton Ave Ste 930
White Plains NY 10601
914 397-1600

(P-10775)
MARSH & MCLENNAN AGENCY LLC
9171 Towne Centre Dr # 500, San Diego (92122-1234)
PHONE...............................858 457-3414
Paul Hering, *CEO*
EMP: 200
SALES (corp-wide): 12.8B Publicly Held
SIC: 6411 Property & casualty insurance agent; life insurance agents
HQ: Marsh & Mclennan Agency Llc
360 Hamilton Ave Ste 930
White Plains NY 10601
914 397-1600

(P-10776)
MARSH RISK & INSURANCE SVCS (HQ)
Also Called: MMC
777 S Figueroa St # 2200, Los Angeles (90017-5800)
PHONE...............................213 624-5555
Fax: 213 346-5999
Paul Gibbs, *Managing Dir*
Melody Schwartz, *Senior VP*
Steve Flynn, *Managing Dir*
Susie Beesley, *Buyer*
Susan Varanese, *Manager*
EMP: 575
SALES (est): 147.6MM
SALES (corp-wide): 12.8B Publicly Held
SIC: 6411 Insurance brokers
PA: Marsh & Mclennan Companies, Inc.
1166 Avenue Of The Americ
New York NY 10036
212 345-5000

6411 - Insurance Agents, Brokers & Svc County (P-10797)

(P-10777)
MARSH USA INC
345 California St # 1300, San Francisco (94104-2606)
PHONE..............................415 743-8000
Fax: 925 743-8080
Mike Kelley, *Office Mgr*
Teri Ferem, *Senior VP*
Michael S Kelly, *Senior VP*
Marilyn Fahey, *VP Mktg*
Mike Finigan, *Manager*
EMP: 64
SALES (corp-wide): 12.8B Publicly Held
WEB: www.marsh.com
SIC: 6411 Insurance brokers
HQ: Marsh Usa Inc.
1166 Ave Of The Americas
New York NY 10036
212 345-6000

(P-10778)
MARSH USA INC
Also Called: Marsh Risk & Insurance Svcs
1735 Tech Dr Ste 790, San Jose (95110)
PHONE..............................408 467-5600
Fax: 408 467-5699
Andrew Haaser, *Manager*
Manpreet S Gill, *Associate*
EMP: 62
SALES (corp-wide): 12.8B Publicly Held
SIC: 6411 Insurance brokers
HQ: Marsh Usa Inc.
1166 Ave Of The Americas
New York NY 10036
212 345-6000

(P-10779)
MAXSON YOUNG ASSOC INC
180 Montgomery St # 2100, San Francisco (94104-4231)
PHONE..............................415 228-6400
Vernon Chalfant, *CEO*
EMP: 120
SALES (est): 12.2MM Privately Held
SIC: 6411 Insurance adjusters

(P-10780)
MC GRAW COMMERCIAL INSUR SVC
Also Called: McGraw Insurance Services
8185 E Kaiser Blvd, Anaheim (92808-2214)
PHONE..............................714 939-9875
Vivian Tafolla, *Principal*
EMP: 51
SALES (corp-wide): 60.6MM Privately Held
SIC: 6411 Insurance agents, brokers & service
PA: Mc Graw Commercial Insurance Service, Inc
3601 Haven Ave
Menlo Park CA 94025
650 780-4800

(P-10781)
MC GRAW COMMERCIAL INSUR SVC (PA)
3601 Haven Ave, Menlo Park (94025-1064)
PHONE..............................650 780-4800
Michael J Mc Graw, *President*
Joan D Mc Graw, *Corp Secy*
John M Mc Graw, *Vice Pres*
John V McGraw Jr, *Director*
EMP: 90
SQ FT: 20,000
SALES (est): 60.6MM Privately Held
SIC: 6411 Insurance agents & brokers

(P-10782)
MC GRAW INSURANCE SERVICES CO
2200 Geng Rd Ste 200, Palo Alto (94303-3358)
PHONE..............................650 780-4800
Fax: 650 780-4848
John V Mc Graw, *Ch of Bd*
Richard Fowler, *CFO*
Timothy Summers, *Exec VP*
EMP: 100
SQ FT: 20,000
SALES (est): 21.4MM Privately Held
SIC: 6411 Insurance agents, brokers & service

(P-10783)
MEDICAL EYE SERVICES INC
345 Baker St E, Costa Mesa (92626-4518)
P.O. Box 25209, Santa Ana (92799-5209)
PHONE..............................714 619-4660
Aspasia Shappet, *President*
Dan Conley, *Regional Mgr*
Dione Billingslea, *Human Resources*
Rodney Mattos, *Sales Mgr*
Silvia Morando, *Sales Staff*
EMP: 100
SQ FT: 12,000
SALES (est): 23.4MM Privately Held
SIC: 6411 Insurance claim processing, except medical
PA: The Eye Care Network Of California Inc
345 Baker St E
Costa Mesa CA 92626
415 362-7771

(P-10784)
MEDICAL INSURANCE EXCHANGE CAL
6250 Claremont Ave, Oakland (94618-1324)
PHONE..............................510 596-4935
Dr Bradford Cohn, *President*
Dr William Donald, *Vice Chairman*
Linda Matson, *Vice Pres*
Patricia Lari, *Executive*
Dr Conrad Anderson, *Admin Sec*
EMP: 74
SQ FT: 13,000
SALES (est): 14.3MM Privately Held
WEB: www.miec.com
SIC: 6411 Loss prevention services, insurance

(P-10785)
METROPOLITAN LIFE INSUR CO
Also Called: MetLife
425 Market St Ste 960, San Francisco (94105-2423)
PHONE..............................415 536-1065
Fax: 415 546-3359
Henry Loubouet, *Director*
Chris Rothering, *Analyst*
Pamela Russo, *Human Resources*
Christina W Chua, *Counsel*
Carol Palmer, *Manager*
EMP: 375
SALES (corp-wide): 69.9B Publicly Held
SIC: 6411 Insurance agents & brokers
HQ: Metropolitan Life Insurance Company (Inc)
2701 Queens Plz N Ste 1
Long Island City NY 11101
212 578-2211

(P-10786)
MICHAEL MAGUIRE & ASSOCIATES
611 Anton Blvd Ste 900, Costa Mesa (92626-7684)
PHONE..............................714 435-7500
Michael Maguire, *Owner*
EMP: 50
SALES (est): 5MM Privately Held
SIC: 6411 8111 Insurance agents, brokers & service; general practice attorney, lawyer

(P-10787)
MITCHELL BUCKMAN INC (PA)
Also Called: Kemper Insurance
500 N Santa Fe St, Visalia (93292-5065)
P.O. Box 629 (93279-0629)
PHONE..............................559 733-1181
Fax: 559 738-5517
Clifford Dunbar, *Ch of Bd*
Stanley S Simpson, *Shareholder*
Lela Turbell, *Shareholder*
Jeffrey Boyle, *President*
Judy A Fussel, *President*
EMP: 80
SQ FT: 16,000
SALES (est): 61.8MM Privately Held
WEB: www.bminc.com
SIC: 6411 Insurance agents

(P-10788)
MOMENTOUS INSURANCE BRKG INC
5990 Sepulvda Blvd # 550, Van Nuys (91411-2536)
PHONE..............................818 933-2700
Diane Brinson Schiele, *President*
David Toth, *COO*
Pam Weiser, *Exec VP*
Susan Brien, *Senior VP*
Erin Gaston, *Senior VP*
EMP: 99
SALES (est): 42.5MM Privately Held
SIC: 6411 Insurance agents, brokers & service

(P-10789)
MONARCH E & S INSURANCE SVCS
2540 Foothill Blvd # 101, La Crescenta (91214-4573)
PHONE..............................559 226-0200
Derek Borisoff, *President*
Helene Briskin, *Vice Pres*
Linda McKee, *Admin Asst*
Linda S Stephens, *Broker*
Stefanie McLeod, *Assistant VP*
EMP: 70
SALES (est): 16.4MM Privately Held
SIC: 6411 Insurance information & consulting services

(P-10790)
MORGAN KLEPPE & NASH
Also Called: Mkni
600 W Acequia Ave, Visalia (93291-6130)
P.O. Box 1390 (93279-1390)
PHONE..............................559 732-3436
Fax: 559 732-3256
Keith Kleppe, *Partner*
Gerry Folmer, *Partner*
Stewart Crain, *Office Admin*
EMP: 58
SQ FT: 2,500
SALES (est): 22MM Privately Held
WEB: www.morgankleppenash.com
SIC: 6411 Insurance agents, brokers & service

(P-10791)
MORRIS GRRITANO INSUR AGCY INC
1122 Laurel Ln, San Luis Obispo (93401-5895)
P.O. Box 1189 (93406-1189)
PHONE..............................805 543-6887
Fax: 805 543-3064
Brendan Morris, *CEO*
David Morgan, *Shareholder*
Kelly Morgan, *Shareholder*
Kerry Pollock, *Shareholder*
John Pullock, *Shareholder*
EMP: 85
SQ FT: 14,000
SALES (est): 27.4MM Privately Held
WEB: www.morrisgarritano.com
SIC: 6411 Insurance agents, brokers & service; insurance brokers

(P-10792)
MULLIN TBG INSUR AGCY SVCS LLC (DH)
Also Called: Mullintbg
100 N Sepulveda Blvd, El Segundo (90245-4359)
PHONE..............................310 203-8770
Fax: 310 203-9268
Michael R Shute, *CEO*
Michael Glickman, *CFO*
Anne Fitzgerald, *Exec VP*
Andrew McGinnis, *Exec VP*
Yong Lee, *Senior VP*
EMP: 185
SALES (est): 128.1MM
SALES (corp-wide): 57.1B Publicly Held
WEB: www.mcg-chi.com
SIC: 6411 Insurance agents, brokers & service
HQ: The Prudential Insurance Company Of America
751 Broad St
Newark NJ 07102
973 802-6000

(P-10793)
NATIONAL CRDTORS CNNECTION INC
Also Called: Ncci
14 Orchard Ste 100, Lake Forest (92630-8311)
PHONE..............................949 461-7540
Fax: 949 581-6080
Richard Rodriguez, *CEO*
Charles Ortiz, *CFO*
Richard Bellows, *Vice Pres*
Jay Loeb, *Vice Pres*
Lori Lynn, *Vice Pres*
EMP: 65
SQ FT: 12,000
SALES (est): 19.3MM Privately Held
WEB: www.nationalcreditors.com
SIC: 6411 Inspection & investigation services, insurance

(P-10794)
NATIONAL RTREMENT PARTNERS INC (PA)
34700 Pacific Coast Hwy, Capistrano Beach (92624-1351)
PHONE..............................949 488-8726
William R Chetney, *CEO*
Sean Ciemiewicz, *Managing Prtnr*
Timothy O'Brien, *President*
Robert France, *COO*
Lawrence Craig Smith, *Officer*
EMP: 53
SALES (est): 17MM Privately Held
WEB: www.n-r-p.com
SIC: 6411 Pension & retirement plan consultants

(P-10795)
NEAR N ENTRMT INSURANCES LLC
1840 Century Park E # 1100, Los Angeles (90067-2101)
PHONE..............................310 556-1900
Fax: 310 556-4702
Tia Porter, *Principal*
Paul Walker, *Software Dev*
EMP: 75 EST: 1997
SALES (est): 8.4MM Privately Held
SIC: 6411 Insurance agents & brokers

(P-10796)
NETWORKED INSURANCE AGENTS LLC
443 Crown Point Cir Ste A, Grass Valley (95945-9557)
PHONE..............................800 682-8476
George Biancardi, *President*
Kelly McRae, *CFO*
Larry Oslie, *Exec VP*
Rocco Demateis, *Vice Pres*
Tammy Magliola, *Vice Pres*
EMP: 150
SQ FT: 20,000
SALES (est): 60.3MM
SALES (corp-wide): 7.3MM Privately Held
WEB: www.nia-ins.com
SIC: 6411 Insurance agents, brokers & service
PA: Networked Holdings, Llc
2711 Cntrvlle Rd Ste 400
Wilmington DE 19808
800 682-8476

(P-10797)
NEW YORK LIFE INSURANCE CO
1300 S El Cmno Real 400, San Mateo (94402)
PHONE..............................650 571-1220
Fax: 650 358-9808
K B Sareen, *Manager*
Debbie Gassaway, *Director*
EMP: 400
SALES (corp-wide): 12.3B Privately Held
WEB: www.newyorklife.com
SIC: 6411 Insurance agents & brokers
PA: New York Life Insurance Company
51 Madison Ave Bsmt 1b
New York NY 10010
212 576-7000

6411 - Insurance Agents, Brokers & Svc County (P-10798)

PRODUCTS & SERVICES SECTION

(P-10798)
NEW YORK LIFE INSURANCE CO
675 Placentia Ave Ste 250, Brea (92821-6171)
PHONE.................714 672-0236
Burritt Anderson, *Branch Mgr*
Yoshio Kinjo, *Agent*
Surinder Sachdev, *Agent*
EMP: 58
SALES (corp-wide): 12.3B **Privately Held**
WEB: www.newyorklife.com
SIC: 6411 Insurance agents & brokers
PA: New York Life Insurance Company
51 Madison Ave Bsmt 1b
New York NY 10010
212 576-7000

(P-10799)
NEW YORK LIFE INSURANCE CO
1731 Tech Dr Ste 400, San Jose (95110)
PHONE.................408 392-9782
Fax: 408 452-6012
Victor Vuong, *Partner*
Todd Langton, *Sales Staff*
Elaine Ly, *Advisor*
Nelson Pinto, *Advisor*
Raymond Triplett, *Advisor*
EMP: 100
SALES (corp-wide): 12.3B **Privately Held**
WEB: www.newyorklife.com
SIC: 6411 Insurance agents & brokers
PA: New York Life Insurance Company
51 Madison Ave Bsmt 1b
New York NY 10010
212 576-7000

(P-10800)
NEW YORK LIFE INSURANCE CO
5329 Office Center Ct # 223, Bakersfield (93309-7419)
PHONE.................559 447-3900
Bert Moosios, *Agent*
EMP: 58
SALES (corp-wide): 12.3B **Privately Held**
WEB: www.newyorklife.com
SIC: 6411 Insurance agents & brokers
PA: New York Life Insurance Company
51 Madison Ave Bsmt 1b
New York NY 10010
212 576-7000

(P-10801)
NEW YORK LIFE INSURANCE CO
2020 Main St Ste 1200, Irvine (92614-8235)
PHONE.................949 797-2400
Fax: 949 797-2490
Christopher Prudhomme, *Owner*
Scott Ziegelmeier, *Sales Associate*
Saurabh Deedwania, *Agent*
Michael L Dodge, *Agent*
Monzur A Mollah, *Agent*
EMP: 70
SALES (corp-wide): 12.3B **Privately Held**
WEB: www.newyorklife.com
SIC: 6411 Insurance agents & brokers
PA: New York Life Insurance Company
51 Madison Ave Bsmt 1b
New York NY 10010
212 576-7000

(P-10802)
NEW YORK LIFE INSURANCE CO
425 Market St Fl 16, San Francisco (94105-2498)
PHONE.................415 393-6060
Kevin Choi, *Manager*
Hanh Nguyen, *Agent*
EMP: 50
SALES (corp-wide): 12.3B **Privately Held**
WEB: www.newyorklife.com
SIC: 6411 Insurance agents & brokers
PA: New York Life Insurance Company
51 Madison Ave Bsmt 1b
New York NY 10010
212 576-7000

(P-10803)
NEW YORK LIFE INSURANCE CO
901 Corporate Center Dr, Pomona (91768-2642)
PHONE.................909 902-1027
Betty Shubin, *Manager*
EMP: 100
SALES (corp-wide): 12.3B **Privately Held**
WEB: www.newyorklife.com
SIC: 6411 Insurance agents & brokers
PA: New York Life Insurance Company
51 Madison Ave Bsmt 1b
New York NY 10010
212 576-7000

(P-10804)
NEW YORK LIFE INSURANCE CO
2999 Douglas Blvd Ste 350, Roseville (95661-3839)
PHONE.................916 774-6200
Fax: 916 786-6327
Mark Ham, *Manager*
Nancy D'Angelo, *Human Resources*
Rick Stivers, *Sales Executive*
Louie Grajeda, *Advisor*
Denise Ash, *Agent*
EMP: 100
SALES (corp-wide): 12.3B **Privately Held**
WEB: www.newyorklife.com
SIC: 6411 Insurance agents & brokers
PA: New York Life Insurance Company
51 Madison Ave Bsmt 1b
New York NY 10010
212 576-7000

(P-10805)
NEW YORK LIFE INSURANCE CO
4365 Executive Dr Ste 800, San Diego (92121-2130)
PHONE.................858 623-8600
Fax: 858 623-9784
Antonio Montalvo, *Branch Mgr*
David J Skinner, *VP Finance*
Mary Barlow, *Manager*
Jayshree Patel, *Agent*
EMP: 140
SALES (corp-wide): 12.3B **Privately Held**
WEB: www.newyorklife.com
SIC: 6411 Insurance agents & brokers
PA: New York Life Insurance Company
51 Madison Ave Bsmt 1b
New York NY 10010
212 576-7000

(P-10806)
NEW YORK LIFE INSURANCE CO
300 E Esplanade Dr # 2050, Oxnard (93036-0267)
PHONE.................805 656-4598
Fax: 805 656-0365
Ashwani Kumarrana, *Principal*
Lonnie Lechelt, *Office Mgr*
Judy Sun, *Advisor*
EMP: 50
SALES (corp-wide): 12.3B **Privately Held**
WEB: www.newyorklife.com
SIC: 6411 Insurance agents & brokers
PA: New York Life Insurance Company
51 Madison Ave Bsmt 1b
New York NY 10010
212 576-7000

(P-10807)
NEW YORK LIFE INSURANCE CO
6300 Wilshire Blvd # 1900, Los Angeles (90048-5221)
PHONE.................323 782-3000
Fax: 323 782-3285
Jerry M Fish, *Managing Prtnr*
Dale Wawracz, *CTO*
Jennie K Alcain, *Manager*
Jeff Beaulieu, *Manager*
Brad Bunker, *Manager*
EMP: 50
SALES (corp-wide): 12.3B **Privately Held**
WEB: www.newyorklife.com
SIC: 6411 Insurance agents & brokers
PA: New York Life Insurance Company
51 Madison Ave Bsmt 1b
New York NY 10010
212 576-7000

(P-10808)
NEW YORK LIFE INSURANCE CO
7112 N Fresno St Ste 100, Fresno (93720-2949)
PHONE.................559 447-3900
Janz Myderup, *Branch Mgr*
Zena Clark, *Manager*
EMP: 100
SALES (corp-wide): 12.3B **Privately Held**
WEB: www.newyorklife.com
SIC: 6411 Insurance agents & brokers
PA: New York Life Insurance Company
51 Madison Ave Bsmt 1b
New York NY 10010
212 576-7000

(P-10809)
NEW YORK LIFE INSURANCE CO
140 Via Verde Ste 200, San Dimas (91773-5117)
PHONE.................909 594-4892
Fax: 909 305-6500
Eddie Chao, *Manager*
EMP: 100
SALES (corp-wide): 12.3B **Privately Held**
WEB: www.newyorklife.com
SIC: 6411 Insurance agents & brokers
PA: New York Life Insurance Company
51 Madison Ave Bsmt 1b
New York NY 10010
212 576-7000

(P-10810)
NHIC CORP
402 Otterson Dr, Chico (95928-8248)
PHONE.................530 332-1168
Jeff Brooks, *Executive*
Anne Bockhoff-Dalton, *Vice Pres*
EMP: 304
SALES (est): 39.9MM
SALES (corp-wide): 34.1B **Publicly Held**
WEB: www.medicarenhic.com
SIC: 6411 6321 Medical insurance claim processing, contract or fee basis; accident & health insurance
HQ: Hp Enterprise Services, Llc
5400 Legacy Dr
Plano TX 75024
972 604-6000

(P-10811)
NNA SERVICES LLC (PA)
Also Called: Nna Insurance Services
9350 De Soto Ave, Chatsworth (91311-4926)
P.O. Box 2402 (91313-2402)
PHONE.................818 739-4071
Milton G Valera, *Ch of Bd*
Thomas A Heymann, *CEO*
Robert A Clarke, *CFO*
Deborah M Thaw, *Exec VP*
Deborah Valera, *Vice Pres*
EMP: 204
SQ FT: 55,000
SALES (est): 103.1MM **Privately Held**
WEB: www.nationalnotary.com
SIC: 6411 Insurance agents, brokers & service

(P-10812)
NORCAL MUTUAL INSURANCE CO (PA)
560 Davis St Fl 2, San Francisco (94111-1974)
PHONE.................415 397-9703
Fax: 415 835-9817
Theodore Scott Diener, *CEO*
Neil Simons, *President*
Jim Sunsari, *President*
Scott Diener, *COO*
Christoph Dugre, *Assoc VP*
EMP: 285
SALES (est): 270.7MM **Privately Held**
SIC: 6411 6331 Insurance agents, brokers & service; fire, marine & casualty insurance

(P-10813)
NORTHWEST INSURANCE AGENCY
Also Called: Bondi-Nderson Assoc Insur Brks
418 B St Ste 100, Santa Rosa (95401-8500)
PHONE.................707 573-1300
Fax: 707 546-8321
Mary Feli, *President*
David Noxon, *IT/INT Sup*
Sam Peterson, *IT/INT Sup*
Shelly Frushour, *Technician*
Mary Fairow, *Financial Exec*
EMP: 55
SALES (est): 4.5MM **Privately Held**
SIC: 6411 Insurance brokers

(P-10814)
OLD REPUBLIC CONSTRUCTION PROG
225 S Lake Ave Ste 900, Pasadena (91101-3011)
PHONE.................626 683-5200
Fax: 626 683-5209
Joan Miles, *CEO*
Dean Clifton, *Vice Pres*
Spencer Leroy III, *Admin Sec*
Mary A Foote, *Controller*
Laurie Murphy, *Human Resources*
EMP: 91
SALES (est): 23.2MM
SALES (corp-wide): 5.2B **Publicly Held**
SIC: 6411 Insurance agents, brokers & service
HQ: Old Republic General Insurance Group, Inc.
307 N Michigan Ave # 1418
Chicago IL 60601
312 346-8100

(P-10815)
OLD REPUBLIC HM PROTECTION INC
2 Annabel Ln Ste 112, San Ramon (94583-1377)
P.O. Box 5017 (94583-0917)
PHONE.................925 866-1500
Fax: 925 866-8038
Gwen M Gallagher, *President*
Pj Cochran, *Vice Pres*
Cathy Hall, *Vice Pres*
Lorna Mello, *Vice Pres*
Jim Mullery, *Vice Pres*
EMP: 305
SQ FT: 39,500
SALES (est): 185.7MM
SALES (corp-wide): 5.2B **Publicly Held**
WEB: www.orhp.com
SIC: 6411 Insurance agents, brokers & service
PA: Old Republic International Corporation
307 N Michigan Ave
Chicago IL 60601
312 346-8100

(P-10816)
OMEGA INSURANCE SERVICES
Also Called: Word and Brown
721 S Parker St Ste 300, Orange (92868-4732)
PHONE.................714 973-0311
Fax: 714 347-3908
D P Thomas, *CEO*
Paula Serios, *Chief Mktg Ofcr*
David Duker, *Senior VP*
Angela Moran, *Senior VP*
Gregg Ratkovic, *Senior VP*
EMP: 50
SQ FT: 2,500
SALES (est): 23.7MM **Privately Held**
SIC: 6411 Insurance brokers

(P-10817)
ONCOR INSURANCE SERVICES LLC
870 Glenn Dr, Folsom (95630-3185)
PHONE.................916 932-3210
Timothy F Kneeland,
Gail Quirk, *Sales Executive*
Brett Hancock, *Marketing Mgr*
James M Flewellen,
EMP: 60
SALES (est): 4.2MM **Privately Held**
SIC: 6411 Insurance agents, brokers & service

PRODUCTS & SERVICES SECTION

6411 - Insurance Agents, Brokers & Svc County (P-10837)

HQ: Transamerica Agency Network, Inc.
4333 Edgewood Rd Ne
Cedar Rapids IA 52499
-

(P-10818)
ONSITE CLIMS APPRISAL TECH INC
Also Called: Onsite-Cat
255 Piedra Springs Rd, Arroyo Grande (93420-6966)
PHONE.................805 474-0893
Jane Rockwell, CEO
EMP: 100 EST: 2000
SALES: 8.9MM Privately Held
SIC: 6411 Insurance claim adjusters, not employed by insurance company

(P-10819)
OWEN & COMPANY
1455 Response Rd Ste 260, Sacramento (95815-5263)
PHONE.................916 993-2700
Jere Owen, President
John Owen, Corp Secy
Kristin Daniel, Executive Asst
Heather Romig, Marketing Staff
EMP: 57
SQ FT: 4,741
SALES (est): 13.3MM Privately Held
SIC: 6411 8111 Insurance brokers; legal services

(P-10820)
OWEN DUNN INSURANCE SERVICES
1455 Response Rd Ste 260, Sacramento (95815-5263)
PHONE.................916 443-0200
Fax: 916 443-0251
Jere Owen, Partner
Donald Dunn, Partner
John Owen, Partner
Owen Taylor, Partner
Mike McIntosh, CTO
EMP: 56
SQ FT: 10,000
SALES (est): 10.9MM Privately Held
WEB: www.owendunn.com
SIC: 6411 Insurance agents

(P-10821)
PACIFIC INDEMNITY COMPANY
Also Called: Chubb
555 S Flower St Ste 300, Los Angeles (90071-2427)
PHONE.................213 622-2334
John Fennigan, President
Kenneth Jones, Vice Pres
Chris Zupko, Info Tech Mgr
Karen Axel, Human Res Mgr
Michael Hoeschen, Marketing Mgr
EMP: 300
SALES (est): 64.8MM
SALES (corp-wide): 17.2B Privately Held
WEB: www.chubb.com
SIC: 6411 6331 6351 Insurance agents, brokers & service; fire, marine & casualty insurance: mutual; surety insurance
HQ: Ina Chubb Holdings Inc
436 Walnut St
Philadelphia PA 19106
215 640-1000

(P-10822)
PACIFIC PIONEER INSUR GROUP (PA)
Also Called: Pacific Pioneer Insur Group
6363 Katella Ave, Cypress (90630-5205)
PHONE.................714 228-7888
Fax: 714 228-7899
Lin W Lan, Founder
Sherri Carlson, Branch Mgr
Ping Chen, Controller
Laurie Eusebio, Marketing Staff
Juli Queen, Manager
EMP: 80
SQ FT: 32,000
SALES (est): 24.7MM Privately Held
SIC: 6411 Insurance agents, brokers & service

(P-10823)
PACIFIC SPECIALTY INSURANCE CO
2200 Geng Rd Ste 200, Palo Alto (94303-3358)
P.O. Box 40, Anaheim (92815-0040)
PHONE.................650 780-4800
Fax: 714 998-3158
Timothy Joel Summers, CEO
John Mc Graw, Shareholder
Ann Mc Graw-Morrical, Shareholder
John Chu, President
Mike Mc Graw, President
EMP: 50
SQ FT: 20,000
SALES (est): 16.6MM
SALES (corp-wide): 17.7MM Privately Held
WEB: www.pacificspecialty.com
SIC: 6411 Insurance agents & brokers
PA: Western Service Contract Corp.
2200 Geng Rd Ste 200
Palo Alto CA 94303
650 780-4800

(P-10824)
PEGASUS RISK MANAGEMENT INC (PA)
Also Called: Status Medical Management
642 Galaxy Way, Modesto (95356-9606)
P.O. Box 5038 (95352-5038)
PHONE.................209 574-2800
Fax: 209 574-2900
Ray Simon, President
Paula Towe, Vice Pres
Michelle Zaldua, Human Res Dir
Sharlene Russell, Director
Debra Burkett, Manager
EMP: 70
SQ FT: 10,000
SALES (est): 24.4MM Privately Held
WEB: www.statusmedical.com
SIC: 6411 Insurance claim processing, except medical

(P-10825)
PERR & KNIGHT INC (PA)
401 Wilshire Blvd Ste 300, Santa Monica (90401-1454)
PHONE.................310 230-9339
Timothy B Perr, CEO
Scott Knight, Admin Mgr
Kathy Holmes, Office Mgr
Paula Rossman, Research
Jaime Polanco, Technology
EMP: 88
SQ FT: 10,098
SALES (est): 47.1MM Privately Held
SIC: 6411 Loss prevention services, insurance; research services, insurance; reporting services, insurance

(P-10826)
PETRA RISK SOLUTIONS
5927 Priestly Dr Ste 112, Carlsbad (92008-8037)
PHONE.................800 466-8951
EMP: 83
SALES (corp-wide): 31.1MM Privately Held
SIC: 6411 Insurance agents, brokers & service
PA: Petra Risk Solutions
13950 Cerritos Corprt Dr A
Cerritos CA
-

(P-10827)
PFS INVESTMENTS INC
1955 W Texas St Ste 1, Fairfield (94533-4462)
PHONE.................707 435-9507
Fax: 707 435-8696
Rich Baker, Manager
EMP: 200 Publicly Held
SIC: 6411 Insurance agents, brokers & service
HQ: Pfs Investments Inc
3120 Breckinridge Blvd # 200
Duluth GA 30096
770 381-1000

(P-10828)
POLISEEK AIS INSUR SLTIONS INC
17785 Center Court Dr N # 250, Cerritos (90703-8573)
PHONE.................866 480-7335
Mark Ribisi, President
Chris Bremer, CFO
Lani Elkin, VP Opers
Romayne Levee, VP Mktg
Mark Casas, VP Sales
EMP: 70 EST: 2008
SALES (est): 9.9MM
SALES (corp-wide): 3B Publicly Held
SIC: 6411 Insurance agents, brokers & service
HQ: Ais Management, Llc
17785 Center Court Dr N # 250
Cerritos CA 90703
562 345-4247

(P-10829)
POLYCOMP ADMINISTRATIVE SVCS
3000 Lava Ridge Ct # 130, Roseville (95661-2800)
PHONE.................916 773-3480
Fax: 916 773-3484
Pamela Constantino, Systems Mgr
Ed Dillon, VP Sales
EMP: 50
SQ FT: 4,500
SALES (corp-wide): 46.7MM Privately Held
WEB: www.polycomp.net
SIC: 6411 Pension & retirement plan consultants
PA: Polycomp Administrative Services Inc
6400 Canoga Ave Ste 250
Woodland Hills CA 91367
818 716-0111

(P-10830)
PORTAL INSURANCE AGENCY INC
Also Called: Ascension Bnfits Insur Sltions
1277 Treat Blvd Ste 650, Walnut Creek (94597-7983)
PHONE.................925 937-8787
Joe Tatum, President
Matthew Niebuhr, Manager
EMP: 450
SALES (est): 94.6MM Privately Held
SIC: 6411 Insurance agents, brokers & service

(P-10831)
PRECEPT INC (DH)
Also Called: Precept Group The
130 Theory Ste 200, Irvine (92617-3065)
PHONE.................949 955-1430
Fax: 949 955-9471
Wade R Olson, President
Roxane Langevin, President
Steve Williams, President
Steve Zarate, COO
Christopher H Coulter, Chief Mktg Ofcr
EMP: 90
SQ FT: 32,000
SALES (est): 34.9MM
SALES (corp-wide): 10.3B Publicly Held
WEB: www.preceptgroup.com
SIC: 6411 Insurance agents & brokers
HQ: Bb&T Insurance Services, Inc.
3605 Glenwood Ave Ste 190
Raleigh NC 27612
919 716-9907

(P-10832)
PREFERRED EMPLOYERS INSUR CO
9797 Aero Dr Ste 200, San Diego (92123-1898)
P.O. Box 85478 (92186-5478)
PHONE.................619 688-3900
Fax: 619 688-3913
Linda R Smith, President
Jan Beaver, Vice Pres
Eric Hansen, Vice Pres
Timothy Wiebe, Vice Pres
Tammy A Ebnet, Executive
EMP: 70
SALES (est): 20MM
SALES (corp-wide): 7.2B Publicly Held
WEB: www.preferredworkcomp.com
SIC: 6411 Insurance information & consulting services
PA: W. R. Berkley Corporation
475 Steamboat Rd Fl 1
Greenwich CT 06830
203 629-3000

(P-10833)
PREMIER DEALER SERVICES INC
9449 Balboa Ave Ste 300, San Diego (92123-4395)
PHONE.................858 810-1700
Fax: 858 282-1647
John R Topits, President
Kurt Wolery, Senior VP
A Kurt Wolery, Admin Sec
Scott Harrington, Administration
Karen Penninger, Manager
EMP: 100
SALES (est): 27.7MM Privately Held
WEB: www.pdsadm.com
SIC: 6411 Insurance agents, brokers & service

(P-10834)
PREMIERE AGENCY OF CALIFORNIA
Also Called: Placer Insurance
5 Sierra Gate Plz Fl 2nd, Roseville (95678-6637)
P.O. Box 619052 (95661-9052)
PHONE.................916 784-1008
Fax: 916 784-8116
Walter Klekowski, President
Dineen Fraser, Opers Mgr
Nanette Rice, Director
Tracey Deatsch, Manager
Noel Beltran, Agent
EMP: 65
SQ FT: 9,600
SALES (est): 15.8MM
SALES (corp-wide): 15.2B Privately Held
WEB: www.placerins.com
SIC: 6411 Insurance agents
HQ: Allied Group, Inc
1100 Locust St
Des Moines IA 50391
515 280-4211

(P-10835)
PRIMERICA FINANCIAL SVCS INC
27470 Jefferson Ave 5a, Temecula (92590-2693)
PHONE.................951 695-4325
Fax: 951 694-0148
Mary Simeta, Manager
EMP: 70 Publicly Held
SIC: 6411 Insurance agents & brokers
HQ: Primerica Financial Services, Inc.
3120 Breckinridge Blvd
Duluth GA 30099
800 544-5445

(P-10836)
PRIMERICA LIFE INSURANCE CO
260 Sheridan Ave Ste B42, Palo Alto (94306-2046)
PHONE.................650 323-2554
Omonike Wesipuryear, Branch Mgr
EMP: 121
SALES (corp-wide): 1MM Privately Held
SIC: 6411 Insurance agents & brokers
PA: Primerica Life Insurance Company
1 Primerica Pkwy
Duluth GA 30099
770 381-1000

(P-10837)
PRIMERICA LIFE INSURANCE CO
41307 12th St W Ste 200, Palmdale (93551-1455)
PHONE.................661 947-9070
Belia Rosales, Branch Mgr
EMP: 126
SALES (corp-wide): 1MM Privately Held
SIC: 6411 Insurance agents & brokers

6411 - Insurance Agents, Brokers & Svc County (P-10838)

PA: Primerica Life Insurance Company
1 Primerica Pkwy
Duluth GA 30099
770 381-1000

(P-10838)
PRIMERICA LIFE INSURANCE CO
175 N Cawston Ave, Hemet (92545-5277)
PHONE................951 652-6190
EMP: 126
SALES (corp-wide): 1MM **Privately Held**
SIC: 6411 6799 Insurance agents & brokers; investors
PA: Primerica Life Insurance Company
1 Primerica Pkwy
Duluth GA 30099
770 381-1000

(P-10839)
PROFESSIONAL INSUR ASSOC INC (PA)
Also Called: Professsional Insurance
1100 Industrial Rd Ste 3, San Carlos (94070-4131)
P.O. Box 1266 (94070-1266)
PHONE................650 592-7333
Fax: 650 592-4939
Paula Hammack, *President*
Paul Hammack, *Vice Pres*
Dennis McClenahan, *Vice Pres*
Lisa Colville, *Executive Asst*
Anna Fernandez, *VP Sales*
EMP: 50
SQ FT: 9,000
SALES (est): 56MM **Privately Held**
WEB: www.piainc.com
SIC: 6411 Insurance agents; insurance brokers

(P-10840)
PROGRESSIVE WEST INSURANCE CO
10940 White Rock Rd, Rancho Cordova (95670-6182)
PHONE................916 864-6000
Mark Niehaus, *President*
Miriam Palevsky, *Treasurer*
Jan Kusner, *Asst Treas*
Jolane Davis, *Human Res Mgr*
Jan Dolohanty, *Assistant VP*
EMP: 400
SQ FT: 750
SALES: 25.6MM
SALES (corp-wide): 20.8B **Publicly Held**
SIC: 6411 Insurance agents, brokers & service
PA: The Progressive Corporation
6300 Wilson Mills Rd
Mayfield Village OH 44143
440 461-5000

(P-10841)
PROVIEW ADVANCED SOLUTIONS INC
130 Theory Ste 200, Irvine (92617-3065)
PHONE................949 752-2484
Alex Wasilewski III, *President*
EMP: 90
SALES (est): 13.8MM
SALES (corp-wide): 10.3B **Publicly Held**
WEB: www.preceptgroup.com
SIC: 6411 Insurance agents, brokers & service
HQ: Precept, Inc
130 Theory Ste 200
Irvine CA 92617
949 955-1430

(P-10842)
PRUDENTIAL INSUR CO OF AMER
3333 Michelson Dr Ste 820, Irvine (92612-0655)
PHONE................949 440-5300
Fax: 949 440-5353
Jay Skolnick, *Manager*
Milton Landes, *Manager*
Bernard O'Hara, *Manager*
Eric Porter, *Manager*
EMP: 50
SALES (corp-wide): 57.1B **Publicly Held**
SIC: 6411 Insurance agents, brokers & service

HQ: The Prudential Insurance Company Of America
751 Broad St
Newark NJ 07102
973 802-6000

(P-10843)
PRUDENTIAL INSUR CO OF AMER
4 Embarcadero Ctr # 2700, San Francisco (94111-4106)
PHONE................415 398-7310
Fax: 415 956-2197
Micheal Jamieson, *Manager*
John Hall, *Managing Dir*
Kenji Tamaoki, *Director*
Stephen Baird, *Associate*
Elizabeth Velazquez, *Associate*
EMP: 80
SALES (corp-wide): 57.1B **Publicly Held**
SIC: 6411 Insurance agents, brokers & service
HQ: The Prudential Insurance Company Of America
751 Broad St
Newark NJ 07102
973 802-6000

(P-10844)
PRUDENTIAL INSUR CO OF AMER
15303 Ventura Blvd # 1550, Sherman Oaks (91403-6624)
PHONE................818 990-2122
Fax: 818 990-1550
Craig Biggf, *Manager*
Walt Danheiser, *Officer*
EMP: 50
SALES (corp-wide): 57.1B **Publicly Held**
SIC: 6411 Insurance agents, brokers & service
HQ: The Prudential Insurance Company Of America
751 Broad St
Newark NJ 07102
973 802-6000

(P-10845)
PRUDENTIAL INSUR CO OF AMER
180 Montgomery St # 1900, San Francisco (94104-4205)
PHONE................415 486-3050
Tom Rhee, *Manager*
EMP: 97
SALES (corp-wide): 57.1B **Publicly Held**
SIC: 6411 6324 6321 6311 Insurance agents, brokers & service; insurance agents; health maintenance organization (HMO), insurance only; accident & health insurance; life insurance
HQ: The Prudential Insurance Company Of America
751 Broad St
Newark NJ 07102
973 802-6000

(P-10846)
PRUDENTIAL INSUR CO OF AMER
5990 Sepulvda Blvd # 300, Van Nuys (91411-2500)
PHONE................818 901-0028
EMP: 60
SALES (corp-wide): 41.4B **Publicly Held**
SIC: 6411
HQ: The Prudential Insurance Company Of America
751 Broad St
Newark NJ 07102
973 802-6000

(P-10847)
QBE FIRST INSURANCE AGENCY INC
9800 Muirlands Blvd, Irvine (92618-2515)
PHONE................949 206-6200
Fax: 949 457-8095
Becky Igo, *Principal*
John D Lock, *COO*
John Lock, *COO*
Tom Bohen, *Vice Pres*
Cindy Mello, *Vice Pres*
EMP: 300 **Publicly Held**
WEB: www.zcsterling.com

SIC: 6411 Insurance agents
HQ: Qbe First Insurance Agency, Inc.
210 Interstate North Pkwy
Atlanta GA 30339
770 690-8400

(P-10848)
QUALIFIED BENEFITS INC
21021 Ventura Blvd # 100, Woodland Hills (91364-2200)
PHONE................818 594-4900
Greg Taylor, *President*
Angelo Mazzone, *Admin Sec*
Ben Lopez, *Director*
EMP: 50
SQ FT: 11,500
SALES (est): 9.1MM
SALES (corp-wide): 10MM **Privately Held**
WEB: www.qben.com
SIC: 6411 Pension & retirement plan consultants
PA: Qbi, Llc
21031 Ventura Blvd # 1200
Woodland Hills CA 91364
818 594-4900

(P-10849)
QUALITY CLAIMS MANAGEMENT CORP
2763 Camino Del Rio S, San Diego (92108-3708)
PHONE................619 450-8600
Ronald Reitz, *President*
Anne Schupack, *President*
Kevin McCarthy, *CFO*
Kelly Barbieri, *Vice Pres*
Robert Hopson, *Vice Pres*
EMP: 60
SQ FT: 8,000
SALES (est): 12.9MM **Privately Held**
WEB: www.qualityclaims.com
SIC: 6411 Insurance claim adjusters, not employed by insurance company

(P-10850)
R MC CLOSKEY INSURANCE AGENCY
Also Called: Tax and Financial Group
4001 Macarthur Blvd # 300, Newport Beach (92660-2505)
PHONE................949 223-8100
Richard Mc Closkey, *President*
Brian McNulty, *Managing Prtnr*
Paul Thomas, *Managing Prtnr*
Brian Freeman, *Senior VP*
Tim Steele, *Vice Pres*
EMP: 120
SQ FT: 15,000
SALES (est): 42.4MM **Privately Held**
WEB: www.tfgroup.com
SIC: 6411 Insurance agents; life insurance agents

(P-10851)
R S I INSURANCE BROKERS INC (PA)
2801 Bristol St Ste 200, Costa Mesa (92626-5996)
PHONE................714 546-6616
Fax: 714 546-4457
Barry Rabune, *President*
Debra Cellini, *CFO*
Ben Thomas, *Vice Pres*
Sandra Taber, *Regional Mgr*
Belinda Hegarty, *Marketing Mgr*
EMP: 50
SQ FT: 6,500
SALES: 55MM **Privately Held**
WEB: www.rsiinsurancebrokers.com
SIC: 6411 Insurance brokers

(P-10852)
RAMKADE INSURANCE SERVICES
Also Called: Time Financial Services
21550 Oxnard St Ste 500, Woodland Hills (91367-7111)
PHONE................818 444-1340
Kate Kinkade, *President*
Patrick Ramsey, *Vice Pres*
Ethel Williams, *Controller*
EMP: 60

SALES (est): 8.9MM
SALES (corp-wide): 88.2B **Publicly Held**
WEB: www.timefin.com
SIC: 6411 Insurance agents, brokers & service
HQ: Citi Investor Services, Inc.
105 Eisenhower Pkwy Ste 2
Roseland NJ 07068
973 461-2500

(P-10853)
RAMSELL PUBLIC HEALTH RX LLC
200 Webster St Ste 300, Oakland (94607-4108)
PHONE................510 587-2600
Eric A Flowers,
Jennifer Klatt, *CFO*
Jason Barnett, *Controller*
Thomas Laker,
EMP: 51 **EST:** 2005
SQ FT: 1,500
SALES (est): 4.3MM
SALES (corp-wide): 12.2MM **Privately Held**
SIC: 6411 Medical insurance claim processing, contract or fee basis
PA: Ramsell Corporation
200 Webster St Ste 200
Oakland CA 94607
510 587-2659

(P-10854)
REGISTRY MONITORING INS SRVCS
Also Called: Rmis
5388 Sterling Center Dr, Westlake Village (91361-4612)
PHONE................818 933-6350
Marvin Landon, *CEO*
Craig H Landon, *President*
Peter Lunenfeld, *Exec VP*
Jodi Santino, *Controller*
Justin Buller, *Natl Sales Mgr*
EMP: 80
SQ FT: 25,000
SALES (est): 10.2MM **Privately Held**
WEB: www.registrymonitoring.com
SIC: 6411 6531 Insurance agents, brokers & service; insurance information & consulting services; real estate agents & managers

(P-10855)
REHAB WEST INC
277 Rancheros Dr Ste 190, San Marcos (92069-2982)
PHONE................619 518-3710
Fax: 760 796-7564
Sharon Douglas, *CEO*
Carol Holub, *CFO*
Tammy Rancourt, *Administration*
EMP: 50
SQ FT: 3,000
SALES: 5.5MM **Privately Held**
WEB: www.rehabwest.com
SIC: 6411 Medical insurance claim processing, contract or fee basis

(P-10856)
ROBERT MORENO INSURANCE SVCS
22860 Savi Ranch Pkwy, Yorba Linda (92887-4610)
P.O. Box 87023 (92885-7023)
PHONE................714 525-5168
Fax: 714 738-1806
Robert B Moreno, *Owner*
Laura Moreno, *COO*
Ana Smith, *Business Mgr*
Benjamen Bailey, *Sls & Mktg Exec*
Omar Gaitan, *Marketing Mgr*
EMP: 140
SQ FT: 28,500
SALES (est): 29.1MM **Privately Held**
WEB: www.rmismga.com
SIC: 6411 Insurance agents & brokers

(P-10857)
RON FILICE ENTERPRISES INC
Also Called: Filice Insurance Agency
738 N 1st St Ste 202, San Jose (95112-6371)
PHONE................408 294-0477
Fax: 408 294-0806
Ron Filice, *President*

PRODUCTS & SERVICES SECTION

6411 - Insurance Agents, Brokers & Svc County (P-10878)

Eric Pogue, *Sr Exec VP*
Mike Chavez, *Vice Pres*
Michelle Filice, *Vice Pres*
Lance Perry, *Vice Pres*
EMP: 50
SQ FT: 3,000
SALES (est): 20.4MM **Privately Held**
SIC: 6411 Insurance agents, brokers & service

(P-10858)
SACRAMNTO HSING RDVLPMENT AGCY
630 I St Fl 3, Sacramento (95814-2404)
PHONE 916 440-1376
Fax: 916 441-2442
La Shelle Dozier, *Branch Mgr*
Jim Hare, *Program Mgr*
Ranjit Rai, *CTO*
Tina McKenney, *Finance*
Annie Chin, *Analyst*
EMP: 160 **Privately Held**
SIC: 6411 Insurance agents, brokers & service
PA: Sacramento Housing And Redevelopment Agency
801 12th St
Sacramento CA 95814
916 440-1390

(P-10859)
SAFECO INSURANCE COMPANY AMER
330 N Brand Blvd Ste 680, Glendale (91203-2385)
PHONE 818 956-4250
Don Chambers, *Manager*
EMP: 160
SALES (corp-wide): 37.6B **Privately Held**
SIC: 6411 Insurance agents, brokers & service
HQ: Safeco Insurance Company Of America
1001 4th Ave Ste 800
Seattle WA 98185
206 545-5000

(P-10860)
SAN DIEGO COUNTY EMPLOYEES RET
2275 Rio Bonito Way # 200, San Diego (92108-1685)
PHONE 619 515-6800
Brian White, *CEO*
David Myers, *Vice Chairman*
Linda Crosland, *Accountant*
Gail Strohl, *Accounts Mgr*
Karen Johanson, *Associate*
EMP: 90
SALES (est): 20.1MM **Privately Held**
SIC: 6411 Pension & retirement plan consultants

(P-10861)
SCC ESA DEPT OF RISK MGMT
Also Called: ESA Risk Management
2310 N 1st St Ste 202, San Jose (95131-1040)
PHONE 408 441-4207
Janet Moody, *Director*
Erwin Sulak, *Mng Member*
EMP: 65
SALES (est): 3.4MM **Privately Held**
WEB: www.esariskmanagement.com
SIC: 6411 Insurance agents, brokers & service

(P-10862)
SCHIRMER FIRE PROTECTION ENG
Also Called: AON
707 Wilshire Blvd # 2600, Los Angeles (90017-3501)
PHONE 213 630-2020
Jacqueline Bychowski, *Office Mgr*
Mark Rochholz, *COO*
Maria Molina, *Human Res Dir*
Lizette Junor, *Director*
Kristine Mendez, *Director*
EMP: 99
SALES (corp-wide): 151.3MM **Privately Held**
SIC: 6411 Insurance brokers

HQ: Schirmer Fire Protection Engineering Corporation
200 E Randolph St
Chicago IL 60601
312 381-1000

(P-10863)
SCOTTISH AMERICAN INSURANCE (PA)
Also Called: Yates & Associates
2002 E Mcfadden Ave # 100, Santa Ana (92705-4766)
P.O. Box B25133 (92799)
PHONE 714 550-5050
Fax: 714 832-1861
Paul A Thomson, *CEO*
Carl Ledbetter, *President*
James M Yates, *President*
Barbara Parkerhatch, *Exec VP*
Klayton Caldiero, *Vice Pres*
EMP: 57
SQ FT: 14,300
SALES (est): 26.3MM **Privately Held**
WEB: www.yates-assoc.com
SIC: 6411 Insurance brokers

(P-10864)
SEABURY & SMITH DELAWARE INC
777 S Figueroa St # 2400, Los Angeles (90017-5800)
PHONE 213 346-5000
Fax: 213 346-5946
Kris Davis, *Branch Mgr*
Scott Fisher, *Executive*
EMP: 80
SALES (corp-wide): 12.8B **Publicly Held**
WEB: www.seabury.com
SIC: 6411 Insurance brokers
HQ: Seabury & Smith (Delaware), Inc.
1166 Ave Of The Americas
New York NY 10036
212 345-9049

(P-10865)
SEDGWICK CLAIMS MGT SVCS
701 S Parker St Ste 5000, Orange (92868-4749)
P.O. Box 14442, Lexington KY (40512-4442)
PHONE 714 245-7800
Fax: 951 245-7673
Marie Woodward, *Manager*
Denise Fleury, *Senior VP*
Maryanne Selly, *Info Tech Dir*
EMP: 70
SALES (corp-wide): 3.2B **Privately Held**
WEB: www.sedgwickcms.com
SIC: 6411 Insurance agents; insurance brokers
HQ: Sedgwick Claims Management Services, Inc.
1100 Ridgeway Loop Rd # 200
Memphis TN 38120
901 415-7400

(P-10866)
SEDGWICK CLAIMS MGT SVCS INC
3280 E Foothill Blvd # 350, Pasadena (91107-3103)
P.O. Box 14435, Lexington KY (40512-4435)
PHONE 626 568-1415
Barbara Jones, *Principal*
EMP: 70
SALES (corp-wide): 3.2B **Privately Held**
SIC: 6411 Insurance claim adjusters, not employed by insurance company
HQ: Sedgwick Claims Management Services, Inc.
1100 Ridgeway Loop Rd # 200
Memphis TN 38120
901 415-7400

(P-10867)
SEDGWICK CLAIMS MGT SVCS INC
5990 Sepulvda Blvd # 500, Sherman Oaks (91411-2500)
PHONE 818 782-8820
Fax: 818 997-3555
Jeremiah Russell, *Branch Mgr*
EMP: 68

SALES (corp-wide): 3.2B **Privately Held**
SIC: 6411 Insurance agents, brokers & service
HQ: Sedgwick Claims Management Services, Inc.
1100 Ridgeway Loop Rd # 200
Memphis TN 38120
901 415-7400

(P-10868)
SEDGWICK CLAIMS MGT SVCS INC
24025 Park Sorrento # 200, Calabasas (91302-4018)
PHONE 818 591-9444
John Gernert, *Manager*
William Bautista, *Technology*
Kevin Hawkins, *Finance*
EMP: 200
SALES (corp-wide): 3.2B **Privately Held**
WEB: www.sedgwickcms.com
SIC: 6411 Insurance claim adjusters, not employed by insurance company
HQ: Sedgwick Claims Management Services, Inc.
1100 Ridgeway Loop Rd # 200
Memphis TN 38120
901 415-7400

(P-10869)
SEDGWICK CLAIMS MGT SVCS INC
2101 Webster St, Oakland (94612-3011)
PHONE 510 302-3000
Fax: 510 847-8205
Athanasios Soha, *Branch Mgr*
David Hocutt, *President*
Robert Shaffer, *Vice Pres*
Baicelia Ortega, *Comp Spec*
Greg Delgado, *Personnel Exec*
EMP: 70
SALES (corp-wide): 3.2B **Privately Held**
WEB: www.sedgwickcms.com
SIC: 6411 Insurance agents, brokers & service
HQ: Sedgwick Claims Management Services, Inc.
1100 Ridgeway Loop Rd # 200
Memphis TN 38120
901 415-7400

(P-10870)
SEDGWICK CLAIMS MGT SVCS INC
1851 Heritage Ln, Sacramento (95815-4926)
PHONE 916 568-7394
EMP: 70
SALES (corp-wide): 3.2B **Privately Held**
SIC: 6411 Insurance agents, brokers & service
HQ: Sedgwick Claims Management Services, Inc.
1100 Ridgeway Loop Rd # 200
Memphis TN 38120
901 415-7400

(P-10871)
SELECTQUOTE INSURANCE SERVICES (PA)
595 Market St Fl 10, San Francisco (94105-2899)
PHONE 415 543-7338
Fax: 415 543-7338
Charan J Singh, *President*
Robert Edwards, *COO*
Steven H Gerber, *Vice Pres*
Kellie Stewart, *Office Mgr*
Michael L Feroah, *CTO*
EMP: 200
SALES (est): 298.1MM **Privately Held**
WEB: www.selectquote.com
SIC: 6411 Life insurance agents

(P-10872)
SIGNATURE RESOURCES INS/FNCL
Also Called: John Hancock
16755 Von Karman Ave # 200, Irvine (92606-4963)
PHONE 949 794-0800
Gary Kaltenbach, *Owner*
Steve Finch, *Exec VP*
Nina Manning, *Office Mgr*
Ward Doherty, *Advisor*

EMP: 60
SQ FT: 1,800
SALES (est): 9.3MM **Privately Held**
WEB: www.signatureresources.net
SIC: 6411 Insurance agents & brokers

(P-10873)
SKYLES INSURANCE AGENCY
9840 Business Park Dr, Sacramento (95827-1704)
PHONE 916 361-9585
Fax: 916 361-9821
Theron Skyles, *Partner*
Cindy Wingard, *Sales Associate*
Michael McFarlane, *Agent*
EMP: 50
SALES (est): 8.2MM **Privately Held**
SIC: 6411 Insurance agents, brokers & service

(P-10874)
SPECIALTY RISK SERVICES INC
1 Pointe Dr Ste 220, Brea (92821-7626)
P.O. Box 7007, La Habra (90632-7007)
PHONE 714 674-1000
Fax: 714 674-4602
Sharon Bartholomew, *Principal*
Brian Gannon, *Business Dir*
EMP: 87
SALES (corp-wide): 3.2B **Privately Held**
SIC: 6411 Insurance agents, brokers & service
HQ: Specialty Risk Services, Inc.
100 Corporate Dr Ste 211
Windsor CT 06095

(P-10875)
SPECIALTY RISK SERVICES INC
6140 Stoneridge Mall Rd # 245, Pleasanton (94588-3233)
PHONE 877 809-9478
Eric Hansen, *Principal*
EMP: 117
SALES (corp-wide): 3.2B **Privately Held**
WEB: www.srsconnect.com
SIC: 6411 Insurance claim processing, except medical; loss prevention services, insurance
HQ: Specialty Risk Services, Inc.
100 Corporate Dr Ste 211
Windsor CT 06095

(P-10876)
SQUARETRADE INC (PA)
360 3rd St Fl 6, San Francisco (94107-2154)
PHONE 415 541-1000
Ahmedulla Khaishgi, *President*
Michael Costanza, *President*
Michael Adler, *CFO*
Randy Heppner, *CFO*
Mike Liberatore, *CFO*
EMP: 146
SQ FT: 54,000
SALES (est): 2.3B **Privately Held**
WEB: www.squaretrade.com
SIC: 6411 Pension & retirement plan consultants

(P-10877)
STATE FARM FIRE AND CSLTY CO
Also Called: State Farm Insurance
5127 W Walnut Ave, Visalia (93277-3472)
PHONE 559 625-4330
Fax: 559 625-2586
Patrick Salazar, *Manager*
Elaine R Rider, *Agent*
EMP: 63
SALES (corp-wide): 37B **Privately Held**
WEB: www.statefarm.com
SIC: 6411 Insurance agents & brokers
HQ: State Farm Fire And Casualty Company
Three State Frm Plz S H-4
Bloomington IL 61710
309 766-2311

(P-10878)
STATE FARM FIRE AND CSLTY CO
Also Called: State Farm Insurance
6400 State Farm Dr, Rohnert Park (94928)
PHONE 707 588-6011

6411 - Insurance Agents, Brokers & Svc County (P-10879)

Fax: 707 588-6075
Glen Dorsett, *Manager*
EMP: 500
SALES (corp-wide): 46B **Privately Held**
WEB: www.statefarm.net
SIC: 6411 Insurance agents & brokers
HQ: State Farm Fire And Casualty Company
Three State Farm Plaza
Bloomington IL 61710
309 766-2311

(P-10879)
STATE FARM MUTL AUTO INSUR CO
Also Called: State Farm Insurance
12122 S Halldale Ave # 200, Los Angeles (90047-5320)
PHONE.................................309 766-2311
Edward Rust, *Branch Mgr*
EMP: 326
SALES (corp-wide): 37B **Privately Held**
WEB: www.statefarm.com
SIC: 6411 Insurance agents & brokers
PA: State Farm Mutual Automobile Insurance Company
1 State Farm Plz
Bloomington IL 61710
309 766-2311

(P-10880)
STATE FARM MUTL AUTO INSUR CO
Also Called: State Farm Insurance
16656 Ventura Blvd # 203, Encino (91436-1918)
PHONE.................................818 849-5126
Fax: 818 906-8210
EMP: 71
SALES (corp-wide): 37B **Privately Held**
SIC: 6411 Insurance agents, brokers & service
PA: State Farm Mutual Automobile Insurance Company
1 State Farm Plz
Bloomington IL 61710
309 766-2311

(P-10881)
STATE FARM MUTL AUTO INSUR CO
Also Called: State Farm Insurance
10350 Hrtg Pk Dr Ste 202, Santa Fe Springs (90670)
P.O. Box 57112, Irvine (92619-7112)
PHONE.................................562 903-2800
Fax: 562 903-2887
Austin Miller, *Manager*
EMP: 50
SALES (corp-wide): 37B **Privately Held**
WEB: www.statefarm.com
SIC: 6411 Insurance agents & brokers
PA: State Farm Mutual Automobile Insurance Company
1 State Farm Plz
Bloomington IL 61710
309 766-2311

(P-10882)
STATE FARM MUTL AUTO INSUR CO
Also Called: State Farm Insurance
900 Old River Rd, Bakersfield (93311-9501)
PHONE.................................661 663-1921
Sen Larry Knight, *Manager*
Jill E Elofson, *Broker*
Diane Williams, *Broker*
Carol Nelson, *HR Admin*
Charlene Worth, *Senior Mgr*
EMP: 72
SALES (corp-wide): 37B **Privately Held**
WEB: www.statefarm.com
SIC: 6411 Insurance agents & brokers
PA: State Farm Mutual Automobile Insurance Company
1 State Farm Plz
Bloomington IL 61710
309 766-2311

(P-10883)
STATE FARM MUTL AUTO INSUR CO
Also Called: State Farm Insurance
5050 El Camino Real # 108, Los Altos (94022-1530)
PHONE.................................650 694-6767
Fax: 650 694-6760
Don M Parker, *Principal*
Jack Flesher, *Manager*
EMP: 72
SALES (corp-wide): 37B **Privately Held**
WEB: www.statefarm.com
SIC: 6411 Insurance agents & brokers
PA: State Farm Mutual Automobile Insurance Company
1 State Farm Plz
Bloomington IL 61710
309 766-2311

(P-10884)
STATE FARM MUTL AUTO INSUR CO
Also Called: State Farm Insurance
200 Corporate Pointe # 210, Culver City (90230-7645)
PHONE.................................310 568-5824
Pete Falcone, *Manager*
CLF C Ward, *Vice Pres*
Patti Adragna, *Social Dir*
Mareva Muchenje, *Social Dir*
EMP: 100
SALES (corp-wide): 37B **Privately Held**
WEB: www.statefarm.com
SIC: 6411 6321 Insurance agents, brokers & service; accident insurance carriers
PA: State Farm Mutual Automobile Insurance Company
1 State Farm Plz
Bloomington IL 61710
309 766-2311

(P-10885)
STATE FARM MUTL AUTO INSUR CO
Also Called: State Farm Insurance
30125 Agoura Rd Ste 200, Agoura Hills (91301-4322)
PHONE.................................818 597-4300
Dennis Pitta, *Branch Mgr*
EMP: 72
SALES (corp-wide): 46B **Privately Held**
WEB: www.statefarm.com
SIC: 6411 Insurance agents & brokers
PA: State Farm Mutual Automobile Insurance Company
1 State Farm Plz
Bloomington IL 61710
309 766-2311

(P-10886)
STATE FARM MUTL AUTO INSUR CO
Also Called: State Farm Insurance
1705 E 10th St Apt 201, Long Beach (90813-6347)
PHONE.................................310 632-9810
Fax: 310 632-8673
Phil Davis, *Manager*
EMP: 72
SALES (corp-wide): 46B **Privately Held**
WEB: www.statefarm.com
SIC: 6411 Insurance agents & brokers
PA: State Farm Mutual Automobile Insurance Company
1 State Farm Plz
Bloomington IL 61710
309 766-2311

(P-10887)
STATE FARM MUTL AUTO INSUR CO
Also Called: State Farm Insurance
17122 Slover Ave Ste 106, Fontana (92337-7588)
PHONE.................................909 349-2050
Fax: 909 349-2054
Lenita Graves, *Manager*
EMP: 72
SALES (corp-wide): 46B **Privately Held**
WEB: www.statefarm.com
SIC: 6411 Insurance agents & brokers
PA: State Farm Mutual Automobile Insurance Company
1 State Farm Plz
Bloomington IL 61710
309 766-2311

(P-10888)
STATE FARM MUTL AUTO INSUR CO
Also Called: State Farm Insurance
2019 24th St, Bakersfield (93301-3814)
PHONE.................................661 324-4077
Fax: 661 324-4025
Roger Hess, *Branch Mgr*
EMP: 72
SALES (corp-wide): 46B **Privately Held**
WEB: www.statefarm.com
SIC: 6411 Insurance agents & brokers
PA: State Farm Mutual Automobile Insurance Company
1 State Farm Plz
Bloomington IL 61710
309 766-2311

(P-10889)
STATE FARM MUTL AUTO INSUR CO
Also Called: State Farm Insurance
2555 Flores St Ste 175, San Mateo (94403-2343)
PHONE.................................650 345-3571
Fax: 650 345-3573
Jake Bursalyan, *Manager*
EMP: 72
SALES (corp-wide): 46B **Privately Held**
WEB: www.statefarm.com
SIC: 6411 Insurance agents & brokers
PA: State Farm Mutual Automobile Insurance Company
1 State Farm Plz
Bloomington IL 61710
309 766-2311

(P-10890)
STATE FARM MUTL AUTO INSUR CO
Also Called: State Farm Insurance
300 Crprate Pinte Ste 200, Culver City (90230)
PHONE.................................310 568-5200
Fax: 310 568-5313
Cathy Rourke, *Branch Mgr*
Eddie Contreras, *Manager*
EMP: 72
SALES (corp-wide): 50.6B **Privately Held**
WEB: www.statefarm.com
SIC: 6411 Insurance agents & brokers
PA: State Farm Mutual Automobile Insurance Company
1 State Farm Plz
Bloomington IL 61710
309 766-2311

(P-10891)
STATE FARM MUTL AUTO INSUR CO
Also Called: State Farm Insurance
3351 Michelson Dr Ste 200, Irvine (92612-4427)
PHONE.................................309 766-2311
Mike Memoly, *Owner*
Don Middleton, *Manager*
EMP: 72
SALES (corp-wide): 46B **Privately Held**
WEB: www.statefarm.com
SIC: 6411 Insurance agents & brokers
PA: State Farm Mutual Automobile Insurance Company
1 State Farm Plz
Bloomington IL 61710
309 766-2311

(P-10892)
STATE FARM MUTL AUTO INSUR CO
Also Called: State Farm Insurance
40315 Junction Dr Ste A, Oakhurst (93644-9159)
PHONE.................................559 683-3467
Fax: 559 683-3410
Marilyn Rigg, *Branch Mgr*
EMP: 72
SALES (corp-wide): 46B **Privately Held**
WEB: www.statefarm.com
SIC: 6411 Insurance agents & brokers
PA: State Farm Mutual Automobile Insurance Company
1 State Farm Plz
Bloomington IL 61710
309 766-2311

(P-10893)
STATE FARM MUTL AUTO INSUR CO
Also Called: State Farm Insurance
5345 Fallbrook Ave, Woodland Hills (91367-6112)
PHONE.................................818 887-1060
Fax: 818 887-6442
Gary Hoover, *Manager*
Vic Nader, *Agent*
EMP: 72
SALES (corp-wide): 46B **Privately Held**
WEB: www.statefarm.com
SIC: 6411 Insurance agents & brokers
PA: State Farm Mutual Automobile Insurance Company
1 State Farm Plz
Bloomington IL 61710
309 766-2311

(P-10894)
STATE FARM MUTL AUTO INSUR CO
Also Called: State Farm Insurance
845 Via De La Paz Ste 12, Pacific Palisades (90272-3627)
PHONE.................................310 454-0349
Vince Gurino, *Manager*
Trish Bowe, *Manager*
EMP: 72
SALES (corp-wide): 46B **Privately Held**
WEB: www.statefarm.com
SIC: 6411 Insurance agents & brokers
PA: State Farm Mutual Automobile Insurance Company
1 State Farm Plz
Bloomington IL 61710
309 766-2311

(P-10895)
STATE FARM MUTL AUTO INSUR CO
Also Called: State Farm Insurance
7944 W 3rd St, Los Angeles (90048-4305)
PHONE.................................323 852-6868
Fax: 323 852-6869
Daniel Williams, *Manager*
EMP: 72
SALES (corp-wide): 46B **Privately Held**
WEB: www.statefarm.com
SIC: 6411 Insurance agents & brokers
PA: State Farm Mutual Automobile Insurance Company
1 State Farm Plz
Bloomington IL 61710
309 766-2311

(P-10896)
STATE FARM MUTL AUTO INSUR CO
Also Called: State Farm Insurance
4600 Ashe Rd Ste 308, Bakersfield (93313-2040)
PHONE.................................661 664-9663
Fax: 661 664-1729
Keith Stonebraker, *Branch Mgr*
Rosie Schweer, *Manager*
EMP: 72
SALES (corp-wide): 46B **Privately Held**
WEB: www.statefarm.com
SIC: 6411 Insurance agents & brokers
PA: State Farm Mutual Automobile Insurance Company
1 State Farm Plz
Bloomington IL 61710
309 766-2311

(P-10897)
STATE FARM MUTL AUTO INSUR CO
Also Called: State Farm Insurance
1558 Fitzgerald Dr, Pinole (94564-2229)
PHONE.................................510 222-1102
Donald L Greco, *Owner*
EMP: 72
SALES (corp-wide): 46B **Privately Held**
WEB: www.statefarm.com
SIC: 6411 Insurance agents & brokers

PRODUCTS & SERVICES SECTION
6411 - Insurance Agents, Brokers & Svc County (P-10917)

PA: State Farm Mutual Automobile Insurance Company
1 State Farm Plz
Bloomington IL 61710
309 766-2311

(P-10898)
STATE FARM MUTL AUTO INSUR CO
Also Called: State Farm Insurance
900 Old River Rd, Bakersfield (93311-9501)
PHONE..................661 663-1313
Beth Long, *Manager*
Linda Vest, *Planning*
Ram Bhat, *Project Mgr*
Patrick Culligan, *Marketing Staff*
Mike Pringle, *Corp Comm Staff*
EMP: 1500
SALES (corp-wide): 46B **Privately Held**
WEB: www.statefarm.com
SIC: 6411 Insurance agents & brokers
PA: State Farm Mutual Automobile Insurance Company
1 State Farm Plz
Bloomington IL 61710
309 766-2311

(P-10899)
STRATEGIC FINANCIAL GROUP
18191 Von Karman Ave # 100, Irvine (92612-7103)
PHONE..................949 622-7200
Fax: 949 622-7222
Shawn Mackey, *Principal*
Kevin Dupree, *Manager*
EMP: 50
SALES (est): 3.9MM **Privately Held**
SIC: 6411 Insurance agents, brokers & service

(P-10900)
SULLIVAN GJ & ASSOCIATES INC (PA)
Also Called: Sullivan Group, The
800 W 6th St Ste 1800, Los Angeles (90017-2701)
PHONE..................213 626-1000
Fax: 213 489-0766
Gerald J Sullivan, *President*
Paul Cunningham, *CFO*
Tom Coleman, *Vice Pres*
Steve Fetchet, *Vice Pres*
Diane Moen, *Vice Pres*
EMP: 175
SQ FT: 24,500
SALES (est): 172.2MM **Privately Held**
SIC: 6411 Insurance brokers

(P-10901)
SUN COAST GEN INSUR AGCY INC
23042 Mill Creek Dr, Laguna Hills (92653-1214)
P.O. Box 30750 (92654-0750)
PHONE..................949 768-1132
Fax: 949 768-4045
Jeffrey Yeskin, *CEO*
David Yeskin, *President*
Larua Gibson, *CFO*
Scott Boren, *Chief Mktg Ofcr*
Rosie Garcia, *Technology*
EMP: 55
SQ FT: 13,000
SALES (est): 13.3MM **Privately Held**
WEB: www.suncoastinsurance.com
SIC: 6411 Insurance agents, brokers & service

(P-10902)
SURVIVAL INSURANCE INC
Also Called: Survival Insurance Brkg A Cal
2550 N Hollywood Way # 120, Burbank (91505-5044)
PHONE..................818 565-1584
Richard Acunto, *Ch of Bd*
Susan Mithoff, *Vice Pres*
EMP: 240
SQ FT: 10,000
SALES (est): 28.1MM **Privately Held**
SIC: 6411 Insurance brokers

(P-10903)
TBG INSURANCE SERVICES CORP
100 N Sepulveda Blvd # 500, El Segundo (90245-4359)
PHONE..................310 203-8770
Michael R Shute, *CEO*
Michael Glickman, *CFO*
Dan Banis, *Exec VP*
Mary B Barrett-Newman, *Exec VP*
Harry Levitt, *Managing Dir*
EMP: 260
SALES (est): 47MM **Privately Held**
SIC: 6411 8111 Insurance agents, brokers & service; legal services

(P-10904)
THOITS INSURANCE SERVICE INC
444 Castro St Ste 200, Mountain View (94041-2051)
PHONE..................408 792-5400
Fax: 650 934-0495
Donald A Way, *CEO*
Eric Nielsen, *CFO*
Michael Solomon, *Vice Pres*
Rena Ebright, *Admin Asst*
Karen Aasen, *Technology*
EMP: 67
SQ FT: 16,250
SALES: 14.3MM **Privately Held**
WEB: www.thoits-insurance.com
SIC: 6411 Insurance agents & brokers

(P-10905)
TOKIO MARINE MANAGEMENT INC
1825 S Grant St Ste 570, San Mateo (94402-2661)
PHONE..................650 295-1180
Tokio Marine, *Principal*
EMP: 144
SALES (corp-wide): 36.4B **Privately Held**
SIC: 6411 Insurance agents, brokers & service
HQ: Tokio Marine America
230 Park Ave Fl 2
New York NY 10169
212 297-6600

(P-10906)
TOKIO MARINE MANAGEMENT INC
800 E Colorado Blvd Ste 8, Pasadena (91101-2103)
P.O. Box 7127 (91109-7127)
PHONE..................626 568-7600
Fax: 626 796-7766
Kaz Takashima, *Manager*
David Brooks, *VP Human Res*
Pattie Evans, *Underwriter*
EMP: 250
SALES (corp-wide): 36.4B **Privately Held**
SIC: 6411 6331 6321 Insurance agents, brokers & service; fire, marine & casualty insurance; accident & health insurance
HQ: Tokio Marine America
230 Park Ave Fl 2
New York NY 10169
212 297-6600

(P-10907)
TRAVELERS INDEMNITY COMPANY
Also Called: Travelers Insurance
21688 Gateway Center Dr # 300, Diamond Bar (91765-2451)
P.O. Box 6510 (91765-8510)
PHONE..................909 612-3000
Annet Ball, *Manager*
John Braddock, *Human Res Mgr*
Kety Lopez, *Opers Staff*
Peggy Smalley, *Manager*
Denise Pineda, *Consultant*
EMP: 200
SALES (corp-wide): 26.8B **Publicly Held**
WEB: www.travelers.com
SIC: 6411 6331 Insurance agents, brokers & service; fire, marine & casualty insurance
HQ: The Travelers Indemnity Company
1 Tower Sq
Hartford CT 06183
860 277-0111

(P-10908)
TRAVELERS PROPERTY CSLTY CORP
Also Called: Travelers Insurance
205 Lennon Ln, Walnut Creek (94598-2420)
P.O. Box 13089, Sacramento (95813-3089)
PHONE..................925 945-4000
Fax: 925 945-4077
Julie Weisert, *Branch Mgr*
Robert Wullner, *Vice Pres*
Kelly Ziemann, *Accounts Exec*
EMP: 300
SALES (corp-wide): 26.8B **Publicly Held**
WEB: www.travelerspc.com
SIC: 6411 Insurance agents, brokers & service
HQ: Travelers Property Casualty Corp.
1 Tower Sq 8ms
Hartford CT 06183

(P-10909)
TRAVELERS PROPERTY CSLTY CORP
Also Called: Travelers Insurance
145 S State College Blvd # 240, Brea (92821-5818)
PHONE..................714 671-8000
Fax: 714 671-8478
Bob Plourde, *Branch Mgr*
Rolf Neuschaefer, *Div Sub Head*
EMP: 116
SALES (corp-wide): 26.8B **Publicly Held**
WEB: www.travelerspc.com
SIC: 6411 Insurance agents, brokers & service
HQ: Travelers Property Casualty Corp.
1 Tower Sq 8ms
Hartford CT 06183

(P-10910)
TRI-AD ACTUARIES INC
221 W Crest St Ste 300, Escondido (92025-1737)
PHONE..................760 743-7555
Curtis Hamilton, *CEO*
Robert Krier, *CFO*
Christopher Cerone, *Vice Pres*
Thad Hamilton, *Vice Pres*
Judy Simons, *Vice Pres*
EMP: 117
SQ FT: 17,500
SALES (est): 40.5MM **Privately Held**
WEB: www.tri-ad.com
SIC: 6411 8742 Pension & retirement plan consultants; human resource consulting services

(P-10911)
TRISTAR RISK MANAGEMENT
203 N Golden Circle Dr # 200, Santa Ana (92705-4011)
PHONE..................714 543-0700
Thomas Veale, *Branch Mgr*
Jon Fujiwara, *Sales Staff*
EMP: 69
SALES (corp-wide): 401.3MM **Privately Held**
WEB: www.tristarrisk.com
SIC: 6411 8742 Inspection & investigation services, insurance; management consulting services
HQ: Tristar Risk Management
100 Oceangate Ste 700
Long Beach CA 90802
562 495-6600

(P-10912)
UNIFAX INSURANCE SYSTEMS INC
26050 Mureau Rd Fl 2, Calabasas (91302-3174)
PHONE..................818 591-9800
Erwin Cheldin, *President*
Lester Aaron, *Treasurer*
Cary Cheldin, *Exec VP*
EMP: 80 EST: 1972
SQ FT: 50,000
SALES (est): 10.8MM
SALES (corp-wide): 33.2MM **Publicly Held**
WEB: www.crusaderinsurance.com
SIC: 6411 Insurance agents, brokers & service
PA: Unico American Corporation
26050 Mureau Rd Fl 2
Calabasas CA 91302
818 591-9800

(P-10913)
UNITED AGENCIES INC (PA)
Also Called: Kemper Insurance
301 E Colo Blvd Ste 200, Pasadena (91101)
P.O. Box 7139 (91109-7139)
PHONE..................626 564-2670
Thomas Hays, *Ch of Bd*
Gary Conkey, *President*
Karen Bader, *CFO*
Robert W Bader, *Vice Pres*
Jeff Chan, *Vice Pres*
EMP: 66 EST: 1962
SQ FT: 5,900
SALES (est): 90.3MM **Privately Held**
WEB: www.unitedagencies.com
SIC: 6411 Insurance agents; insurance brokers

(P-10914)
UNITED CHINESE AMERICAN GENERA (PA)
Also Called: Uca General Insurance
6363 Katella Ave, Cypress (90630-5205)
PHONE..................714 228-7800
Robert Lan, *President*
Lin Lan, *Shareholder*
Ping Chen, *Corp Secy*
Tom Hermstad, *Info Tech Mgr*
EMP: 50
SQ FT: 20,000
SALES: 10MM **Privately Held**
WEB: www.ucageneral.com
SIC: 6411 Insurance agents, brokers & service

(P-10915)
UNITED INSURANCE COMPANY
5601 E Slauson Ave # 105, Commerce (90040-2997)
PHONE..................323 869-9381
Fax: 323 869-9385
Norman Petrousian, *Manager*
EMP: 50
SALES (est): 6.3MM **Privately Held**
SIC: 6411 Insurance agents, brokers & service

(P-10916)
UNITED STATES FIRE INSUR CO
Also Called: Crum Forster
777 S Figueroa St # 1500, Los Angeles (90017-5810)
PHONE..................213 797-3100
Fax: 213 797-3139
Mark Owens, *Manager*
EMP: 53
SALES (corp-wide): 9.5B **Privately Held**
SIC: 6411 Insurance agents, brokers & service
HQ: United States Fire Insurance Company
305 Madison Ave
Morristown NJ 07960
973 490-6600

(P-10917)
UNUM LIFE INSURANCE CO AMER
Also Called: Unumprovident
655 N Central Ave, Glendale (91203-1422)
PHONE..................818 291-4739
Fax: 818 956-2580
Vicki Riggs, *Branch Mgr*
EMP: 195
SALES (corp-wide): 10.7B **Publicly Held**
SIC: 6411 Insurance agents, brokers & service
HQ: Unum Life Insurance Company Of America
2211 Congress St
Portland ME 04122
207 575-2211

6411 - Insurance Agents, Brokers & Svc County (P-10918)

(P-10918)
USI OF SOUTHERN CALIFORNIA INS
21700 Oxnard St Ste 1200, Woodland Hills (91367-7578)
PHONE..................................818 251-3000
Fax: 818 251-1800
Mike Rastigue, *President*
Robert Corenson, *Vice Pres*
Mark Goldberg, *Vice Pres*
Bernadette Jackson, *Vice Pres*
Maria Souza, *Administration*
EMP: 50
SQ FT: 15,000
SALES (est) 14.3MM Privately Held
WEB: www.usicondo.com
SIC: 6411 Insurance agents; life insurance agents
HQ: Usi Service Corporation
555 Plsntvlle Rd Ste 160s
Briarcliff Manor NY 10510
914 747-6300

(P-10919)
USI SOUTH COAST
Also Called: Kemper Insurance
29a Technology Dr 200, Irvine (92618-2302)
PHONE..................................949 790-9200
Randy Joe Hartman, *Vice Pres*
Tim Porreca, *Chairman*
Robert Nesbit, *Officer*
Phil Larson, *Senior VP*
Sandra Usleman, *Senior VP*
EMP: 60
SQ FT: 5,000
SALES (est): 11.3MM Privately Held
SIC: 6411 7513 Insurance agents, brokers & service; property & casualty insurance agent; truck rental & leasing, no drivers

(P-10920)
VALUEOPTIONS OF CALIFORNIA
Also Called: Value Options-V B H
10805 Holder St Ste 300, Cypress (90630-5147)
PHONE..................................800 228-1286
Juan Molina, *VP Opers*
Steve Rockowitz, *Ch of Bd*
Jolene Myrter, *CFO*
EMP: 200
SALES (est): 27.2MM
SALES (corp-wide): 431.2MM Privately Held
WEB: www.fhchealthsystems.com
SIC: 6411 6321 Insurance agents, brokers & service; accident & health insurance
PA: Fhc Health Systems, Inc
240 Corporate Blvd # 100
Norfolk VA 23502
757 459-5100

(P-10921)
VAN BEURDEN INSURANCE SVCS INC (PA)
Also Called: Kemper Insurance
1600 Draper St, Kingsburg (93631-1911)
P.O. Box 67 (93631-0067)
PHONE..................................559 634-7125
Fax: 559 897-4070
William J Van Beurden, *President*
Robin Hankins, *CFO*
Mike Beall, *Vice Pres*
Mark Karlie, *Vice Pres*
Brian Loven, *Vice Pres*
EMP: 67
SQ FT: 20,000
SALES (est): 40.1MM Privately Held
WEB: www.vanbeurden.com
SIC: 6411 Insurance agents & brokers

(P-10922)
VEBA ADMINISTRATORS INC
Also Called: Benefit Planning
4640 Admiralty Way Fl 9, Marina Del Rey (90292-6630)
PHONE..................................310 577-1444
Guy Hocker, *President*
Richard Caplan, *Vice Pres*
Anthony Delfino, *Vice Pres*
Richard L Kapan, *Marketing Staff*
EMP: 50

SALES (est): 7.3MM Privately Held
WEB: www.benplaninc.com
SIC: 6411 6141 Pension & retirement plan consultants; financing: automobiles, furniture, etc., not a deposit bank

(P-10923)
VENBROOK INSURANCE SVCS LLC (PA)
Also Called: Kemper Insurance
6320 Canoga Ave Fl 12, Woodland Hills (91367-2584)
PHONE..................................818 598-8900
Marc Bishara,
Michael Flood, *Senior VP*
Tim Johnston, *Senior VP*
Alan Shetzer, *Senior VP*
Jack Snyder, *Senior VP*
EMP: 86 EST: 2007
SALES (est): 43.6MM Privately Held
SIC: 6411 Insurance information & consulting services

(P-10924)
VETERINARY PET INSUR SVCS INC (DH)
Also Called: Dvm Insurance Agency
1800 E Emperi Hwy Ste 145, Brea (92821)
P.O. Box 2344 (92822-2344)
PHONE..................................714 989-0555
Michael Funk, *CFO*
Mike Miller, *Chairman*
Phil Grevin, *Vice Pres*
Dennis Drent, *Principal*
Charysse Sweet, *Program Mgr*
EMP: 113
SQ FT: 80,000
SALES: 264.2MM
SALES (corp-wide): 15.2B Privately Held
WEB: www.petinsurance.com
SIC: 6411 Insurance agents, brokers & service; insurance agents & brokers
HQ: Scottsdale Insurance Company
8877 N Gainey Center Dr
Scottsdale AZ 85258
480 365-4000

(P-10925)
VISALUS INC
Also Called: Visalus Science
6300 Wilshire Blvd # 610, Los Angeles (90048-5208)
PHONE..................................323 801-2400
Ryan Blair, *Owner*
Connie Lau, *Project Mgr*
Nick Clement, *Director*
Sadie Curry, *Director*
Sophia Lazoen, *Director*
EMP: 420
SALES (corp-wide): 71.4MM Privately Held
SIC: 6411 Insurance agents, brokers & service
PA: Visalus, Inc.
340 E Big Beaver Rd # 400
Troy MI 48083
323 801-2483

(P-10926)
W BROWN & ASSC PROPERTY & CSU
19000 Macarthur Blvd, Irvine (92612-1438)
PHONE..................................949 851-2060
Scott Brown, *President*
EMP: 67
SALES (est): 38MM Privately Held
SIC: 6411 Insurance agents, brokers & service

(P-10927)
WARNER PACIFIC INSUR SVCS INC (PA)
32110 Agoura Rd, Westlake Village (91361-4026)
PHONE..................................408 298-4049
John H Nelson, *CEO*
Matthew Conrow, *CFO*
Stephanie Brown, *Senior VP*
Debbie Vaillancourt, *Senior VP*
David Nelson, *Vice Pres*
EMP: 146
SQ FT: 10,000
SALES (est): 163.3MM Privately Held
SIC: 6411 Insurance brokers

(P-10928)
WELLS FARGO INSUR SVCS USA INC
Also Called: Kemper Insurance
1039 N Mcdowell Blvd A, Petaluma (94954-1173)
PHONE..................................707 769-2900
Fax: 650 413-4491
Wayne Shira, *Manager*
Lisa Kaufman, *Executive*
Dave Rohling, *Technical Staff*
EMP: 80
SALES (corp-wide): 90B Publicly Held
SIC: 6411 Insurance agents, brokers & service
HQ: Wells Fargo Insurance Services Usa, Inc.
150 N Michigan Ave # 3900
Chicago IL 60601
866 294-2571

(P-10929)
WELLS FARGO INSUR SVCS USA INC
5200 N Palm Ave Ste 114, Fresno (93704-2225)
PHONE..................................559 228-6300
Debra Powers, *Branch Mgr*
Craig Takahashi, *Info Tech Dir*
EMP: 70
SALES (corp-wide): 90B Publicly Held
SIC: 6411 Insurance agents, brokers & service
HQ: Wells Fargo Insurance Services Usa, Inc.
150 N Michigan Ave # 3900
Chicago IL 60601
866 294-2571

(P-10930)
WELLS FARGO INSUR SVCS USA INC
15303 Ventura Blvd Fl 7, Sherman Oaks (91403-3197)
PHONE..................................818 464-9300
Alan Boring, *Director*
Ralph Rodriguez, *Info Tech Mgr*
EMP: 123
SALES (corp-wide): 90B Publicly Held
SIC: 6411 Insurance agents, brokers & service; insurance brokers
HQ: Wells Fargo Insurance Services Usa, Inc.
150 N Michigan Ave # 3900
Chicago IL 60601
866 294-2571

(P-10931)
WELLS FARGO INSUR SVCS USA INC
10940 White Rock Rd, Rancho Cordova (95670-6182)
PHONE..................................916 589-8000
Donna Flores, *Branch Mgr*
Samuel Jones, *Sr Corp Ofcr*
Nancy Goldsmith, *Trust Officer*
Anne Walters, *Trust Officer*
Fred Cannon, *Exec VP*
EMP: 210
SALES (corp-wide): 90B Publicly Held
SIC: 6411 Insurance agents, brokers & service; insurance brokers
HQ: Wells Fargo Insurance Services Usa, Inc.
150 N Michigan Ave # 3900
Chicago IL 60601
866 294-2571

(P-10932)
WELLS FARGO INSUR SVCS USA INC
Also Called: Abd Insurance and Fincl Svcs
959 Skyway Rd Ste 200, San Carlos (94070-2719)
PHONE..................................650 413-4499
Fax: 650 839-6050
Samuel Jones, *Branch Mgr*
Erik Stenson, *Senior VP*
Pat Hoefling, *Vice Pres*
Terry Sityar, *Vice Pres*
Joel Graves, *VP Bus Dvlpt*
EMP: 200
SALES (corp-wide): 90B Publicly Held
SIC: 6411 Insurance agents, brokers & service

HQ: Wells Fargo Insurance Services Usa, Inc.
150 N Michigan Ave # 3900
Chicago IL 60601
866 294-2571

(P-10933)
WELLS FARGO INSUR SVCS USA INC
1350 Treat Blvd Ste 550, Walnut Creek (94597-7999)
PHONE..................................925 988-1700
Fax: 925 280-2750
Brian Heatherington, *Director*
EMP: 70
SALES (corp-wide): 90B Publicly Held
SIC: 6411 Insurance agents, brokers & service
HQ: Wells Fargo Insurance Services Usa, Inc.
150 N Michigan Ave # 3900
Chicago IL 60601
866 294-2571

(P-10934)
WELLS FARGO INSURANCE SVCS INC
11017 Cobblerock Dr # 100, Rancho Cordova (95670-6049)
PHONE..................................916 231-3400
Mark Freeman, *District Mgr*
Lisa J Bowen, *Vice Pres*
Greg Vannesn, *Marketing Staff*
Jean Luis, *Accounts Mgr*
EMP: 130
SALES (corp-wide): 90B Publicly Held
SIC: 6411 Insurance agents, brokers & service
HQ: Wells Fargo Insurance Services, Inc.
230 W Monroe St Ste 1950
Chicago IL 60606
312 685-4122

(P-10935)
WELLS FRGO INSUR SVCS MINN INC
4141 Inland Empire Blvd, Ontario (91764-5004)
PHONE..................................909 481-3802
EMP: 103
SALES (corp-wide): 90B Publicly Held
SIC: 6411 Insurance agents, brokers & service
HQ: Wells Fargo Insurance Services Of Minnesota, Inc.
400 Highway 169 S Ste 800
Minneapolis MN 55426
952 563-0600

(P-10936)
WESTERN GENERAL AGENCY INC
12200 Sylvan St Ste 140, North Hollywood (91606-3240)
P.O. Box 7001 (91615-0001)
PHONE..................................818 766-6500
Fax: 818 766-0931
Weldon Wilson, *President*
Chris Stolp, *Network Mgr*
Bill Salkin, *Database Admin*
EMP: 55
SQ FT: 41,000
SALES (est): 6.4MM
SALES (corp-wide): 233.8MM Privately Held
WEB: www.cnico.com
SIC: 6411 Insurance agents
PA: Kramer-Wilson Company, Inc.
6345 Balboa Blvd Ste 190
Encino CA 91316
818 760-0880

(P-10937)
WESTERN UNITED INSURANCE CO
Also Called: Csaa Insur Group Walnut Creek
3349 Michelson Dr Ste 100, Irvine (92612-0688)
P.O. Box 24523, Oakland (94623-1523)
PHONE..................................800 959-9842
Fax: 949 474-4132
James B Schallert, *President*
Nelson Allen, *Vice Pres*
Steven Gilmer, *Engineer*
Bryan Hall, *Engineer*

PRODUCTS & SERVICES SECTION
6512 - Operators Of Nonresidential Bldgs County (P-10959)

Tweeti Nguyen, *Accountant*
EMP: 165
SQ FT: 50,000
SALES (est): 27.6MM
SALES (corp-wide): 1.1B **Privately Held**
WEB: www.californiastateautomobileassociation.c
SIC: 6411 Insurance agents
PA: American Automobile Association Of Northern California, Nevada & Utah
1900 Powell St Ste 1200
Emeryville CA 94608
800 922-8228

(P-10938)
WESTWOOD INSURANCE AGENCY (DH)
8407 Fllbrook Ave Ste 200, Canoga Park (91304)
PHONE..................818 990-9715
Fax: 818 227-0121
John Flynn, *President*
Stephen G Franks, *Treasurer*
Mark Nettleton, *Vice Pres*
Karen Sherman, *Executive Asst*
James P Novak, *Admin Sec*
EMP: 89
SQ FT: 17,765
SALES (est): 24.1MM **Publicly Held**
WEB: www.westwoodinsurance.com
SIC: 6411 Insurance agents
HQ: National General Lender Services, Inc.
210 Interstate N Pkwy
Atlanta GA 30339
770 690-8400

(P-10939)
WILSHIRE INSURANCE COMPANY
Also Called: Accidental Fire & Casualty
1206 W Avenue J Ste 100, Lancaster (93534-2953)
P.O. Box 7006 (93539-7006)
PHONE..................661 940-7300
Fax: 661 723-6799
Stephen Stephano, *President*
Dianna Dantice, *Chief Mktg Ofcr*
Nickie Rowe, *Officer*
Debbie Wrinkle, *Vice Pres*
Grace Sanchez, *Executive*
EMP: 50
SALES (est): 7.5MM **Privately Held**
SIC: 6411 Insurance agents

(P-10940)
WINTERTHUR U S HOLDINGS INC
888 S Figueroa St Ste 570, Los Angeles (90017-5449)
PHONE..................213 228-0281
Ken McClelland, *Branch Mgr*
EMP: 240
SALES (corp-wide): 17.9B **Privately Held**
SIC: 6411 6311 6331 Property & casualty insurance agent; life insurance; fire, marine & casualty insurance
HQ: Winterthur U. S. Holdings Inc
1 General Dr
Sun Prairie WI 53596
608 837-4440

(P-10941)
WINTON IRELAND STROM & GREEN (PA)
Also Called: Winton-Ireland, Strom and Gr
627 E Canal Dr, Turlock (95380-4022)
PHONE..................209 667-0995
Michael Ireland, *President*
Ted Green, *Vice Pres*
Jeff Quinn, *Vice Pres*
Barbara Schmidt, *Admin Asst*
Julie Teran, *Admin Asst*
EMP: 80
SQ FT: 10,000
SALES (est): 39.2MM **Privately Held**
WEB: www.wintonireland.com
SIC: 6411 Insurance agents, brokers & service

(P-10942)
WM MICHAEL STEMLER INC (PA)
Also Called: Delta Health Systems
3244 Brookside Rd Ste 200, Stockton (95219-2384)
P.O. Box 1227 (95201-1227)
PHONE..................209 948-8483
Fax: 209 474-5400
William M Stemler, *CEO*
Richard Rouse, *President*
Patti Silva, *Exec VP*
Ramona Larkin, *Executive*
Susan Elis, *Accountant*
EMP: 110
SQ FT: 30,100
SALES: 24.8MM **Privately Held**
WEB: www.deltahealthsystems.com
SIC: 6411 Medical insurance claim processing, contract or fee basis

(P-10943)
WM MICHAEL STEMLER INC
7110 N Fresno St Ste 350, Fresno (93720-2933)
PHONE..................559 228-4144
Robert Maes, *Branch Mgr*
EMP: 150
SALES (corp-wide): 24.8MM **Privately Held**
SIC: 6411 Medical insurance claim processing, contract or fee basis
PA: Wm. Michael Stemler, Incorporated
3244 Brookside Rd Ste 200
Stockton CA 95219
209 948-8483

(P-10944)
WOOD GUTMANN BOGART INSUR BRKG
Also Called: W G B
15901 Red Hill Ave # 100, Tustin (92780-7318)
PHONE..................714 505-7000
Fax: 714 573-1770
Kevin S Bogart, *CEO*
Angela Mullin, *Vice Pres*
Lisa Doherty, *Personnel*
Norm Hainlen, *Director*
Jackie Morey, *Manager*
EMP: 93
SALES (est): 32.4MM **Privately Held**
WEB: www.wgbib.com
SIC: 6411 Insurance agents

(P-10945)
WOODRUFF-SAWYER & CO (PA)
50 California St Fl 12, San Francisco (94111-4646)
PHONE..................415 391-2141
Fax: 415 989-9923
Charles Rosson, *CEO*
Kristine Furrer, *Senior VP*
Stephen Gaitley, *Senior VP*
Stephen Mork, *Senior VP*
Judy Roberts, *Senior VP*
EMP: 240
SQ FT: 54,000
SALES (est): 212.9MM **Privately Held**
SIC: 6411 Insurance brokers

(P-10946)
WORLDWIDE HOLDINGS INC (PA)
725 S Figueroa St # 1900, Los Angeles (90017-5496)
PHONE..................213 236-4500
Donald R Davis, *Chairman*
Davis D Moore, *President*
Eve Williams, *Officer*
Daniel Colacurcio, *Exec VP*
EMP: 85
SQ FT: 23,000
SALES (est): 51.2MM **Privately Held**
WEB: www.wwfi.com
SIC: 6411 Insurance agents, brokers & service

(P-10947)
WORXSITEHR INSUR SOLUTIONS INC
5000 Parkway Calabasas # 302, Calabasas (91302-1400)
PHONE..................877 479-3591
EMP: 60

SQ FT: 2,500
SALES (est): 4.7MM **Privately Held**
SIC: 6411 7371

(P-10948)
YOURPEOPLE INC
Also Called: Zenefits Ftw insurance Svcs
303 2nd St Ste 401, San Francisco (94107-1366)
PHONE..................415 798-9086
David Sacks, *CEO*
Laks Srini, *Officer*
Yi Ding, *Software Engr*
Tracy Ng, *Tech Recruiter*
Prasanna Sankar, *Engineer*
EMP: 700 **EST:** 2010
SALES (est): 174.2MM **Privately Held**
SIC: 6411 7372 Insurance brokers; business oriented computer software

(P-10949)
ZURICH AMERICAN INSURANCE CO
525 Market St Ste 2900, San Francisco (94105-2737)
PHONE..................415 538-7100
Fax: 415 538-7214
Bill Dougherty, *Marketing Staff*
Jennifer Levine, *Executive*
Chris Omen, *Manager*
EMP: 200
SALES (corp-wide): 62B **Privately Held**
WEB: www.zurichna.com
SIC: 6411 Insurance agents, brokers & service; insurance agents
HQ: Zurich American Insurance Company
1299 Zurich Way
Schaumburg IL 60173
800 987-3373

6512 Operators Of Nonresidential Bldgs

(P-10950)
14545 FRIAR LLC
14545 Friar St Ste 105, Van Nuys (91411-2357)
PHONE..................818 817-0082
Kambiz Merabi,
EMP: 52 **EST:** 2007
SQ FT: 3,000
SALES: 4.6MM **Privately Held**
SIC: 6512 6531 Nonresidential building operators; real estate agent, commercial

(P-10951)
5 DIAMOND PROTECTION INC
2901 W Macarthur Blvd, Santa Ana (92704-6910)
PHONE..................949 466-1367
Mohammad Sayed, *President*
Tupua Loane, *Opers Mgr*
Troy Sims, *Director*
EMP: 99
SALES: 200K **Privately Held**
SIC: 6512 Nonresidential building operators

(P-10952)
AAT TORREY RESERVE 6 LLC
11455 El Cmino Real Ste 2, San Diego (92130)
PHONE..................858 350-2600
John Chamberlain, *Principal*
EMP: 66
SALES (est): 1.7MM
SALES (corp-wide): 21.6MM **Privately Held**
SIC: 6512 Nonresidential building operators
PA: American Assets, Inc.
11455 El Cmino Rl Ste 140
San Diego CA 92130
858 350-2600

(P-10953)
ABBEY-PROPERTIES LLC (PA)
12447 Lewis St Ste 203, Garden Grove (92840-6601)
PHONE..................562 435-2100
Donald G Abbey,
Anne Koegel, *Officer*
Kurt Kaufman, *Exec Dir*
Fred Leland, *Controller*

Omar Howard, *Marketing Staff*
EMP: 75
SQ FT: 276,000
SALES (est): 4.6MM **Privately Held**
WEB: www.theabbeyco.com
SIC: 6512 Commercial & industrial building operation

(P-10954)
ALEXANDER PROPERTIES COMPANY
1 Annabel Ln, San Ramon (94583-4358)
P.O. Box 640 (94583-0640)
PHONE..................925 866-0100
John T Waterhouse, *CEO*
Alexander Mehran, *Principal*
EMP: 50
SALES: 3.1MM **Privately Held**
SIC: 6512 Nonresidential building operators

(P-10955)
ALISAM OXNARD OPERATING
Also Called: Water Drops Express Carwash
212 26th St Ste 246, Santa Monica (90402-2524)
PHONE..................310 877-7179
Bob Bandabi, *Mng Member*
Sam Siam, *Mng Member*
EMP: 116
SALES: 32MM **Privately Held**
SIC: 6512 Nonresidential building operators

(P-10956)
ALLIED SWISS LIMITED
Also Called: Allied Swift
2636 Vista Pacific Dr, Oceanside (92056-3514)
PHONE..................760 941-1702
Wade Prescott, *Partner*
Bruce Damon, *Ltd Ptnr*
Robert Hively, *Ltd Ptnr*
Bonnie Prescott, *Ltd Ptnr*
Chip Prescott, *Ltd Ptnr*
EMP: 112
SQ FT: 21,000
SALES (est): 6.6MM **Privately Held**
WEB: www.alliedswiss.net
SIC: 6512 Commercial & industrial building operation

(P-10957)
ALPINE VILLAGE
Also Called: Alpine Inn Restaurant
833 Torrance Blvd Ste 1a, Torrance (90502-1733)
PHONE..................310 327-4384
Fax: 310 327-6520
Ursula Wilson, *CEO*
EMP: 250
SALES (est): 14.1MM **Privately Held**
WEB: www.alpinevillage.net
SIC: 6512 Commercial & industrial building operation

(P-10958)
AMERICARE HLTH RETIREMENT INC
Also Called: Silvergate San Marcos
1550 Security Pl Ofc, San Marcos (92078-4063)
PHONE..................760 744-4484
Fax: 760 471-4763
Melba Dunn, *Administration*
Beulah Bondi, *Manager*
Marion Byron, *Manager*
Stephen Forsythe, *Manager*
EMP: 100
SQ FT: 51,071
SALES (corp-wide): 10.5MM **Privately Held**
WEB: www.americarehr.com
SIC: 6512 8051 Nonresidential building operators; skilled nursing care facilities
PA: Americare Health & Retirement, Inc.
140 Lomas Santa Fe Dr # 103
Solana Beach CA 92075
858 792-0696

(P-10959)
ANTELOPE VALLEY MALL
1233 W Rancho Vista Blvd # 405, Palmdale (93551-3949)
PHONE..................661 266-9150
Fax: 661 266-9699

6512 - Operators Of Nonresidential Bldgs County (P-10960)

Greg Lenners, *General Mgr*
George D Zamias *Developer, Partner*
Monica Barth, *Manager*
Brian Gardner, *Manager*
EMP: 70
SALES (est): 3.6MM **Privately Held**
WEB: www.av-mall.com
SIC: 6512 Shopping center, property operation only

(P-10960)
ARDEN REALTY INC (DH)
11601 Wilshire Blvd Fl 4, Los Angeles (90025-1740)
PHONE.............................310 966-2600
Fax: 310 966-2699
Joaquin De Monet, *CEO*
Robert Peddicord, *COO*
Kevin Early, *CFO*
Jeffrey A Berger, *Senior VP*
David A Swartz, *Senior VP*
EMP: 68
SALES (est): 12.8MM
SALES (corp-wide): 117.3B **Publicly Held**
WEB: www.ardenrealty.com
SIC: 6512 Commercial & industrial building operation
HQ: G E Commercial Finance Real Estate
292 Long Ridge Rd
Stamford CT 06902
203 373-2211

(P-10961)
ARE- MARYLAND NO 31 LLC
385 E Colo Blvd Ste 299, Pasadena (91101)
PHONE.............................626 578-0777
Lawrence Diamond, *Exec VP*
EMP: 50
SALES (est): 574.7K **Privately Held**
SIC: 6512 Nonresidential building operators

(P-10962)
BAY WEST SHWPLACE INVSTORS LLC (PA)
Also Called: Sheplace Design Center
2 Henry Adams St Ste 450, San Francisco (94103-5000)
PHONE.............................415 490-5800
Fax: 415 553-3963
Tim Threadway, *Chairman*
EMP: 50
SALES (est): 3.4MM **Privately Held**
SIC: 6512 5712 Commercial & industrial building operation; furniture stores

(P-10963)
BRIDGE HOUSING ACQUISITION
1 Hawthorne St Ste 400, San Francisco (94105-3909)
PHONE.............................415 989-1111
Carol Gilante, *President*
Lydia Tan, *Vice Pres*
EMP: 80
SALES: 78.1K **Privately Held**
SIC: 6512 Nonresidential building operators

(P-10964)
BUILDING SERVICES/SYSTEM INC
2575 Stanwell Dr, Concord (94520-4888)
PHONE.............................925 688-1234
Sam Martinovich, *Principal*
Sam Mardinovich, *Principal*
EMP: 99
SALES (est): 5.2MM **Privately Held**
SIC: 6512 Commercial & industrial building operation

(P-10965)
CALIFORNIA MART LLC
Also Called: California Mart Parking
110 E 9th St Ste A727, Los Angeles (90079-1727)
PHONE.............................213 630-3600
Fax: 213 630-3708
Judah Hertz,
Dan Matthews, *Personnel Exec*
EMP: 100
SALES (est): 5.3MM **Privately Held**
WEB: www.californiamarketcenter.com
SIC: 6512 7521 Commercial & industrial building operation; parking garage

(P-10966)
CASDEN BUILDERS LLC
9090 Wilshire Blvd Fl 3, Beverly Hills (90211-1851)
PHONE.............................310 274-5553
Robert Hilderbrand,
Marilley Joe, *Project Mgr*
Mike Murray, *Superintendent*
EMP: 50 EST: 1998
SALES (est): 1.8MM **Privately Held**
SIC: 6512 Nonresidential building operators

(P-10967)
CB RICHARD ELLIS STRTGC PRTNRS
515 S Flower St, Los Angeles (90071-2201)
PHONE.............................213 683-4200
Richard Ellis,
Janet Aston, *Managing Dir*
Let CAM, *Business Anlyst*
Kira Ross, *Business Anlyst*
Akinola Akiwowo, *Technician*
EMP: 100
SALES (est): 20.8MM
SALES (corp-wide): 10.8B **Publicly Held**
WEB: www.cbrichardellis.com
SIC: 6512 Nonresidential building operators
PA: Cbre Group, Inc.
400 S Hope St Ste 25
Los Angeles CA 90071
213 613-3333

(P-10968)
CBRE GROUP INC
101 California St Fl 44, San Francisco (94111-5899)
PHONE.............................415 772-0123
Darin Bosch, *Branch Mgr*
Jack Churton, *Exec VP*
Ham Southworth, *Exec VP*
Meade Boutwell, *Senior VP*
Jay Sholl, *Senior VP*
EMP: 223
SALES (corp-wide): 10.8B **Publicly Held**
SIC: 6512 6531 Nonresidential building operators; real estate agents & managers
PA: Cbre Group, Inc.
400 S Hope St Ste 25
Los Angeles CA 90071
213 613-3333

(P-10969)
CENTURY NATIONAL PROPERTIES (PA)
Also Called: Daytona Surfise
12200 Sylvan St Ste 250, North Hollywood (91606-3229)
PHONE.............................818 760-0880
Weldon Wilson, *President*
Judith Osborne, *Treasurer*
Marie Balicki, *Admin Sec*
EMP: 61
SQ FT: 92,000
SALES (est): 2.9MM **Privately Held**
SIC: 6512 7011 Commercial & industrial building operation; motels

(P-10970)
CESAR CHAVEZ STUDENT CENTER
Also Called: Snackademic
1650 Holloway Ave Rm C134, San Francisco (94132-1722)
PHONE.............................415 338-7362
Guy Dalpe, *Exec Dir*
EMP: 130
SALES: 5MM **Privately Held**
SIC: 6512 Nonresidential building operators

(P-10971)
CITY OF ANAHEIM
Also Called: Anaheim Arena
2695 E Katella Ave, Anaheim (92806-5904)
PHONE.............................714 704-2400
Tim Ryan, *Manager*
Gary Perdew, *Chief Engr*
EMP: 450 **Privately Held**
WEB: www.anaheim.net
SIC: 6512 7941 Nonresidential building operators; sports field or stadium operator, promoting sports events
PA: City Of Anaheim
200 S Anaheim Blvd
Anaheim CA 92805
714 765-5162

(P-10972)
CITY OF FAIRFIELD
Also Called: Fairfield Community Center
1000 Webster St, Fairfield (94533-4883)
PHONE.............................707 428-7435
Fax: 707 428-7437
Karin McMillan, *Mayor*
EMP: 150 **Privately Held**
WEB: www.fairfieldpoa.com
SIC: 6512 Auditorium & hall operation
PA: City Of Fairfield
1000 Webster St
Fairfield CA 94533
707 428-7569

(P-10973)
DAVID D BOHANNON ORGANIZATION (PA)
Also Called: San Lorenzo Village Shopg Ctr
60 31st Ave, San Mateo (94403-3404)
PHONE.............................650 345-8222
David D Bohannon II, *President*
Scott Bohannon, *Senior VP*
Ernest Lotti Jr, *Vice Pres*
Frances E Nelson, *Director*
EMP: 60
SQ FT: 5,000
SALES (est): 4.3MM **Privately Held**
SIC: 6512 6552 Commercial & industrial building operation; subdividers & developers

(P-10974)
DESERT SPRINGS HOTEL
10805 Palm Dr, Desert Hot Springs (92240-2511)
PHONE.............................760 251-3399
Lynn Byrnes, *President*
EMP: 50
SALES (est): 1.6MM **Privately Held**
SIC: 6512 Nonresidential building operators

(P-10975)
DONAHUE SCHRIBER RLTY GROUP LP (PA)
200 Baker St E Ste 100, Costa Mesa (92626-4551)
PHONE.............................714 545-1400
Patrick S Donahue, *CEO*
Lawrence P Casey, *President*
Lisa L Hirose, *Exec VP*
Mark L Whitfield, *Exec VP*
Kathryn Yoshimura, *Info Tech Mgr*
EMP: 100
SQ FT: 44,805
SALES (est): 22.1MM **Privately Held**
WEB: www.donahueschriber.com
SIC: 6512 Shopping center, property operation only

(P-10976)
DONAHUE SCHRIBER RLTY GROUP LP
5082 N Palm Ave, Fresno (93704-2231)
PHONE.............................714 545-1400
Elizabeth Schreiber, *Manager*
Patrick S Donahue, *COO*
Kathy Stepp, *Admin Sec*
Taran Stokes, *Property Mgr*
Laurie Sweeney, *Director*
EMP: 57
SALES (corp-wide): 22.1MM **Privately Held**
SIC: 6512 Shopping center, property operation only
PA: Donahue Schriber Realty Group, L.P.
200 Baker St E Ste 100
Costa Mesa CA 92626
714 545-1400

(P-10977)
DONAHUE SCHRIBER RLTY GROUP LP
8020 E Santa Ana Cyn Rd, Anaheim (92808-1110)
PHONE.............................714 283-3535
Patrick S Donahue, *Branch Mgr*
EMP: 57
SALES (corp-wide): 22.1MM **Privately Held**
SIC: 6512 Shopping center, property operation only
PA: Donahue Schriber Realty Group, L.P.
200 Baker St E Ste 100
Costa Mesa CA 92626
714 545-1400

(P-10978)
DONAHUE SCHRIBER RLTY GROUP LP
12925 El Camino Real J22, San Diego (92130-1891)
PHONE.............................858 793-5757
Pat Snow, *Branch Mgr*
EMP: 57
SALES (corp-wide): 22.1MM **Privately Held**
WEB: www.donahueschriber.com
SIC: 6512 Shopping center, property operation only
PA: Donahue Schriber Realty Group, L.P.
200 Baker St E Ste 100
Costa Mesa CA 92626
714 545-1400

(P-10979)
ENTREPRENEURIAL CAPITAL CORP
4100 Nwport Pl Dr Ste 400, Newport Beach (92660)
PHONE.............................949 809-3900
John K Abel, *Principal*
EMP: 240
SALES (corp-wide): 49.9MM **Privately Held**
SIC: 6512 Commercial & industrial building operation
PA: Entrepreneurial Capital Corporation
4100 Newport Place Dr # 400
Newport Beach CA 92660
949 809-3900

(P-10980)
ESKATON (PA)
5105 Manzanita Ave Ste D, Carmichael (95608-0523)
PHONE.............................916 334-0296
Fax: 916 338-1248
Todd Murch, *CEO*
Trevor Hammond, *COO*
William Pace, *CFO*
Bill Pace, *Senior VP*
Kim Rhinehelder, *Vice Pres*
EMP: 100
SQ FT: 27,000
SALES: 1.4MM **Privately Held**
SIC: 6512 8051 Commercial & industrial building operation; convalescent home with continuous nursing care

(P-10981)
ETHAN CONRAD PROPERTIES INC
1300 National Dr Ste 100, Sacramento (95834-1981)
PHONE.............................916 779-1000
Fax: 916 779-1200
Ethan Conrad, *President*
Kenneth Miller, *CFO*
Vincent Dupavillon, *Vice Pres*
Marissa Todd, *Executive Asst*
Jon Lemos, *Controller*
EMP: 100
SQ FT: 45,063
SALES: 45MM **Privately Held**
WEB: www.ethanconradprop.com
SIC: 6512 Commercial & industrial building operation

(P-10982)
FIVE LONG ISLAND PROPERTIES LL
1 Sun America Ctr Fl 38, Los Angeles (90067-6101)
PHONE.............................310 772-6306
Keith Honig, *Managing Prtnr*
EMP: 50
SALES (est): 1.3MM **Privately Held**
SIC: 6512 Nonresidential building operators

PRODUCTS & SERVICES SECTION
6512 - Operators Of Nonresidential Bldgs County (P-11005)

(P-10983)
FOREST CITY RENTAL PRPTS CORP
Oasis Fd Crt Antelope Vly Mall
1233 W Avenue P Ste 900, Palmdale (93551-3950)
PHONE..................661 266-9150
Brian Gardner, *Manager*
EMP: 80
SALES (corp-wide): 978.2MM **Privately Held**
SIC: 6512 Shopping center, property operation only; commercial & industrial building operation
HQ: Forest City Properties, Llc
50 Public Sq Ste 1360
Cleveland OH 44113
216 621-6060

(P-10984)
FRATERNAL ORDER EAGLES 1582
Also Called: EAGLES HALL
124 Vernon St, Roseville (95678-2631)
P.O. Box 766 (95678-0766)
PHONE..................916 782-2694
Charles Chase, *Admin Sec*
EMP: 120
SALES: 79.3K **Privately Held**
SIC: 6512 8641 Nonresidential building operators; civic social & fraternal associations

(P-10985)
FRED H LUNDBLADE JR
Also Called: Lundblade Builders
939 Koster St Ste B, Eureka (95501-0106)
PHONE..................707 442-8049
Fax: 707 442-6668
Fred H Lundblade, *Owner*
EMP: 58
SALES (est): 2.5MM **Privately Held**
SIC: 6512 6513 1521 1541 Nonresidential building operators; apartment building operators; single-family housing construction; industrial buildings & warehouses

(P-10986)
FREMONT PROPERTIES INC
199 Fremont St Ste 1900, San Francisco (94105-2255)
PHONE..................415 284-8500
Fax: 415 284-8184
Allen Dachs, *CEO*
Debbie Duncan, *CFO*
David Wall, *Exec VP*
Christopher Quiett, *Vice Pres*
Gry Faber, *Principal*
EMP: 50
SALES (est): 3.5MM
SALES (corp-wide): 16.4MM **Privately Held**
SIC: 6512 Nonresidential building operators
PA: Fremont Investors, Inc.
199 Fremont St Fl 19
San Francisco CA 94105
415 284-8500

(P-10987)
GEHR DEVELOPMENT CORPORATION (HQ)
7400 E Slauson Ave, Commerce (90040-3308)
PHONE..................323 728-5558
David Lifschitz, *CFO*
Alfred Somekh, *President*
EMP: 70
SALES (est): 6.1MM
SALES (corp-wide): 76.1MM **Privately Held**
WEB: www.gehr.com
SIC: 6512 6513 Nonresidential building operators; apartment building operators
PA: The Gehr Group Inc
7400 E Slauson Ave
Commerce CA 90040
323 728-5558

(P-10988)
GIRARDI AND KEEFE
1126 Wilshire Blvd, Los Angeles (90017-1904)
PHONE..................213 489-5330
Thomas Girardi, *Partner*
Bob Keefe, *Partner*
John A Girardi,
EMP: 100
SQ FT: 21,000
SALES (est): 3.3MM **Privately Held**
SIC: 6512 Commercial & industrial building operation

(P-10989)
GLENDALE ASSOCIATES LTD
Also Called: Apple Store Glendale Galleria
100 W Broadway Ste 700, Glendale (91210-1225)
PHONE..................818 246-6737
Properties Knickerbocker, *Principal*
Knickerbocker Properties, *Partner*
Joan Brosi, *General Mgr*
Wyan Hursh, *Manager*
EMP: 100
SALES (est): 7.6MM **Privately Held**
SIC: 6512 Property operation, retail establishment

(P-10990)
GONGS MARKET OF SANGER INC (PA)
Also Called: Gong's Ventures
1825 Academy Ave, Sanger (93657-3798)
PHONE..................559 875-5576
Fax: 559 875-7599
William Gong, *President*
Bessie Gong Ohashi, *Corp Secy*
Thomas Gong, *Vice Pres*
EMP: 50
SQ FT: 35,000
SALES (est): 4.7MM **Privately Held**
SIC: 6512 Property operation, retail establishment

(P-10991)
GREENTREE PROPERTY MGT INC
600 California St Fl 19, San Francisco (94108-2710)
PHONE..................415 347-8600
Yat Pang Au, *President*
EMP: 50
SALES (est): 3.2MM **Privately Held**
SIC: 6512 Property operation, retail establishment

(P-10992)
GROSSMONT SHOPPING CENTER CO
Also Called: Grossmont Center Management
5500 Grsmnt Ctr Dr # 213, La Mesa (91942-3016)
PHONE..................619 465-2900
Fax: 619 465-9207
Thomas J Magee, *President*
EMP: 57 **EST:** 1960
SQ FT: 3,000
SALES (est): 5.8MM **Privately Held**
SIC: 6512 Shopping center, property operation only

(P-10993)
GUMBINER & SAVETT INC
Also Called: Gumbiner, Savett, Finkel, Fing
1723 Cloverfield Blvd, Santa Monica (90404-4017)
PHONE..................310 828-9798
Fax: 310 829-7853
Louis Savett, *Ch of Bd*
Charles Gumbiner, *President*
Gary Finkel, *Exec VP*
Ronald Greene, *Exec VP*
Rick Parent, *Exec VP*
EMP: 90
SQ FT: 25,000
SALES (est): 10.7MM **Privately Held**
WEB: www.gscpa.com
SIC: 6512 Nonresidential building operators

(P-10994)
H D S I MANAGMENT
3460 S Broadway, Los Angeles (90007-4409)
PHONE..................323 231-1104
Fax: 323 232-0094
Noel Sweitzer, *Partner*
Michelle Kloman, *Manager*
EMP: 50
SALES (est): 1.9MM **Privately Held**
SIC: 6512 Nonresidential building operators

(P-10995)
HAILWOOD INC
Also Called: Chase Bros Dairy
5755 Valentine Rd Ste 203, Ventura (93003-7460)
PHONE..................805 487-4981
Fax: 805 487-2529
Glywn S Chase Jr, *President*
Miriam Wille, *Corp Secy*
H M Chase, *Vice Pres*
Danny Lopez, *Executive*
Ken Mercer, *General Mgr*
EMP: 75
SQ FT: 1,600,000
SALES (est): 4.2MM **Privately Held**
SIC: 6512 5143 5451 2024 Commercial & industrial building operation; dairy products, except dried or canned; dairy products stores; ice cream & frozen desserts

(P-10996)
HALSTEAD PARTNERSHIP
Also Called: Sundt Construction
2860 Gateway Oaks Dr # 300, Sacramento (95833-3508)
PHONE..................916 830-8000
Fax: 916 830-8015
John Wald, *Managing Prtnr*
Jerrie Waltz, *Administration*
EMP: 60
SALES (est): 8.6MM **Privately Held**
SIC: 6512 Nonresidential building operators

(P-10997)
HARDAGE INVESTMENTS INC
Also Called: Woodfin Suites
39150 Cedar Blvd, Newark (94560-5024)
PHONE..................510 795-1200
Fax: 510 795-8874
Bill Marzonie, *Branch Mgr*
EMP: 50
SQ FT: 100,978
SALES (corp-wide): 7.2MM **Privately Held**
SIC: 6512 Nonresidential building operators
PA: Hardage Investments, Inc.
12671 High Bluff Dr # 300
San Diego CA

(P-10998)
HATHAWAY DINWIDDIE CNSTR CO
565 Laurelwood Rd, Santa Clara (95054-2419)
PHONE..................415 986-2718
Greg Cosko, *President*
David A Lee, *Senior VP*
Monica Treadway, *Project Mgr*
Connie Simpson, *Marketing Staff*
Teresa Conik, *Manager*
EMP: 100
SQ FT: 7,000
SALES (est): 13.6MM **Privately Held**
SIC: 6512 Commercial & industrial building operation

(P-10999)
HATHAWAY DINWIDDIE CNSTR GROUP
565 Laurelwood Rd, Santa Clara (95054-2419)
PHONE..................408 988-4200
Greg Cosko, *President*
EMP: 100 **Privately Held**
SIC: 6512 Commercial & industrial building operation
PA: Hathaway Dinwiddie Construction Group
275 Battery St Ste 300
San Francisco CA 94111

(P-11000)
HEALTH CARE WORKERS UNION (PA)
Also Called: Local 250 Health Care Wkrs Un
560 Thomas L Berkley Way, Oakland (94612-1602)
PHONE..................510 251-1250
Fax: 510 763-2680
Sal Rosselli, *President*
EMP: 70
SQ FT: 25,777
SALES (est): 6MM **Privately Held**
SIC: 6512 8631 Commercial & industrial building operation; labor unions & similar labor organizations

(P-11001)
HFRM II INC (PA)
2051 Hilltop Dr Ste A18, Redding (96002-0234)
PHONE..................530 242-2010
Herbert F R Meyer Jr, *CEO*
Herbert F R Meyer III, *Shareholder*
Isaac Scott Meyer, *Shareholder*
Dara O'Farrell, *CFO*
Jan Pratt, *Admin Sec*
EMP: 260
SALES (est): 6.9MM **Privately Held**
WEB: www.meyercrest.com
SIC: 6512 Nonresidential building operators

(P-11002)
HUDSON TCHMART CMMERCE CTR LLC
5201 Great America Pkwy, Santa Clara (95054-1122)
PHONE..................408 451-4440
Mark Lammas, *COO*
Wendy Contreras, *Exec Sec*
EMP: 99 **EST:** 2015
SQ FT: 284,440
SALES (est): 1MM **Privately Held**
SIC: 6512 Commercial & industrial building operation

(P-11003)
HYDROX PROPERTIES XII LLC
3170 Hilltop Mall Rd, Richmond (94806-1921)
PHONE..................510 262-7200
Mechanics Bank, *Principal*
Peggy Herzog-Mills, *Senior VP*
Mark Corsa, *Vice Pres*
Clayton Lloyd, *Vice Pres*
Michelle Monaco, *Vice Pres*
EMP: 85
SALES (est): 4MM **Privately Held**
SIC: 6512 Nonresidential building operators

(P-11004)
ICW VALENCIA LLC
11455 El Camino Real, San Diego (92130-2088)
PHONE..................858 350-2600
John Chamberlain, *Principal*
EMP: 88
SALES (est): 1.3MM
SALES (corp-wide): 21.6MM **Privately Held**
SIC: 6512 Nonresidential building operators
PA: American Assets, Inc.
11455 El Cmno RI Ste 140
San Diego CA 92130
858 350-2600

(P-11005)
INSIGNIA/ESG HT PARTNERS INC (DH)
11150 Santa Monica Blvd # 220, Los Angeles (90025-3380)
PHONE..................310 765-2600
Mary Ann Tighe, *CEO*
John Powers, *President*
Mike Taylor, *Info Tech Mgr*
Pama Sremado, *Manager*
EMP: 325
SALES (est): 71MM
SALES (corp-wide): 10.8B **Publicly Held**
WEB: www.insigniaesg.com
SIC: 6512 Property operation, retail establishment

6512 - Operators Of Nonresidential Bldgs County (P-11006)

HQ: Cb Richard Ellis Real Estate Services, Llc
200 Park Ave Fl 19
New York NY 10166
212 984-8000

(P-11006)
INTEX RECREATION CORP
1665 Hughes Way, Long Beach (90810-1835)
PHONE..................310 549-5400
Kwai Kenny, *Exec Dir*
Phil Mimaki, *Creative Dir*
Carlos Bartra, *Engineer*
Patrick Chik, *Opers Mgr*
Scott Weir, *Opers Mgr*
EMP: 84
SALES (corp-wide): 192.8MM **Privately Held**
SIC: 6512 Nonresidential building operators
PA: Intex Recreation Corp
4001 Via Oro Ave Ste 210
Long Beach CA 90810
310 549-5400

(P-11007)
INVITATION HOMES
6320 Canoga Ave Ste 150, Woodland Hills (91367-7702)
PHONE..................805 372-2900
Debra Schuster, *Admin Asst*
James Valles, *Manager*
Diego Ruiz, *Assistant*
EMP: 99 EST: 2013
SALES (est): 4.3MM **Privately Held**
SIC: 6512 Nonresidential building operators

(P-11008)
JAMESON PROPERTIES CO INC
3530 Wilshire Blvd # 600, Los Angeles (90010-2328)
PHONE..................213 487-3770
Fax: 213 387-4941
Eric Kim, *General Mgr*
David Lee, *President*
EMP: 50
SQ FT: 4,000
SALES: 159.1K **Privately Held**
WEB: www.jamisonservices.com
SIC: 6512 Commercial & industrial building operation

(P-11009)
LAGUNA COUNTRY MART LTD INC
Also Called: Lumberyard Plaza Mall
12410 Santa Monica Blvd, Los Angeles (90025-2522)
PHONE..................310 826-5635
Michael Koss, *President*
EMP: 50
SALES (est): 2.6MM **Privately Held**
SIC: 6512 Shopping center, property operation only

(P-11010)
LANSING MALL LTD PARTNERSHIP
Also Called: Southland Mall
1 Southland Mall, Hayward (94545-2125)
PHONE..................510 782-3527
Veronica Curley, *General Mgr*
EMP: 50
SALES (corp-wide): 13.6MM **Privately Held**
WEB: www.mallofla.com
SIC: 6512 Shopping center, property operation only
HQ: Lansing Mall Limited Partnership
5330 W Saginaw Hwy
Lansing MI 48917
517 321-0145

(P-11011)
LANSING MALL LTD PARTNERSHIP
Also Called: Northridge Fashion Center
9301 Tampa Ave Ofc, Northridge (91324-5627)
PHONE..................818 885-9700
Daniele Gordon, *General Mgr*
EMP: 75

SALES (corp-wide): 13.6MM **Privately Held**
WEB: www.mallofla.com
SIC: 6512 Shopping center, property operation only
HQ: Lansing Mall Limited Partnership
5330 W Saginaw Hwy
Lansing MI 48917
517 321-0145

(P-11012)
LOS ANGELES CONVENTION AND EXH
Also Called: Convention Center Los Angeles
1201 S Figueroa St, Los Angeles (90015-1308)
PHONE..................213 741-1151
Fax: 213 765-4266
Brad Gessner, *General Mgr*
Annie Bebber, *President*
John Hyde, *CFO*
Estella M Flores, *Bd of Directors*
Kathleen Clariett, *Vice Pres*
EMP: 288
SQ FT: 867,000
SALES: 21.5MM **Privately Held**
WEB: www.laconventioninn.com
SIC: 6512 Commercial & industrial building operation; property operation, auditoriums & theaters

(P-11013)
MACERICH COMPANY
Also Called: Westside Pavilion
10800 W Pico Blvd Ste 312, Los Angeles (90064-2187)
PHONE..................310 474-6255
Fax: 310 466-8155
Ken Raffensberger, *Manager*
Josh Richman, *Technology*
EMP: 75
SALES (corp-wide): 1.2B **Publicly Held**
SIC: 6512 Shopping center, property operation only
PA: Macerich Company
401 Wilshire Blvd Ste 700
Santa Monica CA 90401
310 394-6000

(P-11014)
MACERICH COMPANY
Also Called: Stonewood Ctr Mall Office
251 Stonewood St, Downey (90241-3935)
PHONE..................562 861-9233
Fax: 562 923-7440
Charlie Hallums, *Manager*
Vivian Brogan, *Manager*
EMP: 50
SALES (corp-wide): 1.2B **Publicly Held**
WEB: www.macerich.com
SIC: 6512 Shopping center, property operation only
PA: Macerich Company
401 Wilshire Blvd Ste 700
Santa Monica CA 90401
310 394-6000

(P-11015)
MALIBU CONFERENCE CENTER INC
327 Latigo Canyon Rd, Malibu (90265-2708)
PHONE..................818 889-6440
Fax: 818 879-8130
Glen Gerson, *President*
Julie Milham, *Accountant*
Cindy Liang, *Sales Staff*
Shirley Blackman, *Accounts Mgr*
EMP: 500
SALES (est): 32.4MM **Privately Held**
WEB: www.trainingsites.com
SIC: 6512 Commercial & industrial building operation

(P-11016)
MCCLELLAN FACILITIES SVCS LLC
3140 Peacekeeper Way, McClellan (95652-2508)
PHONE..................916 965-7100
Larry Kelley, *President*
Frank Meyers, *Vice Pres*
EMP: 52
SALES (est): 2.2MM **Privately Held**
SIC: 6512 Property operation, retail establishment

(P-11017)
MEGA MAIL MALL INC
128 Avenida Del Mar, San Clemente (92672-4080)
PHONE..................888 998-6245
Sara Chavez, *Manager*
EMP: 50
SALES (est): 1.6MM **Privately Held**
SIC: 6512 Shopping center, property operation only

(P-11018)
MFW PARTNERS
1120 Silverado St, La Jolla (92037-4524)
PHONE..................858 454-8857
Leah Hurwitz, *Managing Prtnr*
Esther Belinski, *Partner*
Anita Tobias, *Partner*
Evie Weinstock, *Partner*
EMP: 50
SALES (est): 2.2MM **Privately Held**
SIC: 6512 Nonresidential building operators

(P-11019)
MILLS CORPORATION
Also Called: Ontario Mills Shopping Center
1 Mills Cir Ste 1, Ontario (91764-5215)
PHONE..................909 484-8300
Fax: 909 484-8306
Laurence Siegel, *Branch Mgr*
Jim Mance, *Exec Dir*
EMP: 60
SALES (corp-wide): 128MM **Privately Held**
WEB: www.millscorp.com
SIC: 6512 Shopping center, property operation only
HQ: The Mills Corporation
5425 Wisconsin Ave # 300
Chevy Chase MD 20815
301 968-6000

(P-11020)
MULLER TAJ LLC
Also Called: Taj Mahal Building
23521 Paseo De Valencia # 200, Laguna Hills (92653-3107)
PHONE..................949 470-9840
Steven Muller,
EMP: 100 EST: 1972
SQ FT: 82,978
SALES (est): 4.2MM **Privately Held**
WEB: www.vmalaw.com
SIC: 6512 Commercial & industrial building operation

(P-11021)
MULLER-ING-GATEWAY LLC
23521 Paseo De Valencia # 206, Laguna Hills (92653-3107)
PHONE..................951 687-2900
Jon Muller, *President*
EMP: 80
SALES (est): 1.5MM **Privately Held**
SIC: 6512 Nonresidential building operators

(P-11022)
MUTH DEVELOPMENT CO INC
Also Called: Orco Block
11100 Beach Blvd, Stanton (90680-3219)
PHONE..................714 527-2239
Richard Muth, *President*
Dwayne Gleason, *Vice Pres*
Lynn Muth, *Vice Pres*
Tom Ruggeri, *Controller*
EMP: 80
SALES (est): 4.5MM **Privately Held**
SIC: 6512 Nonresidential building operators

(P-11023)
NEDERLANDER OF CALIFORNIA INC
6233 Hollywood Blvd Fl 2, Los Angeles (90028-5310)
PHONE..................323 468-1700
James M Nederlander, *Chairman*
Robert Nederlander, *President*
David Goldberg, *Office Mgr*
Neil Papiano, *Agent*
EMP: 50 EST: 1975
SQ FT: 2,500

SALES (est): 3.7MM **Privately Held**
WEB: www.greektheatrela.com
SIC: 6512 7922 Theater building, ownership & operation; theatrical producers & services

(P-11024)
NEVINS-ADAMS PROPERTIES INC (PA)
Also Called: Nevins Adams Properties
920 Garden St Ste A, Santa Barbara (93101-7465)
PHONE..................805 963-2884
Fax: 805 963-9885
Henry Nevins, *President*
David Adams, *Chairman*
Bob Timur, *Info Tech Mgr*
EMP: 250
SALES (est): 9.2MM **Privately Held**
WEB: www.nevinsadams.com
SIC: 6512 Commercial & industrial building operation

(P-11025)
NORTHRIDGE 07 A LLC
12411 Ventura Blvd, Studio City (91604-2407)
PHONE..................818 505-6777
Cathy Reynolds,
Alan Fox,
EMP: 80
SALES (est): 4MM **Privately Held**
SIC: 6512 Commercial & industrial building operation

(P-11026)
OATES BUZZ ENTERPRISES
Also Called: Folsom Manlove Venture
555 Capitol Mall Fl 9, Sacramento (95814-4601)
PHONE..................916 381-3600
Fax: 916 381-1834
Marvin L Oates, *Partner*
Carl Best, *Partner*
EMP: 100
SALES (est): 5.3MM **Privately Held**
SIC: 6512 6552 6531 Nonresidential building operators; subdividers & developers; real estate agents & managers

(P-11027)
OLEN COMMERCIAL REALTY CORP
Also Called: Olen Residential Realty
7 Corporate Plaza Dr, Newport Beach (92660-7904)
PHONE..................949 644-6536
Igor M Olenicoff, *President*
Andrei Olenicoff, *Corp Secy*
EMP: 400 EST: 1974
SQ FT: 44,000
SALES (est): 23.7MM **Privately Held**
SIC: 6512 Commercial & industrial building operation

(P-11028)
OLTMANS INVESTMENT COMPANY
Also Called: Oltmans Property Management
10005 Mission Mill Rd, Whittier (90601-1739)
P.O. Box 985 (90608-0985)
PHONE..................562 948-4242
J O Oltmans II, *President*
Basil C Johnson, *Managing Prtnr*
Robert Roy, *Managing Prtnr*
Gregory V Grupp, *Controller*
EMP: 50
SQ FT: 56,000
SALES (est): 3.2MM **Privately Held**
SIC: 6512 6552 Commercial & industrial building operation; subdividers & developers

(P-11029)
PACIFIC EAGLE HOLDINGS CORP
353 Sacramento St Ste 360, San Francisco (94111-3688)
PHONE..................415 398-2473
Michael Simons, *Exec VP*
Adriana Leleu, *Executive*
EMP: 85

PRODUCTS & SERVICES SECTION
6512 - Operators Of Nonresidential Bldgs County (P-11053)

SALES (corp-wide): 18.9MM **Privately Held**
SIC: **6512** 6531 Commercial & industrial building operation; real estate managers
PA: Pacific Eagle Holdings Corporation
353 Sacramento St
San Francisco CA 94111
925 866-9662

(P-11030)
PACIFIC STERLING PROPERTIES
2101 Bus Ctr Dr Ste 140, Irvine (92612)
PHONE..................949 222-9911
Nancy Domino, *Post Master*
Anna Jin, *Real Est Agnt*
EMP: 50
SALES (est): 1.2MM **Privately Held**
SIC: **6512** Nonresidential building operators

(P-11031)
PARAMOUNT THEATRE OF ARTS INC
2025 Broadway, Oakland (94612-2303)
PHONE..................510 893-2300
Leslee Stewart, *Director*
EMP: 60
SQ FT: 37,000
SALES: 2.4MM **Privately Held**
SIC: **6512** Theater building, ownership & operation

(P-11032)
PIER 39 LIMITED PARTNERSHIP (PA)
Beach Embarcadero Level 3, San Francisco (94133)
P.O. Box 193730 (94119-3730)
PHONE..................415 705-5500
Fax: 415 981-8808
Robert A Moor, *General Ptnr*
Molly M South, *Partner*
John Luu, *HR Admin*
Maud Castejon, *Sales Mgr*
Lauren Chinn, *Marketing Staff*
EMP: 60 EST: 1968
SQ FT: 200,000
SALES: 40MM **Privately Held**
SIC: **6512** Commercial & industrial building operation

(P-11033)
PROPERTY INSIGHT
1007 E Cooley Dr, Colton (92324-3901)
PHONE..................909 876-6505
Frank Trujillo, *Principal*
Karen Schwartz, *Controller*
Marty Dandrea, *Sales Staff*
EMP: 200
SALES (est): 33.3MM
SALES (corp-wide): 9.1B **Publicly Held**
SIC: **6512** Nonresidential building operators
PA: Fidelity National Financial, Inc.
601 Riverside Ave Fl 4
Jacksonville FL 32204
904 854-8100

(P-11034)
PUBLIC STOR COML PRPTS GROUP
701 Western Ave, Glendale (91201-2349)
P.O. Box 25050 (91221-5050)
PHONE..................818 244-8080
Ronald Havner, *CEO*
EMP: 85
SALES (est): 2MM
SALES (corp-wide): 2.3B **Publicly Held**
WEB: www.publicstorage.com
SIC: **6512** Commercial & industrial building operation
PA: Public Storage
701 Western Ave
Glendale CA 91201
818 244-8080

(P-11035)
PVCC INC (PA)
Also Called: Pacific View Companies
8100 La Mesa Blvd Ste 101, La Mesa (91942-6498)
PHONE..................619 463-4040
Fax: 619 583-0093
Charles I Feurzeig, *President*

Robert Teal, *CFO*
Charles R Swimmer, *Corp Secy*
James M Houck, *Vice Pres*
Robert Houck, *Vice Pres*
EMP: 50
SQ FT: 1,400
SALES (est): 4MM **Privately Held**
WEB: www.pacificviewcompanies.com
SIC: **6512** 6513 Shopping center, property operation only; apartment building operators

(P-11036)
REAL ESTATE LAW CENTER PC
695 S Vt Ave Ste 1100, Los Angeles (90005-1349)
PHONE..................213 201-6384
Erikson Davis, *CEO*
Hector Almansor, *Case Mgr*
Edna Cano, *Accounts Exec*
EMP: 51
SALES (est): 775.2K **Privately Held**
SIC: **6512** Nonresidential building operators

(P-11037)
RP REALTY PARTNERS LLC
990 W 8th St Ste 600, Los Angeles (90017-2831)
PHONE..................310 207-6990
Stuart Ruben, *CEO*
Dan Soussan, *CFO*
Howard Aminoff, *Exec VP*
Richard Costanzo, *Exec VP*
Yashaar Amin, *Vice Pres*
EMP: 50
SALES (est): 4.3MM **Privately Held**
SIC: **6512** Nonresidential building operators

(P-11038)
SAN DEGO CNVNTION CTR CORP INC (PA)
111 W Harbor Dr, San Diego (92101-7822)
PHONE..................619 525-5000
Fax: 619 525-5005
Carol Wallace, *President*
Mark Emch, *CFO*
Alfonso Sanchez, *Officer*
Michael Vile, *Officer*
Andy Mikschl, *Senior VP*
EMP: 70
SALES (est): 101.2MM **Privately Held**
SIC: **6512** Nonresidential building operators

(P-11039)
SAN DIEGO THEATRES INC
Also Called: CIVIC THEATRE
1100 3rd Ave, San Diego (92101-4113)
P.O. Box 124920 (92112-4920)
PHONE..................619 615-4000
Fax: 619 615-4001
Donald M Telford, *CEO*
EMP: 200
SALES: 7.2MM **Privately Held**
WEB: www.sandiegotheatres.org
SIC: **6512** Theater building, ownership & operation

(P-11040)
SANTA MONICA CITY OF
Also Called: Civic Auditorium
1855 Main St, Santa Monica (90401-3209)
PHONE..................310 458-8551
Fax: 310 394-3411
Carole Curtin, *Manager*
Jose Villasenor, *Maint Spvr*
EMP: 50 **Privately Held**
WEB: www.santamonicapd.org
SIC: **6512** 9111 Auditorium & hall operation; mayors' offices
PA: City Of Santa Monica
1685 Main St
Santa Monica CA 90401
310 458-8281

(P-11041)
SDJ GENERAL PARTNERSHIP
2125 N Madera Rd Ste C, Simi Valley (93065-7711)
PHONE..................805 582-3200
Jawahar Tandon, *Partner*
Devinder Tandon, *Partner*
Sirjang Tandon, *Partner*
Thomas Nulman, *CFO*

EMP: 70
SQ FT: 70,000
SALES (est): 2.9MM **Privately Held**
SIC: **6512** 6513 Nonresidential building operators; apartment building operators

(P-11042)
SFI 2365 IRON POINT LLC
260 California St Ste 300, San Francisco (94111-4364)
PHONE..................415 395-9701
Christopher Peatross, *President*
EMP: 50
SALES (est): 574.7K **Privately Held**
SIC: **6512** Nonresidential building operators

(P-11043)
SFI CARLSBAD LLC
260 California St Ste 300, San Francisco (94111-4364)
PHONE..................415 395-9701
Christopher Peatross,
Deborah Abernathy, *Manager*
EMP: 50
SALES (est): 574.7K **Privately Held**
SIC: **6512** Nonresidential building operators

(P-11044)
SHENYANG ZHONG YI TIN-PLATING
Also Called: Professional Services Company
870 Market St Ste 950, San Francisco (94102-2912)
PHONE..................415 788-2280
Fax: 415 399-0338
Ku Hing Pong, *Principal*
EMP: 130
SQ FT: 250
SALES (est): 3.7MM **Privately Held**
SIC: **6512** 5023 Nonresidential building operators; home furnishings

(P-11045)
SHOPPING CENTER MGT CORP
660 Stanford Shopping Ctr, Palo Alto (94304-1400)
PHONE..................650 617-8234
David B Longbine, *President*
EMP: 54
SALES (est): 2MM **Privately Held**
SIC: **6512** Shopping center, property operation only

(P-11046)
SHORENSTEIN COMPANY LLC
235 Montgomery St Fl 15, San Francisco (94104-3102)
PHONE..................415 772-8209
Fax: 415 772-7080
Douglas Shorenstein,
Thomas Rose, *COO*
James Collins, *Vice Pres*
Tom McDonnell, *Vice Pres*
Caitlin Simon, *Vice Pres*
EMP: 50
SALES (est): 5.1MM **Privately Held**
SIC: **6512** Nonresidential building operators

(P-11047)
SHORENSTEIN PROPERTIES LLC (PA)
235 Montgomery St Fl 16, San Francisco (94104-3104)
PHONE..................415 772-7000
Fax: 415 772-7048
Douglas W Shorenstein, *CEO*
Glenn A Shannon, *President*
Norman Lee, *Treasurer*
D Drew Dowsett, *Senior VP*
Katie McGettigan, *Senior VP*
EMP: 125
SQ FT: 20,000
SALES (est): 49.7MM **Privately Held**
SIC: **6512** Commercial & industrial building operation

(P-11048)
SIGNATURE SERVICES
4425 Jamboree Rd Ste 250, Newport Beach (92660-3002)
PHONE..................949 851-9391
Fax: 949 724-3091
Chad Horning, *President*

EMP: 75
SALES (est): 7.5MM **Privately Held**
SIC: **6512** Nonresidential building operators

(P-11049)
SMG
225 E Broadway 312, Glendale (91205-1008)
P.O. Box 572559, Tarzana (91357-2559)
PHONE..................310 432-2893
EMP: 69
SALES (corp-wide): 410.9MM **Privately Held**
SIC: **6512** Nonresidential building operators
PA: Smg Holdings, Inc
300 Cnshohckn State Rd # 450
Conshohocken PA 19428
610 729-7900

(P-11050)
SMG HOLDINGS INC
Also Called: S M G
747 Howard St, San Francisco (94103-3118)
PHONE..................650 738-8737
Allan Crawford, *Finance*
Linda Villa, *Executive Asst*
Pete Castellani, *Technician*
Holly Alderton, *Director*
Ed Ho, *Director*
EMP: 110
SALES (corp-wide): 410.9MM **Privately Held**
WEB: www.smgworld.com
SIC: **6512** 5812 8742 8741 Nonresidential building operators; eating places; management consulting services; management services
PA: Smg Holdings, Inc
300 Cnshohckn State Rd # 450
Conshohocken PA 19428
610 729-7900

(P-11051)
SMG HOLDINGS INC
Also Called: Long Beach Convention Center
300 E Ocean Blvd, Long Beach (90802-4825)
PHONE..................562 436-3636
Charles Berni, *Branch Mgr*
Deann Fruhling, *Sales Mgr*
Ray Blanton, *Facilities Dir*
Veronica Quintero, *Manager*
EMP: 69
SALES (corp-wide): 410.9MM **Privately Held**
WEB: www.smgworld.com
SIC: **6512** Nonresidential building operators
PA: Smg Holdings, Inc
300 Cnshohckn State Rd # 450
Conshohocken PA 19428
610 729-7900

(P-11052)
SOLARI ENTERPRISES INC
1507 W Yale Ave, Orange (92867-3447)
PHONE..................714 282-2520
Fax: 714 282-2521
Johrita Solari, *President*
Bruce Solari, *Vice Pres*
Robb Goldman, *Regional Mgr*
Mary Oliver, *Regional Mgr*
Kara Cappeluti, *Office Mgr*
EMP: 140
SQ FT: 8,400
SALES (est): 17.7MM **Privately Held**
SIC: **6512** Property operation, retail establishment

(P-11053)
SOTOYOME MEDICAL BUILDING LLC
Also Called: Redwood Regional Medical Group
990 Sonoma Ave Ste 15, Santa Rosa (95404-4813)
PHONE..................707 525-4000
Fax: 707 578-6258
Harold Phillips,
Ralph Hanahan, *Senior Partner*
Sharon Debenedetti, *COO*
Kimberly Harbin, *Executive Asst*
Juli Forrestall, *Administration*

6512 - Operators Of Nonresidential Bldgs County (P-11054)

EMP: 80
SQ FT: 27,000
SALES (est): 9.8MM Privately Held
SIC: 6512 Commercial & industrial building operation

(P-11054)
SOUTH COAST PLAZA LLC (PA)
Also Called: South Coast Plaza Village
3333 Bristol St Ofc, Costa Mesa (92626-1811)
PHONE..................................714 546-0110
N R Segerstrom, Mng Member
Nancy Miller, COO
Debra Downing, Exec Dir
Werner Escher, Exec Dir
Karen Wholey, Executive Asst
EMP: 55
SQ FT: 8,000
SALES (est): 23.2MM Privately Held
WEB: www.blackstarrfrost.com
SIC: 6512 Shopping center, property operation only

(P-11055)
SOUTH COAST PLAZA LLC
Also Called: South Coast Plaza Mall
3333 Bristol St Ofc, Costa Mesa (92626-1811)
PHONE..................................714 435-2000
Fax: 714 540-7334
David Grant, Manager
N Segerstrom, Managing Prtnr
Anton Segerstrom, Manager
EMP: 60
SALES (corp-wide): 23.9MM Privately Held
WEB: www.blackstarrfrost.com
SIC: 6512 Shopping center, property operation only
PA: South Coast Plaza, Llc
  3333 Bristol St Ofc
  Costa Mesa CA 92626
  714 546-0110

(P-11056)
SOUTHTOWN INDUSTRIAL PARK
Also Called: Neff Construction
1701 S Bon View Ave 104, Ontario (91761-4412)
PHONE..................................909 947-3768
Kenneth L Neff, President
EMP: 50
SALES (est): 2.1MM Privately Held
SIC: 6512 Nonresidential building operators

(P-11057)
SPECTACOR MANAGEMENT GROUP
300 E Ocean Blvd, Long Beach (90802-4825)
PHONE..................................562 436-3636
Charlie Beirne, General Mgr
EMP: 439
SQ FT: 4,000
SALES (est): 13.6MM Privately Held
SIC: 6512 Nonresidential building operators

(P-11058)
SUN AMERICA HOUSING FUND
Also Called: AIG Sun America
1999 Avenue Of The Stars, Los Angeles (90067-6022)
PHONE..................................310 772-6000
Mike Fowler, General Ptnr
Scott Richland, Vice Pres
Barkev Azadian, Project Dir
Ann Franklin, VP Human Res
Robert Bryant, Director
EMP: 100 EST: 1990
SALES (est): 5.1MM
SALES (corp-wide): 58.3B Publicly Held
SIC: 6512 6513 Nonresidential building operators; apartment building operators
HQ: Sunamerica Inc.
  1 Sun America Ctr Fl 38
  Los Angeles CA 90067
  310 772-6000

(P-11059)
SUNAMERICA HSNG FND 1071
1 Sun America Ctr Fl 36, Los Angeles (90067-6104)
PHONE..................................310 772-6000
Eric Geisler, CFO
EMP: 110
SALES (est): 3.2MM Privately Held
SIC: 6512 6513 Nonresidential building operators; apartment building operators

(P-11060)
TARIFF BUILDING ASSOCIATES LP (PA)
222 Kearny St Ste 200, San Francisco (94108-4537)
PHONE..................................415 397-5572
Michael Depatie, CEO
Cesar Herrera, Project Mgr
Cheryl Lovelace, VP Opers
Michael Thibodeau, Director
EMP: 60 EST: 1998
SALES (est): 1.3MM Privately Held
SIC: 6512 6513 Property operation, retail establishment; residential hotel operation

(P-11061)
TEGTMEIER ASSOCIATES INC
6701 Clark Rd, Paradise (95969-2833)
PHONE..................................530 872-7700
John Tegemeier, President
EMP: 58
SQ FT: 24,000
SALES (corp-wide): 3.7MM Privately Held
SIC: 6512 7841 5049 Theater building, ownership & operation; video disk/tape rental to the general public; theatrical equipment & supplies
PA: Tegtmeier Associates Inc.
  14 Mansion Ct
  Menlo Park CA 94025
  650 847-1639

(P-11062)
TELACU NW FIVE INC (PA)
5400 E Olympic Blvd, Commerce (90022-5147)
PHONE..................................323 721-1655
David Lizarraga, President
Paul Samuel, CFO
John Kingsley, VP Finance
EMP: 50 EST: 1977
SQ FT: 10,000
SALES (est): 319.5K Privately Held
SIC: 6512 Commercial & industrial building operation

(P-11063)
TNPPM NORTH STAFFORD LLC
1900 Main St Ste 700, Irvine (92614-7328)
PHONE..................................949 833-8252
Darryll Goodman,
EMP: 99
SALES: 950K Privately Held
SIC: 6512 Nonresidential building operators

(P-11064)
TOM HOM INVESTMENT CORP
7660 Fay Ave Ste H, La Jolla (92037-4843)
PHONE..................................858 456-5000
Tom Hom, President
William Newbern, President
Les Harvey, CFO
EMP: 100
SQ FT: 2,000
SALES (est): 3.5MM Privately Held
SIC: 6512 Nonresidential building operators

(P-11065)
TOPA MANAGEMENT COMPANY (PA)
1800 Avenue Of The Stars # 1400, Los Angeles (90067-4220)
PHONE..................................310 203-9199
James Brooks, CEO
Jim Brooks, President
Jeanne Gettemy-Lazar, CFO
Darren Bell, Vice Pres
Paul Gienger, Vice Pres
EMP: 158
SALES (est): 9.5MM Privately Held
WEB: www.topamanagement.com
SIC: 6512 Commercial & industrial building operation

(P-11066)
US PROPERTY GROUP INC
Also Called: Manchester Center
1901 E Shields Ave # 203, Fresno (93726-5313)
PHONE..................................559 227-1901
Fax: 559 227-1602
Kevin Mahieu, Manager
Eugene Warner, Branch Mgr
Laura Geuvjehizian, Director
EMP: 50
SALES (est): 4.5MM Privately Held
WEB: www.manchester-center.com
SIC: 6512 Commercial & industrial building operation

(P-11067)
VALLEY PROPERTIES INC
10324 Balboa Blvd Lbby, Granada Hills (91344-7363)
PHONE..................................818 360-3430
Peter J McKinnon, President
EMP: 90
SALES (est): 3.5MM Privately Held
SIC: 6512 Nonresidential building operators

(P-11068)
WATT PROPERTIES INC (PA)
Also Called: Watt Commercial Properties
2716 Ocean Park Blvd # 2025, Santa Monica (90405-5207)
PHONE..................................310 314-2430
Fax: 310 399-6681
Janet Watt Van Huisen, Ch of Bd
Susan Rorison, President
James Maginn, CEO
Melanie Rush, CFO
Jerry Grimaldi, Exec VP
EMP: 78
SQ FT: 8,700
SALES (est): 17.7MM Privately Held
WEB: www.wattcommercial.com
SIC: 6512 6531 6552 Shopping center, property operation only; real estate managers; land subdividers & developers, commercial

(P-11069)
WELLS FARGO BANK NATIONAL ASSN
Also Called: Operations
333 S Hope St Ste D100, Los Angeles (90071-3003)
PHONE..................................213 628-2251
Shaffi Poswal, Branch Mgr
Jeannette Wright, Vice Pres
EMP: 250
SALES (corp-wide): 90B Publicly Held
WEB: www.wellsfargo.com
SIC: 6512 Bank building operation
HQ: Wells Fargo Bank, National Association
  464 California St
  San Francisco CA 94104
  415 396-7392

(P-11070)
WEST SIDE REHAB CORPORATION
1755 E M L King Jr Blvd, Los Angeles (90058)
PHONE..................................323 231-4174
Dean Foley, President
EMP: 200
SQ FT: 1,500
SALES (est): 4.8MM Privately Held
SIC: 6512 Commercial & industrial building operation

(P-11071)
WEST VILLE PALM DESERT
Also Called: Palm Desert Town Center
72840 Highway 111 Ste 115, Palm Desert (92260-3345)
PHONE..................................760 346-2121
Norie Bowlan, Manager
EMP: 50
SQ FT: 373,000
SALES (est): 2.8MM Privately Held
SIC: 6512 Shopping center, property operation only

(P-11072)
WESTFIELD LLC (DH)
2049 Century Park E # 4100, Los Angeles (90067-3101)
PHONE..................................813 926-4600
Fax: 310 277-5809
Peter Lowy, CEO
Gregory Miles, COO
Mark Stefanel, CFO
Mike Skovran, Sr Corp Ofcr
Katy Dickey, Exec VP
EMP: 400
SQ FT: 120,000
SALES (est): 204.2MM
SALES (corp-wide): 1.8B Privately Held
WEB: www.westfieldamerica.com
SIC: 6512 Shopping center, property operation only
HQ: Westfield America, Inc.
  2049 Century Park E Fl 41
  Los Angeles CA 90067
  310 478-4456

(P-11073)
WESTFIELD AMERICA INC (HQ)
2049 Century Park E Fl 41, Los Angeles (90067-3101)
PHONE..................................310 478-4456
Fax: 310 235-0080
Peter S Lowy, CEO
Kenneth Wong, COO
Mark A Stefanek, CFO
Dimitri Vazelakis, Officer
Richard Steets, Sr Exec VP
EMP: 200 EST: 1924
SALES (est): 212.8MM
SALES (corp-wide): 1.8B Privately Held
WEB: www.westfieldamerica.com
SIC: 6512 Nonresidential building operators
PA: Scentre Group Limited
  L 30 80-85 Castlereagh St
  Sydney NSW 2000
  130 013-2211

(P-11074)
WESTFIELD AMERICA LTD PARTNR
2049 Century Park E # 4100, Los Angeles (90067-3101)
PHONE..................................310 277-3898
John Widdup, CEO
Peter Lowy, Partner
Mike Skovaran, CFO
Stan Duncan, VP Human Res
Kurt Stetzer, Safety Dir
EMP: 500
SALES (est): 10MM
SALES (corp-wide): 1.8B Privately Held
SIC: 6512 Nonresidential building operators
HQ: Westfield, Llc
  2049 Century Park E # 4100
  Los Angeles CA 90067

(P-11075)
WESTLAKE DEVELOPMENT GROUP LLC (PA)
520 S El Camino Real # 900, San Mateo (94402-1722)
PHONE..................................650 579-1010
Fax: 650 340-8252
T M Chang, Mng Member
William H C Chang,
M G Wong, Agent
EMP: 75
SQ FT: 80,000
SALES (est): 8.4MM Privately Held
WEB: www.westlake-global.com
SIC: 6512 6513 6531 Shopping center, property operation only; commercial & industrial building operation; apartment building operators; retirement hotel operation; real estate agents & managers

PRODUCTS & SERVICES SECTION

6513 - Operators Of Apartment Buildings County (P-11100)

6513 Operators Of Apartment Buildings

(P-11076)
1658 CAMDEN LLC
12147 Riverside Dr, North Hollywood (91607-3832)
PHONE................................818 769-1944
F Samuel Malik,
EMP: 50
SALES (est): 1.7MM Privately Held
SIC: 6513 Apartment building operators

(P-11077)
2ND FLOOR MAIN STREET CONCEPTS
126 Main St Ste 201, Huntington Beach (92648-8132)
PHONE................................714 969-9000
EMP: 50
SALES (est): 1.1MM Privately Held
SIC: 6513 Apartment building operators

(P-11078)
7410 WOODMAN AVENUE LLC
Also Called: Kaufman Properties
22837 Ventura Blvd # 201, Woodland Hills (91364-1260)
PHONE................................805 496-4336
Mark Kaufman,
Jill Pulido, *Info Tech Mgr*
Eddie Garravillo, *Manager*
David Villagomez, *Manager*
EMP: 100
SALES (est): 4.4MM Privately Held
SIC: 6513 Apartment building operators

(P-11079)
A COMMUNITY OF FRIENDS
3701 Wilshire Blvd # 700, Los Angeles (90010-2813)
PHONE................................213 480-0809
Fax: 213 480-1788
Dora Leong Gallo, *CEO*
Ronald Stewart, *Exec Dir*
Dinde Patrick, *Office Mgr*
Kinette Cager, *Administration*
James Kim, *Project Mgr*
EMP: 60
SQ FT: 5,800
SALES: 9.1MM Privately Held
WEB: www.acof.org
SIC: 6513 Apartment building operators

(P-11080)
AAH HUDSON LP
Also Called: Hudson Gardens
1255 N Hudson Ave, Pasadena (91104-2868)
PHONE................................626 794-9179
Victoria Miranda, *Comms Mgr*
Ellen Guccione, *Exec VP*
Kelly McBride, *Director*
EMP: 3400
SALES: 200K
SALES (corp-wide): 981.3MM Publicly Held
SIC: 6513 Apartment building operators
PA: Apartment Investment & Management Company
4582 S Ulster St Ste 1100
Denver CO 80237
303 757-8101

(P-11081)
ALDERSLY RETIREMENT CENTER
Also Called: ALDERSLY RETIREMENT COMMUNITY
326 Mission Ave, San Rafael (94901-3425)
PHONE................................415 453-9271
Joanne Maxwell, *Administration*
EMP: 75 EST: 1921
SQ FT: 3,000
SALES: 2.4MM Privately Held
WEB: www.aldersly.com
SIC: 6513 Retirement hotel operation

(P-11082)
ALL HALLOWS PRESERVATION LP
Also Called: All Hallows Garden Apartments
54 Navy Rd, San Francisco (94124-2825)
PHONE................................415 285-3909
Fax: 415 285-5712
Leeann Morein, *Senior VP*
George Buchanan, *Partner*
EMP: 3900
SALES: 950K Privately Held
SIC: 6513 Apartment building operators

(P-11083)
ALTENHEIM INC
1720 Macarthur Blvd, Oakland (94602-1766)
PHONE................................510 530-4013
Cathy Hoopaugh, *Director*
Leone Gonzales, *Facilities Dir*
EMP: 64 EST: 1890
SALES: 320.9K Privately Held
SIC: 6513 8051 Retirement hotel operation; skilled nursing care facilities; extended care facility

(P-11084)
AMERICAN BAPTIST HOMES OF WEST
Also Called: American Baptist Homes of West
460 E Fern Ave, Redlands (92373-6040)
PHONE................................909 335-3077
Mildred Makamure, *Manager*
Becky Shearer, *Admin Asst*
EMP: 200
SALES (corp-wide): 129.1MM Privately Held
SIC: 6513 Apartment building operators
PA: American Baptist Homes Of The West
6120 Stoneridge Mall Rd # 300
Pleasanton CA 94588
925 924-7100

(P-11085)
AMERICAN BAPTIST HOMES OF WEST
Also Called: Valle Verde Retirement Center
900 Calle De Los Amigos, Santa Barbara (93105-4435)
PHONE................................805 687-1571
Fax: 805 687-5540
Dawn Norrington, *Branch Mgr*
Ronald Schaefer, *Exec Dir*
Michael A Manley, *Agent*
EMP: 200
SALES (corp-wide): 129.1MM Privately Held
WEB: www.abhow.org
SIC: 6513 8051 8052 Apartment building operators; convalescent home with continuous nursing care; intermediate care facilities
PA: American Baptist Homes Of The West
6120 Stoneridge Mall Rd # 300
Pleasanton CA 94588
925 924-7100

(P-11086)
AR PRESERVATION LP
201 Eddy St, San Francisco (94102-2715)
PHONE................................415 776-2151
Donald Falk, *Principal*
Zachary Lopez, *Manager*
EMP: 99
SALES (est): 2.3MM Privately Held
SIC: 6513 Apartment building operators

(P-11087)
ASPEN APTS I
165 Eddy St, San Francisco (94102)
PHONE................................415 673-5879
EMP: 99
SALES (est): 3.4MM Privately Held
SIC: 6513

(P-11088)
ASPEN GROVE APARTMENTS LLC
450 E 8th St, Gilroy (95020-6650)
PHONE................................408 848-6400
Linda Mandolini, *President*
Jacqueline Javier, *Admin Asst*
EMP: 99
SALES (est): 1.2MM Privately Held
SIC: 6513 Apartment building operators

(P-11089)
ATRIA SENIOR LIVING GROUP INC
Also Called: Montego Heights Lodge
1400 Montego, Walnut Creek (94598-2950)
PHONE................................925 938-6611
Fax: 925 938-5842
Kathy Moore, *Manager*
Guy Haycraft, *Director*
Richard Usaf, *Director*
Lori Gutierrez, *Manager*
EMP: 55
SALES (corp-wide): 3.2B Publicly Held
WEB: www.atriacom.com
SIC: 6513 Apartment building operators
HQ: Atria Senior Living Group Inc
300 E Market St Ste 100
Louisville KY 40202

(P-11090)
ATRIA SENIOR LIVING GROUP INC
Also Called: Willow Glen Villa
1660 Gaton Dr Ofc, San Jose (95125-4599)
PHONE................................408 266-1660
Fax: 408 266-7756
Laurie Becker, *Exec Dir*
Joseph Pollifrone, *Food Svc Dir*
Enrique Donzales, *Director*
Camille Flores, *Director*
Tamberly Mott, *Director*
EMP: 63
SALES (corp-wide): 3.2B Publicly Held
WEB: www.atriacom.com
SIC: 6513 Apartment building operators
HQ: Atria Senior Living Group Inc
300 E Market St Ste 100
Louisville KY 40202

(P-11091)
ATRIA SENIOR LIVING GROUP INC
Also Called: El Camino Gardens
2426 Garfield Ave Ofc, Carmichael (95608-5199)
PHONE................................916 488-5722
Fax: 916 488-1708
Maryann Peterson, *Director*
EMP: 70
SALES (corp-wide): 3.2B Publicly Held
WEB: www.atriacom.com
SIC: 6513 Apartment building operators
HQ: Atria Senior Living Group Inc
300 E Market St Ste 100
Louisville KY 40202

(P-11092)
BAYVIEW PRESERVATION LP
5 Commer Ct, San Francisco (94124-2713)
PHONE................................415 285-7344
Leeann Morein, *Senior VP*
Jennifer Hardee, *Partner*
David Robertson, *Partner*
EMP: 3900 EST: 2008
SALES (est): 30.3MM Privately Held
SIC: 6513 Apartment building operators

(P-11093)
BEAR CREEK MANOR
2929 M St, Merced (95348-3215)
PHONE................................209 723-4674
H Davidson, *Principal*
Robert Bear, *Manager*
Mary Davidson, *Manager*
EMP: 50
SALES (est): 1.7MM Privately Held
SIC: 6513 Apartment building operators

(P-11094)
BELMONT VILLAGE LP
Also Called: Belmont Village of Sunnyvale
1039 E El Camino Real, Sunnyvale (94087-7719)
PHONE................................408 720-8498
Dorothy Passarella, *Manager*
Tom Pembleton, *Manager*
EMP: 60
SALES (corp-wide): 35.2MM Privately Held
SIC: 6513 Retirement hotel operation
PA: Belmont Village, L.P.
8554 Katy Fwy Ste 200
Houston TX 77024
713 463-1700

(P-11095)
BELMONT VILLAGE LP
455 E Angeleno Ave, Burbank (91501-3077)
PHONE................................818 972-2405
Fax: 818 972-2419
Jane Hirsch, *Manager*
Douglas Lessard, *Vice Pres*
Marjorie J Rodriguez, *Manager*
EMP: 60
SALES (corp-wide): 35.2MM Privately Held
SIC: 6513 Retirement hotel operation
PA: Belmont Village, L.P.
8554 Katy Fwy Ste 200
Houston TX 77024
713 463-1700

(P-11096)
BELMONT VILLAGE LP
5701 Crestridge Rd, Rancho Palos Verdes (90275-4962)
PHONE................................310 377-9977
Fax: 310 377-4499
Judith Uy-Dillaruz, *Manager*
Judith Dillaruz, *Manager*
EMP: 60
SALES (corp-wide): 35.2MM Privately Held
SIC: 6513 Retirement hotel operation
PA: Belmont Village, L.P.
8554 Katy Fwy Ste 200
Houston TX 77024
713 463-1700

(P-11097)
BELMONT VILLAGE LP
Also Called: Belmont Village of Hollywood
2051 N Highland Ave, Los Angeles (90068-1373)
PHONE................................323 874-7711
Kevin Ward, *Manager*
Tiffani Jones, *Personnel Exec*
Jacqueline Marques, *Pub Rel Dir*
EMP: 50
SQ FT: 96,800
SALES (corp-wide): 35.2MM Privately Held
SIC: 6513 Retirement hotel operation
PA: Belmont Village, L.P.
8554 Katy Fwy Ste 200
Houston TX 77024
713 463-1700

(P-11098)
BIRTCHER/AETNA LAGUNA HILLS
Also Called: Wellington, The
24903 Moulton Pkwy Ofc, Laguna Hills (92653-6403)
PHONE................................949 458-2311
Scott Mc Nutt, *Vice Pres*
EMP: 100
SQ FT: 292,000
SALES (est): 6.3MM Privately Held
SIC: 6513 Retirement hotel operation

(P-11099)
BRADDOCK & LOGAN INC
Also Called: Mission Pines Apts
3600 Pine St Apt 3600, Martinez (94553-8505)
PHONE................................925 229-1747
Russell Schaadt, *General Mgr*
Lorraine Guerra, *Manager*
Kami Plummer, *Manager*
EMP: 62
SALES (est): 1.7MM Privately Held
SIC: 6513 Apartment building operators

(P-11100)
BROADMOOR HOTEL (PA)
Also Called: The Broadmoore
1499 Sutter St, San Francisco (94109-5417)
PHONE................................415 776-7034
Fax: 415 929-3116
Irene Lieberman, *President*
EMP: 75

6513 - Operators Of Apartment Buildings County (P-11101)

SALES (est): 8.9MM **Privately Held**
WEB: www.granadasf.com
SIC: 6513 Residential hotel operation

(P-11101)
BROOKDALE LVING CMMUNITIES INC
1715 E Alluvial Ave, Fresno (93720-2714)
PHONE..................559 321-8624
EMP: 69
SALES (corp-wide): 4.9B **Publicly Held**
SIC: 6513 Apartment building operators
HQ: Brookdale Living Communities, Inc.
 515 N State St Ste 1750
 Chicago IL 60654

(P-11102)
BROOKDALE SENIOR LIVING INC
72201 Country Club Dr, Rancho Mirage (92270-4001)
PHONE..................760 340-5999
EMP: 95
SALES (corp-wide): 4.9B **Publicly Held**
SIC: 6513 Retirement hotel operation
PA: Brookdale Senior Living
 111 Westwood Pl Ste 400
 Brentwood TN 37027
 615 221-2250

(P-11103)
BROOKDALE SENIOR LIVING INC
201 E Foothill Blvd, Monrovia (91016-5500)
PHONE..................626 301-0204
Fax: 626 303-8655
EMP: 79
SALES (corp-wide): 4.9B **Publicly Held**
SIC: 6513 Apartment building operators
PA: Brookdale Senior Living
 111 Westwood Pl Ste 400
 Brentwood TN 37027
 615 221-2250

(P-11104)
BROWNING APARTMENTS
1104 Browning Blvd, Los Angeles (90037-1662)
PHONE..................213 252-8847
Tina Booth, *Manager*
EMP: 50
SALES: 55.4K **Privately Held**
SIC: 6513 Apartment building operators

(P-11105)
C M I MANAGEMENT INC
Also Called: Harvey Apartments
5640 Santa Monica Blvd # 116, Los Angeles (90038-2962)
P.O. Box 35496 (90035-0496)
PHONE..................323 465-8044
Eric Guefen, *Manager*
EMP: 151
SALES (corp-wide): 6.3MM **Privately Held**
WEB: www.harveyapts.com
SIC: 6513 Apartment building operators
PA: C M I Management Inc
 1436 S La Cienega Blvd
 Los Angeles CA

(P-11106)
CAL SOUTHERN PRESBT HOMES
Also Called: Regents Point
19191 Harvard Ave Ofc, Irvine (92612-8624)
PHONE..................949 854-9500
Fax: 949 725-9132
Melinda Forney, *Manager*
Anita Dominguez, *Exec Dir*
Dax Maddocks, *Tech/Comp Coord*
EMP: 175
SALES (corp-wide): 79.2MM **Privately Held**
WEB: www.scths.com
SIC: 6513 8052 8051 Retirement hotel operation; intermediate care facilities; skilled nursing care facilities
PA: Southern California Presbyterian Homes
 516 Burchett St
 Glendale CA 91203
 818 247-0420

(P-11107)
CAL SOUTHERN PRESBT HOMES
Also Called: Windsor Manor
1230 E Windsor Rd Ofc, Glendale (91205-2674)
PHONE..................818 244-3887
Fax: 818 240-3887
Marc Herrera, *Branch Mgr*
Jeanette D Beurekjian, *Sls & Mktg Exec*
Lim Taw, *Director*
EMP: 110
SQ FT: 139,840
SALES (corp-wide): 79.2MM **Privately Held**
WEB: www.scths.com
SIC: 6513 Retirement hotel operation
PA: Southern California Presbyterian Homes
 516 Burchett St
 Glendale CA 91203
 818 247-0420

(P-11108)
CAL SOUTHERN PRESBT HOMES
Also Called: PARK PASEO
516 Burchett St, Glendale (91203-1014)
PHONE..................818 247-0420
Gerald W Dingivan, *President*
Greg Bearce, *Vice Pres*
Dewayne McMullin, *Principal*
Edwin Racine, *VP Finance*
EMP: 55
SALES: 1.3MM **Privately Held**
WEB: www.parkpaseo.com
SIC: 6513 Retirement hotel operation

(P-11109)
CAL SOUTHERN PRESBT HOMES
Also Called: Royal Oaks
1763 Royal Oaks Dr Ofc, Duarte (91010-1989)
PHONE..................626 357-1632
Tina Heaney, *Manager*
Armida Escobeso, *Executive Asst*
EMP: 161
SALES (corp-wide): 74.7MM **Privately Held**
WEB: www.scths.com
SIC: 6513 Retirement hotel operation
PA: Southern California Presbyterian Homes
 516 Burchett St
 Glendale CA 91203
 818 247-0420

(P-11110)
CALIFORNIA ODD FELLOWS (PA)
Also Called: Meadows of NAPA Valley
1800 Atrium Pkwy, NAPA (94559-4837)
PHONE..................707 257-7885
Fax: 707 257-6915
Wayne Panchesson, *Exec Dir*
Carlos Garcia, *Admin Mgr*
Kent Fry, *Sls & Mktg Exec*
Sharon Borunda, *Director*
Joedna Bohanon, *Manager*
EMP: 100
SQ FT: 219,000
SALES (est): 1.5MM **Privately Held**
WEB: www.meadowsofnapavalley.org
SIC: 6513 8051 8322 Retirement hotel operation; convalescent home with continuous nursing care; old age assistance

(P-11111)
CALIFORNIA ODD FELLOWS
Also Called: Meadows Nappa Valley Care Ctr
1800 Atrium Pkwy, NAPA (94559-4837)
PHONE..................707 257-7885
Wyane Panchesson, *Administration*
Jerry Esparcia, *Exec Dir*
EMP: 65
SQ FT: 30,000
SALES (corp-wide): 1.5MM **Privately Held**
WEB: www.meadowsofnapavalley.org
SIC: 6513 8051 Apartment building operators; skilled nursing care facilities
PA: California Odd Fellows Housing Of Napa, Incorporated
 1800 Atrium Pkwy
 Napa CA 94559
 707 257-7885

(P-11112)
CARMEL VLG RTIREMENT RESIDENCE
17077 San Mateo St # 3113, Fountain Valley (92708-7658)
PHONE..................714 962-6667
Fax: 714 964-0447
S Butts, *President*
EMP: 65
SQ FT: 117,670
SALES (est): 3.8MM **Privately Held**
SIC: 6513 Retirement hotel operation

(P-11113)
CASA SANDOVAL LLC
1200 Russell Way, Hayward (94541-7708)
PHONE..................510 727-1700
Fax: 510 727-0671
Wai Tsin Chang,
Karolina Baban, *Exec Dir*
Luz Falcon, *Food Svc Dir*
Tess Barreto, *Director*
Ann Ibalio, *Director*
EMP: 90
SQ FT: 215,000
SALES (est): 8.4MM **Privately Held**
WEB: www.casasandoval.com
SIC: 6513 Retirement hotel operation

(P-11114)
CHARLES & CYNTHIA EBERLY INC
Also Called: The Eberly Company
8383 Wilshire Blvd # 906, Beverly Hills (90211-2425)
PHONE..................323 937-6468
Charles Eberly, *President*
Cynthia Eberly, *Vice Pres*
Deena Eberly, *Manager*
Jessica Avendano, *Assistant*
John Ene, *Supervisor*
EMP: 90
SALES (est): 7MM **Privately Held**
WEB: www.eberlyco.com
SIC: 6513 Apartment building operators

(P-11115)
CHATEAU LA JOLLA INN
233 Prospect St, La Jolla (92037-4600)
PHONE..................858 459-4451
Toll Free:..................888 -
Fax: 858 459-5708
Robert Collins, *Partner*
Jeff Fee, *Partner*
Danny Gali, *Technology*
Kim Hollingsworth, *Director*
EMP: 50
SQ FT: 40,000
SALES (est): 4.3MM **Privately Held**
WEB: www.chateaulajollainn.com
SIC: 6513 Apartment hotel operation

(P-11116)
CLASSIC PARK LANE PARTNERSHIP
Also Called: Park Lane A Classic Residenc
200 Glenwood Cir Ofc, Monterey (93940-6773)
PHONE..................831 373-0101
Steve Brudnick, *Exec Dir*
Park Lane Investment, *Partner*
Jim Cox, *Director*
EMP: 83
SQ FT: 190,000
SALES (est): 3.1MM **Privately Held**
SIC: 6513 8361 Retirement hotel operation; home for the aged

(P-11117)
COMMERCIAL PROPERTY MANAGEMENT (PA)
3251 W 6th St Ste 109, Los Angeles (90020-5018)
PHONE..................213 739-2000
David Soufer, *President*
EMP: 64
SQ FT: 4,500
SALES (est): 4MM **Privately Held**
WEB: www.cpmusa.com
SIC: 6513 Apartment building operators

(P-11118)
CULVER CITY HSING PARTNERS LP
911 N Studebaker Rd, Long Beach (90815-4900)
PHONE..................562 257-5100
Laverne Joseph, *President*
Deborah Stouff, *Admin Sec*
EMP: 99
SQ FT: 49,185
SALES (est): 789.1K **Privately Held**
SIC: 6513 Apartment building operators

(P-11119)
CYPRESS GARDEN VILLAS
21600 Bloomfield Ave, Hawaiian Gardens (90716-2325)
PHONE..................562 860-9260
Fax: 562 860-7460
Julia Forrester, *President*
Maria Gonzalez, *Manager*
EMP: 70
SALES (est): 1.2MM **Privately Held**
WEB: www.cypressgardensinn.com
SIC: 6513 Apartment building operators

(P-11120)
DOMINICAN OAKS CORPORATION
3400 Paul Sweet Rd Ofc, Santa Cruz (95065-1559)
PHONE..................831 462-6257
Fax: 831 462-6742
Patience Beck, *Manager*
Sister Julie Hyer, *President*
Sally Boyd, *Administration*
EMP: 80
SALES: 10.7MM **Privately Held**
WEB: www.dominicanoaks.com
SIC: 6513 Retirement hotel operation

(P-11121)
DOWNEY RETIREMENT CTR
11500 Dolan Ave, Downey (90241-4900)
PHONE..................562 869-2416
Eddie Rosenberg, *Owner*
EMP: 50
SALES (est): 258.8K **Privately Held**
SIC: 6513 Retirement hotel operation

(P-11122)
E J WILLIAMS PROPERTY MGT
5637 N Pershing Ave Ste D, Stockton (95207-4943)
P.O. Box 7185 (95267-0185)
PHONE..................209 473-4022
Ej Williams, *Principal*
EMP: 60
SALES (est): 270.9K **Privately Held**
SIC: 6513 Apartment building operators

(P-11123)
EAST BAY ASIAN LOCAL DEV CORP
1825 San Pablo Ave # 201, Oakland (94612-1517)
PHONE..................510 267-1917
Jeremy Liu, *Exec Dir*
Judy Graboyes, *Associate Dir*
Joshua Simon, *General Mgr*
Kyle Lee, *Info Tech Mgr*
Lanetha Oliver, *Human Res Dir*
EMP: 109
SQ FT: 78,000
SALES: 10.2MM **Privately Held**
WEB: www.ebaldc.org
SIC: 6513 Apartment building operators

(P-11124)
EMERITUS CORPORATION
Also Called: Villa Del Rey Retirement Inn
1351 E Washington Ave, Escondido (92027-1934)
PHONE..................760 741-3055
Fax: 760 741-3057
Pam Judkins, *Branch Mgr*
Michelle Boylin, *Exec Dir*
EMP: 50

PRODUCTS & SERVICES SECTION

6513 - Operators Of Apartment Buildings County (P-11147)

SQ FT: 60,000
SALES (corp-wide): 4.9B **Publicly Held**
WEB: www.emeraldestatesslc.com
SIC: **6513** Apartment building operators
HQ: Emeritus Corporation
  3131 Elliott Ave Ste 500
  Milwaukee WI 53214
  206 298-2909

(P-11125)
EMERITUS CORPORATION
Also Called: Emeritus At Casa Glendale
426 Piedmont Ave, Glendale (91206-3448)
PHONE.................................818 246-7457
David Wilkens, *Branch Mgr*
EMP: 50
SALES (corp-wide): 4.9B **Publicly Held**
SIC: **6513** Apartment building operators
HQ: Emeritus Corporation
  3131 Elliott Ave Ste 500
  Milwaukee WI 53214
  206 298-2909

(P-11126)
EMERITUS CORPORATION
Also Called: Creston Village
1919 Creston Rd Ofc, Paso Robles (93446-4475)
PHONE.................................805 239-1313
Fax: 805 239-4814
Tonya Hogue, *Director*
EMP: 50
SALES (corp-wide): 4.9B **Publicly Held**
WEB: www.emeraldestatesslc.com
SIC: **6513** Retirement hotel operation
HQ: Emeritus Corporation
  3131 Elliott Ave Ste 500
  Milwaukee WI 53214
  206 298-2909

(P-11127)
EUROPEAN HOTL INVSTRS OF CA (PA)
Also Called: O H I
2532 Dupont Dr, Irvine (92612-1524)
PHONE.................................949 474-7368
Fax: 949 474-7732
Timothy R Busch, *General Ptnr*
T R Busch Realty Corp, *Partner*
John Moody, *Financial Exec*
Gregory Busch, *CPA*
Brian Leip, *Controller*
EMP: 50
SQ FT: 9,000
SALES (est): 13.9MM **Privately Held**
SIC: **6513** Hotels & motels

(P-11128)
FAIRWOOD ASSOCIATES APTS
Also Called: Fairwood Apartments
8893 Fair Oaks Blvd Ofc, Carmichael (95608-2672)
PHONE.................................916 944-0152
Leeann Morein, *Principal*
Arthur F Evans, *Partner*
The National Housing Partnersh, *Partner*
Jennifer Hardee, *Principal*
Joanette Stiron, *Manager*
EMP: 99
SALES: 500K
SALES (corp-wide): 981.3MM **Publicly Held**
WEB: www.fairwoodapartments.com
SIC: **6513** Apartment building operators
PA: Apartment Investment & Management Company
  4582 S Ulster St Ste 1100
  Denver CO 80237
  303 757-8101

(P-11129)
FATHERS OF ST CHARLES
Also Called: Villa Sclabrini Retirement Ctr
10631 Vinedale St, Sun Valley (91352-2825)
PHONE.................................818 768-6500
Fax: 818 767-1410
Ermete Nazzani, *Director*
Father E Nazzini, *Bd of Directors*
Christian Perez, *Office Mgr*
Liana Volpe, *Director*
EMP: 188
SQ FT: 90,000
SALES: 5MM **Privately Held**
SIC: **6513** 8051 Retirement hotel operation; skilled nursing care facilities

(P-11130)
FENTON SCRIPPS LANDING LLC
Also Called: H.G. Fenton Company
9970 Erma Rd, San Diego (92131-2425)
PHONE.................................858 586-0206
Michael Neal,
Andrea Norby, *Manager*
EMP: 99
SALES (est): 2.5MM **Privately Held**
SIC: **6513** Apartment building operators

(P-11131)
FIFTY PENINSULA PARTNERS
Also Called: Sterling Court
850 N El Camino Real Ofc, San Mateo (94401-3787)
PHONE.................................650 344-8200
Fax: 650 344-7395
S St Charles, *Exec Dir*
Sarah St Charles, *Exec Dir*
EMP: 55
SALES (est): 5.3MM **Privately Held**
SIC: **6513** Apartment building operators

(P-11132)
FOREMOST HEALTHCARE CENTERS
Also Called: Health Care Developers
17581 Sultana St, Hesperia (92345-6552)
PHONE.................................760 244-5579
Leonard Crites, *Owner*
Barbara Bandringa, *Owner*
Elizabeth Colon, *Administration*
Tyrone James, *Facilities Dir*
Jason Kears, *Maintence Staff*
EMP: 60
SALES (est): 1.7MM **Privately Held**
SIC: **6513** Apartment building operators

(P-11133)
FRED LEEDS PROPERTIES
1640 S Sepulv Blvd # 320, Los Angeles (90025-7536)
PHONE.................................310 826-2466
Fax: 310 826-3505
Fred Leeds, *President*
EMP: 50
SQ FT: 3,000
SALES (est): 3.3MM **Privately Held**
WEB: www.fredleedsproperties.com
SIC: **6513** Apartment building operators

(P-11134)
FRONT PORCH COMMUNITIES
849 Coast Blvd, La Jolla (92037-4223)
PHONE.................................858 454-2151
Fax: 858 454-7537
Justin Weber, *Exec Dir*
Margo McNeill, *Nursing Dir*
EMP: 100
SALES (corp-wide): 165.1MM **Privately Held**
SIC: **6513** 8052 8361 Retirement hotel operation; intermediate care facilities; residential care
PA: Front Porch Communities And Services - Casa De Manana, Llc
  800 N Brand Blvd Fl 19
  Glendale CA 91203
  818 729-8100

(P-11135)
FSQ RIO LAS PALMAS BUSINESS TR
877 E March Ln Apt 378, Stockton (95207-5880)
PHONE.................................209 957-4711
Sam Ogden, *Exec Dir*
Connie Salinas, *Office Mgr*
Connie Salinas, *Office Mgr*
B T Swearingen, *Administration*
EMP: 54
SALES (est): 2.7MM
SALES (corp-wide): 1.3B **Publicly Held**
WEB: www.fivestarqualitycare.com
SIC: **6513** Retirement hotel operation
PA: Five Star Quality Care, Inc.
  400 Centre St
  Newton MA 02458
  617 796-8387

(P-11136)
GABLES OF OJAI LLC
701 N Montgomery St, Ojai (93023-1844)
PHONE.................................805 646-1446
Fax: 805 646-3720
Sue Collingsworth, *Director*
Barbara Nelson, *Office Mgr*
EMP: 56
SALES (est): 2.7MM
SALES (corp-wide): 5.9MM **Privately Held**
WEB: www.gablesofojai.com
SIC: **6513** Retirement hotel operation
PA: The Parsons Group Inc
  1 N Calle Chavez Ste 200
  Santa Barbara CA 93101
  805 564-3341

(P-11137)
GERSON BAKER & ASSOCIATES
Also Called: Westlake Village Apartments
333 Park Plaza Dr Ofc, Daly City (94015-1538)
PHONE.................................650 756-0959
Fax: 650 755-1081
Gerson Baker, *Owner*
EMP: 100
SQ FT: 5,000
SALES (est): 6MM **Privately Held**
WEB: www.westlakevillageapts.com
SIC: **6513** Apartment building operators

(P-11138)
GRAIG HALL SERVICE COMPANY
Also Called: Gordon Hall Conference Center
1400 W 3rd St, Chico (95928-4825)
PHONE.................................530 345-1393
John Fox, *General Mgr*
Thomas Liotta, *Corp Secy*
EMP: 90
SALES (est): 2.4MM **Privately Held**
SIC: **6513** Residential hotel operation

(P-11139)
HARVEST FACILITY HOLDINGS LP
Also Called: Mission Cmmons Rtrment Rsdence
10 Terracina Blvd Ofc, Redlands (92373-4800)
PHONE.................................909 793-8691
Fax: 909 798-9238
John Degoucvia, *Manager*
David Haskins, *Manager*
EMP: 80
SALES (corp-wide): 1.2B **Publicly Held**
WEB: www.holidaytouch.com
SIC: **6513** Apartment building operators
HQ: Harvest Facility Holdings Lp
  5885 Meadows Rd Ste 500
  Lake Oswego OR 97035
  503 370-7070

(P-11140)
HG FENTON COMPANY
7577 Mission Valley Rd # 200, San Diego (92108-4432)
PHONE.................................619 400-0120
Fax: 619 400-0111
Mike Neal, *CEO*
Robert Gottlieb, *CFO*
Lisa Gaudet, *Vice Pres*
Allen Jones, *Vice Pres*
Kari Prevost, *Vice Pres*
EMP: 93
SALES (est): 13.4MM **Privately Held**
SIC: **6513** 6519 Apartment building operators; real property lessors

(P-11141)
HIGNELL COMPANIES
Also Called: Sierra Manor Apts
1836 Laburnum Ave, Chico (95926-2375)
PHONE.................................530 345-1965
Becky Nelson, *Branch Mgr*
EMP: 80
SALES (corp-wide): 41.1MM **Privately Held**
SIC: **6513** Apartment building operators
PA: Hignell, Incorporated
  1750 Humboldt Rd
  Chico CA 95928
  530 894-0404

(P-11142)
INGLEWOOD MEADOWS KBS LP
1 S Locust St, Inglewood (90301-1808)
PHONE.................................310 820-4888
Thomas Safran, *Partner*
Anthony Yannatta, *Director*
Lade Johnson, *Manager*
EMP: 90
SALES: 1,000K **Privately Held**
SIC: **6513** Apartment building operators

(P-11143)
INVESTORS MGT TR RE GROUP INC (PA)
Also Called: I M T
15303 Ventura Blvd # 200, Sherman Oaks (91403-3110)
PHONE.................................818 784-4700
John M Tesoriero, *President*
Bryan Scher, *COO*
Frank Hutter, *CFO*
Scott Burns, *Senior VP*
Dan Onder, *Vice Pres*
EMP: 50
SQ FT: 8,000
SALES (est): 15.1MM **Privately Held**
SIC: **6513** Apartment building operators

(P-11144)
IRVINE APT COMMUNITIES LP (HQ)
Also Called: I A C
110 Innovation Dr, Irvine (92617-3040)
PHONE.................................949 720-5600
Raymond Watson, *Vice Chairman*
Mike Ellis, *Exec VP*
Mark Henningan, *Vice Pres*
Tom Pleickhardt, *Webmaster*
Lisa Cappel, *Mktg Dir*
EMP: 200
SQ FT: 8,316
SALES (est): 51.3MM
SALES (corp-wide): 2B **Privately Held**
WEB: www.rental-living.com
SIC: **6513** 6552 6798 Apartment building operators; subdividers & developers; real estate investment trusts
PA: The Irvine Company Llc
  550 Newport Center Dr # 160
  Newport Beach CA 92660
  949 720-2000

(P-11145)
JEWISH SENIOR LIVING GROUP
302 Silver Ave, San Francisco (94112-1510)
PHONE.................................415 562-2600
Daniel Ruth, *President*
Olga Strashnaya, *Info Tech Mgr*
Ken Diep, *Engineer*
Terrence Scott, *Controller*
Marilyn McAlister, *Manager*
EMP: 60
SALES: 8.1MM **Privately Held**
SIC: **6513** Retirement hotel operation

(P-11146)
JOHN COLLINS CO INC
5155 Cedarwood Rd Mgr, Bonita (91902-1942)
PHONE.................................818 227-2190
EMP: 97
SALES (corp-wide): 1.6MM **Privately Held**
SIC: **6513** Apartment building operators
PA: The John Collins Co Inc
  5135 N Harbor Dr
  San Diego CA
  -

(P-11147)
JONES & JONES MGT GROUP INC
8220 Topanga Canyon Blvd, Canoga Park (91304-3844)
P.O. Box 6550, Woodland Hills (91365-6550)
PHONE.................................818 594-0019
John D Jones, *President*
Helen Jones, *CEO*
Margaret Jones Dry, *Vice Pres*
Krystal Dry, *Associate*
EMP: 142

6513 - Operators Of Apartment Buildings County (P-11148)

SALES (est): 11.5MM **Privately Held**
SIC: 6513 Apartment building operators

(P-11148)
KINGSLEY APARTMENTS
Also Called: Kingsley Court Apartments
1345 N Kingsley Dr, Los Angeles (90027-5763)
PHONE 323 666-8862
Angelica Hovhannisyan, *Manager*
Gary Weiner, *Director*
Marietta Kartashyan, *Manager*
EMP: 80
SALES (est): 2.6MM **Privately Held**
SIC: 6513 Apartment building operators

(P-11149)
KISCO SENIOR LIVING LLC
Also Called: Drake Terrace
275 Los Ranchitos Rd, San Rafael (94903-3673)
PHONE 415 491-1935
EMP: 117
SALES (corp-wide): 135.3MM **Privately Held**
SIC: 6513 Retirement hotel operation
PA: Senior Kisco Living Llc
5790 Fleet St Ste 300
Carlsbad CA 92008
760 804-5900

(P-11150)
KISCO SENIOR LIVING LLC
1731 W Medical Center Dr, Anaheim (92801-1837)
PHONE 714 778-5100
Carol Bush, *Director*
EMP: 72
SALES (corp-wide): 135.3MM **Privately Held**
SIC: 6513 Retirement hotel operation
PA: Senior Kisco Living Llc
5790 Fleet St Ste 300
Carlsbad CA 92008
760 804-5900

(P-11151)
LA JOLLA COVE HOTEL & MOTEL
Also Called: La Jolla Cove Motel
1155 Coast Blvd, La Jolla (92037-3627)
P.O. Box 1067 (92038-1067)
PHONE 858 459-2621
Fax: 858 551-3405
Helen Jackman, *Vice Pres*
EMP: 78 EST: 1959
SQ FT: 78,000
SALES (est): 5.8MM **Privately Held**
WEB: www.lajollacove.com
SIC: 6513 Apartment hotel operation

(P-11152)
LA SALLE APARTMENTS
Also Called: La Salle Preservation
30 Whitfield Ct Ste 1, San Francisco (94124-2840)
PHONE 415 647-0607
Fax: 415 647-5751
Leeann Morein, *Principal*
Jennifer Hardee, *Principal*
EMP: 99 EST: 2008
SALES (est): 2.6MM **Privately Held**
SIC: 6513 Apartment building operators

(P-11153)
LASSLEY ENTERPRISES INC
Also Called: Western Homes
1289 E Shaw Ave, Fresno (93710-7801)
P.O. Box 26988 (93729-6988)
PHONE 559 226-4300
Fax: 559 226-6115
Larry Lassley, *President*
Floyd Lassley, *President*
Terry Graham, *Corp Secy*
Lorraine Lassley, *Vice Pres*
EMP: 50 EST: 1963
SQ FT: 4,000
SALES (est): 1.8MM **Privately Held**
SIC: 6513 Apartment building operators

(P-11154)
LEGACY PARTNERS HOLLYWOOD
1600 Vine St, Los Angeles (90028-8818)
PHONE 949 930-7706
Tim O'Brien, *Partner*

Scott Walter, *Senior VP*
Mairia Balosteros, *Assistant*
EMP: 91
SALES (est): 2.4MM **Privately Held**
SIC: 6513 Apartment building operators

(P-11155)
LEISURE CARE INC
Also Called: Norlyn Builders Newport Beach
1455 Superior Ave, Newport Beach (92663-6127)
PHONE 949 645-6833
Fax: 949 642-1131
Connie Marvick, *Administration*
Newport Beach Plaza Retirement, *General Ptnr*
M David Green, *Ltd Ptnr*
Jerome Pastor, *Ltd Ptnr*
Chuck Lytle, *CEO*
EMP: 60
SQ FT: 90,000
SALES (est): 4MM **Privately Held**
SIC: 6513 Retirement hotel operation

(P-11156)
LEISURE CARE LLC
Also Called: Heritage Estates-Livermore
800 E Stanley Blvd, Livermore (94550-2800)
PHONE 925 371-2300
Fax: 925 373-7676
EMP: 91
SALES (corp-wide): 138.2MM **Privately Held**
SIC: 6513 Apartment building operators
PA: Leisure Care, Llc
999 3rd Ave Ste 4500
Seattle WA 98104
800 327-3490

(P-11157)
LINCOLN MARINERS ASSOC LTD
Also Called: Mariners Cove Apartments
4392 W Point Loma Blvd, San Diego (92107-1128)
PHONE 619 225-1473
Fax: 619 225-8451
Leeann Morein, *Principal*
Jennifer Hardee, *Principal*
EMP: 99
SALES (est): 3.3MM **Privately Held**
WEB: www.marinerscoveapartments.com
SIC: 6513 Apartment building operators

(P-11158)
LIVING OPPORTUNITIES MGT CO
6900 Seville Ave, Huntington Park (90255-4970)
PHONE 323 589-5956
EMP: 209
SALES (est): 9.1MM **Privately Held**
SIC: 6513 Apartment building operators
PA: Living Opportunities Management Co
3787 Worsham Ave
Long Beach CA 90808
562 595-7567

(P-11159)
LONGWOOD MANAGEMENT CORP
Also Called: California Villa
6728 Sepulveda Blvd, Van Nuys (91411-1248)
PHONE 818 781-6348
Fax: 818 781-8361
Jackie Beltran, *Administration*
Susan Weisbarth, *Exec Dir*
EMP: 50
SALES (corp-wide): 169.4MM **Privately Held**
SIC: 6513 8361 Retirement hotel operation; residential care
PA: Longwood Management Corp.
4032 Wilshire Blvd Fl 6
Los Angeles CA 90010
213 389-6900

(P-11160)
LONGWOOD MANAGEMENT CORP
Also Called: Woodland Park Retirement Hotel
895 E Pasadena St, Pomona (91767-4930)
PHONE 818 884-7100
Susan Weisbarth, *Manager*
EMP: 68
SQ FT: 66,332
SALES (corp-wide): 169.4MM **Privately Held**
SIC: 6513 Retirement hotel operation
PA: Longwood Management Corp.
4032 Wilshire Blvd Fl 6
Los Angeles CA 90010
213 389-6900

(P-11161)
LOS ANGELES SENIOR CITIZEN
Also Called: PICO WOOSTER SENIOR HOUSING
1425 S Wooster St, Los Angeles (90035-3456)
PHONE 310 271-9670
Fax: 310 271-9676
Anne Friedrich, *President*
Angel Jaramillo, *Controller*
Douglas Cope, *Director*
EMP: 55
SALES (est): 608.1K **Privately Held**
SIC: 6513 Retirement hotel operation

(P-11162)
M&M ASSEET MANAGEMENT GNL
2936 W El Segundo Blvd, Gardena (90249-1558)
PHONE 310 769-6669
Ram K Mittal, *Principal*
Lillian Mittal, *Principal*
Evelyn Revellame, *Controller*
EMP: 99
SALES (est): 2.1MM **Privately Held**
SIC: 6513 Apartment building operators

(P-11163)
MARINA CITY CLUB LP A CALI
4333 Admiralty Way, Marina Del Rey (90292-5469)
PHONE 310 822-0611
J H Snyder, *Partner*
Lewis Geyser, *Partner*
Lon Snyder, *Partner*
Milton Swimmer, *Partner*
Eileen Mc Carthy, *Sales Dir*
EMP: 125
SQ FT: 10,000
SALES (est): 8.5MM **Privately Held**
WEB: www.marinacityclub.net
SIC: 6513 7997 4493 Apartment building operators; membership sports & recreation clubs; marinas

(P-11164)
MAYER ASSOCIATES
9090 Wilshire Blvd Fl 3, Beverly Hills (90211-1851)
PHONE 310 274-5553
Alan I Casden, *Partner*
EMP: 100
SALES (est): 2MM **Privately Held**
SIC: 6513 Apartment building operators

(P-11165)
MBK REAL ESTATE LTD A CALFOR
100 Lockewood Ln, Scotts Valley (95066-3900)
PHONE 831 438-7533
Kit Siemer, *Exec Dir*
EMP: 80
SALES (corp-wide): 40.6B **Privately Held**
SIC: 6513 Retirement hotel operation
HQ: Mbk Real Estate Ltd., A California Limited Partnership
4 Park Plz Ste 850
Irvine CA 92614
949 789-8300

(P-11166)
MBK REAL ESTATE LTD A CALIFOR
Also Called: Ocean House Retirement Inn
2107 Ocean Ave Ofc, Santa Monica (90405-2282)
PHONE 310 399-3227
Fax: 310 314-7356
Lesley Henriksen, *Exec Dir*
EMP: 50
SALES (corp-wide): 40.6B **Privately Held**
SIC: 6513 Retirement hotel operation
HQ: Mbk Real Estate Ltd., A California Limited Partnership
4 Park Plz Ste 850
Irvine CA 92614
949 789-8300

(P-11167)
MERCY HSING CALIFORNIA XXXIV
Also Called: Edith Witt Senior Community
66 9th St, San Francisco (94103-1427)
PHONE 415 503-0816
Abelle Cochico, *Manager*
Teresa Walorski, *Administration*
EMP: 99
SALES: 84.9K **Privately Held**
SIC: 6513 Apartment building operators

(P-11168)
MERIDIAN MANAGEMENT GROUP
1145 Bush St, San Francisco (94109-5919)
PHONE 415 434-9700
Fax: 415 782-3833
Randall Chapman, *President*
Gil Dowd, *Vice Pres*
Russell Flynn, *Vice Pres*
James R Wilson, *Admin Sec*
Celine Mayer, *Human Res Mgr*
EMP: 160
SQ FT: 6,200
SALES (est): 14.7MM **Privately Held**
WEB: www.mmgroup.com
SIC: 6513 Apartment building operators

(P-11169)
MONARK LP
2804 W El Segundo Blvd, Gardena (90249-1551)
PHONE 310 769-6669
Evelyn Revellame, *CFO*
EMP: 99
SALES (est): 2.1MM **Privately Held**
SIC: 6513 Apartment building operators

(P-11170)
MONROE RESIDENCE CLUB
Also Called: Kenmore Residence Club
1499 Sutter St, San Francisco (94109-5417)
PHONE 415 771-9119
Irene Lieberman, *Owner*
Vincent Cooper, *Manager*
EMP: 75
SQ FT: 1,000
SALES (est): 2.1MM **Privately Held**
WEB: www.monroeresidenceclub.com
SIC: 6513 Residential hotel operation

(P-11171)
MONTE VISTA RETIREMENT LODGE
Also Called: Monte Vista Village
6458 Lake Tahoe Ct, San Diego (92119-2534)
PHONE 619 465-1331
Fax: 619 465-2426
Sidney Goodman, *Partner*
John Goodman, *Partner*
Donna Hanson, *Partner*
Amos Heilicher, *Partner*
Daniel Heilicher, *Partner*
EMP: 90
SALES (est): 6.3MM **Privately Held**
WEB: www.montevistalodge.com
SIC: 6513 Retirement hotel operation

PRODUCTS & SERVICES SECTION
6513 - Operators Of Apartment Buildings County (P-11196)

(P-11172)
MP SHORELINE ASSOC LTD PARTNR
Also Called: Shorebreeze Apartments
460 N Shoreline Blvd, Mountain View (94043-4661)
PHONE.................650 966-1327
Matt Franklin, *President*
Luina Palchak, *Manager*
EMP: 50
SALES: 2.7MM
SALES (corp-wide): 41.9K **Privately Held**
SIC: 6513 Apartment building operators
PA: Stanford Mid-Peninsula Urban Coalition
303 Vintage Park Dr # 250
Foster City CA 94404
650 356-2900

(P-11173)
MT VIEW APARTMENTS LLC
3170 Crow Canyon Pl # 165, San Ramon (94583-1347)
P.O. Box 308 (94583-0308)
PHONE.................925 866-8429
Dennis Fuller,
EMP: 60
SALES (est): 2.9MM **Privately Held**
SIC: 6513 Apartment building operators

(P-11174)
NORMAND/WLSHIRE RTRMENT HT INC
Also Called: CALIFORNIA HEALTHCARE AND REHA
6700 Sepulveda Blvd, Van Nuys (91411-1248)
PHONE.................818 373-5429
Jerry Catama, *Administration*
EMP: 99
SALES: 21.5MM **Privately Held**
SIC: 6513 8059 Retirement hotel operation; convalescent home

(P-11175)
NORTHERN CALIFORNIA PRESBYTERI
Also Called: Sequoias, The
1400 Geary Blvd, San Francisco (94109-6561)
PHONE.................415 673-2352
Michael Dougherty, *Principal*
Candiece Milford, *Mktg Dir*
EMP: 160
SALES (corp-wide): 69.3MM **Privately Held**
WEB: www.contracostasbdc.com
SIC: 6513 Retirement hotel operation
PA: Northern California Presbyterian Homes And Services, Inc.
1525 Post St
San Francisco CA 94109
415 922-0200

(P-11176)
NORTHGATE TERRACE APTS
1290 Northgate Dr Apt 48, Yuba City (95991-1565)
PHONE.................530 671-2026
Dennis McLear, *President*
EMP: 100
SALES (est): 2.1MM **Privately Held**
SIC: 6513 Apartment building operators

(P-11177)
OAK CREEK APARTMENTS
Also Called: Gerson Bakar & Associates
1600 Sand Hill Rd, Palo Alto (94304-2047)
PHONE.................650 327-1600
Fax: 650 321-4263
Gerson Bakar, *Partner*
A S Wilsey, *General Ptnr*
Tina Dirienzo, *Property Mgr*
Jacqueline Tuato'o, *Manager*
EMP: 50 **EST:** 1968
SQ FT: 300,000
SALES: 2.8MM
SALES (corp-wide): 21.1MM **Privately Held**
WEB: www.oakcreekapts.com
SIC: 6513 Apartment building operators
PA: Jalson Co., Inc.
201 Filbert St Ste 700
San Francisco CA 94133
415 391-1313

(P-11178)
OAKDALE HEIGHTS MGT CORP (PA)
250 Hemsted Dr Ste 100, Redding (96002-0940)
PHONE.................530 222-6797
Fax: 530 222-6725
Michael Loudon, *President*
Jim Koenig, *Shareholder*
EMP: 347
SALES (est): 11.5MM **Privately Held**
SIC: 6513 Retirement hotel operation

(P-11179)
OCONNER WOODS A CALIFORNIA
3400 Wagner Heights Rd, Stockton (95209-4843)
PHONE.................209 956-3400
Scot Sinclair, *President*
EMP: 100
SQ FT: 3,000
SALES (est): 3.6MM
SALES (corp-wide): 24.6MM **Privately Held**
SIC: 6513 Retirement hotel operation
PA: St. Joseph's Regional Housing Corporation
3400 Wagner Heights Rd
Stockton CA 95209
209 956-3400

(P-11180)
OCONNOR WOODS HOUSING CORP
3400 Wagner Heights Rd, Stockton (95209-4843)
PHONE.................209 956-3400
Fax: 209 952-6201
Edward G Schoeder, *President*
Scot Sinclair, *Exec Dir*
Jackie Arnesonm, *Accounting Mgr*
EMP: 100
SALES: 29.1MM
SALES (corp-wide): 24.6MM **Privately Held**
WEB: www.oconnorwoods.org
SIC: 6513 Retirement hotel operation
PA: St. Joseph's Regional Housing Corporation
3400 Wagner Heights Rd
Stockton CA 95209
209 956-3400

(P-11181)
OLIVE GROVE RETIREMENT RESORT
7858 California Ave, Riverside (92504-2599)
PHONE.................951 687-2241
Fax: 951 687-0459
Kendall Jamison, *Director*
EMP: 65 **EST:** 1982
SQ FT: 170,000
SALES (est): 3.7MM **Privately Held**
WEB: www.olivegrove.com
SIC: 6513 Retirement hotel operation

(P-11182)
PAHC APARTMENTS INC
725 Alma St, Palo Alto (94301-2403)
PHONE.................650 321-9709
Marlene Prentergast, *President*
EMP: 50
SALES: 1.4MM **Privately Held**
SIC: 6513 Apartment building operators

(P-11183)
PANORAMA PARK APTS
401 W Columbus St Apt 64, Bakersfield (93301-5819)
PHONE.................661 325-4047
Latanya Gordon, *Manager*
Leeann Morein, *Partner*
EMP: 99
SALES (est): 2.4MM **Privately Held**
SIC: 6513 Apartment building operators

(P-11184)
PARK NEWPORT LTD (PA)
Also Called: Park Newport Apartments
1 Park Newport, Newport Beach (92660-5004)
PHONE.................949 644-1900
Fax: 949 644-5385
Gerson Bakar, *Owner*
Linda Guenther, *Administration*
Craig Capelouto, *Finance Mgr*
EMP: 75
SQ FT: 10,000
SALES (est): 4.7MM **Privately Held**
WEB: www.parknewport.com
SIC: 6513 Apartment building operators

(P-11185)
PARKWAY APARTMENTS LLC
3170 Crow Canyon Pl # 165, San Ramon (94583-1347)
P.O. Box 308 (94583-0308)
PHONE.................925 866-8429
Dennis Fuller, *Owner*
EMP: 50
SALES (est): 1.4MM **Privately Held**
SIC: 6513 Apartment building operators

(P-11186)
PARKWEST APARTMENTS
Also Called: Victoria Management
562 Kendall Ave, Palo Alto (94306-2746)
PHONE.................650 856-0930
Vince Giovannoto, *Owner*
Kent Taylor, *Manager*
EMP: 63
SALES (est): 1.7MM **Privately Held**
SIC: 6513 Apartment building operators

(P-11187)
PIONEER TOWERS RHF PARTNERS LP
515 P St Ofc, Sacramento (95814-6310)
PHONE.................916 443-6548
Laverne R Joseph, *Managing Prtnr*
Deborah Stouff, *Principal*
EMP: 50
SALES (est): 1.4MM **Privately Held**
SIC: 6513 Apartment building operators

(P-11188)
PLB MANAGEMENT LLC
Also Called: Park Labrea Management
6200 W 3rd St, Los Angeles (90036-3157)
PHONE.................323 549-5400
Dan James,
Dave Myers, *Systems Staff*
Greg Holihan,
James Dan, *Manager*
Clifton Dehayward, *Manager*
EMP: 50
SALES (est): 3.8MM **Privately Held**
WEB: www.parklabrea.com
SIC: 6513 Apartment building operators

(P-11189)
PLUMMER VLG PRESERVATION LP
15450 Plummer St, North Hills (91343-2141)
PHONE.................818 891-0646
Leeann Morein, *Partner*
Leeann Moreinm, *Partner*
EMP: 99
SALES: 950K **Privately Held**
SIC: 6513 Apartment building operators

(P-11190)
PROVIDENT GROUP CROWN PNTE LLC
Also Called: Crown Pointe Retirement
737 Magnolia Ave Ofc, Corona (92879-7005)
PHONE.................951 737-7482
Fax: 951 737-1497
Steve Hicks, *Mng Member*
Kathy Franco,
Debra Lockwood,
Gean Walker, *Manager*
EMP: 56
SALES (est): 3.2MM **Privately Held**
SIC: 6513 Retirement hotel operation

(P-11191)
R & B REALTY GROUP
Also Called: Oakwood Garden Apts
3600 Barham Blvd, Los Angeles (90068-1106)
PHONE.................323 851-3450
Fax: 323 851-2639
Tal Amquest, *Manager*
EMP: 100
SALES (corp-wide): 140.1MM **Privately Held**
SIC: 6513 Apartment building operators
PA: R & B Realty Group, A California Limited Partnership
2222 Corinth Ave
Los Angeles CA 90064
800 888-0808

(P-11192)
R & B REALTY GROUP
Also Called: Oakwood Apartments
22122 Victory Blvd, Woodland Hills (91367-1937)
PHONE.................818 710-5400
Fax: 818 595-2200
William Frill, *Manager*
EMP: 80
SALES (corp-wide): 140.1MM **Privately Held**
SIC: 6513 Apartment building operators
PA: R & B Realty Group, A California Limited Partnership
2222 Corinth Ave
Los Angeles CA 90064
800 888-0808

(P-11193)
R & B REALTY GROUP
Also Called: Oakwood Apts
4111 Via Marina, Marina Del Rey (90292-5302)
PHONE.................310 751-4545
Fax: 310 301-8246
Heather Hermann, *Manager*
Jin Heo, *Manager*
EMP: 55
SALES (corp-wide): 140.1MM **Privately Held**
SIC: 6513 Apartment building operators
PA: R & B Realty Group, A California Limited Partnership
2222 Corinth Ave
Los Angeles CA 90064
800 888-0808

(P-11194)
RANCE KING PROPERTIES INC (PA)
Also Called: R K Properties
3737 E Broadway, Long Beach (90803-6104)
PHONE.................562 240-1000
Fax: 562 439-0283
William Rance King Jr, *President*
Steven King, *Vice Pres*
Tanja Pierce, *Admin Asst*
Tanya Peers, *Administration*
Thang Pham, *Controller*
EMP: 104
SQ FT: 5,000
SALES (est): 15.6MM **Privately Held**
WEB: www.rkprop.com
SIC: 6513 Apartment building operators

(P-11195)
REGENCY HILL ASSOCIATES
Also Called: La Mirage
6560 Ambrosia Dr, San Diego (92124-3133)
PHONE.................619 281-5200
Fax: 619 281-6551
David Nethercut, *President*
EMP: 58
SQ FT: 3,000
SALES (est): 3.2MM **Privately Held**
SIC: 6513 Apartment building operators

(P-11196)
RETIREMENT PROJECT-OAKMONT
Also Called: Oakmont Gardens
301 White Oak Dr Apt 293, Santa Rosa (95409-5948)
PHONE.................707 538-1914
Fax: 707 538-9364
Scott Scbissey, *Director*
Transamerica-Products One, *Partner*
Larry Stearley, *Executive*
Scott Bissey, *Exec Dir*
David Peironnet, *Exec Dir*
EMP: 70
SALES (est): 4.7MM **Privately Held**
SIC: 6513 Retirement hotel operation

6513 - Operators Of Apartment Buildings County (P-11197)

HQ: Transamerica Oakmont Corporation
600 Montgomery St Fl 16
San Francisco CA 94111

(P-11197)
RICK WEISS NEW HOPE APARTMENTS
1637 Appian Way, Santa Monica (90401-3249)
PHONE.................310 395-1026
Reint Alberts, Manager
Elsa Reynoso, Manager
EMP: 50
SALES: 707K Privately Held
SIC: 6513 Apartment building operators

(P-11198)
ROOM & BOARD INC
685 7th St, San Francisco (94103-4910)
PHONE.................415 252-9280
Andre Sharp, Senior Mgr
EMP: 121
SALES (corp-wide): 159.1MM Privately Held
SIC: 6513 Apartment building operators
PA: Room & Board, Inc.
4600 Olson Memorial Hwy
Minneapolis MN 55422
763 588-7525

(P-11199)
SAN DIMAS RETIREMENT CENTER (PA)
Also Called: Longwood Management
834 W Arrow Hwy, San Dimas (91773-2418)
PHONE.................909 599-8441
Fax: 909 599-4784
Frankie Ramirez, Administration
EMP: 70
SALES (est): 3.4MM Privately Held
SIC: 6513 8059 Retirement hotel operation; personal care home, with health care

(P-11200)
SENIOR RESOURCE GROUP LLC
Also Called: La Vida Del Mar Associates
850 Del Mar Downs Rd # 338, Solana Beach (92075-2725)
PHONE.................858 519-0890
Fax: 858 755-6239
Terry Oquest, Manager
EMP: 50
SALES (corp-wide): 70.7MM Privately Held
WEB: www.srgseniorliving.com
SIC: 6513 Apartment building operators
PA: Senior Resource Group, Llc
500 Stevens Ave Ste 100
Solana Beach CA 92075
858 792-9300

(P-11201)
SHARON CREST APTS
680 Sharon Park Dr Apt 25, Menlo Park (94025-6932)
PHONE.................650 854-5130
Cheryl Goodwin, General Mgr
EMP: 50 EST: 2001
SALES (est): 1MM Privately Held
SIC: 6513 Apartment building operators

(P-11202)
SHOREVIEW PRESERVATION LP
35 Lillian Ct, San Francisco (94124-2822)
PHONE.................415 647-6922
Fax: 415 647-6962
George Buchanan, Partner
EMP: 99
SALES: 950K Privately Held
SIC: 6513 Apartment building operators

(P-11203)
SIGN OF DOVE
Also Called: Sunrise Retirement Villa
707 Sunrise Ave Ofc, Roseville (95661-4531)
PHONE.................916 786-3277
Debbie Norman, Manager
EMP: 60 Privately Held
WEB: www.signdove.com
SIC: 6513 Retirement hotel operation

PA: Sign Of The Dove
22900 Ventura Blvd # 200
Woodland Hills CA 91364

(P-11204)
SILVERADO ORCHARDS (PA)
Also Called: Management Associates
601 Pope St Ofc, Saint Helena (94574-1275)
P.O. Box 102 (94574-0102)
PHONE.................707 963-1461
Alan Baldwin, General Ptnr
L Meade Baldwin, General Ptnr
EMP: 75
SQ FT: 80,000
SALES (est): 3.8MM Privately Held
WEB: www.silveradoorchards.com
SIC: 6513 Retirement hotel operation

(P-11205)
SNAPDRAGON PLACE 1 LP
702 County Square Dr, Ventura (93003-5450)
PHONE.................805 659-3791
Nancy Conk, Partner
EMP: 86 EST: 2014
SALES (est): 3.3MM Privately Held
SIC: 6513 Apartment building operators

(P-11206)
SOUTH BAY VLLA PRESERVATION LP
13111 S San Pedro St, Los Angeles (90061-2760)
PHONE.................310 516-7325
Leeann Morein, Vice Pres
EMP: 99
SALES: 950K
SALES (corp-wide): 3.5MM Privately Held
SIC: 6513 Apartment building operators
PA: South Bay Villa Preservation,
55 Beattie Pl
Greenville SC

(P-11207)
STATEWIDE ENTERPRISES INC
Also Called: Camelot Apartments
8151 Reseda Blvd Apt 101, Reseda (91335-1259)
PHONE.................818 709-4434
Rebecca Reyes, Manager
Alyssa Zura, Property Mgr
EMP: 90
SALES (corp-wide): 6.5MM Privately Held
SIC: 6513 Apartment building operators
PA: Statewide Enterprises, Inc.
4311 Wilshire Blvd # 600
Los Angeles CA 90010
323 934-5055

(P-11208)
STEADFAST MANAGEMENT CO INC
Also Called: Flanders Pointe Apts
15520 Tustin Village Way, Tustin (92780-4211)
PHONE.................714 542-2229
EMP: 251
SALES (corp-wide): 65.8MM Privately Held
SIC: 6513 6531 Apartment building operators; real estate managers
PA: Steadfast Management Company, Inc.
18100 Von Karman Ave
Irvine CA 92612
949 748-3000

(P-11209)
STERLING-ASE LTD PARTNERSHIP
Also Called: Sterling Inn
17738 Francesca Rd, Victorville (92395-5105)
PHONE.................760 951-9507
Fax: 760 245-0533
Aaron Koelsch, Managing Prtnr
Bill Ziprick, Ltd Ptnr
EMP: 125
SQ FT: 98,000
SALES (est): 5.9MM Privately Held
SIC: 6513 Retirement hotel operation

(P-11210)
SUNRISE RETIREMENT VILLA
707 Sunrise Ave Ofc, Roseville (95661-4531)
PHONE.................916 786-3277
Fax: 916 786-5931
Ed Latin, General Ptnr
Mike Klein, General Ptnr
EMP: 60
SQ FT: 180,000
SALES (est): 2.4MM Privately Held
SIC: 6513 Apartment building operators

(P-11211)
TANTRA LAKE PARTNERS LP
18802 Bardeen Ave, Irvine (92612-1521)
PHONE.................949 756-5959
Sares Regis Holdings, General Ptnr
David J Jacobson, Senior VP
Heiken Michael, E-Business
EMP: 120 EST: 1998
SALES (est): 4MM Privately Held
SIC: 6513 Apartment building operators

(P-11212)
TERRACINA MEADOWS APTS
4500 Tynebourne St F105, Sacramento (95834-2567)
PHONE.................916 419-0925
Fax: 916 419-0958
Gary Benn, COO
EMP: 50
SALES (est): 1.3MM Privately Held
SIC: 6513 Apartment building operators

(P-11213)
THE PINES LTD
1423 E Washington Ave, El Cajon (92019-2559)
PHONE.................619 447-1880
Helen Sue, Partner
Tim Sliger, General Mgr
EMP: 111
SALES (est): 4.1MM Privately Held
SIC: 6513 Apartment building operators

(P-11214)
TOPANGA VILLAS COMPANY
Also Called: Warner Villa
5807 Topanga Canyon Blvd, Woodland Hills (91367-4626)
PHONE.................818 884-8017
Fax: 818 884-8052
Catherine Hayes, Partner
Universal Properties, Partner
EMP: 100
SALES (est): 3.6MM Privately Held
SIC: 6513 Apartment building operators

(P-11215)
TPG REFLECTIONS II LLC
Also Called: Tpg/Calstrs
515 S Flower St, Los Angeles (90071-2201)
PHONE.................213 613-1900
James A Thomas,
Michael McGrath, Manager
EMP: 99
SALES: 950K Privately Held
SIC: 6513 Apartment building operators

(P-11216)
TREES APARTMENTS LLC
7030 Eigleberry St, Gilroy (95020-6465)
PHONE.................408 848-6400
Linda Mandolini, President
Jacqueline Javier, Admin Asst
EMP: 99
SALES (est): 1.3MM Privately Held
SIC: 6513 Apartment building operators

(P-11217)
TUOLUMNE CITY INV GRP II LP
Also Called: Tuolumne Cy Senior Apartments
18402 Tuolumne Rd Apt 31, Tuolumne (95379-9719)
PHONE.................209 928-1567
Rod Moore, Principal
EMP: 50
SALES (est): 872.6K Privately Held
SIC: 6513 Apartment building operators

(P-11218)
TURK & EDDY ASSOCIATES LP
201 Eddy St, San Francisco (94102-2715)
PHONE.................415 474-6524

Donald Falk, Exec Dir
EMP: 65
SALES (est): 548.7K Privately Held
SIC: 6513 Apartment building operators

(P-11219)
VASONA MANAGEMENT INC
Also Called: Marina Breeze
13931 Doolittle Dr, San Leandro (94577-5535)
PHONE.................510 352-8728
Willie Johnson, Principal
EMP: 277
SALES (corp-wide): 31MM Privately Held
SIC: 6513 Apartment building operators
PA: Vasona Management, Inc.
18 E Main St
Los Gatos CA 95030
408 354-4200

(P-11220)
VILLA PASEO SENIOR RESIDENCES
Also Called: Villa Paseo Palms
2818 Ramada Dr, Paso Robles (93446-3981)
PHONE.................805 227-4588
Jim Brooks, Controller
Tesa Doleman,
EMP: 99
SALES: 950K Privately Held
SIC: 6513 Apartment building operators

(P-11221)
VILLA SERRA CORPORATION
1320 Padre Dr Apt 103, Salinas (93901-2162)
PHONE.................831 754-5532
Fax: 831 754-5609
Chuck Major, Vice Pres
Andre Adema, General Mgr
Brenda Baugh, Human Res Dir
Cindy Tacktill, Director
Estelle Melendez, Manager
EMP: 65
SQ FT: 160,000
SALES (est): 5MM Privately Held
SIC: 6513 8361 Retirement hotel operation; geriatric residential care

(P-11222)
VILLAGE GLEN APARTMENTS
633 S Pasadena Ave Apt 45, Glendora (91740-6804)
PHONE.................626 963-4575
Julie Flores, Manager
EMP: 98
SALES (est): 1.5MM Privately Held
SIC: 6513 Apartment building operators

(P-11223)
VINTAGE SENIOR HOUSING LLC
Also Called: Vintage Simi Hills
5300 E Los Angeles Ave, Simi Valley (93063-4136)
PHONE.................805 583-3500
John Peter,
EMP: 325
SALES (corp-wide): 16.9MM Privately Held
SIC: 6513 Retirement hotel operation
PA: Senior Vintage Housing Llc
23 Corporate Plaza Dr # 190
Newport Beach CA 92660
949 719-4080

(P-11224)
VINTAGE SENIOR LIVING CORP
27783 Center Dr, Mission Viejo (92692-3603)
PHONE.................949 364-6210
EMP: 75
SALES (est): 378.6K Privately Held
SIC: 6513 Retirement hotel operation

(P-11225)
VINTAGE SENIOR MANAGEMENT INC
91 Napa Rd, Sonoma (95476-7691)
PHONE.................707 595-0009
EMP: 1163

PRODUCTS & SERVICES SECTION
6519 - Lessors Of Real Estate, NEC County (P-11247)

SALES (corp-wide): 69.9MM **Privately Held**
SIC: 6513 Retirement hotel operation
PA: Senior Vintage Management Inc
23 Corporate Plaza Dr # 190
Newport Beach CA 92660
949 719-4080

(P-11226)
VIVA GROUP INC
Also Called: Rent.com
11766 Wilshire Blvd # 300, Los Angeles (90025-6570)
PHONE 310 449-6400
Bill McKnight, *General Mgr*
Gretchen Humbert, *CFO*
Chris Cousin, *Administration*
Alain Avakian, *CTO*
Peijie Hu, *QA Dir*
EMP: 100
SALES (est): 6.8MM **Privately Held**
SIC: 6513 7375 Apartment building operators; information retrieval services

(P-11227)
WAMC COMPANY INC (PA)
Also Called: Cal West Enterprises
7420 Clairemont Mesa Blvd, San Diego (92111-1546)
PHONE 858 454-2753
Peter Valenti, *President*
James Bashor, *Principal*
EMP: 85
SALES (est): 1.9MM **Privately Held**
SIC: 6513 Apartment building operators

(P-11228)
WILLMARK CMMNTIES UNIV VLG INC (PA)
9948 Hibert St Ste 210, San Diego (92131-1034)
PHONE 858 271-0582
Mark Schmidt, *President*
Cindy Peel, *Executive*
EMP: 78
SQ FT: 2,000
SALES (est): 5.3MM **Privately Held**
SIC: 6513 1522 Apartment building operators; multi-family dwellings, new construction; condominium construction

(P-11229)
WILLOW GLEN VILLA A
1660 Gaton Dr, San Jose (95125-4534)
PHONE 408 266-1660
EMP: 70
SQ FT: 146,000
SALES: 3MM **Privately Held**
SIC: 6513

(P-11230)
WINDHAM AT SAINT AGNES
1100 E Spruce Ave Ofc, Fresno (93720-3314)
PHONE 559 449-8070
Fax: 559 449-0773
Sue Hefty, *Vice Pres*
Transamerica Realty Investment, *Owner*
Tina Barrios, *Asst Admin*
EMP: 66
SQ FT: 200,000
SALES (est): 3.5MM **Privately Held**
SIC: 6513 Retirement hotel operation

(P-11231)
WOODLAND RESIDENTIAL SERVICES
1381 E Gum Ave, Woodland (95776-4275)
PHONE 530 419-0059
Fax: 530 419-0052
Parm Kajley, *CEO*
Jack Kenealy, *Vice Pres*
Debbie Lancaster, *Manager*
EMP: 66
SALES (est): 4.2MM **Privately Held**
SIC: 6513 Apartment building operators

6514 Operators Of Dwellings, Except

(P-11232)
ACTION PROPERTY MANAGEMENT INC (PA)
2603 Main St Ste 500, Irvine (92614-4261)
PHONE 949 450-0202
Fax: 949 450-0303
Matthew Holbrook, *CEO*
Matthew Davidson, *COO*
Nicholas Michaelian, *Officer*
Jenifer Antonelli, *General Mgr*
Corinne Marrinan, *General Mgr*
EMP: 90
SQ FT: 18,000
SALES (est): 76.5MM **Privately Held**
SIC: 6514 8641 Residential building, four or fewer units: operation; homeowners' association

(P-11233)
BOQ
N9 56 Bldg 804 Rm 108, Lemoore (93246-0001)
PHONE 619 556-0266
John Young, *Principal*
Aurora Francisco, *Accounting Mgr*
Shara Bryant, *Manager*
EMP: 60
SALES (est): 2.3MM **Privately Held**
SIC: 6514 Dwelling operators, except apartments

(P-11234)
EAH INC (PA)
Also Called: EAH SAN PABLO
2169 Francisco Blvd E B, San Rafael (94901-5509)
PHONE 415 258-1800
Mary Murtagh, *CEO*
Linn Warren, *Vice Chairman*
Laura Hall, *CEO*
Alvin Bonnett, *Senior VP*
Karen Belanger, *Executive*
EMP: 70 **EST:** 1968
SQ FT: 30,000
SALES: 38.5MM **Privately Held**
WEB: www.centennialvillage.com
SIC: 6514 Residential building, four or fewer units: operation

(P-11235)
HOME PORT INC
5030 Union Ave, San Jose (95124-5432)
PHONE 408 377-4134
Peter Villareal, *Manager*
EMP: 99
SALES: 225.3K
SALES (corp-wide): 41.9K **Privately Held**
SIC: 6514 6513 Residential building, four or fewer units: operation; apartment building operators
PA: Stanford Mid-Peninsula Urban Coalition
303 Vintage Park Dr # 250
Foster City CA 94404
650 356-2900

(P-11236)
MENLO GATEWAY INC
Also Called: MIDPEN HOUSING
303 Vintage Park Dr # 250, Foster City (94404-1166)
PHONE 650 356-2900
Mark Battey, *Chairman*
Peter Villareal, *Principal*
Luina Palchak, *Manager*
EMP: 99
SALES: 1.9MM
SALES (corp-wide): 41.9K **Privately Held**
SIC: 6514 6513 Residential building, four or fewer units: operation; apartment building operators
PA: Stanford Mid-Peninsula Urban Coalition
303 Vintage Park Dr # 250
Foster City CA 94404
650 356-2900

(P-11237)
MERRILL GARDENS
Also Called: Country Suites By Carlson
2860 Country Dr Ofc, Fremont (94536-5338)
PHONE 510 790-1645
Dan Bodily, *Owner*
EMP: 65
SALES (est): 1.7MM **Privately Held**
SIC: 6514 Dwelling operators, except apartments

(P-11238)
MIDPEN RESIDENT SERVICES CORP
303 Vintage Park Dr # 250, Foster City (94404-1166)
PHONE 650 356-2965
Fran Wagstaff, *President*
Lory Candelf, *Vice Pres*
Deena Soulon, *Asst Sec*
EMP: 300
SALES: 5.6MM
SALES (corp-wide): 41.9K **Privately Held**
SIC: 6514 6513 Residential building, four or fewer units: operation; apartment building operators
PA: Stanford Mid-Peninsula Urban Coalition
303 Vintage Park Dr # 250
Foster City CA 94404
650 356-2900

(P-11239)
MP MORSE COURT ASSOCIATES
Also Called: Morse Court Apartments
825 Morse Ave, Sunnyvale (94085-3070)
PHONE 408 734-9442
Matthew O Franklin, *Partner*
Luina Palchak, *Manager*
EMP: 99
SALES: 70K
SALES (corp-wide): 41.9K **Privately Held**
SIC: 6514 6513 Residential building, four or fewer units: operation; apartment building operators
PA: Stanford Mid-Peninsula Urban Coalition
303 Vintage Park Dr # 250
Foster City CA 94404
650 356-2900

(P-11240)
PROFESSIONAL CMNTY MGT CAL INC
Also Called: Pcm
27051 Towne Centre Dr # 200, Foothill Ranch (92610-2819)
PHONE 949 768-7261
Jeffrey Olson, *CEO*
Jim Fraker, *Vice Pres*
Ed Thira, *Info Tech Mgr*
EMP: 80
SALES (corp-wide): 41.3MM **Privately Held**
WEB: www.pcm-ca.com
SIC: 6514 Dwelling operators, except apartments
PA: Professional Community Management Of California
27051 Towne Centre Dr # 200
Foothill Ranch CA 92610
800 369-7260

(P-11241)
SARATOGA COURT INC
Also Called: MID PENN HOUSING
18855 Cox Ave, Saratoga (95070-4159)
PHONE 408 866-1392
Matthew Franklin, *President*
Peter Villareal, *Manager*
EMP: 99
SALES: 318.8K
SALES (corp-wide): 41.9K **Privately Held**
SIC: 6514 6513 Residential building, four or fewer units: operation; apartment building operators
PA: Stanford Mid-Peninsula Urban Coalition
303 Vintage Park Dr # 250
Foster City CA 94404
650 356-2900

(P-11242)
VIVENTE 1 INC
Also Called: MIDPEN HOUSING
2400 Enborg Ln, San Jose (95128-2641)
PHONE 408 279-2706
Matthew O Franklin, *President*
EMP: 99
SALES: 407.5K
SALES (corp-wide): 41.9K **Privately Held**
SIC: 6514 6513 Residential building, four or fewer units: operation; apartment building operators
PA: Stanford Mid-Peninsula Urban Coalition
303 Vintage Park Dr # 250
Foster City CA 94404
650 356-2900

(P-11243)
VIVENTE 2 INC
5347 Dent Ave, San Jose (95118-2900)
PHONE 408 279-2706
Matthew O Franklin, *President*
Peter Villareal, *Manager*
EMP: 99
SALES: 506.8K
SALES (corp-wide): 41.9K **Privately Held**
SIC: 6514 6513 Residential building, four or fewer units: operation; apartment building operators
PA: Stanford Mid-Peninsula Urban Coalition
303 Vintage Park Dr # 250
Foster City CA 94404
650 356-2900

6515 Operators of Residential Mobile Home

(P-11244)
BARBACCIA PROPERTIES
Also Called: Villa Theresa Mobile Home Park
165 Blossom Hill Rd, San Jose (95123-5938)
PHONE 408 225-1010
Fax: 408 365-9834
Cy Barbaccia, *Partner*
Eva Antonio, *Partner*
Lena Barbaccia, *Partner*
Lou Barbaccia, *Partner*
EMP: 80
SQ FT: 5,000
SALES: 7MM **Privately Held**
SIC: 6515 7999 Mobile home site operators; golf driving range

(P-11245)
R C ROBERTS & CO (PA)
Also Called: Sands Rv Resort
801 A St, San Rafael (94901-3010)
PHONE 415 456-8600
Barbel Roberts,
Troy Leach, *Info Tech Mgr*
Niels Roberts,
Scott Roberts,
EMP: 216 **EST:** 1977
SQ FT: 3,000
SALES (est): 11.5MM **Privately Held**
SIC: 6515 7011 6531 Mobile home site operators; resort hotel; real estate agents & managers

(P-11246)
WATERHOUSE MANAGEMENT CORP
500 Giuseppe Ct Ste 2, Roseville (95678-6305)
PHONE 916 772-4918
Fax: 916 772-4923
Kenneth Watershouse, *President*
EMP: 150
SQ FT: 10,000
SALES (est): 9.1MM **Privately Held**
SIC: 6515 Mobile home site operators

6519 Lessors Of Real Estate, NEC

(P-11247)
A G PACEMAN INC
1100 Industrial Rd Ste 11, San Carlos (94070-4131)
PHONE 650 592-7282
Fax: 650 592-7284
Darrell W Leong, *President*
Anna Leong, *Treasurer*
EMP: 55
SQ FT: 30,000
SALES (est): 2.6MM **Privately Held**
SIC: 6519 Real property lessors

6519 - Lessors Of Real Estate, NEC County (P-11248)

(P-11248)
AB/SW 70 S LAKE OWNER LLC
70 S Lake Ave, Pasadena (91101-4703)
PHONE.................................650 571-2200
Nancy Chau, *Vice Pres*
EMP: 50
SALES (est): 468.4K **Privately Held**
SIC: 6519 Real property lessors

(P-11249)
CALIFRN/NVADA DEVELOPMENTS LLC
3010 Old Ranch Pkwy # 330, Seal Beach (90740-2764)
PHONE.................................714 677-5721
James R Wheeler,
EMP: 128
SALES (est): 76.2K
SALES (corp-wide): 6.1B **Publicly Held**
SIC: 6519 Real property lessors
HQ: Ese Land Corporation
300 Liberty St
Peoria IL

(P-11250)
COLTON REAL ESTATE GROUP (PA)
Also Called: Mvp Partners
515 Cabrillo Park Dr # 305, Santa Ana (92701-5016)
PHONE.................................949 475-4200
Dave Colton, *President*
John Clintock, *CFO*
John Mc Clintock, *CFO*
Emma Werlin, *Director*
EMP: 55
SQ FT: 7,000
SALES (est): 6.5MM **Privately Held**
SIC: 6519 Real property lessors

(P-11251)
EASTLAND TOWER PARTNERSHIP
Also Called: Eastland Executive Office
100 N Barranca St Ste 900, West Covina (91791-1662)
PHONE.................................626 858-2000
Ziad Alahassen, *Partner*
EMP: 50
SALES (est): 2.4MM **Privately Held**
SIC: 6519 Real property lessors

(P-11252)
ELEVATE PROPERTY SERVICES LP
19700 Fairchild Ste 150, Irvine (92612-2500)
PHONE.................................562 219-2101
Andrew Layland, *Principal*
Kerrigan Capital LLC, *General Ptnr*
EMP: 50 EST: 2009
SALES (est): 2.5MM **Privately Held**
SIC: 6519 Real property lessors

(P-11253)
ESSEX QUEEN ANNE LLC
Also Called: Essex Property
1100 Park Pl Ste 200, San Mateo (94403-7107)
PHONE.................................650 849-1600
Michael Schall, *President*
Jannah Abdo, *Accountant*
EMP: 531
SALES (est): 14.9MM **Privately Held**
SIC: 6519 Real property lessors
PA: Essex Portfolio, L.P.
925 E Meadow Dr
Palo Alto CA 94303

(P-11254)
EVERETT MALL 01 LLC
12411 Ventura Blvd, Studio City (91604-2407)
PHONE.................................818 505-6777
Alan Fox,
EMP: 50
SALES (est): 1.3MM **Privately Held**
SIC: 6519 Real property lessors

(P-11255)
FREMONT REALTY CAPITAL LP
199 Fremont St Fl 19, San Francisco (94105-2255)
PHONE.................................415 284-8665
Fax: 415 284-8187
Claude J Zinngrabe Jr, *Managing Prtnr*
Victor Kwok, *CFO*
Ashminder Singh, *Vice Pres*
Stuart I Blackie, *Vice Pres*
Kathleen Shurling, *Manager*
EMP: 74
SQ FT: 100,000
SALES (est): 3.8MM
SALES (corp-wide): 38.8MM **Privately Held**
WEB: www.fremontrealtycapital.com
SIC: 6519 8742 Real property lessors; real estate consultant
PA: Fremont Group, L.L.C.
199 Fremont St Ste 2500
San Francisco CA 94105
415 284-8880

(P-11256)
IC BP III HOLDINGS XV LLC
1 Sansome St Fl 15, San Francisco (94104-4449)
PHONE.................................415 273-4250
Ray Kim, *Principal*
Mark Bailey,
EMP: 50 EST: 2015
SALES (est): 832.7K **Privately Held**
SIC: 6519 7389 Sub-lessors of real estate;

(P-11257)
LAACO LTD (PA)
Also Called: Storage West
431 W 7th St, Los Angeles (90014-1601)
PHONE.................................213 622-1254
Fax: 213 622-5643
Karen L Hathaway, *President*
Bryan J Cusworth, *CFO*
John K Hathaway, *Vice Pres*
Steven K Hathaway, *Vice Pres*
Charles Michaels, *Vice Pres*
EMP: 125
SQ FT: 100,000
SALES (est): 18.8MM **Privately Held**
SIC: 6519 7997 7011 5812 Real property lessors; yacht club, membership; hotels; resort hotel; eating places

(P-11258)
LYON REALTY
4330 Golden Center Dr C, Kelsey (95667-6232)
PHONE.................................530 295-4444
Teresa Burroughs, *Broker*
Mary Meyer, *Broker*
Shawn Allan, *Real Est Agnt*
Aaron Bate, *Real Est Agnt*
Andi Wagner, *Real Est Agnt*
EMP: 168
SALES (corp-wide): 4.1MM **Privately Held**
SIC: 6519 6531 Real property lessors; real estate brokers & agents
PA: Lyon Realty
2280 Del Paso Rd Ste 100
Sacramento CA 95834
916 574-8800

(P-11259)
MT EDEN NURSERY CO INC (PA)
2124 Bering Dr, San Jose (95131-2013)
PHONE.................................408 213-5777
Yoshimi Shibata, *President*
EMP: 50
SALES (est): 2.8MM **Privately Held**
SIC: 6519 Farm land leasing

(P-11260)
OCEAN VIEW MANOR LP ◆
Also Called: Ocean View Manor Apartments
3533 Empleo St, San Luis Obispo (93401-7334)
PHONE.................................805 781-3088
John Fowler, *CEO*
Griffin Moore, *General Mgr*
EMP: 70 EST: 2016
SQ FT: 10,000
SALES (est): 587.4K **Privately Held**
SIC: 6519 Real property lessors

(P-11261)
PACIFIC EQUITIES CAPTL
Also Called: V G Pacific Equities
1640 S Sepulveda Blvd # 308, Los Angeles (90025-7536)
P.O. Box 25991 (90025-0991)
PHONE.................................310 477-5300
David S Rosen, *President*
Ron Pelleg, *Exec Dir*
Harvey Rosen, *Admin Sec*
EMP: 75 EST: 1985
SALES (est): 4.7MM **Privately Held**
WEB: www.pacificequities.net
SIC: 6519 Landholding office

(P-11262)
PACIFIC YGNACIO CORPORATION
500 Ygnacio Valley Rd # 340, Walnut Creek (94596-3840)
PHONE.................................925 939-3275
Fax: 925 939-3278
Robin Andrews, *Manager*
EMP: 62 EST: 1998
SQ FT: 105,495
SALES (est): 1.9MM
SALES (corp-wide): 18.9MM **Privately Held**
WEB: www.paceagle.com
SIC: 6519 Real property lessors
PA: Pacific Eagle Holdings Corporation
353 Sacramento St
San Francisco CA 94111
925 866-9662

(P-11263)
PLDA INC
2570 N 1st St 218, San Jose (95131-1035)
PHONE.................................408 273-4528
Jean-Yves Brena, *President*
Owen Lee, *General Mgr*
EMP: 55
SALES (est): 1.7MM **Privately Held**
WEB: www.plda.com
SIC: 6519 Real property lessors

(P-11264)
SAN JACINTO UNIFIED SCHOOL
Also Called: Facilities & Operations
905 Industrial Way, San Jacinto (92582-3890)
PHONE.................................951 654-7769
John I Norman, *President*
Jane Logan, *Executive*
Jennifer Williams, *Executive*
Maria Ramirez, *Office Mgr*
Monica Alcantara, *Admin Sec*
EMP: 64
SALES: 0 **Privately Held**
SIC: 6519 7359 Real property lessors; equipment rental & leasing

6531 Real Estate Agents & Managers

(P-11265)
1370 REALTY CORP
14545 Friar St Ste 101, Van Nuys (91411-2357)
PHONE.................................818 817-0092
Kambiz Merabi, *President*
EMP: 180
SQ FT: 16,400
SALES (est): 4.9MM **Privately Held**
SIC: 6531 Real estate agents & managers

(P-11266)
15TH ISLAND LLC
405 15th St, San Diego (92101-7534)
PHONE.................................619 321-1111
William Persky, *Principal*
Evan Gerber, *Manager*
EMP: 73
SALES (est): 2.6MM **Privately Held**
SIC: 6531 Real estate agents & managers

(P-11267)
1755 EFM 1 LLC
1755 E M L King Jr Blvd, Los Angeles (90058)
PHONE.................................323 231-4174
Tim English,
EMP: 70
SALES (est): 1.8MM **Privately Held**
SIC: 6531 6513 Rental agent, real estate; apartment building operators

(P-11268)
2300 WEST EL SECUNDO LP
11916 Eucalyptus Ave, Hawthorne (90250-2820)
PHONE.................................310 769-6669
Evelyn Revellame, *Controller*
EMP: 99
SALES (est): 2.1MM **Privately Held**
SIC: 6531 Real estate managers

(P-11269)
600B AG-LO OWNER L P
Also Called: LPC West
600 B St Ste 2480, San Diego (92101-4527)
PHONE.................................619 234-7036
Deborah Valdivia, *Manager*
Brig Black, *Senior VP*
Rosanna Orsborn, *Administration*
EMP: 75
SQ FT: 359,217
SALES (est): 4MM **Privately Held**
SIC: 6531 Real estate managers

(P-11270)
A F GILMORE COMPANY
6301 W 3rd St, Los Angeles (90036-3154)
P.O. Box 480314 (90048-1314)
PHONE.................................323 939-1191
Fax: 323 939-5248
Henry Hilty Jr, *President*
Ernest Mauritson, *Vice Pres*
Dawn Aberg, *Executive Asst*
Sherif Barsoum, *Software Dev*
EMP: 55 EST: 1915
SALES (est): 5.8MM **Privately Held**
SIC: 6531 Real estate managers

(P-11271)
A G SPANOS MANAGEMENT INC
10100 Trinity Pkwy Fl 5, Stockton (95219-7242)
P.O. Box 7126 (95267-0126)
PHONE.................................209 478-7954
Alexander G Spanos, *President*
Jeremiah T Murphy, *CFO*
George Spanos, *Corp Secy*
Nanette Hatch, *Admin Sec*
EMP: 50 EST: 1967
SQ FT: 5,000
SALES (est): 1.8MM
SALES (corp-wide): 58.4MM **Privately Held**
SIC: 6531 Real estate managers
PA: A.G. Spanos Companies
10100 Trinity Pkwy Fl 5
Stockton CA 95219
209 478-7954

(P-11272)
ABBEY PARTNER VI
Also Called: Airpark Partners
7207 Arlington Ave Ste D, Riverside (92503-1550)
PHONE.................................951 785-8800
Don Abbey, *Owner*
Brett Alerecht, *Vice Pres*
EMP: 50
SALES (est): 830.9K
SALES (corp-wide): 4.6MM **Privately Held**
WEB: www.theabbeyco.com
SIC: 6531 Real estate managers
PA: Abbey-Properties Llc
12447 Lewis St Ste 203
Garden Grove CA 92840
562 435-2100

(P-11273)
ABINGTON HOMES INC
4364 Bonita Rd Ste 442, Bonita (91902-1421)
PHONE.................................619 208-9486
Richard A Lawson, *CEO*
EMP: 58
SALES (est): 1.5MM **Privately Held**
WEB: www.abingtonhomes.com
SIC: 6531 Real estate brokers & agents

PRODUCTS & SERVICES SECTION
6531 - Real Estate Agents & Managers County (P-11296)

(P-11274)
ABODE COMMUNITIES
1149 S Hill St Fl 7, Los Angeles (90015-2219)
PHONE..................213 629-2702
Robin Hughes, *President*
Rick Saperstein, *CFO*
Kenneth Krug, *Chairman*
Sandra Kulli, *Chairman*
Gio Aliano, *Vice Pres*
EMP: 150
SQ FT: 10,094
SALES: 6.3MM **Privately Held**
SIC: 6531 8712 8711 Housing authority operator; architectural services; engineering services

(P-11275)
ACTUAL REALITY PICTURES INC
Also Called: The Residence
16030 Ventura Blvd # 380, Encino (91436-2778)
PHONE..................818 325-8800
Rj Cutler, *President*
EMP: 50
SALES (est): 1.9MM **Privately Held**
SIC: 6531 Real estate brokers & agents

(P-11276)
ADAMS & BARNES INC
Also Called: Century 21
433 W Foothill Blvd, Monrovia (91016-2025)
PHONE..................626 358-1858
Fax: 626 303-8733
Lou Jean Barnes, *President*
Andrew Barnes, *Treasurer*
Thomas E Adams, *Vice Pres*
Scott Vejar, *Broker*
Ruben Contreras, *Real Est Agnt*
EMP: 50
SALES (est): 4.1MM **Privately Held**
WEB: www.c21ab.com
SIC: 6531 Real estate agent, residential

(P-11277)
AES CORPORATION
1100 N Harbor Dr, Redondo Beach (90277-2017)
PHONE..................310 318-7510
Gogita Gogiberidze, *Branch Mgr*
Sergio Silva, *VP Finance*
Steven Winters, *Senior Mgr*
EMP: 76
SALES (corp-wide): 14.9B **Publicly Held**
SIC: 6531 Real estate brokers & agents
PA: The Aes Corporation
4300 Wilson Blvd Ste 1100
Arlington VA 22203
703 522-1315

(P-11278)
AGUA CALIENTE DEVELOPMENT AUTH
5401 Dinah Shore Dr, Palm Springs (92264-5970)
PHONE..................760 699-6800
Richard M Milanovich, *Chairman*
EMP: 99
SALES (est): 6.5MM
SALES (corp-wide): 182MM **Privately Held**
SIC: 6531 Real estate leasing & rentals
PA: Agua Caliente Band Of Cahuilla Indians
5401 Dinah Shore Dr
Palm Springs CA 92264
760 699-6800

(P-11279)
ALAIN PINEL REALTORS
Junipero Between 5 & 6 # 56, Carmel (93921)
P.O. Box 7249 (93921-7249)
PHONE..................831 622-1040
Fax: 831 622-1050
Ron Kirendole, *Manager*
Jill Rowlette, *Sales Associate*
Lynda M Ballin, *Real Est Agnt*
Mark A Duchesne, *Real Est Agnt*
William Faber, *Real Est Agnt*
EMP: 65
SALES (est): 3.3MM **Privately Held**
SIC: 6531 Real estate brokers & agents

(P-11280)
ALAIN PINEL REALTORS INC
2001 Union St Ste 200, San Francisco (94123-4135)
PHONE..................415 814-6690
Fax: 415 441-1750
Paul Hulme, *CEO*
Carol Burnett, *Vice Pres*
James Morris, *Broker*
Todd Van Laanen, *Broker*
Paul Radcliffe, *Sr Associate*
EMP: 62
SALES (corp-wide): 7.9MM **Privately Held**
SIC: 6531 Real estate brokers & agents
PA: Alain Pinel Realtors, Inc.
12772 Sartga Snyvl Rd # 1000
Saratoga CA 95070
408 741-1111

(P-11281)
ALAIN PINEL REALTORS INC
101 Nellen Ave, Corte Madera (94925-1180)
PHONE..................415 755-1111
Steve Dickason, *Vice Pres*
Judith Belmont, *Real Est Agnt*
Beth Rosener, *Real Est Agnt*
EMP: 62
SALES (corp-wide): 7.9MM **Privately Held**
SIC: 6531 Real estate brokers & agents
PA: Alain Pinel Realtors, Inc.
12772 Sartga Snyvl Rd # 1000
Saratoga CA 95070
408 741-1111

(P-11282)
ALAIN PINEL REALTORS INC
520 S El Camino Real # 100, San Mateo (94402-1714)
PHONE..................650 548-1111
Fax: 650 548-1238
Ron Gable, *Manager*
Karen Gansky, *Treasurer*
Gwen Bridges, *CTO*
Joanne Clark, *Info Tech Dir*
Helen Seeley, *Info Tech Mgr*
EMP: 70
SALES (corp-wide): 7.9MM **Privately Held**
SIC: 6531 Real estate brokers & agents
PA: Alain Pinel Realtors, Inc.
12772 Sartga Snyvl Rd # 1000
Saratoga CA 95070
408 741-1111

(P-11283)
ALAIN PINEL REALTORS INC
750 University Ave # 150, Los Gatos (95032-7697)
PHONE..................408 358-1111
Jeff Barnett, *Manager*
Suzanne Butts, *Office Admin*
Rose Gogarty, *Admin Asst*
Sheila Gennaro, *Human Res Dir*
Mikala Caune, *Sales Associate*
EMP: 55
SALES (corp-wide): 7.9MM **Privately Held**
SIC: 6531 Real estate brokers & agents
PA: Alain Pinel Realtors, Inc.
12772 Sartga Snyvl Rd # 1000
Saratoga CA 95070
408 741-1111

(P-11284)
ALAIN PINEL REALTORS INC
2911 Cleveland Ave, Santa Rosa (95403-2715)
PHONE..................707 636-3800
Dennis Park, *Branch Mgr*
Ellen Crusoe, *Real Est Agnt*
EMP: 51
SALES (corp-wide): 7.9MM **Privately Held**
SIC: 6531 Real estate brokers & agents
PA: Alain Pinel Realtors, Inc.
12772 Sartga Snyvl Rd # 1000
Saratoga CA 95070
408 741-1111

(P-11285)
ALAIN PINEL REALTORS INC
900 Main St Ste 101, Pleasanton (94566-6073)
PHONE..................925 251-1111
Fax: 925 396-6180
Carol Rodoni, *Owner*
Timothy McGuire, *COO*
Daniel Alpher, *Webmaster*
Sally Martin, *Property Mgr*
Linda Traurig, *Property Mgr*
EMP: 62
SALES (corp-wide): 7.9MM **Privately Held**
SIC: 6531 Real estate brokers & agents
PA: Alain Pinel Realtors, Inc.
12772 Sartga Snyvl Rd # 1000
Saratoga CA 95070
408 741-1111

(P-11286)
ALAIN PINEL REALTORS INC
1440 Chapin Ave Ste 200, Burlingame (94010-4011)
PHONE..................650 375-1111
Fax: 650 931-2099
Janice Woods, *Branch Mgr*
Kimberly P Parker, *COO*
Blaise Lofland, *Executive*
Baron J Littleton Sr, *Software Dev*
Cathy Littlefield, *Broker*
EMP: 62
SALES (corp-wide): 7.9MM **Privately Held**
SIC: 6531 Real estate brokers & agents
PA: Alain Pinel Realtors, Inc.
12772 Sartga Snyvl Rd # 1000
Saratoga CA 95070
408 741-1111

(P-11287)
ALAIN PINEL REALTORS INC
578 University Ave, Palo Alto (94301-1901)
PHONE..................650 323-1111
Fax: 650 323-1143
Robert Gerlach, *Manager*
Sandy Harris, *Property Mgr*
Denise Simons, *Property Mgr*
Scott Symon, *Property Mgr*
Ursula Fisher, *Manager*
EMP: 120
SALES (corp-wide): 7.9MM **Privately Held**
SIC: 6531 Real estate brokers & agents
PA: Alain Pinel Realtors, Inc.
12772 Sartga Snyvl Rd # 1000
Saratoga CA 95070
408 741-1111

(P-11288)
ALAIN PINEL REALTORS INC
167 S San Antonio Rd # 1, Los Altos (94022-3055)
PHONE..................650 941-1111
Fax: 650 941-1411
Gary Wheeler, *Manager*
Susan Sweeley, *Trustee*
Cheryl Okuno, *Executive*
Steve Brinkman, *Admin Mgr*
Alex Liu, *Broker*
EMP: 100
SALES (corp-wide): 7.9MM **Privately Held**
SIC: 6531 Real estate brokers & agents
PA: Alain Pinel Realtors, Inc.
12772 Sartga Snyvl Rd # 1000
Saratoga CA 95070
408 741-1111

(P-11289)
ALAIN PINEL REALTORS INC
1550 El Camino Real # 100, Menlo Park (94025-4117)
PHONE..................650 462-1111
Mary Gebhardt, *Manager*
Mary Gephardt, *Executive*
Monica Corman, *Broker*
Anna Park, *Broker*
Dennis Park, *Broker*
EMP: 80
SALES (corp-wide): 7.9MM **Privately Held**
SIC: 6531 Real estate brokers & agents
PA: Alain Pinel Realtors, Inc.
12772 Sartga Snyvl Rd # 1000
Saratoga CA 95070
408 741-1111

(P-11290)
ALAMEDA PRODUCE MARKET LLC
761 Terminal St Ste 2, Los Angeles (90021-1111)
PHONE..................213 221-3400
Richard Meruelo,
Miguel Echemendia, *Vice Pres*
EMP: 80 **EST:** 1997
SQ FT: 22,000
SALES (est): 4.6MM **Privately Held**
SIC: 6531 Real estate agent, commercial

(P-11291)
ALLIANCE BAY FUNDING INC
37600 Central Ct Ste 264, Newark (94560-3440)
PHONE..................510 742-6600
Dawar Lodin, *President*
EMP: 100
SALES (est): 5.4MM **Privately Held**
SIC: 6531 Real estate agents & managers

(P-11292)
ALLIANT ASSET MGT CO LLC (PA)
21600 Oxnard St Ste 1200, Woodland Hills (91367-4949)
PHONE..................818 668-2805
Fax: 310 668-2828
Shawn Horwitz, *Mng Member*
Anil Advani, *Sr Corp Ofcr*
Allan Schnier, *Exec VP*
Elizabeth Briones, *Senior VP*
Melvin Gevisser, *Vice Pres*
EMP: 81
SQ FT: 19,816
SALES (est): 18.4MM **Privately Held**
SIC: 6531 Broker of manufactured homes, on site

(P-11293)
ALLISON DOWDY
1045 College Ave, Santa Rosa (95404-4112)
PHONE..................707 303-3472
Allison Dowdy, *Principal*
EMP: 65
SALES: 300K **Privately Held**
SIC: 6531 Real estate agents & managers

(P-11294)
ALLMARK INC (PA)
10070 Arrow Rte, Rancho Cucamonga (91730-4194)
PHONE..................909 989-7556
Wayne Slavitt, *CEO*
Michael Krcelic, *President*
Pat Price, *CFO*
Steve Strebel, *CFO*
Michael Payne, *Treasurer*
EMP: 65
SQ FT: 3,167
SALES (est): 8.3MM **Privately Held**
WEB: www.allmarkproperties.com
SIC: 6531 Real estate managers

(P-11295)
ALTERA REAL ESTATE
33522 Niguel Rd Ste 200, Dana Point (92629-4009)
PHONE..................949 547-7351
Matt Brabeck, *Principal*
EMP: 356
SALES (est): 7.4MM **Privately Held**
SIC: 6531 Real estate brokers & agents

(P-11296)
AMERICAN HOMEOWNERS & RENTERS
334 W 120th St Apt 7, Los Angeles (90061-1348)
P.O. Box 61175, Pasadena (91116-7175)
PHONE..................310 913-9263
Anthony Brown, *Exec Dir*
EMP: 50
SALES: 950K **Privately Held**
SIC: 6531 Housing authority operator

6531 - Real Estate Agents & Managers County (P-11297)

(P-11297)
AMERICAN MARKETING SYSTEMS INC
Also Called: Amsi Real Estate Services
2800 Van Ness Ave, San Francisco (94109-1426)
PHONE................................800 747-7784
Zoya Lee Smithton, *Director*
Roberto Estrada, *Sales Staff*
Robb Fleischer, *Director*
Ken Valencia, *Director*
Casey Belway, *Manager*
EMP: 75
SQ FT: 8,000
SALES: 20MM **Privately Held**
WEB: www.amsisf.com
SIC: 6531 Real estate brokers & agents

(P-11298)
AMERICAN REALTY CENTRE INC
120 S Glendale Ave, Glendale (91205-1195)
PHONE................................323 666-6111
Fax: 818 507-9157
Peter P Chorebanian, *President*
Alan Artunian, *Real Est Agnt*
Stephen Hampar, *Real Est Agnt*
EMP: 55
SQ FT: 1,961
SALES (est): 2.9MM **Privately Held**
WEB: www.americanrealtycentre.com
SIC: 6531 Real estate brokers & agents

(P-11299)
AMR APPRAISALS INC
Also Called: Got Appraisals
5000 Executive Pkwy # 270, San Ramon (94583-4282)
P.O. Box 2426 (94583-7426)
PHONE................................925 400-6066
Joe M Reid, *President*
Nicole Stefani, *Business Mgr*
Nick Roberson, *Opers Mgr*
EMP: 54
SALES (est): 5.6MM **Privately Held**
SIC: 6531 Appraiser, real estate

(P-11300)
APPRAISER LOFT LLC
3027 Townsgate Rd Ste 140, Westlake Village (91361-5871)
PHONE................................858 832-8334
Aman Makka, *Mng Member*
Dawn Burton, *Natl Sales Mgr*
Brandon Goldstein, *Natl Sales Mgr*
Brad Wulick, *Natl Sales Mgr*
EMP: 50 EST: 2007
SQ FT: 20,000
SALES (est): 2.8MM **Privately Held**
SIC: 6531 Appraiser, real estate

(P-11301)
ARAKELYAN ARAM
2115 Balmain Way, Glendale (91206-1106)
PHONE................................818 247-0191
Aram Arakelyan, *Owner*
EMP: 50
SALES: 4MM **Privately Held**
SIC: 6531 Real estate agents & managers

(P-11302)
ARCADIA MANAGEMENT SERVICE CO
150 Almaden Blvd Ste 1100, San Jose (95113-2030)
P.O. Box 5368 (95150-5368)
PHONE................................408 286-4440
Michael Fletcher, *President*
EMP: 50
SALES (est): 3MM **Privately Held**
SIC: 6531 Cooperative apartment manager

(P-11303)
AREA HOUSING AUTHORITY (PA)
1400 W Hillcrest Dr, Newbury Park (91320-2721)
PHONE................................805 480-9991
Douglas A Tapking, *Exec Dir*
George McGehee, *General Mgr*
Alexandria Banks, *Executive Asst*
Dennise Avila, *Info Tech Mgr*
Denise Howells, *Accounting Mgr*
EMP: 50
SQ FT: 24,000
SALES: 33.7MM **Privately Held**
WEB: www.ahacv.org
SIC: 6531 Housing authority operator

(P-11304)
ARGENT MANAGEMENT CO LLC
2392 Morse Ave, Irvine (92614-6234)
PHONE................................949 777-4070
Rosemarie Dyvig, *Mng Member*
David Cecchele, *Senior VP*
Joe Garcia, *Vice Pres*
Andrew Wilson, *Vice Pres*
Julia Suslavage, *Executive Asst*
EMP: 72
SALES (est): 7.9MM **Privately Held**
SIC: 6531 Rental agent, real estate

(P-11305)
ARGON ENTERPRISES INC
Also Called: Pacific Properties Realty
13658 Hawthorne Blvd # 306, Hawthorne (90250-5824)
PHONE................................310 349-8777
Armando Gonzalez, *President*
EMP: 92
SQ FT: 5,000
SALES (est): 3MM **Privately Held**
SIC: 6531 Multiple listing service, real estate

(P-11306)
ARROYO & COATES INC
425 California St # 2000, San Francisco (94104-2102)
PHONE................................415 445-7800
Tom Coates, *Ch of Bd*
Brad Colton, *President*
Pedro Arroyo, *Corp Secy*
Dan Singer, *Controller*
EMP: 60
SQ FT: 7,500
SALES (est): 3.3MM **Privately Held**
WEB: www.acventures.com
SIC: 6531 Real estate brokers & agents

(P-11307)
ASSOCIATED REALTORS
27411 Viana, Mission Viejo (92692-3211)
PHONE................................949 813-1888
Fax: 949 837-7974
Heleen Chaban, *Partner*
Helene Chaban, *Partner*
Edward Coury, *Partner*
Lee Jacobs, *COO*
Helene Chaben, *Office Mgr*
EMP: 80 EST: 1976
SQ FT: 5,000
SALES: 5MM **Privately Held**
WEB: www.ocrelocate.com
SIC: 6531 Real estate brokers & agents

(P-11308)
ASTRO REALTY INC
Also Called: Century 21
11305 183rd St, Cerritos (90703-5434)
PHONE................................562 924-3381
Fax: 562 924-5951
Louis Rosencrance, *President*
EMP: 65
SALES (est): 2MM **Privately Held**
SIC: 6531 Real estate agent, residential

(P-11309)
AUCHANTE INC
Also Called: Remax VIP
6730 Florence Ave, Bell Gardens (90201-4946)
PHONE................................562 231-1880
Eliazar Felix, *President*
Maria Felix, *Vice Pres*
EMP: 75
SQ FT: 15,000
SALES: 3MM **Privately Held**
SIC: 6531 Real estate agent, commercial

(P-11310)
AUCTIONCOM INC
1 Mauchly Ste 27, Irvine (92618-2305)
PHONE................................800 499-6199
Jeffrey Frieden, *CEO*
Jake Seid, *President*
James Corum, *COO*
Tim Morse, *CFO*
Virginia Pierce, *CFO*
EMP: 200
SQ FT: 18,000
SALES: 15.8MM **Privately Held**
WEB: WWW.AUCTION.COM
SIC: 6531 Auction, real estate

(P-11311)
AVANTRA REAL ESTATE SERVICES
Also Called: Avantra Financial
148 E Fthill Blvd Ste 100, Arcadia (91006)
PHONE................................626 357-7028
Fax: 626 357-2676
Robert B Doeppel, *CEO*
Vicky Hansen, *President*
Debbie Bello, *Treasurer*
Gina Olivares, *Admin Sec*
Richard Faeh, *Manager*
EMP: 50
SQ FT: 1,800
SALES: 35MM **Privately Held**
WEB: www.avantrahomes.com
SIC: 6531

(P-11312)
B F MANAGEMENT
117 N Fuller Ave, Los Angeles (90036-2811)
PHONE................................323 931-7776
Fax: 213 931-0356
Chaim Freeman, *Owner*
EMP: 70
SQ FT: 1,000
SALES (est): 990K **Privately Held**
SIC: 6531 Real estate agents & managers

(P-11313)
BARCELON ASSOCIATES MGT CORP
590 Lennon Ln Ste 110, Walnut Creek (94598-5923)
PHONE................................925 627-7000
Mark Barcelon, *CEO*
Sandy Barcelon, *Co-CEO*
Roland Holz, *Manager*
Fatemeh Winans, *Advisor*
EMP: 250
SQ FT: 3,000
SALES (est): 1.6MM **Privately Held**
WEB: www.barcelon.com
SIC: 6531 Real estate managers

(P-11314)
BAYCO FINANCIAL CORPORATION (PA)
24050 Madison St Ste 101, Torrance (90505-6016)
PHONE................................310 378-8181
Brenda McKenneth, *President*
Robert Cohen, *Ch of Bd*
Sheri Pfau, *Treasurer*
Mary Colin, *Vice Pres*
Michael Gibson, *Agent*
EMP: 53
SALES (est): 3.5MM **Privately Held**
SIC: 6531 Real estate managers

(P-11315)
BEACHSIDE REALTORS (PA)
Also Called: Century 21
19671 Beach Blvd Ste 101, Huntington Beach (92648-5902)
PHONE................................714 969-6100
Thomas Denny, *President*
Christina Dialogu, *Broker*
Lenny Dong, *Marketing Staff*
EMP: 87
SQ FT: 13,000
SALES (est): 10.5MM **Privately Held**
WEB: www.mikelembeck.com
SIC: 6531 Real estate agent, residential

(P-11316)
BEACHSIDE REALTORS
Also Called: Century 21
15820 Whittier Blvd Ste B, Whittier (90603-2572)
PHONE................................562 947-7834
Shelley Reesman, *Manager*
Felipe Reyes, *Real Est Agnt*
Maria Reyes, *Real Est Agnt*
EMP: 80
SALES (corp-wide): 10.5MM **Privately Held**
WEB: www.mikelembeck.com
SIC: 6531 Real estate agent, residential

PA: Beachside Realtors
19671 Beach Blvd Ste 101
Huntington Beach CA 92648
714 969-6100

(P-11317)
BEETHOVEN HOLDINGS INC
Also Called: Keller William Realty
400 E Main St Ste 110, Visalia (93291-6320)
PHONE................................559 733-4100
Albert Meggers, *Principal*
Janet Deering, *Broker*
Michael Benevedes, *Real Est Agnt*
Larry Garcia, *Real Est Agnt*
EMP: 250
SALES (est): 10.1MM **Privately Held**
SIC: 6531 Real estate agent, residential

(P-11318)
BEITLER & ASSOCIATES INC (PA)
Also Called: Beitler Commercial Realty Svcs
825 S Barrington Ave, Los Angeles (90049-6759)
PHONE................................310 820-2955
Fax: 310 820-7224
Barry Beitler, *CEO*
Robert H Sargent, *CFO*
Iris Cohen, *Assoc VP*
Tony Dorn, *Exec VP*
Doug Green, *Vice Pres*
EMP: 50
SQ FT: 13,000
SALES (est): 11.1MM **Privately Held**
WEB: www.beitler.com
SIC: 6531 Real estate agents & agents

(P-11319)
BERKELEY 75 HSING PARTNERS LP
1936 University Ave # 130, Berkeley (94704-1003)
PHONE................................510 705-1488
Jim Brooks, *Controller*
Tesa Doleman, *Manager*
EMP: 50 EST: 2014
SALES (est): 1.8MM **Privately Held**
SIC: 6531 Real estate agents & managers

(P-11320)
BERKSHIRE HATTAWAY HOME SERVCS
Also Called: Mulhearn Group
16404 Colima Rd, Hacienda Heights (91745-5502)
PHONE................................626 913-2808
Bruce Mulhearn, *President*
James Liao, *Admin Sec*
Maria Zeger, *Sales Executive*
Vivian Yan, *Sls & Mktg Exec*
Deviona Pukarta, *Senior Mgr*
EMP: 75
SALES (est): 3MM **Privately Held**
SIC: 6531 Real estate agent, residential

(P-11321)
BETTER HOMES AND GARDENS MASON
5887 Lone Tree Way Ste A, Antioch (94531-8625)
PHONE................................925 776-2740
Melody Royal, *Manager*
Gina Alfaro, *Sales Associate*
Clayton Bowers, *Sales Associate*
Christine Chavez, *Sales Associate*
Diane Grindle, *Sales Associate*
EMP: 60 EST: 2010
SALES (est): 1.6MM **Privately Held**
SIC: 6531 Real estate agents & managers

(P-11322)
BEVERLYWOOD REALTY INC
2800 S Robertson Blvd, Los Angeles (90034-2406)
PHONE................................310 836-8322
Fax: 310 839-6657
Stanley Shapiro, *President*
EMP: 50
SALES (est): 1.7MM **Privately Held**
WEB: www.beverlywoodha.com
SIC: 6531 Real estate brokers & agents

6531 - Real Estate Agents & Managers County (P-11346)

(P-11323)
BIRTCHER ANDRSON PROPERTY SVCS (PA)
27611 La Paz Rd Ste D, Laguna Niguel (92677-3938)
PHONE..................................949 831-0707
Fax: 949 643-7755
Robert Anderson, *President*
Art B Birtcher, *CEO*
David L Afromsky, *Vice Pres*
Sam Parsa, *Asst Controller*
Alan Tuntland, *Consultant*
EMP: 60
SQ FT: 15,000
SALES (est): 9MM **Privately Held**
SIC: 6531 Real estate managers

(P-11324)
BIRTCHER N GOODMAN AMER LLC
18201 Von Karman Ave, Irvine (92612-1000)
PHONE..................................949 407-0100
Fax: 949 502-5505
Brandon Birtcher, *CEO*
Dan Grable, *COO*
Philip Pearce, *Exec Dir*
Charles Crossland, *Managing Dir*
Michael Gimblett, *General Mgr*
EMP: 100
SALES (est): 9.2MM **Privately Held**
SIC: 6531 6552 1542 Real estate managers; land subdividers & developers, commercial; commercial & office building, new construction

(P-11325)
BLACKROCK HOLDCO 2 INC
Also Called: Metrick Property Management
50 California St Ste 200, San Francisco (94111-4605)
PHONE..................................415 678-2000
Ron Zuzack, *Director*
Gil Wimmer, *Technology*
EMP: 80
SALES (corp-wide): 11.4B **Publicly Held**
WEB: www.blackrock.com
SIC: 6531 Real estate managers
HQ: Blackrock Holdco 2, Inc.
40 E 52nd St
New York NY 10022
212 754-5300

(P-11326)
BLAYNE PACELLI
12345 Ventura Blvd Ste A, Studio City (91604-2511)
PHONE..................................310 383-6281
Blayne Joseph Pacelli, *Owner*
EMP: 85
SALES (est): 1.3MM **Privately Held**
SIC: 6531 Real estate agents & managers

(P-11327)
BMR 21 ERIE ST LLC
17190 Bernardo Center Dr, San Diego (92128-7030)
PHONE..................................858 485-9840
Alan D Gold, *CEO*
EMP: 79
SALES (est): 368K
SALES (corp-wide): 674.6MM **Privately Held**
SIC: 6531 Real estate brokers & agents
HQ: Biomed Realty, L.P.
17190 Bernardo Center Dr
San Diego CA 92128
858 485-9840

(P-11328)
BRADLEY MELISSA REAL ESTATE
851 Irwin St Ste 104, San Rafael (94901-3343)
PHONE..................................415 459-1010
Fax: 415 259-2889
Melissa Bradley, *CEO*
Robert Bradley, *President*
Galina Thillois, *Office Admin*
John Bernarding, *Broker*
Brandon Bierke, *Broker*
EMP: 100
SALES (est): 8.8MM **Privately Held**
SIC: 6531 Real estate agents & managers

(P-11329)
BROSAMER & WALL LLC
1777 Oakland Blvd Ste 300, Walnut Creek (94596-4063)
PHONE..................................925 932-7900
Charles Wall, *Mng Member*
Cynthia Lundquist, *Controller*
Robert Brosamer,
EMP: 50
SALES (est): 8.8MM **Privately Held**
SIC: 6531 8711 Rental agent, real estate; construction & civil engineering

(P-11330)
BRUNSWICK CORNER PARTNERSHIP
Also Called: Ray Stone
550 Howe Ave Ste 200, Sacramento (95825-8339)
PHONE..................................916 649-7500
J Todd Stone, *Partner*
ERCI Olsen, *Treasurer*
EMP: 50
SALES (est): 2.3MM **Privately Held**
SIC: 6531 Real estate agents & managers

(P-11331)
BUCHANAN STREET PARTNERS LP
3501 Jamboree Rd Ste 4200, Newport Beach (92660-2958)
PHONE..................................949 721-1414
Robert Brunswick, *CEO*
Timothy Ballard, *COO*
James Gill, *Vice Pres*
Eric Snyder, *Principal*
EMP: 85
SALES (est): 4MM **Privately Held**
SIC: 6531 Real estate agents & managers

(P-11332)
BURKSHIRE HAS A WAY HOME SERVC
Also Called: Prudential
16810 Ventura Blvd Fl 1, Encino (91436-1778)
PHONE..................................818 501-4800
Fax: 818 990-4750
Kathy King, *Manager*
Ash Joshi, *Financial Exec*
William T Taylor, *Asst Mgr*
Michael G Jacobsen, *Real Est Agnt*
Lavondra R Luckey, *Real Est Agnt*
EMP: 70 EST: 2000
SALES (est): 3MM **Privately Held**
WEB: www.homes2estates.net
SIC: 6531 Real estate agent, residential

(P-11333)
BUZZ OATES MANAGEMENT SERVICES
555 Capitol Mall Ste 900, Sacramento (95814-4606)
PHONE..................................916 381-3843
Fax: 916 381-7826
Phil Oates, *Chairman*
Larry Allbaugh, *President*
Mike Stodden, *CFO*
Kiberley Chambers, *Vice Pres*
Dayna Palmer, *Executive*
EMP: 50
SQ FT: 8,630
SALES (est): 5.1MM **Privately Held**
SIC: 6531 Real estate agents & managers

(P-11334)
C B COAST NEWPORT PROPERTIES
Also Called: Coldwell Bnkr Rsdntial
840 Nwport Ctr Dr Ste 100, Newport Beach (92660)
PHONE..................................949 644-1600
Fax: 949 644-1690
Daniel F Bibb, *President*
Tom Queen, *Senior VP*
Bjorn Fundbakken, *Info Tech Dir*
Gary Legrand, *VP Finance*
Phil Malamatenios, *Sls & Mktg Exec*
EMP: 100
SQ FT: 7,300
SALES (est): 4.3MM
SALES (corp-wide): 5.7B **Publicly Held**
WEB: www.cbestates.com
SIC: 6531 Real estate agent, residential; selling agent, real estate
HQ: Coldwell Banker Residential Estate
27271 Las Ramblas
Mission Viejo CA 92691
949 367-1800

(P-11335)
C C CONNECTION INC
Also Called: Re/Maxcc
2950 Buskirk Ave Ste 140, Walnut Creek (94597-7773)
PHONE..................................925 937-0100
Fax: 925 937-0150
Robert Decker, *President*
Debbie Carter, *Treasurer*
EMP: 57
SQ FT: 4,200
SALES (est): 2.8MM **Privately Held**
WEB: www.re-pro.com
SIC: 6531 Real estate agent, residential

(P-11336)
C-21 SUPER STARS
Also Called: 21st Century Super Stars.
22342 Avenida Empresa, Rcho STA Marg (92688-2140)
PHONE..................................949 389-1600
Phillip Romero, *Owner*
EMP: 90
SALES (est): 3.3MM **Privately Held**
SIC: 6531 Real estate agents & managers

(P-11337)
CALDWELL BANKER INC
Also Called: Coldwell Banker
40 Main St Ste E100, Vista (92083-5831)
PHONE..................................760 941-6888
Susan Anderson, *Office Mgr*
Jim Morrow, *President*
Wendy Worcester, *Office Admin*
Sheryl Brown, *Broker*
Mary Cantwell, *Broker*
EMP: 80
SALES (est): 3.3MM **Privately Held**
SIC: 6531 Real estate agent, residential

(P-11338)
CALDWELL REALTY
14831 Whittier Blvd # 102, Whittier (90605-1747)
PHONE..................................562 907-5655
Fax: 562 907-5648
Donald Caldwell, *Owner*
EMP: 60
SALES (est): 1.9MM **Privately Held**
SIC: 6531 Real estate brokers & agents

(P-11339)
CALIFORNIA GOLDEN REALTY
26752 Calaroga Ave, Hayward (94545-3505)
PHONE..................................408 822-6000
Fax: 408 822-4501
Renu Bhardwaj, *Principal*
Igor Feoktistov, *Administration*
Mike Powers, *Software Engr*
EMP: 893
SALES (est): 38.6MM **Privately Held**
SIC: 6531 Real estate brokers & agents

(P-11340)
CANTAMAR PROPERTY MGT INC
Also Called: Meruelo Enterprises
9550 Firestone Blvd # 105, Downey (90241-5560)
PHONE..................................562 862-4470
Alex Meruelo, *President*
EMP: 50
SALES (est): 3.2MM **Privately Held**
SIC: 6531 Real estate managers

(P-11341)
CARITAS MANAGEMENT CORPORATION
1358 Valencia St, San Francisco (94110-3715)
PHONE..................................415 647-7191
Fax: 415 648-3919
Robert Zerrilla, *President*
Karen Olsan, *Manager*
EMP: 55
SQ FT: 3,000
SALES (est): 4.5MM
SALES (corp-wide): 18.6MM **Privately Held**
SIC: 6531 Real estate agents & managers
PA: Mission Housing Development Corporation
474 Valencia St Ste 280
San Francisco CA 94103
415 864-6432

(P-11342)
CARLTON SENIOR LIVING
Also Called: Carlton Plaza of San Leandro
1000 E 14th St, San Leandro (94577-3787)
PHONE..................................510 636-0660
Fax: 510 636-0668
Harry Darrett, *Manager*
EMP: 65
SQ FT: 96,676
SALES (corp-wide): 31.1MM **Privately Held**
SIC: 6531 Real estate agents & managers
PA: Senior Carlton Living Inc
4005 Port Chicago Hwy
Concord CA 94520
925 338-2434

(P-11343)
CARLTON SENIOR LIVING INC
6915 Elk Grove Blvd, Elk Grove (95758-5526)
PHONE..................................916 714-2404
Kimberly Carlton, *Branch Mgr*
EMP: 50
SALES (corp-wide): 31.1MM **Privately Held**
SIC: 6531 Real estate managers
PA: Senior Carlton Living Inc
4005 Port Chicago Hwy
Concord CA 94520
925 338-2434

(P-11344)
CARUSO MGT LTD A CAL LTD PRTNR
Also Called: Commons At Calabasas, The
101 The Grove Dr, Los Angeles (90036-6221)
PHONE..................................323 900-8100
Rick Caruso, *Partner*
Peter Hayden, *President*
David Silva, *Exec VP*
David Williams, *Exec VP*
Chris Baccus, *Senior VP*
EMP: 100
SALES (est): 15.2MM **Privately Held**
SIC: 6531 Rental agent, real estate

(P-11345)
CASBN INVESTMENT INC
Also Called: RE Max Westlake Investments
345 Gellert Blvd Ste A, Daly City (94015-2617)
PHONE..................................650 991-2800
Fax: 650 997-3000
Francis Ng, *President*
EMP: 60
SALES (est): 4.7MM **Privately Held**
SIC: 6531 6163 Real estate agents & managers; mortgage brokers arranging for loans, using money of others

(P-11346)
CASSIDY TRLY PROP MGT SN FRNCS
201 California St Ste 800, San Francisco (94111-5010)
PHONE..................................415 781-8100
Mike Kamm, *CEO*
Daniel Wald, *Managing Prtnr*
Joseph Stettinius Jr, *President*
John J Fleury, *COO*
William J Florent, *CFO*
EMP: 86 EST: 2010
SALES (est): 17.3MM
SALES (corp-wide): 5B **Privately Held**
SIC: 6531 Real estate agent, commercial
HQ: Cushman & Wakefield, Inc.
77 W Wacker Dr Ste 1800
Chicago IL 60601
312 424-8000

6531 - Real Estate Agents & Managers County (P-11347)

(P-11347)
CB C&C PROPERTIES/COMM DI INC
2120 Churn Creek Rd, Redding (96002-0738)
PHONE..................530 221-7551
Steve Craft, *President*
EMP: 70
SALES (est): 2.6MM Privately Held
SIC: 6531 Real estate brokers & agents

(P-11348)
CB RICHARD ELLIS RE SVCS LLC
Also Called: Cbre Valuation and Advisory
355 S Grand Ave Ste 2700, Los Angeles (90071-1596)
PHONE..................213 613-3333
Cicily Dostalek, *Branch Mgr*
Chuck Nixon, *Senior VP*
Sabrina Hunt, *Comms Mgr*
Ellen Rudin, *Managing Dir*
Kathryn Haeusler, *Program Mgr*
EMP: 80
SALES (corp-wide): 10.8B Publicly Held
WEB: www.insigniafinancial.com
SIC: 6531 Real estate agents & managers
HQ: Cb Richard Ellis Real Estate Services, Llc
200 Park Ave Fl 19
New York NY 10166
212 984-8000

(P-11349)
CBABR INC (PA)
Also Called: Coldwell Banker
31620 Rr Cyn Rd Ste A, Canyon Lake (92587-9476)
PHONE..................951 640-7056
Fax: 951 244-4219
Budge Huskey, *CEO*
Dennis M McCoy, *President*
Margaret McCoy, *Treasurer*
Jody Regus, *Vice Pres*
Laura Plasch, *Admin Asst*
EMP: 73
SQ FT: 4,000
SALES (est): 3.4MM Privately Held
WEB: www.margaretmccoy.com
SIC: 6531 Real estate agent, residential

(P-11350)
CBRE INC
500 Capitol Mall Fl 24, Sacramento (95814-4737)
PHONE..................916 446-6800
Fax: 916 446-8750
David Brennan, *Manager*
R Smyth, *Managing Dir*
Angela Carlton, *Manager*
EMP: 80
SALES (corp-wide): 10.8B Publicly Held
SIC: 6531 Real estate agent, commercial
HQ: Cbre, Inc.
400 S Hope St Ste 25
Los Angeles CA 90071
310 477-5876

(P-11351)
CBRE INC
2125 E Katella Ave # 100, Anaheim (92806-6072)
P.O. Box 9410 (92812-7410)
PHONE..................714 939-2100
Jeff Moore, *Branch Mgr*
EMP: 200
SALES (corp-wide): 10.8B Publicly Held
SIC: 6531 8742 Real estate brokers & agents; management consulting services
HQ: Cbre, Inc.
400 S Hope St Ste 25
Los Angeles CA 90071
310 477-5876

(P-11352)
CBRE INC
4900 Rivergrade Rd A110, Baldwin Park (91706-1401)
PHONE..................626 814-7900
Shashi Panat, *Manager*
EMP: 300
SALES (corp-wide): 10.8B Publicly Held
SIC: 6531 Real estate brokers & agents
HQ: Cbre, Inc.
400 S Hope St Ste 25
Los Angeles CA 90071
310 477-5876

(P-11353)
CBRE INC
15303 Ventura Blvd # 200, Van Nuys (91403-3110)
PHONE..................818 907-4600
Fax: 818 907-4688
Don Hudson, *Manager*
EMP: 60
SQ FT: 11,000
SALES (corp-wide): 10.8B Publicly Held
SIC: 6531 Real estate brokers & agents
HQ: Cbre, Inc.
400 S Hope St Ste 25
Los Angeles CA 90071
310 477-5876

(P-11354)
CBRE INC
234 S Brand Blvd Ste 800, Glendale (91204-1362)
PHONE..................818 502-6700
Fax: 818 243-6069
David Josker, *Director*
EMP: 85
SALES (corp-wide): 10.8B Publicly Held
SIC: 6531 Real estate brokers & agents
HQ: Cbre, Inc.
400 S Hope St Ste 25
Los Angeles CA 90071
310 477-5876

(P-11355)
CBRE INC
2221 Rosecrans Ave # 100, El Segundo (90245-4931)
PHONE..................310 363-4900
Myles Helm, *Director*
Bret Quinlan, *Senior VP*
Ken White, *Senior VP*
Ben Knight, *Vice Pres*
Priscilla Nee, *Vice Pres*
EMP: 175
SALES (corp-wide): 10.8B Publicly Held
SIC: 6531 Real estate brokers & agents
HQ: Cbre, Inc.
400 S Hope St Ste 25
Los Angeles CA 90071
310 477-5876

(P-11356)
CBRE INC
1840 Century Park E # 900, Los Angeles (90067-2110)
PHONE..................310 550-2500
Fax: 310 203-9624
Jim Kruse, *Director*
James Donnerstag, *Senior VP*
Marty Barkan, *Vice Pres*
Jeffery Pion, *Vice Pres*
Adrienne Barr, *Sales Executive*
EMP: 90
SALES (corp-wide): 10.8B Publicly Held
SIC: 6531 Real estate brokers & agents
HQ: Cbre, Inc.
400 S Hope St Ste 25
Los Angeles CA 90071
310 477-5876

(P-11357)
CBRE INC
4365 Executive Dr # 1600, San Diego (92121-2101)
PHONE..................858 546-4600
Fax: 619 546-3985
John Frager, *Sales/Mktg Dir*
Kathleen Davis, *Real Est Agnt*
EMP: 160
SALES (corp-wide): 10.8B Publicly Held
SIC: 6531 Real estate brokers & agents
HQ: Cbre, Inc.
400 S Hope St Ste 25
Los Angeles CA 90071
310 477-5876

(P-11358)
CBRE INC
4141 Inland Empire Blvd # 100, Ontario (91764-5025)
PHONE..................909 418-2000
Joe Cesta, *Director*
David Consani, *Exec VP*
Kent Stalwick, *Senior VP*
Jason Chao, *Vice Pres*
Gerald Harvey, *Vice Pres*
EMP: 100
SALES (corp-wide): 10.8B Publicly Held
SIC: 6531 Real estate agents & managers
HQ: Cbre, Inc.
400 S Hope St Ste 25
Los Angeles CA 90071
310 477-5876

(P-11359)
CBRE GROUP INC (PA)
400 S Hope St Ste 25, Los Angeles (90071-2800)
PHONE..................213 613-3333
Fax: 310 606-4701
Robert E Sulentic, *President*
Chadwick McCleskey, *Partner*
Michael Svoboda, *Partner*
Ray Wirta, *Ch of Bd*
Jack Durburg, *CEO*
EMP: 250
SALES: 10.8B Publicly Held
WEB: www.cbrichardellis.com
SIC: 6531 6162 8742 Real estate agent, commercial; real estate managers; appraiser, real estate; mortgage bankers; real estate consultant

(P-11360)
CBRE SERVICES INC
Also Called: CB Richard Ellis Services Inc
400 S Hope St Ste 25, Los Angeles (90071-2800)
PHONE..................213 613-3333
Robert Sulentic, *CEO*
Nathan Bugbee, *Admin Asst*
Lisa Perry, *Admin Asst*
Luke Denmon, *Sales Staff*
Alice Chiang, *Sr Associate*
EMP: 70
SALES (est): 14.6MM
SALES (corp-wide): 10.8B Publicly Held
WEB: www.cbrichardellis.com
SIC: 6531 8742 Real estate agents & managers; real estate agent, commercial; appraiser, real estate; real estate consultant
PA: Cbre Group, Inc.
400 S Hope St Ste 25
Los Angeles CA 90071
213 613-3333

(P-11361)
CBSRR INC
Also Called: Coldwell Banker Sky Ridge Rlty
27206 Hwy 189, Blue Jay (92317)
P.O. Box 189, Lake Arrowhead (92352-0189)
PHONE..................909 336-2131
Steve Keefe, *President*
Stephen Keefe, *President*
Jamie Keefe, *Vice Pres*
Bruce Block, *Marketing Staff*
Jackie Sussell, *Manager*
EMP: 62
SALES (est): 5.8MM Privately Held
WEB: www.cbskyridge.com
SIC: 6531 Real estate agent, residential

(P-11362)
CEDAR MANAGEMENT LLC
Also Called: Cedar Signature
3233 Dnald Douglas Loop S, Santa Monica (90405-3235)
P.O. Box 7484 (90406-7484)
PHONE..................310 396-3100
Fax: 310 396-1240
Adam Pasori,
Maria Castorena, *Controller*
Adam Assori, *Manager*
EMP: 80
SQ FT: 10,000
SALES (est): 3.8MM Privately Held
SIC: 6531 Real estate managers

(P-11363)
CENTURY 21
301 Dickson Hill Rd Ste A, Fairfield (94533-7203)
PHONE..................707 429-2121
Linda Green, *President*
Laura Lee, *Vice Pres*
Susan Sheffer, *Manager*
Lauralee Ensign, *Real Est Agnt*
EMP: 50
SALES (est): 1.3MM Privately Held
SIC: 6531 Real estate agent, residential

(P-11364)
CENTURY 21 A BETTER SVC RLTY
8077 2nd St Fl Fl, Downey (90241-3621)
PHONE..................562 287-0230
David Sarinana, *President*
Nelson Sanchez, *Vice Pres*
EMP: 99
SALES (est): 4MM Privately Held
SIC: 6531 Real estate agent, residential

(P-11365)
CENTURY 21 ABLE INC
3202 Governor Dr Ste 100, San Diego (92122-2939)
PHONE..................858 450-2100
Fax: 858 259-0122
Tom Kumz, *President*
Martha Karelius, *COO*
Kurt Francis, *Office Mgr*
Ann Howard, *Sales Associate*
Elva Rodriguez, *Assistant*
EMP: 56
SALES (est): 1.9MM Privately Held
SIC: 6531 Real estate agent, residential

(P-11366)
CENTURY 21 ALPHA LLC
1630 W Campbell Ave, Campbell (95008-1500)
PHONE..................408 369-2000
Fax: 408 266-2769
Ed Zimbrick, *Mng Member*
Daniel Deasy, *Sales Mgr*
EMP: 89
SALES (est): 2.7MM Privately Held
WEB: www.century21alpha.com
SIC: 6531 Real estate agent, residential

(P-11367)
CENTURY 21 AMBER REALTY INC
21024 Wood Ave Apt A, Torrance (90503-4143)
PHONE..................310 625-4363
David Sheerin, *President*
EMP: 80
SALES (est): 3.1MM Privately Held
WEB: www.c21amber.com
SIC: 6531 Real estate agent, residential

(P-11368)
CENTURY 21 BEACHSIDE
6265 E 2nd St Ste 103, Long Beach (90803-4613)
PHONE..................562 430-2121
Fax: 562 430-4297
Ron Horn, *Manager*
Craig Smith, *Principal*
EMP: 71
SQ FT: 10,000
SALES (est): 1.8MM Privately Held
SIC: 6531 8611

(P-11369)
CENTURY 21 BEVERLYWOOD REALTY
2800 S Robertson Blvd, Los Angeles (90034-2489)
PHONE..................310 836-8321
Fax: 323 839-6657
Stanley Shaprio, *President*
Cheryl Shapiro, *Vice Pres*
Jerald Shapiro, *Vice Pres*
Sheryl Shapiro, *Vice Pres*
Jean S Ferron, *Broker*
EMP: 55
SALES (est): 2.2MM Privately Held
SIC: 6531 7389 Real estate agent, residential; notary publics

(P-11370)
CENTURY 21 CHAMPION
10420 S De Anza Blvd, Cupertino (95014-3032)
PHONE..................408 725-4000
Fax: 650 996-0560
Alan Aoyana, *Senior VP*
Jim Hessling, *Principal*
John Piper, *Principal*
Felix Enow, *Administration*

PRODUCTS & SERVICES SECTION
6531 - Real Estate Agents & Managers County (P-11394)

Kunja Kang, *Marketing Mgr*
EMP: 50
SQ FT: 5,000
SALES (est): 2.2MM **Privately Held**
WEB: www.century21champion.com
SIC: 6531 Real estate agent, residential

(P-11371)
CENTURY 21 CREST
4005 Foothill Blvd, La Crescenta (91214-1623)
PHONE 818 248-9100
Ray Mirzakhanian, *Owner*
EMP: 66
SALES (est): 1.3MM
SALES (corp-wide): 10MM **Privately Held**
SIC: 6531 Real estate agent, residential
PA: E.A.M. Enterprises Inc.
  4005 Foothill Blvd
  La Crescenta CA 91214
  818 248-9100

(P-11372)
CENTURY 21 DSTNCTIVE PRPTS INC
Also Called: Century 21 Green Gable RE
1450 Ary Ln Ste A, Dixon (95620-4413)
PHONE 707 678-9211
Fax: 707 678-1566
Linda Green, *President*
Deborah Belt, *Manager*
Delaine Vargas, *Manager*
EMP: 92
SQ FT: 2,200
SALES: 485K **Privately Held**
SIC: 6531 Real estate agent, residential

(P-11373)
CENTURY 21 EXCELLENCE
5207 Rosemead Blvd Ste 1, Pico Rivera (90660-2734)
PHONE 562 948-4553
Fax: 562 948-2339
Manuel Davila, *Partner*
Mike Oycque, *Partner*
EMP: 50
SQ FT: 5,100
SALES (est): 2.6MM **Privately Held**
SIC: 6531 Real estate agent, residential

(P-11374)
CENTURY 21 EXCLUSIVE REALTORS
22831 Hawthorne Blvd, Torrance (90505-3615)
PHONE 310 373-5252
Ron Karno, *Owner*
EMP: 130 **EST:** 1998
SALES (est): 2.6MM **Privately Held**
SIC: 6531 Real estate agent, residential

(P-11375)
CENTURY 21 GOLDEN REALTY
1332 N Lake Ave, Pasadena (91104-2856)
PHONE 626 204-2400
Fax: 626 204-2401
Carol Gharossian, *Branch Mgr*
Shahe Abrahamian, *Broker*
Luis A Berrios, *Broker*
Setrak Bronzian, *Broker*
Zoe Chapjian, *Broker*
EMP: 50
SALES (corp-wide): 3.9MM **Privately Held**
SIC: 6531 Real estate agent, residential
PA: Century 21 Golden Realty
  482 N Rosemead Blvd
  Pasadena CA 91107
  626 797-6680

(P-11376)
CENTURY 21 HALEY & ASSOCIATES
699 Wshington Blvd Ste B5, Roseville (95678)
PHONE 916 782-1500
Fax: 916 782-1500
James Haley, *President*
Pamela Sekulich, *Human Res Mgr*
Lori Anderson, *Property Mgr*
Kate Berlin, *Real Est Agnt*
EMP: 72
SQ FT: 1,400

SALES: 1.9MM **Privately Held**
SIC: 6531 Real estate agent, residential

(P-11377)
CENTURY 21 HOME REALTORS
Also Called: Century 21 King Realtors
8338 Day Creek Blvd # 101, Rancho Cucamonga (91739-9366)
P.O. Box 3424 (91729-3424)
PHONE 909 980-8000
Julio Cardenas, *Manager*
Andrew Espinoza, *Sales Mgr*
Carol Olivas, *Facilities Mgr*
Carlos Tovar, *Real Est Agnt*
James Tschann, *Real Est Agnt*
EMP: 90
SALES (corp-wide): 4.5MM **Privately Held**
SIC: 6531 Real estate agent, residential
PA: Century 21 Home Realtors
  4110 Edison Ave Ste 210
  Chino CA 91710
  909 591-0158

(P-11378)
CENTURY 21 LANDMARK PROPERTIES
1650 Ximeno Ave Ste 120, Long Beach (90804-2179)
PHONE 562 422-0911
Fax: 562 428-1842
Alan Fasnacht, *Owner*
Rose Melvin, *Administration*
EMP: 50 **EST:** 1960
SALES (est): 2.3MM **Privately Held**
SIC: 6531 Real estate agent, residential

(P-11379)
CENTURY 21 LES RYAN REALTY
1057 College Ave Ofc Ste, Santa Rosa (95404-4128)
PHONE 707 577-7777
Pat Provost, *Partner*
EMP: 75
SALES (corp-wide): 2.8MM **Privately Held**
WEB: www.c21lesryan.com
SIC: 6531 Real estate agent, residential
PA: Century 21 Les Ryan Realty
  495 E Perkins St Ste A
  Ukiah CA 95482
  707 468-0423

(P-11380)
CENTURY 21 LUDECKE INC (PA)
20 E Foothill Blvd # 105, Arcadia (91006-2335)
PHONE 626 445-0123
Michael W Ludecke, *President*
EMP: 55
SALES (est): 3.3MM **Privately Held**
WEB: www.c21ludecke.com
SIC: 6531 Real estate agent, residential

(P-11381)
CENTURY 21 SHOWCASE INC
7835 Church St, Highland (92346-4380)
PHONE 909 936-9334
Jeff Stoffel, *President*
Ed Neighbors, *Manager*
EMP: 60
SALES (est): 2.9MM **Privately Held**
WEB: www.century21showcase.com
SIC: 6531 Real estate agent, residential

(P-11382)
CENTURY ADANALIAN & VASQUEZ
Also Called: Century 21
1415 W Shaw Ave, Fresno (93711-3608)
PHONE 559 244-6000
Fax: 209 248-0425
Bill Adanalian, *President*
Greg Vasquez, *Vice Pres*
Percy Saucedo, *Office Mgr*
Charlie Adanalian, *Agent*
Denise Centeno, *Real Est Agnt*
EMP: 62
SQ FT: 4,250
SALES (est): 3.8MM **Privately Held**
SIC: 6531 Real estate agent, residential

(P-11383)
CENTURY PROPERTIES OWNERS ASSN
Also Called: Century, The
1 W Century Dr, Los Angeles (90067-3401)
PHONE 310 272-8580
Jim Brooks, *Controller*
Tesa Doleman, *Manager*
EMP: 50
SALES (est): 3.9MM **Privately Held**
SIC: 6531 Real estate agent, residential

(P-11384)
CH MARKET CENTER INC
Also Called: Keller Williams Realtors
4200 Chino Health Ste 325, Chino Hills (91709)
PHONE 909 628-9100
Nick Lanza, *President*
David Porchas, *President*
Suzi Moret, *Principal*
EMP: 75
SALES (est): 3.8MM **Privately Held**
SIC: 6531 Real estate agent, residential

(P-11385)
CHARLES DUNN CO INC
Also Called: Charles Dunn Raltor State Svcs
800 W 6th St Ste 800, Los Angeles (90017-2741)
PHONE 213 481-1800
Walter J Conn, *President*
Richard C Dunn, *President*
Eleanor B Dunn, *Vice Pres*
Joseph Dunn, *Admin Sec*
Matthew Dunn, *Assistant VP*
EMP: 200
SALES (est): 4.6MM **Privately Held**
SIC: 6531 Real estate brokers & agents

(P-11386)
CHARLES DUNN RE SVCS INC (PA)
800 W 6th St Ste 600, Los Angeles (90017-2709)
PHONE 213 270-6200
Walter Conn, *CEO*
Patrick Conn, *President*
Jerry Wang, *Exec VP*
Tom Arai, *Vice Pres*
Susan Dunst, *Vice Pres*
EMP: 86
SQ FT: 30,000
SALES (est): 8.7MM **Privately Held**
WEB: www.charlesdunn.com
SIC: 6531 Real estate brokers & agents; real estate managers

(P-11387)
CHICAGO TITLE & ESCROW
316 W Mission Ave Ste 110, Escondido (92025-1731)
PHONE 760 746-3882
Joanne Lockard, *President*
Joann Lockard, *President*
Anne Radstinner, *Vice Pres*
Elaine Lothspeich, *Human Res Mgr*
Shirley Cate, *Manager*
EMP: 50
SALES (est): 8.3MM
SALES (corp-wide): 9.1B **Publicly Held**
WEB: www.fntg.com
SIC: 6531 Real estate brokers & agents
PA: Fidelity National Financial, Inc.
  601 Riverside Ave Fl 4
  Jacksonville FL 32204
  904 854-8100

(P-11388)
CHILD DEVELOPMENT INCORPORATED
17341 Jacquelyn Ln, Huntington Beach (92647-5713)
PHONE 714 842-4064
EMP: 725
SALES (corp-wide): 28MM **Privately Held**
SIC: 6531 Real estate agents & managers
PA: Child Development Incorporated
  20 Great Oaks Blvd # 200
  San Jose CA 95119
  408 556-7300

(P-11389)
CHRISTIAN AND WAKEFIELD (PA)
Also Called: Burnham Real Estate
110 W A St Ste 900, San Diego (92101-3705)
P.O. Box 122910 (92112-2910)
PHONE 619 236-1555
Fax: 619 525-2973
Stath Karras, *President*
Scott W Abell, *Senior VP*
Mike Philben, *Senior VP*
Jon Walz, *Senior VP*
Jeanette Kagan, *Property Mgr*
EMP: 53
SQ FT: 22,000
SALES (est): 6MM **Privately Held**
SIC: 6531 Real estate brokers & agents

(P-11390)
CHRISTIAN CHURCH HOMES
Also Called: Westlake Christian Terrace - E
251 28th St, Oakland (94611-6063)
PHONE 510 893-2998
Fax: 510 893-1848
John Jordan, *Branch Mgr*
EMP: 219
SALES (corp-wide): 13.3MM **Privately Held**
SIC: 6531 Real estate agents & managers
PA: Christian Church Homes
  303 Hegenberger Rd # 201
  Oakland CA 94621
  510 632-6712

(P-11391)
CIM GROUP INC (PA)
Also Called: Commercial Inv MGT Group
4700 Wilshire Blvd Ste 1, Los Angeles (90010-3854)
PHONE 323 860-4900
Fax: 323 860-4901
Avraham Shemesch, *CEO*
David Thompson, *CFO*
Kelly Eppich, *Principal*
Shaul Kuba, *Principal*
Richard Ressler, *Principal*
EMP: 83
SALES: 2.5MM **Privately Held**
WEB: www.cimgroup.com
SIC: 6531 6798 6552 Real estate agents & managers; real estate investment trusts; land subdividers & developers, commercial

(P-11392)
CITISCAPE PRPRTY MGT GROUP LLC
3450 3rd St Ste 1a, San Francisco (94124-1444)
PHONE 415 674-1440
Paul Mora, *Branch Mgr*
EMP: 64
SALES (corp-wide): 15.6MM **Privately Held**
SIC: 6531 Real estate managers
PA: Citiscape Property Management Group Llc
  3450 3rd St Ste 1a
  San Francisco CA 94124
  415 401-2000

(P-11393)
CITIVEST INC
4340 Von Karman Ave # 110, Newport Beach (92660-1201)
PHONE 949 474-0440
Dana Haynes, *President*
Johnathan Loevenguth, *CFO*
Larry Weese, *Exec VP*
Jane Kho, *Controller*
EMP: 90
SQ FT: 4,000
SALES (est): 10.3MM **Privately Held**
WEB: www.citivestinc.com
SIC: 6531 Real estate agents & managers

(P-11394)
CITY VENTURES LLC (PA)
3121 Michelson Dr Ste 150, Irvine (92612-5679)
PHONE 949 258-7555
Mark R Buckland,
Phil Kerr, *Senior VP*
Patrick Hendry, *Vice Pres*

6531 - Real Estate Agents & Managers County (P-11395)

Bill McReynolds, *Vice Pres*
Tony Pauker, *Vice Pres*
EMP: 50
SALES (est): 74.9MM **Privately Held**
SIC: 6531 Real estate agent, residential

(P-11395)
CLARK ENTERPRISES INC
3655 Nobel Dr Ste 500, San Diego (92122-1051)
PHONE.................................858 320-3900
Jennifer Hartwell, *Director*
Greg M Rice, *CFO*
John Bielski, *Exec Dir*
Jack Lester, *Managing Dir*
Steven Seidman, *Managing Dir*
EMP: 239
SALES (corp-wide): 2.2B **Privately Held**
SIC: 6531 6519 Real estate agents & managers; real property lessors
PA: Clark Enterprises, Inc.
7500 Old Georgetown Rd # 7
Bethesda MD 20814
301 657-7100

(P-11396)
CLAYTON PLACE ASSOCIATES INC
Also Called: Re/Max
20412 Elkwood St, Winnetka (91306-2234)
PHONE.................................818 702-0115
William A Clayton, *President*
Darlene Clayton, *Vice Pres*
EMP: 80
SALES (est): 3.2MM **Privately Held**
SIC: 6531 Real estate agent, residential

(P-11397)
CLEARCAPITALCOM INC
10875 Pioneer Trl, Truckee (96161-0235)
PHONE.................................530 550-2500
Valorie Scott, *President*
Becky Andrews, *Bd of Directors*
Kenon Chen, *Exec VP*
James Smith, *Senior VP*
Erin Dodd, *Office Mgr*
EMP: 140
SALES (corp-wide): 143.5MM **Privately Held**
SIC: 6531 Appraiser, real estate
PA: Clearcapital.Com, Inc.
300 E 2nd St Ste 1405
Reno NV 89501
775 470-5656

(P-11398)
CLEARCAPITALCOM INC
1410 Rocky Ridge Dr # 180, Roseville (95661-2811)
PHONE.................................530 582-5011
Duane Andrews, *Branch Mgr*
EMP: 100
SALES (corp-wide): 143.5MM **Privately Held**
SIC: 6531 Real estate agents & managers
PA: Clearcapital.Com, Inc.
300 E 2nd St Ste 1405
Reno NV 89501
775 470-5656

(P-11399)
CLPF - SYCAMORE
6721 Sycamore Canyon Blvd, Riverside (92507-0751)
PHONE.................................212 883-2500
Stacey Magee, *Principal*
Kathy Handlon, *Principal*
EMP: 99
SALES: 950K **Privately Held**
SIC: 6531 Real estate agents & managers

(P-11400)
COAST TO COAST REALTY
Also Called: Century 21
18879 Brasilia Dr, Porter Ranch (91326-1919)
PHONE.................................818 360-2609
Fax: 818 906-8590
Debbie Abeyesinhe, *Owner*
EMP: 80
SALES (est): 2.5MM **Privately Held**
WEB: www.debbisellsthevalley.com
SIC: 6531 Real estate agent, residential

(P-11401)
COASTAL ALLIANCE HOLDINGS INC
Also Called: Coldwell Banker Coastl Aliance
1650 Ximeno Ave Ste 120, Long Beach (90804-2179)
PHONE.................................562 370-1000
Jack Irvin, *President*
Marina Eberwein, *CFO*
Kris Conrad, *Admin Sec*
Ronald Howard, *Info Tech Mgr*
Jennifer Brown, *Director*
EMP: 140
SALES (est): 6.3MM **Privately Held**
SIC: 6531 Real estate agents & managers

(P-11402)
COASTSIDE SENIOR HOUSING LIMIT
925 Main St, Half Moon Bay (94019-2379)
PHONE.................................415 355-7100
Jane Graf,
EMP: 50
SALES (est): 1.7MM **Privately Held**
SIC: 6531 Real estate leasing & rentals

(P-11403)
COLDWELL BANKER
730 Alhambra Blvd Ste 150, Sacramento (95816-3885)
PHONE.................................916 447-5900
Fax: 916 447-5911
Michael Lippi, *Manager*
Malka Khan, *Office Admin*
Sara Moody, *Broker*
Tamara Spillane, *Personnel Exec*
Patti McNulty-Langdon, *Sales Associate*
▲ **EMP:** 60
SALES (est): 2.6MM **Privately Held**
SIC: 6531 Real estate agent, residential

(P-11404)
COLDWELL BANKER
9332 Fuerte Dr, La Mesa (91941-4199)
PHONE.................................619 460-6600
Rick Hoffman, *President*
Antonio Rosselli, *Asst Broker*
Martha A Price, *Broker*
Phillip Meares, *Mktg Dir*
Steve Wilson, *Manager*
EMP: 88
SQ FT: 4,000
SALES (est): 4MM **Privately Held**
SIC: 6531 Real estate agent, residential

(P-11405)
COLDWELL BANKER
740 Garden View Ct # 100, Encinitas (92024-2474)
PHONE.................................760 753-5616
Fax: 760 753-5925
Jeff Hayes, *Manager*
Tatjana Jovanovic, *Asst Broker*
Michael Korn, *Asst Broker*
Nancy J Chodur, *Broker*
Jan Jarboe-Greider, *Broker*
EMP: 75
SALES (est): 3.4MM **Privately Held**
SIC: 6531 Real estate agent, residential

(P-11406)
COLDWELL BANKER
248 Main St Ste 200, Half Moon Bay (94019-7120)
PHONE.................................650 726-1100
Fax: 650 726-8676
Greg Cowen, *Partner*
Stella Johnson, *Partner*
William Mahar, *Principal*
Rose Serdy, *Principal*
EMP: 50
SALES (est): 2.4MM **Privately Held**
SIC: 6531 Real estate agent, residential

(P-11407)
COLDWELL BANKER
1775 Lincoln Ave, NAPA (94558-4706)
PHONE.................................707 257-7673
Carolyn Roberts, *Principal*
EMP: 80
SALES (est): 1.1MM **Privately Held**

(P-11408)
COLDWELL BANKER AFFILIATES
161 S San Antonio Rd # 1, Los Altos (94022-3031)
PHONE.................................650 941-7040
Fax: 650 941-3094
Fred Hibbard, *Manager*
Gary Van Zee, *Info Tech Mgr*
Carrie Deak, *Broker*
Joanne Fraser, *Broker*
Carol Van Zee, *Manager*
EMP: 70
SQ FT: 9,000
SALES (est): 3MM **Privately Held**
SIC: 6531 Real estate agent, residential

(P-11409)
COLDWELL BANKER AMARAL & ASSOC
3775 Main St Ste E, Oakley (94561-5793)
PHONE.................................925 439-7400
Fax: 925 625-4552
Arron Manwos, *Owner*
Craig Boswell, *Manager*
EMP: 65
SALES (est): 1.5MM **Privately Held**
SIC: 6531 Real estate agent, residential

(P-11410)
COLDWELL BANKER PREMIER PRPTS
1498 E Valley Rd, Santa Barbara (93108-1241)
PHONE.................................805 565-2200
Chuck Farish, *President*
Scott McCosker, *Broker*
Steven Richardson, *Manager*
EMP: 70
SALES (est): 1.8MM **Privately Held**
WEB: www.betsyzwick.com
SIC: 6531 Real estate agent, residential

(P-11411)
COLDWELL BANKER PROF GROUP
2860 Zanker Rd Ste 204, San Jose (95134-2120)
PHONE.................................408 383-1044
Fax: 408 383-4801
Kathy Low, *Principal*
Kathleen Chiu, *Executive*
Jeff Barry, *Sales Associate*
Ishrat Khatoon, *Sales Associate*
Daniel Abebe, *Manager*
EMP: 90
SALES (est): 3MM **Privately Held**
WEB: www.kathylow.com
SIC: 6531 Real estate agent, residential

(P-11412)
COLDWELL BANKER RE CORP
15490 Ventura Blvd # 100, Sherman Oaks (91403-3033)
PHONE.................................818 995-2424
Fax: 818 995-7483
Bill Dalton, *Branch Mgr*
Connie Harrison, *Broker*
Lolita James, *Broker*
Syrus Jamneshan, *Sales Associate*
Paulette Zemlicka, *Sales Associate*
EMP: 60
SALES (corp-wide): 5.7B **Publicly Held**
SIC: 6531 Real estate agent, residential
HQ: Coldwell Banker Real Estate Corporation
175 Park Ave
Madison NJ 07940
888 829-0221

(P-11413)
COLDWELL BANKER RE CORP
1000 Sunset Dr Ste 190, Roseville (95678-4056)
PHONE.................................408 981-7200
Maxine Feil, *Manager*
Chuck Farish, *Branch Mgr*
Robert Weber, *Real Est Agnt*
EMP: 50
SALES (corp-wide): 5.7B **Publicly Held**
WEB: www.coldwellbanker.com
SIC: 6531 Real estate agent, residential
HQ: Coldwell Banker Real Estate Corporation
175 Park Ave
Madison NJ 07940
888 829-0221

(P-11414)
COLDWELL BANKER RE CORP
501 W Redlands Blvd Ste A, Redlands (92373-4642)
PHONE.................................909 792-4147
Fax: 909 792-0803
Sheila Cannon, *Owner*
Frank Faxon, *Manager*
Gloria Grochowski, *Manager*
Patricia Seymour, *Manager*
Peggy Wilcox, *Manager*
EMP: 50
SALES (corp-wide): 5.7B **Publicly Held**
WEB: www.coldwellbanker.com
SIC: 6531 Real estate agent, residential
HQ: Coldwell Banker Real Estate Corporation
175 Park Ave
Madison NJ 07940
888 829-0221

(P-11415)
COLDWELL BANKER REAL ESTATE
1045 Willow St, San Jose (95125-2346)
PHONE.................................408 491-1600
Fax: 408 280-1233
Joe Brown, *Manager*
Yvonne Barron, *Asst Broker*
Julia Brittner, *Asst Broker*
Rachel Pham, *Broker*
Michael Uhri, *Broker*
EMP: 75
SALES (est): 2.3MM **Privately Held**
SIC: 6531 Real estate agent, residential

(P-11416)
COLDWELL BANKER RESIDENTIAL RE (DH)
27271 Las Ramblas, Mission Viejo (92691-6392)
PHONE.................................949 367-1800
Fax: 949 367-2040
Robert Becker, *President*
Richard Campbell, *Real Est Agnt*
Jan Palya, *Real Est Agnt*
EMP: 410
SQ FT: 6,000
SALES (est): 107.3MM
SALES (corp-wide): 5.7B **Publicly Held**
WEB: www.cbestates.com
SIC: 6531 Real estate agent, residential

(P-11417)
COLDWELL BANKER RESIDENTIAL RE
15 E Foothill Blvd, Arcadia (91006-2399)
PHONE.................................626 445-5500
Fax: 626 447-0388
Jack Cooley, *Principal*
Cynthia Woo, *Office Mgr*
Brian Peralez, *Asst Broker*
Mary Daniels, *Broker*
Bevin Eustace, *Broker*
EMP: 63
SALES (est): 3MM **Privately Held**
SIC: 6531 Real estate agent, residential

(P-11418)
COLDWELL BANKER TOWN & COUNTRY
345 E Rowland St, Covina (91723-3153)
PHONE.................................626 966-3688
Fax: 626 937-3918
Norman Cox, *Manager*
EMP: 70
SQ FT: 7,000
SALES (est): 3.5MM **Privately Held**
WEB: www.cbtcsocal.com
SIC: 6531 Real estate agent, residential

(P-11419)
COLDWELL BANKERS RESIDENTIAL
21060 Redwood Rd Ste 100, Castro Valley (94546-5931)
PHONE.................................510 583-5400
Fax: 510 583-5480
Nelly Jagroop, *Manager*

PRODUCTS & SERVICES SECTION
6531 - Real Estate Agents & Managers County (P-11439)

Scott Harrison, *Asst Broker*
Willie Campbell, *Consultant*
Richard Dibona, *Consultant*
Arnie Concepcion, *Real Est Agnt*
EMP: 90
SALES (corp-wide): 3.3MM **Privately Held**
WEB: www.laurarivera.com
SIC: 6531 Real estate agent, residential
PA: Coldwell Bankers Residential
604 Lindero Canyon Rd
Agoura Hills CA 91377
818 575-2660

(P-11420)
COLDWELL BANKERS RESIDENTIAL (PA)
604 Lindero Canyon Rd, Agoura Hills (91377-5455)
PHONE.................................818 575-2660
Fax: 805 735-4137
Irma Haldane, *Manager*
Randy Paller, *Admin Sec*
Cheri Herman, *Personnel Exec*
Bill Dalton, *Sales Executive*
Beth Novak, *Real Est Agnt*
EMP: 52
SALES (est): 3.3MM **Privately Held**
WEB: www.sharonberman.com
SIC: 6531 Real estate agent, residential

(P-11421)
COLDWELL BNKR FIRST CLASS RLTY
7825 Florence Ave A, Downey (90240-3727)
PHONE.................................323 721-7430
Richard Estrada, *Manager*
Richard Estarda, *Manager*
EMP: 60
SALES (est): 2.3MM **Privately Held**
SIC: 6531 Real estate agent, residential

(P-11422)
COLDWELL BNKR FRST PRMIER RLTY
537 N Euclid Ave, Ontario (91762-3221)
PHONE.................................909 395-5400
Gil Patcheco, *Manager*
EMP: 63
SALES (est): 2.3MM **Privately Held**
SIC: 6531 Real estate agent, residential

(P-11423)
COLDWELL BNKR RESIDENTIAL BRKG
181 2nd Ave Ste 100, San Mateo (94401-3830)
PHONE.................................650 558-6800
Fax: 650 573-4160
Janine Foey, *Branch Mgr*
Pete Aiello, *Broker*
Bryant McFadyen, *Sales Staff*
Brian Owens, *Consultant*
Victor Aenlle, *Real Est Agnt*
EMP: 52
SALES (corp-wide): 5.7B **Publicly Held**
SIC: 6531 Real estate agent, residential
HQ: Coldwell Banker Residential Brokerage
1855 Gateway Blvd Ste 750
Concord CA 94520
925 275-3000

(P-11424)
COLDWELL BNKR RESIDENTIAL BRKG
500 Auburn Folsom Rd # 300, Auburn (95603-5645)
PHONE.................................530 823-7653
Fax: 916 823-5713
Randi Greene, *Principal*
Charllis W Twilligear, *Real Est Agnt*
EMP: 52
SALES (corp-wide): 5.7B **Publicly Held**
SIC: 6531 Real estate agent, residential
HQ: Coldwell Banker Residential Brokerage
1855 Gateway Blvd Ste 750
Concord CA 94520
925 275-3000

(P-11425)
COLDWELL BNKR RESIDENTIAL BRKG (DH)
Also Called: Valley of California, Inc.
1855 Gateway Blvd Ste 750, Concord (94520-3290)
PHONE.................................925 275-3000
Fax: 925 275-3022
Bruce G Zipf, *CEO*
Avram Goldman, *President*
John Carman, *Office Mgr*
Neil Stanton, *Info Tech Dir*
Diana Jesus, *IT/INT Sup*
EMP: 100
SALES (est): 32.8MM
SALES (corp-wide): 5.7B **Publicly Held**
WEB: www.cbnorcal.com
SIC: 6531 Real estate agent, residential

(P-11426)
COLDWELL BNKR RESIDENTIAL BRKG
2140 41st Ave Ste 100, Capitola (95010-2067)
PHONE.................................831 462-9000
Spencer Hays, *Branch Mgr*
Bryan Mackenzie, *Consultant*
Gabriele Erlach, *Real Est Agnt*
EMP: 52
SALES (corp-wide): 5.7B **Publicly Held**
SIC: 6531 Real estate agent, residential
HQ: Coldwell Banker Residential Brokerage
1855 Gateway Blvd Ste 750
Concord CA 94520
925 275-3000

(P-11427)
COLDWELL BNKR RESIDENTIAL BRKG
1427 Chapin Ave, Burlingame (94010-4002)
PHONE.................................650 558-4200
Rachel Ni, *Branch Mgr*
Joan Saidy, *Broker*
David Virella, *Broker*
Patrick Ho, *Sales Associate*
Joanne Huh, *Sales Associate*
EMP: 52
SALES (corp-wide): 5.7B **Publicly Held**
SIC: 6531 Real estate agent, residential
HQ: Coldwell Banker Residential Brokerage
1855 Gateway Blvd Ste 750
Concord CA 94520
925 275-3000

(P-11428)
COLDWELL BNKR RESIDENTIAL BRKG
1801 Lombard St, San Francisco (94123-2909)
PHONE.................................415 447-8800
Mark Best, *Branch Mgr*
Jennifer Andary, *Broker*
John Oloughlin, *Broker*
Jeff Boonma, *Sales Executive*
Andrew Halpern, *Sales Associate*
EMP: 52
SALES (corp-wide): 5.7B **Publicly Held**
WEB: www.markbest.com
SIC: 6531 Real estate agent, residential
HQ: Coldwell Banker Residential Brokerage
1855 Gateway Blvd Ste 750
Concord CA 94520
925 275-3000

(P-11429)
COLDWELL BNKR RESIDENTIAL BRKG
1081 N Palm Canyon Dr, Palm Springs (92262-4419)
PHONE.................................760 325-4500
Thomas Ogle, *Branch Mgr*
Dominic Godfrey, *Executive*
Cena Rasmussen, *Asst Broker*
Michael Paduano, *Broker*
Chris Kallgren, *Sales Staff*
EMP: 74
SALES (corp-wide): 5.7B **Publicly Held**
WEB: www.bonnieo.com
SIC: 6531 Real estate agent, residential
HQ: Coldwell Banker Residential Brokerage Company
27271 Las Ramblas
Mission Viejo CA 92691
949 367-1800

(P-11430)
COLDWELL BNKR RESIDENTIAL BRKG
5034 Sunrise Blvd, Fair Oaks (95628-4945)
PHONE.................................916 966-8200
Donna Kopp, *Principal*
Mary Grebitus, *Asst Broker*
Barbara McNaught, *Asst Broker*
Svitlana Kravchenko, *Broker*
Lynn Murphy, *Sales Associate*
EMP: 52
SALES (corp-wide): 5.7B **Publicly Held**
WEB: www.kathyfox.com
SIC: 6531 Real estate agent, residential
HQ: Coldwell Banker Residential Brokerage
1855 Gateway Blvd Ste 750
Concord CA 94520
925 275-3000

(P-11431)
COLDWELL BNKR RESIDENTIAL BRKG
21580 Yorba Linda Blvd, Yorba Linda (92887-3748)
PHONE.................................714 832-0020
Fax: 714 832-6984
Tom Iovenitti, *President*
James Cameron, *Office Mgr*
Yolanda Hawkins, *Broker*
Kim Olson, *Broker*
April Bayraktar, *Sales Staff*
EMP: 50
SALES (est): 1.5MM **Privately Held**
SIC: 6531 Real estate agent, residential

(P-11432)
COLDWELL BNKR RESIDENTIAL BRKG
23586 Calabasas Rd # 105, Calabasas (91302-1319)
PHONE.................................818 222-0023
Fax: 818 222-9979
Bill Dalton, *Manager*
Denice Rice, *Broker*
Julie Bate, *Human Res Mgr*
Doug Arbetman, *Sales Staff*
Brian Mallasch, *Sales Associate*
EMP: 100
SALES (corp-wide): 5.7B **Publicly Held**
WEB: www.bonnieo.com
SIC: 6531 Real estate agent, residential
HQ: Coldwell Banker Residential Brokerage Company
27271 Las Ramblas
Mission Viejo CA 92691
949 367-1800

(P-11433)
COLDWELL BNKR RESIDENTIAL BRKG
166 N Canon Dr Ste 200, Beverly Hills (90210-5304)
PHONE.................................310 273-3113
Betty Graham, *Manager*
Loren Judd, *Branch Mgr*
Susan Bliss, *Office Admin*
Tania Ravaei, *Asst Broker*
Emily Fredrick, *Broker*
EMP: 74
SALES (corp-wide): 5.7B **Publicly Held**
WEB: www.bonnieo.com
SIC: 6531 Real estate agent, residential
HQ: Coldwell Banker Residential Brokerage Company
27271 Las Ramblas
Mission Viejo CA 92691
949 367-1800

(P-11434)
COLDWELL BNKR RESIDENTIAL BRKG
72605 Highway 111 Ste B2, Palm Desert (92260-3392)
PHONE.................................760 776-9898
Ron Gerlich, *Manager*
Judy Patti, *Executive*
Brenda Fitch, *Asst Broker*
Michael Maggio, *Asst Broker*
Denise Francis, *Sales Associate*
EMP: 100
SALES (corp-wide): 5.7B **Publicly Held**
WEB: www.bonnieo.com
SIC: 6531 Real estate agent, residential
HQ: Coldwell Banker Residential Brokerage Company
27271 Las Ramblas
Mission Viejo CA 92691
949 367-1800

(P-11435)
COLDWELL BNKR RESIDENTIAL BRKG
45000 Club Dr, Indian Wells (92210-8856)
PHONE.................................760 771-5454
Diane Busch, *Manager*
Jeffrey Fishbein, *Asst Broker*
Jerry Rich, *Asst Broker*
Gailmc Quary, *Broker*
Pamla Abramson, *Sales Staff*
EMP: 74
SALES (corp-wide): 5.7B **Publicly Held**
WEB: www.bonnieo.com
SIC: 6531 Real estate agent, residential
HQ: Coldwell Banker Residential Brokerage Company
27271 Las Ramblas
Mission Viejo CA 92691
949 367-1800

(P-11436)
COLDWELL BNKR RESIDENTIAL BRKG
410 Sims Rd, Santa Cruz (95060-1326)
PHONE.................................831 420-2628
EMP: 59
SALES (corp-wide): 19.1MM **Privately Held**
SIC: 6531 Real estate agent, residential
PA: Coldwell Banker Residential Brokerage
3 Parkway N Ste 400
Deerfield IL 60015
847 313-6500

(P-11437)
COLDWELL BNKR RESIDENTIAL BRKG
3340 Walnut Ave Ste 110, Fremont (94538-2215)
PHONE.................................510 608-7600
Fax: 510 795-7187
Kathy Fox, *Branch Mgr*
Victoria Corpuz, *Office Admin*
Mohua Dey, *Asst Broker*
Jeff Pereyda, *Asst Broker*
Alex Cyriac, *Broker*
EMP: 52
SALES (corp-wide): 5.7B **Publicly Held**
SIC: 6531 Real estate agent, residential
HQ: Coldwell Banker Residential Brokerage
1855 Gateway Blvd Ste 750
Concord CA 94520
925 275-3000

(P-11438)
COLDWELL BNKR RSDENTIAL RE LLC
410 N Santa Cruz Ave, Los Gatos (95030-5321)
PHONE.................................408 355-1500
Karen Trolan, *Manager*
David Metten, *Project Mgr*
Nathera Mawla, *Broker*
Piyawan Rungsuk, *Broker*
Elizabeth Winegar-Howard, *Broker*
EMP: 100
SALES (corp-wide): 5.7B **Publicly Held**
SIC: 6531 Real estate agent, residential
HQ: Coldwell Banker Residential Real Estate Llc
6285 Barfield Rd Ste 100
Atlanta GA 30328
404 705-1500

(P-11439)
COLDWELL BNKR RSDNTIAL RE SVCS
4370 Town Center Blvd # 270, El Dorado Hills (95762-7140)
PHONE.................................916 933-1155
Russ Leiser, *Branch Mgr*
Paulette Lewis, *Broker*
Kim Ross, *Sales Associate*
Theresa Gerety, *Real Est Agnt*
Vick Melancon, *Real Est Agnt*
EMP: 424
SALES (corp-wide): 8MM **Privately Held**
SIC: 6531 Real estate agent, residential

6531 - Real Estate Agents & Managers County (P-11440)

PRODUCTS & SERVICES SECTION

PA: Coldwell Banker Residential Real Estate Services Inc
27271 Las Ramblas
Mission Viejo CA

(P-11440) COLDWER BANKER PREVIEWS
Also Called: Coldwell Banker
9069 W Sunset Blvd # 100, West Hollywood (90069-1828)
PHONE..................310 278-9470
Fran Hughes, Manager
Jessica Lucero, Human Res Dir
Jason Arena, Sales Staff
Damon Barone, Real Est Agnt
Gene Bush, Real Est Agnt
EMP: 120
SALES (est): 3.6MM Privately Held
SIC: 6531 Real estate agent, residential

(P-11441) COLLEGE PARK REALTY INC (PA)
Also Called: Re/Max
10791 Los Alamitos Blvd, Los Alamitos (90720-2309)
PHONE..................562 594-6753
Fax: 562 795-6709
Barry Binder, President
Betty Binder, Treasurer
Carol Treadway, Vice Pres
Josh Jones, Info Tech Dir
Shelly Hemphill, Technology
EMP: 80
SQ FT: 5,000
SALES (est): 9.8MM Privately Held
WEB: www.joannmurphy.com
SIC: 6531 Real estate agent, residential

(P-11442) COLLEGE PARK REALTY INC
Also Called: Remax College Park Realty
2610 Los Coyotes Diagonal, Long Beach (90815-1355)
PHONE..................562 982-0300
Fax: 562 982-0303
Marian Edwards, Principal
Sindy Verdugo, Administration
Bob Slawson, Real Est Agnt
Susan Zaitz, Real Est Agnt
EMP: 50
SALES (corp-wide): 9.8MM Privately Held
WEB: www.joannmurphy.com
SIC: 6531 Real estate agents & managers
PA: College Park Realty Inc
10791 Los Alamitos Blvd
Los Alamitos CA 90720
562 594-6753

(P-11443) COLLIERS INTERNATIONAL
101 2nd St Ste 1100, San Francisco (94105-3652)
PHONE..................415 788-3100
Herbert Damner Jr, Partner
Karen Hoke, Senior VP
Alan Collenette, Managing Dir
Vikki Johnson, Managing Dir
Susan Olinski, Finance Mgr
EMP: 65
SALES (est): 7.2MM
SALES (corp-wide): 1.7B Privately Held
SIC: 6531 Real estate brokers & agents
HQ: Colliers International New England, Llc
160 Federal St Fl 11
Boston MA 02110
617 330-8000

(P-11444) COLLIERS INTERNATIONAL GREATER (HQ)
865 S Figueroa St # 3500, Los Angeles (90017-2543)
PHONE..................213 627-1214
Fax: 213 327-3200
Martin Pupil, Chairman
Jeffrey Thielman, Treasurer
John Hollingsworth, Vice Pres
Hans Mumper, Vice Pres
Michael Arnette, Admin Sec
EMP: 65 EST: 1967
SALES (est): 62.9MM
SALES (corp-wide): 9.4MM Privately Held
SIC: 6531 Real estate brokers & agents
PA: Cmn Calgary Inc
335 8 Ave Sw Suite 1000
Calgary AB T2P 1
403 266-5544

(P-11445) COLLIERS INTL PRPERTY CONS INC
4660 La Jolla Village Dr # 100, San Diego (92122-4601)
PHONE..................858 455-1515
Fax: 858 546-9146
Tony Albin Senior, Vice Pres
EMP: 50
SALES (corp-wide): 527.7MM Privately Held
SIC: 6531 Real estate brokers & agents
HQ: Colliers International Property Consultants Inc.
601 Union St Ste 3320
Seattle WA 98101
206 695-4200

(P-11446) COLLIERS INTL PRPERTY CONS INC
301 University Ave # 100, Sacramento (95825-5537)
PHONE..................916 929-5999
Randy Dixon, Manager
EMP: 100
SALES (corp-wide): 527.7MM Privately Held
SIC: 6531 Real estate agents & managers
HQ: Colliers International Property Consultants Inc.
601 Union St Ste 3320
Seattle WA 98101
206 695-4200

(P-11447) COLLIERS PARRISH INTL INC
Also Called: Colliers Investment Services
450 W Santa Clara St, San Jose (95113-1503)
PHONE..................408 282-3800
Fax: 408 292-8100
Mike Burke, Manager
Jim Beeger, Senior VP
Terry Healy, Senior VP
Marne Michaels, Senior VP
Mike Mixer, Senior VP
EMP: 70
SALES (corp-wide): 20.7MM Privately Held
WEB: www.terraceaustin.com
SIC: 6531 Real estate brokers & agents
PA: Parrish Colliers International Inc
1 Almaden Blvd Ste 300
San Jose CA 95113
408 282-9799

(P-11448) COLLIERS PARRISH INTL INC
1850 Mt Diablo Blvd # 200, Walnut Creek (94596-4476)
PHONE..................925 279-1050
Fax: 925 279-0450
Edward Delbeccaro, Manager
Kevin Van Voorhis, Plan/Corp Dev D
Marie Turrin, Admin Asst
EMP: 51
SALES (corp-wide): 20.7MM Privately Held
WEB: www.terraceaustin.com
SIC: 6531 Real estate agents & managers
PA: Parrish Colliers International Inc
1 Almaden Blvd Ste 300
San Jose CA 95113
408 282-9799

(P-11449) COLONY MANAGEMENT INC
Also Called: Colony Advisors
1999 Ave Of The Ste 1200, Los Angeles (90067)
PHONE..................310 282-8820
Fax: 310 282-8808
Thomas A Barrack, CEO
Mark Hedstrom, CFO
Adrian Stuessy, Manager
EMP: 75

SQ FT: 15,000
SALES (est): 4.4MM
SALES (corp-wide): 1B Privately Held
WEB: www.colonyinc.com
SIC: 6531 Real estate brokers & agents
PA: Colony Capital, Llc
2450 Broadway Ste 600
Santa Monica CA 90404
310 282-8820

(P-11450) COMMUNITY DEVELOPMENT COMM
Also Called: Housing Authority Division
700 W Main St, Alhambra (91801-3312)
PHONE..................626 262-4511
Sean Rogan, Exec Dir
EMP: 150 Privately Held
WEB: www.co.la.ca.us
SIC: 6531 Housing authority operator
HQ: Community Development Commission
700 W Main St
Alhambra CA 91801
626 262-4511

(P-11451) CONAM MANAGEMENT CORPORATION (PA)
3990 Ruffin Rd Ste 100, San Diego (92123-4805)
PHONE..................858 614-7200
Fax: 619 297-5016
J Bradley Forrester, CEO
Scott Dupree, COO
Robert Svatos, CFO
Daniel J Epstein, Chairman
Frazier Crawford, Exec VP
EMP: 142
SQ FT: 45,634
SALES (est): 19.9MM Privately Held
SIC: 6531 Real estate agents & managers

(P-11452) CONTINENTAL 155 5TH CORP
2041 Rosecrans Ave # 200, El Segundo (90245-4707)
PHONE..................310 640-1520
Richard C Lundquist, President
Marcia Helfer, Vice Pres
EMP: 50
SALES (est): 1.6MM
SALES (corp-wide): 37.1MM Privately Held
WEB: www.continentaldevelopment.com
SIC: 6531 Real estate agent, commercial
PA: Continental Development Corporation
2041 Rosecrans Ave # 200
El Segundo CA 90245
310 640-1520

(P-11453) COOK REALTY INC
Also Called: Cook Realty Sales
4305 Freeport Blvd, Sacramento (95822-2045)
PHONE..................916 451-6702
Fax: 916 451-2754
Frank Cook, President
Barbara Cook, Corp Secy
Vickie Hulbert, Marketing Staff
Yvette Goodwin, Agent
Stephen Bacon, Real Est Agnt
EMP: 106
SALES (est): 5.7MM Privately Held
WEB: www.cookrealty.net
SIC: 6531 Real estate brokers & agents

(P-11454) CORE COMMUNICATIONS GROUP LLC
2749 Saturn St, Brea (92821-6705)
PHONE..................714 729-8404
Arnold Valencia,
Laurel Reimer, Planning Mgr
Gina Vandergriff, Office Admin
Karen Tomita, Human Res Mgr
John Koos,
EMP: 58 EST: 2005
SALES (est): 5.9MM Privately Held
SIC: 6531 Real estate agents & managers

(P-11455) CORE REALTY HOLDINGS MGT INC
Also Called: Crh Management
1600 Dove St Ste 450, Newport Beach (92660-2447)
PHONE..................949 863-1031
Dougless Morehead, CEO
Marc Raskulinecz, Senior VP
Tracie Nguyen, Vice Pres
Kirk White, General Mgr
EMP: 99
SALES (est): 5.4MM Privately Held
SIC: 6531 Real estate agents & managers

(P-11456) CORELOGIC INC
201 Spear St Fl 4, San Francisco (94105-1669)
PHONE..................714 250-6400
Dan Berman, Branch Mgr
Manindra Singh, Data Proc Staff
Darren Daukas, Asst Director
Connie Keim, Director
EMP: 50
SALES (corp-wide): 1.5B Publicly Held
SIC: 6531 Real estate agents & managers
PA: Corelogic, Inc.
40 Pacifica Ste 900
Irvine CA 92618
949 214-1000

(P-11457) CORELOGIC INC
40 Pacifica Ste 900, Irvine (92618-7487)
PHONE..................714 250-6400
Fax: 949 800-3352
Doug Lamb, Sr Project Mgr
Tom Alberts, Manager
Joe May, Manager
Adam Paff, Manager
EMP: 50
SALES (corp-wide): 1.5B Publicly Held
SIC: 6531 Real estate brokers & agents
PA: Corelogic, Inc.
40 Pacifica Ste 900
Irvine CA 92618
949 214-1000

(P-11458) CORINTHIAN REALTY LLC
3902 Smith St, Union City (94587-2616)
PHONE..................510 487-8653
Rey Sison, CEO
Eugene Soriano, Marketing Staff
Belinda Gunther, Manager
EMP: 60
SALES (est): 2.6MM Privately Held
SIC: 6531 Real estate brokers & agents

(P-11459) CORONADO FINANCIAL CORP
Also Called: Prudential
940 Eastlake Pkwy, Chula Vista (91914-3558)
PHONE..................619 946-1900
Corey Shepard, President
Jolene Shepard, Treasurer
EMP: 50
SQ FT: 10,000
SALES (est): 3.5MM Privately Held
SIC: 6531 Real estate agent, residential

(P-11460) COSTAR GROUP INC
8910 University Center Ln # 300, San Diego (92122-1029)
PHONE..................858 458-4900
Fax: 858 558-4309
Todd Thelen, Manager
Jim Shreeves, Administration
Martine Baechtel, QA Dir
Victor Marrero, Web Dvlpr
Krystyna Blonska, Software Dev
EMP: 230
SALES (corp-wide): 711.7MM Publicly Held
WEB: www.costar.com
SIC: 6531 Real estate agents & managers
PA: Costar Group, Inc.
1331 L St Nw Ste 2
Washington DC 20005
202 346-6500

PRODUCTS & SERVICES SECTION
6531 - Real Estate Agents & Managers County (P-11483)

(P-11461)
CROCKER GROUP LLC
1101 E Orangewood Ave, Anaheim (92805-6827)
PHONE..................714 221-5621
Peter Barker, *Principal*
EMP: 75
SALES (est): 1MM **Privately Held**
SIC: 6531 Real estate agent, residential

(P-11462)
CUSHMAN & WAKEFIELD INC
Also Called: Terranomics
1350 Bayshore Hwy Ste 900, Burlingame (94010-1818)
PHONE..................650 347-3700
Sheryl Simpson, *Branch Mgr*
John Brackett, *Partner*
Tom Christian, *Partner*
Staci E Cole, *Partner*
Jamie D'Alessandro, *Partner*
EMP: 50
SALES (corp-wide): 5B **Privately Held**
SIC: 6531 8742 Real estate leasing & rentals; real estate consultant
HQ: Cushman & Wakefield, Inc.
77 W Wacker Dr Ste 1800
Chicago IL 60601
312 424-8000

(P-11463)
CUSHMAN & WAKEFIELD CAL INC (DH)
1 Maritime Plz Ste 900, San Francisco (94111-3412)
PHONE..................408 275-6730
Fax: 415 393-1540
Joseph Stettinius Jr, *CEO*
Anthony Sirianni, *COO*
Robert Ballard, *Exec VP*
Robert Rudin, *Exec VP*
Russ Stai, *Senior VP*
EMP: 110 **EST:** 1887
SQ FT: 26,500
SALES (est): 259.8MM
SALES (corp-wide): 5B **Privately Held**
WEB: www.cushwake-nb.com
SIC: 6531 Real estate brokers & agents; real estate agent, commercial; real estate managers; appraiser, real estate
HQ: Cushman & Wakefield, Inc.
77 W Wacker Dr Ste 1800
Chicago IL 60601
312 424-8000

(P-11464)
CUSHMAN & WAKEFIELD CAL INC
2020 Main St Ste 1000, Irvine (92614-8224)
PHONE..................949 474-4004
Fax: 949 474-0405
Dee Shipley, *Sales/Mktg Mgr*
John Tran, *Associate Dir*
EMP: 50
SALES (corp-wide): 5B **Privately Held**
WEB: www.cushwake-nb.com
SIC: 6531 Real estate brokers & agents
HQ: Cushman & Wakefield Of California, Inc.
1 Maritime Plz Ste 900
San Francisco CA 94111
408 275-6730

(P-11465)
DAYMARK REALTY ADVISORS INC
Also Called: Daymark Properties Realty
750 B St Ste 2620, San Diego (92101-8172)
P.O. Box 7369, Newport Beach (92658-7369)
PHONE..................714 975-2999
Todd A Mikles, *CEO*
Meredith Coleman, *Admin Asst*
Tran Jenny, *Controller*
Lori McGhee, *Property Mgr*
EMP: 400
SALES (est): 25.4MM **Privately Held**
SIC: 6531 Real estate brokers & agents

(P-11466)
DEAN GOODMAN INC
10833 Valley View St # 500, Cypress (90630-5054)
PHONE..................714 229-8999
Candice H Miller, *President*
Joyce Barg, *Accounts Mgr*
Staci Hornung, *Advisor*
EMP: 55
SALES (est): 4MM **Privately Held**
WEB: www.goodmandean.com
SIC: 6531 Real estate agents & managers; appraiser, real estate

(P-11467)
DECRON PROPERTIES CORP
8601 Lincoln Blvd, Los Angeles (90045-3554)
PHONE..................310 363-4887
EMP: 87
SALES (corp-wide): 25.7MM **Privately Held**
SIC: 6531 6552 Real estate agent, residential; land subdividers & developers, residential
PA: Decron Properties Corp.
6222 Wilshire Blvd # 400
Los Angeles CA 90048
323 556-6600

(P-11468)
DENOVA HOME SALES INC
Also Called: Denova Homes
1500 Willow Pass Ct, Concord (94520-1009)
PHONE..................925 852-0545
David Sanson, *President*
Lori Sanson, *Vice Pres*
Peter Giles, *Superintendent*
Chris Gust, *Asst Supt*
EMP: 84
SQ FT: 1,850
SALES (est): 10.4MM **Privately Held**
WEB: www.denovahomes.com
SIC: 6531 Real estate brokers & agents

(P-11469)
DESERT RESORT MANAGEMENT
42635 Melanie Pl Ste 103, Palm Desert (92211-9113)
PHONE..................760 831-0172
Fax: 760 346-9918
Mark Dodge, *President*
Gloria Kirkwood, *General Mgr*
Jessica Marsh, *Admin Asst*
Dana Brown, *Property Mgr*
Leann Wallace, *Property Mgr*
EMP: 52
SQ FT: 11,000
SALES (est): 5.3MM **Privately Held**
SIC: 6531 Real estate managers

(P-11470)
DIABLO REALTY INC
Also Called: Pacific Mortgage Resources
975 Ygnacio Valley Rd, Walnut Creek (94596-3825)
PHONE..................925 933-9300
Fax: 925 906-1434
Linda Jean Anderson, *President*
Moses Guillory, *Corp Secy*
EMP: 50
SQ FT: 7,000
SALES (est): 3.5MM **Privately Held**
WEB: www.diablorealty.com
SIC: 6531 6163 Real estate brokers & agents; mortgage brokers arranging for loans, using money of others

(P-11471)
DIEZ & LEIS RE GROUP INC
Also Called: Prudential Norcal Realty
5120 Manzanita Ave # 120, Carmichael (95608-0558)
PHONE..................916 487-4287
Fax: 916 487-4322
Ron Leis, *President*
Dave Alexander, *Real Est Agnt*
Traciann Beaulieu, *Real Est Agnt*
Karla Douglas, *Real Est Agnt*
Richard Hammill, *Real Est Agnt*
EMP: 60
SQ FT: 10,000
SALES (est): 3.8MM
SALES (corp-wide): 57.1B **Publicly Held**
SIC: 6531 Real estate agent, residential
HQ: Brer Affiliates Inc
18500 Von Karman Ave # 400
Irvine CA 92612
949 794-7900

(P-11472)
DILBECK INC (PA)
Also Called: Dilbeck Realtors
1030 Foothill Blvd, La Canada (91011-3285)
PHONE..................818 790-6774
Fax: 818 790-8967
Mark Dilbeck, *Ch of Bd*
Bruce Dilbeck, *Admin Sec*
Gladys Waters, *Administration*
Jennifer D Allen, *Broker*
Leah M Dilbeck, *Broker*
EMP: 70
SQ FT: 9,000
SALES (est): 8.7MM **Privately Held**
WEB: www.lacanadarealestate.com
SIC: 6531 Real estate brokers & agents; real estate managers

(P-11473)
DILBECK INC
2943 Foothill Blvd, La Crescenta (91214-3412)
PHONE..................818 248-2248
Susan Lindsey, *Manager*
Vahe Kabakian, *Broker*
Lynnell Woodward, *Broker*
EMP: 80
SALES (corp-wide): 8.7MM **Privately Held**
WEB: www.lacanadarealestate.com
SIC: 6531 Real estate brokers & agents
PA: Dilbeck Inc.
1030 Foothill Blvd
La Canada CA 91011
818 790-6774

(P-11474)
DILBECK INC
Also Called: Dilbeck Realtors
225 E Colorado Blvd, Pasadena (91101-1903)
PHONE..................626 584-0101
Fax: 626 584-3889
Ray Hayes, *Manager*
EMP: 60
SALES (corp-wide): 8.7MM **Privately Held**
WEB: www.lacanadarealestate.com
SIC: 6531 Real estate brokers & agents
PA: Dilbeck Inc.
1030 Foothill Blvd
La Canada CA 91011
818 790-6774

(P-11475)
DONAHUE SCHRBER RLTY GROUP INC (PA)
200 Baker St E Ste 100, Costa Mesa (92626-4551)
PHONE..................714 545-1400
Thomas Schriber, *Ch of Bd*
Patrick S Donahue, *President*
Larry Casey, *CFO*
Kathy Step, *Asst Sec*
EMP: 80
SQ FT: 20,000
SALES (est): 11MM **Privately Held**
WEB: www.montebellotowncenter.com
SIC: 6531 Real estate agent, commercial

(P-11476)
DOUG ARNOLD REAL ESTATE INC (PA)
Also Called: Coldwell Banker
505 2nd St, Davis (95616-4618)
PHONE..................530 758-3080
Fax: 530 753-8825
Doug Arnold, *President*
J David Taoramino, *Treasurer*
Jimi Faria, *Real Est Agnt*
Scott McLallen, *Real Est Agnt*
Andrew Skaggs, *Real Est Agnt*
EMP: 50
SQ FT: 7,000
SALES (est): 4.4MM **Privately Held**
WEB: www.coldwellbankerdougarnold.com
SIC: 6531 Real estate agent, residential

(P-11477)
DOUGLAS ELLIMAN REAL ESTATE
9440 Santa Monica Blvd # 710, Beverly Hills (90210-4653)
PHONE..................310 595-3888
Collin Keanan, *General Mgr*
EMP: 50
SALES (est): 232.6K **Privately Held**
SIC: 6531 Real estate agents & managers

(P-11478)
DOUGLAS EMMETT REALTY FUND 199
808 Wilshire Blvd Ste 200, Santa Monica (90401-1889)
PHONE..................310 255-7700
Dan Emmett, *Principal*
EMP: 60
SALES (est): 1.4MM
SALES (corp-wide): 635.7MM **Privately Held**
SIC: 6531 Real estate brokers & agents
PA: Douglas Emmett, Inc.
808 Wilshire Blvd Ste 200
Santa Monica CA 90401
310 255-7700

(P-11479)
DPPM INC
Also Called: Zephyr Real Estate
4040 24th St, San Francisco (94114-3716)
PHONE..................415 695-7707
Fax: 415 695-1106
EMP: 80
SALES (corp-wide): 16.4MM **Privately Held**
SIC: 6531
PA: Dppm, Inc.
850 7th St
San Francisco CA 94107
415 348-1212

(P-11480)
DREAM HOME ESTATES INC
2901 W Coast Hwy Ste 200, Newport Beach (92663-4045)
PHONE..................949 415-4646
David Prewitt, *CEO*
EMP: 50
SALES (est): 678.2K **Privately Held**
SIC: 6531 6799 8742 Selling agent, real estate; real estate investors, except property operators; real estate consultant

(P-11481)
DUNLAP PROPERTY GROUP INC
801 E Chapman Ave Ste 233, Fullerton (92831-3847)
P.O. Box 4308 (92834-4308)
PHONE..................714 879-0111
Paul Dunlap, *President*
EMP: 55
SALES (est): 2.9MM **Privately Held**
SIC: 6531 Real estate agents & managers

(P-11482)
DYNAMIC REALTY CORP
800 S Barranca Ave # 260, Covina (91723-3625)
P.O. Box 741, West Covina (91793-0741)
PHONE..................626 931-3200
Henry Melandez, *President*
EMP: 70
SALES (est): 3MM **Privately Held**
SIC: 6531 Real estate agents & brokers

(P-11483)
E R A FIRST STAR REALTY
Also Called: ERA
505 S Villa Real Ste 101a, Anaheim (92807-3432)
PHONE..................714 974-3111
Fax: 714 637-5880
Blake Bartanian, *Owner*
EMP: 50
SALES (est): 1MM **Privately Held**
SIC: 6531 Real estate agents & brokers

6531 - Real Estate Agents & Managers County (P-11484)

(P-11484)
E-N REALTY II
Also Called: Century 21 E
1081 Grand Ave, Diamond Bar (91765-2210)
PHONE 909 597-1736
Fax: 909 860-0133
John Newe, *President*
EMP: 50
SALES (est): 2MM **Privately Held**
SIC: 6531 Real estate agent, residential

(P-11485)
EAGLE ESTATES INC
Also Called: ERA
10175 Rancho Carmel Dr # 124, San Diego (92128-3675)
PHONE 858 484-3829
Fax: 619 484-5961
Donald A Mc Guiness, *President*
Donald A Guiness, *President*
Fred Bradley, *Vice Pres*
Vincent Macisaac, *Agent*
Lori Beaner, *Real Est Agnt*
EMP: 50
SALES (est): 3.8MM **Privately Held**
WEB: www.eraeagle.com
SIC: 6531 Real estate agent, residential

(P-11486)
EAM ENTERPRISES INC (PA)
Also Called: Crest R E O & Relocation
4005 Foothill Blvd, La Crescenta (91214-1623)
PHONE 818 248-9100
Fax: 818 248-9295
Razmik Mirzakhanian, *CEO*
EMP: 100
SQ FT: 5,000
SALES (est): 10MM **Privately Held**
SIC: 6531 Real estate agent, residential

(P-11487)
EAPPRAISEIT LLC (PA)
12395 First American Way, Poway (92064-6897)
PHONE 800 281-6200
Anthony Merlo, *President*
Shawn McGowan, *Exec VP*
Diane Valadez, *Senior VP*
Devid Feildman, *Principal*
Anna Rojas, *Executive Asst*
EMP: 65
SALES (est): 4.6MM **Privately Held**
WEB: www.eappraiseit.com
SIC: 6531 Appraiser, real estate

(P-11488)
EAST CRSON II HSING PRTNERS LP
401 W Carson St, Carson (90745-2616)
PHONE 310 522-9606
Jim Brooks, *Controller*
EMP: 99
SALES (est): 3.5MM **Privately Held**
SIC: 6531 Real estate agents & managers

(P-11489)
EDEN HOUSING MANAGEMENT INC (PA)
22645 Grand St, Hayward (94541-5031)
PHONE 510 582-1460
Fax: 510 582-6523
Linda Mandolini, *President*
Jan Peters, *COO*
Tony MA, *CFO*
Samuel Walker, *Controller*
Tracy Griffin, *Human Res Mgr*
EMP: 50
SALES: 5.6MM **Privately Held**
SIC: 6531 Real estate managers

(P-11490)
ELIZABETH LARSON
3736 Jackson St, San Francisco (94118-1609)
PHONE 415 409-7300
Elizabeth Larson, *Owner*
EMP: 60
SALES (est): 1.4MM **Privately Held**
WEB: www.elarsonphoto.com
SIC: 6531 Auction, real estate

(P-11491)
ELMER F KARPE INC
Also Called: Karpe Real Estate Center
8501 Camino Media Ste 400, Bakersfield (93311-1358)
P.O. Box 1968 (93303-1968)
PHONE 661 847-4800
Fax: 661 832-3417
Raymond Karpe, *President*
Craig Lindsay, *Treasurer*
Jerrold Fisher, *Vice Pres*
Randy Merriman, *Vice Pres*
Tom Teagarden, *Vice Pres*
EMP: 50
SQ FT: 7,200
SALES (est): 4.2MM **Privately Held**
WEB: www.karpe.com
SIC: 6531 6163 Real estate brokers & agents; mortgage brokers arranging for loans, using money of others

(P-11492)
EMPIRE ESTATES INC
Also Called: Prudential
10750 Civic Center Dr # 100, Rancho Cucamonga (91730-3891)
PHONE 909 980-3100
Fax: 909 472-2081
Kim Senecal, *President*
Sheirley Geihm, *Admin Asst*
Patricia Parks, *Administration*
EMP: 100
SQ FT: 4,500
SALES (est): 7.3MM **Privately Held**
WEB: www.kimsenecal.com
SIC: 6531 Real estate agent, residential

(P-11493)
EMPIRE REALTY ASSOCIATES INC
380 Diablo Rd Ste 201, Danville (94526-3468)
PHONE 925 217-5000
Fax: 925 964-0860
Judith Keenholtz, *President*
Barbara Youngman, *Broker*
Elizabeth Cardoza, *Mktg Dir*
Jo Bender, *Real Est Agnt*
Dennis Burow, *Real Est Agnt*
EMP: 60
SALES (est): 5.2MM **Privately Held**
WEB: www.empirera.com
SIC: 6531 Real estate brokers & agents

(P-11494)
EQUITY ONE INCORPORATED
3 Serramonte Ctr, Daly City (94015-2345)
PHONE 415 421-5100
Fax: 415 421-6021
Jeffrey S Olson, *Branch Mgr*
Natalie Chavez, *Property Mgr*
Lissette Costa, *Property Mgr*
Mary Hunter, *Property Mgr*
Jane Schor, *Property Mgr*
EMP: 60
SALES (corp-wide): 29.4MM **Privately Held**
SIC: 6531 Real estate agent, commercial
PA: Equity One Incorporated
410 Park Ave Ste 1220
New York NY 10022
212 796-1760

(P-11495)
ERA REALTY CENTER
49 Placerville Dr, Placerville (95667-3901)
PHONE 530 295-2900
Fax: 530 295-2929
Dan Jacuzzi, *Owner*
Joe Reid, *Manager*
Sally Bobier-Hymes, *Real Est Agnt*
Linda Capone, *Real Est Agnt*
David Hymes, *Real Est Agnt*
EMP: 60
SALES (est): 2MM **Privately Held**
SIC: 6531 Real estate agent, residential

(P-11496)
ESSEX REALTY MANAGEMENT INC
18012 Sky Park Cir # 200, Irvine (92614-6671)
PHONE 949 798-8100
Jim Niger, *President*
Burrel D Magnusson, *Chairman*
Linda Webber, *Vice Pres*
Robyn Sepulveda, *Accounting Mgr*
Susan Carroll, *Accountant*
EMP: 75
SALES (est): 7.3MM **Privately Held**
SIC: 6531 Real estate brokers & agents

(P-11497)
EVANS/SIPES INC (PA)
Also Called: Re/Max
5720 Ralston St Ste 100, Ventura (93003-7845)
PHONE 805 644-1242
Fax: 805 650-9669
Glenn Sipes, *President*
Jerry Beebe, *CFO*
Michael Sipes, *Vice Pres*
Patty Ahrens, *Office Admin*
Mike Fites, *Broker*
EMP: 110
SQ FT: 35,000
SALES (est): 10.5MM **Privately Held**
WEB: www.cynthialoughman.com
SIC: 6531 Real estate agent, residential

(P-11498)
EVOQ PROPERTIES INC
1318 E 7th St 200, Los Angeles (90021-1114)
PHONE 213 988-8890
Fax: 213 627-5979
Martin Caveroy, *CEO*
John Charles Maddux, *President*
Andrew Murray, *CFO*
Miguel Enrique Echemendia, *Officer*
Lynn Beckemeyer, *Exec VP*
EMP: 82
SALES (est): 6.4MM **Privately Held**
WEB: www.meruelomaddux.com
SIC: 6531 Real estate agent, commercial; real estate agent, residential

(P-11499)
EVR LENDING INC
1397 Calle Avanzado, San Clemente (92673-6351)
PHONE 949 492-4868
Fax: 949 492-8965
Shannon Rurup, *Sales Executive*
EMP: 73
SALES (corp-wide): 21.4MM **Privately Held**
SIC: 6531 Real estate brokers & agents
PA: Evr Lending Inc
9901 Irvine Center Dr
Irvine CA 92618
949 753-7888

(P-11500)
EXCELLNCE OF INLAND EMPIRE INC
Also Called: Century 21
9568 Archibald Ave 110, Rancho Cucamonga (91730-5710)
PHONE 909 758-4311
Ramiro Majia, *President*
Luis Oliver, *CFO*
EMP: 106
SQ FT: 8,874
SALES: 3.5MM **Privately Held**
SIC: 6531 7389 Real estate agent, residential; brokers' services

(P-11501)
EXPREAL INC
Also Called: Century 21 Experience
7168 Archibald Ave # 100, Alta Loma (91701-5061)
PHONE 909 373-4400
Peter Gottuso, *Vice Pres*
EMP: 99
SALES: 950K **Privately Held**
SIC: 6531 Real estate agent, residential

(P-11502)
F M TARBELL CO
18295 Collier Ave, Lake Elsinore (92530-2755)
PHONE 951 471-5333
Carol Rounsley, *Manager*
EMP: 70
SALES (corp-wide): 132.4MM **Privately Held**
SIC: 6531 Real estate brokers & agents
HQ: F. M. Tarbell Co
1403 N Tustin Ave Ste 380
Santa Ana CA 92705
714 972-0988

(P-11503)
F M TARBELL CO
Also Called: Tarbel Realtors
39028 Winchester Rd # 101, Murrieta (92563-3505)
PHONE 951 677-3565
Joe McAllen, *General Mgr*
Gay Lyon, *Real Est Agnt*
Michele Metz, *Real Est Agnt*
EMP: 80
SALES (corp-wide): 132.4MM **Privately Held**
SIC: 6531 Real estate brokers & agents
HQ: F. M. Tarbell Co
1403 N Tustin Ave Ste 380
Santa Ana CA 92705
714 972-0988

(P-11504)
F M TARBELL CO
Also Called: Tarbell Realtors
321 S State College Blvd, Anaheim (92806-4118)
PHONE 714 772-8990
Fax: 714 772-3801
EMP: 55
SALES (corp-wide): 134.2MM **Privately Held**
SIC: 6531
HQ: F. M. Tarbell Co
1403 N Tustin Ave Ste 380
Santa Ana CA 92705
714 972-0988

(P-11505)
F M TARBELL CO
Also Called: Tarbell Realtors
6396 E Santa Ana Cyn Rd, Anaheim (92807-2365)
PHONE 714 637-7240
Fax: 714 637-1912
Mercedes Sedano, *Manager*
EMP: 50
SALES (corp-wide): 132.4MM **Privately Held**
WEB: www.tarbell.com
SIC: 6531 Real estate agents & managers
HQ: F. M. Tarbell Co
1403 N Tustin Ave Ste 380
Santa Ana CA 92705
714 972-0988

(P-11506)
F M TARBELL CO (HQ)
Also Called: Tarbell Realtors
1403 N Tustin Ave Ste 380, Santa Ana (92705-8691)
PHONE 714 972-0988
Fax: 714 972-1014
Tina Jimov, *President*
Donald M Tarbell, *CEO*
Jin Lee, *COO*
Carol Red, *Info Tech Mgr*
Nancy Foster, *Manager*
EMP: 110
SQ FT: 60,000
SALES (est): 28.6MM
SALES (corp-wide): 132.4MM **Privately Held**
WEB: www.tarbell.com
SIC: 6531 Real estate brokers & agents
PA: Tarbell Financial Corporation
1403 N Tustin Ave Ste 380
Santa Ana CA 92705
714 972-0988

(P-11507)
F M TARBELL CO
Also Called: Tarbell Realtors
315 Magnolia Ave, Corona (92879-3300)
PHONE 951 280-6040
Fax: 909 280-6050
Danny Vallejo, *Manager*
EMP: 190
SALES (corp-wide): 132.4MM **Privately Held**
WEB: www.tarbell.com
SIC: 6531 Real estate brokers & agents

6531 - Real Estate Agents & Managers County (P-11528)

HQ: F. M. Tarbell Co
1403 N Tustin Ave Ste 380
Santa Ana CA 92705
714 972-0988

(P-11508)
F M TARBELL CO
Also Called: Tarbell Realtors
25201 La Paz Rd, Laguna Hills (92653-5118)
PHONE...............949 830-6030
Fax: 949 830-5867
Dianne Montgomery, *Manager*
Ginny Lavan, *Info Tech Mgr*
Judy Michael, *Info Tech Mgr*
Karen Peters, *Opers Mgr*
David Barr, *Sales Mgr*
EMP: 62
SQ FT: 10,325
SALES (corp-wide): 132.4MM **Privately Held**
WEB: www.tarbell.com
SIC: 6531 Real estate brokers & agents
HQ: F. M. Tarbell Co
1403 N Tustin Ave Ste 380
Santa Ana CA 92705
714 972-0988

(P-11509)
F M TARBELL CO
Also Called: Tarbell Realtors
27701 Scott Rd Ste 103, Menifee (92584-9434)
PHONE...............951 301-5932
Fax: 909 679-1716
Kathy Ranier, *Manager*
EMP: 60
SALES (corp-wide): 132.4MM **Privately Held**
WEB: www.tarbell.com
SIC: 6531 Real estate agents & managers
HQ: F. M. Tarbell Co
1403 N Tustin Ave Ste 380
Santa Ana CA 92705
714 972-0988

(P-11510)
F M TARBELL CO
Also Called: Tarbell Realtors
31990 Temecula Pkwy # 101, Temecula (92592-5897)
PHONE...............951 303-0307
Fax: 951 303-0447
West Ives, *Manager*
Pam McLaurin, *Executive*
Michelle Evans, *Real Est Agnt*
Dwight Griffith, *Real Est Agnt*
EMP: 135
SALES (corp-wide): 132.4MM **Privately Held**
WEB: www.tarbell.com
SIC: 6531 Real estate brokers & agents
HQ: F. M. Tarbell Co
1403 N Tustin Ave Ste 380
Santa Ana CA 92705
714 972-0988

(P-11511)
F M TARBELL CO
Also Called: Tarbell Realtors
22632 Golden Springs Dr # 290, Diamond Bar (91765-4166)
PHONE...............909 861-3100
Fax: 909 861-3152
Martha Figureoa, *Manager*
EMP: 90
SALES (corp-wide): 132.4MM **Privately Held**
WEB: www.tarbell.com
SIC: 6531 Real estate brokers & agents
HQ: F. M. Tarbell Co
1403 N Tustin Ave Ste 380
Santa Ana CA 92705
714 972-0988

(P-11512)
F M TARBELL CO
Also Called: Tarbell Realtors
1001 Avenida Pico Ste N, San Clemente (92673-6956)
PHONE...............949 366-8810
Fax: 949 366-8826
Brent Jorgensen, *Branch Mgr*
Brad Parks, *Agent*
Richelle Redivo, *Real Est Agnt*
EMP: 60
SALES (corp-wide): 132.4MM **Privately Held**
WEB: www.tarbell.com
SIC: 6531 Real estate agents & managers
HQ: F. M. Tarbell Co
1403 N Tustin Ave Ste 380
Santa Ana CA 92705
714 972-0988

(P-11513)
F M TARBELL CO
18295 Collier Ave, Lake Elsinore (92530-2755)
PHONE...............951 471-5333
Carol Rounsley, *Manager*
EMP: 60
SALES (corp-wide): 132.4MM **Privately Held**
WEB: www.tarbell.com
SIC: 6531 Real estate brokers & agents
HQ: F. M. Tarbell Co
1403 N Tustin Ave Ste 380
Santa Ana CA 92705
714 972-0988

(P-11514)
F M TARBELL CO
Also Called: Tarbell Realtors
1403 N Tustin Ave Ste 340, Santa Ana (92705-8691)
PHONE...............714 639-0677
Sherlli Cattish, *Manager*
EMP: 50
SALES (corp-wide): 132.4MM **Privately Held**
WEB: www.tarbell.com
SIC: 6531 Real estate agents & managers
HQ: F. M. Tarbell Co
1403 N Tustin Ave Ste 380
Santa Ana CA 92705
714 972-0988

(P-11515)
F M TARBELL CO
Also Called: Tarbell Realtors
4000 Barranca Pkwy # 160, Irvine (92604-4710)
PHONE...............949 559-8451
Fax: 949 559-1841
Sheila Mayers, *Manager*
Margie Williams, *Real Est Agnt*
EMP: 72
SALES (corp-wide): 132.4MM **Privately Held**
WEB: www.tarbell.com
SIC: 6531 Real estate brokers & agents
HQ: F. M. Tarbell Co
1403 N Tustin Ave Ste 380
Santa Ana CA 92705
714 972-0988

(P-11516)
F M TARBELL CO
2409 S Vineyard Ave Ste A, Ontario (91761-6401)
PHONE...............951 270-1022
Fax: 951 270-1020
Nancy Foster, *Branch Mgr*
George Ibarra, *Real Est Agnt*
EMP: 70
SALES (corp-wide): 132.4MM **Privately Held**
WEB: www.tarbell.com
SIC: 6531 Real estate agents & managers
HQ: F. M. Tarbell Co
1403 N Tustin Ave Ste 380
Santa Ana CA 92705
714 972-0988

(P-11517)
F M TARBELL CO
Also Called: Tarbell Realtors
1365 E 19th St Ste A, Upland (91784-4201)
PHONE...............909 982-8881
Bill Velto, *Manager*
Tina Jimov-Red, *Branch Mgr*
Clement Lai, *Real Est Agnt*
Ken Winter, *Real Est Agnt*
EMP: 102
SALES (corp-wide): 132.4MM **Privately Held**
WEB: www.tarbell.com
SIC: 6531 Real estate agents & managers

(P-11518)
FELSON COMPANIES INC
1290 B St Ste 210, Hayward (94541-2996)
PHONE...............510 538-1150
Joseph Felson, *President*
Joseph Lee Felson, *President*
Elliot Felson, *Corp Secy*
Victor Richard Felson, *Vice Pres*
Elfride Groh, *General Mgr*
EMP: 90
SQ FT: 4,000
SALES (est): 8.4MM **Privately Held**
SIC: 6531 Real estate agents & managers

(P-11519)
FILLMORE MARKETPLACE LP
Also Called: Fillmore Marketplace I
1223 Webster St, San Francisco (94115-5021)
PHONE...............415 921-6514
Jim Brooks, *Controller*
Tesa Doleman, *Manager*
EMP: 50
SALES (est): 1.3MM **Privately Held**
SIC: 6531 Real estate agents & managers

(P-11520)
FIRST & LA REALTY CORP (PA)
Also Called: Century 21 Hill Top Realtors
1301 E Los Angeles Ave, Simi Valley (93065-2882)
PHONE...............805 581-0021
Robert Connlee, *President*
Pat Connlee, *Treasurer*
Susan Hill, *Admin Sec*
Kim M Dennert, *Real Est Agnt*
EMP: 67
SQ FT: 2,600
SALES (est): 4.1MM **Privately Held**
WEB: www.patconlee.com
SIC: 6531 Real estate agent, residential

(P-11521)
FIRST AMERCN PROF RE SVCS INC (PA)
200 Commerce, Irvine (92602-1318)
PHONE...............714 250-1400
Larry Davidson, *President*
Bob Dailey, *COO*
Mickey Allee, *Exec VP*
Andy Hand, *Vice Pres*
Eric Jones, *Vice Pres*
EMP: 240
SQ FT: 28,000
SALES (est): 10MM **Privately Held**
WEB: www.firstamsms.com
SIC: 6531 Real estate agents & managers

(P-11522)
FIRST AMERICAN APPRAISAL SVCS (HQ)
12395 First American Way, Poway (92064-6897)
PHONE...............619 938-7078
Fax: 760 938-7063
Anand Nallathambi, *President*
Joe Cuffaro Jr, *Exec VP*
Michael Fosser, *Senior VP*
George Klinke, *Vice Pres*
Eric Rumsey, *Vice Pres*
EMP: 66
SQ FT: 7,000
SALES (est): 9.5MM
SALES (corp-wide): 1.5B **Publicly Held**
SIC: 6531 Appraiser, real estate
PA: Corelogic, Inc.
40 Pacifica Ste 900
Irvine CA 92618
949 214-1000

(P-11523)
FIRST AMERICAN TEAM REALTY INC (PA)
Also Called: Best Financial, The
2501 Cherry Ave Ste 100, Signal Hill (90755-2039)
PHONE...............562 427-7765
Steve S Vong, *President*
Nita Hahn, *Info Tech Dir*
Veronica Garcia, *Sales Associate*
Jim Bollenbacher, *Consultant*
Jose Alamo, *Real Est Agnt*
EMP: 150
SQ FT: 3,300
SALES (est): 7.1MM **Privately Held**
WEB: www.firstamericanteam.com
SIC: 6531 Real estate brokers & agents

(P-11524)
FIRST AMERICAN TITLE INSUR CO
1001 Galaxy Way Ste 101, Concord (94520-5736)
PHONE...............925 356-7000
Connie Pickett, *Manager*
Kat Steenhuyse, *Officer*
Rich Belente, *Branch Mgr*
Gerri Gilleran, *Branch Mgr*
Paula Mullins, *Branch Mgr*
EMP: 80 **Publicly Held**
WEB: www.fatc.com
SIC: 6531 Real estate agents & managers
HQ: First American Title Insurance Company
1 First American Way
Santa Ana CA 92707
800 854-3643

(P-11525)
FIRST FAMILY HOMES
Also Called: Century 21
12027 Paramount Blvd, Downey (90242-2307)
PHONE...............562 862-7373
Fax: 562 862-7797
William C Park, *President*
Soomi Park, *Corp Secy*
EMP: 50
SALES (est): 2.2MM **Privately Held**
WEB: www.century21prorealty.com
SIC: 6531 6798 Real estate agent, residential; real estate investment trusts

(P-11526)
FIRST MARIN REALTY INC
145 Lomita Dr, Mill Valley (94941-1403)
PHONE...............415 383-9393
Fax: 415 388-6124
Douglas B Engel, *President*
Bruce Engel, *Ch of Bd*
Marcine Engel, *Vice Pres*
Brigetta Engle, *Vice Pres*
John Arthun, *Regional Mgr*
EMP: 60
SQ FT: 10,000
SALES: 3MM **Privately Held**
WEB: www.firstmarin.net
SIC: 6531 Real estate brokers & agents

(P-11527)
FIRST TEAM RE - ORANGE CNTY
74855 Country Club Dr, Palm Desert (92260-1961)
PHONE...............760 340-9911
Todd Banks, *Branch Mgr*
Byron A Clark, *Real Est Agnt*
Mark Dorris, *Real Est Agnt*
Susan Drew, *Real Est Agnt*
Jorge Granados, *Real Est Agnt*
EMP: 64
SALES (corp-wide): 95.7MM **Privately Held**
SIC: 6531 Real estate brokers & agents
PA: First Team Real Estate - Orange County
108 Pacifica Ste 300
Irvine CA 92618
888 236-1943

(P-11528)
FIRST TEAM RE - ORANGE CNTY
Also Called: First Team S S Estate
1950 S Brea Canyon Rd # 1, Diamond Bar (91765-4015)
PHONE...............909 861-1380
Jim Carrescia, *Manager*
Ernie Delgadillo, *Sales Executive*
Paul Monte, *Sales Staff*
Alicia Yong, *Corp Comm Staff*
Michael Chu, *Real Est Agnt*
EMP: 100

6531 - Real Estate Agents & Managers County (P-11529)

SALES (corp-wide): 95.7MM **Privately Held**
WEB: www.coastcitiesescrow.com
SIC: 6531 Real estate agent, residential
PA: First Team Real Estate - Orange County
   108 Pacifica Ste 300
   Irvine CA 92618
   888 236-1943

(P-11529)
FIRST TEAM RE - ORANGE CNTY
18180 Yorba Linda Blvd # 501, Yorba Linda (92886-3901)
PHONE...................714 223-2143
Fax: 714 986-1771
Bob Macculloch, *Manager*
Herman Dowdle, *Broker*
Denise Tash, *Sales Executive*
Herman Andres, *Sales Associate*
Bob Bendat, *Sales Associate*
EMP: 100
SALES (corp-wide): 95.7MM **Privately Held**
WEB: www.coastcitiesescrow.com
SIC: 6531 Real estate agent, residential
PA: First Team Real Estate - Orange County
   108 Pacifica Ste 300
   Irvine CA 92618
   888 236-1943

(P-11530)
FIRST TEAM RE - ORANGE CNTY
12501 Seal Beach Blvd # 100, Seal Beach (90740-2763)
PHONE...................562 596-9911
Fax: 562 596-4661
Judy Sharp, *Manager*
Fred Nassab, *General Mgr*
Philip A Dematteo, *Administration*
Alice Marie, *Software Dev*
Patricia Putnam, *Broker*
EMP: 150
SALES (corp-wide): 95.7MM **Privately Held**
WEB: www.coastcitiesescrow.com
SIC: 6531 Real estate agent, residential
PA: First Team Real Estate - Orange County
   108 Pacifica Ste 300
   Irvine CA 92618
   888 236-1943

(P-11531)
FIRST TEAM RE - ORANGE CNTY
4 Corprate Plz Dr Ste 100, Corona Del Mar (92625)
PHONE...................949 759-5747
Fax: 949 759-5744
Troy Davis, *Manager*
EMP: 55
SALES (corp-wide): 95.7MM **Privately Held**
WEB: www.coastcitiesescrow.com
SIC: 6531 Real estate agents & managers
PA: First Team Real Estate - Orange County
   108 Pacifica Ste 300
   Irvine CA 92618
   888 236-1943

(P-11532)
FIRST TEAM RE - ORANGE CNTY (PA)
Also Called: First Team Walk-In Realty
108 Pacifica Ste 300, Irvine (92618-7435)
PHONE...................888 236-1943
Fax: 714 668-0430
Cameron Merage, *CEO*
Jeff Arcuri, *Senior VP*
Todd Bruechert, *Vice Pres*
Jennifer Chiavetta, *Creative Dir*
Mila Rodriguera, *Office Mgr*
EMP: 160 EST: 1976
SQ FT: 8,000
SALES (est): 95.7MM **Privately Held**
WEB: www.coastcitiesescrow.com
SIC: 6531 Real estate agent, residential

(P-11533)
FIRST TEAM RE - ORANGE CNTY
Also Called: First State
20100 Brookhurst St, Huntington Beach (92646-4938)
PHONE...................714 965-2244
Fax: 714 968-1211
Wally Malesh, *Manager*
Barbara Arrigale, *Real Est Agnt*
Jerry Beusee, *Real Est Agnt*
Maryann Cardullo, *Real Est Agnt*
Ewa Chrzanowska, *Real Est Agnt*
EMP: 100
SALES (corp-wide): 95.7MM **Privately Held**
WEB: www.coastcitiesescrow.com
SIC: 6531 Real estate brokers & agents
PA: First Team Real Estate - Orange County
   108 Pacifica Ste 300
   Irvine CA 92618
   888 236-1943

(P-11534)
FIRST TEAM RE - ORANGE CNTY
4040 Barranca Pkwy # 100, Irvine (92604-4766)
PHONE...................949 857-0414
Fax: 949 857-6403
Dan Sarnecky, *Manager*
Shannon N Jaramillo, *Manager*
Mana Aminian, *Real Est Agnt*
Robert Armstrong, *Real Est Agnt*
Mary Barnes, *Real Est Agnt*
EMP: 90
SALES (corp-wide): 95.7MM **Privately Held**
WEB: www.coastcitiesescrow.com
SIC: 6531 Real estate brokers & agents
PA: First Team Real Estate - Orange County
   108 Pacifica Ste 300
   Irvine CA 92618
   888 236-1943

(P-11535)
FIRST TEAM RE - ORANGE CNTY
42 64th Pl, Long Beach (90803-5676)
PHONE...................562 346-5088
EMP: 78
SALES (corp-wide): 95.7MM **Privately Held**
SIC: 6531 Real estate brokers & agents
PA: First Team Real Estate - Orange County
   108 Pacifica Ste 300
   Irvine CA 92618
   888 236-1943

(P-11536)
FIRST TEAM RE - ORANGE CNTY
32451 Golden Lantern # 210, Laguna Niguel (92677-5344)
PHONE...................949 240-7979
Mark Kojac, *General Mgr*
Geraldine Duarte, *Broker*
Lois Pallone, *Broker*
Brenda Thomas, *Agent*
Beau Beardslee, *Real Est Agnt*
EMP: 140
SALES (corp-wide): 95.7MM **Privately Held**
WEB: www.coastcitiesescrow.com
SIC: 6531 Real estate brokers & agents
PA: First Team Real Estate - Orange County
   108 Pacifica Ste 300
   Irvine CA 92618
   888 236-1943

(P-11537)
FIRST TEAM RE - ORANGE CNTY
Also Called: 1st Team Real Estate
17240 17th St, Tustin (92780-1940)
PHONE...................714 544-5456
Fax: 714 544-4490
Michael Hampton, *Manager*
Misuk Hysen, *Sales Associate*
Heidi Buccola, *Real Est Agnt*
David Caballero, *Real Est Agnt*
Jay Gaylen, *Real Est Agnt*
EMP: 137
SALES (corp-wide): 95.7MM **Privately Held**
WEB: www.coastcitiesescrow.com
SIC: 6531 Real estate brokers & agents
PA: First Team Real Estate - Orange County
   108 Pacifica Ste 300
   Irvine CA 92618
   888 236-1943

(P-11538)
FIRST TEAM RE - ORANGE CNTY
8028 E Santa Ana Cyn Rd, Anaheim (92808-1108)
PHONE...................714 974-9191
Fax: 714 921-9438
Anna Bennet, *Manager*
Sandra Meucci, *Office Admin*
Alexander Thompson, *Broker*
Bruce Brown, *Real Est Agnt*
Jayson Cook, *Real Est Agnt*
EMP: 63
SALES (corp-wide): 99.8MM **Privately Held**
WEB: www.coastcitiesescrow.com
SIC: 6531 Real estate agents & managers
PA: First Team Real Estate - Orange County
   108 Pacifica Ste 300
   Irvine CA 92618
   888 236-1943

(P-11539)
FIRSTSRVICE RSIDENTIAL CAL INC (DH)
195 N Euclid Ave, Upland (91786-6055)
P.O. Box 1510 (91785-1510)
PHONE...................909 981-4131
Fax: 909 981-7631
Glennon Gray, *President*
James Gray, *Vice Pres*
Kathy Johnston, *Division Mgr*
Dana Mathey, *Division Mgr*
Caroylyn Poust, *Executive Asst*
EMP: 69
SQ FT: 16,000
SALES (est): 7.6MM
SALES (corp-wide): 1.2B **Privately Held**
WEB: www.euclidmanagement.com
SIC: 6531 Real estate managers
HQ: Firstservice Residential, Inc.
   1855 Griffin Rd Ste A330
   Dania Beach FL 33004
   954 926-2921

(P-11540)
FKC PARTNERS A CAL LTD PARTNR
Also Called: Fkc Properties
180 N Rverview Dr Ste 100, Anaheim (92808)
PHONE...................714 528-9864
Fax: 714 528-6641
Paul Kramer,
Brett Albrecht, *Director*
EMP: 50
SALES (est): 2.1MM **Privately Held**
SIC: 6531 Real estate agents & managers

(P-11541)
FLYNN PROPERTIES INC
225 Bush St Ste 1470, San Francisco (94104-4226)
PHONE...................415 835-0225
Greg Flynn, *President*
Lorin Cortina, *CFO*
Kristine Equihua, *Manager*
EMP: 50
SALES (est): 5.4MM **Privately Held**
SIC: 6531 Real estate agents & managers

(P-11542)
FOUNTAIN COURT ESSEX
22102 Clarendon St # 200, Woodland Hills (91367-6307)
PHONE...................818 227-2100
Michael Schall, *President*
EMP: 50
SALES (est): 1.2MM **Privately Held**
SIC: 6531 Rental agent, real estate

(P-11543)
FPI MANAGEMENT INC (PA)
800 Iron Point Rd, Folsom (95630-9004)
PHONE...................916 357-5300
Fax: 916 357-5310
Dennis Treadaway, *President*
Ken Hunt, *Shareholder*
Gary Quattrin, *Shareholder*
David Divine, *Vice Pres*
Michelle Fisher, *Vice Pres*
EMP: 50
SQ FT: 18,000
SALES (est): 73.9MM **Privately Held**
WEB: www.fpimgt.com
SIC: 6531 Real estate managers

(P-11544)
FRANK HOWARD ALLEN FINCL CORP
Also Called: Frank Howard Allen Real Estate
1016 Irwin St, San Rafael (94901-3320)
PHONE...................415 456-3000
Fax: 415 457-2359
Fred Angeli, *Manager*
EMP: 55
SALES (corp-wide): 5.7B **Publicly Held**
WEB: www.fhallen.com
SIC: 6531 Real estate brokers & agents
HQ: Frank Howard Allen Financial Corporation
   1013 2nd St
   Novato CA
   415 897-4444

(P-11545)
FRANK HOWARD ALLEN FINCL CORP
460 Mission Blvd, Santa Rosa (95409-5351)
PHONE...................707 523-3000
Fax: 707 537-7427
Brian Connell, *Sales/Mktg Mgr*
Niki Rapp, *Administration*
Judy Freedman, *Real Est Agnt*
Joe Hernandez, *Real Est Agnt*
Mike Stollmeyer, *Real Est Agnt*
EMP: 71
SALES (corp-wide): 5.7B **Publicly Held**
WEB: www.fhallen.com
SIC: 6531 Selling agent, real estate
HQ: Frank Howard Allen Financial Corporation
   1013 2nd St
   Novato CA
   415 897-4444

(P-11546)
FUSION REAL ESTATE NETWORK INC
1300 National Dr Ste 170, Sacramento (95834-1991)
PHONE...................916 448-3174
Gwen Scott, *President*
James Becker, *Vice Pres*
Helen Whitelaw, *Vice Pres*
Aaron Tyler, *Broker*
Renee Wecker, *Exec Sec*
EMP: 90
SQ FT: 4,400
SALES (est): 5.1MM **Privately Held**
SIC: 6531 Real estate agents & managers

(P-11547)
G & K MANAGEMENT CO INC (PA)
5150 Overland Ave, Culver City (90230-4914)
PHONE...................310 204-2050
Carole Glodney, *CEO*
Jona Goldrich, *Vice Pres*
Stephanie Kufhner, *Office Mgr*
Leslie Suder, *Mktg Dir*
Sylvia Rubalcava, *Asst Director*
EMP: 150
SALES (est): 19MM **Privately Held**
WEB: www.gkind.com
SIC: 6531 Real estate managers

(P-11548)
G & K MANAGEMENT CO INC
Also Called: Coronado Royale
299 Prospect Pl, Coronado (92118-1967)
PHONE...................619 437-1777
Rudy Littlefield, *Manager*
EMP: 50

PRODUCTS & SERVICES SECTION
6531 - Real Estate Agents & Managers County (P-11571)

SALES (corp-wide): 19MM **Privately Held**
WEB: www.gkind.com
SIC: **6531** 6513 Real estate managers; retirement hotel operation
PA: G & K Management Co., Inc.
5150 Overland Ave
Culver City CA 90230
310 204-2050

(P-11549)
G & K MANAGEMENT CO INC
Also Called: Kittridge Gardens
6540 Wilbur Ave, Reseda (91335-5927)
PHONE.................................818 705-8834
Fax: 818 705-0029
Jane Pouchino, *Manager*
EMP: 80
SALES (corp-wide): 19MM **Privately Held**
WEB: www.gkind.com
SIC: **6531** 6513 Real estate managers; apartment building operators
PA: G & K Management Co., Inc.
5150 Overland Ave
Culver City CA 90230
310 204-2050

(P-11550)
G M A C-ONE SOURCE REALTY (PA)
898 Jackman St, El Cajon (92020-3057)
PHONE.................................619 405-6231
Greg Seaman, *Owner*
EMP: 56
SALES (est): 2.2MM **Privately Held**
SIC: **6531** Real estate agents & managers

(P-11551)
GEMMM CORP
587 W Los Angeles Ave, Moorpark (93021-1709)
PHONE.................................805 267-2700
Dave Ward, *Branch Mgr*
EMP: 59
SALES (corp-wide): 8.1MM **Privately Held**
SIC: **6531** Real estate agents & managers
PA: Gemmm Corp
2860 E Thousand Oaks Blvd
Thousand Oaks CA 91362
805 496-0555

(P-11552)
GEMMM CORP
2211 Memory Ln, Westlake Village (91361-5524)
PHONE.................................818 522-0740
Chris Doernes, *Branch Mgr*
EMP: 59
SALES (corp-wide): 8.1MM **Privately Held**
SIC: **6531** Real estate brokers & agents
PA: Gemmm Corp
2860 E Thousand Oaks Blvd
Thousand Oaks CA 91362
805 496-0555

(P-11553)
GEMMM CORP (PA)
Also Called: Prudential
2860 E Thousand Oaks Blvd, Thousand Oaks (91362-3201)
PHONE.................................805 496-0555
Fax: 805 374-2126
Robert L Majorino, *President*
Anthony Principe, *CFO*
Natalia Gavrilov, *Senior VP*
Henry Hershkowitz, *Senior VP*
Eric Janssen, *Senior VP*
EMP: 100
SQ FT: 12,500
SALES (est): 8.1MM **Privately Held**
WEB: www.prucalhomes.com
SIC: **6531** Real estate agent, residential

(P-11554)
GENESIS VOCATIONAL SPECIALIST
5200 W Century Blvd 305, Los Angeles (90045-5928)
PHONE.................................213 892-6307
Yzette Page, *President*
EMP: 50
SALES (est): 1.1MM **Privately Held**
SIC: **6531** Real estate agents & managers

(P-11555)
GLENBOROUGH LLC (PA)
400 S El Camino Real # 1100, San Mateo (94402-1706)
PHONE.................................650 343-9300
Fax: 650 343-7438
Andrew Batinovich, *CEO*
Michael Steele, *COO*
Brian S Peay, *CFO*
Chip Burns, *Senior VP*
Terri Garnick, *Senior VP*
EMP: 60
SALES: 7MM **Privately Held**
SIC: **6531** Real estate managers

(P-11556)
GOLD COUNTRY MANAGEMENT INC
1825 Bell St Ste 100, Sacramento (95825-1020)
PHONE.................................916 929-3003
James Gately, *President*
EMP: 70 EST: 1993
SALES (est): 3.3MM **Privately Held**
SIC: **6531** Real estate managers

(P-11557)
GOLDEN RAIN FOUNDATION (PA)
Also Called: Rossmoor
1001 Golden Rain Rd, Walnut Creek (94595-2441)
P.O. Box 2070 (94595-0070)
PHONE.................................925 988-7700
Fax: 925 988-7686
Stephen Adams, *CEO*
Rick Chakoff, *CFO*
Craig Miller, *Treasurer*
Paul Rosenzweig, *Bd of Directors*
Lyle Brown, *Vice Pres*
EMP: 63
SQ FT: 5,000
SALES (est): 24MM **Privately Held**
WEB: www.rossmoornews.com
SIC: **6531** 8011 2711 7997 Real estate managers; offices & clinics of medical doctors; newspapers; golf club, membership

(P-11558)
GOODMAN GROUP INC
Also Called: Alamitos Convalescent Hospital
3902 Katella Ave, Los Alamitos (90720-3304)
PHONE.................................562 596-5561
Kevin Russo, *Exec Dir*
EMP: 65
SALES (corp-wide): 25.5MM **Privately Held**
WEB: www.thepalmsoflargo.com
SIC: **6531** Real estate managers
PA: The Goodman Group Inc
1107 Hazeltine Blvd # 200
Chaska MN 55318
952 361-8000

(P-11559)
GRAND PACIFIC RESORTS INC (PA)
5900 Pasteur Ct Ste 200, Carlsbad (92008-7336)
P.O. Box 4068 (92018-4068)
PHONE.................................760 431-8500
Timothy J Stripe, *CEO*
Diane Proulx, *President*
Sherri Weeks-Rivera, *President*
Nigel Lobo, *COO*
David Brown, *Vice Pres*
EMP: 250
SQ FT: 22,000
SALES (est): 206.1MM **Privately Held**
WEB: www.grandpacificresorts.com
SIC: **6531** 7011 Time-sharing real estate sales, leasing & rentals; hotels & motels

(P-11560)
GREENBRIAR MANAGEMENT COMPANY
Also Called: Greenbriar Homes Community
43160 Osgood Rd, Fremont (94539-5608)
PHONE.................................510 497-8200
Gilbert M Meyer, *CEO*
Carol Meyer, *Vice Pres*
Mort Newman, *Vice Pres*
Brain Cochran, *Administration*
Aslaug Uttenreuther, *Accountant*
EMP: 100
SQ FT: 16,932
SALES (est): 5.4MM **Privately Held**
SIC: **6531** Cooperative apartment manager

(P-11561)
GREGA BROOKE SRA
18501 Riverside Dr, Sonoma (95476-4509)
P.O. Box 268 (95476-0268)
PHONE.................................707 938-3362
Grega Brooke, *Principal*
EMP: 50
SALES (est): 1.3MM **Privately Held**
SIC: **6531** Appraiser, real estate

(P-11562)
GREYSTAR MANAGEMENT SVCS LP
6320 Canoga Ave Ste 1512, Woodland Hills (91367-2526)
PHONE.................................818 596-2180
Grace White, *Owner*
EMP: 521
SALES (corp-wide): 264.3MM **Privately Held**
SIC: **6531** Real estate brokers & agents
PA: Greystar Management Services, L.P.
750 Bering Dr Ste 300
Houston TX 77057
713 966-5000

(P-11563)
GRUBB CO INC
1960 Mountain Blvd, Oakland (94611-2894)
PHONE.................................510 339-0400
D J Grubb Jr, *President*
Grubb John, *COO*
Laura Castillo, *Office Mgr*
Julie Gardner, *Broker*
Kristen Parkinson, *Bookkeeper*
EMP: 53
SQ FT: 2,800
SALES (est): 4.8MM **Privately Held**
WEB: www.grubbco.com
SIC: **6531** Real estate brokers & agents

(P-11564)
GRUPE COMPANY (PA)
3255 W March Ln Ste 400, Stockton (95219-2352)
P.O. Box 7576 (95267-0576)
PHONE.................................209 473-6000
Fax: 209 951-0684
Frank A Passadore, *President*
Greenlaw Grupe Jr, *Ch of Bd*
Frank Paadore, *COO*
Nelson Bahler, *Exec VP*
Chris Conklin, *Vice Pres*
EMP: 60 EST: 1960
SQ FT: 7,000
SALES (est): 82.9MM **Privately Held**
WEB: www.grupe.com
SIC: **6531** 1542 Real estate agent, residential; real estate brokers & agents; commercial & office building, new construction

(P-11565)
GUARANTEE REAL ESTATE
756 W Shaw Ave Ste 105, Fresno (93704-2223)
PHONE.................................559 650-6030
Fax: 559 650-6033
Sandy Darling, *Vice Pres*
J Scott Leonard, *CEO*
Laura Everson, *CFO*
Al Alarcon, *Broker*
Barbara Cox, *Broker*
EMP: 50
SALES (est): 2.6MM **Privately Held**
SIC: **6531** Real estate agents & managers

(P-11566)
GUARANTEE REAL ESTATE CORP
6710 N West Ave Ste 108, Fresno (93711-4300)
PHONE.................................559 431-8600
Fax: 209 432-3346
Allan Atchley, *Manager*
Awremce Reba, *Vice Pres*
Vince Carter, *Manager*
Andy Nazaroff, *Manager*
Taryn Emmett, *Real Est Agnt*
EMP: 65
SALES (corp-wide): 210.8B **Publicly Held**
SIC: **6531** Real estate brokers & agents
HQ: Guarantee Real Estate Corporation
5380 N Fresno St Ste 101
Fresno CA 93710
559 650-6000

(P-11567)
HANNAM CHAIN USA INC
5301 Beach Blvd, Buena Park (90621-1231)
PHONE.................................714 670-0670
Charles Kim, *Owner*
EMP: 82
SALES (corp-wide): 98.8MM **Privately Held**
SIC: **6531** Real estate brokers & agents
PA: Hannam Chain U.S.A., Inc.
2740 W Olympic Blvd
Los Angeles CA 90006
213 382-2922

(P-11568)
HANSEN QUALITY LOAN SVCS INC
9339 Carroll Park Dr # 100, San Diego (92121-3247)
PHONE.................................858 909-4300
Gregory Hansen,
Brian Polchow, *Controller*
Gilbert Vasquez, *Controller*
EMP: 150 EST: 1991
SQ FT: 15,000
SALES (est): 5.7MM
SALES (corp-wide): 9.1B **Publicly Held**
WEB: www.hanqual.com
SIC: **6531** Appraiser, real estate
HQ: Fidelity National Information Solutions Inc
4050 Calle Real
Santa Barbara CA

(P-11569)
HARMONY ESCROW INC
17100 Gillette Ave, Irvine (92614-5603)
PHONE.................................949 474-1134
Rande Johnsen, *President*
Terry Johnsen, *CFO*
Miguel Ochoa, *Trustee*
Debbie Sala, *Executive*
Audrey Bryan, *Office Mgr*
EMP: 60
SALES (est): 950K **Privately Held**
SIC: **6531** Real estate agents & managers

(P-11570)
HELM MANAGEMENT CO (PA)
Also Called: Helm, The
4668 Nebo Dr Ste A, La Mesa (91941-5200)
PHONE.................................619 589-6222
Fax: 619 466-6499
Tom Hensley, *President*
Amena Nawabi, *Admin Asst*
EMP: 70
SQ FT: 1,176
SALES (est): 7MM **Privately Held**
WEB: www.helmmanagement.com
SIC: **6531** Real estate agents & managers; time-sharing real estate sales, leasing & rentals; rental agent, real estate; condominium manager

(P-11571)
HMS AGRICULTURAL CORPORATION
46247 Arabia St, Indio (92201-5840)
P.O. Box 1787 (92202-1787)
PHONE.................................760 347-2335
Fax: 760 342-1043
Ole Fogh-Andersen, *President*
Earline Taylor, *Treasurer*
Linden Anderson, *Vice Pres*
Henry Bastidas, *Vice Pres*
EMP: 70 EST: 1975
SQ FT: 1,600
SALES (est): 4.8MM **Privately Held**
SIC: **6531** Real estate managers

6531 - Real Estate Agents & Managers County (P-11572)

(P-11572)
HOMEGAINCOM INC
12667 Alcosta Blvd # 200, San Ramon (94583-4693)
PHONE..................................888 542-0800
Tim Fagan, *CEO*
Mandy Grace, *CFO*
Kal Deutsch, *Vice Pres*
Gleen Houck, *Vice Pres*
Mark Lieberman, *Vice Pres*
EMP: 65
SQ FT: 13,000
SALES (est): 2.8MM
SALES (corp-wide): 52.5MM **Privately Held**
WEB: www.homegain.com
SIC: 6531 Real estate agents & managers
PA: One Planet Ops Inc.
12667 Alcosta Blvd # 200
San Ramon CA 94583
925 983-3400

(P-11573)
HOUSE OF SEVEN GABLES RE (PA)
12651 Newport Ave, Tustin (92780-2422)
PHONE..................................714 731-3777
Fax: 714 731-4906
Ronald C Douglas, *President*
Felicia Martinez, *Chief Mktg Ofcr*
Barbara Salisbury, *Office Admin*
Mike Hickman, *Info Tech Dir*
Ryan Hildebrant, *Info Tech Mgr*
EMP: 80 **EST:** 1976
SQ FT: 5,900
SALES (est): 14.3MM **Privately Held**
WEB: www.sevengables.com
SIC: 6531 Real estate brokers & agents

(P-11574)
HOUSING ATHRTY OF THE CNTY OF
2931 Mission St, Santa Cruz (95060-5709)
PHONE..................................831 454-9455
Fax: 831 429-3249
Ken Cole, *Exec Dir*
Pam Smith, *Finance*
EMP: 65
SALES (est): 58MM **Privately Held**
SIC: 6531 Real estate managers

(P-11575)
HST LESSEE SAN DIEGO LP
Also Called: Sheraton San Diego Ht & Marina
1380 Harbor Island Dr, San Diego (92101-1007)
PHONE..................................619 291-2900
Fax: 619 692-3241
Joe Tursey, *Principal*
Fred Garcia, *Finance*
Miriam Slack, *Controller*
Karla Britt, *HR Admin*
Sarah Buxbaum, *Manager*
EMP: 800
SQ FT: 75,000
SALES (est): 45.3MM **Privately Held**
WEB: www.sheratonsandiegohotelandmarina.com
SIC: 6531 7011 5812 5947 Real estate agent, commercial; real estate managers; hotels & motels; eating places; gift, novelty & souvenir shop; drinking places; marinas

(P-11576)
HUNT ENTERPRISES INC
Also Called: Shibui Apartments
2270 Sepulveda Blvd # 50, Torrance (90501-5304)
PHONE..................................310 325-1496
EMP: 113
SQ FT: 53,813
SALES (corp-wide): 12.6MM **Privately Held**
SIC: 6531 Real estate leasing & rentals
PA: Hunt Enterprises, Inc.
4416 W 154th St
Lawndale CA 90260
310 675-3555

(P-11577)
HUNTER REALTY INC
Also Called: Prudential
2605 S Miller St Ste 101, Santa Maria (93455-1774)
PHONE..................................805 346-8688
Fax: 805 928-2968
David Cabot, *President*
EMP: 155
SALES (est): 5.9MM **Privately Held**
SIC: 6531 8742 Real estate brokers & agents; real estate consultant

(P-11578)
HYATT VACATION OWNERSHIP INC
9615 Brighton Way M180, Beverly Hills (90210-5140)
PHONE..................................310 285-0990
John Burlingame, *Exec VP*
Larry Shulman, *VP Sales*
EMP: 80
SALES (est): 1.3MM **Privately Held**
SIC: 6531 Real estate leasing & rentals

(P-11579)
I D PROPERTY CORPORATION
Also Called: Property I D
1001 Wilshire Blvd # 100, Los Angeles (90017-2821)
PHONE..................................213 625-0100
Fax: 213 270-7145
Carlos Siderman, *President*
John Cote, *President*
Kitty Krant, *Executive*
Lisa Rembold, *Executive*
Debra Speer, *Executive*
▲ **EMP:** 120
SALES (est): 11.6MM **Privately Held**
SIC: 6531 8742 Real estate listing services; real estate consultant

(P-11580)
IC BP III HOLDINGS XII LLC
1 Sansome St Ste 1500, San Francisco (94104-4449)
PHONE..................................415 549-5054
Aaron Snegg, *Manager*
EMP: 60
SALES (est): 1.9MM **Privately Held**
SIC: 6531 Real estate leasing & rentals

(P-11581)
IDS REAL ESTATE GROUP (PA)
Also Called: I S D
515 S Figueroa St Fl 16, Los Angeles (90071-3301)
PHONE..................................213 627-9937
Murad M Siam, *CEO*
David G Mgrubllan, *President*
Mickey Siam, *COO*
Jeff Newman, *CFO*
James Cain, *Senior VP*
EMP: 60
SQ FT: 20,000
SALES (est): 16.1MM **Privately Held**
SIC: 6531 Real estate brokers & agents; real estate managers

(P-11582)
INLAND EMPIRE RE SOLUTIONS
Also Called: Remax Legends
8794 19th St, Alta Loma (91701-4608)
P.O. Box 129, Rancho Cucamonga (91739-0129)
PHONE..................................909 476-1000
Fax: 909 476-6474
Jodi Lee Nazi, *President*
Jodi Lee Nazir, *President*
Jason Rowe, *Real Est Agnt*
EMP: 76
SQ FT: 5,600
SALES: 4MM **Privately Held**
SIC: 6531 Real estate agent, residential

(P-11583)
INLAND EMPIRE REAL ESTATE
8010 Haven Ave, Rancho Cucamonga (91730-3047)
P.O. Box 1195 (91729-1195)
PHONE..................................909 944-2070
Fax: 909 944-2077
Ruben Mendez, *President*
EMP: 50
SALES (est): 1.7MM **Privately Held**
SIC: 6531 Real estate agents & managers

(P-11584)
INMAN SPINOSA & BUCHAN INC
Also Called: Landmark Realty Center
28901 S Wstn Ave Ste 101, Rancho Palos Verdes (90275)
PHONE..................................310 519-1080
Fax: 310 519-1882
Gordon Inman, *President*
Nancy Inman, *Treasurer*
Donna Buchan, *Vice Pres*
EMP: 58
SALES (est): 3.5MM **Privately Held**
WEB: www.salsorrentino.com
SIC: 6531 6163 Real estate brokers & agents; mortgage brokers arranging for loans, using money of others

(P-11585)
INTERO REAL ESTATE SERVICES
790 1st St, Gilroy (95020-4972)
PHONE..................................408 848-8400
Fax: 408 848-5847
Kathie Kingston, *President*
Angela Kluck, *Personnel Exec*
EMP: 62
SALES (est): 2.3MM **Privately Held**
SIC: 6531 Real estate agent, residential

(P-11586)
INTERO REAL ESTATE SVCS INC
12900 Saratoga Ave, Saratoga (95070-4668)
PHONE..................................408 741-1600
Fax: 408 863-3099
Tom Tagnoli, *General Mgr*
Daniela Bitter, *Real Est Agnt*
Carlos R Cruz, *Real Est Agnt*
Kathleen Daniels, *Real Est Agnt*
Suni Jin, *Real Est Agnt*
EMP: 81
SALES (corp-wide): 210.8B **Publicly Held**
SIC: 6531 Real estate brokers & agents
HQ: Intero Real Estate Services, Inc.
10275 N De Anza Blvd
Cupertino CA 95014
408 342-3000

(P-11587)
INTERO REAL ESTATE SVCS INC
8255 Firestone Blvd # 200, Downey (90241-4877)
PHONE..................................562 861-7242
Oscar Mendoza, *Principal*
EMP: 81
SALES (corp-wide): 210.8B **Publicly Held**
SIC: 6531 Real estate brokers & agents
HQ: Intero Real Estate Services, Inc.
10275 N De Anza Blvd
Cupertino CA 95014
408 342-3000

(P-11588)
INTERO REAL ESTATE SVCS INC
32145 Alvarado Niles Rd # 101, Union City (94587-2930)
PHONE..................................510 489-8989
Joey Anudon, *Branch Mgr*
EMP: 81
SALES (corp-wide): 210.8B **Publicly Held**
SIC: 6531 Real estate brokers & agents
HQ: Intero Real Estate Services, Inc.
10275 N De Anza Blvd
Cupertino CA 95014
408 342-3000

(P-11589)
INTERO REAL ESTATE SVCS INC
5890 Silver Creek Vly Rd, San Jose (95138-1027)
PHONE..................................408 574-5000
Robert Cruz, *Manager*
Gary Tilbury, *Vice Pres*
Joseph Orason, *Network Mgr*
Carole Holcomb, *Real Est Agnt*
EMP: 150
SALES (corp-wide): 210.8B **Publicly Held**
SIC: 6531 6519 Real estate agents & managers; real property lessors
HQ: Intero Real Estate Services, Inc.
10275 N De Anza Blvd
Cupertino CA 95014
408 342-3000

(P-11590)
INTERO REAL ESTATE SVCS INC
Also Called: Intero Silicon Valley
1900 Camden Ave, San Jose (95124-2942)
PHONE..................................408 558-3600
Terry Meyer, *COO*
Chris Stuart, *Vice Pres*
Rafael Noriega, *Exec Dir*
Teressa Francis, *Mktg Dir*
Rob Martin, *Marketing Staff*
EMP: 50
SALES (est): 2.1MM **Privately Held**
SIC: 6531 7389 Real estate brokers & agents; office facilities & secretarial service rental

(P-11591)
INVESERVE CORPORATION
123 S Chapel Ave, Alhambra (91801-3951)
PHONE..................................626 458-3435
Fax: 626 458-5321
Norman Chang, *President*
Amy Chang, *Vice Pres*
Timothy TSE, *Controller*
Michael Fang, *Advisor*
EMP: 80
SQ FT: 1,000
SALES (est): 7.2MM **Privately Held**
WEB: www.inveserve.com
SIC: 6531 Real estate brokers & agents; real estate managers

(P-11592)
IVY REALTY
611 S Wilton Pl, Los Angeles (90005-3220)
PHONE..................................213 386-8888
Fax: 213 386-8183
J D Kym, *CEO*
Joana Chang, *Real Est Agnt*
Micki M Park, *Real Est Agnt*
EMP: 50
SALES (est): 1.8MM **Privately Held**
WEB: www.ivyrealty.com
SIC: 6531 Real estate brokers & agents

(P-11593)
J BARON INC
Also Called: Re/Max
5299 Alton Pkwy, Irvine (92604-8604)
PHONE..................................949 451-1200
Fax: 714 730-7774
Tom Baron, *President*
Lafourcade Jeanne, *Info Tech Dir*
Ruth Watkins, *Info Tech Mgr*
Vanissa Micklethwait, *Broker*
Kathryn Smith, *Sales Executive*
EMP: 96
SALES (est): 6MM **Privately Held**
SIC: 6531 Real estate agent, residential

(P-11594)
J H SYNDER CO LLC
5757 Wilshire Blvd Ph 30, Los Angeles (90036-3690)
PHONE..................................323 857-5546
Jerome Snyder, *Managing Prtnr*
Thomas Dujovne, *Ch Invest Ofcr*
Mina Elliott, *Vice Pres*
Patrick Irvine, *Vice Pres*
Mary Schwei, *Executive*
EMP: 60
SALES (est): 5.2MM **Privately Held**
SIC: 6531 Buying agent, real estate

(P-11595)
JAMBOREE REALTY CORP (PA)
Also Called: Jamboree Management
22982 Mill Creek Dr, Laguna Hills (92653-1214)
PHONE..................................949 380-0300
Fax: 949 900-4950
Fred G Sparks, *President*
Richard M Tucker, *CEO*
Kathleen Tucker, *Treasurer*
Terri Boykin, *Admin Asst*
EMP: 120
SALES (est): 15.9MM **Privately Held**
SIC: 6531 Real estate agents & managers

PRODUCTS & SERVICES SECTION

6531 - Real Estate Agents & Managers County (P-11621)

(P-11596)
JB PARTNERS GROUP INC
18375 Ventura Blvd, Tarzana (91356-4218)
PHONE..................818 668-8201
Robert E Hart, *Principal*
EMP: 110
SALES (est): 4.3MM
SALES (corp-wide): 18MM **Privately Held**
SIC: 6531 Real estate leasing & rentals
PA: The Laramar Group L L C
    222 S Riverside Plz
    Chicago IL 60606
    312 669-1200

(P-11597)
JOE CANPAGNA
Also Called: Prudential
2830 Shelter Island Dr, San Diego (92106-2733)
PHONE..................619 222-0555
Fax: 619 226-6649
Joe Canpagna, *Manager*
Jaime Deblassio, *Executive*
Joe Camphena, *Manager*
Markus Feldmann, *Real Est Agnt*
Alexandria Ghadishah, *Real Est Agnt*
EMP: 90 EST: 1998
SALES (est): 2.2MM **Privately Held**
WEB: www.bythewood.com
SIC: 6531 Real estate agent, residential

(P-11598)
JOHN G SHIPLEY
Also Called: Century 21
100 W Valencia Mesa Dr # 201, Fullerton (92835-3765)
PHONE..................714 626-2000
John G Shipley, *Owner*
EMP: 90
SALES (est): 4MM **Privately Held**
WEB: www.c21discovery.com
SIC: 6531 Real estate agent, residential

(P-11599)
JOHN STEWART COMPANY
191 Heritage Ln, Dixon (95620-4873)
PHONE..................707 676-5660
EMP: 71
SALES (corp-wide): 107.7MM **Privately Held**
SIC: 6531 Real estate agents & managers
PA: John Stewart Company
    1388 Sutter St Ste 1100
    San Francisco CA 94109
    213 833-1860

(P-11600)
JOHN STEWART COMPANY
888 S Figueroa St Ste 700, Los Angeles (90017-5320)
PHONE..................213 787-2700
Monica Salirdano, *Branch Mgr*
Richard Himmelberger, *Regional Mgr*
Monica Solorzano, *Sales Mgr*
Melissa Bayles, *Director*
Marjorie Anderson, *Manager*
EMP: 50
SALES (corp-wide): 107.7MM **Privately Held**
SIC: 6531 6513 Real estate managers; apartment building operators
PA: John Stewart Company
    1388 Sutter St Ste 1100
    San Francisco CA 94109
    213 833-1860

(P-11601)
JOHN STEWART COMPANY (PA)
1388 Sutter St Ste 1100, San Francisco (94109-5454)
PHONE..................213 833-1860
John K Stewart, *Chairman*
Jack D Gardner, *CEO*
Michael Smith-Heimer, *CFO*
Dan Levine, *Senior VP*
Loren Sanborn, *Senior VP*
EMP: 80
SQ FT: 15,000
SALES (est): 107.7MM **Privately Held**
WEB: www.jsco.net
SIC: 6531 6552 6726 Real estate managers; subdividers & developers; investors syndicates

(P-11602)
JONES LANG LASALLE INC
4444 Mkt St Ste 1100, San Francisco (94111)
PHONE..................415 395-4900
Chris Albrow, *Manager*
EMP: 200
SALES (corp-wide): 5.9B **Publicly Held**
WEB: www.joneslanglasalle.com
SIC: 6531 Real estate agents & managers
PA: Jones Lang Lasalle Inc
    200 E Randolph St # 4300
    Chicago IL 60601
    312 782-5800

(P-11603)
JS TAMERS INC
468 N Camden Dr Ste 200, Beverly Hills (90210-4507)
PHONE..................323 609-4101
Jordan T Seltzer, *President*
EMP: 50
SALES (est): 1.2MM **Privately Held**
SIC: 6531 Rental agent, real estate

(P-11604)
JUDY SPIEGEL
Also Called: Coldwell Banker Residential BR
580 El Camino Real, San Carlos (94070-2412)
PHONE..................650 596-5400
Fax: 650 637-9857
Judy Spiegel, *Principal*
Carmichael Patrick, *Info Tech Mgr*
Nohema Fernandez, *Asst Broker*
Loc Phan, *Sales Staff*
Q Buchwald, *Real Est Agnt*
EMP: 60
SALES (est): 1.2MM **Privately Held**
SIC: 6531 Real estate agent, residential

(P-11605)
KAUFMAN & BROAD SAN ANTONIO
10990 Wilshire Blvd 7th, Los Angeles (90024-3913)
PHONE..................310 231-4000
Roger Menard, *President*
EMP: 60
SQ FT: 40,000
SALES (est): 1.7MM
SALES (corp-wide): 3B **Publicly Held**
WEB: www.kbhome.com
SIC: 6531 Real estate agents & managers
PA: Kb Home
    10990 Wilshire Blvd Fl 5
    Los Angeles CA 90024
    310 231-4000

(P-11606)
KELLER WILLIAMS
Also Called: Keller Williams Realtors
770 Paseo Camarillo # 100, Camarillo (93010-6092)
PHONE..................805 389-1919
Maria Vine, *Partner*
EMP: 99
SALES (est): 2.6MM **Privately Held**
SIC: 6531 Real estate agent, residential

(P-11607)
KELLER WILLIAMS REALTY
Also Called: Keller Williams Realtors
39 Calle De Los Ositos, Carmel Valley (93924-9711)
PHONE..................831 622-6200
Fax: 831 626-1534
Bert Aronson, *Principal*
Ben Beesley, *Real Est Agnt*
Kristy Cosmero, *Real Est Agnt*
Christian Haun, *Real Est Agnt*
Judith Midgley, *Real Est Agnt*
EMP: 60
SALES (est): 2.4MM **Privately Held**
SIC: 6531 Real estate agent, residential

(P-11608)
KELLER WILLIAMS REALTY
Also Called: Keller Williams Realtors
100 N Citrus Ave, Covina (91723-2022)
PHONE..................626 384-2803
John Hollander, *Principal*
EMP: 70 EST: 2015
SALES (est): 113.5K **Privately Held**
SIC: 6531 6519 Real estate agent, residential; real property lessors

(P-11609)
KELLER WILLIAMS REALTY
Also Called: Keller Williams Realtors
23670 Hawthorne Blvd # 100, Torrance (90505-5968)
PHONE..................310 375-3511
Fax: 310 375-6860
Kenny Shishido, *Manager*
Aaron Aalcides, *Real Est Agnt*
Rosa Chen, *Real Est Agnt*
Betty Fogg, *Real Est Agnt*
Deian Kazachki, *Real Est Agnt*
EMP: 300
SALES (est): 9.7MM **Privately Held**
SIC: 6531 Real estate agent, residential

(P-11610)
KELLER WILLIAMS REALTY
Also Called: Keller Williams Realtors
12530 Hesperia Rd Ste 110, Victorville (92395-5848)
PHONE..................760 951-5242
Brad Bodell, *Owner*
EMP: 99
SALES (est): 2.7MM **Privately Held**
SIC: 6531 Real estate agent, residential

(P-11611)
KELLER WILLIAMS REALTY INC
Also Called: Keller Williams Realtors
400 E Main St, Visalia (93291-6315)
PHONE..................559 636-1235
Jillian Bos, *Branch Mgr*
Daisy Aldaco, *Real Est Agnt*
Dannelle Blain, *Real Est Agnt*
Jacob Castro, *Real Est Agnt*
Lynne Kendrick, *Real Est Agnt*
EMP: 100
SALES (corp-wide): 127.2MM **Privately Held**
SIC: 6531 Real estate agent, residential
PA: Keller Williams Realty, Inc.
    1221 S Mo Pac Expy # 400
    Austin TX 78746
    512 327-3070

(P-11612)
KELLER WILLIAMS REALTY INC
Also Called: Keller Williams Realtors
400 Auburn Folsom Rd, Auburn (95603-5515)
PHONE..................530 328-1900
Ralph Carpenter, *Branch Mgr*
EMP: 80
SALES (corp-wide): 127.2MM **Privately Held**
SIC: 6531 Real estate agent, residential
PA: Keller Williams Realty, Inc.
    1221 S Mo Pac Expy # 400
    Austin TX 78746
    512 327-3070

(P-11613)
KELLER WLLAMS RLTY BVRLY HILLS
439 N Canon Dr Ste 300, Beverly Hills (90210-3909)
PHONE..................310 432-6400
Fax: 310 432-6401
Paul Morris, *Principal*
Penni Ziers, *Web Dvlpr*
John Harper, *Real Est Agnt*
Kevin Stricklin, *Real Est Agnt*
EMP: 90
SALES (est): 4.8MM **Privately Held**
SIC: 6531 Real estate agent, residential

(P-11614)
KENNEDY-WILSON INC (PA)
151 El Camino Dr, Beverly Hills (90212-2704)
PHONE..................310 887-6400
William McMorrow, *Ch of Bd*
Justin Enbody, *CFO*
Philip Wintner, *CFO*
Clifford Smith, *Senior VP*
John Pradhu, *Vice Pres*
EMP: 103
SALES (est): 48.1MM **Privately Held**
SIC: 6531 6799 Auction, real estate; real estate investors, except property operators

(P-11615)
KENNETH P SLAUGHT INC
200 E Carrillo St Ste 200, Santa Barbara (93101-2144)
PHONE..................805 962-8989
Kenneth P Slaught, *President*
EMP: 50
SALES (est): 1.4MM **Privately Held**
SIC: 6531 Real estate brokers & agents

(P-11616)
KENNY PABST
248 Redondo Ave, Long Beach (90803-5952)
PHONE..................562 439-2147
George Pabst, *Owner*
EMP: 50
SALES (est): 1.5MM **Privately Held**
SIC: 6531 Real estate agents & managers

(P-11617)
KEYSTONE PCF PROPERTY MGT INC (PA)
Also Called: Reflections and Enclave Hoa
16775 Von Karman Ave # 100, Irvine (92606-4966)
PHONE..................949 833-2600
Cary Treff, *President*
Denise Bergstrom, *COO*
Gerry Kay, *CFO*
Jaime Chandler, *Vice Pres*
Sarah Miller, *Vice Pres*
EMP: 55
SALES (est): 29.6MM **Privately Held**
WEB: www.canyonview.net
SIC: 6531 Real estate managers

(P-11618)
KIDDER MATHEWS LLC
12230 El Camino Real # 400, San Diego (92130-2090)
PHONE..................858 509-1200
Mickey Morera, *Manager*
EMP: 142
SALES (corp-wide): 97MM **Privately Held**
SIC: 6531 6519 Real estate agents & managers; real property lessors
PA: Kidder Mathews Llc
    601 Union St Ste 4720
    Seattle WA 98101
    206 296-9600

(P-11619)
KILROY REALTY LP
2211 Michelson Dr Ste 330, Irvine (92612-1388)
PHONE..................949 788-1200
Doug Holte, *Senior VP*
EMP: 147
SALES (corp-wide): 581.2MM **Privately Held**
SIC: 6531 Real estate agent, residential
PA: Kilroy Realty, L.P.
    12200 W Olympic Blvd # 200
    Los Angeles CA 90064
    310 481-8400

(P-11620)
KILROY REALTY LP
100 1st St Ste 250, San Francisco (94105-4640)
PHONE..................415 243-8803
Doug Holte, *Branch Mgr*
Kenneth Church, *Senior VP*
Chris Calimlim, *Facilities Mgr*
Deborah Cho, *Property Mgr*
EMP: 73
SALES (corp-wide): 581.2MM **Privately Held**
SIC: 6531 6519 Real estate agents & managers; real property lessors
PA: Kilroy Realty, L.P.
    12200 W Olympic Blvd # 200
    Los Angeles CA 90064
    310 481-8400

(P-11621)
KING MONSTER INC
Also Called: Realty One Group Solution
25129 The Old Rd Ste 100, Stevenson Ranch (91381-2281)
PHONE..................661 253-3000
Fax: 661 253-3050
Rich Szerman, *President*
Barabara Westover, *Treasurer*

6531 - Real Estate Agents & Managers County (P-11622)

PRODUCTS & SERVICES SECTION

Jean Szerman, *Vice Pres*
Patrick Raach, *Admin Sec*
Arlyne Szerman, *Manager*
EMP: 68
SQ FT: 5,000
SALES: 500K **Privately Held**
WEB: www.silvercreekrealty.com
SIC: 6531 Real estate brokers & agents

(P-11622)
KOLL MANAGEMENT SERVICES INC
4343 Von Karman Ave # 150, Newport Beach (92660-2099)
PHONE.................................949 833-3030
Fax: 949 833-3755
Donald M Koll, *Ch of Bd*
EMP: 2400
SALES (est): 29.1MM **Privately Held**
SIC: 6531 8741 Real estate managers; management services

(P-11623)
KROPA REALTY
Also Called: Century 21
3093 Citrus Cir Ste 150, Walnut Creek (94598-2693)
PHONE.................................925 937-4040
Fax: 925 295-1920
James Kropa, *Partner*
Maxine Chan, *Partner*
Joanne Bickley, *General Mgr*
William Tegge, *CPA*
Tom Legault, *Manager*
EMP: 50
SQ FT: 2,500
SALES (est): 1.9MM **Privately Held**
WEB: www.kroparealty.com
SIC: 6531 Real estate agent, residential

(P-11624)
LA CIENEGA ASSOCIATES
Also Called: Beverly Center
8500 Beverly Blvd Ste 501, Los Angeles (90048-6277)
PHONE.................................310 854-0071
Fax: 310 652-6857
Laurel Crary-Globus, *General Mgr*
Sheldon Gordon, *Partner*
A Alfred Taubman, *Partner*
Charlotte Warner, *Manager*
EMP: 75
SQ FT: 2,500
SALES (est): 5.7MM **Privately Held**
SIC: 6531 6512 Real estate brokers & agents; auditorium & hall operation

(P-11625)
LAGUNA WOODS VILLAGE
24351 El Toro Rd, Laguna Beach (92653)
P.O. Box 2220, Laguna Hills (92654-2220)
PHONE.................................949 597-4267
Fax: 949 598-7030
Milton John, *Director*
Russ Disbro, *Director*
Paul Ortiz, *Manager*
EMP: 1000
SALES (est): 29.4MM **Privately Held**
SIC: 6531 Real estate agents & managers

(P-11626)
LANE STUART COMPANY LLC
740 Lucille Ct, Moorpark (93021-1241)
P.O. Box 364 (93020-0364)
PHONE.................................805 553-9562
Fax: 805 553-9582
Stuart Lane, *Mng Member*
Gail Lane,
EMP: 55
SALES (est): 2.1MM **Privately Held**
SIC: 6531 Real estate agents & managers

(P-11627)
LAPHAM COMPANY INC
Also Called: Lapham Company Management
4844 Telegraph Ave, Oakland (94609-2010)
PHONE.................................510 531-6000
Fax: 510 594-7611
Jon Shahoian, *President*
Jon M Shahoian, *President*
Menna Tesfatsion, *Vice Pres*
Elizabeth Gonzalez, *Administration*
Velina Barnes, *Manager*
EMP: 85 **EST:** 1947
SQ FT: 10,500
SALES (est): 7.2MM **Privately Held**
WEB: www.laphamcompany.com
SIC: 6531 Real estate brokers & agents; real estate managers

(P-11628)
LARRY BLAIR REALTOR
2488 Junipero Serra Blvd, Daly City (94015-1633)
PHONE.................................650 991-5267
Larry Blair, *Principal*
EMP: 50
SALES (est): 2.2MM **Privately Held**
SIC: 6531 Real estate brokers & agents

(P-11629)
LBA REALTY LLC (PA)
3347 Michelson Dr Ste 200, Irvine (92612-0687)
PHONE.................................949 833-0400
Philip A Belling, *Mng Member*
Mike Memoly, *CFO*
Don Shaver, *Senior VP*
Linda Macdonald, *Vice Pres*
Tom Motherway, *Vice Pres*
EMP: 50
SALES (est): 33.3MM **Privately Held**
SIC: 6531 Real estate brokers & agents

(P-11630)
LEE & ASSOC COMM REAL EST SVCS
Also Called: Lee & Associates Coml RE Svcs
3535 Inland Empire Blvd, Ontario (91764-4908)
PHONE.................................909 989-7771
Donald Kazanjian, *President*
Bill Heim, *Exec VP*
Vincent Anthony, *Vice Pres*
Michael Chavez, *Vice Pres*
Douglas Earnhart, *Vice Pres*
EMP: 50
SALES (est): 4.4MM **Privately Held**
WEB: www.lee-assoc.com
SIC: 6531 8742 Real estate agent, commercial; real estate consultant

(P-11631)
LEE & ASSOCIATES COML RE SVCS (PA)
7700 Irvine Center Dr # 600, Irvine (92618-2923)
PHONE.................................949 727-1200
Fax: 949 727-1299
John Matus, *Vice Pres*
Russ Johnson, *President*
Guy La Ferrara, *Corp Secy*
Sonya Grech, *Bd of Directors*
Mike Baker, *Vice Pres*
EMP: 50
SQ FT: 8,500
SALES (est): 6.1MM **Privately Held**
SIC: 6531 Real estate brokers & agents

(P-11632)
LEE & ASSOCIATES REALTY GROUP
Also Called: LEE& Associates
100 Bayview Cir Ste 600, Newport Beach (92660-2982)
PHONE.................................949 724-1000
Fax: 949 833-0608
Steve Jehorek, *President*
Stephen Grossman, *Senior VP*
Bob Sager, *Senior VP*
Sean Ahern, *Vice Pres*
Eric Hill, *Vice Pres*
EMP: 50
SQ FT: 8,600
SALES (est): 3.9MM **Privately Held**
SIC: 6531 Real estate agent, commercial

(P-11633)
LEROY DURBIN
Also Called: Century 21
14620 Lakewood Blvd, Bellflower (90706-2860)
PHONE.................................562 531-2001
Fax: 562 866-9857
Alex Lurchin, *Owner*
Leroy Durbin, *Owner*
Nina Barquero, *Manager*
Roger A Roe, *Real Est Agnt*
EMP: 85

(P-11634)
LION CREEK SENIOR HOUSING PART
6710 Lion Way, Oakland (94621-3370)
PHONE.................................510 878-9120
Jim Brooks, *Controller*
Tesa Doleman,
EMP: 99 **EST:** 2014
SALES (est): 2.6MM **Privately Held**
SIC: 6531 Real estate agents & managers

(P-11635)
LOIS LAUER REALTY
Also Called: Century 21
1998 Orange Tree Ln, Redlands (92374-2841)
PHONE.................................909 748-7000
Fax: 909 748-7132
David Coy, *President*
Lawn Brian, *CEO*
Ann Bryan, *Treasurer*
Brenda Davis, *Bd of Directors*
Shirley Harrington, *Vice Pres*
EMP: 250
SQ FT: 17,000
SALES (est): 14MM **Privately Held**
WEB: www.loislauer.com
SIC: 6531 Real estate agent, residential

(P-11636)
LONG DRAGON REALTY CO INC
Also Called: Long Dragon Financial Service
2633 S Baldwin Ave, Arcadia (91007-8325)
PHONE.................................626 309-7999
Fax: 626 309-7977
Renee Ho, *CEO*
Robert Ho, *President*
George Ho, *Treasurer*
Wen LI, *General Mgr*
John Lee, *Network Tech*
EMP: 120
SQ FT: 5,000
SALES (est): 6.4MM **Privately Held**
WEB: www.longdragonrealty.com
SIC: 6531 6163 6799 Real estate brokers & agents; mortgage brokers arranging for loans, using money of others; real estate investors, except property operators

(P-11637)
LOU BOZIGIAN
5900 Alleppo Ln, Palmdale (93551-2825)
PHONE.................................661 948-4737
Lou Bozigian, *President*
EMP: 60
SALES (est): 1.8MM **Privately Held**
WEB: www.coldwellbanker-bozigian.com
SIC: 6531 8742 Real estate brokers & agents; real estate consultant

(P-11638)
LOWE ENTERPRISES INC (PA)
Also Called: Lei AG Seattle
11777 San Vicente Blvd # 900, Los Angeles (90049-6615)
PHONE.................................310 820-6661
Fax: 310 207-1132
Robert J Lowe, *President*
Brian T Prinn, *Vice Chairman*
Joseph Heredia, *President*
Rachel Pederson, *President*
James Sabatier, *President*
EMP: 125
SQ FT: 20,000
SALES (est): 735.2MM **Privately Held**
WEB: www.ccpavilion.com
SIC: 6531 6552 Real estate managers; subdividers & developers

(P-11639)
LRES CORPORATION (PA)
765 The City Dr S Ste 300, Orange (92868-6916)
PHONE.................................714 520-5737
Fax: 714 520-5499
Roger Beane, *President*
Paul Abbamonto, *COO*
Susheel Mantha, *CFO*
Don Mask, *Officer*
Richard Cimino, *Senior VP*
EMP: 91
SQ FT: 11,000
SALES: 27MM **Privately Held**
WEB: www.lrescorp.com
SIC: 6531 Real estate managers

(P-11640)
LUMINOUS CONSUMER SERVICES INC
25322 Rye Canyon Rd # 106, Valencia (91355-1468)
PHONE.................................661 993-1475
Patrick Davis, *CEO*
EMP: 100 **EST:** 2013
SALES (est): 3.1MM **Privately Held**
SIC: 6531 7381 Real estate brokers & agents; real estate agent, residential; security guard service

(P-11641)
LYON REAL ESTATE
150 Natoma Station Dr # 300, Folsom (95630-7965)
PHONE.................................916 355-7000
Michael Lyon, *CFO*
Carol Kellog, *Office Mgr*
Erin O Nelson, *Office Mgr*
Dave Wilson, *CTO*
Peggie Ryan, *Database Admin*
EMP: 75
SALES (est): 2.8MM **Privately Held**
SIC: 6531 Real estate brokers & agents

(P-11642)
LYON REALTY
2220 Douglas Blvd Ste 100, Roseville (95661-3822)
PHONE.................................916 784-1500
Chris Sheffer, *Principal*
Kathryn Lockhart, *Executive*
Paula Colombo, *Office Mgr*
Mike Johnston, *Broker*
Sherry Bleiweiss, *Human Res Mgr*
EMP: 84
SALES (corp-wide): 4.1MM **Privately Held**
SIC: 6531 Real estate brokers & agents
PA: Lyon Realty
2280 Del Paso Rd Ste 100
Sacramento CA 95834
916 574-8800

(P-11643)
LYON REALTY
2580 Fair Oaks Blvd # 20, Sacramento (95825-7631)
PHONE.................................916 481-3840
Jim Waters, *Office Mgr*
Nancy Arndorfer, *Administration*
Vicki Bourn, *Broker*
Susan Harrold, *Property Mgr*
Thomas Phillips, *Property Mgr*
EMP: 84
SALES (corp-wide): 4.1MM **Privately Held**
SIC: 6531 Real estate brokers & agents
PA: Lyon Realty
2280 Del Paso Rd Ste 100
Sacramento CA 95834
916 574-8800

(P-11644)
LYON REALTY
8814 Madison Ave, Fair Oaks (95628-3908)
PHONE.................................916 962-0111
Fax: 916 962-1435
Kevin Schmicking, *Executive*
Lezlie Agar, *Real Est Agnt*
Peggy Kengle, *Real Est Agnt*
Patricia C Nelson, *Real Est Agnt*
Kelly Stapp, *Real Est Agnt*
EMP: 336
SALES (corp-wide): 4.1MM **Privately Held**
SIC: 6531 Selling agent, real estate
PA: Lyon Realty
2280 Del Paso Rd Ste 100
Sacramento CA 95834
916 574-8800

(P-11645)
LYON REALTY
851 Pleasant Grove Blvd # 150, Roseville (95678-6177)
PHONE.................................916 787-7700
Alan Harry, *Real Est Agnt*
Cheree Hort, *Real Est Agnt*

PRODUCTS & SERVICES SECTION
6531 - Real Estate Agents & Managers County (P-11666)

Erick Johanson, *Real Est Agnt*
Balbir Kajla, *Real Est Agnt*
Dennis L Miller, *Real Est Agnt*
EMP: 84
SALES (corp-wide): 4.1MM **Privately Held**
SIC: 6531 Real estate agents & managers
PA: Lyon Realty
  2280 Del Paso Rd Ste 100
  Sacramento CA 95834
  916 574-8800

(P-11646)
LYON REALTY
3900 Park Dr, El Dorado Hills (95762-4553)
PHONE...................916 939-5300
Brenda Sims, *Broker*
Tony Fennoy, *Agent*
Crystal Bell, *Real Est Agnt*
Liani Davenport, *Real Est Agnt*
Patricia A Heinzer, *Real Est Agnt*
EMP: 84
SALES (corp-wide): 4.1MM **Privately Held**
SIC: 6531 Real estate brokers & agents
PA: Lyon Realty
  2280 Del Paso Rd Ste 100
  Sacramento CA 95834
  916 574-8800

(P-11647)
LYON REALTY (PA)
2280 Del Paso Rd Ste 100, Sacramento (95834-9701)
PHONE...................916 574-8800
Fax: 916 574-9007
Patrick Shey, *President*
Susan S Pierce, *Branch Mgr*
Rod Bouvia, *Broker*
Tim Pierce, *Sales Associate*
Tong Veu, *Property Mgr*
EMP: 60
SALES (est): 4.1MM **Privately Held**
SIC: 6531 6519 Real estate agents & managers; real property lessors

(P-11648)
M & M STONE INC
Also Called: Stone Bros. & Associates
5250 Claremont Ave, Stockton (95207-5700)
PHONE...................209 478-1791
Robert W Romero, *President*
Michael J Minson, *Treasurer*
Lynne Lebouef, *Office Mgr*
EMP: 70
SQ FT: 4,632
SALES (est): 3.5MM **Privately Held**
SIC: 6531 Real estate managers

(P-11649)
M & S ACQUISITION CORPORATION (PA)
707 Wilshire Blvd # 5200, Los Angeles (90017-3501)
PHONE...................213 385-1515
Mark Santarsiero, *CFO*
Robert Kerslake, *Ch of Bd*
Paul Craig, *CFO*
Merle Atkins, *Exec VP*
John Spude, *Exec VP*
EMP: 115
SALES (est): 16.1MM **Privately Held**
SIC: 6531 8742 Appraiser, real estate; management consulting services

(P-11650)
M S E ENTERPRISES INC (PA)
Also Called: Marshall S Ezralow & Assoc
23622 Calabasas Rd # 200, Calabasas (91302-1549)
PHONE...................818 223-3500
Marshall S Ezralow, *President*
Cindy Alangan, *Asst Sec*
EMP: 90
SALES (est): 3.8MM **Privately Held**
WEB: www.ezralow.com
SIC: 6531 Real estate managers

(P-11651)
MACDONALD HOUSING PARTNERS LP
Also Called: Trinity Plaza
350 Macdonald Ave Ste 100, Richmond (94801-3097)
PHONE...................510 620-0865
Jim Brooks, *Controller*
Tesa Doleman, *Manager*
EMP: 50 **EST:** 2009
SALES (est): 1.2MM **Privately Held**
SIC: 6531 Real estate agents & managers

(P-11652)
MACERICH COMPANY
10800 W Pico Blvd Ste 312, Los Angeles (90064-2187)
PHONE...................310 474-5940
Ken Raffensberger, *Manager*
EMP: 52
SALES (corp-wide): 1.2B **Publicly Held**
SIC: 6531 Real estate agent, commercial
PA: Macerich Company
  401 Wilshire Blvd Ste 700
  Santa Monica CA 90401
  310 394-6000

(P-11653)
MAJESTY ONE PROPERTIES INC
6249 Quartz St, Rancho Cucamonga (91701-3437)
PHONE...................909 980-8000
Julio Cardenas, *President*
EMP: 130
SALES (est): 3.7MM **Privately Held**
SIC: 6531 Real estate agents & managers

(P-11654)
MANGOLD PROPERTY MANAGEMENT
575 Calle Principal, Monterey (93940-2811)
PHONE...................831 372-1338
Thomas Mangold, *Owner*
Craig Coming, *Broker*
EMP: 65
SQ FT: 13,000
SALES (est): 5.7MM **Privately Held**
WEB: www.mangoldproperties.com
SIC: 6531 Real estate managers

(P-11655)
MARCUS & MILLICHAP CAPITL CORP
777 S California Ave, Palo Alto (94304-1102)
PHONE...................650 494-1400
George Marcus, *President*
EMP: 50
SALES (est): 4.7MM
SALES (corp-wide): 689MM **Publicly Held**
SIC: 6531 Real estate brokers & agents
HQ: Marcus & Millichap Real Estate Investment Services, Inc.
  23975 Park Sorrento # 400
  Calabasas CA 91302
  818 212-2250

(P-11656)
MARCUS MILLICHAP REIS NEV INC
23975 Park Sorrento # 400, Calabasas (91302-4015)
PHONE...................650 494-1400
EMP: 108
SALES (est): 4.5MM **Privately Held**
SIC: 6531 Buying agent, real estate

(P-11657)
MARCUS MLLCHAP RE INV SVCS INC
Also Called: Ponderosa Mobile Estates
750 Battery St Fl 5, San Francisco (94111-1526)
PHONE...................415 391-9220
Fax: 415 296-0619
Jeffrey M Mishkin, *Sales Mgr*
Jeffrey M Ishkin, *Sales Mgr*
EMP: 50
SALES (corp-wide): 62.6MM **Privately Held**
SIC: 6531 8742 Real estate agents & managers; real estate consultant
HQ: Marcus & Millichap Real Estate Investment Services Of Indiana, Inc.
  2626 Hanover St
  Palo Alto CA 94304
  650 494-1400

(P-11658)
MARRAKESH MANAGEMENT CORP
47000 Marrakesh Dr, Palm Desert (92260-5805)
PHONE...................760 568-2688
Barbara Valdivia, *Controller*
Dan Cooper, *Exec VP*
EMP: 50
SQ FT: 5,000
SALES: 704.3K **Privately Held**
WEB: www.marrakeshcountryclub.com
SIC: 6531 Real estate managers

(P-11659)
MASON-MCDUFFIE REAL ESTATE INC
Also Called: Prudential
2095 Rose St Ste 100, Berkeley (94709-1997)
PHONE...................510 705-8611
Fax: 510 540-9957
Phina Chrisentery, *Manager*
Kristin Roberts, *Real Est Agnt*
Frances E Russell, *Real Est Agnt*
EMP: 70
SALES (corp-wide): 27.3MM **Privately Held**
WEB: www.mohrparkneighbors.com
SIC: 6531 Real estate agent, residential
PA: Mason-Mcduffie Real Estate, Inc.
  1555 Riviera Ave Ste E
  Walnut Creek CA 94596
  925 924-4600

(P-11660)
MASON-MCDUFFIE REAL ESTATE INC
Also Called: Prudential
2051 Mt Diablo Blvd, Walnut Creek (94596-4301)
PHONE...................925 932-1000
Fax: 925 938-4526
Steve Curtis, *Manager*
David Gardner, *Manager*
Robert Georgiou, *Real Est Agnt*
EMP: 78
SALES (corp-wide): 27.3MM **Privately Held**
WEB: www.mohrparkneighbors.com
SIC: 6531 Real estate agent, residential
PA: Mason-Mcduffie Real Estate, Inc.
  1555 Riviera Ave Ste E
  Walnut Creek CA 94596
  925 924-4600

(P-11661)
MASON-MCDUFFIE REAL ESTATE INC
Also Called: Prudential
630 San Ramon Valley Blvd # 100, Danville (94526-4087)
PHONE...................925 837-4281
Fax: 925 837-1529
Julie Hensley, *Manager*
Monina Berestka, *Sales Associate*
Camille Greunke, *Sales Associate*
Manjit Hundle, *Sales Associate*
Michele Landes, *Sales Associate*
EMP: 100
SALES (corp-wide): 27.3MM **Privately Held**
WEB: www.mohrparkneighbors.com
SIC: 6531 Real estate agent, residential
PA: Mason-Mcduffie Real Estate, Inc.
  1555 Riviera Ave Ste E
  Walnut Creek CA 94596
  925 924-4600

(P-11662)
MASON-MCDUFFIE REAL ESTATE INC
Also Called: AAAA Investors
89 Davis Rd Ste 100, Orinda (94563-3032)
PHONE...................925 254-0440
Fax: 925 245-1521
Regina Englehart, *Broker*
Maura Aars, *Sales Associate*
Douglas Faulkner, *Sales Associate*
John Fazel, *Sales Associate*
Tomi Izuno, *Sales Associate*
EMP: 55
SALES (corp-wide): 27.3MM **Privately Held**
WEB: www.mohrparkneighbors.com
SIC: 6531 Real estate agent, commercial; real estate agent, residential
PA: Mason-Mcduffie Real Estate, Inc.
  1555 Riviera Ave Ste E
  Walnut Creek CA 94596
  925 924-4600

(P-11663)
MASON-MCDUFFIE REAL ESTATE INC
Also Called: Prudential
5887 Lone Tree Way Ste A, Antioch (94531-8625)
PHONE...................925 776-2740
Fax: 925 754-6274
Melody Royal, *Manager*
Teresa Carter, *Sales Associate*
EMP: 52
SALES (corp-wide): 27.3MM **Privately Held**
WEB: www.mohrparkneighbors.com
SIC: 6531 Real estate agent, residential
PA: Mason-Mcduffie Real Estate, Inc.
  1555 Riviera Ave Ste E
  Walnut Creek CA 94596
  925 924-4600

(P-11664)
MASON-MCDUFFIE REAL ESTATE INC
21060 Redwood Rd Ste 100, Castro Valley (94546-5931)
PHONE...................510 886-7511
Gretchen Pearson, *Manager*
EMP: 50
SALES (corp-wide): 27.3MM **Privately Held**
WEB: www.mohrparkneighbors.com
SIC: 6531 Real estate brokers & agents
PA: Mason-Mcduffie Real Estate, Inc.
  1555 Riviera Ave Ste E
  Walnut Creek CA 94596
  925 924-4600

(P-11665)
MASON-MCDUFFIE REAL ESTATE INC
Also Called: Predentials
3320 Grand Ave, Oakland (94610-2737)
PHONE...................510 834-2010
Fax: 510 834-3841
Amberson McCulloch, *Manager*
Malaika Randolph, *Real Est Agnt*
Ernest Villafranca, *Real Est Agnt*
EMP: 80
SALES (corp-wide): 27.3MM **Privately Held**
WEB: www.mohrparkneighbors.com
SIC: 6531 Real estate agent, commercial
PA: Mason-Mcduffie Real Estate, Inc.
  1555 Riviera Ave Ste E
  Walnut Creek CA 94596
  925 924-4600

(P-11666)
MASON-MCDUFFIE REAL ESTATE INC
Also Called: Dutra Realty
5950 Stoneridge Dr, Pleasanton (94588-2706)
PHONE...................925 734-5000
Fax: 925 416-1513
Frank Cannella, *Manager*
Sue Condon, *Real Est Agnt*
EMP: 80
SALES (corp-wide): 27.3MM **Privately Held**
WEB: www.mohrparkneighbors.com
SIC: 6531 Real estate brokers & agents
PA: Mason-Mcduffie Real Estate, Inc.
  1555 Riviera Ave Ste E
  Walnut Creek CA 94596
  925 924-4600

6531 - Real Estate Agents & Managers County (P-11667)

(P-11667)
MAX SOMMERS REAL ESTATE
615 Esplanade Unit 312, Redondo Beach (90277-4135)
PHONE.................310 560-1499
Max Sommers, *Owner*
EMP: 75
SALES (est): 2.9MM **Privately Held**
SIC: 6531 Real estate agents & managers

(P-11668)
MBK REAL ESTATE COMPANIES
Also Called: MBK Laguna
4 Park Plz Ste 1000, Irvine (92614-2552)
PHONE.................949 789-8300
Kain Matsumoto, *Chairman*
Kent Crandall, *CFO*
Mike Schmidt, *VP Opers*
Amanda McCann, *Marketing Mgr*
Gabriel Hernandez, *Facilities Mgr*
EMP: 50
SALES (est): 5.9MM
SALES (corp-wide): 40.6B **Privately Held**
WEB: www.mitsui.co.jp
SIC: 6531 Real estate agents & managers
PA: Mitsui & Co., Ltd.
1-1-3, Marunouchi
Chiyoda-Ku TKY 100-0
332 851-111

(P-11669)
MCM PARTNERS INC
Also Called: Prudential
6111 Johnson Ct Ste 110, Pleasanton (94588-3340)
PHONE.................925 463-9500
Fax: 925 463-6145
Janet P Cristano, *President*
Jennifer B Gri, *Manager*
Sandy Parkins, *Real Est Agnt*
Thomas Worster, *Real Est Agnt*
EMP: 65
SALES (est): 2.4MM **Privately Held**
SIC: 6531 Real estate agent, residential

(P-11670)
MCMILLIN RE & MRTG CO INC
320 E H St, Chula Vista (91910-7483)
PHONE.................619 422-4500
Amrian Adan, *Manager*
Jackie Metcalf, *Real Est Agnt*
Patricia Nesbitt, *Real Est Agnt*
EMP: 60
SALES (corp-wide): 4.4MM **Privately Held**
SIC: 6531 Buying agent, real estate
PA: Mcmillin Real Estate & Mortgage Company, Inc.
4210 Bonita Rd Ste B
Bonita CA 91902
619 475-0233

(P-11671)
MEF REALTY LLC
2900 Adams St Ste B30-6, Riverside (92504-4398)
PHONE.................951 687-2900
Jon Muller,
Irene Adelhelm, *Manager*
EMP: 89
SALES (est): 2.4MM **Privately Held**
SIC: 6531 Real estate brokers & agents

(P-11672)
MELISSA BRADLEY RE INC
206 E Blithedale Ave, Mill Valley (94941-2028)
PHONE.................415 388-5113
Mette Shirley, *Branch Mgr*
Lauren Breitenbuecher, *Real Est Agnt*
Noelle X Forfota, *Real Est Agnt*
EMP: 51
SALES (corp-wide): 8.2MM **Privately Held**
SIC: 6531 6519 Real estate agents & managers; real property lessors
PA: Melissa Bradley Real Estate, Inc.
55 Broadway Blvd
Fairfax CA 94930
415 455-1140

(P-11673)
MELISSA BRADLEY RE INC
3249 Browns Valley Rd, NAPA (94558-5424)
PHONE.................707 258-3900
Carol Adler, *Branch Mgr*
EMP: 51
SALES (corp-wide): 8.2MM **Privately Held**
SIC: 6531 Real estate brokers & agents
PA: Melissa Bradley Real Estate, Inc.
55 Broadway Blvd
Fairfax CA 94930
415 455-1140

(P-11674)
MELISSA BRADLEY RE INC
1401 4th St, Santa Rosa (95404-4015)
PHONE.................707 536-0888
Robert Bradley, *Branch Mgr*
EMP: 51
SALES (corp-wide): 8.2MM **Privately Held**
SIC: 6531 Real estate agents & managers
PA: Melissa Bradley Real Estate, Inc.
55 Broadway Blvd
Fairfax CA 94930
415 455-1140

(P-11675)
MELISSA BRADLEY RE INC
1690 Tiburon Blvd, Belvedere Tiburon (94920-2543)
PHONE.................415 435-2705
Arlene Manalo, *Branch Mgr*
Melissa Bradley, *Executive*
Suzanne Agasi, *Real Est Agnt*
Azar Riazi, *Real Est Agnt*
EMP: 51
SALES (corp-wide): 8.2MM **Privately Held**
SIC: 6531 Real estate brokers & agents
PA: Melissa Bradley Real Estate, Inc.
55 Broadway Blvd
Fairfax CA 94930
415 455-1140

(P-11676)
MELISSA BRADLEY RE INC
1701 Novato Blvd Ste 100, Novato (94947-3002)
PHONE.................415 209-1000
Julie Mello, *Branch Mgr*
Jean Tidwell, *Asst Broker*
Melissa Bradley, *Manager*
Jim Armstrong, *Real Est Agnt*
Edward Beckerman, *Real Est Agnt*
EMP: 100
SALES (corp-wide): 8.2MM **Privately Held**
SIC: 6531 Real estate brokers & agents
PA: Melissa Bradley Real Estate, Inc.
55 Broadway Blvd
Fairfax CA 94930
415 455-1140

(P-11677)
MELISSA BRADLEY RE INC
44 Bolinas Rd, Fairfax (94930-1661)
PHONE.................415 485-4300
Fax: 415 454-9250
Vince Sheehan, *Branch Mgr*
EMP: 51
SALES (corp-wide): 8.2MM **Privately Held**
SIC: 6531 Real estate agents & managers
PA: Melissa Bradley Real Estate, Inc.
55 Broadway Blvd
Fairfax CA 94930
415 455-1140

(P-11678)
MERCY HOUSING CALIFORNIA XXVI
Also Called: Mercy Housing Calif Xxv
2512 River Plaza Dr, Sacramento (95833-3673)
PHONE.................916 414-4400
Greg Sparks, *General Ptnr*
Araya Hiranjaruvong, *Admin Sec*
EMP: 60
SALES (est): 532.4K
SALES (corp-wide): 13MM **Privately Held**
SIC: 6531 Real estate agents & managers
HQ: Mercy Housing California Xxv, A California Limited Partnership
1360 Mission St Ste 300
San Francisco CA 94103
415 355-7100

(P-11679)
MERIT PROPERTY MANAGEMENT INC (HQ)
Also Called: Merit Companies The
15241 Laguna Canyon Rd, Irvine (92618-3146)
PHONE.................949 448-6000
Melinda M Masson, *Principal*
Kelly Lee, *Vice Pres*
Judy Krupp, *Admin Asst*
Bob Cardoza, *Info Tech Mgr*
Tony Hart, *Facilities Mgr*
EMP: 200
SQ FT: 21,000
SALES (est): 41.1MM
SALES (corp-wide): 1.2B **Privately Held**
SIC: 6531 Real estate managers
PA: Firstservice Corporation
1140 Bay St Suite 4000
Toronto ON M5S 2
416 960-9500

(P-11680)
MERRILL GARDENS LLC
799 Yellowstone Dr, Vacaville (95687-3449)
PHONE.................707 447-7496
Holly Sullins, *Branch Mgr*
Gary Sebunia, *Manager*
Patrick Ward, *Manager*
EMP: 60
SALES (corp-wide): 85.5MM **Privately Held**
SIC: 6531 Real estate agents & managers
PA: Merrill Gardens L.L.C.
1938 Frview Ave E Ste 300
Seattle WA 98102
206 676-5300

(P-11681)
MERRILL GARDENS LLC
350 Locust Dr Apt L215, Vallejo (94591-4226)
PHONE.................707 553-2698
Frank Cook, *Branch Mgr*
EMP: 62
SALES (corp-wide): 85.5MM **Privately Held**
SIC: 6531 Real estate agents & managers
PA: Merrill Gardens L.L.C.
1938 Frview Ave E Ste 300
Seattle WA 98102
206 676-5300

(P-11682)
MERRILL GARDENS LLC
4855 Snyder Ln Apt 152, Rohnert Park (94928-4863)
PHONE.................707 585-7878
Jason Englehorn, *Branch Mgr*
EMP: 62
SALES (corp-wide): 85.5MM **Privately Held**
SIC: 6531 Real estate agents & managers
PA: Merrill Gardens L.L.C.
1938 Frview Ave E Ste 300
Seattle WA 98102
206 676-5300

(P-11683)
MERRILL GARDENS LLC
Also Called: Merrill Gardens At Bankers Hl
2567 2nd Ave, San Diego (92103-6503)
PHONE.................619 961-4990
EMP: 63
SALES (corp-wide): 85.5MM **Privately Held**
SIC: 6531 Appraiser, real estate
PA: Merrill Gardens L.L.C.
1938 Frview Ave E Ste 300
Seattle WA 98102
206 676-5300

(P-11684)
MERRILL GARDENS LLC
17200 Goldenwest St # 101, Huntington Beach (92647-5412)
PHONE.................714 842-6569
EMP: 52
SALES (corp-wide): 85.5MM **Privately Held**
SIC: 6531 Real estate agents & managers
PA: Merrill Gardens L.L.C.
1938 Frview Ave E Ste 300
Seattle WA 98102
206 676-5300

(P-11685)
MERRILL GARDENS LLC
2115 Winchester Blvd, Campbell (95008-3443)
PHONE.................408 370-6431
Suzanne Russo, *Pub Rel Dir*
EMP: 52
SALES (corp-wide): 85.5MM **Privately Held**
SIC: 6531 Real estate agents & managers
PA: Merrill Gardens L.L.C.
1938 Frview Ave E Ste 300
Seattle WA 98102
206 676-5300

(P-11686)
MERRILL GARDENS LLC
3500 Lake Blvd, Oceanside (92056-4600)
PHONE.................760 414-9880
Dori Lee, *Sls & Mktg Exec*
Camille Bertrand, *Supervisor*
Rhodalyn Dalit, *Supervisor*
EMP: 63
SALES (corp-wide): 85.5MM **Privately Held**
SIC: 6531 Real estate agents & managers
PA: Merrill Gardens L.L.C.
1938 Frview Ave E Ste 300
Seattle WA 98102
206 676-5300

(P-11687)
MESA MANAGEMENT INC
1451 Quail St Ste 201, Newport Beach (92660-2741)
P.O. Box 2990 (92658-9018)
PHONE.................949 851-0995
Fax: 949 250-8574
Steve Mensinger, *President*
Robert Lucas, *Vice Pres*
Linda Nelson, *Info Tech Mgr*
Jim Jenulius, *Manager*
EMP: 70
SQ FT: 5,000
SALES (est): 9.7MM **Privately Held**
WEB: www.mesamanagement.net
SIC: 6531 Real estate managers

(P-11688)
MGR SERVICES INC
1425 W Foothill Blvd # 300, Upland (91786-3689)
PHONE.................909 981-4466
Fax: 909 981-6267
Michael Rademaker, *President*
Jenny Roybal, *CTO*
Terry Padgitt, *Sales Mgr*
Marla Brady, *Real Est Agnt*
Robert A Gonzales, *Real Est Agnt*
EMP: 73
SQ FT: 13,000
SALES (est): 5.7MM **Privately Held**
WEB: www.mgrservices.com
SIC: 6531 Selling agent, real estate; real estate managers

(P-11689)
MOBILONA LLC
601 S Figueroa St # 4050, Los Angeles (90017-5704)
PHONE.................213 260-3200
Jerome Bottari, *CEO*
EMP: 50
SALES (est): 1.5MM **Privately Held**
SIC: 6531 Real estate agents & managers

(P-11690)
MODULAR SYSTEMS INC
Also Called: MSI
800 Garden St Ste K, Santa Barbara (93101-1596)
PHONE.................805 963-9350
Antonio R Romasanta, *President*
Angie Schultz, *Admin Sec*
EMP: 52
SQ FT: 6,000
SALES (est): 3.5MM **Privately Held**
SIC: 6531 8742 Real estate managers; management consulting services

6531 - Real Estate Agents & Managers County (P-11715)

(P-11691)
MONTAGE HOTELS & RESORTS LLC (PA)
Also Called: Montage Laguna Beach
1 Ada Ste 250, Irvine (92618-5340)
P.O. Box 52031, Phoenix AZ (85072-2031)
PHONE 949 715-5002
Alan Fuerstman, CEO
Jason Herthel, President
Iqbal Bashir, Vice Pres
James D Bermingham, Vice Pres
Bill Claypool, Vice Pres
EMP: 640
SQ FT: 586,000
SALES (est): 430.9MM Privately Held
WEB: www.montagehotels.com
SIC: 6531 Real estate managers

(P-11692)
MOONSTONE MANAGEMENT CORP (PA)
Also Called: Moonstone Hotel Properties
2905 Burton Dr, Cambria (93428-4001)
PHONE 805 927-4200
Dirk Winter, President
Matthhew Holder, CIO
Sunshine Rimelen, Controller
Amie Balais, Human Resources
Patty Ehman, Human Resources
EMP: 175
SQ FT: 5,000
SALES (est): 14.1MM Privately Held
SIC: 6531 Real estate managers

(P-11693)
MOSS & COMPANY INC (PA)
15300 Ventura Blvd # 418, Sherman Oaks (91403-3140)
PHONE 310 453-0911
Cindy Gray, President
Don Shields, COO
Chris Gray, Exec VP
Henriette Saffron, Vice Pres
Kelly Cheney, Executive Asst
EMP: 70
SQ FT: 10,000
SALES (est): 2.6MM Privately Held
SIC: 6531 Real estate managers

(P-11694)
MOUNTAIN HIGH RESORT ASSOC LLC
24512 Highway 2, Wrightwood (92397)
P.O. Box 3010 (92397-3010)
PHONE 760 249-5808
Karl Kapuscinski,
Michele Roy, CFO
Judy Pritts, Human Res Dir
John McColly,
Michelle Roy,
EMP: 900
SALES (est): 40.9MM Privately Held
SIC: 6531 Real estate managers

(P-11695)
MOVE INC
8428 Calvin Ave, Northridge (91324-4212)
PHONE 818 701-0012
Dan Laudo, Branch Mgr
EMP: 126
SALES (corp-wide): 8.2B Publicly Held
SIC: 6531 Real estate listing services
HQ: Move, Inc.
3315 Scott Blvd
Santa Clara CA 95054
408 558-7100

(P-11696)
MOVE INC (HQ)
3315 Scott Blvd, Santa Clara (95054-3139)
PHONE 408 558-7100
Steven H Berkowitz, CEO
Sunil Mehrotra, President
Eric Thorkilsen, President
Bryan Charap, CFO
Rachel C Glaser, CFO
EMP: 500
SQ FT: 32,405
SALES: 227MM
SALES (corp-wide): 8.2B Publicly Held
WEB: www.homestore.com
SIC: 6531 Real estate listing services; multiple listing service, real estate

PA: News Corporation
1211 Ave Of The Americas
New York NY 10036
212 416-3400

(P-11697)
MOVE CO
30700 Russell Ranch Rd # 100, Westlake Village (91362-9501)
PHONE 805 557-2300
Lew Delote, CFO
Glen Glesecke, CFO
Robert J Krolik, CFO
Joe F Hanauer, Bd of Directors
Lisa Farris, Chief Mktg Ofcr
EMP: 122
SALES (est): 8.7MM Privately Held
SIC: 6531 Real estate agent, commercial

(P-11698)
MOVOTO LLC
1900 S Norfolk St Ste 310, San Mateo (94403-1171)
PHONE 888 766-8686
Shiro Takeuchi, CEO
Mark Brandemuehl, COO
Ying Xia, Engineer
Chris Kolmar, Director
Sandeep Chaudhary, Manager
EMP: 51
SALES (est): 568K Privately Held
SIC: 6531 Real estate agents & managers

(P-11699)
MP TICE OAKS ASSOCIATES A CA
Also Called: Tice Oaks Apartments
2150 Valley Blvd, Walnut Creek (94595)
PHONE 650 356-2976
Matthew O Franklin, Partner
EMP: 99
SALES: 600K Privately Held
SIC: 6531 Real estate agents & managers

(P-11700)
MULHEARN
Also Called: Tifanny Mulhearn Realtors
11306 183rd St Ste 101, Cerritos (90703-5408)
PHONE 562 860-2443
Fax: 562 924-4060
Bruce Mulhearn, President
Dick Allen, Officer
EMP: 70
SALES (est): 2.3MM Privately Held
WEB: www.prucarealty.com
SIC: 6531 Real estate brokers & agents

(P-11701)
MULHEARN REALTORS INC
Also Called: Prudential
11642 Firestone Blvd, Norwalk (90650-2805)
PHONE 562 462-1055
Fax: 562 867-1425
Terry Robertson, Manager
Guillermo Blanco, Real Est Agnt
EMP: 100
SALES (corp-wide): 18.3MM Privately Held
SIC: 6531 Real estate agents, residential
PA: Mulhearn Realtors, Inc.
18000 Studebaker Rd # 205
Cerritos CA 90703
562 860-2625

(P-11702)
MURCOR INC
Also Called: Pcv Murcor Real Estate Svcs
740 Corp Ctr Dr, Pomona (91768)
PHONE 909 623-4001
Keith D Murray, President
Tim Scherf, COO
Richard J Barkley, Exec VP
Jon D Van Deuren, Exec VP
Frank Obregon, Info Tech Mgr
EMP: 225
SALES (est): 19.4MM Privately Held
SIC: 6531 Appraiser, real estate

(P-11703)
NELSON SHELTON & ASSOCIATES
Also Called: Nelson, Shelton, & Associates
355 N Canon Dr, Beverly Hills (90210-4704)
PHONE 310 271-2229
Mark Shelton, Vice Pres
Elsa Nelson, Vice Pres
Corrina Gonzales, Property Mgr
Louisa Ovanesian, Real Est Agnt
Cindy M Rohrbough, Real Est Agnt
EMP: 200
SALES (est): 7.8MM Privately Held
WEB: www.jeffmarkell.com
SIC: 6531 Real estate brokers & agents

(P-11704)
NEVIN LEVY LLP A PARTNERSHIP
50 California St Ste 1500, San Francisco (94111-4612)
PHONE 415 800-5770
Nathan Diehl, Vice Chairman
EMP: 63
SQ FT: 4,000
SALES (est): 1.5MM Privately Held
SIC: 6531 Buying agent, real estate

(P-11705)
NEW HOME PROFESSIONALS
Also Called: Estate Investment Group
6500 Dublin Blvd Ste 201, Dublin (94568-3152)
P.O. Box 2398 (94568-0239)
PHONE 925 556-1555
Jay Lange, President
EMP: 150 EST: 1984
SALES (est): 6.1MM Privately Held
SIC: 6531 Real estate agents & managers

(P-11706)
NEWMARK & COMPANY RE INC
Also Called: Newmark Grubb Knight Frank
4675 Macarthur Ct # 1600, Newport Beach (92660-1875)
PHONE 949 608-2000
Fax: 949 833-8037
Oliver Fleener, Vice Pres
Kirk Cole, Senior VP
Eva Horton, Vice Pres
Stanley Mullin, Vice Pres
Elizabeth Raiford, Vice Pres
EMP: 96
SALES (corp-wide): 2.5B Publicly Held
SIC: 6531 Real estate brokers & agents
HQ: Newmark & Company Real Estate, Inc.
125 Park Ave
New York NY 10017
212 372-2000

(P-11707)
NIJJAR REALTY INC (PA)
4900 Santa Anita Ave 2b, El Monte (91731-1498)
P.O. Box 6085 (91734-2085)
PHONE 626 575-0062
Fax: 626 575-3084
Daljit Kler, Principal
Mike Nijjar, President
Swaranjit S Nijjar, CEO
Evert Miller, CFO
Peter Nijjar, Treasurer
EMP: 70
SQ FT: 2,000
SALES (est): 6.7MM Privately Held
SIC: 6531 Real estate brokers & agents; real estate agent, commercial; real estate agent, residential

(P-11708)
NINE-TWENTY INC
Also Called: Home Lenders
1040 University Ave B211, San Diego (92103-7328)
PHONE 619 497-4900
Fax: 619 308-2270
Bob J Fields, President
EMP: 60
SALES (est): 3.8MM Privately Held
WEB: www.joansouder.com
SIC: 6531 Real estate agents & managers

(P-11709)
NMMS TWIN PEAKS LLC
Also Called: PBR Twin Peaks
5850 Canoga Ave Ste 650, Woodland Hills (91367-6573)
PHONE 818 710-6100
Sandra Kist,
Sanford Siegal,
EMP: 100
SALES (est): 4.4MM Privately Held
SIC: 6531 Real estate agent, commercial

(P-11710)
NMS PROPERTIES INC
1430 5th St Ste 101, Santa Monica (90401-4423)
PHONE 310 475-7600
Naum Shekhter, CEO
Margot Shekhter, President
Dino Ciarmoli, Exec VP
Scott Walter, Exec VP
EMP: 95
SALES (est): 12MM Privately Held
SIC: 6531 Real estate agents & managers

(P-11711)
NNJ SERVICES INC
9610 Waples St, San Diego (92121-2955)
PHONE 858 550-7900
Lelnor Hugus, CEO
Mike Packard, President
Lil Vanvleet, Office Mgr
Chris Jaeschke, Admin Sec
Andy Robertson, Administration
EMP: 250
SALES (est): 6.1MM Privately Held
WEB: www.nnj.com
SIC: 6531 Real estate agents & managers

(P-11712)
NOBLE TOWER PRESERVATION LP
1515 Lakeside Dr, Oakland (94612-4558)
PHONE 510 444-5228
Larry Lipton, Principal
Tesa Doleman, Manager
EMP: 99
SALES (est): 3.7MM Privately Held
SIC: 6531 Real estate agents & managers

(P-11713)
NORCAL GOLD INC
Also Called: Re/Max
2340 E Bidwell St, Folsom (95630-3455)
PHONE 916 984-8778
Fax: 916 984-8777
Michael Kooken, Manager
Alicia Chamblee, Admin Asst
Connie Chan, Broker
Todd Cackler, Agent
Debbie Woodruff, Consultant
EMP: 50
SALES (corp-wide): 29.8MM Privately Held
SIC: 6531 Real estate agent, residential
PA: Norcal Gold, Inc.
5200 Sunrise Blvd Ste 5
Fair Oaks CA 95628
916 218-6700

(P-11714)
NORTHGATE TER CMNTY PARTNER LP
550 24th St, Oakland (94612-1757)
PHONE 510 465-9346
Fax: 510 465-0604
Leslie Torres, Principal
Barbara Rosenblatt, Admin Asst
EMP: 50
SQ FT: 49,846
SALES (est): 1.5MM Privately Held
SIC: 6531 Real estate agents & managers

(P-11715)
NOURMAND & ASSOCIATES
421 N Beverly Dr Ste 200, Beverly Hills (90210-4643)
PHONE 310 274-4000
Fax: 310 278-9900
Saeed Nourmand, President
Joyce Azria, Agent
EMP: 50
SALES (est): 3.5MM Privately Held
WEB: www.andreabest.net
SIC: 6531 Real estate brokers & agents

6531 - Real Estate Agents & Managers County (P-11716)

(P-11716)
NRT COMMERCIAL UTAH LLC
Also Called: Coldwell Banker
42 S Pasadena Ave, Pasadena
(91105-1943)
PHONE.....................626 449-5222
Fax: 626 568-9507
Dale Williamson, *Manager*
Carol Majors, *Broker*
Armine Tagvoryan, *Marketing Mgr*
Natalie Oginz, *Manager*
Ester Hickman, *Real Est Agnt*
EMP: 100
SALES (corp-wide): 5.7B **Publicly Held**
WEB: www.nrtinc.com
SIC: 6531 Real estate agent, residential
HQ: Nrt Commercial Utah Llc
175 Park Ave
Madison NJ 07940

(P-11717)
NUTEC ENTERPRISES INC
Also Called: Prudential
24200 Magic Mountain Pkwy # 105, Valencia (91355-4887)
PHONE.....................661 287-3200
Fax: 805 255-8849
Roxanna Ramey, *President*
Mark Jenkins, *Vice Pres*
Michael C Hawk, *Personnel Exec*
James W Brent, *Real Est Agnt*
Richard M Knox, *Real Est Agnt*
EMP: 94
SQ FT: 5,000
SALES (est): 3.5MM **Privately Held**
WEB: www.scvfinehomes.com
SIC: 6531 Real estate agent, residential

(P-11718)
OAKTREE REAL ESTATE OPPORTUNIT
333 S Grand Ave Fl 28, Los Angeles (90071-1504)
PHONE.....................213 830-6300
EMP: 1258 **EST:** 2014
SALES (est): 183.2K **Privately Held**
SIC: 6531 Real estate agents & managers
PA: Oaktree Capital Group Holdings, L.P.
333 S Grand Ave Fl 28
Los Angeles CA 90071
-

(P-11719)
OMNINET TWIN TOWERS GP LLC
9420 Wilshire Blvd # 400, Beverly Hills (90212-3151)
PHONE.....................310 300-4118
Jacquie Felan,
EMP: 50 **EST:** 2012
SALES (est): 1.4MM **Privately Held**
SIC: 6531 Real estate agents & managers

(P-11720)
OMNINET TWIN TOWERS LP
9420 Wilshire Blvd # 400, Beverly Hills (90212-3151)
PHONE.....................310 300-4110
Andrea Constantini, *Manager*
EMP: 50
SQ FT: 215,000
SALES (est): 2.8MM **Privately Held**
SIC: 6531 Fiduciary, real estate

(P-11721)
ON CENTRAL REALTY INC
1648 Colorado Blvd, Los Angeles (90041-1403)
PHONE.....................323 543-8500
Vazrik Bonyadi, *Branch Mgr*
EMP: 354
SALES (corp-wide): 9MM **Privately Held**
SIC: 6519 Real estate agents & managers; real property lessors
PA: On Central Realty, Inc.
1625 W Glenoaks Blvd
Glendale CA 91201
818 476-3000

(P-11722)
ORCHARD HOLDINGS GROUP INC
1 Venture Ste 300, Irvine (92618-7416)
PHONE.....................949 502-8300

James Saccacio, *President*
Lauren Guzak, *Vice Pres*
Larry Spencer, *Vice Pres*
Lisa Klages, *Executive Asst*
Bud Reynolds, *Admin Sec*
EMP: 160
SQ FT: 1,300
SALES (est): 7.6MM **Privately Held**
SIC: 6531 Real estate agents & managers

(P-11723)
PACIFIC CITIES MANAGEMENT INC (PA)
Also Called: Westcal Management
6056 Rutland Dr Ste 1, Carmichael (95608-0514)
P.O. Box 417127, Sacramento (95841-7127)
PHONE.....................916 348-1188
Fax: 916 348-1194
Michael Force, *President*
Amanda Friesz, *Property Mgr*
EMP: 55
SQ FT: 2,600
SALES (est): 3.7MM **Privately Held**
SIC: 6531 Real estate managers

(P-11724)
PACIFIC HOUSING MANAGEMENT (PA)
945 Katella St, Laguna Beach (92651-3705)
PHONE.....................714 508-1777
Fax: 714 669-8556
Richard Hall, *President*
EMP: 60
SALES (est): 3.3MM **Privately Held**
WEB: www.sharonmichael.com
SIC: 6531 Real estate managers

(P-11725)
PACIFIC MEDICAL BUILDINGS LP
Also Called: P M B
3394 Carmel Mountain Rd # 200, San Diego (92121-1066)
PHONE.....................858 794-1900
Jeffrey L Rush MD, *Mng Member*
Stephen King, *President*
Hal Sherman, *Vice Pres*
Jennifer Garcia, *Accounting Mgr*
Monica Powell, *Property Mgr*
EMP: 55
SQ FT: 5,000
SALES (est): 7.8MM **Privately Held**
SIC: 6531 Real estate managers

(P-11726)
PACIFIC MONARCH RESORTS INC
7 Grenada St, Laguna Niguel (92677-4825)
PHONE.....................949 228-1396
EMP: 72
SALES (corp-wide): 15.1MM **Privately Held**
SIC: 6531 Real estate agents & managers
PA: Pacific Monarch Resorts, Inc.
4000 Macarthur Blvd # 600
Newport Beach CA 92660
949 609-2400

(P-11727)
PACIFIC MONARCH RESORTS INC
Also Called: Vacation Marketing Group
981 Iowa Ave Ste C, Riverside (92507-1615)
PHONE.....................951 905-5377
Fax: 951 342-7976
Ken Otto, *Manager*
Julian Santos, *Exec Dir*
EMP: 150
SALES (corp-wide): 15.1MM **Privately Held**
SIC: 6531 Time-sharing real estate sales, leasing & rentals
PA: Pacific Monarch Resorts, Inc.
4000 Macarthur Blvd # 600
Newport Beach CA 92660
949 609-2400

(P-11728)
PACIFIC MONARCH RESORTS INC (PA)
Also Called: Vacation Interval Realty
4000 Macarthur Blvd # 600, Newport Beach (92660-2517)
PHONE.....................949 609-2400
Fax: 949 587-2410
Mark D Post, *CEO*
Richard Muller, *President*
Loren Gallagher, *COO*
Nick Baldwin, *Vice Pres*
Wayne Fields, *Info Tech Dir*
EMP: 100
SQ FT: 20,000
SALES (est): 15.1MM **Privately Held**
SIC: 6531 7011 Time-sharing real estate sales, leasing & rentals; vacation lodges

(P-11729)
PACIFIC PREMIER BANK (HQ)
17901 Von Karman Ave, Irvine (92614-6297)
PHONE.....................714 431-4000
Fax: 714 433-3088
Steven R Gardner, *President*
Jeff C Jones, *Ch of Bd*
Angie Filochowski, *COO*
Ronald J Nicolas Jr, *CFO*
John Shindler, *CFO*
EMP: 83
SQ FT: 36,159
SALES: 93MM **Publicly Held**
SIC: 6531 Real estate listing services

(P-11730)
PACIFIC RIM REALTY GROUP
740 Lucille Ct, Moorpark (93021-1241)
P.O. Box 364 (93020-0364)
PHONE.....................805 553-9562
Stuart Groten, *President*
EMP: 50
SALES: 950K **Privately Held**
SIC: 6531 Real estate brokers & agents

(P-11731)
PACIFIC UNION CO
1699 Van Ness Ave, San Francisco (94109-3608)
PHONE.....................415 474-6600
Fax: 415 775-0637
Linda Harrison, *Manager*
Daniel Cronan, *Exec Dir*
Bic Chimjarn, *Admin Asst*
Michelle Fajardo, *Sales Associate*
Doug Shaw, *Director*
EMP: 65
SALES (corp-wide): 99.1MM **Privately Held**
WEB: www.sfcommercial.com
SIC: 6531 6552 Real estate agents & managers; subdividers & developers
PA: Pacific Union Co.
1 Letterman Dr Ste 300
San Francisco CA 94129
415 929-7100

(P-11732)
PACIFIC UNION RE GROUP (DH)
1 Letterman Dr Ste 300, San Francisco (94129-1495)
PHONE.....................415 929-7100
Sandy Shaffer, *President*
Bill Facendini, *Senior VP*
Beth Birgo, *Office Mgr*
Robert James, *IT/INT Sup*
Doug Swanson, *Broker*
EMP: 80
SQ FT: 700
SALES (est): 7.9MM
SALES (corp-wide): 14.9B **Privately Held**
WEB: www.bayarea-newhomes.com
SIC: 6531 6163 8741 Real estate brokers & agents; mortgage brokers arranging for loans, using money of others; financial management for business
HQ: Gmac Home Services, Inc.
4 Walnut Grove Dr
Horsham PA 19044
215 682-4600

(P-11733)
PACIFIC UNION RESIDENTIAL BRKG
1900 Mountain Blvd # 102, Oakland (94611-2800)
PHONE.....................510 339-6460
Fax: 510 339-6519
Pamela Hoffman, *President*
Debra Dryden, *Real Est Agnt*
Sheila Gallagher, *Real Est Agnt*
Barbara Hardacre, *Real Est Agnt*
Robyn Mohr, *Real Est Agnt*
EMP: 72
SALES (est): 2.9MM
SALES (corp-wide): 14.9B **Privately Held**
WEB: www.bayarea-newhomes.com
SIC: 6531 Real estate brokers & agents
HQ: Pacific Union Real Estate Group Ltd
1 Letterman Dr Ste 300
San Francisco CA 94129
415 929-7100

(P-11734)
PACIFICA HOTEL COMPANY (HQ)
1933 Cliff Dr Ste 1, Santa Barbara (93109-1502)
PHONE.....................805 957-0095
Fax: 805 899-2426
Mike Barnard, *President*
Matt Marquis, *President*
Dale J Marquis, *CEO*
Todd Moreau, *Vice Pres*
Christy Edson, *Director*
EMP: 77
SQ FT: 12,500
SALES (est): 38MM
SALES (corp-wide): 154.9MM **Privately Held**
WEB: www.cottage-inn.com
SIC: 6531 7011 Real estate brokers & agents; real estate managers; hotels & motels
PA: Invest West Financial Corp
1933 Cliff Dr Ste 1
Santa Barbara CA 93109
805 957-0095

(P-11735)
PANATTONI DEVELOPMENT CO INC (PA)
20411 Sw Birch St Ste 200, Newport Beach (92660-1797)
PHONE.....................916 381-1561
Carl Panattoni, *Chairman*
Dudley Mitchell, *President*
Greg Thurman, *President*
Adon Panattoni, *CEO*
Jacklyn Shelby, *COO*
EMP: 90
SQ FT: 7,000
SALES (est): 28.1MM **Privately Held**
SIC: 6531 Real estate agent, commercial

(P-11736)
PARAGON REAL ESTATE GROUP
1400 Van Ness Ave, San Francisco (94109-4608)
PHONE.....................415 738-7000
Fax: 415 738-7099
Anita Head, *Owner*
Brian Wilcox, *President*
Sally Stull, *COO*
Patrick Carlisle, *Chief Mktg Ofcr*
Dan McGue, *Exec VP*
EMP: 101
SALES (est): 7.1MM **Privately Held**
SIC: 6531 6519 Real estate agents & managers; real property lessors

(P-11737)
PARAGON REAL ESTATE GROUP
1400 Van Ness Ave, San Francisco (94109-4608)
PHONE.....................415 292-2384
Robert N Dadurka, *President*
France Santos, *Admin Asst*
Shelley Greeves, *VP Mktg*
John Beeney, *Real Est Agnt*
Sharon L Collier, *Real Est Agnt*
EMP: 70
SALES (est): 4MM **Privately Held**
SIC: 6531 Real estate agents & managers

PRODUCTS & SERVICES SECTION
6531 - Real Estate Agents & Managers County (P-11762)

(P-11738)
PARAMUNT CONTRS DEVELOPERS INC
Also Called: Tops Auto Parks
6464 W Sunset Blvd # 700, Los Angeles (90028-8001)
PHONE..................323 464-7050
Fax: 323 462-0863
Brad Folb, *President*
Brian Folb, *Exec VP*
Brad Foldski, *Info Tech Mgr*
EMP: 50
SQ FT: 102,000
SALES (est): 4.9MM Privately Held
WEB: www.folbart.com
SIC: 6531 1541 1521 Real estate managers; industrial buildings & warehouses; single-family housing construction

(P-11739)
PARK REGENCY INC
10146 Balboa Blvd, Granada Hills (91344-7408)
PHONE..................818 363-6116
Fax: 818 360-1770
Joseph Alexander, *President*
Patrick Pace, *CFO*
Ken Engeron, *Vice Pres*
Melody Cutler, *Info Tech Mgr*
Carmen Martinez, *Real Est Agnt*
EMP: 70
SQ FT: 4,500
SALES (est): 5MM Privately Held
WEB: www.parkregency.com
SIC: 6531 Real estate agent, residential; real estate agent, commercial

(P-11740)
PARMA MANAGEMENT CO INC
6390 Greenwich Dr Ste 150, San Diego (92122-5958)
P.O. Box 22209 (92192-2209)
PHONE..................858 457-4999
Leon Parma, *President*
David Kressin, *Vice Pres*
Michael Parma, *Vice Pres*
Debbie Wilmont, *Administration*
EMP: 50
SALES (est): 4.7MM Privately Held
SIC: 6531 Real estate agents & managers

(P-11741)
PARWOOD PRESERVATION LP
Also Called: Northpointe Apartment Homes
5441 N Paramount Blvd, Long Beach (90805-5128)
PHONE..................562 531-7880
Larry Lipton, *Partner*
EMP: 99
SALES (est): 3.9MM Privately Held
SIC: 6531 Real estate agents & managers

(P-11742)
PASEO VLG HSING PARTNERS LP
1115 N Citron St, Anaheim (92801-2328)
PHONE..................714 991-9172
Jim Brooks, *Controller*
Tesa Doleman,
EMP: 50
SALES (est): 1.7MM Privately Held
SIC: 6531 Real estate agents & managers

(P-11743)
PASSCO COMPANIES LLC (PA)
2050 Main St Ste 650, Irvine (92614-8265)
PHONE..................949 442-1000
William O Passo,
William H Winn, *President*
Jeff Fralick, *CFO*
Thomas B Jahncke, *Senior VP*
Paul Mittmann, *Vice Pres*
EMP: 70
SALES (est): 17MM Privately Held
WEB: www.passco.com
SIC: 6531 Real estate agents & managers

(P-11744)
PAUL CALVO AND COMPANY
1619 W Garvey Ave N # 201, West Covina (91790-2147)
PHONE..................626 814-8000
Paul Calvo, *Owner*
Juan Quimi, *Property Mgr*
EMP: 50

SALES (est): 3.1MM Privately Held
WEB: www.calvogroup.com
SIC: 6531 Real estate brokers & agents; real estate managers

(P-11745)
PCS PROPERTY MANAGMENT LLC
11859 Wilshire Blvd # 600, Los Angeles (90025-6616)
PHONE..................310 231-1000
Michael Ross, *Branch Mgr*
EMP: 136 Privately Held
SIC: 6531 Real estate managers
PA: Pcs Property Managment Llc
4500 Woodman Ave Ofc
Sherman Oaks CA 91423

(P-11746)
PETALUMA JINT UN HIGH SCHL DST
333 Casa Grande Rd, Petaluma (94954-5706)
PHONE..................707 778-4677
Fax: 707 778-4687
Linda Scheele, *Administration*
EMP: 77 Privately Held
SIC: 6531 Real estate brokers & agents
PA: Petaluma Joint Union High School District
200 Douglas St
Petaluma CA 94952

(P-11747)
PHOENIX RE INVESTMENT CO
1754 Tech Dr Ste 108, San Jose (95110)
PHONE..................408 213-8600
Gin Song, *President*
EMP: 60
SALES (est): 1.3MM Privately Held
SIC: 6531 Real estate brokers & agents

(P-11748)
PICKFORD REALTY INC
Also Called: Prudential
1015 Nipomo St Ste 100, San Luis Obispo (93401-3890)
PHONE..................805 782-6000
Eric Pinpker, *Branch Mgr*
EMP: 51
SALES (corp-wide): 2.3MM Privately Held
SIC: 6531 Real estate agent, residential
HQ: Pickford Realty, Inc.
12544 High Bluff Dr # 420
San Diego CA 92130
888 995-7575

(P-11749)
PICKFORD REALTY INC
11120 E Ocean Air Dr # 103, San Diego (92130-4683)
PHONE..................858 793-6106
Delorine Jackson, *Branch Mgr*
EMP: 51
SALES (corp-wide): 2.3MM Privately Held
SIC: 6531 Real estate agents & managers
HQ: Pickford Realty, Inc.
12544 High Bluff Dr # 420
San Diego CA 92130
888 995-7575

(P-11750)
PICKFORD REALTY INC
Also Called: Prudential
2365 Northside Dr Ste 200, San Diego (92108-2720)
PHONE..................619 294-3113
Fax: 619 521-0100
Spencer Tenen, *Manager*
Miriam Vildosola, *Executive*
Bohumila Stepankova, *Human Res Mgr*
Nicki Marcellino, *Manager*
Babette Bayless, *Real Est Agnt*
EMP: 120
SALES (corp-wide): 2.3MM Privately Held
WEB: www.dreamhomesrus.com
SIC: 6531 Real estate agent, residential
HQ: Pickford Realty, Inc.
12544 High Bluff Dr # 420
San Diego CA 92130
888 995-7575

(P-11751)
PICKFORD REALTY INC
Also Called: Prudential
101 Orange Ave, Coronado (92118-1408)
PHONE..................619 435-8722
Fax: 619 437-1762
Lou Ann Williams, *Agent*
Harold Caldwell, *Real Est Agnt*
Janice Clements, *Real Est Agnt*
Shawn Dooley, *Real Est Agnt*
Patricia Emrich, *Real Est Agnt*
EMP: 51
SALES (corp-wide): 2.3MM Privately Held
WEB: www.dreamhomesrus.com
SIC: 6531 Real estate agent, residential
HQ: Pickford Realty, Inc.
12544 High Bluff Dr # 420
San Diego CA 92130
888 995-7575

(P-11752)
PINNACLE ESTATE PROPERTIES (PA)
Also Called: Pinnacle Escrow Company
9137 Reseda Blvd, Northridge (91324-3039)
PHONE..................818 993-4707
Fax: 818 701-7576
Dana Potter, *President*
Jeff Black, *CFO*
Diane Hahn, *Office Mgr*
Leila Perwilliger, *Office Mgr*
Kris Carr, *Technical Staff*
EMP: 120
SQ FT: 13,000
SALES (est): 17.4MM Privately Held
WEB: www.billparent.com
SIC: 6531 Real estate brokers & agents; escrow agent, real estate

(P-11753)
PITTS & BACHMANN REALTORS INC
1436 State St, Santa Barbara (93101-2512)
PHONE..................805 963-1391
Fax: 805 966-3622
Patty Tunnicliffe, *Manager*
Loann Barter, *Info Tech Dir*
Lenora Bradley, *Manager*
Carolyn Fryer, *Manager*
Jennifer Mansbach, *Manager*
EMP: 70
SALES (corp-wide): 4.4MM Privately Held
WEB: www.bridgetmurphyhomes.com
SIC: 6531 Real estate agents & managers
PA: Pitts & Bachmann Realtors Inc
1165 Coast Village Rd K
Santa Barbara CA 93108
805 682-6415

(P-11754)
PK NEVADA LLC
1317 5th St Fl 2, Santa Monica (90401-1470)
PHONE..................310 255-0025
Kenneth Pressberg,
Mike Parker, *Sales Mgr*
EMP: 50
SALES (est): 1.9MM Privately Held
WEB: www.pknevada.com
SIC: 6531 Real estate agents & managers

(P-11755)
PLAZA MANOR PRESERVATION LP
Also Called: Summer Crest Apartments
2615 E Plaza Blvd, National City (91950-4017)
PHONE..................619 475-2125
Larry Lipton, *Principal*
Las Palmas Foundation, *Partner*
Michael Herrington, *Partner*
EMP: 1828
SALES (est): 34.4MM Privately Held
SIC: 6531 Real estate agents & managers

(P-11756)
POMONA HOUSING PARTNERS LP
Also Called: Pomona Intergenerational
1731 W Holt Ave, Pomona (91768-3347)
PHONE..................909 622-1010

Jim Brooks, *Controller*
Tesa Doleman,
EMP: 50 EST: 2014
SALES (est): 1.6MM Privately Held
SIC: 6531 Real estate agents & managers

(P-11757)
POWERHOUSE REALTY INC
Also Called: Century 21 Powerhouse Realty
3452 E Florence Ave, Huntington Park (90255-5835)
PHONE..................323 562-7777
Fax: 323 562-7770
Francisco Granadeno, *President*
Andrea Fernando, *Vice Pres*
EMP: 70
SALES (est): 3.9MM Privately Held
WEB: www.powerhouserealty.com
SIC: 6531 Real estate agent, residential

(P-11758)
PPM REAL ESTATE INC
3575 San Pablo Dam Rd, El Sobrante (94803-7205)
P.O. Box 20621 (94820-0621)
PHONE..................510 758-5636
Raymond D Smith, *President*
Ray Smith, *President*
John Pieropti, *Manager*
EMP: 75
SALES (est): 3.1MM Privately Held
WEB: www.samuelchu.com
SIC: 6531 Real estate agent, residential

(P-11759)
PREFERRED BROKERS INC (PA)
Also Called: Coldwell Banker
9100 Ming Ave Ste 100, Bakersfield (93311-1329)
PHONE..................661 836-2345
Fax: 661 836-0744
John Mackessey, *President*
Gary Belter, *Vice Pres*
Jill Pinheiro, *Office Mgr*
Carson Blacklock, *Sales Staff*
Will Chandler, *Agent*
EMP: 70
SQ FT: 8,000
SALES (est): 5.1MM Privately Held
WEB: www.lesliewalters.com
SIC: 6531 Real estate agent, residential

(P-11760)
PRELLIS GROUP INC
Also Called: Prellis Mortgage Company
11011 Balboa Blvd, Granada Hills (91344-5008)
P.O. Box 33755 (91394-3755)
PHONE..................818 363-1717
Ron Prechtl, *President*
Kathy Prechtl, *CFO*
Clark Hill, *Asst Broker*
Barbara Pearson, *Director*
Heidi M Etzger, *Real Est Agnt*
EMP: 136
SQ FT: 7,400
SALES (est): 7.5MM Privately Held
WEB: www.c21allmoves.com
SIC: 6531 8741 Real estate agent, residential; management services

(P-11761)
PRESCOTT COMPANIES (PA)
5950 La Place Ct Ste 200, Carlsbad (92008-8852)
PHONE..................760 634-4700
Gloria Todisco, *President*
Douglas Farrah, *Bd of Directors*
Shelley Leobold, *Vice Pres*
Melissa Vaughan, *General Mgr*
Bonnie Grisandra, *Executive Asst*
EMP: 50
SQ FT: 11,000
SALES (est): 9.6MM Privately Held
SIC: 6531 Real estate agents & managers

(P-11762)
PRITCHETT RAPF AND ASSOCIATES
23732 Malibu Rd, Malibu (90265-4603)
PHONE..................310 456-6771
Fax: 310 456-5688
Jim Rapf, *Partner*
Jack Pritchett, *Partner*
Lisa Yuhasz, *Office Mgr*
Matt Rapf, *Asst Broker*

6531 - Real Estate Agents & Managers County (P-11763)

Robert Lehmkuhl, *Broker*
EMP: 62
SALES (est): 4.2MM **Privately Held**
SIC: 6531 Rental agent, real estate

(P-11763)
PRO GROUP INC
Also Called: Keller Williams Realtors
4160 Temescal Canyon Rd # 500, Corona (92883-4642)
PHONE 951 271-3000
Fax: 951 271-3111
James Brown, *President*
Jim Brown, *President*
Joseph Regan, *CFO*
David Clark, *Vice Pres*
Annie S Petrikin, *Real Est Agnt*
EMP: 195
SQ FT: 18,000
SALES: 6MM **Privately Held**
SIC: 6531 Real estate agent, residential

(P-11764)
PROFESSIONAL CMNTY MGT CAL INC
2335 Avenida Sevilla, Laguna Woods (92637-2391)
P.O. Box 2220, Laguna Hills (92654-2220)
PHONE 949 597-4359
EMP: 134
SALES (corp-wide): 41.3MM **Privately Held**
WEB: www.pcm-ca.com
SIC: 6531 Real estate managers
PA: Professional Community Management Of California
27051 Towne Centre Dr # 200
Foothill Ranch CA 92610
800 369-7260

(P-11765)
PROFESSIONAL CMNTY MGT CAL INC
Also Called: Sun Lakes Country Club
850 Country Club Dr, Banning (92220-5306)
PHONE 951 845-2191
Fax: 951 845-7814
Mike Bennett, *Manager*
EMP: 50
SALES (corp-wide): 41.3MM **Privately Held**
WEB: www.pcm-ca.com
SIC: 6531 Real estate managers
PA: Professional Community Management Of California
27051 Towne Centre Dr # 200
Foothill Ranch CA 92610
800 369-7260

(P-11766)
PROFESSIONAL CMNTY MGT CAL INC
Also Called: Pcm
24351 El Toro Rd, Laguna Woods (92637-4901)
PHONE 949 206-0580
Milt Johns, *Manager*
Judie Zoerhof, *Exec Dir*
Jens Vreeland, *Technology*
Jackie Giacomazzi, *Human Res Mgr*
Barbara Potter, *Manager*
EMP: 134
SALES (corp-wide): 41.3MM **Privately Held**
WEB: www.pcm-ca.com
SIC: 6531 Real estate agents & managers
PA: Professional Community Management Of California
27051 Towne Centre Dr # 200
Foothill Ranch CA 92610
800 369-7260

(P-11767)
PROFESSIONAL CMNTY MGT CAL INC
24351 El Toro Rd, Laguna Hills (92637-4901)
P.O. Box 2220 (92654-2220)
PHONE 949 268-2271
Milton John, *Vice Pres*
EMP: 350

SALES (corp-wide): 41.3MM **Privately Held**
WEB: www.pcm-ca.com
SIC: 6531 Real estate managers
PA: Professional Community Management Of California
27051 Towne Centre Dr # 200
Foothill Ranch CA 92610
800 369-7260

(P-11768)
PROFESSIONAL CMNTY MGT CAL INC
Also Called: Leisure World Resales
23522 Paseo De Valencia, Laguna Hills (92653)
P.O. Box 2220 (92654-2220)
PHONE 949 597-4200
Fax: 949 580-1599
Gabrielle Velten, *Manager*
EMP: 134
SALES (corp-wide): 41.3MM **Privately Held**
WEB: www.pcm-ca.com
SIC: 6531 Real estate agents & managers
PA: Professional Community Management Of California
27051 Towne Centre Dr # 200
Foothill Ranch CA 92610
800 369-7260

(P-11769)
PROFESSIONAL COMMUNITY MGT CAL (PA)
Also Called: P C M
27051 Towne Centre Dr # 200, Foothill Ranch (92610-2819)
PHONE 800 369-7260
Fax: 949 859-3129
Donny Disbro, *CEO*
Russ Disbro, *Senior VP*
Sherri McGillivary, *Vice Pres*
Julia Wilkenson, *Executive Asst*
Julia S Wilkinon, *Admin Sec*
EMP: 50
SQ FT: 12,000
SALES (est): 41.3MM **Privately Held**
WEB: www.pcm-ca.com
SIC: 6531 Real estate managers

(P-11770)
PROLAND PROPERTY MANAGMENT LLC (PA)
Also Called: Hollingshead Management
2510 W 7th St Fl 2, Los Angeles (90057-3802)
PHONE 213 738-8175
Fax: 213 738-8092
Ronald Gregg,
Anna Lee, *Office Mgr*
Peter Zhanvi, *Controller*
James Harris,
EMP: 80
SQ FT: 5,000
SALES (est): 5.2MM **Privately Held**
SIC: 6531 Real estate managers

(P-11771)
PROMETHEUS RE GROUP INC (PA)
1900 S Norfolk St Ste 150, San Mateo (94403-1161)
PHONE 650 931-3400
Fax: 650 931-3401
Sanford N Diller, *CEO*
Bill Levia, *CFO*
Jackie Safier, *Exec VP*
Brian Cox, *Vice Pres*
John Ghio, *Vice Pres*
EMP: 140
SALES (est): 36.4MM **Privately Held**
WEB: www.prometheusreg.com
SIC: 6531 6552 Real estate managers; land subdividers & developers, commercial

(P-11772)
PROPERTY MANAGEMENT ASSOC INC (PA)
Also Called: Capital Commercial Property
6011 Bristol Pkwy, Culver City (90230-6601)
PHONE 323 295-2000
Thomas Spear, *President*
Patrick Lacey, *COO*

Joshua Fein, *CFO*
Helena Kuti, *Administration*
Helena Cueto, *Info Tech Mgr*
EMP: 130
SQ FT: 6,500
SALES (est): 11.8MM **Privately Held**
WEB: www.wemanageproperties.com
SIC: 6531 Real estate managers

(P-11773)
PRUDENTIAL 24 HOUR REAL ESTATE
8635 Florence Ave Ste 101, Downey (90240-4045)
PHONE 562 861-7257
Mel Berdelis, *Owner*
Johanna Soto, *Mktg Dir*
Maria Nicolaou, *Manager*
Kelly Persico, *Consultant*
Lourdes Cue, *Real Est Agnt*
EMP: 80
SALES (est): 3MM **Privately Held**
WEB: www.prudential24hours.com
SIC: 6531 Real estate agents & managers

(P-11774)
PRUDENTIAL CA REALTY
39275 Mssion Blvd Ste 103, Fremont (94539)
PHONE 510 487-6088
William L Salgado, *President*
Grace Pinacate, *Admin Sec*
Celia Goduco, *Marketing Staff*
EMP: 58
SALES (est): 2.3MM **Privately Held**
WEB: www.kensmithrealty.com
SIC: 6531 Real estate agents & managers

(P-11775)
PRUDENTIAL CALIFORNIA REALTY
9003 Reseda Blvd Ste 105, Northridge (91324-3942)
PHONE 818 993-8900
Fax: 818 892-1999
John Maquar, *President*
Sandy Weisberg, *Exec VP*
Jeff Kahn, *Sales Mgr*
Gaye Howard, *Real Est Agnt*
EMP: 50
SALES (est): 2.2MM **Privately Held**
WEB: www.patrussell4re.com
SIC: 6531 Real estate agent, residential

(P-11776)
PRUDENTIAL CALIFORNIA REALTY
29947 Ave De Las Bndra # 150, Rcho STA Marg (92688-2167)
PHONE 949 888-2300
Fax: 949 635-0804
Linda Scarberry, *Manager*
Sandy Mathews, *CFO*
Sandy B Fujiwara, *Senior Mgr*
Roger Iannetta, *Manager*
Brian Byrns, *Supervisor*
EMP: 70
SALES (est): 1.8MM **Privately Held**
SIC: 6531 Real estate agent, residential

(P-11777)
PRUDENTIAL CALIFORNIA REALTY
677 Portola Dr, San Francisco (94127-1207)
PHONE 415 664-9400
Steven Spears, *President*
Rachael Ashley, *Vice Pres*
Sheila Elgart, *Sales Executive*
Martha Beckman, *Real Est Agnt*
Ana J Cadena, *Real Est Agnt*
EMP: 90
SALES (est): 4.3MM **Privately Held**
WEB: www.propertyinsanfrancisco.com
SIC: 6531 Real estate agent, residential

(P-11778)
PRUDENTIAL CALIFORNIA REALTY
976 Main St Ste A, Ramona (92065-1970)
PHONE 858 487-3520
Fax: 858 451-0932
Jon Cook, *President*
Leeann Iacino, *COO*
Kyle Knaphus, *Executive*

Dean Stalter, *Branch Mgr*
Michele Ashbarry, *Broker*
EMP: 81
SQ FT: 1,200
SALES (est): 3.4MM **Privately Held**
WEB: www.wattshername.com
SIC: 6531 Real estate agent, residential

(P-11779)
PRUDENTIAL REALTY CORP
1430 Taraval St, San Francisco (94116-2346)
PHONE 415 566-9800
Sam Cadelinia, *President*
Timothy Chan, *Executive*
EMP: 66
SALES (est): 3.3MM **Privately Held**
SIC: 6531 Real estate agent, residential

(P-11780)
PS BUSINESS PARKS LP
701 Western Ave, Glendale (91201-2349)
PHONE 818 244-8080
Maria Hawthorne, *Partner*
Safu Rana, *Manager*
EMP: 99
SALES (est): 5MM **Privately Held**
SIC: 6531 Real estate agents & managers

(P-11781)
QAL AFFILIATE INC
Also Called: Century 21 Golden Hills
2680 S White Rd Ste 150, San Jose (95148-2079)
PHONE 408 238-5111
Fax: 408 238-6896
Bob Fernandez, *President*
Terry Castro, *Sales Staff*
Lillian Dang, *Agent*
Maria Castro, *Real Est Agnt*
Faye Espejo, *Real Est Agnt*
EMP: 50
SQ FT: 7,000
SALES (est): 2.6MM **Privately Held**
WEB: www.c21goldenhills.com
SIC: 6531 Real estate agent, residential

(P-11782)
R & B REALTY GROUP LP
Also Called: Oakwood Worldwide
2222 Corinth Ave, Los Angeles (90064-1602)
PHONE 310 478-1021
Fax: 310 444-2420
Howard F Ruby, *Partner*
Marina Lubinsky, *Senior VP*
Guinevere Lyster, *Admin Sec*
Larry McClements, *Info Tech Mgr*
Karen Stout, *VP Human Res*
EMP: 1500
SALES (est): 53.6MM **Privately Held**
SIC: 6531 Real estate agents & managers; buying agent, real estate

(P-11783)
RAINBOW PROPERTIES INC
Also Called: Century 21
4812 Ostrom Ave, Lakewood (90713-2812)
PHONE 323 562-0730
Zora Cervantes, *President*
Vince Cervantes, *Vice Pres*
EMP: 55
SALES (est): 2.9MM **Privately Held**
WEB: www.rainbowhomes.net
SIC: 6531 Real estate agent, residential

(P-11784)
RAINBOW REALTY CORPORATION
Also Called: Century 21
24221 Paseo De Valencia, Laguna Woods (92637-3112)
PHONE 949 770-9626
Frank J Hill, *President*
Michele Morris, *Credit Mgr*
Maurice Rouleau,
Steve Bullock, *Agent*
Melanie Callahan, *Agent*
EMP: 55
SALES (est): 3.4MM **Privately Held**
WEB: www.lizhead.net
SIC: 6531 Real estate agent, residential

PRODUCTS & SERVICES SECTION
6531 - Real Estate Agents & Managers County (P-11810)

(P-11785)
RAM COMMERCIAL ENTERPRISES INC
Also Called: Homepointe Property Management
5896 S Land Park Dr, Sacramento (95822-3311)
P.O. Box 221660 (95822-8660)
PHONE..................................916 429-1205
Robert Machado, *President*
Cathy Garcia, *Office Mgr*
Janeen Kimbriel, *Property Mgr*
Jason Pickens, *Property Mgr*
Andy Pokorny, *Property Mgr*
EMP: 50
SALES (est): 4.2MM **Privately Held**
WEB: www.homepointe.com
SIC: 6531 Real estate managers

(P-11786)
RAMSEY-SHILLING RESIDENTIAL RE
3360 Barham Blvd, Los Angeles (90068-1473)
PHONE..................................323 851-5512
Fax: 323 851-6105
Michael Alley, *Owner*
Marti Harlow, *Sales Executive*
Leland E Shilling, *Agent*
Paula Carpenter, *Real Est Agnt*
Dana L Forbes, *Real Est Agnt*
EMP: 75
SALES (est): 1.6MM **Privately Held**
SIC: 6531 Real estate agents & managers

(P-11787)
RANCON REAL ESTATE CORPORATION (PA)
27740 Jefferson Ave # 100, Temecula (92590-2607)
PHONE..................................951 677-1800
Daniel L Stephenson, *Ch of Bd*
Andrew Bell, *Partner*
Michael Diaz, *President*
Sandy Tyler, *Vice Pres*
Corinne Berge, *Real Est Agnt*
EMP: 60
SQ FT: 7,000
SALES (est): 11.4MM **Privately Held**
WEB: www.rancon.com
SIC: 6531 Real estate brokers & agents

(P-11788)
RE MAX ADVANTAGE
Also Called: Re/Max
648 Yerington Ln, Lincoln (95648-8370)
PHONE..................................800 247-4200
Britt Cooper, *President*
EMP: 80
SALES (est): 2.7MM **Privately Held**
SIC: 6531 Real estate agent, residential

(P-11789)
RE MAX ALL CITIES LK ARROWHEAD
28200 Highway 189, Lake Arrowhead (92352-9700)
PHONE..................................909 337-6111
Kelli Todd, *President*
EMP: 50
SALES (est): 2.2MM **Privately Held**
SIC: 6531 Real estate agent, residential

(P-11790)
RE MAX PARKSIDE REAL ESTATE
Also Called: RCA Properties
711 12th St, Paso Robles (93446-2206)
PHONE..................................805 239-3310
Peter Dankin, *President*
Ed Steinbeck, *Broker*
D Stinchfield, *Manager*
Alicia Digrazia, *Real Est Agnt*
Mark Farley, *Real Est Agnt*
EMP: 60
SALES (est): 3.8MM **Privately Held**
WEB: www.janstemperbrown.com
SIC: 6531 Real estate agent, residential

(P-11791)
RE/MAX
201 New Stine Rd Ste 300, Bakersfield (93309-2659)
PHONE..................................661 616-4040

Debra L Craig, *Owner*
Debbie Banducci, *Human Resources*
Carina Martin, *Assistant*
EMP: 50
SALES (est): 1.5MM **Privately Held**
SIC: 6531 Real estate agent, residential

(P-11792)
RE/MAX LLC
Also Called: Remax Champions Real Estate
1071 E 16th St, Upland (91784-9148)
PHONE..................................303 770-5531
None G Brmgr, *Branch Mgr*
EMP: 50
SALES (corp-wide): 176.8MM **Publicly Held**
SIC: 6531 Real estate agent, residential
HQ: Re/Max, Llc
  5075 S Syracuse St
  Denver CO 80237
  303 770-5531

(P-11793)
RE/MAX BEACH CITIES REALTY MAR
400 S Sepulveda Blvd # 100, Manhattan Beach (90266-6814)
PHONE..................................310 376-2225
Fax: 310 372-4296
Robert Kenneth Todd, *Owner*
Patricia Hedstrom, *Executive*
Ismael Reyas, *Admin Sec*
Helena Velasquez, *Technology*
Lupe Andrade, *Broker*
EMP: 150
SQ FT: 15,000
SALES (est): 5.2MM **Privately Held**
SIC: 6531 Real estate agent, residential

(P-11794)
RE/MAX MAGIC
11420 Ming Ave Ste 530, Bakersfield (93311-1369)
PHONE..................................661 616-4040
Fax: 661 616-4041
Debbie Banducci, *Owner*
Walter Bowen, *Broker*
EMP: 50
SALES (est): 410.2K **Privately Held**
SIC: 6531 Real estate agent, residential

(P-11795)
RE/MAX PLOS VRDES RLTY / EXCES
Also Called: Remax Estate Properties
450 Silver Spur Rd, Rancho Palos Verdes (90275-3573)
PHONE..................................310 541-5224
Fax: 310 541-6181
Kevin Mullen, *Manager*
Mary Thomas, *COO*
Jeff Kashanchi, *Info Tech Mgr*
Vicki Longley, *Asst Broker*
Cindy Chaisson, *Sales Associate*
EMP: 50
SALES (corp-wide): 13.2MM **Privately Held**
WEB: www.realestatebymichele.com
SIC: 6531 Real estate agent, residential
PA: Re/Max Palos Verdes Realty / Exces
  63 Malaga Cove Plz
  Palos Verdes Estates CA 90274
  310 378-9494

(P-11796)
REAL ESTATE CALIFORNIA DEPT
Property Management
3737 Main St Ofc, Riverside (92501-3338)
PHONE..................................951 715-0130
Bobie Sanchez, *Manager*
EMP: 100 **Privately Held**
SIC: 6531 9532 Real estate brokers & agents; urban & community development;
HQ: California Department Of Real Estate
  2201 Broadway Lowr
  Sacramento CA
  -

(P-11797)
REAL PROPERTY SYSTEMS INC
1443 E Washington Blvd, Pasadena (91104-2650)
PHONE..................................760 243-1143
Michael Palmer, *President*

Barbara Duran, *Manager*
EMP: 250
SALES (est): 6.9MM **Privately Held**
WEB: www.realpropertysystems.com
SIC: 6531 Real estate agents & managers

(P-11798)
REALOGY HOLDINGS CORP
Also Called: Artisan Sotheby's Intl. Realty
3554 Round Barn Blvd, Santa Rosa (95403-0929)
PHONE..................................707 284-1111
Eric Drew, *Branch Mgr*
Martin Schwartz, *Real Est Agnt*
EMP: 485
SALES (corp-wide): 5.7B **Publicly Held**
SIC: 6531 Real estate brokers & agents
PA: Realogy Holdings Corp.
  175 Park Ave
  Madison NJ 07940
  973 407-2000

(P-11799)
REALTOR SFR GREEN
4090 Mission Blvd, San Diego (92109-5043)
PHONE..................................858 488-4090
Brian Barber, *General Mgr*
EMP: 50 **EST:** 2011
SALES (est): 1MM **Privately Held**
SIC: 6531 Real estate brokers & agents

(P-11800)
REALTY ONE GROUP INC
19322 Jesse Ln, Riverside (92508-5072)
PHONE..................................951 565-8105
EMP: 127
SALES (corp-wide): 22.1MM **Privately Held**
SIC: 6531 Real estate brokers & agents
PA: Realty One Group, Inc.
  4010 Barranca Pkwy # 120
  Irvine CA 92604
  949 596-4300

(P-11801)
REFERRAL REALTY INC
1601 S De Anza Blvd # 150, Cupertino (95014-5358)
PHONE..................................408 996-8100
Fax: 408 253-0983
Morise Nahouraii, *President*
Carl Zanger, *President*
John Faylor, *Administration*
George H Nelson, *Broker*
Keith Walker, *E-Business*
EMP: 55
SQ FT: 5,800
SALES (est): 3.5MM **Privately Held**
WEB: www.referralrealty.com
SIC: 6531 Real estate agents & managers

(P-11802)
REGENCY PARK SENIOR LIVING INC
Also Called: Regency Park El Molino
245 S El Molino Ave, Pasadena (91101-2996)
PHONE..................................626 578-0460
Emil Fish, *President*
EMP: 81
SALES (corp-wide): 10.6MM **Privately Held**
SIC: 6531 Real estate agents & managers
PA: Regency Park Senior Living, Inc.
  150 S Los Robles Ave # 480
  Pasadena CA 91101
  626 773-8800

(P-11803)
RELS LLC
Also Called: Rels Valuation
40 Pacifica Ste 900, Irvine (92618-7487)
PHONE..................................949 214-1000
Anand Nallathambi, *President*
Frank D Martell, *COO*
EMP: 1300
SALES (est): 399K
SALES (corp-wide): 1.5B **Publicly Held**
WEB: www.rels.com
SIC: 6531 7323 Appraiser, real estate; commercial (mercantile) credit reporting bureau

PA: Corelogic, Inc.
  40 Pacifica Ste 900
  Irvine CA 92618
  949 214-1000

(P-11804)
REMAX ACTIVE REALTY
Also Called: Remax Active Teal State
4056 Decoto Rd, Fremont (94555-3201)
PHONE..................................510 505-1660
Fax: 510 505-1666
Fay Louis, *Owner*
Jamie Chan, *Associate*
EMP: 50 **EST:** 2001
SALES (est): 1.8MM **Privately Held**
SIC: 6531 Real estate agent, residential

(P-11805)
REMAX ALL STARS REALTY
765 N Main St, Corona (92880-1440)
PHONE..................................951 739-4000
Fax: 909 739-4060
Bret Meckes, *Owner*
EMP: 64
SALES (est): 2.2MM **Privately Held**
SIC: 6531 Real estate brokers & agents

(P-11806)
REMAX GOLD
Also Called: Re/Max
3620 Fair Oaks Blvd # 300, Sacramento (95864-7266)
PHONE..................................916 609-2800
Fax: 916 609-2830
Pam Porter, *General Mgr*
Johnny Carson, *Real Est Agnt*
Shelly Cruz, *Real Est Agnt*
Sharon L D'Arelli, *Real Est Agnt*
Khou Fang, *Real Est Agnt*
EMP: 85
SALES (est): 2.8MM **Privately Held**
WEB: www.goldcommercial.com
SIC: 6531 7389 Real estate agent, residential; brokers, business: buying & selling business enterprises

(P-11807)
REMAX METRO INC
Also Called: Re/Max
150 Paularino Ave Ste 125, Costa Mesa (92626-3318)
PHONE..................................714 557-2544
Fax: 714 617-8706
Joseph Brodrick, *President*
EMP: 60
SALES (est): 2.3MM **Privately Held**
SIC: 6531 Real estate agent, residential

(P-11808)
REMAX OLSON
Also Called: Re/Max
30699 Russell Ranch Rd, Westlake Village (91362-7315)
PHONE..................................805 267-4929
Fax: 805 267-4949
Todd Olson, *Owner*
Keith Myers, *President*
David Boardman, *Vice Pres*
Michael Laur, *Vice Pres*
Ruiqing Jiang, *CTO*
EMP: 70
SALES (est): 3.7MM **Privately Held**
WEB: www.joedecarlo.com
SIC: 6531 Real estate agent, residential

(P-11809)
REMAX RANCH BEACH
Also Called: Re/Max
16787 Bernardo Center Dr # 6, San Diego (92128-2505)
PHONE..................................858 391-5800
Al Haragely, *Owner*
Robert Adams, *Real Est Agnt*
Mira I Bozanich, *Real Est Agnt*
EMP: 70
SALES (est): 1.9MM **Privately Held**
SIC: 6531 Real estate agent, residential

(P-11810)
RENWOOD REALTYTRAC LLC
Also Called: Attom Data Solutions
1 Venture Ste 300, Irvine (92618-7416)
PHONE..................................949 502-8300
Fax: 949 502-0803
Brandon Moore, *CEO*
Jeff Mattice, *President*

6531 - Real Estate Agents & Managers County (P-11811)

James Moyle, *President*
Cabell Cobbs, *CFO*
Joe Doyle, *Sr Corp Ofcr*
EMP: 63
SALES (est): 8MM **Privately Held**
SIC: 6531 Real estate listing services

(P-11811)
RETIREMENT HOUSING FOUNDATION (PA)
911 N Studebaker Rd # 100, Long Beach (90815-4980)
PHONE 562 257-5100
Fax: 562 257-5200
Rev Laverne R Joseph, *President*
Raymond East, *Ch of Bd*
Christina E Potter, *Vice Chairman*
Darryl M Sexton, *Vice Chairman*
Frank G Jahrling, *Treasurer*
EMP: 65
SALES: 29.7MM **Privately Held**
WEB: www.bixbyknollstowers.com
SIC: 6531 Real estate agents & managers

(P-11812)
RETIREMENT HOUSING FOUNDATION
Also Called: Plymouth Square
1319 N Madison St Ofc, Stockton (95202-1001)
PHONE 209 466-4341
Gary Wiemers, *Administration*
EMP: 100
SALES (corp-wide): 32.1MM **Privately Held**
WEB: www.bixbyknollstowers.com
SIC: 6531 Real estate agents & managers
PA: Retirement Housing Foundation Inc
  911 N Studebaker Rd # 100
  Long Beach CA 90815
  562 257-5100

(P-11813)
RICHARD REALTY GROUP INC
2792 Gateway Rd Ste 103, Carlsbad (92009-1749)
PHONE 760 603-8377
Bill Richard, *CEO*
Jan Richard, *CEO*
Steve Compos, *Real Est Agnt*
EMP: 110 **EST:** 2009
SALES (est): 4.3MM **Privately Held**
SIC: 6531 Real estate agents & managers

(P-11814)
RIPHAGEN & BULLERDICK INC
Also Called: Re/Max
5925 Ball Rd, Cypress (90630-3245)
PHONE 714 763-2100
Fax: 714 763-2101
Gary Riphagen, *President*
Gerry Bullerdick, *Treasurer*
Kerry Louis, *Manager*
Shahid Shaikh, *Associate*
EMP: 50
SQ FT: 2,600
SALES (est): 4MM **Privately Held**
WEB: www.remaxtiffany.com
SIC: 6531 Real estate agent, residential

(P-11815)
RODEO REALTY INC
15300 Ventura Blvd # 101, Sherman Oaks (91403-3103)
PHONE 818 986-7300
Jason Katzman, *Branch Mgr*
Ellen Grosser, *Real Est Agnt*
Ruth Jimenez, *Real Est Agnt*
Brandon Kramer, *Real Est Agnt*
Stefano Militello, *Real Est Agnt*
EMP: 76
SALES (corp-wide): 80.5MM **Privately Held**
SIC: 6531 Real estate brokers & agents
PA: Rodeo Realty, Inc.
  9171 Wilshire Blvd # 321
  Beverly Hills CA 90210
  818 349-9997

(P-11816)
RODEO REALTY INC
11940 San Vicente Blvd, Los Angeles (90049-5004)
PHONE 310 873-0100
Simon Pozi, *Manager*
Shel Kirshner, *Real Est Agnt*

Iris Lee, *Real Est Agnt*
Santiago Sanchez, *Real Est Agnt*
Ryan Trefry, *Real Est Agnt*
EMP: 68
SALES (corp-wide): 80.5MM **Privately Held**
SIC: 6531 Real estate brokers & agents
PA: Rodeo Realty, Inc.
  9171 Wilshire Blvd # 321
  Beverly Hills CA 90210
  818 349-9997

(P-11817)
RODEO REALTY INC
Also Called: Paramount Properties Encino BR
17501 Ventura Blvd, Encino (91316-3836)
PHONE 818 285-3700
Syd Leibovitch, *President*
EMP: 76
SALES (corp-wide): 80.5MM **Privately Held**
SIC: 6531 Real estate agents & managers
PA: Rodeo Realty, Inc.
  9171 Wilshire Blvd # 321
  Beverly Hills CA 90210
  818 349-9997

(P-11818)
RODEO REALTY INC
12345 Ventura Blvd Ste A, Studio City (91604-2511)
PHONE 818 308-8273
Sib Leibovitch, *President*
Todd Jones, *Real Est Agnt*
Paul Orenstein, *Real Est Agnt*
EMP: 80
SALES (corp-wide): 80.5MM **Privately Held**
SIC: 6531 Real estate brokers & agents
PA: Rodeo Realty, Inc.
  9171 Wilshire Blvd # 321
  Beverly Hills CA 90210
  818 349-9997

(P-11819)
RODEO REALTY INC (PA)
Also Called: Paramount Properties
9171 Wilshire Blvd # 321, Beverly Hills (90210-5562)
PHONE 818 349-9997
Fax: 310 471-2602
Sydney Leibovitch, *CEO*
Trudy Swearingen, *Officer*
Barbara Eisner, *Vice Pres*
Linda Leibovitch, *Vice Pres*
Teresa Todd, *Branch Mgr*
EMP: 76
SQ FT: 5,000
SALES (est): 80.5MM **Privately Held**
WEB: www.jennifer4homes.com
SIC: 6531 Real estate brokers & agents

(P-11820)
RODEO REALTY INC
9338 Reseda Blvd Ste 102, Northridge (91324-2986)
PHONE 818 349-9997
Teresa Todd, *Branch Mgr*
Sin S Kim, *Real Est Agnt*
EMP: 100
SALES (corp-wide): 80.5MM **Privately Held**
WEB: www.jennifer4homes.com
SIC: 6531 Real estate agents & managers
PA: Rodeo Realty, Inc.
  9171 Wilshire Blvd # 321
  Beverly Hills CA 90210
  818 349-9997

(P-11821)
RODEO REALTY INC
Also Called: Paramount Properties
21031 Ventura Blvd # 100, Woodland Hills (91364-2208)
PHONE 818 999-2030
Fax: 310 999-0826
Demetra Kalizki, *Manager*
Norma Streams, *Vice Pres*
Donna Schrank, *Engineer*
Donna J Schrank, *Human Res Mgr*
Jason Katznan, *Manager*
EMP: 100
SALES (corp-wide): 80.5MM **Privately Held**
WEB: www.jennifer4homes.com
SIC: 6531 Real estate brokers & agents

PA: Rodeo Realty, Inc.
  9171 Wilshire Blvd # 321
  Beverly Hills CA 90210
  818 349-9997

(P-11822)
RONALD L WOLFE & ASSOC INC
Also Called: Wolfe & Associates
173 Chapel St, Santa Barbara (93111-2333)
PHONE 805 964-6770
Fax: 805 964-8047
Ronald L Wolfe, *President*
Scott Wolfe, *Manager*
Tom McDonald, *Supervisor*
EMP: 50 **EST:** 1971
SQ FT: 5,000
SALES (est): 5MM **Privately Held**
WEB: www.rlwa.com
SIC: 6531 Real estate managers

(P-11823)
ROSANO PARTNERS
700 S Flower St Ste 2526, Los Angeles (90017-4207)
PHONE 213 802-0300
Sagiv Rosano, *CEO*
Michael Chui, *Vice Pres*
Fernando Hernandez, *Broker*
Raymond Aramburu, *Director*
Jimmy Wang, *Director*
EMP: 50
SALES (est): 3.5MM **Privately Held**
WEB: www.rosanopartners.com
SIC: 6531 Real estate brokers & agents

(P-11824)
ROW MANAGEMENT LTD INC
499 N Canon Dr, Beverly Hills (90210-4887)
PHONE 310 887-3671
Kevin Shahin, *Branch Mgr*
EMP: 165
SALES (corp-wide): 5.4MM **Privately Held**
SIC: 6531 Real estate agents & managers
PA: Row Management Ltd. Inc.
  1551 Sawgrs Corp Pkwy
  Sunrise FL 33323
  954 538-8449

(P-11825)
ROXBURY MANAGEMENT COMPANY
P.O. Box 1345 (90213-1345)
PHONE 310 274-4142
Maynard Brittan, *President*
Graydon H Brittan, *Treasurer*
Linda Brittan, *Admin Sec*
EMP: 52
SQ FT: 6,000
SALES (est): 5.4MM **Privately Held**
SIC: 6531 Real estate managers

(P-11826)
RUBICON CORPORATION AMERICA
Also Called: Rubicon Realty
10425 Oklahoma Ave, Chatsworth (91311-2450)
PHONE 818 765-2001
Nicholas M Cariglia, *President*
EMP: 50
SQ FT: 3,000
SALES (est): 1.7MM **Privately Held**
SIC: 6531 6163 Real estate brokers & agents; loan brokers

(P-11827)
RVTLZATION ANAHEIM II PARTNERS
1515 S Calle Del Mar, Anaheim (92802-2607)
PHONE 714 520-4041
Jim Brooks, *Partner*
EMP: 75 **EST:** 2014
SALES (est): 1.8MM **Privately Held**
SIC: 6531 Real estate agents & managers

(P-11828)
S D PROPERTY MANAGEMENT INC
Also Called: Four Seasons Landscaping
14937 Delano St, Van Nuys (91411-2123)
PHONE 323 658-7990

Fax: 323 658-6434
Steve Darrison, *President*
EMP: 60
SQ FT: 1,150
SALES (est): 2.9MM **Privately Held**
SIC: 6531 Real estate managers

(P-11829)
S P R E INC
Also Called: Security Pacific RE Brkg
3223 Blume Dr, Richmond (94806-5782)
PHONE 510 222-8340
Fax: 510 222-8228
Jack Burns Sr, *President*
Betty Couzens, *Corp Secy*
Ray De Gennaro, *Vice Pres*
Colin Davies, *Real Est Agnt*
EMP: 100
SQ FT: 16,000
SALES (est): 5MM **Privately Held**
WEB: www.spre.com
SIC: 6531 Real estate brokers & agents

(P-11830)
SAN DIEGO MORTGAGE & RE
9461 Grsmnt Smt Dr Ste D, La Mesa (91941-4165)
PHONE 619 334-7779
Fax: 619 334-7790
Mark Revetta, *President*
EMP: 50 **EST:** 2001
SALES: 25MM **Privately Held**
SIC: 6531 Real estate brokers & agents

(P-11831)
SAN MAR PROPERTIES INC (PA)
Also Called: Valleywide Maintenance
6356 N Fresno St Ste 101, Fresno (93710-6870)
PHONE 559 439-5500
Fax: 209 439-3727
Marc A Wilson, *President*
Angel Martin, *President*
Sandra Wilson, *Vice Pres*
Stephanie Strobel, *Office Mgr*
Pat Locey, *Supervisor*
EMP: 50
SQ FT: 3,400
SALES (est): 4.4MM **Privately Held**
SIC: 6531 7349 Real estate managers; real estate agent, commercial; building maintenance services

(P-11832)
SAN PEDRO COURT HOUSE
9537 Pettswood Dr, Huntington Beach (92646-4137)
PHONE 562 519-6023
Gena Kelley, *Director*
EMP: 100
SALES (est): 3.4MM **Privately Held**
SIC: 6531 Real estate agent, residential

(P-11833)
SANTA ROSA & SONOMA CO REAL ES
1057 College Ave, Santa Rosa (95404-4128)
PHONE 707 524-1124
EMP: 50
SALES (est): 2MM **Privately Held**
SIC: 6531

(P-11834)
SATELLITE MANAGEMENT CO (PA)
Also Called: Ccts
1010 E Chestnut Ave, Santa Ana (92701-6497)
PHONE 714 558-2411
Fax: 714 558-0927
Ronald Jensen, *CEO*
Mary E Conzelman, *Vice Pres*
Mary E Conzlman, *Vice Pres*
Helen M Jensen, *Vice Pres*
Terri Nolan, *Admin Sec*
EMP: 121
SQ FT: 800
SALES (est): 20MM **Privately Held**
WEB: www.satellitemanagement.com
SIC: 6531 Real estate managers

6531 - Real Estate Agents & Managers County (P-11859)

(P-11835)
SCHWEIZER RENA
Also Called: White House Properties
15720 Ventura Blvd # 100, Encino (91436-2914)
PHONE.................818 501-7100
Fax: 818 386-0977
Marty William, *Owner*
Rena Schweizer, *Owner*
EMP: 60
SALES (est): 1.6MM **Privately Held**
WEB: www.realwinds.com
SIC: 6531 Real estate agents & managers

(P-11836)
SCOTT PLACE ASSOCIATES
60 31st Ave, San Mateo (94403-3404)
PHONE.................650 345-8222
David Bohannon, *General Ptnr*
EMP: 60
SALES (est): 2MM **Privately Held**
SIC: 6531 Real estate managers

(P-11837)
SEC PAC INC
Also Called: Security Pacific Real Estate
1555 Riviera Ave Ste E, Walnut Creek (94596-7321)
PHONE.................925 938-9200
Fax: 925 938-2825
Allan Hibbard, *President*
Michael R Clancy, *Executive*
Richard J Clancy, *Principal*
Cindy Reed, *Finance Mgr*
Michael James, *Senior Mgr*
EMP: 60
SQ FT: 10,000
SALES (est): 3.6MM **Privately Held**
WEB: www.soldbymarian.com
SIC: 6531 Real estate agent, residential

(P-11838)
SECURITY PACIFIC RE BRKG
292 Violet Rd, Hercules (94547-1027)
PHONE.................510 245-9901
Jack Burns Sr, *President*
Bill Prather, *Manager*
EMP: 90
SALES (est): 1.7MM **Privately Held**
WEB: www.billprather.com
SIC: 6531 Real estate agents & managers

(P-11839)
SERVICE CORP INTERNATIONAL
Also Called: SCI
3500 Pacific View Dr, Corona Del Mar (92625-1112)
PHONE.................949 644-2700
Fax: 949 640-6829
Ruby Louis, *Branch Mgr*
Catherine K Wadsworth, *Executive*
Tom Clampitt, *Financial Exec*
EMP: 65
SALES (corp-wide): 2.9B **Publicly Held**
WEB: www.sci-corp.com
SIC: 6531 7261 Cemetery management service; crematory
PA: Service Corporation International
1929 Allen Pkwy
Houston TX 77019
713 522-5141

(P-11840)
SFT REALTY GALWAY DOWNS LLC
Also Called: Kentina
38801 Los Porralitos, Temecula (92592)
P.O. Box 4404 Jeremie Dr
PHONE.................951 232-1880
Kenneth C Smith, *Mng Member*
EMP: 70 EST: 2013
SQ FT: 2,000
SALES: 400K **Privately Held**
SIC: 6531 Real estate agents & managers

(P-11841)
SHEA HOMES ARIZONA LTD PARTNR
655 Brea Canyon Rd, Walnut (91789-3078)
PHONE.................909 594-9500
EMP: 54
SALES (est): 84.3K
SALES (est): 2B **Privately Held**
SIC: 6531 Real estate agents & managers
HQ: Shea Homes Limited Partnership, A California Limited Partnership
655 Brea Canyon Rd
Walnut CA 91789

(P-11842)
SHEA PROPERTIES LLC
130 Vantis Ste 200, Aliso Viejo (92656-2691)
PHONE.................949 389-7000
Fax: 949 389-7300
Colm Macken, *Executive Asst*
Bryan McGowan, *COO*
Janet Bonetto, *CFO*
Peter Culshaw, *Exec VP*
Steve Gilmore, *Senior VP*
EMP: 58
SALES (est): 9.7MM **Privately Held**
SIC: 6531 Real estate agents & managers

(P-11843)
SHEA PROPERTIES MGT CO INC
130 Vantis Ste 200, Aliso Viejo (92656-2691)
P.O. Box 62814, Irvine (92602-6093)
PHONE.................949 389-7000
Colm Macken, *CEO*
Steve Schafenacker, *Senior VP*
Allen Bunch, *Network Mgr*
Marcelo Sandoval, *Marketing Mgr*
Julie Ball, *Manager*
EMP: 347
SQ FT: 48,000
SALES (est): 24.1MM
SALES (corp-wide): 2B **Privately Held**
SIC: 6531 Rental agent, real estate
PA: J. F. Shea Co., Inc.
655 Brea Canyon Rd
Walnut CA 91789
909 594-9500

(P-11844)
SHII LLC
Also Called: Frontier Communities
8300 Utica Ave Ste 300, Rancho Cucamonga (91730-3852)
PHONE.................909 354-8000
James Previti, *Mng Member*
EMP: 50
SALES (est): 5.1MM **Privately Held**
SIC: 6531 Real estate agents & managers

(P-11845)
SKYHILL FINANCIAL INC
7071 Warner Ave Ste F378, Huntington Beach (92647-5495)
PHONE.................714 657-3938
Rosanne Covy, *President*
Angela Hess, *COO*
Debbie Warren, *General Mgr*
Tyrone Helton, *Info Tech Mgr*
Tina Norder, *VP Finance*
EMP: 60 **Privately Held**
SIC: 6531 8741 Real estate managers; administrative management

(P-11846)
SMARTZIP ANALYTICS INC
6210 Stoneridge Mall Rd # 100, Pleasanton (94588-3268)
PHONE.................925 218-1900
Tom Glassanos, *President*
Frank Richards, *Chairman*
Kim McNally, *Office Admin*
Yu Pan, *Sr Software Eng*
Sam Law, *Engineer*
EMP: 58
SALES (est): 6.4MM **Privately Held**
SIC: 6531 Real estate agents & managers

(P-11847)
SMITH & SONS INVESTMENT CO
735 Ohms Way, Costa Mesa (92627-4305)
PHONE.................949 646-9648
Walker Smith III, *President*
Kim S Lazarus, *Treasurer*
Clarke Smith, *Vice Pres*
EMP: 50
SQ FT: 4,700
SALES (est): 2.6MM **Privately Held**
SIC: 6531 Real estate agent, commercial; real estate managers

(P-11848)
SMITH COLEMAN INC
Also Called: Century 21
707 N La Brea Ave, Inglewood (90302-2203)
PHONE.................310 671-8271
Fax: 310 671-4614
Ellis Smith, *President*
EMP: 50
SALES (est): 2.9MM **Privately Held**
WEB: www.joeltaylorrealestate.com
SIC: 6531 Real estate agent, residential

(P-11849)
SNOWCREEK PROPERTY MANAGEMENT
Also Called: Snow Creek Resort
1254 Old Mammoth Rd, Mammoth Lakes (93546)
P.O. Box 1647 (93546-1647)
PHONE.................760 934-3333
Fax: 760 934-1619
Linda Dempsey, *Owner*
Julie Wright, *Vice Pres*
Jodi Melton, *Broker*
Sherry Wishney, *Broker*
Kami Boyer, *Real Est Agnt*
EMP: 50
SALES (est): 2.6MM **Privately Held**
WEB: www.snowcreekresort.com
SIC: 6531 Time-sharing real estate sales, leasing & rentals

(P-11850)
SOLANO PACIFIC CORPORATION
Also Called: Coldwell Banker Solano Pacific
900 1st St, Benicia (94510-3218)
PHONE.................707 745-6000
Fax: 707 746-1337
Richard A Bortolazzo, *CEO*
Joseph Banuat, *President*
EMP: 100
SQ FT: 5,000
SALES (est): 3.3MM **Privately Held**
SIC: 6531 Real estate agent, residential

(P-11851)
SOTHEBYS INTL RLTY INC
23405 Pacific Coast Hwy, Malibu (90265-4824)
PHONE.................310 456-6431
Michael Novotny, *General Mgr*
Amy E Alcini, *Real Est Agnt*
Barry Kinyon, *Real Est Agnt*
Jerel Taylor, *Real Est Agnt*
Jeffrey Thompson, *Real Est Agnt*
EMP: 50
SALES (corp-wide): 5.7B **Publicly Held**
SIC: 6531 Real estate agents & managers
HQ: Sotheby's International Realty, Inc.
38 E 61st St
New York NY 10065
212 606-7660

(P-11852)
SOUTH COUNTY HOUSING CORP (PA)
16500 Monterey St Ste 120, Morgan Hill (95037-5193)
PHONE.................510 582-1460
Fax: 408 842-0277
Dennis Lalor, *CEO*
John Cesare, *CFO*
Sandy Soria, *Finance Dir*
Nestor Nu A EZ, *Finance*
Andy Liese, *Director*
EMP: 50
SQ FT: 13,000
SALES: 10MM **Privately Held**
WEB: www.scounty.com
SIC: 6531 Real estate agent, residential

(P-11853)
SOVEREIGN CAPITL MGT GROUP INC
Also Called: Sovereign Capital MGT Group
750 B St Ste 2620, San Diego (92101-8172)
PHONE.................619 294-8989
Todd A Mikles, *CEO*
William White, *President*
Chad Wardwell, *Vice Pres*
Peter Nguyen, *Info Tech Dir*
Julian Willis, *Director*
EMP: 619
SALES (est): 3.6MM **Privately Held**
SIC: 6531 7389 Real estate agents & managers; financial services

(P-11854)
SPERRY VAN NESS INTL CORP
11999 San Vicente Blvd # 215, Los Angeles (90049-5131)
PHONE.................310 979-0800
David Rich, *Senior VP*
Kanna Sunkara, *Advisor*
EMP: 55 **Privately Held**
WEB: www.kittywallaceteam.com
SIC: 6531 Real estate agent, commercial
PA: Sperry Van Ness International Corp.
1 Center Plz Ste 250
Boston MA 02108

(P-11855)
STAR REAL ESTATE
19440 Goldenwest St, Huntington Beach (92648-2116)
PHONE.................714 500-3300
Fax: 714 500-3333
Terry Reay, *Manager*
Heidi Hoang, *Broker*
Gina Vreeland, *Broker*
Mary Connally, *Real Est Agnt*
Teri Miles, *Real Est Agnt*
EMP: 90
SALES (corp-wide): 9.9MM **Privately Held**
SIC: 6531 Real estate agent, residential
PA: Star Real Estate
10540 Talbert Ave 100w
Fountain Valley CA 92708
714 754-6262

(P-11856)
STAR REAL ESTATE SOUTH COUNTY
26711 Aliso Creek Rd 200a, Aliso Viejo (92656-4822)
PHONE.................949 389-0004
Michelle Williams, *President*
Becky Davis, *Administration*
Pat Gaines, *Asst Broker*
Lynne Bachover-Barz, *Broker*
Debbie Newsome, *Broker*
EMP: 250 EST: 1976
SALES (est): 7.8MM **Privately Held**
SIC: 6531 6519 Real estate brokers & agents; escrow agent, real estate; mine property leasing

(P-11857)
STARPOINT PROPERTY MGT LLC
Also Called: Vision Realty Managements
450 N Roxbury Dr Ste 1050, Beverly Hills (90210-4235)
PHONE.................310 247-0550
Fax: 310 247-0507
Paul Daneshrad,
Pat Haakstad, *Executive Asst*
Ethan Bui, *Info Tech Mgr*
Farahnik Evan, *Financial Exec*
Sheila Dameshrad,
EMP: 110
SALES (est): 9.7MM **Privately Held**
SIC: 6531 Real estate agents & managers

(P-11858)
STEVE ROBERSON
Also Called: Century 21
7825 Florence Ave, Downey (90240-3727)
PHONE.................562 927-2626
Fax: 562 928-1474
Steve Roberson, *Owner*
Angie Pierce, *Office Mgr*
EMP: 65 EST: 1977
SQ FT: 4,000
SALES (est): 2.5MM **Privately Held**
SIC: 6531 Real estate agent, residential

(P-11859)
STONE REAL ESTATE INC (PA)
Also Called: Prudential
1101 Sylvan Ave Ste B25, Modesto (95350-1607)
PHONE.................209 847-1230
Fax: 209 529-0967
Craig Lewis, *President*
Nate Mecham Sr, *Officer*

6531 - Real Estate Agents & Managers County (P-11860)

Cindy Fraze, *Executive Asst*
Donna Pearson, *Human Res Dir*
Ronald Ikenberry, *Human Res Mgr*
EMP: 80
SALES (est): 5.3MM **Privately Held**
SIC: 6531 Real estate agent, residential

(P-11860)
STRATEGIC PROPERTY MANAGEMENT
2055 3rd Ave Ste 200, San Diego (92101-2058)
PHONE...................619 295-2211
Don Claussson, *Principal*
Randy Strauss, *CFO*
Grant Beckwith, *District Mgr*
EMP: 75
SALES (est): 8.6MM **Privately Held**
WEB: www.stratprop.com
SIC: 6531 Real estate managers

(P-11861)
SUNRIZE STAGING INC
2210 Meyers Ave Ste 6b, Escondido (92029-1003)
P.O. Box 300067 (92030-0067)
PHONE...................760 743-2043
Lucian Luly, *President*
Hilda Stark, *Manager*
EMP: 51
SQ FT: 600
SALES (est): 2.6MM **Privately Held**
WEB: www.sunrizestaging.com
SIC: 6531 Rental agent, real estate

(P-11862)
T ROYAL MANAGEMENT (PA)
7419 N Cedar Ave Ste 102, Fresno (93720-3640)
PHONE...................559 447-9887
David Michael Thomas, *CEO*
James Ganson, *Shareholder*
Howard Wayne, *Sales Executive*
EMP: 55
SQ FT: 5,000
SALES (est): 3.6MM **Privately Held**
WEB: www.royaltmanagement.com
SIC: 6531 Real estate managers

(P-11863)
TAHOE SEASONS RESORT TIME INTE
3901 Saddle Rd, South Lake Tahoe (96150-8707)
P.O. Box 16300 (96151-6300)
PHONE...................530 541-6700
Michael Presley, *General Mgr*
EMP: 123
SALES (est): 10.5MM **Privately Held**
WEB: www.tahoeseasons.com
SIC: 6531 7011 5813 5812 Time-sharing real estate sales, leasing & rentals; hotels & motels; drinking places; eating places

(P-11864)
TARBELL FINANCIAL CORPORATION
1440 Industrial Park Ave, Redlands (92374-4517)
PHONE...................909 335-0750
Maria Luevano, *Branch Mgr*
EMP: 60
SALES (corp-wide): 132.4MM **Privately Held**
SIC: 6531 Real estate brokers & agents
PA: Tarbell Financial Corporation
1403 N Tustin Ave Ste 380
Santa Ana CA 92705
714 972-0988

(P-11865)
TEAM SPIRIT REALTY INC
6301 Beach Blvd Ste 225, Buena Park (90621-4031)
PHONE...................714 562-0404
Fax: 714 736-0404
Edward Son, *President*
EMP: 50
SALES (est): 1.4MM **Privately Held**
SIC: 6531 Real estate agents & managers

(P-11866)
TEJON RANCH CO (PA)
4436 Lebec Rd, Lebec (93243-9705)
P.O. Box 1000 (93243-1000)
PHONE...................661 248-3000
Fax: 661 248-1300
Gregory S Bielli, *President*
Richard Daley, *Records Dir*
Norman J Metcalfe, *Ch of Bd*
Allen E Lyda, *CFO*
Hugh McMahon, *Exec VP*
EMP: 60 **EST:** 1936
SALES: 51.1MM **Publicly Held**
WEB: www.tejonfilm.com
SIC: 6531 0173 0172 Real estate agents & managers; real estate brokers & agents; real estate agent, commercial; real estate agent, residential; almond grove; pistachio grove; walnut grove; grapes

(P-11867)
TEN-X LLC
1301 Shoreway Rd Ste 425, Belmont (94002-4154)
PHONE...................800 793-6107
Monte J M Koch, *Branch Mgr*
EMP: 204
SALES (corp-wide): 156.8MM **Privately Held**
SIC: 6531 Real estate agents & managers
PA: Ten-X, Llc
1 Mauchly
Irvine CA 92618
949 859-2777

(P-11868)
TEN-X LLC (PA)
Also Called: Auction.com
1 Mauchly, Irvine (92618-2305)
PHONE...................949 859-2777
Monte J M Koch, *CEO*
Sarah Andrews, *President*
Keith McLane, *President*
Frank Muhlon, *President*
Randy Wallen, *President*
EMP: 83
SALES (est): 156.8MM **Privately Held**
SIC: 6531 Real estate agents & managers

(P-11869)
TERRA COASTAL PROPERTIES INC
Also Called: Prudential Malibu Realty
23405 Pacific Coast Hwy, Malibu (90265-4824)
PHONE...................310 457-2534
Michael Novotny, *CEO*
Kate E Novotny, *Asst Broker*
Rita Simpson, *Real Est Agnt*
EMP: 50
SALES (est): 2.5MM **Privately Held**
SIC: 6531 Real estate agents & managers

(P-11870)
TERRA VISTA MANAGEMENT INC
Also Called: Terra Vista Management
2211 Pacific Beach Dr, San Diego (92109-5626)
PHONE...................858 581-4200
Fax: 858 581-4206
Micheal Gelfand, *Branch Mgr*
EMP: 120
SALES (corp-wide): 13MM **Privately Held**
SIC: 6531 7033 4225 4226 Real estate managers; trailer parks & campsites; general warehousing & storage; special warehousing & storage; nonresidential building operators
PA: Vista Terra Management Inc
6310 San Vicente Blvd # 506
Los Angeles CA 90048
323 954-5900

(P-11871)
TERRY MEYER
Also Called: Coldwell Banker Residential RE
1712 Meridian Ave Ste C, San Jose (95125-5587)
PHONE...................408 723-3300
Terry Meyer, *Principal*
Thuy Duong, *Asst Broker*
Darcus Simmons, *Asst Broker*

Robert Sharrock, *Broker*
Bob Jamello, *Sales Associate*
EMP: 61
SALES (est): 1.7MM **Privately Held**
SIC: 6531 Real estate agents & managers

(P-11872)
TEXACO INC
9525 Camino Media, Bakersfield (93311-1314)
PHONE...................661 654-7000
Gary Wolff, *Manager*
EMP: 300
SALES (corp-wide): 138.4B **Publicly Held**
WEB: www.texaco.com
SIC: 6531 5511 1311 Real estate agents & managers; automobiles, new & used; crude petroleum production
HQ: Texaco Inc.
6001 Bollinger Canyon Rd
San Ramon CA 94583
925 842-1000

(P-11873)
THIRD & MISSION ASSOCIATES LLC
Also Called: Paramount
680 Mission St, San Francisco (94105-4000)
PHONE...................415 341-8457
Fax: 415 227-9680
Jim Brooks, *Controller*
Tesa Doleman,
EMP: 50 **EST:** 2014
SALES (est): 2.2MM **Privately Held**
SIC: 6531 Real estate agents & managers

(P-11874)
THOMAS J HOBAN (PA)
Also Called: Hoban Management
215 W Lexington Ave, El Cajon (92020-4411)
PHONE...................619 442-1665
Fax: 619 442-7636
Thomas J Hoban, *Owner*
Arturo Gonzalez, *Maint Spvr*
Thomas J Castonguay,
Cathy Ketchum, *Director*
Naomi Zuniga, *Manager*
EMP: 50
SQ FT: 1,700
SALES (est): 11.2MM **Privately Held**
WEB: www.hoban-management.com
SIC: 6531 Real estate brokers & agents; real estate managers

(P-11875)
THOMAS M OBINSON JR
7480 N Palm Ave Ste 101, Fresno (93711-5501)
PHONE...................559 432-6200
Thomas Robinson, *Owner*
EMP: 55
SALES (est): 1.2MM **Privately Held**
SIC: 6531 Real estate agent, commercial

(P-11876)
TIM BROWN
Also Called: Coldwell Banker Residential RE
1096 Blossom Hill Rd # 200, San Jose (95123-1237)
PHONE...................408 717-2575
Tim Brown, *Principal*
Erik Bakker, *Sales Staff*
Shirley Boudinot, *Sales Staff*
Jacquelyn Jones, *Sales Staff*
Kerry McCarty, *Sales Staff*
EMP: 90
SALES (est): 2.1MM **Privately Held**
SIC: 6531 Real estate agents & managers

(P-11877)
TOPA BERKELEY LTD
1800 Avenue Of The Stars, Los Angeles (90067-4201)
PHONE...................310 203-9199
John Anderson, *Owner*
Brenda Seuthe, *CFO*
Darren Bell, *Vice Pres*
Elsbeth Rowaan, *Vice Pres*
Curt Nakamura, *General Mgr*
EMP: 100
SALES (est): 2.6MM **Privately Held**

(P-11878)
TRANSPACIFIC MANAGEMENT SVC
647 Camino De Los Mares # 230, San Clemente (92673-2860)
P.O. Box 4169, Santa Ana (92702-4169)
PHONE...................949 248-2822
Bill Sasser, *Owner*
Veronica Lopez, *Director*
EMP: 60
SALES (est): 2.5MM **Privately Held**
SIC: 6531 Real estate managers

(P-11879)
TRANSPACIFIC MANAGEMENT SVC
15661 Red Hill Ave # 205, Tustin (92780-7328)
PHONE...................714 285-2626
William Sasser, *President*
Sherrie Fitchen, *Exec VP*
Michelle Pate, *Vice Pres*
Bill Etienne, *Info Tech Dir*
EMP: 55
SALES (est): 5.1MM **Privately Held**
WEB: www.transpacinc.com
SIC: 6531 Real estate agents & managers

(P-11880)
TRANSWESTERN CORP POINTE LLC
600 Crprate Pinte Ste 250, Culver City (90230)
PHONE...................310 642-1001
Dave Rock,
EMP: 99
SALES: 950K **Privately Held**
SIC: 6531 Real estate agents & managers

(P-11881)
TRG INC
Also Called: Rosenthal Group, The
1350 Abbot Kinney Blvd # 101, Venice (90291-3893)
P.O. Box 837 (90294-0837)
PHONE...................310 396-6750
R J Rosenthal, *President*
EMP: 100
SALES (est): 3.3MM **Privately Held**
WEB: www.trgnational.com
SIC: 6531 Real estate agents & managers

(P-11882)
TRILOGY REALTY GROUP INC
2025 N Mantle Ln, Santa Ana (92705-7614)
PHONE...................937 206-0725
Garrett J Hilseth, *CEO*
EMP: 100 **EST:** 2014
SALES (est): 3MM **Privately Held**
SIC: 6531 Real estate agents & managers

(P-11883)
TRIMONT LAND COMPANY (HQ)
Also Called: Northstar-At-Tahoe
5001 Northstar Dr, Truckee (96161-4236)
P.O. Box 129 (96160-0129)
PHONE...................530 562-2252
Fax: 530 562-2214
Robert A Katz, *CEO*
Tim Silver, *CEO*
Daniel Graves, *CFO*
Brian Pope, *Vice Pres*
Jessica James, *Comms Mgr*
EMP: 300 **EST:** 1966
SALES (est): 28.1MM
SALES (corp-wide): 582.1MM **Privately Held**
SIC: 6531 7011 Real estate managers; ski lodge; resort hotel
PA: The Vail Corporation
390 Interlocken Cres # 1000
Broomfield CO 80021
303 404-1800

(P-11884)
TROOP REAL ESTATE INC
4165 E Thousand Oaks Blvd # 101, Westlake Village (91362-3814)
PHONE...................805 402-3028
Fax: 805 497-4931
Jeff Rosenblum, *Branch Mgr*
Patti Hepple, *Top Exec*
Gaston Estrada, *Broker*
Rodd Feingold, *Broker*

Robert Swanson, *Broker*
EMP: 56
SALES (corp-wide): 23.2MM **Privately Held**
SIC: 6531 Real estate brokers & agents
PA: Troop Real Estate, Inc.
3200 E Los Angeles Ave
Simi Valley CA 93065
805 581-3200

(P-11885)
TROOP REAL ESTATE INC (PA)
3200 E Los Angeles Ave, Simi Valley (93065-3972)
PHONE..................805 581-3200
Fax: 805 581-1854
Brian C Troop, *CEO*
Laura Lee Anthony, *President*
Deborah McCarthy, *COO*
Joann Luce, *Office Admin*
Kenneth W Grech, *Mktg Dir*
EMP: 95
SQ FT: 10,000
SALES (est): 23.2MM **Privately Held**
WEB: www.scottpetto.com
SIC: 6531 Real estate brokers & agents

(P-11886)
TRZ HOLDINGS II INC
Also Called: Brookfield Properties
725 S Figueroa St # 1850, Los Angeles (90017-5524)
PHONE..................213 955-7170
Tim Callahan, *Manager*
EMP: 280
SALES (corp-wide): 14.9B **Privately Held**
SIC: 6531 6552 Real estate managers; subdividers & developers
HQ: Trz Holdings Ii, Inc
3 World Financial Ctr
New York NY 10281
212 693-8150

(P-11887)
TURNSTONE SYSTEMS INC
2220 Central Expy, Santa Clara (95050-2516)
PHONE..................408 907-1400
Richard N Tinsley, *Principal*
Eric Scott Yeaman, *CEO*
Danny Hernandez, *Controller*
Duffie P K, *Director*
EMP: 160
SALES (est): 5.2MM **Privately Held**
SIC: 6531 Real estate brokers & agents

(P-11888)
TWENTIETH CENTURY FOX IN
10201 W Pico Blvd, Los Angeles (90064-2651)
PHONE..................310 369-1000
Peter Chernin, *Ch of Bd*
Maryanne Shivanandan, *VP Sls/Mktg*
EMP: 577
SALES (est): 14.5MM
SALES (corp-wide): 27.3B **Publicly Held**
SIC: 6531 Real estate brokers & agents
HQ: Fox Entertainment Group, Inc.
2029 Century Park E # 1400
Los Angeles CA 90067
310 369-1000

(P-11889)
TWIN ADVANTAGE INC
Also Called: Exit Twin Advantage Realty
39755 Murrieta Hot S Ste G, Murrieta (92563)
PHONE..................951 445-4200
Fax: 951 698-1818
Susan Ebert, *President*
Jason Friend, *General Mgr*
Jacquie Becker, *Real Est Agnt*
Dameon Cook, *Real Est Agnt*
Sam Gyasi, *Real Est Agnt*
EMP: 60
SALES (est): 4.1MM **Privately Held**
SIC: 6531 Real estate agent, residential

(P-11890)
TYSON INVESTMENTS INC
Also Called: Star Estate
26711 Aliso Creek Rd, Aliso Viejo (92656-4820)
PHONE..................949 389-0004
Michele Williams, *CEO*
EMP: 150
SALES (est): 4MM **Privately Held**
SIC: 6531 Real estate brokers & agents

(P-11891)
UNITED CALIFORNIA REALTY INC
12829 Bear Valley Rd, Victorville (92392-9786)
PHONE..................760 949-4040
Fax: 760 949-3912
Bob Gates, *President*
C V Tirone, *President*
Philip Tirone, *Corp Secy*
Richard Trombley, *Administration*
EMP: 65
SQ FT: 3,600
SALES (est): 3.1MM **Privately Held**
WEB: www.ucrproperties.com
SIC: 6531 Real estate brokers & agents

(P-11892)
UNIVERSE HOLDINGS DEV CO LLC
350 S Beverly Dr Ste 210, Beverly Hills (90212-4816)
PHONE..................310 785-0077
Fax: 310 785-0990
Henry Manoucheri,
EMP: 50
SQ FT: 1,100
SALES (est): 1.9MM **Privately Held**
SIC: 6531 Real estate agents & managers

(P-11893)
US REAL ESTATE SERVICES INC
Also Called: Res.net
25520 Commercentre Dr # 1, Lake Forest (92630-8884)
PHONE..................949 598-9920
Fax: 949 598-9950
Keith Guenther, *CEO*
Matt Dohman, *President*
Todd Mobraten, *COO*
Michael Bull, *CFO*
Gregory Metz, *Treasurer*
EMP: 90
SQ FT: 37,000
SALES (est): 14.5MM **Privately Held**
WEB: www.usres.com
SIC: 6531 Real estate managers

(P-11894)
USA MULTIFAMILY MANAGEMENT
3200 Douglas Blvd Ste 200, Roseville (95661-4238)
PHONE..................916 773-6060
Fax: 916 773-1682
Karen McCurdy, *President*
Kristen Hawkins, *Treasurer*
Steven Gall, *Vice Pres*
Vicky Bartley, *Manager*
Vernon Crockett, *Manager*
EMP: 130
SQ FT: 5,020
SALES (est): 11.6MM
SALES (corp-wide): 83MM **Privately Held**
WEB: www.usapropfund.com
SIC: 6531 Real estate managers
PA: Usa Properties Fund, Inc.
3200 Douglas Blvd Ste 200
Roseville CA 95661
916 773-6060

(P-11895)
V TROTH INC
Also Called: Berkshire Hathaway
1801 W Avenue K Ste 101, Lancaster (93534-5999)
P.O. Box 2024 (93539-2024)
PHONE..................661 948-4646
Fax: 661 945-9133
Debra K Anderson, *President*
Patrick J Hunt, *COO*
Donald L Anderson, *Vice Pres*
Mark A Troth, *Admin Sec*
Michelle Bragg, *Real Est Agnt*
EMP: 75
SALES (est): 4.7MM **Privately Held**
SIC: 6531 8742 Real estate agents & managers; real estate consultant

(P-11896)
VALUATION CONCEPTS LLC
Also Called: Appraisal Trend
16350 Ventura Blvd D140, Encino (91436-5300)
PHONE..................818 812-6233
Kendrick Jackson,
EMP: 90
SQ FT: 500
SALES (est): 1.9MM **Privately Held**
SIC: 6531 Appraiser, real estate

(P-11897)
VELOCITY COMMERCIAL CAPITL LLC
30699 Russell Ranch Rd, Westlake Village (91362-7315)
PHONE..................818 532-3700
Fax: 818 532-3800
Christopher D Farrar,
Lou Akel, *Ch Credit Ofcr*
Jay Samtani, *Officer*
Joseph Cowell, *Senior VP*
Chris Wanner, *Loan Officer*
EMP: 50
SQ FT: 15,000
SALES (est): 8.5MM **Privately Held**
WEB: www.velocitycommercial.com
SIC: 6531 Real estate agent, commercial

(P-11898)
VILLAGEWAY MANAGEMENT INC
Also Called: Villageway Property Management
23041 Ave De La Carlta # 270, Laguna Hills (92653-1545)
PHONE..................949 450-1515
Fax: 949 585-0146
Janet Walley, *President*
William Christiansen, *Treasurer*
Melanie Young, *Executive Asst*
Laura Gomez, *Human Res Dir*
EMP: 70 **EST:** 1969
SQ FT: 14,000
SALES (est): 5.9MM **Privately Held**
WEB: www.villageway.com
SIC: 6531 Real estate managers

(P-11899)
VINSON CHASE INC
Also Called: Coldwell Banker
220 Standiford Ave Ste A, Modesto (95350-1159)
PHONE..................209 577-4747
Fax: 209 577-0251
Vinson Chase, *President*
Sandra Chase, *Vice Pres*
Kady Chase, *Administration*
Richard Millentree, *Info Tech Mgr*
Helen Edmonds, *Real Est Agnt*
EMP: 58
SQ FT: 11,000
SALES (est): 3MM **Privately Held**
WEB: www.modestorealestate.com
SIC: 6531 Real estate agent, residential

(P-11900)
VISTA ANGLINA HSING PRTNRS LP
418 E Edgeware Rd, Los Angeles (90026-5693)
PHONE..................213 482-4718
Tesa Doleman,
Jim Brooks, *Controller*
EMP: 50
SALES (est): 1.6MM **Privately Held**
SIC: 6531 Real estate agents & managers

(P-11901)
VISTA VALENCIA GROUP INC
Also Called: Coldwell Banker
25545 Via Paladar, Valencia (91355-3153)
PHONE..................661 255-4600
Fax: 661 297-8698
Carol James, *CEO*
Roy Medows, *Bd of Directors*
Joan Byrd, *General Mgr*
Greg Handy, *General Mgr*
Darlene Halkyard, *Admin Asst*
EMP: 50
SALES (est): 3MM **Privately Held**
WEB: www.cbvista.com
SIC: 6531 Real estate agents, residential

(P-11902)
VOIT REAL ESTATE SERVICES LP
101 Shipyard Way Ste A, Newport Beach (92663-4447)
PHONE..................949 644-8648
Bob Voit, *Managing Prtnr*
EMP: 130
SALES (est): 7.6MM **Privately Held**
WEB: www.voitco.com
SIC: 6531 Real estate agents & managers

(P-11903)
W K G COMPANY
1400 W 3rd St, Chico (95928-4825)
PHONE..................530 345-1393
Rod Platte, *President*
John Rothrock, *Controller*
EMP: 130
SQ FT: 3,000
SALES (est): 4.4MM **Privately Held**
SIC: 6531 Real estate managers

(P-11904)
WAGNER JACOBSON BROKERAGE INC
16400 Ventura Blvd # 333, Encino (91436-2137)
PHONE..................323 872-1636
Fax: 818 995-4055
Michael Wagner, *President*
Charlotte Wagner, *Corp Secy*
EMP: 50
SALES (est): 2.2MM **Privately Held**
SIC: 6531 Real estate brokers & agents

(P-11905)
WALSH VINEYARDS MANAGEMENT INC
1125 Golden Gate Dr, NAPA (94558-6188)
PHONE..................707 255-1650
Tim Rodgers, *President*
Vicki Thorpe, *Corp Secy*
Brian Shepard, *Vice Pres*
Towle Merritt, *General Mgr*
Ruben Flores, *Human Res Mgr*
EMP: 250
SQ FT: 6,000
SALES (est): 26.8MM **Privately Held**
WEB: www.wvmgmt.com
SIC: 6531 Real estate managers

(P-11906)
WALTER E MCGUIRE RE INC
360 Primrose Rd, Burlingame (94010-4005)
PHONE..................650 348-0222
Fax: 650 348-0233
Charles Moore, *President*
EMP: 180
SALES (corp-wide): 35.1MM **Privately Held**
WEB: www.mcguire.com
SIC: 6531 Real estate agents & managers
PA: Walter E. Mcguire Real Estate, Inc.
2001 Lombard St
San Francisco CA 94123
415 929-1500

(P-11907)
WALTER E MCGUIRE RE INC (PA)
2001 Lombard St, San Francisco (94123-2808)
PHONE..................415 929-1500
Fax: 415 922-5958
Charles Moore, *CEO*
Alex Buehlmann, *COO*
Aldo Congi, *Vice Pres*
Dierk Herbermann, *Vice Pres*
Dave Hobson, *Vice Pres*
EMP: 50
SQ FT: 10,000
SALES (est): 35.1MM **Privately Held**
WEB: www.mcguire.com
SIC: 6531 Real estate brokers & agents

(P-11908)
WALTER E MCGUIRE RE INC
Also Called: Raymond Brown Company
17 Bluxome St, San Francisco (94107-1605)
PHONE..................415 296-0123
Aldo Congi, *Manager*
James O'Meara, *Sales Associate*

6531 - Real Estate Agents & Managers County (P-11909)

Kristen Thompson, *Real Est Agnt*
EMP: 50
SALES (corp-wide): 35.1MM **Privately Held**
WEB: www.mcguire.com
SIC: 6531 Real estate brokers & agents
PA: Walter E. Mcguire Real Estate, Inc.
2001 Lombard St
San Francisco CA 94123
415 929-1500

(P-11909)
WALTER VOSS CYNTHIA RE MAX
6695 E Pacific Coast Hwy # 150, Long Beach (90803-4235)
PHONE 562 434-5980
Bob Stallings, *Owner*
EMP: 85
SALES (est): 1.4MM **Privately Held**
SIC: 6531 Real estate agent, residential

(P-11910)
WATERMARK RTRMENT CMMNTIES INC
3890 Nobel Dr, San Diego (92122-5786)
PHONE 858 597-8000
Barbara Wilkinson, *Manager*
EMP: 75
SALES (corp-wide): 116.1MM **Privately Held**
SIC: 6531 Real estate managers
HQ: Watermark Retirement Communities, Inc.
2020 W Rudasill Rd
Tucson AZ 85704
520 797-4000

(P-11911)
WATT INVESTMENT PARTNERS LLC
2716 Ocean Park Blvd, Santa Monica (90405-5207)
PHONE 310 450-3802
J Scott Watt, *Principal*
EMP: 60
SALES (est): 2.2MM **Privately Held**
SIC: 6531 Real estate agent, commercial

(P-11912)
WAYPOINT REAL ESTATE GROUP LLC
1999 Harrison St Fl 22nd, Oakland (94612-4719)
PHONE 510 250-2200
Colin Wiel, *Mng Member*
Scott Gable, *COO*
Nina Tran, *CFO*
Mike Travalini, *Business Dir*
Ali Nazar, *CTO*
EMP: 82
SALES (est): 8.3MM **Privately Held**
SIC: 6531 Real estate brokers & agents

(P-11913)
WELK RESORT GROUP INC (PA)
Also Called: Welk Resort Center
300 Rancheros Dr Ste 450, San Marcos (92069-2969)
PHONE 760 652-4913
Fax: 760 749-5332
Larry Welk, *CEO*
Jonathan Fredricks, *President*
David Rice, *Vice Pres*
Maggie Condiff, *Social Dir*
Anita Perez, *Admin Asst*
EMP: 50
SALES (est): 71.5MM **Privately Held**
WEB: www.welksandiego.com
SIC: 6531 6552 7992 7011 Time-sharing real estate sales, leasing & rentals; subdividers & developers; public golf courses; hotels & motels; eating places; tour operators

(P-11914)
WELLS & BENNETT REALTORS (PA)
1451 Leimert Blvd, Oakland (94602-1896)
PHONE 510 531-7000
Fax: 510 531-2831
Barton W Bennett, *Owner*
Stan Hammond, *CIO*
Catherine Vallee, *Broker*
Jeannine Nelson, *Manager*
James Plumbridge, *Manager*
EMP: 65 **EST:** 1924
SQ FT: 5,000
SALES (est): 4.2MM **Privately Held**
WEB: www.wellsandbennett.com
SIC: 6531 6512 Real estate brokers & agents; real estate managers; nonresidential building operators; commercial & industrial building operation

(P-11915)
WESTCOE REALTORS INC
Also Called: Westcoe Escrow Division
7191 Magnolia Ave, Riverside (92504-3805)
PHONE 951 784-2500
Fax: 951 682-2310
Rich Simonin, *Manager*
Susan Simonin, *President*
Richard Simonin, *Vice Pres*
Scott Beloian, *Real Est Agnt*
April Bolin, *Real Est Agnt*
EMP: 65
SQ FT: 11,200
SALES (est): 4.1MM **Privately Held**
WEB: www.louanneludwig.com
SIC: 6531 Real estate brokers & agents

(P-11916)
WESTERN AMERICA PROPERTIES LLC
111 N Sepulveda Blvd # 330, Manhattan Beach (90266-6813)
P.O. Box 1597 (90267-1597)
PHONE 310 374-4381
James Perley,
EMP: 89
SALES (est): 2.7MM **Privately Held**
SIC: 6531 Real estate agent, commercial

(P-11917)
WESTERN NATIONAL SECURITIES (PA)
8 Executive Cir, Irvine (92614-6746)
P.O. Box 19528 (92623-9528)
PHONE 949 862-6200
Michael K Hayde, *CEO*
James Gilly, *President*
Jerry Lapointe, *Principal*
EMP: 120
SQ FT: 35,000
SALES (est): 12.9MM **Privately Held**
WEB: www.jpi.com
SIC: 6531 Real estate managers

(P-11918)
WESTLAKE REALTY GROUP INC (PA)
520 S El Camino Real 9th, San Mateo (94402-1726)
PHONE 650 579-1010
M Gary Wong, *President*
David Chua, *Vice Pres*
Lin Zhou, *Accounting Mgr*
Richard Ng, *Controller*
EMP: 90
SALES (est): 5MM **Privately Held**
SIC: 6531 Real estate agents & managers

(P-11919)
WESTMINSTER HOUSING PARTENERS
Also Called: Windsor Court/Stratford Place
8140 13th St, Westminster (92683-4794)
PHONE 714 891-3000
Jim Brooks, *Controller*
Tesa Doleman,
EMP: 50
SALES (est): 1.7MM **Privately Held**
SIC: 6531 Real estate agents & managers

(P-11920)
WHEATLAND SCHOOL DISTRICT
Also Called: Realty World
100 Wheatland Park Dr, Wheatland (95692-9286)
PHONE 530 633-3135
Angela Gouker, *Administration*
Jonathan Drury, *Assistant*
EMP: 85
SALES (corp-wide): 14.7MM **Privately Held**
SIC: 6531 Real estate agent, residential
PA: Wheatland School District
111 Main St
Wheatland CA 95692
530 633-3130

(P-11921)
WILDE & GUERNSEY INC
Also Called: Coldwell Banker Property Shop
727 W Ojai Ave, Ojai (93023-3726)
PHONE 805 646-7288
Fax: 805 646-0524
Dennis Guernsey, *President*
Larry Wilde Od, *Owner*
Sharon Maharry, *Real Est Agnt*
Christa Green, *Associate*
EMP: 60
SALES (est): 3.1MM **Privately Held**
WEB: www.ojaicoldwell.com
SIC: 6531 Real estate agent, residential

(P-11922)
WILLIAM L LYON & ASSOC INC
Also Called: Lyon & Associates Realtors
2801 J St, Sacramento (95816-4315)
PHONE 916 447-7878
Fax: 916 447-4051
Laure Woodgundlach, *Manager*
Farah Petrushkin, *Trustee*
Carol Kellogg, *Office Mgr*
James Lutton, *Research*
Lucy Janzer, *Chief Engr*
EMP: 55
SALES (corp-wide): 66.4MM **Privately Held**
WEB: www.lyonre.com
SIC: 6531 Real estate agents & managers
PA: L Lyon William & Associates Inc
3640 American River Dr
Sacramento CA 95864
916 978-4200

(P-11923)
WILLIAM L LYON & ASSOC INC
Also Called: Lyon Realtors
8814 Madison Ave, Fair Oaks (95628-3908)
PHONE 916 535-0356
Fax: 916 535-5156
Clay Sigg, *Manager*
Kyle Thompson, *Office Mgr*
Lyn Gras, *Manager*
Rakesh Bhargava, *Real Est Agnt*
Sigrid Biddle, *Real Est Agnt*
EMP: 70
SALES (corp-wide): 66.4MM **Privately Held**
WEB: www.lyonre.com
SIC: 6531 Real estate managers
PA: L Lyon William & Associates Inc
3640 American River Dr
Sacramento CA 95864
916 978-4200

(P-11924)
WILLIS ALLEN REAL ESTATE (PA)
1131 Wall St, La Jolla (92037-4579)
PHONE 858 459-4033
Andrew E Nelson, *President*
Bud Clark, *Exec VP*
Josie Vara, *Office Mgr*
Terry Courington, *Accounting Mgr*
Bobby Graham, *Broker*
EMP: 50
SQ FT: 6,000
SALES (est): 6.6MM **Privately Held**
SIC: 6531 Real estate brokers & agents

(P-11925)
WILLIS ALLEN REAL ESTATE
6024 Pasco Delicias, Rancho Santa Fe (92067)
P.O. Box 107 (92067-0107)
PHONE 858 756-2444
Fax: 858 756-5773
Gary Wheeler, *Manager*
Debbie Funderburk, *Broker*
Dick Tibbetts, *Real Est Agnt*
EMP: 50
SALES (corp-wide): 6.6MM **Privately Held**
SIC: 6531 Real estate agent, residential
PA: Willis Allen Real Estate
1131 Wall St
La Jolla CA 92037
858 459-4033

(P-11926)
WILLOW GLEN HSING PARTNERS LP
465 Willow Glen Way # 100, San Jose (95125-6513)
PHONE 408 267-7252
Jim Brooks, *Controller*
Tesa Doleman,
EMP: 50 **EST:** 2014
SALES (est): 1.4MM **Privately Held**
SIC: 6531 Real estate agents & managers

(P-11927)
WILMARK MANAGEMENT SERVICES (PA)
Also Called: Wilmark Development
9948 Hibert St Ste 210, San Diego (92131-1034)
PHONE 858 271-0583
Fax: 858 271-0740
Mark S Schmidt, *President*
EMP: 65
SALES (est): 2.9MM **Privately Held**
SIC: 6531 Real estate managers

(P-11928)
WILSHIRE INVESTMENTS CORP
12100 Wilshire Blvd # 1400, Los Angeles (90025-7120)
PHONE 310 207-0704
Deane Earl Ross, *President*
Lawrence Penn, *Treasurer*
Suzanne Magnuson, *Admin Sec*
EMP: 75
SQ FT: 5,000
SALES (est): 3.6MM **Privately Held**
SIC: 6531 Rental agent, real estate

(P-11929)
WINDERMERE REAL ESTATE EAST
71691 Highway 111, Rancho Mirage (92270-4441)
PHONE 760 568-2568
Bob Deville, *Principal*
Nick Mocuta, *Asst Broker*
Pat Smith, *Asst Broker*
Dave Black, *Broker*
Jake Brown, *Broker*
EMP: 67
SALES (corp-wide): 13.8MM **Privately Held**
SIC: 6531 Real estate agents & managers
PA: Windermere Real Estate East Inc
14405 Se 36th St Ste 100
Bellevue WA 98006
425 643-5500

(P-11930)
YORBA PROPERTIES CORP
Also Called: Re/Max
20459 Yorba Linda Blvd, Yorba Linda (92886-3043)
PHONE 714 777-5112
Fax: 714 693-0184
Gerry Bullerdick, *President*
Stefanie Leal, *Manager*
Janet Escobar, *Real Est Agnt*
Nancy Campau, *Associate*
Nancy Dushane-Bank, *Associate*
EMP: 75
SQ FT: 6,000
SALES (est): 3.3MM **Privately Held**
WEB: www.eastlakevillage.net
SIC: 6531 6163 Real estate agent, residential; mortgage brokers arranging for loans, using money of others

(P-11931)
YOUNG ESTATES
971 S Westlke Blvd 100, Westlake Village (91361)
PHONE 805 446-1800
Joan Young, *President*
Bill Carter, *Exec VP*
EMP: 80
SALES (est): 2.1MM **Privately Held**
SIC: 6531 Real estate agents & managers

(P-11932)
YOUNG REALTORS
Also Called: Joan Young Co Realtors
971 S Westlke Blvd # 100, Westlake Village (91361-3115)
PHONE 805 497-0947

PRODUCTS & SERVICES SECTION

6552 - Land Subdividers & Developers County (P-11955)

Fax: 805 374-9898
Joan Young, *Owner*
Marc Schnitman, *Info Tech Mgr*
Michael O Proett, *Human Res Mgr*
Anthony Defranco, *Real Est Agnt*
Michelle Esparza, *Real Est Agnt*
EMP: 53
SALES (est): 1.5MM **Privately Held**
SIC: 6531 Real estate brokers & agents

(P-11933)
Z & M ASSCIATES INC
Also Called: Referral Realty Cupertino
1601 S Danza Blvd Ste 150, Cupertino (95014)
PHONE 408 996-8100
Mois Nahouraii, *President*
EMP: 85
SALES (est): 2.7MM **Privately Held**
SIC: 6531 Real estate brokers & agents

(P-11934)
ZENITH HEALTH CARE
Also Called: Regency Park
245 S El Molino Ave, Pasadena (91101-2905)
PHONE 626 578-0460
Fax: 626 568-8216
Sandy Wooters, *Administration*
Nancy Oconnor, *Administration*
EMP: 70
SALES (est): 1.9MM **Privately Held**
WEB: www.zenithadm.com
SIC: 6531 Real estate agents & managers

(P-11935)
ZIPREALTY INC (DH)
2000 Powell St Ste 300, Emeryville (94608-1838)
PHONE 510 735-2600
Fax: 510 735-2850
Lanny Baker, *CEO*
Eric L Mersch, *CFO*
Jeffrey G Waoner, *Senior VP*
Joe Pucillo, *Vice Pres*
Jaime Wison, *Vice Pres*
EMP: 53 **EST:** 2004
SQ FT: 23,803
SALES (est): 55.5MM
SALES (corp-wide): 5.7B **Publicly Held**
WEB: www.ziprealty.com
SIC: 6531 7375 Real estate brokers & agents; information retrieval services
HQ: Realogy Group Llc
175 Park Ave
Madison NJ 07940
973 407-2000

(P-11936)
ZURICH FINANCIAL RESOURCES (PA)
1110 Kregmont Dr, Glendora (91741-2249)
PHONE 626 963-4398
Ray Parayno, *President*
John Carrie, *CIO*
EMP: 103
SALES: 200K **Privately Held**
SIC: 6531 6163 Real estate brokers & agents; escrow agent, real estate; mortgage brokers arranging for loans, using money of others

6541 Title Abstract Offices

(P-11937)
CHICAGO TITLE INSURANCE CO
3127 Transworld Dr # 103, Stockton (95206-4988)
P.O. Box 7638 (95267-0638)
PHONE 209 952-5500
Fax: 209 478-4063
Lisa Westfall, *Branch Mgr*
EMP: 60
SALES (corp-wide): 9.1B **Publicly Held**
SIC: 6541 6361 6099 Title abstract offices; title insurance; escrow institutions other than real estate
HQ: Chicago Title Insurance Company
4050 Calle Real
Santa Barbara CA 93110
805 565-6900

(P-11938)
ORANGE COAST TITLE COMPANY
2411 W La Palma Ave # 300, Anaheim (92801-2683)
PHONE 714 822-3211
Barbara Kooey, *Manager*
Randy Fernando, *Assoc VP*
Fred Nilsen, *Vice Pres*
Julie Walters, *Accounting Mgr*
Danny De La Torre, *Opers Staff*
EMP: 100
SALES (corp-wide): 160.8MM **Privately Held**
SIC: 6541 Title & trust companies
PA: Orange Coast Title Company Of Southern California
640 N Tustin Ave Ste 106
Santa Ana CA 92705
714 558-2836

(P-11939)
STEWART INFORMATION SVCS CORP
6477 Telephone Rd Ste 8, Ventura (93003-4459)
PHONE 805 677-6915
Craig Martin, *Branch Mgr*
EMP: 83
SALES (corp-wide): 2B **Publicly Held**
WEB: www.stewart.com
SIC: 6541 Title & trust companies
PA: Stewart Information Services Corporation
1980 Post Oak Blvd
Houston TX 77056
713 625-8100

(P-11940)
STEWART INFORMATION SVCS CORP
3888 State St Ste 201, Santa Barbara (93105-5619)
PHONE 805 899-7700
Kelley Cox, *Principal*
EMP: 83
SALES (corp-wide): 2B **Publicly Held**
SIC: 6541 Title & trust companies
PA: Stewart Information Services Corporation
1980 Post Oak Blvd
Houston TX 77056
713 625-8100

(P-11941)
TIMESHARE RELIEF INC
Also Called: Transer America
2239 W 190th St, Torrance (90504-6001)
PHONE 310 755-6434
Dave Halpern, *CEO*
Dave McMillian, *President*
Gina Crittenden, *CFO*
Marcus Gillette, *Vice Pres*
Cindy Martin, *Vice Pres*
EMP: 170
SQ FT: 11,000
SALES (est): 7.1MM **Privately Held**
WEB: www.timesharerelief.com
SIC: 6541 Title abstract offices

(P-11942)
TITLE RECORDS INC
8926 Sunland Blvd, Sun Valley (91352-2843)
PHONE 818 767-9610
Fax: 818 767-2841
Brad Westover, *President*
Timothy Morgan, *Ch of Bd*
Kenneth Sean Pratt, *President*
Sue Daley, *Accounting Mgr*
Linda Smith, *Agent*
EMP: 63
SQ FT: 88,000
SALES (est): 2MM **Privately Held**
SIC: 6541 Title search companies

(P-11943)
WFG NATIONAL TITLE INSUR CO
333 W Santa Clara St # 110, San Jose (95113-1714)
PHONE 408 560-3000
EMP: 51

SALES (corp-wide): 128.2MM **Privately Held**
SIC: 6541 Title abstract offices
PA: Wfg National Title Insurance Company
700 N Brand Blvd Ste 1100
Glendale CA 91203
818 476-4000

6552 Land Subdividers & Developers

(P-11944)
A M S PARTNERSHIP (PA)
Also Called: La Mancha Development
1517 S Sepulveda Blvd, Los Angeles (90025-3311)
PHONE 310 312-6698
Fax: 310 312-0040
Marvin B Levine, *Partner*
Samuel Bachner, *Partner*
EMP: 60
SQ FT: 2,500
SALES (est): 7.3MM **Privately Held**
SIC: 6552 6512 Subdividers & developers; commercial & industrial building operation

(P-11945)
ALLEN DEVELOPMENT PARTNERS LLC (PA)
125 Sbridge 100, Visalia (93291)
PHONE 559 732-5425
Richard S Allen,
Jenny Saubert, *Financial Exec*
Kevin Noell,
EMP: 60
SALES (est): 5.6MM **Privately Held**
SIC: 6552 Subdividers & developers

(P-11946)
AMCAL COMMUNITIES INC
30141 Agoura Rd Ste 100, Agoura Hills (91301-2020)
PHONE 818 706-0694
Percival Vaz, *President*
EMP: 50
SALES (est): 4.4MM **Privately Held**
SIC: 6552 Land subdividers & developers, residential

(P-11947)
AMERICAN NWLAND COMMUNITIES LP (PA)
9820 Towne Centre Dr # 100, San Diego (92121-1912)
PHONE 858 455-7503
Fax: 858 455-7500
Ladonna K Monsees, *CEO*
Dave Wood, *President*
Daniel C Van Epp, *COO*
Vicki R Mullins, *CFO*
Daniel Van Epp, *Exec VP*
EMP: 50
SQ FT: 12,000
SALES (est): 163.7MM **Privately Held**
SIC: 6552 Subdividers & developers

(P-11948)
ANNABEL INVESTMENT COMPANY
Also Called: Sunset Development Company
2600 Camino Ramon Ste 201, San Ramon (94583-5000)
P.O. Box 640 (94583-0640)
PHONE 925 866-0100
Alexander Mehran, *Partner*
EMP: 100
SQ FT: 1,000,000
SALES (est): 5.9MM **Privately Held**
SIC: 6552 Subdividers & developers

(P-11949)
BEVERLY HILLS COUNTRY CLUB
3084 Motor Ave, Los Angeles (90064-4746)
PHONE 310 836-4400
Fax: 310 836-4651
Gene Axelrod, *Partner*
Paul Epner, *Managing Dir*
Ivette Carrero, *Controller*
Doreen Nesher, *Director*
Regina Concepcion, *Manager*
EMP: 130

SQ FT: 100,000
SALES (est): 17.4MM **Privately Held**
WEB: www.beverlyhillscc.com
SIC: 6552 6531 7997 Subdividers & developers; real estate agents & managers; membership sports & recreation clubs

(P-11950)
BIXBY RANCH CO A CALIFORNIA LP
Also Called: Bixby Ranch Company
3901 Lampson Ave, Seal Beach (90740-2756)
PHONE 562 596-4425
Fax: 562 594-0414
Tim King, *President*
Frank Herrera, *General Mgr*
Ken Kelley, *General Mgr*
Diane Orcc, *Controller*
Rene Brion, *Human Res Dir*
EMP: 185
SQ FT: 200,000
SALES (est): 25MM **Privately Held**
WEB: www.bixbyranchcompanycojojalama-ranches.visua
SIC: 6552 6531 6512 Subdividers & developers; real estate managers; commercial & industrial building operation; shopping center, property operation only

(P-11951)
BOSTON PROPERTIES LTD PARTNR
4 Embarcadero Ctr Lbby 1, San Francisco (94111-5906)
PHONE 415 772-0500
Robert Pester, *Manager*
EMP: 61 **Publicly Held**
SIC: 6552 6531 Subdividers & developers; real estate agents & managers
HQ: Boston Properties Limited Partnership
800 Boylston St Ste 1900
Boston MA 02199
617 236-3300

(P-11952)
BRADDOCK & LOGAN GROUP II LP
4155 Blackhawk Plaza Cir # 201, Danville (94506-4903)
PHONE 925 736-4000
Joseph Raphel, *General Ptnr*
Angela Kluver, *Administration*
EMP: 200
SALES (est): 7.7MM **Privately Held**
SIC: 6552 Subdividers & developers

(P-11953)
BRIDGE HOUSING CORPORATION (PA)
600 California St Ste 900, San Francisco (94108-2706)
PHONE 415 989-1111
Cinthia Parker, *President*
Kent Colwell, *Bd of Directors*
Susan Johnson, *Exec VP*
Lydia Tan, *Exec VP*
Katie Hart, *Admin Asst*
EMP: 90
SQ FT: 12,000
SALES (est): 23.8MM **Privately Held**
SIC: 6552 Land subdividers & developers, residential

(P-11954)
BROOKFELD BAY AREA HLDINGS LLC
Also Called: Brookfield Homes
500 La Gonda Way Ste 100, Danville (94526-1747)
PHONE 925 743-8000
John J J Ryan,
Jay Lueckeman,
Casey Schnoor, *Manager*
Marilyn Stone, *Manager*
EMP: 60
SALES (est): 15.1MM **Privately Held**
SIC: 6552 Land subdividers & developers, residential

(P-11955)
BURBANK HOUSING DEV CORP
790 Sonoma Ave, Santa Rosa (95404-4713)
PHONE 707 526-9782

6552 - Land Subdividers & Developers County (P-11956)

Fax: 707 526-9811
David W Spilman, *CEO*
Charles A Cornell, *President*
John Lowry, *President*
Stuart W Martin, *Treasurer*
Chuck Angell, *Info Tech Dir*
EMP: 156
SQ FT: 9,850
SALES: 7.1MM **Privately Held**
SIC: 6552 Land subdividers & developers, residential

(P-11956)
CARLTON SENIOR LIVING INC
Also Called: Chateau Pleasant Hill 2
2770 Pleasant Hill Rd Ofc, Concord (94523-2086)
PHONE....................925 935-1660
Fax: 925 935-8304
Linda Jackson, *Manager*
EMP: 65
SALES (corp-wide): 31.1MM **Privately Held**
SIC: 6552 Subdividers & developers
PA: Senior Carlton Living Inc
4005 Port Chicago Hwy
Concord CA 94520
925 338-2434

(P-11957)
CASDEN COMPANY LLC
9606 Santa Monica Blvd # 3, Beverly Hills (90210-4420)
PHONE....................310 274-5553
Alan I Casden,
EMP: 100
SQ FT: 40,000
SALES (est): 8.1MM **Privately Held**
SIC: 6552 Land subdividers & developers, residential

(P-11958)
CASTLE & COOKE COMMERCIAL CA
10000 Stockdale Hwy # 300, Bakersfield (93311-3604)
PHONE....................661 665-1540
Bruce Freeman, *President*
Bruce Davis, *Vice Pres*
Laura Whitaker, *Vice Pres*
Carol A Stringer, *Admin Sec*
Rosalinda Oasay, *Asst Treas*
EMP: 70
SQ FT: 19,602
SALES: 5.2MM
SALES (corp-wide): 563.1MM **Privately Held**
WEB: www.castlecooke.net
SIC: 6552 Land subdividers & developers, commercial
PA: Castle & Cooke, Inc.
1 Dole Dr
Westlake Village CA 91362

(P-11959)
COLRICH COMMUNITIES INC
444 W Beech St Ste 300, San Diego (92101-2942)
PHONE....................858 350-7672
Richard Gabriel, *Ch of Bd*
Colin Seid, *President*
Dennis Holmes, *CFO*
Maggie Lucas, *Admin Sec*
EMP: 60
SALES (est): 8.1MM **Privately Held**
SIC: 6552 Subdividers & developers

(P-11960)
COMSTOCK CROSSER ASSOC DEV INC
Also Called: Comstock Homes
321 12th St Ste 200, Manhattan Beach (90266-5354)
PHONE....................310 546-5781
Fax: 310 545-2802
David Lauletta, *CEO*
Gary L Lyter, *CFO*
Gary L Yter, *CFO*
Tere Richards, *Senior VP*
Dan Crosser, *Vice Pres*
EMP: 50
SQ FT: 7,000
SALES (est): 13.9MM **Privately Held**
WEB: www.comstock-homes.com
SIC: 6552 Subdividers & developers

(P-11961)
DANCO COMMUNITIES
5251 Ericson Way Ste A, Arcata (95521-9274)
PHONE....................707 822-9000
Daniel J Johnson, *Owner*
EMP: 99
SALES: 1,000K **Privately Held**
SIC: 6552 Subdividers & developers

(P-11962)
DIABLO GRANDE LTD PARTNERSHIP
9521 Morton Davis Dr, Patterson (95363-8610)
PHONE....................209 892-7421
Donald Panoz, *Ltd Ptnr*
Jay Morton Davis, *Ltd Ptnr*
Deborah Agar, *Accounting Mgr*
Stacie Brauch, *Marketing Staff*
Hans Bratt, *Manager*
EMP: 100
SQ FT: 18,000
SALES (est): 7.5MM
SALES (corp-wide): 95.2MM **Privately Held**
WEB: www.diablogrande.com
SIC: 6552 7011 7992 5812 Subdividers & developers; resort hotel; public golf courses; eating places
HQ: Elan Chateau Resorts Llc
100 Rue Charlemagne Dr
Braselton GA 30517

(P-11963)
DYA ASSOC
8335 W Sunset Blvd # 320, Los Angeles (90069-1538)
PHONE....................323 364-4270
David Yashar, *Principal*
EMP: 60 **EST:** 2015
SALES (est): 1.4MM **Privately Held**
SIC: 6552 Subdividers & developers

(P-11964)
EDAW INC (HQ)
300 California St Fl 5, San Francisco (94104-1411)
PHONE....................415 955-2800
Joseph E Brown, *CEO*
Jason Prior, *President*
Dana Waymire, *CFO*
Dennis Carmichael, *Vice Pres*
Richard Dorrier, *Vice Pres*
EMP: 120
SQ FT: 18,072
SALES (est): 68.1MM
SALES (corp-wide): 17.9B **Publicly Held**
WEB: www.edaw.com
SIC: 6552 0781 Subdividers & developers; landscape architects
PA: Aecom
1999 Avenue Of The Stars # 2600
Los Angeles CA 90067
213 593-8000

(P-11965)
ESTANCIA ESTATES
980 Bryant Cyn, Soledad (93960-2830)
PHONE....................707 431-1975
Richard Sands, *President*
EMP: 72
SALES (est): 4.2MM **Privately Held**
WEB: www.estanciaestates.com
SIC: 6552 Land subdividers & developers, residential

(P-11966)
F H ONE INC
1212 Broadway Ste 716, Oakland (94612-1806)
PHONE....................510 832-3240
Farrokh Hosseinyoun, *President*
EMP: 100
SQ FT: 106,210
SALES (est): 3.7MM **Privately Held**
WEB: www.fhone.com
SIC: 6552 Subdividers & developers

(P-11967)
FBC INDUSTRIES (PA)
Also Called: Antelope Valley Distributing
2800 S Reservoir St, Pomona (91766-6525)
PHONE....................909 627-6131
Fax: 909 627-0374
Robert B Lewis, *Ch of Bd*
Jeffrey Lewis, *President*
Patrick Gabriele, *CFO*
▲ **EMP:** 100
SQ FT: 37,000
SALES (est): 20.9MM **Privately Held**
SIC: 6552 5181 5182 5149 Subdividers & developers; beer & other fermented malt liquors; wine & distilled beverages; groceries & related products; water supply

(P-11968)
FC METROPOLITAN LOFTS INC
Also Called: Forrest City Development
949 S Hope St Ste 100, Los Angeles (90015-1455)
PHONE....................213 488-0010
Fax: 213 488-5127
Kevin Ratner, *President*
Ronald A Ratner, *President*
EMP: 80
SALES (est): 5.3MM **Privately Held**
SIC: 6552 Subdividers & developers

(P-11969)
FOOTHILL ESTATES INC
400 Griffin St, Salinas (93901-4344)
PHONE....................831 422-7819
Frederick A Jensen, *President*
E A Jensen, *Agent*
EMP: 90
SALES (est): 4.4MM **Privately Held**
WEB: www.foothillestates.com
SIC: 6552 Land subdividers & developers, residential

(P-11970)
GOLDRICH & KEST INDUSTRIES LLC (PA)
5150 Overland Ave, Culver City (90230-4914)
P.O. Box 3623 (90231-3623)
PHONE....................310 204-2050
Fax: 310 204-1900
Warren Breslow,
Marc Walton, *VP Finance*
Michael Warjias, *Business Mgr*
Robert Oleesky, *Analyst*
Stephanie Kushner, *Manager*
EMP: 750
SQ FT: 5,000
SALES (est): 243.9MM **Privately Held**
SIC: 6552 Subdividers & developers

(P-11971)
GOLDRICH AND KEST CONSTRUCTION (PA)
5150 Overland Ave, Culver City (90230-4914)
P.O. Box 3623 (90231-3623)
PHONE....................310 204-2050
Jona Goldrich, *President*
Sol Kest, *Vice Pres*
EMP: 250
SQ FT: 5,000
SALES: 1.3MM **Privately Held**
SIC: 6552 Land subdividers & developers, commercial

(P-11972)
GROUPE DEVELOPMENT ASSOCIATES
Also Called: Brook Side Development
3255 W March Ln Fl 4, Stockton (95219-2304)
P.O. Box 7576 (95267-0576)
PHONE....................209 473-6000
Fritz Grupe, *Chairman*
EMP: 100
SQ FT: 500
SALES (est): 4MM **Privately Held**
SIC: 6552 Land subdividers & developers, commercial; land subdividers & developers, residential

(P-11973)
HINES GS PROPERTIES INC
101 California St # 1000, San Francisco (94111-5802)
PHONE....................415 982-6200
James B Buie, *Exec VP*
John Carr, *Controller*
EMP: 50
SQ FT: 7,000
SALES (corp-wide): 2B **Privately Held**
SIC: 6552 Subdividers & developers
HQ: Hines Gs Properties, Inc.
2800 Post Oak Blvd
Houston TX 77056
713 621-8000

(P-11974)
IRVINE COMPANY LLC
111 Innovation Dr, Irvine (92617-3040)
PHONE....................949 720-4400
Tim Lynch, *Manager*
Richard Roy, *Vice Pres*
Lindsay Hagen, *Manager*
Florentine Christian, *Asst Mgr*
EMP: 178
SALES (corp-wide): 2B **Privately Held**
WEB: www.irvineco.com
SIC: 6552 6531 Subdividers & developers; real estate managers
PA: The Irvine Company Llc
550 Newport Center Dr # 160
Newport Beach CA 92660
949 720-2000

(P-11975)
KEITH DEVELOPMENT CORPORATION
2777 Cleveland Ave # 109, Santa Rosa (95403-2763)
PHONE....................707 528-8703
Fax: 707 528-6125
Joseph P Keith, *President*
Frank Denney, *Vice Pres*
Chris Coles, *Admin Sec*
EMP: 50
SQ FT: 2,000
SALES: 17MM **Privately Held**
SIC: 6552 1521 Land subdividers & developers, residential; new construction, single-family houses

(P-11976)
KING VENTURES
285 Bridge St, San Luis Obispo (93401-5510)
PHONE....................805 544-4444
Fax: 805 544-5637
John E King, *Owner*
John Sonksen, *Finance Dir*
EMP: 126
SQ FT: 10,000
SALES (est): 10.5MM **Privately Held**
WEB: www.kingventures.net
SIC: 6552 6512 Land subdividers & developers, commercial; land subdividers & developers, residential; commercial & industrial building operation

(P-11977)
KLINGBEIL COMPANY
615 Front St, San Francisco (94111-1913)
PHONE....................415 398-0106
James D Klingbeil, *Ch of Bd*
Mark Mullen, *COO*
EMP: 100
SALES: 7.9MM **Privately Held**
SIC: 6552 6531 1521 Subdividers & developers; buying agent, real estate; real estate managers; single-family housing construction

(P-11978)
LEGACY PRTNERS COML CAPITL INC
2050 Main St Ste 830, Irvine (92614-8260)
PHONE....................949 863-0390
Fax: 949 261-1182
Erik Hansen, *Senior VP*
EMP: 170
SALES (corp-wide): 199.1MM **Privately Held**
WEB: www.legacypartners.com
SIC: 6552 Land subdividers & developers, commercial; land subdividers & developers, residential
PA: Steelwave, Inc.
4000 E 3rd Ave Ste 600
Foster City CA 94404
650 571-2200

PRODUCTS & SERVICES SECTION
6552 - Land Subdividers & Developers County (P-12000)

(P-11979)
LODI DEVELOPMENT INC
Also Called: Anderson Homes
1420 S Mills Ave Ste A, Lodi (95242-4291)
P.O. Box 1237 (95241-1237)
PHONE..................209 367-7600
Larry W Anderson, *President*
Bob Dolliver Sr, *COO*
Craig Barton, *CFO*
EMP: 50
SQ FT: 5,000
SALES (est): 3.7MM **Privately Held**
WEB: www.lodidevelopment.com
SIC: 6552 Land subdividers & developers, commercial

(P-11980)
LOWE ENTERPRISES COML GROUP
11777 San Vicente Blvd # 900, Los Angeles (90049-6615)
PHONE..................310 820-6661
Bob Lowe, *President*
EMP: 90 **EST:** 1994
SQ FT: 10,000
SALES (est): 3.9MM
SALES (corp-wide): 735.2MM **Privately Held**
WEB: www.loweenterprises.com
SIC: 6552 6531 Land subdividers & developers, commercial; real estate managers
PA: Lowe Enterprises, Inc.
11777 San Vicente Blvd # 900
Los Angeles CA 90049
310 820-6661

(P-11981)
LOWE ENTERPRISES INC
11777 San Vincente Blvd S Ste 900, Los Angeles (90049)
PHONE..................310 820-6661
Bob Lowe, *President*
Bill Wethe, *CFO*
EMP: 100
SQ FT: 15,000
SALES (est): 3.7MM
SALES (corp-wide): 735.2MM **Privately Held**
SIC: 6552 Land subdividers & developers, commercial
HQ: Lowe Development Corporation-Reserve Manager
11777 San Vicente Blvd
Los Angeles CA 90049
310 820-6661

(P-11982)
MBK REAL ESTATE LTD A CALFOR (HQ)
4 Park Plz Ste 850, Irvine (92614-8559)
PHONE..................949 789-8300
Stefan Markowitz, *General Ptnr*
Kent Crandall, *CFO*
Dale Kemp, *CFO*
Jonas Dabao, *Asst Controller*
Jonathan Evans, *Analyst*
EMP: 58
SQ FT: 39,985
SALES (est): 14.9MM
SALES (corp-wide): 40.6B **Privately Held**
SIC: 6552 Land subdividers & developers, commercial; land subdividers & developers, residential
PA: Mitsui & Co., Ltd.
1-1-3, Marunouchi
Chiyoda-Ku TKY 100-0
332 851-111

(P-11983)
MEANY WILSON L P
4 Embarcadero Ctr # 3330, San Francisco (94111-4184)
PHONE..................415 905-5300
Thomas P Sullivan, *Partner*
Christoper Meany, *Admin Sec*
Tina Arretche, *Property Mgr*
Keith Orlesky, *Director*
Elaine Lin, *Manager*
EMP: 50
SQ FT: 22,000
SALES (est): 8.6MM **Privately Held**
WEB: www.wmspartners.com
SIC: 6552 6531 Land subdividers & developers, commercial; real estate agents & managers

(P-11984)
MIDPEN HOUSING CORPORATION
303 Vintage Park Dr # 250, Foster City (94404-1176)
PHONE..................650 356-2900
Mark Battey, *CEO*
Matthew O Franklin, *President*
Pam Prasad, *Administration*
Deena Soulon, *Asst Sec*
EMP: 300
SQ FT: 20,000
SALES: 22.3MM **Privately Held**
SIC: 6552 Land subdividers & developers, residential

(P-11985)
MORELAND PCF SNOQUALMIE LLC
5060 California Ave # 1150, Bakersfield (93309-0728)
PHONE..................661 322-1081
Fax: 661 325-1802
Terry L Moreland, *Ch of Bd*
Tammy Fleming, *President*
Sharise Moreland, *Human Res Mgr*
EMP: 150
SQ FT: 3,000
SALES (est): 14.4MM **Privately Held**
SIC: 6552 6512 Land subdividers & developers, commercial; commercial & industrial building operation

(P-11986)
MOUNTAIN RETREAT INCORPORATED
111 Deerwood Rd Ste 100, San Ramon (94583-4445)
P.O. Box 178 (94583-0178)
PHONE..................925 838-7780
Thomas Porter, *President*
Peggy Porter, *Corp Secy*
Christopher Porter, *Vice Pres*
EMP: 100
SQ FT: 8,000
SALES (est): 5.7MM **Privately Held**
SIC: 6552 6531 Subdividers & developers; real estate managers

(P-11987)
NATIONAL CMNTY RENAISSANCE CAL (PA)
9421 Haven Ave Ste 100, Rancho Cucamonga (91730-5890)
PHONE..................909 483-2444
Steven J Pontell, *CEO*
Orlando Cabrera, *President*
Tracy Thomas, *COO*
Richard Whittingham, *CFO*
Sebastiano Sterpa, *Chairman*
EMP: 100
SALES: 53.3K **Privately Held**
SIC: 6552 Subdividers & developers

(P-11988)
NEHEMIAH PROGRESSIVE HOUSING D
424 N 7th St Ste 250, Sacramento (95811-0210)
PHONE..................916 231-1999
Scott Syphax, *CEO*
Walt McDaniel, *COO*
Walt Mc Daniel, *CFO*
EMP: 60
SQ FT: 1,500
SALES (est): 2.8MM **Privately Held**
WEB: www.nehemiahcorp.org
SIC: 6552 Land subdividers & developers, residential
PA: Nehemiah Corporation Of America
640 Bercut Dr Ste A
Sacramento CA 95811

(P-11989)
NEWLAND GROUP INC (PA)
Also Called: Newland Northwest
4790 Eastgate Mall # 150, San Diego (92121-2061)
PHONE..................858 455-7503
Robert B Mc Leod, *President*
Ladonna Monsees, *President*
Mark Sexton, *Administration*
Gary Gagne, *VP Accounting*
Nadine Saia, *Accountant*
EMP: 50
SQ FT: 40,000
SALES (est): 16.9MM **Privately Held**
SIC: 6552 Subdividers & developers

(P-11990)
NW MANOR COMMUNITY PARTNERS LP
17782 Sky Park Cir, Irvine (92614-6404)
PHONE..................714 662-5565
Anand Kannan, *Partner*
Brian Brooks, *General Ptnr*
Perry Harenda, *General Ptnr*
Karen Buckland, *Project Mgr*
Caitlin Marroquin, *Project Mgr*
EMP: 85 **EST:** 2014
SQ FT: 25,000
SALES (est): 5.7MM **Privately Held**
SIC: 6552 Subdividers & developers

(P-11991)
O & S HOLDINGS LLC
11611 San Vicente Blvd, Los Angeles (90049-5106)
PHONE..................310 207-8600
Gary Safady,
Shawna Ellis, *CFO*
Doug Badia, *Exec VP*
Shahla Atabaki, *Broker*
Susan Yates, *Legal Staff*
EMP: 50
SALES: 2MM **Privately Held**
WEB: www.osholdings.com
SIC: 6552 Subdividers & developers

(P-11992)
OCEAN COLONY PARTNERS LLC
Also Called: Half Moon Bay Golf Links
2450 Cabrillo Hwy S # 200, Half Moon Bay (94019-2266)
PHONE..................650 726-5764
Fax: 650 560-9198
William E Barrett, *Partner*
Mary McVay, *Mktg Dir*
Becky Holson, *Manager*
Dan Miller, *Superintendent*
EMP: 175
SQ FT: 6,000
SALES (est): 25MM **Privately Held**
SIC: 6552 7992 7389 Subdividers & developers; public golf courses; telephone services

(P-11993)
OLD FISHERMANS GROTTO
39 Fishermans Wharf, Monterey (93940-2432)
PHONE..................831 375-4604
Chris Shake, *General Ptnr*
Tene Shake, *Partner*
EMP: 75
SALES: 5.8MM **Privately Held**
SIC: 6552 Subdividers & developers

(P-11994)
OLIVERMCMILLAN LLC (PA)
733 8th Ave, San Diego (92101-6407)
PHONE..................619 321-1111
Fax: 619 455-1697
Morgan Dene Oliver, *CEO*
Paul Buss, *President*
Dan Nishikawa, *President*
Bill Persky, *CFO*
Jim McMillan, *Chairman*
EMP: 60
SQ FT: 19,900
SALES (est): 85.9MM **Privately Held**
WEB: www.olivermcmillan.com
SIC: 6552 Land subdividers & developers, commercial

(P-11995)
OLSON URBAN HOUSING LLC
Also Called: Olson Company, The
3010 Old Ranch Pkwy # 100, Seal Beach (90740-2750)
PHONE..................562 596-4770
Steve Olson,
William E Holford, *President*
Todd J Olson, *President*
Stephen E Olson, *CEO*
Scott Laurie, *COO*
EMP: 60
SALES (est): 10.6MM **Privately Held**
SIC: 6552 Subdividers & developers

(P-11996)
PACIFIC COMMUNITIES BLDR INC
1000 Dove St Ste 100, Newport Beach (92660-2809)
PHONE..................949 660-8988
Fax: 949 660-8866
Nelson Chung, *President*
Christine Chung, *CFO*
Shiung Lin, *Admin Sec*
EMP: 87
SQ FT: 21,000
SALES (est): 14.4MM **Privately Held**
WEB: www.pacificcommunities.com
SIC: 6552 Subdividers & developers

(P-11997)
PACIFIC UNION HOMES INC (PA)
675 Hartz Ave Ste 300, Danville (94526-3859)
PHONE..................925 314-3800
Fax: 925 314-3850
Jeffrey W Abramson, *President*
Todd Deutscher, *CFO*
Matt Tunney, *Vice Pres*
Tammy Reyes, *Admin Sec*
Barbara Winter, *Manager*
EMP: 75 **EST:** 1996
SALES (est): 9.8MM **Privately Held**
WEB: www.pacificunionhomes.com
SIC: 6552 Subdividers & developers

(P-11998)
PARDEE HOMES
12220 El Camino Real # 300, San Diego (92130-2091)
PHONE..................858 259-6390
Greg Sorich, *Branch Mgr*
EMP: 50
SALES (corp-wide): 2.4B **Publicly Held**
WEB: www.pardeehomes.com
SIC: 6552 6519 1542 1522 Subdividers & developers; real property lessors; non-residential construction; residential construction; single-family housing construction
HQ: Pardee Homes
177 E Colo Blvd Ste 550
Pasadena CA 91105
310 955-3100

(P-11999)
PARDEE HOMES (DH)
177 E Colo Blvd Ste 550, Pasadena (91105)
PHONE..................310 955-3100
Peter M Orser, *CEO*
Michael V McGee, *President*
Jon Lash, *COO*
Hal Struck, *COO*
William Bryan, *Treasurer*
EMP: 53
SQ FT: 35,000
SALES (est): 35.2MM
SALES (corp-wide): 2.4B **Publicly Held**
WEB: www.pardeehomes.com
SIC: 6552 1531 Subdividers & developers; operative builders

(P-12000)
PBP HOTEL LLC
Also Called: Double Tree Club Ht San Diego
1515 Hotel Cir S, San Diego (92108-3409)
PHONE..................619 881-6900
Fax: 619 260-0346
Bu Patel,
Michael Dejesus, *Sales Dir*
Halle Long, *Sales Staff*
Sunil Madhav,
John Murphy, *Mng Member*
EMP: 60
SQ FT: 6,000
SALES (est): 9.9MM
SALES (corp-wide): 67.4MM **Privately Held**
WEB: www.doubletreeclubsd.com
SIC: 6552 7011 Land subdividers & developers, commercial; hotels & motels
PA: Tarsadia Hotels
620 Newport Center Dr # 1400
Newport Beach CA 92660
949 610-8000

6552 - Land Subdividers & Developers County (P-12001)

(P-12001)
PDC CAPITAL GROUP LLC
250 Fischer Ave, Costa Mesa (92626-4515)
PHONE......................866 500-8550
Emilio Francisco, *CEO*
Joseph N Franscisco, *Admin Sec*
EMP: 52
SQ FT: 25,000
SALES: 50MM Privately Held
SIC: 6552 Subdividers & developers

(P-12002)
PONDEROSA HOMES INC
6130 Stoneridge Mall Rd # 185, Pleasanton (94588-3290)
PHONE......................925 460-8900
Fax: 925 734-9141
Kile Morgan Jr, *CEO*
EMP: 64
SALES (est): 10.5MM Privately Held
SIC: 6552 Land subdividers & developers, residential

(P-12003)
PORTSMOUTH SQUARE INC
10940 Wilshire Blvd, Los Angeles (90024-3915)
PHONE......................310 889-2500
John V Winfield, *Ch of Bd*
David T Nguyen, *CFO*
Clyde W Tinnen, *Admin Sec*
Geoffrey M Palermo, *Asst Sec*
EMP: 314
SALES: 58.5MM
SALES (corp-wide): 72.9MM Publicly Held
SIC: 6552 7011 Subdividers & developers; hotels
HQ: Santa Fe Financial Corporation
10940 Wilshire Blvd Ste 2
Los Angeles CA 90024
310 889-2500

(P-12004)
R F R CORPORATION
Also Called: Biltwell Roofing
3310 Verdugo Rd, Los Angeles (90065-2845)
PHONE......................800 346-7663
Bruce Radenbaugh, *President*
Steven Radenbaugh, *Vice Pres*
EMP: 92
SQ FT: 1,000
SALES (est): 8.8MM Privately Held
WEB: www.biltwell.com
SIC: 6552 Subdividers & developers

(P-12005)
ROCKEFELLER GROUP DEV CORP
4 Park Plz Ste 840, Irvine (92614-3504)
PHONE......................949 468-1800
Kevin Hackett, *President*
Tom McCormick, *Vice Pres*
Audrey Postal, *Admin Asst*
EMP: 104
SALES (est): 6.2MM
SALES (corp-wide): 8.6B Privately Held
SIC: 6552 Land subdividers & developers, commercial
HQ: Rockefeller Group Development Corporation
1221 Ave Of Americas 17th Flr 17
New York NY 10020
212 282-2100

(P-12006)
SCC ACQUISITIONS INC
2392 Morse Ave, Irvine (92614-6234)
PHONE......................949 777-4000
Bruce Elieff, *President*
Steve Elieff, *President*
Tom Rollins, *CFO*
Angela Brown, *Admin Asst*
EMP: 160
SQ FT: 20,392
SALES (est): 14.1MM
SALES (corp-wide): 76.9MM Privately Held
SIC: 6552 Subdividers & developers
PA: Scd Holdings Corporation
2392 Morse Ave
Irvine CA 92614
949 777-4000

(P-12007)
SEECON BUILT HOMES INC
4021 Port Chicago Hwy, Concord (94520-1134)
P.O. Box 4113 (94524-4113)
PHONE......................925 671-7711
Albert Seeno Jr, *President*
EMP: 80
SQ FT: 16,000
SALES (est): 6MM Privately Held
SIC: 6552 1542 1521 Land subdividers & developers, commercial; land subdividers & developers, residential; nonresidential construction; single-family housing construction

(P-12008)
SHAPELL INDUSTRIES LLC (HQ)
Also Called: S & S Construction Co
8383 Wilshire Blvd # 700, Beverly Hills (90211-2425)
PHONE......................323 655-7330
Fax: 323 651-4349
Nathan Shapell, *CEO*
Margaret F Leong, *CFO*
David Shapell, *Exec VP*
Max Webb, *Senior VP*
Karen Synesiou, *Info Tech Mgr*
EMP: 100
SQ FT: 25,000
SALES (est): 87.2MM
SALES (corp-wide): 4.1B Publicly Held
WEB: www.shapell.com
SIC: 6552 6514 1522 Land subdividers & developers, residential; residential building, four or fewer units: operation; residential construction
PA: Toll Brothers, Inc.
250 Gibralter Rd
Horsham PA 19044
215 938-8000

(P-12009)
SIERRA PACIFIC DEVELOPMENT
1470 W Herndon Ave # 100, Fresno (93711-0552)
PHONE......................559 256-1300
Paul Owhadi, *President*
Daniel Baker, *Manager*
EMP: 70
SQ FT: 14,000
SALES (est): 5.4MM Privately Held
SIC: 6552 Land subdividers & developers, commercial; land subdividers & developers, residential

(P-12010)
SIGNATURE PROPERTIES INC
4670 Willow Rd Ste 200, Pleasanton (94588-8588)
PHONE......................925 463-1122
Mike Gielmetti, *President*
Coreen Moore, *Assistant*
EMP: 75
SQ FT: 24,000
SALES (est): 4.9MM Privately Held
SIC: 6552 Subdividers & developers

(P-12011)
SILVER SADDLE RANCH & CLUB INC
20751 Aristotle Dr, California City (93505)
P.O. Box 2518 (93504-0518)
PHONE......................760 373-8617
Fax: 760 373-1897
Debra Nicastro, *Principal*
Clifford Reynolds, *Managing Dir*
EMP: 93
SALES (corp-wide): 6MM Privately Held
WEB: www.silversaddleranch.com
SIC: 6552 7011 Subdividers & developers; hotels & motels
PA: Silver Saddle Ranch & Club, Inc.
7635 N San Fernando Rd
Burbank CA 91505
818 768-8808

(P-12012)
SM 10000 PROPERTY LLC
Also Called: Michelle Pasternak
10000 Santa Monica Blvd, Los Angeles (90067-7002)
PHONE......................305 374-5700
Roman Speron, *CEO*
EMP: 55 **EST:** 2010
SALES (est): 920.7K Privately Held
SIC: 6552 Subdividers & developers

(P-12013)
STEELWAVE INC (PA)
4000 E 3rd Ave Ste 600, Foster City (94404-4828)
PHONE......................650 571-2200
Barry S Diraimondo, *CEO*
C Preston Butcher, *President*
EMP: 175
SALES (est): 199.1MM Privately Held
WEB: www.legacypartners.com
SIC: 6552 8741 6531 Land subdividers & developers, commercial; land subdividers & developers, residential; financial management for business; real estate agents & managers

(P-12014)
STEELWAVE LLC
4000 E 3rd Ave Ste 500, Foster City (94404-4824)
PHONE......................650 571-2200
Fax: 949 833-3062
Preston Butcher, *Mng Member*
Aaron Dwinell, *Vice Pres*
Annabel Chu, *Controller*
Barry S Diraimondo, *Mng Member*
EMP: 1200
SALES (est): 44.9MM Privately Held
SIC: 6552 8741 6531 Land subdividers & developers, commercial; financial management for business; real estate agents & managers

(P-12015)
SUNDANCE FINANCIAL INC
2505 Congress St Ste 220, San Diego (92110-2847)
PHONE......................619 298-9877
Russ R Richard, *President*
Jason Khoury, *Vice Pres*
Noel F Khoury, *Admin Sec*
EMP: 50
SALES (est): 3.1MM Privately Held
WEB: www.legacybldg.com
SIC: 6552 Subdividers & developers

(P-12016)
SUNRISE DESERT PARTNERS
Also Called: Toscana
300 Eagle Cir, Palm Desert (92211)
PHONE......................760 404-1280
Mike Van, *Branch Mgr*
Randall G Bone, *Exec VP*
Thomas Gilbertson, *General Mgr*
Clay Meininger, *General Mgr*
Tina Phillips, *Controller*
EMP: 100
SALES (corp-wide): 36.4MM Privately Held
WEB: www.indianridgecc.com
SIC: 6552 Land subdividers & developers, commercial; land subdividers & developers, residential
PA: Sunrise Desert Partners, A California Limited Partnership
300 Eagle Dance Cir
Palm Desert CA 92211
760 772-7227

(P-12017)
TAHOE LAKE PARTNERS LLC
855 Bordeaux Way Ste 200, NAPA (94558-7568)
P.O. Box 2490 (94558-0523)
PHONE......................707 255-9890
Tim Wilkens,
EMP: 68 **EST:** 2002
SALES (est): 5.1MM Privately Held
SIC: 6552 Land subdividers & developers, commercial

(P-12018)
TD DESERT DEV LTD PARTNR (HQ)
Also Called: Rancho La Quinta Country Club
81570 Carboneras, La Quinta (92253-8219)
PHONE......................760 777-1001
Nolan Sparks, *Vice Pres*
Marc McAlpine, *Senior VP*
Phyllis Mackovic, *Mktg Coord*
David Bowman, *Manager*
EMP: 150
SALES (est): 44.3MM
SALES (corp-wide): 6.5B Privately Held
WEB: www.rancholaquinta.com
SIC: 6552 Land subdividers & developers, residential
PA: Drummond Company, Inc.
1000 Urban Center Dr # 300
Vestavia AL 35242
205 945-6500

(P-12019)
TOSCANA LAND LLC
300 Eagle Dance Cir, Palm Desert (92211-7440)
PHONE......................760 772-7200
Toscana Land LP, *General Ptnr*
Phillip Smith, *President*
EMP: 100
SALES (est): 4.8MM Privately Held
SIC: 6552 Subdividers & developers

(P-12020)
TOWBES GROUP INC (PA)
21 E Victoria St Ste 200, Santa Barbara (93101-2605)
PHONE......................805 962-2121
Michael Towbes, *CEO*
Craig Zimmerman, *President*
R D R Deaver, *CFO*
Michelle Konoske, *CFO*
Robert Skinner, *Exec VP*
EMP: 58
SQ FT: 7,250
SALES (est): 55.8MM Privately Held
SIC: 6552 6512 1542 Subdividers & developers; nonresidential building operators; nonresidential construction

(P-12021)
UNITED DEVELOPMENT GROUP INC
2805 Dickens St Ste 103, San Diego (92106-2764)
PHONE......................858 244-0900
William Ayyad, *President*
Kim Stevenson, *Executive Asst*
Melissa Tollifson, *Controller*
EMP: 50
SQ FT: 3,000
SALES (est): 7.1MM Privately Held
SIC: 6552 Subdividers & developers

(P-12022)
UNIWELL CORPORATION
2233 Ventura St, Fresno (93721-2915)
PHONE......................559 268-1000
Steve Klein, *Manager*
Kristen Read, *Human Resources*
EMP: 90
SALES (corp-wide): 28.3MM Privately Held
WEB: www.uniwell.com
SIC: 6552 Subdividers & developers
PA: Uniwell Corporation
21172 Figueroa St
Carson CA 90745
310 782-8888

(P-12023)
USA PROPERTIES FUND INC (PA)
3200 Douglas Blvd Ste 200, Roseville (95661-4238)
PHONE......................916 773-6060
Fax: 916 773-5866
Geoffrey C Brown, *President*
Kristen Hawkins, *Treasurer*
Edward R Herzog, *Exec VP*
Michael McCleery, *Senior VP*
Karen McCurdy, *Senior VP*
EMP: 80
SQ FT: 10,500
SALES (est): 83MM Privately Held
WEB: www.usapropfund.com
SIC: 6552 6531 Subdividers & developers; real estate agents & managers

(P-12024)
VENTAS INC
2050 Main St Ste 800, Irvine (92614-8260)
PHONE......................949 718-4400
Debra Cafaro, *Principal*
EMP: 60
SALES (corp-wide): 3.2B Publicly Held
SIC: 6552 Subdividers & developers

PRODUCTS & SERVICES SECTION

6712 - Offices Of Bank Holding Co's County (P-12045)

PA: Ventas, Inc.
353 N Clark St Ste 3300
Chicago IL 60654
877 483-6827

(P-12025)
VOIT DEVELOPMENT MANAGER INC
Also Called: Voit Commercial Brokerage
2020 Main St Ste 100, Irvine (92614-8218)
PHONE..................949 851-5110
Fax: 949 261-9092
EMP: 57
SALES (corp-wide): 25.4MM Privately Held
SIC: 6552 6531
PA: Voit Development Manager, Inc.
101 Shipyard Way Ste M
Newport Beach CA 92663
949 644-8648

(P-12026)
WESTFIELD AMERICA LTD PARTNR
2049 Century Park E Fl 41, Los Angeles (90067-3101)
PHONE..................310 478-4456
Peter Lowy, Partner
Stephanie Shieh, Asst Sec
EMP: 99
SQ FT: 81,909
SALES (est): 5.8MM Privately Held
SIC: 6552 Land subdividers & developers, commercial

6553 Cemetery Subdividers & Developers

(P-12027)
ALDERWOODS (DELAWARE) INC
Also Called: Lakewood Memorial Pk & Fnrl HM
900 Santa Fe Ave, Hughson (95326-9240)
PHONE..................209 883-0411
Robin Warn, Admin Mgr
EMP: 50
SALES (corp-wide): 2.9B Publicly Held
WEB: www.memorialparkfuneral.com
SIC: 6553 7261 Cemeteries, real estate operation; funeral home
HQ: Alderwoods (Delaware), Inc.
1929 Allen Pkwy
Houston TX 77019
713 522-5141

(P-12028)
CHAPEL OF CHIMES (DH)
Also Called: Alameda Chapel of The Chimes
32992 Mission Blvd, Hayward (94544-8277)
PHONE..................510 471-3363
Fax: 510 471-8814
Andy Bryant, President
Gordon Swallow, Treasurer
Harry Blakeman, Site Mgr
Stephanie Brooks, Sales Mgr
EMP: 71
SQ FT: 10,000
SALES (est): 23.2MM
SALES (corp-wide): 9.1MM Publicly Held
WEB: www.bailingyuan.com
SIC: 6553 7261 Cemeteries, real estate operation; mausoleum operation; funeral home; crematory
HQ: Skylawn
32992 Mission Blvd
Hayward CA 94544
510 471-3363

(P-12029)
FOREST LAWN MEMORIAL-PARK ASSN
Also Called: Forest Lawn Memorial & Mortuar
4471 Lincoln Ave, Cypress (90630-2507)
P.O. Box 1151, Glendale (91209-1151)
PHONE..................714 828-3131
Fax: 714 220-1369
Don Gras, Branch Mgr
EMP: 80

SALES (corp-wide): 129.4MM Privately Held
SIC: 6553 7261 Cemeteries, real estate operation; funeral service & crematories
PA: Forest Lawn Memorial-Park Association
1712 S Glendale Ave
Glendale CA 91205
323 254-3131

(P-12030)
FOREST LAWN MEMORIAL-PARK ASSN
Also Called: Hollywood Hills
6300 Forest Lawn Dr, Los Angeles (90068-1096)
PHONE..................323 254-7251
Fax: 323 769-7336
Wilma Joanis, Branch Mgr
George Perez, Planning
EMP: 100
SALES (corp-wide): 129.4MM Privately Held
SIC: 6553 7261 Cemetery subdividers & developers; funeral service & crematories
PA: Forest Lawn Memorial-Park Association
1712 S Glendale Ave
Glendale CA 91205
323 254-3131

(P-12031)
FOREST LAWN MEMORIAL-PARK ASSN
1500 E San Antonio Dr, Long Beach (90807-1233)
PHONE..................562 424-1631
Fax: 562 981-8627
Kim Evans, Manager
EMP: 60
SALES (corp-wide): 129.4MM Privately Held
SIC: 6553 7261 Cemeteries, real estate operation; crematory
PA: Forest Lawn Memorial-Park Association
1712 S Glendale Ave
Glendale CA 91205
323 254-3131

(P-12032)
HANIL DEVELOPMENT INC
Also Called: Aroma Wilshire Center
3680 Wilshire Blvd B01, Los Angeles (90010-2708)
PHONE..................213 387-0111
Fax: 213 387-0999
Yeong Ik Kweon, CEO
Kee June Huh, Vice Pres
Joung Ki Kim, Exec Dir
EMP: 50
SALES (est): 3MM Privately Held
WEB: www.aromaresort.com
SIC: 6553 Real property subdividers & developers, cemetery lots only

(P-12033)
LAKEWOOD MEM PK FNRL SVCS INC
Also Called: Lakewood Memorial Pk & Fnrl HM
900 Santa Fe Ave, Hughson (95326-9240)
PHONE..................209 883-4465
Fax: 209 883-2016
Robin Warn, President
EMP: 50 EST: 1988
SALES (est): 2.2MM Privately Held
SIC: 6553 7261 Cemeteries, real estate operation; funeral home

(P-12034)
OAKDALE MEMORIAL PARK (PA)
1401 S Grand Ave, Glendora (91740-5406)
PHONE..................626 335-0281
Fax: 626 335-4142
Genny Delgado, Manager
EMP: 75 EST: 1890
SQ FT: 10,000
SALES (est): 8.1MM Privately Held
SIC: 6553 Cemeteries, real estate operation

(P-12035)
ROMAN CATHOLIC ARCHDIOCESE OF
Also Called: Holy Cross Cemetery
1500 Old Mission Rd, Daly City (94014)
P.O. Box 1577, Colma (94014-0577)
PHONE..................650 756-2060
Kathy Atkinson, Director
EMP: 55
SALES (corp-wide): 57.9MM Privately Held
WEB: www.strita.edu
SIC: 6553 Cemetery association
PA: The Roman Catholic Archdiocese Of San Francisco
1 Peter Yorke Way 1
San Francisco CA 94109
415 614-5500

(P-12036)
ROSE HILLS COMPANY (HQ)
Also Called: Rose Hills Mem Pk & Mortuary
3888 Workman Mill Rd, Whittier (90601-1626)
PHONE..................562 699-0921
Fax: 562 692-4766
Dennis Poulsen, Ch of Bd
Kenton Woods, President
Jackie Jung, Officer
Derrick Stover, Exec VP
Ophelia Camero, Vice Pres
EMP: 595
SQ FT: 143,950
SALES (est): 206MM Privately Held
WEB: www.rosehill.com
SIC: 6553 Real property subdividers & developers, cemetery lots only
PA: Rose Hills Holdings Corp.
3888 Workman Mill Rd
Whittier CA 90601
562 699-0921

(P-12037)
ROSE HILLS HOLDINGS CORP (PA)
Also Called: Rose Hills Mem Pk & Mortuary
3888 Workman Mill Rd, Whittier (90601-1626)
PHONE..................562 699-0921
Fax: 562 699-6372
Pat Monroe, CEO
Gilbert Magallanes, Admin Asst
Jaciel Camacho, Recruiter
Ed Neilson, Natl Sales Mgr
Jolene Webb, Manager
EMP: 500
SQ FT: 143,950
SALES (est): 206MM Privately Held
SIC: 6553 Cemetery subdividers & developers

(P-12038)
SERVICE CORP INTERNATIONAL
Also Called: SCI
1999 S El Camino Real, Oceanside (92054-5754)
PHONE..................760 754-6600
Debra Allen, General Mgr
EMP: 80
SALES (corp-wide): 2.9B Publicly Held
WEB: www.sci-corp.com
SIC: 6553 7261 Cemetery association; funeral service & crematories
PA: Service Corporation International
1929 Allen Pkwy
Houston TX 77019
713 522-5141

6712 Offices Of Bank Holding Co's

(P-12039)
BANAMEX USA BANCORP (DH)
2029 Century Park E Fl 42, Los Angeles (90067-2901)
PHONE..................310 203-3440
Salvador Villar Jr, President
Jorge A Figueroa, Exec VP
Francisco Moreno Sr, Vice Pres
Wasim Khwaja, Controller
Alfredo Sanchez, Agent
EMP: 210

SALES (est): 65MM
SALES (corp-wide): 88.2B Publicly Held
SIC: 6712 6029 6022 Bank holding companies; commercial banks; state commercial banks
HQ: Banco Nacional De Mexico, S.A., Integrante Del Grupo Financiero Banamex
Isabel La Catolica No. 44
Ciudad De Mexico D.F. 06000
552 226-1476

(P-12040)
CENTRAL VALLEY COMMUNITY BANK (HQ)
600 Pollasky Ave, Clovis (93612-1838)
PHONE..................559 323-3384
Fax: 559 298-4153
Daniel J Doyle, CEO
James M Ford, President
David A Kinross, CFO
Thomas L Sommer, Ch Credit Ofcr
Steve Doyel, Officer
EMP: 117
SQ FT: 11,400
SALES: 48MM
SALES (corp-wide): 51.2MM Publicly Held
SIC: 6712 Bank holding companies
PA: Central Valley Community Bancorp
7100 N Fincl Dr Ste 101
Fresno CA 93720
559 298-1775

(P-12041)
CENTRAL VALLEY COMMUNITY BANK
Clovis Community Bank RE Div
7100 N Fincl Dr Ste 101, Fresno (93720)
PHONE..................559 298-1775
Fax: 559 323-3455
Jeffrey Pace, Manager
Lydia Shaw, Vice Pres
Thomas Sommer, Vice Pres
EMP: 230
SALES (corp-wide): 51.2MM Publicly Held
SIC: 6712 Bank holding companies
HQ: Central Valley Community Bank
600 Pollasky Ave
Clovis CA 93612
559 323-3384

(P-12042)
DELTA NATIONAL BANCORP (PA)
Also Called: Delta Bank
611 N Main St, Manteca (95336-3740)
PHONE..................209 824-4000
Fax: 209 823-3837
Warren Wegge, President
Mark Bayhi, Vice Pres
Grant Thornton, Director
EMP: 66
SQ FT: 3,200
SALES (est): 16MM Privately Held
SIC: 6712 6029 Bank holding companies; commercial banks

(P-12043)
K-FED MUTUAL HOLDING COMPANY
1359 N Grand Ave, Covina (91724-1016)
PHONE..................626 339-9663
James L Breeden, Ch of Bd
Nancy Huber, Ch Credit Ofcr
EMP: 110 Privately Held
SIC: 6712 Bank holding companies

(P-12044)
MISSION VALLEY BANCORP
9116 Sunland Blvd, Sun Valley (91352-2052)
PHONE..................818 394-2300
Tamara Gurney, CEO
EMP: 53
SALES: 1,000K Privately Held
WEB: www.missionvalleybank.com
SIC: 6712 Bank holding companies

(P-12045)
SECURITY CALIFORNIA BANCORP
3403 10th St Ste 830, Riverside (92501-3666)
PHONE..................951 368-2265

6719 Offices Of Holding Co's, NEC

James A Robinson, *CEO*
Jim Robinson, *Ch of Bd*
Thomas Ferrer, *CFO*
Dolly L Nugent, *Ch Credit Ofcr*
EMP: 63 **Privately Held**
SIC: 6712

6719 Offices Of Holding Co's, NEC

(P-12046)
ABA HOLDINGS LLC
4777 Ruffner St, San Diego (92111-1519)
PHONE 858 565-4131
Steven B Andrade,
Richard Dine, *Purch Mgr*
Clyde C Blyleven,
EMP: 200 **Privately Held**
SIC: 6719 Investment holding companies, except banks

(P-12047)
ABBEY MANAGEMENT COMPANY LLC
330 Golden Shore Ste 300, Long Beach (90802-4283)
PHONE 562 243-2100
Donald Abbey, *Mng Member*
Kevin Dillard, *Treasurer*
Dennis Loput Jr, *Admin Sec*
EMP: 60 **Privately Held**
SIC: 6719 Investment holding companies, except banks

(P-12048)
ACCRIVA DGNOSTICS HOLDINGS INC (PA)
Also Called: Itc Nexus Holding Company
6260 Sequence Dr, San Diego (92121-4358)
PHONE 858 263-2300
Scott Cramer, *CEO*
Tom Whalen, *COO*
Greg Tibbitts, *CFO*
Frank Laduca PHD, *Officer*
Brett Giffin, *Officer*
EMP: 350
SALES: 80MM **Privately Held**
SIC: 6719 Investment holding companies, except banks

(P-12049)
ARCH BAY HOLDINGS LLC
327 W Maple Ave, Monrovia (91016-3331)
PHONE 949 679-2400
Shawn Miller,
Orisio Becerra, *Info Tech Dir*
Steven Davis,
EMP: 60 **EST:** 2008 **Privately Held**
SIC: 6719 Investment holding companies, except banks

(P-12050)
CCC PROPERTY HOLDINGS LLC
Also Called: Contractors Cargo Company
500 S Alameda St, Compton (90221-3801)
P.O. Box 5290 (90224-5290)
PHONE 310 609-1957
Gerald Wheeler, *Ch of Bd*
Carla Ann Wheeler, *CFO*
Jerry Wheeler, *Chairman*
Andrea Sisneros, *Executive Asst*
Kim Dorio, *Admin Sec*
EMP: 121 **EST:** 2009
SQ FT: 18,000 **Privately Held**
SIC: 6719 Investment holding companies, except banks

(P-12051)
CLEARBALANCE HOLDINGS LLC
3636 Nobel Dr Ste 250, San Diego (92122-1042)
PHONE 858 535-0870
Mitch Patridge, *CEO*
EMP: 50 **Privately Held**
SIC: 6719 Investment holding companies, except banks

(P-12052)
CLUB ASSIST NORTH AMERICA INC (PA)
3550 Wilshire Blvd # 650, Los Angeles (90010-2401)
PHONE 213 388-4333
Brett Davies, *CEO*
Scott Davies, *COO*
Alex Leombruni, *CFO*
Candace Enman, *Treasurer*
Scott Davis, *Branch Mgr*
EMP: 64
SALES (est): 15.1MM **Privately Held**
SIC: 6719 Personal holding companies, except banks

(P-12053)
CONCRETE HOLDING CO CAL INC
15821 Ventura Blvd # 475, Encino (91436-2915)
PHONE 818 788-4228
Don Unmacht, *President*
Dominique Bidet, *Vice Pres*
EMP: 293
SQ FT: 4,000
SALES (corp-wide): 421.1MM **Privately Held**
SIC: 6719 Investment holding companies, except banks
HQ: National Cement Company, Inc.
15821 Ventura Blvd # 475
Encino CA 91436
818 728-5200

(P-12054)
CSU HOLDING COMPANY
531 Stone Rd, Benicia (94510-1113)
PHONE 707 746-0353
Jochen Michalski, *President*
Brian Bernstein, *Sales Staff*
EMP: 50 **Privately Held**
SIC: 6719 Investment holding companies, except banks

(P-12055)
CTC GROUP INC (PA)
Also Called: Torrance Hilton At South Bay
21333 Hawthorne Blvd # 308, Torrance (90503-5602)
PHONE 310 540-0500
John Huang, *CEO*
Andre Koo, *President*
Jose Cano, *Executive*
Tony Mayoral, *Executive*
Daisy Tai, *Office Mgr*
EMP: 145
SALES (est): 37.7MM **Privately Held**
WEB: www.hiltontorrance.com
SIC: 6719 Investment holding companies, except banks

(P-12056)
CYTOSPORT HOLDINGS INC
1340 Treat Blvd Ste 350, Walnut Creek (94597-7581)
PHONE 707 751-3942
Robert King, *CEO*
EMP: 190
SALES (corp-wide): 9.2B **Publicly Held**
SIC: 6719 Investment holding companies, except banks
PA: Hormel Foods Corporation
1 Hormel Pl
Austin MN 55912
507 437-5611

(P-12057)
D Y U INC
223 N Crescent Way, Anaheim (92801-6704)
PHONE 714 239-2433
Young Bae Song, *President*
Hyun Jung Song, *Treasurer*
Yound Hee Song, *Admin Sec*
EMP: 170 **Privately Held**
SIC: 6719 Personal holding companies, except banks

(P-12058)
DELIMEX HOLDINGS INC
7878 Airway Rd, San Diego (92154-8305)
PHONE 619 210-2700
Neil Harrison, *President*
Dori Reap, *CEO*
Christopher J Puma, *Vice Pres*
John B Puma, *Vice Pres*
Greggory R Surabian, *Vice Pres*
EMP: 550
SQ FT: 86,917
SALES (corp-wide): 210.8B **Publicly Held**
WEB: www.delimex.com
SIC: 6719 Personal holding companies, except banks
HQ: H J Heinz Finance Company
1 Ppg Pl Ste 3100
Pittsburgh PA 15222
412 456-5700

(P-12059)
DPR HOLDINGS LLC
Also Called: Massnexus
4804 Laurel Canyon Blvd, Studio City (91607-3717)
PHONE 323 761-9829
Anthony Dickson, *Mng Member*
Mark Burton, *COO*
Chris Burns, *CFO*
EMP: 50 **EST:** 2011 **Privately Held**
SIC: 6719 Investment holding companies, except banks

(P-12060)
EVOLUTION HOLDINGS LLC (PA)
10250 Constellation Blvd, Los Angeles (90067-6200)
PHONE 541 826-2113
Andrew Nikou, *Principal*
EMP: 150
SALES (est): 31.2MM **Privately Held**
SIC: 6719 Investment holding companies, except banks

(P-12061)
FORTRESS HOLDING GROUP LLC
5500 E Sta Ana Cnyn S220, Anaheim (92807-3154)
PHONE 714 202-8710
Loise Perez, *Chairman*
Adam Forbs, *President*
Bryan Keuper, *Vice Pres*
Erica Rodriguez, *Human Res Mgr*
EMP: 90 **Privately Held**
SIC: 6719 Investment holding companies, except banks

(P-12062)
FREEDOM CMMNCTONS HOLDINGS INC (DH)
Also Called: Press Enterprise, The
625 N Grand Ave, Santa Ana (92701-4347)
PHONE 714 796-7000
Richard E Mirman, *CEO*
Aaron Kushner, *CEO*
EMP: 150
SALES (corp-wide): 3.1B **Privately Held**
SIC: 6719 2711 4813 2721 Investment holding companies, except banks; newspapers, publishing & printing; ; magazines: publishing & printing
HQ: 2100 Freedom Inc
625 N Grand Ave
Santa Ana CA 92701
714 796-7000

(P-12063)
FUTURIS GLOBAL HOLDINGS LLC (HQ)
233 Wilshire Blvd Ste 800, Santa Monica (90401-1207)
PHONE 510 771-2333
Mark Gregory Dewit, *CEO*
Eric Rundall, *CFO*
Mervynn Dunn, *Chairman*
EMP: 100
SQ FT: 90,000
SALES: 500MM **Privately Held**
SIC: 6719 Investment holding companies, except banks

(P-12064)
GAF HOLDINGS INC
1300 E Mineral King Ave, Visalia (93292-6913)
P.O. Box 1431 (93279-1431)
PHONE 559 734-3333
Don Groppetti, *President*
EMP: 300 **EST:** 1999 **Privately Held**
SIC: 6719 Personal holding companies, except banks

(P-12065)
GATEWAY FRESH LLC
Also Called: Baja Fresh
3660 Grand Ave Ste A, Chino Hills (91709-1477)
P.O. Box 383 (91709-0013)
PHONE 951 378-5439
Fax: 909 548-6602
Malik Asif, *Mng Member*
Elida Lopez, *Site Mgr*
EMP: 190
SQ FT: 5,000 **Privately Held**
SIC: 6719 Investment holding companies, except banks

(P-12066)
GLOBAL HOLDINGS INC
550 N Brand Blvd Ste 600, Glendale (91203-1983)
PHONE 818 905-6000
Sam Solakyan, *CEO*
AME Gray, *Assistant*
EMP: 150 **Privately Held**
SIC: 6719 Investment holding companies, except banks

(P-12067)
GORES NORMENT HOLDINGS INC (HQ)
10877 Wilshire Blvd # 1805, Los Angeles (90024-4341)
PHONE 310 209-3010
Alex Gores, *Principal*
Stan Sasser, *Manager*
EMP: 246
SALES (corp-wide): 6.8B **Privately Held**
SIC: 6719 Investment holding companies, except banks
PA: The Gores Group Llc
9800 Wilshire Blvd
Beverly Hills CA 90212
310 209-3010

(P-12068)
HCO HOLDING I CORPORATION (HQ)
999 N Sepulveda Blvd, El Segundo (90245-2714)
PHONE 323 583-5000
Mike Kenny, *CEO*
Brian C Strauss, *CEO*
Jason Peel, *CFO*
Dori M Reap, *CFO*
Robert D Armstrong, *Senior VP*
EMP: 100
SALES (est): 235.4MM **Privately Held**
WEB: www.henry.com
SIC: 6719 Investment holding companies, except banks
PA: Hnc Parent, Inc.
999 N Sepulveda Blvd
El Segundo CA 90245
310 955-9200

(P-12069)
HEALTHFUSION HOLDINGS INC (HQ)
100 N Rios Ave, Solana Beach (92075-1238)
PHONE 858 523-2120
Fax: 858 523-2124
Seth M Flam, *President*
Jonathan Flam, *CFO*
Yuri Kormuskins, *Info Tech Mgr*
Aj Eisan, *Web Dvlpr*
Sayali Utekar, *Software Engr*
EMP: 54
SALES (est): 25.4MM
SALES (corp-wide): 492.4MM **Publicly Held**
WEB: www.healthfusion.com
SIC: 6719 Investment holding companies, except banks
PA: Quality Systems, Inc.
18111 Von Karman Ave # 700
Irvine CA 92612
949 255-2600

PRODUCTS & SERVICES SECTION

6719 - Offices Of Holding Co's, NEC County (P-12096)

(P-12070)
IMPAC COMPANIES
19500 Jamboree Rd, Irvine (92612-2401)
PHONE.....................................949 475-3933
Bill Ashmore, *Principal*
Douglas Wilkins, *Senior Engr*
Lynn Linchangco, *Accounting Mgr*
Richard Johnson, *Assistant VP*
Justin Meads, *Accounts Exec*
EMP: 95
SALES: 950K **Privately Held**
SIC: 6719 Holding companies

(P-12071)
LEISURE SPORTS INC
4670 Willow Rd Ste 100, Pleasanton (94588-8587)
PHONE.....................................925 942-6301
Brian Amador, *Branch Mgr*
EMP: 350
SALES (corp-wide): 213MM **Privately Held**
WEB: www.leisuresportsinc.com
SIC: 6719 Investment holding companies, except banks; personal holding companies, except banks
PA: Leisure Sports, Inc.
  4670 Willow Rd Ste 100
  Pleasanton CA 94588
  925 600-1966

(P-12072)
LIVERMORE SNIOR LVING ASSOC LP
Also Called: Leisure Care
900 E Stanley Blvd # 383, Livermore (94550-4089)
PHONE.....................................925 371-2300
Mike Palmer, *General Mgr*
EMP: 50 **Privately Held**
SIC: 6719 Investment holding companies, except banks

(P-12073)
LIZHANG ENTERPRISES CORP
58 Paisley Pl, Irvine (92620-0247)
PHONE.....................................714 734-6683
Charles Riley, *President*
EMP: 50 **Privately Held**
WEB: www.mx0.wwwnew.eu
SIC: 6719 Holding companies

(P-12074)
MAFAB INC (PA)
1925 Century Park E # 650, Los Angeles (90067-2752)
PHONE.....................................714 893-0551
Ronald B Grey, *President*
Ronald Grey, *President*
EMP: 60
SQ FT: 3,600
SALES (est): 15.2MM **Privately Held**
SIC: 6719 Personal holding companies, except banks

(P-12075)
MISSION ENERGY HOLDING COMPANY
2600 Michelson Dr # 1700, Irvine (92612-1550)
PHONE.....................................949 752-5588
Mark C Clarke, *CEO*
Thomas R McDaniel, *President*
W James Scilacci, *CFO*
EMP: 1890
SALES (corp-wide): 11.5B **Publicly Held**
WEB: www.edison.com
SIC: 6719 Personal holding companies, except banks
HQ: Edison Mission Group Inc.
  2244 Walnut Grove Ave
  Rosemead CA 91770
  626 302-2222

(P-12076)
MLIM HOLDINGS LLC
350 Camino De La Reina, San Diego (92108-3003)
PHONE.....................................619 299-3131
Douglas Manchester, *Chairman*
John Lynch, *CEO*
EMP: 768 **Privately Held**
SIC: 6719 Investment holding companies, except banks

(P-12077)
MODERN ALLOYS INC
1925 Century Park E # 650, Los Angeles (90067-2752)
PHONE.....................................714 893-0551
Ronald B Grey, *Vice Pres*
Ron Grey, *Vice Pres*
Scott Squires, *Vice Pres*
EMP: 60
SQ FT: 6,800
SALES (corp-wide): 15.2MM **Privately Held**
SIC: 6719 Personal holding companies, except banks
PA: Mafab Inc
  1925 Century Park E # 650
  Los Angeles CA 90067
  714 893-0551

(P-12078)
NADAVON CAPITAL PARTNERS LLC
3333 W Coast Hwy Ste 300, Newport Beach (92663-4058)
PHONE.....................................714 427-1000
Romir Bosu,
EMP: 130 **EST:** 2013 **Privately Held**
SIC: 6719 Investment holding companies, except banks

(P-12079)
NOVOZYMES US INC
1445 Drew Ave, Davis (95618-4880)
PHONE.....................................530 757-8100
Ejner Bech Jensen, *CEO*
Glen Medwin, *President*
EMP: 675
SALES (corp-wide): 2B **Privately Held**
SIC: 6719 Investment holding companies, except banks
PA: Novozymes A/S
  Krogshojvej 36
  BagsvArd 2880
  444 600-00

(P-12080)
NRP HOLDING CO INC (PA)
1 Mauchly, Irvine (92618-2305)
PHONE.....................................949 583-1000
Jeffrey P Frieden, *President*
Ken Rivkin, *Exec VP*
Robert Friedman, *Vice Pres*
Jason Allnutt, *General Mgr*
Nirvana Alonso, *Graphic Designe*
EMP: 200
SQ FT: 40,000
SALES (est): 50.2MM **Privately Held**
SIC: 6719 Investment holding companies, except banks

(P-12081)
OMNI VENTURES GROUP LLC
300 Pasadena Ave, South Pasadena (91030-2905)
PHONE.....................................510 384-1033
Timothy Naple, *CEO*
EMP: 75 **EST:** 2007
SQ FT: 100,000 **Privately Held**
SIC: 6719 Investment holding companies, except banks

(P-12082)
PACIFIC STATES INVESTORS
1551 Emerson St, Palo Alto (94301-3533)
PHONE.....................................650 326-0990
George James, *Mng Member*
EMP: 200 **Privately Held**
SIC: 6719 Investment holding companies, except banks

(P-12083)
PARPRO HOLDINGS CO LTD
9355 Airway Rd Ste 4, San Diego (92154-7931)
PHONE.....................................619 498-9004
EMP: 250
SALES (corp-wide): 44.8MM **Privately Held**
SIC: 6719 Investment holding companies, except banks
PA: Parpro Corporation
  67-1, Tung Yuan Rd., Chung Li Ind. Park,
  Taoyuan City TAY 32063
  345 255-35

(P-12084)
PLATINUM GROUP COMPANIES INC (PA)
Also Called: Top Finance Company
8407 Fllbrook Ave Ste 250, Canoga Park (91304)
PHONE.....................................818 721-3800
David Mandel, *CEO*
Sandy To, *Treasurer*
Netzel Robert, *Info Tech Mgr*
Marilyn Vateri, *Finance*
EMP: 125
SQ FT: 20,000
SALES (est): 60.6MM **Privately Held**
SIC: 6719 Personal holding companies, except banks

(P-12085)
PROJECT BOAT HOLDINGS LLC
360 N Crescent Dr Bldg S, Beverly Hills (90210-2529)
PHONE.....................................310 712-1850
Tom Gores,
Johnny O Lopez,
EMP: 3174
SALES (corp-wide): 13.2B **Privately Held**
SIC: 6719 Investment holding companies, except banks
PA: Platinum Equity, Llc
  360 N Crescent Dr Bldg S
  Beverly Hills CA 90210
  310 712-1850

(P-12086)
PUBLIC STORAGE PRPTS XVIII INC
701 Western Ave Ste 200, Glendale (91201-2349)
PHONE.....................................818 244-8080
B Wayne Hughes, *Ch of Bd*
Harvey Lenkin, *President*
Orben B Gerich, *CFO*
Ronald L Havner Jr, *Vice Pres*
Hugh W Horne, *Vice Pres*
EMP: 100 **Privately Held**
SIC: 6719 Investment holding companies, except banks

(P-12087)
RIVER ROCK EQUIPMENT LLC
216 Kenroy Ln, Roseville (95678-4202)
PHONE.....................................916 791-1609
Warren Holt,
Bob Lettek,
EMP: 100
SQ FT: 2,500
SALES: 1MM **Privately Held**
SIC: 6719 Investment holding companies, except banks

(P-12088)
SAN FRANCISCO FORTY NINERS
4949 Mrie P Debartolo Way, Santa Clara (95054-1156)
PHONE.....................................408 562-4949
John York, *Owner*
Les Schmidt, *COO*
Debye Whelchel, *Controller*
EMP: 90 **EST:** 1977
SALES: 3.9MM **Privately Held**
SIC: 6719 Investment holding companies, except banks

(P-12089)
SANTA PAULA WATER WORKS LTD
9750 Washburn Rd, Downey (90241-5625)
PHONE.....................................562 923-0711
Henry H Wheeler Jr, *President*
Douglas K Martinet, *CFO*
EMP: 70 **Privately Held**
WEB: www.parkwater.com
SIC: 6719 Investment holding companies, except banks

(P-12090)
SKEFFINGTON ENTERPRISES INC
2200 S Yale St, Santa Ana (92704-4404)
PHONE.....................................714 540-1700
William J Skeffington, *President*
John Skeffington, *CFO*
Tien Nguyen, *Controller*
EMP: 100
SQ FT: 180,000
SALES: 32.1MM **Privately Held**
SIC: 6719 Personal holding companies, except banks

(P-12091)
STANTEC HOLDINGS DEL III INC (PA)
5500 Ming Ave Ste 300, Bakersfield (93309-4627)
PHONE.....................................661 396-3770
Robert Gomes, *President*
EMP: 182
SALES (est): 20.7MM **Privately Held**
SIC: 6719 Investment holding companies, except banks

(P-12092)
STEELRIVER INFRASTURCTURE PART (PA)
1 Letterman Dr, San Francisco (94129-1494)
PHONE.....................................415 512-1515
Christopher P Kinney, *Partner*
John Anderson, *Partner*
Dennis Mahoney, *Partner*
Brian Carmichael, *Commissioner*
Vittorio Lacagnina, *Director*
EMP: 200
SALES (est): 146.3MM **Privately Held**
SIC: 6719 Investment holding companies, except banks

(P-12093)
STURGEON SERVICES INTL INC (PA)
Also Called: Sturgeon & Son
3511 Gilmore Ave, Bakersfield (93308-6205)
PHONE.....................................661 322-4408
Fax: 661 322-7574
Paul H Sturgeon, *President*
Oliver Sturgeon, *Ch of Bd*
Joe D'Angelo, *CFO*
Gina Blankenship, *Vice Pres*
John Powell, *General Mgr*
EMP: 50
SQ FT: 5,000
SALES (est): 189.9MM **Privately Held**
SIC: 6719 Personal holding companies, except banks

(P-12094)
TRADESHIFT HOLDINGS INC (HQ)
612 Howard St Ste 100, San Francisco (94105-3927)
PHONE.....................................800 381-3585
Christian Lanng, *CEO*
Jigish Avalani, *President*
Jeppe Rindom, *CFO*
Peter Van Pruissen, *CFO*
EMP: 80 **EST:** 2011
SALES (est): 30.6MM
SALES (corp-wide): 15MM **Privately Held**
SIC: 6719 Investment holding companies, except banks

(P-12095)
TRANSAMERICA INTL HOLDINGS
600 Montgomery St Fl 16, San Francisco (94111-2718)
PHONE.....................................415 983-4000
EMP: 220 **Privately Held**
SIC: 6719 Personal holding companies, except banks
HQ: Transamerica Corporation
  4333 Edgewood Rd Ne
  Cedar Rapids IA 52499
  319 398-8511

(P-12096)
TREX PARTNERS LLC
10455 Pacific Center Ct, San Diego (92121-4339)
PHONE.....................................858 646-5300
Kenneth Tang,
Doug Bletcher, *Info Tech Dir*
Tod Barrett, *Webmaster*
EMP: 200 **Privately Held**
SIC: 6719 Investment holding companies, except banks

(PA)=Parent Co (HQ)=Headquarters (DH)=Div Headquarters
✪ = New Business established in last 2 years

6719 - Offices Of Holding Co's, NEC County (P-12097)

(P-12097)
USB SOLARCITY MASTER TENANT
393 Vintage Park Dr # 140, Foster City (94404-1140)
PHONE...................650 963-5693
Lyndon Rive, *CEO*
Tara Hobbs,
EMP: 99 **Privately Held**
SIC: 6719 Holding companies

(P-12098)
UTBLO INC
11061 Los Alamitos Blvd, Los Alamitos (90720-3201)
PHONE...................562 493-3664
Wendi Rothman, *President*
Jasmine Cardona, *Manager*
EMP: 120
SQ FT: 12,000
SALES (corp-wide): 3.2B **Publicly Held**
WEB: www.lovinoven.com
SIC: 6719 Personal holding companies, except banks
HQ: Treehouse Private Brands, Inc.
800 Market St
Saint Louis MO 63101
314 877-7300

6722 Management Investment Offices

(P-12099)
ABSOLUTE RETURN PORTFOLIO
700 Newport Center Dr, Newport Beach (92660-6307)
P.O. Box 9000 (92658-9030)
PHONE...................800 800-7646
EMP: 2235
SALES (est): 36.5MM
SALES (corp-wide): 8.6B **Privately Held**
SIC: 6722 Money market mutual funds
HQ: Pacific Life Fund Advisors Llc
700 Newport Center Dr
Newport Beach CA 92660
800 800-7646

(P-12100)
ADVANCED COMMERCIAL CORPORATIO
5900 Pasteur Ct Ste 200, Carlsbad (92008-7336)
P.O. Box 4068 (92018-4068)
PHONE...................760 431-8500
Tim Stripe, *CEO*
David Brown, *President*
Armando Mercado, *Manager*
EMP: 110
SALES (est): 12.2MM **Privately Held**
WEB: www.vacation-resales.com
SIC: 6722 Management investment, open-end

(P-12101)
AMCAP FUND INC
333 S Hope St Ste Levb, Los Angeles (90071-3003)
PHONE...................213 486-9200
Marry Clemeson, *President*
Mary C Hall, *Treasurer*
Gordon Crawford, *Senior VP*
Paul G Haaga Jr, *Senior VP*
Walter Stern, *Principal*
EMP: 300
SQ FT: 2,000
SALES (est): 14.1MM **Privately Held**
SIC: 6722 Mutual fund sales, on own account

(P-12102)
AMERICAN FUNDS DISTRS INC (DH)
333 S Hope St Ste Levb, Los Angeles (90071-3003)
PHONE...................213 486-9200
Fax: 213 486-9571
Mark Freeman, *President*
Larry Clemmensen, *Ch of Bd*
Michael Johnston, *Ch of Bd*
J Kelly Webb, *Treasurer*
Dean Rydquist, *Ch Credit Ofcr*
EMP: 116
SQ FT: 6,000
SALES (est): 57.7MM
SALES (corp-wide): 2.5B **Privately Held**
SIC: 6722 Mutual fund sales, on own account
HQ: Capital Research And Management Company
333 S Hope St Fl 55
Los Angeles CA 90071
213 486-9200

(P-12103)
AMERICAN MUTUAL FUND INC
333 S Hope St Fl 51, Los Angeles (90071-1420)
PHONE...................213 486-9200
Jonathan B Lovelace Jr, *Ch of Bd*
James K Dunton, *Ch of Bd*
Robert G O'Donnell, *President*
Mary C Hall, *Treasurer*
James W Ratzlaff, *Vice Ch Bd*
EMP: 200 **EST:** 1949
SQ FT: 5,000
SALES (est): 13.9MM **Privately Held**
SIC: 6722 Money market mutual funds

(P-12104)
BARCLAYS GLOBL INVESTORS FUNDS
45 Fremont St Bsmt, San Francisco (94105-2214)
PHONE...................415 597-2000
Fax: 415 597-2010
Mike Sobel, *Principal*
Naozer Dadachanji, *COO*
Deborah Ferris, *Principal*
Terri L Slane, *Admin Sec*
Sarah Brydon, *Administration*
EMP: 68
SALES (est): 30.4MM **Privately Held**
SIC: 6722 Management investment, open-end

(P-12105)
BAY GROVE CAPITAL GROUP LLC (PA)
423 Washington St Fl 7, San Francisco (94111-2342)
PHONE...................415 229-7953
Fax: 415 229-7954
Kevin Marchetti,
Adam Janvey, *Vice Pres*
Kristina Hentschel, *Opers Staff*
Michael Billings,
Geoff Colla,
EMP: 50
SALES (est): 71.7MM **Privately Held**
SIC: 6722 Management investment, open-end

(P-12106)
BLACKROCK INSTNL TR NAT ASSN (HQ)
Also Called: Ishares
400 Howard St, San Francisco (94105-2618)
PHONE...................415 597-2000
Laurence D Fink, *CEO*
Robert S Kapito, *President*
James Parsons, *President*
Eric Braithwaite, *Vice Pres*
Scott Thompson, *Managing Dir*
EMP: 600
SQ FT: 65,000
SALES (corp-wide): 11.4B **Publicly Held**
SIC: 6722 Management investment, open-end
PA: Blackrock, Inc.
55 E 52nd St Fl 11
New York NY 10055
212 810-5300

(P-12107)
BROADRACH CPITL PRTNERS FUND I
248 Homer Ave, Palo Alto (94301-2722)
PHONE...................650 331-2500
EMP: 987
SALES (est): 20.2MM
SALES (corp-wide): 407.4MM **Privately Held**
SIC: 6722 Money market mutual funds
PA: Broadreach Capital Partners Llc
248 Homer Ave
Palo Alto CA 94301
650 331-2500

(P-12108)
CAMBRIA GLOBAL TACTICAL FUND 2
2321 Rosecrans Ave # 3225, El Segundo (90245-4903)
PHONE...................310 683-5500
Eric W Richardson, *Principal*
EMP: 53
SALES (est): 3MM
SALES (corp-wide): 15.4MM **Privately Held**
SIC: 6722 Management investment, open-end
PA: Cambria Investment Management Lp
2321 Rosecrans Ave # 3225
El Segundo CA 90245
310 683-5500

(P-12109)
CDCF III PACIFIC CATALINA
320 Golden Shore Ste 320, Long Beach (90802-4281)
PHONE...................562 453-1353
Kristina Beverly, *Property Mgr*
Keisha Freeman, *Manager*
EMP: 99
SALES (est): 2.8MM **Privately Held**
SIC: 6722 Management investment, open-end

(P-12110)
CHURCHILL PCF ASSET MGT LLC
601 S Figueroa St # 2400, Los Angeles (90017-5704)
PHONE...................213 489-3810
William Tomai, *Mng Member*
EMP: 119
SALES (est): 158.4K
SALES (corp-wide): 167.6MM **Publicly Held**
SIC: 6722 Management investment, open-end
PA: Resource Capital Corp.
712 5th Ave Fl 12
New York NY 10019
212 974-1708

(P-12111)
COLFIN ESH FUNDING LLC
2450 Broadway Fl 6, Santa Monica (90404-3570)
PHONE...................310 282-8820
Linda Bodenstein, *Principal*
EMP: 299
SALES (est): 430.8K
SALES (corp-wide): 841.9MM **Publicly Held**
SIC: 6722 Management investment, open-end
PA: Colony Capital, Inc.
515 S Flower St Fl 44
Los Angeles CA 90071
310 282-8820

(P-12112)
DODGE & COX
555 California St Fl 40, San Francisco (94104-1538)
PHONE...................415 981-1710
Fax: 415 986-1369
Dana M Emery, *CEO*
John A Gunn, *Chairman*
John Loll, *Treasurer*
C Bryan Cameron, *Senior VP*
Thomas S Dugan, *Senior VP*
EMP: 195 **EST:** 1930
SQ FT: 45,000
SALES (est): 216.8MM **Privately Held**
WEB: www.dodgeandcox.com
SIC: 6722 Management investment, open-end

(P-12113)
ENCORE FUND LP
555 California St # 2975, San Francisco (94104-1503)
PHONE...................415 676-4000
Jeff Skelton, *President*
EMP: 70
SALES (est): 4.1MM **Privately Held**
SIC: 6722 Management investment, open-end

(P-12114)
FARALLON CAPITAL MGT LLC (PA)
1 Maritime Plz Ste 2100, San Francisco (94111-3528)
PHONE...................415 421-2132
Fax: 415 421-2133
Chun R Ding, *Mng Member*
Paul Caldwell, *Exec Dir*
Charles Gunawan, *Managing Dir*
Bill Seybold, *Managing Dir*
Miranda Cornejo, *Admin Asst*
EMP: 80
SQ FT: 8,000
SALES (est): 47.2MM **Privately Held**
SIC: 6722 Management investment, open-end

(P-12115)
FORTRESS INVESTMENT GROUP LLC
10250 Constellation Blvd, Los Angeles (90067-6200)
PHONE...................310 228-3030
Ian Schnider, *Director*
EMP: 74
SALES (corp-wide): 1.2B **Publicly Held**
SIC: 6722 Management investment, open-end
PA: Fortress Investment Group Llc
1345 Avenue Flr 46
New York NY 10105
212 798-6100

(P-12116)
FORTRESS INVESTMENT GROUP LLC
42 Florida St Flr, San Francisco (94103)
PHONE...................415 284-7400
EMP: 74
SALES (corp-wide): 1.2B **Publicly Held**
SIC: 6722 Management investment, open-end
PA: Fortress Investment Group Llc
1345 Avenue Flr 46
New York NY 10105
212 798-6100

(P-12117)
FRANKLIN RESOURCES INC (PA)
1 Franklin Pkwy, San Mateo (94403-1906)
PHONE...................650 312-2000
Fax: 650 312-4918
Gregory E Johnson, *Ch of Bd*
Vijay C Advani, *President*
Jennifer M Johnson, *President*
Kenneth A Lewis, *CFO*
Rupert H Johnson Jr, *Vice Ch Bd*
EMP: 105
SALES: 7.9B **Publicly Held**
WEB: www.frk.com
SIC: 6722 6726 Management investment, open-end; management investment funds, closed-end

(P-12118)
KAYNE ANDERSON RUDNI
1800 Avenue Of The Stars # 200, Los Angeles (90067-4204)
PHONE...................310 229-9260
Fax: 310 284-6490
Stephen Rigali, *Exec VP*
Sheryl Sadis, *CFO*
Stephanie Gillman, *Bd of Directors*
Doug Foreman, *Ch Invest Ofcr*
Randy Allen, *Senior VP*
EMP: 60
SQ FT: 20,000
SALES: 17MM
SALES (corp-wide): 214.6MM **Privately Held**
WEB: www.kayne.com
SIC: 6722 Management investment, open-end
PA: Virtus Partners, Inc.
100 Pearl St Fl 9
Hartford CT 06103
860 403-5000

PRODUCTS & SERVICES SECTION
6726 - Unit Investment Trusts, Face-Amount Certificate Offices County (P-12142)

(P-12119)
MCMILLIN MANAGEMENT SVCS LP (HQ)
Also Called: McMillin Homes
2750 Womble Rd Ste 200, San Diego (92106-6114)
PHONE..................619 477-4117
Fax: 760 336-3119
Scott McMillin, *General Ptnr*
Mark McMillin, *Partner*
Jerie Sturgeon, *Vice Pres*
Rosa Patrone, *Manager*
EMP: 249
SQ FT: 24,000
SALES (est): 42.1MM
SALES (corp-wide): 50MM **Privately Held**
WEB: www.mcmillin.com
SIC: **6722** 8611 Management investment, open-end; business associations
PA: Mcmillin Companies, Llc
2750 Womble Rd Ste 200
San Diego CA 92106
619 477-4117

(P-12120)
ORANGE COUNTY EMPLOYEES RETIR
2223 S Wellington Ave, Santa Ana (92701)
PHONE..................714 558-6200
Raymond Fleming, *CEO*
Girard Miller, *Ch Invest Ofcr*
Thomas Flanigan, *CIO*
Robert Kinsler, *Info Tech Mgr*
Jenny Sadoski, *Technology*
EMP: 51
SALES (est): 8.5MM **Privately Held**
WEB: www.ocers.org
SIC: **6722** 8111 Management investment, open-end; legal services

(P-12121)
PARKMAN AGENTS
468 N Camden Dr, Beverly Hills (90210-4507)
PHONE..................310 860-7757
John London, *CEO*
Terry Johnson, *CEO*
EMP: 65
SALES (est): 4MM **Privately Held**
SIC: **6722** Management investment, open-end

(P-12122)
PIMCO FUNDS DISTRIBUTION CO
840 Nwport Ctr Dr Ste 100, Newport Beach (92660)
PHONE..................949 720-4761
Bill Gross, *CEO*
Ronnie Trinidad, *Office Mgr*
EMP: 300
SALES (est): 13.5MM **Privately Held**
SIC: **6722** Management investment, open-end

(P-12123)
REO WORLD INC
170 Nwport Ctr Dr Ste 150, Newport Beach (92660)
P.O. Box 1070, Corona Del Mar (92625-6070)
PHONE..................949 478-8000
Fax: 949 720-1206
Mark Cardelucci, *President*
Thomas F Crone, *COO*
EMP: 99
SALES (est): 950K **Privately Held**
WEB: www.reoworld.com
SIC: **6722** Management investment, open-end

(P-12124)
RS INVESTMENT MANAGEMENT LP (PA)
1 Bush St Ste 900, San Francisco (94104-4425)
PHONE..................415 591-2700
Fax: 415 591-2858
Matthew H Scanlan, *CEO*
Ben Douglas, *Partner*
G Randall Hecht, *Partner*
Terry Otten, *Partner*
John Sanders, *Partner*
EMP: 80

SALES (est): 33.7MM **Privately Held**
WEB: www.rsim.com
SIC: **6722** Mutual fund sales, on own account

(P-12125)
SUNAMERICA INVESTMENTS INC
1 Sun America Ctr Fl 38, Los Angeles (90067-6101)
PHONE..................310 772-6000
Jay Wintrob, *President*
EMP: 200
SALES (est): 7.8MM
SALES (corp-wide): 58.3B **Publicly Held**
SIC: **6722** Management investment, open-end
HQ: Sunamerica Inc.
1 Sun America Ctr Fl 38
Los Angeles CA 90067
310 772-6000

(P-12126)
TEMPLETON FRANKLIN INTL TR
Also Called: Templton Fgn Smaller Companies
1 Franklin Pkwy, San Mateo (94403-1906)
PHONE..................650 312-2000
Gregory E Johnson, *CEO*
EMP: 50
SALES (est): 8.5MM **Privately Held**
SIC: **6722** Management investment, open-end

(P-12127)
US SMALL CPITL VALUE PORTFOLIO
1299 Ocean Ave Ste 150, Santa Monica (90401-1002)
PHONE..................310 395-8005
David Booth, *President*
EMP: 70
SALES (est): 6.2MM **Privately Held**
SIC: **6722** Management investment, open-end

(P-12128)
VANTAGEPOINT VENTURE PARTNERS
1001 Bayhill Dr Ste 300, San Bruno (94066-3061)
PHONE..................650 866-3100
Alan E Salzman, *Partner*
EMP: 55
SALES (est): 5.2MM
SALES (corp-wide): 16.9MM **Privately Held**
SIC: **6722** Mutual fund sales, on own account
PA: Vantagepoint Venture Partners
1001 Bayhill Dr Ste 300
San Bruno CA 94066
650 866-3100

(P-12129)
VIHARAS GROUP INC
1919 W Artesia Blvd, Compton (90220-5397)
PHONE..................310 537-6700
Ashok Patel, *President*
EMP: 75 EST: 2007
SALES (est): 4.8MM **Privately Held**
SIC: **6722** Management investment, open-end

(P-12130)
VISTA EQUITY PARTNERS FUND VI-
4 Embarcadero Ctr Fl 20, San Francisco (94111-5982)
PHONE..................415 765-6500
EMP: 5003
SALES (est): 128.8K
SALES (corp-wide): 1.1B **Privately Held**
SIC: **6722** Money market mutual funds
PA: Vista Equity Partners Management, Llc
4 Embarcadero Ctr Fl 20
San Francisco CA

(P-12131)
WELLS FARGO INTL BOND CIT
525 Market St Fl 10, San Francisco (94105-2718)
PHONE..................415 396-4943

Gary Schlossberg, *Vice Pres*
INA Strack, *Vice Pres*
Bruce Olson, *Executive*
Galen Blomster, *Managing Dir*
Larry Fernandes, *Managing Dir*
EMP: 240
SALES (est): 17.2MM
SALES (corp-wide): 90B **Publicly Held**
SIC: **6722** Money market mutual funds
HQ: Wells Capital Management Incorporated
525 Market St Fl 10
San Francisco CA 94105
415 396-8000

(P-12132)
ZILLIONAIRE EMPRESS DANIELLE B
8549 Wilshire Blvd # 817, Beverly Hills (90211-3104)
PHONE..................310 461-9923
Danielle Berhane, *CEO*
EMP: 1000
SQ FT: 300
SALES (est): 44.6MM **Privately Held**
SIC: **6722** Management investment, open-end

6726 Unit Investment Trusts, Face-Amount Certificate Offices

(P-12133)
ASIA PACIFIC CAPITAL
345 Suth Fgroa St Ste 100, Los Angeles (90071)
PHONE..................213 628-8800
Eddy Chao, *CEO*
EMP: 85
SALES (est): 6.4MM **Privately Held**
WEB: www.apccusa.com
SIC: **6726** Investment offices

(P-12134)
AXA ADVISORS LLC
88 Kearny St Fl 20, San Francisco (94108-5548)
PHONE..................415 276-2100
Daniel W Worthington, *Manager*
EMP: 70
SALES (corp-wide): 2.9B **Publicly Held**
WEB: www.axacs.com
SIC: **6726** Unit investment trusts
HQ: Axa Advisors, Llc
1290 Ave Of Amrcs Fl Cnc1
New York NY 10104
212 554-1234

(P-12135)
CAL FED INVESTMENTS INC
3900 Lennane Dr, Sacramento (95834-1909)
PHONE..................916 614-2440
Fax: 916 614-2820
Debra Bernot, *President*
EMP: 100
SALES (est): 8.2MM **Privately Held**
SIC: **6726** Investment offices

(P-12136)
CBRE INC (HQ)
400 S Hope St Ste 25, Los Angeles (90071-2800)
PHONE..................310 477-5876
Bob Sulentic, *President*
Tracy Kennedy, *Vice Chairman*
Jay Wagley, *Vice Chairman*
Steven Swerdlow, *COO*
Kenneth J Kay, *CFO*
EMP: 150
SALES (est): 2.6B
SALES (corp-wide): 10.8B **Publicly Held**
SIC: **6726** 6531 Investment offices; real estate agent, commercial; real estate managers; appraiser, real estate
PA: Cbre Group, Inc.
400 S Hope St Ste 25
Los Angeles CA 90071
213 613-3333

(P-12137)
CENTURY PK CAPITL PARTNERS LLC (PA)
2101 Rosecrans Ave # 4275, El Segundo (90245-4749)
PHONE..................310 867-2210
Fax: 310 867-2212
Martin A Sarafa,
Guy Zaczepinski, *Partner*
Charles W Roellig, *Managing Prtnr*
Martin Sarafa, *Managing Prtnr*
Paul J Wolf, *Managing Prtnr*
EMP: 160
SALES (est): 73.7MM **Privately Held**
WEB: www.cpclp.com
SIC: **6726** 3569 3086 3448 Management investment funds, closed-end; firefighting apparatus & related equipment; carpet & rug cushions, foamed plastic; ramps: prefabricated metal

(P-12138)
CITY OF FRESNO
Also Called: Retirement System
2828 Fresno St Ste 201, Fresno (93721-1327)
PHONE..................559 621-7080
Oscar Williams, *Branch Mgr*
EMP: 112 **Privately Held**
SIC: **6726** Investment offices
PA: City Of Fresno
2600 Fresno St
Fresno CA 93721
559 621-7001

(P-12139)
FFL PARTNERS LLC (PA)
Also Called: F F L
1 Maritime Plz Fl 22, San Francisco (94111-3512)
PHONE..................415 402-2100
Fax: 415 402-2111
Tully M Friedman, *CEO*
Patty Nykodym, *CFO*
Jeremy Thatcher, *CFO*
David Crussell, *Vice Pres*
Abhishek Gupta, *Vice Pres*
EMP: 54
SALES (est): 23.3MM **Privately Held**
WEB: www.fflpartners.com
SIC: **6726** Investment offices

(P-12140)
INTERNATIONAL INDUSTRIAL PARK
5440 Morehouse Dr # 4000, San Diego (92121-1798)
PHONE..................858 623-9000
David Wick, *Vice Pres*
Lindsay Arobone, *Administration*
EMP: 99
SALES (est): 7.8MM **Privately Held**
SIC: **6726** Investment offices

(P-12141)
J ALEXANDER INVESTMENTS INC (PA)
Also Called: Investment Banking
922 S Barrington Ave A, Los Angeles (90049-6519)
PHONE..................213 687-8400
Fax: 213 625-8388
James Alexander, *President*
EMP: 50
SQ FT: 4,500
SALES (est): 12.1MM **Privately Held**
WEB: www.investmentbanking.com
SIC: **6726** Investment offices

(P-12142)
SABAN CAPITAL GROUP INC ✪
10100 Santa Monica Blvd, Los Angeles (90067-4003)
PHONE..................310 557-5100
Adam Chesnoss, *COO*
Bernie Leypold, *Vice Pres*
EMP: 70 EST: 2016
SALES (est): 2.1MM **Privately Held**
SIC: **6726** Investment offices

(PA)=Parent Co (HQ)=Headquarters (DH)=Div Headquarters
✪ = New Business established in last 2 years

6726 - Unit Investment Trusts, Face-Amount Certificate Offices County (P-12143)

PRODUCTS & SERVICES SECTION

(P-12143)
SABAN MUSIC GROUP INC (PA)
Also Called: Saban Capital Group
10100 Santa Monica Blvd # 1050, Los Angeles (90067-4003)
PHONE.................................310 557-5100
Fax: 310 557-5144
Haim Saban, *CEO*
Adam Chesnoff, *President*
Fred Gluckman, *CFO*
Carl Morgan Jr, *CFO*
Chip Morgan, *CFO*
EMP: 51
SALES (est): 44.4MM **Privately Held**
WEB: www.saban.com
SIC: 6726 Investment offices

(P-12144)
SILVER LAKE PARTNERS LP (PA)
2775 Sand Hill Rd Ste 100, Menlo Park (94025-7085)
PHONE.................................650 233-8120
Jim Davidson, *Partner*
Yolande Jun, *Partner*
Tom Conneely, *President*
Angela Jiang, *Vice Pres*
Tezira Nabongo, *Vice Pres*
EMP: 70
SALES (est): 46.3MM **Privately Held**
SIC: 6726 Investment offices

(P-12145)
SILVER LAKE PARTNERS II LP
10080 N Wolfe Rd Sw3190, Cupertino (95014-2544)
PHONE.................................408 454-4732
Fax: 408 454-4734
Andy Wagner, *Branch Mgr*
EMP: 51
SALES (corp-wide): 360.9MM **Privately Held**
SIC: 6726 Investment offices
PA: Silver Lake Partners Ii, L.P.
2775 Sand Hill Rd Ste 100
Menlo Park CA 94025
650 233-8120

(P-12146)
SILVER LAKE PARTNERS II LP
Also Called: Silver Lake Financial
1 Market Plz, San Francisco (94105-1101)
PHONE.................................415 293-4355
Roger Whittlin, *Manager*
Todd Nabi, *Mktg Dir*
EMP: 204
SALES (corp-wide): 360.9MM **Privately Held**
SIC: 6726 Investment offices
PA: Silver Lake Partners Ii, L.P.
2775 Sand Hill Rd Ste 100
Menlo Park CA 94025
650 233-8120

(P-12147)
SPUS7 235 PINE LP
235 Pine St Ste 125, San Francisco (94104-2706)
PHONE.................................231 683-4200
Pamela Craig, *General Ptnr*
Ming Lee, *General Ptnr*
EMP: 99 **EST:** 2014
SQ FT: 25,000
SALES (est): 7.2MM **Privately Held**
SIC: 6726 Investment offices

(P-12148)
SPUS7 MIAMI ACC LP
515 S Flower St Ste 3100, Los Angeles (90071-2233)
PHONE.................................213 683-4200
Mark Zikakis, *Principal*
Pamela Craig, *Partner*
EMP: 50 **EST:** 2014
SQ FT: 25,000
SALES (est): 6.5MM **Privately Held**
SIC: 6726 Investment offices

(P-12149)
STARR INVESTMENT HOLDINGS LLC
101 2nd St Ste 2500, San Francisco (94105-3666)
PHONE.................................415 216-4000
William J Weichold,
EMP: 56
SALES (est): 3.2MM
SALES (corp-wide): 125.3MM **Privately Held**
SIC: 6726 Investment offices
HQ: C. V. Starr & Co.
101 2nd St Ste 2500
San Francisco CA 94105
415 216-4000

(P-12150)
TENNENBAUM CAPITL PARTNERS LLC (PA)
Also Called: T C P
2951 28th St Ste 1000, Santa Monica (90405-2993)
PHONE.................................310 396-5451
Fax: 310 566-1010
Mark Holdsworth, *Managing Prtnr*
Melvin Van Cleave, *CTO*
Andrew Kim, *VP Finance*
Donna Beuchamp, *Finance*
David Adler,
EMP: 64
SQ FT: 15,850
SALES (est): 146.7MM **Privately Held**
SIC: 6726 Management investment funds, closed-end

(P-12151)
TOMAHAWK ACQUISITION LLC
150 California St Fl 19, San Francisco (94111-4550)
PHONE.................................415 765-6500
Charles Boesenberg,
EMP: 1609
SALES (est): 51.3MM
SALES (corp-wide): 1.1B **Privately Held**
SIC: 6726 7371 Investment offices; computer software development
HQ: Vista Equity Partners, Llc
4 Embarcadero Ctr # 2000
San Francisco CA 94111
415 765-6500

6732 Education, Religious & Charitable Trusts

(P-12152)
ASIA FOUNDATION (PA)
465 California St Fl 9, San Francisco (94104-1892)
P.O. Box 193223 (94119-3223)
PHONE.................................415 982-4640
Fax: 415 392-8863
David D Arnold, *President*
Suzanne Siskel, *COO*
Ken Krug, *CFO*
Nadia Ali, *Officer*
Diana Alvord, *Officer*
EMP: 90
SQ FT: 17,207
SALES: 120.5MM **Privately Held**
SIC: 6732 Charitable trust management

(P-12153)
ASSISTANCE LEAG SAN BERNARDINO
Also Called: Childrens Dental Health Center
580 W 6th St, San Bernardino (92410-3002)
PHONE.................................909 885-2045
Nancy Varner, *President*
Dottie Pfeiffer, *President*
Carol Choisnet, *Treasurer*
Jeannie Cox, *Admin Sec*
Donna Call, *Bookkeeper*
EMP: 52
SQ FT: 4,000
SALES: 140.8K **Privately Held**
SIC: 6732 8021 Trusts: educational, religious, etc.; offices & clinics of dentists

(P-12154)
BETHESDA UNIVERSITY CALIFORNIA
Also Called: BETHESDA CHRISTIAN UNIVERSITY
730 N Euclid St Ste 314, Anaheim (92801-4115)
PHONE.................................714 517-1945
Fax: 714 517-1948
Grace Sung Hae Kim, *Chancellor*
Uh Gin Kihm, *CFO*
William Min, *Officer*
Yoomin Kim, *Vice Pres*
Kenneth Walters, *Librarian*
EMP: 70
SQ FT: 34,349
SALES: 4.4MM **Privately Held**
WEB: www.bethesdachristianuniversity.com
SIC: 6732 8221 Trusts: educational, religious, etc.; university

(P-12155)
CALIFORNIA CMNTY FOUNDATION (PA)
221 S Figueroa St Ste 400, Los Angeles (90012-3760)
PHONE.................................213 413-4130
Antonia Hernandez, *President*
Tom Unterman, *Ch of Bd*
Woubzena Jifar, *COO*
Steve Cobb, *CFO*
Elizabeth Hernandez, *CFO*
EMP: 53
SQ FT: 16,000
SALES (est): 270.2MM **Privately Held**
WEB: www.ccf-la.org
SIC: 6732 Charitable trust management

(P-12156)
CALWORKS PARTNR CONFERENCE
5151 Murphy Canyon Rd # 220, San Diego (92123-4440)
PHONE.................................858 292-2900
Pat Rickard, *President*
EMP: 50
SALES (est): 6.2MM **Privately Held**
SIC: 6732 Educational trust management

(P-12157)
HENRY J KAISER FMLY FOUNDATION (PA)
2400 Sand Hill Rd Ste 200, Menlo Park (94025-6910)
PHONE.................................650 854-9400
Fax: 650 854-4800
Drew Altman, *President*
Charles J Ogletree, *Trustee*
Koonal Gandhi, *Senior VP*
Gary Claxton, *Vice Pres*
Tina Hoff, *Vice Pres*
EMP: 67
SQ FT: 185,000
SALES: 26.3MM **Privately Held**
SIC: 6732 Trusts: educational, religious, etc.

(P-12158)
HOUSE OF PRAYER
701 2nd St, Modesto (95351-3353)
PHONE.................................916 410-3349
Charlena Cobb, *Principal*
EMP: 50
SALES (est): 4.8MM **Privately Held**
SIC: 6732 Trusts: educational, religious, etc.

(P-12159)
KRISHNMRTI FOUNDATION OF AMER (PA)
134 Besant Rd, Ojai (93023-2305)
P.O. Box 1560 (93024-1560)
PHONE.................................805 646-2726
Fax: 805 646-6674
Jaap Sluijter, *Exec Dir*
Derek Dodds, *CFO*
John Duncan, *Director*
Jackie Saunders, *Director*
EMP: 50 **EST:** 1969
SQ FT: 10,000
SALES: 4.9MM **Privately Held**
WEB: www.oakgroveschool.com
SIC: 6732 Educational trust management; charitable trust management

(P-12160)
LOS ANGELES COUNTY APPRENTICES
Also Called: ELECTRICAL TRAINING TRUST
6023 Garfield Ave, Commerce (90040-3608)
PHONE.................................323 221-5881
Fax: 323 721-6522
Byron Cummins, *Director*
Don Davis, *Exec Dir*
Mya Thomas, *Administration*
Jean Ngo, *Controller*
Bill Novak, *Manager*
EMP: 75 **EST:** 1964
SQ FT: 50,000
SALES (est): 8.4MM **Privately Held**
WEB: www.laett.com
SIC: 6732 Trusts: educational, religious, etc.

(P-12161)
OAKLAND PUBLIC EDUCATION FUND
1000 Broadway Ste 300, Oakland (94607-4033)
P.O. Box 27148 (94602-0148)
PHONE.................................510 221-6968
Robert Spencer, *President*
Brian Stanley, *Exec Dir*
EMP: 95 **EST:** 2003
SALES (est): 1.9MM **Privately Held**
SIC: 6732 Trusts: educational, religious, etc.

(P-12162)
PENINSULA COMMUNITY FOUNDATION
Also Called: Center For Ventr Philanthropy
1700 S El Camino Real # 300, San Mateo (94402-3047)
PHONE.................................650 358-9369
Fax: 650 358-9817
Sterling K Speirn, *President*
Kathy Lee, *Info Tech Mgr*
Akiko Ebina, *CPA*
George Chong, *Controller*
Sandy Hutchins, *Controller*
EMP: 55
SQ FT: 16,800
SALES: 200MM **Privately Held**
SIC: 6732 Charitable trust management

(P-12163)
PERVERTED JSTICE FUNDATION INC
703 Pier Ave Ste B154, Hermosa Beach (90254-3960)
PHONE.................................310 910-9380
Xavier Von Erck, *President*
Dennis Kerr, *CFO*
EMP: 200
SALES: 65.5K **Privately Held**
SIC: 6732 Trusts: educational, religious, etc.

(P-12164)
UCLA FOUNDATION
10920 Wilshire Blvd # 200, Los Angeles (90024-6502)
PHONE.................................310 794-3193
Fax: 310 794-6921
Peter Hayashida, *Exec Dir*
Neal Axelrod, *Treasurer*
Denise Sloan, *Vice Pres*
Dennis Slon, *Vice Pres*
Jess Tsuei, *Prgrmr*
EMP: 317
SALES: 351.6MM **Privately Held**
SIC: 6732 Educational trust management

(P-12165)
UCR BOTANY AND PLANT SCIENCES
3401 Watkins Dr, Riverside (92507-4633)
PHONE.................................951 827-5133
Michael Roose, *Principal*
Karrin Alstad, *Manager*
EMP: 99
SALES (est): 6.2MM **Privately Held**
SIC: 6732 Trusts: educational, religious, etc.

(P-12166)
US GREEN BUILDING COUNCIL -
Also Called: US GREEN BUILDING COUNCIL INLA
2879 Breezy Meadow Ln, Corona (92883-5915)
P.O. Box 2181, Redlands (92373-0721)
PHONE.................................818 621-4880
Jennifer Ward, *CEO*
EMP: 99
SALES: 48.5K **Privately Held**
SIC: 6732 Trusts: educational, religious, etc.

6733 Trusts Except Educational, Religious & Charitable

(P-12167)
2100 TRUST LLC (PA)
625 N Grand Ave, Santa Ana (92701-4347)
PHONE....................877 469-7344
Erek J Delorenzi, *Principal*
EMP: 200
SALES (est): 3.1B **Privately Held**
SIC: 6733 Trusts

(P-12168)
ANNENBERG FOUNDATION TRUST (PA)
71231 Tamarisk Ln, Rancho Mirage (92270-2366)
PHONE....................760 202-2222
Geoffrey Cowan, *President*
Wallis Annenberg, *CEO*
Debbi Hinton, *CFO*
Charles Annenberg Weingarten, *Vice Pres*
Lisa Prince, *Project Mgr*
EMP: 91
SALES: 14.1MM **Privately Held**
SIC: 6733 Trusts

(P-12169)
CAPITAL GUARDIAN TRUST COMPANY (HQ)
333 S Hope St Fl 52, Los Angeles (90071-3061)
PHONE....................213 486-9200
Richard C Barker, *Ch of Bd*
Robert Ronus, *President*
Martin Romo, *Exec VP*
Hilda Applbaum, *Senior VP*
Ralph Heckert, *Senior VP*
EMP: 100
SQ FT: 6,000
SALES (est): 71.7MM
SALES (corp-wide): 2.5B **Privately Held**
SIC: 6733 Trusts, except educational, religious, charity: management
PA: The Capital Group Companies Inc
333 S Hope St Fl 55
Los Angeles CA 90071
213 486-9200

(P-12170)
CARPENTER FUNDS
265 Hegenberger Rd # 100, Oakland (94621-1443)
PHONE....................510 633-0333
Fax: 510 562-5801
Gene H Price, *Administration*
Maria Gonzalez, *Controller*
Luci Maldonaldo, *Human Res Mgr*
Ford Carlberg, *Asst Director*
Richard Alcantar, *Agent*
EMP: 79
SQ FT: 60,956
SALES (est): 14.6MM **Privately Held**
WEB: www.carpenterfunds.com
SIC: 6733 Trusts, except educational, religious, charity: management

(P-12171)
CHRISTMAS BONUS FUND OF THE PL
501 Shatto Pl Ste 5, Los Angeles (90020-1730)
PHONE....................213 385-6161
Milton D Johnson, *Administration*
Mike Ayre, *Ch of Bd*
E A Norris, *Ch of Bd*
Joel Brick, *CFO*
Allen Jones Jr, *Co-COB*
EMP: 60
SQ FT: 70,000
SALES: 4.7MM **Privately Held**
SIC: 6733 Trusts, except educational, religious, charity: management

(P-12172)
DEFINED CONTRIBUTION TRUST FUN
Also Called: Southern Cal Pipe Trades
501 Shatto Pl Ste 500, Los Angeles (90020-1730)
PHONE....................213 385-6161
Milton D Johnson, *CEO*
Mike Ayre, *Ch of Bd*
Raymond Forman, *Trustee*
Charles La Bouff, *Admin Sec*
EMP: 60
SQ FT: 70,000
SALES (est): 6MM **Privately Held**
SIC: 6733 Trusts, except educational, religious, charity: management

(P-12173)
DEVEREUX FOUNDATION
Also Called: Devereux Center In California
El Colegio Rd, Goleta (93117)
PHONE....................805 968-2525
Amy Evans, *Director*
David Dennis, *Exec Dir*
Evan Soenke, *Administration*
Brian Hersh, *Network Mgr*
Mr David Weisman, *Human Res Dir*
EMP: 350
SALES (corp-wide): 391.5MM **Privately Held**
SIC: 6733 8361 8031 Trusts; group foster home; offices & clinics of osteopathic physicians
PA: Devereux Foundation
444 Devereux Dr
Villanova PA 19085
610 520-3000

(P-12174)
FIRST NATIONAL BANK (PA)
401 W A St Ste 200, San Diego (92101-7917)
PHONE....................619 233-5588
Fax: 619 235-1268
Mike Perdue, *President*
John Eggerman, *Ch of Bd*
Kim Drivas, *Branch Mgr*
EMP: 75
SALES (est): 62.5MM **Privately Held**
SIC: 6733 Trusts

(P-12175)
IMMIGRATION VOICE
3561 Homestead Rd 375, Santa Clara (95051-5161)
PHONE....................408 204-2200
Aman Kapoor, *Owner*
EMP: 99
SALES: 136.3K **Privately Held**
SIC: 6733 Trusts

(P-12176)
IMPAC SECURED ASSETS CORP
19500 Jamboree Rd, Irvine (92612-2401)
PHONE....................949 475-3600
Ronald Martin Morrison, *Administration*
EMP: 92
SALES (est): 112.3K **Publicly Held**
SIC: 6733 Trusts
HQ: Impac Funding Corporation
19500 Jamboree Rd
Irvine CA 92612

(P-12177)
IRA SERVICES INC
1160 Industrial Rd Ste 1, San Carlos (94070-4128)
PHONE....................650 593-2221
Edwin Blue, *President*
Paula Harvey, *COO*
Todd Yancey, *Officer*
Michael McNair, *Vice Pres*
Gary R Shumm, *Vice Pres*
EMP: 101
SQ FT: 16,000
SALES: 20MM **Privately Held**
WEB: www.ierinc.com
SIC: 6733 Trusts

(P-12178)
IRON WORKERS LOCAL 433
Also Called: California Field Ironwrkrs
252 Hillcrest Ave, San Bernardino (92408-2120)
PHONE....................909 884-5500
Fax: 909 885-0047
Mike Sulvi, *General Mgr*
EMP: 50
SALES (est): 1.5MM **Privately Held**
SIC: 6733 Trusts

(P-12179)
IRONWRKER EMPLYEES BENEFT CORP
Also Called: Ironworkers Union
131 N El Molino Ave # 330, Pasadena (91101-1873)
PHONE....................626 792-7337
Dick Zampa, *President*
Glen Cline, *Exec Dir*
Lisanne Negrete, *Admin Asst*
Paul Aragon, *Asst Controller*
Jennifer Janssen, *Exec Sec*
EMP: 65
SQ FT: 19,000
SALES (est): 11.9MM **Privately Held**
SIC: 6733 Trusts, except educational, religious, charity: management; vacation funds for employees

(P-12180)
KAISER FOUNDATION HOSPITALS
Also Called: Otay Mesa Medical Offices
4650 Palm Ave, San Diego (92154-8404)
PHONE....................619 662-5107
William F Luetzow, *Surgeon*
James M Moseman, *Med Doctor*
EMP: 454
SALES (corp-wide): 27.8B **Privately Held**
SIC: 6733 Trusts
HQ: Kaiser Foundation Hospitals Inc
1 Kaiser Plz
Oakland CA 94612
510 271-6611

(P-12181)
KAISER FOUNDATION HOSPITALS
Also Called: Kaiser Permanente
4647 Zion Ave, San Diego (92120-2507)
PHONE....................619 528-5888
Fax: 619 528-3904
Kathy Roper, *Manager*
Lynette Seid, *CFO*
Charles Columbus, *Senior VP*
Elmer Cabrera, *Executive*
Wayne Cherry, *Lab Dir*
EMP: 3000
SALES (corp-wide): 27.8B **Privately Held**
WEB: www.kaiserpermanente.org
SIC: 6733 8062 Trusts; general medical & surgical hospitals
HQ: Kaiser Foundation Hospitals Inc
1 Kaiser Plz
Oakland CA 94612
510 271-6611

(P-12182)
KAISER FOUNDATION HOSPITALS
Also Called: Martinez Medical Offices
200 Muir Rd, Martinez (94553-4672)
PHONE....................925 372-1000
Fax: 925 372-1413
Bryan Fong, *Principal*
Charles Lavadore, *Administration*
Charles Hearey, *Research*
Pablo Baker, *Chief Engr*
Glenn J Ozoa, *Osteopathy*
EMP: 200
SALES (corp-wide): 27.8B **Privately Held**
WEB: www.kaiserpermanente.org
SIC: 6733 8011 Trusts; general & family practice, physician/surgeon
HQ: Kaiser Foundation Hospitals Inc
1 Kaiser Plz
Oakland CA 94612
510 271-6611

(P-12183)
KAISER FOUNDATION HOSPITALS
Also Called: Kaiser Permanente
5119 Pomona Blvd, Los Angeles (90022-1711)
PHONE....................323 881-5516
Judy Nantes, *Manager*
EMP: 50
SALES (corp-wide): 27.8B **Privately Held**
WEB: www.kaiserpermanente.org
SIC: 6733 Trusts
HQ: Kaiser Foundation Hospitals Inc
1 Kaiser Plz
Oakland CA 94612
510 271-6611

(P-12184)
KAISER FOUNDATION HOSPITALS
Also Called: Moreno Valley Heacock Med Offs
12815 Heacock St, Moreno Valley (92553-2836)
PHONE....................951 601-6174
Mark Ituah, *Principal*
Sergio Noriega, *Info Tech Mgr*
Wadih A Hawat, *Internal Med*
Ziaolei Zing, *Internal Med*
EMP: 50
SALES (corp-wide): 27.8B **Privately Held**
WEB: www.kaiserpermanente.org
SIC: 6733 Trusts
HQ: Kaiser Foundation Hospitals Inc
1 Kaiser Plz
Oakland CA 94612
510 271-6611

(P-12185)
KAISER FOUNDATION HOSPITALS
Also Called: Kaiser Permanente
3285 Claremont Way, NAPA (94558-3313)
PHONE....................707 258-2500
Fax: 707 258-4439
Debby Bacon, *Branch Mgr*
Bonnie L Richardson, *Family Practiti*
Donna Dolislager, *Pediatrics*
Lawrence A Mills, *Pediatrics*
Mark A Price, *Plastic Surgeon*
EMP: 200
SALES (corp-wide): 27.8B **Privately Held**
WEB: www.kaiserpermanente.org
SIC: 6733 8093 8062 Trusts, except educational, religious, charity: management; specialty outpatient clinics; general medical & surgical hospitals
HQ: Kaiser Foundation Hospitals Inc
1 Kaiser Plz
Oakland CA 94612
510 271-6611

(P-12186)
KAISER FOUNDATION HOSPITALS
Also Called: Kaiser Permanente
789 E Cooley Dr, Colton (92324-4007)
PHONE....................909 427-5521
Barry A Wolfman, *Principal*
Richard L Henderson, *Psychiatry*
Mike L Hicks, *Physician Asst*
Katherine R Lewis, *Physician Asst*
Jennifer Bautista, *Med Doctor*
EMP: 793
SQ FT: 23,088
SALES (corp-wide): 27.8B **Privately Held**
WEB: www.kaiserpermanente.org
SIC: 6733 Trusts
HQ: Kaiser Foundation Hospitals Inc
1 Kaiser Plz
Oakland CA 94612
510 271-6611

(P-12187)
KAISER FOUNDATION HOSPITALS
Also Called: Kaiser Permanente
2425 Geary Blvd, San Francisco (94115-3358)
PHONE....................415 833-2000
Mike Alexander, *Senior VP*
Mehrnaz Zahiri, *Pharmacy Dir*
Randy Wittorp, *CTO*
Linda Linethan, *Opers Staff*
EMP: 720
SALES (corp-wide): 27.8B **Privately Held**
WEB: www.kaiserpermanente.org
SIC: 6733 Trusts
HQ: Kaiser Foundation Hospitals Inc
1 Kaiser Plz
Oakland CA 94612
510 271-6611

6733 - Trusts Except Educational, Religious & Charitable County (P-12188)

(P-12188)
KAISER FOUNDATION HOSPITALS
Also Called: Corona Medical Offices
182 Granite St, Corona (92879-1288)
PHONE.................................866 984-7483
Randy Florence, *Branch Mgr*
EMP: 793
SALES (corp-wide): 27.8B **Privately Held**
SIC: 6733 8011 Trusts; internal medicine practitioners; general & family practice, physician/surgeon
HQ: Kaiser Foundation Hospitals Inc
   1 Kaiser Plz
   Oakland CA 94612
   510 271-6611

(P-12189)
KAISER FOUNDATION HOSPITALS
Also Called: Orange County-Irvine Med Ctr
6640 Alton Pkwy, Irvine (92618-3734)
PHONE.................................949 932-5000
George Disalvo, *Branch Mgr*
David B Keschner, *Top Exec*
Brian P Kim, *Top Exec*
Julie M Phipps, *Vice Pres*
Jennifer Cody, *Op Rm Dir*
EMP: 379
SALES (corp-wide): 27.8B **Privately Held**
SIC: 6733 Trusts
HQ: Kaiser Foundation Hospitals Inc
   1 Kaiser Plz
   Oakland CA 94612
   510 271-6611

(P-12190)
MAKING WAVES EDUCATION PROGRAM (PA)
3220 Blume Dr Ste 250, San Pablo (94806-5741)
PHONE.................................510 237-3434
Fax: 510 215-6305
Glenn Holsclaw, *Exec Dir*
Sherry Smith, *Managing Dir*
William Turner, *Info Tech Mgr*
Anton Jungherr, *Business Mgr*
Corina Garcia, *Opers Mgr*
EMP: 225
SQ FT: 12,000
SALES: 3.9MM **Privately Held**
SIC: 6733 Trusts, except educational, religious, charity: management

(P-12191)
MANAGEMENT TRUST ASSN INC
100 E Thousand Oaks Blvd, Thousand Oaks (91360-5713)
PHONE.................................805 496-5514
EMP: 134
SALES (corp-wide): 135MM **Privately Held**
SIC: 6733 Trusts
PA: The Management Trust Association Inc
   15661 Red Hill Ave # 201
   Tustin CA 92780
   714 285-2626

(P-12192)
MANAGEMENT TRUST ASSN INC
9815 Carroll Canyon Rd, San Diego (92131-1123)
PHONE.................................858 547-4373
Diane Houston, *Branch Mgr*
EMP: 100
SALES (corp-wide): 135MM **Privately Held**
SIC: 6733 Trusts
PA: The Management Trust Association Inc
   15661 Red Hill Ave # 201
   Tustin CA 92780
   714 285-2626

(P-12193)
MANAGEMENT TRUST ASSN INC
4160 Temescal Canyon Rd # 202, Corona (92883-4625)
PHONE.................................951 694-1758
EMP: 100
SALES (corp-wide): 135MM **Privately Held**
SIC: 6733 Trusts
PA: The Management Trust Association Inc
   15661 Red Hill Ave # 201
   Tustin CA 92780
   714 285-2626

(P-12194)
MANAGEMENT TRUST ASSN INC (PA)
Also Called: Management Trust, The
15661 Red Hill Ave # 201, Tustin (92780-7300)
PHONE.................................714 285-2626
William B Sasser, *CEO*
EMP: 58
SALES (est): 135MM **Privately Held**
SIC: 6733 Trusts

(P-12195)
MTC FINANCIAL INC
Also Called: Trustee Corps
17100 Gillette Ave, Irvine (92614-5603)
PHONE.................................949 252-8300
Fax: 949 634-1011
EMP: 50 **EST:** 1992
SALES (est): 4.7MM **Privately Held**
SIC: 6733

(P-12196)
NORTHERN CAL RET CLKS-EMP FUND
190 N Wiget Ln Ste 110, Walnut Creek (94598-2476)
PHONE.................................925 746-7530
Jeff Chapman, *Administration*
Janet Garner, *Controller*
EMP: 120
SQ FT: 11,000
SALES (est): 4.7MM **Privately Held**
SIC: 6733 Vacation funds for employees

(P-12197)
OPERATING ENGINEERS FUNDS INC (PA)
100 Corson St Ste 222, Pasadena (91103-3892)
P.O. Box 7063 (91109-7063)
PHONE.................................626 792-8900
Mike Roddy, *CEO*
Matt Erieg, *CEO*
Rodney Goodwin, *CFO*
Chuck Killian, *CFO*
Alexander Rados, *Trustee*
EMP: 135
SQ FT: 84,600
SALES (est): 39.5MM **Privately Held**
WEB: www.oefunds.com
SIC: 6733 Trusts, except educational, religious, charity: management

(P-12198)
PROVIDENCE HEALTH SYSTEM
Also Called: Little Co Mary Hosp Pavilion
4320 Maricopa St, Torrance (90503-4314)
PHONE.................................310 543-5900
Fax: 310 370-4875
Mary Ann Young, *Manager*
Chris Nowell, *Chief Engr*
Ray Bruels, *Director*
EMP: 200
SALES (corp-wide): 10.1B **Privately Held**
WEB: www.lcmhs.org
SIC: 6733 8069 8051 Trusts; specialty hospitals, except psychiatric; skilled nursing care facilities
HQ: Providence Health System-Southern California
   1801 Lind Ave Sw
   Renton WA 98057
   425 525-3355

(P-12199)
PROVIDENCE HEALTH SYSTEM
3551 Voyager St Ste 201, Torrance (90503-1674)
PHONE.................................310 370-5895
Agnes Padernal, *Director*
EMP: 200
SALES (corp-wide): 10.1B **Privately Held**
WEB: www.lcmhs.org
SIC: 6733 Trusts
HQ: Providence Health System-Southern California
   1801 Lind Ave Sw
   Renton WA 98057
   425 525-3355

(P-12200)
PROVIDENCE HEALTH SYSTEM
3620 Lomita Blvd, Torrance (90505-3938)
PHONE.................................310 378-8587
Elizabeth Zuanich, *Principal*
EMP: 200
SALES (corp-wide): 10.1B **Privately Held**
WEB: www.lcmhs.org
SIC: 6733 Trusts
HQ: Providence Health System-Southern California
   1801 Lind Ave Sw
   Renton WA 98057
   425 525-3355

(P-12201)
PROVIDENCE HEALTH SYSTEM
511 S Buena Vista St, Burbank (91505-4809)
PHONE.................................818 846-8141
EMP: 200
SALES (corp-wide): 10.1B **Privately Held**
WEB: www.lcmhs.org
SIC: 6733 Trusts
HQ: Providence Health System-Southern California
   1801 Lind Ave Sw
   Renton WA 98057
   425 525-3355

(P-12202)
QUALITY LOAN SERVICE CORP
411 Ivy St, San Diego (92101-2108)
PHONE.................................619 645-7711
Kevin R McCarthy, *CEO*
Thomas J Holthus, *Ch of Bd*
Dave Owen, *COO*
Adriana Banuelos, *Trustee*
Carlos Contreras, *Trustee*
EMP: 384
SQ FT: 4,000
SALES (est): 32.4MM **Privately Held**
WEB: www.qualityloan.com
SIC: 6733 Trusts, except educational, religious, charity: management

(P-12203)
SOUTHERN CAL PIPE TRADES ADM (PA)
Also Called: Southern Cal Pipe Trades ADM
501 Shatto Pl Ste 500, Los Angeles (90020-1705)
PHONE.................................213 385-6161
Milton D Johnson, *President*
Steven Kwan, *Admin Asst*
Southern C Pipe Trade, *Project Mgr*
EMP: 70
SQ FT: 70,000
SALES (est): 19.6MM **Privately Held**
WEB: www.marinavillage.net
SIC: 6733 6513 Trusts, except educational, religious, charity: management; retirement hotel operation

(P-12204)
TCW VALUE ADDED LTD PARTNR
865 S Figueroa St, Los Angeles (90017-2543)
PHONE.................................213 244-0000
EMP: 248
SALES (est): 6.9MM
SALES (corp-wide): 3B **Publicly Held**
SIC: 6733 Private estate, personal investment & vacation fund trusts
HQ: Tcw Asset Management Company
   865 S Figueroa St # 1800
   Los Angeles CA 90017
   213 244-0000

(P-12205)
THE CHARLES SCHWAB TRUST CO (HQ)
425 Market St Fl 7, San Francisco (94105-5405)
PHONE.................................415 371-0518
James McCool, *CEO*
Steven Scheid, *CFO*
Nancy Larget, *Vice Pres*
Libbie Agran,
Andrew Berg,
EMP: 50
SALES (est): 39.5MM
SALES (corp-wide): 6.3B **Publicly Held**
SIC: 6733 Trusts
PA: The Charles Schwab Corporation
   211 Main St Fl 17
   San Francisco CA 94105
   415 667-7000

(P-12206)
UFCW EMPLOYERS BENEFIT PLAN (PA)
2200 Prof Dr Ste 200, Roseville (95661)
PHONE.................................925 746-7530
Jody Osterweil, *Administration*
Bob West, *Controller*
Karen Dyer, *VP Human Res*
EMP: 110
SQ FT: 57,600
SALES (est): 21.9MM **Privately Held**
SIC: 6733 Trusts

(P-12207)
VACATION AND HOLIDAY BENEFIT F
501 Shatto Pl Ste 5, Los Angeles (90020-1730)
PHONE.................................213 385-6161
Milton D Johnson, *Administration*
Mike Ayre, *Ch of Bd*
E A Norris, *Ch of Bd*
Allen Jones Jr, *Co-COB*
Raymond Forman, *Trustee*
EMP: 60
SQ FT: 70,000
SALES (est): 3MM **Privately Held**
SIC: 6733 Trusts, except educational, religious, charity: management

(P-12208)
VARNER FAMILY LTD PARTNERSHIP (PA)
5900 E Lerdo Hwy, Shafter (93263-4023)
PHONE.................................661 399-1163
James Varner, *General Ptnr*
EMP: 80
SALES (est): 111MM **Privately Held**
SIC: 6733 Private estate, personal investment & vacation fund trusts

(P-12209)
WATTS HEALTH FOUNDATION INC
Also Called: Watts Health Center
10300 Compton Ave, Los Angeles (90002-3628)
PHONE.................................323 357-6688
Fax: 323 563-1636
Clyde W Oden, *Manager*
Patricia P Brown, *Office Mgr*
Sylvia Rojas, *Purch Agent*
Carolyn Holmes, *Manager*
Jose Juarez, *Manager*
EMP: 450
SALES (corp-wide): 31.9MM **Privately Held**
WEB: www.sonnytran.com
SIC: 6733 8322 8011 Trusts; individual & family services; offices & clinics of medical doctors
HQ: Watts Health Foundation, Inc.
   3405 W Imperial Hwy # 304
   Inglewood CA 90303
   310 424-2220

6794 Patent Owners & Lessors

(P-12210)
ANTHONY ROBBINS & ASSOCIATES
9888 Carroll Cntre Rd 1 Ste 100, San Diego (92126)
PHONE.................................858 535-9900
Anthony Robbins, *Owner*
Sam Georges, *President*
Mina Shah, *Training Spec*
EMP: 100
SALES: 2.4MM **Privately Held**
WEB: www.anthonyrobbins.com
SIC: 6794 Franchises, selling or licensing

PRODUCTS & SERVICES SECTION
6794 - Patent Owners & Lessors County (P-12231)

(P-12211)
BRER AFFILIATES INC (DH)
Also Called: Prudential
18500 Von Karman Ave # 400, Irvine
(92612-0511)
PHONE 949 794-7900
John Vanderwall, *Ch of Bd*
Larry Goebel, *Senior VP*
Patti Ray, *Senior VP*
David S Beard, *Vice Pres*
Betty Allen, *Asst Broker*
EMP: 208
SQ FT: 55,500
SALES (est): 116.7MM
SALES (corp-wide): 57.1B **Publicly Held**
WEB: www.preacanada.com
SIC: 6794 6531 Franchises, selling or licensing; real estate agents & managers
HQ: The Prudential Insurance Company Of America
751 Broad St
Newark NJ 07102
973 802-6000

(P-12212)
BROOKFIELD RELOCATION INC (DH)
Also Called: Prudential
3333 Michelson Dr # 1000, Irvine
(92612-0625)
PHONE 949 794-7900
Fax: 949 794-7044
Brian McEleney, *Vice Pres*
Dave Benivengo, *Vice Pres*
Marty Capaun, *Info Tech Dir*
Mohammad Kahn, *Info Tech Dir*
Mike Zeffiro, *Info Tech Dir*
EMP: 100
SALES (est): 100.6MM
SALES (corp-wide): 14.9B **Publicly Held**
WEB: www.randalgoodson.net
SIC: 6794 Franchises, selling or licensing
HQ: Brer Services Inc
16260 N 71st St
Scottsdale AZ 85254
949 794-7900

(P-12213)
CHEROKEE INC (PA)
5990 Sepulvda Blvd # 600, Sherman Oaks
(91411-2500)
PHONE 818 908-9868
Fax: 818 908-9191
Henry Stupp, *CEO*
Howard Siegel, *President*
Jason Boling, *CFO*
Mark Disiena, *CFO*
Gene Ellison, *Treasurer*
EMP: 51
SQ FT: 11,399
SALES: 34.6MM **Publicly Held**
WEB: www.cherokeegroup.com
SIC: 6794 Copyright buying & licensing

(P-12214)
DOLBY LABS LICENSING CORP
100 Potrero Ave, San Francisco
(94103-4886)
PHONE 415 558-0200
Ray Dolby, *Chairman*
N William Jasper Jr, *President*
Gita Viswanaathan, *Technology*
Douglas Mandell, *Engineer*
David Gray, *Prdtn Mgr*
EMP: 125
SQ FT: 50,000
SALES (est): 25.9MM
SALES (corp-wide): 970.6MM **Publicly Held**
WEB: www.dolby.net
SIC: 6794 Patent buying, licensing, leasing
PA: Dolby Laboratories, Inc.
1275 Market St
San Francisco CA 94103
415 558-0200

(P-12215)
FARMER BOY FOODS INC (PA)
Also Called: Farmer Boys Restaurants
3452 University Ave, Riverside
(92501-3327)
PHONE 951 275-9900
Fax: 951 275-9930
Karen Eadon, *President*
Judy Lewis, *CFO*
Larry Rusinko, *Chief Mktg Ofcr*
Lawrence Rusinko, *Chief Mktg Ofcr*
Chris Havadjis, *Vice Pres*
EMP: 66
SQ FT: 1,500
SALES (est): 45.3MM **Privately Held**
SIC: 6794 5812 Franchises, selling or licensing; eating places

(P-12216)
FRANDELI GROUP LLC (PA)
20377 Sw Acacia St # 200, Newport Beach
(92660-1780)
PHONE 714 450-7660
Fax: 714 385-1945
Doug Pak, *Sales Executive*
Michael Churchman, *Info Tech Dir*
Jan Miller, *VP Human Res*
Doug Hoffman, *Opers Staff*
EMP: 100
SALES (est): 126.6MM **Privately Held**
SIC: 6794 Franchises, selling or licensing

(P-12217)
HOBBY LOBBY STORES INC
27651 San Bernardino Ave # 140, Redlands
(92374-5031)
PHONE 909 307-0135
EMP: 148
SALES (corp-wide): 4.4B **Privately Held**
SIC: 6794 Patent owners & lessors
PA: Hobby Lobby Stores, Inc.
7707 Sw 44th St
Oklahoma City OK 73179
855 329-7060

(P-12218)
LA BOXING FRANCHISE CORP
1241 E Dyer Rd Ste 100, Santa Ana
(92705-5611)
PHONE 714 668-0911
Anthony Geisler, *President*
Rob McCullough, *Training Dir*
EMP: 309 **EST:** 1992
SALES (est): 38.9MM **Privately Held**
SIC: 6794 Franchises, selling or licensing
PA: U Gym, Llc
1241 E Dyer Rd Ste 100
Santa Ana CA 92705
760 444-0897

(P-12219)
LICENSALE INC
900 Bush St Apt 205, San Francisco
(94109-6379)
PHONE 604 681-6888
Benjamin Arazy, *President*
Mingsheng Qiu, *CFO*
EMP: 100
SALES (est): 25MM **Privately Held**
SIC: 6794 8748 Patent buying, licensing, leasing; business consulting

(P-12220)
ORIGINAL PETES PIZZA INC
2001 J St, Sacramento (95811-3119)
PHONE 916 442-6770
Steve Presson, *President*
David Edminston, *Vice Pres*
EMP: 50
SALES (est): 3.7MM **Privately Held**
SIC: 6794 5812 Franchises, selling or licensing; eating places

(P-12221)
QUALCOMM INTERNATIONAL INC (HQ)
5775 Morehouse Dr, San Diego
(92121-1714)
PHONE 858 587-1121
Steve Altman, *President*
Derek Aberle, *Exec VP*
Christian Thornely, *Business Anlyst*
Ming Kuo, *Design Engr*
EMP: 4000
SALES (est): 315.8MM
SALES (corp-wide): 25.2B **Publicly Held**
SIC: 6794 Patent buying, licensing, leasing
PA: Qualcomm Incorporated
5775 Morehouse Dr
San Diego CA 92121
858 587-1121

(P-12222)
RELIGIOUS TECHNOLOGY CENTER
Also Called: RTC
1710 Ivar Ave Ste 1100, Los Angeles
(90028-5575)
PHONE 323 663-3258
Fax: 323 667-0960
Warren McShane, *President*
Barbara Griffin, *Treasurer*
Laurisse Stuckenbrock, *Admin Sec*
EMP: 67
SQ FT: 1,200
SALES (est): 10.9MM **Privately Held**
WEB: www.rtc.org
SIC: 6794 8661 Copyright buying & licensing; religious organizations

(P-12223)
RISK MANAGEMENT SOLUTIONS INC (DH)
7575 Gateway Blvd, Newark (94560-1193)
PHONE 510 505-2500
Fax: 510 505-2501
Hemant Shah, *CEO*
Paul Dali, *Ch of Bd*
Stephen Robertson, *CFO*
Brad Nichols, *Senior VP*
Alex Barnett, *Vice Pres*
EMP: 140
SQ FT: 55,000
SALES (est): 247.5MM
SALES (corp-wide): 2.8B **Privately Held**
SIC: 6794 6411 Patent owners & lessors; insurance information & consulting services
HQ: Dmgi Land & Property Europe Ltd
5-7 Abbey Court
Exeter
844 844-9966

(P-12224)
RPX CORPORATION (PA)
1 Market Plz Ste 800, San Francisco
(94105-1008)
PHONE 866 779-7641
John A Amster, *President*
Robert H Heath, *CFO*
Mallun Yen, *Exec VP*
Dan McCurdy, *Senior VP*
Martin E Roberts, *Senior VP*
EMP: 70
SQ FT: 67,000
SALES: 291.8MM **Publicly Held**
SIC: 6794 8741 Patent owners & lessors; business management

(P-12225)
TENSILICA INC (HQ)
3393 Octavius Dr, Santa Clara
(95054-3004)
P.O. Box 202769, Dallas TX (75320-2769)
PHONE 408 986-8000
Fax: 408 986-8919
Jack Guedj, *President*
Chris Carney, *CFO*
Keith Van Sickle, *CFO*
Ashish Dixia, *Senior VP*
Beatrice Fu, *Senior VP*
EMP: 80
SQ FT: 20,000
SALES (est): 22.6MM
SALES (corp-wide): 1.7B **Publicly Held**
WEB: www.tensilica.com
SIC: 6794 9621 Patent owners & lessors; licensing agencies
PA: Cadence Design Systems, Inc.
2655 Seely Ave Bldg 5
San Jose CA 95134
408 943-1234

(P-12226)
UNIVERSAL MUSIC ENTERPRISES
2220 Colorado Ave, Santa Monica
(90404-3506)
PHONE 310 865-7857
A Schroeder, *Director*
EMP: 99
SALES (est): 10.3MM **Privately Held**
SIC: 6794 Music licensing & royalties

(P-12227)
UNIVERSAL STDIOS LICENSING INC
Also Called: Universal Studios Consmr Pdts
100 Universal City Plz, Universal City
(91608-1002)
PHONE 818 762-6284
Cynthia C Cleveland, *President*
EMP: 150
SALES (est): 15.8MM
SALES (corp-wide): 74.5B **Publicly Held**
WEB: www.universalstudios.com
SIC: 6794 Copyright buying & licensing
HQ: Universal Studios, Inc.
100 Universal City Plz
North Hollywood CA 91608
818 777-1000

(P-12228)
VIACOM CONSUMER PRODUCTS INC
5555 Melrose Ave, Los Angeles
(90038-3989)
PHONE 323 956-5634
Andrea Hein, *President*
Mike Goldman, *Senior VP*
Terry Helton, *Senior VP*
Jonathan Finn, *Vice Pres*
Abe Wong, *CIO*
EMP: 50
SALES (est): 8MM
SALES (corp-wide): 13.2B **Publicly Held**
WEB: www.viacom.com
SIC: 6794 Patent buying, licensing, leasing
HQ: Paramount Pictures Corporation
5555 Melrose Ave
Los Angeles CA 90038
323 956-5000

(P-12229)
WALT DISNEY MUSIC COMPANY (DH)
500 S Buena Vista St, Burbank
(91521-0007)
P.O. Box 3232, Anaheim (92803-3232)
PHONE 818 560-1000
Fax: 818 848-2610
Chris Montan, *President*
Robert Cavallo, *Ch of Bd*
Cathleen M Taff, *CEO*
Cathleen Tass, *Treasurer*
Luigi-Theo Calabrese, *Vice Pres*
EMP: 53
SALES (est): 112.2MM **Publicly Held**
WEB: www.worldofdisney.com
SIC: 6794 Music royalties, sheet & record
HQ: Disney Enterprises, Inc.
500 S Buena Vista St
Burbank CA 91521
818 560-1000

(P-12230)
WONDERLAND MUSIC COMPANY INC
500 S Buena Vista St, Burbank
(91521-0001)
PHONE 818 840-1671
Chris Montan, *Principal*
EMP: 55
SALES (est): 3.3MM **Publicly Held**
SIC: 6794 Patent owners & lessors
HQ: Disney Enterprises, Inc.
500 S Buena Vista St
Burbank CA 91521
818 560-1000

(P-12231)
WSM INVESTMENTS LLC
Also Called: Topco Sales
3990b Heritage Oak Ct, Simi Valley
(93063-6716)
PHONE 818 332-4600
Fax: 818 332-4700
Scott Tucker, *CEO*
Martin Tucker, *Ch of Bd*
Michael Siegel, *COO*
Jocelyn Centenera, *Executive Asst*
Shelly Hua, *Planning*
▲ **EMP:** 145
SQ FT: 150,000

6798 - Real Estate Investment Trusts County (P-12232)

SALES (est): 23.6MM
SALES (corp-wide): 6.1MM **Privately Held**
WEB: www.topco-sales.com
SIC: 6794 5122 5099 4731 Performance rights, publishing & licensing; cosmetics; novelties, durable; freight forwarding
PA: Lover Health Science And Technology Co.,Ltd.
No.1208, Taihu Ave., Changxing Economic Development Zone
Changxing County 31310
572 603-0621

6798 Real Estate Investment Trusts

(P-12232)
AAT SORRENTO POINTE LLC
11455 El Camino Real, San Diego (92130-2088)
PHONE 858 350-2600
Ernest Rady, *CEO*
Robert Barton, *CFO*
EMP: 80
SALES (est): 4MM **Privately Held**
SIC: 6798 Real estate investment trusts

(P-12233)
AMERICAN ASSETS TRUST INC (PA)
11455 El Camino Real # 200, San Diego (92130-2047)
PHONE 858 350-2600
Ernest S Rady, *Ch of Bd*
Robert F Barton, *CFO*
Adam Wyll, *Senior VP*
Jerry Gammieri, *Vice Pres*
Quyen Dao-Haddock, *Controller*
EMP: 51
SALES: 275.6MM **Privately Held**
SIC: 6798 Real estate investment trusts

(P-12234)
AMERICAN HOMES 4 RENT (PA)
30601 Agoura Rd Ste 200, Agoura Hills (91301-2148)
PHONE 805 413-5300
David P Singelyn, *CEO*
B Wayne Hughes, *Ch of Bd*
John Corrigan, *COO*
Diana M Laing, *CFO*
Sara H Vogt-Lowell,
EMP: 59
SALES: 630.5MM **Publicly Held**
SIC: 6798 Real estate investment trusts

(P-12235)
AMERICAN HOMES TRUST
450 Camino Hermoso, San Marcos (92078-8905)
PHONE 619 694-7821
Jesse Bookheim, *Owner*
EMP: 100
SQ FT: 23,000
SALES: 2MM **Privately Held**
SIC: 6798 Real estate investment trusts

(P-12236)
AMERICAN REALTY ADVISORS
801 N Brand Blvd Ste 800, Glendale (91203-3237)
PHONE 818 545-1152
Stanley Iezman, *President*
Gregory A Blomstrand, *Principal*
Scott Darling, *Principal*
Leanne Cobb, *Marketing Staff*
Robert Samuel, *Marketing Staff*
EMP: 58
SALES (est): 2.8MM **Privately Held**
SIC: 6798 Real estate investment trusts

(P-12237)
AMH PORTFOLIO ONE LLC
Also Called: Beazer Pre-Owned Rental Homes
30601 Agoura Rd Ste 200, Agoura Hills (91301-2148)
PHONE 480 921-4600
David P Singelyn, *CEO*
EMP: 475 **EST:** 2014

SALES (est): 51.8MM
SALES (corp-wide): 630.5MM **Publicly Held**
SIC: 6798 Realty investment trusts
PA: American Homes 4 Rent
30601 Agoura Rd Ste 200
Agoura Hills CA 91301
805 413-5300

(P-12238)
ARPI REIT LLC
Also Called: Sunrise Merger Sub, LLC
30601 Agoura Rd Ste 200, Agoura Hills (91301-2148)
PHONE 805 413-5300
David Singelyn, *CEO*
EMP: 157
SALES (est): 2.6MM
SALES (corp-wide): 630.5MM **Publicly Held**
SIC: 6798 Real estate investment trusts
PA: American Homes 4 Rent
30601 Agoura Rd Ste 200
Agoura Hills CA 91301
805 413-5300

(P-12239)
BROOKFIELD DTLA FUND OFFICE
355 S Grand Ave Ste 3300, Los Angeles (90071-1592)
PHONE 213 626-3300
Dennis Friedrich, *Branch Mgr*
EMP: 70
SALES (corp-wide): 14.9B **Privately Held**
SIC: 6798 Real estate investment trusts
HQ: Brookfield Dtla Fund Office Trust Inc.
4 Wrld Fncl Ctr Fl 15
New York NY 10281
212 417-7064

(P-12240)
CANYON VIEW CAPITAL INC
331 Soquel Ave Ste 100, Santa Cruz (95062-2330)
PHONE 831 480-6335
Robert J Davidson, *CEO*
Alison Ruday, *Principal*
EMP: 80
SALES: 60MM **Privately Held**
SIC: 6798 Real estate investment trusts

(P-12241)
CORE REALTY HOLDINGS LLC (PA)
1600 Dove St Ste 450, Newport Beach (92660-2447)
PHONE 949 863-1031
Fax: 949 863-1022
Doug Morehead, *Mng Member*
Gary Davi, *COO*
Jonathan Harmer, *CFO*
William Russ Colvin, *Chm Emeritus*
Sterling McGregor, *Ch Invest Ofcr*
EMP: 53
SALES (est): 34.1MM **Privately Held**
WEB: www.corerealtyholdings.com
SIC: 6798 Realty investment trusts

(P-12242)
DALLAS UNION HOTEL INC
Also Called: Sheraton
150 Corson St, Pasadena (91103-3839)
PHONE 626 356-1000
Leo Majich, *President*
Rona Bevando, *Treasurer*
Jeff Ford, *Vice Pres*
Helen Sariles, *Executive Asst*
Ali Shiva, *MIS Dir*
EMP: 170
SALES (est): 3.3MM
SALES (corp-wide): 39.5MM **Privately Held**
WEB: www.sheratongranddfw.com
SIC: 6798 Real estate investment trusts
PA: Operating Engineers Funds Inc
100 Corson St Ste 222
Pasadena CA 91103
626 792-8900

(P-12243)
DIGITAL REALTY TRUST INC (PA)
4 Embarcadero Ctr # 3200, San Francisco (94111-4106)
PHONE 415 738-6500
Dennis E Singleton, *Ch of Bd*
A William Stein, *CEO*
Jarrett B Appleby, *COO*
Andrew P Power, *CFO*
William Stein, *CFO*
EMP: 150
SALES: 1.7B **Publicly Held**
WEB: www.digitalrealtytrust.com
SIC: 6798 Real estate investment trusts

(P-12244)
ESSEX MANAGEMENT CORPORATION
925 E Meadow Dr, Palo Alto (94303-4299)
PHONE 650 494-3700
Keith Guericke, *President*
R Guericke, *Vice Chairman*
Marty Brill, *CFO*
Michael J Schall, *CFO*
John Eudy, *Exec VP*
EMP: 60
SALES (est): 8.6MM **Privately Held**
SIC: 6798 Real estate investment trusts

(P-12245)
ESSEX PROPERTY TRUST INC
8795 Folsom Blvd Ste 101, Sacramento (95826-3720)
PHONE 916 381-0345
Fax: 916 381-0770
Laurie Bernhard, *Branch Mgr*
EMP: 70
SALES (corp-wide): 1.1B **Privately Held**
WEB: www.breproperties.com
SIC: 6798 Real estate investment trusts
PA: Essex Property Trust, Inc.
1100 Park Pl Ste 200
San Mateo CA 94403
650 655-7800

(P-12246)
ESSEX PROPERTY TRUST INC (PA)
1100 Park Pl Ste 200, San Mateo (94403-7107)
PHONE 650 655-7800
Fax: 650 494-8743
Michael J Schall, *President*
George M Marcus, *Ch of Bd*
Michael T Dance, *CFO*
Keith R Guericke, *Vice Ch Bd*
Janice Sears, *Bd of Directors*
EMP: 109
SQ FT: 39,600
SALES: 1.1B **Privately Held**
SIC: 6798 Real estate investment trusts

(P-12247)
GR HARDESTER LLC
21088 Calistoga Rd, Middletown (95461-9300)
P.O. Box 308 (95461-0308)
PHONE 707 987-2325
Ross Hardester,
Walter Hardester,
EMP: 127 **EST:** 1999
SALES (est): 5.7MM **Privately Held**
SIC: 6798 Real estate investment trusts

(P-12248)
HCP INC (PA)
1920 Main St Ste 1200, Irvine (92614-7230)
PHONE 949 407-0700
Lauralee E Martin, *President*
Timothy M Schoen, *CFO*
Scott A Anderson, *Exec VP*
Jonathan Bergschneider, *Exec VP*
Thomas D Kirby, *Exec VP*
EMP: 58
SALES: 2.5B **Publicly Held**
WEB: www.hcpi.com
SIC: 6798 Real estate investment trusts

(P-12249)
HUDSON PACIFIC PROPERTIES INC (PA)
11601 Wilshire Blvd Fl 6, Los Angeles (90025-0509)
PHONE 310 445-5700
Fax: 310 445-5710
Victor J Coleman, *Ch of Bd*
Mark T Lammas, *COO*
Alexander Vouvalides, *Ch Invest Ofcr*
Steven M Jaffe, *Officer*
Christopher J Barton, *Exec VP*
EMP: 53
SALES: 520.8MM **Publicly Held**
SIC: 6798 Real estate investment trusts

(P-12250)
IMPAC MORTGAGE HOLDINGS INC (PA)
19500 Jamboree Rd, Irvine (92612-2401)
PHONE 949 475-3600
Joseph R Tomkinson, *Ch of Bd*
William S Ashmore, *President*
Todd R Taylor, *CFO*
Ronald M Morrison, *Exec VP*
EMP: 57
SQ FT: 210,000
SALES: 166.9MM **Publicly Held**
SIC: 6798 Real estate investment trusts

(P-12251)
IMPAC MORTGAGE HOLDINGS INC
Integrated Real Estate Service
19500 Jamboree Rd, Irvine (92612-2401)
PHONE 949 475-3781
Justin Moisio, *Branch Mgr*
EMP: 53 **Publicly Held**
SIC: 6798 Real estate investment trusts
PA: Impac Mortgage Holdings, Inc.
19500 Jamboree Rd
Irvine CA 92612

(P-12252)
IRVINE EASTGATE OFFICE II LLC
Also Called: Irvine Company Office Property
550 Newport Center Dr, Newport Beach (92660-7011)
P.O. Box 2460 (92658-8960)
PHONE 949 720-2000
Fax: 949 720-2161
Pam Van Nort, *Vice Pres*
Coral Lovci, *Opers Staff*
EMP: 3000
SQ FT: 3,000
SALES (est): 329MM **Privately Held**
SIC: 6798 Real estate investment trusts

(P-12253)
JONES LANG LA SALLE
515 S Flower St Fl 13, Los Angeles (90071-2201)
PHONE 213 239-6000
Peter Belisle, *General Mgr*
EMP: 80
SALES (est): 6.1MM **Privately Held**
SIC: 6798 Real estate investment trusts

(P-12254)
KILROY REALTY CORPORATION (PA)
12200 W Olympic Blvd # 200, Los Angeles (90064-1044)
PHONE 310 481-8400
Fax: 310 481-6501
John Kilroy, *Ch of Bd*
Jeffrey Hawken, *COO*
Tyler Rose, *CFO*
Tracy Murphy, *Exec VP*
Heidi Roth, *Exec VP*
EMP: 68
SQ FT: 150,117
SALES: 581.2MM **Publicly Held**
WEB: www.kilroyrealty.com
SIC: 6798 Real estate investment trusts

(P-12255)
LBA REALTY FUND III - III LLC
3347 Michelson Dr Ste 200, Irvine (92612-0687)
PHONE 949 833-0400
Perry Schonfeld, *Principal*

PRODUCTS & SERVICES SECTION
6799 - Investors, NEC County (P-12280)

Aileen Chiang, *Accountant*
EMP: 99
SALES (est): 3.5MM **Privately Held**
SIC: 6798 Real estate investment trusts

(P-12256)
LBA RLTY FUND I-COMPANY IV LLC
3347 Michelson Dr Ste 950, Irvine (92612-1692)
PHONE...................................949 955-9321
Michael Memoly,
Kyung Jang, *Comptroller*
EMP: 99
SALES (est): 7.8MM **Privately Held**
SIC: 6798 Real estate investment trusts

(P-12257)
LUBERT-DLER MNAGEMENT-WEST INC
1401 Ocean Ave Ste 350, Santa Monica (90401-2161)
PHONE...................................310 496-4130
Dean S Adler, *President*
Vesna Dalmatin, *Administration*
EMP: 233
SALES (est): 145.6K
SALES (corp-wide): 81.5MM **Privately Held**
SIC: 6798 Real estate investment trusts
PA: Lubert-Adler Management Company, L.P.
2929 Arch St Ste 1650
Philadelphia PA 19104
215 972-2200

(P-12258)
MACERICH COMPANY (PA)
401 Wilshire Blvd Ste 700, Santa Monica (90401-1452)
PHONE...................................310 394-6000
Fax: 310 395-2791
Arthur M Coppola, *Ch of Bd*
Edward C Coppola, *President*
Olivia Leigh, *President*
Robert D Perlmutter, *COO*
Thomas E O'Hern, *CFO*
EMP: 80 **EST:** 1965
SALES: 1.2B **Publicly Held**
WEB: www.macerich.com
SIC: 6798 Real estate investment trusts

(P-12259)
MAGUIRE PROPERTIES TWR 17 LLC
1733 Ocean Ave Fl 4, Santa Monica (90401-3223)
PHONE...................................310 857-1100
Martin Griffiths,
Anzor Zurhaev, *Vice Pres*
Marguerite Anastassiou, *Technology*
Alain Artin, *Technology*
Clemente Jimenez, *Chief Engr*
EMP: 99
SALES (est): 5MM **Privately Held**
SIC: 6798 Real estate investment trusts

(P-12260)
MERABI & SONS LLC
14545 Friar St Ste 101, Van Nuys (91411-2357)
PHONE...................................818 817-0006
Kambiz Merabi, *Managing Dir*
Nasser Merabi, *CFO*
Tamir Oheb, *Office Mgr*
EMP: 135
SQ FT: 15,000
SALES (est): 1.5MM **Privately Held**
WEB: www.merabiandsons.com
SIC: 6798 Real estate investment trusts

(P-12261)
MERIDIAN INDUSTRIAL TRUST
455 Market St Ste 1700, San Francisco (94105-2456)
PHONE...................................415 281-3900
Fax: 415 284-2840
Allen J Anderson, *CEO*
Milton K Reeder, *President*
Milton Reeder, *Treasurer*
Jaime Suarez, *Treasurer*
Dennis H Higgs, *Senior VP*
EMP: 60
SALES: 66.1MM **Privately Held**
SIC: 6798 Real estate investment trusts

(P-12262)
MYRA INVESTMENT AND DEV CORP
47 W 6th St, Tracy (95376-4109)
PHONE...................................209 834-2343
Abdul Siddiqi, *President*
EMP: 55
SQ FT: 2,500
SALES (est): 3.2MM **Privately Held**
SIC: 6798 Real estate investment trusts

(P-12263)
ONE EMBARCADERO CENTER VENTURE
4 Embarcadero Ctr Ste 1, San Francisco (94111-4106)
PHONE...................................415 772-0700
Bob Pester, *Regional Mgr*
Constance J Yu, *Criminal Law*
EMP: 70
SALES (est): 4.4MM **Privately Held**
SIC: 6798 Real estate investment trusts

(P-12264)
PACIFICA COMPANIES LLC (PA)
1775 Hancock St Ste 200, San Diego (92110-2036)
PHONE...................................619 296-9000
Deepak Israni, *President*
Ashok Israni, *Chairman*
Ian Blake, *Purch Agent*
Stan Clark, *Property Mgr*
Cynthia Martinez, *Asst Sec*
EMP: 63
SALES (est): 486.5MM **Privately Held**
SIC: 6798 6512 Real estate investment trusts; nonresidential building operators

(P-12265)
PRIME ADMINISTRATION LLC
Also Called: Prime Group
357 S Curson Ave, Los Angeles (90036-5201)
P.O. Box 360859 (90036-1359)
PHONE...................................323 549-7155
Daniel H James, *Chairman*
John C Atwater, *CEO*
Christopher Anderson, *Senior VP*
Melisa Bell, *Administration*
Daniel James,
EMP: 522
SALES (est): 95.8MM **Privately Held**
SIC: 6798 Real estate investment trusts

(P-12266)
PROLOGIS INC (PA)
Bay 1 Pier 1, San Francisco (94111)
PHONE...................................415 394-9000
Hamid R Moghadam, *Ch of Bd*
Gary E Anderson, *CEO*
Eugene F Reilly, *CEO*
Thomas S Olinger, *CFO*
Edward S Nekritz,
EMP: 460
SALES: 2.2B **Publicly Held**
WEB: www.amb.com
SIC: 6798 Real estate investment trusts

(P-12267)
PROLOGIS LP (HQ)
Bay 1 Pier 1, San Francisco (94111)
PHONE...................................415 394-9000
Hamid R Moghadam, *Ch of Bd*
Thomas S Olinger, *CFO*
Lori A Palazzolo,
EMP: 452
SALES: 2.2B **Publicly Held**
WEB: www.amb.com
SIC: 6798 6799 Real estate investment trusts; real estate investors, except property operators
PA: Prologis, Inc.
Bay 1 Pier 1
San Francisco CA 94111
415 394-9000

(P-12268)
PS BUSINESS PARKS INC (PA)
701 Western Ave, Glendale (91201-2349)
PHONE...................................818 244-8080
Fax: 818 242-0566
Joseph D Russell Jr, *CEO*
Ronald L Havner Jr, *Ch of Bd*
Maria R Hawthorne, *President*
John W Petersen, *COO*
Edward A Stokx, *CFO*
◆ **SALES:** 373.6MM **Publicly Held**
WEB: www.psbusinessparks.com
SIC: 6798 Real estate investment trusts

(P-12269)
PUBLIC STORAGE (PA)
701 Western Ave, Glendale (91201-2349)
PHONE...................................818 244-8080
Fax: 818 553-2376
Ronald L Havner Jr, *Ch of Bd*
Joseph D Russell, *President*
John Reyes, *CFO*
Lily Y Hughes,
Candace N Krol, *Officer*
EMP: 200 **EST:** 1980
SALES: 2.3B **Publicly Held**
WEB: www.publicstorage.com
SIC: 6798 4225 Real estate investment trusts; miniwarehouse, warehousing

(P-12270)
QUAIL HILL INVESTMENTS INC
Also Called: Remax Value Properties
1124 Meridian Ave, San Jose (95125-4329)
PHONE...................................408 978-9000
EMP: 110
SALES (est): 5.9MM **Privately Held**
WEB: www.colleenanddennisb.com
SIC: 6798

(P-12271)
REALTY INCOME CORPORATION (PA)
11995 El Camino Real, San Diego (92130-2539)
PHONE...................................858 284-5000
Fax: 760 741-8674
John P Case, *President*
Sumit Roy, *President*
Paul M Meurer, *CFO*
Evelyn J Clark, *Treasurer*
Jill Cossaboom, *Assoc VP*
EMP: 52
SALES: 1B **Publicly Held**
WEB: www.realtyincome.com
SIC: 6798 Real estate investment trusts

(P-12272)
REDWOOD TRUST INC (PA)
1 Belvedere Pl Ste 300, Mill Valley (94941-2493)
PHONE...................................415 389-7373
Fax: 415 381-1773
Martin S Hughes, *CEO*
Richard D Baum, *Ch of Bd*
Douglas B Hansen, *Vice Chairman*
Brian Geraghty, *President*
Brett D Nicholas, *President*
EMP: 70
SALES: 284.6MM **Publicly Held**
SIC: 6798 Real estate investment trusts; mortgage investment trusts

(P-12273)
SM BROADWAY CORP
Also Called: Hilton Newark Sremont
710 S Myrtle Ave Ste 285, Monrovia (91016-3423)
PHONE...................................626 301-1198
Wen Shen Chang, *CEO*
Audrey Ho, *Manager*
EMP: 100
SALES (est): 3.1MM **Privately Held**
SIC: 6798 Real estate investment trusts

(P-12274)
SUNSTONE HOTEL INVESTORS INC (PA)
120 Vantis Ste 350, Aliso Viejo (92656-2686)
PHONE...................................949 330-4000
John V Arabia, *President*
Douglas M Pasquale, *Ch of Bd*
Marc A Hoffman, *COO*
Bryan A Giglia, *CFO*
Robert C Springer, *Exec VP*
EMP: 50
SALES: 1.2B **Publicly Held**
SIC: 6798 Real estate investment trusts

(P-12275)
T C W REALTY FUND VI
Also Called: C B Richard Ellis Investors
515 S Flower St Fl 31, Los Angeles (90071-2201)
PHONE...................................213 683-4200
Bob Zerbst, *CEO*
Westmark Realty Advisors LLC, *General Ptnr*
Trust C West, *Trustee*
Neal Golub, *Vice Pres*
Alison Hawkins, *Managing Dir*
EMP: 150
SQ FT: 24,000
SALES (est): 9.5MM **Privately Held**
SIC: 6798 Realty investment trusts

(P-12276)
US ADVISOR LLC
600 Trancas St, NAPA (94558-3083)
PHONE...................................707 253-9953
Fax: 707 253-9954
Kevin Fitzgerald, *Mng Member*
Kathaleen Scanlon,
EMP: 73
SQ FT: 3,200
SALES (est): 3.6MM **Privately Held**
SIC: 6798 Real estate investment trusts

(P-12277)
WEST OAHU MALL ASSOCIATES
1880 Century Park E # 810, Los Angeles (90067-1600)
PHONE...................................310 276-1290
Joseph Daneshgar, *Principal*
Bill Ketcham, *Principal*
EMP: 50
SALES (est): 2.9MM **Privately Held**
SIC: 6798 Real estate investment trusts

(P-12278)
WESTCOAST PERFORMANCE PDTS USA
Also Called: Zantos Living Trust
3100 E Coronado St, Anaheim (92806-1914)
PHONE...................................714 630-4411
Fax: 714 630-4477
Robert Zantos, *President*
Phil Zantos, *General Mgr*
Jose Navas, *Production*
Robert Boult, *Maintence Staff*
A J Bryce, *Manager*
EMP: 70
SALES (corp-wide): 5.9MM **Privately Held**
WEB: www.westcoastinc.com
SIC: 6798 Real estate investment trusts
PA: Westcoast Performance Products (Usa) Inc
3100 E Coronado St
Anaheim CA
714 630-4411

(P-12279)
WESTERN ASSET MRTG CAPITL CORP
385 E Colorado Blvd, Pasadena (91101-1923)
PHONE...................................626 844-9400
Gavin L James, *President*
James W Hirschmann III, *Ch of Bd*
Elliott Neumayer, *COO*
Lisa Meyer, *CFO*
Steven M Sherwyn, *CFO*
EMP: 824
SALES: 40.6MM **Privately Held**
SIC: 6798 Real estate investment trusts

6799 Investors, NEC

(P-12280)
ADG CORPORATION
1871 Market St, San Francisco (94103-1112)
PHONE...................................415 864-4090
David Levy, *President*
Gerald K Dowd, *Admin Sec*
EMP: 50 **EST:** 1977
SALES (est): 2.4MM **Privately Held**
WEB: www.adg.vn
SIC: 6799 Venture capital companies

6799 - Investors, NEC County (P-12281)

(P-12281)
ADMIRALTY PARTNERS INC
1170 Somera Rd, Los Angeles (90077-2628)
PHONE...................................310 471-3772
Jon Kutler, President
EMP: 51
SALES (est): 5.2MM Privately Held
WEB: www.admiraltypartners.com
SIC: 6799 3675 Investors; electronic capacitors

(P-12282)
AG/LPC GRIFFIN TOWERS LP
5 Hutton Cntre Dr Ste 120, Santa Ana (92707)
PHONE...................................714 662-5902
David Binswanger,
EMP: 50
SALES (est): 3MM Privately Held
SIC: 6799 6512 Real estate investors, except property operators; nonresidential building operators

(P-12283)
ARES MANAGEMENT LLC (HQ)
2000 Avenue Of The Stars, Los Angeles (90067-4700)
PHONE...................................310 201-4100
Fax: 310 201-4170
Antony Ressler, Mng Member
Eric Beckman, Senior Partner
Greg Margolies, Senior Partner
Tom Bevan, President
Satya Nayak, President
EMP: 60
SALES (est): 748.9MM
SALES (corp-wide): 814.4MM Publicly Held
SIC: 6799 Venture capital companies
PA: Ares Management, L.P.
    2000 Avenue Of The Stars
    Los Angeles CA 90067
    310 201-4100

(P-12284)
BERTRAM CAPITAL MANAGEMENT LLC
800 Concar Dr Ste 100, San Mateo (94402-7045)
PHONE...................................650 358-5000
Fax: 650 358-5001
Jeff Drazan, Partner
Ryan Craig, Partner
David Hellier, Partner
Jared Ruger, Partner
Ingrid Swenson, Partner
EMP: 136
SQ FT: 9,000
SALES (est): 42.6MM Privately Held
SIC: 6799 Investors

(P-12285)
BIRTCHER ANDRSON INVESTORS LLC
31910 Del Obispo St # 100, San Juan Capistrano (92675-3182)
PHONE...................................949 545-0526
Robert M Anderson,
EMP: 50
SALES (est): 2.4MM Privately Held
SIC: 6799 Investors

(P-12286)
BROADREACH CAPITL PARTNERS LLC
6430 W Sunset Blvd # 504, Los Angeles (90028-7901)
PHONE...................................310 691-5760
Fax: 310 691-5769
EMP: 1645
SALES (corp-wide): 407.4MM Privately Held
SIC: 6799 Investors
PA: Broadreach Capital Partners Llc
    248 Homer Ave
    Palo Alto CA 94301
    650 331-2500

(P-12287)
BROADREACH CAPITL PARTNERS LLC
235 Montgomery St # 1018, San Francisco (94104-2902)
PHONE...................................415 354-4640
John A Foster, Branch Mgr
EMP: 1316
SALES (corp-wide): 407.4MM Privately Held
SIC: 6799 Investors
PA: Broadreach Capital Partners Llc
    248 Homer Ave
    Palo Alto CA 94301
    650 331-2500

(P-12288)
BUCHANAN FUND I LLC
620 Nwport Ctr Dr Ste 850, Newport Beach (92660)
PHONE...................................949 721-1414
Timothy Ballard, Mng Member
EMP: 75 EST: 2000
SQ FT: 5,400
SALES (est): 4.3MM Privately Held
SIC: 6799 Real estate investors, except property operators

(P-12289)
BY-THE-BAY INVESTMENTS INC
37000 Fremont Blvd, Fremont (94536-3604)
PHONE...................................510 793-2581
Fax: 510 793-2581
Javier Samaniego, Branch Mgr
EMP: 287
SALES (corp-wide): 13MM Privately Held
SIC: 6799 Investors
PA: By-The-Bay Investments, Inc.
    360 Kiely Blvd Ste 270
    San Jose CA 95129
    408 243-4700

(P-12290)
CALL TO ACTION LLC
11601 Wilshire Blvd Fl 23, Los Angeles (90025-1759)
PHONE...................................310 996-7200
Colin Sapire, Mng Member
Carol Conley, Marketing Mgr
Melinda Thorne, Sales Staff
Richard Kam,
Lenny Sands,
EMP: 100
SQ FT: 9,500
SALES (est): 4.3MM Privately Held
SIC: 6799 Investors

(P-12291)
CANESSA INVESTMENTS N V
9434 Cherokee Ln, Beverly Hills (90210-1704)
PHONE...................................310 273-8543
Allen Martin, Manager
EMP: 50
SALES (est): 2.8MM Privately Held
SIC: 6799 Investors

(P-12292)
CARFINANCE CAPITAL LLC
7525 Irvine Center Dr # 250, Irvine (92618-3066)
P.O. Box 57053 (92619-7053)
PHONE...................................800 900-5150
Dennis Morris,
Michael Ritter,
EMP: 558
SALES (est): 1.1MM Privately Held
SIC: 6799 6141 Investors; financing: automobiles, furniture, etc., not a deposit bank
PA: Flagship Credit Acceptance Llc
    3 Christy Dr Ste 203
    Chadds Ford PA 19317

(P-12293)
CASTER FAMILY ENTERPRISES INC
4607 Mission Gorge Pl, San Diego (92120-4132)
PHONE...................................619 287-8893
Fax: 619 287-2493
Terrence R Caster, President
Barbara Caster, Vice Pres
Barbara Culver, Executive
Stella Cook, Area Mgr
Gregory Brown, Info Tech Dir
EMP: 125 EST: 1973
SQ FT: 250,000
SALES (est): 14.2MM Privately Held
WEB: www.castergrp.com
SIC: 6799 6512 6531 Real estate investors, except property operators; commercial & industrial building operation; real estate agents & managers

(P-12294)
CB RICHARD ELLIS STRATEGIC PAR
515 S Flower St Ste 3100, Los Angeles (90071-2233)
PHONE...................................213 614-6862
Vance Maddocks, Principal
EMP: 62
SALES (est): 3.9MM Privately Held
SIC: 6799 Investors

(P-12295)
CCCC GROWTH FUND LLC
899 El Centro St, South Pasadena (91030-3101)
PHONE...................................626 441-8770
Carl L Herrmann Jr, Mng Member
Richard L Burnside, Exec VP
Patrick Blandford, Managing Dir
Richard Burnside, Managing Dir
Chris Grekowicz, Associate
EMP: 61
SQ FT: 10,000
SALES (est): 4.8MM Privately Held
SIC: 6799 6411 Investors; insurance agents, brokers & service

(P-12296)
CHEVRON INVESTOR INC (HQ)
6001 Bollinger Canyon Rd, San Ramon (94583-5737)
P.O. Box 5046 (94583-0946)
PHONE...................................925 842-1000
Howard Sheppard, CEO
John S Watson, CEO
Pedro X Gama, Project Mgr
Uriel Oseguera, VP Finance
Trisha Eggleston, Manager
EMP: 300
SALES (est): 87.9MM
SALES (corp-wide): 138.4B Publicly Held
SIC: 6799 Investors
PA: Chevron Corporation
    6001 Bollinger Canyon Rd
    San Ramon CA 94583
    925 842-1000

(P-12297)
CLEARLAKE CAPITAL GROUP LP (PA)
233 Wilshire Blvd Ste 800, Santa Monica (90401-1207)
PHONE...................................310 400-8800
Behdad Eghbali, Partner
Jose Feliciano, Partner
James Pade, Vice Pres
Randy Souza, Accounting Mgr
Fred Ebrahemi, General Counsel
EMP: 258
SALES (est): 781.3MM Privately Held
SIC: 6799 Investors

(P-12298)
COLONY CAPITAL LLC (PA)
Also Called: Colony Management
2450 Broadway Ste 600, Santa Monica (90404-3591)
PHONE...................................310 282-8820
Thomas J Barrack Jr, Chairman
Kevin L Davis, COO
Jeffrey Moore, Exec VP
Brent Elkins, Senior VP
Stefan Jaeger, Senior VP
EMP: 80
SALES (est): 1B Privately Held
SIC: 6799 7999 7011 5813 Real estate investors, except property operators; gambling & lottery services; hotels & motels; drinking places; eating places

(P-12299)
DAVIDON FIVE STAR CORP
Also Called: Davidon Homes
1600 S Main St Ste 150, Walnut Creek (94596-5341)
PHONE...................................925 945-8000
Donald Chaiken, Owner
John Albini, Vice Pres
Linda Allen, Executive
EMP: 80
SALES (est): 5MM Privately Held
SIC: 6799 Real estate investors, except property operators

(P-12300)
EASIA GOLF INVESTMENT LLC
84000 Terra Lago Pkwy, Indio (92203-9706)
PHONE...................................760 775-2000
Jon Lee, General Mgr
EMP: 60
SALES (est): 42MM Privately Held
SIC: 6799 Investors

(P-12301)
EAST HALL INVESTORS INC
Also Called: Keller Williams Realtors
11601 Blocker Dr Ste 200, Auburn (95603-4650)
PHONE...................................530 328-1900
Fax: 530 328-1901
Daryl Rogers, President
Rob Hamilton, Real Est Agnt
Casey Spencer, Real Est Agnt
EMP: 80
SALES (est): 5.3MM Privately Held
SIC: 6799 Investors

(P-12302)
EDISON CAPITAL (DH)
18101 Von Karman Ave, Irvine (92612-1012)
PHONE...................................909 594-3789
Fax: 949 752-6325
Thomas Mc Daniel, President
Oded Rhone, President
Phillip Dandridge, CFO
Steve Dandridge, CFO
Jim Phillipsen, Treasurer
EMP: 92
SQ FT: 12,000
SALES (est): 22.4MM
SALES (corp-wide): 11.5B Publicly Held
WEB: www.edisoncapital.com
SIC: 6799 Investors
HQ: Edison Mission Group Inc.
    2244 Walnut Grove Ave
    Rosemead CA 91770
    626 302-2222

(P-12303)
EMP III INC
Also Called: Duarte Manor
1755 Mrtn Lthr Kng Jr Blv, Los Angeles (90058-1522)
PHONE...................................323 231-4174
Ernie Piltil, President
Tim English, CEO
Scott Mason, Vice Pres
Genifer Fales, Assistant
EMP: 80
SALES (est): 5.8MM Privately Held
SIC: 6799 Real estate investors, except property operators

(P-12304)
END-TIME MESSAGE & SUPPORT
855 W 125th St, Los Angeles (90044-3811)
PHONE...................................323 756-6252
Alvin Labostrie, Vice Pres
EMP: 50
SALES (est): 2.1MM Privately Held
SIC: 6799 Real estate investors, except property operators

(P-12305)
ENGINEERED FOREST PRODUCTS LLC
Also Called: Future Homes International
1340 Bollinger Cyn, Moraga (94556-2742)
P.O. Box 6092 (94570-6092)
PHONE...................................925 376-0881
Fax: 925 376-1381
Gregory L Koepf,
Greg Koepf, President
Anne-Marie Koepf, Admin Sec
EMP: 100
SQ FT: 5,000
SALES: 100K Privately Held
SIC: 6799 Venture capital companies

6799 - Investors, NEC County (P-12330)

(P-12306)
ENTERPRISE PARTNERS MGT LLC
2223 Avenida De Playa 210, La Jolla (92037)
PHONE.................................858 731-0300
Carl Eibl, *Mng Member*
William Stensrud, *Managing Dir*
Robert Conn,
Andrew E Senyei,
Jim Park, *Manager*
EMP: 200
SALES (est): 9.5MM **Privately Held**
WEB: www.epvc.com
SIC: 6799 Venture capital companies

(P-12307)
FNI INTERNATIONAL INC
1300 Ethan Way, Sacramento (95825-2211)
PHONE.................................916 643-1400
Bob Taylor, *Manager*
EMP: 111
SALES (corp-wide): 23.4MM **Privately Held**
SIC: 6799 Investors
PA: Fni International, Inc
200 N Sepulveda Blvd
El Segundo CA 90245
310 326-3100

(P-12308)
FRANCISCO PARTNERS MGT LP (PA)
1 Letterman Dr Ste 410, San Francisco (94129-1495)
PHONE.................................415 418-2900
Fax: 650 233-2999
Dipanjan Deb, *Partner*
Neil Garfinkle, *General Ptnr*
Sanford Robertson, *Partner*
Tom Ludwig, *COO*
Ann Halloran, *CFO*
EMP: 50
SQ FT: 15,000
SALES (est): 1B **Privately Held**
WEB: www.franciscopartners.com
SIC: 6799 7372 Investors; application computer software

(P-12309)
GIC REAL ESTATE INC (HQ)
255 Shoreline Dr Ste 600, Redwood City (94065-1433)
PHONE.................................650 593-3122
Fax: 650 802-1212
Mike Carp, *President*
EMP: 60
SQ FT: 10,000
SALES (est): 42.8MM **Privately Held**
SIC: 6799 6531 Real estate investors, except property operators; real estate managers

(P-12310)
GOLDEN INTERNATIONAL
424 S Los Angeles St # 2, Los Angeles (90013-1470)
PHONE.................................213 628-1388
Gl Hanbae, *Branch Mgr*
EMP: 2968
SALES (corp-wide): 158.3MM **Privately Held**
SIC: 6799 Investors
PA: Golden International
36720 Palmdale Rd
Rancho Mirage CA 92270
760 568-1912

(P-12311)
GRUBB ELLIS RLTY INVESTORS LLC
19700 Fairchild Ste 300, Irvine (92612-2515)
P.O. Box 7369, Newport Beach (92658-7369)
PHONE.................................714 667-8252
Jeffrey T Hanson, *President*
Rick Burnett, *Exec VP*
Jerry Geiger, *Exec VP*
Al Haworth, *Senior VP*
Michael Van Dusen, *Senior VP*
EMP: 458 **EST:** 1998
SQ FT: 18,800
SALES (est): 128K **Privately Held**
SIC: 6799 6531 Investors; real estate managers

(P-12312)
HARVARD GRAND INV INC A CAL
2 Civic Plaza Dr, Carson (90745-2231)
P.O. Box 761458, Los Angeles (90076-1458)
PHONE.................................310 513-7560
Chang Hun Lee, *President*
Kathy Choy, *Controller*
EMP: 99 **EST:** 2007
SALES: 950K **Privately Held**
SIC: 6799 Investors

(P-12313)
HELLMAN & FRIEDMAN CAPITAL IV
1 Maritime Plz Ste 1200, San Francisco (94111-3531)
PHONE.................................415 788-5111
Warren Hellman, *Mng Member*
Allen Thorp,
EMP: 50
SALES (est): 2.5MM
SALES (corp-wide): 2.4B **Privately Held**
WEB: www.hf.com
SIC: 6799 Investors
PA: Hellman & Friedman Llc
1 Maritime Plz Fl 12
San Francisco CA 94111
415 788-5111

(P-12314)
HGGC LLC (PA)
1950 University Ave # 350, East Palo Alto (94303-2286)
PHONE.................................650 321-4910
Rich Lawson, *CEO*
Gary Crittenden, *Managing Prtnr*
James Learner, *Managing Prtnr*
Jay Tabu, *President*
Les Brown, *CFO*
EMP: 253 **EST:** 2007
SALES (est): 350MM **Privately Held**
SIC: 6799 Investors

(P-12315)
HURON DEVELOPMENT INC
19800 Macarthur Blvd, Irvine (92612-2421)
PHONE.................................949 863-9789
John Tait, *President*
EMP: 70
SALES (est): 3.7MM **Privately Held**
WEB: www.coastalmgtinc.com
SIC: 6799 Real estate investors, except property operators

(P-12316)
IDEALAB HOLDINGS LLC (PA)
130 W Union St, Pasadena (91103-3628)
PHONE.................................626 585-6900
Bill Gross, *CEO*
Marcia Goodstein, *President*
Craig Chrisney, *CFO*
Allen Morgan, *Bd of Directors*
Kristen Ding, *Vice Pres*
EMP: 626
SALES (est): 184.6MM **Privately Held**
WEB: www.idealab.com
SIC: 6799 5045 5734 Venture capital companies; computer software; computer software & accessories

(P-12317)
JH CAPITAL PARTNERS LP
451 Jackson St, San Francisco (94111-1615)
PHONE.................................415 364-0300
John Hansen, *Partner*
EMP: 50
SALES (est): 1.5MM **Privately Held**
SIC: 6799 Venture capital companies

(P-12318)
KLEINPARTNERS CAPITAL CORP
400 Continental Blvd # 600, El Segundo (90245-5076)
PHONE.................................310 426-2055
Fax: 310 426-2623
Edward McMahon, *President*
Greg Klein, *Chairman*
EMP: 405
SALES (est): 13.5MM **Privately Held**
SIC: 6799 Investors

(P-12319)
KM FRESNO INVESTORS LLC
6222 Wilshire Blvd # 650, Los Angeles (90048-5123)
PHONE.................................323 556-6600
David J Nagel, *President*
Betania L Luques, *Executive Asst*
EMP: 50
SQ FT: 152,117
SALES (est): 4.8MM **Privately Held**
SIC: 6799 6531 Investors; real estate managers

(P-12320)
KOHLBERG KRAVIS ROBERTS CO LP
Also Called: K K R
2800 Sand Hill Rd Ste 200, Menlo Park (94025-7080)
PHONE.................................650 233-6560
Fax: 650 233-6561
Michael Michelson, *Manager*
Mark Howard, *Officer*
David Herbers, *Vice Pres*
Renee Cunningham, *Executive*
Rachel Lantin, *Admin Asst*
EMP: 55
SALES (corp-wide): 1B **Publicly Held**
WEB: www.kkr.com
SIC: 6799 Investors
HQ: Kohlberg Kravis Roberts & Co. L.P.
9 W 57th St Ste 4200
New York NY 10019
212 750-8300

(P-12321)
LAMSON INVESTMENT CORP
Also Called: McDonald's
806 W Imola Ave, NAPA (94559-4026)
PHONE.................................707 253-7461
Fax: 707 253-8809
Scott Lamson, *President*
Bruce Anderson, *Supervisor*
EMP: 95
SALES (est): 5MM **Privately Held**
SIC: 6799 Investors

(P-12322)
LIGHTHOUSE CAPITAL FUNDING
Also Called: Light House Group, The
15332 Antioch St Ste 540, Pacific Palisades (90272-3628)
PHONE.................................310 230-8335
Gary Leshgold, *President*
EMP: 50
SALES (est): 5.1MM **Privately Held**
WEB: www.lighthousecapitalfunding.net
SIC: 6799 Venture capital companies

(P-12323)
M & H REALTY PARTNERS LP
353 Sacramento St Fl 21, San Francisco (94111-3676)
PHONE.................................415 693-9000
Fax: 415 693-0480
Peter Merlone, *Managing Prtnr*
EMP: 70
SALES (est): 5.1MM **Privately Held**
SIC: 6799 Real estate investors, except property operators

(P-12324)
MATSUSHITA INTERNATIONAL CORP (PA)
1141 Via Callejon, San Clemente (92673-6230)
PHONE.................................949 498-1000
Fax: 949 498-5400
Hiroyuki Matsushita, *President*
Erin Rice, *Accounts Mgr*
EMP: 80
SALES (est): 23.6MM **Privately Held**
SIC: 6799 3711 3714 Real estate investors, except property operators; automobile assembly, including specialty automobiles; motor vehicle parts & accessories

(P-12325)
MCMILLIN COMMUNITIES INC (PA)
Also Called: McMillin Realty
2750 Womble Rd Ste 200, San Diego (92106-6114)
PHONE.................................619 561-5275
Fax: 619 292-7689
Mark McMillin, *President*
Kenneth Baumgartner, *President*
Gary Beason, *CFO*
Bryce Jones, *Vice Pres*
Joe W Shiely, *General Mgr*
EMP: 51
SQ FT: 29,000
SALES (est): 119.8MM **Privately Held**
SIC: 6799 Investors

(P-12326)
MCMILLIN COMPANIES LLC (PA)
Also Called: McMillin Homes
2750 Womble Rd Ste 200, San Diego (92106-6114)
PHONE.................................619 477-4117
Scott McMillin, *CEO*
Mark D McMillin, *President*
Robin Lewis, *Senior VP*
Anthony Glenn, *Technology*
EMP: 80 **EST:** 1998
SQ FT: 60,000
SALES (est): 50MM **Privately Held**
WEB: www.mcmillinrealty.com
SIC: 6799 Real estate investors, except property operators

(P-12327)
MEDIMPACT HOLDINGS INC (PA)
10181 Scripps Gateway Ct, San Diego (92131-5152)
PHONE.................................858 790-6646
Frederick Howe, *Principal*
Jim Gollaher, *CFO*
Debra Minich, *Vice Pres*
Patience Stevens, *Executive*
Francis D Cruz, *Admin Asst*
EMP: 54
SALES (est): 84.1MM **Privately Held**
SIC: 6799 Investors

(P-12328)
N S B N INVESTMENTS LLC
9454 Wilshire Blvd Fl 4, Beverly Hills (90212-2907)
PHONE.................................310 273-2501
Fax: 310 273-4464
Ken Miles,
William Esensten,
Jack Nienstein,
EMP: 75
SALES (est): 3.7MM **Privately Held**
WEB: www.nsbn.com
SIC: 6799 Investors

(P-12329)
NEW CIVIC COMPANY LTD
870 Market St Ste 1168, San Francisco (94102-2916)
PHONE.................................415 986-1668
Zhonggen Ll, *President*
Jun Chen, *Vice Pres*
EMP: 164
SALES (est): 10MM **Privately Held**
SIC: 6799 Investors

(P-12330)
NORTHWEST VNTR PARTNERS VII LP
525 University Ave # 800, Palo Alto (94301-1903)
PHONE.................................650 321-8000
Kurt Betcher, *Partner*
EMP: 60
SALES (est): 2.5MM
SALES (corp-wide): 90B **Publicly Held**
SIC: 6799 Venture capital companies
HQ: Norwest Limited Lp, Lllp
420 Montgomery St
San Francisco CA

6799 - Investors, NEC County (P-12331)

(P-12331)
NORWEST VENTURE PARTNERS VI LP
525 University Ave # 800, Palo Alto (94301-1922)
PHONE..................650 289-2243
George J Still Jr, *Managing Prtnr*
Catherine Paul, *Executive Asst*
Sohil Chand, *Director*
Andy LI, *Manager*
EMP: 60
SALES (est): 2.3MM
SALES (corp-wide): 90B **Publicly Held**
SIC: 6799 Investors
HQ: Norwest Limited Lp, Lllp
420 Montgomery St
San Francisco CA

(P-12332)
NRLL LLC
Also Called: Land Disposition Company
1 Mauchly, Irvine (92618-2305)
PHONE..................949 768-7777
Fax: 949 457-3194
Robert D Friedman,
Jeffrey Friedman,
John Martin, *Manager*
EMP: 50
SQ FT: 18,000
SALES (est): 4MM
SALES (corp-wide): 50.2MM **Privately Held**
WEB: www.landdisposition.com
SIC: 6799 Real estate investors, except property operators
PA: Nrp Holding Co., Inc.
1 Mauchly
Irvine CA 92618
949 583-1000

(P-12333)
NUMERO UNO MARKET
4373 S Vermont Ave, Los Angeles (90037-2411)
PHONE..................323 231-9403
EMP: 83
SALES (corp-wide): 35.2MM **Privately Held**
SIC: 6799 Investors
PA: Numero Uno Market
701 E Jefferson Blvd
Los Angeles CA 90011
323 846-5842

(P-12334)
NUMERO UNO MARKET
9127 S Figueroa St, Los Angeles (90003-3905)
PHONE..................213 381-1734
EMP: 83
SALES (corp-wide): 35.2MM **Privately Held**
SIC: 6799 Investors
PA: Numero Uno Market
701 E Jefferson Blvd
Los Angeles CA 90011
323 846-5842

(P-12335)
OAKTREE HOLDINGS INC
333 S Grand Ave Ste 2800, Los Angeles (90071-1530)
PHONE..................213 830-6300
EMP: 1258 **EST:** 2014
SALES (est): 138.9K **Privately Held**
SIC: 6799 Investors
PA: Oaktree Capital Group Holdings, L.P.
333 S Grand Ave Fl 28
Los Angeles CA 90071

(P-12336)
OCM REAL ESTATE OPPORTUNITIES
333 S Grand Ave Fl 28, Los Angeles (90071-1504)
PHONE..................213 830-6300
EMP: 1258 **EST:** 2014
SALES (est): 224.4K **Privately Held**
SIC: 6799 Investors
PA: Oaktree Capital Group Holdings, L.P.
333 S Grand Ave Fl 28
Los Angeles CA 90071

(P-12337)
P-WAVE HOLDINGS LLC
10877 Wilshire Blvd, Los Angeles (90024-4341)
PHONE..................310 209-3010
Alec Gores,
EMP: 2179 **EST:** 2012
SALES (est): 38.4MM **Privately Held**
SIC: 6799 Investors

(P-12338)
PYRAMID PEAK CORPORATION
450 Nwport Ctr Dr Ste 650, Newport Beach (92660)
PHONE..................949 769-8600
Cindy Ragsdale, *President*
Debbie Hanratty, *Manager*
EMP: 70
SALES (est): 7.9MM **Privately Held**
SIC: 6799 Investors

(P-12339)
R H O CAPITAL PARTNERS INC
525 University Ave # 1350, Palo Alto (94301-1934)
PHONE..................650 463-0300
Mark Leschley, *Principal*
Joshua Ruch, *Partner*
Peter Kalkanis, *CFO*
Kamel Tarazi, *Controller*
Farooq Javed, *Associate*
EMP: 50
SALES (est): 3.3MM **Privately Held**
SIC: 6799 Venture capital companies

(P-12340)
RECURRENT ENRGY DEV HLDNGS LLC (DH)
300 California St Fl 7, San Francisco (94104-1415)
PHONE..................415 675-1500
Mitchell Randall, *President*
Joshua Goldstein, *Vice Pres*
Yumin Liu, *Vice Pres*
Helen Shin, *Vice Pres*
Odessa Cooper, *Admin Sec*
EMP: 150 **EST:** 2009
SALES (est): 178.7K
SALES (corp-wide): 3.4B **Privately Held**
SIC: 6799 Investors
HQ: Recurrent Energy, Llc
300 California St Fl 7
San Francisco CA 94104
415 956-3168

(P-12341)
ROLL PROPERTIES INTL INC
Also Called: Paramount Farms
13646 Highway 33, Lost Hills (93249-9719)
PHONE..................661 797-6500
Bill Bowers, *Manager*
Jay Menon, *Vice Pres*
Alycia Morris, *Executive Asst*
Brent Rogers, *Info Tech Dir*
Robert Misuraca, *Technician*
EMP: 61
SALES (corp-wide): 61.3MM **Privately Held**
WEB: www.roll.com
SIC: 6799 Real estate investors, except property operators
PA: Roll Properties International, Inc.
11444 W Olympic Blvd # 10
Los Angeles CA 90064
310 966-5700

(P-12342)
SBE HOTEL GROUP LLC
8000 Beverly Blvd, Los Angeles (90048-4504)
PHONE..................323 655-8000
Sam Nazarian,
Josh Fluhr, *Vice Pres*
Paulina Yap, *Controller*
Daniel Carillo, *Manager*
EMP: 65
SQ FT: 11,000
SALES (est): 6.2MM
SALES (corp-wide): 23.4MM **Privately Held**
WEB: www.sbehotelgroup.com
SIC: 6799 Venture capital companies
PA: Sbe Entertainment Group, Llc
2535 Las Vegas Blvd S
Los Angeles CA 90036
323 655-8000

(P-12343)
SEQUOIA CAPITAL OPERATIONS LLC
2800 Sand Hill Rd Ste 100, Menlo Park (94025-7079)
PHONE..................650 854-3927
Donald Valentine, *General Ptnr*
Roelof Botha, *General Ptnr*
Doug Leone, *General Ptnr*
Tom McMurray, *General Ptnr*
Thomas Stephenson, *General Ptnr*
EMP: 89
SQ FT: 6,000
SALES (est): 51.9MM **Privately Held**
WEB: www.sequoiacap.com
SIC: 6799 Venture capital companies

(P-12344)
SFI PLEASANTON LLC
260 California St # 1100, San Francisco (94111-4396)
PHONE..................415 395-0960
Deborah Abernathy, *Manager*
EMP: 99
SALES (est): 1.8MM **Privately Held**
SIC: 6799 Investors

(P-12345)
SITUS HOLDINGS LLC
2 Embarcadero Ctr # 1300, San Francisco (94111-3821)
PHONE..................415 374-2820
Steven J Powel, *CEO*
George Wisniewski, *Director*
EMP: 389
SALES (corp-wide): 44MM **Privately Held**
SIC: 6799 6162 Investment clubs; bond & mortgage companies
PA: Situs Holdings, Llc
5065 Westheimer Rd # 700
Houston TX 77056
713 328-4400

(P-12346)
SUNSTONE HOTEL INVESTORS LLC (HQ)
120 Vantis Ste 350, Aliso Viejo (92656-2686)
PHONE..................949 330-4000
Fax: 949 361-4157
Ken Cruse, *CEO*
Robert A Alter, *Ch of Bd*
Jon D Kline, *President*
David Sloan, *President*
Marc A Hoffman, *COO*
EMP: 63
SALES (est): 58.4MM **Privately Held**
WEB: www.sunstonehotels.com
SIC: 6799 7011 Real estate investors, except property operators; hotels & motels
PA: Westbrook Acquisitions, L.L.C.
1370 Ave Of The Americas
New York NY 10019
212 445-0061

(P-12347)
TANO CAPITAL LLC
1 Franklin Pkwy, San Mateo (94403-1906)
PHONE..................650 212-0330
Chuck Johnson, *Director*
Candace Lyche, *Officer*
Peter Dabrowski, *Managing Dir*
Frank Liu, *Managing Dir*
Cfa P Palani, *Managing Dir*
EMP: 50
SALES (est): 5MM **Privately Held**
SIC: 6799 Investors

(P-12348)
TC PROPERTY MGT A CALIFORNI
1224 Cottonwood St Ofc, Woodland (95695-4349)
PHONE..................530 666-5799
Ted Caldwell, *President*
James Olsen, *Vice Pres*
Jim Olsen, *Agent*
EMP: 80 **EST:** 1982
SALES (est): 4.3MM **Privately Held**
SIC: 6799 6531 Real estate investors, except property operators; real estate managers

(P-12349)
TCMI INC (PA)
Also Called: Technology Crossover Ventures
528 Ramona St, Palo Alto (94301-1709)
PHONE..................650 614-8200
Jay Hoag, *President*
Robert Bensky, *General Ptnr*
Christopher Marshall, *General Ptnr*
Richard Kimball, *CEO*
Nari Ansari, *Vice Pres*
EMP: 50 **EST:** 1995
SQ FT: 2,700
SALES (est): 22.7MM **Privately Held**
WEB: www.tcv.com
SIC: 6799 Venture capital companies

(P-12350)
TENEX GREENHOUSE VENTURES LLC
533 Airport Blvd Ste 400, Burlingame (94010-2013)
PHONE..................650 375-7021
Bob Leach,
Timothy Mills, *Managing Prtnr*
Natalie Fay, *Controller*
EMP: 67
SQ FT: 5,000
SALES (est): 3MM **Privately Held**
SIC: 6799 Venture capital companies

(P-12351)
VANTAGEPOINT MANAGEMENT INC (PA)
Also Called: Vantagepoint Capital Partners
1001 Bayhill Dr Ste 300, San Bruno (94066-3061)
PHONE..................650 866-3100
Alan E Salzman, *CEO*
Harold Friedman, *CFO*
Jim Jensen, *Sr Corp Ofcr*
Andrew T Sheehan, *Top Exec*
Jean-David Begin, *Vice Pres*
EMP: 65
SQ FT: 21,166
SALES (est): 11.9MM **Privately Held**
SIC: 6799 Venture capital companies

(P-12352)
WESTAR CAPITAL ASSOC II LLC
949 S Coast Dr, Costa Mesa (92626-7737)
PHONE..................714 481-5160
Fax: 714 481-5166
George Argyros, *Branch Mgr*
John Clark, *VP Human Res*
Keith Bailey, *Manager*
Dale Jabour, *Manager*
EMP: 1184
SALES (corp-wide): 110.4MM **Privately Held**
SIC: 6799 Investors
PA: Westar Capital Associates Ii, Llc
949 S Coast Dr Ste 170
Costa Mesa CA 92626
714 481-5160

(P-12353)
WESTCORE DELTA LLC
Also Called: Westcore Croydon
4435 Estgate Mall Ste 300, San Diego (92121)
P.O. Box 844405, Los Angeles (90084-4405)
PHONE..................858 625-4100
Don Ankeny, *CEO*
Marc Brutten, *Ch of Bd*
EMP: 60
SQ FT: 14,000
SALES (est): 6.6MM **Privately Held**
SIC: 6799 Real estate investors, except property operators

(P-12354)
WESTPORT CAPITAL PARTNERS LLC
2121 Rosecrans Ave # 4325, El Segundo (90245-4744)
PHONE..................310 294-1234
Fax: 310 643-7379
Russel S Bernard, *Branch Mgr*
Marian George, *Assistant VP*
EMP: 62
SALES (corp-wide): 36.2MM **Privately Held**
SIC: 6799 Investors

PRODUCTS & SERVICES SECTION

7011 - Hotels, Motels & Tourist Courts County (P-12379)

PA: Westport Capital Partners Llc
40 Danbury Rd
Wilton CT 06897
203 429-8600

(P-12355)
WNC HOUSING LP
17782 Sky Park Cir, Irvine (92614-6404)
PHONE..................................714 662-5565
Willfred Cooper, *President*
Tom Riha, *CFO*
EMP: 50
SALES (est): 4.4MM **Privately Held**
SIC: 6799 Real estate investors, except property operators

7011 Hotels, Motels & Tourist Courts

(P-12356)
1000 AGUAJITO OP CO LLC
Also Called: Hilton Garden Inn Monterey
1000 Aguajito Rd, Monterey (93940-4801)
PHONE..................................831 373-6141
Jayson Zimmer, *General Mgr*
EMP: 77
SALES (est): 3.2MM **Privately Held**
SIC: 7011 Hotels & motels

(P-12357)
120 SOUTH LOS ANGELES STREET H
Also Called: Kyoto Grand Hotel
120 S Los Angeles St, Los Angeles (90012-3724)
PHONE..................................213 629-1200
Shannon King,
Marvin Love, *Executive*
Joseph Kuhn,
EMP: 99
SALES (est): 4.4MM **Privately Held**
SIC: 7011 Hotels & motels

(P-12358)
1260 BB PROPERTY LLC
Also Called: Four Ssons Rsort Santa Barbara
1260 Channel Dr, Santa Barbara (93108-2805)
PHONE..................................805 969-2261
Isadore Sharp, *Chairman*
J Allen Smith, *President*
David Caffo, *CFO*
Christine Judd, *Chief Mktg Ofcr*
Karen Earp, *General Mgr*
▲ EMP: 500 EST: 1986
SALES (est): 45.6MM **Privately Held**
SIC: 7011 Hotels & motels

(P-12359)
15TH & L INVESTORS LLC
1121 15th St, Sacramento (95814-4011)
PHONE..................................916 267-6805
Anthony R Giannoni, *Mng Member*
Shelly Moranville, *General Mgr*
EMP: 55
SALES (est): 2.2MM **Privately Held**
SIC: 7011 Hotel, franchised

(P-12360)
1835 COLUMBIA STREET LP
Also Called: Porto Vista Hotel
1835 Columbia St, San Diego (92101-2505)
PHONE..................................619 564-3993
Moe Siry,
Greg Keebler, *Executive*
Arnold Ming, *Finance*
Mary Navarro, *Marketing Staff*
Tom McMahan, *Director*
EMP: 60
SALES (est): 4.7MM **Privately Held**
SIC: 7011 Hotels

(P-12361)
425 NORTH POINT STREET LLC
Also Called: Tuscan Inn
101 California St Ste 950, San Francisco (94111-5826)
PHONE..................................800 648-4626
Jan Misch,
EMP: 99
SALES (est): 6MM **Privately Held**
SIC: 7011 Hotels & motels

(P-12362)
4290 EL CAMINO PROPERTIES LP
Also Called: Cabana Hotel
4290 El Camino Real, Palo Alto (94306-4404)
PHONE..................................650 857-0787
Fax: 650 496-1939
Bhupendra B Patel, *Owner*
Tony Balestrieri, *Finance*
John Sesham, *Manager*
EMP: 146
SALES (est): 5.8MM **Privately Held**
SIC: 7011 Hotels & motels

(P-12363)
48123 CA INVESTORS LLC
Also Called: Ventana Inn & Spa
48123 Highway 1, Big Sur (93920-9538)
PHONE..................................831 667-2331
Fax: 831 667-0573
Kent L Colwell, *Mng Member*
Randy Smith, *Vice Pres*
Bruce Card, *Engineer*
Shelly Gaynor, *Business Mgr*
Lisa Sorensen, *Controller*
EMP: 152
SALES (est): 11.6MM **Privately Held**
WEB: www.ventanainn.com
SIC: 7011 5812 Bed & breakfast inn; eating places

(P-12364)
495 GEARY LLC
Also Called: Clift Hotels
495 Geary St, San Francisco (94102-1222)
PHONE..................................415 775-4700
Mary Coller, *Controller*
Alexandra Walterspiel, *General Mgr*
Rachel Grabozi, *Manager*
EMP: 220
SALES (est): 2.7MM
SALES (corp-wide): 219.9MM **Publicly Held**
SIC: 7011 Hotels & motels
PA: Morgans Hotel Group Co.
475 10th Ave Fl 11
New York NY 10018
212 277-4100

(P-12365)
51ST ST & 8TH AVE CORP
Also Called: Loews Coronado Bay Resort
4000 Coronado Bay Rd, Coronado (92118-3290)
PHONE..................................619 424-4000
Fax: 619 424-4400
Johnathan M Tish, *Chairman*
Kim Dopulos, *Associate Dir*
Danielle Lundy, *Admin Asst*
Dennis Coffey, *Info Tech Mgr*
Mellisa Fitzgerald, *Finance*
▲ EMP: 550
SALES (est): 35.9MM **Privately Held**
SIC: 7011 Hotels & motels

(P-12366)
550 FLOWER ST OPERATIONS LLC
Also Called: Standard Hotel, The
550 S Flower St, Los Angeles (90071-2501)
PHONE..................................213 892-8080
Andre Balaz,
Micah Fields, *Executive*
George Taule, *Executive*
George Wu, *Asst Controller*
Mike Sade, *Controller*
EMP: 200
SQ FT: 172,197
SALES (est): 6MM **Privately Held**
WEB: www.standardhotel.com
SIC: 7011 5813 5812 Hotels; drinking places; eating places

(P-12367)
5TH AVENUE PARTNERS LLC
1047 5th Ave, San Diego (92101-5101)
PHONE..................................619 515-3000
Stephen Rebeil,
EMP: 300
SALES (est): 3.4MM **Privately Held**
SIC: 7011 Hotels

(P-12368)
711 HOPE LP
Also Called: Sheraton Los Angeles
711 S Hope St, Los Angeles (90017-3803)
PHONE..................................213 488-3500
Pat Birgham, *Partner*
Eric Guiterrez, *MIS Mgr*
Laura Alvarez, *Human Res Dir*
Patrick Edmonds, *Manager*
EMP: 250
SALES (est): 7.4MM **Privately Held**
SIC: 7011 Hotels & motels

(P-12369)
8110 AERO HOLDING LLC
Also Called: Sheraton
8110 Aero Dr, San Diego (92123-1715)
PHONE..................................858 277-8888
Lucy Burni, *Mng Member*
Nabih Geha, *Principal*
Tes Tanti, *Controller*
Luci Burni, *Manager*
EMP: 200
SALES (est): 14.5MM **Privately Held**
WEB: www.sheratonfourpointshotel.com
SIC: 7011 5813 5812 Hotels & motels; drinking places; eating places

(P-12370)
901 WEST OLYMPIC BLVD LP
Also Called: Courtyard & Residence Inn La
901 W Olympic Blvd, Los Angeles (90015-1327)
PHONE..................................347 992-5707
Greg Steinhauer, *Partner*
Homer Williams, *Partner*
Erik Palmer, *General Mgr*
EMP: 110
SQ FT: 286,000
SALES (est): 11.5MM **Privately Held**
SIC: 7011 Hotels & motels

(P-12371)
A J ESPRIT
Also Called: Comfort Inn
5102 N Harbor Dr, San Diego (92106-2356)
PHONE..................................619 223-8171
A J Esprit, *Manager*
EMP: 50
SALES (est): 2.8MM **Privately Held**
WEB: www.comfortinnattheharbor.com
SIC: 7011 Hotels & motels

(P-12372)
ACCOR BUS & LEISURE N AMER INC
Also Called: Hotel Sofitel
223 Twin Dolphin Dr, Redwood City (94065-1414)
PHONE..................................650 598-9000
Fax: 650 598-9383
John Hutar, *General Mgr*
Philippe Van Der Borght, *Finance*
Gabriela Salazar, *Human Res Mgr*
Adrienn Haidinger, *Marketing Staff*
Chris Wilcox, *Director*
EMP: 200
SALES (corp-wide): 946.2MM **Privately Held**
SIC: 7011 Hotels & motels
HQ: Accor Business And Leisure North America, Inc.
245 Park Ave
New York NY 10167
972 360-9000

(P-12373)
ACCOR CORP
Also Called: Sofitel Los Angeles
8555 Beverly Blvd, Los Angeles (90048-3303)
PHONE..................................310 278-5444
Fax: 310 657-2816
Gunter Zweimuller, *Manager*
Magda Matuskiva, *Human Resources*
EMP: 200
SQ FT: 380,000
SALES (est): 7.7MM
SALES (corp-wide): 946.2MM **Privately Held**
SIC: 7011 5812 Hotels; eating places
PA: Accorhotels
82 Rue Henry Farman
Issy Les Moulineaux 92130

(P-12374)
AGUA CLNTE BAND CHILLA INDIANS
Also Called: Agua Caliente Casino & Resort
32250 Bob Hope Dr, Rancho Mirage (92270-2704)
PHONE..................................760 321-2000
Ken Kettler, *Branch Mgr*
Karen Welmas, *Treasurer*
Cordis Gilliam, *Technology*
Joshua Estrella, *Human Resources*
Kathleen Garrity, *Adv Dir*
EMP: 1000
SALES (corp-wide): 182MM **Privately Held**
WEB: www.hotwatercasino.com
SIC: 7011 Casino hotel
PA: Agua Caliente Band Of Cahuilla Indians
5401 Dinah Shore Dr
Palm Springs CA 92264
760 699-6800

(P-12375)
AGUA CLNTE BAND CHILLA INDIANS
Also Called: Spa Resort Casino
401 E Amado Rd, Palm Springs (92262-6403)
PHONE..................................800 854-1279
Ramona Grinager, *Principal*
Curtis Johnson, *Info Tech Dir*
Lexie Felicidario, *Sales Staff*
Savannah Cook, *Manager*
Greg Rogers, *Manager*
EMP: 1000
SALES (corp-wide): 202.3MM **Privately Held**
SIC: 7011 7991 Casino hotel; spas
PA: Agua Caliente Band Of Cahuilla Indians
5401 Dinah Shore Dr
Palm Springs CA 92264
760 699-6800

(P-12376)
AIRPORT CENTURY INN
Also Called: Travelodge
5547 W Century Blvd, Los Angeles (90045-5913)
PHONE..................................310 649-4000
Lance Libscomb, *General Mgr*
Lance Lipscomb, *General Mgr*
EMP: 59
SQ FT: 60,000
SALES (est): 3.4MM **Privately Held**
WEB: www.travelodgelax.com
SIC: 7011 6519 Hotels & motels; real property lessors

(P-12377)
AL ANWA USA INCORPORATED
Also Called: Marina International Hotel
4200 Admiralty Way, Marina Del Rey (90292-5422)
PHONE..................................310 301-2000
Mohammed Khan, *Manager*
EMP: 120
SALES (corp-wide): 6MM **Privately Held**
WEB: www.marinaintlhotel.com
SIC: 7011 Hotels
PA: Al Anwa Usa Incorporated
2200 Nw 50th St Ste 240
Oklahoma City OK

(P-12378)
ALADDIN SONORA MOTOR INN
14260 Mono Way, Sonora (95370-8654)
PHONE..................................209 533-4971
Fax: 209 532-1522
David E Kalash, *Owner*
EMP: 50
SALES (est): 1.2MM **Privately Held**
WEB: www.aladdininn.com
SIC: 7011 5812 Motor inn; eating places

(P-12379)
ALBION RIVER INN INCORPORATED
3790 N Highway 1, Albion (95410-9781)
P.O. Box 100 (95410-0100)
PHONE..................................707 937-1919
Fax: 707 937-2604
Peter Wells, *President*

7011 - Hotels, Motels & Tourist Courts County (P-12380)

Flurry Healy, Vice Pres
Debbie Desmond, Admin Asst
EMP: 65 EST: 1979
SQ FT: 15,000
SALES (est): 4.9MM Privately Held
WEB: www.albionriverinn.com
SIC: 7011 5812 Resort hotel; eating places

(P-12380)
ALLIANCE RVRSIDE HSPTALITY LLC
Also Called: Courtyard By Mrriott Riverside
21520 Yorba Linda Blvd, Yorba Linda (92887-3762)
PHONE..................949 229-3168
Chiangsun Wang, Mng Member
Alice Hsu, Controller
EMP: 50
SALES: 3.8MM Privately Held
SIC: 7011 Hotels & motels; resort hotel, franchised

(P-12381)
ALOFT ONTARIO-RANCHO CUCAMONGA
Also Called: Ihr Grnbuck Rncho Ccmnga Ventr
10480 4th St, Rancho Cucamonga (91730-5893)
PHONE..................909 484-2018
Fax: 909 484-6491
Cristina Riveroll, Owner
Yani Duran, Director
EMP: 55
SALES (est): 3.3MM Privately Held
SIC: 7011 Hotels & motels

(P-12382)
ALPINE MEADOWS SKI AREA
Also Called: Alpine Meadows Ski Resort
2600 Alpine Meadows Rd, Alpine Meadows (96146-9854)
PHONE..................530 583-4232
Fax: 530 583-0963
John Cumming, President
Richard Defvaux, CFO
Richard N Heywood, CFO
Rick D Vaux, CFO
Rick N Vaux, CFO
EMP: 60
SQ FT: 30,000
SALES (est): 5.7MM
SALES (corp-wide): 243.3MM Privately Held
WEB: www.skialpine.com
SIC: 7011 Ski lodge
HQ: The Squaw Valley Development Company
1960 Squaw Valley Rd
Olympic Valley CA 96146
530 583-6985

(P-12383)
AMERICAN PROPERTY MANAGEMENT
Also Called: Pleasanton Hilton Hotel
7050 Johnson Dr, Pleasanton (94588-3328)
PHONE..................925 463-8000
Fax: 925 463-0649
Han-Ching Lin, President
Hui-Ying Chou, Vice Pres
Ana Carter, Sales Dir
EMP: 190
SQ FT: 191,112
SALES (est): 10.1MM Privately Held
SIC: 7011 5813 5812 Hotels & motels; drinking places; eating places

(P-12384)
AMERICAN PRPRTY-MNAGEMENT CORP
Also Called: U. S. Grant Hotel
326 Broadway, San Diego (92101-4812)
PHONE..................619 232-3121
Fax: 619 239-9517
John Gallegon, Manager
Rita Baca, Opers Mgr
EMP: 200
SALES (corp-wide): 129.4MM Privately Held
WEB: www.americanpropertymanagement-corp.com
SIC: 7011 Hotels & motels

PA: American Property-Management Corporation
8910 University Center Ln # 100
San Diego CA 92122
858 964-5500

(P-12385)
AMSTAR/DAVIDSON ROBLES LLC
Also Called: Hilton Pasadena
168 S Los Robles Ave, Pasadena (91101-2430)
PHONE..................626 577-1000
Fax: 626 584-3127
Larry Mills, Manager
Alma Quintero, Human Res Mgr
Kevin Busch, Marketing Staff
EMP: 99
SQ FT: 199,278
SALES (est): 6.2MM Privately Held
SIC: 7011 Hotels & motels

(P-12386)
ANAHEIM CA LLC
Also Called: Doubltree Ht Anhim-Orange Cnty
100 The City Dr S, Orange (92868-3204)
PHONE..................714 634-4500
Denise Pflum, Manager
Louis Ederes, General Mgr
Jimmy Abadeir, Engineer
Feliza Manzano, Human Res Mgr
Maggie Giddens, Director
EMP: 65
SALES (est): 5.4MM Privately Held
SIC: 7011 Hotels & motels

(P-12387)
ANAHEIM HOTEL LLC
Also Called: Sheraton Pk Ht At Anheim Rsort
1855 S Harbor Blvd, Anaheim (92802-3509)
PHONE..................714 750-1811
Russ Cox, Manager
Your Catering, Comp Spec
EMP: 200
SALES (corp-wide): 7MM Privately Held
SIC: 7011 Hotels & motels
PA: Anaheim Hotel, Llc
575 E Parkcntr Blvd 500
Boise ID 83706
208 343-3439

(P-12388)
ANAHEIM PARK HOTEL
Also Called: Wyndham Hotels & Resorts
222 W Houston Ave, Fullerton (92832-3453)
PHONE..................714 992-1700
Fax: 714 447-3269
Fred Menoufi, Partner
Abdul El Mekligiange, General Mgr
Joe Nolasco, Chief Engr
John Colaco, Accounting Mgr
B Kharwa, Controller
EMP: 101
SQ FT: 174,123
SALES (est): 1.8MM Privately Held
SIC: 7011 YWCA/YWHA hotel

(P-12389)
ANAHEIM PARK INN AND CAMELOT
1520 S Harbor Blvd, Anaheim (92802-2312)
PHONE..................714 635-7275
Fax: 714 635-7276
Suren Badalian, Owner
EMP: 75
SALES (est): 1.6MM Privately Held
WEB: www.bei-hotels.com
SIC: 7011 Hotels & motels

(P-12390)
ANAHEIM PLAZA HOTEL INC
Also Called: Anaheim Plaza Hotel & Suites
1700 S Harbor Blvd, Anaheim (92802-2316)
PHONE..................714 772-5900
Fax: 714 491-8215
Saroj Patel, CEO
Rajni Patel, Vice Pres
Mark Siddiqi, General Mgr
Mark Siddiqui, General Mgr
Evelyn Aspiritu, Human Res Mgr
EMP: 150
SQ FT: 5,600

SALES (est): 4.9MM Privately Held
WEB: www.anaheimplazahotel.com
SIC: 7011 5812 5813 Motels; eating places; drinking places

(P-12391)
ANDERSEN HOTELS INC
Also Called: Hotel Laguna
425 S Coast Hwy, Laguna Beach (92651-2403)
PHONE..................949 494-1151
Fax: 949 497-2163
Claes Andersen, President
Georgia Andersen, Vice Pres
Hannie Darwazeh, Director
Damon Nicholson, Manager
EMP: 80
SQ FT: 40,000
SALES (est): 4.7MM Privately Held
WEB: www.hotellaguna.com
SIC: 7011 5812 5813 Hotels; American restaurant; bar (drinking places)

(P-12392)
APPLE EGHT HOSPITALITY MGT INC
Also Called: Courtyard Cypress
5865 Katella Ave, Cypress (90630-5008)
PHONE..................714 827-1010
Gary Liss, Branch Mgr
Amos Lopez, Director
EMP: 65
SALES (corp-wide): 898.3MM Privately Held
WEB: www.dimdev.com
SIC: 7011 Hotels & motels
HQ: Apple Eight Hospitality Management, Inc.
814 E Main St
Richmond VA 23219

(P-12393)
APPLE HOSPITALITY REIT INC
Also Called: Hilton Garden Inn Sacremento
2540 Venture Oaks Way, Sacramento (95833-3200)
PHONE..................916 568-5400
Jeff Irving, General Mgr
Eduardo Franco, Chief Engr
EMP: 55 EST: 2007
SALES (est): 460.5K Privately Held
SIC: 7011 Hotels & motels

(P-12394)
APPLE INNS INC
68 Monarch Bay Dr, San Leandro (94577-6427)
PHONE..................510 895-1311
Fax: 510 483-4078
Audrey Velasquez, Branch Mgr
Peter Schultz, President
David Miller, Vice Pres
Victoria Aquino, Sales Mgr
Janise Dawson, Sales Staff
EMP: 50
SALES (est): 2.7MM Privately Held
WEB: www.sanleandromarinainn.com
SIC: 7011 Hotels & motels

(P-12395)
ARC HOSP PORTFOLIO II NTC TRS
Also Called: Courtyard San Diego Carlsbad
5835 Owens Ave, Carlsbad (92008-6562)
PHONE..................760 431-9399
Fax: 760 431-9809
Minda Zoloth, Branch Mgr
Patricia Santini, Admin Sec
EMP: 50 Publicly Held
SIC: 7011 Hotels & motels
HQ: Arc Hospitality Portfolio Ii Ntc Trs, Lp
106 York Rd
Jenkintown PA

(P-12396)
ARC HOSPITALITY PORTFOLIO
Also Called: Residence Inn La Lax El Segndo
2135 E El Segundo Blvd, El Segundo (90245-4503)
PHONE..................310 333-0888
EMP: 50 Publicly Held
SIC: 7011 Hotels & motels

HQ: Arc Hospitality Portfolio I Ntc Trs, Lp
106 York Rd
Jenkintown PA
-

(P-12397)
ART PICCADILLY SHAW LLC
Also Called: Piccadilly Inn Airport
5115 E Mckinley Ave, Fresno (93727-2033)
PHONE..................559 375-7760
Kathy Bell, Branch Mgr
EMP: 100
SALES (corp-wide): 12.1MM Privately Held
SIC: 7011 5813 5812 Hotels; drinking places; eating places
PA: Art Piccadilly Shaw Llc
2305 W Shaw Ave
Fresno CA 93711
559 348-5520

(P-12398)
ART PICCADILLY SHAW LLC
Piccadilly Inn-University
4961 N Cedar Ave, Fresno (93726-1062)
PHONE..................559 224-4200
Fax: 559 226-1387
Theresa Cross, Branch Mgr
EMP: 120
SALES (corp-wide): 12.1MM Privately Held
SIC: 7011 Motels
PA: Art Piccadilly Shaw Llc
2305 W Shaw Ave
Fresno CA 93711
559 348-5520

(P-12399)
ATASCADERO HOTEL PARTNERS LLC
900 El Camino Real, Atascadero (93422-1424)
PHONE..................805 462-3500
Elizabeth Eberly, Accounting Mgr
EMP: 52
SALES (est): 189.1K Privately Held
SIC: 7011 Hotels

(P-12400)
ATRIUM HOTELS LP
Also Called: Holiday Inn Bay Bridge
1800 Powell St, Oakland (94608-1808)
PHONE..................510 658-9300
Pat Goss, Manager
Lisa Scott, Purch Dir
EMP: 300
SALES (corp-wide): 593MM Privately Held
WEB: www.embassysuitesoutdoorworld.com
SIC: 7011 5813 5812 7991 Hotels & motels; motels; drinking places; eating places; physical fitness facilities
PA: Tucson Hotels Lp
2711 Centerville Rd # 400
Wilmington DE 19808
678 830-2438

(P-12401)
ATRIUM HOTELS LP
Also Called: Holiday Inn
300 J St, Sacramento (95814-2210)
PHONE..................916 446-0100
Fax: 916 446-0100
Liz Tavernese, Manager
Elizabeth Tavernese, General Mgr
EMP: 165
SALES (corp-wide): 593MM Privately Held
WEB: www.holidayinnportland.com
SIC: 7011 5812 5813 Hotels & motels; restaurant, family: independent; bar (drinking places)
PA: Tucson Hotels Lp
2711 Centerville Rd # 400
Wilmington DE 19808
678 830-2438

(P-12402)
ATRIUM HOTELS LP
Also Called: Holiday Inn Scp
300 J St, Sacramento (95814-2210)
PHONE..................916 446-0100
Liz Tavernese, General Mgr
Lorraine Buckley, Human Res Mgr
Ruthann Haskell, Purch Dir

PRODUCTS & SERVICES SECTION
7011 - Hotels, Motels & Tourist Courts County (P-12423)

EMP: 153
SALES (corp-wide): 593MM **Privately Held**
SIC: 7011 Hotels & motels
PA: Tucson Hotels Lp
2711 Centerville Rd # 400
Wilmington DE 19808
678 830-2438

(P-12403)
ATRIUM HOTELS LP
Also Called: Embassy Stes Monterey Bay Htl
1441 Canyon Del Rey Blvd, Seaside (93955-4729)
PHONE 831 393-1115
Fax: 831 393-1113
Rick Weichert, *General Mgr*
Wright Jim, *Sales Executive*
Erika Boatman, *Manager*
Rob Lettman, *Manager*
EMP: 156
SALES (corp-wide): 593MM **Privately Held**
WEB: www.holidayinnportland.com
SIC: 7011 5813 5812 Hotels & motels; drinking places; eating places
PA: Tucson Hotels Lp
2711 Centerville Rd # 400
Wilmington DE 19808
678 830-2438

(P-12404)
ATRIUM PLAZA LLC
1770 S Amphlett Blvd, San Mateo (94402-2708)
PHONE 650 653-6000
Ron Anderhan,
Stephanie Bauer, *General Mgr*
Mario Urroz, *Data Proc Exec*
Phil Brenzenski, *Manager*
Neil Korsgaard, *Manager*
EMP: 208
SALES (est): 4.2MM **Privately Held**
SIC: 7011 Hotels & motels

(P-12405)
AV COURTYARD SD SPECTRUM
Also Called: San Diego Courtyard Central
8651 Spectrum Center Blvd, San Diego (92123-1489)
PHONE 858 573-0700
Fax: 858 573-9818
Matthew Spencer, *General Mgr*
Alex Wiley, *COO*
EMP: 87
SALES (est): 1.8MM **Privately Held**
SIC: 7011 Hotels

(P-12406)
AVIARA FSRC ASSOCIATES LIMITED
7100 Aviara Resort Dr, Carlsbad (92011-4908)
PHONE 760 603-6800
Robert Cima, *General Mgr*
Aviara Resort Club, *General Ptnr*
Hef IV LLC, *General Ptnr*
EMP: 1200 **EST:** 1995
SALES (est): 12.7MM
SALES (corp-wide): 64.8MM **Privately Held**
SIC: 7011 Resort hotel
PA: Aviara Resort Associates Limited Partnership, A California Limited Partnership
7100 Aviara Resort Dr
Carlsbad CA 92011
760 448-1234

(P-12407)
AVIARA RESORT ASSOCIATES (PA)
Also Called: Park Hyatt Aviara Resort
7100 Aviara Resort Dr, Carlsbad (92011-4908)
PHONE 760 448-1234
Maritz Wolff, *General Ptnr*
Jenny Simonson, *Accountant*
EMP: 900
SALES (est): 64.8MM **Privately Held**
SIC: 7011 Hotels & motels

(P-12408)
AWH BURBANK HOTEL LLC
Also Called: Marriott Burbank
2500 N Hollywood Way, Burbank (91505-1019)
PHONE 813 843-6000
William Deforrest, *CEO*
Chad Cooley, *Vice Pres*
Russell Flicker, *Vice Pres*
Bernard Michael, *Vice Pres*
Jonathan Rosenfeld, *Vice Pres*
EMP: 176 **EST:** 2014
SALES (est): 5.7MM **Privately Held**
SIC: 7011 Hotels & motels

(P-12409)
AYRES GROUP (PA)
355 Bristol St, Costa Mesa (92626-7922)
PHONE 714 540-6060
Bruce F Ayres, *CEO*
Jana Beekman, *Project Mgr*
Gregg Kleminsky, *Controller*
Tom Asnon, *Human Res Dir*
Deanna Garcia, *Human Res Mgr*
EMP: 54
SALES (est): 43.4MM **Privately Held**
SIC: 7011 Hotels & motels

(P-12410)
B H R OPERATIONS LLC
Also Called: Crown Plaza
777 Bellew Dr, Milpitas (95035-7900)
PHONE 408 321-9500
Roy Escobar, *Mng Member*
Winnie Kwok, *General Mgr*
EMP: 100
SQ FT: 250,000
SALES (est): 1.6MM
SALES (corp-wide): 1.8B **Privately Held**
WEB: www.bristolhotels.com
SIC: 7011 Motel, franchised
HQ: Bristol Hotel & Resorts Inc.
3 Ravinia Dr Ste 100
Atlanta GA 30346
770 604-2000

(P-12411)
B S A PARTNERS
Also Called: Residence Inn By Marriott
14419 Firestone Blvd, La Mirada (90638-5912)
PHONE 714 523-2800
Fax: 714 522-5884
Jim Gilbert, *General Mgr*
William Swank, *General Ptnr*
William E Swank Jr, *General Ptnr*
EMP: 80
SQ FT: 102,943
SALES (est): 3.7MM **Privately Held**
SIC: 7011 Hotels & motels

(P-12412)
BADALIAN ENTERPRISES INC
Also Called: Park Inn
1540 S Harbor Blvd, Anaheim (92802-2312)
PHONE 714 635-4082
Fax: 714 635-1535
Ernest Badalian, *President*
Bonny Harutunian, *Corp Secy*
Greg Badalian, *Vice Pres*
Suren Badalian, *Vice Pres*
Ann Mousner, *Vice Pres*
EMP: 90
SQ FT: 55,000
SALES (est): 6.7MM **Privately Held**
SIC: 7011 Hotels & motels

(P-12413)
BAKERSFIELD RODEWAY INN INC
Also Called: Regency Inn
818 Real Rd, Bakersfield (93309-1002)
PHONE 661 324-6666
Fax: 661 324-6670
Robert King, *President*
EMP: 135
SQ FT: 40,000
SALES (est): 1.5MM **Privately Held**
SIC: 7011 5812 5813 7933 Motels; eating places; cocktail lounge; bowling centers

(P-12414)
BALDWIN HOSPITALITY LLC
Also Called: Courtyard By Marriott
14635 Baldwin Ave, Baldwin Park (91706-1739)
PHONE 626 962-6000
Fax: 626 962-6214
Lina Mita, *Branch Mgr*
Henry Zamora, *General Mgr*
Kathy Vicario, *Financial Exec*
EMP: 80
SQ FT: 148,187
SALES (corp-wide): 12.2MM **Privately Held**
SIC: 7011 Hotels & motels
PA: Baldwin Hospitality Llc
411 E Huntington Dr # 305
Arcadia CA 91006
626 446-2988

(P-12415)
BANEY CORPORATION
Also Called: Oxford Suites Chico
2035 Business Ln, Chico (95928-7628)
PHONE 530 899-9090
Chris Coder, *Manager*
Christopher B Coder, *General Mgr*
Jason Olivares, *General Mgr*
Katie Marskey, *Sales Dir*
Nicole Clever, *Assistant*
EMP: 52
SALES (corp-wide): 50.4MM **Privately Held**
WEB: www.oxfordsuites.com
SIC: 7011 Hotels
PA: Baney Corporation
475 Ne Bellevue Dr # 210
Bend OR 97701
541 382-2188

(P-12416)
BARONA RESORT & CASINO
1932 Wildcat Canyon Rd, Lakeside (92040-1553)
PHONE 619 443-2300
Fax: 619 443-1714
Dean Allen, *Senior VP*
Nick Dillon, *Exec VP*
Troy Simpson, *Exec VP*
Linda Devine, *Senior VP*
Linda Jordan, *Senior VP*
EMP: 3500
SALES (est): 118.6MM **Privately Held**
WEB: www.barona.com
SIC: 7011 Resort hotel; casino hotel

(P-12417)
BARTELL HOTELS
Also Called: Humphreys Half Moon Inn
2303 Shelter Island Dr, San Diego (92106-3109)
PHONE 619 224-3411
Fax: 619 224-3478
Sergio Davies, *Manager*
Brandon Knitter, *Info Tech Dir*
Dana Irby, *Sales Dir*
Sarah Stinson, *Sales Staff*
Jody Gilbert, *Manager*
EMP: 200
SALES (corp-wide): 75.9MM **Privately Held**
WEB: www.holinnbayside.com
SIC: 7011 5812 5813 Motels; eating places; cocktail lounge
PA: Bartell Hotels
4875 N Harbor Dr
San Diego CA 92106
619 224-1556

(P-12418)
BARTELL HOTELS
1710 W Mission Bay Dr, San Diego (92109-7810)
PHONE 619 222-6440
Kevin Konopasek, *General Mgr*
EMP: 200
SALES (corp-wide): 75.9MM **Privately Held**
WEB: www.holinnbayside.com
SIC: 7011 4493 5812 Hotels; marinas; eating places
PA: Bartell Hotels
4875 N Harbor Dr
San Diego CA 92106
619 224-1556

(P-12419)
BARTELL HOTELS
Also Called: Pacific Terrace
610 Diamond St, San Diego (92109-2444)
PHONE 858 581-3500
Fax: 858 274-3341
Bob Kingery, *Branch Mgr*
Julie Greb, *Senior VP*
Leeann Bockmier, *Executive*
Jen Watkins, *Director*
EMP: 50
SALES (corp-wide): 75.9MM **Privately Held**
SIC: 7011 Hotels & motels
PA: Bartell Hotels
4875 N Harbor Dr
San Diego CA 92106
619 224-1556

(P-12420)
BARTELL HOTELS
Also Called: Best Western Island Palms
2051 Shelter Island Dr, San Diego (92106-3105)
PHONE 619 222-0561
Fax: 619 222-9760
Jim Finnegan, *Manager*
Andrea Davis, *Sales Staff*
EMP: 70
SQ FT: 56,500
SALES (corp-wide): 75.9MM **Privately Held**
WEB: www.holinnbayside.com
SIC: 7011 Hotels & motels
PA: Bartell Hotels
4875 N Harbor Dr
San Diego CA 92106
619 224-1556

(P-12421)
BARTELL HOTELS
Also Called: Sheraton
3299 Holiday Ct, La Jolla (92037-1830)
PHONE 858 453-5500
Fax: 858 453-9909
Craig Reber, *Owner*
Robert Hillborne, *COO*
Garry Grace, *Vice Pres*
Mark Kuper, *Sales Mgr*
EMP: 81
SQ FT: 68,159
SALES (corp-wide): 75.9MM **Privately Held**
WEB: www.holinnbayside.com
SIC: 7011 5812 Hotels & motels; eating places
PA: Bartell Hotels
4875 N Harbor Dr
San Diego CA 92106
619 224-1556

(P-12422)
BASSLAKE LLC
39255 Marina Dr, Bass Lake (93604)
P.O. Box 90 (93604-0090)
PHONE 559 642-3121
Kyu Sun Choe, *Principal*
Sun Wha Choe, *Principal*
EMP: 99
SALES (est): 984.6K **Privately Held**
SIC: 7011 Resort hotel

(P-12423)
BAVARIAN LION COMPANY CAL (PA)
Also Called: Flamingo Resort Hotel
2777 4th St, Santa Rosa (95405-4795)
PHONE 707 545-8530
Fax: 707 526-1429
Pierre Ehret, *President*
Drew Stegner, *Executive Asst*
Deborah Simon, *Sales Mgr*
Phil Krohn, *Director*
Tony Pace, *Manager*
EMP: 200 **EST:** 1976
SQ FT: 32,000
SALES (est): 19.4MM **Privately Held**
WEB: www.flamingohotel.com
SIC: 7011 7991 Resort hotel; health club

7011 - Hotels, Motels & Tourist Courts County (P-12424)

(P-12424)
BAY CLUB HOTEL AND MARINA A C
Also Called: The Bay Club Hotel and Marina
2131 Shelter Island Dr, San Diego (92106-3106)
PHONE...................................619 222-0314
Fax: 619 225-1604
Frank Hope, *Partner*
Bob Collins, *Partner*
Chuck Hope, *Partner*
Ed Malone, *Partner*
Michael Ardelt, *General Mgr*
EMP: 55
SQ FT: 200,000
SALES (est): 5.2MM **Privately Held**
WEB: www.bayclubhotel.com
SIC: **7011** 6512 5812 5813 Hotels; lessors of piers, docks, associated buildings & facilities; American restaurant; bars & lounges

(P-12425)
BAY ROSIE HOTEL LLP
Also Called: Hilton
1775 E Mission Bay Dr, San Diego (92109-6801)
PHONE...................................619 276-4010
Fax: 619 275-7973
Greg Fracassa, *Mng Member*
Joe Pasint, *Administration*
Bill Kern, *Info Tech Mgr*
Wil Purvis, *Info Tech Mgr*
Kimberlee Guarino, *Human Res Dir*
EMP: 360
SALES (est): 22.3MM **Privately Held**
SIC: **7011** 5812 5947 Hotels & motels; eating places; gift, novelty & souvenir shop

(P-12426)
BAYVIEW PROPERTIES INC
Also Called: Best Western
2600 Sand Dunes Dr, Monterey (93940-3838)
PHONE...................................831 655-7650
Fax: 831 655-7657
Allison Nord, *Manager*
Valerie T Arveson, *Director*
EMP: 65
SALES (corp-wide): 9MM **Privately Held**
WEB: www.montereybeachhotel.com
SIC: **7011** Hotels & motels
PA: Bayview Properties Inc
2600 Sand Dunes Dr
Monterey CA 93940
831 394-3321

(P-12427)
BAYVIEW PROPERTIES INC
Also Called: Carmel Mission Inn
3665 Rio Rd, Carmel (93923-8609)
PHONE...................................831 624-1841
John Elford, *Manager*
EMP: 65
SQ FT: 40,000
SALES (corp-wide): 9MM **Privately Held**
WEB: www.montereybeachhotel.com
SIC: **7011** Motel, franchised
PA: Bayview Properties Inc
2600 Sand Dunes Dr
Monterey CA 93940
831 394-3321

(P-12428)
BCRA RESORT SERVICES INC
Also Called: Bacara Resorts and Spa
8301 Hollister Ave, Santa Barbara (93117-2474)
PHONE...................................805 571-3176
Fax: 805 968-1800
Patrick K Fox, *CEO*
B J Hoppe, *President*
David Brown, *Exec Dir*
Kathleen Cochran, *General Mgr*
Thomas Humphrey, *General Mgr*
EMP: 150
SALES (est): 19.2MM **Privately Held**
SIC: **7011** Hotels
PA: The Adco Group Inc
450 Park Ave Fl 3
New York NY 10022
212 848-0200

(P-12429)
BEACH MOTEL PARTNERS LTD
Also Called: Harbor View Inn
28 W Cabrillo Blvd, Santa Barbara (93101-3504)
PHONE...................................800 755-0222
Fax: 805 963-7967
Antonio R Romasanta, *Partner*
Birgit Romasanta, *Partner*
Silvie Loeback, *Executive*
Irma Singer, *Accounting Mgr*
Mark Romasanta, *Manager*
EMP: 60 EST: 1983
SQ FT: 40,000
SALES (est): 5.8MM **Privately Held**
SIC: **7011** Hotels & motels

(P-12430)
BEAR RIVER CASINO
Also Called: Bear River Casino Hotel
11 Bear Paws Way, Loleta (95551-9684)
PHONE...................................707 733-9644
Fax: 707 733-9611
John McGinnis, *Executive Asst*
Jesse Orr, *Technology*
Jesse Reeves, *Technical Staff*
Craig Morey, *Mktg Dir*
Ashley Moore, *Asst Director*
EMP: 286
SALES (corp-wide): 50MM **Privately Held**
SIC: **7011** Casino hotel
PA: Bear River Casino
27 Bear River Dr
Loleta CA 95551
707 733-9644

(P-12431)
BEHRINGER HARVARD WILSHIRE
10740 Wilshire Blvd, Los Angeles (90024-4493)
PHONE...................................310 475-8711
John Dupont, *Partner*
Ravi Sikand, *Controller*
EMP: 99
SALES (est): 488.1K **Privately Held**
SIC: **7011** 6531 Hotels & motels; real estate agents & managers

(P-12432)
BEHRINGER HARVARD WILSHIRE BLV
Also Called: Hotel Palomar
10740 Wilshire Blvd, Los Angeles (90024-4493)
PHONE...................................310 475-8711
Ravi Sikand, *Partner*
Peter Moore, *Officer*
Matthew Yoakum, *Sales Executive*
EMP: 99
SALES (est): 7.7MM **Privately Held**
SIC: **7011** 6531 Hotels & motels; real estate agents & managers

(P-12433)
BELMONT CORPORATION
Also Called: Best Western
901 Park Ave, South Lake Tahoe (96150-6938)
PHONE...................................530 542-1101
Fax: 530 542-1714
Wilson Williford, *President*
EMP: 60
SALES (est): 3.5MM **Privately Held**
WEB: www.stationhouseinn.com
SIC: **7011** 5012 Hotels & motels; automobiles & other motor vehicles

(P-12434)
BELVEDERE HOTEL PARTNERSHIP
Also Called: Peninsula Beverly Hill's
9882 Santa Monica Blvd, Beverly Hills (90212-1605)
PHONE...................................310 551-2888
Ali Kasikci, *Manager*
Gareth Roberts, *Manager*
EMP: 442
SALES (corp-wide): 15.1MM **Privately Held**
WEB: www.patandmelody.com
SIC: **7011** 6512 5813 5812 Hotels & motels; nonresidential building operators; drinking places; eating places

PA: The Belvedere Hotel Partnership
421 N Beverly Dr Ste 350
Beverly Hills CA 90210
310 275-1001

(P-12435)
BELVEDERE PARTNERSHIP
Also Called: Peninsula Beverly Hills, The
9882 Santa Monica Blvd, Beverly Hills (90212-1605)
PHONE...................................310 551-2888
Fax: 310 788-2319
Robert Zarnegan, *President*
Leslie Mackillop, *Vice Pres*
Albert Rothman, *General Mgr*
Scott Berger, *Admin Asst*
Rossana Nagat, *Auditor*
EMP: 400
SALES (est): 34MM **Privately Held**
SIC: **7011** Bed & breakfast inn

(P-12436)
BERESFORD CORPORATION
Also Called: Beresford Arms, The
635 Sutter St, San Francisco (94102-1017)
PHONE...................................415 673-9900
Fax: 415 474-0449
Richard Osborn, *Branch Mgr*
EMP: 75
SALES (corp-wide): 5.9MM **Privately Held**
WEB: www.beresford.com
SIC: **7011** Hotels & motels
PA: Beresford Corporation
582 Market St Ste 912
San Francisco CA 94104
415 981-7386

(P-12437)
BEST WESTERN HILLTOP INN
2300 Hilltop Dr, Redding (96002-0508)
PHONE...................................530 221-6100
Fax: 530 221-2867
Ed Rullman,
Steve Gaines, *General Ptnr*
Steven Wahrlich, *General Ptnr*
Tracy Wahrlich, *General Ptnr*
Georgia Hurley, *Sales Staff*
EMP: 50
SQ FT: 10,000
SALES (est): 2.5MM **Privately Held**
WEB: www.thehilltopinn.com
SIC: **7011** 5812 5813 Hotels & motels; eating places; drinking places

(P-12438)
BEST WESTERN HOTEL TOMO
1800 Sutter St, San Francisco (94115-3220)
PHONE...................................415 921-4000
Fax: 415 563-1278
Sean Salera, *CFO*
EMP: 50 EST: 2007
SALES (est): 1.3MM
SALES (corp-wide): 5.4MM **Privately Held**
SIC: **7011** Hotels & motels
PA: Khp Iii Sf Sutter Llc
1800 Sutter St
San Francisco CA 94115
415 921-4000

(P-12439)
BEST WESTERN INTERNATIONAL INC
805 S Kaweah Ave, Exeter (93221-9361)
PHONE...................................559 592-8118
Fax: 559 592-5226
Neil Patel, *Manager*
EMP: 80
SALES (corp-wide): 328.7MM **Privately Held**
SIC: **7011** Hotels & motels
PA: Best Western International, Inc.
6201 N 24th Pkwy
Phoenix AZ 85016
602 957-4200

(P-12440)
BEST WESTERN OXNARD INN
1156 S Oxnard Blvd, Oxnard (93030-7418)
PHONE...................................805 483-9581
Fax: 805 483-4072
Pravin Lad, *Owner*
Jace Lad, *Manager*
▲ EMP: 50

SALES (est): 1.8MM **Privately Held**
WEB: www.bestwesternoxnardinn.com
SIC: **7011** Hotels & motels

(P-12441)
BEST WESTERN ROYAL HOST INN
5414 Brook Hollow Ct, Stockton (95219-2440)
PHONE...................................209 810-2619
Pradeep Patel, *Partner*
Chetan Patel, *Partner*
Paresh Patel, *Partner*
Prakash Patel, *Partner*
EMP: 156
SALES (est): 11.4MM **Privately Held**
SIC: **7011** Hotels & motels

(P-12442)
BEST WESTERN STOVALLS INN
Also Called: Best Western Park Place
1544 S Harbor Blvd, Anaheim (92802-2312)
PHONE...................................714 776-4800
Fax: 714 758-1396
Lilian Wright, *General Mgr*
EMP: 50
SALES (corp-wide): 24.7MM **Privately Held**
WEB: www.anaheiminn.com
SIC: **7011** Hotels & motels
PA: Best Western Stovalls Inn
1110 W Katella Ave
Anaheim CA 92802
714 956-4430

(P-12443)
BEST WESTERN STOVALLS INN (PA)
1110 W Katella Ave, Anaheim (92802-2805)
PHONE...................................714 956-4430
Fax: 714 635-9827
James Stovall, *Partner*
Bill O'Connell, *Partner*
Minta Pettis-Stovall, *Partner*
Robert Stovall, *Partner*
William Oconnell, *General Mgr*
EMP: 290
SQ FT: 4,800
SALES (est): 24.7MM **Privately Held**
WEB: www.anaheiminn.com
SIC: **7011** Hotels

(P-12444)
BESTON DEVELOPMENT
Also Called: Bristol, The
1055 1st Ave, San Diego (92101-4808)
PHONE...................................619 232-6315
John Methercutt, *General Mgr*
Scott Woods, *Vice Pres*
EMP: 60
SALES: 2MM **Privately Held**
WEB: www.bristolhotelsandiego.com
SIC: **7011** Hotels & motels

(P-12445)
BEVERLY BLVD LEASECO LLC
Also Called: Sofitel
8555 Beverly Blvd, Los Angeles (90048-3303)
PHONE...................................310 278-5444
Fax: 310 657-4679
Pierre-Louis Renou,
Jim Coleman, *Executive*
Sylvain Harribey, *Executive*
Monica Srinivasa, *Social Dir*
Denis Dupart, *General Mgr*
EMP: 100
SALES (est): 14.7MM
SALES (corp-wide): 946.2MM **Privately Held**
SIC: **7011** Hotels & motels
HQ: Accor North America, Inc.
5055 Kelle Sprin Rd Ste 2
Addison TX 75001
972 360-9000

(P-12446)
BEVERLY HILLS LUXURY HOTEL LLC
1801 Century Park E # 1200, Los Angeles (90067-2334)
PHONE...................................310 274-9999
Fax: 310 860-7801

PRODUCTS & SERVICES SECTION
7011 - Hotels, Motels & Tourist Courts County (P-12469)

Kenneth Bordewick, *Mng Member*
EMP: 450
SALES (est): 21.9MM Privately Held
SIC: 7011 Hotels

(P-12447)
BEVERLY SUNSTONE HILLS LLC
Also Called: Residence Inn By Marriott
1177 S Beverly Dr, Los Angeles (90035-1119)
PHONE..................310 228-4100
Robert Alter, *CEO*
Michael Demorgio, *General Mgr*
Maria More, *Controller*
EMP: 60
SALES (est): 1.3MM Privately Held
SIC: 7011 Hotels & motels

(P-12448)
BH PARTN A CALIF LIMIT PARTNE (PA)
Also Called: Bahia Resort Hotels
998 W Mission Bay Dr, San Diego (92109-7803)
PHONE..................858 539-7635
Fax: 858 488-1512
Anne L Evans, *General Ptnr*
William L Evans, *Partner*
Nancy Kyzer, *Treasurer*
William Evans, *Exec VP*
Janet Dooley, *Risk Mgmt Dir*
EMP: 300
SALES (est): 56.6MM Privately Held
WEB: www.missionbayresorts.com
SIC: 7011 6531 5812 Resort hotel; real estate managers; eating places

(P-12449)
BH PARTN A CALIF LIMIT PARTNE
Also Called: The Lodge At Torrey Pines
11480 N Torrey Pines Rd A, La Jolla (92037-1045)
PHONE..................858 453-4420
Fax: 619 453-0691
Luis Badios, *Manager*
Luis Deniz, *Executive*
Lizeeth Borquez, *Human Res Dir*
Dan Ferbal, *Human Res Dir*
Joe Mancillas, *HR Admin*
EMP: 100
SALES (corp-wide): 56.6MM Privately Held
WEB: www.missionbayresorts.com
SIC: 7011 5813 5812 Hotels & motels; drinking places; eating places
PA: Bh Partnership, A California Limited Partnership
998 W Mission Bay Dr
San Diego CA 92109
858 539-7635

(P-12450)
BICYCLE CASINO LP
Also Called: Bicycle Club
888 Bicycle Casino Dr, Bell Gardens (90201-7617)
PHONE..................562 806-4646
Hashem Minaiy, *General Ptnr*
EMP: 86
SALES (est): 8.9MM Privately Held
SIC: 7011 Casino hotel

(P-12451)
BIG RIVER LTD-DESIGN
Also Called: Big River Lodge
44850 Comptche Ukiah Rd, Mendocino (95460-9007)
P.O. Box 487 (95460-0487)
PHONE..................707 937-5615
Fax: 707 937-0305
Jeff Stanford, *Co-Owner*
Joan Stanford, *Co-Owner*
Lois Scheller, *Administration*
EMP: 70
SQ FT: 40,000
SALES (est): 3.5MM Privately Held
WEB: www.stanfordinn.com
SIC: 7011 5551 5941 5261 Resort hotel; canoes; kayaks; bicycle & bicycle parts; surfing equipment & supplies; nursery stock, seeds & bulbs; antiques; bathing suits; marine apparel

(P-12452)
BILTMORE HOTEL
2151 Laurelwood Rd, Santa Clara (95054-2796)
PHONE..................408 988-8411
Fax: 408 986-9807
Dafney Kang, *Owner*
Kay Gupta, *Executive*
Barbara Radcliff, *General Mgr*
Barbara Ratcliffe, *General Mgr*
Carolina Onoz, *Manager*
▲ **EMP:** 110
SALES (est): 2.5MM Privately Held
SIC: 7011 Hotels

(P-12453)
BLACK MEADOW LANDING
156100 Black Meadow Rd, Parker Dam (92267)
P.O. Box 98 (92267-0098)
PHONE..................760 663-4901
Fax: 760 663-3088
George H Field Jr, *Owner*
EMP: 55
SQ FT: 100,000
SALES (est): 1.6MM Privately Held
WEB: www.blackmeadowlanding.com
SIC: 7011 7033 5411 5812 Motels; recreational vehicle parks; grocery stores, independent; restaurant, family: independent

(P-12454)
BLUE DEVILS LESSEE LLC
Also Called: Le Merdien Dlfina Santa Monica
530 Pico Blvd, Santa Monica (90405-1223)
PHONE..................310 399-9344
Jon Bortz, *Ch of Bd*
Bridgett Billingsley, *Executive*
Arnel Mojica, *Finance Dir*
Raymond Martz, *Executive*
EMP: 170
SALES (est): 29.7MM Privately Held
SIC: 7011 Hotels

(P-12455)
BLUE LAKE CASINO
777 Casino Way Blue Lk Blue Lake, Blue Lake (95525)
P.O. Box 1128 (95525-1128)
PHONE..................707 668-5101
Eric Ramos, *President*
EMP: 51
SALES (est): 4.1MM Privately Held
SIC: 7011 Casino hotel

(P-12456)
BLUE SKY LODGE MOTEL
10 Flight Rd, Carmel Valley (93924-9617)
PHONE..................831 659-2935
Fax: 831 659-1632
Louis Gardner, *Owner*
EMP: 95
SALES (est): 1.8MM Privately Held
SIC: 7011 6513 Motels; apartment hotel operation

(P-12457)
BODEGA BAY ASSOCIATES
Also Called: Bodega Bay Lodge
1100 Alma St Ste 106, Menlo Park (94025-3344)
PHONE..................650 330-8888
Ellis J Alden,
EMP: 95
SALES (est): 6.2MM Privately Held
SIC: 7011 Motels

(P-12458)
BOREAL RIDGE CORPORATION
Also Called: Boreal Ski Area
19749 Boreal Ridge Rd, Soda Springs (95728)
P.O. Box 39, Truckee (96160-0039)
PHONE..................530 426-1012
Fax: 530 426-3173
John Cumming, *President*
Jodi Churich, *Vice Pres*
David Dobbs, *Accounting Dir*
Jon Slaughter, *Mktg Dir*
EMP: 110
SQ FT: 10,000
SALES (est): 11MM
SALES (corp-wide): 96.7MM Privately Held
WEB: www.powdr.com
SIC: 7011 7999 Ski lodge; hotels; ski rental concession
PA: Powdr Corp.
1790 Bonanza Dr Ste W201
Park City UT 84060
435 647-5490

(P-12459)
BOYKIN MGT CO LTD LBLTY CO
Also Called: Hampton Inn
3888 Greenwood St, San Diego (92110-4412)
PHONE..................619 299-6633
Tom Whelan, *Principal*
EMP: 50
SALES (corp-wide): 31.9MM Privately Held
WEB: www.wangyufei.com
SIC: 7011 Hotels & motels
PA: Boykin Management Company Limited Liability Company
8015 W Kenton Cir Ste 220
Huntersville NC 28078
704 896-2880

(P-12460)
BOYKIN MGT CO LTD LBLTY CO
Also Called: Radisson Inn
200 Marina Blvd, Berkeley (94710-1608)
PHONE..................510 548-7920
Neil Pasan, *Manager*
EMP: 300
SALES (corp-wide): 31.9MM Privately Held
WEB: www.wangyufei.com
SIC: 7011 5812 5813 Hotels & motels; eating places; drinking places
PA: Boykin Management Company Limited Liability Company
8015 W Kenton Cir Ste 220
Huntersville NC 28078
704 896-2880

(P-12461)
BOYKIN MGT CO LTD LBLTY CO
Also Called: Mission Valley
875 Hotel Cir S, San Diego (92108-3406)
PHONE..................619 298-8281
Fax: 619 295-5610
Robert Earp, *Ch of Bd*
EMP: 121
SALES (corp-wide): 31.9MM Privately Held
SIC: 7011 5812 5813 Hotels & motels; American restaurant; cocktail lounge
PA: Boykin Management Company Limited Liability Company
8015 W Kenton Cir Ste 220
Huntersville NC 28078
704 896-2880

(P-12462)
BRAEMAR PARTNERSHIP
Also Called: Catamaran Resort Hotel
3999 Mission Blvd, San Diego (92109-6959)
PHONE..................858 539-8600
Robert Gleason, *CFO*
The Trust of W D Evans, *Partner*
Anne L Evans, *Managing Prtnr*
Steven Riemer, *Executive*
Patrick Burkhardt, *Mktg Dir*
EMP: 350
SALES (est): 18MM Privately Held
WEB: www.catamaranresort.com
SIC: 7011 5812 5813 Resort hotel; American restaurant; cocktail lounge

(P-12463)
BRE DIAMOND HOTEL LLC
Also Called: Ritz-Carlton Halfmoon Bay
1 Miramontes Point Rd, Half Moon Bay (94019-2376)
PHONE..................650 712-7000
Fax: 650 712-7070
John Berndt, *Manager*
Stephanie Shaw, *Info Tech Mgr*
Daryl Eicher, *VP Mktg*
Alana Lo, *Sales Mgr*
Stephanie E Velasquez, *Sales Staff*
EMP: 127
SALES (corp-wide): 5.9MM Privately Held
WEB: www.shci.com
SIC: 7011 Hotels & motels
HQ: Bre Diamond Hotel Llc
200 W Madison St Ste 1700
Chicago IL 60606
312 658-5000

(P-12464)
BRE/JAPANTOWN OWNER LLC
Also Called: Hotel Kabuki
1625 Post St, San Francisco (94115-3603)
PHONE..................415 922-3200
Craig Walterman, *General Mgr*
Robert Branconi, *Chief Engr*
EMP: 100
SALES (est): 2MM Privately Held
SIC: 7011 Hotels & motels

(P-12465)
BRIGHT BRISTOL STREET LLC
Also Called: Crowne Plaza Costa Mesa
3131 Bristol St, Costa Mesa (92626-3037)
PHONE..................714 557-3000
Benjamin Shih, *Project Mgr*
Joseph Fan, *Manager*
EMP: 85
SALES (est): 250.9K Privately Held
SIC: 7011 Hotels & motels

(P-12466)
BRILLIANCE INVESTMENT LLC
Also Called: Days Inn
8350 Edes Ave, Oakland (94621-1307)
PHONE..................510 568-1880
Fax: 510 569-4652
Wagner Han,
EMP: 55
SQ FT: 70,000
SALES (est): 3.7MM Privately Held
SIC: 7011 5812 5813 Hotels & motels; restaurant, family: independent; bars & lounges

(P-12467)
BRISAM LAX (DE) LLC
Also Called: Holiday Inn Lax
9901 S La Cienega Blvd, Los Angeles (90045-5915)
PHONE..................310 649-5151
Fax: 310 568-0143
Steve Hostetter, *General Mgr*
Karen Nusenow, *Executive Asst*
EMP: 95
SALES (est): 3.5MM Privately Held
SIC: 7011 Hotels & motels

(P-12468)
BRISTOL HOTEL
1055 1st Ave, San Diego (92101-4808)
PHONE..................619 232-6141
Fax: 619 232-1948
Eric Horodas, *President*
Arlene Laucis, *Sales Dir*
EMP: 100
SQ FT: 56,000
SALES (est): 4.8MM Privately Held
WEB: www.bristol.polhotels.com
SIC: 7011 5812 Hotels; eating places

(P-12469)
BROADMOOR HOTEL
Gaylord Suites
1465 65th St Apt 274, Emeryville (94608-1168)
PHONE..................415 673-8445
Fax: 415 673-8555
Tony Daviduskis, *Branch Mgr*
EMP: 75
SQ FT: 85,619
SALES (corp-wide): 8.9MM Privately Held
WEB: www.granadasf.com
SIC: 7011 6513 Hotels & motels; apartment hotel operation
PA: Broadmoor Hotel
1499 Sutter St
San Francisco CA 94109
415 776-7034

7011 - Hotels, Motels & Tourist Courts County (P-12470)

(P-12470)
BROADMOOR HOTEL
Also Called: Granada Hotel
1000 Sutter St, San Francisco (94109-5818)
PHONE 415 673-2511
Fax: 415 771-4305
Tony Daviduskis, *Manager*
James Purcell, *Manager*
EMP: 70
SALES (corp-wide): 8.9MM **Privately Held**
WEB: www.granadasf.com
SIC: 7011 Hotels
PA: Broadmoor Hotel
   1499 Sutter St
   San Francisco CA 94109
   415 776-7034

(P-12471)
BROOKFIELD DTLA FUND OFFICE
Also Called: Westin Pasadena, The
191 N Los Robles Ave, Pasadena (91101-1707)
PHONE 626 792-2727
Fax: 626 792-3755
Jonathan Litvack, *General Mgr*
Thomas Shuman, *CTO*
Mort Heydari, *Info Tech Mgr*
Wilfredo Rivera, *Engineer*
William Macgregor, *Chief Engr*
EMP: 70
SALES (corp-wide): 14.9B **Privately Held**
WEB: www.maguireproperties.com
SIC: 7011 5812 5813 7299 Hotels & motels; American restaurant; bars & lounges; banquet hall facilities
HQ: Brookfield Dtla Fund Office Trust Inc.
   4 Wrld Fncl Ctr Fl 15
   New York NY 10281
   212 417-7064

(P-12472)
BROOKTRAILS LODGE LLC
24675 Birch St, Willits (95490-8476)
P.O. Box 297 (95490-0297)
PHONE 707 459-1596
Fax: 707 459-1684
Robert S Gitlin, *Manager*
EMP: 54
SQ FT: 87,120
SALES (est): 1.9MM **Privately Held**
SIC: 7011 Tourist camps, cabins, cottages & courts

(P-12473)
BURTON-WAY HOUSE LTD A CA
Also Called: Four Seasons Hotel
2 Dole Dr, Westlake Village (91362-7300)
PHONE 805 214-8075
Robert Cohen, *Branch Mgr*
EMP: 347
SALES (corp-wide): 30.4MM **Privately Held**
SIC: 7011 Hotels
PA: Burton Way Hotels, Ltd., A California Limited Partnership
   2029 Century Park E # 2200
   Los Angeles CA 90067
   310 552-6623

(P-12474)
BURTON-WAY HOUSE LTD A CA
Also Called: Four Seasons Hotel
300 S Doheny Dr, Los Angeles (90048-3704)
PHONE 310 273-2222
Mehdi Efpekari, *General Mgr*
Jennifer Elfenbein, *Controller*
Sarah Cairns, *Pub Rel Dir*
Pete Alles, *Manager*
EMP: 83
SALES (corp-wide): 30.4MM **Privately Held**
SIC: 7011 5812 Hotels; eating places
PA: Burton Way Hotels, Ltd., A California Limited Partnership
   2029 Century Park E # 2200
   Los Angeles CA 90067
   310 552-6623

(P-12475)
BURTON-WAY HOUSE LTD A CA (PA)
Also Called: Four Seasons Hotel
2029 Century Park E # 2200, Los Angeles (90067-2901)
PHONE 310 552-6623
Robert Cohen, *General Ptnr*
Joseph Cohen, *Partner*
Mehdi Estekari, *General Mgr*
Shinglie Lee, *Manager*
EMP: 50
SALES (est): 30.4MM **Privately Held**
SIC: 7011 Hotels

(P-12476)
BY THE BLUE SEA LLC
Also Called: Shutters On The Beach
1 Pico Blvd, Santa Monica (90405-1063)
PHONE 310 458-0030
Fax: 310 587-1788
Tim Dubois, *President*
Armella Stepan, *President*
Ellen Adleman, *COO*
Muzassar Kahell, *CFO*
Klaus Mennekes, *Vice Pres*
EMP: 350
SALES (est): 22.8MM **Privately Held**
SIC: 7011 Hotels & motels

(P-12477)
C N L HOTEL DEL PARTNERS LP
1500 Orange Ave, San Diego (92118-2918)
PHONE 619 522-8299
Todd Shallan, *Partner*
David Nadeau, *CFO*
EMP: 1100
SALES (est): 9.3MM **Privately Held**
SIC: 7011 Hotels & motels

(P-12478)
CABAZON BAND MISSION INDIANS
Fantasy Spring Resort Casino
84245 Indio Springs Dr, Indio (92203-3405)
PHONE 760 342-5000
Jim McCannon, *Manager*
Joni Woltkamp, *Purchasing*
EMP: 520 **Privately Held**
SIC: 7011 Casino hotel
PA: Cabazon Band Of Mission Indians
   84245 Indio Springs Dr
   Indio CA 92203
   760 342-2593

(P-12479)
CACHE CREEK CASINO RESORT
14455 State Highway 16, Brooks (95606-9707)
P.O. Box 65 (95606-0065)
PHONE 530 796-3118
Mike Leonard, *Vice Pres*
Joe Maloney, *Vice Pres*
Daniel Ogden, *Sr Ntwrk Engine*
Tavis Feese, *Info Tech Mgr*
Fran Moore, *Info Tech Mgr*
EMP: 2000
SALES (est): 116.4MM **Privately Held**
SIC: 7011 Casino hotel
PA: Yocha Dehe Wintun Nation
   18960 County Rd 75 A
   Brooks CA 95606
   530 796-2109

(P-12480)
CALHOT ILLINIOS LLC
Also Called: Ramada Inn
5250 W El Segundo Blvd, Hawthorne (90250-4142)
PHONE 310 536-9800
Fax: 310 536-9535
Fred Groth, *General Mgr*
Kairey Choi, *Manager*
Clara Gaeta, *Manager*
EMP: 160
SALES (est): 2.1MM **Privately Held**
SIC: 7011 5812 Hotels & motels; eating places

(P-12481)
CALIFORNIA BISTRO AT FO
Also Called: Four Seasons Resort Aviara
7100 Aviara Resort Dr, Carlsbad (92011-4908)
PHONE 760 603-3700
Fax: 760 603-6801
Vince Parotta, *President*
Paula Swinnerton, *Accountant*
Farzin Khorsandjamal, *Manager*
David Samuel, *Manager*
EMP: 51
SALES (est): 2.1MM **Privately Held**
SIC: 7011 Resort hotel

(P-12482)
CALIFORNIA COMMERCE CLUB INC
Also Called: Commerce Casino
6131 Telegraph Rd, Commerce (90040-2501)
PHONE 323 721-2100
Fax: 323 728-8874
Haig Papaian, *CEO*
Dante Oliveto, *CFO*
Harvey Ross, *Vice Pres*
Andrew Schneiderman, *Vice Pres*
Ralph Wong, *Vice Pres*
EMP: 2600
SQ FT: 350,000
SALES (est): 87.5MM **Privately Held**
WEB: www.commercecasino.com
SIC: 7011 5812 Casino hotel; eating places

(P-12483)
CAMINO REAL GROUP LLC
Also Called: Hilton
840 E El Camino Real, Mountain View (94040-2808)
PHONE 650 964-1700
Fax: 650 964-7900
Garrett Ritter, *Manager*
Tom Lawrence, *Manager*
EMP: 50
SALES (est): 4MM **Privately Held**
SIC: 7011 Hotels & motels

(P-12484)
CAMPBELL HHG HOTEL DEV LP
Also Called: Courtyard By Marriott San Jose
655 Creekside Way, Campbell (95008-0636)
PHONE 408 626-9590
Fax: 408 626-9591
Patricia Santini, *Manager*
EMP: 50
SALES (est): 1.9MM **Privately Held**
SIC: 7011 7389 Hotels & motels; office facilities & secretarial service rental

(P-12485)
CANOGA HOTEL CORPORATION
Also Called: Hilton Wdlnd Hlls / Los Angles
6360 Canoga Ave, Woodland Hills (91367-2501)
PHONE 818 595-1000
James Evans, *CFO*
Deepak Mehra, *General Mgr*
EMP: 200
SALES (est): 4MM **Privately Held**
SIC: 7011 Hotels

(P-12486)
CANTERBURY HOTEL CORP
Also Called: Best Western Canterbury Hotel
750 Sutter St, San Francisco (94109-6417)
PHONE 415 474-1452
Fax: 415 474-5856
Dean Lehr, *President*
Jacqueline W Lehr, *Ch of Bd*
Frederick T Smith, *Treasurer*
Jon Lehr, *Vice Pres*
EMP: 110
SQ FT: 98,410
SALES (est): 3.3MM **Privately Held**
WEB: www.canterbury-hotel.com
SIC: 7011 5812 Hotels & motels; eating places

(P-12487)
CAPITOL REGENCY LLC
Also Called: Hyatt Regency Sacramento
1209 L St, Sacramento (95814-3936)
PHONE 916 443-1234
Fax: 916 321-3099

Randy Verrue,
Denise Morgenstern, *Social Dir*
Brenda F Miller, *General Mgr*
Ulrich Samietz, *General Mgr*
Charlie Bane, *Engineer*
EMP: 360
SALES (est): 28MM **Privately Held**
SIC: 7011 Hotels & motels

(P-12488)
CAPSTAR SAN FRANCISCO CO LLC
Also Called: Sheraton Fisherman's Wharf
2500 Mason St, San Francisco (94133-1450)
PHONE 415 937-6084
David Givens, *General Mgr*
Daniel Monnet, *Finance Dir*
EMP: 250
SALES (est): 11.4MM **Privately Held**
SIC: 7011 Resort hotel

(P-12489)
CARLTON HOTEL PROPERTIES LP
1075 Sutter St, San Francisco (94109-5866)
PHONE 415 673-0242
Fax: 415 673-4904
Diane Feinstein, *Partner*
Richard Blum, *Partner*
Eileen Gartland, *Partner*
EMP: 55
SQ FT: 76,000
SALES (est): 4.3MM **Privately Held**
SIC: 7011 5812 Hotels; eating places

(P-12490)
CARMEL MISSION INN
3665 Rio Rd, Carmel (93923-8609)
PHONE 831 624-1841
Bob Buescher, *General Mgr*
Richard Pierini, *General Mgr*
Denise Morton, *Sales Dir*
Kristen Phillips, *Manager*
EMP: 60
SALES (est): 914.2K **Privately Held**
SIC: 7011 Hotels & motels

(P-12491)
CARMEL VALLEY RANCH
Also Called: Carmel Valley Ranch Hotel
1 Old Ranch Rd, Carmel (93923-8579)
PHONE 831 625-9500
Fax: 831 626-2553
Thomas Becker, *General Mgr*
Cv Ranch, *General Ptnr*
Scott Gill, *Executive*
Tim Wood, *Executive*
Kristina Jetton, *General Mgr*
EMP: 250
SALES (est): 23MM **Privately Held**
SIC: 7011 7997 6552 Resort hotel; tennis club, membership; golf club, membership; subdividers & developers

(P-12492)
CARMEL VLY MRTG BORROWER LLC
Also Called: Carmel Valley Resort
1 Old Ranch Rd, Carmel (93923-8551)
PHONE 831 625-9500
Laura Bell, *Principal*
EMP: 99
SALES (est): 1.5MM **Privately Held**
SIC: 7011 Hotels & motels

(P-12493)
CARNEROS INN LLC
Also Called: Poumtjack Hotels
4048 Sonoma Hwy, NAPA (94559-9745)
PHONE 707 299-4880
Keith Rogal, *CEO*
Krista Galyen, *Managing Prtnr*
Nicholas Monroe, *CFO*
Nick Monroe, *CFO*
Justin Stark, *Executive*
EMP: 350
SQ FT: 50,000
SALES (est): 26.3MM **Privately Held**
SIC: 7011 Resort hotel

PRODUCTS & SERVICES SECTION

7011 - Hotels, Motels & Tourist Courts County (P-12519)

(P-12494)
CARPENTERS SOUTHWEST ADM CORP (PA)
533 S Fremont Ave, Los Angeles (90071-1712)
P.O. Box 17969 (90017-0969)
PHONE 213 386-8590
Douglas McCarron, CEO
Brooke Reid, Officer
EMP: 70
SQ FT: 25,000
SALES (est): 41MM Privately Held
SIC: 7011 Hotels & motels

(P-12495)
CARSON OPERATING COMPANY LLC
Also Called: Doubletree By Hilton Carson
2 Civic Plaza Dr, Carson (90745-2231)
PHONE 310 830-9200
Leroy Russell, Controller
EMP: 90 EST: 2015
SALES (est): 1.3MM Privately Held
SIC: 7011 Hotels & motels

(P-12496)
CASA MADRONA HOTEL AND SPA LLC
801 Bridgeway, Sausalito (94965-2186)
PHONE 415 332-0502
Fax: 415 331-3125
John Warren Mays,
Darren Oliver, General Mgr
Jeremy Stanfield, General Mgr
Brian Kelley, Controller
Willie Villar, Director
EMP: 55
SQ FT: 18,000
SALES (est): 4.5MM
SALES (corp-wide): 33.7MM Privately Held
WEB: www.casamadrona.com
SIC: 7011 5812 Hotels; eating places
PA: Olympus Real Estate Corp
    5080 Spectrum Dr
    Addison TX 75001
    972 980-2200

(P-12497)
CASA MUNRAS HOTEL LLC
700 Munras Ave, Monterey (93940-3110)
PHONE 831 375-2411
Karl K Hoagland III,
EMP: 82
SALES: 950K Privately Held
SIC: 7011 Hotels & motels

(P-12498)
CASA REAL ESTATE LTD PARTNR
Also Called: Estralla Inn & Spa
415 S Belardo Rd, Palm Springs (92262-7307)
PHONE 760 320-4117
Elkor Trio, General Ptnr
EMP: 66
SALES (est): 4.6MM Privately Held
WEB: www.viceroypalmsprings.com
SIC: 7011 Hotels

(P-12499)
CASTLBLACK PISMO BCH OWNER LLC
Also Called: Hilton Garden Inn Pismo
601 James Way, Pismo Beach (93449-3502)
PHONE 805 773-6020
Gordon Jackson, Manager
Laura Benner, Vice Pres
Leonard Levenson, Vice Pres
EMP: 50
SALES (est): 836.6K
SALES (corp-wide): 31.8MM Privately Held
SIC: 7011 Hotels & motels
PA: Castleblack Owner Holdings, Llc
    399 Park Ave Fl 18
    New York NY 10022
    212 547-2609

(P-12500)
CASTLEHILL PROPERTIES INC (PA)
Also Called: Residnce Inn By Mrrott Stckton
3240 W March Ln, Stockton (95219-2341)
PHONE 209 472-9800
Jeff Carpenter, General Mgr
Ramona Ewell, General Mgr
Tanya Sims, Manager
Shawn Williams, Manager
EMP: 63
SALES (est): 5.8MM Privately Held
SIC: 7011 Hotels & motels

(P-12501)
CAVALIER INN INCORPORATED
Also Called: Best Western
250 San Simeon Ave Ste 4c, San Simeon (93452-9715)
PHONE 805 927-6444
Michael R Hanchett, President
Barbara J Hanchett, CFO
EMP: 90
SALES (est): 4.8MM Privately Held
WEB: www.cavalierresort.com
SIC: 7011 Hotels & motels

(P-12502)
CAVALLO POINT LLC (PA)
601 Murray Cir, Sausalito (94965)
PHONE 415 339-4700
Peter Heinmann, Partner
Jacqueline Alcantara, Social Dir
Debbie Coller, Practice Mgr
Lonny Watne, Branch Mgr
Stephanie Simontacchi, Controller
EMP: 80 EST: 2007
SALES (est): 10.4MM Privately Held
SIC: 7011 Hotels & motels

(P-12503)
CB-1 HOTEL
Also Called: Four Seasons Hotel
757 Market St, San Francisco (94103-2001)
PHONE 415 633-3838
Fax: 415 633-3001
Douglas Housley, General Mgr
Phing Thong, Controller
EMP: 99
SQ FT: 59,300
SALES (est): 6.5MM Privately Held
SIC: 7011 Hotels

(P-12504)
CDC SAN FRANCISCO LLC
Also Called: Intercontinental San Francisco
888 Howard St, San Francisco (94103-3011)
PHONE 415 616-6512
Peter Koehler,
EMP: 99 EST: 2007
SALES: 950K Privately Held
SIC: 7011 Hotels & motels

(P-12505)
CECIL HOTEL COMPANY LLC
640 S Main St, Los Angeles (90014-2031)
PHONE 213 213-7829
Fax: 213 627-1629
Peter Cretanian, General Mgr
Janica Tagorda, Accountant
EMP: 65
SQ FT: 180,000
SALES (est): 3.5MM Privately Held
WEB: www.cecilhotel.com
SIC: 7011 Hotels

(P-12506)
CELEBRITY CASINOS INC
Also Called: Crystal Casino & Hotel
123 E Artesia Blvd, Compton (90220-4921)
PHONE 310 631-3838
Mark A Kelegian, President
Haig Kelegian Jr, CFO
Taro Ito, General Mgr
Chip Cartwright, Systs Prg Mgr
EMP: 400
SQ FT: 190,000
SALES (est): 16.5MM Privately Held
SIC: 7011 Hotels & motels

(P-12507)
CENTURY WILSHIRE INC
Also Called: Century Wilshire Hotel
9400 Culver Blvd, Culver City (90232-2617)
PHONE 310 558-9400
Fax: 310 836-7105
Theodora Mallick, President
Monika Mallick, Corp Secy
Maya Mallick, Principal
Seth Horowitz, General Mgr
Ken Giurdanella, Sls & Mktg Exec
EMP: 70
SQ FT: 38,000
SALES (est): 5.1MM Privately Held
WEB: www.centurywilshirehotel.com
SIC: 7011 Hotels

(P-12508)
CH CUPERTINO OWNER LLC
Also Called: Cypress Hotel
10050 S De Anza Blvd, Cupertino (95014-2128)
PHONE 408 253-8900
Fax: 408 253-3800
David Hayes, Marketing Staff
Alanna Wheeler, Executive
Lesley Wilson, Associate Dir
Joshua Hogan, Sales Dir
EMP: 130
SALES (est): 8.9MM Privately Held
WEB: www.thecypresshotel.com
SIC: 7011 Hotels & motels

(P-12509)
CHAMBER MAID LESSEE INC
Also Called: Chamberlain West Hollywood
1000 Westmount Dr, West Hollywood (90069-4142)
PHONE 310 657-7400
Chad Thompson, General Mgr
Christine Rodriguez, Accountant
Bria Padilla, Controller
Gustavo Paredes, Opers Staff
EMP: 51
SALES (est): 3.6MM Privately Held
SIC: 7011 Hotels

(P-12510)
CHAMSON MANAGEMENT INC
Also Called: Doubletree Hotel
7 Hutton Centre Dr, Santa Ana (92707-5753)
PHONE 714 751-2400
Fax: 714 662-7935
Jung-Hsiung Chiu, President
Magaly Marquez, Accounting Mgr
Donna Evans, Sales Executive
Joyce Nissen, Sales Executive
EMP: 90 EST: 1994
SALES (est): 6MM Privately Held
SIC: 7011 Hotels & motels

(P-12511)
CHESAPEAKE LODGING TRUST
Also Called: Le Meridian Hotel
333 Battery St Lbby, San Francisco (94111-3234)
PHONE 415 296-2900
Fax: 415 296-2989
Joel Myers, Director
Michael Cochrane, Data Proc Exec
Michael Cochran, MIS Dir
Frank Metafavage, Controller
Sonia Rollins, Human Res Dir
EMP: 96
SALES (est): 10.6MM Privately Held
SIC: 7011 Hotels

(P-12512)
CHIEF SAN DIEGO HOTEL LLC
601 Pacific Hwy, San Diego (92101-5914)
PHONE 619 239-2400
Andy Slater, Vice Pres
John D Smith, General Mgr
Larry Foster, Controller
EMP: 100
SALES (est): 2MM
SALES (corp-wide): 23.3B Privately Held
SIC: 7011 Hotels & motels
HQ: Barings Real Estate Advisers Llc
    1 Financial Plz Ste 1700
    Hartford CT 06103
    860 509-2200

(P-12513)
CHINA PEAK MOUNTAIN RESORT LLC
59265 Hwy 168, Lakeshore (93634)
P.O. Box 236 (93634-0236)
PHONE 559 233-2500
Tim Cohee, CEO
Michelle Vikupitz, Marketing Staff
Rich Bailey, Manager
Olivia Lyons, Assistant
EMP: 67
SALES (est): 6.7MM Privately Held
SIC: 7011 Resort hotel

(P-12514)
CHIRAG HOSPITALITY INC
Also Called: Super 8 Motel
2440 Lombard St, San Francisco (94123-2604)
PHONE 415 922-0244
Chirag Patel, CEO
Mishan Giri, Manager
EMP: 78
SALES (est): 109.2K Privately Held
SIC: 7011 Hotels & motels

(P-12515)
CHOA HOPE LLC
Also Called: Sioux City Ht & Conference Ctr
515 W Washington Ave, Escondido (92025-1628)
PHONE 712 277-4101
Peter Parsons, General Mgr
Shannon Warengo, Controller
Dan Maher, Sales Staff
Todd Frush, Manager
Frush Todd, Manager
EMP: 50
SALES (est): 1.9MM Privately Held
SIC: 7011 Hotels

(P-12516)
CHOICE HOTELS INTL INC
Also Called: Econo Lodge Inn & Suites
20688 Tracy Ave, Buttonwillow (93206-9782)
PHONE 661 764-5207
EMP: 98
SALES (corp-wide): 859.8MM Publicly Held
SIC: 7011 Hotels & motels
PA: Choice Hotels International, Inc.
    1 Choice Hotels Cir
    Rockville MD 20850
    301 592-5000

(P-12517)
CHSP TRS FISHERMAN WHARF LLC
Also Called: Hyatt Fisherman's Wharf
555 N Point St, San Francisco (94133-1311)
PHONE 415 563-1234
James Francis, President
EMP: 180
SALES (est): 1.5MM Publicly Held
SIC: 7011 5813 5812 Hotels & motels;
    bars & lounges; eating places
PA: Chesapeake Lodging Trust
    1997 Annapolis Exch Pkwy
    Annapolis MD 21401

(P-12518)
CHSP TRS LOS ANGELES LLC
Also Called: Hilton Checkers Los Angeles
535 S Grand Ave, Los Angeles (90071-2601)
PHONE 213 624-0000
Eddie Andre, CEO
Twain Schreiber, Executive
Paul Chambers, Engineer
EMP: 88 Publicly Held
SIC: 7011 Hotels & motels
HQ: Crestline Hotels & Resorts, Llc
    3950 University Dr # 301
    Fairfax VA 22030
    571 529-6100

(P-12519)
CHUKCHANSI GOLD RESORT CASINO
711 Lucky Ln, Coarsegold (93614-8206)
PHONE 866 794-6946
Fax: 559 692-5329

7011 - Hotels, Motels & Tourist Courts County (P-12520)

Richard Williams, *Owner*
Larry King, *CFO*
Chanel Wright, *Officer*
Matt Olin, *General Mgr*
Ken Pottenger, *Administration*
EMP: 1400
SQ FT: 489,000
SALES (est): 46.1MM **Privately Held**
SIC: 7011 Casino hotel

(P-12520)
CIM/J STREET HT SACRAMENTO INC
Also Called: Sheraton Grand Sacramento Ht
1230 J St, Sacramento (95814-2907)
PHONE..................916 447-1700
Fax: 916 447-1701
Avraham Shemesh, *President*
Norbert Hurka, *Opers Staff*
EMP: 280
SALES (est): 1.9MM
SALES (corp-wide): 2.5MM **Privately Held**
SIC: 7011 7389 Hotels & motels; office facilities & secretarial service rental
PA: Cim Group, Inc.
4700 Wilshire Blvd Ste 1
Los Angeles CA 90010
323 860-4900

(P-12521)
CIM/OAKLAND CITY CENTER LLC
Also Called: Marriott
1001 Broadway, Oakland (94607-4019)
PHONE..................510 451-4000
Fax: 510 835-3466
John Mazzoni, *Manager*
Avraham Shemesh, *Principal*
Elie Khoury, *General Mgr*
Keith R Montgomery, *Controller*
Derrick Dawson, *Purch Mgr*
EMP: 99
SALES (est): 10.4MM **Privately Held**
SIC: 7011 Hotels & motels

(P-12522)
CINDERELLA MOTEL
Also Called: Candy Cane Inn
1747 S Harbor Blvd, Anaheim (92802-2315)
PHONE..................559 432-0118
Fax: 714 772-5462
Ralph Kazarian, *President*
Robert Fambrough, *General Mgr*
Marla Johnson, *Office Mgr*
EMP: 81
SQ FT: 65,542
SALES (corp-wide): 744.7K **Privately Held**
WEB: www.candycaneinn.net
SIC: 7011 Motels
PA: Cinderella Motel
2416 W Shaw Ave Ste 109
Fresno CA 93711
559 432-0118

(P-12523)
CITY OF SAN JOSE
Also Called: Dolce Hayes Mansion
200 Edenvale Ave, San Jose (95136-3309)
PHONE..................408 226-6765
Cedric Fasbender, *General Mgr*
Russell Duarte, *Info Tech Mgr*
Jack Jackson, *Chief Engr*
Carol Johnson, *Finance*
Jo Danna, *Sales Mgr*
EMP: 140 **Privately Held**
WEB: www.csjfinance.org
SIC: 7011 Hotels & motels
PA: City Of San Jose
200 E Santa Clara St
San Jose CA 95113
408 535-3500

(P-12524)
CLAREMONT HT PRPTS LTD PARTNR
Also Called: Claremont Hotel Club & Spa
41 Tunnel Rd, Berkeley (94705-2429)
PHONE..................510 843-3000
Len Czarnecki, *Mng Member*
Michael Coughlin, *Finance Dir*
Adrian Larick, *Sales Dir*
Joan Burgess, *Sales Staff*
Alexis Garhammer, *Manager*
EMP: 550
SALES (est): 11.1MM **Privately Held**
SIC: 7011 Hotels

(P-12525)
CLAREMONT STAR LP
Also Called: Doubletree Hotel
555 W Foothill Blvd, Claremont (91711-3478)
PHONE..................909 482-0124
Harry Wu, *Partner*
Shawn Chen, *Partner*
Tom Abercrombie, *Chief Engr*
John Johnson, *Accounts Mgr*
EMP: 50
SALES (est): 3.2MM **Privately Held**
SIC: 7011 Hotels & motels

(P-12526)
CLARION HOTEL SAN JOSE AIRPORT
1355 N 4th St, San Jose (95112-4783)
PHONE..................408 453-5340
Ajay Shingal,
Ram Garg,
Mira Shingal,
Ayelet Morag, *Manager*
EMP: 90
SALES (est): 3MM **Privately Held**
SIC: 7011 Hotels

(P-12527)
CLASSIC RIVERDALE INC
Also Called: Hyatt Hotel
200 Glenwood Cir, Monterey (93940-6741)
PHONE..................831 373-0101
Matt Madison, *Partner*
EMP: 81
SALES (corp-wide): 67.3MM **Privately Held**
WEB: www.hyattclassic.com
SIC: 7011 Hotels & motels
PA: Classic Riverdale, Inc.
200 W Madison St Ste 3700
Chicago IL 60606
312 803-8800

(P-12528)
CLASSIC RSDENCE MGT LTD PARTNR
Also Called: Hyatt Hotel
200 Glenwood Cir Ofc, Monterey (93940-6773)
PHONE..................831 373-0101
Fax: 831 373-0863
Deann Daniel, *Exec Dir*
EMP: 100
SQ FT: 196,000
SALES (est): 4.3MM **Privately Held**
SIC: 7011 Hotels & motels

(P-12529)
CLOCKTOWER INN
Also Called: Ramada Clock Tower Inn
181 E Santa Clara St, Ventura (93001-2715)
PHONE..................805 652-0141
Fax: 805 643-1432
S Patel, *President*
Dianne Calderon, *Sales Dir*
Sara Gregory, *Sales Dir*
David Fox, *Manager*
EMP: 65
SQ FT: 29,000
SALES (est): 3.3MM **Privately Held**
SIC: 7011 Hotels

(P-12530)
CNCML A CALIFORNIA LTD PARTNR
Also Called: Plumpjack The
1920 Squaw Valley Rd, Olympic Valley (96146)
P.O. Box 2407 (96146-2407)
PHONE..................530 583-1578
Fax: 530 583-1734
Hilary Newsom, *President*
Jeremy Scherer, *Vice Pres*
Milham D Wakin, *Vice Pres*
Jessica Grunst, *Human Res Mgr*
Rob McCormick, *Sales Dir*
EMP: 100
SQ FT: 20,000
SALES (est): 5.6MM **Privately Held**
SIC: 7011 5812 Hotels; eating places

(P-12531)
COASTAL HOTEL GROUP INC
Also Called: Inns of Monterey
652 Cannery Row, Monterey (93940-1021)
PHONE..................831 646-8900
Fax: 831 646-5342
Randy Bernard, *Manager*
Sandra Moritz, *Administration*
EMP: 120
SALES (corp-wide): 48.3MM **Privately Held**
WEB: www.coastalhotel.com
SIC: 7011 5813 5812 Hotels & motels; drinking places; eating places
PA: Coastal Hotel Group, Inc.
15375 Se 30th Pl Ste 290
Bellevue WA 98007
206 388-0400

(P-12532)
COASTAL HOTEL GROUP INC
Also Called: Hotel Pacific
300 Pacific St, Monterey (93940-2418)
PHONE..................831 373-5700
Fax: 831 373-1655
Randy Venard, *Manager*
EMP: 55
SALES (corp-wide): 48.3MM **Privately Held**
WEB: www.coastalhotel.com
SIC: 7011 Hotels
PA: Coastal Hotel Group, Inc.
15375 Se 30th Pl Ste 290
Bellevue WA 98007
206 388-0400

(P-12533)
COASTAL HOTEL GROUP INC
Also Called: Victorian Inn
487 Foam St, Monterey (93940-1409)
PHONE..................831 373-8000
Fax: 831 373-4815
Patrick Mallone, *Manager*
EMP: 50
SALES (corp-wide): 48.3MM **Privately Held**
WEB: www.coastalhotel.com
SIC: 7011 Hotels
PA: Coastal Hotel Group, Inc.
15375 Se 30th Pl Ste 290
Bellevue WA 98007
206 388-0400

(P-12534)
COLUMBIA WOODLAKE LLC
500 Leisure Ln, Sacramento (95815-4207)
PHONE..................206 728-9063
Alex Washburn, *President*
Leigh Noble, *CFO*
EMP: 90
SALES (est): 927K **Privately Held**
SIC: 7011 Resort hotel

(P-12535)
COMFORT CALIFORNIA INC
Also Called: Comfort Inn
2775 Van Ness Ave, San Francisco (94109-1423)
PHONE..................415 928-5000
Todd Symynuk, *Branch Mgr*
EMP: 50
SALES (corp-wide): 220.8MM **Privately Held**
WEB: www.clarionanaheim.com
SIC: 7011 Hotels & motels
HQ: Comfort California, Inc.
10750 Columbia Pike # 300
Silver Spring MD 20901
301 592-3800

(P-12536)
COMFORT CALIFORNIA INC
Also Called: Clarion Hotel
616 W Convention Way, Anaheim (92802-3401)
PHONE..................714 750-3131
Mike Thomas, *Branch Mgr*
Cristina Martinez, *Division Mgr*
Jeff Heeth, *General Mgr*
Stephanie Westberg, *Sales Executive*
Cathy Dutton, *Sales Dir*
EMP: 83
SALES (corp-wide): 220.8MM **Privately Held**
WEB: www.clarionanaheim.com
SIC: 7011 Hotels & motels
HQ: Comfort California, Inc.
10750 Columbia Pike # 300
Silver Spring MD 20901
301 592-3800

(P-12537)
COMFORT SUITES
Also Called: Comfort Inn
121 E Grand Ave, South San Francisco (94080-4800)
PHONE..................650 589-7100
Fax: 650 589-7796
David R Lane, *CFO*
Steven Nokes, *Partner*
EMP: 100
SQ FT: 5,000
SALES (est): 3.5MM **Privately Held**
SIC: 7011 Hotels & motels

(P-12538)
COMMUNE HOTELS AND RESORTS LLC (PA)
530 Bush St Ste 501, San Francisco (94108-3633)
PHONE..................415 248-5930
Niki Leondakis, *CEO*
Mary Coller, *President*
Michael J Wisner, *CFO*
Rick Colangelo, *Exec VP*
Phil Keb, *Exec VP*
EMP: 64
SALES (est): 27.9MM **Privately Held**
SIC: 7011 Hotels

(P-12539)
CONCORD HOTEL LLC
Also Called: Crowne Plaza Concord
45 John Glenn Dr, Concord (94520-5604)
PHONE..................925 521-3751
Fax: 925 674-9567
Dave Warner,
Laurant Bertheon, *Executive*
Joe Dumlao, *Chief Engr*
Liz Kibe, *Bookkeeper*
Laura Tyson, *Sales Mgr*
EMP: 95
SALES: 8MM **Privately Held**
SIC: 7011 Hotels & motels

(P-12540)
CONESTOGA HOTEL
Also Called: Holiday Inn
1240 S Walnut St, Anaheim (92802-2241)
PHONE..................714 535-0300
Fax: 714 491-8953
Kevin Clayton, *General Mgr*
Mark Nunneley, *CFO*
Tom Van Winkle, *General Mgr*
EMP: 90
SQ FT: 150,000
SALES (est): 3.1MM **Privately Held**
WEB: www.conestogahotel.com
SIC: 7011 5812 5813 Hotels & motels; American restaurant; drinking places

(P-12541)
COUNTRY INN &SUITE BY CARLSON
231 N Vineyard Ave, Ontario (91764-4427)
PHONE..................909 937-6000
Peter Bhakta, *Owner*
EMP: 50
SALES (est): 751K **Privately Held**
SIC: 7011 Hotels & motels

(P-12542)
COUNTRYSIDE INN-CORONA LP
Also Called: Ayres Hotel Laguna Woods
24341 El Toro Rd, Aliso Viejo (92653)
PHONE..................949 588-0131
Fax: 949 588-1935
Vince Neale, *Manager*
EMP: 60
SALES (corp-wide): 45.4MM **Privately Held**
WEB: www.ayreshotelgroup.com
SIC: 7011 Hotels
PA: Countryside Inn-Corona, L.P.
1900 Frontage Rd
Corona CA 92882
714 540-6060

PRODUCTS & SERVICES SECTION
7011 - Hotels, Motels & Tourist Courts County (P-12566)

(P-12543)
COUNTRYSIDE INN-CORONA LP
Also Called: Countryside Suites By Ayres
325 Bristol St, Costa Mesa (92626-5998)
PHONE...............................714 549-0300
Fax: 714 662-0828
Steve Winning, *General Mgr*
Donald Ayres, *Vice Pres*
Steve Snyder, *Engineer*
Greg Kleminsky, *Controller*
EMP: 100
SALES (corp-wide): 45.4MM **Privately Held**
WEB: www.ayreshotelgroup.com
SIC: 7011 5813 5812 Hotels & motels; drinking places; eating places
PA: Countryside Inn-Corona, L.P.
1900 Frontage Rd
Corona CA 92882
714 540-6060

(P-12544)
COURTYARD BY MARRIOTT
595 Hotel Cir S, San Diego (92108-3403)
PHONE...............................619 291-5720
John Blem, *General Mgr*
Veronica Butler, *Director*
EMP: 60
SALES (est): 2.4MM **Privately Held**
SIC: 7011 Hotels & motels

(P-12545)
COURTYARD BY MARRIOTT
1605 Calle Joaquin, San Luis Obispo (93405-7214)
PHONE...............................805 786-4200
Fax: 805 786-4210
James Flagg,
Tabitha Christensen, *Manager*
EMP: 55
SALES (est): 2.2MM **Privately Held**
SIC: 7011 Hotels & motels

(P-12546)
COURTYARD BY MARRIOTT
2500 Larkspur Landing Cir, Larkspur (94939-1831)
PHONE...............................415 925-1800
Fax: 415 925-1107
Sam Pahlazan, *Principal*
EMP: 80
SALES (est): 2.1MM **Privately Held**
SIC: 7011 Hotels & motels

(P-12547)
COURTYARD BY MARRIOTT
1905 S Azusa Ave, Hacienda Heights (91745-6850)
PHONE...............................626 965-1700
Michael Sweany, *Principal*
Maritza Mejia, *General Mgr*
Man L Tam, *General Mgr*
Michael Swaney, *Office Mgr*
EMP: 80
SALES (est): 2.3MM **Privately Held**
SIC: 7011 Hotels & motels

(P-12548)
COURTYARD MANAGEMENT CORP
21101 Ventura Blvd, Woodland Hills (91364-2104)
PHONE...............................818 999-2200
J Willard Marriott, *Principal*
EMP: 55
SALES (corp-wide): 14.4B **Publicly Held**
SIC: 7011 Hotels & motels
HQ: Courtyard Management Corporation
10400 Fernwood Rd
Bethesda MD 20817
301 380-3000

(P-12549)
COURTYARD MANAGEMENT CORP
Also Called: Courtyard By Marriott
2250 Contra Costa Blvd, Pleasant Hill (94523-3744)
PHONE...............................925 691-1444
Fax: 925 691-0616
Trace Moviel, *Branch Mgr*
EMP: 50
SALES (corp-wide): 14.4B **Publicly Held**
SIC: 7011 Hotels & motels

HQ: Courtyard Management Corporation
10400 Fernwood Rd
Bethesda MD 20817
301 380-3000

(P-12550)
COURTYARD MANAGEMENT CORP
Also Called: Courtyard By Marriott
10683 White Rock Rd, Rancho Cordova (95670-6002)
PHONE...............................916 638-3800
Fax: 916 638-6776
John Lister, *Branch Mgr*
Danielle Decruz, *Accounts Mgr*
EMP: 50
SALES (corp-wide): 14.4B **Publicly Held**
SIC: 7011 Hotels & motels
HQ: Courtyard Management Corporation
10400 Fernwood Rd
Bethesda MD 20817
301 380-3000

(P-12551)
CPH MONARCH HOTEL LLC
Also Called: St Regis Resort Monarch Beach
1 Monarch Beach Resort, Dana Point (92629-4085)
PHONE...............................949 234-3200
Fax: 949 234-3333
Paul Makarechian, *President*
Jaclyn Frost, *Executive Asst*
Denise McConnell, *Sales Mgr*
Tracy Ladsovich, *Manager*
Stephanie Smith, *Manager*
▲ EMP: 1100
SQ FT: 300,000
SALES (est): 62.4MM
SALES (corp-wide): 86.5MM **Privately Held**
SIC: 7011 Resort hotel
PA: Washington Real Estate Holdings Llc
600 University St # 2820
Seattle WA 98101
206 613-5300

(P-12552)
CREEDENCE LESSEE LLC
Also Called: Tuscan and Pescatore, The
425 N Point St, San Francisco (94133-1405)
PHONE...............................415 561-1100
Emily Chung, *Director*
EMP: 99 EST: 2015
SALES (est): 443.6K **Privately Held**
SIC: 7011 Hotels & motels

(P-12553)
CRESTLINE HOTELS & RESORTS INC (DH)
Also Called: Kyoto Grand Hotel and Gardens
120 S Los Angeles St 11, Los Angeles (90012-3724)
PHONE...............................213 629-1200
Richard Gaines, *General Mgr*
Pricilla Alacantara, *Accountant*
John Jedic, *Human Res Dir*
EMP: 130
SALES (est): 3.4MM **Publicly Held**
SIC: 7011 5812 5813 Hotels; restaurant, family: independent; drinking places
HQ: Crestline Hotels & Resorts, Llc
3950 University Dr # 301
Fairfax VA 22030
571 529-6100

(P-12554)
CRESTLINE HOTELS & RESORTS LLC
Also Called: Renaissance Palm Springs Hotel
888 E Tahquitz Canyon Way, Palm Springs (92262-6708)
PHONE...............................760 322-6000
Eric Hill, *Controller*
EMP: 200 **Publicly Held**
WEB: www.crestlinehotels.com
SIC: 7011 Hotels & motels
HQ: Crestline Hotels & Resorts, Llc
3950 University Dr # 301
Fairfax VA 22030
571 529-6100

(P-12555)
CROWN PLAZA SD
Also Called: Islands Restaurant & Lounge
2270 Hotel Cir N, San Diego (92108-2810)
PHONE...............................619 297-1101
Anna Cooper, *Manager*
EMP: 80
SALES (est): 3.3MM **Privately Held**
WEB: www.islandssushi.com
SIC: 7011 5812 Hotels & motels; eating places

(P-12556)
CROWNE PLAZA LAX LLC
Also Called: Intercontntl Hotels Grp Resour
5985 W Century Blvd, Los Angeles (90045-5477)
PHONE...............................310 258-1321
Paul Gibbs, *General Mgr*
Nelson Zager, *Info Tech Mgr*
EMP: 250
SALES (est): 5.3MM
SALES (corp-wide): 1.8B **Privately Held**
WEB: www.crowneplaza.com
SIC: 7011 Hotels & motels
HQ: Intercontinental Hotels Group Resources, Inc.
3 Ravinia Dr Ste 100
Atlanta GA 30346
770 604-5000

(P-12557)
CRP CENTINELA LP
Also Called: Doubltree Los Angeles Westside
6161 W Centinela Ave, Culver City (90230-6306)
PHONE...............................901 821-4117
Larry M Mills, *Partner*
EMP: 152
SALES: 950K
SALES (corp-wide): 3B **Publicly Held**
SIC: 7011 Hotels & motels
PA: The Carlyle Group L P
1001 Pennsylvania Ave Nw 220s
Washington DC 20004
202 729-5626

(P-12558)
CUSTOM HOTEL LLC
8639 Lincoln Blvd, Los Angeles (90045-3503)
PHONE...............................310 645-0400
Alisa Matthews, *General Mgr*
Bruno Vergeynst, *General Mgr*
Jerry Peck, *Controller*
EMP: 100
SALES (est): 5.2MM
SALES (corp-wide): 231.8MM **Privately Held**
SIC: 7011 Hotels & motels
PA: Joie De Vivre Hospitality, Llc
530 Bush St Ste 501
San Francisco CA 94108
415 835-0300

(P-12559)
CUSTOM HOUSE HOTEL LP
Also Called: Portola Hotel & Spa
2 Portola Plz, Monterey (93940-2419)
PHONE...............................831 649-4511
Dan Pollock,
Phillip Pennington, *General Mgr*
Kari Osborne, *Executive Asst*
Daniel Mayer, *Technician*
Stephanie Chrietzberg, *Asst Controller*
EMP: 87
SALES (est): 10.9MM **Privately Held**
SIC: 7011 Bed & breakfast inn

(P-12560)
CWGP LIMITED PARTNERSHIP
Also Called: Le Merigot
1740 Ocean Ave, Santa Monica (90401-3214)
PHONE...............................310 395-9700
Kai Beumer, *General Mgr*
Eileen Bronchick, *Vice Pres*
Paul Hortobagyi, *General Mgr*
Sig K Otloff, *General Mgr*
EMP: 100
SALES (est): 4.8MM **Privately Held**
WEB: www.lemerigotbeachhotel.com
SIC: 7011 Hotels & motels

PA: C W Hotels Ltd
740 Centre View Blvd
Crestview Hills KY 41017
859 578-1100

(P-12561)
CY SAC OPERATOR LLC
Also Called: Courtyard Sacramento-Midtown
4422 Y St, Sacramento (95817-2220)
PHONE...............................916 455-6800
Colleen Jimenez,
Roshan Bhakta,
EMP: 67
SALES (est): 4.9MM **Privately Held**
SIC: 7011 Hotels

(P-12562)
D & W LLC
Also Called: Ramada Inn
3501 Rindge Ln, Redondo Beach (90278-1420)
PHONE...............................310 345-0075
Paul Ding,
Jane Ding,
Jenny Wu,
EMP: 55
SQ FT: 80,000
SALES (est): 2.4MM **Privately Held**
SIC: 7011 Hotels & motels

(P-12563)
DARENSBURG ROGHAIR & RENIER
Also Called: Quailty Inn of Barstow
1520 E Main St, Barstow (92311-3230)
PHONE...............................760 256-6891
Fax: 760 256-3850
Charles Darensburg, *Partner*
T Patel, *Manager*
Nichole Ursry, *Manager*
EMP: 50
SALES (est): 2.4MM **Privately Held**
SIC: 7011 5812 Motel, franchised; American restaurant

(P-12564)
DAVIDSON HOTEL PARTNERS LP
Also Called: Agoura Hills Renaissance Hotel
30100 Agoura Rd, Agoura Hills (91301-2004)
PHONE...............................818 707-1220
Larry Mills, *Partner*
EMP: 120
SALES (corp-wide): 105.4MM **Privately Held**
SIC: 7011 Hotels & motels
PA: Davidson Hotel Partners, L.P
1 Ravinia Dr Ste 1600
Atlanta GA 30346
901 761-4664

(P-12565)
DAVIS HALLMARK PARTNERSHIP
Also Called: Hallmark Inn
110 F St, Davis (95616-4628)
PHONE...............................530 753-3320
Julian M Youmans, *Partner*
John Youmans, *Partner*
Stacey Horigan, *Controller*
EMP: 50
SQ FT: 70,000
SALES (est): 2.7MM **Privately Held**
WEB: www.hallmarkinn.com
SIC: 7011 Hotels

(P-12566)
DAWN RANCH LODGE & RD HSE REST
16467 Hwy 116, Guerneville (95446-8328)
P.O. Box 45 (95446-0045)
PHONE...............................707 869-0656
Michael Clark, *President*
EMP: 65 EST: 1905
SQ FT: 23,226
SALES (est): 3.4MM **Privately Held**
SIC: 7011 5813 5812 Resort hotel; bar (drinking places); eating places

7011 - Hotels, Motels & Tourist Courts County (P-12567)

(P-12567)
DESTINATION RESORT MGT INC
Also Called: Shadow Mnt Rsort/Rcqut CL Tns
45750 San Luis Rey Ave, Palm Desert (92260-4728)
PHONE..................................760 346-4647
Sindy Calhoun, *Manager*
Ted Scharf, *Senior VP*
Cynthia Calquhoun, *General Mgr*
Laura Torres, *Sales Staff*
EMP: 50
SALES (corp-wide): 735.2MM **Privately Held**
WEB: www.destinationhotels.com
SIC: 7011 5699 6531 Resort hotel; sports apparel; condominium manager
HQ: Destination Residences Llc
10333 E Dry Creek Rd
Englewood CO 80112
303 799-3830

(P-12568)
DIAMOND INTL INVESTMENT LLC
3737 N Blackstone Ave, Fresno (93726-5307)
PHONE..................................559 226-2200
Betty Qi,
Alvin Cachaper, *Manager*
EMP: 63 **EST:** 2015
SALES (est): 840.4K **Privately Held**
SIC: 7011 Hotel, franchised

(P-12569)
DIAMOND MOUNTAIN CASINO
900 Skyline Dr, Susanville (96130-6071)
PHONE..................................530 252-1100
Campbell Jamieson, *Manager*
Jill Ault, *CFO*
Bob Nay, *Security Dir*
Nick Padilla, *Administration*
James Myers, *Technology*
EMP: 135
SQ FT: 24,000
SALES (est): 9.4MM **Privately Held**
WEB: www.diamondmountaincasino.com
SIC: 7011 Casino hotel

(P-12570)
DIAMONDROCK SAN DEGO TNANT LLC
Also Called: Westin San Diego
400 W Broadway, San Diego (92101-3504)
PHONE..................................619 239-4500
John Beaton,
Pamela Ford Green, *Accounting Mgr*
Julie Drazan, *Finance*
Stephanie Lee, *Sales Mgr*
Victoria Lewis, *Sales Mgr*
EMP: 300
SQ FT: 337,717
SALES (est): 5.2MM
SALES (corp-wide): 930.9MM **Publicly Held**
SIC: 7011 Hotels & motels
HQ: Diamondrock Hospitality Limited Partnership
3 Bethesda Metro Ctr
Bethesda MD 20814
240 744-1150

(P-12571)
DIMENSION DEVELOPMENT TWO LLC
Also Called: Hampton Inn San Diego-Downtown
1531 Pacific Hwy, San Diego (92101-2413)
PHONE..................................619 233-8408
Fax: 619 233-8418
Dan Danable, *Manager*
Orlando Woods, *Branch Mgr*
Marisela Navarro, *Supervisor*
EMP: 55
SALES (corp-wide): 69.5MM **Privately Held**
WEB: www.dimdev.com
SIC: 7011 Hotels & motels
PA: Dimension Development Two, Llc
769 Highway 494
Natchitoches LA 71457
318 352-9519

(P-12572)
DIMENSION DEVELOPMENT TWO LLC
Also Called: Sheraton
11611 Bernardo Plaza Ct, San Diego (92128-2408)
PHONE..................................858 485-9250
Douglas R Korn, *Branch Mgr*
Aureliano Meave, *Chief Engr*
EMP: 60
SALES (corp-wide): 69.5MM **Privately Held**
WEB: www.dimdev.com
SIC: 7011 Hotels & motels
PA: Dimension Development Two, Llc
769 Highway 494
Natchitoches LA 71457
318 352-9519

(P-12573)
DISNEY ENTERPRISES INC
1150 W Magic Way, Anaheim (92802-2247)
PHONE..................................714 817-7317
Michael D Eisner, *President*
Jennifer Paulo, *Social Dir*
Cyrus Ramtin, *Electrical Engi*
Gregg Haniford, *Sales Dir*
Michele Gendreau, *Director*
EMP: 300 **Publicly Held**
SIC: 7011 Hotels
HQ: Disney Enterprises, Inc.
500 S Buena Vista St
Burbank CA 91521
818 560-1000

(P-12574)
DISNEY ENTERPRISES INC
1717 S Disneyland Dr, Anaheim (92802-2308)
PHONE..................................714 956-6425
Marcy Canner, *Manager*
Stacey Edwards, *Office Mgr*
Charles Clark, *Manager*
James Minor, *Manager*
EMP: 300 **Publicly Held**
SIC: 7011 5813 5812 Hotels; drinking places; eating places
HQ: Disney Enterprises, Inc.
500 S Buena Vista St
Burbank CA 91521
818 560-1000

(P-12575)
DISNEYLAND INTERNATIONAL
1580 S Disneyland Dr, Anaheim (92802-2294)
PHONE..................................714 956-6746
EMP: 300 **Publicly Held**
SIC: 7011 Resort hotel
HQ: Disneyland International
770 The Cy Dr S Ste 6000
Orange CA 92868
714 490-3004

(P-12576)
DISNEYLAND INTERNATIONAL (DH)
770 The Cy Dr S Ste 6000, Orange (92868)
PHONE..................................714 490-3004
Douglas S McGuire, *President*
Joe Schott, *Vice Pres*
EMP: 85
SALES (est): 45.5MM **Publicly Held**
SIC: 7011 Motels
HQ: Walt Disney Music Company
500 S Buena Vista St
Burbank CA 91521
818 560-1000

(P-12577)
DISNEYS GRAND CALIFORNIAN HT
1600 S Disneyland Dr, Anaheim (92802-2317)
PHONE..................................714 635-2300
Fax: 714 300-7300
Dorothy Stratton, *Manager*
EMP: 80
SALES (est): 3.9MM **Privately Held**
WEB: www.disneymouselinks.com
SIC: 7011 Hotels

(P-12578)
DJONT/CMB SSF
Also Called: Embassy Sites-So San Francisco
250 Gateway Blvd, South San Francisco (94080-7018)
PHONE..................................650 589-3400
Fax: 650 876-0305
Rudy Ortiz, *General Mgr*
Dee Bradford, *Executive*
Nathan Duke, *Human Resources*
John Konzem, *Manager*
EMP: 60
SALES (est): 238K
SALES (corp-wide): 886.2MM **Privately Held**
SIC: 7011 Hotels & motels
PA: Felcor Lodging Trust Incorporated
545 E John Carpenter Fwy # 1300
Irving TX 75062
972 444-4900

(P-12579)
DKN HOTEL LLC (PA)
42 Corporate Park Ste 200, Irvine (92606-3104)
PHONE..................................714 427-4320
Kiran Patel, *CEO*
Nilesh Patel, *Co-Owner*
John Jorgensen, *Vice Pres*
Bhalesh Gandhi, *Controller*
Dahya Lal,
EMP: 290
SQ FT: 4,000
SALES (est): 35.5MM **Privately Held**
WEB: www.dknhotels.com
SIC: 7011 Hotels & motels

(P-12580)
DKN HOTEL LLC
Also Called: Holiday Inn
1240 S Walnut St, Anaheim (92802-2241)
PHONE..................................714 535-0300
Niral Munshaw, *Branch Mgr*
EMP: 88
SALES (corp-wide): 35.5MM **Privately Held**
WEB: www.dknhotels.com
SIC: 7011 Hotels & motels
PA: Dkn Hotel, Llc
42 Corporate Park Ste 200
Irvine CA 92606
714 427-4320

(P-12581)
DNC PRKS RSRTS AT YOSEMITE INC
Also Called: Yosemite Concession Services
9001 Village Dr, Yosemite Ntpk (95389-9912)
PHONE..................................209 372-1001
Fax: 209 372-1364
Dan Jensen, *President*
Paul Jensen, *Vice Pres*
Paul Jeppson, *Vice Pres*
Christy Contreras, *Area Mgr*
Audrey Lanting, *Asst Controller*
EMP: 1100
SALES (est): 65MM
SALES (corp-wide): 2.9B **Privately Held**
SIC: 7011 5399 5812 5947 Hotels; vacation lodges; country general stores; eating places; snack shop; gift shop; gasoline service stations; tours, conducted
HQ: Delaware North Companies Parks & Resorts, Inc.
250 Delaware Ave Ste 3
Buffalo NY 14202
716 858-5000

(P-12582)
DODGE RIDGE CORPORATION
Also Called: Dodge Ridge Winter Sports Area
1 Dodge Ridge Rd, Pinecrest (95364)
PHONE..................................209 536-5300
Jason Reed, *CFO*
Bob Hohne, *CFO*
Jason Smith, *Director*
Kenneth Hurst, *Manager*
EMP: 350
SQ FT: 10,000
SALES (est): 13.1MM **Privately Held**
WEB: www.dodgeridge.com
SIC: 7011 7033 Ski lodge; campgrounds

(P-12583)
DOLCE INTERNATIONAL / NAPA LLC
1600 Atlas Peak Rd, NAPA (94558-1425)
PHONE..................................707 257-0200
Steven A Rudnitsky, *President*
EMP: 484
SALES (est): 1.7MM
SALES (corp-wide): 5.5B **Publicly Held**
SIC: 7011 Hotels & motels
HQ: Dolce International Holdings, Inc.
22 Sylvan Way
Parsippany NJ 07054
201 307-8700

(P-12584)
DOLPHIN BAY HT & RESIDENCE INC
Also Called: Dolphin Bay Hotel & Residences
2727 Shell Beach Rd, Shell Beach (93449-1602)
PHONE..................................805 773-4300
Richard J Loughead Jr, *CEO*
Lee McGregor, *Manager*
EMP: 90
SALES (est): 6.1MM **Privately Held**
SIC: 7011 Hostels

(P-12585)
DOLPHINS COVE RESORT LTD
465 W Orangewood Ave, Anaheim (92802-4759)
PHONE..................................714 980-0830
Fax: 714 980-0943
Winners Circle Resort Intnl In, *General Ptnr*
Jessica Mendoza, *Executive*
Jennifer Eaton, *General Mgr*
EMP: 90
SALES (est): 3.2MM **Privately Held**
SIC: 7011 Resort hotel

(P-12586)
DOMINION INTERNATIONAL INC
Also Called: Hampton Inn
2305 Longport Ct, Elk Grove (95758-7127)
PHONE..................................916 683-9545
Fax: 916 683-9546
Perry Ferrera, *General Mgr*
EMP: 100
SALES (est): 3.2MM **Privately Held**
SIC: 7011 Hotels & motels

(P-12587)
DONALD T STERLING CORPORATION
Also Called: Beverly Hills Plaza Hotel
10300 Wilshire Blvd, Los Angeles (90024-4772)
PHONE..................................310 275-5575
Fax: 310 278-3325
Zair Caceres, *Manager*
Khali Guruuchin, *Asst Mgr*
EMP: 80
SALES (corp-wide): 7.1MM **Privately Held**
SIC: 7011 Hotels
PA: Donald T. Sterling Corporation
9411 Wilshire Blvd Ste Pe
Beverly Hills CA 90212
310 278-8000

(P-12588)
DOUBLETREE BY HILTON HOTEL
1985 E Grand Ave, El Segundo (90245-5015)
PHONE..................................310 322-0999
Jordan Austin, *General Mgr*
Mark Lewis, *Vice Pres*
Kenya Bannister, *Director*
EMP: 110 **EST:** 2011
SALES (est): 610.2K **Privately Held**
SIC: 7011 Hotels

(P-12589)
DOUBLETREE HOTEL
888 Montebello Blvd, Rosemead (91770-4303)
PHONE..................................323 722-8800
Fax: 323 722-5207
Frank Huang, *Partner*
Denis Ng, *Info Tech Mgr*
EMP: 86
SQ FT: 110,000

PRODUCTS & SERVICES SECTION
7011 - Hotels, Motels & Tourist Courts County (P-12611)

SALES (est): 5.5MM Privately Held
SIC: 7011 Hotels & motels

(P-12590)
DOUBLETREE LLC
Also Called: Doubletree Hotel
14455 Penasquitos Dr, San Diego (92129-1603)
PHONE 858 485-4145
Fax: 858 672-9166
Russ Tanakaya, *General Mgr*
Andrea Lambert, *Vice Pres*
Brian Dadd, *Manager*
Michael Menager, *Manager*
EMP: 140
SALES (corp-wide): 11.2B Publicly Held
WEB: www.dtwarrenplace.com
SIC: 7011 Hotels & motels
HQ: Doubletree Llc
7930 Jones Branch Dr
Mc Lean VA 22102
703 883-1000

(P-12591)
DOUBLETREE LLC
Also Called: Doubletree Hotel
222 N Vineyard Ave, Ontario (91764-4428)
PHONE 909 605-4222
Fax: 909 937-0900
Herman Haastrup, *Manager*
Zaira Urey, *Financial Exec*
Jim Boitnott, *Sales Mgr*
EMP: 343
SALES (corp-wide): 11.2B Publicly Held
WEB: www.dtwarrenplace.com
SIC: 7011 Hotels & motels
HQ: Doubletree Llc
7930 Jones Branch Dr
Mc Lean VA 22102
703 883-1000

(P-12592)
DOUBLETREE LLC
Also Called: Doubletree Hotel
2050 Gateway Pl, San Jose (95110-1047)
PHONE 408 453-4000
David Costain, *General Mgr*
Ken Kundert, *Bd of Directors*
Aissata S Morton, *Bd of Directors*
Boris Frenkel, *Engineer*
Paul Bielinski, *Director*
EMP: 350
SALES (corp-wide): 11.2B Publicly Held
WEB: www.dtwarrenplace.com
SIC: 7011 5812 Hotels & motels; eating places
HQ: Doubletree Llc
7930 Jones Branch Dr
Mc Lean VA 22102
703 883-1000

(P-12593)
DOUBLETREE LLC
Also Called: Doubltree By Hlton Ht Bkrsfeld
3100 Camino Del Rio Ct, Bakersfield (93308-6245)
PHONE 661 323-7111
Robert Balmer, *Manager*
Bill Murray, *General Mgr*
Erika Chesley, *Sales Dir*
EMP: 234
SALES (corp-wide): 11.2B Publicly Held
WEB: www.doralpalmsprings.com
SIC: 7011 7299 Hotels & motels; banquet hall facilities
HQ: Doubletree Llc
7930 Jones Branch Dr
Mc Lean VA 22102
703 883-1000

(P-12594)
DOUBLETREE LLC
Also Called: Doubletree Hotel
2001 Point West Way, Sacramento (95815-4702)
PHONE 916 929-8855
Chris Mellini, *Manager*
Walter Hopkins, *Engineer*
Melissa Barcelo, *Human Res Dir*
Al Rosales, *Persnl Dir*
Courtney Morgan, *HR Admin*
EMP: 350

(P-12595)
DOUBLETREE LLC
Also Called: Doubletree Hotel
201 E Macarthur Blvd, Santa Ana (92707-5776)
PHONE 714 825-3333
Fax: 714 442-1902
Marsha Hansen, *General Mgr*
Tina Beverly, *Human Res Mgr*
Olga Paz, *Human Res Mgr*
EMP: 182
SALES (corp-wide): 11.2B Publicly Held
WEB: www.dtwarrenplace.com
SIC: 7011 Hotels & motels
HQ: Doubletree Llc
7930 Jones Branch Dr
Mc Lean VA 22102
703 883-1000

(P-12596)
DOUBLETREE LLC
Also Called: Doubletree Hotel
1150 9th St Frnt, Modesto (95354-0823)
PHONE 209 526-6000
Fax: 209 526-6096
Cindy Power, *Manager*
EMP: 270
SALES (corp-wide): 11.2B Publicly Held
WEB: www.dtwarrenplace.com
SIC: 7011 5813 Hotels & motels; drinking places
HQ: Doubletree Llc
7930 Jones Branch Dr
Mc Lean VA 22102
703 883-1000

(P-12597)
DOUBLETREE LLC
Also Called: Doubletree By Hilton
7450 Hazard Center Dr, San Diego (92108-4598)
PHONE 619 297-5466
Karima Zaki, *Manager*
Mark Seetin, *Vice Pres*
Chris Naylor, *General Mgr*
Jessica Puccio, *Admin Asst*
James Le, *CIO*
EMP: 300
SALES (corp-wide): 11.2B Publicly Held
WEB: www.doralpalmsprings.com
SIC: 7011 5812 Hotels & motels; eating places
HQ: Doubletree Llc
7930 Jones Branch Dr
Mc Lean VA 22102
703 883-1000

(P-12598)
DOUBLETREE LLC
Also Called: Doubletree Hotel
835 Airport Blvd, Burlingame (94010-1922)
PHONE 650 344-5500
Fax: 650 340-8851
Liza Normandy, *Branch Mgr*
Bruce Tarlon, *General Mgr*
Romeo Arellano, *Info Tech Dir*
Raymond Wai, *Credit Mgr*
Richard Wall, *Manager*
EMP: 175
SALES (corp-wide): 11.2B Publicly Held
WEB: www.doralpalmsprings.com
SIC: 7011 6512 5813 5812 Hotels & motels; nonresidential building operators; drinking places; eating places
HQ: Doubletree Llc
7930 Jones Branch Dr
Mc Lean VA 22102
703 883-1000

(P-12599)
DOUBLETREE LLC
Also Called: Doubletree Hotel
1 Doubletree Dr, Rohnert Park (94928-1336)
PHONE 707 584-5466
Ted Sakai, *Manager*

SALES (corp-wide): 11.2B Publicly Held
WEB: www.dtwarrenplace.com
SIC: 7011 5812 5813 7991 Hotels & motels; eating places; bar (drinking places); physical fitness facilities
HQ: Doubletree Llc
7930 Jones Branch Dr
Mc Lean VA 22102
703 883-1000

Mary B Parks, *Vice Pres*
Michael Sokulski, *Principal*
Simon McGrath, *General Mgr*
Bill Worcester, *General Mgr*
EMP: 170
SALES (corp-wide): 11.2B Publicly Held
WEB: www.dtwarrenplace.com
SIC: 7011 5813 5812 7991 Hotels & motels; drinking places; eating places; physical fitness facilities
HQ: Doubletree Llc
7930 Jones Branch Dr
Mc Lean VA 22102
703 883-1000

(P-12600)
DOUBLETREE LLC
Also Called: Doubletree Hotel
34402 Pacific Coast Hwy, Dana Point (92624-1211)
PHONE 949 661-1100
Mike Peludo, *Manager*
Rudy Alvarez, *Sales Dir*
EMP: 80
SALES (corp-wide): 11.2B Publicly Held
WEB: www.doralpalmsprings.com
SIC: 7011 Hotels & motels
HQ: Doubletree Llc
7930 Jones Branch Dr
Mc Lean VA 22102
703 883-1000

(P-12601)
DOUBLTREE SUITES BY HILTON LLC
Also Called: Doubletree Hotel
2085 S Harbor Blvd, Anaheim (92802-3513)
PHONE 714 750-3000
Fax: 714 750-3002
Amrit K Patel, *Manager*
Christopher Neilson, *Technology*
Debbie Plueger, *Mktg Dir*
William R O'Connell,
Shirish H Patel,
EMP: 175
SALES (est): 9.2MM Privately Held
WEB: www.orangewood.net
SIC: 7011 5812 Hotels & motels; American restaurant

(P-12602)
DTRS SANTA MONICA LLC
Also Called: Loews Santa Monica Beach Hotel
1700 Ocean Ave, Santa Monica (90401-3214)
PHONE 310 458-6700
Fax: 310 458-2813
Paul Leclerc, *General Mgr*
John Thaeker, *Regional VP*
Jenny Frankel, *Exec VP*
Don Foreman, *Vice Pres*
Gail Paul, *Engineer*
EMP: 300
SQ FT: 300,000
SALES (est): 21.4MM Privately Held
SIC: 7011 Hotels

(P-12603)
DUE WEST LLC
Also Called: Canary Hotel
31 W Carrillo St, Santa Barbara (93101-3212)
PHONE 805 884-0300
Fax: 805 884-8153
Thomas Slatkin,
Dianne Travis-Teague, *Executive*
Connie Rowe, *Controller*
Sierra Trujillo, *Sales Mgr*
Edward Slatkin,
EMP: 55
SALES (est): 5.1MM Privately Held
SIC: 7011 Hotels

(P-12604)
E H SUMMIT INC (PA)
Also Called: Luxe Sunset Boulevard Hotel
11461 W Sunset Blvd, Los Angeles (90049-2031)
PHONE 310 476-6571
Efrem Harkhan, *CEO*
Barbara Shore, *Exec VP*
Carlos Amaya, *Executive*
Fabiola Hernandez, *Executive*
Miguel Cano, *Chief Engr*

EMP: 60
SALES (est): 15.9MM Privately Held
SIC: 7011 Hotels & motels

(P-12605)
E H SUMMIT INC
360 N Rodeo Dr, Beverly Hills (90210-5177)
PHONE 310 273-0300
Efrem Harkhan, *President*
EMP: 65
SALES (corp-wide): 16.7MM Privately Held
SIC: 7011 Hotels & motels
PA: E. H. Summit, Inc.
11461 W Sunset Blvd
Los Angeles CA 90049
310 476-6571

(P-12606)
EAST KATELLA PARTNERSHIP
Also Called: Ramada Inn
525 Cabrillo Park Dr # 220, Santa Ana (92701-5017)
PHONE 714 978-8088
Mickey Tody, *General Mgr*
L A Sofer, *Partner*
EMP: 60
SALES (est): 3.7MM Privately Held
SIC: 7011 Hotels & motels

(P-12607)
EAST PALO ALTO HOTEL DEV INC
Also Called: Four Seasons Hotel Silicon Vly
2050 University Ave, East Palo Alto (94303-2248)
PHONE 650 566-1200
Tracy Mercer, *General Mgr*
EMP: 210
SALES (est): 8.8MM Privately Held
SIC: 7011 7389 Hotels; office facilities & secretarial service rental

(P-12608)
EASUN INC
2001 Point West Way, Sacramento (95815-4702)
PHONE 916 929-8855
Benjamin Shih, *Director*
EMP: 250
SALES (est): 20MM Privately Held
SIC: 7011 Hotels & motels

(P-12609)
ECONOMY INN
1243 E Main St, Barstow (92311-2408)
PHONE 760 256-5601
Mike Patel, *Owner*
EMP: 50
SALES (est): 656K Privately Held
WEB: www.elliott.com
SIC: 7011 Hotels & motels

(P-12610)
EDWARD THOMAS COMPANIES
Also Called: Jolly Roger Inn
640 W Katella Ave, Anaheim (92802-3411)
PHONE 714 782-7500
Fax: 714 772-2308
Fred Kokash, *Branch Mgr*
Richard E Duffy, *Agent*
EMP: 100
SALES (corp-wide): 6.1MM Privately Held
WEB: www.jollyrogerhotel.com
SIC: 7011 5812 Motels; eating places
PA: The Edward Thomas Companies
9950 Santa Monica Blvd
Beverly Hills CA 90212
310 859-9366

(P-12611)
EDWARD THOMAS HOSPITALITY CORP
Also Called: Shutters On The Beach
1 Pico Blvd, Santa Monica (90405-1063)
PHONE 310 458-0030
Klaus Mennekes, *Branch Mgr*
Wendy Bolte, *Info Tech Mgr*
Laura Bloomquist, *Accountant*
Kirk Knudsen, *Controller*
Chuck Craig, *Director*
EMP: 350

7011 - Hotels, Motels & Tourist Courts County (P-12612)

SALES (corp-wide): 18.9MM **Privately Held**
WEB: www.shuttersonthebeach.com
SIC: **7011** 5812 7991 5813 Hotels & motels; eating places; physical fitness facilities; drinking places
PA: The Edward Thomas Hospitality Corp
9950 Santa Monica Blvd
Beverly Hills CA 90212
310 859-9366

(P-12612)
EL CORDOVA HOTEL
Also Called: Pacific Terrace Inn
1351 Orange Ave, Coronado (92118-2916)
PHONE 619 435-4131
Fax: 619 435-0632
Mark Francois, *General Mgr*
Robert Mc Ginnis, *Partner*
Robert Bottomley, *Manager*
Alex Hernandez, *Manager*
Zanete Millar, *Manager*
EMP: 100
SQ FT: 20,000
SALES (est): 2.7MM **Privately Held**
WEB: www.elcordovahotel.com
SIC: **7011** Hotels; motels

(P-12613)
EL DORADO ENTERPRISES INC
Also Called: Hustler Casino
1000 W Redondo Beach Blvd, Gardena (90247-4192)
PHONE 310 719-9800
Fax: 310 515-0293
Larry C Flynt, *CEO*
Michael Laser, *Security Dir*
Tom Candy, *General Mgr*
Alyona Konova, *Info Tech Dir*
Alyona Kononova, *Info Tech Mgr*
EMP: 760
SALES (est): 32MM **Privately Held**
WEB: www.hustlergaming.com
SIC: **7011** Casino hotel

(P-12614)
EL RANCHO MOTEL INC
Also Called: Best Wstn El Rancho Inn Suites
1100 El Camino Real, Millbrae (94030-2098)
PHONE 650 588-8500
Fax: 650 742-5582
John C Wilms, *President*
Paul Wilms, *Vice Pres*
Jim Kiefer, *Information Mgr*
Vicki Venstad, *Human Res Dir*
Corazon Glover, *Manager*
EMP: 168
SQ FT: 23,958
SALES (est): 10.8MM **Privately Held**
WEB: www.elranchoinn.com
SIC: **7011** 5812 5813 7991 Hotels & motels; eating places; drinking places; physical fitness facilities

(P-12615)
ELIZABETHAN INN ASSOCIATES LP
Also Called: The Sterling Hotel
1935 Wright St Apt 231, Sacramento (95825-1191)
PHONE 916 448-1300
Sandra Wasserman, *Partner*
EMP: 90
SQ FT: 15,000
SALES (est): 1.4MM **Privately Held**
WEB: www.sterlinghotel.com
SIC: **7011** 5812 7299 Hotels; ethnic food restaurants; banquet hall facilities

(P-12616)
EMBARCADERO INN ASSOCIATES
Also Called: Hotel Griffon
155 Steuart St, San Francisco (94105-1206)
PHONE 415 495-2100
Fax: 415 495-3522
Edward Marinucci, *General Ptnr*
Pacific Union Investment Corpo, *General Ptnr*
Patrick McAllister, *Controller*
EMP: 125
SALES (est): 5MM **Privately Held**
WEB: www.hotelgriffon.com
SIC: **7011** 5812 Hotels; family restaurants

(P-12617)
EMBASSY SUITES MANAGEMENT LLC
4550 La Jolla Village Dr, San Diego (92122-1248)
PHONE 858 453-0400
Tim Billing, *General Mgr*
EMP: 102 EST: 2007
SALES (est): 789.3K **Privately Held**
SIC: **7011** Hotels & motels

(P-12618)
EMERIK HOTEL CORP
Also Called: Luxe City Center
1020 S Figueroa St, Los Angeles (90015-1305)
PHONE 213 748-1291
Emerson Glazer, *President*
Art Malmgren, *CFO*
John Kelly, *Vice Pres*
Eric Stone, *Vice Pres*
James Jones, *Admin Sec*
EMP: 90
SALES: 8MM **Privately Held**
WEB: www.hicitycenter.com
SIC: **7011** 5813 5812 Hotels & motels; bar (drinking places); American restaurant

(P-12619)
ENCINA PEPPER TREE JOINT VENTR (PA)
Also Called: BEST WESTERN PEPPER TREE INN
3850 State St, Santa Barbara (93105-3112)
PHONE 805 687-5511
Fax: 805 682-2410
Jeanette Webber, *Managing Prtnr*
David Potter, *Partner*
Camille Shaar, *Partner*
Pamela Webber, *Partner*
Chivaun Clark, *General Mgr*
EMP: 70
SQ FT: 100,000
SALES: 12.4MM **Privately Held**
WEB: www.sbhotels.com
SIC: **7011** Hotels & motels

(P-12620)
ENCINA PEPPER TREE JOINT VENTR
Also Called: Best Western
2220 Bath St, Santa Barbara (93105-4322)
PHONE 805 682-7277
Fax: 805 563-9319
Pam Webber, *Manager*
EMP: 80
SALES (corp-wide): 12.4MM **Privately Held**
WEB: www.sbhotels.com
SIC: **7011** Hotels & motels
PA: Pepper Encina Tree Joint Venture
3850 State St
Santa Barbara CA 93105
805 687-5511

(P-12621)
EQUISTAR IRVINE COMPANY LLC
Also Called: Hilton Irvine
18800 Macarthur Blvd, Irvine (92612-1410)
PHONE 949 833-3331
Meristar Mezzanine Borrower, *Manager*
Tricia Wall, *General Mgr*
EMP: 99
SALES (est): 5.2MM **Privately Held**
SIC: **7011** Hotels & motels

(P-12622)
ERGS AIM HOTEL REALTY LLC
Also Called: Embassy Suites Anaheim Orange
400 N State College Blvd, Orange (92868-1708)
PHONE 714 938-1111
Eric Pyland, *Business Mgr*
John Rogers, *CEO*
Manuel Rocha, *Executive*
Cheree Goodall, *Office Mgr*
EMP: 75
SQ FT: 50,000
SALES (est): 1MM **Privately Held**
SIC: **7011** Hotels & motels

(P-12623)
ESA P PRTFOLIO OPER LESSEE LLC
Also Called: Extended Stay America, Inc.
4881 Birch St, Newport Beach (92660-2112)
PHONE 949 851-2711
Fax: 949 851-2733
William Arter, *Branch Mgr*
EMP: 50
SALES (corp-wide): 1.2B **Publicly Held**
WEB: www.weddingbells.net
SIC: **7011** Hotels & motels
HQ: Esa P Portfolio Operating Lessee, Llc
11525 N Community House R
Charlotte NC 28277
980 345-1600

(P-12624)
ESA P PRTFOLIO OPER LESSEE LLC
Also Called: Extended Stay America, Inc.
1635 W Katella Ave, Orange (92867-3412)
PHONE 714 639-8608
Fax: 714 639-8472
Leilani Reynolds, *Branch Mgr*
EMP: 73
SALES (corp-wide): 1.2B **Publicly Held**
WEB: www.weddingbells.net
SIC: **7011** Hotels & motels
HQ: Esa P Portfolio Operating Lessee, Llc
11525 N Community House R
Charlotte NC 28277
980 345-1600

(P-12625)
ET WHITEHALL SEASCAPE LLC
Also Called: Hotel Casa Del Mar
1910 Ocean Way, Santa Monica (90405-1083)
PHONE 310 581-5533
Edward Slatkin,
Ellen Adelman, *General Mgr*
James Borrella, *General Mgr*
James Ayash, *Info Tech Mgr*
Jodi Horwitz, *Controller*
EMP: 202 EST: 1998
SQ FT: 200,000
SALES (est): 11.6MM **Privately Held**
WEB: www.hotelcasadelmar.com
SIC: **7011** 5812 Hotels & motels; eating places

(P-12626)
EUROPEAN HOTL INVSTRS OF CA
Also Called: Doubletree Hotel
1985 E Grandave, El Segundo (90245)
PHONE 310 322-0999
Fax: 310 322-4758
Tim River, *Manager*
Jordan Austin, *General Mgr*
EMP: 50
SALES (corp-wide): 13.9MM **Privately Held**
SIC: **7011** Hotels & motels
PA: European Hotel Investors I I, A California Limited Partnership
2532 Dupont Dr
Irvine CA 92612
949 474-7368

(P-12627)
EVERGREEN DSTNTION HLDINGS LLC
Also Called: Evergreen Lodge
33160 Evergreen Rd, Groveland (95321-9772)
PHONE 209 379-2606
Fax: 209 379-2607
Brian Anderluh,
Donna West, *Financial Exec*
Dan Braun,
Lee Zimmerman,
Julia Convissor, *Manager*
EMP: 75
SQ FT: 6,000
SALES (est): 5.2MM **Privately Held**
SIC: **7011** 5812 Hotels; eating places

(P-12628)
EXECUTIVE INN INC
Also Called: Ramada Inn
1217 Wildwood Ave, Sunnyvale (94089-2701)
PHONE 408 245-5330
Roger Chang, *President*
Jeffry S C Chang, *President*
David C M Chang, *Admin Sec*
Karen Chau, *Manager*
EMP: 97
SQ FT: 15,400
SALES (est): 4.5MM **Privately Held**
SIC: **7011** Hotels & motels

(P-12629)
FAIRFIELD INN SUITES BY M
315 Pittman Rd, Fairfield (94534-6799)
PHONE 707 864-6672
Nash Desai, *Manager*
EMP: 80
SALES (est): 3.8MM **Privately Held**
SIC: **7011** Hotels & motels

(P-12630)
FAIRMONT HOTEL PARTNERS LLC
101 Wilshire Blvd, Santa Monica (90401-1106)
PHONE 310 319-3122
Karl Buchta, *General Mgr*
EMP: 275
SALES (corp-wide): 27.3MM **Privately Held**
SIC: **7011** Hotels
HQ: Fairmont Hotel Partners, Llc
950 Mason St
San Francisco CA 94108
415 772-5000

(P-12631)
FARGO COLONIAL LLC
Also Called: Grande Colonial
910 Prospect St, La Jolla (92037-4144)
PHONE 858 454-2181
Roger Joseph,
Katy Giacalone, *Executive*
Audra Gillespie, *General Mgr*
Terrence D Underwood, *General Mgr*
Aki Tomiyama, *Information Mgr*
EMP: 63
SQ FT: 46,480
SALES: 9.6MM **Privately Held**
WEB: www.thegrandecolonial.com
SIC: **7011** 5812 Hotels; eating places

(P-12632)
FC EL SEGUNDO LLC
Also Called: Cambria El Segundo Lax
199 Continental Blvd, El Segundo (90245-4525)
PHONE 702 439-7945
Milton B Patipa, *Senior VP*
EMP: 75
SQ FT: 86,106
SALES (est): 233.5K **Privately Held**
SIC: **7011** Hotels

(P-12633)
FEDERTED INDANS GRTON RNCHERIA
Graton Resort & Casino
630 Park Ct, Rohnert Park (94928-7906)
PHONE 707 588-7100
Greg Sarris, *Branch Mgr*
EMP: 103 **Privately Held**
SIC: **7011** Casino hotel
PA: Federated Indians Of Graton Rancheria
6400 Redwood Dr Ste 300
Rohnert Park CA 94928
619 917-9566

(P-12634)
FERRADO GARDEN COURT LLC
520 Cowper St Ste 100, Palo Alto (94301-1826)
PHONE 650 543-2224
Ferrado Inmuebles SL, *Mng Member*
Lora Ion, *Sales Executive*
Barbara Gross,
EMP: 60
SQ FT: 63,620
SALES (est): 1MM **Privately Held**
WEB: www.gardencourt.com
SIC: **7011** Hotels & motels

PRODUCTS & SERVICES SECTION
7011 - Hotels, Motels & Tourist Courts County (P-12659)

(P-12635)
FESS PRKER-RED LION GEN PARTNR
Also Called: Doubletree Hotel
633 E Cabrillo Blvd, Santa Barbara (93103-3611)
PHONE.................805 564-4333
Fax: 805 564-1170
Fess Parker, *Partner*
Julie Menicucci, *Exec Dir*
Scott Reams, *Exec Dir*
Raymond Montoya, *Controller*
Darrin Williams, *Security Mgr*
EMP: 325
SALES (est): 19.4MM **Privately Held**
SIC: 7011 Hotels & motels

(P-12636)
FIRST HOTELS INTERNATIONAL INC
Also Called: Radisson Inn
295 N E St, San Bernardino (92401-1507)
P.O. Box 1805 (92402-1805)
PHONE.................909 884-9364
James Deskus, *General Mgr*
Cindy Gardner, *Treasurer*
Chocchet Koski, *Controller*
Ivan Verheijen, *Manager*
EMP: 140
SALES (est): 2.8MM **Privately Held**
SIC: 7011 Hotels & motels

(P-12637)
FITNESS RIDGE MALIBU LLC
Also Called: Biggest Lser Ftnes Rdge Malibu
277 Latigo Canyon Rd, Malibu (90265-2707)
PHONE.................818 874-1300
Michelle Kelsch,
Tami Clark,
Cameron Kelsch,
EMP: 56
SALES (est): 1.4MM **Privately Held**
SIC: 7011 7991 Hotels & motels; physical fitness facilities

(P-12638)
FJS INC
Also Called: Anabella Hotel The
1030 W Katella Ave, Anaheim (92802-3419)
PHONE.................714 905-1050
Francis J Sparolini, *CEO*
C Y Chan, *President*
Nathan Fitzgerald, *General Mgr*
Brandon Jemison, *Office Mgr*
Rachel Moorhead, *Admin Sec*
EMP: 118
SALES (est): 11.7MM **Privately Held**
WEB: www.anabellahotel.com
SIC: 7011 Resort hotel

(P-12639)
FLORENCE VILLA HOTEL
Also Called: The Villa Florence Hotel
225 Powell St, San Francisco (94102-2205)
PHONE.................415 397-7700
Fax: 415 397-1006
Steve Miller, *General Mgr*
Michael Lennon, *Manager*
EMP: 200
SALES (est): 9.4MM
SALES (corp-wide): 1.2B **Privately Held**
WEB: www.villaflorence.com
SIC: 7011 5812 Hotels; eating places
PA: Lasalle Hotel Properties
7550 Wisconsin Ave # 100
Bethesda MD 20814
301 941-1500

(P-12640)
FLORENCE VILLA HOTEL LLC
225 Powell St, San Francisco (94102-2205)
PHONE.................415 397-7700
Sue Hefty,
David Garrin, *General Mgr*
Marit Davey,
Michael Lennon, *Manager*
EMP: 99
SALES (est): 3.6MM **Privately Held**
SIC: 7011 Hotels & motels

(P-12641)
FORCE-OAKLEAF LP
Also Called: Courtyard By Marriott
6333 Bristol Pkwy, Culver City (90230-6904)
PHONE.................310 484-7000
Andy Eklov, *Partner*
EMP: 66
SQ FT: 167,792
SALES (est): 2.2MM **Privately Held**
SIC: 7011 Hotels & motels

(P-12642)
FORGE-VIDOVICH MOTEL LIMITED
Also Called: Cupertino Inn
10889 N De Anza Blvd, Cupertino (95014-0439)
PHONE.................408 996-7700
Fax: 408 257-0578
John Vidovich, *General Ptnr*
Stephen J Vidovich, *General Ptnr*
Barbara Perzigian, *General Mgr*
Leann Hall, *Manager*
EMP: 60
SQ FT: 8,323
SALES (est): 4.8MM **Privately Held**
WEB: www.cupertinoinn.com
SIC: 7011 Hotels

(P-12643)
FORTUNA ENTERPRISES LP
Also Called: Los Angles Arprt Hilton Towers
5711 W Century Blvd, Los Angeles (90045-5672)
PHONE.................310 410-4000
Fax: 310 410-6250
Henry H Hsu, *Partner*
Christine Hsu, *Partner*
David Hsu, *Partner*
Grant Coonley, *General Mgr*
Philip Chao, *Info Tech Mgr*
EMP: 450
SQ FT: 2,700
SALES (est): 30.2MM **Privately Held**
SIC: 7011 5812 5813 Hotels & motels; eating places; bar (drinking places)
HQ: Universal Fortuna Investment, Inc
5711 W Century Blvd # 1628
Los Angeles CA 90045
310 410-6239

(P-12644)
FOUNDERS MANAGEMENT II CORP
Also Called: Crowne Plaza Hotel
1221 Chess Dr, Foster City (94404-1173)
PHONE.................650 570-5700
Fax: 650 295-0540
Solomon Tsai, *Managing Dir*
Scott Castle, *General Mgr*
Deena Castle, *Sales Dir*
Martin Uiberlacker, *Asst Mgr*
EMP: 275
SQ FT: 280,000
SALES (est): 17.2MM **Privately Held**
SIC: 7011 5812 5813 Hotels & motels; eating places; bar (drinking places)

(P-12645)
FOUNTAINGROVE INN LLC
Also Called: Fountngrove Inn Conference Ctr
101 Fountaingrove Pkwy, Santa Rosa (95403-1777)
PHONE.................707 578-6101
Fax: 707 544-3126
Robert Miller,
Russell Hendon, *Human Res Dir*
Brenda Alberigi, *Sales Dir*
Angelo Serro,
Ceclie Kraus, *Director*
EMP: 100
SQ FT: 79,200
SALES (est): 6.3MM **Privately Held**
WEB: www.fountaingroveinn.com
SIC: 7011 5812 Hotels; eating places

(P-12646)
FOUR POINTS BY SHERATON
9750 Airport Blvd, Los Angeles (90045-5404)
PHONE.................310 645-4600
Fax: 310 338-9618
Jonh Vickers, *President*
Gloria Green, *Accountant*
EMP: 57
SALES (est): 3MM **Privately Held**
SIC: 7011 Hotels & motels

(P-12647)
FOUR SEASONS HOTEL INC
Also Called: Four Ssons Hotel-San Francisco
735 Market St Fl 6, San Francisco (94103-2034)
PHONE.................415 633-3441
Stan Bromley, *Branch Mgr*
EMP: 515
SALES (corp-wide): 6.9MM **Privately Held**
SIC: 7011 Hotels & motels
HQ: Four Seasons Hotels Limited
1165 Leslie St
North York ON M3C 2
416 449-1750

(P-12648)
FOUR SEASONS HOTEL INC
2050 University Ave, East Palo Alto (94303-2248)
PHONE.................650 566-1200
Robert Whitfield, *Manager*
EMP: 515
SALES (corp-wide): 6.9MM **Privately Held**
SIC: 7011 Hotels & motels
HQ: Four Seasons Hotels Limited
1165 Leslie St
North York ON M3C 2
416 449-1750

(P-12649)
FOUR SEASONS WESTLAKE
2 Dole Dr, Westlake Village (91362-7300)
PHONE.................818 575-3000
Thomas Gurtner, *Manager*
Bill Thomas, *Human Res Dir*
EMP: 54
SALES (est): 3.1MM **Privately Held**
SIC: 7011 Hotels

(P-12650)
FOUR SISTERS INNS
Also Called: 1906 Lodge
1060 Adella Ave, Coronado (92118-2908)
PHONE.................619 437-1900
Susan Nelson, *General Mgr*
EMP: 168
SALES (corp-wide): 22.1MM **Privately Held**
SIC: 7011 Hotels & motels
PA: Four Sisters Inns
460 Alma St Ste 100
Monterey CA 93940
831 649-0908

(P-12651)
FPL LLC
Also Called: Wyndham Garden Pierpont Inn
550 San Jon Rd, Ventura (93001-3745)
PHONE.................805 643-6144
Nilesh Patel,
EMP: 55
SALES (est): 2.2MM **Privately Held**
SIC: 7011 Hotels & motels

(P-12652)
FREMONT MARRIOTT
46100 Landing Pkwy, Fremont (94538-6437)
PHONE.................510 413-3700
John Ault, *General Mgr*
EMP: 130
SALES (est): 387.6K **Privately Held**
SIC: 7011 Hotels

(P-12653)
FRENCH REDWOOD INC
Also Called: Hotel Sfitel San Francisco Bay
223 Twin Dolphin Dr, Redwood City (94065-1414)
PHONE.................650 598-9000
Fax: 650 598-0459
David O'Shaunessy, *President*
Brian L Monica, *Director*
Carol Sass, *Director*
Carmen Morello, *Manager*
Suzanne Balsamo, *Assistant*
EMP: 228
SALES (est): 9.7MM
SALES (corp-wide): 946.2MM **Privately Held**
WEB: www.hbsaward.com
SIC: 7011 5813 5812 Hotels; drinking places; eating places
PA: Accorhotels
82 Rue Henry Farman
Issy Les Moulineaux 92130

(P-12654)
FRESNO AIRPORT HOTELS LLC
Also Called: Ramada Inn Fresno Airport
5090 E Clinton Way, Fresno (93727-1506)
PHONE.................559 252-3611
Rohit Kumar, *President*
Leslie Beninga, *Director*
EMP: 65
SALES (est): 1MM **Privately Held**
SIC: 7011 Hotels & motels

(P-12655)
FRESNO HOTEL PARTNERS LP
Also Called: Ramada Inn
324 E Shaw Ave, Fresno (93710-7610)
PHONE.................559 224-4040
EMP: 60
SALES (est): 2MM **Privately Held**
SIC: 7011 7991 5812 7999 Hotels & motels; physical fitness facilities; eating places; swimming pool, non-membership

(P-12656)
G5 GLOBAL PARTNERS IX LLC
Also Called: Ramada Plz Ht San Dego/ Ht Cir
2151 Hotel Cir S, San Diego (92108-3314)
PHONE.................619 291-6500
Evan Hitter,
EMP: 75
SALES: 950K **Privately Held**
SIC: 7011 Hotels & motels

(P-12657)
GALLERIA PARK ASSOCIATES LLC
Also Called: Galleria Park Hotel
191 Sutter St, San Francisco (94104-4501)
PHONE.................415 781-3060
Fax: 415 433-4409
James Lim, *General Mgr*
Jane Howard, *Officer*
Linda Palermo, *Officer*
Fred De Stefano, *Exec VP*
Mark Polochak, *Vice Pres*
EMP: 68
SQ FT: 109,673
SALES: 8.5MM **Privately Held**
WEB: www.galleriapark.com
SIC: 7011 6512 5813 5812 Hotels; non-residential building operators; drinking places; eating places

(P-12658)
GARDEN COURT HOTEL
520 Cowper St Ste 100, Palo Alto (94301-1826)
PHONE.................650 322-9000
Fax: 650 322-3440
Norman Rosenblatt, *General Ptnr*
Irwin G Kasle, *General Ptnr*
Nan Rosenblatt, *General Ptnr*
Sanford H Webster, *General Ptnr*
Jesse Bresnahan, *Social Dir*
EMP: 90
SQ FT: 67,000
SALES (est): 6.9MM **Privately Held**
SIC: 7011 5812 Hotels; eating places

(P-12659)
GASLAMP HOTEL MANAGEMENT INC
202 Island Ave, San Diego (92101-6826)
PHONE.................619 234-0977
Dana Blasi, *President*
Joann Myers, *Manager*
EMP: 168
SALES (est): 4MM **Privately Held**
SIC: 7011 8741 Hotels; hotel or motel management

7011 - Hotels, Motels & Tourist Courts County (P-12660)

(P-12660)
GCCFC 2005-GG5 Y ST LTD PARTNR
Also Called: Courtyard By Marriott S
4422 Y St, Sacramento (95817-2220)
PHONE 916 455-6800
Ken Brewer, *General Mgr*
Beth Gamble, *Controller*
EMP: 70
SALES: 950K Privately Held
SIC: 7011 Hotels & motels

(P-12661)
GEARY DARLING LESSEE INC
Also Called: Marker Hotel, The
501 Geary St, San Francisco (94102-1640)
PHONE 415 292-0100
Fax: 415 292-0111
Michael Depatie, *President*
Lisa Krishna, *General Mgr*
James Tyler, *Director*
EMP: 150
SQ FT: 20,000
SALES (est): 13.4MM Privately Held
WEB: www.monaco-sf.com
SIC: 7011 7991 5813 5812 Hotels; physical fitness facilities; drinking places; eating places; banquet hall facilities

(P-12662)
GENTRY ASSOCIATES LLC
Also Called: Park Manor Suites
525 Spruce St, San Diego (92103-5814)
PHONE 619 296-0057
Fax: 619 291-8844
Elizabeth Willis, *Mng Member*
Sandra Speers, *Sales Staff*
Bonnie Gundert, *Manager*
EMP: 80
SALES (est): 4.1MM Privately Held
WEB: www.parkmanorsuites.com
SIC: 7011 5812 Hotels; eating places

(P-12663)
GEORGIAN HOTEL
1415 Ocean Ave, Santa Monica (90401-2101)
PHONE 310 395-9945
Fax: 310 451-3374
Richard Dodrill,
Katherine Guerra, *Senior VP*
Jane M Guerra, *Executive*
Catalina Montoya, *Executive*
Juan Viramontes, *General Mgr*
EMP: 55
SQ FT: 40,000
SALES (est): 4.7MM Privately Held
WEB: www.georgianhotel.com
SIC: 7011 5812 Hotels; American restaurant

(P-12664)
GFP OCEANSIDE BLOCK 21 LLC
Also Called: Springhill Suites Oceanside
110 N Myers St, Oceanside (92054-2603)
PHONE 760 722-1003
Kathleen Maola,
Ryan Smith,
EMP: 99
SQ FT: 110,000
SALES (est): 1.7MM Privately Held
SIC: 7011 5812 Resort hotel, franchised; seafood restaurants

(P-12665)
GGWH LLC
Also Called: Holiday Inn Woodland Hills
9440 Santa Monica Blvd # 610, Beverly Hills (90210-4653)
PHONE 310 786-1700
Emerson Glazer,
Ericka Glazer,
EMP: 50
SALES (est): 1.2MM Privately Held
SIC: 7011 5812 5813 Hotels & motels; eating places; drinking places

(P-12666)
GHG PROPERTIES LLC
7320 Greenleaf Ave, Whittier (90602-1620)
PHONE 562 945-8511
Benjamin Shih, *Exec Sec*
Joseph Fan, *Manager*
EMP: 80
SALES (est): 242.3K Privately Held
SIC: 7011 Hotels & motels

(P-12667)
GOLDEN DOOR PROPERTIES LLC
777 Deer Springs Rd, San Marcos (92069-9757)
PHONE 760 744-5777
Joanne Conway, *Mng Member*
Kathy Van Ness, *COO*
Judy Bird, *Exec Dir*
Ann Duliere, *Finance Dir*
EMP: 139
SQ FT: 50,000
SALES: 13.9MM Privately Held
SIC: 7011 Hotels & motels

(P-12668)
GOLDEN HOTELS LTD PARTNERSHIP
Also Called: Atrium Hotel
18700 Macarthur Blvd, Irvine (92612-1409)
PHONE 949 833-2770
Mike Wang, *Partner*
Pacific Coast Realty Services, *General Ptnr*
John Wang, *Partner*
Sheri Blackwood, *General Mgr*
Steve Hostetter, *General Mgr*
EMP: 140
SQ FT: 120,000
SALES (est): 7.1MM Privately Held
WEB: www.atriumhotel.com
SIC: 7011 Hotels

(P-12669)
GOLDENPARK LLC
Also Called: Norwalk Marriott Hotel
16209 Paramount Blvd # 214, Paramount (90723-5461)
PHONE 562 863-5555
Fax: 562 868-4486
Dae In Kim,
Craig Parker, *General Mgr*
Jiang Frances, *Controller*
Renee Spingola, *Marketing Staff*
Jane N Kim,
EMP: 100
SQ FT: 138,944
SALES (est): 4.7MM Privately Held
SIC: 7011 Hotel, franchised

(P-12670)
GOODRICH LAX A CAL LTD PARTNR
Also Called: Quality Hotel Airport
310 W Longden Ave, Arcadia (91007-8235)
PHONE 626 254-9988
Xi Min Yuan, *Partner*
Alex Salazar, *Controller*
EMP: 80
SALES (est): 4MM Privately Held
SIC: 7011 Hotels & motels

(P-12671)
GRAND DEL MAR RESORT LP
5300 Grand Del Mar Ct, San Diego (92130-4901)
PHONE 858 314-2000
Fax: 858 314-2001
Tom Voss, *Partner*
Jordan Snider, *Executive*
Amy B Butterfield, *Meeting Planner*
Jay Pak, *CTO*
Edward Castillo, *Info Tech Mgr*
EMP: 570
SALES (est): 40.4MM Privately Held
SIC: 7011 Resort hotel

(P-12672)
GRAND PACIFIC CARLSBAD HT LP
Also Called: Sheraton Carlsbad Resort & Spa
5480 Grand Pacific Dr, Carlsbad (92008-4723)
PHONE 760 827-2400
Fax: 760 827-2429
Tim Shinkle, *CFO*
Chef Patrick, *Executive*
Julian Quinones, *Executive*
Darrin Rosenberg, *Executive*
Erin Lindquist, *General Mgr*
EMP: 272
SALES (est): 23.7MM Privately Held
SIC: 7011 Hotels & motels

(P-12673)
GRAND PACIFIC RESORTS SVCS LP
5900 Pasteur Ct Ste 200, Carlsbad (92008-7336)
PHONE 760 431-8500
Timothy Stripe, *Partner*
David Brown, *Partner*
Brenda Caughron, *Executive*
Sherrie McIntosh, *Manager*
EMP: 120
SQ FT: 22,000
SALES (est): 6.2MM Privately Held
SIC: 7011 Hotels & motels

(P-12674)
GRANLIBAKKEN MANAGEMENT CO LTD
Also Called: Granlibakken Ski Racquet Resort
725 Granlibakken Rd, Tahoe City (96145)
P.O. Box 6329 (96145-6329)
PHONE 800 543-3221
Fax: 530 583-7641
Willem G C Parson, *President*
Norma Parson, *Corp Secy*
Ron Eber, *Executive*
Christine Funicella, *Sales Mgr*
EMP: 60
SALES (est): 7MM Privately Held
WEB: www.granlibakken.com
SIC: 7011 Resort hotel

(P-12675)
GRANVILLE HOTEL CORP
13111 Sycamore Dr, Norwalk (90650-8339)
PHONE 562 863-5555
Lawrence Lui, *President*
James Evans, *CFO*
Anthony Carter, *Vice Pres*
Dan Guiles, *Engineer*
EMP: 115
SALES (est): 1.3MM Privately Held
WEB: www.sheratonuptown.com
SIC: 7011 Hotel, franchised

(P-12676)
GREAT WESTERN HOTELS CORP
Also Called: Heritage Inn
1050 N Norma St, Ridgecrest (93555-3151)
PHONE 760 446-6543
Fax: 760 446-2884
Victoria Moore, *Manager*
EMP: 50
SALES (corp-wide): 10.7MM Privately Held
WEB: www.danapointmarinainn.com
SIC: 7011 Hotels
PA: Great Western Hotels Corp
401 W Imperial Hwy
La Habra CA 90631
714 459-7500

(P-12677)
GREEN TREE CAPITAL LP
Also Called: Green Tree Inn
14173 Green Tree Blvd, Victorville (92395-4343)
PHONE 760 245-3461
Cathy Davis, *General Mgr*
Cristina Gordon, *Executive*
Philip Elghanian,
EMP: 55
SQ FT: 52,647
SALES (est): 1.2MM Privately Held
SIC: 7011 Hotels & motels

(P-12678)
GREENLEAF HOTEL INC
Also Called: Radisson Hotel Whittier
7320 Greenleaf Ave, Whittier (90602-1620)
PHONE 562 945-8511
Fax: 562 945-6519
Hui-Ling Chou, *President*
Ron Acaevebo, *Chief Engr*
Christobal Martinez, *Sales Dir*
Todd Raessler, *Manager*
EMP: 139
SQ FT: 143,475
SALES (est): 10MM Privately Held
SIC: 7011 5812 7299 Hotels & motels; eating places; banquet hall facilities

(P-12679)
GROSVENOR PROPERTIES LTD
Also Called: Best Western
380 S Airport Blvd, South San Francisco (94080-6704)
PHONE 650 873-3200
Fax: 650 589-3495
Jim McGuire, *Manager*
Jim Fruuen, *Appctn Conslt*
David Huddleston, *Opers Mgr*
Roland Cinco, *Sales Mgr*
EMP: 160
SALES (corp-wide): 11MM Privately Held
WEB: www.grosvenorsfo.com
SIC: 7011 5813 5812 7299 Hotels & motels; drinking places; eating places; banquet hall facilities
PA: Grosvenor Properties Ltd.
222 Front St Fl 7
San Francisco CA 94111
415 421-5940

(P-12680)
GROSVENOR VISALIA ASSOCIATES
Also Called: Holiday Inn
9000 W Airport Dr, Visalia (93277-9511)
PHONE 559 651-5000
Fax: 559 651-2624
Robert K Werbe, *General Ptnr*
Noemi Sanchez, *Hum Res Coord*
EMP: 58
SQ FT: 163,415
SALES (est): 4.3MM Privately Held
SIC: 7011 Hotels & motels

(P-12681)
H C T INC
Also Called: Hyatt Regency Mission Bay Spa
1441 Quivira Rd, San Diego (92109-7805)
PHONE 619 224-1234
Fax: 619 221-4842
Mohsen Kaleghi, *President*
Mark S Hoplamazian, *President*
Linda Villalobos, *Executive*
Mohsen Khaleghi, *General Mgr*
Bettina Pullum, *Asst Controller*
EMP: 300
SALES (est): 17.9MM Publicly Held
SIC: 7011 4491 5813 5812 Hotels & motels; marine terminals; piers, incl. buildings & facilities: operation & maintenance; drinking places; eating places
PA: Chesapeake Lodging Trust
1997 Annapolis Exch Pkwy
Annapolis MD 21401

(P-12682)
H D G ASSOCIATES
Also Called: Hotel Marmonte
1111 E Cabrillo Blvd, Santa Barbara (93103-3701)
PHONE 805 963-0744
Fax: 805 962-4140
Ruth Grande, *President*
Steve Lindsey, *Controller*
Chris Robinson, *Purch Mgr*
EMP: 125
SQ FT: 150,000
SALES (est): 2.9MM
SALES (corp-wide): 4.3B Publicly Held
WEB: www.hotelmarmonte.com
SIC: 7011 Hotels & motels
HQ: Hyatt Corporation
150 N Riverside Plz
Chicago IL 60606
312 750-1234

(P-12683)
HAMPSTEAD LAFAYETTE HOTEL LLC
Also Called: Innsuites Hotels
2223 El Cajon Blvd, San Diego (92104-1103)
PHONE 619 296-2101
James Green, *Manager*
EMP: 50
SALES (corp-wide): 3.9MM Privately Held
WEB: www.lafayettehotelsd.com
SIC: 7011 Hotels
PA: Lafayette Hampstead Hotel Llc
2223 El Cajon Blvd
San Diego CA 92104
619 296-2101

PRODUCTS & SERVICES SECTION
7011 - Hotels, Motels & Tourist Courts County (P-12707)

(P-12684)
HAMPTON INN NORCO CORONA NORTH
1530 Hamner Ave, Norco (92860-2939)
PHONE 951 279-1111
Mahendra B Desai, *Executive Asst*
Vincent Magallanes, *Manager*
Palvika Patel, *Manager*
EMP: 80
SALES (est): 2.6MM **Privately Held**
SIC: 7011 Hotels & motels

(P-12685)
HANDLERY HOTELS INC
Also Called: Handlery Union Square Hotel
351 Geary St, San Francisco (94102-1801)
PHONE 415 781-7800
Fax: 415 362-9685
John Handlery, *Manager*
Vick Deasy, *Human Res Dir*
EMP: 150
SALES (corp-wide): 34.9MM **Privately Held**
WEB: www.handlery.com
SIC: 7011 Hotels
PA: Handlery Hotels, Inc.
180 Geary St Ste 700
San Francisco CA 94108
415 781-4550

(P-12686)
HANDLERY HOTELS INC
950 Hotel Cir N, San Diego (92108-2995)
PHONE 415 781-4550
Fax: 619 298-3948
John Martin, *Manager*
Millie Tores, *Human Res Mgr*
Jose Curiel, *Director*
EMP: 150
SALES (corp-wide): 34.9MM **Privately Held**
WEB: www.handlery.com
SIC: 7011 5941 5812 5947 Hotels & motels; golf goods & equipment; eating places; gift, novelty & souvenir shop; drinking places
PA: Handlery Hotels, Inc.
180 Geary St Ste 700
San Francisco CA 94108
415 781-4550

(P-12687)
HANFORD HOTELS INC
Also Called: Hotel Hanford, The
3131 Bristol St, Costa Mesa (92626-3037)
PHONE 714 957-6951
Tony Eccher, *Exec Dir*
Tom Van Winkle, *General Mgr*
EMP: 100
SQ FT: 65,311
SALES (corp-wide): 16.2MM **Privately Held**
SIC: 7011 Hotels & motels
PA: Hanford Hotels, Inc.
17542 17th St Ste 450
Tustin CA 92780
714 210-0400

(P-12688)
HANFORD HOTELS LLC
17542 17th St Ste 450, Tustin (92780-1964)
PHONE 714 210-0400
Donald E Sodaro, *Mng Member*
Anthony Eccher, *Controller*
William A Caine Jr,
EMP: 189
SQ FT: 5,000
SALES (est): 2.8MM **Privately Held**
WEB: www.hanfordhotels.com
SIC: 7011 Hotels & motels

(P-12689)
HARBOR ISLAND HOTEL GROUP LP
Also Called: Four Points Sheraton Ventura
1050 Schooner Dr, Ventura (93001-4273)
PHONE 805 658-1212
Joseph Fan, *General Ptnr*
Victor Dollar, *Executive*
Sammi Wang, *Admin Sec*
Rachel Guirguis, *Marketing Staff*
Ben Shih, *Accounts Mgr*
EMP: 80

SALES (est): 4MM **Privately Held**
SIC: 7011 Hotels & motels

(P-12690)
HARBOR VIEW HOTEL VENTURES LLC
Also Called: Doubletree Ht San Diego Dwntwn
1646 Front St, San Diego (92101-2920)
PHONE 619 239-6800
Michael Gallegos, *Mng Member*
Joanie Clapper, *Sales Mgr*
Elizabeth Boman, *Marketing Staff*
Mario Garcia, *Marketing Staff*
Leean Pennapli, *Cust Mgr*
EMP: 100
SALES (est): 7.2MM **Privately Held**
SIC: 7011 Hotels & motels

(P-12691)
HARBOR VIEW HOTELS INC
Also Called: Hilton San Francisco
600 Airport Blvd, Burlingame (94010-1920)
PHONE 650 340-8500
Fax: 650 342-2908
James Evans, *CFO*
Nigel Lor, *General Mgr*
Sandy Lal, *Sales Staff*
EMP: 99
SALES (est): 5.8MM **Privately Held**
WEB: www.sheratonsfo.com
SIC: 7011 Hotels & motels

(P-12692)
HARDAGE GROUP OF COMPANIES
Also Called: Woodfin Suites Hotel Brea
3100 E Imperial Hwy, Brea (92821-6719)
PHONE 714 579-3200
Fax: 714 996-5984
Karla Barges, *Branch Mgr*
Wendi Wolfe, *Admin Asst*
EMP: 55
SALES (corp-wide): 8.2MM **Privately Held**
WEB: www.woodfinsuitehotels.com
SIC: 7011 Hotels & motels
PA: The Hardage Group Of Companies
12730 High Bluff Dr # 250
San Diego CA

(P-12693)
HAVASU LANDING CASINO (PA)
1 Main St, Needles (92363)
PHONE 760 858-5380
Dave Bartlett, *Info Tech Dir*
Mary Betrens, *Human Res Dir*
Vickie Yount, *Marketing Staff*
David Nye, *Manager*
EMP: 71
SALES (est): 3.9MM **Privately Held**
SIC: 7011 Casino hotel

(P-12694)
HAWAIIAN HOTELS & RESORTS INC
2830 Borchard Rd, Newbury Park (91320-3810)
PHONE 805 480-0052
Fax: 805 480-0338
Edward J Hogan, *President*
Tom Bell, *Vice Pres*
Jimmy Banh, *Info Tech Dir*
Pansy Mendez, *Human Res Dir*
Jennifer Carvalho, *Natl Sales Mgr*
EMP: 100
SALES (est): 5.3MM
SALES (corp-wide): 4.8B **Privately Held**
WEB: www.hawaiihotels.com
SIC: 7011 Resort hotel
HQ: Pleasant Holidays, Llc
2404 Townsgate Rd
Westlake Village CA 91361
818 991-3390

(P-12695)
HAYES MANSION CONFERENCE CTR
200 Edenvale Ave, San Jose (95136-3309)
PHONE 408 226-3200
Fax: 408 362-2388
Vickie Leong, *Principal*
Rupas Kumar, *Asst Controller*
Tarol Johnson, *Controller*

Andrew Toledo, *Manager*
EMP: 140
SALES (est): 4.2MM **Privately Held**
WEB: www.hayesmansion.com
SIC: 7011 Hotels & motels

(P-12696)
HAZENS INVESTMENT LLC
Also Called: Sheraton
6101 W Century Blvd, Los Angeles (90045-5310)
PHONE 310 642-1111
Fax: 310 642-4859
Orazio Parisi, *Executive*
Sirenia Liu, *Social Dir*
Pamela Pasley, *Social Dir*
Daniel Ybarra, *Business Dir*
Phyllis McCall, *General Mgr*
EMP: 395
SALES (est): 30.2MM **Privately Held**
WEB: www.edgemastery.com
SIC: 7011 Hotels & motels

(P-12697)
HEI IRVINE LLC
2120 Main St, Irvine (92614-6219)
PHONE 949 553-8332
Gary Mendell, *Principal*
EMP: 78
SALES (est): 1MM
SALES (corp-wide): 238.5MM **Privately Held**
SIC: 7011 Hotels & motels
PA: Hei Hospitality, Llc
101 Merritt 7 Corp
Norwalk CT 06851
203 849-8844

(P-12698)
HEI LONG BEACH LLC
Also Called: Hilton Hotels
701 W Ocean Blvd, Long Beach (90831-3100)
PHONE 562 983-3400
Fax: 562 983-1200
Clark Christopher, *Principal*
Michelle Negrete, *Accountant*
HEI Hospitality Fund Holdings,
EMP: 125
SALES (est): 6.2MM
SALES (corp-wide): 238.5MM **Privately Held**
SIC: 7011 Hotels & motels
PA: Hei Hospitality, Llc
101 Merritt 7 Corp
Norwalk CT 06851
203 849-8844

(P-12699)
HEI MISSION VALLEY LP
Also Called: San Diego Mission Vly Hilton
901 Camino Del Rio S, San Diego (92108-3515)
PHONE 619 299-2729
Dan Weber, *General Ptnr*
Stan Kaminski, *General Mgr*
Jennifer Palessiro, *Meeting Planner*
Reza Shemiran, *Chief Engr*
Dena Hartsuyker, *Controller*
EMP: 220
SQ FT: 219,000
SALES (est): 4.5MM **Privately Held**
SIC: 7011 Hotels

(P-12700)
HHC TRS PORTSMOUTH LLC
Also Called: Renaissance Palm Springs
888 E Tahquitz Canyon Way, Palm Springs (92262-6708)
PHONE 760 322-6000
David Kimichik,
EMP: 95 EST: 2003
SALES (est): 1.9MM **Privately Held**
SIC: 7011 Hotels & motels

(P-12701)
HHLP SAN DIEGO LESSEE LLC
Also Called: Marriott
530 Broadway, San Diego (92101-5206)
PHONE 619 446-3000
Fax: 619 446-3010
Ashish Parikh, *Manager*
Samuel Hoffman, *Admin Asst*
EMP: 90
SQ FT: 1,000,000

SALES (est): 5.1MM **Privately Held**
SIC: 7011 Hotels & motels

(P-12702)
HI FRESNO HOSPITALITY LLC
Also Called: Holiday Inn
1055 Van Ness Ave, Fresno (93721-2006)
PHONE 559 233-6650
Fax: 559 233-6750
Mukesh Shah, *Info Tech Mgr*
Rodolfo Gutierrez, *General Mgr*
Siddharth Shah, *General Mgr*
EMP: 60
SALES (est): 4MM **Privately Held**
SIC: 7011 Hotels & motels

(P-12703)
HIGHLAND HOSPITALITY CORP
Also Called: Palm Springs Hotel
888 E Tahquitz Canyon Way, Palm Springs (92262-6708)
PHONE 760 322-6000
Fax: 760 416-2998
John Daw, *General Mgr*
David Buell, *Chief Engr*
EMP: 200
SALES (corp-wide): 794.8MM **Publicly Held**
WEB: www.highlandhospitality.com
SIC: 7011 5813 5812 Hotels; drinking places; eating places
HQ: Highland Hospitality Corp
8405 Greensboro Dr # 500
Mc Lean VA 22102

(P-12704)
HIGHLANDS INN INVESTORS II LP
Also Called: Hyatt Hotel
120 Highland Dr, Carmel (93923-9607)
PHONE 831 624-3801
Ulrich Samietz, *Principal*
Highlands Inn Investors, *Ltd Ptnr*
Mara Cantor, *Human Res Dir*
EMP: 260
SALES (est): 8.5MM **Privately Held**
SIC: 7011 5812 5813 5947 Hotels & motels; American restaurant; drinking places; gift, novelty & souvenir shop

(P-12705)
HILTON EL SEGUNDO LLC
Also Called: Hiltonm Grdn Inn Lax El Sgundo
2100 E Mariposa Ave, El Segundo (90245-5002)
PHONE 310 726-0100
Brianna Akins,
Mike Powers, *General Mgr*
EMP: 60 EST: 2013
SALES (est): 2.1MM **Privately Held**
SIC: 7011 Hotels & motels

(P-12706)
HILTON GARDEN IN SAN MATEO
Also Called: Hilton Garden Hotel
2000 Bridgepointe Pkwy, Foster City (94404-1586)
PHONE 650 522-9000
Fax: 650 522-9099
Derrick Hudson, *Manager*
EMP: 60
SALES (corp-wide): 4.2MM **Privately Held**
SIC: 7011 Hotels & motels
PA: Hilton Garden In San Mateo
2000 Bridgepointe Pkwy
Foster City CA 94404
650 522-9000

(P-12707)
HILTON GARDEN INN
510 Lewelling Blvd, San Leandro (94579-1803)
PHONE 510 346-5533
Fax: 510 346-5544
Burt Knewson, *Manager*
Ynoee Lee, *General Mgr*
David Schlesinger, *Director*
EMP: 80
SALES (est): 2.3MM **Privately Held**
SIC: 7011 Hotels & motels

7011 - Hotels, Motels & Tourist Courts County (P-12708)

(P-12708)
HILTON GARDEN INNS MGT LLC
6450 Carlsbad Blvd, Carlsbad
(92011-1058)
PHONE..................760 476-0800
Robert Moore, *General Mgr*
Carlos Chang, *Controller*
Jen Sehwani, *Sales Mgr*
EMP: 116
SALES (corp-wide): 11.2B **Publicly Held**
WEB: www.esirvine.com
SIC: **7011** Hotels & motels
HQ: Hilton Garden Inns Management Llc
7930 Jones Branch Dr
Mc Lean VA 22102
703 448-6100

(P-12709)
HILTON GARDEN INNS MGT LLC
2100 E Mariposa Ave, El Segundo
(90245-5002)
PHONE..................310 726-0100
Fax: 310 726-9606
Barbara Bejan, *Manager*
Mike Powers, *General Mgr*
EMP: 67
SQ FT: 87,198
SALES (corp-wide): 11.2B **Publicly Held**
SIC: **7011** Hotels & motels
HQ: Hilton Garden Inns Management Llc
7930 Jones Branch Dr
Mc Lean VA 22102
703 448-6100

(P-12710)
HILTON GARDEN INNS MGT LLC
2801 Constitution Dr Fl 2, Livermore
(94551-7613)
PHONE..................925 292-2000
Fax: 925 292-2100
Joan Baldon, *Manager*
EMP: 50
SALES (corp-wide): 11.2B **Publicly Held**
SIC: **7011** Hotels & motels
HQ: Hilton Garden Inns Management Llc
7930 Jones Branch Dr
Mc Lean VA 22102
703 448-6100

(P-12711)
HILTON LOS ANGLES UNIVERSAL CY
555 Unversal Hollywood Dr, Universal City
(91608-1001)
PHONE..................818 506-2500
Juan Aquinde, *General Mgr*
George Sit, *Executive*
Donna Giordan, *Meeting Planner*
Elsie McDonald, *HR Admin*
Robert Hegel, *Purch Dir*
▲ EMP: 380
SALES (est): 16.7MM **Privately Held**
SIC: **7011** Hotels

(P-12712)
HILTON SUITES INC
Also Called: Anaheim/Orange Hilton Suites
400 N State College Blvd, Orange
(92868-1700)
PHONE..................714 938-1111
Fax: 714 938-0930
John Ault, *Manager*
Kari Lucena, *Human Res Mgr*
Susan Valen, *Marketing Staff*
EMP: 120
SALES (corp-wide): 11.2B **Publicly Held**
WEB: www.hiltondirect.com
SIC: **7011** 5812 Hotels & motels; eating places
HQ: Hilton Suites, Inc
7930 Jones Branch Dr
Mc Lean VA 22102
703 883-1000

(P-12713)
HILTON UNIVERSAL HOTEL
555 Unversal Hollywood Dr, Universal City
(91608-1001)
PHONE..................818 506-2500
Michelle Szeto, *Principal*
Evette Aparicio, *Vice Pres*
LMI Unson, *Associate Dir*
Juan Aquinde, *General Mgr*
Ramon Mejia, *Human Res Mgr*
EMP: 99

SALES (est): 1,000K
SALES (corp-wide): 20.6MM **Privately Held**
SIC: **7011** Hotels & motels
HQ: Sun Hill Properties, Inc.
555 Unversal Hollywood Dr
Universal City CA 91608
818 506-2500

(P-12714)
HILTON WOODLAND HILLS & TOWERS
6360 Canoga Ave, Woodland Hills
(91367-2501)
PHONE..................818 595-1000
Fax: 818 595-1090
Ed Debries, *General Mgr*
Conoga Hotel Corporation, *Partner*
Ed Devries, *General Mgr*
Jim Atwater, *Purch Agent*
Lisa Barbargallo, *Manager*
EMP: 200
SALES (est): 7.9MM **Privately Held**
SIC: **7011** 5813 5812 Hotels; drinking places; eating places

(P-12715)
HILTON WORLDWIDE INC
633 E Cabrillo Blvd, Santa Barbara
(93103-3611)
PHONE..................805 564-4333
Dean Feldmeier, *Manager*
EMP: 300
SALES (corp-wide): 11.2B **Publicly Held**
WEB: www.esirvine.com
SIC: **7011** Hotels & motels
HQ: Park Hotels & Resorts Inc.
7930 Jones Branch Dr # 700
Mc Lean VA 22102
703 883-1000

(P-12716)
HILTON WORLDWIDE INC
Also Called: Embassy Suites
901 E Calaveras Blvd, Milpitas
(95035-5419)
PHONE..................408 942-0400
Bonnie Benson, *Manager*
Tara Weber, *CTO*
Brian Contildes, *Chief Engr*
Anastasia Beals, *Marketing Staff*
Chris Hernandez, *Manager*
EMP: 65
SALES (corp-wide): 11.2B **Publicly Held**
WEB: www.esirvine.com
SIC: **7011** 5813 5812 Hotels & motels; drinking places; eating places
HQ: Park Hotels & Resorts Inc.
7930 Jones Branch Dr # 700
Mc Lean VA 22102
703 883-1000

(P-12717)
HILTON WORLDWIDE INC
Also Called: Hilton
1775 E Mission Bay Dr, San Diego
(92109-6801)
PHONE..................619 276-4010
Patrick Duffy, *Director*
Natalie McNeal, *Analyst*
Dan Gaudreau, *Human Res Dir*
Carlos Nava, *Purch Dir*
Brad Naucler, *Sales Dir*
EMP: 360
SALES (corp-wide): 11.2B **Publicly Held**
SIC: **7011** 5812 5947 Hotels & motels; eating places; gift, novelty & souvenir shop
HQ: Park Hotels & Resorts Inc.
7930 Jones Branch Dr # 700
Mc Lean VA 22102
703 883-1000

(P-12718)
HILTON WORLDWIDE INC
Also Called: Hilton
333 Ofarrell St, San Francisco
(94102-2116)
P.O. Box 420868 (94142-0868)
PHONE..................415 771-1400
Fax: 415 673-6490
Holger B Gantz, *Manager*
William Boring, *Social Dir*
Christine Himpler, *Technical Staff*
Kathy Penick, *Technical Staff*

Malanie Fullove, *Credit Staff*
EMP: 330
SALES (corp-wide): 11.2B **Publicly Held**
WEB: www.esirvine.com
SIC: **7011** 5812 7299 Hotels & motels; eating places; banquet hall facilities
HQ: Park Hotels & Resorts Inc.
7930 Jones Branch Dr # 700
Mc Lean VA 22102
703 883-1000

(P-12719)
HILTON WORLDWIDE INC
Also Called: Hilton
1 Hegenberger Rd, Oakland (94621-1405)
P.O. Box 2549 (94614-0549)
PHONE..................510 635-5000
Fax: 510 383-4026
Mark Clement, *General Mgr*
Anna McKenzie, *Planning*
Tara Capizano, *Marketing Staff*
EMP: 114
SALES (corp-wide): 11.2B **Publicly Held**
WEB: www.esirvine.com
SIC: **7011** 5813 5812 Hotels & motels; drinking places; eating places
HQ: Park Hotels & Resorts Inc.
7930 Jones Branch Dr # 700
Mc Lean VA 22102
703 883-1000

(P-12720)
HILTON WORLDWIDE INC
Also Called: Hilton
10950 N Torrey Pines Rd, La Jolla
(92037-1006)
PHONE..................858 450-4569
Patrick Duffy, *Manager*
Teresa Cram, *Human Res Mgr*
Sandie Lopez, *Mktg Dir*
Cheri Walter, *Manager*
EMP: 50
SALES (corp-wide): 11.2B **Publicly Held**
WEB: www.esirvine.com
SIC: **7011** 5813 5812 Hotels & motels; drinking places; eating places
HQ: Park Hotels & Resorts Inc.
7930 Jones Branch Dr # 700
Mc Lean VA 22102
703 883-1000

(P-12721)
HILTON WORLDWIDE INC
Also Called: Embassy Suites
1075 California Blvd, NAPA (94559-1061)
PHONE..................707 253-9540
Reynaldo Zertuche, *Manager*
Pearl Wright, *General Mgr*
Sheri Kohlenberger, *Controller*
Richard Thornberry, *VP Human Res*
Theresa Ajari, *Sales Mgr*
EMP: 80
SQ FT: 83,251
SALES (corp-wide): 11.2B **Publicly Held**
WEB: www.esirvine.com
SIC: **7011** Hotels & motels
HQ: Park Hotels & Resorts Inc.
7930 Jones Branch Dr # 700
Mc Lean VA 22102
703 883-1000

(P-12722)
HILTON WORLDWIDE INC
Also Called: Hilton Hotels
700 N Haven Ave, Ontario (91764-4902)
PHONE..................909 980-3420
Fax: 909 941-6781
Christopher J Nassetta, *Branch Mgr*
Robert Smith, *Branch Mgr*
Howard Taylor, *General Mgr*
Bette Gill, *Sales Staff*
Chihiro Abe, *Manager*
EMP: 116
SALES (corp-wide): 11.2B **Publicly Held**
SIC: **7011** Hotels & motels
HQ: Park Hotels & Resorts Inc.
7930 Jones Branch Dr # 700
Mc Lean VA 22102
703 883-1000

(P-12723)
HILTON WORLDWIDE INC
Also Called: Hilton
168 S Los Robles Ave, Pasadena
(91101-2430)
PHONE..................626 577-1000

Fax: 626 584-3184
Todd Iacono, *Manager*
Nadine Koch, *General Mgr*
Alma Quintero, *Human Res Dir*
Alma Quinteros, *Human Res Dir*
Linda Hilton, *Sales Dir*
EMP: 248
SALES (corp-wide): 11.2B **Publicly Held**
WEB: www.esirvine.com
SIC: **7011** 5812 7389 7299 Hotels & motels; eating places; hotel & motel reservation service; banquet hall facilities; drinking places
HQ: Park Hotels & Resorts Inc.
7930 Jones Branch Dr # 700
Mc Lean VA 22102
703 883-1000

(P-12724)
HILTON WORLDWIDE INC
55 Cyril Magnin St, San Francisco
(94102-2812)
PHONE..................415 392-8000
Steve Cowan, *General Mgr*
EMP: 500
SALES (corp-wide): 11.2B **Publicly Held**
SIC: **7011** 5812 Hotels; American restaurant
HQ: Park Hotels & Resorts Inc.
7930 Jones Branch Dr # 700
Mc Lean VA 22102
703 883-1000

(P-12725)
HILTON WORLDWIDE INC
Also Called: Embassy Suites
1211 E Garvey St, Covina (91724-3666)
PHONE..................626 915-3441
Fax: 626 331-0773
Seig Heglund, *Manager*
Jose Garcia, *Opers Mgr*
Jeff Gladu, *VP Sales*
EMP: 75
SALES (corp-wide): 11.2B **Publicly Held**
WEB: www.esirvine.com
SIC: **7011** 7991 7359 7299 Hotels & motels; physical fitness facilities; equipment rental & leasing; banquet hall facilities
HQ: Park Hotels & Resorts Inc.
7930 Jones Branch Dr # 700
Mc Lean VA 22102
703 883-1000

(P-12726)
HILTON WORLDWIDE INC
9876 Wilshire Blvd, Beverly Hills
(90210-3115)
PHONE..................310 415-3340
Fax: 310 205-3627
Beverly Hilton, *Principal*
Chris Naylor, *President*
Andy Slater, *President*
Rob Palleschi, *Vice Pres*
Karla Visconti, *Comms Dir*
EMP: 113
SALES (corp-wide): 11.2B **Publicly Held**
WEB: www.esirvine.com
SIC: **7011** Hotels & motels
HQ: Park Hotels & Resorts Inc.
7930 Jones Branch Dr # 700
Mc Lean VA 22102
703 883-1000

(P-12727)
HILTON WORLDWIDE INC
4130 Lake Tahoe Blvd, South Lake Tahoe
(96150-6965)
PHONE..................530 543-2126
John Steinbach, *Manager*
Bill Cottrill, *Sales Dir*
Julie Willis, *Manager*
EMP: 250
SALES (corp-wide): 11.2B **Publicly Held**
WEB: www.esirvine.com
SIC: **7011** Hotels & motels
HQ: Park Hotels & Resorts Inc.
7930 Jones Branch Dr # 700
Mc Lean VA 22102
703 883-1000

(P-12728)
HILTON WORLDWIDE INC
Also Called: Embassy Suites
150 Anza Blvd, Burlingame (94010-1924)
PHONE..................650 342-4600
Christopher Beckman, *General Mgr*

PRODUCTS & SERVICES SECTION
7011 - Hotels, Motels & Tourist Courts County (P-12750)

Melinda Wulf, *Executive*
EMP: 130
SALES (corp-wide): 11.2B **Publicly Held**
WEB: www.esirvine.com
SIC: 7011 5813 5812 Hotels & motels; drinking places; eating places
HQ: Park Hotels & Resorts Inc.
7930 Jones Branch Dr # 700
Mc Lean VA 22102
703 883-1000

(P-12729)
HILTON WORLDWIDE INC
Also Called: Embassy Suites
211 E Huntington Dr, Arcadia (91006-3745)
PHONE..................................626 445-8525
Fax: 626 445-8548
Stig Hedlund, *Manager*
Art Rosales, *Marketing Staff*
EMP: 116
SALES (corp-wide): 11.2B **Publicly Held**
WEB: www.esirvine.com
SIC: 7011 Hotels & motels
HQ: Park Hotels & Resorts Inc.
7930 Jones Branch Dr # 700
Mc Lean VA 22102
703 883-1000

(P-12730)
HILTON WORLDWIDE INC
Also Called: Embassy Suites
8425 Firestone Blvd, Downey (90241-3843)
PHONE..................................562 861-1900
Stig Hedlund, *Systems Staff*
Rudy Segura, *Human Res Mgr*
EMP: 100
SALES (corp-wide): 11.2B **Publicly Held**
WEB: www.esirvine.com
SIC: 7011 5813 5812 Hotels & motels; drinking places; eating places
HQ: Park Hotels & Resorts Inc.
7930 Jones Branch Dr # 700
Mc Lean VA 22102
703 883-1000

(P-12731)
HILTON WORLDWIDE INC
Also Called: Embassy Suites
7762 Beach Blvd, Buena Park (90620-1935)
PHONE..................................714 739-5600
Fax: 714 521-9650
Juergen Oswald, *General Mgr*
EMP: 65
SALES (corp-wide): 11.2B **Publicly Held**
WEB: www.esirvine.com
SIC: 7011 Hotels & motels
HQ: Park Hotels & Resorts Inc.
7930 Jones Branch Dr # 700
Mc Lean VA 22102
703 883-1000

(P-12732)
HILTON WORLDWIDE INC
Also Called: Hilton
700 N Haven Ave, Ontario (91764-4902)
PHONE..................................909 980-0400
Fax: 909 948-9309
Robert Smith, *Branch Mgr*
David Hirsch, *General Mgr*
EMP: 116
SALES (corp-wide): 11.2B **Publicly Held**
WEB: www.esirvine.com
SIC: 7011 5813 5812 Hotels & motels; drinking places; eating places
HQ: Park Hotels & Resorts Inc.
7930 Jones Branch Dr # 700
Mc Lean VA 22102
703 883-1000

(P-12733)
HILTON WORLDWIDE INC
225 W Valley Blvd, San Gabriel (91776-3743)
PHONE..................................626 270-2700
Charles Noh, *Manager*
David Cheng, *Technology*
Amy Au, *Sls & Mktg Exec*
Althea Schaub, *Manager*
EMP: 116
SALES (corp-wide): 11.2B **Publicly Held**
WEB: www.esirvine.com
SIC: 7011 Hotels & motels
HQ: Park Hotels & Resorts Inc.
7930 Jones Branch Dr # 700
Mc Lean VA 22102
703 883-1000

(P-12734)
HILTON WORLDWIDE INC
Also Called: Embassy Suites
2120 Main St, Irvine (92614-6219)
PHONE..................................949 553-8332
Fax: 949 261-5301
Mari Hnatt, *Manager*
Walid Doud, *Vice Pres*
Lorraine Penate, *Human Resources*
EMP: 114
SALES (corp-wide): 11.2B **Publicly Held**
WEB: www.esirvine.com
SIC: 7011 Hotels & motels
HQ: Park Hotels & Resorts Inc.
7930 Jones Branch Dr # 700
Mc Lean VA 22102
703 883-1000

(P-12735)
HILTON WORLDWIDE INC
Also Called: Hilton
3050 Bristol St, Costa Mesa (92626-3036)
PHONE..................................714 540-7000
Shaun Robinson, *General Mgr*
Carlos Nava, *Purch Dir*
Lisa Amick, *Manager*
Scott Bruno, *Manager*
EMP: 307
SALES (corp-wide): 11.2B **Publicly Held**
WEB: www.esirvine.com
SIC: 7011 5812 7299 Hotels & motels; eating places; banquet hall facilities
HQ: Park Hotels & Resorts Inc.
7930 Jones Branch Dr # 700
Mc Lean VA 22102
703 883-1000

(P-12736)
HILTON WORLDWIDE INC
Also Called: Embassy Suites
4550 La Jolla Village Dr, San Diego (92122-1248)
PHONE..................................858 431-2116
Doug Ramsey, *General Mgr*
Gina Reyes, *Human Res Mgr*
Christine Hong, *Sales Staff*
Kathleen Coleman, *Manager*
EMP: 150
SALES (corp-wide): 11.2B **Publicly Held**
WEB: www.esirvine.com
SIC: 7011 5812 5813 Hotels & motels; eating places; drinking places
HQ: Park Hotels & Resorts Inc.
7930 Jones Branch Dr # 700
Mc Lean VA 22102
703 883-1000

(P-12737)
HILTON WORLDWIDE INC
Also Called: Embassy Suites
101 Mcinnis Pkwy, San Rafael (94903-2773)
PHONE..................................415 499-9222
Fax: 415 499-9268
Rudy Otriz, *Manager*
Pat Sorber, *General Mgr*
Michael Vanmeter, *Info Tech Mgr*
David Tewelde, *Sales Dir*
Melissa Patel, *Sales Staff*
EMP: 65
SALES (corp-wide): 11.2B **Publicly Held**
WEB: www.esirvine.com
SIC: 7011 5812 5813 Hotels & motels; eating places; drinking places
HQ: Park Hotels & Resorts Inc.
7930 Jones Branch Dr # 700
Mc Lean VA 22102
703 883-1000

(P-12738)
HILTON WORLDWIDE INC
Also Called: HILTON WORLDWIDE, INC.
333 Ofarrell St, San Francisco (94102-2116)
PHONE..................................415 771-1400
Greg Gurthrie, *VP Mktg*
EMP: 89
SALES (corp-wide): 11.2B **Publicly Held**
WEB: www.hilton.com
SIC: 7011 Hotels

(P-12739)
HILTON WORLDWIDE INC
Also Called: Embassy Suites
5711 W Century Blvd, Los Angeles (90045-5672)
PHONE..................................310 410-4000
Fax: 310 410-6151
David Villarrubia, *General Mgr*
Herschel Goldscher, *Social Dir*
Grant Coonley, *General Mgr*
Phillip Chao, *Info Tech Mgr*
Oshan Ruiz, *Info Tech Mgr*
EMP: 116
SALES (corp-wide): 11.2B **Publicly Held**
WEB: www.esirvine.com
SIC: 7011 5813 5812 Hotels & motels; hotel, franchised; drinking places; eating places
HQ: Park Hotels & Resorts Inc.
7930 Jones Branch Dr # 700
Mc Lean VA 22102
703 883-1000

(P-12740)
HILTON WORLDWIDE INC
Also Called: Hilton
3100 E Frontera St, Anaheim (92806-2820)
PHONE..................................714 632-1221
Margo Gilbert, *Manager*
Tony Murrietta, *Admin Asst*
Carolyn Nonsils, *Manager*
Ana Ruinds, *Manager*
Joseph Lee, *Supervisor*
EMP: 65
SALES (corp-wide): 11.2B **Publicly Held**
WEB: www.esirvine.com
SIC: 7011 8741 6794 Hotels & motels; hotel or motel management; franchises, selling or licensing
HQ: Park Hotels & Resorts Inc.
7930 Jones Branch Dr # 700
Mc Lean VA 22102
703 883-1000

(P-12741)
HILTON WORLDWIDE INC
Also Called: Embassy Suites
250 Gateway Blvd, South San Francisco (94080-7018)
PHONE..................................650 589-3400
Rudy Ortiz, *General Mgr*
Jennifer Busse, *Director*
John Konzem, *Manager*
EMP: 65
SALES (corp-wide): 11.2B **Publicly Held**
WEB: www.esirvine.com
SIC: 7011 Hotels & motels
HQ: Park Hotels & Resorts Inc.
7930 Jones Branch Dr # 700
Mc Lean VA 22102
703 883-1000

(P-12742)
HILTON WORLDWIDE INC
Also Called: Embassy Suites
901 Ski Run Blvd, South Lake Tahoe (96150-8569)
PHONE..................................530 541-6122
Fax: 530 541-2028
Verla Younker, *Manager*
Phil Moulton, *Principal*
EMP: 50
SALES (corp-wide): 11.2B **Publicly Held**
WEB: www.esirvine.com
SIC: 7011 Hotels & motels
HQ: Park Hotels & Resorts Inc.
7930 Jones Branch Dr # 700
Mc Lean VA 22102
703 883-1000

(P-12743)
HISTORICAL PROPERTIES INC (PA)
Also Called: Horton Grand Hotel
311 Island Ave, San Diego (92101-6923)
PHONE..................................619 230-8417
Fax: 619 239-3823
Doris J Rose, *President*
Santiago Ojeda, *CEO*
Paula Ellis, *General Mgr*
Joanna Kay, *Manager*
EMP: 96
SQ FT: 60,000
SALES (est): 8.6MM **Privately Held**
WEB: www.hortongrand.com
SIC: 7011 Hotels

(P-12744)
HLB FUNDING LLC
Also Called: Hilton Hotel Long Beach
701 W Ocean Blvd, Long Beach (90831-3100)
PHONE..................................562 983-3400
John Murphy,
Chris Granados, *Info Tech Mgr*
Ron Brown,
Jenny Magistrado, *Accounts Mgr*
EMP: 97 **EST:** 2013
SALES (est): 4.8MM **Privately Held**
SIC: 7011 Hotels & motels

(P-12745)
HLT OPERATE DTWC LLC
Also Called: Doubletree By Hilton
7450 Hazard Center Dr, San Diego (92108-4539)
PHONE..................................619 297-5466
Owen Wilcox,
Kevin J Jacobs, *CFO*
Sean Dell'orto, *Treasurer*
Kristin Campbell, *Exec VP*
Joseph Berger, *Senior VP*
EMP: 140
SALES: 20.3MM
SALES (corp-wide): 11.2B **Publicly Held**
SIC: 7011 Hotels
HQ: Park Hotels & Resorts Inc.
7930 Jones Branch Dr # 700
Mc Lean VA 22102
703 883-1000

(P-12746)
HMBL LLC
Also Called: Holiday Inn Express and Suites
8400 W Sunset Blvd Ste 3a, West Hollywood (90069-1934)
PHONE..................................323 656-8090
Robert Jackson, *Mng Member*
Glen Grush,
Joel Leebove,
David Rose,
EMP: 125
SQ FT: 1,500
SALES (est): 8MM **Privately Held**
SIC: 7011 Hotels & motels

(P-12747)
HOLIDAY GARDEN SF CORP
Also Called: Residence In Anaheim
1700 S Clementine St, Anaheim (92802-2902)
PHONE..................................714 533-3555
Fax: 714 535-7626
Hai-Ni Chen, *President*
Jeff Virgil, *Manager*
EMP: 50 **EST:** 1997
SALES: 7MM **Privately Held**
SIC: 7011 Hotels & motels

(P-12748)
HOLIDAY INN & SUITES ANNAHEIM
1240 S Walnut St, Anaheim (92802-2241)
PHONE..................................714 535-0300
Eva Huang, *Principal*
EMP: 75
SALES (est): 1.5MM **Privately Held**
SIC: 7011 Hotels & motels

(P-12749)
HOLIDAY INN EXPRESS MERCED
730 Motel Dr, Merced (95341-5151)
PHONE..................................209 383-0333
Fax: 209 383-0643
Kainth Brothers, *Principal*
EMP: 100
SALES (est): 2.1MM **Privately Held**
SIC: 7011

(P-12750)
HOLIDAY INN HOTEL TORRANCE
19800 S Vermont Ave, Torrance (90502-1138)
PHONE..................................310 781-9100

7011 - Hotels, Motels & Tourist Courts County (P-12751)

Fax: 310 217-9178
David Britton, *General Mgr*
EMP: 130
SQ FT: 95,000
SALES: 10.5MM **Privately Held**
SIC: 7011 Hotels & motels

(P-12751)
HOLIDAY INN NORTHEAST
5321 Date Ave, Sacramento (95841-2597)
PHONE..................................916 338-5800
Fax: 916 334-2868
Dwight Miyakawa, *General Mgr*
Parveen Chand, *Director*
Parzeen Phand, *Manager*
EMP: 114
SALES: 8MM **Privately Held**
WEB: www.sacnortheast.com
SIC: 7011 Hotels & motels

(P-12752)
HOLIDAY INN RNCHO BERNARDO LLC
17065 W Bernardo Dr, San Diego (92127-1495)
PHONE..................................858 485-6530
Fax: 858 485-6530
Hsuan Jau Lin,
John Edwen, *General Mgr*
Yon Huang,
EMP: 55
SALES (est): 3.3MM **Privately Held**
SIC: 7011 Hotels & motels

(P-12753)
HOLIDAY INN SELECT
14299 Firestone Blvd, La Mirada (90638-5591)
PHONE..................................714 739-8500
Fax: 714 739-4272
Jeff Brown, *Principal*
Walid Daoud, *Vice Pres*
EMP: 50
SALES: 12MM **Privately Held**
SIC: 7011 Hotels & motels

(P-12754)
HOLLYWOOD STANDARD LLC
Also Called: Standard The
8300 W Sunset Blvd, Los Angeles (90069-1516)
PHONE..................................323 822-3111
Fax: 323 654-0793
Andre Balazs,
Amy Kowallis, *General Mgr*
Yosh Moriwaki, *Controller*
Bradley Frye, *Human Res Mgr*
Yvonne Lopez, *Human Res Mgr*
EMP: 170
SALES (est): 7MM **Privately Held**
SIC: 7011 Hotels

(P-12755)
HOME AWAY INC
54432 Road 432, Bass Lake (93604-9762)
PHONE..................................559 642-3121
Kyusun Choe, *President*
Sun Choe, *Admin Sec*
EMP: 65
SALES: 4MM **Privately Held**
SIC: 7011 Hotels & motels

(P-12756)
HOMEWOOD SUITES MANAGEMENT LLC
1103 Embarcadero, Oakland (94606-5122)
PHONE..................................510 663-2700
Fax: 510 663-2701
Jason Oliveras, *Manager*
Charles G Brown, *General Mgr*
Tiffanie M Caldwell, *General Mgr*
Alfonso Chavez, *General Mgr*
Jason Olivares, *General Mgr*
EMP: 50
SALES (corp-wide): 11.2B **Publicly Held**
WEB: www.esirvine.com
SIC: 7011 Hotels & motels
HQ: Homewood Suites Management Llc
  7930 Jones Branch Dr
  Mc Lean VA 22102
  703 883-1000

(P-12757)
HONEYMOON REAL ESTATE LP
Also Called: Avalon Hotel
9400 W Olympic Blvd, Beverly Hills (90212-4552)
PHONE..................................310 277-5221
Brad Korzen, *Partner*
Fabian Iobbi, *Vice Pres*
Jyoti Dutt, *Executive*
Pradeep Raman, *General Mgr*
Sharon Lahpai, *Office Mgr*
EMP: 90
SQ FT: 400,000
SALES: 5.9MM **Privately Held**
WEB: www.avalonhotel.com
SIC: 7011 Hotels & motels

(P-12758)
HONG KONG & SHANGHAI HOTELS
Also Called: The Peninsula Beverly Hills
9882 Santa Monica Blvd, Beverly Hills (90212-1605)
PHONE..................................310 551-2888
Ali Kasikci, *Branch Mgr*
EMP: 75
SALES (corp-wide): 740.6MM **Privately Held**
WEB: www.hshgroup.com
SIC: 7011 Hotels & motels
PA: Hongkong And Shanghai Hotels, Limited, The
  8/F St George's Bldg
  Central District HK
  284 077-88

(P-12759)
HOSPITALITY SOLUTIONS LLC
Also Called: Holiday Inn
111 E March Ln, Stockton (95207-5854)
PHONE..................................209 474-3301
Fax: 209 474-7612
Ganatra Vasant, *Mng Member*
Munzer Baiseiso, *General Mgr*
Miguel Garsa, *Controller*
EMP: 50
SALES (est): 1.5MM **Privately Held**
SIC: 7011 Hotels & motels

(P-12760)
HOST HOTELS & RESORTS INC
Also Called: Marriott Fisherman's Wharf
1250 Columbus Ave, San Francisco (94133-1327)
PHONE..................................415 775-7555
Fax: 415 474-2099
Michael Promos, *Branch Mgr*
Christy Galati, *Marketing Staff*
EMP: 170
SALES (corp-wide): 5.3B **Publicly Held**
SIC: 7011 Hotels & motels
PA: Host Hotels & Resorts, Inc.
  6903 Rockledge Dr # 1500
  Bethesda MD 20817
  240 744-1000

(P-12761)
HOST HOTELS & RESORTS INC
1 Market Pl, San Diego (92101-7714)
PHONE..................................619 232-1234
Fax: 619 233-6464
Ted Kanatas, *Manager*
Kimmy Bui, *Social Dir*
Richard K Mitrovich, *Meeting Planner*
Michelle Trick, *Credit Mgr*
Jamil Barhoum, *Controller*
EMP: 170
SALES (corp-wide): 5.3B **Publicly Held*
WEB: www.hyatt.com
SIC: 7011 Hotels & motels
PA: Host Hotels & Resorts, Inc.
  6903 Rockledge Dr # 1500
  Bethesda MD 20817
  240 744-1000

(P-12762)
HOST HOTELS & RESORTS LP
Also Called: Newport Bch Marriott Ht & Spa
900 Newport Center Dr, Newport Beach (92660-6206)
PHONE..................................949 640-4000
Fax: 949 640-5055
Paul Cahill, *General Mgr*
John Lado, *Branch Mgr*
Michelle Rhee, *Purchasing*
Greg Paulk, *Director*
EMP: 100
SALES (corp-wide): 5.3B **Publicly Held**
WEB: www.scmarriott.com
SIC: 7011 5813 5812 Hotels & motels; drinking places; eating places
HQ: Host Hotels & Resorts, L.P.
  6903 Rockledge Dr # 1500
  Bethesda MD 20817
  240 744-1000

(P-12763)
HOST HOTELS & RESORTS LP
Also Called: Marriott
8757 Rio San Diego Dr, San Diego (92108-1620)
PHONE..................................619 692-3800
Fax: 619 692-0769
Dennis Bayer, *Manager*
Daryl Rhead, *Finance*
Anabel Valdez, *Human Resources*
Dawn Medina-Amos, *Director*
EMP: 66
SALES (corp-wide): 5.3B **Publicly Held**
WEB: www.scmarriott.com
SIC: 7011 Hotels & motels
HQ: Host Hotels & Resorts, L.P.
  6903 Rockledge Dr # 1500
  Bethesda MD 20817
  240 744-1000

(P-12764)
HOST HOTELS & RESORTS LP
Also Called: Hyatt Rgncy San Frncisco Arprt
1333 Bayshore Hwy, Burlingame (94010-1804)
PHONE..................................650 347-1234
Fax: 650 347-5948
Keith Butz, *Manager*
Sarah Geller, *Marketing Staff*
Haley Murray, *Manager*
EMP: 64
SALES (corp-wide): 5.3B **Publicly Held**
WEB: www.scmarriott.com
SIC: 7011 Hotels & motels
HQ: Host Hotels & Resorts, L.P.
  6903 Rockledge Dr # 1500
  Bethesda MD 20817
  240 744-1000

(P-12765)
HOST HOTELS & RESORTS LP
Also Called: Santa Clara Marriott Hotel
2700 Mission College Blvd, Santa Clara (95054-1218)
PHONE..................................408 988-1500
Fax: 408 727-4353
Dan Keheller, *Manager*
Eric O'Brien, *Principal*
Chuck Pacioni, *Broker*
Shelly Robb, *Director*
EMP: 66
SALES (corp-wide): 5.3B **Publicly Held**
WEB: www.scmarriott.com
SIC: 7011 8742 7991 5813 Hotels & motels; management consulting services; physical fitness facilities; drinking places; eating places
HQ: Host Hotels & Resorts, L.P.
  6903 Rockledge Dr # 1500
  Bethesda MD 20817
  240 744-1000

(P-12766)
HOST HOTELS & RESORTS LP
Also Called: JW Marriott Desert
74855 Country Club Dr, Palm Desert (92260-1961)
PHONE..................................760 341-2211
Ken Forths, *Manager*
Tim Sullivan, *Systems Mgr*
Dale Fox, *Chief Engr*
Gilda Preston, *Purch Mgr*
Joy Smith, *Purch Mgr*
EMP: 64
SALES (corp-wide): 5.3B **Publicly Held**
WEB: www.scmarriott.com
SIC: 7011 Hotels & motels
HQ: Host Hotels & Resorts, L.P.
  6903 Rockledge Dr # 1500
  Bethesda MD 20817
  240 744-1000

(P-12767)
HOST HOTELS & RESORTS LP
Also Called: Marriott
201 World Way, Los Angeles (90045-5807)
PHONE..................................310 417-3807
Fax: 310 646-8058
Ed Wilcox, *Manager*
EMP: 66
SALES (corp-wide): 5.3B **Publicly Held**
WEB: www.scmarriott.com
SIC: 7011 Hotels & motels
HQ: Host Hotels & Resorts, L.P.
  6903 Rockledge Dr # 1500
  Bethesda MD 20817
  240 744-1000

(P-12768)
HOST HOTELS & RESORTS LP
Also Called: Sheraton San Diego Ht & Marina
1380 Harbor Island Dr, San Diego (92101-1007)
PHONE..................................619 291-2900
Joe Terzi, *Branch Mgr*
Kelly Sanders, *General Mgr*
Gary Harkins, *Systs Prg Mgr*
Garry Phillips, *Marketing Staff*
Doug Korn, *Manager*
EMP: 66
SALES (corp-wide): 5.3B **Publicly Held**
WEB: www.scmarriott.com
SIC: 7011 Hotels
HQ: Host Hotels & Resorts, L.P.
  6903 Rockledge Dr # 1500
  Bethesda MD 20817
  240 744-1000

(P-12769)
HOST HOTELS & RESORTS LP
Also Called: San Francisco Marriott Marquis
55 4th St, San Francisco (94103-3156)
PHONE..................................415 896-1600
Fax: 415 486-8101
Dan Kellher, *Manager*
Dan Kelleher, *President*
Chris Giuntoli, *Meeting Planner*
Freida Azanze, *Technology*
Terry Freeman, *Maintence Staff*
EMP: 66
SALES (corp-wide): 5.3B **Publicly Held**
WEB: www.scmarriott.com
SIC: 7011 5813 5812 Hotels & motels; drinking places; eating places
HQ: Host Hotels & Resorts, L.P.
  6903 Rockledge Dr # 1500
  Bethesda MD 20817
  240 744-1000

(P-12770)
HOST HOTELS & RESORTS LP
Also Called: Costa Mesa Marriott Suites
500 Anton Blvd, Costa Mesa (92626-1911)
PHONE..................................714 957-1100
Stephanie Mack, *General Mgr*
EMP: 66
SALES (corp-wide): 5.3B **Publicly Held**
WEB: www.scmarriott.com
SIC: 7011 5813 5812 Hotels & motels; drinking places; eating places
HQ: Host Hotels & Resorts, L.P.
  6903 Rockledge Dr # 1500
  Bethesda MD 20817
  240 744-1000

(P-12771)
HOST HOTELS & RESORTS LP
Also Called: Marriott
500 Bayview Cir, Newport Beach (92660-2933)
PHONE..................................949 854-4500
Pam Ryan, *Manager*
Daniel Romero, *Executive*
Heather Arellano, *Human Resources*
EMP: 66
SALES (corp-wide): 5.3B **Publicly Held**
WEB: www.scmarriott.com
SIC: 7011 7389 Hotels & motels; office facilities & secretarial service rental
HQ: Host Hotels & Resorts, L.P.
  6903 Rockledge Dr # 1500
  Bethesda MD 20817
  240 744-1000

PRODUCTS & SERVICES SECTION
7011 - Hotels, Motels & Tourist Courts County (P-12796)

(P-12772)
HOST HOTELS & RESORTS LP
1800 Old Bayshore Hwy, Burlingame
(94010-1203)
PHONE 650 692-9100
EMP: 66
SALES (corp-wide): 5.3B Publicly Held
WEB: www.scmarriott.com
SIC: 7011 Hotels & motels
HQ: Host Hotels & Resorts, L.P.
6903 Rockledge Dr # 1500
Bethesda MD 20817
240 744-1000

(P-12773)
HOST HOTELS & RESORTS LP
Also Called: Ritz-Carlton Ht Marina Del Rey
4375 Admiralty Way, Venice (90292-5434)
PHONE 310 823-1700
Robert Thomas, *Branch Mgr*
Don Hunington, *Info Tech Dir*
EMP: 66
SALES (corp-wide): 5.3B Publicly Held
WEB: www.scmarriott.com
SIC: 7011 Hotels & motels
HQ: Host Hotels & Resorts, L.P.
6903 Rockledge Dr # 1500
Bethesda MD 20817
240 744-1000

(P-12774)
HOST HOTELS & RESORTS LP
Also Called: Westin Los Angeles Airport
5400 W Century Blvd, Los Angeles
(90045-5975)
PHONE 310 216-5858
Fax: 310 417-4597
Kimbell John, *CEO*
EMP: 66
SALES (corp-wide): 5.3B Publicly Held
WEB: www.scmarriott.com
SIC: 7011 Hotels & motels
HQ: Host Hotels & Resorts, L.P.
6903 Rockledge Dr # 1500
Bethesda MD 20817
240 744-1000

(P-12775)
HOST HOTELS & RESORTS LP
Also Called: Manhattan Beach Marriott
1400 Park View Ave, Manhattan Beach
(90266-3714)
PHONE 310 546-7511
Fax: 310 939-1486
David Brown, *Engineer*
Suzanne Largova, *Controller*
Mynor Alarcon, *Purch Mgr*
EMP: 70
SALES (corp-wide): 5.3B Publicly Held
WEB: www.scmarriott.com
SIC: 7011 7997 Hotels & motels; golf club, membership
HQ: Host Hotels & Resorts, L.P.
6903 Rockledge Dr # 1500
Bethesda MD 20817
240 744-1000

(P-12776)
HOST HOTELS & RESORTS LP
Also Called: Marriott
4100 Admiralty Way, Marina Del Rey
(90292-6207)
PHONE 310 301-3000
Fax: 310 448-4870
Susan Reardon, *Manager*
Steve Thompson, *Engineer*
Rick Spade, *Personnel Exec*
Laura Carr, *Sales Mgr*
Janet Luna, *Director*
EMP: 66
SALES (corp-wide): 5.3B Publicly Held
WEB: www.scmarriott.com
SIC: 7011 5812 7389 Hotels & motels; eating places; office facilities & secretarial service rental
HQ: Host Hotels & Resorts, L.P.
6903 Rockledge Dr # 1500
Bethesda MD 20817
240 744-1000

(P-12777)
HOST HOTELS & RESORTS LP
Also Called: Westin Los Angeles Airport
5400 W Century Blvd, Los Angeles
(90045-5975)
PHONE 310 216-5858

Tyrone Boykin, *Chief Engr*
Terry Morgan, *Financial Exec*
Monique Taylor, *Manager*
EMP: 66
SALES (corp-wide): 5.3B Publicly Held
WEB: www.scmarriott.com
SIC: 7011 Hotels & motels
HQ: Host Hotels & Resorts, L.P.
6903 Rockledge Dr # 1500
Bethesda MD 20817
240 744-1000

(P-12778)
HOST INTERNATIONAL INC
Also Called: Marriott
1661 Airport Blvd Ste 3e, San Jose
(95110-1216)
PHONE 408 294-1702
Fax: 408 294-4260
Broskin Strickland, *Manager*
Ping Lee, *Vice Pres*
EMP: 180
SALES (corp-wide): 9.4MM Privately Held
WEB: www.hostairporthotel.com
SIC: 7011 Hotels & motels
HQ: Host International, Inc.
6905 Rockledge Dr Fl 1
Bethesda MD 20817
240 694-4100

(P-12779)
HOST INTERNATIONAL INC
3835 N Harbor Dr, San Diego
(92101-1073)
PHONE 619 231-5100
Fax: 619 299-1273
Cynthia Lias, *Branch Mgr*
EMP: 193
SALES (corp-wide): 9.4MM Privately Held
SIC: 7011 Hotels
HQ: Host International, Inc.
6905 Rockledge Dr Fl 1
Bethesda MD 20817
240 694-4100

(P-12780)
HOTEL ADVENTURES LLC
17662 Irvine Blvd Ste 4, Tustin
(92780-3132)
PHONE 714 730-7717
Brad Perrin, *Mng Member*
EMP: 75
SALES (est): 2.8MM Privately Held
SIC: 7011 Hotels

(P-12781)
HOTEL BEL-AIR
701 Stone Canyon Rd, Los Angeles
(90077-2909)
PHONE 310 472-1211
Carlos Lopes, *Managing Dir*
Leslie Miller, *Administration*
Ed Anonas, *Controller*
EMP: 265
SQ FT: 30,000
SALES (est): 861.6K
SALES (corp-wide): 17.2MM Privately Held
WEB: www.hotelbelair.com
SIC: 7011 Hotels
PA: Kava Holdings, Inc.
701 Stone Canyon Rd
Los Angeles CA 90077
310 472-1211

(P-12782)
HOTEL CIRCLE INN & SUITES
2201 Hotel Cir S, San Diego (92108-3315)
PHONE 619 851-6800
Fred Sandoval, *Manager*
Cindy Bailey, *General Mgr*
Michael Foster, *Sales Staff*
Betty Cantrell, *Manager*
EMP: 50
SQ FT: 70,000
SALES (est): 3.2MM Privately Held
SIC: 7011 Motels

(P-12783)
HOTEL CIRCLE PROPERTY LLC
500 Hotel Cir N, San Diego (92108-3005)
PHONE 619 291-7131
Kathryn Little, *Credit Staff*
EMP: 500

SALES (est): 5.1MM Privately Held
SIC: 7011 Resort hotel

(P-12784)
HOTEL CONTRACTING SERVICES INC
2140 Prof Dr Ste 150, Roseville (95661)
PHONE 916 865-4204
Ray Burns, *CEO*
Ann Edgerton, *Vice Pres*
James Murray, *Vice Pres*
EMP: 80
SALES (est): 3MM Privately Held
WEB: www.hotelcontractingservices.com
SIC: 7011 5812 7389 Hotels & motels; caterers;

(P-12785)
HOTEL DEL CORONADO LP
1500 Orange Ave, Coronado (92118-2986)
PHONE 619 522-8011
Fax: 619 522-8160
Brian Miller, *Partner*
Andre Zotoff, *Vice Pres*
Pamela Swentek, *Executive*
Salvador Ulloa, *Executive*
Brian Vincent, *Regional Mgr*
EMP: 51
SALES (est): 15.3MM Privately Held
SIC: 7011 Hotels & motels

(P-12786)
HOTEL DIAMOND
220 W 4th St, Chico (95928-5315)
PHONE 530 893-3100
Fax: 530 893-3103
Wayne Cook, *Owner*
Katie O'Donnell, *Social Dir*
Amanda McGowan, *Sales Staff*
EMP: 50
SQ FT: 19,800
SALES (est): 1.6MM Privately Held
SIC: 7011 Hotels & motels

(P-12787)
HOTEL DURANT A LTD PARTNERSHIP
Also Called: Henry's Pub
2600 Durant Ave, Berkeley (94704-1711)
PHONE 510 845-8981
Fax: 510 486-8336
Stephen Wahrlich, *General Ptnr*
Thunderbird Investors, *General Ptnr*
Tracy W Wahrlich Jr, *General Ptnr*
Barbara Ahzade, *Sales Executive*
Rose Farhi-Doss, *Sales Mgr*
EMP: 84
SQ FT: 57,730
SALES (est): 4.5MM Privately Held
WEB: www.hoteldurant.com
SIC: 7011 5812 5813 6512 Hotels; American restaurant; bar (drinking places); nonresidential building operators

(P-12788)
HOTEL HEALDSBURG (PA)
25 Matheson St, Healdsburg (95448-4107)
PHONE 707 431-2800
Aziz Zhari, *Manager*
Most Rev Aziz Zhari, *Manager*
EMP: 79
SQ FT: 57,500
SALES (est): 8.4MM Privately Held
WEB: www.hotelhealdsburg.com
SIC: 7011 Hotels & motels

(P-12789)
HOTEL LA JOLLA
7955 La Jolla Shores Dr, La Jolla
(92037-3301)
PHONE 858 459-0261
Juliana Bancraft, *President*
Lora Hepp, *Finance Dir*
EMP: 82
SALES (est): 5.3MM Privately Held
WEB: www.hotellajolla.com
SIC: 7011 Hotels

(P-12790)
HOTEL MAC RESTAURANT INC
50 Washington Ave, Richmond
(94801-3945)
PHONE 510 233-0576
Fax: 510 233-3904
William Burnett, *President*
EMP: 50 EST: 1978

SQ FT: 4,000
SALES (est): 3.4MM Privately Held
WEB: www.hotelmac.net
SIC: 7011 5812 5813 Hotels & motels; eating places; bar (drinking places)

(P-12791)
HOTEL NIKKO SAN FRANCISCO INC
222 Mason St, San Francisco
(94102-2115)
PHONE 415 394-1111
Fax: 415 394-1179
Hiroshi Oishi, *CEO*
Anna Marie Presutti, *Vice Pres*
Michael Raub, *Executive*
Thuy Tran, *Executive*
David Ng, *Info Tech Dir*
EMP: 260
SQ FT: 540,000
SALES (est): 26.4MM
SALES (corp-wide): 40.9MM Privately Held
WEB: www.hotelnikkosf.com
SIC: 7011 5812 5813 7991 Hotels; eating places; bar (drinking places); health club; banquet hall facilities
HQ: Okura Nikko Hotel Management Co., Ltd.
2-4-11, Higashishinagawa
Shinagawa-Ku TKY 140-0
354 607-334

(P-12792)
HOTEL TONIGHT INC
901 Market St Ste 310, San Francisco
(94103-1752)
PHONE 800 208-2949
Sam Shank, *CEO*
Jared Simon, *COO*
Tony Grimminck, *CFO*
Amanda Richardson, *Vice Pres*
Kelsey Cooper, *Executive*
EMP: 75
SALES (est): 6.6MM Privately Held
SIC: 7011 Hotels

(P-12793)
HOTEL WHITCOMB
1231 Market St, San Francisco
(94103-1400)
PHONE 415 626-8000
Thomas Chan, *Controller*
Damien Jones, *Executive*
Sharon Chism, *Director*
Tim Bell, *Manager*
EMP: 99
SALES (est): 6.1MM Privately Held
SIC: 7011 Hotels

(P-12794)
HOWARD JOHN
Also Called: Chick-Fil-A
7681 Carson Blvd, Long Beach
(90808-2367)
PHONE 562 425-4232
John Howard, *Owner*
EMP: 70
SALES (est): 615.1K Privately Held
SIC: 7011 Hotels & motels

(P-12795)
HPT TRS IHG 2 INC
Also Called: Holiday Inn
19800 S Vermont Ave, Torrance
(90502-1126)
PHONE 310 781-9100
David Britton, *General Mgr*
EMP: 74
SALES (corp-wide): 1.8B Privately Held
SIC: 7011 Hotels & motels
HQ: Intercontinental Hotels Group Resources, Inc.
3 Ravinia Dr Ste 100
Atlanta GA 30346
770 604-5000

(P-12796)
HPT TRS IHG 2 INC
Also Called: Holiday Inn
5650 Calle Real, Goleta (93117-2319)
PHONE 805 964-6241
Fax: 805 964-8467
Gary Opdahl, *General Mgr*
EMP: 65

7011 - Hotels, Motels & Tourist Courts County (P-12797)

PRODUCTS & SERVICES SECTION

SALES (corp-wide): 1.8B **Privately Held**
WEB: www.sixcontinenthotels.com
SIC: **7011** Hotels & motels
HQ: Intercontinental Hotels Group Resources, Inc.
3 Ravinia Dr Ste 100
Atlanta GA 30346
770 604-5000

(P-12797)
HPT TRS IHG-2 INC
Also Called: Candlewood Suites
481 El Camino Real, Santa Clara (95050-4300)
PHONE.................................408 241-9305
Fax: 408 241-9307
Liz Olson, *Owner*
EMP: 74 **Publicly Held**
SIC: **7011** Hotels & motels
HQ: Hpt Trs Ihg-2, Inc.
255 Washington St Ste 300
Newton MA 02458
617 964-8389

(P-12798)
HPT TRS IHG-2 INC
Also Called: Holiday Inn
1915 S Manchester Ave, Anaheim (92802-3802)
PHONE.................................714 748-7777
Fax: 714 748-7300
Sven Grunder, *General Mgr*
EMP: 100
SQ FT: 3,540 **Publicly Held**
WEB: www.sixcontinenthotels.com
SIC: **7011** Hotels & motels
HQ: Hpt Trs Ihg-2, Inc.
255 Washington St Ste 300
Newton MA 02458
617 964-8389

(P-12799)
HPT TRS IHG-2 INC
Also Called: Crowne Plaza
5985 W Century Blvd, Los Angeles (90045-5477)
PHONE.................................310 642-7500
Fax: 310 216-6646
Michael Payton, *Manager*
EMP: 100 **Publicly Held**
WEB: www.sixcontinenthotels.com
SIC: **7011** Hotels & motels
HQ: Hpt Trs Ihg-2, Inc.
255 Washington St Ste 300
Newton MA 02458
617 964-8389

(P-12800)
HPT TRS IHG-2 INC
Also Called: Crowne Plaza
300 N Harbor Dr, Redondo Beach (90277-2552)
PHONE.................................310 318-8888
Fax: 310 376-1930
Paul Gibbs, *Branch Mgr*
Bill Ryburn, *Engineer*
EMP: 300 **Publicly Held**
WEB: www.sixcontinenthotels.com
SIC: **7011** Hotels & motels
HQ: Hpt Trs Ihg-2, Inc.
255 Washington St Ste 300
Newton MA 02458
617 964-8389

(P-12801)
HPT TRS IHG-2 INC
Also Called: Staybridge Suites
900 Hamlin Ct, Sunnyvale (94089-1401)
PHONE.................................408 745-1515
Tina Messenger, *Branch Mgr*
Thomas McEvoy, *Director*
EMP: 50 **Publicly Held**
WEB: www.hptreit.com
SIC: **7011** Hotels & motels
HQ: Hpt Trs Ihg-2, Inc.
255 Washington St Ste 300
Newton MA 02458
617 964-8389

(P-12802)
HST LESSEE BOSTON LLC
Also Called: Sheraton
1380 Harbor Island Dr, San Diego (92101-1007)
PHONE.................................619 692-2255
Fax: 619 296-5297

Joe Tursey, *General Mgr*
Steve Mueller, *Controller*
Eric Holle, *Manager*
EMP: 60
SALES (corp-wide): 14.4B **Publicly Held**
SIC: **7011** Hotels & motels
HQ: Hst Lessee Boston Llc
39 Dalton St
Boston MA 02199
617 236-2000

(P-12803)
HUMNIT HOTEL AT LAX LLC
Also Called: Concourse Hotel At
6225 W Century Blvd, Los Angeles (90045-5311)
PHONE.................................424 702-1234
Jina Luman, *Principal*
EMP: 99 **EST**: 2013
SQ FT: 49,500
SALES (est): 3.1MM **Privately Held**
SIC: **7011** Hotels & motels

(P-12804)
HUNTINGTON HOTEL COMPANY
Also Called: Inn At Rancho Santa Fe, The
5951 Linea Del Cielo, Rancho Santa Fe (92067)
PHONE.................................858 756-1131
Fax: 858 759-1604
Scott Jenkins, *CEO*
Gordon Macmitchell, *General Mgr*
Mary George, *Sales Mgr*
Jeri Smith, *Sales Mgr*
Frank Polinski, *Food Svc Dir*
EMP: 88
SQ FT: 5,000
SALES (est): 8.2MM **Privately Held**
SIC: **7011** 5812 Resort hotel; eating places

(P-12805)
HUOYEN INTERNATIONAL INC
Also Called: Crowne Plaza
1500 S Raymond Ave, Fullerton (92831-5236)
PHONE.................................714 635-9000
Hsi Jung Yang, *President*
Achilles Yang, *General Mgr*
Charles Yang, *General Mgr*
Nina Lien, *CTO*
Alan Ho, *Controller*
EMP: 90
SQ FT: 144,698
SALES (est): 6.1MM **Privately Held**
SIC: **7011** Hotels & motels

(P-12806)
HUSKIES LESSEE LLC
Also Called: Sir Francis Drake Hotel
450 Powell St, San Francisco (94102-1504)
PHONE.................................415 392-7755
John Price, *General Mgr*
Peter Dykes, *General Mgr*
David Shaffer, *Finance Dir*
EMP: 375
SALES: 32MM **Privately Held**
SIC: **7011** Hotels

(P-12807)
HYATT CORPORATION
Also Called: Hyatt Hotel
8401 W Sunset Blvd, Los Angeles (90069-1909)
PHONE.................................323 656-1234
Fax: 323 650-4469
Tim Flodin, *Manager*
Agustin Cruz, *Sales Mgr*
EMP: 165
SALES (corp-wide): 4.3B **Publicly Held**
WEB: www.hyatt.com
SIC: **7011** 5812 5813 Hotels & motels; restaurant, family: independent; bar (drinking places)
HQ: Hyatt Corporation
150 N Riverside Plz
Chicago IL 60606
312 750-1234

(P-12808)
HYATT CORPORATION
4001 Northstar Dr, Truckee (96161-4250)
PHONE.................................530 562-3900
Beryl Guyon, *Branch Mgr*
EMP: 316

SALES (corp-wide): 4.3B **Publicly Held**
SIC: **7011** Vacation lodges
HQ: Hyatt Corporation
150 N Riverside Plz
Chicago IL 60606
312 750-1234

(P-12809)
HYATT CORPORATION
Also Called: Hyatt Los Angeles Airport
6225 W Century Blvd, Los Angeles (90045-5311)
PHONE.................................312 750-1234
Donald J Henderson, *Manager*
Jeff Jorgensen, *Engineer*
Jim Chatelain, *Accounting Dir*
Sharon Heelan, *Persnl Dir*
Philippe Brenot, *Purch Dir*
EMP: 500
SALES (corp-wide): 4.3B **Publicly Held**
SIC: **7011** 5812 5813 Hotels; restaurant, family: chain; bar (drinking places)
HQ: Hyatt Corporation
150 N Riverside Plz
Chicago IL 60606
312 750-1234

(P-12810)
HYATT CORPORATION
3500 Market St, Riverside (92501-2841)
PHONE.................................909 240-9526
EMP: 316
SALES (corp-wide): 4.3B **Publicly Held**
SIC: **7011** Hotels & motels
HQ: Hyatt Corporation
150 N Riverside Plz
Chicago IL 60606
312 750-1234

(P-12811)
HYATT CORPORATION
Also Called: Grand Hyatt San Francisco
345 Stockton St, San Francisco (94108-4606)
PHONE.................................415 848-6050
Fax: 415 403-4882
Steve Trent, *Manager*
Gary Cavalli, *Exec Dir*
Martha Cohen, *Exec Dir*
Ed Randes, *Engineer*
Susan Schafer, *Human Res Dir*
EMP: 500
SALES (corp-wide): 4.3B **Publicly Held**
WEB: www.hyatt.com
SIC: **7011** 5813 5812 6512 Hotels & motels; drinking places; eating places; non-residential building operators
HQ: Hyatt Corporation
150 N Riverside Plz
Chicago IL 60606
312 750-1234

(P-12812)
HYATT CORPORATION
Also Called: Hyatt Hotel
50 Drumm St, San Francisco (94111-4804)
PHONE.................................415 788-1234
Fax: 415 291-6569
Matthew Adams, *Manager*
Arnel Cruz, *Commissioner*
Ellen Saepoff, *Manager*
EMP: 900
SALES (corp-wide): 4.3B **Publicly Held**
WEB: www.hyatt.com
SIC: **7011** 5812 5813 Hotels & motels; eating places; bar (drinking places)
HQ: Hyatt Corporation
150 N Riverside Plz
Chicago IL 60606
312 750-1234

(P-12813)
HYATT CORPORATION
Also Called: Hyatt House San Ramon
2323 San Ramon Vly Blvd, San Ramon (94583-1607)
PHONE.................................925 743-1882
Pam Callahan, *Branch Mgr*
Kerry Knudson, *General Mgr*
Julie Thomas, *Manager*
EMP: 317
SALES (corp-wide): 4.3B **Publicly Held**
SIC: **7011** Hotels & motels

HQ: Hyatt Corporation
150 N Riverside Plz
Chicago IL 60606
312 750-1234

(P-12814)
HYATT CORPORATION
Also Called: Hyatt Hotel
200 S Pine Ave, Long Beach (90802-4537)
PHONE.................................562 432-0161
Fax: 562 432-1972
Steve Smith, *Manager*
Emrah Ozkaya, *Bd of Directors*
Marilyn J Healey, *Meeting Planner*
Grace Catubig, *Info Tech Mgr*
Jim Chatelain, *Controller*
EMP: 500
SALES (corp-wide): 4.3B **Publicly Held**
WEB: www.hyatt.com
SIC: **7011** 7299 Hotels & motels; banquet hall facilities
HQ: Hyatt Corporation
150 N Riverside Plz
Chicago IL 60606
312 750-1234

(P-12815)
HYATT CORPORATION
Also Called: Hyatt Regency Monterey
1 Old Golf Course Rd, Monterey (93940-4908)
PHONE.................................831 372-1234
Fax: 831 375-3960
Michael Koffler, *Manager*
Neal Matsumoto, *Controller*
Paula Calvetti, *Human Res Dir*
Nick Pozzo, *Sales Mgr*
Michael Cuffler, *Manager*
EMP: 420
SALES (corp-wide): 4.3B **Publicly Held**
WEB: www.hyatt.com
SIC: **7011** Hotels & motels
HQ: Hyatt Corporation
150 N Riverside Plz
Chicago IL 60606
312 750-1234

(P-12816)
HYATT CORPORATION
Also Called: Hyatt Hotel
17900 Jamboree Rd, Irvine (92614-6211)
PHONE.................................949 975-1234
Fax: 949 225-6719
Rod T Schinnerer, *General Mgr*
Jodie Ullman, *Treasurer*
Daniel Guiles, *Chief Engr*
Zafar Qureshi, *Chf Purch Ofc*
Lisa Fossen, *Sales Dir*
EMP: 450
SALES (corp-wide): 4.3B **Publicly Held**
WEB: www.hyatt.com
SIC: **7011** 7992 7991 5813 Hotels & motels; public golf courses; physical fitness facilities; drinking places; eating places
HQ: Hyatt Corporation
150 N Riverside Plz
Chicago IL 60606
312 750-1234

(P-12817)
HYATT CORPORATION
Also Called: Hyatt Regency Orange County
11999 Harbor Blvd, Garden Grove (92840-2703)
PHONE.................................714 750-1234
Kevin Kennedy, *Manager*
Brad Marman, *Project Dir*
Glen Wilson, *Engineer*
Nicole Sowers, *Sales Mgr*
Joy Hedrick, *Director*
EMP: 300
SALES (corp-wide): 4.3B **Publicly Held**
WEB: www.hyatt.com
SIC: **7011** Hotels & motels
HQ: Hyatt Corporation
150 N Riverside Plz
Chicago IL 60606
312 750-1234

(P-12818)
HYATT CORPORATION
Also Called: Hyatt Grand Champion Resort
44600 Indian Wells Ln, Indian Wells (92210-8707)
PHONE.................................760 341-1000
Fax: 760 568-2236

PRODUCTS & SERVICES SECTION
7011 - Hotels, Motels & Tourist Courts County (P-12840)

Allan Farwell, *Manager*
Natalie Maupin, *Comms Mgr*
Cathy J Thompson, *Meeting Planner*
Maria Romero, *Sales Mgr*
Lydia Montez, *Assistant*
EMP: 500
SALES (corp-wide): 4.3B **Publicly Held**
WEB: www.hyatt.com
SIC: 7011 5813 5812 Hotels & motels; drinking places; eating places
HQ: Hyatt Corporation
150 N Riverside Plz
Chicago IL 60606
312 750-1234

(P-12819)
HYATT CORPORATION
Also Called: Hyatt Hotel
1107 Jamboree Rd, Newport Beach (92660-6219)
PHONE.................949 729-1234
Fax: 949 644-1552
Cauline Kareti, *General Mgr*
Paul Devitt, *General Mgr*
Randy Goldberg, *CIO*
Mataline Douglas, *Human Res Dir*
Martha Collins, *Sales Associate*
EMP: 300
SALES (corp-wide): 4.3B **Publicly Held**
WEB: www.hyatt.com
SIC: 7011 5813 5812 Hotels & motels; drinking places; eating places
HQ: Hyatt Corporation
150 N Riverside Plz
Chicago IL 60606
312 750-1234

(P-12820)
HYATT CORPORATION
55 E Brokaw Rd, San Jose (95112-4202)
PHONE.................408 453-3006
Fax: 408 453-3066
Frank Palacios, *Principal*
EMP: 314
SALES (corp-wide): 4.3B **Publicly Held**
SIC: 7011 8741 Hotels & motels; hotel or motel management
HQ: Hyatt Corporation
150 N Riverside Plz
Chicago IL 60606
312 750-1234

(P-12821)
HYATT CORPORATION
Also Called: Hyatt Regency San Francisco Ht
5 Embarcadero Ctr, San Francisco (94111-4800)
PHONE.................415 788-1234
Fax: 415 398-2567
Jerry Simmons, *General Mgr*
Duane Bell, *Senior VP*
Pete Sears, *Senior VP*
Victor Litkewycz, *Executive*
Cynthia Motta, *Executive*
EMP: 600
SALES (corp-wide): 4.3B **Publicly Held**
WEB: www.hyatt.com
SIC: 7011 5812 5813 Hotels & motels; eating places; drinking places
HQ: Hyatt Corporation
150 N Riverside Plz
Chicago IL 60606
312 750-1234

(P-12822)
HYATT CORPORATION
Also Called: Andaz Sandiego
600 F St, San Diego (92101-6310)
PHONE.................619 849-1234
Fax: 619 531-7955
Rusty Middleton, *Branch Mgr*
Rebecca Quezada, *Controller*
EMP: 200
SALES (corp-wide): 4.3B **Publicly Held**
SIC: 7011 Hotels
HQ: Hyatt Corporation
150 N Riverside Plz
Chicago IL 60606
312 750-1234

(P-12823)
HYATT CORPORATION
Also Called: Hyatt Hotel
880 S Westlake Blvd, Westlake Village (91361-2905)
PHONE.................805 557-1234
Fax: 805 557-4894
David Coonan, *General Mgr*
Matt Kovac, *Sales Dir*
EMP: 248
SALES (corp-wide): 4.3B **Publicly Held**
WEB: www.hyatt.com
SIC: 7011 5812 5813 Hotels & motels; eating places; drinking places
HQ: Hyatt Corporation
150 N Riverside Plz
Chicago IL 60606
312 750-1234

(P-12824)
HYATT EQUITIES LLC
Also Called: Hyatt Hotel
1740 N 1st St, San Jose (95112-4508)
PHONE.................408 993-1234
Fax: 408 436-8644
Manou Mobesesahi, *Branch Mgr*
Gary Lind, *General Mgr*
Paolo Hutchison, *MIS Dir*
David Kerkeles, *Human Res Dir*
EMP: 253
SALES (corp-wide): 4.3B **Publicly Held**
SIC: 7011 Hotels & motels
HQ: Hyatt Equities, L.L.C.
71 S Wacker Dr Fl 14
Chicago IL 60606
312 750-1234

(P-12825)
HYATT HOTELS CORPORATION
1 Old Golf Course Rd, Monterey (93940-4908)
PHONE.................831 372-1234
Mark Bastis, *General Mgr*
EMP: 500
SQ FT: 10,000
SALES (corp-wide): 4.3B **Publicly Held**
WEB: www.hyattvacations.com
SIC: 7011 Hotels & motels
HQ: Hyatt Hotels Management Corporation
71 S Wacker Dr Ste 1000
Chicago IL 60606
312 750-1234

(P-12826)
HYATT HOTELS MANAGEMENT CORP
24500 Town Center Dr, Valencia (91355-1322)
PHONE.................661 799-1234
Fax: 661 799-1233
Chris Aldiere, *Manager*
EMP: 140
SALES (corp-wide): 4.3B **Publicly Held**
WEB: www.hyattvacations.com
SIC: 7011 5812 5813 Hotels & motels; banquet hall facilities; caterers
HQ: Hyatt Hotels Management Corporation
71 S Wacker Dr Ste 1000
Chicago IL 60606
312 750-1234

(P-12827)
HYATT HOTELS MANAGEMENT CORP
Also Called: Regency Caterers By Hyatt
3777 Lajolla Village Dr, San Diego (92122)
PHONE.................858 552-1234
Chris Alteri, *Manager*
Amy C McIntyre, *Senior VP*
Robert Webb, *VP Human Res*
Arnold Samoi, *Maintence Staff*
EMP: 485
SALES (corp-wide): 4.3B **Publicly Held**
WEB: www.hyattvacations.com
SIC: 7011 5812 5813 Hotels & motels; caterers; drinking places
HQ: Hyatt Hotels Management Corporation
71 S Wacker Dr Ste 1000
Chicago IL 60606
312 750-1234

(P-12828)
HYATT HOTELS MANAGEMENT CORP
285 N Palm Canyon Dr, Palm Springs (92262-5525)
PHONE.................760 322-9000
Fax: 760 416-5573
Dania Duke, *Manager*
Mary J Ginther, *Engineer*
Jamye McLaren, *Engineer*
EMP: 200
SALES (corp-wide): 4.3B **Publicly Held**
WEB: www.hyatt.com
SIC: 7011 7299 5812 Hotels & motels; banquet hall facilities; caterers
HQ: Hyatt Hotels Management Corporation
71 S Wacker Dr Ste 1000
Chicago IL 60606
312 750-1234

(P-12829)
HYATT HOTELS MANAGEMENT CORP
4219 El Camino Real, Palo Alto (94306-4405)
PHONE.................650 352-1234
Fax: 650 424-0836
Colleen Kareti, *General Mgr*
Shari Okumura, *Comms Dir*
Nido Romeo, *Controller*
EMP: 365
SALES (corp-wide): 4.3B **Publicly Held**
WEB: www.hyattvacations.com
SIC: 7011 5813 5812 Hotels & motels; drinking places; eating places
HQ: Hyatt Hotels Management Corporation
71 S Wacker Dr Ste 1000
Chicago IL 60606
312 750-1234

(P-12830)
HYATT REGENCY CENTURY PLAZA
2025 Avenue Of The Stars, Los Angeles (90067-4701)
PHONE.................310 228-1234
Rakesh Sarna, *CEO*
Ken Cruse, *President*
Jay Cosico, *Social Dir*
Elizabeth Borrelli, *Administration*
Richard Ponti, *Purch Dir*
EMP: 650
SALES (est): 25.4MM **Privately Held**
SIC: 7011 Hotels & motels

(P-12831)
HYATT REGENCY SANTA CLARA
5101 Great America Pkwy, Santa Clara (95054-1118)
PHONE.................408 200-1234
Fax: 408 510-6449
Peter Reice, *General Mgr*
Santi Wathinanon, *Asst Controller*
Jovino Navasca, *Purch Mgr*
EMP: 77
SALES (est): 7.8MM **Privately Held**
SIC: 7011 Hotels & motels

(P-12832)
I CYPRESS COMPANY
Also Called: Pebble Beach Company
2700 17 Mile Dr, Pebble Beach (93953-2668)
P.O. Box 1418 (93953-1418)
PHONE.................831 647-7500
Bill Perocchi, *CEO*
Cody Plott, *COO*
David Heuck, *CFO*
Paul Spengler, *Exec VP*
Mark Stilwell, *Exec VP*
EMP: 2500
SALES (est): 106.7MM **Privately Held**
SIC: 7011 Hotels & motels

(P-12833)
I PCA L P
Also Called: Doubletree Suites By Hilton
1707 4th St, Santa Monica (90401-3301)
PHONE.................310 395-3332
Elizabeth Procaccianti,
Ruben Ayala, *Controller*
EMP: 135
SALES (est): 4.3MM **Privately Held**
SIC: 7011 Hotels & motels

(P-12834)
IHG MANAGEMENT (MARYLAND) LLC
Also Called: Crown Plaza Los Angeles
5985 W Century Blvd, Los Angeles (90045-5477)
PHONE.................310 642-7500
Fax: 310 649-4035
William Block, *Finance Dir*
EMP: 250
SQ FT: 14,000
SALES: 30MM **Privately Held**
SIC: 7011 Hotels & motels

(P-12835)
IHMS (SF) LLC
Also Called: Campton Place, A Taj Hotel
340 Stockton St, San Francisco (94108-4609)
PHONE.................415 781-5555
Sanjay Jain,
Puranjay Kumar, *COO*
Dori Portner, *General Mgr*
Leo Ramos, *General Mgr*
Ranju Singh, *General Mgr*
EMP: 150
SALES (est): 12.1MM
SALES (corp-wide): 325MM **Privately Held**
SIC: 7011 Hotels & motels
HQ: International Hotel Management Services Inc.
2 E 61st St
New York NY 10065
212 838-8000

(P-12836)
INDIAN WELLS RESORT HOTEL
76661 Us Highway 111, Indian Wells (92210-8972)
PHONE.................760 345-6466
Fax: 760 772-5083
Brad Weimer, *President*
Willie Cabrera, *Executive*
Manuel Rojo, *Sales Staff*
Wendell Cook, *Med Doctor*
Pete Dourbayan, *Manager*
EMP: 50
SQ FT: 240,000
SALES (est): 3.7MM **Privately Held**
WEB: www.indianwellsresort.com
SIC: 7011 5812 Hotels; eating places

(P-12837)
INN AT SCOTTS VALLEY LLC
Also Called: Hilton Santa Cruz/Scotts Vly
6001 La Madrona Dr, Scotts Valley (95060-1057)
PHONE.................831 440-1000
Fax: 831 440-1111
Rich Higdon, *Mng Member*
EMP: 70
SQ FT: 130,000
SALES (est): 3.1MM **Privately Held**
SIC: 7011 Motels

(P-12838)
INTERCNTNNTAL CLEMENT MONTEREY
750 Cannery Row Ste 100, Monterey (93940-1087)
PHONE.................831 375-4500
Fax: 831 375-4501
Clement Chen, *President*
John Turner, *General Mgr*
Anne Stroul, *Marketing Staff*
Cara Hawran, *Supervisor*
EMP: 54
SALES (est): 4.6MM **Privately Held**
SIC: 7011 Hotels

(P-12839)
INTERCNTNNTAL HT GROUP RSURCES
Also Called: Hotel Indigo San Diego
509 9th Ave, San Diego (92101-7213)
PHONE.................619 727-4000
Pat McTigue, *General Mgr*
Nathile Neeses, *Executive*
Kelsey Shull, *Manager*
EMP: 60
SALES (corp-wide): 1.8B **Privately Held**
SIC: 7011 Hotels
HQ: Intercontinental Hotels Group Resources, Inc.
3 Ravinia Dr Ste 100
Atlanta GA 30346
770 604-5000

(P-12840)
INTERCNTNNTAL HT GROUP RSURCES
Also Called: Holiday Inn
1300 Columbus Ave, San Francisco (94133-1328)
PHONE.................415 771-9000

7011 - Hotels, Motels & Tourist Courts County (P-12841)

Sheila Martin, *General Mgr*
Linda Goulden, *Human Res Mgr*
EMP: 252
SALES (corp-wide): 1.8B **Privately Held**
WEB: www.sixcontinenthotels.com
SIC: **7011** 8741 Hotels; hotel or motel management
HQ: Intercontinental Hotels Group Resources, Inc.
3 Ravinia Dr Ste 100
Atlanta GA 30346
770 604-5000

(P-12841)
INTERCNTNNTAL HT GROUP RSURCES
Also Called: Crowne Plaza Irvine-Orange Cou
17941 Von Karman Ave, Irvine (92614-6253)
PHONE..................................949 863-1999
Martin Driskel, *Opers-Prdtn-Mfg*
EMP: 100
SALES (corp-wide): 1.8B **Privately Held**
WEB: www.southforkhotel.com
SIC: **7011** 5813 5812 Hotels & motels; drinking places; eating places
HQ: Intercontinental Hotels Group Resources, Inc.
3 Ravinia Dr Ste 100
Atlanta GA 30346
770 604-5000

(P-12842)
INTERCONTINENTAL HOTELS GROUP
Also Called: Crowne Plaza
17941 Von Karman Ave, Irvine (92614-6253)
PHONE..................................949 863-1999
Fax: 949 474-7236
Jim Alexander, *Owner*
Cristy Smith, *General Mgr*
Justin Gammon, *Sales Dir*
Tod Makimoto, *Food Svc Dir*
EMP: 180
SALES (corp-wide): 1.8B **Privately Held**
WEB: www.hptreit.com
SIC: **7011** Hotels & motels
HQ: Intercontinental Hotels Group Resources, Inc.
3 Ravinia Dr Ste 100
Atlanta GA 30346
770 604-5000

(P-12843)
INTERCONTINENTAL HOTELS GROUP
Also Called: Holiday Inn
50 8th St, San Francisco (94103-1409)
PHONE..................................415 626-6103
Fax: 415 552-0184
Gino Lazzara, *General Mgr*
EMP: 160
SALES (corp-wide): 1.8B **Privately Held**
SIC: **7011** 5813 5812 6512 Hotels; drinking places; eating places; nonresidential building operators
HQ: Intercontinental Hotels Group Resources, Inc.
3 Ravinia Dr Ste 100
Atlanta GA 30346
770 604-5000

(P-12844)
INTERCONTINENTAL HOTELS GROUP
Also Called: San Francisco Marriott Un Sq
480 Sutter St, San Francisco (94108-3901)
PHONE..................................415 398-8900
John Simonich, *Branch Mgr*
Susan Saucedo, *Director*
Chris Wing, *Manager*
EMP: 210
SALES (corp-wide): 1.8B **Privately Held**
WEB: www.southforkhotel.com
SIC: **7011** Hotels
HQ: Intercontinental Hotels Group Resources, Inc.
3 Ravinia Dr Ste 100
Atlanta GA 30346
770 604-5000

(P-12845)
INTERCONTINENTAL HOTELS GROUP
Also Called: Holiday Inn Express and Suites
550 N Point St, San Francisco (94133-1312)
PHONE..................................415 409-4600
Fax: 415 409-5111
Mike Cunningham, *Manager*
Chris Eng, *Vice Pres*
Martha Flynn, *Manager*
EMP: 50
SALES (corp-wide): 1.8B **Privately Held**
WEB: www.southforkhotel.com
SIC: **7011** Hotels
HQ: Intercontinental Hotels Group Resources, Inc.
3 Ravinia Dr Ste 100
Atlanta GA 30346
770 604-5000

(P-12846)
INTERCONTINENTAL HOTELS GROUP
2280 S Haven Ave, Ontario (91761-0739)
PHONE..................................909 930-5555
Lori Whiting, *Manager*
EMP: 122
SALES (corp-wide): 1.8B **Privately Held**
WEB: www.southforkhotel.com
SIC: **7011** Hotels
HQ: Intercontinental Hotels Group Resources, Inc.
3 Ravinia Dr Ste 100
Atlanta GA 30346
770 604-5000

(P-12847)
INTERCONTINENTAL HOTELS GROUP
Also Called: Intercontinental San Francisco
888 Howard St, San Francisco (94103-3011)
PHONE..................................415 616-6500
Fax: 415 616-6501
Peter Coehler, *General Mgr*
Casey U Neuburger, *General Mgr*
Connie Perez, *Pub Rel Mgr*
EMP: 350
SALES (corp-wide): 1.8B **Privately Held**
WEB: www.southforkhotel.com
SIC: **7011** Hotels & motels
HQ: Intercontinental Hotels Group Resources, Inc.
3 Ravinia Dr Ste 100
Atlanta GA 30346
770 604-5000

(P-12848)
INTERSTATE HOTELS RESORTS INC
Also Called: Sheraton
2500 Mason St, San Francisco (94133-1450)
PHONE..................................415 362-5500
Fax: 415 627-6529
David Gievens, *Manager*
Jim Sega, *Marketing Staff*
Michael Fontanilla, *Manager*
EMP: 250
SALES (corp-wide): 1.7B **Privately Held**
WEB: www.sheratonokc.com
SIC: **7011** Hotels & motels
HQ: Interstate Hotels & Resorts, Inc.
4501 Fairfax Dr Ste 500
Arlington VA 22203
703 387-3100

(P-12849)
INTERSTATE HOTELS RESORTS INC
Also Called: Marriott Los Angeles Downtown
333 S Figueroa St, Los Angeles (90071-1001)
PHONE..................................213 617-1133
Guenet Kelelatchew, *Director*
Joe Aro, *Bd of Directors*
Ann Burckle, *Bd of Directors*
Ahmed Enany, *Bd of Directors*
Alison Maxwell, *Bd of Directors*
EMP: 220
SQ FT: 143,000
SALES (corp-wide): 1.7B **Privately Held**
WEB: www.sheratonokc.com
SIC: **7011** 8741 Hotels & motels; hotel or motel management
HQ: Interstate Hotels & Resorts, Inc.
4501 Fairfax Dr Ste 500
Arlington VA 22203
703 387-3100

(P-12850)
INTERSTATE HOTELS RESORTS INC
Also Called: Westin Bonaventure Ht & Suites
404 S Figueroa St 418a, Los Angeles (90071-1710)
PHONE..................................213 624-1000
Peter Zen, *President*
Randy Gordon, *Vice Pres*
John Worthington, *Social Dir*
Barrie Rerks, *Sales Mgr*
John Marco, *Director*
EMP: 500
SALES (corp-wide): 1.7B **Privately Held**
WEB: www.sheratonokc.com
SIC: **7011** Hotels & motels
HQ: Interstate Hotels & Resorts, Inc.
4501 Fairfax Dr Ste 500
Arlington VA 22203
703 387-3100

(P-12851)
INTERSTATE HOTELS RESORTS INC
Also Called: Claremont Resort
41 Tunnel Rd, Berkeley (94705-2429)
PHONE..................................510 843-3000
Fax: 510 848-6208
Mike Czarcinski, *General Mgr*
Darwin Davis, *CIO*
Yuriy Mukha, *MIS Mgr*
EMP: 99
SALES (corp-wide): 1.7B **Privately Held**
WEB: www.sheratonokc.com
SIC: **7011** Resort hotel
HQ: Interstate Hotels & Resorts, Inc.
4501 Fairfax Dr Ste 500
Arlington VA 22203
703 387-3100

(P-12852)
INTERSTATE HOTELS RESORTS INC
Also Called: Radisson Inn
32083 Alvarado Niles Rd, Union City (94587-2942)
PHONE..................................510 489-2200
Peter San, *General Mgr*
EMP: 140
SALES (corp-wide): 1.7B **Privately Held**
WEB: www.sheratonokc.com
SIC: **7011** 5812 5813 Hotels & motels; eating places; bar (drinking places)
HQ: Interstate Hotels & Resorts, Inc.
4501 Fairfax Dr Ste 500
Arlington VA 22203
703 387-3100

(P-12853)
INTERSTATE HOTELS RESORTS INC
Also Called: Hilton Sacramento Arden West
2200 Harvard St, Sacramento (95815-3306)
PHONE..................................916 922-4700
Howard Harris, *General Mgr*
Robert Simpson, *Branch Mgr*
Hilton West, *Info Tech Mgr*
Kenneth Leone, *Manager*
Cheri Montez, *Manager*
EMP: 200
SALES (corp-wide): 1.7B **Privately Held**
WEB: www.sheratonokc.com
SIC: **7011** 5812 5813 5947 Hotels & motels; eating places; drinking places; gift, novelty & souvenir shop
HQ: Interstate Hotels & Resorts, Inc.
4501 Fairfax Dr Ste 500
Arlington VA 22203
703 387-3100

(P-12854)
IRP LAX HOTEL LLC
Also Called: Four Points by Sheraton LAX
9750 Airport Blvd, Los Angeles (90045-5404)
PHONE..................................310 645-4600
Phil Baxter,
Jairo Alvarez, *Executive*
Justin Jaramillo, *Office Mgr*
Kristi Arndt, *Controller*
Lulu Medina, *Human Res Dir*
EMP: 240
SQ FT: 337,720
SALES (est): 5.5MM
SALES (corp-wide): 17.9B **Publicly Held**
SIC: **7011** Hotels & motels
HQ: Tishman Hotel Corporation
666 5th Ave Fl 38
New York NY 10103
212 399-3600

(P-12855)
ISLAND HOSPITALITY MGT LLC
Residence Inn By Marriott
750 Lakeway Dr, Sunnyvale (94085-4011)
PHONE..................................408 720-1000
Hugo Hernandez, *Branch Mgr*
John Firoe, *Branch Mgr*
Rich Pinto, *VP Opers*
Michelle Mercier, *Sales Executive*
Steve Cotten, *Manager*
EMP: 50
SALES (corp-wide): 634.5MM **Privately Held**
WEB: www.napleshamptoninn.com
SIC: **7011** Hotels & motels
PA: Island Hospitality Management, Llc
222 Lakeview Ave Ste 200
West Palm Beach FL 33401
561 832-6132

(P-12856)
ISLAND HOSPITALITY MGT LLC
Also Called: Residence Inn By Marriott
2000 Winward Way, San Mateo (94404-2472)
PHONE..................................650 574-4700
Fax: 650 572-9084
Omar Paredes, *Branch Mgr*
Leuis Carreno, *Manager*
EMP: 60
SALES (corp-wide): 634.5MM **Privately Held**
WEB: www.napleshamptoninn.com
SIC: **7011** Hotels & motels
PA: Island Hospitality Management, Llc
222 Lakeview Ave Ste 200
West Palm Beach FL 33401
561 832-6132

(P-12857)
ISLAND HOSPITALITY MGT LLC
Residence Inn By Marriott
1080 Stewart Dr, Sunnyvale (94085-3917)
PHONE..................................408 720-8893
Kort Gursu, *Manager*
EMP: 59
SALES (corp-wide): 634.5MM **Privately Held**
WEB: www.napleshamptoninn.com
SIC: **7011** Hotels & motels
PA: Island Hospitality Management, Llc
222 Lakeview Ave Ste 200
West Palm Beach FL 33401
561 832-6132

(P-12858)
ISLAND HOSPITALITY MGT LLC
Also Called: Residence Inn By Marriott
2025 Convention Ctr Way, Ontario (91764-4450)
PHONE..................................909 937-6788
Fax: 909 937-2462
Frank Palacios, *Branch Mgr*
EMP: 50
SALES (corp-wide): 634.5MM **Privately Held**
WEB: www.napleshamptoninn.com
SIC: **7011** Hotels & motels
PA: Island Hospitality Management, Llc
222 Lakeview Ave Ste 200
West Palm Beach FL 33401
561 832-6132

PRODUCTS & SERVICES SECTION

7011 - Hotels, Motels & Tourist Courts County (P-12884)

(P-12859)
ISLAND HOSPITALITY MGT LLC
Also Called: Summerfield Suites By Hyatt
400 Concourse Dr, Belmont (94002-4125)
PHONE.................................650 591-8600
Trinity Nguyen, *Branch Mgr*
Denise Eldrich, *General Mgr*
Alvin Magcale, *General Mgr*
EMP: 80
SALES (corp-wide): 634.5MM **Privately Held**
WEB: www.napleshamptoninn.com
SIC: 7011 Hotels & motels
PA: Island Hospitality Management, Llc
222 Lakeview Ave Ste 200
West Palm Beach FL 33401
561 832-6132

(P-12860)
IWF HALF MOON BAY LP
Also Called: Best Wstn Half Moon Bay Lodge
2400 Cabrillo Hwy S, Half Moon Bay
(94019-2253)
PHONE.................................650 726-9000
Fax: 650 726-7951
Kevin Lanigan, *Manager*
EMP: 50
SALES (est): 2.2MM **Privately Held**
SIC: 7011 Hotels & motels

(P-12861)
J5TH LLC
Also Called: Residence Inn By Mariott
356 6th Ave, San Diego (92101-7186)
PHONE.................................619 487-1200
Fax: 619 487-1202
Rajan Hansji, *Mng Member*
Nicole Masri, *General Mgr*
Sajan Hansji,
Dilip Kanji,
EMP: 55
SALES (est): 2.6MM **Privately Held**
SIC: 7011 7389 Hotels & motels; office facilities & secretarial service rental

(P-12862)
JACK PARKER CORP
Also Called: Le Parker Meridien Palm Sprng
4200 E Palm Canyon Dr, Palm Springs
(92264-5230)
PHONE.................................760 770-5000
Fax: 760 324-2188
Adam Glick, *President*
Brandon McCurley, *General Mgr*
Sherrie McRae, *Manager*
▲ **EMP:** 177
SALES (est): 5.2MM **Privately Held**
SIC: 7011 Motels

(P-12863)
JC RESORTS INN
17550 Bernardo Oaks Dr, San Diego
(92128-2112)
PHONE.................................858 487-0700
Katherine Colachis, *Owner*
EMP: 80
SALES (est): 1.2MM **Privately Held**
SIC: 7011 Hotels

(P-12864)
JCK HOTELS LLC
Also Called: Holiday Inn
9888 Mira Mesa Blvd, San Diego
(92131-1025)
PHONE.................................858 635-5566
Brad Housewoorth,
Napoleon Salinas, *General Mgr*
Judy Fang,
George Liu,
Gloria Liu,
EMP: 55
SQ FT: 4,800
SALES (est): 3.4MM **Privately Held**
WEB: www.mmpcusa.com
SIC: 7011 Hotels & motels

(P-12865)
JHC INVESTMENT INC
Also Called: Dt Club Hotel Santa Ana
7 Hutton Centre Dr, Santa Ana
(92707-5753)
PHONE.................................714 751-2400
Jung-Hsiung Chiu, *President*
Mark Pfeifer, *General Mgr*
EMP: 70
SQ FT: 85,000

SALES (est): 2.7MM **Privately Held**
SIC: 7011 Hotels

(P-12866)
JJ GRAND HOTEL
620 S Harvard Blvd, Los Angeles
(90005-2510)
PHONE.................................213 383-3000
James Lee, *President*
Kuija Kim, *President*
Cho Nicole, *Financial Exec*
EMP: 60
SALES (est): 1.5MM **Privately Held**
WEB: www.jjgrandhotel.com
SIC: 7011 Hotels

(P-12867)
JOIE DE VIVRE HOSPITALITY INC
Also Called: Wild Palms Hotel & Bar
910 E Fremont Ave, Sunnyvale
(94087-3702)
PHONE.................................408 738-0500
Steven C Y Chen, *President*
Ely Malek, *General Mgr*
Greg Duque, *Office Mgr*
Michael Miller, *Asst Controller*
Sandi Liverman, *Accountant*
EMP: 51
SQ FT: 80,000
SALES (est): 4.8MM **Privately Held**
SIC: 7011 Motels

(P-12868)
JOSEPH FAN
Also Called: Clarion Hotel
21725 Gateway Center Dr, Diamond Bar
(91765-2400)
PHONE.................................909 860-5440
Joseph Fan, *Owner*
EMP: 70
SALES (est): 1.2MM **Privately Held**
SIC: 7011 Hotels & motels

(P-12869)
JOYOUS MANAGEMENT INC
Also Called: Residnce Inn Oxnard Rver Ridge
2101 W Vineyard Ave, Oxnard
(93036-2268)
PHONE.................................805 278-2200
Chaohui Liu, *CEO*
Nianyong Wang, *CFO*
Maricela Ayala, *Info Tech Mgr*
Millicent Bennett, *Director*
David WEI, *Accounts Mgr*
EMP: 80
SQ FT: 479,160
SALES (est): 7MM **Privately Held**
SIC: 7011 Hotels

(P-12870)
JP ALLEN EXTENDED STAY
Also Called: Holiday Inn
150 E Angeleno Ave, Burbank
(91502-1911)
PHONE.................................818 841-4770
Fax: 818 566-7886
Chris Haven, *Manager*
EMP: 50
SALES (corp-wide): 9.3MM **Privately Held**
SIC: 7011 Hotels & motels
PA: Jp Allen Extended Stay
450 Pioneer Dr
Glendale CA 91203
818 956-0202

(P-12871)
JP ALLEN EXTENDED STAY (PA)
Also Called: Days Inn
450 Pioneer Dr, Glendale (91203-1713)
PHONE.................................818 956-0202
Joe Perry, *Owner*
EMP: 76
SQ FT: 4,000
SALES (est): 9.3MM **Privately Held**
SIC: 7011 Hotels & motels

(P-12872)
JS HOSPITALITY GROUP LLC
Also Called: Courtyard Oxnard Ventura
600 E Esplanade Dr, Oxnard (93036-2403)
PHONE.................................805 988-3600
Joseph Fan,
EMP: 100

SALES: 5MM **Privately Held**
SIC: 7011 Hotels

(P-12873)
JWMCC LIMITED PARTNERSHIP
Also Called: Hyatt Hotel
2151 Avenue Of The Stars, Los Angeles
(90067-5004)
PHONE.................................310 277-1234
Fax: 310 785-9240
Ulrich Samietz, *General Mgr*
Louisa Rivera, *Manager*
EMP: 353
SQ FT: 4,600
SALES (est): 5.1MM **Privately Held**
SIC: 7011 5812 Hotels & motels; eating places

(P-12874)
KALPANA LLC
Also Called: San Dego Mission Vly Hilton Ht
901 Camino Del Rio S, San Diego
(92108-3515)
PHONE.................................619 543-9000
Fax: 619 296-9561
Jack Giacomini, *General Mgr*
Mark Ziomek, *General Mgr*
Julie Hernandez, *Accounting Mgr*
Margie Jimenez, *Finance*
Dena Hartsuyker, *Controller*
EMP: 250
SALES (corp-wide): 8.4MM **Privately Held**
WEB: www.doralpalmsprings.com
SIC: 7011 5812 7299 Hotels; eating places; banquet hall facilities
PA: Kalpana, Llc
620 Newport Center Dr # 14
Newport Beach CA 92660
949 610-8200

(P-12875)
KANG FAMILY PARTNERS LLC
Also Called: Santa Ynez Valley Marriott
555 Mcmurray Rd, Buellton (93427-9559)
PHONE.................................805 688-1000
Daphne Kang, *Mng Member*
Tammy Gesler, *CFO*
Camden Wirick, *General Mgr*
Thomas Munoz, *Sales Mgr*
EMP: 110
SALES: 6MM **Privately Held**
WEB: www.santaynezhotels.com
SIC: 7011 Hotel, franchised

(P-12876)
KAVA HOLDINGS INC (PA)
Also Called: Hotel Bel-Air
701 Stone Canyon Rd, Los Angeles
(90077-2909)
PHONE.................................310 472-1211
Fax: 310 476-5890
Hj Suharafadzil, *President*
Helen Smith, *President*
Christopher Cowdary, *CEO*
Franois Delahaye, *COO*
Eugenio Pirri, *Vice Pres*
EMP: 200
SQ FT: 30,000
SALES (est): 17.2MM **Privately Held**
WEB: www.hotelbelair.com
SIC: 7011 Resort hotel

(P-12877)
KEARNY VILLA HOTEL VENTURE LLC
Also Called: Courtyard By Marriott
8651 Spectrum Center Blvd, San Diego
(92123-1489)
PHONE.................................858 573-0700
Brnet Andrus, *President*
Yuly Rivera, *Controller*
Sherly Chester, *Manager*
Audun Poulsen, *Manager*
Patricia Santini, *Manager*
EMP: 70
SALES (est): 4.5MM **Privately Held**
WEB: www.cy-kearnymesa.com
SIC: 7011 7389 Hotels & motels; office facilities & secretarial service rental

(P-12878)
KEN REAL ESTATE LEASE LTD
Also Called: Anaheim Majestic Garden Hotel
900 S Disneyland Dr, Anaheim
(92802-1844)
PHONE.................................714 778-1700
Fax: 714 533-7817
Shigeru Sato, *President*
Richard Aragon, *Executive*
Debbie Hodge, *General Mgr*
Cindy Smith, *General Mgr*
Elizabeth Zant, *Technology*
EMP: 99
SALES (est): 9.6MM **Privately Held**
SIC: 7011 Hotels

(P-12879)
KESARI HOSPITALITY LLC
445 Hotel Cir S, San Diego (92108-3402)
PHONE.................................619 298-1291
Kalpesh Kalthia, *Mng Member*
EMP: 72
SQ FT: 18,774
SALES (est): 228K **Privately Held**
SIC: 7011 Resort hotel, franchised

(P-12880)
KEY INN LTD
Also Called: Key Inn & Suites
1611 El Camino Real, Tustin (92780-5203)
PHONE.................................714 832-3220
Fax: 714 838-3481
Armando Robles, *General Mgr*
Ed Pankey, *Partner*
Peter Pankey, *Partner*
EMP: 50
SALES: 3.5MM **Privately Held**
WEB: www.keyinntustin.com
SIC: 7011 Motels

(P-12881)
KHATRI INC
Also Called: Khatri Properties
1608 Sunrise Ave Ste 6, Modesto
(95350-4678)
PHONE.................................209 576-1481
Anil Khatri, *Manager*
EMP: 50
SQ FT: 10,662
SALES (corp-wide): 4.6MM **Privately Held**
SIC: 7011 Hotels & motels
PA: Khatri, Inc.
20700 Manter Rd
Castro Valley CA 94552
510 886-7909

(P-12882)
KHP II SAN DIEGO HOTEL LLC
Also Called: Palomar San Diego
1047 5th Ave, San Diego (92101-5101)
PHONE.................................619 515-3000
Fax: 619 515-3006
Nikki Leondakis, *Mng Member*
Mark Van Cooney,
EMP: 99
SALES (est): 8.4MM **Privately Held**
SIC: 7011 Hotels

(P-12883)
KHP III GOLETA LLC ✪
Also Called: Goodland
5650 Calle Real, Goleta (93117-2319)
PHONE.................................805 964-6241
Wesley Lau, *Principal*
EMP: 99 **EST:** 2016
SALES (est): 610.2K **Privately Held**
SIC: 7011 5812 Resort hotel; American restaurant

(P-12884)
KIMPTON HOTEL & REST GROUP LLC
Also Called: Serrano Hotel
405 Taylor St, San Francisco (94102-1701)
PHONE.................................415 885-2500
Fax: 415 474-4879
John Turner, *General Mgr*
Brenda Ly, *Info Tech Mgr*
Sarah Mendoza, *Asst Controller*
David Von Dinckler, *Opers Staff*
EMP: 100
SALES (corp-wide): 1.8B **Privately Held**
WEB: www.kuletos.com
SIC: 7011 7299 Hotels & motels; banquet hall facilities

7011 - Hotels, Motels & Tourist Courts County (P-12885)

HQ: Kimpton Hotel & Restaurant Group Llc
222 Kearny St Ste 200
San Francisco CA 94108
415 397-5572

(P-12885)
KIMPTON HOTEL & REST GROUP LLC
Also Called: Tuscan Inn
425 N Point St, San Francisco (94133-1405)
PHONE 415 561-1100
Jan Misch, Manager
EMP: 85
SALES (corp-wide): 1.8B Privately Held
WEB: www.kuletos.com
SIC: 7011 7299 5813 Hotels; banquet hall facilities; drinking places
HQ: Kimpton Hotel & Restaurant Group Llc
222 Kearny St Ste 200
San Francisco CA 94108
415 397-5572

(P-12886)
KINGLEDON INC
Also Called: Ventura Beach Marriott Hotel
2055 Harbor Blvd, Ventura (93001-3707)
PHONE 805 643-6000
Chaohui Liu, CEO
Shannon Hillygus, General Mgr
EMP: 150 EST: 2013
SALES (est): 3.7MM Privately Held
SIC: 7011 Hotels

(P-12887)
KINTETSU ENTERPRISES CO AMER (HQ)
Also Called: Kintetsu Enterprises Co Amer
21241 S Wstn Ave Ste 100, Torrance (90501)
PHONE 310 782-9300
Fax: 415 922-3103
Hisao Hiro, President
EMP: 200 EST: 1961
SALES (est): 13.7MM
SALES (corp-wide): 10.4B Privately Held
WEB: www.miyakola.com
SIC: 7011 6512 Hotel, franchised; nonresidential building operators
PA: Kintetsu Group Holdings Co., Ltd.
6-1-55, Uehonmachi, Tennoji-Ku
Osaka OSK 543-0
667 753-355

(P-12888)
KINTETSU ENTERPRISES CO AMER
328 E 1st St, Los Angeles (90012-3902)
PHONE 213 617-2000
Akimasa Yoneda, Branch Mgr
Yasuyuki Suzuki, General Mgr
EMP: 80
SALES (corp-wide): 10.4B Privately Held
WEB: www.miyakola.com
SIC: 7011 Hotels
HQ: Kintetsu Enterprises Company Of America
21241 S Wstn Ave Ste 100
Torrance CA 90501
310 782-9300

(P-12889)
KITTRIDGE HOTELS & RESORTS LLC
Also Called: Hard Rock Hotel Palm Springs
150 S Indian Canyon Dr, Palm Springs (92262-6604)
PHONE 760 325-9676
Stan Kantowski, General Mgr
EMP: 64
SALES (est): 2.2MM Privately Held
WEB: www.hotelzoso.com
SIC: 7011 Hotels

(P-12890)
KMS FISHERMANS WHARF LP
Also Called: Tuscan Inn
425 N Point St, San Francisco (94133-1405)
PHONE 415 561-1100
Fax: 415 292-4549
Laura Meith, Director
Jan Misch, Partner
Lita Tulloch, Marketing Staff
EMP: 110
SQ FT: 97,724
SALES (est): 3.5MM Privately Held
WEB: www.tuscaninn.com
SIC: 7011 Hotel, franchised

(P-12891)
KNOTTS BERRY FARM LLC
Also Called: Knott's Berry Farm Hotel
7675 Crescent Ave, Buena Park (90620-3947)
PHONE 714 995-1111
Stan Dlander, Manager
Katie Leong, General Mgr
Stephanie M Gomez, Meeting Planner
Alberto Ponce, Engineer
Jose Lopez, Purchasing
EMP: 230
SALES (corp-wide): 1.2B Publicly Held
WEB: www.knotts.com
SIC: 7011 Resort hotel
HQ: Berry Knott's Farm Llc
8039 Beach Blvd
Buena Park CA 90620
714 827-1776

(P-12892)
KUMAR HOTELS INC
Also Called: Holiday Inn
545 N Humboldt Ave, Willows (95988-3502)
PHONE 530 934-8900
Pawan Kumar, President
EMP: 150
SALES (est): 6.4MM Privately Held
SIC: 7011 Hotels & motels

(P-12893)
L & S INVESTMENT CO INC
Also Called: Best Western
14173 Green Tree Blvd, Victorville (92395-4343)
PHONE 760 245-3461
Fax: 760 245-7745
Walter Schroeder, Ch of Bd
Pat Taylor, Admin Sec
EMP: 100
SQ FT: 120,000
SALES (est): 7.2MM Privately Held
SIC: 7011 Hotels & motels

(P-12894)
L-O CORONADO HOTEL INC
1500 Orange Ave, Coronado (92118-2918)
PHONE 619 435-6611
Tod Shallon, President
Vic Duvela, Info Tech Mgr
Crelia Hadley, Finance Mgr
Susan Corey-Tuckwell, HR Admin
Wayne Buchta, Training Spec
EMP: 1350 EST: 1886
SALES (est): 8.1MM Privately Held
WEB: www.shopsatthedel.com
SIC: 7011 5812 5813 5941 Hotels; eating places; cocktail lounge; tennis goods & equipment

(P-12895)
L-O SOMA HOTEL INC
Also Called: Argent Hotel, The
50 3rd St, San Francisco (94103-3106)
PHONE 415 974-6400
Charles S Peck, President
Peter A Del Franco, Exec VP
Ronald A Silva, Exec VP
Dean Thong, Controller
Todd Roetler, Manager
EMP: 420
SALES (est): 9.7MM
SALES (corp-wide): 735.2MM Privately Held
WEB: www.destinationhotels.com
SIC: 7011 5812 Hotels; eating places
HQ: Destination Residences Llc
10333 E Dry Creek Rd
Englewood CO 80112
303 799-3830

(P-12896)
LA HOTEL VENTURE LLC
Also Called: Los Angeles Marriott Downtown
333 S Figueroa St, Los Angeles (90071-1001)
PHONE 213 617-1133
HEI Huang,
Carl Sprayberry, General Mgr
Wendy Beemer, Meeting Planner
Ronnie Lamm,
Ezri Manvar,
EMP: 400
SALES (est): 14.1MM Privately Held
SIC: 7011 Hotels & motels

(P-12897)
LA JOLLA BCH & TENNIS CLB INC (PA)
Also Called: Sea Lodge Hotel
2000 Spindrift Dr, La Jolla (92037-3237)
PHONE 858 454-7126
Fax: 619 454-1064
William J Kellogg, CEO
Pierrette Featherby, Admin Asst
Maria Kitty, Admin Asst
Joanne Snodgrass, Admin Asst
Bill Kellogg, CIO
EMP: 165
SQ FT: 3,500
SALES (est): 41.5MM Privately Held
WEB: www.ljbtc.com
SIC: 7011 8742 7997 Hotels; food & beverage consultant; membership sports & recreation clubs

(P-12898)
LA JOLLA BCH & TENNIS CLB INC
Also Called: Shores Restaurant
8110 Camino Del Oro, La Jolla (92037-3108)
PHONE 858 459-8271
Fax: 858 456-9346
John Cambel, Manager
EMP: 155
SALES (corp-wide): 41.5MM Privately Held
WEB: www.ljbtc.com
SIC: 7011 5812 5813 7299 Resort hotel; restaurant, family: independent; cocktail lounge; banquet hall facilities
PA: La Jolla Beach & Tennis Club, Inc.
2000 Spindrift Dr
La Jolla CA 92037
858 454-7126

(P-12899)
LA POSTA CASINO
Also Called: La Posta Band Mission Indians
777 Crestwood Rd, Boulevard (91905)
PHONE 619 824-4100
Dwendolyn Prada, President
James Hill, Corp Secy
EMP: 140
SQ FT: 20,000
SALES (est): 3.3MM Privately Held
SIC: 7011 Casino hotel

(P-12900)
LAGUNA HILLS HOTEL DEV VENTR
Also Called: Holiday Inn
25205 La Paz Rd, Laguna Hills (92653-5105)
PHONE 949 586-5000
Fax: 949 581-7410
June Chen, Partner
Clement Chen, President
EMP: 100
SQ FT: 102,241
SALES (est): 2.7MM Privately Held
WEB: www.holidayinngreaterlosangeles.com
SIC: 7011 5812 7299 Hotels & motels; eating places; banquet hall facilities

(P-12901)
LAKE ARRWHEAD RSORT OPRTOR INC (PA)
27984 Hwy 189, Lake Arrowhead (92352)
P.O. Box 1699 (92352-1699)
PHONE 909 744-3012
Fax: 909 336-3300
Carmen Rodriguez, CEO
Veronique Williams, Administration
Haither Tanzey, Accountant
Gena Richardson, Director
EMP: 115
SALES (est): 14.6MM Privately Held
WEB: www.laresort.com
SIC: 7011 5813 5812 Resort hotel; drinking places; eating places

(P-12902)
LAKE NATOMA LODGING LP
Also Called: Lake Natoma Inn
702 Gold Lake Dr, Folsom (95630-2559)
PHONE 916 351-1500
Robert Leach, Partner
Rick Fenstermaker, General Ptnr
Pat Kunzs, Chief Mktg Ofcr
Lynn Solberg, General Mgr
EMP: 80
SQ FT: 82,000
SALES (est): 4.5MM Privately Held
WEB: www.lakenatomainn.com
SIC: 7011 Hotel, franchised

(P-12903)
LAMP LITER ASSOCIATES
Also Called: Lamp Liter Inn
3130 W Main St Ste A, Visalia (93291-5765)
PHONE 559 733-4328
Fax: 559 732-1840
Robert Lee, General Mgr
Dennis Stout, Director
EMP: 75
SQ FT: 100,000
SALES (est): 3.2MM Privately Held
WEB: www.lampliter.com
SIC: 7011 5812 5813 Motels; eating places; cocktail lounge

(P-12904)
LANDMARK HOTELS LLC
Also Called: Landmark Princess
312 Broadway St Ste 204, Laguna Beach (92651-4335)
PHONE 949 640-5040
EMP: 150 EST: 2001
SALES: 12.9MM Privately Held
SIC: 7011 Hotels

(P-12905)
LANGHAM HOTELS PACIFIC CORP
Also Called: Langham Hotels International
1401 S Oak Knoll Ave, Pasadena (91106-4508)
PHONE 617 451-1900
Ka Shui Lo, President
Brett Butcher, Vice Pres
Rose Santomauro, Finance
EMP: 80
SALES (est): 9.7MM Privately Held
SIC: 7011 Hotels & motels; resort hotel

(P-12906)
LARKSPUR HSPTALITY DEV MGT LLC
Also Called: Hilton Garden Inn San
670 Gateway Blvd, South San Francisco (94080-7014)
PHONE 650 872-1515
Brian Fox, General Mgr
Jeffrey Durkin, Manager
EMP: 100 Privately Held
SIC: 7011 Hotels & motels
PA: Larkspur Hospitality Development And Management Company, Llc
125 E Sir F Drake Blvd
Larkspur CA 94939

(P-12907)
LAV HOTEL CORP
Also Called: Whaling Bar & Grill
1132 Prospect St, La Jolla (92037-4533)
PHONE 858 454-0771
Fax: 858 456-3921
Harry Collins, President
W M Allen Sr, Bd of Directors
W M Allen Jr, Vice Pres
EMP: 250
SQ FT: 1,000
SALES (est): 13.9MM Privately Held
WEB: www.lavalencia.com
SIC: 7011 Hotels & motels

(P-12908)
LAX HOSPITALITY LP
Also Called: Radisson Inn
6225 W Century Blvd, Los Angeles (90045-5311)
PHONE 310 670-9000
EMP: 200
SQ FT: 26,000

PRODUCTS & SERVICES SECTION
7011 - Hotels, Motels & Tourist Courts County (P-12930)

SALES (est): 11MM **Privately Held**
SIC: 7011

(P-12909)
LAX HOTEL VENTURES LLC
Also Called: Four Points Sheraton Lax
9750 Airport Blvd, Los Angeles (90045-5404)
PHONE..................................310 645-4600
EMP: 50
SALES: 950K **Privately Held**
SIC: 7011

(P-12910)
LAX PLAZA HOTEL
6333 Bristol Pkwy, Culver City (90230-6904)
PHONE..................................310 902-2202
Lindsay Butcher, *General Mgr*
Elizabeth Lopez, *Accountant*
EMP: 120
SALES (est): 1MM **Privately Held**
WEB: www.laxplazahotel.com
SIC: 7011 5812 5813 Hotels & motels; eating places; bars & lounges

(P-12911)
LC TRS INC
Also Called: La Costa Resort & Spa
2100 Costa Del Mar Rd, Carlsbad (92009-6823)
PHONE..................................760 438-9111
Fax: 760 929-6305
Mike Shannon, *President*
Scott Dalecio, *Vice Pres*
Chevis Hosea, *Vice Pres*
Hans Wiegand, *Executive*
Dave Nelson, *General Mgr*
EMP: 872
SQ FT: 5,000
SALES (est): 64.1MM **Privately Held**
SIC: 7011 5812 Resort hotel; eating places

(P-12912)
LE MONTROSE HOTEL
Also Called: Le Montrose Suite Hotel
900 Hammond St Apt 434, West Hollywood (90069-4443)
PHONE..................................310 855-1115
John Douponce, *Managing Prtnr*
Joe Monseriete, *CFO*
Wilford Weregdoa, *Controller*
EMP: 69
SQ FT: 1,000
SALES (est): 3.9MM **Privately Held**
WEB: www.lemontrose.com
SIC: 7011 Hotels

(P-12913)
LEE-VICTORVILLE HOTEL CORP
Also Called: Green Tree Inn
14173 Green Tree Blvd, Victorville (92395-4343)
PHONE..................................760 245-3461
Walter M Schroeder, *President*
Dick Bestone, *General Mgr*
Pat Taylor, *Admin Sec*
EMP: 105
SQ FT: 380,000
SALES (est): 5.4MM **Privately Held**
SIC: 7011 Bed & breakfast inn

(P-12914)
LEISURE SPORTS INC
Also Called: Renaissance Clubsport
2805 Jones Rd, Walnut Creek (94597-7848)
PHONE..................................925 938-3058
Fax: 925 938-8707
Brian Amador, *General Mgr*
EMP: 330
SALES (corp-wide): 213MM **Privately Held**
WEB: www.leisuresportsinc.com
SIC: 7011 Hotels & motels
PA: Leisure Sports, Inc.
4670 Willow Rd Ste 100
Pleasanton CA 94588
925 600-1966

(P-12915)
LENEXA HOTEL LP
Also Called: Doubletree
10740 Wilshire Blvd, Los Angeles (90024-4493)
PHONE..................................310 475-8711
Fax: 310 475-5220
Joe Tichizian, *Opers-Prdtn-Mfg*
Tim Weaver, *General Mgr*
EMP: 105
SALES (corp-wide): 22.1MM **Privately Held**
WEB: www.radissonlenexa.com
SIC: 7011 5812 Hotels & motels; eating places
PA: Lenexa Hotel, L.P.
730 New Hampshire St # 206
Lawrence KS 66044
785 841-3100

(P-12916)
LH INDIAN WELLS OPERATING LLC
4500 Indian Wells Ln, Indian Wells (92210)
PHONE..................................760 341-2200
Bob Low, *Principal*
EMP: 220
SALES (est): 4.2MM
SALES (corp-wide): 4.6MM **Privately Held**
SIC: 7011 7991 Resort hotel; spas
PA: Lh Indian Wells Holding, Llc
11777 San Vicente Blvd
Los Angeles CA 90049
760 341-2200

(P-12917)
LH UNIVERSAL OPERATING LLC
Also Called: Sheraton Universal Hotel
333 Universal Hollywood Dr, Universal City (91608-1001)
PHONE..................................818 980-1212
Fax: 818 985-4980
Robert Lowe, *Executive*
Reza Motamednia, *Executive*
Sean Waldron, *Security Dir*
Ryan Laskey, *General Mgr*
Randy Player, *General Mgr*
EMP: 280
SALES (est): 30MM **Privately Held**
SIC: 7011 Hotels

(P-12918)
LHO SANTA CRUZ ONE LESSE INC
Also Called: Chaminade of Santa Cruz
1 Chaminade Ln, Santa Cruz (95065-1524)
PHONE..................................831 475-5600
Michael Barnello, *President*
Alfred Young, *COO*
Hans Weger, *CFO*
Robert Hagan, *Vice Pres*
Michael P Butler, *Controller*
EMP: 193
SQ FT: 50,000
SALES (est): 13.4MM
SALES (corp-wide): 1.2B **Privately Held**
SIC: 7011 Resort hotel
PA: Lasalle Hotel Properties
7550 Wisconsin Ave # 100
Bethesda MD 20814
301 941-1500

(P-12919)
LHOBERGE LESSEE INC
Also Called: L'Auberge Del Mar
1540 Camino Del Mar, Del Mar (92014-2411)
PHONE..................................858 259-1515
Fax: 858 755-4940
Jamie Sabatier, *CEO*
Charles Peck, *President*
Dennis Fischer, *Vice Pres*
Randy Treadway, *IT/INT Sup*
C'Annette N Hussong, *Asst Controller*
EMP: 250
SQ FT: 84,312
SALES (est): 14.2MM **Privately Held**
WEB: www.laubergedelmar.com
SIC: 7011 Hotels

(P-12920)
LIBERTY STATION HHG HOTEL LP
Also Called: Courtyard By Marr San Diego Ai
2592 Laning Rd, San Diego (92106-6418)
PHONE..................................619 221-1900
Fax: 619 221-0900
Kevin Keefer, *Partner*
EMP: 60
SALES (est): 3MM **Privately Held**
SIC: 7011 Hotels & motels

(P-12921)
LIBERTY STATION HHG HOTEL LP
Also Called: Homewood Suites Libery Station
2576 Laning Rd, San Diego (92106-6418)
PHONE..................................619 222-0500
Fax: 619 222-0600
Rick Brown, *General Mgr*
Kevin Keefer, *Partner*
Del Barerra, *Office Mgr*
Alicia Trulles, *Manager*
EMP: 50
SALES (est): 2.8MM **Privately Held**
SIC: 7011 Hotels & motels

(P-12922)
LINCOLN PLAZA HOTEL INC
123 S Lincoln Ave, Monterey Park (91755-2914)
PHONE..................................626 571-8818
Fax: 626 571-4005
Thira Ratanapreukskul, *President*
William H Roach, *Corp Secy*
EMP: 60
SQ FT: 95,600
SALES (est): 2.6MM **Privately Held**
WEB: www.lincolnplazahotel.net
SIC: 7011 Hotels

(P-12923)
LIONSGATE HT & CONFERENCE CTR
3410 Westover St, McClellan (95652-1005)
PHONE..................................916 643-6222
Fax: 916 927-5168
Lary Kelly, *President*
Michael Hutchings, *Executive*
Kathy Irwin, *Project Mgr*
Terry Stewart, *Opers Staff*
Beth Bettencourt, *Manager*
EMP: 90
SALES (est): 5MM **Privately Held**
SIC: 7011 Hotels & motels

(P-12924)
LITTLE RIVER INN INC
Also Called: Little River Inn and Golf Crse
7901 N Highway 1, Little River (95456-9500)
P.O. Box B (95456-0430)
PHONE..................................707 937-5942
Fax: 707 937-3944
Charles D Hervilla, *CEO*
Susan Mc Kinney, *Vice Pres*
Marc Dym, *Executive*
Melissa Pyorre, *Executive*
Cally Dym, *General Mgr*
EMP: 100
SQ FT: 3,000
SALES (est): 10MM **Privately Held**
WEB: www.littleriverinn.com
SIC: 7011 5812 Inns; American restaurant

(P-12925)
LODGE AT TORREY PINES PARTNERS
998 W Mission Bay Dr, San Diego (92109-7803)
PHONE..................................858 550-3908
Anne L Evans, *Partner*
David Cherashore, *Owner*
Philip Spada, *Principal*
CHI Wang, *Info Tech Mgr*
Jamie Cheng, *Adv Mgr*
EMP: 275
SALES (est): 3.9MM **Privately Held**
WEB: www.lodgeattorreypines.com
SIC: 7011 5812 Hotels; coffee shop

(P-12926)
LOEWS HOLLYWOOD HOTEL LLC
1755 N Highland Ave, Hollywood (90028-4403)
PHONE..................................323 450-2235
Jonathan Tisch, *Ch of Bd*
David Orellana, *Executive*
Eileen Daley, *Sales Staff*
Erin McGown, *Assistant*
EMP: 375 EST: 2012
SALES (est): 15.8MM
SALES (corp-wide): 13.4B **Publicly Held**
SIC: 7011 Hotels
PA: Loews Corporation
667 Madison Ave Fl 7
New York NY 10065
212 521-2000

(P-12927)
LOK PETALUMA MARINA HT CO LLC
Also Called: Sheraton Sonoma County Hotel
745 Baywood Dr, Petaluma (94954-5388)
PHONE..................................707 283-2888
Tom Birdsall, *Manager*
Lok Petaluma Marina Developmen, *Mng Member*
EMP: 95
SQ FT: 134,732
SALES (est): 5.4MM **Privately Held**
SIC: 7011 Hotels

(P-12928)
LONE CYPRESS COMPANY LLC
US Open At Pebble Beach
17 Mile Dr, Pebble Beach (93953)
P.O. Box 567 (93953-0567)
PHONE..................................831 624-3811
Fax: 831 647-7496
Robert Lapso, *Branch Mgr*
Paul Spengler, *Exec VP*
Diane Stracuzzi, *Marketing Staff*
EMP: 1500
SALES (corp-wide): 119.8MM **Privately Held**
WEB: www.pebblebeach.com
SIC: 7011 7992 5813 5812 Resort hotel; public golf courses; drinking places; eating places
PA: Pebble Beach Resort Co Dba Lone Cypress Shop
2700 17 Mile Dr
Pebble Beach CA 93953
831 647-7500

(P-12929)
LONG BEACH GOLDEN SAILS INC
Also Called: Best Western Golden Sails Ht
6285 E Pacific Coast Hwy, Long Beach (90803-4803)
PHONE..................................562 795-5241
Fax: 562 594-0623
Yuk N Siu, *President*
Matthew Daniel, *CFO*
Lilian Lai, *General Mgr*
Susan Tayabe, *Manager*
EMP: 90
SQ FT: 150,000
SALES (est): 4.2MM **Privately Held**
WEB: www.goldensailshotel.com
SIC: 7011 5812 5813 Hotels & motels; restaurant, family: independent; bar (drinking places)

(P-12930)
LONG POINT DEVELOPMENT LLC
Also Called: Terranea Resort
100 Terranea Way, Rancho Palos Verdes (90275-1013)
PHONE..................................310 265-2800
Terri Haack, *Mng Member*
Jennifer Yang, *Executive Asst*
Michael Moon, *Asst Mgr*
EMP: 1000 EST: 2004
SALES (est): 59.7MM **Privately Held**
SIC: 7011 Resort hotel

7011 - Hotels, Motels & Tourist Courts County (P-12931)

(P-12931)
LQ MANAGEMENT LLC
Also Called: La Quinta Inn
5249 W Century Blvd, Los Angeles (90045-5917)
PHONE.................310 645-2200
Ryan Thayer, *Branch Mgr*
Marilyn Gams, *Purch Agent*
Shelby Turner, *Sales Dir*
Juan A Navarro-Sig, *Manager*
Juan Navarro-Sigala, *Manager*
EMP: 63
SALES (corp-wide): 1B **Publicly Held**
WEB: www.neubayern.net
SIC: **7011** Hotels & motels
HQ: Lq Management L.L.C.
909 Hidden Rdg Ste 600
Irving TX 75038
214 492-6600

(P-12932)
LQR PROPERTY LLC
Also Called: La Quinta Resort & Club
49499 Eisenhower Dr, La Quinta (92253-2722)
PHONE.................760 564-4111
EMP: 84
SALES (est): 7.7MM **Privately Held**
SIC: **7011** 7999 Hotels & motels; golf driving range

(P-12933)
LUXURY LINK LLC
Also Called: Luxury Link Travel Group
5510 Lincoln Blvd Ste 275, Playa Vista (90094-2097)
P.O. Box 3008, La Mesa (91944-3008)
PHONE.................310 215-8060
Fax: 310 215-8279
James Kaplan,
Bob Bennett, *COO*
Sandra Lattlo, *Senior VP*
Takka McCord, *Office Mgr*
Glenda Okechukw, *Finance Mgr*
EMP: 50
SALES (est): 5.8MM **Privately Held**
WEB: www.luxurylink.com
SIC: **7011** 4724 Hotels; travel agencies

(P-12934)
M&C HOTEL INTERESTS INC
Also Called: Sheraton
530 Pico Blvd, Santa Monica (90405-1223)
PHONE.................310 399-9344
Lisa Nagahori, *Branch Mgr*
Enrique Licona, *Human Res Dir*
Kara Mont, *Manager*
EMP: 55
SALES (corp-wide): 1.2B **Privately Held**
WEB: www.richfield.com
SIC: **7011** Hotels & motels
HQ: M&C Hotel Interests, Inc.
6560 Greenwood Plaza Blvd # 300
Greenwood Village CO 80111
303 779-2000

(P-12935)
MADRONA MNR WINE CNTRY INN
1001 Westside Rd, Healdsburg (95448-9434)
PHONE.................707 433-4231
Fax: 707 258-4003
William R Konrad, *President*
Jesse Mallgren, *Executive*
Kevin West, *General Mgr*
Sarah Azevedo, *Office Mgr*
Gertrude V Konrad,
EMP: 55 EST: 1983
SQ FT: 1,800
SALES (est): 3.7MM **Privately Held**
WEB: www.madronamanor.com
SIC: **7011** 5812 Inns; Italian restaurant; Chinese restaurant; French restaurant; American restaurant

(P-12936)
MAJESTIC INDUSTRY HILLS LLC
Also Called: Pacific Plms Conference Resort
1 Industry Hills Pkwy, City of Industry (91744-5160)
PHONE.................626 810-4455
Scott Huntsman, *Branch Mgr*
John Semcken, *Principal*
John Ordonez, *Purch Dir*
German Jennifer, *Purch Agent*
EMP: 360
SALES (corp-wide): 32MM **Privately Held**
SIC: **7011** 7999 7389 7299 Hotels; tennis courts, outdoor/indoor: non-membership; convention & show services; banquet hall facilities
PA: Majestic Industry Hills, Llc
1 Industry Hills Pkwy
City Of Industry CA 91744
562 692-9581

(P-12937)
MAKAR ANAHEIM LLC
Also Called: Anaheim Hilton & Towers
777 W Convention Way, Anaheim (92802-3425)
PHONE.................714 740-4431
Fax: 714 740-4460
Paul Makarechian,
John Chmara, *Finance Dir*
Lisa McQuillin, *Opers Staff*
Harold Rapoza, *Manager*
EMP: 1200
SQ FT: 1,000,000
SALES (est): 25.9MM **Privately Held**
SIC: **7011** Hotels

(P-12938)
MAMMOTH MOUNTAIN SKI AREA LLC (HQ)
10001 Minaret Rd, Mammoth Lakes (93546)
P.O. Box 24 (93546-0024)
PHONE.................760 934-2571
Fax: 760 934-0604
Rusty Gregory,
David Cummings, *Partner*
Mark Clausen, *CFO*
Erik Forsell, *Officer*
Bruce Burton, *Vice Pres*
EMP: 347
SQ FT: 140,000
SALES: 137.9MM
SALES (corp-wide): 477.6MM **Privately Held**
WEB: www.mammothmotocross.com
SIC: **7011** 5812 Ski lodge; resort hotel; eating places
PA: Starwood Capital Group, L.L.C.
591 W Putnam Ave
Greenwich CT 06830
203 422-7700

(P-12939)
MANAS HOSPITALITY LLC
Also Called: Holiday Inn Express Sacramento
445 Hotel Cir S, San Diego (92108-3402)
PHONE.................619 298-1291
Rajesh Chollera,
Hitesh Kalthia,
EMP: 50
SQ FT: 63,424
SALES (est): 674.6K **Privately Held**
SIC: **7011** Hotels & motels

(P-12940)
MANCHESTER GRAND RESORTS LP
Also Called: Hyatt Hotel
1 Market Pl Fl 33, San Diego (92101-7714)
PHONE.................619 232-1234
Fax: 619 696-7100
Mark S Hoplamazian, *CEO*
Richard V Gibbons, *Partner*
Douglas F Manchester, *Partner*
Gebhard F Rainer, *CFO*
H Charles Floyd, *Exec VP*
EMP: 900
SALES (est): 24MM
SALES (corp-wide): 4.3B **Publicly Held**
WEB: www.hyatt.com
SIC: **7011** Hotels & motels
HQ: Hyatt Corporation
150 N Riverside Plz
Chicago IL 60606
312 750-1234

(P-12941)
MARIANIS INN & RESTAURANT
2500 El Camino Real, Santa Clara (95051-3098)
PHONE.................408 243-0312
Louis Mariani Sr, *President*
Dennis Mariani, *Principal*
Susie Castillo, *Controller*
EMP: 220
SALES: 1.5MM **Privately Held**
SIC: **7011** 5812 Motels; eating places

(P-12942)
MARINE CORPS UNITED STATES
Also Called: Camp Pendleton Billeting Fund
A St Bldg 1341, Camp Pendleton (92055)
PHONE.................760 430-4709
Monique Ramirez, *Director*
Jeanette Naputi, *Accounting Mgr*
EMP: 50 **Publicly Held**
WEB: www.usmc.mil
SIC: **7011** Hotels & motels
HQ: United States Marine Corps
Pentagon Rm 4b544
Washington DC 20380
816 394-7628

(P-12943)
MARITIME HOTEL ASSOCIATES LP
Also Called: Argonaut Hotel
495 Jefferson St, San Francisco (94109-1314)
PHONE.................415 563-0800
Fax: 415 563-2800
Micheal Ditatie, *CEO*
EMP: 175
SALES (est): 7.5MM **Privately Held**
SIC: **7011** Hotels

(P-12944)
MARK HOPKINS IHC
999 California St, San Francisco (94108-2250)
PHONE.................415 616-6991
Nelum Gunewardane, *Partner*
Paul Mitchell, *Finance*
Robert Stevens, *Accountant*
Michelle Gatschet, *Manager*
EMP: 256
SALES (est): 3.8MM **Privately Held**
SIC: **7011** Hotels & motels

(P-12945)
MARRIOT COURTYARD
Also Called: Courtyard By Marriott
580 Beach St, San Francisco (94133-1128)
PHONE.................415 775-1103
James Edmondson, *Owner*
Jon Peterson, *Vice Pres*
Elizabeth Coleman, *General Mgr*
Julia Burton, *Manager*
EMP: 50 EST: 1995
SALES (est): 1.8MM **Privately Held**
SIC: **7011** Hotels & motels

(P-12946)
MARRIOTT
3140 El Camino Real, Carlsbad (92008-2108)
PHONE.................760 720-9898
Fax: 760 720-0175
Carles Bloom, *Principal*
Susan Compton, *Administration*
Bobi Thomas, *Marketing Staff*
David Hernandez, *Facilities Dir*
EMP: 80
SALES (est): 1.5MM **Privately Held**
SIC: **7011** Hotels & motels

(P-12947)
MARRIOTT
10 Morgan, Irvine (92618-2003)
PHONE.................949 380-3000
Fax: 949 588-7743
Camillo Bruce, *Manager*
EMP: 80
SALES (est): 2.4MM **Privately Held**
SIC: **7011** Hotels & motels

(P-12948)
MARRIOTT GRAND RESIDENCE
1001 Heavenly Village Way, South Lake Tahoe (96150-6983)
PHONE.................530 542-8400
Fax: 530 542-8410
Steve Weitz, *President*
Marriot International, *Owner*
EMP: 320
SALES (est): 7.1MM **Privately Held**
SIC: **7011** Hotels & motels

(P-12949)
MARRIOTT HOTELS & RESORTS
1001 Broadway, Oakland (94607-4019)
PHONE.................510 451-4000
Steven Williams, *Director*
Elie Khoury, *Senior VP*
EMP: 80
SALES (est): 1.4MM **Privately Held**
SIC: **7011** Hotels & motels

(P-12950)
MARRIOTT INTERNATIONAL INC
5835 Owens Ave, Carlsbad (92008-6562)
PHONE.................760 431-9399
EMP: 173
SALES (corp-wide): 14.4B **Publicly Held**
SIC: **7011** Hotels & motels
PA: Marriott International, Inc.
10400 Fernwood Rd
Bethesda MD 20817
301 380-3000

(P-12951)
MARRIOTT INTERNATIONAL INC
4381 Myra Ave, Cypress (90630-4131)
PHONE.................714 209-6586
Daryn Benton, *Meeting Planner*
EMP: 175
SALES (corp-wide): 14.4B **Publicly Held**
SIC: **7011** Hotels & motels
PA: Marriott International, Inc.
10400 Fernwood Rd
Bethesda MD 20817
301 380-3000

(P-12952)
MARRIOTT INTERNATIONAL INC
9620 Airport Blvd, Los Angeles (90045-5402)
PHONE.................310 337-2800
Fax: 310 216-6681
Gregory Lehman, *Manager*
Robert Thomas, *General Mgr*
Michael Nott, *Info Tech Mgr*
Jennry Ulch, *Finance*
Stephanie Woo, *Accountant*
EMP: 300
SALES (corp-wide): 14.4B **Publicly Held**
SIC: **7011** 5813 5812 7389 Hotels & motels; drinking places; eating places; office facilities & secretarial service rental
PA: Marriott International, Inc.
10400 Fernwood Rd
Bethesda MD 20817
301 380-3000

(P-12953)
MARRIOTT INTERNATIONAL INC
11966 El Camino Real, San Diego (92130-2592)
PHONE.................858 523-1700
Fax: 858 523-1355
Michael Woldowski, *Branch Mgr*
Lauren Walsh, *Financial Exec*
EMP: 167
SALES (corp-wide): 14.4B **Publicly Held**
SIC: **7011** 5812 Hotels & motels; American restaurant
PA: Marriott International, Inc.
10400 Fernwood Rd
Bethesda MD 20817
301 380-3000

(P-12954)
MARRIOTT INTERNATIONAL INC
5855 W Century Blvd, Los Angeles (90045-5614)
PHONE.................310 641-5700
Fax: 310 337-5358
Jim Burns, *General Mgr*
Alan Watson, *Senior VP*
Steven Hall, *General Mgr*
Tim Cho, *Chief Engr*
Tom Cantora, *Marketing Staff*
EMP: 900
SALES (corp-wide): 14.4B **Publicly Held**
SIC: **7011** 7389 6513 Hotels & motels; office facilities & secretarial service rental; residential hotel operation

▲ = Import ▼=Export
◆ =Import/Export

PRODUCTS & SERVICES SECTION

7011 - Hotels, Motels & Tourist Courts County (P-12975)

PA: Marriott International, Inc.
10400 Fernwood Rd
Bethesda MD 20817
301 380-3000

(P-12955)
MARRIOTT INTERNATIONAL INC
299 2nd St, San Francisco (94105-3123)
PHONE..................................415 947-0700
Fax: 415 947-0800
Lance Rohf, *Manager*
Rich Gagliardi, *General Mgr*
Robert Knigge, *Sales Dir*
EMP: 100
SALES (corp-wide): 14.4B Publicly Held
SIC: 7011 6531 5812 5813 Hotels & motels; real estate managers; eating places; drinking places
PA: Marriott International, Inc.
10400 Fernwood Rd
Bethesda MD 20817
301 380-3000

(P-12956)
MARRIOTT INTERNATIONAL INC
Also Called: Springhill Suites
900 Bayfront Ct, San Diego (92101-3007)
PHONE..................................619 831-0225
Mike Murphy, *General Mgr*
Evangelina Ramirez, *Accountant*
Dawn Myers, *Human Res Mgr*
Zenon Leonor, *Director*
EMP: 100
SALES (corp-wide): 14.4B Publicly Held
SIC: 7011 Hotels & motels
PA: Marriott International, Inc.
10400 Fernwood Rd
Bethesda MD 20817
301 380-3000

(P-12957)
MARRIOTT INTERNATIONAL INC
18000 Von Karman Ave, Irvine (92612-1004)
PHONE..................................949 724-3606
Fax: 949 261-7059
Satinder Palpa, *Branch Mgr*
Rahul Vir, *General Mgr*
Oscar Gamero, *Purchasing*
Pat Chung, *Mfg Staff*
Mike Cooke, *Director*
EMP: 500
SALES (corp-wide): 14.4B Publicly Held
SIC: 7011 7389 Hotels & motels; office facilities & secretarial service rental
PA: Marriott International, Inc.
10400 Fernwood Rd
Bethesda MD 20817
301 380-3000

(P-12958)
MARRIOTT INTERNATIONAL INC
46100 Landing Pkwy, Fremont (94538-6437)
PHONE..................................510 413-3700
Fax: 510 413-3710
Orlando Carrasquillo, *Manager*
Tony Paine, *CTO*
Craig Resnick, *Research*
Eman Nassif, *Director*
EMP: 200
SALES (corp-wide): 14.4B Publicly Held
SIC: 7011 7389 Hotels & motels; office facilities & secretarial service rental
PA: Marriott International, Inc.
10400 Fernwood Rd
Bethesda MD 20817
301 380-3000

(P-12959)
MARRIOTT INTERNATIONAL INC
4240 La Jolla Village Dr, La Jolla (92037-1407)
PHONE..................................858 587-1414
Fax: 858 546-8518
Paul Corsinita, *Manager*
Dan Kaplan, *General Mgr*
Tom Broene, *Engineer*
John Carl, *Chief Engr*
Eddie Huerta, *Finance*
EMP: 337
SALES (corp-wide): 14.4B Publicly Held
SIC: 7011 Hotels & motels
PA: Marriott International, Inc.
10400 Fernwood Rd
Bethesda MD 20817
301 380-3000

(P-12960)
MARRIOTT INTERNATIONAL INC
Also Called: Residence Inn By Marriott
5852 Stadium St, San Diego (92122-3305)
PHONE..................................858 587-1770
Fax: 858 552-0387
Joe Kuhn, *Manager*
Larraine Daniel, *Executive*
Kimberley Boyd, *Director*
Traci Krauser, *Manager*
George Flores, *Asst Mgr*
EMP: 89
SALES (corp-wide): 14.4B Publicly Held
PA: Marriott International, Inc.
10400 Fernwood Rd
Bethesda MD 20817
301 380-3000

(P-12961)
MARRIOTT INTERNATIONAL INC
Also Called: Residence Inn By Marriott
38305 Cook St, Palm Desert (92211-1794)
PHONE..................................760 776-0050
Jim Zeltmer, *Manager*
EMP: 167
SALES (corp-wide): 14.4B Publicly Held
SIC: 7011 Hotels & motels
PA: Marriott International, Inc.
10400 Fernwood Rd
Bethesda MD 20817
301 380-3000

(P-12962)
MARRIOTT INTERNATIONAL INC
Also Called: Residence Inn By Marriott
2135 E El Segundo Blvd, El Segundo (90245-4503)
PHONE..................................310 333-0888
Fax: 310 333-0789
Ray Cruickshanks, *Manager*
EMP: 167
SALES (corp-wide): 14.4B Publicly Held
SIC: 7011 Hotels & motels
PA: Marriott International, Inc.
10400 Fernwood Rd
Bethesda MD 20817
301 380-3000

(P-12963)
MARRIOTT INTERNATIONAL INC
Also Called: Residence Inn By Marriott
5400 Kearny Mesa Rd, San Diego (92111-1303)
PHONE..................................858 278-2100
Doug Former, *Branch Mgr*
Shirley Walker, *President*
Al Meave, *Chief Engr*
Jonathan Correll, *Sales Staff*
EMP: 167
SALES (corp-wide): 14.4B Publicly Held
SIC: 7011 Hotels & motels
PA: Marriott International, Inc.
10400 Fernwood Rd
Bethesda MD 20817
301 380-3000

(P-12964)
MARRIOTT INTERNATIONAL INC
4700 Airport Plaza Dr, Long Beach (90815-1252)
PHONE..................................562 425-5210
Fax: 562 425-2744
Miran Ahmed, *Branch Mgr*
EMP: 210
SALES (corp-wide): 14.4B Publicly Held
SIC: 7011 Hotels & motels
PA: Marriott International, Inc.
10400 Fernwood Rd
Bethesda MD 20817
301 380-3000

(P-12965)
MARRIOTT INTERNATIONAL INC
Also Called: Residence Inn By Marriott
2025 Convention Ctr Way, Ontario (91764-4450)
PHONE..................................909 937-6788
Frank Palacios, *General Mgr*
EMP: 167
SALES (corp-wide): 14.4B Publicly Held
SIC: 7011 Hotels & motels
PA: Marriott International, Inc.
10400 Fernwood Rd
Bethesda MD 20817
301 380-3000

(P-12966)
MARRIOTT INTERNATIONAL INC
21850 Oxnard St, Woodland Hills (91367-3631)
PHONE..................................818 887-4800
Fax: 818 347-0907
Clay Andrews, *Manager*
Aleea A Leblanc, *Executive*
Richard Low, *Planning*
Lee Lehr, *Purch Mgr*
Beth Derange, *Director*
EMP: 167
SALES (corp-wide): 14.4B Publicly Held
SIC: 7011 Hotels & motels
PA: Marriott International, Inc.
10400 Fernwood Rd
Bethesda MD 20817
301 380-3000

(P-12967)
MARRIOTT INTERNATIONAL INC
Also Called: Residence Inn By Marriott
1015 Montecito Dr, Corona (92879-1760)
PHONE..................................951 371-0107
Fax: 951 371-0159
Fred Kokash, *Branch Mgr*
EMP: 167
SALES (corp-wide): 14.4B Publicly Held
SIC: 7011 Hotels & motels
PA: Marriott International, Inc.
10400 Fernwood Rd
Bethesda MD 20817
301 380-3000

(P-12968)
MARRIOTT INTERNATIONAL INC
Also Called: Courtyard By Marriott
2000 E Mariposa Ave, El Segundo (90245-5027)
PHONE..................................310 322-0700
Steve Vandesteeg, *Manager*
EMP: 167
SALES (corp-wide): 14.4B Publicly Held
SIC: 7011 Hotels & motels
PA: Marriott International, Inc.
10400 Fernwood Rd
Bethesda MD 20817
301 380-3000

(P-12969)
MARRIOTT INTERNATIONAL INC
14400 Aviation Blvd, Hawthorne (90250-6654)
PHONE..................................310 725-9696
David Laatz, *Branch Mgr*
Marc Walz, *Regional Mgr*
EMP: 167
SALES (corp-wide): 14.4B Publicly Held
SIC: 7011 Hotels & motels
PA: Marriott International, Inc.
10400 Fernwood Rd
Bethesda MD 20817
301 380-3000

(P-12970)
MARRIOTT INTERNATIONAL INC
Also Called: Courtyard By Marriott
10605 N Wolfe Rd, Cupertino (95014-0613)
PHONE..................................408 252-9100
Fax: 408 252-0632
Mike Gale, *Branch Mgr*
EMP: 167
SALES (corp-wide): 14.4B Publicly Held
SIC: 7011 Hotels & motels
PA: Marriott International, Inc.
10400 Fernwood Rd
Bethesda MD 20817
301 380-3000

(P-12971)
MARRIOTT INTERNATIONAL INC
905 California St, San Francisco (94108-2289)
PHONE..................................415 989-3500
Bill Love, *Branch Mgr*
Michael Baier, *General Mgr*
Scott McCoy, *General Mgr*
Don Brill, *Planning*
Teresa Crooks, *Human Res Dir*
EMP: 167
SALES (corp-wide): 14.4B Publicly Held
SIC: 7011 Hotels & motels
PA: Marriott International, Inc.
10400 Fernwood Rd
Bethesda MD 20817
301 380-3000

(P-12972)
MARRIOTT INTERNATIONAL INC
39802 Cedar Blvd, Newark (94560-5340)
PHONE..................................510 657-4600
Scott Crunk, *Manager*
Pablo Sanchez, *General Mgr*
EMP: 167
SALES (corp-wide): 14.4B Publicly Held
SIC: 7011 Hotels & motels
PA: Marriott International, Inc.
10400 Fernwood Rd
Bethesda MD 20817
301 380-3000

(P-12973)
MARRIOTT INTERNATIONAL INC
4111 E Willow St, Long Beach (90815-1740)
PHONE..................................562 595-0909
Fax: 562 988-0587
Lucas Fiamengo, *Manager*
Rob Johnston, *General Mgr*
Julie Buettner, *Office Mgr*
Eric Torrez, *Info Tech Mgr*
EMP: 167
SALES (corp-wide): 14.4B Publicly Held
SIC: 7011 Hotels & motels
PA: Marriott International, Inc.
10400 Fernwood Rd
Bethesda MD 20817
301 380-3000

(P-12974)
MARRIOTT INTERNATIONAL INC
1325 Broadway, Sonoma (95476-7505)
PHONE..................................707 935-6600
Fax: 707 935-6829
Dave Dolquist, *General Mgr*
Cindy Gagle, *Chief Mktg Ofcr*
Mike Eusanio, *Finance*
EMP: 200
SQ FT: 1,500
SALES (corp-wide): 14.4B Publicly Held
SIC: 7011 Hotels & motels
PA: Marriott International, Inc.
10400 Fernwood Rd
Bethesda MD 20817
301 380-3000

(P-12975)
MARRIOTT INTERNATIONAL INC
3130 S Harbor Blvd # 550, Santa Ana (92704-6862)
PHONE..................................714 545-5261
Fax: 714 641-8372
Wynne Prima, *Branch Mgr*
Theona Simbrat, *Bd of Directors*
Chad Herendeen, *Technology*
Barbara Finch, *Human Resources*
Amanda Wood-Berkholtz, *Human Resources*
EMP: 167
SALES (corp-wide): 14.4B Publicly Held
SIC: 7011 Hotels & motels

7011 - Hotels, Motels & Tourist Courts County (P-12976)

PRODUCTS & SERVICES SECTION

PA: Marriott International, Inc.
10400 Fernwood Rd
Bethesda MD 20817
301 380-3000

(P-12976)
MARRIOTT INTERNATIONAL INC
Also Called: Residence Inn By Marriott
700 Ellinwood Way, Pleasant Hill (94523-4700)
PHONE.....................925 689-1010
Trish Snowden, *Principal*
Juan C Medina, *General Mgr*
Stephanie Martirani, *Manager*
EMP: 167
SALES (corp-wide): 14.4B **Publicly Held**
SIC: 7011 Hotels & motels
PA: Marriott International, Inc.
10400 Fernwood Rd
Bethesda MD 20817
301 380-3000

(P-12977)
MARRIOTT INTERNATIONAL INC (PA)
500 Post St, San Francisco (94102-1229)
PHONE.....................415 929-2030
Lisa Definney, *General Mgr*
Jennifer Randles, *Officer*
Akihito Ikeda, *Principal*
Donna Collings, *General Mgr*
Ryan Callahan, *Sales Mgr*
EMP: 98
SALES (est): 9.6MM **Privately Held**
SIC: 7011 Hotels & motels

(P-12978)
MARRIOTT INTERNATIONAL INC
900 W Olympic Blvd, Los Angeles (90015-1338)
PHONE.....................213 284-3862
EMP: 167
SALES (corp-wide): 14.4B **Publicly Held**
SIC: 7011 Hotels & motels
PA: Marriott International, Inc.
10400 Fernwood Rd
Bethesda MD 20817
301 380-3000

(P-12979)
MARRIOTT INTERNATIONAL INC
1800 Old Bayshore Hwy, Burlingame (94010-1203)
PHONE.....................650 692-9100
Fax: 650 692-9861
Stan Moore, *Manager*
Cliff Clark, *General Mgr*
James Last, *Finance*
Ken Hansen, *Controller*
Raphael Santiago, *Human Res Dir*
EMP: 167
SALES (corp-wide): 14.4B **Publicly Held**
SIC: 7011 7389 Hotels & motels; office facilities & secretarial service rental
PA: Marriott International, Inc.
10400 Fernwood Rd
Bethesda MD 20817
301 380-3000

(P-12980)
MARRIOTT INTERNATIONAL INC
18090 San Ramon Vly Blvd, San Ramon (94583-4405)
PHONE.....................925 866-1228
Barbara Croker, *Branch Mgr*
Jacky Anderson, *Human Resources*
EMP: 167
SALES (corp-wide): 14.4B **Publicly Held**
SIC: 7011 Hotels & motels
PA: Marriott International, Inc.
10400 Fernwood Rd
Bethesda MD 20817
301 380-3000

(P-12981)
MARRIOTT INTERNATIONAL INC ◆
Also Called: Residence Inn By Marriott
900 Bayfront Ct, San Diego (92101-3007)
PHONE.....................619 831-0224
Evangelina Alaniz, *Accountant*

EMP: 99 **EST:** 2016
SALES (est): 301.3K **Privately Held**
SIC: 7011 Hotels & motels

(P-12982)
MARRIOTTS NEWPORT COAST VILLA
23000 Newport Coast Dr, Newport Beach (92657-2100)
PHONE.....................949 464-6000
Fax: 949 464-6010
Eric Penningroth, *Owner*
EMP: 59
SALES (est): 4MM **Privately Held**
SIC: 7011 Resort hotel

(P-12983)
MASON STREET OPCO LLC
Also Called: Fairmont San Francisco
950 Mason St, San Francisco (94108-6000)
PHONE.....................415 772-5000
Seung Geon Kim, *President*
Daniel Kramer, *Asst Sec*
EMP: 850
SQ FT: 750,000
SALES: 112MM **Privately Held**
SIC: 7011 Hotels & motels

(P-12984)
MAYFAIR HOTEL
1430 Amherst Ave Apt 5, Los Angeles (90025-0358)
PHONE.....................213 484-9789
Tung Shui Ng, *President*
Simin Datafari, *Manager*
EMP: 60
SQ FT: 228,800
SALES (est): 3.8MM **Privately Held**
WEB: www.mayfairla.com
SIC: 7011 Hotels

(P-12985)
MBIPCH LLC
Also Called: Malibu Beach Inn
22878 Pacific Coast Hwy, Malibu (90265-5041)
PHONE.....................310 456-6444
Fax: 310 456-1499
Richard Sherman, *CEO*
Jill Jennings, *General Mgr*
Nina Ponte, *Mktg Dir*
EMP: 52
SALES (est): 3.8MM **Privately Held**
SIC: 7011 Resort hotel

(P-12986)
MBP LAND LLC
Also Called: Courtyard Marriott Mission Vly
595 Hotel Cir S, San Diego (92108-3403)
PHONE.....................619 291-5720
John Blem, *Mng Member*
Peter Vermeer, *Vice Pres*
Joshua Roop, *Controller*
Martin Bowen, *Director*
EMP: 56
SALES: 750K
SALES (corp-wide): 265.6MM **Privately Held**
SIC: 7011 Hotels & motels
PA: Evolution Hospitality, Llc
1211 Puerta Del Sol # 170
San Clemente CA 92673
949 498-2056

(P-12987)
MCCLELLAN HOSPITALITY SVCS LLC
3140 Peacekeeper Way, McClellan (95652-2508)
PHONE.....................916 965-7100
Larry Kelley,
Douglas Hart,
EMP: 75
SALES (est): 1.3MM **Privately Held**
SIC: 7011 5812 Hotels & motels; caterers

(P-12988)
MENDOCINO HOTEL & RESORT CORP
45080 Main St, Mendocino (95460)
P.O. Box 587 (95460-0587)
PHONE.....................707 937-0511
Fax: 707 937-0513
Thomas Kravis, *President*

Carlos Pena, *Executive*
Juan C Pena, *Executive*
Dan Clark, *Info Tech Mgr*
Cindy Rhinehart, *Data Proc Staff*
EMP: 70
SQ FT: 12,500
SALES (est): 4.9MM **Privately Held**
WEB: www.mendocinohotel.com
SIC: 7011 5812 5813 7299 Hotels; eating places; bars & lounges; banquet hall facilities

(P-12989)
MERISTAR SAN PEDRO HILTON LLC
Also Called: Hilton Port Los Angls-San Pdro
2800 Via Cabrillo Marina, San Pedro (90731-7223)
PHONE.....................310 514-3344
Fax: 310 514-8945
Paul Whetsell, *Mng Member*
Jeff Milnes, *CEO*
John Emery, *CFO*
Ramon Torres, *Engineer*
Louie Batacan, *CPA*
EMP: 176
SALES (est): 2.1MM
SALES (corp-wide): 1.7B **Privately Held**
WEB: www.sheratonokc.com
SIC: 7011 Hotels & motels
HQ: Interstate Hotels & Resorts, Inc.
4501 Fairfax Dr Ste 500
Arlington VA 22203
703 387-3100

(P-12990)
MERRITT HOSPITALITY LLC
Also Called: Hilton
701 W Ocean Blvd, Long Beach (90831-3100)
PHONE.....................562 983-3400
Fax: 562 983-3477
Grace Sun, *Sales Mgr*
Annette Dhein, *Vice Pres*
James Garcia, *General Mgr*
Rachel Duron, *Human Res Dir*
Helen McCaughan, *Sales Dir*
EMP: 250
SALES (corp-wide): 238.5MM **Privately Held**
SIC: 7011 7991 5813 5812 Hotels & motels; physical fitness facilities; drinking places; eating places
HQ: Merritt Hospitality, Llc
101 Merritt 7 Ste 14
Norwalk CT 06851
203 849-8844

(P-12991)
MERRITT HOSPITALITY LLC
Also Called: Marriott
2701 Nutwood Ave, Fullerton (92831-5400)
PHONE.....................714 738-7800
Tom Beebon, *Manager*
Trica Paige, *Marketing Mgr*
Todd Rogers, *Director*
EMP: 125
SALES (corp-wide): 238.5MM **Privately Held**
SIC: 7011 7991 5813 5812 Hotels & motels; physical fitness facilities; drinking places; eating places
HQ: Merritt Hospitality, Llc
101 Merritt 7 Ste 14
Norwalk CT 06851
203 849-8844

(P-12992)
MERRITT HOSPITALITY LLC
Also Called: Starwood Hotels & Resorts
3555 Round Barn Blvd, Santa Rosa (95403-1763)
PHONE.....................707 523-7555
Fax: 707 569-5555
David Connor, *Branch Mgr*
Heidi Miersemann, *Sales Dir*
EMP: 130
SALES (corp-wide): 238.5MM **Privately Held**
SIC: 7011 Hotels & motels
HQ: Merritt Hospitality, Llc
101 Merritt 7 Ste 14
Norwalk CT 06851
203 849-8844

(P-12993)
MHRP RESORT INC
Also Called: Mountain High Ski Resort
24510 Highway 2, Wrightwood (92397)
P.O. Box 3010 (92397-3010)
PHONE.....................760 249-5808
Fax: 760 316-7895
Russel S Bernard, *President*
W Gregory Geiger, *Vice Pres*
Kenneth Liang, *Vice Pres*
Marc Porosoff, *Vice Pres*
Paul Bauer, *Director*
EMP: 100
SALES (est): 6.3MM **Privately Held**
WEB: www.mountainhighskiresort.com
SIC: 7011 Ski lodge

(P-12994)
MIKADO HOTELS INC
Also Called: Mikado Best Western Hotel
12600 Riverside Dr, North Hollywood (91607-3411)
PHONE.....................818 763-9141
Fax: 818 752-1045
Jerome Frick, *CEO*
Edmond Petrossian, *President*
Diran Yahyayan, *Vice Pres*
EMP: 50
SQ FT: 71,500
SALES (est): 3.5MM **Privately Held**
SIC: 7011 5812 5813 Hotel, franchised; restaurant, lunch counter; cocktail lounge

(P-12995)
MILE POST PROPERTIES LLC
Also Called: La Quinta Inn
1050 Van Ness Ave, San Francisco (94109-6934)
PHONE.....................415 673-4711
Fax: 415 673-9362
Fred Reed, *General Mgr*
Fred Rapp, *General Mgr*
EMP: 100
SQ FT: 100,000
SALES (est): 1.8MM **Privately Held**
SIC: 7011 Hotels & motels

(P-12996)
MILLBRAE WCP HOTEL I LLC
Also Called: Westin Sfo
335 Powell St, San Francisco (94102-1804)
PHONE.....................415 397-7000
Marc Swerdlow, *President*
Mark Zettl, *COO*
Richard Horshington, *Executive*
Mac Nguyen, *Controller*
Debe Cupano, *Human Res Mgr*
EMP: 1000
SALES (est): 33.6MM
SALES (corp-wide): 124.6MM **Privately Held**
WEB: www.westinstfrancis.com
SIC: 7011 Hotels & motels
HQ: Ultima Hospitality, L.L.C.
30 S Wacker Dr Ste 3600
Chicago IL 60606
312 948-4500

(P-12997)
MILLBRAE WCP HOTEL II LLC
Also Called: Aloft Sfo
401 E Millbrae Ave, Millbrae (94030-3111)
PHONE.....................650 443-5500
Fax: 650 443-5501
Marc Swerdlow, *President*
Mark Zettl, *COO*
Chris Offutt, *General Mgr*
John Gilliam, *Chief Engr*
EMP: 50
SQ FT: 288,000
SALES (est): 4.1MM
SALES (corp-wide): 124.6MM **Privately Held**
SIC: 7011 Hotels & motels
HQ: Ultima Hospitality, L.L.C.
30 S Wacker Dr Ste 3600
Chicago IL 60606
312 948-4500

(P-12998)
MISSION RANCH INC
26270 Dolores St, Carmel (93923-9215)
PHONE.....................831 624-6436
Roy Kaufman, *President*
Howard Bernstein, *Treasu*

Sue Carota, *Exec Dir*
Clint Eastwood, *Director*
EMP: 50
SALES (est): 3.9MM **Privately Held**
SIC: 7011 7999 Hotels; tennis club, non-membership

(P-12999)
MISSION STUART HT PARTNERS LLC
Also Called: Hotel Vitale
8 Mission St, San Francisco (94105-1227)
PHONE.................................415 278-3700
Chip Conley,
Jason Kwan, *Controller*
Grace Lok, *Controller*
EMP: 200
SALES (est): 10.5MM **Privately Held**
WEB: www.hotelvitale.com
SIC: 7011 Hotels

(P-13000)
MISSION VALLEY HT OPERATOR INC
595 Hotel Cir S, San Diego (92108-3403)
PHONE.................................619 291-5720
Michael Medzigian, *President*
George Gudgeon, *Treasurer*
EMP: 75
SALES (est): 846.3K **Privately Held**
SIC: 7011 Hotel, franchised

(P-13001)
MIYAKO HOTELS
328 E 1st St Ste 510, Los Angeles (90012-3902)
PHONE.................................213 617-2000
Fax: 213 617-2700
Akimasa Yoneda, *President*
EMP: 56
SALES (est): 2.2MM **Privately Held**
SIC: 7011 Hotels

(P-13002)
MODESTO HOSPITALITY LESSEE LLC
Also Called: Doubletree Hotel Modesto
1150 9th St Ste C, Modesto (95354-0857)
PHONE.................................209 526-6000
EMP: 99
SALES: 950K **Privately Held**
SIC: 7011

(P-13003)
MONO WIND CASINO
Also Called: Big Sandy Rancheria
37302 Rancheria Ln, Auberry (93602-9423)
P.O. Box 1060 (93602-1060)
PHONE.................................559 855-4350
Fax: 559 855-4351
Connie Lewis, *Chairman*
Elizabeth D Kipp, *Principal*
Dave Reynolds, *Info Tech Mgr*
John Robertson, *Maintenance Dir*
EMP: 100
SALES (est): 6.6MM **Privately Held**
WEB: www.monowindcasino.com
SIC: 7011 5812 Casino hotel; restaurant, family: independent

(P-13004)
MONTAGE HOTELS & RESORTS LLC
Also Called: Montage Beverly Hills
225 N Canon Dr, Beverly Hills (90210-5301)
PHONE.................................310 499-4199
Alan Fuerstman, *Branch Mgr*
EMP: 450
SALES (corp-wide): 430.9MM **Privately Held**
SIC: 7011 7991 Hotels & motels; spas
PA: Montage Hotels & Resorts, Llc
    1 Ada Ste 250
    Irvine CA 92618
    949 715-5002

(P-13005)
MONTCLAIR HOTELS MB LLC
Also Called: Holiday Inn Concord
1050 Burnett Ave, Concord (94520-5713)
PHONE.................................925 687-5500
Stephanie Mullen, *General Mgr*
Ela Patel, *Human Res Mgr*
EMP: 75
SALES (corp-wide): 32MM **Privately Held**
WEB: www.montclairhotels.com
SIC: 7011 Hotels & motels
PA: Montclair Hotels Mb, Llc
    6600 Mannheim Rd
    Rosemont IL 60018
    847 457-3900

(P-13006)
MONTECITO SEQUOIA INC
Also Called: Montecito Sequoia Lodge
8000 Generals Hwy, Kings Canyon Nationa (93633)
P.O. Box 858, Kcnp (93633-0858)
PHONE.................................559 565-3388
Fax: 559 565-3223
Virginia C Barnes, *President*
Vasilij Karnickis, *Administration*
EMP: 61 EST: 1960
SALES (est): 2MM **Privately Held**
SIC: 7011 Hotels & motels

(P-13007)
MONTEREY PLAZA HT LTD PARTNR
Also Called: Monterey Plaza Hotel & Spa
400 Cannery Row, Monterey (93940-7501)
PHONE.................................800 334-3999
Fax: 831 646-0285
John V Narigi, *General Ptnr*
Alexa Hickein, *Admin Asst*
Annita Ceoto, *Administration*
Frank Pitpit, *CIO*
Oscar Lopez, *Info Tech Dir*
EMP: 360
SALES (est): 24.4MM **Privately Held**
WEB: www.montereyplazahotel.com
SIC: 7011 Hotels

(P-13008)
MORGANS HOTEL GROUP MGT LLC
Also Called: Mondrian Hotel
8440 W Sunset Blvd, Los Angeles (90069-1912)
PHONE.................................323 650-8999
Fax: 323 650-3718
David Weidlich, *General Mgr*
Daniel Espino, *Vice Pres*
Mich S Reddan, *VP Finance*
Robin Clark, *Sales Dir*
Deborah Lisboa, *Sales Dir*
EMP: 200
SALES (corp-wide): 219.9MM **Publicly Held**
WEB: www.mondrianhotel.com
SIC: 7011 5813 5812 Hotels & motels; drinking places; eating places
HQ: Morgans Hotel Group Management Llc
    475 10th Ave Fl 11
    New York NY 10018

(P-13009)
MORGANS HOTEL GROUP MGT LLC
Also Called: Clift Hotel Four Season
495 Geary St, San Francisco (94102-1222)
PHONE.................................415 775-4700
Fax: 415 441-4621
Alexandra Walterstiel, *General Mgr*
Hicham Mouhsin, *Human Res Mgr*
EMP: 200
SQ FT: 271,387
SALES (corp-wide): 219.9MM **Publicly Held**
WEB: www.mondrianhotel.com
SIC: 7011 5812 7991 5813 Hotels; eating places; physical fitness facilities; drinking places
HQ: Morgans Hotel Group Management Llc
    475 10th Ave Fl 11
    New York NY 10018

(P-13010)
MOTEL 6 OPERATING LP
5101 W Century Blvd, Inglewood (90304-1223)
PHONE.................................310 419-1234
Amad Serhat, *Manager*
Ray Sitzhugh, *General Mgr*
EMP: 53
SQ FT: 112,875
SALES (corp-wide): 365.2MM **Privately Held**
WEB: www.motel6.com
SIC: 7011 Hotels & motels
HQ: Motel 6 Operating L.P.
    4001 Intl Pkwy Ste 500
    Carrollton TX 75007
    972 360-9000

(P-13011)
MOUNTAIN SPRINGS KIRKWOOD LLC
1501 Kirkwood Meadows Dr, Kirkwood (95646)
PHONE.................................209 258-6000
Charles E Cobb Jr, *Mng Member*
Tobin T Cobb,
Bud D Klein,
EMP: 200
SALES (est): 2MM **Privately Held**
SIC: 7011 Ski lodge; resort hotel

(P-13012)
MSR HOTELS & RESORTS INC
Also Called: Embassy Suites- Santa Clara
2885 Lakeside Dr, Santa Clara (95054-2805)
PHONE.................................408 496-6400
Teri Owens, *Branch Mgr*
EMP: 80
SALES (corp-wide): 37.9B **Publicly Held**
SIC: 7011 Hotels & motels
HQ: Msr Hotels & Resorts, Inc.
    450 S Orange Ave
    Orlando FL 32801
    407 650-1000

(P-13013)
NAPA VALLEY LODGE LP
Also Called: Bodega Bay Lodge
103 Coast Highway 1, Bodega Bay (94923-9723)
PHONE.................................707 875-3525
Ellis Alden, *Owner*
EMP: 60
SALES (corp-wide): 6.4MM **Privately Held**
WEB: www.napavalleylodge.com
SIC: 7011 Vacation lodges
PA: Napa Valley Lodge L.P.
    2230 Madison St
    Yountville CA 94599
    707 944-2468

(P-13014)
NARVEN ENTERPRISES INC (PA)
Also Called: Holiday Inn
1430 7th Ave Ste B, San Diego (92101-2815)
PHONE.................................619 239-2261
Behram Baxter, *President*
Micheal Nguyen, *Controller*
Rick Orr, *Sales Mgr*
EMP: 73
SQ FT: 6,000
SALES (est): 5.7MM **Privately Held**
SIC: 7011 Hotels & motels

(P-13015)
NARVEN ENTERPRISES INC
Also Called: Holiday Inn
1430 7th Ave Ste B, San Diego (92101-2815)
PHONE.................................619 232-2261
Sunil Thdaini, *General Mgr*
EMP: 75
SALES (corp-wide): 5.7MM **Privately Held**
SIC: 7011 Hotels & motels
PA: Narven Enterprises Inc.
    1430 7th Ave Ste B
    San Diego CA 92101
    619 239-2261

(P-13016)
NATIONAL HOSPITALITY LLC
Also Called: Royal Scandinavian Inn
400 Alisal Rd, Solvang (93463-3741)
P.O. Box 30 (93464-0030)
PHONE.................................805 688-8000
Fax: 805 688-0761
Cynthia Elwood, *Mng Member*
EMP: 80
SQ FT: 65,000
SALES (est): 3.2MM **Privately Held**
WEB: www.royalscandinavianinn.com
SIC: 7011 5812 7299 5813 Inns; eating places; banquet hall facilities; cocktail lounge

(P-13017)
NBC SUITE HOTEL
Also Called: Embassy Suites
1440 E Imperial Ave, El Segundo (90245-2623)
PHONE.................................310 640-3600
Shar Franklin, *President*
Tariq Saeed, *Executive*
Kimberly Kaneshiro, *Controller*
EMP: 57
SALES (est): 4.5MM **Privately Held**
SIC: 7011 Hotels & motels

(P-13018)
NEW FIGUEROA HOTEL INC
1000 S Hope St Apt 201, Los Angeles (90015-1492)
PHONE.................................213 627-8971
Fax: 213 689-0305
Uno Thimansson, *President*
Elyse Omori, *Vice Pres*
EMP: 70
SQ FT: 200,000
SALES (est): 7.2MM **Privately Held**
SIC: 7011 5812 5813 Hotels; eating places; bars & lounges

(P-13019)
NEWAGE ANAHEIM INN LLC
Also Called: Hotel Menage
1221 S Harbor Blvd, Anaheim (92805-6004)
PHONE.................................714 758-0900
Rob Kaulfonic, *Vice Pres*
Calina Ikhhihfo, *Accountant*
Phil Wolfgramm, *Manager*
Penina Ikahifo, *Assistant*
EMP: 123
SALES (est): 5MM **Privately Held**
SIC: 7011 5813 5812 Hotels & motels; drinking places; eating places

(P-13020)
NEWARK COURTYARD BY MARRIOTT
34905 Newark Blvd, Newark (94560-1215)
PHONE.................................510 792-5200
Melody Lanthorn, *Manager*
Enrique Nepomuceno, *Engineer*
EMP: 60
SALES (est): 2.4MM **Privately Held**
SIC: 7011 Hotels & motels

(P-13021)
NEWPORT HOSPITALITY GROUP INC
Also Called: Holiday Inn
801 Truxtun Ave, Bakersfield (93301-4726)
PHONE.................................661 323-1900
Fax: 661 324-7794
Eric Iokal, *Manager*
EMP: 200
SALES (corp-wide): 97.9MM **Privately Held**
WEB: www.newport-hospitality.com
SIC: 7011 Hotels & motels
PA: Newport Hospitality Group Inc
    1048 Irvine Ave Ste 365
    Newport Beach CA
    949 706-7002

(P-13022)
NHCA INC
Also Called: Crowne Plz Los Angeles Hbr Ht
601 S Palos Verdes St, San Pedro (90731-3329)
PHONE.................................310 519-8200
Fax: 310 521-8053
SM Nasarudin, *CEO*
Mindy Liu, *CFO*
Ramon Torres, *Engineer*
Casey Keong, *Marketing Staff*
EMP: 151
SALES (est): 10.3MM **Privately Held**
WEB: www.sheratonlaharbor.com
SIC: 7011 Hotels

7011 - Hotels, Motels & Tourist Courts County (P-13023)

(P-13023)
NOB HILL PROPERTIES INC
Also Called: Big Four Restaurant
1075 California St, San Francisco (94108-2281)
PHONE.................................415 474-5400
Fax: 415 474-6227
John Cope, *President*
Newton Cope Sr, *Ch of Bd*
Newton Cope Jr, *Vice Pres*
Orlando Mayor, *Controller*
Martina Milnar, *Sales Mgr*
EMP: 280
SALES (est): 19.1MM **Privately Held**
WEB: www.nobhillspa.com
SIC: 7011 5812 Hotels; eating places

(P-13024)
NOBLE AEW VINEYARD CREEK LLC
Also Called: Hyatt Vineyard Creek Ht & Spa
170 Railroad St, Santa Rosa (95401-6266)
PHONE.................................707 284-1234
Josephine Redrico, *Principal*
Brad Calkins, *Purch Dir*
Micheal Russell, *Sales Dir*
EMP: 99
SALES: 950K **Privately Held**
SIC: 7011 Hotels & motels

(P-13025)
NOBLE/UTAH LONG BEACH LLC
Also Called: Westin Long Beach Hotel, The
333 E Ocean Blvd, Long Beach (90802-4827)
PHONE.................................562 436-3000
Mitesh B Shah, *Mng Member*
Jim Conley, *CFO*
Marc Choplick, *General Mgr*
Brooke Vandenbrink, *Finance*
EMP: 250
SQ FT: 51,000
SALES (est): 10MM
SALES (corp-wide): 103MM **Privately Held**
SIC: 7011 Hotels & motels
PA: Noble Investment Group Llc
3424 Peachtree Rd Ne # 2000
Atlanta GA 30326
404 262-9660

(P-13026)
NOIRO WEST LLC
Also Called: Sheraton Suites San Diego
701 A St, San Diego (92101-4611)
PHONE.................................619 819-6620
Fax: 619 696-1555
Richard M Kelleher,
Alex Wilmot, *Controller*
Emily Peda, *Sales Mgr*
EMP: 200
SQ FT: 99,999
SALES (est): 10.2MM **Privately Held**
SIC: 7011 Hotels

(P-13027)
NORTHERN QUEEN INC
Also Called: Northern Queen Inn
400 Railroad Ave, Nevada City (95959-2868)
PHONE.................................530 265-4492
Fax: 530 265-3720
Roy J Ramey, *President*
Jacqueline Ramey, *Corp Secy*
Colleen Flores, *Vice Pres*
Diane Mansfield, *Systems Mgr*
EMP: 65
SQ FT: 32,000
SALES (est): 2.3MM **Privately Held**
SIC: 7011 6552 Motels; subdividers & developers

(P-13028)
NORTHWEST HOTEL CORPORATION (PA)
Also Called: Howard Johnson
1380 S Harbor Blvd, Anaheim (92802-2310)
PHONE.................................714 776-6120
James P Edmondson, *President*
EMP: 68
SQ FT: 50,000
SALES (est): 7.8MM **Privately Held**
SIC: 7011 Hotels & motels

(P-13029)
NPL ANAHEIM INVESTMENTS LLC
Also Called: Homewood Suites Anaheim Resort
2010 S Harbor Blvd, Anaheim (92802-3514)
PHONE.................................714 750-2010
Curtis Olson, *President*
Matthew Kaufman, *Corp Secy*
Ajesh Patel, *Vice Pres*
EMP: 68 EST: 2013
SQ FT: 165,000
SALES (est): 182.2K **Privately Held**
SIC: 7011 Hotels & motels; hotel, franchised; hotels

(P-13030)
NREA-TRC 711 LLC
Also Called: Sheraton Downtown Los Angeles
700 S Flower St Ste 2600, Los Angeles (90017-4213)
PHONE.................................213 486-6500
Rosslyn Bledsoe, *Accountant*
EMP: 200
SQ FT: 470,000
SALES (est): 8MM **Privately Held**
SIC: 7011 Hotels

(P-13031)
OAK CREEK LP
Also Called: Holiday Inn Diamond Bar
21725 Gateway Center Dr, Diamond Bar (91765-2400)
PHONE.................................909 860-5440
Fax: 909 860-8224
Billy Mendez, *Partner*
Sammi Wang, *Principal*
Cesar Aparicio, *Chief Engr*
EMP: 60
SALES (est): 3.3MM **Privately Held**
SIC: 7011 Hotels & motels

(P-13032)
OCEAN AVENUE LLC
Also Called: Fairmont Miramar Hotel
101 Wilshire Blvd, Santa Monica (90401-1106)
PHONE.................................310 576-7777
Ellis O'Connor,
Wolfgang Jonas, *General Mgr*
Mathew Armstrong, *Info Tech Mgr*
Tom Bosak, *Asst Controller*
Walter Moerve, *Controller*
EMP: 275
SQ FT: 209,000
SALES (est): 23.4MM **Privately Held**
SIC: 7011 7299 Hotels; banquet hall facilities

(P-13033)
OCEAN HOLIDAY LP
Also Called: Holiday Inn Oceanside Marina
1401 Carmelo Dr, Oceanside (92054-1012)
PHONE.................................760 231-7000
Joseph Fan, *Partner*
Benjamin Shih, *Executive Asst*
EMP: 55
SALES (est): 1.7MM **Privately Held**
SIC: 7011 Hotels & motels

(P-13034)
OCEAN PARK HOTELS INC
Also Called: Hilton
1000 Aguajito Rd, Monterey (93940-4801)
PHONE.................................831 373-6141
Cherie Davis, *General Mgr*
George Kaplanis, *Admin Mgr*
Emil Agib, *Administration*
Tereza Lee, *Financial Exec*
Laurie Mendoza, *Accounting Mgr*
EMP: 115
SALES (corp-wide): 18.8MM **Privately Held**
WEB: www.ophot.com
SIC: 7011 5813 8741 Hotels & motels; drinking places; hotel or motel management
PA: Ocean Park Hotels, Inc.
9777 Blue Larkspur Ln # 102
Monterey CA 93940
805 544-0812

(P-13035)
OCEAN PARK HOTELS INC
Also Called: Hilton
27710 The Old Rd, Valencia (91355-1036)
PHONE.................................661 284-3200
Angela Peterson, *Branch Mgr*
Maria Theodore, *General Mgr*
EMP: 60
SALES (corp-wide): 18.8MM **Privately Held**
WEB: www.ophot.com
SIC: 7011 Hotels & motels
PA: Ocean Park Hotels, Inc.
9777 Blue Larkspur Ln # 102
Monterey CA 93940
805 544-0812

(P-13036)
OCEAN PARK HOTELS MMEX LLC
Also Called: Holiday Inn
27513 Wayne Mills Pl, Valencia (91355-4980)
PHONE.................................661 284-2101
Fax: 661 284-3550
James Flagg,
EMP: 50
SQ FT: 5,322
SALES (est): 2.1MM **Privately Held**
SIC: 7011 Hotels & motels

(P-13037)
OHI RESORT HOTELS LLC
Also Called: Wyndham Anaheim Garden Grove
12021 Harbor Blvd, Garden Grove (92840-4001)
PHONE.................................714 867-5555
Fax: 714 867-5100
Jeremy Yujuico, *Principal*
Ronnie Delgado, *General Mgr*
Scoot Mathew, *Manager*
EMP: 98
SALES (est): 5.5MM **Privately Held**
SIC: 7011 Hotels & motels

(P-13038)
OJAI VALLEY INN GOLF COURSE
Also Called: Ojai Valley Spa
905 Country Club Rd, Ojai (93023-3789)
PHONE.................................805 646-2420
Thad Hyland, *Director*
Armie Mar, *CTO*
Doug Bowman, *Info Tech Mgr*
Shelly Archer, *Accounts Exec*
EMP: 600
SALES (est): 8.5MM **Privately Held**
WEB: www.ojaivalleyspa.com
SIC: 7011 7992 5941 Resort hotel; public golf courses; sporting goods & bicycle shops

(P-13039)
OLD TOWN FMLY HOSPITALITY CORP
Also Called: Fiesta De Reyes
4962 Concannon Ct, San Diego (92130-2723)
PHONE.................................619 246-8010
Chuck Ross, *President*
EMP: 240 EST: 2009
SQ FT: 1,600
SALES: 16MM **Privately Held**
SIC: 7011 5812 Hotels; eating places

(P-13040)
OLS HOTELS & RESORTS LP
Also Called: Le Parc Suite Hotel
733 W Knoll Dr, West Hollywood (90069-5207)
PHONE.................................310 855-1115
Fax: 310 659-7812
Sam Ebeid, *CEO*
Ira Kleinrock, *General Mgr*
Ojan Ahmad, *Chief Engr*
Barry Podob, *Sales Dir*
EMP: 105
SALES (corp-wide): 84.8MM **Privately Held**
WEB: www.outriggerlodging.com
SIC: 7011 8741 Hotels; hotel or motel management
PA: Ols Hotels & Resorts, Lp
16000 Ventura Blvd # 1010
Encino CA 91436
818 905-8280

(P-13041)
OLS HOTELS & RESORTS LP
Also Called: Marriott
14635 Bldwin Pk Towne Ctr, Baldwin Park (91706-5548)
PHONE.................................626 962-6000
Peter Ehienberg, *Manager*
Henry Zamora, *General Mgr*
Jiyu Liang, *Human Res Dir*
Kym Herzog, *Manager*
EMP: 509
SALES (corp-wide): 84.8MM **Privately Held**
WEB: www.outriggerlodging.com
SIC: 7011 Hotels & motels
PA: Ols Hotels & Resorts, Lp
16000 Ventura Blvd # 1010
Encino CA 91436
818 905-8280

(P-13042)
OMNI HOTELS CORPORATION
41000 Bob Hope Dr, Rancho Mirage (92270-4416)
PHONE.................................760 568-2727
EMP: 256
SALES (corp-wide): 1.2B **Privately Held**
SIC: 7011 Hotels & motels
HQ: Omni Hotels Corporation
4001 Maple Ave Ste 500
Dallas TX 75219
972 730-6664

(P-13043)
OMNI HOTELS CORPORATION
675 L St, San Diego (92101-7022)
PHONE.................................619 231-6664
Ed Netzhammer, *Manager*
Brian Hughes, *General Mgr*
Anna McNamara, *Asst Controller*
Anthony Belef, *Human Res Dir*
Julie Larsen, *Sales Mgr*
EMP: 300
SALES (corp-wide): 1.2B **Privately Held**
WEB: www.omnihotels.com
SIC: 7011 Hotels & motels
HQ: Omni Hotels Corporation
4001 Maple Ave Ste 500
Dallas TX 75219
972 730-6664

(P-13044)
OMNI HOTELS CORPORATION
500 California St, San Francisco (94104-1001)
PHONE.................................415 677-9494
Fax: 415 273-3038
Michael Casey, *Branch Mgr*
Bob Peckenpaugh, *General Mgr*
Ruth Hirtzinger, *Sales Mgr*
EMP: 264
SALES (corp-wide): 1.2B **Privately Held**
WEB: www.omnihotels.com
SIC: 7011 Hotels & motels
HQ: Omni Hotels Corporation
4001 Maple Ave Ste 500
Dallas TX 75219
972 730-6664

(P-13045)
OMNI HOTELS CORPORATION
251 S Olive St Fl 1, Los Angeles (90012-3002)
PHONE.................................213 617-3300
Fax: 213 356-4049
Bob Greeney, *General Mgr*
Bob Graney, *General Mgr*
Edwin Adolfo, *Purch Dir*
Steve Schultze, *Safety Dir*
John Anderson, *Director*
EMP: 250
SALES (corp-wide): 1.2B **Privately Held**
WEB: www.omnihotels.com
SIC: 7011 Hotels & motels
HQ: Omni Hotels Corporation
4001 Maple Ave Ste 500
Dallas TX 75219
972 730-6664

PRODUCTS & SERVICES SECTION
7011 - Hotels, Motels & Tourist Courts County (P-13068)

(P-13046)
ONE NOB HILL ASSOCIATES LLC
Also Called: Intercontinental Mark Hopkins
999 California St, San Francisco (94108-2250)
PHONE................................415 392-3434
Maarten Drenth, *General Mgr*
Mary Ann Gonzales, *General Mgr*
Michael Quan, *Info Tech Dir*
EMP: 86
SALES (est): 1.9MM **Privately Held**
SIC: 7011 Hotels

(P-13047)
ONTARIO AIRPORT HOTEL CORP
Also Called: Hilton Santa Clara
4949 Great America Pkwy, Santa Clara (95054-1216)
PHONE................................408 562-6709
Fax: 408 330-0011
James Evans, *CFO*
Gary Hauck, *Engineer*
Patricia Veron, *Human Res Mgr*
Joseph Jenci, *Sales Dir*
Roy Truitt, *Sales Associate*
EMP: 127
SQ FT: 169,768
SALES (est): 11.1MM **Privately Held**
WEB: www.hiltonsantaclara.com
SIC: 7011 Hotels

(P-13048)
ORCHARD INTERNATIONAL GROUP (PA)
Also Called: Orchard Hotel
665 Bush St, San Francisco (94108-3510)
PHONE................................415 362-8878
Fax: 415 362-8088
S C Huang, *President*
Robert Huang, *CEO*
Amira Causevic, *Executive*
Tony Llanos, *Controller*
EMP: 75
SQ FT: 60,000
SALES: 12.4MM **Privately Held**
SIC: 7011 Hotels & motels

(P-13049)
OTB ACQUISITION LLC
Also Called: Sierra Vista Extended Stay
770 S Brea Blvd Ste 227, Brea (92821-5399)
PHONE................................520 458-0540
EMP: 206 **Privately Held**
SIC: 7011 Hotels & motels
PA: Otb Acquisition Llc
2201 W Royal Ln Ste 240
Irving TX 75063

(P-13050)
OUTRIGGER HOTELS HAWAII
Also Called: Marina International Hotel
4200 Admiralty Way, Venice (90292-5422)
PHONE................................310 301-2000
Fax: 310 301-6687
Mohammed Khan, *General Mgr*
EMP: 80
SALES (corp-wide): 108.6MM **Privately Held**
WEB: www.outriggerhawaii.com
SIC: 7011 6531 Hotels; real estate managers
PA: Outrigger Hotels Hawaii
2375 Kuhio Ave Fl 4
Honolulu HI 96815
808 921-6510

(P-13051)
OUTRIGGER HOTELS HAWAII
Grafton On Sunset, The
8462 W Sunset Blvd, West Hollywood (90069-1912)
PHONE................................323 491-9015
Chad Thompson, *Branch Mgr*
Troy Berry, *Sales Staff*
Michael Spencer, *Sales Staff*
EMP: 98
SALES (corp-wide): 108.6MM **Privately Held**
WEB: www.outriggerhawaii.com
SIC: 7011 Hotels & motels

PA: Outrigger Hotels Hawaii
2375 Kuhio Ave Fl 4
Honolulu HI 96815
808 921-6510

(P-13052)
OVIS LLC
Also Called: Ojai Valley Inn & Spa
905 Country Club Rd, Ojai (93023-3734)
PHONE................................805 646-5511
Toll Free:................................888 -
Fax: 805 646-7969
Stephen Crown, *Mng Member*
Magdalena Morin, *CFO*
Lynne Hayman, *Executive*
Janis Clapoff, *Managing Dir*
Donna Keeter, *General Mgr*
EMP: 600
SALES (est): 36.4MM **Privately Held**
WEB: www.ojairesort.com
SIC: 7011 5813 5812 Resort hotel; drinking places; eating places

(P-13053)
OXFORD PALACE
745 S Oxford Ave, Los Angeles (90005-2909)
PHONE................................213 382-7756
Bowhan Kim, *Principal*
Don W Chang, *Principal*
Bora Park, *Director*
Joann Lee, *Manager*
Weon Moon, *Manager*
EMP: 96
SALES (est): 5.7MM **Privately Held**
WEB: www.oxfordhotel.com
SIC: 7011 5812 Hotels; Korean restaurant

(P-13054)
OXNARD BEACH HOTEL LP
350 E Port Hueneme Rd, Port Hueneme (93041-3209)
PHONE................................805 488-6560
Joseph Fan, *Partner*
EMP: 50 EST: 2012
SALES (est): 1.1MM **Privately Held**
SIC: 7011 Hotels

(P-13055)
PACIFIC CAMBRIA INC
Also Called: Cambria Pines Lodge
2905 Burton Dr, Cambria (93428-4001)
PHONE................................805 927-6114
Fax: 805 927-4016
Dirk Winter, *President*
Tricia Anderson, *CTO*
John Gill, *Info Tech Mgr*
Elizabeth Borges, *Controller*
Kate Cutler, *Sales Dir*
EMP: 90
SQ FT: 70,000
SALES (est): 5.6MM **Privately Held**
WEB: www.cambriapineslodge.com
SIC: 7011 5812 5813 Hotels; resort hotel; restaurant, family: independent; bar (drinking places)

(P-13056)
PACIFIC GROVE ASLMAR OPER CORP
Also Called: Asilomar Conference Center
800 Asilomar Blvd, Pacific Grove (93950-3704)
PHONE................................831 372-8016
Fax: 831 372-7227
David Dornbusch, *General Mgr*
Gary Kimmel, *Finance Dir*
EMP: 250
SQ FT: 20,000
SALES: 13.2MM **Privately Held**
SIC: 7011 Hotels

(P-13057)
PACIFIC HOTEL DEV VENTR LP
Also Called: Sheraton Palo Alto
625 El Camino Real, Palo Alto (94301-2301)
PHONE................................650 347-8260
Clement Chen, *Vice Pres*
EMP: 200
SALES (est): 8.7MM **Privately Held**
SIC: 7011 Hotels & motels

(P-13058)
PACIFIC HOTEL MANAGEMENT LLC
Also Called: Sheraton
1603 Powell St, Emeryville (94608-2436)
PHONE................................510 547-7888
Michelle Sims, *Owner*
EMP: 122
SALES (corp-wide): 64.7MM **Privately Held**
SIC: 7011 Hotels & motels
PA: Pacific Hotel Management, Llc
400 S El Camino Real # 200
San Mateo CA 94402
650 347-8260

(P-13059)
PACIFIC HOTEL MANAGEMENT LLC
Also Called: Courtyard By Marriott
3150 Garrity Way, Richmond (94806-1983)
PHONE................................510 262-0700
Fax: 510 262-0927
Curt Newport, *Branch Mgr*
Becky Ross, *General Mgr*
Chris Rokas, *Chief Engr*
Cecille Francisco, *Accountant*
Anni Sauerlander, *Human Res Dir*
EMP: 122
SALES (corp-wide): 64.7MM **Privately Held**
WEB: www.pacifichotelmanagement.com
SIC: 7011 7389 Hotels & motels; office facilities & secretarial service rental
PA: Pacific Hotel Management, Llc
400 S El Camino Real # 200
San Mateo CA 94402
650 347-8260

(P-13060)
PACIFIC HOTEL MANAGEMENT LLC
Also Called: Sheraton
625 El Camino Real, Palo Alto (94301-2301)
PHONE................................650 328-2800
Jim Rebosio, *General Mgr*
Clement Chen, *Vice Pres*
Annie Tepe, *Social Dir*
Keiko Freese, *Office Mgr*
John Groth, *Info Tech Dir*
EMP: 300
SALES (corp-wide): 58.8MM **Privately Held**
SIC: 7011 Hotels & motels
PA: Pacific Hotel Management, Llc
400 S El Camino Real # 200
San Mateo CA 94402
650 347-8260

(P-13061)
PACIFIC HOTEL MANAGEMENT INC
Also Called: Radison Hotel Newport Beach
4545 Macarthur Blvd, Newport Beach (92660-2022)
PHONE................................949 608-1091
Ron Mavaddat, *President*
Bikas Pandey, *Controller*
Donna Walp, *Marketing Staff*
Bob Williamson, *Manager*
EMP: 99
SALES (est): 6.5MM **Privately Held**
SIC: 7011 Hotels & motels

(P-13062)
PACIFIC SNOW VALLEY RESORT LLC
Also Called: Nor Thowds
1427 W Valley Blvd # 201, Alhambra (91803-2364)
PHONE................................626 588-2889
David Kuo,
May Kay, *Manager*
EMP: 50
SALES (est): 1.4MM **Privately Held**
SIC: 7011 Resort hotel

(P-13063)
PACIFICA HIORANGE LP
Also Called: Hampton Inn
2720 Hotel Ter, Santa Ana (92705-5602)
PHONE................................714 556-3838
Russell Fraser, *General Ptnr*
Arlene Kostock, *CFO*

EMP: 80 EST: 2012
SALES (est): 3.6MM **Privately Held**
SIC: 7011 Hotels & motels

(P-13064)
PACIFICA HOST INC
Also Called: Clarion Hotel
700 16th St, Sacramento (95814-2002)
PHONE................................916 444-8000
Fax: 916 442-8129
Shannon Rossie, *General Mgr*
Lee Barnes, *General Mgr*
Rachelle English, *Food Svc Dir*
Donna Dotti, *Director*
Cindy Ortega, *Manager*
EMP: 50
SALES (est): 2.5MM **Privately Held**
SIC: 7011 Hotels & motels

(P-13065)
PACIFICA HOSTS INC
Also Called: Radisson Inn
6225 W Century Blvd, Los Angeles (90045-5311)
PHONE................................310 670-9000
Ashok Israni, *President*
Evelin Alvarado, *Human Res Mgr*
Sandy Valenci, *Human Res Mgr*
EMP: 249
SALES (corp-wide): 147.9MM **Privately Held**
SIC: 7011 6552 5813 5812 Hotels & motels; subdividers & developers; drinking places; eating places
PA: Pacifica Hosts, Inc.
1775 Hancock St Ste 200
San Diego CA 92110
619 296-9000

(P-13066)
PACIFICA HOTEL & CONFERENCE CE
Also Called: Radisson Hotel La Westside
6161 W Centinela Ave, Culver City (90230-6306)
PHONE................................310 649-1776
Fax: 310 649-4411
Jim Collins, *General Ptnr*
Robert Leonard, *Partner*
David Dowdre, *Chief Engr*
Mark Schwabenbauer, *Sales Executive*
Terry Crump, *General Counsel*
EMP: 190
SALES (est): 4.7MM **Privately Held**
SIC: 7011 6512 5812 7389 Hotels & motels; commercial & industrial building operation; eating places; convention & show services

(P-13067)
PACIFICA HOTEL COMPANY
Also Called: Shelter Point Hotel & Marina
1551 Shelter Island Dr, San Diego (92106-3102)
PHONE................................619 221-8000
Fax: 619 226-5798
Henric Larsen, *General Mgr*
EMP: 200
SALES (corp-wide): 154.9MM **Privately Held**
WEB: www.cottage-inn.com
SIC: 7011 4493 Hotels; marinas
HQ: Pacifica Hotel Company
1933 Cliff Dr Ste 1
Santa Barbara CA 93109
805 957-0095

(P-13068)
PACIFICA HOTEL COMPANY
Also Called: Best Western Half Moon Bay
2400 Cabrillo Hwy S, Half Moon Bay (94019-2253)
PHONE................................650 726-9000
Curt Picillo, *Manager*
EMP: 50
SALES (corp-wide): 154.9MM **Privately Held**
WEB: www.cottage-inn.com
SIC: 7011 Hotels & motels
HQ: Pacifica Hotel Company
1933 Cliff Dr Ste 1
Santa Barbara CA 93109
805 957-0095

7011 - Hotels, Motels & Tourist Courts County (P-13069)   PRODUCTS & SERVICES SECTION

(P-13069)
PACIFICA SAN JOSE LP
Also Called: Wyndham San Jose
1775 Hancock St Ste 100, San Diego
(92110-2035)
PHONE..................619 296-9000
Ashok Israni, *Partner*
Deepak Israni, *Partner*
Sushil Israni, *Partner*
Greer Barnes, *Controller*
EMP: 175
SALES: 12MM **Privately Held**
SIC: 7011 Hotels & motels

(P-13070)
PACKARD REALTY INC
Also Called: Holiday Inn
9901 S La Cienega Blvd, Los Angeles
(90045-5915)
PHONE..................310 649-5151
Tommy Spencer, *General Mgr*
Mihran Kalaydjian, *Manager*
Angela Tuazon, *Manager*
EMP: 85
SALES (corp-wide): 35.9MM **Privately Held**
WEB: www.hilax.com
SIC: 7011 Hotels & motels
PA: Packard Realty Inc.
    9555 Chesapeake Dr # 202
    San Diego CA 92123
    858 277-4305

(P-13071)
PALA MESA LIMITED PARTNERSHIP
Also Called: Pala Mesa Resort
2001 Old Highway 395, Fallbrook
(92028-9771)
PHONE..................760 728-5881
Fax: 760 723-8292
Tray Crayton, *President*
Jay G Lee, *General Mgr*
Kevin Poorbaugh, *General Mgr*
Mark Dixon, *Info Tech Mgr*
Greg Plog, *Research*
EMP: 225
SALES (est): 8.8MM **Privately Held**
WEB: www.palamesa.com
SIC: 7011 Resort hotel

(P-13072)
PALMDALE RESORT INC
Also Called: Holiday Inn
38630 5th St W, Palmdale (93551-4208)
PHONE..................661 947-8055
Fax: 661 947-9957
Toni Vilopas, *Owner*
Tony Zilobaf, *General Mgr*
Kimberly Zilobas, *Sales Dir*
Kimberly Zilobaf, *Director*
EMP: 50
SQ FT: 71,394
SALES (est): 2.9MM **Privately Held**
WEB: www.hipalmdale.com
SIC: 7011 Hotels & motels

(P-13073)
PALMETTO HOSPITALITY
Also Called: Hilton Garden Inn Palo Alto
4216 El Camino Real, Palo Alto
(94306-4404)
PHONE..................650 843-0795
Jason Boehm, *Vice Pres*
EMP: 50
SALES (est): 272.2K **Privately Held**
SIC: 7011 Hotels & motels

(P-13074)
PAN PCFIC HTELS RSRTS AMER INC
Also Called: Pan Pacific San Diego
400 W Broadway, San Diego (92101-3504)
PHONE..................619 239-4500
Fax: 619 239-3274
Jim Hollister, *General Mgr*
EMP: 330
SALES (corp-wide): 18.4MM **Privately Held**
SIC: 7011 5812 Hotels & motels; eating places

PA: Pan Pacific Hotels And Resorts America Inc.
    500 Post St Ste 800
    San Francisco CA 94102
    415 732-7747

(P-13075)
PARK INN BY RADISSON
3737 N Blackstone Ave, Fresno
(93726-5307)
PHONE..................559 226-2200
Betty Qi, *Owner*
EMP: 75 **Privately Held**
SIC: 7011 Hotels & motels

(P-13076)
PARK INN BY READISSON FRESNO
Also Called: Park Central Hotel Fresno
3737 N Blackstone Ave, Fresno
(93726-5307)
PHONE..................559 226-2200
Lori Lascola, *General Mgr*
EMP: 62 EST: 2011
SALES (est): 3.1MM **Privately Held**
SIC: 7011 Hotels & motels

(P-13077)
PARK PLAZA HOTEL
150 Hegenberger Rd, Oakland
(94621-1422)
PHONE..................510 635-5300
Fax: 510 635-4869
Tracy W Wahrlich Jr, *President*
Carl T Doughty, *General Ptnr*
Bert Taprizi, *General Ptnr*
Stephen Wahrlich, *General Ptnr*
EMP: 50
SALES (est): 3MM **Privately Held**
WEB: www.parkplazaoakland.com
SIC: 7011 Hotels

(P-13078)
PASADENA HOTEL DEV VENTR LP
Also Called: Sheraton Pasadena
303 Cordova St, Pasadena (91101-2426)
PHONE..................626 449-4000
Ray Serafin, *Principal*
Ana M Tolces, *Pharmacy Dir*
David Iwane, *Principal*
Howard Haberman, *CIO*
Amita Patel, *Marketing Staff*
EMP: 99
SALES (est): 7.4MM **Privately Held**
SIC: 7011 Hotels & motels

(P-13079)
PASADENA RBLES ACQUISITION LLC
168 S Los Robles Ave, Pasadena
(91101-2430)
PHONE..................626 577-1000
Vince Cuce, *Officer*
Cheree Goodall, *Office Mgr*
EMP: 99
SQ FT: 85,000
SALES (est): 273.9K **Privately Held**
SIC: 7011 Hotels & motels

(P-13080)
PASO ROBLES INN LLC
Also Called: Paso Robles Hotel
1103 Spring St, Paso Robles (93446-2598)
PHONE..................805 238-2660
Fax: 805 238-4707
Paul Wallace, *General Mgr*
Tom Martin, *Owner*
Kim Eady, *Partner*
Andrew Litton, *Partner*
Ken Litton, *Partner*
EMP: 52
SALES (est): 2.5MM **Privately Held**
WEB: www.pasoroblesinn.com
SIC: 7011 5812 5813 Hotels; restaurant, family: independent; cocktail lounge

(P-13081)
PAUL P ORTNER DDS
Also Called: Best Wstn Golden Pheasant Inn
249 N Humboldt Ave, Willows
(95988-2609)
PHONE..................530 934-4603
Fax: 530 934-4275
C Emerson Propps, *Owner*

Michelle Barret, *Manager*
EMP: 65
SALES (corp-wide): 2.3MM **Privately Held**
SIC: 7011 Motel, franchised
PA: Paul P Ortner Dds
    48 Vicente St Ste 1
    San Francisco CA 94127
    415 681-3171

(P-13082)
PAUMA BAND OF MISSION INDIANS
Casino Pauma
777 Pauma Reservation Rd, Pauma Valley
(92061)
P.O. Box 1067 (92061-1067)
PHONE..................760 742-2177
Fax: 760 742-2438
Richard Darder, *CEO*
Marlene Bojorquec, *Vice Chairman*
Anthony Winter, *Administration*
Bud Watkins, *Financial Exec*
D Holland, *Opers Staff*
EMP: 500 **Privately Held**
WEB: www.casinopauma.com
SIC: 7011 Casino hotel
PA: Pauma Band Of Mission Indians
    1010 Pauma Reservation Rd
    Pauma Valley CA 92061
    760 742-1289

(P-13083)
PD HOTEL ASSOCIATES LLC
Also Called: Radisson Hotel Sacramento
500 Leisure Ln, Sacramento (95815-4207)
PHONE..................916 922-2020
Fax: 916 920-7310
Murray Dow,
Jane Dominowski, *Controller*
EMP: 170
SALES (est): 4.2MM
SALES (corp-wide): 153.9MM **Privately Held**
WEB: www.radissonsac.com
SIC: 7011 6514 5812 Hotels & motels; dwelling operators, except apartments; eating places
PA: The Dow Hotel Company Llc
    16400 Southcenter Pkwy # 208
    Tukwila WA 98188
    206 575-3600

(P-13084)
PEACOCK STES RESORT LTD PARTNR
1745 S Anaheim Blvd, Anaheim
(92805-6518)
PHONE..................714 535-8255
Fax: 714 535-8914
Sheldon Ginsburg, *General Ptnr*
Shell Development Corporation-, *General Ptnr*
Perry Snyderman, *General Ptnr*
John Slaughter, *Info Tech Mgr*
Teri Folsom, *Financial Exec*
EMP: 60
SQ FT: 75,000
SALES (est): 2.9MM **Privately Held**
WEB: www.peacocksuitesresort.com
SIC: 7011 Hotels

(P-13085)
PEBBLE BCH RESRT CO DBA LONE C (PA)
Also Called: Pebble Beach Resorts
2700 17 Mile Dr, Pebble Beach
(93953-2668)
P.O. Box 567 (93953-0567)
PHONE..................831 647-7500
Fax: 415 381-3482
Bill Perocchi, *CEO*
Cody Plott, *President*
Dave Heuck, *CFO*
Paul Spengler, *Exec VP*
Mark Stilwell, *Exec VP*
EMP: 134
SQ FT: 2,197
SALES (est): 119.8MM **Privately Held**
WEB: www.pebblebeach.com
SIC: 7011 7992 5941 7991 Resort hotel; public golf courses; golf goods & equipment; tennis goods & equipment; physical fitness facilities

(P-13086)
PEBBLE BEACH CO A LTD PARTNR (PA)
2700 17 Mile Dr, Pebble Beach
(93953-2668)
PHONE..................831 647-7500
Fax: 831 644-7957
Arnold Palmer, *Partner*
Clint Eastwood, *Partner*
Richard Ferris, *Partner*
William Perocchi, *Partner*
Peter Ueberroth, *Partner*
EMP: 51
SALES (est): 4.1MM **Privately Held**
SIC: 7011 Resort hotel

(P-13087)
PECHANGA DEVELOPMENT CORP
Also Called: Pechanga Resort & Casino
45000 Pechanga Pkwy, Temecula
(92592-5810)
P.O. Box 9041 (92589-9041)
PHONE..................951 695-4655
Fax: 951 303-2571
Patrick Murphy, *President*
Jerry Konchar, *CFO*
Jared Munoa, *Treasurer*
Gilbert Mendoza, *Exec VP*
Scott Mallory, *Senior VP*
EMP: 4000
SALES (est): 206.1MM **Privately Held**
WEB: www.pechangarv.com
SIC: 7011 7929 7999 Hotels & motels; entertainment service; gambling establishment

(P-13088)
PELORIA BRIDGE BAY LLC
10300 Bridge Bay Rd, Redding
(96003-9418)
PHONE..................530 275-3021
Shelly Davis, *Accounting Mgr*
EMP: 75
SALES: 5.3MM
SALES (corp-wide): 7MM **Privately Held**
WEB: www.sevencrown.com
SIC: 7011 Resort hotel
PA: Peloria Marinas Llc
    2550 Via Tejon Ste 2b
    Palos Verdes Estates CA 90274
    310 363-7775

(P-13089)
PEPPER TREE INN
Also Called: Rodeway Inn
645 N Lake Blvd, Tahoe City (96145)
P.O. Box 29 (96145-0029)
PHONE..................530 583-3711
Fax: 530 583-6938
Thomas Brown, *Manager*
EMP: 65
SQ FT: 18,609
SALES (corp-wide): 3.1MM **Privately Held**
WEB: www.pismosands.com
SIC: 7011 Hotels & motels
PA: Pepper Tree Inn
    998 Hilmar St
    Santa Clara CA 95050
    408 293-4196

(P-13090)
PEPPERMILL CASINOS INC
4021 Port Chicago Hwy, Concord
(94520-1122)
PHONE..................925 671-7711
Ronald Rives, *Manager*
EMP: 200
SALES (corp-wide): 243.1MM **Privately Held**
WEB: www.thepeppermillcasinonv.com
SIC: 7011 7999 Casino hotel; gambling establishment
PA: Peppermill Casinos, Inc.
    90 W Grove St Ste 600
    Reno NV 89509
    775 689-8900

(P-13091)
PHF II BURBANK LLC
Also Called: Burbank Airport Marriott Hotel
2500 N Hollywood Way, Burbank
(91505-1019)
PHONE..................818 843-6000

PRODUCTS & SERVICES SECTION

7011 - Hotels, Motels & Tourist Courts County (P-13115)

Linda Davey, *Human Res Mgr*
Connie Tejeira, *Controller*
Linda McDonnel, *Human Res Dir*
Sharon Estep, *Sales Mgr*
EMP: 220
SALES (est): 10MM **Privately Held**
SIC: 7011 Hotels & motels

(P-13092)
PHF RUBY LLC
Also Called: Pier 2620 Ht Fishermans Wharf
2620 Jones St, San Francisco (94133-1306)
PHONE....................415 885-4700
Jose L Torres,
Luis Alvarado, *Exec Dir*
Pat Sorber, *Admin Mgr*
Jim Turner, *General Mgr*
Scott Fleming, *Controller*
EMP: 118
SALES (est): 8.4MM **Privately Held**
SIC: 7011 7991 5813 5812 Hotel, franchised; physical fitness facilities; drinking places; eating places

(P-13093)
PHOENIX LOUNGE AND CASINO
5948 Auburn Blvd Ste M, Citrus Heights (95621-6052)
PHONE....................916 334-4225
Fax: 916 334-9261
Jack Cunningham, *Owner*
EMP: 100
SQ FT: 3,500
SALES (est): 4MM **Privately Held**
WEB: www.phoenixlounge.com
SIC: 7011 5813 Casino hotel; cocktail lounge

(P-13094)
PICCADILLY HOSPITALITY LLC
Also Called: Piccadilly Inn Shaw
2305 W Shaw Ave, Fresno (93711-3411)
PHONE....................559 348-5520
Mu-Pien Chien, *President*
Gene Chien, *Vice Pres*
EMP: 50 **EST:** 2012
SALES (est): 1.4MM **Privately Held**
SIC: 7011 Hotels

(P-13095)
PIER PONT HOTEL LP
550 San Jon Rd, Ventura (93001-3745)
PHONE....................805 643-6144
Joseph Fan, *Mng Member*
EMP: 50
SALES (est): 692.9K **Privately Held**
SIC: 7011 Hotels

(P-13096)
PINE & POWELL PARTNERS LLC
Also Called: Stanford Court Hotel
905 California St, San Francisco (94108-2201)
PHONE....................415 989-3500
Naveen Kakarla,
Michael Baier,
Rosanna Harrison,
EMP: 99
SQ FT: 287,000
SALES (est): 273.9K **Privately Held**
SIC: 7011 Hotels & motels

(P-13097)
PINNACLE 1617 LLC
Also Called: Four Points By Sheraton
1617 1st Ave, San Diego (92101-3003)
PHONE....................619 239-9600
Bharat Lall,
Sue Depascale, *Partner*
Hema Lall, *Partner*
EMP: 50
SALES (est): 3.7MM **Privately Held**
SIC: 7011 Hotels & motels

(P-13098)
PINNACLE HOTELS USA INC
8369 Vickers St Ste 101, San Diego (92111-2113)
PHONE....................858 974-8201
Fax: 858 974-8203
Bharat Lall, *CEO*
Hema Lall, *Corp Secy*
Oswin Riquenes, *Executive*
Dominic Chevalier, *General Mgr*

Maria Rebollar, *General Mgr*
EMP: 53 **EST:** 1999
SALES (est): 8.2MM **Privately Held**
SIC: 7011 Hotels & motels

(P-13099)
PINNACLE RVRSIDE HSPITALITY LP
Also Called: Riverside Marriott
3400 Market St, Riverside (92501-2826)
PHONE....................951 784-8000
Dr Bharat Lall, *General Ptnr*
Tom Donaue, *General Mgr*
Rowena Seward, *Controller*
Angelica Rivera, *Human Res Mgr*
Debra Lusby, *Sales Dir*
EMP: 190
SALES (est): 6.2MM **Privately Held**
SIC: 7011 Hotels & motels

(P-13100)
PIONEER SQUARE HOTEL COMPANY
1940 Fillmore St, San Francisco (94115-2745)
PHONE....................415 346-2323
Bart Seidler, *President*
EMP: 50
SALES (est): 1.5MM **Privately Held**
SIC: 7011 Hotels

(P-13101)
PISMO COAST VILLAGE INC
165 S Dolliver St, Pismo Beach (93449-2999)
PHONE....................805 773-5649
Fax: 805 773-1507
Jay Jamison, *General Mgr*
Ronald Nunlist, *President*
Wayne Hardesty, *CFO*
Terris Hughes, *Exec VP*
Dwight Plumley, *Vice Pres*
EMP: 60
SALES (est): 7.6MM **Privately Held**
WEB: www.pismocoastvillage.com
SIC: 7011 Resort hotel

(P-13102)
PLAZA SUITES
3100 Lakeside Dr, Santa Clara (95054-2804)
PHONE....................408 748-9800
Scott Seymore, *Principal*
Rose Criado, *Executive*
Jean Roilet, *General Mgr*
Jean Roilet, *General Mgr*
Michael David, *Mktg Dir*
EMP: 61
SALES (est): 4.8MM **Privately Held**
WEB: www.theplazasuites.com
SIC: 7011 Hotels

(P-13103)
PLEASANT CANYON HOTEL INC
Also Called: Residence Inn By Marriott
11920 Dublin Canyon Rd, Pleasanton (94588-2818)
PHONE....................925 847-0535
Fax: 925 828-1199
James Evans, *CFO*
Samir Zarour, *Vice Pres*
Karen Gum, *General Mgr*
EMP: 50 **EST:** 1996
SQ FT: 98,496
SALES (est): 3.1MM **Privately Held**
SIC: 7011 Hotels & motels

(P-13104)
PONTE VINEYARD INN
35001 Rancho Cal Rd, Temecula (92591-4008)
PHONE....................951 587-6688
Sarah Martinez, *General Mgr*
Crystal Stadel, *Sales Dir*
EMP: 75 **EST:** 2012
SALES (est): 233.5K
SALES (corp-wide): 1.3MM **Privately Held**
SIC: 7011 Hotels
PA: Pointe Family Estate
35001 Rancho Cal Rd
Temecula CA 92591
951 587-6688

(P-13105)
PORTFOLIO HOTELS & RESORTS LLC
Also Called: Casa Munras Garden Hotel
700 Munras Ave, Monterey (93940-3110)
PHONE....................831 375-2411
Meredith Wood, *Principal*
Everett Ely, *General Mgr*
Tom Macdonald, *Administration*
Meridth Wood, *Manager*
EMP: 50
SALES (corp-wide): 3.1MM **Privately Held**
SIC: 7011 Hotels & motels
PA: Portfolio Hotels & Resorts, Llc
601 Oakmont Ln Ste 420
Westmont IL 60559
630 366-2018

(P-13106)
PORTOFINO HOTEL PARTNERS LP
Also Called: Hotel Portofino
260 Portofino Way, Redondo Beach (90277-2033)
PHONE....................310 379-8481
Fax: 310 406-2509
Glenn Bishop, *Principal*
Tanya Firman, *General Mgr*
Malia Osterbauer, *General Mgr*
L Routh, *Director*
Lori Benjamins, *Manager*
EMP: 151
SALES (est): 12.4MM **Privately Held**
WEB: www.hotelportofino.com
SIC: 7011 Hotels & motels

(P-13107)
PORTOFINO INN & SUITES ANAHEIM
1831 S Harbor Blvd, Anaheim (92802-3509)
PHONE....................714 782-7600
Fax: 714 782-7619
Jennifer Reihl, *Director*
Edgar Rosas, *Office Mgr*
Ricardo De La Torre, *Chief Engr*
Matthew Lacy, *Controller*
Esequiel Munoz, *Sales Mgr*
EMP: 727
SALES (est): 22.6MM
SALES (corp-wide): 67.4MM **Privately Held**
SIC: 7011 Inns
PA: Tarsadia Hotels
620 Newport Center Dr # 1400
Newport Beach CA 92660
949 610-8000

(P-13108)
POSADA ROYALE HOTEL & SUITES
1775 Madera Rd, Simi Valley (93065-3049)
PHONE....................805 584-6300
Larry Rogers, *Partner*
Peter Zegers, *Partner*
Miller Vargas, *General Mgr*
Surech Patel, *Manager*
Chavini Patel, *Asst Mgr*
EMP: 50
SQ FT: 55,000
SALES (est): 3.4MM **Privately Held**
WEB: www.posadaroyale.com
SIC: 7011 5812 7389 7299 Hotels; American restaurant; convention & show services; banquet hall facilities

(P-13109)
POST STREET RENAISSANCE
Also Called: Prescott Hotel, The
545 Post St, San Francisco (94102-1228)
PHONE....................415 563-0303
Fax: 415 563-6831
John Dern, *President*
Baltazar Ceja, *Chief Engr*
EMP: 300
SALES (est): 18.1MM
SALES (corp-wide): 1.8B **Privately Held**
WEB: www.prescotthotel.com
SIC: 7011 Hotels
HQ: Kimpton Hotel & Restaurant Group Llc
222 Kearny St Ste 200
San Francisco CA 94108
415 397-5572

(P-13110)
PRESIDIO HOTEL GROUP LLC
Also Called: Fairfield Inn
10713 White Rock Rd, Rancho Cordova (95670-6031)
PHONE....................916 631-7500
Fax: 916 631-7500
Sushil Patel, *Branch Mgr*
David Ho, *Vice Pres*
Jaime Suarez, *Controller*
Dale Harvey, *Director*
Mark Marques, *Manager*
EMP: 67
SALES (corp-wide): 10.5MM **Privately Held**
SIC: 7011 Hotels & motels
PA: Presidio Hotel Group, Llc
1011 10th St
Sacramento CA 95814
707 429-6000

(P-13111)
PROFICIENT LLC
Also Called: Crowne Plz Los Angeles Hbr Ht
601 S Palos Verdes St, San Pedro (90731-3329)
PHONE....................310 519-8200
Joyce Wang, *Principal*
Charlene Tritipeskul, *Director*
Magda Khordoc, *Manager*
EMP: 99
SALES (est): 2.6MM **Privately Held**
SIC: 7011 Hotels & motels

(P-13112)
PRUTEL JOINT VENTURE
Also Called: Ritz-Carlton Laguna Niguel
1 Ritz Carlton Dr, Dana Point (92629-4205)
PHONE....................949 240-2000
Fax: 949 240-0829
W B Johnson, *Partner*
Prudential Realty, *Partner*
Paul Patterson, *CFO*
Brie Jones, *Social Dir*
Mike Williams, *Engineer*
EMP: 700
SALES (est): 32.4MM **Privately Held**
SIC: 7011 Hotels & motels

(P-13113)
PT GAMING LLC
970 W 190th St Ste 400, Torrance (90502-1065)
PHONE....................323 260-5060
Patrick Tierney, *Mng Member*
David Shindle, *COO*
Jamie Breen, *Controller*
EMP: 700
SQ FT: 7,000
SALES (est): 17.1MM **Privately Held**
SIC: 7011 Casino hotel

(P-13114)
PYRAMID ADVISORS LLC
Also Called: Pleasanton Marriott
11950 Dublin Canyon Rd, Pleasanton (94588-2818)
PHONE....................925 847-6000
Norval Nelson, *General Mgr*
Karen Gum, *General Mgr*
Jeffery Blair, *Sales Staff*
EMP: 70
SALES (corp-wide): 175.5MM **Privately Held**
SIC: 7011 Hotels & motels
PA: Pyramid Advisors Llc
1 Post Office Sq Ste 1950
Boston MA 02109
617 202-2033

(P-13115)
Q S H PROPERTIES INC
Also Called: Quality Suites Hotel
2701 Hotel Ter, Santa Ana (92705-5603)
PHONE....................714 957-9200
Vahi M Melkonian, *President*
Donna Walp, *General Mgr*
Gonzalo Rodriguez, *Chief Engr*
Cheng Wu, *Manager*
EMP: 52
SALES (est): 2.6MM **Privately Held**
SIC: 7011 Hotels & motels

7011 - Hotels, Motels & Tourist Courts County (P-13116) PRODUDUCTS & SERVICES SECTION

(P-13116)
Q S SAN LUIS OBISPO LP
Also Called: San Luis Obispo Quality Suites
1631 Monterey St, San Luis Obispo (93401-2929)
PHONE..................805 541-5001
Fax: 805 546-9475
George Newland, *Partner*
Harold Parker, *General Ptnr*
Robert Warmington, *General Ptnr*
Christopher Houston, *Accounts Mgr*
EMP: 50
SALES (est): 2MM **Privately Held**
SIC: 7011 Hotels & motels

(P-13117)
QUAIL LODGE INC
Also Called: Covey, The
8205 Valley Greens Dr, Carmel (93923-9513)
PHONE..................831 624-1581
Fax: 831 624-8481
Clement Kwok, *CEO*
William Lawson Little, *Vice Pres*
Gabriel Braganza, *Controller*
Kerfoot Hughes, *Broker*
Drew Drier, *Sls & Mktg Exec*
▲ **EMP:** 250
SQ FT: 20,000
SALES (est): 25.3MM **Privately Held**
WEB: www.quaillodge.com
SIC: 7011 7997 7389 5941 Resort hotel; golf club, membership; convention & show services; golf goods & equipment; eating places; subdividers & developers

(P-13118)
QUEENSBAY HOTEL LLC
Also Called: Hotel Maya
700 Queensway Dr, Long Beach (90802-6343)
PHONE..................562 481-3910
Cherie Davis, *Manager*
David Aubuchon, *Controller*
EMP: 100
SALES (corp-wide): 6.2MM **Privately Held**
SIC: 7011 Hotels & motels
PA: Queensbay Hotel, Llc
    444 W Ocean Blvd
    Long Beach CA 90802
    562 628-0625

(P-13119)
R C HOTELS INC
Also Called: Hotel On Huntington Beach
7667 Center Ave, Huntington Beach (92647-3073)
PHONE..................714 891-0123
Toll Free:..................877 -
Fax: 714 895-4591
Shu Chin Kou, *President*
Tan Pham, *Engineer*
Joe Tsai, *Accountant*
Christopher Deguzman, *Sales Mgr*
EMP: 60
SQ FT: 114,012
SALES (est): 3.9MM **Privately Held**
SIC: 7011 Hotels

(P-13120)
R P S RESORT CORP
1600 N Indian Canyon Dr, Palm Springs (92262-4602)
PHONE..................760 327-8311
Douglas McCarron, *President*
Robert Bartley, *Info Tech Mgr*
EMP: 250
SALES (est): 2.3MM
SALES (corp-wide): 41MM **Privately Held**
WEB: www.psriv.com
SIC: 7011 Resort hotel
HQ: The San Bernardino Hilton
    285 E Hospitality Ln
    San Bernardino CA 92408
    909 889-0133

(P-13121)
RADISSON HT FISHERMANS WHARF
250 Beach St, San Francisco (94133-1291)
PHONE..................415 392-6700
Fax: 415 392-6700
John Sevilla, *General Mgr*

Ronald Diaz, *Human Resources*
EMP: 100
SALES (est): 6.4MM **Privately Held**
SIC: 7011 Hotels & motels

(P-13122)
RADISSON SUITES HOTEL BUENA PK
7762 Beach Blvd, Buena Park (90620-1935)
PHONE..................714 739-5600
Kevin Clayton, *Principal*
EMP: 65
SALES: 980K **Privately Held**
SIC: 7011 Hotels & motels

(P-13123)
RADLAX GATEWAY HOTEL LLC
Also Called: Radisson Inn
6225 W Century Blvd, Los Angeles (90045-5311)
PHONE..................310 670-9000
Peter Dumon, *Mng Member*
John Lazaro, *Accountant*
Evelin Alvarado, *Human Res Mgr*
Rufino Silviera, *Accounts Mgr*
EMP: 300
SALES (est): 620K
SALES (corp-wide): 3.1MM **Privately Held**
SIC: 7011 Hotels & motels
PA: Portfolio Hotels & Resorts, Llc
    601 Oakmont Ln Ste 420
    Westmont IL 60559
    630 366-2018

(P-13124)
RAFFLES LRMITAGE BEVERLY HILLS
Also Called: L'Ermitage Hotel
9291 Burton Way, Beverly Hills (90210-3709)
PHONE..................310 278-3344
Jack Naderkhani, *General Mgr*
Aaron Traylor, *Finance*
Alfonso Vazquez, *Purch Dir*
EMP: 249
SALES (est): 12.1MM
SALES (corp-wide): 27.3MM **Privately Held**
SIC: 7011 5813 5812 Hotels & motels; drinking places; eating places
HQ: Raffles International Limited
    250 North Bridge Road
    Singapore 17910
    633 983-77

(P-13125)
RALEIGH ENTERPRISES INC (PA)
Also Called: Raleigh Holdings
5300 Melrose Ave Fl 4, Los Angeles (90038-5114)
PHONE..................310 899-8900
Fax: 310 899-8910
Kristen J Raleigh, *CEO*
George I Rosenthal, *Ch of Bd*
Mark Rosenthal, *President*
Michael Donahue, *COO*
Josie Lewis, *Info Tech Mgr*
EMP: 130
SQ FT: 20,000
SALES (est): 34.2MM **Privately Held**
WEB: www.raleighenterprises.com
SIC: 7011 Hotels

(P-13126)
RAMADA PLAZA HT ANAHEIM RESORT
515 W Katella Ave, Anaheim (92802-3609)
PHONE..................714 991-6868
Fax: 714 991-6565
Stephen Hsu, *Owner*
Mimi Jong, *Facilities Mgr*
EMP: 200
SALES (est): 3.2MM **Privately Held**
SIC: 7011 Hotels & motels

(P-13127)
RANCHO BERNARDO PARTNERS LTD
Also Called: Radisson Inn
11520 W Bernardo Ct, San Diego (92127-1602)
P.O. Box 1538, San Marcos (92079-1538)
PHONE..................858 451-6600
Fax: 651 451-5629
Jonathan Jacobs, *Managing Prtnr*
Duke Sobek, *General Mgr*
Rhonda O Leary, *Sales Executive*
Scott Hardison, *Sales Engr*
Tammie Wheatley, *Manager*
EMP: 60
SQ FT: 87,214
SALES (est): 3.5MM **Privately Held**
SIC: 7011 Hotels & motels

(P-13128)
RANCHO LEONERO RESORT
5671 Palmer Way Ste E, Carlsbad (92010-7256)
PHONE..................760 438-2905
Genie Ireland, *Owner*
John Ireland, *Partner*
Eugenie Ireland, *Manager*
EMP: 50
SALES (est): 1.7MM **Privately Held**
SIC: 7011 Resort hotel

(P-13129)
RANCHO VALENCIA RESORT
5921 Valencia Cir, Rancho Santa Fe (92067-9520)
P.O. Box 9126 (92067-4126)
PHONE..................858 756-1123
Fax: 858 756-0165
Jeffrey Essakow, *Mng Member*
Beverley Matthews, *General Mgr*
Mark Blevins, *Finance*
Nicole Sharp, *Mktg Dir*
Hal Jacobs,
EMP: 300
SALES (est): 27.5MM **Privately Held**
WEB: www.ranchovalencia.com
SIC: 7011 Resort hotel

(P-13130)
RBD HOTEL PALM SPRINGS LLC
Also Called: Hyatt Rgency Suites Palm Sprng
285 N Palm Canyon Dr, Palm Springs (92262-5525)
PHONE..................760 322-1383
Larry Mills, *Senior VP*
Jamye Claren, *Engineer*
Jayme McLaren, *Engineer*
Jamye McLaren, *Chief Engr*
EMP: 75
SALES: 950K **Privately Held**
SIC: 7011 Hotels & motels

(P-13131)
RECP CY OXNARD LLC
Also Called: Courtyard By Marriott Oxnard
600 E Esplanade Dr, Oxnard (93036-2403)
PHONE..................805 604-7527
Mary Reece, *Principal*
Maria Zavala, *Financial Exec*
Recp III Cal West Hotels LLC, *Mng Member*
Patrick Mullin, *Manager*
EMP: 70
SQ FT: 103,000
SALES (est): 3.3MM **Privately Held**
SIC: 7011 Hotels & motels

(P-13132)
RECP RI OXNARD LLC
Also Called: Residnce Inn By Mrriott Oxnard
2101 W Vineyard Ave, Oxnard (93036-2268)
PHONE..................805 278-2200
Doug Pflaumer, *Manager*
Millicent Bennett, *Principal*
Recp III Cal West Hotels LLC, *Mng Member*
David Dreher, *Manager*
EMP: 150
SQ FT: 103,000
SALES (est): 4.3MM **Privately Held**
SIC: 7011 Hotels & motels

(P-13133)
RECP/WNDSOR SCRAMENTO VENTR LP
Also Called: Windsor Capital Hotel Group
4422 Y St, Sacramento (95817-2220)
PHONE..................916 455-6800
Mike Cryan, *CEO*
Recp Windsor Rim Sacramento GP, *General Ptnr*
Douglas Warren, *General Mgr*
EMP: 72
SALES (est): 1.9MM **Privately Held**
SIC: 7011 Hotels

(P-13134)
RED EARTH CASINO
3089 Norm Niver Rd, Thermal (92274-6550)
PHONE..................760 395-1200
Fax: 760 395-0408
Andrew Miranda, *General Mgr*
Nigel White, *Owner*
Carl Lucas, *CFO*
John Evanoff, *Info Tech Mgr*
Jose Mariscal, *Engineer*
EMP: 150
SQ FT: 15,000
SALES (est): 9.3MM **Privately Held**
SIC: 7011 Casino hotel

(P-13135)
RED LION HOTELS CORPORATION
Also Called: Red Lion Hotel Anaheim
1850 S Harbor Blvd, Anaheim (92802-3510)
PHONE..................714 750-2801
Joseph Mollerus, *Branch Mgr*
EMP: 86
SALES (corp-wide): 142.9MM **Publicly Held**
WEB: www.westcoasthotels.com
SIC: 7011 5813 5812 7991 Hotels & motels; cocktail lounge; American restaurant; physical fitness facilities
PA: Red Lion Hotels Corporation
    201 W North River Dr # 100
    Spokane WA 99201
    509 459-6100

(P-13136)
REDDING RANCHERIA (PA)
Also Called: Win River Casino Bingo
2000 Redding Rancheria Rd, Redding (96001-5528)
PHONE..................530 225-8979
Fax: 530 241-1879
Tracy Edward, *CEO*
Stacey Carman, *COO*
Christi Hines, *CFO*
Tamra Olson, *CFO*
Renee Wolfe, *Pharmacy Dir*
EMP: 60
SQ FT: 16,360
SALES (est): 40MM **Privately Held**
WEB: www.redding-rancheria.com
SIC: 7011 9131 Hotels & motels

(P-13137)
REICHERT LENGFELD LTD PARTNR
Also Called: RI Properties
725 Folger Ave, Albany (94710-2809)
PHONE..................510 845-1077
Diana R Meyer, *Partner*
Herbert R Meyer, *General Ptnr*
EMP: 90
SQ FT: 1,500
SALES (est): 3.5MM **Privately Held**
SIC: 7011 Hotels & motels

(P-13138)
REMINGTON HOTEL CORPORATION
Also Called: Palm Springs Renaissance
888 E Tahquitz Canyon Way, Palm Springs (92262-6708)
PHONE..................760 322-6000
EMP: 85
SALES (corp-wide): 369.8MM **Privately Held**
SIC: 7011 Hotels & motels

PRODUCTS & SERVICES SECTION
7011 - Hotels, Motels & Tourist Courts County (P-13162)

PA: Remington Hotel Corporation
14185 Dallas Pkwy # 1150
Dallas TX 75254
972 980-2700

(P-13139)
REMINGTON LDGING HSPTALITY LLC
Bardessono Hotel
6526 Yount St, Yountville (94599-1270)
PHONE..........................877 932-5333
Phillip G Sherburne, *Branch Mgr*
Jim Tredway, *General Mgr*
Tess Allen, *VP Mktg*
Kristi Klein, *Sales Dir*
Kini Parente, *Sales Dir*
EMP: 1305
SALES (corp-wide): 115.5MM **Privately Held**
SIC: 7011 Hotels
PA: Remington Lodging & Hospitality Llc
14185 Dallas Pkwy # 1150
Dallas TX 75254
972 980-2700

(P-13140)
RENAISSANCE HOTEL CLUBSPORT
50 Enterprise, Aliso Viejo (92656-6026)
PHONE..........................949 643-6700
Fax: 949 643-7950
Ed Tomlin, *General Mgr*
Julio Garneff, *Executive*
Michell Gullett, *Info Tech Mgr*
Damon Durante, *Sales Staff*
EMP: 61
SALES (est): 4.7MM **Privately Held**
SIC: 7011 Hotels & motels

(P-13141)
RENAISSANCE HOTEL HOLDINGS INC
1325 Broadway, Sonoma (95476-7505)
PHONE..........................707 935-6600
Dave Dalquist, *General Mgr*
Ruth Benett, *Executive Asst*
Patty Field, *Manager*
Gina Thayer, *Manager*
EMP: 99
SALES (est): 1.7MM **Privately Held**
SIC: 7011 Hotels & motels

(P-13142)
RENAISSANCE HOTEL OPERATING CO
Also Called: Renaissance Indian Wells
44400 Indian Wells Ln, Indian Wells (92210-8708)
PHONE..........................760 773-4444
Tom Tabler, *Branch Mgr*
EMP: 600
SALES (corp-wide): 871.6MM **Privately Held**
WEB: www.renaissancehotel.com
SIC: 7011 Hotels
PA: Renaissance Hotel Operating Company, Inc
10400 Fernwood Rd
Bethesda MD 20817
301 380-3000

(P-13143)
RENAISSNCE ESMRALDA RESORT SPA
44400 Indian Wells Ln, Indian Wells (92210-8708)
PHONE..........................760 773-4444
Fax: 760 346-9308
John Kalinski, *Principal*
Terry Venema, *Engineer*
Robert Lander, *Marketing Staff*
Brian Parsons, *Accounts Exec*
EMP: 66
SALES (est): 4.6MM **Privately Held**
SIC: 7011 Hotels & motels

(P-13144)
RENESON HOTELS INC (PA)
Also Called: Carriage Inn
2700 Junipero Serra Blvd, Daly City (94015-1634)
PHONE..........................650 449-5353
Alrene Flynn, *Chairman*
Garrett Grialou, *President*
Doug Sherer, *CFO*
Diane Grialou, *Admin Sec*
Ricky Dang, *Controller*
EMP: 100
SALES (est): 13.6MM **Privately Held**
WEB: www.renesonhotels.com
SIC: 7011 Hotels

(P-13145)
RENESON HOTELS INC
Also Called: Hotel Britton
112 7th St, San Francisco (94103-2809)
PHONE..........................415 621-7001
Norman Onaga, *General Mgr*
Anni Sauerlender, *Human Res Dir*
Marlene Merino, *Sales Staff*
EMP: 150
SALES (corp-wide): 13.6MM **Privately Held**
WEB: www.renesonhotels.com
SIC: 7011 Motels
PA: Reneson Hotels, Inc.
2700 Junipero Serra Blvd
Daly City CA 94015
650 449-5353

(P-13146)
RESIDENCE INN BY MARRIOTT
5322 N Diana St, Fresno (93710-6700)
PHONE..........................559 222-8900
Fax: 559 222-9089
Juliee May, *Principal*
Juliee May, *Manager*
EMP: 80
SALES (est): 2MM **Privately Held**
SIC: 7011 Hotels & motels

(P-13147)
RESIDENCE INN BY MARRIOTT
1700 S Clementine St, Anaheim (92802-2909)
PHONE..........................714 533-3555
Rosa Cook, *General Mgr*
EMP: 80
SALES (est): 1.5MM **Privately Held**
SIC: 7011 Hotels & motels

(P-13148)
RESIDENCE INN BY MARRIOTT
11002 Rancho Carmel Dr, San Diego (92128-4288)
PHONE..........................858 673-1900
Casey Grieme, *Manager*
Ketra Slayton, *Manager*
Ryan Shanahan, *Asst Mgr*
EMP: 80
SALES (est): 1.9MM **Privately Held**
SIC: 7011 Hotels & motels

(P-13149)
RESIDENCE INN BY MARRIOTT
700 W Kimberly Ave, Placentia (92870-6329)
PHONE..........................714 996-0555
Fax: 714 993-1043
Paulette Lombrodi, *Principal*
Audun Poulsen, *General Mgr*
Nancy Medrano, *Manager*
EMP: 80
SALES (est): 2.3MM **Privately Held**
SIC: 7011 Hotels & motels

(P-13150)
RESORT AT PELICAN HILL LLC
22701 Pelican Hill Rd S, Newport Coast (92657-2008)
PHONE..........................949 467-6800
Elia Gutierrez, *Director*
Jean Dubray, *Executive*
Zully Cardona, *Manager*
Jay Colliatie, *Manager*
EMP: 208
SALES (est): 26.1MM **Privately Held**
SIC: 7011 Resort hotel

(P-13151)
REX RISING L P
Also Called: Hotel Rex
562 Sutter St, San Francisco (94102-1102)
PHONE..........................415 273-9790
Chip Conley, *Partner*
Joyce Curley, *Controller*
Nancy Chen, *Manager*
EMP: 58
SALES (est): 2.6MM
SALES (corp-wide): 930.9MM **Publicly Held**
SIC: 7011 Hotels & motels
PA: Diamondrock Hospitality Co
3 Bethesda Metro Ctr # 1500
Bethesda MD 20814
240 744-1150

(P-13152)
RIO VISTA DEVELOPMENT COMPANY (PA)
Also Called: Holiday Inn Universal Studios
4222 Vineland Ave, North Hollywood (91602-3318)
PHONE..........................818 980-8000
Scott Mills, *General Ptnr*
Chef Csotai, *Executive*
Ivan A Fuerte, *Executive*
Lily Swearingen, *Technology*
Steve Eisenberg, *Technical Staff*
EMP: 69
SQ FT: 100,000
SALES (est): 11.3MM **Privately Held**
WEB: www.beverlygarland.com
SIC: 7011 Hotels & motels

(P-13153)
RITZ-CARLTON HOTEL COMPANY LLC
690 Market St, San Francisco (94104-5101)
PHONE..........................415 781-9000
Fax: 415 247-1145
John Fitzgerald, *Branch Mgr*
Erin Lasser, *Mktg Dir*
EMP: 343
SALES (corp-wide): 14.4B **Publicly Held**
SIC: 7011 Hotels & motels
HQ: The Ritz-Carlton Hotel Company Llc
4445 Willard Ave Ste 800
Chevy Chase MD 20815
301 547-4700

(P-13154)
RITZ-CARLTON HOTEL COMPANY LLC
Also Called: Ritz Carlton
68900 Frank Sinatra Dr, Rancho Mirage (92270-5300)
PHONE..........................760 321-8282
Carlton Ritz, *Branch Mgr*
Gary Ardrey, *General Mgr*
Raul Salcido, *General Mgr*
Alaine Lewis, *Office Mgr*
Amy Campbell, *Pub Rel Dir*
EMP: 349
SALES (corp-wide): 14.4B **Publicly Held**
SIC: 7011 Hotels & motels
HQ: The Ritz-Carlton Hotel Company Llc
4445 Willard Ave Ste 800
Chevy Chase MD 20815
301 547-4700

(P-13155)
RITZ-CARLTON HOTEL COMPANY LLC
1 Ritz Carlton Dr, Dana Point (92629-4206)
PHONE..........................949 240-5020
John Dravinski, *General Mgr*
Marguerite Dowd, *Admin Asst*
Paul Sanudo, *Administration*
Wes Kowalczyk, *Chief Engr*
Sara Bodenhamer, *Sales Staff*
EMP: 348
SALES (corp-wide): 14.4B **Publicly Held**
SIC: 7011 Hotels & motels
HQ: The Ritz-Carlton Hotel Company Llc
4445 Willard Ave Ste 800
Chevy Chase MD 20815
301 547-4700

(P-13156)
RITZ-CARLTON HOTEL COMPANY LLC
Also Called: Ritz-Carlton San Francisco
600 Stockton St, San Francisco (94108-2386)
PHONE..........................415 773-6168
Fax: 415 291-0147
Edward Madey, *Manager*
Jo-Anne Hill, *President*
Edward Mady, *COO*
Ed Mady, *General Mgr*
Nickolas Tice, *General Mgr*
EMP: 500
SALES (corp-wide): 14.4B **Publicly Held**
WEB: www.ritz-carlton.com
SIC: 7011 Hotels & motels
HQ: The Ritz-Carlton Hotel Company Llc
4445 Willard Ave Ste 800
Chevy Chase MD 20815
301 547-4700

(P-13157)
RITZ-CARLTON HOTEL COMPANY LLC
Also Called: Ritz Carlton Rancho Mirage
68900 Frank Sinatra Dr, Rancho Mirage (92270-5300)
PHONE..........................760 321-8282
Fax: 760 321-6928
James H Pallin Jr, *Manager*
Herbert Spiegel, *Manager*
Regula Wipf, *Manager*
EMP: 313
SALES (corp-wide): 14.4B **Publicly Held**
WEB: www.ritz-carlton.com
SIC: 7011 Hotels & motels
HQ: The Ritz-Carlton Hotel Company Llc
4445 Willard Ave Ste 800
Chevy Chase MD 20815
301 547-4700

(P-13158)
RITZ-CARLTON MARINA DEL REY
4375 Admiralty Way, Marina Del Rey (90292-5434)
PHONE..........................310 823-1700
Fax: 310 823-2403
Robert Thomas, *Principal*
EMP: 97
SALES (est): 7MM **Privately Held**
SIC: 7011 Hotels & motels

(P-13159)
RIVER ROCK ENTERTAINMENT AUTH
Also Called: River Rock Casino
3250 Highway 128, Geyserville (95441-8908)
PHONE..........................707 857-2777
David Fendrick, *CEO*
Joseph R Callahan, *CFO*
Jerry Arretche, *Info Tech Dir*
Greg Bentall, *Finance Dir*
Steven Delira, *Analyst*
EMP: 616
SALES (est): 19.5MM **Privately Held**
SIC: 7011 Casino hotel

(P-13160)
RIVIERA REINCARNATE LLC
Also Called: Palm Sprng Riviera Resorts Spa
1600 N Indian Canyon Dr, Palm Springs (92262-4602)
PHONE..........................760 327-8311
Fax: 760 778-0305
Jim Manion,
Emely Soto, *Asst Controller*
Adam Sachaffer, *Accountant*
Heidi Walker, *Mktg Coord*
EMP: 87
SALES (est): 10.3MM **Privately Held**
SIC: 7011 Resort hotel

(P-13161)
RL EUREKA LLC
Also Called: Red Lion Hotel Eureka
1929 4th St, Eureka (95501-0725)
PHONE..........................707 268-8341
Fax: 707 445-2752
Joseph Mollerus,
EMP: 64
SALES (est): 2.7MM
SALES (corp-wide): 142.9MM **Publicly Held**
WEB: www.westcoasthotels.com
SIC: 7011 Hotels & motels
HQ: RI Venture Llc
201 W North River Dr # 100
Spokane WA 99201
509 459-6100

(P-13162)
RL REDDING LLC
Also Called: Red Lion Hotel Redding
1830 Hilltop Dr, Redding (96002-0212)
PHONE..........................530 221-8700

7011 - Hotels, Motels & Tourist Courts County (P-13163)

PRODUDUCTS & SERVICES SECTION

Fax: 530 221-0324
Joseph Mollerus,
Chris Korologos, *Director*
EMP: 66
SALES (est): 2.7MM
SALES (corp-wide): 142.9MM **Publicly Held**
WEB: www.westcoasthotels.com
SIC: **7011** Hotels & motels
HQ: Rl Venture Llc
  201 W North River Dr # 100
  Spokane WA 99201
  509 459-6100

(P-13163)
RLJHGN EMERYVILLE LESSEE LP
Also Called: Hilton
1800 Powell St, Emeryville (94608-1808)
PHONE....................510 658-9300
Mark Burden, *CEO*
Jeff Virgil, *CFO*
Dorota Wossner, *Social Dir*
Eduardo Alcocer, *General Mgr*
Elizabeth Goss, *Controller*
EMP: 120
SQ FT: 476
SALES (est): 7.5MM **Privately Held**
SIC: **7011** Hotels & motels

(P-13164)
RMS FOUNDATION INC
Also Called: Queen Mary Hotel
1126 Queens Hwy, Long Beach (90802-6331)
PHONE....................562 435-3511
Fax: 562 436-3185
Joseph F Prevratil, *President*
Edgar Stevens, *COO*
Angela Berrigan, *Vice Pres*
Leo Fuentes, *Executive*
John Adamson, *Exec Dir*
EMP: 650
SQ FT: 750,000
SALES (est): 36.7MM **Privately Held**
WEB: www.queenmary.com
SIC: **7011** Hotels & motels
PA: City Of Long Beach
  333 W Ocean Blvd Fl 10
  Long Beach CA 90802
  562 570-6450

(P-13165)
ROOSEVELT HOTEL LLC
Also Called: Hollywood Roosevelt Hotel
7000 Hollywood Blvd, Los Angeles (90028-6003)
PHONE....................323 466-7000
Fax: 323 432-8056
Goodwin Gaw, *Mng Member*
Brett Blass, *General Mgr*
Muzaffar Khalelli, *Finance Dir*
Muzaffar Khaleeli, *Finance*
Ashley Eberhard, *Human Res Dir*
EMP: 200
SALES (est): 19.5MM **Privately Held**
WEB: www.hollywoodroosevelt.com
SIC: **7011** 5813 5812 Hotels & motels; drinking places; eating places

(P-13166)
ROPPONGI-TAHOE LP A CALIFORNI
Also Called: Lake Tahoe Resort Hotel
4130 Lake Tahoe Blvd, South Lake Tahoe (96150-6965)
PHONE....................530 544-5400
John Steinbach, *General Mgr*
Kunihiro Nakayabu, *Managing Prtnr*
Masaru Saito, *Managing Prtnr*
Charles Lancellotti, *Finance*
Bill Cottrill, *Marketing Staff*
EMP: 200
SALES (est): 12.6MM **Privately Held**
WEB: www.embassytahoe.com
SIC: **7011** Hotels & motels

(P-13167)
ROSANNA INC
Also Called: Avenue of Arts Wyndham Hotel
3350 Avenue Of The Arts, Costa Mesa (92626-1913)
PHONE....................714 751-5100
Nick Price, *General Mgr*
Rachael Moorhead, *President*
Paul Sanford, *CEO*

Rosanna Chan, *Principal*
Robin Reid, *Director*
EMP: 151
SALES (est): 9.4MM **Privately Held**
SIC: **7011** 5812 Hotels; food bars; caterers

(P-13168)
ROSCOE REAL ESTATE LTD PARTNR
Also Called: Elkor Properties
1819 Ocean Ave, Santa Monica (90401-3215)
PHONE....................310 260-7500
Fax: 310 260-7515
Vincent Piro, *General Mgr*
Elkor Trio LL LLC, *General Ptnr*
Lalo Vasquez, *Technical Mgr*
EMP: 80
SALES (est): 3.8MM **Privately Held**
WEB: www.viceroysantamonica.com
SIC: **7011** 7389 Hotels & motels; hotel & motel reservation service

(P-13169)
ROSEVILLE TOWNE PLACE SUITES
10569 Fairway Dr, Roseville (95678-3570)
PHONE....................916 782-2232
Gary Tharaldson, *Principal*
Lynda Abrams, *Principal*
EMP: 99
SALES (est): 1.5MM **Privately Held**
SIC: **7011** Hotel, franchised

(P-13170)
ROSEWOOD HOTELS & RESORTS LLC
Also Called: Rosewood Sand Hill Hotel
2825 Sand Hill Rd, Menlo Park (94025-7022)
PHONE....................650 561-1500
Fax: 650 561-1501
Michael Casey, *Managing Dir*
Sharon Myers, *Marketing Staff*
EMP: 300 EST: 2008
SALES (est): 14.2MM **Privately Held**
SIC: **7011** Hotels

(P-13171)
ROYAL GORGE NORDIC SKI RESORT (PA)
Also Called: Royal Gorge Crss Cntry Ski Rst
9411 Hillside Rd, Soda Springs (95728)
PHONE....................530 426-3871
Fax: 530 426-9221
John Slouber, *President*
Frances Wiesel, *Admin Sec*
EMP: 120 EST: 1971
SQ FT: 50,000
SALES (est): 4.5MM **Privately Held**
SIC: **7011** Ski lodge

(P-13172)
ROYAL HOSPITALITY INCORPORATED
Also Called: Ramada Inn
5550 Kearny Mesa Rd, San Diego (92111-1304)
PHONE....................858 278-0800
Fax: 619 277-6585
Maurice Coreia, *President*
Espie Collier, *Sales Staff*
Maureen Maughan, *Property Mgr*
EMP: 60
SQ FT: 63,000
SALES (est): 4.3MM **Privately Held**
WEB: www.ramadasandiego.com
SIC: **7011** Hotels & motels

(P-13173)
RP SCS WSD HOTEL LLC
Also Called: W San Diego Hotel
421 W B St, San Diego (92101-3501)
PHONE....................619 398-3020
Michael O'Donohue, *General Mgr*
Valerie Valente, *Executive*
Maria Veronica Rodriguez, *Finance Dir*
Cheryl Barba, *Accountant*
Jennifer McDonough, *Director*
EMP: 60
SALES (est): 5MM **Privately Held**
SIC: **7011** Hotels

(P-13174)
RP/KINETIC PARC 55 OWNER LLC
Also Called: Parc 55 Hotel
55 Cyril Magnin St, San Francisco (94102-2812)
PHONE....................415 392-8000
Fax: 415 296-8054
Steve Barick,
Peter Beheda, *Senior VP*
Gary Gutierrez, *Vice Pres*
Rob Gauthier, *General Mgr*
Billy Wuepper, *Info Tech Dir*
EMP: 450
SALES (est): 22.5MM
SALES (corp-wide): 4.6B **Publicly Held**
WEB: www.parc55hotel.com
SIC: **7011** Hotels & motels
PA: The Blackstone Group L P
  345 Park Ave Ste 1100
  New York NY 10154
  212 583-5000

(P-13175)
RPC OLD TOWN AVENUE OWNER LLC
Also Called: Fairfield Inn
3900 Old Town Ave, San Diego (92110-2904)
PHONE....................619 299-7400
Evan Hitter, *Director*
EMP: 55
SALES (est): 1.2MM **Privately Held**
SIC: **7011** Hotels & motels

(P-13176)
RPC OLD TOWN JEFFERSON
Also Called: San Diego Old Town
2435 Jefferson St, San Diego (92110-3026)
PHONE....................619 725-4221
Budd Barmeyer, *General Mgr*
Amanda Frank, *Info Tech Mgr*
Kjersti Roosevelt, *Sales Staff*
Evan Hitter, *Director*
EMP: 60
SQ FT: 5,000
SALES (est): 4.7MM **Privately Held**
WEB: www.sunstonehotels.com
SIC: **7011** Hotels & motels

(P-13177)
RPD HOTELS 18 LLC (PA)
Also Called: Vagabond Inns
2361 Rosecrans Ave # 150, El Segundo (90245-7906)
PHONE....................213 746-1531
Fax: 310 410-5770
Juan Sanchez Llaca, *President*
Les Biggins, *Vice Pres*
Mark Sekelick, *Vice Pres*
Jana Gage, *General Mgr*
Chuck Valentino, *VP Opers*
EMP: 800
SALES (est): 33.6MM **Privately Held**
SIC: **7011** Motels

(P-13178)
RT PASAD HOTEL PARTNERS LP
Also Called: Courtyard By Marriott
180 N Fair Oaks Ave, Pasadena (91103-3614)
PHONE....................626 403-7600
Timothy Bristol, *General Mgr*
Jeff Hart, *General Mgr*
Luis Guzman, *Plant Mgr*
Stephen Blaine, *Sales Staff*
Merlin Wan, *Sales Staff*
EMP: 140
SQ FT: 165,342
SALES (est): 6.6MM **Privately Held**
SIC: **7011** Hotels & motels

(P-13179)
RUBICON B HACIENDA LLC
Also Called: Aloft El Sgnd-Los Angles Arprt
475 N Sepulveda Blvd, El Segundo (90245-4446)
PHONE....................424 290-5555
Louisa Yeung, *Administration*
Marc Gordon,
EMP: 87
SALES (est): 254.3K **Privately Held**
SIC: **7011** Hotels & motels

(P-13180)
RUFFIN HOTEL CORP OF CAL
Also Called: Long Beach Marriott
4700 Airport Plaza Dr, Long Beach (90815-1252)
PHONE....................562 425-5210
Fax: 562 420-7904
Phillip G Ruffin, *President*
Hamid Raza, *CFO*
Jose Lopez, *Executive*
Samantha Perrin, *Executive*
George Maragos, *General Mgr*
EMP: 260
SALES (est): 14.5MM **Privately Held**
WEB: www.lbmarriott.com
SIC: **7011** 5812 5813 Hotels & motels; eating places; coffee shop; drinking places

(P-13181)
RUNNING CREEK CASINO
635 E State Highway 20, Upper Lake (95485-8793)
P.O. Box 788 (95485-0788)
PHONE....................707 275-9209
Mike Caryl, *Finance Dir*
David Schugar, *General Mgr*
EMP: 170 EST: 2011
SALES (est): 8.8MM **Privately Held**
SIC: **7011** 5812 Casino hotel; eating places

(P-13182)
RYDE HOTEL LLC
Also Called: Ryde Motel
14340 State Highway 160, Walnut Grove (95690-9742)
PHONE....................916 776-1318
Toll Free:....................888 -
Janice G Leroy,
EMP: 50 EST: 1997
SALES (est): 1.3MM **Privately Held**
WEB: www.rydehotel.com
SIC: **7011** 5812 Hotels & motels; eating places

(P-13183)
S R H H INC
Also Called: Radisson Inn
1085 E El Camino Real, Sunnyvale (94087-3755)
PHONE....................408 247-0800
Fax: 408 984-7120
Donald Bramer, *President*
Gaylon Patterson, *Treasurer*
John Branagh, *Admin Sec*
Erin Gilchrest, *Manager*
EMP: 50
SQ FT: 150,000
SALES (est): 1.5MM **Privately Held**
SIC: **7011** 5812 5813 Hotels & motels; American restaurant; cocktail lounge

(P-13184)
S W K PROPERTIES LLC
Also Called: Holiday Inn Orange Cnty Arprt
2726 S Grand Ave Lbby, Santa Ana (92705-5404)
PHONE....................714 481-6300
Rod Hurt, *Manager*
Barbara Smith, *Info Tech Mgr*
Annette Anderson, *Sales Mgr*
Britney Taylor, *Sales Mgr*
EMP: 66
SALES (corp-wide): 10MM **Privately Held**
SIC: **7011** Hotels & motels
PA: S W K Properties Llc
  3807 Wilshire Blvd # 1226
  Los Angeles CA 90010
  213 383-9204

(P-13185)
SACRAMENTO HOTEL PARTNERS LLC
100 Capitol Mall, Sacramento (95814-3244)
PHONE....................916 326-5000
Vishwa Nand, *Manager*
Robert Weight, *Manager*
EMP: 90
SALES (corp-wide): 7.9MM **Privately Held**
WEB: www.essacramento.com
SIC: **7011** Hotels & motels

PRODUCTS & SERVICES SECTION

7011 - Hotels, Motels & Tourist Courts County (P-13207)

PA: Sacramento Hotel Partners, Llc
100 Saratoga Ave Ste 300
Santa Clara CA 95051
408 249-2500

(P-13186)
SACRAMNTO FORTY NINER TRVL PLZ
Also Called: Sacramento 49er
2828 El Centro Rd, Sacramento (95833-9602)
PHONE..................916 927-4774
Tristen Griffith, President
Terrace Rust, Vice Pres
EMP: 125 EST: 1976
SQ FT: 27,000
SALES (est): 7.8MM Privately Held
WEB: www.sacramento49er.com
SIC: 7011 5331 5812 5541 Motels; variety stores; restaurant, family: independent; truck stops

(P-13187)
SAGA SEAL CO LTD
Also Called: Pacific Inn, The
600 Marina Dr, Seal Beach (90740-6123)
PHONE..................562 493-7501
Steve Bader, President
Jene Sugita, Manager
EMP: 80
SQ FT: 33,597
SALES (est): 4.3MM Privately Held
SIC: 7011 Hotels

(P-13188)
SAGE HOSPITALITY RESOURCES LLC
Also Called: Courtyard By Marriott
700 W Huntington Dr, Monrovia (91016-3104)
PHONE..................626 357-5211
Fax: 626 359-4862
Dennis Hollingdrake, Manager
EMP: 100
SALES (corp-wide): 438.5MM Privately Held
WEB: www.21chotel.com
SIC: 7011 Hotels & motels
PA: Sage Hospitality Resources L.L.C.
1575 Welton St Ste 300
Denver CO 80202
303 595-7200

(P-13189)
SAGE HOSPITALITY RESOURCES LLC
Also Called: Homewood Suites Hilton Sfo
2000 Shoreline Ct, Brisbane (94005-1870)
PHONE..................650 589-1600
Fax: 650 589-2622
Gina Merz, Branch Mgr
Debbie Goodmenson, Manager
EMP: 67
SALES (corp-wide): 438.5MM Privately Held
WEB: www.21chotel.com
SIC: 7011 Hotels & motels
PA: Sage Hospitality Resources L.L.C.
1575 Welton St Ste 300
Denver CO 80202
303 595-7200

(P-13190)
SAJAHTERA INC
Also Called: Beverly Hills Hotel
9641 Sunset Blvd, Beverly Hills (90210-2938)
PHONE..................310 276-2251
Fax: 310 271-0319
Junaidi Masri, President
Edward Mady, General Mgr
Norma Cuevas, Administration
Porfirio Caamal, Accounting Mgr
Ana Martinez, Credit Mgr
EMP: 550
SQ FT: 10,758
SALES (est): 51MM
SALES (corp-wide): 477.3MM Privately Held
WEB: www.sajahtera.com
SIC: 7011 Hotels
HQ: Dorchester Group Limited
3 Tilney Street
London W1Y 5
207 319-7401

(P-13191)
SALIMAR INC
Also Called: Best Western
2620 Buck Owens Blvd, Bakersfield (93308-6310)
PHONE..................661 327-9651
Fax: 661 334-1820
Sam Parabia, President
Ray Parabia, General Mgr
Jessica Oomeoi, Controller
Diane Hitchcock, Mktg Dir
Cheryl Carter, Accounts Mgr
EMP: 85
SALES (est): 3.3MM Privately Held
WEB: www.bwibakersfield.com
SIC: 7011 Hotels & motels

(P-13192)
SALT LAKE HOTEL ASSOCIATES LP (PA)
222 Kearny St Ste 200, San Francisco (94108-4537)
PHONE..................415 397-5572
Tom Lataur, President
EMP: 111 EST: 1997
SALES (est): 3.6MM Privately Held
SIC: 7011 Hotels & motels

(P-13193)
SAN BERNARDINO HILTON (HQ)
285 E Hospitality Ln, San Bernardino (92408-3411)
PHONE..................909 889-0133
Fax: 909 381-4299
Douglas McCarron, President
Morgan McPherson, Exec Dir
Ronald Schoen, Admin Sec
Kenneth Morris, Finance
Dael Strange, Mktg Dir
EMP: 152
SALES (est): 37MM
SALES (corp-wide): 41MM Privately Held
WEB: www.web66.com
SIC: 7011 6512 5812 Hotels & motels; commercial & industrial building operation; eating places
PA: Carpenters Southwest Administrative Corporation
533 S Fremont Ave
Los Angeles CA 90071
213 386-8590

(P-13194)
SAN CARLOS ASSOCIATES LTD
Also Called: Monterey Marriott
350 Calle Principal, Monterey (93940-2416)
PHONE..................831 649-4234
Rene Boskoff, General Mgr
Renee Onge, Manager
EMP: 225
SALES (corp-wide): 5.7MM Privately Held
SIC: 7011 5813 5812 Hotels; bar (drinking places); grills (eating places)
PA: San Carlos Associates Ltd
1111 3rd Ave Ste 3030
Seattle WA

(P-13195)
SAN DIEGO FARAH PARTNERS
Also Called: Quality Inn
1430 7th Ave Ste B, San Diego (92101-2815)
PHONE..................619 239-2261
Fax: 619 239-0138
Berham Baxter, General Ptnr
EMP: 50
SQ FT: 99,999
SALES (est): 3.1MM Privately Held
SIC: 7011 Hotels & motels

(P-13196)
SAN DIEGO HOTEL CIR OWNER LLC
1515 Hotel Cir S, San Diego (92108-3409)
PHONE..................619 881-6700
Victor Ravago, Manager
Evette Betancourt, Accounting Mgr
EMP: 70 EST: 2015
SALES (est): 1.9MM Privately Held
SIC: 7011 Hotel, franchised

(P-13197)
SAN DIEGO HOTEL COMPANY LLC
Also Called: Marriott San Dego Gslamp Qrter
660 K St, San Diego (92101-7036)
PHONE..................619 696-0234
James Evans, CFO
Marie Palmer-Jeffrey, Info Tech Mgr
Texann Niedzwiecki, Controller
Sheila Buckley, Marketing Mgr
Bill Cheefman, Director
EMP: 135
SALES (est): 6MM Privately Held
WEB: www.sheratonuptown.com
SIC: 7011 Hotels & motels

(P-13198)
SAN DIEGO HOTEL LEASE LLC
Also Called: Courtyard By Marriott
530 Broadway, San Diego (92101-5206)
PHONE..................619 446-3000
J W Marriott, Chairman
Arne M Sorenson, CEO
Carl T Berquist, Exec VP
Will Garber, General Mgr
Allina Boohoff, Mng Member
EMP: 200
SQ FT: 126,742
SALES (est): 4MM Privately Held
SIC: 7011 Hotels & motels

(P-13199)
SAN DIEGO PARADISE PT RESORT
Also Called: Paradise Point Resort & Spa
1404 Vacation Rd, San Diego (92109-7905)
PHONE..................858 274-4630
Fax: 858 581-5922
David Hall, General Mgr
Nicole Conlon, Admin Asst
EMP: 350
SALES (est): 20.9MM Privately Held
WEB: www.paradisepoint.com
SIC: 7011 Resort hotel

(P-13200)
SAN DIEGO SHERATON CORPORATION
Also Called: Starwood Hotels & Resorts
1590 Harbor Island Dr, San Diego (92101-1009)
PHONE..................619 291-6400
Robert Cartwright, General Mgr
Luz Gutierrez, Executive
Andy Simer, Controller
EMP: 850
SALES (est): 17.4MM
SALES (corp-wide): 14.4B Publicly Held
SIC: 7011 5813 5812 4493 Hotels & motels; drinking places; eating places; marinas
HQ: Starwood Hotels & Resorts Worldwide, Llc
1 Star Pt
Stamford CT 06902
203 964-6000

(P-13201)
SAN FRANCISCO HOTEL ASSOCIATES
Also Called: Masa's
650 Bush St, San Francisco (94108-3509)
PHONE..................415 392-4666
Fax: 415 433-4065
Michael Lennon, Partner
EMP: 80
SQ FT: 46,067
SALES (est): 2.4MM Privately Held
WEB: www.vintagecourt.com
SIC: 7011 5812 Hotels; French restaurant

(P-13202)
SAN FRANCISCO HOTEL GROUP LLC
Also Called: Loews Regency San Francisco
222 Sansome St, San Francisco (94104-2703)
PHONE..................415 276-9888
Yue-Tin Chang, President
Jonathan Tisch, Chairman
Shin Shih, Vice Pres
Tracy Lee, Controller
Gordon Yee, Purch Mgr
EMP: 183
SALES (est): 8.3MM
SALES (corp-wide): 13.4B Publicly Held
SIC: 7011 Hotels
HQ: Loews Hotels Holding Corporation
667 Madison Ave
New York NY 10065
212 521-2000

(P-13203)
SAN JOSE AIRPORT GARDEN HOTEL
1740 N 1st St, San Jose (95112-4508)
P.O. Box 2409 (95109-2409)
PHONE..................408 793-3300
Ronald Werner, Partner
Vijay Bhatia, General Mgr
John Stanford, Chief Engr
Charlene Shaughnessy, Sales Mgr
EMP: 99
SALES (est): 3MM Privately Held
SIC: 7011 Hotels & motels

(P-13204)
SAN JOSE AIRPORT HOTEL LLC
Also Called: San Jose Airport Garden Hotel
1740 N 1st St, San Jose (95112-4508)
PHONE..................408 793-3939
Manou Mobedshahi, Mng Member
Harry Engineer,
EMP: 230
SALES (est): 6.9MM Privately Held
SIC: 7011 Hotels & motels; inns

(P-13205)
SAN JOSE FAIRMONT LESSEE LLC
170 S Market St Lbby, San Jose (95113-2361)
PHONE..................408 998-1900
Fax: 408 287-1648
Cirilo Custodio,
Jose Zarate, General Mgr
Adrian Flores, Human Resources
Caroline Grover, Purch Mgr
Lina Broydo, Relations
EMP: 500
SALES: 69MM
SALES (corp-wide): 27.3MM Privately Held
WEB: www.cp.ca
SIC: 7011 5812 5813 Hotels; ethnic food restaurants; cocktail lounge
HQ: Fairmont Hotels & Resorts Inc
155 Wellington St W Suite 3300
Toronto ON M5V 0
416 874-2600

(P-13206)
SAN MARCOS CATERERS INC
Also Called: Quails Inn Motel
1025 La Bonita Dr, San Marcos (92078-5220)
PHONE..................760 744-0120
Gordon N Frazar, President
Ronald Frazar, Corp Secy
Dodi Holiday, General Mgr
EMP: 60
SALES (est): 4.3MM Privately Held
WEB: www.lakesanmarcosresort.com
SIC: 7011 5812 Motels; caterers

(P-13207)
SAN PSQUAL BAND MSSION INDIANS
Also Called: Valley View Casino
16300 Nyemii Pass Rd, Valley Center (92082-6769)
P.O. Box 2379 (92082-2379)
PHONE..................760 291-5500
Toll Free:..................866 -
Bruce Howards, General Mgr
Don Haig, Vice Pres
Larry Chapp, Purchasing
Christina Martinez, Opers Staff
EMP: 500
SALES (corp-wide): 20MM Privately Held
WEB: www.sanpasqualindians.org
SIC: 7011 Casino hotel
PA: San Pasqual Band Of Mission Indians
16400 Kumeyaay Way
Valley Center CA 92082
760 749-3200

7011 - Hotels, Motels & Tourist Courts County (P-13208)

(P-13208)
SAN PSQUAL CSINO DEV GROUP INC
Also Called: Valley View Casino
16300 Nyemii Pass Rd, Valley Center (92082-6769)
PHONE..................760 291-5500
Fax: 760 291-5674
Joe Navarro, *President*
Don Haig, *President*
Jennifer Bryant, *CFO*
Michael Gorczynski, *Treasurer*
Al Cope, *Vice Pres*
EMP: 50
SQ FT: 62,000
SALES (est): 3.4MM
SALES (corp-wide): 20MM **Privately Held**
SIC: 7011 Casino hotel
PA: San Pasqual Band Of Mission Indians
16400 Kumeyaay Way
Valley Center CA 92082
760 749-3200

(P-13209)
SAN YSIDRO BB PROPERTY LLC
Also Called: Stonehouse Restaurant
900 San Ysidro Ln, Santa Barbara (93108-1325)
PHONE..................805 969-5046
Fax: 805 565-1995
Seamus McManus,
Maxine Rutledge, *Officer*
Andrea Gates, *General Mgr*
Duncan Graham, *Director*
Mike Trupiano, *Director*
EMP: 140
SQ FT: 4,415
SALES (est): 9MM **Privately Held**
WEB: www.sanysidroranch.com
SIC: 7011 5812 Hotels; eating places

(P-13210)
SANDWICH SPOT (PA)
1630 18th St, Sacramento (95811-6702)
PHONE..................916 492-2613
Fax: 916 492-2614
Tom Heally, *Principal*
EMP: 57
SALES (est): 3.9MM **Privately Held**
SIC: 7011 Bed & breakfast inn

(P-13211)
SANSPAN CORPORATION
1500 Orange Ave, Coronado (92118-2918)
PHONE..................619 435-6611
Todd Shallan, *President*
Bob Antes, *CFO*
Howart Cho, *Admin Mgr*
Marvin Tayag, *Admin Mgr*
Lauren Cinadr, *Executive Asst*
EMP: 1000
SALES (est): 13.9MM
SALES (corp-wide): 4.6B **Publicly Held**
SIC: 7011 Hotels & motels
PA: The Blackstone Group L P
345 Park Ave Ste 1100
New York NY 10154
212 583-5000

(P-13212)
SANTA CLARA TENANT CORP
Also Called: Embassy Suites- Santa Clara
2885 Lakeside Dr, Santa Clara (95054-2805)
PHONE..................408 496-6400
Fax: 408 492-9121
T Owens, *General Mgr*
Teri Owens, *General Mgr*
EMP: 90
SALES (est): 4.9MM
SALES (corp-wide): 794.8MM **Publicly Held**
SIC: 7011 Hotels & motels
PA: Ashford Hospitality Trust Inc
14185 Dallas Pkwy # 1100
Dallas TX 75254
972 490-9600

(P-13213)
SANTA CRUZ HOTEL ASSOCIATES
Also Called: West Coast Santa Cruz Hotel
175 W Cliff Dr, Santa Cruz (95060-5438)
PHONE..................831 426-4330
Brian Corbell, *President*
EMP: 150
SALES (est): 7.3MM **Privately Held**
SIC: 7011 Hotels

(P-13214)
SANTA CRUZ SEASIDE COMPANY
Also Called: Sea & Sand Inn
201 W Cliff Dr, Santa Cruz (95060-6144)
PHONE..................831 427-3400
Fax: 831 466-9882
Lisa Morley, *Manager*
EMP: 507
SALES (corp-wide): 55.2MM **Privately Held**
WEB: www.scseaside.com
SIC: 7011 Hotels & motels
PA: Santa Cruz Seaside Company Inc
400 Beach St
Santa Cruz CA 95060
831 423-5590

(P-13215)
SANTA MARIA AIRPORT REGENCY
Also Called: Radisson Hotel Santa Maria
3455 Skyway Dr, Santa Maria (93455-2501)
PHONE..................805 928-8000
Fax: 805 928-5251
Jean Luc Garlon, *Manager*
Jean-Luc Garon, *General Mgr*
Sheri Martini, *Controller*
EMP: 60
SQ FT: 60,000
SALES (est): 3.7MM **Privately Held**
SIC: 7011 5812 Hotels & motels; eating places

(P-13216)
SANTA MARIA HOTEL CORP
Also Called: Holiday Inn
2100 N Broadway, Santa Maria (93454-1140)
PHONE..................805 928-6000
Lawrence Lui, *President*
EMP: 88
SALES (est): 4.3MM **Privately Held**
SIC: 7011 5812 7389 Hotels & motels; eating places; convention & show services

(P-13217)
SANTA MONICA HSR LTD PARTNR
Also Called: Doubletree Hotel
1707 4th St, Santa Monica (90401-3301)
PHONE..................310 395-3332
Fax: 310 452-7399
Shashi Poudyal, *Manager*
EMP: 160
SALES (est): 4.4MM **Privately Held**
WEB: www.doubletreesantamonica.com
SIC: 7011 5812 Hotels & motels; eating places

(P-13218)
SANTANA ROW HOTEL PARTNERS LP
355 Santana Row, San Jose (95128-2049)
PHONE..................408 551-0010
Bonnie Best, *General Mgr*
EMP: 200 **Privately Held**
SIC: 7011 Hotels & motels
PA: Santana Row Hotel Partners Lp
4400 Post Oak Pkwy
Houston TX 77027

(P-13219)
SANWA JUTAKU CO LTD
Also Called: Embassy Suites
8425 Firestone Blvd, Downey (90241-3843)
PHONE..................562 861-1900
Fax: 562 923-5847
Yoko Maeda, *President*
Michelle Escobedo, *Manager*
EMP: 50
SALES (est): 3.3MM **Privately Held**
SIC: 7011 Hotels & motels

(P-13220)
SARATOGA CAPITAL INC
Also Called: Hotel De Anza
233 W Santa Clara St, San Jose (95113-1710)
PHONE..................408 286-1000
Fax: 408 286-0500
Alison McAennon, *Manager*
EMP: 65
SALES (corp-wide): 16.9MM **Privately Held**
WEB: www.saratogacapital.net
SIC: 7011 Hotels & motels
HQ: Saratoga Capital, Inc.
66 E Santa Clara St
San Jose CA 95113
408 298-8600

(P-13221)
SAVE QUEEN LLC
Also Called: Queen Mary, The
429 Shoreline Village Dr I, Long Beach (90802-8136)
PHONE..................562 435-3511
Sean Meddock, *Mng Member*
Sabine Dubois, *Vice Pres*
Edgar Stevens, *Technology*
Dic Mitchell, *Controller*
Brian Panozzo, *Opers Staff*
EMP: 500
SALES (est): 17.4MM **Privately Held**
SIC: 7011 Hotels

(P-13222)
SBEHG 465 S LA CIENEGA LLC
Also Called: S L S Hotel
465 S La Cienega Blvd, Los Angeles (90048-4001)
PHONE..................310 247-0400
Fax: 310 246-2067
Manfred Moennich,
Emily Seld, *Admin Asst*
Tom Henbest,
Jaxques Ligne,
Rob White,
EMP: 500
SALES (est): 26.4MM **Privately Held**
WEB: www.granada-learning.com
SIC: 7011 Hotels

(P-13223)
SC HARP EL SEGUNDO LLC
1985 E Grand Ave, El Segundo (90245-5015)
PHONE..................310 322-0999
Dave Harvey, *Mng Member*
Cheryl Gavin, *Controller*
EMP: 84
SALES: 950K **Privately Held**
SIC: 7011 Hotels & motels

(P-13224)
SC HOTEL PARTNERS LLC
Also Called: Hotel Adagio
550 Geary St, San Francisco (94102-1650)
PHONE..................415 775-5000
Fax: 415 775-9388
Paul Frentsos, *Manager*
Jill Plemons, *Sales Dir*
Micheal Pace, *Manager*
EMP: 52
SALES (est): 4.4MM **Privately Held**
SIC: 7011 Hotels

(P-13225)
SD STADIUM HOTEL LLC
Also Called: Hilton Garded
3805 Murphy Canyon Rd, San Diego (92123-4404)
PHONE..................858 278-9300
Mayur Patel,
Margie Padilla, *General Mgr*
Michael Mc Cullough, *Info Tech Dir*
Richard Koll, *Chief Engr*
John Inocentes, *Manager*
EMP: 100
SALES (est): 2.8MM **Privately Held**
WEB: www.hioldtownhotel.com
SIC: 7011 Hotels & motels

(P-13226)
SE SAN DIEGO HOTEL LLC
1047 5th Ave, San Diego (92101-5101)
PHONE..................619 515-3000
Ador Bustamante, *Director*
Rigel Bitterman, *Social Dir*
Joe Velasquez, *Mktg Dir*
Lesley Casemero, *Manager*
EMP: 57
SALES (est): 5MM **Privately Held**
SIC: 7011 Hotels

(P-13227)
SEACLIFF INN INC
Also Called: Best Western
7500 Old Dominion Ct, Aptos (95003-3807)
PHONE..................831 661-4671
Fax: 831 685-3603
Frank Giuliani, *President*
T J Scott, *Treasurer*
Norm BEl, *Vice Pres*
Coleen Giuliani, *Admin Sec*
Nikki Castro, *Human Res Dir*
EMP: 90
SQ FT: 60,000
SALES (est): 3.8MM **Privately Held**
WEB: www.seacliffinn.com
SIC: 7011 Hotels & motels

(P-13228)
SEASCAPE RESORT LTD A CALIF
Also Called: Sanderlings
19 Seascape Vlg, Aptos (95003-6102)
PHONE..................831 662-7120
Fax: 831 685-0615
Mark Holcomb, *General Ptnr*
Karl Staub, *Executive*
EMP: 300
SQ FT: 45,000
SALES (est): 8MM **Privately Held**
WEB: www.seascaperesort.com
SIC: 7011 Resort hotel

(P-13229)
SEASIDE LAGUNA INN & SUITES
1661 S Coast Hwy, Laguna Beach (92651-3228)
PHONE..................949 494-9717
Fax: 949 497-1031
Tino Farjad, *General Mgr*
EMP: 51
SQ FT: 27,500
SALES (est): 2.3MM **Privately Held**
WEB: www.seacliffmotel.com
SIC: 7011 Hotels

(P-13230)
SECOND STREET CORPORATION
Also Called: Huntley Hotel Santa Monica Bch
1111 2nd St, Santa Monica (90403-5003)
PHONE..................310 394-5454
Fax: 310 451-7424
Sohrab Sassounian, *President*
Dora Levy, *Shareholder*
Marschinda Felix, *COO*
Helal M El-Sherif, *CFO*
Shiva Aghaipour, *Vice Pres*
EMP: 250
SQ FT: 185,000
SALES (est): 16.1MM **Privately Held**
SIC: 7011 5812 Hotels; eating places

(P-13231)
SELECT HOTELS GROUP LLC
Also Called: Hyatt Pl Fremont/Silicon Vly
3101 W Warren Ave, Fremont (94538-6428)
PHONE..................510 623-6000
Fax: 510 623-6001
John McEngee, *Manager*
EMP: 50
SALES (corp-wide): 4.3B **Publicly Held**
WEB: www.amerisuites.com
SIC: 7011 Hotels & motels
HQ: Select Hotels Group, L.L.C.
200 W Monroe St Ste 800
Chicago IL 60606
312 750-1234

PRODUCTS & SERVICES SECTION

7011 - Hotels, Motels & Tourist Courts County (P-13258)

(P-13232)
SELECT HOTELS GROUP LLC
Also Called: Hyatt House Rancho Cordova
11260 Point East Dr, Rancho Cordova (95742-6232)
PHONE.................................916 638-4141
Fax: 916 638-1045
Brett Tmekei, *General Mgr*
Brett Peterson, *General Mgr*
EMP: 50
SALES (corp-wide): 4.3B **Publicly Held**
WEB: www.hallmarksuites.com
SIC: 7011 Hotel, franchised
HQ: Select Hotels Group, L.L.C.
200 W Monroe St Ste 800
Chicago IL 60606
312 750-1234

(P-13233)
SELVI-VIDOVICH LP
Also Called: Grand Hotel The
865 W El Camino Real, Sunnyvale (94087-1154)
PHONE.................................408 720-8500
Fax: 408 720-1997
John Vidovich, *Partner*
Al Selvi, *Partner*
Barbara Perzigian, *General Mgr*
Erica Amesbury, *Sales Dir*
Erika Orr, *Sales Mgr*
EMP: 70
SQ FT: 90,805
SALES (est): 4.5MM **Privately Held**
WEB: www.thegrandhotel.com
SIC: 7011 Hotels

(P-13234)
SETHI MANAGEMENT INC
183 Calle Magdalena # 101, Encinitas (92024-3793)
PHONE.................................760 652-4010
J P Sethi, *President*
Ganisha Sethi, *COO*
Laurel Pavlik, *General Mgr*
Gilbert Preciado, *Controller*
EMP: 99
SALES (est): 3.2MM **Privately Held**
SIC: 7011 Hotels & motels

(P-13235)
SEVEN SEAS ASSOCIATES LLC
Also Called: Seven Seas Best Western
411 Hotel Cir S, San Diego (92108-3402)
PHONE.................................619 291-1300
Joe Toczylowski, *CFO*
Jennifer Langham, *Vice Pres*
Sanjay Stokes, *Sales Staff*
Eisler Family Trust,
Orwitz Family Trust,
EMP: 108
SQ FT: 101,000
SALES (est): 8.7MM **Privately Held**
WEB: www.bw7seas.com
SIC: 7011 Motels

(P-13236)
SFD PARTNERS LLC
Also Called: Sir Francis Drake Hotel
450 Powell St, San Francisco (94102-1504)
PHONE.................................415 392-7755
John Price, *General Mgr*
Chuck Brown, *General Mgr*
Richard Thome, *Director*
EMP: 350
SALES (est): 2.8MM **Privately Held**
WEB: www.sirfrancisdrake.com
SIC: 7011 5812 5813 7389 Hotels; eating places; drinking places; hotel & motel reservation service

(P-13237)
SHAMROCK-HOSTMARK PALM DESRT
74700 Highway 111, Palm Desert (92260-3806)
PHONE.................................760 340-6600
Bob Cataldo,
David Hirsch, *General Mgr*
Gerri Lynch,
EMP: 87
SALES (est): 3.1MM **Privately Held**
SIC: 7011 Hotels & motels

(P-13238)
SHAW HOSPITALITY GROUP INC
Also Called: Ramada Inn University
324 E Shaw Ave, Fresno (93710-7610)
PHONE.................................559 224-4040
Raman Patel, *President*
Ashok Patel, *CFO*
EMP: 55
SQ FT: 91,168
SALES (est): 1.4MM **Privately Held**
SIC: 7011 Hotels & motels

(P-13239)
SHC BURBANK II LLC
Also Called: Marriott
2500 N Hollywood Way, Burbank (91505-1019)
PHONE.................................818 843-6000
EMP: 210
SALES (est): 10.7MM **Privately Held**
SIC: 7011

(P-13240)
SHEN ZHEN NEW WORLD II LLC
Also Called: Sheraton Universal Hotel
333 Unversal Hollywood Dr, Universal City (91608-1001)
PHONE.................................818 980-1212
Ming Yu,
Shannon King, *Accountant*
EMP: 99
SALES (est): 3.1MM **Privately Held**
SIC: 7011 Hotels & motels

(P-13241)
SHERATON CORPORATION
2500 Mason St, San Francisco (94133-1450)
PHONE.................................415 362-5500
Fax: 415 391-9451
Jim Sega, *Manager*
Valerie Coats, *General Mgr*
Daniel Monnet, *Finance*
Tom Leeper, *Controller*
Chris Keil, *Manager*
EMP: 300
SALES (corp-wide): 14.4B **Publicly Held**
SIC: 7011 Hotels & motels
HQ: The Sheraton Corporation
1111 Westchester Ave
White Plains NY 10604
800 328-6242

(P-13242)
SHERATON CORPORATION
6101 W Century Blvd, Los Angeles (90045-5310)
PHONE.................................310 642-1111
Michael Washington, *General Mgr*
Blanca Lopez, *Human Res Mgr*
Brandon Swan, *Sales Mgr*
Willem Both, *Manager*
EMP: 500
SALES (corp-wide): 14.4B **Publicly Held**
SIC: 7011 5813 5812 Hotels & motels; drinking places; eating places
HQ: The Sheraton Corporation
1111 Westchester Ave
White Plains NY 10604
800 328-6242

(P-13243)
SHERATON CORPORATION
Also Called: Sheraton Grand Sacramento Ht
1230 J St 13th, Sacramento (95814-2907)
PHONE.................................916 447-1700
Gunter Stannius, *Manager*
Cora Sorensen, *Sales Mgr*
EMP: 328
SALES (corp-wide): 14.4B **Publicly Held**
WEB: www.sheraton.com
SIC: 7011 Hotels & motels
HQ: The Sheraton Corporation
1111 Westchester Ave
White Plains NY 10604
800 328-6242

(P-13244)
SHERATON CORPORATION
11960 Foothill Blvd, Rancho Cucamonga (91739-9370)
PHONE.................................909 204-6100
EMP: 328
SALES (corp-wide): 14.4B **Publicly Held**
SIC: 7011 Hotels & motels

HQ: The Sheraton Corporation
1111 Westchester Ave
White Plains NY 10604
800 328-6242

(P-13245)
SHERATON CORPORATION
5990 Stoneridge Mall Rd, Pleasanton (94588-3229)
PHONE.................................925 463-3330
Marilyn Milligan, *Manager*
EMP: 328
SALES (corp-wide): 14.4B **Publicly Held**
SIC: 7011 Hotels & motels
HQ: The Sheraton Corporation
1111 Westchester Ave
White Plains NY 10604
800 328-6242

(P-13246)
SHERATON PK HT AT ANAHEIM RSORT
Also Called: Franchisee
1855 S Harbor Blvd, Anaheim (92802-3509)
PHONE.................................714 750-1811
Fax: 714 971-3626
Russell Cox, *Principal*
Eric Czech, *Vice Pres*
Rosa Cook, *Principal*
John Medrow, *Office Mgr*
Casaundra Alvarado, *Human Res Mgr*
EMP: 57
SALES (est): 4.9MM **Privately Held**
SIC: 7011 Hotels & motels

(P-13247)
SHERTON GRDN GROVE ANHEIM S HT
12221 Harbor Blvd, Garden Grove (92840-4005)
PHONE.................................714 703-8400
Ronnie Lam, *Owner*
Phil Wolfgramm, *General Mgr*
Jonathan Chitwood, *Manager*
EMP: 80
SALES (est): 1.9MM **Privately Held**
SIC: 7011 Hotels

(P-13248)
SHERWOOD VALLEY RANCHERIA
Also Called: Sherwood Vlley Rnchria Casino
100 Kawi Pl, Willits (95490-4674)
PHONE.................................707 459-7330
Kani Neves, *Manager*
Elizabeth Sadlier, *Chief Mktg Ofcr*
EMP: 60 **Privately Held**
SIC: 7011 Casino hotel
PA: Sherwood Valley Rancheria
190 Sherwood Hill Dr
Willits CA 95490
707 459-9690

(P-13249)
SHOKAWAH CASINO
Also Called: Hopland Sho-Ka-Wah Casino
13101 Nokomis Rd, Hopland (95449-9793)
PHONE.................................707 744-1395
Fax: 707 744-1698
Donna Sallady, *Principal*
EMP: 50
SALES (est): 4.4MM **Privately Held**
SIC: 7011 Casino hotel

(P-13250)
SHORE HOTEL
1515 Ocean Ave, Santa Monica (90401-2118)
PHONE.................................310 458-1515
Julie Ward, *Principal*
Aaron Peaslee, *Director*
Danielle Nathan, *Assistant*
Jennifer Weikel, *Assistant*
EMP: 59
SALES (est): 3.5MM **Privately Held**
SIC: 7011 Hotels

(P-13251)
SHRI LAXMI NARYAN HSPTLTY GRP
Also Called: Hilton
1401 Arden Way, Sacramento (95815-4002)
PHONE.................................916 922-8041

Vinod Kumar Sharma, *President*
Nadder Elkabbany, *General Mgr*
Lisa Liddon, *Sales Staff*
EMP: 99
SALES: 950K **Privately Held**
SIC: 7011 Hotels & motels

(P-13252)
SHRI SIDHI VINAYAKA HOTEL INC
Also Called: Hilton
500 Leisure Ln, Sacramento (95815-4207)
PHONE.................................855 922-5252
Vinod Kumar Sharma, *CEO*
Janet Berger, *General Mgr*
EMP: 197
SALES (est): 6.2MM **Privately Held**
SIC: 7011 Hotels & motels

(P-13253)
SIDJON CORPORATION
Also Called: Livermore Casino
3571 1st St, Livermore (94551-4901)
PHONE.................................925 606-6135
Fax: 925 606-1087
Sidney Ahn, *CEO*
EMP: 100 EST: 2007
SQ FT: 15,000
SALES (est): 3.2MM **Privately Held**
SIC: 7011 Casino hotel

(P-13254)
SIERRA AT TAHO SKI RESORTS
1111 Sierra At Tahoe Rd, Twin Bridges (95735-9505)
PHONE.................................530 659-7519
John Rice, *President*
George Gillette, *President*
Stewart Tattersall, *MIS Dir*
EMP: 50 EST: 1996
SALES (est): 2MM **Privately Held**
SIC: 7011 Resort hotel, franchised

(P-13255)
SILICON VALLEY HWANG LLC
Also Called: Radisson Plaza Hotel Inn
1471 N 4th St, San Jose (95112-4716)
PHONE.................................408 452-0200
John Simpson, *Principal*
EMP: 150
SQ FT: 112,218
SALES (est): 2.4MM **Privately Held**
SIC: 7011 Hotels & motels

(P-13256)
SILVERADO RSORT SVCS GROUP LLC
1600 Atlas Peak Rd, NAPA (94558-1425)
PHONE.................................707 257-0200
Fax: 707 257-2867
Tim Wall, *Mng Member*
Phyllis Branco, *Executive*
Dan Tierney, *Controller*
Sharon Hopkins, *Sales Mgr*
Connie Hagston, *Sales Staff*
EMP: 450
SALES (est): 27.4MM **Privately Held**
SIC: 7011 Resort hotel

(P-13257)
SIMI WEST INC
Also Called: Grand Vista Hotel
999 Enchanted Way, Simi Valley (93065-1998)
PHONE.................................805 583-2000
Fax: 805 579-9172
Tim Lasure, *Branch Mgr*
Teresa Meza, *Executive*
Tawny Byron, *General Mgr*
Marcia Foulks, *General Mgr*
Paul Gale, *Chief Engr*
EMP: 115
SALES (corp-wide): 5.4MM **Privately Held**
SIC: 7011 5812 7299 Hotels & motels; eating places; banquet hall facilities
PA: Simi West Inc
75110 Saint Charles Pl # 14
Palm Desert CA

(P-13258)
SINCLAIR COMPANIES
Also Called: Westgate Hotel
1055 2nd Ave, San Diego (92101-4811)
PHONE.................................619 238-1818

7011 - Hotels, Motels & Tourist Courts County (P-13259)

Richard Cox, *Branch Mgr*
EMP: 160
SALES (corp-wide): 6.9B **Privately Held**
SIC: 7011 Hotels
PA: The Sinclair Companies
550 E South Temple
Salt Lake City UT 84102
801 363-5100

(P-13259)
SISKIYOU DEVELOPMENT COMPANY
Also Called: HI Lo Motel
88 S Weed Blvd, Edgewood (96094-2607)
PHONE.................................530 938-2731
Fax: 530 938-2610
Shawn Zanni, *Manager*
EMP: 65
SALES (corp-wide): 12.4MM **Privately Held**
WEB: www.sisdevco.com
SIC: 7011 Motels
PA: Siskiyou Development Company Inc
79 S Weed Blvd Ste 2
Weed CA 96094
530 938-2904

(P-13260)
SITA RAM LLC
Also Called: Best Western Amador Inn
200 S State Highway 49, Jackson (95642-2548)
PHONE.................................209 223-0211
Fax: 209 223-4836
Kumar Sharma,
Puwan Kumar,
EMP: 100
SQ FT: 8,000
SALES (est): 3.1MM **Privately Held**
WEB: www.sitaram.com
SIC: 7011 5812 5813 7991 Hotels & motels; eating places; bar (drinking places); physical fitness facilities

(P-13261)
SIX CONTINENTS HOTELS INC
Also Called: Staybrdge Sites By Holiday Inn
19901 Prairie Ave, Torrance (90503-1687)
PHONE.................................310 371-8525
John Bvell, *Manager*
EMP: 97
SALES (corp-wide): 1.8B **Privately Held**
SIC: 7011 Hotels & motels; hotel, franchised
HQ: Six Continents Hotels, Inc.
3 Ravinia Dr Ste 100
Atlanta GA 30346
770 604-2000

(P-13262)
SIX CONTINENTS HOTELS INC
Also Called: Holiday Inn Van Nuys
8244 Orion Ave, Van Nuys (91406-1344)
PHONE.................................818 989-5010
Bob Yeager, *General Mgr*
Darrell Stephems, *Chief Engr*
Vilma Regopoulos, *Exec Sec*
EMP: 70
SALES (corp-wide): 1.8B **Privately Held**
SIC: 7011 5812 Hotels & motels; restaurant, family: chain
HQ: Six Continents Hotels, Inc.
3 Ravinia Dr Ste 100
Atlanta GA 30346
770 604-2000

(P-13263)
SIX CONTINENTS HOTELS INC
Also Called: Holiday Inn
1020 S Figueroa St, Los Angeles (90015-1305)
PHONE.................................213 748-1291
Fax: 213 748-6028
Emerson Glazer, *President*
EMP: 100
SALES (corp-wide): 1.8B **Privately Held**
WEB: www.sixcontinenhotels.com
SIC: 7011 5812 5813 Hotels & motels; eating places; bar (drinking places)
HQ: Six Continents Hotels, Inc.
3 Ravinia Dr Ste 100
Atlanta GA 30346
770 604-2000

(P-13264)
SIX CONTINENTS HOTELS INC
Also Called: Holiday Inn
19800 S Vermont Ave, Torrance (90502-1126)
PHONE.................................310 781-9100
David Britton, *General Mgr*
EMP: 140
SALES (corp-wide): 1.8B **Privately Held**
WEB: www.sixcontinenthotels.com
SIC: 7011 Hotels & motels
HQ: Six Continents Hotels, Inc.
3 Ravinia Dr Ste 100
Atlanta GA 30346
770 604-2000

(P-13265)
SIX CONTINENTS HOTELS INC
Also Called: Holiday Inn - San Diego-On Bay
1355 N Harbor Dr, San Diego (92101-3321)
PHONE.................................619 232-3861
Tony Lovoy, *General Mgr*
Sandra Maleck, *Manager*
EMP: 75
SALES (corp-wide): 1.8B **Privately Held**
WEB: www.sixcontinenthotels.com
SIC: 7011 Hotels & motels
HQ: Six Continents Hotels, Inc.
3 Ravinia Dr Ste 100
Atlanta GA 30346
770 604-2000

(P-13266)
SIX CONTINENTS HOTELS INC
Also Called: Crown Plaza
11950 Dublin Canyon Rd # 609, Pleasanton (94588-2818)
PHONE.................................925 847-6000
Cathy Ryle, *Manager*
EMP: 75
SALES (corp-wide): 1.8B **Privately Held**
WEB: www.sixcontinenthotels.com
SIC: 7011 Hotels & motels
HQ: Six Continents Hotels, Inc.
3 Ravinia Dr Ste 100
Atlanta GA 30346
770 604-2000

(P-13267)
SIX CONTINENTS HOTELS INC
Also Called: Staybridge Suites
1110 A St, San Diego (92101-4732)
PHONE.................................619 795-4000
Chris Jones, *Manager*
Michael Schaff, *Manager*
Thomas Stuart, *Manager*
EMP: 97
SALES (corp-wide): 1.8B **Privately Held**
WEB: www.sixcontinenthotels.com
SIC: 7011 Hotels & motels
HQ: Six Continents Hotels, Inc.
3 Ravinia Dr Ste 100
Atlanta GA 30346
770 604-2000

(P-13268)
SIX CONTINENTS HOTELS INC
Also Called: Holiday Inn
700 National City Blvd, National City (91950-1124)
PHONE.................................619 474-2800
Fax: 619 474-1689
Larry Oneal, *General Mgr*
Nicole Hohenstein, *General Mgr*
Zoltan Sarkany, *Info Tech Mgr*
Anh Tran, *Accounting Mgr*
Todd Olson, *Controller*
EMP: 80
SALES (corp-wide): 1.8B **Privately Held**
WEB: www.sixcontinenthotels.com
SIC: 7011 Hotels & motels
HQ: Six Continents Hotels, Inc.
3 Ravinia Dr Ste 100
Atlanta GA 30346
770 604-2000

(P-13269)
SKY COURT USA INC
Also Called: Hyatt Westlake Plaza Hotel
880 S Westlake Blvd, Westlake Village (91361-2905)
PHONE.................................805 497-9991
Tetsuo Nishida, *President*
David Kirkinn, *General Mgr*
Leroy Russel, *Controller*
Kathryn Rhodes, *Human Res Mgr*
EMP: 180
SALES (est): 2.6MM **Privately Held**
SIC: 7011 Hotels

(P-13270)
SMITH RIVER LUCKY 7 CASINO
350 N Indian Rd, Smith River (95567-9474)
PHONE.................................707 487-7777
Fax: 707 487-5007
Terry Westrick, *Partner*
EMP: 70 **EST:** 1997
SALES (est): 5.2MM **Privately Held**
SIC: 7011 Casino hotel

(P-13271)
SMOKE TREE INC
Also Called: Smoke Tree Ranch
1850 Smoke Tree Ln, Palm Springs (92264-1602)
PHONE.................................760 327-1221
Fax: 760 327-9490
Lisa Bell, *Manager*
Dana Fosberg, *Controller*
Brad Poncher, *Manager*
EMP: 85
SALES (est): 6MM **Privately Held**
WEB: www.smoketreeinc.com
SIC: 7011 Resort hotel

(P-13272)
SNOW SUMMIT SKI CORPORATION (PA)
880 Summit Blvd, Big Bear Lake (92315)
P.O. Box 77 (92315-0077)
PHONE.................................909 866-5766
Fax: 909 866-3201
Richard C Kun, *President*
Robert Tarras, *CFO*
Alan Macquoid, *Treasurer*
Robert Law, *Vice Pres*
Janet Evans, *Admin Mgr*
EMP: 150
SQ FT: 10,000
SALES (est): 59MM **Privately Held**
WEB: www.bearmtn.com
SIC: 7011 5812 Ski lodge; American restaurant

(P-13273)
SOULDRIVER LESSEE INC
Also Called: Hotel Solamar
435 6th Ave, San Diego (92101-7007)
PHONE.................................619 819-9500
Maria Streedy, *President*
Jim Gross, *General Mgr*
Pam Richardson, *General Mgr*
Laura Hepp, *Finance*
Eric Manning, *Sales Dir*
EMP: 80
SALES (est): 7.6MM **Privately Held**
SIC: 7011 Hotels & motels

(P-13274)
SOUTH COAST WESTIN HOTEL CO
Also Called: Starwood Hotels & Resorts
686 Anton Blvd, Costa Mesa (92626-1920)
PHONE.................................714 540-2500
Fax: 714 662-6695
Steve Heyer, *CEO*
Bob Jenness, *Vice Pres*
Mike Hall, *Managing Dir*
Vasant Prabhu, *CTO*
Eden Malik, *Controller*
EMP: 99
SALES (est): 10.2MM
SALES (corp-wide): 14.4B **Publicly Held**
SIC: 7011 5812 Hotels & motels; eating places
HQ: Starwood Hotels & Resorts Worldwide, Llc
1 Star Pt
Stamford CT 06902
203 964-6000

(P-13275)
SOUTHBOURNE INC
Also Called: Campton Place Hotel
340 Stockton St, San Francisco (94108-4609)
PHONE.................................415 781-5555
Fax: 415 955-5536
Reymond Dixon, *Director*
Nieves Trejo, *Chief Engr*
Jason Quan, *Controller*
Ruth Dfranco, *Human Res Dir*
Birgit Rapp, *Account Dir*
EMP: 131
SALES (est): 5.6MM **Privately Held**
WEB: www.camptonplace.com
SIC: 7011 Hotels
PA: Taj Hotels
Nandafata Aral Korpana
Wardha MH

(P-13276)
SPA RESORT CASINO (PA)
401 E Amado Rd, Palm Springs (92262-6403)
PHONE.................................760 883-1000
Kato Moy, *General Mgr*
Agvahgue Eahilla Indian, *Owner*
Maria Mendoza, *Executive*
Brat Meier, *Controller*
Steve Burt, *Senior Buyer*
EMP: 99
SALES (est): 59MM **Privately Held**
SIC: 7011 Resort hotel

(P-13277)
SPA RESORT CASINO
100 N Indian Canyon Dr, Palm Springs (92262-6414)
PHONE.................................760 883-1034
Max Ross, *CFO*
Daniel Spencer, *Manager*
EMP: 901
SALES (corp-wide): 59MM **Privately Held**
SIC: 7011 Resort hotel
PA: Spa Resort Casino
401 E Amado Rd
Palm Springs CA 92262
760 883-1000

(P-13278)
SPECTRUM HOTEL GROUP LLC
Also Called: Double Three Htlirvinespectrum
90 Pacifica, Irvine (92618-3312)
PHONE.................................949 471-8888
Wade Branning, *CFO*
Luis Plascencia, *Admin Mgr*
Shef Keto, *Manager*
EMP: 100
SALES (est): 6.1MM **Privately Held**
SIC: 7011 7991 5812 Hotels & motels; physical fitness facilities; eating places

(P-13279)
SPECTRUM HOTEL GROUP LLC
Also Called: Doubletree Hotel
90 Pacifica, Irvine (92618-3312)
PHONE.................................949 471-8888
Fax: 949 471-8600
Tim Busch, *President*
Malcolm Smith, *General Mgr*
John Savage, *Data Proc Staff*
Shef Keto, *Manager*
EMP: 100
SALES (est): 3MM **Privately Held**
WEB: www.doubletreeirvinespectrum.com
SIC: 7011 7991 5812 Hotels & motels; physical fitness facilities; eating places

(P-13280)
SPIRE CONCESSIONS LLC
Also Called: Marriott Burbank
2500 N Hollywood Way, Burbank (91505-1019)
PHONE.................................818 843-6000
William Deforrest, *CEO*
William Keating, *President*
Chad Cooley, *Vice Pres*
Russell Flicker, *Vice Pres*
Bernard Michael, *Vice Pres*
EMP: 80
SALES (est): 1.9MM **Privately Held**
SIC: 7011 Hotels & motels

(P-13281)
SPORTSMENS LODGE HOTEL LLC
12825 Ventura Blvd, Studio City (91604-2397)
PHONE.................................818 769-4700
Fax: 818 766-4093
Mark Harlig,
Ron Silva, *General Mgr*
Michael Dunkel, *Controller*

Tiffany Flowers, *Controller*
Angel Delara, *Sales Mgr*
EMP: 120
SQ FT: 100,000
SALES (est): 9MM **Privately Held**
WEB: www.slhotel.com
SIC: 7011 5812 5813 Hotels; American restaurant; cocktail lounge

(P-13282)
SQUAW CREEK ASSOCIATES LLC
Also Called: Resort At Squaw Creek
400 Squaw Creek Rd, Alpine Meadows (96146-9778)
P.O. Box 3333, Olympic Valley (96146-3333)
PHONE 530 581-6624
Fax: 530 581-5407
Eric Sather, *General Mgr*
Jamie Sabatier, *COO*
Andre Priemer, *General Mgr*
Jorge Melendez, *Controller*
Erika Stohl, *Human Res Dir*
EMP: 600
SALES (est): 40.1MM **Privately Held**
WEB: www.squawcreek.com
SIC: 7011 Resort hotel

(P-13283)
SQUAW VALLEY DEVELOPMENT CO (HQ)
Also Called: Squaw Valley Ski
1960 Squaw Valley Rd, Olympic Valley (96146)
P.O. Box 2007 (96146-2007)
PHONE 530 583-6985
Fax: 530 581-7106
Andy Wirth, *CEO*
Lori Pommerenck, *Treasurer*
Rodney Jones, *Vice Pres*
Carolyn Dee, *Admin Mgr*
Lisa Houghton, *Info Tech Mgr*
EMP: 111
SALES (est): 31.6MM
SALES (corp-wide): 243.3MM **Privately Held**
SIC: 7011 5812 5813 7929 Hostels; ski lodge; eating places; bar (drinking places); entertainment service
PA: Ksl Capital Partners, Llc
100 Saint Paul St Ste 800
Denver CO 80206
720 284-6400

(P-13284)
SQUAW VALLEY SKI CORPORATION (DH)
1960 Squaw Valley Rd, Olympic Valley (96146)
P.O. Box 2007 (96146-2007)
PHONE 530 583-6985
Fax: 530 581-7161
Alexander C Cushing, *Ch of Bd*
Nancy R Wendt, *President*
Andy Wirth, *President*
Mike Livak, *Exec VP*
Mike Degroff, *Vice Pres*
EMP: 80
SQ FT: 200,000
SALES (est): 25.9MM
SALES (corp-wide): 243.3MM **Privately Held**
SIC: 7011 Ski lodge
HQ: The Squaw Valley Development Company
1960 Squaw Valley Rd
Olympic Valley CA 96146
530 583-6985

(P-13285)
STANFORD HOTELS CORPORATION
433 California St Ste 700, San Francisco (94104-2011)
PHONE 415 398-3333
Lawrence Lui, *President*
James Evans, *CFO*
Colman Conneely, *Regional VP*
Candace E Fennell, *Vice Pres*
Joyce Weible, *Office Mgr*
EMP: 245
SQ FT: 12,000
SALES (est): 24.5MM **Privately Held**
WEB: www.sheratonuptown.com
SIC: 7011 Hotels & motels

(P-13286)
STANFORD PARK HOTEL
100 El Camino Real, Menlo Park (94025-5292)
PHONE 650 322-1234
Fax: 650 322-0975
Ellis Alden, *Partner*
Western Lodging Flume Corpor, *Partner*
John Farrington, *General Mgr*
William Lea, *Purchasing*
Wanda Derrig, *Sales Staff*
EMP: 212
SQ FT: 122,000
SALES (est): 14.4MM **Privately Held**
WEB: www.stanfordparkhotel.com
SIC: 7011 5813 5812 Hotels; drinking places; eating places

(P-13287)
STARLIGHT MANAGEMENT GROUP
Also Called: Wyndham Garden Hotel
1355 N 4th St, San Jose (95112-4714)
PHONE 408 334-7456
Ajay Shingal, *Vice Pres*
EMP: 99
SALES (est): 2.4MM **Privately Held**
SIC: 7011 Hotels & motels

(P-13288)
STARWOOD HOTEL
Also Called: Starwood Hotels & Resorts
5990 Green Valley Cir, Culver City (90230-6907)
PHONE 310 641-7740
Ian Gee, *Corp Counsel*
Francisco Amaya, *Executive*
King Natalie, *Sales Executive*
Marcello Gustos, *Manager*
EMP: 60
SALES (est): 3.5MM
SALES (corp-wide): 14.4B **Publicly Held**
SIC: 7011 Hotels & motels
HQ: Starwood Hotels & Resorts Worldwide, Llc
1 Star Pt
Stamford CT 06902
203 964-6000

(P-13289)
STARWOOD HOTELS & RESORTS
10480 4th St, Rancho Cucamonga (91730-5893)
PHONE 909 484-2018
EMP: 195
SALES (corp-wide): 14.4B **Publicly Held**
SIC: 7011 Hotels & motels
HQ: Starwood Hotels & Resorts Worldwide, Llc
1 Star Pt
Stamford CT 06902
203 964-6000

(P-13290)
STARWOOD HOTELS & RESORTS
930 Hilgard Ave, Los Angeles (90024-3033)
PHONE 310 208-8765
Parita Burmee, *Branch Mgr*
Jeff Darnell, *Sales Mgr*
Kelly Beaver, *Account Dir*
EMP: 185
SALES (corp-wide): 14.4B **Publicly Held**
SIC: 7011 Hotels & motels
HQ: Starwood Hotels & Resorts Worldwide, Llc
1 Star Pt
Stamford CT 06902
203 964-6000

(P-13291)
STARWOOD HOTELS & RESORTS
1230 J St, Sacramento (95814-2907)
PHONE 916 447-1700
EMP: 201
SALES (corp-wide): 14.4B **Publicly Held**
SIC: 7011 Hotels & motels

HQ: Starwood Hotels & Resorts Worldwide, Llc
1 Star Pt
Stamford CT 06902
203 964-6000

(P-13292)
STARWOOD HOTELS & RESORTS
15621 Red Hill Ave # 100, Tustin (92780-7322)
PHONE 714 258-4575
EMP: 60
SALES (corp-wide): 5.7B **Publicly Held**
SIC: 7011
PA: Starwood Hotels & Resorts Worldwide, Inc.
1 Star Pt
Stamford CT 06902
203 964-6000

(P-13293)
STARWOOD HOTELS & RESORTS
181 3rd St, San Francisco (94103-3107)
PHONE 415 777-5300
Fax: 415 817-7864
Toni Knorr, *General Mgr*
Kym Evets, *Marketing Staff*
Terry Haney, *Director*
EMP: 100
SALES (corp-wide): 14.4B **Publicly Held**
SIC: 7011 8741 Hotels & motels; casino hotel; resort hotel; motor inn; hotel or motel management
HQ: Starwood Hotels & Resorts Worldwide, Llc
1 Star Pt
Stamford CT 06902
203 964-6000

(P-13294)
STARWOOD HOTELS & RESORTS
404 S Figueroa St, Los Angeles (90071-1710)
PHONE 213 624-1000
Bryan Fitzgerald, *Manager*
Nick F Fisher, *Manager*
EMP: 900
SALES (corp-wide): 14.4B **Publicly Held**
SIC: 7011 Hotels & motels
HQ: Starwood Hotels & Resorts Worldwide, Llc
1 Star Pt
Stamford CT 06902
203 964-6000

(P-13295)
STARWOOD HOTELS & RESORTS
1010 Northgate Dr, San Rafael (94903-2502)
PHONE 415 479-8800
Susan Bell, *General Mgr*
Victor Jimenez, *Chief Engr*
Lori Owles, *Director*
John Monestere, *Manager*
EMP: 140
SALES (corp-wide): 14.4B **Publicly Held**
SIC: 7011 5812 Hotels & motels; eating places
HQ: Starwood Hotels & Resorts Worldwide, Llc
1 Star Pt
Stamford CT 06902
203 964-6000

(P-13296)
STARWOOD HOTELS & RESORTS
401 E Millbrae Ave, Millbrae (94030-3111)
PHONE 650 692-6363
Fax: 650 697-8735
Tim Lucher, *Branch Mgr*
Tim Lessure, *General Mgr*
Jorge Silva, *Finance*
EMP: 99
SALES (corp-wide): 14.4B **Publicly Held**
SIC: 7011 Hotels & motels
HQ: Starwood Hotels & Resorts Worldwide, Llc
1 Star Pt
Stamford CT 06902
203 964-6000

(P-13297)
STARWOOD HOTELS & RESORTS
71333 Dinah Shore Dr, Rancho Mirage (92270-1501)
PHONE 760 328-5955
Fax: 760 770-2170
Ken Pilgrim, *Manager*
Robert Wood, *MIS Dir*
Dawn O'Flannery-Cleveland, *Sales Staff*
EMP: 600
SALES (corp-wide): 14.4B **Publicly Held**
SIC: 7011 Hotels & motels
HQ: Starwood Hotels & Resorts Worldwide, Llc
1 Star Pt
Stamford CT 06902
203 964-6000

(P-13298)
STARWOOD HOTELS & RESORTS
125 3rd St, San Francisco (94103-3107)
PHONE 415 284-4049
Fax: 415 284-4015
EMP: 150
SALES (corp-wide): 14.4B **Publicly Held**
SIC: 7011 Hotels & motels
HQ: Starwood Hotels & Resorts Worldwide, Llc
1 Star Pt
Stamford CT 06902
203 964-6000

(P-13299)
STARWOOD HOTELS & RESORTS
2 New Montgomery St, San Francisco (94105-3402)
PHONE 415 512-1111
T Staramelino, *Business Mgr*
Celeste Repsher, *Human Resources*
EMP: 195
SALES (corp-wide): 14.4B **Publicly Held**
SIC: 7011 Hotels & motels
HQ: Starwood Hotels & Resorts Worldwide, Llc
1 Star Pt
Stamford CT 06902
203 964-6000

(P-13300)
STARWOOD HOTELS & RESORTS
125 3rd St, San Francisco (94103-3107)
PHONE 415 284-4000
Elias Assaly, *Manager*
Richard Thone, *Engineer*
EMP: 195
SALES (corp-wide): 14.4B **Publicly Held**
SIC: 7011 Hotels & motels
HQ: Starwood Hotels & Resorts Worldwide, Llc
1 Star Pt
Stamford CT 06902
203 964-6000

(P-13301)
STARWOOD HOTELS & RESORTS
910 Broadway Cir, San Diego (92101-6114)
PHONE 619 239-2200
Fax: 619 239-0509
Doug Korn, *General Mgr*
EMP: 250
SALES (corp-wide): 14.4B **Publicly Held**
SIC: 7011 7991 6512 5812 Hotels & motels; physical fitness facilities; nonresidential building operators; eating places
HQ: Starwood Hotels & Resorts Worldwide, Llc
1 Star Pt
Stamford CT 06902
203 964-6000

(P-13302)
STARWOOD HOTELS & RESORTS
6250 Hollywood Blvd, Los Angeles (90028-5325)
PHONE 323 798-1300
Leon Young, *General Mgr*
EMP: 195

7011 - Hotels, Motels & Tourist Courts County (P-13303)

PRODUUCTS & SERVICES SECTION

SALES (corp-wide): 14.4B **Publicly Held**
SIC: 7011 Hotels & motels
HQ: Starwood Hotels & Resorts Worldwide, Llc
    1 Star Pt
    Stamford CT 06902
    203 964-6000

(P-13303)
STARWOOD HOTELS & RESORTS
601 W Mckinley Ave, Pomona (91768-1635)
PHONE..................909 622-2220
John Gilbert, *General Mgr*
Cheryl Wheat, *Human Res Dir*
EMP: 195
SALES (corp-wide): 14.4B **Publicly Held**
SIC: 7011 Hotels & motels
HQ: Starwood Hotels & Resorts Worldwide, Llc
    1 Star Pt
    Stamford CT 06902
    203 964-6000

(P-13304)
STARWOOD HOTELS & RESORTS
1617 1st Ave, San Diego (92101-3003)
PHONE..................619 239-9600
Gary Comeaux, *General Mgr*
EMP: 60
SALES (corp-wide): 14.4B **Publicly Held**
SIC: 7011 Hotels & motels
HQ: Starwood Hotels & Resorts Worldwide, Llc
    1 Star Pt
    Stamford CT 06902
    203 964-6000

(P-13305)
STOCKBRIDGE/SBE HOLDINGS LLC
5900 Wilshire Blvd # 3100, Los Angeles (90036-5013)
PHONE..................323 655-8000
Sam Nazarian, *CEO*
EMP: 3000
SALES (est): 61MM **Privately Held**
SIC: 7011 Hotels; casino hotel

(P-13306)
STONEBRIDGE MCWHINNEY LLC
Also Called: Hampton Inn
11747 Harbor Blvd, Garden Grove (92840-2701)
PHONE..................714 703-8800
Fax: 714 703-8900
Thomas Long, *Manager*
Mike Thomas, *Manager*
EMP: 50
SALES (corp-wide): 8.9MM **Privately Held**
WEB: www.sleepinnpueblo.com
SIC: 7011 Hotels & motels
PA: Stonebridge Mcwhinney Llc
    9100 E Panorama Dr # 300
    Englewood CO 80112
    303 785-3100

(P-13307)
STRESS RELIEF SERVICES
12603 Mariposa Rd, Victorville (92395-6004)
PHONE..................760 241-7472
Nicole Williams, *Owner*
EMP: 60
SALES (est): 1.8MM **Privately Held**
SIC: 7011 Hotels

(P-13308)
SUN HILL PROPERTIES INC (HQ)
Also Called: Hilton Los Angls/Nversal Cy Ht
555 Unversal Hollywood Dr, Universal City (91608-1001)
PHONE..................818 506-2500
Fax: 818 509-2031
Denn Hu, *Ch of Bd*
Lewis Henderson, *Vice Pres*
Ziba Javaherpoury, *Telecom Exec*
Thomas Rubcic, *Info Tech Mgr*
Michelle Szeto, *Controller*
EMP: 350

SALES (est): 19.2MM
SALES (corp-wide): 20.6MM **Privately Held**
WEB: www.sfbayleasing.com
SIC: 7011 Hotel, franchised
PA: Universal Paragon Corporation
    150 Executive Park Blvd # 4000
    San Francisco CA 94134
    415 468-6676

(P-13309)
SUNNYSIDE RESORT
1850 W Lake Blvd, Tahoe City (96145)
P.O. Box 5969 (96145-5969)
PHONE..................530 583-7200
Fax: 530 583-7224
Sandy Saxton, *President*
J Robert Thibaut, *Vice Pres*
Jeff Oxandaboure, *General Mgr*
EMP: 75
SALES (est): 4.2MM **Privately Held**
WEB: www.sunnysideresort.com
SIC: 7011 5812 5813 Hotels; American restaurant; bar (drinking places)

(P-13310)
SUNNYVALE SOF-X OWNER L P
Also Called: Sheraton Hotel Sunnyvale
1100 N Mathilda Ave, Sunnyvale (94089-1206)
PHONE..................408 542-8264
Nick Antonopoulos, *Principal*
Anita Evans, *Principal*
Epenesa Pakola, *General Mgr*
Daniel Williams, *General Mgr*
EMP: 50
SQ FT: 120,000
SALES (est): 326K **Privately Held**
SIC: 7011 Seasonal hotel

(P-13311)
SUNSET TOWER HOTEL LLC
8358 W Sunset Blvd, Los Angeles (90069-1516)
PHONE..................323 654-7100
E Peter Krulewitch, *Mng Member*
Matina Lapanaitis, *General Mgr*
Roger Zavala, *Chief Engr*
Limoko Bolia, *Controller*
Douglas Wickard, *Opers Staff*
EMP: 78
SALES (est): 7.2MM **Privately Held**
SIC: 7011 Hotels

(P-13312)
SUNSTONE CENTER CRT LESSEE INC
120 Vantis Ste 350, Aliso Viejo (92656-2686)
PHONE..................949 382-4000
John V Arabia, *CFO*
Lindsay Monge, *Vice Pres*
EMP: 160
SALES (est): 3.8MM
SALES (corp-wide): 1.2B **Publicly Held**
SIC: 7011 5812 5813 Hotels; eating places; drinking places
HQ: Sunstone Hotel Trs Lessee, Inc.
    120 Vantis Ste 350
    Aliso Viejo CA

(P-13313)
SUNSTONE HOTEL INVESTORS INC
Also Called: Holiday Inn
1617 1st Ave Ste 16, San Diego (92101-3003)
PHONE..................619 239-6171
John Ault, *Manager*
EMP: 65
SALES (corp-wide): 58.4MM **Privately Held**
WEB: www.sunstonehotels.com
SIC: 7011 5812 Hotels & motels; eating places
HQ: Sunstone Hotel Investors, L.L.C.
    120 Vantis Ste 350
    Aliso Viejo CA 92656
    949 330-4000

(P-13314)
SUNSTONE HOTEL INVESTORS INC
Also Called: Marriott
3425 Solano Ave, NAPA (94558-2709)
PHONE..................707 253-8600
Micheal George, *Opers-Prdtn-Mfg*
Jason Woods, *Manager*
EMP: 100
SALES (corp-wide): 58.4MM **Privately Held**
WEB: www.sunstonehotels.com
SIC: 7011 Hotels & motels
HQ: Sunstone Hotel Investors, L.L.C.
    120 Vantis Ste 350
    Aliso Viejo CA 92656
    949 330-4000

(P-13315)
SUNSTONE HOTEL INVESTORS INC
Also Called: Embassy Suites
9801 Airport Blvd, Los Angeles (90045-5407)
PHONE..................310 215-1000
Fax: 310 215-1952
Phil Campaneli, *Manager*
Maria Mora, *Executive*
Michael Damodio, *General Mgr*
Darren Vaughn, *Sales Dir*
EMP: 150
SALES (corp-wide): 58.4MM **Privately Held**
WEB: www.sunstonehotels.com
SIC: 7011 Hotels & motels
HQ: Sunstone Hotel Investors, L.L.C.
    120 Vantis Ste 350
    Aliso Viejo CA 92656
    949 330-4000

(P-13316)
SUNSTONE HOTEL INVESTORS INC
Also Called: Fairmont Newport Beach
4500 Macarthur Blvd, Newport Beach (92660-2010)
PHONE..................949 476-2001
Randy Zupnaski, *General Mgr*
Karl Kruger, *General Mgr*
Virginia Bergman, *Controller*
Sarah Newcomer, *Sales Staff*
EMP: 265
SALES (corp-wide): 58.4MM **Privately Held**
WEB: www.sunstonehotels.com
SIC: 7011 5812 Hotels; eating places
HQ: Sunstone Hotel Investors, L.L.C.
    120 Vantis Ste 350
    Aliso Viejo CA 92656
    949 330-4000

(P-13317)
SUNSTONE HOTEL INVESTORS INC
6161 W Century Blvd, Los Angeles (90045-5310)
PHONE..................310 649-1400
Connie White, *Mng Member*
Suthikiati Chirathivat, *President*
Michael Staehelin, *Executive*
Paul Verduin, *Manager*
EMP: 122
SALES (corp-wide): 58.4MM **Privately Held**
WEB: www.sunstonehotels.com
SIC: 7011 Hotels & motels
HQ: Sunstone Hotel Investors, L.L.C.
    120 Vantis Ste 350
    Aliso Viejo CA 92656
    949 330-4000

(P-13318)
SUNSTONE HOTEL INVESTORS LLC
Also Called: Holiday Inn
14299 Firestone Blvd, La Mirada (90638-5523)
PHONE..................714 739-8500
Dalla Rodriguez, *Manager*
EMP: 122

SALES (corp-wide): 58.4MM **Privately Held**
WEB: www.sunstonehotels.com
SIC: 7011 6512 5812 Hotels & motels; nonresidential building operators; eating places
HQ: Sunstone Hotel Investors, L.L.C.
    120 Vantis Ste 350
    Aliso Viejo CA 92656
    949 330-4000

(P-13319)
SUNSTONE HOTEL INVESTORS LLC
Also Called: Embassy Suites
39375 5th St W, Palmdale (93551-3886)
PHONE..................661 267-6587
Fax: 661 266-3625
Randy Keller, *Manager*
EMP: 122
SALES (corp-wide): 58.4MM **Privately Held**
SIC: 7011 Hotels & motels
HQ: Sunstone Hotel Investors, L.L.C.
    120 Vantis Ste 350
    Aliso Viejo CA 92656
    949 330-4000

(P-13320)
SUNSTONE HOTEL INVESTORS LLC
2 Civic Plaza Dr, Carson (90745-2231)
PHONE..................310 830-9200
John Schulv, *General Mgr*
EMP: 75
SALES (corp-wide): 58.4MM **Privately Held**
WEB: www.sunstonehotels.com
SIC: 7011 7991 5812 Hotels; physical fitness facilities; eating places
HQ: Sunstone Hotel Investors, L.L.C.
    120 Vantis Ste 350
    Aliso Viejo CA 92656
    949 330-4000

(P-13321)
SUNSTONE HOTEL INVESTORS LLC
Also Called: Hawthorn Suites
1752 S Clementine St, Anaheim (92802-2902)
PHONE..................714 635-5000
Warren Nocon, *Branch Mgr*
John Desantis, *Financial Analy*
EMP: 122
SALES (corp-wide): 58.4MM **Privately Held**
WEB: www.sunstonehotels.com
SIC: 7011 Hotels & motels
HQ: Sunstone Hotel Investors, L.L.C.
    120 Vantis Ste 350
    Aliso Viejo CA 92656
    949 330-4000

(P-13322)
SUNSTONE HOTEL MANAGEMENT INC
Also Called: Marriott
3400 Market St, Riverside (92501-2826)
PHONE..................951 784-8000
Tom Donahue, *Manager*
EMP: 200
SALES (corp-wide): 35.6MM **Privately Held**
WEB: www.sunstoneshopper.com
SIC: 7011 Hotels & motels
PA: Sunstone Hotel Management Inc
    120 Vantis Ste 350
    Aliso Viejo CA 92656
    949 297-4183

(P-13323)
SUNSTONE HOTEL MANAGEMENT INC (PA)
120 Vantis Ste 350, Aliso Viejo (92656-2686)
PHONE..................949 297-4183
Robert A Alter, *CEO*
Jon D Cline, *CFO*
Ken Cruse, *CFO*
Kenneth K Cruse, *CFO*
Kenneth Biehl, *Vice Pres*
EMP: 50
SQ FT: 1,200

PRODUCTS & SERVICES SECTION 7011 - Hotels, Motels & Tourist Courts County (P-13346)

SALES (est): 35.6MM **Privately Held**
WEB: www.sunstoneshopper.com
SIC: 7011 Hotels & motels

(P-13324)
SUNSTONE HOTEL PROPERTIES INC
Also Called: Residence Inn By Marriott
1177 S Beverly Dr, Los Angeles (90035-1119)
PHONE............................310 228-4100
Fax: 310 277-7488
Tom Beedon, *General Mgr*
Micahel Damido, *Manager*
Pamela Reisman, *Manager*
Ana Martin, *Consultant*
EMP: 79
SALES (corp-wide): 1.7B **Privately Held**
WEB: www.sunstonehotelproperties.com
SIC: 7011 Hotels & motels
HQ: Sunstone Hotel Properties Inc
120 Vantis Ste 350
Aliso Viejo CA 92656

(P-13325)
SUNSTONE HOTEL PROPERTIES INC
Also Called: Residence Inn By Marriott
1700 N Sepulveda Blvd, Manhattan Beach (90266-5015)
PHONE............................310 546-7627
Fax: 310 545-1327
Sandi Rae Kraft, *Branch Mgr*
Richard Davis, *Sales Dir*
Dolores Escobar, *Manager*
EMP: 79
SALES (corp-wide): 1.7B **Privately Held**
WEB: www.sunstonehotelproperties.com
SIC: 7011 Hotels & motels
HQ: Sunstone Hotel Properties Inc
120 Vantis Ste 350
Aliso Viejo CA 92656

(P-13326)
SUNSTONE HOTEL PROPERTIES INC (DH)
Also Called: Hampton Inn
120 Vantis Ste 350, Aliso Viejo (92656-2686)
PHONE............................949 330-4000
Arthur Buser, *President*
John Elston, *Exec VP*
Evan Studer, *Exec VP*
Kenneth Biehl, *Vice Pres*
Olivier Kolpin, *Vice Pres*
EMP: 120
SALES (est): 88.6MM
SALES (corp-wide): 1.7B **Privately Held**
WEB: www.sunstonehotelproperties.com
SIC: 7011 Hotels & motels
HQ: Interstate Hotels & Resorts, Inc.
4501 Fairfax Dr Ste 500
Arlington VA 22203
703 387-3100

(P-13327)
SUNSTONE OCEAN LESSEE INC
120 Vantis Ste 350, Aliso Viejo (92656-2686)
PHONE............................949 382-4000
John V Arabia, *CFO*
Lindsay Monge, *Treasurer*
Juan Lomeli, *Info Tech Mgr*
Judith Morgan, *Controller*
Laura Hoover, *Sales Mgr*
EMP: 275
SQ FT: 302,000
SALES (est): 6.2MM
SALES (corp-wide): 1.2B **Publicly Held**
SIC: 7011 Hotels & motels
HQ: Sunstone Hotel Trs Lessee, Inc.
120 Vantis Ste 350
Aliso Viejo CA

(P-13328)
SUNSTONE TOP GUN LLC
Also Called: Embassy Stes San Dego-La Jolla
4550 La Jolla Village Dr, San Diego (92122-1248)
PHONE............................858 453-0400

Fax: 858 453-4226
Sunstone Holdco,
Paul Brouillette, *General Mgr*
EMP: 100
SALES (est): 2.8MM
SALES (corp-wide): 1.2B **Publicly Held**
SIC: 7011 Hotels & motels
HQ: Sunstone Hotel Partnership, Llc
120 Vantis Ste 350
Aliso Viejo CA 92656
949 330-4000

(P-13329)
SVI LAX LLC
Also Called: Residence Inn By Marriot Lax/C
5933 W Century Blvd, Los Angeles (90045-5471)
PHONE............................310 281-0300
Robert A Alter,
Diana Owen, *CFO*
Tom Beedon, *General Mgr*
EMP: 60
SQ FT: 213,000
SALES: 12MM **Privately Held**
SIC: 7011 Hotels & motels

(P-13330)
SWISS HOTEL GROUP INC
18 W Spain St, Sonoma (95476-5601)
PHONE............................707 938-2884
Fax: 707 938-3298
Henry Marioni, *President*
EMP: 60 EST: 1929
SQ FT: 6,350
SALES: 2.3MM **Privately Held**
WEB: www.swisshotelsonoma.com
SIC: 7011 5813 5812 Hotels; bar (drinking places); steak restaurant

(P-13331)
SWVP DEL MAR HOTEL LLC
Also Called: DoubleTree by Hilton
11915 El Camino Real, San Diego (92130-2539)
PHONE............................858 481-5900
Fax: 858 481-0990
Tom Donahue, *Manager*
EMP: 120 EST: 2005
SALES (est): 6.3MM **Privately Held**
SIC: 7011 Hotels & motels

(P-13332)
SYCAMORE MINERAL SPRING RESORT
1215 Avila Beach Dr, San Luis Obispo (93405-8048)
PHONE............................805 595-7302
Russell Kiessig, *President*
John King, *President*
Steve Gregory, *Vice Pres*
Charles Yates, *Vice Pres*
Tamarah Chancellor, *Accountant*
EMP: 65 EST: 1975
SQ FT: 36,150
SALES (est): 2.9MM **Privately Held**
WEB: www.smsr.com
SIC: 7011 7991 Resort hotel; spas

(P-13333)
SYDELL HOTELS LLC
Also Called: Line Hotel The
3515 Wilshire Blvd, Los Angeles (90010-2301)
PHONE............................213 381-7411
Doug Elpern, *President*
Gary J Thomas, *Principal*
Seth Dubner, *Project Mgr*
Alex Baum-Stein, *Sr Project Mgr*
Steve Harloe, *Director*
EMP: 130
SALES (est): 9.6MM **Privately Held**
SIC: 7011 Hotels

(P-13334)
T I C HOTELS INC
Also Called: Best Western Bayside Inn
555 W Ash St, San Diego (92101-3414)
PHONE............................619 238-7577
Tracey Wicken, *General Mgr*
Emily Tillson, *Manager*
EMP: 55 **Privately Held**
WEB: www.tichotels.com
SIC: 7011 Hotels & motels

HQ: T I C Hotels Inc
1811 State St Ste C
Santa Barbara CA 93101
805 898-0855

(P-13335)
T I C HOTELS INC
Also Called: Shorecliff Properties
2555 Price St, Pismo Beach (93449-2111)
PHONE............................805 773-4671
Fax: 805 773-2341
Edward Brown, *Systems Mgr*
Charles Holden, *General Mgr*
Barbara Parra, *General Mgr*
Karen Fyfe, *Human Res Dir*
Michael Bruce, *Manager*
EMP: 100 **Privately Held**
WEB: www.tichotels.com
SIC: 7011 5813 5812 Hotels & motels; eating places; bar (drinking places)
HQ: T I C Hotels Inc
1811 State St Ste C
Santa Barbara CA 93101
805 898-0855

(P-13336)
T M MIAN & ASSOCIATES INC
Also Called: Hilton Garden Inn Calabasas
24150 Park Sorrento, Calabasas (91302-4101)
PHONE............................818 591-2300
Shawn Nicoles, *General Mgr*
EMP: 55
SALES (corp-wide): 4.2MM **Privately Held**
SIC: 7011 Hotel, franchised
PA: T. M. Mian & Associates, Inc.
1055 Regal Row
Dallas TX 75247
972 960-2024

(P-13337)
T M MIAN & ASSOCIATES INC
Also Called: Hilton
2000 Solar Dr, Oxnard (93036-2694)
PHONE............................805 983-8600
Fax: 805 983-3200
T M Mian, *Partner*
Alan Hurd, *Executive*
Dolores Licon, *Info Tech Mgr*
EMP: 70
SALES (corp-wide): 4.2MM **Privately Held**
SIC: 7011 Hotels & motels
PA: T. M. Mian & Associates, Inc.
1055 Regal Row
Dallas TX 75247
972 960-2024

(P-13338)
T-12 THREE LLC
Also Called: Hard Rock Hotel
207 5th Ave, San Diego (92101-6908)
PHONE............................619 702-3000
Nilesh Madhav, *Mng Member*
Jon Eyer, *Executive*
Jorge Ruiz Jr, *Executive*
Arron Reynolds, *Social Dir*
Luis Bregas, *General Mgr*
EMP: 356
SALES (est): 25.1MM **Privately Held**
SIC: 7011 Hotels & motels

(P-13339)
TACHI PALACE HOTEL & CASINO
17225 Jersey Ave, Lemoore (93245-9760)
PHONE............................559 924-7751
Tachi Yokut, *Owner*
Santa Rosa Rancheria Tachi Yok, *Owner*
Richard Laudale, *CFO*
Jim Snead, *CFO*
Joaquin Amaral, *Analyst*
◆ EMP: 1500
SALES (est): 59.5MM **Privately Held**
SIC: 7011 Casino hotel

(P-13340)
TAHOE BEACH & SKI CLUB
3601 Lake Tahoe Blvd, South Lake Tahoe (96150-8915)
PHONE............................530 541-6220
Roy Fraser, *President*
Tamara Hollingsworth, *Manager*
EMP: 60

SALES (est): 3MM **Privately Held**
WEB: www.tahoebeachandski.com
SIC: 7011 6513 Hotels & motels; apartment hotel operation

(P-13341)
TERRE DU SOLEIL LTD
Also Called: Auberge Du Soleil
180 Rutherford Hill Rd, Rutherford (94573)
P.O. Box B (94573-0902)
PHONE............................707 963-1211
Fax: 707 963-8764
George Goeggel, *General Ptnr*
Robert Harmon, *General Mgr*
Bradley Reynolds, *General Ptnr*
Claude Rouas, *General Ptnr*
Robert Curry, *Executive*
EMP: 280
SQ FT: 20,000
SALES (est): 16.8MM **Privately Held**
WEB: www.aubergedusoleil.com
SIC: 7011 5812 Resort hotel; French restaurant

(P-13342)
TESI INVESTMENT COMPANY LLC
Also Called: Best Western Pasada At Harbor
5005 N Harbor Dr, San Diego (92106-2307)
PHONE............................619 224-3254
Fax: 619 224-2186
Octavio Terrazas, *President*
Teresa Terrazas, *CFO*
Victoria Elizondo, *Vice Pres*
Pilar Terrazas, *Admin Sec*
EMP: 60
SQ FT: 9,825
SALES: 1.8MM **Privately Held**
SIC: 7011 Hotels & motels

(P-13343)
TIBURON HOTEL LLC
Also Called: Lodge At Tiburon, The
1651 Tiburon Blvd, Belvedere Tiburon (94920-2511)
PHONE............................415 435-5996
EMP: 77
SALES (est): 3.9MM **Privately Held**
SIC: 7011 7389 Hotels & motels; office facilities & secretarial service rental

(P-13344)
TIC HOTELS INC
Also Called: Tic Worldwide
555 W Ash St, San Diego (92101-3414)
PHONE............................619 238-7577
Suzy Briggs, *Corp Secy*
Tracey Wicken, *General Mgr*
Margarita Gervacio, *Financial Exec*
Tracy Wickens, *Sales Mgr*
T I C Hotels,
EMP: 50
SALES (est): 3MM **Privately Held**
SIC: 7011 Hotels

(P-13345)
TIC WORLD-WIDE CORP
Also Called: Best Western
555 W Ash St, San Diego (92101-3414)
PHONE............................619 233-7500
Fax: 619 239-8060
Mamo Takeuchi, *President*
EMP: 55
SQ FT: 67,381
SALES (est): 4.1MM **Privately Held**
WEB: www.baysideinn.com
SIC: 7011 Hotels & motels

(P-13346)
TIDES CENTER
124 Turk St, San Francisco (94102-3926)
PHONE............................415 359-9401
EMP: 268 **Privately Held**
SIC: 7011 Hotels & motels
PA: The Tides Center
The Prsdio 1014 Trney Ave
San Francisco CA 94129

7011 - Hotels, Motels & Tourist Courts County (P-13347)

(P-13347)
TODAYS HOTEL CORPORATION (PA)
Also Called: Holiday Inn
1500 Van Ness Ave, San Francisco (94109-4606)
PHONE 415 441-4000
Fax: 415 776-7155
Ming Nin Zen, *President*
Lyn Vuston, *Accountant*
Sita Harding, *Manager*
Alvenia Jeter, *Manager*
EMP: 90
SALES (est): 51.2MM **Privately Held**
WEB: www.goldengatewayhotel.com
SIC: 7011 Hotels & motels

(P-13348)
TODAYS VI LLC
Also Called: Amerisuites
4760 Mills Cir, Ontario (91764-5223)
PHONE 909 980-2200
Fax: 909 980-4433
Peter Zen,
Paul Zen,
Juan Azpeita, *Manager*
EMP: 60
SALES (est): 1.5MM **Privately Held**
SIC: 7011 Hotels & motels

(P-13349)
TORRES-MARTINEZ
Also Called: Red Earth Casino
3089 Norm Niver Rd, Thermal (92274-6550)
PHONE 760 395-1200
David Seufert, *Branch Mgr*
Frank Dwyer, *Director*
Torres Martinez, *Manager*
EMP: 150 **Privately Held**
SIC: 7011 Casino hotel
PA: Torres-Martinez Desert Cahuilla Indians
66725 Martinez Rd
Thermal CA 92274
760 397-0300

(P-13350)
TOWNEPLACE SUITES
Also Called: TownePlace Suites By Marriott
700 E Campbell Ave, Campbell (95008-2104)
PHONE 408 370-4510
Fax: 408 370-4511
Elece Otten, *Owner*
EMP: 80
SALES (est): 1.7MM **Privately Held**
SIC: 7011 Hotel, franchised

(P-13351)
TPG LA COMMERCE LLC
Also Called: Doubletree By Hilton La - Com
5757 Telegraph Rd, Commerce (90040-1513)
PHONE 401 946-4600
Elizabeth Procaccianti,
Michelle Joyal, *Administration*
EMP: 100
SALES (est): 873.7K **Privately Held**
SIC: 7011 Resort hotel, franchised

(P-13352)
TR WARNER CENTER LP
Also Called: Warner Center Marriott Hotel
21850 Oxnard St, Woodland Hills (91367-3631)
PHONE 818 887-4800
Clay Andrews, *Mng Member*
Greg Chensky, *Controller*
Sue Stalley, *Sales Mgr*
EMP: 300
SQ FT: 500,000
SALES (est): 10MM **Privately Held**
SIC: 7011 Hotels

(P-13353)
TRADEWINDS LODGE (PA)
Also Called: Cliff House Restaurant
400 S Main St, Fort Bragg (95437-4806)
PHONE 707 964-4761
Fax: 707 964-0372
Dominic Affinito, *Partner*
EMP: 65
SQ FT: 19,000
SALES: 5MM **Privately Held**
SIC: 7011 5812 5813 6512 Motels; restaurant, family: independent; seafood restaurants; bars & lounges; commercial & industrial building operation; land subdividers & developers, commercial; land subdividers & developers, residential

(P-13354)
TRADEWINDS PARTNERSHIP
Also Called: Tradewinds Lodge Partnership
2920 Arden Way Ste F1, Sacramento (95825-1393)
PHONE 916 333-5239
Michelle V Affinito, *Partner*
EMP: 60
SALES: 950K **Privately Held**
SIC: 7011 1531 Hotels & motels; operative builders

(P-13355)
TREVI PARTNERS A CALIF LP
Also Called: Tollhouse Hotel
140 S Santa Cruz Ave, Los Gatos (95030-6702)
PHONE 408 395-7070
Fax: 408 395-3730
Marie Tallman, *Manager*
EMP: 88
SALES (corp-wide): 19.5MM **Privately Held**
WEB: www.marinholidayinnexpress.com
SIC: 7011 Hotels; eating places
HQ: Trevi Partners, A Calif. L.P.
6680 Regional St
Dublin CA 94568
925 828-7750

(P-13356)
TREVI PARTNERS A CALIF LP (HQ)
Also Called: Holiday Inn Dublin
6680 Regional Rd, Dublin (94568-2916)
PHONE 925 828-7750
Micheal McDavid, *General Mgr*
Tim Hall, *Executive*
Ramon Gonzales, *Info Tech Mgr*
Hamid Elasmar, *Controller*
Kerwin Garcia, *Sales Staff*
EMP: 74
SALES (est): 19.5MM **Privately Held**
WEB: www.marinholidayinnexpress.com
SIC: 7011 Hotels & motels
PA: Trevi Partners, A Calif. L.P.
5955 Coronado Ln
Pleasanton CA 94588
925 225-4000

(P-13357)
TREVI PARTNERS A CALIF LP
Also Called: Best Wstn Carmel Mission Inn
3665 Rio Rd, Carmel (93923-8609)
PHONE 831 624-1841
Fax: 831 624-8684
Bob Bucher, *Manager*
EMP: 76
SALES (corp-wide): 19.5MM **Privately Held**
WEB: www.marinholidayinnexpress.com
SIC: 7011 Hotels & motels
HQ: Trevi Partners, A Calif. L.P.
6680 Regional St
Dublin CA 94568
925 828-7750

(P-13358)
TREVI PARTNERS A CALIF LP (PA)
5955 Coronado Ln, Pleasanton (94588-8518)
PHONE 925 225-4000
Michael Madden, *Partner*
Kerwin Garcia, *Sales Staff*
EMP: 120
SALES (est): 19.5MM **Privately Held**
SIC: 7011 Hotels & motels

(P-13359)
TRI-STAR CCW MANAGEMENT L P
Also Called: Doubletree Hotel-Lax
1985 E Grand Ave, El Segundo (90245-5015)
PHONE 310 322-0999
Harry Wu, *Partner*
Norman Chang, *Partner*
Shau An Chen, *Partner*
Andrew Behnkey, *General Mgr*
EMP: 99
SALES (est): 2.5MM **Privately Held**
SIC: 7011 Hotels & motels

(P-13360)
TRIGILD INTERNATIONAL INC
Also Called: Ramada Inn
2151 Hotel Cir S, San Diego (92108-3314)
PHONE 619 291-6500
Charlie Holiday, *Manager*
Juliet Gonzalez, *Personnel Exec*
Lee Schlendorf, *Manager*
EMP: 80
SALES (corp-wide): 36.7MM **Privately Held**
WEB: www.trigild.com
SIC: 7011 Hotels & motels
PA: Trigild International, Inc.
3323 Carmel Mountain Rd # 2
San Diego CA 92121
858 720-6700

(P-13361)
TROPICANA GARDENS HOLDINGS LLC
6585 El Colegio Rd, Santa Barbara (93117-4614)
PHONE 805 968-4319
Kent W Dunn, *Mng Member*
David Wilcox,
EMP: 50
SALES (est): 2.7MM **Privately Held**
SIC: 7011 Hostels

(P-13362)
TWO BUNCH PALMS LLC
67425 Two Bunch Palms Trl, Desert Hot Springs (92240-6034)
PHONE 760 329-8791
Fax: 760 329-1317
John King, *Mng Member*
Patrick J Sturgeon, *General Mgr*
Michelle Fiorda, *Financial Exec*
Mark Eades, *Manager*
EMP: 53
SALES (est): 4.6MM **Privately Held**
SIC: 7011 7991 Resort hotel; spas

(P-13363)
TYME MAIDU TRIBE-BERRY CREEK
Also Called: Gold Country Casino
4020 Olive Hwy, Oroville (95966-5527)
PHONE 530 538-4560
Fax: 530 538-4569
Jim E Tribal, *CEO*
Leatha C Tribal, *Treasurer*
Grant Townsend, *Vice Pres*
Debra A Tribal, *Vice Pres*
Ed White, *General Mgr*
EMP: 519
SALES (est): 34.4MM **Privately Held**
WEB: www.goldcountrycasino.com
SIC: 7011 Casino hotel

(P-13364)
UA LOCAL 38 BONBELSENT TR FUND
Also Called: Konocti Harbor Resort & Spa
8727 Soda Bay Rd Ofc, Kelseyville (95451-9689)
PHONE 707 279-4281
Fax: 707 279-9680
Gregory J Bennett, *President*
Peter Machi, *Trust Officer*
Jason Lyons, *Engineer*
Stephanie Drake, *Director*
EMP: 275
SALES (est): 4.4MM **Privately Held**
WEB: www.konoctiharbor.com
SIC: 7011 Resort hotel

(P-13365)
UKA LLC
Also Called: Tarsadia Hotels
620 Newport Center Dr # 1400, Newport Beach (92660-8025)
PHONE 949 610-8000
B U Patel, *Mng Member*
L'Auberge Sedona, *Controller*
Pushpa Patel,
EMP: 50
SQ FT: 12,000
SALES (est): 518K **Privately Held**
SIC: 7011 Hotels

(P-13366)
UNITED AUBURN INDIAN COMMUNITY
Also Called: Thunder Valley Casino
1200 Athens Ave, Lincoln (95648-9328)
PHONE 916 408-7777
Fax: 916 408-8370
Scott Garawitz, *Branch Mgr*
John Comeau, *Vice Pres*
George Cvek, *Vice Pres*
Todd Deremer, *Vice Pres*
Jay Duarte, *Vice Pres*
EMP: 1963 **Privately Held**
WEB: www.thundervalleyresort.com
SIC: 7011 Casino hotel
PA: United Auburn Indian Community
10720 Indian Hill Rd
Auburn CA 95603

(P-13367)
UNIWELL CORPORATION
Also Called: Holiday Inn
7000 Beach Blvd, Buena Park (90620-1832)
PHONE 714 522-7000
Fax: 714 522-3230
Tracy Myer, *Branch Mgr*
Sidney Chan, *President*
Elaine Chan, *President*
Teddy Katuari, *Principal*
Fyda Dennis, *Sales Executive*
EMP: 150
SALES (corp-wide): 28.3MM **Privately Held**
WEB: www.uniwell.com
SIC: 7011 5813 5812 Hotels & motels; drinking places; eating places
PA: Uniwell Corporation
21172 Figueroa St
Carson CA 90745
310 782-8888

(P-13368)
UNIWELL FRESNO HOTEL LLC
Also Called: Doubletree By Hilton Fresno
2233 Ventura St, Fresno (93721-2915)
PHONE 559 268-1000
Steve Klein,
Nikki Wheelock, *Human Res Dir*
Wendy Niles, *Sales Executive*
April Newton, *Sales Dir*
Angie Ayon, *Manager*
EMP: 100
SALES (est): 8.4MM **Privately Held**
SIC: 7011 Hotels & motels

(P-13369)
UPHAM HOTEL
1404 De La Vina St # 93101, Santa Barbara (93101-3057)
PHONE 805 962-0058
Fax: 805 963-2825
Carl Johnson, *Owner*
Janice M Winn, *Manager*
EMP: 50
SALES (est): 2.3MM **Privately Held**
WEB: www.uphamhotel.com
SIC: 7011 Hotels

(P-13370)
US GRANT HOTEL VENTURES LLC
326 Broadway, San Diego (92101-4800)
PHONE 619 744-2007
Fax: 619 232-3626
Daniel Tucker,
EMP: 80
SQ FT: 99,999
SALES (est): 6.4MM **Privately Held**
SIC: 7011 Hotels

(P-13371)
US HOTEL AND RESORT MGT INC
Also Called: Regency Inn
2544 Newport Blvd, Costa Mesa (92627-1331)
PHONE 949 650-2988
Fax: 949 650-7820
Peggy Chen, *Manager*

PRODUCTS & SERVICES SECTION

7011 - Hotels, Motels & Tourist Courts County (P-13396)

EMP: 83
SALES (corp-wide): 28MM **Privately Held**
WEB: www.regency-mgmt.com
SIC: 7011 Hotels
HQ: U.S. Hotel And Resort Management, Inc.
3211 W Sencore Dr
Sioux Falls SD 57107
605 334-2371

(P-13372)
VAGABOND INN CORPORATION (HQ)
2361 Rosecrans Ave # 150, El Segundo (90245-7906)
P.O. Box 3455 (90245-8591)
PHONE 213 284-7533
Juan Llaca, *CEO*
Cindy Liao, *Marketing Staff*
Cari Lyall, *Corp Comm Staff*
EMP: 57
SALES (est): 8.2MM
SALES (corp-wide): 13.9MM **Privately Held**
SIC: 7011 Hotels & motels
PA: Vista Investments, Llc
2361 Rosecrans Ave # 150
El Segundo CA 90245
213 284-7500

(P-13373)
VALADON HOTEL LLC
Also Called: Petit Ermitage
8822 Cynthia St, West Hollywood (90069-4502)
PHONE 310 854-1114
Fax: 310 657-9192
Stefan Ashkenazy,
Adrian Ashkenazy,
Kristen Daie, *Director*
EMP: 80
SQ FT: 40,000
SALES (est): 8MM **Privately Held**
WEB: www.valadonhotel.com
SIC: 7011 Hotels & motels

(P-13374)
VALLEY HO HOTELS INC
Also Called: Kings Inn Hotel & Grille
1333 Hotel Cir S, San Diego (92108-3408)
PHONE 619 297-2231
Fax: 619 296-5255
C Andro Petersen, *President*
David Parrent, *Chief Mktg Ofcr*
Richard Camacho, *Exec Dir*
Alfonso Gonzalez, *Financial Exec*
Ana Cabrera, *Manager*
EMP: 70
SALES (est): 5.6MM **Privately Held**
SIC: 7011 Hotels

(P-13375)
VAN NESS HOTEL INC
1050 Van Ness Ave, San Francisco (94109-6934)
PHONE 415 673-4711
John M Scheurer, *President*
Robin Aooneftis, *Manager*
EMP: 90
SALES (est): 3MM **Privately Held**
SIC: 7011 Hotels

(P-13376)
VENTU PARK LLC
Also Called: Palm Garden Hotel
495 N Ventu Park Rd, Thousand Oaks (91320-2707)
PHONE 805 716-4200
Bob Zonitch, *Principal*
Michael Garik, *Principal*
Dave Warner, *Principal*
Steven Ortmann, *General Mgr*
Beth Gamble, *Controller*
EMP: 70
SALES: 4MM **Privately Held**
SIC: 7011 Hotels & motels

(P-13377)
VENTURA HSPTALITY PARTNERS LLC
Also Called: Crowne Plaza Ventura Beach
450 Harbor Blvd, Ventura (93001-2708)
PHONE 805 648-2100
David Storm,
Akemi Shapiro, *Social Dir*

Dougles Wood, *General Mgr*
Ben Vaughn, *Chief Engr*
Jessica Murphy, *Controller*
EMP: 140
SQ FT: 143,000
SALES: 10MM **Privately Held**
SIC: 7011 Hotels & motels

(P-13378)
VERASA MANAGEMENT LLC
1314 Mckinstry St, NAPA (94559-1900)
PHONE 707 257-1800
Stewart Andersen, *Mng Member*
EMP: 94 **EST:** 2010
SALES (est): 3.3MM **Privately Held**
SIC: 7011 Hotels

(P-13379)
VICTORVLLE TRSURE HOLDINGS LLC
Also Called: Holiday Inn Victorville
15494 Palmdale Rd, Victorville (92392-2408)
PHONE 760 245-6565
Benjamin Gonzales, *General Mgr*
EMP: 75 **EST:** 2011
SALES (est): 494.2K **Privately Held**
SIC: 7011 5812 Hotels & motels; American restaurant

(P-13380)
VINTNERS INN
4350 Barnes Rd, Santa Rosa (95403-1514)
PHONE 707 575-7350
Fax: 707 575-1426
Donald Carano,
Elena Reynoso, *Marketing Staff*
EMP: 100
SQ FT: 30,670
SALES: 3.9MM **Privately Held**
WEB: www.vintnersinn.com
SIC: 7011 Motels

(P-13381)
VISCAMAR LLC
Also Called: Presidian Hotel
300 S Court St, Visalia (93291-6214)
PHONE 559 636-1111
H Drake Leddy,
EMP: 91
SQ FT: 134,055
SALES (est): 2.8MM **Privately Held**
SIC: 7011 Hotels & motels

(P-13382)
VISTA INVESTMENTS LLC (PA)
2361 Rosecrans Ave # 150, El Segundo (90245-7906)
PHONE 213 284-7500
Juan Sanchez-llaca,
Les Biggins, *CFO*
Elizabeth Kim, *Controller*
Jaime Suarez, *Controller*
Theodore Cohen, *General Counsel*
EMP: 56 **EST:** 1999
SALES (est): 13.9MM **Privately Held**
SIC: 7011 6726 Hotels; management investment funds, closed-end

(P-13383)
VWI CONCORD LLC
Also Called: Hilton Concord
1970 Diamond Blvd, Concord (94520-5718)
PHONE 925 827-2000
Fax: 925 671-0984
Jack Hlavac, *General Mgr*
Jim Dunbar, *Officer*
Becky Wagner, *Executive*
Edgar Ventura, *Info Tech Mgr*
George Chu, *Finance*
EMP: 130
SALES (est): 10.6MM **Privately Held**
SIC: 7011 Hotels & motels

(P-13384)
W HOTEL
Also Called: Starwood Hotels & Resorts
181 3rd St, San Francisco (94103-3189)
PHONE 415 777-5300
Darren Sturgill, *Manager*
Mike Nettles, *Marketing Mgr*
Lisa Leonor, *Marketing Staff*
Michele Beretta, *Asst Director*
Sacha Chin, *Director*

EMP: 50 **EST:** 2008
SALES (est): 3.5MM **Privately Held**
SIC: 7011 Hotels & motels

(P-13385)
W LOS ANGELES
Also Called: Westwood Marquis Hotel & Grdns
930 Hilgard Ave, Los Angeles (90024-3033)
P.O. Box 14029, Scottsdale AZ (85267-4029)
PHONE 310 208-8765
Fax: 310 824-5062
George I Rosenthal, *President*
Mark Rosenthal, *COO*
Anil Sharma, *CFO*
Seng Yeoh, *Controller*
Alicia Goidich, *Human Res Dir*
EMP: 330
SALES (est): 12MM
SALES (corp-wide): 34.2MM **Privately Held**
SIC: 7011 Hotels
WEB: www.raleighenterprises.com
PA: Raleigh Enterprises, Inc.
5300 Melrose Ave Fl 4
Los Angeles CA 90038
310 899-8900

(P-13386)
W-BEL AGE LLC
1020 N San Vicente Blvd, West Hollywood (90069-3802)
PHONE 310 854-1111
Laura Bell, *Principal*
EMP: 99
SALES (est): 973.2K **Privately Held**
SIC: 7011 Hotels & motels

(P-13387)
W-EMERALD LLC
Also Called: Westin San Diego
400 W Broadway, San Diego (92101-3504)
PHONE 619 239-4500
John Beaton, *General Mgr*
Andrea Visser, *Chief Mktg Ofcr*
EMP: 230
SQ FT: 99,999
SALES (est): 6.3MM **Privately Held**
SIC: 7011 Hotels & motels

(P-13388)
W2005 NEW CNTURY HT PRTFLIO LP
Also Called: Sheraton Hotel Sunnyvale
1100 N Mathilda Ave, Sunnyvale (94089-1206)
PHONE 408 745-6000
Epenesa Pakola, *Manager*
EMP: 53
SALES (corp-wide): 12.9MM **Privately Held**
WEB: www.hicrystallake.com
SIC: 7011 Hotels & motels
PA: W2005 New Century Hotel Portfolio, L.P.
6011 Connection Dr
Irving TX 75039
972 368-2200

(P-13389)
W2005 WYN HOTELS LP
Also Called: Doubletree Hotel
5757 Telegraph Rd, Commerce (90040-1513)
PHONE 323 887-8100
Steve Barick, *COO*
Thomas Smalley, *General Mgr*
EMP: 81 **EST:** 1991
SALES (est): 4.2MM **Privately Held**
SIC: 7011 Hotels & motels

(P-13390)
WALT DISNEY COMPANY
Also Called: Disneyland
1598 S Harbor Blvd, Anaheim (92802-2312)
PHONE 714 781-4278
Ed Greier, *Branch Mgr*
Charlie Lanham, *Program Mgr*
David Greene, *Info Tech Mgr*
Erin Stubbs, *Project Mgr*
EMP: 170 **Publicly Held**
SIC: 7011 Resort hotel

PA: The Walt Disney Company
500 S Buena Vista St
Burbank CA 91521

(P-13391)
WALTERS FAMILY PARTNERSHIP
Also Called: Hilton Resort In Palm Spring
400 E Tahquitz Canyon Way, Palm Springs (92262-6605)
PHONE 760 320-6868
Lance Walters, *Partner*
Lynn Thaonk, *Persnl Mgr*
EMP: 150
SQ FT: 200,000
SALES (est): 8.3MM **Privately Held**
SIC: 7011 5813 5812 Hotels; drinking places; eating places

(P-13392)
WARWICK CALIFORNIA CORPORATION
Also Called: Warwick Hotel San Francisco
490 Geary St, San Francisco (94102-1223)
PHONE 415 992-3809
Richard Chiu, *President*
Joseph Tung, *Vice Pres*
EMP: 60
SQ FT: 23,386
SALES (est): 2.2MM **Privately Held**
WEB: www.warwicksf.com
SIC: 7011 7299 Hotels; banquet hall facilities
PA: Warwick Holdings Sa
Rue Eugene Ruppert 6
Luxembourg

(P-13393)
WASHINGTON INN LLC
Also Called: Holiday Inn
737 Washington Blvd, Marina Del Rey (90292-5542)
PHONE 310 821-4455
Fax: 310 821-8098
John Mathews,
Doug Pflumer, *General Mgr*
EMP: 80
SALES (est): 3.1MM **Privately Held**
SIC: 7011 Hotels & motels

(P-13394)
WATERFALL RESORT
5951 Encina Rd Ste 207, Goleta (93117-6252)
PHONE 805 879-3780
Chuck Beard, *Director*
EMP: 100
SALES (est): 4.6MM **Privately Held**
WEB: www.waterfallresort.com
SIC: 7011 Seasonal hotel

(P-13395)
WATERFRONT HOTEL LLC
Also Called:
21100 Pacific Coast Hwy, Huntington Beach (92648-5307)
PHONE 714 845-8000
Fax: 714 845-8425
John Gilbert, *Manager*
Pat Johnson, *General Mgr*
Tiffany Stewart, *General Mgr*
Glenn Shorr, *Web Proj Mgr*
Candy Fish, *Human Res Dir*
EMP: 298
SALES (corp-wide): 10.4MM **Privately Held**
WEB: www.waterfrontresort.com
SIC: 7011 5813 5812 7299 Hotels & motels; drinking places; eating places; banquet hall facilities
PA: Waterfront Hotel Llc
660 Newport Center Dr
Newport Beach CA
949 759-8091

(P-13396)
WATERFRONT PLAZA HOTEL LLC
10 Washington St, Oakland (94607-3751)
PHONE 510 836-3800
Fax: 510 832-5695
Clyde R Gibb, *General Ptnr*
Thunderbird Investors, *General Ptnr*

7011 - Hotels, Motels & Tourist Courts County (P-13397)

EMP: 65 EST: 1964
SALES (est): 3.4MM Privately Held
SIC: 7011 Hotels

(P-13397)
WELCOME GROUP MANAGEMENT LLC
Also Called: Visalia Mrrott At Cnvntion Ctr
300 S Court St, Visalia (93291-6214)
PHONE..................310 378-6666
Amarjit Shokeen,
Sheri A O'Hara, *Executive*
Joe Kuhn, *General Mgr*
Carrie Groover, *Sales Dir*
Tanja Renzi, *Director*
EMP: 97
SQ FT: 3,224
SALES (est): 71.5K Privately Held
SIC: 7011 Motel, franchised

(P-13398)
WELK GROUP INC (PA)
Also Called: Welk Music Group
8860 Lawrence Welk Dr, Escondido (92026-6403)
PHONE..................760 749-3000
Jon Fredricks, *President*
Marc L Luzzatto, *COO*
Mario Trejo, *Plant Mgr*
Emily Parker, *Manager*
Nicole Turk, *Manager*
EMP: 345
SQ FT: 6,200
SALES (est): 119.4MM Privately Held
SIC: 7011 5099 Resort hotel; compact discs

(P-13399)
WEST HOTEL PARTNERS LP
Also Called: San Jose Hilton and Towers
300 Almaden Blvd, San Jose (95110-2703)
PHONE..................408 947-4450
Fax: 408 947-4489
John Southwell, *Branch Mgr*
Chuck Munch, *Administration*
Angel Arambulo, *MIS Mgr*
Alan Steel, *IT/INT Sup*
Roseann Cuevas-Garcia, *Human Resources*
EMP: 200
SALES (corp-wide): 12.4MM Privately Held
WEB: www.firstconf.com
SIC: 7011 7371 6512 5813 Hotels & motels; custom computer programming services; nonresidential building operators; drinking places; eating places
PA: West Hotel Partners, L.P.
11828 La Grange Ave 200
Los Angeles CA 90025
310 477-3593

(P-13400)
WEST INN & SUITES LLC
4970 Avenida Encinas, Carlsbad (92008-4343)
PHONE..................760 448-4500
Debbie Vought,
Jennifer Grosmark, *Office Mgr*
Veronica Garcia, *Administration*
Linda Fietz, *Sales Dir*
David Calica, *Supervisor*
EMP: 80
SALES (est): 4.2MM Privately Held
WEB: www.westinnandsuites.com
SIC: 7011 Inns

(P-13401)
WEST SAN CRLOS HT PARTNERS LLC
Also Called: Hyatt Place San Jose Hotel
282 Almaden Blvd, San Jose (95113-2003)
PHONE..................408 998-0400
Fax: 408 998-6210
F Matthew Dinapoli,
Michael Lerman, *General Mgr*
Tina Castaneda, *Administration*
EMP: 65
SALES (est): 1B Privately Held
SIC: 7011 Hotels & motels

(P-13402)
WESTERN HOST INC (DH)
Also Called: Starwood Hotels & Resorts
1 Old Bayshore Hwy, Millbrae (94030-3120)
P.O. Box 14019, Scottsdale AZ (85267-4019)
PHONE..................650 692-3500
Fax: 650 872-8104
Michael Dojlidko, *CEO*
Jonathan Wright, *Info Tech Dir*
Kevin Kujawski, *VP Finance*
Alen Schnaid, *Controller*
Steven Gee, *Purch Mgr*
EMP: 50 EST: 1974
SALES (est): 9.7MM
SALES (corp-wide): 14.4B Publicly Held
SIC: 7011 7389 Hotels & motels; office facilities & secretarial service rental
HQ: Starwood Hotels & Resorts Worldwide, Llc
1 Star Pt
Stamford CT 06902
203 964-6000

(P-13403)
WESTGROUP SAN DIEGO ASSOCIATES
Also Called: Paradise Point Resort
1404 Vacation Rd, San Diego (92109-7905)
PHONE..................858 274-4630
David Feeney, *Partner*
Terry Hoppes, *Executive*
Jessie Williams, *Executive*
Ann Patterson, *Executive Asst*
Ihab Sabry, *Finance*
EMP: 500
SALES (est): 18.4MM Privately Held
SIC: 7011 Resort hotel

(P-13404)
WESTIN DESERT WILLOW
75 Willow Ridge, Palm Desert (92260-0305)
PHONE..................760 636-7003
Jim Moran, *General Mgr*
Warren Jerome, *Opers Staff*
EMP: 75
SALES (est): 3.4MM Privately Held
SIC: 7011 Hotels & motels

(P-13405)
WESTLAKE VILLAGE INN
Also Called: Westlake Inn Hotel
31943 Agoura Rd, Westlake Village (91361-4427)
PHONE..................805 496-1667
Fax: 818 889-4815
John Notter, *Owner*
Michael Reardon, *General Mgr*
Heidi Schatz, *Finance Mgr*
Roxanne Stevenson, *Human Res Mgr*
David McCarthy, *VP Sales*
EMP: 150
SALES (est): 8.1MM Privately Held
WEB: www.westlakevillageinn.com
SIC: 7011 Hotels

(P-13406)
WESTLAND HOTEL CORPORATION
Also Called: Best Western Stockton Inn
4219 E Waterloo Rd, Stockton (95215-2304)
PHONE..................209 931-3131
Fax: 209 931-0423
Champ Patel, *Manager*
EMP: 50
SALES (corp-wide): 5.2MM Privately Held
SIC: 7011 Hotels & motels
PA: Westland Hotel Corporation
8885 Rio San Diego Dr
San Diego CA
619 297-4040

(P-13407)
WESTPOST BERKELEY LLC
Also Called: Doubletree By Hilton Brky Mrna
200 Marina Blvd, Berkeley (94710-1608)
PHONE..................510 548-7920
Moez Mangalgi, *Mng Member*
Mohan Persaud, *Controller*
EMP: 99

SALES (est): 5.1MM Privately Held
SIC: 7011 Hotels & motels

(P-13408)
WESTWARD HOSPITALITY MGT
200 Marina Blvd, Berkeley (94710-1608)
PHONE..................510 548-7920
Patrick Birmingham, *Principal*
Rafael Fernandez, *Principal*
EMP: 99
SALES: 15MM Privately Held
SIC: 7011 Hotels & motels

(P-13409)
WHATEVER IT TAKES INC
Also Called: Desert Hot Springs Spa Hotel
10805 Palm Dr, Desert Hot Springs (92240-2511)
PHONE..................760 329-6000
Fax: 760 329-6915
Michael Bickford, *President*
Dave Malstan, *Manager*
EMP: 50 EST: 1970
SQ FT: 50,000
SALES (est): 2.7MM Privately Held
SIC: 7011 5812 Hotels; eating places

(P-13410)
WHB CORPORATION
Also Called: Millennium Biltmore Hotel
506 S Grand Ave, Los Angeles (90071-2602)
PHONE..................213 624-1011
Fax: 213 612-1657
John Demola, *Branch Mgr*
Daniel Desbaillets, *COO*
Sandra Avalos, *Executive*
Beth Dumas, *Executive*
Swietlana Cahill, *General Mgr*
EMP: 630
SALES (corp-wide): 28.1MM Privately Held
SIC: 7011 5812 5813 Hotels & motels; eating places; drinking places
PA: Whb Corporation
7600 E Orchard Rd 230s
Greenwood Village CO 80111
303 779-2000

(P-13411)
WHGCA LLC
Also Called: Hilton Sacramento Arden West
2200 Harvard St, Sacramento (95815-3306)
PHONE..................916 922-4700
Fax: 916 649-1311
Alex Vargas, *Controller*
Lisa Backman, *General Mgr*
EMP: 228
SALES (est): 4.7MM
SALES (corp-wide): 82.1MM Privately Held
SIC: 7011 Hotels & motels
HQ: Westminster Hospitality Inc
5847 San Felipe St # 4650
Houston TX 77057
713 782-9100

(P-13412)
WIN RIVER HOTEL CORPORATION
Also Called: Hilton
5050 Bechelli Ln, Redding (96002-3539)
PHONE..................530 226-5111
Fax: 530 226-5005
Glen Howard, *President*
Kasey Danielson, *Social Dir*
Greg Knoellk, *General Mgr*
EMP: 50
SALES (est): 3.2MM
SALES (corp-wide): 44MM Privately Held
SIC: 7011 Hotels & motels
PA: Redding Rancheria
2000 Redding Rancheria Rd
Redding CA 96001
530 225-8979

(P-13413)
WIN TIME LTD (PA)
Also Called: Holiday Inn
9335 Kearny Mesa Rd, San Diego (92126-4502)
PHONE..................858 695-2300
Fax: 858 578-7925
Herman Lin, *General Ptnr*

Chue-Huang Chiu, *Partner*
Yi-Ho Huang, *Partner*
Pearlette Johnson, *CFO*
Marijo Fabian, *General Mgr*
EMP: 166
SQ FT: 100,000
SALES (est): 16.6MM Privately Held
SIC: 7011 Hotels & motels

(P-13414)
WINDSOR CAPITAL GROUP INC
Also Called: Residence Inn By Marriott
2101 W Vineyard Ave, Oxnard (93036-2268)
PHONE..................805 988-0627
Doug Pflaumer, *Branch Mgr*
Elaine Nieves, *Director*
EMP: 100
SALES (corp-wide): 161.5MM Privately Held
WEB: www.snowbirdpackage.com
SIC: 7011 Hotels & motels
PA: Windsor Capital Group, Inc.
3250 Ocean Park Blvd # 350
Santa Monica CA 90405
310 566-1100

(P-13415)
WINDSOR CAPITAL GROUP INC
Also Called: Pacific Suites Hotel
3250 Ocean Park Blvd # 350, Santa Monica (90405-3257)
PHONE..................310 566-1100
Michael D Cryan, *Manager*
Greg Case, *General Mgr*
Misael Frias, *Chief Engr*
Doug Covell, *Controller*
Shannon Bernard, *Human Res Dir*
EMP: 78
SALES (corp-wide): 161.5MM Privately Held
WEB: www.snowbirdpackage.com
SIC: 7011 Hotels & motels
PA: Windsor Capital Group, Inc.
3250 Ocean Park Blvd # 350
Santa Monica CA 90405
310 566-1100

(P-13416)
WINDSOR CAPITAL GROUP INC
Also Called: Embassy Suites Arcadia
3250 Ocean Park Blvd # 350, Santa Monica (90405-3257)
PHONE..................310 566-1100
EMP: 78
SALES (corp-wide): 161.5MM Privately Held
WEB: www.snowbirdpackage.com
SIC: 7011 Hotels & motels
PA: Windsor Capital Group, Inc.
3250 Ocean Park Blvd # 350
Santa Monica CA 90405
310 566-1100

(P-13417)
WINDSOR CAPITAL GROUP INC
Also Called: Embassy Suites Lompoc
3250 Ocean Park Blvd # 350, Santa Monica (90405-3257)
PHONE..................209 577-3825
David Del Vecchio, *Manager*
EMP: 78
SALES (corp-wide): 161.5MM Privately Held
WEB: www.snowbirdpackage.com
SIC: 7011 Hotels & motels
PA: Windsor Capital Group, Inc.
3250 Ocean Park Blvd # 350
Santa Monica CA 90405
310 566-1100

(P-13418)
WINDSOR CAPITAL GROUP INC
Also Called: Marriott
3250 Ocean Park Blvd # 350, Santa Monica (90405-3257)
PHONE..................209 577-3825
Shawn Williams, *Manager*
EMP: 78
SALES (corp-wide): 161.5MM Privately Held
WEB: www.snowbirdpackage.com
SIC: 7011 Hotels & motels

PRODUCTS & SERVICES SECTION   7011 - Hotels, Motels & Tourist Courts County (P-13440)

PA: Windsor Capital Group, Inc.
3250 Ocean Park Blvd # 350
Santa Monica CA 90405
310 566-1100

(P-13419)
WINDSOR CAPITAL GROUP INC
Also Called: Embassy Suites
900 E Birch St, Brea (92821-5812)
PHONE 714 990-6000
Fax: 714 990-1653
Regina Samy, *Manager*
Carolyn Nonsils, *Manager*
EMP: 74
SQ FT: 48,164
SALES (corp-wide): 161.5MM Privately Held
SIC: 7011 Hotels & motels
PA: Windsor Capital Group, Inc.
3250 Ocean Park Blvd # 350
Santa Monica CA 90405
310 566-1100

(P-13420)
WINDSOR CAPITAL GROUP INC
Also Called: Embassy Suites
29345 Rancho California, Temecula (92591-5201)
PHONE 951 676-5656
Tom Demott, *General Mgr*
Greg Roberts, *General Mgr*
Kellie Hanselman, *Administration*
EMP: 75
SALES (corp-wide): 161.5MM Privately Held
SIC: 7011 Hotels & motels
PA: Windsor Capital Group, Inc.
3250 Ocean Park Blvd # 350
Santa Monica CA 90405
310 566-1100

(P-13421)
WINDSOR CAPITAL GROUP INC
3250 Ocean Park Blvd # 350, Santa Monica (90405-3257)
PHONE 310 566-1100
EMP: 78
SALES (corp-wide): 161.5MM Privately Held
WEB: www.snowbirdpackage.com
SIC: 7011 Hotels & motels
PA: Windsor Capital Group, Inc.
3250 Ocean Park Blvd # 350
Santa Monica CA 90405
310 566-1100

(P-13422)
WINDSOR CAPITAL GROUP INC
Also Called: Embassy Suites El Paso
3250 Ocean Park Blvd # 350, Santa Monica (90405-3257)
PHONE 310 566-1100
Ken Hassett, *Vice Pres*
Regina Samy, *Vice Pres*
Herman Turk, *Vice Pres*
EMP: 78
SALES (corp-wide): 161.5MM Privately Held
WEB: www.snowbirdpackage.com
SIC: 7011 Hotels & motels
PA: Windsor Capital Group, Inc.
3250 Ocean Park Blvd # 350
Santa Monica CA 90405
310 566-1100

(P-13423)
WINDSOR CAPITAL GROUP INC
Also Called: Embassy Suites
1325 E Dyer Rd, Santa Ana (92705-5615)
PHONE 714 241-3800
Samuel Sansone, *Manager*
Louise L Deluca, *Director*
EMP: 87
SALES (corp-wide): 161.5MM Privately Held
SIC: 7011 5813 5812 Hotels & motels; drinking places; eating places
PA: Windsor Capital Group, Inc.
3250 Ocean Park Blvd # 350
Santa Monica CA 90405
310 566-1100

(P-13424)
WINDSOR CAPITAL GROUP INC
Also Called: Marriott
1510 University Ave, Riverside (92507-4468)
PHONE 951 276-1200
Jim Larson, *General Mgr*
Julie Martini, *General Mgr*
EMP: 68
SALES (corp-wide): 161.5MM Privately Held
WEB: www.snowbirdpackage.com
SIC: 7011 Hotels & motels
PA: Windsor Capital Group, Inc.
3250 Ocean Park Blvd # 350
Santa Monica CA 90405
310 566-1100

(P-13425)
WINDSOR CAPITAL GROUP INC
Also Called: Marriott
2355 N Main St, Walnut Creek (94596-3547)
PHONE 925 934-2000
Patrick Nesbitt, *Branch Mgr*
EMP: 140
SALES (corp-wide): 161.5MM Privately Held
SIC: 7011 Hotels & motels
PA: Windsor Capital Group, Inc.
3250 Ocean Park Blvd # 350
Santa Monica CA 90405
310 566-1100

(P-13426)
WMK SACRAMENTO LLC
Also Called: Doubltree By Hilton Scrmento Ht
2001 Point West Way, Sacramento (95815-4702)
PHONE 916 929-8855
Ken Leone, *General Mgr*
Jonathan Wiser, *General Mgr*
EMP: 250
SALES: 17MM Privately Held
SIC: 7011 Hotel, franchised

(P-13427)
WOODFIN SUITE HOTELS LLC
Also Called: Chase Suite and Woodfin Hotels
12555 High Bluff Dr # 330, San Diego (92130-3005)
PHONE 858 314-7910
Sam Hardage, *CEO*
Richard Meza, *CFO*
Mark Penrod, *Sales Staff*
EMP: 780
SQ FT: 10,000
SALES (est): 29.2MM Privately Held
SIC: 7011 Hotels

(P-13428)
WORLD MARK OF OCEANSIDE
Also Called: World Mark By Trend West
1301 Carmelo Dr, Oceanside (92054-1089)
PHONE 760 721-0890
Gene Hensley, *President*
Asael Sandoval, *General Mgr*
EMP: 52
SALES (est): 2.1MM Privately Held
SIC: 7011 Resort hotel

(P-13429)
WORLD TRADE CTR HT ASSOC LTD
Also Called: Long Beach Hilton, The
701 W Ocean Blvd, Long Beach (90831-3100)
PHONE 562 983-3400
Steve Holloway, *Controller*
Greater Los Angeles Trade Cent, *General Ptnr*
Matsushita International Corpo, *Ltd Ptnr*
Nacine Nakakihara, *Controller*
Rachel Duron, *Human Res Dir*
EMP: 250
SALES (est): 8.2MM Privately Held
SIC: 7011 7991 5813 5812 Hotels; physical fitness facilities; drinking places; eating places

(P-13430)
WS HDM LLC
Also Called: Hilton San Diego/Del Mar
15575 Jimmy Durante Blvd, Del Mar (92014-1901)
PHONE 858 792-5200

Al Hatfield, *Partner*
Scott Sloan, *General Mgr*
Kaylee Meyer, *Finance Dir*
EMP: 99 EST: 2012
SQ FT: 240,000
SALES (est): 3.2MM Privately Held
SIC: 7011 Resort hotel, franchised

(P-13431)
WS HDM LLC
Also Called: Hilton San Diego/Del Mar
15575 Jimmy Durante Blvd, Del Mar (92014-1901)
PHONE 858 792-5200
Fax: 858 792-0353
Scott Sloan, *Mng Member*
Damien Proctor, *Principal*
Rowmona Roman, *Asst Controller*
Roxanne McDermott, *Controller*
EMP: 250
SALES (est): 11.8MM Privately Held
SIC: 7011 Hotels & motels

(P-13432)
WW LBV INC
Also Called: Radisson Inn
30100 Agoura Rd, Agoura Hills (91301-2004)
PHONE 818 707-1220
Clay Andrews, *General Mgr*
Dan Monahan, *General Mgr*
Trisha Sheslo, *Office Spvr*
Alex Campbell, *Engineer*
Sandi Gorup, *Sales Dir*
EMP: 103
SALES (corp-wide): 82.1MM Privately Held
SIC: 7011 6022 5812 5813 Hotels & motels; state commercial banks; caterers; drinking places
PA: Ww Lbv Inc.
2000 Hotel Plaza Blvd
Lake Buena Vista FL 32830
407 828-2424

(P-13433)
WW SAN DIEGO HARBOR ISLAND LLC
Also Called: Hilton
1960 Harbor Island Dr, San Diego (92101-1013)
PHONE 619 291-6700
Fax: 619 293-0964
Shahid Kayani, *General Mgr*
Stephanie Sorn, *Info Tech Mgr*
Dickson Ula, *Engineer*
Maria E Pace, *Human Res Mgr*
Pam Richardson, *Human Res Mgr*
EMP: 120
SALES: 11.5MM
SALES (corp-wide): 82.1MM Privately Held
WEB: www.hiltonharborisland.com
SIC: 7011 Hotels & motels
PA: Ww Lbv Inc.
2000 Hotel Plaza Blvd
Lake Buena Vista FL 32830
407 828-2424

(P-13434)
WYNDHAM INTERNATIONAL INC
222 W Houston Ave, Fullerton (92832-3453)
PHONE 714 992-1700
Roger Beard, *Bd of Directors*
Herbert L Peck, *Bd of Directors*
Jason Nate, *Vice Pres*
EMP: 102
SALES (corp-wide): 96.4MM Privately Held
WEB: www.wyndham.com
SIC: 7011 Hotel, franchised
HQ: Wyndham International, Inc
22 Sylvan Way
Parsippany NJ 07054
973 753-6000

(P-13435)
WYNDHAM INTERNATIONAL INC
888 E Tahquitz Canyon Way, Palm Springs (92262-6708)
PHONE 760 322-6000
Jennie Hui, *Branch Mgr*
EMP: 102

SALES (corp-wide): 96.4MM Privately Held
WEB: www.wyndham.com
SIC: 7011 Hotel, franchised
HQ: Wyndham International, Inc
22 Sylvan Way
Parsippany NJ 07054
973 753-6000

(P-13436)
WYNDHAM INTERNATIONAL INC
Also Called: Wyndham San Dego At Emrald Plz
400 W Broadway, San Diego (92101-3504)
PHONE 619 239-4500
Fax: 619 338-3662
John Beaton, *Branch Mgr*
EMP: 102
SALES (corp-wide): 96.4MM Privately Held
WEB: www.wyndham.com
SIC: 7011 Hotel, franchised
HQ: Wyndham International, Inc
22 Sylvan Way
Parsippany NJ 07054
973 753-6000

(P-13437)
WYNDHAM INTERNATIONAL INC
Also Called: Wyndham Hotels & Resorts
1 Old Ranch Rd, Carmel (93923-8551)
PHONE 831 625-9500
Henry Dunwall, *Owner*
EMP: 102
SALES (corp-wide): 96.4MM Privately Held
WEB: www.wyndham.com
SIC: 7011 Hotels & motels
HQ: Wyndham International, Inc
22 Sylvan Way
Parsippany NJ 07054
973 753-6000

(P-13438)
WYNDHAM INTERNATIONAL INC
Also Called: Wyndham Garden Hotel
5757 Telegraph Rd, Commerce (90040-1513)
PHONE 323 887-4331
Fax: 323 887-0779
Swiet Lana Cahill, *Manager*
EMP: 85
SALES (corp-wide): 96.4MM Privately Held
WEB: www.wyndham.com
SIC: 7011 5812 Hotels & motels; eating places
HQ: Wyndham International, Inc
22 Sylvan Way
Parsippany NJ 07054
973 753-6000

(P-13439)
WYNDHAM INTERNATIONAL INC
3350 Ave Of The Arts, Costa Mesa (92626-1913)
PHONE 714 751-5100
Fax: 714 751-2704
Thomas Smalley, *General Mgr*
Atuljeet Singh, *Webmaster*
EMP: 100
SALES (corp-wide): 96.4MM Privately Held
WEB: www.wyndham.com
SIC: 7011 5812 5813 Hotels; eating places; drinking places
HQ: Wyndham International, Inc
22 Sylvan Way
Parsippany NJ 07054
973 753-6000

(P-13440)
WYNDHAM INTERNATIONAL INC
Also Called: Wyndham Hotels & Resorts
400 Concourse Dr, Belmont (94002-4125)
PHONE 650 591-8600
Sylvia Chu, *Manager*
EMP: 50
SALES (corp-wide): 96.4MM Privately Held
WEB: www.wyndham.com
SIC: 7011 Hotels & motels

7011 - Hotels, Motels & Tourist Courts County (P-13441)   PRODUDUCTS & SERVICES SECTION

HQ: Wyndham International, Inc
22 Sylvan Way
Parsippany NJ 07054
973 753-6000

(P-13441)
WYNDHAM INTERNATIONAL INC
Also Called: Wyndham Hotels & Resorts
1350 N 1st St, San Jose (95112-4709)
PHONE.....................408 451-3050
Gary Hageman, *Branch Mgr*
Vianca Rodriguez, *Supervisor*
EMP: 140
SALES (corp-wide): 96.4MM **Privately Held**
WEB: www.wyndham.com
SIC: 7011 5813 5812 Hotels; drinking places; eating places
HQ: Wyndham International, Inc
22 Sylvan Way
Parsippany NJ 07054
973 753-6000

(P-13442)
WYNDHAM RESORT DEV CORP
Also Called: Worldmark Resort
123 Selkirk Ranch Rd, Angels Camp (95222-9593)
PHONE.....................209 736-2999
Bennet Posman, *Manager*
EMP: 50
SALES (corp-wide): 5.5B **Publicly Held**
SIC: 7011 Resort hotel
HQ: Wyndham Resort Development Corporation
9805 Willows Rd Ne
Redmond WA 98052
425 498-2500

(P-13443)
XANTERRA PARKS & RESORTS INC
Also Called: Furnace Creek Ranch & Inn
Hwy 190, Death Valley (92328)
P.O. Box 187 (92328-0187)
PHONE.....................760 786-2345
Fax: 760 786-2307
Dominie Lenz, *Branch Mgr*
EMP: 215
SALES (corp-wide): 390.7MM **Privately Held**
WEB: www.amfac.com
SIC: 7011 Resort hotel
HQ: Parks Xanterra & Resorts Inc
6312 S Fiddlers Green Cir 600n
Greenwood Village CO 80111
303 600-3400

(P-13444)
XLD GROUP LLC
Also Called: Torrance Marriott Hotel
3635 Fashion Way, Torrance (90503-4809)
PHONE.....................310 316-3636
Fax: 310 543-6013
Pam Ryan, *General Mgr*
Sonia Vargas, *Finance*
Christine Delgado, *Director*
Jon Jackson, *Director*
Francis Martin, *Manager*
EMP: 66
SALES (corp-wide): 3.5MM **Privately Held**
WEB: www.scmarriott.com
SIC: 7011 7389 Hotels & motels; office facilities & secretarial service rental
PA: Xld Group, Llc
500 Sansome St Ste 502
San Francisco CA

(P-13445)
YHB LONG BEACH LLC
Also Called: Holiday Inn Long Beach Airport
2640 N Lakewood Blvd, Long Beach (90815-1715)
PHONE.....................562 597-4401
Fax: 562 597-0601
Traycee Mayer, *Principal*
Eillen Labrador, *General Mgr*
Robert Smit, *General Mgr*
Ellen Lee, *Admin Sec*
Chris Mills, *Chief Engr*
EMP: 90
SALES (est): 6MM **Privately Held**
WEB: www.hilongbeach.com
SIC: 7011 Hotels & motels

(P-13446)
YHB SAN FRANCISCO LLC
Also Called: Pickwick Hotel The
85 5th St, San Francisco (94103-1812)
PHONE.....................415 421-7500
Fred Kleisner, *CEO*
Fred Adriano, *Manager*
Karla Cruz, *Manager*
EMP: 65
SALES (est): 3.9MM **Privately Held**
WEB: www.thepickwickhotel.com
SIC: 7011 Hotels & motels

(P-13447)
ZHG INC
Also Called: Monterey Beach Hotel
2600 Sand Dunes Dr, Monterey (93940-3838)
PHONE.....................831 394-3321
Theodore Richter, *President*
Sharon Regan, *Manager*
EMP: 85
SQ FT: 4,996
SALES (est): 2.4MM **Privately Held**
SIC: 7011 Hotels & motels

(P-13448)
ZMC HOTELS LLC
1855 Olympic Blvd Ste 300, Walnut Creek (94596-5019)
PHONE.....................925 933-4000
Kenneth Goldfine, *CEO*
Mark D Hall,
EMP: 233
SALES (est): 493K
SALES (corp-wide): 5.1MM **Privately Held**
SIC: 7011 Hotels & motels
PA: Zmc Hotels, Inc.
2305 W Superior St
Duluth MN 55806
218 723-8433

7021 Rooming & Boarding Houses

(P-13449)
CAL POLY CORPORATION
Also Called: Housing Services
Cal Poly Bldg 31, San Luis Obispo (93407)
PHONE.....................805 756-1587
Alan Pepe, *Manager*
Jeanne Schrader, *Admin Asst*
EMP: 70
SALES (corp-wide): 44.1MM **Privately Held**
WEB: www.calpolyarts.org
SIC: 7021 Dormitory, commercially operated
PA: Cal Poly Corporation
1 Grand Ave Bldg 15
San Luis Obispo CA 93407
805 756-1131

(P-13450)
COLLEGE HOUSING NORTHWEST
Also Called: Craig Hall College Residences
1400 W 3rd St, Chico (95928-4825)
PHONE.....................530 345-1393
Fax: 530 345-1549
Karen Dewall, *Manager*
EMP: 60
SQ FT: 172,962
SALES (corp-wide): 7.3MM **Privately Held**
SIC: 7021 Dormitory, commercially operated; furnished room rental
PA: College Housing Northwest, Llc
1604 Sw Clay St
Portland OR
503 345-4100

(P-13451)
CROCODILE BAY LODGE
Also Called: Lynch Creek Medical Management
731 Southpoint Blvd, Petaluma (94954-1495)
PHONE.....................707 559-7990
Robert T Williams, *Consultant*
John F Galloway, *Exec VP*
Rodrigo Alonso, *Controller*
John Williams, *Agent*
Robert T Willaims, *Consultant*
EMP: 192
SQ FT: 2,500
SALES (est): 3MM **Privately Held**
WEB: www.crocodilebay.com
SIC: 7021 4724 Rooming & boarding houses; travel agencies

(P-13452)
INTERNATIONAL HOUSE
Also Called: Interntnal Hse At U C Berkeley
2299 Piedmont Ave Ste 535, Berkeley (94720-2392)
PHONE.....................510 642-9490
Fax: 510 642-5220
Robert M Berdahl, *Ch of Bd*
Joseph Lurie, *Exec Dir*
Clara Fomich, *Executive Asst*
Mark Phillips, *Data Proc Dir*
Ted Goode, *Sales Staff*
EMP: 162
SQ FT: 100,000
SALES: 17.3MM **Privately Held**
SIC: 7021 Rooming & boarding houses

(P-13453)
OAKWOOD CORPORATE HOUSING INC (PA)
2222 Corinth Ave, Los Angeles (90064-1602)
PHONE.....................310 478-1021
Howard F Ruby, *President*
Gary Grubbs, *Vice Chairman*
Ricardo Villarreal, *President*
Chris Brenk, *CFO*
Hailna Moffatt, *CFO*
EMP: 65
SALES (est): 14.4MM **Privately Held**
SIC: 7021 Furnished room rental

(P-13454)
PACIFIC LABOR SERVICES INC
5690 Cypress Rd, Oxnard (93033-8509)
P.O. Box 824, Buellton (93427-0824)
PHONE.....................805 488-4625
Fax: 805 488-3211
Rafael Ramos, *President*
EMP: 50
SQ FT: 62,000
SALES: 1.1MM **Privately Held**
WEB: www.pacificlaborsourceinc.com
SIC: 7021 7363 7361 Rooming & boarding houses; temporary help service; labor contractors (employment agency)

(P-13455)
RED ROAD SOBRIETY HOUSE
10 Kirk Ave, San Jose (95127-2214)
PHONE.....................408 512-8474
Jennifer Swifteagle, *Owner*
EMP: 50
SALES (est): 306.8K **Privately Held**
SIC: 7021 Rooming & boarding houses

(P-13456)
THE HOUSING AUTHORITY OF
Also Called: Housing Auth Cnty Monterey
1112 Parkside St, Salinas (93906-3642)
PHONE.....................831 449-7268
Elizabeth Williams, *Branch Mgr*
EMP: 80 **Privately Held**
SIC: 7021 Lodging house, except organization
PA: The Housing Authority Of The County Of Monterey
123 Rico St
Salinas CA 93907
831 775-5000

7032 Sporting & Recreational Camps

(P-13457)
ADVENTRES RLLING CROSS-COUNTRY
Also Called: Adventures Cross-Country
242 Redwd Hwy Frntge 1, Mill Valley (94941-6613)
PHONE.....................415 332-5075
Fax: 415 332-2130
Scott A Von Eschen, *President*
Jacob Swarsen, *Mktg Dir*
Kristin Eschen, *Hlthcr Dir*
Lisa Halsted, *Director*
Bridget Murphy, *Director*
EMP: 133
SQ FT: 2,500
SALES (est): 3.5MM **Privately Held**
WEB: www.adventurescrosscountry.com
SIC: 7032 Sporting & recreational camps

(P-13458)
ALISAL PROPERTIES (PA)
Also Called: Alisal Guest Ranch
1054 Alisal Rd, Solvang (93463-3033)
PHONE.....................805 688-6411
Fax: 805 688-2510
Palmer Jackson, *President*
Susanne Powell, *Corp Secy*
Joan Y Jackson, *Vice Pres*
John Hardy, *CTO*
Tracy Frost, *Controller*
EMP: 165
SQ FT: 10,000
SALES (est): 19.1MM **Privately Held**
WEB: www.alisal.com
SIC: 7032 7997 Sporting camps; golf club, membership

(P-13459)
ALLIANCE RDWODS CNFRNCE GRNDS
6250 Bohemian Hwy, Occidental (95465-9105)
PHONE.....................707 874-3507
Fax: 707 874-2509
James Blake, *Exec Dir*
Tim Welch, *Info Tech Dir*
EMP: 65
SQ FT: 1,392
SALES (est): 3.6MM **Privately Held**
WEB: www.allianceredwoods.com
SIC: 7032 Recreational camps; youth camps; Bible camp

(P-13460)
BEACHSPORTS INC
600 N Catalina Ave, Redondo Beach (90277-2134)
PHONE.....................310 372-2202
Jack Tingley, *President*
Lisa Jarrett, *Director*
EMP: 50
SALES: 437K **Privately Held**
SIC: 7032 Summer camp, except day & sports instructional

(P-13461)
BIG LGUE DREAMS CONSULTING LLC
33700 Date Palm Dr, Cathedral City (92234-4731)
PHONE.....................760 324-5600
Steve Navarro, *Vice Pres*
Sherrye Ryan, *General Mgr*
EMP: 145
SALES (corp-wide): 37.8MM **Privately Held**
SIC: 7032 Sporting & recreational camps
PA: Big League Dreams Consulting, Llc
16333 Fairfield Ranch Rd
Chino Hills CA 91709
909 287-1700

(P-13462)
CITY OF LOS ANGELES
Also Called: Parks & Recreation Dept
3200 Canyon Dr, Los Angeles (90068-2422)
PHONE.....................323 467-7193
Fax: 323 957-4526
Kathrynn Penny, *Director*
EMP: 50 **Privately Held**
WEB: www.lacity.org
SIC: 7032 9512 7999 Sporting & recreational camps; recreational program administration, government; ; recreation center
PA: City Of Los Angeles
200 N Spring St Ste 303
Los Angeles CA 90012
213 978-0600

(P-13463)
EASTER SEALS INC
Also Called: Camp Harmon Easter Seal Soc
16403 Highway 9, Boulder Creek (95006-9696)
PHONE.....................831 338-3383
Fax: 831 338-0200

PRODUCTS & SERVICES SECTION
7033 - Trailer Parks & Camp Sites County (P-13484)

Jennifer Whalen, *Manager*
EMP: 60
SALES (corp-wide): 73MM **Privately Held**
WEB: www.eastersealsinc.com
SIC: 7032 7033 Sporting & recreational camps; trailer parks & campsites
PA: Easter Seals, Inc.
233 S Wacker Dr Ste 2400
Chicago IL 60606
312 726-6200

(P-13464)
GUIDED DISCOVERIES INC
Also Called: Desert Sun Science Center, The
26800 Saunders Meadows Rd, Idyllwild (92549)
P.O. Box 3399 (92549-3399)
PHONE 951 659-6062
Fax: 951 659-9843
Allen Tiso, *Director*
EMP: 50
SALES (corp-wide): 14.7MM **Privately Held**
SIC: 7032 8299 Sporting & recreational camps; educational services
PA: Guided Discoveries, Inc.
27282 Calle Arroyo
San Juan Capistrano CA 92675
800 645-1423

(P-13465)
HARMONIUM INC
Also Called: San Diego Regional Teen Center
8450 Mira Mesa Blvd, San Diego (92126-2311)
PHONE 858 271-4000
Rosa Ana Lozada, *Branch Mgr*
Jerry Figueroa, *Manager*
EMP: 635
SQ FT: 6,438
SALES (corp-wide): 9.3MM **Privately Held**
SIC: 7032 Youth camps
PA: Harmonium Inc
9245 Activity Rd Ste 200
San Diego CA 92126
858 684-3080

(P-13466)
HUME LAKE CHRISTIAN CAMPS INC
64144 Hume Lake Rd Ofc, Miramonte (93628-9600)
PHONE 559 305-7770
Genie Coe, *Accountant*
Dathan Brown, *Exec Dir*
Deanne Douglass, *Office Admin*
Cameron Cadiz, *Admin Asst*
Mike Drake, *Opers Dir*
EMP: 97
SALES (corp-wide): 14.4MM **Privately Held**
SIC: 7032 Bible camp
PA: Hume Lake Christian Camps Inc
5545 E Hedges Ave
Fresno CA 93727
559 251-6055

(P-13467)
MAMMOTH MOUNTAIN LAKE CORP
10001 Minaret Rd, Mammoth Lakes (93546)
P.O. Box 24 (93546-0024)
PHONE 760 934-2571
Alan Gregory, *CEO*
Rusty Gregory, *Principal*
Colleen Gaunt, *Human Resources*
EMP: 450
SALES (est): 2.6MM
SALES (corp-wide): 477.6MM **Privately Held**
SIC: 7032 Sporting & recreational camps
HQ: Mammoth Mountain Ski Area, Llc
10001 Minaret Rd
Mammoth Lakes CA 93546
760 934-2571

(P-13468)
MOUNT HERMON ASSOCIATION INC
2500 Smith Rd, Bradley (93426-9653)
P.O. Box 413, Mount Hermon (95041-0413)
PHONE 805 472-9201
Fax: 805 335-9218
Trevor Van Laar, *Branch Mgr*
Ron Demolar, *Associate Dir*
Lorie Heerwagen, *Admin Asst*
Joshua Bootz, *Graphic Designe*
Lisa Olson, *Program Dir*
EMP: 75
SALES (corp-wide): 12.3MM **Privately Held**
SIC: 7032 Recreational camps
PA: Mount Hermon Association Inc
37 Conference Dr
Mount Hermon CA 95041
831 335-4466

(P-13469)
MOUNT HERMON ASSOCIATION INC (PA)
Also Called: Christian Conference Grounds
37 Conference Dr, Mount Hermon (95041)
PHONE 831 335-4466
Roger E Williams, *Exec Dir*
Jon Wilcox, *Executive*
Kerry Phibbs, *Associate Dir*
David Talbott, *Associate Dir*
Roger Williams, *Exec Dir*
EMP: 100
SQ FT: 10,000
SALES (est): 12.3MM **Privately Held**
WEB: www.mhcamps.org
SIC: 7032 5942 Bible camp; books, religious

(P-13470)
SILICON VALLEY MONTEREY BAY CO
29211 Highway 108, Long Barn (95335-9737)
PHONE 209 965-3432
Alan Buscaglia, *Branch Mgr*
EMP: 54
SALES (corp-wide): 4MM **Privately Held**
WEB: www.scouting.org
SIC: 7032 Boys' camp
PA: Silicon Valley Monterey Bay Council, Inc., Boy Scouts Of America
970 W Julian St
San Jose CA 95126
408 279-2086

(P-13471)
SILVER SPUR CHRISTIAN CAMP
17301 Silver Spur Dr, Tuolumne (95379-9638)
PHONE 209 928-4248
Stephen Johnson, *Director*
Marie Johnson, *Administration*
Jim Britt, *IT/INT Sup*
EMP: 60
SALES (est): 2.1MM **Privately Held**
WEB: www.silverspur.com
SIC: 7032 7011 Recreational camps; hotels & motels

(P-13472)
UNITED CMPS CNFRENCES RETREATS (PA)
Also Called: Uccr
1304 Sthpint Blvd Ste 200, Petaluma (94954)
PHONE 707 762-3220
Mike Carr, *President*
Carolyn Briggs, *Bookkeeper*
Doug Stairs, *Sales Mgr*
Michelle Scanlon, *Director*
Jonnie Arellanes, *Manager*
EMP: 50
SQ FT: 1,700
SALES: 1.8MM **Privately Held**
WEB: www.uccr.org
SIC: 7032 Recreational camps; youth camps

(P-13473)
WESTMINSTER WOODS CAMP & CONFE
6510 Bohemian Hwy, Occidental (95465-9101)
PHONE 707 874-2426
Sheila Denton, *Principal*
EMP: 50
SALES (est): 187.5K **Privately Held**
SIC: 7032 Sporting & recreational camps

(P-13474)
WILSHIRE BOULEVARD TEMPLE
11495 Pacific Coast Hwy, Malibu (90265-2006)
PHONE 310 457-7861
EMP: 213
SALES (corp-wide): 13.7MM **Privately Held**
SIC: 7032 Sporting & recreational camps
PA: Wilshire Boulevard Temple
3663 Wilshire Blvd
Los Angeles CA 90010
213 388-2401

7033 Trailer Parks & Camp Sites

(P-13475)
BURLINGAME INDUSTRIES INC (PA)
Also Called: Eagle Roofing Products
3546 N Riverside Ave, Rialto (92377-3878)
PHONE 909 355-7000
Fax: 909 822-5940
Robert C Burlingame, *Ch of Bd*
Kevin C Burlingame, *President*
Rich Jones, *CFO*
Seamus P Burlingame, *Exec VP*
William L Robinson, *Admin Sec*
EMP: 100 **EST:** 1989
SQ FT: 100,000
SALES (est): 71.2MM **Privately Held**
SIC: 7033 0971 3559 3259 Campgrounds; hunting preserve; tile making machines; roofing tile, clay; asphalt felts & coatings

(P-13476)
BURLINGAME INDUSTRIES INC
Also Called: Resort Campground Intl
277 Lytle Creek Rd, Lytle Creek (92358-9751)
PHONE 909 887-7038
Fax: 909 880-2430
Bob Boyter, *Manager*
Alan Monteleone, *Manager*
EMP: 103
SALES (corp-wide): 71.2MM **Privately Held**
SIC: 7033 Campgrounds; campsite
PA: Burlingame Industries, Incorporated
3546 N Riverside Ave
Rialto CA 92377
909 355-7000

(P-13477)
CALIFORNIA LAND MGT SVCS CORP
Also Called: Calif Land Management
2165 Fallen Leaf Rd, South Lake Tahoe (96150)
PHONE 530 544-5994
Gayle Ellis, *General Mgr*
Larry Chapman, *Manager*
EMP: 50
SALES (corp-wide): 12.7MM **Privately Held**
WEB: www.clm-services.com
SIC: 7033 Trailer parks & campsites
PA: California Land Management Services Corporation
675 Gilman St
Palo Alto CA 94301
650 322-1181

(P-13478)
COLORADO RIVER ADVENTURES INC (PA)
Also Called: Yuma Lakes Resort
2715 Parker Dam Rd, Earp (92242-9712)
P.O. Box 1088, Parker AZ (85344-1088)
PHONE 760 663-3737
Phil Younis, *President*
Tina Givens, *Human Res Mgr*
Randy Wright, *Mktg Dir*
EMP: 112
SQ FT: 6,500
SALES (est): 6.1MM **Privately Held**
WEB: www.coloradoriveradventures.com
SIC: 7033 8641 7032 Campgrounds; social club, membership; recreational camps

(P-13479)
COUNTY OF SAN MATEO
Also Called: Parks Department
455 County Ctr Fl 4, Redwood City (94063-1663)
PHONE 650 363-4020
Fax: 650 599-1721
Jim Natell, *Director*
Sara Medina, *Admin Mgr*
Cecily Harris, *General Mgr*
Luther Perry, *CIO*
Gary Lockman, *Info Tech Mgr*
EMP: 55 **Privately Held**
WEB: www.ci.sanmateo.ca.us
SIC: 7033 9199 Trailer park;
PA: County Of San Mateo
400 County Ctr
Redwood City CA 94063
650 363-4123

(P-13480)
EL CAPITAN RANCH LLC
Also Called: El Capitan Canyon
11560 Calle Real, Santa Barbara (93117-9789)
PHONE 805 685-3887
Fax: 805 968-6772
Roger Himovitz,
Terri Bowman, *Sales Dir*
Kendra Summers, *Sales Dir*
Robert Hansen, *Sales Mgr*
Kali McDonald, *Sales Mgr*
EMP: 62
SALES (est): 5.2MM **Privately Held**
WEB: www.elcapitanranch.com
SIC: 7033 Trailer parks & campsites

(P-13481)
EMERALD BROOK LLC
Also Called: Emerald Desert Rv Resort
76000 Frank Sinatra Dr, Palm Desert (92211-5031)
PHONE 760 345-4770
Fax: 619 345-0460
Neil Brandom,
EMP: 50
SQ FT: 8,000
SALES (est): 2.1MM **Privately Held**
WEB: www.emeralddesert.com
SIC: 7033 7997 Recreational vehicle parks; golf club, membership

(P-13482)
SAN FRNCSCO NORTH/PETALUMA KOA
20 Rainsville Rd, Petaluma (94952-8121)
PHONE 707 763-1492
Fax: 707 763-2668
William Wood, *President*
Judith Wood, *Corp Secy*
EMP: 50
SQ FT: 2,000
SALES (est): 2.1MM **Privately Held**
WEB: www.petalumakoakampground.com
SIC: 7033 4119 Campgrounds; sightseeing bus

(P-13483)
SILENT VALLEY CLUB INC
46305 Poppet Flats Rd, Banning (92220-9636)
PHONE 951 849-4501
Fax: 951 849-2527
Nellie Afana, *President*
Brenda Mejia, *CFO*
Jo A Prosper, *Human Res Dir*
Joann Trosper, *Agent*
Jane Bryant, *Relations*
EMP: 70
SQ FT: 2,200
SALES: 3.5MM **Privately Held**
WEB: www.silentvalleyclub.com
SIC: 7033 Campgrounds

(P-13484)
THOUSAND TRAILS INC
Also Called: N A C O
31191 Hardin Flat Rd, Groveland (95321-9716)
PHONE 209 962-0100
John Kimbrough, *Manager*
EMP: 50
SALES (corp-wide): 821.6MM **Publicly Held**
WEB: www.indianpt.com
SIC: 7033 Trailer parks & campsites

7033 - Trailer Parks & Camp Sites County (P-13485)

PRODUCTS & SERVICES SECTION

HQ: Thousand Trails, Inc.
2325 Highway 90
Gautier MS 39553
228 497-3594

(P-13485)
TRAILER PARK INC
4300 Soquel Dr Spc 90, Soquel (95073-2140)
PHONE.....................831 462-3271
Mark Kalemos, *Principal*
EMP: 120
SALES (corp-wide): 41.9MM **Privately Held**
SIC: 7033 Trailer park
PA: Trailer Park, Inc.
6922 Hollywood Blvd Fl 12
Los Angeles CA 90028
310 845-3000

7041 Membership-Basis Hotels

(P-13486)
AIRBNB INC (PA)
888 Brannan St Ste 400, San Francisco (94103-4932)
PHONE.....................415 800-5959
Brian Chesky, *CEO*
Nathan Blecharczyk, *Founder*
Joe Gebbia,
Jacob Lama, *Trust Officer*
Kim Roth, *Trust Officer*
EMP: 1032 **EST:** 2008
SALES (est): 198.1MM **Privately Held**
SIC: 7041 Residence club, organization

(P-13487)
ASSOCIATED STUDENTS INC
333 S Twin Oaks Valley Rd, San Marcos (92096-0001)
PHONE.....................760 750-4990
Fax: 760 750-3149
Susana Figueroa, *President*
Laura Poggi, *Exec Dir*
Ghazala Rehan, *Psychiatry*
EMP: 50 **EST:** 1991
SALES (est): 1.3MM **Privately Held**
SIC: 7041 Boarding house, fraternity & sorority

(P-13488)
BERKELEY STUDENT COOP INC
2424 Ridge Rd, Berkeley (94709-1212)
PHONE.....................510 848-1936
Janette E Stokley, *Exec Dir*
Palmer Buchholz, *President*
Marjorie Greene, *CFO*
Steve Catano, *Administration*
Zach Gottesman, *Network Mgr*
EMP: 100
SQ FT: 18,000
SALES (est): 10.9MM **Privately Held**
WEB: www.usca.org
SIC: 7041 Boarding house, organization

(P-13489)
CALIFORNIA OMICRON CHAPTER
1990 S Bundy Dr Ste 500, Los Angeles (90025-5245)
PHONE.....................310 979-3857
Justin Schnuelle, *President*
EMP: 85
SALES: 529.4K **Privately Held**
SIC: 7041 Fraternities & sororities

(P-13490)
CITY OF SUNNYVALE
Also Called: Housing Division
456 W Olive Ave, Sunnyvale (94086-7661)
P.O. Box 3707 (94088-3707)
PHONE.....................408 730-7451
Gary Luebbers, *Principal*
Katrina Ardina, *Admin Sec*
EMP: 99 **Privately Held**
SIC: 7041 Rooming houses
PA: City Of Sunnyvale
456 W Olive Ave
Sunnyvale CA 94086
408 730-7415

(P-13491)
CLUB QUARTERS SAN FRANCISCO
424 Clay St, San Francisco (94111-3207)
PHONE.....................415 268-3606
Sanj Rai, *Manager*
Patrick Jackson, *General Mgr*
EMP: 99
SALES (est): 1.9MM **Privately Held**
SIC: 7041 Membership-basis organization hotels

(P-13492)
GAMMA PHI BETA SORORITY INC
Also Called: DELTA PHI CHAPTER
890 Camino Pescadero, Goleta (93117-4768)
PHONE.....................805 968-4221
Amber Setrakain, *President*
EMP: 90
SALES: 240.7K **Privately Held**
WEB: www.gammaphibetaucsb.com
SIC: 7041 8641 7011 Membership-basis organization hotels; university club; hotels & motels

(P-13493)
HEART CONSCIOUSNESS CHURCH (PA)
Also Called: Harbin Hot Springs
18424 Harbin Springs Rd, Middletown (95461-9687)
P.O. Box 782 (95461-0782)
PHONE.....................707 987-2477
Robert F Hartley, *President*
Suzie Lecavalier, *Treasurer*
Julie Adams, *Vice Pres*
Sajjad Mahmud, *Vice Pres*
Elaine Watt, *Accounting Mgr*
EMP: 110
SQ FT: 4,000
SALES: 23.7MM **Privately Held**
WEB: www.harbinhotsprings.com
SIC: 7041 Membership-basis organization hotels

(P-13494)
NATIONAL COMMUNITY RENAISSANCE (PA)
9421 Haven Ave Ste 100, Rancho Cucamonga (91730-5890)
PHONE.....................909 483-2444
Steve Pontell, *President*
Joe Vanbalen, *Ch of Bd*
Tracy Thomas, *CFO*
Ciriaco Pinedo, *Exec VP*
Michael M Ruane, *Exec VP*
EMP: 51 **EST:** 1997
SALES (est): 6MM **Privately Held**
SIC: 7041 Lodging house, organization

(P-13495)
NAVY EXCHANGE SERVICE COMMAND
Also Called: Navy Bachelor Quarters
1395 Hussey Rd, Ridgecrest (93555)
PHONE.....................760 939-8681
Mike Biddlingmeier, *Business Dir*
EMP: 95 **Publicly Held**
WEB: www.navy-nex.com
SIC: 7041 Lodging house, organization
HQ: Navy Exchange Service Command
3280 Virginia Beach Blvd
Virginia Beach VA 23452
800 448-3996

(P-13496)
PHI DELTA THETA INC
17740 Halsted St, Northridge (91325-2025)
P.O. Box 34082, Granada Hills (91394-4082)
PHONE.....................818 885-9940
Jason McKnight, *President*
Bryan Guerrero, *Treasurer*
Evan Press, *Principal*
EMP: 50
SALES (est): 809.2K **Privately Held**
WEB: www.redarc.com
SIC: 7041 8641 Fraternities & sororities; fraternal associations

(P-13497)
RLJ HGN EMERYVILLE LESSEE LP
Also Called: Hilton Garden Inn Emeryville
1800 Powell St, Emeryville (94608-1808)
PHONE.....................510 658-9300
Hank Artime, *Agent*
Lakeisha Walker, *Agent*
EMP: 99
SQ FT: 89,000
SALES (est): 287.1K **Privately Held**
SIC: 7041 Membership-basis organization hotels

(P-13498)
SIGMA KAPPA SORORITY
2409 Warring St, Berkeley (94704-2593)
PHONE.....................510 540-9142
Donna Jollymour, *President*
EMP: 80
SALES (est): 1.7MM **Privately Held**
SIC: 7041 Sorority residential house

7211 Power Laundries, Family & Commercial

(P-13499)
AMERICAN ETC INC
Also Called: Royal Laundry
1140 San Mateo Ave, South San Francisco (94080-6602)
PHONE.....................650 873-5353
Kenn T Edwards, *CEO*
Don Luckenbach, *President*
Michael Levy, *Vice Pres*
Martha Guzman, *Controller*
Darlene Bell, *Opers Mgr*
EMP: 325
SQ FT: 70,000
SALES (est): 21.3MM **Privately Held**
SIC: 7211 Power laundries, family & commercial

(P-13500)
ANITSA INC
Also Called: Valet Services
6032 Shull St, Bell Gardens (90201-6237)
PHONE.....................213 237-0533
Margo Minisiam, *President*
Gary Von, *Executive*
Daniel Soussa, *Administration*
Paul Chaney, *Manager*
EMP: 135
SQ FT: 65,000
SALES (est): 7.9MM **Privately Held**
WEB: www.anitsa.com
SIC: 7211 8742 Power laundries, family & commercial; industry specialist consultants

(P-13501)
BRAUN LINEN SERVICE INC
A-1 Pomona Linen
396 La Mesa St, Pomona (91766-2129)
P.O. Box 317 (91769-0317)
PHONE.....................909 623-2678
Jim Moore, *Manager*
Peter Uy, *Manager*
EMP: 100
SALES (corp-wide): 10.4MM **Privately Held**
SIC: 7211 7213 5947 Power laundries, family & commercial; linen supply; gifts & novelties
PA: Braun Linen Service, Inc.
16514 Garfield Ave
Paramount CA 90723
909 623-2678

(P-13502)
DEL MAR FRENCH LAUNDRY
508 Del Monte Ave, Monterey (93940-2405)
P.O. Box 1141 (93942-1141)
PHONE.....................831 375-9597
Cedo Godspodnetich, *President*
Cynthia Godspodnetich, *Admin Sec*
EMP: 50
SQ FT: 12,150
SALES (est): 1MM **Privately Held**
SIC: 7211 Power laundries, family & commercial

(P-13503)
EMERALD TEXTILES LLC
1725 Dornoch Ct Ste 101, San Diego (92154-7206)
PHONE.....................619 690-7353
Philip Gildred, *CEO*
EMP: 252
SALES (est): 14.5MM **Privately Held**
SIC: 7211 Power laundries, family & commercial

(P-13504)
MONTEREY BAY ACADAMY LAUNDRY
Also Called: Campus Laundry
675 Beach Dr, Watsonville (95076-1904)
PHONE.....................831 728-1481
Tim Kuprock, *Principal*
Jay Ketelsen, *General Mgr*
Gina Jett, *Manager*
Jay Ketelson, *Manager*
EMP: 70
SALES (est): 4MM **Privately Held**
SIC: 7211 7213 Power laundries, family & commercial; linen supply

(P-13505)
PRO-WASH INC
9117 S Main St, Los Angeles (90003-3722)
PHONE.....................323 756-6000
Steve Koo, *President*
EMP: 70
SQ FT: 20,000
SALES (est): 2.4MM **Privately Held**
WEB: www.prowashconsulting.com
SIC: 7211 Laundry collecting & distributing outlet

(P-13506)
RADIANT SERVICES CORP (PA)
651 W Knox St, Gardena (90248-4409)
PHONE.....................310 327-6300
Fax: 310 323-4030
Mina Keywanfar, *CEO*
Shahrokh Keywanfar, *President*
Jamshid Beroukhim, *Vice Pres*
EMP: 235
SALES (est): 13.4MM **Privately Held**
WEB: www.radiantservices.com
SIC: 7211 7216 Power laundries, family & commercial; drycleaning plants, except rugs

(P-13507)
ROYAL AIRLINE LINEN INC
125 N Ash Ave, Inglewood (90301-1648)
PHONE.....................310 677-9885
Fax: 310 677-9593
Norman Magidow, *CEO*
Tony Griffin, *President*
Kay Cunningham, *Vice Pres*
EMP: 100
SQ FT: 12,800
SALES: 5.8MM **Privately Held**
SIC: 7211 7218 7213 Laundry collecting & distributing outlet; industrial launderers; linen supply

(P-13508)
YUEN YEE LAUNDRY & CLEANERS
Also Called: Yee Yuen Linen Service
2575 S Normandie Ave, Los Angeles (90007-1598)
PHONE.....................323 734-7205
Deborah Morikawa, *President*
Luis Lee, *Corp Secy*
Cynthia Louie, *Vice Pres*
EMP: 80
SQ FT: 20,000
SALES (est): 4.8MM **Privately Held**
WEB: www.yeeyuenlinen.com
SIC: 7211 Laundry collecting & distributing outlet

7212 Garment Pressing & Cleaners' Agents

▲ = Import ▼=Export
◆ =Import/Export

PRODUCTS & SERVICES SECTION

7213 - Linen Sply County (P-13530)

(P-13509)
JOSEPH DIPUZO
Also Called: Superclean America
601 E Tahquitz Canyon Way # 120, Palm Springs (92262-6700)
P.O. Box 3006 (92263-3006)
PHONE..................760 325-1200
Joseph Dipuzo, *Owner*
EMP: 50
SALES (est): 701.6K **Privately Held**
SIC: 7212 Laundry & drycleaner agents

7213 Linen Sply

(P-13510)
ALSCO INC
1009 Factory St, Richmond (94801-2166)
PHONE..................510 237-9634
EMP: 84
SALES (corp-wide): 658.7MM **Privately Held**
SIC: 7213
PA: Alsco Inc.
505 E South Temple
Salt Lake City UT 84102
801 328-8831

(P-13511)
ALSCO INC
900 N Highland Ave, Los Angeles (90038-2413)
PHONE..................323 465-5111
Mike Keller, *Branch Mgr*
EMP: 180
SALES (corp-wide): 683.4MM **Privately Held**
WEB: www.amlinen.com
SIC: 7213 Linen supply
PA: Alsco Inc.
505 E South Temple
Salt Lake City UT 84102
801 328-8831

(P-13512)
ALSCO INC
2215 Palma Dr, Ventura (93003-6437)
PHONE..................805 650-6578
John Mc Carty, *Branch Mgr*
EMP: 85
SALES (corp-wide): 683.4MM **Privately Held**
SIC: 7213 5087 Linen supply; laundry equipment & supplies
PA: Alsco Inc.
505 E South Temple
Salt Lake City UT 84102
801 328-8831

(P-13513)
ALSCO INC
705 W Grape St, San Diego (92101-2212)
P.O. Box 122671 (92112-2671)
PHONE..................619 234-7291
Mike Scacco, *Branch Mgr*
Roberta Carleton, *Office Mgr*
EMP: 110
SALES (corp-wide): 683.4MM **Privately Held**
WEB: www.amlinen.com
SIC: 7213 Linen supply
PA: Alsco Inc.
505 E South Temple
Salt Lake City UT 84102
801 328-8831

(P-13514)
ALSCO INC
1575 Indiana St, San Francisco (94107-3529)
PHONE..................415 648-9266
Jonathan Silver, *Branch Mgr*
Nick Axsom, *General Mgr*
David Torres, *Chief Engr*
Van Van De Graaf, *Sales Associate*
EMP: 100
SALES (corp-wide): 683.4MM **Privately Held**
WEB: www.amlinen.com
SIC: 7213 Linen supply
PA: Alsco Inc.
505 E South Temple
Salt Lake City UT 84102
801 328-8831

(P-13515)
ALSCO INC
1750 S Zeyn St, Anaheim (92802-2904)
P.O. Box 25068 (92825-5068)
PHONE..................714 774-4165
Scott Norris, *Manager*
Ray Schroeder, *District Mgr*
Shawn Swingholm, *General Mgr*
Princess Gaoay, *Office Mgr*
John Alvarez, *Chief Engr*
EMP: 100
SQ FT: 16,008
SALES (corp-wide): 683.4MM **Privately Held**
SIC: 7213 7218 Linen supply; industrial launderers
PA: Alsco Inc.
505 E South Temple
Salt Lake City UT 84102
801 328-8831

(P-13516)
ALSCO INC
3311 Industrial Dr, Santa Rosa (95403-2094)
PHONE..................707 523-3311
Denny Bunch, *General Mgr*
Terry Sachs, *Chief Mktg Ofcr*
EMP: 100
SQ FT: 36,448
SALES (corp-wide): 683.4MM **Privately Held**
WEB: www.amlinen.com
SIC: 7213 Linen supply
PA: Alsco Inc.
505 E South Temple
Salt Lake City UT 84102
801 328-8831

(P-13517)
ALSCO INC
2275 Junction Ave, San Jose (95131-1211)
PHONE..................408 279-2345
Paul Johnson, *Manager*
Bob Warford, *Personnel Exec*
Balvina Gonzalez, *Human Resources*
EMP: 110
SQ FT: 53,760
SALES (corp-wide): 683.4MM **Privately Held**
WEB: www.amlinen.com
SIC: 7213 7218 Uniform supply; industrial launderers
PA: Alsco Inc.
505 E South Temple
Salt Lake City UT 84102
801 328-8831

(P-13518)
ALSCO INC
5159 Commercial Cir, Concord (94520-8597)
PHONE..................707 751-0652
Fax: 707 676-7803
Norman Underwood, *Branch Mgr*
EMP: 150
SALES (corp-wide): 683.4MM **Privately Held**
WEB: www.amlinen.com
SIC: 7213 Uniform supply
PA: Alsco Inc.
505 E South Temple
Salt Lake City UT 84102
801 328-8831

(P-13519)
ALSCO INC
3391 Lanatt St, Sacramento (95819-1917)
PHONE..................916 454-5545
Fax: 916 454-9397
Michael Hollemdeck, *Branch Mgr*
EMP: 100
SALES (corp-wide): 683.4MM **Privately Held**
WEB: www.amlinen.com
SIC: 7213 Uniform supply
PA: Alsco Inc.
505 E South Temple
Salt Lake City UT 84102
801 328-8831

(P-13520)
AMERICAN TEXTILE MAINT CO
Also Called: Medico Professional Linen Svc
1705 Hooper Ave, Los Angeles (90021-3111)
P.O. Box 4928, Long Beach (90804-0928)
PHONE..................213 749-4433
Fax: 562 256-2434
Kenny Immazumi, *Manager*
EMP: 50
SALES (corp-wide): 30.1MM **Privately Held**
WEB: www.amtextile.net
SIC: 7213 Linen supply
PA: American Textile Maintenance Company
1667 W Washington Blvd
Los Angeles CA 90007
323 731-3132

(P-13521)
AMERICAN TEXTILE MAINT CO
Also Called: Republic Uniform
3001 E Anaheim St, Long Beach (90804-3810)
PHONE..................562 438-7656
Lawrence Pallan, *Manager*
EMP: 75
SALES (corp-wide): 30.1MM **Privately Held**
WEB: www.amtextile.net
SIC: 7213 Linen supply
PA: American Textile Maintenance Company
1667 W Washington Blvd
Los Angeles CA 90007
323 731-3132

(P-13522)
AMERICAN TEXTILE MAINT CO
Also Called: Master-Chef's Linen Rental
1664 W Washington Blvd, Los Angeles (90007-1115)
PHONE..................323 735-1661
Fax: 323 731-1622
Bob Brill, *Branch Mgr*
Brad Shames, *Vice Pres*
EMP: 130
SALES (corp-wide): 30.1MM **Privately Held**
WEB: www.amtextile.net
SIC: 7213 Towel supply; uniform supply
PA: American Textile Maintenance Company
1667 W Washington Blvd
Los Angeles CA 90007
323 731-3132

(P-13523)
AMERICAN TEXTILE MAINT CO
2201 E Carson St, Long Beach (90807-3043)
PHONE..................562 424-1607
Steve Jones, *Manager*
EMP: 180
SALES (corp-wide): 30.1MM **Privately Held**
WEB: www.amtextile.net
SIC: 7213 7218 Linen supply; uniform supply; industrial launderers
PA: American Textile Maintenance Company
1667 W Washington Blvd
Los Angeles CA 90007
323 731-3132

(P-13524)
AMERIPRIDE SERVICES INC
109 Calle Propano Ste C, Paso Robles (93446-5950)
PHONE..................805 239-9449
Matt Wenzel, *Branch Mgr*
Keith Jones, *Site Mgr*
EMP: 100
SALES (corp-wide): 383.2MM **Privately Held**
WEB: www.ameripride.com
SIC: 7213 Uniform supply
PA: Ameripride Services, Inc.
10801 Wayzata Blvd # 100
Hopkins MN 55305
952 738-4200

(P-13525)
AMERIPRIDE SERVICES INC
3750 Eastside Rd, Redding (96001-3807)
PHONE..................530 242-0564
J Oldham, *Branch Mgr*
EMP: 50
SALES (corp-wide): 383.2MM **Privately Held**
SIC: 7213 Uniform supply
PA: Ameripride Services, Inc.
10801 Wayzata Blvd # 100
Hopkins MN 55305
952 738-4200

(P-13526)
AMERIPRIDE SERVICES INC
Also Called: Ameripride Uniform Svcs
335 Washington St, Bakersfield (93307-2719)
PHONE..................661 324-7941
Mike Beckwith, *General Mgr*
Jerry Hill, *Sales Staff*
EMP: 110
SQ FT: 34,000
SALES (corp-wide): 383.2MM **Privately Held**
WEB: www.ameripride.com
SIC: 7213 7218 Linen supply; industrial launderers
PA: Ameripride Services, Inc.
10801 Wayzata Blvd # 100
Hopkins MN 55305
952 738-4200

(P-13527)
AMERIPRIDE SERVICES INC
4206 S B St, Stockton (95206-3990)
PHONE..................209 982-0020
Walter Locke, *Branch Mgr*
EMP: 50
SALES (corp-wide): 383.2MM **Privately Held**
WEB: www.ameripride.com
SIC: 7213 7218 Linen supply; industrial launderers
PA: Ameripride Services, Inc.
10801 Wayzata Blvd # 100
Hopkins MN 55305
952 738-4200

(P-13528)
AMERIPRIDE SERVICES INC
2230 W Chapman Ave, Orange (92868-2316)
PHONE..................714 385-8991
Frank Saldana, *Branch Mgr*
EMP: 50
SALES (corp-wide): 383.2MM **Privately Held**
WEB: www.ameripride.com
SIC: 7213 7218 Linen supply; industrial launderers
PA: Ameripride Services, Inc.
10801 Wayzata Blvd # 100
Hopkins MN 55305
952 738-4200

(P-13529)
AMERIPRIDE SERVICES INC
3701 Collins Ave Ste 5b, Richmond (94806-2079)
PHONE..................800 748-6178
John Galletta, *Manager*
EMP: 50
SALES (corp-wide): 383.2MM **Privately Held**
WEB: www.ameripride.com
SIC: 7213 7218 Linen supply; industrial launderers
PA: Ameripride Services, Inc.
10801 Wayzata Blvd # 100
Hopkins MN 55305
952 738-4200

(P-13530)
AMERIPRIDE SERVICES INC
1356 Dayton St Ste R, Salinas (93901-4427)
PHONE..................800 882-5326
Elizabeth Ledford, *Ch Credit Ofcr*
EMP: 50
SALES (corp-wide): 383.2MM **Privately Held**
WEB: www.ameripride.com
SIC: 7213 7218 Linen supply; industrial launderers

7213 - Linen Sply County (P-13531)

PA: Ameripride Services, Inc.
10801 Wayzata Blvd # 100
Hopkins MN 55305
952 738-4200

(P-13531)
ANGELICA CORPORATION
Also Called: Angelica Textile
701 Willow Pass Rd Ste 10, Pittsburg
(94565-1803)
PHONE.................................925 473-2520
John Burskens, *Office Mgr*
EMP: 200 **Privately Held**
SIC: 7213 Linen supply
HQ: Angelica Corporation
1105 Lakewood Pkwy # 210
Alpharetta GA 30009
678 823-4100

(P-13532)
ANGELICA TEXTILE SERVICES INC
1575 N Case St, Orange (92867-3635)
PHONE.................................714 998-6109
Fax: 714 637-5239
Alicia Silva, *Branch Mgr*
Phillip Bellot, *IT/INT Sup*
EMP: 240 **Privately Held**
SIC: 7213 7218 Linen supply; uniform supply; industrial launderers
HQ: Angelica Textile Services, Inc.
1105 Lakewood Pkwy # 210
Alpharetta GA 30009
678 823-4100

(P-13533)
ANGELICA TEXTILE SERVICES INC
300 E Commercial St, Pomona
(91767-5506)
PHONE.................................909 623-5135
Fax: 909 622-0411
Albert Cunningham, *General Mgr*
Saundra Huerta, *Human Res Dir*
EMP: 80 **Privately Held**
SIC: 7213 Linen supply; uniform supply
HQ: Angelica Textile Services, Inc.
1105 Lakewood Pkwy # 210
Alpharetta GA 30009
678 823-4100

(P-13534)
ARAMARK UNF & CAREER AP LLC
15525 Garfield Ave, Paramount
(90723-4033)
P.O. Box 1799 (90723-1799)
PHONE.................................323 774-4216
Fax: 323 531-1765
Dave Canzani, *Owner*
Allen Lee, *Manager*
EMP: 71
SALES (corp-wide): 14.3B **Publicly Held**
WEB: www.aramark-uniform.com
SIC: 7213 Uniform supply
HQ: Aramark Uniform & Career Apparel, Llc
115 N First St Ste 203
Burbank CA 91502
818 973-3700

(P-13535)
ARAMARK UNF & CAREER AP LLC
855 Mckendrie St, San Jose (95126-1295)
P.O. Box 28383 (95159-8383)
PHONE.................................408 243-9824
Brett Borba, *Manager*
EMP: 100
SALES (corp-wide): 14.3B **Publicly Held**
WEB: www.aramark-uniform.com
SIC: 7213 7218 Uniform supply; industrial launderers
HQ: Aramark Uniform & Career Apparel, Llc
115 N First St Ste 203
Burbank CA 91502
818 973-3700

(P-13536)
ARAMARK UNF & CAREER AP LLC
3333 N Sabre Dr, Fresno (93727-7816)
P.O. Box 1289, Clovis (93613-1289)
PHONE.................................559 291-6631
Fax: 559 291-6180
Anthony Mollica, *Sales/Mktg Mgr*
Norma Campbell, *Office Mgr*
Janis Hill, *Info Tech Mgr*
Mike E Elmore, *Manager*
Homer Gray, *Accounts Mgr*
EMP: 200
SQ FT: 130,449
SALES (corp-wide): 14.3B **Publicly Held**
WEB: www.aramark-uniform.com
SIC: 7213 Uniform supply
HQ: Aramark Uniform & Career Apparel, Llc
115 N First St Ste 203
Burbank CA 91502
818 973-3700

(P-13537)
ARAMARK UNF & CAREER AP LLC
5665 Eastgate Dr, San Diego
(92121-2817)
P.O. Box 919007 (92191-9007)
PHONE.................................858 550-1131
Stephen M Donly, *President*
Kady Aun, *Info Tech Mgr*
Gene West, *Manager*
Vigny Sonzeu, *Accounts Mgr*
EMP: 50
SALES (corp-wide): 14.3B **Publicly Held**
WEB: www.aramark-uniform.com
SIC: 7213 Uniform supply
HQ: Aramark Uniform & Career Apparel, Llc
115 N First St Ste 203
Burbank CA 91502
818 973-3700

(P-13538)
ARAMARK UNF & CAREER AP LLC
440 Carolina St, San Francisco
(94107-2304)
PHONE.................................415 244-8332
Deborah Hupp, *Manager*
EMP: 250
SALES (corp-wide): 14.3B **Publicly Held**
WEB: www.aramark-uniform.com
SIC: 7213 Uniform supply
HQ: Aramark Uniform & Career Apparel, Llc
115 N First St Ste 203
Burbank CA 91502
818 973-3700

(P-13539)
BRAUN LINEN SERVICE INC (PA)
Also Called: A-1 Pomona Linen
16514 Garfield Ave, Paramount
(90723-5304)
P.O. Box 348 (90723-0348)
PHONE.................................909 623-2678
Fax: 562 531-2050
Richard A Cornwell, *CEO*
William S Cornwell, *Vice Pres*
EMP: 125
SQ FT: 28,000
SALES (est): 10.4MM **Privately Held**
SIC: 7213 Towel supply; table cover supply

(P-13540)
CAL SOUTHERN SERVICES
Also Called: Socal Uniform Rental
419 Mcgroarty St, San Gabriel
(91776-2302)
PHONE.................................626 281-5942
Theodore W Doll Jr, *President*
James L Brittain, *Admin Sec*
Elaine Martinez, *Accountant*
Elaine Martinuz, *Manager*
EMP: 99
SALES (est): 3.1MM **Privately Held**
SIC: 7213 Linen supply

(P-13541)
CALIFORNIA LINEN SERVICES INC
40 E California Blvd, Pasadena
(91105-3203)
PHONE.................................626 564-4576
Brian O'Neil, *President*
Linda Harman, *Cust Mgr*
Angel Camarena, *Associate*
EMP: 60
SALES (est): 2.6MM **Privately Held**
SIC: 7213 Linen supply

(P-13542)
CINTAS CORPORATION
3201 Dnville Blvd Ste 285, Alamo (94507)
PHONE.................................925 743-1745
EMP: 54
SALES (corp-wide): 4.9B **Publicly Held**
SIC: 7213 5999 5912 5699 Uniform supply; alarm & safety equipment stores; drug stores & proprietary stores; uniforms & work clothing
PA: Cintas Corporation
6800 Cintas Blvd
Cincinnati OH 45262
513 459-1200

(P-13543)
CINTAS CORPORATION NO 3
2829 Workman Mill Rd, Whittier
(90601-1549)
PHONE.................................562 692-8741
Bryce Littlejohn, *General Mgr*
Vinil Ramachandran, *General Mgr*
EMP: 100
SALES (corp-wide): 4.9B **Publicly Held**
WEB: www.cintas-corp.com
SIC: 7213 7218 Uniform supply; industrial launderers
HQ: Cintas Corporation No 3
6800 Cintas Blvd
Mason OH 45040

(P-13544)
CINTAS CORPORATION NO 3
2150 Proforma Ave, Ontario (91761-8518)
PHONE.................................909 930-9096
Fax: 909 930-0348
Jim Ewald, *President*
Eric Curtis, *Site Mgr*
EMP: 150
SQ FT: 49,705
SALES (corp-wide): 4.9B **Publicly Held**
SIC: 7213 Uniform supply
HQ: Cintas Corporation No 3
6800 Cintas Blvd
Mason OH 45040

(P-13545)
CINTAS CORPORATION NO 3
28334 Industry Dr, Valencia (91355-4103)
PHONE.................................661 310-7400
Fax: 661 310-7401
Eric Curtis, *Branch Mgr*
EMP: 94
SALES (corp-wide): 4.9B **Publicly Held**
WEB: www.cintas-corp.com
SIC: 7213 Uniform supply
HQ: Cintas Corporation No 3
6800 Cintas Blvd
Mason OH 45040

(P-13546)
CITY TOWEL & DUST SERVICE INC
Also Called: Sunset Linen Service
3016 Dutton Ave, Santa Rosa
(95407-7886)
PHONE.................................707 542-0391
Fax: 707 542-0130
Michael Erwin, *President*
EMP: 50
SQ FT: 5,000
SALES (est): 3.9MM **Privately Held**
SIC: 7213 7211 Linen supply, clothing; linen supply, non-clothing; laundry collecting & distributing outlet

(P-13547)
DOMESTIC LINEN SUPPLY CO INC (HQ)
1600 Compton Ave, Los Angeles
(90021-3142)
P.O. Box 21326 (90021-0326)
PHONE.................................213 749-6300
Bruce L Colton, *President*
Leonard Colton, *Treasurer*
Jeson McCarbell, *General Mgr*
David J Colton, *Admin Sec*
EMP: 50
SQ FT: 49,454
SALES (est): 3.4MM
SALES (corp-wide): 36.9MM **Privately Held**
SIC: 7213 Uniform supply
PA: Domestic Linen Supply And Laundry Company
30555 Northwestern Hwy
Farmington Hills MI 48334
248 737-2000

(P-13548)
FOASBERG LAUNDRY & CLRS INC (PA)
Also Called: Crdn of Southern La County
640 E Wardlow Rd, Long Beach
(90807-4696)
PHONE.................................562 426-7345
Fax: 562 595-9693
James W Foasberg, *CEO*
Lynn Vavrick, *CFO*
Richard Foasberg, *Vice Pres*
Lynnette Vavrek, *Info Tech Mgr*
EMP: 68
SQ FT: 40,000
SALES (est): 4.4MM **Privately Held**
SIC: 7213 7216 7211 7218 Uniform supply; drycleaning collecting & distributing agency; laundry collecting & distributing outlet; industrial launderers

(P-13549)
GBS LINENS INC (PA)
Also Called: GBS Party Linens
305 N Muller St, Anaheim (92801-5445)
PHONE.................................714 778-6448
Fax: 714 533-4271
Pravin Mody, *President*
Ameer P Mody, *Vice Pres*
Sudha Mody, *Vice Pres*
Carol Trapschuh, *Social Dir*
Anthony Poploski, *Admin Mgr*
EMP: 100
SQ FT: 57,000
SALES (est): 12.3MM **Privately Held**
WEB: www.gbslinens.com
SIC: 7213 2392 7211 5023 Linen supply; household furnishings; power laundries, family & commercial; home furnishings; textile mill waste & remnant processing

(P-13550)
LA TAVOLA LLC (PA)
2655 Napa Valley Corp Dr, NAPA (94558)
PHONE.................................707 257-3358
Betsy Stone, *President*
Alegndra Mareno, *Accountant*
EMP: 80
SALES (est): 3.5MM **Privately Held**
SIC: 7213 Linen supply

(P-13551)
MEDICAL LINEN SERVICES INC
Also Called: Complete Linen Services
290 S Maple Ave, South San Francisco
(94080-6304)
PHONE.................................650 873-1221
Fax: 650 873-3676
Steve Bruni, *President*
Patrice Bruni, *Treasurer*
Colin Morf, *Vice Pres*
EMP: 100
SQ FT: 14,000
SALES (est): 6MM **Privately Held**
WEB: www.completelinen.com
SIC: 7213 Linen supply

(P-13552)
MISSION LINEN SUPPLY
Also Called: Mission Linen & Uniform Svc
2727 Industry St, Oceanside (92054-4810)
PHONE.................................760 757-9099
Fax: 760 757-0589
Graig Rogers, *Principal*
Randy Garrett, *General Mgr*
David Speaks, *General Mgr*
Rob Weilhammer, *Sales Executive*
EMP: 108
SALES (corp-wide): 169.8MM **Privately Held**
WEB: www.missions.com
SIC: 7213 7218 Linen supply; industrial launderers
PA: Mission Linen Supply
717 E Yanonali St
Santa Barbara CA 93103
805 730-3620

PRODUCTS & SERVICES SECTION
7215 - Coin Operated Laundries & Cleaning County (P-13573)

(P-13553)
MISSION LINEN SUPPLY
Mission Linen & Uniform Svc
399 Errol St, Morro Bay (93442-1896)
PHONE..................805 772-4451
Fax: 805 772-7826
David Hergenroeder, *General Mgr*
EMP: 50
SALES (corp-wide): 169.8MM **Privately Held**
WEB: www.missions.com
SIC: 7213 Linen supply
PA: Mission Linen Supply
   717 E Yanonali St
   Santa Barbara CA 93103
   805 730-3620

(P-13554)
MISSION LINEN SUPPLY
Also Called: Mission Linen & Uniform Svc
7520 Reese Rd, Sacramento (95828-3707)
PHONE..................916 423-3179
Fax: 916 689-8375
Peppy Secaile, *Manager*
Pepi Scalise, *Sales Staff*
Mark Rogers, *Manager*
EMP: 125
SALES (corp-wide): 169.8MM **Privately Held**
WEB: www.missions.com
SIC: 7213 7218 Linen supply; industrial launderers
PA: Mission Linen Supply
   717 E Yanonali St
   Santa Barbara CA 93103
   805 730-3620

(P-13555)
MISSION LINEN SUPPLY
Also Called: Mission Linen & Uniform Svc
315 Kern St, Salinas (93905-2595)
PHONE..................831 424-1707
Fax: 831 424-3439
Mark Rogers, *Manager*
Linda Bartoli, *General Mgr*
EMP: 59
SALES (corp-wide): 169.8MM **Privately Held**
WEB: www.missions.com
SIC: 7213 Uniform supply
PA: Mission Linen Supply
   717 E Yanonali St
   Santa Barbara CA 93103
   805 730-3620

(P-13556)
MISSION LINEN SUPPLY
Also Called: Mission Linen & Uniform Svc
2555 S Orange Ave, Fresno (93725-1398)
PHONE..................559 268-0647
Fax: 559 229-2948
Allen Gregory, *Manager*
EMP: 75
SALES (corp-wide): 169.8MM **Privately Held**
WEB: www.missions.com
SIC: 7213 Linen supply
PA: Mission Linen Supply
   717 E Yanonali St
   Santa Barbara CA 93103
   805 730-3620

(P-13557)
MISSION LINEN SUPPLY
Also Called: Mission Linen Supply & Svcs
1401 Summer St, Eureka (95501-2246)
PHONE..................707 443-8681
Fax: 707 443-6945
Jack Anderson, *General Mgr*
Dennis Piper, *Executive*
Walter Rowley, *Area Mgr*
Ruth Clark, *Manager*
Robert Zankowski, *Manager*
EMP: 58
SALES (corp-wide): 169.8MM **Privately Held**
WEB: www.missions.com
SIC: 7213 Linen supply
PA: Mission Linen Supply
   717 E Yanonali St
   Santa Barbara CA 93103
   805 730-3620

(P-13558)
MISSION LINEN SUPPLY
Also Called: Mission Linen & Uniform Svc
505 Maulhardt Ave, Oxnard (93030-7925)
PHONE..................805 485-6794
Fax: 805 983-6534
Matthew Aguelli, *Manager*
Nina Zinn, *General Mgr*
EMP: 55
SALES (corp-wide): 169.8MM **Privately Held**
WEB: www.missions.com
SIC: 7213 Towel supply
PA: Mission Linen Supply
   717 E Yanonali St
   Santa Barbara CA 93103
   805 730-3620

(P-13559)
MISSION LINEN SUPPLY
Also Called: Mission Linen & Uniform Svc
30305 Union City Blvd, Union City (94587-1513)
PHONE..................510 429-7305
Ken Eggers, *Manager*
Mike Galloni, *Manager*
EMP: 120
SALES (corp-wide): 169.8MM **Privately Held**
WEB: www.missions.com
SIC: 7213 5699 Linen supply, non-clothing; linen supply, clothing; industrial launderers
PA: Mission Linen Supply
   717 E Yanonali St
   Santa Barbara CA 93103
   805 730-3620

(P-13560)
MISSION LINEN SUPPLY
Also Called: Mission Linen & Uniform Svc
712 E Montecito St, Santa Barbara (93103-3295)
PHONE..................805 962-7687
Fax: 805 963-0856
Curtos Lopez, *Manager*
Rebecca Hillan, *Office Mgr*
Sarah Larson, *Office Mgr*
Viet Pham, *Chief Engr*
Albert Vanderhoeven, *Benefits Mgr*
EMP: 50
SALES (corp-wide): 169.8MM **Privately Held**
WEB: www.missions.com
SIC: 7213 Linen supply
PA: Mission Linen Supply
   717 E Yanonali St
   Santa Barbara CA 93103
   805 730-3620

(P-13561)
MISSION LINEN SUPPLY
Also Called: Mission Linen & Uniform Svc
1340 W 7th St, Chico (95928-4907)
PHONE..................530 342-4110
Fax: 530 342-7499
Nick Katzenstein, *Manager*
David Simcox, *Area Mgr*
EMP: 50
SALES (corp-wide): 169.8MM **Privately Held**
WEB: www.missions.com
SIC: 7213 5699 Uniform supply; uniforms & work clothing
PA: Mission Linen Supply
   717 E Yanonali St
   Santa Barbara CA 93103
   805 730-3620

(P-13562)
MISSION LINEN SUPPLY
Also Called: Mission Linen & Uniform Svc
801 Sunset Dr, Pacific Grove (93950-4713)
PHONE..................831 375-2491
Fax: 831 375-8325
Bill McCreary, *Manager*
EMP: 90
SALES (corp-wide): 169.8MM **Privately Held**
WEB: www.missions.com
SIC: 7213 Linen supply
PA: Mission Linen Supply
   717 E Yanonali St
   Santa Barbara CA 93103
   805 730-3620

(P-13563)
MISSION LINEN SUPPLY
Also Called: Mission Linen & Uniform Svc
619 W Avenue I, Lancaster (93534-2585)
PHONE..................661 948-5051
Bud McGuire, *General Mgr*
EMP: 100
SALES (corp-wide): 169.8MM **Privately Held**
SIC: 7213 2841 Linen supply; soap & other detergents
PA: Mission Linen Supply
   717 E Yanonali St
   Santa Barbara CA 93103
   805 730-3620

(P-13564)
MISSION LINEN SUPPLY
Also Called: Mission Linen & Uniform Svc
7524 Reese Rd, Sacramento (95828-3707)
PHONE..................916 423-3135
Fax: 916 423-3171
Ed Morrow, *Manager*
Doug Snyder, *Area Mgr*
EMP: 150
SALES (corp-wide): 169.8MM **Privately Held**
WEB: www.missions.com
SIC: 7213 7218 Linen supply; uniform supply; towel supply; apron supply; industrial launderers
PA: Mission Linen Supply
   717 E Yanonali St
   Santa Barbara CA 93103
   805 730-3620

(P-13565)
MISSION LINEN SUPPLY
Also Called: Mission Linen & Uniform Svc
602 S Western Ave, Santa Maria (93458-5496)
PHONE..................805 922-3579
Fax: 805 922-8991
Bill Bently, *General Mgr*
EMP: 80
SALES (corp-wide): 169.8MM **Privately Held**
WEB: www.missions.com
SIC: 7213 Linen supply
PA: Mission Linen Supply
   717 E Yanonali St
   Santa Barbara CA 93103
   805 730-3620

(P-13566)
MISSION LINEN SUPPLY
Also Called: Mission Linen & Uniform Svc
5400 Alton Way, Chino (91710-7601)
PHONE..................909 393-5589
Fax: 909 597-0468
Mike Keller, *Manager*
John Rubalcaba, *Branch Mgr*
Jaime Brockamp, *Manager*
EMP: 400
SALES (corp-wide): 169.8MM **Privately Held**
WEB: www.missions.com
SIC: 7213 Linen supply, non-clothing; linen supply, clothing; industrial launderers
PA: Mission Linen Supply
   717 E Yanonali St
   Santa Barbara CA 93103
   805 730-3620

(P-13567)
MORGAN SERVICES INC
Also Called: Morgan Linen Service
905 Yale St, Los Angeles (90012-1724)
PHONE..................213 485-9666
Fax: 213 621-3199
Mark Smith, *Branch Mgr*
Michelle Valenzuela, *Admin Asst*
Todd Smith, *Sales Mgr*
EMP: 100
SQ FT: 51,339
SALES (corp-wide): 35.1MM **Privately Held**
WEB: www.morganservices.com
SIC: 7213 7218 Linen supply; industrial launderers
PA: Morgan Services, Inc.
   323 N Michigan Ave
   Chicago IL 60601
   312 346-3181

(P-13568)
PARK CLEANERS INC (PA)
Also Called: Park Uniform Rentals
419 Mcgroarty St, San Gabriel (91776-2302)
PHONE..................626 281-5942
Fax: 626 281-4539
James L Brittain, *President*
Ted Doll, *Vice Pres*
Sidney Tinberg, *Agent*
EMP: 75
SQ FT: 7,000
SALES (est): 2.4MM **Privately Held**
SIC: 7213 7216 Uniform supply; cleaning & dyeing, except rugs

(P-13569)
SOCAL AUTO SUPPLY INC
21418 Osborne St, Canoga Park (91304-1520)
PHONE..................302 360-8373
EMP: 59 **Privately Held**
SIC: 7213 2676 Towel supply; towels, napkins & tissue paper products
PA: Socal Auto Supply Inc
   16192 Postal Hwy
   Lewes DE 19958

(P-13570)
SYNERGY HEALTH NORTH AMER INC
2240 E Artesia Blvd, Long Beach (90805-1739)
PHONE..................562 428-5858
Gary Metz, *Manager*
Carol Kelly, *Office Admin*
EMP: 72
SALES (corp-wide): 622.8MM **Privately Held**
SIC: 7213 Linen supply
HQ: Synergy Health North America, Inc.
   401 E Jackson St Ste 3100
   Tampa FL 33602
   813 891-9550

(P-13571)
UNIFIRST CORPORATION
4630 Beloit Dr Ste 40, Sacramento (95838-2449)
PHONE..................916 929-3766
Jerald Satterlfield, *Branch Mgr*
Tony Salinas, *Marketing Staff*
EMP: 50
SALES (corp-wide): 1.4B **Publicly Held**
SIC: 7213 5949 5699 Uniform supply; needlework goods & supplies; uniforms
PA: Unifirst Corporation
   68 Jonspin Rd
   Wilmington MA 01887
   978 658-8888

7215 Coin Operated Laundries & Cleaning

(P-13572)
ALL VALLEY WASHER SERVICE INC
15008 Delano St, Van Nuys (91411-2016)
PHONE..................818 787-1100
Fax: 818 989-7378
Ron Feinstein, *President*
Billy Feinstein, *Treasurer*
Robert Feinstein, *Vice Pres*
John Cottrell, *Mktg Dir*
Steve Wyard, *Sales Dir*
EMP: 70
SQ FT: 11,000
SALES (est): 9.8MM **Privately Held**
WEB: www.allvalleywasher.com
SIC: 7215 6531 7359 5087 Laundry, coin-operated; real estate agents & managers; appliance rental; laundry equipment & supplies

(P-13573)
CLEAN KING LAUNDRY SYSTEMS INC
15431 Chatsworth St, Mission Hills (91345-1905)
P.O. Box 8689, Northridge (91327-8689)
PHONE..................818 363-5500
Brian Merkel, *President*

7215 - Coin Operated Laundries & Cleaning County (P-13574)

EMP: 50
SALES (est): 1.3MM **Privately Held**
SIC: 7215 Coin-operated laundries & cleaning

(P-13574)
COINMACH CORPORATION (PA)
Also Called: Reliable Co
3628 San Fernando Rd, Glendale (91204-2944)
PHONE..................818 637-4300
Hal Savzmann, *Vice Pres*
Stephan Kerrigan, *Ch of Bd*
Rick Carr, *COO*
Matt Craig, *Executive*
Brianne Tallo, *Administration*
EMP: 80
SQ FT: 22,000
SALES (est): 5.9MM **Privately Held**
SIC: 7215 7211 5087 Laundry, coin-operated; power laundries, family & commercial; laundry equipment & supplies

(P-13575)
COINMACH CORPORATION
Also Called: Kwik Wash Laundries
32910 Alvarado Niles Rd # 150, Union City (94587-3173)
PHONE..................510 429-0900
Mike Hagen, *Manager*
EMP: 150
SALES (corp-wide): 5.9MM **Privately Held**
SIC: 7215 Coin-operated laundries & cleaning
PA: Coinmach Corporation
3628 San Fernando Rd
Glendale CA 91204
818 637-4300

(P-13576)
OCEANSIDE LAUNDRY LLC
Also Called: Campus Laundry
675 Beach Dr, Watsonville (95076-1904)
PHONE..................831 722-4358
Fax: 831 722-2260
Gregory Anderson, *President*
Gary Schmidt, *Financial Exec*
EMP: 100
SALES (est): 8.2MM **Privately Held**
SIC: 7215 Coin-operated laundries & cleaning

(P-13577)
PACIFIC CONCEPT LAUNDRY INC
1370 Esperanza St, Los Angeles (90023-3912)
PHONE..................323 980-3800
Moohan Bae, *President*
EMP: 204
SALES (est): 2.7MM **Privately Held**
WEB: www.pacific-club-phuket.com
SIC: 7215 Laundry, coin-operated

(P-13578)
WASH MLTFMILY LDRY SYSTEMS LLC (PA)
100 N Sepulveda Blvd, El Segundo (90245-4359)
PHONE..................310 643-8491
Fax: 310 297-9494
Adam E Coffey, *President*
Vivian Hung, *Exec VP*
Miles OH, *Vice Pres*
Greg Hernandez, *Info Tech Dir*
Karen Hongyu, *Accounting Mgr*
EMP: 150
SQ FT: 130,000
SALES (est): 59.9MM **Privately Held**
WEB: www.weblaundry.com
SIC: 7215 Laundry, coin-operated

7216 Dry Cleaning Plants, Except Rug Cleaning

(P-13579)
COIT SERVICES INC
1297 Logan Ave, Costa Mesa (92626-4004)
PHONE..................949 760-0760
Fax: 714 303-2306
John Comer, *Branch Mgr*
Jan Carney, *Administration*
EMP: 50
SALES (corp-wide): 51.9MM **Privately Held**
SIC: 7216 7217 Drycleaning plants, except rugs; carpet & upholstery cleaning
PA: Coit Services, Inc.
865 Hinckley Rd
Burlingame CA 94010
650 342-6023

(P-13580)
CUSTOM COMMERCIAL DRY CLRS INC (PA)
Also Called: Frsteam By Custom Commercial
3201 Investment Blvd, Hayward (94545-3813)
PHONE..................510 723-1000
Fax: 510 723-1010
Courtney Nicholas, *CEO*
Jim Nicholas, *President*
Ryan Meekma, *Vice Pres*
Holly Murry, *Vice Pres*
Sheri White, *Area Mgr*
EMP: 50
SALES (est): 3.6MM **Privately Held**
SIC: 7216 Drycleaning plants, except rugs

(P-13581)
GOLDENWEST LDRY & VALET SVCS
17862 Jamestown Ln, Huntington Beach (92647-7135)
PHONE..................714 843-0723
Fax: 714 843-5273
Ezra Schley, *President*
Mellisa Brown, *Services*
EMP: 50
SQ FT: 7,500
SALES (est): 1.7MM **Privately Held**
SIC: 7216 Drycleaning plants, except rugs

(P-13582)
INTER-CITY CLEANERS
438 S Airport Blvd, South San Francisco (94080-6908)
PHONE..................650 875-9200
Fax: 650 875-9380
Hans Gelfand, *Co-Owner*
Vera Gelfand, *Co-Owner*
EMP: 68
SQ FT: 9,000
SALES (est): 5.7MM **Privately Held**
WEB: www.intercitycleaners.com
SIC: 7216 7219 Drycleaning plants, except rugs; laundry, except power & coin-operated

(P-13583)
PICO CLEANER INC (PA)
9150 W Pico Blvd, Los Angeles (90035-1320)
PHONE..................310 274-2431
Sharam Jahanbani, *CEO*
Simon Djahanbani, *President*
EMP: 80
SQ FT: 10,000
SALES (est): 5.4MM **Privately Held**
WEB: www.picocleaners.com
SIC: 7216 Drycleaning plants, except rugs; curtain cleaning & repair

(P-13584)
RICHARD K NEWMAN AND ASSOC INC (PA)
Also Called: Sparkle Uniform & Linen Svc
121 Monterey St, Bakersfield (93305-3406)
PHONE..................661 634-1130
Fax: 661 325-2922
Jeffrey C Newman Sr, *Ch of Bd*
Jeffrey C Newman Jr, *President*
Mike Daniel, *COO*
Kelley Brown, *Human Res Dir*
EMP: 50
SQ FT: 26,000
SALES (est): 7.8MM **Privately Held**
WEB: www.sparklerental.com
SIC: 7216 7213 Drycleaning plants, except rugs; drycleaning collecting & distributing agency; linen supply, non-clothing; uniform supply

(P-13585)
SANTA BARBARA FABRICARE INC
Also Called: Ablitt's Fine Cleaners
14 W Gutierrez St, Santa Barbara (93101-3423)
PHONE..................805 963-6677
Fax: 805 966-3799
Neil Ablitt, *President*
R Neil Ablitt, *President*
Sue Ablitt, *Vice Pres*
Sean Nguyen, *General Mgr*
EMP: 50
SQ FT: 12,500
SALES (est): 2.7MM **Privately Held**
SIC: 7216 7211 7212 Drycleaning plants, except rugs; power laundries, family & commercial; valet apparel service

(P-13586)
SHADKOR INC
Also Called: Milt & Michael Master Dry Clrs
4021 W Alameda Ave, Burbank (91505-4335)
PHONE..................818 953-4627
Fax: 818 972-2739
Thomas Agha, *President*
Milton Shortkoff, *Corp Secy*
Tom Ajhammian, *General Mgr*
EMP: 60
SQ FT: 4,345
SALES (est): 3.2MM **Privately Held**
SIC: 7216 Drycleaning plants, except rugs

(P-13587)
SHUD WCV INC
Also Called: West Coast Valet Services
855 Malcolm Rd, Burlingame (94010-1406)
PHONE..................650 692-7380
Hamid S Noori, *President*
Hamid B Noori, *President*
EMP: 85
SQ FT: 20,000
SALES (est): 3.9MM **Privately Held**
SIC: 7216 7211 Drycleaning plants, except rugs; laundry collecting & distributing outlet

(P-13588)
STERLING WESTWOOD INC
Also Called: Sterling Dry Cleaners
3405 Overland Ave, Los Angeles (90034-5405)
PHONE..................310 287-2431
Harry Gershenson, *Manager*
EMP: 55
SALES (corp-wide): 1.8MM **Privately Held**
SIC: 7216 Drycleaning plants, except rugs
PA: Sterling Westwood Inc
1600 Westwood Blvd
Los Angeles CA 90024
310 474-8525

(P-13589)
VALETOR INC
Also Called: Hollyway Cleaners
8359 Santa Monica Blvd, Los Angeles (90069-4312)
PHONE..................323 654-1271
Fax: 323 656-9428
Fatehali Amersi, *President*
EMP: 50
SQ FT: 4,000
SALES (est): 1.6MM **Privately Held**
SIC: 7216 7215 Drycleaning plants, except rugs; laundry, coin-operated

7217 Carpet & Upholstery Cleaning

(P-13590)
BONDED INC (PA)
Also Called: Bonded Carpet
7831 Ostrow St, San Diego (92111-3602)
P.O. Box 23910 (92193-3910)
PHONE..................858 576-8400
Fax: 858 576-9500
Mitch Adler, *President*
Sherri Adler, *Vice Pres*
Mary Nelson, *Executive*
Melissa Almaguer, *Engineer*
Elva Espinoza, *Human Res Dir*
EMP: 80
SQ FT: 16,500
SALES (est): 6.1MM **Privately Held**
WEB: www.bondedcarpet.com
SIC: 7217 5713 Carpet & furniture cleaning on location; floor covering stores; carpets

(P-13591)
C & S DRAPERIES INC
Also Called: Coit Restoration Services
4210 Kiernan Ave, Modesto (95356-9758)
PHONE..................209 466-5371
Fax: 209 545-6319
Pete Bakker, *CEO*
Helen Bakker, *CEO*
Alice Canas, *Executive*
EMP: 150
SQ FT: 50,000
SALES (est): 10.5MM **Privately Held**
SIC: 7217 Carpet & furniture cleaning on location; carpet & rug cleaning plant; carpet & rug cleaning & repairing plant

(P-13592)
CARPET SOLUTIONS
17100 Margay Ave, Carson (90746-1224)
PHONE..................310 886-3800
Yenling Huan, *Owner*
EMP: 50 **EST:** 2011
SALES (est): 1.6MM **Privately Held**
SIC: 7217 1752 Carpet & upholstery cleaning; carpet laying

(P-13593)
CHROMA SYSTEMS
Also Called: Southcoast Dyeing & Finishing
3201 S Susan St, Santa Ana (92704-6838)
PHONE..................714 557-8480
Peer Vinther, *Partner*
Monterey Carpets, *Partner*
Camelot Carpet Mills, *Partner*
Ryan Menna, *Administration*
Kevin Moridian, *Controller*
EMP: 100
SQ FT: 200,000
SALES (est): 3.3MM **Privately Held**
SIC: 7217 2273 Carpet & rug dyeing plant; carpets & rugs

(P-13594)
CLEANING SERVICES
7828 Monterey St, Gilroy (95020-4537)
PHONE..................408 778-9251
Fax: 408 842-1770
Michael Jones, *President*
EMP: 50
SALES (est): 1.4MM **Privately Held**
WEB: www.makeitclean.com
SIC: 7217 Upholstery cleaning on customer premises

(P-13595)
COIT CLG & RESTORATION SVCS
1080 N Marshall Ave, El Cajon (92020-1829)
PHONE..................619 726-4734
James Garner, *Principal*
EMP: 600
SALES: 950K **Privately Held**
SIC: 7217 Upholstery cleaning on customer premises

(P-13596)
COLT SERVICES INC
Also Called: Stanley Steemer Carpet Cleaner
9655 Via Excelencia, San Diego (92126-4555)
PHONE..................858 271-9988
Toll Free: 888 -
Fax: 619 566-9988
Steven R Thompson, *President*
Lian Walters, *Executive Asst*
Sylvia Cortez, *Human Res Mgr*
Kathy Arthman, *Accounts Mgr*
EMP: 100
SQ FT: 33,000
SALES (est): 8.9MM **Privately Held**
SIC: 7217 Carpet & furniture cleaning on location

PRODUCTS & SERVICES SECTION

7218 - Industrial Launderers County (P-13616)

(P-13597)
DUN-RITE MAINTENANCE INC
438 Petaluma Blvd N, Petaluma (94952-2873)
P.O. Box 455 (94953-0455)
PHONE.................707 765-2434
Fax: 707 765-0539
Richard Wallenstein, *President*
EMP: 100
SQ FT: 8,000
SALES (est): 2.3MM **Privately Held**
SIC: 7217 7349 5087 Carpet & upholstery cleaning; janitorial service, contract basis; janitors' supplies

(P-13598)
EXPRESS CONTRACTORS INC
11625 Industry Ave, Fontana (92337-6931)
P.O. Box 310279 (92331-0279)
PHONE.................951 360-6500
Amaer Alhamwi, *President*
Mireya Quirarte, *Accounting Mgr*
Beulah Alarcon, *Controller*
Ladawn Zavadil, *Controller*
Nicholas Rodriguez, *Supervisor*
EMP: 100
SQ FT: 10,000
SALES (est): 10MM **Privately Held**
SIC: 7217 1752 1721 1743 Carpet & rug cleaning & repairing plant; carpet & rug cleaning plant; carpet & rug dyeing plant; carpet laying; painting & paper hanging; terrazzo, tile, marble, mosaic work

(P-13599)
J&M KEYSTONE INC
2709 Via Orange Way Ste A, Spring Valley (91978-1708)
PHONE.................619 466-9876
Ronald D Martin, *CEO*
Joe Welsh, *CFO*
Dale Whittle, *Corp Secy*
James Bronson, *Vice Pres*
Kristie Nelson, *Office Mgr*
EMP: 80
SQ FT: 9,100
SALES: 9.2MM **Privately Held**
WEB: www.jmkeystone.com
SIC: 7217 1542 1799 8744 Carpet & furniture cleaning on location; commercial & office buildings, renovation & repair; steam cleaning of building exteriors; ; air duct cleaning; floor waxing; repairing fire damage, single-family houses

(P-13600)
STANLEY STEEMER OF LOS ANGLES (PA)
841 W Foothill Blvd, Azusa (91702-2815)
PHONE.................626 791-9400
Fax: 626 812-5462
Kevin Pucci, *President*
Jeff Pucci, *Vice Pres*
Ryan Jourdain, *Opers Mgr*
EMP: 63
SQ FT: 100,000
SALES (est): 6.3MM **Privately Held**
SIC: 7217 1799 Carpet & furniture cleaning on location; post-disaster renovations

7218 Industrial Launderers

(P-13601)
AMERIPRIDE SERVICES INC
Also Called: Ameripride Uniform Services
1050 W Whites Bridge Ave, Fresno (93706-1328)
P.O. Box 11884 (93775-1884)
PHONE.................559 266-0627
Matt Wencel, *Manager*
Deborah Money, *Officer*
Carl Anderson, *Sales Executive*
Steve Plescia, *Sales Executive*
EMP: 100
SALES (corp-wide): 383.2MM **Privately Held**
WEB: www.ameripride.com
SIC: 7218 7213 Radiation protective garment supply; linen supply
PA: Ameripride Services, Inc.
10801 Wayzata Blvd # 100
Hopkins MN 55305
952 738-4200

(P-13602)
ARAMARK UNF & CAREER AP LLC
1617 Jim Way, Modesto (95358-5703)
P.O. Box 5164 (95352-5164)
PHONE.................209 368-9785
Fax: 209 537-5846
Manny Martinez, *General Mgr*
Jerry Gibson, *Manager*
Randy Hoover, *Accounts Mgr*
Greg Moyers, *Accounts Exec*
EMP: 60
SALES (corp-wide): 14.3B **Publicly Held**
WEB: www.aramark-uniform.com
SIC: 7218 Industrial launderers
HQ: Aramark Uniform & Career Apparel, Llc
115 N First St Ste 203
Burbank CA 91502
818 973-3700

(P-13603)
ARAMARK UNF & CAREER AP LLC
115 N First St, Burbank (91502-1856)
P.O. Box 7891 (91510-7891)
PHONE.................818 973-3700
Fax: 818 953-4502
David Michaelson, *Controller*
Monica Justus, *Accounts Exec*
EMP: 62
SALES (corp-wide): 14.3B **Publicly Held**
SIC: 7218 Industrial launderers
HQ: Aramark Uniform & Career Apparel, Llc
115 N First St Ste 203
Burbank CA 91502
818 973-3700

(P-13604)
ARAMARK UNF & CAREER AP LLC
330 Chestnut St, Oakland (94607-2528)
PHONE.................510 835-9285
Art Wake, *Branch Mgr*
EMP: 200
SQ FT: 10,000
SALES (corp-wide): 14.3B **Publicly Held**
WEB: www.aramark-uniform.com
SIC: 7218 Wiping towel supply
HQ: Aramark Uniform & Career Apparel, Llc
115 N First St Ste 203
Burbank CA 91502
818 973-3700

(P-13605)
ARAMARK UNF & CAREER AP LLC
4422 Dunham St, Los Angeles (90023-4113)
PHONE.................323 266-0555
Fax: 323 261-2749
Alice Stewart, *General Mgr*
Boris Mezhebovsky, *Administration*
Charles McCready, *Network Mgr*
David Lincoln, *Director*
Gonzalez Sal, *Director*
EMP: 230
SALES (corp-wide): 14.3B **Publicly Held**
WEB: www.aramark-uniform.com
SIC: 7218 Industrial launderers
HQ: Aramark Uniform & Career Apparel, Llc
115 N First St Ste 203
Burbank CA 91502
818 973-3700

(P-13606)
ARAMARK UNF & CAREER AP LLC
755 Butte St, Redding (96001-0928)
PHONE.................530 241-6433
Fax: 530 241-0885
Michael Brodeur, *Manager*
EMP: 70
SALES (corp-wide): 14.3B **Publicly Held**
WEB: www.aramark-uniform.com
SIC: 7218 7213 Industrial launderers; uniform supply
HQ: Aramark Uniform & Career Apparel, Llc
115 N First St Ste 203
Burbank CA 91502
818 973-3700

(P-13607)
ARAMARK UNF & CAREER AP LLC (DH)
115 N First St Ste 203, Burbank (91502-1857)
P.O. Box 7891 (91510-7891)
PHONE.................818 973-3700
Brad Drummond, *President*
Bruce Hausman, *CFO*
Chris Holland, *Treasurer*
Mike Fadden, *Exec VP*
Caralee Brown, *Vice Pres*
EMP: 250
SQ FT: 63,000
SALES (est): 939.3MM
SALES (corp-wide): 14.3B **Publicly Held**
WEB: www.aramark-uniform.com
SIC: 7218 Industrial uniform supply; treated equipment supply: mats, rugs, mops, cloths, etc.; wiping towel supply
HQ: Aramark Uniform & Career Apparel Group, Inc.
1101 Market St Ste 45
Philadelphia PA 19107
215 238-3000

(P-13608)
ARAMARK UNF & CAREER AP LLC
1419 National Dr, Sacramento (95834-1946)
P.O. Box 340910 (95834-0910)
PHONE.................916 286-4100
Jeff Black, *Manager*
EMP: 300
SALES (corp-wide): 14.3B **Publicly Held**
WEB: www.aramark-uniform.com
SIC: 7218 7213 Industrial launderers; uniform supply
HQ: Aramark Uniform & Career Apparel, Llc
115 N First St Ste 203
Burbank CA 91502
818 973-3700

(P-13609)
ARAMARK UNF & CAREER AP LLC
31148 San Antonio St, Hayward (94544-7906)
P.O. Box 5034 (94540-5034)
PHONE.................510 487-1855
Dave Tyquiengco, *Manager*
EMP: 70
SALES (corp-wide): 14.3B **Publicly Held**
WEB: www.aramark-uniform.com
SIC: 7218 Industrial uniform supply; treated equipment supply: mats, rugs, mops, cloths, etc.; wiping towel supply
HQ: Aramark Uniform & Career Apparel, Llc
115 N First St Ste 203
Burbank CA 91502
818 973-3700

(P-13610)
ARAMARK UNF & CAREER AP LLC
3101 W Adams St, Santa Ana (92704-5807)
P.O. Box 20378, Fountain Valley (92728-0378)
PHONE.................714 545-4877
Fax: 714 545-3834
Mark Papapendorf, *Manager*
Amy Nguyen, *Site Mgr*
John Bos, *Director*
Tom Hergenrohder, *Manager*
Jerry Robinson, *Manager*
EMP: 80
SQ FT: 15,317
SALES (corp-wide): 14.3B **Publicly Held**
WEB: www.aramark-uniform.com
SIC: 7218 7213 Industrial launderers; uniform supply
HQ: Aramark Uniform & Career Apparel, Llc
115 N First St Ste 203
Burbank CA 91502
818 973-3700

(P-13611)
ARAMARK UNF & CAREER AP LLC
5000 Forni Dr, Concord (94520-1223)
P.O. Box 5826 (94524-0826)
PHONE.................925 827-3782
Ray Rhode, *Manager*
Randy Yray, *General Mgr*
Franck Perrotti, *Sales Mgr*
EMP: 69
SALES (corp-wide): 14.3B **Publicly Held**
WEB: www.aramark-uniform.com
SIC: 7218 7213 Industrial launderers; uniform supply
HQ: Aramark Uniform & Career Apparel, Llc
115 N First St Ste 203
Burbank CA 91502
818 973-3700

(P-13612)
ARAMARK UNF & CAREER AP LLC
1135 Hall Ave, Riverside (92509-1870)
P.O. Box 33470 (92519-0470)
PHONE.................909 888-4272
Gene West, *Manager*
Mark Papapendorf, *Manager*
EMP: 100
SALES (corp-wide): 14.3B **Publicly Held**
WEB: www.aramark-uniform.com
SIC: 7218 7213 Industrial launderers; uniform supply
HQ: Aramark Uniform & Career Apparel, Llc
115 N First St Ste 203
Burbank CA 91502
818 973-3700

(P-13613)
ARAMARK UNF & CAREER AP LLC
15372 Cobalt St, Sylmar (91342-2729)
PHONE.................818 364-8272
Brad Drummond, *Principal*
Guy Verdugo, *District Mgr*
Jon Anderson, *VP Sales*
Jordan Lippel, *Manager*
EMP: 63
SALES (corp-wide): 14.3B **Publicly Held**
SIC: 7218 Industrial launderers
HQ: Aramark Uniform & Career Apparel, Llc
115 N First St Ste 203
Burbank CA 91502
818 973-3700

(P-13614)
ARAMARK UNF & CAREER AP LLC
440 N Canal St, South San Francisco (94080-4603)
PHONE.................650 244-9332
Fax: 650 244-9317
David Techlingco, *Manager*
EMP: 70
SALES (corp-wide): 14.3B **Publicly Held**
WEB: www.aramark-uniform.com
SIC: 7218 Industrial launderers
HQ: Aramark Uniform & Career Apparel, Llc
115 N First St Ste 203
Burbank CA 91502
818 973-3700

(P-13615)
ARAMARK UNF SVCS MIDWEST LLC
115 N First St, Burbank (91502-1856)
PHONE.................800 388-3300
EMP: 52
SALES (est): 4.8MM
SALES (corp-wide): 14.3B **Publicly Held**
SIC: 7218 Industrial launderers
HQ: Aramark Services, Inc.
1101 Market St Ste 45
Philadelphia PA 19107
215 238-3000

(P-13616)
ARAMARK UNIFORM SERVICES
1419 National Dr, Sacramento (95834-1946)
PHONE.................916 286-4100
Fax: 916 286-4190
Gary Koolhof, *Principal*
Bill Ledbetter, *Purch Agent*
Brian Morris, *Director*
Gary Smith, *Director*
Nancy Meyers, *Manager*
EMP: 99
SALES (est): 7.2MM
SALES (corp-wide): 14.3B **Publicly Held**
SIC: 7218 Industrial launderers

7218 - Industrial Launderers County (P-13617)

PA: Aramark Corporation
1101 Market St Ste 45
Philadelphia PA 19107
215 238-3000

(P-13617)
BOWSMITH INC (PA)
131 2nd St, Exeter (93221-1947)
P.O. Box 428 (93221-0428)
PHONE..................559 592-9485
Fax: 559 592-2314
Allan L Smith, *President*
Tonnie Garnett, *Purchasing*
Victor Gonzales, *Safety Mgr*
Richard Phillips, *Mfg Mgr*
Kenneth Berg, *Director*
EMP: 55
SQ FT: 14,400
SALES (est): 8.9MM **Privately Held**
WEB: www.bowsmith.com
SIC: 7218 4971 Industrial equipment launderers; irrigation systems

(P-13618)
CINTAS CORPORATION NO 2
2188 Del Franco St Ste 70, San Jose (95131-1583)
PHONE..................408 292-6700
Scott Douglas Farmer, *Branch Mgr*
Melissa Jacobs, *Sales Executive*
Reese Dole, *Regl Sales Mgr*
Michael McNany, *Sales Mgr*
Justin Simpson, *Sales Mgr*
EMP: 88
SALES (corp-wide): 4.9B **Publicly Held**
WEB: www.cintas-corp.com
SIC: 7218 Industrial uniform supply
HQ: Cintas Corporation No. 2
6800 Cintas Blvd
Mason OH 45040

(P-13619)
CINTAS CORPORATION NO 3
5500 Young St, Bakersfield (93311-9648)
PHONE..................661 282-4300
EMP: 79
SALES (corp-wide): 4.9B **Publicly Held**
SIC: 7218 Industrial uniform supply
HQ: Cintas Corporation No. 3
6800 Cintas Blvd
Mason OH 45040

(P-13620)
CINTAS CORPORATION NO 3
675 32nd St, San Diego (92102-3301)
PHONE..................619 239-1001
Kevin Nolan, *Branch Mgr*
Matt Haley, *Opers Mgr*
Travis Vasquez, *Sales Staff*
EMP: 150
SQ FT: 7,000
SALES (corp-wide): 4.9B **Publicly Held**
WEB: www.cintas-corp.com
SIC: 7218 7213 Industrial uniform supply; uniform supply
HQ: Cintas Corporation No. 3
6800 Cintas Blvd
Mason OH 45040

(P-13621)
CINTAS CORPORATION NO 3
904 Holloway Rd, Gilroy (95020-7006)
PHONE..................408 337-2910
Aldrin Leonardo, *Manager*
Paganelli Veronica, *Personnel Exec*
Gregg Pichler, *Sales Executive*
EMP: 101
SQ FT: 28,154
SALES (corp-wide): 4.9B **Publicly Held**
WEB: www.cintas-corp.com
SIC: 7218 Industrial uniform supply
HQ: Cintas Corporation No. 3
6800 Cintas Blvd
Mason OH 45040

(P-13622)
CINTAS CORPORATION NO 3
20929 Cabot Blvd, Hayward (94545-1155)
PHONE..................510 352-6330
Stephen Dee, *Branch Mgr*
EMP: 79
SALES (corp-wide): 4.9B **Publicly Held**
WEB: www.cintas-corp.com
SIC: 7218 Industrial uniform supply
HQ: Cintas Corporation No. 3
6800 Cintas Blvd
Mason OH 45040

(P-13623)
CINTAS CORPORATION NO 3
20100 S Susana Rd, Compton (90221-5722)
PHONE..................310 725-2850
Bryce Littlejohn, *Branch Mgr*
EMP: 79
SALES (corp-wide): 4.9B **Publicly Held**
SIC: 7218 Industrial uniform supply
HQ: Cintas Corporation No. 3
6800 Cintas Blvd
Mason OH 45040

(P-13624)
CINTAS CORPORATION NO 3
1231 National Dr, Sacramento (95834-1902)
PHONE..................916 419-8519
Fax: 916 576-2862
Doyle Denny, *Manager*
EMP: 150
SALES (corp-wide): 4.9B **Publicly Held**
WEB: www.cintas-corp.com
SIC: 7218 Industrial uniform supply
HQ: Cintas Corporation No. 3
6800 Cintas Blvd
Mason OH 45040

(P-13625)
CINTAS CORPORATION NO 3
1851 S Wineville Ave, Ontario (91761-3667)
PHONE..................909 390-4912
Adrian Sandoval, *Manager*
EMP: 79
SALES (corp-wide): 4.9B **Publicly Held**
WEB: www.cintas-corp.com
SIC: 7218 Industrial launderers
HQ: Cintas Corporation No. 3
6800 Cintas Blvd
Mason OH 45040

(P-13626)
CINTAS CORPORATION NO 3
370 Shaw Rd, South San Francisco (94080-6606)
PHONE..................650 278-4004
Chris Hines, *Manager*
John Auer, *Manager*
Jenn Wong, *Manager*
EMP: 85
SALES (corp-wide): 4.9B **Publicly Held**
SIC: 7218 2326 5136 5137 Industrial uniform supply; work uniforms, uniforms, men's & boys'; uniforms, women's & children's; uniform supply
HQ: Cintas Corporation No. 3
6800 Cintas Blvd
Mason OH 45040

(P-13627)
CINTAS CORPORATION NO 3
220 Demeter St, East Palo Alto (94303-1303)
PHONE..................650 589-4300
EMP: 79
SALES (corp-wide): 4.9B **Publicly Held**
SIC: 7218 Industrial uniform supply
HQ: Cintas Corporation No. 3
6800 Cintas Blvd
Mason OH 45040

(P-13628)
CINTAS CORPORATION NO 3
45133 Industrial Dr, Fremont (94538-6412)
PHONE..................510 573-5300
Hall Dansbury, *General Mgr*
Hal Stansbury, *Branch Mgr*
Amy Kissee, *Marketing Staff*
EMP: 79
SALES (corp-wide): 4.9B **Publicly Held**
SIC: 7218 Industrial uniform supply
HQ: Cintas Corporation No. 3
6800 Cintas Blvd
Mason OH 45040

(P-13629)
G&K SERVICES INC
5900 Alder Ave, Sacramento (95828-1110)
PHONE..................916 381-5500
Fax: 916 381-5525
Rich Pland, *Branch Mgr*
Mark Howard, *Vice Pres*
Eva Garcia, *Executive*
Alberto Robles, *Plant Mgr*
Joe Brownholtz, *Sales Executive*
EMP: 80
SALES (corp-wide): 978MM **Publicly Held**
WEB: www.gkservices.com
SIC: 7218 5699 7213 Industrial uniform supply; uniforms; uniform supply
PA: G&K Services, Inc.
5995 Opus Pkwy Ste 500
Minnetonka MN 55343
952 912-5500

(P-13630)
GARMENT INDUSTRY LAUNDRY
710 W 58th St, Los Angeles (90037-4034)
PHONE..................323 752-8335
Fax: 323 752-0112
Lyle Dean Foreman, *President*
Bjarne Schmidt, *Vice Pres*
EMP: 200
SQ FT: 30,000
SALES (est): 7.6MM **Privately Held**
SIC: 7218 7211 Industrial launderers; power laundries, family & commercial

(P-13631)
IMAGE FIRST HEALTHCRE LNDRY SP
Also Called: Image 1st
17818 S Figueroa St, Gardena (90248-4214)
PHONE..................310 819-1463
Bryan Cunningham, *Manager*
Gino Giannettino, *Asst Mgr*
EMP: 332
SALES (corp-wide): 30.9MM **Privately Held**
SIC: 7218 Industrial clothing launderers
PA: Image First Healthcare Laundry Specialists, Inc.
900 E 8th Ave Ste 300
King Of Prussia PA 19406
484 253-7200

(P-13632)
INTERNATIONAL GARMENT FINISHER
Also Called: I G F
2144 W Gaylord St, Long Beach (90813-1034)
PHONE..................562 983-7400
Richard Kim, *President*
EMP: 100
SALES (est): 3.4MM **Privately Held**
WEB: www.igf.com
SIC: 7218 Industrial launderers

(P-13633)
MISSION LINEN SUPPLY
Also Called: Mission Linen & Uniform Svc
435 W Market St, Salinas (93901-1498)
PHONE..................831 424-1753
Fax: 831 424-1072
Bill McCreary, *Manager*
EMP: 150
SALES (corp-wide): 169.8MM **Privately Held**
WEB: www.missions.com
SIC: 7218 7213 Industrial launderers; linen supply
PA: Mission Linen Supply
717 E Yanonali St
Santa Barbara CA 93103
805 730-3620

(P-13634)
PRUDENTIAL OVERALL SUPPLY
6920 Bandini Blvd, Commerce (90040-3382)
PHONE..................323 724-4888
Fax: 323 726-7251
Mark Albertson, *Manager*
Mitch Cummins, *Sales Mgr*
Jennifer Shearer, *Sales Staff*
EMP: 100
SQ FT: 40,000
SALES (corp-wide): 158.2MM **Privately Held**
WEB: www.pos-clean.com
SIC: 7218 7213 5087 Industrial launderers; uniform supply; janitors' supplies
PA: Prudential Overall Supply
1661 Alton Pkwy
Irvine CA 92606
949 250-4855

(P-13635)
PRUDENTIAL OVERALL SUPPLY (PA)
1661 Alton Pkwy, Irvine (92606-4877)
P.O. Box 11210, Santa Ana (92711-1210)
PHONE..................949 250-4855
Fax: 949 261-1947
Dan Clark, *CEO*
Thomas C Watts, *President*
Dean Killion, *COO*
John Thompson, *CFO*
Donald C Lahn, *Vice Ch Bd*
EMP: 95
SQ FT: 20,000
SALES: 158.2MM **Privately Held**
WEB: www.pos-clean.com
SIC: 7218 Industrial launderers; wiping towel supply; clean room apparel supply; industrial uniform supply

(P-13636)
PRUDENTIAL OVERALL SUPPLY
Also Called: Prudential Dust Control
6997 Jurupa Ave, Riverside (92504-1009)
PHONE..................951 687-0440
Fax: 951 354-8110
Jay Boyer, *Manager*
John Thompson, *CFO*
Karen Stewart, *Manager*
EMP: 127
SALES (corp-wide): 158.2MM **Privately Held**
WEB: www.pos-clean.com
SIC: 7218 Industrial launderers
PA: Prudential Overall Supply
1661 Alton Pkwy
Irvine CA 92606
949 250-4855

(P-13637)
PRUDENTIAL OVERALL SUPPLY
Also Called: Prudential Cleanroom Services
1437 N Milpitas Blvd, Milpitas (95035-3154)
PHONE..................408 719-0886
Fax: 408 719-0887
Tim Bleigh, *Manager*
Joe Sharma, *Asst Mgr*
EMP: 99
SQ FT: 30,201
SALES (corp-wide): 158.2MM **Privately Held**
WEB: www.pos-clean.com
SIC: 7218 Industrial launderers; wiping towel supply; clean room apparel supply; industrial uniform supply
PA: Prudential Overall Supply
1661 Alton Pkwy
Irvine CA 92606
949 250-4855

(P-13638)
PRUDENTIAL OVERALL SUPPLY
Also Called: Prudential Cleanroom Services
6948 Bandini Blvd, Commerce (90040-3326)
PHONE..................323 722-0636
Fax: 323 722-2346
Chris Wealch, *General Mgr*
Gary Oien, *Business Mgr*
Sandra Sepulveda, *Plant Supt*
Gina Torres, *Manager*
EMP: 65
SQ FT: 21,925
SALES (corp-wide): 158.2MM **Privately Held**
WEB: www.pos-clean.com
SIC: 7218 7213 5085 Industrial launderers; uniform supply; clean room supplies

PRODUCTS & SERVICES SECTION

7221 - Photographic Studios, Portrait County (P-13661)

PA: Prudential Overall Supply
1661 Alton Pkwy
Irvine CA 92606
949 250-4855

(P-13639)
PRUDENTIAL OVERALL SUPPLY
1260 E North Ave, Fresno (93725-1930)
PHONE...................................559 264-8231
Fax: 559 264-2860
Rick Ponce, *Branch Mgr*
Donna Aguilar, *Assistant*
EMP: 80
SQ FT: 42,704
SALES (corp-wide): 158.2MM **Privately Held**
WEB: www.pos-clean.com
SIC: 7218 7213 Industrial launderers; linen supply
PA: Prudential Overall Supply
1661 Alton Pkwy
Irvine CA 92606
949 250-4855

(P-13640)
PRUDENTIAL OVERALL SUPPLY
16901 Aston, Irvine (92606-4829)
PHONE...................................760 717-6803
Chris Kalert, *Manager*
James Murray, *Treasurer*
Terry Lahn, *Vice Pres*
Sandra Quezada, *Office Mgr*
Hack Huges, *Info Tech Mgr*
EMP: 85
SALES (corp-wide): 158.2MM **Privately Held**
WEB: www.pos-clean.com
SIC: 7218 7213 5087 Industrial launderers; uniform supply; janitors' supplies
PA: Prudential Overall Supply
1661 Alton Pkwy
Irvine CA 92606
949 250-4855

(P-13641)
PRUDENTIAL OVERALL SUPPLY
Also Called: Store 17
5300 Gabbert Rd, Moorpark (93021-1772)
P.O. Box 11210, Santa Ana (92711-1210)
PHONE...................................805 529-0833
Fax: 805 529-3447
Mark Stanton, *Manager*
Jerry Martin, *Sales Executive*
Mike Blazek, *Manager*
EMP: 56
SALES (corp-wide): 158.2MM **Privately Held**
WEB: www.pos-clean.com
SIC: 7218 7213 5087 Industrial launderers; wiping towel supply; clean room apparel supply; industrial uniform supply; uniform supply; janitors' supplies
PA: Prudential Overall Supply
1661 Alton Pkwy
Irvine CA 92606
949 250-4855

(P-13642)
PRUDENTIAL OVERALL SUPPLY INC
2485 Ash St, Vista (92081-8424)
PHONE...................................760 727-7163
Fax: 760 727-8472
Jason Thaffin, *Branch Mgr*
Scott Chafin, *General Mgr*
EMP: 95
SQ FT: 38,476
SALES (corp-wide): 158.2MM **Privately Held**
WEB: www.pos-clean.com
SIC: 7218 7213 5699 Industrial launderers; uniform supply; uniforms & work clothing
PA: Prudential Overall Supply
1661 Alton Pkwy
Irvine CA 92606
949 250-4855

(P-13643)
STONE BLUE INC
Also Called: Pink Diamonds
2501 E 28th St, Vernon (90058-1429)
PHONE...................................323 277-0008
Fax: 323 277-0009
Judy OH, *President*
EMP: 100
SQ FT: 70,000
SALES (est): 4.1MM **Privately Held**
SIC: 7218 Industrial clothing launderers

(P-13644)
UNIFIRST CORPORATION
819 N Hunter St, Stockton (95202-1706)
PHONE...................................209 941-8364
Peter Bernadicou, *Principal*
Joe Chiatello, *General Mgr*
Cindy Saucier, *Manager*
EMP: 50
SALES (corp-wide): 1.4B **Publicly Held**
WEB: www.unifirst.com
SIC: 7218 7213 Industrial launderers; uniform supply
PA: Unifirst Corporation
68 Jonspin Rd
Wilmington MA 01887
978 658-8888

(P-13645)
UNIFIRST CORPORATION
4041 Market St, San Diego (92102-4593)
PHONE...................................619 263-6116
Jesse Sandoval, *Manager*
Reginald Avalos, *Engineer*
Ty Gaydish, *Site Mgr*
Roy Cella, *Regl Sales Mgr*
Christina Humphrey, *Manager*
EMP: 60
SQ FT: 22,685
SALES (corp-wide): 1.4B **Publicly Held**
WEB: www.unifirst.com
SIC: 7218 7213 Industrial uniform supply; work clothing supply; radiation protective garment supply; uniform supply
PA: Unifirst Corporation
68 Jonspin Rd
Wilmington MA 01887
978 658-8888

(P-13646)
UNIFIRST CORPORATION
700 Etiwanda Ave Ste C, Ontario (91761-8608)
PHONE...................................909 390-8670
Fax: 909 390-8679
Jeff Martin, *Manager*
Ben Childers, *President*
EMP: 130
SALES (corp-wide): 1.4B **Publicly Held**
WEB: www.unifirst.com
SIC: 7218 7213 Industrial uniform supply; work clothing supply; radiation protective garment supply; uniform supply
PA: Unifirst Corporation
68 Jonspin Rd
Wilmington MA 01887
978 658-8888

(P-13647)
UNIFIRST CORPORATION
4730 E Commerce Ave, Fresno (93752-2222)
PHONE...................................559 233-0400
James Pirson, *Branch Mgr*
EMP: 60
SALES (corp-wide): 1.4B **Publicly Held**
SIC: 7218 Radiation protective garment supply
PA: Unifirst Corporation
68 Jonspin Rd
Wilmington MA 01887
978 658-8888

(P-13648)
UNIFIRST CORPORATION
2016 Zanker Rd, San Jose (95131-2110)
PHONE...................................408 297-8101
EMP: 60
SALES (corp-wide): 1.4B **Publicly Held**
SIC: 7218 Radiation protective garment supply
PA: Unifirst Corporation
68 Jonspin Rd
Wilmington MA 01887
978 658-8888

(P-13649)
WORKRITE UNIFORM COMPANY INC (HQ)
1701 Lombard St Ste 200, Oxnard (93030-8235)
PHONE...................................805 483-0175
Philip C Williamson, *CEO*
Keith Suddaby, *President*
Mark Adler, *Vice Pres*
David Bass, *Finance Dir*
Lucien Jervis, *Human Res Mgr*
EMP: 385
SALES (est): 22.7MM
SALES (corp-wide): 2.3B **Privately Held**
SIC: 7218 Flame & heat resistant clothing supply
PA: Williamson-Dickie Manufacturing Company
509 W Vickery Blvd
Fort Worth TX 76104
817 336-7201

7219 Laundry & Garment Svcs, NEC

(P-13650)
ARAMARK SERVICES INC
1405 E 58th Pl, Los Angeles (90001-1207)
PHONE...................................323 587-7661
Barry Eastill, *Manager*
Jeanette Mendoza, *Sales Mgr*
EMP: 100
SQ FT: 22,000
SALES (corp-wide): 14.3B **Publicly Held**
SIC: 7219 7218 Laundry, except power & coin-operated; industrial launderers
HQ: Aramark Services, Inc.
1101 Market St Ste 45
Philadelphia PA 19107
215 238-3000

(P-13651)
CM LAUNDRY LLC
14919 S Figueroa St, Gardena (90248-1720)
PHONE...................................310 436-6170
Luis Rodriguez,
Anthony Millar,
Ernesto Munoz, *Mng Member*
EMP: 100
SQ FT: 26,500
SALES (est): 4.6MM **Privately Held**
SIC: 7219 Laundry, except power & coin-operated

(P-13652)
DY-DEE SERVICE PASADENA INC
Also Called: California Linen Service
40 E California Blvd, Pasadena (91105-3203)
PHONE...................................626 792-6183
Fax: 626 792-4337
Brian O'Neil, *President*
EMP: 60
SQ FT: 15,000
SALES (est): 4.6MM **Privately Held**
WEB: www.calinen.com
SIC: 7219 7213 Diaper service; linen supply

(P-13653)
DYDEE SERVICE OF PASEDENA
Also Called: California Linen
40 E California Blvd, Pasadena (91105-3203)
PHONE...................................626 240-0115
Fax: 323 792-4337
Bryan O'Nell, *Owner*
EMP: 100 EST: 1938
SALES: 8MM **Privately Held**
SIC: 7219 Diaper service

(P-13654)
JOB OPTIONS INCORPORATED
1110 S Washington Ave, San Bernardino (92408-2244)
PHONE...................................909 890-4612
Fax: 909 890-4673
Jeff Still, *Manager*
EMP: 820
SQ FT: 35,800
SALES (corp-wide): 50.4MM **Privately Held**
WEB: www.joboptionsinc.org
SIC: 7219 Fur garment cleaning, repairing & storage
PA: Job Options, Incorporated
3465 Camino Di Rio S 30
San Diego CA 92108
619 688-1784

(P-13655)
KL CUTTING SERVICE INC
2250 Maple Ave, Los Angeles (90011-1190)
PHONE...................................213 742-9001
Alex Palomino, *General Mgr*
Mark Feldman, *President*
EMP: 164 EST: 1997
SQ FT: 78,200
SALES (est): 7.8MM **Privately Held**
SIC: 7219 Garment making, alteration & repair

(P-13656)
PENINOU FRENCH LDRY & CLRS INC (PA)
101 S Maple Ave, South San Francisco (94080-6303)
PHONE...................................800 392-2532
Todd Edwards, *CEO*
Carly Grima, *Accounting Dir*
Tiffany Klinkner, *Manager*
Dina Viviani, *Manager*
EMP: 90
SQ FT: 25,000
SALES (est): 5.7MM **Privately Held**
WEB: www.peninou.com
SIC: 7219 7216 French hand laundry; drycleaning collecting & distributing agency

(P-13657)
SPECIALIZED LAUNDRY SVCS INC
Also Called: 1st Class Laundry Services
33483 Western Ave, Union City (94587-3201)
PHONE...................................510 487-8297
Jefferey Lee Schlagel, *CEO*
EMP: 50
SALES (est): 3.6MM **Privately Held**
SIC: 7219 Garment making, alteration & repair

(P-13658)
T POINTS INC
350 W Mrtn Lthr King Jr, Los Angeles (90037-4529)
PHONE...................................323 846-9176
EMP: 50
SALES (est): 695.8K **Privately Held**
SIC: 7219

7221 Photographic Studios, Portrait

(P-13659)
BAY PHOTO INC
2959 Park Ave Ste A, Soquel (95073-2863)
PHONE...................................831 475-6090
Fax: 831 475-5275
Larry Abitbol, *Principal*
EMP: 122
SALES (corp-wide): 33MM **Privately Held**
SIC: 7221 Photographer, still or video
PA: Bay Photo, Inc
900 Disc Dr
Scotts Valley CA
831 475-6686

(P-13660)
LIFETOUCH INC
7916 Alta Sunrise Ln, Citrus Heights (95610-7904)
PHONE...................................916 535-7733
Chris Rousso, *Branch Mgr*
Chris Risso, *Site Mgr*
EMP: 80
SALES (corp-wide): 874.7MM **Privately Held**
WEB: www.lifetouch.com
SIC: 7221 Photographic studios, portrait
PA: Lifetouch Inc.
11000 Viking Dr
Eden Prairie MN 55344
952 826-4000

(P-13661)
LIFETOUCH NAT SCHL STUDIOS INC
2860 Fair St, Chico (95928-8804)
PHONE...................................530 345-3993

7221 - Photographic Studios, Portrait County (P-13662)

PRODUDUCTS & SERVICES SECTION

Fax: 530 879-4910
Robert Evans, *Manager*
Phil Lawry, *Technology*
Ryan Cranney, *Engineer*
Mark Pereira, *Senior Mgr*
Bob Evans, *Manager*
EMP: 100
SQ FT: 53,000
SALES (corp-wide): 874.7MM **Privately Held**
SIC: 7221 Photographer, still or video
HQ: Lifetouch National School Studios Inc.
11000 Viking Dr Ste 300
Eden Prairie MN 55344
952 826-4000

(P-13662)
LIFETOUCH NAT SCHL STUDIOS INC
30351 Huntwood Ave, Hayward (94544-7015)
PHONE..................510 293-1818
Fax: 510 293-0407
John Capistrant, *Manager*
Capistrant John, *Manager*
EMP: 50
SALES (corp-wide): 874.7MM **Privately Held**
SIC: 7221 School photographer
HQ: Lifetouch National School Studios Inc.
11000 Viking Dr Ste 300
Eden Prairie MN 55344
952 826-4000

(P-13663)
LIFETOUCH NAT SCHL STUDIOS INC
2122 Porter Field Way, Upland (91786-2111)
PHONE..................909 985-3532
Gary Anderson, *Manager*
EMP: 50
SALES (corp-wide): 874.7MM **Privately Held**
SIC: 7221 School photographer
HQ: Lifetouch National School Studios Inc.
11000 Viking Dr Ste 300
Eden Prairie MN 55344
952 826-4000

(P-13664)
LIFETOUCH PORTRAIT STUDIOS INC
9770 Carroll Centre Rd C, San Diego (92126-6504)
PHONE..................858 693-9197
Kim Clark, *Manager*
EMP: 50
SQ FT: 1,200
SALES (corp-wide): 874.7MM **Privately Held**
WEB: www.jcpportraits.com
SIC: 7221 Photographer, still or video; school photographer
HQ: Lifetouch Portrait Studios Inc.
11000 Viking Dr
Eden Prairie MN 55344
952 826-4335

(P-13665)
SCHOOL PORTRAITS BY KRANZ
9992 Center Dr, Villa Park (92861-2715)
PHONE..................714 545-1775
Fax: 714 545-5914
Gary Kranz, *President*
Judy Kranz, *Vice Pres*
EMP: 82
SQ FT: 14,455
SALES (est): 5.3MM **Privately Held**
SIC: 7221 School photographer

7231 Beauty Shops

(P-13666)
ALEXANDERS GRAND SALON
Also Called: Alexander's Grand Salon & Spa
5579 E Santa Ana Cyn Rd, Anaheim (92807-3143)
PHONE..................714 282-6438
Fax: 714 282-6446
Sanda Morse, *Owner*
EMP: 65
SALES (est): 1.1MM **Privately Held**
SIC: 7231 Beauty shops

(P-13667)
BEAUTY BAZAR INC
Also Called: La Belle Days Spas and Salons
36 Stanford Shopping Ctr, Palo Alto (94304-1423)
PHONE..................650 326-8522
Fax: 650 326-8125
Vella Schner, *Owner*
Anh Le, *Manager*
EMP: 80
SALES (corp-wide): 3MM **Privately Held**
WEB: www.labelledayspas.com
SIC: 7231 5999 Beauty shops; toiletries, cosmetics & perfumes
PA: Beauty Bazar Inc
233 Grant Ave Fl 4
San Francisco CA 94108
415 433-7644

(P-13668)
BEAUTY RECOGNIZED LP
224 Via Rodeo Dr, Beverly Hills (90210-5142)
PHONE..................310 278-7646
Fax: 310 278-4296
Jose Eber,
EMP: 70
SALES (est): 909.8K **Privately Held**
SIC: 7231 Unisex hair salons

(P-13669)
BEAUTY SERVICE INC
2946 State St Ste F, Carlsbad (92008-2336)
P.O. Box 2804 (92018-2804)
PHONE..................760 434-4141
Fax: 760 434-4154
Elizabeth Ferguson, *President*
Marvin Ferguson, *Vice Pres*
EMP: 50
SQ FT: 1,000
SALES (est): 1.9MM **Privately Held**
SIC: 7231 Hairdressers

(P-13670)
CLASS ACT HAIR & NAIL SALON
2795 Bechelli Ln, Redding (96002-1924)
PHONE..................530 223-3442
EMP: 69
SALES (est): 598.4K **Privately Held**
SIC: 7231

(P-13671)
CREATIVE NAIL DESIGN INC
Also Called: Revlon Professional
9560 Towne Centre Dr # 200, San Diego (92121-1972)
PHONE..................760 599-2900
Fax: 760 599-4005
James A Nordstrom, *CEO*
Jan Bragulla, *President*
Sennen Pamich, *President*
Chris Christopher, *CFO*
Mary Nordstrom, *Treasurer*
EMP: 105
SQ FT: 60,000
SALES (est): 8.9MM
SALES (corp-wide): 1.9B **Publicly Held**
SIC: 7231 Manicurist, pedicurist
PA: Revlon, Inc.
1 New York Plz
New York NY 10004
212 527-4000

(P-13672)
DIANAS MEXICAN FOOD PDTS INC
Also Called: Diana's Beauty Salon
5841 S Figueroa St, Los Angeles (90003-1061)
PHONE..................323 758-4845
EMP: 114
SALES (corp-wide): 104.5MM **Privately Held**
SIC: 7231 Beauty shops
PA: Diana's Mexican Food Products, Inc.
16330 Pioneer Blvd
Norwalk CA 90650
562 926-5802

(P-13673)
ESALONCOM LLC
10361 Jefferson Blvd, Culver City (90232-3511)
PHONE..................310 846-9100
Francisco Gimenec,
Lani Kuramoto, *Vice Pres*
Tass Gunthelaka, *Sales Dir*
Ameann Dejohn, *Director*
EMP: 56
SALES (est): 3.9MM **Privately Held**
SIC: 7231 Unisex hair salons

(P-13674)
FEDERICO BEAUTY INSTITUTE
1515 Sports Dr Ste 100, Sacramento (95834-1905)
PHONE..................916 929-4242
Jeremy Frederico, *President*
EMP: 50
SALES (est): 1.2MM **Privately Held**
SIC: 7231 Beauty schools

(P-13675)
FERGUSON SALON MANAGEMENT INC
1104 Knowles Ave, Carlsbad (92008-1459)
P.O. Box 2804 (92018-2804)
PHONE..................760 434-5008
Elizabeth Ferguson, *President*
Marvin Ferguson, *CFO*
EMP: 50
SALES (est): 2MM **Privately Held**
SIC: 7231 7241 Beauty shops; barber shops

(P-13676)
FLORIDA BEAUTY FLORA INC
6205 Ventura Blvd, Ventura (93003-7226)
PHONE..................805 642-1633
Ronen Koubi, *Branch Mgr*
EMP: 296
SALES (corp-wide): 55.9MM **Privately Held**
SIC: 7231 Beauty shops
PA: Florida Beauty Flora, Inc.
3100 Nw 74th Ave
Miami FL 33122
305 503-1200

(P-13677)
GATES OF SPAIN WIBEL
2545 Mission St, Pasadena (91108-1691)
PHONE..................626 441-3078
William J Bell, *President*
Susan Bell, *Co-Owner*
Vicki Lanzarotta, *Admin Sec*
EMP: 50 EST: 1959
SALES: 1MM **Privately Held**
SIC: 7231 Cosmetology & personal hygiene salons

(P-13678)
HAIR FASHION INC
Also Called: Cristophe Salon
348 N Beverly Dr, Beverly Hills (90210-4701)
PHONE..................310 274-0851
Fax: 310 274-0682
Cristopher Schatteman, *President*
Cristophe Schatteman, *President*
EMP: 80
SQ FT: 7,000
SALES (est): 2.4MM **Privately Held**
WEB: www.cristophesalon.com
SIC: 7231 Unisex hair salons

(P-13679)
HOSHALL CORPORATION
Also Called: Hoshall Designer Group
6608 Folsom Auburn Rd # 4, Folsom (95630-2147)
PHONE..................916 987-1995
William C Hoshall, *President*
EMP: 50 EST: 1964
SALES (est): 1.1MM **Privately Held**
WEB: www.hoshallssalonandspa.com
SIC: 7231 5621 5999 Cosmetology & personal hygiene salons; ready-to-wear apparel, women's; cosmetics

(P-13680)
JURLIQUE HLISTIC SKIN CARE INC
Also Called: Jurlique Wellness Day Spa
1230 Montana Ave Ste 105, Santa Monica (90403-5986)
PHONE..................310 899-1923
Dianna Ralws, *Branch Mgr*
Sara Labree, *Manager*
EMP: 450
SALES (corp-wide): 6.6MM **Privately Held**
SIC: 7231 Facial salons
PA: Jurlique Holistic Skin Care, Inc.
1411 5th St Ste 501
Santa Monica CA 90401
914 998-8800

(P-13681)
JURLIQUE HLISTIC SKIN CARE INC (PA)
1411 5th St Ste 501, Santa Monica (90401-2481)
PHONE..................914 998-8800
Fax: 310 264-6899
Sam McKay, *CEO*
EMP: 50
SALES (est): 6.6MM **Privately Held**
SIC: 7231 Beauty shops

(P-13682)
NAILAGIO
Also Called: Nailissimo
23677 Calabasas Rd, Calabasas (91302-1502)
P.O. Box 2601, Winnetka (91396-2601)
PHONE..................818 222-6633
Judy Tran, *Owner*
EMP: 50
SALES (est): 1.4MM **Privately Held**
SIC: 7231 Manicurist, pedicurist

(P-13683)
ORGANIC & SUSTAINABLE BUTY INC
5933 Bowcroft St, Los Angeles (90016-4301)
PHONE..................310 815-8201
Jessica Iclisoy, *President*
Arthur Iclisoy, *Managing Dir*
EMP: 50 EST: 2006
SALES (est): 1.9MM **Privately Held**
SIC: 7231 2844 Beauty shops; hair preparations, including shampoos; suntan lotions & oils; face creams or lotions

(P-13684)
PERSONLIZED BUTY DISCOVERY INC
Also Called: Ipsy
201 Baldwin Ave Fl 2, San Mateo (94401-3914)
PHONE..................888 769-4526
Marcelo Camberos, *CEO*
Jennifer Goldfarb, *President*
Jorge Esteban Ochoa, *Vice Pres*
Nicole Collins, *Manager*
EMP: 200
SALES (est): 504.8K **Privately Held**
SIC: 7231 Beauty shops

(P-13685)
PILGRIM PLACE IN CLAREMONT
Also Called: Pilgrim Place Beauty Salon
721 Harrison Ave, Claremont (91711-4539)
PHONE..................909 621-9581
Fax: 909 625-6830
Will Cunitz, *Sales/Mktg Dir*
Bernie Valek, *CFO*
Steve Rogers, *Vice Pres*
Cathy Brown, *Social Dir*
Lindsey Hafemann, *Social Dir*
EMP: 180
SALES (corp-wide): 19.5MM **Privately Held**
WEB: www.pilgrimplace.org
SIC: 7231 Beauty shops
PA: Pilgrim Place In Claremont
625 Mayflower Rd
Claremont CA 91711
909 399-5500

(P-13686)
PLATINUM STRANDS SALON
3443 E Chapman Ave, Orange (92869-3812)
PHONE..................714 532-2633
Fax: 714 363-0806
Donald Anderson, *Owner*
Sam Ardalan, *Owner*
Thomas Penna, *Manager*
EMP: 65
SALES (est): 2.7MM **Privately Held**
SIC: 7231 Hairdressers

PRODUCTS & SERVICES SECTION
7261 - Funeral Svcs & Crematories County (P-13711)

(P-13687)
REGIS CORPORATION
Also Called: Vidal Sassoon Salon
9403 Santa Monica Blvd, Beverly Hills (90210-4604)
PHONE 310 274-8791
Stephen Taenaka, *Manager*
EMP: 50
SALES (corp-wide): 1.7B **Publicly Held**
SIC: 7231 Beauty shops
PA: Regis Corporation
7201 Metro Blvd
Edina MN 55439
952 947-7777

(P-13688)
ROMEO CECYLIA K BEAUTY SALON
11740 Carmel Mountain Rd # 198, San Diego (92128-4636)
PHONE 858 946-0179
Joe Roccaforte, *Owner*
EMP: 50
SALES (est): 231.8K **Privately Held**
SIC: 7231 Beauty shops

(P-13689)
SALON LUJON INC
216 N Harbor Blvd, Fullerton (92832-3604)
PHONE 714 738-1882
Fax: 714 446-0151
Rale Whitesell, *Manager*
Lulu Poore, *Admin Sec*
EMP: 60
SQ FT: 3,000
SALES (est): 1.3MM **Privately Held**
SIC: 7231 7991 Beauty shops; spas

(P-13690)
SALON-SALON
1700 Mchenry Ave Ste 29, Modesto (95350-4340)
PHONE 209 571-3500
Norma Foster Maddy, *Partner*
Chris Johnson, *Partner*
Kathy Houret, *Controller*
Jessica Stanfield, *Manager*
EMP: 55
SQ FT: 10,500
SALES (est): 2.3MM **Privately Held**
SIC: 7231 5621 5999 Hairdressers; boutiques; hair care products

(P-13691)
SPA GREGORIES LLC
Also Called: Spa Blue
2710 Via De Vly Ste B, Del Mar (92014)
PHONE 858 481-6672
Brenda Bladow, *Owner*
EMP: 62
SALES (corp-wide): 2.6MM **Privately Held**
SIC: 7231 Beauty shops
PA: Spa Gregorie's Llc
200 Nwport Ctr Dr Ste 111
Newport Beach CA 92660
949 644-6672

(P-13692)
TONI & GUY HAIRDRESSING (PA)
1177 Newport Center Dr, Newport Beach (92660-6950)
PHONE 949 721-1666
Fax: 949 751-4442
Frank Chirico, *Partner*
Olivia Price, *Manager*
EMP: 50
SALES (est): 1.6MM **Privately Held**
SIC: 7231 Unisex hair salons

(P-13693)
TRILOGY SQUAW SPA LLC
Also Called: Trilogy Day Spa
451 Manhattan Beach Blvd B108, Manhattan Beach (90266-5345)
PHONE 310 760-0044
Fax: 310 760-0053
Shandra Shaw,
EMP: 50
SALES (est): 1.8MM **Privately Held**
SIC: 7231 Cosmetology & personal hygiene salons

(P-13694)
ULTA SALON COSMT FRAGRANCE INC
1229 S Lone Hill Ave, Glendora (91740-4507)
PHONE 909 592-5393
EMP: 147
SALES (corp-wide): 3.9B **Publicly Held**
SIC: 7231 Beauty shops
PA: Ulta Salon, Cosmetics & Fragrance, Inc.
1000 Remington Blvd # 120
Bolingbrook IL 60440
630 410-4800

(P-13695)
ULTA SALON COSMT FRAGRANCE INC
9000 Ming Ave, Bakersfield (93311-1318)
PHONE 661 664-1402
EMP: 155
SALES (corp-wide): 3.9B **Publicly Held**
SIC: 7231 5999 Beauty shops; toiletries, cosmetics & perfumes
PA: Ulta Salon, Cosmetics & Fragrance, Inc.
1000 Remington Blvd # 120
Bolingbrook IL 60440
630 410-4800

(P-13696)
ULTA SALON COSMT FRAGRANCE INC
2841 Countryside Dr, Turlock (95380-8403)
PHONE 209 664-1725
EMP: 155
SALES (corp-wide): 3.9B **Publicly Held**
SIC: 7231 Beauty shops
PA: Ulta Salon, Cosmetics & Fragrance, Inc.
1000 Remington Blvd # 120
Bolingbrook IL 60440
630 410-4800

(P-13697)
ULTA SALON COSMT FRAGRANCE INC
185 S Las Posas Rd, San Marcos (92078-2419)
PHONE 760 744-0853
EMP: 155
SALES (corp-wide): 3.9B **Publicly Held**
SIC: 7231 Beauty shops
PA: Ulta Salon, Cosmetics & Fragrance, Inc.
1000 Remington Blvd # 120
Bolingbrook IL 60440
630 410-4800

7241 Barber Shops

(P-13698)
CUTTING EDGE PROTECTION I
381 Crosby St, Altadena (91001-5569)
PHONE 949 307-1596
Anthony Beaty, *President*
Greg Hammond, *Vice Pres*
EMP: 50
SALES (est): 321.2K **Privately Held**
WEB: www.tmbhollywood.com
SIC: 7241 Barber shops

(P-13699)
HAIRCUTTERS
1230 W Imperial Hwy Ste A, La Habra (90631-6961)
PHONE 562 690-2217
Johnny Shin, *Manager*
EMP: 92
SALES (corp-wide): 13.5MM **Privately Held**
SIC: 7241 7231 Barber shops; beauty shops
PA: The Haircutters
5160 Van Nuys Blvd
Sherman Oaks CA 91403
818 716-5319

(P-13700)
UPTOWNERS BARBER SHOP
134 E Main St, Barstow (92311-2219)
PHONE 760 256-5813
Lyn Lightle, *Owner*
EMP: 69
SALES (est): 317.3K **Privately Held**
SIC: 7241 Barber shops

7251 Shoe Repair & Shoeshine Parlors

(P-13701)
NAFTA SHOES INC
14632 Nelson Ave, City of Industry (91744-4346)
PHONE 626 369-9681
Fax: 626 369-0121
Ralph Chen, *President*
Angel Chen, *Vice Pres*
Grace Chen, *Manager*
EMP: 100
SQ FT: 40,000
SALES (est): 2.4MM **Privately Held**
WEB: www.naftashoehospital.com
SIC: 7251 3144 3143 5139 Shoe repair shop; women's footwear, except athletic; men's footwear, except athletic; shoes

7261 Funeral Svcs & Crematories

(P-13702)
CHAPEL OF CHIMES
Also Called: Chapel of Memories Crematorium
4499 Piedmont Ave, Oakland (94611-4293)
PHONE 510 654-1288
Daniel F Shaw, *Manager*
Harley Forrey, *Manager*
EMP: 50
SALES (corp-wide): 9.1MM **Publicly Held**
WEB: www.bailingyuan.com
SIC: 7261 Crematory
HQ: Chapel Of The Chimes
32992 Mission Blvd
Hayward CA 94544
510 471-3363

(P-13703)
CREMATION SPCLISTS LOS ANGELES
6000 Santa Monica Blvd, Los Angeles (90038-1864)
PHONE 323 469-9933
Tyler Cassity, *President*
EMP: 60 **EST:** 1998
SALES (est): 3.2MM **Privately Held**
WEB: www.cremationkansascity.com
SIC: 7261 Crematory

(P-13704)
CYPRESS FUNERAL SERVICES INC
Also Called: Cypress Lawn Funeral Home
1370 El Camino Real, Colma (94014-3239)
PHONE 650 550-8808
Fax: 650 755-5610
Kenneth E Varner, *President*
Armando Santana, *Managing Dir*
Teresa Chen, *Director*
Ben Chin, *Director*
Alvin Dougharty, *Director*
EMP: 150
SALES (est): 4.7MM **Privately Held**
SIC: 7261 Funeral service & crematories

(P-13705)
DESERT VIEW FUNERAL HOME
11478 Amargosa Rd, Victorville (92392-8125)
PHONE 760 244-0007
Fax: 760 949-4106
Jim Larkin, *CEO*
Terry Harmon, *Vice Pres*
Nanette Fernandez, *Director*
EMP: 50
SALES (est): 1.1MM **Privately Held**
SIC: 7261 Funeral home

(P-13706)
F R A LP
1702 Fairhaven Ave, Santa Ana (92705-6821)
PHONE 714 633-1442
Fred Forgy Jr, *Partner*
Jack Stanley, *Partner*
EMP: 70 **EST:** 1911
SQ FT: 12,000
SALES (est): 6.2MM **Privately Held**
SIC: 7261 6512 6553 5999 Crematory; commercial & industrial building operation; mausoleum operation; gravestones, finished; flowers, fresh

(P-13707)
NEPTUNE MANAGEMENT CORPORATION
150 W 6th St Ste 100, San Pedro (90731-3300)
PHONE 310 832-6923
EMP: 55
SALES (corp-wide): 11.3MM **Privately Held**
WEB: www.tridentsociety.com
SIC: 7261 Crematory
PA: Neptune Management Corporation
1250 S Pine Island Rd # 500
Plantation FL 33324
954 556-9400

(P-13708)
NEPTUNE MANAGEMENT CORPORATION
4065 Mowry Ave, Fremont (94538-1339)
PHONE 510 797-2269
EMP: 55
SALES (corp-wide): 11.3MM **Privately Held**
SIC: 7261 Funeral service & crematories
PA: Neptune Management Corporation
1250 S Pine Island Rd # 500
Plantation FL 33324
954 556-9400

(P-13709)
NEPTUNE MANAGEMENT CORPORATION
9650 Fairway Dr 120, Roseville (95678-3537)
PHONE 916 771-5300
EMP: 73
SALES (corp-wide): 11.3MM **Privately Held**
SIC: 7261 Funeral service & crematories
PA: Neptune Management Corporation
1250 S Pine Island Rd # 500
Plantation FL 33324
954 556-9400

(P-13710)
PIERCE BROTHERS (DH)
Also Called: SCI
10621 Victory Blvd, North Hollywood (91606-3918)
PHONE 818 763-9121
Fax: 818 760-0463
Oliver Yeo, *Manager*
R L Waltrip, *Ch of Bd*
David Anderson, *President*
Curtis Briggs, *Vice Pres*
Ray Gipson, *Vice Pres*
EMP: 80 **EST:** 1902
SQ FT: 10,000
SALES (est): 9.5MM
SALES (est): 2.9B **Publicly Held**
SIC: 7261 6553 Crematory; cemeteries, real estate operation
HQ: Sci Funeral Services Of New York, Inc.
1929 Allen Pkwy
Houston TX 77019
713 522-5141

(P-13711)
R A F LP
Also Called: Fairhaven Mem Pk & Mortuary
1702 Fairhaven Ave, Santa Ana (92705-6821)
PHONE 714 633-1442
Fax: 714 633-5471
Marla Noel, *Partner*
Liz Welch, *Human Res Dir*
Michael Casey, *Manager*
Cynthia Adair, *Relations*
EMP: 85
SQ FT: 11,000
SALES (est): 7MM **Privately Held**
WEB: www.fairhavenmemorial.com
SIC: 7261 5992 5999 6512 Funeral home; flowers, fresh; gravestones, finished; commercial & industrial building operation; mausoleum operation

7261 - Funeral Svcs & Crematories County (P-13712)

PRODUCDUCTS & SERVICES SECTION

(P-13712)
ROMAN CATH ARCH OF LOS ANGELES
Also Called: Holy Cross Cemetary & Masoleum
5835 W Slauson Ave, Culver City (90230-6505)
PHONE.................................310 836-5500
Maria Arascor, *Manager*
EMP: 50
SALES (corp-wide): 373.2MM **Privately Held**
WEB: www.smes.com
SIC: 7261 6553 Funeral service & crematories; cemetery subdividers & developers
PA: The Roman Catholic Archbishop Of Los Angeles
3424 Wilshire Blvd
Los Angeles CA 90010
213 637-7000

(P-13713)
ROMAN CATH ARCH OF LOS ANGELES
Also Called: Calvary Cemetery
199 N Hope Ave, Santa Barbara (93110-1609)
PHONE.................................805 687-8811
Gwen Hueston, *Branch Mgr*
EMP: 697
SALES (corp-wide): 373.2MM **Privately Held**
SIC: 7261 6553 Funeral service & crematories; cemetery subdividers & developers
PA: The Roman Catholic Archbishop Of Los Angeles
3424 Wilshire Blvd
Los Angeles CA 90010
213 637-7000

(P-13714)
ROSE HILLS MORTUARY INC
Also Called: Rose Hills Co
3888 Workman Mill Rd, Whittier (90601-1626)
P.O. Box 110 (90608-0110)
PHONE.................................562 699-0921
Dennis Poulsen, *Ch of Bd*
Mary C Guzman, *CFO*
Greg Williamson, *VP Sales*
EMP: 850
SQ FT: 230,000
SALES (est): 15.5MM **Privately Held**
SIC: 7261 6553 Funeral service & crematories; cemetery subdividers & developers

(P-13715)
SINAI TEMPLE
Also Called: Mt Sinai Mem Pk & Mortuary
5950 Forest Lawn Dr, Los Angeles (90068-1010)
PHONE.................................323 469-6000
Fax: 323 469-2372
Len Lawrence, *Manager*
Karen Fink, *Financial Exec*
Marc Granirer, *Finance Mgr*
Christine Olliff, *Asst Controller*
Gail Levy, *Marketing Mgr*
EMP: 125
SQ FT: 22,633
SALES (corp-wide): 26.1MM **Privately Held**
WEB: www.mt-sinai.com
SIC: 7261 6553 Funeral home; cemeteries, real estate operation
PA: Temple Sinai
10400 Wilshire Blvd
Los Angeles CA 90024
310 475-6401

(P-13716)
STEWART ENTERPRISES INC
Also Called: El Camino Mem Pk & Mortuary
5600 Carroll Canyon Rd, San Diego (92121-1702)
PHONE.................................858 453-2121
Virginia McCuyston, *Manager*
EMP: 50
SALES (corp-wide): 2.9B **Publicly Held**
WEB: www.stewartenterprises.com
SIC: 7261 Funeral service & crematories
HQ: Stewart Enterprises, Inc.
1333 S Clearview Pkwy
New Orleans LA 70121
504 729-1400

(P-13717)
TEMPLE ISRAEL OF HOLLYWOOD (PA)
Also Called: Hillside Mem Pk & Mortuary
7300 Hollywood Blvd, Los Angeles (90046-2999)
PHONE.................................323 876-8330
Fax: 323 876-6341
Steve Sloan, *President*
David Cremin, *Treasurer*
Renee Mochkatel, *Vice Pres*
Stephanie Bressler, *Exec Dir*
Jane Zuckerman, *Exec Dir*
EMP: 83
SQ FT: 15,000
SALES (est): 10MM **Privately Held**
SIC: 7261 8299 Funeral service & crematories; religious school

7291 Tax Return Preparation Svcs

(P-13718)
AKAMAI HOLDING INC
Also Called: H & R Block
515 W Ramsey St Ste A, Banning (92220-4813)
P.O. Box 1297 (92220-0009)
PHONE.................................951 922-2419
Esosa Ogunbor, *CEO*
EMP: 52 EST: 2010
SALES (est): 1.2MM **Privately Held**
SIC: 7291 Tax return preparation services

(P-13719)
ANDERSEN TAX LLC
400 Suth Hope St Ste 2000, Los Angeles (90071)
PHONE.................................213 593-2300
Kurt Brune, *Managing Dir*
EMP: 80
SALES (corp-wide): 24MM **Privately Held**
SIC: 7291 Tax return preparation services
PA: Andersen Tax Llc
100 1st St Ste 1600
San Francisco CA 94105
415 764-2700

(P-13720)
EXACTAX INC (PA)
1100 E Orangethorpe Ave # 100, Anaheim (92801-5168)
P.O. Box 61048 (92803-6148)
PHONE.................................714 284-4802
Fax: 714 284-4814
Kevin Love, *President*
Franklin Pang, *Shareholder*
Richard Johnson, *Treasurer*
Michael Leonetti, *Vice Pres*
Bob Lynch, *Vice Pres*
EMP: 74
SQ FT: 18,000
SALES (est): 2.5MM **Privately Held**
WEB: www.exactax.com
SIC: 7291 7371 Tax return preparation services; computer software development

(P-13721)
H & R BLOCK INC
401 N Broadway Ste B, Santa Maria (93454-4121)
PHONE.................................805 349-9266
Bill Norris, *Branch Mgr*
EMP: 70
SALES (corp-wide): 3B **Publicly Held**
WEB: www.hrblock.com
SIC: 7291 Tax return preparation services
PA: H&R Block, Inc.
1 H&R Block Way
Kansas City MO 64105
816 854-3000

(P-13722)
H & R BLOCK INC
4300 Sonoma Blvd Ste 600, Vallejo (94589-2211)
PHONE.................................707 643-1856
Vince Largo, *Manager*
EMP: 200
SALES (corp-wide): 3B **Publicly Held**
WEB: www.hrblock.com
SIC: 7291 Tax return preparation services
PA: H&R Block, Inc.
1 H&R Block Way
Kansas City MO 64105
816 854-3000

(P-13723)
H&R BLOCK INC
Also Called: H & R Block
4038 S Western Ave, Los Angeles (90062-1634)
PHONE.................................323 292-8836
Fax: 323 386-2799
Henry York, *Manager*
EMP: 50
SALES (corp-wide): 3B **Publicly Held**
WEB: www.hrblock.com
SIC: 7291 Tax return preparation services
PA: H&R Block, Inc.
1 H&R Block Way
Kansas City MO 64105
816 854-3000

(P-13724)
J B LAQUINDANUM & ASSOCIATES
2608 Springs Rd, Vallejo (94591-5713)
PHONE.................................707 648-0501
Fax: 707 554-9824
J B Laquindanum, *Owner*
EMP: 50
SQ FT: 9,156
SALES (est): 940K **Privately Held**
SIC: 7291 Tax return preparation services

(P-13725)
MODERN HR INC
9000 W Sunset Blvd # 900, West Hollywood (90069-5801)
PHONE.................................310 270-9800
Harold Walt, *CEO*
Faith Branvold, *President*
Grace Drulias, *CFO*
Marie Hyde, *Accountant*
EMP: 400
SALES: 1MM **Privately Held**
SIC: 7291 8721 8742 Tax return preparation services; payroll accounting service; human resource consulting services

(P-13726)
OPTIMA TAX RELIEF LLC
3100 S Harbor Blvd # 250, Santa Ana (92704-6823)
PHONE.................................714 361-4636
Fax: 714 333-9327
Jesse Torres,
Jarrod Bassin, *Vice Pres*
Leandro Amado, *Technician*
Mick Cotten, *Technology*
Megan Bitney, *Marketing Staff*
EMP: 180
SQ FT: 30,000
SALES (est): 16.2MM **Privately Held**
WEB: www.optimataxrelief.com
SIC: 7291 Tax return preparation services

(P-13727)
STOPIRSDEBTCOM INC
10100 Santa Monica Blvd, Los Angeles (90067-4003)
PHONE.................................323 857-5809
Fax: 323 857-6759
Light Silver, *President*
EMP: 50
SQ FT: 3,500
SALES (est): 1.2MM **Privately Held**
WEB: www.stopirsdebt.com
SIC: 7291 Tax return preparation services

(P-13728)
THOMSON RTERS TAX ACCNTING INC
1300 Clay St Ste 810, Oakland (94612-1428)
PHONE.................................510 452-6900
Jim Tom, *Branch Mgr*
EMP: 135
SALES (corp-wide): 3.8B **Publicly Held**
SIC: 7291 Tax return preparation services
HQ: Thomson Reuters (Tax & Accounting) Inc.
2395 Midway Rd
Carrollton TX 75006
800 431-9025

7299 Miscellaneous Personal Svcs, NEC

(P-13729)
A-1 EVENT & PARTY RENTALS
Also Called: A1 Event & Party Rentals
251 E Front St, Covina (91723-1613)
PHONE.................................626 967-0500
Fax: 626 967-7572
Chet Fortney, *President*
Rene Martinez, *Vice Pres*
Albert Funfstuck, *General Mgr*
Jerry Hinds, *Financial Exec*
Steven Martinez, *Opers Mgr*
EMP: 55
SQ FT: 40,000
SALES (est): 4.2MM **Privately Held**
SIC: 7299 7359 Party planning service; party supplies rental services

(P-13730)
ADIR MONEY TRANSFER CORP
Also Called: Curacao Financial
1605 W Olympic Blvd, Los Angeles (90015-3808)
PHONE.................................213 639-2195
Francisco Moreno, *Vice Pres*
EMP: 50
SALES (est): 732.1K **Privately Held**
SIC: 7299 Personal financial services

(P-13731)
AMERICAN CONSERVATORY THEATER
1117 Market St, San Francisco (94103-1513)
PHONE.................................415 439-2379
Heather Kitchen, *Principal*
EMP: 109 **Privately Held**
SIC: 7299 Costume rental
PA: American Conservatory Theater
30 Grant Ave Fl 7
San Francisco CA 94108

(P-13732)
AMERICAN DATAMED (PA)
325 Maple Ave, Torrance (90503-2602)
PHONE.................................949 250-4000
Robb Howard, *President*
Darren Testa, *COO*
Ron Fisk, *Administration*
Jon Stapp, *Controller*
EMP: 100
SQ FT: 7,000
SALES: 18MM **Privately Held**
SIC: 7299 Information services, consumer

(P-13733)
APPLE VLLEY/ VCTRVLLE CNSRTIUM
14955 Dale Evans Pkwy, Apple Valley (92307-3061)
PHONE.................................760 240-7000
Keneth J Henderson, *Exec Dir*
EMP: 65
SALES (est): 469.9K **Privately Held**
SIC: 7299 Information services, consumer

(P-13734)
AT YOUR HOME FAMILYCARE
6540 Lusk Blvd Ste C266, San Diego (92121-2783)
PHONE.................................858 625-0406
Laurie Edwards-Tate, *President*
EMP: 200
SQ FT: 2,000
SALES (est): 6.7MM **Privately Held**
WEB: www.atyourhomefamilycare.com
SIC: 7299 8082 Babysitting bureau; home health care services

(P-13735)
BABYCENTER LLC (DH)
163 Freelon St, San Francisco (94107-1624)
PHONE.................................415 537-0900
Fax: 415 537-0909
Mary Baker,
Gerald G Briggs, *Bd of Directors*
Traci Burgess, *Bd of Directors*
Suzanne Dixon, *Bd of Directors*
Dawn Rosenberg, *Bd of Directors*

PRODUCTS & SERVICES SECTION
7299 - Miscellaneous Personal Svcs, NEC County (P-13759)

EMP: 52
SALES (est): 4.8MM
SALES (corp-wide): 70B Publicly Held
WEB: www.babycenter.com
SIC: 7299 5999 Information services, consumer; infant furnishings & equipment
HQ: Johnson & Johnson Consumer Inc.
199 Grandview Rd
Skillman NJ 08558
908 874-1000

(P-13736)
BANQUET FACILITIES
Also Called: Indian Hills Golf Club
6000 Camino Real, Riverside (92509-5310)
PHONE 951 360-2081
John De Zoetez, Manager
EMP: 50
SALES (est): 510.6K Privately Held
SIC: 7299 Banquet hall facilities

(P-13737)
BELCAMPO BUTCHERY
Also Called: Belcampo Meat
329 N Phillipe Ln, Yreka (96097-9413)
PHONE 530 842-5200
Anya Sernald, President
EMP: 50
SALES (est): 1.1MM Privately Held
SIC: 7299 5421 Butcher service, processing only; meat markets, including freezer provisioners

(P-13738)
BEST VALET PARKING CORPORATION
12792 Valley View St # 201, Garden Grove (92845-2510)
PHONE 800 708-2538
Fax: 714 894-6140
Michael Raemer, President
EMP: 100
SQ FT: 650
SALES (est): 5MM Privately Held
SIC: 7299 Valet parking

(P-13739)
BUCKINGHAM PROPERTY MANAGEMENT
Also Called: Coventry Cove Apartments
12609 Moffatt Ln, Fresno (93730-9704)
PHONE 559 322-1105
Cher Cha, Principal
EMP: 93
SALES (corp-wide): 13MM Privately Held
SIC: 7299 Apartment locating service
PA: Buckingham Property Management Inc
2170 N Winery Ave
Fresno CA 93703
559 452-8250

(P-13740)
CALIFORNIA SUN CENTERS INC
8265 Sierra College Blvd, Roseville (95661-9403)
PHONE 916 789-9767
Michael Blore, CEO
EMP: 80
SALES (est): 3.1MM Privately Held
SIC: 7299 5651 Tanning salon; family clothing stores

(P-13741)
CAPITAL ATHLETIC CLUB INC
1515 8th St, Sacramento (95814-5503)
PHONE 916 442-3927
Fax: 916 442-3826
Ken Hoffman, President
Jane Coolidge, Admin Mgr
Bruce Coolidge, Director
EMP: 64
SQ FT: 52,000
SALES (est): 2.6MM Privately Held
WEB: www.capitalac.com
SIC: 7299 Personal appearance services

(P-13742)
CARFAX STUDIOS
3937 Carfax Ave, Long Beach (90808-2210)
PHONE 562 377-0223
Paul Levitt, Principal
EMP: 62 EST: 2009

SALES (est): 1.8MM Privately Held
SIC: 7299 Apartment locating service

(P-13743)
CATTLEMENS
Also Called: Cattlemens Restaurant
2882 Kitty Hawk Rd, Livermore (94551-7666)
PHONE 925 447-1224
Fax: 925 447-1801
Jackie Gibson, General Mgr
EMP: 70
SALES (corp-wide): 20.6MM Privately Held
WEB: www.beststeakinthewest.com
SIC: 7299 5812 Banquet hall facilities; American restaurant
PA: Cattlemens
250 Dutton Ave
Santa Rosa CA 95407
707 528-1040

(P-13744)
CHOURA VENUE SERVICES
Also Called: Choura Vnue Svcs At Carson Ctr
4101 E Willow St, Long Beach (90815-1740)
PHONE 562 426-0555
James Choura, CEO
Sandra Valdovinos, Sales Executive
EMP: 99
SALES (est): 7.1MM Privately Held
SIC: 7299 5812 Information services, consumer; caterers

(P-13745)
CINTAS CORPORATION NO 2
18050 Central Ave, Carson (90746-4006)
PHONE 310 635-8713
Cluadia Sanchez, Manager
EMP: 69
SALES (corp-wide): 4.9B Publicly Held
WEB: www.cintas-corp.com
SIC: 7299 Personal appearance services
HQ: Cintas Corporation No. 2
6800 Cintas Blvd
Mason OH 45040

(P-13746)
CINTAS CORPORATION NO 3
777 139th Ave, San Leandro (94578-3218)
PHONE 510 352-6330
Fax: 510 352-0348
Brian Delbecq, General Mgr
Mark Bassett, Office Mgr
Katharina Chaname, Office Mgr
Marisela Fuentes, Human Res Mgr
EMP: 50
SQ FT: 25,000
SALES (corp-wide): 4.9B Publicly Held
WEB: www.cintas-corp.com
SIC: 7299 2326 Clothing rental services; men's & boys' work clothing
HQ: Cintas Corporation No. 3
6800 Cintas Blvd
Mason OH 45040

(P-13747)
CLASSMATES MEDIA CORPORATION
21301 Burbank Blvd, Woodland Hills (91367-6679)
PHONE 818 287-3600
Mark R Goldston, Ch of Bd
Paul J Pucino, CFO
Frederic A Randall Jr, Exec VP
Sally McKenzie, Senior VP
Sarah Pynchon, Vice Pres
EMP: 346
SALES (est): 6.5MM
SALES (corp-wide): 112.5MM Publicly Held
WEB: www.classmatesmedia.com
SIC: 7299 7389 Personal document & information services; advertising, promotional & trade show services
HQ: United Online, Inc.
21255 Burbank Blvd # 400
Woodland Hills CA 91367
818 287-3000

(P-13748)
CONDUIT LNGAGE SPECIALISTS INC
22720 Ventura Blvd # 100, Woodland Hills (91364-1305)
PHONE 859 299-3178
Art Mathews, Branch Mgr
EMP: 93
SALES (corp-wide): 6.9MM Privately Held
SIC: 7299 Personal appearance services
PA: Conduit Language Specialists, Inc.
206 Winchester St
Paris KY 40361
859 299-3178

(P-13749)
CONSUMER CREDIT COUNSELING SVC (PA)
Also Called: Credit Counselor of California
595 Market St Ste 1500, San Francisco (94105-2824)
PHONE 415 788-0288
Fax: 415 527-5163
Kathryn Davis, CEO
Arnold Pasco, Office Mgr
Viken Demirjian, Info Tech Mgr
Kenneth Crone, Director
EMP: 60 EST: 1969
SQ FT: 14,000
SALES (est): 6.9MM Privately Held
WEB: www.cccssf.org
SIC: 7299 Debt counseling or adjustment service, individuals

(P-13750)
CORINTHIAN INTL PRKG SVCS INC
Also Called: Corinthian Parking Services
19925 Stevens Creek Blvd, Cupertino (95014-2300)
PHONE 408 867-7275
Fax: 408 370-7262
Douglas E Knapp, CEO
Todd Fedde, Vice Pres
Brian King, Analyst
Kyle Baldasano, Director
Laura Gomes, Manager
EMP: 500
SQ FT: 6,000
SALES (est): 15.3MM Privately Held
WEB: www.corinthianparking.com
SIC: 7299 7521 4119 Valet parking; parking garage; limousine rental, with driver

(P-13751)
CORPORATE SOUL LLC
433 Hudson St, Healdsburg (95448-4461)
PHONE 707 431-7781
Michele Boudreaux, Mng Member
EMP: 270
SQ FT: 2,000
SALES (est): 3.8MM Privately Held
WEB: www.corporatesoul.net
SIC: 7299 Massage parlor

(P-13752)
CP OPCO LLC (HQ)
Also Called: Classic Party Rentals
901 W Hillcrest Blvd, Inglewood (90301-2100)
PHONE 310 966-4900
Brent Mumford, President
Charles Brown, CFO
Ing Eden, Controller
EMP: 2300
SALES: 250MM
SALES (corp-wide): 1.1MM Privately Held
SIC: 7299 Facility rental & party planning services

(P-13753)
CRYSTAL VALET PARKING INC
4477 Hollywood Blvd 209, Los Angeles (90027-6006)
P.O. Box 27386 (90027-0386)
PHONE 323 663-7275
Greg Gee, President
EMP: 70
SALES (est): 2.5MM Privately Held
SIC: 7299 Valet parking

(P-13754)
DANERICA ENTERPRISES INC
Also Called: Tax Resolution Services, Co
6345 Balboa Blvd Ste 285, Encino (91316-5238)
PHONE 818 201-3300
Fax: 818 774-9361
Michael Rozbruch, CEO
R Brian Compton, President
Becky Stephens, Executive Asst
Michael Castaneda, Manager
Romy Tcherkezian, Manager
EMP: 100 EST: 1998
SQ FT: 15,000
SALES (est): 6.5MM Privately Held
WEB: www.taxresolution.com
SIC: 7299 Personal financial services

(P-13755)
DEBTMERICA LLC
Also Called: Debtmerica Relief
3100 S Harbor Blvd # 250, Santa Ana (92704-6823)
PHONE 714 389-4200
Jesse Torres,
Harry Langenberg, Executive
Sonia Duenas, Human Res Mgr
Jarrod Bassin, Sales Dir
Charles Hughes, Marketing Staff
EMP: 65
SQ FT: 15,000
SALES (est): 5MM Privately Held
WEB: www.debtmerica.com
SIC: 7299 Debt counseling or adjustment service, individuals

(P-13756)
DESTINATION RESIDENCES LLC
Also Called: Tesancia La Jlla Ht Spa Resort
9700 N Torrey Pines Rd, La Jolla (92037-1102)
PHONE 858 550-1000
Fax: 858 550-1001
Charlie Peck, President
Kim Ponsoll, Sales Mgr
Tanya Torrence, Sales Mgr
Claudia Wehrman, Sales Staff
Dreux Jacques, Asst Director
EMP: 256
SALES (corp-wide): 735.2MM Privately Held
WEB: www.destinationhotels.com
SIC: 7299 7389 7991 7011 Banquet hall facilities; convention & show services; spas; hotels
HQ: Destination Residences Llc
10333 E Dry Creek Rd
Englewood CO 80112
303 799-3830

(P-13757)
DEVELOP POINT EDUCATION
9909 Topanga Canyon Blvd # 346, Chatsworth (91311-3602)
PHONE 805 624-6171
Jim Negrete, Principal
EMP: 50
SALES (est): 439.5K Privately Held
SIC: 7299 Miscellaneous personal service

(P-13758)
EVEREST WTRPRFING RSTRTION INC
1270 Missouri St, San Francisco (94107-3310)
PHONE 415 282-9800
Fax: 415 282-1205
Keith Goldstein, President
Mark Murray, Vice Pres
Seth Acharya, Opers Mgr
Jeannie Savage, Manager
EMP: 64
SQ FT: 5,000
SALES (est): 4.9MM Privately Held
WEB: www.everestsf.com
SIC: 7299 Home improvement & renovation contractor agency

(P-13759)
FLUXX LABS INC
77 Maiden Ln Fl 4, San Francisco (94108-5426)
PHONE 855 358-9946
Jason Ricci, CEO
Kerrin Mitchell, COO
Eric Hansen,

7299 - Miscellaneous Personal Svcs, NEC County (P-13760)

PRODUDUCTS & SERVICES SECTION

John Joyce, *Manager*
EMP: 50 **EST:** 2010
SALES (est): 184.2K **Privately Held**
SIC: 7299 Information services, consumer

(P-13760)
FREEDOM FINANCIAL NETWORK LLC (PA)
Also Called: Freedom Debt Relief
1875 S Grant St Ste 400, San Mateo (94402-2676)
PHONE..................................650 393-6619
Fax: 650 292-2227
Bradford Stroh,
Rich Ransom, *CFO*
Sean Fox, *Officer*
Andy Dull, *Vice Pres*
Benjamin Sloop, *Vice Pres*
EMP: 70
SQ FT: 20,000
SALES (est): 17.4MM **Privately Held**
WEB: www.freedomfinancialnetwork.com
SIC: 7299 Debt counseling or adjustment service, individuals

(P-13761)
FRESNO AG HARDWARE INC
4590 N 1st St, Fresno (93726-1987)
PHONE..................................559 224-6441
James Rosetta, *President*
Rae R Rosetta, *CEO*
Vicki Bassett, *Executive*
Vikki Klusener, *Manager*
EMP: 65
SQ FT: 50,000
SALES (est): 5.2MM **Privately Held**
WEB: www.fresnoag.com
SIC: 7299 Home improvement & renovation contractor agency

(P-13762)
GALKOS CONSTRUCTION INC (PA)
15262 Pipeline Ln, Huntington Beach (92649-1136)
PHONE..................................714 373-8545
Fax: 714 373-8540
Frank E Gialketsis, *President*
Lonnie Gialketsis, *Vice Pres*
Lonnie Gialketsis, *Branch Mgr*
Christopher Gialketsis, *Info Tech Mgr*
EMP: 61
SALES (est): 10MM **Privately Held**
WEB: www.galkos.com
SIC: 7299 Home improvement & renovation contractor agency

(P-13763)
GLEN IVY HOT SPRINGS
1001 Brea Mall, Brea (92821-5721)
PHONE..................................714 990-2090
Jen Breakey, *Manager*
EMP: 190
SALES (corp-wide): 11.1MM **Privately Held**
SIC: 7299 7991 5812 5699 Massage parlor; spas; cafe; bathing suits; toiletries, cosmetics & perfumes
PA: Glen Ivy Hot Springs
  25000 Glen Ivy Rd
  Corona CA 92883
  951 277-3529

(P-13764)
HOMETOWN BUFFET INC
Also Called: Hometown Buffet 261
11471 South St, Cerritos (90703-6600)
PHONE..................................562 402-8307
Fax: 562 402-8318
Mary Woods, *General Mgr*
EMP: 51
SALES (corp-wide): 848.5MM **Privately Held**
WEB: www.hometownbuffet.com
SIC: 7299 Banquet hall facilities
HQ: Hometown Buffet Inc.
  120 Chula Vis
  San Antonio TX 78232
  651 994-8608

(P-13765)
HORNBLOWER YACHTS LLC
200 Marina Blvd, Berkeley (94710-1608)
PHONE..................................916 446-1185
Daniel Montoya, *Manager*
Cameron Clark, *Vice Pres*

Christopher Schlerf, *Food Svc Dir*
EMP: 102
SALES (corp-wide): 104.6MM **Privately Held**
SIC: 7299 Banquet hall facilities
PA: Hornblower Yachts, Llc
  On The Embarcadero Pier 3 St Pier
  San Francisco CA 94111
  415 788-8866

(P-13766)
HOTPADS COM
225 Bush St Ste 1100, San Francisco (94104-4250)
PHONE..................................563 289-7368
Douglas Pope, *Director*
Tim Licata, *Technology*
Cameron Swiggett, *Manager*
EMP: 57 **EST:** 2008
SALES (est): 1.7MM
SALES (corp-wide): 644.6MM **Publicly Held**
SIC: 7299 Apartment locating service
HQ: Zillow, Inc.
  1301 2nd Ave Fl 31
  Seattle WA 98101
  206 470-7000

(P-13767)
IDENTITY THEFT RECOVERY & MONI
1990 N Calif Blvd Fl 8, Walnut Creek (94596-3742)
PHONE..................................888 269-2314
Jamall Robinson, *Chairman*
EMP: 60
SALES: 13MM **Privately Held**
SIC: 7299 Debt counseling or adjustment service, individuals

(P-13768)
INFORMATION & REFERRAL FED LOS
Also Called: 211 La County
526 W Las Tunas Dr, San Gabriel (91776-1111)
P.O. Box 726 (91778-0726)
PHONE..................................626 350-1841
Maribel Marin, *CEO*
Amy Latzer, *COO*
Sharun Luu, *CFO*
Laura Mejia, *Program Mgr*
Catherine Abbott, *QA Dir*
EMP: 100
SQ FT: 23,000
SALES: 8.6MM **Privately Held**
WEB: www.211-la.net
SIC: 7299 Information services, consumer

(P-13769)
INTERNATIONAL MISSING PERSONS
609 S Broder St, Anaheim (92804-3232)
P.O. Box 2542 (92814-0542)
PHONE..................................714 827-1947
Arthur Suchesk, *President*
Robert W Pershelli, *CFO*
J Cullins, *Admin Sec*
EMP: 55
SALES: 4.3MM **Privately Held**
SIC: 7299 Personal document & information services

(P-13770)
JENNY CRAIG INC (HQ)
5770 Fleet St, Carlsbad (92008-4700)
PHONE..................................760 696-4000
Fax: 760 696-4607
Monty Sharma, *CEO*
Patricia Larchet, *Ch of Bd*
Paul Britton, *CFO*
Jim Kelly, *CFO*
Leesa Eichberger, *Chief Mktg Ofcr*
EMP: 220
SQ FT: 75,000
SALES (est): 130.7MM
SALES (corp-wide): 170.7MM **Privately Held**
WEB: www.jennycraig.com
SIC: 7299 6794 5149 5499 Diet center, without medical staff; franchises, selling or licensing; diet foods; dietetic foods
PA: North Castle Partners, L.L.C.
  183 E Putnam Ave
  Greenwich CT 06830
  203 485-0216

(P-13771)
JENNY CRAIG WGHT LOSS CTRS INC (DH)
5770 Fleet St, Carlsbad (92008-4700)
PHONE..................................760 696-4000
Dana Fiser, *President*
Kent Kreh, *Ch of Bd*
Patti Larchet, *President*
Jenny Craig, *CEO*
James Kelly, *CFO*
EMP: 130
SQ FT: 50,000
SALES (est): 55MM
SALES (corp-wide): 170.7MM **Privately Held**
SIC: 7299 7991 Diet center, without medical staff; weight reducing clubs
HQ: Jenny Craig, Inc.
  5770 Fleet St
  Carlsbad CA 92008
  760 696-4000

(P-13772)
JN PROJECTS INC
Also Called: Hellosign
944 Market St Ste 400, San Francisco (94102-4023)
PHONE..................................415 766-0273
Joseph Hartman Walla, *CEO*
Whitney Bouck, *COO*
Jack Dauer, *Executive*
Neil Omara, *CTO*
Jacques Benkoski, *Director*
EMP: 50
SQ FT: 5,000
SALES (est): 1.1MM **Privately Held**
SIC: 7299 Personal document & information services

(P-13773)
MAC PRO INC
12300 Washington Blvd R, Whittier (90606-2599)
PHONE..................................562 623-4300
David Machado, *President*
Mellisa Moreno, *Admin Sec*
EMP: 50
SALES (est): 2.1MM **Privately Held**
SIC: 7299 Home improvement & renovation contractor agency

(P-13774)
MASSAGE PLACE
2516 Overland Ave, Los Angeles (90064-3333)
PHONE..................................310 204-3004
Michael Marylander, *Branch Mgr*
EMP: 200
SALES (corp-wide): 1.9MM **Privately Held**
SIC: 7299 Massage parlor
PA: The Massage Place
  245 Main St
  Venice CA 90291
  310 399-5566

(P-13775)
MASTROIANNI FAMILY ENTPS LTD
Also Called: Jay's Catering
10581 Garden Grove Blvd, Garden Grove (92843-1128)
PHONE..................................310 952-1700
Fax: 714 636-6045
Jay Mastroiannis, *President*
EMP: 78
SALES (corp-wide): 34.9MM **Privately Held**
WEB: www.jayscatering.com
SIC: 7299 Banquet hall facilities
PA: Mastroianni Family Enterprises Ltd.
  10581 Garden Grove Blvd
  Garden Grove CA 92843
  714 636-6045

(P-13776)
MCH ELECTRIC INC
4923 W 11th St, Tracy (95340-9579)
PHONE..................................209 835-9755
James Humphrey, *Branch Mgr*
EMP: 89
SALES (corp-wide): 24.4MM **Privately Held**
SIC: 7299 Personal shopping service

PA: Mch Electric, Inc.
  7693 Longard Rd
  Livermore CA 94551
  209 835-9755

(P-13777)
MICHAEL GROVE
Also Called: California Exteriors
3260 N E St Ste C, San Bernardino (92405-2618)
PHONE..................................909 883-5398
Fax: 909 883-5498
Michael Grove, *Owner*
Maurisa Harris, *Office Mgr*
EMP: 50
SALES (est): 2.1MM **Privately Held**
SIC: 7299 Handyman service

(P-13778)
MOGL LOYALTY SERVICES INC
9645 Scranton Rd Ste 110, San Diego (92121-1764)
PHONE..................................858 436-7036
Jon Carder, *President*
Tracy Neumann, *Vice Pres*
James Smith, *Controller*
Thiago Saza, *Cust Svc Mgr*
Leslie Miller, *Marketing Mgr*
EMP: 65
SALES (est): 5.7MM **Privately Held**
SIC: 7299 Tax refund discounting

(P-13779)
MOUNTASIA OF SANTA CLARITA
Also Called: Mountasia Family Fun Center
21516 Golden Triangle Rd, Saugus (91350-2612)
PHONE..................................661 253-4386
Michael Fleming, *Partner*
David Fleming, *Partner*
EMP: 60
SALES (est): 1.6MM **Privately Held**
SIC: 7299 7999 Party planning service; skating rink operation services

(P-13780)
MOVE SALES INC (DH)
Also Called: Homestore Apartments & Rentals
30700 Russell Ranch Rd # 100, Westlake Village (91362-9501)
PHONE..................................805 557-2300
Steve Berkowitz, *CEO*
Maria Pietrosorte, *President*
Daniel Woods, *President*
Barbara O'Connor, *Exec VP*
Errol Samuelson, *Exec VP*
EMP: 75
SALES (est): 9MM
SALES (corp-wide): 8.2B **Publicly Held**
SIC: 7299 Apartment locating service
HQ: Move, Inc.
  3315 Scott Blvd
  Santa Clara CA 95054
  408 558-7100

(P-13781)
OCB RESTAURANT COMPANY LLC
Also Called: Hometown Buffet 269
3617 W Shaw Ave, Fresno (93711-3206)
PHONE..................................559 271-1927
Fax: 559 271-2684
Craig Vike, *General Mgr*
Craig Vikey, *Office Mgr*
EMP: 55
SQ FT: 9,000
SALES (corp-wide): 848.5MM **Privately Held**
WEB: www.buffet.com
SIC: 7299 Banquet hall facilities
HQ: Ocb Restaurant Company Llc
  120 Chula Vis
  San Antonio TX 78232
  210 403-3725

(P-13782)
OCB RESTAURANT COMPANY LLC
Also Called: Hometown Buffet
8629 S Sepulveda Blvd # 310, Los Angeles (90045-4001)
PHONE..................................310 216-9208
Ralph Miller, *Manager*
EMP: 66

PRODUCTS & SERVICES SECTION

7311 - Advertising Agencies County (P-13807)

SALES (corp-wide): 848.5MM **Privately Held**
WEB: www.buffet.com
SIC: 7299 Banquet hall facilities
HQ: Ocb Restaurant Company Llc
120 Chula Vis
San Antonio TX 78232
210 403-3725

(P-13783)
PACIFICA HEALTH AND MEDICAL
2650 Cmino Del Rio N 21, San Diego (92108)
PHONE.................................619 688-1848
Fax: 619 688-1898
Jeff Sternberg, *President*
Jamie Danielian, *Manager*
EMP: 104
SQ FT: 1,000
SALES (est): 2.2MM **Privately Held**
SIC: 7299 Diet center, without medical staff

(P-13784)
PALMDALE WOMANS CLUB
2141 E Avenue Q, Palmdale (93550-4040)
P.O. Box 901825 (93590-1825)
PHONE.................................661 266-3008
Shirley Haning, *President*
Helen Cleveland, *President*
Jackie Lawslo, *President*
EMP: 52
SQ FT: 3,215
SALES: 15.9K **Privately Held**
WEB: www.palmdalewomansclub.com
SIC: 7299 8699 Personal appearance services; charitable organization

(P-13785)
PALO ALTO HILLS GOLF AN
3000 Alexis Dr, Palo Alto (94304-1303)
PHONE.................................650 948-1800
Fax: 650 948-9532
Padmanabhan Srinagesh, *CEO*
Katelyn Pavao, *Admin Asst*
Marcela Tannenbergova, *Accountant*
Marian Paragas, *Controller*
Kelli Tsai, *Corp Comm Staff*
EMP: 75
SQ FT: 25,000
SALES (est): 7.7MM **Privately Held**
WEB: www.pahgcc.com
SIC: 7299 7997 Banquet hall facilities; golf club, membership

(P-13786)
PARTY PANTRY GARDEN ROOM
12777 Knott St, Garden Grove (92841-3903)
PHONE.................................714 899-0626
Lisa Waddell, *Owner*
EMP: 50 EST: 1971
SALES (est): 641.1K **Privately Held**
SIC: 7299 Banquet hall facilities

(P-13787)
PPS PARKING INC
1800 E Garry Ave Ste 107, Santa Ana (92705-5803)
P.O. Box 16635, Irvine (92623-6635)
PHONE.................................949 223-8707
Steve Paliska, *President*
Paul Paliska, *Exec VP*
Karen Such, *Senior VP*
EMP: 506
SQ FT: 5,000
SALES (est): 10.2MM **Privately Held**
SIC: 7299 8748 Valet parking; business consulting

(P-13788)
PRAETORIAN USA
Also Called: Praetorian Event Services
925 Lakeville St 129, Petaluma (94952-3329)
PHONE.................................707 780-8020
Kathy J Kingman, *President*
Mark Solum, *Manager*
EMP: 99
SALES: 200K **Privately Held**
SIC: 7299 7389 Party planning service;

(P-13789)
PROGRESS ADVOCATES GROUP LLC
Also Called: Student Advocates
3100 Bristol St Ste 300, Costa Mesa (92626-7331)
PHONE.................................800 279-9319
Sean Lucero,
Brad Hunt,
Louise Matthews, *Director*
EMP: 145 EST: 2014
SQ FT: 19,000
SALES (est): 1.4MM **Privately Held**
SIC: 7299 Personal document & information services

(P-13790)
REGENT CORP
Also Called: Piccadilly Inn
2305 W Shaw Ave, Fresno (93711-3411)
PHONE.................................559 226-3850
Lela Forstez, *General Mgr*
EMP: 50
SALES (est): 1.9MM **Privately Held**
WEB: www.regentcorp.com
SIC: 7299 Banquet hall facilities

(P-13791)
RETREAT & CONFERENCE CENTER
Also Called: De Lasalle Institute
4401 Redwood Rd, NAPA (94558-9708)
PHONE.................................707 252-3810
Linda Bausch, *Director*
Jennifer Contreras, *Administration*
EMP: 50 EST: 2001
SALES (est): 471.9K **Privately Held**
SIC: 7299 8661 Wedding chapel, privately operated; community church

(P-13792)
SALON TECHNIQUE
101 N Harbor Blvd, Fullerton (92832-3608)
PHONE.................................714 871-4247
Lynette Coryell, *Partner*
Pamela Coryell, *Partner*
EMP: 50
SALES: 1.4MM **Privately Held**
SIC: 7299 7231 Massage parlor; facial salons; hairdressers

(P-13793)
SAN MARCOS COUNTRY CLUB
Also Called: GORDON'S ON THE GREEN
1750 San Pablo Dr, San Marcos (92078-4718)
PHONE.................................760 744-9385
Ronald Frazer, *President*
EMP: 50
SALES: 15K **Privately Held**
SIC: 7299 Banquet hall facilities

(P-13794)
SKYPARK INC
Also Called: Airport Parking Services
1000 San Mateo Ave, San Bruno (94066-1594)
PHONE.................................650 875-6655
Fax: 650 873-7040
Kim Kasser, *President*
Joe Galligan, *Ch of Bd*
Joel Kull, *Treasurer*
Essayas Araya, *Office Mgr*
Shirley Krouse, *Admin Sec*
EMP: 75
SQ FT: 430,000
SALES (est): 5MM **Privately Held**
WEB: www.skypark.com
SIC: 7299 Valet parking

(P-13795)
SLC OPERATING LTD PARTNERSHIP
Also Called: Sheraton Universal Hotel
333 Unversal Hollywood Dr, North Hollywood (91608-1001)
PHONE.................................818 980-1212
Silvio Campos, *Branch Mgr*
Cesar Encarnacion, *Engineer*
EMP: 350
SALES (corp-wide): 14.4B **Publicly Held**
SIC: 7299 7011 6512 5813 Banquet hall facilities; hotels; nonresidential building operators; drinking places; eating places
HQ: Slc Operating Limited Partnership
2231 E Camelback Rd # 400
Phoenix AZ 85016

(P-13796)
SOIREE VALET PARKING SERVICE
1470 Howard St, San Francisco (94103-2523)
PHONE.................................415 284-9700
Fax: 415 284-9770
Jamie Dyos, *President*
Katie Dyos, *Business Dir*
EMP: 150
SQ FT: 3,000
SALES (est): 2.8MM **Privately Held**
WEB: www.soireevalet.com
SIC: 7299 7521 Personal item care & storage services; automobile parking

(P-13797)
SPARK NETWORKS INC (PA)
11150 Santa Monica Blvd # 600, Los Angeles (90025-0479)
PHONE.................................310 893-0550
Fax: 323 658-3001
Michael J McConnell, *Ch of Bd*
Michael S Egan, *CEO*
Robert W O'Hare, *CFO*
John R Volturo, *Chief Mktg Ofcr*
Gregory J Franchina, *CIO*
EMP: 98
SQ FT: 16,000
SALES (est): 48.1MM **Publicly Held**
WEB: www.spark.net
SIC: 7299 Dating service

(P-13798)
SPECTRUM BRANDS INC
Also Called: Spectrum Brands Hhi
19701 Da Vinci, Foothill Ranch (92610-2622)
PHONE.................................949 672-4003
Phil Szuba, *Senior VP*
Jan Van Leyen, *Manager*
EMP: 500
SALES (corp-wide): 5.8B **Publicly Held**
SIC: 7299 Home improvement & renovation contractor agency
HQ: Spectrum Brands, Inc.
3001 Deming Way
Middleton WI 53562
608 275-3340

(P-13799)
SPRIN NONPR CONSU CREDI MANAG
1605 Spruce St Ste 100, Riverside (92507-2400)
PHONE.................................951 684-3168
Lori Lamb, *Principal*
Shyam Medandrao, *Software Dev*
EMP: 350
SALES (corp-wide): 29MM **Privately Held**
SIC: 7299 Debt counseling or adjustment service, individuals
PA: Springboard Nonprofit Consumer Credit Management, Inc.
4351 Latham St
Riverside CA 92501
951 781-0114

(P-13800)
TURTLE ENTERTAINMENT AMERICA
Also Called: Esl
1212 Chestnut St, Burbank (91506-1627)
PHONE.................................818 861-7315
Han Park, *President*
Craig Levine, *Exec VP*
EMP: 50
SALES (est): 962K
SALES (corp-wide): 19.8MM **Privately Held**
SIC: 7299 Party planning service
PA: Turtle Entertainment Gmbh
Siegburger Str. 189
Koln 50679
221 880-4490

(P-13801)
UNIFIED VALET PARKING INC
99 S Chester Ave Fl 2, Pasadena (91106-5805)
PHONE.................................818 822-5807
Mike Madjid Sabet, *President*
EMP: 57 EST: 2009
SALES: 6.5MM **Privately Held**
SIC: 7299 Valet parking

(P-13802)
USA VALET PARKING LLC
980 9th St Ste 1620, Sacramento (95814-2719)
PHONE.................................916 792-1055
Steven Baver, *Mng Member*
EMP: 50
SALES: 126.9K **Privately Held**
SIC: 7299 7521 Valet parking; outdoor parking services

(P-13803)
VISIONEERING STUDIOS INC
2050 Main St Ste 400, Irvine (92614-8270)
P.O. Box 19700 (92623-9700)
PHONE.................................949 417-5800
Melvin E McGowan, *President*
John Parker, *COO*
Robert Bergmann, *Vice Pres*
Greg Ahmann, *Executive*
Steven A Chaparro, *Executive*
EMP: 75
SALES (est): 8.9MM **Privately Held**
SIC: 7299 Apartment locating service

(P-13804)
WATERCOURSE WAY
Also Called: Water Course Way
165 Channing Ave, Palo Alto (94301-2409)
PHONE.................................650 462-2000
Fax: 650 462-2020
John Roberts, *Partner*
Watercourse Way, *Partner*
EMP: 120
SALES (est): 3.8MM **Privately Held**
WEB: www.watercourseway.com
SIC: 7299 Massage parlor & steam bath services

(P-13805)
WESTERN COSTUME LEASING
11041 Vanowen St, North Hollywood (91605-6314)
PHONE.................................818 760-0900
Eddie Marks, *President*
Kristin Holbak, *Executive Asst*
EMP: 60
SQ FT: 150,000
SALES (est): 1.1MM
SALES (corp-wide): 6.5MM **Privately Held**
WEB: www.westerncostume.com
SIC: 7299 Costume rental
HQ: Western Costume Co.
11041 Vanowen St
North Hollywood CA 91605
818 760-0900

(P-13806)
Z VALET INC
Also Called: Z Valet & Shuttle Service
4221 Wilshire Blvd 170-11, Los Angeles (90010-3519)
PHONE.................................323 954-3700
Fax: 323 954-3733
Daniel Ziv, *President*
EMP: 225
SQ FT: 1,500
SALES (est): 4.9MM **Privately Held**
WEB: www.zvalet.com
SIC: 7299 7363 8748 Valet parking; chauffeur service; business consulting

7311 Advertising Agencies

(P-13807)
180LA LLC
1733 Ocean Ave Ste 400, Santa Monica (90401-3270)
PHONE.................................310 382-1400
Michael Allen, *Mng Member*
William Gelner, *Executive*
Adam Groves, *Creative Dir*
Pierre Janneau, *Creative Dir*

7311 - Advertising Agencies County (P-13808)

Karen Quinn, *Finance Dir*
EMP: 110
SQ FT: 13,000
SALES: 24.4MM
SALES (corp-wide): 15.1B **Publicly Held**
WEB: www.180la.com
SIC: 7311 Advertising agencies
HQ: Tbwa Worldwide Inc.
488 Madison Ave
New York NY 10022
212 804-1000

(P-13808)
72ANDSUNNY LLC
12101 Bluff Creek Dr, Playa Vista (90094-2627)
PHONE....................310 215-9009
Fax: 310 215-9012
John Boiler,
Sedef Onar, *Officer*
Josh Fell, *Creative Dir*
Eric Steele, *Creative Dir*
Kate Ruppert, *Office Mgr*
EMP: 140
SALES (est): 40.6MM **Privately Held**
SIC: 7311 Advertising agencies

(P-13809)
A S I CORPORATION
Also Called: Bridgford Foods
1308 N Patt St, Anaheim (92801-2551)
PHONE....................714 526-5533
Allan L Bridgford, *Chairman*
Robert E Schulze, *President*
Richard A Foster, *Bd of Directors*
Dan R Yost, *Senior VP*
Allan L Bridgeford, *Vice Pres*
EMP: 200
SQ FT: 95,000
SALES (est): 51.4MM
SALES (corp-wide): 133.8MM **Publicly Held**
WEB: www.bridgford.com
SIC: 7311 2711 Advertising consultant; newspapers
HQ: Bridgford Foods Corporation
1308 N Patt St
Anaheim CA 92801
714 526-5533

(P-13810)
AAAZA INC
3250 Wilshire Blvd # 1901, Los Angeles (90010-1609)
PHONE....................213 380-8333
Fax: 213 380-5331
Zan Ng, *CEO*
Jeanine Kim, *Shareholder*
Peter Huang, *President*
Ko Gibilterra, *Production*
Kevin Vu, *Mktg Dir*
EMP: 60
SQ FT: 3,000
SALES (est): 9.7MM **Privately Held**
WEB: www.aaaza.com
SIC: 7311 Advertising agencies

(P-13811)
ADCONION MEDIA INC (PA)
Also Called: Adconion Media Group
3301 Exposition Blvd Fl 1, Santa Monica (90404-5082)
PHONE....................310 382-5521
Kristian Wilson, *President*
Bruce Wiseman, *COO*
Ramazan Demir, *Officer*
Patrick Meininger, *Officer*
Glenn Lingle, *Sr Software Eng*
EMP: 75
SALES (est): 23.7MM **Privately Held**
SIC: 7311 Advertising agencies; advertising consultant

(P-13812)
ADLINK CABLE ADVERTISING LLC
11150 Santa Monica Blvd # 100, Los Angeles (90025-2398)
PHONE....................310 477-3994
Fax: 310 477-8139
Bob McCauley,
Bright Kim, *CFO*
Lisa Palmer, *General Mgr*
Andrew Sewall, *Sales Associate*
Tom Laky, *Director*
EMP: 120

SALES (est): 13.4MM **Privately Held**
WEB: www.adlink.com
SIC: 7311 Advertising agencies

(P-13813)
ADMARKETING INC
Also Called: Add Media
1801 Century Park E # 2100, Los Angeles (90067-2330)
PHONE....................310 203-8400
Fax: 310 277-7621
Jack Roth, *President*
Tim Balzer, *CFO*
Robert Roth, *Treasurer*
Marty Cagan, *Exec VP*
Dianne Thomas, *VP Mktg*
EMP: 55
SQ FT: 16,000
SALES (est): 12.4MM **Privately Held**
WEB: www.admarketingcreative.com
SIC: 7311 Advertising agencies

(P-13814)
ADROLL INC (PA)
972 Mission St Fl 3, San Francisco (94103-2992)
PHONE....................877 723-7655
Aaron Bell, *CEO*
Adam Berke, *President*
Peter Krivkovich, *COO*
Suresh Khanna, *Officer*
Neil Coleman, *Managing Dir*
EMP: 108
SALES (est): 29.7MM **Privately Held**
SIC: 7311 Advertising agencies

(P-13815)
AIRPUSH INC
11400 W Olympic Blvd, Los Angeles (90064-1550)
PHONE....................877 944-2490
Asher Delug, *CEO*
David K Awamoto, *President*
Shawn Sires, *President*
Inman Breaux, *COO*
Matt Shaw, *Officer*
EMP: 140
SALES (est): 18.4MM **Privately Held**
SIC: 7311 Advertising agencies

(P-13816)
ALCONE MARKETING GROUP INC (HQ)
Also Called: Jeep Gear
4 Studebaker, Irvine (92618-2012)
PHONE....................949 595-5322
Fax: 949 770-2957
William Hahn, *CEO*
Carolyn Capshaw, *Ch Credit Ofcr*
Sean Conciatore, *Ch Credit Ofcr*
Peter Viento, *Ch Credit Ofcr*
Jim Zebruski, *Chief Mktg Ofcr*
EMP: 100
SQ FT: 90,000
SALES (est): 28.8MM
SALES (corp-wide): 15.1B **Publicly Held**
WEB: www.alconemarketing.com
SIC: 7311 Advertising agencies
PA: Omnicom Group Inc.
437 Madison Ave
New York NY 10022
212 415-3600

(P-13817)
AVIA TECH LLC
7220 Trade St Ste 300, San Diego (92121-2334)
PHONE....................858 777-5000
Dwight Gould, *CEO*
Margaret McAllister, *Exec VP*
Chris Pravato, *Vice Pres*
Mark Royer, *CTO*
Cheryl Gould,
EMP: 56
SQ FT: 8,000
SALES (est): 10.2MM **Privately Held**
SIC: 7311 Advertising agencies

(P-13818)
AYZENBERG GROUP INC
49 E Walnut St, Pasadena (91103-3832)
PHONE....................626 584-4070
Fax: 626 584-3954
Eric Ayzenberg, *President*
Claudia Llanos, *CFO*
Steve Fowler, *Vice Pres*

Joey Jones, *Vice Pres*
Matt Rice, *Vice Pres*
EMP: 65
SQ FT: 10,000
SALES (est): 17.6MM **Privately Held**
WEB: www.ayzenberg.com
SIC: 7311 7336 Advertising consultant; commercial art & graphic design

(P-13819)
BBDO WORLDWIDE INC
600 California St Fl 8, San Francisco (94108-2726)
PHONE....................415 808-6200
Linda D Merrick, *Senior VP*
Steve Sanchez, *Senior VP*
Crockett Jeffers, *Creative Dir*
Amber Justis, *Creative Dir*
Linda Domercq, *Controller*
EMP: 60
SALES (corp-wide): 15.1B **Publicly Held**
WEB: www.bbdo.com
SIC: 7311 Advertising agencies
HQ: Bbdo Worldwide Inc.
1285 Ave Of The Amer
New York NY 10019
212 459-5000

(P-13820)
BDS MARKETING INC (PA)
10 Holland, Irvine (92618-2504)
PHONE....................949 472-6700
Fax: 949 597-2220
Mark Dean, *Principal*
Kristen Cook, *Managing Prtnr*
Kristen D Chatelets, *Chief Mktg Ofcr*
Mike Britton, *Exec VP*
Larry Dorr, *Vice Pres*
EMP: 120
SQ FT: 41,000
SALES (est): 120.9MM **Privately Held**
WEB: www.bdsmarketing.com
SIC: 7311 8743 8732 Advertising agencies; promotion service; commercial nonphysical research

(P-13821)
BRIGHTROLL INC (HQ)
343 Sansome St Ste 600, San Francisco (94104-5603)
PHONE....................415 677-9222
Fax: 415 677-0895
Tod Sacerdoti, *CEO*
Bruce Falck, *COO*
Ron Will, *CFO*
Christopher Amen-Kroeger, *Senior VP*
Tim Avila, *Senior VP*
EMP: 241
SALES (est): 78.5MM
SALES (corp-wide): 4.9B **Publicly Held**
WEB: www.brightroll.com
SIC: 7311 Advertising agencies
PA: Yahoo Inc.
701 First Ave
Sunnyvale CA 94089
408 349-3300

(P-13822)
BUTLER SHINE STERN PRTNERS LLC
Also Called: Bssp
20 Liberty Ship Way, Sausalito (94965-3312)
PHONE....................415 331-6049
Fax: 415 331-3524
Greg Stern,
Dennis Moore, *CFO*
Jordan Kretchmer, *Creative Dir*
Mark Winn, *Design Engr*
Cassandra Bates, *Mktg Dir*
EMP: 139
SALES (est): 46.3MM **Privately Held**
SIC: 7311 Advertising agencies

(P-13823)
CASANOVA PNDRILL PBLICIDAD INC (PA)
275 Mccormick Ave Ste 1a, Costa Mesa (92626-3325)
PHONE....................949 474-5001
Fax: 714 918-8295
Daniel Nance, *President*
Laura Marella, *Vice Pres*
Vivian Pagan, *Admin Asst*
Chantal Tran, *Accounting Mgr*
Pilar Matallana, *Prdtn Mgr*

EMP: 55
SQ FT: 12,000
SALES (est): 10.5MM **Privately Held**
WEB: www.casanova.com
SIC: 7311 Advertising agencies

(P-13824)
COLOR AD INC
18601 S Santa Fe Ave, Compton (90221-5901)
PHONE....................310 632-5500
Fax: 310 632-2300
Daryl Oldenkamp, *President*
Rose Oldenkamp, *Vice Pres*
EMP: 50
SQ FT: 33,000
SALES (est): 17.8MM **Privately Held**
WEB: www.gocolorad.com
SIC: 7311 2752 Advertising agencies; commercial printing, lithographic

(P-13825)
COMCAST SPOTLIGHT INC
50 Francisco St Fl 3, San Francisco (94133-2134)
PHONE....................415 675-2300
Jackie Canas, *Manager*
EMP: 90
SALES (corp-wide): 74.5B **Publicly Held**
WEB: www.cablecomcast.com
SIC: 7311 7313 Advertising agencies; television & radio time sales
HQ: Comcast Spotlight, Inc.
5 Times Sq
New York NY 10036
212 278-8156

(P-13826)
CONILL ADVERTISING INC
2101 Rosecrans Ave Fl 2, El Segundo (90245-4749)
PHONE....................424 290-4400
Carlos Martinez, *President*
Federico Duran, *Creative Dir*
Courtney Corbett, *Accounting Mgr*
Julia Sanchez, *Accounting Mgr*
Viviana Suarez, *Accounting Mgr*
EMP: 160
SQ FT: 18,000
SALES (est): 1.3MM **Privately Held**
SIC: 7311 Advertising agencies

(P-13827)
CONILL ADVERTISING INC
2101 Rosecrans Ave Fl 2, El Segundo (90245-4749)
PHONE....................424 290-4400
Fax: 310 214-6409
Carlos Martinez, *Manager*
Ana Rodriguez, *Vice Pres*
Sohemia Morales, *Executive Asst*
Beatrice S Rossi, *Accounting Mgr*
Delia Lopez, *Pub Rel Mgr*
EMP: 100
SQ FT: 30,000
SALES (corp-wide): 65.7MM **Privately Held**
WEB: www.conill-ideas.com
SIC: 7311 Advertising agencies
HQ: Conill Advertising, Inc.
800 Brickell Ave Ste 400
Miami FL 33131
305 351-2901

(P-13828)
CREW CREATIVE ADVERTISING LLC
7966 Beverly Blvd, Los Angeles (90048-4511)
PHONE....................310 451-3225
Damon Wolf, *Mng Member*
John Cain, *COO*
Andrew Crane, *Finance Dir*
Jennifer Cain,
Charles Reimers,
EMP: 165
SQ FT: 65,000
SALES (est): 10.7MM **Privately Held**
WEB: www.crewcreative.com
SIC: 7311 Advertising agencies

PRODUCTS & SERVICES SECTION

7311 - Advertising Agencies County (P-13850)

(P-13829)
D AUGUSTINE & ASSOCIATES
Also Called: Augustine Ideas
532 Gibson Dr Ste 250, Roseville (95678-5879)
PHONE 916 774-9600
Debra Augustine, *CEO*
Robert Nelson, *COO*
Marlene Navarro, *Executive*
Michael Mezzanotte, *Creative Dir*
Brian Carey, *Business Dir*
EMP: 52
SQ FT: 7,500
SALES: 9.7MM **Privately Held**
SIC: 7311 Advertising agencies

(P-13830)
DAILEY & ASSOCIATES
Also Called: Interpublic Group of Companies
8687 Melrose Ave Ste G300, Los Angeles (90069-5705)
PHONE 310 360-3100
Thomas Lehr, *CEO*
Michael Perdigao, *Managing Prtnr*
Eugene Alejo Jr, *CFO*
Helen Benaza, *CFO*
Jim Lorden, *Exec VP*
EMP: 100 EST: 1964
SALES (est): 27.2MM
SALES (corp-wide): 7.6B **Publicly Held**
WEB: www.daileyads.com
SIC: 7311 Advertising agencies
PA: The Interpublic Group Of Companies Inc
   909 3rd Ave Fl 7
   New York NY 10022
   212 704-1200

(P-13831)
DAVID & GOLIATH LLC
909 N Sepulveda Blvd # 700, El Segundo (90245-2724)
PHONE 310 445-5200
David Angelo, *Mng Member*
Brian Dunbar, *Managing Prtnr*
Colin Jeffery, *Managing Prtnr*
Jerry Duran, *CFO*
Mike Geiger, *Officer*
EMP: 130
SQ FT: 1,000
SALES (est): 31.8MM **Privately Held**
WEB: www.dngla.com
SIC: 7311 Advertising agencies

(P-13832)
DAVISELEN ADVERTISING INC (PA)
865 S Figueroa St # 1200, Los Angeles (90017-2543)
PHONE 213 688-7000
Mark Davis, *CEO*
Robert Elen, *President*
Steven Orenstein, *CFO*
Terry Sullivan, *CFO*
Terian Hughes, *Exec VP*
EMP: 172
SQ FT: 32,000
SALES (est): 37.7MM **Privately Held**
WEB: www.daviselen.com
SIC: 7311 Advertising agencies

(P-13833)
DAVISELEN ADVERTISING INC
420 Stevens Ave Ste 240, Solana Beach (92075-2079)
PHONE 858 847-0789
Fax: 858 847-0790
Jim Kelly, *Branch Mgr*
Jennifer Wiles, *Accounts Exec*
EMP: 61
SALES (corp-wide): 37.7MM **Privately Held**
SIC: 7311 Advertising consultant
PA: Daviselen Advertising, Inc.
   865 S Figueroa St # 1200
   Los Angeles CA 90017
   213 688-7000

(P-13834)
DDB WORLDWIDE
10960 Wilshire Blvd Fl 16, Los Angeles (90024-3802)
PHONE 310 907-1500
Fax: 310 907-1990
Nick Bishop, *Manager*
Joanne Howes, *Partner*
Darrell Loden, *Creative Dir*
Cherese Brown, *Human Res Mgr*
EMP: 175
SALES (corp-wide): 15.1B **Publicly Held**
SIC: 7311 Advertising agencies
HQ: Ddb Worldwide Communications Group, Inc.
   437 Madison Ave Fl 11
   New York NY 10022
   212 415-2000

(P-13835)
DDB WORLDWIDE
600 California St Fl 7, San Francisco (94108-2731)
PHONE 415 732-3600
Fax: 415 732-3636
Mary Moudry, *President*
Larissa Acosta, *Managing Prtnr*
Geoffrey Gougion, *Managing Dir*
Stefan Hawes, *Managing Dir*
Elizabeth Ross, *Managing Dir*
EMP: 160
SALES (corp-wide): 15.1B **Publicly Held**
SIC: 7311 Advertising consultant
HQ: Ddb Worldwide Communications Group, Inc.
   437 Madison Ave Fl 11
   New York NY 10022
   212 415-2000

(P-13836)
DEDICATED MEDIA INC (PA)
909 N Sepulveda Blvd # 320, El Segundo (90245-2734)
PHONE 310 524-9400
Scott Yamano, *CEO*
Chris Berman, *COO*
Ryan Becker, *Vice Pres*
Brian Malone, *Vice Pres*
Holly Martin, *Vice Pres*
EMP: 65
SQ FT: 45,000
SALES (est): 18.9MM **Privately Held**
WEB: www.dedicatedla.com
SIC: 7311 Advertising consultant

(P-13837)
DEUTSCH LA INC
5454 Beethoven St, Los Angeles (90066-7017)
PHONE 310 862-3000
Fax: 310 862-3100
Mike Sheldon, *CEO*
Brian McManus, *Vice Pres*
Dana Commandatore, *Creative Dir*
Gil Parkin, *Executive Asst*
Drew Brooks, *Graphic Designe*
EMP: 100
SALES (est): 37.5MM
SALES (corp-wide): 7.6B **Publicly Held**
SIC: 7311 Advertising agencies
PA: The Interpublic Group Of Companies Inc
   909 3rd Ave Fl 7
   New York NY 10022
   212 704-1200

(P-13838)
DGWB INC
Also Called: Dgwb Advg & Communications
217 N Main St Ste 200, Santa Ana (92701-4843)
PHONE 714 881-2300
Fax: 714 881-2443
Mike Wiseman, *CEO*
Mark Weinfeld, *Plan/Corp Dev D*
John Gothold, *Principal*
Sindy De Jong, *Executive Asst*
Cindy Melton, *Controller*
EMP: 70
SALES (est): 20.3MM **Privately Held**
SIC: 7311 Advertising consultant

(P-13839)
DGWB VENTURES LLC
Also Called: Advertising
217 N Main St Ste 200, Santa Ana (92701-4843)
PHONE 714 881-2308
Mike Weisman,
Jeanzaudre Vauderuil, *Sr Corp Ofcr*
Alma Gonsalez, *Office Mgr*
Joseph Servia, *Project Mgr*
Madeline Dossin,
EMP: 95
SQ FT: 25,839
SALES (est): 625.7K **Privately Held**
SIC: 7311 Advertising consultant

(P-13840)
DIRECT PARTNERS INC (HQ)
12777 W Jefferson Blvd # 120, Los Angeles (90066-7038)
PHONE 310 482-4200
Fax: 310 482-4201
Tom Harrison, *President*
Tom Parr, *CFO*
Hans Forsman, *Senior VP*
Jeff Braucher, *Vice Pres*
Edward J Gillespie, *Vice Pres*
EMP: 52
SQ FT: 31,000
SALES (est): 16.1MM
SALES (corp-wide): 15.1B **Publicly Held**
WEB: www.directpartners.com
SIC: 7311 Advertising agencies
PA: Omnicom Group Inc.
   437 Madison Ave
   New York NY 10022
   212 415-3600

(P-13841)
DOREMUS & COMPANY
550 3rd St, San Francisco (94107-1805)
PHONE 415 398-5699
Fax: 415 398-0854
Garrett Lawrence, *Manager*
Mike Goefft, *Exec Dir*
Thomas Lee, *Admin Asst*
Sal Allababidi, *Info Tech Mgr*
Eric Liu, *Graphic Designe*
EMP: 50
SALES (corp-wide): 15.1B **Publicly Held**
WEB: www.doremus.com
SIC: 7311 7319 Advertising agencies; sky writing
HQ: Doremus & Company
   200 Varick St Fl 11
   New York NY 10014
   212 366-3000

(P-13842)
ELEVEN INC
Also Called: Eleven Communications
500 Sansome St, San Francisco (94111-3211)
PHONE 415 707-1111
Fax: 415 707-1100
Courtney Buechert, *CEO*
Michael Borosky, *Partner*
Alison Fowler, *Partner*
Jarett Hausske, *Partner*
Mike McKay, *Partner*
EMP: 140
SALES (est): 48.1MM **Privately Held**
WEB: www.eleveninc.com
SIC: 7311 Advertising agencies

(P-13843)
ELEVEN AGENCY LLC
4 Studebaker, Irvine (92618-2012)
PHONE 949 679-1182
Graeme S Bradley,
Natalie Miller, *Accountant*
Jackie Kim, *Opers Staff*
Timothy C Regan,
Dana Twyman, *Director*
EMP: 50
SQ FT: 10,000
SALES (est): 8MM
SALES (corp-wide): 15.1B **Publicly Held**
WEB: www.elevenagency.com
SIC: 7311 Advertising agencies
PA: Omnicom Group Inc.
   437 Madison Ave
   New York NY 10022
   212 415-3600

(P-13844)
ENGAGE BDR INC
9000 W Sunset Blvd, West Hollywood (90069-5801)
PHONE 310 954-0751
Ted Dhanik, *President*
Kurtis Rintala, *COO*
Ryan Davidson, *Senior VP*
Ed Lee, *Senior VP*
Andy Dhanik, *Vice Pres*
EMP: 50
SALES (est): 175.4K **Privately Held**
SIC: 7311 Advertising agencies

(P-13845)
EPICENTRO ADVERTISING MKTG SVC
2370 Qume Dr Ste B, San Jose (95131-1842)
PHONE 408 453-0353
Maria Schabbing, *Owner*
EMP: 50
SALES (est): 4.7MM **Privately Held**
SIC: 7311 Advertising agencies

(P-13846)
EQAL INC
5250 Lankershim Blvd # 720, North Hollywood (91601-3188)
PHONE 818 276-6300
Miles Beckett, *CEO*
Greg Goodfried, *President*
Robert Weiss, *COO*
Tyler Rubin, *CFO*
Elizabeth Tomasulo, *Senior VP*
EMP: 216
SALES (est): 16.1MM
SALES (corp-wide): 231.9MM **Publicly Held**
SIC: 7311 Advertising consultant
PA: Everyday Health, Inc.
   345 Hudson St Rm 1600
   New York NY 10014
   646 728-9500

(P-13847)
EVANS HARDY & YOUNG INC
829 De La Vina St Ste 100, Santa Barbara (93101-3285)
PHONE 805 963-5841
Fax: 805 564-4279
Jim L Evans, *President*
Sue Andrews, *CFO*
Dennis Hardy, *Exec VP*
John O'Brien, *Senior VP*
John Stranger, *Vice Pres*
EMP: 50
SQ FT: 5,000
SALES (est): 11.3MM **Privately Held**
WEB: www.ehy.com
SIC: 7311 Advertising agencies

(P-13848)
EXPONENTIAL INTERACTIVE INC (HQ)
5858 Horton St Ste 300, Emeryville (94608-2183)
PHONE 510 250-5500
Dilip Dasilva, *President*
Marvin Tseu, *COO*
Tim Brown, *Officer*
Philip Buxton, *Officer*
Gill Brown, *Vice Pres*
EMP: 90 EST: 2000
SALES (est): 43.4MM
SALES (corp-wide): 6.8MM **Privately Held**
WEB: www.tribalfusion.com
SIC: 7311 Advertising agencies

(P-13849)
FCB WORLDWIDE INC
Also Called: Draftfcb
1160 Battery St Ste 250, San Francisco (94111-1216)
PHONE 415 820-8545
Ian Beavis, *Branch Mgr*
M B Bralye, *Associate Dir*
Tom Glowicki, *Info Tech Dir*
Ken Copen, *Prdtn Dir*
Joann Olsen, *Manager*
EMP: 524
SALES (corp-wide): 7.6B **Publicly Held**
SIC: 7311 Advertising agencies
HQ: Fcb Worldwide, Inc.
   100 W 33rd St Fl 5
   New York NY 10001
   212 885-3000

(P-13850)
FCB WORLDWIDE INC
1160 Battery St Ste 250, San Francisco (94111-1216)
PHONE 415 820-8000
Dominic Whittles, *President*
Kass Sells, *COO*
Tara Charf, *CFO*
Vicki Wagner, *Senior VP*
Brian Bacino, *Director*

7311 - Advertising Agencies County (P-13851)

PRODUDUCTS & SERVICES SECTION

EMP: 180
SALES (corp-wide): 7.6B Publicly Held
WEB: www.pezzano.com
SIC: 7311 Advertising agencies
HQ: Fcb Worldwide, Inc.
100 W 33rd St Fl 5
New York NY 10001
212 885-3000

(P-13851)
FORTY FOUR GROUP LLC
Also Called: Origaudio
16351 Gothard St Ste B, Huntington Beach (92647-3633)
PHONE...................................949 407-6360
Michael Szymczak,
Jason Lucash,
EMP: 58
SQ FT: 2,000
SALES (est): 275K Privately Held
SIC: 7311 7389 Advertising agencies;

(P-13852)
FULLSCREEN INC (HQ)
12180 Millennium Ste 100, Playa Vista (90094-2951)
PHONE...................................310 202-3333
George Strompolos, CEO
Jonathan Barr, Senior Partner
Ted Otte, Senior Partner
Damon Berger, President
Beau Bryant, Senior VP
EMP: 70 EST: 2011
SALES (est): 49.7MM
SALES (corp-wide): 1.2MM Privately Held
SIC: 7311 Advertising agencies
PA: Otter Media Holdings, Llc
12180 Millennium
Playa Vista CA 90094
310 202-3333

(P-13853)
GIANT CREATIVE STRATEGY LLC
1700 Montgomery St # 485, San Francisco (94111-1021)
PHONE...................................415 655-5200
Fax: 415 227-4464
Steven Gold, CEO
Alyse Sukalski, Managing Prtnr
Adam Gelling, President
Jeffrey Nemy, CFO
Eric Steckelman, Officer
EMP: 230
SQ FT: 24,000
SALES (est): 55.5MM Privately Held
WEB: www.giantagency.com
SIC: 7311 Advertising agencies; advertising consultant

(P-13854)
GL NEMIROW INC
Also Called: Terry Hines & Assoc
2550 N Hollywood Way, Burbank (91505-1055)
PHONE...................................818 562-9433
Fax: 818 562-9438
Grant W Nemirow, President
Ralph Terraciano, CFO
Paul Feldman, Administration
Norm Hayes, Technology
EMP: 97
SALES (est): 14MM Privately Held
WEB: www.thatrailers.com
SIC: 7311 Advertising agencies

(P-13855)
GL NEWMIROW INC
Also Called: Terry Hines & Assoicates
2550 N Hollywood Way, Burbank (91505-1055)
PHONE...................................818 562-9433
Fax: 323 562-9476
Renee Rascoe, President
Grant Nemirow, President
Jimmy Sogg, Vice Pres
Kristina Calas, Admin Asst
Paul Feldman, Info Tech Mgr
EMP: 100
SALES (est): 8.6MM Privately Held
SIC: 7311 Advertising agencies

(P-13856)
GOODBY SLVERSTEIN PARTNERS INC (HQ)
Also Called: Goodby Silverstein & Partners
720 California St, San Francisco (94108-2440)
PHONE...................................415 392-0669
Fax: 415 296-1628
Rich Silverstein, CEO
Robert Riccardi, Managing Prtnr
Derek Robson, Managing Prtnr
Jeff Goodby, President
Brady Baltezore, Creative Dir
EMP: 134
SQ FT: 60,000
SALES (est): 28.4MM
SALES (corp-wide): 15.1B Publicly Held
WEB: www.omnicomgroup.com
SIC: 7311 Advertising agencies
PA: Omnicom Group Inc.
437 Madison Ave
New York NY 10022
212 415-3600

(P-13857)
HAGGIN MARKETING INC (PA)
Also Called: Stereomax
100 Shoreline Hwy A200, Mill Valley (94941-3650)
PHONE...................................415 289-1110
Steve Freedman, President
Valter Calamita, CFO
Mike Wychcoki, Exec VP
Mike Lapchick, Senior VP
Betsy Wetthorn, Vice Pres
EMP: 170 EST: 2001
SQ FT: 33,000
SALES (est): 15.6MM Privately Held
WEB: www.hagginmarketing.com
SIC: 7311 Advertising consultant

(P-13858)
HAVAS EDGE LLC (PA)
2386 Faraday Ave Ste 200, Carlsbad (92008-7223)
PHONE...................................760 929-1357
Ron Bess, Mng Member
Greg Johnson, President
Dalton Mangin, President
Eric Bush, CFO
Shannon Ellis, Exec VP
EMP: 102
SALES (est): 28MM Privately Held
WEB: www.eurorscg-drtv.com
SIC: 7311 Advertising agencies

(P-13859)
HOBBS HERDER ADVERTISING
Also Called: Hobbs/Herder Training
419 Main St, Huntington Beach (92648-5199)
PHONE...................................800 999-6090
Fax: 949 515-5005
Greg Herder, Ch of Bd
John Surge, President
Dennis Leblanc, Vice Pres
Jack Desbouillons, Info Tech Dir
Monica St Duran, Info Tech Mgr
EMP: 85
SQ FT: 18,500
SALES (est): 13.3MM Privately Held
WEB: www.hobbsherder.com
SIC: 7311 Advertising agencies

(P-13860)
HVSF TRANSITION LLC
Also Called: Heat Ventures LLC
1100 Sansome St, San Francisco (94111-1205)
PHONE...................................415 477-1999
John Elder, President
Warren Cockrel, Creative Dir
EMP: 60
SQ FT: 12,000
SALES (est): 14.5MM
SALES (corp-wide): 9.5B Privately Held
WEB: www.sfheat.com
SIC: 7311 Advertising agencies
HQ: Deloitte Consulting Llp
30 Rockefeller Plz
New York NY 10112
212 492-4000

(P-13861)
I MEAN IT CREATIVE INC
10000 Venice Blvd, Culver City (90232-2720)
PHONE...................................310 287-1000
Emrah Yucel, President
EMP: 50
SALES (est): 8.5MM Privately Held
SIC: 7311 Advertising agencies

(P-13862)
IGNITE HEALTH LLC (PA)
7535 Irvine Center Dr # 200, Irvine (92618-4951)
PHONE...................................949 861-3200
Matt Brown, President
Brian Lefkowitz, Officer
Aj Triano, Vice Pres
Nico Coetzee, Finance
Richard E Fair,
EMP: 99
SQ FT: 15,000
SALES (est): 7.4MM Privately Held
WEB: www.ignitehealth.com
SIC: 7311 Advertising agencies

(P-13863)
IGNITED LLC (PA)
2150 Park Pl Ste 100, El Segundo (90245-4714)
PHONE...................................310 773-3100
Fax: 310 773-3101
Eric Johnson, CEO
William Rosenthal, COO
Dave Martin, Vice Pres
David Lock, Executive
Ted Williams, Technology
EMP: 115 EST: 1999
SQ FT: 55,000
SALES (est): 180MM Privately Held
WEB: www.ignitedminds.com
SIC: 7311 Advertising agencies

(P-13864)
INNOCEAN WRLDWIDE AMERICAS LLC (PA)
180 5th St Ste 200, Huntington Beach (92648-7107)
PHONE...................................714 861-5200
Yun Jong Beak, CFO
Cynthia Jensen, Senior VP
Fabrizia Cannalonga, Vice Pres
Jonathan Farjo, Vice Pres
Ben Gogley, Vice Pres
EMP: 140
SALES (est): 49.6MM Privately Held
WEB: www.worldmarketinggroup.com
SIC: 7311 Advertising agencies

(P-13865)
INTER/MEDIA TIME BUYING CORP (PA)
Also Called: Inter/Media Advertising
22120 Clarendon St # 300, Woodland Hills (91367-6315)
PHONE...................................818 995-1455
Fax: 818 995-6093
Robert B Yallen, President
James Christensen, Vice Pres
Malena Cruz, Vice Pres
Joseph Poulose, Vice Pres
Grant Rosenquist, Vice Pres
EMP: 80
SQ FT: 12,000
SALES (est): 25.6MM Privately Held
WEB: www.intermedia-advertising.com
SIC: 7311 Advertising agencies

(P-13866)
INTERACTIVE MEDIA HOLDINGS (PA)
Also Called: Viant
4 Park Plz Ste 1500, Irvine (92614-3516)
PHONE...................................949 861-8888
Timothy C Vanderhook, President
Chris Vanderhook, COO
Roy E Luna, CFO
Larry Madden, CFO
Jon Schulz, Exec VP
EMP: 56
SALES (est): 37.5MM Privately Held
SIC: 7311 7313 Advertising agencies; newspaper advertising representative

(P-13867)
INTERTREND COMMUNICATIONS INC
228 E Broadway, Long Beach (90802-4840)
PHONE...................................562 733-1888
Julia Huang, CEO
Susanna Jue, General Mgr
Jenny Wang, Planning Mgr
Stacy Liu, Executive Asst
Tate Allen, Administration
EMP: 70
SQ FT: 10,000
SALES (est): 17.3MM Privately Held
WEB: www.intertrend.com
SIC: 7311 Advertising agencies

(P-13868)
ISEARCH MEDIA LLC
1710 S Amphlett Blvd # 320, San Mateo (94402-2706)
PHONE...................................415 358-0882
Maury Domengeaux, CEO
Scott Rayden, President
Charles Hentrich, CTO
EMP: 66
SALES (est): 212.5K
SALES (corp-wide): 495.3MM Publicly Held
SIC: 7311 Advertising agencies
HQ: 3q Digital, Inc.
155 Bovet Rd Ste 480
San Mateo CA 94402
650 539-4124

(P-13869)
IW GROUP (PA)
8687 Melrose Ave Ste G540, West Hollywood (90069-5715)
PHONE...................................310 289-5500
Fax: 310 289-5501
Bill Imada, CEO
Nita Song, President
Tan Vu, Accounting Mgr
Mary Delacruz, Manager
Joanna Lin, Manager
EMP: 54
SQ FT: 7,500
SALES (est): 30MM Privately Held
WEB: www.iwgroupinc.com
SIC: 7311 8743 Advertising agencies; public relations services

(P-13870)
J WALTER THOMPSON USA LLC
303 2nd St, San Francisco (94107-1366)
PHONE...................................415 268-5555
Greg Rowan, Branch Mgr
EMP: 66
SALES (corp-wide): 18.4B Privately Held
SIC: 7311 Advertising agencies
HQ: J. Walter Thompson U.S.A., Llc
466 Lexington Ave Ste 6r
New York NY 10017
212 210-7000

(P-13871)
JACK MORTON WORLDWIDE INC
8687 Melrose Ave Ste G700, West Hollywood (90069-5721)
PHONE...................................310 967-2400
Fax: 310 967-2450
Gemma Roskam, Principal
Jodi Minehan, Mktg Coord
EMP: 53
SALES (corp-wide): 7.6B Publicly Held
SIC: 7311 7812 Advertising agencies; audio-visual program production
HQ: Jack Morton Worldwide Inc.
142 Berkeley St Ste 6
Boston MA 02116
617 585-7000

(P-13872)
KANE & FINKEL LLC
Also Called: Kane Fnkle Hlthcare Cmmnctions
534 4th St, San Francisco (94107-1621)
P.O. Box 128, Corte Madera (94976-0128)
PHONE...................................415 777-4990
Fax: 415 777-5019
Robert Finkel,
Lisa McMillan, Controller

PRODUCTS & SERVICES SECTION
7311 - Advertising Agencies County (P-13894)

John Kane,
Elisa Widjaja, *Art Dir*
EMP: 70 **EST:** 1997
SQ FT: 15,000
SALES (est): 10MM **Privately Held**
WEB: www.kaneandfinkel.com
SIC: 7311 Advertising agencies

(P-13873)
KATCH
2381 Rosecrans Ave # 400, El Segundo (90245-4917)
PHONE....................310 219-6200
Patrick Quigley, *CEO*
Patrick Cross, *Chief Mktg Ofcr*
Hector Hung, *Accountant*
Betsy Niksefat, *Controller*
Robert Chrone,
EMP: 70
SALES: 140MM **Privately Held**
WEB: www.vantagemedia.com
SIC: 7311 Advertising agencies

(P-13874)
KERN ORGANIZATION INC
Also Called: Kern Direct Marketing
20955 Warner Center Ln, Woodland Hills (91367-6511)
PHONE....................818 703-8775
Russell Kern, *President*
Ezequiel Ibarbia, *CFO*
Zeke Ibarbia, *CFO*
Steven Orenstein, *CFO*
David Azulay, *Senior VP*
EMP: 80
SQ FT: 11,350
SALES (est): 26.3MM
SALES (corp-wide): 15.1B **Publicly Held**
WEB: www.thekernorg.com
SIC: 7311 Advertising agencies
PA: Omnicom Group Inc.
437 Madison Ave
New York NY 10022
212 415-3600

(P-13875)
KOVEL/FULLER LLC
9925 Jefferson Blvd, Culver City (90232-3505)
PHONE....................310 841-4444
Fax: 310 841-4599
John Fuller, *President*
J Reilly, *Vice Pres*
Leila Reynolds, *Vice Pres*
Len Zimmelman, *Vice Pres*
Bob Dashtizad, *Executive*
EMP: 55
SQ FT: 40,000
SALES (est): 14.2MM **Privately Held**
WEB: www.kovelfuller.com
SIC: 7311 Advertising agencies

(P-13876)
LOCAL CORPORATION (PA)
Also Called: Local.com
7555 Irvine Center Dr, Irvine (92618-2930)
P.O. Box 50700 (92619-0700)
PHONE....................949 784-0800
Frederick G Thiel, *Ch of Bd*
Kenneth S Cragun, *CFO*
Scott Reinke, *Officer*
Erick Herring, *Senior VP*
Peter Hutto, *Senior VP*
EMP: 93 **EST:** 1999
SQ FT: 34,612
SALES: 83.1MM **Privately Held**
SIC: 7311 Advertising agencies

(P-13877)
LOS DEFENSORES INC
1010 S Cabrillo Ave, San Pedro (90731-4030)
PHONE....................310 519-4050
Mary Ann Walker, *President*
EMP: 50
SQ FT: 3,000
SALES (est): 3.6MM **Privately Held**
SIC: 7311 8111 Advertising agencies; general practice attorney, lawyer

(P-13878)
LOWCOM LLC
818 W 7th St Ste 700, Los Angeles (90017-3430)
PHONE....................213 408-0080
Lawrence Ng,

Fred Hsu,
Kia Singleton, *Manager*
EMP: 150
SALES (est): 9MM **Privately Held**
WEB: www.lowermybills.com
SIC: 7311 Advertising agencies

(P-13879)
MACHINTEL CORPORATION
4225 Executive Sq, La Jolla (92037-9122)
PHONE....................617 517-3090
Mark Choudhari, *Ch of Bd*
EMP: 60 **EST:** 2010
SALES (est): 3.2MM **Privately Held**
SIC: 7311 Advertising agencies

(P-13880)
MARTIN MEDIA INC (PA)
Also Called: Martini Media Network
415 Brannan St, San Francisco (94107-1703)
PHONE....................415 913-7446
Erik Pavelka, *CEO*
Tom Oregan, *President*
Gagan Saksena, *Officer*
Bill Rowley, *Senior VP*
JD Ambati, *Vice Pres*
EMP: 50
SALES (est): 12.4MM **Privately Held**
SIC: 7311 Advertising agencies

(P-13881)
MCCANN WORLD GROUP INC (PA)
Also Called: Universal McCann
653 Front St, San Francisco (94111-1913)
PHONE....................415 262-5500
Daryl Lee, *CEO*
Sarah Personette, *President*
Gary Barsky, *Senior VP*
Loukia Brattain, *Senior VP*
Stacy Malone, *Senior VP*
EMP: 70 **EST:** 2009
SALES (est): 17MM **Privately Held**
SIC: 7311 Advertising agencies

(P-13882)
MCCANN-ERICKSON CORPORATION (HQ)
135 Main St Fl 21, San Francisco (94105-8115)
PHONE....................415 348-5600
Don Hov, *CFO*
Hans Ullmark, *Div Sub Head*
Bettsy Sperry, *Managing Dir*
Pierrette Fleury, *Accounting Mgr*
Fred Raimondo, *Director*
EMP: 100
SQ FT: 37,000
SALES (est): 15.8MM
SALES (corp-wide): 7.6B **Publicly Held**
SIC: 7311 Advertising agencies
PA: The Interpublic Group Of Companies Inc
909 3rd Ave Fl 7
New York NY 10022
212 704-1200

(P-13883)
MEA DIGITAL WORX LLC
Also Called: Piston Agency
530 B St Ste 1900, San Diego (92101-4472)
PHONE....................619 238-8923
Michael Chaney, *CEO*
John Hartman, *President*
Andrew Resnick, *CFO*
Megan Black, *Vice Pres*
Colin Ayres, *Creative Dir*
EMP: 50
SALES (est): 13.2MM **Privately Held**
WEB: www.meadigital.com
SIC: 7311 8742 Advertising agencies; marketing consulting services

(P-13884)
MEDIAPLEX INC (DH)
30699 Russell Ranch Rd # 250, Westlake Village (91362-7315)
PHONE....................818 575-4500
Gregory R Raifman, *Ch of Bd*
Costa John, *COO*
Francis P Patchel, *CFO*
Ruiqing Jiang, *CTO*
Mark Joseph, *CTO*
EMP: 100

SALES (est): 5.1MM
SALES (corp-wide): 6.4B **Publicly Held**
WEB: www.mediaplex.com
SIC: 7311 Advertising agencies
HQ: Conversant, Llc
30699 Russell Ranch Rd # 250
Westlake Village CA 91362
818 575-4500

(P-13885)
MENDELSOHN/ZIEN ADVG LLC
11901 Santa Monica Blvd # 618, Los Angeles (90025-2767)
PHONE....................310 444-1990
Fax: 310 444-9888
Richard Zien,
Melissa Cottingham, *Producer*
Jordin Mendelsohn,
EMP: 75 **EST:** 1982
SQ FT: 7,000
SALES (est): 10.8MM
SALES (corp-wide): 10.3B **Privately Held**
WEB: www.mzad.com
SIC: 7311 Advertising agencies
HQ: Hakuhodo Incorporated
5-3-1, Akasaka
Minato-Ku TKY 107-0
364 418-111

(P-13886)
METRO ONE TELECOM INC
4900 Rivergrade Rd B210, Irwindale (91706-1401)
PHONE....................626 337-8100
Fax: 626 337-8347
Gary Brent, *Manager*
EMP: 150
SALES (corp-wide): 37.1MM **Publicly Held**
WEB: www.metro1.com
SIC: 7311 7389 Advertising agencies; telephone services
PA: Metro One Telecommunications, Inc.
1331 Nw Lovejoy St # 900
Portland OR 97209
503 643-9500

(P-13887)
MOB SCENE LLC
Also Called: Mob Scene Creative Productions
8447 Wilshire Blvd # 100, Beverly Hills (90211-3228)
PHONE....................323 648-7200
Fax: 310 286-2234
Brian Daly,
Matt McDonald, *Creative Dir*
Michelle Holt, *Controller*
Tom Grane,
Laney Gutstein,
EMP: 65
SALES: 16.1MM **Privately Held**
WEB: www.mobscene.com
SIC: 7311 7929 3993 7812 Advertising agencies; entertainment service; advertising artwork; television film production

(P-13888)
MYPOINTSCOM LLC (HQ)
Also Called: My Points.com
44 Montgomery St Ste 250, San Francisco (94104-4630)
PHONE....................415 615-1100
Fax: 415 829-6122
Jeff Goldstein, *CFO*
Mark Harrington, *Exec VP*
Edward Zinser, *Exec VP*
Seth Barnes, *Senior VP*
John Heffernan, *Senior VP*
EMP: 60
SALES (est): 10.9MM
SALES (corp-wide): 50.8MM **Privately Held**
WEB: www.mypoints.com
SIC: 7311 Advertising agencies
PA: Prodege, Llc
100 N Sepulveda Blvd Fl 8
El Segundo CA 90245
310 294-9599

(P-13889)
OGILVY & MATHER WORLDWIDE INC
2425 Olympic Blvd 2200w, Santa Monica (90404-4095)
PHONE....................310 280-2200
Hugh Branigan, *Sales & Mktg St*

Richard Salas, *Office Mgr*
Ruth Fogleman, *Executive Asst*
Jerry McGee, *Manager*
Sam Pierce, *Account Dir*
EMP: 75
SALES (corp-wide): 18.4B **Privately Held**
SIC: 7311 Advertising agencies
HQ: Ogilvy & Mather Worldwide, Inc.
636 11th Ave
New York NY 10036
212 237-4000

(P-13890)
ONE PLANET OPS INC (PA)
12667 Alcosta Blvd # 200, San Ramon (94583-5272)
PHONE....................925 983-3400
Payam Zamani, *CEO*
Debi Coleman, *Ch of Bd*
Chris Cooley, *Vice Pres*
Nina Chow, *Executive Asst*
Minh Le, *Software Dev*
EMP: 121
SALES (est): 52.5MM **Privately Held**
WEB: www.reply.com
SIC: 7311 Advertising agencies

(P-13891)
OPENX TECHNOLOGIES INC (DH)
888 E Walnut St Fl 2, Pasadena (91101-1897)
PHONE....................855 673-6948
Tim Cadogan, *CEO*
John Gentry, *President*
Tom Fuelling, *CFO*
Deborah Roth, *Ch Credit Ofcr*
Tish Whitcraft, *Ch Credit Ofcr*
EMP: 148
SALES (est): 99.7MM
SALES (corp-wide): 141.2MM **Privately Held**
SIC: 7311 Advertising agencies
HQ: Openx Limited
1 Maple Place
London W1T 4
800 587-3690

(P-13892)
ORGANIC HOLDINGS INC
Also Called: Organic On
600 California St Fl 8, San Francisco (94108-2726)
PHONE....................415 581-5300
Jonathan Nelson, *CEO*
Deborah Charapaty, *Officer*
Tom Weisz, *Officer*
EMP: 350
SALES (est): 24MM **Privately Held**
SIC: 7311 7374 8742 7375 Advertising consultant; computer graphics service; management consulting services; information retrieval services

(P-13893)
OVERSEENET (PA)
550 S Hope St Ste 200, Los Angeles (90071-2672)
PHONE....................213 408-0080
Debra Domeyer, *CEO*
Lawrence Ng, *President*
Dwayne Walker, *President*
Elizabeth Murray, *CFO*
Gene Chuang, *CTO*
EMP: 170
SQ FT: 54,000
SALES (est): 25.4MM **Privately Held**
WEB: www.oversee.net
SIC: 7311 Advertising agencies

(P-13894)
PEREIRA & ODELL LLC (PA)
215 2nd St Ste 100, San Francisco (94105-3141)
PHONE....................415 284-9916
Nancy Daum, *CFO*
Andrew O'Dell, *CEO*
Nancy Ruggeiro, *COO*
Pj Pereira, *Ch Credit Ofcr*
Joshua Brandau, *Vice Pres*
EMP: 81
SALES (est): 20MM **Privately Held**
WEB: www.pereiraodell.com
SIC: 7311 Advertising agencies

7311 - Advertising Agencies County (P-13895)
PRODUCTS & SERVICES SECTION

(P-13895)
PETROL ADVERTISING INC
443 N Varney St, Burbank (91502-1733)
PHONE..................323 644-3720
Alan J Hunter, *President*
Karl Stewart, *Partner*
Ben Granados, *Senior VP*
Art Babayan, *Vice Pres*
Simon Bollier, *Creative Dir*
EMP: 70
SALES (est): 17MM **Privately Held**
WEB: www.foodallergycure.com
SIC: 7311 Advertising agencies

(P-13896)
PHELPS GROUP
12121 W Bluff Dr Ste 200, Los Angeles (90094)
PHONE..................310 752-4400
Joe Phelps, *CEO*
Ed Chambliss, *President*
Schieke Glen, *COO*
Glenn Schieke, *COO*
Bob Berry, *CFO*
EMP: 65
SQ FT: 17,000
SALES (est): 21.2MM **Privately Held**
WEB: www.phelpsgroup.com
SIC: 7311 Advertising agencies

(P-13897)
POP-TENT INC
34221 Golden Lantern St # 202, Dana Point (92629-2850)
PHONE..................949 313-7160
Rick Parkhill, *Chairman*
Andrew Jedynak, *CEO*
Sandy Dondici, *COO*
Tony Romeo, *Exec VP*
Dave Mann, *Vice Pres*
EMP: 55
SALES (est): 6.7MM **Privately Held**
SIC: 7311 Advertising agencies

(P-13898)
PORTER CRISPIN & BOGUSKY LLC
2110 Colorado Ave Ste 200, Santa Monica (90404-3763)
PHONE..................305 859-2070
Ryan Skubic, *Manager*
Kent Carmichael, *Creative Dir*
Kat Street, *Graphic Designe*
Meredith Schneider, *Recruiter*
Darryl Tait, *QC Mgr*
EMP: 125
SALES (corp-wide): 1.3B **Publicly Held**
SIC: 7311 Advertising agencies
HQ: Crispin Porter & Bogusky Llc
3390 Mary St Ste 300
Miami FL 33133
305 859-2070

(P-13899)
POSTAER RUBIN AND ASSOCIATES (PA)
Also Called: R P Direct
2525 Colorado Ave Ste 100, Santa Monica (90404-5576)
PHONE..................310 394-4000
Fax: 310 260-4622
Willam C Hagelstein, *CEO*
Gerrold R Rubin, *Ch of Bd*
Gus Campos, *President*
Vincent Mancuso, *CFO*
Larry Postaer, *Exec VP*
EMP: 148
SQ FT: 130,000
SALES (est): 76.4MM **Privately Held**
SIC: 7311 Advertising agencies

(P-13900)
PRICE ASSOCIATES
Also Called: Price, Stuart
15760 Ventura Blvd # 1100, Encino (91436-3000)
PHONE..................818 995-9216
Stuart Price, *Owner*
Karen Tahler, *Opers Staff*
Mari Cervantes, *Legal Staff*
EMP: 50
SALES (est): 4.3MM **Privately Held**
SIC: 7311 Advertising agencies

(P-13901)
PUBLICIS & HAL RINEY (HQ)
2001 The Embarcadero, San Francisco (94133-5200)
PHONE..................415 981-0950
Fax: 415 955-4267
Kristi Vandenbosch, *CEO*
Lyn Muegge, *CFO*
Debbie Chin, *Vice Pres*
Cornelia Enders, *Vice Pres*
Mark Sweeney, *Vice Pres*
EMP: 120
SQ FT: 60,000
SALES (est): 11.4MM
SALES (corp-wide): 65.7MM **Privately Held**
WEB: www.hrp.com
SIC: 7311 Advertising agencies
PA: Publicis Groupe S A
133 Avenue Des Champs Elysees
Paris 75008
144 437-000

(P-13902)
PUBMATIC INC (PA)
305 Main St Fl 1, Redwood City (94063-1729)
PHONE..................650 351-9162
Fax: 650 331-2810
Rajeev Goel, *CEO*
Amar Goel, *Ch of Bd*
Mukul Kumar, *President*
Kirk McDonald, *President*
Steve Pantelick, *CFO*
EMP: 99
SQ FT: 4,000
SALES (est): 76.6MM **Privately Held**
SIC: 7311 Advertising agencies

(P-13903)
QUAD/GRAPHICS INC
Also Called: Sacramento Div
1201 Shore St, West Sacramento (95691-3510)
PHONE..................916 371-9500
Dan Coffee, *Administration*
Barbara Callaghan, *Human Res Dir*
Barbara Callahan, *Human Res Mgr*
Bob Boone, *Opers Mgr*
CAM McAtee, *Mfg Staff*
EMP: 250
SALES (corp-wide): 4.6B **Publicly Held**
WEB: www.vertisinc.com
SIC: 7311 2759 2752 Advertising agencies; commercial printing; commercial printing, lithographed
PA: Quad/Graphics Inc.
N61w23044 Harrys Way
Sussex WI 53089
414 566-6000

(P-13904)
QUIGLY-SIMPSON HEPPELWHITE INC
11601 Wilshire Blvd, Los Angeles (90025-0509)
PHONE..................818 444-3450
Angela Zepeda, *CEO*
Renee Hill, *COO*
Renee Hill Young, *COO*
Kathryn Browne, *CFO*
Duryea Ruffins, *Exec VP*
EMP: 100
SQ FT: 10,500
SALES (est): 32MM **Privately Held**
WEB: www.quigleysimpson.com
SIC: 7311 Advertising agencies

(P-13905)
RANKER INC
6420 Wilshire Blvd # 880, Los Angeles (90048-5538)
PHONE..................323 782-1448
Clark Benson, *CEO*
EMP: 50
SALES (est): 1.7MM **Privately Held**
SIC: 7311 Advertising consultant

(P-13906)
RAPP WORLDWIDE INC
12777 W Jefferson Blvd, Los Angeles (90066-7048)
PHONE..................310 563-7200
Collins Rapp, *Branch Mgr*
Dave Churilla, *Art Dir*
EMP: 100

SALES (corp-wide): 15.1B **Publicly Held**
SIC: 7311 Advertising agencies
HQ: Rapp Worldwide Inc.
437 Madison Ave
New York NY 10022
212 817-6800

(P-13907)
REACHLOCAL INC (HQ)
21700 Oxnard St Ste 1600, Woodland Hills (91367-7586)
PHONE..................818 274-0260
Fax: 818 708-2467
Sharon T Rowlands, *CEO*
Ross G Landsbaum, *CFO*
Kris Barton,
Becky Grosser, *Senior VP*
Scott Whitt, *Vice Pres*
EMP: 148
SQ FT: 38,592
SALES: 382.6MM
SALES (corp-wide): 5.7B **Publicly Held**
SIC: 7311 7375 Advertising agencies; on-line data base information retrieval
PA: Gannett Co., Inc.
7950 Jones Branch Dr
Mc Lean VA 22102
703 854-6000

(P-13908)
REAL BRANDING LLC
77 Maiden Ln Fl 4, San Francisco (94108-5426)
PHONE..................415 522-1516
Steve Raives,
Mark Olsen, *Controller*
Christopher Compton, *Marketing Staff*
Pat Hagerman,
Mark Silva,
EMP: 50
SALES (est): 4.9MM **Privately Held**
WEB: www.realbranding.com
SIC: 7311 Advertising agencies

(P-13909)
RED DOOR INTERACTIVE INC (PA)
350 10th Ave Ste 100, San Diego (92101-8706)
PHONE..................619 398-2670
Fax: 619 398-2671
Reid Carr, *CEO*
Amy Carr, *CFO*
Josh Fleming, *Web Dvlpr*
Andrew Bower, *Opers Staff*
Whitney Gandara, *Marketing Staff*
EMP: 57
SQ FT: 10,167
SALES (est): 17MM **Privately Held**
WEB: www.alliancelumber.com
SIC: 7311 Advertising agencies

(P-13910)
RED SKY INTERACTIVE
201 Mission St Fl 8, San Francisco (94105-1834)
PHONE..................415 430-3200
Tim Smith, *CEO*
Howard Belk, *President*
Robert Murray, *CTO*
EMP: 110
SALES (est): 7MM **Privately Held**
SIC: 7311 Advertising agencies

(P-13911)
REMITWARE PAYMENTS INC
2600 El Camino Real, Palo Alto (94306-1705)
PHONE..................650 843-9192
Rajiv Parikh, *CEO*
EMP: 170
SALES (est): 2.9MM **Privately Held**
SIC: 7311 Advertising agencies

(P-13912)
RICHARDS GROUP INC
Also Called: Metro Pcs
888 S Figueroa St # 1400, Los Angeles (90017-5449)
PHONE..................214 891-5700
Gene Howe, *Owner*
EMP: 175
SALES (corp-wide): 118.5MM **Privately Held**

PA: The Richards Group Inc
2801 N Cntl Expy Ste 100
Dallas TX 75204
214 891-5700

(P-13913)
ROCKET FUEL INC (PA)
1900 Seaport Blvd, Redwood City (94063-5587)
PHONE..................650 595-1300
Fax: 650 595-1274
E Randolph Wootton III, *CEO*
Rex S Jackson, *CFO*
Rick Song, *Officer*
Richard A Frankel, *Exec VP*
Joann C Covington, *Senior VP*
EMP: 148
SQ FT: 140,000
SALES: 461.6MM **Publicly Held**
SIC: 7311 Advertising agencies

(P-13914)
ROE HOLDINGS LLC
8437 Warner Dr, Culver City (90232-2428)
PHONE..................310 559-9222
Adam Roe, *Partner*
Lorraine Dahlinger, *Partner*
EMP: 62
SQ FT: 13,000
SALES (est): 5.2MM **Privately Held**
SIC: 7311 Advertising agencies

(P-13915)
RUBICON PROJECT INC (PA)
12181 Bluff Creek Dr Fl 4, Los Angeles (90094-3234)
PHONE..................310 207-0272
Fax: 310 207-0528
Frank Addant, *Ch of Bd*
Gregory R Raifman, *President*
David L Day, *Officer*
Adam Chandler, *Senior VP*
Mari Kim Novak, *Senior VP*
EMP: 120
SQ FT: 47,000
SALES: 248.4MM **Publicly Held**
SIC: 7311 Advertising agencies

(P-13916)
RUNYON SALTZMAN EINHORN INC
Also Called: Rse
2020 L St Ste 100, Sacramento (95811-4260)
PHONE..................916 446-9900
Fax: 916 446-3619
Christopher Holben, *President*
Estelle Saltzman, *Ch of Bd*
Jane Einhorn, *Senior VP*
Paul McClure, *Vice Pres*
Scott Rose, *Vice Pres*
EMP: 65
SQ FT: 14,000
SALES: 39MM **Privately Held**
WEB: www.rs-e.com
SIC: 7311 8743 Advertising agencies; public relations & publicity

(P-13917)
RW LYNCH CO INC (PA)
2333 San Ramon Valley Blv, San Ramon (94583-4429)
P.O. Box 5159 (94583-5159)
PHONE..................925 837-3877
Fax: 925 837-4734
Randall W Lynch, *CEO*
Brian Lynch, *President*
Stephen Grazzini, *CFO*
C L Darrow, *Admin Sec*
Ed Holtz, *Business Mgr*
EMP: 58
SQ FT: 19,000
SALES (est): 20MM **Privately Held**
WEB: www.lawonline.com
SIC: 7311 Advertising agencies

(P-13918)
SAATCHI & SAATCHI N AMER INC
Team One Advertising
13031 W Jefferson Blvd, Los Angeles (90094-7000)
PHONE..................310 437-2500
Brian Sheesan, *CEO*
Amanda Taft, *President*
Leonard Pearlstein, *Info Systems*

PRODUCTS & SERVICES SECTION

7311 - Advertising Agencies County (P-13941)

Lew Katz, *Finance*
Ellen F November, *Director*
EMP: 250
SALES (corp-wide): 65.7MM **Privately Held**
WEB: www.saatchila.com
SIC: 7311 Advertising agencies
HQ: Saatchi & Saatchi North America, Inc.
375 Hudson St Fl 16
New York NY 10014
212 463-2000

(P-13919)
SEARCH AGENCY INC (PA)
11150 W Olym Blvd Ste 600, Los Angeles (90064)
PHONE 310 582-5706
David Hughes, *CEO*
Barbra Palmer, *President*
Matt Kain, *CEO*
Peter Harington, *CFO*
Brian McCarthy, *Senior VP*
EMP: 55
SALES (est): 15.6MM **Privately Held**
SIC: 7311

(P-13920)
SHARETHIS INC (PA)
4005 Miranda Ave Ste 100, Palo Alto (94304-1221)
PHONE 650 641-0191
Tim Schigel, *Ch of Bd*
Kurt Abrahamson, *CEO*
Matt Gallatin, *CFO*
Beezer Clarkson, *Bd of Directors*
Julie Greenhouse, *Senior VP*
EMP: 50 **EST:** 2004
SALES (est): 14.7MM **Privately Held**
SIC: 7311 7313 7372 Advertising agencies; electronic media advertising representatives; prepackaged software

(P-13921)
SIERRA WEATHERIZATION CO INC
43 E Main St Ste B, Los Gatos (95030-6907)
PHONE 408 354-1900
Peter Hofmann, *President*
Amy Diffenderfer, *Corp Secy*
EMP: 99
SALES: 12MM **Privately Held**
SIC: 7311 Advertising agencies

(P-13922)
SOLUTION SET LLC
100 Montgomery St # 1500, San Francisco (94104-4300)
PHONE 415 367-6300
Fax: 415 367-6301
Tim Ross, *CEO*
Christopher R Averill, *CFO*
Libby Demeo, *Senior VP*
Adam Trissel, *Vice Pres*
Roland Ambrose, *Creative Dir*
EMP: 200
SALES (est): 37.2MM
SALES (corp-wide): 6.4B **Publicly Held**
SIC: 7311 Advertising agencies
HQ: Hyper Marketing Incorporated
104 S Michigan Ave # 1500
Chicago IL
312 263-2558

(P-13923)
STEEL HOUSE INC
3644 Eastham Dr, Culver City (90232-2411)
PHONE 310 773-3331
Mark Douglas, *CEO*
Ted Rupp, *Senior VP*
Vin Bhardwaj, *Vice Pres*
Lindsey Breeden, *Vice Pres*
Chris Innes, *Vice Pres*
EMP: 51 **EST:** 2009
SALES (est): 12.7MM **Privately Held**
SIC: 7311 Advertising agencies

(P-13924)
STUDIO 13
800 S Pacific Coast Hwy # 8, Redondo Beach (90277-4700)
PHONE 310 837-8107
Dale Bowman, *President*
Marie Naron, *President*
EMP: 50

SALES (est): 5.8MM **Privately Held**
WEB: www.danse-studio13.com
SIC: 7311 Advertising agencies

(P-13925)
SUISSA MILLER ADVERTISING LLC
8687 Melrose Ave, West Hollywood (90069-5701)
PHONE 310 392-9666
David Suissa,
Nobbie Kim, *Production*
Bruce Miller,
EMP: 100
SQ FT: 40,000
SALES (est): 5.2MM **Privately Held**
SIC: 7311

(P-13926)
TAPJOY INC (PA)
111 Sutter St Fl 13, San Francisco (94104-4541)
PHONE 415 766-6900
Fax: 415 296-9007
Steve Wadsworth, *President*
Matthew Service, *COO*
Al Wood, *CFO*
George Garrick, *Chairman*
Peter Dille, *Chief Mktg Ofcr*
EMP: 54 **EST:** 2007
SALES (est): 18MM **Privately Held**
SIC: 7311 Advertising agencies

(P-13927)
TBWA WORLDWIDE INC
Also Called: Media Arts Lab
12539 Beatrice St, Los Angeles (90066-7001)
PHONE 310 305-4400
Larry Kelly, *Owner*
Paul Wysocan, *Art Dir*
EMP: 133
SALES (corp-wide): 15.1B **Publicly Held**
SIC: 7311 Advertising agencies
HQ: Tbwa Worldwide Inc.
488 Madison Ave
New York NY 10022
212 804-1000

(P-13928)
TMP WORLDWIDE ADVERTISING & CO
330 N Brand Blvd Ste 1050, Glendale (91203-2875)
PHONE 818 539-2000
Fax: 818 539-2112
Gretchen Edwards, *Vice Pres*
Wendy De Haas, *Manager*
EMP: 74
SALES (corp-wide): 122.3MM **Privately Held**
SIC: 7311 Advertising agencies
PA: Tmp Worldwide Advertising & Communications, Llc
125 Broad St Fl 10
New York NY 10004
646 613-2000

(P-13929)
TRADE DESK INC (PA)
Also Called: Thetradedesk
42 N Chestnut St, Ventura (93001-2662)
PHONE 805 585-3434
Jeff T Green, *President*
Robert D Perdue, *COO*
Paul E Ross, *CFO*
Brian J Stempeck, *Ch Credit Ofcr*
David R Pickles, *CTO*
EMP: 79
SQ FT: 12,200
SALES: 113.8MM **Publicly Held**
SIC: 7311 Advertising agencies

(P-13930)
TRAILER PARK INC
6922 Hollywood Blvd # 1200, Los Angeles (90028-6132)
PHONE 310 845-8400
Joel Johnston, *President*
Neal Spector, *Exec VP*
Denise Baldwin, *Administration*
EMP: 60
SALES (corp-wide): 41.9MM **Privately Held**
SIC: 7311 7812 Advertising agencies; motion picture & video production

PA: Trailer Park, Inc.
6922 Hollywood Blvd Fl 12
Los Angeles CA 90028
310 845-3000

(P-13931)
TRAILER PARK INC (PA)
6922 Hollywood Blvd Fl 12, Los Angeles (90028-6132)
P.O. Box 2950 (90078-2950)
PHONE 310 845-3000
Tim Nett, *President*
James Hale, *Shareholder*
Doug Troy, *COO*
Bob Bouknight, *Senior VP*
Chris Park, *Senior VP*
EMP: 100
SQ FT: 8,000
SALES (est): 43.1MM **Privately Held**
SIC: 7311 Advertising agencies

(P-13932)
UNDERGROUND ELEPHANT INC
600 B St Ste 1300, San Diego (92101-4588)
PHONE 800 466-4178
Jason Kulpa, *President*
Lauren Alexander, *Chief Mktg Ofcr*
Nicole McGuire, *Senior VP*
John Todd, *Senior VP*
Lindsay Estrada, *Vice Pres*
EMP: 100
SQ FT: 14,000
SALES (est): 25.8MM **Privately Held**
SIC: 7311 7371 Advertising agencies; computer software development

(P-13933)
UPWORK INC (PA)
Also Called: Elance-Odesk
441 Logue Ave Ste 150, Mountain View (94043-4018)
PHONE 650 316-7500
Fax: 650 316-7501
Stephane Kasriel, *Vice Pres*
Raymond J Lane, *Ch of Bd*
Murali Murugan, *President*
Servaes Tholen, *CFO*
Rich Pearson, *Chief Mktg Ofcr*
EMP: 55
SQ FT: 20,000
SALES (est): 28.9MM **Privately Held**
WEB: www.elance.com
SIC: 7311 Advertising agencies

(P-13934)
US INTERACTIVE CORP DELAWARE
1270 Oakmead Pkwy Ste 318, Sunnyvale (94085-4044)
PHONE 408 863-7500
Sunil Mathur, *Branch Mgr*
Sunanda Kothapalli, *Office Mgr*
EMP: 130
SALES (corp-wide): 10.2MM **Privately Held**
SIC: 7311 Advertising consultant
PA: U.S. Interactive Corp Delaware
1270 Oakmead Pkwy Ste 318
Sunnyvale CA 94085
408 863-7500

(P-13935)
VENABLES/BELL & PARTNERS LLC
Also Called: Vbp Orange
201 Post St Fl 2, San Francisco (94108-5027)
PHONE 415 288-3300
Fax: 415 421-3683
Paul Venables, *Mng Member*
Gary Brown, *CFO*
Harley Griffiths, *Senior VP*
Will McGinness, *Creative Dir*
Erich Pfeifer, *Creative Dir*
EMP: 190
SQ FT: 30,000
SALES (est): 57.6MM **Privately Held**
WEB: www.venablesbell.com
SIC: 7311 Advertising agencies

(P-13936)
VERTICAL SEARCH WORKS INC
1808 Aston Ave Ste 170, Carlsbad (92008-7367)
PHONE 212 967-9502
EMP: 60
SALES (corp-wide): 12.3MM **Privately Held**
SIC: 7311
PA: Vertical Search Works, Inc.
336 W 37th St Rm 100
New York NY 10018
212 967-9502

(P-13937)
VISIONAIRE GROUP INC
Also Called: Tvgla
5340 Alla Rd Ste 100, Los Angeles (90066-7036)
PHONE 310 823-1800
Dimitry Ioffe, *CEO*
Bryan Pettigrew, *President*
Matthew Lipson, *Vice Pres*
Francisco Camberos, *Creative Dir*
Jonathan Cook, *Creative Dir*
EMP: 52
SALES (est): 9.6MM **Privately Held**
SIC: 7311 Advertising agencies; advertising consultant

(P-13938)
VITRO LLC
2305 Historic Decatur Rd # 205, San Diego (92106-6073)
PHONE 619 234-0408
Tom Sullivan, *President*
Mike Brower, *Creative Dir*
Kt Thayer, *Creative Dir*
John Hickman, *Comms Dir*
Stefanie Meehan, *Office Admin*
EMP: 90
SALES (est): 17.8MM **Privately Held**
SIC: 7311 Advertising agencies

(P-13939)
VITROROBERTSON LLC
2305 Historic Decatur Rd, San Diego (92106-6050)
PHONE 619 234-0408
Fax: 619 234-4015
John Vitro, *Principal*
Tom Sullivan, *President*
Alan Bonine, *Exec VP*
Dan Consiglio, *Associate Dir*
Dave Huerta, *Associate Dir*
EMP: 89
SQ FT: 12,000
SALES (est): 21.1MM
SALES (corp-wide): 1.3B **Publicly Held**
WEB: www.vitrorobertson.com
SIC: 7311 Advertising agencies
PA: Mdc Partners Inc.
745 5th Ave Fl 19
New York NY 10151
646 429-1800

(P-13940)
VUNGLE INC
185 Clara St Ste 100, San Francisco (94107-4505)
PHONE 415 800-1400
Zain Jaffer, *CEO*
Wayne Chan, *President*
Jack Smith, *President*
Mike Pilawski, *Vice Pres*
Colin Behr, *Business Dir*
EMP: 160 **EST:** 2011
SQ FT: 4,500
SALES (est): 5.8MM **Privately Held**
SIC: 7311 7319 7313 Advertising agencies; display advertising service; electronic media advertising representatives

(P-13941)
WALKER ADVERTISING INC
1010 S Cabrillo Ave, San Pedro (90731-4030)
PHONE 310 519-4050
Fax: 310 519-4090
Mary Ann Walker, *CEO*
Alfonso Martinez, *Creative Dir*
Melissa Briceno, *Managing Dir*
Nereiba Casarez, *General Mgr*
Amir Tamjidi, *Info Tech Mgr*
EMP: 50

7311 - Advertising Agencies County (P-13942)
PRODUDUCTS & SERVICES SECTION

SALES (est): 12.3MM **Privately Held**
WEB: www.walkeradvertising.com
SIC: **7311** Advertising agencies

(P-13942)
WINKLER ADVERTISING INC
301 Howard St Ste 2100, San Francisco (94105-6616)
PHONE..................415 957-0242
Agnieszka Winkler, *President*
Chuck Maggio, *CFO*
Jim Robinson, *Info Tech Mgr*
Tad Zgoda, *Systems Mgr*
EMP: 55
SQ FT: 19,000
SALES (est): 3.8MM **Privately Held**
WEB: www.winklerad.com
SIC: **7311** Advertising agencies

(P-13943)
XAD INC
440 N Wolfe Rd, Sunnyvale (94085-3869)
PHONE..................415 480-6366
Stephen McCarthy, *Owner*
EMP: 300
SALES (corp-wide): 52.8MM **Privately Held**
SIC: **7311** Advertising agencies
PA: Xad, Inc.
 1 World Trade Ctr Fl 60
 New York NY 10007
 347 271-2258

(P-13944)
YOUNG & RUBICAM INC
Also Called: Y & R
303 2nd St Ste N300, San Francisco (94107-3638)
PHONE..................415 882-0600
Fax: 415 371-6879
Michael Reese, *Branch Mgr*
Jim Rotant, *Officer*
Austin McHie, *Div Sub Head*
Dave Chapman, *Admin Mgr*
EMP: 120
SALES (corp-wide): 18.4B **Privately Held**
SIC: **7311** Advertising agencies
HQ: Young & Rubicam Inc.
 3 Columbus Cir Fl 8
 New York NY 10019
 212 210-3000

(P-13945)
YUME INC (PA)
1204 Middlefield Rd, Redwood City (94063-2059)
PHONE..................650 591-9400
Fax: 650 591-9401
Jayant Kadambi, *President*
Anthony Carvalho, *CFO*
Hardeep Bindra, *Exec VP*
Paul Porrini, *Exec VP*
Ayyappan Sankaran, *Exec VP*
EMP: 148 EST: 2004
SQ FT: 26,900
SALES: 173.2MM **Publicly Held**
SIC: **7311** Advertising agencies

(P-13946)
Z57 INC (DH)
10045 Mesa Rim Rd, San Diego (92121-2913)
PHONE..................858 623-5577
Fax: 858 558-1736
Steve Weber, *President*
Ryan Whitlock, *CEO*
Erin Todd, *Assoc VP*
Cynthia Sener, *Vice Pres*
Tom Springer, *Executive*
EMP: 55
SALES (est): 11.5MM
SALES (corp-wide): 1.8B **Privately Held**
WEB: www.z57.com
SIC: **7311** Advertising agencies

(P-13947)
ZEETOGROUP LLC
Also Called: Zeeto Media
925 B St Fl 5, San Diego (92101-4697)
PHONE..................888 771-9194
Matthew Marcin, *Software Dev*
Stephan Goss, *CEO*
Bob Frady, *Vice Pres*
Greg Kuchcik, *Human Res Dir*
Brian Jones, *Pub Rel Dir*
EMP: 55 EST: 2007

SALES: 17.2MM **Privately Held**
SIC: **7311** Advertising agencies

(P-13948)
ZUBI ADVERTISING SERVICES INC
11601 Wilshire Blvd Fl 5, Los Angeles (90025-1995)
PHONE..................310 575-4839
Fax: 310 575-1808
EMP: 68
SALES (corp-wide): 24.1MM **Privately Held**
SIC: **7311** Advertising agencies
PA: Zubi Advertising Services Inc
 2990 Ponce De Leon Blvd # 600
 Coral Gables FL 33134
 305 448-9824

(P-13949)
ZVENTS INC
199 Fremont St Fl 4, San Francisco (94105-6634)
PHONE..................408 376-7346
Ethan Stock, *President*
Derek Hansen, *Vice Pres*
Dell Reibenschuh, *Office Mgr*
Grace Lin, *QA Dir*
Ivan Small, *Info Tech Mgr*
EMP: 50
SALES (est): 7.5MM **Privately Held**
WEB: www.zvents.com
SIC: **7311** Advertising agencies

7312 Outdoor Advertising Svcs

(P-13950)
BAMKO INC
11620 Wilshire Blvd # 610, Los Angeles (90025-1267)
PHONE..................310 470-5859
▲ EMP: 150
SALES (est): 33.2MM **Privately Held**
WEB: www.bamko.net
SIC: **7312** **7311**

(P-13951)
LAMBDA LAMBDA SIGMA LLC
Also Called: National Promotions & Advg
3434 Overland Ave, Los Angeles (90034-5406)
PHONE..................310 558-8555
Greta Gallas, *CFO*
Carlos Centeno, *Controller*
EMP: 51
SQ FT: 25,000
SALES (est): 1MM **Privately Held**
SIC: **7312** Poster advertising, outdoor

(P-13952)
MARKETSHARE INC (PA)
2001 Tarob Ct, Milpitas (95035-6825)
PHONE..................408 262-0677
Frederick R Wilhelm, *CEO*
Alexis Bybel, *CFO*
Steve Simpson, *Exec VP*
Jonathan Wilhelm, *CTO*
Lew Wilhelm, *Info Tech Dir*
EMP: 92
SQ FT: 16,000
SALES (est): 9.5MM **Privately Held**
WEB: www.marketlineonline.com
SIC: **7312** **3993** Outdoor advertising services; electric signs

(P-13953)
MOBPARTNER INC
625 2nd St Ste 280, San Francisco (94107-2184)
PHONE..................415 813-1202
Jamel Agaoua, *CEO*
EMP: 60
SALES (est): 2.5MM
SALES (corp-wide): 32.1MM **Privately Held**
SIC: **7312** Outdoor advertising services
PA: Mobpartner
 89 Avenue Ledru Rollin
 Paris 75011
 967 089-477

(P-13954)
OUTDOOR SYSTEMS ADVERTISING
Also Called: Roberts Outdoor Advertising
1731 Workman St, Los Angeles (90031-3334)
PHONE..................323 222-7171
Denis Kuhl, *General Mgr*
Artie Moreno, *CEO*
Tom Weiss, *Credit Mgr*
Denise Thompson, *Credit Staff*
Pamela Winters, *Human Res Dir*
EMP: 250
SALES (est): 10MM **Privately Held**
SIC: **7312** Outdoor advertising services

(P-13955)
OUTFRONT MEDIA INC
2100 W Orangewood Ave, Orange (92868-1952)
PHONE..................657 221-2760
EMP: 486
SALES (corp-wide): 1.5B **Publicly Held**
SIC: **7312** Outdoor advertising services
PA: Outfront Media Inc.
 405 Lexington Ave Fl 17
 New York NY 10174
 212 297-6400

(P-13956)
OUTFRONT MEDIA LLC
1695 Eastshore Hwy, Berkeley (94710-1733)
PHONE..................510 527-3350
Patrick Roche, *Branch Mgr*
Greg Donner, *Vice Pres*
Gary Duckworth, *Div Sub Head*
Christian Grimshaw, *Accounts Exec*
EMP: 100
SQ FT: 13,068
SALES (corp-wide): 1.5B **Publicly Held**
SIC: **7312** Outdoor advertising services
HQ: Outfront Media Llc
 405 Lexington Ave Fl 14
 New York NY 10174
 212 297-6400

7313 Radio, TV & Publishers Adv Reps

(P-13957)
101COMMUNICATIONS HOLDINGS LLC (HQ)
Also Called: 1105 Government Group
9201 Oakdale Ave Ste 101, Chatsworth (91311-6546)
PHONE..................818 734-1520
Fax: 818 734-1522
Neal Vitale, *President*
Jeffrey S Klein, *President*
Richard Vitale, *CFO*
Michael Valenti, *Exec VP*
Bonnie Dowd, *Vice Pres*
EMP: 64
SQ FT: 21,000
SALES (est): 15.1MM
SALES (corp-wide): 147.9MM **Privately Held**
WEB: www.adtmag.com
SIC: **7313** **7389** Printed media advertising representatives; convention & show services
PA: 1105 Media, Inc.
 9201 Oakdale Ave Ste 101
 Chatsworth CA 91311
 818 814-5200

(P-13958)
APPSFLYER LTD
111 New Montgomery St, San Francisco (94105-3605)
PHONE..................415 636-9430
Armando Osuna, *Partner*
EMP: 80
SALES (est): 3.5MM **Privately Held**
SIC: **7313** Electronic media advertising representatives

(P-13959)
BEACHBODY LLC (PA)
Also Called: Product Partners
3301 Exposition Blvd Fl 3, Santa Monica (90404-5082)
PHONE..................310 883-9000
Carl Daikeler,
William E Wheeler, *Officer*
Babak Azad, *Vice Pres*
Louise Bak, *Vice Pres*
Erica Cruz, *Vice Pres*
EMP: 148
SALES (est): 158.2MM **Privately Held**
SIC: **7313** **7999** Electronic media advertising representatives; physical fitness instruction

(P-13960)
BRITE MEDIA GROUP LLC
Also Called: Gsa Media
50 1st St Ste 600, San Francisco (94105-2418)
PHONE..................877 479-7777
Art Baer,
EMP: 113
SALES (est): 11.2MM **Privately Held**
SIC: **7313** Electronic media advertising representatives

(P-13961)
BRITE MEDIA LLC
Also Called: Brite Promotions
16027 Ventura Blvd # 210, Encino (91436-2876)
PHONE..................818 849-3560
Greg Martin, *Branch Mgr*
Tobin Hartman, *VP Sales*
Mike Christensen, *Sales Staff*
EMP: 142
SALES (corp-wide): 25.6MM **Privately Held**
SIC: **7313** Radio, television, publisher representatives
PA: Brite Media Llc
 475 14th St Ste 200
 Oakland CA 94612
 877 479-7777

(P-13962)
COMCAST CORPORATION
50 Francisco St Fl 3, San Francisco (94133-2134)
PHONE..................415 835-5700
Craig Coane, *General Mgr*
Drew Bruno, *Sales Dir*
Julien Cornil, *Manager*
James Dykstra, *Manager*
Michael Denatale, *Supervisor*
EMP: 100
SALES (corp-wide): 74.5B **Publicly Held**
WEB: www.comcast.com
SIC: **7313** Radio, television, publisher representatives
PA: Comcast Corporation
 1701 Jfk Blvd
 Philadelphia PA 19103
 215 286-1700

(P-13963)
DAILY JOURNAL CORPORATION
915 E 1st St, Los Angeles (90012-4042)
PHONE..................213 229-5500
Tu To, *Controller*
EMP: 50
SALES (corp-wide): 43.9MM **Publicly Held**
WEB: www.dailyjournal.com
SIC: **7313** Newspaper advertising representative
PA: Daily Journal Corporation
 915 E 1st St
 Los Angeles CA 90012
 213 229-5300

(P-13964)
DANIEL J EDELMAN INC
75 Enterprise, Aliso Viejo (92656-2629)
PHONE..................949 330-6760
EMP: 53
SALES (corp-wide): 868.7MM **Privately Held**
SIC: **7313** **8743** Electronic media advertising representatives; public relations services

PRODUCTS & SERVICES SECTION

7319 - Advertising, NEC County (P-13986)

HQ: Daniel J. Edelman, Inc.
200 E Randolph St Fl 63
Chicago IL 60601
312 240-3000

(P-13965)
DANIEL J EDELMAN INC
Also Called: Edelman Public Relations
201 Baldwin Ave, San Mateo (94401-3914)
PHONE.............................650 762-2800
Bob Angus, *Branch Mgr*
Victoria Brown, *Vice Pres*
Travis Murdock, *Vice Pres*
Maria Amundson, *General Mgr*
Todd Irwin, *General Mgr*
EMP: 100
SALES (corp-wide): 868.7MM Privately Held
SIC: 7313 8743 Electronic media advertising representatives; public relations & publicity
HQ: Daniel J. Edelman, Inc.
200 E Randolph St Fl 63
Chicago IL 60601
312 240-3000

(P-13966)
DANIEL J EDELMAN INC
Also Called: Edelman Public Relations
5900 Wilshire Blvd # 2400, Los Angeles (90036-5022)
PHONE.............................323 857-9100
EMP: 53
SALES (corp-wide): 790.4MM Privately Held
SIC: 7313 8743
HQ: Daniel J. Edelman, Inc.
200 E Randolph St Fl 63
Chicago IL 60601
312 240-3000

(P-13967)
DEMAND MEDIA INC (PA)
1655 26th St, Santa Monica (90404-4016)
PHONE.............................310 656-6253
Sean Moriarty, *CEO*
James R Quandt, *Ch of Bd*
Brian Pike, *COO*
Rachel Glaser, *CFO*
Daniel Weinrot, *Exec VP*
EMP: 116
SQ FT: 52,000
SALES: 125.9MM Publicly Held
WEB: www.demandmedia.com
SIC: 7313 7336 Electronic media advertising representatives; creative services to advertisers, except writers

(P-13968)
EL CLASIFICADO (PA)
11205 Imperial Hwy, Norwalk (90650-2229)
PHONE.............................323 837-4095
Martha C Dela Torre, *President*
Joseph Badame, *President*
Gil Garcia, *CFO*
Mike Wong, *Info Tech Dir*
Rebecca German, *Opers Staff*
EMP: 100
SALES (est): 12.3MM Privately Held
SIC: 7313 Newspaper advertising representative

(P-13969)
GHOST MANAGEMENT GROUP LLC
41 Discovery, Irvine (92618-3150)
PHONE.............................949 870-1400
Justin Hartfield, *CEO*
Doug Francis, *President*
Albert Lopez, *CFO*
Chris Beals, *General Counsel*
EMP: 175
SQ FT: 44,820
SALES: 40MM Privately Held
SIC: 7313 7371 Electronic media advertising representatives; computer software development & applications; custom computer programming services

(P-13970)
JAYLANE ENTERTAINMENT CORP ✪
585 Fernando Dr, Novato (94945-3333)
PHONE.............................707 820-2773
EMP: 65 EST: 2016

SALES (est): 941.1K Privately Held
SIC: 7313

(P-13971)
M CHANNEL INC
2015 S Westgate Ave, Los Angeles (90025-6118)
PHONE.............................310 231-5124
David Teichner, *CEO*
Eric Hebel, *President*
Dennis Quinn, *President*
Peter Lee, *Security Dir*
Valentino Gorelik, *Finance*
EMP: 54
SQ FT: 5,000
SALES (est): 2.9MM
SALES (corp-wide): 58.7MM Privately Held
WEB: www.channelm.com
SIC: 7313 8743 Television & radio time sales; sales promotion
PA: Playnetwork, Inc.
8727 148th Ave Ne Bldg D
Redmond WA 98052
425 497-8100

(P-13972)
MEDIASHIFT INC
600 N Brand Blvd Ste 230, Glendale (91203-4234)
PHONE.............................949 407-8488
David Grant, *Ch of Bd*
Brendon Kensel, *President*
Mike Spalter, *COO*
Rick Baran, *CFO*
Sanjeev Kuwadekar, *CTO*
EMP: 60
SALES: 6.9MM Privately Held
SIC: 7313 Electronic media advertising representatives

(P-13973)
MODE MEDIA CORPORATION (PA)
Also Called: Project Y
2000 Sierra Point Pkwy # 10, Brisbane (94005-1845)
PHONE.............................650 244-4000
Fax: 650 244-4004
Samir Arora, *Ch of Bd*
John C Small, *COO*
Ernie Cicogna, *CFO*
Stephen E Recht, *CFO*
Jeanne Seeley, *CFO*
EMP: 128
SQ FT: 5,000
SALES (est): 56.9MM Privately Held
SIC: 7313 7311 Electronic media advertising representatives; advertising agencies

(P-13974)
NAPASTYLE INC (PA)
360 Industrial Ct Ste A, NAPA (94558)
PHONE.............................707 251-5100
Renee Thomas Jacobs, *President*
Christy Logan, *Creative Dir*
Karen Janssen, *Info Tech Dir*
John Hanna, *Technology*
Mike Arnaud, *Manager*
▲ EMP: 80
SALES (est): 15.1MM Privately Held
SIC: 7313 Radio, television, publisher representatives

(P-13975)
OBSCURA DIGITAL INCORPORATED
729 Tennessee St, San Francisco (94107-3031)
PHONE.............................415 227-9979
Fax: 415 227-9494
Travis Threlkel, *Co-CEO*
Chris Lejeune, *Co-CEO*
Kimber Sterling, *Vice Pres*
Alex Ilten, *Creative Dir*
Josh Buchbinder, *Software Dev*
EMP: 50 EST: 2000
SQ FT: 40,000
SALES (est): 8.7MM Privately Held
WEB: www.obscuradigital.com
SIC: 7313 Electronic media advertising representatives; printed media advertising representatives

(P-13976)
PAC-12 ENTEPRISES LLC
360 3rd St Ste 300, San Francisco (94107-2163)
PHONE.............................415 580-4200
Fax: 925 932-4601
Lydia Murphy Stevens, *President*
Jamie Zaninovich, *COO*
Ron McQuate, *CFO*
Ronald McQuate, *CFO*
Lydia Murphy-Stephans, *Exec VP*
EMP: 120
SQ FT: 11,000
SALES (est): 26.3MM Privately Held
WEB: www.pac-10.org
SIC: 7313 Electronic media advertising representatives

(P-13977)
QW MEDIA INTERNATIONAL LLC
620 Newport Center Dr # 11, Newport Beach (92660-6420)
PHONE.............................949 200-4616
Marianne Moy, *Chairman*
Drian Hirabayashi, *Vice Pres*
Brian Hirabayashi, *Principal*
EMP: 50
SALES: 2MM Privately Held
SIC: 7313 Printed media advertising representatives

(P-13978)
SHED MEDIA US INC
3800 Barham Blvd Ste 410, Los Angeles (90068-1042)
PHONE.............................323 904-4680
Nick Emmerson, *President*
Mark Blatty, *Senior VP*
Daniel D Helberg, *Senior VP*
John Hesling, *Senior VP*
Dan Snook, *Senior VP*
EMP: 55
SALES (est): 9.8MM Privately Held
SIC: 7313 Electronic media advertising representatives

(P-13979)
STUDIO 71 LP
Also Called: Collective Digital Studio, LLC
8383 Wilshire Blvd Ste 10, Beverly Hills (90211-2425)
PHONE.............................323 370-1500
Reza Isad,
Andrew Reyes, *Executive*
Nicole Andrewin,
Michael Green,
Jordan Toplitzky,
EMP: 150 EST: 2011
SQ FT: 15,000
SALES: 60MM
SALES (corp-wide): 3.5B Privately Held
SIC: 7313 Electronic media advertising representatives
PA: Prosiebensat.1 Media Se
Medienallee 7
Unterfohring 85774
899 507-1150

(P-13980)
THOUGHTFUL MEDIA GROUP INC
Also Called: Thoughtful Asia Limited
14724 Ventura Blvd # 1110, Sherman Oaks (91403-3511)
PHONE.............................818 465-7500
Jak C Severson, *President*
Daniel T Thorman, *Vice Pres*
Michelle Merino, *Business Dir*
EMP: 70
SALES (est): 4.4MM Privately Held
SIC: 7313 Electronic media advertising representatives

(P-13981)
TIME INC
2 Embarcadero Ctr # 1900, San Francisco (94111-3914)
PHONE.............................415 982-5000
Fax: 415 434-5256
Tim Richards, *Manager*
Teri Everett, *Exec VP*
John Griffin, *Exec VP*
James Jacovides, *Vice Pres*
Kevin Binder, *Info Tech Mgr*

EMP: 60
SALES (corp-wide): 3.1B Publicly Held
SIC: 7313 Magazine advertising representative
PA: Time Inc.
225 Liberty St
New York NY 10281
212 522-1212

(P-13982)
TIME INC
Time Magazine
11766 Wilshire Blvd # 1700, Los Angeles (90025-6542)
PHONE.............................310 268-7200
Fax: 310 268-7203
Sally Masters, *Branch Mgr*
Jim McMicken, *Info Tech Dir*
Tony Toubia, *Network Enginr*
EMP: 200
SALES (corp-wide): 3.1B Publicly Held
SIC: 7313 Magazine advertising representative
PA: Time Inc.
225 Liberty St
New York NY 10281
212 522-1212

(P-13983)
TRAVELZOO USA INC
800 W El Camino Re, Mountain View (94040)
PHONE.............................650 316-6956
Chris Loughlin, *CEO*
Ralph Bartel, *President*
Wayne Lee, *CFO*
Mary A Dickerson, *General Mgr*
Lisa Su, *Controller*
EMP: 81
SALES (est): 16.6MM
SALES (corp-wide): 141.7MM Publicly Held
WEB: www.travelzoo.com
SIC: 7313 Electronic media advertising representatives
PA: Travelzoo Inc.
590 Madison Ave Rm 3700
New York NY 10022
212 484-4900

(P-13984)
ULTRADOT MEDIA
9908 Bell Ranch Dr, Santa Fe Springs (90670-2972)
PHONE.............................562 906-0737
Bill Shears, *President*
EMP: 75
SALES (est): 3.7MM Privately Held
WEB: www.ultradotmedia.com
SIC: 7313 7336 Printed media advertising representatives; commercial art & graphic design

(P-13985)
WGA WEST INC
7000 W 3rd St, Los Angeles (90048-4321)
PHONE.............................323 782-4512
Chris Keyser, *President*
Natalie Fong, *Exec Sec*
EMP: 100
SALES (est): 3.6MM Privately Held
SIC: 7313 Electronic media advertising representatives

7319 Advertising, NEC

(P-13986)
ADVERTISING CONSULTANTS INC (PA)
Also Called: American Crclation Innovations
330 Golden Shore Ste 410, Long Beach (90802-4271)
PHONE.............................310 233-2750
Keith Somers, *President*
John G Walsh, *COO*
Kent Brown, *CFO*
Robert Somers, *Chairman*
Randall S Brant, *VP Sls/Mktg*
EMP: 50 EST: 1966
SQ FT: 60,000
SALES (est): 13.4MM Privately Held
WEB: www.acicirculation.com
SIC: 7319 Distribution of advertising material or sample services

---

(PA)=Parent Co (HQ)=Headquarters (DH)=Div Headquarters
✪ = New Business established in last 2 years

7319 - Advertising, NEC County (P-13987)

(P-13987)
AEGIS SOFTWARE INC
Also Called: Destination Webcam
5580 La Jolla Blvd # 436, La Jolla (92037-7651)
PHONE..................................858 551-1652
Alan Edwards, *President*
EMP: 50
SALES (est): 3MM **Privately Held**
WEB: www.ecodb.com
SIC: 7319 Media buying service

(P-13988)
AMERICAN MDSG SPECIALISTS INC
958 Dainty Ave, Brentwood (94513-1206)
P.O. Box 2047 (94513-9047)
PHONE..................................925 516-3220
Steve Nozet, *Branch Mgr*
Erica Humphrey, *Executive Asst*
Gregory Cummings, *Training Dir*
Lynette Urban, *Human Resources*
Benjamin Berni, *Sales Mgr*
EMP: 234
SALES (corp-wide): 24.1MM **Privately Held**
SIC: 7319 Display advertising service
PA: American Merchandising Specialists, Inc.
  177 Barley Park Ln
  Mooresville NC 28115
  704 235-0144

(P-13989)
BAY AREA NEWS GROUP E BAY LLC (HQ)
6270 Houston Pl Ste A, Dublin (94568-3161)
PHONE..................................925 302-1683
William Dean Singleton,
Jason Cross, *Vice Pres*
Erin Day, *Mktg Coord*
Joseph J Lodovic IV,
Michael Tully,
EMP: 82
SALES (est): 11.6MM
SALES (corp-wide): 21.6MM **Privately Held**
SIC: 7319 Media buying service
PA: California Newspapers Partnership
  4 N 2nd St Fl 8
  San Jose CA 95113
  408 920-5333

(P-13990)
CARAT USA INC
2700 Penn Ave Fl 2, Santa Monica (90404-5431)
PHONE..................................310 255-1000
John Barnes, *Branch Mgr*
Tiffany Srisook, *Associate*
EMP: 150
SALES (corp-wide): 5.7B **Privately Held**
SIC: 7319 7313 Media buying service; printed media advertising representatives
HQ: Carat Usa, Inc.
  150 E 42nd St
  New York NY 10017
  212 591-9100

(P-13991)
CBS INTERACTIVE INC
2900 W Alameda Ave, Burbank (91505-4220)
PHONE..................................818 556-1538
EMP: 127
SALES (corp-wide): 27.6B **Publicly Held**
SIC: 7319
HQ: Cbs Interactive Inc.
  235 2nd St
  San Francisco CA 94105
  415 344-2000

(P-13992)
CBS INTERACTIVE INC (DH)
Also Called: Cbsi
235 2nd St, San Francisco (94105-3124)
PHONE..................................415 344-2000
Fax: 310 322-8957
Jarl Mohn, *Ch of Bd*
Eric Foote, *Partner*
Barry Briggs, *President*
Jim Lanzone, *President*
Serious Pie, *Bd of Directors*
EMP: 600

SQ FT: 283,000
SALES (est): 328.5MM
SALES (corp-wide): 27.1B **Publicly Held**
WEB: www.mysimon.com
SIC: 7319 7375 4832 Distribution of advertising material or sample services; on-line data base information retrieval; radio broadcasting stations
HQ: Cbs Corporation
  51 W 52nd St Bsmt 1
  New York NY 10019
  212 975-4321

(P-13993)
CIE DIGITAL LABS LLC (PA)
Also Called: Choice Internet
19900 Macarthur Blvd # 1000, Irvine (92612-8415)
PHONE..................................949 381-6200
Anderee Berengian, *CEO*
Alvin Fong, *Senior VP*
Miriam Ferreira, *Controller*
Jennifer Meza, *Human Resources*
Jennifer Walter, *VP Prdtn*
EMP: 50 **EST:** 1999
SQ FT: 13,500
SALES (est): 9.9MM **Privately Held**
SIC: 7319 Display advertising service

(P-13994)
DELIVERY AGENT INC (PA)
300 California St Fl 3, San Francisco (94104-1413)
PHONE..................................415 696-5800
Fax: 415 358-8033
Michael Fitzsimmons, *CEO*
Subhashini Gajjala, *Senior Partner*
Peter Lai, *President*
James Peters, *President*
Mike Fitzsimmons, *CEO*
EMP: 61
SQ FT: 12,000
SALES (est): 50.9MM **Privately Held**
WEB: www.deliveryagent.com
SIC: 7319 Media buying service

(P-13995)
FASTCLICK INC
Also Called: Fastclick.com
530 E Montecito St, Santa Barbara (93103-3252)
PHONE..................................805 689-9839
Kurt A Johnson, *President*
Fred Krupica, *CFO*
James Aviani, *CTO*
Fredric Harman, *Director*
EMP: 87
SQ FT: 14,900
SALES (est): 4.8MM
SALES (corp-wide): 6.4B **Publicly Held**
WEB: www.fastclick.com
SIC: 7319 Circular & handbill distribution; coupon distribution
HQ: Conversant, Llc
  30699 Russell Ranch Rd # 250
  Westlake Village CA 91362
  818 575-4500

(P-13996)
HORIZON MEDIA INC
1940 Century Park E Fl 3, Los Angeles (90067-1742)
PHONE..................................310 282-0909
Fax: 310 229-8104
Zach Rosenberg, *Branch Mgr*
Dave Masen, *Buyer*
April Minsky, *Buyer*
Oury Tamboura, *Buyer*
Peter Bhusiririt, *Supervisor*
EMP: 70
SALES (corp-wide): 179.4MM **Privately Held**
SIC: 7319 Media buying service
PA: Horizon Media, Inc.
  75 Varick St Ste 1404
  New York NY 10013
  212 220-5000

(P-13997)
ICON MEDIA DIRECT INC (PA)
5910 Lemona Ave, Van Nuys (91411-3006)
PHONE..................................818 995-6400
Nancy Lazkani, *CEO*
Leslie Williams, *Office Mgr*
Kali Howard, *Executive Asst*
Meg Howard, *Executive Asst*

Lindsay Pritikin, *Executive Asst*
EMP: 81
SQ FT: 16,445
SALES (est): 16.2MM **Privately Held**
WEB: www.iconmediadirect.com
SIC: 7319 Media buying service

(P-13998)
IMAGE OPTIONS
80 Icon, Foothill Ranch (92610-3000)
PHONE..................................949 586-7665
Fax: 949 586-8655
Tim Bennett, *CEO*
Brian Hite, *President*
Dave Bales, *Vice Pres*
Dave Brewer, *Vice Pres*
Kathy Guerineau, *Vice Pres*
EMP: 101
SQ FT: 22,000
SALES (est): 22MM **Privately Held**
SIC: 7319 7336 Display advertising service; commercial art & graphic design

(P-13999)
KSL MEDIA INC
15910 Ventura Blvd # 900, Encino (91436-2809)
PHONE..................................212 468-3395
Fax: 818 461-1373
Kalman Liebowitz, *Ch of Bd*
Hank Cohen, *President*
Russell Meisels, *CFO*
Tyler Liebowitz, *Senior VP*
Christina Selberis, *Vice Pres*
EMP: 130
SQ FT: 13,000
SALES (est): 365.9MM **Privately Held**
WEB: www.kslmedia.com
SIC: 7319 Media buying service

(P-14000)
LEGGETT & PLATT INCORPORATED
Beeline Group
30955 Huntwood Ave, Hayward (94544-7005)
PHONE..................................510 487-8063
Fax: 510 441-1782
Scott Tiedemann, *Branch Mgr*
Philip Green, *Vice Pres*
Meghan Mitchell, *Project Mgr*
Mario Orsi, *Controller*
Kim Eggert, *Human Res Mgr*
EMP: 100
SALES (corp-wide): 3.9B **Publicly Held**
WEB: www.leggett.com
SIC: 7319 Display advertising service
PA: Leggett & Platt, Incorporated
  1 Leggett Rd
  Carthage MO 64836
  417 358-8131

(P-14001)
MEDIABRANDS WORLDWIDE INC
5700 Wilshire Blvd # 400, Los Angeles (90036-3659)
PHONE..................................323 370-8000
Fax: 323 370-8950
Guy Walker, *CFO*
Bret Leece, *Senior VP*
Christiana Messina, *Vice Pres*
Kat Chung, *Associate Dir*
Bryan Andrews, *Social Dir*
EMP: 300
SALES (corp-wide): 7.6B **Publicly Held**
WEB: www.wimc.com
SIC: 7319 Media buying service
HQ: Mediabrands Worldwide, Inc.
  100 W 33rd St
  New York NY 10001
  212 605-7000

(P-14002)
NATIONAL CBLE CMMNICATIONS LLC
Also Called: Nca
11150 Santa Monica Blvd # 900, Los Angeles (90025-3380)
PHONE..................................310 231-0745
Fax: 310 996-1034
Dori Wilde, *Manager*
Lee Winikoff, *Manager*
Tim Curry, *Accounts Exec*
Justin Ehly, *Accounts Exec*
Annie Joh, *Accounts Exec*

EMP: 75
SALES (corp-wide): 74.5B **Publicly Held**
SIC: 7319 1799 7313 Transit advertising services; cable splicing service; radio, television, publisher representatives
HQ: National Cable Communications Llc
  405 Lexington Ave Fl 6
  New York NY 10174
  212 548-3300

(P-14003)
NATIONAL DISTRIBUTION CENTERS
Also Called: Ontario Distribution Center
5140 Santa Ana St, Ontario (91761-8632)
PHONE..................................909 390-5696
Andy Traupman, *General Mgr*
EMP: 76 **EST:** 2012
SALES (est): 3.5MM **Privately Held**
SIC: 7319 Advertising

(P-14004)
ND SYSTEMS INC
5750 Hellyer Ave, San Jose (95138-1000)
PHONE..................................408 776-0085
Jim Ciardella, *CFO*
Kees Poot, *Vice Pres*
Trina Cirauollo, *Director*
EMP: 75
SALES (est): 4.6MM **Privately Held**
WEB: www.nationaldisplay.com
SIC: 7319 Display advertising service

(P-14005)
PALISADES MEDIA GROUP INC (PA)
Also Called: Palisades Interactive
1620 26th St Ste 200s, Santa Monica (90404-4143)
PHONE..................................310 564-5400
Fax: 310 828-9117
Roger Schaffner, *Ch of Bd*
Laura Jean Bracken, *President*
Bruce Dennler, *President*
Bruce Dennier, *COO*
Jean Brooks, *Exec VP*
EMP: 58
SQ FT: 13,000
SALES (est): 16.7MM **Privately Held**
WEB: www.palisadesmedia.com
SIC: 7319 Media buying service

(P-14006)
PINTEREST INC
808 Brannan St, San Francisco (94103-4904)
PHONE..................................415 400-4645
Ben Silbermann, *Branch Mgr*
EMP: 257
SALES (corp-wide): 120.7MM **Privately Held**
SIC: 7319 Display advertising service
PA: Pinterest, Inc.
  808 Brannan St
  San Francisco CA 94103
  650 561-5407

(P-14007)
QUANTCAST CORPORATION (PA)
201 3rd St Ste 2, San Francisco (94103-3154)
PHONE..................................415 738-4755
Fax: 415 738-2318
Konrad Feldman, *President*
Christina Cubeta, *Senior Partner*
Stephen Collins, *President*
Michael Kamprath, *President*
Julio Pekarovic, *CFO*
EMP: 125
SALES (est): 50.8MM **Privately Held**
SIC: 7319 Display advertising service

(P-14008)
QUOTIENT TECHNOLOGY INC (PA)
400 Logue Ave, Mountain View (94043-4019)
PHONE..................................650 605-4600
Fax: 650 605-4700
Steven R Boal, *CEO*
Mir Aamir, *President*
Ron J Fior, *CFO*
Connie Chen, *General Counsel*
EMP: 141

PRODUCTS & SERVICES SECTION

7322 - Adjustment & Collection Svcs County (P-14029)

SQ FT: 110,000
SALES: 237.3MM **Publicly Held**
SIC: 7319 Coupon distribution

(P-14009)
REVENUE FRONTIER LLC
Also Called: Media Design Group
6922 Hollywood Blvd 2, Los Angeles
(90028-6117)
PHONE..................................310 584-9200
Fax: 310 584-9230
Greg Thomas, *CEO*
Patrick Romagnano, *COO*
Michael Marrone, *Vice Pres*
Daniel Tieman, *Technology*
Mike Scott, *Director*
EMP: 55
SALES (est): 8.7MM
SALES (corp-wide): 28MM **Privately Held**
WEB: www.revenuefrontier.com
SIC: 7319 Media buying service
PA: Havas Edge Llc
   2386 Faraday Ave Ste 200
   Carlsbad CA 92008
   760 929-1357

(P-14010)
SAATCHI & SAATCHI NORTH AMER
3501 Sepulveda Blvd, Torrance
(90505-2540)
PHONE..................................310 214-6000
Fax: 310 214-6160
David Murphy, *President*
Rich Anderman, *COO*
John Lisko, *Exec VP*
Katherine Jaris, *Senior VP*
Leo Circo, *Vice Pres*
EMP: 400
SALES (corp-wide): 65.7MM **Privately Held**
WEB: www.saatchila.com
SIC: 7319 Transit advertising services
HQ: Saatchi & Saatchi North America, Inc.
   375 Hudson St Fl 16
   New York NY 10014
   212 463-2000

(P-14011)
SUPERMEDIA SALES INC
300 E Esplanade Dr # 600, Oxnard
(93036-1238)
PHONE..................................805 278-3400
Mike Walden, *Branch Mgr*
Jeffrey Kearney, *Sales Staff*
EMP: 100
SALES (corp-wide): 1.8B **Privately Held**
SIC: 7319 Display advertising service
HQ: Supermedia Sales, Inc.
   2200 W Airfield Dr
   Dfw Airport TX 75261
   972 453-7000

(P-14012)
TURN INC (PA)
901 Marshall St 200, Redwood City
(94063-2026)
PHONE..................................650 353-4399
Fax: 650 556-1955
Bill Demas, *President*
Mark Liao, *CFO*
Joe Nemeth, *CFO*
Wendy Macgregor, *Officer*
Bryan Busse, *Senior VP*
EMP: 148
SQ FT: 14,000
SALES (est): 66.7MM **Privately Held**
WEB: www.turn.com
SIC: 7319 Display advertising service

(P-14013)
US INTERNATIONAL MEDIA LLC (PA)
Also Called: US Outdoor
1201 Alta Loma Rd, Los Angeles
(90069-2403)
PHONE..................................310 482-6700
Dennis Holt, *CEO*
Alicia Nelson, *President*
Doug Livingston, *COO*
Robyn Campbell, *Exec VP*
Sixto Castillo, *Exec VP*
EMP: 118
SQ FT: 5,000
SALES (est): 20.6MM **Privately Held**
WEB: www.usintlmedia.com
SIC: 7319 Media buying service

(P-14014)
WEST COAST COUPON INC
9400 Oso Ave, Chatsworth (91311-6020)
PHONE..................................818 341-2400
Fax: 818 341-5953
Mark Fischer, *President*
Doug Rewers, *Vice Pres*
Trono Robertson, *Manager*
EMP: 50
SQ FT: 30,000
SALES (est): 8.9MM **Privately Held**
SIC: 7319 2731 5961 Coupon distribution; books: publishing & printing; computer software; mail order

---

7322 Adjustment & Collection Svcs

(P-14015)
ACCOUNT CONTROL TECHNOLOGY INC
5531 Bus Park S Ste 100, Bakersfield
(93309-1656)
PHONE..................................661 395-5702
Sam Shawwa, *Manager*
Lynn Heineman, *VP Sales*
EMP: 50
SALES (corp-wide): 222.8MM **Privately Held**
WEB: www.accountcontrol.com
SIC: 7322 Collection agency, except real estate
HQ: Account Control Technology Inc.
   21700 Oxnard St Ste 1400
   Woodland Hills CA 91367
   818 712-4999

(P-14016)
ALLIED INTERSTATE INC (DH)
30699 Russell Ranch Rd # 250, Westlake Village (91362-7315)
PHONE..................................818 575-5400
Marwan Kashou, *General Mgr*
Bret Langdoser, *Manager*
Michelle Mc Laughling, *Manager*
Jim Pond, *Manager*
Chris Reynolds, *Manager*
EMP: 51
SQ FT: 10,000
SALES (est): 4MM **Privately Held**
SIC: 7322 8742 Adjustment & collection services; financial consultant
HQ: Intellirisk Management Corporation
   335 Madison Ave Fl 27
   New York NY 10017
   646 274-3030

(P-14017)
ARS NATIONAL SERVICES INC (PA)
201 W Grand Ave, Escondido
(92025-2603)
P.O. Box 463023 (92046-3023)
PHONE..................................800 456-5053
Jason Howerton, *President*
John Watson, *COO*
John Howerton, *Chairman*
Jim Beck, *Vice Pres*
Kathy Howerton, *Admin Sec*
EMP: 150
SQ FT: 33,000
SALES (est): 26.8MM **Privately Held**
WEB: www.arsnational.com
SIC: 7322 Collection agency, except real estate

(P-14018)
ATTORNEY RECOVERY SYSTEMS INC (PA)
18757 Burbank Blvd # 300, Tarzana
(91356-6329)
PHONE..................................818 774-1420
Gene Bloom, *President*
Debbie Delgado, *Manager*
EMP: 70
SALES (est): 5.5MM **Privately Held**
WEB: www.legalcollection.com
SIC: 7322 8111 Adjustment & collection services; legal services

(P-14019)
BAY AREA CREDIT SERVICE LLC (PA)
1901 W 10th St, Antioch (94509-1380)
PHONE..................................408 392-4425
Fax: 408 392-4420
Par Chadha, *Mng Member*
Sunil Rajadhyksha, *Info Tech Dir*
Scott Zimmerman, *Human Res Mgr*
Sunil Rajadhyaksha,
Taylor Pensoneau, *Manager*
EMP: 150
SQ FT: 14,000
SALES (est): 27MM **Privately Held**
WEB: www.bayareacredit.com
SIC: 7322 Collection agency, except real estate

(P-14020)
CAINE & WEINER COMPANY INC (PA)
21210 Erwin St, Woodland Hills
(91367-3714)
P.O. Box 5010 (91365-5010)
PHONE..................................818 226-6000
Greg A Cohen, *President*
Mark Milstein, *COO*
Sunny Caine, *CFO*
Brad Schaffer, *Senior VP*
Frank Dispensa, *Vice Pres*
EMP: 90
SQ FT: 14,400
SALES (est): 23.9MM **Privately Held**
WEB: www.caine-weiner.com
SIC: 7322 Collection agency, except real estate

(P-14021)
CALIFORNIA BUSINESS BUREAU INC (PA)
Also Called: Medical Billing Services
1711 S Mountain Ave, Monrovia
(91016-4256)
P.O. Box 5010 (91017-7110)
PHONE..................................626 303-1515
Fax: 626 303-2339
Michael J Sigal, *President*
Kathy Tree, *Vice Pres*
Rafael Ramirez, *Info Tech Dir*
Angie Faulkner, *Manager*
Fatima Nunez, *Manager*
EMP: 132 EST: 1973
SQ FT: 24,000
SALES (est): 11.9MM **Privately Held**
WEB: www.cbbinc.com
SIC: 7322 Collection agency, except real estate

(P-14022)
CALIFORNIA PHARMACY MGT LLC
3198 Arprt Loop Dr Ste F, Costa Mesa
(92626)
PHONE..................................714 777-3100
Vonda Ray, *Mng Member*
EMP: 85
SALES (est): 5.1MM **Privately Held**
SIC: 7322 Collection agency, except real estate

(P-14023)
CB ASSOCIATES INC
11659 Haynes St, North Hollywood
(91606-2530)
PHONE..................................818 284-3699
Candie Fernandez, *President*
Branden Fernandez, *COO*
Daniel Pettway Jr, *CFO*
EMP: 50
SALES (est): 1.8MM **Privately Held**
SIC: 7322 Collection agency, except real estate

(P-14024)
CBSJ FINANCIAL CORPORATION
1735 N 1st St Ste 250, San Jose
(95112-4531)
PHONE..................................408 792-4600
Bertha Martin, *President*
EMP: 100
SALES (est): 4.4MM **Privately Held**
WEB: www.cbsj.com
SIC: 7322 Collection agency, except real estate

(P-14025)
CMRE FINANCIAL SERVICES INC
3075 E Imperial Hwy # 200, Brea
(92821-6753)
PHONE..................................714 528-3200
Fax: 714 528-5863
Jack C Nixon, *CEO*
John Nixon, *Shareholder*
Sandy Lawrence, *President*
Andrea Parr, *Corp Secy*
Patrick Nixon, *Vice Pres*
EMP: 300
SQ FT: 35,000
SALES (est): 38.4MM **Privately Held**
WEB: www.cmrefsi.com
SIC: 7322 Collection agency, except real estate

(P-14026)
COLLECTECH SYSTEMS INC (DH)
2290 Agate Ct 1a, Simi Valley
(93065-1935)
PHONE..................................818 597-7500
Steve Kent, *Exec VP*
EMP: 175
SQ FT: 19,376
SALES (est): 10.7MM **Privately Held**
SIC: 7322 Collection agency, except real estate
HQ: Intellirisk Management Corporation
   335 Madison Ave Fl 27
   New York NY 10017
   646 274-3030

(P-14027)
COLLECTION TECHNOLOGY INC
Also Called: C T I
10801 6th St Ste 200, Rancho Cucamonga
(91730-5904)
P.O. Box 2200 (91729-2200)
PHONE..................................800 743-4284
Chris Van Dellen, *CEO*
Paul Van Dellen, *President*
Ricardo Rubio, *Info Tech Mgr*
Sean Teng, *Info Tech Mgr*
Divina Balli, *Financial Exec*
EMP: 100
SALES (est): 3.3MM **Privately Held**
WEB: www.collectiontechnology.com
SIC: 7322 Adjustment & collection services

(P-14028)
CONRAD CREDIT CORPORATION
476 W Vermont Ave, Escondido
(92025-6529)
P.O. Box 770 (92033-0770)
PHONE..................................760 735-5000
Fax: 760 735-5010
Keith Richenbacher, *President*
Charlie Hawk, *CFO*
John Page, *Vice Pres*
Bob Pranik, *Admin Sec*
EMP: 50
SQ FT: 6,000
SALES (est): 6.1MM
SALES (corp-wide): 11.9MM **Privately Held**
SIC: 7322 Collection agency, except real estate
PA: Conrad Corporation
   476 W Vermont Ave
   Escondido CA 92025
   800 826-6723

(P-14029)
CREDIT BUREAU NAPA COUNTY INC
Also Called: Chase Receivables
1247 Broadway, Sonoma (95476-7503)
PHONE..................................707 940-3000
Fax: 707 933-3613
Fred Merrill, *Chairman*
EMP: 145
SQ FT: 1,357
SALES (est): 12.9MM **Privately Held**
WEB: www.chaserec.com
SIC: 7322 Collection agency, except real estate

7322 - Adjustment & Collection Svcs County (P-14030)

(P-14030)
CREDIT MANAGEMENT ASSOCIATION (PA)
40 E Verdugo Ave, Burbank (91502-1931)
P.O. Box 7740 (91510-7740)
PHONE..................................818 972-5300
Michael G Mitchell, *President*
Michael Mitchell, *President*
David Macomber, *CFO*
James Clark, *Vice Pres*
Robert Hoder, *Vice Pres*
EMP: 52
SQ FT: 22,811
SALES (est): 12.4MM **Privately Held**
SIC: 7322 7323 8742 7389 Adjustment bureau, except insurance; collection agency, except real estate; commercial (mercantile) credit reporting bureau; administrative services consultant; estimating service, construction; auction, appraisal & exchange services; educational services

(P-14031)
FCI LENDER SERVICES INC
Also Called: F C I
8180 E Kaiser Blvd, Anaheim (92808-2277)
PHONE..................................714 974-1945
Michael W Griffith, *President*
Vicky Nelson, *Trustee*
Teri Snyder, *Exec VP*
Jean Smith, *Vice Pres*
Vivian Prieto, *Office Mgr*
EMP: 105
SQ FT: 19,000
SALES (est): 10.2MM **Privately Held**
WEB: www.trustfci.com
SIC: 7322 Adjustment & collection services

(P-14032)
FINANCIAL CREDIT NETWORK INC (PA)
1300 W Main St, Visalia (93291-5825)
P.O. Box 3084 (93278-3084)
PHONE..................................559 733-7550
Fax: 559 733-0588
Alicia Sundstrom, *President*
Kris Davisson, *Vice Pres*
Joe Halford, *Info Tech Mgr*
Paul Flannery, *Director*
EMP: 50
SQ FT: 11,000
SALES (est): 6.5MM **Privately Held**
WEB: www.fcnetwork.com
SIC: 7322 Collection agency, except real estate

(P-14033)
GC SERVICES LTD PARTNERSHIP
4900 Rivergrade Rd # 210, Irwindale (91706-1401)
PHONE..................................626 851-8227
David Jacques, *Manager*
EMP: 149
SALES (corp-wide): 423.1MM **Privately Held**
SIC: 7322 7373 7375 Adjustment & collection services; computer integrated systems design; information retrieval services
PA: Gc Services Limited Partnership
6330 Gulfton St
Houston TX 77081
713 777-4441

(P-14034)
GRANT & WEBER (PA)
Also Called: Grant & Weber Travel
26610 Agoura Rd Ste 209, Calabasas (91302-2975)
P.O. Box 8669 (91372-8669)
PHONE..................................818 878-7700
Fax: 818 878-7777
Jimi Bingham, *CEO*
Spencer Weinerman, *CFO*
Gene Grossblatt, *Treasurer*
Omar Perez, *Vice Pres*
Mary Kempski, *CIO*
EMP: 96
SQ FT: 30,000
SALES (est): 26.8MM **Privately Held**
WEB: www.grantweber.com
SIC: 7322 Collection agency, except real estate

(P-14035)
INTELLIRISK MANAGEMENT CORP
31229 Cedar Valley Dr, Westlake Village (91362-4036)
PHONE..................................818 575-5400
Jim Pond, *Branch Mgr*
EMP: 50 **Privately Held**
SIC: 7322 Adjustment & collection services
HQ: Intellirisk Management Corporation
335 Madison Ave Fl 27
New York NY 10017
646 274-3030

(P-14036)
J & L COLLECTIONS SERVICES INC
Also Called: J&L Teamworks
651 N Cherokee Ln Ste B2, Lodi (95240-4267)
PHONE..................................800 481-6006
Donald R Johnsen, *President*
Kenneth M Lamont, *CFO*
Charlene Wyche, *Executive*
Jason Baumgarte, *Info Tech Dir*
Jan Major, *Bookkeeper*
EMP: 85
SQ FT: 11,200
SALES: 6.5MM **Privately Held**
SIC: 7322 Collection agency, except real estate

(P-14037)
JJ MAC INTYRE CO INC (PA)
4160 Temescal Canyon Rd, Corona (92883-4625)
P.O. Box 78150 (92877-0138)
PHONE..................................951 898-4300
Fax: 951 898-4398
Scott M Hall, *CEO*
Kenneth A Lee, *President*
Tim Dodd, *MIS Mgr*
Peter Schuvie, *Opers Mgr*
EMP: 115
SQ FT: 28,254
SALES: 7.5MM **Privately Held**
WEB: www.jjmac.com
SIC: 7322 Collection agency, except real estate

(P-14038)
KINGS CREDIT SERVICES
96 Shaw Ave Ste 221, Clovis (93612-3842)
PHONE..................................559 322-2550
Randall Burchfield, *Owner*
Jeffrey Adams, *Director*
EMP: 55
SALES (est): 3.6MM **Privately Held**
SIC: 7322 Adjustment & collection services

(P-14039)
NATIONAL COMMERCIAL SERVICES
6644 Valjean Ave Ste 100, Van Nuys (91406-5816)
PHONE..................................818 701-4400
Zoran Jovanoski, *President*
Zoran Jovanovski, *President*
Natalie Mansour, *Vice Pres*
EMP: 52
SQ FT: 4,500
SALES: 1.2MM **Privately Held**
WEB: www.ncslegalservices.com
SIC: 7322 Adjustment & collection services

(P-14040)
PCI COLLECTIONS INC
Also Called: P C I & Associates
402 W Broadway Fl 4, San Diego (92101-3554)
P.O. Box 3206, Gardena (90247-1406)
PHONE..................................619 595-3114
Emanuel Theodore Davis, *CEO*
EMP: 262
SALES (est): 10.8MM **Privately Held**
SIC: 7322 Collection agency, except real estate

(P-14041)
PERFORMANT RECOVERY INC
Also Called: DCS
17080 S Harlan Rd, Lathrop (95330-8729)
PHONE..................................209 858-3500
James Tracey, *Principal*
EMP: 200
SALES (corp-wide): 159.3MM **Publicly Held**
SIC: 7322 Collection agency, except real estate
HQ: Performant Recovery, Inc.
333 N Canyons Pkwy # 100
Livermore CA 94551
209 858-3994

(P-14042)
PERFORMANT RECOVERY INC (HQ)
Also Called: D C S
333 N Canyons Pkwy # 100, Livermore (94551-9478)
PHONE..................................209 858-3994
Lisa Im, *CEO*
Hakan Orvell, *CFO*
Lara Crapo, *General Mgr*
Linda Cipolla, *Executive Asst*
Bruce Calvin, *Admin Sec*
EMP: 118
SQ FT: 31,000
SALES (est): 52.2MM
SALES (corp-wide): 159.3MM **Publicly Held**
SIC: 7322 8742 7371 Adjustment & collection services; financial consultant; custom computer programming services
PA: Performant Financial Corporation
333 N Canyons Pkwy # 100
Livermore CA 94551
925 960-4800

(P-14043)
QUALIFIED BLLING CLLCTIONS LLC
Also Called: Q B C
4601 Wilshire Blvd Fl 3, Los Angeles (90010-3884)
PHONE..................................323 556-3470
Thomas Baker, *COO*
Peter Yeh, *COO*
EMP: 200 **EST:** 1982
SALES (est): 2.6MM **Privately Held**
SIC: 7322 Collection agency, except real estate

(P-14044)
RM GALICIA INC
Also Called: Progressive Management Systems
1521 W Cameron Ave # 100, West Covina (91790-2738)
P.O. Box 2220 (91793-2220)
PHONE..................................626 813-6200
Fax: 626 813-6230
Timothy Chase Banta, *CEO*
Juan Vargas, *Vice Pres*
Olga Diaz, *Technology*
EMP: 125 **EST:** 1978
SQ FT: 20,000
SALES (est): 19.4MM **Privately Held**
WEB: www.pmscollects.com
SIC: 7322 Collection agency, except real estate

(P-14045)
RUTLEDGE CLAIMS MANAGEMENT INC
14286 Danielson St # 103, Poway (92064-8819)
PHONE..................................858 888-2000
Thomas W Rutledge, *CEO*
EMP: 100
SALES (est): 1.2MM **Privately Held**
SIC: 7322 Adjustment bureau, except insurance

(P-14046)
SANTA CLARA COUNTY OF
Also Called: Revenue, Dept of
1555 Berger Dr Fl 1, San Jose (95112-2716)
P.O. Box 1897 (95109-1897)
PHONE..................................408 282-3200
Robert McGrath, *Branch Mgr*
Chris Elias, *Treasurer*
Tony Arata, *Admin Mgr*
Ed Bagsik,
Jeff Draper, *Manager*
EMP: 75 **Privately Held**
WEB: www.countyairports.org
SIC: 7322 9311 Adjustment & collection services; taxation department, government;
PA: County Of Santa Clara
3180 Newberry Dr Ste 150
San Jose CA 95118
408 299-5105

(P-14047)
SEQUOIA CONCEPTS INC
Also Called: Sequoia Financial Services
28632 Roadside Dr Ste 110, Agoura Hills (91301-6074)
PHONE..................................818 409-6000
Roy Duplessis, *President*
Denise Duplessis, *Vice Pres*
Roy Deplessis II, *Admin Sec*
King Bechtel, *Mktg Dir*
Tonette Hayes, *Marketing Staff*
EMP: 75
SQ FT: 9,100
SALES (est): 8.5MM **Privately Held**
WEB: www.sequoiafinancial.com
SIC: 7322 Collection agency, except real estate

(P-14048)
TD SERVICE FINANCIAL CORP (PA)
4000 W Metro Dr Ste 400, Orange (92868)
PHONE..................................714 543-8372
Dale Dykema, *Ch of Bd*
Dale L Dykema, *Ch of Bd*
Mark Crafford, *CFO*
Sandra J Medina, *Exec VP*
Chris Breakfield, *Senior VP*
EMP: 141
SALES: 45.2MM **Privately Held**
SIC: 7322 6531 Adjustment & collection services; escrow agent, real estate

(P-14049)
UNIVERSAL ACCOUNTS INC
690 E Green St Ste 300, Pasadena (91101-2121)
PHONE..................................626 356-7900
Lon Yatman, *President*
Esther Yatman, *Exec VP*
Guy Jameson, *Manager*
Weng Tang, *Manager*
Weng L Tang, *Agent*
EMP: 60
SQ FT: 14,000
SALES (est): 5.1MM **Privately Held**
WEB: www.fhs-unifi.com
SIC: 7322 Collection agency, except real estate

(P-14050)
USCB INC
3535 Wilshire Blvd # 700, Los Angeles (90010-2303)
PHONE..................................213 387-6181
Rose Erin, *Manager*
EMP: 75
SALES (corp-wide): 27.1MM **Privately Held**
WEB: www.uscbinc.com
SIC: 7322 Collection agency, except real estate
PA: Uscb, Inc.
3333 Wilshire Blvd Fl 7
Los Angeles CA 90010
213 985-2111

(P-14051)
USCB INC (PA)
Also Called: Uscb America
3333 Wilshire Blvd Fl 7, Los Angeles (90010-4109)
PHONE..................................213 985-2111
Albert Cadena, *Sales Executive*
Melvin F Shaw, *President*
John McCrosky, *CFO*
Thomas Isgrigg, *Exec VP*
Astrid Blackmon, *Senior VP*
EMP: 213
SQ FT: 34,000

PRODUCTS & SERVICES SECTION

7331 - Direct Mail Advertising Svcs County (P-14072)

SALES (est): 27.1MM **Privately Held**
WEB: www.uscbinc.com
SIC: 7322 8741 Adjustment & collection services; management services

(P-14052)
VENGROFF WILLIAMS & ASSOC INC
2099 S State College Blvd # 300, Anaheim (92806-6149)
PHONE..................714 889-6200
Robert Sherman, *Branch Mgr*
Joseph Torba, *President*
Michael Heinz, *Manager*
EMP: 213
SALES (corp-wide): 19.1MM **Privately Held**
SIC: 7322 Collection agency, except real estate
PA: Vengroff, Williams & Associates, Inc.
  8440 N Tamiami Trl
  Sarasota FL 34243
  941 363-5200

7323 Credit Reporting Svcs

(P-14053)
A-CHECK AMERICA INC (PA)
Also Called: A-Check America, Member Act 1
1501 Research Park Dr, Riverside (92507-2114)
P.O. Box 5615 (92517-5615)
PHONE..................951 750-1501
Fax: 951 750-1301
Janice B Howroyd, *CEO*
Carlos Lacambra, *President*
Michael Hoyal, *Vice Pres*
Gregg Hassler, *Vice Pres*
Christine Folmer, *Admin Asst*
EMP: 170
SQ FT: 30,000
SALES (est): 27.9MM **Privately Held**
WEB: www.acheckamerica.com
SIC: 7323 7375 Credit reporting services; information retrieval services

(P-14054)
A-CHECK AMERICA INC
1501 Research Park Dr, Riverside (92507-2114)
P.O. Box 29048, Glendale (91209-9048)
PHONE..................800 872-2677
Carlos Lacambra, *Branch Mgr*
Michael A Hoyal, *Admin Sec*
Sonia Torchia, *Admin Asst*
Steve Cheatham, *Info Tech Dir*
Jay Narang, *Info Tech Mgr*
EMP: 141
SALES (corp-wide): 27.9MM **Privately Held**
WEB: www.acheckamerica.com
SIC: 7323 7389 Credit reporting services; personal investigation service
PA: A-Check America, Inc.
  1501 Research Park Dr
  Riverside CA 92507
  951 750-1501

(P-14055)
ACEVA TECHNOLOGIES INC
1810 Gateway Dr Ste 360, San Mateo (94404-4063)
PHONE..................650 227-5500
Fax: 650 227-5501
Sundeep Jain, *Principal*
EMP: 200
SALES (est): 7MM
SALES (corp-wide): 6.6B **Publicly Held**
WEB: www.aceva.com
SIC: 7323 Credit clearinghouse
HQ: Fis Data Systems Inc.
  680 E Swedesford Rd
  Wayne PA 19087
  484 582-2000

(P-14056)
CREDIT INTERLINK AMERICA
6 Harris Ct, Monterey (93940-5799)
P.O. Box 452, Pebble Beach (93953-0452)
PHONE..................831 655-7890
Tor Matheson, *President*
Phil Karbo, *Vice Pres*
William Mangione-Smith, *Technical Mgr*
EMP: 50

SQ FT: 9,500
SALES (est): 3.5MM **Privately Held**
SIC: 7323 Commercial (mercantile) credit reporting bureau

(P-14057)
DUN & BRADSTREET INC
Also Called: D&B
1 Embarcadero Ctr # 2060, San Francisco (94111-3628)
PHONE..................415 343-6540
EMP: 76
SALES (corp-wide): 1.6B **Publicly Held**
SIC: 7323 Commercial (mercantile) credit reporting bureau
HQ: Dun & Bradstreet, Inc
  103 Jfk Pkwy
  Short Hills NJ 07078
  973 921-5500

(P-14058)
EXPERIAN CORPORATION
475 Anton Blvd, Santa Ana (92704)
PHONE..................714 830-7000
Rick Cortese, *President*
Craig Smith, *Ch of Bd*
Thomas Newkirk, *Vice Chairman*
Chris Callero, *President*
Margaret B Smith, *President*
EMP: 7710
SQ FT: 323,000
SALES (est): 98.4MM
SALES (corp-wide): 4.5B **Privately Held**
SIC: 7323 Credit bureau & agency; commercial (mercantile) credit reporting bureau
HQ: Experian Na Unlimited
  Landmark House
  Nottingham NOTTS NG80
  844 481-8000

(P-14059)
EXPERIAN INFO SOLUTIONS INC (DH)
475 Anton Blvd, Costa Mesa (92626-7037)
P.O. Box 5001 (92628-5001)
PHONE..................714 830-2444
Fax: 714 830-2444
Chris Callero, *CEO*
Craig Halley, *President*
Gary Kearns, *President*
Daniel Schotland, *President*
Jennifer Schulz, *President*
EMP: 3700 EST: 1996
SQ FT: 323,000
SALES (est): 4.7B
SALES (corp-wide): 4.5B **Privately Held**
WEB: www.experian.com
SIC: 7323 Credit bureau & agency; commercial (mercantile) credit reporting bureau
HQ: Experian Holdings, Inc.
  475 Anton Blvd
  Costa Mesa CA 92626
  714 830-7000

(P-14060)
EXPERIAN INFO SOLUTIONS INC
18500 Von Karman Ave # 400, Irvine (92612-0511)
PHONE..................949 567-3731
Ed Ojdana, *President*
Hung Huynh, *Manager*
Patricia Grissom, *Supervisor*
EMP: 200
SALES (corp-wide): 4.5B **Privately Held**
WEB: www.experian.com
SIC: 7323 Commercial (mercantile) credit reporting bureau
HQ: Experian Information Solutions, Inc.
  475 Anton Blvd
  Costa Mesa CA 92626
  714 830-7000

(P-14061)
INFORMATIVE RESEARCH (PA)
13030 Euclid St Ste 209, Garden Grove (92843-1334)
P.O. Box 2379 (92842-2379)
PHONE..................714 638-2855
Fax: 714 636-2510
Randy Buckner, *CEO*
Sean Buckner, *President*
Stan Baldwin, *COO*
Patrick Buckner, *Vice Pres*

Amy Montgomery, *Vice Pres*
EMP: 50 EST: 1946
SALES (est): 11.7MM **Privately Held**
WEB: www.informativeresearch.com
SIC: 7323 Credit reporting services

(P-14062)
MONTRENES FINANCIAL SVCS INC
Also Called: U S Merchant Services
27 Montpellier, Newport Beach (92660-6844)
PHONE..................562 795-0450
Fax: 714 827-7711
Dan Montrenes, *President*
Nancy Newton, *Human Res Dir*
Kelly Nelson, *Sales Mgr*
Pat Means, *Accounts Exec*
EMP: 100
SQ FT: 30,000
SALES (est): 5.3MM **Privately Held**
SIC: 7323 Credit reporting services

(P-14063)
MORTGAGE FAX INC
18685 Main St Ste 101, Huntington Beach (92648-1719)
PHONE..................714 899-2656
Joanne Ahmadi, *President*
EMP: 65
SQ FT: 8,500
SALES (est): 4.4MM **Privately Held**
WEB: www.mortgagefaxinc.com
SIC: 7323 Credit bureau & agency

7331 Direct Mail Advertising Svcs

(P-14064)
ADVANTAGE MAILING INC (PA)
Also Called: Advantage Mailing Service
1600 N Kraemer Blvd, Anaheim (92806-1410)
P.O. Box 66013 (92816-6013)
PHONE..................714 538-3881
Tom Ling, *President*
Thomas C Ling, *President*
Brett Noss, *CFO*
Cara Cohan, *VP Mktg*
Tom Duchene, *Sales Dir*
EMP: 125
SQ FT: 60,000
SALES (est): 39.3MM **Privately Held**
WEB: www.advmailing.com
SIC: 7331 Direct mail advertising services

(P-14065)
ALL DIRECT MAIL SERVICES INC
Also Called: Mr Mailer
5091 4th St, Baldwin Park (91706-2173)
PHONE..................818 833-7773
Fax: 818 765-6960
Dennis Zetting, *CEO*
Doug Zetting, *President*
Theresa Elkins, *Vice Pres*
John Momeyer, *Vice Pres*
Shirley Stephens, *Admin Sec*
EMP: 102
SQ FT: 50,000
SALES (est): 8.3MM **Privately Held**
WEB: www.admsi.com
SIC: 7331 Direct mail advertising services

(P-14066)
BUSINESS SERVICES NETWORK
1275 Fairfax Ave Ste 103, San Francisco (94124-1759)
PHONE..................415 282-8161
Fax: 415 282-8176
Harry Yue, *President*
Cindy Yue, *Vice Pres*
Steven Voris, *Marketing Mgr*
EMP: 72
SQ FT: 31,120
SALES (est): 8.8MM **Privately Held**
WEB: www.bsnc.com
SIC: 7331 2752 7374 Mailing service; commercial printing, offset; data processing service

(P-14067)
CENTRAL VALLEY PRESORT INC
Also Called: Presort Center, The
1931 G St, Fresno (93706-1618)
PHONE..................559 498-6151
Eric Kozlowski, *President*
Robert Kahle, *CEO*
Elga Acosta-Boccardo, *Vice Pres*
Bert Myers, *Vice Pres*
EMP: 85
SQ FT: 52,000
SALES (est): 22.1MM **Privately Held**
WEB: www.thepresort.com
SIC: 7331 2752 Mailing service; promotional printing, lithographic; business form & card printing, lithographic

(P-14068)
DATABASE MARKETING GROUP INC
5 Peters Canyon Rd # 150, Irvine (92606-1793)
PHONE..................714 727-0800
John A Engstrom, *President*
Craig Engstrom, *Vice Pres*
Sharon M Engstrom, *Vice Pres*
Scott Humphrey, *Business Dir*
Gabe Netty, *Sr Software Eng*
EMP: 200
SQ FT: 12,000
SALES (est): 37.6MM **Privately Held**
WEB: www.dbmgroup.com
SIC: 7331 8742 Direct mail advertising services; marketing consulting services

(P-14069)
EURO RSCG SAN FRANCISCO LLC
1355 Sansome St Fl 4, San Francisco (94111-6213)
PHONE..................415 345-7700
Fax: 415 345-7701
Alen Vergis,
Alen Burgis, *CEO*
Jim Lighter, *CFO*
Ed Stevens, *Senior VP*
Jim Lightner, *Vice Pres*
EMP: 50
SALES (est): 3.4MM **Privately Held**
SIC: 7331 Direct mail advertising services

(P-14070)
FINANCIAL STATEMENT SVCS INC (PA)
Also Called: Fssi
3300 S Fairview St, Santa Ana (92704-7004)
PHONE..................714 436-3326
Fax: 714 436-3396
Jennifer Dietz, *CEO*
Henry Perez, *COO*
Karen Elsbury, *CFO*
Dick O'Neil, *Senior VP*
Charles Ragusa, *Vice Pres*
EMP: 144
SQ FT: 167,000
SALES: 19.2MM **Privately Held**
WEB: www.fssi-ca.com
SIC: 7331 7374 2759 Mailing service; data processing & preparation; laser printing

(P-14071)
GLOBAL MAIL INC
921 W Artesia Blvd, Compton (90220-5105)
PHONE..................310 735-0800
Eric Ricardo, *Branch Mgr*
Rick Nordblad, *General Mgr*
EMP: 200
SALES (corp-wide): 63.6B **Privately Held**
SIC: 7331 Mailing service
HQ: Global Mail, Inc.
  2700 S Comm Pkwy Ste 300
  Weston FL 33331
  800 805-9306

(P-14072)
GRIZZARD CMMNCATIONS GROUP INC
110 N Maryland Ave, Glendale (91206-4235)
PHONE..................818 543-1315
Fax: 818 543-1306

7331 - Direct Mail Advertising Svcs County (P-14073)
PRODUDUCTS & SERVICES SECTION

Philip Stolberg, *Branch Mgr*
Pat Sabatelle, *Senior VP*
James Read, *Creative Dir*
Christina Grigg, *Director*
Mayra Oyaga, *Accounts Mgr*
EMP: 55
SALES (corp-wide): 15.1B **Publicly Held**
SIC: 7331 Direct mail advertising services
HQ: Grizzard Communications Group, Inc.
 3500 Lenox Rd Ne Ste 1900
 Atlanta GA 30326
 404 522-8330

(P-14073)
HARTE-HANKS DIRECT MAIL/CALIFO
2337 W Commonwealth Ave, Fullerton (92833-2997)
PHONE.....................714 738-5478
Fax: 714 992-8228
Larry Franklin, *Ch of Bd*
Richard Hockhouser, *President*
Donald R Crews, *Vice Pres*
EMP: 85
SQ FT: 65,000
SALES (est): 5.9MM
SALES (corp-wide): 495.3MM **Publicly Held**
SIC: 7331 Direct mail advertising services
PA: Harte Hanks, Inc.
 9601 Mcallister Fwy # 610
 San Antonio TX 78216
 210 829-9000

(P-14074)
INFOGROUP INC
951 Mariners Island Blvd # 130, San Mateo (94404-1558)
PHONE.....................650 389-0700
Fax: 650 389-0707
EMP: 75
SALES (corp-wide): 151.6MM **Privately Held**
SIC: 7331 2741
PA: Infogroup Inc.
 1020 E 1st St
 Papillion NE 68046
 402 836-4500

(P-14075)
IRON MOUNTAIN FULFILLMENT (HQ)
Also Called: Iron Mountain Assurance Corp
565 Sinclair Frontage Rd, Milpitas (95035-5413)
PHONE.....................408 945-1600
Mike Smith, *President*
William Brown, *Vice Pres*
Stephen P Golden, *Vice Pres*
Fred Garcia, *Executive*
Mike Westin, *Managing Dir*
EMP: 50
SALES (est): 15MM
SALES (corp-wide): 3B **Publicly Held**
WEB: www.comac.com
SIC: 7331 Direct mail advertising services
PA: Iron Mountain Incorporated
 1 Federal St Fl 7
 Boston MA 02110
 617 535-4766

(P-14076)
K/P LLC
13947 Washington Ave, San Leandro (94578-3220)
PHONE.....................510 614-7800
Rich De Senglau, *Branch Mgr*
EMP: 50
SALES (corp-wide): 110.3MM **Privately Held**
WEB: www.kpcorporation.com
SIC: 7331 Direct mail advertising services
PA: Kp Llc
 13951 Washington Ave
 San Leandro CA 94578
 510 346-0729

(P-14077)
KINECTA ALTERNATIVE FIN
2750 E 1st St, Los Angeles (90033-3634)
PHONE.....................323 269-3929
Fax: 323 980-8992
Tom Nix, *Branch Mgr*
EMP: 53

SALES (corp-wide): 27.8MM **Privately Held**
SIC: 7331 6099 Addressing service; check cashing agencies
PA: Kinecta Alternative Financial Solutions, Inc.
 1440 Rosecrans Ave
 Manhattan Beach CA 90266
 310 538-2242

(P-14078)
KP LLC
Also Called: Hunter Advertising Mail Co
13951 Washington Ave, San Leandro (94578-3220)
PHONE.....................510 346-0729
Rich De Senglau, *President*
Aaron Hunt, *Administration*
Shane Morgan, *Info Tech Mgr*
Don Miller, *Project Mgr*
Tom Stoneback, *Opers Mgr*
EMP: 140
SALES (corp-wide): 110.3MM **Privately Held**
WEB: www.kpcorporation.com
SIC: 7331 Direct mail advertising services
PA: Kp Llc
 13951 Washington Ave
 San Leandro CA 94578
 510 346-0729

(P-14079)
KP LLC
13951 Washington Ave, San Leandro (94578-3220)
PHONE.....................510 614-7800
Scott Kane, *Manager*
EMP: 60
SQ FT: 6,000
SALES (corp-wide): 110.3MM **Privately Held**
WEB: www.kpcorporation.com
SIC: 7331 Mailing service
PA: Kp Llc
 13951 Washington Ave
 San Leandro CA 94578
 510 346-0729

(P-14080)
LOMITA LOGISTICS LLC
Also Called: Xpo
3541 Lomita Blvd, Torrance (90505-5016)
PHONE.....................310 784-8485
Fax: 310 784-0554
Kelly Herold, *Mng Member*
David Gomes, *Info Tech Dir*
Fabrizio Alvear, *Info Tech Mgr*
Julie Martin, *Sales Mgr*
Barbara Rousch, *Sales Mgr*
EMP: 100
SQ FT: 15,000
SALES: 16.8MM
SALES (corp-wide): 11.2B **Publicly Held**
WEB: www.xpomail.com
SIC: 7331 Mailing service
PA: R.R. Donnelley & Sons Company
 35 W Wacker Dr Ste 3650
 Chicago IL 60601
 312 326-8000

(P-14081)
M M DIRECT MARKETING INC
14271 Corporate Dr, Garden Grove (92843-4937)
PHONE.....................714 265-4100
Godfred P Otueye, *President*
Godfred P Otuteye, *Admin Sec*
Kevin Fournier, *IT/INT Sup*
Dawn Croasmun, *Opers Staff*
Joanna Valigura, *Marketing Staff*
EMP: 300
SALES (est): 9.8MM
SALES (corp-wide): 3.9B **Privately Held**
WEB: www.moneymailer.com
SIC: 7331 6794 Mailing service; franchises, selling or licensing
HQ: Money Mailer, Llc
 12131 Western Ave
 Garden Grove CA 92841
 714 889-3800

(P-14082)
MAILMARK ENTERPRISES LLC
8587 Canoga Ave, Canoga Park (91304-2609)
PHONE.....................818 407-0660

Fax: 818 407-0901
Barry Silver,
Will Shatford, *CTO*
Leon Sturman, *Software Dev*
Megan Lincavage, *Opers Staff*
Elmer Gomez, *Sales Mgr*
EMP: 50
SQ FT: 15,500
SALES (est): 6.1MM **Privately Held**
WEB: www.mailmark.com
SIC: 7331 Direct mail advertising services

(P-14083)
MERCURY MAILING SYSTEMS INC
2727 Exposition Blvd, Los Angeles (90018-4119)
PHONE.....................323 730-0307
Fax: 323 730-1548
Paul Hood, *President*
Cynthia Garcia, *VP Sales*
EMP: 70
SQ FT: 20,000
SALES (est): 3.3MM **Privately Held**
SIC: 7331 Mailing service

(P-14084)
MONEY MAILER LLC (HQ)
Also Called: Mm Advertising
12131 Western Ave, Garden Grove (92841-2914)
PHONE.....................714 889-3800
Fax: 714 889-1590
Gary Mulloy,
Tom Cimino, *Vice Pres*
Doug Cunningham, *Vice Pres*
Mike Hiskett, *Vice Pres*
Stephen Lee, *Vice Pres*
EMP: 250
SQ FT: 60,000
SALES (est): 63.4MM
SALES (corp-wide): 3.9B **Privately Held**
WEB: www.moneymailer.com
SIC: 7331 6794 Mailing service; franchises, selling or licensing
PA: Roark Capital Group Inc.
 1180 Peachtree St Ne # 2500
 Atlanta GA 30309
 404 591-5200

(P-14085)
MOPAR ENTERPRISES
Also Called: West Coast Mailing & Dist
1710 Dornoch Ct Ste A, San Diego (92154-7235)
PHONE.....................858 492-1123
Fax: 858 492-1277
Parvin Salehi, *President*
EMP: 60
SQ FT: 49,278
SALES (est): 4.3MM **Privately Held**
SIC: 7331 Mailing service

(P-14086)
POMONA COLLEGE
333 N College Way, Claremont (91711-4429)
PHONE.....................909 621-8000
Fax: 909 621-8952
David W Oxtoby, *President*
David Alexander, *Trustee*
Amy Marcus-Newhall, *Vice Pres*
Ann Quinley, *Vice Pres*
Jordan Snedcof, *Associate Dir*
EMP: 97
SALES (corp-wide): 275.5MM **Privately Held**
SIC: 7331 8221 Addressing service; college, except junior
PA: Pomona College
 550 N College Ave
 Claremont CA 91711
 909 621-8135

(P-14087)
PSI GROUP
125 Valley Dr, Brisbane (94005-1317)
PHONE.....................415 468-1660
Fax: 415 468-0169
Nicholas Saribalis, *Owner*
EMP: 70
SALES (est): 5.9MM **Privately Held**
SIC: 7331 Direct mail advertising services

(P-14088)
REAL ESTATE IMAGE
Also Called: Advanced Image Direct
1415 S Acacia Ave, Fullerton (92831-5317)
PHONE.....................714 502-3900
Fax: 714 502-3901
Ty McMillin, *President*
Michael Shevitz, *CFO*
Hugo Solorio, *Vice Pres*
Perry Wilson, *VP Sales*
Brett Furlong, *Cust Mgr*
EMP: 150
SQ FT: 136,000
SALES (est): 22MM **Privately Held**
WEB: www.advancedimagedirect.com
SIC: 7331 2752 Direct mail advertising services; commercial printing, lithographic

(P-14089)
RR DONNELLEY & SONS COMPANY
3541 Lomita Blvd, Torrance (90505-5016)
PHONE.....................310 784-8485
Eric Fernandez, *Manager*
EMP: 100
SALES (corp-wide): 11.2B **Publicly Held**
SIC: 7331 Mailing service
PA: R.R. Donnelley & Sons Company
 35 W Wacker Dr Ste 3650
 Chicago IL 60601
 312 326-8000

(P-14090)
SPECTRUM INFORMATION SERVICES (PA)
16 Technology Dr Ste 107, Irvine (92618-2323)
PHONE.....................949 752-7070
Curtis Pilon, *President*
Mike Buttke, *COO*
Jim Bradford, *CFO*
Glenn Odell, *Senior VP*
Glenn O Dell, *Vice Pres*
EMP: 70
SQ FT: 142,000
SALES: 10MM **Privately Held**
SIC: 7331 7375 4731 Mailing service; information retrieval services; shipping documents preparation

(P-14091)
STAMPSCOM INC (PA)
1990 E Grand Ave, El Segundo (90245-5013)
PHONE.....................310 482-5800
Kenneth McBride, *Ch of Bd*
James Bortnak, *President*
Kyle Huebner, *President*
Seth Weisberg,
EMP: 148
SQ FT: 99,600
SALES: 213.9MM **Publicly Held**
WEB: www.stamps.com
SIC: 7331 5961 4813 Mailing service; catalog & mail-order houses;

(P-14092)
T G T ENTERPRISES INC
Also Called: Anderson Direct Marketing
12650 Danielson Ct, Poway (92064-6822)
PHONE.....................858 413-0300
Ted Tietge, *CEO*
Randy Dale, *President*
Vicky Ruegsegger, *Officer*
Scott Hopkins, *Exec VP*
Mike Campbell, *Vice Pres*
EMP: 130
SQ FT: 77,000
SALES (est): 32.8MM **Privately Held**
WEB: www.andersondirectmail.com
SIC: 7331 2759 Mailing service; commercial printing

(P-14093)
TOWNE INC
Also Called: Towne Advertising
3441 W Macarthur Blvd, Santa Ana (92704-6805)
PHONE.....................714 540-3095
Fax: 714 540-4192
Tarek Elkomi, *Branch Mgr*
EMP: 100

PRODUCTS & SERVICES SECTION
7334 - Photocopying & Duplicating Svcs County (P-14113)

SALES (corp-wide): 20.5MM **Privately Held**
SIC: 7331 7311 Mailing service; advertising agencies
PA: Towne, Inc.
3441 W Macarthur Blvd
Santa Ana CA 92704
714 540-3095

(P-14094)
TRANSMRCAN MLING FLFLLMENT INC
355 State Pl, Escondido (92029-1359)
PHONE 760 745-5343
Fax: 760 745-0162
Paul Barron, *CEO*
Heather Benjamin, *Vice Pres*
Eleanor Monica, *Vice Pres*
Erik Martinez, *Prgrmr*
David Graner, *Programmer Anys*
EMP: 100
SALES (est): 18.6MM **Privately Held**
WEB: www.transamericanmailing.com
SIC: 7331 Mailing service

(P-14095)
UPS EXPEDITED MAIL SVCS INC
3004 Alvarado St Ste G, San Leandro (94577-5729)
PHONE 510 297-4600
Mike Frete, *General Mgr*
EMP: 50
SALES (corp-wide): 58.3B **Publicly Held**
SIC: 7331 Mailing service
HQ: Ups Expedited Mail Services, Inc.
12380 Morris Rd
Alpharetta GA 30005
404 828-6000

(P-14096)
VALASSIS COMMUNICATIONS INC
1575 Corporate Dr, Costa Mesa (92626-1426)
PHONE 714 751-4006
Steve Scott, *Manager*
Lyjune Carter, *Human Res Mgr*
Jenny Pado, *Human Resources*
EMP: 52
SALES (corp-wide): 5.3B **Privately Held**
WEB: www.valassis.com
SIC: 7331 Direct mail advertising services
HQ: Valassis Communications, Inc.
19975 Victor Pkwy
Livonia MI 48152
734 591-3000

(P-14097)
VALASSIS DIRECT MAIL INC
6955 Mowry Ave, Newark (94560-4924)
PHONE 510 505-6500
Debra Robinson, *Manager*
EMP: 100
SALES (corp-wide): 5.3B **Privately Held**
WEB: www.advo.com
SIC: 7331 Direct mail advertising services
HQ: Valassis Direct Mail, Inc.
1 Targeting Ctr
Windsor CT 06095
800 437-0479

7334 Photocopying & Duplicating Svcs

(P-14098)
ABI ATTORNEYS SERVICE INC (PA)
Also Called: ABI VIP Attorney Service
2015 W Park Ave, Redlands (92373-6271)
P.O. Box 9240 (92375-2440)
PHONE 909 793-0613
Fax: 909 792-2590
Alice J Benge, *President*
Chuck Benge, *Corp Secy*
Michael Chudy, *Opers Staff*
EMP: 80
SQ FT: 7,500
SALES (est): 6MM **Privately Held**
WEB: www.abivip.com
SIC: 7334 Photocopying & duplicating services

(P-14099)
AMERICAN LEGAL COPY-OR LLC
98 Battery St Ste 220, San Francisco (94111-5509)
PHONE 415 777-4449
Fax: 415 777-4474
Kevin Brooks, *Manager*
EMP: 100 **Privately Held**
WEB: www.alcweb.com
SIC: 7334 Photocopying & duplicating services
PA: American Legal Copy-Or, Llc
1001 4th Ave Ste 300
Seattle WA 98154

(P-14100)
AMERICAN REPROGRAPHICS CO LLC
Also Called: Ford Graphics
934 Venice Blvd, Los Angeles (90015-3230)
PHONE 213 745-3145
Fax: 213 745-3160
Juan Carlos, *Principal*
Jorge Avalos, *Officer*
EMP: 100
SALES (corp-wide): 428.6MM **Publicly Held**
WEB: www.e-arc.com
SIC: 7334 7336 7374 Photocopying & duplicating services; commercial art & graphic design; computer graphics service
HQ: American Reprographics Company, L.L.C.
1981 N Broadway Ste 385
Walnut Creek CA 94596
925 949-5100

(P-14101)
AMERICAN REPROGRAPHICS CO LLC
Also Called: Brownie's Digital Imaging
1322 V St, Sacramento (95818-1418)
PHONE 916 443-1322
Jack Anderson, *Manager*
Rochon John, *Technology*
Allenby Lori, *Technology*
EMP: 80
SALES (corp-wide): 428.6MM **Publicly Held**
WEB: www.e-arc.com
SIC: 7334 Blueprinting service
HQ: American Reprographics Company, L.L.C.
1981 N Broadway Ste 385
Walnut Creek CA 94596
925 949-5100

(P-14102)
AMERICAN REPROGRAPHICS CO LLC
Also Called: ARC Imaging Resources
616 Monterey Pass Rd, Monterey Park (91754-2419)
PHONE 626 289-5021
Doug Elffers, *Mng Member*
J Dieterich, *Manager*
EMP: 52
SALES (corp-wide): 428.6MM **Publicly Held**
WEB: www.e-arc.com
SIC: 7334 Photocopying & duplicating services
HQ: American Reprographics Company, L.L.C.
1981 N Broadway Ste 385
Walnut Creek CA 94596
925 949-5100

(P-14103)
AMERICAN REPROGRAPHICS CO LLC
San Jose Blueprint
821 Martin Ave, Santa Clara (95050-2903)
PHONE 408 295-5770
Norma Mathews, *Human Res Mgr*
Doug Koch, *Business Mgr*
Rick Ferry, *Manager*
EMP: 90

SALES (corp-wide): 428.6MM **Publicly Held**
WEB: www.e-arc.com
SIC: 7334 Photocopying & duplicating services
HQ: American Reprographics Company, L.L.C.
1981 N Broadway Ste 385
Walnut Creek CA 94596
925 949-5100

(P-14104)
AMERICAN REPROGRAPHICS CO LLC
Also Called: Consolidated Reprographics
345 Clinton St, Costa Mesa (92626-6011)
PHONE 714 751-2680
Fax: 714 662-7655
Erick Hazell, *Vice Pres*
Darrell Seng, *Info Tech Dir*
Lindsey Smith, *Director*
EMP: 150
SQ FT: 42,000
SALES (corp-wide): 428.6MM **Publicly Held**
WEB: www.e-arc.com
SIC: 7334 Photocopying & duplicating services; blueprinting service; multigraphing
HQ: American Reprographics Company, L.L.C.
1981 N Broadway Ste 385
Walnut Creek CA 94596
925 949-5100

(P-14105)
AMERICAN REPROGRAPHICS CO LLC
Also Called: Ocb Riverside
4295 Main St, Riverside (92501-3822)
PHONE 951 686-0530
Jesse De La Cruz, *General Mgr*
EMP: 75
SALES (corp-wide): 428.6MM **Publicly Held**
WEB: www.ocbinc.com
SIC: 7334 Photocopying & duplicating services
HQ: American Reprographics Company, L.L.C.
1981 N Broadway Ste 385
Walnut Creek CA 94596
925 949-5100

(P-14106)
ARC
Riot Color- Region 3
1740 Stanford St, Santa Monica (90404-4116)
PHONE 310 857-5759
Richard Waters, *President*
EMP: 217
SALES (corp-wide): 25.6MM **Privately Held**
SIC: 7334 Blueprinting service
PA: Arc
345 Clinton St
Costa Mesa CA 92626
714 424-8500

(P-14107)
ARC DOCUMENT SOLUTIONS INC
655 N Central Ave, Glendale (91203-1422)
PHONE 818 242-6555
Michael Cohanzard, *CEO*
EMP: 120
SALES (corp-wide): 428.6MM **Publicly Held**
SIC: 7334 Blueprinting service
PA: Arc Document Solutions, Inc.
1981 N Broadway Ste 385
Walnut Creek CA 94596
925 949-5100

(P-14108)
ARC DOCUMENT SOLUTIONS INC
1207 John Reed Ct Ste A, City of Industry (91745-2421)
PHONE 626 333-7005
Steve Ostrander, *Manager*
EMP: 92

SALES (corp-wide): 428.6MM **Publicly Held**
SIC: 7334 Photocopying & duplicating services
PA: Arc Document Solutions, Inc.
1981 N Broadway Ste 385
Walnut Creek CA 94596
925 949-5100

(P-14109)
ARC DOCUMENT SOLUTIONS INC
2430 Mariner Square Loop, Alameda (94501-1074)
PHONE 415 495-8700
Kumar Suriyakumar, *CEO*
Kumarakulasingam Suriyakumar, *CEO*
EMP: 50
SALES (est): 11MM **Privately Held**
SIC: 7334 Photocopying & duplicating services; blueprinting service

(P-14110)
ARC DOCUMENT SOLUTIONS INC
Elite Reprographics
945 Bryant St Ste 1000, San Francisco (94103-4523)
PHONE 415 495-8700
Fax: 415 957-1211
Soren Goodman, *General Mgr*
Suri Suriyakumar, *CEO*
Rick Ferry, *Principal*
EMP: 50
SALES (corp-wide): 428.6MM **Publicly Held**
WEB: www.e-arc.com
SIC: 7334 Photocopying & duplicating services; blueprinting service
PA: Arc Document Solutions, Inc.
1981 N Broadway Ste 385
Walnut Creek CA 94596
925 949-5100

(P-14111)
ARC DOCUMENT SOLUTIONS INC
Also Called: Reliable Graphics
15019 Califa St, Van Nuys (91411-3003)
PHONE 818 908-0222
Fax: 818 785-9352
Danny Mesa, *Branch Mgr*
Danny Meza, *Manager*
EMP: 120
SQ FT: 15,727
SALES (corp-wide): 428.6MM **Publicly Held**
SIC: 7334 Blueprinting service
PA: Arc Document Solutions, Inc.
1981 N Broadway Ste 385
Walnut Creek CA 94596
925 949-5100

(P-14112)
ASSOCTED REPRODUCTION SVCS INC
Also Called: ARS
13925 Whittier Blvd, Whittier (90605-2037)
PHONE 562 696-1181
John A Antonelli, *CEO*
John W Antonelli, *President*
Marsha Antonelli, *Vice Pres*
Dan Jakle, *Vice Pres*
Ron Weingarten, *Info Tech Mgr*
EMP: 160
SQ FT: 25,000
SALES (est): 17.3MM **Privately Held**
WEB: www.arslegal.com
SIC: 7334 Photocopying & duplicating services

(P-14113)
AUXILIO INC (PA)
27271 Las Ramblas Ste 200, Mission Viejo (92691-8042)
PHONE 949 614-0700
Fax: 949 614-0701
Joseph J Flynn, *President*
JD Abouchar, *Ch of Bd*
John D Pace, *Ch of Bd*
Paul T Anthony, *CFO*
Sean Hughes, *Exec VP*
EMP: 105
SQ FT: 17,000

7334 - Photocopying & Duplicating Svcs County (P-14114)

SALES: 61.2MM **Publicly Held**
WEB: www.auxilio.net
SIC: 7334 8748 Photocopying & duplicating services; business consulting

(P-14114)
AUXILIO SOLUTIONS INC
27271 Las Ramblas Ste 200, Mission Viejo (92691-8042)
PHONE.....................949 614-0700
Joseph J Flynn, *President*
EMP: 214 EST: 2004
SQ FT: 10,000
SALES (est): 2.9MM **Publicly Held**
SIC: 7334 8741 Photocopying & duplicating services; management services
PA: Auxilio, Inc.
  27271 Las Ramblas Ste 200
  Mission Viejo CA 92691

(P-14115)
C2 IMAGING (PA)
3180 Pullman St, Costa Mesa (92626-3323)
PHONE.....................714 668-5955
Fax: 714 545-2850
Gary Crisp, *CEO*
William Govaars II, *Shareholder*
Arthur Gregory Lundeen III, *Shareholder*
Barry Malkin, *COO*
Julie Crisp, *Exec VP*
EMP: 60
SQ FT: 28,000
SALES (est): 29.2MM **Privately Held**
WEB: www.c2repro.com
SIC: 7334 Photocopying & duplicating services

(P-14116)
CONCORD DOCUMENT SERVICES INC (PA)
1321 W 12th St, Los Angeles (90015-2008)
PHONE.....................213 745-3175
Fernando B Flores, *CEO*
Hector Flores, *President*
Jenny Flores, *Manager*
EMP: 51 EST: 1996
SQ FT: 9,000
SALES (est): 7.4MM **Privately Held**
WEB: www.concorddoc.com
SIC: 7334 3577 Photocopying & duplicating services; optical scanning devices

(P-14117)
FAR WESTERN GRAPHICS INC
Also Called: Denevi Digital
2642 Heritage Park Cir, San Jose (95132-2211)
PHONE.....................408 481-9777
Fax: 408 481-9780
Serena Dawn Motekaitis, *CEO*
David Motekaitis, *President*
Brian Cruzen, *Opers Mgr*
Terry Curry, *Sales Mgr*
Gene Smyth, *Maintence Staff*
EMP: 65 EST: 1973
SQ FT: 38,600
SALES (est): 15.5MM **Privately Held**
WEB: www.farwesterngraphics.com
SIC: 7334 2752 Photocopying & duplicating services; commercial printing, offset

(P-14118)
FEDEX OFFICE & PRINT SVCS INC
2799 E Thousand Oaks Blvd, Thousand Oaks (91362-3257)
PHONE.....................805 379-1552
Chris O'Neil, *Manager*
Christina Davis, *Sales Executive*
Maria Gonzales, *Sales Executive*
Andrew Dalto, *Accounts Exec*
Andrew Morales, *Accounts Exec*
EMP: 50
SALES (corp-wide): 50.3B **Publicly Held**
WEB: www.kinkos.com
SIC: 7334 Photocopying & duplicating services
HQ: Fedex Office And Print Services, Inc.
  7900 Legacy Dr
  Plano TX 75024
  214 550-7000

(P-14119)
FEDEX OFFICE & PRINT SVCS INC
13488 Maxella Ave, Marina Del Rey (90292-4300)
PHONE.....................310 827-2297
Greg Johnson, *Manager*
EMP: 50
SALES (corp-wide): 50.3B **Publicly Held**
WEB: www.kinkos.com
SIC: 7334 Photocopying & duplicating services
HQ: Fedex Office And Print Services, Inc.
  7900 Legacy Dr
  Plano TX 75024
  214 550-7000

(P-14120)
FEDEX OFFICE & PRINT SVCS INC
4360 E Main St Ste A, Ventura (93003-8279)
PHONE.....................805 339-2000
Rick Schaub, *Manager*
Leslie Benners, *CFO*
Lance Pury, *Technician*
EMP: 60
SALES (corp-wide): 50.3B **Publicly Held**
WEB: www.kinkos.com
SIC: 7334 Photocopying & duplicating services
HQ: Fedex Office And Print Services, Inc.
  7900 Legacy Dr
  Plano TX 75024
  214 550-7000

(P-14121)
FEDEX OFFICE & PRINT SVCS INC
800 Wilshire Blvd, Los Angeles (90017-2604)
P.O. Box Shire Blvd (90017)
PHONE.....................213 892-1700
Shawn Pendergast, *Branch Mgr*
EMP: 50
SALES (corp-wide): 50.3B **Publicly Held**
WEB: www.kinkos.com
SIC: 7334 Photocopying & duplicating services
HQ: Fedex Office And Print Services, Inc.
  7900 Legacy Dr
  Plano TX 75024
  214 550-7000

(P-14122)
KNOX ATTORNEY SERVICE INC (PA)
Also Called: Knox Copy Centers
2250 4th Ave Ste 200, San Diego (92101-2124)
PHONE.....................619 233-9700
Fax: 619 685-4290
Steve Knox, *President*
Steve Todd, *CFO*
John Maguire, *Vice Pres*
Marilyn Menard, *Executive*
Shelly Griffin, *Executive Asst*
EMP: 165
SQ FT: 165,929
SALES (est): 26.3MM **Privately Held**
WEB: www.knoxservices.com
SIC: 7334 8111 7389 Photocopying & duplicating services; legal aid service; courier or messenger service

(P-14123)
NOVITEX ENTP SOLUTIONS INC
71 Park Ln, Brisbane (94005-1309)
PHONE.....................415 528-2960
EMP: 174
SALES (corp-wide): 478.3MM **Privately Held**
SIC: 7334 Photocopying & duplicating services
PA: Novitex Enterprise Solutions, Inc.
  300 First Stamford Pl # 2
  Stamford CT 06902
  844 668-4839

(P-14124)
OPTISOURCE TECHNOLOGIES INC
1855 W Katella Ave # 170, Orange (92867-3441)
PHONE.....................714 288-0825

Trang Nguyen, *President*
David Nguyen, *President*
EMP: 50 EST: 1997
SQ FT: 5,500
SALES (est): 2.1MM **Privately Held**
WEB: www.optisource.com
SIC: 7334 Photocopying & duplicating services

(P-14125)
RICOH USA INC
Also Called: Nightrider Overnite Copy Svc
333 S Hope St Ste E200, Los Angeles (90071-1467)
PHONE.....................213 489-1700
Fax: 213 489-7880
Mark Nunokawa, *Manager*
Mark Wentworth, *Engineer*
Manuel Valle, *Manager*
EMP: 50
SALES (corp-wide): 18.8B **Privately Held**
WEB: www.ikon.com
SIC: 7334 Photocopying & duplicating services
HQ: Ricoh Usa, Inc.
  70 Valley Stream Pkwy
  Malvern PA 19355
  610 296-8000

(P-14126)
RICOH USA INC
Also Called: Nightrider Overnite Copy Svc
1300 Clay St Ste 165, Oakland (94612-1421)
PHONE.....................510 839-6399
Fax: 510 839-7834
Charles Dickinson, *Manager*
Anthony Edwards, *Sr Ntwrk Engine*
Matt Heekin, *Project Mgr*
Kristine Fakhimi, *Mktg Dir*
Cindy Marshall, *Sales Staff*
EMP: 50
SALES (corp-wide): 18.8B **Privately Held**
WEB: www.ikon.com
SIC: 7334 Photocopying & duplicating services
HQ: Ricoh Usa, Inc.
  70 Valley Stream Pkwy
  Malvern PA 19355
  610 296-8000

(P-14127)
SAN JOSE BLUPRT SVC & SUP CO (PA)
821 Martin Ave, Santa Clara (95050-2903)
PHONE.....................408 295-5770
Fax: 408 971-3299
David Dignam, *President*
Bernice E Cowherd, *Treasurer*
Miles Cowherd, *Vice Pres*
EMP: 90
SQ FT: 10,000
SALES (est): 3.9MM **Privately Held**
SIC: 7334 5999 Photocopying & duplicating services; blueprinting service; drafting equipment & supplies

(P-14128)
UCLA COPY SERVICES
555 Westwood Plz Ste B, Los Angeles (90095-8351)
PHONE.....................310 794-6371
James Muh, *Director*
David Aberbush, *Director*
EMP: 50
SALES (est): 3.4MM **Privately Held**
SIC: 7334 2759 Photocopying & duplicating services; commercial printing

(P-14129)
V A ANDERSON ENTERPRISES INC
2680 Bishop Dr Ste 140, San Ramon (94583-4453)
PHONE.....................925 866-6150
Fax: 925 866-6664
EMP: 73
SALES (corp-wide): 8.3MM **Privately Held**
SIC: 7334
PA: V. A. Anderson Enterprises, Inc.
  400 Atlas St
  Brea CA 92821
  714 990-6100

(P-14130)
XEROX CORPORATION
914 S Victory Blvd, Burbank (91502-2429)
PHONE.....................818 848-8676
Michael Simenian, *Branch Mgr*
EMP: 77
SALES (corp-wide): 18B **Publicly Held**
WEB: www.xerox.com
SIC: 7334 Photocopying & duplicating services
PA: Xerox Corporation
  45 Glover Ave Ste 700
  Norwalk CT 06850
  203 968-3000

7335 Commercial Photography

(P-14131)
CDM FIELD SERVICES INC
25 Crescent Dr 253a, Pleasant Hill (94523-5508)
PHONE.....................936 537-7786
Steven Smith, *Principal*
EMP: 125 EST: 2013
SQ FT: 700
SALES (est): 8.1MM **Privately Held**
SIC: 7335 Commercial photography

(P-14132)
PRIMARY COLOR SYSTEMS CORP
401 Coral Cir, El Segundo (90245-4622)
PHONE.....................310 841-0250
Ed Phillips, *Branch Mgr*
Dennis Daniels, *Opers Dir*
Billy Siah, *Manager*
EMP: 130
SALES (corp-wide): 60MM **Privately Held**
SIC: 7335 7384 Photographic studio, commercial; photofinishing laboratory
PA: Primary Color Systems Corporation
  265 Briggs Ave
  Costa Mesa CA 92626
  949 660-7080

(P-14133)
SECOND IMAGE NATIONAL LLC
700 E Bonita Ave, Pomona (91767-1906)
PHONE.....................909 445-8080
EMP: 72
SALES (corp-wide): 23.2MM **Privately Held**
SIC: 7335 Photographic studio, commercial
PA: Second Image National, Llc
  170 E Arrow Hwy
  San Dimas CA 91773
  800 229-7477

7336 Commercial Art & Graphic Design

(P-14134)
BLT & ASSOCIATES INC
6430 W Sunset Blvd # 800, Los Angeles (90028-7911)
PHONE.....................323 860-4000
Fax: 323 860-0890
Clive Baillie, *President*
Kaz Dugandzic, *President*
Dawn Baillie, *CFO*
Andi Delott, *Senior VP*
Rick Lynch, *Vice Pres*
EMP: 170
SQ FT: 15,000
SALES (est): 22.5MM **Privately Held**
WEB: www.bltomato.com
SIC: 7336 Commercial art & graphic design

(P-14135)
BROAD BEACH FILMS INC
1438 N Gower St Ste 48, Los Angeles (90028-8362)
PHONE.....................323 468-5120
Malek Akkad, *President*
Keren Shane, *Accounting Staf*
EMP: 200

PRODUCTS & SERVICES SECTION
7336 - Commercial Art & Graphic Design County (P-14157)

SALES (est): 6.2MM **Privately Held**
SIC: 7336 Film strip, slide & still film production

(P-14136)
CHAMPION SIGNS INCORPORATED
7835 Wilkerson Ct, San Diego (92111-3606)
PHONE..................................858 751-2900
Fax: 858 751-2901
Ron Johnson, *President*
EMP: 50
SQ FT: 8,000
SALES (est): 3.2MM **Privately Held**
WEB: www.championsigns.net
SIC: 7336 Silk screen design

(P-14137)
CINNABAR
4571 Electronics Pl, Los Angeles (90039-1007)
PHONE..................................818 842-8190
Jonathan Katz, *President*
Alexandra Demilner, *Project Mgr*
Brian Whittier, *Manager*
Larry Hymes, *Agent*
EMP: 200
SQ FT: 60,000
SALES (est): 15.6MM **Privately Held**
SIC: 7336 3999 7819 Graphic arts & related design; theatrical scenery; sound (effects & music production), motion picture; visual effects production

(P-14138)
CINNABAR CALIFORNIA INC
4571 Electronics Pl, Los Angeles (90039-1007)
PHONE..................................818 842-8190
Jonathan Katz, *Ch of Bd*
Leslie Crawford, *Vice Pres*
Kip Katz, *Vice Pres*
Jeannie Lomma, *General Mgr*
EMP: 60
SQ FT: 55,000
SALES (est): 6.7MM **Privately Held**
SIC: 7336 Art design services

(P-14139)
CONSOLIDATED DESIGN WEST INC
Also Called: Cdw
1345 S Lewis St, Anaheim (92805-6431)
PHONE..................................714 999-1476
Fax: 714 999-2863
Victor John Perrillo, *CEO*
Debbie Racy, *Controller*
Michael Brown, *Marketing Staff*
Jon Templeton, *Marketing Staff*
Chantel Heath, *Receptionist*
EMP: 80
SQ FT: 7,500
SALES (est): 19MM **Privately Held**
SIC: 7336 2754 Package design; commercial printing, gravure

(P-14140)
COUNTY OF LOS ANGELES
Also Called: Gateway
1 Gateway Plz, Los Angeles (90012-3745)
P.O. Box 90012 (90009-0012)
PHONE..................................213 922-6210
Roger Snoball, *Owner*
Frank Alejandro, *COO*
Ted Montoya, *Director*
Young Chang, *Manager*
Lilian D Gutierrez, *Manager*
EMP: 1000 **Privately Held**
WEB: www.co.la.ca.us
SIC: 7336 9621 Commercial art & graphic design; transportation department: government, non-operating;
PA: County Of Los Angeles
500 W Temple St Ste 375
Los Angeles CA 90012
213 974-1101

(P-14141)
CUSTOMLINE PROFESSIONAL
567 S Melrose St, Placentia (92870-6305)
PHONE..................................714 996-1333
Fax: 714 996-4513
Dan Mattox, *President*
John Immanuel, *Controller*
EMP: 300

SQ FT: 60,000
SALES (est): 35.8MM **Privately Held**
WEB: www.customlinescreenprint.com
SIC: 7336 Silk screen design

(P-14142)
DANDREA GRAPHIC CORPORTION
Also Called: D'Andrea Graphics
6341 Arizona Cir, Los Angeles (90045-1201)
PHONE..................................310 642-0260
David D'Andrea, *CEO*
EMP: 80
SQ FT: 25,000
SALES (est): 15.4MM **Privately Held**
SIC: 7336 Commercial art & graphic design

(P-14143)
DSH WEST INC
Also Called: Dsh Graphics
5455 Camino De Bryant, Yorba Linda (92887-4209)
PHONE..................................714 692-8777
Ron Herrera, *President*
Donna Herrera, *President*
EMP: 75
SALES (est): 7.8MM **Privately Held**
SIC: 7336 Creative services to advertisers, except writers; graphic arts & related design

(P-14144)
E21 CORP
39111 Paseo Padre Pkwy # 208, Fremont (94538-1672)
PHONE..................................510 818-9600
Joseph Sun, *President*
CJ Chen, *President*
William Walker, *Vice Pres*
Amy Sun, *Admin Sec*
EMP: 120
SALES (est): 9.4MM **Privately Held**
WEB: www.e21mm.com
SIC: 7336 Graphic arts & related design

(P-14145)
FINAL FILM
Also Called: Flash Point Graphix
3620 W Valhalla Dr, Burbank (91505-1127)
PHONE..................................323 467-0700
Fax: 323 461-9980
Thomas L Saliba, *Ch of Bd*
Guy S Claudy, *President*
Ron Dejesus, *President*
Gregory D Davidiian, *CEO*
Gary Gross, *CFO*
EMP: 62
SQ FT: 20,000
SALES (est): 10MM **Privately Held**
WEB: www.finalfilm.com
SIC: 7336 Graphic arts & related design

(P-14146)
FROG DESIGN INC (DH)
660 3rd St Fl 4, San Francisco (94107-1921)
PHONE..................................415 442-4804
Fax: 415 442-4803
Doreen Lorenzo, *CEO*
Andy Zimmerman, *President*
Craig Ayers, *CFO*
Theodore Forbath, *Vice Pres*
Eric Hummel, *Vice Pres*
EMP: 148
SALES (est): 36.6MM
SALES (corp-wide): 1B **Publicly Held**
WEB: www.frogdesign.com
SIC: 7336 Graphic arts & related design
HQ: Aricent Us Inc.
1 Tower Center Blvd Fl 18
East Brunswick NJ 08816
732 514-6654

(P-14147)
GEL PAK LLC
31398 Huntwood Ave, Hayward (94544-7818)
PHONE..................................510 576-2220
Jeanne Beacham, *Principal*
EMP: 75
SALES (est): 163.4K
SALES (corp-wide): 22.6MM **Privately Held**
SIC: 7336 Package design

PA: Delphon Industries, Llc
31398 Huntwood Ave
Hayward CA 94544
510 576-2220

(P-14148)
HARDING MKTG CMMUNICATIONS INC (PA)
Also Called: Harding & Associates
377 S Daniel Way, San Jose (95128-5120)
PHONE..................................408 345-4545
Fax: 408 345-4550
James F Harding, *CEO*
Maria Richard, *CFO*
Karen Scordino, *Executive*
Ryan Luders, *Administration*
Lambert Lee, *Info Tech Mgr*
EMP: 70
SQ FT: 10,000
SALES (est): 11MM **Privately Held**
WEB: www.hardingmarketing.com
SIC: 7336 Graphic arts & related design

(P-14149)
IDEO LP (PA)
150 Forest Ave, Palo Alto (94301-1614)
PHONE..................................650 289-3400
Fax: 650 289-3707
Tim Brown, *President*
Davide Agnelli, *Managing Dir*
Manish Kelley, *General Mgr*
Sally Clerk, *Admin Sec*
Megan Weibler, *Planning*
EMP: 135
SQ FT: 60,000
SALES (est): 55.3MM **Privately Held**
WEB: www.ideo.com
SIC: 7336 7389 8711 Commercial art & graphic design; design, commercial & industrial; engineering services

(P-14150)
LANDOR ASSOCIATES INTL LTD (DH)
1001 Front St, San Francisco (94111-1467)
PHONE..................................415 365-1700
Lois Jacobs, *CEO*
Cheryl Giovannoni, *President*
Ran Wadleigh, *CFO*
Craig Branigan, *Chairman*
Peter Law-Gisiko, *Principal*
EMP: 200
SQ FT: 44,000
SALES (est): 52.3MM
SALES (corp-wide): 18.4B **Privately Held**
SIC: 7336 Commercial art & graphic design
HQ: Young & Rubicam Inc.
3 Columbus Cir Fl 8
New York NY 10019
212 210-3000

(P-14151)
LATERAL DESIGNS INC
Also Called: Logo Design Pros
639 Front St Fl 3, San Francisco (94111-1970)
PHONE..................................415 847-6618
Cliff Kaplan, *President*
EMP: 100
SALES: 5MM **Privately Held**
SIC: 7336 Graphic arts & related design

(P-14152)
MARKET TECH MEDIA CORPORATION
27220 Turnberry Ln # 190, Valencia (91355-1018)
PHONE..................................661 257-4745
Thomas Rice, *President*
Vance Kirby, *COO*
Brian Greenburg, *Senior VP*
Mike Tubek, *Vice Pres*
Richard Van Slyke, *Manager*
EMP: 100
SQ FT: 54,000
SALES (est): 8.8MM **Privately Held**
WEB: www.addcart.com
SIC: 7336 7311 Graphic arts & related design; advertising agencies

(P-14153)
MARVEL STUDIOS LLC
Marvel Eastern Productions
1600 Rosecrans Ave, Manhattan Beach (90266-3708)
PHONE..................................310 727-2700
David Maisel, *Branch Mgr*
EMP: 58
SALES (corp-wide): 5.6MM **Privately Held**
SIC: 7336 Film strip, slide & still film production
PA: Marvel Studios, Llc
1600 Rosecrans Ave Bldg 7
Manhattan Beach CA 90266
310 727-2700

(P-14154)
MIRUM INC
Also Called: Digitaria
350 10th Ave Ste 1200, San Diego (92101-8702)
PHONE..................................619 237-5552
Fax: 619 237-5269
Daniel Khabie, *CEO*
Doug Hecht, *President*
Doug Ruhl, *President*
Gary Correia, *CFO*
Mark Newcomer, *Vice Pres*
EMP: 200
SQ FT: 4,000
SALES (est): 30.5MM
SALES (corp-wide): 18.4B **Privately Held**
WEB: www.digitaria.com
SIC: 7336 Commercial art & graphic design
HQ: J. Walter Thompson U.S.A., Llc
466 Lexington Ave Ste 6r
New York NY 10017
212 210-7000

(P-14155)
MOTION THEORY INC
Also Called: Mirada
4235 Redwood Ave, Los Angeles (90066-5605)
PHONE..................................310 396-9433
Andrew Merkin,
Janell Perez, *CFO*
Christopher Leone, *Bd of Directors*
Brian Clark, *Administration*
Tina Van Delden, *Human Res Dir*
EMP: 110 EST: 2000
SQ FT: 25,000
SALES: 27MM **Privately Held**
WEB: www.motiontheory.com
SIC: 7336 7371 7812 Graphic arts & related design; computer software development & applications; motion picture production

(P-14156)
MOTIVATIONAL SYSTEMS INC (PA)
2200 Cleveland Ave, National City (91950-6412)
PHONE..................................619 474-8246
Fax: 619 474-0678
Robert D Yound, *CEO*
Joe Jordan, *Treasurer*
Debra Bennett, *Vice Pres*
Andrew Cabrera, *Vice Pres*
Bob Charette, *Vice Pres*
EMP: 100 EST: 1975
SQ FT: 50,000
SALES (est): 24.8MM **Privately Held**
WEB: www.motivationalsystems.com
SIC: 7336 3993 Commercial art & graphic design; signs & advertising specialties

(P-14157)
ONE K STUDIOS LLC
Also Called: 1k Studios
3400 W Olive Ave Ste 300, Burbank (91505-5408)
PHONE..................................818 531-3800
Fax: 818 531-3801
Matt Kennedy,
Jason Miller, *Vice Pres*
Mike Gottschalk, *Creative Dir*
Steve Klinenberg, *Financial Exec*
Mitchell Rubinstein,
EMP: 50
SQ FT: 25,000

7336 - Commercial Art & Graphic Design County (P-14158)

PRODUDUCTS & SERVICES SECTION

SALES (est): 5.7MM Privately Held
WEB: www.one-k.com
SIC: 7336 Commercial art & graphic design

(P-14158)
PARS PUBLISHING CORP
Also Called: Grapheex
4485 Runway St, Simi Valley (93063-3436)
PHONE.................................818 280-0540
Mehran Kiankarimi, *President*
Mike Kian, *President*
Allan Yegani, *Treasurer*
Mahnaz Shidfar, *Vice Pres*
Vincent Fisher, *Admin Sec*
EMP: 54 EST: 1996
SQ FT: 40,000
SALES (est): 7.3MM Privately Held
WEB: www.grapheex.com
SIC: 7336 Commercial art & graphic design

(P-14159)
PLEASANTON UNIFIED SCHOOL DST
4665 Bernal Ave, Pleasanton (94566-7449)
PHONE.................................925 462-5500
Fax: 925 462-4635
Lee Pomplin, *Branch Mgr*
EMP: 259
SALES (corp-wide): 80.8MM Privately Held
SIC: 7336 Commercial art & graphic design
PA: Pleasanton Unified School District
4665 Bernal Ave
Pleasanton CA 94566
925 462-5500

(P-14160)
PULP STUDIO INCORPORATED (PA)
Also Called: CGB
2100 W 139th St, Gardena (90249-2412)
P.O. Box 16231, Beverly Hills (90209-2231)
PHONE.................................310 815-4999
Bernard Lax, *CEO*
Lynda N Lax, *President*
Mercy Vellamaria, *Controller*
Gary Benson, *Purchasing*
Katie Grimes, *Sales Associate*
EMP: 60
SQ FT: 36,000
SALES (est): 17.1MM Privately Held
WEB: www.pulpstudio.com
SIC: 7336 3229 Commercial art & graphic design; glass furnishings & accessories

(P-14161)
SCREENWORKS LLC
1580 Magnolia Ave, Corona (92879-2053)
PHONE.................................951 279-8877
Kevin Rabbitt, *CEO*
Tom McCracken, *Manager*
EMP: 75 EST: 2012
SALES (est): 403.3K
SALES (corp-wide): 76.5MM Privately Held
SIC: 7336 Graphic arts & related design
HQ: Nep Supershooters, L.P.
2 Beta Dr
Pittsburgh PA 15238
412 826-1414

(P-14162)
TECH FLEX PACKAGE
12624 Daphne Ave, Hawthorne (90250-3310)
PHONE.................................323 241-1800
Neil Kinney, *President*
EMP: 50
SALES (est): 1.8MM Privately Held
SIC: 7336 Package design

(P-14163)
THE DESIGNORY INC (HQ)
211 E Ocean Blvd Ste 100, Long Beach (90802-4850)
PHONE.................................562 624-0200
Fax: 562 436-0470
Paul Hosea, *CEO*
Matt Radigan, *CFO*
Joel Fuller, *Exec VP*
Kevin Lane, *Executive*
Jay Brida, *Creative Dir*

EMP: 115
SALES (est): 18.2MM
SALES (corp-wide): 15.1B Publicly Held
WEB: www.designory.com
SIC: 7336 Graphic arts & related design
PA: Omnicom Group Inc.
437 Madison Ave
New York NY 10022
212 415-3600

(P-14164)
TURNER DUCKWORTH LLC
831 Montgomery St, San Francisco (94133-5108)
PHONE.................................415 675-7777
Fax: 415 675-7778
David Turner, *COO*
Bruce Duckworth, *COO*
Greet Hods, *Creative Dir*
Joanne Chan, *General Mgr*
Jessica Rodgers, *Director*
EMP: 70
SQ FT: 5,600
SALES (est): 7MM
SALES (corp-wide): 65.7MM Privately Held
SIC: 7336 Graphic arts & related design
HQ: Leo Burnett Company, Inc.
35 W Wacker Dr Fl 21
Chicago IL 60601
312 220-5959

(P-14165)
WILD SIDE WEST (PA)
Also Called: Wildside
311 Parkside Dr, San Fernando (91340-3036)
PHONE.................................818 837-5000
Faruk Gizatullin, *President*
Bernard Eveler, *Vice Pres*
Sean Gizatullin, *Vice Pres*
EMP: 80
SQ FT: 50,000
SALES (est): 5.9MM Privately Held
WEB: www.thewildside.com
SIC: 7336 Silk screen design

7338 Secretarial & Court Reporting Svcs

(P-14166)
ATKINSON-BAKER INC (PA)
Also Called: Depo.com
500 N Brand Blvd Fl 3, Glendale (91203-1945)
P.O. Box 29054 (91209-9054)
PHONE.................................818 551-7300
Fax: 818 551-7330
Alan Atkinson Baker, *CEO*
Sheila Atkinson-Baker, *President*
Deborah J Ackema, *Vice Pres*
April Hill, *Vice Pres*
Laura Medina, *Vice Pres*
EMP: 150
SQ FT: 23,000
SALES: 34MM Privately Held
WEB: www.atkinsonbaker.com
SIC: 7338 Court reporting service

(P-14167)
RETT INC
Also Called: Canedy Court Reporting
402 W Broadway Ste 400, San Diego (92101-3554)
PHONE.................................619 231-0403
Fax: 619 231-0983
Vicki Canedy, *President*
Blake Canedy, *CEO*
Mj Mansan, *Executive Asst*
EMP: 100
SQ FT: 1,500
SALES: 2MM Privately Held
SIC: 7338 Court reporting service

(P-14168)
ROSE OX INC (DH)
Also Called: Esquire
402 W Broadway Ste 1600, San Diego (92101-8522)
PHONE.................................619 239-4111
Fax: 619 239-4117
Alexander Gallo, *President*
Kevin Littlejohn, *CFO*
Andrew Sams, *CFO*

Lynn Evers, *Executive Asst*
Paul O Jones, *Info Tech Dir*
EMP: 53
SALES (est): 5.2MM
SALES (corp-wide): 99.6MM Privately Held
SIC: 7338 Court reporting service
HQ: Aga Associates, Inc.
101 Marietta St Nw # 2700
Atlanta GA 30303
404 495-0777

(P-14169)
SOFTSCRIPT INC
2215 Campus Dr, El Segundo (90245-0001)
PHONE.................................310 451-2110
Howard Wisnicki, *CEO*
Ruien Shu, *Exec VP*
Brandon Phillips, *Senior VP*
Todd Krim, *Vice Pres*
Michael Iverson, *Software Dev*
EMP: 1200
SALES (est): 58.1MM Privately Held
WEB: www.softscript.com
SIC: 7338 Secretarial & court reporting

7342 Disinfecting & Pest Control Svcs

(P-14170)
A-ABLE INC (PA)
Also Called: Fume-A-Pest & Termite Control
17801 Ventura Blvd, Encino (91316-3616)
PHONE.................................323 658-5779
Michael Herson, *President*
Jack Herson, *Vice Pres*
EMP: 65
SQ FT: 9,026
SALES (est): 5.2MM Privately Held
SIC: 7342 1799 Pest control in structures; termite control; steam cleaning of building exteriors

(P-14171)
ABLE EXTERMINATORS INC
68 N Sunset Ave, San Jose (95116-2036)
P.O. Box 5339 (95150-5339)
PHONE.................................408 251-6500
Fax: 408 251-3652
Don Petree, *Vice Pres*
Shawna Petree, *Vice Pres*
Tammy Petree, *Manager*
EMP: 51
SQ FT: 4,000
SALES (est): 4.3MM Privately Held
WEB: www.ablexterm.com
SIC: 7342 Termite control; exterminating & fumigating

(P-14172)
ANTIMITE ASSOCIATES INC
5458 Complex St 401, San Diego (92123-1118)
PHONE.................................619 231-2900
Fax: 619 528-0086
Doug Lewis, *Branch Mgr*
EMP: 53
SALES (corp-wide): 19.8MM Privately Held
SIC: 7342 Pest control in structures; termite control
PA: Antimite Associates Inc.
6770 N Sunrise Blvd G200
Glendale AZ 85305
909 606-2300

(P-14173)
CARTWRIGHT TERMITE & PEST CTRL
51360 Calle Guatemala, La Quinta (92253-2916)
P.O. Box 658 (92247-0658)
PHONE.................................760 771-6091
Fax: 760 771-4881
Will Cartwright, *Owner*
EMP: 50
SALES (est): 3.1MM Privately Held
SIC: 7342 Pest control in structures

(P-14174)
CATS USA INC
Also Called: Cats U S A Pest Control
5683 Whitnall Hwy, North Hollywood (91601-2213)
P.O. Box 151 (91603-0151)
PHONE.................................818 506-1000
Fax: 818 506-6385
Hirotaka Otomo, *Ch of Bd*
Bob Wall, *Vice Pres*
EMP: 100
SQ FT: 3,900
SALES (est): 7.1MM
SALES (corp-wide): 813.6K Privately Held
SIC: 7342 Pest control in structures
HQ: Cats,Inc.
15-13, Nampeidaicho
Shibuya-Ku TKY 150-0
354 575-101

(P-14175)
CLARK PEST CTRL STOCKTON INC (PA)
555 N Guild Ave, Lodi (95240-0809)
P.O. Box 1480 (95241-1480)
PHONE.................................209 368-7152
Joseph Clark, *CEO*
Jeffrey Clark, *Vice Pres*
Terry Clark, *Vice Pres*
Bryan Alger, *Branch Mgr*
Cathie Larkin, *Admin Asst*
EMP: 70
SQ FT: 2,500
SALES: 108.2MM Privately Held
SIC: 7342 Exterminating & fumigating; pest control in structures; termite control

(P-14176)
CLARK PEST CTRL STOCKTON INC
480 E Service Rd, Modesto (95358-9491)
PHONE.................................209 524-6384
Fax: 209 556-5210
Ron Fair, *Manager*
Jennifer Mora, *Executive*
Bill Fernandez, *General Mgr*
James Roque, *Mktg Dir*
Rhonda Mills, *Manager*
EMP: 60
SALES (corp-wide): 108.2MM Privately Held
SIC: 7342 Exterminating & fumigating
PA: Clark Pest Control Of Stockton, Inc.
555 N Guild Ave
Lodi CA 95240
209 368-7152

(P-14177)
CLARK PEST CTRL STOCKTON INC
811 U Banks, Vacaville (95688)
PHONE.................................707 446-9748
Fax: 707 446-1042
Ron Gardner, *Manager*
EMP: 50
SQ FT: 1,300
SALES (corp-wide): 108.2MM Privately Held
SIC: 7342 Exterminating & fumigating
PA: Clark Pest Control Of Stockton, Inc.
555 N Guild Ave
Lodi CA 95240
209 368-7152

(P-14178)
CLARK PEST CTRL STOCKTON INC
4750 Beloit Dr, Sacramento (95838-2428)
PHONE.................................916 723-3390
Steven Adams, *Manager*
Nona Bradley, *Financial Exec*
EMP: 100
SQ FT: 3,100
SALES (corp-wide): 108.2MM Privately Held
SIC: 7342 Exterminating & fumigating; pest control in structures
PA: Clark Pest Control Of Stockton, Inc.
555 N Guild Ave
Lodi CA 95240
209 368-7152

PRODUCTS & SERVICES SECTION
7349 - Building Cleaning & Maintenance Svcs, NEC County (P-14200)

(P-14179)
CLARK PEST CTRL STOCKTON INC
4816 Clowes St, Stockton (95210-3506)
P.O. Box 1480, Lodi (95241-1480)
PHONE...............................209 474-3204
Fax: 209 474-2512
Joe Dinubilo, *Manager*
EMP: 50
SALES (corp-wide): 108.2MM **Privately Held**
SIC: 7342 Pest control in structures
PA: Clark Pest Control Of Stockton, Inc.
   555 N Guild Ave
   Lodi CA 95240
   209 368-7152

(P-14180)
CLARK PEST CTRL STOCKTON INC
2313 Research Dr, Livermore (94550-3824)
PHONE...............................925 449-6203
Fax: 925 426-0966
Dave Erichsen, *Manager*
Harold Lewis, *Sales Staff*
EMP: 60
SALES (corp-wide): 108.2MM **Privately Held**
SIC: 7342 Disinfecting & pest control services
PA: Clark Pest Control Of Stockton, Inc.
   555 N Guild Ave
   Lodi CA 95240
   209 368-7152

(P-14181)
CLARK PEST CTRL STOCKTON INC
199 Topaz St, Milpitas (95035-5430)
PHONE...............................408 945-3600
Joe Gatto, *Branch Mgr*
EMP: 70
SALES (corp-wide): 108.2MM **Privately Held**
SIC: 7342 Pest control in structures
PA: Clark Pest Control Of Stockton, Inc.
   555 N Guild Ave
   Lodi CA 95240
   209 368-7152

(P-14182)
CLARK PEST CTRL STOCKTON INC
11285 White Rock Rd, Rancho Cordova (95742-6504)
PHONE...............................916 635-7770
Robert Golubski, *Manager*
Bob Golubski, *General Mgr*
EMP: 50
SALES (corp-wide): 108.2MM **Privately Held**
SIC: 7342 Pest control services
PA: Clark Pest Control Of Stockton, Inc.
   555 N Guild Ave
   Lodi CA 95240
   209 368-7152

(P-14183)
CORKYS PEST CONTROL INC
909 Rancheros Dr, San Marcos (92069-3028)
PHONE...............................760 432-8801
Fax: 760 432-8215
Corky Mizer, *President*
Stephanie Crognale, *Sales Executive*
Francisca Bautista, *Manager*
Glenn Erath, *Manager*
Lorenzo Llamas, *Manager*
EMP: 60
SQ FT: 5,000
SALES (est): 6.6MM **Privately Held**
SIC: 7342 0782 2879 5211 Pest control in structures; lawn & garden services; insecticides & pesticides; insulation material, building; landscape services; handyman service

(P-14184)
CRANE ACQUISITION INC
Also Called: Crane Pest Control
2700 Geary Blvd, San Francisco (94118-3406)
PHONE...............................415 922-1666
Fax: 415 922-1789
Harold Stein, *President*
Harry J Cynkus, *Treasurer*
Deborah Hoffman, *Officer*
Ken Ward, *Vice Pres*
Eugene Iarocci, *Admin Sec*
EMP: 86
SQ FT: 6,000
SALES (est): 6.5MM
SALES (corp-wide): 1.4B **Publicly Held**
WEB: www.cranepestcontrol.com
SIC: 7342 Pest control services
PA: Rollins, Inc.
   2170 Piedmont Rd Ne
   Atlanta GA 30324
   404 888-2000

(P-14185)
ECOLA SERVICES INC
15314 Devonshire St Ste C, Mission Hills (91345-2773)
PHONE...............................818 920-7301
Susan Fries, *President*
EMP: 52
SQ FT: 10,000
SALES (est): 5.7MM **Privately Held**
WEB: www.ecolatermite.com
SIC: 7342 Termite control

(P-14186)
HOMEGUARD INCORPORATED (PA)
Also Called: Redrocks Fumigation
510 Madera Ave, San Jose (95112-2918)
PHONE...............................408 993-1900
James Steffenson Jr, *President*
Jim Hessling, *Treasurer*
Jessica Morgan, *Admin Asst*
Corina Reefe, *Bookkeeper*
Susan Dillard, *Manager*
EMP: 56
SQ FT: 6,000
SALES (est): 11.2MM **Privately Held**
SIC: 7342 Termite control

(P-14187)
LLOYD PEST CONTROL CO
19161 Newhall St, North Palm Springs (92258)
P.O. Box 580490 (92258-0490)
PHONE...............................951 232-9687
EMP: 87
SALES (corp-wide): 21.3MM **Privately Held**
SIC: 7342 Pest control services
PA: The Lloyd Pest Control Co
   935 Sherman St
   San Diego CA 92110
   619 298-9865

(P-14188)
LLOYD PEST CONTROL CO
566 E Dyer Rd, Santa Ana (92707-3737)
PHONE...............................714 979-6021
Fax: 714 979-3512
Mike Magnuson, *Manager*
EMP: 50
SALES (corp-wide): 23.7MM **Privately Held**
SIC: 7342 Pest control in structures; termite control
PA: The Lloyd Pest Control Co
   935 Sherman St
   San Diego CA 92110
   619 298-9865

(P-14189)
MCCLENAHAN PEST CONTROL INC
1 Arastradero Rd, Portola Valley (94028-8012)
PHONE...............................650 326-8781
James M Mc Clenahan, *President*
John H McClenahan, *Agent*
EMP: 50
SALES (est): 1.5MM **Privately Held**
SIC: 7342 Pest control services

(P-14190)
MIKES VINEYARD SPRAY INC
Also Called: Mikes Bopps Ranches
5156 W Minarets Ave, Fresno (93722-3454)
PHONE...............................559 269-7109
Michael Bopp, *President*
EMP: 140

SALES: 750K **Privately Held**
SIC: 7342 Exterminating & fumigating

(P-14191)
TERMINIX INTL CO LTD PARTNR
3055 N California St, Burbank (91504-2005)
PHONE...............................818 972-2037
Fax: 818 840-2775
Tarvis Braun, *Manager*
EMP: 50
SALES (corp-wide): 2.5B **Publicly Held**
SIC: 7342 Pest control services
HQ: The Terminix International Company Limited Partnership
   860 Ridge Lake Blvd
   Memphis TN 38120
   901 766-1400

(P-14192)
TERMINIX INTL CO LTD PARTNR
649 S Waterman Ave Ste A, San Bernardino (92408-2365)
PHONE...............................909 332-2479
Fax: 909 884-2436
Rodney Prince, *Principal*
EMP: 50
SALES (corp-wide): 2.5B **Publicly Held**
SIC: 7342 Pest control services
HQ: The Terminix International Company Limited Partnership
   860 Ridge Lake Blvd
   Memphis TN 38120
   901 766-1400

(P-14193)
TERMINIX INTL CO LTD PARTNR
6678 Owens Dr Ste 100, Pleasanton (94588-3324)
PHONE...............................925 460-5063
Fax: 408 283-0230
Robert Castillo, *Sales/Mktg Mgr*
Rick Campbell, *Manager*
Mike Dawson, *Manager*
Tony Doyle, *Manager*
Vance Miller, *Manager*
EMP: 70
SALES (corp-wide): 2.5B **Publicly Held**
SIC: 7342 Pest control services
HQ: The Terminix International Company Limited Partnership
   860 Ridge Lake Blvd
   Memphis TN 38120
   901 766-1400

(P-14194)
WESTERN EXTERMINATOR COMPANY
3333 W Temple St, Los Angeles (90026-4523)
PHONE...............................310 274-9244
Fax: 213 386-6458
Paul Trammell, *Manager*
Edith Anderson, *Personnel Exec*
Angela Ortiz, *Human Res Dir*
EMP: 85
SQ FT: 10,264
SALES (corp-wide): 2.6B **Privately Held**
WEB: www.west-ext.com
SIC: 7342 Disinfecting & pest control services
HQ: Western Exterminator Company
   305 N Crescent Way
   Anaheim CA 92801
   714 517-9000

(P-14195)
WESTERN EXTERMINATOR COMPANY
1985 W Wardlow Rd, Long Beach (90810-2037)
PHONE...............................310 835-3513
Sandi Quintana, *Manager*
EMP: 50
SALES (corp-wide): 2.6B **Privately Held**
WEB: www.west-ext.com
SIC: 7342 Pest control services
HQ: Western Exterminator Company
   305 N Crescent Way
   Anaheim CA 92801
   714 517-9000

(P-14196)
WESTERN EXTERMINATOR COMPANY
Also Called: Target Specialty Products
15415 Marquardt Ave, Santa Fe Springs (90670-5711)
P.O. Box 3408 (90670-1408)
PHONE...............................562 802-2238
Rich Records, *Manager*
Gary Singh, *Administration*
Harry Upasena, *Systems Staff*
John Longhurst, *Manager*
EMP: 100
SALES (corp-wide): 2.6B **Privately Held**
WEB: www.west-ext.com
SIC: 7342 Disinfecting & pest control services
HQ: Western Exterminator Company
   305 N Crescent Way
   Anaheim CA 92801
   714 517-9000

(P-14197)
YOUR WAY FUMIGATION INC
41880 Kalmia St Ste 170, Murrieta (92562-8838)
PHONE...............................951 699-9116
Jose Manuel Aguilar, *President*
Sandy Huffman, *Opers Staff*
EMP: 90
SALES (est): 9.2MM **Privately Held**
SIC: 7342 Exterminating & fumigating

7349 Building Cleaning & Maintenance Svcs, NEC

(P-14198)
A1 BUILDING MANAGEMENT INC
2461 E Orangethorpe Ave # 200, Fullerton (92831-5302)
PHONE...............................714 447-3800
Trent Pollack, *President*
EMP: 125
SALES (est): 2MM **Privately Held**
SIC: 7349 Building maintenance services

(P-14199)
ABM ELECTRICAL & LTG SOLUTIONS (DH)
152 Technology Dr, Irvine (92618-2401)
PHONE...............................877 546-2937
Fax: 949 888-2350
Henrick C Slipsager, *CEO*
Sue Bremner, *Partner*
Michael Brennan, *Partner*
Joe Franz, *Partner*
Tracy K Price, *Partner*
EMP: 50
SQ FT: 4,803
SALES (est): 9.5MM
SALES (corp-wide): 4.9B **Publicly Held**
WEB: www.sundownlighting.com
SIC: 7349 Lighting maintenance service
HQ: Abm Facility Solutions Group, Llc
   1221 Lamar St Ste 1500
   Houston TX 77010
   832 214-5500

(P-14200)
ABM FACILITY SERVICES INC (HQ)
Also Called: ABM Engineering
1266 14th St Ste 103, Oakland (94607-2211)
PHONE...............................510 251-0381
Fax: 510 286-8565
Mike Latham, *CEO*
J E Benton III, *President*
Cornel Sneekes, *Exec VP*
George Sundby, *Senior VP*
Charlie Booth, *Vice Pres*
EMP: 100
SALES (est): 37.1MM
SALES (corp-wide): 4.9B **Publicly Held**
SIC: 7349 Building maintenance services
PA: Abm Industries Incorporated
   1 Liberty Plz Fl Con1
   New York NY 10006
   212 297-0200

7349 - Building Cleaning & Maintenance Svcs, NEC County (P-14201)

PRODUDUCTS & SERVICES SECTION

(P-14201)
ABM INDUSTRIES INCORPORATED
5300 S Eastrn Ave Ste 110, Los Angeles (90040)
PHONE.................323 720-4020
Brian Holt, *Prgrmr*
EMP: 50
SALES (corp-wide): 4.9B **Publicly Held**
SIC: 7349 Building maintenance services
PA: Abm Industries Incorporated
1 Liberty Plz Fl Con1
New York NY 10006
212 297-0200

(P-14202)
ABM JANITORIAL SERVICES INC
4747 N Bendel Ave Ste 104, Fresno (93722-3962)
PHONE.................559 276-9096
Fax: 559 276-0451
Tony Bautista, *Manager*
EMP: 325
SALES (corp-wide): 4.9B **Publicly Held**
SIC: 7349 Janitorial service, contract basis
HQ: Abm Janitorial Services, Inc.
1111 Fannin St Ste 1500
Houston TX 77002
713 654-8924

(P-14203)
ABM JANITORIAL SERVICES INC
6671 Owens Dr, Pleasanton (94588-3335)
PHONE.................925 924-0270
Greg Bu Puis, *Manager*
EMP: 267
SALES (corp-wide): 4.9B **Publicly Held**
SIC: 7349 Cleaning service, industrial or commercial
HQ: Abm Janitorial Services, Inc.
1111 Fannin St Ste 1500
Houston TX 77002
713 654-8924

(P-14204)
ABM JANITORIAL SERVICES INC
830 Riverside Pkwy Ste 40, West Sacramento (95605-1505)
PHONE.................916 374-1739
Sean Petone, *Manager*
EMP: 320
SALES (corp-wide): 4.9B **Publicly Held**
SIC: 7349 Janitorial service, contract basis
HQ: Abm Janitorial Services, Inc.
1111 Fannin St Ste 1500
Houston TX 77002
713 654-8924

(P-14205)
ABM JANITORIAL SERVICES INC
11955 Jack Benny Dr # 104, Rancho Cucamonga (91739-9231)
PHONE.................909 987-3700
EMP: 105
SALES (corp-wide): 4.9B **Publicly Held**
SIC: 7349 Janitorial service, contract basis
HQ: Abm Janitorial Services, Inc.
1111 Fannin St Ste 1500
Houston TX 77002
713 654-8924

(P-14206)
ABM JANITORIAL SERVICES INC
2385 Arch Airport Rd # 100, Stockton (95206-4404)
PHONE.................209 983-3923
Fax: 209 576-0904
Tony McGrat, *Manager*
EMP: 105
SALES (corp-wide): 4.9B **Publicly Held**
SIC: 7349 Building maintenance services
HQ: Abm Janitorial Services, Inc.
1111 Fannin St Ste 1500
Houston TX 77002
713 654-8924

(P-14207)
ABM JNTRIAL SVCS - STHWEST INC
1400 Easton Dr Ste 149, Bakersfield (93309-9406)
PHONE.................661 322-3280
Javier Vasquez, *Manager*
EMP: 100
SALES (corp-wide): 4.9B **Publicly Held**
SIC: 7349 Building maintenance services
HQ: Abm Janitorial Services - Southwest, Inc.
5300 S Eastern Ave
Los Angeles CA 90040
323 720-4020

(P-14208)
ABM JNTRIAL SVCS - STHWEST INC
4747 N Bendel Ave, Fresno (93722-3962)
PHONE.................559 276-9096
Clayton Olson, *Branch Mgr*
EMP: 77
SALES (corp-wide): 4.9B **Publicly Held**
SIC: 7349 Building maintenance services
HQ: Abm Janitorial Services - Southwest, Inc.
5300 S Eastern Ave
Los Angeles CA 90040
323 720-4020

(P-14209)
ACCELERATED ENVMTL SVCS INC
23601 Taft Hwy, Bakersfield (93311)
P.O. Box 398, Taft (93268-0398)
PHONE.................661 765-4003
Fax: 661 765-4001
John E Neumann, *President*
Sovanna Wilke, *Accountant*
EMP: 100
SQ FT: 25,440
SALES (est): 4.7MM **Privately Held**
SIC: 7349 Cleaning service, industrial or commercial

(P-14210)
ACCENT SERVICE COMPANY INC
2770 S Harbor Blvd Ste J, Santa Ana (92704-5835)
P.O. Box 9495, Newport Beach (92658-9495)
PHONE.................714 557-2837
Dan Yasui, *President*
Dan Davis, *Mktg Dir*
EMP: 99
SQ FT: 200
SALES: 6MM **Privately Held**
WEB: www.accentsc.com
SIC: 7349 Building maintenance services

(P-14211)
ACME BUILDING MAINTENANCE CO (HQ)
941 Catherine St, Alviso (95002)
PHONE.................408 263-5911
Fax: 408 946-6484
Richard Sanchez, *President*
Henry Sanchez, *Ch of Bd*
Solomon Wong, *Treasurer*
Luz Pardl, *Finance Mgr*
EMP: 80
SQ FT: 8,000
SALES (est): 48.4MM
SALES (corp-wide): 800MM **Privately Held**
SIC: 7349 Building & office cleaning services; building component cleaning service
PA: Gca Services Group, Inc.
1350 Euclid Ave Ste 1500
Cleveland OH 44115
216 535-4900

(P-14212)
ACME BUILDING MAINTENANCE CO
Also Called: Acme-Cisco Systems
3750 Zanker Rd, San Jose (95134-1408)
PHONE.................408 526-5939
Karen Loria, *Manager*
Eric Cusack, *Info Tech Mgr*
Asha Patidar, *Info Tech Mgr*
Diana Colin, *Project Mgr*
Liz Segura, *Project Mgr*
EMP: 125
SQ FT: 151,400
SALES (corp-wide): 800MM **Privately Held**
SIC: 7349 Janitorial service, contract basis
HQ: Acme Building Maintenance Co., Inc
941 Catherine St
Alviso CA 95002
408 263-5911

(P-14213)
ADHEI ENTERPRISES INC
Also Called: Knudtson Building Maint Svc
4627 Lemona Ave, Sherman Oaks (91403-2428)
PHONE.................818 788-7680
Fax: 818 986-3836
Jacqueline Campbell, *President*
Dayna Campbell, *Principal*
EMP: 50
SALES (est): 1.1MM **Privately Held**
SIC: 7349 Janitorial service, contract basis

(P-14214)
ADVANCE BUILDING MAINTENANCE
9601 Wilshire Blvd Gl25, Beverly Hills (90210-5217)
PHONE.................310 247-0077
Fax: 310 247-0089
Forrest I Nolin, *President*
EMP: 500
SALES (est): 8.9MM **Privately Held**
WEB: www.advancemaintenance.com
SIC: 7349 Janitorial service, contract basis

(P-14215)
ADVANCED CLNROOM MCRCLEAN CORP
Also Called: A C M
3250 S Susan St Ste A, Santa Ana (92704-6807)
PHONE.................714 751-1152
Fax: 714 754-4088
Janet Ford, *CEO*
Troy Woodard, *Regional Mgr*
Norma Lopez, *Accountant*
EMP: 200
SQ FT: 3,500
SALES (est): 8.7MM **Privately Held**
WEB: www.advcleanroom.com
SIC: 7349 8734 Cleaning service, industrial or commercial; testing laboratories

(P-14216)
AESTHETIC MAINTENANCE CORP
Also Called: AMC
1625 Palo Alto St Ste 301, Los Angeles (90026-5050)
PHONE.................213 353-1525
Fax: 213 353-1529
Curtiss Pierose, *President*
Vicki Stuart, *Office Mgr*
EMP: 50
SQ FT: 1,000
SALES (est): 1.8MM **Privately Held**
SIC: 7349 Building maintenance services

(P-14217)
AIRCRAFT SERVICE INTL INC
5720 Avion Dr, Los Angeles (90045-5620)
P.O. Box 90156 (90009-0156)
PHONE.................310 646-2990
Fax: 310 645-0879
Rick Cortez, *Opers-Prdtn-Mfg*
Brook James, *Manager*
EMP: 70
SALES (corp-wide): 2.2B **Privately Held**
WEB: www.asig.com
SIC: 7349 Building maintenance services
HQ: Aircraft Service International, Inc.
201 S Orange Ave Ste 1100
Orlando FL 32801
407 648-7373

(P-14218)
ALL CARE INDUSTRIES INC
16747 1/2 Parkside Ave, Cerritos (90703-1840)
PHONE.................562 623-4000
Fax: 562 623-4039
Christopher Kim, *President*
Charles Lee, *Vice Pres*
William Bark, *General Mgr*
Labrenda Ramos, *Manager*
EMP: 100
SALES: 1.7MM **Privately Held**
SIC: 7349 Janitorial service, contract basis

(P-14219)
ALL CONTROL CLEANING INC
124 N Aviador St Ste 1, Camarillo (93010-8321)
P.O. Box 341, Newbury Park (91319-0341)
PHONE.................805 987-4210
Lee Parrilla, *President*
Syeda Parrilla, *Admin Sec*
EMP: 52 **EST:** 2009
SQ FT: 5,000
SALES: 1.5MM **Privately Held**
SIC: 7349 Building maintenance services

(P-14220)
ALL-RITE LEASING COMPANY INC
3420 Bristol St Ste 210, Costa Mesa (92626-7222)
PHONE.................714 530-7074
Chris Schran, *President*
Pauline Rosenberg, *Corp Secy*
EMP: 269
SALES (est): 6.6MM **Privately Held**
SIC: 7349 Building maintenance services

(P-14221)
ALLSTAR COMMERCIAL CLEANING
4805 Mercury St Ste H, San Diego (92111-2110)
PHONE.................858 715-0500
Michael Paul McCarthy, *CEO*
Adam Bolio, *Co-Owner*
EMP: 50
SALES (est): 1.3MM **Privately Held**
SIC: 7349 Cleaning service, industrial or commercial

(P-14222)
ALLSTATE BUILDING MAINTENANCE
4890 Saint Andrews Ave, Buena Park (90621-1072)
P.O. Box 3144, La Habra (90632-3144)
PHONE.................714 739-8080
Mike Ko, *Owner*
EMP: 100
SQ FT: 3,000
SALES (est): 1.4MM **Privately Held**
SIC: 7349 Building maintenance services

(P-14223)
AMERI-KLEEN
Also Called: Ameri-Kleen Building Services
313 W Beach St, Watsonville (95076-4508)
P.O. Box 2167 (95077-2167)
PHONE.................831 722-8888
Fax: 805 761-6385
Marisol Tavera, *Branch Mgr*
EMP: 450
SALES (corp-wide): 48.1MM **Privately Held**
SIC: 7349 Building maintenance services
PA: Ameri-Kleen
328 E Lake Ave
Watsonville CA 95076
831 722-8888

(P-14224)
AMERI-KLEEN
Also Called: Ameri-Kleen Building Services
1023 E Grand Ave, Arroyo Grande (93420-2504)
PHONE.................805 546-0706
Dan Erpenbach, *Branch Mgr*
EMP: 250
SALES (corp-wide): 48.1MM **Privately Held**
SIC: 7349 Janitorial service, contract basis
PA: Ameri-Kleen
328 E Lake Ave
Watsonville CA 95076
831 722-8888

(P-14225)
AMERICAN BLDG MAINT CO OF ILL
44870 Osgood Rd, Fremont (94539-6101)
PHONE.................510 573-1618

PRODUCTS & SERVICES SECTION
7349 - Building Cleaning & Maintenance Svcs, NEC County (P-14248)

EMP: 50
SALES (corp-wide): 4.9B Publicly Held
SIC: 7349 Building maintenance services
HQ: American Building Maintenance Co Of
Illinois, Inc
420 Taylor St 200
San Francisco CA 94102
415 351-4386

(P-14226)
AMERICAN BLDG MAINT CO-WEST (HQ)
75 Broadway Ste 111, San Francisco
(94111-1423)
PHONE 415 733-4000
Henrik Slipsager, *President*
Douglas Bowlus, *Treasurer*
Harry H Kahn, *Admin Sec*
Alex Paiavi, *Bookkeeper*
EMP: 150
SALES (est): 21.8MM
SALES (corp-wide): 4.9B Publicly Held
SIC: 7349 Janitorial service, contract basis
PA: Abm Industries Incorporated
1 Liberty Plz Fl Con1
New York NY 10006
212 297-0200

(P-14227)
AMERICAN BUILDING MAINT CO NY
101 California St, San Francisco
(94111-5802)
PHONE 415 733-4000
Henrik Slipsager, *President*
Douglas Bowlus, *Treasurer*
Scott Salmirs, *Exec VP*
Catherine Myers, *Accountant*
EMP: 4530
SALES (est): 39.1MM
SALES (corp-wide): 4.9B Publicly Held
SIC: 7349 Janitorial service, contract basis
PA: Abm Industries Incorporated
1 Liberty Plz Fl Con1
New York NY 10006
212 297-0200

(P-14228)
AMERICAN BUILDING SERVICE
4578 Crow Canyon Pl, Castro Valley
(94552-4804)
P.O. Box 32, San Leandro (94577-0003)
PHONE 510 483-5120
Rui Donaldo Teixeira Canha, *President*
EMP: 100
SALES (est): 3.1MM Privately Held
SIC: 7349 Janitorial service, contract basis

(P-14229)
AMERICAN SERVICES AND PRODUCTS
Also Called: American Janitor Services
949 Camino Dos Rios, Thousand Oaks
(91360-2360)
PHONE 805 375-2858
Dorothy Clemen, *President*
Mel Clemen, *Vice Pres*
Ron Clemen, *Admin Sec*
Walter Coelho, *Sales Mgr*
Patrick McNaughton, *Consultant*
EMP: 60
SQ FT: 800
SALES: 1.4MM Privately Held
WEB: www.greenstoyotadirect.com
SIC: 7349 Janitorial service, contract basis

(P-14230)
ANDOVER MAINTENANCE INC
Also Called: Specialty Services
45 La Porte St, Arcadia (91006-2826)
PHONE 626 254-1651
Daniel Tellez, *President*
Peter Richards, *Vice Pres*
Bob Daly, *Manager*
Felix Morales, *Manager*
EMP: 73
SQ FT: 3,500
SALES (est): 3MM Privately Held
SIC: 7349 Janitorial service, contract basis

(P-14231)
APPLEBEE & SHEEHAN INC (PA)
Also Called: Airtek Indoor Air Solutions
978 W 10th St, Azusa (91702-1936)
PHONE 800 200-8872
Joseph McLean, *CEO*
Matt Kelly, *Branch Mgr*
Melissa Asplund, *Marketing Staff*
EMP: 55
SALES (est): 10.9MM Privately Held
SIC: 7349 Cleaning service, industrial or commercial; air duct cleaning

(P-14232)
ARAMARK FACILITY SERVICES LLC
941 W 35th St, Los Angeles (90007-4002)
PHONE 213 740-8968
Ron Cote, *Manager*
EMP: 200
SALES (corp-wide): 14.3B Publicly Held
SIC: 7349 Building maintenance services
HQ: Aramark Facility Services, Llc
1101 Market St
Philadelphia PA 19107
215 238-3000

(P-14233)
ARAMARK FACILITY SERVICES LLC
5301 Bolsa Ave Bldg 10, Huntington Beach
(92647-2048)
PHONE 714 372-0683
Christopher Olsen-Bates, *Manager*
EMP: 50
SALES (corp-wide): 14.3B Publicly Held
SIC: 7349 Janitorial service, contract basis; building maintenance, except repairs
HQ: Aramark Facility Services, Llc
1101 Market St
Philadelphia PA 19107
215 238-3000

(P-14234)
ARAMARK MGT SVCS LTD PARTNR
Also Called: ServiceMaster
2401 E Wardlow Rd Ste C, Long Beach
(90807-5309)
PHONE 562 593-2724
Rick Carnado, *Manager*
EMP: 50
SALES (corp-wide): 14.3B Publicly Held
SIC: 7349 Building maintenance services
HQ: Aramark Management Services Limited Partnership
2300 Warrenville Rd
Downers Grove IL 60515
630 271-2000

(P-14235)
ATL SERVICES
2390 E Orangewood Ave, Anaheim
(92806-6141)
PHONE 714 712-4220
Fax: 714 940-4090
James P McClure, *CEO*
Jess E Benton III, *Ch of Bd*
Douglas Bowlus, *Treasurer*
David L Farwell, *Treasurer*
Mark Binns, *Exec VP*
EMP: 317
SQ FT: 10,000
SALES (est): 5.3MM
SALES (corp-wide): 6.1B Publicly Held
SIC: 7349 Lighting maintenance service
HQ: Sylvania Lighting Services Corp.
200 Ballardvale St
Wilmington MA 01887
978 570-3000

(P-14236)
AVALON BUILDING MAINTENANCE (PA)
3148 E La Palma Ave Ste A, Anaheim
(92806-2805)
PHONE 714 693-2407
Steve J Healis, *CEO*
Tom Poston, *CFO*
Tom Devlin, *Admin Sec*
Aldrey Postman, *Admin Sec*
EMP: 220
SQ FT: 5,000
SALES (est): 9.2MM Privately Held
WEB: www.avaloncorona.com
SIC: 7349 Building maintenance services

(P-14237)
BERGENSONS PROPERTY SVCS INC
Also Called: Solve All Facility Services
3605 Ocean Ranch Blvd # 200, Oceanside
(92056-2695)
PHONE 760 631-5111
Fax: 760 941-5723
Mark M Minasian, *CEO*
Philip Hobaugh, *President*
Aram Minasian, *President*
John Parrish, *President*
James Braun, *CFO*
EMP: 2000
SQ FT: 2,000
SALES (est): 52.1MM Privately Held
WEB: www.bergensons.com
SIC: 7349 Building maintenance, except repairs; janitorial service, contract basis

(P-14238)
BISSELL BROTHERS JANITORIAL
Also Called: Bissell Bros Bldg Maint Servic
3207 Luyung Dr, Rancho Cordova
(95742-6862)
PHONE 916 635-1852
Fax: 916 635-1875
David Bissell, *CEO*
EMP: 80
SQ FT: 2,400
SALES (est): 2.1MM Privately Held
WEB: www.cleaningcrew.com
SIC: 7349 Janitorial service, contract basis

(P-14239)
BRADFORD BUILDING SERVICES
5200 S Eastern Ave, Los Angeles
(90040-2940)
PHONE 323 720-4020
Larry Smith, *Senior VP*
Fred Iseli, *Vice Pres*
Justin Dedeaux, *VP Mktg*
EMP: 50
SALES (est): 742K
SALES (corp-wide): 4.9B Publicly Held
WEB: www.bradfordbuildingservices.com
SIC: 7349 Building service, contract basis
PA: Abm Industries Incorporated
1 Liberty Plz Fl Con1
New York NY 10006
212 297-0200

(P-14240)
BRILLIANT GENERAL MAINT INC
Also Called: Bgm
954 Chestnut St, San Jose (95110-1504)
PHONE 408 287-6708
Fax: 408 271-6679
Daniel Montes, *CEO*
Joel Sanchez, *CFO*
Adalet Aguiar, *Opers Mgr*
Eleuterio Pacheco, *Opers Mgr*
Alberto Delgadillo, *Accounts Mgr*
EMP: 200
SQ FT: 6,000
SALES (est): 7.8MM Privately Held
SIC: 7349 Building maintenance, except repairs; janitorial service, contract basis

(P-14241)
BRITEWORKS INC
620 N Commercial Ave, Covina
(91723-1309)
PHONE 626 337-0099
Fax: 626 337-3399
Anita Ron, *President*
Gracie Corona, *Office Mgr*
Lance Nass, *Info Tech Dir*
EMP: 75
SQ FT: 4,800
SALES (est): 3.1MM Privately Held
WEB: www.briteworks.com
SIC: 7349 Janitorial service, contract basis

(P-14242)
C E B M INC
3100 E Cedar St Ste 17, Ontario
(91761-7695)
PHONE 909 975-4440
William Dazalla, *President*
Robert Dazalla, *Vice Pres*
EMP: 50
SQ FT: 2,000
SALES (est): 1.2MM Privately Held
WEB: www.cebm.net
SIC: 7349 Janitorial service, contract basis

(P-14243)
CALDERON BUILDING MAINTENANCE
3822 Sherman St, San Diego (92110-4322)
P.O. Box 3550 (92163-1550)
PHONE 619 269-5940
Fax: 619 297-0554
Andres J Calderon, *President*
Maria Calderon, *Admin Sec*
EMP: 90
SALES (est): 3.3MM Privately Held
WEB: www.calderoninc.com
SIC: 7349 Building maintenance services

(P-14244)
CALIFORNIA BUILDING MAINT
11315 Rancho Bernardo Rd, San Diego
(92127-1402)
P.O. Box 270342 (92198-2342)
PHONE 858 451-9111
Fax: 858 451-9023
Sally Walker, *Owner*
Dave Walker, *Co-Owner*
EMP: 50
SALES (est): 785.7K Privately Held
SIC: 7349 Building maintenance services

(P-14245)
CARRASCO HELEO
Also Called: Building Cleaning Systems
2510 N Grand Ave Ste 102, Santa Ana
(92705-8753)
PHONE 714 639-1759
Fax: 714 639-7657
Heleo Carrasco, *President*
EMP: 130
SALES (est): 4.7MM Privately Held
WEB: www.buildingcleaningsystems.com
SIC: 7349 Building maintenance services

(P-14246)
CENTURY CONTRACT SERVICES INC
15815 Camino Codorniz, San Diego
(92127-5825)
P.O. Box 270589 (92198-2589)
PHONE 858 672-4118
Edmund Rhee, *President*
Linda Lee, *Office Mgr*
Demain Arny, *Director*
EMP: 125
SQ FT: 3,000
SALES (est): 3.4MM Privately Held
SIC: 7349 Janitorial service, contract basis

(P-14247)
CITY OF LOS ANGELES
Also Called: General Services
3330 W 36th St, Los Angeles (90018-3610)
PHONE 213 847-2799
Melody McCormick, *Branch Mgr*
EMP: 60 Privately Held
WEB: www.lacity.org
SIC: 7349 9611 Building maintenance services; administration of general economic programs;
PA: City Of Los Angeles
200 N Spring St Ste 303
Los Angeles CA 90012
213 978-0600

(P-14248)
CITY OF PALMDALE
Also Called: Public Works Dept
39101 3rd St E, Palmdale (93550-3209)
PHONE 661 267-5338
Gene Trevail, *Superintendent*
Marleen Mizanin, *Manager*
Lonnie Shpman, *Manager*
Jennifer Tallakson, *Manager*
Dave Realder, *Supervisor*
EMP: 135 Privately Held
SIC: 7349 9111 Building maintenance services; mayors' offices
PA: City Of Palmdale
38300 Sierra Hwy
Palmdale CA 93550
661 267-5115

7349 - Building Cleaning & Maintenance Svcs, NEC County (P-14249)

(P-14249)
CITY OF PASADENA
Also Called: Mayor Office
117 E Colorado Blvd, Pasadena (91105-1938)
PHONE 626 744-4311
Fax: 626 744-7093
Bill Bogaard, *Mayor*
Dan Rix, *Executive*
David Garcia, *Admin Asst*
Beverly Wykoff, *Analyst*
Takashi Hata, *Human Res Dir*
EMP: 70 **Privately Held**
WEB: www.cityofpasadena.net
SIC: **7349** 9111 Building maintenance services; mayors' offices
PA: City Of Pasadena
100 N Garfield Ave
Pasadena CA 91101
626 744-4386

(P-14250)
CITY OF SALINAS
426 Work St, Salinas (93901-4308)
PHONE 831 758-7233
Fax: 831 758-7940
Denise Estrada, *Director*
EMP: 89 **Privately Held**
WEB: www.co.monterey.ca.us
SIC: **7349** 9224 Building maintenance services; fire department, not including volunteer
PA: City Of Salinas
200 Lincoln Ave
Salinas CA 93901
831 758-7256

(P-14251)
CITY OF SAN MATEO
Also Called: Corporate Yard
1949 Pacific Blvd, San Mateo (94403-1430)
PHONE 650 522-7300
Vernon Ficklind, *Manager*
EMP: 60 **Privately Held**
WEB: www.cityarts-sm.org
SIC: **7349** 9111 Building maintenance services; mayors' offices
PA: City Of San Mateo
330 W 20th Ave
San Mateo CA 94403
650 522-7000

(P-14252)
CJ MODEL HOME MAINTENANCE INC
240 Spring St, Pleasanton (94566-6626)
P.O. Box 5547 (94566-1547)
PHONE 925 485-3280
Fax: 925 485-3296
Carrie Wevill, *President*
Richard Wevill, *Admin Sec*
EMP: 70
SQ FT: 2,200
SALES (est): 4.5MM **Privately Held**
WEB: www.cjsmodelhome.com
SIC: **7349** Building component cleaning service

(P-14253)
CLEAN ENVIROMENT
4570 Alvarado Canyon Rd C, San Diego (92120-4317)
PHONE 619 521-0543
Fax: 619 521-1492
Steve G Ottman, *Owner*
Gloria Fernandes, *Admin Sec*
EMP: 60
SALES (est): 1.3MM **Privately Held**
SIC: **7349** Building maintenance services

(P-14254)
CLEAN-A-RAMA MAINTENANCE CO
526 Columbus Ave, San Francisco (94133-2802)
PHONE 415 495-5298
Fax: 415 495-4933
Piero Sebastiani, *Partner*
EMP: 60
SQ FT: 800
SALES (est): 1.3MM **Privately Held**
SIC: **7349** Janitorial service, contract basis

(P-14255)
COAST TO COAST WATER DAMAGE
Also Called: Coast To Coast Restoration
10881 La Tuna Canyon Rd, Sun Valley (91352-2010)
PHONE 818 255-3323
Hayko Aldzhikyan, *President*
Marina Demirchyan, *Vice Pres*
Rubina Tumanian, *Manager*
EMP: 50
SQ FT: 9,000
SALES (est): 1.4MM **Privately Held**
WEB: www.c2crestoration.com
SIC: **7349** Building maintenance services

(P-14256)
COASTAL BUILDING SERVICES INC
718 N Hariton St, Orange (92868-1314)
PHONE 714 775-2855
Fax: 714 630-4499
Hipolito G Arias, *CEO*
Brett Dunstan, *CFO*
Polo Arias, *Officer*
Alberto Melendez, *Opers Staff*
Rafael Perez, *Manager*
EMP: 300
SQ FT: 5,300
SALES (est): 9.9MM **Privately Held**
WEB: www.coastalbuildingservice.com
SIC: **7349** Building cleaning service

(P-14257)
COBB WATERBLASTING INC
Also Called: Cobb Property Services
1145 W Shelley Ct, Orange (92868-1200)
PHONE 714 769-2622
Mark Cobb, *President*
Dorothy Cobb, *Vice Pres*
William Roche, *Admin Sec*
EMP: 82
SALES (est): 3.4MM **Privately Held**
SIC: **7349** Building cleaning service

(P-14258)
COME LAND MAINT SVC CO INC
1419 N San Fernando Blvd # 250, Burbank (91504-4185)
PHONE 818 567-2455
Grace H Lee, *President*
William Lee, *Admin Sec*
Edward Lee, *Opers Mgr*
EMP: 513
SQ FT: 12,750
SALES (est): 3.9MM
SALES (corp-wide): 4MM **Privately Held**
SIC: **7349** Building maintenance services
PA: Come Land, Inc.
1419 N San Fernando Blvd # 250
Burbank CA 91504
818 567-2455

(P-14259)
COMMON AREA MAINT SVCS INC (PA)
Also Called: CAM Services
5664 Selmaraine Dr, Culver City (90230-6120)
PHONE 310 390-3552
Jim Swindle, *CEO*
David A Herrera, *President*
Sidney Young, *Principal*
Gardy Brill, *Manager*
Jesse Medina, *Manager*
EMP: 89
SQ FT: 4,000
SALES (est): 14.7MM **Privately Held**
WEB: www.camservices.com
SIC: **7349** Building maintenance, except repairs

(P-14260)
CONSOLIDATED CLEANING SERVICES
2515 Willow St, Oakland (94607-1710)
PHONE 510 663-2585
Fax: 510 250-1845
Joanne King, *President*
Michael Herling, *COO*
Onoria Luna, *Manager*
Sebastian Desio, *Bookkeeper*
Carlos Umana, *Opers Mgr*
EMP: 100
SQ FT: 7,500
SALES (est): 3.4MM **Privately Held**
SIC: **7349** Building maintenance, except repairs; janitorial service, contract basis

(P-14261)
CONTRACT SERVICES GROUP INC
Also Called: Celex Solutions
480 Capricorn St, Brea (92821-3203)
P.O. Box 8815 (92822-5815)
PHONE 714 582-1800
John Pearce, *CEO*
Casey Pearce, *President*
Jorge Carpio, *Vice Pres*
EMP: 250
SALES (est): 9.7MM **Privately Held**
SIC: **7349** Building & office cleaning services

(P-14262)
CONTRLLED CNTMINATION SVCS LLC
Also Called: Controlled Contamination Svcs
6150 Lusk Blvd Ste 205, San Diego (92121-2739)
PHONE 858 457-3157
Fax: 858 457-7598
Christopher Zines, *Mng Member*
Steve Richards, *CFO*
Debra Guzman, *Admin Asst*
Dana Barton, *Business Mgr*
Debbie Jensen, *Business Mgr*
EMP: 140
SQ FT: 2,000
SALES (est): 8.3MM **Privately Held**
SIC: **7349** Cleaning service, industrial or commercial

(P-14263)
CONTROLLED CONTAMINATION SVCS
Also Called: CCS
23595 Cabot Blvd Ste 115, Hayward (94545-1681)
PHONE 510 728-1106
Brian Thaler, *Manager*
Roland Deleon, *Opers Mgr*
Debbie Jensen, *Marketing Staff*
EMP: 66
SALES (est): 1.9MM **Privately Held**
SIC: **7349** Cleaning service, industrial or commercial

(P-14264)
CORPORATE BUILDING SVCS INC
3325 Wilshire Blvd # 1240, Los Angeles (90010-1728)
PHONE 213 252-0999
Bruce Kim, *President*
Cindy Kim, *Admin Sec*
EMP: 200
SQ FT: 2,000
SALES: 3.5MM **Privately Held**
SIC: **7349** Janitorial service, contract basis

(P-14265)
CORPORATION SERVICE COMPANY
Also Called: Prentice Hall Legal Fincl Svcs
2710 Gateway Oaks Dr, Sacramento (95833-3505)
PHONE 302 636-5400
EMP: 100
SQ FT: 12,000
SALES (corp-wide): 454.7MM **Privately Held**
WEB: www.incspot.com
SIC: **7349** Building maintenance services
PA: Corporation Service Company Inc
2711 Centerville Rd # 400
Wilmington DE 19808
302 636-5400

(P-14266)
COSTLESS MAINTENANCE SVCS CO
Also Called: Cmsc
3254 19th St, San Francisco (94110-1917)
PHONE 415 550-8819
Fax: 415 550-8831
Marlene Samson, *President*
Norma Edar, *CFO*
Guillermo Guzman, *Vice Pres*
EMP: 55
SALES: 1.8MM **Privately Held**
SIC: **7349** Building maintenance services

(P-14267)
COUNTY OF CONTRA COSTA
Also Called: General Services
2099 Arnold Industrial Wa, Concord (94520-5321)
PHONE 925 646-5877
Jerry Redic, *Manager*
EMP: 100 **Privately Held**
SIC: **7349** 9199 Building maintenance services; general government administration;
PA: County Of Contra Costa
625 Court St Ste 100
Martinez CA 94553
925 957-5280

(P-14268)
COUNTY OF CONTRA COSTA
Also Called: General Services
2467 Waterbird Way, Martinez (94553-1457)
PHONE 925 313-7052
Roland Hindsman, *Manager*
John Abraham, *Manager*
EMP: 100 **Privately Held**
SIC: **7349** 9199 Building maintenance services; general government administration;
PA: County Of Contra Costa
625 Court St Ste 100
Martinez CA 94553
925 957-5280

(P-14269)
COUNTY OF EL DORADO
El Dorado Cnty Bldg & Grounds
3000 Fairlane Ct Ste 2, Placerville (95667-4100)
PHONE 530 621-5845
Fax: 530 295-2540
Bruce Pease, *Manager*
EMP: 76 **Privately Held**
WEB: www.filmtahoe.com
SIC: **7349** 9111 Building maintenance services; executive offices
PA: County Of El Dorado
330 Fair Ln
Placerville CA 95667
530 621-5830

(P-14270)
COUNTY OF SACRAMENTO
Also Called: Airfield Maintenance
7207 Earhart Dr, Sacramento (95837-1104)
PHONE 916 874-0746
Terry Sutton, *Branch Mgr*
EMP: 80 **Privately Held**
WEB: www.sna.com
SIC: **7349** 9311 Building maintenance services;
PA: County Of Sacramento
700 H St Ste 7650
Sacramento CA 95814
916 874-5544

(P-14271)
CREATIVE MAINTENANCE SYSTEMS
1340 Reynolds Ave Ste 111, Irvine (92614-5503)
PHONE 949 852-2871
Fax: 949 852-2869
Bill Koop, *President*
Christina Alexander, *Vice Pres*
Jenny Valenzuela, *Accounts Mgr*
EMP: 100
SQ FT: 2,000
SALES (est): 2.3MM **Privately Held**
SIC: **7349** Building cleaning service

(P-14272)
CROSSROADS FACILITY SVCS INC
9300 Tech Center Dr # 100, Sacramento (95826-2565)
PHONE 916 568-5230
David Deleonardis, *President*
Robert Bennett Jr, *Vice Chairman*
Bill Walters, *Corp Secy*
EMP: 57
SQ FT: 5,700

PRODUCTS & SERVICES SECTION
7349 - Building Cleaning & Maintenance Svcs, NEC County (P-14296)

SALES (est): 1MM Privately Held
SIC: 7349 1752 0781 Janitorial service, contract basis; wood floor installation & refinishing; landscape services

(P-14273)
CROWN BUILDING MAINTENANCE CO
1832 Tribute Rd Ste J, Sacramento (95815-4309)
PHONE.................................916 920-9556
Jeff Marquis, *Principal*
Epigmenio Montenegro, *Supervisor*
EMP: 1214
SALES (corp-wide): 258.4MM Privately Held
SIC: 7349 1623 Building maintenance services; water, sewer & utility lines
PA: Crown Building Maintenance Co.
868 Folsom St
San Francisco CA 94107
415 981-8070

(P-14274)
CROWN BUILDING MAINTENANCE CO
Also Called: Able Building Maintenance
3300 W Macarthur Blvd, Santa Ana (92704-6804)
PHONE.................................714 434-9494
Robert Hughes, *CEO*
Kurt Sitzman, *Accounts Mgr*
EMP: 50
SALES (corp-wide): 258.4MM Privately Held
SIC: 7349 Building maintenance services
PA: Crown Building Maintenance Co.
868 Folsom St
San Francisco CA 94107
415 981-8070

(P-14275)
CROWN BUILDING MAINTENANCE CO
235 Pine St Ste 600, San Francisco (94104-2745)
PHONE.................................303 680-3713
Dan Jaster, *Branch Mgr*
EMP: 270
SALES (corp-wide): 258.4MM Privately Held
SIC: 7349 8711 Janitorial service, contract basis; engineering services
PA: Crown Building Maintenance Co.
868 Folsom St
San Francisco CA 94107
415 981-8070

(P-14276)
CROWN BUILDING MAINTENANCE CO
5482 Complex St Ste 108, San Diego (92123-1125)
PHONE.................................858 560-5785
Dan Jaster, *Branch Mgr*
EMP: 270
SALES (corp-wide): 258.4MM Privately Held
SIC: 7349 8711 Janitorial service, contract basis; engineering services
PA: Crown Building Maintenance Co.
868 Folsom St
San Francisco CA 94107
415 981-8070

(P-14277)
CROWN BUILDING MAINTENANCE CO
Also Called: Able Building Maintenance
2601 S Figueroa St # 299, Los Angeles (90007-3254)
PHONE.................................213 765-7800
Brian Pagac, *Principal*
EMP: 50
SALES (corp-wide): 258.4MM Privately Held
WEB: www.ableserve.com
SIC: 7349 8711 Janitorial service, contract basis; engineering services
PA: Crown Building Maintenance Co.
868 Folsom St
San Francisco CA 94107
415 981-8070

(P-14278)
CROWN ENERGY SERVICES INC
Also Called: Able Engineering Services
2601 S Figueroa St Fl 1, Los Angeles (90007-3254)
PHONE.................................213 765-7800
Fax: 213 763-0509
Ed Figueroa, *Manager*
Marlon Jarrett, *Engineer*
Steven Vertrees, *Engineer*
Moses Kibuye, *Chief Engr*
Brian Pagac, *Manager*
EMP: 800
SALES (corp-wide): 403.7MM Privately Held
SIC: 7349 Building maintenance services
PA: Crown Energy Services, Inc.
868 Folsom St
San Francisco CA 94107
415 546-6534

(P-14279)
D S P SERVICE INC
Also Called: D S P Janitorial Service
23762 Foley St Ste 3, Hayward (94545-1662)
PHONE.................................510 782-2200
Don Wallace, *President*
Dawn Wallace, *Corp Secy*
Gloria Wallace, *Vice Pres*
EMP: 50
SQ FT: 2,000
SALES: 1MM Privately Held
WEB: www.dspjanitorial.com
SIC: 7349 Janitorial service, contract basis

(P-14280)
DAN LOFGREN
Also Called: Central Cleaning Co
7707 Forsythia Ct, Pleasanton (94588-4818)
PHONE.................................925 846-6632
Fax: 510 485-9181
Dan Lofgren, *Owner*
EMP: 60
SALES: 1.5MM Privately Held
SIC: 7349 Building maintenance services

(P-14281)
DANISH ENVIRONMENT INC
31125 Via Colinas, Chatsworth (91311)
PHONE.................................818 992-6722
Jens Grau, *President*
Christina Johansen, *Office Mgr*
EMP: 70
SALES (est): 1.7MM Privately Held
WEB: www.danishenvironment.com
SIC: 7349 Janitorial service, contract basis

(P-14282)
DANLIL ENTERPRISE INC
Also Called: Sterling Building Services
1440 S State College Blvd, Anaheim (92806-5724)
PHONE.................................714 776-7705
Dan Rubio, *President*
EMP: 75
SQ FT: 2,000
SALES: 2.5MM Privately Held
WEB: www.jabezbs.com
SIC: 7349 Janitorial service, contract basis

(P-14283)
DMS FACILITY SERVICES INC
Also Called: D M S
3137 Skyway Ct, Fremont (94539-5910)
PHONE.................................510 656-9400
Loren Dotts, *Manager*
EMP: 800
SALES (corp-wide): 60.6MM Privately Held
WEB: www.dms-services.com
SIC: 7349 0782 Building maintenance, except repairs; lawn & garden services
PA: Dms Facility Services, Inc.
1040 Arroyo Dr
South Pasadena CA 91030
626 305-8500

(P-14284)
DYNAMIC MAINTENANCE SVCS INC
837 Arnold Dr Ste 220, Martinez (94553-6534)
PHONE.................................925 228-7434
Fax: 925 228-7402
Arturo Ramos, *President*
Susan K Moore, *CFO*
Violet Ramos, *Corp Secy*
Maria L Ramos, *Vice Pres*
Pablo Juarez, *General Mgr*
EMP: 52
SQ FT: 536
SALES: 1.8MM Privately Held
SIC: 7349 Building maintenance services

(P-14285)
E&S BUILDING MAINTENANCE INC
3315 E Miraloma Ave # 116, Anaheim (92806-1924)
PHONE.................................714 961-8078
Fax: 714 961-0137
Ernesto Diedrich, *President*
Sylvia Diedrich, *Vice Pres*
EMP: 85
SQ FT: 5,000
SALES (est): 2.3MM Privately Held
SIC: 7349 7359 Janitorial service, contract basis; carpet & upholstery cleaning equipment rental

(P-14286)
EBM INC
Also Called: Express Building Maint Co
3200 Wilshire Blvd # 1000, Los Angeles (90010-1333)
PHONE.................................213 365-4905
Fax: 213 465-4906
Alex T Wang, *President*
EMP: 75
SQ FT: 1,175
SALES (est): 2.1MM Privately Held
WEB: www.expressbm.com
SIC: 7349 Building maintenance services

(P-14287)
EBM JANITORIAL SERVICES INC
Also Called: Excellent Building Maintenance
5260 Bonsai St Ste E, Moorpark (93021-1768)
P.O. Box 204, Newbury Park (91319-0204)
PHONE.................................805 523-3700
Fax: 805 498-3138
Matt Mullen, *President*
EMP: 70
SALES (est): 1.4MM Privately Held
SIC: 7349 Janitorial service, contract basis

(P-14288)
ELITE CRAFTSMAN (PA)
Also Called: Stockmar Industrial
2763 South St Louis Ave, Long Beach (90755-2025)
P.O. Box 90458 (90809-0458)
PHONE.................................562 989-3511
Fax: 562 989-1198
William C Stockmar, *President*
George N Negrete, *Vice Pres*
Linda Pierson, *Admin Sec*
EMP: 130
SQ FT: 10,000
SALES (est): 8.7MM Privately Held
SIC: 7349 Building maintenance services

(P-14289)
ELITE MAINTENANCE SERVICES INC
7770 Regents Rd Ste 113, San Diego (92122-1967)
PHONE.................................619 516-7000
Fax: 619 516-7077
Heidi Anderson, *President*
EMP: 55
SALES (est): 1.3MM Privately Held
SIC: 7349 Building maintenance services; building cleaning service

(P-14290)
EMPIRE BUILDING SERVICES INC
1570 E Edinger Ave Ste D, Santa Ana (92705-4909)
P.O. Box 26, Tustin (92781-0026)
PHONE.................................714 836-7700
Fax: 714 836-9538
Suzanne De Rossett, *President*
Katie Doweling, *Admin Asst*
EMP: 80
SALES (est): 3.8MM Privately Held
SIC: 7349 Building cleaning service

(P-14291)
ENVIRONMENT CONTROL
1849 N Helm Ave Ste 105, Fresno (93727-1624)
PHONE.................................559 456-9791
Fax: 559 456-9795
Dick Johns, *Partner*
Kit Seals, *Partner*
EMP: 50
SQ FT: 6,000
SALES (est): 1.5MM Privately Held
SIC: 7349 Janitorial service, contract basis

(P-14292)
EVERGREEN CLEANING SYSTEMS INC
3325 Wilshire Blvd # 622, Los Angeles (90010-1747)
PHONE.................................213 386-3260
Fax: 213 386-3268
John Lee, *President*
EMP: 50
SALES (est): 1.4MM Privately Held
SIC: 7349 Building & office cleaning services

(P-14293)
EXCEL BUILDING SERVICES LLC
1061 Serpentine Ln Ste H, Pleasanton (94566-4793)
P.O. Box 5040, San Jose (95150-5040)
PHONE.................................650 755-0900
Jenn Fabrique, *CEO*
Jack Fabrique, *President*
Steve Sui, *CFO*
Gabe Costello, *Exec VP*
Scott Henley, *Exec VP*
EMP: 1300 EST: 1998
SQ FT: 3,000
SALES (est): 52.8MM Privately Held
SIC: 7349 Janitorial service, contract basis

(P-14294)
EXPERT BUILDING MAINT LLC
4596 Ish Dr Ste 200, Simi Valley (93063-7690)
PHONE.................................805 520-1580
Fax: 805 520-7432
Robert Pedder,
Jennifer Duarte, *Admin Asst*
Alberto Duarte,
Carolyn Pedder, *Manager*
EMP: 100
SQ FT: 1,000
SALES (est): 4.4MM Privately Held
WEB: www.thebuildingexperts.com
SIC: 7349 Janitorial service, contract basis

(P-14295)
FACILITY MASTERS INC (PA)
1604 Kerley Dr, San Jose (95112-4815)
PHONE.................................408 436-9090
Ramsin Bitmansour, *CEO*
James Machado, *President*
Osvaldo Almeida, *Vice Pres*
Youra Tarverdi, *Data Proc Exec*
Touboul Yoel, *Info Tech Dir*
EMP: 230
SQ FT: 7,000
SALES (est): 14MM Privately Held
SIC: 7349 Building & office cleaning services

(P-14296)
FAME SYSTEMS INC
301 Hearst Dr, Oxnard (93030-5158)
PHONE.................................805 485-0808
Sal Mejia, *President*
Jesus Mejia, *Vice Pres*
Antonia Mejia, *Manager*

7349 - Building Cleaning & Maintenance Svcs, NEC County (P-14297)

PRODUDUCTS & SERVICES SECTION

Melina Mejia, *Manager*
Diana Ornelas, *Accounts Mgr*
EMP: 50
SALES: 2.5MM **Privately Held**
WEB: www.famesystems.com
SIC: 7349 Janitorial service, contract basis

(P-14297)
FIELDS CONSTRUCTION SERVICES
Also Called: Fields Win Clg Win Protection
5715 Southfront Rd Ste B1, Livermore (94551-7807)
PHONE.....................925 294-8183
Fax: 925 294-8157
Daniel Fields, *President*
EMP: 60
SALES (est): 1.5MM **Privately Held**
SIC: 7349 1799 Cleaning service, industrial or commercial; coating, caulking & weather, water & fireproofing

(P-14298)
FLAIR BUILDING SERVICES
Also Called: Flair Building Maintenance
3470 Edward Ave, Santa Clara (95054-2130)
PHONE.....................408 987-4040
Fax: 408 987-4045
John McEvoy, *CEO*
Oscar Pena, *President*
Shirely McEvoy, *Treasurer*
Maria Souza, *Director*
Fatima Delgado, *Manager*
EMP: 90
SQ FT: 2,400
SALES: 3.7MM **Privately Held**
SIC: 7349 Building maintenance services

(P-14299)
FLUOR FACILITY & PLANT SVCS
124 Blossom Hill Rd 1524h, San Jose (95123-2308)
PHONE.....................408 256-1333
Brett Heckel, *Finance*
EMP: 250
SALES (corp-wide): 18.1B **Publicly Held**
SIC: 7349 Building maintenance services
HQ: Fluor Facility & Plant Services, Inc
3 Polaris Way
Aliso Viejo CA
949 349-2000

(P-14300)
FLUOR INDUSTRIAL SERVICES INC
1 Enterprise, Aliso Viejo (92656-2606)
PHONE.....................949 439-2000
David T Seaton, *CEO*
EMP: 1000
SALES (est): 9.6MM
SALES (corp-wide): 18.1B **Publicly Held**
SIC: 7349 Building maintenance services
HQ: Fluor Enterprises, Inc.
6700 Las Colinas Blvd
Irving TX 75039
469 398-7000

(P-14301)
FOUNTAIN VALLEY SCHOOL DST
Also Called: South Valley School District
17330 Mount Herrmann St, Fountain Valley (92708-4104)
PHONE.....................714 668-5882
Fax: 714 668-5895
Joe Hastie, *Supervisor*
Pat Minnesang, *Data Proc Exec*
Traci Castaneda, *Education*
EMP: 75
SALES (corp-wide): 38.4MM **Privately Held**
SIC: 7349 Building maintenance services
PA: Fountain Valley School District
10055 Slater Ave
Fountain Valley CA 92708
714 668-5886

(P-14302)
FRANCOIS ANNAIE
Also Called: Roses Maid Service
29131 Escalante Rd, Quail Valley (92587-7241)
PHONE.....................619 846-3438
Annaie Francois, *Owner*

EMP: 50
SALES (est): 850K **Privately Held**
SIC: 7349 7342 Building & office cleaning services; office cleaning or charring; building cleaning service; rest room cleaning service

(P-14303)
FREMONT UNIFIED SCHOOL DST
43772 S Grimmer Blvd, Fremont (94538-6308)
PHONE.....................510 657-0761
EMP: 64
SALES (corp-wide): 189.7MM **Privately Held**
SIC: 7349 Building maintenance services
PA: Fremont Unified School District
4210 Technology Dr
Fremont CA 94538
510 657-2350

(P-14304)
FRESNO UNIFIED SCHOOL DISTRICT
Also Called: Maintenance Department
4600 N Brawley Ave, Fresno (93722-3921)
PHONE.....................559 457-3074
Ron Tessada, *Director*
Jose Alvarado, *Telecomm Mgr*
Brad Johnson, *IT/INT Sup*
Chuck Braun, *Opers Staff*
John Klang, *Manager*
EMP: 170
SALES (corp-wide): 458.3MM **Privately Held**
WEB: www.fresno.k12.ca.us
SIC: 7349 Building maintenance services
PA: Fresno Unified School District
2309 Tulare St
Fresno CA 93721
559 457-3000

(P-14305)
GALAXY BUILDING SYSTEMS INC
23978 Craftsman Rd, Calabasas (91302-1437)
PHONE.....................818 340-6557
Fax: 818 340-7800
Gerald C Baggett, *President*
Maydie Encinas, *Human Res Mgr*
Mark Baggette, *Sales Staff*
EMP: 150 **EST:** 1968
SALES (est): 3.2MM **Privately Held**
WEB: www.galaxyservicesca.com
SIC: 7349 Janitorial service, contract basis

(P-14306)
GAMBOA SERVICE INC
Also Called: Corporate Image Maintenance
2116 S Wright St, Santa Ana (92705-5314)
PHONE.....................714 966-5325
Fax: 714 966-5329
Gilbert Gamboa, *President*
EMP: 55
SQ FT: 2,800
SALES (est): 1.8MM **Privately Held**
SIC: 7349 Building maintenance services

(P-14307)
GARCIA ASSET MANAGEMENT INC
Also Called: Empire Building & Envmtl Svcs
740 S Corrida Dr, Covina (91724-3563)
PHONE.....................626 289-8755
Elaina Garcia, *President*
Ronnie Garcia, *Vice Pres*
EMP: 150
SQ FT: 8,000
SALES: 4MM **Privately Held**
SIC: 7349 Building maintenance services

(P-14308)
GENERAL SERVICES CAL DEPT
9645 Butterfield Way # 1503, Sacramento (95827-1501)
P.O. Box 277376 (95827-7376)
PHONE.....................916 845-4942
Jeff Henninger, *Director*
EMP: 120 **Privately Held**
WEB: www.4c.net
SIC: 7349 9199 Building maintenance services; general government administration;

HQ: California Department Of General Services
707 3rd St
West Sacramento CA 95605

(P-14309)
GENERAL SERVICES CAL DEPT
1304 O St Ste 301, Sacramento (95814-5906)
PHONE.....................916 445-4566
Fred Lucy, *Principal*
EMP: 2000 **Privately Held**
WEB: www.4c.net
SIC: 7349 9199 Building maintenance services; general government administration;
HQ: California Department Of General Services
707 3rd St
West Sacramento CA 95605

(P-14310)
GENERAL SERVICES CAL DEPT
Also Called: Building and Property MGT BR
300 S Spring St Ste 1726, Los Angeles (90013-1256)
PHONE.....................213 897-2241
Christopher Robles, *Regional Mgr*
Genny Estrada, *Supervisor*
EMP: 65 **Privately Held**
WEB: www.4c.net
SIC: 7349 9199 Building maintenance services; general government administration;
HQ: California Department Of General Services
707 3rd St
West Sacramento CA 95605

(P-14311)
GHOSSAIN & TRUELOCK ENTPS INC
Also Called: Custom Service Systems
783 Palmyrita Ave Ste A, Riverside (92507-1817)
P.O. Box 5596 (92517-5596)
PHONE.....................951 781-9345
Fax: 951 787-0123
Kenneth Truelock, *President*
David L Truelock, *CEO*
Robert K Ghossain, *Bd of Directors*
Bob Ghossain, *Manager*
EMP: 80
SALES (est): 3.1MM **Privately Held**
WEB: www.cssclean.com
SIC: 7349 Janitorial service, contract basis

(P-14312)
GLEN ALPINE BUILDING SVCS INC
24685 Oneil Ave, Hayward (94544-1627)
P.O. Box 738 (94543-0738)
PHONE.....................510 582-7400
Fax: 510 582-7415
Janice Lynn Slade, *President*
EMP: 60
SALES: 1.8MM **Privately Held**
SIC: 7349 Janitorial service, contract basis

(P-14313)
GLENN BUILDING SERVICES INC
1148 N Lake Ave Apt 1, Pasadena (91104-3729)
PHONE.....................626 398-8000
Fax: 626 398-1290
Christopher Garcia, *President*
Yvonne Pico, *Vice Pres*
EMP: 85
SALES: 600K **Privately Held**
SIC: 7349 Building & office cleaning services

(P-14314)
GLOBAL BUILDING SERVICES INC (PA)
25129 The Old Rd Ste 102, Stevenson Ranch (91381-2287)
PHONE.....................661 288-5733
Julio Belloso, *President*
Tony Martinez, *Asst Mgr*
EMP: 802

SALES (est): 37.3MM **Privately Held**
WEB: www.globalbuildingservices.com
SIC: 7349 Janitorial service, contract basis

(P-14315)
GMG JANITORIAL INC
2237 Palou Ave, San Francisco (94124-1504)
PHONE.....................415 642-2100
Fax: 415 642-2101
Gina Gregori, *President*
EMP: 220
SALES (est): 8.7MM **Privately Held**
SIC: 7349 Janitorial service, contract basis; building maintenance, except repairs

(P-14316)
GMI BUILDING SERVICES INC
8001 Vickers St, San Diego (92111-1917)
PHONE.....................858 279-6262
Fax: 858 279-2721
Larry Abrams, *President*
Liza Pasko, *Human Res Mgr*
EMP: 225
SQ FT: 15,000
SALES (est): 9.2MM **Privately Held**
SIC: 7349 5087 Janitorial service, contract basis; janitors' supplies

(P-14317)
GMS JANITORIAL SERVICES INC
8316 Clairemont Mesa Blvd # 201, San Diego (92111-1316)
PHONE.....................858 569-6009
Fax: 858 569-6006
Rene Gonzalez, *President*
EMP: 66
SALES (est): 2.3MM **Privately Held**
SIC: 7349 Janitorial service, contract basis

(P-14318)
H U S D MAINTENANCE OPERATION
24400 Amador St, Hayward (94544-1302)
PHONE.....................510 784-2666
Joseph Zanini, *Director*
JAS Sohal, *Purch Mgr*
EMP: 80
SALES (est): 1.9MM **Privately Held**
SIC: 7349 Building maintenance services

(P-14319)
HARBOR BUILDING SERVICES
2701 Plaza Del Amo # 706, Torrance (90503-7314)
PHONE.....................310 320-2966
Fax: 310 320-2971
Peter Lescord, *Owner*
Toni Deaso, *Administration*
EMP: 86
SQ FT: 3,000
SALES (est): 2.7MM **Privately Held**
SIC: 7349 Janitorial service, contract basis

(P-14320)
HAYNES BUILDING SERVICE LLC
16027 Arrow Hwy Ste I, Baldwin Park (91706-2064)
PHONE.....................626 359-6100
Fax: 626 359-7008
John P Scharler, *President*
Michael Franco, *Vice Pres*
Mark Scharler, *Manager*
EMP: 175
SQ FT: 20,000
SALES (est): 5.3MM **Privately Held**
WEB: www.haynesservices.com
SIC: 7349 Janitorial service, contract basis

(P-14321)
HOSPITAL HOUSEKEEPING
1300 N Vermont Ave, Los Angeles (90027-6098)
PHONE.....................323 913-4820
Maria Carlos, *Director*
David Taylor, *Director*
EMP: 66
SALES (est): 1.6MM **Privately Held**
WEB: www.hospitalhousekeeping.com
SIC: 7349 Building maintenance services

7349 - Building Cleaning & Maintenance Svcs, NEC County (P-14344)

(P-14322)
HUNTER EASTERDAY CORPORATION
1475 N Hundley St, Anaheim (92806-1323)
PHONE.................714 238-3400
Fax: 714 238-3409
Sam Easterday, *CEO*
Manny Jones, *President*
Joanne Easterday, *CFO*
Gilbert Anzaldua, *Vice Pres*
Jannet Chris, *Manager*
EMP: 135
SQ FT: 4,400
SALES (est): 4.2MM **Privately Held**
WEB: www.ebmcorp.com
SIC: 7349 5087 Janitorial service, contract basis; building maintenance, except repairs; janitors' supplies

(P-14323)
HYDROCHEM LLC
Also Called: Hydro Chem Industrial Services
901 Loveridge Rd 592, Pittsburg (94565-2811)
P.O. Box 1859 (94565-0859)
PHONE.................925 432-1749
Fax: 925 432-5549
Jodi White, *Manager*
EMP: 65
SALES (corp-wide): 700.3MM **Privately Held**
WEB: www.hydrochem.com
SIC: 7349 Cleaning service, industrial or commercial
HQ: Hydrochem Llc
   900 Georgia Ave
   Deer Park TX 77536
   713 393-5600

(P-14324)
IMPEC GROUP INC
3350 Scott Blvd Bldg 8, Santa Clara (95054-3108)
PHONE.................408 330-9350
Raffy Espiritu, *President*
Andy Fuhrman, *COO*
Christine Chen, *Vice Pres*
Leonard Liang, *Business Dir*
Jason Fang, *Admin Sec*
EMP: 230 EST: 1991
SQ FT: 5,000
SALES (est): 9.9MM **Privately Held**
WEB: www.cleaninnovation.com
SIC: 7349 Building maintenance services

(P-14325)
INTEGRATED CLG SOLUTIONS INC
Also Called: I C S
3043 Mission St, San Francisco (94110-4501)
PHONE.................415 821-6757
Fax: 415 821-6871
Nicholas Mettler, *President*
Guillermo Guajardo, *Office Mgr*
Edith Cuares, *Human Res Mgr*
EMP: 50
SQ FT: 2,500
SALES: 8MM **Privately Held**
WEB: www.nomoredirt.com
SIC: 7349 Building maintenance services

(P-14326)
INTEGRITY MANAGEMENT SVCS INC
141 W Dana St Ste 100, Nipomo (93444-9152)
P.O. Box 976 (93444-0976)
PHONE.................805 238-0905
Fax: 805 929-8404
Raul Torres, *President*
EMP: 200
SALES (est): 6.1MM **Privately Held**
SIC: 7349 Janitorial service, contract basis

(P-14327)
ISS FACILITY SERVICES INC
Also Called: Loma Cleaning Service
541 Taylor Way Ste 5, San Carlos (94070-6254)
PHONE.................650 593-9774
Peter Beck, *Vice Pres*
EMP: 300
SALES (corp-wide): 11.4B **Privately Held**
SIC: 7349 Janitorial service, contract basis
HQ: Iss Facility Services, Inc.
   1019 Central Pkwy N # 139
   San Antonio TX 78232
   210 495-6021

(P-14328)
J & J MAINTENANCE INC
100 Hangar Ave Bldg 785, Fairfield (94535-1812)
PHONE.................707 423-7453
Tom Jobin, *Branch Mgr*
EMP: 175
SALES (corp-wide): 356.9MM **Privately Held**
SIC: 7349 Building maintenance services
PA: J & J Maintenance, Inc.
   7710 Rialto Blvd Unit 200
   Austin TX 78735
   512 444-7271

(P-14329)
JABEZ BUILDING SERVICES INC
2094 Orange Ave, Costa Mesa (92627-2101)
PHONE.................714 776-7705
Fax: 714 641-7394
Daniel Rubio, *President*
Mary Rubio, *Vice Pres*
Erika Lopez, *Office Mgr*
Fidel Reyes, *Opers Mgr*
EMP: 60
SALES (est): 1.6MM **Privately Held**
SIC: 7349 Building maintenance services

(P-14330)
JAN PRO CLG SYSTEMS STHERN CAL
2401 E Katella Ave # 525, Anaheim (92806-5939)
PHONE.................714 220-0500
Fax: 714 220-0243
Dave Rhodes, *Manager*
EMP: 50
SALES (corp-wide): 526K **Privately Held**
SIC: 7349 5087 Building maintenance services; service establishment equipment
PA: Jan Pro Cleaning Systems Of Southern California
   3875 Hopyard Rd Ste 194
   Pleasanton CA 94588
   714 220-0500

(P-14331)
JANICO BUILDING MAINTENANCE
3001 Red Hill Ave 2-221, Costa Mesa (92626-4546)
PHONE.................714 444-4339
Shawn Dawson, *President*
Heather Brown, *Manager*
EMP: 412
SQ FT: 5,000
SALES (est): 3.5MM **Privately Held**
SIC: 7349 Janitorial service, contract basis

(P-14332)
JANITORIAL EQUIPMENT SVCS INC
Also Called: King Janitorial Equipment Svcs
11752 Garden Grove Blvd # 100, Garden Grove (92843-1477)
PHONE.................951 205-8937
Javier Brito, *CFO*
EMP: 55
SALES: 950K **Privately Held**
SIC: 7349 Building maintenance services

(P-14333)
K & P JANITORIAL SERVICES
412 S Pacific Coast Hwy # 200, Redondo Beach (90277-3712)
PHONE.................310 540-8878
Fax: 310 791-4408
Kelly Lynch, *President*
EMP: 100
SALES (est): 3.2MM **Privately Held**
SIC: 7349 Building maintenance services

(P-14334)
KBM FCLITY SLTONS HOLDINGS LLC
Also Called: Kbm Fclity Sltons Holdings LLC
7976 Engineer Rd Ste 200, San Diego (92111-1935)
PHONE.................858 467-0202
Brian Snow, *CEO*
Omar Lopez, *COO*
Susan Cologna, *CFO*
John Mullen, *CFO*
Norma Autry, *Vice Pres*
EMP: 500
SQ FT: 10,000
SALES (est): 23.3MM
SALES (corp-wide): 33.2MM **Privately Held**
SIC: 7349 Janitorial service, contract basis
PA: Pristine Environments Inc
   7925 Jones Branch Dr Ll330
   Mc Lean VA 22102
   703 245-4751

(P-14335)
KM INDUSTRIAL INC
2375 W Esther St, Long Beach (90813-1029)
PHONE.................562 786-6200
Fax: 562 786-6299
Will Colon, *CEO*
Rich Bartel, *President*
Kenny Sephus, *Project Mgr*
Holly Wickenhagen, *Manager*
EMP: 128
SALES (est): 4.5MM
SALES (corp-wide): 170.5MM **Privately Held**
SIC: 7349 Cleaning service, industrial or commercial
PA: K2 Industrial Services, Inc.
   4527 Columbia Ave 2
   Hammond IN 46327
   708 928-4765

(P-14336)
LANDMARK SERVICES INC
410 N Fairview St, Santa Ana (92703-3412)
PHONE.................714 547-6308
Dan Rogers, *President*
Don Voska, *CFO*
Nancy Quarles, *Vice Pres*
EMP: 60
SQ FT: 130,000
SALES: 3.8MM **Privately Held**
SIC: 7349 Janitorial service, contract basis

(P-14337)
LEES MAINTENANCE SERVICE INC
14740 Keswick St, Van Nuys (91405-1205)
PHONE.................818 988-6644
Fax: 818 988-7922
Tyrone P Ingram, *President*
EMP: 275 EST: 1961
SQ FT: 3,000
SALES (est): 8.4MM **Privately Held**
WEB: www.leesmaint.com
SIC: 7349 5087 Janitorial service, contract basis; laundry & dry cleaning equipment & supplies

(P-14338)
LEWIS & TAYLOR LLC
Also Called: Lewis & Taylor Bldg Svc Contrs
440 Bryant St, San Francisco (94107-1303)
PHONE.................415 781-3496
Fax: 415 227-4868
Michael L Milstein, *President*
Dennis Sakurai, *Manager*
EMP: 150 EST: 1945
SQ FT: 4,000
SALES: 6.4MM **Privately Held**
WEB: www.lewistaylor.com
SIC: 7349 Building maintenance, except repairs; janitorial service, contract basis; window cleaning; chemical cleaning services

(P-14339)
LIFE CYCLE ENGINEERING INC
2535 Camino Del Rio S # 250, San Diego (92108-3780)
PHONE.................619 785-5990
John Spencer, *Manager*
Susan Colvin, *Executive Asst*
Victoria Hood, *Administration*
Adam B Duncan, *Engineer*
Ron Leonard, *Sr Consultant*
EMP: 80
SALES (corp-wide): 91.1MM **Privately Held**
WEB: www.lcesd.com
SIC: 7349 Building maintenance, except repairs
PA: Life Cycle Engineering, Inc.
   4360 Corporate Rd Ste 100
   North Charleston SC 29405
   843 744-7110

(P-14340)
LITTLE GIANT BLDG MAINT INC
15 Brooks Pl, Pacifica (94044-4403)
PHONE.................415 508-0282
David Dellanini, *President*
EMP: 231
SALES (corp-wide): 8.4MM **Privately Held**
SIC: 7349 7217 Window cleaning; carpet & upholstery cleaning
PA: Little Giant Building Maintenance, Inc.
   1485 Bay Shore Blvd # 117
   San Francisco CA 94124
   415 508-0282

(P-14341)
LODI UNIFIED SCHOOL DISTRICT
Also Called: Maintenance & Operations
1305 E Vine St, Lodi (95240-3179)
PHONE.................209 331-7181
Mike Matranga, *Manager*
EMP: 65
SALES (corp-wide): 297MM **Privately Held**
WEB: www.lodiusd.net
SIC: 7349 Building maintenance services
PA: Lodi Unified School District
   1305 E Vine St
   Lodi CA 95240
   209 331-7000

(P-14342)
LONG BEACH UNIFIED SCHOOL DIST
Also Called: Maintenance
2425 Webster Ave, Long Beach (90810-3204)
PHONE.................562 997-7550
Joe Rasch, *Director*
Cheryl Caldwell, *Admin Sec*
Lisa Dutra, *Administration*
Chris Eftychiou, *CTO*
Edith Florence, *Project Mgr*
EMP: 200
SALES (corp-wide): 810.4MM **Privately Held**
WEB: www.lbusd.k12.ca.us
SIC: 7349 School custodian, contract basis
PA: Long Beach Unified School District
   1515 Hughes Way
   Long Beach CA 90810
   562 997-8000

(P-14343)
LOS ANGELES UNIFIED SCHOOL DST
Also Called: Maintenance Dept
17729 S Figueroa St, Gardena (90248-4237)
PHONE.................310 808-1500
Roger Finstad, *Director*
EMP: 50
SALES (corp-wide): 4.4B **Privately Held**
WEB: www.lausd.k12.ca.us
SIC: 7349 School custodian, contract basis
PA: Los Angeles Unified School District
   333 S Beaudry Ave Ste 209
   Los Angeles CA 90017
   213 241-1000

(P-14344)
LUXERA INC
39300 Civic Center Dr # 140, Fremont (94538-2338)
PHONE.................510 456-7690
Leonard Simon Livschitz, *CEO*
Anatoly Shteynberg, *Med Doctor*
EMP: 50

7349 - Building Cleaning & Maintenance Svcs, NEC County (P-14345)

PRODUDUCTS & SERVICES SECTION

SALES (est): 1.2MM Privately Held
SIC: 7349 Lighting maintenance service

(P-14345)
M-N-Z JANITORIAL SERVICES INC
2109 W Burbank Blvd, Burbank (91506-1231)
PHONE..............................323 851-4115
Fax: 323 851-4303
Marc De Mauregne, *Exec VP*
Dennis Krebs, *Shareholder*
Zorina Russell Kroop, *President*
EMP: 110
SQ FT: 1,000
SALES (est): 3.1MM Privately Held
WEB: www.mnz.com
SIC: 7349 1799 Building maintenance, except repairs; construction site cleanup

(P-14346)
MAIN SOURCE GROUP INC
3255 Wilshire Blvd # 1806, Los Angeles (90010-1404)
P.O. Box 8628, Northridge (91327-8628)
PHONE..............................213 387-1001
Charles Hong, *President*
Michelle Hong, *Treasurer*
Michael Adams, *Sales Dir*
June Kim, *Manager*
EMP: 100
SQ FT: 3,000
SALES: 2.1MM Privately Held
SIC: 7349 Building maintenance services

(P-14347)
MAINTENANCE SERVICE FOR THE CY
Also Called: Public Works Superintendent
1616 Fortmann Way, Alameda (94501-1274)
PHONE..............................510 865-3778
Fax: 510 521-8762
Lance Bryant, *Superintendent*
EMP: 51
SALES (est): 1MM Privately Held
SIC: 7349 Building maintenance services

(P-14348)
MAINTENANCE STAFF INC
122 W 8th St, Long Beach (90813-4371)
PHONE..............................562 493-3982
Vivian M Frahm, *President*
EMP: 2600
SALES (est): 18MM Privately Held
WEB: www.maintenancestaff.com
SIC: 7349 Janitorial service, contract basis

(P-14349)
MARK GARCIA
Also Called: All In One Complete Bldg Svcs
5131 Ellsworth Rd Ste B, Vacaville (95688-9483)
P.O. Box 2383 (95696-2383)
PHONE..............................707 446-4529
Fax: 707 446-4529
Mark Garcia, *Owner*
Diane Garcia, *Office Mgr*
EMP: 60
SQ FT: 4,000
SALES: 250K Privately Held
SIC: 7349 1799 1521 Building maintenance services; cleaning new buildings after construction; cleaning building exteriors; repairing fire damage, single-family houses

(P-14350)
MAROTTO CORPORATION
Also Called: All American Maintenance
9620 Topanga Canyon Pl D, Chatsworth (91311-4139)
PHONE..............................818 775-0320
Fax: 818 775-0335
Mario Marotto, *President*
Nancy Stout, *Vice Pres*
EMP: 319
SQ FT: 11,700
SALES (est): 10.1MM Privately Held
SIC: 7349 1771 Building maintenance, except repairs; flooring contractor

(P-14351)
MASTER CLEAN USA INC
Also Called: Janitorial
5511 Ekwill St Ste D, Santa Barbara (93111-2361)
P.O. Box 8032, Goleta (93118-8032)
PHONE..............................805 681-0950
Jessica Sanchez Hoseler, *CEO*
Brandee Hostler, *Info Tech Mgr*
EMP: 50
SALES (est): 1.8MM Privately Held
SIC: 7349 7389 1799 Maid services, contract or fee basis; ; construction site cleanup

(P-14352)
MCKOWSKIS MAINT SYSTEMS INC
10979 San Dego Mission Rd, San Diego (92108-2431)
PHONE..............................619 269-4600
Fax: 858 679-4180
James R McElwee, *President*
Natalie McElwee, *Manager*
EMP: 147 EST: 1979
SQ FT: 7,000
SALES (est): 5.1MM Privately Held
WEB: www.mckowskis.com
SIC: 7349 Janitorial service, contract basis

(P-14353)
MERCHANTS BUILDING MAINT CO
1639 E Edinger Ave Ste C, Santa Ana (92705-5013)
PHONE..............................714 973-9272
Fax: 714 973-2124
George Rodriguez, *Branch Mgr*
Antonio Torre, *CTO*
EMP: 300
SALES (corp-wide): 112.5MM Privately Held
WEB: www.mbmonline.com
SIC: 7349 Building maintenance, except repairs
PA: Merchants Building Maintenance Company
1190 Monterey Pass Rd
Monterey Park CA 91754
323 881-6701

(P-14354)
MERCHANTS BUILDING MAINT CO (PA)
1190 Monterey Pass Rd, Monterey Park (91754-3615)
PHONE..............................323 881-6701
Fax: 323 263-7141
Theodore Haas, *CEO*
David Haas, *President*
Karen T Haas, *Treasurer*
Wayne Eames, *Vice Pres*
Krista M Haas, *Vice Pres*
EMP: 148
SQ FT: 8,000
SALES (est): 112.5MM Privately Held
WEB: www.mbmonline.com
SIC: 7349 Building maintenance services

(P-14355)
MERCHANTS BUILDING MAINT CO
1995 W Holt Ave, Pomona (91768-3352)
PHONE..............................909 622-8260
Fax: 909 622-2217
Angel Meza, *General Mgr*
Lupe Lumes, *Office Mgr*
Sharon Godinez, *Manager*
Fidel Merchants, *Manager*
EMP: 220
SALES (corp-wide): 112.5MM Privately Held
WEB: www.mbmonline.com
SIC: 7349 7381 Building maintenance services; security guard service
PA: Merchants Building Maintenance Company
1190 Monterey Pass Rd
Monterey Park CA 91754
323 881-6701

(P-14356)
MERCHANTS BUILDING MAINT CO
606 Monterey Paca Rd 20 Ste 202, Monterey Park (91754)
PHONE..............................323 881-8902
Michael Anthony Palma,
Wallace Reid, *Vice Pres*
Cesar Prado, *Branch Mgr*
EMP: 130
SALES (corp-wide): 112.5MM Privately Held
WEB: www.mbmonline.com
SIC: 7349 7381 Building maintenance services; detective & armored car services
PA: Merchants Building Maintenance Company
1190 Monterey Pass Rd
Monterey Park CA 91754
323 881-6701

(P-14357)
MERCHANTS BUILDING MAINT CO
1190 Monterey Pass Rd, Los Angeles (90065)
PHONE..............................800 560-6700
Veronica Corona, *Branch Mgr*
EMP: 280
SALES (corp-wide): 112.5MM Privately Held
WEB: www.mbmonline.com
SIC: 7349 7381 Building maintenance services; detective & armored car services
PA: Merchants Building Maintenance Company
1190 Monterey Pass Rd
Monterey Park CA 91754
323 881-6701

(P-14358)
METRO SERVICE SOUTH INC
3605 Cahuenga Blvd W, Los Angeles (90068-1205)
PHONE..............................310 995-8950
Michael Oddo, *President*
EMP: 100
SQ FT: 2,000
SALES (est): 1.2MM Privately Held
SIC: 7349 Building maintenance services

(P-14359)
MIDA INDUSTRIES INC
6101 Obispo Ave, Long Beach (90805-3799)
PHONE..............................562 616-1020
Fax: 562 616-1028
Michael T Drake, *President*
Dawit Kidane, *CFO*
John Valencia, *Vice Pres*
Lysbeth Merida, *Project Mgr*
Francisco Solis, *Project Mgr*
EMP: 250
SQ FT: 10,000
SALES (est): 14MM Privately Held
WEB: www.midaindustries.com
SIC: 7349 1799 Janitorial service, contract basis; asbestos removal & encapsulation

(P-14360)
MINTIE CORPORATION (PA)
Also Called: Mintie Technologies
1114 N San Fernando Rd, Los Angeles (90065-1126)
PHONE..............................323 225-4111
Fax: 323 222-7853
Kevin J Mintie, *CEO*
James M Mintie, *Exec VP*
Ahmed Ashqar, *General Mgr*
Colleen Cooks, *Financial Exec*
Tom Aoki, *Sales Dir*
EMP: 80
SQ FT: 8,000
SALES (est): 15MM Privately Held
WEB: www.mintie.com
SIC: 7349 Building cleaning service; air duct cleaning

(P-14361)
MOBLEY ENTERPRISES INC
Also Called: ServiceMaster
1771 Grogan Ave, Merced (95341-6455)
P.O. Box 3528 (95344-1528)
PHONE..............................209 726-9185
Jack Mobley, *President*
Amy Davis, *Manager*
EMP: 81
SQ FT: 3,000
SALES (est): 2.8MM Privately Held
SIC: 7349 Building maintenance services

(P-14362)
MOLLY MAID
24412 Muirlands Blvd A, Lake Forest (92630-3900)
PHONE..............................949 367-8000
Fax: 949 367-2811
Stephen Schatan, *Owner*
EMP: 50
SQ FT: 2,000
SALES (est): 1.2MM Privately Held
SIC: 7349 7363 7299 Maid services, contract or fee basis; domestic help service; handyman service

(P-14363)
MONTEBELLO UNIFIED SCHOOL DST
Also Called: Maintenance & Operation Dept
500 Hendricks St Fl 2, Montebello (90640-1566)
PHONE..............................323 887-2140
Virgil Downs, *Principal*
EMP: 100
SALES (corp-wide): 296.9MM Privately Held
SIC: 7349 Building maintenance services
PA: Montebello Unified School District Protective League
123 S Montebello Blvd
Montebello CA 90640
323 887-7900

(P-14364)
MORENO & ASSOCIATES INC
1260 Birchwood Dr, Sunnyvale (94089-2205)
PHONE..............................408 924-0353
Fax: 408 924-0373
Ernie Moreno, *President*
Paul Lima, *Vice Pres*
Christopher Moreno, *Administration*
Alfredo Cortez, *Opers Spvr*
Felipe Moreno, *Manager*
EMP: 60
SQ FT: 1,100
SALES (est): 2.8MM Privately Held
WEB: www.morenoclean.com
SIC: 7349 Building maintenance services

(P-14365)
NATIONAL MAINTENANCE INC
355 Foxen Ln, Los Alamos (93440)
PHONE..............................805 680-6779
Fax: 805 925-0142
Paul S Morgan, *President*
Curtis A Golier Jr, *Vice Pres*
Judith Goller, *Principal*
Andrew Allen, *Controller*
EMP: 168
SQ FT: 2,000
SALES (est): 4.6MM Privately Held
WEB: www.nationalmaintenance.com
SIC: 7349 Building cleaning service

(P-14366)
NATIONAL REAL ESTATE SOLUTIONS
Also Called: Pacific Preservation Services
299 W Hillcrest Dr # 117, Thousand Oaks (91360-4264)
PHONE..............................805 496-1084
Brian Mingham, *President*
Britney Smith, *Manager*
EMP: 80
SALES (est): 3.2MM Privately Held
SIC: 7349 1521 0782 1522 Building maintenance services; maid services, contract or fee basis; single-family home remodeling, additions & repairs; garden maintenance services; lawn care services; remodeling, multi-family dwellings

7349 - Building Cleaning & Maintenance Svcs, NEC County (P-14391)

(P-14367)
NEALS JANITORIAL SERVICE
1588 Calco Creek Dr, San Jose (95127-4372)
PHONE......................408 271-9944
Ralph B Neal, *Owner*
Martez Cratch, *General Mgr*
EMP: 50
SQ FT: 3,000
SALES (est): 1.2MM **Privately Held**
SIC: 7349 Janitorial service, contract basis; window cleaning

(P-14368)
NEXSENTIO
3071 Muirdrum Pl, San Jose (95148-2024)
PHONE......................408 392-9249
Danielle Bunel, *President*
Renee Velazquez, *COO*
Vagish Kapila, *Security Dir*
Araceli Reyes, *Marketing Staff*
EMP: 50
SQ FT: 3,500
SALES: 2MM **Privately Held**
SIC: 7349 Janitorial service, contract basis

(P-14369)
NEXSENTIO INC
1346 Ridder Park Dr, San Jose (95131-2313)
PHONE......................408 392-9249
Danielle Bunel, *President*
Rene Velazquez, *Vice Pres*
EMP: 85 EST: 2006
SALES (est): 1.9MM **Privately Held**
SIC: 7349 7299 Janitorial service, contract basis; handyman service

(P-14370)
NMS MANAGEMENT INC
155 W 35th St Ste A, National City (91950-7922)
PHONE......................619 425-0440
David Guaderrama, *President*
Sophia Guaderrama, *Exec VP*
EMP: 75
SQ FT: 8,300
SALES: 3MM **Privately Held**
SIC: 7349 0781 Building maintenance, except repairs; janitorial service, contract basis; landscape services

(P-14371)
NORTH STAR BUILDING MAINT INC
2828 Cochran St Ste 214, Simi Valley (93065-2780)
PHONE......................805 518-0417
Glenn Rose, *President*
Jamie Rose, *Vice Pres*
EMP: 60
SQ FT: 800
SALES: 1MM **Privately Held**
SIC: 7349 Building & office cleaning services

(P-14372)
NOVA COMMERCIAL COMPANY INC (PA)
24683 Oneil Ave, Hayward (94544-1627)
P.O. Box 759 (94543-0759)
PHONE......................510 728-7000
Fax: 510 728-7001
James L Slade Jr, *President*
Janice Slade, *Vice Pres*
Gabriela Gonzalez, *Executive*
Eleanor Anglin, *Manager*
Mindy Gottlibe, *Manager*
EMP: 54
SQ FT: 8,544
SALES (est): 10.1MM **Privately Held**
SIC: 7349 Janitorial service, contract basis

(P-14373)
OAKLAND UNIFIED SCHOOL DST
Also Called: Facilities Management
955 High St, Oakland (94601-4404)
PHONE......................510 535-2717
Timothy White, *Asst Supt*
Madeleine Clarke, *Vice Pres*
Maxine Jasper, *Office Mgr*
Ethel C Turner, *Office Mgr*
Ron Chandler, *Info Tech Dir*
EMP: 150
SALES (corp-wide): 460.6MM **Privately Held**
WEB: www.ousd.k12.ca.us
SIC: 7349 Building maintenance services
PA: Oakland Unified School District
1000 Broadway Fl 4
Oakland CA 94607
510 434-7790

(P-14374)
OPTIMA BUILDING SERVICES MAINT
210 Mountain View Ave, Santa Rosa (95407-8203)
PHONE......................707 586-6640
Adolfo Mendoza, *President*
EMP: 100
SALES (est): 2.3MM **Privately Held**
SIC: 7349 Building cleaning service

(P-14375)
PACIFIC BUILDING MAINT INC (PA)
Also Called: Servicmster Clean By Integrity
1601 Ives Ave Ste E, Oxnard (93033-1908)
PHONE......................805 642-0214
Fax: 805 654-0554
Aaron Shia, *President*
Aaron Shiah, *President*
Katie Sebenius, *Business Mgr*
Omar Lopez, *Analyst*
Jennifer Furst, *Manager*
EMP: 81
SQ FT: 1,600
SALES (est): 2.3MM **Privately Held**
WEB: www.pacificbuildingmaintenance.com
SIC: 7349 Cleaning service, industrial or commercial

(P-14376)
PACIFIC CLEANING SERVICE INC
3334 Pacific Coast Hwy # 205, Corona Del Mar (92625-2328)
PHONE......................949 829-8790
Jeff Murray, *President*
Aureo Tellez, *Sales Executive*
EMP: 50
SQ FT: 1,500
SALES (est): 1.8MM **Privately Held**
WEB: www.pacificwindow.com
SIC: 7349 Window cleaning

(P-14377)
PACIFIC MAINTENANCE SVCS INC
1902 Verde Vista Dr, Redlands (92373-7322)
PHONE......................909 793-7111
David Schulte, *President*
EMP: 200
SQ FT: 2,800
SALES (est): 3.1MM **Privately Held**
SIC: 7349 Building maintenance services

(P-14378)
PANAMA-BUENA VISTA UN SCHL DST
Also Called: District Office East
5901 Schirra Ct, Bakersfield (93313-2161)
PHONE......................661 397-2205
Fax: 661 831-7704
Diane McConnell, *Administration*
EMP: 413
SALES (corp-wide): 152.3MM **Privately Held**
SIC: 7349 Building maintenance services
PA: Panama-Buena Vista Union School District
4200 Ashe Rd
Bakersfield CA 93313
661 831-8331

(P-14379)
PARADISE BUILDING SERVICES
9664 Hermosa Ave, Rancho Cucamonga (91730-5812)
PHONE......................909 399-0707
Fax: 909 399-0627
Chris Clifton, *President*
Susan Cutshaw, *Vice Pres*
EMP: 115
SQ FT: 5,500
SALES (est): 3MM **Privately Held**
SIC: 7349 Janitorial service, contract basis

(P-14380)
PARAGON COML BLDG MAINT INC
6731 32nd St Ste J, North Highlands (95660-3042)
PHONE......................916 334-8801
Dwayne Willis, *President*
Robert Calberon, *Manager*
EMP: 80
SALES (est): 2.9MM **Privately Held**
SIC: 7349 Building maintenance services

(P-14381)
PARAMOUNT BLDG SOLUTIONS LLC
2045 California Ave, Corona (92881-7231)
PHONE......................951 272-4001
Glen Kucera, *Branch Mgr*
EMP: 418
SALES (corp-wide): 154.2MM **Privately Held**
SIC: 7349 Janitorial service, contract basis
PA: Paramount Building Solutions, Llc
10235 S 51st St Ste 185
Phoenix AZ 85044
480 348-1177

(P-14382)
PBM MAINTENANCE CORP
Also Called: Professional Building Maint
8523 Lankershim Blvd, Sun Valley (91352-3127)
PHONE......................818 771-1100
Fernando Real, *President*
David Lorin, *President*
Adrian Schmotolocha, *CFO*
EMP: 400
SQ FT: 40,000
SALES (est): 9.7MM **Privately Held**
WEB: www.pbmco.net
SIC: 7349 1799 Building maintenance services; steam cleaning of building exteriors

(P-14383)
PBMS INC
Also Called: Premier Building Maint Svcs
1909 Wilshire Blvd, Los Angeles (90057-3604)
PHONE......................213 386-2552
Fax: 213 386-2546
Bryant S Kim, *President*
Kim Bryant, *Owner*
Yun Wallis, *Manager*
EMP: 100 EST: 1996
SQ FT: 1,400
SALES (est): 3.3MM **Privately Held**
SIC: 7349 Janitorial service, contract basis

(P-14384)
PEERLESS BUILDING MAINT INC
4665 Mountain Lakes Blvd, Redding (96003-1450)
PHONE......................530 222-6369
Fax: 530 222-6393
Jan Pauline Tuttle, *CEO*
Terry Tuttle, *President*
EMP: 100
SQ FT: 8,000
SALES: 3MM **Privately Held**
SIC: 7349 Janitorial service, contract basis

(P-14385)
PEERLESS MAINTENANCE SERVICE
1100 S Euclid St, La Habra (90631-6807)
P.O. Box 3900 (90632-3900)
PHONE......................714 871-3380
Fax: 562 871-2232
Linda Gabriel, *President*
David Gabriel, *Corp Secy*
Badawi Naffer, *Manager*
Nasser Badawi, *Supervisor*
EMP: 300
SQ FT: 2,000
SALES (est): 9.8MM **Privately Held**
WEB: www.peerlesssvc.com
SIC: 7349 Janitorial service, contract basis

(P-14386)
PEGASUS BUILDING SVCS CO INC
7554 Trade St, San Diego (92121-2412)
PHONE......................858 457-8201
Fax: 858 457-8256
Jeffery Baker, *Manager*
EMP: 105
SALES (corp-wide): 15.9MM **Privately Held**
SIC: 7349 Building maintenance services
PA: Pegasus Building Services Company, Inc.
2343 Mira Mar Ave
Long Beach CA 90815
562 961-1998

(P-14387)
PEGASUS BUILDING SVCS CO INC (PA)
2343 Mira Mar Ave, Long Beach (90815-1755)
PHONE......................562 961-1998
Fax: 562 961-1116
Judith Becker, *President*
Anna Corona, *Regional Mgr*
Laura Cortez, *Regional Mgr*
Betty Hernandez, *District Mgr*
Rosy Rodriguez, *Admin Asst*
EMP: 245
SQ FT: 12,800
SALES (est): 15.9MM **Privately Held**
SIC: 7349 Janitorial service, contract basis

(P-14388)
PERFORMANCE BUILDING SERVICES
Also Called: Performance Cleanroom Services
22642 Lambert St Ste 409, Lake Forest (92630-1645)
PHONE......................949 364-4364
Fax: 949 364-6474
James Chriss, *President*
Robert Lynch, *Vice Pres*
Ron Matthews, *Vice Pres*
EMP: 104
SALES: 5MM **Privately Held**
WEB: www.performance-now.com
SIC: 7349 7699 Building maintenance services; cleaning services

(P-14389)
PLATINUM CLG INDIANAPOLIS LLC
1522 2nd St, Santa Monica (90401-2303)
PHONE......................310 584-8000
William Hertz,
EMP: 460 EST: 2008
SALES (est): 10.6MM **Privately Held**
SIC: 7349 Building & office cleaning services

(P-14390)
PLATINUM FACILITIES SERVICES
1530 Oakland Rd Ste 120, San Jose (95112-1241)
PHONE......................408 998-9004
Roger K Daniels, *President*
EMP: 150
SALES (est): 4.4MM **Privately Held**
SIC: 7349 Janitorial service, contract basis

(P-14391)
POLARIS BUILDING MAINTENANCE
2580 Wyandotte St Ste E, Mountain View (94043-2366)
PHONE......................650 964-9400
Fax: 650 964-0605
Frank Schwarb, *President*
Roger Gomez, *Vice Pres*
EMP: 80
SQ FT: 2,700
SALES (est): 3.4MM **Privately Held**
SIC: 7349 Janitorial service, contract basis; building maintenance, except repairs

7349 - Building Cleaning & Maintenance Svcs, NEC County (P-14392)

(P-14392)
PONDEROSA BUILDERS INC
Also Called: United Building Services
3300 W Macarthur Blvd, Santa Ana (92704-6804)
PHONE..................714 434-9494
Robert Hughes, *President*
Luisa Hughes, *Treasurer*
EMP: 800
SQ FT: 10,000
SALES (est): 11.8MM **Privately Held**
WEB: www.ubservices.com
SIC: 7349 Janitorial service, contract basis; window cleaning

(P-14393)
PRIORITY BUILDING SERVICES LLC
Also Called: Priority Landscape Services
521 Mercury Ln, Brea (92821-4831)
PHONE..................714 255-2940
Simon Rocha, *President*
Lucia Vargas, *Branch Mgr*
David Kraushaar, *Sales Mgr*
Rosa Alcala, *Sales Staff*
Scott Nankervis,
EMP: 375
SQ FT: 6,000
SALES (est): 13.8MM **Privately Held**
WEB: www.prioritybuildingservices.com
SIC: 7349 Cleaning service, industrial or commercial

(P-14394)
PRO BUILDING MAINTENANCE INC
149 N Maple St Ste H, Corona (92880-1773)
PHONE..................951 279-3386
Carl Hoff, *CEO*
Christina L Hoff, *Principal*
EMP: 120
SQ FT: 1,600
SALES: 7.5MM **Privately Held**
SIC: 7349 Building maintenance services

(P-14395)
PROFESSIONAL JANITORIAL SVC
234 Eucalyptus Dr B, El Segundo (90245-3820)
P.O. Box 646 (90245-0646)
PHONE..................310 410-1452
Michael Mc Grath, *President*
EMP: 50
SALES (est): 706.8K **Privately Held**
SIC: 7349 Building maintenance services

(P-14396)
PROFESSIONAL MAINT SYSTEMS INC
Also Called: Professional Maint Systems
4912 Naples St, San Diego (92110-3820)
P.O. Box 80038 (92138-0038)
PHONE..................619 276-1150
Fax: 619 276-1150
Karen Berry, *CEO*
Hector Romero, *Opers Mgr*
Phil Senescall, *Sales Mgr*
Laura Iascon, *Manager*
EMP: 800
SQ FT: 9,000
SALES: 19.8MM **Privately Held**
WEB: www.pmsjanitorial.com
SIC: 7349 Janitorial service, contract basis

(P-14397)
PROTEC ASSOCIATION SERVICES (PA)
Also Called: Protec Building Services
10180 Willow Creek Rd, San Diego (92131-1636)
PHONE..................858 569-1080
Fax: 858 569-1088
J David Rauch, *President*
Scot Clark, *Shareholder*
Russ Piccoli, *Shareholder*
Libbey Rauch, *Shareholder*
George Vanoofbree, *Shareholder*
EMP: 140
SQ FT: 12,500
SALES (est): 20.3MM **Privately Held**
SIC: 7349 Building maintenance services

(P-14398)
PYRAMID BUILDING MAINT CORP (PA)
Also Called: Pacific Maintenance Company
2175 Martin Ave, Santa Clara (95050-2701)
PHONE..................408 727-9393
Fax: 408 727-9344
Hazel B Chioini, *CEO*
Kari Hus, *President*
Larry Wishart, *COO*
Brandon Fitzpatrick, *Exec VP*
Monique Romero, *Area Mgr*
EMP: 603
SQ FT: 14,000
SALES (est): 35.9MM **Privately Held**
WEB: www.pmc-ibm.com
SIC: 7349 Janitorial service, contract basis

(P-14399)
PYRAMID BUILDING MAINT CORP
600 Eubanks Ct Ste C, Vacaville (95688-9409)
PHONE..................707 454-2020
Larry Wishart, *Branch Mgr*
EMP: 152
SALES (corp-wide): 35.9MM **Privately Held**
WEB: www.pmc-ibm.com
SIC: 7349 Janitorial service, contract basis
PA: Pyramid Building Maintenance Corporation
2175 Martin Ave
Santa Clara CA 95050
408 727-9393

(P-14400)
QUALITY COAST INCORPORATED
2462 Main St Ste H, Chula Vista (91911-4671)
PHONE..................619 443-9192
Fax: 619 443-9492
Consuelo Rosengreen, *President*
Richard Rosengreen, *Treasurer*
EMP: 50
SALES (est): 1.9MM **Privately Held**
WEB: www.qualitycoast.com
SIC: 7349 Janitorial service, contract basis

(P-14401)
RAINBOW - BRITE INDUS SVCS LLC
16998 Kent Ave, Lemoore (93245-5235)
PHONE..................559 925-2580
Fax: 559 294-8603
Diana Tutson-Snowden, *CEO*
EMP: 100
SALES: 3.5MM **Privately Held**
SIC: 7349 Building maintenance services; janitorial service, contract basis
PA: Santa Rosa Indian Community Of The Santa Rosa Rancheria
16835 Alkali Dr
Lemoore CA 93245
559 924-1278

(P-14402)
RANSCAPES INC
30 Hughes Ste 209, Irvine (92618-1916)
P.O. Box 50580 (92619-0580)
PHONE..................866 883-9297
Ran Tomaino, *President*
Susan Tomaino, *Corp Secy*
Kelly Kimberly, *Office Mgr*
Daniel Martin, *Safety Mgr*
Joel Conchas, *Accounts Mgr*
EMP: 50
SQ FT: 2,000
SALES (est): 2.5MM **Privately Held**
WEB: www.ranscapes.com
SIC: 7349 Janitorial service, contract basis

(P-14403)
RECOLOGY CLEANSCAPES
2265 Revere Ave, San Francisco (94124-1925)
PHONE..................415 626-5685
Chris Husband, *Branch Mgr*
EMP: 171
SALES (corp-wide): 17.6MM **Privately Held**
SIC: 7349 Office cleaning or charring
PA: Recology Cleanscapes
117 S Main St Ste 300
Seattle WA 98104
206 859-6700

(P-14404)
REDWOOD BUILDING MAINT CO
1364 N Mcdowell Blvd B, Petaluma (94954-1116)
P.O. Box 750985 (94975-0985)
PHONE..................707 782-9100
Robert Stanley, *Owner*
Sarah Burnham, *Office Mgr*
Sarah Powers, *Finance Mgr*
Tim Johnson, *Opers Staff*
Layne Bowen, *Accounts Mgr*
EMP: 75
SQ FT: 2,000
SALES (est): 2.7MM **Privately Held**
WEB: www.rbmco.com
SIC: 7349 Janitorial service, contract basis

(P-14405)
RELIABLE INTERNATIONAL SVCS
Also Called: Reliable Building Maint Co
P.O. Box 12249, Palm Desert (92255-2249)
PHONE..................760 772-1377
Robert Barr, *President*
EMP: 200
SQ FT: 4,500
SALES (est): 4.6MM **Privately Held**
SIC: 7349 Janitorial service, contract basis

(P-14406)
RESOURCE COLLECTION INC
Also Called: Command Guard Services
3771 W 242nd St Ste 205, Torrance (90505-6566)
PHONE..................310 219-3272
Martin Benom, *Ch of Bd*
Steven Jacobson, *Corp Secy*
Paula Benom, *Vice Pres*
Marilyn Jacobson, *Vice Pres*
EMP: 1400
SQ FT: 15,000
SALES (est): 16.4MM **Privately Held**
WEB: www.resourcecollection.com
SIC: 7349 7381 0782 3564 Air duct cleaning; guard services; lawn & garden services; air cleaning systems

(P-14407)
REYNOLDS CLEANING SERVICES INC
1472 Oddstad Dr, Redwood City (94063-2607)
PHONE..................650 599-0202
Fax: 650 568-7171
James R Reynolds Jr, *President*
Charles Chantaca, *General Mgr*
Helen Vargas, *Administration*
Josh Juarbe, *Business Mgr*
Norma Orozco, *Accountant*
EMP: 110
SQ FT: 1,800
SALES: 3.2MM **Privately Held**
WEB: www.reynoldscleaning.com
SIC: 7349 Janitorial service, contract basis

(P-14408)
RHINO BUILDING SERVICES INC
6650 Flanders Dr Ste K, San Diego (92121-3908)
PHONE..................858 455-1440
Cody Sears, *President*
EMP: 120
SQ FT: 110
SALES (est): 3.6MM **Privately Held**
WEB: www.rhinoliningsindustrial.com
SIC: 7349 Janitorial service, contract basis

(P-14409)
ROGAN BUILDING SERVICES INC
1531 7th St, Riverside (92507-4454)
P.O. Box 5787 (92517-5787)
PHONE..................951 248-1261
Fax: 951 248-1226
Byron Lee Rogan, *President*
Anne Rogan, *Admin Sec*
EMP: 50
SQ FT: 5,000
SALES (est): 1.6MM **Privately Held**
SIC: 7349 Building maintenance, except repairs; janitorial service, contract basis

(P-14410)
ROY JORGENSEN ASSOCIATES INC
19001 S Western Ave, Torrance (90501-1106)
PHONE..................310 468-2478
Mark Thomas, *Principal*
EMP: 65
SALES (corp-wide): 77.3MM **Privately Held**
SIC: 7349 Building maintenance services
PA: Roy Jorgensen Associates, Inc.
3735 Buckeystown Pike
Buckeystown MD 21717
301 831-1000

(P-14411)
ROYAL CREST BUILDING MAINT
8601 Roland St Ste E, Buena Park (90621-4809)
P.O. Box 391 (90621-0391)
PHONE..................714 562-5034
Fax: 714 562-5036
Robert Young, *President*
Carry Young, *Vice Pres*
Shaun Black, *Manager*
EMP: 50
SQ FT: 2,400
SALES (est): 1.6MM **Privately Held**
SIC: 7349 Janitorial service, contract basis

(P-14412)
RUBICON ENTERPRISES INC
Also Called: RUBICON PROGRAMS
2500 Bissell Ave, Richmond (94804-1815)
PHONE..................510 235-1516
Richard Aubry PHD, *Exec Dir*
Lindy Hahn, *Senior VP*
Kelly Dunn, *Vice Pres*
John Tammen, *General Mgr*
Cate Stean, *Facilities Mgr*
EMP: 220
SALES: 2.9MM **Privately Held**
SIC: 7349 8322 8331 Building maintenance services; social service center; job training & vocational rehabilitation services

(P-14413)
RUBICON PROGRAMS INCORPORATED (PA)
2500 Bissell Ave, Richmond (94804-1815)
PHONE..................510 235-1516
Fax: 510 235-2025
Jane Fischberg, *President*
Victoria Gratton, *Office Mgr*
Mike Keller, *Office Mgr*
Adrienne Kimball, *Admin Sec*
Matthew Ball, *Admin Asst*
EMP: 75
SQ FT: 14,500
SALES: 16.1MM **Privately Held**
SIC: 7349 8322 8331 Building maintenance services; social service center; job training & vocational rehabilitation services

(P-14414)
RUIZ JANITORIAL CO INC
446 Heller St, Redwood City (94063-2207)
PHONE..................650 361-1303
Fax: 650 299-9670
Guadalupe Ruiz, *President*
EMP: 50
SALES: 1.5MM **Privately Held**
SIC: 7349 Janitorial service, contract basis

(P-14415)
S J GENERAL BUILDING MAINT
919 Berryessa Rd Ste 10, San Jose (95133-1087)
PHONE..................408 392-0800
Armando Lamas, *President*
EMP: 60
SALES (est): 2.4MM **Privately Held**
SIC: 7349 Janitorial service, contract basis

PRODUCTS & SERVICES SECTION 7349 - Building Cleaning & Maintenance Svcs, NEC County (P-14440)

(P-14416)
SAN BERNARDINO CITY UNF SCHOOL
Also Called: Building Services
956 W 9th St, San Bernardino (92411-2844)
PHONE..................909 388-6100
Bob Leon, *Director*
EMP: 220
SALES (corp-wide): 331.5MM Privately Held
WEB: www.sbcusd.k12.ca.us
SIC: 7349 8741 8211 Building maintenance services; management services; elementary & secondary schools
PA: San Bernardino City Unified School District
777 N F St
San Bernardino CA 92410
909 381-1100

(P-14417)
SAN DIEGO UNIFIED SCHOOL DST
Also Called: Maintenance Unit
4860 Ruffner St, San Diego (92111-1522)
PHONE..................858 627-7130
William Fantos, *Director*
EMP: 1000
SALES (corp-wide): 713.3MM Privately Held
WEB: www.sdcs.k12.ca.us
SIC: 7349 Building maintenance services
PA: San Diego Unified School District
4100 Normal St
San Diego CA 92103
619 725-8000

(P-14418)
SANTA CLARA COUNTY OF
Also Called: Facilities and Fleet
2310 N 1st St Ste 200, San Jose (95131-1040)
PHONE..................408 993-4700
Fax: 408 993-4695
Larry Jinkins, *Branch Mgr*
EMP: 50 Privately Held
WEB: www.countyairports.org
SIC: 7349 Building maintenance services
PA: County Of Santa Clara
3180 Newberry Dr Ste 150
San Jose CA 95118
408 299-5105

(P-14419)
SANTA CLARA VALLEY CORPORATION
Also Called: Swenson Developers and Contrs
715 N 1st St Ste 27, San Jose (95112-6309)
PHONE..................408 947-1100
Fax: 408 742-7432
Case Swenson, *President*
Lisa Swenson, *Admin Sec*
Heather Solis, *Project Mgr*
Craig Cameron, *Controller*
Hugo Ponce, *Property Mgr*
EMP: 85
SQ FT: 1,200
SALES (est): 3.9MM Privately Held
SIC: 7349 0782 7623 7699 Building maintenance, except repairs; janitorial service, contract basis; lawn services; refrigeration service & repair; elevators: inspection, service & repair

(P-14420)
SBM MANAGEMENT SERVICES LP
5241 Arnold Ave, McClellan (95652-1025)
PHONE..................866 855-2211
Charles Somers, *CEO*
Ken Silva, *CFO*
Donald Tracy, *Exec VP*
Don Tracy, *Principal*
Ronald Alvarado, *Administration*
EMP: 6000
SALES (est): 98.4MM Privately Held
SIC: 7349 Janitorial service, contract basis

(P-14421)
SBM SITE SERVICES LLC (PA)
Also Called: S B M
5241 Arnold Ave, McClellan (95652-1025)
PHONE..................916 922-7600
Fax: 916 565-3609
Charles Somers, *Mng Member*
Chris Geyer, *COO*
Ken Silva, *Officer*
Mary B Fort, *Executive*
Bill Early, *Program Mgr*
EMP: 100
SQ FT: 25,000
SALES (est): 264.3MM Privately Held
SIC: 7349 Building maintenance services

(P-14422)
SBRM INC (PA)
Also Called: Servicmster Cmplete Rstoration
2342 Meyers Ave, Escondido (92029-1008)
PHONE..................760 480-0208
Barbara Robert, *President*
Mike Gamez, *Admin Sec*
Jack Asbury, *Controller*
EMP: 70
SQ FT: 20,000
SALES (est): 11MM Privately Held
WEB: www.smsos.com
SIC: 7349 1521 Building maintenance services; repairing fire damage, single-family houses

(P-14423)
SEAFUS CORPORATION
Also Called: ServiceMaster
439 Eccles Ave, South San Francisco (94080-1902)
PHONE..................415 584-6100
David Decker, *President*
Beth Decker, *CFO*
EMP: 50
SQ FT: 4,500
SALES: 1,000K Privately Held
SIC: 7349 7217 Building maintenance services; carpet & upholstery cleaning

(P-14424)
SERVI-TEK INC
Also Called: Servi-Tek Janitorial Services
3970 Sorrento Valley Blvd, San Diego (92121-1416)
PHONE..................858 638-7735
Bryan McMinn,
Eric S Friz,
Kurt G Lester,
Bryan D McMinn,
Kim Paterson, *Associate*
EMP: 300
SQ FT: 2,000
SALES (est): 11.3MM Privately Held
WEB: www.servitek.org
SIC: 7349 Janitorial service, contract basis

(P-14425)
SERVICE BY MEDALLION
Also Called: Medallion Cnstr Clean-Up
455 National Ave, Mountain View (94043-2219)
PHONE..................650 625-1010
Fax: 650 625-1043
Roland H Strick, *CEO*
David Godinez, *Shareholder*
Roland F Strick, *Vice Pres*
Maria E Strick, *Admin Sec*
Maria Strick, *Admin Sec*
EMP: 490 EST: 1978
SQ FT: 7,000
SALES (est): 22.4MM Privately Held
WEB: www.servicebymedallion.com
SIC: 7349 Janitorial service, contract basis

(P-14426)
SERVICEMASTER COMPANY LLC
1003 Hi Point St, Los Angeles (90035-2607)
PHONE..................760 298-7001
Samuel Druhora, *Branch Mgr*
EMP: 85
SALES (corp-wide): 2.5B Publicly Held
SIC: 7349 Building maintenance services
HQ: The Servicemaster Company Llc
860 Ridge Lake Blvd
Memphis TN 38120
901 597-1400

(P-14427)
SERVICEMASTER COMPANY LLC
216 N Clara St, Santa Ana (92703-3518)
PHONE..................714 245-1465
Gregg Gills, *Manager*
EMP: 200
SALES (corp-wide): 2.5B Publicly Held
WEB: www.servicemaster.com
SIC: 7349 Building maintenance services
HQ: The Servicemaster Company Llc
860 Ridge Lake Blvd
Memphis TN 38120
901 597-1400

(P-14428)
SERVICO BUILDING MAINT CO
13732b Carmel Ave, Glen Ellen (95442)
P.O. Box 25 (95442-0025)
PHONE..................707 935-1224
Fax: 707 935-1567
Gary D'Acquisto, *President*
EMP: 100
SQ FT: 800
SALES (est): 2MM Privately Held
SIC: 7349 7217 Janitorial service, contract basis; window cleaning; carpet & furniture cleaning on location

(P-14429)
SFUSD BUILDING GROUND
834 Toland St, San Francisco (94124-1314)
PHONE..................415 695-5508
John Bitoff, *Director*
EMP: 100
SALES (est): 3.5MM Privately Held
SIC: 7349 Building maintenance services

(P-14430)
SIGNATURE BUILDING MAINT INC
1330 White Oaks Rd, Campbell (95008-6723)
P.O. Box 110340 (95011-0340)
PHONE..................408 377-8066
Fax: 408 879-1103
Anna Murphy, *President*
Jeff Loiyd, *CFO*
Patrick Murphy, *General Mgr*
Tony Reyes, *Admin Sec*
Jessica Noyer, *Admin Asst*
EMP: 80 EST: 1999
SQ FT: 1,800
SALES (est): 3.9MM Privately Held
WEB: www.signaturefacilities.com
SIC: 7349 Building maintenance services

(P-14431)
SIGNIFICANT CLEANING SVCS LLC
1855 Hamilton Ave Ste 104, San Jose (95125-5672)
P.O. Box 7702 (95150-7702)
PHONE..................408 559-5959
Larry Lovaglia,
Jeff Davidson, *Branch Mgr*
Nelson Celada, *Facilities Mgr*
John Ornales, *Manager*
Anthony Lovaglia, *Asst Mgr*
EMP: 105 EST: 1988
SQ FT: 250
SALES (est): 4.1MM Privately Held
WEB: www.significantcleaning.com
SIC: 7349 Cleaning service, industrial or commercial

(P-14432)
SITE CREW INC
3185 Airway Ave Ste G, Costa Mesa (92626-4601)
PHONE..................714 668-0100
Tina Manavi, *CEO*
Maria Candle, *Relations*
EMP: 300
SQ FT: 2,160
SALES (est): 8MM Privately Held
WEB: www.sitecrewinc.com
SIC: 7349 Janitorial service, contract basis

(P-14433)
SKYLSTAD-SCHOELEN CO INC
Also Called: ServiceMaster
3130 Skyway Dr Ste 701, Santa Maria (93455-1800)
PHONE..................805 349-0503
Fax: 805 352-1025
Linda Schoelen, *President*
Jeffrey Hopson, *Principal*
EMP: 80

SALES (est): 2.5MM Privately Held
SIC: 7349 Building maintenance services

(P-14434)
SODEXO OPERATIONS LLC
1325 Iris Ave Bldg 181, Imperial Beach (91932-3751)
PHONE..................619 429-5692
Rodrigo Domingo, *Branch Mgr*
EMP: 52
SALES (corp-wide): 96.3MM Privately Held
SIC: 7349 Building maintenance services
HQ: Sodexo Operations, Llc
9801 Washingtonian Blvd
Gaithersburg MD 20878
301 987-4000

(P-14435)
SOUTHERN BUILDING MAINT INC
836 Crenshaw Blvd Ste 102, Los Angeles (90005-3631)
PHONE..................213 598-7071
Charles Chung, *CEO*
Kimberly Paek, *Principal*
Janet Cho, *Exec Dir*
EMP: 70
SALES (est): 950K Privately Held
SIC: 7349 Building maintenance services

(P-14436)
SOUTHERN CAL MAID SVC CRPT CLG
14909 Crenshaw Blvd # 209, Gardena (90249-3665)
P.O. Box 1653 (90249-0653)
PHONE..................310 675-0585
Rueben Trejo, *President*
EMP: 98
SALES (est): 2.7MM Privately Held
SIC: 7349 7217 Maid services, contract or fee basis; carpet & furniture cleaning on location

(P-14437)
SPENCER BUILDING MAINTENANCE
1336 Dixieanne Ave, Sacramento (95815-2717)
PHONE..................916 922-1900
Fax: 916 922-8290
Aaron D Spencer, *President*
Jose Yanez, *Opers Staff*
Joan Spencer, *Marketing Staff*
Julie Bizal, *Manager*
Gordon Platt, *Accounts Mgr*
EMP: 307
SQ FT: 5,000
SALES (est): 12.6MM Privately Held
WEB: www.spencerservices.com
SIC: 7349 Building maintenance services

(P-14438)
STAR BRITE BUILDING MAINT
2688 Dawson Ave, Long Beach (90755-2020)
PHONE..................562 988-2829
Fax: 562 988-2879
Eric E Jenderko, *President*
EMP: 329
SALES: 500K Privately Held
SIC: 7349 Janitorial service, contract basis

(P-14439)
STEVE AND BETH CHAPUT
Also Called: Molly Maid
1025 Sentinel Dr Ste 103, La Verne (91750-3281)
PHONE..................909 596-9994
Steve Chaput, *Partner*
Beth Chaput, *Partner*
EMP: 50
SALES (est): 1MM Privately Held
SIC: 7349 Maid services, contract or fee basis

(P-14440)
SUNSET BUILDING MAINTANCE INC
Also Called: Sunset Building Maintenance
1920 Lafayette St Ste E, Santa Clara (95050-3956)
PHONE..................408 727-3408
Fax: 408 727-7967

7349 - Building Cleaning & Maintenance Svcs, NEC County (P-14441)

Marisela Del Rio, *President*
Shella Delrio, *Office Mgr*
EMP: 50
SQ FT: 1,000
SALES (est): 1.2MM **Privately Held**
SIC: 7349 Janitorial service, contract basis

(P-14441)
SUPERIOR ENVMTL SVCS INC
Also Called: SES
6383 Lake Arrowhead Dr, San Diego (92119-3534)
P.O. Box 19784 (92159-0784)
PHONE...................................619 462-7079
Kevin Tullgren, *President*
EMP: 50
SQ FT: 2,000
SALES: 1MM **Privately Held**
SIC: 7349 Cleaning service, industrial or commercial

(P-14442)
SWAYZERS INCORPORATED
Also Called: Swayzer A-1 Sanitizing
1663 E Del Amo Blvd, Carson (90746-2937)
P.O. Box 4365 (90749-4365)
PHONE...................................323 979-7223
Samuel Swayzer, *President*
Regina Swayzer, *Vice Pres*
EMP: 60
SALES (est): 1.7MM **Privately Held**
SIC: 7349 Building cleaning service

(P-14443)
THOREAU JANITORIAL SVCS INC
Also Called: Thoreau Services Nationwide
5301 Beethoven St Ste 109, Los Angeles (90066-7066)
PHONE...................................310 822-8017
Nicki Frank, *President*
Dan Firestone, *Shareholder*
Robert Firestone, *Shareholder*
Peter Cormier, *General Mgr*
Velia Ortega, *Admin Asst*
EMP: 150
SQ FT: 1,300
SALES (est): 5.9MM **Privately Held**
SIC: 7349 Building cleaning service

(P-14444)
TIM HOFER INC
Also Called: Environment Control
148 N Akers St, Visalia (93291-5121)
P.O. Box 6445 (93290-6445)
PHONE...................................559 732-6676
Fax: 559 732-6670
Timothy Hofer, *President*
Suzanne Hofer, *Admin Sec*
EMP: 103
SQ FT: 5,700
SALES: 2.6MM **Privately Held**
SIC: 7349 Janitorial service, contract basis

(P-14445)
TOTAL QUALITY MAINTENANCE INC
895 Commercial St, Palo Alto (94303-4906)
PHONE...................................650 846-4700
Peter Vesanovic, *President*
Dee Vesanovic, *Admin Sec*
Liz Vesanovic, *Manager*
EMP: 180
SQ FT: 2,000
SALES (est): 5.5MM **Privately Held**
SIC: 7349 Building maintenance services

(P-14446)
TRINITY BUILDING SERVICES
430 N Canal St Ste 2, South San Francisco (94080-4665)
PHONE...................................650 873-2121
Mike A Boschetto, *President*
Manuel Espinoza, *Supervisor*
Maria Guevara, *Supervisor*
EMP: 275
SALES (est): 9.5MM **Privately Held**
WEB: www.trinityservices.com
SIC: 7349 Janitorial service, contract basis

(P-14447)
TSCM CORPORATION
17791 Jamestown Ln, Huntington Beach (92647-7134)
PHONE...................................714 841-1988
Fax: 714 841-3222
Margaret Pappano, *President*
Frank Pappano, *Vice Pres*
Carlos Mendez, *Info Tech Dir*
Norma J Burch, *Agent*
EMP: 55
SALES: 4.7MM **Privately Held**
WEB: www.tscmcorp.com
SIC: 7349 1799 Building maintenance services; steam cleaning of building exteriors

(P-14448)
TSI
789 W 20th St, Costa Mesa (92627-3487)
PHONE...................................949 515-7800
Thomas P Salazar, *President*
EMP: 100
SQ FT: 1,500
SALES (est): 1.8MM **Privately Held**
SIC: 7349 Building maintenance services

(P-14449)
TUTTLE FAMILY ENTERPRISES INC
Also Called: Peerless Building Maint Co
21020 Superior St, Chatsworth (91311-4321)
PHONE...................................818 534-2566
Tim Tuttle, *CEO*
Joseph Russo, *Sales Staff*
EMP: 350 **EST:** 1948
SALES (est): 11.2MM **Privately Held**
SIC: 7349 Building maintenance, except repairs

(P-14450)
ULTIMATE MAINTENANCE SVCS INC
4237 Redondo Beach Blvd, Lawndale (90260-3341)
PHONE...................................310 542-1474
Fax: 310 542-0073
Claudia Salomon, *CFO*
Paul Marmol, *President*
Sherly Garcia, *Office Mgr*
EMP: 50
SALES (est): 2MM **Privately Held**
WEB: www.ultimatemaintenanceservices.com
SIC: 7349 Building maintenance services

(P-14451)
UNISERVE FACILITIES SVCS CORP (PA)
Also Called: Union Building Maintenance
2363 S Atlantic Blvd, Commerce (90040-1256)
PHONE...................................213 533-1000
Sam M Hwang, *Ch of Bd*
Anthony Santana, *COO*
Eugene Hwang, *Mktg Dir*
EMP: 500
SQ FT: 5,000
SALES: 8.5MM **Privately Held**
SIC: 7349 Janitorial service, contract basis

(P-14452)
UNISERVE FACILITIES SVCS CORP
1200 Getty Center Dr, Los Angeles (90049-1657)
PHONE...................................310 440-6747
F Jackson, *Opers Staff*
EMP: 620
SALES (corp-wide): 8.5MM **Privately Held**
SIC: 7349 Janitorial service, contract basis
PA: Uniserve Facilities Services Corporation
2363 S Atlantic Blvd
Commerce CA 90040
213 533-1000

(P-14453)
UNITED BUILDING MAINTENANCE
8211 Sierra College Blvd # 420, Roseville (95661-9406)
PHONE...................................916 772-8101
Fax: 916 772-3203
Valerie Sherman, *President*
Donna Gregory, *President*
Tony Rosiles, *Mktg Dir*
EMP: 110
SALES (est): 4.2MM **Privately Held**
WEB: www.unitedfullservice.com
SIC: 7349 Janitorial service, contract basis

(P-14454)
UNIVERSAL
Also Called: Clean Up
4632 Acacia Ave, San Bernardino (92407-3539)
PHONE...................................909 882-5337
EMP: 100
SALES (est): 729.6K **Privately Held**
SIC: 7349 Building & office cleaning services

(P-14455)
UNIVERSAL BLDG SVCS & SUP CO (PA)
3120 Pierce St, Richmond (94804-5996)
PHONE...................................510 527-1078
Fax: 510 526-7289
Grace Brusseau, *CEO*
Leonard Brusseau, *President*
Arty Tong, *Opers Mgr*
EMP: 250 **EST:** 1963
SQ FT: 20,000
SALES (est): 39.5MM **Privately Held**
WEB: www.ubsco.com
SIC: 7349 5087 5169 Janitorial service, contract basis; janitors' supplies; chemicals & allied products

(P-14456)
UNIVERSAL BLDG SVCS & SUP CO
421 N Buchanan Cir, Pacheco (94553-5142)
PHONE...................................925 934-5533
Frank Batra, *Controller*
EMP: 125
SALES (corp-wide): 40.3MM **Privately Held**
WEB: www.ubsco.com
SIC: 7349 Building maintenance services
PA: Universal Building Services And Supply Co.
3120 Pierce St
Richmond CA 94804
510 527-1078

(P-14457)
UNIVERSAL BLDG SVCS & SUP CO
430 Roberson Ln, San Jose (95112-1125)
PHONE...................................408 995-5111
Su Miles, *Branch Mgr*
EMP: 125
SALES (corp-wide): 40.3MM **Privately Held**
WEB: www.ubsco.com
SIC: 7349 Building maintenance services
PA: Universal Building Services And Supply Co.
3120 Pierce St
Richmond CA 94804
510 527-1078

(P-14458)
UNIVERSAL BUILDING MAINT LLC
1551 N Tustin Ave Ste 650, Santa Ana (92705-8664)
PHONE...................................714 619-9700
Mark Olivas, *President*
Scott Savoie, *CFO*
EMP: 5003
SALES (est): 66.2K
SALES (corp-wide): 2B **Privately Held**
SIC: 7349 Janitorial service, contract basis
PA: Universal Services Of America, Lp
1551 N Tustin Ave
Santa Ana CA 92705
714 619-9700

(P-14459)
UNIVERSAL SITE SERVICES INC
760 E Capitol Ave, Milpitas (95035-6812)
P.O. Box 28010, San Jose (95159-8010)
PHONE...................................408 295-9688
Fax: 408 263-2382
Gina Vella, *President*
Joseph Vella, *Vice Pres*
Denise Barone, *Controller*
EMP: 110
SQ FT: 20,000
SALES (est): 6.7MM **Privately Held**
WEB: www.universalsweeping.com
SIC: 7349 4959 0782 Building maintenance, except repairs; road, airport & parking lot maintenance services; lawn services

(P-14460)
US METRO GROUP INC
Also Called: Metro Building Maintenance
605 S Wilton Pl, Los Angeles (90005-3220)
PHONE...................................213 382-6435
Fax: 213 382-6401
Charles Kim, *CEO*
Gene Vargars, *Shareholder*
Jennifer Park, *CFO*
Peter Wang, *CFO*
Mark Clark, *Chief Mktg Ofcr*
EMP: 800
SQ FT: 40,000
SALES (est): 31.3MM **Privately Held**
SIC: 7349 Janitorial service, contract basis

(P-14461)
VALLEY FLOOR MAINTENANCE INC
Also Called: Valley Sanitary Supply
1945 N Helm Ave Ste 102, Fresno (93727-1670)
P.O. Box 27246 (93729-7246)
PHONE...................................559 495-3083
Steven Rosso, *President*
Jeffrey N Lundeen, *Vice Pres*
EMP: 95
SQ FT: 1,120
SALES (est): 3.3MM **Privately Held**
WEB: www.valleysanitary.com
SIC: 7349 5087 Janitorial service, contract basis; janitors' supplies

(P-14462)
VARSITY CONTRACTORS INC
24155 Laguna Hills Mall # 900, Laguna Hills (92653-3667)
PHONE...................................949 586-8283
Jolynn Burr, *Manager*
EMP: 67
SALES (corp-wide): 85MM **Privately Held**
SIC: 7349 Building maintenance services
PA: Varsity Contractors, Inc.
315 S 5th Ave
Pocatello ID 83201
208 232-8598

(P-14463)
VEOLIA ES INDUSTRIAL SVCS INC
Also Called: Brand Precision Services
511 E Channel Rd, Benicia (94510-1158)
PHONE...................................707 745-0501
Michael Hanrigan, *Manager*
Lindsay West, *Data Proc Exec*
EMP: 55
SALES (corp-wide): 507.8MM **Privately Held**
WEB: www.onyxindustrial.com
SIC: 7349 Building component cleaning service
HQ: Veolia Es Industrial Services, Inc.
3180 N Highway 146
Baytown TX 77032
713 307-2100

(P-14464)
WARD ENTERPRISES
2679 Buhach Rd, Atwater (95301-2504)
P.O. Box 413 (95301-0413)
PHONE...................................209 358-0445
Fax: 209 358-0483
Waverly Pryor, *Partner*
Dennis Williams, *Partner*
EMP: 358
SQ FT: 5,284

PRODUCTS & SERVICES SECTION
7353 - Heavy Construction Eqpt Rental & Leasing County (P-14486)

SALES: 941K **Privately Held**
SIC: 7349 7217 5999 Janitorial service, contract basis; maid services, contract or fee basis; carpet & furniture cleaning on location; cleaning equipment & supplies

(P-14465)
WEST COAST MAINTENANCE INC
16312 S Main St, Gardena (90248-2822)
PHONE 310 324-2511
Christopher Mehl, *President*
Mari Guzman, *Director*
Alice Robledo, *Manager*
Sandy Rodriguez, *Manager*
EMP: 65
SALES: 840K **Privately Held**
WEB: www.westcoastmaintenance.com
SIC: 7349 Building maintenance services

(P-14466)
WURMS JANITORIAL SERVICE INC
544 Bateman Cir, Corona (92880-2011)
PHONE 951 582-0003
Larry Stewart, *President*
Pam Costa, *Vice Pres*
EMP: 80
SALES: 1.4MM **Privately Held**
SIC: 7349 Janitorial service, contract basis

(P-14467)
ZWS/ABS JOINT VENTURE LLC
39899 Balentine Dr # 200, Newark (94560-5355)
P.O. Box 1485 (94560-6485)
PHONE 510 461-1433
Shavila Singh, *Mng Member*
EMP: 60
SALES: 2MM **Privately Held**
SIC: 7349 Building maintenance services

7352 Medical Eqpt Rental & Leasing

(P-14468)
ADVANTACARE HEALTH INC (PA)
Also Called: Advantacare Medical
5 Mandeville Ct, Monterey (93940-5745)
PHONE 831 373-1111
Fax: 831 476-4699
Elizabeth McCarter, *President*
Duncan L McCarter, *Shareholder*
Ann Greeninger, *Manager*
Trisha New, *Manager*
EMP: 54
SQ FT: 10,000
SALES (est): 15MM **Privately Held**
SIC: 7352 5999 Medical equipment rental; medical apparatus & supplies

(P-14469)
APRIA HEALTHCARE LLC
2150 Trabajo Dr Ste B, Oxnard (93030-8800)
PHONE 805 278-6700
Fax: 805 983-1756
Tammy Martin, *Manager*
EMP: 115
SALES (corp-wide): 2.4B **Privately Held**
WEB: www.apria.com
SIC: 7352 5999 7359 5047 Medical equipment rental; medical apparatus & supplies; equipment rental & leasing; medical & hospital equipment
HQ: Apria Healthcare Llc
26220 Enterprise Ct
Lake Forest CA 92630
949 616-2606

(P-14470)
APRIA HEALTHCARE LLC
10090 Willow Creek Rd, San Diego (92131-1623)
PHONE 858 653-6800
Bruce Bowman, *Branch Mgr*
Christopher Fishman, *Manager*
Frank Kennedy, *Manager*
Leticia Estrada, *Accounts Exec*
EMP: 89
SALES (corp-wide): 2.4B **Privately Held**
WEB: www.apria.com
SIC: 7352 Medical equipment rental
HQ: Apria Healthcare Llc
26220 Enterprise Ct
Lake Forest CA 92630
949 616-2606

(P-14471)
APRIA HEALTHCARE LLC
15091 Bake Pkwy, Irvine (92618-2501)
PHONE 714 508-3000
Fax: 714 508-0120
Kristopher Fishman, *Principal*
Shakar RAO, *Development*
Ahmad Guest, *Marketing Staff*
Alexander Zaslavsky, *Director*
EMP: 290
SALES (corp-wide): 2.4B **Privately Held**
WEB: www.apria.com
SIC: 7352 Medical equipment rental
HQ: Apria Healthcare Llc
26220 Enterprise Ct
Lake Forest CA 92630
949 616-2606

(P-14472)
APRIA HEALTHCARE LLC
2040 Corporate Ct, San Jose (95131-1753)
PHONE 408 383-4400
Fax: 408 432-9484
Josepf Ware, *Manager*
EMP: 55
SALES (corp-wide): 2.4B **Privately Held**
WEB: www.apria.com
SIC: 7352 5999 Medical equipment rental; medical apparatus & supplies
HQ: Apria Healthcare Llc
26220 Enterprise Ct
Lake Forest CA 92630
949 616-2606

(P-14473)
APRIA HEALTHCARE LLC
3636 N Laughlin Rd # 190, Santa Rosa (95403-1063)
PHONE 707 543-0979
Fax: 707 543-5852
Jennifier Lasiter, *Principal*
EMP: 53
SALES (corp-wide): 2.4B **Privately Held**
WEB: www.apria.com
SIC: 7352 Medical equipment rental
HQ: Apria Healthcare Llc
26220 Enterprise Ct
Lake Forest CA 92630
949 616-2606

(P-14474)
DYNAMIC MEDICAL SYSTEMS LLC (HQ)
2811 E Ana St, Compton (90221-5601)
PHONE 310 928-0251
Fax: 310 928-0259
Mark Ludwig, *Manager*
Kristen Dephilipis, *Exec Dir*
Richard Stempson, *Opers Staff*
Nicole Hill, *VP Sales*
Marco Carreon, *Sales Staff*
EMP: 70
SQ FT: 25,000
SALES (est): 14.3MM **Privately Held**
WEB: www.godynamic.com
SIC: 7352 Medical equipment rental
PA: Joerns Healthcare Parent Llc
2430 Whitehall Park Dr # 100
Charlotte NC 28273
800 966-6662

(P-14475)
OPTION ONE HOME MED EQP INC
1220 Research Dr Ste A, Redlands (92374-4563)
P.O. Box 40700, Mesa AZ (85274-0700)
PHONE 909 478-5413
Fax: 562 946-5955
David Scheven, *CEO*
Nicole Mangiapelo, *Admin Asst*
Annette Rosas, *Manager*
▲ EMP: 117
SQ FT: 36,000

SALES (est): 13.2MM **Privately Held**
WEB: www.lifecaresoln.com
SIC: 7352 5999 Medical equipment rental; medical apparatus & supplies

(P-14476)
SCHAEFER AMBULANCE SERVICE INC
2215 S Bristol St, Santa Ana (92704-5124)
PHONE 714 545-8486
Ron Beyer, *Manager*
EMP: 50
SALES (corp-wide): 44.7MM **Privately Held**
WEB: www.schaeferamb.com
SIC: 7352 4119 Medical equipment rental; ambulance service
PA: Schaefer Ambulance Service, Inc.
4627 Beverly Blvd
Los Angeles CA 90004
323 469-1473

(P-14477)
WOUNDCO HOLDINGS INC
10877 Wilshire Blvd, Los Angeles (90024-4341)
PHONE 310 551-0101
Timothy J Hart, *CEO*
Robert Owen, *CFO*
EMP: 500
SALES (est): 20MM **Privately Held**
SIC: 7352 Medical equipment rental

7353 Heavy Construction Eqpt Rental & Leasing

(P-14478)
BIGRENTZ INC
Also Called: Bigrentz.com
1063 Mcgaw Ave Ste 200, Irvine (92614-5553)
PHONE 855 999-5438
Dallas Imbimbo, *CEO*
Brandon Huff, *President*
Joseph Dixon, *COO*
Stephen Jesson, *Exec VP*
Robert Gray, *Vice Pres*
EMP: 75
SQ FT: 15,852
SALES (est): 12.7MM **Privately Held**
SIC: 7353 Heavy construction equipment rental

(P-14479)
D&D EQUIPMENT RENTAL LLC
9016 Norwalk Blvd, Santa Fe Springs (90670-2532)
P.O. Box 2369 (90670-0369)
PHONE 562 595-4555
Gary Darnell,
John Allaire,
EMP: 50
SALES (est): 5.5MM **Privately Held**
WEB: www.ddrental.com
SIC: 7353 Earth moving equipment, rental or leasing

(P-14480)
DOWNS EQUIPMENT RENTALS INC (PA)
4800 Saco Rd, Bakersfield (93308-9626)
P.O. Box 80536 (93380-0536)
PHONE 661 615-6119
Fax: 661 399-9555
Gordon L Downs, *President*
Joyce M Downs, *Vice Pres*
Alexander R Ambrose, *Marketing Mgr*
Kristine Hudson, *Manager*
Theresa Martin, *Manager*
EMP: 58 EST: 1976
SALES (est): 9.6MM **Privately Held**
WEB: www.downsequip.com
SIC: 7353 1794 Earth moving equipment, rental or leasing; excavation work

(P-14481)
EXTERRAN INC
3449 Santa Anita Ave, El Monte (91731-2424)
PHONE 626 455-0739
EMP: 51
SALES (corp-wide): 3.1B **Publicly Held**
SIC: 7353

HQ: Exterran, Inc.
16666 Northchase Dr
Houston TX 77060
281 836-7000

(P-14482)
GALENA EQUIPMENT RENTAL LLC
Also Called: Biggie Crane and Ritting
10700 Bigge St, San Leandro (94577-1032)
PHONE 510 638-8100
Brock Settlemier,
Ed Wanat, *Data Proc Staff*
Robert Fredrickson, *Human Res Mgr*
Reid Settlemeier,
Marlene Settlemier,
EMP: 50
SALES (est): 7.1MM **Privately Held**
SIC: 7353 Cranes & aerial lift equipment, rental or leasing

(P-14483)
HARBOR INDUSTRIAL SERVICES
211 N Marine Ave, Wilmington (90744-5724)
PHONE 310 522-1193
Fax: 310 522-9283
W Michael Hawk, *President*
Billie Noble, *Admin Mgr*
EMP: 80 EST: 1993
SALES (est): 9.6MM **Privately Held**
WEB: www.harborindustrial.com
SIC: 7353 Cranes & aerial lift equipment, rental or leasing

(P-14484)
HAWTHORNE MACHINERY CO (PA)
Also Called: Caterpillar Authorized Dealer
16945 Camino San Bernardo, San Diego (92127-2499)
PHONE 858 674-7000
Fax: 858 674-3291
Tee K Ness, *President*
David Ness, *COO*
Brian Verhoeven, *CFO*
Stephen E Wittman, *Vice Pres*
Ken Emerick, *Branch Mgr*
EMP: 200
SQ FT: 130,000
SALES (est): 175.7MM **Privately Held**
SIC: 7353 7699 5082 7359 Heavy construction equipment rental; construction equipment repair; construction & mining machinery; equipment rental & leasing

(P-14485)
HAWTHORNE MACHINERY CO (HQ)
Also Called: Caterpillar Authorized Dealer
16945 Camino San Bernardo, San Diego (92127-2499)
PHONE 858 674-7000
Fax: 858 674-7095
Tee K Ness, *CEO*
Bob Price, *Exec VP*
Kirk Fowkes, *Vice Pres*
Paul Hawthorne, *Vice Pres*
Mike Johnson, *Vice Pres*
EMP: 100
SQ FT: 130,000
SALES (est): 12.3MM
SALES (corp-wide): 175.7MM **Privately Held**
WEB: www.hawthornelift.com
SIC: 7353 5084 Heavy construction equipment rental; industrial machinery & equipment
PA: Hawthorne Machinery Co.
16945 Camino San Bernardo
San Diego CA 92127
858 674-7000

(P-14486)
M T M & M INC
Also Called: Pick-A-Part
3333 Peck Rd, Monrovia (91016-5001)
PHONE 626 445-2922
Thomas Hutton, *President*
EMP: 100
SQ FT: 1,100

7353 - Heavy Construction Eqpt Rental & Leasing County (P-14487)

SALES (est): 8MM
SALES (corp-wide): 7.1B **Publicly Held**
WEB: www.pickapart.com
SIC: 7353 5093 Heavy construction equipment rental; scrap & waste materials
HQ: Pick-Your-Part Auto Wrecking
1235 S Beach Blvd
Anaheim CA 92804
714 385-1200

(P-14487)
MARCO CRANE & RIGGING CO
10168 Channel Rd, Lakeside (92040-1704)
PHONE................................619 938-8080
Fax: 619 938-8081
George Wheeler, *Sales/Mktg Mgr*
EMP: 70
SALES (corp-wide): 20.1MM **Privately Held**
WEB: www.marcocrane.com
SIC: 7353 Cranes & aerial lift equipment, rental or leasing
PA: Marco Crane & Rigging Co.
221 S 35th Ave
Phoenix AZ 85009
602 272-2671

(P-14488)
MAXIM CRANE WORKS LP
2373 E Mariposa Rd, Stockton (95205-7811)
PHONE................................209 464-7635
Darrel Sudduth, *Manager*
EMP: 150 **Publicly Held**
WEB: www.maximcrane.com
SIC: 7353 Heavy construction equipment rental
HQ: Maxim Crane Works, L.P.
1225 Wash Pike Ste 100
Bridgeville PA 15017
412 504-0200

(P-14489)
NATIONAL BUSINESS GROUP INC (PA)
Also Called: National Tube & Steel
15319 Chatsworth St, Mission Hills (91345-2040)
PHONE................................818 221-6000
James Mooneyham, *President*
◆ EMP: 85
SQ FT: 24,000
SALES (est): 98.4MM **Privately Held**
WEB: www.fence-rental.com
SIC: 7353 5039 7359 3496 Earth moving equipment, rental or leasing; wire fence, gates & accessories; garage facility & tool rental; fencing, made from purchased wire; utility trailer rental

(P-14490)
NATIONAL CNSTR RENTALS INC (HQ)
15319 Chatsworth St, Mission Hills (91345-2040)
PHONE................................818 221-6000
Fax: 818 221-6099
James R Mooneyham, *President*
W Robert Mooneyham, *President*
Elaine Boast, *Admin Asst*
Rod Dizon, *Administration*
Joseph Young, *Info Tech Dir*
EMP: 85
SQ FT: 23,000
SALES (est): 98.4MM **Privately Held**
WEB: www.rentnational.com
SIC: 7353 Heavy construction equipment rental
PA: The National Business Group Inc
15319 Chatsworth St
Mission Hills CA 91345
818 221-6000

(P-14491)
NOBLE RENTS INC
8314 Slauson Ave, Pico Rivera (90660-4323)
PHONE................................855 767-4424
Nabil Kassam, *CEO*
Suzy Taherian, *Corp Secy*
Aurora Lucatero, *Admin Asst*
Robina Ali, *Controller*
David Hitchcock, *Manager*
EMP: 65 EST: 2011
SQ FT: 62,766
SALES (est): 13.4MM **Privately Held**
SIC: 7353 Heavy construction equipment rental

(P-14492)
NORTHWEST EXCAVATING INC
18201 Napa St, Northridge (91325-3374)
PHONE................................818 349-5861
Fax: 818 701-9326
Susan Groff, *CEO*
Robbie Groff, *Vice Pres*
Cecille Bandalaria, *Executive Asst*
Cecilia Bandalia, *Manager*
EMP: 72
SQ FT: 2,500
SALES (est): 13.8MM **Privately Held**
WEB: www.nwexc.com
SIC: 7353 1794 Heavy construction equipment rental; excavation & grading, building construction

(P-14493)
OFFSHORE CRANE & SERVICE CO (PA)
Also Called: T & T Truck & Crane Service
1375 N Olive St Ste A, Ventura (93001-1375)
P.O. Box 1748 (93002-1748)
PHONE................................805 648-3348
Earl G Holder, *CEO*
Tim Holder, *President*
Kimberly A Loft, *Treasurer*
Shawn Paul, *Vice Pres*
Christine Bowen, *Office Mgr*
EMP: 52 EST: 1970
SQ FT: 11,000
SALES (est): 15.5MM **Privately Held**
SIC: 7353 4212 Cranes & aerial lift equipment, rental or leasing; truck rental with drivers

(P-14494)
PEED EQUIPMENT COMPANY
1480 Nandina Ave, Perris (92571-7008)
PHONE................................951 657-0900
Carolyn Peed, *President*
Michael Peed, *Treasurer*
Misty Brailey, *Office Mgr*
David Peed, *Admin Sec*
Tom Loeb, *Agent*
EMP: 50
SQ FT: 17,000
SALES (est): 12.1MM **Privately Held**
SIC: 7353 7699 Heavy construction equipment rental; construction equipment repair

(P-14495)
RALPH D MITZEL INC
Also Called: Mitzel Company
1520 N Fairview St, Santa Ana (92706-3111)
PHONE................................714 554-4745
Fax: 714 554-6831
Ralph D Mitzel Jr, *President*
Bill Stehle, *CFO*
Arlene Mitzel, *Corp Secy*
John K Mitzel, *Vice Pres*
EMP: 100
SQ FT: 1,000
SALES (est): 13.5MM **Privately Held**
SIC: 7353 1794 Heavy construction equipment rental; excavation & grading, building construction

(P-14496)
RDO CONSTRUCTION EQUIPMENT CO
Also Called: John Deere Authorized Dealer
10108 Riverford Rd, Lakeside (92040-2740)
PHONE................................619 443-3758
Fax: 619 443-3274
Ron Offets, *President*
Christopher Scott, *General Mgr*
Robert Wheelington, *General Mgr*
Ashley Triplett, *Accountant*
Bruce Johnson, *Manager*
EMP: 60
SQ FT: 2,200
SALES (est): 12.4MM **Privately Held**
WEB: www.bbrental.com
SIC: 7353 5082 Heavy construction equipment rental; general construction machinery & equipment

(P-14497)
RJ ALLEN INC
10392 Stanford Ave, Garden Grove (92840-6301)
PHONE................................714 539-1022
Fax: 714 590-6955
Andrew Allen, *President*
Deanna Allen, *Treasurer*
Ron Markham, *Vice Pres*
Wendi Bennett, *Office Admin*
Liz Wood, *Human Res Mgr*
EMP: 65
SQ FT: 20,000
SALES (est): 15MM **Privately Held**
WEB: www.rjalleninc.com
SIC: 7353 Heavy construction equipment rental

(P-14498)
SHEEDY DRAYAGE CO (PA)
1215 Michigan St, San Francisco (94107-3518)
P.O. Box 77004 (94107-0004)
PHONE................................415 648-7171
Fax: 415 648-1535
Don Russell, *Chairman*
Richard Battaini, *President*
Michael A Battaini, *CEO*
Peter Hogan, *Corp Secy*
Ed Hollenbeck, *Division Mgr*
EMP: 80 EST: 1925
SQ FT: 25,000
SALES (est): 21.3MM **Privately Held**
WEB: www.sheedycrane.com
SIC: 7353 Cranes & aerial lift equipment, rental or leasing

(P-14499)
SONSRAY MACHINERY LLC (HQ)
23935 Madison St, Torrance (90505-6010)
PHONE................................323 319-1900
Matthew Hoelscher, *President*
James Martinez, *Manager*
EMP: 102
SQ FT: 30,000
SALES: 60MM **Privately Held**
SIC: 7353 5082 Heavy construction equipment rental; road construction equipment
PA: Tk Services, Inc.
23935 Madison St
Torrance CA 90505
323 585-1271

(P-14500)
TONY R CRISALLI INC
3468 Campbell St, Riverside (92509-1029)
PHONE................................951 727-0110
Fax: 951 727-0130
Tony R Crisalli, *President*
EMP: 50
SALES (est): 5.2MM **Privately Held**
SIC: 7353 Heavy construction equipment rental

(P-14501)
TRITON CONT INTL INC N AMER (DH)
55 Green St Ste 500, San Francisco (94111-1412)
PHONE................................415 956-6311
Fax: 415 421-5318
Edward P Schneider, *CEO*
Dean Bonomo, *Vice Pres*
Terry Fast, *Vice Pres*
Susan Morrison, *Vice Pres*
Glen Regier, *Vice Pres*
EMP: 111
SALES (est): 16.1MM **Privately Held**
SIC: 7353 7359 Heavy construction equipment rental; shipping container leasing
HQ: Triton Container International Limited
C/O Appleby
Hamilton
441 295-2287

(P-14502)
WASTE MGT COLLECTN RECYCL INC
1800 S Grand Ave, Santa Ana (92705-4800)
PHONE................................714 637-3010
Fax: 714 836-0668
David Steiner, *President*
Lee Hicks, *Principal*
David Ross, *District Mgr*
Paula Davey, *Project Mgr*
Angelica Hernandez, *Hum Res Coord*
EMP: 350
SALES (est): 111.5MM
SALES (corp-wide): 12.9B **Publicly Held**
SIC: 7353 4953 Heavy construction equipment rental; refuse collection & disposal services
PA: Waste Management, Inc.
1001 Fannin St Ste 4000
Houston TX 77002
713 512-6200

7359 Equipment Rental & Leasing, NEC

(P-14503)
(A) TOOL SHED INC (PA)
Also Called: A Tool Shed Equipment Rentals
3700 Soquel Ave, Santa Cruz (95062-1774)
PHONE................................831 477-7133
Robert Pedersen, *President*
Eric Pedersen, *Treasurer*
Lars Pedersen, *Vice Pres*
Bonnie Pedersen, *Admin Sec*
Tim Heer, *Manager*
EMP: 72
SQ FT: 2,500
SALES (est): 22MM **Privately Held**
WEB: www.atoolshed.com
SIC: 7359 Equipment rental & leasing

(P-14504)
A-THRONE CO INC
1850 E 33rd St, Long Beach (90807-5208)
PHONE................................562 981-1197
Fax: 562 426-9896
Michael L Rice, *President*
Minerva Songco, *General Mgr*
Dixie Vane, *Project Mgr*
Nikki Hussein, *Controller*
EMP: 55
SALES (est): 8.4MM **Privately Held**
WEB: www.athrone.com
SIC: 7359 1799 Portable toilet rental; fence construction

(P-14505)
ADVANCED TEST EQUIPMENT CORP
Also Called: ADVANCED TEST EQUIPMENT RENTAL
10401 Roselle St, San Diego (92121-1523)
PHONE................................858 558-6500
Fax: 858 558-6570
James P Berg, *CEO*
Jill Berg, *President*
Enrique Gonzales, *CFO*
Deana Stout, *CFO*
Jill Ryan, *Executive*
EMP: 60
SQ FT: 25,000
SALES: 19.3MM **Privately Held**
WEB: www.atecorp.com
SIC: 7359 Equipment rental & leasing

(P-14506)
AFTER-PARTY2 INC (HQ)
Also Called: Classic Party Rentals
901 W Hillcrest Blvd, Inglewood (90301-2100)
PHONE................................310 202-0011
Fax: 310 202-8542
Jeff Black, *President*
Cesar Torres, *President*
Matt Wiltshire, *Vice Pres*
Luis Flores, *Social Dir*
Ryan Presern, *Social Dir*
EMP: 200
SALES (est): 81.9MM **Publicly Held**
SIC: 7359 Party supplies rental services

(P-14507)
AFTER-PARTY2 INC
2310 E Imperial Hwy, El Segundo (90245-2813)
PHONE................................310 535-3660
Michael Stern, *Manager*
Andrew Platts, *Network Enginr*
EMP: 59 **Publicly Held**
SIC: 7359 Tent & tarpaulin rental

PRODUCTS & SERVICES SECTION

7359 - Equipment Rental & Leasing, NEC County (P-14528)

HQ: After-Party2, Inc.
901 W Hillcrest Blvd
Inglewood CA 90301
310 202-0011

(P-14508)
AIR LEASE CORPORATION (PA)
2000 Avenue Of The Stars 1000n, Los Angeles (90067-4734)
PHONE..................................310 553-0555
Fax: 310 553-0999
Steven F Udvar-Hazy, *Ch of Bd*
Sabrina Lemmens, *President*
John L Plueger, *President*
Gregory B Willis, *CFO*
Carol H Forsyte, *Ch Credit Ofcr*
EMP: 74
SALES: 1.2B **Publicly Held**
SIC: 7359 7389 Equipment rental & leasing; aircraft & industrial truck rental services; aircraft rental; financial services

(P-14509)
AJAX PORTABLE SERVICES
Also Called: Waste Management
11240 Commercial Pkwy, Castroville (95012-3206)
PHONE..................................831 384-5000
Fax: 831 632-0181
David Steiner, *President*
Lyndon Ferrer, *Program Mgr*
Steve Boe, *District Mgr*
Sandra Landy, *District Mgr*
Stephen Miceli, *District Mgr*
EMP: 50
SALES (est): 5.4MM **Privately Held**
SIC: 7359 Portable toilet rental

(P-14510)
ALTA EQUIPMENT LEASING COMPANY
50 California St Fl 24, San Francisco (94111-4796)
PHONE..................................415 875-1000
Michael J Sangiacomo, *President*
Archie L Humphrey, *COO*
Mark Lomele, *CFO*
Tim Daleiden, *Project Mgr*
Oscar Campos, *Technology*
EMP: 55
SALES (est): 3.4MM
SALES (corp-wide): 1.6B **Privately Held**
WEB: www.norcalwastesystemsofbutte-county.com
SIC: 7359 Equipment rental & leasing
PA: Recology Inc.
50 California St Fl 24
San Francisco CA 94111
415 875-1000

(P-14511)
AMADA CAPITAL CORPORATION
7025 Firestone Blvd, Buena Park (90621-1869)
PHONE..................................714 739-2111
Mike Guerin, *President*
Koji Tschimoto, *Treasurer*
David Kehrli, *Vice Pres*
Eisuke Aoki, *Admin Sec*
Mitsuaki Amada, *Director*
EMP: 100
SQ FT: 103,000
SALES (est): 11.9MM
SALES (corp-wide): 2.6B **Privately Held**
SIC: 7359 Equipment rental & leasing
HQ: Amada North America, Inc
7025 Firestone Blvd
Buena Park CA 90621

(P-14512)
AMES TAPING TOOLS
Also Called: Ames Taping Tool Systems
1842 Herndon Rd Ste A, Ceres (95307-4422)
PHONE..................................209 538-0113
Carl Winn, *Vice Pres*
Rany Niemann, *Manager*
EMP: 99 EST: 1974
SALES: 600K **Privately Held**
SIC: 7359 5032 Tool rental; drywall materials

(P-14513)
ANDY GUMP INC
11551 Hart St, North Hollywood (91605-6204)
PHONE..................................818 255-0650
Gary Wood, *Manager*
Thomas Field, *Sales Mgr*
EMP: 70
SALES (corp-wide): 16.9MM **Privately Held**
WEB: www.andygump.com
SIC: 7359 Portable toilet rental
PA: Andy Gump, Inc.
26410 Summit Cir
Santa Clarita CA 91350
661 251-7721

(P-14514)
AUDIO VISUAL HEADQUARTERS (DH)
Also Called: Psav
16320 Arthur St, Cerritos (90703-2129)
PHONE..................................310 603-0652
Michael O'Brien, *President*
Pat Gephardt, *CFO*
Hong Chae, *Info Tech Mgr*
Nicholas Jackson, *Project Mgr*
EMP: 50
SQ FT: 70,000
SALES (est): 16.9MM
SALES (corp-wide): 677.8MM **Privately Held**
WEB: www.avhq.com
SIC: 7359 7389 Audio-visual equipment & supply rental; convention & show services
HQ: Audio Visual Services Group, Inc.
111 W Ocean Blvd Ste 1110
Long Beach CA 90802
562 366-0620

(P-14515)
AUTO-CHLOR SYSTEM LLC
450 Ferguson Dr, Mountain View (94043-5214)
PHONE..................................650 967-3085
Jerry Ivy, *Mng Member*
Deborah Ivy, *Principal*
Edward Ivy, *Mng Member*
Kirk Greenwood, *Manager*
EMP: 56
SALES (est): 9.7MM **Privately Held**
SIC: 7359 Equipment rental & leasing

(P-14516)
BA LEASING & CAPITAL CORP (DH)
555 California St Fl 4, San Francisco (94104-1506)
PHONE..................................415 765-1804
Fax: 415 622-7915
Richard Harris, *President*
K Thomas Rose, *COO*
Rod Hurd, *Treasurer*
Richard C Walter, *Vice Pres*
Oliver James Warner, *Vice Pres*
EMP: 130 EST: 1955
SALES (est): 7.2MM
SALES (corp-wide): 93B **Publicly Held**
SIC: 7359 Equipment rental & leasing
HQ: Banc Of America Leasing & Capital, Llc
555 California St Fl 4
San Francisco CA 94104
415 765-7349

(P-14517)
BAKERCORP (HQ)
3020 Old Ranch Pkwy # 220, Seal Beach (90740-2765)
PHONE..................................562 430-6262
Bob Craycraft, *President*
Raymond Aronoff, *COO*
David Ignata, *CFO*
Bruce Lux, *CFO*
John Friend, *Senior VP*
EMP: 120
SQ FT: 7,500
SALES (est): 230.6MM **Privately Held**
WEB: www.bakercorp.com
SIC: 7359 Equipment rental & leasing
PA: Ftt Holdings, Inc.
3020 Old Ranch Pkwy
Seal Beach CA 90740
562 430-6262

(P-14518)
BBAM ARCFT HOLDINGS 137 LABUAN
50 California St Fl 14, San Francisco (94111-4683)
PHONE..................................415 267-1600
Steve Zissis, *CEO*
Renee Reuter, *Executive Asst*
Jackie Lam, *Controller*
EMP: 100
SALES (est): 9.5MM **Privately Held**
SIC: 7359 Aircraft rental

(P-14519)
BROOK FURNITURE RENTAL INC
Also Called: Brook Furniture Clearance Ctr
30985 Santana St, Hayward (94544-7029)
PHONE..................................510 487-4440
Fax: 510 487-2904
Robert W Crawford, *Owner*
EMP: 50
SALES (corp-wide): 53.4MM **Privately Held**
WEB: www.bfr.com
SIC: 7359 Furniture rental
HQ: Brook Furniture Rental, Inc.
100 N Field Dr Ste 220
Lake Forest IL 60045
847 810-4000

(P-14520)
CAI INTERNATIONAL INC (PA)
1 Market Plz Ste 900, San Francisco (94105-1009)
PHONE..................................415 788-0100
Victor M Garcia, *President*
Hiromitsu Ogawa, *Ch of Bd*
Timothy B Page, *CFO*
Timothy Page, *CFO*
Daniel J Hallahan, *Senior VP*
EMP: 95
SALES: 249.6MM **Publicly Held**
WEB: www.capps.com
SIC: 7359 Shipping container leasing

(P-14521)
CAL WEST GENERAL ENGRG INC
5480 Baltimore Dr Ste 215, La Mesa (91942-2066)
PHONE..................................619 469-5811
Fax: 619 469-1707
Ronald E Provience, *CEO*
Frank A Passiglia, *President*
Kally Teck, *Accounts Mgr*
EMP: 50
SQ FT: 2,000
SALES (est): 4.6MM **Privately Held**
SIC: 7359 Equipment rental & leasing

(P-14522)
CHOURA EVENTS
540 Hawaii Ave, Torrance (90503-5148)
PHONE..................................310 320-6200
James Ryan Choura, *CEO*
Howard Tabackman, *Exec VP*
Joey Sparks, *Sales Associate*
Sandra Valdovinos, *Sales Staff*
EMP: 80 EST: 2014
SALES: 8MM **Privately Held**
SIC: 7359 Equipment rental & leasing

(P-14523)
CLAIRMONT CAMERA INC (PA)
4343 Lankershim Blvd, North Hollywood (91602-2705)
PHONE..................................818 761-4440
Fax: 818 761-0861
Denny Clairmont, *President*
Alan Albert, *Exec VP*
Tom Boelens, *Vice Pres*
Michael Condon, *Vice Pres*
Irving Correa, *Vice Pres*
EMP: 54
SQ FT: 33,000
SALES (est): 14.8MM **Privately Held**
WEB: www.clairmont.com
SIC: 7359 Audio-visual equipment & supply rental

(P-14524)
COMPASS GROUP USA INC
Also Called: Canteen Vending
12640 Knott St, Garden Grove (92841-3902)
PHONE..................................714 899-2520
Fax: 310 637-0001
Ron Wanamaker, *Vice Pres*
EMP: 125
SALES (corp-wide): 27.3B **Privately Held**
WEB: www.compass-usa.com
SIC: 7359 7699 5962 Vending machine rental; vending machine repair; merchandising machine operators
HQ: Compass Group Usa, Inc.
2400 Yorkmont Rd
Charlotte NC 28217
704 329-4000

(P-14525)
CORT BUSINESS SERVICES CORP
14350 Grfield Ave Ste 500, Paramount (90723)
PHONE..................................562 582-1515
Fax: 562 582-1516
Pat Bockenstette, *Branch Mgr*
Mike Jimenez, *Admin Mgr*
Keith Souhrada, *Assistant*
EMP: 70
SALES (corp-wide): 210.8B **Publicly Held**
SIC: 7359 Home appliance, furniture & entertainment rental services
HQ: Cort Business Services Corporation
15000 Conference Ste 440
Chantilly VA 20151
703 968-8500

(P-14526)
CP OPCO LLC
Also Called: Classic Party Rentals
745 Skyway Ct, NAPA (94558-7510)
PHONE..................................707 253-2332
Michael Prichett, *Manager*
Megan Balaguy, *Sales Associate*
Don Ross, *Manager*
Christine Schindewolf, *Receptionist*
EMP: 59
SALES (corp-wide): 1.1MM **Privately Held**
SIC: 7359 Equipment rental & leasing
HQ: Cp Opco, Llc
901 W Hillcrest Blvd
Inglewood CA 90301
310 966-4900

(P-14527)
CP OPCO LLC
Also Called: Classic Party Rentals
7069 Cnsld Way Ste 300, San Diego (92121)
PHONE..................................858 496-9700
Sean Carlton, *Manager*
Erin Regan, *Social Dir*
Blake Richards, *Social Dir*
Daniel Lopez, *Opers Mgr*
Leah Cafagna, *Manager*
EMP: 59
SALES (corp-wide): 1.1MM **Privately Held**
SIC: 7359 Party supplies rental services
HQ: Cp Opco, Llc
901 W Hillcrest Blvd
Inglewood CA 90301
310 966-4900

(P-14528)
CP OPCO LLC
Also Called: Classic Party Rentals
4623 Mchenry Ave, Modesto (95356-9562)
PHONE..................................209 524-1966
Ross Condit, *Branch Mgr*
Lynda Cremin, *Manager*
EMP: 59
SALES (corp-wide): 1.1MM **Privately Held**
SIC: 7359 Equipment rental & leasing
HQ: Cp Opco, Llc
901 W Hillcrest Blvd
Inglewood CA 90301
310 966-4900

7359 - Equipment Rental & Leasing, NEC County (P-14529)

(P-14529)
CP OPCO LLC
Also Called: Classic Party Rentals
1828 State St, Santa Barbara (93101-2420)
PHONE................805 563-3800
Nicole Charuvastra, *Sales Staff*
Berenice Mora, *Manager*
EMP: 59
SALES (corp-wide): 1.1MM **Privately Held**
SIC: 7359 Equipment rental & leasing
HQ: Cp Opco, Llc
901 W Hillcrest Blvd
Inglewood CA 90301
310 966-4900

(P-14530)
CP OPCO LLC
Also Called: Classic Party Rentals
1120 Mark Ave, Carpinteria (93013-2918)
PHONE................805 566-3566
Fax: 805 566-3599
Richard Good, *Manager*
Shila Crabtree, *Accounts Exec*
EMP: 59
SALES (corp-wide): 1.1MM **Privately Held**
SIC: 7359 Equipment rental & leasing
HQ: Cp Opco, Llc
901 W Hillcrest Blvd
Inglewood CA 90301
310 966-4900

(P-14531)
CP OPCO LLC
Also Called: Classic Party Rentals
1635 Rollins Rd Ste A, Burlingame (94010-2301)
PHONE................650 652-0300
Fax: 650 697-9090
Susan Kidwell, *Branch Mgr*
Bruce Wellman, *Opers Mgr*
Valerie Hopple, *Sales Mgr*
Donald Macneil, *Director*
Bernadette Pisani, *Assistant*
EMP: 59
SALES (corp-wide): 1.1MM **Privately Held**
SIC: 7359 Party supplies rental services
HQ: Cp Opco, Llc
901 W Hillcrest Blvd
Inglewood CA 90301
310 966-4900

(P-14532)
CP OPCO LLC
Also Called: Classic Party Rentals
11766 Wilshire Blvd # 380, Los Angeles (90025-6538)
PHONE................310 966-4900
Pedro Mata, *President*
EMP: 59
SALES (corp-wide): 1.1MM **Privately Held**
SIC: 7359 Party supplies rental services
HQ: Cp Opco, Llc
901 W Hillcrest Blvd
Inglewood CA 90301
310 966-4900

(P-14533)
CP OPCO LLC
Also Called: Classic Party Rentals
3101 S Harbor Blvd, Santa Ana (92704-6826)
PHONE................714 540-6111
Tony Alvares, *Manager*
Mari Barron, *Sales Associate*
Nicole Bunjovac, *Sales Staff*
EMP: 100
SALES (corp-wide): 1.1MM **Privately Held**
SIC: 7359 Party supplies rental services
HQ: Cp Opco, Llc
901 W Hillcrest Blvd
Inglewood CA 90301
310 966-4900

(P-14534)
CWF INC
Also Called: A-1 Party Rentals
251 E Front St, Covina (91723-1613)
PHONE................626 967-0500
Chet Fortney, *President*
Jerry Hinds, *Controller*
Rosa Laurel, *Marketing Staff*
EMP: 51
SALES: 950K **Privately Held**
SIC: 7359 Party supplies rental services

(P-14535)
DIAMOND ENVIRONMENTAL SVCS LP
807 E Mission Rd, San Marcos (92069-3002)
PHONE................760 744-7191
Eric De Jong,
Eric Jong, *Project Mgr*
Tanno Gomolka, *Sales Mgr*
Cindy Mellon, *Manager*
Cindy Packer, *Manager*
EMP: 100 **EST:** 1997
SQ FT: 2,000
SALES (est): 17.6MM **Privately Held**
SIC: 7359 Portable toilet rental

(P-14536)
EAGLE HIGH REACH EQUIPMENT LLC
14241 Alondra Blvd, La Mirada (90638-5501)
PHONE................619 265-2637
Fax: 714 522-6591
John Benjamin,
EMP: 70
SQ FT: 22,000
SALES (est): 4.1MM **Privately Held**
SIC: 7359 7353 5084 Equipment rental & leasing; cranes & aerial lift equipment, rental or leasing; materials handling machinery

(P-14537)
EL CAMINO RENTAL
1833 Oceanside Blvd Ste D, Oceanside (92054-3456)
PHONE................760 722-7368
Fax: 760 722-7821
Bill Mahalic, *Owner*
EMP: 50
SALES (est): 3.4MM **Privately Held**
WEB: www.elcaminorental.com
SIC: 7359 Equipment rental & leasing

(P-14538)
ELECTRO RENT CORPORATION (PA)
6060 Sepulveda Blvd # 300, Van Nuys (91411-2512)
P.O. Box 605, Newbury Park (91319-0605)
PHONE................818 786-2525
Fax: 818 786-4354
Steven Markheim, *CEO*
Allen Sciarillo, *CFO*
EMP: 148
SQ FT: 84,500
SALES: 175.3MM **Privately Held**
SIC: 7359 7377 5065 5045 Electronic equipment rental, except computers; computer rental & leasing; electronic parts & equipment; computers & accessories, personal & home entertainment

(P-14539)
EPIC PRODUCTION TECH US INC
1401 Maulhardt Ave Ste A, Oxnard (93030-7960)
P.O. Box 454, Lake Oswego OR (97034-0049)
PHONE................805 278-2400
Ted Fowler, *CEO*
Katie Boyd, *Office Admin*
Michelle M Fowler, *Admin Sec*
Justin Freeman, *Technical Mgr*
Dario Lucciola, *Controller*
EMP: 65 **EST:** 2008
SQ FT: 15,000
SALES (est): 5.8MM **Privately Held**
WEB: www.edandted.com
SIC: 7359 Sound & lighting equipment rental
PA: Epic Holding Company Inc.
1401 Maulhardt Ave A
Oxnard CA 93030

(P-14540)
EZ ACCEPTANCE INC
7651 Ronson Rd, San Diego (92111-1511)
PHONE................858 278-8351
Ronald Zagami, *President*
Mike Toomey, *Vice Pres*
EMP: 140
SALES (est): 4.2MM **Privately Held**
SIC: 7359 Equipment rental & leasing

(P-14541)
FIFTH & SUNSET ENTERPRISES LLC
Also Called: 5th & Sunset Productions
12322 Exposition Blvd, Los Angeles (90064-1014)
PHONE................310 979-0212
Bruce E Kramer, *President*
Barry Gernstein, *Vice Pres*
John Blakely, *Manager*
Pat Brown, *Manager*
EMP: 85
SQ FT: 19,000
SALES: 12.5MM **Privately Held**
SIC: 7359 7335 Equipment rental & leasing; still & slide file production

(P-14542)
FREEMAN AUDIO VISUAL INC
901 E South St, Anaheim (92805-5347)
PHONE................714 254-3400
Gabriele Buonacorsi, *Branch Mgr*
Bob Laing, *Info Tech Dir*
EMP: 200
SALES (corp-wide): 2B **Privately Held**
WEB: www.avwtelav.com
SIC: 7359 Audio-visual equipment & supply rental
HQ: Freeman Audio Visual, Inc.
1600 Viceroy Dr Ste 100
Dallas TX 75235
214 445-1000

(P-14543)
GRAND EVENTS INC
4623 Mchenry Ave, Modesto (95356-9562)
PHONE................209 569-0399
Ross Condit, *President*
EMP: 50
SQ FT: 37,000
SALES (est): 3.4MM **Privately Held**
WEB: www.grand-events.com
SIC: 7359 5947 Party supplies rental services; gifts & novelties

(P-14544)
H&E EQUIPMENT SERVICES INC
14241 Alondra Blvd, La Mirada (90638-5501)
PHONE................714 522-6590
David Harkey, *Manager*
Amanda Dow, *Parts Mgr*
EMP: 110
SALES (corp-wide): 1B **Publicly Held**
WEB: www.engquist.com
SIC: 7359 7353 5084 Equipment rental & leasing; cranes & aerial lift equipment, rental or leasing; materials handling machinery
PA: H&E Equipment Services, Inc.
7500 Pecue Ln
Baton Rouge LA 70809
225 298-5200

(P-14545)
HANA FINANCIAL INC (PA)
1000 Wilshire Blvd Fl 20, Los Angeles (90017-5645)
PHONE................213 240-1234
Fax: 213 482-1212
Sunnie S Kim, *CEO*
Michelle Yue, *Officer*
Joseph Choe, *Senior VP*
Ken Lee, *Senior VP*
Susan Lee, *Senior VP*
EMP: 85
SQ FT: 24,000
SALES (est): 28.3MM **Privately Held**
SIC: 7359 6153 6159 Equipment rental & leasing; factoring services; small business investment companies

(P-14546)
HOLZMUELLER CORPORATION
Also Called: Holzmueller Productions
1000 25th St, San Francisco (94107-3509)
PHONE................415 826-8383
Fax: 415 826-2608
Richard P Gentschel, *President*
Carol Gentschel, *Vice Pres*
Michael Hamlin, *Sales Mgr*
Damon Hope, *Sales Staff*
Jim Schelstrate, *Manager*
EMP: 50
SQ FT: 30,000
SALES (est): 6.8MM **Privately Held**
WEB: www.holzmueller.com
SIC: 7359 5719 1731 Sound & lighting equipment rental; lighting fixtures; electrical work

(P-14547)
HUB CONSTRUCTION SPC INC (PA)
Also Called: Hub Construction Sups & Eqp
379 S I St, San Bernardino (92410-2409)
P.O. Box 1269 (92402-1269)
PHONE................909 235-4100
Fax: 909 885-0983
Robert T Gogo, *President*
Edward Dainko, *CFO*
Bernice Gogo, *Corp Secy*
Roberto Pedregon, *Branch Mgr*
Tom Holod, *Opers Mgr*
EMP: 50
SQ FT: 25,000
SALES (est): 48.4MM **Privately Held**
SIC: 7359 5082 Equipment rental & leasing; construction & mining machinery

(P-14548)
IDEAL EQUIPMENT RENTAL INC
Also Called: Eagle High Reach
14241 Alondra Blvd, La Mirada (90638-5501)
PHONE................714 237-9232
John Benjamin, *President*
Mary Jo RE, *Controller*
Fernando Castillo, *Manager*
EMP: 100
SALES (est): 5.2MM **Privately Held**
SIC: 7359 Equipment rental & leasing

(P-14549)
IMPERIAL MRIDIAN COMPANIES INC
Also Called: Imca Capital
11901 Santa Monica Blvd # 338, Los Angeles (90025-2767)
PHONE................310 447-3460
Blake B Johnson, *President*
Emma Cabildo, *CFO*
EMP: 85
SQ FT: 10,200
SALES: 10MM **Privately Held**
SIC: 7359 Equipment rental & leasing

(P-14550)
INTERNATIONAL LEASE FIN CORP (HQ)
10250 Constellation Blvd, Los Angeles (90067-6200)
PHONE................310 788-1999
Henri Courpron, *CEO*
Elias Habayeb, *CFO*
Pamela Hendry, *Treasurer*
Kurt H Schwarz, *Senior VP*
Philip Scruggs, *Senior VP*
EMP: 128
SQ FT: 149,000
SALES (est): 95.5MM
SALES (corp-wide): 131MM **Privately Held**
WEB: www.ilfc.com
SIC: 7359 8741 5599 Aircraft rental; business management; aircraft dealers
PA: Aercap U.S. Global Aviation Llc
10250 Constellation Blvd
Los Angeles CA 90067
310 788-1999

(P-14551)
J M EQUIPMENT COMPANY INC (PA)
Also Called: John Deere Authorized Dealer
321 Spreckels Ave, Manteca (95336-6007)
PHONE................209 522-3271

PRODUCTS & SERVICES SECTION

7359 - Equipment Rental & Leasing, NEC County (P-14573)

Ray Azevedo, *CEO*
Dave Baiocchi, *President*
Ed Henriquez, *President*
Vincent C Victorine, *CFO*
Jacqueline Gonzalez, *Treasurer*
EMP: 80
SQ FT: 7,000
SALES (est): 34.9MM **Privately Held**
WEB: www.jmequipment.com
SIC: 7359 5084 5999 Equipment rental & leasing; materials handling machinery; farm equipment & supplies; farm machinery; farm tractors

(P-14552)
JALUX AMERICAS INC (HQ)
390 N Sepulveda Blvd # 2000, El Segundo (90245-4475)
PHONE.................................310 524-1000
Osamu Yamaguchi, *CEO*
Shinichi Matsuyama, *President*
Naohiko Habuki, *Corp Secy*
Hidebumi Mori, *Exec VP*
Hideko Payton, *Controller*
EMP: 50
SQ FT: 15,000
SALES: 20.3MM
SALES (corp-wide): 1.2B **Privately Held**
WEB: www.jaluxam.com
SIC: 7359 5088 5199 Aircraft rental; office machine rental, except computers; aircraft equipment & supplies; variety store merchandise
PA: Jalux Inc.
  1-2-70, Konan
  Minato-Ku TKY 108-0
  363 678-800

(P-14553)
JC PARTY RENTALS INC
11562 Vanowen St, North Hollywood (91605-6229)
PHONE.................................818 765-4819
Delmy Chavarria, *CEO*
Jose Urquilla, *President*
Jeeza Arriola, *Office Mgr*
Ivan Olivas, *Sales Mgr*
EMP: 52
SQ FT: 6,600
SALES: 653K **Privately Held**
SIC: 7359 Party supplies rental services

(P-14554)
KING EQUIPMENT LLC
1690 Ashley Way, Colton (92324-4000)
P.O. Box 1080, Ontario (91762-0080)
PHONE.................................909 986-5300
Ernie Quijada,
Diane Quijada, *Admin Sec*
Drew Cavanagh, *Marketing Staff*
Brad Santi, *Sales Staff*
Mike Burns, *Manager*
EMP: 73
SALES: 32MM **Privately Held**
SIC: 7359 Business machine & electronic equipment rental services

(P-14555)
L A PARTY RENTS INC
13520 Saticoy St, Van Nuys (91402-6428)
PHONE.................................818 989-4300
Fax: 818 989-3593
Gerome Nehus, *President*
Kevin Dwyer, *Admin Asst*
Jerry Nehus, *CIO*
Richard Davidson, *Info Tech Mgr*
Jerry O Dean, *Info Tech Mgr*
EMP: 100
SALES (est): 10.3MM **Privately Held**
WEB: www.lapartyrents.com
SIC: 7359 Party supplies rental services

(P-14556)
MACQURIE ARCFT LSG SVCS US INC
2 Embarcadero Ctr Ste 200, San Francisco (94111-3801)
PHONE.................................415 829-6600
John R Willingham, *CEO*
Harry Forsythe, *Exec VP*
Nora Bergman, *Senior VP*
Bruce Hogarth, *Vice Pres*
Zenaida L Lawhon, *Vice Pres*
EMP: 60
SALES: 12.6MM **Privately Held**
SIC: 7359 Aircraft rental

PA: Macquarie Airfinance Holdings Limited
  South Bank House
  Dublin
  -

(P-14557)
MCGRATH RENTCORP
Adler Tank Rentals
5700 Las Positas Rd, Livermore (94551-7806)
PHONE.................................925 453-3312
Steve Adler, *Principal*
EMP: 94
SALES (corp-wide): 404.5MM **Publicly Held**
SIC: 7359 Equipment rental & leasing
PA: Mcgrath Rentcorp
  5700 Las Positas Rd
  Livermore CA 94551
  925 606-9200

(P-14558)
MCGRATH RENTCORP
Also Called: Mobile Modular
5700 Las Positas Rd, Livermore (94551-7806)
PHONE.................................877 221-2813
Kay Dashner, *Executive*
Tom Sauer, *Administration*
Dave Whitney, *CIO*
Mark Rowell, *Info Tech Dir*
Jay Lovett, *Technology*
EMP: 102
SALES (corp-wide): 404.5MM **Publicly Held**
SIC: 7359 5084 Equipment rental & leasing; electronic equipment rental, except computers; rental store, general; measuring & testing equipment, electrical
PA: Mcgrath Rentcorp
  5700 Las Positas Rd
  Livermore CA 94551
  925 606-9200

(P-14559)
MCGRATH RENTCORP (PA)
5700 Las Positas Rd, Livermore (94551-7806)
PHONE.................................925 606-9200
Dennis C Kakures, *President*
Ronald H Zech, *Ch of Bd*
Joseph F Hanna, *COO*
Keith E Pratt, *CFO*
John P Skenesky, *Treasurer*
EMP: 148 **EST:** 1979
SQ FT: 26,160
SALES: 404.5MM **Publicly Held**
SIC: 7359 5084 Equipment rental & leasing; electronic equipment rental, except computers; rental store, general; measuring & testing equipment, electrical

(P-14560)
MEETING SERVICES INC
Also Called: MSI PRODUCTION SERVICES
10895 Thornmint Rd Ste A, San Diego (92127-2420)
PHONE.................................858 348-0100
Fax: 858 503-0993
John Brinkman, *CEO*
Tom Bollard, *Shareholder*
Ed Lafever, *Shareholder*
Ray Lucy, *Shareholder*
Greg Hurst, *Executive*
EMP: 90
SQ FT: 20,000
SALES: 13.4MM **Privately Held**
WEB: www.msiprod.com
SIC: 7359 7629 5049 Audio-visual equipment & supply rental; electrical equipment repair, high voltage; theatrical equipment & supplies

(P-14561)
MICROFINANCIAL INCORPORATED
2801 Townsgate Rd, Westlake Village (91361-3003)
PHONE.................................805 367-8900
Richard Latour, *CEO*
EMP: 139
SALES (corp-wide): 62.5MM **Privately Held**
SIC: 7359 Business machine & electronic equipment rental services

HQ: Microfinancial Incorporated
  16 New England Executive
  Burlington MA 01803
  781 994-4800

(P-14562)
OES EQUIPMENT LLC (PA)
37421 Centralmont Pl, Fremont (94536-6536)
PHONE.................................510 284-1900
Peter Nosler,
Bob Logar, *General Mgr*
Doug Woods,
EMP: 53
SQ FT: 20,000
SALES (est): 22.1MM **Privately Held**
SIC: 7359 Equipment rental & leasing

(P-14563)
OHANA PARTNERS INC (PA)
Also Called: Stuart Rental Company
454 S Abbott Ave, Milpitas (95035-5258)
PHONE.................................408 856-3220
Fax: 408 856-3233
Michael Berman, *CEO*
Andrew Sutton, *Vice Pres*
R Andrew Sutton, *Vice Pres*
Gwen Anderson, *Planning*
Marcelo Figueroa, *Opers Mgr*
EMP: 71
SALES (est): 11.2MM **Privately Held**
WEB: www.stuartrental.com
SIC: 7359 5947 Party supplies rental services; tent & tarpaulin rental; gifts & novelties

(P-14564)
P J J ENTERPRISES INC
1250 Delevan Dr, San Diego (92102-2437)
PHONE.................................619 232-6136
John Lenore, *President*
Dorothy Lenore, *Treasurer*
Roger Carey, *Director*
EMP: 70 **EST:** 1966
SQ FT: 20,000
SALES (est): 2.7MM
SALES (corp-wide): 143.9MM **Privately Held**
WEB: www.johnlenore.com
SIC: 7359 Rental store, general
PA: Lenore John & Co
  1250 Delevan Dr
  San Diego CA 92102
  619 232-6136

(P-14565)
PANAVISION INC (PA)
Also Called: Panavision Group
6101 Variel Ave, Woodland Hills (91367-3722)
PHONE.................................818 316-1000
Fax: 818 316-1111
Ronald O Perelman, *Ch of Bd*
William C Bevins, *President*
Kimberly Snyder, *CEO*
Ross Landsbaum, *COO*
Will Paice, *COO*
EMP: 440
SQ FT: 150,000
SALES (est): 202.1MM **Privately Held**
WEB: www.panastore.com
SIC: 7359 3861 3648 5063 Equipment rental & leasing; cameras & related equipment; stage lighting equipment; lighting fixtures

(P-14566)
PARKMERCED INVESTORS LLC
3711 19th Ave, San Francisco (94132-2641)
PHONE.................................877 243-5544
Bruce Ward,
Brandi Mille, *General Mgr*
Ryan Owens, *Director*
EMP: 50
SALES (est): 8.1MM **Privately Held**
SIC: 7359 Lawn & garden equipment rental

(P-14567)
PENSKE LEASING
15050 Northam St, La Mirada (90638-5757)
PHONE.................................714 522-3330
Shawna McCormick, *Manager*
Liza Bardemi, *Administration*

EMP: 80
SALES (est): 3.1MM **Privately Held**
SIC: 7359 Equipment rental & leasing

(P-14568)
PICO RENTS INC
Also Called: Pico Party Rents
13414 S Figueroa St, Los Angeles (90061-1144)
PHONE.................................310 275-9431
Fax: 323 939-3823
William Edwards Jr, *President*
Penny Rangel, *Treasurer*
Darren G Edwards, *Admin Sec*
EMP: 60
SQ FT: 24,500
SALES (est): 8.1MM **Privately Held**
WEB: www.picopartyrents.com
SIC: 7359 Party supplies rental services

(P-14569)
PINAMAR LLC
Also Called: Special Events
6909 Las Positas Rd Ste D, Livermore (94551-5113)
PHONE.................................925 243-8979
Fax: 925 243-8799
Weston Cook,
Jose Lazo, *Production*
Elizabeth Clark, *Sales Mgr*
Troy Porras, *Manager*
EMP: 60
SALES (est): 6.6MM **Privately Held**
WEB: www.pinamar.com
SIC: 7359 Party supplies rental services

(P-14570)
PRG LIGHTING
1245 Aviation Pl, San Fernando (91340-1459)
PHONE.................................818 252-1268
Susan Tesh, *Manager*
Barry Claxton, *Executive*
Tom Force, *Manager*
EMP: 50 **Privately Held**
SIC: 7359 Sound & lighting equipment rental
HQ: Prg Lighting
  8617 Ambassador Row # 120
  Dallas TX 75247
  214 630-1963

(P-14571)
PROFESSIONAL BUREAU OF COLLECT
9675 Elk Grv Florin Rd, Elk Grove (95624-2225)
PHONE.................................916 685-3399
Fax: 916 685-3729
Travis Justus, *Branch Mgr*
EMP: 115
SALES (corp-wide): 13.2MM **Privately Held**
SIC: 7359 Work zone traffic equipment (flags, cones, barrels, etc.)
PA: Professional Bureau Of Collections Of Maryland, Inc.
  5295 Dtc Pkwy
  Greenwood Village CO 80111
  303 488-2500

(P-14572)
PSAV HOLDINGS LLC
111 W Ocean Blvd Ste 1110, Long Beach (90802-4688)
PHONE.................................562 366-0138
J Michael McIlwain, *Exec Dir*
James Whitney Markowitz, *Admin Sec*
EMP: 8200
SALES (est): 98.4MM **Privately Held**
SIC: 7359 Equipment rental & leasing

(P-14573)
QUIXOTE STUDIOS LLC (PA)
Also Called: Quixote Production Vehicles
1011 N Fuller Ave, West Hollywood (90046-6651)
PHONE.................................323 851-5030
Fax: 323 851-5029
Jordan T Kitaen,
Kaye Michaelson, *CFO*
Jeff Arnone, *Vice Pres*
Michael Matus, *Info Tech Mgr*
Michael Sundstrom, *Accounting Mgr*
EMP: 50
SQ FT: 32,000

7359 - Equipment Rental & Leasing, NEC County (P-14574) — PRODUDUCTS & SERVICES SECTION

SALES (est): 22.4MM **Privately Held**
WEB: www.quixotestudios.com
SIC: 7359 Sound & lighting equipment rental

(P-14574)
R & D LEASING INC
Also Called: Blare's Air & Ground Services
19101 Kent Ave, Lemoore (93245-9137)
PHONE..................................559 924-1276
Fax: 559 924-7139
Roger Hewett, *President*
Diana Hewett, *Principal*
EMP: 67
SALES (est): 4MM **Privately Held**
SIC: 7359 Equipment rental & leasing

(P-14575)
RAPHAELS PARTY RENTALS INC (PA)
8606 Miramar Rd, San Diego (92126-4326)
PHONE..................................858 444-1692
Fax: 858 689-8040
Raphael Silverman, *President*
Phillip Silverman, *Vice Pres*
Kitty Silverman, *Admin Sec*
Theresa Canuo, *Bookkeeper*
EMP: 175
SQ FT: 60,000
SALES (est): 11.5MM **Privately Held**
WEB: www.raphaels.com
SIC: 7359 Party supplies rental services

(P-14576)
S & S PORTABLE SERVICES INC
4511 Rowland Ave, El Monte (91731-1123)
PHONE..................................626 967-9300
Sergio D Diez, *President*
EMP: 99
SALES (est): 10.8MM **Privately Held**
SIC: 7359 Equipment rental & leasing

(P-14577)
S & S RENT-A-FENCE INC
Also Called: S & S Construction Services
4511 Rowland Ave, El Monte (91731-1123)
P.O. Box 367, Glendora (91740-0367)
PHONE..................................818 896-7710
Sergio Diez, *CEO*
Steve Lakie, *Principal*
Steven R Parsell, *Principal*
EMP: 60 EST: 1978
SQ FT: 1,800
SALES (est): 5.6MM **Privately Held**
WEB: www.sandsrentafence.com
SIC: 7359 Equipment rental & leasing; portable toilet rental

(P-14578)
SEACASTLE INC
4000 Executive Pkwy # 240, San Ramon (94583-4257)
PHONE..................................925 480-3000
Kathleen Francis, *Vice Pres*
EMP: 65
SALES (corp-wide): 102MM **Privately Held**
SIC: 7359 Equipment rental & leasing
HQ: Seacastle, Inc
123 Tice Blvd Ste 210
Woodcliff Lake NJ 07677
201 391-0800

(P-14579)
SIERRA EQUIPMENT LEASING INC
Also Called: Sierra Mountain Express
1140 Suncast Ln, El Dorado Hills (95762-9313)
PHONE..................................925 676-7300
Murray Zwicker, *President*
Carol Zwicker, *Treasurer*
EMP: 50
SALES (est): 10.1MM **Privately Held**
SIC: 7359 Industrial truck rental

(P-14580)
SILICATEC RENTALS INC
800 Mossdale Rd, Lathrop (95330-8650)
P.O. Box 1429 (95330-1429)
PHONE..................................209 234-1500
Robert H Brown Sr, *President*
Jana Bolter, *Controller*
EMP: 50
SALES (est): 1.6MM **Privately Held**
SIC: 7359 Equipment rental & leasing

(P-14581)
SR BRAY LLC
Also Called: Power Plus
2750 N Perris Blvd, Perris (92571-3234)
PHONE..................................951 436-2920
Tony Maldonado, *Manager*
Nick Quinn, *Sales Mgr*
EMP: 50
SALES (corp-wide): 120.3MM **Privately Held**
SIC: 7359 Equipment rental & leasing
PA: S.R. Bray Llc
1210 N Red Gum St
Anaheim CA 92806
714 765-7551

(P-14582)
TEXTAINER EQUIPMENT MGT US LTD (DH)
650 California St Fl 16, San Francisco (94108-2720)
PHONE..................................415 434-0551
Ernest Furtado, *CFO*
Grace Young, *CFO*
Brian Hogan, *Vice Pres*
Ernest Hawkins, *Technology*
Phillip Rigling, *Manager*
EMP: 55
SQ FT: 15,000
SALES (est): 9.9MM **Privately Held**
WEB: www.textainer.com
SIC: 7359 Shipping container leasing
HQ: Textainer Group Holdings Ltd
650 California St Fl 16
San Francisco CA 94108
415 434-0551

(P-14583)
TEXTANER EQP INCOME FUND II LP
650 California St Fl 16, San Francisco (94108-2720)
PHONE..................................415 434-0551
Ernest J Furtado, *CFO*
EMP: 80
SQ FT: 15,000
SALES (est): 2.6MM **Privately Held**
SIC: 7359 Shipping container leasing

(P-14584)
TOWN & COUNTRY EVENT RENTALS (PA)
Also Called: Tacer
7725 Airport Bus Pkwy, Van Nuys (91406)
PHONE..................................818 908-4211
Fax: 818 908-4219
Richard Loguercio, *CEO*
Evan Warshawsky, *CFO*
Chris Mackey, *Vice Pres*
Sherry Stimatz, *Branch Mgr*
Camille Conroy, *Office Mgr*
EMP: 400
SQ FT: 1,100
SALES (est): 28MM **Privately Held**
WEB: www.townandcountryeventrentals.com
SIC: 7359 Party supplies rental services

(P-14585)
UNITED RENTALS NORTH AMER INC
2911 E Fremont St, Stockton (95205-3913)
P.O. Box 8810 (95208-0810)
PHONE..................................209 948-9500
Joe Doran, *Manager*
Mohammed Sayeed, *General Mgr*
Jeff Parker, *Marketing Staff*
EMP: 61
SALES (corp-wide): 5.8B **Publicly Held**
WEB: www.ur.com
SIC: 7359 Tool rental
HQ: United Rentals (North America), Inc.
100 Frist Stamford Rd
Stamford CT 06902
203 622-3131

(P-14586)
UNITED RENTALS NORTH AMER INC
3455 San Gbriel Rver Pkwy, Pico Rivera (90660-1450)
PHONE..................................562 695-0748
Donnie Richardson, *Manager*
Scott Rucinski, *Branch Mgr*
Andy Hamrock, *Financial Exec*
Annette Ramerez, *Sales Associate*
John Packard, *Sales Staff*
EMP: 125
SALES (corp-wide): 5.8B **Publicly Held**
WEB: www.unitedrentals.com
SIC: 7359 Equipment rental & leasing
HQ: United Rentals (North America), Inc.
100 Frist Stamford 700
Stamford CT 06902
203 622-3131

(P-14587)
UNITED SITE SERVICES CAL INC (PA)
242 Live Oak Ave, Irwindale (91706-1311)
PHONE..................................626 462-9110
Debbi Thornton, *Manager*
EMP: 50
SQ FT: 2,400
SALES (est): 5.4MM **Privately Held**
WEB: www.americanclassicsanitation.com
SIC: 7359 Portable toilet rental

(P-14588)
UNITED SITE SERVICES CAL INC
3408 Hillcap Ave, San Jose (95136-1306)
PHONE..................................408 295-2263
Ron Carapezzi, *CEO*
Frank Youngblood, *President*
Terence P Moriarty, *CFO*
Jim Youngblood, *Exec VP*
Dan Youngblood, *Vice Pres*
EMP: 200
SALES (est): 15.6MM
SALES (corp-wide): 724.3MM **Privately Held**
WEB: www.acmeandsons.com
SIC: 7359 Equipment rental & leasing; portable toilet rental
PA: United Site Services, Inc.
50 Washington St 1000
Westborough MA 01581
508 594-2655

(P-14589)
VCI EVENT TECHNOLOGY INC
Also Called: Videocam
1261 S Simpson Cir, Anaheim (92806-5530)
PHONE..................................714 772-2002
Toll Free:..................................888 -
Fax: 714 772-0259
Evan H Goldschlag, *President*
Kirk Rhinehart, *Vice Pres*
Patrick Phaneuf, *General Mgr*
Bryan Cook, *IT/INT Sup*
Michael Cruz, *Manager*
EMP: 166
SALES (est): 20.1MM **Privately Held**
WEB: www.videocam.net
SIC: 7359 Audio-visual equipment & supply rental

(P-14590)
WESTERN OILFIELDS SUPPLY CO (PA)
Also Called: Westside Pump
3404 State Rd, Bakersfield (93308-4538)
P.O. Box 2248 (93303-2248)
PHONE..................................661 399-9058
Fax: 661 393-1424
Robert Lake, *CEO*
Mark Lasswell, *CEO*
Maston Cunningham, *CFO*
Frank Bozarth, *Vice Pres*
Chris Lake, *Vice Pres*
EMP: 150 EST: 1934
SQ FT: 57,000
SALES (est): 15.7MM **Privately Held**
WEB: www.rainforrent.com
SIC: 7359 3523 5083 Equipment rental & leasing; farm machinery & equipment; irrigation equipment

(P-14591)
WESTERN PRECOOLING SYSTEMS
761 Commercial Ave, Oxnard (93030-7233)
PHONE..................................805 486-6371
Don Dearmond, *Branch Mgr*
EMP: 60
SALES (corp-wide): 57MM **Privately Held**
WEB: www.wpsox.com
SIC: 7359 Equipment rental & leasing
PA: Western Precooling Systems
43990 Fremont Blvd
Fremont CA 94538
510 656-2220

(P-14592)
WOW PARTY RENTAL INC
14575 Firestone Blvd, La Mirada (90638-5914)
PHONE..................................714 367-3380
Kevin Rahimi, *President*
Rodrigo Rodrigues, *Vice Pres*
EMP: 52
SQ FT: 22,000
SALES (est): 1.5MM **Privately Held**
SIC: 7359 Party supplies rental services

7361 Employment Agencies

(P-14593)
40 HRS INC
Also Called: 40 Hours Staffing
1669 Flanigan Dr, San Jose (95121-1682)
PHONE..................................408 414-0158
Bryan Phan, *President*
EMP: 60
SQ FT: 3,000
SALES (est): 34.3MM **Privately Held**
SIC: 7361 Employment agencies

(P-14594)
A S A P PROFESSIONAL SERVICES
Also Called: ASAP Professional Services
2440 Camino Ramon Ste 313, San Ramon (94583-4391)
P.O. Box 1224 (94583-6224)
PHONE..................................800 303-2727
Pam Sullivan, *President*
Matthew Feltz, *Vice Pres*
William Sullivan, *Vice Pres*
Andy Dazevedo, *Department Mgr*
Joe Sullivan, *Safety Mgr*
EMP: 80
SQ FT: 2,500
SALES (est): 4.7MM **Privately Held**
WEB: www.asapps.com
SIC: 7361 Employment agencies

(P-14595)
A-STAR STAFFING INC
2835 Camino Del Rio S # 220, San Diego (92108-3825)
PHONE..................................619 574-7600
Fax: 619 574-6700
Diana M Barnes, *President*
Daniel R Barnes, *Admin Sec*
Jessica Melton, *Admin Asst*
EMP: 250
SQ FT: 2,400
SALES (est): 11.4MM **Privately Held**
WEB: www.astarstaffing.com
SIC: 7361 7363 Employment agencies; placement agencies; help supply services; temporary help service

(P-14596)
AB CLOSING CORPORATION
Also Called: Kavaliro
1304 Southpoint Blvd, Petaluma (94954-7464)
PHONE..................................707 766-1777
Jane E Hynes, *Branch Mgr*
Marc Dimaio, *Manager*
EMP: 133
SALES (corp-wide): 25.3MM **Privately Held**
SIC: 7361 Employment agencies
PA: A.B. Closing Corporation
12001 Res Pkwy Ste 344
Orlando FL 32826
407 243-6006

PRODUCTS & SERVICES SECTION
7361 - Employment Agencies County (P-14620)

(P-14597)
ABSO
101 Creekside Ridge Ct # 2, Roseville (95678-3595)
PHONE.................................800 943-2589
Fax: 916 788-1745
William Greenblatt, *CEO*
Bradley Landin, *Vice Pres*
Natalie Voros, *Principal*
Jim Dabney, *Info Tech Mgr*
Jeniffer Hess, *Manager*
EMP: 135
SQ FT: 19,000
SALES (est): 5.8MM
SALES (corp-wide): 785.9MM **Privately Held**
WEB: www.absolutehire.com
SIC: 7361 Executive placement
PA: Sterling Infosystems, Inc.
1 State St Fl Plaza24
New York NY 10004
800 899-2272

(P-14598)
ACCELON INC
2603 Camino Ramon Ste 200, San Ramon (94583-9137)
PHONE.................................925 216-5735
Aizad Kamal, *CEO*
Unsa Kazmi Kamal, *CFO*
EMP: 50
SQ FT: 1,500
SALES (est): 2MM **Privately Held**
SIC: 7361 8742 Placement agencies; labor contractors (employment agency); construction project management consultant; business consultant

(P-14599)
ACCESS NURSES INC
5935 Cornerstone Ct W, San Diego (92121-3737)
PHONE.................................858 458-4400
Alan Braynin, *CEO*
Benjamin Greenberg, *CFO*
Thomas Johnson, *Vice Pres*
Thomas Lee, *Division Mgr*
Nicole Barbano, *Director*
EMP: 100
SQ FT: 20,000
SALES (est): 5.6MM **Privately Held**
WEB: www.accessnurses.com
SIC: 7361 Employment agencies

(P-14600)
ACT 1 GROUP INC
Agile 1
1999 W 190th St, Torrance (90504-6202)
PHONE.................................310 532-1529
Janice Bryant Howard, *CEO*
Eric Forst, *Manager*
EMP: 75
SALES (corp-wide): 294.4MM **Privately Held**
WEB: www.act-1.com
SIC: 7361 8741 Employment agencies; management services
PA: The Act 1 Group Inc
1999 W 190th St
Torrance CA 90504
310 532-1529

(P-14601)
ACT 1 GROUP INC (PA)
Also Called: Agile 1
1999 W 190th St, Torrance (90504-6202)
P.O. Box 2886 (90509-2886)
PHONE.................................310 532-1529
Fax: 310 750-1100
Janice B Howroyd, *CEO*
Bernard Howroyd, *President*
Jeff Kornreich, *CFO*
Carlton Bryant, *Exec VP*
Patricia Bryant, *Vice Pres*
EMP: 90
SQ FT: 18,026
SALES (est): 294.4MM **Privately Held**
WEB: www.act-1.com
SIC: 7361 8741 Employment agencies; administrative management

(P-14602)
ADDUS HEALTHCARE INC
817 Coffee Rd Ste B1, Modesto (95355-4241)
PHONE.................................209 526-8451
Fax: 209 574-6116
Linda Stinson, *Branch Mgr*
EMP: 100
SALES (corp-wide): 336.8MM **Publicly Held**
WEB: www.addus.com
SIC: 7361 Nurses' registry
HQ: Addus Healthcare, Inc.
2300 Warrenville Rd
Downers Grove IL 60515
630 296-3400

(P-14603)
ALL HEALTH SERVICES CORP (PA)
206 W 8th St, Hanford (93230-4532)
PHONE.................................559 583-9101
Dave Matthews, *President*
Michael Ross, *Vice Pres*
Jeremy Matthews, *Admin Sec*
Robert Garcia, *Director*
Jacquelyn Franco, *Manager*
EMP: 65
SALES: 9MM **Privately Held**
WEB: www.allhs.net
SIC: 7361 Employment agencies

(P-14604)
ALLEN LEE ROSE INC
Also Called: Legalstaff of San Diego
9370 Sky Park Ct Ste 250, San Diego (92123-5380)
PHONE.................................858 587-3100
Richard Hackett Jr, *President*
Richard Hackett Sr, *Treasurer*
Stephanie Hackett, *Vice Pres*
Deanna Hackett, *Admin Sec*
EMP: 50
SQ FT: 1,900
SALES: 3MM **Privately Held**
SIC: 7361 7812 Employment agencies; motion picture & video production

(P-14605)
ALTA HOME CARE INC
1740 W Katella Ave Ste B, Orange (92867-3434)
PHONE.................................714 744-8191
Fax: 951 346-4140
Jake Fackrell, *Branch Mgr*
EMP: 50
SALES (corp-wide): 9.2MM **Privately Held**
WEB: www.altahomecare.com
SIC: 7361 Nurses' registry
PA: Alta Home Care Inc.
1315 Crona Pinte Ct 201
Corona CA 92879
714 744-8191

(P-14606)
AMERICAN LABOR POOL INC
1725 De La Cruz Blvd # 2, Santa Clara (95050-3011)
PHONE.................................408 496-9950
Doug Boom, *Branch Mgr*
Abraham Romo, *Manager*
EMP: 50
SALES (corp-wide): 4.9MM **Privately Held**
SIC: 7361 7363 Employment agencies; temporary help service
PA: American Labor Pool Inc.
8898 Clairemont Mesa Blvd A
San Diego CA 92123
858 569-7977

(P-14607)
AMERICAN UNIQUE STAFF PROVIDER
14545 Victory Blvd # 404, Van Nuys (91411-4133)
PHONE.................................818 908-9051
Soloman Gochin, *President*
Guaga Lupe, *Manager*
EMP: 50
SQ FT: 1,600
SALES (est): 1.6MM **Privately Held**
SIC: 7361 8331 7363 Employment agencies; job training & vocational rehabilitation services; help supply services

(P-14608)
APPLE ONE SERVICE ARIZONA INC
16371 Beach Blvd Ste 22, Huntington Beach (92647-4108)
PHONE.................................714 848-2610
EMP: 94
SALES (corp-wide): 8.5MM **Privately Held**
SIC: 7361 Employment agencies
PA: Apple One Service Arizona Inc.
327 W Broadway
Glendale CA 91204
818 240-8688

(P-14609)
ASAP STAFFING INC
11 Golden Shore Ste 360, Long Beach (90802-4280)
PHONE.................................562 499-2120
Fax: 562 499-2192
Dan O Callaghan, *CEO*
F Simon Zaman, *President*
Simon F Zaman, *COO*
Christian Kelbiche, *Info Tech Mgr*
Richard Ueligitone, *Info Tech Mgr*
EMP: 50
SQ FT: 5,200
SALES (est): 2.7MM **Privately Held**
SIC: 7361 Employment agencies

(P-14610)
ASSISTED HOME RECOVERY INC (PA)
Also Called: Assisted Home Care
8550 Balboa Blvd Lbby, Northridge (91325-5808)
PHONE.................................818 894-8117
Elaine S Donley, *President*
Bill Donley, *Ch of Bd*
Jim Gladfelter, *CFO*
Steve Souza, *General Mgr*
Carolynn Cody, *Human Res Dir*
EMP: 110
SQ FT: 4,000
SALES (est): 10.9MM **Privately Held**
WEB: www.assistedca.com
SIC: 7361 Nurses' registry

(P-14611)
AYALA CORPORATION
Also Called: Ayala Farms
21510 S Chteau Fresno Ave, Riverdale (93656-9673)
P.O. Box 187 (93656-0187)
PHONE.................................559 867-5700
Piedad Ayala, *President*
Norma Chesma, *Manager*
Liona Williams, *Manager*
EMP: 150
SQ FT: 2,000
SALES (est): 9.2MM **Privately Held**
SIC: 7361 Labor contractors (employment agency)

(P-14612)
B & R FARM LABOR CONTRACTOR
422 Mockingbird Ln, Fillmore (93015-1673)
P.O. Box 366 (93016-0366)
PHONE.................................805 524-1346
Birtha Delara, *Owner*
EMP: 200
SALES (est): 7MM **Privately Held**
SIC: 7361 0761 Labor contractors (employment agency); farm labor contractors

(P-14613)
BARONHR LLC
13085 Central Ave Ste 4, Chino (91710-4184)
PHONE.................................909 517-3800
EMP: 55
SALES (corp-wide): 47.6MM **Privately Held**
SIC: 7361 Employment agencies
PA: Baronhr, Llc
8101 E Kaiser Blvd # 110
Anaheim CA 92808
714 202-8710

(P-14614)
BAY AREA TECHWORKERS
2000 Crow Canyon Pl # 150, San Ramon (94583-1383)
PHONE.................................925 359-2200
Fax: 925 359-2201
Don Peed, *CEO*
HB Drake, *Vice Pres*
Gordon Jones, *Vice Pres*
Ronald Lom, *Vice Pres*
Rob Olsen, *Vice Pres*
EMP: 400
SQ FT: 8,500
SALES (est): 52MM **Privately Held**
WEB: www.techworkers.com
SIC: 7361 Placement agencies

(P-14615)
BOILING POINT REST SCA INC
13668 Valley Blvd Unit C2, City of Industry (91746-2572)
PHONE.................................626 551-5181
CHI How Chou, *Chairman*
Michael Lin, *Vice Pres*
Christopher Brown, *Human Resources*
EMP: 300
SALES: 9.2MM **Privately Held**
SIC: 7361 Employment agencies

(P-14616)
BRENNER INFO TECH STAFFING INC
Also Called: Ocj Group, The
21300 Victory Blvd # 240, Woodland Hills (91367-2525)
PHONE.................................818 705-7500
Mark Brenner, *President*
Dave Colvin, *Manager*
EMP: 50
SQ FT: 2,150
SALES (est): 3.1MM **Privately Held**
SIC: 7361 Employment agencies

(P-14617)
BULMARO CASTRO CONTRACTORS
Also Called: Bc Contractors
349 Belden St, Gonzales (93926)
P.O. Box 779 (93926-0779)
PHONE.................................831 675-2927
Bulmaro Castro, *President*
Alicia Lopez, *Office Mgr*
EMP: 200
SQ FT: 1,500
SALES: 3.5MM **Privately Held**
SIC: 7361 0761 Labor contractors (employment agency); farm labor contractors

(P-14618)
BUSINESS CONNECTIONS
Also Called: California Search Services
332 Pine St, Red Bluff (96080-3312)
PHONE.................................530 527-6229
Fax: 530 529-2645
Lynne Moule, *Owner*
EMP: 92
SALES (est): 3.8MM **Privately Held**
SIC: 7361 7363 Employment agencies; temporary help service

(P-14619)
CAMPOS DMETRIO FRM LABOR CONTR
Also Called: Campos Dmetrio Frm Labor Contr
117 W Main St Ste 19, Woodland (95695-2988)
P.O. Box 1288 (95776-1288)
PHONE.................................530 662-4143
Demetrio Campos, *President*
EMP: 100
SQ FT: 650
SALES (est): 4.9MM **Privately Held**
SIC: 7361 0761 Labor contractors (employment agency); farm labor contractors

(P-14620)
CANOGA PARK WORKSOURCE CENTER
Also Called: Arbor Employment & Training
21010 Vanowen St, Canoga Park (91303-2804)
PHONE.................................818 596-4448
Gabe Ross, *President*
EMP: 50

7361 - Employment Agencies County (P-14621)

PRODUDUCTS & SERVICES SECTION

SALES (est): 2MM **Privately Held**
SIC: 7361 Employment agencies

(P-14621)
CARE PLUS NORTH OF SAN DIEGO
2337 Eastridge Loop, Chula Vista (91915-1111)
PHONE..............................619 421-0807
George Khoury, *Owner*
EMP: 67
SALES (est): 4MM **Privately Held**
WEB: www.careplusinternational.com
SIC: 7361 Nurses' registry

(P-14622)
CAREER GROUP INC (PA)
Also Called: Fourthfloor Fashion Talent
10100 Santa Monica Blvd # 900, Los Angeles (90067-4138)
PHONE..............................310 277-8188
Michael B Levine, *CEO*
Susan Levine, *President*
Scott H Pick, *CFO*
Sarah Mendel, *Executive Asst*
Ian Lockhart, *Credit Staff*
EMP: 2100 EST: 1980
SQ FT: 11,986
SALES (est): 88.6MM **Privately Held**
SIC: 7361 Executive placement

(P-14623)
CERTIFIED NURSING REGISTRY INC
2707 E Valley Blvd # 309, West Covina (91792-3198)
PHONE..............................626 912-1877
Maria Cristina C Sy, *President*
Wilson Sy, *Vice Pres*
Cathy Chua, *Manager*
EMP: 125
SQ FT: 2,000
SALES (est): 2.5MM **Privately Held**
SIC: 7361 Registries

(P-14624)
CHIPTON-ROSS INC (WISCONSIN)
343 Main St, El Segundo (90245-3814)
PHONE..............................310 414-7800
Sharon King, *President*
John Koch, *Accountant*
Patricia Padilla, *Human Res Mgr*
EMP: 450
SQ FT: 4,000
SALES (est): 103.1MM **Privately Held**
WEB: www.chiptonross.com
SIC: 7361 Executive placement

(P-14625)
CITY OF SUNNYVALE NOVA
505 W Olive Ave Ste 550, Sunnyvale (94086-7626)
PHONE..............................408 730-7232
Fax: 408 730-7643
Kris Stabelman, *Director*
Cathy Haynes, *Program Mgr*
Jasmine Khosravian, *Training Spec*
Luther Jackson, *Manager*
Pat Richards, *Manager*
EMP: 60 EST: 2011
SALES (est): 2.1MM **Privately Held**
SIC: 7361 Labor contractors (employment agency)

(P-14626)
CLC INCORPORATED (PA)
3001 Lava Ridge Ct # 250, Roseville (95661-2838)
PHONE..............................916 789-7600
Fax: 916 724-2228
Brad Barron, *President*
Doug Abbott, *Senior VP*
Duncan Hay, *Vice Pres*
Katie Winkler, *Vice Pres*
Joanne Hawley, *Executive Asst*
EMP: 50
SQ FT: 20,000
SALES (est): 10MM **Privately Held**
WEB: www.clclegalplans.com
SIC: 7361 Employment agencies

(P-14627)
COLONIAL HOME CARE SVCS INC
1224 E Katella Ave # 101, Orange (92867-5049)
PHONE..............................714 289-7220
Catherina Bertaina, *President*
Trevor O'Neil, *Administration*
EMP: 180
SQ FT: 1,200
SALES (est): 2.5MM **Privately Held**
WEB: www.colonialhomecareservices.com
SIC: 7361 Nurses' registry

(P-14628)
CONTEMPORARY SERVICES CORP (PA)
Also Called: C S C
17101 Superior St, Northridge (91325-1961)
PHONE..............................818 885-5150
Fax: 818 885-0609
Damon Zumwalt, *CEO*
Jim Granger, *President*
Jonathan Fleming, *COO*
Mark Camillo, *Vice Pres*
Malik Jones, *Executive*
EMP: 133
SQ FT: 20,000
SALES (est): 304.3MM **Privately Held**
WEB: www.csc-usa.com
SIC: 7361 Employment agencies

(P-14629)
CORPORATE RESOURCE SERVICES
2414 S Grove Ave, Ontario (91761-6224)
PHONE..............................909 230-4510
Phil Leblanc, *Owner*
EMP: 67
SALES (corp-wide): 663.9MM **Privately Held**
SIC: 7361 Employment agencies
PA: Corporate Resource Services, Inc.
  160 Broadway Rm 1300
  New York NY 10038
  646 443-2380

(P-14630)
COVENANT INDUSTRIES INC
Also Called: People Onesource
110 Pine Ave Ste 910, Long Beach (90802-9447)
P.O. Box 7045, La Puente (91744-7045)
PHONE..............................951 808-3708
Statney Lattin, *CEO*
Joseph Randle El, *President*
Anna Roque, *Admin Sec*
Maria Lopez, *Human Res Mgr*
Casandra Lattin, *Manager*
EMP: 75
SQ FT: 2,500
SALES (est): 4.7MM **Privately Held**
WEB: www.covenantindustries.net
SIC: 7361 Employment agencies

(P-14631)
CREATIVE CIRCLE LLC (DH)
5900 Wilshire Blvd # 1100, Los Angeles (90036-5036)
PHONE..............................323 634-0156
Lawrence Serf, *Mng Member*
Tanya Marcus, *Area Mgr*
Jamie Brasier, *Admin Asst*
Malerie Diamante, *City Mgr*
Jon Giunta, *City Mgr*
EMP: 146
SALES (est): 26.2MM
SALES (corp-wide): 2B **Publicly Held**
SIC: 7361 Employment agencies
HQ: Mscp V Cc Parent, Llc
  5900 Wilshire Blvd # 1100
  Los Angeles CA 90036
  323 634-0156

(P-14632)
CROSS COUNTRY HEALTHCARE INC
1700 Iowa Ave Ste 210, Riverside (92507-2403)
PHONE..............................951 786-7683
EMP: 95
SALES (corp-wide): 767.4MM **Publicly Held**
SIC: 7361 Employment agencies
PA: Cross Country Healthcare, Inc.
  6551 Pk Of Cmmrce Blvd Nw
  Boca Raton FL 33487
  561 998-2232

(P-14633)
CUTTING EDGE STAFFING INC
27715 Jefferson Ave, Temecula (92590-2660)
P.O. Box 1510 (92593-1510)
PHONE..............................951 587-0550
Fax: 951 587-0555
Lisa Fuess, *President*
EMP: 75
SALES (est): 3.2MM **Privately Held**
SIC: 7361 Employment agencies

(P-14634)
CVPARTNERS INC (HQ)
505 Sansome St Ste 1100, San Francisco (94111-3174)
PHONE..............................415 543-8600
Kent Gray, *President*
Nancy Gray, *Vice Pres*
Ann King, *Vice Pres*
EMP: 161
SALES (est): 7.3MM
SALES (corp-wide): 181.8MM **Privately Held**
SIC: 7361 Executive placement
PA: Addison Professional Financial Search Llc
  125 S Wacker Dr Fl 27
  Chicago IL 60606
  312 424-0300

(P-14635)
CYBERCODERS INC
Also Called: Cyberscientific
6591 Irvine Center Dr # 200, Irvine (92618-2129)
PHONE..............................949 885-5151
Heidi Golledge, *CEO*
Matt Miller, *COO*
Shane Lamb, *Senior VP*
Gino Aielli, *Executive*
Peter Bakey, *Executive*
EMP: 140
SALES (est): 23.1MM
SALES (corp-wide): 2B **Publicly Held**
WEB: www.cyberscientific.com
SIC: 7361 Executive placement
PA: On Assignment, Inc.
  26745 Malibu Hills Rd
  Calabasas CA 91301
  818 878-7900

(P-14636)
DEPLOY HR INC
5870 Stoneridge Mall Rd # 208, Pleasanton (94588-3267)
PHONE..............................925 426-1010
Larry T James, *President*
Andre Douzdjian, *CFO*
Melba Bachem, *Controller*
Nora Schild, *Assistant*
EMP: 100
SALES (est): 41.2MM **Privately Held**
SIC: 7361 Employment agencies

(P-14637)
DIRECT WAY PERSONNEL
7300 Alondra Blvd Ste 103, Paramount (90723-4000)
PHONE..............................562 531-8808
Felipe Rivas, *Owner*
▲ EMP: 70
SQ FT: 1,201
SALES (est): 2.9MM **Privately Held**
SIC: 7361 Employment agencies

(P-14638)
DIVERSE STAFFING INC
211 Imperial Hwy Ste 200, Fullerton (92835-1047)
PHONE..............................714 525-8477
Fred S Flores, *Branch Mgr*
EMP: 1173
SALES (corp-wide): 26.8MM **Privately Held**
SIC: 7361 Employment agencies
PA: Diverse Staffing, Inc.
  1800 E Lambert Rd Ste 100
  Brea CA 92821
  714 482-0499

(P-14639)
DURAN HUMAN CAPITAL PARTNERS
300 Orchard Cy Dr Ste 142, Campbell (95008)
PHONE..............................408 540-0070
James Duran, *President*
M Steve, *Recruiter*
Jo A Andre, *Sales Executive*
EMP: 50
SALES (est): 3.2MM **Privately Held**
SIC: 7361 Placement agencies

(P-14640)
E Z STAFFING INC (PA)
333 E Glenoaks Blvd # 200, Glendale (91207-2095)
PHONE..............................818 845-2500
Abraham ABI-Rafeh, *President*
Abraham Rafeh, *Exec VP*
Chadia ABI-Rafeh, *Vice Pres*
Abraham Abirafeh, *Info Tech Dir*
EMP: 298
SALES (est): 13.6MM **Privately Held**
SIC: 7361 Employment agencies

(P-14641)
EAGLE RESOURCES INC
516 W Boone St, Santa Maria (93458-5614)
P.O. Box 6510 (93456-6510)
PHONE..............................805 922-0000
Guadalupe Castillo, *President*
Daniel Castillo Jr, *Vice Pres*
EMP: 100
SQ FT: 3,600
SALES (est): 4.2MM **Privately Held**
SIC: 7361 Labor contractors (employment agency)

(P-14642)
EAST LOS ANGELES EMPLOYMENT
5301 Whittier Blvd Ste G, Los Angeles (90022-4038)
PHONE..............................323 838-5710
Manny Cons, *Manager*
EMP: 50
SALES (est): 1.3MM **Privately Held**
SIC: 7361 Employment agencies

(P-14643)
EASTRDGE PRSONNEL OF LAS VEGAS
530 Davis St, San Francisco (94111-1902)
PHONE..............................415 248-2567
EMP: 65
SALES (corp-wide): 9.3MM **Privately Held**
SIC: 7361 Employment agencies
PA: Eastridge Personnel Of Las Vegas Inc
  2355 Northside Dr Ste 120
  San Diego CA 92108
  619 260-2000

(P-14644)
EASTRDGE PRSONNEL OF LAS VEGAS (PA)
Also Called: Eastridge Infotech
2355 Northside Dr Ste 120, San Diego (92108-2714)
PHONE..............................619 260-2000
Fax: 619 285-5810
Robert Svet, *President*
Cynthia Lopez, *Managing Dir*
Rio Wagner, *Tech Recruiter*
Rick Whitaker, *CPA*
Debra Thompson, *Controller*
EMP: 50
SALES (est): 9.3MM **Privately Held**
WEB: www.eastridge-infotech.com
SIC: 7361 Employment agencies

(P-14645)
ELITE NURSING SERVICES INC
1700 E Garry Ave Ste 103, Santa Ana (92705-5828)
PHONE..............................949 475-0700
Fax: 949 475-0701
Lee Hadfield, *President*
EMP: 50
SALES: 2.3MM **Privately Held**
SIC: 7361 Nurses' registry

PRODUCTS & SERVICES SECTION
7361 - Employment Agencies County (P-14670)

(P-14646)
ELITECARE MEDICAL STAFFING LLC
761 E Locust Ave Ste 103, Fresno (93720-3023)
PHONE..................................559 438-7700
Fax: 559 446-2170
Steve Poggi,
Stacey Green, *Opers Mgr*
EMP: 60
SALES (est): 3.2MM **Privately Held**
SIC: 7361 Nurses' registry

(P-14647)
ELVIRA SANDOVAL
Also Called: Sandoval Labor Contractor
2154 Hill Rd, Williams (95987-5123)
P.O. Box 81 (95987-0081)
PHONE..................................530 473-5718
Elvira Sandoval, *Owner*
EMP: 170 **EST:** 1985
SALES (est): 7.4MM **Privately Held**
SIC: 7361 Employment agencies

(P-14648)
EMPLOYMENT DEV CAL DEPT
Also Called: Workforce Resource Center
1410 S Broadway Ste E, Santa Maria (93454-6971)
PHONE..................................805 614-1550
Fax: 805 614-1230
Judy Kelley, *Branch Mgr*
Andrea McGrath, *Chief Mktg Ofcr*
EMP: 100 **Privately Held**
WEB: www.mpic.org
SIC: 7361 9441 8331 7338 Employment agencies; administration of social & manpower programs; ; job training & vocational rehabilitation services; secretarial & court reporting
HQ: California Department Of Employment Development
800 Capitol Mall 83
Sacramento CA 95814
916 654-8210

(P-14649)
EMPLOYMENT DEV CAL DEPT
Also Called: Edd Payroll Services
751 N St Fl 6, Sacramento (95814-4763)
P.O. Box 826880 (94280-0001)
PHONE..................................916 654-7867
Tina Campbell, *Chief*
Harish Kumar, *Accounting Dir*
EMP: 100 **Privately Held**
WEB: www.mpic.org
SIC: 7361 9441 Employment agencies; administration of social & manpower programs;
HQ: California Department Of Employment Development
800 Capitol Mall 83
Sacramento CA 95814
916 654-8210

(P-14650)
EMPLOYMENT DEV CAL DEPT
1550 W Main St, El Centro (92243-2105)
P.O. Box 3187 (92244-3187)
PHONE..................................760 339-2709
Norma Jauregui, *Manager*
EMP: 50 **Privately Held**
WEB: www.mpic.org
SIC: 7361 9441 Employment agencies; administration of social & manpower programs;
HQ: California Department Of Employment Development
800 Capitol Mall 83
Sacramento CA 95814
916 654-8210

(P-14651)
EMPOLYMENT DEVELOPMENT DEPT
750 N St, Sacramento (95814)
PHONE..................................916 653-2065
Patrick Henning, *Owner*
Ellen Morton, *Analyst*
EMP: 99
SALES (est): 3.7MM **Privately Held**
SIC: 7361 Employment agencies

(P-14652)
ESPARZA ENTERPRISES INC (PA)
3851 Fruitvale Ave Ste A, Bakersfield (93308-5111)
PHONE..................................661 831-0002
Luis Esparza, *President*
Irene Borland, *Controller*
EMP: 50
SQ FT: 4,800
SALES (est): 56.6MM **Privately Held**
WEB: www.esparzaenterprises.com
SIC: 7361 7363 Labor contractors (employment agency); help supply services

(P-14653)
ESPARZA ENTERPRISES INC
3851 Fruitvale Ave A, Bakersfield (93308-5111)
PHONE..................................661 831-0002
Irene Borland, *Manager*
EMP: 55
SALES (corp-wide): 56.6MM **Privately Held**
WEB: www.esparzaenterprises.com
SIC: 7361 Labor contractors (employment agency)
PA: Esparza Enterprises, Inc.
3851 Fruitvale Ave Ste A
Bakersfield CA 93308
661 831-0002

(P-14654)
ESPARZA ENTERPRISES INC
51335 Harrison St Ste 112, Coachella (92236-1528)
PHONE..................................760 398-0349
Manuel Padilla, *Manager*
EMP: 230
SALES (corp-wide): 56.6MM **Privately Held**
SIC: 7361 Employment agencies
PA: Esparza Enterprises, Inc.
3851 Fruitvale Ave Ste A
Bakersfield CA 93308
661 831-0002

(P-14655)
FINEZI INC
31080 Blvd Ste 212, Union City (94587)
PHONE..................................510 790-4768
Madhu Puttur, *President*
Vijendra Shetty, *Technology*
Dhanraj Devadiga, *Recruiter*
Manjunath Hebbar, *Recruiter*
Vikas Naik, *Recruiter*
EMP: 90
SALES (est): 5.5MM **Privately Held**
SIC: 7361 8742 Executive placement; management consulting services

(P-14656)
FIRST CALL NURSING SVCS INC
1313 N Milpitas Blvd # 210, Milpitas (95035-3182)
PHONE..................................408 262-1533
Fax: 408 941-9458
Franklin Camillo, *CEO*
Celina Salazar-Camillo, *President*
Celina Salazar, *CFO*
Celina Camillo, *General Mgr*
EMP: 180
SALES (est): 10.4MM **Privately Held**
WEB: www.firstcallnursingservices.com
SIC: 7361 Nurses' registry

(P-14657)
FOSTER MOORE INC
650 Page Mill Rd, Palo Alto (94304-1001)
PHONE..................................650 819-3042
Stephen Robb, *Manager*
Joel Foster, *CEO*
EMP: 99 **EST:** 2012
SALES (est): 4.2MM **Privately Held**
SIC: 7361 Registries

(P-14658)
FOWLER LABOR SERVICE INC
633 W Fresno St, Fowler (93625-9697)
PHONE..................................559 834-3723
Fax: 559 834-5949
EMP: 300
SQ FT: 3,250
SALES (est): 8.8MM **Privately Held**
SIC: 7361 0783

(P-14659)
FUENTES FARMS AG INC
2346 Glen Ave, Merced (95340-4059)
PHONE..................................209 722-7201
Edward Fuentes, *President*
EMP: 500
SALES (est): 13.8MM **Privately Held**
SIC: 7361 7363 0761 Labor contractors (employment agency); help supply services; farm labor contractors

(P-14660)
GARICH INC (PA)
Also Called: The Tristaff Group
6336 Greenwich Dr Ste A, San Diego (92122-5922)
PHONE..................................858 453-1331
Fax: 858 453-6022
Gary O Van Eik, *President*
Rick Kail, *COO*
Amy Moser, *Vice Pres*
Alex Papike, *Vice Pres*
Chris Papike, *Vice Pres*
EMP: 295
SQ FT: 9,000
SALES (est): 40.3MM **Privately Held**
SIC: 7361 8742 Employment agencies; management consulting services

(P-14661)
GARICH INC
Also Called: Tristaff Group
504 E Alvarado St Ste 201, Fallbrook (92028-2364)
PHONE..................................951 302-4750
Fax: 714 513-9401
Trevor Nevis, *Manager*
EMP: 365
SALES (corp-wide): 40.3MM **Privately Held**
SIC: 7361 Employment agencies
PA: Garich Inc
6336 Greenwich Dr Ste A
San Diego CA 92122
858 453-1331

(P-14662)
GLOBAL HORIZONS INC
Also Called: Domestic Horizons
468 N Camden Dr Ste 200, Beverly Hills (90210-4507)
PHONE..................................310 234-8475
Mordechai Orian, *President*
Robert Rutt, *CFO*
EMP: 400
SALES (est): 14.6MM **Privately Held**
WEB: www.gmpusa.com
SIC: 7361 Labor contractors (employment agency)

(P-14663)
GLOBAL STAFFING INC
Also Called: G T Global Staffing
5301 Beethoven St Ste 101, Los Angeles (90066-7066)
P.O. Box 33025, Denver CO (80233-0025)
PHONE..................................303 451-5602
Fax: 303 451-5642
Ronald M Telanoff, *CEO*
Debbie Westmoreland, *Admin Sec*
EMP: 200
SALES (est): 6.7MM **Privately Held**
WEB: www.gtglobalstaffing.com
SIC: 7361 7363 Employment agencies; temporary help service

(P-14664)
GO-STAFF INC
9878 Complex Dr, Oceanside (92054)
PHONE..................................760 730-8520
EMP: 2443
SALES (corp-wide): 44.5MM **Privately Held**
SIC: 7361 Employment agencies
PA: Go-Staff, Inc.
8798 Complex Dr
San Diego CA 92123
858 292-8562

(P-14665)
GRANITE SOLUTIONS GROUPE INC
235 Montgomery St Ste 430, San Francisco (94104-2907)
P.O. Box 3399, Diamond Springs (95619-3399)
PHONE..................................415 963-3999
Daniel Hector L'Abbe, *CEO*
Ann Bauer, *CFO*
John Henning, *Vice Pres*
Dana Ziegler, *Admin Asst*
Kara King, *Accounts Mgr*
EMP: 100
SQ FT: 3,582
SALES (est): 8.3MM **Privately Held**
WEB: www.granitesolutionsgroup.com
SIC: 7361 Executive placement

(P-14666)
GROWERS COMPANY INC
21570 Potter Rd, Salinas (93908-9727)
P.O. Box 6217 (93912-6217)
PHONE..................................831 424-3850
Jesse Garcia, *Director*
EMP: 100
SALES (corp-wide): 20MM **Privately Held**
WEB: www.thegrowerscompany.com
SIC: 7361 Labor contractors (employment agency)
PA: The Growers Company Inc
15834 S Avenue G
Somerton AZ 85350
928 627-8080

(P-14667)
GTE CORPORATION
Also Called: Verizon
1800 Solar Dr, Oxnard (93030-2655)
PHONE..................................805 988-5760
Tina Curts, *Principal*
EMP: 900
SALES (corp-wide): 131.6B **Publicly Held**
WEB: www.gte.com
SIC: 7361 Employment agencies
HQ: Gte Corporation
140 West St
New York NY 10007
212 395-1000

(P-14668)
HARDESTY LLC (PA)
19800 Macar Boule Ste 820, Irvine (92612)
PHONE..................................949 407-6625
Karl Hardesty, *CEO*
Natl Arthur Cohen, *Partner*
Dan Corredor, *Partner*
Skip D'Orazio, *Partner*
David Tiffany, *Managing Dir*
EMP: 50
SQ FT: 5,000
SALES: 6MM **Privately Held**
SIC: 7361 Executive placement

(P-14669)
HARVEST TECHNICAL SERVICE INC
1839 Ygnacio Valley Rd # 390, Walnut Creek (94598-3214)
PHONE..................................925 937-4874
Fax: 925 937-8090
Judy Fick, *President*
Chris Fick, *Admin Sec*
Carla Adcock, *HR Admin*
Samantha Gatewood, *Recruiter*
Jen Lindsey, *Recruiter*
EMP: 150 **EST:** 1997
SQ FT: 1,000
SALES (est): 8.6MM **Privately Held**
WEB: www.harvtech.com
SIC: 7361 Employment agencies

(P-14670)
HEIDRICK & STRUGGLES INTL INC
1 California St Ste 2400, San Francisco (94111-5435)
PHONE..................................415 981-2854
Fax: 415 981-0482
Lee Hanson, *Branch Mgr*
Regina Oconnell, *Executive Asst*
Jenny Torres, *Admin Asst*
Thomas Friel, *Director*

Robert Knowling, *Director*
EMP: 55
SALES (corp-wide): 548.3MM **Publicly Held**
WEB: www.heidrick.com
SIC: 7361 Employment agencies
PA: Heidrick & Struggles International, Inc.
233 S Wacker Dr Ste 4900
Chicago IL 60606
312 496-1200

(P-14671)
HIRED HANDS INC
1754 2nd St Ste D, NAPA (94559-2452)
PHONE 707 265-6400
April Jacek, *Branch Mgr*
EMP: 127
SALES (corp-wide): 4.4MM **Privately Held**
SIC: 7361 Employment agencies
PA: Hired Hands Inc
10 Commercial Blvd # 102
Novato CA 94949
415 884-4343

(P-14672)
HOLISTIC APPROACH INC
Also Called: Holistic Approach HM Hlth Care
4505 Precissi Ln Ste B, Stockton (95207-6240)
PHONE 209 956-7050
Alice Sepulveda, *President*
Julian Sepulveda, *CFO*
Mary J Sepulveda, *Exec Dir*
Mary Supelvede, *Exec Dir*
Sylvia Sanchez, *Admin Sec*
EMP: 80
SQ FT: 6,000
SALES (est): 3.6MM **Privately Held**
SIC: 7361 8082 Nurses' registry; home health care services

(P-14673)
HORIZON GOVERNMENT SVCS INC
4600 Northgate Blvd # 120, Sacramento (95834-1159)
PHONE 916 760-7913
Hasnain Ali, *CEO*
EMP: 80
SALES (est): 1.7MM **Privately Held**
SIC: 7361 Nurses' registry

(P-14674)
HOWARD FISCHER ASSOCIATES INC
254 E Hacienda Ave, Campbell (95008-6617)
PHONE 408 374-0580
Howard Fisher, *President*
Theodore Stein, *Vice Pres*
EMP: 50 EST: 1977
SALES (est): 2.7MM **Privately Held**
SIC: 7361 Executive placement

(P-14675)
HOWROYD-WRIGHT EMPLYMNT AGCY (HQ)
Also Called: Apple One Employment
327 W Broadway, Glendale (91204-1301)
PHONE 818 240-8688
Janice Bryant Howroyd, *CEO*
Bernard Howroyd, *President*
Michael Hoyal, *CFO*
Bill Lindsay, *Division VP*
Rachel Borowski, *Vice Pres*
EMP: 175
SQ FT: 27,000
SALES (est): 122.7MM
SALES (corp-wide): 294.4MM **Privately Held**
WEB: www.appleone.com
SIC: 7361 Labor contractors (employment agency); executive placement
PA: The Act 1 Group Inc
1999 W 190th St
Torrance CA 90504
310 532-1529

(P-14676)
HOWROYD-WRIGHT EMPLYMNT AGCY
Also Called: Appleone Employment Services
327 W Broadway, Glendale (91204-1301)
PHONE 818 240-8688

Fax: 800 539-2228
Marie Rounsavell, *Manager*
Michael A Hoyal, *Exec VP*
Suzanne Jolcover, *Branch Mgr*
Megan Kennedy, *Branch Mgr*
Joi Biggers, *Office Admin*
EMP: 120
SALES (corp-wide): 294.4MM **Privately Held**
WEB: www.appleone.com
SIC: 7361 Labor contractors (employment agency)
HQ: Howroyd-Wright Employment Agency, Inc.
327 W Broadway
Glendale CA 91204
818 240-8688

(P-14677)
HYRIAN LLC
2355 Westwood Blvd, Los Angeles (90064-2109)
PHONE 212 590-2567
Daniel Solmons,
Martin Brody, *CFO*
Pauline Kwan, *Exec VP*
Kris Ellenberg, *Vice Pres*
Jason Berkowitz,
EMP: 110
SQ FT: 15,000
SALES (est): 4.3MM **Privately Held**
SIC: 7361 Employment agencies

(P-14678)
IDC TECHNOLOGIES INC
1851 Mccarthy Blvd # 116, Milpitas (95035-7448)
PHONE 408 376-0212
Prateek Gattani, *President*
Yogen Malvia, *CFO*
Aparna Shukla, *Executive*
Roma Singh, *Managing Dir*
Sangita Pandey, *General Mgr*
EMP: 200
SQ FT: 4,000
SALES (est): 33.6MM **Privately Held**
SIC: 7361 Placement agencies

(P-14679)
IGATE CORPORATION
Chen & McGinley
1 Market Plz Ste 1800, San Francisco (94105-1018)
PHONE 415 836-8800
Fax: 415 356-1464
Myriam Chen, *Branch Mgr*
Vickie Fan, *COO*
David Mysona, *Manager*
EMP: 260
SALES (corp-wide): 277.5MM **Privately Held**
SIC: 7361 Employment agencies; labor contractors (employment agency)
HQ: Igate Corporation
100 Somerset Corp Blvd # 5000
Bridgewater NJ 08807
908 219-8050

(P-14680)
IMPACT LOGISTICS
1155 S Milliken Ave Ste I, Ontario (91761-8158)
PHONE 909 937-9035
Fax: 909 937-0223
David Hamilton, *Principal*
EMP: 50
SALES (est): 1.6MM **Privately Held**
WEB: www.impactlogistics.com
SIC: 7361 Labor contractors (employment agency)

(P-14681)
IMPACT SOLUTIONS LLC
3604 Ocean Ranch Blvd, Oceanside (92056-2669)
PHONE 760 231-0450
Toby Copeland,
EMP: 50
SQ FT: 3,000
SALES: 3.1MM **Privately Held**
SIC: 7361 Employment agencies

(P-14682)
INCLINE INCORPORATED
Also Called: Hireforces
560 S Winchester Blvd # 500, San Jose (95128-2500)
PHONE 408 454-1140
Ray Ghamous, *President*
Kevin Foder, *Personnel*
EMP: 120
SALES (est): 4.6MM **Privately Held**
WEB: www.inclineinc.com
SIC: 7361 Labor contractors (employment agency)

(P-14683)
INDOSYS CORPORATION
3315 San Felipe Rd Ste 37, San Jose (95135-2000)
PHONE 408 705-1953
Sunil Kumar Bagai, *President*
Naina Bagai, *Vice Pres*
Sanjay Sarkar, *Tech Recruiter*
Prathvi Shetty, *Tech Recruiter*
Rajeev Kumar, *Finance Mgr*
EMP: 140
SALES: 2.4MM **Privately Held**
WEB: www.indosys.com
SIC: 7361 Employment agencies

(P-14684)
INDUSTRIAL LABOR MGT GROUP INC
Also Called: Ilm Group, The
647 E E St Ste 105, Ontario (91764-4200)
PHONE 323 582-4100
Fax: 323 582-8314
Gina Mendoza, *CEO*
Georgina Mendoza, *Owner*
Andrea Banuelos, *Manager*
Dolores Domez, *Manager*
EMP: 250
SQ FT: 2,000
SALES (est): 12.4MM **Privately Held**
SIC: 7361 Employment agencies

(P-14685)
INNOVTIVE SCNTFIC SLUTIONS INC
Also Called: Innovative Staffing Resources
17581 Irvine Blvd Ste 202, Tustin (92780-3124)
PHONE 714 508-8620
Arlene Key Auster, *CEO*
Keith A Fiscus, *COO*
Anita Schoen, *Treasurer*
Paul Chadman, *Vice Pres*
Darius Farrelly, *Vice Pres*
EMP: 120
SQ FT: 1,518
SALES: 7MM **Privately Held**
WEB: www.innstaff.com
SIC: 7361 Employment agencies

(P-14686)
INTERNET BOOKING AGENCYCOM INC
Also Called: Santa For Hire.com
232 Via Eboli, Newport Beach (92663-4604)
PHONE 949 673-7707
Robert Mindte, *CEO*
Felicia Mindte, *COO*
Donna Camp, *Opers Mgr*
EMP: 500
SQ FT: 1,700
SALES (est): 16MM **Privately Held**
WEB: www.hireasanta.com
SIC: 7361 7922 Employment agencies; theatrical producers & services

(P-14687)
INTERNTIONAL LONGSHORE WHSE UN
Also Called: Ilwu Local 46
Bldng 608 Port Heneme Hbr, Port Hueneme (93041)
P.O. Box 100 (93044-0100)
PHONE 805 488-2944
Fax: 805 488-1242
Larry Carlton, *Manager*
EMP: 100

SALES (corp-wide): 7.4MM **Privately Held**
WEB: www.ilwu10.org
SIC: 7361 4491 Labor contractors (employment agency); marine cargo handling
PA: International Longshore & Warehouse Union
1188 Franklin St Fl 4
San Francisco CA 94109
415 775-0533

(P-14688)
JACKIE HOOFRING
Also Called: Avalon Staffing
3390 Auto Mall Dr, Westlake Village (91362-3629)
PHONE 818 961-7272
Jackie Hoofring, *Owner*
EMP: 50
SQ FT: 200
SALES: 1MM **Privately Held**
SIC: 7361 Employment agencies

(P-14689)
JOSEPHINES PROF STAFFING (PA)
Also Called: Josephine's Personnel Services
2158 Ringwood Ave, San Jose (95131-1720)
PHONE 408 943-0111
Josephine Hughes, *President*
Victoria Picard, *Administration*
Melanie Abuyo, *Accounting Mgr*
Ellen Burrell, *HR Admin*
EMP: 225
SQ FT: 4,000
SALES (est): 11.1MM **Privately Held**
WEB: www.jps-inc.com
SIC: 7361 8742 8721 7363 Employment agencies; management consulting services; accounting, auditing & bookkeeping; help supply services

(P-14690)
JST FONTANA
16730 Arrow Blvd, Fontana (92335-3802)
PHONE 909 854-4062
Anthony Luck, *Manager*
EMP: 65
SALES (est): 3.3MM **Privately Held**
SIC: 7361 Employment agencies

(P-14691)
JUNO HEALTHCARE REGISTRY INC
4401 Wilshire Blvd # 230, Los Angeles (90010-3703)
PHONE 323 937-7210
Nonita Teodoro, *CEO*
Dante Raul Teodoro, *Shareholder*
EMP: 98 EST: 2008
SALES (est): 3.2MM **Privately Held**
SIC: 7361 Nurses' registry

(P-14692)
KENT DANIELS & ASSOCIATES INC
Also Called: Daniels Kent Personnel Agency
100 N Citrus St Ste 435, West Covina (91791-1655)
PHONE 626 859-5018
Fax: 626 962-3200
Kimberly Ann Feith, *President*
Rick Feith, *Vice Pres*
Laura Vieyra, *HR Admin*
Madeline Zapanta, *Recruiter*
Susan Martin, *Manager*
EMP: 150
SALES: 1MM **Privately Held**
WEB: www.kentdaniels.com
SIC: 7361 Employment agencies

(P-14693)
KFORCE INC
4510 Executive Dr Ste 325, San Diego (92121-3069)
PHONE 858 550-1645
Fax: 858 552-9071
Maryland Kaforey, *Manager*
EMP: 66
SALES (corp-wide): 1.3B **Publicly Held**
WEB: www.kforce.com
SIC: 7361 Employment agencies

PRODUCTS & SERVICES SECTION

7361 - Employment Agencies County (P-14716)

PA: Kforce Inc.
1001 E Palm Ave
Tampa FL 33605
813 552-5000

(P-14694)
KINETICOM INC (PA)
701 B St Ste 1350, San Diego (92101-8170)
PHONE 619 330-3100
Michael Wager, *CEO*
Casey Marquand, *CFO*
Blair Bode, *Vice Pres*
William Coyman, *Vice Pres*
Michael Steadman, *Vice Pres*
EMP: 92
SQ FT: 6,000
SALES (est): 32MM **Privately Held**
WEB: www.kineticom.com
SIC: 7361 Employment agencies

(P-14695)
LA JOLLA NURSES HOME CARE
2223 Avenida De La Playa, La Jolla (92037-3200)
PHONE 858 454-9339
Fax: 760 454-5010
Brittany Solerno, *Director*
William J Mara, *Chairman*
Martin Murphy, *Treasurer*
Sonia Cantor, *Personnel*
Billie Davis, *VP Opers*
EMP: 240
SALES (est): 2.2MM
SALES (corp-wide): 6.5MM **Privately Held**
WEB: www.carehealthservices.com
SIC: 7361 8742 8082 Nurses' registry; management consulting services; home health care services
PA: Care Health Services, Inc
2290 10th Ave N Ste 304
Lake Worth FL 33461
561 433-8800

(P-14696)
LAUREL LABOR SERVICES INC
727 Richmind Ct, Santa Maria (93455-7133)
P.O. Box 5792 (93456-5792)
PHONE 805 928-0113
Lucy Laurel, *President*
Marianita Edralin, *Office Mgr*
EMP: 99
SQ FT: 950
SALES (est): 4.5MM **Privately Held**
SIC: 7361 Employment agencies

(P-14697)
LOAN ADMINISTRATION NETWRK INC
Also Called: Lani
18952 Macarthur Blvd # 315, Irvine (92612-1401)
PHONE 949 752-5246
Fax: 949 752-5329
Charlene Nichols, *President*
Catherine L Anderson, *Vice Pres*
Thomas A Seavey, *Managing Dir*
Susana Moreno, *Admin Asst*
Mila Fernandez, *Accounting Mgr*
EMP: 100
SALES (est): 5.9MM **Privately Held**
WEB: www.lani.com
SIC: 7361 8742 Employment agencies; financial consultant; training & development consultant; banking & finance consultant

(P-14698)
LONG BEACH UNIFIED SCHOOL DST
Also Called: Long Bch Unfied Schl Dst Lbusd
999 Atlantic Ave Fl 3, Long Beach (90813-4514)
PHONE 562 491-1281
Ramon Curiel, *Branch Mgr*
EMP: 331
SALES (corp-wide): 810.4MM **Privately Held**
SIC: 7361 Employment agencies
PA: Long Beach Unified School District
1515 Hughes Way
Long Beach CA 90810
562 997-8000

(P-14699)
LUIS ESPARZA SERVICES INC
183 Hwy 33, Maricopa (93252)
PHONE 661 766-2344
Luis Esparza, *President*
EMP: 500
SALES (est): 7MM **Privately Held**
SIC: 7361 8631 Labor contractors (employment agency); labor unions & similar labor organizations

(P-14700)
M C M HARVESTERS INC
1585 Lirio Ave, Ventura (93004-3227)
P.O. Box 4731 (93007-0731)
PHONE 805 659-6833
Dennis Mc Murray, *President*
EMP: 300
SQ FT: 4,000
SALES (est): 9.4MM **Privately Held**
SIC: 7361 Labor contractors (employment agency)

(P-14701)
MAGANA LABOR SERVICES
2896 W Telegraph Rd, Fillmore (93015-9642)
PHONE 805 524-0446
Fax: 805 524-0446
Juvenal Magana, *Owner*
Rowe Burgett, *Manager*
EMP: 200
SALES (est): 9.4MM **Privately Held**
SIC: 7361 8631 Labor contractors (employment agency); labor unions & similar labor organizations

(P-14702)
MED-LINK NURSING SERVICES INC
1307 W 6th St Ste 121, Corona (92882-1642)
PHONE 951 279-6333
Larry Latinwo, *CEO*
Olayinka Latinwo, *Admin Sec*
EMP: 100 **EST:** 2005
SQ FT: 1,000
SALES (est): 3.3MM **Privately Held**
SIC: 7361 Employment agencies

(P-14703)
MEGA FARM LABOR SERVICES INC
110 S Montclair St # 103, Bakersfield (93309-3118)
P.O. Box 744, Delano (93216-0744)
PHONE 661 229-8077
Belen Casimiro, *President*
EMP: 151
SALES (est): 4.4MM **Privately Held**
SIC: 7361 Labor contractors (employment agency)

(P-14704)
MHS CUSTOMER SERVICE INC
7586 Trade St Ste C, San Diego (92121-2427)
PHONE 858 695-2151
Fax: 858 695-2361
Don T Fryer, *President*
Theresa Phebes, *Vice Pres*
Kip Meyer, *Project Mgr*
Cameron Thompson, *Project Mgr*
Denise Meyer, *VP Finance*
EMP: 75
SQ FT: 8,600
SALES (est): 6.3MM **Privately Held**
SIC: 7361 1542 1531 7299 Labor contractors (employment agency); nonresidential construction; operative builders; handyman service

(P-14705)
MID-VALLEY LABOR SERVICES INC
19358 Avenue 18 1/2, Madera (93637-9709)
P.O. Box 899 (93639-0899)
PHONE 559 661-6390
Fax: 559 661-0574
Samuel Mascarenas, *President*
Ben Mascarenas, *CFO*
EMP: 500
SQ FT: 2,132
SALES: 27MM **Privately Held**
WEB: www.midvalleybirthingservices.com
SIC: 7361 Labor contractors (employment agency)

(P-14706)
NETPOLARITY INC
900 E Campbell Ave, Campbell (95008-2366)
PHONE 408 971-1100
Fax: 408 971-0806
Haixia Zhang, *CEO*
David Chuang, *President*
Cathleen Lariviere, *General Mgr*
Nathan Chase, *CTO*
Rakesh Agarwal, *Tech Recruiter*
EMP: 500
SQ FT: 5,000
SALES (est): 54.6MM **Privately Held**
WEB: www.netpolarity.com
SIC: 7361 Employment agencies

(P-14707)
NETSOURCE INC
5955 Geary Blvd, San Francisco (94121-2006)
P.O. Box 590665 (94159-0665)
PHONE 415 831-3681
Lana Bondar, *President*
Riva Bondar, *Treasurer*
Eren Bondar, *Controller*
EMP: 55
SALES: 6MM **Privately Held**
WEB: www.netsourceweb.com
SIC: 7361 Employment agencies

(P-14708)
NORTHWEST STAFFING RESOURCES
Also Called: Resource Staffing Group
701 University Ave # 120, Sacramento (95825-6700)
PHONE 916 960-2668
Fax: 916 960-2669
Windy Richard, *Manager*
Amber Villegas, *Manager*
EMP: 1097
SALES (corp-wide): 140.2MM **Privately Held**
WEB: www.nwstaffing.com
SIC: 7361 7363 Labor contractors (employment agency); temporary help service
PA: Northwest Staffing Resources, Inc.
851 Sw 6th Ave Ste 300
Portland OR 97204
503 323-9190

(P-14709)
NOVATIME TECHNOLOGY INC (PA)
1440 Bridgegate Dr # 300, Diamond Bar (91765-3932)
PHONE 909 895-8100
Fax: 323 980-1878
Frank Su, *President*
Ian Sexton, *Senior VP*
Gil Sidhom, *Vice Pres*
Dharmesh Shah, *Administration*
Andri Gunawan, *Software Dev*
EMP: 60
SQ FT: 6,000
SALES (est): 24.9MM **Privately Held**
WEB: www.novatime.com
SIC: 7361 Executive placement

(P-14710)
NPH MEDICAL SERVICES
Also Called: Nurses & Prof Hlth Care
2639 Forest Ave Ste 110, Chico (95928-4393)
PHONE 530 899-2255
SIS Gilmore, *President*
Jim Gilmore, *Vice Pres*
EMP: 76
SALES: 80K **Privately Held**
SIC: 7361 Nurses' registry

(P-14711)
NURSE PROVIDERS INC
Also Called: Nursing Registry
355 Gellert Blvd Ste 110, Daly City (94015-2668)
PHONE 650 992-8559
Fax: 650 301-3257
Sherri Burke, *President*
EMP: 800
SQ FT: 1,400
SALES (est): 19.3MM **Privately Held**
SIC: 7361 Nurses' registry

(P-14712)
NURSEFINDERS LLC
1832 Commercenter Cir B, San Bernardino (92408-3430)
PHONE 909 890-2286
Toll Free: .... 877 -
Fax: 909 890-2346
Diane Booth, *Manager*
EMP: 150
SALES (corp-wide): 1.4B **Publicly Held**
WEB: www.nursefinders.com
SIC: 7361 7363 Employment agencies; temporary help service
HQ: Nursefinders, Llc
12400 High Bluff Dr
San Diego CA 92130
858 314-7427

(P-14713)
NURSEFINDERS LLC (HQ)
12400 High Bluff Dr, San Diego (92130-3077)
P.O. Box 919024 (92191-9024)
PHONE 858 314-7427
Susan Salka, *CEO*
Ralph S Henderson, *President*
Denise L Jackson, *Senior VP*
John Dillon, *Finance*
Ryan Anne, *Human Res Mgr*
EMP: 110
SQ FT: 22,000
SALES (est): 83.2MM
SALES (corp-wide): 1.4B **Publicly Held**
WEB: www.nursefinders.com
SIC: 7361 8082 7363 8049 Employment agencies; home health care services; help supply services; temporary help service; nurses, registered & practical
PA: Amn Healthcare Services, Inc.
12400 High Bluff Dr
San Diego CA 92130
866 871-8519

(P-14714)
ODESK CORPORATION
Also Called: Elance-Odesk
441 Logue Ave, Mountain View (94043-4018)
PHONE 650 853-4100
Fax: 650 853-4101
Gary Swart, *President*
Jeff Jackson, *President*
Nilesh Lakhani, *CFO*
Shoshana Deutschkron, *Comms Dir*
Michelle Anderson, *Software Dev*
EMP: 50
SQ FT: 16,000
SALES (est): 5.7MM **Privately Held**
SIC: 7361 7371 Employment agencies; computer software development & applications

(P-14715)
OFFICEWORKS INC
11801 Pierce St Fl 2, Riverside (92505-4400)
PHONE 951 784-2534
EMP: 57
SALES (corp-wide): 18.3MM **Privately Held**
SIC: 7361 Employment agencies
PA: Officeworks, Inc.
5877 Pine Ave Ste 250
Chino Hills CA 91709
818 758-1555

(P-14716)
ORANGE COUNTY ONE STOP CENTER
Also Called: Coastal Community College
5405 Grdn Rd Blvd Ste 100, Westminster (92683)
PHONE 714 241-4900
Lois Wilkerson, *Director*
EMP: 55
SALES (est): 1.9MM **Privately Held**
WEB: www.coastalcommunitycollege.com
SIC: 7361 8742 Employment agencies; human resource consulting services

7361 - Employment Agencies County (P-14717)

(P-14717)
P & P AGRILABOR
Highway 101 Floretta Rd, Chualar (93925)
PHONE 831 679-2307
P Concepcion Baclig, *Owner*
Purisima Concepcion Baclig, *Owner*
EMP: 80
SALES (est): 2.1MM **Privately Held**
SIC: 7361 Labor contractors (employment agency)

(P-14718)
PACIFIC GTWY WRKFRCE PRTNR INC
3447 Atlantic Ave, Long Beach (90807-4513)
PHONE 562 570-3700
Nick Schultz, *Exec Dir*
EMP: 50
SALES (est): 1.6MM **Privately Held**
SIC: 7361 Labor contractors (employment agency)

(P-14719)
PACIFIC RIM RSRCES SEARCH AGCY
14148 Brookhurst St, Garden Grove (92843-4656)
PHONE 714 638-0307
Trang Diem Tran, *Owner*
EMP: 200
SALES (est): 6.5MM **Privately Held**
WEB: www.prresources.net
SIC: 7361 Employment agencies

(P-14720)
PARADIGM STAFFING SOLUTIONS
1970 Broadway Ste 615, Oakland (94612-2218)
PHONE 510 663-7860
Fax: 510 663-7866
Kelvin Marshall, *President*
Christina Van Buskirk, *Recruiter*
EMP: 50
SALES (est): 2.3MM **Privately Held**
WEB: www.parastaffing.com
SIC: 7361 Employment agencies

(P-14721)
PDS TECH INC
1798 Tech Dr Ste 130, San Jose (95110)
PHONE 408 916-4848
EMP: 1504
SALES (corp-wide): 321.4MM **Privately Held**
SIC: 7361 Employment agencies
PA: Pds Tech, Inc.
  1925 W J Carpentr Fwy 5
  Irving TX 75063
  214 647-9600

(P-14722)
PDS TECH INC
3100 S Harbor Blvd # 135, Santa Ana (92704-6813)
PHONE 214 647-9600
Dj Englert, *Manager*
EMP: 82
SALES (corp-wide): 321.4MM **Privately Held**
WEB: www.pdstech.com
SIC: 7361 Employment agencies
PA: Pds Tech, Inc.
  1925 W J Carpentr Fwy 5
  Irving TX 75063
  214 647-9600

(P-14723)
PEMER PACKING CO INC
20260 Spence Rd, Salinas (93908-9507)
P.O. Box 4783 (93912-4783)
PHONE 831 758-8586
Pedro Mercado, *President*
EMP: 800
SQ FT: 3,000
SALES (est): 32.9MM **Privately Held**
SIC: 7361 Labor contractors (employment agency)

(P-14724)
PEOPLE SCIENCE INC
951 Mariners Island Blvd, San Mateo (94404-1558)
PHONE 888 924-1004
Christine Nichlos, *CEO*
EMP: 50
SALES (corp-wide): 3.2MM **Privately Held**
SIC: 7361 Executive placement
PA: People Science Inc
  595 Shrewsbury Ave # 102
  Shrewsbury NJ 07702
  888 924-1004

(P-14725)
PEOPLES CHOICE STAFFING INC
4218 Green River Rd # 101, Corona (92880-1635)
PHONE 951 735-0550
Denise Peoples, *President*
Wendell Peoples, *COO*
Candice Handley, *Manager*
EMP: 100
SALES (est): 14.5MM **Privately Held**
WEB: www.peopleschoicestaffing.com
SIC: 7361 Employment agencies

(P-14726)
PEOPLEWARE TECHNICAL RESOURCES
302 W Grand Ave Ste 4, El Segundo (90245-5108)
PHONE 310 640-2406
Fax: 310 640-2629
Sheryl Rooker, *President*
Jeff Thaler, *CFO*
Dane Encarnacion, *Recruiter*
EMP: 60
SQ FT: 3,000
SALES (est): 3.1MM **Privately Held**
WEB: www.peoplewareinc.com
SIC: 7361 7363 Placement agencies; help supply services

(P-14727)
PHASE 1 TELE-TEAM
1119 Electric St, Gardena (90248-3345)
PHONE 562 746-8734
Keisha Joseph-Beard, *Partner*
EMP: 50
SALES: 60K **Privately Held**
SIC: 7361 Employment agencies

(P-14728)
PLANETPRO INC (PA)
2410 Camino Ramon Ste 275, San Ramon (94583-4278)
PHONE 925 277-0727
Fax: 925 277-0729
Ravi Thota, *Chairman*
Camir Khosla, *President*
Jackie Zweck, *Treasurer*
Johnson Boru, *Vice Pres*
Adrian Tay, *General Mgr*
EMP: 100
SQ FT: 2,000
SALES: 16MM **Privately Held**
WEB: www.planetpro.com
SIC: 7361 Labor contractors (employment agency)

(P-14729)
PLUS GROUP INC
Also Called: Jobs Plus
2551 Sn Rmn Vlly Blvd 2 Ste 201, San Ramon (94583)
PHONE 925 831-8551
Fax: 925 831-0265
Patrick O'Donnell, *Branch Mgr*
Rosemarie Ardire, *Branch Mgr*
Kelly Kramer, *Branch Mgr*
Vince Gavin, *MIS Mgr*
Kelly Karmer, *Recruiter*
EMP: 100
SALES (corp-wide): 12MM **Privately Held**
WEB: www.tpgstaffing.com
SIC: 7361 7363 Employment agencies; executive placement; temporary help service
PA: The Plus Group Inc
  7425 Janes Ave Ste 201
  Woodridge IL 60517
  630 515-0500

(P-14730)
POSITIVE SOLUTION STAFFING LLC
15949 Oak Hill Dr, Chino Hills (91709-2467)
PHONE 909 606-7512
Grace Rojas, *Mng Member*
Mary Rodriguez,
EMP: 106
SALES (est): 2.8MM **Privately Held**
SIC: 7361 Employment agencies

(P-14731)
PRECISE FIT LIMITED ONE LLC
Also Called: Pfitech
959 Suth Cast Dr Ste 200, Costa Mesa (92626)
PHONE 310 824-1800
Richard Hernandez,
Donald Zamba, *COO*
Carl Chadwell, *Vice Pres*
Carl Cook, *Executive*
Orianna Pacchioni, *Human Res Mgr*
EMP: 380
SQ FT: 10,000
SALES (est): 20.5MM **Privately Held**
SIC: 7361 Employment agencies

(P-14732)
PREMIER HEALTHCARE SVCS LLC
2020 Camino Del Rio N # 600, San Diego (92108-1545)
PHONE 619 491-0300
Kelly Johnson, *Branch Mgr*
Wesley Tomsick, *Manager*
EMP: 200
SALES (corp-wide): 26.8MM **Privately Held**
SIC: 7361 Nurses' registry
PA: Premier Healthcare Services, Llc
  815 Colorado Blvd Ste 400
  Los Angeles CA 90041
  626 204-7930

(P-14733)
PREMIER HEALTHCARE SVCS LLC (PA)
Also Called: Phs Staffing
815 Colorado Blvd Ste 400, Los Angeles (90041-1745)
PHONE 626 204-7930
Kelly Johnson, *Mng Member*
Jacob Henley, *Regional Mgr*
Tyeshia Dunwoddie, *Administration*
Natasha Taylor, *Accountant*
Steve Mena, *VP Opers*
EMP: 200
SALES (est): 26.8MM **Privately Held**
WEB: www.phs-staffing.com
SIC: 7361 Nurses' registry

(P-14734)
PREMIER INSITE GROUP INC
111 W Ocean Blvd Ste 400, Long Beach (90802-4633)
PHONE 562 741-5018
Jose Castellanos, *President*
Juan Calderon, *Treasurer*
Sandra Picos, *Exec Dir*
EMP: 99
SQ FT: 1,628
SALES (est): 3.7MM **Privately Held**
SIC: 7361 Labor contractors (employment agency)

(P-14735)
PROFESSIONAL CIR STAFFING INC (PA)
Also Called: Creative Circle
5900 Wilshire Blvd # 1100, Los Angeles (90036-5013)
PHONE 323 930-2333
Lawrence Serf, *CEO*
Michelle Sorto, *Project Mgr*
Anne Tyrrell, *Opers Mgr*
Michelle Moore, *Manager*
EMP: 56
SALES (est): 8.8MM **Privately Held**
WEB: www.creativecircle.com
SIC: 7361 Employment agencies

(P-14736)
PROFESSNAL RGISTRY NETWRK CORP
20132 Canyon Dr, Yorba Linda (92886-6058)
PHONE 714 394-4071
George Makridis, *President*
EMP: 105
SALES (est): 5.3MM **Privately Held**
WEB: www.prncorp.net
SIC: 7361 Registries

(P-14737)
PROFILE OF SANTA CRUZ
Also Called: Experience Unlimited
2045 40th Ave Ste B, Capitola (95010-2549)
PHONE 831 479-0393
Fax: 831 462-4369
Lance Vera, *Exec Dir*
EMP: 70
SALES (est): 2.9MM **Privately Held**
WEB: www.santacruzprofile.org
SIC: 7361 Placement agencies

(P-14738)
PROLINX SERVICES INC
2033 Gateway Pl Ste 500, San Jose (95110-3712)
PHONE 408 689-5777
Bryan Dunlap, *President*
Gerardo Ballester, *CFO*
Lisa Hannon, *Manager*
EMP: 65 **EST:** 2008
SALES (est): 4.5MM
SALES (corp-wide): 9.6MM **Privately Held**
SIC: 7361 Employment agencies
PA: Tiffany Stuart Solutions, Inc.
  390 Diablo Rd Ste 220
  Danville CA 94526
  925 855-3600

(P-14739)
PS NATIONAL INC
Also Called: Professional Staffing
17645 Chatsworth St, Granada Hills (91344-5602)
PHONE 818 366-1300
Fax: 818 366-7385
Lee Leatherman, *President*
Ruth Leatherman, *Vice Pres*
EMP: 300 **EST:** 1977
SQ FT: 4,000
SALES (est): 12.7MM **Privately Held**
SIC: 7361 7363 Nurses' registry; help supply services

(P-14740)
PSINAPSE TECHNOLOGY LTD
5820 Stnrge Mall Rd # 212, Pleasanton (94588-3200)
PHONE 925 225-0400
Fax: 925 225-0600
Sylvia Luneau, *President*
Noel Luneau, *Vice Pres*
Kesha Boyd, *Admin Asst*
Nicole Foster, *Tech Recruiter*
Julia Barnes, *Manager*
EMP: 90
SQ FT: 4,000
SALES (est): 3MM **Privately Held**
WEB: www.psinapse.com
SIC: 7361 Placement agencies

(P-14741)
RAMCO ENTERPRISES LP
325 Plaza Dr Ste 1, Santa Maria (93454-6929)
PHONE 805 922-9888
EMP: 740
SALES (corp-wide): 85MM **Privately Held**
SIC: 7361 Employment agencies
PA: Ramco Enterprises, L.P.
  320 Airport Blvd
  Salinas CA 93905
  831 758-5272

(P-14742)
RAMCO ENTERPRISES LP
585 Auto Center Dr, Watsonville (95076-3764)
PHONE 831 722-3370
EMP: 740

PRODUCTS & SERVICES SECTION

7361 - Employment Agencies County (P-14765)

SALES (corp-wide): 85MM **Privately Held**
SIC: 7361 Employment agencies
PA: Ramco Enterprises, L.P.
   320 Airport Blvd
   Salinas CA 93905
   831 758-5272

(P-14743)
RANDSTAD NORTH AMERICA INC
7014 N Cedar Ave, Fresno (93720-3300)
PHONE..................559 297-0054
Tammy Wallace, *Branch Mgr*
EMP: 200
SALES (corp-wide): 20.6B **Privately Held**
SIC: 7361 Employment agencies
HQ: Randstad North America, Inc.
   3625 Cumberland Blvd Se
   Atlanta GA 30339
   770 937-7000

(P-14744)
RANDSTAD PROFESSIONALS US LP
Also Called: Randstad Finance & Accounting
111 Anza Blvd Ste 202, Burlingame (94010-1932)
PHONE..................650 343-5111
Jimmy Alradaideh, *Financial Exec*
Anna Santiago, *HR Admin*
Chandra Pappas, *VP Opers*
Vick Thomas, *Opers Mgr*
Angelo Hatzistratis, *Director*
EMP: 235
SALES (corp-wide): 20.6B **Privately Held**
SIC: 7361 Employment agencies
HQ: Randstad Professionals Us, Lp
   150 Presidential Way # 300
   Woburn MA 01801
   781 213-1500

(P-14745)
RCSN INC
10221 Slater Ave Ste 214, Fountain Valley (92708-4751)
PHONE..................714 965-0244
Catherin Long, *CEO*
Ann Lee, *CFO*
Erick Nguyen, *Accounts Mgr*
Luke Nguyen, *Accounts Mgr*
EMP: 150
SQ FT: 400
SALES (est): 4.2MM **Privately Held**
SIC: 7361 Employment agencies

(P-14746)
READYLINK HEALTHCARE
72030 Metroplex Dr, Thousand Palms (92276)
P.O. Box 1047 (92276-1047)
PHONE..................760 343-7000
Fax: 760 343-7076
Barry L Treash, *President*
Christy Marshall, *Executive Asst*
Roberta Crncic, *Info Tech Mgr*
Jennifer Amundson, *Manager*
Roberta Derrington, *Manager*
EMP: 85
SALES (est): 7.2MM **Privately Held**
WEB: www.readylinkhealthcare.com
SIC: 7361 Labor contractors (employment agency)

(P-14747)
REAL TIME STAFFING SERVICES
Also Called: Select Staffing
3820 State St Ste A, Santa Barbara (93105-3182)
PHONE..................805 882-2200
Steve Sorensen, *Principal*
Robin Doran, *President*
Paul Sorenson, *Vice Pres*
EMP: 99
SALES: 950K **Privately Held**
SIC: 7361 Employment agencies

(P-14748)
REDLANDS EMPLOYMENT SERVICES
Also Called: Redlands Staffing Services
4295 Jurupa St Ste 110, Ontario (91761-1429)
PHONE..................951 688-0083
Fax: 951 688-0087
Matt Tahlmeyer, *President*
Debbie Jahn, *Controller*
EMP: 355
SALES (corp-wide): 14.9MM **Privately Held**
SIC: 7361 Employment agencies
PA: Redlands Employment Services Inc
   499 W State St
   Redlands CA 92373
   909 792-3413

(P-14749)
RELIABLE NURSING SOLUTIONS
16057 Kamana Rd Ste B, Apple Valley (92307-0841)
PHONE..................760 946-9191
Carol Grigsby, *President*
EMP: 85
SQ FT: 1,200
SALES (est): 2.7MM **Privately Held**
WEB: www.reliablenursing.com
SIC: 7361 Placement agencies

(P-14750)
RENTERIA SANTIAGO J FARM LABO
137 W Kern Ave, Mc Farland (93250-1348)
PHONE..................661 792-0052
Fax: 661 792-3722
Santiago J Renteria, *Owner*
EMP: 150
SQ FT: 768
SALES (est): 6MM **Privately Held**
SIC: 7361 Labor contractors (employment agency)

(P-14751)
RESOURCES CONNECTION LLC (HQ)
Also Called: Resources Global Professionals
17101 Armstrong Ave, Irvine (92614-5730)
PHONE..................714 430-6400
Donald B Murray, *Ch of Bd*
Anthony Cherbak, *President*
Tracy Stephens, *COO*
Nathan W Franke, *CFO*
Tanja Cebula, *Exec VP*
EMP: 60 EST: 1999
SQ FT: 16,366
SALES (est): 30.1MM
SALES (corp-wide): 598.5MM **Publicly Held**
WEB: www.resourcesconnection.com
SIC: 7361 8742 Employment agencies; management consulting services
PA: Resources Connection, Inc.
   17101 Armstrong Ave
   Irvine CA 92614
   714 430-6400

(P-14752)
RESPONSE 1 MEDICAL STAFFING
1101 Inv Blvd Ste 140, El Dorado Hills (95762)
PHONE..................916 932-0430
Cheree Love, *CEO*
Gordon Helm, *Shareholder*
Gary Slavit, *Shareholder*
Tyler Covey, *COO*
Lajuan Knorr, *CFO*
EMP: 150
SQ FT: 3,000
SALES: 12MM **Privately Held**
WEB: www.response1.com
SIC: 7361 Nurses' registry

(P-14753)
RICHARD M GONZALEZ
Also Called: Valley Agricultural Labor Svcs
11450 Avenue 388, Cutler (93615-9744)
PHONE..................559 591-2207
Richard M Gonzalez, *Owner*
Richard Gonzalez, *Owner*
EMP: 100
SALES: 600K **Privately Held**
WEB: www.gonet.com
SIC: 7361 Labor contractors (employment agency)

(P-14754)
RIGHT CHOICE A HEALTH CARE
620 S Glendora Ave Ste A, Glendora (91740-6815)
P.O. Box 127 (91740-0127)
PHONE..................626 335-1318
Fax: 626 335-1554
Mike Dababneh, *President*
EMP: 300
SQ FT: 3,000
SALES (est): 9MM **Privately Held**
WEB: www.right-choicestaffing.com
SIC: 7361 Employment agencies

(P-14755)
ROBERT HALF INTERNATIONAL INC
10 Almaden Blvd Ste 900, San Jose (95113-2268)
PHONE..................408 961-2975
Catrina Simbe, *Branch Mgr*
EMP: 92
SALES (corp-wide): 5B **Publicly Held**
SIC: 7361 Employment agencies
PA: Robert Half International Inc.
   2884 Sand Hill Rd Ste 200
   Menlo Park CA 94025
   650 234-6000

(P-14756)
ROBERT HALF INTERNATIONAL INC
865 S Figueroa St # 2600, Los Angeles (90017-5486)
PHONE..................213 270-6731
Alicia Arzola, *Principal*
EMP: 92
SALES (corp-wide): 5B **Publicly Held**
WEB: www.rhii.com
SIC: 7361 Placement agencies
PA: Robert Half International Inc.
   2884 Sand Hill Rd Ste 200
   Menlo Park CA 94025
   650 234-6000

(P-14757)
ROBERT HALF INTERNATIONAL INC
50 California St Fl 10, San Francisco (94111-4613)
PHONE..................415 434-2429
Fax: 415 434-4217
MA Woods, *Manager*
EMP: 92
SALES (corp-wide): 5B **Publicly Held**
SIC: 7361 Employment agencies
PA: Robert Half International Inc.
   2884 Sand Hill Rd Ste 200
   Menlo Park CA 94025
   650 234-6000

(P-14758)
ROBERT HALF INTERNATIONAL INC
39141 Civic Center Dr # 205, Fremont (94538-5823)
PHONE..................510 744-6486
Harold M Messmer Jr, *Branch Mgr*
EMP: 92
SALES (corp-wide): 5B **Publicly Held**
SIC: 7361 Employment agencies
PA: Robert Half International Inc.
   2884 Sand Hill Rd Ste 200
   Menlo Park CA 94025
   650 234-6000

(P-14759)
ROBERT HALF INTERNATIONAL INC
4 Lower Ragsdale Dr # 101, Monterey (93940-7835)
PHONE..................831 241-9042
Fax: 831 333-1361
Gabby Ayala, *Manager*
Mary King, *Manager*
EMP: 94
SALES (corp-wide): 5B **Publicly Held**
SIC: 7361 Employment agencies
PA: Robert Half International Inc.
   2884 Sand Hill Rd Ste 200
   Menlo Park CA 94025
   650 234-6000

(P-14760)
ROBERT HALF INTERNATIONAL INC
1 City Blvd W Ste 1115, Orange (92868-3605)
PHONE..................714 450-9838
Tina Fox, *Branch Mgr*
EMP: 92
SALES (corp-wide): 5B **Publicly Held**
SIC: 7361 Labor contractors (employment agency)
PA: Robert Half International Inc.
   2884 Sand Hill Rd Ste 200
   Menlo Park CA 94025
   650 234-6000

(P-14761)
ROBERT HALF INTERNATIONAL INC
Also Called: Accountemps
17871 Park Plaza Dr # 100, Cerritos (90703-9335)
PHONE..................562 356-1031
Fax: 562 860-4280
Tricia Howard, *Branch Mgr*
Ba Tran, *Branch Mgr*
EMP: 92
SALES (corp-wide): 5B **Publicly Held**
SIC: 7361 Employment agencies
PA: Robert Half International Inc.
   2884 Sand Hill Rd Ste 200
   Menlo Park CA 94025
   650 234-6000

(P-14762)
ROBERT HALF INTERNATIONAL INC
2280 Market St Ste 220, Riverside (92501-2120)
PHONE..................951 779-9081
Jason Buchbinder, *Manager*
EMP: 92
SALES (corp-wide): 5B **Publicly Held**
SIC: 7361 Employment agencies
PA: Robert Half International Inc.
   2884 Sand Hill Rd Ste 200
   Menlo Park CA 94025
   650 234-6000

(P-14763)
ROBERT HALF INTERNATIONAL INC
3100 Zinfandel Dr Ste 260, Rancho Cordova (95670-6391)
PHONE..................916 852-1705
Chris Gardiner, *Branch Mgr*
EMP: 92
SALES (corp-wide): 5B **Publicly Held**
SIC: 7361 Employment agencies
PA: Robert Half International Inc.
   2884 Sand Hill Rd Ste 200
   Menlo Park CA 94025
   650 234-6000

(P-14764)
ROBERT HALF INTERNATIONAL INC
3000 Oak Rd Ste 625, Walnut Creek (94597-2280)
PHONE..................925 930-7766
Heath Harris, *Branch Mgr*
Theresa Walsh-Arietta, *Vice Pres*
EMP: 92
SALES (corp-wide): 5B **Publicly Held**
SIC: 7361 Employment agencies
PA: Robert Half International Inc.
   2884 Sand Hill Rd Ste 200
   Menlo Park CA 94025
   650 234-6000

(P-14765)
ROBERT HALF INTERNATIONAL INC
Also Called: Accountemps
50 California St Fl 10, San Francisco (94111-4613)
PHONE..................415 434-1900
Fax: 415 986-7446
Katy Giggere, *Branch Mgr*
Jean Thoreson, *Manager*
EMP: 140

7361 - Employment Agencies County (P-14766)

SALES (corp-wide): 5B **Publicly Held**
WEB: www.rhii.com
SIC: 7361 7363 Executive placement; help supply services
PA: Robert Half International Inc.
2884 Sand Hill Rd Ste 200
Menlo Park CA 94025
650 234-6000

(P-14766)
ROBERT HALF INTERNATIONAL INC
Also Called: Accountemps
2884 Sand Hill Rd Ste 200, Menlo Park (94025-7059)
PHONE..............................650 234-6000
Paul Gentzkow, *President*
Bob Glass, *Exec VP*
Kristi Larson, *Admin Asst*
Marisol Rincon, *Administration*
Lisa Coker, *Business Mgr*
EMP: 99
SALES (corp-wide): 5B **Publicly Held**
WEB: www.rhii.com
SIC: 7361 Placement agencies
PA: Robert Half International Inc.
2884 Sand Hill Rd Ste 200
Menlo Park CA 94025
650 234-6000

(P-14767)
ROBERT HALF INTERNATIONAL INC
Also Called: Creative Group, The
2884 Sand Hill Rd Ste 200, Menlo Park (94025-7059)
PHONE..............................650 234-6000
Paul Gentzkow, *President*
Rene McDonald, *Project Mgr*
Sarah Greenhill, *Graphic Designe*
Michael Guy, *Graphic Designe*
Judy Sakai, *Graphic Designe*
EMP: 100
SALES (corp-wide): 5B **Publicly Held**
WEB: www.rhii.com
SIC: 7361 7363 Placement agencies; temporary help service
PA: Robert Half International Inc.
2884 Sand Hill Rd Ste 200
Menlo Park CA 94025
650 234-6000

(P-14768)
ROBERT HALF INTERNATIONAL INC
Also Called: Office Team
2884 Sand Hill Rd Ste 200, Menlo Park (94025-7059)
PHONE..............................650 234-6000
Chris Hoffmann, *President*
Tom Valentine, *Branch Mgr*
Jenny Lemus, *Office Admin*
Erica Bradshaw, *Admin Asst*
Felecia Elliott, *Admin Asst*
EMP: 92
SALES (corp-wide): 5B **Publicly Held**
SIC: 7361 Employment agencies
PA: Robert Half International Inc.
2884 Sand Hill Rd Ste 200
Menlo Park CA 94025
650 234-6000

(P-14769)
ROBERT HALF INTERNATIONAL INC
Also Called: Officeteam
18200 Von Karman Ave # 800, Irvine (92612-7158)
PHONE..............................949 476-3199
Tina Fox, *Director*
EMP: 92
SALES (corp-wide): 5B **Publicly Held**
SIC: 7361 8721 Employment agencies; ship crew agency; auditing services
PA: Robert Half International Inc.
2884 Sand Hill Rd Ste 200
Menlo Park CA 94025
650 234-6000

(P-14770)
ROBERT HALF INTERNATIONAL INC
790 E Colo Blvd Ste 650, Pasadena (91101)
PHONE..............................626 463-2037
Tania Hablian, *Branch Mgr*
Debra Nunes, *Administration*
Ameri Ramirez, *Manager*
EMP: 92
SALES (corp-wide): 5B **Publicly Held**
WEB: www.rhii.com
SIC: 7361 7363 Employment agencies; temporary help service
PA: Robert Half International Inc.
2884 Sand Hill Rd Ste 200
Menlo Park CA 94025
650 234-6000

(P-14771)
ROBERT HALF INTERNATIONAL INC
990 W 190th St Ste 290, Torrance (90502-1046)
PHONE..............................310 719-1400
Steve Higginbotham, *Manager*
EMP: 92
SALES (corp-wide): 5B **Publicly Held**
WEB: www.rhii.com
SIC: 7361 Placement agencies
PA: Robert Half International Inc.
2884 Sand Hill Rd Ste 200
Menlo Park CA 94025
650 234-6000

(P-14772)
ROBERT HALF INTERNATIONAL INC
3600 W Byshore Rd Ste 103, Palo Alto (94303)
PHONE..............................650 812-9790
Christina Marinovich, *Principal*
Eric Lesniak, *Manager*
EMP: 92
SALES (corp-wide): 5B **Publicly Held**
SIC: 7361 Employment agencies
PA: Robert Half International Inc.
2884 Sand Hill Rd Ste 200
Menlo Park CA 94025
650 234-6000

(P-14773)
ROBERT HALF INTERNATIONAL INC
Also Called: Office Team
2613 Camino Ramon, San Ramon (94583-4289)
PHONE..............................925 913-1000
Max Messner, *Manager*
Marvin Williams, *Administration*
Emmendo Legaspi, *Sr Software Eng*
Stephen Radomski, *Info Tech Dir*
Anurita Biswas, *Software Engr*
EMP: 50
SALES (corp-wide): 5B **Publicly Held**
WEB: www.rhii.com
SIC: 7361 7363 Placement agencies; temporary help service
PA: Robert Half International Inc.
2884 Sand Hill Rd Ste 200
Menlo Park CA 94025
650 234-6000

(P-14774)
ROBERT QUINTERO LABOR CONTG
1827 S Bardo St, Visalia (93277-4848)
PHONE..............................559 732-6954
Robert Quintero, *Owner*
EMP: 50
SALES: 1MM **Privately Held**
SIC: 7361 Employment agencies

(P-14775)
ROBERTAS LABOR CONTRACTING
137 Main St, Soledad (93960-3023)
P.O. Box I (93960-0860)
PHONE..............................831 678-8176
Fax: 831 678-8189
Roberta Urquidez, *Owner*
EMP: 300
SALES (est): 9.2MM **Privately Held**
SIC: 7361 Labor contractors (employment agency)

(P-14776)
RYDEK ELETRONICS LLC
898 N Sepulveda Blvd # 475, El Segundo (90245-2705)
PHONE..............................310 641-9800
Doug Browning, *Principal*
Eric Uliano, *IT/INT Sup*
EMP: 100
SALES (est): 3.2MM **Privately Held**
WEB: www.rydek.com
SIC: 7361 Employment agencies

(P-14777)
SANDOVAL BROTHERS INC
36503 Mile End Rd, Soledad (93960-9689)
P.O. Box 1183 (93960-1183)
PHONE..............................831 678-1465
Fax: 831 678-1522
Antonio Sandoval, *President*
EMP: 60 **EST:** 1997
SALES (est): 3.9MM **Privately Held**
SIC: 7361 Labor contractors (employment agency)

(P-14778)
SANTA ANA CITY OF
1000 E Santa Ana Blvd # 108, Santa Ana (92701-3900)
PHONE..............................714 565-2600
Gus Chamoro, *Manager*
Gerardo Mouet, *Exec Dir*
Joe Supe, *Training Spec*
Michele Martinez, *City Council*
EMP: 50 **Privately Held**
SIC: 7361 9111 Employment agencies; mayors' offices
PA: City Of Santa Ana
20 Civic Center Plz Fl 8
Santa Ana CA 92701
714 647-5400

(P-14779)
SANTA CLARA VLY JOB CAREER CTR
725 E Main St Ste 101, Santa Paula (93060-2748)
PHONE..............................805 933-8300
Art Hernandez, *Director*
EMP: 60
SALES (est): 1.4MM **Privately Held**
SIC: 7361 Employment agencies

(P-14780)
SCOTTS LABOR LEASING CO INC
Also Called: Scott's Glass Service
22560 Lucerne St, Carson (90745-4303)
P.O. Box 3683, Long Beach (90803-0683)
PHONE..............................310 835-8388
Tom Scott, *President*
Cheri Scott, *Admin Sec*
EMP: 80
SQ FT: 1,000
SALES: 1.5MM **Privately Held**
SIC: 7361 Employment agencies

(P-14781)
SE SCHER CORPORATION
Also Called: Acrobat Staffing
2525 Camino Del Rio S, San Diego (92108-3717)
PHONE..............................858 546-8300
Marc Caplan, *Branch Mgr*
Jessica Cox, *Assistant*
EMP: 332
SALES (corp-wide): 16MM **Privately Held**
SIC: 7361 Employment agencies
PA: S.E. Scher Corporation
665 3rd St Ste 415
San Francisco CA 94107
415 431-8826

(P-14782)
SE SCHER CORPORATION
Also Called: Acrobat Staffing
6731 Five Star Blvd Ste C, Rocklin (95677-2680)
PHONE..............................916 632-1363
Steve Scher, *CEO*
EMP: 332
SALES (corp-wide): 16MM **Privately Held**
SIC: 7361 Employment agencies
PA: S.E. Scher Corporation
665 3rd St Ste 415
San Francisco CA 94107
415 431-8826

(P-14783)
SECURE NURSING SERVICE INC
3333 Wilshire Blvd # 625, Los Angeles (90010-4106)
PHONE..............................213 736-6771
Fax: 213 736-7334
Haesook Kim, *President*
Angelo Legasse, *Admin Mgr*
EMP: 350 **EST:** 2001
SQ FT: 2,500
SALES: 6.5MM **Privately Held**
WEB: www.securenursing.com
SIC: 7361 Nurses' registry

(P-14784)
SELECT TEMPORARIES LLC (DH)
Also Called: Select Personnel Services
3820 State St, Santa Barbara (93105-3182)
PHONE..............................805 882-2200
Fax: 805 964-2811
Thomas A Bickes, *President*
Shawn W Poole, *CFO*
Paul Galleberg, *Admin Sec*
Nancy Vigil, *Personnel*
John Rinaldi, *Purch Agent*
EMP: 90
SQ FT: 30,000
SALES (est): 50.3MM
SALES (corp-wide): 391.2MM **Privately Held**
SIC: 7361 Employment agencies
HQ: Employment Solutions Management, Inc.
1040 Crown Pointe Pkwy
Atlanta GA 30338
770 671-1900

(P-14785)
SHARF WOODWARD & ASSOCIATES
5900 Sepulvda Blvd # 104, Van Nuys (91411-2511)
PHONE..............................818 989-2200
Bernard Sharf, *Co-President*
Robert Bell, *Manager*
Terrence Crook, *Accounts Mgr*
EMP: 90
SALES: 10MM **Privately Held**
WEB: www.swjobs.com
SIC: 7361 Employment agencies

(P-14786)
SIRACUSA ENTERPRISES INC
Also Called: Quality Temp Staffing
17737 Chtswrth St Ste 200, Granada Hills (91344-5628)
PHONE..............................818 831-1130
Joe Alas, *President*
Marie Alas, *Vice Pres*
Michelle Stetz, *Administration*
EMP: 70
SALES: 3.7MM **Privately Held**
SIC: 7361 Employment agencies

(P-14787)
SISKIYOU OPPORTUNITY CENTER
Also Called: Yreka Employment Services
321 N Gold St, Yreka (96097-2307)
P.O. Box 594 (96097-0594)
PHONE..............................530 842-4110
EMP: 60
SALES (corp-wide): 1.7MM **Privately Held**
SIC: 7361 Employment agencies
PA: Siskiyou Opportunity Center Inc
1516 S Mount Shasta Blvd
Mount Shasta CA 96067
530 926-4698

(P-14788)
SMART CHOICE INVESTMENTS INC
Also Called: Brightstar Health
23332 Hawthorne Blvd # 203, Torrance (90505-3749)
PHONE..............................310 944-6985
Maurice Geyen, *President*
EMP: 80 **EST:** 2008
SALES (est): 3.5MM **Privately Held**
SIC: 7361 8082 Nurses' registry; home health care services

PRODUCTS & SERVICES SECTION

7361 - Employment Agencies County (P-14815)

(P-14789)
SMARTRECRUITERS INC
56 Tehama St, San Francisco (94105-3110)
PHONE 415 508-3755
Jerome Ternynck, *CEO*
David Hurwitz, *Chief Mktg Ofcr*
Bjorn Eriksson, *Officer*
Charlie Nelson, *Business Dir*
Caitlin Rolla, *Marketing Mgr*
EMP: 60
SALES (est): 5MM **Privately Held**
SIC: 7361 Placement agencies

(P-14790)
SNELLING EMPLOYMENT LLC
2203 Harvbor Bay Pkwy, Alameda (94502)
PHONE 510 769-4400
Fax: 510 769-4404
Michelle Berkovich, *Manager*
EMP: 100
SALES (corp-wide): 4.2B **Privately Held**
SIC: 7361 7363 Employment agencies; temporary help service
HQ: Snelling Employment, Llc
12801 N Cntl Expy Ste 600
Dallas TX 75243
972 239-7575

(P-14791)
SOCAL SERVICES INC
Also Called: Tsg
6336 Greenwich Dr Ste 100, San Diego (92122-5922)
PHONE 858 453-1331
Fax: 858 453-6021
Rich Papike, *President*
Gary Van Eik, *CEO*
EMP: 250
SQ FT: 3,000
SALES: 15MM **Privately Held**
WEB: www.socalservices.com
SIC: 7361 7363 Employment agencies; temporary help service; office help supply service

(P-14792)
SPEC PERSONNEL LLC
Also Called: Spectra
1900 La Fytte St Unit 125, Santa Clara (95050)
PHONE 408 727-8000
Andrew Bergen, *Branch Mgr*
EMP: 150
SALES (corp-wide): 35MM **Privately Held**
SIC: 7361 Employment agencies
PA: Spec Personnel, Llc
4625 Creekstone Dr # 130
Durham NC 27703
203 254-9935

(P-14793)
SPECIAL EVENTS STAFFING
1015 N Lake Ave Ste 202, Pasadena (91104-4575)
PHONE 626 296-6771
Frank Barnes, *CEO*
EMP: 626
SQ FT: 900
SALES: 3.3MM **Privately Held**
SIC: 7361 Employment agencies

(P-14794)
STAFFCHEX INC
20537 Devonshire St, Chatsworth (91311-3208)
PHONE 818 709-6100
Steven Zingerman, *Principal*
EMP: 1956
SALES (corp-wide): 68.4MM **Privately Held**
SIC: 7361 Employment agencies
PA: Staffchex, Inc.
790 The City Dr S Ste 180
Orange CA 92868
714 912-7500

(P-14795)
STAFFING SOLUTIONS INC
Also Called: Balance Staffing
2142 Bering Dr, San Jose (95131-2013)
PHONE 408 980-9000
Fax: 408 980-9950
John Moss, *CEO*
Robert Feinstein, *President*
Lily Rappeport, *Branch Mgr*
Linda Pulido, *Admin Asst*
Adriana Guicho, *Administration*
EMP: 80
SQ FT: 4,000
SALES (est): 6.6MM **Privately Held**
SIC: 7361 7363 Employment agencies; help supply services

(P-14796)
STAR H-R
1822 Jefferson St, NAPA (94559-1618)
PHONE 707 265-9911
Fax: 707 265-9900
Lisa Rogeldstad, *Manager*
EMP: 1012
SALES (corp-wide): 38.9MM **Privately Held**
SIC: 7361 Employment agencies
PA: Star H-R
3820 Cypress Dr Ste 2
Petaluma CA 94954
707 762-4447

(P-14797)
STAR H-R
105 E 1st St, Cloverdale (95425-3701)
PHONE 707 894-4404
EMP: 1012
SALES (corp-wide): 38.9MM **Privately Held**
SIC: 7361 Employment agencies
PA: Star H-R
3820 Cypress Dr Ste 2
Petaluma CA 94954
707 762-4447

(P-14798)
SUNSHINE CLEARING CORPORATION
Also Called: Paragon Personel Services
1215 W Imperial Hwy # 210, Brea (92821-3738)
PHONE 714 829-0273
Brandy Rae Guzman, *President*
EMP: 50
SQ FT: 1,000
SALES (est): 1MM **Privately Held**
SIC: 7361 Placement agencies

(P-14799)
SWS2 INC
Also Called: Ryte Professionals
4141 Ball Rd Ste 517, Cypress (90630-3465)
PHONE 714 821-6699
Wende Morishige, *President*
Steve J Sjostrom, *Senior VP*
Pam Kimura, *Admin Asst*
EMP: 70
SQ FT: 1,000
SALES: 6MM **Privately Held**
SIC: 7361 Employment agencies

(P-14800)
T W R FRAMING
1661 Railroad St, Corona (92880-2503)
PHONE 951 279-2000
Tom Rhodes, *Owner*
Debbie Diter, *Controller*
Yesenia Salazar, *Human Res Mgr*
Amy Strommer, *Director*
EMP: 100 **EST:** 2001
SALES (est): 3.4MM **Privately Held**
WEB: www.twrframing.com
SIC: 7361 Labor contractors (employment agency)

(P-14801)
TALENT SPACE INC
2570 N 1st St Ste 400, San Jose (95131-1045)
PHONE 408 330-1900
Lisa Flores, *President*
Maida Lecours, *Accounts Exec*
EMP: 80
SALES: 15MM **Privately Held**
SIC: 7361 Employment agencies

(P-14802)
TEAM-ONE EMPLYMENT SPCLSTS LLC
Also Called: Team One
2999 Overland Ave Ste 212, Los Angeles (90064-4243)
PHONE 310 481-4482
Fax: 310 607-0974
Frank Moran,
Daniel Cox, *CFO*
Raymond Barajas, *General Mgr*
EMP: 5000
SQ FT: 4,500
SALES: 35MM **Privately Held**
SIC: 7361 Employment agencies

(P-14803)
TECHNICAL TEMPS INC
Also Called: TTI
1096 Pecten Ct, Milpitas (95035-6805)
P.O. Box 610190, San Jose
PHONE 408 956-8256
Fax: 408 956-8260
Judith Kalune, *President*
EMP: 100
SQ FT: 1,000
SALES (est): 3.8MM **Privately Held**
WEB: www.technicaltemps.com
SIC: 7361 Executive placement

(P-14804)
TETRA TECH EXECUTIVE SVCS INC
3475 E Foothill Blvd, Pasadena (91107-6024)
PHONE 626 470-2400
Sam Box, *Principal*
Patrick Haun, *Vice Pres*
Eric Gerritsen, *Info Tech Mgr*
Julian Paez, *Info Tech Mgr*
Cheryl Johnson, *Data Proc Staff*
EMP: 162
SALES (est): 7.6MM
SALES (corp-wide): 2.3B **Publicly Held**
WEB: www.tetratech.com
SIC: 7361 Employment agencies
PA: Tetra Tech, Inc.
3475 E Foothill Blvd
Pasadena CA 91107
626 351-4664

(P-14805)
TOTAL PROFESSIONAL NETWORK
Also Called: Core Medstaff
3275 Wilshire Blvd # 100, Los Angeles (90010-1406)
PHONE 213 382-5550
Elizabeth Ann Poe, *President*
Therese Nery, *Vice Pres*
EMP: 100
SALES (est): 5.4MM **Privately Held**
WEB: www.coremedstaff.com
SIC: 7361 Nurses' registry

(P-14806)
TQ INC (PA)
Also Called: Total Quality Staffing Service
13191 Crocaroad Pkwy N Ste 143, City of Industry (91746)
P.O. Box 60586, Pasadena (91116-6586)
PHONE 562 908-9655
Douglas Duong, *President*
Belinda Duong, *Admin Sec*
Simon Woods, *Engineer*
EMP: 75
SALES (est): 4.6MM **Privately Held**
WEB: www.tq.com
SIC: 7361 Employment agencies

(P-14807)
TRI-STATE EMPLOYMENT SVC INC
450 Westmont Dr, San Pedro (90731-1010)
PHONE 310 521-9616
Neftali Torres, *Branch Mgr*
EMP: 465
SALES (corp-wide): 192.9MM **Privately Held**
SIC: 7361 Employment agencies
PA: Tri-State Employment Service Inc.
160 Broadway Fl 15
New York NY 10038
212 346-7960

(P-14808)
TRINET GROUP INC (PA)
1100 San Leandro Blvd # 300, San Leandro (94577-1599)
PHONE 510 352-5000
Burton M Goldfield, *President*
H Raymond Bingham, *Ch of Bd*
William Porter, *CFO*
Brady Mickelsen,
Edward Griese, *Senior VP*
EMP: 120
SALES: 2.6B **Publicly Held**
WEB: www.trinet.com
SIC: 7361 8721 Employment agencies; accounting, auditing & bookkeeping

(P-14809)
TRUE NORTH AR LLC
10971 Sun Center Dr 200, Rancho Cordova (95670-6115)
PHONE 916 369-9850
Manoj Sharma, *Branch Mgr*
EMP: 50
SALES (corp-wide): 6.4MM **Privately Held**
SIC: 7361 Employment agencies
PA: True North Ar, Llc
100 Wood Hllow Dr Ste 200
Novato CA 94945
415 878-2200

(P-14810)
UAW-LBOR EMPLYMENT TRNING CORP
Also Called: One Stop Program
3965 S Vermont Ave, Los Angeles (90037-1937)
PHONE 323 730-7900
Audrey Holmes, *Branch Mgr*
EMP: 125
SALES (corp-wide): 7.7MM **Privately Held**
SIC: 7361 Employment agencies
PA: Uaw-Labor Employment And Training Corporation
11010 Artesia Blvd # 100
Cerritos CA 90703
562 989-7700

(P-14811)
UNITED TEMP SERVICES INC
694 Albanese Cir, San Jose (95111-1001)
PHONE 408 472-4309
EMP: 100
SALES: 1.5MM **Privately Held**
SIC: 7361 7363

(P-14812)
UPWORK INC
441 Logue Ave, Mountain View (94043-4018)
PHONE 650 316-7500
Stephane Kasriel, *CEO*
Brian Levey, *CFO*
Daphne LI, *Senior VP*
Rich Pearson, *Senior VP*
Han Yuan, *Senior VP*
EMP: 300
SALES (est): 2MM **Privately Held**
SIC: 7361 Executive placement

(P-14813)
VACO LAJOLLA LLC
Also Called: Vaco Technology
4250 Executive Sq Ste 750, La Jolla (92037-9105)
PHONE 858 642-0000
Brandy Sloatermen, *Mng Member*
Todd Sweat, *CFO*
Jerry Bostelman,
Jay Hollaman,
Brian Waller,
EMP: 58
SALES: 12.4MM **Privately Held**
SIC: 7361 Executive placement

(P-14814)
VALIDUS GROUP INC
Also Called: Ahr Professionals
1 Orchard Ste 210, Lake Forest (92630-8314)
PHONE 949 457-7606
Brian Demeo, *CEO*
EMP: 75
SALES (est): 3.2MM **Privately Held**
SIC: 7361 Employment agencies

(P-14815)
VALLEY LABOR SERVICE INC
39678 Road 84, Dinuba (93618-9588)
P.O. Box 775 (93618-0775)
PHONE 559 591-5591

7361 - Employment Agencies County (P-14816)

Fax: 559 591-2214
Jane Hobbs, *President*
Salvador Romero, *Vice Pres*
EMP: 100
SQ FT: 1,100
SALES (est): 5MM **Privately Held**
SIC: 7361 Labor contractors (employment agency)

(P-14816)
VOTUM STAFFING INC
515 W Whittier Blvd, Montebello (90640-5233)
PHONE..................................310 499-4902
Giuseppe Veneziano, *CEO*
EMP: 450
SALES (est): 14.1MM **Privately Held**
SIC: 7361 Employment agencies

(P-14817)
WEDRIVEU HOLDINGS INC
700 Airport Blvd Ste 250, Burlingame (94010-1937)
PHONE..................................650 579-5800
Dennis Carlson, *CEO*
Brian F Sours, *Vice Pres*
Erick Vanwagenen, *Vice Pres*
Robert Miller, *General Mgr*
EMP: 99
SALES (est): 1MM **Privately Held**
SIC: 7361 Employment agencies

(P-14818)
WEST VALLEY ENGINEERING INC
3875 Hopyard Rd Ste 130, Pleasanton (94588-8505)
PHONE..................................925 416-9707
Mike Williams, *Branch Mgr*
Charlie Allport, *Vice Pres*
EMP: 70
SALES (corp-wide): 48.8MM **Privately Held**
SIC: 7361 Employment agencies
PA: West Valley Engineering, Inc.
390 Potrero Ave
Sunnyvale CA 94085
408 735-1420

(P-14819)
WESTERN STAFFING SOLUTIONS LLC
1235 Carbide Dr, Corona (92881-7269)
PHONE..................................951 545-4349
Steve Whitworth, *Principal*
EMP: 123
SALES: 450K **Privately Held**
SIC: 7361 Employment agencies

(P-14820)
WMBE PAYROLLING INC
Also Called: Target Cw
9475 Chesapeake Dr Ste A, San Diego (92123-1337)
PHONE..................................858 810-3000
Samer Khouli, *CEO*
Benjamin Jack, *Office Mgr*
Erika Thomas, *Info Tech Mgr*
Andrew Proctor, *Web Dvlpr*
Joyce Jordan, *Tech Recruiter*
EMP: 75
SALES (est): 3MM **Privately Held**
SIC: 7361 Employment agencies

(P-14821)
WORKFORCELOGIC
425 California St, San Francisco (94104-2102)
PHONE..................................707 939-4300
Fax: 707 933-0530
Catherine Candland, *CEO*
Steve Furtado, *CFO*
Gary D Nelson, *Chairman*
Stuart Thompto, *Senior VP*
Catherine Wingate, *Senior VP*
EMP: 100
SALES (est): 5.2MM
SALES (corp-wide): 214.2MM **Privately Held**
SIC: 7361 7371 Employment agencies; executive placement; computer software development
PA: Zerochaos, Llc
420 S Orange Ave Ste 600
Orlando FL 32801
407 770-6161

(P-14822)
XL STAFFING INC
Also Called: Excell Staffing & SEC Svcs
450 Fletcher Pkwy Ste 204, El Cajon (92020-2520)
PHONE..................................619 579-0442
Fax: 619 579-0531
William Mackey, *President*
EMP: 200
SQ FT: 1,100
SALES (est): 11.8MM **Privately Held**
SIC: 7361 7381 Employment agencies; security guard service

(P-14823)
YANG C PARK
Also Called: Cal Facilities Management Co
3703 Payne Ave, San Jose (95117-3413)
P.O. Box 9306 (95157-0306)
PHONE..................................408 260-8066
Toll Free:..................................888 -
Fax: 408 260-8067
Yang C Park, *Owner*
EMP: 100
SALES (est): 4.7MM **Privately Held**
SIC: 7361 7349 Labor contractors (employment agency); building maintenance services

(P-14824)
YOUR EXECUTIVE SOLUTIONS
9054 Slauson Ave, Pico Rivera (90660-4521)
PHONE..................................562 388-4150
Gani Gjonbalaj, *CEO*
EMP: 650
SQ FT: 2,000
SALES (est): 8.6MM **Privately Held**
SIC: 7361 Employment agencies

(P-14825)
ZENITH TALENT CORPORATION
3315 San Felipe Rd Ste 37, San Jose (95135-2000)
PHONE..................................844 467-2300
Sunil Bagai, *CEO*
Naina Bagai, *Vice Pres*
Jude Birnbaum, *Executive Asst*
Bharath BT, *Tech Recruiter*
Yashasvi Agrawal, *Recruiter*
EMP: 240
SALES: 9MM **Privately Held**
SIC: 7361 Employment agencies

(P-14826)
ZOEL HOLDING COMPANY INC
2143 Hurley Way, Sacramento (95825-3253)
PHONE..................................916 646-3100
Ryan Johnson, *Branch Mgr*
EMP: 150
SALES (corp-wide): 55.7MM **Privately Held**
SIC: 7361 Employment agencies
PA: Zoe Holding Company, Inc.
3131 E Camelback Rd # 200
Phoenix AZ 85016
602 508-1883

7363 Help Supply Svcs

(P-14827)
24-HOUR MED STAFFING SVCS LLC
21700 Copley Dr Ste 270, Diamond Bar (91765-5489)
PHONE..................................909 895-8960
Erlinda R Stone,
Krystle Garcia, *Manager*
EMP: 110
SALES (est): 4.4MM **Privately Held**
SIC: 7363 Temporary help service

(P-14828)
A P R INC
Also Called: Alpha Professional Resources
100 E Thsnd Oaks Blvd Ste 240, Thousand Oaks (91360)
PHONE..................................805 379-3400
Fax: 805 435-7472
Salvador Ramirez, *President*
Cliff Goodwin, *CFO*
Jackie Turner, *Office Mgr*
Dennis Dunn, *Recruiter*
Marquita Thomas, *Recruiter*
EMP: 125
SQ FT: 1,100
SALES: 6.3MM **Privately Held**
WEB: www.alphaprofessionals.com
SIC: 7363 7361 Temporary help service; employment agencies

(P-14829)
AARDVARK STAFFING INC
3017 Douglas Blvd Fl 3, Roseville (95661-3848)
PHONE..................................916 774-7115
Laura O'Boyle, *Principal*
EMP: 50
SALES: 2.5MM **Privately Held**
SIC: 7363 Help supply services

(P-14830)
ACCOUNTABLE HEALTH STAFF INC
Also Called: Hrn Services
7777 Greenback Ln Ste 205, Citrus Heights (95610-5800)
PHONE..................................916 286-7667
Tina Wilson, *Branch Mgr*
EMP: 535
SALES (corp-wide): 119.6MM **Privately Held**
SIC: 7363 Employee leasing service
PA: Accountable Healthcare Staffing, Inc.
999 Yamato Rd Ste 210
Boca Raton FL 33431
561 235-7810

(P-14831)
ADVANCE STAFFING INC
189 Easy St Unit C, Mountain View (94043-3783)
P.O. Box 391447 (94039-1447)
PHONE..................................408 205-6154
Colleen Murphy, *President*
EMP: 75
SALES: 800K **Privately Held**
SIC: 7363 Help supply services

(P-14832)
ADVANCED MEDICAL REVIEWS INC
2950 31st St Ste 100, Santa Monica (90405-3047)
PHONE..................................310 575-0900
Barak Mevorak, *CEO*
Abigail M Mosley, *Admin Asst*
Amanda Marfise, *Business Mgr*
Megan Kaufman, *Opers Staff*
Reva Sober, *Director*
EMP: 61
SQ FT: 10,000
SALES (est): 4MM
SALES (corp-wide): 819.5MM **Privately Held**
WEB: www.advancedmedicalreviews.com
SIC: 7363 Medical help service
HQ: Examworks Group, Inc.
3280 Peachtree Rd Ne # 2625
Atlanta GA 30305

(P-14833)
AFFILIATED TEMPORARY HELP
4359 Florence Ave, Bell (90201-3525)
P.O. Box 124 (90201-0124)
PHONE..................................323 771-1383
Fax: 323 771-8300
John G Carbett, *President*
Ron Thomas, *Vice Pres*
EMP: 400
SQ FT: 1,100
SALES (est): 9.9MM **Privately Held**
SIC: 7363 8322 Temporary help service; individual & family services

(P-14834)
AGOSTINI AND ASSOCIATES INC
Also Called: Agostini Health Care Staffing
1470 Civic Ct Ste 1760, Concord (94520-7949)
P.O. Box 6337, Moraga (94570-6337)
PHONE..................................925 691-7300
Linda Hughes Agostini, *President*
Jules Agostini, *Corp Secy*
EMP: 50
SQ FT: 1,300
SALES (est): 1.7MM **Privately Held**
SIC: 7363 Medical help service

(P-14835)
ALLEGIS GROUP INC
1 Waters Park Dr, San Mateo (94403-1157)
PHONE..................................650 425-6950
EMP: 158
SALES (corp-wide): 10.8B **Privately Held**
SIC: 7363 Temporary help service
PA: Allegis Group, Inc.
7301 Parkway Dr
Hanover MD 21076
410 579-3000

(P-14836)
AMERICAN EAGLE SERVICES INC
1320 Arrow Hwy, La Verne (91750-5218)
PHONE..................................574 859-2055
Fax: 909 596-5497
Jeni Bartolotti, *President*
John Bartolotti, *Vice Pres*
EMP: 70
SQ FT: 1,100
SALES: 3.7MM **Privately Held**
SIC: 7363 7513 Labor resource services; truck rental & leasing, no drivers

(P-14837)
AMN HEALTHCARE SERVICES INC (PA)
12400 High Bluff Dr, San Diego (92130-3077)
PHONE..................................866 871-8519
Douglas D Wheat, *Ch of Bd*
Diana Bowden, *President*
Ralph Henderson, *President*
Susan R Salka, *President*
Brian M Scott, *CFO*
EMP: 120
SQ FT: 199,418
SALES: 1.4B **Publicly Held**
WEB: www.amnhealthcare.com
SIC: 7363 Help supply services; medical help service

(P-14838)
ANDERSON ASSOCIATES STAFFING (PA)
8200 Wilshire Blvd # 200, Beverly Hills (90211-2328)
PHONE..................................323 930-3170
Fax: 310 652-2105
Tom Anderson, *President*
EMP: 200 **EST:** 1997
SALES (est): 6.2MM **Privately Held**
WEB: www.andersonstaff.com
SIC: 7363 Temporary help service

(P-14839)
APEX STAFFING SERVICE
10134 6th St Ste A, Rancho Cucamonga (91730-5856)
PHONE..................................909 941-0267
Cynthia L Pacheco, *Partner*
Nick Saucedo, *Partner*
EMP: 50
SALES (est): 2.6MM **Privately Held**
SIC: 7363 Temporary help service

(P-14840)
ARCADIA SERVICES INC
4340 Redwood Hwy Ste 123, San Rafael (94903-2104)
PHONE..................................248 352-7530
John E Elliott II, *Branch Mgr*
Cathy Sparling, *COO*
EMP: 51
SALES (corp-wide): 168.8MM **Privately Held**
SIC: 7363 8082 Medical help service; home health care services
PA: Arcadia Services, Inc.
20750 Civic Center Dr # 100
Southfield MI 48076
248 352-7530

(P-14841)
AYA HEALTHCARE INC
5930 Cornerstone Ct W # 300, San Diego (92121-3741)
PHONE..................................858 458-4410
Alan Braynin, *President*
Shelley Donovan, *President*

PRODUCTS & SERVICES SECTION

7363 - Help Supply Svcs County (P-14866)

Dan Walter, *Vice Pres*
Ashli Nelson, *Finance Mgr*
Neely Falgout, *Accountant*
EMP: 500
SQ FT: 20,000
SALES (est): 141MM **Privately Held**
SIC: 7363 8049 Temporary help service; nurses, registered & practical

(P-14842)
B2B STAFFING SERVICES INC
Also Called: B2b Payroll Services
4141 Ball Rd Ste 150, Cypress (90630-3465)
PHONE..................714 243-4104
Brian Wigdor, *President*
Bruce Underwood, *CFO*
Cathy Underwood, *Human Res Dir*
Albert Garcia, *HR Admin*
Yvette Calzada, *Sales Staff*
EMP: 300
SALES (est): 10MM **Privately Held**
SIC: 7363 8721 Temporary help service; payroll accounting service

(P-14843)
BANYAN SOLUTIONS INC
Also Called: Banyon Transcription
1067 Bryant Way, Sunnyvale (94087-3705)
PHONE..................650 766-9338
Jyoti Challi, *Principal*
EMP: 63
SALES (est): 3.3MM **Privately Held**
SIC: 7363 Medical help service

(P-14844)
BAY SPAN INC
260 Link Rd Ste D, Fairfield (94534-1674)
PHONE..................707 863-4949
Fax: 707 863-4943
Dana Carnes, *President*
Krista Perata, *Manager*
EMP: 92
SQ FT: 3,500
SALES: 1.5MM **Privately Held**
WEB: www.bayspan.com
SIC: 7363 Temporary help service; industrial help service

(P-14845)
BAYSIDE SOLUTIONS INC
1917 Palomar Oaks Way # 130, Carlsbad (92008-5512)
PHONE..................760 448-2970
Bob Klotz, *President*
Nick Skaric, *Manager*
EMP: 50
SALES (est): 1.1MM **Privately Held**
SIC: 7363 Manpower pools

(P-14846)
BEHAVIORAL INTERVENTION ASSN
Also Called: B I A
2354 Powell St A, Emeryville (94608-1738)
PHONE..................510 652-7445
Fax: 510 652-9288
Hilary Stubblefield, *Exec Dir*
Sonia Newton, *Officer*
Fred Baldi, *Business Dir*
Deanne Detmers, *Program Dir*
Hilary S Baldi, *Director*
EMP: 50
SALES: 3.4MM **Privately Held**
WEB: www.bia4autism.org
SIC: 7363 Domestic help service

(P-14847)
BUTLER INTERNATIONAL INC (PA)
3820 State St Ste A, Santa Barbara (93105-3182)
PHONE..................805 882-2200
Edward M Kopko, *Ch of Bd*
Mark Koscinski, *CFO*
James J Beckley, *Senior VP*
Barbara Spindel, *Human Res Dir*
Ren E Ward, *Marketing Mgr*
EMP: 200
SALES (est): 88.4MM **Privately Held**
WEB: www.butler.com
SIC: 7363 8742 Help supply services; management consulting services

(P-14848)
BUTLER SERVICE GROUP INC (HQ)
3820 State St Ste A, Santa Barbara (93105-3182)
PHONE..................201 891-5312
Edward M Kopko, *President*
Michael C Hellriegel, *CFO*
R Scott Silver Hill, *Senior VP*
EMP: 100
SQ FT: 82,000
SALES (est): 29.1MM
SALES (corp-wide): 88.4MM **Privately Held**
SIC: 7363 8711 8748 3661 Engineering help service; engineering services; communications consulting; telephone & telegraph apparatus; general automotive repair shops
PA: Butler International, Inc.
3820 State St Ste A
Santa Barbara CA 93105
805 882-2200

(P-14849)
CALIFORNIA SCHL EMPLOYEES ASSN
4600 Santa Anita Ave, El Monte (91731-1320)
PHONE..................626 258-3300
Michael Leon, *Branch Mgr*
EMP: 295
SQ FT: 8,286
SALES (corp-wide): 65.6MM **Privately Held**
SIC: 7363 Help supply services
PA: California School Employees' Association
2045 Lundy Ave
San Jose CA 95131
408 473-1000

(P-14850)
CANON RECRUITING GROUP LLC
26531 Summit Cir, Santa Clarita (91350-3049)
PHONE..................661 252-7400
Fax: 661 252-7880
Laurie Grayem, *CEO*
Tim Grayem, *President*
William Rivera, *Manager*
Ryan McAhren, *Accounts Mgr*
EMP: 400
SQ FT: 7,500
SALES (est): 21.8MM **Privately Held**
SIC: 7363 7361 Office help supply service; executive placement

(P-14851)
CARDINAL POINT CAPTAINS INC
3508 Seagate Way Ste 140, Oceanside (92056-2685)
PHONE..................760 438-7361
Jordan E Cousino,
Jordan Cousino, *General Mgr*
EMP: 56
SQ FT: 3,200
SALES (est): 890K **Privately Held**
SIC: 7363 Boat crew service

(P-14852)
CARE MEDICAL TRNSP INC
Also Called: Care Ambulance
9770 Candida St, San Diego (92126-4536)
PHONE..................858 653-4520
Fax: 858 653-4538
Kelvin Carlisle, *President*
EMP: 190
SQ FT: 14,000
SALES (est): 13.4MM **Privately Held**
SIC: 7363 Medical help service

(P-14853)
CHILDCARE CAREERS LLC
1700 S El Camino Real # 201, San Mateo (94402-3065)
PHONE..................650 372-0211
Fax: 650 345-8837
Jason Jones,
Sabah Raza, *Opers Staff*
Dominique Ridley, *Teacher*
Cecilia De Ment, *Director*
Jessica Guttenbeil, *Supervisor*
EMP: 1000 **EST:** 2010
SQ FT: 4,000
SALES (est): 5.2MM **Privately Held**
SIC: 7363 7361 Temporary help service; teachers' agency

(P-14854)
CLEARPATH WORKFORCE MGT INC
1215 W Center St Ste 102, Manteca (95337-4280)
PHONE..................209 239-8700
Renee Fink, *CEO*
Judy Gnade, *CFO*
Jason Posel, *Senior VP*
Sue Ortiz, *Vice Pres*
EMP: 275 **EST:** 2001
SQ FT: 3,171
SALES: 28.8MM **Privately Held**
SIC: 7363 Help supply services
PA: Clearpath Management Group, Inc.
1215 W Center St Ste 102
Manteca CA 95337
209 239-8700

(P-14855)
CLP RESOURCES INC
1485 Bay Shore Blvd # 138, San Francisco (94124-4002)
PHONE..................415 508-0910
Richard Webb, *Branch Mgr*
Toby Karlitz, *Executive*
EMP: 50
SALES (corp-wide): 2.7B **Publicly Held**
SIC: 7363 Temporary help service
HQ: Clp Resources, Inc.
1015 A St
Tacoma WA 98402
775 321-8000

(P-14856)
CLP RESOURCES INC
1260 N Dutton Ave, Santa Rosa (95401-4659)
PHONE..................707 569-0200
Dan Rosiak, *Branch Mgr*
EMP: 50
SALES (corp-wide): 2.7B **Publicly Held**
SIC: 7363 Temporary help service
HQ: Clp Resources, Inc.
1015 A St
Tacoma WA 98402
775 321-8000

(P-14857)
CLP RESOURCES INC
1000 Sunrise Ave Ste 8a, Roseville (95661-5471)
PHONE..................916 788-0300
EMP: 60
SALES (corp-wide): 2.1B **Publicly Held**
SIC: 7363
HQ: Clp Resources, Inc.
1015 A St
Tacoma WA 98402
775 321-8000

(P-14858)
CLP RESOURCES INC
570 El Cmino Real Ste 170, Redwood City (94067)
PHONE..................650 261-2100
Vince Vargas, *Director*
EMP: 200
SALES (corp-wide): 2.7B **Publicly Held**
SIC: 7363 Temporary help service
HQ: Clp Resources, Inc.
1015 A St
Tacoma WA 98402
775 321-8000

(P-14859)
CLP RESOURCES INC
4460 Redwood Hwy Ste 14, San Rafael (94903-1953)
PHONE..................415 446-7000
EMP: 50
SALES (corp-wide): 2.1B **Publicly Held**
SIC: 7363
HQ: Clp Resources, Inc.
1015 A St
Tacoma WA 98402
775 321-8000

(P-14860)
CLP RESOURCES INC
741 E Ball Rd Ste 100, Anaheim (92805-5952)
PHONE..................714 300-0510
Brian Rogers, *Manager*
EMP: 100
SALES (corp-wide): 2.7B **Publicly Held**
SIC: 7363 Help supply services
HQ: Clp Resources, Inc.
1015 A St
Tacoma WA 98402
775 321-8000

(P-14861)
CLP RESOURCES INC
Also Called: Contractors Labor Pool of La
111 N First St Ste 100, Burbank (91502-1851)
PHONE..................818 260-9190
Fax: 310 558-7909
Guan Santos, *Manager*
Jesse Remer, *Manager*
Hopen Wolf, *Manager*
EMP: 85
SALES (corp-wide): 2.7B **Publicly Held**
SIC: 7363 7361 Help supply services; employment agencies
HQ: Clp Resources, Inc.
1015 A St
Tacoma WA 98402
775 321-8000

(P-14862)
CO TEAM STAFFING
1608 Sunrise Ave Ste D, Modesto (95350-4678)
PHONE..................209 578-4286
Hilario Vieyra, *Principal*
EMP: 90
SALES (est): 1.5MM **Privately Held**
SIC: 7363 Help supply services

(P-14863)
COAST PERSONNEL SERVICES INC (PA)
2295 De La Cruz Blvd, Santa Clara (95050-3020)
P.O. Box 328 (95052-0328)
PHONE..................408 653-2100
Fax: 408 653-2109
Larry K Bunker, *CEO*
Michael Avidano, *Vice Pres*
Larry Broun, *Vice Pres*
Janet Marchel, *Vice Pres*
Sonya Hopson, *Director*
EMP: 1895
SQ FT: 7,500
SALES (est): 58MM **Privately Held**
WEB: www.coastjobs.com
SIC: 7363 Temporary help service

(P-14864)
COMPUTERIZED MANAGEMENT
40 W Cochran St, Simi Valley (93065-6251)
P.O. Box 190 (93062-0190)
PHONE..................805 522-5999
Daryl Favale, *Owner*
Dale Fazvale, *President*
Thomas Brajkovich, *Info Tech Mgr*
EMP: 60
SALES (est): 1.3MM **Privately Held**
WEB: www.cmsmanagement.net
SIC: 7363 8721 Medical help service; billing & bookkeeping service

(P-14865)
CORPORATE DRIVER SERVICES INC
1820 Pasadena Glen Rd, Pasadena (91107-1217)
PHONE..................626 791-9020
Warren Williams, *President*
Linda Williams, *Vice Pres*
EMP: 150
SALES: 500K **Privately Held**
SIC: 7363 Truck driver services

(P-14866)
CPE PEO INC
9200 W Sunset Blvd # 700, West Hollywood (90069-3502)
PHONE..................310 385-1000
Lee C Samson, *CEO*

7363 - Help Supply Svcs County (P-14867)

Jay Cober, *President*
Grace Drulius, *CFO*
Harold Walt, *CFO*
Larry Feigen, *Vice Ch Bd*
EMP: 90
SQ FT: 11,000
SALES (est): 3MM **Privately Held**
SIC: 7363 Employee leasing service

(P-14867)
CRAFT RESOURCES INC
220 S Pcifc Cst Hwy 112, Redondo Beach (90277)
P.O. Box 7000 (90277-8710)
PHONE..................310 937-3744
Stephen A Lawrence, *President*
Ginny Griewig, *Mng Officer*
Melissa Jaimes, *Office Mgr*
Ginny Striewig, *Office Mgr*
EMP: 150
SQ FT: 2,000
SALES (est): 4.6MM **Privately Held**
WEB: www.craft-resources.com
SIC: 7363 7361 Industrial help service; employment agencies

(P-14868)
CULINARY SERVICES AMERICA INC
Also Called: Culinary Staffing Service
6363 Wilshire Blvd # 305, Los Angeles (90048-5726)
PHONE..................323 965-7582
Fax: 323 965-7599
Randy Hopp, *President*
EMP: 50
SQ FT: 1,200
SALES (est): 2.1MM **Privately Held**
SIC: 7363 7361 Temporary help service; employment agencies

(P-14869)
CW HEALTHCARE INC
7700 Edgewater Dr Ste 728, Oakland (94621-3009)
PHONE..................510 636-9000
Russell Jones, *President*
Judy Mejia, *Manager*
EMP: 50
SQ FT: 900
SALES (est): 1.5MM **Privately Held**
WEB: www.cwhealthcare.com
SIC: 7363 Medical help service

(P-14870)
DELTA PERSONNEL SERVICES INC
Also Called: Guardian Security Agency
1820 Galindo St Ste 3, Concord (94520-2447)
PHONE..................925 356-3034
Fax: 925 356-3031
Judith Travers, *CEO*
Heather Travers, *Vice Pres*
EMP: 80
SQ FT: 4,300
SALES (est): 5.5MM **Privately Held**
SIC: 7363 Temporary help service

(P-14871)
DISCHARGE RESOURCE GROUP
Also Called: DRG Health Care Staffing
400 Oyster Point Blvd # 440, South San Francisco (94080-1979)
PHONE..................650 877-8111
Fax: 650 877-8129
Lawrence Hix, *CEO*
Nancy Jacobson, *COO*
Marsha Hix, *Treasurer*
Lorie Descala, *Exec Dir*
Lucinda Ip, *Info Tech Mgr*
EMP: 250
SQ FT: 2,000
SALES (est): 12.4MM **Privately Held**
WEB: www.drgstaffing.com
SIC: 7363 7361 Temporary help service; medical help service; employment agencies

(P-14872)
ECORPTECH LLC
4732 Travertino St, Dublin (94568-4251)
PHONE..................408 216-8116
Sudhakar Reddy,
Seema Vashist,
EMP: 50
SALES: 1.5MM **Privately Held**
WEB: www.ecorptech.com
SIC: 7363 Temporary help service

(P-14873)
EMPLOYBRIDGE LLC (HQ)
Also Called: Select Staffing
3820 State St, Santa Barbara (93105-3182)
PHONE..................805 882-2200
Fax: 805 898-7111
Thomas A Bickes, *President*
Fred R Herbert, *President*
Steve Mills, *President*
Paul J Sorensen, *President*
Mark R McComb, *COO*
EMP: 148
SALES (est): 304MM
SALES (corp-wide): 391.2MM **Privately Held**
WEB: www.selectpersonnel.com
SIC: 7363 Temporary help service
PA: Employbridge Holding Company
1040 Crown Pointe Pkwy # 1040
Atlanta GA 30338
770 671-1900

(P-14874)
EPLICA INC (PA)
Also Called: Eastridge ADM Staffing
2355 Northside Dr Ste 120, San Diego (92108-2714)
PHONE..................619 260-2000
Robert Svet, *President*
Avrom Laverne, *Admin Sec*
Brad Taylor, *Engineer*
Debbie Thompson, *Accounting Dir*
Debra Thompson, *Controller*
EMP: 175 **EST:** 1971
SQ FT: 1,500
SALES (est): 179.4MM **Privately Held**
WEB: www.hr-solutions.com
SIC: 7363 7361 Temporary help service; employment agencies

(P-14875)
EXPRESS PERSONNEL SERVICES
870 W Onstott Frontage Rd E, Yuba City (95991-3500)
PHONE..................530 671-9202
Tina Williams, *President*
Tom Williams, *Vice Pres*
EMP: 60
SALES (est): 2.4MM **Privately Held**
SIC: 7363 Temporary help service

(P-14876)
EXPRESS SERVICES INC
Also Called: Express Personnel Services
1433 N Montebello Blvd, Montebello (90640-2584)
PHONE..................323 832-9405
EMP: 5002
SALES (corp-wide): 2.6B **Privately Held**
SIC: 7363 Temporary help service
PA: Express Services Inc
9701 Boardwalk Blvd
Oklahoma City OK 73162
405 840-5000

(P-14877)
FAMILY SVC AGCY SAN FRANCISCO (PA)
Also Called: Felton Institute
1500 Franklin St, San Francisco (94109-4523)
PHONE..................415 474-7310
Fax: 415 563-2097
Albert Gilbert III, *President*
Nina Cartee, *CFO*
Marvin L Davis, *CFO*
Resa Peay-Wainwright, *Vice Pres*
Charles Ward, *Vice Pres*
EMP: 70
SQ FT: 14,000
SALES: 16MM **Privately Held**
SIC: 7363 Help supply services

(P-14878)
FERNANDES & SONS GEN CONTRS
2110 S Bascom Ave Ste 201, Campbell (95008-3299)
PHONE..................408 626-9090
Larry Fernandes, *President*
Linda Gonzalez, *Project Engr*
Christine Kleinsmid, *Manager*
EMP: 55
SALES (est): 4.8MM **Privately Held**
SIC: 7363 8299 Medical help service; educational services

(P-14879)
FLEXCARE LLC
Also Called: Flexcare Medical Staffing
990 Reserve Dr Ste 200, Roseville (95678-1391)
PHONE..................866 564-3589
Nate Porter, *Mng Member*
EMP: 1000
SALES (est): 231.8K **Privately Held**
SIC: 7363 Help supply services

(P-14880)
FREEDOM STAFF LEASING INC
3142 Pacific Coast Hwy, Torrance (90505-6746)
P.O. Box 1689, Wilmington (90748-1689)
PHONE..................310 834-6621
Fax: 310 513-0446
Lofton Ryan Burris, *President*
EMP: 300
SQ FT: 1,000
SALES (est): 6.6MM **Privately Held**
WEB: www.freedompeo.com
SIC: 7363 Employee leasing service

(P-14881)
G R HELM INC
Also Called: Helm Technical Services
5050 Rbert J Mathews Pkwy, El Dorado Hills (95762-5761)
PHONE..................916 933-9697
Fax: 916 933-9692
Gordon Helm, *President*
Denise Deagon, *Sales Mgr*
EMP: 85
SQ FT: 1,050
SALES (est): 3.3MM **Privately Held**
WEB: www.helmtech.com
SIC: 7363 7371 Labor resource services; computer software development

(P-14882)
GENESIS HOME HEALTH INC
1687 Erringer Rd Ste 202, Simi Valley (93065-6509)
PHONE..................805 520-7100
EMP: 50
SALES (est): 2.9MM **Privately Held**
SIC: 7363 7361

(P-14883)
GO-STAFF INC (PA)
Also Called: G S I
8798 Complex Dr, San Diego (92123-1402)
PHONE..................858 292-8562
Fax: 858 292-0230
Scott Crumrine, *CEO*
Stacey Crumrine, *Vice Pres*
Brooke Velazquez, *Regional Mgr*
Jacques Albarran, *Division Mgr*
Justine March, *Admin Asst*
EMP: 54
SQ FT: 12,000
SALES (est): 44.5MM **Privately Held**
WEB: www.gsica.com
SIC: 7363 8721 Temporary help service; payroll accounting service

(P-14884)
GOODWILL OF SILICON VALLEY (PA)
1080 N 7th St, San Jose (95112-4425)
PHONE..................408 998-5774
Fax: 408 283-9093
Michael E Fox, *CEO*
Frank Kent, *CEO*
Christopher King, *COO*
Christopher Baker, *CFO*
Dale Achabal, *Treasurer*
EMP: 100
SQ FT: 180,000
SALES: 39.4MM **Privately Held**
SIC: 7363 5932 Help supply services; used merchandise stores

(P-14885)
HEALTHLINK STAFFING INC
4444 W Riverside Dr # 105, Burbank (91505-4073)
PHONE..................818 972-2140
Diane Wagner, *President*
EMP: 74
SQ FT: 700
SALES: 400K **Privately Held**
SIC: 7363 8742 8399 Medical help service; hospital & health services consultant; health systems agency

(P-14886)
I N C BUILDERS INC
Also Called: Acme Staffing
1560 Ocotillo Dr Ste L, El Centro (92243-4237)
PHONE..................760 352-4200
Fax: 760 352-5202
Rebecca Deal, *Manager*
EMP: 350
SALES (corp-wide): 6.6MM **Privately Held**
SIC: 7363 Help supply services
PA: I N C Builders, Inc.
550 E 32nd St Ste 2
Yuma AZ 85365
928 344-8367

(P-14887)
INFINITY NURSES CARE INC
39159 Paseo Padre Pkwy # 111, Fremont (94538-1608)
PHONE..................510 713-8892
Fax: 510 713-8246
Angeles Santos, *President*
Richard Santos, *Vice Pres*
Jack Shahin, *Manager*
Joseph Visconti, *Manager*
EMP: 100
SQ FT: 1,500
SALES: 15K **Privately Held**
SIC: 7363 8082 Medical help service; home health care services

(P-14888)
INFINITY STAFFING SERVICE
710 Kirkpatric Ct, Hollister (95023-2817)
PHONE..................831 638-0360
Ramiro Rodriguez, *President*
Trisha Tafoya, *Business Mgr*
Esequiel Arrizon, *Sales Executive*
EMP: 260 **EST:** 2007
SALES (est): 854.9K **Privately Held**
SIC: 7363 Help supply services

(P-14889)
INTERACTIVE MEDICAL SPECIALIST
454 Las Gallinas Ave # 287, San Rafael (94903-3618)
PHONE..................415 472-4204
Jaleh Ebrahimi, *President*
Oranous Ebrahimi, *Treasurer*
Ghazaleh Ebrahimi, *Vice Pres*
Jaleh Ory, *Human Res Mgr*
EMP: 70
SALES: 1.8MM **Privately Held**
WEB: www.imsspecialists.com
SIC: 7363 Medical help service

(P-14890)
IQ PIPELINE LLC
1550 Hotel Cir N Ste 270, San Diego (92108-2908)
PHONE..................858 483-7400
Chris Oberle,
Angie Bisone, *Vice Pres*
Kyle Luken, *Recruiter*
Nate Hockett, *Director*
Eunji Kim, *Director*
EMP: 100
SALES (est): 6.2MM **Privately Held**
SIC: 7363 Temporary help service

PRODUCTS & SERVICES SECTION

7363 - Help Supply Svcs County (P-14914)

(P-14891)
JUNE GROUP LLC
Also Called: Qualstaff Resources
9444 Waples St Ste 100, San Diego
(92121-2940)
PHONE.................................858 450-4290
Fax: 858 450-4292
R Scott Silver-Hill, *Mng Member*
Kerry Walker, *Tech Recruiter*
Brent Robertson, *Business Mgr*
Michelle Barron, *HR Admin*
Amber Boytis-Barriga, *Recruiter*
EMP: 100
SQ FT: 4,200
SALES (est): 4.1MM **Privately Held**
SIC: 7363 Temporary help service

(P-14892)
KAMPS COMPANY
1262 Dupont Ct, Manteca (95336-6003)
PHONE.................................209 823-8924
John Paul, *President*
John Kamps, *Shareholder*
EMP: 160
SQ FT: 3,000
SALES (est): 3.4MM **Privately Held**
SIC: 7363 Employee leasing service
PA: Kamps Propane, Inc.
1262 Dupont Ct
Manteca CA 95336

(P-14893)
KENSINGTON AGENCY INC
Also Called: Kensington Nursing Agency
8469 La Mesa Blvd, La Mesa
(91942-5335)
PHONE.................................619 280-6993
Fax: 619 283-6049
David Keyte, *General Mgr*
Deaydre Pulliam, *COO*
EMP: 50
SQ FT: 1,000
SALES (est): 3.2MM **Privately Held**
SIC: 7363 Temporary help service

(P-14894)
L&T STAFFING INC
Also Called: Staffing Solutions
2122 W Whittier Blvd, Montebello
(90640-4013)
PHONE.................................323 727-9056
Fortino Rivera, *Branch Mgr*
EMP: 354
SALES (corp-wide): 7MM **Privately Held**
SIC: 7363 Temporary help service
PA: L&T Staffing, Inc
400 N Tustin Ave Ste 140
Santa Ana CA 92705
714 558-1821

(P-14895)
LABOR FNDERS OF THE PALM BCHES
Also Called: Labor Finders Staffing
4325 N Blackstone Ave, Fresno
(93726-1902)
PHONE.................................559 221-2023
Fax: 559 221-4204
David Fritz, *Manager*
EMP: 60
SALES (corp-wide): 2.6MM **Privately Held**
SIC: 7363 Help supply services
PA: Labor Finders Of The Palm Beaches Inc
1401 S Military Trl H-1
West Palm Beach FL 33415
561 439-0605

(P-14896)
LABOR READY SOUTHWEST INC
1405 S El Camno Real 51, Oceanside
(92054)
PHONE.................................760 433-4980
Frank Guttierez, *Manager*
EMP: 50
SALES (corp-wide): 2.7B **Publicly Held**
SIC: 7363 Temporary help service
HQ: Labor Ready, Inc.
1015 A St Unit A
Tacoma WA 98402
253 680-8487

(P-14897)
LANDMARK EVENT STAFFING
7700 Edgewater Dr Ste 555, Oakland
(94621-3093)
PHONE.................................510 632-9000
Peter Kranske, *Branch Mgr*
EMP: 504
SALES (corp-wide): 14.1MM **Privately Held**
SIC: 7363 Help supply services
PA: Landmark Event Staffing Services, Inc.
4131 Harbor Walk Dr
Fort Collins CO 80525
714 293-4248

(P-14898)
LEAD STAFFING CORPORATION
216 S Citrus St Ste 397, West Covina
(91791-2144)
PHONE.................................800 928-5561
Lilian Nyamoita, *CEO*
EMP: 225
SALES (est): 6.8MM **Privately Held**
SIC: 7363 8049 Help supply services; medical help service; temporary help service; office help supply service; nurses & other medical assistants

(P-14899)
LESCONCIERGES INC (PA)
200 Pine St Fl 2, San Francisco
(94104-2712)
PHONE.................................415 905-6088
Fax: 415 772-9971
Linda Jenkinson, *Ch of Bd*
Ramesh Patel, *President*
Paul McKnight, *CFO*
Sneha Jhaveri, *Vice Pres*
Sophie Davis, *Social Dir*
EMP: 88
SQ FT: 26,000
SALES (est): 39.1MM **Privately Held**
WEB: www.lesconcierges.com
SIC: 7363 Help supply services

(P-14900)
LIVEOPS INC (PA)
555 Twin Dolphin Dr # 400, Redwood City
(94065-2132)
PHONE.................................650 453-2700
Vasili Triant, *CEO*
Marty Beard, *President*
Suresh Duddi, *President*
Bill Slakely, *CFO*
William Slakey, *CFO*
EMP: 148
SQ FT: 59,000
SALES (est): 65.9MM **Privately Held**
WEB: www.liveops.com
SIC: 7363 Help supply services

(P-14901)
LOS ANGLES CNSRVTION CORPS INC (PA)
605 W Olympic Blvd # 450, Los Angeles
(90015-1400)
P.O. Box 15868 (90015-0868)
PHONE.................................213 362-9000
Fax: 213 362-7958
Mercedes Morton, *President*
Wendy Butts, *CEO*
Albert Chavez, *Treasurer*
Teresa Cisneros Burton, *Admin Sec*
Adewole Williams, *Admin Asst*
EMP: 115
SQ FT: 6,000
SALES: 20.4MM **Privately Held**
SIC: 7363 Temporary help service

(P-14902)
M K TECHNICAL SERVICES INC
4349 San Felipe Rd, San Jose
(95135-1507)
PHONE.................................408 528-0401
Fax: 408 528-0793
Margie Menz King, *President*
Janice Yoshimoto, *Vice Pres*
Johnie Staggs, *Administration*
Cathy Short, *Accounts Mgr*
EMP: 50
SQ FT: 1,000
SALES: 5MM **Privately Held**
SIC: 7363 Temporary help service

(P-14903)
MAHLER ENTERPRISES INC
2121 E Tahquitz Canyon Wa, Palm Springs
(92262-7021)
PHONE.................................760 537-7690
EMP: 336
SALES (corp-wide): 20.2MM **Privately Held**
SIC: 7363 Help supply services
PA: Mahler Enterprises, Inc.
600 N Broadway Ste 200
Milwaukee WI 53202
414 347-1350

(P-14904)
MAXIM HEALTHCARE SERVICES INC
Also Called: Riverside Companion Services
1845 Bus Ctr Dr Ste 112, San Bernardino
(92408)
PHONE.................................951 684-4148
Fax: 951 369-0601
Elijah Hall, *Manager*
EMP: 304
SALES (corp-wide): 1.2B **Privately Held**
WEB: www.maximstaffing.com
SIC: 7363 Medical help service
PA: Maxim Healthcare Services, Inc.
7227 Lee Deforest Dr
Columbia MD 21046
410 910-1500

(P-14905)
MCG SERVICES CORPORATION
Also Called: Management Consulting Group
1010 B St Ste 425, San Rafael
(94901-2921)
PHONE.................................415 721-1444
Todd Ghanizadeh, *President*
Jacqueline Webb, *COO*
Paul Fernandes, *Admin Sec*
EMP: 50
SQ FT: 3,000
SALES (est): 2.3MM **Privately Held**
WEB: www.mcgsf.net
SIC: 7363 Temporary help service

(P-14906)
ME AND ME INC
Also Called: Employee Solutions
14536 Roscoe Blvd Ste 112, Van Nuys
(91402-4103)
P.O. Box 801795, Santa Clarita (91380-1795)
PHONE.................................818 891-0197
Michael E Socha, *President*
EMP: 76
SALES: 2MM **Privately Held**
SIC: 7363 Medical help service

(P-14907)
MED STAFFING LLC
39039 Paseo Padre Pkwy # 208, Fremont
(94538-1618)
PHONE.................................510 795-0114
Ramesh C Karipineni MD,
Karen Parsons, *Opers Mgr*
EMP: 50
SALES: 750K **Privately Held**
SIC: 7363 Help supply services

(P-14908)
MEDICAL HOME SPECIALISTS INC
Also Called: Medical HM Care Professionals
2115 Churn Creek Rd, Redding
(96002-0732)
PHONE.................................530 226-5577
Fax: 530 246-5585
Kathy A McKillop, *CEO*
Elaine Flores, *COO*
Gayle S Shton, *Admin Asst*
EMP: 160
SQ FT: 1,600
SALES (est): 7.9MM **Privately Held**
WEB: www.medicalhomecarepros.com
SIC: 7363 Medical help service

(P-14909)
MEDICAL MANAGEMENT CONS INC (PA)
Also Called: MMC
8150 Beverly Blvd, Los Angeles
(90048-4513)
PHONE.................................310 659-3835
Fax: 323 659-0868
Mashi Rahmani, *President*
Charles Chatelain, *Executive Asst*
Crystal Obrien, *CTO*
Paul Rahmani, *Info Tech Mgr*
Fan Wong, *Accountant*
EMP: 50
SQ FT: 21,000
SALES (est): 71.4MM **Privately Held**
WEB: www.mmchr.com
SIC: 7363 8742 8748 8721 Help supply services; hospital & health services consultant; employee programs administration; payroll accounting service

(P-14910)
MEDICAL SUPPORT SERVICES
6660 W Sunset Blvd Ste J, Los Angeles
(90028-7161)
PHONE.................................323 860-7994
Fax: 323 860-7996
Raynoldo Fernandez, *President*
Riza O Sazon, *Manager*
EMP: 100
SQ FT: 1,000
SALES (est): 2.8MM **Privately Held**
WEB: www.mssregistryinc.com
SIC: 7363 7361 Medical help service; employment agencies

(P-14911)
MERRITT HAWKINS & ASSOC LLC (HQ)
12400 High Bluff Dr, San Diego
(92130-3077)
PHONE.................................858 792-0711
Susan Salka Fka Nowakowski, *CEO*
Brian Scott, *CFO*
John Dillon, *Treasurer*
Mike Belkin, *Vice Pres*
Denise Jackson, *Vice Pres*
EMP: 120
SQ FT: 96,000
SALES: 13.5MM
SALES (corp-wide): 1.4B **Publicly Held**
WEB: www.mhagroup.com
SIC: 7363 Medical help service
PA: Amn Healthcare Services, Inc.
12400 High Bluff Dr
San Diego CA 92130
866 871-8519

(P-14912)
MGA HEALTHCARE CALIFORNIA INC
879 W 190th St Ste 260, Gardena
(90248-4267)
PHONE.................................310 324-5591
David T Zowine, *President*
Jennifer Deporzio, *Controller*
Ian Kohlenscin, *Manager*
EMP: 50
SQ FT: 1,111
SALES: 2.5MM **Privately Held**
SIC: 7363 Help supply services

(P-14913)
MSS NURSES REGISTRY INC
Also Called: Medical Support Services
6660 W Sunset Blvd Ste J, Los Angeles
(90028-7161)
PHONE.................................323 467-5717
Reynaldo Fernandez, *President*
Teresita Fernandez, *Principal*
EMP: 99
SALES (est): 1.4MM **Privately Held**
SIC: 7363 Temporary help service

(P-14914)
MURRAY ENTPS STAFFING SVCS
23250 Lawrence Rd, Fiddletown
(95629-9744)
PHONE.................................530 409-5703
Mike Murray, *President*
Shannon T Murray, *Treasurer*
EMP: 100 **EST:** 1976
SQ FT: 2,300
SALES: 60K **Privately Held**
SIC: 7363 Temporary help service

7363 - Help Supply Svcs County (P-14915)

PRODUDUCTS & SERVICES SECTION

(P-14915)
NATIONAL BUILDER SERVICES INC
3835 E Thousand Oaks Blvd R, Westlake Village (91362-3637)
PHONE..................714 634-7800
Joseph M Wiseman, *President*
Jeff Spooner, *Regional Mgr*
Cindy Stindle, *Personnel Exec*
EMP: 100
SQ FT: 1,700
SALES (est): 3.6MM **Privately Held**
WEB: www.tti-nbs.com
SIC: 7363 Employee leasing service

(P-14916)
NEW DAY STAFFING INC
5920 Friars Rd Ste 104, San Diego (92108-1077)
PHONE..................619 481-5400
Julie Laurice, *President*
EMP: 150
SALES (est): 4.2MM **Privately Held**
SIC: 7363 Help supply services

(P-14917)
NEWPORT BEACH FBO LLC
Also Called: Atlantic Aviation
19711 Campus Dr Ste 100, Santa Ana (92707-5203)
PHONE..................949 851-0049
Steven Hershfer, *Manager*
Sandra Zarate, *Executive*
Deborah Clark, *Sales Executive*
Peter Hershfer, *Manager*
EMP: 64
SQ FT: 125,000
SALES (est): 2.9MM **Privately Held**
SIC: 7363 4581 4522 Pilot service, aviation; airports, flying fields & services; air transportation, nonscheduled

(P-14918)
NOW MEDICAL SERVICES INC
1641 1/2 Westwood Blvd, Los Angeles (90024-5603)
PHONE..................310 479-4520
Fax: 310 778-2615
Larry Schapiro, *President*
EMP: 55
SQ FT: 1,700
SALES (est): 2.9MM **Privately Held**
SIC: 7363 4212 Help supply services; delivery service, vehicular

(P-14919)
NURSEFINDERS INC (PA)
12400 High Bluff Dr, San Diego (92130-3077)
P.O. Box 919024 (92191-9024)
PHONE..................800 445-0459
Rovert Livonius, *Exec Dir*
EMP: 50
SALES (est): 6.8MM **Privately Held**
SIC: 7363 Temporary help service

(P-14920)
ON ASSIGNMENT INC (PA)
26745 Malibu Hills Rd, Calabasas (91301-5355)
PHONE..................818 878-7900
Fax: 818 878-7930
Peter T Dameris, *President*
Jeremy M Jones, *Ch of Bd*
Randolph C Blazer, *President*
Michael J McGowan, *COO*
Edward L Pierce, *CFO*
EMP: 146
SQ FT: 37,200
SALES: 2B **Publicly Held**
WEB: www.onassignment.com
SIC: 7363 7361 Help supply services; temporary help service; employment agencies

(P-14921)
ON CALL EMPLOYEE SOLUTIONS INC
895 Dove St Ste 300, Newport Beach (92660-2996)
PHONE..................949 955-4994
Derrick Broekema, *Branch Mgr*
EMP: 107

SALES (corp-wide): 7.2MM **Privately Held**
SIC: 7363 Help supply services
PA: On Call Employee Solutions, Inc.
110 W A St Ste 650
San Diego CA
619 238-3300

(P-14922)
PERSONNEL PREFERENCE INC
150 Boles St Ste A, Weed (96094-2586)
PHONE..................530 938-3909
Jill Tillinghast, *President*
EMP: 150
SALES (est): 5.7MM **Privately Held**
SIC: 7363 7361 Temporary help service; employment agencies

(P-14923)
PHARMACY TEMPS INC
Also Called: Nor-Cal Medical Temps
2125 Paradise Dr, Belvedere Tiburon (94920-1939)
P.O. Box 736 (94920-0736)
PHONE..................415 459-5211
Kristina Glaves, *President*
EMP: 50
SALES: 700K **Privately Held**
SIC: 7363 Temporary help service

(P-14924)
PHOENIX ENGINEERING CO INC
Also Called: Phoenix Personnel
20630 Leapwood Ave Ste B, Carson (90746-3662)
P.O. Box 66395, Los Angeles (90066-0395)
PHONE..................310 532-1134
Fax: 310 631-8446
Silvia Lugo, *President*
Blanca Maron, *Manager*
EMP: 100
SQ FT: 1,700
SALES: 5.5MM **Privately Held**
WEB: www.phoenix-engineering.com
SIC: 7363 7361 Office help supply service; employment agencies

(P-14925)
PLANT MAINTENANCE INC
Also Called: Temporary Plant Cleaners
1330 Arnold Dr Ste 147, Martinez (94553-6538)
P.O. Box 48 (94553-0115)
PHONE..................925 228-3285
Fax: 925 370-2005
Tim Hollz, *President*
Bill Carter, *Officer*
Kenneth B Johnson, *Vice Pres*
EMP: 150 **EST:** 1996
SQ FT: 2,800
SALES: 2.3MM
SALES (corp-wide): 86.9MM **Privately Held**
WEB: www.montmech.com
SIC: 7363 Industrial help service
PA: Monterey Mechanical Co.
8275 San Leandro St
Oakland CA 94621
510 632-3173

(P-14926)
PREFERRED HLTHCARE RGISTRY INC
9089 Clairemont Mesa Blvd # 200, San Diego (92123-1234)
P.O. Box 17860 (92177-7860)
PHONE..................800 462-1896
Fax: 858 505-0949
Melanie Reiten, *President*
Rebecca Edwards Diata, *Vice Pres*
Karen Horais, *Accountant*
Tasya Quintero, *Controller*
Sally Dale, *Director*
EMP: 170
SQ FT: 2,100
SALES (est): 9MM **Privately Held**
WEB: www.preferredregistry.com
SIC: 7363 7361 Help supply services; temporary help service; medical help service; employment agencies

(P-14927)
PROCEL TEMPORARY SERVICES INC
222 W 6th St Ste 370, San Pedro (90731-3348)
PHONE..................310 372-0560
Fax: 310 372-6067
Marilyn Stephens, *President*
Robert Stephens, *CFO*
Laura Beyer, *Department Mgr*
EMP: 500
SQ FT: 4,600
SALES (est): 19.1MM **Privately Held**
SIC: 7363 Medical help service

(P-14928)
PROVIDIAN STAFFING CORPORATION
1801 Excise Ave Ste 112, Ontario (91761-8556)
PHONE..................909 456-7529
Rosa Gonzalez, *Branch Mgr*
EMP: 598
SALES (corp-wide): 11.7MM **Privately Held**
SIC: 7363 Help supply services
PA: Providian Staffing Corporation
1249 S Diamond Bar Blvd
Diamond Bar CA 91765
909 598-9099

(P-14929)
QUEST DISCOVERY SERVICES INC
1515 W 190th St Ste 410, Gardena (90248-4912)
PHONE..................310 769-5557
Tina Hicks, *Manager*
EMP: 58
SALES (corp-wide): 14.5MM **Privately Held**
SIC: 7363 7334 Help supply services; photocopying & duplicating services
PA: Quest Discovery Services, Inc.
981 Ridder Park Dr
San Jose CA 95131
408 441-7000

(P-14930)
R L KLEIN & ASSOCIATES
3553 Atlantic Ave Ste A, Long Beach (90807-5605)
PHONE..................562 427-5577
Fax: 562 427-1807
Bob Klein, *Owner*
EMP: 60
SQ FT: 2,100
SALES: 1,000K **Privately Held**
SIC: 7363 Temporary help service

(P-14931)
RANDSTAD NORTH AMERICA INC
106 E 7th St, Hanford (93230-4642)
PHONE..................559 582-2700
Fawn Perryman, *Branch Mgr*
EMP: 104
SALES (corp-wide): 20.6B **Privately Held**
WEB: www.placementpros.com
SIC: 7363 Help supply services
HQ: Randstad North America, Inc.
3625 Cumberland Blvd Se
Atlanta GA 30339
770 937-7000

(P-14932)
RANDSTAD NORTH AMERICA INC
1110 W Visalia Rd Ste 116, Exeter (93221-1481)
PHONE..................559 592-6700
Wendy Attaway, *Manager*
EMP: 254
SALES (corp-wide): 20.6B **Privately Held**
WEB: www.placementpros.com
SIC: 7363 Help supply services
HQ: Randstad North America, Inc.
3625 Cumberland Blvd Se
Atlanta GA 30339
770 937-7000

(P-14933)
RANDSTAD NORTH AMERICA INC
27 Maiden Ln Ste 202, San Francisco (94108-5440)
PHONE..................415 397-3384
Mark Rivard, *Branch Mgr*
Dave Lindberg, *Info Tech Mgr*
EMP: 177
SALES (corp-wide): 20.6B **Privately Held**
WEB: www.placementpros.com
SIC: 7363 Help supply services
HQ: Randstad North America, Inc.
3625 Cumberland Blvd Se
Atlanta GA 30339
770 937-7000

(P-14934)
REDWOOD HEALTHCARE STAFFING
600 B St Ste 1570, San Diego (92101-4560)
PHONE..................619 238-4180
EMP: 60 **Privately Held**
SIC: 7363 Temporary help service
PA: Redwood Healthcare Staffing
1015 Gayley Ave
Los Angeles CA 90024

(P-14935)
RELIABLE HEALTH CARE SVCS INC
5705 Sepulveda Blvd, Culver City (90230-6406)
PHONE..................310 397-2229
Fax: 323 398-0155
William A Benbassat, *President*
Scott G Krueger, *Manager*
EMP: 50
SALES (est): 2.5MM **Privately Held**
WEB: www.reliablehealthcare.com
SIC: 7363 Temporary help service

(P-14936)
REMEDYTEMP INC (DH)
Also Called: Remedy Intelligent Staffing
101 Enterprise Ste 100, Aliso Viejo (92656-2604)
PHONE..................949 425-7600
Fax: 949 425-7800
David Stephen Sorensen, *CEO*
Jeff R Mitchell, *CFO*
Richard Hulme, *Exec VP*
Tracy Obrien, *Area Mgr*
Annette Souza, *Area Mgr*
EMP: 143
SQ FT: 51,000
SALES (est): 38.5MM
SALES (corp-wide): 391.2MM **Privately Held**
WEB: www.remedystaff.com
SIC: 7363 7361 Temporary help service; employment agencies
HQ: Employbridge, Llc
3820 State St
Santa Barbara CA 93105
805 882-2200

(P-14937)
RIGHTSOURCING INC (DH)
1150 Iron Point Rd # 100, Folsom (95630-8305)
PHONE..................800 660-9544
Andrew Schultz, *Ch of Bd*
Laurie Bertolacci, *Senior VP*
Martha White, *Vice Pres*
Bill Blatnik, *Business Dir*
Yolanda Hubbard, *Director*
EMP: 53
SALES (est): 14.1MM **Privately Held**
SIC: 7363 Help supply services
HQ: Pro Unlimited, Inc.
7777 W Glades Rd Ste 208
Boca Raton FL 33434
800 291-1099

(P-14938)
RNCMBA INC
Also Called: Interim Services
4801 Truxtun Ave, Bakersfield (93309-0605)
PHONE..................661 395-1700
Fax: 661 395-1800
Darlyn Baker, *President*

PRODUCTS & SERVICES SECTION

7363 - Help Supply Svcs County (P-14963)

Chuck Baker, *Vice Pres*
EMP: 125
SQ FT: 5,000
SALES (est): 6.9MM **Privately Held**
SIC: 7363 Temporary help service

(P-14939)
ROBERT A HALL
Also Called: Straight Edge
9769 Dawn Way, Windsor (95492-8879)
PHONE.................................707 837-8564
Robert Hall, *President*
Leslie Hall, *CFO*
Leslie A Hall, *Manager*
EMP: 60
SALES: 442.1K **Privately Held**
SIC: 7363 Manpower pools

(P-14940)
ROBERT HALF INTERNATIONAL INC (PA)
2884 Sand Hill Rd Ste 200, Menlo Park (94025-7059)
PHONE.................................650 234-6000
Fax: 650 854-9735
Harold M Messmer Jr, *Ch of Bd*
Paul F Gentzkow, *President*
Stacey Hartt, *President*
M Keith Waddell, *President*
Michael C Buckley, *Officer*
EMP: 100 **EST:** 1948
SALES: 5B **Publicly Held**
WEB: www.rhii.com
SIC: 7363 7361 8748 8721 Temporary help service; placement agencies; business consulting; auditing services

(P-14941)
ROBERT HALF INTERNATIONAL INC
Accountemps
10 Almaden Blvd Ste 900, San Jose (95113-2268)
PHONE.................................408 293-8611
Fax: 408 293-1509
Monique Cruz, *Principal*
EMP: 50
SALES (corp-wide): 5B **Publicly Held**
WEB: www.rhii.com
SIC: 7363 Help supply services
PA: Robert Half International Inc.
2884 Sand Hill Rd Ste 200
Menlo Park CA 94025
650 234-6000

(P-14942)
ROBERT HALF INTERNATIONAL INC
4225 Executive Sq Ste 300, La Jolla (92037-9212)
PHONE.................................888 744-9202
Paige Thomas, *Manager*
EMP: 92
SALES (corp-wide): 5B **Publicly Held**
WEB: www.rhii.com
SIC: 7363 Help supply services
PA: Robert Half International Inc.
2884 Sand Hill Rd Ste 200
Menlo Park CA 94025
650 234-6000

(P-14943)
ROBERT HALF INTERNATIONAL INC
Accountemps
1850 Gateway Dr Ste 200, San Mateo (94404-4061)
PHONE.................................650 574-8200
Fax: 650 574-7779
Stephanie Vinske, *Branch Mgr*
Myers Ken, *Technology*
Susan Thomson, *Recruiter*
Christine Pardi, *Pub Rel Mgr*
Janelle Bowman, *Manager*
EMP: 50
SALES (corp-wide): 5B **Publicly Held**
SIC: 7363 Help supply services
PA: Robert Half International Inc.
2884 Sand Hill Rd Ste 200
Menlo Park CA 94025
650 234-6000

(P-14944)
ROTH STAFFING COMPANIES LP (PA)
Also Called: Ultimate Staffing Services
450 N State College Blvd, Orange (92868-1708)
PHONE.................................714 939-8600
Fax: 714 939-8688
Ben Roth, *CEO*
Adam Roth, *President*
Pam Sexauer, *Exec VP*
Julie Hagan, *Senior VP*
Kristi Kennedy, *Senior VP*
EMP: 50
SALES: 258.6MM **Privately Held**
WEB: www.ultimatestaffing.com
SIC: 7363 Help supply services

(P-14945)
RX PRO HEALTH LLC
12400 High Bluff Dr, San Diego (92130-3077)
PHONE.................................858 369-4050
Fax: 720 921-0208
Susan R Salka, *CEO*
EMP: 1800
SQ FT: 175,000
SALES (est): 93.5K
SALES (corp-wide): 1.4B **Publicly Held**
WEB: www.amnhealthcare.com
SIC: 7363 Medical help service
PA: Amn Healthcare Services, Inc.
12400 High Bluff Dr
San Diego CA 92130
866 871-8519

(P-14946)
SE SCHER CORPORATION
1585 The Alameda, San Jose (95126-2310)
PHONE.................................408 844-0772
William Friedeberg,
EMP: 1327
SALES (corp-wide): 16MM **Privately Held**
SIC: 7363 Help supply services
PA: S.E. Scher Corporation
665 3rd St Ste 415
San Francisco CA 94107
415 431-8826

(P-14947)
SFN GROUP INC
114 Pacifica Ste 210, Irvine (92618-3320)
PHONE.................................949 727-8500
Tammy Hawkins, *Manager*
EMP: 75
SALES (corp-wide): 20.6B **Privately Held**
SIC: 7363 Temporary help service
HQ: Sfn Group, Inc.
2050 Spectrum Blvd
Fort Lauderdale FL 33309
954 308-7600

(P-14948)
SFN GROUP INC
Also Called: Spherion Staffing Group
3050 Bictor Ave Ste A, Redding (96002)
PHONE.................................530 222-3434
Fax: 530 226-0941
Sheryl Lakowski, *Branch Mgr*
Cheryl Laskosky, *Office Mgr*
EMP: 150
SALES (corp-wide): 20.6B **Privately Held**
SIC: 7363 Temporary help service
HQ: Sfn Group, Inc.
2050 Spectrum Blvd
Fort Lauderdale FL 33309
954 308-7600

(P-14949)
SOCIAL VOCATIONAL SERVICES INC
3601 Union Ave, Bakersfield (93305-2939)
PHONE.................................661 323-0533
Laurie Hughey, *Branch Mgr*
EMP: 56
SALES (corp-wide): 80.6MM **Privately Held**
SIC: 7363 Temporary help service
PA: Social Vocational Services, Inc.
3555 Torrance Blvd
Torrance CA 90503
310 944-3303

(P-14950)
SPECTRUM PROF STAFFING INC
13520 Evening Creek Dr N # 300, San Diego (92128-8105)
PHONE.................................800 644-1150
Raymond Lucia, *President*
Dorothy Contreras, *Finance Dir*
Jannifer Baker, *Controller*
EMP: 200
SALES (est): 4.6MM **Privately Held**
SIC: 7363 Employee leasing service

(P-14951)
ST JOSEPH HOSPITAL
Community Resource Center
2700 Dolbeer St, Eureka (95501-4799)
PHONE.................................707 268-0190
Maureen Lawlor, *Manager*
EMP: 699
SALES (corp-wide): 248.2MM **Privately Held**
SIC: 7363 Manpower pools
PA: St. Joseph Hospital
2700 Dolbeer St
Eureka CA 95501
707 445-8121

(P-14952)
STAFF TODAY INCORPORATED
212 E Rowland St 313, Covina (91723-3146)
PHONE.................................800 928-5561
Paul Mwangi, *President*
EMP: 150
SALES (est): 578.7K **Privately Held**
SIC: 7363 7361 Temporary help service; employment agencies

(P-14953)
STENO EMPLOYMENT SERVICES INC
8560 Vineyard Ave Ste 208, Rancho Cucamonga (91730-4394)
PHONE.................................909 476-1404
Jaime Silguero, *CEO*
Ahmad Jackson, *President*
EMP: 2000
SALES (est): 46.5MM **Privately Held**
SIC: 7363 Employee leasing service

(P-14954)
SURGICAL STAFF INC
Surgical Staff, The
1523 G St, Sacramento (95814-1618)
PHONE.................................916 444-4424
Fax: 916 444-8971
Maryann Lesbirel, *Manager*
EMP: 200
SALES (corp-wide): 30.7MM **Privately Held**
WEB: www.mcnealtech.com
SIC: 7363 7361 Temporary help service; employment agencies
PA: Surgical Staff, Inc.
120 Saint Matthews Ave
San Mateo CA 94401
650 558-3999

(P-14955)
TAOS MOUNTAIN INC
1 Market St Fl 36, San Francisco (94105-1420)
PHONE.................................888 826-7686
Geoff White, *Consultant*
EMP: 66
SALES (corp-wide): 118.8MM **Privately Held**
SIC: 7363 Temporary help service
PA: Taos Mountain, Llc
121 Daggett Dr
San Jose CA 95134
408 324-2800

(P-14956)
TEG STAFFING INC
2604 El Camino Real Ste B, Carlsbad (92008-1205)
PHONE.................................619 584-3444
Nanci Porter, *President*
EMP: 1600
SALES (est): 18.2MM
SALES (corp-wide): 179.4MM **Privately Held**
SIC: 7363 Temporary help service
PA: Eplica, Inc.
2355 Northside Dr Ste 120
San Diego CA 92108
619 260-2000

(P-14957)
TEGP INC
2375 Northside Dr Ste 360, San Diego (92108-2713)
PHONE.................................619 584-3408
Michael Santos, *President*
EMP: 1500
SALES: 28.9MM
SALES (corp-wide): 179.4MM **Privately Held**
SIC: 7363 Temporary help service
PA: Eplica, Inc.
2355 Northside Dr Ste 120
San Diego CA 92108
619 260-2000

(P-14958)
TEMP UNLIMITED LLC
11306 183rd St Ste 301, Cerritos (90703-5440)
P.O. Box 661358, Arcadia (91066-1358)
PHONE.................................562 860-3340
Fax: 562 860-3390
Carol Forrest, *President*
Robin Campbell, *Vice Pres*
EMP: 80 **EST:** 2001
SALES (est): 2.7MM **Privately Held**
SIC: 7363 Temporary help service

(P-14959)
THERASTAFF INC
Also Called: Socal Staffing
2355 Northside Dr Ste 140, San Diego (92108-4705)
PHONE.................................858 569-7555
Fax: 858 569-4165
William Stone, *President*
Kristy Gargano, *Manager*
EMP: 160
SQ FT: 3,600
SALES: 5.8MM **Privately Held**
WEB: www.therastaff.com
SIC: 7363 Medical help service

(P-14960)
TRANSFORCE INC
965 E Yosemite Ave Ste 7, Manteca (95336-5943)
PHONE.................................209 952-2573
EMP: 50
SALES (est): 2.7MM **Privately Held**
SIC: 7363

(P-14961)
TRANSPORT DRIVERS INC
620 N Dmnd Bar Blvd Ste B, Diamond Bar (91765-1037)
PHONE.................................800 497-6345
Ed Boyes, *Branch Mgr*
EMP: 500
SALES (corp-wide): 67.2MM **Privately Held**
WEB: www.transportdrivers.com
SIC: 7363 Medical help service
PA: Transport Drivers, Inc.
3540 Seven Bridges Dr # 300
Woodridge IL 60517
630 766-2721

(P-14962)
TRANSPORT DRIVERS INC
2131 S Grove Ave Ste D, Ontario (91761-5697)
PHONE.................................909 937-3312
EMP: 89
SALES (corp-wide): 67.2MM **Privately Held**
SIC: 7363 Truck driver services
PA: Transport Drivers, Inc.
3540 Seven Bridges Dr # 300
Woodridge IL 60517
630 766-2721

(P-14963)
TRUEBLUE INC
Also Called: Labor Ready
1362 Colusa Hwy, Yuba City (95993-9001)
PHONE.................................530 755-3291
Fax: 530 755-3251
Carol Pate, *Manager*
EMP: 125

7363 - Help Supply Svcs County (P-14964)

(P-14964)
TRUEBLUE INC
Also Called: Labor Ready
123 E Carrillo St, Santa Barbara
(93101-2110)
PHONE..................805 963-5370
Adam Lockhart, *Manager*
Charles Johnson, *Manager*
EMP: 50
SALES (corp-wide): 2.7B **Publicly Held**
WEB: www.laborready.com
SIC: 7363 Help supply services
PA: Trueblue, Inc.
 1015 A St
 Tacoma WA 98402
 253 383-9101

(P-14965)
TURNING PT RVNUE CYCLE SLTIONS
1255 Treat Blvd Ste 300, San Diego
(92131)
PHONE..................800 360-2300
Jennifer Hays, *CEO*
Debra Heiser, *CFO*
Corinne Egle, *Exec VP*
EMP: 50
SALES (est): 1.4MM **Privately Held**
SIC: 7363 Employee leasing service

(P-14966)
TWO ROADS PROF RESOURCES INC
5122 Bolsa Ave Ste 112, Huntington Beach
(92649-1050)
PHONE..................714 901-3804
Fax: 714 901-3814
Tammy Gottschalk, *President*
Chris Hoff, *Vice Pres*
Michele Hoff, *Vice Pres*
Barry Vince, *Vice Pres*
Jamie Brogdon, *Administration*
EMP: 110
SQ FT: 4,000
SALES (est): 5.9MM **Privately Held**
WEB: www.2roads.com
SIC: 7363 Temporary help service

(P-14967)
UNITED STATES DEPT OF NAVY
Also Called: Manpower
32444 Echo Ln Fl 3, San Diego
(92147-5100)
PHONE..................619 524-1069
EMP: 175 **Publicly Held**
SIC: 7363 Manpower pools
HQ: United States Department Of The Navy
 1200 Navy Pentagon
 Washington DC 20350
 703 545-6700

(P-14968)
VANPIKE INC (PA)
6336 Greenwich Dr Ste 100, San Diego
(92122-5922)
PHONE..................858 453-1331
Gary Van Eik, *President*
Rick Kail, *CFO*
Richard Papike, *Vice Pres*
EMP: 60
SQ FT: 9,000
SALES: 26MM **Privately Held**
WEB: www.tristaff.com
SIC: 7363 7361 Temporary help service; executive placement

(P-14969)
VETERNARY MED SRGCAL GROUP INC
Also Called: Vmsg
2199 Sperry Ave, Ventura (93003-7426)
PHONE..................805 339-2290
Fax: 805 339-2291
Kenneth A Bruecker, *CEO*
Rodney Ayl,
Claude Lessard,
Edward Maher,
Nancy Scott,
EMP: 80
SQ FT: 6,500
SALES (est): 5.6MM **Privately Held**
WEB: www.vmsg.com
SIC: 7363 Medical help service

(P-14970)
VOLT MANAGEMENT CORP
Also Called: Volt Workforce Solutions
19191 S Vt Ave Ste 950, Torrance
(90502-1098)
PHONE..................310 316-8523
Rhona Driggs, *Branch Mgr*
EMP: 130
SALES (corp-wide): 1.1B **Privately Held**
SIC: 7363 Help supply services
PA: Volt Management Corp.
 1133 Ave Of The Americas
 New York NY 10036
 212 704-2400

(P-14971)
VOLT MANAGEMENT CORP
Also Called: Volt Temporary Services
2411 N Glassell St, Orange (92865-2705)
PHONE..................714 921-7460
Fax: 714 921-7483
Rhona Driggs, *Branch Mgr*
Jeff Bakke, *Vice Pres*
Mike King, *Vice Pres*
Tony Trombetta, *Vice Pres*
Ryan Hooper, *Program Mgr*
EMP: 300
SALES (corp-wide): 1.1B **Privately Held**
SIC: 7363 7373 Help supply services; computer integrated systems design
PA: Volt Management Corp.
 1133 Ave Of The Americas
 New York NY 10036
 212 704-2400

(P-14972)
VOLT MANAGEMENT CORP
Also Called: Volt Workforce Solutions
7676 Hazard Center Dr # 1000, San Diego
(92108-4503)
PHONE..................858 576-3140
Fax: 858 576-1513
Rhona Driggs, *Branch Mgr*
EMP: 130
SALES (corp-wide): 1.1B **Privately Held**
SIC: 7363 Help supply services
PA: Volt Management Corp.
 1133 Ave Of The Americas
 New York NY 10036
 212 704-2400

(P-14973)
VOLT MANAGEMENT CORP
Also Called: Volt Workforce Solutions
7676 Hazard Center Dr # 1000, San Diego
(92108-4503)
PHONE..................858 578-0920
Fax: 858 695-6920
Rhona Driggs, *Branch Mgr*
EMP: 130
SALES (corp-wide): 1.1B **Privately Held**
SIC: 7363 Temporary help service
PA: Volt Management Corp.
 1133 Ave Of The Americas
 New York NY 10036
 212 704-2400

(P-14974)
VOLT MANAGEMENT CORP
Also Called: Volt Workforce Solutions
7330 N Palm Ave Ste 105, Fresno
(93711-5768)
PHONE..................559 435-1255
Fax: 559 226-4415
Scott Giroux, *Branch Mgr*
EMP: 130
SALES (corp-wide): 1.1B **Privately Held**
SIC: 7363 7361 Temporary help service; employment agencies
PA: Volt Management Corp.
 1133 Ave Of The Americas
 New York NY 10036
 212 704-2400

(P-14975)
VOLT MANAGEMENT CORP
Also Called: Volt Workforce Solutions
2401 N Glassell St, Orange (92865-2705)
P.O. Box 3708 (92857-0708)
PHONE..................714 921-8800
Fax: 714 974-5601
Scott Giroux, *Branch Mgr*
Cy Hashemi, *CTO*
Frank Sahanas, *Info Tech Mgr*
Mike Huynh, *Technology*
Chris Vega, *Engineer*
EMP: 130
SALES (corp-wide): 1.1B **Privately Held**
SIC: 7363 Help supply services
PA: Volt Management Corp.
 1133 Ave Of The Americas
 New York NY 10036
 212 704-2400

(P-14976)
VOLT MANAGEMENT CORP
Also Called: Volt Workforce Solutions
3001 Lava Ridge Ct # 160, Roseville
(95661-3094)
PHONE..................916 923-0454
Tim Chapman, *Branch Mgr*
EMP: 56
SALES (corp-wide): 1.1B **Privately Held**
WEB: www.volt.com
SIC: 7363 Help supply services
PA: Volt Management Corp.
 1133 Ave Of The Americas
 New York NY 10036
 212 704-2400

(P-14977)
VOLT MANAGEMENT CORP
Also Called: Volt Workforce Solutions
1650 Iowa Ave Ste 140, Riverside
(92507-2432)
PHONE..................951 789-8133
Scott Giroux, *Branch Mgr*
EMP: 56
SALES (corp-wide): 1.1B **Privately Held**
WEB: www.volt.com
SIC: 7363 Help supply services
PA: Volt Management Corp.
 1133 Ave Of The Americas
 New York NY 10036
 212 704-2400

(P-14978)
VOLT MANAGEMENT CORP
Also Called: Volt Workforce Solutions
3558 Deer Park Dr 2, Stockton
(95219-2350)
PHONE..................209 952-5627
Fax: 209 952-5687
Scott Giroux, *Branch Mgr*
EMP: 130
SALES (corp-wide): 1.1B **Privately Held**
SIC: 7363 Help supply services
PA: Volt Management Corp.
 1133 Ave Of The Americas
 New York NY 10036
 212 704-2400

(P-14979)
VOLT MANAGEMENT CORP
Also Called: Volt Workforce Solutions
1701 Solar Dr Ste 145, Oxnard
(93030-0137)
PHONE..................805 485-0506
Fax: 805 983-3381
Scott Giroux, *Branch Mgr*
EMP: 130
SALES (corp-wide): 1.1B **Privately Held**
SIC: 7363 Help supply services
PA: Volt Management Corp.
 1133 Ave Of The Americas
 New York NY 10036
 212 704-2400

(P-14980)
WANNAJOB INC
Also Called: Construction Temps
2710 Saint Louis Ave, Signal Hill
(90755-2026)
PHONE..................562 426-5272
William Davis,
EMP: 75
SQ FT: 300
SALES (est): 4.9MM **Privately Held**
SIC: 7363 7361 Temporary help service; employment agencies

(P-14981)
WEAVE INCORPORATED (PA)
Also Called: Weave
1900 K St Ste 200, Sacramento
(95811-4187)
PHONE..................916 448-2321
Fax: 916 443-7183
Beth Hassett, *Exec Dir*
Garry Maisel, *Ch of Bd*
Priya Batra, *Principal*
Neil Forester, *Principal*
Bryan Merica, *Principal*
EMP: 95
SALES: 3.5MM **Privately Held**
WEB: www.weaveinc.org
SIC: 7363 8322 Domestic help service; individual & family services

(P-14982)
WEST VALLEY ENGINEERING INC (PA)
Also Called: West Valley Staffing Group
390 Potrero Ave, Sunnyvale (94085-4116)
PHONE..................408 735-1420
Michael F Williams, *President*
Teresa Kossayian, *CFO*
Janet Macaulay, *CFO*
Rovilla Wetle, *Sr Exec VP*
Careen Jensen, *Asst Admin*
EMP: 83
SALES (est): 48.8MM **Privately Held**
SIC: 7363 Temporary help service

(P-14983)
WIGHTMAN ENTERPRISES INC
Also Called: Csl Solutions
8017 Sacramento St, Fair Oaks
(95628-7526)
PHONE..................916 961-2959
Michelle Wightman, *President*
EMP: 60
SQ FT: 1,176
SALES (est): 3.3MM **Privately Held**
WEB: www.cslweb.com
SIC: 7363 Employee leasing service

(P-14984)
WILLIAMS AND WILLIAMS HOMECARE
Also Called: Williams & Williams Home Care
4756 Hazelnut Ave, Seal Beach
(90740-3017)
PHONE..................562 597-1006
Fax: 562 597-1874
Lynda Williams, *Vice Pres*
Doug Williams, *President*
Nancy Hanna, *Office Mgr*
EMP: 59
SQ FT: 1,500
SALES (est): 1.9MM **Privately Held**
WEB: www.whomecare.org
SIC: 7363 8011 Medical help service; offices & clinics of medical doctors

(P-14985)
WORK FORCE SERVICES INC
Also Called: Work Force Staffing
300 Truxtun Ave, Bakersfield (93301-5314)
PHONE..................661 327-5019
Fax: 661 328-0386
Brooks Whitehead, *President*
Larry Williams, *Exec VP*
Pamela Cook, *Branch Mgr*
Brenda Bynum, *Accounting Dir*
Virgil Pattarino, *Safety Dir*
EMP: 250
SQ FT: 1,600
SALES (est): 8.9MM **Privately Held**
WEB: www.workforcestaffing1.com
SIC: 7363 Temporary help service

(P-14986)
YOUTH UPRISING
8711 Macarthur Blvd, Oakland
(94605-4000)
PHONE..................510 777-9909
Katherine Seabrooks, *President*
Olive Simmons, *CEO*
Kevin McGahan, *CFO*
Chloe Mays, *Program Mgr*
Sharon Brown, *Executive Asst*
EMP: 53
SALES: 7MM **Privately Held**
SIC: 7363 8299 Medical help service; educational services

(P-14987)
ZB REHAB STAFFING INC
Also Called: Thera Home Care
650 El Camino Real Ste M, Redwood City
(94063-1345)
PHONE.................................650 396-2207
Greg McCarthy, *CEO*
EMP: 75
SQ FT: 1,100
SALES: 2.5MM **Privately Held**
SIC: 7363 Help supply services

7371 Custom Computer Programming Svcs

(P-14988)
314E CORPORATION
47102 Mission Falls Ct # 219, Fremont
(94539-7829)
PHONE.................................510 371-6736
Abhishek Begerhotta, *President*
Alok Sharma, *Senior VP*
Eileen Ha, *Office Admin*
Christine Vo, *Administration*
Sagar Baruah, *Tech Recruiter*
EMP: 97
SQ FT: 10,078
SALES (est): 11.3MM **Privately Held**
WEB: www.314e.com
SIC: 7371 Custom computer programming services

(P-14989)
3DNA CORP
Also Called: Nationbuilder
520 S Grand Ave Fl 2, Los Angeles
(90071-2600)
PHONE.................................213 394-4623
Jim H Gilliam, *President*
Kara Barlow, *Vice Pres*
Gina Davis, *Vice Pres*
Hilary DOE, *Vice Pres*
Michael Moshella, *Vice Pres*
EMP: 100
SALES (est): 14.7MM **Privately Held**
SIC: 7371 Computer software development & applications

(P-14990)
3SHARE ACQUISITION INC
1902 Wright Pl, Carlsbad (92008-6583)
PHONE.................................888 505-1625
Joseph Tomasulo, *CEO*
Jess Moore, *President*
Christine Warner, *CFO*
Brian Johnson, *Vice Pres*
Joshua Goodman, *Admin Sec*
EMP: 50
SALES (est): 3.1MM
SALES (corp-wide): 65.7MM **Privately Held**
SIC: 7371 Software programming applications
HQ: Digitas, Inc.
  33 Arch St Fl 8
  Boston MA 02110
  617 369-8000

(P-14991)
4D INC
95 S Market St Ste 240, San Jose
(95113-2311)
PHONE.................................408 557-4600
Fax: 408 557-4645
Brendan Coveney, *President*
Tracy Roberts, *President*
Brendan Conveney, *CFO*
Vincent Migayrou, *CFO*
Jeffrey Kain, *Exec VP*
EMP: 101
SALES (est): 13.4MM
SALES (corp-wide): 12.3MM **Privately Held**
WEB: www.4d.com
SIC: 7371 7372 Custom computer programming services; prepackaged software
PA: 4d
  Parc Des Erables Batiment 4
  Le Pecq 78230
  -

(P-14992)
5 NINE GROUP INC
Also Called: Franklin Data
1125 Lindero Canyon Rd, Westlake Village
(91362-5474)
PHONE.................................805 880-2948
Matthew Blake, *Exec VP*
Henry Dicker, *Officer*
John Aben, *Exec VP*
Slava Bobryakov, *Network Mgr*
Ryan Schnieber, *Director*
EMP: 250
SQ FT: 14,000
SALES: 48MM **Privately Held**
SIC: 7371 Custom computer programming services

(P-14993)
ABACUS SERVICE CORPORATION
1725 23rd St, Sacramento (95816-7100)
PHONE.................................916 288-8948
Michelle Reuter, *Branch Mgr*
EMP: 300
SALES (corp-wide): 36.8MM **Privately Held**
SIC: 7371 Custom computer programming services
PA: Abacus Service Corporation
  35055 W 12 Mile Rd # 215
  Farmington Hills MI
  248 324-9200

(P-14994)
ABBYY USA SOFTWARE HOUSE INC (PA)
880 N Mccarthy Blvd # 220, Milpitas
(95035-5126)
PHONE.................................408 457-9777
Fax: 408 457-9778
Ding Yuan Tang, *CEO*
Peter Meechan, *COO*
Judy Hsu, *CFO*
Francis Patchell, *CFO*
Arthur Whipple, *CFO*
EMP: 56
SQ FT: 17,000
SALES (est): 31.9MM **Privately Held**
SIC: 7371 5045 Computer software development; computers

(P-14995)
ABZOOBA INC
1551 Mccarthy Blvd # 204, Milpitas
(95035-7437)
PHONE.................................650 453-8760
Vivek Vipul, *CEO*
EMP: 121 **EST:** 2010
SALES (est): 182.3K **Privately Held**
SIC: 7371 Computer software development & applications

(P-14996)
ACCEL-KKR COMPANY LLC (PA)
2500 Sand Hill Rd Ste 300, Menlo Park
(94025-7063)
PHONE.................................650 233-9723
Fax: 650 289-2461
Thomas Barnes,
Rachel Spasser, *Chief Mktg Ofcr*
David Crisp, *Vice Pres*
David Cusimano, *Vice Pres*
Park Durrett, *Vice Pres*
EMP: 61
SQ FT: 7,000
SALES (est): 78.3MM **Privately Held**
WEB: www.accel-kkr.com
SIC: 7371 Computer software systems analysis & design, custom

(P-14997)
ACCESS SYSTEMS AMERICAS INC
1188 E Arques Ave, Sunnyvale
(94085-4602)
PHONE.................................408 400-3000
Kiyo Oishi, *CEO*
Jeanne Seeley, *CFO*
Annette Derksen, *Vice Pres*
Neale Foster, *Vice Pres*
Michael Kelley, *Vice Pres*
EMP: 518
SQ FT: 71,000
SALES (est): 37.2MM
SALES (corp-wide): 56.5MM **Privately Held**
WEB: www.palmsource.com
SIC: 7371 7372 Computer software development; software programming applications; prepackaged software
PA: Access Co.,Ltd.
  3, Kandaneribeicho
  Chiyoda-Ku TKY 101-0
  368 539-088

(P-14998)
ACHIEVO CORPORATION (PA)
1400 Terra Bella Ave E, Mountain View
(94043-3062)
PHONE.................................925 498-8864
Sandy Wai-Yan Chau, *CEO*
Robert P Lee, *President*
Bernard Mathaisel, *COO*
Julio Leung, *CFO*
Darryl Quan, *CFO*
EMP: 66
SALES (est): 61MM **Privately Held**
WEB: www.achievo.com
SIC: 7371 Custom computer programming services

(P-14999)
ACTIVISION BLIZZARD INC
3420 Ocean Park Blvd # 2000, Santa Monica (90405-3304)
PHONE.................................310 581-4700
Monica Temperly, *Information Mgr*
EMP: 140
SALES (corp-wide): 4.6B **Publicly Held**
WEB: www.blizzard.com
SIC: 7371 Computer software development
PA: Activision Blizzard, Inc.
  3100 Ocean Park Blvd
  Santa Monica CA 90405
  310 255-2000

(P-15000)
ADDEPAR INC (PA)
1215 Terra Bella Ave, Mountain View
(94043-1849)
PHONE.................................855 692-3337
Eric Poirier, *CEO*
Karen White, *President*
Joe Lonsdale, *Chairman*
Randi Lo, *Admin Asst*
Jason Mirra, *CTO*
EMP: 85
SALES (est): 18MM **Privately Held**
SIC: 7371 Computer software development

(P-15001)
ADVANCED SOFTWARE DESIGN INC
Also Called: Advanced Software Dynamics Inc
1371 Oakland Blvd Ste 100, Walnut Creek
(94596-8407)
PHONE.................................925 975-0691
Manu Chatterjee, *CEO*
Salig Chada, *Vice Pres*
Sonali Singh, *VP Engrg*
Shikha Chatterjee, *VP Opers*
EMP: 59
SQ FT: 1,200
SALES: 3MM **Privately Held**
WEB: www.asdglobal.com
SIC: 7371 7373 8711 8742 Computer software development; computer integrated systems design; engineering services; management consulting services

(P-15002)
ADVENT RESOURCES INC
235 W 7th St, San Pedro (90731-3321)
PHONE.................................310 241-1500
Fax: 310 241-0011
Ysidro Salinas, *Ch of Bd*
Timothy Gill, *CEO*
Benjamin Gill, *Vice Pres*
Mike Mungiello, *Exec Dir*
Rob Ford, *General Mgr*
EMP: 80
SQ FT: 22,000
SALES (est): 11.7MM **Privately Held**
WEB: www.adventresources.com
SIC: 7371 Computer software development

(P-15003)
ADVENT SOFTWARE INC (HQ)
600 Townsend St Fl 5, San Francisco
(94103-5696)
PHONE.................................415 543-7696
Fax: 415 543-8511
David Peter Hess Jr, *President*
Stephanie Dimarco, *Ch of Bd*
James Cox, *CFO*
Todd Gottula, *Exec VP*
Chris Momsen, *Exec VP*
EMP: 148
SQ FT: 158,264
SALES (est): 335.8MM
SALES (corp-wide): 1B **Publicly Held**
WEB: www.advent.com
SIC: 7371 7373 7372 6722 Custom computer programming services; computer integrated systems design; systems software development services; computer systems analysis & design; prepackaged software; management investment, open-end
PA: Ss&C Technologies Holdings, Inc.
  80 Lamberton Rd
  Windsor CT 06095
  860 298-4500

(P-15004)
AESTIVA SOFTWARE INC
3551 Voyager St Ste 201, Torrance
(90503-1674)
PHONE.................................310 697-0338
David M Silverberg, *President*
Camden Yumori, *Accountant*
Eric Villicana, *Assistant*
EMP: 50
SALES (est): 3.2MM **Privately Held**
SIC: 7371 Computer software development

(P-15005)
ALTIUM INC (HQ)
4275 Executive Sq Ste 825, La Jolla
(92037-1478)
PHONE.................................858 864-1661
Aram Mirkazemi, *CEO*
Gerry Gaffney, *Exec VP*
Kim Besharati, *Vice Pres*
Frank Kraemer, *Vice Pres*
William Markey, *Admin Asst*
EMP: 112
SQ FT: 11,000
SALES: 38MM
SALES (corp-wide): 80.5MM **Privately Held**
SIC: 7371 Computer software development
PA: Altium Limited
  'tower B The Zenith' Level 6
  Chatswood NSW 2067
  180 003-0949

(P-15006)
ALTSCHOOL INC
1245 Folsom St, San Francisco
(94103-3816)
PHONE.................................415 255-9766
Max Ventilla, *President*
Jay Ho, *Engineer*
Jaqi Ruiz-Garcia, *Teacher*
Neil Toomey, *General Counsel*
Lake Phillips, *Director*
EMP: 180 **EST:** 2013
SALES (est): 1.4MM **Privately Held**
SIC: 7371 Custom computer programming services

(P-15007)
AMBER HOLDING INC
150 California St, San Francisco
(94111-4500)
PHONE.................................415 765-6500
Robert F Smith, *President*
Brian N Sheth, *Vice Pres*
EMP: 1010
SALES (est): 23.4MM
SALES (corp-wide): 1.1B **Privately Held**
SIC: 7371 Computer software development; computer software development & applications
HQ: Vista Equity Partners Fund Iii, L.P.
  4 Embarcadero Ctr # 2000
  San Francisco CA 94111
  415 765-6500

7371 - Custom Computer Programming Svcs County (P-15008)

PRODUCTS & SERVICES SECTION

(P-15008)
AMDOCS INC
Innovis
1104 Investment Blvd, El Dorado Hills (95762-5710)
PHONE..........................916 934-7000
Fax: 916 934-7054
Michael Saeger, *Manager*
Nancy Doerer, *Admin Asst*
Terry Gill, *MIS Dir*
Joe Barker, *Info Tech Mgr*
Debbie Knowles, *Software Dev*
EMP: 336
SALES (corp-wide): 3.5B **Privately Held**
WEB: www.amdocs.com
SIC: 7371 7389 7374 Computer software systems analysis & design, custom; computer software development; software programming applications; financial services; data processing & preparation
HQ: Amdocs, Inc.
1390 Timberlake Manor Pkw
Chesterfield MO 63017
314 212-7000

(P-15009)
AMDOCS BCS INC
1104 Investment Blvd, El Dorado Hills (95762-5710)
PHONE..........................916 934-7000
Michael McGrail, *President*
Jim Alexander, *Vice Pres*
Ric Brown, *Vice Pres*
Alan Forman, *Vice Pres*
Bill Guinn, *Vice Pres*
EMP: 336
SALES (est): 557.9K
SALES (corp-wide): 3.5B **Privately Held**
SIC: 7371 7389 7374 Computer software systems analysis & design, custom; computer software development; software programming applications; financial services; data processing & preparation
HQ: Amdocs, Inc.
1390 Timberlake Manor Pkw
Chesterfield MO 63017
314 212-7000

(P-15010)
AMERICAN SUNRISE INC
7404 Santa Fe Canyon Pl, San Diego (92129)
PHONE..........................858 610-4766
John Zhang, *President*
EMP: 100
SQ FT: 4,000
SALES: 1MM **Privately Held**
SIC: 7371 7361 7379 Computer software development; employment agencies; computer related consulting services

(P-15011)
AMOBEE INC (HQ)
950 Tower Ln Ste 2000, Foster City (94404-4255)
PHONE..........................650 802-8871
Fax: 650 802-8951
Mark Strecker, *CEO*
Kim Reed Perell, *President*
Steve Hoffman, *CFO*
Gabi Schindler, *Chief Mktg Ofcr*
Yoad Gonen, *Vice Pres*
EMP: 60
SALES (est): 43.8MM
SALES (corp-wide): 23.9MM **Privately Held**
WEB: www.amobee.com
SIC: 7371 Computer software development
PA: Amobee Group Pte. Ltd.
31 Exeter Road
Singapore 23973
634 010-20

(P-15012)
AMP TECHNOLOGIES LLC (PA)
2420 Camino Ramon Ste 210, San Ramon (94583-4207)
PHONE..........................877 442-2824
Neel Naicker, *CEO*
Arvind Sathyamoorthy, *CTO*
EMP: 133
SALES (est): 4.9MM **Privately Held**
SIC: 7371 Computer software development & applications

(P-15013)
AMPLIFY EDUCATION INC
1032 Irving St Ste 445, San Francisco (94122-2216)
PHONE..........................562 209-7875
EMP: 82
SALES (corp-wide): 179.7MM **Privately Held**
SIC: 7371 Computer software development
PA: Amplify Education, Inc.
55 Washington St Ste 900
Brooklyn NY 11201
212 213-8177

(P-15014)
ANIMOTO LLC
333 Kearny St Fl 6, San Francisco (94108-3269)
PHONE..........................415 987-3139
Bradley C Jefferson, *CEO*
Russell G Keefe, *CFO*
EMP: 60
SQ FT: 15,000
SALES (est): 4.9MM **Privately Held**
SIC: 7371 Computer software development

(P-15015)
ANJANA SOFTWARE SOLUTIONS INC
1445 E Los Angeles Ave # 305, Simi Valley (93065-7818)
PHONE..........................805 583-0121
Saravana Kumarasamy, *President*
Kritik A Govindan, *Treasurer*
Venkatesh Ramachandran, *Vice Pres*
EMP: 75
SQ FT: 3,000
SALES: 20MM
SALES (corp-wide): 8.6MM **Privately Held**
SIC: 7371 Computer software systems analysis & design, custom
PA: Anjana Software Solutions Private Limited
Module No. 306, Nsic Software Technology Park,
Chennai TN 60003
805 583-0121

(P-15016)
ANNIE APP INC (PA)
23 Geary St Ste 400800, San Francisco (94108-5701)
PHONE..........................844 277-2664
Bertrand Schmitt, *CEO*
Marshall Nu, *COO*
Mark Vranesh, *CFO*
Al Campa, *Officer*
Danielle Levitas, *Vice Pres*
EMP: 53
SALES (est): 6.9MM **Privately Held**
SIC: 7371 Computer software development & applications

(P-15017)
ANOMALI INCORPORATED
2317 Broadway St Fl 3, Redwood City (94063-1659)
PHONE..........................408 800-4050
Hugh Njemanze, *CEO*
Nancy Bush, *CFO*
Dan Barahona, *Chief Mktg Ofcr*
Anthony Aragues, *Vice Pres*
WEI Huang, *Vice Pres*
EMP: 100 EST: 2013
SALES: 4.9MM **Privately Held**
SIC: 7371 Computer software development

(P-15018)
APPCELERATOR INC (HQ)
1732 N 1st St Ste 150, San Jose (95112-4540)
PHONE..........................650 200-4255
Jeffrey Haynie, *CEO*
Spencer Punter, *COO*
Mario Cavagnari, *Vice Pres*
Gamiel Gran, *Vice Pres*
Doug Norton-Bilsby, *Vice Pres*
EMP: 50
SQ FT: 12,000
SALES (est): 20.8MM
SALES (corp-wide): 184.9MM **Privately Held**
WEB: www.recallmediagroup.com
SIC: 7371 Computer software systems analysis & design, custom
PA: Axway Software
Petite Avenue Les Glaisins
Annecy Le Vieux 74940
450 333-030

(P-15019)
APPDYNAMICS INC (PA)
303 2nd St Ste N450, San Francisco (94107-3636)
PHONE..........................415 442-8400
Fax: 415 442-8499
David Wadhwani, *CEO*
Joe Sexton, *President*
Randy Gottfried, *CFO*
Jyoti Bansal, *Founder*
Kendall Collins, *Chief Mktg Ofcr*
EMP: 148
SQ FT: 41,718
SALES (est): 119.6MM **Privately Held**
SIC: 7371 Computer software development

(P-15020)
APPERIENCE CORPORATION
665 3rd St Ste 150, San Francisco (94107-1926)
PHONE..........................415 813-2995
Hugo Dong, *CEO*
EMP: 100 EST: 2013
SQ FT: 5,000
SALES (est): 6.9MM **Privately Held**
SIC: 7371 Software programming applications

(P-15021)
APPFABRIX SOFTWARE INC
691 S Milpitas Blvd # 210, Milpitas (95035-5476)
PHONE..........................408 834-4435
Satyanarayana Raju, *President*
EMP: 52 EST: 2013
SQ FT: 3,500
SALES (est): 2MM **Privately Held**
SIC: 7371 Software programming applications

(P-15022)
APPIRIO INC (PA)
760 Market St Ste 1150, San Francisco (94102-2306)
PHONE..........................415 663-4433
Chris Barbin, *President*
Mike Pav, *President*
Rick Gross, *CFO*
Mark O'Connor, *CFO*
Catherine Lang,
EMP: 118
SQ FT: 12,521
SALES: 180MM **Privately Held**
SIC: 7371 7379 Computer software development & applications; computer related consulting services

(P-15023)
APPLIED COMPUTER SOLUTIONS (PA)
Also Called: ACS
15461 Springdale St, Huntington Beach (92649-1335)
PHONE..........................714 861-2200
Fax: 714 842-8795
Sandy Davis, *President*
Michael Davis, *COO*
Warren Barnes, *CFO*
Daniel Hamm, *CFO*
Traci Malone, *Chief Mktg Ofcr*
EMP: 70
SQ FT: 60,000
SALES (est): 81.8MM **Privately Held**
WEB: www.acs-g.com
SIC: 7371 Custom computer programming services; computer software development

(P-15024)
APPLIED ENGINEERING MGT CORP
760 Paseo Camarillo # 101, Camarillo (93010-6000)
P.O. Box 1263 (93011-1263)
PHONE..........................805 484-1909

Anne Morgan, *Branch Mgr*
Sharon Demonsabert, *President*
Kelly Lanier, *Assistant*
EMP: 250
SALES (corp-wide): 32.8MM **Privately Held**
WEB: www.aemcorp.com
SIC: 7371 Computer software development & applications
PA: Virginia Aem Corporation
13880 Dulles Corner Ln # 300
Herndon VA 20171
805 484-1909

(P-15025)
APPSTER INC
180 Sansome St Fl 4, San Francisco (94104-3741)
PHONE..........................415 926-2741
Esther Humphrey, *Administration*
EMP: 80
SALES (est): 3.2MM
SALES (corp-wide): 4.6MM **Privately Held**
SIC: 7371 Computer software development & applications
PA: Appster Pty Ltd
Level 2
Melbourne VIC 3000
180 070-9291

(P-15026)
APPTIVO INC
34364 Eucalyptus Ter, Fremont (94555-1983)
PHONE..........................650 906-1034
Bastin S Gerald, *President*
Mary Jacintha, *CFO*
Randy Jacobs, *Manager*
EMP: 200 EST: 2009
SALES (est): 60K **Privately Held**
SIC: 7371 7389 Computer software development;

(P-15027)
APTELIGENT
760 Market St Ste 1101, San Francisco (94102-2321)
PHONE..........................415 371-1402
Dave Robbins, *CEO*
Lar Kamp, *President*
Kalyan Ramanathan, *Chief Mktg Ofcr*
Yoav Boaz, *Vice Pres*
Frank Swain, *Risk Mgmt Dir*
EMP: 60
SALES (est): 8.8MM **Privately Held**
SIC: 7371 Computer software development & applications

(P-15028)
APTTUS CORPORATION
1400 Fashi Islan Blvd Ste, San Mateo (94404)
PHONE..........................650 445-7700
Kirk Krappe, *CEO*
Neehar Giri, *President*
Chandra Kanive, *President*
Jim Willis, *President*
Sydney Carey, *CFO*
EMP: 121 EST: 2012
SALES (est): 36.6MM **Privately Held**
SIC: 7371 Computer software development

(P-15029)
ARCSIGHT LLC
5 Results Way, Cupertino (95014-5924)
PHONE..........................408 864-2600
Fax: 408 342-1615
Meg Whitman, *President*
Chris Hsu, *COO*
Tim Stonesifer, *CFO*
John Hinshaw, *Ch Credit Ofcr*
Henry Gomez, *Chief Mktg Ofcr*
EMP: 108 EST: 2000
SQ FT: 80,000
SALES (est): 24.6MM
SALES (corp-wide): 34.1B **Publicly Held**
WEB: www.arcsight.com
SIC: 7371 7382 Computer software development & applications; protective devices, security; burglar alarm maintenance & monitoring; fire alarm maintenance & monitoring; confinement surveillance systems maintenance & monitoring

PRODUCTS & SERVICES SECTION
7371 - Custom Computer Programming Svcs County (P-15051)

PA: Hewlett Packard Enterprise Company
3000 Hanover St
Palo Alto CA 94304
650 857-5817

(P-15030)
ARCSOFT INC (PA)
46601 Fremont Blvd, Fremont (94538-6410)
PHONE..................510 440-9901
Fax: 510 440-1270
Michael Deng, *President*
David Nagel, *Ch of Bd*
Todd Peters, *President*
Sean Bi, *Senior VP*
Rene Buhay, *Vice Pres*
EMP: 86
SQ FT: 26,000
SALES (est): 76.7MM **Privately Held**
WEB: www.arcsoft.com
SIC: 7371 5734 Computer software development; computer & software stores

(P-15031)
ARCTOUCH LLC
340 Brannan St Ste 302, San Francisco (94107-1836)
PHONE..................415 944-2000
Eric Shapiro, *CEO*
Jeremy Stephan, *Partner*
Joseph Carrolo, *President*
Paulo Michels, *President*
Adam Fingerman, *Officer*
EMP: 200
SALES (est): 16.6MM
SALES (corp-wide): 18.4B **Privately Held**
SIC: 7371 Computer software development & applications
HQ: Grey Global Group Llc
200 5th Ave Bsmt B
New York NY 10010
212 546-2000

(P-15032)
ARENA SOLUTIONS INC (PA)
989 E Hillsdale Blvd # 250, Foster City (94404-4201)
PHONE..................650 513-3500
Fax: 650 513-3511
Craig Livingston, *CEO*
Ken Bozzini, *COO*
Steve Chalgren, *Exec VP*
Hans Hartmann, *Vice Pres*
Nathan Martin, *Vice Pres*
EMP: 65
SALES (est): 27.5MM **Privately Held**
WEB: www.arenasolutions.com
SIC: 7371 Computer software development & applications

(P-15033)
ARICENT INC (DH)
303 Twin Dolphin Dr # 600, Redwood City (94065-1422)
PHONE..................650 632-4310
Sudip Nandy, *CEO*
Doreen Lorenzo, *President*
Dinesh Singh, *President*
Theodore Forbath, *Vice Pres*
Vikash Agarwal, *Sr Software Eng*
EMP: 108
SALES (est): 143.6MM
SALES (corp-wide): 1B **Publicly Held**
SIC: 7371 Computer software development
HQ: Kohlberg Kravis Roberts & Co. L.P.
9 W 57th St Ste 4200
New York NY 10019
212 750-8300

(P-15034)
ARTIFICIAL SOLUTIONS INC
800 W El Camino Real, Mountain View (94040-2567)
PHONE..................650 943-2325
EMP: 51
SALES (est): 30.7K **Privately Held**
SIC: 7371 Computer software development & applications

(P-15035)
ARTIZEN INCORPORATED
101 Golf Course Dr # 300, Rohnert Park (94928-1718)
PHONE..................650 261-9400
Parker Painter, *President*

Rosanna Medernach, *CFO*
EMP: 150
SQ FT: 2,200
SALES (est): 11.9MM **Privately Held**
SIC: 7371 Custom computer programming services

(P-15036)
ASCENDIFY CORPORATION
530 Bush St Ste 104, San Francisco (94108-3610)
PHONE..................415 528-5503
Matt Hendrickson, *CEO*
Lauren Smith, *Vice Pres*
EMP: 50
SALES (est): 177.6K **Privately Held**
SIC: 7371 Computer software development

(P-15037)
ASHUNYA INC
642 N Eckhoff St, Orange (92868-1004)
PHONE..................714 385-1900
Melanie Merchant, *Principal*
EMP: 88
SALES (est): 7.1MM **Privately Held**
SIC: 7371 7372 7373 Custom computer programming services; application computer software; office computer automation systems integration; turnkey vendors, computer systems; value-added resellers, computer systems

(P-15038)
ASTORIA SOFTWARE
160 Spear St Ste 1100, San Francisco (94105-1546)
PHONE..................415 956-3917
Michael Rosinski, *Branch Mgr*
George Hoyem, *Sales Executive*
EMP: 50
SALES (est): 1.9MM **Privately Held**
SIC: 7371 Computer software development

(P-15039)
ATHOC INC
2988 Campus Dr Ste 200, San Mateo (94403-2558)
PHONE..................650 685-3000
Fax: 650 685-3010
Guy Miasnik, *President*
Douglas Doyle, *Officer*
Aviv Siegel, *Exec VP*
Ly Tran, *Exec VP*
Andy Anderson, *Vice Pres*
EMP: 61
SQ FT: 10,000
SALES (est): 687.8K
SALES (corp-wide): 3.3B **Privately Held**
WEB: www.athoc.com
SIC: 7371 Computer software development & applications
HQ: Blackberry Corp.
3001 Bishop Dr
San Ramon CA 94583
972 650-6126

(P-15040)
ATLAS DATABASE SOFTWARE CORP (PA)
Also Called: Atlas Development
26679 Agoura Rd Ste 200, Calabasas (91302-3812)
PHONE..................818 340-7080
Robert D Atlas, *CEO*
Ana Villafane, *President*
Steven Atlas, *Vice Pres*
Lori Markey, *Vice Pres*
Dan Nelson, *Vice Pres*
EMP: 99
SQ FT: 15,000
SALES (est): 37.5MM **Privately Held**
WEB: www.atlasdev.com
SIC: 7371 Custom computer programming services

(P-15041)
ATLAZ INC
914 S St, Sacramento (95811-7025)
PHONE..................415 671-6142
Mark Fedin, *CEO*
EMP: 70 **EST:** 2015

SALES (est): 1MM **Privately Held**
SIC: 7371 Custom computer programming services; computer software systems analysis & design, custom

(P-15042)
ATRENTA INC (HQ)
690 E Middlefield Rd, Mountain View (94043-4010)
PHONE..................408 453-3333
Fax: 408 453-3322
Ajoy K Bose, *President*
Bert Clement, *COO*
Tim Cheng, *Admin Sec*
Mary Amrine, *Admin Asst*
Oleg Esimov, *Info Tech Mgr*
EMP: 70
SQ FT: 8,000
SALES (est): 67.4MM
SALES (corp-wide): 2.2B **Publicly Held**
WEB: www.atrenta.com
SIC: 7371 Computer software systems analysis & design, custom
PA: Synopsys, Inc.
690 E Middlefield Rd
Mountain View CA 94043
650 584-5000

(P-15043)
AVAMAR TECHNOLOGIES INC
135 Technology Dr, Irvine (92618-2402)
PHONE..................949 743-5100
Fax: 949 743-5190
Edward J Walsh, *CEO*
Hoshi Printer, *CFO*
Clint McVey, *Senior VP*
Gail Greener, *Vice Pres*
Riley Keown, *Credit Mgr*
EMP: 100
SALES (est): 6.4MM
SALES (corp-wide): 72.7B **Publicly Held**
WEB: www.avamar.com
SIC: 7371 Computer software development
HQ: Emc Corporation
176 South St
Hopkinton MA 01748
508 435-1000

(P-15044)
AVANQUEST NORTH AMERICA INC (HQ)
Also Called: Nova Development
23801 Calabasas Rd # 2005, Calabasas (91302-1547)
PHONE..................818 223-8967
Fax: 818 591-8563
Roger Bloxberg, *CEO*
Todd Helfstein, *President*
Sharon Chiu, *CFO*
Michael Addante, *Exec VP*
Sheryl Moss, *Vice Pres*
EMP: 80
SQ FT: 12,000
SALES (est): 56.3MM
SALES (corp-wide): 30MM **Privately Held**
WEB: www.novareg.com
SIC: 7371 Computer software development
PA: Avanquest
Immeuble Vision Defense
La Garenne Colombes Cedex 92257
141 271-970

(P-15045)
AVENUESOCIAL INC
440 N Wolfe Rd, Sunnyvale (94085-3869)
PHONE..................510 275-4485
Salman Ghaznavi, *President*
Seemi Munir, *Office Mgr*
Michele Heath, *Manager*
EMP: 135
SQ FT: 1,000
SALES: 3MM **Privately Held**
SIC: 7371 Software programming applications

(P-15046)
AWAREPOINT CORPORATION (PA)
Also Called: Aware Point
600 W Broadway Ste 250, San Diego (92101-3357)
PHONE..................858 345-5000
Fax: 858 535-1808

Tim Roche, *CEO*
Thomas Warlan, *Senior VP*
Carlene Anteau, *Vice Pres*
Erica Davidson, *VP Human Res*
Bernard Lee, *Mktg Dir*
EMP: 70
SALES (est): 19.9MM **Privately Held**
WEB: www.awarepoint.com
SIC: 7371 Software programming applications

(P-15047)
AXCIENT INC (PA)
1161 San Antonio Rd, Mountain View (94043-1028)
PHONE..................650 314-7300
Justin Moore, *CEO*
John Finegan, *CFO*
Steve Farnfworth, *Vice Pres*
Julie Gibbs, *Vice Pres*
Pam Lyra, *Vice Pres*
EMP: 88
SALES (est): 48.2MM **Privately Held**
WEB: www.axcient.com
SIC: 7371 Software programming applications

(P-15048)
B JACQUELINE AND ASSOC INC
Also Called: J B A
1192 N Lake Ave, Pasadena (91104-3739)
PHONE..................626 844-1400
Jacqueline Buickians, *President*
Gary Buickians, *Admin Sec*
Hyon Kim, *Assistant*
EMP: 300
SQ FT: 4,000
SALES (est): 16.8MM **Privately Held**
SIC: 7371 7379 Computer software development & applications; computer related consulting services

(P-15049)
BAJA LIFE ONLINE PARTNERS
P.O. Box 4917 (92652-4917)
PHONE..................949 376-4619
Fax: 949 376-7575
Erik Cutter, *Partner*
EMP: 50
SALES (est): 1.8MM **Privately Held**
WEB: www.bajalife.com
SIC: 7371 4724 Custom computer programming services; travel agencies

(P-15050)
BAKBONE SOFTWARE INC (DH)
9540 Towne Centre Dr # 100, San Diego (92121-1989)
PHONE..................858 450-9009
Fax: 858 450-9929
Michael S Dell, *CEO*
Stephen J Felice, *President*
Roy Hogsed, *Senior VP*
Kenneth Horner, *Senior VP*
Brian Tgladden, *Senior VP*
EMP: 72
SQ FT: 22,600
SALES (est): 23.6MM
SALES (corp-wide): 72.7B **Publicly Held**
WEB: www.bakbone.com
SIC: 7371 7375 Custom computer programming services; information retrieval services
HQ: Dell Software Inc.
4 Polaris Way
Aliso Viejo CA 92656
949 754-8000

(P-15051)
BEA SYSTEMS INC (HQ)
2315 N 1st St, San Jose (95131-1010)
PHONE..................650 506-7000
Fax: 408 570-8901
Alfred S Chuang, *Ch of Bd*
Alan Button, *Partner*
Ted Kimes, *President*
William Kline, *CFO*
John Knightlys, *Chief Mktg Ofcr*
EMP: 1000
SQ FT: 236,000
SALES (est): 160.8MM
SALES (corp-wide): 37B **Publicly Held**
WEB: www.beasys.com
SIC: 7371 7372 Computer software development; prepackaged software

7371 - Custom Computer Programming Svcs County (P-15052)   PRODUDUCTS & SERVICES SECTION

PA: Oracle Corporation
500 Oracle Pkwy
Redwood City CA 94065
650 506-7000

(P-15052)
BENTLEY SYSTEMS INCORPORATED
1600 Riviera Ave Ste 300, Walnut Creek (94596-3570)
PHONE..................925 933-2525
EMP: 80
SALES (corp-wide): 854.3MM Privately Held
SIC: 7371 8711
PA: Bentley Systems, Incorporated
685 Stockton Dr
Exton PA 19341
610 458-5000

(P-15053)
BIG BULB IDEAS INC
Also Called: Installmonetizer
5655 Silver Creek Vlley R, San Jose (95138-2473)
PHONE..................408 888-2346
Vince Mundy, *CEO*
Lloyd Jacob, *Risk Mgmt Dir*
Jerry Kil, *Project Mgr*
EMP: 50
SQ FT: 400
SALES: 20MM Privately Held
SIC: 7371 Computer software systems analysis & design, custom

(P-15054)
BIRST INC (PA)
45 Fremont St Ste 1800, San Francisco (94105-2219)
PHONE..................415 766-4800
Fax: 415 762-4115
Jay Larson, *CEO*
Samuel Wolff, *CFO*
Carl Tsukahara, *Chief Mktg Ofcr*
Brad Peters, *Officer*
Paul Staelin, *Officer*
EMP: 134
SQ FT: 36,171
SALES (est): 109.9MM Privately Held
SIC: 7371 Computer software development

(P-15055)
BITFONE CORPORATION (PA)
32451 Golden Lantern # 301, Laguna Niguel (92677-5344)
PHONE..................949 234-7000
Gene Wang, *President*
Hang Michael Xu, *CFO*
Harri Okkonen, *Senior VP*
Chris Cassapakis, *Vice Pres*
Carla Fitzgerald, *Vice Pres*
EMP: 50 EST: 2000
SQ FT: 11,000
SALES (est): 4.2MM Privately Held
WEB: www.bitfone.com
SIC: 7371 Computer software development

(P-15056)
BLACKARROW INC (HQ)
65 N San Pedro St, San Jose (95110-2414)
PHONE..................408 642-6400
Nick Troiano, *CEO*
Stephanie Mitchko-Beale, *COO*
Tracy Martin, *CFO*
Chris Hock, *Senior VP*
Tricia Iboshi, *Senior VP*
EMP: 55
SQ FT: 10,000
SALES (est): 13.4MM
SALES (corp-wide): 30.6MM Privately Held
SIC: 7371 Custom computer programming services
PA: Cross Mediaworks, Llc
1450 Broadway Rm 502
New York NY 10018
267 443-2547

(P-15057)
BLACKHAWK INFORMATION SERVICES
22 Beta Ct, San Ramon (94583-1202)
P.O. Box 3592, Danville (94526-8592)
PHONE..................925 244-6701
Fax: 925 830-4252
Jason Yi, *President*
Julie Yi, *CFO*
EMP: 50
SQ FT: 6,000
SALES (est): 1.8MM Privately Held
WEB: www.blackhawkis.com
SIC: 7371 Custom computer programming services

(P-15058)
BLACKLINE INC
21300 Victory Blvd Fl 12, Woodland Hills (91367-7734)
PHONE..................818 223-9008
Therese Tucker, *CEO*
Martin Dixon, *President*
Martin Partin, *CFO*
Stephen Bartels, *Admin Sec*
Austin Pittman, *Admin Asst*
EMP: 490
SALES (est): 168K Privately Held
SIC: 7371 Computer software systems analysis & design, custom

(P-15059)
BLUEYIELD INC
Also Called: Blue Harbor
15 Enterprise Ste 520, Aliso Viejo (92656-2656)
PHONE..................949 385-6219
Jeffrey Danford, *CEO*
Jennifer Heil, *President*
Curtis Kuboyama, *Exec VP*
Ryan Cowan, *Manager*
Jose Fajardo, *Consultant*
EMP: 52
SQ FT: 4,500
SALES: 5MM Privately Held
SIC: 7371 Computer software development

(P-15060)
BLUFOCUS INC
10911 Riverside Dr 200, North Hollywood (91602-2209)
PHONE..................818 294-7695
Paulette E Pantoja, *CEO*
Jake Ramirez, *Business Dir*
Paul Chang, *Office Mgr*
Juan Reyes, *CTO*
EMP: 60
SQ FT: 7,000
SALES (est): 4.5MM Privately Held
WEB: www.blufocus.com
SIC: 7371 8748 7379 Software programming applications; systems analysis & engineering consulting services; computer related consulting services

(P-15061)
BOKU INC (PA)
Also Called: Mobillcash
735 Battery St Fl 2, San Francisco (94111-1536)
P.O. Box 190725 (94119-0725)
PHONE..................415 375-3160
Mark J Britto, *CEO*
Ron Hirson, *President*
Aura Motiska, *COO*
Christian Hinrichs, *CFO*
Stuart Neal, *CFO*
EMP: 60
SALES (est): 36.4MM Privately Held
SIC: 7371 7322 Computer software development & applications; collection agency, except real estate

(P-15062)
BPO MANAGEMENT SERVICES INC (PA)
8175 E Kaiser Blvd 100, Anaheim (92808-2214)
PHONE..................714 972-2670
Patrick A Dolan, *Ch of Bd*
James Cortens, *President*
Donald W Rutherford, *CFO*
Larry Carver, *Vice Pres*
Vernon E Sheppard, *Vice Pres*
EMP: 73
SQ FT: 5,871
SALES: 28.1MM Privately Held
SIC: 7371 Computer software development

(P-15063)
BRACKET GLOBAL LLC
303 2nd St Ste 700, San Francisco (94107-1366)
PHONE..................415 293-1340
Kristen Dellaroca, *Branch Mgr*
Tony Puppo, *Info Tech Mgr*
Simone Robinson, *Human Res Dir*
Mania Shahvekilian, *Manager*
Dony Unardi, *Manager*
EMP: 100
SALES (corp-wide): 78.7MM Privately Held
SIC: 7371 8748 Computer software development; telecommunications consultant
PA: Bracket Global Llc
575 E Swedesford Rd # 200
Wayne PA 19087
610 225-5900

(P-15064)
BRIENCE INC (DH)
Also Called: A Development Stage Company
128 Spear St Fl 3, San Francisco (94105-5147)
PHONE..................415 974-5300
Roderick McGeary, *Ch of Bd*
James Drumright, *COO*
Stephen E Recht, *CFO*
Keyur Patel, *Officer*
Mark Losh, *Senior VP*
EMP: 90
SQ FT: 15,000
SALES (est): 10.5MM
SALES (corp-wide): 861.4MM Privately Held
WEB: www.brience.com
SIC: 7371 Computer software development & applications
HQ: Syniverse Technologies, Llc.
8125 Highwoods Palm Way
Tampa FL 33647
813 637-5000

(P-15065)
BRIGHTEDGE TECHNOLOGIES INC (PA)
999 Baker Way Ste 500, San Mateo (94404-1583)
PHONE..................800 578-8023
Jim Yu, *President*
Jim Emerich, *CFO*
Joshua Crossman, *Vice Pres*
Barrett Foster, *Vice Pres*
Fred Fried, *Vice Pres*
EMP: 134
SALES (est): 13MM Privately Held
SIC: 7371 5045 Computer software development; computers, peripherals & software

(P-15066)
BRIGHTERION INC
150 Spear St Fl 10, San Francisco (94105-5116)
PHONE..................415 986-5600
Fax: 415 986-5691
Akli Adjaoute, *CEO*
Raymond Kendall, *President*
Richard Stiener, *Senior VP*
Thomas Rand-Nash, *General Mgr*
Francois Stehlin, *Info Tech Dir*
EMP: 62
SQ FT: 15,000
SALES: 4MM Privately Held
WEB: www.brighterion.com
SIC: 7371 Computer software development

(P-15067)
BRISTLECONE INCORPORATED
10 Almaden Blvd Ste 600, San Jose (95113-2226)
PHONE..................650 386-4000
Fax: 650 961-2369
Irfan A Khan, *President*
Zhooben Bhiwandiwala, *CFO*
Nadir Godrej, *Bd of Directors*
Joerg Sperling, *Bd of Directors*
Sankha Bhowmick, *Vice Pres*
EMP: 1300 EST: 1998
SQ FT: 10,000
SALES (est): 55MM
SALES (corp-wide): 5.9B Privately Held
WEB: www.bcone.com
SIC: 7371 8742 Software programming applications; management consulting services
PA: Mahindra And Mahindra Limited
Mahindra Towers,
Mumbai MH 40001
222 493-1441

(P-15068)
BROADSOFT CONTACT CENTER INC
930 Hamlin Ct, Sunnyvale (94089-1401)
PHONE..................408 338-0900
Prem Uppaluru, *CEO*
Arnab Mishra, *President*
Mike Shannahan, *CFO*
Brad Mack, *Senior VP*
Gaya Vukkadala, *Senior VP*
EMP: 50
SQ FT: 15,000
SALES (est): 5.7MM
SALES (corp-wide): 278.8MM Publicly Held
SIC: 7371 8742 Computer software systems analysis & design, custom; management information systems consultant
PA: Broadsoft, Inc.
9737 Washingtonian Blvd # 350
Gaithersburg MD 20878
301 977-9440

(P-15069)
BUNCHBALL INC
1820 Gateway Dr Ste 300, San Mateo (94404-4024)
PHONE..................408 215-2924
Jim Scullion, *CEO*
Rajat Paharia, *President*
Brad Clark, *COO*
David Overmyer, *CFO*
Caroline Japic, *Senior VP*
EMP: 60
SALES (est): 9.9MM Privately Held
SIC: 7371 7379 Computer software development & applications;

(P-15070)
BYND LLC
Also Called: Beyond International Corp
100 Montgomery St # 1102, San Francisco (94104-4388)
PHONE..................415 944-2293
Aedhmar Hynes, *Principal*
Julie Swing, *Design Engr*
Seth Duncan, *Research*
Cody Elam, *Research*
Amin Falguni, *Controller*
EMP: 100 EST: 2004
SALES (est): 319.2K
SALES (corp-wide): 197.4MM Privately Held
SIC: 7371 Computer software development & applications
PA: Next Fifteen Communications Group Plc
The Triangle
London

(P-15071)
CAKE CORPORATION
101 Redwood Ave, Redwood City (94061-3020)
PHONE..................650 215-7777
Mani Kulasooriya, *CEO*
Paul Kelaita, *President*
Ned Taylor, *President*
Brian Beach, *Senior VP*
Jim Oconnor, *Senior VP*
EMP: 100 EST: 2010
SALES (est): 886.9K Privately Held
SIC: 7371 Computer software development & applications

(P-15072)
CALLFIRE INC
1410 2nd St Ste 200, Santa Monica (90401-3349)
PHONE..................213 221-2289
Fax: 310 943-0415
Ron Burr, *CEO*

Komnieve Singh, *President*
Tj Thinakaran, *COO*
Tridivesh Kidambi, *CFO*
Vijesh Mehta, *Corp Secy*
EMP: 61
SALES (est): 13.6MM **Privately Held**
WEB: www.skyyconsulting.com
SIC: 7371 Custom computer programming services

(P-15073)
CALLIDUS SOFTWARE INC (PA)
Also Called: Callicuscloud
4140 Dublin Blvd Ste 400, Dublin (94568-7757)
PHONE.................................925 251-2200
Fax: 925 251-0525
Leslie J Stretch, *President*
Charles M Boesenberg, *Ch of Bd*
Bob L Corey, *CFO*
Robert C Conti, *Senior VP*
Jimmy Duan, *Senior VP*
EMP: 148
SQ FT: 75,000
SALES (est): 173MM **Publicly Held**
WEB: www.callidussoftware.com
SIC: 7371 7372 Custom computer programming services; business oriented computer software

(P-15074)
CAPE CLEAR SOFTWARE INC
Also Called: Capeconnect
900 E Hamilton Ave # 100, Campbell (95008-0664)
PHONE.................................408 879-7365
Annrai O'Toole, *CEO*
David Clark, *Vice Pres*
John McGuire, *Vice Pres*
Rich Navok, *Vice Pres*
James Pasley, *CTO*
EMP: 85 **EST:** 1999
SALES (est): 3.1MM **Privately Held**
WEB: www.capeclear.com
SIC: 7371 Computer software development

(P-15075)
CARBONFIVE INCORPORATED
Also Called: Carbon Five
585 Howard St Fl 2, San Francisco (94105-4677)
PHONE.................................415 546-0500
Don Thompson, *Principal*
Mike Wynholds, *CEO*
Alex Cruikshank, *Software Dev*
Thomas Fisher, *Software Dev*
Laura Ku, *Software Engr*
EMP: 62
SALES (est): 6.4MM **Privately Held**
WEB: www.carbonfive.com
SIC: 7371 Custom computer programming services

(P-15076)
CARRIER IQ INC (HQ)
1100 La Avenida St, Mountain View (94043-1452)
PHONE.................................650 625-5400
Fax: 650 625-5435
Larry Lenhart, *Ch of Bd*
Linda Khachooni, *CFO*
Kelly Sharpe, *CFO*
Konstantin Othmer, *Corp Secy*
Magnolia Mansourkia Mobley, *Officer*
EMP: 50
SQ FT: 17,000
SALES (est): 15.3MM **Privately Held**
WEB: www.coremobility.com
SIC: 7371 Computer software development & applications

(P-15077)
CATAPHORA INC (PA)
3425 Edison Way, Menlo Park (94025-1813)
P.O. Box 2007 (94026-2007)
PHONE.................................650 622-9840
Elizabeth B Charnock, *President*
Steve Gupta, *CFO*
Philip Carruthers, *Vice Pres*
Mathieu Feulvarch, *Vice Pres*
Robert Artisst, *Business Dir*
EMP: 60
SQ FT: 25,000
SALES (est): 10.5MM **Privately Held**
WEB: www.cataphora.com
SIC: 7371 Computer software development

(P-15078)
CENTRIFY CORPORATION
3300 Tannery Way, Santa Clara (95054-2828)
PHONE.................................669 444-5200
Tom Kemp, *President*
Timothy Steinkopf, *CFO*
Bilhar Mann, *Adam Au*, *Senior VP*
Adam Au, *Senior VP*
Bill Mann, *Senior VP*
EMP: 300
SQ FT: 8,300
SALES (est): 71.1MM **Privately Held**
WEB: www.centrify.com
SIC: 7371 Computer software development & applications

(P-15079)
CERTAIN INC (PA)
75 Hawthorne St Ste 550, San Francisco (94105-3938)
PHONE.................................415 353-5330
Peter Micciche, *CEO*
Jasvinder Matharu, *President*
Brian Bailard, *Officer*
David Burton, *Vice Pres*
Mark Jauregui, *Vice Pres*
EMP: 53
SALES (est): 13.8MM **Privately Held**
SIC: 7371 Computer software development & applications

(P-15080)
CHASE CREDIT SYSTEMS INC
300 E Magnolia Blvd # 502, Burbank (91502-1178)
PHONE.................................818 762-6262
Perry Cohan, *President*
Ben Cohan, *Vice Pres*
Ron Singer, *Technical Mgr*
Gerd Kerswill, *IT/INT Sup*
EMP: 95
SALES (est): 3.7MM
SALES (corp-wide): 5.2B **Publicly Held**
SIC: 7371 Computer software systems analysis & design, custom
PA: Fiserv, Inc.
255 Fiserv Dr
Brookfield WI 53045
262 879-5000

(P-15081)
CHELSIO COMMUNICATIONS INC
209 N Fair Oaks Ave, Sunnyvale (94085-4423)
PHONE.................................408 962-3600
Kianoosh Naghshineh, *President*
William Delaney, *CFO*
Sean Conlon, *Vice Pres*
Danny Gur, *Vice Pres*
Mehdi Mohtashemi, *Vice Pres*
EMP: 130
SQ FT: 20,000
SALES (est): 28.2MM **Privately Held**
WEB: www.chelsio.com
SIC: 7371 Computer software systems analysis & design, custom

(P-15082)
CHROME RIVER TECHNOLOGIES INC
5757 Wilshire Blvd # 270, Los Angeles (90036-5814)
PHONE.................................323 857-5800
Alan Richeimer, *President*
Dave Terry, *COO*
Daniel Machock, *CFO*
Julie Norquist Roy, *Officer*
Aviva Kram, *Vice Pres*
EMP: 200
SALES (est): 25.1MM **Privately Held**
SIC: 7371 Computer software development & applications

(P-15083)
CIE GAMES LLC
500 Howard St Ste 300, San Francisco (94105-3027)
PHONE.................................415 800-6100
Niccolo De Masi, *CEO*
Dennis Suggs, *President*
Eric Ludwig, *CFO*
Jobe Lloyd, *Software Dev*
EMP: 50
SALES (est): 2.8MM
SALES (corp-wide): 249.9MM **Publicly Held**
SIC: 7371 Custom computer programming services
PA: Glu Mobile Inc.
500 Howard St Ste 300
San Francisco CA 94105
415 800-6100

(P-15084)
CIGNEX DATAMATICS INC (PA)
2350 Mission College Blvd, Santa Clara (95054-1532)
PHONE.................................408 327-9900
Fax: 408 273-6785
Paul Anthony Parokkaran, *CEO*
Munwar Shariff, *Co-Owner*
Amit Babaria, *President*
Dave Malhotra, *COO*
Rajesh Devidasani, *CFO*
EMP: 108
SQ FT: 5,000
SALES (est): 55.1MM **Privately Held**
WEB: www.cignex.com
SIC: 7371 8742 Custom computer programming services; management consulting services

(P-15085)
CIMATRON GIBBS LLC
Also Called: Gibbs & Associates
323 Science Dr, Moorpark (93021-2092)
PHONE.................................805 523-0004
Fax: 805 523-0006
Bill Gibbs, *Owner*
Robb Weinstein, *Senior VP*
Jerry Foglesong, *Admin Asst*
Jeff Castanon, *Sr Software Eng*
James Shisley, *Sr Software Eng*
EMP: 61
SQ FT: 22,500
SALES (est): 8.7MM **Privately Held**
WEB: www.gibbsnc.com
SIC: 7371 Computer software development

(P-15086)
CITRIX SYSTEMS INC
7414 Hollister Ave, Goleta (93117-2583)
PHONE.................................805 690-6400
Albert Alexandrov, *Vice Pres*
David Iuele, *Admin Asst*
Sam Kryder, *Admin Asst*
Deepam Joshi, *Sr Ntwrk Engine*
Frank Zhou, *Sr Ntwrk Engine*
EMP: 500
SALES (corp-wide): 3.2B **Publicly Held**
SIC: 7371 Computer software development
PA: Citrix Systems, Inc.
851 W Cypress Creek Rd
Fort Lauderdale FL 33309
954 267-3000

(P-15087)
CITRIX SYSTEMS INC
4988 Great America Pkwy, Santa Clara (95054-1200)
PHONE.................................408 790-8000
Klaus Oerstermann, *Principal*
Ray Fritz, *CFO*
Sakthi Chandra, *Vice Pres*
Rajiv Sinha, *Vice Pres*
Tammy Forte, *Admin Asst*
EMP: 95
SALES (corp-wide): 3.2B **Publicly Held**
WEB: www.citrix.com
SIC: 7371 Computer software development
PA: Citrix Systems, Inc.
851 W Cypress Creek Rd
Fort Lauderdale FL 33309
954 267-3000

(P-15088)
CLICK LABS INC
315 Montgomery St Fl 8, San Francisco (94104-1803)
PHONE.................................415 658-5227
EMP: 501

(P-15089)
CLICKABILITY INC
250 Montgomery St Ste 300, San Francisco (94104-3428)
PHONE.................................415 200-0410
Fax: 415 538-0839
John McDonald, *CEO*
Darlene Mann, *COO*
John Jerrehian, *Vice Pres*
Rob Lamb, *Vice Pres*
Sean Noonan, *Vice Pres*
EMP: 50
SALES (est): 9.6MM **Publicly Held**
WEB: www.clickability.com
SIC: 7371 7311 Software programming applications; advertising agencies
PA: Upland Software, Inc.
401 Congress Ave Ste 1850
Austin TX 78701

(P-15090)
CLINAPPS INC
9530 Towne Centre Dr # 120, San Diego (92121-1981)
PHONE.................................858 866-0228
Timothy W Elliott, *President*
Michelle Elliott, *Vice Pres*
Terri Fisher, *Vice Pres*
Tom Alvarez, *Manager*
EMP: 57
SQ FT: 7,000
SALES (est): 4.1MM **Privately Held**
SIC: 7371 Computer software development

(P-15091)
CLOUD4WI INC
22 Cleveland St, San Francisco (94103-4014)
PHONE.................................415 852-3900
Andrea Calcagno, *CEO*
Ed Tomlinson, *President*
Elena Briola, *Chief Mktg Ofcr*
Gianni Altamura, *Vice Pres*
Brodie Kirkeby, *Vice Pres*
EMP: 55
SQ FT: 3,500
SALES (est): 900.3K **Privately Held**
SIC: 7371 8748 Computer software development & applications; telecommunications consultant

(P-15092)
CLOUDERA INC (PA)
1001 Page Mill Rd Bldg 3, Palo Alto (94304-1009)
PHONE.................................650 644-3900
Tom Reilly, *President*
Jim Frankola, *CFO*
Wayne Kimber, *CFO*
Patrick Ball, *Vice Pres*
Peter Cooper-Ellis, *Vice Pres*
EMP: 148
SQ FT: 27,443
SALES (est): 214.8MM **Privately Held**
SIC: 7371 5734 8331 Custom computer programming services; software, business & non-game; skill training center

(P-15093)
CLOUDMARK INC (PA)
128 King St Fl 2, San Francisco (94107-1914)
PHONE.................................415 946-3800
Fax: 415 543-1233
George A Riedel, *CEO*
Thomas G Ream, *CFO*
Olivier Lemari, *Vice Pres*
Leon Rishniw, *Vice Pres*
Jacinta Tobin, *Vice Pres*
EMP: 86
SQ FT: 15,000
SALES (est): 41MM **Privately Held**
WEB: www.cloudmark.com
SIC: 7371 Computer software development

7371 - Custom Computer Programming Svcs County (P-15094)

(P-15094)
CLOUDPASSAGE INC
180 Townsend St Fl 3, San Francisco (94107-1909)
PHONE....................800 215-7404
Fax: 650 989-1317
Carson Sweet, *President*
Steve Shevick, *CFO*
Mitch Bishop, *Chief Mktg Ofcr*
Brian Harmon, *Exec VP*
Kent Erickson, *Senior VP*
EMP: 80
SQ FT: 10,000
SALES (est): 2.1MM **Privately Held**
SIC: 7371 Software programming applications

(P-15095)
COLSA CORPORATION
Digital Wizards Division
2727 Camino Del Rio S, San Diego (92108-3750)
PHONE....................619 260-1100
Patricia Hodges, *Principal*
Steve Stamper, *Info Tech Mgr*
Roberta Fender, *Accounts Mgr*
EMP: 110
SALES (corp-wide): 190.1MM **Privately Held**
SIC: 7371 8711 Computer software development; engineering services
PA: Colsa Corporation
   6728 Odyssey Dr Nw
   Huntsville AL 35806
   256 964-5361

(P-15096)
COMMISSION JUNCTION INC (DH)
530 E Montecito St, Santa Barbara (93103-3252)
PHONE....................805 730-8000
Fax: 805 730-8001
James R Zarley, *CEO*
Matthew Gordon, *Partner*
Kerri Pollard, *President*
Jeffrey A Pullen, *President*
Jim Buckley, *CFO*
EMP: 81
SQ FT: 16,000
SALES (est): 17.2MM
SALES (corp-wide): 6.4B **Publicly Held**
WEB: www.cj.com
SIC: 7371 Custom computer programming services
HQ: Conversant, Llc
   30699 Russell Ranch Rd # 250
   Westlake Village CA 91362
   818 575-4500

(P-15097)
COMPULAW LLC
200 Crprate Pinte Ste 400, Culver City (90230)
PHONE....................310 553-3355
Fax: 310 553-7660
David Kalmick, *Mng Member*
Michael Armstrong,
Stephanie Hall,
Lois Kalmick,
Alex Manners,
EMP: 50
SQ FT: 15,000
SALES (est): 3MM **Privately Held**
WEB: www.compulaw.com
SIC: 7371 Computer software development; computer software development & applications; software programming applications
PA: Aderant Holdings, Inc.
   500 Northridge Rd Ste 800
   Atlanta GA 30350

(P-15098)
COMPUTER PROC UNLIMITED INC
Also Called: Cpu Medical Management Systems
9235 Activity Rd Ste 104, San Diego (92126-4440)
PHONE....................858 530-0875
Fax: 858 530-2615
Michael Stringer, *President*
Brian Castle, *CFO*
Doug Allem, *Treasurer*
Jean Campbell, *Senior VP*
Herald Bing, *Vice Pres*
EMP: 65
SQ FT: 11,250
SALES (est): 12MM
SALES (corp-wide): 190.8B **Publicly Held**
WEB: www.cpumms.com
SIC: 7371 5045 Computer software systems analysis & design, custom; computer peripheral equipment
PA: Mckesson Corporation
   1 Post St Fl 18
   San Francisco CA 94104
   415 983-8300

(P-15099)
COMPUTER RESOURCES GROUP INC
275 Battery St Ste 800, San Francisco (94111-3364)
PHONE....................415 398-3535
Fax: 415 399-1405
Richard D Green, *Ch of Bd*
Allen Prestegard, *President*
Jackie Autry, *Vice Pres*
Dave Hanson, *Vice Pres*
Christina Iwamura, *Vice Pres*
EMP: 250
SQ FT: 12,000
SALES (est): 9.3MM **Privately Held**
SIC: 7371 7379 Custom computer programming services; computer related consulting services

(P-15100)
COMPUTER TASK GROUP INC
2033 Gateway Pl Fl 5, San Jose (95110-3709)
PHONE....................408 573-6070
Randolph A Marks, *Branch Mgr*
EMP: 230
SALES (corp-wide): 369.4MM **Publicly Held**
SIC: 7371 Custom computer programming services
PA: Computer Task Group, Incorporated
   800 Delaware Ave
   Buffalo NY 14209
   716 882-8000

(P-15101)
COMPUTER TASK GROUP INC
Also Called: Ctg
101 Metro Dr Ste 530, San Jose (95110-1341)
PHONE....................800 992-5350
Fax: 408 441-8148
Larry Comstock, *Sales/Mktg Mgr*
EMP: 300
SALES (corp-wide): 369.4MM **Publicly Held**
WEB: www.ctg.com
SIC: 7371 7373 Custom computer programming services; computer systems analysis & design
PA: Computer Task Group, Incorporated
   800 Delaware Ave
   Buffalo NY 14209
   716 882-8000

(P-15102)
COMPUTRITION INC (HQ)
8521 Fllbrook Ave Ste 100, Canoga Park (91304)
P.O. Box 4689, Chatsworth (91313-4689)
PHONE....................818 961-3999
Fax: 818 701-1702
Scott Saklad, *President*
Scott R Saklad, *COO*
Kim C Goldberg, *Vice Pres*
Ronald Abarca, *Technology*
Nursen Celebi, *Human Res Mgr*
EMP: 60
SQ FT: 16,763
SALES (est): 12.4MM
SALES (corp-wide): 1.8B **Privately Held**
WEB: www.computrition.com
SIC: 7371 7372 Computer software development; prepackaged software
PA: Constellation Software Inc
   20 Adelaide St E Suite 1200
   Toronto ON M5C 2
   416 861-2279

(P-15103)
COMPUWARE CORPORATION
15303 Ventura Blvd Fl 9, Sherman Oaks (91403-3199)
PHONE....................818 380-3019
Que Hirschi, *Principal*
EMP: 69
SALES (corp-wide): 1.4B **Privately Held**
SIC: 7371 Computer software development & applications
HQ: Compuware Corporation
   1 Campus Martius Fl 4
   Detroit MI 48226
   313 227-7300

(P-15104)
COMPUWARE CORPORATION
5375 Mira Sorrento Pl # 500, San Diego (92121-3809)
PHONE....................858 824-5200
Rob Mills, *Principal*
Kenneth Grossman, *Info Tech Dir*
Michael Donner, *VP Mktg*
EMP: 50
SALES (corp-wide): 1.4B **Privately Held**
WEB: www.compuware.com
SIC: 7371 7372 Computer software development; software programming applications; prepackaged software
HQ: Compuware Corporation
   1 Campus Martius Fl 4
   Detroit MI 48226
   313 227-7300

(P-15105)
COMPVUE INC
440 N Wolfe Rd, Sunnyvale (94085-3869)
PHONE....................408 892-9909
Rakesh Gupta, *CEO*
Velu P Padmanabhan, *Technology*
Aishwarya Srinivasan, *Director*
EMP: 70
SALES: 981.7K **Privately Held**
SIC: 7371 Custom computer programming services

(P-15106)
CONCERRO INC (DH)
9276 Scranton Rd Ste 400, San Diego (92121-7714)
PHONE....................858 882-8500
Graham Barnes, *CEO*
Cindy Watson, *COO*
Derrick Clackenbush, *CFO*
Steven Bartell, *Vice Pres*
Michael E Meisel, *Vice Pres*
EMP: 50
SQ FT: 16,000
SALES: 5.2MM
SALES (corp-wide): 117.3B **Publicly Held**
SIC: 7371 Computer software development & applications
HQ: Api Healthcare Corporation
   1550 Innovation Way
   Hartford WI 53027
   262 673-6815

(P-15107)
CONNOTATE TECHNOLOGIES INC
2601 Main St Ste 830, Irvine (92614-5219)
PHONE....................949 270-1916
Keith Cooper, *CEO*
EMP: 50
SALES (corp-wide): 15.2MM **Privately Held**
SIC: 7371 Computer software writing services
PA: Connotate Technologies Inc.
   100 Albany St Ste 250
   New Brunswick NJ 08901
   732 296-8844

(P-15108)
CONVERTRO INC
13031 W Jeff Blvd 900, Playa Vista (90094)
PHONE....................800 797-0176
Jeffrey Zwelling, *CEO*
Sanjog Misra, *Ch of Bd*
David Feldman, *CFO*
Quinn Collins, *Senior VP*
Paul Bates, *Vice Pres*
EMP: 50
SALES (est): 5.3MM
SALES (corp-wide): 131.6MM **Publicly Held**
SIC: 7371 8732 Computer software development & applications; business analysis; business research service; market analysis or research
HQ: Aol Inc.
   770 Broadway Fl 4
   New York NY 10003
   212 652-6400

(P-15109)
CORELYNX INC
11501 Dublin Blvd Ste 200, Dublin (94568-2827)
PHONE....................877 267-3599
Fax: 510 742-5417
Manash Chaudhuri, *CEO*
Shiv Guha, *Business Mgr*
Amit Roy, *Opers Mgr*
EMP: 103
SQ FT: 500
SALES: 3MM **Privately Held**
SIC: 7371 Custom computer programming services; computer software development

(P-15110)
CORETECHS STAFFING INC
50 Woodside Plz Ste 604, Redwood City (94061-2500)
PHONE....................650 363-7960
Fax: 408 442-1166
Andrew Adelman, *President*
Randall Stratton, *Principal*
Jon Brose, *Manager*
EMP: 55
SALES (est): 5.1MM **Privately Held**
SIC: 7371 Computer software systems analysis & design, custom

(P-15111)
CORPTAX
21550 Oxnard St Ste 700, Woodland Hills (91367-7170)
PHONE....................818 316-2400
Arnold Cosme, *Info Tech Mgr*
Jovelt Jeune, *Engineer*
EMP: 60 **Privately Held**
SIC: 7371 Computer software development
PA: Corptax
   1751 Lake Cook Rd Ste 100
   Deerfield IL 60015

(P-15112)
COVANSYS CORPORATION
34740 Tuxedo Cmn, Fremont (94555-2746)
PHONE....................510 304-3430
Chris Pensy, *Manager*
EMP: 150
SALES (corp-wide): 7.1B **Publicly Held**
SIC: 7371 Custom computer programming services
HQ: Covansys Corporation
   3170 Fairview Park Dr
   Falls Church VA 22042
   703 876-1000

(P-15113)
COVERITY LLC (HQ)
185 Berry St Ste 6500, San Francisco (94107-1728)
PHONE....................415 321-5200
Fax: 415 541-9521
Anthony Bettencourt, *President*
Mike Conti, *President*
Jennifer Johnson, *Chief Mktg Ofcr*
Dave Peterson, *Chief Mktg Ofcr*
Sunil Nagdev, *Senior VP*
EMP: 80
SALES (est): 37.6MM
SALES (corp-wide): 2.2B **Publicly Held**
WEB: www.coverity.com
SIC: 7371 7372 Custom computer programming services; computer software development; software programming applications; prepackaged software
PA: Synopsys, Inc.
   690 E Middlefield Rd
   Mountain View CA 94043
   650 584-5000

PRODUCTS & SERVICES SECTION
7371 - Custom Computer Programming Svcs County (P-15134)

(P-15114)
CRESCENT STAFFING INC (PA)
Also Called: Crescent Solutions
17871 Mitchell N Ste 100, Irvine (92614-6050)
PHONE..............................949 724-0304
Fax: 949 724-1511
Brian Fischbein, *CEO*
Keith McDonald, *President*
Mitchell Balzer, *Vice Pres*
Pj Viloski, *Vice Pres*
Matthew Fristoe, *Admin Sec*
EMP: 195
SALES (est): 33.6MM **Privately Held**
WEB: www.crescent-enterprise.com
SIC: 7371 8748 7379 Custom computer programming services; business consulting; computer related consulting services

(P-15115)
CSRA LLC
2727 Hamner Ave, Norco (92860-1927)
PHONE..............................951 898-3015
Dennis Plambeck, *Manager*
Donna King, *Admin Asst*
Patricia Plambeck, *Administration*
Ralph Whittington, *Engineer*
Kathy Whitfield, *Human Res Mgr*
EMP: 100
SALES (corp-wide): 4.2B **Publicly Held**
WEB: www.csc.com
SIC: 7371 Custom computer programming services
HQ: Csra Llc
3170 Fairview Park Dr
Falls Church VA 22042
703 876-1000

(P-15116)
CSS HOLDINGS INC
Also Called: Live Pos
7486 La Jolla Blvd, La Jolla (92037-5029)
PHONE..............................866 343-7185
Liad Biton, *CEO*
Sammy Kahen, *President*
Sia Kahen, *CFO*
Shiran Biton, *Admin Sec*
Dekel Ezri, *Regl Sales Mgr*
EMP: 70
SQ FT: 5,000
SALES: 5.8MM **Privately Held**
SIC: 7371 7379 Computer software development; computer related consulting services

(P-15117)
CU DIRECT CORPORATION (PA)
Also Called: Cudc
2855 E Guasti Rd Ste 500, Ontario (91761-1253)
P.O. Box 51482 (91761-0082)
PHONE..............................909 481-2300
Antony Boutelle, *President*
Craig S Montesanti, *CFO*
Jerry Neemann, *Officer*
Kip Haas, *Exec VP*
Joe Greenwald, *Senior VP*
EMP: 175
SQ FT: 30,000
SALES: 60MM **Privately Held**
SIC: 7371 Computer software development

(P-15118)
D P TECHNOLOGY CORP (PA)
Also Called: Esprit
1150 Avenida Acaso, Camarillo (93012-8719)
PHONE..............................805 388-6000
Fax: 805 388-3085
Daniel Frayssinet, *CEO*
Paul Ricard, *President*
Keith Jablonowski, *Regional Mgr*
Mike Gustafson, *Sr Software Eng*
Zhenyu Cheng, *Software Engr*
EMP: 60
SQ FT: 12,000
SALES (est): 23.4MM **Privately Held**
WEB: www.dptechnology.com
SIC: 7371 7373 7372 Custom computer programming services; computer integrated systems design; prepackaged software

(P-15119)
DAQRI LLC (PA)
1201 W 5th St Ste T800, Los Angeles (90017-1452)
PHONE..............................213 375-8830
Troy West, *President*
Sam Aborne, *Vice Pres*
Josh Littlefield, *Business Dir*
Sean McCabe, *Administration*
Timothy Deputy, *CIO*
EMP: 57 EST: 2007
SALES (est): 37.9MM **Privately Held**
SIC: 7371 Computer software development

(P-15120)
DASSAULT SYSTEMES AMERICAS
6320 Canoga Ave Fl 3, Woodland Hills (91367-2573)
PHONE..............................818 999-2500
Fax: 818 999-3535
Kendall Pond, *Vice Pres*
Holly Stratford, *President*
Thibault De Tersant, *CFO*
Allen Kathy, *CFO*
Frederic Tardif, *CFO*
EMP: 133
SALES (corp-wide): 13.3MM **Privately Held**
SIC: 7371 Computer software development
HQ: Dassault Systemes Americas Corp
175 Wyman St
Waltham MA 02451
781 810-3000

(P-15121)
DATABRICKS INC
160 Spear St Fl 13, San Francisco (94105-1546)
PHONE..............................415 494-7672
Ion Stoica, *CEO*
John Engler, *Sr Software Eng*
Matei Zaharia, *CTO*
Arsalan Tavakoli, *Marketing Staff*
Scott Walent, *Manager*
EMP: 55
SQ FT: 18,000
SALES (est): 3.5MM **Privately Held**
SIC: 7371 Computer software systems analysis & design, custom

(P-15122)
DATAMEER INC (PA)
1550 Bryant St Ste 490, San Francisco (94103-4869)
PHONE..............................650 286-9100
Stefan Groschupf, *CEO*
Lance Walter, *Chief Mktg Ofcr*
Kenneth Jakobsen, *Officer*
Ralf Eiling, *Vice Pres*
Linda Esperance, *Vice Pres*
EMP: 57
SALES (est): 15.3MM **Privately Held**
SIC: 7371 Computer software development

(P-15123)
DAYBREAK GAME COMPANY LLC
15051 Avenue Of Science, San Diego (92128-3430)
PHONE..............................858 239-0500
Fax: 858 577-3200
Russell Shanks, *President*
Don Vercelli, *Senior VP*
John Blakely, *Vice Pres*
Jens Andersen, *Creative Dir*
Louis A Figueroa, *Business Dir*
EMP: 450
SALES (est): 98.1MM **Privately Held**
SIC: 7371 Computer software development

(P-15124)
DAZ SYSTEMS INC (PA)
Also Called: D A Z
880 Apollo St Ste 201, El Segundo (90245-4783)
PHONE..............................310 640-1300
Fax: 310 640-9900
Walt Zipperman, *CEO*
Deborah Arnold, *Vice Pres*
Kevin Koontz, *Vice Pres*
Srinivas Lakkaraju, *Vice Pres*
Adam Stafford, *Vice Pres*
EMP: 73
SQ FT: 2,600
SALES (est): 40.9MM **Privately Held**
SIC: 7371 7372 Computer software development & applications; prepackaged software

(P-15125)
DCM TECHNOLOGIES INC
Also Called: D C M Data Systems
39159 Paseo Padre Pkwy # 303, Fremont (94538-1698)
PHONE..............................510 791-2182
Janakiram Kaki, *CEO*
Ashok Choudhury, *Executive*
Pradeep Arora, *Admin Mgr*
Sanjeev Jain, *Senior Mgr*
Shilpa Kumari, *Manager*
EMP: 100
SALES (est): 11.5MM **Privately Held**
WEB: www.dcmds.com
SIC: 7371 Computer software systems analysis & design, custom
PA: Baap Technologies India Private Limited
No. 7
Coimbatore TN
422 259-0095

(P-15126)
DEALERSOCKET INC (PA)
100 Avenida La Pata, San Clemente (92673-6304)
P.O. Box 74866 (92673-0163)
PHONE..............................949 900-0300
Jonathan Ord, *President*
Cameron Darby, *COO*
Jim Habig, *Vice Pres*
Matthew Redden, *Vice Pres*
Jacinto Delarosa, *Analyst*
EMP: 60
SALES (est): 112MM **Privately Held**
WEB: www.firesocket.com
SIC: 7371 Computer software systems analysis & design, custom

(P-15127)
DECARTA INC
1455 Market St Fl 4, San Francisco (94103-1355)
PHONE..............................408 294-8400
Kim J Fennell, *President*
Michael Seifert, *CFO*
Brent Hamby, *Vice Pres*
Yonh Shin, *Vice Pres*
Franco Lucando, *Administration*
EMP: 96
SQ FT: 17,000
SALES (est): 9.6MM
SALES (corp-wide): 68.2MM **Privately Held**
WEB: www.decarta.com
SIC: 7371 Computer software development
HQ: Uber Technologies, Inc.
1455 Market St Fl 4
San Francisco CA 94103
415 986-2715

(P-15128)
DECISION SCIENCES INTL CORP
12345 First American Way # 100, Poway (92064-6828)
P.O. Box 328, Middleburg VA (20118-0328)
PHONE..............................858 571-1900
Stanton D Sloane, *President*
Konstantin Borozdin, *President*
Dwight Johnson, *CEO*
Michael Goll, *CFO*
Jay Cohen, *Principal*
EMP: 60
SALES (est): 7.7MM **Privately Held**
WEB: www.decisionsciencescorp.com
SIC: 7371 Software programming applications

(P-15129)
DELL SOFTWARE INC
9540 Towne Centre Dr # 100, San Diego (92121-1989)
PHONE..............................858 450-7153
Archibald Nesbitt, *Branch Mgr*
EMP: 65
SALES (corp-wide): 72.7B **Publicly Held**
SIC: 7371 5734 5045 Software programming applications; computer software & accessories; computers, peripherals & software
HQ: Dell Software Inc.
4 Polaris Way
Aliso Viejo CA 92656
949 754-8000

(P-15130)
DEMANDFORCE INC
22 4th St Fl 12, San Francisco (94103-3108)
PHONE..............................415 904-8080
Fax: 415 532-2800
Richard E Berry, *President*
Keith Conte, *CFO*
Sam Osman, *Vice Pres*
Brian Persons, *Area Mgr*
Tim Blair, *Sr Software Eng*
EMP: 100
SQ FT: 10,000
SALES (est): 17MM
SALES (corp-wide): 4.6B **Publicly Held**
WEB: www.demandforce.com
SIC: 7371 Computer software development & applications
PA: Intuit Inc.
2700 Coast Ave
Mountain View CA 94043
650 944-6000

(P-15131)
DENA CORP
185 Berry St Ste 3000, San Francisco (94107-1799)
PHONE..............................415 375-3170
Shintaro Asako, *Principal*
Kelly Karpenske, *Administration*
Nicolas Troncoso, *Software Engr*
Hiroaki Tokuda, *Asst Controller*
Lois Wang, *Manager*
EMP: 99 EST: 2014
SALES (est): 7.2MM **Privately Held**
SIC: 7371 Computer software development & applications

(P-15132)
DESTINATIONRX INC (HQ)
Also Called: D R X
600 Wilshire Blvd # 1100, Los Angeles (90017-3212)
PHONE..............................800 379-9060
Randell P Herman, *President*
Yury Furman, *Director*
Janie Kim, *Manager*
EMP: 69
SALES: 17.3MM
SALES (corp-wide): 95.8MM **Publicly Held**
WEB: www.drx.com
SIC: 7371 Custom computer programming services
PA: Connecture, Inc.
18500 W Corp Dr Ste 250
Brookfield WI 53045
262 432-8282

(P-15133)
DEVICE ANYWHERE
777 Mariners Isl Blvd # 250, San Mateo (94404-5008)
PHONE..............................650 655-6400
Faraz Syed, *Principal*
Christopher C Callahan, *Senior VP*
Mark A Dirsa, *Vice Pres*
Robert Kleinschmidt, *Vice Pres*
Rachel Obstler, *Vice Pres*
EMP: 75
SALES (est): 4.6MM **Privately Held**
SIC: 7371 Computer software development

(P-15134)
DEWMOBILE USA INC
2901 Tasman Dr Ste 107, Santa Clara (95054-1137)
PHONE..............................408 550-2818
Shangpin Chang, *CTO*
EMP: 50
SALES (est): 3.3MM **Privately Held**
SIC: 7371 Computer software development & applications

7371 - Custom Computer Programming Svcs County (P-15135)

(P-15135)
DFUSION SOFTWARE INC
Also Called: Total Immersion
5900 Wilshire Blvd # 2550, Los Angeles (90036-5035)
PHONE...............323 617-5577
Didier Lesteven, *CEO*
Mike Cohen, *Vice Pres*
Bruno Uzzan, *Principal*
EMP: 50
SQ FT: 3,000
SALES (est): 3.8MM **Privately Held**
WEB: www.t-immersion.com
SIC: 7371 Computer software development

(P-15136)
DHAP DIGITAL INC
465 California St Ste 600, San Francisco (94104-1816)
PHONE...............415 962-4900
Philip Dzilvelis, *President*
Dave McKew, *Office Mgr*
Rocio Reyes, *Technical Mgr*
Tim Irvin, *Technology*
Jason Swierk, *Technology*
EMP: 50 **EST:** 1997
SQ FT: 12,000
SALES: 5MM **Privately Held**
WEB: www.dhap.com
SIC: 7371 Custom computer programming services

(P-15137)
DIGICASH INCORPORATED
2656 E Bayshore Rd, Palo Alto (94303-3211)
PHONE...............650 321-0300
Michael Nash, *CEO*
Scott Loftesnes, *CEO*
Thomas Lerrone, *CFO*
David Chaum, *CTO*
EMP: 50
SALES (est): 4.1MM **Privately Held**
SIC: 7371 Computer software development

(P-15138)
DIGICENTURY CORPORATION
2303 Camino Ramon Ste 202, San Ramon (94583-1175)
P.O. Box 12935 (94583)
PHONE...............408 213-0146
Emily Zhang, *CEO*
Weikai Xie, *President*
Jeana Nishihara, *Manager*
EMP: 67
SALES (est): 2.9MM **Privately Held**
WEB: www.digicentury.com
SIC: 7371 Computer software development

(P-15139)
DIGITAL FOUNDRY INC
1707 Tiburon Blvd, Belvedere Tiburon (94920-2513)
PHONE...............415 789-1600
Fax: 415 789-5054
Bradley W Stauffer, *President*
Robert Fraik, *Chairman*
Bonnie Albin Fraik, *Vice Pres*
Joe Carpenter, *Business Dir*
Ryan Robinett, *CTO*
EMP: 50
SQ FT: 7,500
SALES (est): 4.5MM **Privately Held**
WEB: www.digitalfoundry.com
SIC: 7371 7379 Custom computer programming services; computer software development & applications; computer related consulting services

(P-15140)
DIGITE INC
21060 Homestead Rd # 220, Cupertino (95014-0204)
PHONE...............408 418-3834
Suhas S Patil, *Ch of Bd*
A V Sridhar, *CEO*
Raghunath Basavanahalli, *Senior VP*
Sudipta Lahiri, *Senior VP*
Mahesh Singh, *Senior VP*
EMP: 87
SQ FT: 3,000
SALES (est): 7MM **Privately Held**
WEB: www.digite.com
SIC: 7371 Computer software development

(P-15141)
DIMENSION DATA CLOUD SOLUTIONS (DH)
5201 Great America Pkwy # 122, Santa Clara (95054-1125)
PHONE...............408 567-2000
Fax: 408 982-8902
Robert J Ryan, *CEO*
Rick Dyer, *President*
Ray Solnik, *President*
Barry Wyse, *President*
Bryan Tolls, *CFO*
EMP: 75
SALES (est): 46.4MM
SALES (corp-wide): 98.6B **Privately Held**
WEB: www.opsource.net
SIC: 7371 Computer software development & applications
HQ: Dimension Data (Pty) Ltd
The Campus, 57 Sloane Street
Johannesburg GP
115 750-000

(P-15142)
DISNEY INTERACTIVE STUDIOS INC
601 Circle Seven Dr, Glendale (91201-2332)
PHONE...............818 560-1000
Fax: 818 637-2869
Peter Casciani, *Manager*
Sean Ratcliffe, *Technical Staff*
EMP: 120 **Publicly Held**
SIC: 7371 Computer software development
HQ: Disney Interactive Studios, Inc.
500 S Buena Vista St
Burbank CA 91521
818 560-1000

(P-15143)
DISNEY INTERACTIVE STUDIOS INC
622 Circle Seven Dr, Glendale (91201-2333)
PHONE...............801 595-1020
John Blackburn, *Branch Mgr*
Jeff Gosztyla, *General Mgr*
EMP: 120 **Publicly Held**
SIC: 7371 Computer software development
HQ: Disney Interactive Studios, Inc.
500 S Buena Vista St
Burbank CA 91521
818 560-1000

(P-15144)
DISNEY INTERACTIVE STUDIOS INC
681 W Buena Vista St, Burbank (91521-0001)
PHONE...............818 553-5000
Gram Hoper, *Branch Mgr*
EMP: 120 **Publicly Held**
SIC: 7371 Computer software development
HQ: Disney Interactive Studios, Inc.
500 S Buena Vista St
Burbank CA 91521
818 560-1000

(P-15145)
DOLPHIN IMAGING SYSTEMS LLC
9200 Eton Ave, Chatsworth (91311-5807)
PHONE...............818 435-1368
Chester H Wang,
Hollman I Puccini, *President*
Otto Colette, *Vice Pres*
Miquel Mayol, *Regional Mgr*
Michael Quick, *CTO*
EMP: 50
SALES (est): 5.5MM
SALES (corp-wide): 4.3B **Publicly Held**
WEB: www.dolphinimaging.com
SIC: 7371 Computer software development & applications

(P-15146)
DORADO SOFTWARE INC
Also Called: Visiworks Software
4805 Golden Foothill Pkwy, El Dorado Hills (95762-9651)
PHONE...............916 673-1100
Timothy Sebring, *President*
Mitch Carlsen, *Vice Pres*
Ed Kucala, *Vice Pres*
Laurie Baser, *Admin Sec*
David Phong, *QA Dir*
EMP: 80
SALES (est): 12.2MM **Privately Held**
WEB: www.doradosoftware.com
SIC: 7371 Computer software development

(P-15147)
DOUBLETWIST INC
1849 Sawtelle Blvd # 543, Los Angeles (90025-7006)
PHONE...............510 628-0100
Robert F Williamson, *President*
John Couch, *Ch of Bd*
Greg Thayer, *CFO*
H Ward Wolff, *CFO*
Simon Tomlinson, *Vice Pres*
EMP: 149
SALES: 4MM **Privately Held**
SIC: 7371 5961 5045 Computer software development; catalog & mail-order houses; computers, peripherals & software

(P-15148)
DRCHRONOCOM INC
1001 N Rengstorff Ave # 200, Mountain View (94043-1748)
PHONE...............650 600-2079
Michael Nusimow, *CEO*
Daniel Kivatinos, *COO*
Nick Meharry, *Software Dev*
Craig Silverman, *VP Sales*
Kyle Morham, *Sales Staff*
EMP: 50
SALES (est): 3.2MM **Privately Held**
SIC: 7371 Computer software development

(P-15149)
DTECNET INC
2600 W Olive Ave Ste 910, Burbank (91505-4568)
PHONE...............208 685-1810
Thomas Sehested, *CEO*
Lars U Diemer, *COO*
Kristian Lakkegaard, *CTO*
EMP: 308
SALES (est): 6.6MM
SALES (corp-wide): 3.8B **Publicly Held**
SIC: 7371 Computer software development & applications
HQ: Markmonitor Inc.
425 Market St Ste 500
San Francisco CA 94105
415 278-8400

(P-15150)
DTEX SYSTEMS INC
300 Santana Row Ste 400, San Jose (95128-2423)
PHONE...............408 418-3786
Christy Wyatt, *CEO*
Bahman Mahbod, *COO*
Steve Hewitt, *Vice Pres*
Mohan Koo, *CTO*
Bill Lauritzen, *Director*
EMP: 50
SALES (est): 3.7MM **Privately Held**
SIC: 7371 Computer software development

(P-15151)
E A COM INC
209 Redwood Shores Pkwy, Redwood City (94065-1175)
PHONE...............650 628-1500
Fax: 650 628-1380
E Stanton Mc Kee, *Exec VP*
Ruth A Kennedy, *Senior VP*
Bryan Neider, *Vice Pres*
Christian Brodda, *Manager*
Darren Perfonic, *Manager*
EMP: 140
SALES (est): 26.7MM
SALES (corp-wide): 4.4B **Publicly Held**
WEB: www.ea.com
SIC: 7371 Computer software development
PA: Electronic Arts Inc.
209 Redwood Shores Pkwy
Redwood City CA 94065
650 628-1500

(P-15152)
E Z DATA INC (HQ)
251 S Lake Ave Ste 200, Pasadena (91101-3075)
PHONE...............626 585-3505
Fax: 626 440-9097
Dale Okuno, *President*
Muthu Arumugham, *Vice Pres*
Adolfo Perez, *CIO*
Prajacta Gandre, *Business Anlyst*
Marlon Urias, *Manager*
EMP: 51
SALES (est): 5.9MM
SALES (corp-wide): 265.4MM **Publicly Held**
WEB: www.ez-data.com
SIC: 7371 Computer software development
PA: Ebix, Inc.
1 Ebix Way Ste 100
Duluth GA 30097
678 281-2020

(P-15153)
E-INFOCHIPS INC
1230 Midas Way Ste 200, Sunnyvale (94085-4068)
PHONE...............408 496-1882
Pratul Shroff, *CEO*
Raj Sirohi, *COO*
Sribash Dey, *Vice Pres*
Girish Sharma, *Sr Software Eng*
Jimit Doshi, *QA Dir*
EMP: 149
SQ FT: 6,178
SALES (est): 2.7B
SALES (corp-wide): 40MM **Privately Held**
SIC: 7371 7373 Computer software development; systems software development services; computer systems analysis & design; computer-aided system services; computer-aided design (CAD) systems service
PA: E-Infochips Limited
11/A-B, 'e-Infochips House' Chandra Colony,
Ahmedabad GUJ 38000
792 656-3705

(P-15154)
ECONOSOFT INC
2375 Zanker Rd Ste 250, San Jose (95131-1143)
PHONE...............408 324-1203
Chander Shaiker, *President*
Usman Khan, *Sales Mgr*
Abhijeet Tiwari, *Sales Mgr*
Himanshu Kakkar, *Senior Mgr*
Anudeep Maheshwari, *Manager*
EMP: 72 **EST:** 2000
SALES (est): 4.6MM
SALES (corp-wide): 18MM **Privately Held**
SIC: 7371 Computer software systems analysis & design, custom
PA: Ace Technologies, Inc.
2375 Zanker Rd Ste 250
San Jose CA 95131
408 324-1203

(P-15155)
EGNYTE INC (PA)
1350 W Middlefield Rd, Mountain View (94043-3061)
PHONE...............650 968-4018
Vineet Jain, *President*
Kevin Patterson, *Senior Partner*
Ben Rice, *President*
Benjamin Rice, *President*
Ian Whiting, *President*
EMP: 133 **EST:** 2008

PRODUCTS & SERVICES SECTION
7371 - Custom Computer Programming Svcs County (P-15178)

SALES (est): 61.4MM Privately Held
SIC: 7371 Computer software development & applications

(P-15156)
EHEALTHINSURANCE SERVICES INC
Also Called: Ehealth Insurance.com
11919 Foundation Pl # 100, Gold River (95670-4537)
PHONE.................................916 608-6101
Robert Hurley, *Branch Mgr*
Gary Matalucci, *Vice Pres*
Robert Boyajan, *Administration*
Robin Haider, *Accountant*
Hollie Watson, *Sales Dir*
EMP: 120
SALES (corp-wide): 189.5MM Publicly Held
WEB: www.anysure.com
SIC: 7371 Computer software development
HQ: Ehealthinsurance Services, Inc.
  440 E Middlefield Rd
  Mountain View CA 94043
  650 584-2700

(P-15157)
EINSTEIN INDUSTRIES INC
Also Called: Einstein Dental
6675 Mesa Ridge Rd, San Diego (92121-2907)
PHONE.................................858 459-1182
Fax: 858 430-5239
Robert C Silkey, *President*
Sergiy Zubatiy, *COO*
Dean Hecker, *CFO*
Ted Ricasa, *Vice Pres*
Amir Nurani, *Regional Mgr*
EMP: 180
SALES (est): 22.3MM Privately Held
WEB: www.einsteindental.com
SIC: 7371 8742 8732 Computer software development & applications; marketing consulting services; referral service for personal & social problems

(P-15158)
ELASTICA INC ✪
3055 Olin Ave Ste 2000, San Jose (95128-2069)
PHONE.................................925 699-6714
Lee Khan, *VP Opers*
Rehan Jalil, *CEO*
Kevin Thompson, *CFO*
EMP: 90 EST: 2016
SALES (est): 1.8MM
SALES (corp-wide): 3.6B Publicly Held
SIC: 7371 Computer software development & applications
HQ: Blue Coat Systems Llc
  384 Santa Trinita Ave
  Sunnyvale CA 94085
  408 220-2200

(P-15159)
ELLATION INC
Also Called: Crunchyroll
835 Market St Ste 700, San Francisco (94103-1906)
PHONE.................................415 796-3560
EMP: 200
SALES (est): 2.3MM Privately Held
SIC: 7371 5932 Computer software development & applications; used merchandise stores

(P-15160)
ELLIE MAE INC (PA)
4420 Rosewood Dr Ste 500, Pleasanton (94588-3059)
PHONE.................................925 227-7000
Jonathan H Corr, *President*
Dee Khullar, *Senior Partner*
Sigmund Anderman, *Ch of Bd*
Edgar A Luce, *CFO*
Cathleen Schreiner Gates, *Exec VP*
EMP: 120 EST: 1997
SQ FT: 137,170
SALES: 253.9MM Publicly Held
WEB: www.elliemae.com
SIC: 7371 Computer software systems analysis & design, custom; computer software development & applications

(P-15161)
ELLIE MAE INC
24025 Park Sorrento # 210, Calabasas (91302-4025)
PHONE.................................818 223-2000
EMP: 228
SALES (corp-wide): 253.9MM Publicly Held
SIC: 7371 Computer software systems analysis & design, custom
PA: Ellie Mae, Inc.
  4420 Rosewood Dr Ste 500
  Pleasanton CA 94588
  925 227-7000

(P-15162)
EMBARCADERO SYSTEMS CORP
1601 Harbor Bay Pkwy # 120, Alameda (94502-3039)
PHONE.................................510 749-7400
Fax: 510 749-3800
Christopher R Redlich Jr, *Chairman*
Richard Beedenbender, *President*
John Sullivan, *Admin Sec*
Nina Troth, *Human Res Dir*
Adele Richards, *Manager*
EMP: 140
SQ FT: 27,000
SALES (est): 11.9MM Privately Held
WEB: www.esystem.com
SIC: 7371 Computer software development

(P-15163)
EMBRANE INC
2350 Mission College Blvd # 703, Santa Clara (95054-1556)
PHONE.................................408 550-2700
Bill Burns, *President*
Marco Di Benedetto, *CTO*
Emanuela Todaro, *Human Resources*
EMP: 50
SQ FT: 7,300
SALES (est): 5.3MM Privately Held
SIC: 7371 Computer software development

(P-15164)
EMETER CORPORATION
4000 E 3rd Ave Fl 4, Foster City (94404-4824)
PHONE.................................650 227-7770
Lisa Caswell, *President*
Guido Frantzen, *CFO*
Chris King, *Risk Mgmt Dir*
Harman Birdi, *Sr Software Eng*
Larsh Johnson, *CTO*
EMP: 130
SQ FT: 30,000
SALES (est): 20.8MM
SALES (corp-wide): 83.5B Privately Held
WEB: www.emeter.com
SIC: 7371 Computer software development
HQ: Siemens Industry, Inc.
  1000 Deerfield Pkwy
  Buffalo Grove IL 60089
  847 215-1000

(P-15165)
ENGINE YARD INC
580 Market St Ste 150, San Francisco (94104-5427)
P.O. Box 77130 (94107-0130)
PHONE.................................866 518-9273
Lance Walley, *CEO*
Dawn Nott, *Human Res Mgr*
Sara Gardner, *VP Mktg*
Ankur Jariwala, *Marketing Staff*
EMP: 87
SALES (est): 5.1MM Privately Held
SIC: 7371 Computer software development

(P-15166)
ENMETRIC SYSTEMS INC
617 Mountain View Ave # 5, Belmont (94002-2581)
PHONE.................................650 489-4441
Dave Bagshaw, *Chairman*
Jake Masters, *CEO*
Bob Larson, *COO*
Walter Shimoon, *Vice Pres*
Josh Emert, *Manager*
EMP: 50

SALES (est): 3.5MM Privately Held
SIC: 7371 Custom computer programming services; computer software development

(P-15167)
ENTERPRISE TECH GROUP INC
13428 Maxella Ave 788, Marina Del Rey (90292-5620)
PHONE.................................972 373-8800
Phillip Hyun, *President*
EMP: 204
SALES (est): 2MM
SALES (corp-wide): 896.3MM Publicly Held
SIC: 7371 Computer software systems analysis & design, custom
PA: Nexstar Broadcasting Group, Inc.
  545 E John Carpenter Fwy # 700
  Irving TX 75062
  972 373-8800

(P-15168)
ENVIANCE INC (HQ)
5780 Fleet St Ste 200, Carlsbad (92008-4714)
PHONE.................................760 496-0200
Fax: 760 496-0202
Amy Stelling, *CEO*
David McCurdy, *COO*
Jeffrey Pownell, *CFO*
Paul Baier, *Vice Pres*
Michele B Hincks, *Vice Pres*
EMP: 117
SQ FT: 10,000
SALES (est): 12.8MM Privately Held
WEB: www.enviance.com
SIC: 7371 7374 Custom computer programming services; data processing & preparation

(P-15169)
EPITOME ENTERPRISES LLC
821 Mary Pl, Claremont (91711-2273)
PHONE.................................909 625-4728
Uma Reddy, *President*
EMP: 60
SALES: 1.8MM Privately Held
WEB: www.epitomeenterprises.com
SIC: 7371 Computer software development

(P-15170)
EQUATOR LLC (HQ)
Also Called: Equator Business Solutions
6060 Center Dr Ste 500, Los Angeles (90045-1587)
PHONE.................................310 469-9500
Fax: 310 347-4261
Chris Saitta, *CEO*
Robert McKinley, *President*
John Vella, *COO*
Ashley Bean, *Vice Pres*
Dirk Meillinger, *Vice Pres*
EMP: 200
SALES: 45.4MM Privately Held
SIC: 7371 Computer software development & applications

(P-15171)
ESCALATE INC (DH)
Also Called: Escalate Retail
10680 Treena St Ste 170, San Diego (92131-2443)
PHONE.................................858 457-3888
Stewart M Bloom, *CEO*
Mike Larkin, *CFO*
Ron Franks, *Vice Pres*
Richard Harmatiuk, *Vice Pres*
Michael Julson, *Vice Pres*
EMP: 290
SQ FT: 59,000
SALES (est): 25.6MM
SALES (corp-wide): 1.3B Privately Held
SIC: 7371 7373 5045 Custom computer programming services; computer integrated systems design; computers, peripherals & software

(P-15172)
ESI PUBLISHING INC
16920 S Main St, Gardena (90248-3124)
PHONE.................................310 768-1800
Fax: 310 768-1822
Michael Bell, *CEO*
Michael Wegmann, *President*
Allen Breiter, *Creative Dir*

Todd Coleman, *Admin Sec*
Ivette Santiago, *Finance*
EMP: 52
SALES (est): 4.3MM Privately Held
SIC: 7371 Computer software development

(P-15173)
ESTUATE INC
1183 Bordeaux Dr Ste 22, Sunnyvale (94089-1201)
PHONE.................................408 400-0680
Fax: 408 400-0683
Prakash Balebail, *President*
Marc Hebert, *COO*
Nagaraja Kini, *CFO*
Sunil Kumaran, *Vice Pres*
Subbarao Satyavolu, *Vice Pres*
EMP: 67
SALES (est): 12.3MM Privately Held
SIC: 7371 Computer software development & applications

(P-15174)
ETRIGUE CORP
6399 San Ignacio Ave # 200, San Jose (95119-1244)
PHONE.................................408 490-2900
Sharon Coleman, *Principal*
EMP: 50
SQ FT: 43,000
SALES (est): 4.1MM Privately Held
SIC: 7371 Computer software development

(P-15175)
EVEREST CONSULTING GROUP INC
39650 Mission Blvd, Fremont (94539-3000)
PHONE.................................510 494-8440
Fax: 510 494-8151
Raj Kamalanathan, *Manager*
EMP: 85
SALES (corp-wide): 24.2MM Privately Held
WEB: www.everestconsulting.net
SIC: 7371 Computer software development
PA: Everest Consulting Group Inc.
  3840 Park Ave Ste 203
  Edison NJ 08820
  732 548-2700

(P-15176)
EVISIONS INC (PA)
440 Exchange Ste 200, Irvine (92602-1390)
PHONE.................................949 833-1384
Kevin Jones, *CEO*
Penny Dobbs, *CFO*
Marianne D Jones, *Treasurer*
Matt McLellan, *VP Sls/Mktg*
Lynn Crist, *Manager*
EMP: 57
SQ FT: 15,000
SALES (est): 12.3MM Privately Held
SIC: 7371 Computer software development

(P-15177)
EVOX PRODUCTIONS LLC (PA)
2363 E Pacifica Pl 305, Compton (90220-6212)
PHONE.................................310 605-1400
Fax: 310 605-1429
David Falstrup,
Carol Falstrup, *CFO*
Peter Avildsen, *Chief Mktg Ofcr*
Chris Williams, *Vice Pres*
Kate Dugam, *Admin Sec*
EMP: 58
SQ FT: 37,500
SALES (est): 11.4MM Privately Held
SIC: 7371 7335 Custom computer programming services; commercial photography

(P-15178)
EXIGEN (USA) INC (PA)
Also Called: Exigen Group
345 California St Fl 22, San Francisco (94104-2606)
PHONE.................................415 402-2600
Fax: 415 402-2038
Greg Shenkman, *CEO*

7371 - Custom Computer Programming Svcs County (P-15179)
PRODUDUCTS & SERVICES SECTION

Tsvi Gal, *General Ptnr*
Alec Miloslavsky, *Ch of Bd*
Alex Kolt, *President*
Rick Koo, *Senior VP*
EMP: 320
SQ FT: 26,000
SALES (est): 56.3MM **Privately Held**
WEB: www.exigengroup.com
SIC: 7371 Computer software development & applications

(P-15179)
EYEFINITY INC
10875 Intl Dr Fl 2 200, Rancho Cordova (95670)
PHONE...................877 481-4455
Fax: 916 463-8087
Steve Baker, *President*
Kevin Kane, *Exec VP*
Suzanne Brehm, *Senior VP*
Troy Eberlein, *Senior VP*
Sam Nasser, *Senior VP*
EMP: 74
SALES (est): 12.6MM
SALES (corp-wide): 4.9B **Privately Held**
WEB: www.eyefinity.com
SIC: 7371 Computer software systems analysis & design, custom
PA: Vision Service Plan
  3333 Quality Dr
  Rancho Cordova CA 95670
  916 851-5000

(P-15180)
FAMOUS SOFTWARE LLC (PA)
8080 N Palm Ave Ste 210, Fresno (93711-5797)
PHONE...................559 438-3600
Fax: 559 447-6339
Kirk Parrish,
Santanu Banerjee, *Exec Dir*
Kate Macbean, *QA Dir*
Christopher Craft, *Software Dev*
Jason Bezerra, *Software Engr*
EMP: 53
SQ FT: 8,300
SALES: 10MM **Privately Held**
WEB: www.famoussoftware.com
SIC: 7371 7372 Custom computer programming services; business oriented computer software

(P-15181)
FASTLY INC
475 Brannan St Ste 320, San Francisco (94107-5420)
P.O. Box 78266 (94107-8266)
PHONE...................415 488-6329
Artur Bergman's, *CEO*
Hooman Beheshti, *President*
Bill Kaufmann, *COO*
Steve Souders, *Officer*
Lori Beedle, *Senior VP*
EMP: 128
SALES (est): 25.4MM **Privately Held**
SIC: 7371 Computer software development & applications

(P-15182)
FCS SOFTWARE SOLUTIONS LIMITED
2375 Zanker Rd Ste 250, San Jose (95131-1143)
PHONE...................408 324-1203
Dalip Kumar, *President*
Hemant Singh, *Executive*
Rahul Singh, *Executive*
Mohit Pandey, *Software Dev*
Gurpreet Baidan, *Tech Recruiter*
EMP: 99
SALES (est): 10.7MM **Privately Held**
SIC: 7371 Custom computer programming services

(P-15183)
FENDER DIGITAL LLC
1575 N Gower St, Los Angeles (90028-6487)
PHONE...................480 845-5452
EMP: 75
SQ FT: 25,000
SALES: 50MM
SALES (corp-wide): 806.8MM **Privately Held**
SIC: 7371 Computer software development & applications

PA: Fender Musical Instruments Corporation
  17600 N Perimeter Dr # 100
  Scottsdale AZ 85255
  480 596-7195

(P-15184)
FINANCIAL INFORMATION NETWORK
Also Called: F I N
6656 Valjean Ave, Van Nuys (91406-5816)
P.O. Box 7954 (91409-7954)
PHONE...................818 782-0331
Fax: 818 376-4095
Jerry Sears, *President*
Alan Shepoiser, *CFO*
Frank Proietti, *Executive*
Kathy Tarr, *Executive*
Gail Curtis, *Sales Dir*
EMP: 60
SQ FT: 6,000
SALES (est): 6.9MM **Privately Held**
WEB: www.fingps.com
SIC: 7371 7372 Custom computer programming services; prepackaged software

(P-15185)
FINANCIALFORCECOM INC (DH)
595 Market St Ste 2700, San Francisco (94105-2840)
PHONE...................866 743-2220
Jeremy Roche, *CEO*
Joe Fuca, *President*
John Bonney, *CFO*
John Moss, *Senior VP*
Johnny Ola, *Vice Pres*
EMP: 71
SALES (est): 80MM **Privately Held**
SIC: 7371 Computer software development
HQ: Unit4 N.V.
  Stationspark 1000
  Sliedrecht 3364
  184 444-444

(P-15186)
FINJAN INC
Also Called: Finjan Software
828 W Taft Ave, Orange (92865-4232)
PHONE...................408 452-9700
John Vigouroux, *President*
Bessemer Ventures, *Shareholder*
Eric Benhamou, *Ch of Bd*
David Aber, *CFO*
Dennis P Wolf, *CFO*
EMP: 150
SALES (est): 5MM **Privately Held**
WEB: www.finjan.com
SIC: 7371 Computer software development
HQ: Tw Security Corp
  8845 Irvine Center Dr # 101
  Irvine CA 92618

(P-15187)
FLEXERA SOFTWARE LLC
25 Orinda Way Ste 101, Orinda (94563-4402)
PHONE...................847 466-4000
EMP: 70
SALES (corp-wide): 236.4MM **Privately Held**
SIC: 7371 Computer software development
PA: Flexera Software Llc
  300 Park Blvd Ste 500
  Itasca IL 60143
  847 466-4000

(P-15188)
FLEXERA SOFTWARE LLC
101 Metro Dr Ste 375, San Jose (95110-1400)
PHONE...................408 642-3700
Fax: 408 642-3764
Emmitt John, *Branch Mgr*
Brent Pietrzak, *Vice Pres*
David Znidarsic, *Vice Pres*
John Emmitt, *Sls & Mktg Exec*
Chris Herter, *Manager*
EMP: 70

SALES (corp-wide): 236.4MM **Privately Held**
SIC: 7371 Computer software development
PA: Flexera Software Llc
  300 Park Blvd Ste 500
  Itasca IL 60143
  847 466-4000

(P-15189)
FLUID INC (PA)
222 Sutter St Fl 8, San Francisco (94108-4459)
PHONE...................415 263-7700
Andy Lloyd, *CEO*
Kent Deverell, *CEO*
Kent Price, *CFO*
Larry Bernstein, *Vice Pres*
Angela Flynn, *Vice Pres*
EMP: 61
SQ FT: 7,000
SALES (est): 22.8MM **Privately Held**
SIC: 7371 Computer software development

(P-15190)
FNC INC
40 Pacifica Ste 900, Irvine (92618-7487)
PHONE...................714 866-1099
Neil Olsen, *Security Dir*
Neil Olson, *Officer*
Dennis Tosh Jr, *Officer*
David Johnson, *Executive*
Christopher Floyd, *Admin Asst*
EMP: 52
SALES (corp-wide): 59.1MM **Privately Held**
SIC: 7371 Custom computer programming services
PA: Fnc, Inc.
  1214 Office Park Dr
  Oxford MS 38655
  662 236-2020

(P-15191)
FOCUS 360 INC
27721 La Paz Rd Ste B, Laguna Niguel (92677-3949)
PHONE...................949 234-0008
Steven G Ormonde, *President*
Brent C Chase, *Vice Pres*
Peggy Chase, *Human Resources*
Steven Greco, *Mktg Dir*
Mike Gentile, *Supervisor*
EMP: 54
SQ FT: 18,300
SALES (est): 5.3MM **Privately Held**
WEB: www.focus360.com
SIC: 7371 Custom computer programming services

(P-15192)
FORESCOUT TECHNOLOGIES INC (PA)
190 W Tasman Dr, San Jose (95134-1700)
PHONE...................408 213-3191
Fax: 408 213-2283
T Kent Elliott, *CEO*
Tom Dolan, *President*
Christopher Harms, *CFO*
Pedro Abreu, *Officer*
Darren Milliken, *Officer*
EMP: 148
SALES (est): 125.8MM **Privately Held**
WEB: www.forescout.com
SIC: 7371 Computer software development

(P-15193)
FRANKLY CO
333 Bryant St Ste 240, San Francisco (94107-1443)
PHONE...................415 861-9797
Steve Chung, *CEO*
Jungsoo Park, *Vice Pres*
Harrison Shih, *Vice Pres*
Amanda Warren, *Manager*
EMP: 100
SQ FT: 3,000
SALES: 1MM **Privately Held**
SIC: 7371 Computer software development & applications

(P-15194)
FRONT PORCH INC (PA)
14520 Mono Way Ste 200, Sonora (95370-7829)
PHONE...................209 288-5500
Fax: 209 288-5505
Zachary Britton, *President*
Robert Hohne Jr, *CFO*
Ned Sudduth, *Vice Pres*
Derek Maxson, *CTO*
Robert Powser, *QA Dir*
EMP: 60
SQ FT: 1,022
SALES (est): 11.3MM **Privately Held**
WEB: www.adfirst.com
SIC: 7371 Computer software development

(P-15195)
FRONTECH N FUJITSU AMER INC
2933 Bunker Hill Ln # 101, Santa Clara (95054-1124)
PHONE...................408 982-3697
John Mullerworth, *Manager*
EMP: 100
SALES (corp-wide): 40.5B **Privately Held**
WEB: www.fjicl.com
SIC: 7371 Computer software development
HQ: Fujitsu Frontech North America, Inc.
  27121 Towne Centre Dr # 100
  Foothill Ranch CA 92610
  949 855-5500

(P-15196)
FUJITSU GLOVIA INC (HQ)
2250 E Imperial Hwy # 200, El Segundo (90245-3543)
PHONE...................310 563-7000
Fax: 310 563-7300
Chikara Ono, *CEO*
Paul Hughes, *COO*
Masahiro Cho, *CFO*
Robert Luth, *CFO*
James Gorham, *Vice Pres*
EMP: 150
SQ FT: 53,000
SALES (est): 36.5MM
SALES (corp-wide): 40.5B **Privately Held**
SIC: 7371 7372 Computer software development; prepackaged software
PA: Fujitsu Limited
  1-5-2, Higashishimbashi
  Minato-Ku TKY 105-0
  362 522-220

(P-15197)
FUSIONONE INC
55 Almaden Blvd Ste 500, San Jose (95113-1612)
PHONE...................408 282-1200
Fax: 408 282-2345
Mike Mulica, *CEO*
Rick Onyon, *Ch of Bd*
Leighton Ridgard, *President*
Ed Battle, *CFO*
Jay Burrell, *Exec VP*
EMP: 90
SQ FT: 13,000
SALES: 3MM
SALES (corp-wide): 457.3MM **Publicly Held**
WEB: www.fusionone.com
SIC: 7371 Custom computer programming services
PA: Synchronoss Technologies, Inc.
  200 Crossing Blvd Fl 8
  Bridgewater NJ 08807
  866 620-3940

(P-15198)
FUSIONOPS INC
707 California St, Mountain View (94041-2005)
PHONE...................408 524-2222
Ram Mohan, *President*
Travis Adlman, *CFO*
Tony Wessels, *Chief Mktg Ofcr*
Chris Bernhoft, *Vice Pres*
Allen Jacques, *Vice Pres*
EMP: 105
SALES (est): 923.5K **Privately Held**
WEB: www.fusionops.com
SIC: 7371 Computer software development

PRODUCTS & SERVICES SECTION   7371 - Custom Computer Programming Svcs County (P-15221)

(P-15199)
FUTURENET TECHNOLOGIES CORP
1320 Valley Vista Dr # 202, Diamond Bar (91765-3956)
PHONE 909 396-4000
Tom Liu, *President*
Dale Kivi, *Business Dir*
Lee Zhu, *CIO*
EMP: 123
SQ FT: 9,650
SALES (est): 7.9MM **Privately Held**
WEB: www.futurenet-tech.com
SIC: 7371 Computer software development

(P-15200)
G2 DIRECT AND DIGITAL
Also Called: Grey Direct-E Marketing
612 Howard St Ste 400, San Francisco (94105-3944)
PHONE 415 421-1000
EMP: 50
SALES (corp-wide): 18.4B **Privately Held**
WEB: www.greydirect.com
SIC: 7371 Custom computer programming services
HQ: G2 Direct And Digital
  777 3rd Ave Ste 37
  New York NY 10017
  212 537-3700

(P-15201)
GEHRY TECHNOLOGIES INC (HQ)
12181 Bluff Creek Dr # 200, Playa Vista (90094-3232)
PHONE 310 862-1200
Meaghan Lloyd, *CEO*
Michael Lin, *CFO*
Deep Bhattacharya, *Exec VP*
Matt Reid, *Senior VP*
Laurence Sotsky, *Senior VP*
EMP: 57
SQ FT: 2,000
SALES (est): 16.6MM
SALES (corp-wide): 2.2B **Publicly Held**
WEB: www.foga.com
SIC: 7371 Computer software development & applications
PA: Trimble Inc.
  935 Stewart Dr
  Sunnyvale CA 94085
  408 481-8000

(P-15202)
GENEX (HQ)
800 Corporate Pointe # 100, Culver City (90230-7667)
PHONE 424 672-9500
Fax: 424 672-9501
Walter Schild, *CEO*
Gretchen Humbert, *CFO*
Ian Burns, *Creative Dir*
Chip McCarthy, *Creative Dir*
Eric Sanders, *Info Tech Dir*
EMP: 130
SQ FT: 12,000
SALES (est): 15.1MM
SALES (corp-wide): 1.6B **Publicly Held**
WEB: www.genex.com
SIC: 7371 7379 4813 Custom computer programming services; computer related consulting services;
PA: Meredith Corporation
  1716 Locust St
  Des Moines IA 50309
  515 284-3000

(P-15203)
GENUENT USA LLC
2240 Douglas Blvd Ste 100, Roseville (95661-3874)
PHONE 916 772-3700
Greg Abel, *Manager*
Lawanna Katz, *Manager*
EMP: 68
SALES (corp-wide): 12MM **Privately Held**
SIC: 7371 Custom computer programming services
HQ: Genuent Usa, Llc
  1400 Post Oak Blvd # 200
  Houston TX 77056
  713 547-4444

(P-15204)
GIVA INC
1030 E El Camino Real, Sunnyvale (94087-3759)
PHONE 408 260-9000
Ronald Avignone, *Founder*
EMP: 60 EST: 1999
SALES (est): 4.7MM **Privately Held**
SIC: 7371 Computer software development

(P-15205)
GLOBALLOGIC INC (PA)
1741 Tech Dr Ste 400, San Jose (95110)
PHONE 408 273-8900
Shashank Samant, *CEO*
Glenn Rusinak, *President*
Sameer Tikoo, *President*
Jim Dellamore, *COO*
Doug Ahrens, *CFO*
EMP: 213
SALES (est): 424.6MM **Privately Held**
WEB: www.globallogic.com
SIC: 7371 7379 7373 Computer software development & applications; computer related consulting services; systems engineering, computer related

(P-15206)
GLOBANT LLC
875 Howard St Fl 3, San Francisco (94103-3027)
PHONE 877 798-8104
Martin Migoya, *CEO*
Sandeep Chawda, *Exec VP*
Andres Angelani, *Security Dir*
EMP: 67
SALES (est): 100MM **Privately Held**
SIC: 7371 Computer software development

(P-15207)
GLOVIA INC
2250 E Imperial Hwy # 200, El Segundo (90245-3543)
PHONE 310 563-7000
Howard Goldman, *Controller*
Masahiro Cho, *Officer*
EMP: 200
SALES (est): 8MM **Privately Held**
SIC: 7371 Computer software development & applications

(P-15208)
GLU MOBILE INC (PA)
500 Howard St Ste 300, San Francisco (94105-3027)
PHONE 415 800-6100
Fax: 650 532-2500
Niccolo M De Masi, *President*
William J Miller, *Ch of Bd*
Nick Earl, *President*
Eric R Ludwig, *COO*
Eric Ball, *Bd of Directors*
EMP: 142
SQ FT: 29,000
SALES: 249.9MM **Publicly Held**
WEB: www.glu.com
SIC: 7371 3944 Custom computer programming services; computer software writing services; computer code authors; electronic games & toys

(P-15209)
GOOD SPORTS PLUS LTD
Also Called: ARC
370 Amapola Ave Ste 208, Torrance (90501-7241)
PHONE 310 671-4400
Brad Lupien, *President*
Gary Lipsky, *President*
Kitty Cohen, *Vice Pres*
Claudia Mendoza, *Director*
EMP: 300
SQ FT: 3,500
SALES (est): 7.5MM **Privately Held**
SIC: 7371 7997 Custom computer programming services; outdoor field clubs

(P-15210)
GOOD TECHNOLOGY CORPORATION (HQ)
430 N Mary Ave Ste 200, Sunnyvale (94085-2923)
PHONE 408 212-7500
Fax: 408 212-7505
Christy Wyatt, *President*
Ronald J Fior, *CFO*
Cheryln Chin, *Senior VP*
Fr D Ric ARI S, *Senior VP*
Aira Cook, *Vice Pres*
EMP: 160 EST: 2014
SQ FT: 80,000
SALES: 160.3MM
SALES (corp-wide): 3.3B **Privately Held**
WEB: www.good.com
SIC: 7371 7382 Computer software development & applications; custom computer programming services; protective devices, security
PA: Blackberry Limited
  2200 University Ave E
  Waterloo ON N2K 0
  519 888-7465

(P-15211)
GRACENOTE INC (HQ)
2000 Powell St Ste 1500, Emeryville (94608-1820)
PHONE 510 428-7200
Fax: 510 596-7671
Stephen White, *President*
Ben Ceschi, *President*
Dominique Schurman, *COO*
Mike Novelly, *CFO*
Eric Allen, *Senior VP*
EMP: 148
SALES (est): 98.7MM
SALES (corp-wide): 2B **Publicly Held**
WEB: www.gracenote.com
SIC: 7371 Software programming applications
PA: Tribune Media Company
  435 N Michigan Ave Fl 2
  Chicago IL 60611
  212 210-2786

(P-15212)
GRAND INTELLIGENCE LLC
2880 Zanker Rd Ste 203, San Jose (95134-2122)
PHONE 408 954-7368
Marylyn Lin, *Mng Member*
Dongyan Wang, *COO*
EMP: 100 EST: 2012
SALES: 10MM **Privately Held**
SIC: 7371 Computer software development

(P-15213)
GREE INTERNATIONAL INC
185 Berry St Ste 590, San Francisco (94107-9105)
PHONE 415 409-5159
Naoki Aoyagi, *CEO*
Neil Haldar, *President*
Andrew Sheppard, *COO*
Eiji Araki, *Senior VP*
Shanti Bergel, *Senior VP*
EMP: 250
SALES (est): 37.3MM
SALES (corp-wide): 642.7MM **Privately Held**
SIC: 7371 Computer software development & applications; computer software systems analysis & design, custom; software programming applications
PA: Gree, Inc.
  6-10-1, Roppongi
  Minato-Ku TKY 106-0
  357 709-500

(P-15214)
GRIDIRON SYSTEMS INC
4555 Great America Pkwy # 150, Santa Clara (95054-1243)
PHONE 201 502-0512
Javed Patel, *CEO*
David Wright, *President*
EMP: 179
SALES (est): 3.6MM
SALES (corp-wide): 50.8MM **Publicly Held**
SIC: 7371 Computer software development & applications
PA: Violin Memory, Inc.
  4555 Great America Pkwy # 150
  Santa Clara CA 95054
  650 396-1500

(P-15215)
GROUP AVANTICA INC
Also Called: Avantica Technologies
2680 Bayshore Pkwy # 416, Mountain View (94043-1022)
PHONE 650 248-9678
Mario Chaves, *CEO*
Luis C Chaves, *President*
Luis G Avila, *Info Tech Mgr*
John Hitchcock, *Director*
Rodrigo Vargas, *Manager*
EMP: 260
SALES (est): 17.3MM **Privately Held**
WEB: www.avantica.net
SIC: 7371 Computer software development

(P-15216)
GTXCEL INC
2855 Telg Ave Ste 600, Berkeley (94705)
PHONE 800 609-8994
Becky Zehr, *Vice Pres*
Peter Stilson, *President*
Matthew McGinty, *COO*
Aaron Johnson, *Business Dir*
Tom Munson, *Business Dir*
EMP: 80
SQ FT: 10,000
SALES: 10MM **Privately Held**
SIC: 7371 Computer software development

(P-15217)
GUIDEBOOK INC
1 Zoe St, San Francisco (94107-1709)
PHONE 650 319-7233
Jeff Lewis, *CEO*
Chris Hart, *CFO*
Wayne Morris, *Vice Pres*
Dan Lyon, *Admin Asst*
Sarah Kostas, *Finance Mgr*
EMP: 90 EST: 2011
SQ FT: 6,500
SALES (est): 9.7MM **Privately Held**
SIC: 7371 Computer software development & applications

(P-15218)
H & R ACCOUNTS INC
Also Called: Avadyne Health
3131 Camino Del Rio N, San Diego (92108-5701)
PHONE 619 819-8844
Linda Hevern, *Branch Mgr*
Rob Ayer, *Technology*
EMP: 65
SALES (corp-wide): 29.6MM **Privately Held**
SIC: 7371 Computer software development
PA: H & R Accounts, Inc.
  7017 John Deere Pkwy
  Moline IL 61265
  309 736-2255

(P-15219)
HEWLETT PACKARD
3000 Hanover St, Palo Alto (94304-1185)
PHONE 650 857-1501
EMP: 1835
SALES (est): 98.4MM **Privately Held**
SIC: 7371

(P-15220)
HMOINTERFACECOM LLC
Also Called: Solartis
1601 N Sepulveda Blvd, Manhattan Beach (90266-5111)
PHONE 310 251-4861
Nicholas Richardson, *President*
Srinivasan Alagarsamy, *COO*
Gerald Williams, *Program Mgr*
Siby Nidhiry, *CTO*
EMP: 238
SALES (est): 12.3MM **Privately Held**
SIC: 7371 Computer software development

(P-15221)
HONEYBOOK INC
539 Bryant St Ste 200, San Francisco (94107-1269)
PHONE 770 403-9234
Oz Eliyahu, *CEO*
John Kramer, *COO*
Leslie Wong, *Director*

7371 - Custom Computer Programming Svcs County (P-15222)

PRODUCTS & SERVICES SECTION

Sara Raines, *Accounts Mgr*
Hema Padhu, *Advisor*
EMP: 55
SALES: 1MM **Privately Held**
SIC: 7371 Computer software development & applications

(P-15222)
HORIZON TECHNOLOGIES INC
Also Called: Horizon Systems
1270 Oakmead Pkwy Ste 115, Sunnyvale (94085-4031)
PHONE 408 733-1530
Fax: 408 716-3366
Santosh Addagulla, *President*
Noah Shashialegala, *Info Tech Mgr*
EMP: 213
SALES (est): 16.7MM **Privately Held**
WEB: www.horizontechnol.com
SIC: 7371 Computers, peripherals & software

(P-15223)
HOUZZ INC (PA)
285 Hamilton Ave Fl 4, Palo Alto (94301-2540)
PHONE 650 326-3000
ADI Tatarko, *CEO*
Alon Cohen, *President*
Liza Hausman, *Vice Pres*
Jerry Kingkade, *Vice Pres*
Sam Veazey, *Vice Pres*
EMP: 86
SALES (est): 67.1MM **Privately Held**
SIC: 7371 Computer software development

(P-15224)
HP INC
2525 Colorado Ave Ste 310, Santa Monica (90404-3552)
PHONE 310 255-3000
Chuck Smith, *Manager*
EMP: 80
SALES (corp-wide): 103.3B **Publicly Held**
SIC: 7371 5734 Computer software development; computer & software stores
PA: Hp Inc.
   1501 Page Mill Rd
   Palo Alto CA 94304
   650 857-1501

(P-15225)
HTEC GROUP INC
222 Kearny St Ste 800, San Francisco (94108-4513)
PHONE 650 949-4880
Aleksandar Cabrilo, *President*
Timothy Gens, *Admin Sec*
EMP: 99
SALES: 5MM **Privately Held**
SIC: 7371 Custom computer programming services

(P-15226)
HUMANITYCOM INC
235 Montgomery St Ste 500, San Francisco (94104-2908)
PHONE 415 230-0108
Ryan Fyfe, *CEO*
David Charron, *President*
EMP: 50
SALES: 2.5MM **Privately Held**
SIC: 7371 Computer software development

(P-15227)
HYLAND SOFTWARE INC
2355 Main St Ste 100, Irvine (92614-4290)
PHONE 949 242-3100
Lloyd Warman, *Principal*
Fred Davisson, *Admin Asst*
Pam Johnston, *Regl Sales Mgr*
EMP: 60
SALES (corp-wide): 590.3MM **Privately Held**
WEB: www.onbase.com
SIC: 7371 Computer software development
HQ: Hyland Software, Inc.
   28500 Clemens Rd
   Westlake OH 44145
   440 788-5000

(P-15228)
HYUNDAI ATVER TLMTICS AMER INC
10550 Talbert Ave Fl 2, Fountain Valley (92708-6032)
PHONE 949 381-6000
SOO Dong Park, *CEO*
Ui Chul Shi, *CFO*
Hyunho Lee, *Executive*
Changkick Sohn, *Executive*
Jonathan Piol, *Manager*
EMP: 56
SALES (est): 7.7MM **Privately Held**
SIC: 7371 Computer software systems analysis & design, custom; computer software development & applications; software programming applications

(P-15229)
IBOSS INC
Also Called: Iboss Security
4110 Campus Point Ct, San Diego (92121-1513)
PHONE 877 742-6832
Paul Martini, *CEO*
Peter Martini, *President*
Mike Crawford, *COO*
Justin Sollenne, *CFO*
Frank McLallen, *Senior VP*
EMP: 100
SQ FT: 13,445
SALES (est): 22.5MM **Privately Held**
WEB: www.iphantom.com
SIC: 7371 Computer software development & applications

(P-15230)
IBS ENTERPRISE USA INC (HQ)
Also Called: I B S
915 Highland Pointe Dr # 250, Roseville (95678-5421)
PHONE 916 542-2820
Fax: 916 985-4922
Doug Braun, *CEO*
Christian Paulsson, *COO*
Aimee J Lasserre, *CFO*
Fredrik Sandelin, *CFO*
Mark Vincenzini, *CFO*
EMP: 153
SQ FT: 55,000
SALES (est): 29MM
SALES (corp-wide): 6.6MM **Privately Held**
WEB: www.ibsus.com
SIC: 7371 5045 Custom computer programming services; computer software
PA: Iptor Supply Chain Systems Ab
   Hemvarnsgatan 8
   Solna 171 5
   862 723-00

(P-15231)
IC COMPLIANCE LLC (PA)
Also Called: Icon Professional Services
1065 E Hillsdale Blvd # 300, Foster City (94404-1613)
PHONE 650 378-4150
Fax: 650 378-4157
Teresa Creech, *CEO*
Dana Shaw, *COO*
Keith Corbin, *CFO*
Michael Soffel, *Vice Pres*
Catherine Chidyausiku, *Administration*
EMP: 2500
SQ FT: 5,100
SALES (est): 274.6MM **Privately Held**
WEB: www.gotoicon.com
SIC: 7371 8721 Computer software development & applications; payroll accounting service

(P-15232)
ILLUMIO INC
160 San Gabriel Dr, Sunnyvale (94086-5125)
PHONE 669 800-5000
Andrew Rubin, *CEO*
Remo Canessa, *CFO*
Alan Cohen, *Ch Credit Ofcr*
Denis Maynard, *Senior VP*
Emily Couey, *Vice Pres*
EMP: 140 **EST:** 2012
SALES (est): 2.8MM **Privately Held**
SIC: 7371 Custom computer programming services

(P-15233)
IMPERVA INC (PA)
3400 Bridge Pkwy Ste 200, Redwood City (94065-1195)
PHONE 650 345-9000
Anthony J Bettencourt, *Ch of Bd*
Terrence J Schmid, *CFO*
Michael D Mooney, *Officer*
Meg Bear, *Senior VP*
Merav Davidson, *Senior VP*
EMP: 146
SQ FT: 50,500
SALES: 234.3MM **Publicly Held**
WEB: www.imperva.com
SIC: 7371 Computer software development & applications

(P-15234)
INFOSYS LIMITED
7707 Gateway Blvd Ste 110, Newark (94560-1160)
PHONE 510 742-3000
Basab Pradhan, *Branch Mgr*
Venkateswarlu Pallapothu, *COO*
S D Shibulal, *COO*
Tim Pai, *CFO*
Manish Kumar, *Top Exec*
EMP: 100
SALES (corp-wide): 7.9B **Privately Held**
WEB: www.itinfrastructureoutsourcinginfy.com
SIC: 7371 Custom computer programming services
HQ: Infosys Limited
   6100 Tennyson Pkwy # 200
   Plano TX 75024
   469 229-9400

(P-15235)
INNOPATH SOFTWARE INC (PA)
333 W El Camino Real # 230, Sunnyvale (94087-1973)
PHONE 408 962-9200
John Fazio, *President*
Adrian Chan, *President*
Naresh Bansal, *Vice Pres*
Mark Fazio, *Vice Pres*
Eric King, *Vice Pres*
EMP: 100
SALES (est): 36.3MM **Privately Held**
WEB: www.innopath.com
SIC: 7371 Computer software development

(P-15236)
INNOVASYSTEMS INTL LLC
850 Beech St Unit 1006, San Diego (92101-2895)
PHONE 619 955-5890
EMP: 71
SALES (corp-wide): 52.9MM **Privately Held**
SIC: 7371 Custom computer programming services
PA: Innovasystems International Llc
   2385 Northside Dr Ste 300
   San Diego CA 92108
   619 756-6500

(P-15237)
INNOVASYSTEMS INTL LLC (PA)
2385 Northside Dr Ste 300, San Diego (92108-2716)
PHONE 619 756-6500
Fax: 619 955-5801
Lynn Hutton, *Mng Member*
Jan Rhu, *Exec VP*
Mike Lawrence, *Program Mgr*
Anthony Campbell, *Sr Software Eng*
Ian Chase, *Info Tech Mgr*
EMP: 124
SALES (est): 52.7MM **Privately Held**
WEB: www.innovasi.com
SIC: 7371 7373 7379 7376 Custom computer programming services; computer integrated systems design; computer related maintenance services; computer facilities management

(P-15238)
INSPIRA INC
4125 Blackford Ave # 255, San Jose (95117-1711)
PHONE 408 247-9500
Fax: 408 247-9600
Ravindra Gudapati, *President*

EMP: 60
SQ FT: 2,908
SALES: 3MM **Privately Held**
SIC: 7371 Software programming applications

(P-15239)
INSTART LOGIC INC
Also Called: Instart Labs
450 Lambert Ave, Palo Alto (94306-2219)
PHONE 888 418-5044
Manav Ratan Mital, *CEO*
Peter Blum, *Vice Pres*
Robert Dunn, *Vice Pres*
Justin Fitzhugh, *Vice Pres*
Josh Leslie, *Vice Pres*
EMP: 95 **EST:** 2010
SALES (est): 16.3MM **Privately Held**
SIC: 7371 Computer software development & applications

(P-15240)
INSTILL CORPORATION
777 Mariners Island Blvd # 400, San Mateo (94404-5059)
PHONE 650 645-2600
Robert Bonavito, *CEO*
Michael Devries, *President*
Michael R Peckham, *CFO*
Shermann Min, *Officer*
William Yaglou, *Vice Pres*
EMP: 115
SQ FT: 28,427
SALES (est): 7.4MM **Privately Held**
WEB: www.instill.com
SIC: 7371 Computer software development

(P-15241)
INTEGRATED DATA SERVICES INC (PA)
2141 Rosecrans Ave # 2050, El Segundo (90245-4747)
PHONE 310 647-3439
Fax: 310 416-9897
Jerry Murray, *CEO*
Maureen Abdelsayed, *General Mgr*
John Cole, *CTO*
Michelle Bergeron, *QA Dir*
Algis Basiulis, *Info Tech Mgr*
EMP: 52
SALES (est): 16.5MM **Privately Held**
WEB: www.get-integrated.com
SIC: 7371 Computer software development

(P-15242)
INTEGRATED DYNMC SOLUTIONS INC
31194 La Baya Dr Ste 203, Westlake Village (91362-6433)
PHONE 818 707-8797
Nasrollah Gashtili, *CEO*
John Bryant, *Vice Pres*
Joseph Varghese, *VP Human Res*
EMP: 50
SQ FT: 6,000
SALES: 2MM **Privately Held**
WEB: www.idspage.com
SIC: 7371 Computer software systems analysis & design, custom

(P-15243)
INTEGRIEN CORPORATION
3401 Hillview Ave, Palo Alto (94304-1320)
PHONE 323 810-6870
Alfred Eisaian, *CEO*
Mark Smialowicz, *CFO*
Roy Agostino, *Chief Mktg Ofcr*
Dale Quayle, *Exec VP*
Phil Rugani, *Exec VP*
EMP: 50
SQ FT: 14,000
SALES (est): 2.7MM
SALES (corp-wide): 72.7B **Publicly Held**
WEB: www.integrien.com
SIC: 7371 Computer software development
HQ: Vmware, Inc.
   3401 Hillview Ave
   Palo Alto CA 94304
   650 427-5000

PRODUCTS & SERVICES SECTION

7371 - Custom Computer Programming Svcs County (P-15265)

(P-15244)
INTELEX SYSTEMS INC
7728 Ducor Ave, West Hills (91304-4507)
PHONE.................818 518-1100
Sreenath Bangar, *CEO*
EMP: 84 EST: 2006
SALES (est): 3MM **Privately Held**
SIC: 7371 7379 Computer software development; computer related services

(P-15245)
INTELLECTSOFT LLC
721 Colorado Ave Ste 101, Palo Alto (94303-3973)
PHONE.................650 300-4335
Paul Bach,
Uri Soroka, *COO*
Dmitry Evdokimovich, *CIO*
Mikhail Halubtsou, *CTO*
Max Mironchik, *CTO*
EMP: 120
SQ FT: 1,000
SALES (est): 7.9MM **Privately Held**
SIC: 7371 Computer software development & applications

(P-15246)
INTELLISYNC CORPORATION (HQ)
313 Fairchild Dr, Mountain View (94043-2215)
PHONE.................650 625-2185
Woodson Hobbs, *President*
Clyde Foster, *COO*
David Eichler, *CFO*
Kelly J Hicks, *CFO*
Robert Gerber, *Chief Mktg Ofcr*
EMP: 55
SQ FT: 33,821
SALES (est): 25.4MM
SALES (corp-wide): 13.4B **Privately Held**
SIC: 7371 7372 Computer software development; prepackaged software
PA: Nokia Oyj
Karaportti 3
Espoo 02610
104 488-000

(P-15247)
INTERACTIVE DATA CORPORATION
CMS Bondedge
2901 28th St Ste 300, Santa Monica (90405-2972)
PHONE.................310 664-2500
Andrew Hausman, *Manager*
Andrew Hajducky, *Vice Pres*
Laili Agus, *Network Enginr*
Philippe Rasborn, *Manager*
Laurie Adami, *Accounts Mgr*
EMP: 75
SALES (corp-wide): 4.6B **Publicly Held**
WEB: www.interactivedata.com
SIC: 7371 7372 Custom computer programming services; prepackaged software
HQ: Interactive Data Corporation
32 Crosby Dr
Bedford MA 01730
781 687-8500

(P-15248)
INTERNATIONAL BUS MCHS CORP
Also Called: IBM
555 Bailey Ave, San Jose (95141-1003)
PHONE.................408 463-2000
Fax: 408 463-3114
Lou Gerstner, *Manager*
Andy Ho, *Executive*
Steve Mink, *Executive*
Gary Robinson, *Sr Software Eng*
Craig Dew, *Info Tech Dir*
EMP: 1500
SALES (corp-wide): 81.7B **Publicly Held**
WEB: www.ibm.com
SIC: 7371 7372 5961 Computer software development & applications; prepackaged software; catalog & mail-order houses
PA: International Business Machines Corporation
1 New Orchard Rd Ste 1
Armonk NY 10504
914 499-1900

(P-15249)
INTERNATIONAL BUS MCHS CORP
Also Called: IBM
2350 Mission College Blvd, Santa Clara (95054-1532)
PHONE.................408 850-8999
Tuan Nguyen, *Technology*
EMP: 529
SALES (corp-wide): 81.7B **Publicly Held**
SIC: 7371 Computer software development
PA: International Business Machines Corporation
1 New Orchard Rd Ste 1
Armonk NY 10504
914 499-1900

(P-15250)
INTERNATIONAL BUS MCHS CORP
Also Called: IBM
1480 64th St Ste 200, Emeryville (94608-1292)
PHONE.................510 652-6700
May Yang, *Manager*
EMP: 300
SALES (corp-wide): 81.7B **Publicly Held**
SIC: 7371 Computer software development
PA: International Business Machines Corporation
1 New Orchard Rd Ste 1
Armonk NY 10504
914 499-1900

(P-15251)
INTERNATIONAL NETWORK CORP
124 Via De La Vlle Unit 3, Solana Beach (92075)
PHONE.................858 794-2610
Joseph Galante, *President*
EMP: 50
SALES (est): 4.7MM **Privately Held**
SIC: 7371 7373 6799 Custom computer programming services; computer integrated systems design; venture capital companies

(P-15252)
INTERNET BLUEPRINT INC
Also Called: Bidmail
1177 Warner Ave, Tustin (92780-6458)
PHONE.................714 673-6000
Fax: 714 258-9359
Daniel Stapleton, *President*
Peter Amaraphornkul, *Info Tech Dir*
Jared Plumb, *Marketing Mgr*
Juan Duarte, *Manager*
EMP: 50
SALES (est): 5MM **Privately Held**
SIC: 7371 Computer software development & applications

(P-15253)
INTERNET SECURITY SYSTEMS INC
28350 Tamarack Ln, Santa Clarita (91390-4038)
PHONE.................661 296-5752
Lonny Esposito, *Manager*
EMP: 116
SALES (corp-wide): 81.7B **Publicly Held**
WEB: www.issx.com
SIC: 7371 Custom computer programming services
HQ: Internet Security Systems Inc
6303 Barfield Rd
Atlanta GA 30328
404 236-2600

(P-15254)
INVENSYS PROCESSS SYSTEMS INC
26561 Rancho Pkwy S, Lake Forest (92630-8301)
PHONE.................949 727-3200
Fax: 949 455-8151
Yvette Khan, *Principal*
Jim Motes, *Vice Pres*
Aravind Yarlagadda, *Vice Pres*
Dan Carrie, *General Mgr*
Derrick Jones, *Info Tech Dir*
EMP: 114
SALES (corp-wide): 224.4K **Privately Held**
SIC: 7371 Computer software development
HQ: Invensys Processs Systems, Inc.
10900 Equity Dr
Houston TX 77041
713 329-1600

(P-15255)
IQMS (PA)
2231 Wisteria Ln, Paso Robles (93446-9820)
PHONE.................805 227-1122
Randall C Flamm, *President*
Karen Sked, *President*
Nancy Flamm, *Vice Pres*
Jon Gabelica, *Vice Pres*
Glenn Nowak, *Vice Pres*
EMP: 130
SQ FT: 60,000
SALES: 37MM **Privately Held**
WEB: www.iqms.com
SIC: 7371 Computer software development

(P-15256)
IRDETO USA INC (DH)
3255 Scott Blvd Ste 3-101, Santa Clara (95054-3019)
PHONE.................760 268-7299
Fax: 760 795-2626
Barry Douglas Coleman, *CEO*
Loefie Engelbrecht, *President*
Gram Kill, *President*
Keddy Perry, *President*
Jan Hofmeyr, *Exec VP*
EMP: 70
SALES (est): 18.8MM
SALES (corp-wide): 370.9MM **Privately Held**
SIC: 7371 Computer software development
HQ: Mih Holdings Ltd
251 Oak Avenue
Johannesburg GP
112 893-024

(P-15257)
IRISE (PA)
2381 Rosecrans Ave # 100, El Segundo (90245-7903)
PHONE.................800 556-0399
Fax: 310 356-3509
Emmet B Keeffe III, *CEO*
Martin Brunk, *Managing Prtnr*
Maurice Martin, *President*
Lionel Etrillard, *CFO*
Mitch Bishop, *Chief Mktg Ofcr*
EMP: 94
SALES (est): 44.5MM **Privately Held**
SIC: 7371 Computer software development

(P-15258)
ISAAC FAIR CORPORATION
Also Called: Mindwave Software
3661 Valley Centre Dr, San Diego (92130-3321)
PHONE.................858 369-8000
Fax: 858 369-8001
Steve Gutschow, *Principal*
Scott Zoldi, *Vice Pres*
Dawn Davis, *Info Tech Mgr*
Michael Balon, *Director*
Cindy White, *Director*
EMP: 88
SALES (corp-wide): 838.7MM **Publicly Held**
WEB: www.fairisaac.com
SIC: 7371 Computer software development
PA: Fair Isaac Corporation
181 Metro Dr Ste 700
San Jose CA 95110
408 535-1500

(P-15259)
ISCS INC
100 Great Oaks Blvd # 100, San Jose (95119-1462)
PHONE.................408 362-3000
Fax: 408 362-3010
Andy J Scurto, *President*
Tim R Shelton, *CFO*
Jeff Bingham, *Vice Pres*
Leslie Holden-Mikeseli, *Vice Pres*
Myron Meier, *Vice Pres*
EMP: 201
SQ FT: 11,000
SALES (est): 15.5MM **Privately Held**
SIC: 7371 Software programming applications

(P-15260)
ISHERIFF INC
555 Twin Dolphin Dr, Redwood City (94065-2129)
PHONE.................650 412-4300
Paul Lipman, *CEO*
Jon Botter, *President*
Eric Jenny, *CFO*
Marcus Smith, *CFO*
James Socas, *Chairman*
EMP: 85
SALES (est): 9.9MM **Privately Held**
SIC: 7371 Software programming applications

(P-15261)
ITSEEZ INC
548 Market St 82363, San Francisco (94104-5401)
PHONE.................832 781-7169
Alexey Myakov, *Chief Mktg Ofcr*
EMP: 80
SALES: 2.5MM **Privately Held**
SIC: 7371 Computer software development & applications

(P-15262)
JIANGSU JUWANG INFO TECH CO
901 Tasman Dr, Santa Clara (95054)
PHONE.................510 967-3729
Song Han, *Branch Mgr*
EMP: 70
SALES (corp-wide): 2.9MM **Privately Held**
SIC: 7371 Computer software development
PA: Jiangsu Juwang Information Tech Co
195 Recino St
Fremont CA 94539
510 967-3729

(P-15263)
JIRBO INC
Also Called: Adcolony
11440 San Vicente Blvd # 100, Los Angeles (90049-6217)
PHONE.................310 775-8085
William Kassoy, *CEO*
Matt Barash, *President*
Ivan Kwok, *President*
Abe Pralle, *President*
Jonathan Zweig, *President*
EMP: 100
SALES (est): 15.5MM
SALES (corp-wide): 573.2MM **Privately Held**
SIC: 7371 Computer software development
HQ: Opera Software Americas, Llc
1875 S Grant St Ste 800
San Mateo CA 94402
650 625-1262

(P-15264)
JM DRIVER LLC
10620 Treena St Ste 230, San Diego (92131-1140)
PHONE.................858 663-6226
John Driver, *Owner*
Ben Johnson, *Finance Dir*
EMP: 51 EST: 2015
SALES (est): 1.5MM **Privately Held**
SIC: 7371 Computer software development

(P-15265)
KABAM INC (PA)
795 Folsom St Fl 6, San Francisco (94107-4226)
PHONE.................415 391-0817
Kevin Chou, *President*
Nick Earl, *President*
Peter Jackson, *President*
Chris Carvalho, *COO*
Steve Klei, *CFO*
EMP: 148 EST: 2006

7371 - Custom Computer Programming Svcs County (P-15266)

SALES (est): 127.6MM Privately Held
SIC: 7371 Computer software development & applications

(P-15266)
KALLIDUS INC
Also Called: Skava
425 Market St Ste 2200, San Francisco (94105-2434)
PHONE...................................877 554-2176
Arish Ali, *President*
Sudha KV, *President*
Vivek Agrawal, *Vice Pres*
Sudha Varadarajan, *Vice Pres*
Kirk Richards, *Program Mgr*
EMP: 100
SALES (est): 3.1MM
SALES (corp-wide): 7.9B Privately Held
WEB: www.skava.com
SIC: 7371 Computer software development
PA: Infosys Limited
  Plot No. 44 & 97a, Electronics City,
  Bengaluru KAR 56010
  803 987-2222

(P-15267)
KAZEON SYSTEMS INC
2841 Mission College Blvd, Santa Clara (95054-1838)
PHONE...................................650 641-8100
Fax: 650 641-8195
Sudhakar Muddu, *President*
Fred W Patton, *CFO*
Fred Patton, *CFO*
Ed Bauer, *Vice Pres*
Michael Marchi, *Vice Pres*
EMP: 80
SQ FT: 24,000
SALES (est): 3.9MM Privately Held
WEB: www.kazeon.com
SIC: 7371 7379 Computer software development; computer related maintenance services

(P-15268)
KINGSOFT OFFICE SOFTWARE INC
530 Lytton Ave Fl 2, Palo Alto (94301-1541)
PHONE...................................408 806-0998
Angela Zhou, *Finance*
Sun Shaw, *CTO*
EMP: 800
SALES (est): 28.8MM Privately Held
SIC: 7371 Computer software development

(P-15269)
KINNSER SOFTWARE INC
Also Called: Adlware
11 Calle Portofino, San Clemente (92673-6708)
PHONE...................................949 478-0890
Chris Hester, *President*
EMP: 69
SALES (corp-wide): 36MM Privately Held
SIC: 7371 Computer software development & applications
PA: Kinnser Software, Inc.
  2600 Via Fortuna Ste 150
  Austin TX 78746
  512 879-3135

(P-15270)
KRG TECHNOLOGIES INC
Also Called: K R G
25000 Ave Stnford Ste 243, Valencia (91355)
PHONE...................................661 257-9967
Muthuramalingam Umapathi, *President*
Hemalatha Rajagopala, *Owner*
Balamurugan Subbiah, *Principal*
Shyam Krg, *Tech Recruiter*
Vijay Technologies, *Tech Recruiter*
EMP: 400
SQ FT: 780
SALES: 35MM Privately Held
WEB: www.krgtech.com
SIC: 7371 8748 Software programming applications; industrial development planning

(P-15271)
KST DATA INC
3699 Wilshire Blvd # 680, Los Angeles (90010-2740)
PHONE...................................213 384-9555
Torres Tansobing, *President*
Mark Edson, *Vice Pres*
Michael Krueger, *Program Mgr*
Eugene Jacobowitz, *General Mgr*
Brittany Moon, *Executive Asst*
EMP: 52
SQ FT: 11,000
SALES (est): 23.3MM Privately Held
WEB: www.kstdata.com
SIC: 7371 7378 Computer software development & applications; computer maintenance & repair

(P-15272)
LANGUAGE WEAVER INC
Also Called: Sdl
6060 Center Dr Ste 150, Los Angeles (90045-8808)
PHONE...................................310 437-7300
Fax: 310 437-7307
Mark Tapling, *CEO*
Daniel Marcu, *COO*
Laurie Gerber, *Vice Pres*
Kevin Knight, *Vice Pres*
Howard Smith, *Vice Pres*
EMP: 55
SQ FT: 6,000
SALES (est): 8.7MM
SALES (corp-wide): 402.4MM Privately Held
WEB: www.languageweaver.com
SIC: 7371 Computer software development
PA: Sdl Plc
  Globe House
  Maidenhead BERKS SL6 7
  162 841-0100

(P-15273)
LAXMI GROUP INC
Also Called: Importers Software
4699 Old Ironsides Dr # 100, Santa Clara (95054-1824)
PHONE...................................408 329-7733
Gopal RAO, *President*
Shankar Ram, *Principal*
Steve Martel, *VP Finance*
EMP: 60
SQ FT: 2,900
SALES: 6.4MM Privately Held
WEB: www.laxmigroup.com
SIC: 7371 7363 Custom computer programming services; help supply services

(P-15274)
LIGHTBEND INC
625 Market St Ste 1000, San Francisco (94105-3312)
PHONE...................................877 989-7372
Mark Brewer, *Ch of Bd*
Steve Bean, *CFO*
Martin Odersky, *Chairman*
Kathleen Hayes, *Vice Pres*
Derek Henninger, *Vice Pres*
EMP: 68
SALES (est): 7.3MM Privately Held
SIC: 7371 Computer software development & applications

(P-15275)
LIMINEX INC
Also Called: Goguardian
200 N Sepulveda Blvd Ste, Hermosa Beach (90254)
PHONE...................................310 963-3031
Aza Steel, *CEO*
Advait Shinde, *CTO*
EMP: 60 EST: 2014
SQ FT: 16,000
SALES (est): 705.6K Privately Held
SIC: 7371 Computer software development

(P-15276)
LINDEN RESEARCH INC (PA)
Also Called: Linden Lab
945 Battery St, San Francisco (94111-1305)
PHONE...................................415 243-9000
Fax: 415 243-9045
Ebbe Altberg, *CEO*
Bill Gurley, *Partner*
Bob Komin, *COO*
Malcolm Dunne, *CFO*
John Zdanowski, *CFO*
EMP: 103
SALES (est): 51.4MM Privately Held
WEB: www.lindenlab.com
SIC: 7371 Computer software development

(P-15277)
LIVEFYRE INC (PA)
360 3rd St Ste 700, San Francisco (94107-2164)
PHONE...................................415 800-0900
Jordan Kretchmer, *CEO*
Kenneth Grosso, *Senior VP*
David Rodriguez, *Senior VP*
Bruce Ableson, *Vice Pres*
Jenna Langer, *Vice Pres*
EMP: 68
SQ FT: 4,464
SALES (est): 27.2MM Privately Held
SIC: 7371 Computer software development

(P-15278)
LOCKHEED MARTIN CORPORATION
505 W Woodbury Rd, Altadena (91001-5409)
PHONE...................................626 296-7977
Jim Scherer, *Director*
Charles Myles, *Personnel Exec*
Jim Sherrer, *Manager*
EMP: 80
SALES (corp-wide): 46.1B Publicly Held
WEB: www.lockheedmartin.com
SIC: 7371 Custom computer programming services
PA: Lockheed Martin Corporation
  6801 Rockledge Dr
  Bethesda MD 20817
  301 897-6000

(P-15279)
LOCKHEED MARTIN CORPORATION
10325 Meanley Dr, San Diego (92131-3011)
PHONE...................................858 740-5100
Mike Berdeguez, *Manager*
Ryan Jennings, *Human Resources*
Jim Filby, *Facilities Mgr*
Kim Ulrich, *Manager*
EMP: 250
SALES (corp-wide): 46.1B Publicly Held
WEB: www.lockheedmartin.com
SIC: 7371 Custom computer programming services
PA: Lockheed Martin Corporation
  6801 Rockledge Dr
  Bethesda MD 20817
  301 897-6000

(P-15280)
LOCKHEED MARTIN ORINCON
10325 Meanley Dr, San Diego (92131-3011)
PHONE...................................858 455-5530
Larry Cox, *President*
EMP: 70
SALES: 20MM
SALES (corp-wide): 46.1B Publicly Held
SIC: 7371 Computer software development
HQ: Lockheed Martin Orincon Corporation
  10325 Meanley Dr
  San Diego CA 92131
  858 455-5530

(P-15281)
LOCKHEED MARTIN ORINCON CORP (HQ)
10325 Meanley Dr, San Diego (92131-3011)
PHONE...................................858 455-5530
Fax: 858 795-2537
Daniel Alspach, *Ch of Bd*
Thomas P O'Hara, *CFO*
Terry Magee, *Info Tech Dir*
EMP: 200 EST: 1973
SQ FT: 41,000
SALES (est): 42MM
SALES (corp-wide): 46.1B Publicly Held
SIC: 7371 8731 Computer software development & applications; commercial physical research
PA: Lockheed Martin Corporation
  6801 Rockledge Dr
  Bethesda MD 20817
  301 897-6000

(P-15282)
LOGICOR
17752 Mitchell N Ste H, Irvine (92614-6802)
PHONE...................................949 260-2260
C Eugene Cook II, *CEO*
Diane Ermatinger, *Controller*
Greg Bourdon, *Sales Staff*
EMP: 50
SQ FT: 20,000
SALES: 5MM Privately Held
WEB: www.pfastship.com
SIC: 7371 5734 Computer software development; software, business & non-game

(P-15283)
LOGIX DEVELOPMENT CORPORATION
473 Post St, Camarillo (93010-8553)
PHONE...................................888 505-6449
David K Howington, *CEO*
Pauline Malysko, *President*
Anne Howington, *Vice Pres*
Carla Wheeler, *Executive Asst*
Michael Chapman, *Administration*
EMP: 83
SALES (est): 5.2MM Privately Held
WEB: www.pop3.com
SIC: 7371 Computer software development

(P-15284)
LOGLOGIC INC
110 Rose Orchard Way, San Jose (95134-1358)
PHONE...................................408 215-5900
Fax: 408 321-8717
Guy Churchward, *CEO*
Joseph Consul, *CFO*
Joe Garma, *CFO*
Jean Dechant, *Vice Pres*
Kyle Hourihan, *Info Tech Mgr*
EMP: 170
SALES (est): 16.7MM
SALES (corp-wide): 1.2B Privately Held
WEB: www.loglogic.com
SIC: 7371 Computer software development
PA: Tibco Software Inc.
  3303 Hillview Ave
  Palo Alto CA 94304
  650 846-1000

(P-15285)
LOLAPPS INC
122 2nd Ave Ste 201, San Mateo (94401-3855)
PHONE...................................415 243-0749
Kavin Stewart, *CEO*
Kamo Asatryan, *Shareholder*
Brain Rue, *Treasurer*
Annie Change, *Admin Sec*
Jennifer Garcia, *Manager*
EMP: 230
SQ FT: 6,000
SALES (est): 10.4MM Privately Held
SIC: 7371 Computer software development & applications

(P-15286)
MAGMA DESIGN AUTOMATION INC (HQ)
1650 Tech Dr Ste 100, San Jose (95110)
PHONE...................................408 565-7500
Rajeev Madhavan, *CEO*
Noriaki Kikuchi, *President*
Sumit Roy, *President*
Peter S Teshima, *CFO*
Gregory C Walker, *Senior VP*
EMP: 410
SQ FT: 106,854

SALES (est): 37.3MM
SALES (corp-wide): 2.2B **Publicly Held**
WEB: www.magma-da.com
SIC: 7371 7373 Computer software development; computer integrated systems design
PA: Synopsys, Inc.
690 E Middlefield Rd
Mountain View CA 94043
650 584-5000

(P-15287)
MAGNUS TECH SOLUTIONS INC
2600 Ei Camino Real Ste 601, Palo Alto (94306)
PHONE 650 320-0073
Anurag Pal, *CEO*
Satya Edusumiila, *Human Res Mgr*
EMP: 100
SALES (est): 3.1MM **Privately Held**
SIC: 7371 Custom computer programming services

(P-15288)
MAINTECH INCORPORATED
2401 N Glassell St, Orange (92865-2705)
P.O. Box 13500 (92857-8500)
PHONE 714 921-8000
Fax: 714 974-0292
Tony Donato, *Vice Pres*
Adnan Alsamari, *Senior VP*
Noel Hughes, *Managing Dir*
Timothy Campagna, *Admin Asst*
Jariel Torres, *Admin Asst*
EMP: 200
SQ FT: 1,200
SALES (corp-wide): 1.5B **Publicly Held**
SIC: 7371 3577 Computer software systems analysis & design, custom; computer peripheral equipment
HQ: Maintech, Incorporated
14 Commerce Dr Ste 104
Cranford NJ 07016
800 426-8324

(P-15289)
MAPR TECHNOLOGIES INC (PA)
Also Called: Mapr Technology
350 Holger Way, San Jose (95134-1362)
PHONE 408 428-9472
Matt Mills, *CEO*
John Schroeder, *Ch of Bd*
Dan Atler, *CFO*
Steve Fitz, *Senior VP*
Anil Gadre, *Senior VP*
EMP: 98
SALES (est): 65.8MM **Privately Held**
SIC: 7371 Computer software development & applications

(P-15290)
MARKET SCAN INFO SYSTEMS INC (PA)
811 Camarillo Springs Rd B, Camarillo (93012-9465)
PHONE 805 823-4258
Stephen Smythe, *CEO*
Rusty West, *President*
Rustie G West, *CEO*
Nick Kulyk, *CTO*
Steven Saigeon, *Director*
EMP: 80
SQ FT: 14,000
SALES (est): 23.3MM **Privately Held**
SIC: 7371 8732 Computer software development & applications; market analysis, business & economic research

(P-15291)
MARKETO INC (HQ)
901 Mariners Island Blvd, San Mateo (94404-1592)
PHONE 650 376-2300
Fax: 650 376-2331
Phillip M Fernandez, *CEO*
Jason L Holmes, *COO*
Brian K Kinion, *CFO*
Chandar Pattabhiram, *Chief Mktg Ofcr*
Lynne Biggar, *Exec VP*
EMP: 148
SQ FT: 102,670

SALES: 209.8MM
SALES (est): 27.2MM **Privately Held**
SIC: 7371 7372 Custom computer programming services; computer software writing services; prepackaged software
PA: Milestone Holdco, Inc.
901 Mariners Island Blvd
San Mateo CA 94404
650 376-2300

(P-15292)
MARKLOGIC CORPORATION (PA)
999 Skyway Rd Ste 200, San Carlos (94070-2722)
PHONE 650 655-2300
Fax: 650 655-2310
Gary Bloom, *President*
Peter Norman, *CFO*
Dave Ponzini, *CFO*
Michaline Todd, *Chief Mktg Ofcr*
Catherine Chan, *Officer*
EMP: 148
SQ FT: 40,000
SALES (est): 161.3MM **Privately Held**
WEB: www.cerisent.com
SIC: 7371 Computer software development & applications

(P-15293)
MARKMONITOR HOLDINGS INC
425 Market St Ste 500, San Francisco (94105-2464)
PHONE 415 278-8400
Irfan Salim, *President*
Tom Ryden, *Vice Pres*
EMP: 427
SALES (est): 22.8MM **Privately Held**
WEB: www.ftftech.com
SIC: 7371 Computer software development & applications

(P-15294)
MATTEL INC
909 N Sepulveda Blvd # 540, El Segundo (90245-2724)
PHONE 310 227-8230
Lance M Ralls, *Vice Pres*
Jessica Chen, *Executive*
Jonathon Lui, *Info Tech Dir*
John Sagara, *Sales Dir*
Linda Choi, *Marketing Mgr*
EMP: 85
SALES (corp-wide): 5.7B **Publicly Held**
SIC: 7371 7379 Computer software development & applications;
PA: Mattel, Inc.
333 Continental Blvd
El Segundo CA 90245
310 252-2000

(P-15295)
MAVENIR INTL HOLDINGS INC
Also Called: Stoke
2890 Zanker Rd Ste 207, San Jose (95134-2118)
PHONE 408 855-2900
Vikash Varma, *President*
Sue Agopian, *Partner*
Magnus Almquist, *Vice Pres*
Dave Arnold, *Vice Pres*
Paul Cianci, *Vice Pres*
EMP: 60
SQ FT: 35,000
SALES (est): 9.7MM
SALES (corp-wide): 623.3K **Privately Held**
WEB: www.stoke.com
SIC: 7371 Computer software development & applications
HQ: Mavenir Holdings, Inc.
1700 International Pkwy
Richardson TX 75081
469 916-4393

(P-15296)
MBLOX INCORPORATED (HQ)
Also Called: Zoove
1901 S Bascom Ave Ste 400, Campbell (95008-2238)
PHONE 408 617-3700
Fax: 408 617-3799
Thomas M Cotney, *CEO*
David Bernstein, *President*
Steve Love, *CFO*

Katherine Stoltz, *Exec VP*
Bruce Bales, *Senior VP*
EMP: 73
SALES (est): 23.8MM
SALES (corp-wide): 102.4MM **Privately Held**
WEB: www.mblox.com
SIC: 7371 Computer software development & applications

(P-15297)
MEGA PROFESSIONAL INTL
Also Called: Mpic
995 Montague Expy Ste 121, Milpitas (95035-6827)
PHONE 408 946-1500
Monali Mehta, *CEO*
Bob Mehta, *President*
Hemang Trivedi, *Marketing Mgr*
EMP: 52
SALES (est): 3.2MM **Privately Held**
WEB: www.mpic.com
SIC: 7371 Computer software systems analysis & design, custom

(P-15298)
MELLMO INC (DH)
Also Called: Roambi
120 S Sierra Ave, Solana Beach (92075-1811)
PHONE 858 847-3272
Fax: 858 847-3375
Quinton Alsbury, *CEO*
Thibaut De Lataillade, *President*
Jaime Zuluaga, *President*
Claire Remillard, *CFO*
Steve Neat, *Exec VP*
EMP: 51 **EST:** 2008
SALES (est): 10MM
SALES (corp-wide): 22.3B **Privately Held**
SIC: 7371 Custom computer programming services
HQ: Sap America, Inc.
3999 West Chester Pike
Newtown Square PA 19073
610 661-1000

(P-15299)
MERA SOFTWARE SERVICES INC
2350 Mission College Blvd # 340, Santa Clara (95054-1532)
PHONE 650 703-7226
James Hymel, *CEO*
Konstantin Nikashov, *Exec VP*
Yury Menkov, *Vice Pres*
Sergey Drozhilkin, *Principal*
Andrey Ladygin, *Principal*
EMP: 1300
SALES: 18.6MM **Privately Held**
SIC: 7371 Computer software writing services

(P-15300)
MERAKI INC
500 Terry A Francois Blvd, San Francisco (94158-2354)
PHONE 415 632-5800
Joshua Ward, *CEO*
James Ensten, *Senior Partner*
Daniel Atler, *CFO*
Todd Nightingale, *Vice Pres*
Hans Robertson, *Vice Pres*
EMP: 121 **EST:** 2015
SALES (est): 15.2MM **Privately Held**
SIC: 7371 8731 Computer software development & applications; computer (hardware) development

(P-15301)
META COMPANY
2855 Campus Dr Ste 300, San Mateo (94403-2512)
PHONE 844 638-2266
Meron Gribetz, *CEO*
EMP: 70 **EST:** 2013
SALES (est): 13.5MM **Privately Held**
SIC: 7371 Computer software development & applications

(P-15302)
METASWITCH NETWORKS
1751 Harbor Bay Pkwy, Alameda (94502-3001)
PHONE 415 513-1500
John Lazar, *CEO*

Thomas L Cronan III, *CFO*
Stephen Halstead, *CFO*
Carol Copland, *Officer*
Graeme Macarthur, *Exec VP*
EMP: 50
SALES (est): 9.5MM **Privately Held**
SIC: 7371 Computer software development
HQ: Metaswitch Limited
100 Church Street
Enfield MIDDX EN2 6
208 366-1177

(P-15303)
MIDOKURA USA INC
235 Montgomery St Ste 850, San Francisco (94104-2928)
PHONE 888 512-0460
Dan Dumitriu, *CEO*
Adam Johnson, *Vice Pres*
Jim Lenox, *Vice Pres*
Christiane Holtzman, *Social Dir*
Ashish Mukharji, *Business Dir*
EMP: 50
SALES (est): 4MM **Privately Held**
SIC: 7371 Computer software development

(P-15304)
MINDSOURCE INC
555 Clyde Ave Ste 100, Mountain View (94043-2269)
PHONE 650 314-6400
Fax: 650 254-8907
David Clark, *President*
Gabriel Meza, *CFO*
Jaynee Castro, *Recruiter*
Jon Miller, *Recruiter*
David Orsburn, *Director*
EMP: 55
SQ FT: 3,200
SALES (est): 5.3MM **Privately Held**
WEB: www.mindsource.com
SIC: 7371 7372 Computer software development & applications; application computer software

(P-15305)
MINERVA NETWORKS INC (PA)
2150 Gold St, Alviso (95002-3700)
PHONE 800 806-9594
Mauro Bonomi, *President*
Dr Jean-Georges Fritsch, *COO*
John Doerner, *CFO*
Chris Bowick, *Bd of Directors*
Sebastiano Tevarotto, *Bd of Directors*
EMP: 100
SQ FT: 25,600
SALES (est): 25.9MM **Privately Held**
SIC: 7371 Software programming applications

(P-15306)
MIRNAVSEH INC
Also Called: World For US
8436 Florissant Ct, San Diego (92129-4408)
PHONE 858 335-2470
Vitaly Serov, *CEO*
Michael Morozov, *Chief Engr*
EMP: 90
SQ FT: 2,500
SALES (est): 5MM **Privately Held**
SIC: 7371 Computer software development

(P-15307)
MISSION CRITICAL TECH INC
2041 Rosecrans Ave # 220, El Segundo (90245-4789)
PHONE 310 246-4455
Yorgos Stylianos, *CEO*
Beata Stylianos, *General Mgr*
Freddie Flores, *Accountant*
EMP: 50
SQ FT: 3,000
SALES (est): 7.8MM **Privately Held**
WEB: www.mctinc.com
SIC: 7371 8331 7361 7379 Computer software development; job training & vocational rehabilitation services; executive placement; computer related consulting services

7371 - Custom Computer Programming Svcs County (P-15308)

(P-15308)
MITCHELL INTERNATIONAL INC (HQ)
6220 Greenwich Dr, San Diego (92122-5913)
P.O. Box 229001 (92192-9001)
PHONE..................858 368-7000
Fax: 858 578-4252
James Lindner, *Vice Ch Bd*
Jack Farnan, *President*
Alex Sun, *President*
Arthur J Long, *CFO*
Elias Olmeta, *CFO*
EMP: 148
SQ FT: 141,000
SALES (est): 954.7MM
SALES (corp-wide): 1B **Publicly Held**
WEB: www.mitchell.com
SIC: 7371 Computer software development & applications
PA: Kkr & Co. L.P.
  9 W 57th St Ste 4200
  New York NY 10019
  212 750-8300

(P-15309)
MIXPANEL INC
405 Howard St Fl 2, San Francisco (94105-2670)
PHONE..................415 528-2827
Suhail M Doshi, *President*
Mason Yarnell, *Creative Dir*
Caitlin Quinlan, *Finance Mgr*
Rachael Norman, *Opers Dir*
Ryan Toben, *VP Sales*
EMP: 53
SALES (est): 10.1MM **Privately Held**
SIC: 7371 Computer software systems analysis & design, custom

(P-15310)
MOBILE PROGRAMMING LLC
30300 Agoura Rd Ste 140, Agoura Hills (91301-5406)
PHONE..................310 584-6300
Fax: 310 606-2154
Ishwari Singh, *President*
Craig Ford, *Managing Dir*
EMP: 51
SALES (est): 4.6MM **Privately Held**
SIC: 7371 Computer software systems analysis & design, custom

(P-15311)
MOBILITYWARE INC
440 Exchange Ste 100, Irvine (92602-1390)
PHONE..................949 788-9900
John Libby, *President*
Robert Jackson, *Vice Pres*
Natasha Dressler, *Executive Asst*
Claudia Avtabile, *Administration*
Steve Chang, *Sr Software Eng*
EMP: 58
SALES (est): 6.4MM **Privately Held**
SIC: 7371 Computer software development

(P-15312)
MOG INC
2607 7th St Ste C, Berkeley (94710-2571)
PHONE..................510 883-7100
David Rotenberg, *Principal*
Marni Greenberg, *Comms Dir*
John McGlinchey, *Business Mgr*
Kurt Mattia, *Analyst*
Don Proctor, *Materials Mgr*
EMP: 375 EST: 2010
SALES (est): 21.3MM
SALES (corp-wide): 233.7B **Publicly Held**
SIC: 7371 Custom computer programming services
HQ: Beats Electronics, Llc
  8600 Hayden Pl
  Culver City CA 90232

(P-15313)
MONITISE AMERICAS INC
1 Embrcdero Cntre Fl 9, San Francisco (94111)
PHONE..................415 526-7000
Fax: 415 526-7099
Elizabeth Buse, *CEO*
Anna Howard, *President*
Lisa Stanton, *President*
Lee Cameron, *CEO*
Brad Petzer, *CFO*
EMP: 61
SQ FT: 9,000
SALES (est): 13.7MM
SALES (corp-wide): 138.3MM **Privately Held**
WEB: www.clairmail.com
SIC: 7371 Computer software development
PA: Monitise Plc
  Medius House, 3rd Floor
  London W1F 8
  203 657-0900

(P-15314)
MONTAVISTA SOFTWARE LLC (HQ)
2315 N 1st St Fl 4, San Jose (95131-1010)
PHONE..................408 572-8000
Fax: 408 572-8005
Art Landro, *President*
Sanjay Uppal, *CFO*
Sanjay Uppao, *CFO*
Derek Howard, *Vice Pres*
John Phillips, *Vice Pres*
EMP: 100
SALES (est): 15.3MM
SALES (corp-wide): 412.7MM **Publicly Held**
WEB: www.mvista.com
SIC: 7371 Computer software development
PA: Cavium, Inc.
  2315 N 1st St
  San Jose CA 95131
  408 943-7100

(P-15315)
MOODYS WALL ST ANALYTICS INC
395 Oyster Point Blvd # 215, South San Francisco (94080-1930)
PHONE..................650 266-9660
Fax: 650 266-9661
Mark Ferraris, *President*
Adrian Cooper, *Chairman*
Ron Unz, *Co-COB*
EMP: 50
SQ FT: 6,500
SALES (est): 2.9MM
SALES (corp-wide): 3.4B **Publicly Held**
SIC: 7371 Computer software development
PA: Moody's Corporation
  250 Greenwich St
  New York NY 10007
  212 553-0300

(P-15316)
MOOV CORPORATION
Also Called: Moovweb
123 Mission St Ste 1000, San Francisco (94105-5126)
PHONE..................877 666-8932
Ajay Kapur, *CEO*
Gina Jackson, *Info Tech Mgr*
EMP: 105
SALES (est): 11.8MM **Privately Held**
SIC: 7371 Computer software development & applications

(P-15317)
MSHIFT INC
39899 Balentine Dr # 235, Newark (94560-5358)
PHONE..................408 437-2740
Scott Moeller, *CEO*
Jeff Chen, *Vice Pres*
Alan Finke, *Vice Pres*
Eric Buchbinder, *CTO*
Andrew Yee, *Software Engr*
EMP: 50
SALES (est): 6.8MM **Privately Held**
WEB: www.mobileshift.com
SIC: 7371 Computer software development & applications

(P-15318)
MULESOFT INC (PA)
77 Geary St Fl 400, San Francisco (94108-5707)
PHONE..................415 229-2009
Greg Schott, *President*
James Donelan, *President*
Ken Yagen, *President*
Matt Langdon, *CFO*
Mark Dao, *Officer*
EMP: 148
SALES (est): 191.1MM **Privately Held**
WEB: www.mulesource.com
SIC: 7371 Computer software development

(P-15319)
N A ARICENT INC
Also Called: Smartplay, Inc.
2580 N 1st St Ste 480, San Jose (95131-1043)
PHONE..................408 324-1800
Fax: 408 324-1810
Pradeep Vajram, *President*
Sanjay Palasamudram, *COO*
Vijay Krishnamurthy, *CFO*
Vinod Kaushik, *Vice Pres*
Mike Ingester, *General Mgr*
EMP: 60
SALES (est): 5.9MM **Privately Held**
WEB: www.tforceinc.com
SIC: 7371 Custom computer programming services
PA: Lendpro Entertainment Private Limited
  5th Floor, Golden Towers,
  Bengaluru KAR
  804 350-4444

(P-15320)
N MODEL INC (PA)
1600 Seaport Blvd Ste 400, Redwood City (94063-5564)
PHONE..................650 610-4600
Zack Rinat, *Ch of Bd*
Mark Tisdel, *CFO*
Amelia Generalis,
Christopher Larsen, *Officer*
Mark Anderson, *Senior VP*
EMP: 148
SQ FT: 34,600
SALES: 93.7MM **Publicly Held**
WEB: www.modeln.com
SIC: 7371 Custom computer programming services; computer software development & applications

(P-15321)
NANTMOBILE LLC
9920 Jefferson Blvd, Culver City (90232-3506)
PHONE..................310 883-7888
Patrick Soon-Shiong,
EMP: 200
SALES (est): 2.7MM **Privately Held**
SIC: 7371 Computer software development & applications

(P-15322)
NAVIS HOLDINGS LLC
55 Harrison St, Oakland (94607-3790)
PHONE..................510 267-5000
Fax: 510 763-2516
John Dillon, *CEO*
Julia CU, *Vice Pres*
Jonathan Shields PHD, *CTO*
Cody Cerf, *Sales Staff*
Erik Tiemroth PHD,
EMP: 139
SALES (est): 8.4MM
SALES (corp-wide): 4B **Privately Held**
SIC: 7371 Computer software development
HQ: Hiab Usa Inc.
  12233 Williams Rd
  Perrysburg OH 43551
  419 482-6000

(P-15323)
NCIRCLE NETWORK SECURITY INC (DH)
101 2nd St Ste 400, San Francisco (94105-3645)
PHONE..................415 625-5900
Fax: 415 625-5982
Abe Kleinfeld, *President*
Kelly E Lang, *CEO*
Mark Elchinoff, *CFO*
Karl Hutter, *Senior VP*
Jim Acquaviva, *Vice Pres*
EMP: 63
SQ FT: 20,000
SALES (est): 14.6MM
SALES (corp-wide): 2.3B **Publicly Held**
WEB: www.ncircle.com
SIC: 7371 Computer software development & applications
HQ: Tripwire, Inc.
  101 Sw Main St Ste 1500
  Portland OR 97204
  503 276-7500

(P-15324)
NEC CORPORATION OF AMERICA
Also Called: Necam
10850 Gold Center Dr # 200, Rancho Cordova (95670-6117)
PHONE..................916 636-5740
Kelly Gallagher, *Manager*
EMP: 53
SALES (corp-wide): 24.1B **Privately Held**
WEB: www.necam.com
SIC: 7371 5734 Custom computer programming services; computer & software stores
HQ: Nec Corporation Of America
  3929 W John Carpenter Fwy
  Irving TX 75063
  214 262-6000

(P-15325)
NETPACE INC
12657 Alcosta Blvd # 410, San Ramon (94583-4600)
PHONE..................925 543-7760
Fax: 925 543-7765
Omar Khan, *President*
Vajih Khan, *Co-CEO*
Rudy Aguirre, *Creative Dir*
Yousuf Vaid, *Software Engr*
Annie Sen, *Tech Recruiter*
EMP: 55 EST: 1996
SQ FT: 4,000
SALES (est): 3.6MM **Privately Held**
WEB: www.netpace.com
SIC: 7371 Custom computer programming services

(P-15326)
NETSKOPE INC
270 3rd St, Los Altos (94022-3617)
PHONE..................800 979-6988
Sanjay Beri, *CEO*
Chris Andrews, *Senior VP*
Rajneesh Chopra, *Vice Pres*
Rick Holden, *Vice Pres*
Paul Oshan, *Vice Pres*
EMP: 100
SALES (est): 22.1MM **Privately Held**
SIC: 7371 Computer software development

(P-15327)
NETWORKFLEET INC
Also Called: Verizon Networkfleet
9868 Scranton Rd Ste 1000, San Diego (92121-1791)
PHONE..................858 450-3245
Keith Schneider, *President*
Joshua Haims, *Exec VP*
Alan Lewin, *Vice Pres*
Jose Batlle, *District Mgr*
Brad Lackey, *Administration*
EMP: 95
SQ FT: 13,000
SALES (est): 31MM
SALES (corp-wide): 131.6B **Publicly Held**
WEB: www.networkcar.com
SIC: 7371 Computer software development & applications
HQ: Verizon Telematics Inc.
  2002 Summit Blvd Ste 1800
  Brookhaven GA 30319
  404 573-5800

(P-15328)
NETZERO INC (DH)
21301 Burbank Blvd Fl 3, Woodland Hills (91367-6697)
P.O. Box 5004 (91365-5004)
PHONE..................805 418-2000
Fax: 805 418-2075
Mark R Goldston, *Ch of Bd*
Charles S Hilliard, *CFO*
Gerald Popek, *CTO*
Byron Darrah, *Info Tech Dir*

PRODUCTS & SERVICES SECTION
7371 - Custom Computer Programming Svcs County (P-15349)

Larrye Boykin, *Auditor*
EMP: 250
SQ FT: 48,000
SALES (est): 28.1MM
SALES (corp-wide): 112.5MM **Publicly Held**
WEB: www.netzero.net
SIC: 7371 Computer software systems analysis & design, custom
HQ: United Online, Inc.
21255 Burbank Blvd # 400
Woodland Hills CA 91367
818 287-3000

(P-15329)
NEVERSOFT ENTERTAINMENT INC
21255 Burbank Blvd # 600, Woodland Hills (91367-6744)
PHONE.................................818 610-4100
Fax: 818 610-4101
Joel Jewett, *President*
Robert G Solomon, *Incorporator*
James Bryant, *Software Dev*
Sandy Jewett, *Software Dev*
Joe Kirchoff, *Software Engr*
EMP: 170
SALES (est): 13.1MM
SALES (corp-wide): 4.6B **Publicly Held**
WEB: www.blizzard.com
SIC: 7371 7372 Computer code authors; prepackaged software
PA: Activision Blizzard, Inc.
3100 Ocean Park Blvd
Santa Monica CA 90405
310 255-2000

(P-15330)
NEXA TECHNOLOGIES INC (HQ)
18552 Macarthur Blvd # 100, Irvine (92612-1235)
PHONE.................................972 590-8669
Eric Stoop, *President*
David Burnham, *Senior VP*
Kirk Lynn, *Vice Pres*
Mark Munoz, *Vice Pres*
Gerry Cardwell, *Network Enginr*
EMP: 65
SALES (est): 8.8MM **Privately Held**
WEB: www.nexatech.com
SIC: 7371 Computer software development

(P-15331)
NEXGENIX INC (PA)
2 Peters Canyon Rd # 200, Irvine (92606-1798)
PHONE.................................714 665-6240
Rick Dutta, *CEO*
Don Ganguly, *Ch of Bd*
Mark Iwanowski, *COO*
Dave R Andrade, *Vice Pres*
Carol Munroe, *Vice Pres*
EMP: 258
SQ FT: 14,264
SALES (est): 25.1MM **Privately Held**
SIC: 7371 8748 4813 Computer software development; systems analysis or design;

(P-15332)
NIELSEN CLARITAS INC
9444 Waples St Ste 280, San Diego (92121-2985)
PHONE.................................858 622-0800
Michael Schorr, *VP Sales*
Michael Youmans, *VP Sales*
Elizabeth V Phillips, *Director*
EMP: 455
SALES (est): 15.6MM **Privately Held**
WEB: www.claritas.com
SIC: 7371 8742 Computer software development; marketing consulting services

(P-15333)
NITAI PARTNERS INC
1761 Reichert Way, Chula Vista (91913-4345)
PHONE.................................855 879-2847
Aditya Satsangi, *CEO*
Konisha Satsangi, *Principal*
EMP: 80

SALES (est): 5MM **Privately Held**
SIC: 7371 7373 7372 7374 Computer software systems analysis & design, custom; systems integration services; business oriented computer software; data processing & preparation

(P-15334)
NLYTE SOFTWARE AMERICAS LTD (DH)
2800 Campus Dr Ste 135, San Mateo (94403-2554)
PHONE.................................650 561-8200
Fax: 650 642-2701
Doug Sabella, *President*
Fred Dirla, *COO*
Owen Nisbett, *CFO*
Moshe Benjo, *Vice Pres*
Kelvin Clibbon, *Vice Pres*
EMP: 52
SALES (est): 27.4MM
SALES (corp-wide): 23.7MM **Privately Held**
SIC: 7371 Computer software systems analysis & design, custom
HQ: Nlyte Software Americas Limited
26 Osiers Road
London SW18
208 877-7200

(P-15335)
NOMINUM INC (PA)
800 Bridge Pkwy Ste 100, Redwood City (94065-1156)
PHONE.................................650 381-6000
Fax: 650 381-6055
Garry Messiana, *CEO*
Paul Mockapetris, *Ch of Bd*
Gopala Tumuluri, *COO*
Kenton Chow, *CFO*
Bob Verheecke, *CFO*
EMP: 50
SQ FT: 15,000
SALES (est): 53.1MM **Privately Held**
WEB: www.nominum.com
SIC: 7371 Computer software development

(P-15336)
NORTHROP GRMMN SPCE & MSSN SYS
1762 Glenn Curtiss St, Carson (90746-4034)
PHONE.................................310 764-3000
Neil Siegel, *Branch Mgr*
EMP: 150 **Publicly Held**
WEB: www.trw.com
SIC: 7371 Computer software development
HQ: Northrop Grumman Space & Mission Systems Corp.
6377 San Ignacio Ave
San Jose CA 95119
703 280-2900

(P-15337)
NORTHROP GRMMN SPCE & MSSN SYS
9326 Spectrum Center Blvd, San Diego (92123-1443)
PHONE.................................858 514-9000
Mike Twyman, *Branch Mgr*
Christine Clements, *Executive*
Sam Yacoub, *Technology*
EMP: 220 **Publicly Held**
WEB: www.trw.com
SIC: 7371 Computer code authors
HQ: Northrop Grumman Space & Mission Systems Corp.
6377 San Ignacio Ave
San Jose CA 95119
703 280-2900

(P-15338)
NORTHROP GRUMMAN SYSTEMS CORP
9326 Spectrum Center Blvd, San Diego (92123-1443)
PHONE.................................858 514-0400
James F Harvey, *General Mgr*
EMP: 260 **Publicly Held**
SIC: 7371 7379 Computer software development; computer related consulting services

HQ: Northrop Grumman Systems Corporation
2980 Fairview Park Dr
Falls Church VA 22042
703 280-2900

(P-15339)
NORTHROP GRUMMAN SYSTEMS CORP
243 Ames Res Ctr Bldg N, Mountain View (94035)
P.O. Box 81, Moffett Field (94035-0081)
PHONE.................................650 604-5381
James Blount, *Director*
EMP: 106 **Publicly Held**
SIC: 7371 Computer software development & applications
HQ: Northrop Grumman Systems Corporation
2980 Fairview Park Dr
Falls Church VA 22042
703 280-2900

(P-15340)
NPARIO INC
350 Cambridge Ave Ste 330, Palo Alto (94306-1578)
PHONE.................................650 461-9696
Bassel Ojjeh, *CEO*
EMP: 53
SALES (est): 2.8MM **Privately Held**
SIC: 7371 Computer software systems analysis & design, custom

(P-15341)
NTENT INC
1808 Aston Ave Ste 170, Carlsbad (92008-7367)
PHONE.................................760 930-7600
Fax: 760 804-8134
Patti Stewart, *Manager*
EMP: 60
SALES (corp-wide): 11.2MM **Privately Held**
WEB: www.concera.com
SIC: 7371 Custom computer programming services
PA: Ntent, Inc.
342 W 37th St
New York NY 10018
212 967-9502

(P-15342)
NTRUST INFOTECH PRIVATE LTD
2700 N Main St Ste 300, Santa Ana (92705-6638)
PHONE.................................562 207-1610
Srikanth Ramachandran, *President*
EMP: 150
SALES (est): 4.8MM **Privately Held**
SIC: 7371 8748 Computer software development; computer software development & applications; systems analysis & engineering consulting services
PA: Ntrust Infotech Private Limited
152, 3rd Floor Ganesh Tower
Chennai TN

(P-15343)
NTS IT CARE INC
1605 S Main St Ste 125, Milpitas (95035-6270)
PHONE.................................408 480-4083
Jagsaet Sinds, *President*
EMP: 180
SALES (est): 2MM **Privately Held**
SIC: 7371 Computer software development

(P-15344)
NUANCE COMMUNICATIONS INC
1005 Hamilton Ct, Menlo Park (94025-1422)
PHONE.................................650 847-0000
Doug Neilsson, *Principal*
Doug Sharp, *Vice Pres*
Jerry Lanni, *Software Engr*
Geoffrey Myers, *Project Mgr*
Katy Hasek, *Sales Staff*
EMP: 150

SALES (corp-wide): 1.9B **Publicly Held**
WEB: www.nuance.com
SIC: 7371 Computer software development & applications
PA: Nuance Communications, Inc.
1 Wayside Rd
Burlington MA 01803
781 565-5000

(P-15345)
NUNA INCORPORATED
Also Called: Nuna Health
650 Townsend St Ste 425, San Francisco (94103-6221)
PHONE.................................650 390-7745
Jini Kim, *CEO*
David Chen, *General Mgr*
EMP: 66
SQ FT: 25,000
SALES: 5MM **Privately Held**
SIC: 7371 Custom computer programming services

(P-15346)
OBJECTIVE SYSTEMS INTEGRATORS (HQ)
Also Called: OSI
35 Iron Point Cir Ste 250, Folsom (95630-8597)
PHONE.................................916 467-1500
John Travs, *President*
Cheri Simko, *Vice Pres*
Rajveer Singh, *Administration*
Curtis Crum, *Software Dev*
Danny Ho, *Software Engr*
EMP: 50
SQ FT: 14,000
SALES (est): 26.2MM
SALES (corp-wide): 6.5MM **Privately Held**
SIC: 7371 Custom computer programming services
PA: Mycom France
6 Rue Jean Jaures
Puteaux 92800
147 730-651

(P-15347)
OBLONG INDUSTRIES INC (PA)
923 E 3rd St Ste 111, Los Angeles (90013-1867)
PHONE.................................213 683-8863
John Underkoffler, *CEO*
Mary Ann De Lares Norris, *COO*
Stewart Armstrong, *CFO*
Michael Brown, *Vice Pres*
David Kung, *Vice Pres*
EMP: 68
SALES (est): 22.7MM **Privately Held**
SIC: 7371 Computer software development & applications

(P-15348)
OKTA INC (PA)
301 Brannan St Fl 1, San Francisco (94107-3816)
PHONE.................................415 494-8029
Todd McKinnon, *CEO*
Frederic Kerrest, *COO*
Bill Losch, *CFO*
Krista Anderson, *Ch Credit Ofcr*
Bill Fitzgerald, *Vice Pres*
EMP: 134
SALES (est): 58.6MM **Privately Held**
SIC: 7371 Software programming applications

(P-15349)
OMNITEK INFORMATION SYSTEMS
24081 Lindley St, Mission Viejo (92691-3716)
PHONE.................................949 581-5895
Ashok C Dudakia, *President*
Janak Dudakia, *President*
EMP: 65
SQ FT: 2,600
SALES (est): 3.2MM **Privately Held**
WEB: www.omnitekinc.com
SIC: 7371 7375 7374 8711 Computer software development; data base information retrieval; optical scanning data service; engineering services

7371 - Custom Computer Programming Svcs County (P-15350)

(P-15350)
OMNIUPDATE INC
1320 Flynn Rd Ste 100, Camarillo (93012-8745)
PHONE.................805 484-9400
Lance Merker, *President*
Craig Weaver, *CFO*
Tom Nalevanko, *Vice Pres*
Andrew Soderberg, *Vice Pres*
Michael Adams, *Administration*
EMP: 60
SQ FT: 6,600
SALES: 10MM **Privately Held**
WEB: www.omniedit.com
SIC: 7371 7372 Computer software development; prepackaged software

(P-15351)
ONEBILL SOFTWARE INC
3080 Olcott St Ste D230, Santa Clara (95054-3271)
PHONE.................844 462-7638
Jk Chelladurai, *CEO*
Rajesh Jadhev, *Vice Pres*
Bob Maguire, *Vice Pres*
Kathy Mori, *Vice Pres*
Raj Padmanabhan, *Vice Pres*
EMP: 70
SALES (est): 4.9MM **Privately Held**
SIC: 7371 5734 Computer software development & applications; computer software & accessories

(P-15352)
OOYALA INC (DH)
4750 Patrick Henry Dr, Santa Clara (95054-1851)
PHONE.................650 961-3400
Ramesh Srinivasan, *CEO*
Jay Fulcher, *President*
David Wilson, *CFO*
Dave Hare, *Senior VP*
Scott Smith, *Senior VP*
EMP: 110
SALES (est): 124.4MM
SALES (corp-wide): 19B **Privately Held**
SIC: 7371 Software programming applications
HQ: Ooyala Holdings, Inc.
4750 Patrick Henry Dr
Santa Clara CA 95054
650 961-3400

(P-15353)
OPERATION TECHNOLOGY INC (PA)
Also Called: Etap
17 Goodyear Ste 100, Irvine (92618-1822)
PHONE.................949 462-0100
Farrokh Shokooh, *President*
Bill Wooton, *Senior VP*
Ben Boronow, *Vice Pres*
Jaykumar Desai, *Department Mgr*
Nikta Nikzad Shokooh, *Admin Sec*
EMP: 79
SQ FT: 32,000
SALES (est): 21.2MM **Privately Held**
WEB: www.etap.com
SIC: 7371 8732 8249 Computer software development; research services, except laboratory; business training services

(P-15354)
OPTIMIZELY INC (PA)
631 Howard St Ste 100, San Francisco (94105-3934)
PHONE.................415 376-4598
Dan Siroker, *CEO*
Julie Ritchie, *Senior Partner*
Wyatt Jenkins, *Vice Pres*
Kristin Brey, *Executive*
Sarah Lubecki, *Executive Asst*
EMP: 280
SQ FT: 76,000
SALES (est): 77.9MM **Privately Held**
SIC: 7371 Computer software development

(P-15355)
OPUS INSPECTION INC
1410 S Acacia Ave Ste A, Fullerton (92831-5309)
PHONE.................714 999-6727
Mike Golway, *Branch Mgr*
EMP: 55 **Privately Held**
WEB: www.esp-global.com
SIC: 7371 Computer software development
PA: Opus Inspection, Inc.
7 Kripes Rd
East Granby CT 06026

(P-15356)
ORACLE AMERICA INC
Also Called: Sun Microsystems
4220 Network Cir, Santa Clara (95054-1780)
PHONE.................408 276-4300
Mark Toliver, *President*
Aurelio G Ribeyro, *Vice Pres*
Pai Prasad, *Sr Software Eng*
Sundar Yamunachari, *Sr Software Eng*
Daniel Lord, *Info Tech Mgr*
EMP: 187
SALES (corp-wide): 37B **Publicly Held**
SIC: 7371 Custom computer programming services
HQ: Oracle America, Inc.
500 Oracle Pkwy
Redwood City CA 94065
650 506-7000

(P-15357)
ORACLE AMERICA INC
4120 Network Cir, Santa Clara (95054-1778)
PHONE.................408 276-3331
Fax: 408 329-5611
Scott G McNealy, *Ch of Bd*
Ashok Krishnamurthi, *CEO*
Karen Willem, *CFO*
Bruce Fingles, *Exec VP*
Will Rahim, *Vice Pres*
EMP: 150
SALES (est): 15MM **Privately Held**
WEB: www.xsigo.com
SIC: 7371 Custom computer programming services

(P-15358)
ORACLE SYSTEMS CORPORATION
102 Santa Barbara Ave, Daly City (94014-1045)
PHONE.................650 506-8648
EMP: 92
SALES (corp-wide): 37B **Publicly Held**
WEB: www.forcecapital.com
SIC: 7371 Computer software development
HQ: Oracle Systems Corporation
500 Oracle Pkwy
Redwood City CA 94065
650 506-7000

(P-15359)
ORACLE SYSTEMS CORPORATION
17527 Via Sereno, Monte Sereno (95030-3201)
PHONE.................650 506-4060
Russ Rutledge, *Manager*
EMP: 92
SALES (corp-wide): 37B **Publicly Held**
WEB: www.forcecapital.com
SIC: 7371 Computer software development
HQ: Oracle Systems Corporation
500 Oracle Pkwy
Redwood City CA 94065
650 506-7000

(P-15360)
ORACLE SYSTEMS CORPORATION
500 Oracle Pkwy, San Mateo (94403)
PHONE.................650 506-6780
Sayekumar Arumugam, *Principal*
Susan Prusak, *QA Dir*
Alan Iodice, *Sales Staff*
Bill Fox, *Director*
Christina Heyel, *Manager*
EMP: 108
SALES (corp-wide): 37B **Publicly Held**
WEB: www.forcecapital.com
SIC: 7371 Computer software development
HQ: Oracle Systems Corporation
500 Oracle Pkwy
Redwood City CA 94065
650 506-7000

(P-15361)
ORACLE SYSTEMS CORPORATION
2010 Main St Ste 450, Irvine (92614-7260)
PHONE.................949 224-1000
Dawn Lotez, *Manager*
EMP: 100
SALES (corp-wide): 37B **Publicly Held**
WEB: www.forcecapital.com
SIC: 7371 Computer software development
HQ: Oracle Systems Corporation
500 Oracle Pkwy
Redwood City CA 94065
650 506-7000

(P-15362)
ORIGIN SYSTEMS INC
209 Redwood Shores Pkwy, Redwood City (94065-1175)
PHONE.................650 628-1500
EMP: 270
SQ FT: 175,000
SALES (est): 9.1MM
SALES (corp-wide): 4.5B **Publicly Held**
SIC: 7371
PA: Electronic Arts Inc.
209 Redwood Shores Pkwy
Redwood City CA 94065
650 628-7272

(P-15363)
P MURPHY & ASSOCIATES INC
2301 W Olive Ave, Burbank (91506-2627)
PHONE.................818 841-2002
Fax: 818 841-0082
Phyliss Murphy, *President*
Martha Ferrer, *Vice Pres*
Frank Liggett, *VP Mktg*
EMP: 121
SQ FT: 1,200
SALES (est): 10.7MM
SALES (corp-wide): 96MM **Privately Held**
WEB: www.pmurphy.com
SIC: 7371 7361 Custom computer programming services; employment agencies; executive placement
PA: Intelliswift Software, Inc.
2201 Walnut Ave Ste 180
Fremont CA 94538
510 490-9240

(P-15364)
PACKET DESIGN INC
1 Almaden Blvd Ste 1150, San Jose (95113-2249)
PHONE.................408 490-1000
Fax: 408 562-0080
Judy Estrin, *Chairman*
Bart Kelly, *President*
Jack Bradley, *CEO*
Steve Ackley, *Exec VP*
Jeff Raice, *Exec VP*
EMP: 56
SALES (est): 5.4MM **Privately Held**
WEB: www.packetdesign.com
SIC: 7371 Computer software development

(P-15365)
PACKETVIDEO CORPORATION
1901 Avenue Of The Stars # 390, Los Angeles (90067-6001)
PHONE.................310 526-5200
James Carol, *President*
Wilson Carey, *Engineer*
EMP: 80
SALES (corp-wide): 98.6B **Publicly Held**
WEB: www.packetvideo.com
SIC: 7371 Computer software development
HQ: Packetvideo Corporation
10350 Science Center Dr
San Diego CA 92121
858 731-5300

(P-15366)
PACKETVIDEO CORPORATION (DH)
10350 Science Center Dr, San Diego (92121-1129)
PHONE.................858 731-5300
Fax: 858 731-5301
James C Brailean, *CEO*

John Driver, *Chief Mktg Ofcr*
Corbett Kull, *Vice Pres*
Kazunori Takagi, *Vice Pres*
Jouni Leinonen, *Executive*
EMP: 100 **EST:** 1998
SQ FT: 22,000
SALES (est): 25MM
SALES (corp-wide): 98.6B **Privately Held**
WEB: www.packetvideo.com
SIC: 7371 7374 4812 Computer software development; data processing & preparation; radio telephone communication
HQ: Ntt Docomo, Inc.
2-11-1, Nagatacho
Chiyoda-Ku TKY 100-0
351 561-111

(P-15367)
PALANTIR TECHNOLOGIES INC (PA)
100 Hamilton Ave Ste 300, Palo Alto (94301-1651)
PHONE.................650 815-0200
Alex Karp, *President*
Jonty Kelt, *Executive*
Eric Poirier, *Business Dir*
Lori Baylor, *Administration*
Kristina Huey, *Administration*
EMP: 148
SQ FT: 65,000
SALES (est): 555.9MM **Privately Held**
WEB: www.palantirtech.com
SIC: 7371 Computer software development

(P-15368)
PALANTIR USG INC
635 Waverley St, Palo Alto (94301-2550)
PHONE.................650 815-0240
Akash Jain, *President*
Lori Baylor, *Administration*
EMP: 190
SQ FT: 4,000
SALES: 3MM **Privately Held**
SIC: 7371 Computer software development

(P-15369)
PANASAS INC (PA)
969 W Maude Ave, Sunnyvale (94085-2802)
PHONE.................408 215-6800
Fax: 408 215-6801
Faye Pairman, *President*
Tom Shea, *COO*
Stephanie Vinella, *CFO*
Jim Donovan, *Chief Mktg Ofcr*
Barbara Murphy, *Chief Mktg Ofcr*
EMP: 100
SQ FT: 20,000
SALES (est): 38.2MM **Privately Held**
WEB: www.panasas.com
SIC: 7371 Computer software development

(P-15370)
PATIENTSAFE SOLUTIONS INC (PA)
5375 Mira Sorrento Pl, San Diego (92121-3809)
PHONE.................858 746-3100
Si Luo, *President*
Mark Young, *COO*
Balaji Sekar, *CFO*
Peter Longo, *Officer*
Cheryl D Parker, *Officer*
EMP: 83
SALES (est): 28MM **Privately Held**
WEB: www.patientsafesolutions.com
SIC: 7371 Software programming applications

(P-15371)
PATTERSON DENTAL SUPPLY INC
Also Called: Dolphin Imaging MGT Solutions
9200 Eton Ave, Chatsworth (91311-5807)
PHONE.................818 435-1368
Sonya Lester, *Branch Mgr*
Michael Quick, *CIO*
Joseph Bautista, *Tech/Comp Coord*
Linda Homel, *Sales Staff*
Joanna Tavanlar, *Manager*
EMP: 50

PRODUCTS & SERVICES SECTION

7371 - Custom Computer Programming Svcs County (P-15392)

SALES (corp-wide): 4.3B Publicly Held
SIC: 7371 Computer software development & applications; computer software development
HQ: Patterson Dental Supply, Inc.
1031 Mendota Heights Rd
Saint Paul MN 55120
651 686-1600

(P-15372)
PEOPLEFLUENT INC
201 N Calle Cesar Chavez # 100, Santa Barbara (93103-3256)
PHONE..................805 730-1450
Fax: 805 730-1453
Charles S Jones, President
Karen Badger, Executive
EMP: 60
SALES (corp-wide): 7.6MM Privately Held
SIC: 7371 Computer software development
HQ: Peoplefluent Inc.
300 5th Ave Ste 4
Waltham MA 02451
781 530-2000

(P-15373)
PEPPERJAM LLC
Also Called: Adassured
408 Cassidy St Ste 101, Oceanside (92054-5316)
PHONE..................760 585-7150
EMP: 166
SALES (corp-wide): 5.7MM Privately Held
SIC: 7371 Computer software development & applications
PA: Pepperjam Llc
7 S Main St
Wilkes Barre PA 18701
877 796-5700

(P-15374)
PERFICIENT INC
2000 Alameda De Las Pulga, San Mateo (94403-1269)
PHONE..................877 654-0033
Alex Sefanov, General Mgr
EMP: 69
SALES (corp-wide): 473.6MM Publicly Held
SIC: 7371 Computer software development
PA: Perficient, Inc.
555 Maryville Univ Dr 6
Saint Louis MO 63141
314 529-3600

(P-15375)
PERNIXDATA INC
1745 Tech Dr Ste 800, San Jose (95110)
PHONE..................408 724-8413
Poojan Kumar, CEO
Kristin Carnes, Vice Pres
Mike Munoz, Risk Mgmt Dir
Satyam Vaghani, CIO
Eric Cohen, CTO
EMP: 75
SALES (est): 14.3MM Publicly Held
SIC: 7371 Computer software development & applications
PA: Nutanix, Inc.
1740 Tech Dr Ste 150
San Jose CA 95110

(P-15376)
PERSISTENT SYSTEMS INC (HQ)
2055 Laurelwood Rd # 210, Santa Clara (95054-2729)
PHONE..................408 216-7010
Fax: 408 451-9177
Anand Despande, CEO
Mritunjay Singh, President
Neeraj Sinha, President
Raj Sirohi, President
Rohit Kamat, CFO
EMP: 65
SALES (est): 59.6MM
SALES (corp-wide): 213.7MM Privately Held
WEB: www.persistentsystems.com
SIC: 7371 Computer software development

PA: Persistent Systems Limited
No-402 Bhageerath
Pune MH 41101
206 703-4542

(P-15377)
PETZ ENTERPRISES INC (PA)
Also Called: P E I
7575 W Linne Rd, Tracy (95304-9290)
P.O. Box 611 (95378-0611)
PHONE..................209 835-1360
Fax: 209 835-2758
Leroy E Petz Sr, President
Charles W Petz, Treasurer
Reynold F Sbrilli, Officer
Leroy E Petz Jr, Vice Pres
Elizabeth Early, Office Admin
EMP: 88
SALES (est): 23.6MM Privately Held
WEB: www.petzent.com
SIC: 7371 Software programming applications; computer software development & applications; computer software development

(P-15378)
PHACIL INC
601 California St # 1710, San Francisco (94108-2822)
PHONE..................415 901-1600
Fax: 415 366-2900
Sascha Mornell, Principal
EMP: 550
SALES (corp-wide): 121.7MM Privately Held
WEB: www.phacil.com
SIC: 7371 Custom computer programming services
PA: Phacil, Inc.
800 N Glebe Rd Ste 700
Arlington VA 22203
703 526-1800

(P-15379)
PHILIPS HLTHCARE INFRMTICS INC (HQ)
4100 E 3rd Ave Ste 101, Foster City (94404-4819)
PHONE..................650 293-2300
Deborah Disanzo, CEO
Davidi Gilo, Ch of Bd
Oran Muduroglu, President
Tim Kleckner, CFO
Douglas Sinclair, CFO
EMP: 146
SQ FT: 31,523
SALES (est): 68.9MM
SALES (corp-wide): 26B Privately Held
WEB: www.stentor.com
SIC: 7371 Computer software development & applications
PA: Koninklijke Philips N.V.
High Tech Campus 5
Eindhoven 5656
402 791-111

(P-15380)
PHILOTIC INC
524 3rd St, San Francisco (94107-1805)
PHONE..................510 730-1740
Jimmy Kittiyachavalit, Mng Member
EMP: 62
SALES (est): 4MM Privately Held
SIC: 7371 Custom computer programming services

(P-15381)
PIVOT SYSTEMS INC
4320 Stevens Creek Blvd, San Jose (95129-1202)
PHONE..................408 435-1000
Rajesh Nair, CEO
Smita Nair, Admin Sec
Sajin Mathew, Manager
EMP: 160
SQ FT: 40,000
SALES (est): 10.9MM Privately Held
WEB: www.pivotsys.com
SIC: 7371 Computer software development & applications

(P-15382)
PIVOTAL SOFTWARE INC (DH)
3495 Deer Creek Rd, Palo Alto (94304-1316)
PHONE..................650 846-1600

Paul Maritz, CEO
Suhail Ansari, President
Bill Cook, COO
Rob Mee, Senior VP
Jeff Nick, Senior VP
EMP: 97
SALES (est): 57.6MM
SALES (corp-wide): 72.7B Publicly Held
SIC: 7371 3572 3577 Custom computer programming services; computer storage devices; computer peripheral equipment
HQ: Emc Corporation
176 South St
Hopkinton MA 01748
508 435-1000

(P-15383)
PIVOTCLOUD INC
1230 Midas Way Ste 210, Sunnyvale (94085-4068)
P.O. Box 620094, Redwood City (94062-0094)
PHONE..................408 475-6090
Richard Gorman, CEO
Lorne Boden, Vice Pres
EMP: 50 EST: 2011
SALES (est): 2MM Privately Held
SIC: 7371 Computer software development & applications

(P-15384)
PIXELMAGS INC
1800 Century Park E # 600, Los Angeles (90067-1508)
PHONE..................310 598-7303
Mark Stubbs, CEO
Ryan Marquis, COO
Philip Lunn, Chairman
Claudia Jinkins, Executive Asst
Benjamin Miller, CTO
EMP: 70
SQ FT: 5,425
SALES: 48MM Privately Held
WEB: www.pixelmags.com
SIC: 7371 Software programming applications

(P-15385)
PLAYHAVEN LLC
1447 2nd St Ste 200, Santa Monica (90401-3404)
PHONE..................310 308-9668
Mike Jones, President
Tom Dare, Treasurer
Greg Gilman, Admin Sec
EMP: 59 EST: 2014
SQ FT: 15,000
SALES (est): 704K
SALES (corp-wide): 53.1MM Privately Held
SIC: 7371 7311 Computer software development & applications; advertising agencies
PA: Rockyou, Inc.
303 2nd St Ste S600
San Francisco CA 94107
415 580-6400

(P-15386)
PLAYPHONE INC (PA)
345 S B St Fl 2, San Mateo (94401-4019)
PHONE..................408 261-6200
Takahito Yasuki, Chairman
Ron Czerny, CEO
Andrew Page, CFO
Bhaskar Roy,
Richard Hancock, Officer
EMP: 54
SQ FT: 3,000
SALES (est): 15.1MM Privately Held
WEB: www.playphone.com
SIC: 7371 Computer software development & applications

(P-15387)
POINT OF VIEW INC
947 N Del Sol Ln, Diamond Bar (91765-1108)
PHONE..................909 860-0705
Chris Warner, President
Mark Nausha, Vice Pres
Michael Terlecki, Vice Pres
Vince Lee, Info Tech Dir
EMP: 54
SQ FT: 10,000

SALES (est): 6.2MM Privately Held
WEB: www.pov-inc.com
SIC: 7371 Computer software development

(P-15388)
POLARIS NETWORKS INCORPORATED
14856 Holden Way, San Jose (95124-4515)
PHONE..................408 625-7273
Buddhadeb Biswas, CEO
Paramita Saha, Admin Asst
Arindam Ghosh, Sr Software Eng
Namrata Palit, Sr Software Eng
Dhiman Dhar, Software Engr
EMP: 70
SQ FT: 2,000
SALES: 2MM Privately Held
SIC: 7371 Computer software development & applications

(P-15389)
POLARIS WIRELESS INC
301 N Whisman Rd, Mountain View (94043-3969)
PHONE..................408 492-8900
Manlio Allegra, President
Victor C Chun, CFO
Victor Hwang, Principal
Don Weigel, Exec Dir
Jahan Ahmadifard, QA Dir
EMP: 50
SALES (est): 9MM Privately Held
WEB: www.polariswireless.com
SIC: 7371 8711 Computer software development; engineering services

(P-15390)
POLEXIS INC
4820 Eastgate Mall, San Diego (92121-1993)
PHONE..................858 812-7300
Eric M Demarco, President
Deanna H Lund, CFO
Laura L Siegal, Treasurer
Michael W Fink, Vice Pres
Deborah Butera, Admin Sec
EMP: 55
SQ FT: 20,000
SALES (est): 2.9MM
SALES (corp-wide): 657.1MM Publicly Held
WEB: www.polexis.com
SIC: 7371 8742 Computer software development; management consulting services
HQ: Kratos Technology & Training Solutions, Inc.
4820 Estgate Mall Ste 200
San Diego CA 92121
858 812-7300

(P-15391)
POLTEX COMPANY INC
Also Called: Interpoltex
14748 Wild Colt Pl, Jamul (91935-2121)
PHONE..................619 669-1846
Andy Denysiak, President
Andy Novak, Vice Pres
EMP: 96
SALES: 6.8MM Privately Held
SIC: 7371 Computer software development

(P-15392)
POWERREVIEWS OC LLC
180 Montgomery St # 1800, San Francisco (94104-4205)
PHONE..................415 315-9208
Ken Comee, President
Matt Parsons, Vice Pres
Cathy Halligan,
Rosanne Massimino,
Sheila Doolittle, Director
EMP: 95
SALES: 6.1MM
SALES (corp-wide): 9.5MM Privately Held
WEB: www.powerreviews.com
SIC: 7371 Computer software development
PA: Powerreviews, Inc.
180 N Lasalle St Fl 5
Chicago IL 60601
312 447-6100

7371 - Custom Computer Programming Svcs County (P-15393)

(P-15393)
PRACTICE FUSION INC (PA)
Also Called: Ringadoc
731 Market St Ste 400, San Francisco (94103-2009)
PHONE 415 346-7700
Tom Langan, *CEO*
Joe Priest, *Partner*
Lisa Bari, *President*
Steve Filler, *COO*
Robert Park, *CFO*
▲ **EMP:** 120
SALES (est): 58.4MM **Privately Held**
WEB: www.practicefusion.com
SIC: 7371 Computer software development

(P-15394)
PRN LLC (HQ)
600 Montgomery St Fl 18, San Francisco (94111-2720)
PHONE 415 805-2525
Fax: 415 808-3535
Kevin Carbone, *CEO*
Jonathan Rosen, *Senior VP*
Chuck Billups, *Vice Pres*
Chip Hansel, *Vice Pres*
Katie Harless, *Vice Pres*
EMP: 51
SQ FT: 46,000
SALES: 12MM
SALES (corp-wide): 111MM **Privately Held**
SIC: 7371 Computer software development & applications
PA: Stratacache, Inc.
2 Emmet St Ste 200
Dayton OH 45405
937 224-0485

(P-15395)
PROCERA NETWORKS INC (HQ)
47448 Fremont Blvd, Fremont (94538-6503)
PHONE 510 230-2777
Fax: 510 656-1355
Lyndon Cantor, *CEO*
Andrew Kowal, *President*
Charles Constanti, *CFO*
Andy Lovit, *Senior VP*
Debra Machado, *Vice Pres*
EMP: 78
SQ FT: 18,000
SALES (est): 61MM **Privately Held**
WEB: www.proceranetworks.com
SIC: 7371 7372 Custom computer programming services; prepackaged software
PA: Kdr Holding, Inc.
47448 Fremont Blvd
Fremont CA 94538
510 230-2777

(P-15396)
PROCESSWEAVER INC
5201 Great America Pkwy # 300, Santa Clara (95054-1140)
PHONE 888 932-8373
Kumar Vidadala, *CEO*
Ramya Gowda, *Programmer Anys*
Process Weaver, *Human Resources*
Bhargav Chiranjeevi, *Manager*
EMP: 92
SALES: 9.1MM **Privately Held**
SIC: 7371 Computer software development

(P-15397)
PROCORE TECHNOLOGIES INC
6309 Carpinteria Ave # 100, Carpinteria (93013-2931)
PHONE 866 477-6267
Craig F Courtemanche Jr, *CEO*
Steve Zahm, *President*
Robert Reed, *CFO*
Matthew Reid, *Chief Mktg Ofcr*
Matt Brinza, *Software Engr*
EMP: 450
SALES: 23.7MM **Privately Held**
SIC: 7371 Computer software development

(P-15398)
PROLIFICS TESTING INC
4637 Chabot Dr Ste 210, Pleasanton (94588-2805)
PHONE 925 485-9535
Danis Yadegar, *President*
Dick O'Donnell, *Bd of Directors*
Claude Fenner, *Vice Pres*
Dale Lampson, *Vice Pres*
Rutesh Shah, *Vice Pres*
EMP: 60
SQ FT: 6,500
SALES (est): 6MM
SALES (corp-wide): 23.5MM **Privately Held**
SIC: 7371 7372 Custom computer programming services; prepackaged software
HQ: Prolifics Application Services, Inc.
24025 Park Sorrento # 405
Calabasas CA 91302
646 201-4967

(P-15399)
PROOFPOINT INC (PA)
892 Ross Dr, Sunnyvale (94089-1443)
PHONE 408 517-4710
Fax: 408 517-4711
Gary Steele, *CEO*
Eric Hahn, *Ch of Bd*
Paul Auvil, *CFO*
David Knight, *Exec VP*
Tracey Newell, *Exec VP*
EMP: 148
SQ FT: 95,557
SALES: 265.4MM **Publicly Held**
WEB: www.proofpoint.com
SIC: 7371 Custom computer programming services; computer software systems analysis & design, custom; computer software development & applications

(P-15400)
PSI FIRE
820 Eschenburg Dr, Gilroy (95020-5613)
PHONE 408 842-9308
Thomas Strickland, *Partner*
EMP: 50
SALES (est): 2.6MM **Privately Held**
WEB: www.psifire.com
SIC: 7371 Computer software development

(P-15401)
PTC INC
Also Called: P T C
2550 N 1st St Ste 500, San Jose (95131-1038)
PHONE 408 434-8500
David Reeves, *Vice Pres*
Lieberman Allen, *IT/INT Sup*
Steven Payne, *Advisor*
EMP: 50
SALES (corp-wide): 1.2B **Publicly Held**
WEB: www.ptc.com
SIC: 7371 Computer software development
PA: Ptc Inc.
140 Kendrick St
Needham MA 02494
781 370-5000

(P-15402)
PUBLIC BELL INC
9755 Garden Grove Blvd, Garden Grove (92844-1693)
PHONE 818 396-1675
Nelson Rasiah, *CTO*
EMP: 60
SALES (est): 891.1K **Privately Held**
SIC: 7371 Computer software development & applications

(P-15403)
PULSE SECURE LLC (HQ)
2700 Zanker Rd Ste 200, San Jose (95134-2140)
PHONE 408 372-9600
Sudhakar Ramakrishna, *CEO*
Doug Erickson, *Partner*
Jeffrey C Key, *CFO*
David Goldschlag, *Senior VP*
Jeff Green, *Senior VP*
EMP: 85 **EST:** 2014

PRODUCTS & SERVICES SECTION

SALES (est): 33.8MM
SALES (corp-wide): 600.8MM **Privately Held**
SIC: 7371 4899 Computer software development & applications; communication signal enhancement network system
PA: Siris Capital Group, Llc
601 Lexington Ave Rm 5901
New York NY 10022
212 231-0095

(P-15404)
QUALYS INC (PA)
1600 Bridge Pkwy Ste 201, Redwood City (94065-6127)
PHONE 650 801-6100
Fax: 650 801-6101
Philippe F Courtot, *Ch of Bd*
Melissa B Fisher, *CFO*
Sumedh S Thakar, *Vice Pres*
Amer S Deeba, *Vice Pres*
Bruce K Posey, *Vice Pres*
EMP: 148
SQ FT: 50,000
SALES: 164.2MM **Publicly Held**
WEB: www.qualys.com
SIC: 7371 7372 Custom computer programming services; software programming applications; prepackaged software

(P-15405)
RADIANT LOGIC INC (PA)
75 Rowland Way Ste 300, Novato (94945-5060)
PHONE 415 892-7085
Fax: 415 892-7085
Michel Prompt, *President*
Claude Samuelson, *Vice Pres*
Sergiy Alymov, *Software Dev*
Joseph Caplan, *Software Dev*
Nicolas Guyot, *Software Dev*
EMP: 54 **EST:** 1995
SQ FT: 10,718
SALES (est): 11.9MM **Privately Held**
WEB: www.radiantlogic.com
SIC: 7371 Computer software development

(P-15406)
RAICO INC
Also Called: Qasource
73 Ray St, Pleasanton (94566-6643)
PHONE 925 271-5555
Rajeev Rai, *CEO*
Sonia Singh, *CFO*
Nitin Singh, *Business Dir*
Joann Gira, *Executive Asst*
Sumit Jaitly, *Manager*
EMP: 175
SQ FT: 6,900
SALES (est): 12.3MM **Privately Held**
WEB: www.qasource.com
SIC: 7371 Computer software development

(P-15407)
RAINTREE SYSTEMS INC
27307 Via Industria, Temecula (92590-3699)
PHONE 951 252-9400
Richard V Welty, *CEO*
Terrence Sims, *COO*
Yvonne Long, *Office Mgr*
Grace Rodriguez, *Executive Asst*
Justin Buck, *Technology*
EMP: 58
SQ FT: 4,500
SALES (est): 8.2MM **Privately Held**
SIC: 7371 5045 5734 Computer software development; computer software; computer & software stores

(P-15408)
RAPID SOLUTIONS CONSULTING LLC
1900 S Norfolk St Ste 350, San Mateo (94403-1171)
PHONE 801 755-7828
Philip Martin, *CEO*
Mark Israelsen, *Vice Pres*
EMP: 50
SQ FT: 6,500
SALES (est): 1MM **Privately Held**
SIC: 7371 Computer software development & applications

(P-15409)
RAY A MORGAN COMPANY
7042 Commerce Cir Ste A, Pleasanton (94588-8019)
PHONE 925 400-4160
Jim Scarff, *Branch Mgr*
EMP: 60
SALES (corp-wide): 78.6MM **Privately Held**
SIC: 7371 Computer software development & applications
PA: Ray A. Morgan Company
3131 Esplanade
Chico CA 95973
530 343-6065

(P-15410)
REAL-TIME INNOVATIONS INC
Also Called: R T I
232 E Java Dr, Sunnyvale (94089-1318)
PHONE 408 990-7400
Stanley Aaron Schneider, *President*
Supreet Oberoi, *President*
Jody Schneider, *CFO*
Mekler Catherine, *Vice Pres*
Robert Kindel, *Vice Pres*
EMP: 90
SQ FT: 1,000
SALES (est): 12MM **Privately Held**
WEB: www.scopetools.com
SIC: 7371 7379 Computer software development; computer related consulting services

(P-15411)
RED CONDOR INC
1300 Valley House Dr # 115, Rohnert Park (94928-4930)
PHONE 707 569-7419
Ron Longo, *President*
Christy Kenyon, *Marketing Mgr*
Kathy Gegx, *Manager*
EMP: 60
SALES (est): 4.3MM **Privately Held**
WEB: www.redcondor.com
SIC: 7371 Custom computer programming services

(P-15412)
REDIS LABS INC
700 E El Camino Real # 170, Mountain View (94040-2805)
PHONE 415 930-9666
Ofer Bengal, *CEO*
Manish Gupta, *Chief Mktg Ofcr*
Jason Forget, *Risk Mgmt Dir*
Yiftach Shoolman, *CTO*
Regev Yativ, *VP Sales*
EMP: 51
SALES (est): 166.3K **Privately Held**
SIC: 7371 Computer software development & applications

(P-15413)
RELTIO INC
100 Marine Pkwy Ste 275, Redwood City (94065-5234)
PHONE 855 360-3282
Manish Sood, *CEO*
Bob More, *Senior VP*
Gary Ryan, *Vice Pres*
Vasu Vallurupalli, *Vice Pres*
Gary Wong, *Vice Pres*
EMP: 120
SQ FT: 900
SALES: 3MM **Privately Held**
WEB: www.reltio.com
SIC: 7371 Custom computer programming services

(P-15414)
RENOVATE AMERICA INC
Also Called: Hero
15073 Ave Of Science # 200, San Diego (92128-3453)
PHONE 858 605-5333
John Paul McNeill, *CEO*
Thomas Hemmings, *CFO*
Howard Green, *Vice Pres*
Mark Rodgers, *Vice Pres*
Bashiri Cooper, *Program Mgr*
EMP: 119
SQ FT: 23,500

PRODUCTS & SERVICES SECTION
7371 - Custom Computer Programming Svcs County (P-15436)

SALES (est): 26.7MM **Privately Held**
SIC: **7371** 8742 Computer software development & applications; banking & finance consultant

(P-15415)
RESOLVE SYSTEMS LLC (PA)
2302 Martin Ste 300, Irvine (92612-1496)
PHONE..................................949 325-0120
Casey Kindiger,
Erika Reinert, *CTO*
Thomas Daniel, *Technology*
Sean Ryan, *Technology*
Jasjit Singh, *Engineer*
EMP: 65
SQ FT: 6,000
SALES (est): 9.1MM **Privately Held**
WEB: www.generationetech.com
SIC: **7371** Computer software development & applications

(P-15416)
RESONATE INC (PA)
16360 Monterey St Ste 260, Morgan Hill (95037-5496)
PHONE..................................408 545-5500
Peter R Watkins, *Ch of Bd*
Richard Hornstein, *CFO*
Christopher Marino, *Founder*
Stanley L Chin, *Vice Pres*
David R Guecio, *Vice Pres*
EMP: 160
SQ FT: 38,000
SALES (est): 11.6MM **Privately Held**
SIC: **7371** 7372 Custom computer programming services; business oriented computer software

(P-15417)
RESPONSYS INC (DH)
Also Called: Responsys.com
1100 Grundy Ln Ste 300, San Bruno (94066-3066)
PHONE..................................650 745-1700
Fax: 650 745-1701
Daniel D Springer, *CEO*
Christian A Paul, *CFO*
Scott V Olrich, *Chief Mktg Ofcr*
Julian Ong, *Senior VP*
Michael Della Penna, *Senior VP*
EMP: 148
SQ FT: 72,000
SALES: 103MM
SALES (corp-wide): 37B **Publicly Held**
WEB: www.responsys.com
SIC: **7371** 7372 Computer software development; business oriented computer software
HQ: Oc Acquisition Llc
500 Oracle Pkwy
Redwood City CA 94065
650 506-7000

(P-15418)
RESTAURANT IN A BOX LLC
3191 Red Hill Ave, Costa Mesa (92626-3451)
PHONE..................................800 676-1281
Mitesh Gala, *CEO*
EMP: 50
SQ FT: 24,000
SALES (est): 1.2MM **Privately Held**
SIC: **7371** Computer software development & applications

(P-15419)
RETAIL PRO INTERNATIONAL LLC
Also Called: Retail Pro Software
400 Plaza Dr Ste 200, Folsom (95630-4746)
PHONE..................................916 605-7200
Kerry Lemos, *CEO*
William Colley, *Senior VP*
Shaff Kassam, *Vice Pres*
Richard Kolodynski, *Vice Pres*
Peter Latona, *Vice Pres*
EMP: 70
SQ FT: 7,500
SALES (est): 14MM **Privately Held**
WEB: www.retailpro.com
SIC: **7371** 7372 Computer software development; prepackaged software

(P-15420)
RETAILNEXT INC (PA)
60 S Market St Ste 1000, San Jose (95113-2336)
PHONE..................................408 884-2162
Alexei Agratchev, *CEO*
Michael Manlapas, *President*
Kenton D Chow, *COO*
David Tognotti, *COO*
Marc Dietz, *Chief Mktg Ofcr*
EMP: 94
SQ FT: 12,000
SALES (est): 60.3MM **Privately Held**
SIC: **7371** Computer software development & applications

(P-15421)
RHYTHMONE LLC
800 W El Camino Real, Mountain View (94040-2567)
PHONE..................................650 961-9024
EMP: 70
SALES (corp-wide): 214.9MM **Privately Held**
SIC: **7371**
HQ: Rhythmone, Llc
1 Market St Ste 1810
San Francisco CA 94105
415 655-1450

(P-15422)
RICOH USA INC
Also Called: Data-Image Systems
3046 Prospect Park Dr # 100, Rancho Cordova (95670-6356)
PHONE..................................916 638-3333
Fax: 916 630-0909
Merlin Shoemaker, *CEO*
Jack Fisher, *General Mgr*
EMP: 75
SALES (corp-wide): 18.8B **Privately Held**
WEB: www.ikon.com
SIC: **7371** Computer software development & applications
HQ: Ricoh Usa, Inc.
70 Valley Stream Pkwy
Malvern PA 19355
610 296-8000

(P-15423)
RIGHTSCALE INC
402 E Gutierrez St, Santa Barbara (93101-1709)
PHONE..................................805 500-4164
Michael Crandel, *President*
Josh Fraser, *President*
Kane Ida, *CFO*
Ida Kane, *CFO*
Betsy Zikakis, *Vice Pres*
EMP: 112 EST: 2007
SALES (est): 22.2MM **Privately Held**
SIC: **7371** Custom computer programming services

(P-15424)
RIOSOFT HOLDINGS INC
Also Called: Rio Seo
9255 Towne Centre Dr, San Diego (92121-3033)
PHONE..................................858 529-5005
Dema Zlotin, *CEO*
Bill Connard, *Vice Pres*
Amanda Hill, *Marketing Staff*
Sarah Phillips, *Marketing Staff*
Tom Lynch, *Account Dir*
EMP: 50 EST: 2012
SALES (est): 114.7K **Privately Held**
SIC: **7371** Computer software development & applications

(P-15425)
RIOT GAMES INC (DH)
12333 W Olympic Blvd, Los Angeles (90064-1021)
PHONE..................................310 828-7953
Brandon Beck, *CEO*
Mark Marrill, *President*
A Dyoan Jadeja, *CFO*
Dustin Beck, *Vice Pres*
Sean Bender, *Vice Pres*
EMP: 148 EST: 2006
SALES (est): 542.9MM **Privately Held**
SIC: **7371** 7993 Custom computer programming services; video game arcade

HQ: Tencent Holdings Limited
29/F Three Pacific Place
Wan Chai HK
314 851-00

(P-15426)
ROBERT BOSCH HEALTHCARE
2400 Geng Rd Ste 200, Palo Alto (94303-3350)
PHONE..................................650 690-9100
Fax: 650 798-3770
Jasper Zu Putlitz, *President*
Klaus Bachmann, *CFO*
Laura Papenhagen, *Officer*
Heiko Kuehne, *Vice Pres*
Larry Stevens, *Vice Pres*
EMP: 138
SQ FT: 25,000
SALES (est): 27.4MM
SALES (corp-wide): 268.9MM **Privately Held**
WEB: www.boschservice.com
SIC: **7371** Computer software development
HQ: Robert Bosch Llc
2800 S 25th Ave
Broadview IL 60155
248 876-1000

(P-15427)
ROBERT BOSCH START-UP PLATF
Also Called: Mayfield Robotics
400 Convention Way, Redwood City (94063-1445)
PHONE..................................248 876-6430
Michael Beebe, *Mng Member*
EMP: 50 EST: 2015
SALES (est): 772K
SALES (corp-wide): 10.8B **Privately Held**
SIC: **7371** Computer software development & applications
PA: Robert Bosch North America Holding Corporation
38 Thousand Hills Tech Dr
Farmington Hills MI
-

(P-15428)
ROBOCA TECHNOLOGY
245 E Main St Ste 115, Alhambra (91801-7507)
PHONE..................................561 501-3999
Yang Xiaoyan, *Owner*
EMP: 200
SALES: 20MM **Privately Held**
SIC: **7371** Computer software development & applications

(P-15429)
ROSE INTERNATIONAL INC
450 N Brand Blvd Fl 6, Glendale (91203-2349)
PHONE..................................636 812-4000
EMP: 151
SALES (corp-wide): 293.5MM **Privately Held**
SIC: **7371** 8748 Computer software development; systems engineering consultant, ex. computer or professional
PA: Rose International, Inc.
16401 Swingley Ridge Rd
Chesterfield MO 63017
636 812-4000

(P-15430)
ROVI CORPORATION
Also Called: Macrovision
150 Menard Dr, San Jose (95138-1907)
PHONE..................................408 445-8100
John Ryan, *Branch Mgr*
EMP: 70
SALES (corp-wide): 526.2MM **Privately Held**
WEB: www.macrovision.com
SIC: **7371** Computer software development
PA: Rovi Corporation
2 Circle Star Way
San Carlos CA 94070
408 562-8400

(P-15431)
RSA SECURITY LLC
Also Called: R S A Laboratories
2831 Mission College Blvd, Santa Clara (95054-1838)
PHONE..................................650 529-9992
Carl Miller, *Branch Mgr*
C V Chang, *President*
James M Horn, *Principal*
EMP: 200
SALES (corp-wide): 72.7B **Publicly Held**
SIC: **7371** Computer software development
HQ: Rsa Security Llc
174 Middlesex Tpke
Bedford MA 01730
781 515-5000

(P-15432)
SAAB SENSIS CORPORATION
1700 Dell Ave, Campbell (95008-6902)
PHONE..................................315 445-0550
Doug Sweet, *Director*
Mike Gerry, *Vice Pres*
Dave Bordonaro, *Program Mgr*
Paul Ciciriello, *Program Mgr*
Sarah Fitzgerald, *Program Mgr*
EMP: 99
SALES (corp-wide): 3.1B **Privately Held**
SIC: **7371** 8711 Computer software development; consulting engineer
HQ: Saab Sensis Corporation
85 Collamer Crossings
East Syracuse NY 13057
315 445-0550

(P-15433)
SAAMA TECHNOLOGIES INC (PA)
900 E Hamilton Ave, Campbell (95008-0664)
PHONE..................................408 371-1900
Fax: 408 371-1901
Suresh Katta, *President*
Ken Coleman, *Ch of Bd*
Simon Ho, *CFO*
Scott Kleinberg, *CFO*
Rajeev Dadia, *Officer*
EMP: 237
SQ FT: 10,000
SALES (est): 81.9MM **Privately Held**
SIC: **7371** Computer software development & applications

(P-15434)
SAMBREEL SERVICES LLC
5857 Owens Ave Ste 300, Carlsbad (92008-5507)
PHONE..................................760 266-5090
Kai Hankinson, *CEO*
Shawn E Bridgeman, *President*
EMP: 50
SALES (est): 6MM **Privately Held**
WEB: www.finialservices.com
SIC: **7371** Computer software development

(P-15435)
SAMSUNG SDS AMERICA INC
1732 N 1st St Ste 100, San Jose (95112-4543)
PHONE..................................408 638-8800
Jh Kim, *Manager*
Jaedoo Lee, *Project Mgr*
David Park, *Marketing Staff*
Kevin Gould, *Counsel*
Youngrak Cho, *Senior Mgr*
EMP: 72
SALES (corp-wide): 4.2B **Privately Held**
SIC: **7371** Computer software development
HQ: Samsung Sds America, Inc.
100 Challenger Rd
Ridgefield Park NJ 07660
201 229-4456

(P-15436)
SANZARU GAMES INC
1065 E Hillsdale Blvd, Foster City (94404-1613)
PHONE..................................650 312-1000
Glen Egan, *President*
Judah Baron, *Principal*
Martin Gerarro, *Principal*
Dave Grace, *Principal*
Paul Murray, *Principal*

7371 - Custom Computer Programming Svcs County (P-15437)   PRODUDUCTS & SERVICES SECTION

EMP: 50 EST: 2006
SALES (est): 4.7MM **Privately Held**
SIC: 7371 Computer software development

(P-15437)
SAP AMERICA INC
2121 Palomar Airport Rd # 350, Carlsbad (92011-1449)
PHONE..................760 603-8034
EMP: 136
SALES (corp-wide): 22.3B **Privately Held**
SIC: 7371 Computer software development
HQ: Sap America, Inc.
3999 West Chester Pike
Newtown Square PA 19073
610 661-1000

(P-15438)
SAP LABS LLC
3475 Deer Creek Rd, Palo Alto (94304-1316)
PHONE..................650 849-4129
Fax: 650 849-4200
Ben Frommherz, *Manager*
Renu Raman, *Vice Pres*
Jon Reeves, *Vice Pres*
Peggy Gallar, *Admin Asst*
Jedd Go, *Administration*
EMP: 53
SALES (corp-wide): 22.3B **Privately Held**
SIC: 7371 Computer software development & applications
HQ: Sap Labs, Llc
3410 Hillview Ave
Palo Alto CA 94304
-

(P-15439)
SAP LABS LLC (DH)
3410 Hillview Ave, Palo Alto (94304-1395)
PHONE..................650 849-4000
Fax: 650 849-4240
Heinz Roggenkemper,
Gaurav Tewari, *Officer*
Kevin Diestel, *Vice Pres*
Joy Hirayama, *Vice Pres*
David Hu, *Vice Pres*
◆ EMP: 300
SQ FT: 200,000
SALES (est): 46MM
SALES (corp-wide): 22.3B **Privately Held**
WEB: www.saplabs.com
SIC: 7371 Computer software development & applications
HQ: Sap America, Inc.
3999 West Chester Pike
Newtown Square PA 19073
610 661-1000

(P-15440)
SAT CORPORATION (DH)
3200 Patrick Henry Dr # 150, Santa Clara (95054-1875)
PHONE..................402 208-9200
Fax: 408 530-1030
Eric Demarco, *CEO*
Deanna Lund, *CEO*
Laura Siegal, *Treasurer*
Michael Fink, *Vice Pres*
Deborah Butera, *Admin Sec*
EMP: 65
SQ FT: 15,000
SALES (est): 13.6MM
SALES (corp-wide): 657.1MM **Publicly Held**
WEB: www.sat.com
SIC: 7371 Computer software development
HQ: Integral Systems, Inc.
4820 Estgate Mall Ste 200
San Diego CA 92121
443 539-5330

(P-15441)
SATMETRIX SYSTEMS INC (PA)
3 Twin Dolphin Dr Ste 225, Redwood City (94065-1514)
PHONE..................650 227-8300
Fax: 650 227-8301
Richard Owen, *President*
Gary Potts, *CFO*
Andre O'Schwager, *Vice Pres*
Ken Goldman, *Administration*
Gu Kavitharani, *Info Tech Mgr*

EMP: 90
SQ FT: 20,000
SALES (est): 58.8MM **Privately Held**
SIC: 7371 Software programming applications

(P-15442)
SAVVIUS INC (PA)
1340 Treat Blvd Ste 500, Walnut Creek (94597-7961)
PHONE..................925 937-3200
Fax: 925 937-3211
Larry Zulch, *CEO*
Lawrence A Zulch, *President*
Mahboud Zabetian, *CEO*
Jeffrey F Wheeler, *CFO*
Jeffrey Wheeler, *CFO*
EMP: 55
SQ FT: 30,000
SALES (est): 17.8MM **Privately Held**
WEB: www.wildpackets.com
SIC: 7371 Custom computer programming services

(P-15443)
SCENE7 INC
6 Hamilton Landing # 150, Novato (94949-8264)
PHONE..................415 506-6000
Douglas Mack, *CEO*
Peter Noel, *President*
Willie Dorssers, *Controller*
EMP: 75
SALES (est): 4.5MM **Privately Held**
WEB: www.scene7.com
SIC: 7371 Computer code authors

(P-15444)
SECUREAUTH CORPORATION (PA)
8845 Irvine Center Dr # 200, Irvine (92618-4247)
PHONE..................949 777-6959
Craig J Lund, *CEO*
Jeffrey Kukowski, *COO*
Thomas C Stewart, *CFO*
Soumya Das, *Chief Mktg Ofcr*
Nick Mansour, *Exec VP*
EMP: 78
SQ FT: 4,700
SALES (est): 12MM **Privately Held**
SIC: 7371 Computer software development

(P-15445)
SELECT DATA INC
4155 E La Palma Ave # 250, Anaheim (92807-1863)
PHONE..................714 577-1000
Fax: 714 577-1033
Edward A Buckley, *CEO*
Daniel Smuts, *COO*
Pete Poulis, *CFO*
Susan Carmichael, *Officer*
Stacy Ashworth, *Exec VP*
EMP: 121
SQ FT: 18,000
SALES (est): 19.9MM **Privately Held**
WEB: www.selectdata.com
SIC: 7371 7372 Computer code authors; prepackaged software

(P-15446)
SENTIENT TECHNOLOGIES USA LLC
1 California St Ste 2300, San Francisco (94111-5424)
PHONE..................415 422-9886
Antoine Blondeau, *CEO*
Fabrice Fischer, *CFO*
Peter Harrigan,
Babak Hodjat,
Jeff Sanpore, *Director*
EMP: 50
SALES (est): 100K **Privately Held**
SIC: 7371 Computer software development & applications
PA: Sentient Technologies (Hk) Limited
Dominion Ctr
Wan Chai HK
-

(P-15447)
SEQUOIA GREEN
P.O. Box 67517 (90067-0517)
PHONE..................310 753-0728

Wakelin McNeel, *Owner*
EMP: 100
SALES (est): 1.3MM **Privately Held**
SIC: 7371 7389 Computer software development & applications;

(P-15448)
SEQUOIA RETAIL SYSTEMS INC (DH)
660 W Dana St, Mountain View (94041-1302)
PHONE..................650 237-9000
Jim Zaorski, *CEO*
John Diaz, *COO*
Natallia Taradzei, *QA Dir*
Wen Batiz-Vegas, *Info Tech Mgr*
Ocean Dadgari, *Info Tech Mgr*
EMP: 52
SQ FT: 9,000
SALES (est): 11.2MM **Privately Held**
WEB: www.sequoiap.com
SIC: 7371 5942 5961 4813 Computer software development; college book stores; ;
HQ: Blackboard Inc.
1111 19th St Nw
Washington DC 20036
202 463-4860

(P-15449)
SERVICEMAX INC (PA)
4450 Rosewood Dr Ste 200, Pleasanton (94588-3050)
PHONE..................925 965-7859
David Yarnold, *CEO*
Scott Berg, *COO*
Rick Gustafson, *CFO*
David Milam, *Officer*
Don Schleicher, *Exec VP*
EMP: 91
SQ FT: 7,000
SALES (est): 60.8MM **Privately Held**
WEB: www.maxplore.com
SIC: 7371 Computer software development

(P-15450)
SES LLC
26561 Rancho Pkwy S, Lake Forest (92630-8301)
PHONE..................949 727-3200
Jim Griffith, *VP Finance*
Rashesh Mody, *Senior VP*
Mike Pring, *Vice Pres*
Andrew Shipley, *General Mgr*
Patrick Bouzan, *Info Tech Dir*
EMP: 748
SALES (est): 12.2MM
SALES (corp-wide): 224.4K **Privately Held**
SIC: 7371 Computer software development & applications
HQ: Invensys Processs Systems, Inc.
10900 Equity Dr
Houston TX 77041
713 329-1600

(P-15451)
SFUSD JROTC BRIGADE
2162 24th Ave, San Francisco (94116-1723)
PHONE..................415 242-2546
Robert Powell, *Director*
EMP: 55
SALES (est): 2.3MM **Privately Held**
SIC: 7371 Computer software development

(P-15452)
SHOPKICK INC
900 Middlefield Rd Ste 3, Redwood City (94063-1681)
PHONE..................650 763-8727
Cyriac Roeding, *CEO*
Alexis Rask, *CFO*
Ashley Smith, *Office Mgr*
Amelia Gonsalves, *Executive Asst*
Vivek Nyayapathy, *QA Dir*
EMP: 70
SQ FT: 8,000
SALES (est): 18MM **Privately Held**
SIC: 7371 Computer software development

(P-15453)
SIEMENS PRODUCT LIFE MGMT SFTW
Also Called: Siemens PLM Software
10824 Hope St, Cypress (90630-5214)
PHONE..................714 952-6500
Mike Sayen, *Manager*
Jeff Trom, *Data Proc Staff*
Linda Cuttingham, *Accounting Dir*
Mia Fujii, *Director*
Yery Camacho, *Manager*
EMP: 75
SALES (corp-wide): 83.5B **Privately Held**
WEB: www.ugs.com
SIC: 7371 3695 Custom computer programming services; magnetic & optical recording media
HQ: Siemens Product Lifecycle Management Software Inc.
5800 Granite Pkwy Ste 600
Plano TX 75024
972 987-3000

(P-15454)
SIGNALDEMAND INC
101 Montgomery St Ste 400, San Francisco (94104-4145)
PHONE..................415 356-0800
Fax: 415 356-0806
Mark Tice, *CEO*
Scott C Friend, *Partner*
Douglas Hickey, *Partner*
John G Simon, *Partner*
Bill Rupp, *President*
EMP: 50
SALES (est): 8.1MM
SALES (corp-wide): 168.2MM **Publicly Held**
WEB: www.signaldemand.com
SIC: 7371 Computer software development
PA: Pros Holdings, Inc.
3100 Main St Ste 900
Houston TX 77002
713 335-5151

(P-15455)
SILICON PRIME TECHNOLOGIES INC
4154 W 172nd St, Torrance (90504-1002)
PHONE..................310 279-0222
Quoc Dinh Tran Dinh, *CEO*
EMP: 50
SALES: 200K **Privately Held**
SIC: 7371 Computer software development & applications

(P-15456)
SILICON SPACE INC
8765 Aero Dr Ste 226, San Diego (92123-1767)
P.O. Box 160937, Austin TX (78716-0937)
PHONE..................858 751-0200
Curt Nelson, *CEO*
Dema Zlotin, *President*
Dan Joseph, *Vice Pres*
Fred Nicholson, *CTO*
Celia Flores, *Manager*
EMP: 85
SQ FT: 3,200
SALES (est): 5.6MM **Privately Held**
WEB: www.siliconspace.com
SIC: 7371 5045 8742 Custom computer programming services; computers, peripherals & software; training & development consultant

(P-15457)
SKIRE INC
500 Oracle Pkwy, Redwood City (94065-1677)
PHONE..................650 289-2600
Massy Mendipour, *CEO*
Steve Apfelberg, *Chief Mktg Ofcr*
Linda Burnett, *Executive*
Deborah Levis, *Executive*
Michael Lin, *Data Proc Exec*
EMP: 70
SALES (est): 6.5MM
SALES (corp-wide): 37B **Publicly Held**
WEB: www.skire.com
SIC: 7371 Computer software development

PRODUCTS & SERVICES SECTION

7371 - Custom Computer Programming Svcs County (P-15478)

PA: Oracle Corporation
500 Oracle Pkwy
Redwood City CA 94065
650 506-7000

(P-15458)
SLEEPY GIANT ENTERTAINMENT INC
4 San Joaquin Plz Ste 200, Newport Beach (92660-5934)
PHONE..................................949 464-7986
EMP: 150 **EST:** 2007
SALES (est): 11.2MM **Privately Held**
SIC: 7371

(P-15459)
SMART ENERGY SYSTEMS LLC (PA)
19900 Macarthur Blvd, Irvine (92612-2445)
PHONE..................................909 703-9609
Ray Howlett,
EMP: 122
SALES: 70MM **Privately Held**
SIC: 7371 Computer software development & applications

(P-15460)
SMART ENERGY SYSTEMS LLC
Michelson Dr Ste 3370, Irvine (92612)
PHONE..................................909 703-9609
Ray Howlett,
EMP: 150
SALES (corp-wide): 70MM **Privately Held**
SIC: 7371 Computer software development & applications
PA: Smart Energy Systems Llc
19900 Macarthur Blvd
Irvine CA 92612
909 703-9609

(P-15461)
SOFFRONT SOFTWARE INC
45437 Warm Springs Blvd, Fremont (94539-6104)
P.O. Box 14175 (94539-1375)
PHONE..................................510 413-9000
Fax: 510 413-9027
Manu Das, *CEO*
Therese Trapasso, *Regional Mgr*
Sarah Bond, *Office Mgr*
Joe Hofman, *Technical Mgr*
Mike Chantigian, *Business Mgr*
EMP: 100
SQ FT: 10,300
SALES (est): 9.2MM **Privately Held**
WEB: www.soffront.com
SIC: 7371 Custom computer programming services

(P-15462)
SOFTSOL RESOURCES INC (HQ)
46755 Fremont Blvd, Fremont (94538-6539)
PHONE..................................510 824-2000
Fax: 510 824-2098
Srini Madala, *President*
Bob Hersh, *CFO*
Kumar Talluri, *Vice Pres*
Kris Yalavarthy, *Vice Pres*
Kishore Peddeti, *Project Mgr*
EMP: 100
SQ FT: 12,000
SALES (est): 15.2MM
SALES (corp-wide): 578.6K **Privately Held**
WEB: www.softsolusa.com
SIC: 7371 Computer software development & applications
PA: Softsol India Limited
Plot No-4
Hyderabad TS 500 0
403 071-9500

(P-15463)
SOFTWARE AG USA INC
1198 E Arques Ave, Sunnyvale (94085-4602)
P.O. Box 2000, Alviso (95002-2000)
PHONE..................................703 860-5050
Phillip Merrick, *CEO*
MAI Lu, *Administration*
Bindu Nair, *Sr Software Eng*
Andrea Plesnarski, *Sr Software Eng*
Michelle Yen, *Sr Software Eng*
EMP: 160
SALES (corp-wide): 937.7MM **Privately Held**
SIC: 7371 Computer software development
HQ: Software Ag Usa, Inc.
11700 Plaza America Dr # 700
Reston VA 20190
703 860-5050

(P-15464)
SOFTWARE MANAGEMENT CONS INC
Also Called: Smci
959 S Coast Dr Ste 415, Costa Mesa (92626-7839)
PHONE..................................714 662-1841
Cesar Sanchez, *Principal*
April Patterson, *Tech Recruiter*
EMP: 66
SALES (corp-wide): 53.2MM **Privately Held**
SIC: 7371 Custom computer programming services
PA: Software Management Consultants, Inc.
500 Nth Brn Blvd Ste 1100
Glendale CA 91203
818 240-3177

(P-15465)
SOLIDCORE SYSTEMS INC (DH)
3965 Freedom Cir, Santa Clara (95054-1206)
PHONE..................................408 387-8400
Anne Bonaparte, *President*
David Walker, *Senior VP*
Steve Albertolle, *Vice Pres*
Jack Biggane, *Vice Pres*
Monico Mallari, *Vice Pres*
EMP: 100
SQ FT: 2,000
SALES (est): 12.4MM
SALES (corp-wide): 55.3B **Publicly Held**
WEB: www.solidcore.com
SIC: 7371 Computer software development
HQ: Mcafee, Inc.
2821 Mission College Blvd
Santa Clara CA 95054
408 346-3832

(P-15466)
SOLIMAR SYSTEMS INC (PA)
1515 2nd Ave, San Diego (92101-3005)
PHONE..................................619 849-2800
Fax: 619 294-2801
Drew Sprague, *President*
Todd Sprague, *COO*
Steven Bailey, *Vice Pres*
Deanne Demner, *Admin Asst*
John Carrieri, *CTO*
EMP: 77
SQ FT: 5,414
SALES (est): 12.5MM **Privately Held**
WEB: www.solimarsystems.com
SIC: 7371 Computer software development

(P-15467)
SOLIX TECHNOLOGIES INC (PA)
4701 Patrick Henry Dr # 2001, Santa Clara (95054-1864)
PHONE..................................408 654-6400
SAI Gundavelli, *CEO*
Kishore Gadiraju, *President*
Dinendra Joshi, *President*
Mark Lee, *Senior VP*
Neeraj Chawla, *Vice Pres*
▼ **EMP:** 60
SQ FT: 7,000
SALES: 10MM **Privately Held**
WEB: www.solix.com
SIC: 7371 Computer software development

(P-15468)
SONATA SOFTWARE NORTH AMER INC (HQ)
2201 Walnut Ave Ste 180, Fremont (94538-2334)
PHONE..................................510 791-7220
Fax: 510 578-2101
Amit Kumar, *President*
Srikar Reddy, *COO*
Marcelo Da-AZ, *Officer*
N E Devasahayam, *Assoc VP*
N Sridhara, *Assoc VP*
EMP: 66
SQ FT: 2,500
SALES: 47.2MM
SALES (corp-wide): 74.5MM **Privately Held**
WEB: www.odsi.com
SIC: 7371 Computer software development
PA: Sonata Software Limited
Aps Trust Building, Bull Temple Road,
Bengaluru KAR 56001
806 778-2473

(P-15469)
SONIC BOOM WELLNESS INC
Also Called: Sonicboomwellness.com
5963 La Place Ct Ste 100, Carlsbad (92008-8822)
PHONE..................................760 438-1600
Danna Korn, *CEO*
Bryan Van Noy, *President*
Dan V Dague, *Officer*
Geoff Richey, *Web Dvlpr*
Matthew Duggan, *Accountant*
EMP: 76
SQ FT: 11,000
SALES (est): 9.6MM **Privately Held**
WEB: www.sonicboomwellness.com
SIC: 7371 5734 Computer software development & applications; computer peripheral equipment

(P-15470)
SONY CORPORATION OF AMERICA
Sony Interactive Studios Amer
2207 Bridgepointe Pkwy, Foster City (94404-5060)
PHONE..................................650 655-8000
Kelly Flock, *Manager*
Kazuo Hirai, *COO*
Steve Turvey, *General Mgr*
John Tokarek, *Administration*
Eric Lam, *Systs Prg Mgr*
EMP: 200
SALES (corp-wide): 69.2B **Privately Held**
SIC: 7371 Computer software development
HQ: Sony Corporation Of America
25 Madison Ave Fl 27
New York NY 10010
212 833-8000

(P-15471)
SOUNDHOUND INC (PA)
Also Called: Mobile Application
3979 Freedom Cir Ste 400, Santa Clara (95054-1257)
PHONE..................................408 441-3200
Keyvan Mohajer, *CEO*
Cheryl Lucanegro, *President*
Kamran Elahian, *Officer*
Jay Eum, *Officer*
Larry Marcus, *Officer*
EMP: 61
SQ FT: 24,907
SALES (est): 15.7MM **Privately Held**
WEB: www.melodis.com
SIC: 7371 Software programming applications

(P-15472)
SOURCE INTERLINK MEDIA LLC
Also Called: Mind Over Eye
2221 Rosecrans Ave # 195, El Segundo (90245-4931)
PHONE..................................310 531-9394
Daniel Lin, *Branch Mgr*
Dave Wein, *Vice Pres*
Damian Fulton, *Creative Dir*
Paul Babb, *Director*
Scott McNeff, *Director*
EMP: 55
SALES (corp-wide): 1.3B **Privately Held**
SIC: 7371 7812 Computer software development & applications; motion picture & video production
HQ: Ten The Enthusiast Network, Llc
831 S Douglas St Ste 100
El Segundo CA 90245
310 531-9900

(P-15473)
SOURCEBITS INC
2191 E Byshore Rd Ste 200, Palo Alto (94303)
PHONE..................................650 433-7920
EMP: 142
SALES (corp-wide): 16.4MM **Privately Held**
SIC: 7371 Custom computer programming services
PA: Sourcebits, Inc.
211 Sutter St Fl 2
San Francisco CA 94108
415 288-3697

(P-15474)
SPARK UNLIMITED INC
15000 Ventura Blvd # 202, Sherman Oaks (91403-2443)
PHONE..................................818 788-1005
Fax: 818 788-8240
Craig Allen, *CEO*
Cynthia Boone, *Manager*
EMP: 68
SALES (est): 7.5MM **Privately Held**
WEB: www.sparkunlimited.com
SIC: 7371 Computer software development

(P-15475)
SPRUCE TECHNOLOGY INC
3516 Browntail Way, San Ramon (94582-5245)
PHONE..................................925 415-8160
Muttu Nagubandi, *Branch Mgr*
EMP: 75
SALES (corp-wide): 10.3MM **Privately Held**
SIC: 7371 Computer software development & applications
PA: Spruce Technology Inc
1149 Bloomfield Ave Ste G
Clifton NJ 07012
201 693-8843

(P-15476)
STARTEL CORPORATION (PA)
16 Goodyear B-125, Irvine (92618-3758)
PHONE..................................949 863-8700
Fax: 949 863-9650
William Lane, *President*
David Abrams, *Purch Mgr*
Steve Newell, *Manager*
Myrna Nunez, *Manager*
EMP: 60
SQ FT: 27,000
SALES (est): 10.5MM **Privately Held**
WEB: www.startelcorp.com
SIC: 7371 3661 Computer software development; communication headgear, telephone

(P-15477)
STARTUP FARMS INTL LLC
Also Called: Sufi
45690 Northport Loop E, Fremont (94538-6477)
PHONE..................................510 440-0110
Jasvir Gill, *President*
Kaval Kaur, *CFO*
Terri Kareeson, *Human Res Mgr*
EMP: 50
SALES (est): 162K **Privately Held**
WEB: www.startupfarms.com
SIC: 7371 Computer software development

(P-15478)
STRANDS INC A DELAWARE CORP
999 Baker Way Ste 430, San Mateo (94404-1581)
P.O. Box 331639, Miami FL (33233-1639)
PHONE..................................541 753-4426
Edward Chang, *CEO*
David Silverman, *President*
Michael Martin, *CFO*
Kevin Gartner, *Vice Pres*
Eduardo Criado, *Business Dir*
EMP: 50
SQ FT: 3,000
SALES (est): 3.8MM **Privately Held**
WEB: www.strands.com
SIC: 7371 Software programming applications

7371 - Custom Computer Programming Svcs County (P-15479)

(P-15479)
STRANDS LABS INC
Also Called: Strands Finance
999 Baker Way Ste 430, San Mateo (94404-1581)
PHONE 415 398-4333
EMP: 50
SALES (est): 3.1MM Privately Held
SIC: 7371

(P-15480)
STRATACARE LLC
17838 Gillette Ave Ste D, Irvine (92614-6502)
P.O. Box 19600 (92623-9600)
PHONE 949 743-1200
Scott R Green, *CEO*
Steve Ditman, *CFO*
Robert McCaffrey, *Officer*
John Zavoli, *Officer*
Michael Josephs, *Vice Pres*
▲ EMP: 250 EST: 1998
SALES (est): 614K
SALES (corp-wide): 18B Publicly Held
WEB: www.gensourcecorp.com
SIC: 7371 Computer software development & applications
HQ: Isg Holdings, Inc.
20 Waterside Dr
Farmington CT 06032
860 678-7877

(P-15481)
SUCCESSFACTORS INC (DH)
Also Called: Success Factors
1 Tower Pl Fl 11, South San Francisco (94080-1828)
PHONE 800 845-0395
Fax: 650 645-2099
Price Shawn, *President*
Mike Ettling, *President*
Matt Leone, *COO*
Klein Christian, *CFO*
Bruce C Felt, *CFO*
EMP: 148
SQ FT: 58,700
SALES (est): 75.3MM
SALES (corp-wide): 22.3B Privately Held
SIC: 7371 Computer software development
HQ: Sap America, Inc.
3999 West Chester Pike
Newtown Square PA 19073
610 661-1000

(P-15482)
SUGARCRM INC (PA)
10050 N Wolfe Rd Sw2130, Cupertino (95014-2528)
PHONE 408 454-6900
Fax: 408 873-2872
Larry Augustin, *Ch of Bd*
Andrew Chmyz, *CFO*
Steve Valenzuela, *CFO*
Kathy L Woodard, *CFO*
Nick Halsey, *Chief Mktg Ofcr*
EMP: 110
SQ FT: 40,000
SALES (est): 82.3MM Privately Held
WEB: www.sugarcrm.com
SIC: 7371 Computer software development

(P-15483)
SUNGARD BI-TECH INC (DH)
890 Fortress St, Chico (95973-9023)
PHONE 530 891-5281
Fax: 530 891-5011
Aaron Johnson, *President*
Bruce Langston, *CFO*
Brian Robins, *Chief Mktg Ofcr*
Jeff Abbott, *Vice Pres*
Connie Schmaljohann, *Business Anlyst*
EMP: 50
SALES (est): 16.4MM
SALES (corp-wide): 6.6B Publicly Held
WEB: www.bi-tech.com
SIC: 7371 Computer software development
HQ: Fis Data Systems Inc.
680 E Swedesford Rd
Wayne PA 19087
484 582-2000

(P-15484)
SUSHI NOZAWA LLC
Also Called: Sugarfish
11628 Santa Monica Blvd, Los Angeles (90025-2900)
PHONE 310 963-7377
Cameron Broumand,
EMP: 150
SALES (est): 15MM Privately Held
SIC: 7371 5812 Computer software development & applications; eating places

(P-15485)
SYMITAR SYSTEMS INC
8985 Balboa Ave, San Diego (92123-1507)
PHONE 619 542-6700
Kathy Burress, *Principal*
Julian Botero, *Admin Asst*
Ramon Macias, *Administration*
Audrey Macy, *Administration*
Michael Belie, *Sr Software Eng*
EMP: 220
SALES (est): 27.9MM
SALES (corp-wide): 1.3B Publicly Held
SIC: 7371 Computer software development
PA: Jack Henry & Associates, Inc.
663 W Highway 60
Monett MO 65708
417 235-6652

(P-15486)
SYNOPSYS INC (PA)
690 E Middlefield Rd, Mountain View (94043-4033)
PHONE 650 584-5000
Fax: 650 584-4396
Aart J De Geus, *Ch of Bd*
Shankar Hemmady, *Vice Chairman*
CHI-Foon Chan, *President*
Terry MA, *President*
Brian M Beattie, *CFO*
EMP: 500
SQ FT: 341,000
SALES (est): 2.2B Publicly Held
WEB: www.synopsys.com
SIC: 7371 Computer software development

(P-15487)
SYSINTELLI INC
9466 Black Mountain Rd # 200, San Diego (92126-4550)
PHONE 858 271-1600
Ravindra Hanumara, *President*
Padma Seetala, *Manager*
Nithya Sudhakar, *Manager*
EMP: 123
SQ FT: 2,400
SALES: 4.5MM Privately Held
WEB: www.sysintelli.com
SIC: 7371 7379 Custom computer programming services; computer related consulting services

(P-15488)
SYSTEMS AND SOFTWARE ENTPS LLC (HQ)
Also Called: Zodiac Inflight Innovations US
2929 E Imperial Hwy # 170, Brea (92821-6716)
PHONE 714 854-8600
Matt Smith, *CEO*
Ed Barrera, *CFO*
Steve Hawkins, *CTO*
Harry Gray, *VP Sales*
Josette Mollica, *General Counsel*
EMP: 73
SQ FT: 90,000
SALES (est): 54.6MM
SALES (corp-wide): 121MM Privately Held
WEB: www.imsinflight.com
SIC: 7371 Computer software systems analysis & design, custom
PA: Zodiac Aerospace
61 Rue Pierre Curie
Plaisir Cedex 78373
161 342-323

(P-15489)
TAMTRON CORPORATION (DH)
6203 San Ignacio Ave # 110, San Jose (95119-1371)
PHONE 408 323-3303
Fax: 408 246-5415

Steven R Tablak, *President*
Bob Tablak, *Treasurer*
Heather Boatright, *Admin Asst*
EMP: 60
SQ FT: 2,600
SALES (est): 3.7MM
SALES (corp-wide): 1.3B Privately Held
SIC: 7371 Computer software development
HQ: Impac Medical Systems, Inc
100 Mathilda Pl Fl 5
Sunnyvale CA 94086
408 830-8000

(P-15490)
TAPESTRY SOLUTIONS INC (HQ)
5643 Copley Dr, San Diego (92111-7903)
PHONE 858 503-1990
Fax: 858 503-1999
Geoff Evans, *President*
Jeremy Lowe, *President*
Roy Deford, *COO*
Mary Ann Wagner, *COO*
Mark Young, *CFO*
EMP: 125
SQ FT: 36,073
SALES (est): 82MM
SALES (corp-wide): 96.1B Publicly Held
SIC: 7371 5045 Custom computer programming services; computer software
PA: The Boeing Company
100 N Riverside Plz
Chicago IL 60606
312 544-2000

(P-15491)
TAULIA INC (PA)
201 Mssion St Fl9 Ste 900, San Francisco (94105)
PHONE 415 376-8280
Cedric Bru, *CEO*
Jonathan Lowenhar, *President*
Courtney Ring, *President*
Rik Thorbecke, *CFO*
Tony Schopen, *Vice Pres*
EMP: 73
SALES (est): 45.9MM Privately Held
SIC: 7371 Computer software development

(P-15492)
TAVANT TECHNOLOGIES INC (PA)
3965 Freedom Cir Ste 750, Santa Clara (95054-1285)
PHONE 408 519-5400
Fax: 408 519-5401
Sarvesh Mahesh, *CEO*
Venkata Devana, *CFO*
Krishnan Pp, *Officer*
Hassan Rashid, *Senior VP*
Arun Balaraman, *Executive*
EMP: 112
SALES (est): 35MM Privately Held
WEB: www.tavant.com
SIC: 7371 Custom computer programming services; computer software development; computer software systems analysis & design, custom

(P-15493)
TAX COMPLIANCE INC
10089 Willow Creek Rd # 300, San Diego (92131-1699)
PHONE 858 547-4100
Fax: 858 547-4101
Carl Melcher, *Chairman*
Dave Shea, *CEO*
Ed Wallace, *Vice Pres*
Sandy Good, *Executive*
Joy Trebbien, *QA Dir*
EMP: 52
SQ FT: 10,000
SALES (est): 8MM
SALES (corp-wide): 48.2MM Privately Held
WEB: www.taxcomp.com
SIC: 7371 Computer software development
HQ: Mlm Information Services, Llc
780 3rd Ave
New York NY 10017
212 245-5310

(P-15494)
TCG SOFTWARE SERVICES INC
320 Commerce Ste 200, Irvine (92602-1363)
PHONE 714 665-6200
Greg Blevins, *Branch Mgr*
EMP: 50 Privately Held
SIC: 7371 Custom computer programming services; computer software development
PA: Tcg Software Services, Inc.
265 Davidson Ave Ste 220
Somerset NJ 08873

(P-15495)
TECH MAHINDRA (AMERICAS) INC
23461 S Pointe Dr Ste 370, Laguna Hills (92653-1571)
PHONE 949 462-0640
EMP: 80
SALES (corp-wide): 3.1B Privately Held
SIC: 7371 Computer software development & applications
HQ: Tech Mahindra (Americas) Inc.
4965 Preston Park Blvd
Plano TX 75093

(P-15496)
TECHEXCEL INC (PA)
3675 Mt Diablo Blvd # 330, Lafayette (94549-3792)
PHONE 925 871-3900
Tieren Zhou, *President*
James Zhou, *CFO*
Ken Tang, *Sr Software Eng*
Tingjin Xu, *Sr Software Eng*
Xiaojie Liu, *Software Engr*
EMP: 51
SQ FT: 11,187
SALES (est): 12.5MM Privately Held
WEB: www.techexcel.com
SIC: 7371 Computer software development

(P-15497)
TELESYS SOFTWARE
1900 S Norfolk St Ste 221, San Mateo (94403-1172)
PHONE 650 522-9922
Bobby Bahl, *President*
Lee Ed, *CFO*
Ed Lee, *Vice Pres*
Peter Salerno, *Vice Pres*
Sankar Chanda, *CTO*
EMP: 50
SQ FT: 4,000
SALES (est): 5.3MM Privately Held
WEB: www.telesys.com
SIC: 7371 Computer software development

(P-15498)
TERADATA CORPORATION
999 Skyway Rd Ste 100, San Carlos (94070-2722)
PHONE 650 232-2400
Mayank Bawa, *Branch Mgr*
Holly Stephenson, *Director*
EMP: 67
SALES (corp-wide): 2.5B Publicly Held
SIC: 7371 Computer software development
PA: Teradata Corporation
10000 Innovation Dr
Miamisburg OH 45342
866 548-8348

(P-15499)
THINK PASSENGER INC (PA)
12100 Wilshire Blvd # 1950, Los Angeles (90025-7126)
PHONE 323 556-5400
Fax: 323 556-5490
Bahram Nour-Omid, *CEO*
Ramesh Pidikiti, *President*
Anthony Tam, *President*
Steve Howe, *COO*
Michael Winner, *Senior VP*
EMP: 52
SQ FT: 15,000
SALES (est): 9.5MM Privately Held
SIC: 7371 Computer software development

PRODUCTS & SERVICES SECTION

7371 - Custom Computer Programming Svcs County (P-15520)

(P-15500)
THISMOMENT INC
221 Kearny St Fl 4, San Francisco (94108-4524)
PHONE..................415 200-4730
Vince Broady, *CEO*
Trey Walker, *President*
John Walliser, *President*
Steve Bach, *CFO*
John Bara, *Chief Mktg Ofcr*
EMP: 135
SQ FT: 15,000
SALES (est): 19.9MM **Privately Held**
SIC: 7371 Computer software development

(P-15501)
THOMAS GALLAWAY CORPORATION (PA)
Also Called: Technologent
100 Spectrum Center Dr # 700, Irvine (92618-4962)
PHONE..................949 716-9500
Fax: 949 716-9600
Lezlie L Gallaway, *CEO*
Tom Gallaway, *President*
Peter Frankovsky, *CFO*
Marco Mohajer, *Exec VP*
Jim Bevis, *Vice Pres*
EMP: 68
SQ FT: 4,500
SALES (est): 132.7MM **Privately Held**
WEB: www.technologent.com
SIC: 7371 5045 Custom computer programming services; computers & accessories, personal & home entertainment

(P-15502)
THOMSON REUTERS CORPORATION
800 W California Ave # 100, Sunnyvale (94086-3608)
PHONE..................408 524-4628
Fax: 408 524-4798
Stephenie Dixon, *Branch Mgr*
EMP: 50
SALES (corp-wide): 3.8B **Publicly Held**
SIC: 7371 Computer software development
HQ: Thomson Reuters Corporation
3 Times Sq Lbby Mailroom
New York NY 10036
646 223-4000

(P-15503)
TIBCO SOFTWARE INC (PA)
3303 Hillview Ave, Palo Alto (94304-1279)
PHONE..................650 846-1000
Fax: 650 864-1064
Murray Rhode, *CEO*
Thomas Berquist, *CFO*
William Hughes, *Officer*
Bill Hughes, *Exec VP*
Tom Laffey, *Exec VP*
EMP: 148
SQ FT: 292,000
SALES (est): 1.2B **Privately Held**
WEB: www.tibco.com
SIC: 7371 7373 Custom computer programming services; systems integration services

(P-15504)
TIMBRE TECHNOLOGIES INC
3100 W Warren Ave, Fremont (94538-6423)
P.O. Box 270478, Saint Louis MO (63127-0478)
PHONE..................510 624-3300
Fax: 510 624-3301
Jim Hamajima, *President*
Joanne Zhu, *Software Engr*
Jennifer Lintz, *Accountant*
Kiyoshi Sato, *Director*
EMP: 59
SALES (est): 5.1MM
SALES (corp-wide): 5.6B **Privately Held**
WEB: www.tel.co.jp
SIC: 7371 Software programming applications
HQ: Tokyo Electron U.S. Holdings, Inc.
2400 Grove Blvd
Austin TX 78741
512 424-1000

(P-15505)
TIVO SOLUTIONS INC (HQ)
2160 Gold St, Alviso (95002-3700)
P.O. Box 2160, San Jose (95109-2160)
PHONE..................408 519-9100
Fax: 408 519-5330
Thomas S Rogers, *President*
Charles Phillips, *COO*
Dan Phillips, *COO*
Matthew Zinn,
Jeffrey Klugman, *Exec VP*
▲ **EMP:** 148
SQ FT: 164,269
SALES: 489.6MM
SALES (corp-wide): 526.2MM **Privately Held**
WEB: www.tivo.com
SIC: 7371 Computer software development & applications
PA: Rovi Corporation
2 Circle Star Way
San Carlos CA 94070
408 562-8400

(P-15506)
TK CARSITES INC
2975 Red Hill Ave Ste 175, Costa Mesa (92626-1209)
PHONE..................714 937-1239
Richard J Valenta, *CEO*
James Bradford, *President*
James Rucker, *Chief Mktg Ofcr*
Brandon Turnbull, *Admin Asst*
Robert Pryke, *Administration*
EMP: 60
SQ FT: 8,000
SALES (est): 3.2MM
SALES (corp-wide): 26.3MM **Privately Held**
WEB: www.tkcarsites.com
SIC: 7371 Computer software development
PA: Search Optics, Llc
5770 Oberlin Dr
San Diego CA 92121
858 678-0707

(P-15507)
TOOLWIRE INC (PA)
7031 Koll Center Pkwy # 220, Pleasanton (94566-3128)
PHONE..................925 227-8500
Fax: 925 227-8501
John Valencia, *President*
John Catanzaro, *Vice Pres*
Cameron Crowe, *Vice Pres*
Graeme Johnston, *Vice Pres*
Ofelia Hopson, *Admin Asst*
EMP: 56
SQ FT: 12,500
SALES (est): 13.6MM **Privately Held**
WEB: www.toolwire.com
SIC: 7371 Computer software development

(P-15508)
TOWNS END STUDIOS LLC
699 8th St, San Francisco (94103-4901)
PHONE..................415 802-7936
Mark Pincus,
EMP: 1000
SALES (est): 8.1MM
SALES (corp-wide): 764.7MM **Publicly Held**
SIC: 7371 Computer software development & applications
PA: Zynga Inc.
699 8th St
San Francisco CA 94103
855 449-9642

(P-15509)
TRENDSHIFT LLC
435 N Oakhurst Dr, Beverly Hills (90210-3981)
PHONE..................866 644-8877
Ryan Weirich, *VP Finance*
EMP: 55
SALES (est): 832.1K **Privately Held**
SIC: 7371 Computer software development & applications

(P-15510)
TRINUS CORPORATION
177 E Colorado Blvd 200, Pasadena (91105-1986)
PHONE..................818 246-1143
Sanjay Kucheria, *CEO*
Harshada Kucheria, *President*
Sanjeev Sehgal, *Vice Pres*
Ram Vyas, *General Mgr*
Bharat Sain, *Sr Software Eng*
EMP: 50
SALES (est): 10MM **Privately Held**
SIC: 7371 Custom computer programming services

(P-15511)
TUNARI CORP INC
Also Called: Hara Software Inc
2755 Campus Dr Ste 300, San Mateo (94403-2538)
PHONE..................650 249-6740
Rodrigo J Prudencio, *CEO*
EMP: 59
SALES (est): 4.2MM **Privately Held**
SIC: 7371 Computer software development
HQ: Verisae, Inc.
730 2nd Ave S Ste 600
Minneapolis MN 55402
612 455-2300

(P-15512)
TWILIO INC
399 W El Camino Real, Mountain View (94040-2680)
PHONE..................877 889-4546
Ott Kaukver, *Branch Mgr*
EMP: 335
SALES (corp-wide): 166.9MM **Publicly Held**
SIC: 7371 Computer software development
PA: Twilio Inc.
645 Harrison St Fl 3
San Francisco CA 94107
415 390-2337

(P-15513)
UBICS INC
1050 Bridgeway, Sausalito (94965-2173)
PHONE..................415 289-1400
Vijay Mallya, *Branch Mgr*
EMP: 140 **Privately Held**
SIC: 7371 Custom computer programming services
PA: Ubics, Inc.
400 Sthpinte Blvd Ste 425
Canonsburg PA 15317

(P-15514)
UBISOFT HOLDINGS INC (DH)
Also Called: Red Storm
625 3rd St Fl 3, San Francisco (94107-1918)
PHONE..................415 547-4000
Yves Guillemot, *President*
Laurent Detoc, *Vice Pres*
Patrick Fung, *Data Proc Exec*
Benoit Frappier, *Software Dev*
Francois Roy, *Prdtn Mgr*
EMP: 191
SQ FT: 20,000
SALES (est): 38.7MM
SALES (corp-wide): 854.8MM **Privately Held**
SIC: 7371 Computer software writing services
HQ: Ubisoft France
Montreuil Sous Bois
Montreuil Cedex 93108
148 185-000

(P-15515)
ULTIMO SOFTWARE SOLUTIONS INC
2860 Zanker Rd Ste 203, San Jose (95134-2120)
PHONE..................408 943-1490
Fax: 408 943-5180
Venkatasubhash Pasumarthy, *President*
Smita Pasumarthi, *President*
Saurabh Srivastava, *Consultant*
EMP: 127
SQ FT: 4,000
SALES (est): 9.4MM **Privately Held**
WEB: www.ultimosoft.com
SIC: 7371 Computer software development & applications

(P-15516)
UNISYS CORPORATION
9701 Jeronimo Rd Ste 100, Irvine (92618-2076)
PHONE..................949 380-5000
Fax: 949 380-5044
Carmen Lynch, *Manager*
Robert Eichers, *Vice Pres*
Mike Irving, *Vice Pres*
Robert Johnson, *Vice Pres*
David Meyers, *Systs Prg Mgr*
EMP: 1000
SALES (corp-wide): 3B **Publicly Held**
WEB: www.unisys.com
SIC: 7371 Custom computer programming services
PA: Unisys Corporation
801 Lakeview Dr Ste 100
Blue Bell PA 19422
215 986-4011

(P-15517)
UNX INC A DELAWARE CORP
Also Called: Universal Network Exchange
175 E Olive Ave Fl 2, Burbank (91502-1821)
PHONE..................818 333-3300
Fax: 818 559-5586
J Scott Harrison, *CEO*
Andre Perold, *Ch of Bd*
David Collett, *CFO*
Loren Grant, *Officer*
Scott Harrison, *Officer*
EMP: 95 **EST:** 1997
SQ FT: 16,000
SALES (est): 6.5MM **Privately Held**
WEB: www.unx.com
SIC: 7371 4813 6211 Computer software development & applications; ; security brokers & dealers

(P-15518)
UST GLOBAL INC (PA)
5 Polaris Way, Aliso Viejo (92656-5356)
PHONE..................949 716-8757
Dan Gupta, *Chairman*
Joe Nalkara, *President*
Sajan Pillai, *CEO*
Arun Narayanan, *COO*
Saurabh Ranjan, *COO*
EMP: 100
SQ FT: 20,000
SALES (est): 1.3B **Privately Held**
WEB: www.ust-global.com
SIC: 7371 Computer software development

(P-15519)
UTC FIRE SEC AMERICAS CORP INC
Also Called: Utc, Mas
2955 Red Hill Ave Ste 100, Costa Mesa (92626-1207)
PHONE..................949 737-7800
Shin Voeks, *General Mgr*
Anup Khattar, *Vice Pres*
Richard Triplett, *Vice Pres*
Chris Huynh, *Executive*
Ron Darley, *District Mgr*
EMP: 60
SALES (corp-wide): 56.1B **Publicly Held**
SIC: 7371 5063 Computer software development & applications; computer software systems analysis & design, custom; alarm systems
HQ: Utc Fire & Security Americas Corporation, Inc.
1200 S Pine Island Rd
Plantation FL 33324
941 739-4200

(P-15520)
UTILITY SYSTEMS SCIENCE (PA)
601 Parkcenter Dr Ste 209, Santa Ana (92705-3542)
PHONE..................714 542-1004
Gabriel A Chavez, *CEO*
Anthony Chavez, *CFO*
Mark Serres, *Vice Pres*
Bret Houston, *Software Engr*
EMP: 65

7371 - Custom Computer Programming Svcs County (P-15521)

SALES (est): 6.5MM **Privately Held**
SIC: 7371 Computer software development

(P-15521)
VARMOUR NETWORKS INC
800 W El Cam, Mountain View (94040)
PHONE....................................650 564-5100
Jia-Jyi Roger Lian, *CEO*
Demetrios Lazarikos, *Officer*
Julia Tran, *Vice Pres*
Kelly Huang, *Creative Dir*
Becky Brown, *Office Mgr*
EMP: 75
SALES (est): 14.8MM **Privately Held**
SIC: 7371 Computer software development & applications

(P-15522)
VENDINI INC (PA)
660 Market St Ste 400, San Francisco (94104-5004)
PHONE....................................415 693-9611
Mark Tacchi, *President*
Mark A Dirsa, *CFO*
Keith Goldberg, *Officer*
Mark Guarnera, *Exec VP*
Tricia Baker, *Vice Pres*
EMP: 55
SQ FT: 7,000
SALES (est): 20MM **Privately Held**
SIC: 7371 Computer software development

(P-15523)
VERINT AMERICAS INC
Blue Pumpkin
2250 Walsh Ave Ste 120, Santa Clara (95050-2514)
PHONE....................................408 830-5400
Doron Aspitz, *Branch Mgr*
Ron Conway, *Bd of Directors*
Michael Maoz, *Vice Pres*
Elizabeth Ussher, *Vice Pres*
Israel Sanchez, *Administration*
EMP: 100
SALES (corp-wide): 1.1B **Publicly Held**
WEB: www.witness.com
SIC: 7371 8742 7372 Computer software writers, freelance; management consulting services; prepackaged software
HQ: Verint Americas Inc.
800 North Point Pkwy
Alpharetta GA 30005
770 754-1900

(P-15524)
VERITAS TECHNOLOGIES LLC (HQ)
500 E Middlefield Rd, Mountain View (94043-4000)
P.O. Box 7011 (94039-7011)
PHONE....................................650 933-1000
Bill Coleman, *CEO*
Mick Lopez, *CFO*
Ben Gibson, *Chief Mktg Ofcr*
Matt Cain,
John Gannon, *Exec VP*
EMP: 101
SALES (est): 128.4MM
SALES (corp-wide): 1.2B **Publicly Held**
SIC: 7371 7375 Computer software development & applications; information retrieval services; data base information retrieval
PA: Veritas Us Inc.
500 E Middlefield Rd
Mountain View CA 94043
650 933-1000

(P-15525)
VERITAS US INC (PA)
500 E Middlefield Rd, Mountain View (94043-4000)
PHONE....................................650 933-1000
William T Coleman, *CEO*
EMP: 180 EST: 2014
SALES: 1.2B **Privately Held**
SIC: 7371 Computer software development & applications

(P-15526)
VERTAFORE FSC INC
Also Called: Stoneriver Fsc, Inc.
28038 Dorothy Dr, Agoura Hills (91301-2687)
PHONE....................................800 433-2550
Paul Areida, *President*
John Heitman, *Treasurer*
Ben Moulton, *Prgrmr*
EMP: 130
SALES (est): 4.7MM
SALES (corp-wide): 538.5MM **Privately Held**
SIC: 7371 Custom computer programming services
PA: Vertafore, Inc.
11724 Ne 195th St
Bothell WA 98011
425 402-1000

(P-15527)
VIDHWAN INC
2 N Market St Ste 410, San Jose (95113-1211)
PHONE....................................408 521-0167
EMP: 111
SALES (corp-wide): 19.5MM **Privately Held**
SIC: 7371 Custom computer programming services
PA: Vidhwan, Inc.
2 N Market St Ste 400
San Jose CA 95113
408 289-8200

(P-15528)
VISION SOLUTIONS INC (HQ)
15300 Barranca Pkwy # 100, Irvine (92618-2256)
PHONE....................................949 253-6500
Nicolaas Vlok, *President*
Don Scott, *CFO*
Wm Edward Vesely, *Chief Mktg Ofcr*
Alan Arnold, *Exec VP*
Robert Johnson, *Exec VP*
EMP: 90
SQ FT: 25,000
SALES: 145MM **Privately Held**
WEB: www.visionsolutions.com
SIC: 7371 7373 Computer software development; systems integration services

(P-15529)
VISUAL CONCEPTS ENTERTAINMENT
10 Hamilton Landing, Novato (94949-8207)
PHONE....................................415 479-3634
Gregory Thomas, *President*
Scott Patterson, *Vice Pres*
Brian Ramagli, *Software Engr*
Tim Schroeder, *Software Engr*
Matthew Crysdale, *Director*
EMP: 200
SALES (est): 15.5MM
SALES (corp-wide): 1.4B **Publicly Held**
SIC: 7371 Computer software development
PA: Take-Two Interactive Software, Inc.
622 Broadway Fl 6
New York NY 10012
646 536-2842

(P-15530)
VM SERVICES INC
1051 S East St, Anaheim (92805-5749)
PHONE....................................714 678-5200
Bernie Chong, *Branch Mgr*
Michael Webb, *Info Tech Dir*
EMP: 50
SALES (corp-wide): 1.8B **Privately Held**
WEB: www.venturemfg-usa.com
SIC: 7371 5734 3999 Computer software development; computer & software stores; barber & beauty shop equipment
HQ: Vm Services, Inc.
6701 Mowry Ave
Newark CA 94560
510 744-3720

(P-15531)
VM SERVICES INC (DH)
6701 Mowry Ave, Newark (94560-4927)
PHONE....................................510 744-3720
Fax: 510 744-3730
Chin Tong Wong, *CEO*
Wiwit Handayani, *CFO*
Jennifer Thomas, *CFO*
Robert Rios, *Executive*
Kok S Wun, *IT Specialist*
▲ EMP: 120
SQ FT: 4,300
SALES (est): 88.1MM
SALES (corp-wide): 1.8B **Privately Held**
WEB: www.venturemfg-usa.com
SIC: 7371 Computer software development

(P-15532)
VM WARE
3401 Hillview Ave, Palo Alto (94304-1383)
PHONE....................................650 424-8193
Shakir Hussain, *Business Anlyst*
Raja Raj, *Technology*
LI Cui, *Senior Mgr*
Andrew Condon, *Director*
Bhupinder Saluja, *Director*
EMP: 68 EST: 2014
SALES (est): 4.3MM **Privately Held**
SIC: 7371 Custom computer programming services

(P-15533)
VMWARE INC
Springsource
3400 Hillview Ave Lbby, Palo Alto (94304-1343)
PHONE....................................650 427-2100
Peter Cooper, *Principal*
Brian Byun, *Vice Pres*
Mark Fisher, *Sr Software Eng*
Filip Hanik, *Sr Software Eng*
Amee Cooper, *Technical Mgr*
EMP: 180
SALES (corp-wide): 72.7B **Publicly Held**
SIC: 7371 Custom computer programming services
HQ: Vmware, Inc.
3401 Hillview Ave
Palo Alto CA 94304
650 427-5000

(P-15534)
VMWARE INC (DH)
3401 Hillview Ave, Palo Alto (94304-1383)
PHONE....................................650 427-5000
Fax: 650 855-6531
Patrick P Gelsinger, *CEO*
Michael S Dell, *Ch of Bd*
Zane Rowe, *CFO*
S Dawn Smith,
Dirk Hohndel, *Officer*
EMP: 148
SQ FT: 1,499,836
SALES: 6.5B
SALES (corp-wide): 72.7B **Publicly Held**
SIC: 7371 7375 Computer software development & applications; information retrieval services
HQ: Emc Corporation
176 South St
Hopkinton MA 01748
508 435-1000

(P-15535)
VMWARE INC
3305 Hillview Ave, Palo Alto (94304-1204)
P.O. Box 52100 (94303-0751)
PHONE....................................650 812-8200
George Symons, *Branch Mgr*
Sachin Prasad, *Administration*
Vikas Sharma, *Technology*
James Smith,
Jason Cockroft, *Director*
EMP: 180
SALES (corp-wide): 72.7B **Publicly Held**
SIC: 7371 7375 Computer software development & applications; information retrieval services
HQ: Vmware, Inc.
3401 Hillview Ave
Palo Alto CA 94304
650 427-5000

(P-15536)
VMWARE INC
3210 Porter Dr, Palo Alto (94304-1214)
P.O. Box 10009 (94303-0901)
PHONE....................................650 812-8200
Louis Cole, *Manager*
Vivian Hu, *Research*
Hristo Belchev, *Technology*
Jeff Godfrey, *Technology*
Kurt Niska, *Engineer*
EMP: 180
SALES (corp-wide): 72.7B **Publicly Held**
SIC: 7371 Custom computer programming services
HQ: Vmware, Inc.
3401 Hillview Ave
Palo Alto CA 94304
650 427-5000

(P-15537)
VOXIFY INC
1151 Marina Village Pkwy, Alameda (94501-1017)
PHONE....................................510 545-3011
Fax: 510 545-5055
Madhu Ranganathan, *President*
John Gengarella, *President*
John Longinotti, *CFO*
Mike Fuella, *Info Tech Mgr*
Wayne Gale, *Engineer*
EMP: 65
SALES (est): 7.2MM **Privately Held**
WEB: www.voxify.com
SIC: 7371 Computer software development

(P-15538)
WALKME INC
22 4th St Fl 14, San Francisco (94103-3178)
PHONE....................................855 492-5563
Dan Adika, *CEO*
Rephael Sweary, *President*
Eyal Cohen, *Exec VP*
Boaz Maor, *Exec VP*
Richard Woolf, *Senior VP*
EMP: 60 EST: 2012
SALES (est): 5.6MM **Privately Held**
SIC: 7371 Computer software development & applications

(P-15539)
WALZ GROUP LLC (HQ)
Also Called: Walz Postal Solutions
27398 Via Industria, Temecula (92590-3699)
PHONE....................................951 491-6800
Fax: 951 491-6595
Rod Walz, *President*
Kevin Miller, *CFO*
Maria Moskver, *Ch Credit Ofcr*
Brad Knapp, *Exec VP*
Oya Babur, *Vice Pres*
EMP: 117
SQ FT: 40,000
SALES (est): 30.9MM
SALES (corp-wide): 136.2MM **Privately Held**
SIC: 7371 Computer software development & applications
PA: Lenderlive Network, Inc.
710 S Ash St Ste 200
Denver CO 80246
303 226-8000

(P-15540)
WAY FORWARD TECHNOLOGY INC
28738 The Old Rd, Valencia (91355-1084)
PHONE....................................661 286-2769
Voldi Way, *President*
John Beck, *COO*
Mallory Isham, *Human Resources*
EMP: 50
SQ FT: 10,000
SALES: 8.2MM **Privately Held**
WEB: www.wayforward.com
SIC: 7371 Computer software development

(P-15541)
WAZE MARKET INC (PA)
Also Called: Location Labs
5980 Horton St Ste 675, Emeryville (94608-2068)
PHONE....................................510 469-3123
Tasso Roumeliotis, *President*
Steven Ginn, *President*
Joel Grossman, *COO*
Andy Ruff, *Vice Pres*
Vincent Rosso, *Engineer*
EMP: 52 EST: 2000
SALES (est): 18.7MM **Privately Held**
SIC: 7371 Computer software development & applications

PRODUCTS & SERVICES SECTION

7372 - Prepackaged Software County (P-15564)

(P-15542)
WEB SPIDERS INC
180 Snsome St Rocketspace, San Francisco (94104)
PHONE.................................415 230-2202
EMP: 87
SALES (corp-wide): 7.7MM Privately Held
SIC: 7371 Custom computer programming services
PA: Web Spiders, Inc.
22 Cortlandt St Ste 1635
New York NY 10007
917 373-3950

(P-15543)
WEBYOG INC
2900 Gordon Ave 100-7p, Santa Clara (95051-0718)
PHONE.................................408 512-1434
Rohit Nadhani, CEO
John Smittherson, Sales Mgr
EMP: 250
SALES (est): 6.8MM Privately Held
SIC: 7371 Computer software development

(P-15544)
WIDEORBIT INC (PA)
1160 Battery St Ste 300, San Francisco (94111-1212)
PHONE.................................415 675-6700
Fax: 415 675-6701
Eric Mathewson, CEO
Nathan Gans, COO
Margaret McCarthy, CFO
Mickey McClay Wilson, Officer
Brian Burdick, Exec VP
EMP: 88
SQ FT: 9,000
SALES (est): 77.4MM Privately Held
WEB: www.wideorbit.com
SIC: 7371 Computer software development & applications

(P-15545)
WINMAX SYSTEMS CORPORATION
1551 Mccarthy Blvd # 101, Milpitas (95035-7437)
PHONE.................................408 894-9000
Suparna Bhattacharya, President
Vinnie Bandla, Principal
Afton Usry, Opers Mgr
Afton Usry-Papesh, Opers Staff
Hannah Reyes, Sales Dir
EMP: 120
SQ FT: 1,900
SALES (est): 10.5MM Privately Held
WEB: www.winmaxcorp.com
SIC: 7371 8742 Computer software development & applications; management consulting services

(P-15546)
WISE COMMERCE INC
267 8th St, San Francisco (94103-3910)
PHONE.................................855 469-4737
Arie Shpanya, CEO
Miles Kersten, Controller
Brendan Short, Director
Perry Stallings, Director
Jennifer Perez, Manager
EMP: 90
SALES (est): 157.4K Privately Held
SIC: 7371 Computer software development

(P-15547)
WORKDAY INC (PA)
6230 Stoneridge Mall Rd, Pleasanton (94588-3260)
PHONE.................................925 951-9000
Aneel Bhusri, CEO
David A Duffield, Ch of Bd
Randy Hendricks, President
Mark S Peek, President
Philip Wilmington, President
EMP: 132
SQ FT: 322,088
SALES: 1.1B Publicly Held
WEB: www.workday.com
SIC: 7371 Custom computer programming services; computer software development

(P-15548)
WSO2 INC (PA)
787 Castro St, Mountain View (94041-2013)
PHONE.................................650 745-4499
Sanjiva Weerawarana, President
Douglas Garn, Exec VP
Jonathan Marsh, Vice Pres
Dmitry Sotnikov, Vice Pres
Chanaka Jayasena, Sr Software Eng
EMP: 56
SQ FT: 48,000
SALES (est): 11MM Privately Held
WEB: www.wso2.com
SIC: 7371 Computer software development & applications

(P-15549)
WYNNE SYSTEMS INC (DH)
2603 Main St Ste 710, Irvine (92614-4263)
PHONE.................................949 224-6300
Fax: 949 225-6540
John Bureau, President
Mike Stilwagner, Vice Pres
John Daniels, Planning
Alka More, Software Dev
Craig Stanley, Prgrmr
EMP: 95
SALES (est): 5.9MM
SALES (corp-wide): 1.8B Privately Held
WEB: www.unitedrentals.com
SIC: 7371 7372 Computer software development; prepackaged software
HQ: Volaris Group Inc
5800 Explorer Dr Suite 500
Mississauga ON L4W 5
905 629-8727

(P-15550)
XACTLY CORPORATION (PA)
300 Park Ave Ste 1700, San Jose (95110-2774)
PHONE.................................408 977-3132
Fax: 408 977-1261
Christopher W Cabrera, CEO
Carol G Mills, Ch of Bd
L Evan Ellis Jr, President
Joseph C Consul, CFO
EMP: 148
SQ FT: 40,000
SALES: 75.9MM Publicly Held
WEB: www.xactlycorp.com
SIC: 7371 7372 Software programming applications; prepackaged software

(P-15551)
XAMARIN INC (PA)
394 Pacific Ave Fl 4, San Francisco (94111-1719)
PHONE.................................855 926-2746
Nat Friedman, CEO
Derek Drennan, President
Bryan Morris, CFO
Stephanie Schatz, Senior VP
Keith Ballinger, Vice Pres
EMP: 203 EST: 2011
SALES (est): 58.5MM Privately Held
SIC: 7371 Computer software development & applications

(P-15552)
XAP CORPORATION (PA)
100 Crprate Pinte Ste 350, Culver City (90230)
PHONE.................................310 743-0450
Fax: 310 842-9898
Eddie Monnier, CEO
Paul Seo, Human Resources
Farzin Samadani, Opers Mgr
EMP: 50
SQ FT: 14,757
SALES: 10MM Privately Held
WEB: www.xap.com
SIC: 7371 Computer software development

(P-15553)
XCOMMERCE INC (PA)
Also Called: Magento Commerce
54 N Central Ave Ste 200, Campbell (95008-2085)
PHONE.................................310 954-8012
Mark Lavelle, CEO
EMP: 50

SALES: 120MM **Privately Held**
SIC: 7371 Computer software development & applications

(P-15554)
XYKA INC
5201 Great America Pkwy # 320, Santa Clara (95054-1122)
PHONE.................................408 340-1923
Rakesh Hegde, CEO
Nirav Chhaprapati, President
Noel Delaffon, Project Mgr
EMP: 50
SQ FT: 1,500
SALES (est): 2.7MM Privately Held
WEB: www.xyka.com
SIC: 7371 Computer software development & applications

(P-15555)
YARDI SYSTEMS INC (PA)
430 S Fairview Ave, Santa Barbara (93117-3637)
PHONE.................................805 699-2040
Fax: 805 699-2044
Anant Yardi, President
Jonathan Delong, President
Gordon Morrell, COO
Jason Alfano, CFO
John Pendergast, Senior VP
EMP: 380
SQ FT: 160,000
SALES (est): 782.5MM Privately Held
SIC: 7371 Computer software development & applications

(P-15556)
ZANTAZ INC (DH)
5758 W Las Positas Blvd, Pleasanton (94588-4083)
PHONE.................................925 598-3000
Christopher Yelland, CEO
Gautam Bhattacharyya, Partner
Steven Klei, CFO
Roger Erickson, Senior VP
Steve Kennedy, Senior VP
EMP: 51
SQ FT: 29,000
SALES (est): 28.3MM
SALES (corp-wide): 34.1B Publicly Held
WEB: www.zantaz.com
SIC: 7371 Computer software systems analysis & design, custom
HQ: Autonomy Corporation Limited
Amen Corner
Bracknell BERKS
345 270-4567

(P-15557)
ZEND TECHNOLOGIES USA INC
19200 Stevens Creek Blvd, Cupertino (95014-2530)
PHONE.................................408 253-8800
Fax: 408 253-8801
Andi Gutmans, CEO
Stu Schmidt, President
Curt Disibio, CFO
Daniel Moskowitz, Treasurer
Elaine Lennox, Chief Mktg Ofcr
EMP: 130
SALES (corp-wide): 89.3MM Privately Held
SIC: 7371 Computer software development
PA: Rogue Wave Software, Inc
1315 W Century Dr Ste 150
Louisville CO 80027
303 473-9118

(P-15558)
ZENTEK CORPORATION
3031 Stnfrd Rnch Rd 2, Rocklin (95765)
PHONE.................................916 749-3610
Kristi Woehl, Principal
Michael Prendergast, Business Mgr
EMP: 100
SALES (est): 4.8MM Privately Held
SIC: 7371 8741 Computer software development & applications; management services

(P-15559)
ZESTFINANCE INC
6636 Hollywood Blvd, Los Angeles (90028-6208)
PHONE.................................323 450-3000

Douglas Merrill, CEO
Mike Armstrong, Chief Mktg Ofcr
Tori Horton, Marketing Mgr
Laura Gowen, General Counsel
EMP: 61
SALES (est): 10.7MM Privately Held
SIC: 7371 Computer software development

(P-15560)
ZIGNAL LABS INC
995 Market St Fl 2, San Francisco (94103-1732)
PHONE.................................415 683-7871
Bob Deppisch, Director
Andy Ballard, Vice Chairman
Josh Ginsberg, CEO
Alyson Welch, Vice Pres
Loretta Jimenez, QA Dir
EMP: 60 EST: 2011
SALES (est): 8.1MM Privately Held
SIC: 7371 Custom computer programming services

(P-15561)
ZSCALER INC
110 Rose Orchard Way, San Jose (95134-1358)
PHONE.................................408 533-0288
Jay Chaudhry, CEO
Rajnish Mishra, Vice Pres
Lalit Sharma, Software Engr
Ilya Akinfiev, Engineer
Paul Whittenburg, Engineer
EMP: 600
SALES (est): 98.4MM Privately Held
SIC: 7371 Computer software development & applications

(P-15562)
ZYNX HEALTH INCORPORATED (DH)
10880 Wilshire Blvd, Los Angeles (90024-4101)
PHONE.................................310 954-1950
Fax: 310 598-4556
Scott Weingarten, President
Kevin Daly, President
Richard P Malloch, Treasurer
Robert D Wilbanks, Treasurer
Bertina Yen, Exec VP
EMP: 64
SQ FT: 9,422
SALES: 10.8MM
SALES (corp-wide): 4.9B Privately Held
WEB: www.zynx.com
SIC: 7371 Custom computer programming services; custom computer programming services
HQ: Hearst Business Media Corp
2620 Barrett Rd
Gainesville GA 30507
770 532-4111

7372 Prepackaged Software

(P-15563)
ABB ENTERPRISE SOFTWARE INC
60 Spear St, San Francisco (94105-1506)
PHONE.................................415 527-2850
Greg Dukat, Branch Mgr
EMP: 175
SALES (corp-wide): 692.8MM Privately Held
WEB: www.indusinternational.com
SIC: 7372 Business oriented computer software
HQ: Abb Enterprise Software Inc.
400 Perimeter Ctr Ter 5
Atlanta GA 30346
678 830-1000

(P-15564)
ACCELA INC (PA)
2633 Camino Ramon Ste 500, San Ramon (94583-9149)
PHONE.................................925 659-3200
Fax: 925 659-3201
Maury Blackman, CEO
Mark Jung, Ch of Bd
Jerald Lo, President
Jeffrey Toung, COO
John Alves, CFO

7372 - Prepackaged Software County (P-15565)

PRODUDUCTS & SERVICES SECTION

EMP: 150
SALES: 80MM Privately Held
WEB: www.accela.com
SIC: 7372 Prepackaged software

(P-15565)
ACTION TECHNOLOGIES INC
21 Orinda Way Ste 124c, Orinda (94563-2530)
PHONE..................................510 638-8300
Fax: 510 638-8115
William B Welty, *Ch of Bd*
EMP: 60
SQ FT: 12,000
SALES: 2.2MM Privately Held
WEB: www.actiontech.com
SIC: 7372 Prepackaged software; business oriented computer software

(P-15566)
ACTIVISION BLIZZARD INC
4 Hamilton Landing, Novato (94949-8256)
PHONE..................................415 881-9100
EMP: 209
SALES (corp-wide): 4.6B Publicly Held
SIC: 7372 Home entertainment computer software
PA: Activision Blizzard, Inc.
3100 Ocean Park Blvd
Santa Monica CA 90405
310 255-2000

(P-15567)
ACTIVISION BLIZZARD INC (PA)
3100 Ocean Park Blvd, Santa Monica (90405-3032)
PHONE..................................310 255-2000
Robert A Kotick, *President*
Brian G Kelly, *Ch of Bd*
Pete Vlastelica, *President*
Thomas Tippl, *COO*
Dennis Durkin, *CFO*
EMP: 333 EST: 1979
SQ FT: 139,085
SALES: 4.6B Publicly Held
WEB: www.blizzard.com
SIC: 7372 Prepackaged software; home entertainment computer software

(P-15568)
ACTIVISION BLIZZARD INC
Blizzard Entertainment
16205 Alton Pkwy, Irvine (92618-3616)
P.O. Box 18979 (92623-8979)
PHONE..................................949 955-1380
Frank Pearce, *Principal*
Erik Jensen, *Creative Dir*
Michael Maggio, *Sr Software Eng*
Michael Gilmartin, *Data Proc Dir*
Damon Osgood, *Software Engr*
EMP: 85
SALES (corp-wide): 4.6B Publicly Held
WEB: www.blizzard.com
SIC: 7372 Prepackaged software
PA: Activision Blizzard, Inc.
3100 Ocean Park Blvd
Santa Monica CA 90405
310 255-2000

(P-15569)
ADAPTIVE INSIGHTS INC (PA)
Also Called: Adaptive Consolidation
3350 W Byshore Rd Ste 200, Palo Alto (94303)
PHONE..................................800 303-6346
Thomas F Bogan, *CEO*
Carolee Gearhart, *Partner*
Rob Hull, *Ch of Bd*
Mike Conti, *President*
Jim Johnson, *CFO*
EMP: 200
SQ FT: 8,700
SALES (est): 144.6MM Privately Held
WEB: www.adaptiveplanning.com
SIC: 7372 Business oriented computer software

(P-15570)
ADEXA INC (PA)
5777 W Century Blvd # 1100, Los Angeles (90045-5643)
PHONE..................................310 642-2100
Fax: 310 338-9878
Khosrow Cyrus Hadavi, *CEO*
Cameron Hadavi, *Vice Pres*
Kameron Hadavi, *Vice Pres*

John Hosford, *Vice Pres*
Tim Field, *CTO*
EMP: 50
SQ FT: 31,000
SALES (est): 21.5MM Privately Held
WEB: www.adexa.com
SIC: 7372 Business oriented computer software

(P-15571)
ADOBE SYSTEMS INCORPORATED
601 And 625 Townsend St, San Francisco (94103)
PHONE..................................415 832-2000
Fax: 415 832-2020
Les Schmidt, *Vice Pres*
Bridget Perry, *Vice Pres*
Michael Newman, *Program Mgr*
Peter Nguyen, *Administration*
Daniel Marcus, *Network Mgr*
EMP: 1000
SALES (corp-wide): 4.8B Publicly Held
SIC: 7372 Prepackaged software
PA: Adobe Systems Incorporated
345 Park Ave
San Jose CA 95110
408 536-6000

(P-15572)
ADOBE SYSTEMS INCORPORATED (PA)
345 Park Ave, San Jose (95110-2704)
PHONE..................................408 536-6000
Fax: 408 537-6000
Shantanu Narayen, *President*
Charles M Geschke, *Ch of Bd*
John E Warnock, *Ch of Bd*
Mark Garrett, *CFO*
Michael A Dillon, *Exec VP*
EMP: 600
SQ FT: 391,000
SALES: 4.8B Publicly Held
WEB: www.adobe.com
SIC: 7372 Prepackaged software

(P-15573)
AGENCYCOM LLC (HQ)
5353 Grosvenor Blvd, Los Angeles (90066-6913)
PHONE..................................415 817-3800
Fax: 415 817-3801
Chan Suh, *CEO*
Vincent Deven, *Managing Prtnr*
Dawn Furey, *Managing Prtnr*
Jordan Warren, *President*
Charles Dickson, *CFO*
EMP: 100
SQ FT: 130,000
SALES (est): 23.1MM
SALES (corp-wide): 15.1B Publicly Held
WEB: www.agency.com
SIC: 7372 Application computer software
PA: Omnicom Group Inc.
437 Madison Ave
New York NY 10022
212 415-3600

(P-15574)
AGILEPOINT INC
1916 Old Middlefield Way, Mountain View (94043-2555)
PHONE..................................650 968-6789
Jesse Shiah, *President*
Vincent Chau, *Vice Pres*
Kin Yim, *Office Mgr*
Shahaji Gole, *Sr Software Eng*
Kyle Hansen, *Director*
EMP: 115
SQ FT: 2,000
SALES (est): 14.3MM Privately Held
WEB: www.ascentn.com
SIC: 7372 Prepackaged software

(P-15575)
ALEKS CORPORATION
Also Called: Aleks Educational Systems
15640 Laguna Canyon Rd, Irvine (92618)
PHONE..................................714 245-7191
Fax: 714 245-7190
R G Wilmot Lampros, *President*
Nicolas Thiery, *President*
Jean-Claude Falmagne, *Chairman*
Melissa Deveikis, *Marketing Staff*
Emily Wennerberg, *Marketing Staff*
EMP: 130

SQ FT: 50,000
SALES (est): 11.7MM Privately Held
WEB: www.aris.ss.uci.edu
SIC: 7372 Educational computer software

(P-15576)
ALFRESCO SOFTWARE INC (PA)
1825 S Grant St Ste 900, San Mateo (94402-2675)
PHONE..................................888 317-3395
Doug Dennerline, *CEO*
Paul Holmes-Higgin, *President*
Carlton Baab, *CFO*
Bernadette Nixon, *Officer*
Barry Duplantis, *Vice Pres*
EMP: 80
SALES (est): 32.9MM Privately Held
SIC: 7372 Prepackaged software

(P-15577)
ALIENVAULT LLC (PA)
1875 S Grant St Ste 200, San Mateo (94402-2668)
PHONE..................................650 713-3333
Fax: 650 212-7637
Barmak Meftah, *President*
J Alberto Yepez, *Ch of Bd*
Cayce Ullman, *President*
Brian Robins, *CFO*
Rita Selvaggi, *Chief Mktg Ofcr*
EMP: 80
SALES (est): 39.5MM Privately Held
SIC: 7372 Business oriented computer software

(P-15578)
ALLDATA LLC (HQ)
9650 W Taron Dr Ste 100, Elk Grove (95757-8197)
PHONE..................................916 684-5200
Fax: 916 684-5225
Stephen Odland,
Kevin Scott, *Admin Asst*
Cameron Pierce, *Administration*
Scott Reed, *Engineer*
Pat Webb, *VP Finance*
EMP: 114
SQ FT: 35,000
SALES (est): 57.5MM
SALES (corp-wide): 10.1B Publicly Held
WEB: www.alldata.com
SIC: 7372 Business oriented computer software
PA: Autozone, Inc.
123 S Front St
Memphis TN 38103
901 495-6500

(P-15579)
ALTIUM LLC
4225 Executive Sq Ste 700, La Jolla (92037-9181)
PHONE..................................858 864-1500
Aram Mirkazemi,
Martin Ive, *Treasurer*
EMP: 75
SALES (est): 1.2MM Privately Held
SIC: 7372 Prepackaged software

(P-15580)
APPDIRECT INC (PA)
650 California St Fl 25, San Francisco (94108-2606)
PHONE..................................415 852-3924
Nicolas Desmarais, *Ch of Bd*
Daniel Saks, *President*
John Moffett, *CFO*
Stephen Banbury, *Vice Pres*
Mark Beebe, *Vice Pres*
EMP: 59
SQ FT: 10,000
SALES (est): 30.6MM Privately Held
SIC: 7372 7371 Application computer software; computer software development & applications

(P-15581)
APPERY LLC
1340 Treat Blvd Ste 375, Walnut Creek (94597-7590)
PHONE..................................925 602-5504
Lynne Walter, *CFO*
EMP: 60
SQ FT: 7,200

SALES (est): 999.5K Privately Held
SIC: 7372 Application computer software

(P-15582)
APPFOLIO INC (PA)
50 Castilian Dr Ste 101, Goleta (93117-5578)
PHONE..................................805 364-6093
Brian Donahoo, *President*
Andreas Von Blottnitz, *Ch of Bd*
Ida Kane, *CFO*
Jason Randall, *Senior VP*
Jonathan Walker, *CTO*
EMP: 148
SQ FT: 69,800
SALES: 74.9MM Publicly Held
SIC: 7372 Prepackaged software

(P-15583)
APTIV DIGITAL INC
2210 W Olive Ave Fl 2, Burbank (91506-2626)
PHONE..................................818 295-6789
Neil Jones, *President*
Michael Buchheim, *Senior VP*
Sean Rosqvist, *Sr Software Eng*
EMP: 85
SALES (est): 4.9MM
SALES (corp-wide): 526.2MM Privately Held
WEB: www.tvguideinc.com
SIC: 7372 Home entertainment computer software
HQ: Gemstar-Tv Guide International, Inc.
2233 N Ontario St Ste 100
Burbank CA 91504

(P-15584)
ARIBA INC (DH)
3420 Hillview Ave Bldg 3, Palo Alto (94304-1355)
PHONE..................................650 849-4000
Fax: 650 390-1000
Alex Atzberger, *CEO*
Marc Malone, *CFO*
Alicia Tillman, *Chief Mktg Ofcr*
Joseph Fox, *Vice Pres*
Brad Brubaker, *Admin Sec*
EMP: 105
SQ FT: 86,000
SALES (est): 175.1MM
SALES (corp-wide): 22.3B Privately Held
WEB: www.ariba.com
SIC: 7372 Business oriented computer software
HQ: Sap America, Inc.
3999 West Chester Pike
Newtown Square PA 19073
610 661-1000

(P-15585)
ASPECT SOFTWARE INC
101 Academy Ste 130, Irvine (92617-3081)
PHONE..................................408 595-5002
James Foy, *Owner*
EMP: 50 Privately Held
SIC: 7372 Prepackaged software
HQ: Aspect Software, Inc.
2325 E Camelback Rd # 700
Phoenix AZ 85016
978 250-7900

(P-15586)
ATHENAHEALTH INC
50 Hawthorne St, San Francisco (94105-3902)
PHONE..................................415 416-3500
EMP: 153
SALES (corp-wide): 924.7MM Publicly Held
SIC: 7372 Prepackaged software; business oriented computer software
PA: Athenahealth, Inc.
311 Arsenal St Ste 14
Watertown MA 02472
617 402-1000

(P-15587)
ATLASSIAN INC (DH)
1098 Harrison St, San Francisco (94103-4521)
PHONE..................................415 701-1110
Scott Farquhar, *CEO*
Doug Burgum, *Ch of Bd*
Anthony Rethans, *President*

PRODUCTS & SERVICES SECTION

7372 - Prepackaged Software County (P-15608)

Jay Simons, *President*
Murray Demo, *CFO*
EMP: 101
SALES (est): 51.1MM
SALES (corp-wide): 319.4MM **Privately Held**
WEB: www.atlassian.com
SIC: 7372 Prepackaged software
HQ: Atlassian Pty Ltd
L 6 341 George St
Sydney NSW 2000
292 621-443

(P-15588)
AUDATEX NORTH AMERICA INC (DH)
Also Called: Audaexplore
15030 Ave Of Ste 100, San Diego (92128)
PHONE.................................858 946-1900
Tony Aquila, *CEO*
Jack Pearlstein, *CFO*
Mark Porter, *Vice Pres*
Patrick Schmidlin, *Vice Pres*
Don Tartre, *Vice Pres*
EMP: 200
SQ FT: 35,000
SALES (est): 139.5MM
SALES (corp-wide): 227.8MM **Privately Held**
SIC: 7372 Business oriented computer software
HQ: Solera Holdings, Inc.
1301 Solana Blvd Ste 2100
Westlake TX 76262
817 961-2100

(P-15589)
AUTODESK INC
1 Market St, San Francisco (94105-1420)
PHONE.................................415 356-0700
Chris Bradshaw, *Branch Mgr*
Catalina Caba, *Executive Asst*
Arthur Harsuvanakit, *Admin Asst*
Elisabeth Swanson, *Admin Asst*
Michael Russo, *Software Dev*
EMP: 61
SALES (corp-wide): 2.5B **Publicly Held**
WEB: www.autodesk.com
SIC: 7372 Application computer software
PA: Autodesk, Inc.
111 Mcinnis Pkwy
San Rafael CA 94903
415 507-5000

(P-15590)
AUTODESK INC (PA)
111 Mcinnis Pkwy, San Rafael (94903-2700)
PHONE.................................415 507-5000
Fax: 415 507-5100
Carl Bass, *President*
Crawford W Beveridge, *Ch of Bd*
R Scott Herren, *CFO*
Andrew Anagnost, *Senior VP*
Jan Becker, *Senior VP*
EMP: 400 **EST:** 1982
SQ FT: 220,000
SALES: 2.5B **Publicly Held**
WEB: www.autodesk.com
SIC: 7372 Application computer software

(P-15591)
AUTODESK INC
3950 Civic Center Dr, San Rafael (94903-5901)
PHONE.................................415 507-5000
Kathryn Najafi-Tagol, *Manager*
Rebecca Dunn, *Admin Asst*
Ranger Harke, *Sr Software Eng*
EMP: 250
SALES (corp-wide): 2.5B **Publicly Held**
WEB: www.autodesk.com
SIC: 7372 Application computer software
PA: Autodesk, Inc.
111 Mcinnis Pkwy
San Rafael CA 94903
415 507-5000

(P-15592)
AVOLENT INC
444 De Haro St Ste 100, San Francisco (94107-2350)
PHONE.................................415 553-6400
Doug Roberts, *CEO*
Mike Seashols, *Ch of Bd*
Bhupi Singh, *CFO*

Kevin Han, *Exec VP*
Robin Ducot, *Vice Pres*
EMP: 80 **EST:** 1995
SQ FT: 60,000
SALES (est): 5.6MM **Privately Held**
SIC: 7372 Prepackaged software

(P-15593)
AXOLOTL CORP
160 W Santa Clara St, San Jose (95113-1701)
PHONE.................................408 920-0800
Raymond W Scott, *CEO*
Glenn Keet, *President*
Lalo A Valdez, *COO*
Steve Williams, *Sr Software Eng*
Neeraj Jain, *Technology*
EMP: 50
SQ FT: 10,000
SALES (est): 5.9MM
SALES (corp-wide): 157.1B **Publicly Held**
WEB: www.axolotl.com
SIC: 7372 Business oriented computer software
HQ: Optumisight, Inc.
13625 Technology Dr
Eden Prairie MN 55344
952 833-7100

(P-15594)
BADGEVILLE INC
805 Veterans Blvd Ste 307, Redwood City (94063-1737)
P.O. Box 2367 (94064-2367)
PHONE.................................650 323-6668
Jon Shalowitz, *President*
Stephanie Vinella, *CFO*
Kevin Akeroyd, *Senior VP*
Shane Anastasi, *Vice Pres*
Ted Farrell, *Vice Pres*
EMP: 50
SALES (est): 10.2MM **Privately Held**
SIC: 7372 Prepackaged software

(P-15595)
BARRA LLC (HQ)
Also Called: Barra, Inc.
2100 Milvia St, Berkeley (94704-1113)
PHONE.................................510 548-5442
Fax: 510 548-1709
Kamal Duggirala, *CEO*
Andrew Rudd, *Ch of Bd*
Aamir Sheikh, *President*
Robert L Honeycutt, *COO*
Greg Stockett, *CFO*
EMP: 280
SQ FT: 35,000
SALES (est): 27MM
SALES (corp-wide): 1B **Publicly Held**
WEB: www.barra.com
SIC: 7372 8741 6282 Business oriented computer software; financial management for business; investment advisory service
PA: Msci Inc.
250 Greenwich St Fl 49
New York NY 10007
212 804-3900

(P-15596)
BARRACUDA NETWORKS INC (PA)
3175 Winchester Blvd, Campbell (95008-6557)
PHONE.................................408 342-5400
William D Jenkins Jr, *President*
David Faugno, *CFO*
Michael D Perone, *Chief Mktg Ofcr*
Zachary S Levow, *Exec VP*
Diane C Honda, *Senior VP*
EMP: 225
SQ FT: 61,400
SALES: 320.1MM **Publicly Held**
WEB: www.barracudanetworks.com
SIC: 7372 7373 Prepackaged software; computer integrated systems design

(P-15597)
BDNA CORPORATION (PA)
339 Bernardo Ave Ste 206, Mountain View (94043-5232)
PHONE.................................650 625-9530
Fax: 650 625-9533
Constantin Delivanis, *CEO*
Ossama Hassanein, *Ch of Bd*
Walker White, *President*

Fred Hessabi, *CEO*
Dave Pomeroy, *CFO*
EMP: 73
SQ FT: 7,000
SALES (est): 22.2MM **Privately Held**
WEB: www.bdnacorp.com
SIC: 7372 Prepackaged software

(P-15598)
BEATS MUSIC LLC
235 2nd St, San Francisco (94105-3124)
PHONE.................................415 590-5104
Timothy Cook, *CEO*
EMP: 95
SALES (est): 8.3MM
SALES (corp-wide): 233.7B **Publicly Held**
SIC: 7372 Prepackaged software
PA: Apple Inc.
1 Infinite Loop
Cupertino CA 95014
408 996-1010

(P-15599)
BILLCOM INC
1810 Embarcadero Rd, Palo Alto (94303-3308)
PHONE.................................650 353-3301
Fax: 650 644-0293
Rene Lacerte, *CEO*
Mark Orttung, *COO*
John Rettig, *CFO*
Carol Glover, *Senior VP*
Sanjeev Kriplani, *Senior VP*
EMP: 140
SALES (est): 29.2MM **Privately Held**
SIC: 7372 Prepackaged software

(P-15600)
BIZMATICS INC (PA)
4010 Moorpark Ave Ste 222, San Jose (95117-1843)
PHONE.................................408 873-3030
Vinay Deshpande, *CEO*
Sneha Baing, *Executive*
Amreen Shaikh, *Executive*
Nitin Uchibagale, *Web Dvlpr*
Suvarna Gaikwad, *Software Engr*
EMP: 50
SQ FT: 2,000
SALES: 5.9MM **Privately Held**
SIC: 7372 Prepackaged software

(P-15601)
BLACKLINE SYSTEMS INC (PA)
21300 Victory Blvd Fl 12, Woodland Hills (91367-7734)
PHONE.................................818 746-4700
Therese Tucker, *CEO*
Mark Partin, *CFO*
David Downing, *Chief Mktg Ofcr*
Karole Morgan-Prager,
Charles Best, *Officer*
EMP: 108
SQ FT: 66,447
SALES (est): 66.6MM **Privately Held**
WEB: www.blackline.com
SIC: 7372 Prepackaged software

(P-15602)
BLIZZARD ENTERTAINMENT INC (HQ)
16215 Alton Pkwy, Irvine (92618-3616)
P.O. Box 18979 (92623-8979)
PHONE.................................949 955-1380
Fax: 949 737-2000
Mike Morhaime, *President*
Paul Sams, *President*
Frank Pearce, *Exec VP*
Chris Metzen, *Senior VP*
Mark Almeida, *Vice Pres*
EMP: 85
SALES (est): 99.5MM
SALES (corp-wide): 4.6B **Publicly Held**
SIC: 7372 5734 7819 Prepackaged software; software, computer games; reproduction services, motion picture production
PA: Activision Blizzard, Inc.
3100 Ocean Park Blvd
Santa Monica CA 90405
310 255-2000

(P-15603)
BLUE COAT SYSTEMS LLC (DH)
384 Santa Trinita Ave, Sunnyvale (94085-3911)
PHONE.................................408 220-2200
Gregory S Clark, *CEO*
Donald W Alford, *President*
Michael Fey, *President*
David Yntemai, *President*
Thomas Seifert, *CFO*
EMP: 488
SQ FT: 234,000
SALES (est): 726.7MM
SALES (corp-wide): 3.6B **Publicly Held**
WEB: www.cacheflow.com
SIC: 7372 Prepackaged software
HQ: Blue Coat, Inc.
384 Santa Trinita Ave
Sunnyvale CA 94085
408 220-2200

(P-15604)
BMC SOFTWARE INC
10620 Treena St Ste 130, San Diego (92131-1140)
PHONE.................................713 918-8800
Ali Hedayati, *Assoc VP*
Kevin Rice, *President*
Dave Gravley, *Consultant*
Robert Bongo, *Accounts Exec*
Shane Collins, *Accounts Exec*
EMP: 100
SALES (corp-wide): 2.7B **Privately Held**
SIC: 7372 Prepackaged software
HQ: Bmc Software, Inc.
2103 Citywest Blvd # 2100
Houston TX 77042
713 918-8800

(P-15605)
BOPS INC
1200 Charleston Rd, Mountain View (94043-1330)
PHONE.................................650 254-2800
Carl Schlachte, *CEO*
Victor Young, *CFO*
Dan Hauck, *Exec VP*
David Strube', *CTO*
EMP: 100
SQ FT: 11,780
SALES (est): 3.2MM **Privately Held**
SIC: 7372 Prepackaged software

(P-15606)
BORLAND SOFTWARE CORPORATION
951 Mariners Isl Blvd # 460, San Mateo (94404-1558)
PHONE.................................650 286-1900
Gina Rosenberger, *Branch Mgr*
EMP: 100
SALES (corp-wide): 834.5MM **Privately Held**
WEB: www.borland.com
SIC: 7372 Business oriented computer software
HQ: Borland Software Corporation
8310 N Cptl Of Texas Hwy
Austin TX 78731
512 340-2200

(P-15607)
BOX INC (PA)
900 Jefferson Ave, Redwood City (94063-1837)
PHONE.................................877 729-4269
Aaron Levie, *Ch of Bd*
Dan Levin, *President*
Dylan Smith, *CFO*
Carrie Palin, *Chief Mktg Ofcr*
Jim Herbold, *Exec VP*
EMP: 148 **EST:** 2005
SQ FT: 340,000
SALES: 302.7MM **Publicly Held**
SIC: 7372 Prepackaged software

(P-15608)
BQE SOFTWARE INC
3825 Del Amo Blvd Trrance Torrance, Torrance (90503)
PHONE.................................310 602-4020
Fax: 310 784-8482
Shafat Qazi, *CEO*
Taya Pocock, *Manager*
EMP: 95
SQ FT: 20,000

7372 - Prepackaged Software County (P-15609)

SALES (est): 14.6MM **Privately Held**
WEB: www.billquick.com
SIC: 7372 5734 Application computer software; software, business & non-game

(P-15609)
BRIGHTSCOPE INC
9191 Towne Centre Dr # 400, San Diego (92122-1230)
PHONE..................858 452-7500
Mike Alfred, *CEO*
Ryan Alfred, *President*
Dan Weeks, *COO*
Bruce Hansen, *Chairman*
Sonia Ahuja, *Exec VP*
EMP: 65
SALES (est): 8.4MM **Privately Held**
SIC: 7372 Business oriented computer software

(P-15610)
BROADVISION INC (PA)
1700 Seaport Blvd Ste 210, Redwood City (94063-5579)
PHONE..................650 331-1000
Fax: 650 364-3425
Pehong Chen, *Ch of Bd*
Robert Wang, *COO*
Robert H Wang, *COO*
Peter Chu, *CFO*
Peter Downs, *Treasurer*
EMP: 99
SQ FT: 16,399
SALES: 9.4MM **Publicly Held**
WEB: www.broadvision.com
SIC: 7372 Prepackaged software

(P-15611)
C3 INC
Also Called: C3 Iot
1300 Seaport Blvd Ste 500, Redwood City (94063-5592)
PHONE..................650 503-2200
Thomas M Siebel, *CEO*
Ed Abbo, *President*
Peter Eidelman, *CFO*
Jessica Reiter, *Chief Mktg Ofcr*
William Daniher, *Vice Pres*
EMP: 125
SQ FT: 35,000
SALES (est): 23.6MM **Privately Held**
SIC: 7372 Business oriented computer software

(P-15612)
CA INC
3965 Freedom Cir Fl 6, Santa Clara (95054-1286)
PHONE..................800 225-5224
Phil Sheridan, *Mktg Dir*
EMP: 166
SALES (corp-wide): 4B **Publicly Held**
SIC: 7372 Business oriented computer software
PA: Ca, Inc.
  520 Madison Ave Fl 22
  New York NY 10022
  800 225-5224

(P-15613)
CA INC
10180 Telesis Ct Ste 500, San Diego (92121-2787)
PHONE..................631 342-6000
Greg Fox, *Manager*
Lar Kress, *Executive*
Nany Luce, *Branch Mgr*
Jeno Bonetti, *Administration*
Brian Dyson, *Sr Software Eng*
EMP: 100
SALES (corp-wide): 4B **Publicly Held**
WEB: www.cai.com
SIC: 7372 Prepackaged software
PA: Ca, Inc.
  520 Madison Ave Fl 22
  New York NY 10022
  800 225-5224

(P-15614)
CADENCE DESIGN SYSTEMS INC (PA)
2655 Seely Ave Bldg 5, San Jose (95134-1931)
PHONE..................408 943-1234
Lip-Bu Tan, *President*
John B Shoven, *Ch of Bd*
Geoffrey G Ribar, *CFO*
Thomas P Beckley, *Senior VP*
James J Cowie, *Senior VP*
EMP: 700
SALES: 1.7B **Publicly Held**
WEB: www.cadence.com
SIC: 7372 Prepackaged software; application computer software

(P-15615)
CARPARTS TECHNOLOGIES
32122 Camn Capistrano # 100, San Juan Capistrano (92675-3734)
PHONE..................949 488-8860
Charles Ruban, *CEO*
Cynthia Robbins, *President*
Habib Kairouz, *Bd of Directors*
Marc Singer, *Bd of Directors*
Angela Husted, *Info Tech Mgr*
EMP: 163 EST: 2004
SQ FT: 1,400
SALES (est): 6.5MM **Privately Held**
WEB: www.crcs.com
SIC: 7372 Prepackaged software

(P-15616)
CATALYST DEVELOPMENT CORP
56925 Yucca Trl, Yucca Valley (92284-7913)
PHONE..................760 228-9653
Fax: 760 369-1185
Cary Harwin, *President*
Mike Stefanik, *Senior VP*
Sherry Harwin, *General Mgr*
EMP: 50
SALES (est): 3MM **Privately Held**
WEB: www.catalyst.com
SIC: 7372 Prepackaged software

(P-15617)
CFS TAX SOFTWARE
Also Called: CFS Income Tax
1445 E Los Angeles Ave # 214, Simi Valley (93065-2828)
P.O. Box 879 (93062-0879)
PHONE..................805 522-1157
Fax: 805 522-0187
Ted Sullivan, *President*
Nolan Stacey, *Software Dev*
Juliana Caizzo, *Technology*
Roger Stock, *Technical Staff*
Juliana Caiazzo, *Sales Staff*
EMP: 60
SALES (est): 4.5MM **Privately Held**
WEB: www.taxtools.com
SIC: 7372 8721 Prepackaged software; accounting, auditing & bookkeeping

(P-15618)
CHECK POINT SOFTWARE TECH INC (HQ)
959 Skyway Rd Ste 300, San Carlos (94070-2723)
PHONE..................800 429-4391
Fax: 650 654-4233
John Slavitt, *CEO*
Marius Nacht, *Ch of Bd*
Rafael Alegre, *President*
Jorge Steinfeld, *President*
Jerry Ungerman, *President*
EMP: 120
SALES (est): 312.7MM
SALES (corp-wide): 1.6B **Privately Held**
WEB: www.checkpoint.com
SIC: 7372 Operating systems computer software
PA: Check Point Software Technologies Ltd.
  5 Hasolelim
  Tel Aviv-Jaffa
  361 152-64

(P-15619)
CHOWNOW INC
12181 Bluff Creek Dr # 200, Playa Vista (90094-3232)
PHONE..................888 707-2469
Eric Jaffe, *President*
Stuart Hathaway, *CFO*
Ha Lam, *Software Engr*
Fabian Segura, *Graphic Designe*
Jessica Springer, *Marketing Mgr*
EMP: 100
SQ FT: 25,000

SALES (est): 10.3MM **Privately Held**
SIC: 7372 Business oriented computer software

(P-15620)
CISCO IRONPORT SYSTEMS LLC (HQ)
170 W Tasman Dr, San Jose (95134-1706)
PHONE..................650 989-6500
Fax: 650 249-0490
Scott Weiss, *CEO*
Tom Peterson, *President*
Craig Collins, *CFO*
Bob Kavner, *Chairman*
Kelly Bodnar Battles, *Vice Pres*
EMP: 260
SALES (est): 68.7MM
SALES (corp-wide): 49.2B **Publicly Held**
WEB: www.ironport.com
SIC: 7372 5045 Prepackaged software; computers, peripherals & software
PA: Cisco Systems, Inc.
  170 W Tasman Dr
  San Jose CA 95134
  408 526-4000

(P-15621)
CLEARSLIDE INC (PA)
45 Fremont St Ste 3200, San Francisco (94105-2258)
PHONE..................877 360-3366
Jim Benton, *President*
Lawrence Bruhmuller, *President*
Adam Lieb, *CEO*
Dustin Grosse, *COO*
Mark Lambert, *CFO*
EMP: 99
SALES (est): 27.8MM **Privately Held**
SIC: 7372 Business oriented computer software

(P-15622)
CLEARWELL SYSTEMS INC
350 Ellis St, Mountain View (94043-2202)
PHONE..................877 253-2793
Aaref Hilaly, *CEO*
Anup Singh, *CFO*
Venkat Rangan, *CTO*
Bob Nigh, *Recruiter*
Ron Best, *Legal Staff*
▼ **EMP:** 110
SQ FT: 17,000
SALES (est): 9.1MM
SALES (corp-wide): 3.6B **Publicly Held**
WEB: www.clearwellsystems.com
SIC: 7372 Prepackaged software
PA: Symantec Corporation
  350 Ellis St
  Mountain View CA 94043
  650 527-8000

(P-15623)
COLLABNET INC (PA)
4000 Shoreline Ct, South San Francisco (94080-1993)
PHONE..................650 228-2500
Fax: 650 228-2501
Flint Brenton, *President*
Richard Cook, *President*
Louis Suarez-Potts, *President*
Amir Ameri, *CFO*
Maria Carlile, *Senior VP*
EMP: 80
SQ FT: 30,000
SALES (est): 75.4MM **Privately Held**
WEB: www.collab.net
SIC: 7372 Application computer software

(P-15624)
COMMERCE VELOCITY LLC
1 Technology Dr Ste J725, Irvine (92618-2353)
PHONE..................949 756-8950
Umesh Verma,
Jim Schwegman, *Vice Pres*
Ajay Chopra,
EMP: 50
SQ FT: 5,000
SALES (est): 8.3MM
SALES (corp-wide): 9.1B **Publicly Held**
WEB: www.cvelocity.com
SIC: 7372 Business oriented computer software

PA: Fidelity National Financial, Inc.
  601 Riverside Ave Fl 4
  Jacksonville FL 32204
  904 854-8100

(P-15625)
COMPOSITE SOFTWARE LLC (HQ)
755 Sycamore Dr, Milpitas (95035-7411)
PHONE..................800 553-6387
Fax: 650 227-8199
Jim Green, *CEO*
Jon Bode, *CFO*
Marc Breissinger, *Exec VP*
Robert Eve, *Exec VP*
Che Wijesinghe, *Exec VP*
EMP: 74
SQ FT: 14,000
SALES: 16.3MM
SALES (corp-wide): 49.2B **Publicly Held**
WEB: www.compositesw.com
SIC: 7372 Prepackaged software
PA: Cisco Systems, Inc.
  170 W Tasman Dr
  San Jose CA 95134
  408 526-4000

(P-15626)
COMPULINK BUSINESS SYSTEMS INC
1100 Business Center Cir, Newbury Park (91320-1129)
PHONE..................805 446-2050
Fax: 805 497-4983
Link Wilson, *President*
Mary Fitzhugh, *Vice Pres*
Cole Galbarith, *Info Tech Mgr*
Michael Asgariani, *Engineer*
Rod Baker, *Regl Sales Mgr*
EMP: 120
SQ FT: 15,000
SALES (est): 17.7MM **Privately Held**
WEB: www.compulink-software.com
SIC: 7372 Prepackaged software

(P-15627)
COMPULINK MANAGEMENT CTR INC
Also Called: Laserfiche Document Imaging
3545 Long Beach Blvd, Long Beach (90807-3941)
PHONE..................562 988-1688
Fax: 562 988-1886
Nien-Ling Wacker, *President*
Gerald Bengtson, *Sr Corp Ofcr*
Hedy Belttary, *Vice Pres*
Hank Eisner, *Vice Pres*
Jim Haney, *Vice Pres*
EMP: 170
SQ FT: 30,000
SALES (est): 33.6MM **Privately Held**
WEB: www.laserfiche.com
SIC: 7372 Prepackaged software

(P-15628)
CONDUSIV TECHNOLOGIES CORP (PA)
7590 N Glenoaks Blvd, Burbank (91504-1003)
PHONE..................818 771-1600
Craig Jensen, *CEO*
Jeff Medina, *President*
Brian Olson, *President*
Frederic T Boyer, *CFO*
Gary Quan, *Senior VP*
EMP: 102
SQ FT: 72,000
SALES (est): 34MM **Privately Held**
WEB: www.diskeeper.com
SIC: 7372 5734 Prepackaged software; utility computer software; software, business & non-game

(P-15629)
COPLEY PRESS INC
Also Called: Signon San Diego
2375 Northside Dr Ste 300, San Diego (92108-2700)
PHONE..................619 718-5200
Ron James, *Manager*
Debi Rosen, *Sales Mgr*
Thomas Harris, *Director*
Scott Whitley, *Director*
EMP: 80

PRODUCTS & SERVICES SECTION

7372 - Prepackaged Software County (P-15651)

SALES (corp-wide): 92.6MM **Privately Held**
WEB: www.copleynewspapers.com
SIC: **7372** 2711 Prepackaged software; newspapers
PA: The Copley Press Inc
 7776 Ivanhoe Ave
 La Jolla CA 92037
 858 454-0411

(P-15630)
CORNERSTONE ONDEMAND INC (PA)
1601 Cloverfield Blvd 620s, Santa Monica (90404-4178)
PHONE..................................310 752-0200
Fax: 310 752-0199
Adam L Miller, *President*
Mike Erlin, *President*
Kirsten Helvey, *COO*
Brian Swartz, *CFO*
Brian L Swartz, *CFO*
EMP: 120
SQ FT: 108,000
SALES: 339.6MM **Publicly Held**
WEB: www.cornerstoneondemand.com
SIC: **7372** Prepackaged software

(P-15631)
COUPA SOFTWARE INCORPORATED (PA)
1855 S Grant St Fl 4, San Mateo (94402-7034)
PHONE..................................650 931-3200
Fax: 650 230-7126
Rob Bernshteyn, *CEO*
Craig Bittner, *President*
Roger Goulart, *President*
Sean Simpson, *President*
Todd Ford, *CFO*
EMP: 114
SALES: 83.6MM **Publicly Held**
WEB: www.coupa.com
SIC: **7372** Prepackaged software; business oriented computer software

(P-15632)
CRYSTAL DYNAMICS INC
1600 Seaport Blvd Ste 500, Redwood City (94063-5583)
PHONE..................................650 421-7600
Philip Rogers, *CEO*
Robert Dyer, *President*
John Horsley, *President*
John Miller, *President*
Timothy Longo, *Creative Dir*
EMP: 90
SQ FT: 26,000
SALES (est): 12.7MM
SALES (corp-wide): 1.8B **Privately Held**
WEB: www.crystald.com
SIC: **7372** Prepackaged software
HQ: Square Enix Limited
 240 Blackfriars Road
 London SE1 8
 208 636-3000

(P-15633)
CUMULUS NETWORKS INC (PA)
185 E Dana St, Mountain View (94041-1507)
PHONE..................................650 383-6700
Jame Rivers, *CEO*
Nolan Leake, *Co-Owner*
Reza Malekzadeh, *Vice Pres*
Shrijeet Mukherjee, *Vice Pres*
Edward Leake, *Principal*
EMP: 124
SALES (est): 34.1MM **Privately Held**
SIC: **7372** 7371 Publishers' computer software; computer software development

(P-15634)
D+H USA CORPORATION
3 Hutton Cntre Dr Ste 700, Santa Ana (92707)
PHONE..................................714 427-1000
Gladys Gutierrez, *Branch Mgr*
EMP: 173
SALES (corp-wide): 997.8MM **Privately Held**
SIC: **7372** Prepackaged software
HQ: D+H Usa Corporation
 605 Crescent Executive Ct # 600
 Lake Mary FL 32746
 407 804-6600

(P-15635)
D+H USA CORPORATION
5000 Franklin Dr, Pleasanton (94588-3354)
PHONE..................................925 463-8356
Jim Berthelsen, *Manager*
Niles Bay, *Vice Pres*
Michael Hill, *Administration*
Betsy Leeth, *CTO*
Darnelle Huus, *Sales Staff*
EMP: 300
SALES (corp-wide): 997.8MM **Privately Held**
WEB: www.harlandfinancialsolutions.com
SIC: **7372** 7389 Prepackaged software; personal service agents, brokers & bureaus
HQ: D+H Usa Corporation
 605 Crescent Executive Ct # 600
 Lake Mary FL 32746
 407 804-6600

(P-15636)
D3PUBLISHER OF AMERICA INC
11500 W Olympic Blvd, Los Angeles (90064-1524)
PHONE..................................310 268-0820
Yoji Takenaka, *President*
Yuji ITOH, *Ch of Bd*
Hidetaka Tachibana, *CFO*
Peter Andrew, *Vice Pres*
Bill Anker, *Vice Pres*
EMP: 63
SQ FT: 6,129
SALES (est): 9.8MM
SALES (corp-wide): 4.9B **Privately Held**
SIC: **7372** Home entertainment computer software
HQ: D3 Publisher Inc.
 1-9-5, Dogenzaka
 Shibuya-Ku TKY 150-0
 354 283-455

(P-15637)
DELPHIX CORP (PA)
1400 Saport Blvd Ste 200a, Redwood City (94063)
PHONE..................................650 494-1645
Fax: 650 494-1676
Chris Cook, *CEO*
Jedidiah Yueh, *Ch of Bd*
Stewart Grierson, *CFO*
Marco Aurelio, *Vice Pres*
Chris Fuller, *Vice Pres*
EMP: 50 EST: 2008
SQ FT: 18,000
SALES (est): 30.2MM **Privately Held**
SIC: **7372** Business oriented computer software

(P-15638)
DEMANDBASE INC (PA)
680 Folsom St Ste 400, San Francisco (94107-2159)
PHONE..................................415 683-2660
Chris Golec, *President*
Peter Isaacson, *Chief Mktg Ofcr*
Tat Ng, *Senior VP*
George Rekouts, *Senior VP*
Lisa Cleary, *Vice Pres*
EMP: 73
SALES (est): 36.7MM **Privately Held**
WEB: www.demandbase.com
SIC: **7372** Prepackaged software

(P-15639)
DINCLOUD INC
27520 Hawthorne Blvd, Rling HLS Est (90274-3576)
PHONE..................................424 286-2300
Bob Din, *CEO*
Mike Chase, *Exec VP*
Ali M Din, *Vice Pres*
Walid Elemary, *Research*
Khurram Shafique, *Accountant*
EMP: 53
SQ FT: 1,500
SALES: 4MM **Privately Held**
SIC: **7372** 4813 Business oriented computer software;

(P-15640)
DISTILLERY INC
90 Heron Ct, San Quentin (94964)
PHONE..................................415 505-5446
Adrian Szwarcburg, *President*

EMP: 55
SALES (est): 1.9MM **Privately Held**
SIC: **7372** Prepackaged software

(P-15641)
DOCTOR ON DEMAND INC
275 Battery St Ste 650, San Francisco (94111-3332)
PHONE..................................415 935-4447
Adam Jackson, *CEO*
EMP: 100
SALES (est): 204K **Privately Held**
SIC: **7372** Application computer software

(P-15642)
DOCUMENT SCIENCES CORPORATION (DH)
5958 Priestly Dr, Carlsbad (92008-8812)
PHONE..................................760 602-0809
Fax: 760 602-1450
John L McGannon, *President*
Thomas L Ringer, *Ch of Bd*
J Douglas Winter, *COO*
Walker Marine, *CFO*
Todd W Schmidt, *CFO*
EMP: 95
SQ FT: 20,300
SALES (est): 2MM
SALES (corp-wide): 72.7B **Publicly Held**
WEB: www.docscience.com
SIC: **7372** 7371 Prepackaged software; computer software development & applications
HQ: Emc Corporation
 176 South St
 Hopkinton MA 01748
 508 435-1000

(P-15643)
DOCUMENTUM INC
6801 Koll Center Pkwy, Pleasanton (94566-7047)
PHONE..................................925 600-6800
Fax: 925 600-6850
David Dewalt, *President*
Rob Tarkoff, *Exec VP*
Michael Decesare, *Vice Pres*
Mark Garrett, *Vice Pres*
Janet Scott, *Executive Asst*
EMP: 1155
SALES: 61.8MM
SALES (corp-wide): 72.7B **Publicly Held**
WEB: www.documentum.com
SIC: **7372** 7371 Business oriented computer software; custom computer programming services
HQ: Emc Corporation
 176 South St
 Hopkinton MA 01748
 508 435-1000

(P-15644)
DORADO NETWORK SYSTEMS CORP
Also Called: Corelogic Dorado
555 12th St Ste 1100, Oakland (94607-4049)
PHONE..................................650 227-7300
Dain Ehring, *CEO*
Karen Camp, *CFO*
Ravi Balwada, *Senior VP*
Steve Poppe PHD, *Senior VP*
Adam Springer, *Senior VP*
EMP: 140
SQ FT: 19,000
SALES (est): 14.5MM
SALES (corp-wide): 1.5B **Publicly Held**
WEB: www.dorado.com
SIC: **7372** Application computer software
PA: Corelogic, Inc.
 40 Pacifica Ste 900
 Irvine CA 92618
 949 214-1000

(P-15645)
DOUBLE DUTCH INC
2601 Mission St Ste 800, San Francisco (94110-3138)
PHONE..................................800 748-9024
Lawrence Coburn, *CEO*
Brad Roberts, *CFO*
Lucian Beebe, *Vice Pres*
Russ Hearl, *Vice Pres*
Ken Kamada, *Executive*
EMP: 250

SALES: 28MM **Privately Held**
SIC: **7372** Application computer software

(P-15646)
DWA NOVA LLC
1000 Flower St, Glendale (91201-3007)
PHONE..................................818 695-5000
Lincoln Wallen, *CEO*
Derek Chan, *COO*
EMP: 75
SQ FT: 10,000
SALES (est): 1.1MM **Privately Held**
SIC: **7372** Business oriented computer software

(P-15647)
ECRIO INC
19925 Stevens Creek Blvd, Cupertino (95014-2384)
PHONE..................................408 973-7290
Fax: 408 366-8817
Randy Granovetter, *CEO*
Tad Bogdan, *COO*
Nagesh Challa, *Officer*
Ted Goldstein, *Officer*
Lina Martin, *Vice Pres*
EMP: 90
SALES (est): 6.1MM **Privately Held**
WEB: www.ecrio.com
SIC: **7372** Prepackaged software

(P-15648)
EDGEWAVE INC
15333 Ave Of Sci Ste 100, San Diego (92128)
PHONE..................................858 676-2277
Steve Orenberg, *CEO*
Humphrey P Polanen, *Ch of Bd*
Louis E Ryan, *Ch of Bd*
Brian Nugent, *COO*
Thalia R Gietzen, *CFO*
EMP: 100
SQ FT: 37,000
SALES (est): 23MM **Privately Held**
WEB: www.edgewave.com
SIC: **7372** Operating systems computer software

(P-15649)
EGAIN CORPORATION (PA)
1252 Borregas Ave, Sunnyvale (94089-1309)
PHONE..................................408 636-4500
Fax: 408 636-4400
Ashutosh Roy, *Ch of Bd*
Eric Smit, *CFO*
Eric N Smit, *CFO*
Aj Berkeley, *Senior VP*
Ram Kedlaya, *Senior VP*
EMP: 148 EST: 1997
SQ FT: 42,541
SALES: 69.3MM **Publicly Held**
WEB: www.egain.com
SIC: **7372** 7371 Prepackaged software; custom computer programming services

(P-15650)
EGL HOLDCO INC
18200 Von Karman Ave # 1000, Irvine (92612-1023)
PHONE..................................800 678-7423
Pervez Qureshi, *President*
EMP: 4000
SALES (est): 98.4MM
SALES (corp-wide): 185.6MM **Privately Held**
SIC: **7372** Prepackaged software
HQ: Egl Midco, Inc.
 4120 Dublin Blvd
 Dublin CA 94568
 800 678-7423

(P-15651)
EIS GROUP INC
345 California St Fl 10, San Francisco (94104-2606)
PHONE..................................415 402-2622
Fax: 415 402-2022
Gwen Spertell, *President*
Alec Miloslavsky, *CEO*
Sergiy Synyanskyy, *CFO*
Glenn Lim, *Senior VP*
Chris Pigott, *Senior VP*
EMP: 128
SQ FT: 16,803

7372 - Prepackaged Software County (P-15652) — PRODUDUCTS & SERVICES SECTION

SALES (est): 19MM **Privately Held**
SIC: 7372 Business oriented computer software

(P-15652)
ELECTRONIC ARTS INC (PA)
209 Redwood Shores Pkwy, Redwood City (94065-1175)
PHONE..................................650 628-1500
Andrew Wilson, *CEO*
Lawrence F Probst III, *Ch of Bd*
Blake Jorgensen, *CFO*
Peter R Moore, *Ch Credit Ofcr*
Christopher Bruzzo, *Chief Mktg Ofcr*
EMP: 475
SQ FT: 660,000
SALES: 4.4B **Publicly Held**
WEB: www.ea.com
SIC: 7372 Home entertainment computer software

(P-15653)
ELECTRONIC CLEARING HOUSE INC (HQ)
730 Paseo Camarillo, Camarillo (93010-6064)
PHONE..................................805 419-8700
Charles J Harris, *President*
Alice L Cheung, *CFO*
Alice Cheung, *CFO*
Karl Asplund, *Senior VP*
Patricia Williams, *Senior VP*
EMP: 100
SQ FT: 32,669
SALES (est): 12.4MM
SALES (corp-wide): 4.6B **Publicly Held**
WEB: www.echo-inc.com
SIC: 7372 Business oriented computer software
PA: Intuit Inc.
2700 Coast Ave
Mountain View CA 94043
650 944-6000

(P-15654)
EMC CORPORATION
Also Called: Softworks
17011 Beach Blvd, Huntington Beach (92647-5946)
PHONE..................................866 438-3622
Fax: 714 375-1387
Thomas A Cammarano, *Exec VP*
Daryl A Cole, *Branch Mgr*
R C Verbeck, *Consultant*
EMP: 50
SALES (corp-wide): 72.7B **Publicly Held**
WEB: www.emc.com
SIC: 7372 Prepackaged software
HQ: Emc Corporation
176 South St
Hopkinton MA 01748
508 435-1000

(P-15655)
EMC CORPORATION
2841 Mission College Blvd, Santa Clara (95054-1838)
PHONE..................................408 566-2000
William Schroeder, *President*
Lee Schulz, *Vice Pres*
Natasha Skok, *Vice Pres*
Jan Anderson, *Managing Dir*
Kiran Bachu, *CTO*
EMP: 200
SQ FT: 105,000
SALES (corp-wide): 72.7B **Publicly Held**
WEB: www.emc.com
SIC: 7372 Prepackaged software
HQ: Emc Corporation
176 South St
Hopkinton MA 01748
508 435-1000

(P-15656)
EMULEX COMMUNICATIONS CORP
2560 N 1st St Ste 300, San Jose (95131-1041)
PHONE..................................408 434-6064
Ameesh Divatia, *CEO*
Amit Parikh, *CFO*
Chris McBride, *Exec VP*
Bill Huber, *Senior VP*
Tony Gaddis, *Vice Pres*
EMP: 50

SALES (est): 4MM **Privately Held**
WEB: www.aarohicommunications.com
SIC: 7372 Publishers' computer software

(P-15657)
EPICOR SOFTWARE CORPORATION
4120 Dublin Blvd Ste 300, Dublin (94568-7759)
PHONE..................................925 361-9900
Pervez Qureshi, *Branch Mgr*
John Ireland, *Officer*
Donna Troy, *Exec VP*
Noel Goggin, *Senior VP*
Matthew Christus, *Vice Pres*
EMP: 101 **Privately Held**
SIC: 7372 Prepackaged software
PA: Epicor Software Corporation
804 Las Cimas Pkwy
Austin TX 78746

(P-15658)
EPICOR SOFTWARE CORPORATION
3394 Carmel Mountain Rd # 100, San Diego (92121-1065)
PHONE..................................858 352-1600
Fax: 858 352-1777
L George Klaus, *CEO*
Robert L Moore, *Technology*
Elie Salem, *Technology*
Priscilla Wang, *Technology*
Stuart Clifton,
EMP: 60 **Privately Held**
WEB: www.epicor.com
SIC: 7372 Business oriented computer software
PA: Epicor Software Corporation
804 Las Cimas Pkwy
Austin TX 78746

(P-15659)
EUCALYPTUS SYSTEMS INC
6755 Hollister Ave # 200, Goleta (93117-5551)
PHONE..................................805 845-8000
Marten Mickos, *President*
Ning Wang, *CFO*
Woody Rollins, *Officer*
Greg Dekoenigsberg, *Vice Pres*
Barry Duplantis, *Vice Pres*
EMP: 50
SALES (est): 7.4MM **Privately Held**
SIC: 7372 Prepackaged software

(P-15660)
EXADEL INC (PA)
1340 Treat Blvd Ste 375, Walnut Creek (94597-7590)
PHONE..................................925 363-9510
Fima Katz, *President*
Lynne Walter, *CFO*
Dmitry Binunsky, *Vice Pres*
Yvonne Siebert, *Admin Asst*
Sergey Kucherenosov, *Sr Software Eng*
EMP: 57
SALES (est): 22.5MM **Privately Held**
WEB: www.exadel.com
SIC: 7372 Prepackaged software

(P-15661)
FAIR ISAAC CORPORATION (PA)
181 Metro Dr Ste 700, San Jose (95110-1346)
PHONE..................................408 535-1500
William J Lansing, *CEO*
Robert M Berini, *Partner*
A George Battle, *Ch of Bd*
Michael Campbell, *COO*
Michael J Pung, *CFO*
▲ **EMP:** 142
SQ FT: 55,000
SALES: 838.7MM **Publicly Held**
WEB: www.fairisaac.com
SIC: 7372 8748 7389 Prepackaged software; business oriented computer software; business consulting; financial services

(P-15662)
FAIR ISAAC INTERNATIONAL CORP (HQ)
200 Smith Ranch Rd, San Rafael (94903-5551)
PHONE..................................415 446-6000
Thomas G Grudnowski, *President*
Robert Oliver, *Chairman*
George Battle, *Bd of Directors*
Bryant Brooks, *Bd of Directors*
Guy Henshaw, *Bd of Directors*
EMP: 600
SALES (est): 38.5MM
SALES (corp-wide): 838.7MM **Publicly Held**
SIC: 7372 Business oriented computer software
PA: Fair Isaac Corporation
181 Metro Dr Ste 700
San Jose CA 95110
408 535-1500

(P-15663)
FILEMAKER INC (HQ)
5201 Patrick Henry Dr, Santa Clara (95054-1164)
PHONE..................................408 987-7000
Fax: 408 987-3853
Dominique Philippe Goupil, *President*
Bill Epling, *Officer*
Lucy Chen, *Vice Pres*
Brad Freitag, *Vice Pres*
Scott Lewis, *Vice Pres*
EMP: 230
SQ FT: 128,000
SALES (est): 106.2MM
SALES (corp-wide): 233.7B **Publicly Held**
WEB: www.filemaker.com
SIC: 7372 Prepackaged software
PA: Apple Inc.
1 Infinite Loop
Cupertino CA 95014
408 996-1010

(P-15664)
FIORANO SOFTWARE INC
230 S California Ave # 103, Palo Alto (94306-1637)
PHONE..................................650 326-1136
Atul Saini, *CEO*
Madhav Vodnala, *President*
Anjali Saini, *CFO*
William La Forge, *Vice Pres*
Supreme Patida, *Administration*
EMP: 75
SALES (est): 8MM **Privately Held**
SIC: 7372 7371 Prepackaged software; custom computer programming services; computer software development

(P-15665)
FIREEYE INC (PA)
1440 Mccarthy Blvd, Milpitas (95035-7438)
PHONE..................................408 321-6300
David G Dewalt, *Ch of Bd*
Kevin R Mandia, *President*
Michael J Berry, *COO*
Alison Cramer, *Officer*
Julie Cullivan, *Senior VP*
EMP: 148
SQ FT: 223,000
SALES: 622.9MM **Publicly Held**
WEB: www.fireeye.com
SIC: 7372 Prepackaged software

(P-15666)
FITSTAR INC
80 Langton St, San Francisco (94103-3916)
PHONE..................................415 409-8348
Mike Maser, *CEO*
EMP: 589 **EST:** 2004
SALES (est): 105.1K
SALES (corp-wide): 1.8B **Publicly Held**
SIC: 7372 Application computer software
PA: Fitbit, Inc.
405 Howard St Ste 550
San Francisco CA 94105
415 513-1000

(P-15667)
FIVE9 INC (PA)
4000 Executive Pkwy # 400, San Ramon (94583-4257)
PHONE..................................925 201-2000

Fax: 925 469-0172
Michael Burkland, *Ch of Bd*
Barry Zwarenstein, *CFO*
Daniel Burkland, *Exec VP*
Michael Crane, *Exec VP*
Gaurav Passi, *Exec VP*
EMP: 133
SQ FT: 68,000
SALES: 128.8MM **Publicly Held**
WEB: www.five9.com
SIC: 7372 Prepackaged software

(P-15668)
FORGEROCK INC (PA)
201 Mission St Ste 2900, San Francisco (94105-1858)
PHONE..................................415 599-1100
Mike Ellis, *CEO*
Mike Shirley, *President*
John Fernandez, *CFO*
Aled Miles, *Exec VP*
Jamie Dudley, *Senior VP*
EMP: 60
SQ FT: 15,000
SALES (est): 31MM **Privately Held**
SIC: 7372 5045 Prepackaged software; computer software

(P-15669)
FORTINET INC (PA)
899 Kifer Rd, Sunnyvale (94086-5205)
PHONE..................................408 235-7700
Fax: 408 235-7737
Ken Xie, *Ch of Bd*
Jane Zhu,
Rob Atherton, *President*
Michael Xie, *President*
Andrew Del Matto, *CFO*
EMP: 118
SQ FT: 164,000
SALES: 1B **Publicly Held**
WEB: www.fortinet.com
SIC: 7372 Prepackaged software

(P-15670)
FOUNDATION 9 ENTERTAINMENT INC (PA)
30211 A De Las Bandera200 Ste 200, Rancho Santa Margari (92688)
PHONE..................................949 698-1500
James N Hearn, *CEO*
John Goldman, *Ch of Bd*
David Mann, *President*
Steve Sardegna, *CFO*
Patti Torres, *Office Mgr*
EMP: 200
SALES (est): 52.3MM **Privately Held**
SIC: 7372 Home entertainment computer software

(P-15671)
FOUNDSTONE INC
27201 Puerta Real Ste 400, Mission Viejo (92691-8517)
PHONE..................................949 297-5600
Fax: 949 297-5575
George Kurtz, *CEO*
Stuart McClure, *President*
Larry McIntosh, *Chief Mktg Ofcr*
William Chan, *Vice Pres*
Chris Prosise, *Vice Pres*
EMP: 80
SQ FT: 15,000
SALES (est): 6.4MM
SALES (corp-wide): 55.3B **Publicly Held**
WEB: www.foundstone.com
SIC: 7372 Prepackaged software; application computer software; business oriented computer software
HQ: Mcafee, Inc.
2821 Mission College Blvd
Santa Clara CA 95054
408 346-3832

(P-15672)
FRONTRANGE HOLDING INC
490 N Mccarthy Blvd, Milpitas (95035-5118)
PHONE..................................408 601-2800
Jon Temple, *CEO*
Melissa Nelson, *COO*
Karen Rogge, *CFO*
Stephen Baker, *Vice Pres*
Ian Mc Ewan, *Vice Pres*
EMP: 383

▲ = Import ▼ = Export
◆ = Import/Export

PRODUCTS & SERVICES SECTION

7372 - Prepackaged Software County (P-15694)

SALES (est): 12.6MM **Privately Held**
SIC: 7372 7371 Prepackaged software; computer software systems analysis & design, custom

(P-15673)
G7 PRODUCTIVITY SYSTEMS
Also Called: Versacheck
16885 W Bernardo Dr # 290, San Diego (92127-1618)
P.O. Box 270459 (92198-2459)
PHONE.............................858 675-1095
Thomas Priebus, *President*
Teri Pfarr, *COO*
Jim Danforth, *CFO*
EMP: 60
SQ FT: 18,000
SALES (est): 3.9MM **Privately Held**
WEB: www.g7ps.com
SIC: 7372 Prepackaged software

(P-15674)
GAIKAI INC
65 Enterprise, Aliso Viejo (92656-2705)
PHONE.............................949 330-6850
David Perry, *CEO*
Careen Yapp, *President*
Mark Anderson, *COO*
Jamie Cook, *Exec VP*
Robert Stevenson, *Senior VP*
EMP: 53
SALES (est): 12.9MM
SALES (corp-wide): 69.2B **Privately Held**
SIC: 7372 Home entertainment computer software
HQ: Sony Interactive Entertainment America Llc
2207 Bridgepointe Pkwy
Foster City CA 94404
650 655-8000

(P-15675)
GAZILLION INC (PA)
Also Called: Slipgate Ironworks
475 Concar Dr, San Mateo (94402-2650)
PHONE.............................650 393-6500
Robert Hutter, *CEO*
David Brevik, *President*
Bhavin Shah, *COO*
Eric Garay, *CFO*
Christine Legg, *Senior VP*
EMP: 60
SQ FT: 50,000
SALES (est): 51.5MM **Privately Held**
SIC: 7372 Publishers' computer software

(P-15676)
GENERAL ELECTRIC COMPANY
2623 Camino Ramon, San Ramon (94583-9130)
PHONE.............................925 242-6200
Holly Gilthorpe, *Ch Credit Ofcr*
Daniel Camacho, *Marketing Mgr*
EMP: 61
SALES (corp-wide): 117.3B **Publicly Held**
SIC: 7372 Prepackaged software; business oriented computer software
PA: General Electric Company
41 Farnsworth St
Boston MA 02210
617 443-3000

(P-15677)
GENESYS TELECOM LABS (HQ)
Also Called: Genesys Telecom Labs
2001 Junipero Serra Blvd, Daly City (94014-3891)
PHONE.............................650 466-1100
Fax: 415 466-1260
Paul Segre, *CEO*
Tom Eggemeier, *President*
James W Budge, *COO*
David Sudbey, *Ch Credit Ofcr*
Reed Henry, *Chief Mktg Ofcr*
EMP: 450
SQ FT: 156,000
SALES (est): 763.2MM
SALES (corp-wide): 72MM **Privately Held**
WEB: www.genesyslabs.com
SIC: 7372 Business oriented computer software

PA: Permira Advisers Llp
80 Pall Mall
London SW1Y
207 632-1000

(P-15678)
GIGAMON INC (PA)
3300 Olcott St, Santa Clara (95054-3005)
PHONE.............................408 831-4000
Fax: 408 263-2023
Paul A Hooper, *CEO*
Corey M Mulloy, *Ch of Bd*
Michael J Burns, *CFO*
Sachi Sambandan, *Senior VP*
Paul B Shinn, *Senior VP*
EMP: 148
SQ FT: 105,600
SALES: 221.9MM **Publicly Held**
WEB: www.gigamon.com
SIC: 7372 3577 Prepackaged software; computer peripheral equipment

(P-15679)
GIGYA INC
2513 E Char Rd Ste 200, Mountain View (94043)
PHONE.............................650 353-7230
Patrick Salyer, *President*
Rooly Elieverov, *President*
Jeff Bergstrom, *CFO*
Paul Farmer, *CFO*
Jean-Francois Hervy, *CFO*
EMP: 235
SQ FT: 16,000
SALES: 11MM **Privately Held**
WEB: www.gigya-inc.com
SIC: 7372 Application computer software;

(P-15680)
GLOBALEX CORPORATION (PA)
Also Called: Revo Payments
2100 Abbot Kinney Blvd A, Venice (90291-7003)
PHONE.............................310 593-4833
Mike Corbera, *CEO*
Jose Corbera, *Executive*
Lolita Carrico, *Mktg Dir*
Jesse Ohliger, *Sales Dir*
EMP: 60 EST: 2003
SALES (est): 8MM **Privately Held**
SIC: 7372 Prepackaged software

(P-15681)
GOOD TECHNOLOGY SOFTWARE INC
430 N Mary Ave Ste 200, Sunnyvale (94085-2923)
PHONE.............................408 212-7500
Christy Wyatt, *President*
Karen Reynolds, *President*
Ron Fior, *CFO*
Doug Whitman, *Treasurer*
Lynn Lucas, *Chief Mktg Ofcr*
EMP: 600
SALES (est): 65.1MM
SALES (corp-wide): 3.3B **Privately Held**
SIC: 7372 3661 Prepackaged software; telephones & telephone apparatus
HQ: Good Technology Corporation
430 N Mary Ave Ste 200
Sunnyvale CA 94085
408 212-7500

(P-15682)
GOVERNMENTJOBSCOM INC
Also Called: Neogov
222 N Sepulveda Blvd, El Segundo (90245-5648)
PHONE.............................310 426-6304
Damir Davidovic, *CEO*
Scott Letourneau, *President*
Arun K Ganesan, *Sr Software Eng*
Robert Nishimuta, *Sr Software Eng*
Neha Bhardwaj, *QA Dir*
EMP: 98
SQ FT: 5,000
SALES (est): 14.9MM **Privately Held**
WEB: www.governmentjobs.com
SIC: 7372 Prepackaged software

(P-15683)
GRAYPAY LLC
6345 Balboa Blvd Ste 115, Encino (91316-1517)
PHONE.............................818 387-6735
Marc Geolina, *Mng Member*

Bryan Rainey,
EMP: 60 EST: 2015
SALES (est): 2.4MM **Privately Held**
SIC: 7372 Business oriented computer software

(P-15684)
GUAVUS INC (PA)
1800 Gateway Dr Ste 160, San Mateo (94404-4072)
PHONE.............................650 243-3400
Anukool Lakhina, *CEO*
Mike Lajoie, *Ch of Bd*
Ty Nam, *COO*
Mike Staiger, *CFO*
Anupam Rastogi, *Officer*
EMP: 100
SALES (est): 63.6MM **Privately Held**
WEB: www.guavus.com
SIC: 7372 Prepackaged software

(P-15685)
GUIDANCE SOFTWARE INC (PA)
1055 E Colo Blvd Ste 400, Pasadena (91106)
PHONE.............................626 229-9191
Fax: 626 229-9199
Patrick Dennis, *President*
Robert Van Schoonenberg, *Ch of Bd*
Barry Plaga, *COO*
Michael Harris, *Chief Mktg Ofcr*
Ken Basore, *Senior VP*
EMP: 215 EST: 1997
SQ FT: 90,000
SALES: 107MM **Publicly Held**
WEB: www.guidancesoftware.com
SIC: 7372 3572 Prepackaged software; computer storage devices

(P-15686)
GUIDEWIRE SOFTWARE INC (PA)
1001 E Hillsdale Blvd # 800, Foster City (94404-1643)
PHONE.............................650 357-9100
Fax: 650 357-9101
Marcus S Ryu, *President*
John Cavoores, *Ch of Bd*
Richard Hart, *CFO*
Ali Kheirolomoom,
Priscilla Hung, *Officer*
EMP: 148
SQ FT: 97,674
SALES: 424.4MM **Publicly Held**
WEB: www.guidewire.com
SIC: 7372 Prepackaged software

(P-15687)
H2 WELLNESS INCORPORATED
1801 Century Park E # 480, Los Angeles (90067-2306)
PHONE.............................310 362-1888
Hooman Sakki, *CEO*
Houman Arasteh, *COO*
Randy Foliente, *Vice Pres*
Kimberly Jennings, *Director*
EMP: 55
SALES (est): 3.4MM **Privately Held**
SIC: 7372 Application computer software

(P-15688)
HEALTHLINE SYSTEMS LLC (HQ)
17085 Camino San Bernardo, San Diego (92127-5709)
P.O. Box 420399 (92142-0399)
PHONE.............................858 673-1700
Dan E Littrell, *President*
Lisa Hillman, *Vice Pres*
Terrie Sterling, *Vice Pres*
Philip Helmer, *Software Dev*
Ann Linn, *Human Res Dir*
EMP: 80
SQ FT: 20,800
SALES (est): 11.2MM
SALES (corp-wide): 209MM **Publicly Held**
WEB: www.healthlinesystem.com
SIC: 7372 7371 Prepackaged software; computer software development
PA: Healthstream, Inc.
209 10th Ave S Ste 450
Nashville TN 37203
615 301-3100

(P-15689)
HEALTHSTREAM INC
Also Called: Echo, A Healthstream Company
17085 Camino San Bernardo, San Diego (92127-5709)
PHONE.............................800 733-8737
Robert A Frist Jr, *Ch of Bd*
EMP: 165
SALES (corp-wide): 209MM **Publicly Held**
SIC: 7372 7371 Prepackaged software; custom computer programming services
PA: Healthstream, Inc.
209 10th Ave S Ste 450
Nashville TN 37203
615 301-3100

(P-15690)
HEARSAY SOCIAL INC (PA)
185 Berry St Ste 3800, San Francisco (94107-1725)
PHONE.............................888 990-3777
Clara Shih, *CEO*
Michael H Lock, *President*
William Salisbury, *CFO*
Mark Gilbert, *Vice Pres*
Caitlin Haberberger, *Vice Pres*
EMP: 60
SALES (est): 21.1MM **Privately Held**
SIC: 7372 Publishers' computer software

(P-15691)
HEWLETT PACKARD ENTERPRISE CO (PA)
3000 Hanover St, Palo Alto (94304-1185)
PHONE.............................650 857-5817
Margaret C Whitman, *President*
Patricia F Russo, *Ch of Bd*
Christopher P Hsu, *COO*
Timothy C Stonesifer, *CFO*
Kirt P Karros, *Treasurer*
EMP: 148 EST: 2015
SALES (est): 34.1B **Publicly Held**
SIC: 7372 7379 3572 Prepackaged software; computer related maintenance services; computer storage devices

(P-15692)
HORTONWORKS INC
5470 Great America Pkwy, Santa Clara (95054-3644)
PHONE.............................408 916-4121
Robert Bearden, *Ch of Bd*
Herbert Cunitz, *President*
Steven Dean, *President*
Ferguson Mitch, *President*
Scott Davidson, *CFO*
EMP: 150
SQ FT: 65,000
SALES: 121.9MM **Privately Held**
SIC: 7372 Prepackaged software

(P-15693)
HP INC
4209 Technology Dr, Fremont (94538-6339)
PHONE.............................650 265-5448
Debra Getto, *Executive Asst*
Jennifer Osuna, *Manager*
EMP: 51
SALES (corp-wide): 103.3B **Publicly Held**
SIC: 7372 Prepackaged software
PA: Hp Inc.
1501 Page Mill Rd
Palo Alto CA 94304
650 857-1501

(P-15694)
HP INC
250 University Ave Lbby, Palo Alto (94301-1725)
PHONE.............................650 617-3330
Vehbi Tasar, *Engineer*
Dick Doerr, *Sales Dir*
EMP: 100
SALES (corp-wide): 103.3B **Publicly Held**
SIC: 7372 Prepackaged software
PA: Hp Inc.
1501 Page Mill Rd
Palo Alto CA 94304
650 857-1501

7372 - Prepackaged Software County (P-15695)

PRODUDCTS & SERVICES SECTION

(P-15695)
HYTRUST INC (PA)
1975 W El Camino Real # 203, Mountain View (94040-2218)
PHONE.....................650 681-8100
Fax: 650 681-8101
John De Santis, *CEO*
Eric Chiu, *President*
Mercy Caprara, *CFO*
Rudolfo Cifolelli, *Senior VP*
Fred Kost, *Senior VP*
EMP: 52
SQ FT: 12,000
SALES: 4.4MM **Privately Held**
SIC: 7372 Educational computer software

(P-15696)
IFWE INC (PA)
Also Called: Tegged.com
848 Battery St, San Francisco (94111-1504)
PHONE.....................415 946-1850
Dash Gopinath, *CEO*
Greg Tseng, *CEO*
Louis Willacy, *Senior VP*
Devin Dworak, *Vice Pres*
Bill Lewis, *Vice Pres*
EMP: 110
SQ FT: 13,000
SALES (est): 42MM **Privately Held**
WEB: www.tagged.com
SIC: 7372 Application computer software

(P-15697)
IMAGEWARE SYSTEMS INC (PA)
10815 Rncho Brnrdo Rd 3 Ste 310, San Diego (92127)
PHONE.....................858 673-8600
Fax: 858 673-1770
S James Miller Jr, *Ch of Bd*
Wayne Wetherell, *CFO*
Bill Willis, *Exec VP*
David Harding, *Vice Pres*
Mike Rerick, *Vice Pres*
EMP: 62
SQ FT: 9,927
SALES: 4.7MM **Publicly Held**
WEB: www.iwsinc.com
SIC: 7372 3699 Prepackaged software; security control equipment & systems

(P-15698)
INDIUM SOFTWARE INC
1250 Oakmead Pkwy Ste 210, Sunnyvale (94085-4037)
PHONE.....................408 501-8844
Harsha Nutalapati, *CEO*
Vijay Shankar Balaji, *President*
Mani Rvs, *VP Mktg*
EMP: 250
SALES (est): 14.8MM **Privately Held**
WEB: www.indiumsoft.com
SIC: 7372 Prepackaged software

(P-15699)
INFOR (US) INC
Also Called: MAI Systems
26250 Entp Way Ste 220, Lake Forest (92630)
PHONE.....................678 319-8000
Brannon Smith, *Admin Asst*
EMP: 190
SALES (corp-wide): 2.6B **Privately Held**
SIC: 7372 Prepackaged software
HQ: Infor (Us), Inc.
13560 Morris Rd Ste 4100
Alpharetta GA 30004
678 319-8000

(P-15700)
INFOR (US) INC
Also Called: Hansen Information Tech
11000 Olson Dr Ste 201, Rancho Cordova (95670-5642)
PHONE.....................916 921-0883
Charles Hansen, *Manager*
Max Cordero, *QA Dir*
Steven McKillip, *Software Dev*
Jill Yamanaka, *Software Dev*
Doug Schierer, *Business Anlyst*
EMP: 225
SALES (corp-wide): 3.3B **Privately Held**
SIC: 7372 Prepackaged software
HQ: Infor (Us), Inc.
13560 Morris Rd Ste 4100
Alpharetta GA 30004
678 319-8000

(P-15701)
INFOR PUBLIC SECTOR INC (DH)
Also Called: Hansen Information Tech
11092 Sun Center Dr, Rancho Cordova (95670-6109)
PHONE.....................916 921-0883
Fax: 916 921-6620
Charles Hansen, *CEO*
Mark Watts, *President*
Richard Lee, *Vice Pres*
Bob Benstead, *Principal*
Janine Mullinix, *Office Mgr*
EMP: 160
SQ FT: 28,000
SALES (est): 18.1MM
SALES (corp-wide): 2.6B **Privately Held**
SIC: 7372 Prepackaged software
HQ: Infor (Us), Inc.
13560 Morris Rd Ste 4100
Alpharetta GA 30004
678 319-8000

(P-15702)
INFORMATICA LLC (HQ)
2100 Seaport Blvd, Redwood City (94063-5596)
PHONE.....................650 385-5000
Fax: 650 385-5500
Anil Chakravarthy, *CEO*
David Rye, *President*
Jo Stoner, *Officer*
Paul J Hoffman, *Exec VP*
Charles Race, *Exec VP*
EMP: 146
SQ FT: 290,000
SALES: 1B
SALES (corp-wide): 102.5MM **Privately Held**
WEB: www.metadataexchange.com
SIC: 7372 Prepackaged software

(P-15703)
INFORMATION RESOURCES INC
525 Market St Fl 24, San Francisco (94105-2732)
PHONE.....................415 227-4500
Jeanine East, *Manager*
Preeti Gupta, *Info Tech Mgr*
Monica Brown, *Director*
Mary Miller, *Manager*
Sarah Olczyk, *Manager*
EMP: 50
SALES (corp-wide): 663.9MM **Privately Held**
WEB: www.infores.com
SIC: 7372 7371 8732 Prepackaged software; custom computer programming services; market analysis or research
PA: Information Resources, Inc
150 N Clinton St
Chicago IL 60661
312 726-1221

(P-15704)
INFRASCALE INC
Also Called: SOS Hosting
999 N Sepulveda Blvd # 100, El Segundo (90245-2714)
PHONE.....................310 878-2621
Ken Shaw Jr, *Principal*
Michael Bell, *President*
Kenneth Shaw, *CEO*
Hardy Parungao, *CFO*
Robert C Woolery, *Chief Mktg Ofcr*
EMP: 140
SQ FT: 8,000
SALES: 14MM **Privately Held**
SIC: 7372 5045 Prepackaged software; business oriented computer software; computers, peripherals & software; computer software

(P-15705)
INSTANT SYSTEMS INC
Also Called: Instantsys
40211 Dolerita Ave, Fremont (94539-3015)
PHONE.....................510 657-8100
Vipin K Chawla, *President*
Uzay Takaoglu, *Vice Pres*
Mamta Chawla, *Admin Sec*
▲ EMP: 60
SALES (est): 2.1MM **Privately Held**
WEB: www.instantsys.com
SIC: 7372 7371 Prepackaged software; business oriented computer software; custom computer programming services; computer software development & applications

(P-15706)
INTAPP INC (PA)
200 Portage Ave, Palo Alto (94306-2242)
PHONE.....................650 852-0400
John Hall, *CEO*
Daniel Harsell, *President*
Dan Tacone, *President*
Don Coleman, *COO*
Steve Robertson, *CFO*
EMP: 57
SALES (est): 26.9MM **Privately Held**
WEB: www.intapp.com
SIC: 7372 Prepackaged software

(P-15707)
INTEGRAL DEVELOPMENT CORP (PA)
Also Called: Integral Engineering
3400 Hillview Ave, Palo Alto (94304-1346)
PHONE.....................650 424-4500
Fax: 650 903-9077
Harpal Sandhu, *President*
Jay Kronberg, *President*
Albert Yau, *CFO*
Pranab Das, *Software Engr*
Ankur Garg, *Rsch/Dvlpt Dir*
EMP: 50
SQ FT: 35,000
SALES (est): 48.3MM **Privately Held**
WEB: www.integral.com
SIC: 7372 Prepackaged software

(P-15708)
INTERACTIVE SOLUTIONS INC (HQ)
Also Called: Web Traffic School
283 4th St Ste 301, Oakland (94607-4320)
P.O. Box 209 (94604-0209)
PHONE.....................510 214-9002
Isaak Tsifrin, *CEO*
Gary Golduber, *President*
Gary Tsifrin, *COO*
Mercy Gitau, *General Mgr*
EMP: 67
SQ FT: 3,800
SALES (est): 14.7MM
SALES (corp-wide): 20.7MM **Privately Held**
WEB: www.drivered.com
SIC: 7372 Prepackaged software
PA: Edriving Llc
283 4th St Ste 301
Oakland CA 94607
800 243-4008

(P-15709)
INTERWOVEN INC (HQ)
Also Called: Autonomy Interwoven
1140 Enterprise Way, Sunnyvale (94089-1412)
PHONE.....................312 580-9100
Fax: 408 774-2002
Anthony Bettencourt, *CEO*
John E Calonico Jr, *CFO*
Benjamin E Kiker Jr, *Chief Mktg Ofcr*
Shams Rashid, *Exec VP*
Jeff Kissling, *Senior VP*
EMP: 500
SQ FT: 110,000
SALES: 125.1MM
SALES (corp-wide): 34.1B **Publicly Held**
WEB: www.iwov.com
SIC: 7372 Business oriented computer software
PA: Hewlett Packard Enterprise Company
3000 Hanover St
Palo Alto CA 94304
650 857-5817

(P-15710)
INTOUCH TECHNOLOGIES INC
Also Called: Intouch Health
6330 Hollister Ave, Goleta (93117-3115)
PHONE.....................805 562-8686
Fax: 805 562-8663
Yulun Wang, *CEO*
Susan Wang, *Shareholder*
David Adornetto, *COO*
Stephen L Wilson, *CFO*
Paul Evans, *Exec VP*
EMP: 54
SQ FT: 1,600
SALES: 33.4MM **Privately Held**
WEB: www.intouchhealth.com
SIC: 7372 Prepackaged software; business oriented computer software

(P-15711)
INTUIT INC (PA)
2700 Coast Ave, Mountain View (94043-1140)
P.O. Box 7850 (94039-7850)
PHONE.....................650 944-6000
Fax: 650 944-3699
Brad D Smith, *Ch of Bd*
R Neil Williams, *CFO*
Scott D Cook, *Chairman*
Laura A Fennell, *Exec VP*
Sasan K Goodarzi, *Exec VP*
EMP: 70
SQ FT: 711,000
SALES: 4.6B **Publicly Held**
WEB: www.intuit.com
SIC: 7372 Business oriented computer software

(P-15712)
INTUIT INC
2700 Coast Ave Bldg 7, Mountain View (94043-1140)
PHONE.....................650 944-6000
Brad Smith, *Branch Mgr*
EMP: 128
SALES (corp-wide): 4.6B **Publicly Held**
WEB: www.intuit.com
SIC: 7372 Prepackaged software; business oriented computer software
PA: Intuit Inc.
2700 Coast Ave
Mountain View CA 94043
650 944-6000

(P-15713)
INTUIT INC
2535 Garcia Ave, Mountain View (94043-1111)
PHONE.....................650 944-6000
Connie Berg, *Branch Mgr*
Matt Rhodes, *Shareholder*
Thomas Allanson, *Senior VP*
Gordon D Whitten, *Vice Pres*
Susan Lewis, *Executive*
EMP: 128
SALES (corp-wide): 4.6B **Publicly Held**
WEB: www.intuit.com
SIC: 7372 Business oriented computer software
PA: Intuit Inc.
2700 Coast Ave
Mountain View CA 94043
650 944-6000

(P-15714)
INTUIT INC
141 Corona Way, Portola Valley (94028-7437)
PHONE.....................650 944-2840
EMP: 136
SALES (corp-wide): 4.6B **Publicly Held**
WEB: www.intuit.com
SIC: 7372 Prepackaged software
PA: Intuit Inc.
2700 Coast Ave
Mountain View CA 94043
650 944-6000

(P-15715)
INTUIT INC
180 Jefferson Dr, Menlo Park (94025-1115)
PHONE.....................650 944-6000
Brad Smith, *Branch Mgr*
Arthur Velasquez, *Vice Pres*
Ray Kiuchi, *Sr Software Eng*
Jennifer Hall, *VP Info Sys*
Ramya Narisetty, *Business Anlyst*
EMP: 128
SALES (corp-wide): 4.6B **Publicly Held**
WEB: www.intuit.com
SIC: 7372 Business oriented computer software

▲ = Import ▼ = Export
◆ = Import/Export

PRODUCTS & SERVICES SECTION

7372 - Prepackaged Software County (P-15737)

PA: Intuit Inc.
2700 Coast Ave
Mountain View CA 94043
650 944-6000

(P-15716)
INTUIT INC
7535 Torrey Santa Fe Rd, San Diego
(92129-5704)
PHONE.................................858 215-8000
Jason Jackson, *Branch Mgr*
Kelly Parrish, *Vice Pres*
Matthew Lisowski, *Plan/Corp Dev D*
Naomi Colvan, *Program Mgr*
Stacey Pagiatakis, *Executive Asst*
EMP: 300
SALES (corp-wide): 4.6B **Publicly Held**
WEB: www.intuit.com
SIC: 7372 Prepackaged software
PA: Intuit Inc.
2700 Coast Ave
Mountain View CA 94043
650 944-6000

(P-15717)
IPOLIPO INC
Also Called: Jifflenow
440 N Wolfe Rd, Sunnyvale (94085-3869)
PHONE.................................408 916-5290
Hari Shetty, *President*
Parth Mukherjee, *Mktg Dir*
Lou Mendoza, *Sales Staff*
Shekhar Kirani,
Rajesh Setty,
EMP: 75 **EST:** 2006
SALES (est): 3MM **Privately Held**
SIC: 7372 Application computer software

(P-15718)
ISOLUTECOM INC (PA)
9 Northam Ave, Newbury Park
(91320-3323)
PHONE.................................805 498-6259
Byron Nutley, *Ch of Bd*
Don Hyun, *President*
Thomas Mangle, *CFO*
Kelly Tapp, *Officer*
Michael Brown, *CTO*
EMP: 50
SALES (est): 5.1MM **Privately Held**
WEB: www.isolute.com
SIC: 7372 Business oriented computer software

(P-15719)
IXSYSTEMS INC
2490 Kruse Dr, San Jose (95131-1234)
PHONE.................................408 943-4100
Mike Lauth, *CEO*
Andrew Madrid, *COO*
Jeff Kaminsky, *General Mgr*
Valerie Tran, *Admin Asst*
Erin Clark, *Administration*
EMP: 60
SQ FT: 20,000
SALES (est): 50MM **Privately Held**
WEB: www.ixsystems.com
SIC: 7372 Operating systems computer software

(P-15720)
JIVE SOFTWARE INC (PA)
325 Lytton Ave Ste 200, Palo Alto
(94301-1431)
PHONE.................................650 319-1920
Elisa A Steele, *President*
Anthony Zingale, *Ch of Bd*
Jeff Lautenbach, *President*
Bryan J Leblanc, *CFO*
David Puglia, *Chief Mktg Ofcr*
EMP: 148 **EST:** 2001
SQ FT: 18,500
SALES: 195.7MM **Publicly Held**
WEB: www.jivesoftware.com
SIC: 7372 Prepackaged software; application computer software

(P-15721)
KANA SOFTWARE INC (HQ)
Also Called: Verint
2550 Walsh Ave Ste 120, Santa Clara
(95051-1345)
PHONE.................................650 614-8300
Fax: 408 736-7613
Mark Duffell, *CEO*
William A Bose, *President*
Brett White, *President*
Brian Allen, *CFO*
Jeff Wylie, *CFO*
EMP: 100
SQ FT: 40,000
SALES (est): 109.3MM
SALES (corp-wide): 1.1B **Publicly Held**
SIC: 7372 Prepackaged software
PA: Verint Systems Inc.
175 Broadhollow Rd # 100
Melville NY 11747
631 962-9600

(P-15722)
KHAN ACADEMY INC
1200 Villa St Ste 200, Mountain View
(94041-2922)
P.O. Box 1630 (94042-1630)
PHONE.................................650 336-5426
Salman Khan, *Exec Dir*
Shantanu Sinha, *President*
Esther Cho, *Executive Asst*
EMP: 85
SALES (est): 8.3MM **Privately Held**
SIC: 7372 Educational computer software

(P-15723)
KINTERA INC (HQ)
Also Called: Blackbaud Internet Solutions
9605 Scranton Rd Ste 200, San Diego
(92121-1768)
PHONE.................................858 795-3000
Fax: 858 795-3010
Marc E Chardon, *CEO*
Alfred R Berkeley III, *Ch of Bd*
Richard Labarbera, *President*
Richard Davidson, *CFO*
James A Rotherham, *CFO*
EMP: 83
SQ FT: 38,000
SALES (est): 34.5MM
SALES (corp-wide): 637.9MM **Publicly Held**
WEB: www.kintera.org
SIC: 7372 Prepackaged software
PA: Blackbaud, Inc.
2000 Daniel Island Dr
Daniel Island SC 29492
843 216-6200

(P-15724)
KNO INC
2200 Mission College Blvd, Santa Clara
(95054-1537)
PHONE.................................408 844-8120
Ronald D Dickel, *CEO*
Babur Habib, *CTO*
EMP: 70
SQ FT: 35,000
SALES (est): 10.9MM
SALES (corp-wide): 55.3B **Publicly Held**
SIC: 7372 Educational computer software
PA: Intel Corporation
2200 Mission College Blvd
Santa Clara CA 95054
408 765-8080

(P-15725)
KNOVA SOFTWARE INC (HQ)
10201 Torre Ave Ste 350, Cupertino
(95014-2131)
PHONE.................................408 863-5800
Bruce Armstrong, *President*
Kent Heyman, *Ch of Bd*
Thomar Muise, *CFO*
Andy Feit, *Officer*
Sham Chotai, *Vice Pres*
EMP: 50
SQ FT: 16,800
SALES (est): 9.9MM
SALES (corp-wide): 594.3MM **Privately Held**
WEB: www.knova.com
SIC: 7372 Business oriented computer software
PA: Aptean, Inc.
4325 Alexander Dr Ste 100
Alpharetta GA 30022
770 351-9600

(P-15726)
KONAMI DIGITAL ENTRMT INC
2381 Rosecrans Ave # 200, El Segundo
(90245-4922)
PHONE.................................310 220-8100
Tomohiro Uesugi, *President*
Takahiro Azuma, *Vice Pres*
Yumi Hoashi, *Vice Pres*
Careen Yapp, *Vice Pres*
Chris Bartee, *Principal*
▲ **EMP:** 101
SQ FT: 53,596
SALES (est): 24.2MM
SALES (corp-wide): 2.1B **Privately Held**
SIC: 7372 Home entertainment computer software
PA: Konami Holdings Corporation
9-7-2, Akasaka
Minato-Ku TKY 107-0
357 700-573

(P-15727)
KPISOFT INC
50 California St Ste 1500, San Francisco
(94111-4612)
PHONE.................................415 439-5228
Ravee Ramamoothie, *CEO*
EMP: 80
SQ FT: 4,000
SALES (est): 1.9MM **Privately Held**
SIC: 7372 Prepackaged software

(P-15728)
KRANEM CORPORATION
560 S Winchester Blvd, San Jose
(95128-2560)
PHONE.................................650 319-6743
Ajay Batheja, *Ch of Bd*
Edward Miller, *CFO*
Luigi Caramico, *Vice Pres*
Christopher L Rasmussen, *Admin Sec*
EMP: 190
SALES: 8.3MM **Privately Held**
SIC: 7372 Business oriented computer software

(P-15729)
KRATOS TECH TRNING SLTIONS INC (HQ)
4820 Estgate Mall Ste 200, San Diego
(92121)
PHONE.................................858 812-7300
Fax: 858 715-5510
Eric M Demarco, *President*
Kenneth Reagan, *President*
Deanna H Lund, *CFO*
Laura L Siegal, *Treasurer*
Ben Goodwin, *Senior VP*
EMP: 148
SQ FT: 25,000
SALES (est): 72.8MM
SALES (corp-wide): 657.1MM **Publicly Held**
WEB: www.sys.com
SIC: 7372 Business oriented computer software
PA: Kratos Defense & Security Solutions, Inc.
4820 Estgate Mall Ste 200
San Diego CA 92121
858 812-7300

(P-15730)
KRONOS INCORPORATED
50 Corporate Park, Irvine (92606-5105)
PHONE.................................800 580-7374
Kaylee Uribe, *Branch Mgr*
Marianne Morrison, *Executive*
Mark Julien, *Branch Mgr*
Brooke McMillin, *Admin Asst*
Jennifer Phillips, *Admin Asst*
EMP: 56
SALES (corp-wide): 1.8B **Privately Held**
SIC: 7372 Prepackaged software
HQ: Kronos Incorporated
297 Billerica Rd
Chelmsford MA 01824
978 250-9800

(P-15731)
LASTLINE INC
6950 Hollister Ave # 101, Goleta
(93117-2896)
PHONE.................................805 456-7075
EMP: 164
SALES (corp-wide): 12.5MM **Privately Held**
SIC: 7372 Prepackaged software
PA: Lastline, Inc.
203 Redwood Shores Pkwy # 620
Redwood City CA 94065
805 456-7075

(P-15732)
LAWINFOCOM INC
5901 Priestly Dr Ste 200, Carlsbad
(92008-8825)
PHONE.................................760 510-3000
Gunter Enz, *President*
William J Amey, *COO*
Cara Mae Harrison, *COO*
Judd Azulay, *Admin Sec*
EMP: 68 **EST:** 1989
SQ FT: 10,000
SALES: 4.6MM **Privately Held**
WEB: www.lawinfo.com
SIC: 7372 8111 7375 Publishers' computer software; legal services; information retrieval services

(P-15733)
LITHIUM TECHNOLOGIES INC (PA)
225 Bush St Fl 15, San Francisco
(94104-4249)
PHONE.................................510 653-6800
Fax: 510 653-6801
Robert Tarkoff, *CEO*
Carlton Baab, *CFO*
Jim Cox, *CFO*
Mark Culhane, *CFO*
Mike Dinsdale, *CFO*
EMP: 92
SALES (est): 71MM **Privately Held**
WEB: www.lithium.com
SIC: 7372 Prepackaged software

(P-15734)
LIVEOFFICE LLC
Also Called: Advisorsquare
900 Corporate Pointe, Culver City
(90230-7609)
PHONE.................................877 253-2793
Alexander Rusich,
Angella Gavic, *Vice Pres*
Dean Nicolls, *Vice Pres*
Jim O'Hara, *Vice Pres*
Leena Saraf, *Prgrmr*
EMP: 77
SQ FT: 15,000
SALES (est): 5.9MM
SALES (corp-wide): 3.6B **Publicly Held**
WEB: www.advisorsquare.com
SIC: 7372 Prepackaged software
PA: Symantec Corporation
350 Ellis St
Mountain View CA 94043
650 527-8000

(P-15735)
LIVETIME SOFTWARE INC
276 Avocado St Apt C102, Costa Mesa
(92627-7302)
PHONE.................................415 905-4009
Darren Williams, *President*
Antoinette Fox, *Manager*
EMP: 50
SALES (est): 3MM **Privately Held**
SIC: 7372 Prepackaged software

(P-15736)
LPA INSURANCE AGENCY INC
Also Called: Sat
4030 Truxel Rd Ste B, Sacramento
(95834-3767)
PHONE.................................916 286-7850
Michael Winkel, *President*
Terri Tatge, *Human Res Mgr*
EMP: 56
SQ FT: 8,000
SALES: 3.7MM
SALES (corp-wide): 6.6B **Publicly Held**
WEB: www.sungard.com
SIC: 7372 Application computer software
HQ: Fis Data Systems Inc.
680 E Swedesford Rd
Wayne PA 19087
484 582-2000

(P-15737)
LYNX SOFTWARE TECHNOLOGIES INC (PA)
855 Embedded Way, San Jose
(95138-1030)
PHONE.................................408 979-3900
Fax: 408 979-3920
Inder Singh, *Chairman*
Reza R Soliman-Noo, *Vice Chairman*

7372 - Prepackaged Software County (P-15738)

Gurjot Singh, *President*
David Witkowski, *Vice Pres*
Oleg Orel, *Software Engr*
EMP: 52
SQ FT: 30,000
SALES (est): 14.8MM **Privately Held**
WEB: www.lynuxworks.com
SIC: 7372 Prepackaged software

(P-15738)
MALIKCO LLC
2121 N Calif Blvd Ste 290, Walnut Creek (94596-7351)
PHONE....................925 974-3555
Stephynie R Malik, *CEO*
David Gellerman, *CFO*
Alexandra O'Leary, *Business Mgr*
Jan Button, *Opers Mgr*
Devyn Wood, *Marketing Staff*
EMP: 50
SQ FT: 1,000
SALES (est): 4.4MM **Privately Held**
WEB: www.malikco.com
SIC: 7372 Operating systems computer software

(P-15739)
MARKETLINX INC
4 First American Way, Santa Ana (92707-5913)
PHONE....................714 250-6751
Bryan Foreman, *Branch Mgr*
EMP: 50
SALES (corp-wide): 1.5B **Publicly Held**
SIC: 7372 2741 Business oriented computer software; directories: publishing & printing
HQ: Marketlinx, Inc.
1951 Kidwell Dr Ste 300
Vienna VA 22182
703 610-5000

(P-15740)
MCAFEE INC
6707 Barnhurst Dr, San Diego (92117-4208)
PHONE....................858 967-2342
EMP: 82
SALES (corp-wide): 55.3B **Publicly Held**
SIC: 7372 Prepackaged software
HQ: Mcafee, Inc.
2821 Mission College Blvd
Santa Clara CA 95054
408 346-3832

(P-15741)
MCAFEE INC (HQ)
2821 Mission College Blvd, Santa Clara (95054-1838)
PHONE....................408 346-3832
Michael Decesare, *President*
Jean-Claude Broido, *President*
Tom Miglis, *President*
Mark Wyman, *President*
Peter Watkins, *COO*
EMP: 700
SQ FT: 208,000
SALES (est): 1.5B
SALES (corp-wide): 55.3B **Publicly Held**
WEB: www.mcafee.com
SIC: 7372 Prepackaged software; application computer software; business oriented computer software
PA: Intel Corporation
2200 Mission College Blvd
Santa Clara CA 95054
408 765-8080

(P-15742)
MCAFEE SECURITY LLC
2821 Mission College Blvd, Santa Clara (95054-1838)
PHONE....................866 622-3911
Michael Decesare, *President*
Bob Kelly, *CFO*
Edward Hayden, *Senior VP*
Louis Riley, *Senior VP*
EMP: 6210 **EST:** 2006
SQ FT: 208,000
SALES (est): 98.4MM
SALES (corp-wide): 55.3B **Publicly Held**
SIC: 7372 Prepackaged software; application computer software; business oriented computer software

HQ: Mcafee, Inc.
2821 Mission College Blvd
Santa Clara CA 95054
408 346-3832

(P-15743)
MEDALLIA INC (PA)
395 Page Mill Rd Ste 100, Palo Alto (94306-2066)
PHONE....................650 321-3000
Borge Hald, *CEO*
Amy Pressman-Hald, *President*
Nick Thomas, *President*
Jane Thompson, *President*
Chris Watts, *CFO*
EMP: 145
SQ FT: 10,000
SALES (est): 94.9MM **Privately Held**
WEB: www.medallia.com
SIC: 7372 8732 Business oriented computer software; market analysis, business & economic research

(P-15744)
MEDATA INC (HQ)
2741 Walnut Ave Fl 2, Irvine (92606)
PHONE....................714 918-1310
Fax: 714 918-1325
Cy King, *CEO*
Tom Herndon, *President*
Thomas Herndon, *COO*
Bryan Lowe, *CFO*
T Don Theis, *Senior VP*
EMP: 51
SQ FT: 17,192
SALES (est): 46.2MM
SALES (corp-wide): 2.7B **Publicly Held**
WEB: www.medata.com
SIC: 7372 6411 Business oriented computer software; medical insurance claim processing, contract or fee basis
PA: Mednax, Inc.
1301 Concord Ter
Sunrise FL 33323
954 384-0175

(P-15745)
MEDICAL TRANSCRIPTION BILLING
405 Kenyon St Ste 300, San Diego (92110)
PHONE....................800 869-3700
EMP: 504
SALES (corp-wide): 23MM **Publicly Held**
SIC: 7372 Prepackaged software
PA: Medical Transcription Billing, Corp.
7 Clyde Rd
Somerset NJ 08873
732 873-5133

(P-15746)
MEDITAB SOFTWARE INC
333 Hegenberger Rd # 800, Oakland (94621-1416)
PHONE....................510 632-2021
Mike Patel, *President*
Kal Patel, *COO*
Feros Khan, *Info Tech Mgr*
Prakash Rajput, *Software Engr*
Byron Smith, *Regl Sales Mgr*
EMP: 250
SQ FT: 10,000
SALES (est): 31.1MM **Privately Held**
SIC: 7372 Prepackaged software

(P-15747)
MEDRIO INC
345 California St Ste 325, San Francisco (94104-2658)
PHONE....................415 963-3700
Fax: 415 962-2089
Michael Richard Novotny, *CEO*
Raymond Letulle, *COO*
Richard H Scheller, *Exec VP*
Scott Weidley, *Vice Pres*
EMP: 57
SALES (est): 9.7MM **Privately Held**
SIC: 7372 Business oriented computer software

(P-15748)
MERCURY INTERACTIVE LLC (HQ)
3000 Hanover St, Palo Alto (94304-1112)
P.O. Box 60069, Sunnyvale (94088-0069)
PHONE....................650 857-1501
Anthony Zingale, *President*

Moshe Egert, *President*
Jon E Flaxman, *Treasurer*
Scott Bradley, *Vice Pres*
▲ **EMP:** 350
SALES (est): 80.4MM
SALES (corp-wide): 34.1B **Publicly Held**
WEB: www.svca.mercuryinteractive.com
SIC: 7372 Prepackaged software
PA: Hewlett Packard Enterprise Company
3000 Hanover St
Palo Alto CA 94304
650 857-5817

(P-15749)
MERIDIAN PROJECT SYSTEMS INC (HQ)
Also Called: Meridian Systems
1720 Pririe Cy Rd Ste 120, Folsom (95630)
PHONE....................916 294-2000
Fax: 916 294-2001
Steven W Berglund, *CEO*
Chris Carruth, *President*
Thomas Burke, *Senior VP*
Toni Smith, *Program Mgr*
Eric Chan, *Admin Asst*
EMP: 61
SQ FT: 170,000
SALES (est): 25.4MM
SALES (corp-wide): 2.2B **Publicly Held**
SIC: 7372 Business oriented computer software; application computer software
PA: Trimble Inc.
935 Stewart Dr
Sunnyvale CA 94085
408 481-8000

(P-15750)
METRICSTREAM INC (PA)
Also Called: Complianceonline
2600 E Bayshore Rd, Palo Alto (94303-3241)
PHONE....................650 620-2900
Fax: 650 637-1953
Shellye Archambeau, *CEO*
Gaurave Kapoor, *COO*
Bert Clement, *CFO*
Jeffrey Z Zellmer, *CFO*
Gunjan Sinha, *Chairman*
EMP: 130
SQ FT: 10,000
SALES (est): 329.6MM **Privately Held**
SIC: 7372 Application computer software

(P-15751)
MICROSOFT CORPORATION
7007 Friars Rd, San Diego (92108-1148)
PHONE....................619 849-5872
Sarah Forrest, *Manager*
Mika Kunto, *Manager*
William Martin, *Manager*
EMP: 100
SALES (corp-wide): 85.3B **Publicly Held**
SIC: 7372 Prepackaged software
PA: Microsoft Corporation
1 Microsoft Way
Redmond WA 98052
425 882-8080

(P-15752)
MICROSOFT CORPORATION
1020 Entp Way Bldg B, Sunnyvale (94089)
PHONE....................650 693-1009
William H Gates III, *Branch Mgr*
EMP: 103
SALES (corp-wide): 85.3B **Publicly Held**
SIC: 7372 Prepackaged software
PA: Microsoft Corporation
1 Microsoft Way
Redmond WA 98052
425 882-8080

(P-15753)
MICROSOFT CORPORATION
3 Park Plz Ste 1800, Irvine (92614-8541)
PHONE....................949 263-3000
Fax: 949 252-8618
Sandy Thomas, *General Mgr*
Douglas Brown, *Program Mgr*
Warren Kerby, *Info Tech Mgr*
Andy Gottlieb, *Consultant*
EMP: 125
SALES (corp-wide): 85.3B **Publicly Held**
WEB: www.microsoft.com
SIC: 7372 Prepackaged software

PA: Microsoft Corporation
1 Microsoft Way
Redmond WA 98052
425 882-8080

(P-15754)
MICROSOFT CORPORATION
13031 W Jefferson Blvd # 200, Playa Vista (90094-7001)
PHONE....................213 806-7300
Evelyn Morgan, *Opers Mgr*
Monica Delrosario, *Accounts Mgr*
EMP: 100
SALES (corp-wide): 85.3B **Publicly Held**
WEB: www.microsoft.com
SIC: 7372 Application computer software
PA: Microsoft Corporation
1 Microsoft Way
Redmond WA 98052
425 882-8080

(P-15755)
MICROSOFT CORPORATION
555 California St Ste 200, San Francisco (94104-1504)
PHONE....................415 972-6400
Teeka Miller, *Branch Mgr*
EMP: 160
SALES (corp-wide): 85.3B **Publicly Held**
WEB: www.microsoft.com
SIC: 7372 Application computer software
PA: Microsoft Corporation
1 Microsoft Way
Redmond WA 98052
425 882-8080

(P-15756)
MICROSOFT CORPORATION
2045 Lafayette St, Santa Clara (95050-2901)
PHONE....................408 987-9608
EMP: 100
SALES (corp-wide): 85.3B **Publicly Held**
WEB: www.microsoft.com
SIC: 7372 Prepackaged software
PA: Microsoft Corporation
1 Microsoft Way
Redmond WA 98052
425 882-8080

(P-15757)
MINDBODY INC (PA)
4051 Broad St Ste 220, San Luis Obispo (93401-8723)
PHONE....................877 755-4279
Richard L Stollmeyer, *Ch of Bd*
Brett White, *COO*
Chet Brandenburg,
Jill Shah, *Senior VP*
Bradford L Wills, *Security Dir*
EMP: 109
SQ FT: 170,000
SALES: 101.3MM **Publicly Held**
SIC: 7372 8741 Business oriented computer software; business management

(P-15758)
MINDJET LLC (HQ)
275 Battery St Ste 1000, San Francisco (94111-3333)
PHONE....................415 229-4344
Fax: 415 229-4201
Scott Raskin, *CEO*
Steve Anderson, *CFO*
Amy Millard, *Chief Mktg Ofcr*
Todd Clyde, *Exec VP*
Mario Tarantino, *General Mgr*
EMP: 111
SQ FT: 15,140
SALES (est): 41.5MM
SALES (corp-wide): 52.5MM **Privately Held**
SIC: 7372 Business oriented computer software; educational computer software
PA: Mindjet Corporation
275 Battery St Ste 1000
San Francisco CA 94111
415 229-4200

(P-15759)
MITEK SYSTEMS INC (PA)
8911 Balboa Ave Ste B, San Diego (92123-6503)
PHONE....................858 309-1700
Fax: 858 503-7820
James B Debello, *President*

PRODUCTS & SERVICES SECTION

7372 - Prepackaged Software County (P-15780)

Russell C Clark, *CFO*
Michael Diamond, *Senior VP*
David Pintsov PHD, *Senior VP*
Julie Cunningham, *Vice Pres*
EMP: 80 **EST:** 1986
SQ FT: 22,523
SALES: 25.3MM **Publicly Held**
WEB: www.miteksys.com
SIC: 7372 Prepackaged software; business oriented computer software

(P-15760)
MOBILEIRON INC (PA)
415 E Middlefield Rd, Mountain View (94043-4005)
PHONE.....................650 919-8100
Barry Mainz, *President*
Tae Hea Nahm, *Ch of Bd*
Simon Biddiscombe, *CFO*
Laurel Finch, *Ch Credit Ofcr*
Daniel Fields, *Senior VP*
EMP: 148
SQ FT: 123,000
SALES: 149.3MM **Publicly Held**
SIC: 7372 Prepackaged software

(P-15761)
MOBSOC MEDIA LLC
855 Folsom St Apt 523, San Francisco (94107-1181)
PHONE.....................415 974-5429
Steven Duane Wick,
EMP: 65
SALES: 2K **Privately Held**
SIC: 7372 Publishers' computer software

(P-15762)
MODUSLINK CORPORATION
2111 Eastridge Ave, Riverside (92507-0778)
PHONE.....................951 571-8300
Robert Zelis, *Branch Mgr*
EMP: 132
SALES (corp-wide): 459MM **Publicly Held**
SIC: 7372 Prepackaged software
HQ: Moduslink Corporation
1601 Trapelo Rd Ste 170
Waltham MA 02451
781 663-5000

(P-15763)
MOVARIS INC
1901 S Bascom Ave Ste 500, Campbell (95008-2238)
PHONE.....................408 213-3400
Jeffrey Miller, *Chairman*
Eric Keller, *President*
Kevin Shea, *COO*
Ed Porter, *Officer*
Chris Abate, *Vice Pres*
EMP: 50
SQ FT: 10,000
SALES (est): 5.9MM **Privately Held**
WEB: www.movaris.com
SIC: 7372 Business oriented computer software

(P-15764)
MSCSOFTWARE CORPORATION (DH)
4675 Macarthur Ct Ste 900, Newport Beach (92660-1845)
PHONE.....................714 540-8900
Fax: 714 784-4056
Dominic Gallello, *President*
Douglas Lubben, *President*
Kevin Rubin, *CFO*
Kais Bouchiba, *Senior VP*
Douglas W Peterson, *Senior VP*
EMP: 245 **EST:** 1963
SQ FT: 203,500
SALES (est): 195MM
SALES (corp-wide): 915MM **Privately Held**
WEB: www.mscsoftware.com
SIC: 7372 Prepackaged software
HQ: Maximus Holdings Inc.
2475 Hanover St
Palo Alto CA 94304
650 935-9500

(P-15765)
MSCSOFTWARE CORPORATION
Also Called: Marc
4370 La Jolla Village Dr, San Diego (92122-1249)
PHONE.....................858 546-4414
William Markham, *Branch Mgr*
EMP: 90
SALES (corp-wide): 915MM **Privately Held**
SIC: 7372 Business oriented computer software
HQ: Msc.Software Corporation
4675 Macarthur Ct Ste 900
Newport Beach CA 92660
714 540-8900

(P-15766)
MUSICMATCH INC
16935 W Bernardo Dr # 270, San Diego (92127-1634)
PHONE.....................858 485-4300
Fax: 858 485-4300
Dennis Mudd, *CEO*
Peter Csathy, *President*
Gary Acord, *CFO*
Chris Allen, *Senior VP*
Don Leigh, *Senior VP*
EMP: 140
SQ FT: 20,000
SALES (est): 6.4MM
SALES (corp-wide): 4.9B **Publicly Held**
WEB: www.musicmatch.com
SIC: 7372 5734 Prepackaged software; software, business & non-game
PA: Yahoo Inc.
701 First Ave
Sunnyvale CA 94089
408 349-3300

(P-15767)
MY EYE MEDIA LLC
2211 N Hollywood Way, Burbank (91505-1113)
PHONE.....................818 559-7200
Fax: 818 475-1934
Michael Kadenacy,
Rodd Feingold, *CFO*
Kenneth Kiers, *Exec VP*
Jane C Hawley, *Senior VP*
Craig Leener, *Vice Pres*
EMP: 65
SQ FT: 12,000
SALES (est): 11.4MM **Privately Held**
WEB: www.myeyemedia.com
SIC: 7372 Business oriented computer software

(P-15768)
NATIONAL INSTRUMENTS CORP
Also Called: Ni Microwave Components
4600 Patrick Henry Dr, Santa Clara (95054-1817)
PHONE.....................408 610-6800
Dirk De Mol, *Branch Mgr*
EMP: 338
SALES (corp-wide): 1.2B **Publicly Held**
SIC: 7372 Application computer software
PA: National Instruments Corporation
11500 N Mopac Expy
Austin TX 78759
512 338-9119

(P-15769)
NC INTERACTIVE LLC ✪
1900 S Norfolk St Ste 125, San Mateo (94403-1175)
PHONE.....................650 393-2200
Songyee Yoon, *CEO*
Eric Garay, *President*
Janet Lin, *General Counsel*
EMP: 99 **EST:** 2016
SQ FT: 16,692
SALES (est): 1.3MM **Privately Held**
SIC: 7372 Prepackaged software

(P-15770)
NET OPTICS INC
Also Called: Ixia
5303 Betsy Ross Dr, Santa Clara (95054-1102)
PHONE.....................408 737-7777
Thomas B Miller, *CEO*
Robert Shaw, *President*
Dennis Omanoff, *COO*
Burt Podbere, *CFO*
Nadine Matityahu, *Corp Secy*
EMP: 85
SQ FT: 39,000
SALES (est): 15.2MM
SALES (corp-wide): 516.9MM **Publicly Held**
WEB: www.netoptics.com
SIC: 7372 Operating systems computer software
PA: Ixia
26601 Agoura Rd
Calabasas CA 91302
818 871-1800

(P-15771)
NETCUBE SYSTEMS INC
1275 Arbor Ave, Los Altos (94024-5330)
PHONE.....................650 862-7858
Mallikarjuna Reddy, *President*
Suresh Kumar, *Manager*
EMP: 75
SQ FT: 1,000
SALES: 35MM **Privately Held**
SIC: 7372 7379 7371 7361 Application computer software; computer related consulting services; custom computer programming services; employment agencies

(P-15772)
NETSUITE INC (PA)
2955 Campus Dr Ste 100, San Mateo (94403-2539)
PHONE.....................650 627-1000
Zachary Nelson, *CEO*
Evan M Goldberg, *Ch of Bd*
Peter Daffern, *President*
James McGeever, *President*
Ronald Gill, *CFO*
EMP: 148
SQ FT: 165,000
SALES: 741.1MM **Privately Held**
SIC: 7372 Prepackaged software

(P-15773)
NETWORK AUTOMATION INC
3530 Wilshire Blvd # 1800, Los Angeles (90010-2335)
PHONE.....................213 738-1700
Fax: 213 738-7665
Dustin Snell, *CEO*
Graham Taylor, *CTO*
Faith Gabriel, *Human Res Mgr*
Morgan Harvey, *Marketing Staff*
EMP: 50
SQ FT: 9,000
SALES (est): 5.4MM
SALES (corp-wide): 80.1MM **Privately Held**
WEB: www.networkautomation.com
SIC: 7372 Prepackaged software
PA: Help/Systems, Llc
6455 City West Pkwy
Eden Prairie MN 55344
952 933-0609

(P-15774)
NEW BI US GAMING LLC
10920 Via Frontera # 420, San Diego (92127-1729)
PHONE.....................858 592-2472
Ian Bonner, *CEO*
Kimberly Armstrong, *Vice Pres*
Russell Schechter, *Vice Pres*
EMP: 92 **EST:** 2012
SALES (est): 4.8MM **Privately Held**
SIC: 7372 Prepackaged software

(P-15775)
NEW RELIC INC (PA)
188 Spear St Ste 1200, San Francisco (94105-1750)
PHONE.....................650 777-7600
Lewis Cirne, *CEO*
Peter Fenton, *Ch of Bd*
Hilarie Koplow-Mcadams, *President*
Bill Lapcevic, *President*
Mark Sachleben, *COO*
EMP: 148
SQ FT: 73,591
SALES: 181.3MM **Publicly Held**
SIC: 7372 Prepackaged software; application computer software

(P-15776)
NEWS DISTRIBUTION NETWORK INC
Also Called: Ndn
437 Lytton Ave Ste 200, Palo Alto (94301-1533)
PHONE.....................773 426-5938
Gregory A Peters, *CEO*
EMP: 97
SALES (corp-wide): 26.7MM **Privately Held**
SIC: 7372 Educational computer software
PA: News Distribution Network, Inc.
3445 Peachtree Rd Ne # 1000
Atlanta GA 30326
404 962-7400

(P-15777)
NEXENTA SYSTEMS INC
451 El Cmino Real Ste 201, Santa Clara (95050)
PHONE.....................408 791-3341
Fax: 408 791-3305
Tarkan Maner, *Ch of Bd*
Rick Martig, *CFO*
Tim Guleri, *Bd of Directors*
Evan Powell, *Officer*
Jon Ash, *Vice Pres*
EMP: 230
SALES (est): 46.8MM **Privately Held**
SIC: 7372 Operating systems computer software

(P-15778)
NIGHTINGALE VANTAGEMED CORP (HQ)
10670 White Rock Rd, Rancho Cordova (95670-6095)
PHONE.....................916 638-4744
Steven Curd, *CEO*
Mark Cameron, *COO*
Liesel Loesch, *CFO*
David Toews, *CFO*
Mark Crerar, *Exec VP*
EMP: 55
SALES (est): 11.4MM
SALES (corp-wide): 19.6MM **Privately Held**
WEB: www.vantagemed.com
SIC: 7372 Prepackaged software
PA: Nightingale Informatix Corporation
55 Renfrew Dr Suite 200
Markham ON L3R 8
905 943-2600

(P-15779)
NITRO SOFTWARE INC
225 Bush St Ste 700, San Francisco (94104-4221)
PHONE.....................415 632-4894
Sam Chandler, *President*
Gina O Reilly, *COO*
Peter Bardwick, *CFO*
Richard Wenzel, *Treasurer*
Dan Keefe, *Vice Pres*
EMP: 125
SQ FT: 6,000
SALES (est): 24.3MM
SALES (corp-wide): 22.4MM **Privately Held**
WEB: www.nitropdf.com
SIC: 7372 Operating systems computer software
PA: Nitro Software Pty Ltd
L 4 246 Bourke St
Melbourne VIC 3000
399 290-400

(P-15780)
NTRUST INFOTECH INC
230 Commerce Ste 180, Irvine (92602-1336)
PHONE.....................562 207-1600
Srikanth Ramachandran, *CEO*
Ramesh Narayanan, *Vice Pres*
Radhakrishnan Krishnaraj, *Technical Mgr*
Raghavendra Sridhar, *Software Dev*
Krishnan Sundararajan, *Programmer Anys*
EMP: 65 **EST:** 2003
SALES (est): 6.6MM **Privately Held**
SIC: 7372 7371 Business oriented computer software; computer software development & applications

---

(PA)=Parent Co (HQ)=Headquarters (DH)=Div Headquarters
✪ = New Business established in last 2 years

7372 - Prepackaged Software County (P-15781)

PA: Ntrust Infotech Private Limited
152, 3rd Floor Ganesh Tower
Chennai TN
-

(P-15781)
NUANCE COMMUNICATIONS INC
1198 E Arques Ave, Sunnyvale
(94085-4602)
PHONE..................................408 245-5358
Fax: 408 992-6101
Charles Berger, *President*
Remi Duchesneau, *Sr Software Eng*
Aparna Subramanian, *Sr Software Eng*
Fang LI, *Database Admin*
Katalin Vonberg, *Technology*
EMP: 150
SQ FT: 60,000
SALES (corp-wide): 1.9B **Publicly Held**
SIC: 7372 Prepackaged software; application computer software; business oriented computer software
PA: Nuance Communications, Inc.
1 Wayside Rd
Burlington MA 01803
781 565-5000

(P-15782)
NWP SERVICES CORPORATION (HQ)
535 Anton Blvd Ste 1100, Costa Mesa
(92626-7699)
P.O. Box 19661, Irvine (92623-9661)
PHONE..................................949 253-2500
Ron Reed, *President*
Southron Scott, *CFO*
Lana Reeve,
Mike Haviken, *Exec VP*
Randy Gorrell, *Senior VP*
▲ EMP: 141
SQ FT: 21,171
SALES (est): 61.9MM
SALES (corp-wide): 468.5MM **Publicly Held**
WEB: www.nwpco.com
SIC: 7372 8721 Utility computer software; billing & bookkeeping service
PA: Realpage, Inc.
2201 Lakeside Blvd
Richardson TX 75082
972 820-3000

(P-15783)
ODDWORLD INHABITANTS INC
869 Monterey St, San Luis Obispo
(93401-3224)
PHONE..................................805 503-3000
Fax: 510 503-3030
Sherry McKenna, *CEO*
Lorne Lanning, *President*
Maurice Konkle, *COO*
EMP: 60
SQ FT: 15,000
SALES (est): 5.1MM **Privately Held**
WEB: www.oddworld.com
SIC: 7372 Prepackaged software

(P-15784)
OPENTV INC (DH)
Also Called: Nagra
275 Sacramento St Ste Sl1, San Francisco
(94111-3831)
PHONE..................................415 962-5000
Fax: 415 962-5300
Yves Pitton, *CEO*
Adam Benson, *President*
Vic K Finney, *President*
Ben Bennett, *CEO*
Andr Kudelski, *CEO*
EMP: 150
SALES (est): 70.4MM
SALES (corp-wide): 946.1MM **Privately Held**
SIC: 7372 Prepackaged software
HQ: Opentv Corp.
275 Sacramento St Ste Sl1
San Francisco CA 94111
415 962-5000

(P-15785)
OPENWAVE MOBILITY INC
400 Seaport Ct Ste 104, Redwood City
(94063-2799)
PHONE..................................650 480-7200
Fax: 650 480-4452

Tony Condino, *Principal*
Poh Sim Gan, *CFO*
Martin B Dunsby, *Senior VP*
Paul Kennedy, *Info Tech Mgr*
Nuala Drumm, *Human Res Mgr*
EMP: 70
SALES (est): 14.6MM **Privately Held**
SIC: 7372 Prepackaged software

(P-15786)
OPOWER INC
680 Folsom St Ste 300, San Francisco
(94107-2158)
PHONE..................................415 848-4700
EMP: 57
SALES (corp-wide): 37B **Publicly Held**
SIC: 7372 Prepackaged software
HQ: Opower, Inc.
1515 N Courthouse Rd Fl 8
Arlington VA 22201
703 778-4544

(P-15787)
OPTIMUM SOLUTIONS GROUP LLC (HQ)
419 Ponderosa Ct, Lafayette (94549-1812)
PHONE..................................415 954-7100
G John Houtary,
Todd Randolph, *Business Mgr*
Lisa Massman,
EMP: 100
SQ FT: 3,300
SALES (est): 9.1MM
SALES (corp-wide): 5.2B **Privately Held**
WEB: www.optimumsolutions.com
SIC: 7372 7371 8243 7374 Prepackaged software; computer software systems analysis & design, custom; data processing schools; computer graphics service
PA: Kpmg Llp
345 Park Ave Lowr L-4
New York NY 10154
212 758-9700

(P-15788)
ORACLE CORPORATION
279 Barnes Rd, Tustin (92782-3748)
PHONE..................................713 654-0919
Fax: 713 654-8743
John Czapko, *Branch Mgr*
Diana Juneau, *Recruiter*
Johnny Nguyen, *Sales Associate*
Eric Brown, *Sales Staff*
Michael Trudell, *Senior Mgr*
EMP: 191
SALES (corp-wide): 37B **Publicly Held**
SIC: 7372 Prepackaged software
PA: Oracle Corporation
500 Oracle Pkwy
Redwood City CA 94065
650 506-7000

(P-15789)
ORACLE CORPORATION
214 Clarence Ave, Sunnyvale
(94086-5907)
PHONE..................................650 607-5402
Jitendra Chinthakindi, *Principal*
EMP: 302
SALES (corp-wide): 37B **Publicly Held**
SIC: 7372 Prepackaged software
PA: Oracle Corporation
500 Oracle Pkwy
Redwood City CA 94065
650 506-7000

(P-15790)
ORACLE CORPORATION
1408 Antigua Ln, Foster City (94404-3970)
PHONE..................................650 678-3612
ARA Michaelian, *Principal*
Joseph Tomassini, *Manager*
EMP: 302
SALES (corp-wide): 37B **Publicly Held**
SIC: 7372 Prepackaged software
PA: Oracle Corporation
500 Oracle Pkwy
Redwood City CA 94065
650 506-7000

(P-15791)
ORACLE CORPORATION
1490 Newhall St, Santa Clara
(95050-6135)
PHONE..................................408 421-2890
Stephanie Camarda, *Principal*

EMP: 302
SALES (corp-wide): 37B **Publicly Held**
SIC: 7372 Prepackaged software
PA: Oracle Corporation
500 Oracle Pkwy
Redwood City CA 94065
650 506-7000

(P-15792)
ORACLE CORPORATION
231 Kerry Dr, Santa Clara (95050-6603)
PHONE..................................408 276-5552
Annie Van Dalen, *Principal*
EMP: 302
SALES (corp-wide): 37B **Publicly Held**
SIC: 7372 Prepackaged software
PA: Oracle Corporation
500 Oracle Pkwy
Redwood City CA 94065
650 506-7000

(P-15793)
ORACLE CORPORATION
3084 Thurman Dr, San Jose (95148-3143)
PHONE..................................408 276-3822
Alasdair Rendall, *Principal*
EMP: 302
SALES (corp-wide): 37B **Publicly Held**
SIC: 7372 Prepackaged software
PA: Oracle Corporation
500 Oracle Pkwy
Redwood City CA 94065
650 506-7000

(P-15794)
ORACLE CORPORATION
9515 Towne Centre Dr, San Diego
(92121-1973)
PHONE..................................858 587-5374
EMP: 191
SALES (corp-wide): 38.2B **Publicly Held**
SIC: 7372
PA: Oracle Corporation
500 Oracle Pkwy
Redwood City CA 94065
610 407-5150

(P-15795)
ORACLE CORPORATION
3532 Eastin Pl, Santa Clara (95051-2600)
PHONE..................................650 506-9864
Maneesh Jain, *Principal*
EMP: 302
SALES (corp-wide): 37B **Publicly Held**
SIC: 7372 Prepackaged software
PA: Oracle Corporation
500 Oracle Pkwy
Redwood City CA 94065
650 506-7000

(P-15796)
ORACLE CORPORATION
372 Calero Ave, San Jose (95123-4315)
PHONE..................................408 390-8623
Aileen F Casanave, *Principal*
EMP: 302
SALES (corp-wide): 37B **Publicly Held**
SIC: 7372 Prepackaged software
PA: Oracle Corporation
500 Oracle Pkwy
Redwood City CA 94065
650 506-7000

(P-15797)
ORACLE CORPORATION
475 Sansome St Fl 15, San Francisco
(94111-3166)
PHONE..................................415 402-7200
Victor Coskey, *Principal*
Guerry Waters, *Senior VP*
Trey Parsons, *Vice Pres*
Richard Cheung, *Program Mgr*
Rohit Koul, *Sr Software Eng*
EMP: 191
SALES (corp-wide): 37B **Publicly Held**
SIC: 7372 Prepackaged software
PA: Oracle Corporation
500 Oracle Pkwy
Redwood City CA 94065
650 506-7000

(P-15798)
ORACLE CORPORATION
6224 Hummingbird Ln, Rocklin
(95765-5929)
P.O. Box 3442 (95677-8469)
PHONE..................................916 435-8342
Richard Gless, *Principal*
Kevin Amrine, *Director*
Kenneth Zeng, *Director*
EMP: 302
SALES (corp-wide): 37B **Publicly Held**
SIC: 7372 Prepackaged software
PA: Oracle Corporation
500 Oracle Pkwy
Redwood City CA 94065
650 506-7000

(P-15799)
ORACLE CORPORATION
5805 Owens Dr, Pleasanton (94588-3939)
PHONE..................................877 767-2253
Clement Sciammas, *Vice Pres*
Allison Carter, *Sr Software Eng*
Grace Chen, *Sr Software Eng*
Ricky Frost, *Sr Software Eng*
Allan Gore, *Sr Software Eng*
EMP: 315
SALES (corp-wide): 37B **Publicly Held**
SIC: 7372 Prepackaged software
PA: Oracle Corporation
500 Oracle Pkwy
Redwood City CA 94065
650 506-7000

(P-15800)
ORACLE CORPORATION
3925 Emerald Isle Ln, San Jose
(95135-1708)
PHONE..................................925 694-6258
Johnson Aremu, *Principal*
EMP: 306
SALES (corp-wide): 37B **Publicly Held**
SIC: 7372 Prepackaged software
PA: Oracle Corporation
500 Oracle Pkwy
Redwood City CA 94065
650 506-7000

(P-15801)
ORACLE CORPORATION
5863 Carmel Way, Union City
(94587-5170)
PHONE..................................510 471-6971
Renzo Zagni, *Principal*
EMP: 302
SALES (corp-wide): 37B **Publicly Held**
SIC: 7372 Prepackaged software
PA: Oracle Corporation
500 Oracle Pkwy
Redwood City CA 94065
650 506-7000

(P-15802)
ORACLE CORPORATION
5750 Hannum Ave Ste 200, Culver City
(90230-6666)
PHONE..................................310 258-7500
EMP: 302
SALES (corp-wide): 37B **Publicly Held**
SIC: 7372 Business oriented computer software
PA: Oracle Corporation
500 Oracle Pkwy
Redwood City CA 94065
650 506-7000

(P-15803)
ORACLE CORPORATION
200 N Sepulveda Blvd # 400, El Segundo
(90245-5628)
PHONE..................................310 343-7405
EMP: 306
SALES (corp-wide): 37B **Publicly Held**
SIC: 7372 Business oriented computer software
PA: Oracle Corporation
500 Oracle Pkwy
Redwood City CA 94065
650 506-7000

(P-15804)
ORACLE CORPORATION
1001 Sunset Blvd, Rocklin (95765-3702)
PHONE..................................916 315-3500
Fax: 916 315-3000
Chris Wilson, *Branch Mgr*

PRODUCTS & SERVICES SECTION

7372 - Prepackaged Software County (P-15824)

Greg Tennyson, *Vice Pres*
Nancy Peters, *VP Admin*
Stephen Johnston, *Branch Mgr*
Nicole Stokes, *Admin Asst*
EMP: 500
SALES (corp-wide): 37B **Publicly Held**
SIC: 7372 7371 Prepackaged software; custom computer programming services
PA: Oracle Corporation
500 Oracle Pkwy
Redwood City CA 94065
650 506-7000

(P-15805)
ORACLE CORPORATION (PA)
500 Oracle Pkwy, Redwood City (94065-1675)
PHONE.................................650 506-7000
Fax: 650 506-7304
Safra A Catz, *CEO*
Lawrence J Ellison, *Ch of Bd*
Jeffrey O Henley, *Vice Chairman*
Thomas Kurian, *President*
Mark V Hurd, *CEO*
EMP: 2300
SQ FT: 2,000,000
SALES: 37B **Publicly Held**
WEB: www.oracle.com
SIC: 7372 7379 8243 3571 Prepackaged software; business oriented computer software; application computer software; computer related consulting services; software training, computer; minicomputers; microprocessors

(P-15806)
ORACLE SYSTEMS CORPORATION
15760 Ventura Blvd # 1400, Encino (91436-3000)
PHONE.................................818 817-2900
Fax: 818 922-2300
Elizabeth Deitz, *General Mgr*
EMP: 70
SALES (corp-wide): 37B **Publicly Held**
WEB: www.forcecapital.com
SIC: 7372 Prepackaged software
HQ: Oracle Systems Corporation
500 Oracle Pkwy
Redwood City CA 94065
650 506-7000

(P-15807)
ORACLE SYSTEMS CORPORATION
10 Twin Dolphin Dr, Redwood City (94065-1035)
PHONE.................................650 506-0300
Richard Grogan, *Branch Mgr*
Leena Prasad, *Project Mgr*
Michael Grassi, *Marketing Staff*
Yaldah Hakim, *Marketing Staff*
Warren Parti, *Marketing Staff*
EMP: 252
SALES (corp-wide): 37B **Publicly Held**
WEB: www.forcecapital.com
SIC: 7372 Prepackaged software
HQ: Oracle Systems Corporation
500 Oracle Pkwy
Redwood City CA 94065
650 506-7000

(P-15808)
ORACLE SYSTEMS CORPORATION (HQ)
500 Oracle Pkwy, Redwood City (94065-1677)
PHONE.................................650 506-7000
Fax: 650 506-7171
Safra A Catz, *CEO*
Lawrence J Ellison, *Ch of Bd*
Jeffrey O Henley, *Ch of Bd*
Mark V Hurd, *President*
Mark Hurd, *CEO*
EMP: 2300
SQ FT: 2,200,000
SALES (est): 3.9B
SALES (corp-wide): 37B **Publicly Held**
WEB: www.forcecapital.com
SIC: 7372 7379 8243 Prepackaged software; business oriented computer software; application computer software; data processing consultant; software training, computer
PA: Oracle Corporation
500 Oracle Pkwy
Redwood City CA 94065
650 506-7000

(P-15809)
ORACLE SYSTEMS CORPORATION
5840 Owens Dr, Pleasanton (94588-3900)
PHONE.................................925 694-3000
Fax: 925 468-1206
Apu Gupta, *Principal*
Jerry Druce, *Bd of Directors*
Jay Fulcher, *Exec VP*
Randall Geyer, *Sr Software Eng*
Ramani Gujjula, *Sr Software Eng*
EMP: 252
SALES (corp-wide): 37B **Publicly Held**
WEB: www.forcecapital.com
SIC: 7372 5734 Prepackaged software; software, business & non-game
HQ: Oracle Systems Corporation
500 Oracle Pkwy
Redwood City CA 94065
650 506-7000

(P-15810)
ORACLE SYSTEMS CORPORATION
17901 Von Karman Ave # 800, Irvine (92614-6297)
PHONE.................................949 623-9460
Fran Bracey, *Manager*
Chimon Yeung, *Admin Asst*
Tony Hsu, *Sr Software Eng*
Debraj Sinha, *Software Dev*
Chuck Anderson, *Software Engr*
EMP: 275
SALES (corp-wide): 37B **Publicly Held**
WEB: www.forcecapital.com
SIC: 7372 5045 Prepackaged software; computers, peripherals & software
HQ: Oracle Systems Corporation
500 Oracle Pkwy
Redwood City CA 94065
650 506-7000

(P-15811)
ORACLE USA INC
500 Oracle Pkwy, Redwood City (94065-1677)
PHONE.................................650 506-7000
Safra A Catz, *President*
Mark Hurd, *President*
Charles Phillips, *President*
Judson Althoff, *Senior VP*
Matthew Mills, *Senior VP*
EMP: 526 **EST:** 1987
SALES (est): 85.8MM
SALES (corp-wide): 37B **Publicly Held**
SIC: 7372 Prepackaged software
HQ: Oracle Systems Corporation
500 Oracle Pkwy
Redwood City CA 94065
650 506-7000

(P-15812)
OSISOFT LLC (PA)
Also Called: OSI Software
777 Davis St Ste 250, San Leandro (94577-6950)
P.O. Box 727 (94577-0427)
PHONE.................................510 297-5800
Dr J Patrick Kennedy, *Ch of Bd*
Jenny Linton, *President*
Susanna Kass, *COO*
Bob Guilbault, *CFO*
Gary Zies S, *Officer*
EMP: 100
SQ FT: 55,000
SALES (est): 305.7MM **Privately Held**
WEB: www.osisoft.com
SIC: 7372 7371 7373 Application computer software; custom computer programming services; computer integrated systems design

(P-15813)
PACIOLAN INC
5171 California Ave # 200, Irvine (92617-3068)
PHONE.................................949 476-2050
Dave Butler, *CEO*
Jane Kleinberger, *Ch of Bd*
Amit Kothari, *COO*
Megan Dorritiz, *Executive*
Peter Luukko, *Executive*
EMP: 132 **EST:** 1980
SALES (est): 28.3MM
SALES (corp-wide): 74.5B **Publicly Held**
WEB: www.paciolan.com
SIC: 7372 5045 Prepackaged software; computers
PA: Comcast Corporation
1701 Jfk Blvd
Philadelphia PA 19103
215 286-1700

(P-15814)
PATIENTPOP INC
1221 2nc St, Santa Monica (90401-1117)
PHONE.................................310 260-3968
Travis Schneider, *CEO*
Jason Gardner, *CFO*
Luke Kervin, *Co-CEO*
Thomas Le Blan, *Vice Pres*
Taylor Timmer, *Vice Pres*
EMP: 51
SALES (est): 760.8K **Privately Held**
SIC: 7372 Business oriented computer software

(P-15815)
PAXATA INC
305 Walnut St Fl 2, Redwood City (94063-1731)
P.O. Box 5346 (94063-0346)
PHONE.................................650 542-7897
Prakasa Nanduri, *CEO*
David Brewster, *Co-Owner*
Nenshad Bardoliwalla, *Vice Pres*
Christopher Maddox, *Vice Pres*
Rebecca Glenn, *Executive Asst*
EMP: 90
SQ FT: 18,000
SALES (est): 5.4MM **Privately Held**
SIC: 7372 Business oriented computer software

(P-15816)
PAYLOCITY HOLDING CORPORATION
2107 Livingston St, Oakland (94606-5218)
PHONE.................................847 956-4850
EMP: 415
SALES (corp-wide): 230.7MM **Publicly Held**
SIC: 7372 Prepackaged software
PA: Paylocity Holding Corporation
3850 N Wilke Rd
Arlington Heights IL 60004
847 463-3200

(P-15817)
PLANGRID INC
2111 Mission St Ste 400, San Francisco (94110-6349)
PHONE.................................415 349-7440
Tracy Young, *CEO*
Hana Turley, *General Mgr*
Leslie Francisco, *Manager*
EMP: 85
SQ FT: 16,000
SALES (est): 12.3MM **Privately Held**
SIC: 7372 Application computer software

(P-15818)
PLUMGRID INC
5155 Old Ironsides Dr # 100, Santa Clara (95054-1117)
PHONE.................................408 800-7586
Larry Lang, *CEO*
Awais Nemat, *Ch of Bd*
Faisal Mushtaq, *President*
Marty Bradford, *CFO*
Wendy Cartee, *Vice Pres*
EMP: 100 **EST:** 2011
SQ FT: 11,000
SALES (est): 5.3MM **Privately Held**
SIC: 7372 7371 Prepackaged software; computer software development

(P-15819)
POLARION SOFTWARE INC
1001 Marina Village Pkwy # 403, Alameda (94501-6401)
PHONE.................................877 572-4005
Frank Schrder, *CEO*
George Briner, *CFO*
Stefano Rizzo, *Senior VP*
Nikolay Entin, *Vice Pres*
Jiri Walek, *Vice Pres*
EMP: 90
SALES (est): 7.2MM **Privately Held**
SIC: 7372 Prepackaged software

(P-15820)
PORTELLUS INC
2522 Chambers Rd Ste 100, Tustin (92780-6962)
PHONE.................................949 250-9600
John Le, *President*
Brenda Arnold, *Project Mgr*
Jill Malcolm, *Manager*
EMP: 80
SALES (est): 3.6MM **Privately Held**
WEB: www.portellus.com
SIC: 7372 Prepackaged software

(P-15821)
QAD INC (PA)
100 Innovation Pl, Santa Barbara (93108-2268)
PHONE.................................805 566-6000
Fax: 805 565-4202
Karl F Lopker, *CEO*
Pamela M Lopker, *Ch of Bd*
Daniel Lender, *CFO*
Anton Chilton, *Exec VP*
Kara Bellamy, *Senior VP*
EMP: 148
SQ FT: 120,000
SALES: 277.8MM **Publicly Held**
WEB: www.qad.com
SIC: 7372 7371 Prepackaged software; custom computer programming services

(P-15822)
QUALCOMM INNOVATION CENTER INC (HQ)
4365 Executive Dr # 1100, San Diego (92121-2123)
PHONE.................................858 587-1121
Rob Chandhok, *President*
Steven Mair, *Program Mgr*
Joonwoo Park, *Sr Software Eng*
Vikas Das, *Software Engr*
Gordon Thomas, *Software Engr*
EMP: 53 **EST:** 2009
SALES (est): 5MM
SALES (corp-wide): 25.2B **Publicly Held**
SIC: 7372 Prepackaged software
PA: Qualcomm Incorporated
5775 Morehouse Dr
San Diego CA 92121
858 587-1121

(P-15823)
QUALITY SYSTEMS INC (PA)
18111 Von Karman Ave # 700, Irvine (92612-7110)
PHONE.................................949 255-2600
Fax: 949 255-2605
John R Frantz, *President*
Jeffrey H Margolis, *Ch of Bd*
Daniel J Morefield, *COO*
James R Arnold, *CFO*
Craig A Barbarosh, *Vice Ch Bd*
EMP: 148
SQ FT: 71,800
SALES: 492.4MM **Publicly Held**
WEB: www.qsii.com
SIC: 7372 7373 Prepackaged software; computer integrated systems design

(P-15824)
QUMU INC
1100 Grundy Ln Ste 110, San Bruno (94066-3072)
PHONE.................................650 396-8530
Fax: 650 871-8375
Jim Stewart, *CFO*
Ron Evans, *President*
John Page, *Vice Pres*
Mike Poindexter, *Vice Pres*
David Yockelson, *Vice Pres*
EMP: 56
SQ FT: 13,000
SALES (est): 12.8MM
SALES (corp-wide): 34.4MM **Publicly Held**
WEB: www.mediapublisher.com
SIC: 7372 Prepackaged software
PA: Qumu Corporation
510 1st Ave N Ste 305
Minneapolis MN 55403
612 638-9100

7372 - Prepackaged Software County (P-15825) — PRODUDUCTS & SERVICES SECTION

(P-15825)
REAL SOFTWARE SYSTEMS LLC (PA)
21255 Burbank Blvd # 220, Woodland Hills (91367-6610)
PHONE..................818 313-8000
Fax: 818 313-8095
Kent Sahin, *Mng Member*
Michael Stevens, *Manager*
EMP: 50
SALES (est): 11.9MM **Privately Held**
WEB: www.realsoftwaresystems.com
SIC: 7372 Prepackaged software

(P-15826)
REDSEAL INC
940 Stewart Dr Ste 101, Sunnyvale (94085-3912)
PHONE..................408 641-2200
Ray Rothrock, *Ch of Bd*
Pete Sinclair, *COO*
Bob Finley, *CFO*
Vincent A McCord, *CFO*
Gordon Adams, *Officer*
EMP: 100
SQ FT: 6,500
SALES (est): 22MM **Privately Held**
WEB: www.redseal.net
SIC: 7372 Prepackaged software

(P-15827)
RELOADED GAMES INC
17011 Beach Blvd Ste 320, Huntington Beach (92647-7420)
PHONE..................714 333-1420
Bjorn Book-Larsson, *CEO*
EMP: 70 EST: 2011
SQ FT: 16,700
SALES (est): 5.9MM **Privately Held**
SIC: 7372 Home entertainment computer software

(P-15828)
RINGCENTRAL INC (PA)
20 Davis Dr, Belmont (94002-3002)
PHONE..................650 472-4100
Vladimir Shmunis, *Ch of Bd*
Marty Piombo, *Partner*
Clyde Hosein, *CFO*
Riadh Dridi, *Chief Mktg Ofcr*
Dave Sipes, *Officer*
EMP: 80
SQ FT: 84,000
SALES: 296.2MM **Publicly Held**
WEB: www.ringcentral.com
SIC: 7372 4899 Prepackaged software; data communication services

(P-15829)
ROVI CORPORATION (PA)
2 Circle Star Way, San Carlos (94070-6200)
PHONE..................408 562-8400
Fax: 408 567-1800
Thomas Carson, *President*
James E Meyer, *Ch of Bd*
John Burke, *COO*
Peter Halt, *CFO*
James O'Shaughnessy, *Bd of Directors*
▲ **EMP:** 150
SQ FT: 87,000
SALES: 526.2MM **Privately Held**
WEB: www.macrovision.com
SIC: 7372 Home entertainment computer software

(P-15830)
SABA SOFTWARE INC (HQ)
2400 Bridge Pkwy, Redwood City (94065-1166)
PHONE..................650 581-2500
Fax: 650 581-2581
Pervez Qureshi, *CEO*
Phil Saunders, *President*
Edward Hayden, *CFO*
Mark Robinson, *CFO*
Paige Newcombe, *Ch Credit Ofcr*
EMP: 100
SQ FT: 36,000
SALES (est): 297.8MM **Privately Held**
WEB: www.saba.com
SIC: 7372 7371 Application computer software; computer software development & applications

PA: Vector Talent Ii Llc
1 Market St Ste 2300
San Francisco CA 94105
415 293-5000

(P-15831)
SAGE SOFTWARE INC
1380 Tatan Trail Rd, Burlingame (94010)
PHONE..................650 579-3628
Mau Chung Chang, *Branch Mgr*
EMP: 245
SALES (corp-wide): 2.2B **Privately Held**
SIC: 7372 Prepackaged software
HQ: Sage Software, Inc.
271 17th St Nw Ste 1100
Atlanta GA 30363
866 996-7243

(P-15832)
SAGE SOFTWARE HOLDINGS INC (HQ)
6561 Irvine Center Dr, Irvine (92618-2118)
PHONE..................866 530-7243
Stev Swenson, *CEO*
Mack Lout, *CFO*
Doug Meyer, *Vice Pres*
Steven Fritz, *Finance*
EMP: 400
SALES (est): 543.7MM
SALES (corp-wide): 2.2B **Privately Held**
SIC: 7372 7371 Business oriented computer software; custom computer programming services
PA: The Sage Group Plc.
North Park Avenue
Newcastle-Upon-Tyne NE13
800 447-777

(P-15833)
SALESFORCECOM INC (PA)
1 Market Ste 300, San Francisco (94105-5188)
PHONE..................415 901-7000
Fax: 415 901-7040
Marc Benioff, *Ch of Bd*
Keith G Block, *Vice Chairman*
Keith Block, *President*
Alexandre Dayon, *President*
Maria Martinez, *President*
EMP: 600
SALES: 6.6B **Publicly Held**
WEB: www.salesforce.com
SIC: 7372 7375 Business oriented computer software; information retrieval services

(P-15834)
SAS INSTITUTE INC
Salesstock.com
1148 N Lemon St, Orange (92867-4709)
PHONE..................949 250-9999
Shawn Anthony Stiltz, *Vice Pres*
EMP: 56
SALES (corp-wide): 2.9B **Privately Held**
SIC: 7372 Application computer software; business oriented computer software; educational computer software
PA: Sas Institute Inc.
100 Sas Campus Dr
Cary NC 27513
919 677-8000

(P-15835)
SCHOOL INNOVATIONS ACHIEVEMENT (PA)
5200 Golden Foothill Pkwy, El Dorado Hills (95762-9610)
PHONE..................916 933-2290
Fax: 916 487-6441
Jeffrey C Williams, *CEO*
Susan Cook, *COO*
Peter Birdsall, *Exec Dir*
Grace Spencer, *Division Mgr*
Sharon Gillmore, *Executive Asst*
EMP: 95
SQ FT: 25,000
SALES: 14.8MM **Privately Held**
WEB: www.sia-us.com
SIC: 7372 8742 Prepackaged software; management consulting services

(P-15836)
SHAREDATA INC
Also Called: Sharedta/E Trade Bus Solutions
2465 Augustine Dr, Santa Clara (95054-3002)
PHONE..................408 490-2500
Fax: 408 492-0840
Laura Fay, *President*
Nancy Yoneda, *Controller*
Christine Cornwall, *Marketing Staff*
Nancy Bartels, *Director*
Mark Borges, *Director*
EMP: 53
SALES (est): 1.9MM **Privately Held**
SIC: 7372 Business oriented computer software

(P-15837)
SLACK TECHNOLOGIES INC
155 5th St Fl 6, San Francisco (94103-2919)
PHONE..................415 373-8825
Daniel Stewart Butterfield, *CEO*
Tina Gee, *Manager*
EMP: 600
SALES (est): 11.4MM **Privately Held**
SIC: 7372 Business oriented computer software

(P-15838)
SMITH MICRO SOFTWARE INC (PA)
51 Columbia, Aliso Viejo (92656-1456)
PHONE..................949 362-5800
Fax: 949 362-2300
William W Smith Jr, *CEO*
Steven M Yasbek, *CFO*
Mark Lisby, *Treasurer*
Carla Fitzgerald, *Chief Mktg Ofcr*
Rick Carpenter, *Senior VP*
▲ **EMP:** 148
SQ FT: 33,600
SALES: 39.5MM **Publicly Held**
WEB: www.smithmicro.com
SIC: 7372 Prepackaged software

(P-15839)
SNAP INC
579 Toyopa Dr, Pacific Palisades (90272-4470)
PHONE..................310 745-0632
EMP: 651
SALES (corp-wide): 7.4MM **Privately Held**
SIC: 7372 Application computer software
PA: Snap Inc.
63 Market St
Venice CA 90291
310 399-3339

(P-15840)
SNAP INC (PA)
Also Called: Snapchat
63 Market St, Venice (90291-3603)
PHONE..................310 399-3339
Evan T Spiegel, *CEO*
Mary Ritti, *President*
Drew Vollero, *CFO*
Bobby Murphy, *CTO*
Yunao Liu, *Software Engr*
EMP: 88
SALES (est): 7.4MM **Privately Held**
SIC: 7372 Application computer software

(P-15841)
SOCIALIZE INC
450 Townsend St 102, San Francisco (94107-1510)
PHONE..................415 529-4019
Daniel R Odio, *CEO*
Sean Shadmani, *President*
Isaac Mosquera, *CTO*
EMP: 50
SALES (est): 2.7MM
SALES (corp-wide): 14.7MM **Privately Held**
SIC: 7372 Prepackaged software
PA: Sharethis, Inc.
4005 Miranda Ave Ste 100
Palo Alto CA 94304
650 641-0191

(P-15842)
SOFTWARE AG INC
Also Called: Software AG of Virginia
2901 Tasman Dr Ste 219, Santa Clara (95054-1138)
PHONE..................408 490-5300
Karl-Heinz Streibich, *Branch Mgr*
Artie Alvidrez, *Senior Mgr*
EMP: 119
SALES (corp-wide): 937.7MM **Privately Held**
SIC: 7372 Application computer software
HQ: Software Ag, Inc.
11700 Plaza America Dr # 700
Reston VA 20190
703 860-5050

(P-15843)
SPIRALEDGE INC (PA)
Also Called: Swimoutlet.com
1919 S Bascom Ave Fl 3, Campbell (95008-2220)
PHONE..................800 691-4065
AVI Benaroya, *CEO*
Kristopher Kunisch, *Vice Pres*
Laurie Kirchner, *Principal*
Sangeeta Prashar, *Human Res Dir*
Sarah Watt, *Senior Buyer*
EMP: 56
SALES (est): 22.8MM **Privately Held**
SIC: 7372 5137 Prepackaged software; sportswear, women's & children's

(P-15844)
SPLUNK INC (PA)
250 Brannan St, San Francisco (94107-2007)
PHONE..................415 848-8400
Doug Merritt, *President*
Godfrey Sullivan, *Ch of Bd*
Douglas Merritt, *President*
David F Conte, *CFO*
Steven R Sommer, *Chief Mktg Ofcr*
EMP: 160
SQ FT: 95,000
SALES: 668.4MM **Publicly Held**
WEB: www.splunk.com
SIC: 7372 Prepackaged software

(P-15845)
SQUARE INC (PA)
1455 Market St Ste 600, San Francisco (94103-1357)
PHONE..................415 375-3176
Jack Dorsey, *Ch of Bd*
Sarah Friar, *CFO*
Robert Andersen, *Creative Dir*
Scott Gaylord, *Program Mgr*
Dana Wagner, *Admin Sec*
EMP: 50
SQ FT: 333,570
SALES: 1.2B **Publicly Held**
SIC: 7372 Prepackaged software

(P-15846)
SRA OSS INC
5201 Great America Pkwy # 419, Santa Clara (95054-1143)
PHONE..................408 855-8200
Fax: 408 855-8206
RAO Papolu, *President*
Siva Krishna, *Executive*
Teresa Alster, *Administration*
Kirk Vansicklen, *Data Proc Exec*
Kirti Baliga, *Business Mgr*
EMP: 160
SQ FT: 5,000
SALES (est): 16.8MM
SALES (corp-wide): 334.6MM **Privately Held**
WEB: www.sraoss.com
SIC: 7372 Publishers' computer software
HQ: Software Research Associates, Inc.
2-32-8, Minamiikebukuro
Toshima-Ku TKY 171-0
359 792-111

(P-15847)
STALKER SOFTWARE INC
Also Called: Communigate Systems
1100 Larkspur Landing Cir # 355, Larkspur (94939-1826)
PHONE..................415 569-2280
Fax: 415 383-7461
Vladimir Butenko, *President*
John Hart, *Vice Pres*

▲ = Import ▼ = Export
◆ = Import/Export

PRODUCTS & SERVICES SECTION
7372 - Prepackaged Software County (P-15872)

Naomi Nelson, *Vice Pres*
Philip Slater, *Executive*
Thomas Fleissner, *Managing Dir*
EMP: 50
SALES (est) 5.5MM **Privately Held**
WEB: www.communigate.com
SIC: 7372 7371 Prepackaged software; custom computer programming services

(P-15848)
STEELWEDGE SOFTWARE INC (PA)
3875 Hopyard Rd Ste 300, Pleasanton (94588-8527)
PHONE 925 460-1700
Fax: 925 460-1701
Pervinder Johar, *CEO*
Thomas W Williams Jr, *CFO*
Tom Williams, *CFO*
Terrie Hanlon, *Officer*
Glenn Jones, *Exec VP*
EMP: 70
SQ FT: 5,000
SALES (est) 25.3MM **Privately Held**
WEB: www.steelwedge.com
SIC: 7372 Prepackaged software

(P-15849)
STRATCITYCOM LLC
1317 Monterosso St, Danville (94506-1960)
PHONE 408 858-0006
Alfy Louis, *Mng Member*
EMP: 74
SQ FT: 3,400
SALES (est) 1.6MM **Privately Held**
SIC: 7372 Prepackaged software

(P-15850)
STRATEGY COMPANION CORP
3240 El Camino Real # 120, Irvine (92602-1384)
PHONE 714 460-8398
Robert Sterling, *President*
Bill Tang, *Manager*
EMP: 70
SALES (est) 5.2MM **Privately Held**
SIC: 7372 Prepackaged software
PA: Strategy Companion Corp.
Scotia Centre 4th Floor
George Town GR CAYMAN

(P-15851)
STREVUS INC
455 Market St Ste 1670, San Francisco (94105-2472)
PHONE 415 704-8182
Ken Hoang, *CEO*
Gregg Loos, *President*
Dmitri Korablev, *Vice Pres*
Ken Price, *Vice Pres*
Jennifer Turcotte, *Vice Pres*
EMP: 60
SALES (est) 5.5MM **Privately Held**
SIC: 7372 7371 Business oriented computer software; computer software development

(P-15852)
SYMANTEC CORPORATION (PA)
350 Ellis St, Mountain View (94043-2202)
PHONE 650 527-8000
Greg Clark, *CEO*
Daniel H Schulman, *Ch of Bd*
Michael Fey, *President*
Mark S Garfield, *President*
Ajei S Gopal, *President*
EMP: 400
SQ FT: 793,000
SALES: 3.6B **Publicly Held**
WEB: www.symantec.com
SIC: 7372 7379 Prepackaged software; application computer software; utility computer software; business oriented computer software; computer related consulting services

(P-15853)
SYNERGEX INTERNATIONAL CORP
2330 Gold Meadow Way, Gold River (95670-4471)
PHONE 916 635-7300
Michele C Wong, *CEO*
Serena Channel, *Partner*
Vigfus A Asmundson, *Shareholder*
Georgia Petersen, *Shareholder*
Thomas J Powers, *Shareholder*
EMP: 55
SQ FT: 26,000
SALES (est) 10.7MM **Privately Held**
WEB: www.synergex.com
SIC: 7372 Business oriented computer software

(P-15854)
SYNOPSYS INC
199 S Los Robles Ave # 400, Pasadena (91101-4634)
PHONE 626 795-9101
George Bayz, *CEO*
Akash Jain, *Engineer*
Mustafa Kamal, *Engineer*
Geoff Suzuki, *Sales Staff*
Jake Jacobsen, *Manager*
EMP: 90
SALES (corp-wide): 2.2B **Publicly Held**
SIC: 7372 8711 Application computer software; engineering services
PA: Synopsys, Inc.
690 E Middlefield Rd
Mountain View CA 94043
650 584-5000

(P-15855)
SYNPLICITY INC (HQ)
600 W California Ave, Sunnyvale (94086-2486)
P.O. Box 3803 (94088-3803)
PHONE 408 215-6000
Fax: 408 222-0268
Gary Meyers, *President*
Alisa Yaffa, *Ch of Bd*
Andrew Dauman, *President*
John J Hanlon, *CFO*
Andrew Haines, *Senior VP*
EMP: 160
SQ FT: 66,212
SALES (est) 20.6MM
SALES (corp-wide): 2.2B **Publicly Held**
WEB: www.synplicity.com
SIC: 7372 Prepackaged software
PA: Synopsys, Inc.
690 E Middlefield Rd
Mountain View CA 94043
650 584-5000

(P-15856)
TALEO CORPORATION
4140 Dublin Blvd Ste 400, Dublin (94568-7757)
PHONE 925 452-3000
Fax: 510 452-3001
Dorian Daley, *President*
Eric Ball, *CFO*
Martin Dubois, *Officer*
Guy Gauvin, *Exec VP*
Neil Hudspith, *Exec VP*
EMP: 100
SQ FT: 47,500
SALES (est) 93MM
SALES (corp-wide): 37B **Publicly Held**
WEB: www.taleo.com
SIC: 7372 Prepackaged software; business oriented computer software
PA: Oracle Corporation
500 Oracle Pkwy
Redwood City CA 94065
650 506-7000

(P-15857)
TALIX INC
660 3rd St, San Francisco (94107-1927)
PHONE 415 281-3100
Derek Gordon, *President*
Paul Clip, *Vice Pres*
EMP: 70
SALES (est) 1.2MM **Privately Held**
SIC: 7372 8099 Application computer software; blood related health services

(P-15858)
TANGOE INC
9920 Pcf Hts Blvd Ste 200, San Diego (92121)
PHONE 858 452-6800
Sandy Jimenez, *Branch Mgr*
EMP: 100
SALES (corp-wide): 212.4MM **Publicly Held**
SIC: 7372 Application computer software
PA: Tangoe, Inc.
35 Executive Blvd
Orange CT 06477
203 859-9300

(P-15859)
TEKEVER CORPORATION
5201 Great America Pkwy, Santa Clara (95054-1122)
PHONE 408 730-2617
Michael L Margolis, *CEO*
Andre O Oliveira, *Vice Pres*
EMP: 70
SALES (est) 3MM **Privately Held**
WEB: www.tekever.com
SIC: 7372 Prepackaged software

(P-15860)
TELESIGN HOLDINGS INC ✪
13274 Fiji Way Ste 600, Marina Del Rey (90292-7293)
PHONE 310 742-8228
Matthew Hardy, *CFO*
EMP: 70 **EST:** 2016
SALES (est) 1.4MM **Privately Held**
SIC: 7372 Prepackaged software

(P-15861)
THOUSANDEYES INC
301 Howard St Ste 1700, San Francisco (94105-6613)
PHONE 415 513-4526
Mohit Lad, *CEO*
Mike Staiger, *CFO*
Sanjay Mehta, *Chief Mktg Ofcr*
Johnny Bartlett, *Creative Dir*
Ricardo Oliviera, *CTO*
EMP: 75
SALES (est) 5.5MM **Privately Held**
SIC: 7372 Prepackaged software; business oriented computer software; application computer software

(P-15862)
TOTAL DEFENSE INC
100 W San Fernando St # 565, San Jose (95113-1787)
PHONE 408 598-4299
Robert Walters, *CEO*
Lawrence Guerin, *Vice Pres*
EMP: 65
SQ FT: 3,947
SALES (est) 4.2MM **Privately Held**
SIC: 7372 Prepackaged software

(P-15863)
TRAVIDIA INC (PA)
265 Airpark Blvd Ste 500, Chico (95973-9519)
PHONE 530 343-6400
Fax: 530 893-6199
Rand Hutchison, *CEO*
Robert Clark, *Vice Pres*
James Green, *Vice Pres*
Viv Neti, *Vice Pres*
Ed Villescas, *Vice Pres*
EMP: 50
SQ FT: 10,000
SALES (est) 12.7MM **Privately Held**
WEB: www.travidia.com
SIC: 7372 Prepackaged software

(P-15864)
TRIBEWORX LLC
4 San Joaquin Plz Ste 150, Newport Beach (92660-5934)
PHONE 800 949-3432
EMP: 75
SQ FT: 10,000
SALES (est) 4.9MM **Privately Held**
SIC: 7372

(P-15865)
TRION WORLDS INC (PA)
1200 Bridge Pkwy, Redwood City (94065-1159)
PHONE 650 631-9800
Scott Hartsman, *CEO*
Malcolme Dunne, *CFO*
John Burns, *Senior VP*
Nicholas Beliaeff, *Vice Pres*
David Luehmann, *Vice Pres*
EMP: 90
SALES (est) 59.4MM **Privately Held**
WEB: www.trionworld.com
SIC: 7372 Prepackaged software

(P-15866)
TUBEMOGUL INC (PA)
1250 53rd St Ste 2, Emeryville (94608-2965)
PHONE 510 653-0126
Brett Wilson, *President*
Rob Gatto, *COO*
Robert Gatto, *COO*
Ron Will, *CFO*
Keith Eadie, *Chief Mktg Ofcr*
EMP: 112
SQ FT: 49,000
SALES: 180.7MM **Publicly Held**
SIC: 7372 Prepackaged software

(P-15867)
TWILIO INC (PA)
645 Harrison St Fl 3, San Francisco (94107-3624)
PHONE 415 390-2337
Jeff Lawson, *Ch of Bd*
Roy Ng, *COO*
Lee Kirkpatrick, *CFO*
Lee T Kirkpatrick, *CFO*
Robert Van Brewster, *Vice Pres*
EMP: 98
SQ FT: 50,000
SALES: 166.9MM **Publicly Held**
SIC: 7372 4812 Prepackaged software; business oriented computer software; cellular telephone services

(P-15868)
TZ HOLDINGS LP
567 San Nicolas Dr # 120, Newport Beach (92660-6513)
PHONE 949 719-2200
Regina Paolillo, *Principal*
EMP: 2000
SALES (est) 64.4MM **Privately Held**
SIC: 7372 Prepackaged software

(P-15869)
UBER TECHNOLOGIES INC (DH)
1455 Market St Fl 4, San Francisco (94103-1355)
PHONE 415 986-2715
Margaret E Walsh, *Chairman*
Travis Kalanick, *CEO*
Pallav Basu, *Vice Pres*
David Hughes, *Sr Software Eng*
Jesse Lucas, *Finance*
EMP: 75
SALES (est) 1.1B
SALES (corp-wide): 68.2MM **Privately Held**
SIC: 7372 4729 Application computer software; carpool/vanpool arrangement

(P-15870)
UNITY SOFTWARE INC
Also Called: Unity Technologies
30 3rd St, San Francisco (94103-3104)
PHONE 415 848-2533
Oren Tversky, *Vice Pres*
Clive Downie, *Chief Mktg Ofcr*
Elliot Solomon, *Vice Pres*
Cindy Yang, *Business Dir*
Karsten Nielsen, *Administration*
EMP: 173 **EST:** 2009
SALES (est) 12.9MM **Privately Held**
SIC: 7372 Prepackaged software

(P-15871)
URBAN TRADING SOFTWARE INC
21227 Foothill Blvd, Hayward (94541-1517)
PHONE 877 633-6171
Soufyan Abouahmed, *Principal*
EMP: 50
SALES (est) 1.1MM **Privately Held**
SIC: 7372 Prepackaged software

(P-15872)
VEEVA SYSTEMS INC (PA)
4280 Hacienda Dr, Pleasanton (94588-2719)
PHONE 925 452-6500
Fax: 925 452-6504
Peter P Gassner, *CEO*
Gordon Ritter, *Ch of Bd*
Matthew J Wallach, *President*
Timothy S Cabral, *CFO*
E Nitsa Zuppas, *Chief Mktg Ofcr*
EMP: 148

7372 - Prepackaged Software County (P-15873)

SALES: 409.2MM **Publicly Held**
SIC: 7372 7371 7379 Prepackaged software; software programming applications; computer related consulting services

(P-15873)
VELTI INC (PA)
Also Called: Velti USA
150 California St Fl 10, San Francisco (94111-4556)
PHONE.................................415 362-2077
Alex Moukas, *CEO*
Sally Rau, *President*
Wilson W Cheung, *CFO*
Steve Bair, *Vice Pres*
David Staas, *Vice Pres*
EMP: 53
SALES (est): 16.3MM **Privately Held**
WEB: www.adinfuse.com
SIC: 7372 Prepackaged software

(P-15874)
VENDAVO INC (HQ)
401 E Middlefield Rd, Mountain View (94043-4005)
PHONE.................................650 960-4300
Bruno Slosse, *President*
Jim Dianuzzo, *President*
Joshua Sommer, *COO*
John Oosterhouse, *CFO*
Christine Russell, *CFO*
EMP: 129
SALES (est): 70.1MM
SALES (corp-wide): 1B **Privately Held**
WEB: www.vendavo.com
SIC: 7372 Prepackaged software
PA: Francisco Partners Management, L.P.
1 Letterman Dr Ste 410
San Francisco CA 94129
415 418-2900

(P-15875)
VERIFAYA CORPORATION
650 Castro St Ste 120-264, Mountain View (94041-2055)
PHONE.................................408 566-0220
William Heye, *CEO*
Cathy Rosano, *Administration*
Stacy Drumm, *Accounts Exec*
EMP: 160
SALES (est): 5.4MM **Privately Held**
SIC: 7372 Prepackaged software

(P-15876)
VERTICAL COMMUNICATIONS INC (PA)
3900 Freedom Cir Ste 110, Santa Clara (95054-1222)
PHONE.................................408 404-1600
William Tauscher, *Ch of Bd*
Peter Bailey, *President*
Rick Dell, *COO*
Kenneth M Clinebell, *CFO*
David Krietzberg, *CFO*
EMP: 71
SQ FT: 11,202
SALES (est): 74.9MM **Privately Held**
WEB: www.vertical.com
SIC: 7372 Business oriented computer software

(P-15877)
VINDICIA INC
303 Twin Dolphin Dr # 200, Redwood City (94065-1424)
PHONE.................................650 264-4700
Fax: 650 264-4701
Gene Hoffman Jr, *CEO*
Trace Galloway, *President*
Mark Resnick, *COO*
Mark B Elrod, *Exec VP*
Charles Breed, *Senior VP*
EMP: 75
SQ FT: 9,000
SALES (est): 12.6MM **Privately Held**
SIC: 7372 Business oriented computer software

(P-15878)
WARGAMING AMERICA INC (HQ)
1480 64th St Ste 300, Emeryville (94608-1291)
PHONE.................................510 962-6747
Evgueni Kislyi, *CEO*
Andrei Yarantsau, *Vice Pres*
Alex Hart, *Office Mgr*
Vadim Burak, *Executive Asst*
Marcus Diemer, *Manager*
EMP: 53
SQ FT: 1,000
SALES (est): 26.5MM **Privately Held**
SIC: 7372 Application computer software
PA: Wargaming (Usa), Inc.
651 W Washington Blvd # 600
Chicago IL 60661
312 258-0500

(P-15879)
WEST COAST CONSULTING LLC (PA)
9233 Research Dr Ste 200, Irvine (92618-4294)
PHONE.................................949 250-4102
Rajat Khurana,
Daria Price, *Vice Pres*
Tierney Lenahan, *Office Mgr*
Sagar Chand, *Tech Recruiter*
Priti Bajoria, *Technology*
EMP: 100
SALES (est): 15.4MM **Privately Held**
WEB: www.westcoastllc.com
SIC: 7372 Prepackaged software

(P-15880)
WIND RIVER SYSTEMS INC (HQ)
500 Wind River Way, Alameda (94501-1162)
PHONE.................................510 748-4100
Fax: 510 749-2010
Elmar Degenhardt, *CEO*
Kenneth R Klein, *Ch of Bd*
Barry Mainz, *President*
Scot Morrision, *President*
Barry R Mainz, *COO*
EMP: 148
SQ FT: 273,000
SALES (est): 267.2MM
SALES (corp-wide): 55.3B **Publicly Held**
WEB: www.windriver.com
SIC: 7372 7373 Application computer software; systems software development services
PA: Intel Corporation
2200 Mission College Blvd
Santa Clara CA 95054
408 765-8080

(P-15881)
WORDSMART CORPORATION
10025 Mesa Rim Rd, San Diego (92121-2913)
P.O. Box 1167, La Jolla (92038-1167)
PHONE.................................858 565-8068
David Kay, *CEO*
Linda Sullivan, *Administration*
Subhash Katbamna, *Controller*
Lila McKenna, *Human Res Dir*
Vicki Brewer, *Personnel Assit*
EMP: 70
SQ FT: 12,375
SALES (est): 8.8MM **Privately Held**
WEB: www.wordsmart.com
SIC: 7372 Educational computer software

(P-15882)
XAVIENT INFO SYSTEMS INC
2125 N Madera Rd Ste B, Simi Valley (93065-7710)
PHONE.................................805 955-4111
Fax: 805 955-4144
Rajeev Tandon, *CEO*
Mohd Khan, *Top Exec*
Brooke Colegrove, *Senior VP*
Alex Salamon, *Senior VP*
Bob Stankosh, *Senior VP*
EMP: 1800 **Privately Held**
SIC: 7372 Business oriented computer software

(P-15883)
XCELMOBILITY INC
2225 E Byshore Rd Ste 200, Palo Alto (94303)
PHONE.................................650 632-4210
Renyan GE, *CEO*
Ronald Edward Strauss, *Ch of Bd*
Xili Wang, *CFO*
EMP: 98
SALES: 384.5K **Privately Held**
SIC: 7372 7999 Prepackaged software; gambling & lottery services

(P-15884)
ZENDESK INC (PA)
1019 Market St, San Francisco (94103-1612)
PHONE.................................415 418-7506
Mikkel Svane, *Ch of Bd*
Elena Gomez, *CFO*
Rick Rigoli, *CFO*
Toke Nygaard, *Officer*
Marcus A Bragg, *Senior VP*
EMP: 148
SALES: 208.7MM **Publicly Held**
SIC: 7372 Prepackaged software

(P-15885)
ZINIO SYSTEMS INC
114 Sansome St Fl 4, San Francisco (94104-3810)
PHONE.................................415 494-2700
Fax: 415 494-2701
Rusty Lewis, *CEO*
Michelle Bottomley, *President*
Richard A Maggiotto, *President*
Virendra Vase, *COO*
Tom Nofziger, *CFO*
EMP: 75
SALES (est): 9.8MM **Privately Held**
WEB: www.zinio.com
SIC: 7372 Publishers' computer software

(P-15886)
ZYNGA INC (PA)
699 8th St, San Francisco (94103-4901)
PHONE.................................855 449-9642
Frank Gibeau, *CEO*
Mark Pincus, *Ch of Bd*
Matt Bromberg, *COO*
Michelle Quejado, *CFO*
Lincoln Brown, *Senior VP*
EMP: 240
SQ FT: 660,000
SALES: 764.7MM **Publicly Held**
SIC: 7372 7374 Prepackaged software; application computer software; data processing & preparation

(P-15887)
ZYRION INC
440 N Wolfe Rd, Sunnyvale (94085-3869)
PHONE.................................408 524-7424
EMP: 75
SQ FT: 6,000
SALES (est): 4.7MM **Privately Held**
SIC: 7372
PA: Kaseya Global Ireland Limited
Commerzbank House
Dublin

7373 Computer Integrated Systems Design

(P-15888)
10UP LLC
2765 Carradale Dr, Roseville (95661-4089)
PHONE.................................888 571-7130
Jacob Goldman, *Owner*
Pat Silvia, *Manager*
EMP: 80
SQ FT: 1,300
SALES (est): 5.5MM **Privately Held**
SIC: 7373 Systems software development services

(P-15889)
3K TECHNOLOGIES LLC
1114 Cadillac Ct, Milpitas (95035-3058)
PHONE.................................408 716-5900
Fax: 408 884-2420
Sireesha Chittabbathini,
Pamela Jacobs, *Marketing Staff*
Krishna Chittabbathini,
Subrahmanyam Nadikatla, *Manager*
EMP: 76
SQ FT: 2,000
SALES (est): 10.9MM **Privately Held**
SIC: 7373 Systems software development services

(P-15890)
3M COGENT INC (HQ)
639 N Rosemead Blvd, Pasadena (91107-2147)
PHONE.................................626 325-9600
Fax: 626 325-9700
Ming Hsieh, *President*
Paul Kim, *CFO*
Michael Hollowich, *Exec VP*
Roger Lacey, *Vice Pres*
Jian Xie, *Vice Pres*
EMP: 148
SQ FT: 151,000
SALES (est): 57.8MM
SALES (corp-wide): 30.2B **Publicly Held**
WEB: www.cogentsystem.com
SIC: 7373 Computer-aided system services
PA: 3m Company
3m Center Bldg 22011w02
Saint Paul MN 55144
651 733-1110

(P-15891)
A10 NETWORKS INC (PA)
3 W Plumeria Dr, San Jose (95134-2111)
PHONE.................................408 325-8668
Fax: 408 325-8666
Lee Chen, *Ch of Bd*
Greg Straughn, *CFO*
Neil Wu Becker, *Vice Pres*
James Cai, *Vice Pres*
Robert Cochran, *Vice Pres*
EMP: 146
SQ FT: 79,803
SALES: 198.9MM **Publicly Held**
WEB: www.a10networks.com
SIC: 7373 Computer integrated systems design; systems software development services; computer system selling services

(P-15892)
ABX ENGINEERING INC
875 Stanton Rd, Burlingame (94010-1403)
PHONE.................................650 552-2300
Fax: 650 259-8750
Paul Leininger II, *CEO*
Hector Scritzky, *Engineer*
Felice Roberts, *Manager*
John Turner, *Manager*
EMP: 100
SQ FT: 16,000
SALES (est): 24.1MM **Privately Held**
WEB: www.abxengr.com
SIC: 7373 5065 Turnkey vendors, computer systems; electronic parts

(P-15893)
ACMA COMPUTERS INC
1565 Reliance Way, Fremont (94539-6103)
PHONE.................................214 587-1829
CHI Lei Ni, *President*
Jerry Shih, *Shareholder*
Jean Shih, *CEO*
Margaret Huang, *Controller*
Jodie Nie, *Purch Mgr*
EMP: 150
SQ FT: 23,000
SALES (est): 17.1MM **Privately Held**
WEB: www.acma.com
SIC: 7373 Systems integration services

(P-15894)
ACOM SOLUTIONS INC (PA)
2850 E 29th St, Long Beach (90806-2313)
PHONE.................................562 424-7899
Fax: 562 424-2669
Patrick S McMahon, *President*
Edward J Kennedy, *Chairman*
Mark Firmin, *Vice Pres*
Joe Torano, *Vice Pres*
Claude Rosay, *Regional Mgr*
EMP: 50
SQ FT: 23,000
SALES (est): 38.5MM **Privately Held**
WEB: www.acom.com
SIC: 7373 Value-added resellers, computer systems

(P-15895)
ACTIAN CORPORATION (PA)
2300 Geng Rd Ste 150, Palo Alto (94303-3353)
PHONE.................................650 587-5500
Fax: 650 587-5550
Steve Shine, *CEO*
Darya Nasr, *President*
Steven Springsteel, *CFO*
Tony Kavanagh, *Chief Mktg Ofcr*
Kevin Edmiston, *Senior VP*

PRODUCTS & SERVICES SECTION
7373 - Computer Integrated Systems Design County (P-15915)

EMP: 70
SQ FT: 20,000
SALES (est): 207.3MM **Privately Held**
WEB: www.ingres.com
SIC: **7373** 7372 Systems software development services; business oriented computer software

(P-15896)
ACUMEN LLC
Also Called: Medric
500 Airport Blvd Ste 365, Burlingame (94010-1936)
PHONE..................650 558-8882
Fax: 650 558-3981
Thomas Macurdy, *Mng Member*
Michael Bernstam, *Treasurer*
Vicky Wheeler, *Executive*
Sung Park, *Admin Asst*
David Barnes, *Administration*
EMP: 166 EST: 1996
SALES (est): 33.9MM **Privately Held**
WEB: www.acumenllc.com
SIC: **7373** 7379 8742 Systems software development services; computer related consulting services; data processing consultant; management consulting services; administrative services consultant

(P-15897)
ADSTREAM NORTH AMERICA INC
Also Called: Deluxe Ad Services Inc
2400 W Empire Ave, Burbank (91504-3331)
PHONE..................212 459-0290
Gerry Sutton, *CEO*
Anjani Esguerra, *Finance Dir*
EMP: 120
SALES (est): 4.1MM **Privately Held**
SIC: **7373** Systems software development services

(P-15898)
AEROHIVE NETWORKS INC
2899 Toyon Dr, Santa Clara (95051-6836)
PHONE..................408 988-9918
Sheen Khoury, *Exec VP*
George Frie, *CFO*
Doyle Westley, *Technology*
Ray Clounch, *Engineer*
Speros Pavlatos, *Sales Dir*
EMP: 289
SALES (corp-wide): 151.6MM **Publicly Held**
SIC: **7373** Computer integrated systems design
PA: Aerohive Networks, Inc.
1011 Mccarthy Blvd
Milpitas CA 95035
408 510-6100

(P-15899)
AEROHIVE NETWORKS INC (PA)
1011 Mccarthy Blvd, Milpitas (95035-7920)
PHONE..................408 510-6100
David K Flynn, *Ch of Bd*
John Ritchie, *CFO*
David Greene, *Chief Mktg Ofcr*
Raphael Gernez, *Senior VP*
Efstathios Papaefstathiou, *Senior VP*
EMP: 148
SALES: 151.6MM **Publicly Held**
WEB: www.aerohive.com
SIC: **7373** Local area network (LAN) systems integrator

(P-15900)
AGILYSYS INC
5383 Hollister Ave # 120, Santa Barbara (93111-2304)
PHONE..................805 692-6339
EMP: 108
SALES (corp-wide): 120.3MM **Publicly Held**
WEB: www.pios.com
SIC: **7373** Computer systems analysis & design
PA: Agilysys, Inc.
425 Walnut St Ste 1800
Cincinnati OH 45202
770 810-7800

(P-15901)
AMSNET INC (PA)
502 Commerce Way, Livermore (94551-7812)
PHONE..................925 245-6100
Fax: 925 245-6150
Robert Tocci, *CEO*
John Stott, *Vice Pres*
Tom Vasconi, *Vice Pres*
Danielle Escamilla, *Administration*
Britney Hansen, *Administration*
EMP: 50
SQ FT: 15,000
SALES: 52.3MM **Privately Held**
SIC: **7373** 1731 7378 Systems integration services; computer installation; computer maintenance & repair

(P-15902)
APIGEE CORPORATION
10 Almaden Blvd Ste 1600, San Jose (95113-2275)
PHONE..................408 343-7300
Chet Kapoor, *CEO*
Tim Wan, *CFO*
Denise Persson, *Chief Mktg Ofcr*
Meenakshi Singh, *Exec VP*
Stacey Giamalis, *Senior VP*
EMP: 374
SALES: 92MM **Privately Held**
WEB: www.sonoasystems.com
SIC: **7373** Computer integrated systems design

(P-15903)
APRISO CORPORATION
301 E Ocean Blvd Ste 1200, Long Beach (90802-4839)
PHONE..................562 951-8000
James Henderson, *CEO*
Carey Tokirio, *CFO*
Chris Brecher, *Exec VP*
Thomas A Comstock, *Exec VP*
Tom Comstock, *Exec VP*
EMP: 200
SALES (est): 5.1MM
SALES (corp-wide): 13.3MM **Privately Held**
WEB: www.apriso.com
SIC: **7373** Computer integrated systems design
HQ: Dassault Systemes
10 Rue Marcel Dassault
Velizy Villacoublay Cedex 78946
161 626-162

(P-15904)
ART & LOGIC INC
Also Called: Artlogic
2 N Lake Ave Ste 1050, Pasadena (91101-1872)
PHONE..................818 500-1933
Fax: 818 405-9802
Bob Bajoras, *President*
Paul Hershenson, *Co-Owner*
Tom Bajoras, *Owner*
Andrew Sherbrooke, *Vice Pres*
Tendel Wyman, *Office Mgr*
EMP: 55
SQ FT: 1,500
SALES (est): 8.9MM **Privately Held**
WEB: www.artlogic.com
SIC: **7373** 7371 7379 Systems software development services; custom computer programming services; computer related consulting services

(P-15905)
AT ROAD INC (HQ)
888 Tasman Dr, Milpitas (95035-7439)
PHONE..................510 668-1638
Ken Colby, *President*
Michael Walker, *Exec VP*
Ian Gray, *Vice Pres*
Carol Rice-Murphy, *Vice Pres*
Nicole Jurado, *Sales Associate*
EMP: 350
SQ FT: 102,544
SALES (est): 16.3MM
SALES (corp-wide): 2.2B **Publicly Held**
SIC: **7373** 7372 Systems integration services; prepackaged software; business oriented computer software

PA: Trimble Inc.
935 Stewart Dr
Sunnyvale CA 94085
408 481-8000

(P-15906)
ATAC (PA)
2770 De La Cruz Blvd, Santa Clara (95050-2624)
PHONE..................408 736-8447
Fax: 408 736-8447
Scott Simcox, *President*
Charles Winkleman, *CFO*
John Bobick, *Chairman*
Don Crisp, *Vice Pres*
David Holl, *Executive*
EMP: 65
SQ FT: 31,000
SALES: 18.1MM **Privately Held**
WEB: www.atac.com
SIC: **7373** 7376 7379 8711 Computer integrated systems design; computer facilities management; computer related maintenance services; engineering services; physical research, noncommercial

(P-15907)
AUTOMATION ENGRG SYSTEMS INC
Also Called: AES
3520 Seagate Way Ste 115, Oceanside (92056-2681)
PHONE..................858 967-8650
Leo Castaneda, *President*
EMP: 80
SALES (est): 1.9MM **Privately Held**
SIC: **7373** Systems integration services

(P-15908)
BEAR DATA SOLUTIONS INC
11189 Sorrento Valley Rd # 103, San Diego (92121-1341)
PHONE..................858 824-2920
Fax: 858 824-2921
Ramon Samaniego, *Manager*
EMP: 52
SALES (corp-wide): 764.7MM **Publicly Held**
WEB: www.bdata.com
SIC: **7373** 5045 Computer integrated systems design; computers, peripherals & software
HQ: Bear Data Solutions, Inc.
10050 Crosstown Cir
Eden Prairie MN 55344
925 389-1320

(P-15909)
BEAR DATA SOLUTIONS INC
2485 Mccabe Way Ste 100, Irvine (92614-4225)
PHONE..................949 833-3282
Fax: 949 271-2347
EMP: 52
SALES (corp-wide): 764.7MM **Publicly Held**
WEB: www.bdata.com
SIC: **7373** 5045 Computer integrated systems design; computers, peripherals & software
HQ: Bear Data Solutions, Inc.
10050 Crosstown Cir
Eden Prairie MN 55344
925 389-1320

(P-15910)
BRILLIANT SFTWR SOLUTIONS INC
39350 Civic Center Dr # 310, Fremont (94538-2343)
PHONE..................510 742-5120
Narendra Punati, *President*
Sreenivas Veerapaneni, *Vice Pres*
EMP: 75 EST: 2000
SALES (est): 5.1MM **Privately Held**
WEB: www.brilliantsoft.com
SIC: **7373** Systems integration services

(P-15911)
CACI INC - FEDERAL
1455 Frazee Rd Ste 700, San Diego (92108-4308)
PHONE..................619 881-6000
J P London, *Ch of Bd*
EMP: 50

SALES (corp-wide): 3.7B **Publicly Held**
WEB: www.inventure.com
SIC: **7373** Computer integrated systems design
HQ: Caci, Inc. - Federal
1100 N Glebe Rd Ste 200
Arlington VA 22201
703 841-7800

(P-15912)
CADENT INC
Also Called: Orthocad
2560 Orchard Pkwy, San Jose (95131-1033)
PHONE..................408 470-1000
Timothy Mack, *President*
Roger Blanchette, *CFO*
AVI Kopelman, *Exec VP*
Dan N Pitkowsky, *Senior VP*
Nancy Sudo, *Human Res Mgr*
EMP: 130
SQ FT: 24,000
SALES (est): 14.3MM
SALES (corp-wide): 845.4MM **Publicly Held**
WEB: www.orthocad.com
SIC: **7373** Computer systems analysis & design
HQ: Cadent Holdings, Inc.
2560 Orchard Pkwy
San Jose CA

(P-15913)
CALSOFT LABS INC (HQ)
Also Called: Alten Calsoftlabs
2903 Bunker Hill Ln, Santa Clara (95054-1141)
PHONE..................408 755-3001
Ramandeep Singh, *CEO*
SAI Sathiamoorthy, *CFO*
SAI Satyam, *CFO*
Narendra Dhara, *Senior VP*
Glen Baylor, *Vice Pres*
EMP: 269
SQ FT: 4,303
SALES (est): 15.5MM
SALES (corp-wide): 594MM **Privately Held**
SIC: **7373** Systems software development services
PA: Alten
40 Avenue Andre Morizet
Boulogne Billancourt Cedex 92513
155 198-836

(P-15914)
CAPTIVA SOFTWARE CORPORATION (DH)
10145 Pacific Hts Blvd, San Diego (92121-4234)
PHONE..................858 320-1000
Fax: 858 320-1010
Reynolds C Bish, *President*
Patrick L Edsell, *Ch of Bd*
Rick E Russo, *CFO*
Mel S Lavitt, *Bd of Directors*
Howard Dratler, *Exec VP*
EMP: 80
SQ FT: 25,000
SALES (est): 5.4MM
SALES (corp-wide): 72.7B **Publicly Held**
SIC: **7373** 7372 Office computer automation systems integration; prepackaged software
HQ: Emc Corporation
176 South St
Hopkinton MA 01748
508 435-1000

(P-15915)
CARLISLE RESEARCH CORPORATION
7100 Hayvenhurst Ave Ph F, Van Nuys (91406-3804)
PHONE..................818 785-8677
Fax: 818 785-8429
Jimmy Carlisle, *President*
Barbara Gravett, *Manager*
EMP: 54
SQ FT: 52,250

7373 - Computer Integrated Systems Design County (P-15916)

PRODUDUCTS & SERVICES SECTION

SALES (est): 4MM **Privately Held**
WEB: www.cri-corp.com
SIC: **7373** 7379 7372 7371 Computer integrated systems design; data processing consultant; prepackaged software; computer software systems analysis & design, custom; software, business & non-game

(P-15916)
CAVAYA INC
100 Marine Pkwy Ste 400, Redwood City (94065-5204)
PHONE 831 338-1008
Sudhir Saxena, *President*
Sreen Munukutla, *Vice Pres*
Ellen Terwilliger, *Vice Pres*
EMP: 50
SALES (est): 4.6MM **Privately Held**
WEB: www.cavaya.com
SIC: **7373** Systems integration services

(P-15917)
CELLMATICS
2309 Masters Rd, Carlsbad (92008-3843)
PHONE 760 692-2424
Rose Thomas, *CEO*
EMP: 50
SALES: 250K **Privately Held**
SIC: **7373** Computer integrated systems design

(P-15918)
CENTRO INC
115 Sansome St, San Francisco (94104-3601)
PHONE 415 788-6190
Fax: 312 988-9397
EMP: 112
SALES (corp-wide): 23.6MM **Privately Held**
SIC: **7373** Systems software development services
PA: Centro, Inc.
  11 E Madison St Ste 300
  Chicago IL 60602
  312 642-7348

(P-15919)
CGTECH (PA)
9000 Research Dr, Irvine (92618-4214)
PHONE 949 753-1050
Fax: 949 753-1053
Jon L Prun, *President*
Bill Hasenjaeger, *CIO*
Eduard Vaysleb, *Software Engr*
Tim Andrews, *Research*
Frank Bakanau, *Technical Staff*
EMP: 50
SQ FT: 27,000
SALES (est): 16MM **Privately Held**
WEB: www.cgtech.com
SIC: **7373** Computer-aided design (CAD) systems service; computer-aided manufacturing (CAM) systems service

(P-15920)
CHECKFREE CORPORATION
IDS
1640 S Sepulveda Blvd # 400, Los Angeles (90025-7510)
PHONE 310 954-5600
Phillip Alford, *Branch Mgr*
EMP: 75
SALES (corp-wide): 5.2B **Publicly Held**
WEB: www.checkfree.com
SIC: **7373** 7372 Systems software development services; prepackaged software
HQ: Checkfree Corporation
  2900 Westside Pkwy
  Alpharetta GA 30004
  678 375-3000

(P-15921)
CITADEL GROUP SOLUTIONS LLC
Also Called: Paysys
6601 Center Dr W Fl 5, Los Angeles (90045-1594)
PHONE 310 649-7500
Gerald Marshall, *Mng Member*
Jenny Ho, *CFO*
EMP: 63 **EST:** 2014
SQ FT: 22,000
SALES (est): 60MM **Privately Held**
SIC: **7373** Systems software development services

(P-15922)
CLINICOMP INTERNATIONAL INC (PA)
9655 Towne Centre Dr, San Diego (92121-1964)
PHONE 858 546-8202
Fax: 858 546-1801
Chris Haudenschild, *Ch of Bd*
Eloisa Haudenschild, *CFO*
Sarah Crouch Chavez, *Vice Pres*
Jiao Fan, *Vice Pres*
Phillip Lajoie, *Vice Pres*
EMP: 100
SQ FT: 42,000
SALES (est): 23.9MM **Privately Held**
WEB: www.clinicomp.com
SIC: **7373** 7371 3571 Systems software development services; custom computer programming services; electronic computers

(P-15923)
CNET NETWORKS INC
Also Called: Cnetinc
101 California St, San Francisco (94111-5802)
PHONE 415 344-2000
Mehdi Maghsoodnia, *Bd of Directors*
Debbie Andrews, *Vice Pres*
Greg Brannan, *Vice Pres*
Katie Kulik, *Vice Pres*
Wayne Silverman, *Vice Pres*
EMP: 98
SALES (est): 10.8MM
SALES (corp-wide): 13.9B **Publicly Held**
SIC: **7373** 7371 Systems software development services; computer software development & applications
HQ: Cbs Interactive Inc.
  235 2nd St
  San Francisco CA 94105
  415 344-2000

(P-15924)
COMGLOBAL SYSTEMS INC (DH)
1315 Dell Ave, Campbell (95008-6609)
PHONE 619 321-6000
Fax: 408 374-5209
EMP: 68
SQ FT: 600
SALES (est): 14.9MM
SALES (corp-wide): 335.6MM **Privately Held**
WEB: www.comglobal.com
SIC: **7373**
HQ: Analex Corporation
  11091 Sunset Hills Rd # 200
  Reston VA 20171
  703 956-8243

(P-15925)
CORDOBA CORPORATION
1401 N Broadway, Los Angeles (90012-1410)
PHONE 213 895-0224
George Pla, *President*
Maria Mehranian, *COO*
EMP: 65
SALES (est): 5.4MM **Privately Held**
SIC: **7373** Computer integrated systems design

(P-15926)
CUBIC CORPORATION
Also Called: Cubic Defense Systems
9233 Balboa Ave, San Diego (92123-1513)
PHONE 858 277-6780
Brigitte Jen, *Branch Mgr*
John Moran, *Officer*
William C David, *Vice Pres*
John Naff, *Vice Pres*
Dominic Zullo, *Risk Mgmt Dir*
EMP: 2000
SALES (corp-wide): 1.4B **Publicly Held**
SIC: **7373** Computer integrated systems design
PA: Cubic Corporation
  9333 Balboa Ave
  San Diego CA 92123
  858 277-6780

(P-15927)
DATA CONTROL CORPORATION
P.O. Box 2069, Granite Bay (95746-2069)
PHONE 916 774-4000
J Dale Debber, *President*
Dale Debber, *Manager*
David Mitchell, *Manager*
EMP: 67
SQ FT: 15,000
SALES (est): 3.9MM **Privately Held**
SIC: **7373** Systems software development services

(P-15928)
DATA DOMAIN LLC (DH)
2421 Mission College Blvd, Santa Clara (95054-1214)
PHONE 408 980-4800
Frank Slootman, *President*
Michael P Scarpelli, *CFO*
Nick Bacica, *Senior VP*
Daniel R McGee, *Senior VP*
David L Schneider, *Senior VP*
EMP: 131
SQ FT: 200,000
SALES (est): 93.3K
SALES (corp-wide): 72.7B **Publicly Held**
WEB: www.datadomain.com
SIC: **7373** Computer integrated systems design
HQ: Emc Corporation
  176 South St
  Hopkinton MA 01748
  508 435-1000

(P-15929)
DATAPARK INC
1631 Neptune Dr, San Leandro (94577-3162)
PHONE 510 483-7275
Steve Haralambiew, *President*
Lorenza Tomaz, *CFO*
EMP: 60
SQ FT: 9,900
SALES (est): 8.7MM **Privately Held**
WEB: www.dataparkgroup.com
SIC: **7373** Computer integrated systems design

(P-15930)
DELEGATA CORPORATION
2450 Venture Oaks Way # 400, Sacramento (95833-4226)
PHONE 916 609-5400
Kais Menoufy, *President*
Stacy Huffmon, *Administration*
Charles Dunn, *Info Tech Dir*
Albert Nong, *Info Tech Dir*
Mahmoud Abotaleb, *Software Dev*
EMP: 100
SQ FT: 5,000
SALES (est): 13.8MM **Privately Held**
WEB: www.delegata.com
SIC: **7373** Computer integrated systems design

(P-15931)
DELL SOFTWARE INC (DH)
4 Polaris Way, Aliso Viejo (92656-5356)
PHONE 949 754-8000
Michael S Dell, *CEO*
Jeffrey W Clarke, *President*
Stephen J Felice, *President*
Marius A Haas, *President*
Stephen F Schuckenbrock, *President*
EMP: 600
SQ FT: 170,000
SALES (est): 1B
SALES (corp-wide): 72.7B **Publicly Held**
WEB: www.quest.com
SIC: **7373** 7372 7379 Computer integrated systems design; business oriented computer software; computer related consulting services
HQ: Dell Inc.
  1 Dell Way
  Round Rock TX 78682
  512 338-4400

(P-15932)
DIGIMARC CORPORATION
1825 S Grant St Ste 600, San Mateo (94402-2662)
PHONE 888 300-9114
Maricar Baylon, *Technology*
EMP: 155

SALES (corp-wide): 22.1MM **Publicly Held**
SIC: **7373** Computer integrated systems design
PA: Digimarc Corporation
  9405 Sw Gemini Dr
  Beaverton OR 97008
  503 469-4800

(P-15933)
DIGITAL KEYSTONE INC
21631 Stevns Crk Blvd A, Cupertino (95014-1169)
PHONE 650 938-7301
Paolo Siccardo, *CEO*
Luc Vantalon, *CTO*
Freddie Bose, *QA Dir*
EMP: 50
SQ FT: 27,000
SALES (est): 4MM **Privately Held**
WEB: www.dkeystone.com
SIC: **7373** Computer integrated systems design

(P-15934)
DIMENSION DATA NORTH AMER INC
5000 Hopyard Rd, Pleasanton (94588-3348)
PHONE 925 226-8378
Scott Chudy, *Branch Mgr*
Todd Gill, *Technology*
EMP: 89
SALES (corp-wide): 98.6B **Privately Held**
SIC: **7373** Computer integrated systems design
HQ: Dimension Data North America, Inc.
  1 Penn Plz Ste 1600
  New York NY 10119
  212 613-1220

(P-15935)
DOCUSIGN INC (PA)
221 Main St Ste 1000, San Francisco (94105-1925)
PHONE 415 489-4940
Keith Krach, *CEO*
Rinisha Jha, *Senior Partner*
Gordon Payne, *COO*
Mike Dinsdale, *CFO*
Michael Sheridan, *CFO*
EMP: 50
SALES (est): 243.3MM **Privately Held**
WEB: www.docusign.com
SIC: **7373** Systems software development services

(P-15936)
DYNCORP
Nas Nrth Is Bldg 1479, San Diego (92135)
P.O. Box 189002, Coronado (92178-9002)
PHONE 619 522-2222
Mike Johnson, *Manager*
EMP: 115
SALES (corp-wide): 7.1B **Publicly Held**
WEB: www.dyncorp.com
SIC: **7373** Systems software development services
HQ: Dyncorp
  1700 Old Meadow Rd
  Mc Lean VA 22102
  571 722-0210

(P-15937)
E2 CORP
Also Called: E2 Solutions
8121 Van Nuys Blvd # 308, Panorama City (91402-5105)
PHONE 818 904-5660
Fax: 818 904-5666
Sonia Keshap, *President*
Lolita Munsayac, *Accountant*
Kevin Ragan, *Director*
EMP: 75
SQ FT: 1,550
SALES (est): 6.8MM **Privately Held**
WEB: www.e2solutions.com
SIC: **7373** 7371 Computer integrated systems design; computer software systems analysis & design, custom

PRODUCTS & SERVICES SECTION
7373 - Computer Integrated Systems Design County (P-15958)

(P-15938)
ELECTRONIC DATA CARE INC
Also Called: E D C
23670 Hawthorne Blvd # 208, Torrance (90505-8207)
PHONE.................................310 791-2600
Fax: 310 373-5232
Nabil Salem, *President*
Jeff Woods, *Vice Pres*
Amy Riddle, *VP Human Res*
Robert Jones, *Purchasing*
Ali Eissawy, *Director*
EMP: 70
SQ FT: 2,500
SALES: 800K **Privately Held**
WEB: www.edatacare.com
SIC: 7373 8299 Systems integration services; educational services

(P-15939)
ELECTRONIC ONLINE SYSTEMS INTL
Also Called: E O S International
2292 Faraday Ave Frnt, Carlsbad (92008-7237)
PHONE.................................760 431-8400
Scot Cheatham, *President*
Salvatore Provenza, *Top Exec*
Jeff Goodwin, *Vice Pres*
Greg Leiser, *Vice Pres*
Jeff Smith, *Vice Pres*
EMP: 64
SQ FT: 22,000
SALES (est): 9.8MM **Privately Held**
WEB: www.eosintl.com
SIC: 7373 7371 7372 Turnkey vendors, computer systems; computer software development; prepackaged software

(P-15940)
ELITE INFORMATION GROUP INC (DH)
5100 W Goldleaf Cir # 100, Los Angeles (90056-1284)
PHONE.................................323 642-5200
Christopher K Poole, *President*
Daniel Tacone, *COO*
Barry D Emerson, *CFO*
Keith Hall, *Vice Pres*
Steve Krantz, *CTO*
EMP: 400
SQ FT: 40,000
SALES (est): 29MM
SALES (corp-wide): 3.8B **Publicly Held**
WEB: www.eliteis.com
SIC: 7373 7372 Computer integrated systems design; systems software development services; systems integration services; business oriented computer software
HQ: Thomson Reuters Corporation
3 Times Sq Lbby Mailroom
New York NY 10036
646 223-4000

(P-15941)
ENQUERO INC
1851 Mccarthy Blvd # 115, Milpitas (95035-7448)
PHONE.................................408 406-3203
Arvinder Pal Singh, *CEO*
Kabir Singh, *Managing Prtnr*
Hemant Asher, *CFO*
EMP: 80
SALES (est): 199.8K **Privately Held**
SIC: 7373 7379 Systems software development services;

(P-15942)
EPLUS TECHNOLOGY INC
2355 Main St Ste 140, Irvine (92614-4290)
PHONE.................................949 417-7000
William B Uncapher, *President*
Alison Dimick, *Vice Pres*
EMP: 52 **Publicly Held**
SIC: 7373 Computer integrated systems design
HQ: Eplus Technology, Inc.
13595 Dulles Tech Dr
Herndon VA 20171
703 984-8400

(P-15943)
EPSON PORTLAND INC
Also Called: Epson Research Center
150 River Oaks Pkwy, San Jose (95134-1948)
PHONE.................................408 678-0100
Fax: 408 474-0511
Tak Shiozaki, *Branch Mgr*
Yuki Kurumizawa, *Info Tech Mgr*
Keena Doerner, *Human Res Mgr*
EMP: 50
SALES (corp-wide): 9.3B **Privately Held**
WEB: www.epi.epson.com
SIC: 7373 Computer systems analysis & design
HQ: Epson Portland Inc.
3950 Nw Aloclek Pl
Hillsboro OR 97124
503 645-1118

(P-15944)
ERICSSON INC
300 Holger Way, San Jose (95134-1362)
PHONE.................................408 750-5000
Kevin A Denuccio, *Manager*
Stacie Pham, *Chief Mktg Ofcr*
William Sherry, *Vice Pres*
Dwight Witherspoon, *Vice Pres*
Roland Tecson, *Business Dir*
EMP: 1100
SALES (corp-wide): 28.2B **Privately Held**
WEB: www.redbacknetworks.com
SIC: 7373 Computer integrated systems design
HQ: Ericsson Inc.
6300 Legacy Dr
Plano TX 75024
972 583-0000

(P-15945)
ERICSSON INC
100 Headquarters Dr, San Jose (95134-1370)
PHONE.................................408 597-3600
Kevin A Denuccio, *Branch Mgr*
Ebrahim Abbassi, *Senior VP*
Julu Aryasomayajula, *Sr Software Eng*
Namit Dhameja, *Sr Software Eng*
Santosh Mamidi, *Sr Software Eng*
EMP: 1100
SALES (corp-wide): 28.2B **Privately Held**
SIC: 7373 Computer integrated systems design
HQ: Ericsson Inc.
6300 Legacy Dr
Plano TX 75024
972 583-0000

(P-15946)
EXCELA TECHNOLOGY INC
1960 E Grand Ave Ste 1260, El Segundo (90245-5023)
PHONE.................................310 607-9400
Truman Prewitt, *CEO*
EMP: 60
SALES: 950K **Privately Held**
SIC: 7373 Computer integrated systems design

(P-15947)
EXCELFORE CORPORATION
3155 Kearney St Ste 200, Fremont (94538-2268)
PHONE.................................510 868-2500
Shrikant Acharya, *President*
Anoop Balakrishnan, *Vice Pres*
John Crosbie, *Technology*
Neil Page, *Human Res Mgr*
Latha Yogish, *Recruiter*
EMP: 50
SQ FT: 7,000
SALES (est): 5.2MM **Privately Held**
SIC: 7373 Computer integrated systems design

(P-15948)
FRANCISCO PARTNERS LP (HQ)
Also Called: FP
1 Letterman Dr Bldg C, San Francisco (94129-2402)
PHONE.................................415 418-2900
Dipanjan Deb, *Managing Prtnr*
Chris Adams, *Partner*
Ben Ball, *Partner*
Peter Christodoulo, *Partner*
Neil Garfinkel, *Partner*
EMP: 60
SALES (est): 375.5MM
SALES (corp-wide): 1B **Privately Held**
SIC: 7373 7372 Systems integration services; prepackaged software
PA: Francisco Partners Management, L.P.
1 Letterman Dr Ste 410
San Francisco CA 94129
415 418-2900

(P-15949)
FRANCONNECT LLC
300 Carlsbad Village Dr, Carlsbad (92008-2900)
PHONE.................................760 720-5354
EMP: 100
SALES (corp-wide): 16MM **Privately Held**
SIC: 7373 Systems software development services
PA: Franconnect, Llc
11800 Sunrise Valley Dr
Reston VA 20191
703 390-9300

(P-15950)
FRONTECH N FUJITSU AMER INC (DH)
Also Called: Ffna
27121 Towne Centre Dr # 100, Foothill Ranch (92610-2826)
PHONE.................................949 855-5500
Yoshihiko Masuda, *President*
Tatsuo Horibe, *CFO*
Norman Salvesen, *Treasurer*
Anne Prine, *Sr Corp Ofcr*
Pat Cathey, *Senior VP*
EMP: 210
SQ FT: 90,000
SALES (est): 114.8MM
SALES (corp-wide): 40.5B **Privately Held**
WEB: www.fjicl.com
SIC: 7373 Computer systems analysis & design
HQ: Fujitsu Frontech Limited
1776, Yanokuchi
Inagi TKY 206-0
423 775-111

(P-15951)
FUJITSU AMERICA INC (DH)
1250 E Arques Ave, Sunnyvale (94085-5401)
P.O. Box 3470 (94088-3470)
PHONE.................................408 746-6000
Fax: 408 992-2674
Mike Foster, *CEO*
Robert D Pryor, *President*
Maureen McLean, *COO*
ARI Hovsepyan, *CFO*
Daniel Schembri, *Treasurer*
EMP: 400
SALES (est): 1.1B
SALES (corp-wide): 40.5B **Privately Held**
SIC: 7373 Computer integrated systems design; systems software development services; systems integration services
HQ: Fujitsu North America Holdings, Inc.
1250 E Arques Ave
Sunnyvale CA 94085
408 737-5600

(P-15952)
FUJITSU AMERICA INC
3113 Knights Bridge Rd, San Jose (95132-1734)
PHONE.................................408 746-8419
Ratan Mohla, *Principal*
EMP: 100
SALES (corp-wide): 40.5B **Privately Held**
SIC: 7373 Computer integrated systems design
HQ: Fujitsu America Inc
1250 E Arques Ave
Sunnyvale CA 94085
408 746-6000

(P-15953)
FUJITSU AMERICA INC
317 Eureka St, San Francisco (94114-2712)
PHONE.................................408 992-3561
EMP: 140
SALES (corp-wide): 40.5B **Privately Held**
SIC: 7373 Computer integrated systems design
HQ: Fujitsu America Inc
1250 E Arques Ave
Sunnyvale CA 94085
408 746-6000

(P-15954)
FUJITSU AMERICA INC
2250 E Imperial Hwy # 200, El Segundo (90245-3543)
PHONE.................................310 563-7000
Bob Pryor, *Branch Mgr*
EMP: 140
SALES (corp-wide): 40.5B **Privately Held**
SIC: 7373 Computer integrated systems design
HQ: Fujitsu America Inc
1250 E Arques Ave
Sunnyvale CA 94085
408 746-6000

(P-15955)
GROUPWARE TECHNOLOGY INC (PA)
541 Division St, Campbell (95008-6934)
PHONE.................................408 540-0090
Fax: 408 866-5040
Mike Thompson, *CEO*
Scott Sutter, *Exec VP*
Josh Avila, *Vice Pres*
John Barnes, *Vice Pres*
Anthony Miley, *Vice Pres*
EMP: 50
SQ FT: 14,000
SALES: 400MM **Privately Held**
WEB: www.groupwaretechnology.com
SIC: 7373 5045 Computer-aided system services; computers, peripherals & software; computer software

(P-15956)
HANDS-ON MOBILE AMERICAS INC (PA)
208 Utah St Ste 300, San Francisco (94103-4890)
PHONE.................................415 580-6400
Fax: 415 399-1966
Jonathan Sacks, *CEO*
Dan Kranzler, *Ch of Bd*
Dave Arnold, *President*
Niccolo De Masi, *President*
Kevin Dent, *President*
EMP: 50 EST: 2001
SALES (est): 35.2MM **Privately Held**
WEB: www.mforma.com
SIC: 7373 Computer system selling services

(P-15957)
HEARTFLOW INC (PA)
1400 Seaport Blvd Bldg B, Redwood City (94063-5594)
PHONE.................................650 241-1221
John Stevens, *CEO*
Yoshiki Kawabata, *President*
Baird Radford, *CFO*
Brent Ness, *Ch Credit Ofcr*
Campbell Rogers, *Chief Mktg Ofcr*
EMP: 67
SQ FT: 3,400
SALES (est): 22.8MM **Privately Held**
SIC: 7373 Systems software development services

(P-15958)
HENRY BROS ELECTRONICS INC
Also Called: National Safe
1511 E Orangethorpe Ave A, Fullerton (92831-5204)
PHONE.................................714 525-4350
Eric Demarco, *President*
Deanna Lund, *CEO*
Laura Siegal, *Treasurer*
Michael Fink, *Vice Pres*
Gary Marcinkowski, *Vice Pres*
EMP: 200
SQ FT: 10,000

7373 - Computer Integrated Systems Design County

SALES (est): 20.1MM
SALES (corp-wide): 657.1MM **Publicly Held**
WEB: www.hbe-ca.com
SIC: 7373 7382 5063 Computer integrated systems design; security systems services; burglar alarm systems
HQ: Henry Bros. Electronics, Inc.
17-01 Pollitt Dr Ste 5
Fair Lawn NJ 07410
201 794-6500

(P-15959)
HP INC
575 Anton Blvd Ste 300, Costa Mesa (92626-7161)
PHONE.................................714 432-6588
Fax: 714 432-6574
Deborah Michaels, *Owner*
Julie Jones, *Officer*
EMP: 150
SALES (corp-wide): 103.3B **Publicly Held**
WEB: www.3com.com
SIC: 7373 Local area network (LAN) systems integrator
PA: Hp Inc.
1501 Page Mill Rd
Palo Alto CA 94304
650 857-1501

(P-15960)
HP INC
980 9th St Fl 16, Sacramento (95814-2736)
PHONE.................................916 449-9553
Mark Jenkins, *Manager*
EMP: 150
SALES (corp-wide): 103.3B **Publicly Held**
WEB: www.3com.com
SIC: 7373 Local area network (LAN) systems integrator
PA: Hp Inc.
1501 Page Mill Rd
Palo Alto CA 94304
650 857-1501

(P-15961)
HP INC
6320 Canoga Ave Ste 1500, Woodland Hills (91367-2563)
PHONE.................................818 227-5033
EMP: 125
SALES (corp-wide): 103.3B **Publicly Held**
WEB: www.3com.com
SIC: 7373 Local area network (LAN) systems integrator
PA: Hp Inc.
1501 Page Mill Rd
Palo Alto CA 94304
650 857-1501

(P-15962)
HUBB SYSTEMS LLC
Also Called: Data 911
2021 Challenger Dr, Alameda (94501-1038)
PHONE.................................510 865-9100
Donald R Hubbard, *President*
Brian McCown, *CFO*
Doug Mosby, *General Mgr*
Bret Martin, *Sr Software Eng*
Jim Strehlow, *Prgrmr*
EMP: 75
SALES (est): 19.2MM
SALES (corp-wide): 25.4MM **Privately Held**
SIC: 7373 7379 Turnkey vendors, computer systems; computer related consulting services
PA: Broadcast Microwave Services, Inc
12305 Crosthwaite Cir
Poway CA 92064
858 391-3050

(P-15963)
I LAN SYSTEMS INC
237 S Raymond Ave, Alhambra (91801-3131)
PHONE.................................626 304-9021
Tom Reynolds, *President*
Virginia Reynolds, *Treasurer*
Mae LI Woo, *Admin Sec*
EMP: 55

SQ FT: 1,000
SALES (est): 3.4MM **Privately Held**
SIC: 7373 Computer integrated systems design

(P-15964)
ICYGEN LLC
940 Dwight Way Ste 13b, Berkeley (94710-2528)
PHONE.................................510 540-7122
Milena Badjova,
Irina Tsanova, *Manager*
EMP: 80 EST: 1999
SALES (est): 4.6MM **Privately Held**
WEB: www.icygen.com
SIC: 7373 8742 Computer systems analysis & design; marketing consulting services

(P-15965)
INDEPENDA INC
11455 El Camino Real # 365, San Diego (92130-3036)
PHONE.................................800 815-7829
Kian Saneii, *CEO*
Maria Myers, *Executive*
EMP: 50
SALES (est): 5.9MM **Privately Held**
SIC: 7373 Systems software development services

(P-15966)
INTEGRATED DECISION SYSTEMS
11150 W Olympic Blvd # 600, Los Angeles (90064-1817)
PHONE.................................310 954-5530
Fax: 310 473-4352
Jerald Jackrel, *President*
Donald Potter, *CEO*
Philip Alford, *CFO*
Shahram Zaman, *Vice Pres*
Lawrence Kramer, *Principal*
EMP: 75
SALES (est): 4.4MM **Privately Held**
SIC: 7373 7372 Systems software development services; prepackaged software

(P-15967)
INTELLICUS TECH PVT LTD
720 University Ave # 130, Los Gatos (95032-7609)
PHONE.................................408 213-3314
Praveen Kankiria, *CEO*
Jerry Malec, *President*
Anand Raman, *Vice Pres*
Pankaj Mittal, *CTO*
Rajesh Murthy, *VP Engrg*
EMP: 60
SQ FT: 1,000
SALES: 2MM **Privately Held**
SIC: 7373 Computer integrated systems design

(P-15968)
INTERNATIONAL BUS MCHS CORP
Also Called: IBM
30501 Agoura Rd Ste 100, Agoura Hills (91301-4399)
PHONE.................................914 499-1900
Ricky Kurtz, *Manager*
Steve Canepa, *Vice Pres*
Carol Cronin, *Manager*
EMP: 61
SALES (corp-wide): 81.7B **Publicly Held**
WEB: www.ibm.com
SIC: 7373 7379 Systems software development services; computer systems analysis & design; computer related consulting services
PA: International Business Machines Corporation
1 New Orchard Rd Ste 1
Armonk NY 10504
914 499-1900

(P-15969)
INTERNET CORP FOR ASSIGNED NAM (PA)
Also Called: I C A Nn
12025 Waterfront Dr # 300, Los Angeles (90094-3220)
PHONE.................................310 823-9358
Fax: 310 823-8649

Fadi Chehad, *CEO*
Paul Twomey, *President*
Akram Atallah, *COO*
Xavier Calvez, *CFO*
Ram Mohan, *Bd of Directors*
EMP: 148
SALES: 127.8MM **Privately Held**
WEB: www.icann.org
SIC: 7373 Systems software development services

(P-15970)
INTERNTNAL COMMUNICATIONS CORP
Also Called: ICC Networking
11801 Pierce St Fl 2, Riverside (92505-4400)
PHONE.................................951 934-0531
Keith M Alexis, *President*
Amanda Frazier, *COO*
Amada Frazier, *Vice Pres*
Joy Camacho, *Manager*
EMP: 50
SALES (est): 6.1MM **Privately Held**
SIC: 7373 4812 7389 3663 Local area network (LAN) systems integrator; radio telephone communication;; mobile communication equipment

(P-15971)
INTERSTATE ELECTRONICS CORP
3033 Science Park Rd, San Diego (92121-1101)
PHONE.................................858 552-9500
Andrew Leuthe, *Principal*
Kim Dressle, *Accountant*
Cathy Hilton, *Accounts Mgr*
EMP: 53
SALES (corp-wide): 10.4B **Publicly Held**
SIC: 7373 7379 5045 Systems engineering, computer related; computer related consulting services; computer software
HQ: Interstate Electronics Corporation
602 E Vermont Ave
Anaheim CA 92805
714 758-0500

(P-15972)
INTERVISION SYSTEMS TECH INC (PA)
2270 Martin Ave, Santa Clara (95050-2704)
PHONE.................................408 980-8550
Fax: 408 980-8893
Jeff Kaiser, *CEO*
Jason Gress, *President*
Craig Parks, *Vice Pres*
James Whitemore, *Vice Pres*
Rashel Cramer, *Sales Staff*
EMP: 50
SQ FT: 13,130
SALES (est): 49.1MM **Privately Held**
WEB: www.intervision.com
SIC: 7373 8712 Systems integration services; computer systems analysis & design; architectural services

(P-15973)
IP INFUSION INC (HQ)
3965 Freedom Cir Ste 200, Santa Clara (95054-1293)
PHONE.................................408 400-1900
Fax: 408 400-1500
Koichi Narasaki, *Chairman*
Amit Chatterjee, *President*
Kiyo Oishi, *CEO*
Atsushi Ogata, *COO*
Shane Rigby, *COO*
EMP: 53
SQ FT: 11,900
SALES (est): 13.2MM
SALES (corp-wide): 56.5MM **Privately Held**
WEB: www.ipinfusion.com
SIC: 7373 Systems software development services
PA: Access Co.,Ltd.
3, Kandaneribeicho
Chiyoda-Ku TKY 101-0
368 539-088

(P-15974)
IPASS INC
15241 Laguna Canyon Rd # 100, Irvine (92618-3146)
PHONE.................................650 232-4100
Fax: 949 851-7080
John Drosshan, *Manager*
Daniel Fairfax, *CFO*
Greg Carver, *Vice Pres*
Hui Cheong, *Vice Pres*
John Grosshans, *Vice Pres*
EMP: 90 **Publicly Held**
SIC: 7373 Computer integrated systems design
PA: Ipass Inc.
3800 Bridge Pkwy
Redwood City CA 94065

(P-15975)
IXONOS USA LIMITED
85 2nd St, San Francisco (94105-3459)
PHONE.................................949 278-1354
Jo Javier, *Vice Pres*
Mikko Patrakka, *Business Dir*
EMP: 1000
SALES (est): 50.1MM **Privately Held**
SIC: 7373 8731 Systems software development services; computer (hardware) development
HQ: Ixonos Oyj
Hitsaajankatu 24
Helsinki 00810
505 814-075

(P-15976)
JACKSON TULL CHRTRED ENGINEERS
550 Continental Blvd # 195, El Segundo (90245-5049)
PHONE.................................310 658-2132
Fax: 310 658-3121
Knox Tull, *President*
EMP: 50
SALES (corp-wide): 16.9MM **Privately Held**
WEB: www.jacksonandtull.com
SIC: 7373 8711 Systems engineering, computer related; civil engineering
PA: Jackson And Tull Chartered Engineers
2705 Bladensburg Rd Ne
Washington DC 20018
202 333-9100

(P-15977)
JADE GLOBAL INC
1731 Tech Dr Ste 350, San Jose (95110)
PHONE.................................408 899-7200
Fax: 408 436-8399
Karan Yaramada, *CEO*
Harmeet Bhatia, *President*
Rajeev Handa, *President*
Sandeep Suryavanshi, *COO*
Anant Soni, *Exec VP*
EMP: 125
SQ FT: 2,200
SALES (est): 19.5MM **Privately Held**
WEB: www.usjadecorp.com
SIC: 7373 Systems software development services

(P-15978)
JUNIPER NETWORKS INC
600 Anton Blvd Fl 11, Costa Mesa (92626-7221)
PHONE.................................949 584-4591
Ron Touchard, *Branch Mgr*
EMP: 72 **Publicly Held**
WEB: www.juniper.net
SIC: 7373 Computer integrated systems design
PA: Juniper Networks, Inc.
1133 Innovation Way
Sunnyvale CA 94089

(P-15979)
JUNIPER NETWORKS INC
1215 K St Fl 17, Sacramento (95814-3954)
PHONE.................................916 503-1518
Gerald Chavez, *Branch Mgr*
EMP: 72 **Publicly Held**
WEB: www.juniper.net
SIC: 7373 Computer integrated systems design

PRODUCTS & SERVICES SECTION
7373 - Computer Integrated Systems Design County (P-15999)

PA: Juniper Networks, Inc.
1133 Innovation Way
Sunnyvale CA 94089
-

(P-15980)
KOAM ENGINEERING SYSTEMS INC
Also Called: K E S
7807 Convoy Ct Ste 200, San Diego (92111-1213)
PHONE.................................858 292-0922
John S Yi, *President*
Richard Comber, *Vice Pres*
Erica Tofson, *Vice Pres*
Kimberly Bailey, *Controller*
Brandon Yi, *Opers Staff*
EMP: 105
SQ FT: 5,700
SALES (est): 21.6MM **Privately Held**
SIC: 7373 Computer integrated systems design

(P-15981)
KRAFT & KENNEDY INC
1 Post St Ste 2600, San Francisco (94104-5230)
PHONE.................................415 956-4000
Peter Kennedy, *CEO*
Paul Linhan, *Purch Mgr*
EMP: 60
SALES (corp-wide): 16.3MM **Privately Held**
WEB: www.kklsystems.com
SIC: 7373 7379 Computer integrated systems design; computer related consulting services
PA: Kraft & Kennedy, Inc.
630 3rd Ave Rm 1400
New York NY 10017
212 986-4700

(P-15982)
KUTIR CORPORATION
37600 Central Ct Ste 280, Newark (94560-3438)
PHONE.................................510 402-4526
Gerry Ignatius, *President*
Ranjine Ramachandran, *CFO*
Prathiba Kalyan, *Vice Pres*
G L Kluttz, *Vice Pres*
Bhanu Morampudi, *Vice Pres*
EMP: 50
SALES (est): 7.4MM **Privately Held**
WEB: www.kutirtech.com
SIC: 7373 Systems software development services

(P-15983)
L-3 COMMUNICATIONS CORPORATION
117 S Gold Canyon St, Ridgecrest (93555-4121)
PHONE.................................760 375-0390
Jai Gupta, *Manager*
EMP: 100
SALES (corp-wide): 10.4B **Publicly Held**
SIC: 7373 8731 3761 1731 Systems engineering, computer related; computer systems analysis & design; systems integration services; commercial physical research; guided missiles & space vehicles; electrical work
HQ: L-3 Communications Corporation
600 3rd Ave
New York NY 10016
212 697-1111

(P-15984)
LEIDOS INC
1299 Prospect St, La Jolla (92037-3623)
PHONE.................................858 826-6000
EMP: 350
SALES (corp-wide): 5B **Publicly Held**
WEB: www.saic.com
SIC: 7373 Systems engineering, computer related
HQ: Leidos, Inc.
11951 Freedom Dr Ste 300
Reston VA 20190
571 526-6000

(P-15985)
LIFERAY INC (PA)
1400 Montefino Ave # 100, Diamond Bar (91765-5501)
PHONE.................................877 543-3729
Bryan Cheung, *CEO*
Jorge Ferrer, *President*
Scott Tachiki, *CFO*
Paul Hinz, *Chief Mktg Ofcr*
Brian Endo, *Vice Pres*
EMP: 98
SALES (est): 71.2MM **Privately Held**
WEB: www.liferay.com
SIC: 7373 Systems software development services

(P-15986)
LIGHTCREST LLC
12424 Wilshire Blvd Ste 9, Los Angeles (90025-1071)
PHONE.................................888 320-8495
Zachary Fierstadt,
Michael Hughes, *COO*
Chris Hansen, *Vice Pres*
Evan Alexander, *Business Dir*
Denice Legree, *Admin Asst*
EMP: 50
SALES (est): 8MM **Privately Held**
SIC: 7373 Computer integrated systems design

(P-15987)
LILIEN LLC (HQ)
17 E Sir Francis Dr # 110, Larkspur (94939-1708)
PHONE.................................415 389-7500
Geoffrey I Lilien, *Mng Member*
Eric Borsky, *President*
Kevin Garrison, *Vice Pres*
Craig Gieringer, *Vice Pres*
A Osterfeld, *Managing Dir*
EMP: 50
SQ FT: 6,200
SALES (est): 10.8MM
SALES (corp-wide): 62.9MM **Privately Held**
SIC: 7373 Computer integrated systems design
PA: Sysorex International, Inc
335 E Middlefield Rd
Mountain View CA 94043
650 967-2200

(P-15988)
LIQUIDATE DIRECT LLC
Also Called: Solid Commerce
2929 Washington Blvd Fl 2, Marina Del Rey (90292-5546)
PHONE.................................800 750-7617
Eran Pick, *CEO*
Alon Berkovich, *COO*
Shawna Snukst, *Bus Dvlpt Dir*
Jason Hall, *Sales Staff*
EMP: 50
SALES (est): 6.2MM **Privately Held**
SIC: 7373 7371 7379 Computer integrated systems design; custom computer programming services; computer related maintenance services

(P-15989)
LOCKHEED MARTIN CORPORATION
2770 De La Cruz Blvd, Santa Clara (95050-2624)
PHONE.................................408 734-4980
Fax: 408 450-7194
Ed Novak, *Director*
Carol Crose, *Director*
Rick Craig, *Coordinator*
EMP: 1018
SALES (corp-wide): 46.1B **Publicly Held**
WEB: www.lockheedmartin.com
SIC: 7373 Systems integration services
PA: Lockheed Martin Corporation
6801 Rockledge Dr
Bethesda MD 20817
301 897-6000

(P-15990)
LUCID DESIGN GROUP INC
304 12th St Ste 3c, Oakland (94607-4531)
PHONE.................................510 907-0400
Will Coleman, *CEO*
Vladisov Shunturov, *President*
Scott Boutwell, *Senior VP*
Kevin Burns, *Vice Pres*
Shelly Davenport, *Vice Pres*
EMP: 80
SALES (est): 15.8MM **Privately Held**
WEB: www.luciddesigngroup.com
SIC: 7373 Computer integrated systems design

(P-15991)
MANTECH INTERNATIONAL CORP
615 N Nash St Ste 200, El Segundo (90245-2851)
PHONE.................................310 765-9324
EMP: 200
SALES (corp-wide): 1.5B **Publicly Held**
SIC: 7373 Systems software development services
PA: Mantech International Corporation
12015 Lee Jackson Hwy
Fairfax VA 22033
703 218-6000

(P-15992)
MANTECH INTERNATIONAL CORP
8328 Clairemont Mesa Blvd, San Diego (92111-1328)
PHONE.................................858 492-9938
Rais Ahmed, *Administration*
EMP: 200
SALES (corp-wide): 1.5B **Publicly Held**
SIC: 7373 Systems software development services
PA: Mantech International Corporation
12015 Lee Jackson Hwy
Fairfax VA 22033
703 218-6000

(P-15993)
MAVENT INC
Also Called: Assured Regulatory Compliance
3 Park Plz Ste 700, Irvine (92614-8530)
PHONE.................................949 223-6424
Fax: 949 474-4701
Louis Pizante, *CEO*
Paul Nidenberg, *CFO*
Joe Chang, *Senior VP*
Angela Cheek, *Senior VP*
Ryder Todd Smith, *Senior VP*
EMP: 58
SQ FT: 9,400
SALES (est): 4.5MM
SALES (corp-wide): 253.9MM **Publicly Held**
WEB: www.mavent.com
SIC: 7373 Systems software development services
PA: Ellie Mae, Inc.
4420 Rosewood Dr Ste 500
Pleasanton CA 94588
925 227-7000

(P-15994)
MILESTONE TECHNOLOGIES INC (PA)
3101 Skyway Ct, Fremont (94539-5910)
PHONE.................................510 651-2454
Prem Chand, *CEO*
James Schultz, *CFO*
Jim Andersen, *Vice Pres*
Gary Bilovesky, *Vice Pres*
Kristi H Ledwein, *Vice Pres*
EMP: 138
SQ FT: 6,500
SALES (est): 173.5MM **Privately Held**
WEB: www.milestn.com
SIC: 7373 7374 Computer integrated systems design; data processing & preparation

(P-15995)
MIRO TECHNOLOGIES INC
5643 Copley Dr, San Diego (92111-7903)
PHONE.................................858 677-2100
Fax: 858 554-0862
Vincent Monteparte, *President*
Gregory Jasenovec, *CFO*
Steve Offen, *Officer*
Raj Makwana, *Admin Sec*
Jeff Kennedy, *Systs Engr*
EMP: 150
SQ FT: 18,000

SALES (est): 20.3MM
SALES (corp-wide): 96.1B **Publicly Held**
SIC: 7373 Turnkey vendors, computer systems
PA: The Boeing Company
100 N Riverside Plz
Chicago IL 60606
312 544-2000

(P-15996)
MOBICA US INC
2570 N 1st St Fl 2, San Jose (95131-1035)
PHONE.................................650 450-6654
Marcin Kloda, *CEO*
Rafael Janczyk, *COO*
Anna Orlova, *Administration*
EMP: 900 EST: 2012
SALES (est): 398.6K **Privately Held**
SIC: 7373 Systems software development services
HQ: Mobica Limited
Crown House
Wilmslow SK9 1
162 544-6140

(P-15997)
MORPHOTRAK LLC (DH)
Also Called: Safran
5515 E La Palma Ave # 100, Anaheim (92807-2116)
PHONE.................................714 238-2000
Celeste Thomasson, *CEO*
Florian Hebras, *CFO*
Clark Nelson, *Vice Pres*
Hieu Tran, *Vice Pres*
Katie Murphy, *Admin Sec*
EMP: 175
SQ FT: 32,000
SALES (est): 98.5MM
SALES (corp-wide): 604.7MM **Privately Held**
WEB: www.morpho.com
SIC: 7373 Computer integrated systems design
HQ: Morpho
11 Boulevard Gallieni
Issy Les Moulineaux Cedex 92445
158 112-500

(P-15998)
MOZILLA CORPORATION (HQ)
331 E Evelyn Ave Ste 100, Mountain View (94041-1538)
PHONE.................................650 903-0800
Mitchell Baker, *Ch of Bd*
Chris Beard, *CEO*
James Cook, *CFO*
Christopher Beard, *Exec VP*
Kathleen Wilson, *Program Mgr*
EMP: 425
SQ FT: 15,000
SALES (est): 19.3MM **Privately Held**
WEB: www.mozilla.com
SIC: 7373 Systems software development services
PA: Mozilla Foundation
331 E Evelyn Ave
Mountain View CA 94041
650 903-0800

(P-15999)
MSCSOFTWARE CORPORATION
Costa Mesa Office
4675 Macarthur Ct Ste 900, Newport Beach (92660-1845)
PHONE.................................714 540-8900
Frank Perna, *President*
M J Morgan, *Vice Pres*
Tom Curry, *Marketing Mgr*
Tarik Dsoki, *Sales Staff*
Geetha Bharatram, *Consultant*
EMP: 350
SQ FT: 81,000
SALES (corp-wide): 915MM **Privately Held**
SIC: 7373 8711 7372 7371 Computer-aided engineering (CAE) systems service; engineering services; prepackaged software; custom computer programming services
HQ: Msc.Software Corporation
4675 Macarthur Ct Ste 900
Newport Beach CA 92660
714 540-8900

7373 - Computer Integrated Systems Design County (P-16000)

(P-16000)
NAGARRO INC (PA)
Also Called: Projistics
2001 Gateway Pl Ste 100w, San Jose (95110-1046)
PHONE..................408 436-6170
Fax: 408 436-7508
Vikas Sehgal, *CEO*
Manmohan Gupta, *President*
Michel Dorochevsky, *CTO*
Shishir Basant, *Technology*
Rajiv Srinath, *Director*
EMP: 67 **EST:** 1999
SQ FT: 1,200
SALES (est): 42.3MM **Privately Held**
WEB: www.nagarro.com
SIC: 7373 Computer-aided system services

(P-16001)
NANTWORKS LLC (PA)
9920 Jefferson Blvd, Culver City (90232-3506)
PHONE..................310 405-7539
Charles N Kenworthy, *Mng Member*
EMP: 72
SALES (est): 87.3MM **Publicly Held**
SIC: 7373 Computer-aided system services

(P-16002)
NET EXPRESS
32 Snyder Way, Fremont (94536-1675)
PHONE..................510 887-4395
Roland H Baker III, *President*
EMP: 65
SALES (est): 4.8MM **Privately Held**
SIC: 7373 Computer systems analysis & design

(P-16003)
NETAPP INC
300 Spectrum Center Dr # 900, Irvine (92618-4925)
PHONE..................949 754-6600
Chris White, *Branch Mgr*
Jeff Goldstein, *Vice Pres*
Dieter Boehm, *Program Mgr*
Aaron Copeland, *Administration*
Matthew Hall, *Software Engr*
EMP: 209
SALES (corp-wide): 5.5B **Publicly Held**
SIC: 7373 Computer integrated systems design
PA: Netapp, Inc.
495 E Java Dr
Sunnyvale CA 94089
408 822-6000

(P-16004)
NETAPP INC
1299 Orleans Dr, Sunnyvale (94089-1138)
PHONE..................408 822-3402
Joe McKinney, *Accounts Mgr*
EMP: 215
SALES (corp-wide): 5.5B **Publicly Held**
SIC: 7373 Computer integrated systems design
PA: Netapp, Inc.
495 E Java Dr
Sunnyvale CA 94089
408 822-6000

(P-16005)
NETAPP INC
6320 Canoga Ave Ste 1500, Woodland Hills (91367-2563)
PHONE..................818 227-5025
EMP: 209
SALES (corp-wide): 6.3B **Publicly Held**
SIC: 7373
PA: Netapp, Inc.
495 E Java Dr
Sunnyvale CA 94089
408 822-6000

(P-16006)
NETAPP INC
1345 Crossman Ave, Sunnyvale (94089-1114)
PHONE..................408 419-5301
Pam Teshera, *Branch Mgr*
Justin Rojas, *Sales Staff*
Robert McDonald, *Senior Mgr*
Garry Wyndham, *Senior Mgr*
Fadel Hamed, *Director*
EMP: 209
SALES (corp-wide): 5.5B **Publicly Held**
WEB: www.netapp.com
SIC: 7373 Computer integrated systems design
PA: Netapp, Inc.
495 E Java Dr
Sunnyvale CA 94089
408 822-6000

(P-16007)
NETAPP INC
3334 Meadowlands Ln, San Jose (95135-1624)
PHONE..................408 822-3803
EMP: 203
SALES (corp-wide): 6.3B **Publicly Held**
SIC: 7373
PA: Netapp, Inc.
495 E Java Dr
Sunnyvale CA 94089
408 822-6000

(P-16008)
NETAPP INC
222 N Sepulveda Blvd, El Segundo (90245-5648)
PHONE..................310 426-1700
Jeff Herr, *Regional Mgr*
Adrian Vrcic, *Info Tech Mgr*
Del Burke, *Engineer*
Audrey Payne, *Accounts Mgr*
John Ridgway, *Accounts Mgr*
EMP: 50
SALES (corp-wide): 6.1B **Publicly Held**
WEB: www.netapp.com
SIC: 7373 Computer integrated systems design
PA: Netapp, Inc.
495 E Java Dr
Sunnyvale CA 94089
408 822-6000

(P-16009)
NETWORK INTGRTION PARTNERS INC
Also Called: Nic Partners
11981 Jack Benny Dr # 103, Rancho Cucamonga (91739-9232)
PHONE..................909 919-2800
Franklin P Spaeth, *President*
David Cassidy, *CFO*
Sonia Camacho, *Admin Asst*
Nancy Dibella, *Administration*
Elaine Helm, *Administration*
EMP: 80
SQ FT: 6,000
SALES (est): 21.1MM **Privately Held**
SIC: 7373 Systems integration services

(P-16010)
NETWORK PHYSICS INC
333 S Grand Ave Ste 4070, Los Angeles (90071-1544)
PHONE..................240 497-3000
Kenny Frerichs, *President*
Fred Runco, *CFO*
Tom Dunn, *Vice Pres*
Rob Hon, *Vice Pres*
Bob Quillin, *Vice Pres*
EMP: 50
SQ FT: 14,614
SALES (est): 3.5MM **Privately Held**
WEB: www.networkphysics.com
SIC: 7373 Computer systems analysis & design

(P-16011)
NEW DIRECTIONS TECH INC (PA)
Also Called: Ndti
137 Drummond Ave Ste A, Ridgecrest (93555-3583)
PHONE..................760 384-2444
Fax: 760 384-2455
Cedric Knight, *President*
Bert Belisch, *CFO*
Michele E Hoopes, *Exec VP*
Ann Bucharelli, *Executive*
John Dermatas, *Business Dir*
EMP: 65
SQ FT: 6,000
SALES (est): 26.8MM **Privately Held**
WEB: www.ndti.net
SIC: 7373 7374 8711 7371 Systems software development services; data processing & preparation; engineering services; computer software development & applications; computer facilities management

(P-16012)
NORTHROP GRMMN SPCE & MSSN SYS (HQ)
6377 San Ignacio Ave, San Jose (95119-1200)
PHONE..................703 280-2900
Fax: 310 201-3023
Robert M Hamje, *President*
Jeanne Usher, *President*
William K Maciven, *Exec VP*
Nick Barnes, *Senior VP*
Ron Foudray, *Vice Pres*
EMP: 600 **EST:** 1901
SALES (est): 1.3B **Publicly Held**
WEB: www.trw.com
SIC: 7373 3663 3661 3812 Computer integrated systems design; radio & TV communications equipment; telephone & telegraph apparatus; defense systems & equipment; guided missiles & space vehicles

(P-16013)
NORTHROP GRMMN SPCE & MSSN SYS
862 E Hospitality Ln, San Bernardino (92408-3530)
PHONE..................909 382-6800
Dave Davis, *Branch Mgr*
Ron Pipes, *Manager*
EMP: 241 **Publicly Held**
WEB: www.trw.com
SIC: 7373 Computer integrated systems design
HQ: Northrop Grumman Space & Mission Systems Corp.
6377 San Ignacio Ave
San Jose CA 95119
703 280-2900

(P-16014)
NORTHROP GRUMMAN SYSTEMS CORP
Also Called: Technical Services
P.O. Box 81, Moffett Field (94035-0081)
PHONE..................650 604-6056
James R Blount, *Manager*
EMP: 120 **Publicly Held**
SIC: 7373 7374 Computer systems analysis & design; computer processing services
HQ: Northrop Grumman Systems Corporation
2980 Fairview Park Dr
Falls Church VA 22042
703 280-2900

(P-16015)
NORTHROP GRUMMAN SYSTEMS CORP
5161 Verdugo Way, Camarillo (93012-8603)
PHONE..................805 987-9739
Jim Lueck, *Systems Staff*
Rian Hawkins, *Branch Mgr*
EMP: 60 **Publicly Held**
WEB: www.logicon.com
SIC: 7373 8731 8711 7371 Computer systems analysis & design; commercial physical research; engineering services; custom computer programming services
HQ: Northrop Grumman Systems Corporation
2980 Fairview Park Dr
Falls Church VA 22042
703 280-2900

(P-16016)
NTT DATA INC
1000 Corporate Center Dr # 140, Monterey Park (91754-7610)
PHONE..................213 228-2500
Fax: 323 261-3030
EMP: 93
SALES (corp-wide): 93.3B **Privately Held**
SIC: 7373
HQ: Ntt Data, Inc.
5601 Gran Pkwy Ste 1000
Plano TX 75024
800 745-3263

(P-16017)
NTT DATA INC
Healthcare Services Division
4553 Glencoe Ave Ste 350, Marina Del Rey (90292-7929)
PHONE..................310 301-7835
Fax: 310 417-3260
Kathy Haynes, *Manager*
Dave Plunkett, *Manager*
EMP: 110
SALES (corp-wide): 98.6B **Privately Held**
WEB: www.keane.com
SIC: 7373 7371 Computer integrated systems design; custom computer programming services
HQ: Ntt Data, Inc.
5601 Gran Pkwy Ste 1000
Plano TX 75024
800 745-3263

(P-16018)
NURLOGIC DESIGN INC (DH)
5580 Morehouse Dr, San Diego (92121-1709)
PHONE..................858 455-7570
Rich Shine, *Manager*
David Matty, *President*
Hugh D Gerfin, *Treasurer*
Mike Brunolli, *CTO*
EMP: 60
SQ FT: 34,000
SALES (est): 3.5MM
SALES (corp-wide): 1.4B **Privately Held**
SIC: 7373 Computer integrated systems design
HQ: Arm Inc.
150 Rose Orchard Way
San Jose CA 95134
408 576-1500

(P-16019)
NUTANIX INC (PA)
1740 Tech Dr Ste 150, San Jose (95110)
PHONE..................408 216-8360
Dheeraj Pandey, *President*
Duston Williams, *CFO*
Eric Whitaker,
Pranesh Anthapur, *Officer*
Sunil Potti, *Senior VP*
EMP: 623
SQ FT: 165,000
SALES: 241.4MM **Publicly Held**
SIC: 7373 Systems engineering, computer related

(P-16020)
O2 MICRO INC
3118 Patrick Henry Dr, Santa Clara (95054-1850)
PHONE..................408 987-5920
Lynn Lin, *CEO*
Scott Anderson, *Shareholder*
Sterling Du, *President*
Alex Hartular, *COO*
Perry Kuo, *CFO*
EMP: 100
SQ FT: 37,000
SALES (est): 14.6MM **Privately Held**
WEB: www.o2micro.com
SIC: 7373 Computer integrated systems design

(P-16021)
OASIS TECHNOLOGY INC
601 E Daily Dr Ste 226, Camarillo (93010-5840)
PHONE..................805 445-4833
Fax: 805 445-4839
George M Baldonado, *President*
Deborah Johnson, *Vice Pres*
Violeta Baldonado, *Admin Sec*
EMP: 65
SQ FT: 2,800
SALES: 3MM **Privately Held**
WEB: www.oasistechnology.com
SIC: 7373 7372 5734 Computer system selling services; prepackaged software; personal computers

PRODUCTS & SERVICES SECTION
7373 - Computer Integrated Systems Design County (P-16044)

(P-16022)
OBERMAN TIVOLI MILLER PICKERT
Also Called: MEDIA SERVICES
500 S Sepulveda Blvd # 500, Los Angeles (90049-3551)
PHONE..................310 440-9600
Robert Oberman, *President*
Barry Oberman, *CEO*
Sanaa Wadsworth, *CFO*
Gieanna Taylor, *Accountant*
EMP: 230
SALES (est): 30.5MM **Privately Held**
WEB: www.media-services.com
SIC: 7373 8721 8741 Systems software development services; payroll accounting service; business management

(P-16023)
OMNITROL NETWORKS INC
4580 Auto Mall Pkwy # 121, Fremont (94538-3992)
PHONE..................408 919-1100
EMP: 50
SQ FT: 5,000
SALES (est): 5.4MM **Privately Held**
WEB: www.omnitrol.com
SIC: 7373

(P-16024)
ORACLE SYSTEMS CORPORATION
301 Island Pkwy, Belmont (94002-4109)
PHONE..................650 654-7606
EMP: 304
SALES (corp-wide): 37B **Publicly Held**
SIC: 7373 Computer integrated systems design
HQ: Oracle Systems Corporation
500 Oracle Pkwy
Redwood City CA 94065
650 506-7000

(P-16025)
P-COVE ENTERPRISES INC
8745 Remmet Ave, Canoga Park (91304-1519)
PHONE..................818 341-1101
Jonathan Manhan, *CEO*
EMP: 59
SALES: 17MM **Privately Held**
SIC: 7373 Value-added resellers, computer systems

(P-16026)
PACIFIC CROSSING LLC
95 Argonaut Ste 100, Aliso Viejo (92656-4139)
PHONE..................949 679-2588
Phyllis Johnson,
Walter Johnson,
Arlene Stratton, *Manager*
EMP: 225
SQ FT: 1,500
SALES (est): 10.5MM **Privately Held**
WEB: www.pacificcrossing.com
SIC: 7373 Computer integrated systems design

(P-16027)
PANZURA INC
695 Campbell Tech Pkwy, Campbell (95008-5073)
PHONE..................408 457-8504
Randy Chou, *CEO*
Mark Santora, *Ch of Bd*
Darren Daugherty, *Principal*
Susie Lines, *Area Mgr*
Krishna Bhimavarapu, *Engineer*
EMP: 63
SALES (est): 13.6MM **Privately Held**
SIC: 7373 5734 Computer integrated systems design; computer software & accessories

(P-16028)
PARIVEDA SOLUTIONS INC
100 Pine St Ste 375, San Francisco (94111-5140)
PHONE..................415 946-6100
Eric Wells, *Principal*
EMP: 197
SALES (corp-wide): 83.1MM **Privately Held**
SIC: 7373 Computer systems analysis & design
PA: Pariveda Solutions, Inc.
2811 Mckinney Ave Ste 220
Dallas TX 75204
214 777-4600

(P-16029)
PHASE 3 COMMUNICATIONS INC
224 N 27th St Ste B, San Jose (95116-1120)
PHONE..................408 946-9011
Nicolas Dezubiria, *CEO*
Ruben N Yusi, *CFO*
Ruben Yusi, *CFO*
Micheal Marshall, *Opers Mgr*
Joe Steeves, *Sales Staff*
EMP: 55
SQ FT: 3,500
SALES (est): 13.8MM **Privately Held**
WEB: www.p3com.net
SIC: 7373 1731 Fiber optic cable installation; cable splicing service

(P-16030)
PINNACLE TELECOM INC
Also Called: Pti Solutions
7066 Las Positas Rd, Livermore (94551-5121)
PHONE..................916 426-1032
EMP: 75
SALES (corp-wide): 33.1MM **Privately Held**
SIC: 7373 8741 1731 1623 Computer integrated systems design; management services; electrical work; water, sewer & utility lines; computer facilities management;
PA: Pinnacle Telecommunications, Inc.
4242 Forcum Ave Ste 200
Mcclellan CA 95652
916 426-1000

(P-16031)
PINNACLE TELECOM INC (PA)
Also Called: Pti Solutions
4242 Forcum Ave Ste 200, McClellan (95652-2109)
PHONE..................916 426-1000
Cecelia Lakatos Sullivan, *CEO*
Darin Salk, *CFO*
Barbara Winters, *Chairman*
Robert Bobar, *IT/INT Sup*
Eileen Arr, *Director*
EMP: 50
SQ FT: 20,000
SALES (est): 33.1MM **Privately Held**
WEB: www.pinnacle-telecom.com
SIC: 7373 8741 1731 1623 Computer integrated systems design; management services; electronic controls installation; electric power line construction; computer facilities management; computer related maintenance services

(P-16032)
PIXIM INC
1730 N 1st St, San Jose (95112-4508)
PHONE..................650 934-0550
Chris Adams, *CEO*
Randy Strahan, *President*
David Dury, *Treasurer*
Bob Feyen, *Vice Pres*
John Monh, *Vice Pres*
EMP: 51
SQ FT: 13,560
SALES (est): 7MM **Privately Held**
WEB: www.pixim.com
SIC: 7373 7361 Computer integrated systems design; employment agencies

(P-16033)
PLANET TECHNOLOGIES INC
1215 K St Fl 17, Sacramento (95814-3954)
PHONE..................631 269-6140
EMP: 53
SALES (corp-wide): 23.3MM **Privately Held**
SIC: 7373 Systems integration services
PA: Planet Technologies, Inc.
20400 Observation Dr # 107
Germantown MD 20876

(P-16034)
PRIMITIVE LOGIC INC
704 Sansome St, San Francisco (94111-1704)
PHONE..................415 391-8080
Fax: 415 391-8085
Jill P Reber, *CEO*
Kevin Moos, *President*
Mike McDermott, *Senior VP*
Andy Lin, *Vice Pres*
Deborah Metzger, *Vice Pres*
EMP: 63 EST: 1984
SQ FT: 10,000
SALES (est): 14MM **Privately Held**
WEB: www.primitivelogic.com
SIC: 7373 Computer integrated systems design

(P-16035)
QCT LLC
1010 Rincon Cir, San Jose (95131-1325)
PHONE..................510 270-6111
Alan Lam, *Mng Member*
EMP: 1000
SALES (est): 4.8MM
SALES (corp-wide): 31B **Privately Held**
SIC: 7373 Computer integrated systems design
PA: Quanta Computer Inc.
188, Wen Hwa 2nd Rd.,
Taoyuan City TAY 33383
332 723-45

(P-16036)
QUANTUM SECURE INC
100 Century Center Ct # 800, San Jose (95112-4537)
PHONE..................408 453-1008
Fax: 408 853-1009
Ajay Jain, *President*
Steve De Lima, *CFO*
Vik Ghai, *Vice Pres*
Shailendra Sharma, *Vice Pres*
John Skowronski, *Vice Pres*
EMP: 55
SALES (est): 10.8MM
SALES (corp-wide): 7.8B **Privately Held**
WEB: www.quantumsecure.com
SIC: 7373 7371 Systems software development services; computer software development & applications
HQ: Hid Global Corporation
611 Center Ridge Dr
Austin TX 78753
800 237-7769

(P-16037)
QUEST MEDIA & SUPPLIES INC (PA)
5822 Roseville Rd, Sacramento (95842-3071)
P.O. Box 41039 (95841-0039)
PHONE..................916 338-7070
Fax: 916 338-3289
Cindy P Burke, *President*
Timothy Burke, *CEO*
Kathy Campbell, *COO*
Francine Walrath, *CFO*
Etienne Gadient, *Practice Mgr*
EMP: 92
SQ FT: 9,500
SALES: 168MM **Privately Held**
WEB: www.questsys.com
SIC: 7373 Computer integrated systems design

(P-16038)
RAVENSWOOD SOLUTIONS INC
3065 Skyway Ct, Fremont (94539-5909)
PHONE..................650 241-3661
Daniel Donoghue, *CEO*
Christopher Terndrup, *Exec Dir*
John Prausa,
Charlene Galanty, *Manager*
EMP: 99 EST: 2015
SQ FT: 12,878
SALES (est): 3.5MM **Privately Held**
SIC: 7373 7379 Systems engineering, computer related; computer related maintenance services

(P-16039)
REAL TIME LOGIC INC
4820 Estgate Mall Ste 200, San Diego (92121)
PHONE..................858 812-7300
EMP: 88
SALES (corp-wide): 657.1MM **Publicly Held**
SIC: 7373 Computer integrated systems design
HQ: Real Time Logic, Inc.
12515 Academy Ridge Vw
Colorado Springs CO 80921
719 598-2801

(P-16040)
RESULT GROUP INC
2603 Main St Ste 710, Irvine (92614-4263)
PHONE..................480 777-7130
William Derick Robson, *President*
Alex Beric, *Vice Pres*
David Griffiths, *Admin Sec*
Clare McColmick, *Manager*
EMP: 70
SALES (est): 4.4MM
SALES (corp-wide): 1.8B **Privately Held**
SIC: 7373 7372 Systems software development services; business oriented computer software
HQ: Wynne Systems, Inc.
2603 Main St Ste 710
Irvine CA 92614
949 224-6300

(P-16041)
S1 CORPORATION
Also Called: Software Dynamics
8501 Filbrook Ave Ste 200, Canoga Park (91304)
PHONE..................818 992-3299
Tom Shen, *Branch Mgr*
Victor Syracuse, *Vice Pres*
Charles Whitley, *Vice Pres*
Lena Will, *Human Res Dir*
Nick Culolias, *Sales Staff*
EMP: 141
SALES (corp-wide): 1B **Publicly Held**
WEB: www.s1.com
SIC: 7373 7372 7371 Computer systems analysis & design; prepackaged software; computer software development
HQ: S1 Corporation
705 Westech Dr
Norcross GA 30092
678 966-9499

(P-16042)
SAUCE LABS INC
539 Bryant St Ste 303, San Francisco (94107-1269)
PHONE..................415 946-1117
Fax: 415 373-9385
Charles Ramsey, *CEO*
Jim Cerna, *CFO*
Joe Alfaro, *Vice Pres*
John Coyle, *Vice Pres*
Lubos Parobek, *Vice Pres*
EMP: 100
SALES (est): 22.3MM **Privately Held**
SIC: 7373 Systems software development services

(P-16043)
SAVVIS COMMUNICATIONS CORP
200 N Nash St, El Segundo (90245-4529)
PHONE..................310 726-1166
Travis Payton, *Manager*
EMP: 62
SALES (corp-wide): 17.9B **Publicly Held**
SIC: 7373 Computer integrated systems design
HQ: Savvis Communications Corporation
1 Solutions Pkwy
Town And Country MO 63017
314 628-7000

(P-16044)
SCHNEIDER ELECTRIC SFTWR LLC (PA)
26561 Rancho Pkwy S, Lake Forest (92630-8301)
PHONE..................949 727-3200
Ravi Gopinath, *President*
James Danley, *Treasurer*
Paul Forney, *Vice Pres*
Jim Griffith, *Vice Pres*
Robert Murray, *Vice Pres*
EMP: 350

7373 - Computer Integrated Systems Design County (P-16045)

PRODUDUCTS & SERVICES SECTION

SALES: 260MM **Privately Held**
SIC: **7373** Computer integrated systems design

(P-16045)
SCIENCE APPLICATIONS INTL CORP
Also Called: Saic
4015 Hancock St, San Diego (92110-5121)
PHONE..............................858 826-3061
Gordon Saakamodo, *Manager*
Jeff Ferguson, *CEO*
Anthony Moraco, *CEO*
Nancy Aitkenhead, *Vice Pres*
Tom Sears, *Vice Pres*
EMP: 600
SALES (corp-wide): 4.3B **Publicly Held**
WEB: www.saic.com
SIC: **7373** Systems engineering, computer related
PA: Science Applications International Corporation
1710 Saic Dr Ste B
Mc Lean VA 22102
703 676-6942

(P-16046)
SCIENCE APPLICATIONS INTL CORP
Also Called: Saic
4242 Campus Point Ct, San Diego (92121-1513)
PHONE..............................858 826-6000
Raj Seksaria, *President*
Dave Clemons, *Vice Pres*
Amanda Albert, *Software Engr*
Kristen McBride, *Software Engr*
Gary Mills, *Software Engr*
EMP: 350
SALES (corp-wide): 4.3B **Publicly Held**
WEB: www.saic.com
SIC: **7373** Systems engineering, computer related
PA: Science Applications International Corporation
1710 Saic Dr Ste B
Mc Lean VA 22102
703 676-6942

(P-16047)
SEAGATE SERVICES
6121 I C 365 Ste 2, Emeryville (94608)
PHONE..............................510 903-7100
Greg Carson, *CFO*
EMP: 90
SALES (est): 5MM **Privately Held**
SIC: **7373** Systems software development services

(P-16048)
SECOM INTERNATIONAL (PA)
9610 Bellanca Ave, Los Angeles (90045-5508)
PHONE..............................310 641-1290
Fax: 310 216-6693
Ted Burton, *President*
Amir Behic, *CFO*
Terry Bixler, *Vice Pres*
John Martin, *Regional Mgr*
Linda Vose, *Admin Sec*
EMP: 52
SQ FT: 30,000
SALES (est): 9.9MM **Privately Held**
WEB: www.secomintl.com
SIC: **7373** 3446 Turnkey vendors, computer systems; architectural metalwork

(P-16049)
SECURITY ON-DEMAND INC
12121 Scripps Summit Dr # 320, San Diego (92131-4609)
PHONE..............................858 563-5655
Peter Bybee, *CEO*
Gayle Bybee, *CFO*
Tara Quick, *General Mgr*
Sunia Tajik, *Technology*
Heather Antoinetti, *VP Mktg*
EMP: 50
SQ FT: 12,000
SALES: 3MM **Privately Held**
SIC: **7373** Computer integrated systems design

(P-16050)
SECURONIX INC
5777 W Century Blvd # 838, Los Angeles (90045-5673)
PHONE..............................310 641-1000
Sachin Nayyar, *CEO*
Rishma Shariff, *COO*
Sharon Vardi, *Chief Mktg Ofcr*
Amit Lal, *Vice Pres*
Praful Ilamkar, *Project Mgr*
EMP: 61
SQ FT: 1,000
SALES (est): 13.9MM **Privately Held**
SIC: **7373** Systems software development services

(P-16051)
SELLIGENT INC (HQ)
1300 Island Dr Ste 200, Redwood City (94065-5171)
PHONE..............................650 421-4200
Fax: 650 421-4201
William Wagner, *CEO*
Frank Addante, *President*
Tricia Robinson-Pridemore, *President*
Bill Griffin, *CFO*
Steve Pantelick, *CFO*
EMP: 130
SALES (est): 41.5MM
SALES (corp-wide): 350MM **Privately Held**
WEB: www.strongmailsystems.com
SIC: **7373** Computer integrated systems design
PA: Hggc, Llc
1950 University Ave # 350
East Palo Alto CA 94303
650 321-4910

(P-16052)
SEMANTIC RESEARCH INC (PA)
4922 N Harbor Dr, San Diego (92106-2306)
PHONE..............................619 222-4050
Richard Harrison, *CEO*
Tim Lamarca, *President*
Charles Gillespie, *COO*
Jim Hindle, *Exec VP*
Eric Newman, *Vice Pres*
EMP: 70
SQ FT: 2,600
SALES (est): 11.8MM **Privately Held**
WEB: www.semanticresearch.com
SIC: **7373** Computer integrated systems design

(P-16053)
SEZZO LABS INC
2336 Walsh Ave Ste A, Santa Clara (95051-1313)
P.O. Box 18928, San Jose (95158-8928)
PHONE..............................408 562-0081
Walter Simon, *President*
Raman Mirzapour, *COO*
Edwin Chan, *CFO*
EMP: 50 EST: 2004
SQ FT: 5,000
SALES (est): 4.6MM **Privately Held**
WEB: www.ansi.com
SIC: **7373** Computer integrated systems design

(P-16054)
SOFT MACHINES INC
Also Called: Smachines
3920 Freedom Cir, Santa Clara (95054-1240)
PHONE..............................408 969-0215
Mahesh Lingareddy, *CEO*
Mohammad Abdallah, *President*
Rajesh Khanna, *President*
Damodar Thummalapally, *President*
Tom Kais, *CFO*
EMP: 65
SQ FT: 5,000
SALES (est): 11.1MM **Privately Held**
SIC: **7373** Computer integrated systems design

(P-16055)
SOFTWARE DYNAMICS INCORPORATED
8501 Fllbrook Ave Ste 200, Canoga Park (91304)
PHONE..............................818 992-3299
Fax: 818 992-3398

Matthew Hale, *President*
Christopher J Stein, *Treasurer*
Richard Dobb, *Admin Sec*
EMP: 164
SQ FT: 40,000
SALES (est): 6.1MM
SALES (corp-wide): 1B **Publicly Held**
WEB: www.s1.com
SIC: **7373** **7371** Computer systems analysis & design; computer software development
HQ: S1 Corporation
705 Westech Dr
Norcross GA 30092
678 966-9499

(P-16056)
SONICS INC (PA)
2570 N 1st St Ste 100, San Jose (95131-1035)
PHONE..............................408 457-2800
Grant Pierce, *CEO*
James Mac Hale, *Vice Pres*
Mark McMillan, *Vice Pres*
Visal Hak, *Administration*
Grigor Yeghiazaryan, *Software Engr*
EMP: 54
SALES (est): 11.4MM **Privately Held**
SIC: **7373** Computer integrated systems design

(P-16057)
SONICWALL LLC (DH)
Also Called: Dell Sonicwall
5455 Great America Pkwy, Santa Clara (95054-3645)
PHONE..............................800 509-1265
Matt Medeiros, *President*
Robert D Selvi, *CFO*
Gary Bacon, *Vice Pres*
Marvin Blough, *Vice Pres*
Edward Cohen, *Vice Pres*
▲ EMP: 148
SQ FT: 86,000
SALES (est): 114.8MM
SALES (corp-wide): 72.7B **Publicly Held**
WEB: www.sonicwall.com
SIC: **7373** Computer integrated systems design; systems software development services; computer systems analysis & design
HQ: Dell Inc.
1 Dell Way
Round Rock TX 78682
512 338-4400

(P-16058)
SSINFOTEK INC
15615 Alton Pkwy Ste 450, Irvine (92618-3308)
PHONE..............................949 732-3100
Prabhakara Pelluru, *President*
EMP: 50
SALES (est): 3.8MM **Privately Held**
SIC: **7373** Systems software development services

(P-16059)
STEELKIWI INC
1025 Alameda De Las Ste 535, Belmont (94002)
PHONE..............................415 449-8696
Anton Baterikov, *President*
EMP: 66
SALES (est): 1.1MM **Privately Held**
SIC: **7373** **7371** Systems engineering, computer related; computer software development & applications

(P-16060)
STRATEGIC DATA SYSTEMS
Also Called: SDS
610 W Ash St Ste 1100, San Diego (92101-3335)
PHONE..............................619 546-7200
James Christopher, *President*
Donna Locke, *Treasurer*
Eaton Jones, *Vice Pres*
Matthew Heavel, *Administration*
Michael Berg, *Tech Recruiter*
EMP: 125
SQ FT: 3,000

SALES (est): 20MM **Privately Held**
WEB: www.sdatasystems.com
SIC: **7373** **7379** Computer integrated systems design; computer related consulting services

(P-16061)
SYSOREX USA (HQ)
17 E Sir Francis Drake, Larkspur (94939-1727)
PHONE..............................415 389-7500
Fax: 415 388-7510
Nadir Ali, *CEO*
Dhruv Gulati, *Exec VP*
Rick Rutledge, *Executive*
Scott Arnold, *Managing Dir*
Laura Rubeck, *Admin Asst*
EMP: 147
SQ FT: 2,800
SALES (est): 44.9MM
SALES (corp-wide): 66.9MM **Publicly Held**
WEB: www.lilien.com
SIC: **7373** Computer integrated systems design
PA: Sysorex Global
2479 E Byshore Rd Ste 195
Palo Alto CA 94303
408 702-2167

(P-16062)
SYSTEM INTEGRATORS INC (HQ)
Also Called: Netlinx Publishing Solutions
1740 N Market Blvd, Sacramento (95834-1997)
PHONE..............................916 830-2400
Fax: 916 830-2416
Paul Donlan, *President*
Albert Bruijn, *Vice Pres*
Allan Katzen, *Vice Pres*
Joe Dimeglio, *Software Engr*
Rajeev Goonewardene, *Engng Exec*
EMP: 140
SQ FT: 70,000
SALES (est): 8.8MM **Privately Held**
SIC: **7373** **7372** **7371** Computer integrated systems design; prepackaged software; custom computer programming services
PA: Net-Linx Ag
Kathe-Kollwitz-Ufer 76-79
Dresden
351 318-750

(P-16063)
TALEND INC (HQ)
800 Bridge Pkwy Ste 200, Redwood City (94065-1156)
PHONE..............................650 539-3200
Fax: 650 941-5997
Mike Tuchen, *CEO*
Thomas Tuchscherer, *CFO*
Ashley Stirrup, *Chief Mktg Ofcr*
Mike Sheridan, *Exec VP*
Kamal Brar, *Senior VP*
EMP: 74
SQ FT: 1,200
SALES (est): 20.3MM
SALES (corp-wide): 27.3MM **Privately Held**
SIC: **7373** Computer systems analysis & design; systems integration services
PA: Talend
9 Rue Pages
Suresnes 92150
140 999-704

(P-16064)
THREE RVERS PRVIDER NETWRK INC
910 Hale Pl Ste 101, Chula Vista (91914-3598)
PHONE..............................619 230-0508
Todd Breeden, *President*
Frank Whelan, *CFO*
Matthew Jacobs, *Vice Pres*
Josh Lund, *Marketing Staff*
Cande Quintana, *Manager*
EMP: 60
SALES (est): 6.8MM **Privately Held**
SIC: **7373** Local area network (LAN) systems integrator

▲ = Import ▼ = Export
◆ = Import/Export

PRODUCTS & SERVICES SECTION
7373 - Computer Integrated Systems Design County (P-16085)

(P-16065)
TIBCO FINANCE TECHNOLOGY INC
3375 Hillview Ave, Palo Alto (94304-1204)
PHONE 650 461-3000
Robert Knourek, *Ch of Bd*
Richard Murray, *Vice Pres*
Terry U Drymonacos, *Prgrmr*
Jennifer Casillas, *IT/INT Sup*
Eric Ko, *IT/INT Sup*
EMP: 300
SQ FT: 93,000
SALES (est): 17.2MM
SALES (corp-wide): 1.1B **Privately Held**
SIC: 7373 7371 Systems integration services; custom computer programming services
HQ: Vista Equity Partners, Llc
4 Embarcadero Ctr # 2000
San Francisco CA 94111
415 765-6500

(P-16066)
TIBURON INC
9477 Waples St Ste 100, San Diego (92121-2934)
PHONE 858 799-7000
Toney Eales, *CEO*
Blake Clark, *CFO*
Cliff Micham, *Senior VP*
Chris Firth, *Vice Pres*
Larry Helms, *Vice Pres*
EMP: 100
SQ FT: 18,647
SALES (est): 262.7K
SALES (corp-wide): 139.6MM **Privately Held**
WEB: www.tiburoninc.com
SIC: 7373 Computer integrated systems design
PA: Tritech Software Systems
9477 Waples St Ste 100
San Diego CA 92121
858 799-7000

(P-16067)
TRAMS INC (DH)
5777 W Century Blvd # 1200, Los Angeles (90045-5674)
PHONE 310 641-8726
Fax: 310 641-8571
Lee B Rosen, *President*
Jeanne Fick, *Manager*
EMP: 65
SQ FT: 14,500
SALES (est): 6.7MM
SALES (corp-wide): 2.9B **Publicly Held**
WEB: www.clientbase.com
SIC: 7373 Systems software development services
HQ: Sabre Glbl Inc.
3150 Sabre Dr
Southlake TX 76092
682 605-1000

(P-16068)
TRINITY TECHNOLOGY GROUP INC
2015 J St Ste 105, Sacramento (95811-3124)
PHONE 916 779-0201
Randall E Duart, *CEO*
Timothy Purdy, *CFO*
Jane Duart, *Treasurer*
Stephen Williamson, *Vice Pres*
Raelyn Sweebe, *Manager*
EMP: 67
SQ FT: 2,800
SALES: 14.1MM **Privately Held**
WEB: www.trinitytg.com
SIC: 7373 Systems software development services

(P-16069)
UBIQUITI NETWORKS INC (PA)
2580 Orchard Pkwy, San Jose (95131-1033)
PHONE 408 942-3085
Robert J Pera, *Ch of Bd*
Benjamin Moore, *Vice Pres*
Kevin Radigan,
John Sanford, *CTO*
EMP: 85
SQ FT: 64,512
SALES: 666.4MM **Publicly Held**
SIC: 7373 Local area network (LAN) systems integrator

(P-16070)
UNITEK INC
47333 Warm Springs Blvd, Fremont (94539-7462)
PHONE 510 623-8544
Fax: 510 623-8970
Philip Kim, *President*
Eric Driz, *Engineer*
Howard Lee, *CPA*
EMP: 65
SQ FT: 20,000
SALES (est): 9.8MM **Privately Held**
WEB: www.unitekinc.com
SIC: 7373 3679 3672 Turnkey vendors, computer systems; electronic circuits; printed circuit boards

(P-16071)
UPEK INC
2000 Powell St, Emeryville (94608-1804)
PHONE 510 868-0800
Fax: 510 420-2699
Alan Kramer, *President*
Gary Martell, *CFO*
Rajesh Bhakta, *Info Tech Dir*
Marco Mancini, *Engineer*
Michael Allred, *Controller*
EMP: 120
SQ FT: 4,000
SALES (est): 9.6MM **Privately Held**
WEB: www.upek.com
SIC: 7373 Computer-aided design (CAD) systems service

(P-16072)
US DEPT OF THE AIR FORCE
Also Called: 61st Communication Squadron
2420 Vela Way Ste 1467, El Segundo (90245)
PHONE 310 363-1155
EMP: 200 **Publicly Held**
WEB: www.af.mil
SIC: 7373 9711 Computer integrated systems design; Air Force;
HQ: United States Department Of The Air Force
1000 Air Force Pentagon
Washington DC 20330
703 545-6700

(P-16073)
USER ZOOM INC
10 Almaden Blvd Ste 250, San Jose (95113-2226)
PHONE 408 533-8619
Alfonso De La Nuez, *CEO*
Xavier Mestres, *COO*
Brian Gupton, *Vice Pres*
Arthur Moan, *Vice Pres*
Matt Paulus, *Executive*
EMP: 80 **EST:** 2007
SALES (est): 16.7MM **Privately Held**
SIC: 7373 Systems software development services

(P-16074)
V-TEK SYSTEMS CORPORATION
21045 Ridge Park Dr, Yorba Linda (92886-7808)
PHONE 909 396-5355
Fax: 909 396-5360
Bernard D Abrams, *President*
Cliff Veasey, *Engineer*
Mary Ellen Turino, *Human Resources*
Mary E Tourino, *Director*
Benjamin Harvey, *Manager*
EMP: 65
SQ FT: 19,000
SALES (est): 9.6MM **Privately Held**
WEB: www.v-tek.com
SIC: 7373 Computer integrated systems design

(P-16075)
VENCORE INC
1315 Dell Ave, Campbell (95008-6609)
PHONE 408 961-3250
Joe Harris, *General Mgr*
Takeshi Hovie, *Manager*
EMP: 100

SALES (corp-wide): 326.3MM **Privately Held**
WEB: www.comglobal.com
SIC: 7373 1731 Systems software development services; electrical work
HQ: Vencore, Inc.
15052 Conference Ctr Dr
Chantilly VA 20151
571 313-6000

(P-16076)
VENCORE INC
1315 Dell Ave, Campbell (95008-6609)
PHONE 619 321-6000
EMP: 68
SALES (corp-wide): 326.3MM **Privately Held**
SIC: 7373 Systems software development services
HQ: Vencore, Inc.
15052 Conference Ctr Dr
Chantilly VA 20151
571 313-6000

(P-16077)
VENCORE SVCS & SOLUTIONS INC
1315 Dell Ave, Campbell (95008-6609)
PHONE 408 961-3200
EMP: 50
SALES (corp-wide): 326.3MM **Privately Held**
SIC: 7373 Computer integrated systems design
HQ: Vencore Services And Solutions, Inc.
1835 Alexander Bell Dr
Reston VA 20191
703 391-7017

(P-16078)
VERTISYSTEM INC
39300 Civic Center Dr # 230, Fremont (94538-2338)
PHONE 510 794-8099
Shaloo Jeswani, *CEO*
Rakesh Sadhwani, *President*
Deebali Syed, *Vice Pres*
Smitha Prabhakaran, *Admin Asst*
Vikas Sharda, *Technical Staff*
EMP: 110
SQ FT: 2,744
SALES (est): 9.8MM **Privately Held**
SIC: 7373 Systems software development services

(P-16079)
VICOR INC
855 Marina Bay Pkwy # 100, Richmond (94804-6413)
PHONE 510 621-2000
Robert Kirk, *CEO*
Garry Mah, *CFO*
Jack Mangan, *Vice Pres*
John Lynch, *Engineer*
Paul Reppucci, *Senior Mgr*
EMP: 72
SALES (est): 7.9MM
SALES (corp-wide): 6.6B **Publicly Held**
WEB: www.vicor.com
SIC: 7373 7371 Systems engineering, computer related; computer software development
HQ: Metavante Corporation
4900 W Brown Deer Rd
Milwaukee WI 53223
904 438-6000

(P-16080)
WESCON TECHNOLOGY INC
4655 Old Ironsides Dr # 170, Santa Clara (95054-1808)
PHONE 408 727-8818
Fred MA, *President*
Jason Huang, *Vice Pres*
Julie Wang, *Vice Pres*
David Zhuang, *Software Engr*
Joanna Hsu, *Manager*
EMP: 140
SQ FT: 1,610
SALES (est): 15.3MM **Privately Held**
WEB: www.wescongroup.com
SIC: 7373 7371 Computer integrated systems design; computer software writing services

(P-16081)
WEST PUBLISHING CORPORATION
Also Called: Elite
800 Crprate Pinte Ste 150, Culver City (90230)
P.O. Box 51606, Los Angeles (90051-5906)
PHONE 424 243-2100
Salim Sunderji, *Vice Pres*
EMP: 174
SALES (corp-wide): 3.8B **Publicly Held**
WEB: www.rutergroup.com
SIC: 7373 7371 Computer integrated systems design; custom computer programming services
HQ: West Publishing Corporation
610 620 Opperman Dr
Eagan MN 55123
651 687-7000

(P-16082)
XDIMENSIONAL TECHNOLOGIES INC
145 S State College Blvd # 160, Brea (92821-5824)
PHONE 714 672-8960
Michael Walther, *Branch Mgr*
Ryan Gillispie, *Vice Pres*
Rodney Gist, *CTO*
Ken Hansen, *VP Sales*
Jeffrey Glazer, *Director*
EMP: 60
SALES (corp-wide): 8.7MM **Privately Held**
WEB: www.xdimensional.com
SIC: 7373 Systems integration services
PA: Xdimensional Technologies Inc
450a Apollo St Ste A
Brea CA 92821
714 814-4579

(P-16083)
XP SYSTEMS CORPORATION (HQ)
405 Science Dr, Moorpark (93021-2247)
PHONE 805 532-9100
Fax: 805 532-9140
John Edwards, *President*
James Branson, *Administration*
Barbara Hoyt, *Info Tech Mgr*
Frank McQuaid, *Controller*
Karen Clark, *VP Human Res*
EMP: 200
SQ FT: 109,256
SALES (est): 22.6MM
SALES (corp-wide): 5.2B **Publicly Held**
WEB: www.xpsystems.com
SIC: 7373 Computer integrated systems design
PA: Fiserv, Inc.
255 Fiserv Dr
Brookfield WI 53045
262 879-5000

(P-16084)
YAHOO INC (PA)
701 First Ave, Sunnyvale (94089-1019)
PHONE 408 349-3300
Fax: 408 349-3301
Marissa A Mayer, *President*
Phil Lynch, *Partner*
Maynard G Webb Jr, *Ch of Bd*
Kenneth Goldman, *CFO*
Scott Burke, *Senior VP*
EMP: 135
SQ FT: 1,000,000
SALES: 4.9B **Publicly Held**
WEB: www.yahoo.com
SIC: 7373 7375 Computer integrated systems design; systems software development services; information retrieval services; data base information retrieval; on-line data base information retrieval

(P-16085)
ZENITH INFOTECH LIMITED
39675 Cedar Blvd Ste 240b, Newark (94560-8541)
PHONE 510 687-1943
Alok Goel, *Vice Pres*
Raj Saraf, *President*
Dave Mills, *General Mgr*
Suman Vejandla, *Manager*
EMP: 145

7373 - Computer Integrated Systems Design County (P-16086)

PRODUDCTS & SERVICES SECTION

SALES: 7.5MM **Privately Held**
WEB: www.zenithinfotech.com
SIC: 7373 Systems software development services
PA: Zenith Infotech Limited
   29 & 30 Zenith House
   Mumbai MH 40009
   -

(P-16086)
ZMICRO INC (PA)
Also Called: Z Microsystems
9820 Summers Ridge Rd, San Diego (92121-3083)
PHONE.................858 831-7000
Jack Wade, *CEO*
Randall S Millar, *President*
Jason Wade, *COO*
Richard Schmidt, *CFO*
Rick Elliott, *Vice Pres*
EMP: 57
SQ FT: 36,800
SALES (est): 23.4MM **Privately Held**
WEB: www.zmicro.com
SIC: 7373 3577 3572 Computer integrated systems design; computer peripheral equipment; computer storage devices

---
7374 Data & Computer Processing & Preparation

(P-16087)
A S E C INTERNATIONAL INC
Also Called: Asec Group
11400 W Olympic Blvd, Los Angeles (90064-1550)
PHONE.................803 939-4809
Fax: 310 478-4927
Evan Green, *President*
Del Snyder, *Exec VP*
Steve Seiler, *Admin Sec*
AMR Aref, *Research*
Brian Johnson, *VP Sls/Mktg*
EMP: 700
SQ FT: 25,000
SALES (est): 24.2MM **Privately Held**
WEB: www.asecusa.com
SIC: 7374 Data processing service

(P-16088)
ACTIV IDENTITY CORPORATION
6623 Dumbarton Cir, Fremont (94555-3603)
PHONE.................510 574-0100
Fax: 510 574-0101
Grant Evans, *Ch of Bd*
Jacques Kerrest, *COO*
John Boyer, *Senior VP*
Robert Brandewie, *Senior VP*
Jerome Becquart, *Vice Pres*
EMP: 218
SQ FT: 41,000
SALES (est): 14.6MM
SALES (corp-wide): 7.8B **Privately Held**
WEB: www.actividentity.com
SIC: 7374 Data verification service
HQ: Assa Abloy Inc.
   110 Sargent Dr
   New Haven CT 06511
   203 624-5225

(P-16089)
ADVANCED DATA TRANSCRIBING CTR
Also Called: Advanced Data Center
1401 Cuesta Way, Montebello (90640-3218)
PHONE.................626 571-1570
Fax: 626 571-5364
Patty Lay Kwan, *President*
Steve Dinse, *Vice Pres*
EMP: 60
SALES: 2MM **Privately Held**
SIC: 7374 Data processing service

(P-16090)
AUTOMATIC DATA PROCESSING INC
Also Called: ADP
7000 Village Dr Ste 200, Buena Park (90621-2287)
PHONE.................714 690-7000
Fax: 714 690-7054
Joseph Leung, *Principal*
Lily Fan, *President*
Matt Hackett, *District Mgr*
Lauren Komppa, *District Mgr*
Monique Villalobos, *District Mgr*
EMP: 117
SALES (corp-wide): 11.6B **Publicly Held**
SIC: 7374 8721 Data processing service; payroll accounting service
PA: Automatic Data Processing, Inc.
   1 Adp Blvd Ste 1
   Roseland NJ 07068
   973 974-5000

(P-16091)
AUTOMATIC DATA PROCESSING INC
Also Called: ADP
9445 Fairway View Pl # 200, Rancho Cucamonga (91730-0931)
PHONE.................909 477-4266
Fax: 909 477-4919
Bill Crawford, *Manager*
Angela Roundtree, *Human Resources*
EMP: 200
SALES (corp-wide): 11.6B **Publicly Held**
SIC: 7374 Data processing service
PA: Automatic Data Processing, Inc.
   1 Adp Blvd Ste 1
   Roseland NJ 07068
   973 974-5000

(P-16092)
AUTOMATIC DATA PROCESSING INC
Also Called: ADP
5153 Camino Ruiz Ste 100, Camarillo (93012-8656)
PHONE.................805 383-8630
Fax: 805 383-8600
Erich Hillig, *Director*
Jeff Vlach, *Info Tech Mgr*
Jon Rust, *Technology*
Randy Fishwick, *Analyst*
Michelle Benedict, *Marketing Staff*
EMP: 117
SALES (corp-wide): 11.6B **Publicly Held**
SIC: 7374 Data processing service
PA: Automatic Data Processing, Inc.
   1 Adp Blvd Ste 1
   Roseland NJ 07068
   973 974-5000

(P-16093)
AUTOMATIC DATA PROCESSING INC
Also Called: ADP
601 Gateway Blvd Ste 900, South San Francisco (94080-7070)
PHONE.................650 829-6900
Fax: 650 330-6711
Steve Kapusta, *Manager*
Scott Loose, *Sales Executive*
Kate Veprek, *Director*
Audrey Bincarousky, *Manager*
Vicki Sanders, *Manager*
EMP: 50
SALES (corp-wide): 11.6B **Publicly Held**
SIC: 7374 Data processing service
PA: Automatic Data Processing, Inc.
   1 Adp Blvd Ste 1
   Roseland NJ 07068
   973 974-5000

(P-16094)
AUTOMATIC DATA PROCESSING INC
Also Called: ADP
620 W Covina Blvd, San Dimas (91773-2956)
PHONE.................909 592-6411
Melanie Hardin, *Branch Mgr*
Victor Mak, *Vice Pres*
Ranjini Lingam, *Controller*
Cecilia Vazquez, *HR Admin*
Rick Weber, *VP Mktg*
EMP: 130
SALES (corp-wide): 11.6B **Publicly Held**
SIC: 7374 Data processing service
PA: Automatic Data Processing, Inc.
   1 Adp Blvd Ste 1
   Roseland NJ 07068
   973 974-5000

(P-16095)
AUTOMATIC DATA PROCESSING INC
Also Called: ADP
720 Bay Rd, Redwood City (94063-2479)
PHONE.................800 225-5237
EMP: 130
SALES (corp-wide): 11.6B **Publicly Held**
SIC: 7374 Data processing service
PA: Automatic Data Processing, Inc.
   1 Adp Blvd Ste 1
   Roseland NJ 07068
   973 974-5000

(P-16096)
AUTOMATIC DATA PROCESSING INC
Also Called: ADP
505 San Marin Dr Ste A110, Novato (94945-1302)
PHONE.................415 899-7300
Fax: 415 899-7312
EMP: 130
SALES (corp-wide): 11.6B **Publicly Held**
SIC: 7374 Data processing service
PA: Automatic Data Processing, Inc.
   1 Adp Blvd Ste 1
   Roseland NJ 07068
   973 974-5000

(P-16097)
AUTOMATIC DATA PROCESSING INC
Also Called: ADP
820 N Mccarthy Blvd # 120, Milpitas (95035-5115)
PHONE.................408 876-6600
Robert Thomas, *Branch Mgr*
Mike Testa, *Vice Pres*
Abella Jalocon, *Technology*
Alison Baird, *Human Resources*
Maria Sandoval, *Sales Executive*
EMP: 450
SALES (corp-wide): 11.6B **Publicly Held**
SIC: 7374 8721 Data processing service; accounting, auditing & bookkeeping
PA: Automatic Data Processing, Inc.
   1 Adp Blvd Ste 1
   Roseland NJ 07068
   973 974-5000

(P-16098)
AUTOMATIC DATA PROCESSING INC
Also Called: ADP
5355 Orangethorpe Ave, La Palma (90623-1095)
PHONE.................714 994-2000
Fax: 714 228-4103
Jim Wassik, *Branch Mgr*
Laureen Ball, *Executive*
Sean Mackay, *District Mgr*
Hugh Cunning, *CTO*
Kyle Kauss, *CTO*
EMP: 78
SALES (corp-wide): 11.6B **Publicly Held**
SIC: 7374 Data processing service
PA: Automatic Data Processing, Inc.
   1 Adp Blvd Ste 1
   Roseland NJ 07068
   973 974-5000

(P-16099)
AUTOMATIC DATA PROCESSING INC
ADP
4125 Hopyard Rd, Pleasanton (94588-8534)
PHONE.................925 251-5300
Russ Deloach, *Officer*
Kuzminian James, *CIO*
Robert Schneider, *CTO*
Kenneth Wong, *Info Tech Mgr*
Andrew Lucas, *IT/INT Sup*
EMP: 78
SALES (corp-wide): 11.6B **Publicly Held**
SIC: 7374 8741 8742 Data processing service; personnel management; management consulting services
PA: Automatic Data Processing, Inc.
   1 Adp Blvd Ste 1
   Roseland NJ 07068
   973 974-5000

(P-16100)
AUTOMATIC DATA PROCESSING INC
Also Called: ADP
400 W Covina Blvd, San Dimas (91773-2954)
PHONE.................800 225-5237
Fax: 909 592-6508
Rodney Hroblak, *Principal*
Kelly Kaufman, *CFO*
Lina Sierra, *Exec VP*
Robert Barnett, *Vice Pres*
Timothy Corcoran, *Vice Pres*
EMP: 117
SALES (corp-wide): 11.6B **Publicly Held**
SIC: 7374 8721 Data processing service; accounting, auditing & bookkeeping
PA: Automatic Data Processing, Inc.
   1 Adp Blvd Ste 1
   Roseland NJ 07068
   973 974-5000

(P-16101)
AUTOMATIC DATA PROCESSING INC
Also Called: ADP
6300 Canoga Ave Ste 400, Woodland Hills (91367-8008)
PHONE.................661 631-1456
Fax: 818 592-3601
Vicki Fitch, *Branch Mgr*
Gretchen Hundling, *Sales Staff*
Josh Paugh, *Manager*
EMP: 117
SALES (corp-wide): 11.6B **Publicly Held**
SIC: 7374 Data processing & preparation
PA: Automatic Data Processing, Inc.
   1 Adp Blvd Ste 1
   Roseland NJ 07068
   973 974-5000

(P-16102)
AUTOMATIC DATA PROCESSING INC
Also Called: ADP
600 Crprate Pinte Ste 450, Culver City (90230)
PHONE.................800 226-5237
Kevin Gramian, *Manager*
Ashley Witzer, *Sales Executive*
Breeda Desmond, *Manager*
EMP: 70
SALES (corp-wide): 11.6B **Publicly Held**
SIC: 7374 8721 Data processing service; payroll accounting service
PA: Automatic Data Processing, Inc.
   1 Adp Blvd Ste 1
   Roseland NJ 07068
   973 974-5000

(P-16103)
AUTOMATIC DATA PROCESSING INC
Also Called: ADP
1450 Frazee Rd Ste 601, San Diego (92108-4340)
PHONE.................619 293-4800
Fax: 619 688-2780
David Manriquez, *Branch Mgr*
Renee Luke, *Admin Sec*
EMP: 100
SALES (corp-wide): 11.6B **Publicly Held**
SIC: 7374 Data processing service
PA: Automatic Data Processing, Inc.
   1 Adp Blvd Ste 1
   Roseland NJ 07068
   973 974-5000

(P-16104)
BLEACHER REPORT INC
609 Mission St, San Francisco (94105-3506)
PHONE.................415 777-5505
Mike Jacobsen, *CFO*
Kevin Conti, *Software Dev*
Chris Pederick, *Engineer*
Tim Benton, *Producer*
Josh Abrams, *VP Sales*
EMP: 65
SALES: 5.4MM **Privately Held**
SIC: 7374 Data processing & preparation

PRODUCTS & SERVICES SECTION
7374 - Data & Computer Processing & Preparation County (P-16125)

(P-16105)
CALIFORNIA SURVEY RES SVCS
15350 Sherman Way Ste 480, Van Nuys (91406-4268)
PHONE..................818 780-2777
Fax: 818 780-0329
William Kaplan, *CEO*
Kenneth Gross, *President*
Margarita Rodriguez, *Executive*
Lawrence Manayan, *Technology*
Margarita Rivera, *VP Opers*
EMP: 125
SQ FT: 10,000
SALES (est): 8.4MM **Privately Held**
WEB: www.calsurvey.com
SIC: 7374 8732 Data processing service; market analysis or research

(P-16106)
CALIFRNIA HLTH HUMN SRVCS AGCY
Also Called: Hhsa Data Center
3301 S St, Sacramento (95816-7019)
PHONE..................916 739-7640
John Moise, *Director*
Raymond Perkins, *Technology*
EMP: 500 **Privately Held**
SIC: 7374 9431 Data processing & preparation; administration of public health programs;
HQ: California Health & Human Servcs Agency
1600 9th St Ste 460
Sacramento CA 95814
916 654-3454

(P-16107)
CASTLIGHT HEALTH INC
150 Spear St Ste 400, San Francisco (94105-1537)
PHONE..................415 829-1400
Giovanni M Colella, *CEO*
Bryan Roberts, *Ch of Bd*
John C Doyle, *President*
Mark Sarbiewski, *Chief Mktg Ofcr*
Jonathan Rende, *Officer*
EMP: 464
SQ FT: 32,571
SALES: 75.3MM **Privately Held**
SIC: 7374 7372 Data processing & preparation; prepackaged software

(P-16108)
CCH INCORPORATED
Also Called: Cch Computax
20101 Hamilton Ave # 200, Torrance (90502-1371)
PHONE..................310 800-9800
Fax: 310 543-6456
Jessica Perez, *Human Res Mgr*
Rajkumar Govindaraj, *Info Tech Mgr*
Ernie Zoumot, *Marketing Staff*
Peter Kovic, *Sales Staff*
Malatcha Pigott, *Sales Staff*
EMP: 350
SQ FT: 280,000
SALES (corp-wide): 4.5B **Privately Held**
WEB: www.cch.com
SIC: 7374 7372 7371 Data processing & preparation; prepackaged software; custom computer programming services
HQ: Cch Incorporated
2700 Lake Cook Rd
Riverwoods IL 60015
847 267-7000

(P-16109)
CELERITY CONSULTING GROUP INC (PA)
2 Gough St Ste 300, San Francisco (94103-5420)
PHONE..................415 986-8850
Rachelle Yowell, *CEO*
Christopher Yowell, *President*
Norman Yee, *COO*
Steffani Aranas, *Vice Pres*
Dr Bruce V Hartley, *Vice Pres*
EMP: 74
SQ FT: 28,000
SALES (est): 23.8MM **Privately Held**
WEB: www.celerityconsulting.net
SIC: 7374 8742 7371 7379 Data processing & preparation; data processing service; management consulting services; management information systems consultant; computer software development & applications; data processing consultant; on-line data base information retrieval

(P-16110)
CHANGE HEALTHCARE INC
241 Lombard St, Thousand Oaks (91360-5807)
PHONE..................805 777-7773
Bob Ashworth, *Branch Mgr*
EMP: 75
SALES (corp-wide): 1.4B **Privately Held**
SIC: 7374 8742 Data processing service; hospital & health services consultant
HQ: Change Healthcare Holdings, Inc.
3055 Lebanon Pike # 1000
Nashville TN 37214
615 932-3000

(P-16111)
CORRECTONS RHBLTATION CAL DEPT
Also Called: Data Center
1920 Alabama Ave, Sacramento (95825)
P.O. Box 942883 (94283-0001)
PHONE..................916 358-2319
Joe Penora, *Director*
Dennis Dearbugh, *Director*
Scott McDonald, *Manager*
EMP: 200 **Privately Held**
SIC: 7374 9223 Data processing service; correctional institutions;
HQ: California Department Of Corrections & Rehabilitation
1515 S St
Sacramento CA 95811
916 341-7066

(P-16112)
COUNTY OF KERN
Information Technology Svcs
1215 Truxtun Ave, Bakersfield (93301-4619)
PHONE..................661 868-2000
Bill Fawns, *Director*
Robert Hardt, *Purch Dir*
EMP: 61 **Privately Held**
WEB: www.kccfc.org
SIC: 7374 9431 Data processing service; administration of public health programs;
PA: County Of Kern
1115 Truxtun Ave Rm 505
Bakersfield CA 93301
661 868-3690

(P-16113)
COUNTY OF LOS ANGELES
Also Called: Voter Precinct Voter Reg Off
12400 Imperial Hwy, Norwalk (90650-3134)
PHONE..................562 462-2094
Connie McCormack, *Branch Mgr*
EMP: 800 **Privately Held**
WEB: www.co.la.ca.us
SIC: 7374 9111 Data entry service; executive offices
PA: County Of Los Angeles
500 W Temple St Ste 375
Los Angeles CA 90012
213 974-1101

(P-16114)
COUNTY OF MARIN
Also Called: Computer Programming Dept
371 Bel Marin Keys Blvd # 100, Novato (94949-5662)
PHONE..................415 499-7060
Fax: 415 499-3792
Daze Hill, *Director*
Barbara Layton, *Telecomm Mgr*
Jalal Kazemi, *Comp Tech*
EMP: 80 **Privately Held**
SIC: 7374 9111 Data processing service; county supervisors' & executives' offices
PA: County Of Marin
1600 Los Gamos Dr Ste 200
San Rafael CA 94903
415 473-6358

(P-16115)
COUNTY OF SONOMA
Also Called: Sonoma County Data Processing
2615 Paulin Dr, Santa Rosa (95403-2804)
PHONE..................707 527-2911
Bosb Keyser, *Info Systems*
Sabrina Doss, *Project Mgr*
Daniel Fruchey, *Manager*
George Kemmerer, *Manager*
John Sestok, *Manager*
EMP: 150
SQ FT: 13,000 **Privately Held**
WEB: www.sonomacompost.com
SIC: 7374 Data processing service
PA: County Of Sonoma
585 Fiscal Dr 100
Santa Rosa CA 95403
707 565-2431

(P-16116)
COUNTY OF SONOMA
Also Called: Information Systems Department
2300 Prof Dr Rear Door B, Santa Rosa (95403)
PHONE..................707 527-2911
Fax: 707 527-3200
Mark Walsh, *Branch Mgr*
Hector Velasquez, *Network Analyst*
EMP: 75 **Privately Held**
WEB: www.sonomacompost.com
SIC: 7374 Data processing & preparation
PA: County Of Sonoma
585 Fiscal Dr 100
Santa Rosa CA 95403
707 565-2431

(P-16117)
COUNTY OF TUOLUMNE
Also Called: Information Systems & Services
2 S Green St, Sonora (95370-4618)
PHONE..................209 533-5561
Fax: 209 533-5988
Gregg Jacob, *Manager*
Jacob Gregg, *Manager*
EMP: 500 **Privately Held**
WEB: www.tuolumne.courts.ca.gov
SIC: 7374 9111 7376 Data processing & preparation; county supervisors' & executives' offices; computer facilities management
PA: County Of Tuolumne
2 S Green St
Sonora CA 95370
209 533-5521

(P-16118)
CROWDFLOWER INC
2111 Mission St Ste 302, San Francisco (94110-6350)
PHONE..................415 471-1920
Lukas Biewald, *CEO*
Jeff Auston, *President*
Robin Bordoli, *COO*
Christopher Van Pelt, *COO*
Gary Kremen, *Bd of Directors*
EMP: 60
SQ FT: 8,400
SALES (est): 7.6MM **Privately Held**
SIC: 7374 Data processing & preparation

(P-16119)
CYBERSOURCE CORPORATION (HQ)
900 Metro Center Blvd, Foster City (94404-2172)
P.O. Box 8999, San Francisco (94128-8999)
PHONE..................650 432-7350
Michael Walsh, *President*
Scott R Cruickshank, *President*
Steven D Pellizzer, *CFO*
Robert J Ford, *Exec VP*
Robert Ford, *Exec VP*
EMP: 140
SALES (est): 147.2MM
SALES (corp-wide): 13.8B **Publicly Held**
WEB: www.cybersource.com
SIC: 7374 Data processing & preparation
PA: Visa Inc.
900 Metro Center Blvd
Foster City CA 94404
650 432-3200

(P-16120)
DATAPROSE INC
1451 N Rice Ave Ste A, Oxnard (93030-7991)
P.O. Box 451902, Omaha NE (68145-9002)
PHONE..................805 278-7430
Fax: 805 278-7420
Glenn Carter, *President*
John Ray, *President*
Fred Fleet, *CFO*
Bill Murray, *Vice Pres*
Paul Orfalea, *Principal*
EMP: 65
SQ FT: 25,000
SALES (est): 3MM
SALES (corp-wide): 751.2MM **Publicly Held**
SIC: 7374 7389 Service bureau, computer; fund raising organizations
PA: Csg Systems International, Inc.
9555 Maroon Cir
Englewood CO 80112
303 200-2000

(P-16121)
DELUXE MEDIA SERVICES
2130 N Hollywood Way, Burbank (91505-1522)
PHONE..................818 526-3700
Joe Bigley, *General Mgr*
EMP: 500
SALES (est): 36.5MM **Privately Held**
SIC: 7374 Computer graphics service

(P-16122)
DOCLER MEDIA LLC (DH)
720 N Cahuenga Blvd, Los Angeles (90038-3702)
PHONE..................424 777-3999
Balazs Sipocz, *CEO*
EMP: 62
SQ FT: 30,000
SALES: 6.7MM **Privately Held**
SIC: 7374 8741 Computer graphics service; computer processing services; administrative management
HQ: Docler Holding Sarl
Avenue John F. Kennedy 44
Luxembourg
261 118-

(P-16123)
EMERALD CONNECT LLC (HQ)
15050 Avenue Of Sci 200, San Diego (92128)
PHONE..................800 233-2834
Fax: 858 592-6286
Adam D Amsterdam, *Mng Member*
Sharon Greener, *Exec VP*
Heather Hinkle, *Exec VP*
Heidi Saucier, *Exec VP*
Dave Briggs, *Vice Pres*
EMP: 100
SQ FT: 35,000
SALES (est): 20.6MM
SALES (corp-wide): 2.9B **Publicly Held**
WEB: www.emeraldconnect.com
SIC: 7374 7331 Data processing service; mailing service
PA: Broadridge Financial Solutions, Inc.
5 Dakota Dr Ste 300
New Hyde Park NY 11042
516 472-5400

(P-16124)
EMOVE EXPRESS COMPANY
Also Called: Emovexpress.com
688 Matsonia Dr, Foster City (94404-1337)
PHONE..................650 377-0913
Fax: 650 578-0691
Anthony Chiu, *Ch of Bd*
Steve Argyres, *President*
Teresa Hall, *CFO*
EMP: 56
SQ FT: 2,760
SALES (est): 2.1MM **Privately Held**
WEB: www.emoveexpress.com
SIC: 7374 Computer graphics service

(P-16125)
ENCLARITY INC
16815 Von Karman Ave # 125, Irvine (92606-2412)
PHONE..................949 614-8110
Sean Downs, *CEO*

7374 - Data & Computer Processing & Preparation County (P-16126)

Paul Perleberg, *President*
Warren Gouk Andrea, *CFO*
Scott Marber, *Vice Pres*
Brian Smith, *Vice Pres*
EMP: 57
SQ FT: 3,500
SALES (est): 3.9MM
SALES (corp-wide): 9B **Privately Held**
WEB: www.enclarity.com
SIC: 7374 Data processing & preparation
HQ: Lexisnexis Risk Solutions Inc.
1000 Alderman Dr
Alpharetta GA 30005
678 694-6000

(P-16126)
EPOCHCOM LLC
2644 30th St Fl 2, Santa Monica (90405-3061)
PHONE 310 664-5700
Joel Hall, *Mng Member*
Esther Martinez, *COO*
Sanath Fernando, *Vice Pres*
Christine Hull, *Vice Pres*
David Bonsukan, *Risk Mgmt Dir*
EMP: 150
SQ FT: 22,000
SALES (est): 14.7MM **Privately Held**
SIC: 7374 Data processing service

(P-16127)
ESP COMPUTER SERVICES INC (PA)
12444 Victory Blvd Fl 4, North Hollywood (91606-3156)
PHONE 818 487-4500
Jack Miller, *President*
Jeremy Sardoma, *Software Dev*
Dawn Robles, *Prgrmr*
Yesenia Linares, *Hum Res Coord*
Mark Curcio, *HR Admin*
EMP: 59 **EST:** 1969
SALES (est): 14MM **Privately Held**
WEB: www.espcomp.com
SIC: 7374 7371 Data processing service; custom computer programming services

(P-16128)
FIRST DATABANK INC
701 Gateway Blvd Ste 600, San Francisco (94188)
PHONE 650 588-5454
Joe Hirshmann, *Branch Mgr*
Joseph Palermo, *President*
James Wilson, *COO*
Marck Dubois, *Vice Pres*
Joseph Hirschmann, *Administration*
EMP: 100
SQ FT: 3,000
SALES (corp-wide): 4.9B **Privately Held**
WEB: www.firstdatabank.com
SIC: 7374 Data processing service
HQ: First Databank, Inc.
701 Gateway Blvd Ste 600
South San Francisco CA 94080
800 633-3453

(P-16129)
FISERV INC
19935 E Walnut Dr N, City of Industry (91789-2818)
PHONE 909 595-9074
Mark Breithaupt, *Manager*
Ellen Kobzeff, *Executive*
Beth Eppler, *Manager*
EMP: 79
SALES (corp-wide): 5.2B **Publicly Held**
WEB: www.fiserv.com
SIC: 7374 Data processing service
PA: Fiserv, Inc.
255 Fiserv Dr
Brookfield WI 53045
262 879-5000

(P-16130)
FISERV INC
19935 E Walnut Dr N, Walnut (91789-2818)
PHONE 909 598-8700
Bill Costello, *Manager*
EMP: 72
SALES (corp-wide): 5.2B **Publicly Held**
SIC: 7374 Data processing service

PA: Fiserv, Inc.
255 Fiserv Dr
Brookfield WI 53045
800 879-5000

(P-16131)
FISERV INC
525 Almanor Ave, Sunnyvale (94085-3542)
PHONE 408 242-3011
EMP: 70
SALES (corp-wide): 5.2B **Publicly Held**
PA: Fiserv, Inc.
255 Fiserv Dr
Brookfield WI 53045
800 879-5000

(P-16132)
FISERV INC
405 Science Dr, Moorpark (93021-2247)
PHONE 805 532-9100
Fax: 805 532-9137
John Edwards, *Branch Mgr*
EMP: 71
SALES (corp-wide): 5.2B **Publicly Held**
SIC: 7374 7371 Data processing service; computer software development & applications
PA: Fiserv, Inc.
255 Fiserv Dr
Brookfield WI 53045
800 879-5000

(P-16133)
FISERV INC
19935 E Walnut Dr N, Walnut (91789-2818)
PHONE 909 595-9074
Jeff Conte, *Manager*
Martha Bonanno, *Branch Mgr*
Mike Pihulic, *Director*
Kathy Cadic, *Manager*
Gonzalo Maldonado, *Manager*
EMP: 62
SALES (corp-wide): 5.2B **Publicly Held**
WEB: www.fiserv.com
SIC: 7374 Data processing service
PA: Fiserv, Inc.
255 Fiserv Dr
Brookfield WI 53045
800 879-5000

(P-16134)
GENERAL SERVICES CAL DEPT
Office Physical Plg & Dev Csu
4665 Lampson Ave, Los Alamitos (90720-5187)
P.O. Box 3842, Seal Beach (90740-7842)
PHONE 562 342-7212
James K Hightower, *Branch Mgr*
EMP: 100 **Privately Held**
WEB: www.4c.net
SIC: 7374 9199 Data processing service; general government administration
HQ: California Department Of General Services
707 3rd St
West Sacramento CA 95605

(P-16135)
GOODHIRE LLC
555 Twin Dolphin Dr, Redwood City (94065-2129)
P.O. Box 391403, Omaha NE (68139-1403)
PHONE 650 618-9910
Matthew Monahan, *Mng Member*
Jeremy Wood, *Executive*
EMP: 50
SQ FT: 7,000
SALES: 5MM **Privately Held**
SIC: 7374 Data processing & preparation

(P-16136)
GREENPLUM INC
1900 S Norfolk St Ste 224, San Mateo (94403-1166)
PHONE 650 286-8023
Fax: 650 286-8010
Bill Cook, *President*
Ed Jones, *COO*
Ronaldo Amy, *Senior VP*
Ronaldo AMA, *Vice Pres*
Frank Bien, *Vice Pres*
EMP: 123

SALES (est): 7.5MM
SALES (corp-wide): 72.B **Publicly Held**
WEB: www.greenplum.net
SIC: 7374 Data processing & preparation
HQ: Emc Corporation
176 South St
Hopkinton MA 01748
508 435-1000

(P-16137)
GREENSOFT TECHNOLOGY INC
155 S El Molino Ave # 100, Pasadena (91101-2563)
PHONE 323 254-5961
Larry Yen, *President*
Jon Wu, *Vice Pres*
Amber Lee, *Project Engr*
Raja Balu, *Engineer*
EMP: 121
SALES (est): 1.2MM **Privately Held**
SIC: 7374 Data processing service

(P-16138)
HARTE HANKS INC
2337 W Commonwealth Ave, Fullerton (92833-2997)
PHONE 210 829-9000
Maria Koebel, *Manager*
Matthew Pfeifer, *Manager*
EMP: 100
SALES (corp-wide): 495.3MM **Publicly Held**
SIC: 7374 4225 7389 Data processing & preparation; calculating service (computer); general warehousing; telemarketing services
PA: Harte Hanks, Inc.
9601 Mcallister Fwy # 610
San Antonio TX 78216
210 829-9000

(P-16139)
HARTE-HANKS MKT INTELLIGENCE (PA)
Also Called: Aberdeen Group, The
15015 Ave Of Science # 110, San Diego (92128-3435)
PHONE 858 450-1667
Robert G Brown, *President*
Randall W Wussler, *Exec VP*
Lisa Torres, *Sls & Mktg Exec*
Tim Savitt, *VP Mktg*
Robert Mackey, *VP Sales*
EMP: 150
SQ FT: 45,000
SALES (est): 32.7MM **Privately Held**
WEB: www.hartehanksmi.com
SIC: 7374 Data processing & preparation

(P-16140)
HP ENTERPRISE SERVICES LLC
3215 Prospect Park Dr, Rancho Cordova (95670-6017)
PHONE 916 636-1000
Dennis Dormen, *Manager*
Andy Boehl, *Data Proc Staff*
EMP: 800
SALES (corp-wide): 34.1B **Publicly Held**
WEB: www.eds.com
SIC: 7374 Data processing service
HQ: Hp Enterprise Services, Llc
5400 Legacy Dr
Plano TX 75024
972 604-6000

(P-16141)
HP ENTERPRISE SERVICES LLC
3990 Sherman St, San Diego (92110-4324)
PHONE 619 817-3851
Javier Berellez, *Manager*
Marc Robinson, *Engineer*
EMP: 350
SALES (corp-wide): 34.1B **Publicly Held**
WEB: www.eds.com
SIC: 7374 Data processing & preparation
HQ: Hp Enterprise Services, Llc
5400 Legacy Dr
Plano TX 75024
972 604-6000

(P-16142)
HP ENTERPRISE SERVICES LLC
1 Hornet Way, El Segundo (90245-2804)
PHONE 310 331-1074
Nelson Lee, *Branch Mgr*
Tommy Jackson, *Administration*
Linda Gonzales, *IT/INT Sup*
Wanda Slade, *Marketing Staff*
EMP: 138
SALES (corp-wide): 34.1B **Publicly Held**
WEB: www.eds.com
SIC: 7374 Data processing service
HQ: Hp Enterprise Services, Llc
5400 Legacy Dr
Plano TX 75024
972 604-6000

(P-16143)
HYVE SOLUTIONS CORPORATION
44201 Nobel Dr, Fremont (94538-3178)
PHONE 864 349-4415
Kevin Murai, *CEO*
Peter Larocque, *President*
Michael Mason, *Engineer*
Terry Coker, *Traffic Mgr*
Nicole Lin, *Sales Mgr*
EMP: 5000
SALES (est): 2MM
SALES (corp-wide): 13.3B **Publicly Held**
SIC: 7374 Data processing & preparation
PA: Synnex Corporation
44201 Nobel Dr
Fremont CA 94538
510 656-3333

(P-16144)
I HOT LEADS
19671 Beach Blvd Ste 204, Huntington Beach (92648-5905)
PHONE 714 960-8028
Michael Beardon, *CEO*
EMP: 56
SALES (est): 1.7MM **Privately Held**
WEB: www.ihotleads.com
SIC: 7374 Computer graphics service

(P-16145)
IKANO COMMUNICATIONS INC (PA)
Also Called: A & S Technologies
9221 Corbin Ave Ste 260, Northridge (91324-1625)
PHONE 801 924-0900
Jim Murphy, *CEO*
Sam Ghahremanpour, *President*
George Mitsopoulos, *COO*
Kevin Childre, *Exec VP*
Dean Russ, *Vice Pres*
EMP: 91
SQ FT: 50,000
SALES (est): 36.3MM **Privately Held**
WEB: www.ikano.com
SIC: 7374 Data processing & preparation

(P-16146)
IMAGESCAN INC
390 S Fair Oaks Ave, Pasadena (91105-2540)
PHONE 626 844-2050
Fax: 626 844-2055
Basker S Krishnan, *President*
Andy Len, *Marketing Staff*
Meher Kateli, *Manager*
EMP: 90
SQ FT: 4,000
SALES: 5MM **Privately Held**
WEB: www.imagescan-inc.com
SIC: 7374 Data entry service

(P-16147)
INFLECTION LLC
555 Twin Dolphin Dr # 200, Redwood City (94065-2134)
PHONE 650 618-9910
Matthew Monahan,
Donald Landwirth, *COO*
Clarke Christiansen, *Sr Software Eng*
Brent Etiz, *Business Mgr*
Lauren Small, *Marketing Staff*
EMP: 136
SQ FT: 22,914
SALES (est): 13MM **Privately Held**
SIC: 7374 Data processing & preparation

PRODUCTS & SERVICES SECTION
7374 - Data & Computer Processing & Preparation County (P-16171)

(P-16148)
INFOBLOX INC (PA)
3111 Coronado Dr, Santa Clara (95054-3206)
PHONE..................................408 986-4000
Fax: 408 625-4201
Jesper Andersen, *President*
Richard E Belluzzo, *Ch of Bd*
Janesh Moorjani, *CFO*
Scott J Fulton, *Exec VP*
Sonya Andreae, *Vice Pres*
EMP: 125
SQ FT: 127,000
SALES: 358.2MM **Privately Held**
WEB: www.infoblox.com
SIC: **7374** 7371 7379 Data processing & preparation; data processing service; custom computer programming services; computer software development & applications; software programming applications; computer related consulting services

(P-16149)
INKO INDUSTRIAL CORPORATION
695 Vaqueros Ave, Sunnyvale (94085-3524)
PHONE..................................408 830-1040
Fax: 408 830-1058
George Kuo, *President*
Juliet Ng, *Office Mgr*
Frank Ye, *Manager*
Kathy H Chiang, *Agent*
EMP: 100
SQ FT: 80,000
SALES (est): 8.2MM **Privately Held**
WEB: www.pellicle-inko.com
SIC: **7374** Computer graphics service

(P-16150)
INTERNET BRANDS INC (PA)
909 N Sepulveda Blvd # 11, El Segundo (90245-2727)
PHONE..................................310 280-4000
Fax: 310 280-5201
Robert N Brisco, *CEO*
Gregory T Perrier, *President*
Lisa Morita, *COO*
Lisa Vila, *COO*
Scott Friedman, *CFO*
▲ EMP: 148 EST: 1998
SQ FT: 54,000
SALES (est): 275.5MM **Privately Held**
WEB: www.carsdirect.com
SIC: **7374** Computer graphics service

(P-16151)
LEIDOS INC
Also Called: Sissc
1550 N Norma St, Ridgecrest (93555-2556)
PHONE..................................858 826-7670
Doreen Ross, *Branch Mgr*
EMP: 253
SALES (corp-wide): 5B **Publicly Held**
WEB: www.saic.com
SIC: **7374** 7373 Data processing & preparation; systems integration services
HQ: Leidos, Inc.
11951 Freedom Dr Ste 500
Reston VA 20190
571 526-6000

(P-16152)
LENDER PROCESSING SERVICES INC
3100 New York Dr Ste 200, Pasadena (91107-1524)
PHONE..................................626 808-9000
Brian Mushaney, *Vice Pres*
Monty Marcus, *Vice Pres*
Aimee Hartmann, *Principal*
Anthony Higuera, *Administration*
EMP: 99
SALES (est): 6MM **Privately Held**
SIC: **7374** Data processing & preparation

(P-16153)
LOS ANGELES UNIFIED SCHOOL DST
Also Called: Information Technology Agency
200 N Main St Ste 1400, Los Angeles (90012-4127)
PHONE..................................213 847-6911
Jesse Juarros, *Manager*
Henry Lee, *Info Tech Mgr*
EMP: 700
SALES (corp-wide): 4.4B **Privately Held**
WEB: www.lausd.k12.ca.us
SIC: **7374** Data processing service
PA: Los Angeles Unified School District
333 S Beaudry Ave Ste 209
Los Angeles CA 90017
213 241-1000

(P-16154)
MAGNET IN SAND INC
17011 Beach Blvd Ste 900, Huntington Beach (92647-5998)
PHONE..................................623 703-5650
Keisha Freswick, *Principal*
EMP: 200 EST: 2014
SALES (est): 3.9MM **Privately Held**
SIC: **7374** Computer graphics service

(P-16155)
MANAGED NETWORK SERVICES LLC
3800 Bridge Pkwy, Redwood City (94065-1171)
PHONE..................................650 232-4287
Christopher Linden,
EMP: 294
SALES (est): 3.2MM
SALES (corp-wide): 310.2MM **Privately Held**
SIC: **7374** 5734 Data processing service; computer & software stores
HQ: Tolt Solutions, Inc.
3550 Rutherford Rd
Taylors SC 29687
864 322-4200

(P-16156)
MANAGEMENT APPLIED PROGRAMMING (PA)
Also Called: Benefit Programs ADM
13191 Crossroads Pkwy N # 205, City of Industry (91746-3434)
PHONE..................................562 463-5000
Fax: 310 398-6105
Phiroze Dalal, *CEO*
Hormazd Dalal, *CFO*
Blaise Liu, *CFO*
EMP: 50
SALES (est): 19.1MM **Privately Held**
SIC: **7374** Data processing service

(P-16157)
MARIN SOFTWARE INCORPORATED (PA)
123 Mission St Fl 27, San Francisco (94105-1681)
PHONE..................................415 399-2580
Christopher A Lien, *CEO*
David A Yovanno, *Ch of Bd*
Catriona M Fallon, *CFO*
John A Kaelle, *CFO*
Russell Wirth, *Officer*
EMP: 145
SQ FT: 43,000
SALES: 108.5MM **Publicly Held**
SIC: **7374** Data processing & preparation

(P-16158)
MARKETLIVE INC
617 2nd St Ste B, Petaluma (94952-5160)
PHONE..................................707 780-1600
Fax: 707 773-3592
Ken Burke, *CEO*
Josh Baumrind, *Partner*
James Miller, *Exec VP*
Jeff Kreutz, *Senior VP*
Angela Bandlow, *Vice Pres*
EMP: 110
SQ FT: 35,000
SALES (est): 19.9MM
SALES (corp-wide): 52.1MM **Privately Held**
WEB: www.mmlive.com
SIC: **7374** Computer graphics service
PA: Kibo Software, Inc.
717 N Harwood St Ste 1800
Dallas TX 75201
707 780-1600

(P-16159)
MERCHANT SERVICES INC (PA)
1 S Van Ness Ave Fl 5, San Francisco (94103-5416)
PHONE..................................817 725-0900
Lorraine Stimmell, *CEO*
Le Tran-Tl, *Senior VP*
Carrie Gale, *Executive Asst*
Tad Scales, *Controller*
EMP: 400
SQ FT: 58,336
SALES (est): 34MM **Privately Held**
WEB: www.msimerchantservices.com
SIC: **7374** Data processing service

(P-16160)
MERCURY TECHNOLOGY GROUP INC
6430 Oak Cyn Ste 100, Irvine (92618-5227)
PHONE..................................949 417-0260
Fax: 949 417-0261
Brian W Day, *President*
Jeff Cromwell, *COO*
Anthony Kendziorski, *Project Mgr*
Kevin Greenlee, *Engineer*
Kirk Bromberg, *Business Mgr*
EMP: 70
SALES (est): 12MM **Privately Held**
WEB: www.mercurytechnology.com
SIC: **7374** Data processing & preparation

(P-16161)
MESSAGESOLUTION INC
1851 Mccarthy Blvd # 105, Milpitas (95035-7448)
PHONE..................................408 383-0100
Jing Liang, *Branch Mgr*
EMP: 86
SALES (corp-wide): 3MM **Privately Held**
SIC: **7374** Data processing & preparation
PA: Messagesolution, Inc.
1851 Mccarthy Blvd # 105
Milpitas CA 95035
408 383-0100

(P-16162)
MICRO HOLDING CORP
1 Maritime Plz Fl 12, San Francisco (94111-3502)
PHONE..................................415 788-5111
Warren Hellman, *President*
EMP: 650
SALES (corp-wide): 17.9MM
SALES (corp-wide): 2.4B **Privately Held**
SIC: **7374** 7389 Computer graphics service; advertising, promotional & trade show services
PA: Hellman & Friedman Llc
1 Maritime Plz Fl 12
San Francisco CA 94111
415 788-5111

(P-16163)
MOCANA CORPORATION
20 California St Ste 400, San Francisco (94111-4832)
PHONE..................................415 617-0055
Fax: 415 617-0056
James Isaacs, *CEO*
Sandy Taylor, *CFO*
Pat Ivers, *Exec VP*
John Aisien, *Senior VP*
Alan Brenner, *Senior VP*
EMP: 96
SALES (est): 13.7MM **Privately Held**
WEB: www.mocana.com
SIC: **7374** 7379 Computer graphics service;

(P-16164)
MOCEAN LLC
2440 S Sepulveda Blvd # 150, Los Angeles (90064-1786)
PHONE..................................310 481-0808
Fax: 310 481-0807
Craig R Murray, *Mng Member*
Michael McIntyre, *President*
Roshone Harmon, *Vice Pres*
Alan Ireland, *Vice Pres*
Adam Rosenblatt, *Vice Pres*
EMP: 200 EST: 2000
SALES (est): 28MM **Privately Held**
SIC: **7374** 7822 Computer graphics service; motion picture distribution

(P-16165)
NASDAQ INFORMATION TECH CTR
1000 23rd Ave Bldg 2, Port Hueneme (93043-4300)
PHONE..................................805 982-2707
Al Hauwert, *Manager*
Penny Pentecost, *Comp Spec*
Joseph Wilson, *Comp Spec*
EMP: 85 EST: 1999
SALES (est): 2.7MM **Privately Held**
SIC: **7374** Computer processing services

(P-16166)
OERLIKON USA INC
18881 Von Karman Ave # 200, Irvine (92612-1500)
PHONE..................................949 863-1857
Alfred Wein, *Manager*
Mark Gore, *President*
Charles Palmer, *Vice Pres*
EMP: 65
SQ FT: 39,400
SALES (est): 5.7MM **Privately Held**
SIC: **7374** Data processing service

(P-16167)
OSHYN INC
200 Pine Ave Ste 503, Long Beach (90802-3040)
PHONE..................................213 483-1770
Diego Rebosio, *CEO*
Marcello Davalos, *Senior Engr*
EMP: 75
SQ FT: 1,500
SALES (est): 4MM **Privately Held**
WEB: www.oshyn.com
SIC: **7374** Computer graphics service

(P-16168)
PINE DATA PROCESSING INC
Also Called: Pine Company
10559 Jefferson Blvd, Culver City (90232-3526)
P.O. Box 641836, Los Angeles (90064-6836)
PHONE..................................310 815-5700
Fax: 310 815-5599
Ben Pine, *Chairman*
Ken Holsenbeck, *President*
Daniel H Dickson, *CFO*
Carol Lewis, *Vice Pres*
Lynn Blackburn, *MIS Staff*
EMP: 72
SQ FT: 11,500
SALES (est): 3.9MM **Privately Held**
WEB: www.pinedata.com
SIC: **7374** Data processing service

(P-16169)
PLANET LABS INC
Also Called: Cosmogia
346 9th St, San Francisco (94103-3809)
PHONE..................................415 829-3313
William Marshall, *CEO*
Robert Schingler Jr, *President*
Tom Barton, *COO*
Richard Leshner, *General Mgr*
Raymond Murillo, *Administration*
EMP: 150
SQ FT: 25,000
SALES (est): 5.8MM **Privately Held**
SIC: **7374** Data processing service

(P-16170)
PLEX SYSTEMS INC
4305 Hacienda Dr Ste 500, Pleasanton (94588-8586)
PHONE..................................248 391-8001
EMP: 196 **Privately Held**
SIC: **7374** Data processing & preparation
PA: Plex Systems, Inc.
900 Tower Dr Ste 1400
Troy MI 48098

(P-16171)
PRICEMETRIX USA INC
3 Bridgeport Rd, Newport Coast (92657-1014)
PHONE..................................714 357-6192
Brent Geddes, *CFO*
Doug Trott, *President*
EMP: 50
SALES (est): 1.5MM **Privately Held**
SIC: **7374** Data processing service

7374 - Data & Computer Processing & Preparation County (P-16172)

(P-16172)
PROSUM INC (PA)
Also Called: Prosum Technology Services
2321 Rosecrans Ave # 4225, El Segundo (90245-4958)
PHONE.................310 404-1545
Ravi Chatwani, *CEO*
John Petri, *CFO*
Ken Aster, *Vice Pres*
Anne Ponzio, *Vice Pres*
Josh Tofteland, *Vice Pres*
EMP: 57 **EST:** 1996
SALES (est): 37.1MM **Privately Held**
WEB: www.prosum.com
SIC: 7374 8748 Data processing & preparation; systems engineering consultant, ex. computer or professional

(P-16173)
PROTOSOURCE CORPORATION
2511 W Shaw Ave Ste 102, Fresno (93711-3325)
PHONE.................559 490-8600
Fax: 559 448-8050
Andy Chu, *Principal*
EMP: 54
SALES (corp-wide): 8.8MM **Publicly Held**
SIC: 7374 Data processing service
PA: Protosource Corporation
1236 Main St Ste 3
Hellertown PA 18055
610 814-0550

(P-16174)
QUALITY INVESTMENT SANTA CLARA
2807 Mission College Blvd, Santa Clara (95054-1838)
PHONE.................408 844-6000
Chad Williams, *CEO*
EMP: 55
SALES (est): 352K
SALES (corp-wide): 311MM **Privately Held**
SIC: 7374 Data processing & preparation
HQ: Qualitytech, Lp
12851 Foster St
Overland Park KS 66213
877 787-3282

(P-16175)
QUESTUS INC (PA)
675 Davis St, San Francisco (94111-1903)
PHONE.................415 677-5700
Fax: 415 677-9517
Jordan Berg, *CEO*
Linda Berliant, *Controller*
Maya Karmanova, *Controller*
EMP: 50
SQ FT: 4,000
SALES (est): 15.6MM **Privately Held**
WEB: www.questus.com
SIC: 7374 Computer graphics service

(P-16176)
RAINBOW NETWORKING
Also Called: E-Move Express
688 Matsonia Dr, Foster City (94404-1337)
PHONE.................650 377-0913
Anthony Chie, *Owner*
EMP: 55
SALES: 2MM **Privately Held**
SIC: 7374 Data processing & preparation

(P-16177)
REGULUS GROUP LLC (DH)
Also Called: Regulus West
860 Latour Ct, NAPA (94558-6258)
PHONE.................707 259-7100
Lynn Boggs, *Mng Member*
Adrian Gonzalez, *Sr Corp Ofcr*
Howard Mergelkamp, *Vice Pres*
Scott Henry, *Executive*
Darlene Devault, *Creative Dir*
EMP: 175
SALES (est): 196.6MM
SALES (corp-wide): 1.8B **Privately Held**
SIC: 7374 Data processing service
HQ: Transcentra, Inc.
4855 Peachtree Industrial
Berkeley Lake GA 30092
678 728-2500

(P-16178)
RESEARCH OF AMERICA
1232 Q St Ste 100, Sacramento (95811-5801)
PHONE.................916 443-4722
Fax: 916 443-3829
Rob Porber, *Owner*
Robert Proctor, *Vice Pres*
EMP: 135
SQ FT: 7,300
SALES (est): 8.2MM **Privately Held**
WEB: www.emhopinions.com
SIC: 7374 Data verification service

(P-16179)
ROCKSTAR SAN DIEGO
2200 Faraday Ave Ste 200, Carlsbad (92008-7233)
PHONE.................760 929-0700
Allan Wasserman, *President*
Eugene Foss, *Prgrmr*
Chris Wells, *Finance*
Kelly Gibson, *Human Res Dir*
EMP: 125
SQ FT: 24,000
SALES (est): 7.6MM
SALES (corp-wide): 1.4B **Publicly Held**
WEB: www.rockstarsandiego.com
SIC: 7374 7372 Computer graphics service; prepackaged software
PA: Take-Two Interactive Software, Inc.
622 Broadway Fl 6
New York NY 10012
646 536-2842

(P-16180)
SAN DIEGO DATA PROC CORP INC
202 C St Fl 3, San Diego (92101-4806)
PHONE.................858 581-9600
Fax: 858 581-9606
Larry Morgan, *CEO*
Reed Vickerman, *Ch of Bd*
Mary Erlenborn, *CFO*
Bill Martin, *Officer*
Linda Brogdon, *Admin Asst*
EMP: 130
SQ FT: 40,000
SALES: 461.2K **Privately Held**
SIC: 7374 Data processing service
PA: City Of San Diego
202 C St
San Diego CA 92101
619 236-6330

(P-16181)
SANRISE INC
7950 Dublin Blvd Ste 101, Dublin (94568-2936)
PHONE.................925 560-3900
EMP: 160 **EST:** 2000
SQ FT: 13,000
SALES (est): 18.7MM **Privately Held**
SIC: 7374

(P-16182)
SANTA CRUZ COUNTY OF
Also Called: Information Services
701 Ocean St Rm 530, Santa Cruz (95060-4015)
PHONE.................831 454-2030
Kevin Bowling, *Director*
Don Bussey, *Project Mgr*
Jan Beautz, *VP Mktg*
EMP: 70 **Privately Held**
WEB: www.scsheriff.com
SIC: 7374 Computer processing services
PA: County Of Santa Cruz
701 Ocean St Rm 520
Santa Cruz CA 95060
831 454-2100

(P-16183)
SECURE ONE DATA SOLUTIONS LLC
11090 Artesia Blvd Ste D, Cerritos (90703-2545)
PHONE.................562 924-7056
David Sandobal, *President*
Dave Sandoval, *Software Dev*
EMP: 50
SALES (corp-wide): 14.4MM **Privately Held**
SIC: 7374 Data punch service; data processing service
PA: Secure One Data Solutions, Llc
2801 N 33rd Ave Ste 1
Phoenix AZ 85009
602 415-1111

(P-16184)
SENDGRID INC
814 W Chapman Ave, Orange (92868-2823)
PHONE.................888 985-7363
EMP: 92
SALES (corp-wide): 69.4MM **Privately Held**
SIC: 7374 Data processing service
PA: Sendgrid, Inc.
1401 Walnut St Ste 500
Boulder CO 80302
303 552-0653

(P-16185)
SHOPPINGCOM INC
8000 Marina Blvd Ste 500, Brisbane (94005-1886)
PHONE.................650 616-6500
Gautam Thakar, *CEO*
Amir Ashkenazi, *President*
Hendrik Krampe, *CFO*
Robert J Krolik, *CFO*
Lance Podell, *Vice Pres*
EMP: 230 **EST:** 1997
SALES (est): 23.4MM **Publicly Held**
SIC: 7374 Data processing & preparation
PA: Ebay Inc.
2065 Hamilton Ave
San Jose CA 95125

(P-16186)
SIGNALFX INC
60 E 3rd Ave Ste 400, San Mateo (94401-4098)
PHONE.................888 958-5950
Karthik Rau, *CEO*
Heidi Olson, *Executive Asst*
Phillip Liu, *CTO*
EMP: 50
SALES (est): 28.5K **Privately Held**
SIC: 7374 Data processing & preparation

(P-16187)
SIGOS LLC (HQ)
Also Called: Keynote Systems
777 Mariners Island Blvd, San Mateo (94404-5008)
PHONE.................650 376-3033
Fax: 650 403-5500
John Van Siclen, *CEO*
Curtis Smith, *CFO*
Ken Stillwell, *CFO*
Nick Halsey, *Chief Mktg Ofcr*
Simon Huang, *Chief Mktg Ofcr*
EMP: 148
SQ FT: 183,000
SALES (est): 144.5MM **Privately Held**
WEB: www.keynote.com
SIC: 7374 7373 Data processing & preparation; computer system selling services
PA: Hawaii Parent Corp.
600 Montgomery St Fl 32
San Francisco CA 94111
415 263-3660

(P-16188)
SILICONEXPERT TECHNOLOGIES
2975 Scott Blvd Ste 100, Santa Clara (95054-3314)
PHONE.................408 330-7575
Omar Ahmad, *President*
Jeffrey Williams, *Vice Pres*
Bobby Holbrook, *General Mgr*
Ahmad Salama, *Engineer*
Erika Abella, *Director*
EMP: 50
SQ FT: 1,800
SALES (est): 4.9MM
SALES (corp-wide): 23.2B **Publicly Held**
SIC: 7374 Computer graphics service
PA: Arrow Electronics, Inc.
9201 E Dry Creek Rd
Centennial CO 80112
303 824-4000

(P-16189)
SOCIABLE LABS INC
25 Division St, San Mateo (94402)
PHONE.................415 225-8740
Naifan Gabbay, *President*
Peter O'Leary, *Vice Pres*
Ramil Nobleza, *Software Engr*
James Donelan, *VP Engrg*
Jeff Steiner, *Accounting Mgr*
EMP: 50
SQ FT: 1,500
SALES: 3MM **Privately Held**
SIC: 7374 Computer graphics service

(P-16190)
SOCIETY6 LLC
1655 26th St, Santa Monica (90404-4016)
PHONE.................310 394-6400
Sean Moriarty,
Patrick Schwarz, *Manager*
EMP: 50
SQ FT: 25,000
SALES (est): 1.7MM
SALES (corp-wide): 125.9MM **Publicly Held**
SIC: 7374 Data processing & preparation
PA: Demand Media, Inc.
1655 26th St
Santa Monica CA 90404
310 656-6253

(P-16191)
SONY PICTURES IMAGEWORKS INC
9050 Washington Blvd, Culver City (90232-2518)
PHONE.................310 840-8000
Bob Osher, *President*
Ken Ralston, *President*
David C Hendler, *Sr Exec VP*
Leah Weil, *Sr Exec VP*
Pam Marsden, *Exec VP*
EMP: 1000 **EST:** 1992
SALES (est): 98.4MM
SALES (corp-wide): 69.2B **Privately Held**
WEB: www.sonypictures.com
SIC: 7374 Computer graphics service
HQ: Sony Pictures Entertainment, Inc.
10202 Washington Blvd
Culver City CA 90232
310 244-4000

(P-16192)
SOUTHBAY WEBSITE DESIGN LLC
Also Called: Phone App Company, The
1601 Pcf Cast Hwy Ste 290, Hermosa Beach (90254)
PHONE.................310 370-4043
Allen Rubin,
EMP: 60
SQ FT: 250
SALES: 500K **Privately Held**
SIC: 7374 7371 Computer graphics service; computer software development & applications

(P-16193)
STARK SERVICES
12444 Victory Blvd # 300, North Hollywood (91606-3173)
PHONE.................818 985-2003
Fax: 818 985-1213
Maricel Zabel, *President*
Steve Pugh, *Vice Pres*
EMP: 75
SALES (est): 5.6MM **Privately Held**
WEB: www.starkservices.com
SIC: 7374 Data processing service

(P-16194)
STUBHUB INC (HQ)
Also Called: Stubhub.com
199 Fremont St Fl 4, San Francisco (94105-6634)
PHONE.................415 222-8400
Fax: 415 222-8552
Chris Tsakalakis, *President*
Noah Goldberg, *COO*
Ajay Gopal, *CFO*
Jennifer Betka, *Chief Mktg Ofcr*
Raji Arasu, *Vice Pres*
EMP: 140
SQ FT: 20,000

PRODUCTS & SERVICES SECTION
7375 - Information Retrieval Svcs County (P-16216)

SALES (est): 87.4MM **Publicly Held**
SIC: 7374 7999 7922 Data processing & preparation; ticket sales office for sporting events, contract; ticket agency, theatrical

(P-16195)
SUPPORTCOM INC (PA)
900 Chesapeake Dr Fl 2, Redwood City (94063-4727)
PHONE..............................650 556-9440
Elizabeth M Cholawsky, *President*
Jim Stephens, *Ch of Bd*
Roop Lakkaraju, *COO*
Robert C Barnum, *Senior VP*
Shaun Donnelly, *Senior VP*
EMP: 202
SQ FT: 21,620
SALES: 77.3MM **Publicly Held**
WEB: www.supportsoft.com
SIC: 7374 7372 Data processing & preparation; business oriented computer software

(P-16196)
TASKUS INC
3233 Donald, Santa Monica (90405)
PHONE..............................888 400-8275
Bryce Maddock, *CEO*
Jaspar Weir, *President*
Balaji Sekar, *CFO*
Lital Gilad-Shaoulian, *Senior VP*
Michael Epsenhart, *Surgery Dir*
EMP: 5000
SQ FT: 17,000
SALES (est): 854.9K **Privately Held**
SIC: 7374 Data processing service

(P-16197)
TEALIUM INC
11085 Torreyana Rd Fl 2, San Diego (92121-1104)
PHONE..............................858 779-1344
Jeffrey W Lunsford, *CEO*
Ali Behnam, *President*
Doug Lindroth, *CFO*
Tracy Hansen, *Chief Mktg Ofcr*
Ty Gavin, *Vice Pres*
EMP: 198
SQ FT: 4,000
SALES: 20MM **Privately Held**
SIC: 7374 7371 Computer graphics service; computer software development

(P-16198)
TECHNOLOGY SERVICES CAL DEPT
Also Called: Teale Data Center
10860 Gold Center Dr # 100, Rancho Cordova (95670-6024)
P.O. Box 1810 (95741-1810)
PHONE..............................916 464-3747
Fax: 916 464-4025
Carlos Ramos, *Exec Dir*
Dennis Barbough, *Director*
EMP: 50 **Privately Held**
WEB: www.osi.ca.gov
SIC: 7374 9199 Data processing & preparation; general government administration;
HQ: California Department Of Technology Services
1325 J St Ste 1600
Sacramento CA 95814
916 319-9223

(P-16199)
TECHNOSOCIALWORKCOM LLC
Also Called: Stria
4300 Resnik Ct Unit 103, Bakersfield (93313-4836)
P.O. Box 21660 (93390-1660)
PHONE..............................661 617-6601
Fax: 661 215-5097
Jim Damian, *Mng Member*
Robert Cleveland, *General Mgr*
Julie Seaberg, *Office Mgr*
Nick Billingsley, *Production*
Scott Garrison, *VP Sales*
EMP: 75
SQ FT: 10,000
SALES (est): 9.6MM **Privately Held**
WEB: www.goodsamaritanhospital.net
SIC: 7374 Data processing & preparation

(P-16200)
TELOGIS INC (DH)
20 Enterprise Ste 100, Aliso Viejo (92656-7104)
PHONE..............................949 389-5500
Ralph Mason, *CTO*
Jason Koch, *President*
A Newth Morris IV, *President*
Susan Heystee, *Exec VP*
Chris Belden, *Senior VP*
EMP: 150 EST: 2001
SQ FT: 55,700
SALES: 89MM
SALES (corp-wide): 131.6B **Publicly Held**
WEB: www.telogis.com
SIC: 7374 Data processing & preparation
HQ: Verizon Telematics Inc.
2002 Summit Blvd Ste 1800
Brookhaven GA 30319
404 573-5800

(P-16201)
TERIS LLC
600 W Broadway Ste 300, San Diego (92101-3352)
PHONE..............................619 231-3282
Adam Wells, *Branch Mgr*
EMP: 50
SALES (corp-wide): 7.7MM **Privately Held**
SIC: 7374 Data processing & preparation
PA: Teris, Llc
2455 Faber Pl Ste 200
Palo Alto CA 94303
650 213-9922

(P-16202)
TRIFACTA INC
575 Market St Fl 11, San Francisco (94105-5816)
PHONE..............................415 429-7570
Adam Wilson, *CEO*
Sachin Chawla, *President*
Stephanie McReynolds, *Vice Pres*
Dan Niemann, *Vice Pres*
WEI Zheng, *Vice Pres*
EMP: 95
SQ FT: 3,000
SALES (est): 2.2MM **Privately Held**
SIC: 7374 7379 Data processing & preparation; data processing consultant

(P-16203)
TRULIA INC (HQ)
535 Mission St Fl 7, San Francisco (94105-3223)
PHONE..............................415 648-4358
Peter Flint, *CEO*
Lloyd Frink, *President*
Paul Levine, *COO*
Prashant Aggarwal, *CFO*
Larry Illg, *Vice Pres*
EMP: 357
SQ FT: 32,000
SALES: 251.9MM
SALES (corp-wide): 644.6MM **Publicly Held**
SIC: 7374 Data processing & preparation
PA: Zillow Group, Inc.
1301 2nd Ave Fl 31
Seattle WA 98101
206 470-7000

(P-16204)
UCC DIRECT SERVICES INC
330 N Brand Blvd Ste 700, Glendale (91203-2336)
PHONE..............................818 662-4100
Fax: 818 662-4141
Walt Powell, *President*
EMP: 80
SALES (est): 2.4MM **Privately Held**
WEB: www.uccdirectservices.com
SIC: 7374 Data processing service

(P-16205)
UNITAS GLOBAL LLC (PA)
453 S Spring St Ste 201, Los Angeles (90013-2566)
PHONE..............................213 785-6200
Patrick Shutt, *CEO*
Bob Pollan, *COO*
Grant A Kirkwood, *Founder*
Farrah Kashef, *Vice Pres*
Steve Neiger, *Risk Mgmt Dir*

EMP: 54 EST: 2009
SQ FT: 9,000
SALES (est): 42.2MM **Privately Held**
SIC: 7374 Service bureau, computer

(P-16206)
UNIVERSITY CAL SAN DIEGO
Also Called: San Diego Supercomputer Center
10100 Hopkins Dr, La Jolla (92093-0001)
P.O. Box 85608, San Diego (92186-5608)
PHONE..............................858 534-5000
Fax: 858 534-5113
Michael Norman, *Director*
Barbara Carsteens, *Vice Pres*
John Helly, *Lab Dir*
Warren Froelich, *Exec Dir*
Michelle Feiock, *Program Mgr*
EMP: 300 **Privately Held**
WEB: www.generalatomics.com
SIC: 7374 8731 Data processing & preparation; commercial physical research
HQ: University Of California, San Diego
9500 Gilman Dr
La Jolla CA 92093
858 534-2230

(P-16207)
USA VILY GROUP
4301 Valley Blvd Ste D2, Los Angeles (90032-3632)
PHONE..............................323 457-6888
Yuka Chong, *Owner*
EMP: 50
SALES: 5MM **Privately Held**
SIC: 7374 Computer graphics service

(P-16208)
VITESSE LLC
1601 Willow Rd, Menlo Park (94025-1452)
PHONE..............................650 543-4800
Christopher R Gardner, *CEO*
EMP: 3000
SALES (est): 49.9MM
SALES (corp-wide): 17.9B **Publicly Held**
SIC: 7374 Data processing service
PA: Facebook, Inc.
1 Hacker Way Bldg 10
Menlo Park CA 94025
650 543-4800

(P-16209)
VOICE MAIL BROADCASTING CORP
Also Called: Vmbc
5 Columbia, Aliso Viejo (92656-1460)
PHONE..............................714 437-0600
Jesse Crowe, *CEO*
Melinda Chelliah, *CFO*
Andrea Atef, *Executive*
Diego Kellner, *Opers Staff*
Molly Patterson, *Manager*
EMP: 76
SALES (est): 7.6MM **Privately Held**
SIC: 7374 Service bureau, computer

(P-16210)
VOICE PRINT INTERNATIONAL INC (PA)
Also Called: V P I
160 Camino Ruiz, Camarillo (93012-6700)
PHONE..............................805 389-5200
Fax: 805 389-5202
Andrew D Marsh, *CEO*
Patrick Botz, *Vice Pres*
Darryl Corrigan, *Vice Pres*
Stephen O'Neil, *Vice Pres*
Stephen O'Neile, *Vice Pres*
EMP: 53
SALES (est): 23.9MM **Privately Held**
SIC: 7374 7389 Data processing & preparation; recording studio, noncommercial records

(P-16211)
WYLE INFORMATION SYSTEMS LLC
1960 E Grand Ave Ste 900, El Segundo (90245-5092)
PHONE..............................310 563-6694
Robert Gullinese, *Administration*
EMP: 77
SALES (corp-wide): 5.1B **Publicly Held**
SIC: 7374 Data processing & preparation

HQ: Wyle Information Systems, Llc
1600 Intl Dr Ste 800
Mc Lean VA 22102

(P-16212)
XEROX EDUCATION SERVICES LLC (DH)
2277 E 220th St, Long Beach (90810-1639)
PHONE..............................310 830-9847
Fax: 310 847-5052
J Michael Peffer, *Mng Member*
Lynn Blodgett, *COO*
John Fassbender, *Vice Pres*
Imelda Julian, *Vice Pres*
Bill Krouss, *Vice Pres*
EMP: 90 EST: 1970
SALES (est): 111.8MM
SALES (corp-wide): 18B **Publicly Held**
WEB: www.acseducationservices.com
SIC: 7374 Data processing service
HQ: Xerox Business Services, Llc
2828 N Haskell Ave Fl 1
Dallas TX 75204
214 841-6111

(P-16213)
ZEPHYR HEALTH INC
450 Mission St Ste 201, San Francisco (94105-2513)
PHONE..............................415 529-7649
William King, *President*
Sven Junkergard, *Info Tech Dir*
Clifford Tham, *Software Engr*
Aaron Chaiclin, *Director*
Darren Farrugia, *Director*
EMP: 68
SALES (est): 798.9K **Privately Held**
SIC: 7374 Data processing & preparation

7375 Information Retrieval Svcs

(P-16214)
ACCESS INFO MGT SHRED SVCS LLC (PA)
Also Called: Rhinodox
6818 Patterson Pass Rd A, Livermore (94550-4230)
PHONE..............................925 461-5352
Rob Alston, *CEO*
John Chendo, *President*
Nathan Campbell, *COO*
Judd Feldman, *CFO*
Tony Skarupa, *CFO*
EMP: 50
SQ FT: 16,000
SALES: 12MM **Privately Held**
SIC: 7375 Information retrieval services

(P-16215)
ACCURATE BACKGROUND LLC
Also Called: Selectforce
7515 Irvine Center Dr, Irvine (92618-2930)
PHONE..............................800 784-3911
Fax: 949 609-0166
David C Dickerson, *CEO*
Tim Dowd, *President*
Simon Raff, *COO*
Piero Broccardo, *CFO*
Aaron Charbonnet, *Senior VP*
EMP: 315
SQ FT: 58,649
SALES: 44.8MM **Privately Held**
WEB: www.accuratebackground.com
SIC: 7375 Information retrieval services

(P-16216)
ACXIOM CORPORATION
100 Redwood Shores Pkwy, Redwood City (94065-1155)
PHONE..............................650 356-3400
Michael Gorman, *Senior VP*
Scott Prather, *Administration*
Julie Harty, *Engineer*
Linda Moore, *Manager*
EMP: 72
SALES (corp-wide): 850MM **Publicly Held**
SIC: 7375 Information retrieval services

7375 - Information Retrieval Svcs County (P-16217)

PA: Acxiom Corporation
601 E 3rd St
Little Rock AR 72201
501 342-1000

(P-16217)
AMBULNZ HEALTH LLC
12527 Vanowen St, North Hollywood
(91605-5321)
PHONE 310 968-3999
Andre Oberholzer, *CFO*
EMP: 75
SALES (est): 1MM **Privately Held**
SIC: 7375 4119 Information retrieval services; ambulance service

(P-16218)
AUTOBYTEL INC (PA)
18872 Macarthur Blvd # 200, Irvine
(92612-1448)
PHONE 949 225-4500
Fax: 949 225-4541
Jeffrey H Coats, *President*
Michael J Fuchs, *Ch of Bd*
Kimberly S Boren, *CFO*
John M Markovich, *CFO*
Lee Sage, *Officer*
EMP: 133
SQ FT: 26,000
SALES: 133.2MM **Publicly Held**
WEB: www.autobytel.com
SIC: 7375 Information retrieval services; on-line data base information retrieval

(P-16219)
AUTOWEBCOM INC
18872 Macarthur Blvd, Irvine (92612-1408)
PHONE 949 862-1371
Jeffrey Schwartz, *CEO*
Hoshi Printer, *CFO*
Ariel Amir, *Exec VP*
EMP: 297
SQ FT: 40,000
SALES (est): 7.5MM **Publicly Held**
WEB: www.autoweb.com
SIC: 7375 On-line data base information retrieval
PA: Autobytel Inc.
18872 Macarthur Blvd # 200
Irvine CA 92612

(P-16220)
BAYNOTE INC
333 W San Carlos St # 700, San Jose
(95110-2711)
PHONE 866 921-0919
Fax: 408 973-9484
Doug Merritt, *President*
Dario Calia, *President*
John Kelly, *COO*
Anurag Wadehra, *Chief Mktg Ofcr*
Mike Backlund, *Senior VP*
EMP: 55
SALES (est): 7.7MM
SALES (corp-wide): 52.1MM **Privately Held**
SIC: 7375 Information retrieval services
PA: Kibo Software, Inc.
717 N Harwood St Ste 1800
Dallas TX 75201
707 780-1600

(P-16221)
BROWSERCAM
915 Cole St Ste 220, San Francisco
(94117-4315)
PHONE 415 378-6936
John Witchel, *President*
EMP: 243
SALES (est): 73.9K
SALES (corp-wide): 1.4B **Privately Held**
WEB: www.gomez.com
SIC: 7375 Information retrieval services
HQ: Gomez, Inc.
10 Maguire Rd Ste 250
Lexington MA
781 778-2700

(P-16222)
CHANGEORG INC
383 Rhode Island St Fl 3, San Francisco
(94103-5178)
PHONE 415 817-1840
Benj Rattay, *CEO*
Jennifer Dulski, *President*

Benj Rattray, *CEO*
Amanda Levy, *Vice Pres*
Ellen Krouss, *Business Dir*
EMP: 250
SQ FT: 10,000
SALES: 22MM **Privately Held**
SIC: 7375 On-line data base information retrieval

(P-16223)
COMPS INC
4535 Towne Centre Ct, San Diego
(92121-1900)
PHONE 858 658-0576
Andrew Florance, *President*
Craig Farrington, *COO*
Brian Radecki, *CFO*
Kerry Vierra, *Human Res Dir*
EMP: 175
SALES (est): 6MM
SALES (corp-wide): 711.7MM **Publicly Held**
SIC: 7375 Information retrieval services
PA: Costar Group, Inc.
1331 L St Nw Ste 2
Washington DC 20005
202 346-6500

(P-16224)
CONVERSANT LLC (HQ)
30699 Russell Ranch Rd # 250, Westlake Village (91362-7319)
PHONE 818 575-4500
John Giuliani, *President*
Oded Benyo, *President*
David Yovanno, *COO*
John Pitstick, *CFO*
Scott Eagle, *Chief Mktg Ofcr*
EMP: 148
SQ FT: 41,500
SALES: 573.1MM
SALES (corp-wide): 6.4B **Publicly Held**
WEB: www.valueclick.com
SIC: 7375 4813 On-line data base information retrieval;
PA: Alliance Data Systems Corporation
7500 Dallas Pkwy Ste 700
Plano TX 75024
214 494-3000

(P-16225)
CORVENTIS INC (PA)
2033 Gateway Pl Ste 100, San Jose
(95110-3713)
PHONE 408 790-9300
John Russell, *President*
Abhi Chavan, *Vice Pres*
Kathy Lundberg, *Vice Pres*
Murali Srivathsa, *Vice Pres*
Vijaya Kuppa, *Manager*
EMP: 76
SALES (est): 17.3MM **Privately Held**
SIC: 7375 Information retrieval services

(P-16226)
COUNTY OF LOS ANGELES
Also Called: Chief Executive Office
500 W Temple St Ste 493, Los Angeles
(90012-2723)
PHONE 213 974-1102
Fax: 310 626-6941
William T Fujioka, *CEO*
Frank Cheng, *Associate*
EMP: 7000 **Privately Held**
WEB: www.co.la.ca.us
SIC: 7375 9131 Information retrieval services;
PA: County Of Los Angeles
500 W Temple St Ste 375
Los Angeles CA 90012
213 974-1101

(P-16227)
DIGITAL INSIGHT CORPORATION
5601 Lindero Canyon Rd # 100, Westlake Village (91362-6494)
PHONE 818 879-1010
Paul Nieman, *Principal*
Debbie Walker, *Executive*
Paul Mitsuuchi, *Administration*
Atif Alam, *Info Tech Dir*
Mike Medina, *MIS Mgr*
EMP: 150

SALES (corp-wide): 6.3B **Publicly Held**
WEB: www.digitalinsight.com
SIC: 7375 Information retrieval services
HQ: Digital Insight Corporation
1300 Seaport Blvd Ste 300
Redwood City CA 94063

(P-16228)
DIGITAL INSIGHT CORPORATION (HQ)
Also Called: Intuit Financial Services
1300 Seaport Blvd Ste 300, Redwood City
(94063-5591)
PHONE 818 879-1010
Fax: 818 878-7555
Jeffrey E Stiefler, *President*
Joseph M McDoniel, *Exec VP*
Tom Shen, *Exec VP*
Vincent R Brennan, *Senior VP*
Robert R Surridge, *Senior VP*
EMP: 200
SQ FT: 46,000
SALES (est): 202.4MM
SALES (corp-wide): 6.3B **Publicly Held**
WEB: www.digitalinsight.com
SIC: 7375 7372 7371 Information retrieval services; prepackaged software; custom computer programming services
PA: Ncr Corporation
3097 Satellite Blvd # 100
Duluth GA 30096
937 445-5000

(P-16229)
DRIVESAVERS INC
Also Called: Drivesavers Data Recovery
400 Bel Marin Keys Blvd, Novato
(94949-5642)
PHONE 415 382-2000
Fax: 415 883-0780
Jay Hagan, *CEO*
Scott Moyer, *President*
Jacqueline Cunningham, *Executive*
Michael Hall, *CIO*
Rich Ambrise, *Info Tech Dir*
EMP: 90
SQ FT: 4,400
SALES: 20MM **Privately Held**
WEB: www.drivesavers.com
SIC: 7375 Information retrieval services

(P-16230)
E-TIMES CORPORATION LTD
601 S Figueroa St # 5000, Los Angeles
(90017-3883)
PHONE 213 452-6720
Chiharu Nakahara, *President*
EMP: 300
SALES (est): 12.5MM **Privately Held**
WEB: www.etimesltd.com
SIC: 7375 7374 8742 Information retrieval services; computer graphics service; administrative services consultant

(P-16231)
EDMUNDS HOLDING COMPANY (PA)
Also Called: Edmunds.com
1620 26th St Ste 400s, Santa Monica
(90404-4063)
PHONE 310 309-6300
AVI Steinlauf, *CEO*
Seth Berkowitz, *President*
Charles Farrell, *CFO*
Laura Perlman, *Vice Pres*
Megan Jay, *Associate Dir*
EMP: 350
SALES (est): 102.1MM **Privately Held**
SIC: 7375 Information retrieval services

(P-16232)
ELAVON INC
1281 9th Ave Unit 706, San Diego
(92101-4645)
PHONE 954 776-7990
Kimberly Layton, *Manager*
EMP: 514
SALES (corp-wide): 21.4B **Publicly Held**
SIC: 7375 Information retrieval services
HQ: Elavon, Inc.
2 Cncourse Pkwy Ste 800
Atlanta GA 30328
678 731-5000

(P-16233)
ELAVON INC
4234 Hacienda Dr Ste 250, Pleasanton
(94588-2789)
PHONE 925 734-8939
Karen Sonobe, *Manager*
EMP: 400
SALES (corp-wide): 21.4B **Publicly Held**
SIC: 7375 Information retrieval services
HQ: Elavon, Inc.
2 Cncourse Pkwy Ste 800
Atlanta GA 30328
678 731-5000

(P-16234)
EMC CORPORATION
2101 Rosecrans Ave # 3200, El Segundo
(90245-7512)
PHONE 310 341-1600
Fax: 310 414-1625
Tina Thompson, *Owner*
David Harris, *Managing Dir*
Michael Fox, *Administration*
Steve Flor, *Engng Exec*
Sean Cardenas, *Sales Dir*
EMP: 50
SALES (corp-wide): 72.7B **Publicly Held**
WEB: www.emc.com
SIC: 7375 Data base information retrieval
HQ: Emc Corporation
176 South St
Hopkinton MA 01748
508 435-1000

(P-16235)
EXABLOX CORPORATION
1156 Sonora Ct, Sunnyvale (94086-5308)
PHONE 408 773-8477
Douglas Brockett, *CEO*
Ramesh Iyer Balan, *Vice Pres*
Shridar Subramanian, *Risk Mgmt Dir*
Tad Hunt, *CTO*
Ginger Perng, *Web Dvlpr*
EMP: 51 **EST:** 2010
SALES (est): 8.6MM **Privately Held**
SIC: 7375 Data base information retrieval

(P-16236)
FACEBOOK INC (PA)
1 Hacker Way Bldg 10, Menlo Park
(94025-1456)
PHONE 650 543-4800
Mark Zuckerberg, *Ch of Bd*
Sheryl K Sandberg, *COO*
Christopher K Cox, *Officer*
Ajay Shah, *Top Exec*
Jorissen Alexandra, *Vice Pres*
EMP: 800
SQ FT: 2,000,000
SALES: 17.9B **Publicly Held**
SIC: 7375 On-line data base information retrieval

(P-16237)
GLOBAL RISK MGT SOLUTIONS LLC
660 Nwport Ctr Dr Ste 600, Newport Beach
(92660)
PHONE 949 759-8500
Gerard Smith, *President*
Jeff Burkett, *Business Dir*
Joseph Fabiani, *Manager*
EMP: 200 **EST:** 2010
SQ FT: 2,700
SALES (est): 14MM **Privately Held**
SIC: 7375 Information retrieval services

(P-16238)
GO2 SYSTEMS INC
Also Called: Go2systems
18400 Von Karman Ave Fl 9, Irvine
(92612-1514)
PHONE 949 553-0800
Fax: 949 553-0088
S Lee Hancock, *President*
Scott Goldman, *COO*
Mark Buckner, *CFO*
Ward Kennedy, *CFO*
Michael Dobson, *Exec VP*
EMP: 75
SQ FT: 18,955
SALES (est): 3.2MM **Privately Held**
SIC: 7375 Information retrieval services

PRODUCTS & SERVICES SECTION   7375 - Information Retrieval Svcs County (P-16260)

(P-16239)
GOOGLE INC
1945 Charleston Rd, Mountain View
(94043-1201)
PHONE......................................650 253-7323
Ryan Spurlock, *Branch Mgr*
David Tam, *Network Enginr*
Tom REA, *Project Mgr*
Tony Fagan, *Director*
Mohit Kalra, *Associate*
EMP: 99
SALES (corp-wide): 74.9B **Publicly Held**
SIC: 7375 Information retrieval services; data base information retrieval; on-line data base information retrieval
HQ: Google Inc.
  1600 Amphitheatre Pkwy
  Mountain View CA 94043
  650 253-0000

(P-16240)
GOPLUS CORP
3900 E Philadelphia St, Ontario
(91761-2941)
PHONE......................................909 483-1220
WEI Wu, *CEO*
Juan Arista, *Principal*
Daniel A Bailey, *Principal*
Jose M Canchola, *Principal*
Sergio V Carillo, *Principal*
EMP: 60
SALES: 71.4MM **Privately Held**
SIC: 7375 On-line data base information retrieval
PA: Costway.Com, Inc
  3900 E Philadelphia St
  Ontario CA 91761
  909 483-1200

(P-16241)
GROUNDWORK OPEN SOURCE INC
333 Bryant St Ste 100, San Francisco
(94107-4103)
PHONE......................................415 992-4500
Dave Lilly, *CEO*
Alan Cooke, *Vice Pres*
Stuart Thompto, *Vice Pres*
Roger Ruttimann, *Sr Software Eng*
Hans Kriel, *Opers Staff*
EMP: 100
SQ FT: 15,000
SALES (est): 10.4MM
SALES (corp-wide): 12.5MM **Privately Held**
WEB: www.groundworkopensource.com
SIC: 7375 7371 On-line data base information retrieval; custom computer programming services
PA: Fox Technologies, Inc.
  3300 Eagle Run Dr Ne
  Grand Rapids MI
  -

(P-16242)
GUIDANCE SOLUTIONS INC
4134 Del Rey Ave, Marina Del Rey
(90292-5604)
PHONE......................................310 754-4000
Fax: 310 754-4010
Jason Meugniot, *CEO*
John Provisor, *President*
Mike Hill, *Exec VP*
Deborah Blackwell, *Vice Pres*
Jim Caldarola, *Vice Pres*
EMP: 50
SQ FT: 10,000
SALES (est): 10.2MM **Privately Held**
WEB: www.guidance.com
SIC: 7375 4813 Information retrieval services;

(P-16243)
HIRERIGHT LLC (HQ)
3349 Michelson Dr Ste 150, Irvine
(92612-8881)
PHONE......................................949 428-5800
Fax: 949 224-6020
John Fennelly, *CEO*
Brian Pierson, *COO*
Richard Little, *CFO*
Thomas Spaeth, *CFO*
Jim Weber, *Officer*
EMP: 148
SQ FT: 63,440

SALES (est): 287.3MM **Privately Held**
WEB: www.hireright.com
SIC: 7375 7374 Data base information retrieval; data verification service

(P-16244)
IAC SEARCH & MEDIA INC (HQ)
Also Called: Ask.com
555 12th St Ste 500, Oakland
(94607-3699)
PHONE......................................510 985-7400
Fax: 510 985-7412
Doug Leeds, *CEO*
Oliver Hill, *President*
George S Lichter, *President*
Shane McGilloway, *COO*
Dominic Butera, *CFO*
EMP: 200
SQ FT: 76,000
SALES (est): 148.9MM
SALES (corp-wide): 3.2B **Publicly Held**
WEB: www.ask.com
SIC: 7375 Information retrieval services
PA: Iac/Interactivecorp
  555 W 18th St
  New York NY 10011
  212 314-7300

(P-16245)
INSURANCE SERVICES OFFICE INC
388 Market St Ste 750, San Francisco
(94111-5352)
PHONE......................................415 874-4361
Jim Masek, *Branch Mgr*
Mark Bronson, *Accounts Mgr*
EMP: 326
SALES (corp-wide): 2B **Publicly Held**
SIC: 7375 Information retrieval services
HQ: Insurance Services Office, Inc.
  545 Washington Blvd Fl 12
  Jersey City NJ 07310
  201 469-2000

(P-16246)
INTERNET ARCHIVE
300 Funston Ave, San Francisco
(94118-2116)
PHONE......................................415 561-6767
Brewster Kahle, *Director*
Andy Bezella, *Administration*
Hunter Stern, *QA Dir*
Jeremy Anthony, *Software Engr*
Kelsey Hawley, *Software Engr*
EMP: 173
SALES: 12.5MM **Privately Held**
SIC: 7375 On-line data base information retrieval

(P-16247)
ISYNDICATE INC
455 9th St, San Francisco (94103-4410)
PHONE......................................415 896-1900
Joel Mask, *CEO*
Ann-Marie McGowan, *COO*
Steven Dietsch, *CFO*
Ralph Barhydt, *Senior VP*
Eric Kelly, *Senior VP*
EMP: 54
SALES (est): 3.3MM **Privately Held**
SIC: 7375 On-line data base information retrieval

(P-16248)
JEPPESEN DATAPLAN INC
225 W Santa Clara St # 1600, San Jose
(95113-1752)
PHONE......................................408 961-2825
Fax: 408 961-5362
Mark Van Tine, *President*
Jepson Fuller, *CFO*
Ann Bozeman, *Vice Pres*
Judy Graun, *Administration*
John Arensberg, *MIS Staff*
EMP: 118
SQ FT: 20,000
SALES (est): 8.8MM
SALES (corp-wide): 96.1MM **Publicly Held**
WEB: www.jetplan.com
SIC: 7375 Information retrieval services
HQ: Jeppesen Sanderson, Inc.
  55 Inverness Dr E
  Englewood CO 80112
  303 799-9090

(P-16249)
LINKEDIN CORPORATION (PA)
2029 Stierlin Ct Ste 200, Mountain View
(94043-4655)
PHONE......................................650 687-3600
Fax: 650 687-0505
Jeffrey Weiner, *CEO*
Reid Hoffman, *Ch of Bd*
Steven Sordello, *CFO*
Rick Monson, *Treasurer*
Jack Walsh, *Exec VP*
EMP: 124
SQ FT: 373,000
SALES: 2.9B **Publicly Held**
WEB: www.linkedin.com
SIC: 7375 On-line data base information retrieval

(P-16250)
LOGICMONITOR INC
12 E Carrillo St, Santa Barbara
(93101-2707)
PHONE......................................805 617-3884
Kevin McGibben, *CEO*
Steven Francis,
Yasmeen Farukh, *Executive*
Andrew Martin, *Admin Asst*
Jie Song, *CTO*
EMP: 85
SALES (est): 17.5MM **Privately Held**
SIC: 7375 Information retrieval services

(P-16251)
LOWERMYBILLS INC (HQ)
Also Called: Lowermybills.com
12181 Bluff Creek Dr, Playa Vista
(90094-2992)
PHONE......................................310 348-6800
Steve Krazer, *President*
Nancyjane Goldston, *Bd of Directors*
David Razavi, *Vice Pres*
Patricia Tobin, *Vice Pres*
Ricardo Espergue, *Software Dev*
EMP: 71
SALES (est): 45.8MM
SALES (corp-wide): 200MM **Privately Held**
SIC: 7375 Information retrieval services
PA: Cpl Holdings, Llc
  12181 Bluff Creek Dr # 250
  Playa Vista CA 90094
  310 348-6800

(P-16252)
PERFORMANT FINANCIAL CORP (PA)
333 N Canyons Pkwy # 100, Livermore
(94551-9478)
PHONE......................................925 960-4800
Lisa C Im, *Ch of Bd*
Michael Sullivan, *President*
Jeff Haughton, *COO*
Jeffrey R Haughton, *COO*
Hakan L Orvell, *CFO*
EMP: 128
SQ FT: 50,291
SALES: 159.3MM **Publicly Held**
WEB: www.performantcorp.com
SIC: 7375 Information retrieval services

(P-16253)
PINTEREST INC (PA)
808 Brannan St, San Francisco
(94103-4904)
PHONE......................................650 561-5407
Benjamin Silbermann, *CEO*
Evan Sharp, *Co-Founder*
Amanda Cusumano, *Executive Asst*
Kacy Meza-Ashley, *Executive Asst*
Derrick Diaz, *Administration*
EMP: 143 EST: 2008
SALES (est): 120.7MM **Privately Held**
SIC: 7375 On-line data base information retrieval

(P-16254)
QUALITY SPEAKS LLC
Also Called: Phonepower
9221 Corbin Ave Ste 260, Northridge
(91324-1625)
PHONE......................................818 264-4400
Jim Murphy, *CEO*
Sam Ghahremanpour, *President*
Shawn Jones, *President*
Doreen Paisano, *Accounting Mgr*
EMP: 140

SALES: 18MM **Privately Held**
SIC: 7375 Data base information retrieval

(P-16255)
QUORA INC
261 Hamilton Ave Ste 212, Palo Alto
(94301-2534)
PHONE......................................650 485-2464
Adam D Angelo, *CEO*
Steven Trieu, *CFO*
Charlie Cheever, *Principal*
Nadia Singer, *Recruiter*
Yair Livne, *Manager*
EMP: 50
SALES (est): 4MM **Privately Held**
SIC: 7375 Information retrieval services

(P-16256)
RELX INC
Also Called: Lexisnexis
555 W 5th St Ste 4500, Los Angeles
(90013-3003)
PHONE......................................213 627-1130
Fax: 213 683-8600
Tim Dawson, *Branch Mgr*
Jennifer Stevenson, *Mktg Dir*
Sharon T Crosby, *Sales Mgr*
Chris Chang, *Consultant*
EMP: 70
SALES (corp-wide): 9B **Privately Held**
WEB: www.lexis-nexis.com
SIC: 7375 Information retrieval services
HQ: Relx Inc.
  230 Park Ave
  New York NY 10169
  212 309-8100

(P-16257)
REPRINTS DESK INC
5435 Balboa Blvd Ste 202, Encino
(91316-1570)
PHONE......................................310 477-0354
Peter Derycz, *President*
Alan Urban, *CFO*
Atila Arel, *Project Leader*
Brock Andersen, *Technology*
Timothy Burleson, *Technology*
EMP: 92
SQ FT: 2,500
SALES (est): 28.5MM
SALES (corp-wide): 34.3MM **Publicly Held**
SIC: 7375 Information retrieval services
PA: Research Solutions, Inc.
  5435 Balboa Blvd Ste 202
  Encino CA 91316
  310 477-0354

(P-16258)
RESEARCH LIBRARIES GROUP INC
Also Called: R L G
777 Mariners Island Blvd # 550, San Mateo
(94404-5048)
PHONE......................................650 288-1288
James P Michalko, *President*
John Sundell, *CFO*
Robert J Scott, *Treasurer*
EMP: 100
SQ FT: 25,000
SALES (est): 4.6MM **Privately Held**
WEB: www.rlg.com
SIC: 7375 8731 7372 On-line data base information retrieval; commercial physical research; prepackaged software

(P-16259)
ROCKYOU INC (PA)
303 2nd St Ste S600, San Francisco
(94107-3633)
PHONE......................................415 580-6400
Liza Marino, *CEO*
Sean Crawford, *Chief Mktg Ofcr*
Josh Grant, *Senior VP*
Jonathan Knight, *Senior VP*
MEI Castello, *Surgery Dir*
EMP: 67
SALES (est): 53.1MM **Privately Held**
SIC: 7375 Information retrieval services

(P-16260)
SAVVIS COMMUNICATIONS CORP
2101 Tasman Dr Ste 100, Santa Clara
(95054-1016)
PHONE......................................408 884-6269

7375 - Information Retrieval Svcs County (P-16261)

Shannon Gordon, *Branch Mgr*
Michelle Montgomery, *Executive*
Henry Tilton, *Senior Engr*
Mark Goldenberg, *Security Mgr*
Wai Wong, *Sales Executive*
EMP: 150
SALES (corp-wide): 17.9B **Publicly Held**
WEB: www.savvis.net
SIC: 7375 Information retrieval services
HQ: Savvis Communications Corporation
1 Solutions Pkwy
Town And Country MO 63017
314 628-7000

(P-16261)
SCRIBD INC
333 Bush St Ste 2400, San Francisco
(94104-2851)
PHONE 415 896-9890
John Adler, *CEO*
Simon Bond, *Chief Mktg Ofcr*
Hilla Whiting, *Executive*
Kevin Hwang, *Software Engr*
Trip Adler, *Senior Mgr*
EMP: 60
SALES (est): 12.3MM **Privately Held**
SIC: 7375 Information retrieval services

(P-16262)
TEUTONIC HOLDINGS LLC
9221 Corbin Ave Ste 260, Northridge
(91324-1625)
PHONE 818 264-4400
James Murphy, *CEO*
Sam Ghahremanpour, *President*
Doreen Paisano, *Human Resources*
EMP: 140 **EST:** 2012
SALES: 41.7MM **Privately Held**
SIC: 7375 Data base information retrieval

(P-16263)
TINTRI INC
303 Ravendale Dr, Mountain View
(94043-5228)
PHONE 650 810-8200
Ken Klein, *Ch of Bd*
Kieran John Harty, *CEO*
Ian Halifax, *CFO*
Yael Zheng, *Chief Mktg Ofcr*
Tony Chang, *Exec VP*
EMP: 200
SALES (est): 13.8MM **Privately Held**
SIC: 7375 Data base information retrieval; on-line data base information retrieval

(P-16264)
TRI-TECH INTERNET SERVICES INC
3465 Ocean View Blvd, Glendale
(91208-1508)
PHONE 818 548-5400
Jack Guiragosian, *President*
Gayle Butler, *CFO*
David Dginguerian, *Admin Sec*
Linda Carmona, *Info Tech Mgr*
Mario Carmona, *Info Tech Mgr*
EMP: 50 **EST:** 1998
SQ FT: 25,000
SALES: 20.5MM **Privately Held**
SIC: 7375 Information retrieval services

(P-16265)
TROJAN PROFESSIONAL SVCS INC
4410 Cerritos Ave, Los Alamitos
(90720-2549)
P.O. Box 1270 (90720-1270)
PHONE 714 816-7169
Mark Dunn, *CEO*
Ingrid M Kidd, *President*
Chris Iseri, *Admin Sec*
Alvin Gonzalez, *Administration*
Christine Lyons, *Manager*
EMP: 99
SQ FT: 12,000
SALES (est): 11.8MM **Privately Held**
WEB: www.trojanonline.com
SIC: 7375 Data base information retrieval

(P-16266)
TWITTER INC (PA)
1355 Market St Ste 900, San Francisco
(94103-1337)
PHONE 415 222-9670
Fax: 415 222-0922
Jack Dorsey, *CEO*

Omid Kordestani, *Ch of Bd*
Adam Bain, *COO*
Anthony Noto, *CFO*
Vijaya Gadde, *Admin Sec*
EMP: 129 **EST:** 2006
SQ FT: 839,000
SALES: 2.2B **Publicly Held**
SIC: 7375 On-line data base information retrieval

(P-16267)
VESTEK SYSTEMS INC (DH)
425 Market St Fl 6, San Francisco
(94105-2470)
PHONE 415 344-6000
Sam Campopiano, *President*
Virginia Chung, *Exec VP*
Brian Houston, *IT/INT Sup*
Patrick Richmond, *IT/INT Sup*
Lynn Roy PH, *Director*
EMP: 79
SQ FT: 18,000
SALES (est): 4.4MM **Privately Held**
WEB: www.vestek.com
SIC: 7375 On-line data base information retrieval
HQ: Primark Information Services U.K. Limited
First Floor
London W1F 8
207 638-2400

(P-16268)
WATER RESOURCES CAL DEPT
1416 9th St Rm 1225, Sacramento
(95814-5511)
PHONE 916 324-3812
Karen Bates, *President*
EMP: 50 **Privately Held**
WEB: www.water.ca.gov
SIC: 7375 9511 Data base information retrieval; water control & quality agency, government;
HQ: California Department Of Water Resources
1416 9th St
Sacramento CA 95814
916 653-9394

(P-16269)
WIKIA INC
360 3rd St Ste 750, San Francisco
(94107-2165)
PHONE 415 762-0780
Craig Palmer, *CEO*
Walker Jacobs, *COO*
Bud Austin, *CFO*
Jennifer Betka, *Senior VP*
Bob Huseby, *Senior VP*
EMP: 60
SALES (est): 7.7MM **Privately Held**
SIC: 7375 Information retrieval services; on-line data base information retrieval

(P-16270)
WOMENCOM NETWORKS INC
1820 Gateway Dr Ste 150, San Mateo
(94404-2471)
PHONE 650 378-6500
Marleen McDaniel, *President*
Greg Panawek, *CFO*
Gerry A Simone, *Ch Credit Ofcr*
Gina Garrubbo, *Exec VP*
David Brandin, *Senior VP*
EMP: 206
SQ FT: 15,000
SALES (est): 7MM
SALES (corp-wide): 74.5B **Publicly Held**
SIC: 7375 On-line data base information retrieval
HQ: Ivillage Inc.
500 Fashion Ave
New York NY 10018
212 600-6000

(P-16271)
WORLD ACCEPTANCE GROUP CORP (PA)
Also Called: Secure Data Recovery Services
8271 Melrose Ave Ste 205, Los Angeles
(90046-6826)
PHONE 800 388-1266
Dmitri T Kardashev, *President*
Yelena Tselenchuk, *Mktg Dir*
Shane Botwin, *Manager*
Daniel Shultz, *Manager*

EMP: 72
SQ FT: 1,800
SALES: 7.5MM **Privately Held**
WEB: www.securedatarecovery.com
SIC: 7375 7371 Data base information retrieval; computer software development

(P-16272)
YELP INC (PA)
140 New Montgomery St # 900, San Francisco (94105-3821)
PHONE 415 908-3801
Jeremy Stoppelman, *CEO*
Diane M Irvine, *Ch of Bd*
Geoff Donaker, *COO*
Charles Baker, *CFO*
Charles C Baker, *CFO*
EMP: 93
SALES: 549.7MM **Publicly Held**
SIC: 7375 Information retrieval services; on-line data base information retrieval

(P-16273)
ZYME SOLUTIONS INC (PA)
240 Twin Dolphin Dr Ste D, Redwood City
(94065-1403)
PHONE 650 585-2258
Chandran Sankaran, *President*
Rajashree Majumdar, *CFO*
Adam Brenner, *Senior VP*
Edward Dimbero, *Senior VP*
Daryl Miller, *Controller*
EMP: 100
SALES (est): 19.6MM **Privately Held**
SIC: 7375 Information retrieval services

7376 Computer Facilities Management Svcs

(P-16274)
AEROSPACE FCLITIES SUPPORT LLC
244 E Avenue K4, Lancaster (93535-4500)
PHONE 661 723-3148
Archie Moore,
EMP: 99
SQ FT: 150
SALES (est): 2.4MM **Privately Held**
SIC: 7376 Computer facilities management

(P-16275)
ALLIED DIGITAL SERVICES LLC (HQ)
680 Knox St Ste 200, Torrance
(90502-1358)
PHONE 310 431-2375
Paresh Shah, *CEO*
Kapil Mehta, *CFO*
Milind Telawane, *CFO*
Gaurav Bahirvani, *Chief Mktg Ofcr*
Michael Allen, *Senior VP*
EMP: 145
SQ FT: 14,516
SALES (est): 39.7MM
SALES (corp-wide): 20.1MM **Privately Held**
WEB: www.allieddigital.net
SIC: 7376 Computer facilities management
PA: Allied Digital Services Limited
5th Floor,
Mumbai MH 40000
226 681-6681

(P-16276)
COMPUTER SCIENCES CORPORATION
1520 Railroad Ave, Walnut Creek (94595)
PHONE 702 558-8092
Paul Branske, *CEO*
EMP: 145
SALES (corp-wide): 7.1B **Publicly Held**
SIC: 7376 Computer facilities management
PA: Computer Sciences Corporation
1775 Tysons Blvd
Tysons Corner VA 22102
703 245-9675

(P-16277)
COUNTY OF SACRAMENTO
Also Called: Communication & Info Tech
799 G St, Sacramento (95814-1212)
PHONE 916 874-7752
Fax: 916 874-5077

Rami Zakaria, *Branch Mgr*
Brian Richards, *Program Mgr*
Daryl Junnila, *Info Tech Dir*
Jim Hicks, *Info Tech Mgr*
George Gomez, *Network Analyst*
EMP: 395 **Privately Held**
WEB: www.sna.com
SIC: 7376 9631 Computer facilities management; communications commission, government;
PA: County Of Sacramento
700 H St Ste 7650
Sacramento CA 95814
916 874-5544

(P-16278)
CSRA LLC
4045 Hancock St, San Diego (92110-5126)
PHONE 619 225-2600
Art Schrubb, *Manager*
Tim Sheahan, *Vice Pres*
Thomas Volmer, *Department Mgr*
Donna King, *Admin Asst*
Lee Taylor, *MIS Dir*
EMP: 600
SALES (corp-wide): 4.2B **Publicly Held**
WEB: www.csc.com
SIC: 7376 Computer facilities management
HQ: Csra Llc
3170 Fairview Park Dr
Falls Church VA 22042
703 876-1000

(P-16279)
CSRA LLC
1520 Rr Ave Marie Is, Vallejo (94592)
PHONE 703 876-1026
Paul Branske, *CEO*
Katherine Mann, *Director*
EMP: 147
SALES (corp-wide): 4.2B **Publicly Held**
SIC: 7376 Computer facilities management
HQ: Csra Llc
3170 Fairview Park Dr
Falls Church VA 22042
703 876-1000

(P-16280)
HCL AMERICA INC (HQ)
330 Potrero Ave, Sunnyvale (94085-4194)
PHONE 408 733-0480
Shiv Nadar, *Chairman*
Vineet Nayar, *Vice Chairman*
Saurav Adhikari, *President*
Manish Anand, *CEO*
Roshni Nadar Malhotra, *CEO*
EMP: 200
SQ FT: 31,000
SALES: 2.8B
SALES (corp-wide): 1.9B **Privately Held**
SIC: 7376 7371 8741 Computer facilities management; computer software development; management services
PA: Hcl Technologies Limited
A-10/11, Sector 3
Noida UP 20130
120 252-8155

(P-16281)
PEROT SYSTEMS CORPORATION
6701 Center Dr W Ste 1000, Los Angeles
(90045-1566)
PHONE 310 342-3200
Sherry Cowan, *Manager*
Mike Metzinger, *Info Tech Mgr*
Ves Aghajanian, *Manager*
EMP: 70
SALES (corp-wide): 72.7B **Publicly Held**
WEB: www.perotsystems.com
SIC: 7376 7379 Computer facilities management; computer related consulting services
HQ: Perot Systems Corporation
2300 W Plano Pkwy
Plano TX 75075
972 577-0000

(P-16282)
RAGINGWIRE DATA CENTERS INC (DH)
Also Called: Raging Wire
1200 Striker Ave, Sacramento
(95834-1157)
P.O. Box 348060 (95834-8060)
PHONE 916 286-3000

George Macricostas, *President*
Douglas S Adams, *President*
Jason Weckworth, *COO*
Doug Adams, *Officer*
William Dougherty, *Senior VP*
EMP: 275
SALES (est): 198.8MM
SALES (corp-wide): 98.6B **Privately Held**
WEB: www.ragingwire.com
SIC: 7376 Computer facilities management
HQ: Ntt Communications Corporation
1-1-6, Uchisaiwaicho
Chiyoda-Ku TKY 100-0
335 008-111

(P-16283)
VERIZON BUS NETWRK SVCS INC
4340 Solar Way, Fremont (94538-6335)
PHONE 510 497-2500
Randy Cade, *Manager*
EMP: 75
SALES (corp-wide): 131.6MM **Publicly Held**
WEB: www.gtl.net
SIC: 7376 Computer facilities management
HQ: Verizon Business Network Services Inc.
22001 Loudoun County Pkwy
Ashburn VA 20147
703 729-5615

7377 Computer Rental & Leasing

(P-16284)
INSIGHT INVESTMENTS LLC (HQ)
Also Called: Insight Systems Exchange
611 Anton Blvd Ste 700, Costa Mesa (92626-7050)
PHONE 714 939-2300
John W Ford, *CEO*
Richard Heard, *President*
David Wang, *CFO*
Christopher Czaja, *Exec VP*
Carol Boldt, *Vice Pres*
EMP: 148
SQ FT: 30,000
SALES (est): 161.8MM **Privately Held**
WEB: www.insightinvestments.com
SIC: 7377 5045 Computer peripheral equipment rental & leasing; computer peripheral equipment

7378 Computer Maintenance & Repair

(P-16285)
AMKOTRON INC
12620 Hiddencreek Way, Cerritos (90703-2116)
PHONE 562 921-3330
Sunja Lee, *Branch Mgr*
EMP: 60
SALES (corp-wide): 7.7MM **Privately Held**
SIC: 7378 5065 Computer peripheral equipment repair & maintenance; electronic parts & equipment
PA: Amkotron, Inc.
16220 Bloomfield Ave
Cerritos CA 90703
562 921-3330

(P-16286)
APEX COMPUTER SYSTEMS INC
13875 Cerritos Corprt Dr A, Cerritos (90703-2470)
PHONE 562 926-6820
Fax: 562 926-0825
Philip C Chen, *CEO*
Dennis Rice, *President*
Jessica C Chow, *CFO*
Michael Da Silva, *Vice Pres*
Mark Aiken, *District Mgr*
EMP: 60
SQ FT: 18,146
SALES: 23.6MM **Privately Held**
WEB: www.acsi2000.com
SIC: 7378 5734 Computer maintenance & repair; computer & software stores

(P-16287)
BCP SYSTEMS INC
1560 S Sinclair St, Anaheim (92806-5933)
PHONE 714 202-3900
Carlos P Torres, *CEO*
William W Price, *President*
Dianna Rodriguez, *Vice Pres*
Heather Dicarlo, *QA Dir*
Trace Dibble, *Engineer*
EMP: 60
SALES (est): 9.4MM **Privately Held**
WEB: www.bcpsystems.com
SIC: 7378 3571 5063 Computer maintenance & repair; computer peripheral equipment repair & maintenance; electronic computers; electrical apparatus & equipment

(P-16288)
BIGBYTE CORPORATION
47430 Seabridge Dr, Fremont (94538-6548)
PHONE 510 249-1100
Gary D Logan, *President*
Michael Franklin, *COO*
Norman Jordan, *Info Tech Mgr*
Hon Leu, *Controller*
Chuck Le, *Opers Staff*
EMP: 55
SQ FT: 7,500
SALES (est): 4MM **Privately Held**
WEB: www.bigbytecorp.com
SIC: 7378 Computer peripheral equipment repair & maintenance

(P-16289)
COKEVA INC
Also Called: Applied Materials
9000 Foothills Blvd, Roseville (95747-4411)
PHONE 916 462-6001
Ann D Nguyen, *CEO*
Ken Ueltzen, *President*
Dominick Derosa, *CFO*
Joseph Valdivieso, *Officer*
Mark Anderson, *Vice Pres*
EMP: 181
SQ FT: 175,000
SALES (est): 26MM **Privately Held**
SIC: 7378 Computer maintenance & repair

(P-16290)
CONVOY INC
Also Called: Myconvoy
463 Pacific Ave, San Francisco (94133-4614)
P.O. Box 20091, Stanford (94309-0091)
PHONE 415 403-2770
Colin Barceloux, *CEO*
Scott Hasbrouck, *CTO*
EMP: 50 **EST:** 2014
SQ FT: 5,000
SALES (est): 486.1K **Privately Held**
SIC: 7378 Computer maintenance & repair

(P-16291)
DST OUTPUT CALIFORNIA INC
5220 Rbert J Mathews Pkwy, El Dorado Hills (95762-5705)
PHONE 916 939-4617
Fax: 916 983-9212
Kenneth Taylor, *Manager*
Timothy Ross, *President*
Robert Baker, *Exec VP*
Scott Shelton, *Senior VP*
Lino Carnesecca, *Vice Pres*
EMP: 145
SALES (est): 35.5MM
SALES (corp-wide): 2.9B **Publicly Held**
SIC: 7378 Computer maintenance & repair
HQ: Broadridge Customer Communications, Llc
2600 Southwest Blvd
Kansas City MO 64108
816 221-1234

(P-16292)
ESL TECHNOLOGIES INC
8875 Washington Blvd B, Roseville (95678-6214)
PHONE 916 677-4500
Donna Kwidzinski, *CEO*
Tjeu Blommaert, *President*
Greg Dominguez, *Treasurer*
▲ **EMP:** 350
SQ FT: 100,000
SALES (est): 24.2MM **Privately Held**
WEB: www.eslt.com
SIC: 7378 Computer peripheral equipment repair & maintenance
HQ: Teleplan Holding Usa, Inc.
8875 Washington Blvd B
Roseville CA 95678
916 677-4500

(P-16293)
FAKOURI ELECTRICAL ENGRG INC
Also Called: F E E
30001 Comercio, Rcho STA Marg (92688-2106)
PHONE 949 888-2400
Fax: 949 669-0372
Maryam Ewalt, *President*
Charles Ewalt, *COO*
John Oveisi, *CFO*
Bijan Ewalt, *Vice Pres*
Martin Schneyer, *Agent*
EMP: 79 **EST:** 1979
SQ FT: 15,000
SALES (est): 10MM **Privately Held**
WEB: www.fee-ups.com
SIC: 7378 8742 Computer maintenance & repair; maintenance management consultant

(P-16294)
FALCONWOOD INC
1011 Camino Del Rio S, San Diego (92108-3531)
PHONE 619 297-9080
Bill Severi, *Principal*
EMP: 61
SALES (corp-wide): 21MM **Privately Held**
SIC: 7378 8741 Computer & data processing equipment repair/maintenance; management services
PA: Falconwood, Inc.
2231 Crystal Dr Ste 801
Arlington VA 22202
703 888-4300

(P-16295)
GENERAL ELECTRIC COMPANY
1303 Bloomdale St, Duarte (91010-2501)
PHONE 626 359-7988
Katherine B McCarthy, *Vice Pres*
Monika Sywak, *Vice Pres*
Kenneth G Kindl, *Finance Mgr*
Albert King, *Marketing Mgr*
Hao Dinh, *Manager*
EMP: 200
SALES (corp-wide): 117.3B **Publicly Held**
SIC: 7378 Computer maintenance & repair
PA: General Electric Company
41 Farnsworth St
Boston MA 02210
617 443-3000

(P-16296)
GRAY SYSTEMS INC
5173 Waring Rd, San Diego (92120-2705)
P.O. Box 601583 (92160-1583)
PHONE 619 285-5848
Fax: 619 285-9533
Michelle G Gray, *CEO*
Darleen G Parrish, *CFO*
Sharon Hall, *Manager*
EMP: 50
SQ FT: 2,074
SALES (est): 2.8MM **Privately Held**
SIC: 7378 7373 7371 5045 Computer maintenance & repair; local area network (LAN) systems integrator; custom computer programming services; computers, peripherals & software

(P-16297)
GUARDIAN COMPUTER SUPPORT
7075 Commerce Cir Ste D, Pleasanton (94588-8015)
P.O. Box 5440, Walnut Creek (94596-1440)
PHONE 925 251-8800
David Costa, *Principal*
Randy Swanson, *Principal*
EMP: 125
SQ FT: 24,000
SALES (est): 5.9MM **Privately Held**
WEB: www.guardiancomputer.com
SIC: 7378 Computer maintenance & repair

(P-16298)
HP INC
130 Lytton Ave, Palo Alto (94301-1065)
PHONE 650 857-1501
Mark S Manasse, *Principal*
EMP: 80
SALES (corp-wide): 103.3B **Publicly Held**
SIC: 7378 7371 Computer maintenance & repair; custom computer programming services
PA: Hp Inc.
1501 Page Mill Rd
Palo Alto CA 94304
650 857-1501

(P-16299)
INFINITE COMPUTER GROUP LLC
21300 Superior St, Chatsworth (91311-4312)
PHONE 800 922-8075
David Harmon,
Steve Burkett,
Tom Diaz,
EMP: 81
SQ FT: 10,000
SALES (est): 2MM
SALES (corp-wide): 243.3MM **Privately Held**
WEB: www.infinitecomputer.com
SIC: 7378 7379 Computer maintenance & repair; computer related consulting services
PA: Sms Systems Maintenance Services, Inc.
10420 Harris Oak Blvd C
Charlotte NC 28269
704 921-1620

(P-16300)
INHOUSEIT INC
3193 Red Hill Ave, Costa Mesa (92626-3432)
PHONE 949 660-5655
Glen Ackerman, *CEO*
Steve Bender, *President*
Leonard Dimiceli, *General Mgr*
Chris Richner, *CTO*
Christina Karanick, *Accounting Mgr*
EMP: 70
SQ FT: 8,000
SALES (est): 14.4MM **Privately Held**
WEB: www.inhouseit.com
SIC: 7378 Computer maintenance & repair

(P-16301)
LOS ANGELES UNIFIED SCHOOL DST
Also Called: Information Technology
200 N Main St Ste 1400, Los Angeles (90012-4127)
PHONE 213 485-3691
Marry K Kotzman, *Manager*
EMP: 150
SALES (corp-wide): 4.4B **Privately Held**
WEB: www.lausd.k12.ca.us
SIC: 7378 Computer & data processing equipment repair/maintenance
PA: Los Angeles Unified School District
333 S Beaudry Ave Ste 209
Los Angeles CA 90017
213 241-1000

(P-16302)
MG COMPUTERS INC
436 S Dawes Ave, Stockton (95215-5236)
PHONE 831 970-3231
Miguel Santana, *Owner*
EMP: 55
SALES (est): 3.5MM **Privately Held**
WEB: www.mgcomputers.com
SIC: 7378 Computer maintenance & repair

7378 - Computer Maintenance & Repair County (P-16303)

PRODUDUCTS & SERVICES SECTION

(P-16303)
PRINTRAK INTERNATIONAL INC (DH)
1250 N Tustin Ave, Anaheim (92807-1617)
PHONE.....................714 238-2000
Daniel A Crawford, *President*
Dave McNeff, *Exec VP*
Mike Lyons, *Vice Pres*
Charlene Mullen, *CTO*
Wes Thoroughman, *Info Tech Mgr*
EMP: 270
SQ FT: 86,000
SALES (est): 25.3MM
SALES (corp-wide): 604.7MM **Privately Held**
WEB: www.printrak.com
SIC: 7378 7371 Computer maintenance & repair; computer software development
HQ: Morpho
11 Boulevard Gallieni
Issy Les Moulineaux Cedex 92445
158 112-500

(P-16304)
QUEST INTL MONITOR SVC INC (PA)
65 Parker, Irvine (92618-1605)
PHONE.....................949 581-9900
Fax: 949 581-4011
Shahnam Arshadi, *President*
Kamyar Katouzian, *Vice Pres*
Ben Arshadi, *General Mgr*
Nancy Bautista, *Accounting Mgr*
Tim Lee, *Accountant*
EMP: 60
SQ FT: 30,000
SALES (est): 25.5MM **Privately Held**
WEB: www.questinc.com
SIC: 7378 7379 7371 7373 Computer maintenance & repair; computer related maintenance services; custom computer programming services; systems integration services; cathode ray tubes, including rebuilt; computer & software stores

(P-16305)
TELEPLAN SERVICE SOLUTIONS INC
8875 Washington Blvd B, Roseville (95678-6214)
PHONE.....................916 677-4619
Russell Sproull, *CEO*
Pk Bala, *COO*
Jan Piet Valk, *CFO*
Jack Rockwood, *Vice Pres*
Larry Worden, *Vice Pres*
EMP: 75
SALES (est): 14.4MM **Privately Held**
SIC: 7378 Computer maintenance & repair
HQ: Teleplan Holding Usa, Inc.
8875 Washington Blvd B
Roseville CA 95678
916 677-4500

(P-16306)
THIRDWAVE TECHNOLOGY SERVICES
4054 Del Rey Ave Ste 207, Marina Del Rey (90292-5680)
PHONE.....................310 563-2160
Sharmila Herr, *President*
EMP: 50
SALES (est): 3.4MM **Privately Held**
WEB: www.thirdwavets.com
SIC: 7378 Computer maintenance & repair

(P-16307)
TURNER TECHTRONICS INC
17845 Sky Park Cir, Irvine (92614-6112)
PHONE.....................949 724-1339
Randy Hower, *Branch Mgr*
EMP: 118
SALES (corp-wide): 19.6MM **Privately Held**
WEB: www.turnertech.com
SIC: 7378 7372 Computer maintenance & repair; prepackaged software
PA: Turner Techtronics, Inc.
3200 W Burbank Blvd
Burbank CA 91505
818 973-1060

(P-16308)
TUSA INC (PA)
Also Called: Terix Computer Service
388 Oakmead Pkwy, Sunnyvale (94085-5407)
PHONE.....................888 848-3749
EMP: 105
SALES: 30MM **Privately Held**
SIC: 7378 Computer maintenance & repair

(P-16309)
XEROX CORPORATION
2665 N 1st St Ste 200, San Jose (95134-2034)
PHONE.....................408 953-2700
Fax: 408 953-2100
Tom Long, *Manager*
Margo Shrack, *Development*
EMP: 200
SALES (corp-wide): 18B **Publicly Held**
WEB: www.xerox.com
SIC: 7378 7629 3861 5044 Computer peripheral equipment repair & maintenance; business machine repair, electric; photographic equipment & supplies; copying equipment; photocopy machines
PA: Xerox Corporation
45 Glover Ave Ste 700
Norwalk CT 06850
203 968-3000

7379 Computer Related Svcs, NEC

(P-16310)
24/7 CUSTOMER INC (PA)
910 E Hamilton Ave # 240, Campbell (95008-0625)
PHONE.....................650 385-2247
Pallipuram V Kannan, *Ch of Bd*
Matt Sato, *President*
Bill Robbins, *COO*
Tim Pebworth, *CFO*
Martin Puttock, *Exec VP*
EMP: 84
SQ FT: 5,000
SALES (est): 756.1MM **Privately Held**
WEB: www.247customer.com
SIC: 7379

(P-16311)
ABACUS BUSINESS SOLUTIONS INC
3333 Bowers Ave Ste 130, Santa Clara (95054-2928)
P.O. Box 153, Los Altos (94023-0153)
PHONE.....................408 200-0977
Jay S Belur, *President*
David Joffe, *CFO*
Alex Marzano, *Vice Pres*
Daharmesh Rikh, *Vice Pres*
Rabindra Srikantan, *Managing Dir*
EMP: 65
SQ FT: 500
SALES (est): 4.9MM
SALES (corp-wide): 9.3MM **Privately Held**
SIC: 7379 Computer related consulting services
HQ: Advanced Synergic Pte Ltd
8 Jurong Town Hall Road
Singapore 60943
627 057-37

(P-16312)
ABTECH TECHNOLOGIES INC
Also Called: Abtech Support
2042 Corte Del Nogal D, Carlsbad (92011-1438)
PHONE.....................760 827-5100
Robert Russell, *President*
Paul Storck, *President*
Michael Rodriguez, *Project Mgr*
Dave Hurst, *Technology*
Chris Abegglen, *Technical Staff*
EMP: 88
SALES (est): 17.8MM **Privately Held**
WEB: www.abtechsupport.com
SIC: 7379 Computer related consulting services

(P-16313)
ACER AMERICA CORPORATION (DH)
333 W San Carlos St, San Jose (95110-2726)
PHONE.....................408 533-7700
Fax: 408 533-4555
Emmanuel Fromont, *CEO*
Ted Lai, *CFO*
Ming Wang, *CFO*
Jeff Lenz, *Program Mgr*
Howard Cheung, *CIO*
EMP: 100
SALES (est): 85.6MM
SALES (corp-wide): 8.1B **Privately Held**
WEB: www.acersupport.com
SIC: 7379
HQ: Gateway, Inc.
7565 Irvine Center Dr # 150
Irvine CA 92618
949 471-7000

(P-16314)
ADCOM INTERACTIVE MEDIA INC
Also Called: Ad Media
901 W Alameda Ave 102, Burbank (91506-2801)
PHONE.....................800 296-7104
Lacey Stanford, *Principal*
AVI Bibi, *COO*
Sumeet Kamat, *Software Dev*
Ryan Meloy, *Marketing Staff*
Nicole Keffer, *Accounts Exec*
EMP: 52
SALES (est): 8.2MM **Privately Held**
SIC: 7379

(P-16315)
ADVANCED DISCOVERY INC
115 E Gish Rd Ste 500, San Jose (95112-4719)
PHONE.....................408 294-0091
Myron Jadwin, *Exec VP*
Chuck Sutterfield, *General Mgr*
Tanner Ohman, *Project Mgr*
Michael Patterson, *Project Mgr*
Ray Verastegui, *Project Mgr*
EMP: 58
SALES (corp-wide): 42.2MM **Privately Held**
SIC: 7379
PA: Advanced Discovery Inc.
13915 N Mo Pac Expy # 210
Austin TX 78728
512 828-6558

(P-16316)
ADVANCED RSRVATION SYSTEMS INC
2445 Truxtun Rd Ste 205, San Diego (92106-6154)
PHONE.....................858 300-8600
Fax: 619 234-6600
Alec House, *President*
Dan Rhoads, *Shareholder*
Alan Suchodolski, *President*
Alan Suchdolski, *CEO*
Wayne Blum, *Vice Pres*
EMP: 65
SQ FT: 3,000
SALES (est): 9.6MM **Privately Held**
WEB: www.aresdirect.com
SIC: 7379

(P-16317)
ADVANTIS GLOBAL INC (PA)
301 Howard St Ste 1400, San Francisco (94105-6669)
PHONE.....................415 395-4444
Bryan Barber, *CEO*
Jeff Taylor, *COO*
Sabrina Bennett, *Finance Asst*
Sophia Butler, *Human Resources*
Michael Palia, *Human Resources*
EMP: 110 **EST:** 2007
SQ FT: 4,500
SALES: 40MM **Privately Held**
WEB: www.advantisglobal.com
SIC: 7379 Computer related consulting services;

(P-16318)
AGILIANCE INC
845 Stewart Dr Ste D, Sunnyvale (94085-4504)
PHONE.....................408 200-0400
Fax: 408 200-0401
Joe Fantuzzi, *President*
Linda Gallagher, *Vice Pres*
Torsten George, *Vice Pres*
Bob Horn, *Vice Pres*
Ed King, *Vice Pres*
EMP: 50
SQ FT: 8,000
SALES (est): 6.6MM **Privately Held**
SIC: 7379 7376 7373 Computer related consulting services; computer facilities management; computer integrated systems design

(P-16319)
AICENT INC
900 E Hamilton Ave # 600, Campbell (95008-0671)
PHONE.....................408 324-1316
Lynn Lui, *CEO*
Kallen Chan, *CFO*
Eric Weiss, *General Mgr*
Golten Yen, *Engineer*
EMP: 106
SALES (est): 218.1K **Privately Held**
WEB: www.aicent.net
SIC: 7379 Data processing consultant

(P-16320)
AMOS OF AMERICA INC
1465 N Mcdowell Blvd, Petaluma (94954-6516)
PHONE.....................899 415-2000
Axel Shell, *CEO*
Olav Spiegel, *COO*
Otto Halpoth, *CFO*
Ryan Gibson, *Admin Sec*
Wayne Boothby, *Accountant*
EMP: 120 **EST:** 2013
SQ FT: 15,000
SALES: 40MM **Privately Held**
SIC: 7379
HQ: Amos International B.V.
Keizersgracht 484
Amsterdam
205 569-715

(P-16321)
ANAPLAN INC (PA)
625 2nd St Ste 101, San Francisco (94107-2050)
PHONE.....................415 742-8199
Frederic Andre Laluyaux, *CEO*
James Budge, *CFO*
Anthony Reynolds, *Exec VP*
Doug Smith, *Exec VP*
Scott Armstrong, *Vice Pres*
EMP: 56 **EST:** 2008
SALES (est): 42.6MM **Privately Held**
SIC: 7379

(P-16322)
APN SOFTWARE SERVICES INC (PA)
39899 Balentine Dr # 385, Newark (94560-5391)
PHONE.....................510 623-5050
Fax: 510 623-5055
Aslam Chandiwalli, *President*
Charlotte Henson, *Vice Pres*
Poonam Bhatti, *Executive*
Aslam Chandiwalla, *Executive*
Mayur Paranjpe, *CTO*
EMP: 88
SQ FT: 3,500
SALES (est): 32.3MM **Privately Held**
WEB: www.apninc.com
SIC: 7379 Computer related consulting services

(P-16323)
APTTUS CORPORATION
560 S Winchester Blvd, San Jose (95128-2560)
PHONE.....................650 722-1619
Kirk G Krappe, *President*
Barbara Competello, *Senior VP*
Rahul Parikh, *Senior VP*
Nagi Prabhu, *Senior VP*
Jeff Santelices, *Senior VP*
EMP: 60

PRODUCTS & SERVICES SECTION
7379 - Computer Related Svcs, NEC County (P-16348)

SALES (est): 6.5MM **Privately Held**
SIC: **7379** Computer related consulting services

(P-16324)
ARC PARTNERS INC
3 Vanderbilt, Irvine (92618-2039)
PHONE..................703 757-0402
Marjan Hakimi, *President*
Peter Ghassemi, *Vice Pres*
EMP: 63
SALES (est): 4MM **Privately Held**
SIC: **7379** 8999 Computer related maintenance services; communication services

(P-16325)
ASCENT SERVICES GROUP INC
3000 Oak Rd Ste 200, Walnut Creek (94597-4506)
PHONE..................925 627-4900
Fax: 925 627-4910
Joseph Nordlinger, *President*
W Todd Peterson, *CFO*
Sudhir Sahu, *Chairman*
Max Levine, *Exec VP*
Michelle Miller, *Vice Pres*
EMP: 450
SQ FT: 7,000
SALES (est): 71.4MM **Privately Held**
WEB: www.itascent.com
SIC: **7379** 7363 Computer related consulting services; help supply services

(P-16326)
ASSIGN CORPORATION
801 N Brand Blvd Ste 905, Glendale (91203-1236)
PHONE..................818 247-7100
Umesh Lalwani, *CEO*
Tanuj Nigam, *Vice Pres*
Jordan Vazquez, *Office Admin*
Rachel Wagoner, *Admin Asst*
Sharad Singh, *Sr Software Eng*
EMP: 120
SQ FT: 1,300
SALES (est): 8.9MM **Privately Held**
WEB: www.assigncorp.com
SIC: **7379**

(P-16327)
ATI INC
2123 Ringwood Ave, San Jose (95131-1725)
PHONE..................408 942-1780
John Knight, *CEO*
Timothy L Plette, *CFO*
David L Walker, *Vice Pres*
EMP: 50
SQ FT: 8,000
SALES (est): 3.1MM **Privately Held**
SIC: **7379** Disk & diskette conversion service

(P-16328)
BENCHMARK INTERNET GROUP LLC
10621 Calle Lee Ste 141, Los Alamitos (90720-6798)
PHONE..................562 286-6820
Denise Keller,
EMP: 100 EST: 2005
SALES (est): 6.1MM **Privately Held**
SIC: **7379** Computer related consulting services

(P-16329)
BESTITCOM INC (PA)
1464 Madera Rd, Simi Valley (93065-3077)
PHONE..................602 667-5613
Harry Curtin, *CEO*
Susan Silberstein, *COO*
Rich Hybner, *CFO*
Jeff Haisley, *Vice Pres*
Fred Chen, *CTO*
EMP: 65
SQ FT: 20,000
SALES (est): 14.6MM **Privately Held**
WEB: www.bestit.com
SIC: **7379** Computer related consulting services; computer related maintenance services

(P-16330)
BMR APPS INC
548 Market St, San Francisco (94104-5401)
PHONE..................954 651-1412
William Schonbrun, *President*
EMP: 68
SALES (est): 4.9MM **Privately Held**
SIC: **7379**

(P-16331)
BRICSNET FM AMERICA INC
1820 Harvest Rd, Pleasanton (94566-5417)
PHONE..................202 756-1840
Farid Jinian, *CEO*
Hector Rodriguez, *Ch of Bd*
Stuart Turner, *President*
Brian Haines, *Comp Tech*
Christian Fernandez, *Sales Engr*
EMP: 70
SALES (est): 6.2MM **Privately Held**
SIC: **7379** Computer related maintenance services

(P-16332)
CAPIOT SOFTWARE INC
2820 Ramona St, Palo Alto (94306-2364)
PHONE..................650 766-2469
Anil Kshirsagar, *CEO*
Vasudeva Anumukonda, *COO*
Ashish Kapoor, *Vice Pres*
Hitesh Salla, *Vice Pres*
Sandil Srinivasan, *VP Sales*
EMP: 110 EST: 2014
SALES: 1.5MM **Privately Held**
SIC: **7379** 7371 7389 Computer related consulting services; computer software development;

(P-16333)
CERIUM SYSTEMS INC
4701 Patrick Henry Dr, Santa Clara (95054-1819)
PHONE..................408 623-0787
Venkat Arunarthi, *Director*
EMP: 79 EST: 2014
SALES (est): 1.1MM **Privately Held**
SIC: **7379**

(P-16334)
CGI TECHNOLOGIES SOLUTIONS INC
505 14th St Fl 9, Oakland (94612-1406)
PHONE..................510 238-5300
Fax: 510 268-8545
Shelley Bergum, *Branch Mgr*
EMP: 56
SALES (corp-wide): 9.6B **Privately Held**
SIC: **7379** Computer related consulting services
HQ: Cgi Technologies And Solutions Inc.
11325 Random Hills Rd
Fairfax VA 22030
703 267-8000

(P-16335)
CLARABRIDGE INC
Also Called: Market Metrix
900 Larkspur Landing Cir, Larkspur (94939-1757)
PHONE..................415 721-1300
Yuchun Lee, *Branch Mgr*
Mike Pharis, *Vice Pres*
Karen Simoneau, *Business Dir*
Loren Gill, *General Mgr*
Lenny Nash, *General Mgr*
EMP: 86
SALES (corp-wide): 54MM **Privately Held**
SIC: **7379** Computer related consulting services
PA: Clarabridge, Inc.
11400 Commerce Park Dr 500a
Reston VA 20191
571 299-1800

(P-16336)
CLOSINGCORP INC
6165 Greenwich Dr Ste 300, San Diego (92122-5912)
PHONE..................858 551-1500
Brian Benson, *CEO*
James Bolger, *CFO*
Michael D Reynolds, *CFO*
Pat Carney, *Officer*

Dave Petro, *Senior VP*
EMP: 63
SQ FT: 13,823
SALES (est): 13MM **Privately Held**
SIC: **7379** 7375 4813 ; information retrieval services;

(P-16337)
CLOUDIKE INC
3003 N 1st St, San Jose (95134-2004)
P.O. Box 10188, Newark NJ (07101-3188)
PHONE..................609 910-0911
Maxim Azarov, *President*
EMP: 60
SALES: 509.4K **Privately Held**
SIC: **7379** Computer related consulting services

(P-16338)
COMERIT INC
2201 Francisco Dr #140283, El Dorado Hills (95762-3713)
PHONE..................888 556-5990
Greg Clark, *CEO*
Jesper Christensen, *Senior Partner*
Jeff Johnston, *CFO*
Bjarne Berg, *CIO*
EMP: 120
SQ FT: 3,500
SALES (est): 4MM **Privately Held**
SIC: **7379** Computer related consulting services

(P-16339)
COMMERCIAL PRGRM SYSTEMS INC (PA)
Also Called: CPS
4400 Coldwater Canyon Ave # 200, Studio City (91604-1480)
PHONE..................818 308-8560
Alan Strong, *CEO*
Phil Sawyer, *President*
Ed Stevenson, *President*
Marjorie Kram, *Vice Pres*
Michele Stewart, *Vice Pres*
EMP: 146
SQ FT: 8,000
SALES (est): 15.2MM **Privately Held**
SIC: **7379** Data processing consultant

(P-16340)
COMPUTER SCIENCES CORPORATION
1111 Broadway Fl 13, Oakland (94607-4139)
PHONE..................510 645-3000
William Cunningham, *Manager*
EMP: 100
SALES (corp-wide): 7.1B **Publicly Held**
WEB: www.csc.com
SIC: **7379** 7373 Computer related consulting services; systems integration services
PA: Computer Sciences Corporation
1775 Tysons Blvd
Tysons Corner VA 22102
703 245-9675

(P-16341)
CONCENTRIX CORPORATION
44201 Nobel Dr, Fremont (94538-3178)
PHONE..................510 668-3717
John Vitalie, *Branch Mgr*
Rex B Alcoba, *Director*
Ramil Cabaces, *Director*
EMP: 59
SALES (corp-wide): 13.3B **Publicly Held**
SIC: **7379** 8742 7331 7311 Computer related maintenance services; management consulting services; direct mail advertising services; advertising agencies
HQ: Concentrix Corporation
3750 Monroe Ave
Pittsford NY 14534
585 218-5300

(P-16342)
CONNECTX INC
909 N Avi Blvd Unit 6, Manhattan Beach (90266)
PHONE..................310 702-8686
Lance Arthur Parker, *President*
EMP: 50
SQ FT: 4,000
SALES (est): 766.2K **Privately Held**
SIC: **7379** Computer data escrow service

(P-16343)
COUNTY OF RIVERSIDE
4080 Lemon St Fl 3, Riverside (92501-3609)
PHONE..................951 486-7700
Kevin Crawford, *Branch Mgr*
EMP: 50 **Privately Held**
SIC: **7379** Computer related consulting services
PA: County Of Riverside
4080 Lemon St Fl 11
Riverside CA 92501
951 955-1110

(P-16344)
COYOTE CREEK CONSULTING INC
1551 Mccarthy Blvd # 115, Milpitas (95035-7437)
PHONE..................408 383-9200
Michael R Faster, *CEO*
Candi Faster, *Office Mgr*
Derrick Sakai, *Administration*
Nikki Motas, *Tech Recruiter*
Terri Carney, *Sales Dir*
EMP: 65
SQ FT: 3,000
SALES (est): 11.4MM **Privately Held**
WEB: www.coyotecrk.com
SIC: **7379** Computer related consulting services

(P-16345)
CROWDSTRIKE HOLDINGS INC
15440 Laguna Canyon Rd # 250, Irvine (92618-2142)
PHONE..................949 954-6785
George Kurtz, *CEO*
Donald Marston, *CFO*
Dmitri Alperovitch, *Vice Pres*
Dave Cole, *Vice Pres*
Wendi Rafferty, *Vice Pres*
EMP: 120
SQ FT: 5,000
SALES (est): 10.3MM **Privately Held**
SIC: **7379** Computer related consulting services

(P-16346)
CSC CONSULTING INC
2100 E Grand Ave B360, El Segundo (90245-5055)
PHONE..................310 563-2062
Alan Young, *Manager*
EMP: 75
SALES (corp-wide): 12.1B **Publicly Held**
SIC: **7379** Computer related consulting services
HQ: Csc Consulting, Inc.
404 Wyman St Ste 355
Waltham MA 02451
781 890-7446

(P-16347)
CSRA LLC
2100 E Grand Ave, El Segundo (90245-5055)
PHONE..................310 615-0311
Sheryl Bennett, *Manager*
Richard Trice, *Administration*
Katherine Mann, *Director*
EMP: 50
SALES (corp-wide): 4.2B **Publicly Held**
WEB: www.csc.com
SIC: **7379** Computer related consulting services
HQ: Csra Llc
3170 Fairview Park Dr
Falls Church VA 22042
703 876-1000

(P-16348)
CSRA SYSTEM AND SOLUTIONS LLC
2727 Hamner Ave, Norco (92860-1927)
PHONE..................951 735-3300
Kenneth Gunn, *Manager*
Yancy Bradford, *IT/INT Sup*
EMP: 50
SALES (corp-wide): 7.1B **Publicly Held**
SIC: **7379** Computer related consulting services

7379 - Computer Related Svcs, NEC County (P-16349)

HQ: Csra Systems And Solutions Llc
15000 Conference Ctr Dr
Chantilly VA 20151

(P-16349)
CUSTOMER SRVC DLVRY PLTFRM CRP
Also Called: C S D P
15615 Alton Pkwy Ste 310, Irvine (92618-3308)
PHONE................................717 896-8489
Jerry Edinger, *President*
David Englund, *CFO*
Dave Dorret, *CTO*
EMP: 50
SQ FT: 5,000
SALES (est): 3.6MM **Privately Held**
WEB: www.csdpcorp.com
SIC: 7379 7373 Computer related consulting services; systems software development services

(P-16350)
DCM LIMITED
Also Called: Dcm Data Systems
39159 Paseo Padre Pkwy # 303, Fremont (94538-1698)
PHONE................................510 494-2321
Ashok Choudhury, *President*
Jayant Pant, *Marketing Staff*
EMP: 60
SQ FT: 1,500
SALES (corp-wide): 87.5MM **Privately Held**
WEB: www.dcmusa.com
SIC: 7379 Computer related consulting services
PA: D C M Limited
6th Floor, Vikrant Tower
New Delhi DEL 11000
112 571-9967

(P-16351)
DEALERTRACK COLLTE MANAG SERVI
Also Called: Fdi Collateral Management
9750 Goethe Rd, Sacramento (95827-3500)
PHONE................................916 368-5300
Mark O'Neil, *CEO*
Daniel L Wollenberg, *President*
Beverly Devine, *Exec VP*
Chris Hodge, *Senior VP*
Robert Gasser, *Vice Pres*
EMP: 220
SQ FT: 84,900
SALES (est): 31.8MM
SALES (corp-wide): 33.6B **Privately Held**
WEB: www.fdielt.com
SIC: 7379 Computer related consulting services
HQ: Trivin, Inc.
115 Poheganut Dr Ste 201
Groton CT 06340
860 448-3177

(P-16352)
DECLARA INC
977 Commercial St, Palo Alto (94303-4908)
PHONE................................650 800-7695
Ramona Pierson, *CEO*
Pankaj Anand, *President*
Debra Chrapaty, *Executive*
Nelson Gonzalez, *Security Dir*
Bixia Ji, *Sr Software Eng*
EMP: 68
SQ FT: 3,000
SALES (est): 3.6MM **Privately Held**
SIC: 7379 Data processing consultant

(P-16353)
DEFENSEWEB TECHNOLOGIES INC
Also Called: Nliven
10188 Telesis Ct Ste 300, San Diego (92121-4779)
PHONE................................858 272-8505
Fax: 858 272-8565
Robert Nascenzi, *CEO*
Marc Willard, *CEO*
Tonya Torgeson, *COO*
Kevin J Herdman, *CFO*
Jim Kesaris, *CFO*
EMP: 90
SQ FT: 21,352
SALES: 11.3MM
SALES (corp-wide): 54.2B **Publicly Held**
WEB: www.defenseweb.com
SIC: 7379 7371 Computer related consulting services; computer software development
PA: Humana Inc.
500 W Main St Ste 300
Louisville KY 40202
502 580-1000

(P-16354)
DELTA COMPUTER CONSULTING
25550 Hawthorne Blvd # 106, Torrance (90505-6831)
PHONE................................310 541-9440
Marzieh Daneshvar, *President*
Masih Hakimpour, *Vice Pres*
EMP: 180
SQ FT: 2,000
SALES (est): 14.5MM **Privately Held**
WEB: www.deltacomputerconsulting.com
SIC: 7379 Computer related consulting services

(P-16355)
DELTA MAX
23 Curl Dr, Corona Del Mar (92625-1416)
P.O. Box 7188, Newport Beach (92658-7188)
PHONE................................949 759-8529
Robert Swanson, *Owner*
Kenny KAO, *Sales Executive*
EMP: 50
SALES (est): 2.2MM **Privately Held**
WEB: www.deltamax.com
SIC: 7379 Computer related consulting services

(P-16356)
DHARNE & COMPANY
19200 Von Karman Ave # 400, Irvine (92612-8553)
PHONE................................949 293-5675
Nitin Dharne, *President*
Sahil Borate, *Officer*
Gina Wu, *Officer*
EMP: 80
SALES (est): 2.5MM **Privately Held**
SIC: 7379 Computer related services

(P-16357)
DIRECTAPPS INC (PA)
Also Called: Direct Technology
3009 Douglas Blvd Ste 300, Roseville (95661-3895)
PHONE................................916 787-2200
Rick Nelson, *CEO*
Federico Michanie, *President*
Dan Konieczny, *COO*
Casey Stenzel, *CFO*
John Sercu, *Treasurer*
EMP: 125
SQ FT: 19,000
SALES: 38MM **Privately Held**
WEB: www.directapps.com
SIC: 7379 Computer related consulting services

(P-16358)
DTI SERVICES INC (PA)
601 S Figueroa St # 4300, Los Angeles (90017-5757)
PHONE................................213 670-1100
Satoru Amano, *President*
Chad D Harmon, *CEO*
Ken Yasuda, *CFO*
Michael C Frick, *Info Tech Dir*
Kevin Ballard, *Engineer*
EMP: 60 **EST:** 1996
SALES (est): 9.7MM **Privately Held**
WEB: www.dtiserv.com
SIC: 7379 4813 7374 7389 ; ; telephone communications broker; computer graphics service;

(P-16359)
DYNTEK INC (PA)
4440 Von Karman Ave # 200, Newport Beach (92660-2011)
PHONE................................949 271-6700
Ron Ben-Yishay, *CEO*
Wade Stevenson, *President*
Karen S Rosenberger, *COO*
Dave Berry, *CFO*
James Linesch, *CFO*
EMP: 105
SQ FT: 10,250
SALES (est): 68MM **Publicly Held**
WEB: www.dyntek.com
SIC: 7379 Computer related consulting services

(P-16360)
EA CONSULTING INC
1024 Iron Point Rd, Folsom (95630-8013)
PHONE................................916 357-6767
Fax: 916 200-0368
Chin K Wong, *CEO*
Michael Beatty, *Senior Partner*
Robitah Mohd-Khatib, *President*
Mark Burt, *Vice Pres*
Lip P Wang, *Vice Pres*
EMP: 50
SQ FT: 12,000
SALES (est): 3.6MM **Privately Held**
WEB: www.ea-inc.com
SIC: 7379 8748 Computer related consulting services; business consulting

(P-16361)
ECLIPSE SOLUTIONS INC
2150 River Plaza Dr # 380, Sacramento (95833-4138)
PHONE................................916 565-8090
Fax: 916 565-5126
John Willis, *CEO*
Mike Watson, *President*
Paul Baldwin, *CFO*
Lori Duff, *Manager*
EMP: 84
SALES (est): 6.5MM
SALES (corp-wide): 341.4MM **Privately Held**
WEB: www.eclipsesolutions.com
SIC: 7379 8748 8742 8322 Computer related consulting services; business consulting; management consulting services; disaster service
PA: Public Consulting Group, Inc.
148 State St Fl 10
Boston MA 02109
617 426-2026

(P-16362)
EDMIN OPEN SYSTEMS INC (PA)
5471 Krny Vlla Rd Ste 310, San Diego (92123)
PHONE................................858 712-9341
Peter Sibley, *CEO*
Rick Wells, *CFO*
Richard Datz, *Vice Pres*
Clayton D Hoyle, *Vice Pres*
D Clayton Hoyle, *Vice Pres*
EMP: 54
SQ FT: 15,000
SALES (est): 12.4MM **Privately Held**
WEB: www.edmin.com
SIC: 7379 7373 7371 Computer related consulting services; value-added resellers, computer systems; software programming applications

(P-16363)
ELITE TEK SERVICES INC
131 Mercer Way, Costa Mesa (92627-3797)
PHONE................................714 881-5301
Stephanie Duplex, *President*
Scott Duplex, *Vice Pres*
EMP: 54
SALES (est): 4.8MM **Privately Held**
SIC: 7379 7361 Computer related consulting services; employment agencies

(P-16364)
ENCORE SOFTWARE SERVICES INC
2025 Gateway Pl Ste 290, San Jose (95110-1094)
PHONE................................408 573-7337
Radha Krishnan, *President*
Muralee Bhaskar, *CEO*
Rajan Jeyakumar, *Senior VP*
Nirav Doshi, *Admin Asst*
EMP: 72
SALES (est): 7.2MM **Privately Held**
SIC: 7379

(P-16365)
EPAIRS INC
20370 Town Center Ln # 255, Cupertino (95014-3213)
PHONE................................408 973-8466
Fax: 408 973-8499
Kumar Nathan, *President*
Uma Swaiminathan, *Vice Pres*
EMP: 78
SALES (est): 2.7MM
SALES (corp-wide): 473.6MM **Publicly Held**
WEB: www.epairs.com
SIC: 7379 Computer related consulting services
PA: Perficient, Inc.
555 Maryville Univ Dr 6
Saint Louis MO 63141
314 529-3600

(P-16366)
EQUITY FIRM GOLDEN GATE CAPITL
1 Embarcadero Ctr Fl 39th, San Francisco (94111-3628)
PHONE................................415 983-2703
Jake Mizrahi, *Director*
EMP: 201
SALES (est): 4.1MM **Privately Held**
SIC: 7379 Computer related consulting services

(P-16367)
ETAIROS CONSULTING
6711 Studio Pl, Riverside (92509-5900)
PHONE................................844 219-7027
Daniel Salisbury, *CEO*
EMP: 50
SQ FT: 4,000
SALES (est): 2.3MM **Privately Held**
SIC: 7379 Computer related consulting services

(P-16368)
ETHERWAN SYSTEMS INC
2301 E Winston Rd, Anaheim (92806-5542)
PHONE................................714 779-3800
Mitch Yang, *President*
Sal Tassone, *Regional Mgr*
Cara Rising, *Admin Asst*
Lizzeth Alvarazo, *Administration*
David Kuo, *Comp Spec*
EMP: 100 **EST:** 1996
SQ FT: 5,000
SALES (est): 12.4MM
SALES (corp-wide): 147.4MM **Privately Held**
WEB: www.etherwan.com
SIC: 7379 Computer related maintenance services
HQ: Etherwan Systems, Inc.
8f, 2, Alley 6, Lane 235, Pao Chiao Rd.,
New Taipei City 23145
266 298-986

(P-16369)
EXPERTS EXCHANGE LLC
Also Called: Experts Exch Exprts-Xchange-com
2701 Mcmillan Ave Ste 160, San Luis Obispo (93401-4744)
P.O. Box 1229 (93406-1229)
PHONE................................805 787-0603
Randy Redberg, *VP Sales*
Eric Peterson, *Administration*
Gene Richardson, *CIO*
Brian Bermingham, *Info Tech Mgr*
Jack Frost, *Web Dvlpr*
EMP: 55
SQ FT: 13,400
SALES (est): 7.3MM **Privately Held**
SIC: 7379 Computer related consulting services

(P-16370)
FLITE INC
23 Geary St, San Francisco (94108-5701)
PHONE................................415 992-5870
Will Price, *CEO*
Giles Goodwin, *President*
Matt Peake, *President*
Caitlin Haberberger, *CFO*
Chris Krueger, *CFO*
EMP: 60

PRODUCTS & SERVICES SECTION
7379 - Computer Related Svcs, NEC County (P-16394)

SQ FT: 20,000
SALES: 5MM Privately Held
WEB: www.flite.com
SIC: 7379

(P-16371)
FMT CONSULTANTS LLC
Also Called: F M T
2310 Camino Vida Roble # 101, Carlsbad (92011-1561)
PHONE.................760 930-6400
Eric Casazza, *CEO*
Jim O'Grady, *Principal*
Jeff Fenn, *Practice Mgr*
Linh Nguyen, *Finance*
Alice Chen, *Marketing Staff*
EMP: 53
SQ FT: 6,500
SALES: 9MM Privately Held
WEB: www.fmtconsultants.com
SIC: 7379

(P-16372)
FOODBUZZ INC
72 Townsend St, San Francisco (94107-2185)
PHONE.................415 321-1200
Ben Dehan, *CEO*
Devon Odonnell, *Director*
EMP: 77
SALES (est): 2.8MM
SALES (corp-wide): 674.9MM Publicly Held
SIC: 7379
HQ: Federated Media Publishing, Llc
350 Sansome St Ste 925
San Francisco CA 94104
415 332-6955

(P-16373)
FORSYS INC
5994 W Las Positas Blvd # 221, Pleasanton (94588-8525)
PHONE.................844 409-0510
Jayaprasad Vejendla, *President*
EMP: 75 EST: 2015
SQ FT: 3,000
SALES: 20MM Privately Held
SIC: 7379 Computer related consulting services

(P-16374)
FORSYTHE SOLUTIONS GROUP INC
222 N Sepulveda Blvd # 1426, El Segundo (90245-5674)
PHONE.................424 217-6500
EMP: 64
SALES (corp-wide): 3.1B Privately Held
SIC: 7379 Computer related maintenance services
HQ: Forsythe Solutions Group, Inc.
7770 Frontage Rd
Skokie IL 60077
847 213-7000

(P-16375)
FUNNY OR DIE INC
159 2nd Ave, San Mateo (94401-3801)
PHONE.................650 461-3929
Dick Glover, *CEO*
Richard Glover, *CEO*
Mitch Galbraith, *COO*
Peter Morris, *Vice Pres*
Rob Miller, *Producer*
EMP: 50
SALES (est): 7.6MM Privately Held
SIC: 7379

(P-16376)
FUSIONSTORM (PA)
Also Called: Adexis
2 Bryant St Ste 150, San Francisco (94105-1641)
PHONE.................415 623-2626
John Varel, *CEO*
Bill Dougherty, *President*
Daniel Serpico, *President*
Michael Soja, *CFO*
Doug Adams, *Vice Pres*
EMP: 148

SALES (est): 277.2MM Privately Held
WEB: www.fusionstorm.com
SIC: 7379 7371 7374 7376 Computer related maintenance services; computer software systems analysis & design, custom; data processing service; computer facilities management

(P-16377)
FUSIONZONE AUTOMOTIVE INC
1011 Swarthmore Ave, Pacific Palisades (90272-2552)
PHONE.................888 576-1136
Brett Sutherlin, *CEO*
Kevin Maloy, *CFO*
Karen Sutherlin, *CFO*
Leanne McNamee, *Graphic Designe*
Jonas Weirtz, *Director*
EMP: 50
SQ FT: 3,000
SALES (est): 2.7MM Privately Held
SIC: 7379 Computer related consulting services

(P-16378)
FUTURE STATE
2101 Webster St, Oakland (94612-3011)
PHONE.................925 956-4200
Steven Laine, *President*
Carla Gallinat, *Accounting Mgr*
Jim Sherwood, *Controller*
Bill McDaniel, *Director*
Rose Healy, *Accounts Mgr*
EMP: 90
SALES: 19.2MM Privately Held
SIC: 7379 8742 Data processing consultant; management consulting services

(P-16379)
GA SERVICES LLC
1681 Kettering, Irvine (92614-5613)
PHONE.................949 752-6515
Fax: 949 606-1990
Charles S Strauch,
Kim Scherer, *Controller*
George J Harris,
EMP: 50
SQ FT: 10,500
SALES (est): 3.6MM Privately Held
WEB: www.gasllc.com
SIC: 7379 7378 Computer related consulting services; computer maintenance & repair

(P-16380)
GAMEFLY INC (PA)
6080 Center Dr Fl 8, Los Angeles (90045-9205)
PHONE.................310 568-8224
Dave Hodess, *President*
Stacey M Peterson, *CFO*
Shosannah Bacura, *Vice Pres*
Neil Seth, *Vice Pres*
Christopher Tearpak, *Software Dev*
EMP: 115
SALES (est): 33MM Privately Held
SIC: 7379

(P-16381)
GDR GROUP INC
6430 Oak Cyn Ste 200, Irvine (92618-5234)
PHONE.................949 453-8818
Fax: 949 753-1535
Ellen Dorse, *Principal*
Lisa Salinger, *Business Dir*
Bruce Greenburg, *Principal*
Robert Redwitz, *Principal*
David Donaldson, *Admin Asst*
EMP: 100
SALES (est): 16.5MM Privately Held
WEB: www.gdrgroup.com
SIC: 7379 Computer related consulting services

(P-16382)
GEBBS SOFTWARE INTL INC
4640 Admiralty Way Fl 9, Marina Del Rey (90292-6630)
PHONE.................201 227-0088
Nitin Thakor, *CEO*
Nayan Rane, *IT/INT Sup*
Avesh Shaikh, *VP Opers*
EMP: 85
SQ FT: 2,500

SALES: 15.4MM Privately Held
WEB: www.gebbs.com
SIC: 7379 Computer related consulting services
PA: Gebbs Software International Private Limited
Gebbs House
Mumbai MH
222 838-6303

(P-16383)
GEEK SQUAD INC
1490 Fitzgerald Dr, Pinole (94564-2227)
PHONE.................800 433-5778
Fax: 510 758-0285
Rex Santacera, *Branch Mgr*
EMP: 88
SALES (corp-wide): 39.5B Publicly Held
SIC: 7379 Computer related consulting services
HQ: Geek Squad, Inc
1213 Washington Ave N
Minneapolis MN 55401

(P-16384)
GEEK SQUAD INC
2300 N Rose Ave, Oxnard (93036-2628)
PHONE.................805 278-9555
Jonathan Roach, *Manager*
EMP: 88
SALES (corp-wide): 39.5B Publicly Held
SIC: 7379 Computer related consulting services
HQ: Geek Squad, Inc
1213 Washington Ave N
Minneapolis MN 55401

(P-16385)
GEEK SQUAD INC
120 Imperial Hwy, Fullerton (92835-1019)
PHONE.................800 433-5778
EMP: 88
SALES (corp-wide): 39.5B Publicly Held
SIC: 7379 Computer related consulting services
HQ: Geek Squad, Inc
1213 Washington Ave N
Minneapolis MN 55401

(P-16386)
GEEK SQUAD INC
901 S Coast Dr Ste F, Costa Mesa (92626-1783)
PHONE.................714 434-0132
EMP: 88
SALES (corp-wide): 39.5B Publicly Held
SIC: 7379 Computer related consulting services
HQ: Geek Squad, Inc
1213 Washington Ave N
Minneapolis MN 55401

(P-16387)
GEEK SQUAD INC
181 Curtner Ave, San Jose (95125-1014)
PHONE.................408 297-2520
EMP: 88
SALES (corp-wide): 39.5B Publicly Held
SIC: 7379 Computer related consulting services
HQ: Geek Squad, Inc
1213 Washington Ave N
Minneapolis MN 55401

(P-16388)
GEEK SQUAD INC
3741 W Chapman Ave, Orange (92868-1608)
PHONE.................714 938-0380
EMP: 88
SALES (corp-wide): 39.5B Publicly Held
SIC: 7379 Computer related consulting services
HQ: Geek Squad, Inc
1213 Washington Ave N
Minneapolis MN 55401

(P-16389)
GENERAL NETWORKS CORPORATION
3524 Ocean View Blvd, Glendale (91208-1212)
PHONE.................818 249-1962
Fax: 818 249-1024
Robert Todd Withers, *President*
Randall C Wise, *Ch of Bd*
Todd Withers, *President*
Cort Baker, *Vice Pres*
David Horwatt, *Vice Pres*
EMP: 60
SQ FT: 3,600
SALES: 12MM Privately Held
WEB: www.gennet.com
SIC: 7379 5045 7372 Computer related consulting services; terminals, computer; prepackaged software

(P-16390)
GENIUSCOM INCORPORATED
6200 Stoneridge Mall Rd # 500, Pleasanton (94588-3702)
PHONE.................650 931-1382
Fax: 650 212-2051
Sam Weber, *CEO*
Dave Hunsinger, *Vice Pres*
Omer Saeed, *Vice Pres*
Dapeng LI, *Administration*
Yina Mersy, *Finance*
EMP: 61
SQ FT: 20,000
SALES (est): 6MM Privately Held
SIC: 7379 Computer related consulting services

(P-16391)
GLOBAL BUSINESS SOLUTIONS INC
600 Anton Blvd Ste 1050, Costa Mesa (92626-7055)
PHONE.................714 257-1488
Johnnie R Carlin, *CEO*
John R Carlin, *CEO*
David H Gleit, *COO*
EMP: 258
SALES (est): 23.9MM Privately Held
WEB: www.gbscs.com
SIC: 7379 8741 8742 Computer related consulting services; construction management; construction project management consultant

(P-16392)
GLOBAL DATA PUBLICATIONS INC
425 California St # 1300, San Francisco (94104-2102)
PHONE.................415 800-0336
EMP: 480
SALES (corp-wide): 68.6MM Privately Held
SIC: 7379 Data processing consultant
PA: Global Data Publications Inc.
441 Lexington Ave Fl 3
New York NY 10017
646 395-5460

(P-16393)
GLOBALWAYS INC (PA)
42808 Christy St Ste 202, Fremont (94538-3119)
PHONE.................510 580-1974
Uma Uppalapati, *President*
Yi Guo, *Webmaster*
Kailash Reddy, *IT/INT Sup*
Jithendra Anne, *Tech Recruiter*
Raj Kumar, *Manager*
EMP: 68
SQ FT: 3,500
SALES (est): 5.8MM Privately Held
WEB: www.globalways.com
SIC: 7379 Computer related consulting services

(P-16394)
GRID DYNAMICS INTL INC (PA)
4600 Bohannon Dr Ste 220, Menlo Park (94025-1044)
PHONE.................650 523-5000
David Gimpelevich, *President*
Sylvia Kainz, *COO*
Chris Munson, *CFO*
Victoria Livschitz, *Exec Dir*

7379 - Computer Related Svcs, NEC County (P-16395)

Igor Egorov, *Info Tech Dir*
EMP: 50
SQ FT: 1,700
SALES: 2.5MM **Privately Held**
SIC: 7379 Computer related consulting services

(P-16395)
HACKETT GROUP INC
Mednick, Scott & Associates
8522 National Blvd # 101, Culver City (90232-2400)
PHONE.................................310 842-8444
Fax: 310 842-8063
Scott Mednick, *CEO*
EMP: 90
SALES (corp-wide): 260.9MM **Publicly Held**
WEB: www.answerthink.com
SIC: 7379 8748 Computer related consulting services; business consulting
  PA: The Hackett Group Inc
    1001 Brickell Bay Dr # 3000
    Miami FL 33131
    305 375-8005

(P-16396)
HEADSTRONG CORPORATION
150 Mathilda Pl Ste 200, Sunnyvale (94086-6011)
PHONE.................................408 732-8700
Sandip Sahai, *Manager*
EMP: 60 **Privately Held**
WEB: www.headstrong.com
SIC: 7379 8711 1731 Computer related consulting services; engineering services; electrical work
  HQ: Headstrong Corporation
    11921 Freedom Dr Ste 550
    Reston VA 20190
    703 272-6761

(P-16397)
HOMESTAR SYSTEMS INC
Also Called: Izmocars
230 California St Ste 510, San Francisco (94111-4331)
PHONE.................................415 694-6000
Tej Soni, *CEO*
Layton Judd, *Principal*
Noman Saied, *Info Tech Mgr*
Jayakumar Hariharan, *Marketing Mgr*
Rod Lampart, *Director*
EMP: 85
SQ FT: 500
SALES (est): 7MM **Privately Held**
WEB: www.izmocars.com
SIC: 7379 Computer related consulting services

(P-16398)
HYPERMEDIA SYSTEMS INC
700 S Flower St Ste 3210, Los Angeles (90017-4219)
PHONE.................................213 908-2214
Michael Frick, *President*
Yumi Bustillos, *Admin Sec*
Kelvin Mok, *Admin Asst*
John Lee, *Administration*
Jamie Monma, *Administration*
EMP: 85
SQ FT: 800
SALES: 7.3MM **Privately Held**
WEB: www.hypermediasystems.com
SIC: 7379 Computer related consulting services

(P-16399)
IBASET FEDERAL SERVICES LLC (PA)
27442 Portola Pkwy # 300, Foothill Ranch (92610-2823)
PHONE.................................949 598-5200
Ladeira Poonian, *Chairman*
Vic Sial, *President*
Elizabeth Conley, *CFO*
Louis Columbus, *Vice Pres*
Bob Joyce, *Vice Pres*
EMP: 75
SQ FT: 30,000
SALES (est): 55.3MM **Privately Held**
SIC: 7379 Computer related maintenance services

(P-16400)
IDRIVE INC
Also Called: Ibackup.com
26115 Mureau Rd Ste A, Calabasas (91302-3179)
PHONE.................................818 594-5972
Raghu Kulkarni, *President*
Vilabh Mishra, *President*
Pankti Shah, *Human Resources*
EMP: 70
SALES (est): 12.3MM **Privately Held**
WEB: www.pro-softnet.com
SIC: 7379 Computer related maintenance services

(P-16401)
INFOGAIN CORPORATION (PA)
485 Alberto Way Ste 100, Los Gatos (95032-5476)
PHONE.................................408 355-6000
Fax: 408 355-7000
Sunil Bhatia, *CEO*
Kapil K Nanda, *President*
Brian Rogan, *President*
Phil Johnson, *CFO*
Dean Wohlwend, *CFO*
EMP: 186
SQ FT: 15,000
SALES: 85.2MM **Privately Held**
WEB: www.infogain.com
SIC: 7379 7373 8742 8748 Computer related consulting services; computer integrated systems design; management information systems consultant; systems engineering consultant, ex. computer or professional; data processing & preparation; electrical work

(P-16402)
INNOVA SOLUTIONS INC
4633 Old Ironsides Dr # 320, Santa Clara (95054-1846)
PHONE.................................408 889-2020
Rajkumar Velagapudi, *CEO*
Fadi Baaklini, *Senior VP*
Matthew Degel, *Senior VP*
Dheeraj Nallagatla, *Senior VP*
Rich Marino, *Principal*
EMP: 130 EST: 2014
SQ FT: 3,300
SALES: 43MM **Privately Held**
SIC: 7379 Computer related consulting services

(P-16403)
INTEGRITS CORPORATION (PA)
5205 Kearny Villa Way # 200, San Diego (92123-1420)
PHONE.................................858 300-1600
Fax: 858 300-1640
Clarence M Carter Jr, *President*
Ivy Y Carter, *Vice Pres*
Michael Sosamon, *Vice Pres*
Joni Shirley, *Executive*
Nick Enriquez, *CTO*
EMP: 50
SQ FT: 12,600
SALES: 6MM **Privately Held**
WEB: www.integrits.com
SIC: 7379 Computer related consulting services

(P-16404)
INTELLIPRO GROUP INC
2905 Stender Way Ste 42, Santa Clara (95054-3224)
PHONE.................................408 200-9891
Grace MA, *CEO*
Luoyin Zhao, *Director*
EMP: 380
SALES (est): 16.6MM **Privately Held**
SIC: 7379 Computer related consulting services

(P-16405)
INTELLISWIFT SOFTWARE INC (PA)
Also Called: Magagnini
2201 Walnut Ave Ste 180, Fremont (94538-2334)
PHONE.................................510 490-9240
Parag Patel, *CEO*
Rahul Garg, *Exec VP*
John Magagnini, *Vice Pres*
Bob Patel, *Principal*
Rekha Shetty, *Info Tech Mgr*
EMP: 225
SQ FT: 5,200
SALES (est): 96MM **Privately Held**
WEB: www.intelliswift.com
SIC: 7379 Computer related consulting services

(P-16406)
INTERACTIVATE INC
707 Broadway Ste 1000, San Diego (92101-5324)
PHONE.................................619 814-1999
Fax: 619 814-1998
Jack Abbott Jr, *President*
Morgan Brown, *Executive*
Josh Ettwein, *Software Dev*
Alisa Vargas, *Accountant*
Michelle Linhardt, *Controller*
EMP: 90
SALES (est): 5.5MM **Privately Held**
SIC: 7379

(P-16407)
INTERMEDIA HOLDINGS INC (PA)
825 E Middlefield Rd, Mountain View (94043-4025)
PHONE.................................650 641-4000
Michael Gold, *CEO*
Jonathan McCormick, *COO*
Scott Allen, *CFO*
Bob Tirva, *CFO*
Andrew Gachechiladze, *Senior VP*
EMP: 70
SALES (est): 46.5MM **Privately Held**
SIC: 7379

(P-16408)
INTERNATIONAL BUS MCHS CORP
Also Called: IBM
1540 Scenic Ave, Costa Mesa (92626-1408)
PHONE.................................714 327-3501
William Kreidler, *Branch Mgr*
Alexander Kuang, *Lab Dir*
Derek Ricci, *Manager*
EMP: 381
SALES (corp-wide): 81.7B **Publicly Held**
SIC: 7379 Computer related consulting services
  PA: International Business Machines Corporation
    1 New Orchard Rd Ste 1
    Armonk NY 10504
    914 499-1900

(P-16409)
INTERNATIONAL BUS MCHS CORP
Also Called: IBM
1001 E Hillsdale Blvd, Foster City (94404-1643)
PHONE.................................800 426-4968
Richard Baird, *Director*
EMP: 396
SALES (corp-wide): 81.7B **Publicly Held**
SIC: 7379 7371 3571 3572 Computer related consulting services; computer software development; software programming applications; minicomputers; mainframe computers; personal computers (microcomputers); computer storage devices; drum drives, computer; tape storage units, computer; semiconductors & related devices; microcircuits, integrated (semiconductor)
  PA: International Business Machines Corporation
    1 New Orchard Rd Ste 1
    Armonk NY 10504
    914 499-1900

(P-16410)
INTERNET-JOURNALS INC
Also Called: Berkeley Electronic Press
2100 Milvia St 300, Berkeley (94704-1113)
PHONE.................................510 665-1200
Aaron Edlin, *Ch of Bd*
Jean-Gabriel Bankier, *President*
Arianna Pretto, *Executive*
Romeo Mata, *Accountant*
Kenneth Gleason, *Manager*
EMP: 52

SALES (est): 5.4MM **Privately Held**
WEB: www.bepress.com
SIC: 7379

(P-16411)
INTRATEK COMPUTER INC
9950 Irvine Center Dr, Irvine (92618-4357)
PHONE.................................949 334-4200
Fax: 714 892-0845
Allen Fahami, *Chairman*
Anthony Battey, *Shareholder*
Mohsen Fahami, *Shareholder*
Rodney Holdren, *Shareholder*
Jeffrey Shyshka, *CEO*
EMP: 310
SQ FT: 9,800
SALES: 25.4MM **Privately Held**
WEB: www.intrapc.com
SIC: 7379

(P-16412)
IP ACCESS INTERNATIONAL
31831 Cmno Capistrno 300a Ste 300 A, San Juan Capistrano (92675)
PHONE.................................949 655-1000
Fax: 949 240-8072
Bryan Hill, *President*
Bill Pitz, *Vice Pres*
Alan Rich, *Vice Pres*
Ginger Gadberry, *Admin Asst*
Barbara Coleman, *Director*
EMP: 50
SQ FT: 10,000
SALES (est): 6.5MM **Privately Held**
WEB: www.ipinternational.net
SIC: 7379 Computer related consulting services

(P-16413)
IP INTERNATIONAL INC
Also Called: Info Plus International
1510 Fashion Island Blvd # 104, San Mateo (94404-1596)
PHONE.................................650 403-7800
Fax: 650 378-2875
Margaret Schaninger, *President*
Agustin Ramirez, *CFO*
John Wroten, *CTO*
Patti Kozlovsky, *Sr Consultant*
Michael Welton, *Sr Consultant*
EMP: 50
SQ FT: 2,500
SALES (est): 5.9MM **Privately Held**
WEB: www.infoplusintl.com
SIC: 7379 8748 Computer related consulting services; business consulting

(P-16414)
ISPACE INC
2381 Rosecrans Ave # 110, El Segundo (90245-4920)
PHONE.................................310 563-3800
Fax: 310 563-3801
Suresh Kothapalli, *CEO*
Lisa Flores, *Exec VP*
Ram Davaloor, *Vice Pres*
Mark Bonifacio, *Admin Mgr*
Kiran Kumar, *Admin Asst*
EMP: 120
SALES (est): 17.5MM **Privately Held**
WEB: www.ispace.com
SIC: 7379 Computer related consulting services

(P-16415)
ISTS WORLDWIDE INC
2201 Walnut Ave Ste 210, Fremont (94538-2355)
PHONE.................................510 794-1400
Viren Rana, *CEO*
Akash Jain, *President*
Linda S Perry, *Exec VP*
EMP: 106
SALES (est): 8.3MM **Privately Held**
WEB: www.istsinc.com
SIC: 7379 Computer related consulting services

(P-16416)
ITCO SOLUTIONS INC
1003 Whitehall Ln, Redwood City (94061-3687)
P.O. Box 610090 (94061-0090)
PHONE.................................650 367-0514
Ryan Edwards, *Director*
Chris Middleton, *Vice Pres*

PRODUCTS & SERVICES SECTION
7379 - Computer Related Svcs, NEC County (P-16439)

Laura Simonds, *Recruiter*
Brad Ravin, *Regl Sales Mgr*
Tom Kramer, *Manager*
EMP: 295
SALES (est): 21.7MM **Privately Held**
WEB: www.itcosolutions.com
SIC: 7379 Computer related consulting services

(P-16417)
ITEK SERVICES INC
25501 Arctic Ocean Dr, Lake Forest (92630-8827)
PHONE.....................949 770-4835
Donald W Rowley, *CEO*
John Curl, *President*
Maris Krigens, *Software Engr*
Adrian Mauricio, *Engineer*
Diana Bridges, *VP Finance*
EMP: 100
SQ FT: 12,000
SALES: 24MM **Privately Held**
WEB: www.iteksservice.com
SIC: 7379 Computer related maintenance services

(P-16418)
JASS & ASSOCIATES INC
2099 Gateway Pl Ste 304, San Jose (95110-1017)
PHONE.....................408 436-1624
Chakradhar Paturi, *President*
Suresh Venna, *COO*
Jayprasad Vejendla, *CTO*
Michael Maldonado, *Marketing Staff*
Dilip Kondiparti, *Director*
EMP: 325
SALES (est): 14.5MM **Privately Held**
SIC: 7379 Computer related consulting services

(P-16419)
KIOSKED
220 Main St Ste C, Venice (90291-5218)
PHONE.....................310 392-2470
Micke Paqvalen, *CEO*
EMP: 90
SALES (est): 3.9MM **Privately Held**
SIC: 7379

(P-16420)
KORE1 INC
47 Discovery Ste 210, Irvine (92618-3205)
PHONE.....................949 706-6990
Brian Hunt, *CEO*
Steven Quarles, *Managing Dir*
Maryn Harvey, *Accounts Exec*
EMP: 100
SQ FT: 2,000
SALES: 8MM **Privately Held**
SIC: 7379

(P-16421)
LATTICE ENGINES INC (PA)
1820 Gateway Dr Ste 200, San Mateo (94404-4059)
PHONE.....................877 460-0010
Shashi Upadhyay, *CEO*
Andrew Dong, *President*
Kent McCormick, *President*
Howie Shohet, *CFO*
Patrick Donnelly, *Senior VP*
EMP: 85
SALES (est): 39.1MM **Privately Held**
SIC: 7379 Computer related consulting services

(P-16422)
LEIDOS INC
4035 Hancock St, San Diego (92110-5105)
PHONE.....................858 826-5552
Diane Malito, *Branch Mgr*
Nancy Aitkenhead, *Vice Pres*
Laverne Cose, *Vice Pres*
Barbara Drinkwar, *Division Mgr*
Ken Bickel, *Engineer*
EMP: 377
SALES (corp-wide): 5B **Publicly Held**
WEB: www.saic.com
SIC: 7379 Computer related consulting services
HQ: Leidos, Inc.
11951 Freedom Dr Ste 500
Reston VA 20190
571 526-6000

(P-16423)
LIFFEY THAMES GROUP LLC
Also Called: Discovia
465 California St Fl 14, San Francisco (94104-1832)
PHONE.....................415 392-2900
Christian Lawrence, *CEO*
Gregory J Mazares, *President*
Ciaran Power, *President*
Kristopher Taylor, *President*
Paige Hunt Wojcik, *Officer*
EMP: 108
SQ FT: 21,800
SALES: 19.6MM **Privately Held**
WEB: www.sanfranciscolegal.com
SIC: 7379 Data processing consultant

(P-16424)
LOCKHEED MARTIN GOVERNMENT SER
500 N Via Val Verde, Montebello (90640-2358)
PHONE.....................323 721-6979
Nate Sadorian, *Branch Mgr*
EMP: 50
SALES (corp-wide): 5B **Publicly Held**
SIC: 7379 7372 Computer related consulting services; prepackaged software
HQ: Leidos Government Services, Inc.
700 N Frederick Ave
Gaithersburg MD 20879
856 486-5156

(P-16425)
LOGICTIER INC
7 41st Ave 76, San Mateo (94403-5105)
PHONE.....................650 235-6600
Mary Ann Byrnes, *CEO*
Omar Ahmad, *President*
Bill Zerella, *CFO*
Amanda Reed, *Exec VP*
Patrick Whalen, *Exec VP*
EMP: 200
SALES (est): 8.1MM **Privately Held**
SIC: 7379 1731 ; electrical work

(P-16426)
LOGIN CONSULTING SERVICES INC
300 Continental Blvd # 530, El Segundo (90245-5042)
PHONE.....................310 607-9091
Fax: 310 607-9818
Elece J Otten, *President*
Dan McKee, *Officer*
Lisa Borsa, *Executive*
Richard Cole, *Network Mgr*
Marvin Johnson, *Prgrmr*
EMP: 75
SQ FT: 3,200
SALES (est): 8.1MM **Privately Held**
WEB: www.loginconsult.com
SIC: 7379 Computer related consulting services

(P-16427)
MACHINIMA INC
3500 W Olive Ave, Burbank (91505-4628)
P.O. Box 692200, West Hollywood (90069-9257)
PHONE.....................323 872-5300
Chad E Gutstein, *CEO*
Allen Debevoise, *Ch of Bd*
Philip Debevoise, *President*
Stephen Semprevivo, *CEO*
James Glasscock, *Senior VP*
EMP: 98
SALES (est): 21.8MM **Privately Held**
SIC: 7379 Computer related consulting services

(P-16428)
MAGMA CONSULTING GROUP LLC
Also Called: Magmalabs
830 Traction Ave 3a, Los Angeles (90013-1816)
PHONE.....................415 315-9364
Carlos Rocha, *CEO*
EMP: 61 **EST:** 2015
SALES: 2MM **Privately Held**
SIC: 7379 Computer related consulting services

(P-16429)
MARKMONITOR INC (DH)
425 Market St Ste 500, San Francisco (94105-2464)
PHONE.....................415 278-8400
Fax: 415 278-8445
Mark Frost, *CEO*
Frederick Felman, *Chief Mktg Ofcr*
Tom Ryden, *Senior VP*
Ariel Zach, *Senior VP*
Charlie Abrahams, *Vice Pres*
EMP: 86
SQ FT: 25,500
SALES (est): 35.4MM
SALES (corp-wide): 3.8B **Publicly Held**
WEB: www.markmonitor.com
SIC: 7379
HQ: Thomson Reuters Corporation
3 Times Sq Lbby Mailroom
New York NY 10036
646 223-4000

(P-16430)
MAXONIC INC
2041 Mission College Blvd # 140, Santa Clara (95054-1589)
PHONE.....................408 777-6825
Ajay Narain, *CEO*
Nitin Khanna, *President*
Meenal Bagora, *Regional Mgr*
Tracia Chan, *Regional Mgr*
Ambrish Damani, *Regional Mgr*
EMP: 65
SQ FT: 3,499
SALES (est): 14.5MM **Privately Held**
WEB: www.maxonic.com
SIC: 7379 7371 Computer related consulting services; computer software development & applications

(P-16431)
METABYTE INC
Also Called: Hotdoodle.com
39350 Civic Center Dr # 200, Fremont (94538-2343)
PHONE.....................510 494-9700
Fax: 510 494-9100
Manu Mehta, *President*
Monica Miu, *Tech Recruiter*
Bill Ruge, *Accounting Mgr*
Aradhana Mehta, *Client Mgr*
Khalid Akhter, *Manager*
EMP: 100
SQ FT: 15,000
SALES: 12MM **Privately Held**
WEB: www.metabyte.com
SIC: 7379

(P-16432)
METAMOR ENTP SOLUTIONS LLC
18350 Mount Langley St # 1, Fountain Valley (92708-6900)
PHONE.....................866 565-4746
Sumeet Sonu Singh, *CEO*
Arnold Nel, *COO*
Jai Saboo, *CTO*
EMP: 50
SALES (est): 1.7MM
SALES (corp-wide): 786.9MM **Publicly Held**
SIC: 7379 7373 Computer related consulting services; systems integration services
PA: Ciber, Inc.
6312 S Fiddlers Green Cir 320n
Greenwood Village CO 80111
303 220-0100

(P-16433)
METIER LTD
1083 Vine St Ste 511, Healdsburg (95448-4830)
PHONE.....................707 546-9300
Douglas Clark, *CEO*
Sandra Richardson, *COO*
Simmons Lough, *Vice Pres*
Erin Baker, *Business Dir*
Edward Kwok, *Software Dev*
EMP: 55 **EST:** 1998
SALES (est): 7.4MM **Privately Held**
WEB: www.metier.com
SIC: 7379 Computer related consulting services

(P-16434)
MICROTEL COMPUTER SYSTEMS INC
5545 Daniels St, Chino (91710-9026)
PHONE.....................626 839-6038
Juliet Chui, *President*
EMP: 70
SQ FT: 17,000
SALES (est): 6.4MM **Privately Held**
WEB: www.microtelinc.com
SIC: 7379 Computer related consulting services

(P-16435)
MULTIVEN INC
303 Twin Dolphin Dr # 600, Redwood City (94065-1497)
P.O. Box 394, San Carlos (94070-0394)
PHONE.....................408 828-2715
EMP: 50
SQ FT: 2,000
SALES (est): 2.2MM **Privately Held**
WEB: www.multiven.com
SIC: 7379

(P-16436)
MURPHY MCKAY & ASSOCIATES INC
3468 Mt Diablo Blvd B108, Lafayette (94549-7103)
PHONE.....................925 283-9555
David D McKay, *Ch of Bd*
Timothy J Murphy, *President*
Marianne McKay, *CFO*
Renee Laperle, *Administration*
Allen Arthur, *Manager*
EMP: 50
SQ FT: 2,000
SALES (est): 6.8MM **Privately Held**
WEB: www.murphymckay.com
SIC: 7379 Computer related consulting services

(P-16437)
NCC GROUP INC (HQ)
123 Mission St Ste 1020, San Francisco (94105-5126)
PHONE.....................415 268-9300
Rob Cotton, *President*
Craig Motta, *President*
Craig Foster, *CFO*
Maximilian Burkhardt, *IT/INT Sup*
Sal Pineda, *Credit Staff*
EMP: 90
SQ FT: 12,000
SALES: 33.4MM
SALES (corp-wide): 196.5MM **Privately Held**
SIC: 7379 Computer data escrow service
PA: Ncc Group Plc
Manchester Technology Centre
Manchester M1 7E
161 209-5200

(P-16438)
NEUDESIC LLC (PA)
100 Spectrum Center Dr # 1200, Irvine (92618-4962)
PHONE.....................949 754-4500
Fax: 949 754-6800
Parsa Rohani, *CEO*
Steve Oprian, *Executive*
Jason Noble, *General Mgr*
Marty Wasznicky, *General Mgr*
Mike Collins, *VP Opers*
EMP: 125
SQ FT: 15,150
SALES (est): 83.6MM **Privately Held**
SIC: 7379 Computer related consulting services

(P-16439)
NORLAND GROUP
3350 Scott Blvd Ste 6502, Santa Clara (95054-3125)
PHONE.....................408 855-8255
Fax: 408 855-8255
Mayling Liang, *President*
Sophie Kuo, *Accounting Mgr*
Reginald Malla, *Recruiter*
Artem Bagdasaryan, *Accounts Mgr*
EMP: 105
SQ FT: 2,200

7379 - Computer Related Svcs, NEC County (P-16440)

SALES (est): 9.3MM **Privately Held**
WEB: www.norlandgroup.com
SIC: **7379** 7361 Computer related consulting services; employment agencies

(P-16440)
NOWCOM CORPORATION
Also Called: Hankey Group
4751 Wilshire Blvd # 205, Los Angeles (90010-3860)
PHONE..................323 938-6449
Fax: 323 954-5250
Don R Hankey, *President*
Rob Lekstrom, *COO*
Paul Kerwin, *CFO*
Matt M Lee, *Senior VP*
Vaibhav Deshpande, *Vice Pres*
EMP: 54
SQ FT: 4,800
SALES (est): 11.8MM **Privately Held**
WEB: www.nowcom.com
SIC: **7379**

(P-16441)
NRI SECURE TECHNOLOGIES LTD
26 Executive Park Ste 150, Irvine (92614-4744)
PHONE..................949 537-2957
Naoshi Matsushita, *COO*
EMP: 200
SQ FT: 1,700
SALES (est): 5.9MM
SALES (corp-wide): 3.6B **Privately Held**
SIC: **7379** 1731 Computer related maintenance services; ; access control systems specialization
HQ: Nri Secure Technologies, Ltd.
1-7-2, Otemachi
Chiyoda-Ku TKY 100-0
367 060-500

(P-16442)
OLSON & ASSOC
3448 Lupine Cir Ste 102, Costa Mesa (92626-1723)
PHONE..................714 878-6649
Steven Olson, *CEO*
EMP: 60
SQ FT: 1,500
SALES (est): 4.7MM **Privately Held**
WEB: www.strategicgrowthsolutions.com
SIC: **7379** 7389 Computer related consulting services; personal service agents, brokers & bureaus

(P-16443)
OMNIKRON SYSTEMS INC
20920 Warner Center Ln A, Woodland Hills (91367-6526)
PHONE..................818 591-7890
Fax: 818 591-7891
Sudipta K Ghosh, *President*
Robin Rorough, *Business Dir*
Mindy Peterson, *Admin Sec*
Jim Henson, *Training Spec*
Robin Borough, *VP Sales*
EMP: 100
SALES: 4.9MM **Privately Held**
WEB: www.omnikron.com
SIC: **7379** 7375 5045 8243 Computer related consulting services; information retrieval services; computer software; operator training, computer; software training, computer; computer software systems analysis & design, custom; computer systems analysis & design

(P-16444)
ONEHEALTH SOLUTIONS INC
420 Stevens Ave Ste 200, Solana Beach (92075-2078)
PHONE..................858 947-6333
Fax: 858 481-4332
Bruce Springer, *President*
John Shade, *COO*
Wes Staggs, *Exec VP*
Jeff Goe, *Senior VP*
Chuck Mitchell, *Vice Pres*
EMP: 100
SALES (est): 8.4MM
SALES (corp-wide): 31.6MM **Privately Held**
SIC: **7379**

PA: Viverae, Inc.
10670 N Cntl Expy Ste 700
Dallas TX 75231
214 827-4400

(P-16445)
OPAL SOFT INC
Also Called: Opalsoft
1288 Kifer Rd Ste 201, Sunnyvale (94086-5326)
PHONE..................408 267-2211
Omprakash Choudhary, *President*
Alkesh Choudhary, *CFO*
EMP: 80
SQ FT: 2,450
SALES: 13.3MM **Privately Held**
WEB: www.opalsoft.com
SIC: **7379** 7371 8748 8713 Computer related consulting services; computer software systems analysis & design, custom; business consulting; photogrammetric engineering; service bureau, computer; computer facilities management

(P-16446)
ORACLE AMERICA INC
Also Called: Sun Microsystems
80 Railroad Ave, Milpitas (95035-4333)
PHONE..................408 635-3072
Bruce Webbe, *Manager*
Sengquee Liang, *Engineer*
EMP: 251
SALES (corp-wide): 37B **Publicly Held**
SIC: **7379** Computer related consulting services
HQ: Oracle America, Inc.
500 Oracle Pkwy
Redwood City CA 94065
650 506-7000

(P-16447)
ORGANIC INC
390 Amapola Ave Ste 8, Torrance (90501-1400)
PHONE..................310 543-4600
EMP: 71
SALES (corp-wide): 15.3B **Publicly Held**
SIC: **7379**
HQ: Organic, Inc.
600 California St Fl 8
San Francisco CA 94108
415 581-5300

(P-16448)
ORGANIC INC (HQ)
600 California St Fl 8, San Francisco (94108-2726)
PHONE..................415 581-5300
Conor Brady, *Ch Credit Ofcr*
David Bryant, *Officer*
Mark Murata, *Officer*
Danica Remy, *Vice Pres*
Dave Sylvestre, *Exec Dir*
EMP: 142
SQ FT: 23,000
SALES (est): 39.1MM
SALES (corp-wide): 15.1B **Publicly Held**
WEB: www.organic.com
SIC: **7379** 8742 ; computer related consulting services; marketing consulting services
PA: Omnicom Group Inc.
437 Madison Ave
New York NY 10022
212 415-3600

(P-16449)
OSI CONSULTING INC
2525 Main St Ste 350, Irvine (92614-6685)
PHONE..................949 724-8300
Kumar Yamani, *Owner*
Tony Reyes, *Business Anlyst*
Adam Ruthruff, *Technology*
EMP: 50 **Privately Held**
SIC: **7379** Computer related consulting services
PA: Osi Consulting, Inc.
5950 Canoga Ave Ste 300
Woodland Hills CA 91367
-

(P-16450)
OUTLOOK AMUSEMENTS INC
2900 W Alameda Ave # 400, Burbank (91505-4220)
PHONE..................818 433-3800

Jason Freeland, *CEO*
Cyrus Pejoumand, *President*
Tim Youd, *Co-President*
Tom Wszalek, *Senior VP*
Thomas Wszalek, *Vice Pres*
EMP: 150
SQ FT: 8,000
SALES (est): 28.8MM **Privately Held**
SIC: **7379**

(P-16451)
PACIFIC WEST CORPORATION (PA)
10369 Regis Ct, Rancho Cucamonga (91730-3055)
PHONE..................515 270-8181
Girish Reddy, *President*
EMP: 55
SQ FT: 2,500
SALES (est): 9.6MM **Privately Held**
SIC: **7379** Computer related consulting services

(P-16452)
PACTRON
3000 Patrick Henry Dr, Santa Clara (95054-1814)
PHONE..................408 329-5500
Fax: 408 747-1239
Sriram Iyer, *CEO*
K Prakash, *COO*
Lokesh Verma, *COO*
Clara Park, *Admin Asst*
Anand Dhanasekharan, *Technology*
EMP: 99
SQ FT: 35,000
SALES (est): 25MM **Privately Held**
WEB: www.pactroninc.com
SIC: **7379** Computer related maintenance services

(P-16453)
PALOMINO DB INC
Also Called: Blackbird
222 8th St, San Francisco (94103-3911)
PHONE..................775 572-8854
Laine Campbell, *CEO*
Vicki Vance, *COO*
Craig Irwin, *Vice Pres*
Aaron Lee, *General Mgr*
Jay Edwards, *CTO*
EMP: 51
SALES (est): 2.4MM
SALES (corp-wide): 6MM **Privately Held**
SIC: **7379** 7374 ; data processing & preparation; data processing service
PA: Pythian Group Inc, The
1200 St. Laurent Blvd Suite 261
Ottawa ON K1K 3
613 565-8696

(P-16454)
PARTNERS INFORMATION TECH INC (HQ)
Also Called: Calance
7101 Village Dr, Buena Park (90621-2260)
PHONE..................714 736-4487
Fax: 714 573-7470
Amit Govil, *Chairman*
Nancy Stubbs, *Vice Chairman*
Bill Darden, *CFO*
Asit Govil, *Treasurer*
Mark Goedde, *Vice Pres*
EMP: 100
SQ FT: 46,000
SALES (est): 60MM
SALES (corp-wide): 1MM **Privately Held**
SIC: **7379** Computer related consulting services
PA: Calance Software Private Limited
Suite No 201, Greenwood Plaza,
Gurgaon HAR 12200
991 032-0773

(P-16455)
PDS TECH INC
370 N Wstlake Blvd Stw120 Stw, Westlake Village (91362)
PHONE..................805 418-9862
Fax: 805 418-9866
Tony Mian, *Branch Mgr*
Ashley Aman, *Executive*
EMP: 2257

SALES (corp-wide): 321.4MM **Privately Held**
SIC: **7379** 7373 7371 Computer related consulting services; computer integrated systems design; computer software systems analysis & design, custom
PA: Pds Tech, Inc.
1925 W J Carpentr Fwy 5
Irving TX 75063
214 647-9600

(P-16456)
PERFORMANCE TECH PARTNERS LLC
11341 Gold Ex Dr Ste 160, Gold River (95670)
PHONE..................916 307-5669
John Podlipnik, *Vice Pres*
Ronald Hamilton, *Vice Pres*
John McNeal, *Software Dev*
Chris Menard, *Software Dev*
Charles Phillips, *Engineer*
EMP: 106
SQ FT: 4,971
SALES (est): 30MM **Privately Held**
WEB: www.performtechnology.com
SIC: **7379** Computer related consulting services

(P-16457)
PIVOT TECHNOLOGY SOLUTIONS LTD
11988 El Camino Real, San Diego (92130-3579)
PHONE..................647 788-2034
Kevin Shank, *CEO*
Shaun Maine, *COO*
John Flores, *Vice Pres*
EMP: 750
SALES (est): 69.9K **Privately Held**
SIC: **7379** 7373 ; systems integration services

(P-16458)
POINTSPEED INC
135 Wyndham Dr, Portola Valley (94028-7240)
PHONE..................650 638-3720
Norman Goldfarb, *President*
Ron Croce, *COO*
Michael Baltazar, *Vice Pres*
Sabet Chowdbury, *Vice Pres*
Jonathan Lewis, *Vice Pres*
EMP: 71
SALES (est): 5.4MM **Privately Held**
SIC: **7379** Computer related consulting services

(P-16459)
POUNCE CONSULTING INC
6080 Center Dr Ste 600, Los Angeles (90045-1540)
PHONE..................714 774-3500
Roger Viera, *CEO*
Josa A Velasco, *Treasurer*
Thania Herrera, *Office Admin*
Eric Dibella, *Finance Dir*
Maria Jos Viera, *Legal Staff*
EMP: 250
SQ FT: 4,000
SALES (est): 13.5MM
SALES (corp-wide): 16.9MM **Privately Held**
SIC: **7379** 7361 Computer related consulting services; employment agencies
PA: Pounce Consulting, S.A. De C.V.
Av. 8 De Julio No. 1295
Guadalajara JAL. 44190
333 942-2505

(P-16460)
PRAETORIAN GROUP
Also Called: Policeone Academy
200 Green St Ste 200, San Francisco (94111-1356)
PHONE..................415 962-8310
Fax: 415 962-8340
Mike Herning, *Ch of Bd*
Alex Ford, *CEO*
Paul Andrews, *Vice Pres*
Julia Siedlaczek, *Opers Mgr*
Barry Hickerson, *Director*
EMP: 50
SALES (est): 8.5MM **Privately Held**
WEB: www.policeone.com
SIC: **7379**

PRODUCTS & SERVICES SECTION
7379 - Computer Related Svcs, NEC County (P-16484)

(P-16461)
PRAMIRA INC
1422 Edinger Ave Ste 250, Tustin (92780-6299)
PHONE.................................800 678-1169
Omar Houari, *CEO*
EMP: 125 **EST:** 2014
SQ FT: 6,000
SALES (est): 5.9MM **Privately Held**
SIC: 7379 8711 Computer related consulting services; engineering services

(P-16462)
PRO-TEK CONSULTING (PA)
21300 Victory Blvd # 240, Woodland Hills (91367-2525)
PHONE.................................805 807-5571
Raj Kessireddy, *CEO*
Divya Reddy Pyreddy, *Chairman*
Ravi Nizampuram, *Business Mgr*
Jeevan Vikas, *Business Mgr*
Paul Singh, *Sales Mgr*
EMP: 110 **EST:** 2010
SQ FT: 2,400
SALES (est): 11.4MM **Privately Held**
SIC: 7379 Computer related consulting services

(P-16463)
PRODUCT QUALITY PARTNERS INC
450 Main St Ste 207, Pleasanton (94566-7071)
PHONE.................................925 484-6491
Fax: 925 484-2631
Debra Levesque, *President*
Debra Hodtens, *President*
Heather Keyser, *Executive Asst*
EMP: 54
SQ FT: 20,000
SALES: 600K **Privately Held**
WEB: www.qpqa.com
SIC: 7379 Computer related maintenance services

(P-16464)
PROLIFICS INC (DH)
24025 Park Sorrento # 450, Calabasas (91302-9990)
PHONE.................................212 267-7722
Satya Bolli, *CEO*
Sam Ourfalian, *President*
K Ewanyk, *Vice Pres*
David Mogel, *Admin Sec*
Fred Grossman, *Controller*
EMP: 255
SQ FT: 7,000
SALES: 90MM
SALES (corp-wide): 23.5MM **Privately Held**
WEB: www.jyacc.com
SIC: 7379 7371 Computer related consulting services; computer software development
HQ: Prolifics Application Services, Inc.
24025 Park Sorrento # 405
Calabasas CA 91302
646 201-4967

(P-16465)
PROPEL SOFTWARE CORPORATION
1010 Rincon Cir, San Jose (95131-1325)
PHONE.................................408 571-1070
Fax: 408 577-1070
Steven T Kirsch, *President*
Steven Manser, *COO*
Kim Kuan-Louie, *Accounting Mgr*
EMP: 130
SQ FT: 30,000
SALES (est): 9.6MM **Privately Held**
WEB: www.propel.com
SIC: 7379 Computer related consulting services

(P-16466)
QUANTUM SOLUTIONS INC
5146 Douglas Fir Rd # 205, Calabasas (91302-1405)
PHONE.................................818 577-4555
Hamid Akhavan, *CEO*
Guy Mizrachi, *Manager*
EMP: 50
SQ FT: 14,641
SALES (est): 4.9MM **Privately Held**
SIC: 7379 8742 ; business consultant

(P-16467)
QUBERA SOLUTIONS INC
676 Gail Ave Apt 26, Sunnyvale (94086-8134)
PHONE.................................650 294-4460
Prasad Jayaraman, *President*
Jacob Pszonowsky, *Vice Pres*
Scott Smith, *Program Mgr*
Manoj Kumar, *Director*
EMP: 50
SQ FT: 2,900
SALES: 8MM **Privately Held**
SIC: 7379 Computer related consulting services

(P-16468)
R S SOFTWARE INDIA LIMITED
1900 Mccarthy Blvd # 103, Milpitas (95035-7413)
PHONE.................................408 382-1200
Fax: 408 382-0083
Rajnit Jain, *President*
Bibek Das, *Vice Pres*
Biswanath Gupta, *Vice Pres*
Vivek Chaturvedi, *VP Finance*
Kim Van, *Finance*
EMP: 96
SQ FT: 3,100
SALES (est): 12.4MM
SALES (corp-wide): 25.3MM **Privately Held**
WEB: www.rssoftware.com
SIC: 7379 7371 Computer related consulting services; computer software development
PA: R S Software (India) Limited
A - 2, Fmc Fortuna,
Kolkata WB 70002
332 287-6255

(P-16469)
R SYSTEMS INC (HQ)
5000 Windplay Dr Ste 5, El Dorado Hills (95762-9319)
PHONE.................................916 939-9696
Satinder S Rekhi, *CEO*
Lt Gen Baldev Singh, *President*
Ralph Kenney, *COO*
Adheesh Prabhavalkar, *COO*
Raj Swaminathan, *COO*
EMP: 200
SQ FT: 7,000
SALES (est): 89.1MM
SALES (corp-wide): 43.9MM **Privately Held**
WEB: www.rsystems.com
SIC: 7379 7373 7374 Computer related consulting services; systems software development services; data processing & preparation
PA: R Systems International Limited
C 40, Sector 59, Greater Noida,
Noida UP 20130
120 430-3500

(P-16470)
RANDSTAD TECHNOLOGIES LP
8880 Rio San Diego Dr # 107, San Diego (92108-1634)
PHONE.................................619 798-7300
Charity Cescolini, *Branch Mgr*
EMP: 64
SALES (corp-wide): 20.6B **Privately Held**
SIC: 7379 Computer hardware requirements analysis
HQ: Randstad Technologies, Lp
150 Presidential Way # 300
Woburn MA 01801
781 938-1910

(P-16471)
RED OAK TECHNOLOGIES INC
2001 Gateway Pl Ste 150w, San Jose (95110-1055)
PHONE.................................408 200-3500
Brad Gordon, *President*
Yasir Naseer, *Tech Recruiter*
Manni Alvarez, *Recruiter*
Peter Rodil, *Recruiter*
Rashmi Singhal, *Recruiter*
EMP: 100
SQ FT: 2,000
SALES: 112.8K **Privately Held**
WEB: www.redoaktech.com
SIC: 7379 Computer related consulting services

(P-16472)
RISKALYZE INC
373 Elm Ave, Auburn (95603-4524)
PHONE.................................530 748-1660
Allison Harvey, *Administration*
Aaron Klein, *CEO*
Micaela Pope, *Executive Asst*
Matt Pistone, *CTO*
Evan Pope, *Persnl Dir*
EMP: 85
SALES (est): 3.2MM **Privately Held**
SIC: 7379 Computer related services

(P-16473)
SADA SYSTEMS INC
5250 Lankershim Blvd # 620, North Hollywood (91601-3188)
PHONE.................................818 766-2400
Fax: 818 766-0090
Tony Safoian, *CEO*
Matt Lawrence, *COO*
Annie Safoian, *CFO*
David Brown, *Program Mgr*
Suwency Centeno, *Office Admin*
EMP: 106
SQ FT: 10,503
SALES: 28MM **Privately Held**
SIC: 7379 Computer related services

(P-16474)
SCALEMATRIX HOLDINGS INC
5775 Kearny Villa Rd, San Diego (92123-1111)
PHONE.................................888 349-9994
Paul G Marble, *Ch of Bd*
Mark Ortenzi, *CEO*
Emily Stebing, *CFO*
Linnette Hollman, *Admin Asst*
Teresa Schelley, *Software Dev*
EMP: 75
SQ FT: 85,461
SALES (est): 12.8MM **Privately Held**
SIC: 7379 Computer related consulting services

(P-16475)
SCIENCE APPLICATIONS INTL CORP
Also Called: Saic Government Solutions
4015 Hancock St Ste 1000, San Diego (92110-5121)
PHONE.................................703 676-4300
Fax: 619 686-5626
Anthony Moraco, *Branch Mgr*
Jeff Ferguson, *CEO*
Anthony Morraco, *CEO*
Brittany Skaff, *Administration*
EMP: 99
SALES (corp-wide): 4.3B **Publicly Held**
SIC: 7379 Computer related consulting services
PA: Science Applications International Corporation
1710 Saic Dr Ste B
Mc Lean VA 22102
703 676-6942

(P-16476)
SEATECH CONSULTING GROUP INC
609 Deep Valley Dr # 200, Rllng HLS Est (90274-3614)
PHONE.................................310 356-6828
Chairul Irawan, *CEO*
EMP: 50
SALES: 3.5MM **Privately Held**
SIC: 7379 Computer related consulting services

(P-16477)
SEAVER INTERNATIONAL
4169 Green Valley Schl Rd, Sebastopol (95472-8944)
PHONE.................................707 291-4929
Jesse Seaver, *Owner*
EMP: 89
SALES (est): 2.6MM **Privately Held**
SIC: 7379 Computer related consulting services

(P-16478)
SENTEK CONSULTING INC
Also Called: Sentek Global
2811 Nimitz Blvd Ste G, San Diego (92106-4311)
PHONE.................................619 543-9550
Eric Basu, *CEO*
Jason Galetti, *COO*
Robin Ash, *CFO*
Jesse Hamilton, *Exec VP*
Steve Burfield, *Program Mgr*
EMP: 132
SALES (est): 27.9MM **Privately Held**
WEB: www.sentekconsulting.com
SIC: 7379 Computer related consulting services

(P-16479)
SITELITE HOLDINGS INC
111 Theory Fl 2, Irvine (92617-3039)
PHONE.................................949 265-6200
Reddy Marri, *CEO*
Kumar Yamani, *Chairman*
EMP: 135 **EST:** 1999
SQ FT: 30,000
SALES (est): 6.2MM **Privately Held**
SIC: 7379 8742 Computer related consulting services; management consulting services

(P-16480)
SK HYNIX MEMORY SOLUTIONS INC
3103 N 1st St, San Jose (95134-1934)
PHONE.................................408 514-3500
Y J Choi, *CEO*
Steve Son, *CFO*
Mustafiz Choudhury, *Senior VP*
George Kaldani, *Senior VP*
Bumsoo Kim, *Senior VP*
EMP: 270
SALES (est): 46.8MM **Privately Held**
SIC: 7379

(P-16481)
SMASHON INC
1754 Tech Dr Ste 234, San Jose (95110)
PHONE.................................855 762-7466
Tasawar Jalali, *CEO*
EMP: 50
SALES (est): 2.8MM **Privately Held**
SIC: 7379 Computer related maintenance services; computer related consulting services

(P-16482)
SOASTA INC
444 Castro St Ste 400, Mountain View (94041-2053)
PHONE.................................650 210-4941
Tom Lounibis, *President*
Buddy Brewer, *President*
Mike Hemmert, *President*
Pete Boyes, *CFO*
Ken Holcomb, *CFO*
EMP: 89
SALES (est): 16.2MM **Privately Held**
WEB: www.soasta.com
SIC: 7379

(P-16483)
SOFTHQ
6494 Weathers Pl Ste 200, San Diego (92121-2938)
PHONE.................................858 658-9200
Sindhura Thummalasetty, *Principal*
Richa Garg, *Admin Asst*
Satya Saty, *Tech Recruiter*
Murali Golagani, *Technology*
Samuel Bekliph, *Human Res Mgr*
EMP: 89
SALES (est): 9.5MM **Privately Held**
SIC: 7379 Computer related consulting services

(P-16484)
SOFTWARE MANAGEMENT CONS INC (PA)
Also Called: Smci
500 Nth Brn Blvd Ste 1100, Glendale (91203)
PHONE.................................818 240-3177
Spencer L Karpf, *CEO*
Jeff Elsasser, *President*
Deborah House, *President*

7379 - Computer Related Svcs, NEC County (P-16485)

Melinda Oliver, *President*
Clara Nersissian, *CFO*
EMP: 320
SQ FT: 4,450
SALES (est): 53.2MM **Privately Held**
WEB: www.smci.com
SIC: 7379 7361 Computer related consulting services; placement agencies

(P-16485)
SOLUGENIX CORPORATION
225 N Barranca St, West Covina (91791-1688)
PHONE..................866 749-7658
Solugenix Corporation, *Recruiter*
Praveen Mallavarapu, *Manager*
EMP: 59
SALES (corp-wide): 50.7MM **Privately Held**
SIC: 7379 Computer related maintenance services
PA: Solugenix Corporation
 601 Valencia Ave
 Brea CA 92823
 866 749-7658

(P-16486)
SONICOCOM INC
2202 S Figueroa St, Los Angeles (90007-2049)
PHONE..................213 291-0475
Rodrigo Teijeiro, *President*
Gustavo Victorica, *CFO*
EMP: 90
SQ FT: 400
SALES (est): 4MM **Privately Held**
SIC: 7379

(P-16487)
SPARTA CONSULTING INC
111 Woodmere Rd Ste 200, Folsom (95630-4750)
PHONE..................916 985-0300
Lokesh Sikaria, *CEO*
Paul Freudenberg, *Ch of Bd*
Vaibhav Nadgauda, *President*
Denise Ferre, *CFO*
Charu Singh, *CFO*
EMP: 300
SQ FT: 7,200
SALES (est): 41MM **Privately Held**
SIC: 7379 Computer related consulting services
PA: Kpit Technologies Limited
 Plot No. 35 & 36,
 Pune MH 41105
 206 652-5000

(P-16488)
SRK GLOBAL CONSULTING
7225 Crescent Park W # 255, Los Angeles (90094-2718)
PHONE..................310 295-2524
Steven Kahn, *Exec Dir*
EMP: 60
SALES: 500K **Privately Held**
SIC: 7379 Computer related consulting services

(P-16489)
SRS CONSULTING INC
39465 Paseo Padre P Ste 1100, Fremont (94538)
PHONE..................510 252-0625
Sangeetha Chowhan, *CEO*
Shankar Chowhan, *President*
EMP: 58
SQ FT: 1,250
SALES (est): 8MM **Privately Held**
WEB: www.srsconsultinginc.com
SIC: 7379 7371 Computer related consulting services; computer software development

(P-16490)
STRATA INFORMATION GROUP INC
3935 Harney St Ste 203, San Diego (92110-2849)
PHONE..................619 296-0170
Fax: 619 296-0171
Henry A Eimstad, *President*
Frank Vaskelis, *Corp Secy*
Kari Blinn, *Executive*
A J Frank, *Office Mgr*
Edward Ahrens, *Database Admin*
EMP: 93
SQ FT: 2,000
SALES: 17.4MM **Privately Held**
WEB: www.sigcorp.com
SIC: 7379 Computer related consulting services

(P-16491)
SYNECTIC SOLUTIONS INC (PA)
Also Called: S S I
1701 Pacific Ave Ste 260, Oxnard (93033-1887)
PHONE..................805 483-4800
Lynn Dines, *President*
Toby Doane, *President*
Joel Dines, *President*
Richard Martinez, *Officer*
Joann Siros, *Human Res Dir*
EMP: 78 **EST:** 1997
SQ FT: 5,000
SALES (est): 15.9MM **Privately Held**
WEB: www.synecsolu.com
SIC: 7379 8331 Computer related consulting services; job training services

(P-16492)
SYNERGY LABS
135 Townsend St Ste 608, San Francisco (94107-1907)
PHONE..................415 291-8080
Dan Mapes, *Owner*
EMP: 50
SALES (est): 1MM **Privately Held**
SIC: 7379 Computer related consulting services

(P-16493)
SYNIVERSE TECHNOLOGIES LLC
181 Metro Dr Ste 450, San Jose (95110-1344)
PHONE..................408 324-1830
EMP: 106
SALES (corp-wide): 861.4MM **Privately Held**
SIC: 7379 Data processing consultant
HQ: Syniverse Technologies, Llc.
 8125 Highwoods Palm Way
 Tampa FL 33647
 813 637-5000

(P-16494)
SYNOPTEK LLC (PA)
19520 Jamboree Rd Ste 110, Irvine (92612-2429)
PHONE..................949 241-8600
Tim Britt, *CEO*
Ricardo Ordonez, *CFO*
Mike Bank, *Vice Pres*
Tim Becker, *Vice Pres*
Eric Condorniz, *Vice Pres*
EMP: 67
SALES (est): 79.8MM **Privately Held**
WEB: www.netsolutionsinc.com
SIC: 7379 Computer related consulting services

(P-16495)
SYSTECH INTEGRATORS INC
2050 Gateway Pl, San Jose (95110-1011)
PHONE..................408 441-2700
Sam Tyagi, *CEO*
Rajeev Tyagi, *COO*
Jinesh Jain, *Vice Pres*
Jonathan Cowie, *VP Finance*
Bejoy Unnikrishnan, *Director*
EMP: 240
SALES (est): 18.1MM **Privately Held**
WEB: www.systechi.com
SIC: 7379 Computer related consulting services
HQ: Valores Corporativos Softtek, S.A. De C.V.
 Jaime Balmes No. 11
 Ciudad De Mexico D.F. 11510
 811 932-4400

(P-16496)
T & T SOLUTIONS INC
7018 Owensmouth Ave # 201, Canoga Park (91303-2073)
PHONE..................818 676-1786
Fax: 818 676-1272
EMP: 70
SQ FT: 2,100

PRODUDUCTS & SERVICES SECTION

SALES (est): 6.2MM **Privately Held**
WEB: www.ttsus.com
SIC: 7379

(P-16497)
TACIT KNOWLEDGE INC
27 Maiden Ln Fl 4, San Francisco (94108-5444)
PHONE..................415 694-4322
Christopher Andrasick, *President*
Chase Hill, *COO*
Mike Hardy, *CFO*
DEA Hartz, *Office Mgr*
Gilberto Alvarado, *Sr Software Eng*
EMP: 93
SALES (est): 11.3MM **Privately Held**
WEB: www.tacitknowledge.com
SIC: 7379 Computer related consulting services
HQ: Newgistics, Inc.
 2700 Via Fortuna Ste 300
 Austin TX 78746

(P-16498)
TACTICAL ENGRG & ANALIS INC (PA)
6050 Santo Rd Ste 250, San Diego (92124-6104)
P.O. Box 421425 (92142-1425)
PHONE..................858 573-9869
Fax: 858 573-9874
Robert Rosado, *President*
Lawrence Massaro, *CFO*
Julie Rapolla, *Executive*
David Andersen, *Pharmacy Dir*
Marcos Canales, *Engineer*
EMP: 82
SQ FT: 8,500
SALES (est): 18.1MM **Privately Held**
WEB: www.tac-eng.com
SIC: 7379 8711 Computer related consulting services; engineering services

(P-16499)
TANG E TSE INC
3001 S Croddy Way, Santa Ana (92704-6304)
PHONE..................714 957-4000
Augustine TSE, *President*
EMP: 50
SALES (est): 1.8MM **Privately Held**
SIC: 7379 Computer related consulting services

(P-16500)
TAOS MOUNTAIN LLC (PA)
121 Daggett Dr, San Jose (95134-2110)
PHONE..................408 324-2800
Ricardo Urrutia, *CEO*
Katherine Brown, *President*
Jeff Lucchesi, *COO*
Mary Hale, *CFO*
Carrina Cappadona, *Vice Pres*
EMP: 335
SQ FT: 45,000
SALES (est): 118.8MM **Privately Held**
SIC: 7379 Computer related consulting services

(P-16501)
TATA AMERICA INTL CORP
Also Called: Tata Consulting Services
5201 Great America Pkwy # 522, Santa Clara (95054-1122)
PHONE..................408 569-5845
S K Bhattacharjee, *Manager*
Vinod Vishnumurthy, *Business Dir*
Amitava Dutta, *Admin Asst*
Niladri Bhattacharjee, *Technical Mgr*
Sanjay Kumar, *Database Admin*
EMP: 100
SALES (corp-wide): 1.9B **Privately Held**
SIC: 7379 Computer related consulting services
HQ: Tata America International Corporation
 101 Park Ave Rm 2603
 New York NY 10178
 212 557-8038

(P-16502)
TECH-ED NETWORKS INC
10000 Allantown Dr # 175, Roseville (95678-5996)
PHONE..................916 784-2005
Fax: 916 784-3117

Stephen Fassler, *President*
Ross Ramsey, *Vice Pres*
Michael McLaughlin, *Program Mgr*
Donny Johnson, *Executive Asst*
Keith Deary, *Sales Staff*
EMP: 111
SQ FT: 67,800
SALES (est): 6.8MM **Privately Held**
WEB: www.technednetworks.com
SIC: 7379 Computer related consulting services

(P-16503)
TECHNOLOGY RESOURCE CENTER INC
2101 E 4th St Ste 130a, Santa Ana (92705-3843)
PHONE..................714 542-1004
Gabriel Chavez, *President*
Anthony Chavez, *CFO*
Mark Serres, *Vice Pres*
EMP: 60
SQ FT: 2,000
SALES (est): 4.8MM **Privately Held**
WEB: www.trcinc.net
SIC: 7379 7361 Computer related consulting services; employment agencies

(P-16504)
TECHNOLOGY SERVICES CAL DEPT (DH)
Also Called: Dts
1325 J St Ste 1600, Sacramento (95814-2941)
P.O. Box 1810, Rancho Cordova (95741-1810)
PHONE..................916 319-9223
Carlos Ramos, *CEO*
Chris Cruz, *CFO*
Deborah F Decker, *CFO*
Martin Lafon, *Exec Dir*
Susan Ferguson, *General Mgr*
EMP: 130
SALES (est): 39.2MM **Privately Held**
WEB: www.osi.ca.gov
SIC: 7379
HQ: California Government Operations Agency
 915 Capitol Mall Ste 200
 Sacramento CA 95814
 916 651-9011

(P-16505)
TECTURA CORPORATION (PA)
951 Old County Rd 2-317, Belmont (94002-2773)
PHONE..................650 273-4249
Duane W Bell, *CEO*
Duane Bell, *CFO*
Dave Kempski, *CFO*
Steve Goveia, *Vice Pres*
Nicklas Larsson, *Software Dev*
EMP: 50
SALES (est): 78.4MM **Privately Held**
SIC: 7379 Computer related consulting services

(P-16506)
THREATMETRIX INC
160 W Santa Clara St # 1400, San Jose (95113-1735)
PHONE..................408 200-5700
Fax: 408 200-5799
Reed Taussig, *President*
Huanjin Chen, *President*
Neil Katz, *CFO*
Frank Teruel, *CFO*
Samuel A Hageman, *Treasurer*
EMP: 165
SQ FT: 10,000
SALES (est): 33.4MM **Privately Held**
SIC: 7379 7374 Computer related consulting services; computer processing services

(P-16507)
TIGERTEXT INC
2110 Bradway Santa Monica, Santa Monica (90404)
PHONE..................310 401-1820
Jeffrey Evans, *CEO*
Sheila Saldana, *President*
Marc Ladin, *Chief Mktg Ofcr*
Justin Nelson, *Officer*
Karen Greenwood, *Vice Pres*
EMP: 50

PRODUCTS & SERVICES SECTION
7379 - Computer Related Svcs, NEC County (P-16528)

SALES (est): 646.6K **Privately Held**
SIC: 7379 Computer related maintenance services

(P-16508)
TILLSTER INC (PA)
Also Called: Emn8
5959 Cornerstone Ct W # 100, San Diego (92121-3764)
PHONE..................................858 784-0800
Perse Faily, *CEO*
John Redding, *CFO*
Hope W Neiman, *Chief Mktg Ofcr*
Trevor Chong, *Senior VP*
Michael Crawford, *Senior VP*
EMP: 70
SQ FT: 18,642
SALES (est): 33.1MM **Privately Held**
WEB: www.emn8.com
SIC: 7379 7373 Computer related maintenance services; systems integration services; computer system selling services

(P-16509)
TRADEBEAM INC
303 Twin Dolphin Dr # 600, Redwood City (94065-1422)
PHONE..................................650 653-4800
Fax: 650 653-4801
Edward R Flaherty, *CEO*
Buff Jones, *President*
Douglas F Harrison, *CFO*
Bill Stensrud, *Bd of Directors*
Jerry Dolinsky, *Exec VP*
EMP: 100
SQ FT: 26,000
SALES (est): 6MM
SALES (corp-wide): 594.3MM **Privately Held**
WEB: www.tradebeam.com
SIC: 7379 Computer related maintenance services; computer related consulting services
HQ: Cdc Software, Inc.
4325 Alexander Dr
Alpharetta GA 30022
770 351-9600

(P-16510)
TRIAGE PARTNERS LLC
15717 Texaco Ave, Paramount (90723-3923)
PHONE..................................562 634-0058
EMP: 78
SALES (corp-wide): 25.6MM **Privately Held**
SIC: 7379
PA: Triage Partners, L.L.C.
1715 N West Shore Blvd # 250
Tampa FL 33607
813 801-9869

(P-16511)
TRIALPAY INC (PA)
800 California St Ste 300, Mountain View (94041-2810)
PHONE..................................650 318-0000
Alastair M Rampell, *President*
Alastair Rampell, *President*
Terry Angelos, *COO*
Daniel Greenberg, *Chief Mktg Ofcr*
James Gerber, *Senior VP*
EMP: 58
SQ FT: 17,600
SALES (est): 11.9MM **Privately Held**
SIC: 7379

(P-16512)
TRIANZ (HQ)
3979 Freedom Cir Ste 210, Santa Clara (95054-1248)
PHONE..................................408 387-5800
Fax: 408 387-5702
Srikanth Manchala, *President*
Anusuya Chaman, *CFO*
Ganesh Venkataraman, *CFO*
Keshav Gupta, *Vice Pres*
Vivek Gupta, *Vice Pres*
EMP: 115 EST: 2000
SQ FT: 18,000
SALES (est): 88.1MM
SALES (corp-wide): 46.3MM **Privately Held**
WEB: www.trianz.com
SIC: 7379
PA: Trianz Holdings Private Limited
165/2, 6th Floor,
Bengaluru KAR
802 238-8000

(P-16513)
TRUE ULTIMATE STANDARDS
Also Called: Truste
835 Market St Ste 800, San Francisco (94103-1906)
PHONE..................................415 520-3400
Fax: 415 520-3420
Christopher Babel, *CEO*
Tim Sullivan, *CFO*
Bob Bahramipour, *Vice Pres*
Cathy Bump, *Vice Pres*
David Currie, *Vice Pres*
EMP: 100
SQ FT: 7,000
SALES (est): 11.7MM **Privately Held**
WEB: www.truste.com
SIC: 7379 Computer related consulting services

(P-16514)
UNEC SOLUTIONS INC
655 Lewelling Blvd, San Leandro (94579-1831)
PHONE..................................510 851-2808
Danielle Hailne, *President*
EMP: 75
SQ FT: 2,700
SALES (est): 3.8MM **Privately Held**
SIC: 7379 7361 Computer related consulting services; employment agencies

(P-16515)
UNISH CORPORATION
4300 Stevens Creek Blvd, San Jose (95129-1263)
PHONE..................................408 708-9300
Basavaraj Ullagaddi, *President*
EMP: 50
SALES (est): 2.4MM **Privately Held**
SIC: 7379

(P-16516)
UNITED STATES TECHNICAL SVCS
Also Called: Usts
16541 Gothard St Ste 214, Huntington Beach (92647-4436)
PHONE..................................714 374-6300
Fax: 714 242-1346
Bob Polk, *President*
John Courtney, *CEO*
Cynthia Dugger, *Treasurer*
Dawyn Price, *Engineer*
Diane Cooper, *Manager*
EMP: 122
SQ FT: 2,500
SALES (est): 21.7MM **Privately Held**
WEB: www.usts.net
SIC: 7379 Computer related consulting services

(P-16517)
UNITEK INFORMATION SYSTEMS INC (PA)
Also Called: Unitek It Education
4670 Auto Mall Pkwy, Fremont (94538-3197)
PHONE..................................510 249-1060
Janis Paulson, *CEO*
Shiva Jahan, *CFO*
Navraj Bawa, *Vice Pres*
John Lyttle, *Managing Dir*
Charlie Messemer, *Technical Staff*
EMP: 55
SQ FT: 27,000
SALES (est): 29.5MM **Privately Held**
WEB: www.abriasoft.com
SIC: 7379 7371 Computer related consulting services; custom computer programming services

(P-16518)
US DATA MANAGEMENT LLC (PA)
Also Called: Usdm
1746 S Victoria Ave Ste F, Ventura (93003-6190)
PHONE..................................888 231-0816
Kevin Brown, *Mng Member*
Amy Bakken, *Administration*
Justin Ott, *Sales Executive*
EMP: 100
SQ FT: 4,000
SALES: 20MM **Privately Held**
WEB: www.usdatamanagement.com
SIC: 7379 Computer related consulting services

(P-16519)
VALLEY US INC
888 Saratoga Ave Ste 201, San Jose (95129-2639)
PHONE..................................408 260-7342
Sunita Kumari, *President*
Nital Wadhavkar, *Human Res Mgr*
EMP: 70
SALES (est): 3.1MM **Privately Held**
SIC: 7379 Computer related consulting services

(P-16520)
VENTRUM LLC
2033 Gateway Pl Ste 500, San Jose (95110-3712)
PHONE..................................510 304-0852
Rahul Misra,
Sunil Joshi, *Executive*
Sam Shoute, *Tech Recruiter*
Gagan Jha, *Recruiter*
Rohita Misra,
EMP: 75
SALES (est): 8MM **Privately Held**
WEB: www.ventrum.com
SIC: 7379 Computer related consulting services

(P-16521)
VERIZON DIGITAL MEDIA SVCS INC
13031 W Jefferson Blvd # 900, Los Angeles (90094-7002)
PHONE..................................310 396-7400
Alex Kleiman, *President*
Philip Goldsmith, *COO*
John Powers, *CFO*
Lior Elazary, *Senior VP*
Ted Middleton, *Vice Pres*
EMP: 501
SQ FT: 50,000
SALES (est): 36.1MM
SALES (corp-wide): 131.6B **Publicly Held**
WEB: www.edgecast.com
SIC: 7379 Computer related consulting services
PA: Verizon Communications Inc.
1095 Ave Of The Americas
New York NY 10036
212 395-1000

(P-16522)
VIRTUAL INSTRUMENTS CORP
25 Metro Dr, San Jose (95110-1316)
PHONE..................................408 579-4000
Fax: 408 579-4001
John W Thompson, *CEO*
Bo Barker, *President*
Ray Villeneuve, *President*
George W Harrington, *CFO*
Nick Batzdorf, *Sr Corp Ofcr*
EMP: 80
SALES (est): 24.9MM **Privately Held**
SIC: 7379 7371 Computer related consulting services; computer software development

(P-16523)
VISION SOLUTIONS INC
Also Called: Itera Software
15300 Barranca Pkwy # 100, Irvine (92618-2256)
PHONE..................................949 253-6500
Daniel Neville, *Branch Mgr*
Rick Ayres, *CTO*
Darren Sumter, *Finance*
Bob Davis, *Sales Dir*
Brian Neville, *Sales Dir*
EMP: 52 **Privately Held**
WEB: www.visionsolutions.com
SIC: 7379 7371 Computer related consulting services; data processing consultant; computer software development & applications
HQ: Vision Solutions, Inc.
15300 Barranca Pkwy # 100
Irvine CA 92618
949 253-6500

(P-16524)
VORMETRIC INC (HQ)
Also Called: AES Networks
2860 Junction Ave, San Jose (95134-1922)
PHONE..................................408 433-6000
Fax: 408 844-8638
Alan Kessler, *President*
Greg Paulsen, *CFO*
Roman Baudrit, *Vice Pres*
George Chew, *Vice Pres*
Stephen Driggers, *Vice Pres*
EMP: 79
SQ FT: 56,000
SALES (est): 49.9MM
SALES (corp-wide): 224MM **Privately Held**
WEB: www.vormetric.com
SIC: 7379 Computer related maintenance services

(P-16525)
WHITEGOLD SOLUTIONS INC
43 Fernwood Way Ste 210, San Rafael (94901-2528)
PHONE..................................415 456-4493
Jack Zoken, *President*
EMP: 50
SALES (est): 3MM **Privately Held**
WEB: www.sift.com
SIC: 7379 Data processing consultant

(P-16526)
WHITEHAT SECURITY INC
3970 Freedom Cir, Santa Clara (95054-1204)
PHONE..................................408 343-8300
Fax: 408 904-7142
Craig Hinkley, *CEO*
Mark Schulte, *CFO*
John Dean, *Chairman*
Tamir Hardof, *Chief Mktg Ofcr*
Johannes Hoech, *Chief Mktg Ofcr*
EMP: 55
SALES (est): 15.5MM **Privately Held**
WEB: www.whitehatsec.com
SIC: 7379 Computer related consulting services

(P-16527)
WINCERE INC
2350 Mission College Blvd # 290, Santa Clara (95054-1575)
PHONE..................................408 841-4355
Himanshi Kansara, *President*
Pete Cooney, *Vice Pres*
Helen Matharu, *Technology*
Shobha Kothapalli, *Director*
EMP: 210
SQ FT: 3,000
SALES (est): 13.3MM **Privately Held**
SIC: 7379 Computer related consulting services
PA: Wincere Solutions Private Limited
Regus Business Centre, Level 2
New Delhi DEL 11002

(P-16528)
WYNDGATE TECHNOLOGIES
4925 Robert J Mathews Pkw, El Dorado Hills (95762-5700)
PHONE..................................916 404-8400
Fax: 916 404-8484
Michael Ruxnin, *Ch of Bd*
Tom Marcinek, *COO*
Morgan Polcheni, *Vice Pres*
Miklos Csore, *Administration*
Ed Simler, *Engineer*
EMP: 83
SALES (est): 5.9MM
SALES (corp-wide): 908.8MM **Publicly Held**
WEB: www.sttx.net
SIC: 7379 7371 7372 Computer related consulting services; custom computer programming services; prepackaged software
HQ: Global Med Technologies, Inc.
4925 Robert J Mathews Pkw
El Dorado Hills CA 95762
916 404-8400

7379 - Computer Related Svcs, NEC County (P-16529)

PRODUDUCTS & SERVICES SECTION

(P-16529)
XANTRION INCORPORATED
651 Thomas L Berkley Way, Oakland
(94612-1344)
PHONE......................510 272-4701
Fax: 510 763-0342
Tom Snyder, *COO*
Anne Bisagno, *President*
Sean Cameron, *Administration*
Royden S Luis, *Administration*
Adam Martin, *Applctn Conslt*
EMP: 50 **EST:** 2000
SQ FT: 10,000
SALES: 15.1MM **Privately Held**
SIC: 7379 Computer related consulting services

(P-16530)
XAVOR CORPORATION
8925 Research Dr, Irvine (92618-4237)
PHONE......................949 529-7372
Humayun Rashid, *President*
Dr Das Gupta, *Vice Pres*
Amara Masood, *Vice Pres*
Khurram S Malik, *Project Mgr*
Kashif Munir, *Project Mgr*
EMP: 100
SQ FT: 14,000
SALES (est): 8.7MM **Privately Held**
SIC: 7379 1731 Computer related consulting services; electrical work

(P-16531)
XORIANT CORPORATION (PA)
1248 Reamwood Ave, Sunnyvale
(94089-2225)
PHONE......................408 743-4427
Girish Gaitonde, *CEO*
Anirban Chakraborty, *President*
Raj Nataraj, *President*
Arun Tendulkar, *COO*
Mahesh Nalavade, *CFO*
EMP: 120
SALES: 134.6MM **Privately Held**
WEB: www.xoriant.com
SIC: 7379 7371 Computer related consulting services; computer software development

(P-16532)
YAMMER INC
410 Townsend St, San Francisco
(94107-1537)
PHONE......................415 796-7401
Fax: 415 777-5977
Keith R Dolliver, *CEO*
Samantha Loveland, *Vice Pres*
Dee Anna McPherson, *Vice Pres*
David Obrand, *Vice Pres*
David Stewart, *Vice Pres*
EMP: 160
SALES (est): 28.6MM
SALES (corp-wide): 85.3B **Publicly Held**
WEB: www.yammer.com
SIC: 7379 Computer related maintenance services
PA: Microsoft Corporation
    1 Microsoft Way
    Redmond WA 98052
    425 882-8080

(P-16533)
ZIONTECH SOLUTIONS INC
2665 N 1st St Ste 200, San Jose
(95134-2034)
PHONE......................408 434-6001
Hymavathi Pentaparthi, *Principal*
Ashok Anumandla, *CEO*
Jyothi Veam, *Tech Recruiter*
EMP: 79 **EST:** 2008
SALES (est): 269.6K **Privately Held**
SIC: 7379 Computer related consulting services

7381 Detective & Armored Car Svcs

(P-16534)
A SUTTON CARLOS
Also Called: Bel Air Security Solutions
9903 Santa Monica Blvd, Beverly Hills
(90212-1671)
PHONE......................310 286-0010
Carlos Sutton, *Owner*
EMP: 60 **EST:** 1991
SALES (est): 545.5K **Privately Held**
SIC: 7381 Security guard service

(P-16535)
A1 PROTECTIVE SERVICES INC
7000 Franklin Blvd # 665, Sacramento
(95823-1881)
PHONE......................916 421-3000
Cecilia Ochoa, *Branch Mgr*
EMP: 83
SALES (corp-wide): 2MM **Privately Held**
SIC: 7381 Security guard service
PA: A1 Protective Services, Inc.
    5 Thomas Mellon Cir # 155
    San Francisco CA 94134
    415 467-7200

(P-16536)
ABC SECURITY SERVICE INC
3065 Freeport Blvd, Sacramento
(95818-4347)
PHONE......................916 442-7001
Ana Chretien, *Branch Mgr*
EMP: 200
SALES (corp-wide): 7.4MM **Privately Held**
SIC: 7381 Guard services
PA: Abc Security Service, Inc.
    1840 Embarcadero
    Oakland CA 94606
    510 436-0666

(P-16537)
ACTION FORCE SECURITY
1212 W Gardena Blvd Ste C, Gardena
(90247-4896)
PHONE......................310 715-6053
Pedro Villatoro, *Owner*
EMP: 50
SALES (est): 880K **Privately Held**
SIC: 7381 Security guard service

(P-16538)
AGGRESSIVE ACTION SECURITY
17489 Plaza Del Curtidor, San Diego
(92128-2275)
PHONE......................858 829-2516
Mena Salama, *Partner*
EMP: 50
SALES (est): 536.5K **Privately Held**
SIC: 7381 Detective & armored car services

(P-16539)
AI INC/CSC GROU ◆
28001 Smyth Dr Ste 107, Valencia
(91355-4032)
PHONE......................661 775-8400
Randy Andrews, *Partner*
Ingrid Vialla-Davies, *Exec Sec*
EMP: 52 **EST:** 2016
SALES (est): 235K **Privately Held**
SIC: 7381 Guard services

(P-16540)
ALL ACTION SECURITY INC
20501 Ventura Blvd # 275, Woodland Hills
(91364-6413)
PHONE......................800 482-7371
Fax: 818 996-0090
John Ayam, *President*
Maryam Ayam, *General Mgr*
Susan Brennan, *IT/INT Sup*
Abbas Kosh, *Human Res Mgr*
Zia Mohsen, *Opers Mgr*
EMP: 75
SALES (est): 2.1MM **Privately Held**
WEB: www.allactionsecurity.com
SIC: 7381 Security guard service

(P-16541)
ALLIED PROTECTION SERVICES INC
5757 W Century Blvd, Los Angeles
(90045-6401)
PHONE......................310 330-8314
Leon Brooks, *President*
Osumby Kuti, *CFO*
Shavon Dee, *Executive Asst*
Renee Williams, *Admin Sec*
EMP: 78
SQ FT: 1,550
SALES (est): 3MM **Privately Held**
WEB: www.alliedprotection.com
SIC: 7381 Security guard service

(P-16542)
ALLIED RISK MANAGEMENT INC
2010 W Avenue K 395, Lancaster
(93536-5229)
PHONE......................661 305-0455
Howard Fuchs, *Director*
Eric Taylor, *General Mgr*
EMP: 99
SALES: 950K **Privately Held**
SIC: 7381 Security guard service

(P-16543)
ALLIEDBARTON SECURITY SVCS LLC
765 The City Dr S Ste 150, Orange
(92868-6920)
PHONE......................626 213-3100
Fax: 626 213-3140
Janet Melendez, *Manager*
EMP: 127
SALES (corp-wide): 10.5MM **Privately Held**
SIC: 7381 Detective & armored car services
HQ: Alliedbarton Security Services Llc
    8 Tower Bridge 161 Wshgtn
    Conshohocken PA 19428
    610 239-1100

(P-16544)
ALLIEDBARTON SECURITY SVCS LLC
3120 Chicago Ave Ste 190, Riverside
(92507-3431)
PHONE......................951 801-7300
Paul Scrankowski, *Manager*
EMP: 127
SALES (corp-wide): 10.5MM **Privately Held**
SIC: 7381 Guard services
HQ: Alliedbarton Security Services Llc
    8 Tower Bridge 161 Wshgtn
    Conshohocken PA 19428
    610 239-1100

(P-16545)
ALLIEDBARTON SECURITY SVCS LLC
637 E Albertoni St # 202, Carson
(90746-1539)
PHONE......................310 324-1219
EMP: 127
SALES (corp-wide): 10.5MM **Privately Held**
SIC: 7381 Guard services
HQ: Alliedbarton Security Services Llc
    8 Tower Bridge 161 Wshgtn
    Conshohocken PA 19428
    610 239-1100

(P-16546)
ALLIEDBARTON SECURITY SVCS LLC
8950 Cal Center Dr # 150, Sacramento
(95826-3259)
PHONE......................916 489-8280
Fax: 916 784-9762
Rodney Carter, *Branch Mgr*
EMP: 150
SALES (corp-wide): 10.5MM **Privately Held**
WEB: www.alliedsecurity.com
SIC: 7381 Security guard service
HQ: Alliedbarton Security Services Llc
    8 Tower Bridge 161 Wshgtn
    Conshohocken PA 19428
    610 239-1100

(P-16547)
ALLIEDBARTON SECURITY SVCS LLC
3529 Old Conejo Rd # 119, Newbury Park
(91320-2155)
PHONE......................805 480-3563
Fax: 805 480-3564
Tyna Sorenson, *Manager*
EMP: 127
SALES (corp-wide): 10.5MM **Privately Held**
SIC: 7381 Guard services
HQ: Alliedbarton Security Services Llc
    8 Tower Bridge 161 Wshgtn
    Conshohocken PA 19428
    610 239-1100

(P-16548)
ALLIEDBARTON SECURITY SVCS LLC
2540 N 1st St Ste 101, San Jose
(95131-1016)
PHONE......................408 954-8274
Fax: 408 954-8452
Chris Deguzman, *Vice Pres*
EMP: 500
SALES (corp-wide): 10.5MM **Privately Held**
WEB: www.alliedsecurity.com
SIC: 7381 Security guard service; protective services, guard; private investigator; detective agency
HQ: Alliedbarton Security Services Llc
    8 Tower Bridge 161 Wshgtn
    Conshohocken PA 19428
    610 239-1100

(P-16549)
ALLIEDBARTON SECURITY SVCS LLC
7670 Opportunity Rd # 210, San Diego
(92111-2274)
PHONE......................858 874-8200
Fax: 619 874-1895
Melone Widy, *Manager*
EMP: 400
SALES (corp-wide): 10.5MM **Privately Held**
WEB: www.alliedsecurity.com
SIC: 7381 Guard services
HQ: Alliedbarton Security Services Llc
    8 Tower Bridge 161 Wshgtn
    Conshohocken PA 19428
    610 239-1100

(P-16550)
ALLIEDBARTON SECURITY SVCS LLC
3701 Wilshire Blvd # 600, Los Angeles
(90010-2814)
PHONE......................800 418-6423
Fax: 323 937-5893
Veroin Higbee, *Manager*
EMP: 300
SALES (corp-wide): 10.5MM **Privately Held**
WEB: www.alliedsecurity.com
SIC: 7381 Security guard service; protective services, guard; private investigator
HQ: Alliedbarton Security Services Llc
    8 Tower Bridge 161 Wshgtn
    Conshohocken PA 19428
    610 239-1100

(P-16551)
ALLIEDBARTON SECURITY SVCS LLC
Also Called: Allied Barton Security Svcs
41 945 Boardwalk Ste T, Palm Desert
(92211)
PHONE......................760 568-5550
Candice Chriss, *Principal*
EMP: 139
SALES (corp-wide): 10.5MM **Privately Held**
SIC: 7381 Security guard service
HQ: Alliedbarton Security Services Llc
    8 Tower Bridge 161 Wshgtn
    Conshohocken PA 19428
    610 239-1100

(P-16552)
AMERICAN COMMERCIAL SEC SVCS
Also Called: American Loss Prevention Svcs
420 Taylor St Fl 2, San Francisco
(94102-1702)
PHONE......................415 856-1020
Larry T Smith, *President*
EMP: 5000
SALES (est): 37MM
SALES (corp-wide): 4.9B **Publicly Held**
SIC: 7381 Security guard service; private investigator

▲ = Import ▼=Export
◆ =Import/Export

PRODUCTS & SERVICES SECTION

7381 - Detective & Armored Car Svcs County (P-16576)

PA: Abm Industries Incorporated
1 Liberty Plz Fl Con1
New York NY 10006
212 297-0200

(P-16553)
AMERICAN CORPORATE SEC INC (PA)
1 World Trade Ctr # 1240, Long Beach (90831-1240)
PHONE 562 216-7440
Fax: 562 684-0308
Larry J Saye, *CEO*
Dina Christopher, *Officer*
Tim Lovette, *Human Res Mgr*
EMP: 76
SALES (est): 34.5MM **Privately Held**
SIC: 7381 8721 Security guard service; payroll accounting service

(P-16554)
AMERICAN CSTM PRIVATE SEC INC
446 E Vine St Ste A, Stockton (95202-1116)
P.O. Box 8513 (95208-0513)
PHONE 209 369-1200
Rajesh Patti, *President*
EMP: 80
SQ FT: 1,100
SALES: 300K **Privately Held**
SIC: 7381 Security guard service

(P-16555)
AMERICAN FORCE PRIVATE SEC INC
1585 S D St Ste 208, San Bernardino (92408-3236)
PHONE 909 384-9820
Shehab Abdelazim, *CEO*
EMP: 75
SALES (est): 1MM **Privately Held**
SIC: 7381 Guard services

(P-16556)
AMERICAN GUARD SERVICES INC (PA)
1299 E Artesia Blvd # 200, Carson (90746-1667)
PHONE 310 645-6200
Sherine Assal, *President*
Sherif Assal, *Vice Pres*
Nick Komarov, *Admin Mgr*
Carla Obannon, *Executive Asst*
Demian Casey, *Counsel*
EMP: 400
SQ FT: 1,500
SALES: 54.5MM **Privately Held**
SIC: 7381 Detective & armored car services; security guard service

(P-16557)
AMERICAN PATRIOT SECURITY
10293 Rockingham Dr # 104, Sacramento (95827-2521)
P.O. Box 980071, West Sacramento (95798-0071)
PHONE 916 706-2449
Scott Jacobs, *President*
Kelly Rochester, *Vice Pres*
EMP: 75
SQ FT: 1,200
SALES (est): 2.1MM **Privately Held**
WEB: www.americanpatriotsecurity.com
SIC: 7381 Security guard service

(P-16558)
AMERICAN PROFESSIONAL SECURITY
2500 Wilshire Blvd # 1030, Los Angeles (90057-4303)
PHONE 213 487-2100
Shola Ayodele, *President*
Johnson Ayodele, *Vice Pres*
Tunde Ogun, *General Mgr*
EMP: 50
SQ FT: 1,500
SALES (est): 1.2MM **Privately Held**
SIC: 7381 Guard services

(P-16559)
AMERICAN SECURITY FORCE INC
5400 E Olympic Blvd # 225, Commerce (90022-5154)
PHONE 323 722-8585
Albert Williams, *President*
EMP: 157
SQ FT: 3,700
SALES (est): 1.9MM **Privately Held**
SIC: 7381 7382 Protective services, guard; private investigator; guard dog rental; detective agency; burglar alarm maintenance & monitoring

(P-16560)
AMERICAN-1 AIRTIGHT SEC CO
2510 N Grand Ave Ste 207, Santa Ana (92705-8754)
PHONE 714 997-0605
Sid Asghari, *President*
EMP: 50
SALES: 1,000K **Privately Held**
WEB: www.spearsecurity.com
SIC: 7381 Detective & armored car services

(P-16561)
ANDREWS INTERNATIONAL INC
455 N Moss St, Burbank (91502-1727)
PHONE 818 260-9586
Fax: 818 487-4061
John Adams, *Principal*
Tom Walton, *Senior VP*
Steve Aborn, *Exec Dir*
Sean Turner, *Exec Dir*
Lee Watson, *Exec Dir*
EMP: 177
SALES (corp-wide): 270.6MM **Privately Held**
SIC: 7381 Guard services
PA: Andrews International, Inc.
28001 Smyth Dr Ste 107
Valencia CA 91355
661 775-8400

(P-16562)
ANDREWS INTERNATIONAL INC
455 N Moss St, Burbank (91502-1727)
PHONE 805 409-4160
Fax: 805 777-1750
Frank Alverez, *Branch Mgr*
EMP: 177
SALES (corp-wide): 270.6MM **Privately Held**
SIC: 7381 Security guard service
PA: Andrews International, Inc.
28001 Smyth Dr Ste 107
Valencia CA 91355
661 775-8400

(P-16563)
ANDREWS INTERNATIONAL INC (PA)
28001 Smyth Dr Ste 107, Valencia (91355-4032)
PHONE 661 775-8400
Fax: 661 775-8794
Randy Andrews, *President*
Ty Richmond, *COO*
James Wood, *COO*
Michael Topf, *CFO*
Francis Coates Jr, *Officer*
EMP: 1700
SQ FT: 5,000
SALES: 270.6MM **Privately Held**
WEB: www.andrewinternational.com
SIC: 7381 Protective services, guard; private investigator

(P-16564)
ANDREWS INTERNATIONAL INC
455 N Moss St, Burbank (91502-1727)
PHONE 626 407-2290
Fax: 626 407-2286
Mike Wibben, *Vice Pres*
Javier Acuna, *Opers Mgr*
EMP: 200
SALES (corp-wide): 270.6MM **Privately Held**
SIC: 7381 Security guard service
PA: Andrews International, Inc.
28001 Smyth Dr Ste 107
Valencia CA 91355
661 775-8400

(P-16565)
ATLAS SECURITY & PATROL INC
39465 Paseo Padre Pkwy # 2800, Fremont (94538-1631)
PHONE 510 791-7380
Fax: 510 791-2129
Jason Solorzano, *Manager*
EMP: 50
SALES (corp-wide): 4MM **Privately Held**
SIC: 7381 Security guard service; private investigator
PA: Atlas Security & Patrol, Inc.
3851 Charter Park Dr V
San Jose CA
408 972-2099

(P-16566)
AUSTIN SECURITY PATROL INC
11300 Sanders Dr Ste 24, Rancho Cordova (95742-6822)
P.O. Box 1617 (95741-1617)
PHONE 916 631-9877
Fax: 916 631-0407
Mike Boswell, *President*
Bob Skay, *Executive*
EMP: 65
SALES (est): 1.3MM **Privately Held**
WEB: www.austinsecuritypatrol.com
SIC: 7381 Protective services, guard; security guard service

(P-16567)
BACO REALTY CORPORATION
6310 Stockton Blvd, Sacramento (95824-4003)
PHONE 916 974-9898
Fax: 916 393-1960
EMP: 170
SALES (corp-wide): 42.6MM **Privately Held**
SIC: 7381 Guard services
PA: Baco Realty Corporation
51 Federal St Ste 202
San Francisco CA 94107
415 281-3700

(P-16568)
BAECHLER INVESTIGATIVE SVCS
4910 70th St, San Diego (92115-1801)
P.O. Box 19727 (92159-0727)
PHONE 619 464-5600
Fax: 619 464-5651
Anthony Baechler, *President*
EMP: 53
SQ FT: 5,200
SALES (est): 1.7MM **Privately Held**
WEB: www.junes.com
SIC: 7381 Detective & armored car services

(P-16569)
BALD EAGLE SECURITY SVCS INC
3626 Main St, San Diego (92113-3805)
P.O. Box 131350 (92170-1350)
PHONE 619 230-0022
Andrea Robinson, *President*
Dean Heilmann, *Manager*
EMP: 75
SALES (est): 234.2K **Privately Held**
SIC: 7381 Security guard service

(P-16570)
BARCOTT FRANK A SEC INVSTGTONS
Also Called: Barcott SEC & Investigations
6446 San Andres Ave, Cypress (90630-5324)
P.O. Box 2278 (90630-1778)
PHONE 714 891-8556
Fax: 714 430-1742
Frank A Barcott, *President*
Carolyn Barcott, *Vice Pres*
EMP: 200
SALES (est): 5.2MM **Privately Held**
SIC: 7381 Security guard service; detective services

(P-16571)
BARRYS SECURITY SERVICES INC (PA)
16739 Van Buren Blvd, Riverside (92504-5744)
PHONE 951 789-7575
Fax: 951 776-9692
Michelle Barry, *CEO*
Martin Morales, *Vice Pres*
Chase Blakney, *Human Res Dir*
EMP: 188
SQ FT: 5,000
SALES: 8.3MM **Privately Held**
WEB: www.weguard.biz
SIC: 7381 Guard services

(P-16572)
BARRYS SECURITY SERVICES INC
5480 Katella Ave Ste 203, Los Alamitos (90720-6823)
PHONE 562 493-7007
Carlos Nunez, *Branch Mgr*
EMP: 125
SALES (corp-wide): 8.3MM **Privately Held**
WEB: www.weguard.biz
SIC: 7381 Guard services
PA: Barry's Security Services, Inc.
16739 Van Buren Blvd
Riverside CA 92504
951 789-7575

(P-16573)
BEACH CITIES INVEST & PROTCTN
2500 Via Cabrillo Marina, San Pedro (90731-7224)
PHONE 310 322-4724
Kevin R Hackie, *CEO*
Norma Chavarria, *Treasurer*
Nicholas Hackie, *Vice Pres*
Shana Alexander, *Admin Sec*
Tom Greszcyk, *Manager*
EMP: 300
SQ FT: 2,000
SALES (est): 4MM **Privately Held**
SIC: 7381 Detective services; private investigator

(P-16574)
BELL PRIVATE SECURITY INC
Also Called: R M B SEC Cnslting Invstgtions
18030 Brookhurst St, Fountain Valley (92708-6756)
PHONE 714 964-9381
Fax: 714 842-0375
Robert M Bell, *President*
Dwight J Griffith, *Agent*
EMP: 90
SALES (est): 2MM **Privately Held**
WEB: www.bellprivatesecurity.com
SIC: 7381 Security guard service; private investigator

(P-16575)
BLACK BEAR SECURITY SERVICES
Also Called: Montana Investigation
2016 Oakdale Ave Ste B, San Francisco (94124-2041)
PHONE 415 559-5159
Fax: 415 647-0300
Moura Borisova, *President*
William Mercer, *CFO*
Bob Borissoff, *IT/INT Sup*
Nick Kartinski, *Manager*
EMP: 125
SQ FT: 3,000
SALES (est): 3.3MM **Privately Held**
WEB: www.blackbearsecurity.com
SIC: 7381 7382 Detective & armored car services; security systems services

(P-16576)
BLACKTALON ENTERPRISES INC
Also Called: Blacktalon Security Solutions
481 Technology Way, NAPA (94558-7571)
P.O. Box 300 (94559-0300)
PHONE 707 256-1810
Brent D Morgan, *President*
Nicole Haggadone, *Office Mgr*
EMP: 105

7381 - Detective & Armored Car Svcs County (P-16577)

SALES (est): 3.5MM **Privately Held**
WEB: www.blacktalon.com
SIC: **7381** 7382 Detective & armored car services; security guard service; protective services, guard; private investigator; security systems services; protective devices, security

(P-16577)
BORGENS & BORGENS INC
Also Called: Delta Protective Services
141 E Acacia St Ste D, Stockton (95202-1400)
P.O. Box 8633 (95208-0633)
PHONE..................209 547-2980
Fax: 209 948-6533
L D Borgens, *President*
K R Borgens, *Vice Pres*
EMP: 85 EST: 1993
SQ FT: 2,475
SALES (est): 1.8MM **Privately Held**
WEB: www.deltaprotectiveservices.com
SIC: **7381** Detective & armored car services

(P-16578)
BORUNDA PRIVATE SEC PATROL INC
1070 Brookhaven Dr, Clovis (93612-1913)
PHONE..................559 299-2662
Ben Borunda, *CEO*
EMP: 50
SALES (est): 94.3K **Privately Held**
SIC: **7381** Guard services

(P-16579)
BOYD & ASSOCIATES
445 E Esplanade Dr # 210, Oxnard (93036-2126)
PHONE..................805 988-8298
Fax: 805 278-0564
Kathy Correll, *Manager*
EMP: 100
SALES (corp-wide): 21.1MM **Privately Held**
WEB: www.boydsecurity.com
SIC: **7381** Security guard service
PA: Boyd & Associates
2191 E Thompson Blvd
Ventura CA 93001
818 752-1888

(P-16580)
BOYD & ASSOCIATES (PA)
2191 E Thompson Blvd, Ventura (93001-3538)
PHONE..................818 752-1888
Fax: 818 985-7442
Raymond G Boyd Sr, *Ch of Bd*
Daniel Boyd, *President*
Barbara K Boyd, *Vice Pres*
EMP: 160
SQ FT: 8,000
SALES (est): 21.1MM **Privately Held**
WEB: www.boydsecurity.com
SIC: **7381** 7382 Guard services; detective services; security systems services

(P-16581)
BOYD & ASSOCIATES
3151 Airway Ave Ste K105, Costa Mesa (92626-4613)
PHONE..................714 835-5423
Fax: 714 835-5641
EMP: 150
SQ FT: 3,012
SALES (corp-wide): 19.4MM **Privately Held**
SIC: **7381**
PA: Boyd & Associates
2191 E Thompson Blvd
Ventura CA 93001
818 752-1888

(P-16582)
BRINKS INCORPORATED
1120 Venice Blvd, Los Angeles (90015-3289)
PHONE..................818 503-8630
Fax: 213 747-8205
Dennis Dwyer, *Manager*
EMP: 136
SALES (corp-wide): 3B **Publicly Held**
WEB: www.brinksinc.com
SIC: **7381** Armored car services
HQ: Brink's, Incorporated
1801 Bayberry Ct Ste 400
Richmond VA 23226
804 289-9600

(P-16583)
BRINKS INCORPORATED
4520 Federal Blvd Ste A, San Diego (92102-2516)
PHONE..................619 263-6615
Eric Holman, *Manager*
Matthew Martinez, *Executive*
EMP: 120
SALES (corp-wide): 3B **Publicly Held**
WEB: www.brinksinc.com
SIC: **7381** Armored car services
HQ: Brink's, Incorporated
1801 Bayberry Ct Ste 400
Richmond VA 23226
804 289-9600

(P-16584)
BRINKS INCORPORATED
8178 Alpine Ave Unit A, Sacramento (95826-4707)
PHONE..................916 452-5279
Fax: 916 452-0173
Steve Morss, *Manager*
Jamie Acaylar, *Personnel Exec*
EMP: 133
SALES (corp-wide): 3B **Publicly Held**
WEB: www.brinksinc.com
SIC: **7381** Armored car services
HQ: Brink's, Incorporated
1801 Bayberry Ct Ste 400
Richmond VA 23226
804 289-9600

(P-16585)
BRINKS INCORPORATED
1630 Old Bayshore Hwy, San Jose (95112-4304)
PHONE..................408 436-7717
Fax: 408 436-8096
George Geovanni, *Manager*
Linh Giang, *Administration*
EMP: 80
SALES (corp-wide): 3B **Publicly Held**
WEB: www.brinksinc.com
SIC: **7381** Armored car services
HQ: Brink's, Incorporated
1801 Bayberry Ct Ste 400
Richmond VA 23226
804 289-9600

(P-16586)
BRINKS INCORPORATED
1821 S Soto St, Los Angeles (90023-4210)
PHONE..................323 262-2646
Fax: 323 262-0650
Eva Salas, *Manager*
Julian Moreira, *General Mgr*
EMP: 50
SALES (corp-wide): 3B **Publicly Held**
WEB: www.brinksinc.com
SIC: **7381** Detective & armored car services
HQ: Brink's, Incorporated
1801 Bayberry Ct Ste 400
Richmond VA 23226
804 289-9600

(P-16587)
C & C SECURITY PATROL INC
4600 Willow Rd, Pleasanton (94588-2710)
PHONE..................925 227-1400
EMP: 90
SALES (corp-wide): 7.2MM **Privately Held**
SIC: **7381** Guard services
PA: C & C Security Patrol, Inc.
4615 Enterprise Cmn
Fremont CA 94538
510 713-1260

(P-16588)
C S I PATROL SERVICES
3605 Long Beach Blvd # 205, Long Beach (90807-4013)
PHONE..................562 981-8988
Dennis Cook, *President*
EMP: 55
SQ FT: 600
SALES (est): 1.5MM **Privately Held**
WEB: www.csipatrol.com
SIC: **7381** Protective services, guard

(P-16589)
CALIFORNIA GUARD INC
Also Called: Ad Force Private Security
3108 N Cherryland Ave, Stockton (95215-2222)
P.O. Box 55331 (95205-8831)
PHONE..................209 465-8420
Fax: 209 931-1794
George Garcia, *CEO*
Surinder Singh Sandhu, *President*
EMP: 100
SALES (est): 3.5MM **Privately Held**
SIC: **7381** Security guard service

(P-16590)
CALIFORNIA SAFETY AGENCY
8932 Katella Ave Ste 108, Anaheim (92804-6299)
PHONE..................866 996-6990
EMP: 50
SALES (est): 1MM **Privately Held**
SIC: **7381**

(P-16591)
CALIFORNIA SECURITY CONS
3108 N Cherryland Ave, Stockton (95215-2222)
P.O. Box 55331 (95205-8831)
PHONE..................209 465-8420
George Garcia, *President*
EMP: 200
SALES (est): 2.6MM **Privately Held**
SIC: **7381** Security guard service

(P-16592)
CENTRAL COAST PUB SAFETY INC
222 Carmen Ln Ste 202, Santa Maria (93458-7777)
PHONE..................805 556-4450
Carl Dougherty, *CEO*
EMP: 84
SALES (est): 968K **Privately Held**
SIC: **7381** 8249 Protective services, guard; security guard service; medical training services

(P-16593)
CENTURION SECURITY INC
Also Called: Centurion Group, The
11454 San Vicente Blvd, Los Angeles (90049-6208)
PHONE..................818 755-0202
Steven Lemmer, *President*
David Rosenberg, *Corp Secy*
Daniel Cambell, *Vice Pres*
EMP: 200
SQ FT: 3,200
SALES (est): 6.4MM **Privately Held**
SIC: **7381** Security guard service

(P-16594)
CENTURION SECURITY SERVICES
20102 Sw Cypress St, Newport Beach (92660-0713)
PHONE..................949 474-0444
Robyn Hamilton, *President*
EMP: 70
SALES (est): 1.3MM **Privately Held**
SIC: **7381** Security guard service

(P-16595)
CHAMELEON GROUP INC
Also Called: Chameleon Associates
22020 Clarendon St # 112, Woodland Hills (91367-6361)
PHONE..................818 734-8448
Fax: 818 734-8454
Moshe Cohen, *President*
Kim Storms, *Administration*
Anna Polishuk, *Business Mgr*
Amotz Brandes, *Director*
EMP: 60
SQ FT: 3,500
SALES (est): 1.5MM **Privately Held**
WEB: www.chameleon1.com
SIC: **7381** Private investigator

(P-16596)
CHIEF PROTECTIVE SERVICES INC
Also Called: Assure Detective Agency
1344 W 6th St Ste 300, Corona (92882-1641)
P.O. Box 1806 (92878-1806)
PHONE..................951 738-0881
Fax: 951 738-0885
Steven Fernandez, *President*
EMP: 100
SQ FT: 3,000
SALES: 2.9MM **Privately Held**
SIC: **7381** Security guard service; private investigator

(P-16597)
CITADEL SECURITY INC
5199 E Pacific Cst Hwy # 200, Long Beach (90804-3304)
PHONE..................562 248-2300
Brian Kelley, *CEO*
Scott Hartwyk, *Opers Spvr*
EMP: 150
SQ FT: 4,500
SALES (est): 2.4MM **Privately Held**
WEB: www.citadelsecurityinc.com
SIC: **7381** Security guard service

(P-16598)
CITY NATIONAL SEC SVCS INC
6151 W Century Blvd # 916, Los Angeles (90045-5307)
PHONE..................310 641-6666
Fax: 310 252-9977
Chiraz Zouaoui, *Manager*
EMP: 80
SALES: 950K **Privately Held**
SIC: **7381** Security guard service

(P-16599)
CITY SECURITY CO INC
430 S Grfield Ave Ste 401, Alhambra (91801)
PHONE..................626 458-2325
Bob Rysdon, *President*
EMP: 70
SALES (est): 1.3MM **Privately Held**
SIC: **7381** Security guard service

(P-16600)
CLASSIC PROTECTION INC
3208 Royal St, Los Angeles (90007-3657)
PHONE..................213 742-1238
Richard Ullman, *President*
Catherine Ullman, *Administration*
EMP: 50
SQ FT: 1,000
SALES (est): 1.3MM **Privately Held**
SIC: **7381** Guard services; security guard service

(P-16601)
COMMAND INTERNATIONAL SEC SVCS
6819 Sepulveda Blvd, Van Nuys (91405-4463)
PHONE..................818 997-1666
Nafees Memon, *Owner*
Nick Memon, *Opers Mgr*
EMP: 55
SQ FT: 700
SALES: 1.2MM **Privately Held**
SIC: **7381** Guard services

(P-16602)
COMMAND SECURITY CORPORATION
1630 S Sunkist St Ste O, Anaheim (92806-5816)
PHONE..................714 557-9355
John Dunlevy, *Regl Sales Mgr*
EMP: 168
SALES (corp-wide): 133.1MM **Publicly Held**
SIC: **7381** Guard services
PA: Command Security Corporation
512 Herndon Pkwy Ste A
Herndon VA 20170
703 464-4735

PRODUCTS & SERVICES SECTION
7381 - Detective & Armored Car Svcs County (P-16626)

(P-16603)
COMMAND SECURITY CORPORATION
890 Hillview Ct Ste 100, Milpitas (95035-4573)
PHONE..................................510 623-2355
EMP: 168
SALES (corp-wide): 133.1MM **Publicly Held**
SIC: 7381 Guard services
PA: Command Security Corporation
512 Herndon Pkwy Ste A
Herndon VA 20170
703 464-4735

(P-16604)
COMMAND SECURITY CORPORATION
Also Called: Aviation Safeguards
8929 S Sepulveda Blvd # 300, Los Angeles (90045-3616)
PHONE..................................310 981-4530
Fax: 310 568-0433
Sunny Williams, *Vice Pres*
Joe Conlon, *President*
EMP: 800
SALES (corp-wide): 133.1MM **Publicly Held**
WEB: www.cscny.com
SIC: 7381 7382 Security guard service; security systems services
PA: Command Security Corporation
512 Herndon Pkwy Ste A
Herndon VA 20170
703 464-4735

(P-16605)
COMMAND SECURITY CORPORATION
Also Called: Aviation Safeguards
1701 Airport Blvd Ste 205, San Jose (95110-1236)
PHONE..................................650 574-0911
Fax: 408 977-1605
Earl Hartfield, *Manager*
EMP: 80
SALES (corp-wide): 133.1MM **Publicly Held**
WEB: www.cscny.com
SIC: 7381 Security guard service
PA: Command Security Corporation
512 Herndon Pkwy Ste A
Herndon VA 20170
703 464-4735

(P-16606)
COMMERCIAL PROTECTIVE SVCS INC
436 W Walnut St, Gardena (90248-3137)
PHONE..................................310 515-5290
Christopher Coffey, *President*
William R Babcock, *CFO*
EMP: 200 **EST:** 1997
SQ FT: 10,000
SALES: 3.5MM **Privately Held**
SIC: 7381 Protective services, guard

(P-16607)
COMMONWEALTH INTERNATIONAL
968 Durfee Ave, South El Monte (91733-4408)
PHONE..................................626 279-9201
Fax: 626 279-9240
Jose Velasco, *President*
Emil Ayad, *Vice Pres*
Karman Pina, *Office Mgr*
EMP: 50
SALES (est): 1.5MM **Privately Held**
SIC: 7381 Armored car services

(P-16608)
COMPREHENSIVE SEC SVCS INC (PA)
10535 E Stockton Blvd, Elk Grove (95624-9753)
P.O. Box 246719, Sacramento (95824-6719)
PHONE..................................916 683-3605
Fax: 916 732-2203
Bashir A Choudry, *President*
Jamal-Eddine Kabbaj, *Exec VP*
Tawfiq Almassiri, *Opers Mgr*
Tawfiq Alnassiri, *Opers Mgr*

Yakoub Nash, *Manager*
EMP: 75
SQ FT: 3,300
SALES: 8.7MM **Privately Held**
WEB: www.comprehensivesecurity.net
SIC: 7381 7382 Guard services; security systems services

(P-16609)
COMPREHENSIVE SEC SVCS INC
1734 Linda Ave Ste B, Marysville (95901-6413)
PHONE..................................530 743-6762
Fax: 530 743-5456
Bashir A Choudry, *Regional Mgr*
EMP: 85
SALES (corp-wide): 8.7MM **Privately Held**
SIC: 7381 Security guard service
PA: Comprehensive Security Services, Inc.
10535 E Stockton Blvd
Elk Grove CA 95624
916 683-3605

(P-16610)
CONTACT SECURITY INC
3000 E Birch St Ste 111, Brea (92821-6261)
PHONE..................................714 572-6760
Fax: 714 572-6766
Michelle Quesada, *President*
Kerry Phipps, *Supervisor*
EMP: 250
SQ FT: 2,500
SALES (est): 4MM **Privately Held**
WEB: www.contactsecurity.com
SIC: 7381 Security guard service

(P-16611)
CONTEMPORARY SERVICES CORP
Also Called: Crowd Management
2650 E Shaw Ave, Fresno (93710-8284)
PHONE..................................559 225-9325
Robert Humphrey, *Manager*
Devraj URS, *Technology*
Shawna Benjamin, *Human Res Mgr*
EMP: 200
SALES (corp-wide): 304.3MM **Privately Held**
WEB: www.csc-usa.com
SIC: 7381 Protective services, guard
PA: Contemporary Services Corporation
17101 Superior St
Northridge CA 91325
818 885-5150

(P-16612)
CORPORATE SECURITY SERVICE INC
5 3rd St Ste 314, San Francisco (94103-3295)
PHONE..................................415 626-9271
Fax: 415 541-0464
Joseph Mc Reynolds, *CEO*
Judy Mc Reynolds, *President*
Ave Seltsam, *Vice Pres*
EMP: 150
SQ FT: 3,000
SALES (est): 3.6MM **Privately Held**
WEB: www.csssecurity.com
SIC: 7381 Security guard service

(P-16613)
COVENANT AVIATION SECURITY LLC
274 Michelle Ct, South San Francisco (94080-6201)
PHONE..................................650 219-3473
Brian O Apos, *Manager*
EMP: 1100
SALES (corp-wide): 39.4MM **Privately Held**
SIC: 7381 Security guard service
HQ: Covenant Aviation Security, Llc
400 Quadrangle Dr Ste A
Bolingbrook IL 60440
630 771-0800

(P-16614)
CPS SECURITY SOLUTIONS INC (PA)
436 W Walnut St, Gardena (90248-3137)
PHONE..................................310 818-1030

Chris Coffey, *President*
William Babcock, *CFO*
Scott R Barnes, *Exec VP*
Charlie Nelson, *Area Mgr*
Patricia Pillittere, *Manager*
EMP: 74
SQ FT: 14,000
SALES (est): 53.2MM **Privately Held**
SIC: 7381 Security guard service

(P-16615)
CREATIVE SECURITY COMPANY INC
150 S Autumn St Ste B, San Jose (95110-2515)
PHONE..................................408 295-2600
Charles H Wall, *President*
James H Caddell, *Vice Pres*
Robert Hinckley, *Director*
EMP: 350
SQ FT: 12,000
SALES (est): 13.1MM **Privately Held**
WEB: www.creativesecurity.com
SIC: 7381 Security guard service; private investigator

(P-16616)
CRIME IMPACT SECURITY PATROL
Also Called: Crime Impact Security & Patrol
3860 Crenshaw Blvd # 223, Los Angeles (90008-1816)
PHONE..................................323 296-6406
Fax: 323 296-6408
Darrin Jenkins, *President*
EMP: 55
SALES (est): 1.3MM **Privately Held**
SIC: 7381 Security guard service

(P-16617)
CRIMETEK SECURITY
3448 N Golden Ste Bl St G, Turlock (95382)
P.O. Box 845 (95381-0845)
PHONE..................................209 668-6208
Fax: 209 668-6703
Edward Esmaili, *President*
Ed Esmaili, *Partner*
Rosy Esmaili, *Partner*
Joseph Givargis, *Manager*
EMP: 420 **EST:** 1999
SQ FT: 2,200
SALES (est): 11.5MM **Privately Held**
SIC: 7381 Security guard service

(P-16618)
CYPRESS SECURITY LLC (PA)
478 Tehama St, San Francisco (94103-4141)
PHONE..................................415 240-4494
Fax: 415 352-1910
Kes Narbutas,
Veronica Brown, *Accountant*
EMP: 92
SQ FT: 3,500
SALES (est): 29.3MM **Privately Held**
WEB: www.cypress-security.com
SIC: 7381 Security guard service

(P-16619)
CYPRESS SECURITY LLC
Also Called: Cypress Private Security
1762 Tech Dr Ste 122, San Jose (95110)
PHONE..................................408 217-6063
Jason Berckart, *Mng Member*
EMP: 76
SALES (corp-wide): 29.3MM **Privately Held**
SIC: 7381 Security guard service
PA: Cypress Security, Llc
478 Tehama St
San Francisco CA 94103
415 240-4494

(P-16620)
CYPRESS SECURITY LLC
9926 Pioneer Blvd Ste 106, Santa Fe Springs (90670-6243)
PHONE..................................562 222-4197
Kes Narbutas, *CEO*
EMP: 80
SALES (corp-wide): 29.3MM **Privately Held**
SIC: 7381 Security guard service

PA: Cypress Security, Llc
478 Tehama St
San Francisco CA 94103
415 240-4494

(P-16621)
DAN CONNOLLY INC
Also Called: Armed Courier Service
855 Civic Center Dr Ste 5, Santa Clara (95050-3962)
PHONE..................................408 241-0910
Fax: 408 241-0996
Dan Connolly, *President*
EMP: 60
SQ FT: 6,000
SALES (est): 1.7MM **Privately Held**
WEB: www.armedcourierservice.com
SIC: 7381 Armored car services

(P-16622)
DANSK ENTERPRISES INC
Also Called: Nordic Security Services
3419 Via Lido 345, Newport Beach (92663-3908)
PHONE..................................714 751-0347
Peter Jensen, *President*
Eric Reinholtz, *Executive*
Wayne K Spurlock, *General Mgr*
Katrina Hernandez, *Office Mgr*
EMP: 100
SALES (est): 2.8MM **Privately Held**
WEB: www.nordicsec.com
SIC: 7381 Security guard service

(P-16623)
DELTA HAWKEYE SECURITY INC
7400 Shoreline Dr Ste 2, Stockton (95219-5498)
PHONE..................................209 957-3333
Fax: 209 235-6058
Dallas Faulkner, *Vice Pres*
Frank Passadore, *President*
Brian Millin, *Vice Pres*
EMP: 58
SQ FT: 2,000
SALES (est): 1.6MM
SALES (corp-wide): 82.9MM **Privately Held**
WEB: www.deltahawkeye.com
SIC: 7381 Security guard service
PA: The Grupe Company
3255 W March Ln Ste 400
Stockton CA 95219
209 473-6000

(P-16624)
DELTA ONE SECURITY INC
342 Acacia St, Fairfield (94533-3766)
PHONE..................................707 425-9346
Fax: 707 552-5044
Robert Edwards, *President*
Betty Edwards, *CFO*
EMP: 60
SALES (est): 1.2MM **Privately Held**
SIC: 7381 Security guard service

(P-16625)
DESERT SERVICES INC
41921 Beacon Hl, Palm Desert (92211-5191)
PHONE..................................760 837-2000
Fax: 760 775-0229
Richard Bradford, *Branch Mgr*
EMP: 93
SALES (corp-wide): 9.6MM **Privately Held**
SIC: 7381 Guard services
PA: Desert Services, Inc.
770 W Main St
El Centro CA
760 370-5700

(P-16626)
DIPLOMATIC SECURITY SVCS LLC
7581 Etiwanda Ave, Rancho Cucamonga (91739)
PHONE..................................909 463-8409
Iyke U Harrison, *Principal*
EMP: 99 **EST:** 2014
SQ FT: 1,500
SALES (est): 713.1K **Privately Held**
SIC: 7381 Security guard service

7381 - Detective & Armored Car Svcs County (P-16627)

(P-16627)
DLO ENTERPRISES INC
Also Called: Colt Security Services
41865 Boardwalk Ste 216, Palm Desert (92211-9033)
PHONE..................760 346-8033
Fax: 760 773-3083
Dennis L Oliver, *President*
EMP: 55
SALES (est): 1.8MM **Privately Held**
WEB: www.coltsecurity.com
SIC: 7381 Protective services, guard; security guard service

(P-16628)
DRUM SECURITY SERVICE INC
45530 Pelican Hill Ct, Indio (92201-0936)
PHONE..................818 708-7914
Charles R Drum, *President*
EMP: 60
SALES (est): 1.4MM **Privately Held**
SIC: 7381 Security guard service

(P-16629)
DUNBAR ARMORED INC
629 Whitney St, San Leandro (94577-1115)
PHONE..................510 569-7400
Fax: 510 569-1474
Ted Nguyen, *Manager*
EMP: 100
SALES (corp-wide): 612MM **Privately Held**
WEB: www.dunbararmored.com
SIC: 7381 Armored car services
PA: Dunbar Armored, Inc.
    50 Schilling Rd
    Hunt Valley MD 21031
    410 584-9800

(P-16630)
EAGLE SECURITY SERVICE INC
12903 S Normandie Ave, Gardena (90249-2123)
PHONE..................310 532-1626
Mohsen Kamel, *President*
Lina Keissieh, *Manager*
EMP: 150
SQ FT: 5,000
SALES (est): 4.2MM **Privately Held**
SIC: 7381 Detective & armored car services

(P-16631)
EASTSIDE GROUP CORPORATION
Also Called: Prudential Security Services
1830 W Olympic Blvd # 202, Los Angeles (90006-3734)
P.O. Box 531, Lynwood (90262-0531)
PHONE..................213 368-9777
Fax: 213 368-9772
Fernando Gonzales, *President*
Manny Martinez, *Vice Pres*
EMP: 125
SALES: 2.5MM **Privately Held**
SIC: 7381 Security guard service

(P-16632)
ELITE ENFRCMENT SEC SLTONS INC
29970 Technology Dr, Murrieta (92563-2645)
PHONE..................866 354-8308
Kevin Roncevich, *Branch Mgr*
EMP: 50
SALES (corp-wide): 5.1MM **Privately Held**
SIC: 7381 Security guard service
PA: Elite Enforcement Security Solutions, Inc.
    1290 N Hancock St Ste 101
    Anaheim CA 92807
    866 354-8308

(P-16633)
ELITE SECURITY SERVICES INC
18006 Sky Park Cir # 205, Irvine (92614-6406)
P.O. Box 18073 (92623-8073)
PHONE..................949 222-2203
Betty Kaminski, *President*
Gene Kaminski, *Exec VP*
Laura Writer, *Administration*
EMP: 450
SQ FT: 2,400
SALES (est): 5.2MM **Privately Held**
WEB: www.elitesecurityservices.net
SIC: 7381 7382 Guard services; security systems services

(P-16634)
ELITE SHOW SERVICES INC
2878 Camino Del Rio S # 260, San Diego (92108-3855)
PHONE..................619 574-1589
John Kontopuls, *President*
Nicole Stichka, *Senior VP*
Gus Kontopuls, *Vice Pres*
Demond Gooch, *Business Mgr*
Diane Yoshida, *Sales Executive*
EMP: 3123
SALES (est): 77.1MM **Privately Held**
WEB: www.eliteshowservices.com
SIC: 7381 Security guard service

(P-16635)
ET SECURITY INC
Also Called: Et Security
7100 Hayvenhurst Ave # 318, Van Nuys (91406-3804)
P.O. Box 2931 (91404-2931)
PHONE..................818 988-9617
Fax: 818 376-0615
Eddie Tucker, *President*
EMP: 200 EST: 1998
SALES (est): 5.3MM **Privately Held**
SIC: 7381 Guard services

(P-16636)
EVENT GUARD SERVICES INC
1823 Business Center Dr, Duarte (91010-2902)
P.O. Box 26794, Los Angeles (90026-0794)
PHONE..................626 531-6772
Kelly Martin, *President*
Tina Gonzalez, *Payroll Mgr*
Ana Vigo, *Marketing Staff*
Randy Wingard, *Director*
Chris Clausen, *Manager*
EMP: 99
SALES (est): 2.5MM **Privately Held**
SIC: 7381 Guard services

(P-16637)
EXECUSHELD PRTECTION GROUP LLC
301 Georgia St Ste 307, Vallejo (94590-5993)
PHONE..................707 439-6351
Michael Manibusan, *Principal*
Richard Berrios, *Principal*
Daniel Gonzalez, *Principal*
EMP: 75
SALES (est): 512.3K **Privately Held**
SIC: 7381 9221 Protective services, guard; security guard service; police protection

(P-16638)
EXECUSHIELD INC
4104 24th St Ste 501, San Francisco (94114-3615)
PHONE..................415 508-0825
Fax: 415 508-0852
Daniel Gonzalez, *President*
Justin White, *Human Res Mgr*
EMP: 55
SALES (est): 1.6MM **Privately Held**
WEB: www.execushield.com
SIC: 7381 Security guard service

(P-16639)
EXECUTIVE PROTECTION AGENCY K-
Also Called: Epak9
1175 N 2nd St Ste 102, El Cajon (92021-5033)
PHONE..................619 442-5771
Frank Whiteley, *President*
EMP: 50
SQ FT: 3,600
SALES (est): 1MM **Privately Held**
SIC: 7381 Security guard service

(P-16640)
FIDELITY SECURITY SERVICES INC
25133 Avenue Tibbitts H, Valencia (91355-3494)
PHONE..................661 295-5007
Ahmadshah Ahmadi, *President*
Nazifa Ahmadi, *CFO*
EMP: 105
SQ FT: 1,000
SALES: 675K **Privately Held**
WEB: www.fidelitysecurityservices.com
SIC: 7381 Guard services

(P-16641)
FIRST ALARM SEC & PATROL INC (HQ)
1731 Tech Dr Ste 800, San Jose (95110)
PHONE..................831 685-1110
Fax: 831 685-6629
Cal Horton, *President*
Jarl E Saal, *Chairman*
Audrey Pierson, *Executive*
Teresa H Larkin, *Business Dir*
Beverly Deshazer, *Finance Mgr*
EMP: 150
SALES (est): 28.4MM
SALES (corp-wide): 60.7MM **Privately Held**
SIC: 7381 Security guard service
PA: First Alarm
    1111 Estates Dr
    Aptos CA 95003
    831 476-1111

(P-16642)
FIRST INTERSTATE SECURITY INC
16200 Ventura Blvd # 209, Encino (91436-2205)
PHONE..................818 995-6664
Fax: 818 995-6855
Mike Ahmed, *President*
EMP: 210
SQ FT: 5,000
SALES (est): 3.6MM **Privately Held**
WEB: www.firstinterstateinc.com
SIC: 7381 Detective & armored car services; security guard service

(P-16643)
FIRSTLINE TRNSP SEC INC
1250 Sutterville Rd, Sacramento (95822-1101)
PHONE..................916 456-5166
EMP: 120
SALES (corp-wide): 891.5MM **Privately Held**
SIC: 7381 Guard services
HQ: Firstline Transportation Security, Inc..
    7135 Charlotte Pike # 100
    Nashville TN 37209
    216 674-5300

(P-16644)
FOCUSPOINT INTERNATIONAL
4660 La Jolla Village Dr, San Diego (92122-4601)
PHONE..................415 446-9418
Craig Colburn, *COO*
Craig Pearson, *President*
EMP: 400
SALES: 12MM **Privately Held**
WEB: focuspointintl.com/index.php
SIC: 7381 8322 Private investigator; crisis intervention center

(P-16645)
FOUR STAR PRIVATE PATROL INC
Also Called: Custom Security Services
28441 Rancho Ca Rd 105, Temecula (92590-3618)
PHONE..................951 695-4245
Michael E Berumen, *President*
Carol Y Berumen, *Corp Secy*
EMP: 100
SQ FT: 3,000
SALES: 3MM **Privately Held**
WEB: www.fourstarinc.com
SIC: 7381 Security guard service

(P-16646)
FPK SECURITY INC
Also Called: Fpk Investigaions
28348 Constellation Rd # 880, Valencia (91355-5097)
P.O. Box 55597 (91385-0597)
PHONE..................661 702-9091
Mark David, *CEO*
Robert Esquivel, *President*
Joe Madick, *Asst Director*
Mando Esquivel, *Manager*
EMP: 365
SQ FT: 1,200
SALES (est): 8.9MM **Privately Held**
SIC: 7381 Private investigator

(P-16647)
FRASCO INC (PA)
Also Called: Frasco Investigative Services
215 W Alameda Ave, Burbank (91502-3060)
PHONE..................818 848-3888
Fax: 818 846-9995
John C Simmers, *President*
Laura Pfaffman, *CFO*
Noelle Harling, *Vice Pres*
Steven Schulmeister, *Vice Pres*
Jason Simmers, *Vice Pres*
EMP: 65
SQ FT: 10,000
SALES (est): 17.5MM **Privately Held**
WEB: www.frasco.com
SIC: 7381 Private investigator

(P-16648)
FRESNO COUNTY PRIVATE SECURITY
2150 Tulare St, Fresno (93721-2103)
PHONE..................559 233-9800
Fax: 559 438-3010
Ronald Sawl, *President*
David McDonald, *Admin Mgr*
EMP: 100
SALES (est): 2.2MM **Privately Held**
SIC: 7381 Security guard service

(P-16649)
G4S SECURE SOLUTIONS (USA)
4400 Ashe Rd Ste 206, Bakersfield (93313-2036)
PHONE..................661 834-3454
Fax: 661 324-3186
Thomas Robinson, *Branch Mgr*
EMP: 125
SALES (corp-wide): 10.3B **Privately Held**
SIC: 7381 Security guard service
HQ: G4s Secure Solutions (Usa) Inc
    1395 University Blvd
    Jupiter FL 33458
    561 622-5656

(P-16650)
G4S SECURE SOLUTIONS (USA)
5030 Camino De La Siesta, San Diego (92108-3116)
PHONE..................619 295-2394
Steven Fisher, *Branch Mgr*
Camille Bangayan, *Administration*
EMP: 250
SQ FT: 1,500
SALES (corp-wide): 10.3B **Privately Held**
SIC: 7381 Detective & armored car services
HQ: G4s Secure Solutions (Usa) Inc
    1395 University Blvd
    Jupiter FL 33458
    561 622-5656

(P-16651)
G4S SECURE SOLUTIONS (USA)
4929 Wilshire Blvd # 601, Los Angeles (90010-3808)
PHONE..................323 938-9100
Yvonne Herod, *Manager*
EMP: 300
SALES (corp-wide): 10.3B **Privately Held**
SIC: 7381 Security guard service
HQ: G4s Secure Solutions (Usa) Inc
    1395 University Blvd
    Jupiter FL 33458
    561 622-5656

(P-16652)
G4S SECURE SOLUTIONS (USA)
1450 Iowa Ave, Riverside (92507-0522)
PHONE..................951 341-3000
Fax: 951 341-3030
Richard McDale, *Manager*
Bob Schriener, *Business Mgr*
EMP: 300
SALES (corp-wide): 10.3B **Privately Held**
SIC: 7381 Security guard service

PRODUCTS & SERVICES SECTION
7381 - Detective & Armored Car Svcs County (P-16677)

HQ: G4s Secure Solutions (Usa) Inc
1395 University Blvd
Jupiter FL 33458
561 622-5656

(P-16653)
G4S SECURE SOLUTIONS (USA)
200 Pine St Fl 7, San Francisco
(94104-2707)
PHONE..............................415 591-0780
Stanley Lee, *Branch Mgr*
EMP: 119
SALES (corp-wide): 10.3B **Privately Held**
SIC: 7381 Detective & armored car services
HQ: G4s Secure Solutions (Usa) Inc
1395 University Blvd
Jupiter FL 33458
561 622-5656

(P-16654)
G4S SECURE SOLUTIONS (USA)
2300 E Katella Ave # 150, Anaheim
(92806-6061)
PHONE..............................714 939-4900
John Mc Elhaney, *Manager*
Brandon Joffe, *Manager*
EMP: 119
SALES (corp-wide): 10.3B **Privately Held**
SIC: 7381 Detective & armored car services
HQ: G4s Secure Solutions (Usa) Inc
1395 University Blvd
Jupiter FL 33458
561 622-5656

(P-16655)
G4S SECURE SOLUTIONS (USA)
1 Annabel Ln Ste 208, San Ramon
(94583-4360)
PHONE..............................925 543-0008
EMP: 119
SALES (corp-wide): 11.8B **Privately Held**
SIC: 7381
HQ: G4s Secure Solutions (Usa) Inc
1395 University Blvd
Jupiter FL 33458
561 622-5656

(P-16656)
G4S SECURE SOLUTIONS (USA)
5655 Lindero Canyon Rd # 504, Westlake
Village (91362-4016)
PHONE..............................818 889-1113
Yvonne Herrod, *Manager*
EMP: 119
SALES (corp-wide): 10.3B **Privately Held**
SIC: 7381 Detective & armored car services
HQ: G4s Secure Solutions (Usa) Inc
1395 University Blvd
Jupiter FL 33458
561 622-5656

(P-16657)
GARDA CL TECHNICAL SVCS INC
15640 Roxford St, Sylmar (91342-1265)
PHONE..............................818 362-7011
Fax: 818 362-2111
Ken Krogman, *Manager*
EMP: 55
SALES (corp-wide): 1.3B **Privately Held**
WEB: www.gocashlink.com
SIC: 7381 Armored car services
HQ: Garda Cl Technical Services, Inc.
700 S Federal Hwy Ste 300
Boca Raton FL 33432
561 939-7000

(P-16658)
GARDA CL WEST INC
Also Called: Continental Security Guards
1602 W Orange Grove Ave, Orange
(92868-1117)
PHONE..............................714 771-6010
Steve Struck, *Manager*
EMP: 100
SALES (corp-wide): 1.3B **Privately Held**
SIC: 7381 Armored car services
HQ: Garda Cl West, Inc.
1612 W Pico Blvd
Los Angeles CA 90015
213 383-3611

(P-16659)
GARDA CL WEST INC
372 S Arrowhead Ave, San Bernardino
(92408-1307)
PHONE..............................909 574-2676
Jim Chadwick, *Manager*
EMP: 50
SALES (corp-wide): 1.3B **Privately Held**
SIC: 7381 Armored car services
HQ: Garda Cl West, Inc.
1612 W Pico Blvd
Los Angeles CA 90015
213 383-3611

(P-16660)
GARDA CL WEST INC (DH)
Also Called: Gcl W
1612 W Pico Blvd, Los Angeles
(90015-2410)
PHONE..............................213 383-3611
Stephan Cretier, *President*
Chris W Jamroz, *President*
John Mandish, *Administration*
EMP: 375
SQ FT: 25,000
SALES (est): 41.2MM
SALES (corp-wide): 1.3B **Privately Held**
SIC: 7381 Armored car services
HQ: Garda Cl Technical Services, Inc.
700 S Federal Hwy Ste 300
Boca Raton FL 33432
561 939-7000

(P-16661)
GARDA CL WEST INC
301 N Lake Ave Ste 600, Pasadena
(91101-5129)
PHONE..............................800 883-8305
Duncan Longworth, *Branch Mgr*
Vincent Mordarelli, *Senior VP*
Hugues Trottier, *VP Finance*
Miriam Khris, *Finance*
Ken Rose, *Human Res Mgr*
EMP: 70
SALES (corp-wide): 18.6MM **Privately Held**
SIC: 7381 Armored car services; security guard service
PA: Garda Cl West Inc
3021 Gilroy St
Los Angeles CA 90039
323 668-2712

(P-16662)
GATEWAY SECURITY INC
5757 W Century Blvd, Los Angeles
(90045-6401)
PHONE..............................310 410-0790
Stephan Glassman, *Branch Mgr*
EMP: 975
SALES (corp-wide): 87.5MM **Privately Held**
SIC: 7381 Guard services
PA: Gateway Security Inc.
604 Market St 608
Newark NJ 07105
973 465-8006

(P-16663)
GATEWAY SECURITY INC
100 World Way, Los Angeles (90045-5870)
PHONE..............................310 642-0529
EMP: 487
SALES (corp-wide): 87.5MM **Privately Held**
SIC: 7381 Security guard service
PA: Gateway Security Inc.
604 Market St 608
Newark NJ 07105
973 465-8006

(P-16664)
GEIL ENTERPRISES INC (PA)
Also Called: CIS Security
1945 N Helm Ave Ste 102, Fresno
(93727-1670)
PHONE..............................559 495-3000
Fax: 559 256-8872
Sam Geil, *CEO*
Ryan Geil, *President*
Jason Geil, *Manager*
EMP: 107
SQ FT: 10,000
SALES (est): 36.4MM **Privately Held**
WEB: www.geilenterprises.com
SIC: 7381 7349 Protective services, guard; janitorial service, contract basis; building maintenance, except repairs

(P-16665)
GLOBAL SHIELD SECURITY INC
4924 Balboa Blvd Ste 639, Encino
(91316-3402)
PHONE..............................818 988-9010
Zabihullah Kator, *President*
EMP: 50 **EST:** 2006
SALES (est): 746K **Privately Held**
SIC: 7381 Guard services

(P-16666)
GREEN VALLEY SECURITY INC
6049 Douglas Blvd Ste 28, Granite Bay
(95746-6275)
PHONE..............................916 797-4058
Fax: 916 797-2699
Anthony Urbancic, *President*
Jack Johnson, *Manager*
EMP: 60
SQ FT: 300
SALES (est): 1.2MM **Privately Held**
SIC: 7381 Security guard service

(P-16667)
GS1 GROUP INC
70 S Lake Ave Ste 945, Pasadena
(91101-4991)
PHONE..............................626 844-4377
Michael Vincent Severo, *CEO*
Ernesto Garcia, *President*
EMP: 68 **EST:** 2011
SALES: 1.2MM **Privately Held**
SIC: 7381 Security guard service; private investigator

(P-16668)
GUARD MANAGEMENT INC
Also Called: G M I
8001 Vickers St, San Diego (92111-1917)
PHONE..............................858 279-8282
Larry Abrams, *President*
Jason Wingert, *Admin Asst*
Bryan Allen, *Administration*
Stephen Claxton, *Portfolio Mgr*
Sherie Darden, *Human Res Dir*
EMP: 510
SALES (est): 12.6MM **Privately Held**
SIC: 7381 Guard services

(P-16669)
GUARD-SYSTEMS INC
1910 S Archibald Ave M2, Ontario
(91761-8502)
PHONE..............................909 947-5400
Patrick Crawford, *Manager*
EMP: 300
SALES (corp-wide): 7.9MM **Privately Held**
WEB: www.guardsystemsinc.com
SIC: 7381 Protective services, guard; guard services; security guard service
PA: Guard-Systems, Inc.
1190 Monterey Pass Rd
Monterey Park CA 91754
626 443-0031

(P-16670)
GUARD-SYSTEMS INC
1190 Monterey Pass Rd, Monterey Park
(91754-3615)
PHONE..............................323 881-6711
Theodore Haas, *Branch Mgr*
Anita Teh, *Executive*
Morten Syverud, *CIO*
EMP: 300
SALES (corp-wide): 7.9MM **Privately Held**
WEB: www.guardsystemsinc.com
SIC: 7381 Detective & armored car services
PA: Guard-Systems, Inc.
1190 Monterey Pass Rd
Monterey Park CA 91754
626 443-0031

(P-16671)
GUARD-SYSTEMS INC
Also Called: Guard Systems District 1
1190 Monterey Pass Rd, Monterey Park
(91754-3615)
PHONE..............................323 881-6715
Fax: 323 263-7351
Theodore Haas, *Owner*
EMP: 300
SALES (corp-wide): 7.9MM **Privately Held**
WEB: www.guardsystemsinc.com
SIC: 7381 Detective & armored car services
PA: Guard-Systems, Inc.
1190 Monterey Pass Rd
Monterey Park CA 91754
626 443-0031

(P-16672)
GUARDCO SECURITY SERVICES
1360 W 18th St, Merced (95340-4402)
PHONE..............................209 723-4273
Fax: 209 723-7106
David Williams, *Owner*
Max Hernandez, *Manager*
EMP: 71
SQ FT: 1,000
SALES: 1.7MM **Privately Held**
WEB: www.guardcosecurity.com
SIC: 7381 Security guard service

(P-16673)
GUARDIAN EAGLE SECURITY INC
11400 W Olympic Blvd Fl 2, Los Angeles
(90064-1579)
PHONE..............................888 990-0002
Hassan M Galal, *CEO*
Fadwa Galal, *President*
Hassan Galal, *CEO*
Fathi M Galal, *Vice Pres*
EMP: 675
SQ FT: 3,000
SALES (est): 8.3MM **Privately Held**
WEB: www.ges.net
SIC: 7381 Security guard service

(P-16674)
GUARDIAN NATIONAL INC
Also Called: Guardian National Security
20361 Prairie St Ste 1, Chatsworth
(91311-8100)
PHONE..............................800 700-1467
Mohammad Ramzan, *President*
EMP: 50
SALES (est): 1.2MM **Privately Held**
SIC: 7381 Security guard service

(P-16675)
GUARDNOW INC (PA)
18663 Ventura Blvd # 217, Tarzana
(91356-4162)
PHONE..............................877 482-7366
Mike Kator, *President*
EMP: 50 **EST:** 2011
SQ FT: 115
SALES: 5MM **Privately Held**
SIC: 7381 Security guard service

(P-16676)
GUARDSMARK LLC
1225 W 190th St Ste 280, Gardena
(90248-4305)
PHONE..............................310 522-9603
Rebecca Wells, *Manager*
EMP: 60
SALES (corp-wide): 950.8MM **Privately Held**
WEB: www.guardsmark.com
SIC: 7381 Security guard service
HQ: Guardsmark, Llc
1551 N Tustin Ave Ste 650
Santa Ana CA 92705
714 619-9700

(P-16677)
GUARDSMARK LLC
3000 S Robertson Blvd # 150, Los Angeles
(90034-3144)
PHONE..............................310 216-9081
Rebekah Wells, *Principal*
EMP: 111

7381 - Detective & Armored Car Svcs County (P-16678)

SALES (corp-wide): 950.8MM **Privately Held**
WEB: www.guardsmark.com
SIC: 7381 Detective & armored car services
HQ: Guardsmark, Llc
1551 N Tustin Ave Ste 650
Santa Ana CA 92705
714 619-9700

(P-16678)
GUARDSMARK LLC
4713 1st St Ste 215, Pleasanton (94566-7363)
PHONE.....................925 484-4412
Charles Parker, *Manager*
EMP: 350
SALES (corp-wide): 950.8MM **Privately Held**
WEB: www.guardsmark.com
SIC: 7381 Security guard service
HQ: Guardsmark, Llc
1551 N Tustin Ave Ste 650
Santa Ana CA 92705
714 619-9700

(P-16679)
GUARDSMARK LLC (DH)
1551 N Tustin Ave Ste 650, Santa Ana (92705-8664)
PHONE.....................714 619-9700
Fax: 212 265-5466
Steven S Jones, *CEO*
Michelle Craine, *Officer*
Toni Ippolito, *Executive Asst*
EMP: 102
SQ FT: 32,107
SALES (est): 270.5MM
SALES (corp-wide): 950.8MM **Privately Held**
WEB: www.guardsmark.com
SIC: 7381 8742 2721 Security guard service; private investigator; industry specialist consultants; periodicals: publishing only
HQ: Universal Protection Service, Lp
1551 N Tustin Ave Ste 650
Santa Ana CA 92705
714 619-9700

(P-16680)
GUARDSMARK LLC
350 Sansome St, San Francisco (94104-1304)
PHONE.....................415 956-6070
Coley Buellesfeld, *Vice Pres*
EMP: 300
SALES (corp-wide): 950.8MM **Privately Held**
WEB: www.guardsmark.com
SIC: 7381 Security guard service
HQ: Guardsmark, Llc
1551 N Tustin Ave Ste 650
Santa Ana CA 92705
714 619-9700

(P-16681)
GUARDSMARK LLC
1600 Dove St Ste 201, Newport Beach (92660-2469)
PHONE.....................949 757-4693
William Armstrong, *Manager*
Jim Crum, *Manager*
Bob Pietrusiak, *Manager*
EMP: 250
SALES (corp-wide): 950.8MM **Privately Held**
WEB: www.guardsmark.com
SIC: 7381 Security guard service
HQ: Guardsmark, Llc
1551 N Tustin Ave Ste 650
Santa Ana CA 92705
714 619-9700

(P-16682)
GUARDSMARK LLC
4970 Ocamino Ste 110, Los Altos (94022)
PHONE.....................408 241-1493
Rania Terry, *Mng Member*
EMP: 400
SQ FT: 1,949
SALES (corp-wide): 950.8MM **Privately Held**
WEB: www.guardsmark.com
SIC: 7381 Security guard service

HQ: Guardsmark, Llc
1551 N Tustin Ave Ste 650
Santa Ana CA 92705
714 619-9700

(P-16683)
GUARDSMARK LLC
1816 Tribute Rd Ste 150, Sacramento (95815-4317)
PHONE.....................209 575-4972
Ron Resurreccion, *Branch Mgr*
EMP: 112
SALES (corp-wide): 950.8MM **Privately Held**
HQ: Universal Protection Service, Lp
1551 N Tustin Ave Ste 650
Santa Ana CA 92705
714 619-9700

(P-16684)
GUARDSMARK LLC
505 Alexis Ct, NAPA (94558-7526)
PHONE.....................415 898-9022
Roy Sheets, *Branch Mgr*
EMP: 112
SALES (corp-wide): 950.8MM **Privately Held**
SIC: 7381 Security guard service
HQ: Universal Protection Service, Lp
1551 N Tustin Ave Ste 650
Santa Ana CA 92705
714 619-9700

(P-16685)
GUARDSMARK LLC
100 Hegenberger Rd # 130, Oakland (94621-1447)
PHONE.....................510 562-7606
Fax: 510 562-1463
Ben Atkins, *Manager*
Maria Villanueva, *Human Res Mgr*
EMP: 250
SALES (corp-wide): 950.8MM **Privately Held**
WEB: www.guardsmark.com
SIC: 7381 Security guard service; private investigator
HQ: Guardsmark, Llc
1551 N Tustin Ave Ste 650
Santa Ana CA 92705
714 619-9700

(P-16686)
GUARDSMARK LLC
101 S 1st St Ste 408, Burbank (91502-1938)
PHONE.....................818 841-0288
Fax: 213 480-4881
Bob Carpenter, *Manager*
Gustave Lipman, *Exec VP*
Jonathan Escalante, *Branch Mgr*
EMP: 118
SALES (corp-wide): 950.8MM **Privately Held**
WEB: www.guardsmark.com
SIC: 7381 7382 Security guard service; security systems services
HQ: Guardsmark, Llc
1551 N Tustin Ave Ste 650
Santa Ana CA 92705
714 619-9700

(P-16687)
GUARDSMARK LLC
4970 El Camino Real, Los Altos (94022-1460)
PHONE.....................800 238-5878
Fax: 650 864-9130
Rania Terry, *Manager*
EMP: 118
SALES (corp-wide): 950.8MM **Privately Held**
SIC: 7381 Security guard service
HQ: Universal Protection Service, Lp
1551 N Tustin Ave Ste 650
Santa Ana CA 92705
714 619-9700

(P-16688)
GUARDSMARK LLC
5095 Murphy Canyon Rd # 301, San Diego (92123-4346)
PHONE.....................858 499-0025
Ira Lipman, *Branch Mgr*
EMP: 111

SALES (corp-wide): 950.8MM **Privately Held**
WEB: www.guardsmark.com
SIC: 7381 Guard services
HQ: Guardsmark, Llc
1551 N Tustin Ave Ste 650
Santa Ana CA 92705
714 619-9700

(P-16689)
GUARDSMARK LLC
600 W Shaw Ave Ste 200, Fresno (93704-2420)
PHONE.....................559 243-1217
Ricardo Franco, *Branch Mgr*
EMP: 111
SALES (corp-wide): 950.8MM **Privately Held**
WEB: www.guardsmark.com
SIC: 7381 Guard services
HQ: Guardsmark, Llc
1551 N Tustin Ave Ste 650
Santa Ana CA 92705
714 619-9700

(P-16690)
GUARDSMARK LLC
101 S 1st St Ste 408, Burbank (91502-1938)
PHONE.....................818 841-0288
Scott Carpenter, *Manager*
Michael Montgomery, *Sales Executive*
EMP: 111
SALES (corp-wide): 950.8MM **Privately Held**
WEB: www.guardsmark.com
SIC: 7381 Guard services
HQ: Guardsmark, Llc
1551 N Tustin Ave Ste 650
Santa Ana CA 92705
714 619-9700

(P-16691)
GUARDSMARK LLC
505 Alexis Ct, NAPA (94558-7526)
PHONE.....................415 898-9020
Roy Sheets, *Manager*
EMP: 111
SALES (corp-wide): 950.8MM **Privately Held**
WEB: www.guardsmark.com
SIC: 7381 Guard services
HQ: Guardsmark, Llc
1551 N Tustin Ave Ste 650
Santa Ana CA 92705
714 619-9700

(P-16692)
GUARDSMARK LLC
30 E San Joaquin St # 204, Salinas (93901-2947)
PHONE.....................831 769-8981
Ira Litman,
EMP: 111
SALES (corp-wide): 950.8MM **Privately Held**
WEB: www.guardsmark.com
SIC: 7381 Guard services
HQ: Guardsmark, Llc
1551 N Tustin Ave Ste 650
Santa Ana CA 92705
714 619-9700

(P-16693)
GUARDSMARK LLC
77725 Enfield Ln Ste 170, Palm Desert (92211-6227)
PHONE.....................760 328-8320
Steve Glantz, *Manager*
Margaret McCoy, *Human Resources*
Lee Weigel, *Manager*
EMP: 111
SALES (corp-wide): 950.8MM **Privately Held**
WEB: www.guardsmark.com
SIC: 7381 Guard services
HQ: Guardsmark, Llc
1551 N Tustin Ave Ste 650
Santa Ana CA 92705
714 619-9700

(P-16694)
GUARDSMARK LLC
533 Airport Blvd Ste 303, Burlingame (94010-2040)
PHONE.....................650 685-2400

Fax: 650 685-2401
David Connor, *Manager*
EMP: 111
SALES (corp-wide): 950.8MM **Privately Held**
WEB: www.guardsmark.com
SIC: 7381 Guard services
HQ: Guardsmark, Llc
1551 N Tustin Ave Ste 650
Santa Ana CA 92705
714 619-9700

(P-16695)
GUARDSMARK LLC
5300 Lennox Ave Ste 102, Bakersfield (93309-1662)
PHONE.....................661 325-5906
EMP: 111
SALES (corp-wide): 928.7MM **Privately Held**
SIC: 7381
HQ: Guardsmark, Llc
6363 Poplar Ave Ste 300
Memphis TN 92705
901 761-2288

(P-16696)
GUARDSMARK LLC
1225 W 190th St Ste 280, Gardena (90248-4305)
PHONE.....................310 225-3977
Rebecca Wells, *Manager*
EMP: 111
SALES (corp-wide): 950.8MM **Privately Held**
WEB: www.guardsmark.com
SIC: 7381 Security guard service; private investigator
HQ: Guardsmark, Llc
1551 N Tustin Ave Ste 650
Santa Ana CA 92705
714 619-9700

(P-16697)
GUARDSMARK LLC
1601 Bayshore Hwy Ste 350, Burlingame (94010-1522)
PHONE.....................650 652-9130
EMP: 145
SALES (corp-wide): 928.7MM **Privately Held**
SIC: 7381
HQ: Guardsmark, Llc
6363 Poplar Ave Ste 300
Memphis TN 92705
901 761-2288

(P-16698)
GUARDSMARK LLC
101 S 1st St Ste 408, Burbank (91502-1938)
PHONE.....................818 841-0288
Seth Rapaport, *Manager*
EMP: 175
SALES (corp-wide): 950.8MM **Privately Held**
WEB: www.guardsmark.com
SIC: 7381 Security guard service
HQ: Guardsmark, Llc
1551 N Tustin Ave Ste 650
Santa Ana CA 92705
714 619-9700

(P-16699)
GUARDSMARK LLC
2900 Adams St Ste C10a, Riverside (92504-8315)
PHONE.....................909 989-5345
Gary Parks, *Manager*
Marissa Straabe, *Human Res Dir*
Karen Rashid, *Sales Staff*
Glenda Eades, *Manager*
Lisa Micucci, *Manager*
EMP: 295
SALES (corp-wide): 950.8MM **Privately Held**
WEB: www.guardsmark.com
SIC: 7381 7382 Security guard service; security systems services
HQ: Guardsmark, Llc
1551 N Tustin Ave Ste 650
Santa Ana CA 92705
714 619-9700

PRODUCTS & SERVICES SECTION

7381 - Detective & Armored Car Svcs County (P-16726)

(P-16700)
HAL-MAR-JAC ENTERPRISES
Also Called: McCoy's Patrol Service
6271 3rd St, San Francisco (94124-3133)
PHONE.................................415 467-1470
Fax: 415 467-2837
Harold McCoy, *President*
Opal McCoy, *Admin Sec*
EMP: 110
SALES (est): 3.9MM Privately Held
SIC: 7381 Security guard service

(P-16701)
HARVEST V CITIZENS PATROL
25098 Avenida Valencia, Homeland (92548-9318)
P.O. Box 2255 (92548-2255)
PHONE.................................951 926-9763
Robert Gibbons, *Chairman*
Laura Daniels, *Treasurer*
Winn Barker, *Vice Pres*
John Lauda, *Principal*
Roy Yost, *Principal*
EMP: 127
SALES (est): 3.3MM Privately Held
SIC: 7381 Protective services, guard

(P-16702)
HIGHCOM SECURITY SERVICES
1900 Webster St Ste B, Oakland (94612-2946)
PHONE.................................510 893-7600
Sammy Joselewitz, *President*
Jen Wallace, *Info Tech Mgr*
Greg Unger, *Sales Dir*
John Mean, *Sales Mgr*
Logan Presnell, *Manager*
EMP: 60
SALES (est): 1.9MM Privately Held
WEB: www.highcomsecurityservices.com
SIC: 7381 8742 Security guard service; management consulting services

(P-16703)
HMI ASSOCIATES INC
6800 Owensmouth Ave # 330, Canoga Park (91303-3159)
PHONE.................................818 887-6800
Andrew Heider, *President*
Michael Moen, *Vice Pres*
EMP: 200
SALES (est): 1.8MM Privately Held
SIC: 7381 Security guard service; detective agency

(P-16704)
HORSEMEN INC
16911 Algonquin St, Huntington Beach (92649-3812)
PHONE.................................714 847-4243
Patrick Carroll, *President*
Rich Ramirez, *Human Res Mgr*
Andy Crimmins, *Opers Staff*
Cheryl Gall, *Consultant*
EMP: 100
SALES (est): 4.3MM Privately Held
WEB: www.horsemeninc.com
SIC: 7381 Private investigator

(P-16705)
HYLTON SECURITY INC
1015 2nd St Fl 2, Sacramento (95814-3255)
PHONE.................................916 442-1000
Fax: 916 442-2790
David J Hylton, *President*
Mindy A Hylton, *Senior VP*
EMP: 107
SQ FT: 1,500
SALES (est): 250K Privately Held
WEB: www.hyltonsecurity.com
SIC: 7381 Guard services; security guard service

(P-16706)
INTELLIGUARD SECURITY SERVICES
Also Called: Safety Dynamics
4663 Harbord Dr, Oakland (94618-2210)
PHONE.................................510 547-7656
John Weir, *President*
EMP: 130
SALES (est): 5MM Privately Held
SIC: 7381 Detective & armored car services

(P-16707)
INTER-CON INVESTIGATORS INC
Also Called: Inter Con Systems
210 S De Lacey Ave, Pasadena (91105-2048)
PHONE.................................626 535-2200
Enrique Hernandez Jr, *President*
Roland Hernandez, *Vice Pres*
EMP: 100
SQ FT: 17,000
SALES (est): 2.5MM Privately Held
SIC: 7381 Security guard service

(P-16708)
INTER-CON SECURITY SYSTEMS INC (PA)
210 S De Lacey Ave # 200, Pasadena (91105-2048)
PHONE.................................626 535-2200
Fax: 626 535-9111
Enrique Hernandez, *Ch of Bd*
Neil Martau, *President*
Lance Mueller, *COO*
Paul Miller, *CFO*
Robin Simpson, *CFO*
EMP: 120
SQ FT: 17,000
SALES (est): 562.5MM Privately Held
SIC: 7381 Guard services; protective services, guard; security guard service

(P-16709)
INTERNATIONAL SEC SVCS INC
3350 Scott Blvd Bldg 36a, Santa Clara (95054-3100)
PHONE.................................925 634-1935
Michael Luddy, *President*
Michael E Luddy, *President*
EMP: 80
SQ FT: 950
SALES (est): 1.1MM Privately Held
WEB: www.intlsec.com
SIC: 7381 Security guard service; private investigator

(P-16710)
INTERSTATE PROTECTIVE SERVICES
Also Called: Ips
16200 Ventura Blvd # 210, Encino (91436-4644)
PHONE.................................818 995-6664
Nabila Helal, *CEO*
Michael Ahmed, *President*
Wil Hanna, *Principal*
Nancy Saenz, *Principal*
EMP: 99
SALES (est): 4.8MM Privately Held
SIC: 7381 Security guard service

(P-16711)
IPS INC
14413 Glenoak Pl, Fontana (92337-2892)
PHONE.................................909 428-2647
Rodney Cavanaugh, *President*
EMP: 50
SALES (est): 444.6K Privately Held
SIC: 7381 Security guard service

(P-16712)
IRONCLAD SECURITY SERVICES INC
3561 Homestead Rd Ste 600, Santa Clara (95051-5161)
PHONE.................................408 773-2800
Bruce McAllister, *President*
EMP: 75
SQ FT: 4,000
SALES (est): 1MM Privately Held
SIC: 7381 7389 Protective services, guard; security guard service; personal investigation service

(P-16713)
IUNLIMITED INCORPORATED
7801 Folsom Blvd Ste 203, Sacramento (95826-2620)
PHONE.................................916 218-6198
Todd M Tano, *CEO*
Keith Jacobs, *President*
Jeff Walters, *Officer*
EMP: 115
SALES: 8MM Privately Held
SIC: 7381 Private investigator

(P-16714)
J WATERS INC
Also Called: Achates Security Agency
75 San Miguel Ave Ste 5, Salinas (93901-3059)
P.O. Box 418 (93902-0418)
PHONE.................................831 424-1946
Fax: 831 424-1805
Mary Waters, *President*
Jeffrey S Waters, *Vice Pres*
EMP: 50
SALES (est): 1.2MM Privately Held
WEB: www.achatessecurity.com
SIC: 7381 Security guard service

(P-16715)
K TECH SECURITY & PROTECT SVC
665 Alvin St, San Diego (92114-1817)
PHONE.................................619 858-5832
Kelly J Steppe, *Owner*
Keiko A Arroyo, *Director*
EMP: 127
SALES (est): 2.9MM Privately Held
WEB: www.k-techsecurity.com
SIC: 7381 Security guard service

(P-16716)
KAISER MED SECURITY SERVICES
2241 Geary Blvd, San Francisco (94115-3415)
PHONE.................................415 833-3683
Dennis Hyams, *Director*
EMP: 100
SALES (est): 1.3MM Privately Held
SIC: 7381 Security guard service

(P-16717)
KING SECURITY SERVICES INC
1159 7th St, Novato (94945-2207)
PHONE.................................415 556-5464
Kimberly King, *President*
Jolanta King, *CFO*
Louis Siracusa, *Vice Pres*
James Mahoney, *Office Admin*
Ruth Plumley, *Administration*
EMP: 528
SQ FT: 2,000
SALES (est): 13.1MM Privately Held
WEB: www.kingsecurity.com
SIC: 7381 Security guard service; private investigator

(P-16718)
LAKE TAHOE SECRET WITNESS
1051 Al Tahoe Blvd, South Lake Tahoe (96150-4502)
P.O. Box 14282 (96151-4282)
PHONE.................................530 541-6800
Pam Sullivan, *Owner*
EMP: 90 EST: 1997
SALES (est): 979.7K Privately Held
SIC: 7381 Detective services

(P-16719)
LANDMARK EVENT STAFFING
4790 Irvine Blvd Ste 105, Irvine (92620-1998)
PHONE.................................714 293-4248
Peter Kranske, *President*
Paul E Meyer, *Manager*
EMP: 1008
SALES (corp-wide): 14.1MM Privately Held
SIC: 7381 Security guard service
PA: Landmark Event Staffing Services, Inc.
4131 Harbor Walk Dr
Fort Collins CO 80525
714 293-4248

(P-16720)
LANTZ SECURITY SYSTEMS INC
101 N Westlake Blvd # 200, Westlake Village (91362-3753)
PHONE.................................805 496-5775
Terry Oestreich, *Manager*
EMP: 300
SALES (corp-wide): 11.7MM Privately Held
WEB: www.lantzsecurity.com
SIC: 7381 7382 Security guard service; security systems services
PA: Lantz Security Systems Inc
43440 Sahuayo St
Lancaster CA 93535
661 949-3565

(P-16721)
LANTZ SECURITY SYSTEMS INC (PA)
43440 Sahuayo St, Lancaster (93535-4659)
PHONE.................................661 949-3565
Fax: 661 940-1943
Jack E Lantz, *President*
Jose Reyes, *Vice Pres*
EMP: 60
SQ FT: 2,100
SALES (est): 11.7MM Privately Held
WEB: www.lantzsecurity.com
SIC: 7381 Security guard service

(P-16722)
LEGIONS PROTECTIVE SVCS LLC
17201 S Figueroa St, Gardena (90248-3022)
PHONE.................................310 819-8881
Gregorio Campos, *CEO*
Armando Ojeda Jr, *Vice Pres*
EMP: 50
SQ FT: 1,000
SALES (est): 250.6K Privately Held
SIC: 7381 Security guard service

(P-16723)
LEVEL 9 SECURITY SERVICES
9020 Slauson Ave Ste 206, Pico Rivera (90660-4578)
PHONE.................................562 949-7180
Jose Tellez, *Owner*
EMP: 50
SALES (est): 908.7K Privately Held
SIC: 7381 Security guard service

(P-16724)
LOCATOR SERVICES INC
Also Called: Able Patrol & Guard
4616 Mission Gorge Pl, San Diego (92120-4133)
PHONE.................................619 229-6100
Fax: 619 229-6106
George Grauer, *President*
Diane G Edwards, *Vice Pres*
George Grauer Jr, *Vice Pres*
Deborah L Kopki, *Vice Pres*
Christine Lowe, *Admin Asst*
EMP: 120
SQ FT: 4,500
SALES: 1.9MM Privately Held
WEB: www.ablepatrolandguard.com
SIC: 7381 Security guard service

(P-16725)
LOOMIS ARMORED US INC
897 Wrigley Way, Milpitas (95035-5407)
PHONE.................................408 273-1101
Fax: 408 941-9680
Ted Crane, *General Mgr*
Joe Bagonif, *Branch Mgr*
EMP: 90
SALES (corp-wide): 1.8B Privately Held
WEB: www.loomisfargo.com
SIC: 7381 Armored car services
HQ: Loomis Armored Us, Llc
2500 Citywest Blvd # 900
Houston TX 77042
713 435-6700

(P-16726)
LOOMIS ARMORED US LLC
3200 Regatta Blvd Ste B, Richmond (94804-6415)
PHONE.................................510 233-1055
Fax: 510 225-0544
Karen Coady, *Manager*
Karen Cody, *Branch Mgr*
EMP: 100
SALES (corp-wide): 1.8B Privately Held
WEB: www.loomisfargo.com
SIC: 7381 Detective & armored car services
HQ: Loomis Armored Us, Llc
2500 Citywest Blvd # 900
Houston TX 77042
713 435-6700

7381 - Detective & Armored Car Svcs County (P-16727)

(P-16727)
LOOMIS ARMORED US LLC
3555 Aero Ct, San Diego (92123-1710)
PHONE.................................619 232-5106
Fax: 619 232-2105
Tim Bong, *Manager*
Frances Gipson, *Manager*
James Moore, *Manager*
EMP: 70
SALES (corp-wide): 1.8B **Privately Held**
WEB: www.loomisfargo.com
SIC: 7381 Armored car services
HQ: Loomis Armored Us, Llc
   2500 Citywest Blvd # 900
   Houston TX 77042
   713 435-6700

(P-16728)
LOOMIS ARMORED US LLC
315 12th St, Sacramento (95814-0900)
PHONE.................................916 441-1091
Fax: 916 441-3526
Daryl Balko, *General Mgr*
EMP: 70
SALES (corp-wide): 1.8B **Privately Held**
WEB: www.loomisfargo.com
SIC: 7381 Armored car services
HQ: Loomis Armored Us, Llc
   2500 Citywest Blvd # 900
   Houston TX 77042
   713 435-6700

(P-16729)
M & S SECURITY SERVICES INC
Also Called: Westside Security Patrol
2900 L St, Bakersfield (93301-2351)
PHONE.................................661 397-9616
Fax: 661 397-8162
Marvin Fuller Jr, *President*
Steve Fuller, *President*
Darlene Fuller, *Corp Secy*
Jimmy Watters, *Executive*
EMP: 100
SQ FT: 3,000
SALES (est): 3.4MM **Privately Held**
WEB: www.mssecurityservices.com
SIC: 7381 7382 1731 Protective services, guard; security systems services; burglar alarm maintenance & monitoring; fire detection & burglar alarm systems specialization

(P-16730)
MADERA PRIVATE SECURITY PATROL
910 W Yosemite Ave, Madera (93637-4555)
PHONE.................................559 662-1546
Fax: 559 673-4323
Timothy Supple, *Partner*
Michael Gonzalez, *Partner*
Rebecca Supple, *Partner*
EMP: 78
SALES (est): 1.6MM **Privately Held**
WEB: www.maderaprivatesecurity.com
SIC: 7381 Protective services, guard

(P-16731)
MAGNUS SECURITY
2667 Camino Del Rio S, San Diego (92108-3707)
PHONE.................................619 546-7789
Marques Oliver, *Principal*
Marcus Oliver, *Owner*
EMP: 50 EST: 2013
SALES (est): 117.3K **Privately Held**
SIC: 7381 Guard services

(P-16732)
MASTER LIGHTNING SEC SOLUTIONS
1509 W Cameron Ave # 230, West Covina (91790-2725)
PHONE.................................310 419-2915
Peter Suaez, *Principal*
EMP: 70
SALES (est): 1.2MM **Privately Held**
SIC: 7381 Guard services

(P-16733)
MAZAR CORP
Also Called: Gladiator Security Services
3200 E Guasti Rd Ste 100, Ontario (91761-8661)
PHONE.................................909 292-8269

Mukhtar Ahmad Peerzay, *President*
Hares Kabir, *CFO*
Lamonte Sanders, *Vice Pres*
EMP: 62
SALES (est): 1.8MM **Privately Held**
SIC: 7381 Armored car services; security guard service

(P-16734)
MEMON AAMIR
Also Called: American Hritg Protection Svcs
20832 Roscoe Blvd Ste 207, Winnetka (91306-2058)
PHONE.................................818 339-8810
Aamir Memon, *Owner*
EMP: 50 EST: 2011
SQ FT: 500
SALES (est): 751.7K **Privately Held**
SIC: 7381 Security guard service

(P-16735)
METROPOLITAN DST PRIVATE SEC
44262 Division St Ste A, Lancaster (93535-3548)
PHONE.................................661 942-3999
Frederick Porras, *President*
EMP: 93
SQ FT: 1,200
SALES: 696.5K **Privately Held**
SIC: 7381 Security guard service

(P-16736)
MICHAEL MCCARTHY
Also Called: Loyal Svc Unt Spec Team
211 S Shiplan Ave, La Puente (91744)
PHONE.................................310 800-5367
Michael McCarthy, *Owner*
EMP: 50
SQ FT: 1,500
SALES: 200K **Privately Held**
SIC: 7381 4119 7361 Security guard service; local passenger transportation; employment agencies

(P-16737)
MISSION SECURITY AND PATROL
27 W Anapamu St Ste 141, Santa Barbara (93101-3107)
PHONE.................................805 899-3039
Fax: 805 899-3055
Marcus Abundis, *President*
Brian Fairrington, *Director*
EMP: 100
SALES (est): 2.1MM **Privately Held**
SIC: 7381 Security guard service

(P-16738)
MONUMENT SECURITY INC
7700 Edgewater Dr Ste 630, Oakland (94621-3022)
PHONE.................................510 430-3540
Fax: 510 430-3546
Uatisone Nasaniai, *Manager*
EMP: 150 **Privately Held**
SIC: 7381 Detective & armored car services
PA: Monument Security, Inc
   4926 43rd St Ste 10
   Mcclellan CA 95652

(P-16739)
MONUMENT SECURITY INC
12016 Telg Rd Ste 201, Santa Fe Springs (90670)
PHONE.................................562 944-2666
Scott McDonald, *Principal*
EMP: 300 **Privately Held**
SIC: 7381 Guard services
PA: Monument Security, Inc
   4926 43rd St Ste 10
   Mcclellan CA 95652

(P-16740)
MONUMENT SECURITY INC (PA)
4926 43rd St Ste 10, McClellan (95652-2618)
PHONE.................................916 564-4234
Fax: 702 410-6373
Scott Mc Donald, *President*
Lory Reyes, *Controller*
Katie McDonald, *Director*
EMP: 150

SQ FT: 2,500
SALES (est): 27.8MM **Privately Held**
SIC: 7381 Security guard service

(P-16741)
MULHOLLAND SEC & PATROL INC
Also Called: Centurion Group, The
11454 San Vicente Blvd Fi, Los Angeles (90049-6208)
PHONE.................................818 755-0202
Fax: 818 755-0728
David Rosenberg, *President*
Daniel Campbell, *Vice Pres*
Steven Lemmer, *Vice Pres*
EMP: 350
SQ FT: 2,500
SALES (est): 8.4MM **Privately Held**
WEB: www.mulhollandsecurity.com
SIC: 7381 Protective services, guard

(P-16742)
NATIONAL PUBLIC SAFETY
490 N Magnolia Ave, El Cajon (92020-3607)
P.O. Box 1136, Lemon Grove (91946-1136)
PHONE.................................619 401-9431
Natasha Frost, *CEO*
Douglas Frost, *President*
EMP: 56
SALES (est): 1.9MM **Privately Held**
SIC: 7381 Security guard service

(P-16743)
NATIONAL SECURITY TECH LLC
5520 Ekwill St Ste B, Santa Barbara (93111-2335)
PHONE.................................805 681-2488
Stephen M Younger, *Branch Mgr*
James Capelle, *Engineer*
EMP: 1329
SALES (corp-wide): 584.5MM **Privately Held**
SIC: 7381 Guard services
PA: National Security Technologies, Llc
   2621 Losee Rd
   North Las Vegas NV 89030
   702 295-1000

(P-16744)
NATIONWIDE GUARD SERVICES INC
299 W Fthill Blvd Ste 124, Upland (91786)
PHONE.................................909 608-1112
John Woolen, *President*
EMP: 56
SALES (est): 1.3MM **Privately Held**
WEB: www.nationwideguardservices.com
SIC: 7381 Security guard service

(P-16745)
NEW-JACK INDUSTRIES INC
2613 Manhattan Beach Blvd # 100, Redondo Beach (90278-1604)
PHONE.................................310 297-3605
W Tom Bragg, *President*
Ramon Rodriguez, *Vice Pres*
Lammar Lee, *Director*
Diana Marez, *Manager*
EMP: 400
SQ FT: 5,000
SALES (est): 4.5MM **Privately Held**
SIC: 7381 Security guard service

(P-16746)
NORTH AMERICAN SECURITY INC
550 E Carson St P, Carson (90745-2714)
PHONE.................................310 630-4840
Fax: 323 634-9111
Arthur L Lopez, *President*
Kenneth Hillman, *Vice Pres*
Atzi Camarena, *Office Mgr*
Gillian Watanabe, *Accounting Mgr*
Kim Jackson, *Analyst*
EMP: 420
SQ FT: 1,000
SALES (est): 12.8MM **Privately Held**
SIC: 7381 Security guard service

(P-16747)
NORTH AMRCN SEC INVSTGTONS INC
550 E Carson Plaza Dr, Carson (90746-3229)
PHONE.................................323 634-1911
Arthur Lopez, *CEO*
EMP: 500
SQ FT: 6,000
SALES (est): 5.2MM **Privately Held**
SIC: 7381 Private investigator

(P-16748)
NORTH STATE SECURITY INC
1242 Oregon St, Redding (96001-0451)
P.O. Box 991348 (96099-1348)
PHONE.................................530 243-0295
Fax: 530 243-3870
Lance Boek, *President*
EMP: 100
SQ FT: 1,500
SALES: 1.4MM **Privately Held**
SIC: 7381 Security guard service

(P-16749)
NORTHEAST PROTECTIVE SVCS INC
Also Called: Neps Worldwide
16040 Peppertree Ln, La Mirada (90638-3460)
PHONE.................................800 577-0899
Alan Burton, *President*
Frank Widder, *CFO*
EMP: 65
SALES: 1.5MM **Privately Held**
WEB: www.northeastprotectiveservices.com
SIC: 7381 Protective services, guard; security guard service

(P-16750)
OC SPECIAL EVENTS SEC INC
Also Called: Firearms Academy
1232 Village Way Ste K, Santa Ana (92705-4746)
PHONE.................................714 541-4111
Richard Allum, *President*
David S Andersen, *Shareholder*
EMP: 102
SALES (est): 1.4MM **Privately Held**
SIC: 7381 Guard services

(P-16751)
ODONA CENTRAL SECURITY INC
71 N San Gabriel Blvd, Pasadena (91107-3749)
PHONE.................................323 728-8818
Fax: 323 890-0088
Fred Chen, *President*
EMP: 150
SQ FT: 2,000
SALES (est): 3.1MM **Privately Held**
WEB: www.odona.com
SIC: 7381 Security guard service

(P-16752)
OMEGA SECURITY SERVICES & CONS
10611 Garden Grove Ave # 2, Northridge (91326-3211)
PHONE.................................818 831-1100
Fax: 818 831-1101
Motti Ben-Haim, *President*
Motti S Benhaim, *Office Mgr*
EMP: 70
SALES (est): 1.7MM **Privately Held**
WEB: www.omegasec.net
SIC: 7381 Guard services; security guard service

(P-16753)
ON-SCENE SECURITY SERVICES INC
P.O. Box 800147, Santa Clarita (91380-0147)
PHONE.................................661 263-2343
Fax: 661 263-0636
Larry Wilson, *President*
Deborah Wilson, *Vice Pres*
EMP: 50
SALES (est): 747.7K **Privately Held**
SIC: 7381 Security guard service

PRODUCTS & SERVICES SECTION

7381 - Detective & Armored Car Svcs County (P-16779)

(P-16754)
OPSEC SPECIALIZED PROTECTION
44262 Division St Ste A, Lancaster (93535-3548)
PHONE.................................661 942-3999
Fax: 661 942-6331
Anthony Cheval, *Exec Dir*
EMP: 99
SALES: 950K Privately Held
WEB: www.opsecspecializedprotection.com
SIC: 7381 Detective & armored car services

(P-16755)
PACIFIC PROTECTION SERVICES
22144 Clarendon St # 110, Woodland Hills (91367-8201)
PHONE.................................818 313-9369
Melvin Staples, *Branch Mgr*
EMP: 194
SALES (corp-wide): 9MM Privately Held
SIC: 7381 Detective & armored car services
PA: Pacific Protection Services Inc
   22144 Clarendon St # 110
   Woodland Hills CA 91367
   818 313-9369

(P-16756)
PATROL MASTERS INC
1651 E 4th St Ste 150, Santa Ana (92701-5173)
PHONE.................................714 426-2526
Samir Ahmad, *President*
EMP: 150
SALES (est): 5.1MM Privately Held
SIC: 7381 Security guard service

(P-16757)
PEACE KEEPERS PRIVATE SECURITY
2734b Delta Fair Blvd, Antioch (94509-4100)
PHONE.................................925 978-4140
Stuart M Welch, *President*
Stuart Welch, *President*
Janet Brown, *Administration*
EMP: 60 EST: 1993
SALES: 800K Privately Held
SIC: 7381 Security guard service

(P-16758)
PLATINUM PROTECTION GROUP INC
8018 E Santa Ana Cyn Rd, Anaheim (92808-1102)
PHONE.................................800 824-1097
Mark V Holt, *President*
Ronan Collins, *Officer*
Mike Bogosian, *Manager*
EMP: 90
SALES: 500K Privately Held
WEB: www.platinumprotectiongroup.com
SIC: 7381 Detective & armored car services; protective services, guard

(P-16759)
PLATT SECURITY SYSTEMS INC
Also Called: Platt Security Services
3275 E Grant St Ste D, Long Beach (90755-1293)
PHONE.................................562 986-4484
Fax: 562 986-4487
Robert E Platt, *President*
Tamara Platt, *Treasurer*
Mark Platt, *Vice Pres*
Anna Platt, *Human Resources*
EMP: 150
SQ FT: 2,200
SALES (est): 4MM Privately Held
WEB: www.plattsecurity.com
SIC: 7381 7382 Detective & armored car services; security systems services

(P-16760)
PRE-EMPLOYCOM
3655 Meadow View Dr, Redding (96002-9715)
P.O. Box 491570 (96049-1570)
PHONE.................................800 300-1821
Robert Mather, *CEO*
Micheal Hough, *Director*
EMP: 100
SALES: 10MM Privately Held
SIC: 7381 Private investigator

(P-16761)
PRE-EMPLOYCOM INC
2301 Balls Ferry Rd, Anderson (96007-3502)
P.O. Box 491570, Redding (96049-1570)
PHONE.................................530 378-7680
Robert V Mather, *President*
Nancy Van Voris, *Executive*
Kerri Sorber, *Project Mgr*
Jason Dunn, *Controller*
Michael Hough, *Controller*
EMP: 75
SQ FT: 10,500
SALES (est): 3.7MM Privately Held
WEB: www.pre-employ.com
SIC: 7381 Detective services

(P-16762)
PRESTIGE SECURITY SERVICE INC
5855 Green Valley Cir # 207, Culver City (90230-6968)
PHONE.................................310 670-5999
George Bernaba, *Owner*
EMP: 400
SALES (est): 6.9MM Privately Held
SIC: 7381 Security guard service

(P-16763)
PRIME INTERNATIONAL SECURITY
Also Called: Prime Security
1630 Centinela Ave # 209, Inglewood (90302-6948)
P.O. Box 18348, Los Angeles (90018-0348)
PHONE.................................310 670-4565
Akubuo Okorie, *President*
Boniesace Nworgu, *Vice Pres*
EMP: 60
SALES (est): 1.5MM Privately Held
SIC: 7381 Security guard service

(P-16764)
PROBE INFORMATION SERVICES INC
6375 Auburn Blvd, Citrus Heights (95621-5270)
P.O. Box 418429, Sacramento (95841-8429)
PHONE.................................916 676-1826
Ross O Stewart, *President*
Renea Abdin, *Vice Pres*
Dalene Bartholomew, *Vice Pres*
Emily Wingo, *HR Admin*
Van Haas, *VP Opers*
EMP: 101
SQ FT: 6,000
SALES: 7.3MM Privately Held
WEB: www.probeinfo.com
SIC: 7381 Private investigator

(P-16765)
PROFESSIONAL SECURITY CONS (PA)
11454 San Vicente Blvd # 2, Los Angeles (90049-6208)
PHONE.................................310 207-7729
Fax: 310 207-6621
Moshe Alon, *President*
Ilene Alon, *Vice Pres*
Michael Lambos, *Vice Pres*
Sam Adlerstein, *Business Dir*
Grant Erickson, *Exec Dir*
EMP: 148
SALES (est): 76.6MM Privately Held
SIC: 7381 7382 8742 Security guard service; security systems services; management consulting services

(P-16766)
PROFESSIONAL TECHNICAL SEC SVCS
Also Called: Protech
625 Market St Fl 9, San Francisco (94105-3311)
PHONE.................................415 243-2100
Fax: 415 243-4467
Sergio Reyes, *President*
Mike Harrison, *President*
Debra Reyes, *Vice Pres*
Thomas Petersen, *Admin Sec*
Jarmel Mayweather, *Facilities Mgr*
EMP: 400
SQ FT: 1,800
SALES (est): 7.3MM Privately Held
WEB: www.protech.name
SIC: 7381 Guard services

(P-16767)
PROTECTED OUTCOMES CORPORATION
9663 Santa Monica Blvd, Beverly Hills (90210-4303)
PHONE.................................203 545-9565
EMP: 87
SALES: 950K Privately Held
SIC: 7381

(P-16768)
PROTECTION SPECIALISTS
Also Called: Chad Garrett Investigations
6841 Whitsett Ave Apt 104, North Hollywood (91605-5456)
PHONE.................................818 503-1306
Chad Garrett, *Principal*
EMP: 500
SALES (est): 3.5MM Privately Held
SIC: 7381 Protective services, guard

(P-16769)
R STANLEY SECURITY SERVICE
403 18th St, Bakersfield (93301-4930)
PHONE.................................661 634-9283
Rachelle Stanley, *President*
Charles Thompson, *Vice Pres*
EMP: 65
SQ FT: 3,000
SALES: 1MM Privately Held
SIC: 7381 7389 Security guard service; convention & show services

(P-16770)
RANCHO SANTA FE PROTECTIVE SVC
Also Called: Rsf Protective Services
1991 Village Park Way # 100, Encinitas (92024-1994)
PHONE.................................760 433-8887
Ron Boever, *President*
Denise Mueller, *Shareholder*
Richard Crooks, *Opers Staff*
Lance Sutherland, *Opers Staff*
Navio Bains, *Marketing Staff*
EMP: 50
SQ FT: 4,000
SALES (est): 1.2MM Privately Held
SIC: 7381 Security guard service

(P-16771)
RAPID ARMADA SEC SVCS RASS LLC
6774 Kaiser Ave, Fontana (92336-1559)
PHONE.................................909 609-4370
Mayor Ndubisi Ezee, *Mng Member*
EMP: 135
SALES (est): 2.9MM Privately Held
SIC: 7381 Security guard service

(P-16772)
REV ENTERPRISES
Also Called: O & R
417 Arden Ave Ste 103, Glendale (91203-4046)
PHONE.................................818 551-7111
J Antonio Revilla, *Principal*
EMP: 50
SALES: 1.1MM Privately Held
SIC: 7381 Detective & armored car services

(P-16773)
RJN INVESTIGATIONS INC
360 E 1st St Ste 696, Tustin (92780-3211)
P.O. Box 55451, Riverside (92517-0451)
PHONE.................................951 686-7638
Fax: 951 275-5036
Robert Nagle, *President*
Fred Martino, *Administration*
Bob Nagle, *Financial Exec*
Mariam Lawrence, *Manager*
EMP: 70
SALES: 6MM Privately Held
SIC: 7381 Detective agency

(P-16774)
RMI INTERNATIONAL INC
Also Called: Rodbat Security Services
1919 Torrance Blvd, Torrance (90501-2722)
PHONE.................................310 781-6768
Elena Rabinovich, *Branch Mgr*
EMP: 65
SALES (corp-wide): 21.1MM Privately Held
WEB: www.rmiintl.com
SIC: 7381 Guard services; protective services, guard
PA: Rmi International Inc
   8125 Somerset Blvd
   Paramount CA 90723
   562 806-9098

(P-16775)
RORY V PARKER
Also Called: Bmt International SEC Svcs
818 27th St Ste 101, Oakland (94607-3424)
PHONE.................................510 595-5543
Rory Parker, *Owner*
Patrick Charles, *Principal*
EMP: 222 EST: 2009
SQ FT: 2,200
SALES (est): 5.4MM Privately Held
SIC: 7381 Guard services

(P-16776)
ROYAL INVESTIGATION PATROL INC
2950 Merced St Ste 108, San Leandro (94577-5636)
PHONE.................................510 352-6800
Fax: 510 352-1246
Edmund Young, *President*
EMP: 58
SQ FT: 2,000
SALES (est): 1.3MM Privately Held
SIC: 7381 Protective services, guard

(P-16777)
S C SECURITY INC
Also Called: Copper Eagle Patrol & Security
26752 Oak Ave Ste C, Santa Clarita (91351-6620)
PHONE.................................661 251-6999
Fax: 661 251-8661
Isaiah Tally, *President*
William Corbett, *President*
George Streb, *Exec VP*
Deborah Corbett, *Admin Sec*
Maura Corbett, *Sales Dir*
EMP: 50
SQ FT: 2,000
SALES (est): 1.7MM Privately Held
SIC: 7381 Guard services

(P-16778)
SAFETY SECURITY PATROL LLC
560 N Arrowhead Ave 3b, San Bernardino (92401-1219)
PHONE.................................909 888-7778
Carlos Conde, *CEO*
EMP: 63
SALES (est): 78.3K Privately Held
SIC: 7381 Guard services

(P-16779)
SECTRAN SECURITY INCORPORATED (PA)
Also Called: Sectran Armored Truck Service
7633 Industry Ave, Pico Rivera (90660-4301)
P.O. Box 7267, Los Angeles (90022-0967)
PHONE.................................562 948-1446
Fax: 562 949-4327
Fred Kunik, *President*
Rony Ghaby, *General Mgr*
Erryna Pinon, *General Mgr*
Irving Barr, *Admin Sec*
Leonard Karsana, *CIO*
EMP: 141
SQ FT: 19,736
SALES (est): 14.1MM Privately Held
SIC: 7381 Armored car services

7381 - Detective & Armored Car Svcs County (P-16780)

(P-16780)
SECURE NET PROTECTION
Also Called: Security Company
217 E Alameda Ave Ste 301, Burbank
(91502-2622)
PHONE.................818 848-4900
Fax: 818 848-4909
Levi Quintana, *CEO*
Jonathan Kraut, *Partner*
Katie Fogg, *Vice Pres*
Jonathon Kraut, *Manager*
EMP: 50
SALES (est): 828.9K **Privately Held**
SIC: **7381** Guard services; security guard service; protective services, guard

(P-16781)
SECURITAS CRITICAL INFRASTRUCT
3914 Murphy Canyon Rd A120, San Diego
(92123-4491)
PHONE.................858 560-0448
John Tucke, *Branch Mgr*
EMP: 868
SALES (corp-wide): 9.2B **Privately Held**
SIC: **7381** Detective & armored car services
HQ: Securitas Critical Infrastructure Services, Inc.
6850 Versar Ctr Ste 400
Springfield VA 22151

(P-16782)
SECURITAS CRITICAL INFRASTRUCT
19701 Hamilton Ave # 180, Torrance
(90502-1352)
PHONE.................310 817-2177
Elijah Kimble, *Manager*
EMP: 1002
SALES (corp-wide): 9.2B **Privately Held**
SIC: **7381** Security guard service
HQ: Securitas Critical Infrastructure Services, Inc.
6850 Versar Ctr Ste 400
Springfield VA 22151

(P-16783)
SECURITAS CRITICAL INFRASTRUCT
360 N Sepulveda Blvd, El Segundo
(90245-4460)
PHONE.................310 426-3300
Michael Kemppainen, *Branch Mgr*
EMP: 1750
SALES (corp-wide): 9.2B **Privately Held**
SIC: **7381** Detective & armored car services
HQ: Securitas Critical Infrastructure Services, Inc.
6850 Versar Ctr Ste 400
Springfield VA 22151

(P-16784)
SECURITAS CRITICAL INFRASTRUCT
Rm 117 Bldg 7525, Vandenberg Afb
(93437)
PHONE.................805 685-1100
Paul Jensen, *Branch Mgr*
EMP: 885
SALES (corp-wide): 9.2B **Privately Held**
SIC: **7381** Security guard service
HQ: Securitas Critical Infrastructure Services, Inc.
6850 Versar Ctr Ste 400
Springfield VA 22151

(P-16785)
SECURITAS SEC SVCS USA INC
5700 Ralston St Ste 105, Ventura
(93003-7889)
PHONE.................805 650-6285
Silvia Portillo, *Manager*
Michael Perenchio, *Branch Mgr*
Mike Turner, *Manager*
EMP: 116
SALES (corp-wide): 9.2B **Privately Held**
SIC: **7381** Guard services

(P-16786)
SECURITAS SEC SVCS USA INC
Also Called: Northern California Region
3115 W March Ln Ste A, Stockton
(95219-2393)
PHONE.................209 943-1401
Kelly Davis, *Manager*
Diane Harris, *Vice Pres*
Bob Wayco, *Branch Mgr*
Mike Poullos, *Controller*
Allison Bacchus, *Human Res Dir*
EMP: 120
SALES (corp-wide): 9.2B **Privately Held**
WEB: www.securitasinc.com
SIC: **7381** Protective services, guard
HQ: Securitas Security Services Usa, Inc.
9 Campus Dr
Parsippany NJ 07054
973 267-5300

(P-16787)
SECURITAS SEC SVCS USA INC
2045 Hurley Way, Sacramento
(95825-3220)
PHONE.................916 564-2009
Fax: 916 569-4553
Pete Niles, *President*
Joe Saputo, *President*
Kevin Lanius, *Vice Pres*
Manuel Andrade, *Manager*
Wallace Lavery, *Manager*
EMP: 181
SALES (corp-wide): 9.2B **Privately Held**
SIC: **7381** Guard services
HQ: Securitas Security Services Usa, Inc.
9 Campus Dr
Parsippany NJ 07054
973 267-5300

(P-16788)
SECURITAS SEC SVCS USA INC
Also Called: Northern California Region
155 E Shaw Ave Ste 315, Fresno
(93710-7619)
PHONE.................559 221-2302
Fax: 559 221-2318
Christopher Lewis, *Manager*
Harold Mosher, *Manager*
EMP: 116
SALES (corp-wide): 9.2B **Privately Held**
WEB: www.securitasinc.com
SIC: **7381** Security guard service
HQ: Securitas Security Services Usa, Inc.
9 Campus Dr
Parsippany NJ 07054
973 267-5300

(P-16789)
SECURITAS SEC SVCS USA INC
750 Terrado Plz Ste 107, Covina
(91723-3419)
PHONE.................571 321-0913
Michael Persaud, *Branch Mgr*
EMP: 185
SALES (corp-wide): 9.2B **Privately Held**
SIC: **7381** Security guard service
HQ: Securitas Security Services Usa, Inc.
9 Campus Dr
Parsippany NJ 07054
973 267-5300

(P-16790)
SECURITAS SEC SVCS USA INC
425 Bush St Ste 400, San Francisco
(94108-3724)
PHONE.................510 568-6818
Brad Lauer, *Assoc VP*
EMP: 188
SALES (corp-wide): 9.2B **Privately Held**
SIC: **7381** Security guard service
HQ: Securitas Security Services Usa, Inc.
9 Campus Dr
Parsippany NJ 07054
973 267-5300

(P-16791)
SECURITAS SEC SVCS USA INC
Also Called: Northern California Region
407 Lake Blvd, Redding (96003-2406)
PHONE.................530 245-0256
Fax: 530 245-0431
Keith Adams, *Branch Mgr*
Michael Rodrigues, *Human Res Mgr*
EMP: 75
SALES (corp-wide): 9.2B **Privately Held**
WEB: www.securitasinc.com
SIC: **7381** Security guard service; protective services, guard; detective services
HQ: Securitas Security Services Usa, Inc.
9 Campus Dr
Parsippany NJ 07054
973 267-5300

(P-16792)
SECURITAS SEC SVCS USA INC
Also Called: Southern California / Hawa Reg
2344 S 2nd St Ste C, El Centro
(92243-5606)
PHONE.................760 353-8177
Fax: 760 353-9440
Manuel Andrade, *Branch Mgr*
EMP: 116
SALES (corp-wide): 9.2B **Privately Held**
WEB: www.securitasinc.com
SIC: **7381** Security guard service
HQ: Securitas Security Services Usa, Inc.
9 Campus Dr
Parsippany NJ 07054
973 267-5300

(P-16793)
SECURITAS SEC SVCS USA INC
Also Called: Automotive Services Division
402 S Milliken Ave Ste Gh, Ontario
(91761-7850)
PHONE.................909 974-3160
Dave Knutson, *Branch Mgr*
Andrew Morey, *Branch Mgr*
Mark De Ville, *Human Res Mgr*
John Mildew, *Manager*
Sean Nobles, *Manager*
EMP: 100
SALES (corp-wide): 9.2B **Privately Held**
WEB: www.securitasinc.com
SIC: **7381** Security guard service
HQ: Securitas Security Services Usa, Inc.
9 Campus Dr
Parsippany NJ 07054
973 267-5300

(P-16794)
SECURITAS SEC SVCS USA INC
Southern California / Hawa Reg
1550 Hotel Cir N Ste 440, San Diego
(92108-2933)
PHONE.................619 641-0049
Fax: 619 285-8220
Kelly Senados, *Branch Mgr*
Pat Macarthur, *Human Res Mgr*
Charles McMaulaughlin, *Manager*
EMP: 178
SQ FT: 2,600
SALES (corp-wide): 9.2B **Privately Held**
WEB: www.securitasinc.com
SIC: **7381** Security guard service
HQ: Securitas Security Services Usa, Inc.
9 Campus Dr
Parsippany NJ 07054
973 267-5300

(P-16795)
SECURITAS SEC SVCS USA INC
Also Called: Western Operations Center
4330 Park Terrace Dr, Westlake Village
(91361-4630)
PHONE.................818 706-4909
Edie Stafford, *Manager*
Paul R Amour, *President*
Minot B Dodson, *Exec VP*
Pamela Williams, *Vice Pres*
Paul Johnson, *Executive*
EMP: 350
SALES (corp-wide): 9.2B **Privately Held**
WEB: www.securitasinc.com
SIC: **7381** Security guard service
HQ: Securitas Security Services Usa, Inc.
9 Campus Dr
Parsippany NJ 07054
973 267-5300

(P-16796)
SECURITAS SEC SVCS USA INC
Also Called: Northern California Region
1304 Sthpint Blvd Ste 110, Petaluma
(94954)
PHONE.................707 586-1393
Michael Jack, *Branch Mgr*
EMP: 172
SALES (corp-wide): 9.2B **Privately Held**
WEB: www.securitasinc.com
SIC: **7381** Security guard service
HQ: Securitas Security Services Usa, Inc.
9 Campus Dr
Parsippany NJ 07054
973 267-5300

(P-16797)
SECURITAS SEC SVCS USA INC
Also Called: Southern California / Hawa Reg
5276 Hollister Ave # 204, Goleta
(93111-2073)
PHONE.................805 967-8987
Fax: 805 967-2326
Linda Garcia, *Manager*
EMP: 116
SALES (corp-wide): 9.2B **Privately Held**
WEB: www.securitasinc.com
SIC: **7381** Security guard service
HQ: Securitas Security Services Usa, Inc.
9 Campus Dr
Parsippany NJ 07054
973 267-5300

(P-16798)
SECURITAS SEC SVCS USA INC
Also Called: Northern California Region
1606 Koster St Ste A, Eureka
(95501-0179)
PHONE.................707 445-5463
Fax: 707 445-4638
Chris Peters, *Branch Mgr*
John Dunmire, *Personnel Exec*
EMP: 82
SALES (corp-wide): 9.2B **Privately Held**
WEB: www.securitasinc.com
SIC: **7381** Security guard service
HQ: Securitas Security Services Usa, Inc.
9 Campus Dr
Parsippany NJ 07054
973 267-5300

(P-16799)
SECURITAS SEC SVCS USA INC
Northern California Region
2045 Hurley Way Ste 175, Sacramento
(95825-3220)
PHONE.................916 569-4500
Fax: 916 569-4552
Wallace Lavery, *Principal*
Bernadette McCurdy, *Accounting Mgr*
Linda Brewer, *Human Res Mgr*
Fran Mengell, *Human Res Mgr*
Steven N Marks, *Agent*
EMP: 200
SALES (corp-wide): 9.2B **Privately Held**
WEB: www.securitasinc.com
SIC: **7381** Security guard service
HQ: Securitas Security Services Usa, Inc.
9 Campus Dr
Parsippany NJ 07054
973 267-5300

(P-16800)
SECURITAS SEC SVCS USA INC
27450 Ynez Rd Ste 315, Temecula
(92591-4681)
PHONE.................951 676-3954
Fax: 951 676-3624
Pat Mac Arthur, *Manager*
Jeff Barron, *Manager*
EMP: 116
SALES (corp-wide): 9.2B **Privately Held**
SIC: **7381** Security guard service
HQ: Securitas Security Services Usa, Inc.
9 Campus Dr
Parsippany NJ 07054
973 267-5300

(P-16801)
SECURITAS SEC SVCS USA INC
Also Called: Northern California Region
43 100 Cook St Ste 204, Palm Desert
(92211)
PHONE.................760 779-0728
Fax: 760 674-5913
Kiet Phan, *Branch Mgr*
Douglas Robinson, *Managing Dir*
April Cornwall, *Human Res Mgr*
EMP: 200
SALES (corp-wide): 9.2B **Privately Held**
WEB: www.securitasinc.com
SIC: **7381** Security guard service

PRODUCTS & SERVICES SECTION
7381 - Detective & Armored Car Svcs County (P-16825)

HQ: Securitas Security Services Usa, Inc.
2 Campus Dr
Parsippany NJ 07054
973 267-5300

(P-16802)
SECURITAS SEC SVCS USA INC
Also Called: Northern California Region
1611 Bunker Hill Way # 100, Salinas
(93906-6004)
PHONE..............................831 444-9607
Joseph Santos, Manager
EMP: 116
SALES (corp-wide): 9.2B Privately Held
WEB: www.securitasinc.com
SIC: 7381 Security guard service
HQ: Securitas Security Services Usa, Inc.
2 Campus Dr
Parsippany NJ 07054
973 267-5300

(P-16803)
SECURITAS SEC SVCS USA INC
Also Called: Northern California Region
7677 Oakport St Ste 725, Oakland
(94621-1962)
PHONE..............................925 746-0552
Nathan Wolfe, Vice Pres
Patricia Armstrong, Human Res Mgr
Anna Michael, Manager
EMP: 116
SALES (corp-wide): 9.2B Privately Held
WEB: www.securitasinc.com
SIC: 7381 Security guard service
HQ: Securitas Security Services Usa, Inc.
2 Campus Dr
Parsippany NJ 07054
973 267-5300

(P-16804)
SECURITAS SEC SVCS USA INC
Also Called: Southern California / Hawa Reg
1101 W Mckinley Ave, Pomona
(91768-1639)
PHONE..............................909 865-4356
Barry Gillies, Branch Mgr
EMP: 116
SALES (corp-wide): 9.2B Privately Held
WEB: www.securitasinc.com
SIC: 7381 Security guard service
HQ: Securitas Security Services Usa, Inc.
2 Campus Dr
Parsippany NJ 07054
973 267-5300

(P-16805)
SECURITAS SEC SVCS USA INC
Also Called: Southern California / Hawa Reg
6055 E Wash Blvd Ste 155, Commerce
(90040-2418)
PHONE..............................323 832-9074
Mike Kelly, Branch Mgr
EMP: 116
SALES (corp-wide): 9.2B Privately Held
WEB: www.securitasinc.com
SIC: 7381 Security guard service
HQ: Securitas Security Services Usa, Inc.
2 Campus Dr
Parsippany NJ 07054
973 267-5300

(P-16806)
SECURITAS SEC SVCS USA INC
Also Called: Southern California / Hawa Reg
3325 Wilshire Blvd # 11000, Los Angeles
(90010-1703)
PHONE..............................213 217-7489
Richard Heckler, Branch Mgr
Daiva Savickiene, Project Mgr
EMP: 13000
SALES (corp-wide): 9.2B Privately Held
WEB: www.securitasinc.com
SIC: 7381 Security guard service
HQ: Securitas Security Services Usa, Inc.
2 Campus Dr
Parsippany NJ 07054
973 267-5300

(P-16807)
SECURITAS SEC SVCS USA INC
Also Called: Southern California / Hawa Reg
1055 Wilshire Blvd, Los Angeles
(90017-2431)
PHONE..............................213 580-8825
Fax: 213 580-8849
Jeff Winter, Principal

John Grover, Branch Mgr
Jessica Fitzsimmons, Administration
John Gill, Database Admin
Daniel Ramirez, Technology
EMP: 116
SALES (corp-wide): 9.2B Privately Held
WEB: www.securitasinc.com
SIC: 7381 Security guard service
HQ: Securitas Security Services Usa, Inc.
2 Campus Dr
Parsippany NJ 07054
973 267-5300

(P-16808)
SECURITAS SEC SVCS USA INC
Also Called: Southern California / Hawa Reg
1500 W Carson St Ste 109, Long Beach
(90810-1401)
PHONE..............................562 427-2737
Ivory Phillips, Assoc VP
EMP: 116
SALES (corp-wide): 9.2B Privately Held
WEB: www.securitasinc.com
SIC: 7381 Security guard service
HQ: Securitas Security Services Usa, Inc.
9 Campus Dr
Parsippany NJ 07054
973 267-5300

(P-16809)
SECURITAS SEC SVCS USA INC
2099 S State College Blvd, Anaheim
(92806-6142)
PHONE..............................714 385-9745
Steven Lindsey, Owner
Scott Denault, Branch Mgr
Jorge Moreno, Branch Mgr
EMP: 116
SALES (corp-wide): 9.2B Privately Held
WEB: www.securitasinc.com
SIC: 7381 Guard services
HQ: Securitas Security Services Usa, Inc.
2 Campus Dr
Parsippany NJ 07054
973 267-5300

(P-16810)
SECURITAS SEC SVCS USA INC
Also Called: Shared Services
400 Crenshaw Blvd Ste 200, Torrance
(90503-1736)
PHONE..............................310 787-0747
EMP: 181
SALES (corp-wide): 9.4B Privately Held
SIC: 7381
HQ: Securitas Security Services Usa, Inc.
2 Campus Dr
Parsippany NJ 07054
973 267-5300

(P-16811)
SECURITAS SEC SVCS USA INC
Also Called: Southern California / Hawa Reg
15428 Civic Dr Ste 305, Victorville
(92392-9772)
PHONE..............................760 245-1915
Bob Dorian, Branch Mgr
EMP: 150
SALES (corp-wide): 9.2B Privately Held
WEB: www.securitasinc.com
SIC: 7381 Security guard service
HQ: Securitas Security Services Usa, Inc.
2 Campus Dr
Parsippany NJ 07054
973 267-5300

(P-16812)
SECURITAS SEC SVCS USA INC
Also Called: Automotive Services Division
16909 Parthenia St # 202, Northridge
(91343-4551)
PHONE..............................818 891-0458
Fax: 818 891-6380
Pat Salter, Branch Mgr
EMP: 150
SALES (corp-wide): 9.2B Privately Held
WEB: www.securitasinc.com
SIC: 7381 8742 8741 Security guard
service; industry specialist consultants;
management services
HQ: Securitas Security Services Usa, Inc.
9 Campus Dr
Parsippany NJ 07054
973 267-5300

(P-16813)
SECURITAS SEC SVCS USA INC
4330 Park Terrace Dr, Westlake Village
(91361-4630)
PHONE..............................818 706-6800
Steve Lyndsay, Branch Mgr
Miguel F Garuz, Officer
Stefanie Hennig, Officer
Beth Hansen, Vice Pres
Lou Caravelli, Security Dir
EMP: 116
SALES (corp-wide): 9.4B Privately Held
SIC: 7381 Security guard service
HQ: Securitas Security Services Usa, Inc.
2 Campus Dr
Parsippany NJ 07054
973 267-5300

(P-16814)
SECURITAS SECURITY SVCS USA
Southern California / Hawa Reg
402 S Milliken Ave Ste Gh, Ontario
(91761-7850)
PHONE..............................909 974-3160
John W Muldoon III, Principal
Mark De Ville, Financial Exec
EMP: 500
SALES (corp-wide): 9.2B Privately Held
WEB: www.securitasinc.com
SIC: 7381 Security guard service
HQ: Securitas Security Services Usa, Inc.
9 Campus Dr
Parsippany NJ 07054
973 267-5300

(P-16815)
SECURITY AMERICA INC
18105 La Salle Ave, Gardena
(90248-3608)
PHONE..............................310 532-0121
Mary Garnica, President
Fred Garnica, CEO
Mark Carreno, Vice Pres
EMP: 84
SALES (est): 2.1MM Privately Held
WEB: www.securityamericainc.com
SIC: 7381 Security guard service

(P-16816)
SECURITY INDUST SPCIALISTS INC (PA)
6071 Bristol Pkwy, Culver City
(90230-6601)
PHONE..............................310 215-5100
Fax: 310 215-5115
John Spesak, President
Kit Knudsen, COO
Tom Seltz, CFO
Rossell Valerio, Officer
Tom Stevens, Vice Pres
EMP: 148
SQ FT: 9,000
SALES (est): 55.8MM Privately Held
WEB: www.securityindustryspecialists.com
SIC: 7381 5065 7382 Guard services; security control equipment & systems; security systems services

(P-16817)
SECURITY OFFICERS & INVESTIGAT
21 Orinda Way Ste 145c, Orinda
(94563-2530)
PHONE..............................817 386-6947
Sharronda Wheat,
Jai Khan, Manager
EMP: 99
SALES: 950K Privately Held
SIC: 7381 Detective & armored car services

(P-16818)
SECURITY ONE INC
1859 Streiff Ln, Santa Rosa (95403-2326)
PHONE..............................800 778-3017
Tom Kasnick, President
Troy Bohannan, Vice Pres
Valerie Kasnick, Vice Pres
EMP: 65 EST: 1998
SQ FT: 1,000
SALES (est): 1.4MM Privately Held
SIC: 7381 Guard services; security guard service; private investigator

(P-16819)
SHARP GUARD SERVICES INC
3450 Wilshire Blvd # 1000, Los Angeles
(90010-2208)
PHONE..............................213 739-1900
Fax: 213 739-2800
Ilham Chaouir, President
Mike Thabet, Treasurer
EMP: 521 EST: 1999
SALES (est): 4.4MM Privately Held
WEB: www.sharpgs.com
SIC: 7381 Security guard service

(P-16820)
SHERMAN SECURITY
7218 Hermosa Ave, Rancho Cucamonga
(91701-5929)
PHONE..............................909 941-4167
Daryl Enoch, Partner
Clarence Tanner, Partner
EMP: 102
SALES (est): 106.7K Privately Held
SIC: 7381 7389 Guard services;

(P-16821)
SHIELD SECURITY INC (DH)
1551 N Tustin Ave Ste 650, Santa Ana
(92705-8664)
PHONE..............................714 210-1501
Fax: 714 210-5203
Ed Klosterman Jr, President
Kenneth Klosterman, Vice Pres
EMP: 300
SQ FT: 5,500
SALES (est): 25.7MM
SALES (corp-wide): 950.8MM Privately Held
SIC: 7381 Security guard service
HQ: Universal Protection Service, Lp
1551 N Tustin Ave Ste 650
Santa Ana CA 92705
714 619-9700

(P-16822)
SHIELD SECURITY INC
21110 Vanowen St, Canoga Park
(91303-2821)
PHONE..............................818 239-5800
Kenneth Klosterman, Branch Mgr
EMP: 200
SALES (corp-wide): 950.8MM Privately Held
SIC: 7381 Security guard service
HQ: Shield Security, Inc.
1551 N Tustin Ave Ste 650
Santa Ana CA 92705
714 210-1501

(P-16823)
SHIELD SECURITY INC
150 E Wardlow Rd, Long Beach
(90807-4417)
PHONE..............................562 283-1100
Fax: 562 387-9043
Leo Green, Manager
EMP: 450
SALES (corp-wide): 950.8MM Privately Held
SIC: 7381 Security guard service
HQ: Shield Security, Inc.
1551 N Tustin Ave Ste 650
Santa Ana CA 92705
714 210-1501

(P-16824)
SHIELD SECURITY INC
265 N Euclid Ave, Upland (91786-6038)
PHONE..............................909 920-1173
Fax: 909 920-3334
Paul Srankowski, Manager
EMP: 300
SALES (corp-wide): 950.8MM Privately Held
SIC: 7381 Security guard service
HQ: Shield Security, Inc.
1551 N Tustin Ave Ste 650
Santa Ana CA 92705
714 210-1501

(P-16825)
SILICON VLY SEC & PATROL INC (PA)
1131 Luchessi Dr Ste 2, San Jose
(95118-3770)
PHONE..............................408 267-1539
Fax: 408 978-2197

7381 - Detective & Armored Car Svcs County (P-16826)

Ray Higdon, *CEO*
Lisa Higdon, *President*
Gary Mills, *Vice Pres*
Kimberly Robinson, *Admin Asst*
Julianne Hinson, *Finance Mgr*
EMP: 150
SQ FT: 4,000
SALES (est): 10.8MM **Privately Held**
WEB: www.svsp.com
SIC: 7381 Security guard service

(P-16826)
SOS SECURITY INCORPORATED
2601 Ocean Park Blvd # 208, Santa Monica (90405-5229)
PHONE 310 392-9600
Doug Hamilton, *Manager*
EMP: 140
SALES (corp-wide): 102.4MM **Privately Held**
SIC: 7381 Security guard service; detective agency
PA: Sos Security Incorporated
  1915 Us Highway 46 Ste 1
  Parsippany NJ 07054
  973 402-6600

(P-16827)
SOS SECURITY INCORPORATED
26250 Industrial Blvd # 48, Hayward (94545-2922)
PHONE 510 782-4900
Michael Boone, *Vice Pres*
EMP: 140
SALES (corp-wide): 102.4MM **Privately Held**
SIC: 7381 Security guard service; detective agency
PA: Sos Security Incorporated
  1915 Us Highway 46 Ste 1
  Parsippany NJ 07054
  973 402-6600

(P-16828)
SOS SECURITY LLC
331 N Beverly Dr Ste 3, Beverly Hills (90210-4729)
PHONE 310 859-8248
EMP: 70
SALES (corp-wide): 107MM **Privately Held**
SIC: 7381 Security guard service
PA: Sos Security Llc
  1915 Us Highway 46
  Parsippany NJ 07054
  973 402-6600

(P-16829)
SPEAR MANAGEMENT COMPANY
1642 N Cahuenga Blvd, Los Angeles (90028-6252)
PHONE 323 963-7515
Hossein Geramipour, *President*
Josephine Delapaz, *Administration*
EMP: 51
SALES: 1,000K **Privately Held**
SIC: 7381 Detective & armored car services

(P-16830)
SRS PROTECTION INC
4464 Mcgrath St Ste 103, Ventura (93003-7764)
PHONE 805 744-7122
James Allen Rita, *CEO*
Robin Neubert, *Vice Pres*
EMP: 75
SQ FT: 1,200
SALES: 500K **Privately Held**
SIC: 7381 Security guard service

(P-16831)
STAFF PRO INC
675 Convention Way, San Diego (92101-7805)
PHONE 619 544-1774
Mike Hernandez, *Manager*
EMP: 198
SALES (corp-wide): 81.2MM **Privately Held**
WEB: www.staffpro.com
SIC: 7381 Security guard service

PA: Staff Pro Inc.
  15272 Jason Cir
  Huntington Beach CA 92649
  714 230-7200

(P-16832)
STEELE INTERNATIONAL INC (PA)
Also Called: Steele Corp SEC Advisory Svcs
1 Sansome St Ste 3500, San Francisco (94104-4436)
PHONE 415 781-4300
Kenneth Kurtz, *CEO*
Richard N Ilmot, *Exec Dir*
Murray Rouse, *Regional Mgr*
Dennis Haist, *Marketing Mgr*
EMP: 138
SQ FT: 5,000
SALES (est): 41.9MM **Privately Held**
SIC: 7381 8742 8748 Detective & armored car services; management consulting services; agricultural consultant

(P-16833)
TOP NOTCH SECURITY
4312 Woodman Ave Ste 202, Sherman Oaks (91423-5524)
PHONE 818 528-2875
Lou Franzini, *Owner*
John Rolin, *Principal*
EMP: 50 **EST:** 1999
SALES (est): 669.6K **Privately Held**
SIC: 7381 Security guard service

(P-16834)
TRANS WEST INVESTIGATIONS INC
3255 Wilshire Blvd, Los Angeles (90010-1404)
PHONE 213 381-1500
Edward W Beyer, *President*
James T Walsh, *CEO*
EMP: 57
SQ FT: 2,900
SALES (est): 1.2MM **Privately Held**
SIC: 7381 8111 Private investigator; legal services

(P-16835)
TRANS-WEST SECURITY SVCS INC
8503 Crippen St, Bakersfield (93311-8993)
PHONE 661 381-2900
Fax: 661 834-0752
Brooke L Antonioni, *President*
Duane Williams, *Exec VP*
Katy Williams, *Vice Pres*
Monique Williams, *Manager*
EMP: 300
SQ FT: 8,500
SALES (est): 10.2MM **Privately Held**
WEB: www.twsecurity.com
SIC: 7381 Security guard service

(P-16836)
TURNER SECURITY SYSTEMS INC
Also Called: Don Turner and Associates
120 W Shields Ave, Fresno (93705-4101)
PHONE 559 486-3466
Donald A Turner, *President*
Michael Garaffa, *Office Mgr*
Gary Gannon, *Financial Exec*
EMP: 190
SQ FT: 3,700
SALES (est): 7.2MM **Privately Held**
WEB: www.turnersec.com
SIC: 7381 Security guard service

(P-16837)
TYAN INC
Also Called: Security Specialists
1500 Glenoaks Blvd, San Fernando (91340-1780)
P.O. Box 3472, Van Nuys (91407-3472)
PHONE 818 785-5831
Fax: 818 785-7801
Nick Tsotsikyan, *President*
Steve Leon, *Executive*
EMP: 55
SQ FT: 2,000
SALES (est): 1.6MM **Privately Held**
WEB: www.capatrol.com
SIC: 7381 Security guard service

(P-16838)
U S PRIVATE PROTECTION SEC INC
5555 Inglewood Blvd # 205, Culver City (90230-6250)
PHONE 310 301-0010
Dave Solomon, *President*
Omar Vasquez, *Opers Mgr*
EMP: 180
SALES (est): 3.8MM **Privately Held**
SIC: 7381 Protective services, guard

(P-16839)
UNITY SEC & PROTECTIVE SVC
619 E Washington Blvd, Pasadena (91104-2260)
PHONE 323 695-7234
Fax: 213 368-1360
Jayson Lee, *President*
EMP: 78
SQ FT: 3,000
SALES (est): 1.3MM **Privately Held**
WEB: www.unitedprotection.com
SIC: 7381 Security guard service

(P-16840)
UNIVERSAL PROTECTION SVC LP
Also Called: Prestige Protection
2415 San Ramon Vly Blvd, San Ramon (94583-5381)
PHONE 805 496-4401
Tim Elsasser, *Branch Mgr*
EMP: 61
SALES (corp-wide): 950.8MM **Privately Held**
SIC: 7381 Detective & armored car services
HQ: Universal Protection Service, Lp
  1551 N Tustin Ave Ste 650
  Santa Ana CA 92705
  714 619-9700

(P-16841)
UNIVERSAL PROTECTION SVC LP
340 Golden Shore Ste 100, Long Beach (90802-4237)
PHONE 562 981-5700
Fax: 323 981-5701
Steve Salyer, *Owner*
EMP: 58
SALES (corp-wide): 950.8MM **Privately Held**
SIC: 7381 Detective & armored car services
HQ: Universal Protection Service, Lp
  1551 N Tustin Ave Ste 650
  Santa Ana CA 92705
  714 619-9700

(P-16842)
UNIVERSAL PROTECTION SVC LP
21300 Victory Blvd # 230, Woodland Hills (91367-2525)
PHONE 818 227-1240
Fax: 818 227-1245
Jerry McConnell, *Branch Mgr*
EMP: 58
SALES (corp-wide): 950.8MM **Privately Held**
SIC: 7381 Security guard service
HQ: Universal Protection Service, Lp
  1551 N Tustin Ave Ste 650
  Santa Ana CA 92705
  714 619-9700

(P-16843)
UNIVERSAL PROTECTION SVC LP (HQ)
1551 N Tustin Ave Ste 650, Santa Ana (92705-8664)
PHONE 714 619-9700
Fax: 714 619-9701
Brian Cescolini, *Mng Member*
Steve Jones, *CEO*
Jeremy Diggs, *Officer*
Jim Moses, *Senior VP*
Roger Langner, *Vice Pres*
EMP: 148
SALES (est): 950.8MM **Privately Held**
SIC: 7381 Security guard service

PA: Universal Protection Gp, Llc
  1551 N Tustin Ave Ste 650
  Santa Ana CA 92705
  714 619-9700

(P-16844)
UNIVERSAL PROTECTION SVC LP
1208 Vicente St, San Francisco (94116-3044)
PHONE 415 759-5056
David Nagle, *CEO*
EMP: 250
SALES (corp-wide): 950.8MM **Privately Held**
SIC: 7381 Security guard service
HQ: Universal Protection Service, Lp
  1551 N Tustin Ave Ste 650
  Santa Ana CA 92705
  714 619-9700

(P-16845)
UNIVERSAL SERVICES AMERICA LP (PA)
1551 N Tustin Ave, Santa Ana (92705-8634)
P.O. Box 101034, Pasadena (91189-0003)
PHONE 714 619-9700
Steven Jones, *CEO*
Steve Claton, *President*
Mark Olivas, *President*
Jason Stapleton, *President*
Toni Ippolito, *CEO*
EMP: 100
SALES: 2B **Privately Held**
SIC: 7381 7349 Security guard service; janitorial service, contract basis

(P-16846)
UNLIMITED SECURITY SPECIALIST
13636 Ventura Blvd # 206, Sherman Oaks (91423-3700)
PHONE 877 310-4877
Jose Cardona, *Principal*
Michael Laperruque, *Co-Owner*
EMP: 50
SALES: 2.5MM **Privately Held**
SIC: 7381 Guard services

(P-16847)
US SECURITY ASSOCIATES INC
555 W Benjamin Holt Dr # 222, Stockton (95207-3860)
PHONE 209 476-7062
Perry Crawford, *Principal*
Randy Huscher, *Security Dir*
EMP: 108
SALES (corp-wide): 1.7B **Privately Held**
SIC: 7381 Guard services
PA: U.S. Security Associates, Inc.
  200 Mansell Ct E Ste 500
  Roswell GA 30076
  770 625-1500

(P-16848)
US SECURITY ASSOCIATES INC
495 E Rincon St Ste 207, Corona (92879-1379)
PHONE 951 256-4601
Richard Wyckoff, *Branch Mgr*
EMP: 112
SALES (corp-wide): 1.7B **Privately Held**
SIC: 7381 Guard services
PA: U.S. Security Associates, Inc.
  200 Mansell Ct E Ste 500
  Roswell GA 30076
  770 625-1500

(P-16849)
VINCENT LOZANO INVESTIGATIONS
P.O. Box 205 (91785-0205)
PHONE 909 949-0179
Fax: 909 949-4204
Vincent Lozano, *Owner*
EMP: 50 **EST:** 1984
SALES (est): 667.8K **Privately Held**
SIC: 7381 Private investigator

(P-16850)
W S B & ASSOCIATES INC
519 17th St Ste 230, Oakland (94612-1529)
PHONE 510 444-6266

PRODUCTS & SERVICES SECTION

7382 - Security Systems Svcs County (P-16874)

Bobby Sisk, *President*
EMP: 100
SALES (corp-wide): 5MM **Privately Held**
SIC: 7381 Security guard service
PA: W S B & Associates Inc
1390 Market St Ste 314
San Francisco CA 94102
415 864-3510

(P-16851)
W S B & ASSOCIATES INC (PA)
1390 Market St Ste 314, San Francisco (94102-5404)
PHONE.....................................415 864-3510
Bobby Sisk, *CEO*
Derek Dixon, *Mktg Coord*
EMP: 77
SQ FT: 1,600
SALES (est): 5MM **Privately Held**
SIC: 7381 Security guard service

(P-16852)
WHELAN SECURITY CO
400 Continental Blvd, El Segundo (90245-5076)
PHONE.....................................310 343-8628
EMP: 674
SALES (corp-wide): 186.2MM **Privately Held**
SIC: 7381 Guard services
PA: Whelan Security Co.
1699 S Hanley Rd Ste 350
Saint Louis MO 63114
314 644-3227

(P-16853)
WINDWALKER SECURITY PATROL INC
23987 Nw Frontage Rd, Acampo (95220)
P.O. Box 488 (95220-0488)
PHONE.....................................209 333-3953
Fax: 209 333-3954
Richard V Edwards, *CEO*
Bb Edwards, *Shareholder*
EMP: 75
SALES (est): 1.8MM **Privately Held**
SIC: 7381 Detective & armored car services

(P-16854)
WORLD PRIVATE SECURITY INC
16921 Parthenia St # 201, Northridge (91343-4568)
PHONE.....................................818 894-1800
Fax: 818 894-1877
Fred Youssif, *President*
Jeannette Youssif, *Co-Owner*
EMP: 200
SALES: 4MM **Privately Held**
SIC: 7381 Security guard service

(P-16855)
WORLDWIDE SECURITY ASSOCIATES (HQ)
10311 S La Cienega Blvd, Los Angeles (90045-6109)
PHONE.....................................310 743-3000
Fax: 310 743-3005
Andres Martinez, *President*
Richard Rodriguez, *Vice Pres*
Pattie Paquette, *Manager*
EMP: 300
SQ FT: 5,000
SALES (est): 23.2MM
SALES (corp-wide): 30.4MM **Privately Held**
WEB: www.wsainc.net
SIC: 7381 Security guard service
PA: Wsa Group Inc
19208 S Vermont Ave 200
Gardena CA 90248
310 743-3000

(P-16856)
WSA GROUP INC (PA)
19208 S Vermont Ave 200, Gardena (90248-4414)
PHONE.....................................310 743-3000
Andres Martinez, *President*
William Maggio, *Senior VP*
James E Bush, *Vice Pres*
EMP: 50
SQ FT: 10,000
SALES (est): 30.4MM **Privately Held**
WEB: www.wsagroup.com
SIC: 7381 7349 Security guard service; janitorial service, contract basis

(P-16857)
YOSH ENTERPRISES INC
Also Called: Orion Security
675 E Gish Rd, San Jose (95112-2708)
PHONE.....................................408 287-4411
Fax: 408 287-4424
Yosh Gahramani, *President*
Donald Upasena, *Opers Mgr*
EMP: 400
SQ FT: 6,800
SALES (est): 8.8MM **Privately Held**
WEB: www.orionsecurity.com
SIC: 7381 6531 8742 0782 Security guard service; private investigator; real estate managers; industrial & labor consulting services; lawn & garden services

7382 Security Systems Svcs

(P-16858)
3VR SECURITY INC
814 Mission St Fl 4, San Francisco (94103-3034)
PHONE.....................................415 513-4577
Fax: 415 495-5797
Robert A Shipp, *CEO*
Skip Dorazio, *CFO*
Charles F Ryan III, *CFO*
Bob Vallone, *Exec VP*
Masayuki Karahashi, *Senior VP*
EMP: 90
SALES (est): 19.8MM **Privately Held**
WEB: www.3vrsecurity.com
SIC: 7382 Security systems services

(P-16859)
ACS SECURITY INDUSTRIES INC
Also Called: A C S Security
100 Bel Air Rd, Los Angeles (90077-3809)
PHONE.....................................310 475-9016
Al Radi, *President*
Melissa King, *Admin Asst*
Sander Kaufman, *IT/INT Sup*
Kenzie Kimura, *Recruiter*
Carl Converse, *Sales Mgr*
EMP: 60
SALES (est): 6.4MM **Privately Held**
SIC: 7382 Security systems services

(P-16860)
ADMIRAL SECURITY SERVICES INC
2151 Salvio St Ste 260, Concord (94520-2406)
PHONE.....................................888 471-1128
Mohamed S Ahmed, *CEO*
Youssef Abdallah, *President*
EMP: 400
SQ FT: 1,500
SALES (est): 31.1MM **Privately Held**
SIC: 7382 7381 Security systems services; protective services, guard; security guard service; guard services

(P-16861)
ADVANCED PROTECTION INDS INC
Also Called: National Monitoring Center
25341 Commercentre Dr # 100, Lake Forest (92630-8856)
PHONE.....................................949 215-8000
Fax: 949 215-8141
Michael Schubert, *President*
Scott Schubert, *Shareholder*
Woodie George Andrawos, *Exec VP*
Joanna Garcia, *Opers Spvr*
Phea Phann, *Regl Sales Mgr*
EMP: 50
SALES (est): 8.7MM **Privately Held**
WEB: www.nmccentral.com
SIC: 7382 Burglar alarm maintenance & monitoring

(P-16862)
AERO PORT SERVICES INC (PA)
216 W Florence Ave, Inglewood (90301-1213)
PHONE.....................................310 623-8230
Chris Paik, *President*
Stephan Park, *CFO*
Jake Yoon, *CFO*
Julie Hong, *Treasurer*
Robert Yim, *Vice Pres*
EMP: 56
SALES (est): 32.8MM **Privately Held**
WEB: www.aeroportservices.com
SIC: 7382 Security systems services

(P-16863)
ALLIEDBARTON SECURITY SVCS LLC
Also Called: Initial Security
10330 Pioneer Blvd # 235, Santa Fe Springs (90670-6012)
PHONE.....................................562 906-4800
Larry Link, *Vice Pres*
EMP: 500
SALES (corp-wide): 10.5MM **Privately Held**
SIC: 7382 Protective devices, security
HQ: Alliedbarton Security Services Llc
8 Tower Bridge 161 Wshgtn
Conshohocken PA 19428
610 239-1100

(P-16864)
ALLIEDBARTON SECURITY SVCS LLC
1600 Riviera Ave Ste 375, Walnut Creek (94596-7377)
PHONE.....................................510 839-4041
Fax: 510 839-5632
Kiet Phan, *District Mgr*
EMP: 300
SALES (corp-wide): 10.5MM **Privately Held**
WEB: www.alliedsecurity.com
SIC: 7382 Security systems services
HQ: Alliedbarton Security Services Llc
8 Tower Bridge 161 Wshgtn
Conshohocken PA 19428
610 239-1100

(P-16865)
ALLIEDBARTON SECURITY SVCS LLC
765 The City Dr S Ste 105, Orange (92868-6911)
PHONE.....................................714 260-0805
Fax: 714 260-0801
Larry Crowl, *Principal*
EMP: 160
SALES (corp-wide): 10.5MM **Privately Held**
WEB: www.alliedsecurity.com
SIC: 7382 Security systems services
HQ: Alliedbarton Security Services Llc
8 Tower Bridge 161 Wshgtn
Conshohocken PA 19428
610 239-1100

(P-16866)
AMERICAN SERVICE INDUSTRIES
2930 W Imperial Hwy # 332, Inglewood (90303-3143)
PHONE.....................................323 779-4000
Fax: 323 779-4044
Tony Caminiti, *President*
Stephen E Kulp, *CEO*
John Congleton, *Senior VP*
EMP: 100
SQ FT: 1,200
SALES (est): 3.9MM **Privately Held**
SIC: 7382 7349 Protective services, security; janitorial service, contract basis

(P-16867)
ASSERTIVE SECURITY SERVICES &
20501 Ventura Blvd # 150, Woodland Hills (91364-2330)
PHONE.....................................818 888-2405
Maryam Ayam, *President*
Daniel Charron, *Marketing Mgr*
EMP: 550
SALES (est): 28.7MM **Privately Held**
WEB: www.assertivesecurity.com
SIC: 7382 7381 Security systems services; security guard service

(P-16868)
ATLAS SECURITY INC
11862 Balboa Blvd Ste 395, Granada Hills (91344-2753)
PHONE.....................................323 876-1401
Jack Boyd, *President*
EMP: 50
SALES (est): 2.2MM **Privately Held**
SIC: 7382 Security systems services

(P-16869)
AUTHORIZED TAXI CAB
Also Called: A T S
6150 W 96th St, Los Angeles (90045-5218)
PHONE.....................................323 776-5324
Behzad Bitaraf, *President*
EMP: 60
SALES (est): 5.3MM **Privately Held**
SIC: 7382 Security systems services

(P-16870)
BAYER PROTECTIVE SERVICES INC
3436 Amrcn Rver Dr Ste 10, Sacramento (95864)
PHONE.....................................916 486-5800
Fax: 916 486-5803
Bryon A Bayer, *President*
Bryon Bayer, *President*
EMP: 165
SQ FT: 1,600
SALES (est): 12MM
SALES (corp-wide): 14.7MM **Privately Held**
WEB: www.bayerprotectiveservices.com
SIC: 7382 Security systems services
PA: First Security Services
850 San Jose Ave Ste 128
Clovis CA 93612
559 297-1444

(P-16871)
BLUEGILL TECHNOLOGIES LLC
Also Called: Bluegill Solar
11884 Welby Pl Ste 101, Moreno Valley (92557-6444)
PHONE.....................................877 765-2770
Aman Chowdhry, *President*
EMP: 60
SQ FT: 1,100
SALES (est): 12MM **Privately Held**
SIC: 7382 7373 Security systems services; systems integration services

(P-16872)
BRIGHTCLOUD INC
4370 La Jolla Village Dr # 820, San Diego (92122-1277)
PHONE.....................................858 652-4803
Quinn Curtis, *President*
EMP: 125
SALES (est): 3.7MM
SALES (corp-wide): 121MM **Privately Held**
SIC: 7382 Security systems services
PA: Webroot Inc.
385 Interlocken Cres # 800
Broomfield CO 80021
303 442-3813

(P-16873)
CALLAN MANAGEMENT CORPORATION
Also Called: Western Area Security Services
2919 W Burbank Blvd Ste C, Burbank (91505-2351)
PHONE.....................................818 846-2215
Fax: 818 846-8748
Michael Butler, *President*
Joseph Wolf, *Manager*
EMP: 300
SQ FT: 2,000
SALES (est): 16.1MM **Privately Held**
WEB: www.westernarea.com
SIC: 7382 7381 Security systems services; detective & armored car services

(P-16874)
CLOUDFLARE INC (PA)
101 Townsend St, San Francisco (94107-1934)
PHONE.....................................650 319-8930
Matthew Prince, *President*
Amy Kux, *Exec Officer*
Judy Hoctor, *Executive Asst*

7382 - Security Systems Svcs County (P-16875)

Slava Mudry, *Prgrmr*
Eli Staykova, *Research*
EMP: 60
SQ FT: 6,000
SALES (est): 24.3MM **Privately Held**
SIC: 7382 Security systems services

(P-16875)
CONVERGINT TECHNOLOGIES LLC
5860 W Las Positas Blvd # 7, Pleasanton (94588-8557)
PHONE 510 300-2800
Fax: 650 968-1831
Doug Lyle, *Branch Mgr*
Fred Michel, *Project Mgr*
Barry Woodward, *Project Mgr*
Lance Simpson, *Technology*
Bob Tom, *Accounts Exec*
EMP: 50
SALES (corp-wide): 469.1MM **Privately Held**
SIC: 7382 Security systems services
PA: Convergint Technologies Llc
1 Commerce Dr
Schaumburg IL 60173
847 620-5000

(P-16876)
COURIER LEASING INC
1260 Morena Blvd Ste 200, San Diego (92110-3850)
PHONE 619 275-7000
Lawrence Richman, *President*
David Hall, *CFO*
Ken Moller, *Exec VP*
EMP: 560
SQ FT: 4,500
SALES (est): 14.1MM **Privately Held**
SIC: 7382 7359 Security systems services; equipment rental & leasing

(P-16877)
DELTA SCIENTIFIC CORPORATION (PA)
40355 Delta Ln, Palmdale (93551-3616)
PHONE 661 575-1100
Fax: 661 575-1109
Harry D Dickinson, *CEO*
Bill Brunty, *President*
John Friend, *President*
Richard I Winger, *CFO*
Richard Wringer, *CFO*
EMP: 188 **EST:** 1974
SQ FT: 200,000
SALES (est): 28.8MM **Privately Held**
WEB: www.deltascientific.com
SIC: 7382 Security systems services

(P-16878)
DIAL SECURITY (PA)
Also Called: Dial Communications
760 W Ventura Blvd, Camarillo (93010-8382)
P.O. Box 34781, Bethesda MD (20827-0781)
PHONE 805 389-6700
Fax: 805 383-3401
William F Dundas, *President*
EMP: 250
SQ FT: 12,000
SALES (est): 17.8MM **Privately Held**
WEB: www.dialcomm.com
SIC: 7382 7381 Security systems services; detective & armored car services

(P-16879)
DIGITAL PERIPH SOLUTIONS INC
Also Called: Q-See
8015 E Crystal Dr, Anaheim (92807-2523)
PHONE 714 998-3440
Priti Sharma, *President*
Raj Sharma, *President*
Kamal Polani, *Office Mgr*
Ana Hernandez, *Accounting Mgr*
Terry McConnell, *Controller*
EMP: 75
SQ FT: 30,000
SALES (est): 58MM **Privately Held**
WEB: www.q-see.com
SIC: 7382 3651 Confinement surveillance systems maintenance & monitoring; video camera-audio recorders, household use

(P-16880)
DREW CHAIN SECURITY CORP
55 S Raymond Ave Ste 303, Alhambra (91801-7100)
PHONE 626 457-8626
Fax: 626 457-8223
Kenneth Y Lee, *President*
David Young, *General Mgr*
EMP: 71
SQ FT: 800
SALES (est): 1MM **Privately Held**
WEB: www.alhambrahospital.com
SIC: 7382 Protective devices, security

(P-16881)
DRIVE THRU TECHNOLOGY INC
Also Called: Dtt
1755 N Main St, Los Angeles (90031-2516)
PHONE 323 576-1400
Sam Naficy, *President*
Jeff Moran, *CFO*
Mark Simson, *CFO*
Thomas M Moran, *Exec VP*
Michael Sutton, *Exec VP*
EMP: 150
SQ FT: 17,000
SALES (est): 28.8MM **Privately Held**
WEB: www.dttusa.com
SIC: 7382 Confinement surveillance systems maintenance & monitoring

(P-16882)
DTT SURVEILLANCE HOLDINGS INC
1755 N Main St, Los Angeles (90031-2516)
PHONE 323 576-1400
Sam Naficy, *CEO*
Jeffrey Naficy, *CFO*
Thomas M Moran, *Exec VP*
Michael Sutton, *Exec VP*
Scott Greenwald, *Vice Pres*
EMP: 59
SALES (est): 8.2MM **Privately Held**
SIC: 7382 Confinement surveillance systems maintenance & monitoring

(P-16883)
EMAGINED SECURITY INC
2816 San Simeon Way, San Carlos (94070-3611)
PHONE 415 944-2977
David Sockol, *President*
David Zuckerman, *Senior VP*
Eugene Schultz, *CTO*
Julianna Sockol, *Info Tech Mgr*
Yvonne Vega, *Business Mgr*
EMP: 50
SALES (est): 8.6MM **Privately Held**
WEB: www.emagined.com
SIC: 7382 Security systems services

(P-16884)
FED AIR SECURITY CORPORATION
210 S De Lacey Ave, Pasadena (91105-2048)
PHONE 626 535-2200
Enrique Hernandez Jr, *CEO*
Chris R Sherman, *CFO*
EMP: 100
SQ FT: 16,000
SALES (est): 3.7MM **Privately Held**
SIC: 7382 Security systems services

(P-16885)
FIRST ALARM (PA)
1111 Estates Dr, Aptos (95003-3572)
PHONE 831 476-1111
Fax: 831 685-6625
Jarl E Saal, *Chairman*
David Hood, *President*
Chris Guzman, *COO*
Santos Tenorio, *Executive*
Shea Ackerly, *Branch Mgr*
EMP: 120
SQ FT: 14,000
SALES (est): 60.7MM **Privately Held**
WEB: www.firstalarm.com
SIC: 7382 Burglar alarm maintenance & monitoring

(P-16886)
HARRISON IYKE
Also Called: Diplomatic Security Services
7611 Etiwanda Ave, Rancho Cucamonga (91739-9715)
PHONE 909 463-8409
Iyke Harrison, *Owner*
EMP: 99
SALES (est): 4.7MM **Privately Held**
SIC: 7382 Security systems services

(P-16887)
HIKVISION USA INC (HQ)
Also Called: Hikvision Usa, Inc.
908 Canada Ct, City of Industry (91748-1136)
PHONE 909 895-0400
Jeffrey He, *CEO*
Polo Cai, *Vice Pres*
Ning Tang, *Admin Sec*
Albert Lin, *CTO*
Marcus Ching, *Business Anlyst*
EMP: 175 **EST:** 2007
SALES: 75MM
SALES (corp-wide): 1.9B **Privately Held**
SIC: 7382 Confinement surveillance systems maintenance & monitoring
PA: Hangzhou Hikvision Digital Technology Co., Ltd.
No.555 Qianmo Road, Binjiang District
Hangzhou 31005
571 880-7599

(P-16888)
HOMELAND SECURITY SERVICES INC
31805 Temecula Pkwy, Temecula (92592-8203)
P.O. Box 26052, Anaheim (92825-6052)
PHONE 714 956-2200
Leonard Bacani, *President*
Florencia Bacani, *Vice Pres*
EMP: 400
SQ FT: 250
SALES: 437.9K **Privately Held**
WEB: www.homelandsecurityservices.com
SIC: 7382 7381 Protective devices, security; detective & armored car services; detective services

(P-16889)
HONEYWELL INTERNATIONAL INC
22 Centerpointe Dr # 100, La Palma (90623-2504)
PHONE 714 562-8713
Phil O'Leary, *Manager*
EMP: 200
SALES (corp-wide): 38.5B **Publicly Held**
WEB: www.honeywell.com
SIC: 7382 Security systems services
PA: Honeywell International Inc.
115 Tabor Rd
Morris Plains NJ 07950
973 455-2000

(P-16890)
HP INC
20400 Stevens Creek Blvd, Cupertino (95014-2296)
PHONE 408 886-3200
Lisa Viso, *Branch Mgr*
EMP: 90
SALES (corp-wide): 103.3B **Publicly Held**
SIC: 7382 7373 Protective devices, security; systems engineering, computer related
PA: Hp Inc.
1501 Page Mill Rd
Palo Alto CA 94304
650 857-1501

(P-16891)
ID ANALYTICS LLC
15253 Ave Of Science, San Diego (92128-3437)
PHONE 858 312-6200
Scott Carter, *CEO*
Peter Boyes, *COO*
George Gelly, *Officer*
Daniel Rawlings, *Officer*
Steve Dyrhall, *Vice Pres*
EMP: 140 **EST:** 2002
SQ FT: 32,000
SALES (est): 22MM
SALES (corp-wide): 587.4MM **Publicly Held**
WEB: www.idanalytics.com
SIC: 7382 Protective devices, security
PA: Lifelock, Inc.
60 E Rio Salado Pkwy # 400
Tempe AZ 85281
480 682-5100

(P-16892)
INTREPID SECURITY SOLUTIONS
1999 S Bascom Ave Ste 700, Campbell (95008-2205)
PHONE 855 379-2223
Rico Sciaky, *CEO*
EMP: 50
SQ FT: 150
SALES: 1MM **Privately Held**
SIC: 7382 Security systems services

(P-16893)
KERN SECURITY CORPORATION
Also Called: Kern Security Systems
2701 Fruitvale Ave, Bakersfield (93308-5905)
PHONE 661 363-6874
John Affeld, *President*
Ronald C McVicar, *CFO*
EMP: 100
SQ FT: 4,000
SALES (est): 7.6MM
SALES (corp-wide): 39.6MM **Privately Held**
WEB: www.kernsecurity.com
SIC: 7382 5999 1731 Burglar alarm maintenance & monitoring; fire alarm maintenance & monitoring; alarm signal systems; closed circuit television installation
PA: Security Signal Devices, Inc.
1740 N Lemon St
Anaheim CA 92801
714 888-6230

(P-16894)
KIMBERLITE CORPORATION
Sonitrol of Stockton
3728 Imperial Way, Stockton (95215-9686)
PHONE 209 948-2551
Russ Borse, *Manager*
Kenneth Berry, *General Mgr*
EMP: 55
SQ FT: 6,500
SALES (corp-wide): 11.5MM **Privately Held**
SIC: 7382 1731 7359 5063 Burglar alarm maintenance & monitoring; fire detection & burglar alarm systems specialization; electronic equipment rental, except computers; burglary alarm systems
PA: Kimberlite Corporation
3621 W Beechwood Ave
Fresno CA 93711
559 264-9730

(P-16895)
KIMBERLITE CORPORATION (PA)
Also Called: Sonitrol Security Systems
3621 W Beechwood Ave, Fresno (93711-0648)
P.O. Box 9189 (93791-9189)
PHONE 559 264-9730
Joey RAO Russell, *CEO*
Thomas Patterson, *Ch of Bd*
Debbie Brown, *Principal*
Steve Deedon, *Principal*
Rachel Esquivel, *General Mgr*
EMP: 52
SQ FT: 3,500
SALES (est): 11.5MM **Privately Held**
SIC: 7382 Burglar alarm maintenance & monitoring; fire alarm maintenance & monitoring; protective devices, security

(P-16896)
KRATOS PUBLIC SAFETY & SECURIT (HQ)
4820 Estgate Mall Ste 200, San Diego (92121)
PHONE 858 812-7300
Eric M Demarco, *President*
David Knutson, *COO*
Deanna H Lund, *CFO*

PRODUCTS & SERVICES SECTION

7382 - Security Systems Svcs County (P-16920)

Laura L Siegal, *Treasurer*
Carol Clay, *Vice Pres*
EMP: 99
SALES (est): 38.1MM
SALES (corp-wide): 657.1MM **Publicly Held**
WEB: www.kratosdefense.com
SIC: 7382 Security systems services
PA: Kratos Defense & Security Solutions, Inc.
 4820 Estgate Mall Ste 200
 San Diego CA 92121
 858 812-7300

(P-16897)
LANTZ SECURITY SYSTEMS INC
4111 Las Virgenes Rd # 202, Calabasas (91302-1886)
PHONE.................................818 871-0193
EMP: 114
SALES (corp-wide): 9.7MM **Privately Held**
SIC: 7382
PA: Lantz Security Systems Inc
 43440 Sahuayo St
 Lancaster CA 93535
 661 949-3565

(P-16898)
LAW ENFORCEMENT OFFICERS INC
24000 Alicia Pkwy 17-229, Mission Viejo (92691-3929)
PHONE.................................855 477-3536
Erick Reyes, *CEO*
Chris Dancel, *Exec Dir*
EMP: 130
SALES (est): 4.5MM **Privately Held**
SIC: 7382 Protective devices, security

(P-16899)
LIFE ALERT EMERGENCY RESPONSE (PA)
16027 Ventura Blvd # 400, Encino (91436-2728)
PHONE.................................800 247-0000
Fax: 818 386-6393
Isaac Shepher, *President*
Felix Leung, *CFO*
Miriam Shepher, *Senior VP*
Richard Chen, *Vice Pres*
Tom Homsy, *Business Dir*
EMP: 175
SQ FT: 29,489
SALES (est): 42.7MM **Privately Held**
WEB: www.lifealert.com
SIC: 7382 5731 Confinement surveillance systems maintenance & monitoring; consumer electronic equipment

(P-16900)
LYONS SECURITY SERVICE INC
P.O. Box 18955 (92817-8955)
PHONE.................................714 401-4850
Kathleen Guidice, *President*
EMP: 75
SALES (est): 2.7MM **Privately Held**
SIC: 7382 Security systems services

(P-16901)
MOJO NETWORKS INC (PA)
339 Bernardo Ave Ste 200, Mountain View (94043-5232)
PHONE.................................650 961-1111
Fax: 650 961-1169
Rick Wilmer, *CEO*
Tushar Saxena, *Partner*
Gopinath Kn, *President*
Mike Anthofer, *CFO*
Freddy Mangum, *Chief Mktg Ofcr*
EMP: 118
SQ FT: 10,000
SALES (est): 23.7MM **Privately Held**
WEB: www.airtightnetworks.net
SIC: 7382 Protective devices, security

(P-16902)
NATIONAL SECURITY INDUSTRIES
1217 Del Paso Blvd Ste A, Sacramento (95815-3660)
PHONE.................................916 779-0640
EMP: 279 **Privately Held**
SIC: 7382 Security systems services

PA: National Security Industries
 940 Park Ave Frnt Frnt
 San Jose CA 95126
 -

(P-16903)
NAVTRAK LLC
20 Enterprise Ste 100, Aliso Viejo (92656-7104)
PHONE.................................410 548-2337
David Cozzens, *CEO*
Jack L Messman, *Ch of Bd*
Tim Taylor, *COO*
Kyle A Messman, *CFO*
Douglas Hawley, *Vice Pres*
EMP: 97
SQ FT: 8,000
SALES (est): 4.5MM
SALES (corp-wide): 131.6B **Publicly Held**
WEB: www.navtrak.net
SIC: 7382 Security systems services; protective devices, security
HQ: Telogis, Inc.
 20 Enterprise Ste 100
 Aliso Viejo CA 92656
 949 389-5500

(P-16904)
NETCONTINUUM INC
1454 Almaden Valley Dr, San Jose (95120-3801)
PHONE.................................408 961-5600
Varun Nagaraj, *CEO*
Gene Banman, *President*
Kurt Roemer, *Officer*
Pete Abrams, *Vice Pres*
Howard Doherty, *Vice Pres*
EMP: 80
SQ FT: 31,000
SALES: 7.4MM **Privately Held**
SIC: 7382 Security systems services

(P-16905)
NORSE CORP
Also Called: North Federal
104 La Mesa Dr, Portola Valley (94028-7510)
PHONE.................................650 513-2881
Howard A Bain III, *CEO*
Henry Marx, *President*
EMP: 94
SQ FT: 33,000
SALES (est): 3.4MM **Privately Held**
SIC: 7382 Protective devices, security

(P-16906)
ONTEL SECURITY SERVICES INC
708 L St, Modesto (95354-2240)
P.O. Box 579730 (95357-9730)
PHONE.................................209 521-0200
David Ackerman, *CEO*
David McCann, *COO*
Michael Ackerman, *CFO*
Roberta Gray, *Treasurer*
EMP: 71
SQ FT: 2,500
SALES: 2.4MM **Privately Held**
WEB: www.ontelsecurity.com
SIC: 7382 Security systems services

(P-16907)
OVERTON SECURITY SERVICES INC
39300 Civic Center Dr # 370, Fremont (94538-2338)
PHONE.................................510 791-7380
Andrew Overton, *President*
Vicki Greiner, *CFO*
Sandra Overton, *Vice Pres*
Keith Gonzales, *Security Dir*
Tyson Kanalulu, *Security Dir*
EMP: 215
SALES (est): 20MM **Privately Held**
SIC: 7382 Security systems services

(P-16908)
PACIFIC UNIFIED PD INC
Also Called: Pacific Unified Railroad Co
678 S Indian Hill Blvd, Claremont (91711-6002)
PHONE.................................310 817-3346
Aaron Echols, *CEO*
Jennifer Echols, *Vice Pres*
Micheal Garcia, *Director*

Pamela Pitre, *Manager*
EMP: 59
SQ FT: 12,500
SALES: 4.5MM **Privately Held**
SIC: 7382 Security systems services

(P-16909)
PACIFIC WEST SECURITY INC
Also Called: Sonitrol
1587 Schallenberger Rd, San Jose (95131-2434)
PHONE.................................801 748-1034
Fax: 408 293-0252
Paul Schumate, *President*
Sandra Oswalt, *Corp Secy*
Paul Shumate, *Exec VP*
Bill Powers, *IT/INT Sup*
Al Lujan, *Manager*
EMP: 60
SQ FT: 8,000
SALES (est): 6.1MM **Privately Held**
WEB: www.sonitrolsafetyzone.com
SIC: 7382 1731 Burglar alarm maintenance & monitoring; fire alarm maintenance & monitoring; fire detection & burglar alarm systems specialization

(P-16910)
PALADIN PRTCTION SPCALISTS INC
Also Called: Paladin Private Security
4741 Watt Ave Ste B, North Highlands (95660-5526)
PHONE.................................916 331-3175
Louis G Aljens, *CEO*
Trinidad Batad, *Officer*
Brandon Hefner, *Officer*
Matthew Carroll, *Vice Pres*
M Scott Johnson, *Vice Pres*
EMP: 135
SALES (est): 10.4MM **Privately Held**
WEB: www.paladinprivatesecurity.com
SIC: 7382 Security systems services

(P-16911)
PLEXICOR INC (PA)
3598 Cadillac Ave, Costa Mesa (92626-1416)
PHONE.................................714 918-8700
Robert Klemme, *CEO*
EMP: 50
SALES (est): 4MM **Privately Held**
SIC: 7382 5063 1731 Security systems services; electric alarms & signaling equipment; safety & security specialization

(P-16912)
POST ALARM SYSTEMS (PA)
Also Called: Post Alarm Systems Patrol Svcs
47 E Saint Joseph St, Arcadia (91006-2861)
PHONE.................................626 446-7159
William Post, *President*
Bill Post, *Owner*
Lois Post, *Treasurer*
Robert Jennison, *Business Dir*
Gina Post-Franco, *General Mgr*
EMP: 98
SQ FT: 10,500
SALES (est): 11.5MM **Privately Held**
WEB: www.postalarm.com
SIC: 7382 1731 5063 Burglar alarm maintenance & monitoring; fire alarm maintenance & monitoring; protective devices, security; fire detection & burglar alarm systems specialization; electrical apparatus & equipment

(P-16913)
PROTECT-FOR-LESS SECURITY SVCS
Also Called: Pfl Security
72877 Dinah Shore Dr, Rancho Mirage (92270-2763)
PHONE.................................760 343-1192
Norman Southerby, *CEO*
Evelyn Frances Southerby, *President*
EMP: 50
SALES (est): 2.8MM **Privately Held**
SIC: 7382 Security systems services

(P-16914)
PROTECTION ONE INC
6691 Owens Dr, Pleasanton (94588-3335)
PHONE.................................925 251-9088

Pete Sitch, *Branch Mgr*
Joshua Lartigue, *Consultant*
EMP: 50
SALES (corp-wide): 513.8MM **Privately Held**
WEB: www.protectionone.com
SIC: 7382 5063 Security systems services; alarm systems
PA: Protection One, Inc.
 1267 Windham Pkwy
 Romeoville IL 60446
 877 938-2214

(P-16915)
PUBLIC SECURITY INC
3860 Crenshaw Blvd # 223, Los Angeles (90008-1816)
PHONE.................................323 293-9884
Darrin Jenkins, *Principal*
Gen Anderl, *Director*
EMP: 50
SALES: 950K **Privately Held**
SIC: 7382 Protective devices, security

(P-16916)
REPUTATIONCOM INC (PA)
1001 Marshall St Fl 2, Redwood City (94063-2054)
PHONE.................................650 381-3056
Shrey Bhatia, *CEO*
Mark Phillips, *CFO*
Howard Bragman, *Vice Ch Bd*
Colleen McCreary, *Officer*
Rich Matta, *Senior VP*
EMP: 64
SALES (est): 25.1MM **Privately Held**
SIC: 7382 Security systems services

(P-16917)
SAFE SECURITY INC
2440 Camino Ramon Ste 200, San Ramon (94583-4326)
P.O. Box 5164 (94583-5164)
PHONE.................................925 830-4777
Paul F Sargenti, *President*
Jess Alvarado, *CFO*
Karen McQueen, *Marketing Mgr*
EMP: 455
SALES (est): 45.3MM **Privately Held**
SIC: 7382 7539 Burglar alarm maintenance & monitoring; automotive sound system service & installation

(P-16918)
SECTEK INC
Bldg 15, Mountain View (94035)
PHONE.................................650 604-1785
Wilfred D Blood, *Branch Mgr*
EMP: 55
SALES (corp-wide): 70.7MM **Privately Held**
WEB: www.sectek.com
SIC: 7382 Security systems services
PA: Sectek, Inc.
 1930 Isaac Newton Sq W # 100
 Reston VA 20190
 703 435-0970

(P-16919)
SECURITAS SEC SVCS USA INC
Also Called: Northern California Region
1650 Borel Pl Ste 227, San Mateo (94402-3508)
PHONE.................................650 358-1556
Fax: 650 341-1804
George King, *Branch Mgr*
Sanford White, *Branch Mgr*
Alexamaria Najarro, *Admin Asst*
EMP: 114
SALES (corp-wide): 9.2B **Privately Held**
WEB: www.securitasinc.com
SIC: 7382 Security systems services
HQ: Securitas Security Services Usa, Inc.
 9 Campus Dr
 Parsippany NJ 07054
 973 267-5300

(P-16920)
SECURITECH SECURITY SERVICES
3550 Wilshire Blvd # 920, Los Angeles (90010-2401)
P.O. Box 65097 (90065-0097)
PHONE.................................213 387-5050
Fax: 213 387-5044
Serge Tachdjian, *President*

7382 - Security Systems Svcs County (P-16921)

Marianna Amirkhanyan, *CFO*
Adriana Alvarez, *Admin Sec*
EMP: 110
SALES (est): 11.4MM **Privately Held**
WEB: www.securitechguards.com
SIC: 7382 Security systems services

(P-16921)
SECURITY ALARM FING ENTPS INC
2440 Camino Ramon Ste 200, San Ramon (94583-4326)
P.O. Box 5164 (94583-5164)
PHONE.................................925 830-4777
Fax: 925 830-5122
Paul Sargenti, *President*
Yolanda Zara, *Vice Pres*
EMP: 70
SQ FT: 20,000
SALES (est): 9.7MM **Privately Held**
WEB: www.safefinancial.com
SIC: 7382 6141 Security systems services; financing: automobiles, furniture, etc., not a deposit bank

(P-16922)
SECURITY ON-SITE SERVICES INC
8999 Greenback Ln Fl 2, Orangevale (95662-4650)
PHONE.................................916 988-6500
Martin A Steiner, *CEO*
Michael A McConnell, *COO*
EMP: 75 **EST:** 2013
SALES (est): 271.2K **Privately Held**
SIC: 7382 Security systems services

(P-16923)
SECURITY SIGNAL DEVICES INC (PA)
Also Called: Ssd Systems
1740 N Lemon St, Anaheim (92801-1047)
PHONE.................................714 888-6230
Fax: 714 449-9595
John F Affeld, *CEO*
Sheila Rossi, *Admin Sec*
Ron Texeira, *Opers Mgr*
EMP: 50 **EST:** 1969
SQ FT: 20,000
SALES (est): 39.6MM **Privately Held**
WEB: www.ssdsystems.com
SIC: 7382 1731 Security systems services; safety & security specialization; access control systems specialization; closed circuit television installation; fire detection & burglar alarm systems specialization

(P-16924)
SEGURA ENTERPRISES INC
Also Called: Segura Security Services
1011 W Mccoy Ln, Santa Maria (93455-1107)
PHONE.................................805 349-0550
Fax: 805 922-7286
Raul Segura Sr, *CEO*
EMP: 100
SQ FT: 1,500
SALES (est): 7.7MM **Privately Held**
SIC: 7382 7381 Security systems services; security guard service

(P-16925)
SENTINEL MONITORING CORP
220 Technology Dr Ste 200, Irvine (92618-2424)
PHONE.................................949 453-1550
Robert Contestabile, *President*
EMP: 100
SALES (est): 3.8MM
SALES (corp-wide): 76.7MM **Privately Held**
WEB: www.sentrak.com
SIC: 7382 Confinement surveillance systems maintenance & monitoring
PA: Sentinel Offender Services Llc
  201 Technology Dr
  Irvine CA 92618
  949 453-1550

(P-16926)
SENTINEL OFFENDER SERVICES LLC (PA)
201 Technology Dr, Irvine (92618-2400)
PHONE.................................949 453-1550

Mr Robert Contestabile, *CEO*
Tim Lewis, *Vice Pres*
Leo Carson, *Info Tech Mgr*
Julie Hunt, *Human Resources*
Hans Kintsch, *Manager*
EMP: 85
SQ FT: 20,000
SALES (est): 76.7MM **Privately Held**
WEB: www.sentrak.com
SIC: 7382 Confinement surveillance systems maintenance & monitoring

(P-16927)
SIMPLEXGRINNELL LP
12728 Shoemaker Ave, Santa Fe Springs (90670-6345)
PHONE.................................562 405-3817
Andy Bernot, *Manager*
Donna Talley, *Executive*
Richard Krapil, *Technology*
Stephanie Rheaume, *Sales Staff*
Rosi Zuloaga, *Sales Staff*
EMP: 150 **Privately Held**
WEB: www.simplexgrinnell.com
SIC: 7382 1731 1711 Security systems services; fire detection & burglar alarm systems specialization; plumbing, heating, air-conditioning contractors
HQ: Simplexgrinnell Lp
  4700 Exchange Ct
  Boca Raton FL 33431
  561 988-7200

(P-16928)
SKYHIGH NETWORKS INC
900 E Hamilton Ave # 400, Campbell (95008-0670)
PHONE.................................408 564-0278
Rajiv Gupta, *CEO*
Chris Cesio, *President*
Danielle Murcray, *CFO*
Trevor Eddy, *Vice Pres*
Srini Gurrapu, *Vice Pres*
EMP: 99
SALES (est): 1.3MM **Privately Held**
SIC: 7382 Security systems services
PA: Skyhigh Networks Technologies Private Limited
  No - 53 / B, Ward - 57
  Bengaluru KAR

(P-16929)
STAFF PRO INC (PA)
15272 Jason Cir, Huntington Beach (92649-1238)
PHONE.................................714 230-7200
Cory Meredith, *CEO*
Pete Wachob, *CFO*
Michael Absher, *Vice Pres*
Michelle Kidder, *Marketing Staff*
Otto Holz, *Director*
EMP: 700
SQ FT: 10,000
SALES (est): 81.2MM **Privately Held**
WEB: www.staffpro.com
SIC: 7382 8741 Security systems services; management services

(P-16930)
TALON EXECUTIVE SERVICES INC
151 Kalmus Dr Ste A103, Costa Mesa (92626-5900)
PHONE.................................714 434-7476
Ronald William, *CEO*
Jennifer Bales, *Office Mgr*
EMP: 50
SQ FT: 2,000
SALES (est): 4.7MM **Privately Held**
WEB: www.talonexec.com
SIC: 7382 8742 Security systems services; management consulting services

(P-16931)
TYCO INTEGRATED SECURITY LLC
104 E Graham Pl, Burbank (91502-2027)
PHONE.................................818 428-6669
Carlo Alarc, *Branch Mgr*
April Sumague, *Administration*
EMP: 200 **Privately Held**
WEB: www.adt.com
SIC: 7382 Burglar alarm maintenance & monitoring

HQ: Tyco Integrated Security Llc
  4700 Exchange Ct Ste 300
  Boca Raton FL 33431
  561 226-8201

(P-16932)
TYCO INTEGRATED SECURITY LLC
1120 Palmyrita Ave # 280, Riverside (92507-1744)
PHONE.................................951 787-0420
Fax: 951 787-8275
Tom Mannon, *Manager*
Gordon Gober, *Data Proc Staff*
EMP: 100 **Privately Held**
WEB: www.adt.com
SIC: 7382 Burglar alarm maintenance & monitoring; fire alarm maintenance & monitoring
HQ: Tyco Integrated Security Llc
  4700 Exchange Ct Ste 300
  Boca Raton FL 33431
  561 226-8201

(P-16933)
TYCO INTEGRATED SECURITY LLC
3870 Murphy Canyon Rd # 140, San Diego (92123-4446)
PHONE.................................561 988-3600
Greg Pavlicek, *Manager*
John Halverson, *Sales Staff*
EMP: 122 **Privately Held**
WEB: www.adt.com
SIC: 7382 Burglar alarm maintenance & monitoring; fire alarm maintenance & monitoring
HQ: Tyco Integrated Security Llc
  4700 Exchange Ct Ste 300
  Boca Raton FL 33431
  561 226-8201

(P-16934)
TYCO INTEGRATED SECURITY LLC
4650 Beloit Dr, Sacramento (95838-2426)
PHONE.................................916 565-2061
Fax: 916 922-3915
Amanda Matthews, *Sales/Mktg Mgr*
Mark Earl, *MIS Dir*
Jeff Murch, *IT/INT Sup*
Denise Capaldi, *Human Res Dir*
Rick Collins, *Sales Mgr*
EMP: 100 **Privately Held**
WEB: www.adt.com
SIC: 7382 Burglar alarm maintenance & monitoring; fire alarm maintenance & monitoring
HQ: Tyco Integrated Security Llc
  4700 Exchange Ct Ste 300
  Boca Raton FL 33431
  561 226-8201

(P-16935)
TYCO INTEGRATED SECURITY LLC
150 N Hill Dr Ste 3, Brisbane (94005-1024)
PHONE.................................650 634-9000
Dan Zahhos, *Manager*
Cara Denecour, *Opers Staff*
Brent Weber, *Sales Mgr*
EMP: 60 **Privately Held**
WEB: www.adt.com
SIC: 7382 Security systems services
HQ: Tyco Integrated Security Llc
  4700 Exchange Ct Ste 300
  Boca Raton FL 33431
  561 226-8201

(P-16936)
TYCO INTEGRATED SECURITY LLC
3825 Bay Center Pl B, Hayward (94545-3619)
PHONE.................................510 785-2912
EMP: 70 **Privately Held**
WEB: www.adt.com
SIC: 7382 Burglar alarm maintenance & monitoring; fire alarm maintenance & monitoring
HQ: Tyco Integrated Security Llc
  4700 Exchange Ct Ste 300
  Boca Raton FL 33431
  561 226-8201

(P-16937)
TYCO INTEGRATED SECURITY LLC
4725 Enterprise Way Ste 5, Modesto (95356-8967)
PHONE.................................209 574-2704
Damine Lee, *Manager*
Mike Farnsworth, *Div Sub Head*
Debbie Pearce, *Manager*
Rich Perez, *Manager*
EMP: 70 **Privately Held**
WEB: www.adt.com
SIC: 7382 Burglar alarm maintenance & monitoring; fire alarm maintenance & monitoring
HQ: Tyco Integrated Security Llc
  4700 Exchange Ct Ste 300
  Boca Raton FL 33431
  561 226-8201

(P-16938)
TYCO INTEGRATED SECURITY LLC
7565 Irvine Center Dr # 100, Irvine (92618-4919)
PHONE.................................714 223-2300
Fax: 714 256-6520
Nels Jenson, *Manager*
EMP: 135 **Privately Held**
WEB: www.adt.com
SIC: 7382 Burglar alarm maintenance & monitoring
HQ: Tyco Integrated Security Llc
  4700 Exchange Ct Ste 300
  Boca Raton FL 33431
  561 226-8201

(P-16939)
UCLA ASSOC STDNTS EVENT SERVS
308 Westwood Plz Rm A262a, Los Angeles (90095-8355)
PHONE.................................310 206-0832
Karen Noh, *Principal*
EMP: 50
SALES (est): 2MM **Privately Held**
SIC: 7382 Security systems services

(P-16940)
UDP USA
3003 N 1st St Ste 324, San Jose (95134-2004)
PHONE.................................408 519-5774
Chales Kwak, *President*
James Ahn, *President*
EMP: 50
SALES (est): 1.4MM **Privately Held**
SIC: 7382 Security systems services

(P-16941)
UNIVERSAL SERVICES AMERICA LP
777 N 1st St Ste 150, San Jose (95112-6347)
PHONE.................................408 993-1965
Darryl Coleman, *Branch Mgr*
EMP: 5011
SALES (corp-wide): 2B **Privately Held**
SIC: 7382 Security systems services
PA: Universal Services Of America, Lp
  1551 N Tustin Ave
  Santa Ana CA 92705
  714 619-9700

(P-16942)
VERNON SECURITY INC
15317 Parmnt Blvd Ste 201, Paramount (90723)
PHONE.................................562 790-8993
Fax: 562 790-8995
Jay Ellsworth, *President*
Dan Vincent, *Vice Pres*
Anissa Vincent, *Business Dir*
Alex Emeterio, *Business Mgr*
Elizabeth Getten, *Manager*
EMP: 100
SALES (est): 6.4MM **Privately Held**
SIC: 7382 Security systems services

PRODUCTS & SERVICES SECTION

7389 - Business Svcs, NEC County (P-16964)

(P-16943)
WARREN SECURITY SYSTEMS INC
1305 Francisco Blvd E, San Rafael (94901-5501)
P.O. Box 3210 (94912-3210)
PHONE.....................415 456-7034
Warren V Glass III, *President*
EMP: 50
SALES (est): 2.6MM **Privately Held**
SIC: 7382 1731 Burglar alarm maintenance & monitoring; protective devices, security; electrical work

7383 News Syndicates

(P-16944)
ASSOCIATED PRESS
221 S Figueroa St Ste 300, Los Angeles (90012-2553)
PHONE.....................213 626-1200
Fax: 213 346-0200
Anthony Marquez, *Manager*
Cecilia Land, *Executive*
Blair Godbout, *Admin Asst*
Eric Klimek, *Administration*
Roy Wu, *CIO*
EMP: 60
SALES (corp-wide): 568MM **Privately Held**
WEB: www.apme.com
SIC: 7383 News reporting services for newspapers & periodicals
PA: The Associated Press
450 W 33rd St Fl 16
New York NY 10001
212 621-1500

(P-16945)
BLOOMBERG LP
345 California St Fl 35, San Francisco (94104-2624)
PHONE.....................415 912-2960
Fax: 415 912-2961
Curtis McCool, *Manager*
Yuri Paholiouk, *Software Dev*
Ebru Boysan, *Sales Executive*
Joseph Ducote, *Director*
Jeff Taylor, *Editor*
EMP: 100
SALES (corp-wide): 3.6B **Privately Held**
WEB: www.bloomberg.com
SIC: 7383 News syndicates
PA: Bloomberg L.P.
731 Lexington Ave Fl Ll2
New York NY 10022
212 318-2000

(P-16946)
BUENA VISTA TELEVISION (DH)
Also Called: Buena Vista TV Advg Sls
500 S Buena Vista St, Burbank (91521-0001)
PHONE.....................818 560-1878
Fax: 818 566-6566
Janice Marinelli, *CEO*
Mort Marcus, *President*
Sal Sardo, *President*
Anne L Buettner, *CFO*
Jed Cohen, *Exec VP*
EMP: 129
SALES (est): 5.7MM **Publicly Held**
SIC: 7383 News feature syndicate
HQ: Disney Enterprises, Inc.
500 S Buena Vista St
Burbank CA 91521
818 560-1000

(P-16947)
GIGA OMNI MEDIA INC
1613a Lyon St, San Francisco (94115-2414)
PHONE.....................415 974-6355
Paul Walborsky, *CEO*
Surj Patel, *Vice Pres*
Michael Wolf, *Vice Pres*
Alison Murdock, *VP Mktg*
Nomaan Latif, *Sales Dir*
EMP: 75
SALES (est): 8.6MM **Privately Held**
SIC: 7383 News pictures, gathering & distributing; press service

(P-16948)
MARKETWATCH INC (DH)
Also Called: C B S Marketwatch
201 California St Fl 13, San Francisco (94111-5015)
PHONE.....................415 439-6400
Fax: 415 392-1972
Larry S Kramer, *Ch of Bd*
Kathleen B Yates, *President*
Jeni Halpern, *CFO*
Paul Mattison, *CFO*
Joan Platt, *CFO*
EMP: 51
SQ FT: 24,000
SALES (est): 12.9MM
SALES (corp-wide): 8.2B **Publicly Held**
WEB: www.marketwatch.com
SIC: 7383 News ticker service
HQ: Dow Jones & Company, Inc.
1211 Avenue Of The Americ
New York NY 10036
609 627-2999

(P-16949)
MARKETWIRE INC (DH)
100 N Sepulveda Blvd, El Segundo (90245-4359)
PHONE.....................310 765-3200
Fax: 310 765-3297
Michael Nowlan, *President*
James H Delaney, *COO*
Stephen Devito, *CFO*
Michael Shuler, *Senior VP*
Suresh Kumar, *Vice Pres*
EMP: 55 **EST:** 1998
SALES (est): 15.9MM **Privately Held**
WEB: www.marketwire.com
SIC: 7383 Press service
HQ: Marketwired Canada Limited
25 York St Suite 900
Toronto ON M5J 2
416 362-0885

7384 Photofinishing Labs

(P-16950)
ICON EXPOSURE INC
5450 Wilshire Blvd, Los Angeles (90036-4218)
PHONE.....................323 933-1666
Ramesh Venugopal, *President*
Jim Ostermann, *Manager*
EMP: 57 **EST:** 1998
SQ FT: 11,600
SALES (est): 4.7MM **Privately Held**
SIC: 7384 Photofinishing laboratory

(P-16951)
IDEA BITS LLC
Also Called: Behappy.me
19749 Dearborn St, Chatsworth (91311-6510)
PHONE.....................818 736-5361
Lauris Liberts, *Mng Member*
Davis Siksnans, *Founder*
EMP: 60
SQ FT: 5,000
SALES (est): 900K **Privately Held**
SIC: 7384 Film developing & printing

(P-16952)
J H MADDOCKS PHOTOGRAPHY
Also Called: Photocenter Imaging
40 E Verdugo Ave, Burbank (91502-1931)
PHONE.....................818 842-7150
Fax: 818 842-7423
Joe H Maddocks, *President*
Janet Maddocks, *Shareholder*
Vance Maddocks, *CEO*
Scott Maddocks, *Vice Pres*
Boris Winogradow, *Vice Pres*
EMP: 61
SQ FT: 15,000
SALES (est): 4.1MM **Privately Held**
WEB: www.photocenter.net
SIC: 7384 Film processing & finishing laboratory; film developing & printing

(P-16953)
JAKE HEY INCORPORATED (PA)
Also Called: A & I Color Laboratory
257 S Lake St, Burbank (91502-2111)
PHONE.....................323 856-5255
Fax: 323 461-7154

EMP: 80
SQ FT: 16,000
SALES (est): 6.7MM **Privately Held**
SIC: 7384

(P-16954)
PHOTO TLC INC
3925 Cypress Dr, Petaluma (94954-5900)
PHONE.....................415 462-0010
Fax: 415 241-7243
Ed Bernstein, *CEO*
Mike Bishop, *Vice Pres*
Barbara Day, *Office Mgr*
Laura McHugh, *Human Res Dir*
Joe Ording, *Cust Svc Dir*
EMP: 125
SQ FT: 30,000
SALES (est): 4.8MM **Privately Held**
SIC: 7384 Photographic services

(P-16955)
PICTURE IT ON CANVAS INC
12525 Stowe Dr, Poway (92064-6805)
PHONE.....................858 679-1200
Robert McKeon, *CEO*
Monica Denosta, *Senior VP*
Merete McCarthy, *Human Res Mgr*
Veronica Velarde, *Cust Mgr*
Tricia Barnes, *Manager*
EMP: 65
SQ FT: 33,000
SALES (est): 10MM **Privately Held**
SIC: 7384 Photograph developing & retouching

(P-16956)
SHAKE SMART INC
4640 Cass St Unit 90488, San Diego (92169-7101)
PHONE.....................661 993-7383
Kevin Gelfand, *President*
EMP: 74
SALES (est): 950K **Privately Held**
SIC: 7384 Home movies, developing & processing

(P-16957)
SHUTTERFLY INC (PA)
2800 Bridge Pkwy Ste 100, Redwood City (94065-1193)
PHONE.....................650 610-5200
Fax: 650 654-1299
Christopher North, *President*
Michael Pope, *CFO*
Michael W Pope, *CFO*
John Boris, *Chief Mktg Ofcr*
Ishantha Lokuge,
EMP: 148
SQ FT: 100,000
SALES: 1B **Publicly Held**
WEB: www.shutterfly.com
SIC: 7384 Photofinish laboratories; film developing & printing

(P-16958)
SUPER PHOTO LABORATORY INC
Also Called: Super Color Labs
979 N La Brea Ave, West Hollywood (90038-2321)
PHONE.....................323 512-0247
Fax: 323 436-0588
Richard Kung, *President*
Josephine Kung, *Treasurer*
David Chang, *Vice Pres*
Wendy Hwang, *Executive*
May Chang, *Admin Sec*
EMP: 55
SQ FT: 7,500
SALES (est): 4MM **Privately Held**
SIC: 7384 Photofinish laboratories

(P-16959)
TECHNICOLOR INC
Also Called: Technicolor Lab
2255 N Ontario St Ste 180, Burbank (91504-4509)
PHONE.....................818 260-4577
Joe Berchtold, *President*
Jordan Jacobs, *Vice Pres*
Vina Villavivencio, *Human Res Mgr*
EMP: 400
SALES (est): 38.4MM **Privately Held**
SIC: 7384 Photofinish laboratories

7389 Business Svcs, NEC

(P-16960)
A F EVANS COMPANY INC
Also Called: Byron Park
1700 Tice Valley Blvd Ofc, Walnut Creek (94595-1654)
PHONE.....................925 937-1700
Fax: 925 937-0348
Kirsten Korhsege, *Manager*
EMP: 70
SALES (corp-wide): 74.7MM **Privately Held**
WEB: www.afevans.com
SIC: 7389 Personal service agents, brokers & bureaus
PA: A. F. Evans Company, Inc.
2033 N Main St Ste 340
Walnut Creek CA 94596
510 891-9400

(P-16961)
A J PARENT COMPANY INC (PA)
Also Called: Americas Printer.com
6910 Aragon Cir Ste 6, Buena Park (90620-8103)
PHONE.....................714 521-1100
Arthur Parent, *CEO*
Melynda Bryan, *Human Res Dir*
Ray West, *Opers Mgr*
Michael Santoro, *Sales Mgr*
Greg Johnson, *Manager*
EMP: 67 **EST:** 1997
SALES (est): 17.5MM **Privately Held**
WEB: www.americaprinter.com
SIC: 7389 2752 Printers' services: folding, collating; commercial printing, lithographic

(P-16962)
AAA RESTAURANT FIRE CTRL INC
Also Called: AAA Fire Protection Service
30113 Union City Blvd, Union City (94587-1511)
P.O. Box 3626, Hayward (94540-3626)
PHONE.....................510 786-9555
Fax: 650 785-6717
Brent Patterson, *President*
Jeanne Patterson, *Treasurer*
Karen Patterson, *Treasurer*
Brian Patterson, *Vice Pres*
Charisse Filteau, *Office Mgr*
EMP: 90
SQ FT: 10,000
SALES (est): 10.6MM **Privately Held**
WEB: www.aaafireprotection.com
SIC: 7389 Fire extinguisher servicing

(P-16963)
AARON THOMAS COMPANY INC (PA)
7421 Chapman Ave, Garden Grove (92841-2115)
PHONE.....................714 894-4468
James T Chang, *Ch of Bd*
Thomas Bacon, *President*
Linda Bacon, *Treasurer*
Brian Robinson, *Principal*
Jim McCornack, *Division Mgr*
EMP: 125
SQ FT: 207,000
SALES (est): 44.4MM **Privately Held**
WEB: www.packaging.com
SIC: 7389 Packaging & labeling services

(P-16964)
ABSOLUTDATA TECHNOLOGIES INC
1851 Harbor Bay Pkwy # 125, Alameda (94502-3016)
PHONE.....................510 748-9922
Anil Kaul, *President*
Gaurav Rastogi, *Senior VP*
Rangan Bandyopadhyay, *Vice Pres*
Sudeshna Datta, *Vice Pres*
Suhale Kapoor, *Vice Pres*
EMP: 75
SQ FT: 1,600
SALES (est): 7.4MM **Privately Held**
WEB: www.absolutdata.com
SIC: 7389 7374 Personal service agents, brokers & bureaus; data processing service

7389 - Business Svcs, NEC County (P-16965)

PRODUUCTS & SERVICES SECTION

(P-16965)
ABSOLUTE EXHIBITS INC (PA)
Also Called: Meroform Systems USA
1382 Valencia Ave Ste H, Tustin (92780-6472)
PHONE.................................714 685-2800
Todd Koren, *President*
Kirk Cole, *CFO*
Jan Koren, *Co-President*
Sharon Allstun, *Office Mgr*
Tracy Huynh, *Controller*
EMP: 65
SQ FT: 15,500
SALES (est): 12MM **Privately Held**
WEB: www.absoluteexhibits.com
SIC: 7389 Promoters of shows & exhibitions

(P-16966)
ACCO ENGINEERED SYSTEMS INC
6446 E Washington Blvd, Commerce (90040-1820)
PHONE.................................323 201-0931
Matt Deluca, *Principal*
EMP: 50
SALES (corp-wide): 765MM **Privately Held**
SIC: 7389 Automobile recovery service
PA: Acco Engineered Systems, Inc.
   6265 San Fernando Rd
   Glendale CA 91201
   818 244-6571

(P-16967)
ACCT HOLDINGS LLC
5949 Fair Oaks Blvd, Carmichael (95608-5221)
PHONE.................................916 971-1981
EMP: 594
SALES (corp-wide): 347.8MM **Privately Held**
SIC: 7389 Telemarketing services
PA: Acct Holdings Llc
   1235 Westlakes Dr Ste 160
   Berwyn PA 19312
   610 695-0500

(P-16968)
ACCU-COUNT INVENTORY SVCS INC
Also Called: MSI Invntory Srvce-Los Angeles
1024 N Citrus Ave, Covina (91722-2739)
P.O. Box 814, Moorpark (93020-0814)
PHONE.................................805 231-6310
Mike M Naderi, *President*
EMP: 59
SQ FT: 800
SALES: 945.5K **Privately Held**
SIC: 7389 Inventory computing service

(P-16969)
ACTION SPORTS RETAILER
Also Called: Asr
31910 Del Obispo St # 200, San Juan Capistrano (92675-3182)
PHONE.................................949 226-5744
Greg Farrar, *Principal*
Michael Alicea, *Vice Pres*
Derek Irwin, *Vice Pres*
Mary Sustek, *Vice Pres*
EMP: 60
SALES (est): 1.6MM **Privately Held**
SIC: 7389 Trade show arrangement

(P-16970)
ACTIVE STORAGE INC
2295 Jefferson St, Torrance (90501-3302)
PHONE.................................818 709-1133
Alex Grossman, *CEO*
Steve Rizzone, *CEO*
Jane Wike, *CFO*
Mark Lonsdale, *Senior VP*
Jim Wayda, *Vice Pres*
EMP: 50
SALES (est): 6.3MM **Privately Held**
SIC: 7389 Document storage service

(P-16971)
ADMINISTRATIVE SYSTEMS INC
1651 Response Rd Ste 350, Sacramento (95815-5255)
P.O. Box 15437 (95851-0437)
PHONE.................................916 563-1121
Fax: 916 929-2939
Donald J Robinson, *President*
Geraldine M Fong, *Corp Secy*
Chip Moore, *Senior VP*
Keith Crane, *Vice Pres*
James R Powell, *Vice Pres*
EMP: 75
SALES (est): 11.5MM **Privately Held**
WEB: www.asipay.com
SIC: 7389 Personal service agents, brokers & bureaus

(P-16972)
ADVANCED COMMUNICATION SERVICE
Also Called: Fphs2
2650 Flora Spiegel Way, Corona (92881-3560)
PHONE.................................909 210-9328
Eddie Feghali, *President*
Jason Mokbel, *Exec VP*
William Scruggs, *Vice Pres*
Jon Harb, *Council Mbr*
EMP: 121
SQ FT: 2,400
SALES (est): 3.1MM **Privately Held**
SIC: 7389 Personal service agents, brokers & bureaus

(P-16973)
AFFILIATED COMMUNICATIONS INC
Also Called: Alert Communications
3601 Calle Tecate Ste 200, Camarillo (93012-5058)
P.O. Box 5720, Ventura (93005-0720)
PHONE.................................805 650-4949
Richard Starr, *President*
Monte L Widders, *Vice Pres*
Jona Sanford, *Engineer*
Sandra Mondragon,
Frances Starr, *Sales Dir*
EMP: 50
SQ FT: 5,000
SALES (est): 8.3MM **Privately Held**
WEB: www.alertcommunications.com
SIC: 7389 5999 Telephone answering service; telephone & communication equipment

(P-16974)
AFFINITY AUTO PROGRAMS INC
Also Called: Costco Auto Program
10251 Vista Cerento Pkwy Ste 300, San Diego (92121)
PHONE.................................858 643-9324
Jeff Skeen, *President*
Bill Gregory, *President*
Gary Drean, *COO*
Chris Moreno, *Web Dvlpr*
Huyen Huynh, *Technician*
EMP: 80
SQ FT: 34,000
SALES (est): 7.8MM **Privately Held**
WEB: www.costcoauto.com
SIC: 7389 Advertising, promotional & trade show services

(P-16975)
AGENCY FOR PERFORMING ARTS INC (PA)
405 S Beverly Dr Ste 500, Beverly Hills (90212-4425)
PHONE.................................310 557-9049
James Gosnell, *President*
Julie Shapiro, *Senior VP*
Manfred Westphal, *Senior VP*
Lindsay Howard, *Vice Pres*
Nikki Angel, *Executive Asst*
EMP: 100 **EST:** 1962
SALES (est): 28.6MM **Privately Held**
WEB: www.apa-agency.com
SIC: 7389 Artists' agents & brokers

(P-16976)
ALBANY INVENTORY SERVICES
11490 Burbank Blvd Ste 1, North Hollywood (91601-2391)
PHONE.................................818 505-8138
Fax: 818 461-1765
Marykay Connors, *President*
EMP: 50
SALES (est): 3.2MM **Privately Held**
SIC: 7389 Inventory stocking service

(P-16977)
ALEGRECARE INC
1375 Sutter St Ste 110, San Francisco (94109-5465)
PHONE.................................415 974-3530
Charles Symes II, *President*
EMP: 400 **EST:** 2014
SALES (est): 258K **Privately Held**
SIC: 7389

(P-16978)
ALFREDS PICTURES FRAMES INC
Also Called: Heather Ann Creations
1580 Sunflower Ave, Costa Mesa (92626-1511)
PHONE.................................714 434-4838
Fax: 714 434-4842
Pat Cochrane, *President*
Ron Thomas, *Marketing Mgr*
Sandra Adams, *Manager*
EMP: 50
SQ FT: 40,000
SALES (est): 5.5MM **Privately Held**
WEB: www.heatherann.com
SIC: 7389 Interior decorating

(P-16979)
ALL-PRO BAIL BONDS INC (PA)
512 Via De La Valle # 301, Solana Beach (92075-2715)
PHONE.................................858 481-1200
Steffan Gibbs, *President*
EMP: 56
SALES (est): 13.7MM **Privately Held**
SIC: 7389 Bail bonding

(P-16980)
ALL-PRO BAIL BONDS INC
530 Hacienda Dr Ste 104d, Vista (92081-6640)
PHONE.................................760 941-4100
Steffan Gibbs, *President*
Angela Jennings, *Controller*
Susan Shapiro, *Director*
Boon Ray, *Manager*
EMP: 100
SALES (est): 6.9MM **Privately Held**
SIC: 7389 Bail bonding

(P-16981)
ALORICA INC (PA)
Also Called: Priority One Support
5 Park Plz Ste 1100, Irvine (92614-8502)
PHONE.................................949 527-4600
Fax: 909 606-7708
Andy Lee, *President*
Kyle Baker, *President*
Gregory Hopkins, *Officer*
James Molloy, *Officer*
Art Dibari, *Exec VP*
EMP: 100
SALES (est): 4.8B **Privately Held**
WEB: www.alorica.com
SIC: 7389 Telephone services

(P-16982)
ALPHA SWIMMING POOL & SPA
2600 Athena Pl, Fullerton (92833-2005)
PHONE.................................714 879-4667
Kim Moon, *Owner*
EMP: 51
SALES (est): 1.6MM **Privately Held**
SIC: 7389 Swimming pool & hot tub service & maintenance

(P-16983)
ALTA RESOURCES CORP
Also Called: Tmw Marketing
975 W Imperial Hwy # 200, Brea (92821-3846)
PHONE.................................714 672-9700
Fax: 714 257-4299
Jim Maguire, *Manager*
Lorraine Alberts, *Technology*
EMP: 100
SALES (corp-wide): 138.2MM **Privately Held**
SIC: 7389 8742 Telemarketing services; training & development consultant; marketing consulting services
PA: Alta Resources Corp.
   120 N Commercial St
   Neenah WI 54956
   877 464-2582

(P-16984)
ALTAF ZAHID ENGINEERING SVCS
42051 Orange Blossom Dr, Temecula (92591-5543)
PHONE.................................760 481-9072
Shafiq Rassuli, *Director*
EMP: 50
SALES (est): 1.7MM **Privately Held**
SIC: 7389 Pipeline & power line inspection service

(P-16985)
ALTEC PRODUCTS INC (PA)
23422 Mill Creek Dr # 225, Laguna Hills (92653-7910)
PHONE.................................949 727-1248
Fax: 949 597-1200
Mark Ford, *CEO*
Brandt Morell, *President*
Frank Sansone, *CFO*
Mark Tague, *CFO*
Bill Brown, *Exec VP*
EMP: 80
SQ FT: 12,500
SALES (est): 18.2MM **Privately Held**
SIC: 7389 Telemarketing services; printing broker

(P-16986)
AMERICAN DEPT OF INSPECTIONS
Also Called: North America Marine Serveyers
1550 Washington Blvd, Fremont (94539-5100)
P.O. Box 3086 (94539-0308)
PHONE.................................510 683-9360
Gary Lee, *General Mgr*
EMP: 100
SALES (est): 3.1MM **Privately Held**
SIC: 7389 Industrial & commercial equipment inspection service

(P-16987)
AMERICAN HEALTH CONNECTION
8484 Wilshire Blvd # 501, Beverly Hills (90211-3243)
PHONE.................................424 226-0420
Yuriy Koltyar, *CEO*
Azabeh Williamson, *President*
EMP: 350
SQ FT: 3,000
SALES (est): 11.2MM **Privately Held**
SIC: 7389 Telemarketing services

(P-16988)
AMERICAS LEMONADE STAND INC
Also Called: Institutional Financing Svcs
5100 Park Rd, Benicia (94510-1136)
PHONE.................................707 745-1274
Fax: 707 746-1437
James M Cascino, *CEO*
Jose Ferreira Jr, *Ch of Bd*
Jack Hood, *CFO*
Marie Coppola, *Vice Pres*
Laura Kerkes, *Human Res Dir*
EMP: 250
SQ FT: 140,000
SALES (est): 14.5MM **Privately Held**
SIC: 7389 5094 5199 5145 Fund raising organizations; jewelry & precious stones; gifts & novelties; calendars; candy

(P-16989)
AMOEBA MUSIC INC
1855 Haight St, San Francisco (94117-2790)
PHONE.................................415 831-1200
Fax: 415 831-3585
Joe Goldmark, *Manager*
Allen Lewites, *Manager*
EMP: 70
SALES (corp-wide): 18.2MM **Privately Held**
WEB: www.ameebamusic.com
SIC: 7389 5999 5932 5735 Personal service agents, brokers & bureaus; posters; records, secondhand; video discs & tapes, prerecorded
PA: Amoeba Music Inc.
   2455 Telegraph Ave
   Berkeley CA 94704
   510 549-1125

PRODUCTS & SERVICES SECTION

7389 - Business Svcs, NEC County (P-17013)

(P-16990)
ANAHEIM/ORANGE CNTY VISITOR BU (PA)
Also Called: Visit Anaheim
800 W Katella Ave, Anaheim (92802-3415)
P.O. Box 4270 (92803-4270)
PHONE 714 765-8888
Fax: 714 991-8963
Jay Burress, *CEO*
Charles Ahlers, *President*
Christina Dawson, *Vice Pres*
Nancy Decious, *Vice Pres*
Amanda Sudduth, *Admin Asst*
EMP: 56
SQ FT: 3,000
SALES: 13.9MM **Privately Held**
SIC: 7389 Convention & show services; tourist information bureau

(P-16991)
ANDREW LAUREN COMPANY INC
15225 Alton Pkwy Unit 300, Irvine (92618-2345)
PHONE 949 861-4222
Mark Noonan, *Principal*
EMP: 189
SALES (corp-wide): 106.2MM **Privately Held**
SIC: 7389 5713 Interior design services; carpets
PA: The Andrew Lauren Company Inc
8909 Kenamar Dr Ste 101
San Diego CA 92121
858 793-5319

(P-16992)
ANDREW M MARTIN COMPANY INC
16539 S Main St, Gardena (90248-2720)
PHONE 310 323-2000
Ron Spoltore, *CEO*
Mike Gioseffi, *COO*
Lori Rieder, *Controller*
Anjali Desai, *Sales Associate*
Michael Gioseffi,
EMP: 50
SQ FT: 40,000
SALES (est): 6.1MM **Privately Held**
SIC: 7389 Packaging & labeling services

(P-16993)
ANSIRA PARTNERS INC
Also Called: Co-Optimum
5000 Van Nuys Blvd, Sherman Oaks (91403-1793)
PHONE 818 461-6100
Larry Feder, *Manager*
EMP: 60
SALES (corp-wide): 91.4MM **Privately Held**
SIC: 7389 7331 Press clipping service; direct mail advertising services
PA: Ansira Partners, Inc.
2300 Locust St
Saint Louis MO 63103
314 783-2300

(P-16994)
ANSWER FINANCIAL INC (HQ)
Also Called: Insurance Answer Center
15910 Ventura Blvd Fl 6, Encino (91436-2803)
PHONE 818 644-4000
Fax: 818 644-4466
Robert J Slingerland, *CEO*
Darren Howard, *Chief Mktg Ofcr*
Daniel John Bryce, *Senior VP*
Tom Capp, *Senior VP*
Peter Foley, *Senior VP*
EMP: 80
SQ FT: 45,000
SALES (est): 39.7MM
SALES (corp-wide): 35.6B **Publicly Held**
WEB: www.answerfinancial.com
SIC: 7389 6411 Brokers, business: buying & selling business enterprises; property & casualty insurance agent
PA: The Allstate Corporation
2775 Sanders Rd
Northbrook IL 60062
847 402-5000

(P-16995)
APAC CUSTOMER SERVICES INC
8885 Rio San Diego Dr, San Diego (92108-1624)
PHONE 619 298-7103
EMP: 563
SALES (corp-wide): 4.8B **Privately Held**
SIC: 7389 Telemarketing services
HQ: Egs Customer Care, Inc.
5085 W Park Blvd Ste 300
Plano TX 75093
972 943-7000

(P-16996)
APERIO GROUP LLC
3 Harbor Dr Ste 315, Sausalito (94965-2843)
PHONE 415 339-4300
Fax: 415 339-4301
Paul Solli,
Sandeep Gangadhara, *Opers Staff*
Patrick Geddes,
Guy Lampard,
Robert L Newman,
EMP: 56
SALES (est): 2.7MM **Privately Held**
WEB: www.aperiogroup.com
SIC: 7389 Financial services

(P-16997)
APPLEBEE LEASING INC
4 Maidstone Dr, Newport Beach (92660-4271)
P.O. Box 9878 (92658-1878)
PHONE 818 612-6218
William Applebee, *Administration*
EMP: 56
SALES (est): 3.1MM **Privately Held**
SIC: 7389 Personal service agents, brokers & bureaus

(P-16998)
APPLIED LANGUAGE SOLUTIONS LLC
1250 W Sunflower, La Habra (90631-9286)
PHONE 800 579-5010
Gavin Wheeldon, *Mng Member*
Simon Patrick, *CTO*
Kate Popova, *Project Mgr*
Liza Gardner, *Business Mgr*
Rick Kurick, *Business Mgr*
EMP: 102
SALES (est): 4.3MM **Privately Held**
WEB: www.appliedlanguage.com
SIC: 7389 Translation services

(P-16999)
AQUAMATIC FIRE PROTECTION INC (PA)
540 Garcia Ave Ste A, Pittsburg (94565-4950)
PHONE 925 753-0420
Wes Bookout, *CEO*
James Mason, *Vice Pres*
Robin Bookout, *Office Mgr*
Mary Bookout, *Admin Sec*
Teresa Lovos, *Admin Asst*
EMP: 50
SQ FT: 11,000
SALES (est): 10.6MM **Privately Held**
WEB: www.aquamaticfire.com
SIC: 7389 Fire extinguisher servicing

(P-17000)
AQUANTIA CORP (PA)
105 E Tasman Dr, San Jose (95134-1616)
PHONE 408 228-8300
Fax: 408 228-1190
Faraj Aalaei, *President*
Linda Reddick, *CFO*
Kamal Dalmia, *Senior VP*
Phil Delansay, *Senior VP*
Darren Engelkemier, *Vice Pres*
EMP: 72
SALES (est): 39.6MM **Privately Held**
WEB: www.aquantia.com
SIC: 7389 Design services

(P-17001)
ARCANA CORPORATION
118 Nopalitos Way, Santa Barbara (93103-3629)
P.O. Box 4400 (93140-4400)
PHONE 805 882-1305
Scot Smigel, *President*
EMP: 50
SALES (est): 3.3MM **Privately Held**
SIC: 7389 Hotel & motel reservation service

(P-17002)
ARRIVAL COMMUNICATIONS INC (DH)
1800 19th St, Bakersfield (93301-4315)
PHONE 661 322-7375
Fax: 661 281-2110
Richard Jalkut, *CEO*
Warren Heffelfinger, *President*
David Riordan, *COO*
Geoffrey Whynot, *CFO*
Tony Distefano, *Principal*
EMP: 75
SQ FT: 4,000
SALES (est): 6MM
SALES (corp-wide): 494.6MM **Privately Held**
SIC: 7389 Design services
HQ: U.S. Telepacific Corp.
515 S Flower St Fl 47
Los Angeles CA 90071
213 213-3000

(P-17003)
ASPIRIANT LLC
50 California St Ste 2600, San Francisco (94111-4704)
PHONE 415 371-7800
Raymond Edwards, *Branch Mgr*
EMP: 50 **Privately Held**
SIC: 7389 Financial services
PA: Aspiriant, Llc
11100 Santa Monica Blvd
Los Angeles CA 90025

(P-17004)
ASSIST 65 PLUS
111 W 7th St Ste 211, Los Angeles (90014-3933)
PHONE 323 557-4426
Kirbi Toure, *Partner*
EMP: 50
SALES (est): 1.1MM **Privately Held**
SIC: 7389

(P-17005)
ASSOCIATED LANDSCAPE
Also Called: Associated Group
2420 S Eastern Ave, Commerce (90040-1415)
PHONE 714 558-6100
Fax: 714 558-6175
Laurie Resnick, *President*
Patrick Skalka, *COO*
Lydia Monroe, *Vice Pres*
Greg Salmeri, *Vice Pres*
Sherri Cuono, *CIO*
EMP: 90
SQ FT: 30,000
SALES (est): 11.9MM **Privately Held**
WEB: www.associatedgroup.biz
SIC: 7389 0781 Plant care service; decoration service for special events; landscape services

(P-17006)
AT&T CORP
Rm 620, Anaheim (92805)
PHONE 714 284-2878
EMP: 311
SALES (corp-wide): 146.8B **Publicly Held**
WEB: www.swbell.com
SIC: 7389 Telephone services
HQ: At&T Corp.
1 At&T Way
Bedminster NJ 07921
800 403-3302

(P-17007)
AT&T CORP
5130 Hacienda Dr Fl 1, Dublin (94568-7598)
PHONE 925 560-5011
Louis Casali, *Principal*
Lloyd Van Antwerp, *Senior Mgr*
Kim Nguyen, *Director*
EMP: 305
SALES (corp-wide): 146.8B **Publicly Held**
SIC: 7389 Personal service agents, brokers & bureaus
HQ: At&T Corp.
1 At&T Way
Bedminster NJ 07921
800 403-3302

(P-17008)
ATLANTIC RECORDING CORPORATION
3400 W Olive Ave, Burbank (91505-5538)
PHONE 818 238-6800
Aaron Bay-Schuck, *Manager*
Carrie West, *Executive Asst*
EMP: 325
SALES (corp-wide): 2.9B **Privately Held**
WEB: www.ledzep.com
SIC: 7389 Music & broadcasting services
HQ: Atlantic Recording Corp
1633 Broadway Lowr 2c1
New York NY 10019
212 707-2000

(P-17009)
AUGMEDIX INC
1161 Mission St Ste 210, San Francisco (94103-1571)
PHONE 954 903-4993
Ian Shakil, *CEO*
Pelu Tran, *President*
Harisimran Khalsa, *Vice Pres*
Reda Dehy, *CTO*
EMP: 92
SQ FT: 6,636
SALES (est): 3MM **Privately Held**
SIC: 7389 Handwriting analysis

(P-17010)
AUTHORITY TAX SERVICES LLC
Also Called: Tax Problem Center
777 S Figueroa St # 1900, Los Angeles (90017-5817)
PHONE 213 486-5135
Wayne R Johnson, *President*
EMP: 60 **EST:** 2009
SALES (est): 3.9MM **Privately Held**
SIC: 7389 Legal & tax services

(P-17011)
AUTO BUYLINE SYSTEMS INC (PA)
Also Called: A B S Auto Auctions
1620 Fairway Dr, Colton (92324-3102)
P.O. Box 78086, Corona (92877-0136)
PHONE 909 881-7828
Thomas Harmon, *President*
Annette Harmon, *Admin Sec*
Bill Palmer, *Administration*
Gloria Orona, *Opers Mgr*
Kevin Skeldon, *VP Sales*
EMP: 50
SQ FT: 4,500
SALES (est): 21.9MM **Privately Held**
WEB: www.absbidsales.com
SIC: 7389 Authors' agents & brokers

(P-17012)
AUTOCRIB INC
2882 Dow Ave, Tustin (92780-7258)
PHONE 714 274-0400
Fax: 714 274-0399
Stephen Pixley, *CEO*
Wendy Perales, *Admin Asst*
Jennie Rose, *Administration*
Alane Pixley, *Info Tech Mgr*
Jim McMahon, *VP Opers*
EMP: 150 **EST:** 1999
SQ FT: 25,000
SALES (est): 25.4MM **Privately Held**
SIC: 7389 3581 Inventory computing service; automatic vending machines

(P-17013)
AUTUMN LP
1 Kaiser Plz Ste 505, Oakland (94612-3611)
PHONE 415 277-1245
John Menke, *President*
Mathew Foster, *Info Tech Dir*
Charles Bachman, *Counsel*
Laurence Lyon, *Manager*
Francis McCaffery, *Manager*
EMP: 60

7389 - Business Svcs, NEC County (P-17014)

SALES (est): 1.7MM **Privately Held**
SIC: 7389 Brokers, business: buying & selling business enterprises

(P-17014)
AVANTI AGENCY CORPORATION
282 S Anita Dr, Orange (92868-3308)
P.O. Box 5406 (92863-5406)
PHONE..............................714 935-0900
Kenneth Thompson, *President*
EMP: 400
SALES (est): 14.6MM **Privately Held**
SIC: 7389 Personal service agents, brokers & bureaus

(P-17015)
AVANTI HOSPITALS LLC
4060 Whittier Blvd, Los Angeles (90023-2526)
PHONE..............................323 268-5514
EMP: 660
SALES (corp-wide): 139.1MM **Privately Held**
SIC: 7389 Personal service agents, brokers & bureaus
PA: Avanti Hospitals, Llc
  222 N Splvd Blvd Ste 950
  El Segundo CA 90245
  310 356-0550

(P-17016)
AVANTI HOSPITALS LLC
2623 E Slauson Ave, Huntington Park (90255-2926)
PHONE..............................323 583-1931
EMP: 495
SALES (corp-wide): 139.1MM **Privately Held**
SIC: 7389 Personal service agents, brokers & bureaus
PA: Avanti Hospitals, Llc
  222 N Splvd Blvd Ste 950
  El Segundo CA 90245
  310 356-0550

(P-17017)
B RILEY FINANCIAL INC (PA)
21860 Burbank Blvd, Woodland Hills (91367-6477)
PHONE..............................818 884-3737
Bryant R Riley, *Ch of Bd*
Andrew Gumaer, *President*
Thomas J Kelleher, *President*
Phillip J Ahn, *COO*
Alan N Forman, *Exec VP*
EMP: 119
SALES: 112.5MM **Publicly Held**
SIC: 7389 Financial services; merchandise liquidators

(P-17018)
BAD BOYS BAIL BONDS INC (PA)
595 Park Ave Ste 200, San Jose (95110-2641)
PHONE..............................408 298-3333
Fax: 408 453-9993
Clifford J Stanley, *President*
Craig A Stanley, *Vice Pres*
Robert Venn, *General Mgr*
George Wallace, *General Mgr*
Bing Xu, *Controller*
◆ EMP: 75
SQ FT: 3,000
SALES (est): 16.9MM **Privately Held**
SIC: 7389 Bail bonding

(P-17019)
BAE SYSTEMS INC
10920 Technology Pl, San Diego (92127-1874)
PHONE..............................619 788-5000
Fax: 858 592-4400
Malcolm Homan, *Branch Mgr*
Jon Dorn, *Business Dir*
Steven Kelley, *Business Dir*
Bob Swenson, *Program Mgr*
Morgan Welch, *Program Mgr*
EMP: 600
SALES (corp-wide): 25.3B **Privately Held**
SIC: 7389 Personal service agents, brokers & bureaus
HQ: Bae Systems, Inc.
  1101 Wilson Blvd Ste 2000
  Arlington VA 22209
  703 312-6100

(P-17020)
BAKERSFIELD FAMILY MED GROUP
4570 California Ave, Bakersfield (93309-1143)
PHONE..............................661 861-1835
Alan Antiporda, *Branch Mgr*
EMP: 87
SALES (corp-wide): 24.4MM **Privately Held**
SIC: 7389 Personal service agents, brokers & bureaus
PA: Bakersfield Family Medical Group, Inc
  4580 California Ave
  Bakersfield CA 93309
  661 327-4411

(P-17021)
BAMKO LLC
11620 Wilshire Blvd # 610, Los Angeles (90025-1267)
PHONE..............................310 470-5859
Philip Koosed, *CEO*
Joey Chan, *Project Mgr*
Erin Flynn, *Project Mgr*
Emily Beach, *Human Res Mgr*
Sona Ross, *Marketing Staff*
EMP: 150
SALES (est): 1.6MM
SALES (corp-wide): 210.3MM **Publicly Held**
SIC: 7389 Advertising, promotional & trade show services
PA: Superior Uniform Group, Inc.
  10055 Seminole Blvd
  Seminole FL 33772
  727 397-9611

(P-17022)
BANKCARD SERVICES (PA)
21281 S Western Ave, Torrance (90501-2958)
PHONE..............................213 365-1122
EMP: 110
SALES (est): 19.7MM **Privately Held**
SIC: 7389 Financial services

(P-17023)
BATES SAMPLE CASE COMPANY INC
Also Called: Bates Display & Packaging
5995 W Park Dr, Chino Hills (91709-6301)
PHONE..............................951 371-4922
Fax: 951 371-5567
Robert Sherman, *President*
Emmagene Sherman, *Corp Secy*
EMP: 60
SQ FT: 36,000
SALES (est): 8MM **Privately Held**
WEB: www.batesdisplay.com
SIC: 7389 Packaging & labeling services

(P-17024)
BATTERY VENTURES LP
2884 Sand Hill Rd Ste 101, Menlo Park (94025-7072)
PHONE..............................650 372-3939
Chelsea Stoner, *General Ptnr*
Neeraj Agrawal, *General Ptnr*
Michael Brown, *General Ptnr*
Jesse Feldman, *General Ptnr*
Russell Fleischer, *General Ptnr*
EMP: 75
SALES (est): 3.2MM **Privately Held**
SIC: 7389 6799 Financial services; venture capital companies

(P-17025)
BAY AREA INTL TRANSLATION SVCS
46921 Warm Springs Blvd # 111, Fremont (94539-7933)
PHONE..............................510 673-8912
Nargis Radjatoba, *Owner*
EMP: 50 EST: 2014
SALES (est): 45.4K **Privately Held**
SIC: 7389 Translation services

(P-17026)
BENCHMARK-TECH CORPORATION
Also Called: Chaminade of Santa Cruz
1 Chaminade Ln, Santa Cruz (95065-1524)
PHONE..............................831 475-5600
Tom O'Shea, *Vice Pres*
Matt Tomaro, *Info Tech Mgr*
Mike P Butler, *Controller*
Michelle Reynolds, *Human Res Dir*
EMP: 200
SQ FT: 61,000
SALES (est): 11.6MM **Privately Held**
SIC: 7389 Convention & show services

(P-17027)
BENEFICENT TECHNOLOGY INC
Also Called: Benetech
480 S California Ave # 201, Palo Alto (94306-1609)
PHONE..............................650 644-3400
James R Fruchterman, *CEO*
Betsy Beaumon, *President*
Rob Brandon, *President*
Teresa L Throckmorton, *CFO*
Ann Harrison, *Comms Dir*
EMP: 50
SALES (est): 13.7MM **Privately Held**
WEB: www.benetech.org
SIC: 7389 Personal service agents, brokers & bureaus

(P-17028)
BERLITZ LANGUAGES INC
Also Called: Berlitz Language Center
9454 Wilshire Blvd # 100, Beverly Hills (90212-2931)
PHONE..............................310 858-8931
Anne Kelly, *President*
EMP: 50
SALES (corp-wide): 3.8B **Privately Held**
SIC: 7389 8299 Translation services; public speaking school
HQ: Berlitz Languages, Inc.
  7 Roszel Rd Fl 3
  Princeton NJ 08540
  207 828-3768

(P-17029)
BERSHTEL ENTERPRISES LLC (PA)
Also Called: We Pack It All
2745 Huntington Dr, Duarte (91010-2302)
PHONE..............................626 301-9214
Jack Bershtel, *President*
Sharon Bershtel, *CFO*
Gaby Gaiz, *Treasurer*
George Gellert, *Vice Pres*
Robert Gellert, *Vice Pres*
EMP: 145
SQ FT: 50,000
SALES (est): 33.7MM **Privately Held**
WEB: www.wepackitall.com
SIC: 7389 Packaging & labeling services

(P-17030)
BET-NAHRAIN INC
Also Called: Assyrian Cultural Center
3119 Central Ave, Ceres (95307-3632)
P.O. Box 4116, Modesto (95352-4116)
PHONE..............................209 538-4111
William Dadesho, *President*
Lydia Kino, *President*
Stanley Shummon, *Vice Pres*
EMP: 70
SQ FT: 19,179
SALES: 255.8K **Privately Held**
WEB: www.betnahrain.org
SIC: 7389 Personal service agents, brokers & bureaus

(P-17031)
BETTER LIVING BRANDS LLC
11555 Dublin Canyon Rd, Pleasanton (94588-2815)
P.O. Box 99 (94566-0009)
PHONE..............................888 723-3929
Shannon Mahler, *Manager*
Sean Barrett, *Vice Pres*
EMP: 200
SQ FT: 20,000
SALES: 20MM **Privately Held**
SIC: 7389 Packaging & labeling services

(P-17032)
BLAINE CONVENTION SERVICES INC
114 S Berry St, Brea (92821-4826)
PHONE..............................714 522-8270
Fax: 714 522-8271
Thomas W Blaine Sr, *President*
John Lucas, *General Mgr*
Marvin Castellaw, *VP Sls/Mktg*
Wendy Blaine, *Marketing Mgr*
EMP: 960
SALES (est): 72.7MM **Privately Held**
WEB: www.blaineconventionservices.com
SIC: 7389 7359 2542 Exhibit construction by industrial contractors; trade show arrangement; equipment rental & leasing; partitions & fixtures, except wood

(P-17033)
BLUE CHIP INVENTORY SERVICE
14852 Ventura Blvd # 112, Sherman Oaks (91403-3499)
PHONE..............................818 461-1765
Fax: 818 385-2900
Gerard J Walsh, *President*
Jeff Pitts, *CFO*
Carol F Edgington, *Vice Pres*
EMP: 70
SQ FT: 1,800
SALES (est): 3.8MM **Privately Held**
WEB: www.inventoryalliance.com
SIC: 7389 Inventory computing service

(P-17034)
BONHAMS BTTRFLDS ACTNEERS CORP (DH)
220 San Bruno Ave, San Francisco (94103-5018)
PHONE..............................415 861-7500
Robert Brooks, *CEO*
Malcom Barber, *CEO*
Pactric Meade, *COO*
Lydia Ganley, *Trust Officer*
Hadji Rahimipour, *Vice Pres*
EMP: 150 EST: 1793
SQ FT: 45,000
SALES (est): 36.8MM **Privately Held**
SIC: 7389 Auctioneers, fee basis
HQ: Bonhams 1793 Limited
  101 New Bond Street
  London W1S 1
  207 468-8214

(P-17035)
BONHAMS CORPORATION
220 San Bruno Ave, San Francisco (94103-5018)
PHONE..............................415 861-7500
Malcom Barber, *President*
EMP: 140
SALES (est): 8.7MM **Privately Held**
SIC: 7389 Auction, appraisal & exchange services

(P-17036)
BOOST MOBILE LLC (PA)
6316 Irvine Blvd, Irvine (92620-2102)
PHONE..............................949 451-1563
Fax: 949 789-4810
Matt Carter, *Mng Member*
Neil Lindsay, *Vice Pres*
Chun N Lian, *Program Mgr*
Ron N Comeau, *Web Proj Mgr*
Daryl Butler, *Mktg Dir*
EMP: 148
SALES (est): 35MM **Privately Held**
WEB: www.boostmobile.com
SIC: 7389 Telephone services

(P-17037)
BOSHART AUTOMOTIVE TSTG SVCS
1840 S Carlos Ave 15, Ontario (91761-8005)
PHONE..............................909 466-1602
Ken Boshart, *President*
Lynn Boshart, *Vice Pres*
EMP: 54
SQ FT: 13,567
SALES (est): 3.2MM **Privately Held**
SIC: 7389 7549 Inspection & testing services; emissions testing without repairs, automotive

(P-17038)
BOULEVARD ENTERTAINMENT INC
903 S Lake St Ste 202, Burbank (91502-2435)
P.O. Box 1188 (91507-1188)
PHONE..............................818 840-6969

PRODUCTS & SERVICES SECTION

7389 - Business Svcs, NEC County (P-17061)

Scott Jacobson, *President*
David Jacobson, *Vice Pres*
B R Axton, *Agent*
EMP: 108
SALES (est): 4.5MM **Privately Held**
WEB: www.blvdent.com
SIC: 7389 Telephone services

(P-17039)
BOX BROS CORP
825 Wilshire Blvd, Santa Monica
(90401-1809)
PHONE.............................310 394-8660
Mark Frydman, *Branch Mgr*
Konstantine Ossit, *Manager*
EMP: 50
SQ FT: 6,930
SALES (corp-wide): 14.1MM **Privately Held**
SIC: 7389 Mailbox rental & related service
PA: Box Bros. Corp.
  22124 Ventura Blvd Fl 2
  Woodland Hills CA 91364
  818 703-9193

(P-17040)
BRADFORD MESSENGER SERVICE
4955 E Andersen Ave # 118, Fresno
(93727-1543)
PHONE.............................559 252-0775
Fax: 559 252-8698
Liner Bluron, *Manager*
EMP: 60
SQ FT: 1,500
SALES (est): 1.6MM **Privately Held**
SIC: 7389 Courier or messenger service

(P-17041)
BRAGG INVESTMENT COMPANY INC (PA)
Also Called: Bragg Crane & Rigging
6251 N Paramount Blvd, Long Beach
(90805-3713)
P.O. Box 727 (90801-0727)
PHONE.............................562 984-2400
Fax: 562 984-2405
Marilynn Bragg, *CEO*
Mike Roy, *COO*
Mary A Pool, *Corp Secy*
Michael Willer, *Officer*
Scott Bragg, *Vice Pres*
◆ **EMP:** 580
SQ FT: 50,000
SALES (est): 278.7MM **Privately Held**
SIC: 7389 7353 1791 Crane & aerial lift service; heavy construction equipment rental; structural steel erection

(P-17042)
BROKER SOLUTIONS INC
11820 Pierce St, Riverside (92505-4403)
PHONE.............................951 637-2300
Neil Wachsberger, *Manager*
EMP: 68
SALES (corp-wide): 107.4MM **Privately Held**
SIC: 7389 Personal service agents, brokers & bureaus
PA: Broker Solutions, Inc.
  14511 Myford Rd
  Tustin CA 92780
  800 450-2010

(P-17043)
BURBANK WATER & POWER
164 W Magnolia Blvd, Burbank
(91502-1720)
P.O. Box 631 (91503-0631)
PHONE.............................818 238-3706
Fax: 818 238-3560
Ron Davis, *General Mgr*
John Hames, *Principal*
Evilia Waloejo, *Marketing Mgr*
Chris Friesen, *Supervisor*
EMP: 63
SALES (est): 9.7MM **Privately Held**
SIC: 7389 Decoration service for special events

(P-17044)
BUTTER PADDLE
Also Called: Butter Paddle, The
33 N Santa Cruz Ave, Los Gatos
(95030-5916)
PHONE.............................408 395-1678
Fax: 408 867-3601
Doris Beccia, *President*
Mumuna Ali, *President*
Mary Ann Jeffri, *Store Mgr*
EMP: 70 **EST:** 1967
SQ FT: 2,000
SALES (est): 5.5MM **Privately Held**
SIC: 7389 Fund raising organizations

(P-17045)
CADFORCE INC
10811 Wash Blvd Ste 302, Culver City
(90232-3660)
PHONE.............................310 876-1800
Fax: 310 437-7696
James Katz, *Vice Pres*
Robert W Vanech, *Principal*
Cliff Moser, *Manager*
EMP: 800
SALES (est): 35MM **Privately Held**
WEB: www.cadforce.com
SIC: 7389 Drafting service, except temporary help

(P-17046)
CALIFORNIA CREDITS GROUP LLC
251 S Lake Ave Ste 400, Pasadena
(91101-3051)
PHONE.............................626 584-9800
John Simpson,
Richard Mayer, *Info Tech Mgr*
Esmeralda Rivera, *Tax Mgr*
Heather Smith, *Opers Staff*
Karing Pao, *Manager*
EMP: 50
SALES (est): 6.2MM **Privately Held**
WEB: www.ccg.com
SIC: 7389 Personal service agents, brokers & bureaus

(P-17047)
CALIFORNIA HLTH COLLABORATIVE (PA)
1680 W Shaw Ave, Fresno (93711-3504)
PHONE.............................559 221-6315
Gary Erickson, *Chairman*
Deanne Blankenship, *Exec Dir*
Catherine Quinn, *Exec Dir*
Stephen Ramirez, *Exec Dir*
Daisy Lopez, *Program Mgr*
EMP: 68
SQ FT: 11,400
SALES (est): 7.6MM **Privately Held**
WEB: www.california.hometownlocator.com
SIC: 7389 Fund raising organizations

(P-17048)
CALIFORNIA SKATEPARKS
285 N Benson Ave, Upland (91786-5614)
PHONE.............................909 949-1601
Joseph M Ciaglia Jr, *President*
Bill Minadeo, *Vice Pres*
Colby Carter, *Design Engr*
Brian Pino, *Project Mgr*
Ashley Ciaglia, *Marketing Mgr*
EMP: 150
SALES (est): 4.2MM **Privately Held**
SIC: 7389

(P-17049)
CALIFORNIA TRAFFIC CONTROL
Also Called: California Traffic Ctrl Svcs
3333 Cherry Ave, Long Beach
(90807-4901)
PHONE.............................562 595-7575
Fax: 562 595-7797
Delores Kepl, *CFO*
Alan Jordan, *Opers Mgr*
EMP: 70
SALES (est): 5.9MM **Privately Held**
SIC: 7389 Flagging service (traffic control)

(P-17050)
CAMARILLO RANCH FOUNDATION
201 Camarillo Ranch Rd, Camarillo
(93012-5081)
PHONE.............................805 389-8182
Bruce Fuhrman, *Vice Pres*
EMP: 75
SALES (est): 520.8K **Privately Held**
SIC: 7389 Fund raising organizations

(P-17051)
CANON SOLUTIONS AMERICA INC
203 S Waterman Ave, El Centro
(92243-2228)
PHONE.............................800 323-4827
EMP: 80
SALES (corp-wide): 30.8B **Privately Held**
SIC: 7389 Advertising, promotional & trade show services
HQ: Canon Solutions America, Inc.
  1 Canon Park
  Melville NY 11747
  631 330-5000

(P-17052)
CANON SOLUTIONS AMERICA INC
2382 Faraday Ave Ste 250, Carlsbad
(92008-7262)
PHONE.............................760 438-6990
EMP: 79
SALES (corp-wide): 43.8B **Privately Held**
SIC: 7389
HQ: Canon Solutions America, Inc.
  1 Canon Park
  Melville NY 11747
  631 330-5000

(P-17053)
CARDFLEX INC
2900 Bristol St Bldg F, Costa Mesa
(92626-5981)
PHONE.............................714 361-1900
Andrew M Phillips, *President*
Bruce Quigley, *Controller*
EMP: 75
SALES (est): 9.3MM **Privately Held**
SIC: 7389 Financial services

(P-17054)
CARDSERVICE INTERNATIONAL INC
Also Called: C S I
4565 Industrial St Ste 7k, Simi Valley
(93063-3464)
PHONE.............................800 217-4622
Chuck Burtzloft, *Branch Mgr*
EMP: 650
SALES (corp-wide): 11.4B **Publicly Held**
WEB: www.creditcardresults.com
SIC: 7389 7371 6153 Credit card service; custom computer programming services; short-term business credit
HQ: Cardservice International, Inc.
  5898 Condor Dr 220
  Moorpark CA 93021
  805 648-1425

(P-17055)
CARDSERVICE INTERNATIONAL INC
Also Called: Csi
1538 W Commonwealth Ave, Fullerton
(92833-2754)
PHONE.............................714 773-1778
EMP: 56
SALES (corp-wide): 2B **Privately Held**
SIC: 7389
HQ: Cardservice International, Inc.
  5898 Condor Dr 220
  Moorpark CA 93021
  805 648-1425

(P-17056)
CARDSERVICE INTERNATIONAL INC (HQ)
5898 Condor Dr 220, Moorpark
(93021-2603)
PHONE.............................805 648-1425
Don Headlund, *President*
Charles Burtzloff, *CEO*
Brian Layfield, *CFO*
Lori Monaco, *Vice Pres*
Chris Palmer, *Administration*
EMP: 450
SQ FT: 34,000
SALES (est): 29.1MM
SALES (corp-wide): 11.4B **Publicly Held**
WEB: www.creditcardresults.com
SIC: 7389 6153 Credit card service; short-term business credit
PA: First Data Corporation
  225 Liberty St Fl 29
  New York NY 10281
  800 735-3362

(P-17057)
CARECREDIT LLC
2995 Red Hill Ave Ste 100, Costa Mesa
(92626-5984)
PHONE.............................800 300-3046
Kurt Grossheim, *Principal*
Mario Cozzi, *President*
Margarita Garza, *Comp Spec*
Melanie Graves, *Project Mgr*
Sean Temple, *Analyst*
EMP: 120
SQ FT: 12,000
SALES (est): 9.7MM
SALES (corp-wide): 13.6B **Publicly Held**
WEB: www.carecredit.com
SIC: 7389 8742 Financial services; banking & finance consultant
PA: Synchrony Financial
  777 Long Ridge Rd
  Stamford CT 06902
  203 585-2400

(P-17058)
CASECENTRAL INC (HQ)
Also Called: Casecentral.com
1055 E Colo Blvd Ste 400, Pasadena
(91106)
PHONE.............................415 989-2300
Fax: 415 989-2373
Christopher S Kruse, *President*
Jud Coleman, *Exec VP*
Randy Burrows, *Vice Pres*
Peter H Kruse, *Vice Pres*
Jay O'Connor, *Vice Pres*
EMP: 60
SALES (est): 9.4MM
SALES (corp-wide): 107MM **Publicly Held**
WEB: www.casecentral.com
SIC: 7389 4813 4226 Legal & tax services; ; document & office records storage
PA: Guidance Software, Inc.
  1055 E Colo Blvd Ste 400
  Pasadena CA 91106
  626 229-9191

(P-17059)
CASHEDGE INC
525 Almanor Ave Ste 150, Sunnyvale
(94085-3545)
PHONE.............................408 541-3900
McKenzie Lyons, *Principal*
David Cooper, *CTO*
Ron Pimental, *CTO*
Vijayamma Neena, *QC Mgr*
EMP: 100
SALES (corp-wide): 5.2B **Publicly Held**
WEB: www.cashedge.com
SIC: 7389 Financial services
HQ: Cashedge Inc.
  215 Park Ave S Ste 1300
  New York NY 10003
  212 656-9000

(P-17060)
CATATI ROHNERT PARK INC
1400 Magnolia Ave, Rohnert Park
(94928-8129)
PHONE.............................707 792-4531
Fax: 707 792-4513
Jane Wheeler, *Principal*
Alicia Cartwright, *Librarian*
Monica Fong, *Assistant*
EMP: 75
SALES (est): 2MM **Privately Held**
SIC: 7389 Personal service agents, brokers & bureaus

(P-17061)
CENTRAL PAYMENT CO LLC
2350 Kerner Blvd Ste 300, San Rafael
(94901-5597)
PHONE.............................415 462-8335
Matthew Hyman, *Managing Prtnr*
Zachary Hyman, *Managing Prtnr*
Eric Barth, *COO*
John Hinkle, *CFO*
Raymond Butner, *Vice Pres*
EMP: 99

7389 - Business Svcs, NEC County (P-17062)

PRODUDUCTS & SERVICES SECTION

SALES (est): 17.5MM **Privately Held**
WEB: www.centralpaymentcorp.com
SIC: 7389 Credit card service

(P-17062)
CENTRELINK INSUR & FINCL SVCS
Also Called: Centrelink Ins & Fincl Svcs
20750 Ventura Blvd # 300, Woodland Hills (91364-2338)
PHONE..................................818 587-2001
Fax: 818 704-9442
Barry Wolfe, *President*
Larry Shrednick, *IT/INT Sup*
EMP: 90
SALES (est): 3.7MM **Privately Held**
SIC: 7389 8741 Financial services; financial management for business

(P-17063)
CENTURY BANKCARD SERVICES
25129 The Old Rd Ste 222, Stevenson Ranch (91381-2281)
PHONE..................................818 700-3100
Fax: 818 700-3106
Scott Scherr, *President*
EMP: 55
SQ FT: 4,200
SALES (est): 3.7MM **Privately Held**
WEB: www.centurybankcard.com
SIC: 7389 Credit card service
PA: Pace Payment Systems, Inc.
    30 Burton Hills Blvd # 100
    Nashville TN 37215
    -

(P-17064)
CERAMIC DECORATING COMPANY INC
4900 Zambrano St, Commerce (90040-3034)
PHONE..................................323 268-5135
Chad A Johnson, *CEO*
Allan Johnson, *President*
W Allan Johnson, *CEO*
Burnell D Johnson, *Admin Sec*
Rita Ruiz, *Bookkeeper*
EMP: 50 EST: 1934
SQ FT: 30,290
SALES (est): 8.4MM **Privately Held**
WEB: www.ceramicdecoratingco.com
SIC: 7389 2396 Labeling bottles, cans, cartons, etc.; lettering service; automotive & apparel trimmings

(P-17065)
CESARS PRODUCTIONS
91 Miguel St, San Francisco (94131-2605)
PHONE..................................415 821-1156
Fax: 415 829-2278
Cesar Ascarrunz, *Owner*
EMP: 50
SALES (est): 2MM **Privately Held**
WEB: www.cesarsproductions.com
SIC: 7389 Music recording producer

(P-17066)
CETERA FINANCIAL GROUP INC (HQ)
200 N Sepulveda Blvd # 1200, El Segundo (90245-5605)
PHONE..................................800 879-8100
R Lawrence Roth, *CEO*
Adam Antoniades, *President*
Jon C Frojen, *CFO*
Susan Theder, *Chief Mktg Ofcr*
David Ballard, *Exec VP*
EMP: 148
SQ FT: 70,000
SALES (est): 270.2MM
SALES (corp-wide): 2.1B **Privately Held**
SIC: 7389 6282 Financial services; investment advisory service
PA: Aretec Group, Inc.
    405 Park Ave Fl 12
    New York NY 10022
    866 904-2988

(P-17067)
CHAMINADE LTD
Also Called: Chaminade At Santa Cruz
1 Chaminade Ln, Santa Cruz (95065-1524)
PHONE..................................831 475-5600
Fax: 831 476-4798

Tom O'Shea, *General Mgr*
James Birpo, *General Ptnr*
James Greggs, *General Ptnr*
Don Murchanson, *General Ptnr*
EMP: 200 EST: 1979
SQ FT: 12,000
SALES (est): 10.3MM **Privately Held**
SIC: 7389 Convention & show services

(P-17068)
CHAPMAN UNIVERSITY
625 N Glassell St, Orange (92867-6749)
PHONE..................................714 997-6821
Sukbae Tim, *Director*
EMP: 197
SALES (corp-wide): 400.1MM **Privately Held**
SIC: 7389 Printers' services: folding, collating
PA: Chapman University
    1 University Dr
    Orange CA 92866
    714 997-6815

(P-17069)
CHARLES SCHWAB CORPORATION
27580 Ynez Rd Ste A, Temecula (92591-4667)
PHONE..................................951 587-2840
EMP: 91
SALES (corp-wide): 6.3B **Publicly Held**
SIC: 7389 6282 6211 Financial services; investment advice; stock brokers & dealers
PA: The Charles Schwab Corporation
    211 Main St Fl 17
    San Francisco CA 94105
    415 667-7000

(P-17070)
CHERRY AVENUE AUCTION INC
4640 S Cherry Ave, Fresno (93706-5717)
PHONE..................................559 266-9856
Fax: 559 266-9439
William Mitchell, *President*
Neil Burson, *CFO*
Margaret Mitchell, *Treasurer*
EMP: 50
SQ FT: 1,500
SALES (est): 3.2MM **Privately Held**
WEB: www.cherryavenueauction.com
SIC: 7389 Auctioneers, fee basis

(P-17071)
CHICO CSU RESEARCH FOUNDATION
Csuc Bldg 25 Ste 203, Chico (95929-0001)
PHONE..................................530 898-6811
Richard Jackson, *Exec Dir*
Tony Peterson, *Administration*
Dan Devine, *Data Proc Staff*
Gail Hildebrand, *Project Mgr*
Fred Woodmansee, *Finance*
EMP: 2000
SQ FT: 15,000
SALES (est): 41MM **Privately Held**
SIC: 7389 Fund raising organizations

(P-17072)
CISCO WEBEX LLC (HQ)
Also Called: Webex.com
3979 Freedom Cir Ste 100, Santa Clara (95054-1248)
PHONE..................................408 435-7000
Fax: 408 435-7004
Subrah S Iyar,
Yugantar Saikia, *Exec VP*
Hesham Eassa, *Vice Pres*
Morris Porter, *Vice Pres*
Mitch Tarica, *Vice Pres*
EMP: 1108
SQ FT: 160,000
SALES (est): 169MM
SALES (corp-wide): 49.2B **Publicly Held**
WEB: www.webex.com
SIC: 7389 4813 Teleconferencing services; data telephone communications; voice telephone communications
PA: Cisco Systems, Inc.
    170 W Tasman Dr
    San Jose CA 95134
    408 526-4000

(P-17073)
CITY OF CHULA VISTA
276 4th Ave, Chula Vista (91910-2699)
PHONE..................................619 691-5137
EMP: 118
SALES (est): 7.2MM **Privately Held**
SIC: 7389 Financial services

(P-17074)
CITY OF FRESNO
Also Called: Fresno Convention Center
700 M St, Fresno (93721-2715)
PHONE..................................559 445-8200
Fax: 559 488-4634
Michael Swinney, *Director*
Gale Ash, *Social Dir*
Stephanie Carreiro, *Office Admin*
Raquel Gutierrez, *Accountant*
Stephanie Hoang, *Accountant*
EMP: 60 **Privately Held**
WEB: www.fresnocitizencorps.org
SIC: 7389 9111 Convention & show services; mayors' offices
PA: City Of Fresno
    2600 Fresno St
    Fresno CA 93721
    559 621-7001

(P-17075)
CITY OF LONG BEACH
Also Called: Building Inspection
333 W Ocean Blvd Fl 4, Long Beach (90802-4664)
PHONE..................................562 570-7298
Albert Sanchez, *Branch Mgr*
Craig Beck, *Director*
EMP: 300 **Privately Held**
SIC: 7389 Inspection & testing services
PA: City Of Long Beach
    333 W Ocean Blvd Fl 10
    Long Beach CA 90802
    562 570-6450

(P-17076)
CITY OF LONG BEACH
Also Called: Long Bch Convention Entrmt Ctr
300 E Ocean Blvd, Long Beach (90802-4825)
PHONE..................................562 436-3636
David Gordon, *Manager*
Penny Meloche, *Accounting Mgr*
Eric Schriver, *Finance*
Nathan Nguyen, *Controller*
Robert Samuelson, *Training Dir*
EMP: 300 **Privately Held**
WEB: www.polb.com
SIC: 7389 8611 6512 Convention & show services; business associations; nonresidential building operators
PA: City Of Long Beach
    333 W Ocean Blvd Fl 10
    Long Beach CA 90802
    562 570-6450

(P-17077)
CITY OF PALO ALTO
Also Called: Water Quality Control Plant
2501 Embarcadero Way, Palo Alto (94303-3326)
PHONE..................................650 329-2598
Richard Wetzel, *Branch Mgr*
Alice Ringer, *COO*
Jamie Allen, *Plant Mgr*
EMP: 70 **Privately Held**
SIC: 7389 9111 8748 Sewer inspection service; cloth cutting, bolting or winding; city & town managers' offices; ; business consulting
PA: City Of Palo Alto
    250 Hamilton Ave
    Palo Alto CA 94301
    650 329-2571

(P-17078)
CITY OF RIVERSIDE
Also Called: Riverside Convention Center
3485 Mission Inn Ave, Riverside (92501-3304)
PHONE..................................951 346-4700
Scott Megna, *General Mgr*
EMP: 100 **Privately Held**
SIC: 7389 Convention & show services
PA: City Of Riverside
    3900 Main St Fl 7
    Riverside CA 92522
    951 826-5311

(P-17079)
CITY OF SAN JOSE
Also Called: Conventions Arts & Entrmt
408 Almaden Blvd, San Jose (95110-2709)
PHONE..................................408 277-5277
Fax: 408 277-3535
Nancy Johnson, *Branch Mgr*
Janette Divoll, *CFO*
Nancy Kilgore, *Manager*
EMP: 300 **Privately Held**
WEB: www.csjfinance.org
SIC: 7389 9512 Convention & show services; land, mineral & wildlife conservation;
PA: City Of San Jose
    200 E Santa Clara St
    San Jose CA 95113
    408 535-3500

(P-17080)
CITY OF SUNNYVALE
221 Commercial St, Sunnyvale (94085-4509)
P.O. Box 3707 (94088-3707)
PHONE..................................408 730-7510
Fax: 408 736-1611
James Craig, *Superintendent*
EMP: 200 **Privately Held**
SIC: 7389 Field warehousing
PA: City Of Sunnyvale
    456 W Olive Ave
    Sunnyvale CA 94086
    408 730-7415

(P-17081)
CITY OF VISALIA
Also Called: Visalia Convention Center
303 E Acequia Ave, Visalia (93291-6341)
PHONE..................................559 713-4000
Fax: 559 713-4804
Wally Roeben, *General Mgr*
Brent Miller, *Officer*
Mike McCarthy, *Executive*
Teresa Villarrial, *Branch Mgr*
Kathy Fraga, *Systs Prg Mgr*
EMP: 60 **Privately Held**
SIC: 7389 Convention & show services
PA: Visalia, City Of (Inc)
    707 W Acequia Ave
    Visalia CA 93291
    559 713-4565

(P-17082)
CK ENTERPRISES INC
Also Called: World Tuned Radio
110 Copperwood Way Ste K, Oceanside (92058-3869)
PHONE..................................760 967-8863
Christopher Parks, *President*
EMP: 87
SALES (est): 2.5MM **Privately Held**
SIC: 7389

(P-17083)
CLUB SPORT OF FREMONT
46650 Landing Pkwy, Fremont (94538-6420)
PHONE..................................510 226-8500
Fax: 510 770-8945
Angela Grissar, *Business Mgr*
Guin Cloninger, *Partner*
EMP: 200
SALES (est): 13.8MM **Privately Held**
SIC: 7389 Artists' agents & brokers

(P-17084)
CMG FINANCIAL SERVICES
3160 Crow Canyon Rd # 400, San Ramon (94583-1368)
PHONE..................................925 983-3073
Christopher M George, *CEO*
Marshall Griffin, *CFO*
Todd Hempstead, *Senior VP*
Adam Millstein, *Senior VP*
Karen Queenan, *Senior VP*
EMP: 83
SALES (est): 15MM **Privately Held**
SIC: 7389 Financial services

(P-17085)
COACHELLA VALLEY MOSQUITO ABAT
43420 Trader Pl, Indio (92201-2089)
PHONE..................................760 342-8287
Fax: 760 342-8110
Branka Lothrop, *General Mgr*
Veronica Montoya, *Accountant*

PRODUCTS & SERVICES SECTION

7389 - Business Svcs, NEC County (P-17106)

Don Gomsi, *Manager*
EMP: 70
SQ FT: 23,000
SALES (est): 6.6MM **Privately Held**
WEB: www.cvmvcd.org
SIC: 7389 Personal service agents, brokers & bureaus

(P-17086)
COAST ENVIRONMENTAL INC
2221 Las Palmas Dr Ste J, Carlsbad (92011-1528)
PHONE 760 929-9570
Dan Hughes, *President*
Christopher Heitman, *General Mgr*
Andrew Laverty, *Project Engr*
Lisa Smith, *Manager*
Rich Nadeau, *Assistant*
EMP: 60
SQ FT: 25,000
SALES (est): 7.5MM **Privately Held**
WEB: www.coastenvironmental.com
SIC: 7389 Safety inspection service

(P-17087)
COASTAL CLOSEOUTS INC
Also Called: West Coast Rags
100 Oceangate Ste 1200, Long Beach (90802-4324)
PHONE 323 589-7900
Carl Jones, *President*
Walter Levoff, *COO*
Charles Bates, *Vice Pres*
Werner Werwie, *Vice Pres*
EMP: 52
SQ FT: 68,000
SALES (est): 4.1MM **Privately Held**
SIC: 7389 Textile & apparel services

(P-17088)
COASTAL INTERNATIONAL INC (PA)
Also Called: Coastal Intl Cnstr Svcs
3 Harbor Dr Ste 211, Sausalito (94965-1491)
PHONE 415 339-1700
Bruce Green, *CEO*
Bob Hill, *Vice Pres*
Rich Rebecky, *Vice Pres*
Shelley Cowperthwait, *Admin Asst*
Daniel Lecour, *Info Tech Dir*
EMP: 65
SQ FT: 12,000
SALES (est): 33.8MM **Privately Held**
WEB: www.coastlintl.com
SIC: 7389 1542 1522 Trade show arrangement; nonresidential construction; residential construction

(P-17089)
COMPUMAIL INFORMATION SVCS INC
4057 Port Chicago Hwy # 300, Concord (94520-1160)
P.O. Box 6756 (94524-1756)
PHONE 925 689-7100
Monte G Bish, *President*
Frank Fribley, *CFO*
Robert Hayashida, *Admin Asst*
Michelle Lee Chung, *Controller*
Kathy Butler, *Personnel Exec*
EMP: 75
SQ FT: 22,000
SALES (est): 11.1MM **Privately Held**
WEB: www.compumailinc.com
SIC: 7389 Printers' services: folding, collating

(P-17090)
COMWORK
Also Called: My Display Work
6489 Oak Cyn, Irvine (92618-5202)
PHONE 405 703-8889
Fax: 949 654-0401
Robin Wilson, *CEO*
Phil Pageau, *CFO*
Alice Raymond, *Director*
EMP: 50
SALES (est): 2.3MM **Privately Held**
SIC: 7389 Trade show arrangement

(P-17091)
CONCEPT GREEN ENRGY SLTONS INC
13824 Yorba Ave, Chino (91710-5518)
PHONE 855 459-6535
Liang Gao, *President*
Henry F Hsieh, *Principal*
EMP: 4000 **EST:** 2010
SALES (est): 98.4MM **Privately Held**
SIC: 7389 5211 Design services; energy conservation products

(P-17092)
CONSOLDTED FIRE PROTECTION LLC (HQ)
153 Technology Dr Ste 200, Irvine (92618-2461)
PHONE 949 727-3277
Fax: 949 727-3297
Rob Salek, *CEO*
Keith Fielding, *President*
Maddy Malin, *Executive*
Madie Melaan, *Admin Sec*
Jeff Murtari, *Info Tech Dir*
EMP: 800
SALES (est): 110.4MM
SALES (corp-wide): 400.9MM **Privately Held**
SIC: 7389 Fire protection service other than forestry or public
PA: Mx Holdings Us
153 Technology Dr Ste 200
Irvine CA 92618
949 727-3277

(P-17093)
CONTI LIFE COMM PLEA LLC
Also Called: Stoneridge Creek Pleasanton
3300 Stoneridge Creek Way, Pleasanton (94588-2200)
PHONE 925 227-6800
Francis X Rodgers, *Exec Dir*
Troy Bourne, *Vice Pres*
Eileen Rose, *Admin Asst*
Jodee Ayers, *Safety Mgr*
EMP: 51
SALES (est): 8.1MM **Privately Held**
SIC: 7389 Personal service agents, brokers & bureaus

(P-17094)
CONTINENTAL EXCH SOLUTIONS INC (HQ)
Also Called: Ria Financial Service
6565 Knott Ave, Buena Park (90620-1139)
PHONE 714 522-7044
Fax: 562 345-1828
Juan C Bianchi, *CEO*
Timothy A Fanning, *COO*
Mehdi Mahbavi, *CFO*
Anthony Grandidge, *Senior VP*
Cindy Ashcraft, *Vice Pres*
EMP: 148
SALES (est): 206.6MM **Publicly Held**
SIC: 7389 3578 6099 Credit card service; billing machines; money order issuance

(P-17095)
CONVERSE CONSULTANTS INC (HQ)
222 E Huntington Dr # 211, Monrovia (91016-8012)
PHONE 626 930-1200
Richard Gilbert, *President*
Thomas C Benson, *President*
Hashmi S Quazi, *President*
Steven O'Neil, *CFO*
Ruben L Romero, *CFO*
EMP: 50
SALES (est): 12.4MM
SALES (corp-wide): 16.5MM **Privately Held**
WEB: www.converseconsultants.com
SIC: 7389 8711 Inspection & testing services; consulting engineer
PA: The Converse Professional Group
717 S Myrtle Ave
Monrovia CA 91016
626 930-1200

(P-17096)
CORPORATE RISK HLDINGS III INC
Also Called: Hireright
3349 Michelson Dr Ste 150, Irvine (92612-8881)
PHONE 949 428-5839
John Fennelley, *CEO*
Stefano Malnati, *President*
Thomas Spaeth, *CFO*
Jim Weber, *Officer*
Brian Pierson, *Senior VP*
EMP: 1700
SALES (est): 10.2MM **Privately Held**
SIC: 7389 Personal investigation service

(P-17097)
COSCO FIRE PROTECTION INC
Also Called: 76
4990 Greencraig Ln, San Diego (92123-1673)
PHONE 858 444-2000
Fax: 858 444-2056
Alexander Hernandez, *Manager*
Rory Low, *Manager*
EMP: 75
SALES (corp-wide): 400.9MM **Privately Held**
WEB: www.coscofireprotection.com
SIC: 7389 Fire protection service other than forestry or public
HQ: Cosco Fire Protection, Inc.
29222 Rancho Viejo Rd # 205
San Juan Capistrano CA 92675
714 974-8770

(P-17098)
COUNTY OF LOS ANGELES
Also Called: Internal Services Dept
1100 N Eastern Ave, Los Angeles (90063-3200)
PHONE 323 267-2771
Linnette Bookman, *Superintendent*
Garrett Mayer, *Division Mgr*
Wanda Stjulian, *Division Mgr*
EMP: 200 **Privately Held**
WEB: www.co.la.ca.us
SIC: 7389 9631 Telephone services; communications commission, government;
PA: County Of Los Angeles
500 W Temple St Ste 375
Los Angeles CA 90012
213 974-1101

(P-17099)
COUNTY OF MODOC
Also Called: Treasurer/Tax Collector
204 S Court St Ste 6, Alturas (96101-4138)
PHONE 530 233-6223
Fax: 530 233-6500
Cheryl Knoch, *Treasurer*
Linda Wilson, *General Mgr*
EMP: 250 **Privately Held**
WEB: www.modoccounty.us
SIC: 7389 Tax collection agency
PA: County Of Modoc
202 W 4th St Ste A
Alturas CA 96101
530 233-6400

(P-17100)
COUNTY OF MONTEREY
Also Called: Telecommunications Dept
855 E Laurel Dr Ste D, Salinas (93905-1300)
PHONE 831 755-4944
Chin Lavonne, *Branch Mgr*
EMP: 100 **Privately Held**
WEB: www.montereycountyfarmbureau.org
SIC: 7389 Personal service agents, brokers & bureaus
PA: County Of Monterey
168 W Alisal St Fl 3
Salinas CA 93901
831 755-5040

(P-17101)
COUNTY OF MONTEREY
Also Called: Dept of Building Inspection
240 Church St Ste 116, Salinas (93901-2683)
P.O. Box 1208 (93902-1208)
PHONE 831 755-5027
Fax: 831 757-5792
Scott Hennessy, *Director*
EMP: 100 **Privately Held**
WEB: www.montereycountyfarmbureau.org
SIC: 7389 9111 8111 Building inspection service; county supervisors' & executives' offices; legal services
PA: County Of Monterey
168 W Alisal St Fl 3
Salinas CA 93901
831 755-5040

(P-17102)
CRAFTWORKS REST BREWERIES INC
600 Polk St, San Francisco (94102-3328)
PHONE 415 292-5800
EMP: 1829 **Privately Held**
SIC: 7389 Personal service agents, brokers & bureaus
PA: Craftworks Restaurants & Breweries, Inc.
8001 Arista Pl Unit 500
Broomfield CO 80021

(P-17103)
CREATIVE DESIGN CONS INC (PA)
Also Called: C D C
2915 Red Hill Ave G201, Costa Mesa (92626-7948)
PHONE 714 641-4868
Fax: 714 545-1834
Dana Eggerts, *CEO*
Brian Richardson, *Info Tech Mgr*
Shawna Bong, *Project Mgr*
Kelli Burbridge, *Draft/Design*
Jen Nelson, *Mktg Coord*
EMP: 95
SQ FT: 9,988
SALES (est): 21MM **Privately Held**
WEB: www.cdcdesigns.com
SIC: 7389 Interior design services

(P-17104)
CREATIVE TECHNOLOGY GROUP INC (HQ)
14000 Arminta St, Panorama City (91402-6080)
PHONE 818 779-2400
Fax: 818 779-2401
Graham Andrews, *President*
Stephen Gray, *COO*
Andy Reardon, *Managing Dir*
Simon Tibble, *Managing Dir*
Sim Elwood, *General Mgr*
EMP: 80
SALES (est): 40.8MM
SALES (corp-wide): 208.1MM **Privately Held**
WEB: www.avesco.com
SIC: 7389 Teleconferencing services
PA: Avesco Group Plc
Unit E2
Crawley W SUSSEX RH10
129 358-3400

(P-17105)
CREDIT CARD SERVICES INC (PA)
Also Called: Bankcard Services
21281 S Western Ave, Torrance (90501-2958)
PHONE 213 365-1122
Fax: 213 365-1131
Patrick S Hong, *CEO*
Dennis M Lee, *CFO*
Michelle Shin, *Vice Pres*
Paul Cheong, *Executive*
Eric Yeo, *Branch Mgr*
EMP: 95
SQ FT: 17,000
SALES (est): 21.8MM **Privately Held**
WEB: www.e-bankcard.com
SIC: 7389 Credit card service

(P-17106)
CRISPY SEWING INC
3437 E Pico Blvd, Los Angeles (90023-3032)
PHONE 323 262-9639
Fax: 323 262-9778
Maria Saenz, *President*
EMP: 70
SQ FT: 6,400
SALES (est): 3MM **Privately Held**
SIC: 7389 Apparel designers, commercial

7389 - Business Svcs, NEC County (P-17107)
PRODUDCTS & SERVICES SECTION

(P-17107)
CROSSROAD SERVICES INC
2360 Alvarado St, San Leandro
(94577-4314)
PHONE 510 895-5055
Steven Scheiner, *President*
Feroun Khan, *Vice Pres*
EMP: 419
SQ FT: 5,000
SALES: 21MM **Privately Held**
SIC: 7389 Inventory stocking service

(P-17108)
CRUZ HOFFSTETTER LLC
Also Called: Royal Crest Healthcare
519 W Badillo St, Covina (91722-3763)
PHONE 626 915-5621
Fax: 626 915-5621
Lydia Cruz, *President*
Anil Gupta, *Director*
EMP: 60
SALES (est): 3.3MM **Privately Held**
SIC: 7389 Personal service agents, brokers & bureaus

(P-17109)
CSUB NURSING CLASS OF 2006
9001 Stockdale Hwy, Bakersfield
(93311-1022)
PHONE 408 219-5914
Michelle Concuora, *President*
EMP: 71
SALES: 2.3MM **Privately Held**
SIC: 7389 Fund raising organizations

(P-17110)
CURRENT TV LLC
118 King St, San Francisco (94107-1905)
PHONE 415 995-8328
David Bohrman,
Sean Fassett, *Vice Pres*
Peter Dao, *Admin Asst*
Bob Bacon, *Administration*
Theresa Pepe, *CTO*
EMP: 200
SQ FT: 27,000
SALES (est): 6.2MM **Privately Held**
WEB: www.currentmedia.com
SIC: 7389 Field audits, cable television
PA: Al Jazeera Media Network
Qatar Television Building Khalifa Street
Doha
448 242-79

(P-17111)
CUSTOMFAB INC
Also Called: Fullclip USA
7345 Orangewood Ave, Garden Grove
(92841-1411)
PHONE 714 891-9119
Donald Martin Alhanati, *President*
Sharon Benson, *Office Mgr*
Jill Alhanati, *Purch Mgr*
Howard Alhanati, *Sales Mgr*
EMP: 250
SQ FT: 47,000
SALES (est): 31.4MM **Privately Held**
SIC: 7389 Sewing contractor

(P-17112)
CUTLER GROUP LP
101 Montgomery St Ste 700, San Francisco
(94104-4125)
PHONE 415 645-6745
Trent Cutler, *Managing Prtnr*
Alex Budilovsky, *Risk Mgmt Dir*
Windsor Chan, *Analyst*
EMP: 50
SALES (est): 5.1MM **Privately Held**
SIC: 7389 Financial services

(P-17113)
CWPFL INC
1682 Langley Ave, Irvine (92614-5620)
PHONE 714 564-7900
Matthew K Stewart, *President*
Jeff Gunhus, *CEO*
Spencer Pepe, *CEO*
Jason Reed, *CEO*
Tracy Meneses, *Treasurer*
EMP: 50
SALES (est): 1.6MM **Privately Held**
WEB: www.kleen-sales.com
SIC: 7389 Personal service agents, brokers & bureaus

(P-17114)
D2J INC
6351 Regent St Ste 100, Huntington Park
(90255-3567)
PHONE 323 589-1374
Richard Kim, *President*
EMP: 90
SALES (est): 4MM **Privately Held**
SIC: 7389 Sewing contractor

(P-17115)
DAIOHS USA INC (HQ)
Also Called: First Choice Coffee Services
13030 Alondra Blvd # 202, Cerritos
(90703-2249)
PHONE 562 293-2888
Shinichi Ohkubo, *CEO*
Hiroshi Ohkubo, *President*
Charles Brewer, *Regional Mgr*
Sean M Doyle, *Branch Mgr*
Josh James, *Branch Mgr*
EMP: 130
SQ FT: 50,000
SALES: 71.3MM
SALES (corp-wide): 217.1MM **Privately Held**
SIC: 7389 Coffee service
PA: Daiohs Corporation
2-4-1, Hamamatsucho
Minato-Ku TKY 105-0
334 385-511

(P-17116)
DAVID SANTOS FARMING
720 Jefferson Ave, Los Banos
(93635-4713)
PHONE 209 826-1065
David Santos, *Owner*
EMP: 60
SALES (est): 5.6MM **Privately Held**
SIC: 7389 Personal service agents, brokers & bureaus

(P-17117)
DEDICATED MANAGEMENT GROUP LLC
3876 E Childs Ave, Merced (95341-9520)
PHONE 209 385-0694
EMP: 141
SALES (corp-wide): 15.7MM **Privately Held**
SIC: 7389
PA: Dedicated Management Group Llc
3651 Mars Hill Rd Ste 400
Watkinsville GA 30677
404 564-1201

(P-17118)
DEE SIGN CO
Also Called: American Sign
7950 Woodley Ave, Van Nuys
(91406-1260)
PHONE 818 904-3400
Fax: 818 988-4511
Braden Huenefeld, *Principal*
EMP: 55
SQ FT: 28,900
SALES: 3.2MM **Privately Held**
SIC: 7389 3993 Sign painting & lettering shop; signs & advertising specialties

(P-17119)
DEKRA-LITE INDUSTRIES INC
Also Called: Dl Imaging
3102 W Alton Ave, Santa Ana
(92704-6817)
PHONE 714 436-0705
Fax: 714 436-0612
Jeffrey Lopez, *CEO*
Micheal Sterling, *General Mgr*
Stephen Leal, *Purch Agent*
George Sanchez, *Opers Mgr*
Steven Castaneda, *Marketing Mgr*
EMP: 80
SQ FT: 30,000
SALES (est): 13.4MM **Privately Held**
WEB: www.dekra-lite.com
SIC: 7389 5999 3999 Decoration service for special events; art, picture frames & decorations; Christmas lights & decorations; advertising curtains

(P-17120)
DELPHI PRODUCTIONS INC (PA)
Also Called: Group Delphi
950 W Tower Ave, Alameda (94501-5049)
PHONE 510 748-7494
Fax: 510 749-6899
Justin Hersh, *President*
Pete Bowes, *CFO*
Tony Erpelding, *Vice Pres*
Debbie Parrott, *Vice Pres*
Mary A Dickinson, *Info Tech Mgr*
EMP: 102
SQ FT: 148,000
SALES (est): 53.7MM **Privately Held**
WEB: www.delphiproductions.com
SIC: 7389 Trade show arrangement

(P-17121)
DFA OF CALIFORNIA
1050 Diamond St, Stockton (95205-7020)
P.O. Box 1727 (95201-1727)
PHONE 209 465-2289
Fax: 209 467-6704
Debra Pennell, *Principal*
Matt Yost, *Vice Pres*
Gene Clark, *Engineer*
Doug Nesbit, *VP Mktg*
Tim Cannon, *Marketing Staff*
EMP: 60
SALES (corp-wide): 9.5MM **Privately Held**
WEB: www.dfaofca.com
SIC: 7389 Inspection & testing services
PA: Dfa Of California
710 Striker Ave
Sacramento CA 95834
916 561-5900

(P-17122)
DIABLO VLY COLLEGE FOUNDATION (PA)
321 Golf Club Rd, Pleasant Hill
(94523-1544)
PHONE 925 685-1230
Fax: 925 685-1551
Mark G Edelstein, *President*
Katherine Guptill, *CEO*
Newin Orante, *Vice Pres*
Julie Kadalano, *Accountant*
Chrisanne Knox, *Mktg Dir*
EMP: 136
SQ FT: 1,000
SALES: 1.3MM **Privately Held**
WEB: www.dvc.edu
SIC: 7389 8221 Fund raising organizations; colleges universities & professional schools

(P-17123)
DIBA FASHIONS INC
472 N Bowling Green Way, Los Angeles
(90049-2820)
PHONE 323 232-3775
John Gir Daneshrad, *President*
Shahin Daneshrad, *Treasurer*
EMP: 70
SQ FT: 22,400
SALES (est): 3.8MM **Privately Held**
SIC: 7389 2339 Sewing contractor; women's & misses' outerwear

(P-17124)
DIGITAL INTERNATIONAL CORP
2424 N Ontario St, Burbank (91504-3119)
PHONE 818 847-1157
Ed Ceja, *CEO*
Maria Elena Lopez, *Controller*
EMP: 80
SQ FT: 40,000
SALES (est): 3.6MM **Privately Held**
WEB: www.digital-p.com
SIC: 7389 Music & broadcasting services; audio cassette duplication services

(P-17125)
DIRECT PACK INC
Also Called: D P I
1025 W 8th St, Azusa (91702-2248)
PHONE 626 380-2360
Fax: 626 969-5555
Craig Snedden, *President*
Gandhi Sifuentes, *Vice Pres*
Laura Murphy, *VP Sales*
EMP: 100 **EST:** 2006
SALES (est): 15.9MM **Privately Held**
SIC: 7389 2671 Packaging & labeling services; thermoplastic coated paper for packaging

(P-17126)
DISC MARKETING IN FLIGHT DIV
35 W Dayton St, Pasadena (91105-2001)
PHONE 626 795-9510
Fax: 626 405-2370
Tena Clark, *Owner*
EMP: 90
SALES (est): 2.8MM **Privately Held**
SIC: 7389 Music distribution systems

(P-17127)
DISPLAY WORKS LLC
854 Stewart Dr Ste B, Sunnyvale
(94085-4513)
PHONE 408 746-9654
Edward Pak, *Branch Mgr*
EMP: 89
SALES (corp-wide): 60MM **Privately Held**
SIC: 7389 Trade show arrangement
PA: Display Works, Llc
1 Gatehall Dr Ste 210
Parsippany NJ 07054
201 327-1260

(P-17128)
DMCG INC (PA)
Also Called: Bail Hotline Bail Bonds
3605 10th St, Riverside (92501-3619)
PHONE 951 683-9685
Daniel McGuire, *CEO*
Ben Srinivas, *CFO*
Cesar McGuire, *Exec VP*
Gilbert McGuire, *Exec VP*
Marco McGuire, *Exec VP*
EMP: 50
SQ FT: 15,000
SALES (est): 10MM **Privately Held**
SIC: 7389 Bail bonding

(P-17129)
DOCMAGIC INC
Also Called: Document Systems
1800 W 213th St, Torrance (90501-2832)
PHONE 800 649-1362
Fax: 310 564-1362
Dominic Iannitti, *President*
Gavin Ales, *Officer*
Laurie Spira, *Officer*
Jay Hornick, *Vice Pres*
Kathy Moore, *Executive*
EMP: 79
SQ FT: 20,000
SALES (est): 18.3MM **Privately Held**
WEB: www.docmagic.com
SIC: 7389 Legal & tax services

(P-17130)
DOCUMENT TECHNOLOGIES LLC
275 Battery St Ste 250, San Francisco
(94111-3318)
PHONE 415 495-4100
Jonathan Kafka, *Branch Mgr*
EMP: 63
SALES (corp-wide): 472.3MM **Privately Held**
SIC: 7389 Document storage service
PA: Document Technologies, Llc
2 Ravinia Dr Ste 850
Atlanta GA 30346
770 390-2700

(P-17131)
DOCUMENT TECHNOLOGIES LLC
350 S Figueroa St Ste 750, Los Angeles
(90071-1313)
PHONE 213 892-9000
John Davenport Jr, *Branch Mgr*
Gilbert Santos, *Office Mgr*
EMP: 71
SALES (corp-wide): 472.3MM **Privately Held**
SIC: 7389 Document storage service
PA: Document Technologies, Llc
2 Ravinia Dr Ste 850
Atlanta GA 30346
770 390-2700

PRODUCTS & SERVICES SECTION

7389 - Business Svcs, NEC County (P-17155)

(P-17132)
DOCUMENT TECHNOLOGIES LLC
3600 W Bayshore Rd, Palo Alto (94303-4239)
PHONE..................................650 485-2705
Victor Tan, *Branch Mgr*
EMP: 71
SALES (corp-wide): 472.3MM **Privately Held**
SIC: 7389 Document storage service
PA: Document Technologies, Llc
   2 Ravinia Dr Ste 850
   Atlanta GA 30346
   770 390-2700

(P-17133)
DOUBLELINE CAPITAL LP
333 S Grand Ave Fl 18, Los Angeles (90071-1504)
PHONE..................................213 633-8200
Jeffery E Gundlach, *Partner*
Philip A Barach, *Partner*
Henry V Chase, *Partner*
Louis Lucido, *COO*
Joel Damiani, *CFO*
EMP: 111
SQ FT: 35,000
SALES (est): 15.6MM **Privately Held**
SIC: 7389 6719 Financial services; investment holding companies, except banks

(P-17134)
DRIVER SPG
1501 S Harris Ct, Anaheim (92806-5932)
PHONE..................................626 351-8800
Carl Kreutziger, *President*
Karl Kreutziger, *President*
Cecilia Ulloa, *Office Mgr*
Michael Bolda, *Project Mgr*
Frank Bruce, *Project Mgr*
EMP: 50
SALES (est): 6.3MM **Privately Held**
SIC: 7389 Drive-a-way automobile service

(P-17135)
DROISYS INC
4657 Hedgewick Ave, Fremont (94538-3327)
PHONE..................................408 329-1761
Sanjiv Goyal, *Branch Mgr*
EMP: 199
SALES (corp-wide): 26.9MM **Privately Held**
SIC: 7389
PA: Droisys Inc.
   4800 Patrick Henry Dr
   Santa Clara CA 95054
   408 874-8333

(P-17136)
DUFF & PHELPS LLC
345 California St # 2100, San Francisco (94104-2663)
PHONE..................................415 693-5300
Michael Lloyd, *Director*
David Larsen, *Managing Dir*
Peter Rosenberg, *Managing Dir*
EMP: 53
SALES (corp-wide): 377.4MM **Privately Held**
SIC: 7389 Financial services
HQ: Duff & Phelps, Llc
   55 E 52nd St Fl 31
   New York NY 10055
   212 871-2000

(P-17137)
DUN & BRADSTREET EMERGING (DH)
Also Called: Dun & Brdstreet Crdbility Corp
22761 Pacific Coast Hwy # 226, Malibu (90265-5064)
PHONE..................................310 456-8271
Robert Carrigan, *CEO*
Wisdom Lu, *CFO*
Kathleen M Guinnessey, *Treasurer*
Susan D Beriont, *Vice Pres*
Kristin R Kaldor, *Admin Sec*
EMP: 145
SALES (est): 101.7MM
SALES (corp-wide): 1.6B **Publicly Held**
SIC: 7389 Financial services
HQ: Dun & Bradstreet, Inc
   103 Jfk Pkwy
   Short Hills NJ 07078
   973 921-5500

(P-17138)
E & C FASHION INC
Also Called: Pacific Concept Laundry
3600 E Olympic Blvd, Los Angeles (90023-3121)
PHONE..................................323 262-0099
Fax: 323 582-0007
William Moo Han Bae, *CEO*
Maria Bae, *President*
Elizabeth Bae, *Vice Pres*
Claudia Kye, *Vice Pres*
EMP: 300
SQ FT: 111,000
SALES (est): 34MM **Privately Held**
SIC: 7389 Sewing contractor

(P-17139)
E TRADESHOWGIRLSCOM
1 Ocean Rdg, Laguna Niguel (92677-9231)
PHONE..................................949 661-4177
Shelley Tippetts, *Owner*
EMP: 100 **EST:** 2000
SALES (est): 2.7MM **Privately Held**
SIC: 7389 Advertising, promotional & trade show services

(P-17140)
EAST BAY INNOVATIONS
2450 Washington Ave # 240, San Leandro (94577-5943)
PHONE..................................510 618-1580
Tom Heinz, *Director*
Sabrina Sehwartz, *Office Mgr*
Kiera Swan, *Payroll Mgr*
Lisa Zinza, *Co-Director*
Patrick Havel, *Asst Director*
EMP: 60
SALES: 6.1MM **Privately Held**
WEB: www.eastbayinnovations.com
SIC: 7389 Personal service agents, brokers & bureaus

(P-17141)
ECONTACTLIVE INC
Also Called: Telecontact Resource Services
6436 Oakdale Rd, Riverbank (95367-9648)
PHONE..................................209 863-8547
Julie Hutchings, *CEO*
John Werthly, *CFO*
Alice Martinez, *CTO*
Natalie Cron-Tiffany, *Human Res Dir*
Tammy Camarena, *Sales Mgr*
EMP: 80
SQ FT: 6,000
SALES (est): 7.6MM **Privately Held**
WEB: www.eContactLive.com
SIC: 7389 Telemarketing services

(P-17142)
EDCO HEALTH INFO SOLUTION
Also Called: ABI Document Support Service
1804 Tribute Rd Ste F, Sacramento (95815-4313)
PHONE..................................909 793-0613
Maggie Dragna, *Branch Mgr*
EMP: 50
SALES (corp-wide): 68.8MM **Privately Held**
SIC: 7389 5044 Microfilm recording & developing service; office equipment
PA: Edco Health Information Solution Inc
   10411 Clayton Rd Ste 211
   Saint Louis MO 63131
   417 862-4351

(P-17143)
EDCO HEALTH INFO SOLUTION
Also Called: ABI Document Support Services
2015 W Park Ave Ste 13, Redlands (92373-6276)
PHONE..................................909 793-0613
David Benge, *Branch Mgr*
Debra Palazuelos, *Supervisor*
EMP: 100
SALES (corp-wide): 68.8MM **Privately Held**
SIC: 7389 5044 Microfilm recording & developing service; office equipment
PA: Edco Health Information Solution Inc
   10411 Clayton Rd Ste 211
   Saint Louis MO 63131
   417 862-4351

(P-17144)
EDG INTERIOR ARCH & DESIGN INC
Also Called: E D G
7 Hamilton Landing # 200, Novato (94949-8209)
PHONE..................................415 454-2277
Fax: 415 454-2278
Jennifer Johanson, *CEO*
Eric Engstrom, *President*
David Barth, *CFO*
Laurene Schlosser, *Executive Asst*
Nicole Belluomini, *Admin Asst*
EMP: 60
SQ FT: 12,500
SALES (est): 7.4MM **Privately Held**
WEB: www.engstromdesign.com
SIC: 7389 8712 Interior designer; architectural services

(P-17145)
EFINANCE CORPORATION
Also Called: Identrus
795 Folsom St Fl 1, San Francisco (94107-4226)
PHONE..................................866 433-6878
Karen Wendel, *CEO*
Pablo Luther, *CFO*
Marshall Murphy, *Vice Pres*
Andrew Thompson, *Vice Pres*
Eugene Woo, *Vice Pres*
EMP: 50
SALES (est): 3.4MM
SALES (corp-wide): 7.8B **Privately Held**
WEB: www.efinance.com
SIC: 7389 Financial services
HQ: Identrust, Inc.
   55 Hawthorne St Ste 400
   San Francisco CA 94105
   415 486-2900

(P-17146)
ELEVATE EXPO INC
1361 Lowrie Ave, South San Francisco (94080-6403)
PHONE..................................415 625-2821
Dominic Villeggiante, *President*
EMP: 50
SQ FT: 10,000
SALES (est): 1.4MM **Privately Held**
SIC: 7389 Convention & show services

(P-17147)
ELLIE FASHION GROUP INC
1735 Stewart St Fl 2, Santa Monica (90404-4021)
PHONE..................................818 355-3812
Marcus Greinke, *CEO*
EMP: 56
SQ FT: 7,000
SALES (est): 4MM **Privately Held**
SIC: 7389 Apparel designers, commercial

(P-17148)
ELLISON BINER
2685 S Melrose Dr, Vista (92081-8783)
PHONE..................................760 598-6500
Fax: 760 598-7600
Edward Chocholek, *President*
Drake Chochran, *Info Tech Dir*
Joe Golden, *Mktg Dir*
Nick Bird, *Marketing Staff*
EMP: 55
SALES (est): 10MM **Privately Held**
SIC: 7389 Packaging & labeling services

(P-17149)
EMAGIA CORPORATION
4500 Great America Pkwy # 120, Santa Clara (95054-1283)
PHONE..................................408 654-6575
Veena Gundavelli, *CEO*
John Symons, *Director*
Marlene Arabia, *Manager*
Gss Prabhakar, *Manager*
EMP: 50
SALES (est): 3.1MM **Privately Held**
WEB: www.emagia.com
SIC: 7389 Financial services

(P-17150)
EMERALD EXPOSITIONS LLC (HQ)
Also Called: Contract
31910 Del Obispo St # 200, San Juan Capistrano (92675-3195)
PHONE..................................949 226-5700
Kosty Gilis, *CEO*
Sabrina Crow, *Senior VP*
Howard Appelbaum, *Vice Pres*
Rob Carstens, *Vice Pres*
Christine Cassidy, *Vice Pres*
EMP: 650
SQ FT: 6,500
SALES (est): 197.1MM
SALES (corp-wide): 4.1B **Privately Held**
SIC: 7389 Advertising, promotional & trade show services
PA: Onex Corporation
   161 Bay St 49 Fl
   Toronto ON M5J 2
   416 362-7711

(P-17151)
ENTREPRENEURIAL HOSPITALITY
Also Called: Riverside Convention Center
3485 Mission Inn Ave, Riverside (92501-3304)
PHONE..................................951 346-4700
Fax: 951 222-4706
Duane Roberts, *Ch of Bd*
Richard Shippie, *President*
Ted Weggeland, *President*
Scott Megna, *Vice Pres*
EMP: 200
SQ FT: 75,000
SALES (est): 9.1MM **Privately Held**
SIC: 7389 Convention & show services

(P-17152)
EPHONAMATIONCOM INC
Also Called: Ansafone Contact Centers
145 E Columbine Ave, Santa Ana (92707-4401)
P.O. Box 264 (92702-0264)
PHONE..................................714 560-1000
Randy Harmat, *CEO*
Jennifer Oliveros, *Vice Pres*
Ivan Martinez, *Admin Asst*
Veronica Zepeda, *Admin Asst*
Matthew Harless, *CTO*
EMP: 175
SQ FT: 18,900
SALES (est): 21.8MM **Privately Held**
SIC: 7389 Telephone answering service

(P-17153)
EQUILAR INC
1100 Marshall St, Redwood City (94063-2595)
PHONE..................................650 241-6600
Fax: 650 701-0993
David Chun, *CEO*
Timothy Ranzetta, *President*
Thomas L Deitrich, *Exec VP*
Michael Bendorf, *Vice Pres*
Linda Chen, *Vice Pres*
EMP: 112 **EST:** 2000
SALES (est): 19.6MM **Privately Held**
SIC: 7389 Financial services

(P-17154)
EREPUBLIC INC (PA)
Also Called: Government Technology
100 Blue Ravine Rd, Folsom (95630-4509)
PHONE..................................916 932-1300
Fax: 916 932-1470
Dennis McKenna, *CEO*
Erica Hall, *COO*
Margaret Mohr, *Chief Mktg Ofcr*
Beth Niblock, *Officer*
John Flynn, *Vice Pres*
EMP: 120
SQ FT: 36,000
SALES (est): 33.1MM **Privately Held**
WEB: www.erepublic.com
SIC: 7389 2759 2721 Convention & show services; publication printing; magazines: printing; periodicals

(P-17155)
EVERGREEN COMPANY INC
847 E Turner Rd, Lodi (95240-0734)
PHONE..................................916 257-5994

7389 - Business Svcs, NEC County (P-17156)

Thomas W Bors, *CEO*
EMP: 60
SALES (est): 4MM **Privately Held**
SIC: 7389

(P-17156)
EXCELLENCE VENTURES INC
149 S Mednik Ave, Los Angeles (90022-1606)
PHONE.................................323 262-6800
Recardo Davila, *CEO*
Manuel Davila, *President*
Ricardo Davila, *CEO*
EMP: 70
SQ FT: 4,000
SALES (est): 3.1MM **Privately Held**
SIC: 7389 Financial services

(P-17157)
FACT FOUNDATION
Also Called: FREDERICKA MANOR CARE CENTER
303 N Glenoaks Blvd, Burbank (91502-1116)
PHONE.................................818 729-8105
Fax: 818 729-8216
Donna Shaw, *Principal*
Tim Detmen, *President*
EMP: 75
SALES: 816.1K
SALES (corp-wide): 165.1MM **Privately Held**
SIC: 7389 Fund raising organizations
PA: Front Porch Communities And Services - Casa De Manana, Llc
800 N Brand Blvd Fl 19
Glendale CA 91203
818 729-8100

(P-17158)
FACTER DIRECT LTD
4751 Wilshire Blvd # 140, Los Angeles (90010-3827)
PHONE.................................323 634-1999
Larry Keefer, *Controller*
Anju Singh, *Manager*
EMP: 170
SALES (corp-wide): 8.8MM **Privately Held**
WEB: www.giftplanningdirect.com
SIC: 7389 8742 Telemarketing services; marketing consulting services
PA: Facter Direct Ltd
11500 W Olympic Blvd
Los Angeles CA
310 788-9000

(P-17159)
FAITH T & B PLATING INC
Also Called: Faith Bumper Service
8475 Forest St, Gilroy (95020-3646)
PHONE.................................408 986-1226
Fax: 408 986-1983
Robert Foote, *President*
William Foote, *Vice Pres*
Simanta Racine, *Manager*
EMP: 66 **EST:** 1957
SQ FT: 22,000
SALES (est): 7.4MM **Privately Held**
SIC: 7389 Automobile recovery service

(P-17160)
FALLBROOK FIRE PROTECTION DST
315 E Ivy St, Fallbrook (92028-2138)
PHONE.................................760 723-2010
Kermit Harrison, *President*
Herbert A Gaetjens, *Director*
Jsteve Johnson, *Director*
Pete Merritt, *Director*
Arlan H Peterson, *Director*
EMP: 69
SALES (est): 3.8MM **Privately Held**
SIC: 7389 Fire protection service other than forestry or public

(P-17161)
FAMILY PLG ASSOC MED GROUP
2777 Long Beach Blvd # 150, Long Beach (90806-1571)
PHONE.................................562 595-5653
Edward C Allred, *Branch Mgr*
Elizabeth Williams, *Manager*
EMP: 73

SALES (corp-wide): 25.6MM **Privately Held**
SIC: 7389 Personal service agents, brokers & bureaus
PA: Family Planning Associates Medical Group
3050 E Airport Way
Long Beach CA 90806
213 738-7283

(P-17162)
FARMEX LAND MANAGEMENT INC
11156 E Annadale Ave, Sanger (93657-9727)
PHONE.................................559 875-7181
James Yakligian, *President*
EMP: 125
SALES (est): 9MM **Privately Held**
SIC: 7389 Packaging & labeling services

(P-17163)
FEDERAL EXPRESS CORPORATION
Also Called: Fedex
2495 Faraday Ave, Carlsbad (92010-7225)
PHONE.................................800 463-3339
Diane Coale, *Branch Mgr*
EMP: 167
SALES (corp-wide): 50.3B **Publicly Held**
WEB: www.federalexpress.com
SIC: 7389 Personal service agents, brokers & bureaus
HQ: Federal Express Corporation
3610 Hacks Cross Rd
Memphis TN 38125
901 369-3600

(P-17164)
FEDERAL EXPRESS CORPORATION
Also Called: Fedex
200 N Sepulveda Blvd # 800, El Segundo (90245-4340)
PHONE.................................310 563-4176
Fay Lester, *Manager*
William D Wacht, *Analyst*
Mary Gonzales, *Manager*
EMP: 500
SALES (corp-wide): 50.3B **Publicly Held**
WEB: www.federalexpress.com
SIC: 7389 Mailing & messenger services
HQ: Federal Express Corporation
3610 Hacks Cross Rd
Memphis TN 38125
901 369-3600

(P-17165)
FEDERAL EXPRESS CORPORATION
Also Called: Fedex
7275 Johnson Dr, Pleasanton (94588-3861)
PHONE.................................800 463-3339
Tina Bier, *Manager*
EMP: 99
SALES (corp-wide): 50.3B **Publicly Held**
SIC: 7389 Courier or messenger service
HQ: Federal Express Corporation
3610 Hacks Cross Rd
Memphis TN 38125
901 369-3600

(P-17166)
FEDERAL EXPRESS CORPORATION
Also Called: Fedex
7000 Barranca Pkwy, Irvine (92618-3112)
PHONE.................................800 463-3339
EMP: 350
SALES (corp-wide): 47.4B **Publicly Held**
SIC: 7389 4731 4581 4513
HQ: Federal Express Corporation
3610 Hacks Cross Rd
Memphis TN 38125
901 369-3600

(P-17167)
FEDERAL EXPRESS CORPORATION
Also Called: Fedex
3371 E Francis St, Ontario (91761-2914)
PHONE.................................800 463-3339
Manny Vivamaco, *Manager*
EMP: 275

SALES (corp-wide): 50.3B **Publicly Held**
WEB: www.federalexpress.com
SIC: 7389 4513 4215 Courier or messenger service; air courier services; courier services, except by air
HQ: Federal Express Corporation
3610 Hacks Cross Rd
Memphis TN 38125
901 369-3600

(P-17168)
FEDEX CORPORATION
50 Cypress Ln, Brisbane (94005-1217)
PHONE.................................415 657-0403
EMP: 50
SALES (corp-wide): 47.4B **Publicly Held**
SIC: 7389
PA: Fedex Corporation
942 Shady Grove Rd S
Memphis TN 38120
901 818-7500

(P-17169)
FIRST AMERICAN CARD SERVICE
25060 Hancock Ave Ste 103, Murrieta (92562-5959)
PHONE.................................951 677-8720
Fax: 951 698-7263
Brian Rommele, *President*
Alexis Watson, *Controller*
Mike Maxon, *Personnel Exec*
EMP: 50
SALES (est): 1.5MM **Privately Held**
WEB: www.1stamericancardservice.com
SIC: 7389 Charge account service

(P-17170)
FLAGSHIP CREDIT ACCEPTANCE LLC
7525 Irvine Center Dr, Irvine (92618-3066)
PHONE.................................949 748-7172
EMP: 58 **Privately Held**
SIC: 7389 Financial services
PA: Flagship Credit Acceptance Llc
3 Christy Dr Ste 203
Chadds Ford PA 19317

(P-17171)
FLEETCOR TECHNOLOGIES INC
1140 Galaxy Way, Concord (94520-5760)
PHONE.................................800 877-9019
EMP: 259
SALES (corp-wide): 1.7B **Publicly Held**
SIC: 7389 Charge account service
PA: Fleetcor Technologies, Inc.
5445 Triangle Pkwy # 400
Norcross GA 30092
770 449-0479

(P-17172)
FOXCONN
46750 Winema Cmn, Fremont (94539-7992)
PHONE.................................510 226-0822
Maria Chen, *Managing Dir*
Rosa Lucio, *Program Mgr*
Moises De La Cruz, *Sr Software Eng*
Carl Chan, *Project Mgr*
Denise Cunha, *Technology*
EMP: 56
SALES (est): 3.2MM **Privately Held**
SIC: 7389

(P-17173)
FRAMING ASSOCIATES INC
1320 Coolidge Ave, National City (91950-4334)
PHONE.................................619 336-9991
Bruce Mc Dowell, *President*
Ruth Jaffe, *Administration*
EMP: 150
SALES (est): 7.2MM **Privately Held**
SIC: 7389 Personal service agents, brokers & bureaus

(P-17174)
FREEMAN EXPOSITIONS INC
901 E South St, Anaheim (92805-5347)
PHONE.................................714 254-3400
Fax: 714 563-8064
Pattie Balding, *Manager*
Albert Chew, *Senior VP*

Richard Pabst, *Vice Pres*
Tom Bui, *Info Tech Mgr*
Mike Kurz, *Info Tech Mgr*
EMP: 200
SALES (corp-wide): 1.9B **Privately Held**
SIC: 7389 Advertising, promotional & trade show services
PA: Freeman Expositions, Inc.
1600 Viceroy Dr Ste 100
Dallas TX 75235
214 445-1000

(P-17175)
FREEMAN EXPOSITIONS INC
245 S Spruce Ave, South San Francisco (94080-4581)
PHONE.................................650 871-1597
Glenn Wyer, *Manager*
EMP: 95
SALES (corp-wide): 1.9B **Privately Held**
SIC: 7389 Trade show arrangement
PA: Freeman Expositions, Inc.
1600 Viceroy Dr Ste 100
Dallas TX 75235
214 445-1000

(P-17176)
FRESNO CNTY ECONOMIC OPPORTUNT
Also Called: Eoc Resource Development
1920 Mariposa Mall, Fresno (93721-2504)
PHONE.................................559 263-1013
Roger Palomino, *Manager*
EMP: 500
SALES (corp-wide): 108.8MM **Privately Held**
SIC: 7389 Office facilities & secretarial service rental
PA: Fresno County Economic Opportunities Commission
1920 Mariposa Mall # 300
Fresno CA 93721
559 263-1010

(P-17177)
FRESNO METRO FLOOD CTRL DST
5469 E Olive Ave, Fresno (93727-2541)
PHONE.................................559 456-3292
Fax: 559 456-3194
Bob Van Wyk, *General Mgr*
Jerry Lakeman, *Principal*
Wendell Lum, *Admin Asst*
Molly Stone, *Admin Asst*
Ricky Hara, *Systs Prg Mgr*
EMP: 75 **EST:** 1955
SQ FT: 12,965
SALES (est): 8.2MM **Privately Held**
SIC: 7389 Personal service agents, brokers & bureaus

(P-17178)
FUSION CONTACT CENTERS LLC
1288 W Mccoy Ln Ste C, Santa Maria (93455-1054)
PHONE.................................805 922-2999
Dan Ater, *Branch Mgr*
EMP: 188
SALES (corp-wide): 32.9MM **Privately Held**
WEB: www.callfusion.com
SIC: 7389 Personal service agents, brokers & bureaus
PA: Fusion Contact Centers, Llc
11333 N Scottsdale Rd # 130
Scottsdale AZ 85254
866 991-3888

(P-17179)
G INSTRUMENTS
14425 N Church Sq, San Diego (92128-3752)
PHONE.................................858 231-5156
Venko Gyokov, *Principal*
EMP: 65
SALES (est): 3.5MM **Privately Held**
SIC: 7389

(P-17180)
GALICE INC
30140 Tuttle Ct, Tehachapi (93561-7483)
PHONE.................................323 731-8200
Cathrine A Lutz, *President*
EMP: 69 **EST:** 1991

PRODUCTS & SERVICES SECTION

7389 - Business Svcs, NEC County (P-17205)

SALES (est): 3.6MM **Privately Held**
WEB: www.galice.com
SIC: 7389 Interior decorating

(P-17181)
GARY R EDWARDS INC
3930 Utah St Ste C, San Diego
(92104-2939)
PHONE................................619 299-8700
Fax: 619 299-8739
Gary R Edwards, *President*
Buddy Dennis, *Administration*
EMP: 70
SALES (est) 3.5MM **Privately Held**
WEB: www.greinc.com
SIC: 7389 Subscription fulfillment services: magazine, newspaper, etc.

(P-17182)
GBS FINANCIAL CORP
Also Called: Wagner Financials
904 Manhattan Ave Ste 3, Manhattan Beach (90266-5538)
PHONE................................310 937-0073
Donald Gloisten, *CEO*
EMP: 60
SALES (est): 1.9MM **Privately Held**
SIC: 7389 Financial services

(P-17183)
GDF PARENT LLC
Also Called: Import Whl Univ Fund Raising
7119 W Sunset Blvd, Los Angeles
(90046-4411)
PHONE................................646 262-9635
Yoelie Barag,
EMP: 75
SALES (est): 2.3MM **Privately Held**
SIC: 7389 Fund raising organizations

(P-17184)
GENTLE GIANT STUDIOS INC
7511 N San Fernando Rd, Burbank
(91505-1044)
PHONE................................818 504-3555
Fax: 818 504-3554
Karl Z Meyer, *President*
Jewell Morson, *Admin Asst*
Ashly Powell, *Senior Mgr*
Paulie Schrier, *Director*
Dev Gilmore, *Manager*
EMP: 56
SQ FT: 20,000
SALES (est): 6.7MM
SALES (corp-wide): 666.1MM **Publicly Held**
WEB: www.gentlegiantstudios.com
SIC: 7389 Design services
HQ: 3d Systems, Inc.
   333 Three D Systems Cir
   Rock Hill SC 29730
   803 326-3900

(P-17185)
GETTY IMAGES INC
Also Called: Gettyone Image Bank
6300 Wilshire Blvd # 1600, Los Angeles
(90048-5227)
PHONE................................323 202-4200
Anne Marion, *Branch Mgr*
EMP: 100
SALES (corp-wide): 3B **Publicly Held**
WEB: www.getty-images.com
SIC: 7389 Photography brokers
HQ: Getty Images, Inc.
   605 5th Ave S Ste 400
   Seattle WA 98104
   206 925-5000

(P-17186)
GILBERT BARCO
Also Called: Barco Fashions
9034 Terhune Ave, Sun Valley
(91352-2019)
PHONE................................323 232-7672
Fax: 323 232-0419
Gilbert Barco, *Owner*
EMP: 65
SALES (est): 3.3MM **Privately Held**
SIC: 7389 Sewing contractor

(P-17187)
GLOBAL ASCENT INC
36 Waterworks Way, Irvine (92618-3107)
PHONE................................714 930-6860
Gareth Ashworth, *CEO*
Heather Wright, *Office Mgr*
Edgar Barrera, *Safety Mgr*
EMP: 50
SALES (est): 2.6MM
SALES (corp-wide): 842MM **Publicly Held**
SIC: 7389 8711 Petroleum refinery inspection service; civil engineering
PA: Team, Inc.
   13131 Dar Ashford Ste 600
   Sugar Land TX 77478
   281 331-6154

(P-17188)
GLOBAL CHECK SERVICE
1524 Graves Ave Ste C, El Cajon
(92021-2991)
PHONE................................619 449-5150
Fax: 619 593-6527
David James Homoki, *Partner*
Dalila Homoki, *Partner*
EMP: 200 **EST:** 1994
SQ FT: 2,500
SALES (est): 10.3MM **Privately Held**
WEB: www.globalcheck.com
SIC: 7389 Check validation service; credit card service

(P-17189)
GLOBAL EXCHANGE MARKETING INC
26691 Plaza Ste 100, Mission Viejo
(92691-8575)
PHONE................................949 367-0388
Rick Sargent, *President*
Dj Kelly, *VP Opers*
EMP: 100
SQ FT: 3,000
SALES: 15MM **Privately Held**
SIC: 7389 Personal service agents, brokers & bureaus

(P-17190)
GLOBAL EXPRNCE SPECIALISTS INC
5560 Katella Ave, Cypress (90630-5001)
PHONE................................562 370-1500
EMP: 64 **Publicly Held**
SIC: 7389 Convention & show services
HQ: Global Experience Specialists, Inc.
   7000 Lindell Rd
   Las Vegas NV 89118
   702 515-5500

(P-17191)
GLOBAL EXPRNCE SPECIALISTS INC
500 N Brand Blvd Ste 1860, Glendale
(91203-3375)
PHONE................................818 638-5959
Experience Global, *Manager*
EMP: 65 **Publicly Held**
WEB: www.beckergroup.com
SIC: 7389 Design services
HQ: Global Experience Specialists, Inc.
   7000 Lindell Rd
   Las Vegas NV 89118,
   702 515-5500

(P-17192)
GLOBAL EXPRNCE SPECIALISTS INC
Also Called: Ges
491 C St, Chula Vista (91910-1604)
PHONE................................619 498-6300
Tom Robins, *Manager*
Vivian Alvillar, *Executive*
McClaine Hughe, *General Mgr*
EMP: 170 **Publicly Held**
WEB: www.gesexpo.com
SIC: 7389 Convention & show services
HQ: Global Experience Specialists, Inc.
   7000 Lindell Rd
   Las Vegas NV 89118
   702 515-5500

(P-17193)
GLOBAL INNOVATION PARTNERS LLC
Also Called: GI Partners
188 The Embarcadero # 700, San Francisco (94105-1231)
PHONE................................650 233-3600
Rick Magnuson, *Mng Member*
Cary Anderson, *Vice Pres*
Alfred Foglio, *Director*
Stacy Avalos, *Manager*
EMP: 100
SALES (est): 4.5MM **Privately Held**
SIC: 7389 Brokers, business: buying & selling business enterprises

(P-17194)
GLOBAL LANGUAGE SOLUTIONS LLC
19800 Macarthur Blvd # 750, Irvine
(92612-2402)
PHONE................................949 798-1400
Olga Smirnova, *CEO*
Inna Kassatkina, *President*
Jared Bickell, *Vice Pres*
Mariam Mohamdi, *Project Mgr*
Laura Moro, *Project Mgr*
EMP: 100
SQ FT: 7,500
SALES (est): 7.1MM **Privately Held**
WEB: www.globallanguages.com
SIC: 7389 Translation services
PA: Welocalize, Inc.
   241 E 4th St Ste 207
   Frederick MD 21701
   -

(P-17195)
GOOGLE PAYMENT CORP
Also Called: Google Checkout
1600 Amphitheatre Pkwy, Mountain View
(94043-1351)
PHONE................................650 253-0000
EMP: 50
SALES (est): 6.6MM
SALES (corp-wide): 74.9B **Publicly Held**
SIC: 7389
HQ: Google Inc.
   1600 Amphitheatre Pkwy
   Mountain View CA 94043
   650 253-0000

(P-17196)
GORDON & SCHWENKMEYER INC
1418 Howe Ave E, Sacramento
(95825-3230)
PHONE................................916 569-1740
Fax: 916 569-1748
Brett Carter, *Exec VP*
EMP: 70
SALES (corp-wide): 11.7MM **Privately Held**
WEB: www.gsitel.com
SIC: 7389 Personal service agents, brokers & bureaus
PA: Gordon & Schwenkmeyer Inc
   360 N Sepulveda Blvd
   El Segundo CA 90245
   310 615-2300

(P-17197)
GORES CAPITAL PARTNERS LP
10877 Wilshire Blvd Fl 18, Los Angeles
(90024-4373)
PHONE................................310 209-3010
Alex Gores,
EMP: 80
SALES (est): 3.1MM **Privately Held**
SIC: 7389 Financial services

(P-17198)
GRAND PACIFIC RESORTS INC
Also Called: Resortime.com
5900 Pasteur Ct Ste 200, Carlsbad
(92008-7336)
PHONE................................760 431-8500
Sherri Weks, *Manager*
Timothy J Stripe, *Treasurer*
Sabrina Lockemaston, *Info Tech Dir*
Jane McKahan-Jones, *Info Tech Dir*
Kathy Gordon, *Purch Mgr*
EMP: 200
SALES (corp-wide): 206.1MM **Privately Held**
WEB: www.grandpacificresorts.com
SIC: 7389 Personal service agents, brokers & bureaus
PA: Grand Pacific Resorts, Inc.
   5900 Pasteur Ct Ste 200
   Carlsbad CA 92008
   760 431-8500

(P-17199)
GRAND PERFORMANCES
350 S Grand Ave Ste A4, Los Angeles
(90071-3461)
PHONE................................213 687-2190
Fax: 213 687-2191
Craig Bloomgardner, *President*
Craig Bloomgarden, *President*
Amanda Wah, *Marketing Mgr*
EMP: 55
SALES: 1.5MM **Privately Held**
SIC: 7389 Promoters of shows & exhibitions

(P-17200)
GRILL ON THE ALLEY THE INC
6801 Hollywood Blvd, Los Angeles
(90028-6136)
PHONE................................323 856-5530
Fax: 323 856-5533
Katherine Sy, *Branch Mgr*
EMP: 1125
SALES (corp-wide): 25.8MM **Privately Held**
SIC: 7389 Design services
PA: Grill On The Alley, The, Inc
   11661 San Vicente Blvd # 404
   Los Angeles CA 90049
   310 820-5559

(P-17201)
GRILL RECORDING STUDIO
4770 San Pablo Ave Ste C, Emeryville
(94608-3028)
PHONE................................510 531-4351
Levberlak Mhg, *Owner*
EMP: 51
SALES (est): 2MM **Privately Held**
SIC: 7389 Recording studio, noncommercial records

(P-17202)
GSA DESIGN INC
4551 San Fernando Rd # 102, Glendale
(91204-3227)
PHONE................................818 241-2558
Fax: 818 241-2598
Grigor Grigoryan, *President*
Narine Khachatryan, *CFO*
Vartanian Mike, *Human Res Dir*
EMP: 150
SQ FT: 20,000
SALES: 7MM **Privately Held**
SIC: 7389 2386 Sewing contractor; garments, leather

(P-17203)
GTE CORPORATION
Also Called: Verizon
2001 Broadway Fl 1, Santa Monica
(90404-2909)
PHONE................................310 315-7597
Steve Campanion, *Principal*
Daniel Boyan, *Sales Mgr*
Suzanne L Haskell, *Director*
EMP: 60
SALES (corp-wide): 131.6B **Publicly Held**
WEB: www.gte.com
SIC: 7389 Telephone services
HQ: Gte Corporation
   140 West St
   New York NY 10007
   212 395-1000

(P-17204)
GURU KNITS INC
225 W 38th St, Los Angeles (90037-1405)
PHONE................................323 235-9424
Kevin Port, *CEO*
Sarah Chavez, *Bookkeeper*
Chelsea Ferrell, *Accounts Exec*
EMP: 60
SALES: 35.2MM **Privately Held**
SIC: 7389

(P-17205)
GUTHY-RENKER LLC
25892 Towne Centre Dr, Foothill Ranch
(92610-3437)
PHONE................................949 454-1400
Olly Efthyvoulos, *Branch Mgr*
Daniel Lin, *Administration*
Nalene Coker, *Human Res Dir*
Santo Polito, *Director*
Olly Efphyvoulos, *Manager*

7389 - Business Svcs, NEC County (P-17206)

EMP: 100
SALES (corp-wide): 325.8MM **Privately Held**
SIC: 7389 7374 Telemarketing services; data processing service
PA: Guthy-Renker Llc
3340 Ocean Park Blvd # 3055
Santa Monica CA 90405
760 773-9022

(P-17206)
H P SEARS CO INC
Also Called: HP Sears Co.
2000 18th St, Bakersfield (93301-4292)
P.O. Box 2307 (93303-2307)
PHONE 661 325-5981
James P Sears, *President*
Chris Thompson, *General Mgr*
Tania Montoya, *Bookkeeper*
Marshall Sanders, *Accounts Exec*
EMP: 60
SALES (est): 2.5MM **Privately Held**
SIC: 7389 Personal service agents, brokers & bureaus

(P-17207)
HARINGA INC (PA)
Also Called: Premier Packaging/Assembly
14422 Best Ave, Santa Fe Springs (90670-5133)
P.O. Box 4707, Cerritos (90703-4707)
PHONE 800 499-9991
Victoria Haringa, *CEO*
Vicki Haringa, *President*
Randy Haringa, *General Mgr*
EMP: 77
SQ FT: 200,000
SALES (est): 15MM **Privately Held**
WEB: www.premierpkg.com
SIC: 7389 Packaging & labeling services

(P-17208)
HARRIS DIRECT
21250 Califa St Ste 114, Woodland Hills (91367-5023)
PHONE 818 357-2040
Fax: 818 222-3480
James Harris, *President*
EMP: 62
SQ FT: 3,800
SALES: 1.8MM **Privately Held**
SIC: 7389 7331 Telemarketing services; direct mail advertising services

(P-17209)
HARTMANN STUDIOS INCORPORATED
Also Called: Impact Lighting & Production
70 W Ohio Ave Ste H, Richmond (94804-2033)
PHONE 510 232-5060
Matt Guelfi, *President*
Matthew Guelfi, *Vice Pres*
Michael Guelfi, *Vice Pres*
Scott Lowry, *Vice Pres*
Margarita Arroyo, *Creative Dir*
EMP: 150
SQ FT: 105,000
SALES (est): 23.7MM **Privately Held**
WEB: www.hartmann-studios.com
SIC: 7389 Convention & show services

(P-17210)
HEALTHCARE BARTON SYSTEM
Also Called: Barton Ski Clinic At Sierra
1111 Sierra At Tahoe Rd, Twin Bridges (95735-9505)
PHONE 530 543-5575
Richard Derby, *Branch Mgr*
EMP: 242
SALES (corp-wide): 162.4MM **Privately Held**
SIC: 7389 Personal service agents, brokers & bureaus
PA: Barton Healthcare System
2170 South Ave
South Lake Tahoe CA 96150
530 541-3420

(P-17211)
HEARTLAND PAYMENT SYSTEMS INC
Also Called: HEARTLAND PAYMENT SYSTEMS, INC.
548 Shorebird Cir # 3101, Redwood City (94065-1038)
PHONE 650 678-2824
Gary Friedman, *Principal*
EMP: 99
SALES (corp-wide): 2.9B **Publicly Held**
SIC: 7389 Personal service agents, brokers & bureaus
HQ: Heartland Payment Systems, Llc
300 Carnegie Ctr Ste 300
Princeton NJ 08540
609 683-3831

(P-17212)
HEARTLAND PAYMENT SYSTEMS INC
510 Cerritos Way, Cathedral City (92234-1617)
PHONE 760 324-0133
EMP: 97
SALES (corp-wide): 2B **Publicly Held**
SIC: 7389
PA: Heartland Payment Systems, Inc.
90 Nassau St
Princeton NJ 08540
609 683-3831

(P-17213)
HEARTLAND PAYMENT SYSTEMS INC
Also Called: HEARTLAND PAYMENT SYSTEMS, INC.
1007 W College Ave Ste B, Santa Rosa (95401-5046)
PHONE 707 338-0510
Gregory Arena, *Principal*
EMP: 99
SALES (corp-wide): 2.9B **Publicly Held**
SIC: 7389 Personal service agents, brokers & bureaus
HQ: Heartland Payment Systems, Llc
300 Carnegie Ctr Ste 300
Princeton NJ 08540
609 683-3831

(P-17214)
HEARTLAND PAYMENT SYSTEMS INC
Also Called: HEARTLAND PAYMENT SYSTEMS, INC.
4701 Petit Ave, Encino (91436-1910)
PHONE 818 784-6665
Jeff Zander, *Principal*
EMP: 97
SALES (corp-wide): 2.9B **Publicly Held**
SIC: 7389 Personal service agents, brokers & bureaus
HQ: Heartland Payment Systems, Llc
300 Carnegie Ctr Ste 300
Princeton NJ 08540
609 683-3831

(P-17215)
HEARTLAND PAYMENT SYSTEMS INC
Also Called: HEARTLAND PAYMENT SYSTEMS, INC.
1460 Golden Gate Ave # 5, San Francisco (94115-4658)
PHONE 415 518-4810
David Evan, *Principal*
EMP: 99
SALES (corp-wide): 2.9B **Publicly Held**
SIC: 7389 Personal service agents, brokers & bureaus
HQ: Heartland Payment Systems, Llc
300 Carnegie Ctr Ste 300
Princeton NJ 08540
609 683-3831

(P-17216)
HEARTLAND PAYMENT SYSTEMS INC
Also Called: HEARTLAND PAYMENT SYSTEMS, INC.
5325 Elkhorn Blvd, Sacramento (95842-2526)
PHONE 916 844-9548
James Bramblet, *Principal*

EMP: 99
SALES (corp-wide): 2.9B **Publicly Held**
SIC: 7389 Personal service agents, brokers & bureaus
HQ: Heartland Payment Systems, Llc
300 Carnegie Ctr Ste 300
Princeton NJ 08540
609 683-3831

(P-17217)
HENLEY ENTERPRISES INC
230 N Brea Blvd, Brea (92821-4002)
PHONE 714 990-1900
EMP: 535
SALES (corp-wide): 52.3MM **Privately Held**
SIC: 7389 Personal service agents, brokers & bureaus
PA: Henley Enterprises Inc.
54 Jaconnet St Ste 100
Newton MA 02461

(P-17218)
HERBS POOL SERVICE INC
3769 Redwood Hwy, San Rafael (94903-3998)
PHONE 415 479-4040
Fax: 415 479-6823
Sandra Louise Scott, *CEO*
Steve Heneise, *Sales Mgr*
Cris Diaz, *Marketing Staff*
Bill Dougan, *Manager*
Tim Lindelli, *Manager*
EMP: 55 EST: 1958
SQ FT: 3,000
SALES (est): 6.3MM **Privately Held**
SIC: 7389 Swimming pool & hot tub service & maintenance

(P-17219)
HILTON RESORT PALM SPRINGS
400 E Tahquitz Canyon Way, Palm Springs (92262-6605)
PHONE 760 320-6868
Fax: 760 320-2126
Aftab Dada, *General Mgr*
Patty Clark, *Executive Asst*
Barbara Perkins, *Meeting Planner*
Lin Pajonk, *Human Resources*
Catherine Bacher, *Director*
EMP: 200
SALES (est): 19.6MM **Privately Held**
WEB: www.hiltonpalmsprings.com
SIC: 7389 Hotel & motel reservation service

(P-17220)
HIRSCH BEDNER ASSOCIATES (PA)
Also Called: H B A
3216 Nebraska Ave, Santa Monica (90404-4214)
PHONE 310 829-9087
Fax: 310 453-1182
Howard Pharr, *Principal*
Rene Kaerskov, *CFO*
Michael Bedner, *Executive*
Lemor Moses, *Comms Dir*
Paul Fialkowski, *Business Dir*
EMP: 53
SALES (est): 13.8MM **Privately Held**
SIC: 7389 Interior designer

(P-17221)
HIRSCH/BEDNER INTL INC (PA)
Also Called: Hba International
3216 Nebraska Ave, Santa Monica (90404-4214)
PHONE 310 829-9087
Rene G Kaerskov, *CEO*
Michael J Bedner, *Ch of Bd*
Howard Pharr, *President*
Bruce Jones, *Exec VP*
Horace Lee, *Systs Prg Mgr*
EMP: 70
SQ FT: 14,000
SALES (est): 41MM **Privately Held**
WEB: www.hbadesign.com
SIC: 7389 Interior designer; interior design services

(P-17222)
HOBBY LOBBY STORES INC
4635 Chino Hills Pkwy, Chino Hills (91709-5848)
PHONE 909 393-8727
Steven -President Green, *Branch Mgr*
EMP: 148
SALES (corp-wide): 4.4B **Privately Held**
SIC: 7389 5999 5945 5023 Interior design services; art, picture frames & decorations; hobbies; frames & framing, picture & mirror
PA: Hobby Lobby Stores, Inc.
7707 Sw 44th St
Oklahoma City OK 73179
855 329-7060

(P-17223)
HOBBY LOBBY STORES INC
26565 Bouquet Canyon Rd, Santa Clarita (91350-2359)
PHONE 661 513-0005
EMP: 148
SALES (corp-wide): 4.4B **Privately Held**
SIC: 7389 5999 5945 5023 Interior design services; art, picture frames & decorations; hobbies; frames & framing, picture & mirror
PA: Hobby Lobby Stores, Inc.
7707 Sw 44th St
Oklahoma City OK 73179
855 329-7060

(P-17224)
HOLLISTER PROCESS SERVICE
Also Called: Steven Snyder
341 Tres Pinos Rd Ste 201, Hollister (95023-5582)
PHONE 831 634-1479
Stephen Snyder, *Owner*
Gawnette Snyder, *Co-Owner*
EMP: 50
SALES: 65K **Privately Held**
SIC: 7389 Process serving service

(P-17225)
HOLLYWOOD SPORTS PARK LLC
Also Called: Giant Sportz Paintball Park
9030 Somerset Blvd, Bellflower (90706-3402)
PHONE 562 867-9600
Fax: 562 920-0718
Dennis Bukowski, *Mng Member*
Omar Pinuelas, *General Mgr*
Sara Robertson, *Admin Asst*
Noel Castillo, *Accountant*
Judy Bukowski,
EMP: 100
SQ FT: 20,000
SALES (est): 8.3MM **Privately Held**
WEB: www.hollywoodsportspark.com
SIC: 7389 Personal service agents, brokers & bureaus

(P-17226)
HOSPITAL BUSINESS SERVICES INC
3300 E Guasti Rd, Ontario (91761-8655)
PHONE 909 235-4400
Mike Sarian, *President*
Ken Wheeler, *Vice Pres*
Connie Burke, *Human Resources*
EMP: 101
SALES (est): 3.6MM **Privately Held**
SIC: 7389 7349 Financial services; building maintenance services

(P-17227)
HUBZONE-CW DRIVER JOINT VENTR
9300 Santa Anita Ave, Rancho Cucamonga (91730-6145)
PHONE 909 484-0933
Charmaine Burnett, *Partner*
EMP: 99
SALES: 950K **Privately Held**
SIC: 7389 Business services

(P-17228)
HUSTLE DIGITAL INC
12777 W Jefferson Blvd, Los Angeles (90066-7048)
PHONE 310 882-2680
Josh Mandel, *Vice Pres*

PRODUCTS & SERVICES SECTION
7389 - Business Svcs, NEC County (P-17252)

EMP: 50
SALES (est): 1.2MM **Privately Held**
SIC: 7389 Advertising, promotional & trade show services

(P-17229)
HYDE & HYDE INC (PA)
300 El Sobrante Rd, Corona (92879-5757)
PHONE..................................951 279-5239
Tim Hyde, *President*
Veronica Fritsch, *Human Res Dir*
Connie Brezinski, *Purch Mgr*
Ryan Hyde, *Purch Mgr*
Kevin Hyde, *Buyer*
EMP: 200
SQ FT: 70,000
SALES (est): 63.9MM **Privately Held**
WEB: www.hydeandhyde.com
SIC: 7389 Packaging & labeling services

(P-17230)
HYDROPROCESSING ASSOCIATES LLC
Also Called: Hpa-USA
19122 S Santa Fe Ave, Compton (90221-5910)
PHONE..................................310 667-6456
Kees Ooms, *Branch Mgr*
EMP: 50 **Privately Held**
SIC: 7389 Petroleum refinery inspection service
HQ: Hydroprocessing Associates, Llc
6016 Highway 63
Moss Point MS 39563
228 475-2971

(P-17231)
IDEO LP
780 High St, Palo Alto (94301-2420)
PHONE..................................650 289-3400
Tim Brown, *CEO*
EMP: 150
SALES (corp-wide): 55.3MM **Privately Held**
SIC: 7389 Design services
PA: Ideo Lp
150 Forest Ave
Palo Alto CA 94301
650 289-3400

(P-17232)
IDEO LP
The Embarcadero Pier 28 St Pier, San Francisco (94105)
PHONE..................................415 615-5000
Fax: 415 615-5001
Gretchen Addi, *Partner*
John Dito, *Network Mgr*
Chioma Ume, *Manager*
EMP: 52
SALES (corp-wide): 55.3MM **Privately Held**
WEB: www.ideo.com
SIC: 7389 Design, commercial & industrial
PA: Ideo Lp
150 Forest Ave
Palo Alto CA 94301
650 289-3400

(P-17233)
ILANGUAGECOM INC
901 Wilshire Blvd Ste 300, Santa Monica (90401-1884)
PHONE..................................310 899-6800
Marc J Bautil, *CEO*
EMP: 50
SALES (est): 2.7MM **Privately Held**
WEB: www.ilanguage.com
SIC: 7389 Translation services

(P-17234)
IMG (PA)
Also Called: Demo Deluxe
4560 Dorinda Rd, Yorba Linda (92887-1800)
PHONE..................................714 974-1700
Fax: 714 974-0807
Jim Smith, *Partner*
Jerry Smith, *Partner*
Pat Stamatelatos, *Info Tech Mgr*
EMP: 50
SQ FT: 3,600
SALES (est): 76.8MM **Privately Held**
WEB: www.demodeluxe.com
SIC: 7389 Demonstration service

(P-17235)
IMPACT MKTG SPECIALISTS INC
19781 Pauling, Foothill Ranch (92610-2606)
PHONE..................................949 348-2292
Milton Naylor, *President*
Wayne Ybarra, *Info Tech Mgr*
Chyrle Vermylia, *VP Finance*
Favor Kirkland, *Regl Sales Mgr*
Elizabeth Stevens, *Sales Mgr*
EMP: 50
SQ FT: 18,000
SALES (est): 5.6MM **Privately Held**
WEB: www.impactorder.com
SIC: 7389 Printing broker

(P-17236)
INAPP
Also Called: Internet Applications Group
999 Commercial St Ste 210, Palo Alto (94303-4909)
PHONE..................................650 424-0496
Rakesh Puri, *Owner*
Satish Babu, *COO*
Dona Peter, *Executive*
Krishnakumar Nair, *Sales Staff*
Manju Puri, *Director*
EMP: 52 **EST:** 1996
SALES (est): 2.9MM **Privately Held**
WEB: www.inapp.com
SIC: 7389 Business services

(P-17237)
INDUSTRIAL STITCHTECH INC
520 Library St, San Fernando (91340-2524)
PHONE..................................818 361-6319
Ed Perez, *President*
Amber Quinn, *Administration*
Adriana Pena, *Manager*
EMP: 150
SQ FT: 35,000
SALES (est): 12.3MM **Privately Held**
WEB: www.industrialstitchtech.com
SIC: 7389 Sewing contractor

(P-17238)
INGENIO LLC
201 Mission St Ste 200, San Francisco (94105-1832)
PHONE..................................415 992-8220
Devina Whitley, *Mng Member*
EMP: 57
SALES (est): 5.1MM **Privately Held**
SIC: 7389

(P-17239)
INLAND-METRO SERVICES INC
1059 W 14th St, Upland (91786-2678)
PHONE..................................909 373-6810
Robert Ayala Sr, *President*
EMP: 55 **EST:** 2010
SQ FT: 750
SALES (est): 4.6MM **Privately Held**
SIC: 7389

(P-17240)
INNOVATED PACKAGING COMPANY
38505 Cherry St Ste C, Newark (94560-4700)
PHONE..................................510 713-3560
Fax: 510 745-8294
Ben F Polando, *President*
Adele Daszko, *Exec VP*
Donna Fernandez, *Senior VP*
Santina Polando, *Exec Sec*
EMP: 148
SQ FT: 110,000
SALES (est): 14.7MM **Privately Held**
WEB: www.innovpak.com
SIC: 7389 3086 Packaging & labeling services; packaging & shipping materials, foamed plastic

(P-17241)
INNOVATIVE SILICON INC
4800 Great America Pkwy # 500, Santa Clara (95054-1221)
P.O. Box 391657, Mountain View (94039-1657)
PHONE..................................408 572-8700
Mark-Eric Jones, *CEO*
Michael Van Buskirk, *COO*
Jeff Lewis, *Senior VP*
Craig Factor, *Vice Pres*
Daniel Labouve, *Vice Pres*
EMP: 80
SQ FT: 11,000
SALES (est): 3.5MM **Privately Held**
WEB: www.innovativesilicon.com
SIC: 7389 Personal service agents, brokers & bureaus

(P-17242)
INSIKT INC
225 Bush St Ste 1840, San Francisco (94104-4280)
PHONE..................................415 391-2431
James Michael Gutierrez, *CEO*
EMP: 60
SALES (est): 2.3MM **Privately Held**
SIC: 7389 Financial services

(P-17243)
INTEGRA TELECOM INC
101 Metro Dr, San Jose (95110-1314)
PHONE..................................408 758-7700
Robert Guth, *President*
Michael Sharpe, *COO*
Jesse Selnick, *CFO*
Joseph Harding, *Chief Mktg Ofcr*
Karen L Clauson, *Senior VP*
EMP: 72
SALES (corp-wide): 468.8MM **Privately Held**
SIC: 7389 4813 Telephone services; telephone communication, except radio
PA: Electric Lightwave Communications, Inc.
18110 Se 34th St Bldg 1s
Vancouver WA 98683
360 558-6900

(P-17244)
INTEGRA TELECOM INC
3700 Old Redwood Hwy # 100, Santa Rosa (95403-5738)
PHONE..................................707 284-4000
Shawn Shaw, *Branch Mgr*
Robert Guth, *President*
Michael Sharpe, *COO*
Jesse Selnick, *CFO*
Joseph Harding, *Chief Mktg Ofcr*
EMP: 72
SALES (corp-wide): 468.8MM **Privately Held**
SIC: 7389 4813 Telephone services; local & long distance telephone communications
PA: Electric Lightwave Communications, Inc.
18110 Se 34th St Bldg 1s
Vancouver WA 98683
360 558-6900

(P-17245)
INTERIOR OFFICE SOLUTIONS INC (PA)
17800 Mitchell N, Irvine (92614-6004)
PHONE..................................949 724-9444
Jesse Bagley, *President*
Brian Airth, *Vice Pres*
Paula Ray, *Business Mgr*
Richard Reid, *Controller*
EMP: 50
SQ FT: 11,000
SALES: 46MM **Privately Held**
WEB: www.iosinc.com
SIC: 7389 5712 Design services; office furniture

(P-17246)
INTERIOR OFFICE SOLUTIONS INC
444 S Flower St Ste 200, Los Angeles (90071-2903)
PHONE..................................310 726-9067
Shireen Nadjlessi, *Branch Mgr*
EMP: 50
SALES (corp-wide): 46MM **Privately Held**
SIC: 7389 5712 Design services; office furniture
PA: Interior Office Solutions, Inc.
17800 Mitchell N
Irvine CA 92614
949 724-9444

(P-17247)
INTERIORS BY LINDA
49585 Brian Ct, La Quinta (92253-8127)
PHONE..................................760 341-9651
Linda Martin, *Owner*
EMP: 50 **EST:** 1999
SALES (est): 1.8MM **Privately Held**
SIC: 7389 Interior design services

(P-17248)
INTERPAC TECHNOLOGIES INC
Also Called: Interpac Distribution Center
260 N Pioneer Ave, Woodland (95776-5934)
PHONE..................................530 662-6363
Fax: 530 662-6886
Roderick W Miner, *President*
Corinne Christenson, *Vice Pres*
Michael Croker, *Buyer*
Stephen Cosenza, *Opers Mgr*
Lacie Peterman, *Manager*
EMP: 75 **EST:** 2000
SALES (est): 9.7MM **Privately Held**
WEB: www.interpactechnologies.com
SIC: 7389 Packaging & labeling services

(P-17249)
INTERTEK TESTING SVCS NA INC
25791 Commercentre Dr, Lake Forest (92630-8803)
PHONE..................................949 349-1684
Richard Adams, *Branch Mgr*
EMP: 60
SALES (corp-wide): 3.2B **Privately Held**
SIC: 7389 Inspection & testing services
HQ: Intertek Testing Services Na, Inc.
3933 Us Route 11
Cortland NY 13045
607 753-6711

(P-17250)
INTERTEK USA INC
Also Called: Intertek Caleb Brett
1941 Freeman Ave Ste A, Signal Hill (90755-1236)
PHONE..................................562 494-4999
Fax: 562 494-4498
Mark Phoreson, *Branch Mgr*
Mark Thoreson, *Branch Mgr*
John Mulder, *Project Mgr*
EMP: 50
SQ FT: 1,600
SALES (corp-wide): 3.2B **Privately Held**
WEB: www.itscb.com
SIC: 7389 Pipeline & power line inspection service
HQ: Intertek Usa Inc.
2 Riverway Ste 500
Houston TX 77056
713 543-3600

(P-17251)
IPAC INC
7600 Dublin Blvd Ste 240, Dublin (94568-2908)
PHONE..................................925 556-5530
Fax: 925 556-5531
Brian Cereghino, *President*
Jeff Melendez, *Sales Associate*
EMP: 69
SALES (est): 6.8MM **Privately Held**
SIC: 7389

(P-17252)
IPAYMENT HOLDINGS INC (HQ)
30721 Russell Ranch Rd # 200, Westlake Village (91362-7383)
PHONE..................................310 436-5294
Greg Cohen, *COO*
Robert Purcell, *VP Finance*
Dante Croupe, *Director*
Courtney Lester, *Director*
Gabe Grimstad, *Manager*
EMP: 53
SALES: 666.8MM **Privately Held**
SIC: 7389 Credit card service
PA: Ipayment Investors, Inc
40 Burton Hills Blvd
Nashville TN 37215
615 665-1858

7389 - Business Svcs, NEC County (P-17253)

(P-17253)
ISI INSPECTION SERVICES INC (PA)
1798 University Ave, Berkeley (94703-1514)
PHONE.....................415 243-3265
Fax: 415 243-3266
Leslie A Sakai, President
Ed King, Exec VP
Cheryl Childs, Business Dir
Jeff Roe, Division Mgr
Terri Klepp, Office Mgr
EMP: 70
SQ FT: 9,700
SALES (est): 14MM Privately Held
WEB: www.inspectionservices.net
SIC: 7389 Inspection & testing services

(P-17254)
J & J PRODUCTIONS INCORPORATED
1775 E Lincoln Ave # 205, Anaheim (92805-4324)
PHONE.....................714 535-0951
Fax: 714 535-0641
Jack D George, President
Jessica George, Vice Pres
EMP: 50
SQ FT: 1,800
SALES (est): 2.7MM Privately Held
SIC: 7389 Fund raising organizations

(P-17255)
JAPANESE ASSISTANCE NETWRK INC
Also Called: Jan
11135 Magnolia Blvd # 140, North Hollywood (91601-3183)
PHONE.....................818 505-6080
Fax: 818 505-9430
Genichi Kadono, President
Jj Nishikawa, Controller
EMP: 298
SQ FT: 1,700
SALES (est): 12.6MM
SALES (corp-wide): 1.5B Privately Held
WEB: www.jannetwork.com
SIC: 7389 Translation services
HQ: Relocation International,Inc.
4-3-25, Shinjuku
Shinjuku-Ku TKY 160-0
353 128-702

(P-17256)
JD WESSON & ASSOCIATES INC
3212 Jefferson St Ste 206, NAPA (94558-3436)
PHONE.....................707 255-8667
Jim Wesson, President
EMP: 52
SALES (est): 2.7MM Privately Held
WEB: www.jdwesson.com
SIC: 7389 Personal investigation service

(P-17257)
JENCO PRODUCTIONS INC (PA)
401 S J St, San Bernardino (92410-2605)
PHONE.....................909 381-9453
Fax: 909 381-5762
Jennifer Imbriani, President
Nelson Escobar, COO
Roger Imbriani, Mktg Dir
Alicia Garcia, Manager
EMP: 160 EST: 1995
SQ FT: 50,000
SALES (est): 50.8MM Privately Held
WEB: www.jencoprod.com
SIC: 7389 Packaging & labeling services

(P-17258)
JILLIANS SAN FRANCISCO CA
101 4th St Ste 170, San Francisco (94103-3003)
PHONE.....................415 369-6100
Fax: 415 369-6103
Darren Daroches, General Mgr
Dan Smith, President
Marty Ryan, General Mgr
Bryan Galope, Manager
EMP: 60
SQ FT: 50,000
SALES (est): 2.9MM Privately Held
SIC: 7389 Personal service agents, brokers & bureaus

(P-17259)
JIMMYS FASHIONS
3135 Chadney Dr, Glendale (91206-1004)
PHONE.....................818 790-8932
Fax: 213 748-6510
Young Seok OH, Owner
EMP: 50
SALES (est): 2.3MM Privately Held
SIC: 7389 Sewing contractor

(P-17260)
JOHN HANCOCK LIFE INSUR CO USA (DH)
865 S Figueroa St # 3320, Los Angeles (90017-2543)
PHONE.....................213 689-0813
Emeritus D'Alessandro, CEO
David F D'Alessandro, President
Ross Fryer, President
Steve Finch, CFO
Gregory P Winn, Treasurer
▲ EMP: 2000 EST: 1862
SQ FT: 3,600,000
SALES (est): 906.9MM
SALES (corp-wide): 25.8MM Privately Held
WEB: www.jhcases.com
SIC: 7389 6351 6371 6321 Financial services; mortgage guarantee insurance; pensions; accident insurance carriers; health insurance carriers
HQ: John Hancock Financial Services, Inc.
200 Clarendon St
Boston MA 02116
617 572-6000

(P-17261)
JOMAR INDUSTRIES INC
1500 W 139th St, Gardena (90249-2604)
PHONE.....................323 770-0505
Fax: 310 217-1155
John H Stern, President
Margaret H Stern, Corp Secy
Jeff Stern, Vice Pres
▲ EMP: 50
SQ FT: 25,000
SALES (est): 3.3MM Privately Held
SIC: 7389 3089 Packaging & labeling services; coloring & finishing of plastic products

(P-17262)
JONES DAY LIMITED PARTNERSHIP
555 S Flower St Fl 50, Los Angeles (90071-2452)
PHONE.....................213 489-3939
Fax: 213 243-2539
Chris Lovrien, Principal
Erin L Burke, Partner
Lisa Takata, Office Admin
Lisa Y Takata, Office Admin
Lynette Telles, Admin Sec
EMP: 53
SALES (corp-wide): 992.1MM Privately Held
SIC: 7389 8111 Personal service agents, brokers & bureaus; legal services
PA: Jones Day Limited Partnership
901 Lakeside Ave E Ste 2
Cleveland OH 44114
216 586-3939

(P-17263)
JOPARI SOLUTIONS INC
1855 Gateway Blvd Ste 500, Concord (94520-3277)
PHONE.....................925 459-5200
Fax: 925 459-5222
John Stevens II, CEO
Nancy Larget, CFO
Scott A Hefner, Senior VP
Sherry Wilson, Senior VP
Jeannie Yu, Software Dev
EMP: 65
SALES (est): 9.7MM Privately Held
WEB: www.jopari.com
SIC: 7389 Financial services

(P-17264)
JPMORGAN CHASE BANK NAT ASSN
20 Hallcrest Dr, Ladera Ranch (92694-1084)
PHONE.....................949 429-6071
EMP: 103
SALES (corp-wide): 101B Publicly Held
SIC: 7389 Personal service agents, brokers & bureaus
HQ: Jpmorgan Chase Bank, National Association
1111 Polaris Pkwy
Columbus OH 43240
614 436-3055

(P-17265)
JPMORGAN CHASE BANK NAT ASSN
502 Las Posas Rd, Camarillo (93010-5705)
PHONE.....................805 482-2902
Jane Morel, Branch Mgr
EMP: 223
SALES (corp-wide): 101B Publicly Held
SIC: 7389 6029 Financial services; commercial banks
HQ: Jpmorgan Chase Bank, National Association
1111 Polaris Pkwy
Columbus OH 43240
614 436-3055

(P-17266)
JPMORGAN CHASE BANK NAT ASSN
10790 Rancho Bernardo Rd, San Diego (92127-5705)
PHONE.....................858 605-3300
Cindy Dunks, Principal
Cheryl Hassoun, Project Mgr
EMP: 223
SALES (corp-wide): 101B Publicly Held
WEB: www.chase.com
SIC: 7389 Financial services
HQ: Jpmorgan Chase Bank, National Association
1111 Polaris Pkwy
Columbus OH 43240
614 436-3055

(P-17267)
KDS MARKETING
965 N Todd Ave, Azusa (91702-2226)
PHONE.....................818 240-7000
Fax: 626 305-0208
Christopher Burks, President
Fred Burks, Shareholder
EMP: 110
SQ FT: 10,340
SALES (est): 7.4MM Privately Held
SIC: 7389 8742 Demonstration service; management consulting services

(P-17268)
KDS PRINTING AND PACKAGING INC
13397 Marlay Ave Ste A, Fontana (92337-6946)
PHONE.....................909 770-5400
Raymond Fecteau, President
Phyllis Saly, Office Mgr
Cathy Hilton, Accounts Mgr
EMP: 50
SQ FT: 35,000
SALES (est): 3MM Privately Held
WEB: www.kdspackaging.com
SIC: 7389 Printing broker

(P-17269)
KENEDCO INC
29363 Rancho Cal Rd, Temecula (92591-5201)
PHONE.....................951 699-9339
Kenneth G Miskam, CEO
Donna Wright, Administration
EMP: 51
SALES (est): 2.1MM Privately Held
SIC: 7389

(P-17270)
KENNETH BRDWICK INTR DSGNS INC
Also Called: Beverly Hills Luxury Interiors
1801 Century Park E # 1200, Los Angeles (90067-2302)
PHONE.....................310 274-9999
Kenneth Bordewick, CEO
EMP: 73
SALES (est): 3.2MM Privately Held
WEB: www.kennethbordewickinteriordesigns.com
SIC: 7389 Interior design services

(P-17271)
KILCREW PRODUCTIONS
32811 Wesley St, Wildomar (92595-9759)
PHONE.....................619 564-2080
Robert G Kilbride, CEO
Debora Kilbride, CFO
EMP: 57
SALES (est): 3.8MM Privately Held
SIC: 7389 Advertising, promotional & trade show services

(P-17272)
KIM CHONG
Also Called: Sean's Embroidery
2419 E 28th St, Vernon (90058-1401)
PHONE.....................323 581-4700
Fax: 323 581-4747
Chong Kim, Owner
EMP: 59
SQ FT: 10,300
SALES (est): 4.3MM Privately Held
SIC: 7389 2395 Embroidering of advertising on shirts, etc.; embroidery products, except schiffli machine

(P-17273)
KING-REYNOLDS VENTURES LLC
Also Called: Costanoa
2001 Rossi Rd, Pescadero (94060-9732)
PHONE.....................650 879-2136
Fax: 650 879-2275
John King,
Teri Giordani, Sales Dir
Thomas Reynolds,
Sharon Carpenter, Manager
Eron Swedberg, Manager
EMP: 75
SALES (est): 5.7MM Privately Held
WEB: www.costanoa.com
SIC: 7389 Financial services

(P-17274)
KIRSCHENMAN ENTERPRISES SLS LP
12826 Edison Hwy, Edison (93220)
PHONE.....................661 366-5736
Wayde Kirschenman, General Ptnr
EMP: 300
SQ FT: 5,000
SALES: 100MM Privately Held
SIC: 7389 Brokers, business: buying & selling business enterprises

(P-17275)
KOBEY CORPORATION INC (PA)
Also Called: Kobey Swap Meet At Spt Arena
3740 Sports Arena Blvd # 2, San Diego (92110-5132)
P.O. Box 81492 (92138-1492)
PHONE.....................619 523-2700
Fax: 619 523-2715
Kimberly Kobey Pretto, President
Eric Millman, CFO
Charles J Pretto, Vice Pres
Chuck Pretto, Vice Pres
Chris Haesloop, General Mgr
EMP: 55
SQ FT: 1,800
SALES (est): 6.3MM Privately Held
SIC: 7389 Flea market

(P-17276)
KOOS MANUFACTURING INC
Also Called: Big Star
2741 Seminole Ave, South Gate (90280-5550)
PHONE.....................323 249-1000
Fax: 323 564-3141
U Yul Ku, President
Kee H Fong, Vice Pres
John Hur, Vice Pres
Christy Meleon, Executive
Janet Kemp, Admin Sec
▲ EMP: 800
SQ FT: 180,000
SALES (est): 98.4MM Privately Held
WEB: www.koos.com
SIC: 7389 Sewing contractor

PRODUCTS & SERVICES SECTION
7389 - Business Svcs, NEC County (P-17301)

(P-17277)
KOURY ENGRG TSTG & INSPTN
14280 Euclid Ave, Chino (91710-8803)
PHONE..................310 851-8685
Richard Koury, *President*
Deborah Marcotte, *Personnel Exec*
Debra Marcott, *Human Res Mgr*
EMP: 75
SQ FT: 5,000
SALES: 9MM **Privately Held**
WEB: www.kouryengineering.com
SIC: 7389 Building inspection service

(P-17278)
KSI CORP
839 Mitten Rd, Burlingame (94010-1303)
PHONE..................650 952-0815
Carl Bellante, *CEO*
Dennis Siu, *CFO*
Michael Ford, *Senior VP*
Chris Ramos, *Vice Pres*
Glynis Takalo, *Supervisor*
EMP: 60
SALES (est): 3.9MM **Privately Held**
SIC: 7389

(P-17279)
KSM MARKETING INC
Also Called: Keystone Marketing Specialists
10 Holland, Irvine (92618-2504)
PHONE..................949 597-2222
Karen Settle, *President*
Sandra Ambrozio, *Opers Mgr*
EMP: 200
SQ FT: 12,000
SALES (est): 6.8MM **Privately Held**
WEB: www.keystone2000.com
SIC: 7389 Advertising, promotional & trade show services

(P-17280)
L LYON DISTRIBUTING INC
254 W Stuart Ave, Redlands (92374-3136)
P.O. Box 8968 (92375-2168)
PHONE..................909 798-7129
Michael Lyon, *President*
Lori Lyon, *Vice Pres*
EMP: 50
SQ FT: 5,000
SALES (est): 4.1MM **Privately Held**
SIC: 7389 Merchandise liquidators

(P-17281)
LA IMPACT
5700 S Eastern Ave, Commerce (90040-2924)
PHONE..................323 869-6874
Tony Ybarra, *Director*
Silvia Larson, *Admin Asst*
Jaime Robinson, *Admin Asst*
Lisa Vidra, *General Counsel*
David King, *Director*
EMP: 100
SALES (est): 6.7MM **Privately Held**
WEB: www.lacrcic.com
SIC: 7389 Personal service agents, brokers & bureaus

(P-17282)
LA INC CONVENTION VISTORS BUR
333 S Hope St Ste 1800, Los Angeles (90071-1430)
PHONE..................213 236-2301
Mark Liberman, *Exec Dir*
Tia Sanford, *Sales Staff*
EMP: 75
SALES: 19.4MM **Privately Held**
WEB: www.lacvb.com
SIC: 7389 Advertising, promotional & trade show services

(P-17283)
LA JOLLA GROUP INC (PA)
Also Called: Ljg
14350 Myford Rd, Irvine (92606-1002)
PHONE..................949 428-2800
Daniel Neukomm, *CEO*
Tobye Lovelace, *Senior VP*
Tunia Kaawa, *Vice Pres*
Ryan Rush, *Vice Pres*
Brett Hanlon, *Info Tech Dir*
EMP: 58

(P-17284)
LA JOLLA GROUP INC
14350 Myford Rd, Irvine (92606-1002)
PHONE..................949 428-2800
Toby Bost, *Owner*
EMP: 81
SALES (corp-wide): 37.8MM **Privately Held**
SIC: 7389 Apparel designers, commercial
PA: La Jolla Group, Inc.
14350 Myford Rd
Irvine CA 92606
949 428-2800

(P-17285)
LAKESIDE FIRE PROTECTION DST
12216 Lakeside Ave, Lakeside (92040-1715)
PHONE..................619 390-2350
Andy Parr, *Chief*
Robert Schiwitz, *Comptroller*
Jim Kirkpatrick, *Senior Mgr*
Pete Liebig, *Director*
Mark Baker, *Manager*
EMP: 70
SALES (est): 5.6MM **Privately Held**
WEB: www.lakesidefire.com
SIC: 7389 Fire protection service other than forestry or public

(P-17286)
LAKEWOOD PARK HEALTH CENTER (PA)
12023 Lakewood Blvd, Downey (90242-2699)
PHONE..................562 869-0978
Fax: 323 869-5376
Daniel Zilafro, *President*
EMP: 285
SALES (est): 11.1MM **Privately Held**
SIC: 7389 Personal service agents, brokers & bureaus

(P-17287)
LANDMARK ENTERTAINMENT GROUP
466 Foothill Blvd, La Canada (91011-3518)
PHONE..................818 952-6292
Tony Christofer, *President*
Gary Goddard, *Ch of Bd*
Anthony Christopher, *President*
EMP: 50
SQ FT: 46,000
SALES (est): 3.3MM **Privately Held**
WEB: www.landmarkusa.com
SIC: 7389 7812 6794 Design services; motion picture production; television film production; copyright buying & licensing

(P-17288)
LARK INDUSTRIES INC (PA)
Also Called: Residential Design Service
4900 E Hunter Ave, Anaheim (92807-2057)
PHONE..................714 701-4200
Richard D Scholten, *CEO*
Kip Cruze, *Exec VP*
Scott Cheeseman, *Vice Pres*
Kelli A Finale, *Vice Pres*
Paul Forgay, *Vice Pres*
EMP: 113
SALES (est): 67.4MM **Privately Held**
WEB: www.larkindustries.com
SIC: 7389 Interior design services

(P-17289)
LAS VEGAS INTRNTNL TOURS
Also Called: La City Tours.com
18147 Coastline Dr Apt 1, Malibu (90265-5748)
PHONE..................310 581-0718
Monique Chu, *President*
Jan Sherwood, *Principal*
EMP: 81
SQ FT: 129,800
SALES: 750K **Privately Held**
SIC: 7389 Tourist information bureau

(P-17290)
LAX INTERNATIONAL SERVICE CTR
Also Called: Worldway Airmail Center
5800 W Century Blvd, Los Angeles (90009-5601)
PHONE..................310 337-8764
Karen Padden, *General Mgr*
EMP: 65
SALES (est): 1.7MM **Privately Held**
SIC: 7389 Post office contract stations

(P-17291)
LEGAL SUPPORT NETWORK LLC
Also Called: Express Network
1533 Wilshire Blvd, Los Angeles (90017-2205)
PHONE..................213 975-9850
Gary Camara, *Owner*
Nathan Melendrez, *Info Tech Mgr*
EMP: 53
SALES (est): 3.3MM **Privately Held**
SIC: 7389 Courier or messenger service

(P-17292)
LEGEND MERCHANT GROUP INC
201 Mission St Ste 230, San Francisco (94105-1883)
PHONE..................415 957-9555
Chip Unsworth, *President*
EMP: 50
SALES (est): 3.2MM **Privately Held**
SIC: 7389 Financial services

(P-17293)
LEIDOS INC
9455 Towne Centre Dr # 200, San Diego (92121-3079)
PHONE..................858 535-4499
Jim Taylor, *Manager*
John Jumper, *CEO*
Dana Diferdinando, *Vice Pres*
EMP: 112
SALES (corp-wide): 5B **Publicly Held**
WEB: www.saic.com
SIC: 7389 Personal service agents, brokers & bureaus
HQ: Leidos, Inc.
11951 Freedom Dr Ste 500
Reston VA 20190
571 526-6000

(P-17294)
LENNAR PARTNERS OF LOS ANGELES (PA)
4350 Von Karman Ave # 200, Newport Beach (92660-2041)
PHONE..................949 885-8500
Fax: 949 442-6175
David Team, *Division Pres*
Christopher J Martin, *Treasurer*
Erik Hansen, *Senior VP*
Eric Payne, *Risk Mgmt Dir*
Rick Liebermann, *Managing Dir*
EMP: 50
SALES (est): 9.5MM **Privately Held**
WEB: www.lennarpartners.com
SIC: 7389 Personal service agents, brokers & bureaus

(P-17295)
LINDSAY FRUIT COMPANY LLC
Also Called: Yokohl Valley Packing
247 N Mount Vernon Ave, Lindsay (93247-2440)
P.O. Box 907 (93247-0907)
PHONE..................559 562-1327
Fax: 559 562-6732
Tim Bentley,
Larry Larson, *Sales Mgr*
Henry Howison, *Manager*
Ronald Vandeldon, *Manager*
EMP: 75
SALES (est): 6.6MM **Privately Held**
SIC: 7389 Packaging & labeling services

(P-17296)
LITIGTION RSRCES OF AMERICA-CA (PA)
Also Called: Legal Enterprise
4232-1 Las Virgenes Rd, Calabasas (91302-3589)
PHONE..................818 878-9227
Fax: 818 878-0229
Tony Maddocks, *President*
Rick Matsumoto, *Manager*
EMP: 75
SALES (est): 6.1MM **Privately Held**
SIC: 7389 8111 Document storage service; general practice attorney, lawyer

(P-17297)
LIVE NATION ENTERTAINMENT INC
6255 W Sunset Blvd Fl 16, Los Angeles (90028-7403)
PHONE..................323 468-1160
Greg Trojan, *Principal*
Jim Cheung, *President*
John Hopmans, *Exec VP*
Darren McInnes, *Senior VP*
Geoffrey Collins, *Vice Pres*
EMP: 70
SALES (corp-wide): 7.2B **Publicly Held**
SIC: 7389 Promoters of shows & exhibitions
PA: Live Nation Entertainment, Inc.
9348 Civic Center Dr Lbby
Beverly Hills CA 90210
310 867-7000

(P-17298)
LIVE NATION ENTERTAINMENT INC
151 El Camino Dr Fl 3, Beverly Hills (90212-2704)
PHONE..................323 462-4785
Brooke Stanley, *Branch Mgr*
EMP: 70
SALES (corp-wide): 7.2B **Publicly Held**
SIC: 7389 Promoters of shows & exhibitions
PA: Live Nation Entertainment, Inc.
9348 Civic Center Dr Lbby
Beverly Hills CA 90210
310 867-7000

(P-17299)
LMS CORPORATION
300 Crprate Pinte Ste 301, Culver City (90230)
PHONE..................310 641-4222
Nola G Conway, *President*
Vickie Zabi, *General Mgr*
EMP: 50
SQ FT: 2,712
SALES (est): 3.8MM **Privately Held**
WEB: www.thelmscorp.com
SIC: 7389 8742 Telemarketing services; marketing consulting services

(P-17300)
LOCKHEED MARTIN CORPORATION
Also Called: Lockheed Martin Space Sys
16020 Empire Grade, Santa Cruz (95060-9628)
PHONE..................831 425-6375
Byron Ravenscraft, *Manager*
Raleigh Long, *Engineer*
Cary Viktor, *Director*
EMP: 85
SALES (corp-wide): 46.1B **Publicly Held**
WEB: www.lockheedmartin.com
SIC: 7389 Fire protection service other than forestry or public
PA: Lockheed Martin Corporation
6801 Rockledge Dr
Bethesda MD 20817
301 897-6000

(P-17301)
LONG BEACH UNIFIED SCHOOL DST
Also Called: Newcomb Academy
3351 Val Verde Ave, Long Beach (90808-4456)
PHONE..................562 493-3596
Dorothy Colby, *Librarian*
Ryan Noble, *Librarian*
Gayle Maher-Hall, *Assistant*

7389 - Business Svcs, NEC County (P-17302)

PRODUDUCTS & SERVICES SECTION

EMP: 331
SALES (corp-wide): 810.4MM **Privately Held**
SIC: 7389 Fund raising organizations
PA: Long Beach Unified School District
1515 Hughes Way
Long Beach CA 90810
562 997-8000

(P-17302)
LOS ANGELES UNIFIED SCHOOL DST
Also Called: L A U S D
8525 Rex Rd, Pico Rivera (90660-6702)
PHONE..................................562 654-9007
Marc Monforte, *Branch Mgr*
Mar Tigno, *Principal*
Andrew Guerrero, *HR Admin*
Myron Bowens, *Buyer*
EMP: 59
SALES (corp-wide): 4.4B **Privately Held**
WEB: www.lausd.k12.ca.us
SIC: 7389 Purchasing service
PA: Los Angeles Unified School District
333 S Beaudry Ave Ste 209
Los Angeles CA 90017
213 241-1000

(P-17303)
LOS ANGLES TRISM CONVENTION BD (PA)
333 S Hope St Ste 1800, Los Angeles (90071-1430)
PHONE..................................213 624-7300
Fax: 213 624-9746
Ernest Wooden Jr, *CEO*
Bob Graziano, *Managing Prtnr*
Alan I Rothenberg, *Ch of Bd*
Stefan J Dietrich, *CFO*
Don Orris, *Exec VP*
EMP: 50 EST: 1971
SALES: 38.3MM **Privately Held**
SIC: 7389 Convention & show services; tourist information bureau

(P-17304)
LOYAL3 HOLDINGS INC
150 California St Ste 400, San Francisco (94111-4566)
P.O. Box 26027 (94126-6027)
PHONE..................................415 981-0700
Barry L Schneider, *CEO*
Peter Coleman, *CFO*
Jack Thrift, *CFO*
Dana Schmidt, *Ch Credit Ofcr*
Bill Blais, *Exec VP*
EMP: 80
SQ FT: 8,900
SALES (est): 11.8MM **Privately Held**
SIC: 7389 Financial services

(P-17305)
MABIE MARKETING GROUP INC
Also Called: California Marketing
8352 Clairemont Mesa Blvd, San Diego (92111-1302)
PHONE..................................858 279-5585
Fax: 858 279-2079
John Mabie, *President*
Ramyar Ravansari, *CFO*
Samantha Galarneau, *Vice Pres*
Nate Ames, *Info Tech Dir*
Donald Kirchner, *Technology*
EMP: 200
SALES (est): 21MM **Privately Held**
WEB: www.calmarketing.com
SIC: 7389 Telemarketing services

(P-17306)
MACRO-PRO INC (PA)
Also Called: Micro-Pro Microfilming Svcs
2400 Grand Ave, Long Beach (90815-1762)
P.O. Box 90459 (90809-0459)
PHONE..................................562 595-0900
Fax: 562 595-8937
Patty Waldeck, *President*
Graciella Flores, *CFO*
Eric Neitzel, *CFO*
Andrea Kivo, *Manager*
EMP: 140
SQ FT: 24,000

SALES (est): 12.8MM **Privately Held**
WEB: www.macropro.com
SIC: 7389 7334 Legal & tax services; microfilm recording & developing service; photocopying & duplicating services

(P-17307)
MACRO-PRO INC
14764 Wicks Blvd, San Leandro (94577-6718)
P.O. Box 4217 (94579-0217)
PHONE..................................510 483-2679
Fax: 510 483-1470
Patty Waldeck, *Branch Mgr*
Diann Cohen, *Mktg Dir*
EMP: 100
SALES (corp-wide): 12.8MM **Privately Held**
WEB: www.macropro.com
SIC: 7389 Legal & tax services
PA: Macro-Pro, Inc.
2400 Grand Ave
Long Beach CA 90815
562 595-0900

(P-17308)
MADDEN CORPORATION
Also Called: Pam's Delivery Svc & Nat Msgnr
733 W Taft Ave, Orange (92865-4229)
PHONE..................................714 922-1670
Donald L Madden, *President*
Robert Tillmans, *Accountant*
EMP: 100
SQ FT: 7,000
SALES (est): 10.3MM **Privately Held**
SIC: 7389 Courier or messenger service

(P-17309)
MADRIGAL VINEYARD MANAGEMENT
Also Called: Madrigal Vineyards
3718 Saint Helena Hwy, Calistoga (94515-9651)
P.O. Box 937 (94515-0937)
PHONE..................................707 942-8691
Jesus Madrigal, *Owner*
Chris Madrigal, *CEO*
Justin Ovard, *CFO*
Rob Higginfs, *Manager*
EMP: 50
SALES (est): 4.5MM **Privately Held**
WEB: www.madrigalvineyards.com
SIC: 7389 Personal service agents, brokers & bureaus

(P-17310)
MAGNOLIA VENTURES LTD
Also Called: C/O Longwood Management
4032 Wilshire Blvd Fl 6, Los Angeles (90010-3425)
PHONE..................................213 389-6900
Jacob Freedman, *President*
EMP: 100
SALES (est): 3.7MM **Privately Held**
SIC: 7389 Personal service agents, brokers & bureaus

(P-17311)
MARINE TECHNICAL SERVICES INC
Also Called: Dockside Machine & Ship Repair
211 N Marine Ave, Wilmington (90744-5724)
P.O. Box 1301, San Pedro (90733-1301)
PHONE..................................310 549-8030
Fax: 310 549-7365
Dianne Marie Hawke, *President*
Yen Tran, *Accountant*
EMP: 75
SQ FT: 20,000
SALES (est): 11.5MM **Privately Held**
WEB: www.marinetechserv.com
SIC: 7389 7699 Crane & aerial lift service; nautical repair services

(P-17312)
MARINER SYSTEMS INC (PA)
114 C Ave, Coronado (92118-1435)
PHONE..................................305 266-7255
Carlos M Collazo, *President*
Neil Park, *CEO*
Edwin Borja, *Accountant*
EMP: 50

SALES (est): 4.3MM **Privately Held**
WEB: www.marinersystems.net
SIC: 7389 7374 7372 7371 Telephone services; data processing service; prepackaged software; custom computer programming services

(P-17313)
MARMALADE LLC
Also Called: Marmalade Cafes
3894 Cross Creek Rd, Malibu (90265-4933)
PHONE..................................310 317-4242
Fax: 310 317-4242
Paul McGinley, *Branch Mgr*
Barbara Chapin, *Manager*
EMP: 50
SALES (corp-wide): 19.5MM **Privately Held**
WEB: www.marmaladecafe.com
SIC: 7389 Personal service agents, brokers & bureaus
PA: Marmalade, Llc
21300 Victory Blvd # 740
Woodland Hills CA 91367
310 829-0093

(P-17314)
MARQUEZ BROTHERS ADVG AGCY
5801 Rue Ferrari, San Jose (95138-1857)
PHONE..................................408 960-2700
Gustavo Marquez, *President*
EMP: 100
SALES (est): 3.4MM **Privately Held**
SIC: 7389 Advertising, promotional & trade show services

(P-17315)
MARTYS CUTTING INC
Also Called: Marty's Cutting Service
2615 Fruitland Ave, Vernon (90058-2219)
PHONE..................................323 582-5758
Fax: 323 582-5272
Martin Anaya, *President*
Francisco Anaya, *Vice Pres*
EMP: 80
SQ FT: 57,000
SALES (est): 3.8MM **Privately Held**
WEB: www.marty-howard.com
SIC: 7389 Cloth cutting, bolting or winding

(P-17316)
MASTER-SORT INC
245 W Carl Karcher Way, Anaheim (92801-2499)
PHONE..................................714 258-7678
Jeff Stevens, *CEO*
John Makoff, *Officer*
Carlos Aguirre, *Vice Pres*
Eric Norful, *Opers Staff*
John Szozda, *Sales Mgr*
EMP: 150 EST: 1999
SALES (est): 6.4MM
SALES (corp-wide): 3.5B **Publicly Held**
WEB: www.psigroupinc.com
SIC: 7389 Mailbox rental & related service
HQ: Pitney Bowes Presort Services, Inc.
10110 I St
Omaha NE 68127
402 339-6500

(P-17317)
MAVERICK RECORDS LLC
Also Called: Maverick Entertainment
3300 Warner Blvd, Burbank (91505-4632)
PHONE..................................212 275-2000
Madonna Ciccone,
Xavier Ramos, *Mktg Dir*
Frederick Demann,
EMP: 50
SALES (est): 1.6MM
SALES (corp-wide): 2.9B **Privately Held**
WEB: www.maverick.com
SIC: 7389 Music recording producer
HQ: Warner Music Group Corp.
1633 Broadway
New York NY 10019
212 275-2000

(P-17318)
MB COATINGS INC
571 N Poplar St Ste G, Orange (92868-1023)
PHONE..................................714 625-2118
Michael Bartle, *President*

Amanda Bartle, *Vice Pres*
EMP: 80
SQ FT: 2,000
SALES: 5.9MM **Privately Held**
SIC: 7389 Hand painting, textile

(P-17319)
MCCLATCHY NEWSPAPERS INC
Also Called: El Sol
1325 H St, Modesto (95354-2427)
P.O. Box 3928 (95352-3928)
PHONE..................................209 238-4636
Fax: 209 238-4641
Olivia Ruiz, *Manager*
Cecil Jarvis, *Vice Pres*
Robert J Weil, *Vice Pres*
Tom Shaw, *Foreman/Supr*
Frank J Bolyard, *Director*
EMP: 500
SALES (corp-wide): 1B **Publicly Held**
WEB: www.sacbee.com
SIC: 7389 Subscription fulfillment services: magazine, newspaper, etc.
HQ: Mcclatchy Newspapers, Inc.
2100 Q St
Sacramento CA 95816
916 321-1000

(P-17320)
MCKESSON TECHNOLOGIES INC
5110 E Clinton Way # 101, Fresno (93727-2040)
PHONE..................................559 455-4000
Glenda Josey, *Principal*
Denise Thompson, *Manager*
EMP: 120
SALES (corp-wide): 190.8B **Publicly Held**
WEB: www.per-se.com
SIC: 7389 Personal service agents, brokers & bureaus
HQ: Mckesson Technologies Inc.
11475 Great Oaks Way # 400
Alpharetta GA 30022
404 338-6000

(P-17321)
MD7 LLC (PA)
10590 W Ocean Air Dr # 300, San Diego (92130-4682)
PHONE..................................858 799-7850
Michael D Gianni, *CEO*
Tom Leddo, *VP Opers*
Michael Francis, *General Counsel*
Michael G Francis,
Cheryl Bovvitt, *Manager*
EMP: 58
SQ FT: 23,000
SALES (est): 14.7MM **Privately Held**
WEB: www.md7.com
SIC: 7389 Telemarketing services

(P-17322)
MECS INC
1778 Monsanto Way, Martinez (94553-1448)
PHONE..................................925 313-0681
Carl Casale, *Vice Pres*
Wayne Fulghum, *Plant Mgr*
Odis Johnson, *Production*
EMP: 51
SALES (corp-wide): 25.1B **Publicly Held**
SIC: 7389 Personal service agents, brokers & bureaus
HQ: Mecs, Inc.
14522 South Outer 40 Rd # 1
Chesterfield MO 63017
314 275-5700

(P-17323)
MEDIA ALL STARS INC
8525 Gibbs Dr Ste 206, San Diego (92123-1765)
PHONE..................................858 300-9600
Buddy Cummings, *President*
Joel Davies, *COO*
Daniel Smith, *Opers Staff*
Mike McIntosh, *Sales Mgr*
Leah Baltz, *Manager*
EMP: 53
SALES (est): 5.6MM **Privately Held**
WEB: www.mediaallstars.com
SIC: 7389 Fund raising organizations

PRODUCTS & SERVICES SECTION
7389 - Business Svcs, NEC County (P-17347)

(P-17324)
MEDUSIND SOLUTIONS INC
31103 Rancho Viejo Rd, San Juan Capistrano (92675-1759)
PHONE..................949 240-8895
Rajiv Sahney, *Chairman*
Robert Beck, *President*
Vipul Bansal, *CEO*
Dhiren Kapadia, *CFO*
Kranti Munje, *Senior VP*
EMP: 900
SALES (est): 49.1MM
SALES (corp-wide): 20MM **Privately Held**
WEB: www.medusind.com
SIC: 7389 Personal service agents, brokers & bureaus
PA: Medusind Solutions India Private Limited
6th Floor, The Great Oasis, D-13,
Street 21
Mumbai MH 40009
226 666-4701

(P-17325)
MEGA APPRAISERS INC
14724 Ventura Blvd # 800, Sherman Oaks (91403-3508)
PHONE..................818 246-7370
Fax: 818 246-7367
Levon Hairapetian, *President*
EMP: 50
SALES: 1.2MM **Privately Held**
SIC: 7389 Appraisers, except real estate

(P-17326)
MELISSA & DOUG LLC
4718 Newcastle Rd, Stockton (95215-9454)
PHONE..................209 830-7900
EMP: 50
SALES (corp-wide): 153.4MM **Privately Held**
SIC: 7389
PA: Melissa & Doug, Llc
141 Danbury Rd
Wilton CT 06897
203 762-4500

(P-17327)
MERCHANT OF TENNIS INC
1118 S La Cienega Blvd, Los Angeles (90035-2519)
PHONE..................310 855-1946
Fax: 310 855-1949
Jay Banks, *Branch Mgr*
Sung Pak, *Human Res Mgr*
Jeff Green, *Agent*
EMP: 189
SALES (corp-wide): 143.9MM **Privately Held**
SIC: 7389 Packaging & labeling services
PA: The Merchant Of Tennis Inc
8737 Wilshire Blvd
Beverly Hills CA 90211
310 228-4000

(P-17328)
MERCHANT OF TENNIS INC
1625 Proforma Ave, Ontario (91761-7607)
PHONE..................909 923-3388
Larry Khemlani, *Principal*
EMP: 1136
SALES (corp-wide): 143.9MM **Privately Held**
SIC: 7389 Packaging & labeling services
PA: The Merchant Of Tennis Inc
8737 Wilshire Blvd
Beverly Hills CA 90211
310 228-4000

(P-17329)
MERCURY MESSENGER SERVICE INC
Also Called: Bestway Delivery
16735 Saticoy St Ste 104, Van Nuys (91406-2700)
PHONE..................818 989-3115
Lionel Senker, *President*
Jim Gilbertson, *Vice Pres*
EMP: 50
SQ FT: 1,500
SALES (est): 6.3MM **Privately Held**
SIC: 7389 4212 Courier or messenger service; delivery service, vehicular

(P-17330)
MERIBEAR PRODUCTIONS INC
Also Called: Meredith Baer & Associates
4100 Ardmore Ave, South Gate (90280-3246)
PHONE..................323 588-7421
Fax: 310 204-5453
Meridith Baer, *President*
Caleb Morse, *CFO*
Duane Lynch, *Vice Pres*
Anna Viola, *Office Mgr*
Ruben Ibarra, *Accounting Mgr*
EMP: 90
SQ FT: 55,000
SALES (est): 12.7MM **Privately Held**
SIC: 7389 Interior design services; interior decorating

(P-17331)
MERICAL LLC (PA)
2995 E Miraloma Ave, Anaheim (92806-1805)
PHONE..................714 238-7225
Fax: 714 238-7249
Jeffrey Stallings, *President*
Michael Schlinger, *CEO*
D Dean Baltzell, *CFO*
Tom Bovich, *Vice Pres*
Deborah Lingenfelter, *Vice Pres*
EMP: 100
SQ FT: 92,000
SALES (est): 52.6MM **Privately Held**
SIC: 7389 Packaging & labeling services

(P-17332)
MESSAGE BROADCASTCOM LLC
4685 Macarthur Ct Ste 250, Newport Beach (92660-1893)
PHONE..................949 428-3111
William H Potter, *Mng Member*
Juan Gutierrez, *Administration*
Nick Lott, *Technology*
Ato Manuud, *Financial Exec*
Kyle Manchester, *Opers Mgr*
EMP: 50
SQ FT: 8,000
SALES (est): 6.7MM **Privately Held**
SIC: 7389 Telemarketing services

(P-17333)
MESSAGE CENTER COMMUNICATION
6779 Mesa Ridge Rd # 100, San Diego (92121-2996)
PHONE..................858 974-7419
Gary Schaumann, *Owner*
EMP: 50
SALES (est): 2.7MM **Privately Held**
SIC: 7389 Telephone answering service

(P-17334)
METRICUS INC
P.O. Box 458 (94302-0458)
PHONE..................650 328-2500
Jeanne J Fleming, *President*
Leonard C Schwarz, *CFO*
EMP: 119
SALES (est): 3.1MM **Privately Held**
WEB: www.metricus.com
SIC: 7389 Legal & tax services

(P-17335)
MICKWEE GROUP INC
Also Called: Mgi
5600 Mowry School Rd # 230, Newark (94560-5806)
PHONE..................510 651-5527
Fax: 510 651-5892
Ronald Mickwee, *President*
EMP: 52
SALES (est): 3.1MM **Privately Held**
WEB: www.mickwee.com
SIC: 7389 8742 Telemarketing services; management consulting services

(P-17336)
MINIMALISMS INC
49 Missouri St Apt 10, San Francisco (94107-2484)
PHONE..................415 309-3108
George Arriola, *President*
EMP: 52 **EST:** 2014
SALES: 250K **Privately Held**
SIC: 7389 Design services

(P-17337)
MISSION COURIER INC
3204 Orange Grove Ave, North Highlands (95660-5806)
PHONE..................916 484-1992
Fax: 916 484-2096
Marc Raty, *President*
Andy French, *Vice Pres*
Doug Brothers, *Manager*
EMP: 55
SQ FT: 11,000
SALES (est): 6.1MM **Privately Held**
SIC: 7389 Courier or messenger service

(P-17338)
MOBILE MESSENGER AMERICAS INC (PA)
6601 Center Dr W Ste 700, Los Angeles (90045-1545)
PHONE..................310 957-3300
Fax: 310 496-2873
Darcy Wedd, *CEO*
Daniel Machock, *CFO*
Amy Dudman, *Senior VP*
Edward McCormick, *Senior VP*
Israel Niezen, *Senior VP*
EMP: 64
SALES (est): 22.2MM **Privately Held**
WEB: www.mobilemessenger.com
SIC: 7389 Courier or messenger service

(P-17339)
MODERN DEV CO A LTD PARTNR
Also Called: Paramount Swap Meet
7900 All America City Way, Paramount (90723-3400)
PHONE..................949 646-6400
Fax: 562 633-6631
Darren Kurkowski, *Branch Mgr*
EMP: 98
SALES (corp-wide): 20.5MM **Privately Held**
SIC: 7389 Flea market
PA: Modern Development Co, A Limited Partnership
3333 W Coast Hwy Ste 400
Newport Beach CA 92663
949 646-6400

(P-17340)
MOLD TESTING AND INSPECTION
Also Called: MT&i
4785 Sequoia Pl, Oceanside (92057-6126)
PHONE..................760 643-1834
K W Huntington, *President*
Keith William Huntington, *President*
EMP: 75
SALES (est): 3.7MM **Privately Held**
SIC: 7389 Inspection & testing services

(P-17341)
MOTIVATIONAL MARKETING INC
Also Called: Motivational Fulfillment
15820 Euclid Ave, Chino (91708-9162)
PHONE..................909 517-2200
Hal Altman, *CEO*
Andrea Stuhley, *Exec VP*
Anthony Altman, *Senior VP*
Tony Altman, *Vice Pres*
Cheryl Nataren, *Vice Pres*
▲ **EMP:** 400
SQ FT: 300,000
SALES (est): 55.7MM **Privately Held**
WEB: www.mfpsinc.com
SIC: 7389 8748 8742 Telephone services; mailing & messenger services; business consulting; management consulting services

(P-17342)
MOULTON LOGISTICS MANAGEMENT (PA)
7850 Ruffner Ave, Van Nuys (91406-1619)
P.O. Box 8191 (91409-8191)
PHONE..................818 997-1800
Fax: 818 442-0342
Lawrence Moulton, *President*
Tom Moulton, *Vice Pres*
Elizabeth Dermendjian, *Admin Asst*
Shaida Motaghy, *Admin Asst*
Jameson Setzer, *Admin Asst*
◆ **EMP:** 100
SQ FT: 108,000
SALES (est): 52.1MM **Privately Held**
WEB: www.moultonlogistics.com
SIC: 7389 4822 Subscription fulfillment services: magazine, newspaper, etc.; electronic mail

(P-17343)
MULTIVISION INC (DH)
Also Called: Bacon's Multivision
66 Franklin St Fl 3, Oakland (94607-3728)
PHONE..................510 740-5600
Babak Farahi, *President*
Farid Badiee, *Vice Pres*
Caitriona Goss, *Vice Pres*
EMP: 70
SALES (est): 7.1MM **Privately Held**
WEB: www.multivision.com
SIC: 7389 Press clipping service
HQ: Cision Us Inc.
130 E Randolph St Fl 7
Chicago IL 60601
312 922-2400

(P-17344)
MUSCOLINO INVENTORY SVC INC
1620 N Carptr Rd Ste D50, Modesto (95351)
PHONE..................209 576-8469
Fax: 209 576-8469
EMP: 50
SALES (corp-wide): 67MM **Privately Held**
SIC: 7389
HQ: Muscolino Inventory Service, Inc.
320 W Chestnut Ave
Monrovia CA 91016
626 357-8600

(P-17345)
MVENTIX INC
25129 The Old Rd Ste 112, Stevenson Ranch (91381-2293)
PHONE..................661 263-1768
Kristian Fatzov, *CEO*
Andrey Lyutykh, *Program Mgr*
Margaret Aragon, *Office Mgr*
Pavel Monev, *CTO*
Geoffry Shreckengost, *Technology*
EMP: 386
SQ FT: 4,000
SALES (est): 21.3MM **Privately Held**
WEB: www.mventix.com
SIC: 7389 Advertising, promotional & trade show services

(P-17346)
MX COURIER SYSTEMS INC
Also Called: Medical Ex Courier Systems
990 N Tustin St, Orange (92867-5903)
PHONE..................714 288-8622
Fax: 714 288-8626
Mohammad A Zadsham, *President*
Akbar Heidarinia, *President*
EMP: 50
SQ FT: 1,200
SALES: 1.5MM **Privately Held**
SIC: 7389 4212 Courier or messenger service; delivery service, vehicular

(P-17347)
NATIONAL BUS INVSTIGATIONS INC
Also Called: MPS Security
25020 Las Brisas Rd Ste A, Murrieta (92562-4064)
PHONE..................951 677-3500
Michael D Julian, *President*
Lisa Pons, *Administration*
Corrine Day, *Controller*
Rafael Cisneros, *Security Mgr*
Dennis Varhall, *Security Mgr*
EMP: 60 **EST:** 1967
SQ FT: 2,000
SALES (est): 6MM **Privately Held**
SIC: 7389 7381 Personal investigation service; private investigator

7389 - Business Svcs, NEC County (P-17348)

(P-17348)
NATIONAL LGAL STUDIES INST INC
Also Called: Nlsi
23962 Alssndro Blvd Ste P, Moreno Valley (92553-8806)
P.O. Box 7562, Riverside (92513-7562)
PHONE..................951 653-4240
Thersea Thompson, *CEO*
EMP: 50
SQ FT: 2,000
SALES (est): 2.2MM **Privately Held**
SIC: 7389 Paralegal service

(P-17349)
NATIONS DIRECT LENDER & IN
160 S Old Springs Rd # 260, Anaheim (92808-1229)
PHONE..................800 969-7779
Jeff Store, *President*
Hal Lamm, *CFO*
Danielle Strengberg, *Mktg Dir*
Gerrod Daniel, *Manager*
Erica Cornejo, *Accounts Mgr*
EMP: 114
SQ FT: 18,000
SALES (est): 9MM **Privately Held**
WEB: www.signing-services.com
SIC: 7389 Drafting service, except temporary help

(P-17350)
NEFAB PACKAGING WEST LLC
8477 Central Ave, Newark (94560-3431)
PHONE..................408 678-2516
Fredrik Solspher,
Chris Collins, *Accountant*
Anna Gonzalez, *Accounts Mgr*
EMP: 50
SALES: 10MM
SALES (corp-wide): 23.7MM **Privately Held**
SIC: 7389 Packaging & labeling services
HQ: Nefab Companies, Inc.
204 Airline Dr Ste 100
Coppell TX 75019
469 444-5320

(P-17351)
NESTWISE LLC
9785 Towne Centre Dr, San Diego (92121-1968)
PHONE..................855 444-6378
Esther Stearns, *CEO*
Beth Stelluto, *Chief Mktg Ofcr*
Burt White, *Ch Invest Ofcr*
Kandis Bates, *Officer*
Rudy Bethea, *Officer*
EMP: 662
SALES (est): 14.5MM
SALES (corp-wide): 4.2B **Publicly Held**
SIC: 7389 Financial services
PA: Lpl Financial Holdings Inc.
75 State St Ste 2401
Boston MA 02109
617 423-3644

(P-17352)
NETBALL AMERICA INC
4686 Oceano Cir, Huntington Beach (92649-3224)
PHONE..................949 307-4455
Sonya Ottaway, *President*
EMP: 50 **EST:** 2013
SALES (est): 81.4K **Privately Held**
SIC: 7389

(P-17353)
NEW CAM COMMERCE SOLUTIONS LLC
17075 Newhope St Ste 3, Fountain Valley (92708-4299)
PHONE..................714 241-9241
Doug Roberson, *Mng Member*
Nadine Arona, *Info Tech Mgr*
Brent Melbye, *Info Tech Mgr*
Ann Gao, *Controller*
Sherree Lucas, *Sls & Mktg Exec*
EMP: 97
SQ FT: 26,000
SALES (est): 5.8MM **Privately Held**
SIC: 7389 Credit card service

(P-17354)
NEW CREW PRODUCTION CORP
200 W 138th St, Los Angeles (90061-1004)
PHONE..................323 234-8880
Fax: 323 234-0989
Kris Park, *President*
Glen Park, *CFO*
Joseph Park, *Admin Sec*
Tuyet Ha, *Accountant*
EMP: 110
SQ FT: 20,000
SALES (est): 11.3MM **Privately Held**
WEB: www.newcrewproductioncorp.com
SIC: 7389 Sewing contractor

(P-17355)
NEW GLOBAL TELECOM INC
624 S Grand Ave Ste 2900, Los Angeles (90017-3881)
PHONE..................213 489-3708
Fax: 213 438-1313
David Richardson, *Branch Mgr*
EMP: 56 **Privately Held**
WEB: www.ngt.com
SIC: 7389 Telephone services
PA: New Global Telecom, Inc.
143 Union Blvd Ste 400
Lakewood CO 80228

(P-17356)
NEWPORT DIVERSIFIED INC
Santa Fe Springs Swap Meet
13963 Alondra Blvd, Santa Fe Springs (90670-5814)
PHONE..................562 921-4359
Rick Landis, *Sales & Mktg Str*
Erika Garcia, *Human Resources*
Ed Collins, *Asst Mgr*
EMP: 200
SQ FT: 10,846
SALES (corp-wide): 1.1MM **Privately Held**
WEB: www.nd-inc.com
SIC: 7389 5932 Flea market; used merchandise stores
PA: Newport Diversified, Inc.
2301 Dupont Dr Ste 500
Irvine CA 92612
949 851-1355

(P-17357)
NEWPORT DIVERSIFIED INC
Also Called: The Boardwalk
1286 Fletcher Pkwy, El Cajon (92020-1826)
PHONE..................619 449-7800
Ron Westphal, *Manager*
EMP: 100
SALES (corp-wide): 1.1MM **Privately Held**
WEB: www.nd-inc.com
SIC: 7389 7996 Flea market; amusement parks
PA: Newport Diversified, Inc.
2301 Dupont Dr Ste 500
Irvine CA 92612
949 851-1355

(P-17358)
NEWPORT DIVERSIFIED INC
Also Called: Boardwalk and Parkway Bowl
1280 Fletcher Pkwy, El Cajon (92020-1826)
PHONE..................619 448-3147
Ron Westphal, *Manager*
EMP: 115
SALES (corp-wide): 1.2MM **Privately Held**
WEB: www.nd-inc.com
SIC: 7389 7933 Flea market; ten pin center
PA: Newport Diversified Inc.
2301 Dupont Dr Ste 500
Irvine CA 92612
949 851-1355

(P-17359)
NI KI CRUZ LLC
5255 Stevens Creek Blvd, Santa Clara (95051-6664)
PHONE..................408 332-7616
Carlos R Cruz Jr, *Partner*
EMP: 99
SALES (est): 36.6K **Privately Held**
SIC: 7389 Business services

(P-17360)
NIELSEN MOBILE LLC (DH)
1010 Battery St, San Francisco (94111-1202)
PHONE..................917 435-9301
Sid Gorham, *President*
Tom Stahl, *COO*
Jim Wandrey, *Treasurer*
Nick Rau, *Vice Pres*
Timothy Gray, *Engng Exec*
EMP: 180 **EST:** 2000
SQ FT: 38,000
SALES (est): 19.4MM
SALES (corp-wide): 43.6K **Privately Held**
WEB: www.telephia.com
SIC: 7389 Inspection & testing services

(P-17361)
NLC ENTERPRISES INCORPORATED
15710 Leffingwell Rd, Whittier (90604-3325)
PHONE..................562 693-3590
Norman Carter, *Principal*
EMP: 50
SALES (est): 1.6MM **Privately Held**
SIC: 7389 Business services

(P-17362)
NNNCC RANCH
7602 Monson Ave, Orange Cove (93646-9307)
PHONE..................559 626-4890
Richard Nicholas, *Partner*
Richard M Nicholas, *Owner*
EMP: 100 **EST:** 2000
SQ FT: 2,238
SALES (est): 3.5MM **Privately Held**
SIC: 7389 Packaging & labeling services

(P-17363)
NOR-CAL BEVERAGE CO INC
Also Called: Norcal Beverage Co
1226 N Olive St, Anaheim (92801-2543)
PHONE..................714 526-8600
William McFarland, *Manager*
EMP: 200
SALES (corp-wide): 245.3MM **Privately Held**
SIC: 7389 2033 Packaging & labeling services; canned fruits & specialties
PA: Nor-Cal Beverage Co., Inc.
2150 Stone Blvd
West Sacramento CA 95691
916 372-0600

(P-17364)
NORCO DELIVERY SERVICE INC
3082 N Lima St, Burbank (91504-2012)
PHONE..................818 558-4810
Fax: 818 558-4814
Ernie Zuniga, *Branch Mgr*
Rey Mesa, *Manager*
EMP: 134
SALES (corp-wide): 36.7MM **Privately Held**
SIC: 7389 Courier or messenger service
PA: Norco Delivery Service, Inc.
851 E Cerritos Ave
Anaheim CA 92805
714 520-8600

(P-17365)
NORTHERN SHEETS LLC
4841 Urbani Ave Ste D, McClellan (95652-2025)
PHONE..................916 437-2800
David Demeter, *General Mgr*
EMP: 68
SALES (est): 10.1MM **Privately Held**
SIC: 7389 Packaging & labeling services

(P-17366)
NORTHGATE GONZALEZ INC
Also Called: Northgate Market 11
1120 S Bricol St, Santa Ana (92704)
PHONE..................714 957-2529
Rita Roman, *Branch Mgr*
Ben Hashemi, *Manager*
EMP: 120
SALES (corp-wide): 266.7MM **Privately Held**
WEB: www.northgatemarkets.com
SIC: 7389 Personal service agents, brokers & bureaus
PA: Northgate Gonzalez, Inc.
1201 N Magnolia Ave
Anaheim CA 92801
714 778-3784

(P-17367)
NORTHROP GRUMMAN SYSTEMS CORP
6411 W Imperial Hwy, Los Angeles (90045-6307)
PHONE..................310 556-4911
Mark Shea, *Principal*
EMP: 303 **Publicly Held**
SIC: 7389 Personal service agents, brokers & bureaus
HQ: Northrop Grumman Systems Corporation
2980 Fairview Park Dr
Falls Church VA 22042
703 280-2900

(P-17368)
NOVATO FIRE PROTECTION DIST
95 Rowland Way, Novato (94945-5001)
PHONE..................415 878-2690
Daniel Hom, *Finance*
Lisa Maccubbin, *Human Res Dir*
Marc Revere, *Fire Chief*
EMP: 90
SALES (est): 5MM **Privately Held**
SIC: 7389 Fire protection service other than forestry or public

(P-17369)
NSW REAL ESTATE HOLDINGS LLC
99 S Hill Dr Ste A, Brisbane (94005-1282)
PHONE..................415 467-7600
EMP: 90
SALES (est): 12.6MM **Privately Held**
SIC: 7389

(P-17370)
NTH CONNECT TELECOM INC
2371 Bering Dr, San Jose (95131-1125)
PHONE..................408 922-0800
Steven Chen, *President*
Laura McDonnell, *Accounting Mgr*
EMP: 60
SALES (est): 7.1MM **Privately Held**
SIC: 7389 Telephone services

(P-17371)
NTH DEGREE INC
Also Called: N Th Degree
27092 Burbank, Foothill Ranch (92610-2508)
PHONE..................714 734-4155
Fax: 714 573-8609
Scott Bennett, *Branch Mgr*
EMP: 50
SALES (corp-wide): 45.9MM **Privately Held**
WEB: www.nthdegree.com
SIC: 7389 Advertising, promotional & trade show services
PA: Nth Degree, Inc.
2675 Breckinridge Blvd # 200
Duluth GA 30096
404 296-5282

(P-17372)
OAKTREE STRATEGIC INCOME LLC
333 S Grand Ave Fl 28, Los Angeles (90071-1504)
PHONE..................213 830-6300
EMP: 315 **EST:** 2015
SALES (est): 47.6K **Privately Held**
SIC: 7389 Business services
PA: Oaktree Capital Group Holdings, L.P.
333 S Grand Ave Fl 28
Los Angeles CA 90071

PRODUCTS & SERVICES SECTION
7389 - Business Svcs, NEC County (P-17396)

(P-17373)
OCEAN BREEZE MANUFACTURING
1961 Hawkins Cir, Los Angeles (90001-2255)
PHONE 323 586-8760
Fax: 323 586-8757
Jamshid Daneshrad, *President*
Jackline Daneshrad, *Shareholder*
John Daneshrad, *Shareholder*
Shain Daneshrad, *Shareholder*
EMP: 80
SQ FT: 60,000
SALES: 1.5MM **Privately Held**
SIC: 7389 Sewing contractor

(P-17374)
OFFICE OF SPECIAL SERVICES
8633 Arbor Dr, El Cerrito (94530-2728)
PHONE 510 524-9559
Joseph Levit, *Deputy Dir*
EMP: 79
SALES (est): 1.6MM **Privately Held**
SIC: 7389 Personal service agents, brokers & bureaus

(P-17375)
ON LINK TECHNOLOGIES INC
2207 Bridgepointe Pkwy, Foster City (94404-5060)
PHONE 650 477-5000
Tom Siebel, *President*
EMP: 61
SALES (est): 3.6MM **Privately Held**
SIC: 7389 Business services

(P-17376)
ON-SITE MANAGER INC (PA)
307 Orchard Cy Dr Ste 110, Campbell (95008)
PHONE 866 266-7483
Jonathan T Harrington, *CEO*
Scott Jones, *Vice Pres*
Janna Erichsen, *Admin Sec*
Geri Zerbini, *Administration*
Holly Fahn, *Cust Svc Mgr*
EMP: 50
SALES (est): 12.4MM **Privately Held**
WEB: www.on-sitemanager.com
SIC: 7389 Tenant screening service

(P-17377)
ONE LEGAL INC
350 S Figueroa St Ste 385, Los Angeles (90071-1208)
PHONE 213 617-1212
Fax: 213 617-4717
Robert Battaglia, *President*
EMP: 60
SALES (est): 4.2MM **Privately Held**
SIC: 7389 Legal & tax services

(P-17378)
ONTARIO CONVENTION CENTER CORP
Also Called: Smg Management Facility
2000 E Convention Ctr Way, Ontario (91764-5633)
PHONE 909 937-3000
Dick Walsh, *Mayor*
Michael K Krouse, *CEO*
Nancy Hall, *Executive Asst*
EMP: 130
SQ FT: 225,000
SALES (est): 8.1MM **Privately Held**
WEB: www.ontariocc.com
SIC: 7389 9111 Convention & show services; city & town managers' offices
PA: City Of Ontario
    303 E B St
    Ontario CA 91764
    909 395-2012

(P-17379)
OPENTABLE INC (HQ)
1 Montgomery St Ste 700, San Francisco (94104-4536)
PHONE 415 344-4200
Christa Quarles, *CEO*
Matthew Roberts, *Ch of Bd*
Jeff McCombs, *CFO*
I Duncan Robertson, *CFO*
Prasad Gune, *Senior VP*
EMP: 105
SQ FT: 50,965
SALES: 190MM
SALES (corp-wide): 9.2B **Publicly Held**
WEB: www.opentable.com
SIC: 7389 Restaurant reservation service
PA: The Priceline Group Inc
    800 Connecticut Ave 3w01
    Norwalk CT 06854
    203 299-8000

(P-17380)
OPERATIX INC
111 N Market St Ste 300, San Jose (95113-1116)
PHONE 408 332-5796
Graham Curme, *CEO*
Aurelien Mottier, *Vice Pres*
EMP: 65 EST: 2013
SALES (est): 3.2MM **Privately Held**
SIC: 7389

(P-17381)
ORANGE CAST TITLE SOUTHERN CAL (PA)
640 N Tustin Ave Ste 106, Santa Ana (92705-3731)
P.O. Box 11825 (92711-1825)
PHONE 714 558-2836
Fax: 714 667-6017
John L Marconi, *CEO*
William Fajardo, *President*
Rich Mac Aluso, *President*
Fred Nilsen, *President*
Rich Macaluso, *COO*
EMP: 100
SQ FT: 24,000
SALES (est): 160.8MM **Privately Held**
SIC: 7389 6361 6541 Personal service agents, brokers & bureaus; title insurance; title & trust companies

(P-17382)
ORANGE COURIER INC
3731 W Warner Ave, Santa Ana (92704-5218)
P.O. Box 5308 (92704-0308)
PHONE 714 384-3600
Fax: 909 384-3552
Evell T Stanley, *President*
Brandon Ruben, *Manager*
T O Thompson, *Manager*
EMP: 300
SQ FT: 150,000
SALES (est): 36.4MM **Privately Held**
WEB: www.orangecourier.com
SIC: 7389 4213 4225 Courier or messenger service; trucking, except local; general warehousing & storage

(P-17383)
OST TRUCKS AND CRANES INC
Also Called: Ost Crane Service
2951 N Ventura Ave, Ventura (93001-1210)
P.O. Box 237 (93002-0237)
PHONE 805 643-9963
Fax: 805 643-7618
L Dennis Zermeno, *President*
Don D Zermeno, *Vice Pres*
Ron J Zermeno, *Vice Pres*
Kyley Andrews, *Manager*
EMP: 73
SQ FT: 3,000
SALES (est): 11.2MM **Privately Held**
WEB: www.ostcranes.com
SIC: 7389 4212 4225 Crane & aerial lift service; local trucking, without storage; general warehousing & storage

(P-17384)
OSTERHOUT GROUP INC
Also Called: Osterhout Design Group
153 Townsend St Ste 570, San Francisco (94107-1976)
PHONE 415 644-4000
Ralph F Osterhout, *President*
Pete Jameson, *COO*
Robert Radke, *CFO*
Patrick Carroll, *Vice Pres*
Bobby King, *Vice Pres*
EMP: 50
SQ FT: 2,200
SALES (est): 10MM **Privately Held**
SIC: 7389 Design, commercial & industrial

(P-17385)
OUR LADY OF GRACE P T G
2766 Navajo Rd, El Cajon (92020-2121)
PHONE 619 466-0055
Fax: 619 459-0575
Susan Husc, *President*
Kathleen Malinosky, *President*
Gloria Green, *Treasurer*
Stephanie Hagenburger, *Treasurer*
Timothy Phariss, *Vice Pres*
EMP: 50
SALES (est): 3.5MM **Privately Held**
WEB: www.ourladyofkazanchurch.org
SIC: 7389 Fund raising organizations

(P-17386)
OVERLAND PACIFIC & CUTLER (PA)
Also Called: Pacific Relocation Consultants
3750 Schaufele Ave # 150, Long Beach (90808-1779)
PHONE 562 429-9391
Fax: 562 495-0889
Ray Armstrong, *CEO*
Barry McDaniel, *Vice Pres*
Steve Oliver, *Vice Pres*
Min Saysay, *Program Mgr*
Kathy Raven, *Office Mgr*
EMP: 55
SQ FT: 7,000
SALES (est): 17.9MM **Privately Held**
WEB: www.opcservices.com
SIC: 7389 Relocation service

(P-17387)
OXNARD PERFRMN ARTS & CONVTN
Also Called: City Oxnard Prfrmg Arts Ctr
800 Hobson Way, Oxnard (93030-6723)
PHONE 805 486-2424
Robert Holden, *CEO*
Marie A Alarcon, *General Mgr*
EMP: 50
SALES (est): 1.5MM **Privately Held**
SIC: 7389 Convention & show services; tourist information bureau

(P-17388)
OZOO INC
4662 E 49th St, Vernon (90058-3226)
PHONE 323 585-4383
Felix Chavez, *President*
EMP: 120
SALES (est): 5.6MM **Privately Held**
WEB: www.ozoo.com
SIC: 7389 Sewing contractor

(P-17389)
PACIFIC BONDING CORPORATION (PA)
1959 Palomar Oaks Way # 200, Carlsbad (92011-1314)
PHONE 760 431-9911
Robert Hayes, *CEO*
Said Etemad, *Shareholder*
Stefan Gibbs, *Shareholder*
Tracy Miller, *Manager*
EMP: 150
SQ FT: 15,000
SALES (est): 20.9MM **Privately Held**
SIC: 7389 Bail bonding

(P-17390)
PACIFIC COAST COMPANIES INC
10600 White Rock Rd # 100, Rancho Cordova (95670-6294)
P.O. Box 419074 (95741-9074)
PHONE 916 631-6500
David J Lucchetti, *President*
Dale Waldschmitt, *COO*
Joshua Kimerer, *CFO*
Daniel Yanagihara, *Vice Pres*
Ken Kerrick, *CIO*
EMP: 125
SALES (est): 17.6MM
SALES (corp-wide): 926.8MM **Privately Held**
SIC: 7389 8742 Legal & tax services; human resource consulting services
PA: Pacific Coast Building Products, Inc.
    10600 White Rock Rd # 100
    Rancho Cordova CA 95670
    916 631-6500

(P-17391)
PACIFIC COAST PRODUCERS
650 S Guild Ave, Lodi (95240-3114)
PHONE 209 365-9982
Jim Farmer, *Branch Mgr*
Jaime Garcia, *Safety Mgr*
EMP: 500
SALES (corp-wide): 630.7MM **Privately Held**
SIC: 7389 5141 Packaging & labeling services; groceries, general line
PA: Pacific Coast Producers
    631 N Cluff Ave
    Lodi CA 95240
    209 367-8800

(P-17392)
PACIFIC EVENT PRODUCTIONS INC (PA)
6989 Corte Santa Fe, San Diego (92121-3260)
PHONE 858 458-9908
Fax: 858 458-1173
Lawrence J Toll, *CEO*
George Duff, *President*
Stephen Conley, *CFO*
Amy Berner, *Social Dir*
Nancy Bologna, *Social Dir*
EMP: 71
SQ FT: 30,000
SALES (est): 23.6MM **Privately Held**
WEB: www.pacificevents.com
SIC: 7389 Convention & show services

(P-17393)
PACIFIC MEDICAL INC (PA)
1700 N Chrisman Rd, Tracy (95304-9314)
P.O. Box 149 (95378-0149)
PHONE 800 726-9180
John M Petlansky, *CEO*
Brandon Faulk, *President*
Scott Combs, *CFO*
Jeffrey Leonard, *CFO*
Bob McCune, *Vice Pres*
EMP: 148
SQ FT: 18,000
SALES (est): 47.9MM **Privately Held**
WEB: www.pacmedical.com
SIC: 7389 7352 Brokers, contract services; medical equipment rental

(P-17394)
PARADIGM INDUSTRIES INC
13344 S Main St Ste C, Los Angeles (90061-1638)
PHONE 310 965-1900
William Jun, *CEO*
Chu Kim, *President*
EMP: 80
SALES (est): 4.7MM **Privately Held**
WEB: www.paradigmindustries.com
SIC: 7389 Textile & apparel services

(P-17395)
PARCHMENT INC
3000 Lava Ridge Ct # 210, Roseville (95661-2800)
PHONE 480 719-1646
Louis Delzompo, *Manager*
EMP: 61
SALES (corp-wide): 41.7MM **Privately Held**
SIC: 7389
PA: Parchment Inc.
    6263 N Scotts Rd Ste 330
    Scottsdale AZ 85250
    480 719-1646

(P-17396)
PARKING CONCEPTS INC
18601 Airport Way Ste 7, Santa Ana (92707-5210)
PHONE 949 752-5558
Fax: 949 252-6263
Adrian Gonzales, *Branch Mgr*
EMP: 244
SALES (corp-wide): 53.2MM **Privately Held**
SIC: 7389 Personal service agents, brokers & bureaus
PA: Parking Concepts, Inc.
    12 Mauchly Ste I
    Irvine CA 92618
    949 753-7525

7389 - Business Svcs, NEC County (P-17397)

PRODUDUCTS & SERVICES SECTION

(P-17397)
PARKING CONCEPTS INC
601 S Ross St, Santa Ana (92701-5564)
PHONE....................714 836-6009
EMP: 163
SALES (corp-wide): 53.2MM Privately Held
SIC: 7389 Design services
PA: Parking Concepts, Inc.
 12 Mauchly Ste I
 Irvine CA 92618
 949 753-7525

(P-17398)
PARTNER HERO INC
1001 Avenida Pico C260, San Clemente (92673-6957)
PHONE....................888 968-2767
Shervin Talieh, CEO
EMP: 50 EST: 2014
SALES (est): 775.8K Privately Held
SIC: 7389 Telephone answering service

(P-17399)
PARTNERS CAPITAL GROUP INC
201 Sandpointe Ave, Santa Ana (92707-5778)
PHONE....................949 916-3900
Mark Harmond, Branch Mgr
EMP: 120
SALES (corp-wide): 37.3MM Privately Held
SIC: 7389 Financial services
PA: Partners Capital Group, Inc.
 65 Enterprise Ste 455
 Aliso Viejo CA 92656
 949 916-3900

(P-17400)
PARTNERS CAPITAL GROUP INC (PA)
65 Enterprise Ste 455, Aliso Viejo (92656-2705)
PHONE....................949 916-3900
Mark Davin, CEO
Mark Harmond, Mktg Dir
Mike Geske, Sales Dir
Jared Berggren, Accounts Exec
EMP: 80
SQ FT: 20,000
SALES (est): 37.3MM Privately Held
SIC: 7389 Financial services

(P-17401)
PARTOS COMPANY
Also Called: Partos Company, The
227 Broadway Ste 204, Santa Monica (90401-2370)
PHONE....................310 458-7800
Walter Partos,
Laura Roman, Office Mgr
Samantha Taylor, Manager
Ajay Ghosh, Agent
Martijn Hostetler, Commercial
EMP: 70
SQ FT: 2,000
SALES (est): 3.7MM Privately Held
WEB: www.partos.com
SIC: 7389 7922 Authors' agents & brokers; talent agent, theatrical

(P-17402)
PASADENA CENTER OPERATING CO
Also Called: PASADENA CONVENTION CENTER
300 E Green St, Pasadena (91101-2399)
PHONE....................626 795-9311
Fax: 626 793-8014
Michael Ross, CEO
Thomas Corralez, Officer
Gloria Conrad, Principal
Eileen Collins, Executive Asst
Mary Collins, Executive Asst
EMP: 116
SQ FT: 32,000
SALES: 20.4MM Privately Held
WEB: www.pasadenacal.com
SIC: 7389 Convention & show services

(P-17403)
PASSPORT ACCEPTANCE FACILITY
Also Called: Usps
2300 Redondo Ave, Long Beach (90809-9998)
PHONE....................562 494-2296
Jennie Enriquez, Principal
Robin Walker, Treasurer
Daniel Mastren, Info Tech Dir
EMP: 75
SALES (est): 3.7MM Privately Held
SIC: 7389 Mailbox rental & related service

(P-17404)
PASSPRT ACCEPT FCLTY LOS ANGEL
Also Called: Sunset Station
1425 N Cherokee Ave, Los Angeles (90093-2108)
PHONE....................323 460-4811
Gerald Padilla, General Mgr
EMP: 60
SALES (est): 1MM Privately Held
SIC: 7389 Post office contract stations

(P-17405)
PATRICK K WILLIS AND CO INC
Also Called: American Recovery Service
5118 Rbert J Mathews Pkwy, El Dorado Hills (95762-5703)
PHONE....................800 398-6480
Fax: 916 673-3211
David Baker, Senior VP
Johan Lai, Officer
Christian Beyer, Vice Pres
Steven Schelk, Risk Mgmt Dir
Andrew Lynch, Analyst
EMP: 300
SQ FT: 10,000
SALES (est): 2MM Privately Held
SIC: 7389 Repossession service

(P-17406)
PAYMENT RESOURCES INTL
620 Newport Center Dr # 150, Newport Beach (92660-6420)
PHONE....................949 729-1400
Fax: 949 655-4141
John S Blaugrund, President
Andrew Phillips, President
EMP: 50
SQ FT: 14,000
SALES (est): 2MM Privately Held
WEB: www.payflex.net
SIC: 7389 Credit card service

(P-17407)
PB CAR MOVERS
5510 W 120th St, Hawthorne (90250-3406)
PHONE....................310 283-2741
Jose Desiderio, Owner
EMP: 60
SALES (est): 2.5MM Privately Held
SIC: 7389 Automobile recovery service

(P-17408)
PERFORMANCE TEAM FRT SYS INC
1898 Marigold Ave, Redlands (92374-5010)
PHONE....................801 301-1732
EMP: 118
SALES (corp-wide): 435.6MM Privately Held
SIC: 7389 Personal service agents, brokers & bureaus
PA: Performance Team Freight Sys, Inc.
 2240 E Maple Ave
 El Segundo CA 90245
 562 345-2200

(P-17409)
PERMITS TODAY LLC
140 S Lake Ave Ste 323, Pasadena (91101-4787)
PHONE....................626 585-2931
Scott Daves,
Margaret Sargent,
Carla Street,
Mario Zelaya, Manager
EMP: 75 EST: 1998
SALES: 2.5MM Privately Held
WEB: www.permitstoday.com
SIC: 7389 Personal service agents, brokers & bureaus

(P-17410)
PETE HELLING
Also Called: P D Rabbit Messenger Service
11600 Wash Pl Ste 117, Los Angeles (90066-5000)
PHONE....................310 390-2710
Fax: 310 390-4611
Pete Helling, President
EMP: 60
SALES: 2.5MM Privately Held
SIC: 7389 Courier or messenger service

(P-17411)
PHOENIX INTL HOLDINGS INC
127 Press Ln, Chula Vista (91910-1011)
PHONE....................619 207-0871
Kelvin Hall, Branch Mgr
Arealya Evans, Buyer
Mark Ehrnschwender, Assistant
EMP: 143
SALES (corp-wide): 55.3MM Privately Held
SIC: 7389 Marine reporting
PA: Phoenix International Holdings, Inc.
 9301 Largo Dr W
 Largo MD 20774
 301 341-7800

(P-17412)
PHOENIX TEXTILE INC
910 S Los Angeles St, Los Angeles (90015-1726)
PHONE....................213 239-9640
Fax: 213 228-1109
EMP: 70
SALES (corp-wide): 42.4MM Privately Held
SIC: 7389
PA: Phoenix Textile, Inc.
 14600 S Broadway
 Gardena CA 90248
 310 715-7090

(P-17413)
PHONE WARE INC
8902 Activity Rd Ste A, San Diego (92126-4471)
PHONE....................858 530-8550
Fax: 858 964-3079
William J Nassir, President
Jim Rochford, President
Bolden Ellen, CFO
Hazel Nassir, Exec VP
Amy Santos, Regional Mgr
EMP: 366 EST: 1974
SQ FT: 20,000
SALES (est): 36.6MM Privately Held
WEB: www.phoneware.com
SIC: 7389 8742 Telemarketing services; marketing consulting services

(P-17414)
PIONEER THEATRES INC
Also Called: Roadium Open Air Market
2500 Redondo Beach Blvd, Torrance (90504-1529)
PHONE....................310 532-8183
Fax: 323 321-0114
William Fleischman, President
William Warnick, Vice Pres
Tina Weaver, Executive
Christina Weaver, Controller
Mike Romo, Opers Staff
EMP: 110
SQ FT: 3,000
SALES (est): 10.3MM Privately Held
WEB: www.pioneertheatre.org
SIC: 7389 5431 Flea market; fruit & vegetable markets

(P-17415)
PITNEY BOWES PRESORT SVCS INC
18550 S Broadwick St, Compton (90220-6439)
PHONE....................310 763-4615
Lori Butcher, Branch Mgr
Edgar Merida, Technician
Chinh Vu, Technician
Robert Vu, Technician
Luz Zepeda, Cust Mgr
EMP: 115
SALES (corp-wide): 3.5B Publicly Held
WEB: www.psigroupinc.com
SIC: 7389 Presorted mail service
HQ: Pitney Bowes Presort Services, Inc.
 10110 I St
 Omaha NE 68127
 402 339-6500

(P-17416)
PITNEY BOWES PRESORT SVCS INC
125 Valley Dr, Brisbane (94005-1317)
PHONE....................415 468-1660
Nick Saribalis, Vice Pres
Nicholas Saribalis, President
EMP: 70
SALES (corp-wide): 3.5B Publicly Held
WEB: www.pioneusinc.com
SIC: 7389 Presorted mail service
HQ: Pitney Bowes Presort Services, Inc.
 10110 I St
 Omaha NE 68127
 402 339-6500

(P-17417)
PIXIOR LLC (PA)
5901 S Eastern Ave, Commerce (90040-4003)
PHONE....................323 721-2221
Yassine Amallal, Mng Member
Simon Bouzaglou, COO
Elena Pickett, Senior VP
Galina Turetskaya, Accountant
Gloria Harris, Controller
EMP: 122
SQ FT: 192,000
SALES (est): 12MM Privately Held
WEB: www.pixior.com
SIC: 7389 Advertising, promotional & trade show services

(P-17418)
PLASTIFLEX COMPANY INC (DH)
601 E Palomar St Ste 424, Chula Vista (91911-6976)
PHONE....................619 662-8792
Gerald Green, President
Robert Sakiyama, President
David McIvor, CEO
Peter Dirkx, COO
Sal Kiema, CFO
EMP: 130
SQ FT: 48,000
SALES (est): 26.2MM
SALES (corp-wide): 701.9K Privately Held
WEB: www.plastiflex.com
SIC: 7389 Swimming pool & hot tub service & maintenance
HQ: Plastiflex Suzhou Co., Ltd.
 Block 10,Yangshan Science And Technology Industrial Park,No.8,Ji Suzhou
 512 667-2673

(P-17419)
PLUM HEALTHCARE GROUP LLC
Also Called: Redlands Health Care Group
1620 W Fern Ave, Redlands (92373-4918)
PHONE....................909 793-2609
Mark Baliff,
Novi Sitagang, Administration
Eddie Cook, Technology
EMP: 80
SALES (est): 3.9MM Privately Held
WEB: www.plum.ca
SIC: 7389 Personal service agents, brokers & bureaus

(P-17420)
PRECISION IDEO INC
150 Forest Ave, Palo Alto (94301-1614)
PHONE....................650 688-3400
Tim Brown, President
Jane F Suri, Creative Dir
Gopi Krishnaswamy, Managing Dir
Christina Mariani, Office Mgr
Greg Wasson, Info Tech Dir
EMP: 400
SALES (est): 20.5MM Privately Held
SIC: 7389 Design services

PRODUCTS & SERVICES SECTION

7389 - Business Svcs, NEC County (P-17444)

(P-17421)
PRECISION INSPECTION CO INC (PA)
1247 Main St, Newman (95360-1324)
PHONE..................209 862-9511
Kelly Hislop, *President*
Crickett Brinkman, *CFO*
Greg Johnsen, *Vice Pres*
William Martin, *Vice Pres*
Ronald Stevens, *Manager*
EMP: 51
SQ FT: 1,496
SALES: 4.6MM **Privately Held**
WEB: www.precision-inspection.com
SIC: 7389 Building inspection service

(P-17422)
PRECISION RELOCATION INC
16055 Heron Ave Ste B, La Mirada (90638-5514)
PHONE..................714 690-9344
Fax: 714 690-9345
Kirk O O'Gilvy, *CEO*
Douglas Piersant, *President*
Patsy O'Gilvy, *Administration*
Patsy Ogilvy, *Controller*
EMP: 120
SQ FT: 60,000
SALES (est): 8.2MM **Privately Held**
WEB: www.precisionrelocation.com
SIC: 7389 Relocation service

(P-17423)
PREMIER DISP & EXHIBITS INC (PA)
11261 Warland Dr, Cypress (90630-5033)
PHONE..................562 431-2731
Fax: 562 598-3320
Christopher J Bullard, *CEO*
Stephen Amato, *Principal*
Kris Parker, *Controller*
EMP: 89
SQ FT: 170,000
SALES (est): 25.1MM **Privately Held**
WEB: www.premierdisplays.com
SIC: 7389 Trade show arrangement

(P-17424)
PREMIER OFFICE CENTERS LLC (PA)
Also Called: Premier Business Centers
2102 Bus Ctr Dr Ste 130, Irvine (92612)
PHONE..................949 253-4147
Fax: 949 253-4148
Jeffrey Reinstein, *CEO*
Willie Gutierrez, *CFO*
Jenny Shin, *Officer*
Katie Gallicchio, *Regional Mgr*
Laura Allen, *General Mgr*
EMP: 50
SALES (est): 70.7MM **Privately Held**
SIC: 7389 Office facilities & secretarial service rental

(P-17425)
PREVENT LIFE SAFETY SVCS INC
1410 Stealth St, Livermore (94551-9358)
PHONE..................925 667-2088
Carol D Cohan, *President*
Beverly Boff, *Administration*
Jodi Come, *Manager*
EMP: 50
SALES (est): 3.8MM **Privately Held**
SIC: 7389 Fire protection service other than forestry or public

(P-17426)
PRIME MARKETING HOLDINGS LLC
11620 Wilshire Blvd B, Los Angeles (90025-1706)
PHONE..................888 991-6412
Nirit Rubenstein, *CEO*
EMP: 75 **EST:** 2014
SQ FT: 10,000
SALES: 11MM **Privately Held**
SIC: 7389 Financial services

(P-17427)
PRO-TECH DESIGN & MFG INC
14561 Marquardt Ave, Santa Fe Springs (90670-5137)
PHONE..................562 207-1680
Fax: 562 207-1698
Pamela Mc Master, *CEO*
Aaron Swanson, *President*
David Mc Master, *CFO*
Jeff Swanson, *Vice Pres*
Pamela McMaster, *Executive*
EMP: 60
SALES (est): 10MM **Privately Held**
WEB: www.protechdesign.net
SIC: 7389 8711 Packaging & labeling services; industrial engineers

(P-17428)
PROCALL SOLUTIONS INC
20 Ragsdale Dr Ste 100, Monterey (93940-7812)
PHONE..................800 733-9675
Dennis Hill, *Senior VP*
EMP: 120
SQ FT: 10,000
SALES: 5MM
SALES (corp-wide): 110MM **Privately Held**
WEB: www.procallonline.com
SIC: 7389 Telemarketing services
PA: Product Development Corp
20 Ragsdale Dr Ste 100
Monterey CA 93940
831 333-1100

(P-17429)
PRODUCT DEVELOPMENT CORP (PA)
20 Ragsdale Dr Ste 100, Monterey (93940-7812)
PHONE..................831 333-1100
Fax: 831 333-0110
Tim Dinovo, *President*
David Forey, *CFO*
Ed King, *Senior VP*
David Hersey, *CIO*
Adam Rose, *Business Anlyst*
EMP: 148
SQ FT: 10,700
SALES (est): 110MM **Privately Held**
WEB: www.pdceast.com
SIC: 7389 Telephone directory distribution, contract or fee basis

(P-17430)
PRODUCT SLINGSHOT INC
Also Called: Forecast 3d
2221 Rutherford Rd, Carlsbad (92008-8815)
PHONE..................760 929-9380
Fax: 760 929-9357
Corey Douglas Weber, *President*
Alex Fima, *CFO*
Donovan Weber, *Vice Pres*
Norma Martinez, *Executive*
Matt Nebo, *Project Mgr*
EMP: 96
SQ FT: 28,000
SALES (est): 11.5MM **Privately Held**
WEB: www.forecast3d.com
SIC: 7389 3544 3082 3089 Design, commercial & industrial; industrial molds; unsupported plastics profile shapes; casting of plastic; coloring & finishing of plastic products; injection molded finished plastic products

(P-17431)
PROFESSIONAL COIN GRADING SVC
Also Called: Pcgs
1921 E Alton Ave Ste 100, Santa Ana (92705-5845)
P.O. Box 9458, Newport Beach (92658-9458)
PHONE..................949 567-1246
Fax: 949 833-7660
Don Willis, *President*
Stephen H Mayer, *COO*
Laura A Kessler, *Vice Pres*
David Rosenberg, *Info Tech Mgr*
Mike Brandow, *Mktg Dir*
EMP: 75
SQ FT: 15,000
SALES (est): 4.2MM
SALES (corp-wide): 60.9MM **Publicly Held**
WEB: www.pcgs.com
SIC: 7389 Commodity inspection

PA: Collectors Universe, Inc.
1921 E Alton Ave Ste 100
Santa Ana CA 92705
949 567-1234

(P-17432)
PROFESSIONAL EXCHANGE SVC
4747 N 1st St Ste 140, Fresno (93726-0517)
P.O. Box 1071 (93714-1071)
PHONE..................559 229-6249
Fax: 559 227-1463
Cynthia Downing, *CEO*
Peggy Matsoura, *CFO*
Russell Nakaguchio, *Corp Secy*
Matt Haas, *Vice Pres*
Paul Bateman, *Principal*
EMP: 50 **EST:** 1980
SQ FT: 3,700
SALES (est): 5.4MM **Privately Held**
WEB: www.pesc.com
SIC: 7389 Telephone answering service

(P-17433)
PROJECT SIX
13130 Burbank Blvd, Sherman Oaks (91401-6037)
PHONE..................818 781-0360
Barbera Firestone, *President*
Edna Ramos, *Controller*
EMP: 55
SALES: 3MM **Privately Held**
SIC: 7389 Tax title dealers

(P-17434)
PROLOGIC RDMPTION SLUTIONS INC (PA)
2121 Rosecrans Ave, El Segundo (90245-4743)
PHONE..................310 322-7774
William Atkinson, *CEO*
Paul Cooley, *President*
Robb Warwick, *CFO*
Kelly Fuller, *Ch Credit Ofcr*
Ross Ely, *Chief Mktg Ofcr*
EMP: 700
SALES (est): 39.5MM **Privately Held**
SIC: 7389 Coupon redemption service

(P-17435)
PS ENVIRONMENTAL SVCS INC
23775 Madison St, Torrance (90505-6006)
P.O. Box 7000-897, Redondo Beach (90277)
PHONE..................310 373-6259
Fax: 310 373-6269
Joseph Gaglione, *President*
EMP: 62
SALES (est): 3.8MM **Privately Held**
WEB: www.psenvironmental.com
SIC: 7389 Air pollution measuring service

(P-17436)
QUALFAX INC
3605 Long Beach Blvd # 428, Long Beach (90807-6020)
PHONE..................562 988-1272
Daniel Wayne, *Vice Pres*
Jim Wolf, *CEO*
EMP: 60
SALES (est): 2.4MM **Privately Held**
WEB: www.qualfax.com
SIC: 7389 8741 Tenant screening service; management services

(P-17437)
QUICKSILVER DELIVERY INC
Also Called: Quicksilver Delivery Service
129 Kissling St, San Francisco (94103-3726)
PHONE..................415 431-1600
Phil Mc Cafee, *President*
EMP: 65
SQ FT: 5,000
SALES (est): 3.3MM **Privately Held**
SIC: 7389 Courier or messenger service

(P-17438)
QUICKSORT INC (PA)
Also Called: Quicksort Bus Mailing Svcs
100 Ryan Industrial Ct, San Ramon (94583-1527)
PHONE..................925 820-8272
Fax: 925 838-6905
Celina Gonzales, *President*

Mauro Rivero, *President*
Sam Ghaben, *CFO*
Jim Tetzloff, *Vice Pres*
Celina Gonzalez, *Financial Exec*
EMP: 75
SQ FT: 10,000
SALES (est): 14.4MM **Privately Held**
WEB: www.quicksort.com
SIC: 7389 Mailing & messenger services

(P-17439)
QUINSTREET INC (PA)
950 Tower Ln Ste 600, Foster City (94404-4253)
PHONE..................650 578-7700
Fax: 650 578-7604
Douglas Valenti, *Ch of Bd*
Gregory Wong, *CFO*
Martin J Collins, *Ch Credit Ofcr*
Peter Brooks, *Senior VP*
Edton Mock, *Vice Pres*
EMP: 50
SQ FT: 63,998
SALES: 297.7MM **Publicly Held**
WEB: www.quinstreet.com
SIC: 7389 7372 Advertising, promotional & trade show services; prepackaged software; business oriented computer software

(P-17440)
R G CANNING ENTERPRISES INC
4515 E 59th Pl, Maywood (90270-3201)
PHONE..................323 560-7469
Richard G Canning, *President*
Charles R Canning, *Vice Pres*
Tim Ellis, *General Mgr*
EMP: 215
SQ FT: 50,000
SALES (est): 12.1MM **Privately Held**
WEB: www.rgcshows.com
SIC: 7389 Promoters of shows & exhibitions

(P-17441)
RABIN WORLDWIDE INC
21 Locust Ave 2a, Mill Valley (94941-2852)
PHONE..................415 522-5700
Fax: 415 522-5701
Richard Reese, *President*
Shira Weissman, *COO*
Micheal Bank, *Vice Pres*
Morgan Pierce, *Executive*
Marisol Tria, *Opers Mgr*
▼ **EMP:** 51
SALES (est): 6MM **Privately Held**
SIC: 7389 Auctioneers, fee basis; appraisers, except real estate; auction, appraisal & exchange services

(P-17442)
RAILPROS FIELD SERVICES
1 Ada Ste 200, Irvine (92618-5341)
PHONE..................877 315-0513
Johnny Johnson, *CEO*
EMP: 50
SQ FT: 900
SALES (est): 6.4MM **Privately Held**
SIC: 7389

(P-17443)
RAINIER FINANCIAL GROUP LLC
2321 Rosecrans Ave # 4270, El Segundo (90245-4964)
PHONE..................310 335-9200
Kevin Neustadt, *Managing Prtnr*
EMP: 50
SALES (est): 3.8MM **Privately Held**
SIC: 7389 Financial services

(P-17444)
RALIS SERVICES CORP
1 City Blvd W Ste 600, Orange (92868-3639)
PHONE..................844 347-2547
Delbert O Meeks, *CEO*
Mike Chiang, *Admin Sec*
Shawna Parks, *Controller*
EMP: 150
SALES: 6MM **Privately Held**
SIC: 7389 Automobile recovery service

(P-17445)
RALPH COLLAZO PACKING INC
72 E Main St Ste A, Heber (92249)
P.O. Box 271 (92249-0271)
PHONE 760 353-0856
Fax: 760 353-0999
Ralph Collazo, *President*
EMP: 100
SALES (est): 9.8MM **Privately Held**
SIC: 7389 Packaging & labeling services

(P-17446)
RAYTHEON COMPANY
75 Coromar Dr, Goleta (93117-3088)
PHONE 805 562-2941
Mike Allgeier, *Branch Mgr*
Salvador R Ortega, *General Mgr*
Wolin Roger, *Administration*
Stefan Baur, *Info Tech Dir*
Samantha Caballero, *Info Tech Mgr*
EMP: 66
SALES (corp-wide): 23.2B **Publicly Held**
SIC: 7389 Personal service agents, brokers & bureaus
PA: Raytheon Company
    870 Winter St
    Waltham MA 02451
    781 522-3000

(P-17447)
REAL ESTATE DIGITAL LLC
27081 Aliso Creek Rd # 200, Aliso Viejo (92656-5365)
PHONE 800 234-2139
Jay Gaskill, *President*
Mike Kovar, *CFO*
Walt Clark, *Senior VP*
Larry Ross, *Senior VP*
Laura Buser, *Vice Pres*
EMP: 108
SALES (est): 10MM **Privately Held**
SIC: 7389 Advertising, promotional & trade show services

(P-17448)
REGENTS OF THE UNIV OF CAL
Materiel Management
616 Forbes Blvd, San Francisco (94143-2008)
PHONE 510 987-0700
Diana Hopper, *Principal*
EMP: 100 **Privately Held**
SIC: 7389 4225 Purchasing service; general warehousing & storage
HQ: The Regents Of The University Of California
    1111 Franklin St Fl 12
    Oakland CA 94607
    510 987-0700

(P-17449)
REGISTRATION CTRL SYSTEMS INC (PA)
Also Called: Rcs World Travel
1833 Portola Rd Unit B, Ventura (93003-7797)
PHONE 805 654-0171
Fax: 805 654-1676
Edgar A Bolton, *President*
Duane Smeckert, *President*
Gary Palmer, *Vice Pres*
Nancy Devine, *Executive*
Jim Ross, *Info Tech Dir*
EMP: 55
SQ FT: 15,000
SALES (est): 6.3MM **Privately Held**
WEB: www.rcsreg.com
SIC: 7389 Advertising, promotional & trade show services

(P-17450)
RGIS LLC
9663 Tierra Grande St # 205, San Diego (92126-4571)
PHONE 858 653-0355
Stephanie Smith, *Branch Mgr*
EMP: 82
SALES (corp-wide): 4.6B **Publicly Held**
SIC: 7389 Personal service agents, brokers & bureaus
HQ: Rgis, Llc
    2000 Taylor Rd
    Auburn Hills MI 48326
    248 651-2511

(P-17451)
RGIS LLC
8801 Folsom Blvd Ste 173, Sacramento (95826-3249)
PHONE 916 387-9692
Fax: 916 387-9935
Chris Massoni, *Vice Pres*
Marcus Duran, *Manager*
EMP: 100
SALES (corp-wide): 4.6B **Publicly Held**
WEB: www.rgisinv.com
SIC: 7389 Inventory computing service
HQ: Rgis, Llc
    2000 Taylor Rd
    Auburn Hills MI 48326
    248 651-2511

(P-17452)
RGIS LLC
500 E Olive Ave Ste 240, Burbank (91501-2171)
PHONE 248 651-2511
Fax: 818 303-0048
Bruce Hemingway, *Branch Mgr*
EMP: 140
SALES (corp-wide): 4.6B **Publicly Held**
WEB: www.rgisinv.com
SIC: 7389 Inventory computing service
HQ: Rgis, Llc
    2000 Taylor Rd
    Auburn Hills MI 48326
    248 651-2511

(P-17453)
RGIS LLC
7567 Amador Valley Blvd, Dublin (94568-2441)
PHONE 925 829-2875
Majid Jafarkhani, *Branch Mgr*
EMP: 85
SALES (corp-wide): 4.6B **Publicly Held**
WEB: www.rgisinv.com
SIC: 7389 Inventory computing service
HQ: Rgis, Llc
    2000 Taylor Rd
    Auburn Hills MI 48326
    248 651-2511

(P-17454)
RGIS LLC
6153 Fairmount Ave, San Diego (92120-3443)
PHONE 619 624-9882
Tom Seidel, *Manager*
EMP: 60
SALES (corp-wide): 4.6B **Publicly Held**
WEB: www.rgisinv.com
SIC: 7389 Inventory computing service
HQ: Rgis, Llc
    2000 Taylor Rd
    Auburn Hills MI 48326
    248 651-2511

(P-17455)
RGIS LLC
25115 Avenue Stanford, Valencia (91355-1290)
PHONE 661 702-8987
Becky Conde, *Manager*
EMP: 79
SALES (corp-wide): 4.6B **Publicly Held**
WEB: www.rgisinv.com
SIC: 7389 Inventory stocking service
HQ: Rgis, Llc
    2000 Taylor Rd
    Auburn Hills MI 48326
    248 651-2511

(P-17456)
RGIS LLC
20 Landing Cir Ste 100, Chico (95973-7889)
PHONE 530 898-1015
Fax: 530 898-1017
Eric Pearson, *Manager*
EMP: 65
SALES (corp-wide): 4.6B **Publicly Held**
WEB: www.rgisinv.com
SIC: 7389 Inventory computing service
HQ: Rgis, Llc
    2000 Taylor Rd
    Auburn Hills MI 48326
    248 651-2511

(P-17457)
RGIS LLC
1041 W Badillo St, Covina (91722-4194)
PHONE 626 974-4841
James Roseman, *Manager*
Kristin Mitchell, *Manager*
EMP: 79
SALES (corp-wide): 4.6B **Publicly Held**
WEB: www.rgisinv.com
SIC: 7389 Inventory computing service
HQ: Rgis, Llc
    2000 Taylor Rd
    Auburn Hills MI 48326
    248 651-2511

(P-17458)
RGIS LLC
2000 E 4th St Ste 350, Santa Ana (92705-3936)
PHONE 714 541-1431
Fax: 714 541-3714
Majel Becarra, *Branch Mgr*
EMP: 65
SALES (corp-wide): 4.6B **Publicly Held**
WEB: www.rgisinv.com
SIC: 7389 Inventory computing service
HQ: Rgis, Llc
    2000 Taylor Rd
    Auburn Hills MI 48326
    248 651-2511

(P-17459)
RGIS LLC
2171 Junipero Serra Blvd # 400, Daly City (94014-1984)
PHONE 650 757-6770
Fax: 650 757-9972
Alice Souza, *Manager*
EMP: 130
SALES (corp-wide): 4.6B **Publicly Held**
WEB: www.rgisinv.com
SIC: 7389 Inventory computing service
HQ: Rgis, Llc
    2000 Taylor Rd
    Auburn Hills MI 48326
    248 651-2511

(P-17460)
RGIS LLC
5500 Ming Ave Ste 185, Bakersfield (93309-4623)
PHONE 661 827-9195
Fax: 661 827-0331
Laine Martin, *Manager*
EMP: 51
SALES (corp-wide): 4.6B **Publicly Held**
WEB: www.rgisinv.com
SIC: 7389 Inventory computing service
HQ: Rgis, Llc
    2000 Taylor Rd
    Auburn Hills MI 48326
    248 651-2511

(P-17461)
RGIS LLC
1787 Mesa Verde Ave, Ventura (93003-6531)
PHONE 805 644-0454
Fax: 805 644-0345
Darin Coupland, *Manager*
EMP: 75
SALES (corp-wide): 4.6B **Publicly Held**
WEB: www.rgisinv.com
SIC: 7389 Inventory computing service
HQ: Rgis, Llc
    2000 Taylor Rd
    Auburn Hills MI 48326
    248 651-2511

(P-17462)
RGIS LLC
4320 Stevens Creek Blvd, San Jose (95129-1202)
PHONE 408 243-9141
Carol Willis, *Branch Mgr*
EMP: 65
SALES (corp-wide): 4.6B **Publicly Held**
WEB: www.rgisinv.com
SIC: 7389 Inventory computing service
HQ: Rgis, Llc
    2000 Taylor Rd
    Auburn Hills MI 48326
    248 651-2511

(P-17463)
RGIS LLC
1322 E Shaw Ave Ste 170, Fresno (93710-7923)
PHONE 559 224-5898
Fax: 559 224-4869
Tim Butters, *Manager*
EMP: 60
SALES (corp-wide): 4.6B **Publicly Held**
WEB: www.rgisinv.com
SIC: 7389 Inventory computing service
HQ: Rgis, Llc
    2000 Taylor Rd
    Auburn Hills MI 48326
    248 651-2511

(P-17464)
RGIS LLC
876 N Mountain Ave # 103, Upland (91786-4166)
PHONE 909 605-1893
Fax: 909 605-1896
Donna Stuit, *Manager*
EMP: 175
SALES (corp-wide): 4.6B **Publicly Held**
WEB: www.rgisinv.com
SIC: 7389 Inventory computing service
HQ: Rgis, Llc
    2000 Taylor Rd
    Auburn Hills MI 48326
    248 651-2511

(P-17465)
RIVER CITY AUTO RECOVERY INC
3401 Fitzgerald Rd, Rancho Cordova (95742-6815)
PHONE 916 851-1100
Fax: 916 851-9203
David Schmidt, *CFO*
Jennifer Nelson, *Administration*
EMP: 71
SQ FT: 15,000
SALES (est): 2.2MM
SALES (corp-wide): 1.6B **Privately Held**
WEB: www.unitedroad.com
SIC: 7389 Repossession service
HQ: United Road Services, Inc.
    10701 Middlebelt Rd
    Romulus MI 48174
    734 946-3232

(P-17466)
ROAD SAFETY INC
4335 Pacific St Ste A, Rocklin (95677-2104)
PHONE 916 543-4600
Melissa L Bamberg, *President*
Jason Bamberg, *CEO*
Mick Ibanev, *Sales Mgr*
Anthony Cancilla, *Director*
Sanea Simpson, *Accounts Mgr*
EMP: 120
SQ FT: 6,000
SALES (est): 13.9MM **Privately Held**
SIC: 7389 Flagging service (traffic control)

(P-17467)
RONSIN PHOTOCOPY INC (PA)
215 Lemon Creek Dr, Walnut (91789-2643)
PHONE 909 594-5995
Dennis Grant, *President*
Robert Alkema, *Ch of Bd*
Cheryl Alkema, *Corp Secy*
Darren Wong, *Mktg Dir*
Dave Thomas, *Marketing Mgr*
EMP: 60
SQ FT: 12,000
SALES (est): 9.4MM **Privately Held**
WEB: www.ronsinphotocopy.com
SIC: 7389 Microfilm recording & developing service

(P-17468)
ROSE & SHORE INC
5151 Alcoa Ave, Vernon (90058-3715)
P.O. Box 58225 (90058-0225)
PHONE 323 826-2144
Irwin Miller, *President*
Larry V Bos, *Vice Pres*
James Craig, *Vice Pres*
Carol Miller, *Admin Sec*
Lluvia Serrano, *QA Dir*
EMP: 320
SQ FT: 60,000

PRODUCTS & SERVICES SECTION

7389 - Business Svcs, NEC County (P-17492)

SALES: 54MM Privately Held
WEB: www.rose-shore.com
SIC: 7389 5147 Packaging & labeling services; meats, cured or smoked

(P-17469)
RR DONNELLEY & SONS COMPANY
Moore Data Graphics
8925 Carroll Way, San Diego (92121-3421)
PHONE..................................858 693-6662
Roger Bowman, Manager
Bill Bowen, Human Res Mgr
EMP: 70
SALES (corp-wide): 11.2B Publicly Held
WEB: www.moore.com
SIC: 7389 2741 2789 Printing broker; miscellaneous publishing; bookbinding & related work
PA: R.R. Donnelley & Sons Company
35 W Wacker Dr Ste 3650
Chicago IL 60601
312 326-8000

(P-17470)
SALT OF EARTH PRODUCTIONS INC
Also Called: Salt Catering
1437 S Robertson Blvd, Los Angeles (90035-3414)
PHONE..................................818 399-1860
Tomas Rivera, President
EMP: 108
SALES: 1.5MM Privately Held
SIC: 7389 Decoration service for special events

(P-17471)
SAN DIEGO TOURISM AUTHORITY (PA)
750 B St Ste 1500, San Diego (92101-8131)
PHONE..................................619 232-3101
Fax: 619 231-9783
Joseph Terzi, CEO
Reint Reinders, President
Rick Meza, CFO
Christine Shimasaki, Exec VP
Sal Giametta, Vice Pres
EMP: 65
SQ FT: 2,100
SALES: 22.2MM Privately Held
SIC: 7389 Convention & show services; tourist information bureau

(P-17472)
SAN FRANCISCO FOUNDATION
1 Embarcadero Ctr # 4150, San Francisco (94111-3740)
PHONE..................................415 733-8500
Fax: 415 477-2783
Sandra Hernandez MD, Director
Jeremy Madsen, Bd of Directors
Raquel Donoso, Exec Dir
Teresa Mejia, Exec Dir
Fred Jacobs, Info Tech Dir
EMP: 60
SQ FT: 22,000
SALES: 182.8MM Privately Held
SIC: 7389 Fund raising organizations

(P-17473)
SAN FRANCISCO TRAVEL ASSN
Also Called: Ss Travel
1 Front St Ste 2900, San Francisco (94111-5333)
PHONE..................................415 974-6900
Fax: 415 227-2602
Joe D'Alessandro, President
Tina Wu, CFO
Bill Poland, Treasurer
Howard Pickett, Chief Mktg Ofcr
Paul Frentsos, Exec VP
EMP: 70
SQ FT: 15,000
SALES: 23.6MM Privately Held
SIC: 7389 Convention & show services; tourist information bureau

(P-17474)
SANTA BARBARA CITY OF
Also Called: Pub Works/Community Dev
630 Garden St, Santa Barbara (93101-1656)
PHONE..................................805 564-5485

Fax: 805 564-5476
Paul Casey, Director
Brenda Nielsen, Admin Asst
Larry Cassidy, Supervisor
EMP: 200 Privately Held
WEB: www.citytv18.com
SIC: 7389 Safety inspection service
PA: City Of Santa Barbara
735 Anacapa St
Santa Barbara CA 93101
805 564-5334

(P-17475)
SANTA BARBARA PC USERS GROUP
462 S San Marcos Rd, Santa Barbara (93101-2726)
PHONE..................................805 964-5411
Gerard L F Ching, President
EMP: 50 EST: 2001
SALES (est): 1.2MM Privately Held
SIC: 7389 Business services

(P-17476)
SARPA-FELDMAN ENTERPRISES INC
Also Called: Progressive Solutions
650 N King Rd, San Jose (95133-1715)
PHONE..................................408 982-1790
Mark E Sarpa, CEO
Scott R Feldman, CFO
Trang Nguyen, Accountant
Jack Tanowitz, Sales Staff
▲ EMP: 56
SQ FT: 13,000
SALES (est): 9.3MM Privately Held
WEB: www.printhq.com
SIC: 7389 Printing broker

(P-17477)
SCA ENTERPRISES INC (PA)
Also Called: Southern Cal Appraisal Co
3817 W Magnolia Blvd, Burbank (91505-2820)
P.O. Box 1455 (91507-1455)
PHONE..................................818 845-7621
Timothy S Davis, CEO
Paula Davis, CFO
Dan Karlson, Info Tech Mgr
Monica Warner, Accountant
Jaynie Castillo, Recruiter
EMP: 65
SQ FT: 1,200
SALES (est): 18.9MM Privately Held
SIC: 7389 Appraisers, except real estate

(P-17478)
SCHERZER INTERNATIONAL CORP (PA)
6351 Owensmouth Ave # 213, Woodland Hills (91367-2291)
PHONE..................................818 227-2770
Fax: 818 227-2750
Larry S Scherzer, President
Jeffrey Hauptman, Exec VP
David J Lazar, Managing Dir
Carol Scherzer, Admin Sec
Marina Camarillo, Admin Asst
EMP: 60
SQ FT: 11,400
SALES (est): 11.1MM Privately Held
SIC: 7389 Financial services

(P-17479)
SCHURMAN FINE PAPERS
Also Called: Papyrus
1002 S 2nd St, San Jose (95112-5827)
PHONE..................................408 971-8843
Quang Van Tran, Branch Mgr
EMP: 158
SALES (corp-wide): 1.2B Privately Held
SIC: 7389 Printers' services: folding, collating
PA: Schurman Fine Papers
500 Chadbourne Rd
Fairfield CA 94534
707 425-8006

(P-17480)
SCREEN GEMS-EMI MUSIC INC
Also Called: EMI Publishing
2700 Colorado Ave Ste 100, Santa Monica (90404-3581)
PHONE..................................310 586-2700
Martin N Bandier, CEO

EMP: 50
SALES (corp-wide): 72.1MM Privately Held
SIC: 7389 Music recording producer
HQ: Screen Gems-Emi Music Inc.
150 5th Ave Fl 7
New York NY 10011
212 786-8000

(P-17481)
SCRIP ADVANTAGE INC
4273 W Richert Ave # 110, Fresno (93722-6333)
P.O. Box 13238 (93794-3238)
PHONE..................................559 320-0052
John Coyle, President
Robert Coyle, CFO
Bob Coyle, Vice Pres
Fred McIntosh, Controller
Teri Carey, Senior Buyer
EMP: 54 EST: 1999
SQ FT: 2,000
SALES: 136MM Privately Held
WEB: www.scripadvantage.com
SIC: 7389 Fund raising organizations

(P-17482)
SEARCH ENGINE OPTIMIZATION INC
5841 Edison Pl Ste 140, Carlsbad (92008-5510)
PHONE..................................760 929-0039
Garry Grant, CEO
Krishnan Coughran, President
Steve Boccone, CFO
Kimberly Pitcher, Vice Pres
Gary R Berg, Project Mgr
EMP: 58
SQ FT: 15,000
SALES (est): 4.9MM Privately Held
WEB: www.seoinc.com
SIC: 7389 8742 Office facilities & secretarial service rental; marketing consulting services

(P-17483)
SEASIDE HOTEL LESSEE INC
Also Called: Viceroy Santa Monica
1819 Ocean Ave, Santa Monica (90401-3215)
PHONE..................................310 260-7500
Janne Clare, General Mgr
Todd Yamakoa, General Mgr
Jay Thorson, Finance
EMP: 178
SALES: 26MM Privately Held
SIC: 7389 Hotel & motel reservation service; restaurant reservation service

(P-17484)
SEAVIEW INDUSTRIES
2501 Harbor Blvd, Costa Mesa (92626-6143)
PHONE..................................714 957-5073
Fax: 714 957-5572
Tom Thomas, Manager
EMP: 50
SALES (est): 1.5MM Privately Held
WEB: www.seaviewgolf.com
SIC: 7389 Packaging & labeling services

(P-17485)
SEMAFONE
496 Quail Glen Dr, Oakley (94561-3942)
PHONE..................................925 855-7400
EMP: 60
SALES (est): 2.1MM Privately Held
SIC: 7389

(P-17486)
SERVICE CONTAINER COMPANY LLC
1754 Carr Rd Ste 204, Calexico (92231-9509)
PHONE..................................310 223-1666
Michael Fiterman, Ch of Bd
Daniel Zdon, COO
Byron Wieberdink, CFO
David Lenzen, Exec VP
Ronda Bayer, Vice Pres
EMP: 75
SQ FT: 30,000

SALES (est): 4.6MM
SALES (corp-wide): 652.6MM Privately Held
WEB: www.servicecontainer.com
SIC: 7389 Packaging & labeling services
PA: Liberty Diversified International, Inc.
5600 Highway 169 N
New Hope MN 55428
763 536-6600

(P-17487)
SERVICE MASTER INDUSTRIES INC
2342 Meyers Ave, Escondido (92029-1008)
PHONE..................................760 480-0208
Mark Bower, General Mgr
Philip Fitzpatrick, President
Eylse Fitzpatrick, Vice Pres
Gerald Farley, Principal
EMP: 60
SALES (est): 4.1MM Privately Held
SIC: 7389 Personal service agents, brokers & bureaus

(P-17488)
SEVEN ONE INC (PA)
Also Called: Professional Tele Answering Svc
21540 Prairie St Ste E, Chatsworth (91311-5814)
PHONE..................................818 904-3435
James Thompson, President
EMP: 83
SALES (est): 5.1MM Privately Held
WEB: www.sevenone.com
SIC: 7389 Telephone answering service

(P-17489)
SIGNET TESTING LABS INC (HQ)
3526 Breakwater Ct, Hayward (94545-3611)
PHONE..................................510 887-8484
Fax: 510 783-4295
Robert V Tadlock, President
Carrie Ferreira, Mktg Dir
EMP: 50
SALES (est): 16.4MM Privately Held
SIC: 7389 Inspection & testing services
PA: United Engineering Resources, Inc.
498 N 3rd St
Sacramento CA 95811
916 375-6700

(P-17490)
SIGUE CORPORATION (PA)
13190 Telfair Ave, Sylmar (91342-3573)
PHONE..................................818 837-5939
Guillermo Dela Vina, CEO
Christina M Pappas, President
Alfredo Dela Vina, CFO
Jennifer Leo, Officer
Enrique Carvajal, Vice Pres
EMP: 100
SQ FT: 3,000
SALES (est): 70.8MM Privately Held
SIC: 7389 4822 Financial services; telegraph & other communications

(P-17491)
SKYBLUE SEWING MANUFACTURING
960 Mission St Fl 2, San Francisco (94103-2911)
PHONE..................................415 777-9978
Fax: 415 777-9938
Huang Zhem, President
Freda Lau, Vice Pres
EMP: 50
SALES (est): 3MM Privately Held
SIC: 7389 Sewing contractor

(P-17492)
SMG FOOD AND BEVERAGE LLC (PA)
Also Called: Ontario Convention Center
2000 E Convention Ctr Way, Ontario (91764-5633)
PHONE..................................909 937-3000
Fax: 909 937-3080
Victoria Van Damme, Mng Member
Arlette Zavala, Social Dir
Rod Blackwood, Human Res Mgr
John Burns,
Maureen Ginty,
EMP: 86

7389 - Business Svcs, NEC County (P-17493)

SALES (est): 15.2MM **Privately Held**
SIC: 7389 Convention & show services

(P-17493)
SMG HOLDINGS INC
848 M St Fl 2nd, Fresno (93721-2760)
PHONE..................................559 445-8100
William Overfelt, *General Mgr*
EMP: 336
SALES (corp-wide): 410.9MM **Privately Held**
SIC: 7389 Convention & show services
PA: Smg Holdings, Inc
   300 Cnshohckn State Rd # 450
   Conshohocken PA 19428
   610 729-7900

(P-17494)
SMITH-EMERY SAN FRANCISCO INC
1940 Oakdale Ave, San Francisco (94124-2004)
P.O. Box 880550 (94188-0550)
PHONE..................................415 642-7326
James E Partridge, *President*
Helen Choe, *CFO*
Alfreda Lee, *General Mgr*
Leonard Cross, *Manager*
EMP: 113
SQ FT: 10,160
SALES (est): 11.4MM **Privately Held**
SIC: 7389 8711 Inspection & testing services; engineering services

(P-17495)
SOBOBA BAND LUISENO INDIANS
Also Called: Soboba Casino
23333 Soboba Rd, San Jacinto (92583)
P.O. Box 817 (92581-0817)
PHONE..................................951 665-1000
Toll Free:..................................888 -
Fax: 951 487-1375
Richard Kline, *General Mgr*
Phillip Frazer, *CFO*
Patrick Placencia, *Officer*
Bob Frear, *General Mgr*
Leanna Johnson, *Info Tech Mgr*
EMP: 900 **Privately Held**
WEB: www.soboba.com
SIC: 7389 7011 Personal service agents, brokers & bureaus; casino hotel
PA: Soboba Band Of Luiseno Indians
   23906 Soboba Rd
   San Jacinto CA 92583
   951 654-2765

(P-17496)
SONY INTERACTIVE ENTRMT LLC (DH)
Also Called: Sony Interactve Entertnmnt Net
6080 Center Dr Fl 10, Los Angeles (90045-9205)
PHONE..................................310 981-1500
Sangita Patel, *Vice Pres*
Fumi Kanagawa, *Exec VP*
Ron Cushey, *Vice Pres*
Dian Gavanarov, *Admin Asst*
Emily Nahmanson, *Admin Asst*
EMP: 76
SALES (est): 50.9MM
SALES (corp-wide): 69.2B **Privately Held**
SIC: 7389 Music distribution systems
HQ: Sony Corporation Of America
   25 Madison Ave Fl 27
   New York NY 10010
   212 833-8000

(P-17497)
SOUTHWEST INSPECTION AND TSTG
Also Called: Southwest Inspection Testing
441 Commercial Way, La Habra (90631-6168)
PHONE..................................562 941-2990
Steven L Godbey, *President*
Kathy Godbey, *Treasurer*
Charles L Godbey, *Vice Pres*
Jay Dresner, *Supervisor*
EMP: 75
SQ FT: 2,400
SALES (est): 8MM **Privately Held**
SIC: 7389 Building inspection service

(P-17498)
STACCATO COMMUNICATIONS INC
6195 Lusk Blvd Ste 200, San Diego (92121-3723)
PHONE..................................858 812-0981
Rick Kornfeld, *President*
Marty Colombatto, *Ch of Bd*
Colin Macnab, *COO*
Lars Mucke, *Sr Corp Ofcr*
Larry Taylor, *Sr Corp Ofcr*
EMP: 65
SALES (est): 2.6MM **Privately Held**
WEB: www.staccatocommunications.com
SIC: 7389 Personal service agents, brokers & bureaus

(P-17499)
STAGE II INC
Also Called: Stage II Design & Production
1100 Mar West St Ste F, Belvedere Tiburon (94920-1861)
PHONE..................................415 285-8400
Fax: 415 255-9590
Chris McGregor, *President*
Kenneth Fiskin, *Manager*
EMP: 50
SQ FT: 3,800
SALES (est): 3.1MM **Privately Held**
SIC: 7389 Decoration service for special events

(P-17500)
STANISLAUS CONSOL FIRE PROT
321 E St, Waterford (95386-9006)
PHONE..................................209 549-8404
Fax: 209 552-3705
Steve Mayotte, *Principal*
Lyn Rambo, *Manager*
EMP: 50
SQ FT: 3,632
SALES (corp-wide): 3.9MM **Privately Held**
SIC: 7389 Fire protection service other than forestry or public
PA: Stanislaus Consolidated Fire Protection District
   3324 Topeka St
   Riverbank CA 95367
   209 869-7470

(P-17501)
STANTON HOLDINGS AMERICAS
6595 Fairlynn Blvd, Yorba Linda (92886-6414)
PHONE..................................714 689-9551
Brent Author Stenton, *Partner*
EMP: 50
SALES (est): 2.1MM **Privately Held**
SIC: 7389 Brokers' services

(P-17502)
STERICYCLE COMM SOLUTIONS INC
2255 Watt Ave Ste 50, Sacramento (95825-0504)
PHONE..................................888 370-6711
Gail Dawson, *Branch Mgr*
EMP: 54
SALES (corp-wide): 2.9B **Publicly Held**
SIC: 7389 Telephone answering service
HQ: Stericycle Communication Solutions, Inc.
   4010 Commercial Ave
   Northbrook IL 60062
   866 783-9820

(P-17503)
STERICYCLE COMM SOLUTIONS INC
612 S Harbor Blvd, Anaheim (92805-4526)
PHONE..................................714 991-9595
Jamie Lloyd, *Branch Mgr*
EMP: 50
SALES (corp-wide): 2.9B **Publicly Held**
SIC: 7389 Telemarketing services
HQ: Stericycle Communication Solutions, Inc.
   4010 Commercial Ave
   Northbrook IL 60062
   866 783-9820

(P-17504)
STERLING HSA INC
475 14th St Ste 120, Oakland (94612-1900)
P.O. Box 71107 (94612-7207)
PHONE..................................800 617-4729
Cora M Tellez, *President*
Duarte Vatista, *COO*
Mark Maltun, *CFO*
Chris Bettner, *Exec VP*
Michael Robinson, *CTO*
EMP: 50
SALES (est): 8MM **Privately Held**
WEB: www.sterlinghsa.com
SIC: 7389 Financial services

(P-17505)
STITCHES INC
2838 Vail Ave, Commerce (90040-2697)
P.O. Box 1086, Studio City (91614-0086)
PHONE..................................323 622-0175
Robert Reed, *President*
EMP: 150
SQ FT: 30,000
SALES (est): 2MM **Privately Held**
SIC: 7389 Sewing contractor

(P-17506)
STOCKTON UNLIMITED COMPANY
2481 E Main St, Stockton (95205-6521)
PHONE..................................209 464-2200
Emily Salam, *Principal*
Henry Fox, *Treasurer*
EMP: 99
SALES (est): 950K **Privately Held**
SIC: 7389 Business services

(P-17507)
STRIPE PAYMENTS COMPANY
3180 18th St Ste 100, San Francisco (94110-2042)
PHONE..................................888 963-8955
John Collison, *Principal*
EMP: 77 EST: 2014
SALES (est): 8.9MM **Privately Held**
SIC: 7389 Financial services

(P-17508)
SUGAR FOODS CORPORATION
Also Called: Sygma Network, The
9500 El Dorado Ave, Sun Valley (91352-1339)
P.O. Box 1220 (91353-1220)
PHONE..................................818 768-7900
Fax: 818 768-7619
Stephen Odell, *Partner*
EMP: 200
SALES (corp-wide): 323.9MM **Privately Held**
WEB: www.sugarfoods.com
SIC: 7389 2099 2062 Packaging & labeling services; food preparations; cane sugar refining
PA: Sugar Foods Corporation
   950 3rd Ave Fl 21
   New York NY 10022
   212 753-6900

(P-17509)
SUGAR FOODS CORPORATION
Also Called: General Brands Packing
9500 El Dorado Ave, Sun Valley (91352-1339)
P.O. Box 1220 (91353-1220)
PHONE..................................818 768-7900
Steven Odell, *Branch Mgr*
EMP: 100
SQ FT: 60,000
SALES (corp-wide): 323.9MM **Privately Held**
WEB: www.sugarfoods.com
SIC: 7389 Packaging & labeling services
PA: Sugar Foods Corporation
   950 3rd Ave Fl 21
   New York NY 10022
   212 753-6900

(P-17510)
SUN LIGHT & POWER
1035 Folger Ave, Berkeley (94710-2819)
PHONE..................................510 845-2997
Fax: 510 845-1133
Gary Gerber, *President*
Adam Lockert, *Technician*
Charly Bray, *Engng Exec*
Erinne Davis, *Project Mgr*
Pam Lopinto, *Project Mgr*
EMP: 63
SQ FT: 10,000
SALES (est): 11.9MM **Privately Held**
WEB: www.sunlightandpower.com
SIC: 7389 1796 3433 Design services; power generating equipment installation; solar heaters & collectors

(P-17511)
SUPER CENTER CONCEPTS INC
Also Called: Superior Grocers
133 W Avenue 45, Los Angeles (90065-3022)
PHONE..................................323 223-3878
Chris Gonzalez, *District Mgr*
EMP: 195 **Privately Held**
SIC: 7389 Design services
PA: Super Center Concepts, Inc.
   15510 Carmenita Rd
   Santa Fe Springs CA 90670

(P-17512)
SWISSTEX CALIFORNIA INC (PA)
13660 S Figueroa St, Los Angeles (90061-1023)
PHONE..................................310 516-6800
Fax: 310 516-0672
Henry Bassett, *President*
Michel Morger, *Vice Pres*
Thomas Schrieder, *Vice Pres*
Pam Bennett, *Purch Mgr*
EMP: 50
SALES (est): 23MM **Privately Held**
WEB: www.swisstex-ca.com
SIC: 7389 Textile & apparel services

(P-17513)
SYSTEM ONE HOLDINGS LLC
21221 S Wstrn Ave Ste 110, Torrance (90501)
PHONE..................................310 483-7800
Kati Duggleby, *Office Admin*
Joe Wells, *Business Mgr*
Joyce Vasick, *Recruiter*
Geo Daguer, *Manager*
Cristina Lewis, *Manager*
EMP: 208
SALES (corp-wide): 306.2MM **Privately Held**
SIC: 7389 Automobile recovery service
PA: System One Holdings, Llc
   12 Federal St Ste 205
   Pittsburgh PA 15212
   412 995-1900

(P-17514)
TACTICAL TELESOLUTIONS INC
550 Kearny St Ste 210, San Francisco (94108-2592)
PHONE..................................415 788-8808
Fax: 415 788-8848
Laura Hylton, *President*
Kurt Stenzel, *Vice Pres*
Niko Wenner, *Admin Asst*
Michael Hylton, *QA Dir*
Eric Wicklund, *Info Tech Mgr*
EMP: 130
SQ FT: 15,000
SALES (est): 12.8MM **Privately Held**
WEB: www.tts-sf.com
SIC: 7389 Telemarketing services

(P-17515)
TALENTBURST INC
575 Market St Ste 3025, San Francisco (94105-5840)
PHONE..................................415 813-4011
EMP: 115
SALES (corp-wide): 22.3MM **Privately Held**
SIC: 7389 7375 Check validation service; information retrieval services
PA: Talentburst, Inc.
   679 Worcester St
   Natick MA 01760
   508 628-7516

PRODUCTS & SERVICES SECTION   7389 - Business Svcs, NEC County (P-17538)

(P-17516)
TAP WORLDWIDE LLC
2360 Boswell Rd, Chula Vista (91914-3510)
PHONE..................619 216-1444
Daniel Atkins, *President*
EMP: 100 **Privately Held**
SIC: 7389
PA: Tap Worldwide, Llc
    400 W Artesia Blvd
    Compton CA 90220

(P-17517)
TATA COMMUNICATIONS AMER INC
Also Called: Bitgravity
700 Airport Blvd Ste 100, Burlingame (94010-1931)
PHONE..................650 262-0004
Fax: 650 344-9861
Srinivasan Cr, *Vice Pres*
Mehul Kapadia, *Managing Dir*
Adam Buecher, *Sr Software Eng*
Steve Eng, *Software Dev*
Michael Smith, *Software Engr*
EMP: 62
SALES (corp-wide): 700.2MM **Privately Held**
SIC: 7389 Music & broadcasting services
HQ: Tata Communications (America) Inc.
    2355 Dulles Corner Blvd # 700
    Herndon VA 20171
    703 657-8400

(P-17518)
TBWA CHIAT/DAY INC
5353 Grosvenor Blvd, Los Angeles (90066-6913)
PHONE..................310 305-5000
Fax: 310 305-6000
Lee Clow, *Branch Mgr*
Taj Singh, *Vice Pres*
Robin Rossi, *Executive*
Chris King, *Associate Dir*
Brent Anderson, *Creative Dir*
EMP: 126
SALES (corp-wide): 15.1B **Publicly Held**
SIC: 7389 Interior design services
HQ: Tbwa Chiat/Day Inc.
    488 Madison Ave Fl 7
    New York NY 10022
    212 804-1000

(P-17519)
TD SERVICE COMPANY
4000 W Metro Dr Ste 400, Orange (92868)
P.O. Box 11988, Santa Ana (92711-1988)
PHONE..................714 543-8372
Dale L Dykema, *Ch of Bd*
Patrick J Dobiesz, *President*
Kraig Kirtley, *President*
Mark Crofford, *CFO*
Janina Hoak, *Trustee*
EMP: 165
SQ FT: 45,000
SALES: 49.5MM
SALES (corp-wide): 45.2MM **Privately Held**
WEB: www.tdsf.com
SIC: 7389 Personal service agents, brokers & bureaus
PA: T.D. Service Financial Corporation
    4000 W Metro Dr Ste 400
    Orange CA 92868
    714 543-8372

(P-17520)
TEAM SAN JOSE
408 Almaden Blvd, San Jose (95110-2709)
PHONE..................408 295-9600
Karolyn Kirchgesler, *CEO*
Dave Costain, *COO*
Janette Divol, *CFO*
Janette Sutton, *CFO*
Sue Murphy, *Admin Asst*
EMP: 900
SQ FT: 300,000
SALES: 6.4MM **Privately Held**
SIC: 7389 Convention & show services

(P-17521)
TECHNICON DESIGN CORPORATION
32238 Paseo Adelanto A, San Juan Capistrano (92675-3624)
PHONE..................949 218-1300
David Shall, *President*
Helen Thomas, *Exec VP*
Frank Goodchild, *Business Mgr*
Monica Chavez, *Recruiter*
Brenda Ramirez, *Recruiter*
EMP: 120
SQ FT: 1,000
SALES (est): 9.7MM
SALES (corp-wide): 61.2MM **Privately Held**
WEB: www.techniconims.com
SIC: 7389 Design services
PA: Technicon Design Limited
    Technicon House
    Luton BEDS

(P-17522)
TEKWORKS INC (PA)
13000 Gregg St Ste B, Poway (92064-7151)
PHONE..................858 668-1705
Fax: 858 668-3320
William E Bourgeois, *CEO*
Dale Bourgeois, *Vice Pres*
Dave Novak, *Vice Pres*
Brandon Watson, *Vice Pres*
Christina Kinzer, *Executive Asst*
EMP: 130
SALES (est): 62.5MM **Privately Held**
WEB: www.tekworkscomm.com
SIC: 7389 1731 Advertising, promotional & trade show services; electrical work

(P-17523)
TELE-DIRECT COMMUNICATIONS
4741 Madison Ave Ste 200, Sacramento (95841-2580)
PHONE..................916 348-2170
A James Puff, *Chairman*
Thomas Coshow, *CEO*
Sandra Coggeshall, *Exec VP*
Jamei Puff, *Sales/Mktg Mgr*
EMP: 75
SQ FT: 6,000
SALES (est): 7.4MM **Privately Held**
WEB: www.tele-direct.com
SIC: 7389 5999 Telephone services; telephone & communication equipment

(P-17524)
TELE-INTERPRETERS LLC
1 Lower Ragsdale Dr # 2, Monterey (93940-5747)
P.O. Box 202572, Dallas TX (75320-2572)
PHONE..................800 811-7881
Melanie Coto-Trevor,
Michelle Johansen, *Info Tech Mgr*
Bart Zygmond, *Controller*
EMP: 500
SQ FT: 10,000
SALES (est): 14.9MM
SALES (corp-wide): 76.1MM **Privately Held**
WEB: www.teleinterpreters.com
SIC: 7389 Translation services
HQ: Language Line, Llc
    1 Lower Ragsdale Dr # 2
    Monterey CA 93940
    831 648-5800

(P-17525)
TELECOM EVOLUTIONS LLC
9221 Corbin Ave Ste 260, Northridge (91324-1625)
PHONE..................818 264-4400
James Murphy, *Mng Member*
EMP: 50 EST: 2010
SALES: 22MM **Privately Held**
SIC: 7389 Telephone services

(P-17526)
TELECOM INC
2201 Broadway Ste 103, Oakland (94612-3028)
PHONE..................510 873-8283
Fax: 510 873-8293
Jon Martin, *President*

Greg Haggerty, *CTO*
Roffel Ferraz, *Project Mgr*
LI Tao, *Bookkeeper*
Lani Stackel, *Mktg Dir*
EMP: 100
SALES (est): 9.3MM **Privately Held**
WEB: www.telecominc.com
SIC: 7389 4813 8742 Telemarketing services; data telephone communications; marketing consulting services

(P-17527)
TELMATE LLC
655 Montgomery St # 1800, San Francisco (94111-2635)
PHONE..................415 300-4314
Vance A Johnson, *President*
Reuben Garcia, *Tech/Comp Coord*
Kathryn Jarrell, *Opers Staff*
Danny Martinez, *Sales Engr*
Alexis Sneed, *Marketing Staff*
EMP: 153 **Privately Held**
SIC: 7389 Telemarketing services
PA: Telmate, Llc
    1096 Se 6th St
    Ontario OR 97914

(P-17528)
TEXAS INSTRUMENTS SUNNYVALE
165 Gibraltar Ct, Sunnyvale (94089-1301)
PHONE..................408 541-9900
Andrew Hartland, *CFO*
Bruce Kendall, *Engineer*
EMP: 50
SQ FT: 12,070
SALES (est): 1.9MM
SALES (corp-wide): 13B **Publicly Held**
WEB: www.ti.com
SIC: 7389 Design services
PA: Texas Instruments Incorporated
    12500 Ti Blvd
    Dallas TX 75243
    214 479-3773

(P-17529)
THOMPSON & RICH CRANE SERVICE
2373 E Mariposa Rd, Stockton (95205-7811)
P.O. Box 30035 (95213-0035)
PHONE..................209 465-3161
EMP: 50 EST: 1988
SALES (est): 2.5MM **Privately Held**
SIC: 7389

(P-17530)
THOMSON REUTERS (MARKETS) LLC
1 Sansome St Ste 3650, San Francisco (94104-4460)
PHONE..................415 677-2500
Fax: 415 398-6593
Ben Silverman, *Manager*
EMP: 60
SALES (corp-wide): 3.8B **Publicly Held**
WEB: www.reuters.com
SIC: 7389 Personal service agents, brokers & bureaus
HQ: Reuters America Llc
    3 Times Sq
    New York NY 10036
    646 223-4000

(P-17531)
TIDAVATER INC
Also Called: Le Courier
2107 W Alameda Ave, Burbank (91506-2934)
PHONE..................818 848-4151
Fax: 818 848-5294
EMP: 150
SQ FT: 3,000
SALES (est): 5.2MM **Privately Held**
SIC: 7389 4513 4215

(P-17532)
TIMESHARERENTORSELL COM LLC
1685 E Main St Ste 201, El Cajon (92021-5225)
PHONE..................888 872-2517
Sandra Tracy, *Principal*
EMP: 50

SALES (est): 2.4MM **Privately Held**
SIC: 7389 Time-share condominium exchange

(P-17533)
TOMMY BAHAMA GROUP INC
610 Ventura Blvd Ste 1340, Camarillo (93010-5869)
PHONE..................805 482-8868
Janet Infante, *Branch Mgr*
EMP: 112
SALES (corp-wide): 969.2MM **Publicly Held**
SIC: 7389 Apparel designers, commercial
HQ: Tommy Bahama Group, Inc.
    400 Fairview Ave N # 488
    Seattle WA 98109
    206 622-8688

(P-17534)
TOMMY BAHAMA GROUP INC
1720 Redwood Hwy Spc A019, Corte Madera (94925-1249)
PHONE..................415 737-0400
EMP: 112
SALES (corp-wide): 969.2MM **Publicly Held**
SIC: 7389 Apparel designers, commercial
HQ: Tommy Bahama Group, Inc.
    400 Fairview Ave N # 488
    Seattle WA 98109
    206 622-8688

(P-17535)
TOMMY BAHAMA GROUP INC
4061 Camino De La Plz # 480, San Diego (92173-5931)
PHONE..................619 651-2200
EMP: 112
SALES (corp-wide): 969.2MM **Publicly Held**
SIC: 7389 Apparel designers, commercial
HQ: Tommy Bahama Group, Inc.
    400 Fairview Ave N # 488
    Seattle WA 98109
    206 622-8688

(P-17536)
TOWN & COUNTRY EVENT RENTALS
1 N Calle Cesar Chavez # 7, Santa Barbara (93103-5614)
PHONE..................805 770-5729
Kirk Pallotto, *Sales Staff*
Nikki Keller, *Manager*
EMP: 400
SALES (corp-wide): 28MM **Privately Held**
SIC: 7389 Personal service agents, brokers & bureaus
PA: Town & Country Event Rentals, Inc
    7725 Airport Bus Pkwy
    Van Nuys CA 91406
    818 908-4211

(P-17537)
TRAFFIC MANAGEMENT INC (PA)
2435 Lemon Ave, Signal Hill (90755-3462)
PHONE..................562 595-4278
Fax: 562 424-0266
Christopher H Spano, *CEO*
Jonathan Spano, *COO*
Vincent Nathan, *Area Mgr*
Jeff Rehkopf, *Area Mgr*
Liene Dica, *Admin Asst*
EMP: 144
SQ FT: 20,000
SALES (est): 97.5MM **Privately Held**
SIC: 7389 8741 Flagging service (traffic control); business management

(P-17538)
TRAILBLAZER TECHNOLOGIES
Also Called: Transcription Company, The
4100 W Burbank Blvd Fl 3, Burbank (91505-2121)
PHONE..................818 848-6500
Rich Brownstein, *President*
EMP: 60
SALES (est): 1.9MM **Privately Held**
SIC: 7389 Music & broadcasting services

7389 - Business Svcs, NEC County (P-17539)

(P-17539)
TRANS-PAK INCORPORATED (PA)
520 Marburg Way, San Jose (95133-1619)
PHONE 408 254-0500
Fax: 408 254-0551
Arlene Inch, *Chairman*
Bob Lally, *President*
Bert Inch, *CEO*
Ray Horner, *COO*
Chris Lee, *CFO*
EMP: 175
SALES (est): 84.1MM **Privately Held**
WEB: www.transpak.com
SIC: 7389 Packaging & labeling services

(P-17540)
TRANS-PAK INCORPORATED
Also Called: Transpak Los Angeles
2111 Abalone Ave, Torrance (90501-3710)
PHONE 310 618-6937
Charles Frasier, *Principal*
EMP: 108
SALES (corp-wide): 84.1MM **Privately Held**
SIC: 7389 Packaging & labeling services
PA: Trans-Pak, Incorporated
   520 Marburg Way
   San Jose CA 95133
   408 254-0500

(P-17541)
TRANSITION CONNECTION
2740 Fulton Ave Ste 101, Sacramento (95821-5184)
PHONE 916 481-3470
Fax: 916 481-3066
Robin Delong, *Owner*
Pat Orner, *Owner*
EMP: 500
SALES (est): 10MM **Privately Held**
WEB: www.sacrelo.com
SIC: 7389 Relocation service

(P-17542)
TRAP
Also Called: Task Force For Reg Autostaff
9040 Telstar Ave Ste 115, El Monte (91731-2838)
PHONE 626 572-5610
Terence Judge,
EMP: 80
SALES (est): 2.5MM **Privately Held**
SIC: 7389 Personal service agents, brokers & bureaus

(P-17543)
TRILLIANT NETWORKS INC (PA)
1100 Island Dr Ste 201, Redwood City (94065-5187)
PHONE 650 204-5050
Andy White, *President*
Salin Khan, *COO*
Mike Mortimer, *Exec VP*
Norma Formanek, *Senior VP*
Ryan Gerbrandt, *Senior VP*
EMP: 65
SALES (est): 45.6MM **Privately Held**
SIC: 7389 Meter readers, remote

(P-17544)
TRILOGY FINANCIAL SERVICES INC
12526 High Bluff Dr # 150, San Diego (92130-2064)
PHONE 858 755-6696
Fax: 858 755-1116
Doug Stroot, *Manager*
Scott Babbitt, *Vice Pres*
Michael Barrows, *Vice Pres*
Bob Chitrathorn, *Vice Pres*
Joe Fischman, *Vice Pres*
EMP: 50
SALES (corp-wide): 22.1MM **Privately Held**
WEB: www.asktrilogy.com
SIC: 7389 Financial services
PA: Trilogy Financial Services, Inc.
   17011 Beach Blvd Ste 800
   Huntington Beach CA 92647
   714 843-9977

(P-17545)
TRIMARK RAYGAL INC
Also Called: TRIMARK UNITED EAST
2801 Mcgaw Ave, Irvine (92614-5835)
PHONE 949 474-1000
Fax: 949 474-7298
Jack Howard Mervis, *President*
Eric Smith, *Vice Pres*
Dirk Hallett, *Admin Sec*
Mary Stubler, *Admin Asst*
EMP: 83
SQ FT: 21,000
SALES (est): 14MM
SALES (corp-wide): 6.7B **Privately Held**
WEB: www.raygal.com
SIC: 7389 1799 Interior designer; kitchen & bathroom remodeling
HQ: Trimark Usa, Llc
   505 Collins St
   Attleboro MA 02703
   508 399-2400

(P-17546)
TRINCHERO FAMILY ESTATES INC
18667 Jacob Brack Rd, Lodi (95242-9185)
PHONE 707 963-5928
EMP: 163
SALES (corp-wide): 201.2MM **Privately Held**
SIC: 7389 Automobile recovery service
PA: Sutter Home Winery, Inc.
   100 Saint Helena Hwy S
   Saint Helena CA 94574
   707 963-3104

(P-17547)
TWO JINN INC
Also Called: Aladdin Bail Bonds
325 Texas St, Fairfield (94533-5624)
PHONE 707 421-9600
Fax: 707 421-9559
Christian Velazquez, *Principal*
Jim Nules, *Manager*
EMP: 88
SALES (corp-wide): 47.1MM **Privately Held**
SIC: 7389 Bail bonding
PA: Two Jinn, Inc.
   1000 Aviara Dr Ste 300
   Carlsbad CA 92011
   760 431-9911

(P-17548)
TWO JINN INC (PA)
Also Called: Aladdin Bail Bonds
1000 Aviara Dr Ste 300, Carlsbad (92011-4218)
PHONE 760 431-9911
Robert H Hayes, *Ch of Bd*
Herb Mutter, *CFO*
Dave Edwards, *Info Tech Dir*
Kayton Tomaszyk, *Info Tech Mgr*
Leah Taniguchi, *Controller*
EMP: 75
SALES (est): 47.1MM **Privately Held**
WEB: www.twojinn.com
SIC: 7389 Bail bonding

(P-17549)
UBS FINANCIAL SERVICES INC
3801 University Ave # 300, Riverside (92501-3264)
PHONE 951 684-6300
James Gallegos, *Manager*
Scott Morris, *Branch Mgr*
Gary Roth, *Advisor*
EMP: 50
SALES (corp-wide): 28.9B **Privately Held**
SIC: 7389 Brokers, business: buying & selling business enterprises; authors' agents & brokers; speakers' bureau
HQ: Ubs Financial Services, Inc.
   1285 Ave Of The Americas
   New York NY 10019
   212 713-2000

(P-17550)
UBS FINANCIAL SERVICES INC
1200 Prospect St Ste 500, La Jolla (92037-3653)
P.O. Box 2268 (92038-2268)
PHONE 858 454-9181
Lee Tripodi, *Manager*
John Seiber, *Senior VP*
Stephen Seiber, *Senior VP*
Reed Thompson, *Senior VP*
Gary Goldmann, *Vice Pres*
EMP: 60
SALES (corp-wide): 28.9B **Privately Held**
SIC: 7389 Financial services; authors' agents & brokers; speakers' bureau
HQ: Ubs Financial Services Inc.
   1285 Ave Of The Americas
   New York NY 10019
   212 713-2000

(P-17551)
UCDAVIS
1820 Point Reyes Pl, Davis (95616-6652)
PHONE 530 757-3322
Beth Moeller, *Principal*
Carol Schnitter, *Social Dir*
Sharon Ree, *Office Mgr*
Leeann Luttrell, *Office Admin*
Cathy Oliver, *Office Admin*
EMP: 99
SALES (est): 8.6MM **Privately Held**
SIC: 7389

(P-17552)
UCLA HEALTH SYSTEM
1250 15th St Ste 111, Santa Monica (90404-1102)
PHONE 310 393-5153
EMP: 66
SALES (est): 6.5MM **Privately Held**
SIC: 7389 Business services

(P-17553)
UFS INTERNATIONAL LLC
16871 Millikan Ave, Irvine (92606-5011)
PHONE 714 713-6311
Travis Phan, *Owner*
Robert Hrifko, *COO*
EMP: 150
SQ FT: 17,000
SALES (est): 10.8MM **Privately Held**
SIC: 7389 5044 7371 Financial services; office equipment; custom computer programming services

(P-17554)
UNITED EXPRESS MESSENGERS INC
1801 Century Park E # 520, Los Angeles (90067-2307)
PHONE 310 261-2000
Fax: 213 556-7700
Shahin Abrishamchian, *President*
EMP: 60
SQ FT: 3,000
SALES (est): 4.5MM **Privately Held**
SIC: 7389 4212 Courier or messenger service; delivery service, vehicular

(P-17555)
UNITED PARCEL SERVICE INC
Also Called: UPS
14592 Palmdale Rd, Victorville (92392-2754)
PHONE 760 241-5540
Hannah Chung, *Principal*
EMP: 1700
SALES (corp-wide): 58.3B **Publicly Held**
SIC: 7389 Mailing & messenger services
PA: United Parcel Service, Inc.
   55 Glenlake Pkwy
   Atlanta GA 30328
   404 828-6000

(P-17556)
UNITED PARCEL SERVICE INC OH
Also Called: UPS
3331 Industrial Dr Ste C, Santa Rosa (95403-2062)
PHONE 678 339-3171
EMP: 635
SALES (corp-wide): 58.3B **Publicly Held**
SIC: 7389 Mailing & messenger services
HQ: United Parcel Service, Inc. (Oh)
   55 Glenlake Pkwy
   Atlanta GA 30328
   404 828-6000

(P-17557)
UNITED PARCEL SERVICE INC OH
Also Called: UPS
2747 Vail Ave, Commerce (90040-2611)
PHONE 323 837-1220
Steven Hill, *Principal*
EMP: 316
SALES (corp-wide): 58.3B **Publicly Held**
SIC: 7389 Mailing & messenger services
HQ: United Parcel Service, Inc. (Oh)
   55 Glenlake Pkwy
   Atlanta GA 30328
   404 828-6000

(P-17558)
UNITED PARCEL SERVICE INC OH
Also Called: UPS
3221 E Jurupa, Ontario (91764)
PHONE 909 974-7250
Richard Ricardo, *General Mgr*
EMP: 635
SALES (corp-wide): 58.3B **Publicly Held**
WEB: www.upsscs.com
SIC: 7389 Mailing & messenger services
HQ: United Parcel Service, Inc. (Oh)
   55 Glenlake Pkwy
   Atlanta GA 30328
   404 828-6000

(P-17559)
UNITED PARCEL SERVICE INC OH
Also Called: UPS
1746 D St, South Lake Tahoe (96150-6227)
PHONE 800 742-5877
EMP: 316
SALES (corp-wide): 58.3B **Publicly Held**
SIC: 7389 Personal service agents, brokers & bureaus
HQ: United Parcel Service, Inc. (Oh)
   55 Glenlake Pkwy
   Atlanta GA 30328
   404 828-6000

(P-17560)
UNITED PARCEL SERVICE INC OH
Also Called: UPS
201 W Garvey Ave Ste 102, Monterey Park (91754-7425)
PHONE 626 280-8012
Fax: 626 280-8007
Francis Fong, *Owner*
EMP: 635
SALES (corp-wide): 58.3B **Publicly Held**
WEB: www.upsscs.com
SIC: 7389 Mailing & messenger services
HQ: United Parcel Service, Inc. (Oh)
   55 Glenlake Pkwy
   Atlanta GA 30328
   404 828-6000

(P-17561)
UNITED PARCEL SERVICE INC OH
Also Called: UPS
4607 Lakeview Canyon Rd, Westlake Village (91361-4028)
PHONE 818 735-0945
Jim Penna, *Manager*
Jim Latenna, *Manager*
Howard Silber, *Manager*
EMP: 635
SALES (corp-wide): 58.3B **Publicly Held**
WEB: www.upsscs.com
SIC: 7389 Mailing & messenger services
HQ: United Parcel Service, Inc. (Oh)
   55 Glenlake Pkwy
   Atlanta GA 30328
   404 828-6000

(P-17562)
UNITED PARCEL SERVICE INC OH
Also Called: UPS
11811 Landon Dr, Mira Loma (91752-4002)
PHONE 951 749-3400
Paul Slater, *Principal*
Robert Sheldon, *Opers Mgr*
Merdad Motamedi, *Plant Engr*
EMP: 316

PRODUCTS & SERVICES SECTION

7389 - Business Svcs, NEC County (P-17584)

SALES (corp-wide): 58.3B **Publicly Held**
SIC: 7389 Mailing & messenger services
HQ: United Parcel Service, Inc. (Oh)
   55 Glenlake Pkwy
   Atlanta GA 30328
   404 828-6000

(P-17563)
UNITED PARCEL SERVICE INC
OH
Also Called: UPS
48921 Warm Springs Blvd, Fremont (94539-7767)
PHONE..........................800 742-5877
EMP: 316
SALES (corp-wide): 58.3B **Publicly Held**
SIC: 7389 Personal service agents, brokers & bureaus
HQ: United Parcel Service, Inc. (Oh)
   55 Glenlake Pkwy
   Atlanta GA 30328
   404 828-6000

(P-17564)
UNITED PARCEL SERVICE INC
OH
Also Called: UPS
91 W Easy St, Simi Valley (93065-1601)
PHONE..........................866 553-1069
Louis Moody, *Principal*
EMP: 316
SALES (corp-wide): 58.3B **Publicly Held**
SIC: 7389 Mailing & messenger services
HQ: United Parcel Service, Inc. (Oh)
   55 Glenlake Pkwy
   Atlanta GA 30328
   404 828-6000

(P-17565)
UNITED PAYMENT SERVICES
INC
3537 Old Conejo Rd # 113, Newbury Park (91320-2157)
PHONE..........................866 886-4833
Fax: 818 494-3874
Scott Rosen, *President*
Craig Rosen, *COO*
EMP: 480
SQ FT: 15,000
SALES: 4.1MM **Privately Held**
WEB: www.unitedpaymentservices.com
SIC: 7389 Credit card service

(P-17566)
UNITED TRANSPORT SERVICE
INC
6750 Black Forest Dr, Corona (92880-3922)
PHONE..........................951 258-2262
Felipe Mercado, *CEO*
EMP: 50 EST: 1990
SALES (est): 997.3K **Privately Held**
SIC: 7389

(P-17567)
UNITY COURIER SERVICE INC
1132 Beecher St, San Leandro (94577-1252)
PHONE..........................510 568-8890
Michael Wynant, *Branch Mgr*
Albert Trinh, *Financial Analy*
Byron Harrold, *Regl Sales Mgr*
EMP: 60
SALES (corp-wide): 52.8MM **Privately Held**
WEB: www.unitycourier.com
SIC: 7389 Courier or messenger service
PA: Unity Courier Service, Inc.
   3231 Fletcher Dr
   Los Angeles CA 90065
   323 255-9800

(P-17568)
UNIVERSAL CARD INC
Also Called: Merchant Services
9012 Research Dr Ste 200, Irvine (92618-4254)
PHONE..........................949 861-4000
Jason W Moore, *President*
Nathan Jurczyk, *VP Opers*
Michael Kimball, *Opers Mgr*
James Minor, *Opers Mgr*
Kelly Miller, *QC Mgr*
EMP: 400
SQ FT: 40,000
SALES (est): 32.5MM **Privately Held**
WEB: www.merchantsvcs.com
SIC: 7389 Credit card service

(P-17569)
UNIVERSAL MUS INVESTMENTS
INC (HQ)
2220 Colorado Ave, Santa Monica (90404-3506)
PHONE..........................818 577-4700
Fax: 818 577-4740
Lucian C Grainge, *CEO*
Marcella Gaither, *Principal*
Jenna Roher, *Production*
Maria Abuiysa, *Senior Mgr*
Joe Arambula, *Director*
EMP: 80
SALES (est): 32.6MM
SALES (corp-wide): 45.2MM **Privately Held**
SIC: 7389 7929 Music recording producer; musical entertainers; musicians
PA: Vivendi
   42 Avenue De Friedland
   Paris Cedex 08 75380
   171 711-000

(P-17570)
UNIVERSAL MUSIC GROUP INC
(HQ)
2220 Colorado Ave, Santa Monica (90404-3506)
PHONE..........................310 865-4000
Fax: 310 777-6431
Lucian Grainge, *Co-CEO*
Mauro Deceglie, *Partner*
Jules Ferree, *Partner*
Joie Manda, *President*
Steve Barnett, *CEO*
EMP: 100 EST: 1996
SALES (est): 404.7MM
SALES (corp-wide): 45.2MM **Privately Held**
SIC: 7389 2741 Music recording producer; miscellaneous publishing
PA: Vivendi
   42 Avenue De Friedland
   Paris Cedex 08 75380
   171 711-000

(P-17571)
UNIVERSAL MUSIC GROUP INC
10 Universal City Plz, Universal City (91608-1002)
PHONE..........................818 286-4000
Kent Earls, *Branch Mgr*
Frank Chiocchi, *Exec VP*
Andrew Turk, *Network Enginr*
Jane Peterson, *Opers Staff*
Clifton Lancaster, *Litigation*
EMP: 50
SALES (corp-wide): 45.2MM **Privately Held**
SIC: 7389 Music recording producer
HQ: Universal Music Group, Inc.
   2220 Colorado Ave
   Santa Monica CA 90404
   310 865-4000

(P-17572)
UNIVERSAL SERVICES
AMERICA LP
141 Auburn St, Salinas (93901-2601)
PHONE..........................831 751-3230
EMP: 5003
SALES (corp-wide): 2B **Privately Held**
SIC: 7389 Brokers' services
PA: Universal Services Of America, Lp
   1551 N Tustin Ave
   Santa Ana CA 92705
   714 619-9700

(P-17573)
UNIVERSITY OF SAN
FRANCISCO
California Poison Control Sys
3333 California St Ste 11, San Francisco (94118-1944)
P.O. Box 1262 Ucsf (94143)
PHONE..........................415 502-8600
Fax: 415 502-8620
Stuart Heard, *Manager*
Kristine A Madsen, *Pediatrics*
Jacqueline A Nemer, *Med Doctor*
John Rootenberg, *Director*
EMP: 150
SALES (corp-wide): 371.2MM **Privately Held**
WEB: www.usfca.edu
SIC: 7389 8221 Personal service agents, brokers & bureaus; university
PA: University Of San Francisco Inc
   2130 Fulton St
   San Francisco CA 94117
   415 422-5555

(P-17574)
UNIVERSITY OF SAN
FRANCISCO
Also Called: Medicl-Srgcal Nrsing Cnference
275 S Airport Blvd, San Francisco (94115)
PHONE..........................415 422-2028
Patricia Lynch, *Branch Mgr*
EMP: 150
SALES (corp-wide): 371.2MM **Privately Held**
SIC: 7389 Convention & show services
PA: University Of San Francisco Inc
   2130 Fulton St
   San Francisco CA 94117
   415 422-5555

(P-17575)
UNIVERSITY STUDENT UNION
INC
5151 State University Dr, Los Angeles (90032-4226)
PHONE..........................323 343-2450
Joseph Aguirre, *Exec Dir*
Sarah Figueroa, *Exec Dir*
Rowena Tran, *Asst Director*
Martin Sandoval, *Director*
EMP: 110
SALES (est): 3.6MM **Privately Held**
SIC: 7389 Personal service agents, brokers & bureaus

(P-17576)
UPLOAD DEMO INC
9663 Santa Monica Blvd, Beverly Hills (90210-4303)
PHONE..........................818 983-2395
Dino Awadisian, *President*
EMP: 57 EST: 2012
SALES: 80MM **Privately Held**
SIC: 7389 Music recording producer

(P-17577)
UPS STORE INC (HQ)
Also Called: Mail Boxes Etc
6060 Cornerstone Ct W, San Diego (92121-3712)
PHONE..........................858 455-8800
Fax: 619 597-6076
Walter T Davis, *CEO*
Tim Davis, *President*
Susan Chae, *COO*
Jose Ferro, *CFO*
Jennifer Jonson, *CFO*
EMP: 148
SQ FT: 66,000
SALES (est): 88.4MM
SALES (corp-wide): 58.3B **Publicly Held**
WEB: www.ups.com
SIC: 7389 8742 4783 Mailbox rental & related service; printers' services: folding, collating; packaging & labeling services; business consultant; packing goods for shipping
PA: United Parcel Service, Inc.
   55 Glenlake Pkwy
   Atlanta GA 30328
   404 828-6000

(P-17578)
US BANKCARD SERVICES INC
17171 Gale Ave Ste 110, City of Industry (91745-1822)
PHONE..........................888 888-8872
Christopher J Chang, *President*
Jeff Huang, *Purch Agent*
EMP: 75
SQ FT: 3,000
SALES (est): 9MM **Privately Held**
WEB: www.topmsp.com
SIC: 7389 Credit card service

(P-17579)
US MERCHANTS FINCL GROUP
INC
1625 Proforma Ave, Ontario (91761-7607)
PHONE..........................909 923-3388
Larry Khemlani, *Manager*
Larry Khenlani, *Manager*
Cynthia Mayen, *Manager*
EMP: 150
SALES (corp-wide): 170.9MM **Privately Held**
SIC: 7389 7922 Personal service agents, brokers & bureaus; theatrical producers & services
PA: U.S. Merchants Financial Group, Inc.
   1118 S La Cienega Blvd
   Los Angeles CA 90035
   310 855-1946

(P-17580)
V A ANDERSON ENTERPRISES
INC (PA)
Also Called: Kopy Kat Attorney Service
400 Atlas St, Brea (92821-3117)
P.O. Box 1029 (92822-1029)
PHONE..........................714 990-6100
Pat Flynn, *President*
Bob Flynn, *Vice Pres*
Chuck Cunningham, *Sales Executive*
Perry Miller, *Manager*
EMP: 62
SQ FT: 10,000
SALES (est): 9.1MM **Privately Held**
WEB: www.kopykat.net
SIC: 7389 Microfilm recording & developing service

(P-17581)
V G CARELLI INTERNATIONAL
CORP
1 Park Plz Ste 600, Irvine (92614-5987)
PHONE..........................310 247-8410
Vittorio G Carelli, *President*
Rebecca Mansdorf, *Director*
EMP: 50
SALES (est): 1.7MM **Privately Held**
SIC: 7389 Personal service agents, brokers & bureaus

(P-17582)
VALLEY INVENTORY SERVICE
INC
1180 Horizon Dr Ste B, Fairfield (94533-1693)
P.O. Box 503 (94533-0050)
PHONE..........................707 422-6050
Fax: 707 422-7045
Jeffrey J Link, *President*
Veronica Link, *President*
Darian Dixon, *Info Tech Dir*
EMP: 100 EST: 1970
SALES (est): 8.2MM **Privately Held**
WEB: www.valleycount.com
SIC: 7389 Inventory computing service

(P-17583)
VALLEY PRODUCTIONS INC
17247 La Canada Rd, Madera (93636-9249)
PHONE..........................559 661-6121
Fax: 559 675-6624
John Paye,
Steve Arsenault,
EMP: 50
SQ FT: 3,000
SALES: 1.5MM **Privately Held**
SIC: 7389 7922 Fund raising organizations; entertainment promotion

(P-17584)
VENTURE DESIGN SERVICES
INC
451 Aviation Blvd Ste 215, Santa Rosa (95403-1055)
PHONE..........................707 524-8368
Fax: 707 524-8368
Robert Eves, *Branch Mgr*
Robert Armantrout, *Plant Mgr*
EMP: 64
SALES (corp-wide): 15.7MM **Privately Held**
SIC: 7389 Design services

(PA)=Parent Co (HQ)=Headquarters (DH)=Div Headquarters
○ = New Business established in last 2 years

7389 - Business Svcs, NEC County (P-17585) — PRODUDUCTS & SERVICES SECTION

PA: Venture Design Services Inc.
1051 S East St
Anaheim CA 92805
714 765-3740

(P-17585)
VERA BRADLEY INC
356 Santana Row Ste 1020, San Jose (95128-2034)
PHONE..............................408 615-8370
Bradley Vera, *Principal*
EMP: 76
SALES (corp-wide): 502.6MM **Publicly Held**
SIC: 7389 Design services
PA: Vera Bradley, Inc.
12420 Stonebridge Rd
Roanoke IN 46783
877 708-8372

(P-17586)
VERIZON COMMUNICATIONS INC
2801 Townsgate Rd Ste 300, Westlake Village (91361-3040)
PHONE..............................805 390-5417
Connie Murphree, *General Mgr*
Julie Fisher, *Data Proc Exec*
Randy Gromlich, *Marketing Mgr*
EMP: 120
SALES (corp-wide): 131.6B **Publicly Held**
WEB: www.verizon.com
SIC: 7389 4812 Telemarketing services; radio telephone communication
PA: Verizon Communications Inc.
1095 Ave Of The Americas
New York NY 10036
212 395-1000

(P-17587)
VERIZON COMMUNICATIONS INC
18442 Arminta St, Reseda (91335-2012)
PHONE..............................818 438-1104
Randy Green, *Principal*
EMP: 744
SALES (corp-wide): 131.6B **Publicly Held**
SIC: 7389 Personal service agents, brokers & bureaus
PA: Verizon Communications Inc.
1095 Ave Of The Americas
New York NY 10036
212 395-1000

(P-17588)
VERIZON COMMUNICATIONS INC
18850 Orange St, Bloomington (92316-2425)
PHONE..............................909 421-5053
David Edmund, *Branch Mgr*
Stephen Swiecki, *Engineer*
EMP: 776
SALES (corp-wide): 131.6B **Publicly Held**
WEB: www.verizon.com
SIC: 7389 Personal service agents, brokers & bureaus
PA: Verizon Communications Inc.
1095 Ave Of The Americas
New York NY 10036
212 395-1000

(P-17589)
VERIZON COMMUNICATIONS INC
700 S Flower St Ste 1700, Los Angeles (90017-4200)
PHONE..............................213 330-2556
Steve McNeely, *Branch Mgr*
Jaime Quiroga, *Info Tech Dir*
Ross Nosrat, *Sales Engr*
Lynne M Donahue, *Director*
Eric Cabrera, *Accounts Exec*
EMP: 776
SALES (corp-wide): 131.6B **Publicly Held**
WEB: www.verizon.com
SIC: 7389 Personal service agents, brokers & bureaus

PA: Verizon Communications Inc.
1095 Ave Of The Americas
New York NY 10036
212 395-1000

(P-17590)
VIAD CORP
5560 Katella Ave, Cypress (90630-5001)
PHONE..............................562 370-1500
Frank Carbone, *Branch Mgr*
Julie Walters, *Analyst*
Carrie Moreno, *Benefits Mgr*
Bill Kindig, *Opers Staff*
EMP: 85 **Publicly Held**
WEB: www.viad.com
SIC: 7389 Promoters of shows & exhibitions
PA: Viad Corp
1850 N Central Ave # 1900
Phoenix AZ 85004

(P-17591)
VIAN ENTERPRISES INC
1501 Industrial Dr, Auburn (95603-9018)
PHONE..............................530 885-1997
Fax: 530 885-1998
Christopher R Vian, *CEO*
Liz Popsicle, *President*
William Kirby, *CFO*
Carol Ann Vian, *Vice Pres*
Elizabeth Vian, *Financial Exec*
EMP: 50
SALES (est): 8.5MM **Privately Held**
WEB: www.vianenterprises.com
SIC: 7389 Personal service agents, brokers & bureaus

(P-17592)
VISA INTERNATIONAL SVC ASSN
3125 Clearview Way, San Mateo (94402-3711)
PHONE..............................650 432-3579
Rich Sheffield, *Manager*
Carl Pascarella, *Manager*
EMP: 500
SALES (corp-wide): 13.8B **Publicly Held**
WEB: www.visa.com
SIC: 7389 Financial services
HQ: Visa International Service Association
900 Metro Center Blvd
Foster City CA 94404
650 432-3200

(P-17593)
VISA INTERNATIONAL SVC ASSN (HQ)
900 Metro Center Blvd, Foster City (94404-2172)
P.O. Box 8999, San Francisco (94128-8999)
PHONE..............................650 432-3200
Charles W Scharf, *CEO*
William I Campbell, *Ch of Bd*
Byron H Pollitt, *CFO*
Terence Milholland, *Officer*
John Elkins, *Exec VP*
◆ **EMP:** 400 **EST:** 1974
SQ FT: 200,000
SALES (est): 315MM
SALES (corp-wide): 13.8B **Publicly Held**
WEB: www.visa.com
SIC: 7389 Financial services
PA: Visa Inc.
900 Metro Center Blvd
Foster City CA 94404
650 432-3200

(P-17594)
VISA USA INC (HQ)
900 Metro Center Blvd, Foster City (94404-2172)
P.O. Box 8999, San Francisco (94128-8999)
PHONE..............................650 432-3200
Fax: 650 432-3631
Charles W Scharf, *CEO*
Victor W Dahir, *CFO*
Byron H Pollitt, *CFO*
Kevin Burke, *Chief Mktg Ofcr*
Fred Bauer, *Exec VP*
EMP: 275

SALES (est): 392.3MM
SALES (corp-wide): 13.8B **Publicly Held**
WEB: www.moneychoices.com
SIC: 7389 Financial services
PA: Visa Inc.
900 Metro Center Blvd
Foster City CA 94404
650 432-3200

(P-17595)
VISIONFUND INTERNATIONAL
800 W Chestnut Ave, Monrovia (91016-3106)
PHONE..............................626 303-8811
Scott Brown, *CEO*
Brad Stave, *Marketing Staff*
EMP: 85
SALES (est): 1.7MM
SALES (corp-wide): 1B **Privately Held**
SIC: 7389 Financial services
HQ: World Vision International
800 W Chestnut Ave
Monrovia CA 91016
626 303-8811

(P-17596)
VIVA VINA INC
Also Called: Ampac
2702 Media Center Dr, Los Angeles (90065-1733)
PHONE..............................323 225-4984
Steve Lim, *CEO*
Angie Clapier, *Exec VP*
Jason Sells, *Exec VP*
Steven Worton, *Senior VP*
EMP: 100
SALES (est): 3.9MM **Privately Held**
SIC: 7389 8742 Financial services; business consultant

(P-17597)
VIVID SOLUTION
5959 W Century Blvd, Los Angeles (90045-6517)
PHONE..............................310 498-2559
Steve Huwang, *Principal*
EMP: 99
SALES (est): 2.4MM **Privately Held**
SIC: 7389 Business services

(P-17598)
VIVOPOOLS INC
825 S Primrose Ave Ste H, Monrovia (91016-3413)
PHONE..............................818 952-2121
William Johnson, *CEO*
EMP: 55
SQ FT: 1,300
SALES: 5MM **Privately Held**
SIC: 7389 Swimming pool & hot tub service & maintenance

(P-17599)
VIVOPOOLS LLC
Also Called: North Bay Pool and Spa
825 S Primrose Ave Ste H, Monrovia (91016-3413)
PHONE..............................888 702-8486
William Johnson, *Mng Member*
EMP: 63
SQ FT: 1,300
SALES (est): 7.2MM **Privately Held**
SIC: 7389 Swimming pool & hot tub service & maintenance

(P-17600)
VOLCOM LLC (DH)
Also Called: Stone Entertainment
1740 Monrovia Ave, Costa Mesa (92627-4407)
PHONE..............................949 646-2175
Fax: 949 646-5247
Jason Steris, *CEO*
Richard R Woolcott, *President*
Jina Park, *COO*
Douglas P Collier, *CFO*
David Unter, *CFO*
EMP: 200
SQ FT: 104,000

SALES (est): 90.7MM
SALES (corp-wide): 10.7MM **Privately Held**
WEB: www.volcment.com
SIC: 7389 2253 7822 5136 Design services; music & broadcasting services; bathing suits & swimwear, knit; motion picture & tape distribution; men's & boys' clothing; women's & children's clothing

(P-17601)
VORWALLER & BROOKS INC
72182 Corporate Way, Thousand Palms (92276-3324)
PHONE..............................760 262-6300
Eugene Sheldon Vorwaller, *President*
Jason Brooks, *Vice Pres*
Sandy Rodriguez, *Headmaster*
EMP: 55
SALES (est): 7.3MM **Privately Held**
SIC: 7389

(P-17602)
VXI GLOBAL SOLUTIONS LLC (PA)
220 W 1st St Fl 3, Los Angeles (90012-4105)
PHONE..............................213 739-4720
Fax: 213 637-1068
Eva Yi Hui Wang, *President*
Mark Hauge, *President*
David Zhou, *COO*
Stephen Choi, *CFO*
Steven Wang, *CFO*
EMP: 1200
SALES (est): 274.7MM **Privately Held**
WEB: www.vxi.com
SIC: 7389 Telemarketing services

(P-17603)
W P MEDIA COMPLEX
Also Called: Complex The
2323 Corinth Ave, Los Angeles (90064-1701)
PHONE..............................310 477-1938
Walter Ulloa, *Owner*
Jeff Ingber, *Agent*
EMP: 50
SQ FT: 19,000
SALES (est): 3.4MM **Privately Held**
SIC: 7389 Recording studio, noncommercial records

(P-17604)
W SCOTT BLLARD DSIGN ARCH INC
Also Called: Ballard Clothing Design
1800 Century Park E # 600, Los Angeles (90067-1501)
PHONE..............................323 386-4740
W Scott Ballard, *CEO*
EMP: 50
SALES (est): 1.3MM **Privately Held**
SIC: 7389 Design services

(P-17605)
WALKER BROTHERS MCHY MVG INC (PA)
3839 E Coronado St, Anaheim (92807-1606)
PHONE..............................714 630-5957
David E Walker, *President*
Curtis Walker, *Vice Pres*
Regina Ruiz, *Office Mgr*
EMP: 50
SQ FT: 67,500
SALES (est): 12.3MM **Privately Held**
WEB: www.walkerbro.com
SIC: 7389 1796 Relocation service; machine moving & rigging

(P-17606)
WALLIS FASHIONS INC
1100 8th Ave, Oakland (94606-3613)
PHONE..............................510 763-8018
Fax: 510 832-6882
EMP: 110
SALES (est): 5.2MM **Privately Held**
WEB: www.wallisfashions.com
SIC: 7389

PRODUCTS & SERVICES SECTION

7389 - Business Svcs, NEC County (P-17629)

(P-17607)
WARNER BROS ENTERTAINMENT INC
Also Called: Warner Bros. Television
300 Tlvsion Plz Bldg 137, Burbank (91505)
PHONE..................818 954-6901
Barry Meyers, *Branch Mgr*
Mary J Lawler,
Rachel D Young,
EMP: 5000
SALES (corp-wide): 28.1B **Publicly Held**
SIC: 7389 7812 Financial services; motion picture & video production
HQ: Warner Bros. Entertainment Inc.
4000 Warner Blvd
Burbank CA 91522
818 954-6000

(P-17608)
WARNER BROS RECORDS INC (DH)
3300 Warner Blvd, Burbank (91505-4694)
PHONE..................818 953-3378
Fax: 818 953-3276
Todd Moscowitz, *President*
Maria Gonzales, *Managing Prtnr*
Rob Cavallo, *Ch of Bd*
Livia Tortella, *President*
Marty Greenfield, *CFO*
EMP: 460
SQ FT: 85,000
SALES (est): 135.5MM
SALES (corp-wide): 2.9B **Privately Held**
WEB: www.warnerbrosrecords.com
SIC: 7389 Music recording producer; recording studio, noncommercial records
HQ: Warner Music Inc.
75 Rockefeller Plz Bsmt 1
New York NY 10019
212 275-2000

(P-17609)
WASHINGTON INVENTORY SERVICE
Also Called: W I S
13800 Heacock St D135c, Moreno Valley (92553-6262)
PHONE..................951 653-1472
Fax: 951 653-5902
Jeff Ferririak, *Manager*
EMP: 80
SALES (corp-wide): 671MM **Publicly Held**
WEB: www.wisusa.com
SIC: 7389 Inventory computing service
HQ: Washington Inventory Service Inc
9265 Sky Park Ct Ste 100
San Diego CA 92123
858 565-8111

(P-17610)
WASHINGTON INVENTORY SERVICE
Also Called: W I S
9080 Telstar Ave Ste 313, El Monte (91731-2840)
PHONE..................626 288-1200
Fax: 626 288-1424
Tony Toledo, *Manager*
EMP: 60
SALES (corp-wide): 671MM **Publicly Held**
WEB: www.wisusa.com
SIC: 7389 Inventory computing service
HQ: Washington Inventory Service Inc
9265 Sky Park Ct Ste 100
San Diego CA 92123
858 565-8111

(P-17611)
WASHINGTON INVENTORY SERVICE (DH)
9265 Sky Park Ct Ste 100, San Diego (92123-4375)
PHONE..................858 565-8111
Fax: 858 565-8406
Jim Rose, *CEO*
Howard L Madden, *President*
Trey Graham, *CFO*
Chris Forsberg, *Exec VP*
Tom Compogiannis, *Vice Pres*
EMP: 135
SQ FT: 30,000
SALES (est): 74.5MM
SALES (corp-wide): 671MM **Publicly Held**
WEB: www.wisusa.com
SIC: 7389 Inventory computing service
HQ: Western Inventory Service Ltd
3770 Nashua Dr Suite 5
Mississauga ON L4V 1
905 677-1947

(P-17612)
WASHINGTON INVENTORY SERVICE
Also Called: Wis
3800 Watt Ave Ste 101, Sacramento (95821-2622)
PHONE..................916 485-3427
Fax: 916 485-6754
Craig Rust, *President*
EMP: 120
SALES (corp-wide): 671MM **Publicly Held**
WEB: www.wisusa.com
SIC: 7389 Inventory stocking service
HQ: Washington Inventory Service Inc
9265 Sky Park Ct Ste 100
San Diego CA 92123
858 565-8111

(P-17613)
WASHINGTON INVENTORY SERVICE
Also Called: Wis
7150 El Cajon Blvd, San Diego (92115-1895)
PHONE..................619 461-8198
Fax: 619 465-0362
EMP: 70
SALES (corp-wide): 671MM **Publicly Held**
SIC: 7389
HQ: Washington Inventory Service Inc
9265 Sky Park Ct Ste 100
San Diego CA 92123
858 565-8111

(P-17614)
WASHINGTON INVENTORY SERVICE
43068 Christy St, Fremont (94538-3166)
PHONE..................510 498-5979
Fax: 510 252-1837
Trey Graham, *Manager*
EMP: 50
SALES (corp-wide): 671MM **Publicly Held**
WEB: www.wisusa.com
SIC: 7389 Inventory computing service
HQ: Washington Inventory Service Inc
9265 Sky Park Ct Ste 100
San Diego CA 92123
858 565-8111

(P-17615)
WASHINGTON INVENTORY SERVICE
19420 Business Center Dr, Northridge (91324-3541)
PHONE..................818 407-2680
Fax: 818 407-2672
Scott Lopez, *Manager*
Kathleen McCormick, *Manager*
Tana Trinchero, *Manager*
Myra Zuniga, *Manager*
EMP: 80
SALES (corp-wide): 671MM **Publicly Held**
WEB: www.wisusa.com
SIC: 7389 Inventory computing service
HQ: Washington Inventory Service Inc
9265 Sky Park Ct Ste 100
San Diego CA 92123
858 565-8111

(P-17616)
WAWONA PACKING CO LLC
12133 Avenue 408, Cutler (93615-2056)
PHONE..................559 528-4699
Brent Smittcamp,
Lisa Goeas,
Brandon Smittcamp,
Robert Smittcamp,
Georgia Griffin, *Manager*
EMP: 400
SQ FT: 85,000
SALES (est): 19.3MM **Privately Held**
SIC: 7389 Packaging & labeling services

(P-17617)
WEBLY SYSTEMS INC
2603 Camino Ramon Ste 200, San Ramon (94583-9137)
PHONE..................888 444-6400
Taj Reneau, *CEO*
Jim Calandra, *CFO*
Bob McConell, *CFO*
Bob McConnell, *CFO*
Susan Kelley, *Senior VP*
EMP: 50
SALES (est): 2.5MM **Privately Held**
SIC: 7389 Telephone services

(P-17618)
WELLS FARGO CAPITAL FIN INC (DH)
Also Called: Wfcf Technology E2040-030
2450 Colo Ave 3000w 3rd 3000 3rd, Santa Monica (90404)
PHONE..................310 453-7300
Fax: 213 443-6001
Henry K Jordan, *President*
Peter E Schwab, *Ch of Bd*
Steve Macko, *President*
Guy Fuchs, *COO*
Mike Sadilek, *Ch Credit Ofcr*
EMP: 170 **EST**: 1971
SALES (est): 3.5MM
SALES (corp-wide): 90B **Publicly Held**
WEB: www.wffoothill.com
SIC: 7389 Financial services
HQ: The Foothill Group Inc
2450 Colo Ave Ste 3000w
Santa Monica CA 90404
310 453-7300

(P-17619)
WEST COAST LEGAL SERVICE INC
1245 S Winchester Blvd # 208, San Jose (95128-3908)
PHONE..................408 938-6520
Donald Russi, *President*
Kathy Sivongxay, *Office Mgr*
Susan Wertz, *Admin Sec*
Mary McDowell, *Manager*
EMP: 50 **EST**: 1972
SQ FT: 4,000
SALES (est): 3.3MM **Privately Held**
WEB: www.westcoastlegal.com
SIC: 7389 Legal & tax services; process serving service

(P-17620)
WEST CORPORATION
170 N Church Ln, Los Angeles (90049-2044)
PHONE..................310 481-7878
Rick Patten, *Branch Mgr*
EMP: 198 **Publicly Held**
SIC: 7389 Telephone services; telemarketing services
PA: West Corporation
11808 Miracle Hills Dr
Omaha NE 68154

(P-17621)
WEST CORPORATION
3063 W Chapman Ave # 2353, Orange (92868-1738)
PHONE..................949 294-2801
Gavino D Bautista, *Principal*
EMP: 198 **Publicly Held**
SIC: 7389 Telephone services
PA: West Corporation
11808 Miracle Hills Dr
Omaha NE 68154

(P-17622)
WEST UNIFIED CMMNCTONS SVCS INC
1676 N California Blvd, Walnut Creek (94596-4144)
PHONE..................925 988-7112
Scott Etzler, *President*
Mia M Navarro, *District Mgr*
EMP: 70 **Publicly Held**
SIC: 7389 Teleconferencing services
HQ: West Unified Communications Services, Inc.
8420 W Bryn Mawr Ave # 1100
Chicago IL 60631
773 399-1600

(P-17623)
WESTERN PACIFIC PACKAGING INC
2715 Adelaida Rd, Paso Robles (93446-9765)
PHONE..................805 239-1188
Andrew R Martin, *President*
Andrew Sandy R Martin, *President*
EMP: 65
SQ FT: 27,600
SALES (est): 2.6MM **Privately Held**
WEB: www.e-wppi.com
SIC: 7389 Packaging & labeling services

(P-17624)
WESTERN REPACKING LLLP
Also Called: Custom Pak West
8371 Carbide Ct Ste 200, Sacramento (95828-5636)
P.O. Box 3088, Immokalee FL (34143-3088)
PHONE..................916 688-8443
Fax: 916 688-9304
Maxwell Press, *Partner*
Toby Purse, *Partner*
Paul Hoker, *Controller*
EMP: 57
SQ FT: 40,000
SALES (est): 3.1MM **Privately Held**
WEB: www.custompakwest.com
SIC: 7389 Packaging & labeling services

(P-17625)
WESTPOINT MARKETING INTL INC
5901 Avalon Blvd, Los Angeles (90003-1309)
PHONE..................323 233-0233
Kee Sung Hong, *President*
John Hong, *Vice Pres*
Maria Lora, *Asst to Pres*
EMP: 85
SALES (est): 5.5MM **Privately Held**
SIC: 7389 Sewing contractor

(P-17626)
WET (PA)
10847 Sherman Way, Sun Valley (91352-4829)
PHONE..................818 769-6200
Mark W Fuller, *CEO*
Shemi Hart, *CFO*
Tania Avedissian, *Senior VP*
Helen Park, *Senior VP*
Maria Villamil, *Senior VP*
EMP: 148
SQ FT: 112,000
SALES: 56.7MM **Privately Held**
WEB: www.wetdesign.com
SIC: 7389 8711 3443 Design services; engineering services; metal parts

(P-17627)
WILLITS PERPETUAL LLC
21600 Oxnard St, Woodland Hills (91367-4976)
PHONE..................818 668-6800
EMP: 75
SALES (est): 3.2MM **Privately Held**
SIC: 7389

(P-17628)
WILMAY INC
893 Oak Ave, Fillmore (93015-9621)
PHONE..................805 524-2603
Wilbur Mayhew, *President*
EMP: 80
SALES (est): 2.7MM **Privately Held**
SIC: 7389 Packaging & labeling services

(P-17629)
WINDSOR REDWOODS LP
790 Sonoma Ave, Santa Rosa (95404-4713)
PHONE..................707 526-1020
John Lowry, *Partner*
Chaney Delaire, *Director*
EMP: 52

7389 - Business Svcs, NEC County (P-17630) PRODUDUCTS & SERVICES SECTION

SALES (est): 1.7MM **Privately Held**
SIC: **7389** Personal service agents, brokers & bureaus

(P-17630)
WINNING PERFORMANCE PDTS INC
Also Called: Diplomat Packaging
13010 Bradley Ave, Sylmar (91342-3831)
PHONE..................818 367-1041
Fax: 818 362-6541
Todd J Harding, *President*
Kim Harding, *Officer*
Barbara Rogers, *Officer*
EMP: 50
SQ FT: 60,000
SALES (est): 5.7MM **Privately Held**
WEB: www.diplomatpackaging.com
SIC: **7389** 5013 Packaging & labeling services; motorcycle parts

(P-17631)
WIS INTERNATIONAL
9265 Sky Park Ct Ste 100, San Diego (92123-4375)
PHONE..................858 565-8111
Fax: 858 492-2751
Sean P Davoren, *CEO*
Lee Lafleur, *President*
Tom Compogiannis, *CFO*
Mark Hubbard, *Vice Pres*
Tom Jones, *Vice Pres*
EMP: 64 EST: 1998
SALES (est): 14.3MM **Privately Held**
SIC: **7389** 7374 Inventory stocking service; data processing & preparation

(P-17632)
WORLDLINK LLC (PA)
Also Called: Worldlink East
6100 Wilshire Blvd # 1400, Los Angeles (90048-5111)
PHONE..................323 866-5900
Fax: 323 965-7422
Toni E Knight, *Mng Member*
Steve Voleti, *CFO*
Monique McLurkin, *Manager*
Lindsay Davis, *Accounts Exec*
Alex Gusavac, *Accounts Exec*
EMP: 60
SQ FT: 20,000
SALES (est): 12.5MM **Privately Held**
WEB: www.worldlinkmedia.com
SIC: **7389** Personal service agents, brokers & bureaus

(P-17633)
WYNDHAM RESORT DEV CORP
Also Called: World Mark The Club
1177 N Palm Canyon Dr, Palm Springs (92262-4401)
PHONE..................760 864-8726
William Peare, *Principal*
EMP: 150
SALES (corp-wide): 5.5B **Publicly Held**
SIC: **7389** Time-share condominium exchange
HQ: Wyndham Resort Development Corporation
9805 Willows Rd Ne
Redmond WA 98052
425 498-2500

(P-17634)
WYNDHAM RESORT DEV CORP
Also Called: World Mark The Club
140 Via Verde, San Dimas (91773-5116)
PHONE..................909 484-8500
Jeff Peterson, *Manager*
EMP: 60
SALES (corp-wide): 5.5B **Publicly Held**
SIC: **7389** Time-share condominium exchange
HQ: Wyndham Resort Development Corporation
9805 Willows Rd Ne
Redmond WA 98052
425 498-2500

(P-17635)
YAPSTONE INC (PA)
Also Called: Rentpayment.com
2121 N Calif Blvd Ste 400, Walnut Creek (94596-7305)
PHONE..................866 289-5977
Fax: 415 861-9006

Tom Villante, *Ch of Bd*
Kelly Kay, *President*
Bryan Murphy, *President*
Mary Hentges, *CFO*
John Malnar, *CFO*
EMP: 125
SALES (est): 52.6MM **Privately Held**
WEB: www.rentpayment.com
SIC: **7389** Credit card service

(P-17636)
YC CABLE USA INC (HQ)
44061 Nobel Dr, Fremont (94538-3162)
PHONE..................510 824-2788
Gary Hsu, *President*
KAO Y Fang, *Shareholder*
Tony Wu, *Executive*
Grace Chang, *Engineer*
Alan Ngo, *Engineer*
▲ EMP: 70
SQ FT: 45,000
SALES (est): 21.2MM
SALES (corp-wide): 5.1MM **Privately Held**
SIC: **7389** 3643 Field audits, cable television; power line cable
PA: Y.C. Cable Co., Ltd.
5f, 12, Lane 270, Pei Shen Rd., Sec. 3,
New Taipei City 22205
226 629-656

(P-17637)
YPCOM LLC (HQ)
Also Called: AT&T Interactive
611 N Brand Blvd Fl 3, Glendale (91203-3286)
PHONE..................818 937-5500
David Krantz,
Williams Clenney, *CFO*
Sandra Barcena, *Treasurer*
John Vernagus, *Treasurer*
Deborah Slavin, *Senior VP*
EMP: 260
SALES (est): 83.8MM
SALES (corp-wide): 33.1B **Publicly Held**
WEB: www.yellowpages.com
SIC: **7389** Telephone directory distribution, contract or fee basis; telephone services
PA: Cerberus Capital Management, L.P.
875 3rd Ave
New York NY 10022
212 891-2100

(P-17638)
YUCCA VALLEY FIRE PROTECTION
57485 Aviation Dr A, Yucca Valley (92284-3009)
PHONE..................760 365-3335
Fax: 760 365-3337
Michael Snow, *Chief*
EMP: 50 EST: 2009
SALES (est): 1.5MM **Privately Held**
SIC: **7389** Fire protection service other than forestry or public

(P-17639)
ZS ASSOCIATES INC
400 S El Camino Real # 1500, San Mateo (94402-1733)
PHONE..................650 762-7800
Fax: 650 762-7801
Ty Curry, *Manager*
Craig Stinebaugh, *Admin Mgr*
Roxanne Ortega, *Admin Asst*
Timur Shalizi, *Technical Mgr*
Caitlin McDonnell, *Business Anlyst*
EMP: 80
SALES (corp-wide): 469.9MM **Privately Held**
WEB: www.zsassociates.com
SIC: **7389** 8742 Mapmaking services; marketing consulting services
PA: Zs Associates, Inc.
1800 Sherman Ave Ste 37
Evanston IL 60201
858 677-2200

7513 Truck Rental & Leasing, Without Drivers

(P-17640)
COUNTY OF INYO
224 N Edwards St, Independence (93526)
P.O. Box N (93526-0613)
PHONE..................760 878-0292
Fax: 760 878-2241
Ron Juliff, *Manager*
EMP: 73
SQ FT: 4,173 **Privately Held**
SIC: **7513** Truck leasing, without drivers
PA: County Of Inyo
168 N Edwards
Independence CA 93526
760 878-0292

(P-17641)
EL CAMINO RENTAL
5701 El Camino Real, Carlsbad (92008-7202)
PHONE..................760 438-7368
Mike Taylor, *Manager*
EMP: 50
SALES (est): 378.9K **Privately Held**
SIC: **7513** 7519 7359 5261 Truck rental & leasing, no drivers; trailer rental; tool rental; nurseries & garden centers; ready-mixed concrete

(P-17642)
PACCAR LEASING CORPORATION
Also Called: PacLease
2892 E Jensen Ave, Fresno (93706-5111)
PHONE..................559 268-4344
Fax: 559 233-7148
Warren Auwae, *Manager*
Dave Laird, *Vice Pres*
Dan Hertel, *Opers Mgr*
Randy Neuman, *Manager*
EMP: 160
SALES (corp-wide): 19.1B **Publicly Held**
WEB: www.glsayre.com
SIC: **7513** Truck leasing, without drivers
HQ: Paccar Leasing Corporation
777 106th Ave Ne
Bellevue WA 98004
425 468-7877

(P-17643)
PARTS
2445 Evergreen Ave, West Sacramento (95691-3011)
P.O. Box 716 (95691-0716)
PHONE..................916 371-3115
Tim Hollman, *Principal*
Eric Basset, *Manager*
EMP: 82
SALES (est): 1.1MM **Privately Held**
SIC: **7513** Truck rental & leasing, no drivers

(P-17644)
PENSKE AUTOMOTIVE GROUP INC
17 Woodland Ave, San Rafael (94901-5301)
PHONE..................415 492-1922
Jason Golpad, *Principal*
EMP: 50
SALES (corp-wide): 19.2B **Publicly Held**
SIC: **7513** Truck rental & leasing, no drivers
PA: Penske Automotive Group, Inc.
2555 S Telegraph Rd
Bloomfield Hills MI 48302
248 648-2500

(P-17645)
PENSKE AUTOMOTIVE GROUP INC
803 S 1st St, San Jose (95110-3123)
PHONE..................408 293-7688
Ngoc Tran, *Branch Mgr*
EMP: 50
SALES (corp-wide): 19.2B **Publicly Held**
SIC: **7513** Truck rental & leasing, no drivers

PA: Penske Automotive Group, Inc.
2555 S Telegraph Rd
Bloomfield Hills MI 48302
248 648-2500

(P-17646)
PENSKE TRUCK LEASING CO LP
2300 E Olympic Blvd, Los Angeles (90021-2537)
PHONE..................213 628-1255
Fax: 213 488-1590
Alfred McCandless, *Vice Pres*
Fred McMillan, *Office Mgr*
EMP: 50
SALES (corp-wide): 12.5B **Privately Held**
WEB: www.pensketruckleasing.com
SIC: **7513** Truck rental & leasing, no drivers
HQ: Penske Truck Leasing Co., L.P.
2675 Morgantown Rd
Reading PA 19607
610 775-6000

(P-17647)
PENSKE TRUCK LEASING CO LP
19646 Figueroa St, Long Beach (90745-1001)
PHONE..................310 327-3116
Chris Reynolds, *Manager*
EMP: 60
SQ FT: 9,680
SALES (corp-wide): 12.5B **Privately Held**
WEB: www.pensketruckleasing.com
SIC: **7513** Truck rental, without drivers
HQ: Penske Truck Leasing Co., L.P.
2675 Morgantown Rd
Reading PA 19607
610 775-6000

(P-17648)
PENSKE TRUCK LEASING CO LP
3080 E Malaga Ave, Fresno (93725-9212)
PHONE..................559 486-7000
Fax: 559 268-0503
Adam Hemmes, *Principal*
Humberto Rios, *Manager*
EMP: 50
SALES (corp-wide): 12.5B **Privately Held**
WEB: www.pensketruckleasing.com
SIC: **7513** Truck rental & leasing, no drivers
HQ: Penske Truck Leasing Co., L.P.
2675 Morgantown Rd
Reading PA 19607
610 775-6000

(P-17649)
PENSKE TRUCK RENTAL INC
11200 Peoria St, Sun Valley (91352-1632)
PHONE..................818 718-2536
Fax: 818 252-5831
Roger Penske, *President*
EMP: 50
SALES: 21MM **Privately Held**
SIC: **7513** Truck rental & leasing, no drivers

(P-17650)
RYDER INTEGRATED LOGISTICS INC
19133 Parthenia St, Northridge (91324-3626)
PHONE..................818 701-9332
Jerry Conrrad, *Branch Mgr*
EMP: 50
SQ FT: 12,100
SALES (corp-wide): 6.5B **Publicly Held**
SIC: **7513** Truck rental, without drivers
HQ: Ryder Integrated Logistics, Inc.
11690 Nw 105th St
Medley FL 33178
305 500-3726

(P-17651)
RYDER TRUCK RENTAL INC
2700 3rd St, San Francisco (94107-3101)
PHONE..................415 285-0756
Fax: 415 648-4920
Don Kelley, *Manager*
Kim Morrow, *Manager*
EMP: 110
SQ FT: 14,320

PRODUCTS & SERVICES SECTION

7514 - Passenger Car Rental County (P-17674)

SALES (corp-wide): 6.5B **Publicly Held**
SIC: 7513 Truck rental, without drivers
HQ: Ryder Truck Rental, Inc.
11690 Nw 105th St
Medley FL 33178
305 500-3726

(P-17652)
RYDER TRUCK RENTAL INC
13630 Firestone Blvd, Santa Fe Springs (90670-5600)
PHONE..................562 921-0033
Fax: 562 926-4838
Adrianna Ducante, *Manager*
Dee Walker, *Site Mgr*
EMP: 100
SQ FT: 15,680
SALES (corp-wide): 6.5B **Publicly Held**
SIC: 7513 Truck rental, without drivers
HQ: Ryder Truck Rental, Inc.
11690 Nw 105th St
Medley FL 33178
305 500-3726

(P-17653)
RYDER TRUCK RENTAL INC
9608 Santa Anita Ave, Rancho Cucamonga (91730-6121)
PHONE..................909 980-5084
Doreen Coddington, *Branch Mgr*
Warren Weaver, *Maintence Staff*
Donna Kehl, *Manager*
Pete Provanso, *Manager*
EMP: 75
SALES (corp-wide): 6.5B **Publicly Held**
SIC: 7513 4212 4213 4225 Truck leasing, without drivers; truck rental, without drivers; local trucking, without storage; trucking, except local; general warehousing; school buses; management services
HQ: Ryder Truck Rental, Inc.
11690 Nw 105th St
Medley FL 33178
305 500-3726

(P-17654)
TOMS TRUCK CENTER INC
Also Called: Isuzu Truck Services
1008 E 4th St, Santa Ana (92701-4751)
P.O. Box 88 (92702-0088)
PHONE..................714 835-1978
Fax: 714 835-3405
Kc Heidler, *Manager*
Tim Bui, *Info Tech Mgr*
James Bustamante, *Technician*
EMP: 150
SALES (corp-wide): 93.7MM **Privately Held**
SIC: 7513 5511 5012 Automobiles, new & used; automobiles & other motor vehicles
PA: Tom's Truck Center, Inc.
12221 Monarch St
Garden Grove CA 92841
714 835-5070

(P-17655)
U-HAUL CO OF CALIFORNIA (DH)
44511 S Grimmer Blvd, Fremont (94538-6309)
PHONE..................800 528-0463
Fax: 510 656-2501
Dave Adams, *President*
Danny Chan, *Manager*
Pat Fidazzo, *Manager*
Isabelle Wohl, *Accounts Mgr*
EMP: 150
SALES (est): 53.6MM
SALES (corp-wide): 3.2B **Publicly Held**
SIC: 7513 7519 4226 Truck rental & leasing, no drivers; trailer rental; special warehousing & storage
HQ: U-Haul International, Inc.
2727 N Central Ave
Phoenix AZ 85004
602 263-6011

(P-17656)
UNITED HAULING CORP
Also Called: National Cement
2620 Buena Vista St, Duarte (91010-3338)
PHONE..................626 358-9417
Fax: 626 359-3279
Alfred Delmonte, *Branch Mgr*
Sam Hild, *Executive*
EMP: 70

SALES (est): 1.8MM **Privately Held**
SIC: 7513 Truck rental & leasing, no drivers

(P-17657)
WILLIAM WARREN GROUP INC (PA)
201 Wilshire Blvd Ste 102, Santa Monica (90401-1220)
P.O. Box 2034 (90406-2034)
PHONE..................310 451-2130
Fax: 310 451-7821
William Warren Hobin, *President*
Kent Christensen, *COO*
Clark W Porter, *CFO*
Gerald Valle, *Vice Pres*
Sandra Villarreal, *Vice Pres*
EMP: 52
SQ FT: 1,500
SALES (est): 16MM **Privately Held**
SIC: 7513 Truck rental & leasing, no drivers

(P-17658)
WINNRESIDENTIAL LTD PARTNR
2350 W Shaw Ave Ste 148, Fresno (93711-3400)
PHONE..................559 435-3434
EMP: 763
SALES (corp-wide): 5.3MM **Privately Held**
SIC: 7513 Truck rental & leasing, no drivers
PA: Winnresidential Limited Partnership
6 Faneuil Hall Market Pl
Boston MA 02109
617 742-4500

7514 Passenger Car Rental

(P-17659)
ALAMO RENTAL (US) INC
Also Called: Alamo Rent A Car
9020 Aviation Blvd, Inglewood (90301-2907)
PHONE..................310 649-2242
Cesar Saurez, *Manager*
Joe Sowan, *Manager*
EMP: 100
SALES (corp-wide): 6.1B **Privately Held**
WEB: www.area-code-330.info
SIC: 7514 Rent-a-car service
HQ: Alamo Rental (Us) Inc.
600 Corporate Park Dr
Saint Louis MO 63105
314 512-5000

(P-17660)
ALAMO RENTAL (US) INC
Also Called: Alamo Rent A Car
4361 Birch St, Newport Beach (92660-1910)
PHONE..................949 852-0403
Fax: 949 852-0149
Gordon Schmierer, *Manager*
EMP: 50
SALES (corp-wide): 6.1B **Privately Held**
WEB: www.area-code-330.info
SIC: 7514 Passenger car rental
HQ: Alamo Rental (Us) Inc.
600 Corporate Park Dr
Saint Louis MO 63105
314 512-5000

(P-17661)
AVIS BUDGET GROUP INC
513 Eccles Ave Ste A, South San Francisco (94080-1906)
PHONE..................650 616-0150
Bob Salermo, *Branch Mgr*
Jim Curran, *Vice Pres*
Andrew Jaksich, *Technology*
Jeff Eisenbarth, *VP Opers*
Lao Vue, *Manager*
EMP: 100
SALES (corp-wide): 8.5B **Publicly Held**
WEB: www.cendant.com
SIC: 7514 Passenger car rental
PA: Avis Budget Group, Inc.
6 Sylvan Way Ste 1
Parsippany NJ 07054
973 496-4700

(P-17662)
AVIS RENT A CAR SYSTEM INC
3450 E Airport Dr Ste 500, Ontario (91761-7681)
PHONE..................909 974-2192
Fax: 909 390-1318
Richard Kuehner, *Manager*
Sal Vargas, *Branch Mgr*
Dan Diem, *Manager*
Michael Stephens, *Manager*
EMP: 80
SALES (corp-wide): 8.5B **Publicly Held**
WEB: www.avis.com
SIC: 7514 Rent-a-car service
HQ: Avis Rent A Car System, Inc.
6 Sylvan Way Ste 1
Parsippany NJ 07054
973 496-3500

(P-17663)
AVIS RENT A CAR SYSTEM INC
Also Called: Avis Budget Car Rentals
390 Doolittle Dr, San Leandro (94577-1015)
PHONE..................510 562-8828
Marie Peraida, *Manager*
Helen Akkawi, *Manager*
John Edwards, *Manager*
EMP: 200
SALES (corp-wide): 8.5B **Publicly Held**
WEB: www.avis.com
SIC: 7514 Rent-a-car service
HQ: Avis Rent A Car System, Inc.
6 Sylvan Way Ste 1
Parsippany NJ 07054
973 496-3500

(P-17664)
AVIS RENT A CAR SYSTEM INC
Also Called: Avis Rent A Car Systems
6520 Mcnair Cir, Sacramento (95837-1120)
PHONE..................916 922-5601
Fax: 916 920-5360
David McMillan, *Manager*
Christine McDaniel, *Executive*
Craig Lorentz, *Manager*
EMP: 200
SALES (corp-wide): 8.5B **Publicly Held**
WEB: www.avis.com
SIC: 7514 Rent-a-car service
HQ: Avis Rent A Car System, Inc.
6 Sylvan Way Ste 1
Parsippany NJ 07054
973 496-3500

(P-17665)
AVIS RENT A CAR SYSTEM INC
4209 W Vanowen Pl, Burbank (91505-1139)
PHONE..................818 566-3001
Fax: 818 566-3012
Don Shelton, *Branch Mgr*
EMP: 80
SALES (corp-wide): 8.5B **Publicly Held**
WEB: www.avis.com
SIC: 7514 Rent-a-car service
HQ: Avis Rent A Car System, Inc.
6 Sylvan Way Ste 1
Parsippany NJ 07054
973 496-3500

(P-17666)
BHRAC LLC
Also Called: Beverly
9777 Wilshire Blvd # 517, Beverly Hills (90212-1910)
PHONE..................310 862-1933
David Sajasi,
Hugo Vargas, *Controller*
Ani Bsiabanian,
Allan Jerry Siemons,
Blair Stover,
EMP: 65
SALES (est): 13MM **Privately Held**
SIC: 7514 7515 Passenger car rental; passenger car leasing

(P-17667)
BW-BUDGET-SDA LLC
Also Called: Budget Rent-A-Car
3125 Pacific Hwy, San Diego (92101-1128)
PHONE..................619 542-8686
Richard Eddy, *Vice Pres*
Scott Kreit,
EMP: 50
SQ FT: 5,000

SALES (est): 3.7MM **Privately Held**
SIC: 7514 Rent-a-car service

(P-17668)
C AND E INC
3103 W Vallejo Dr, Anaheim (92804-1772)
PHONE..................714 236-5790
Antonio Chase, *President*
EMP: 70 EST: 2015
SALES (est): 763.1K **Privately Held**
SIC: 7514 7336 8699 Rent-a-car service; film strip, slide & still film production; charitable organization

(P-17669)
DOLLAR THRIFTY AUTO GROUP INC
4420 Pacific Hwy, San Diego (92110-3107)
PHONE..................619 298-7635
EMP: 722
SALES (corp-wide): 13.3B **Publicly Held**
SIC: 7514 Rent-a-car service
HQ: Dollar Thrifty Automotive Group, Inc.
5330 E 31st St
Tulsa OK 74135
918 660-7700

(P-17670)
ENTERPRISE HOLDINGS INC
780 W Pinedale Ave, Fresno (93711-5744)
PHONE..................559 261-9221
Al Buroquez, *Branch Mgr*
EMP: 53
SALES (corp-wide): 6.1B **Privately Held**
SIC: 7514 Passenger car rental
HQ: Enterprise Holdings, Inc.
600 Corporate Park Dr
Saint Louis MO 63105
314 512-5000

(P-17671)
ENTERPRISE RENT-A-CAR
78385 Varner Rd Ste D, Palm Desert (92211-4118)
PHONE..................760 772-0281
Fax: 760 772-0598
Jennifer Apruzzesie, *Manager*
EMP: 51
SALES (corp-wide): 6.1B **Privately Held**
SIC: 7514 Passenger car rental
HQ: Enterprise Rent-A-Car Company Of Los Angeles, Llc
333 City Blvd W Ste 1000
Orange CA 92868
657 221-4400

(P-17672)
ENTERPRISE RENT-A-CAR
2942 Kettner Blvd, San Diego (92101-1111)
PHONE..................619 297-0311
Fax: 619 297-8701
Doreen Bonner, *City Mgr*
Yvonne Prieto, *Clerk*
EMP: 60
SALES (corp-wide): 6.1B **Privately Held**
WEB: www.area-code-330.info
SIC: 7514 Rent-a-car service
HQ: Enterprise Rent-A-Car Company Of Los Angeles, Llc
333 City Blvd W Ste 1000
Orange CA 92868
657 221-4400

(P-17673)
ENTERPRISE RENT-A-CAR
28112 Camino Capistrano, Laguna Niguel (92677-1136)
PHONE..................949 373-9350
Fax: 714 841-7165
Sebrina Rokozit, *Manager*
Aileen Jao, *Info Tech Mgr*
EMP: 100
SALES (corp-wide): 6.1B **Privately Held**
SIC: 7514 Passenger car rental
HQ: Enterprise Rent-A-Car Company Of Los Angeles, Llc
333 City Blvd W Ste 1000
Orange CA 92868
657 221-4400

(P-17674)
ENTERPRISE RENT-A-CAR COMPAN
6320 Mcnair Cir, Sacramento (95837-1118)
PHONE..................916 576-3164

7514 - Passenger Car Rental County (P-17675)

Alfred Husary, *Manager*
EMP: 65
SALES (corp-wide): 6.1B **Privately Held**
WEB: www.area-code-330.info
SIC: 7514 Rent-a-car service
HQ: Enterprise Rent-A-Car Company Of Sacramento, Llc
150 N Sunrise Ave
Roseville CA 95661
916 787-4500

(P-17675)
FORD MOTOR COMPANY
2060 Harbor Blvd, Costa Mesa (92627-2673)
P.O. Box 5055 (92628-5055)
PHONE..................................949 642-1291
Theodore Robin, *Owner*
Denise Glass, *Controller*
EMP: 100
SALES (corp-wide): 149.5B **Publicly Held**
WEB: www.ford.com
SIC: 7514 Rent-a-car service
PA: Ford Motor Company
1 American Rd
Dearborn MI 48126
313 322-3000

(P-17676)
FOX RENT A CAR INC (PA)
5500 W Century Blvd, Los Angeles (90045-5914)
PHONE..................................310 342-5155
Allen Rezapour, *President*
Sean Busking, *COO*
Richard Wolff, *CFO*
Mike Jaberi, *Treasurer*
Jerame Jackson, *Vice Pres*
EMP: 50
SQ FT: 73,500
SALES (est): 172.7MM **Privately Held**
SIC: 7514 Passenger car rental

(P-17677)
HERC RENTALS INC
5500 Commerce Blvd, Rohnert Park (94928-1607)
PHONE..................................707 586-4444
Mark Hobson, *Regional Mgr*
EMP: 58
SALES (corp-wide): 13.3B **Publicly Held**
SIC: 7514 Rent-a-car service
HQ: Herc Rentals Inc.
27500 Rverview Ctr Bldg 7
Bonita Springs FL 34134
239 301-1001

(P-17678)
HERC RENTALS INC
Also Called: Hertz
22422 S Alameda St, Carson (90810-1903)
PHONE..................................310 233-5000
Brian Dorte, *Manager*
Elvis Aguilar, *Branch Mgr*
EMP: 50
SQ FT: 19,494
SALES (corp-wide): 13.3B **Publicly Held**
WEB: www.hertzequip.com
SIC: 7514 Rent-a-car service
HQ: Herc Rentals Inc.
27500 Rverview Ctr Bldg 7
Bonita Springs FL 34134
239 301-1001

(P-17679)
HERC RENTALS INC
1025 16th St, Sacramento (95814-4012)
PHONE..................................916 448-2228
Jerry Weiss, *Branch Mgr*
EMP: 51
SALES (corp-wide): 13.3B **Publicly Held**
SIC: 7514 Rent-a-car service
HQ: Herc Rentals Inc.
27500 Rverview Ctr Bldg 7
Bonita Springs FL 34134
239 301-1001

(P-17680)
HERC RENTALS INC
Also Called: Hertz
6315 Snow Rd, Bakersfield (93308-9531)
PHONE..................................661 392-3661
Matt Hudnall, *Branch Mgr*
Viola Pitcher, *Executive*
EMP: 225

SALES (corp-wide): 13.3B **Publicly Held**
SIC: 7514 Rent-a-car service
HQ: Herc Rentals Inc.
27500 Rverview Ctr Bldg 7
Bonita Springs FL 34134
239 301-1001

(P-17681)
HERC RENTALS INC
5251 Industrial Way, Benicia (94510-1034)
PHONE..................................707 747-4444
Fax: 707 747-4460
John Moyer, *Manager*
Elvis Aguilar, *Branch Mgr*
Bryan Murphy, *Manager*
EMP: 50
SALES (corp-wide): 13.3B **Publicly Held**
SIC: 7514 Rent-a-car service
HQ: Herc Rentals Inc.
27500 Rverview Ctr Bldg 7
Bonita Springs FL 34134
239 301-1001

(P-17682)
HERC RENTALS INC
Also Called: Herc Rentals Prosolutions
7727 Oakport St, Oakland (94621-2026)
PHONE..................................510 633-2040
Ted Oshea, *Manager*
EMP: 225
SALES (corp-wide): 13.3B **Publicly Held**
SIC: 7514 Rent-a-car service
HQ: Herc Rentals Inc.
27500 Rverview Ctr Bldg 7
Bonita Springs FL 34134
239 301-1001

(P-17683)
HERTZ CLAIM MANAGEMENT CORP
2923 Bradley St Ste 190, Pasadena (91107-1502)
P.O. Box 7857, Burbank (91510-7857)
PHONE..................................626 296-4760
Fax: 626 296-4799
Jack McDonald, *Principal*
EMP: 84
SALES (corp-wide): 13.3B **Publicly Held**
SIC: 7514 Rent-a-car service
HQ: Hertz Claim Management Corporation
225 Brae Blvd
Park Ridge NJ 07656
201 307-2000

(P-17684)
HERTZ CORPORATION
2627 N Hollywood Way # 8, Burbank (91505-1062)
PHONE..................................818 997-0414
Fax: 818 842-6394
James D Botsch, *Manager*
EMP: 50
SALES (corp-wide): 13.3B **Publicly Held**
WEB: www.hertz.com
SIC: 7514 Rent-a-car service
HQ: The Hertz Corporation
8501 Williams Rd
Estero FL 33928
239 301-7000

(P-17685)
HERTZ CORPORATION
1000 Walsh Ave, Santa Clara (95050-2615)
PHONE..................................408 450-6025
Fax: 408 450-6029
Orland Savio, *Manager*
EMP: 100
SQ FT: 12,230
SALES (corp-wide): 13.3B **Publicly Held**
WEB: www.hertz.com
SIC: 7514 Rent-a-car service
HQ: The Hertz Corporation
8501 Williams Rd
Estero FL 33928
239 301-7000

(P-17686)
HERTZ CORPORATION
30 S Buchanan Cir, Pacheco (94553-5116)
PHONE..................................925 680-0316
Gerry Plescia, *President*
Todd Ransonet, *Sales Mgr*
EMP: 99
SALES (corp-wide): 13.3B **Publicly Held**
SIC: 7514 Rent-a-car service

HQ: The Hertz Corporation
8501 Williams Rd
Estero FL 33928
239 301-7000

(P-17687)
HERTZ CORPORATION
177 S Airport Blvd, South San Francisco (94080-6003)
PHONE..................................650 624-6391
Chuck Paterson, *Manager*
Chantal D Wulf, *Vice Pres*
Brian Wong, *CTO*
EMP: 82
SALES (corp-wide): 13.3B **Publicly Held**
WEB: www.hertz.com
SIC: 7514 Rent-a-car service
HQ: The Hertz Corporation
8501 Williams Rd
Estero FL 33928
239 301-7000

(P-17688)
HERTZ CORPORATION
3111 N Kenwood St, Burbank (91505-1041)
PHONE..................................818 569-6900
Rashida Barner, *Manager*
EMP: 99
SALES (corp-wide): 13.3B **Publicly Held**
SIC: 7514 Rent-a-car service
HQ: The Hertz Corporation
8501 Williams Rd
Estero FL 33928
239 301-7000

(P-17689)
MIDWAY RENT A CAR INC
Also Called: Midway Clinic Cars
1800 S Sepulveda Blvd, Los Angeles (90025-4314)
PHONE..................................310 445-4355
Fax: 310 826-7228
Steve Rosen, *Manager*
EMP: 55
SALES (corp-wide): 90MM **Privately Held**
WEB: www.midway-group.com
SIC: 7514 Rent-a-car service
PA: Midway Rent A Car, Inc.
4751 Wilshire Blvd # 120
Los Angeles CA 90010
323 692-4000

(P-17690)
NATIONAL RENTAL (US) INC
Also Called: National Rent A Car
7600 Earhart Rd Ste 4, Oakland (94621-4558)
PHONE..................................510 877-4507
Fax: 510 639-2416
Babara Chappelle, *Principal*
Gayle Frazier, *Administration*
EMP: 65
SALES (corp-wide): 6.1B **Privately Held**
WEB: www.specialtyrentals.com
SIC: 7514 Rent-a-car service
HQ: National Rental (Us) Inc.
6929 N Lakewood Ave # 100
Tulsa OK 74117
918 401-6000

(P-17691)
NATIONAL RENTAL (US) INC
Also Called: National Rent A Car
2752 De La Cruz Blvd, Santa Clara (95050-2624)
PHONE..................................408 492-0501
Fax: 408 980-5251
Thomas Currier, *Principal*
EMP: 100
SALES (corp-wide): 6.1B **Privately Held**
WEB: www.specialtyrentals.com
SIC: 7514 Rent-a-car service
HQ: National Rental (Us) Inc.
6929 N Lakewood Ave # 100
Tulsa OK 74117
918 401-6000

(P-17692)
RENZENBERGER INC
433 S Sierra Way, San Bernardino (92408-1424)
PHONE..................................909 888-8858
Fax: 909 885-0662
Phil Filmco, *Manager*

EMP: 200
SALES (corp-wide): 449.7MM **Privately Held**
WEB: www.renzenberger.com
SIC: 7514 4119 Hearse or limousine rental, without drivers; local passenger transportation
HQ: Renzenberger, Inc.
14325 W 95th St
Lenexa KS 66215
913 631-0450

(P-17693)
STAR LAX LLC
Also Called: Budget Rent-A-Car
150 S Doheny Dr, Beverly Hills (90211-2545)
PHONE..................................310 642-4500
Jeffery Mirkin,
James Reid, *COO*
David Muinos, *CFO*
Linda King, *Principal*
EMP: 125
SALES (est): 10MM **Privately Held**
SIC: 7514 Rent-a-car service

(P-17694)
T C R LIMITED PARTNERSHIP
Also Called: Thrifty Car Rental
5440 W Century Blvd, Los Angeles (90045-5912)
PHONE..................................310 645-1881
Brett Thomas, *Partner*
Janine Burlin, *Project Mgr*
Venito Corona, *Business Mgr*
Randall Lowe, *Controller*
EMP: 120
SQ FT: 5,000
SALES (est): 3.6MM **Privately Held**
SIC: 7514 Rent-a-car service

(P-17695)
THRIFTY CAR RENTAL
780 Mcdonnell Rd Ste 1, San Francisco (94128-3152)
PHONE..................................415 788-8111
Fax: 415 788-5810
James S Tennant, *President*
John Tennant, *Treasurer*
EMP: 140
SQ FT: 6,000
SALES (est): 5.5MM **Privately Held**
SIC: 7514 7513 7519 Rent-a-car service; truck rental, without drivers; recreational vehicle rental

(P-17696)
THRIFTY RENT-A-CAR SYSTEM INC
Also Called: Thrifty Car Rental
3500 Irvine Ave, Newport Beach (92660-3106)
PHONE..................................949 757-0659
Fax: 949 442-0704
Marion Landazuri, *Manager*
EMP: 50
SALES (corp-wide): 13.3B **Publicly Held**
WEB: www.casinomagic.com
SIC: 7514 Rent-a-car service
HQ: Thrifty Rent-A-Car System, Inc.
14501 Hertz Quail Spgs
Oklahoma City OK 73134
918 665-3930

(P-17697)
THRIFTY RENT-A-CAR SYSTEM INC
Also Called: Thrifty Car Rental
780 Mcdonald Rd, San Carlos (94070)
PHONE..................................650 737-8084
Victor Abalos, *Manager*
EMP: 50
SALES (corp-wide): 13.3B **Publicly Held**
WEB: www.casinomagic.com
SIC: 7514 Rent-a-car service
HQ: Thrifty Rent-A-Car System, Inc.
14501 Hertz Quail Spgs
Oklahoma City OK 73134
918 665-3930

7515 Passenger Car Leasing

(P-17698)
CITY LEASING & RENTALS
2111 Morena Blvd, San Diego (92110-3440)
PHONE..............619 276-6171
John Nieman, *President*
Dick Paullin, *Vice Pres*
Steve Brownell, *Finance Mgr*
Jack Atkins, *Pub Rel Dir*
Josh Irvine, *Pub Rel Dir*
EMP: 200
SALES (est): 4.3MM **Privately Held**
SIC: 7515 7514 5521 Passenger car leasing; passenger car rental; used car dealers

(P-17699)
EL CAJON MOTORS (PA)
Also Called: El Cajon Ford
1595 E Main St, El Cajon (92021-5902)
P.O. Box 1236 (92022-1236)
PHONE..............619 579-8888
Fax: 619 579-3725
Paul F Leader, *President*
Andrew Breech, *Vice Pres*
John Blake, *Admin Sec*
Rob Slater, *Sales Mgr*
Ian Jaffe, *Sales Staff*
▲ EMP: 100
SQ FT: 311,226
SALES (est): 12MM **Privately Held**
WEB: www.elcajonford.com
SIC: 7515 5511 Passenger car leasing; automobiles, new & used; pickups, new & used; vans, new & used

(P-17700)
ENTERPRISE RENT-A-CAR (DH)
333 City Blvd W Ste 1000, Orange (92868-5917)
PHONE..............657 221-4400
Jack C Taylor, *Ch of Bd*
Pamela Nicholson, *COO*
William W Snyder, *CFO*
Andrew C Taylor, *Chairman*
Rose Langhorst, *Treasurer*
EMP: 90
SQ FT: 30,000
SALES (est): 127.6MM
SALES (corp-wide): 6.1B **Privately Held**
SIC: 7515 7513 5511 7514 Passenger car leasing; truck rental & leasing, no drivers; trucks, tractors & trailers: new & used; passenger car rental
HQ: Enterprise Holdings, Inc.
600 Corporate Park Dr
Saint Louis MO 63105
314 512-5000

(P-17701)
ENTERPRISE RENT-A-CAR COMPAN (DH)
150 N Sunrise Ave, Roseville (95661-2905)
PHONE..............916 787-4500
Susan M Irwin, *Vice Pres*
Theo Curtis, *Controller*
Allen Moody, *Sales Staff*
Gina Charette, *Manager*
Lisa Holmes, *Manager*
▲ EMP: 50
SALES (est): 57.7MM
SALES (corp-wide): 6.1B **Privately Held**
SIC: 7515 7514 5511 Passenger car leasing; rent-a-car service; automobiles, new & used
HQ: Enterprise Holdings, Inc.
600 Corporate Park Dr
Saint Louis MO 63105
314 512-5000

(P-17702)
MARTY FRANICH LEASING CO
Also Called: Chrysler Plymouth Dodge Jeep
555 Auto Center Dr, Watsonville (95076-3745)
PHONE..............831 724-2463
Fax: 831 724-6897
Steven Franich, *President*
Robert H Culbertson, *Vice Pres*
Tony Ziegler, *Sales Staff*
Chris Cerrato, *Manager*
Tonia Martinez, *Manager*
EMP: 50
SQ FT: 15,500
SALES (est): 4.3MM **Privately Held**
SIC: 7515 7513 Passenger car leasing; truck leasing, without drivers

(P-17703)
MIDWAY RENT A CAR INC
Also Called: Midway Car Rental
4201 Lankershim Blvd, North Hollywood (91602-2856)
PHONE..............818 985-9770
Fax: 818 985-9437
Tommy Henderson, *Area Mgr*
Dave Ross, *Area Mgr*
Cynthia Tejeda, *Office Mgr*
Beth Ayjian, *Manager*
EMP: 151
SALES (corp-wide): 90MM **Privately Held**
SIC: 7515 7514 Passenger car leasing; passenger car rental
PA: Midway Rent A Car, Inc.
4751 Wilshire Blvd # 120
Los Angeles CA 90010
323 692-4000

(P-17704)
MISSION TRUCK SALES
Also Called: Mission Valley Truck Center
780 E Brokaw Rd, San Jose (95112-1007)
PHONE..............408 436-2920
Ernie Speno, *President*
Jeff Speno, *Vice Pres*
EMP: 75
SALES (est): 2.2MM **Privately Held**
WEB: www.missionvalleyford.com
SIC: 7515 5511 5083 Passenger car leasing; automobiles, new & used; farm & garden machinery

(P-17705)
REYNOLDS BUICK/GMC TRUCKS
Also Called: Reynolds Leasing Co
345 N Citrus St, West Covina (91791-1675)
P.O. Box 400 (91793-0400)
PHONE..............626 966-4461
Fax: 626 332-8118
Iric G Reyolds, *President*
Donald M Reynolds, *President*
Lisa Lidle, *Sales Mgr*
Chuck Rhodes, *Sales Mgr*
EMP: 70
SQ FT: 30,000
SALES (est): 11MM **Privately Held**
WEB: www.reynolds1915.com
SIC: 7515 Passenger car leasing

7519 Utility Trailers & Recreational Vehicle Rental

(P-17706)
EL MONTE RENTS INC (PA)
Also Called: El Monte Rv
12818 Firestone Blvd, Santa Fe Springs (90670-5404)
PHONE..............972 562-1900
Fax: 562 404-2021
Ken Schork, *President*
Sharon Schork, *Corp Secy*
Richard Schork, *Senior VP*
Tucker Schork, *Senior VP*
Todd Schork, *Vice Pres*
EMP: 80
SALES (est): 33.3MM **Privately Held**
WEB: www.elmontev.com
SIC: 7519 5561 Motor home rental; motor homes

(P-17707)
QUIXOTE STUDIOS LLC
11473 Penrose St, Sun Valley (91352-3922)
PHONE..............818 252-7722
Mikel Elliott, *Mng Member*
EMP: 50
SALES (corp-wide): 22.4MM **Privately Held**
SIC: 7519 5561 Trailer rental; travel trailers: automobile, new & used

PA: Quixote Studios Llc
1011 N Fuller Ave
West Hollywood CA 90046
323 851-5030

7521 Automobile Parking Lots & Garages

(P-17708)
ABM PARKING SERVICES (PA)
3585 Corporate Ct, San Diego (92123-2415)
PHONE..............619 235-4500
Paul Chacon, *General Mgr*
EMP: 67
SQ FT: 3,300
SALES (est): 9.2MM **Privately Held**
SIC: 7521 Parking lots

(P-17709)
ACE PARKING MANAGEMENT INC
71 Fortune Dr Ste 916, Irvine (92618-2927)
PHONE..............949 727-1470
Fax: 949 727-1477
John Duanno, *Manager*
Kyle Schulze, *Site Mgr*
EMP: 130
SALES (corp-wide): 273.2MM **Privately Held**
WEB: www.aceparking.com
SIC: 7521 Automobile parking
PA: Ace Parking Management, Inc.
645 Ash St
San Diego CA 92101
619 233-6624

(P-17710)
ACE PARKING MANAGEMENT INC (PA)
645 Ash St, San Diego (92101-3299)
PHONE..............619 233-6624
Scott A Jones, *Chairman*
Steve Burton, *President*
John Baumgardner, *CEO*
Charles Blottin, *CFO*
Matt Griesheimer, *Exec VP*
EMP: 50
SQ FT: 10,000
SALES (est): 273.2MM **Privately Held**
WEB: www.aceparking.com
SIC: 7521 Parking lots; parking structure

(P-17711)
AUTOMATE PARKING INC
8405 Pershing Dr Ste 100, Playa Del Rey (90293-7870)
PHONE..............310 674-3396
Leo Mejia, *President*
EMP: 60
SQ FT: 1,000
SALES (est): 3.8MM **Privately Held**
SIC: 7521 Parking lots

(P-17712)
CENTRAL PARKING CORPORATION
1624 Franklin St Ste 722, Oakland (94612-2823)
PHONE..............510 832-7227
EMP: 100
SALES (corp-wide): 1.5B **Publicly Held**
SIC: 7521
HQ: Central Parking Corporation
507 Mainstream Dr
Nashville TN 37228
615 297-4255

(P-17713)
CENTRAL PARKING SYSTEM INC
3420 Bristol St Ste 225, Costa Mesa (92626-7136)
PHONE..............714 751-2855
Fax: 714 751-6350
Peter Cho, *Manager*
Will Folz, *Manager*
EMP: 70
SALES (corp-wide): 1.6B **Publicly Held**
SIC: 7521 Automobile parking

HQ: Central Parking System, Inc.
507 Mainstream Dr
Nashville TN 37228
615 297-4255

(P-17714)
CENTRAL PARKING SYSTEM INC
716 10th St Ste 101, Sacramento (95814-1807)
PHONE..............916 441-1074
John Webster, *Branch Mgr*
EMP: 60
SALES (corp-wide): 1.6B **Publicly Held**
SIC: 7521 Parking lots
HQ: Central Parking System Inc
1225 I St Nw Ste C100
Washington DC 20005
202 496-9650

(P-17715)
CENTURY PLAZA GARAGE
Also Called: American Building Maintenance
2049 Century Park E Ste D, Los Angeles (90067-3104)
PHONE..............310 226-7495
Fax: 310 556-0397
Jose Ramos, *General Mgr*
Johnny Bermeo, *Opers Mgr*
JP Morgan Investment Mgmnt.
EMP: 135
SQ FT: 2,000
SALES (est): 3MM **Privately Held**
SIC: 7521 Outdoor parking services

(P-17716)
CITY OF BEVERLY HILLS
342 Foothill Rd, Beverly Hills (90210-3608)
PHONE..............310 285-2552
Dan Pack, *Branch Mgr*
EMP: 500 **Privately Held**
WEB: www.bhcpr.org
SIC: 7521 9111 Automobile parking; mayors' offices
PA: City Of Beverly Hills
455 N Rexford Dr
Beverly Hills CA 90210
310 285-1000

(P-17717)
CLASSIC PARKING INC
34 S Autumn St, San Jose (95110-2513)
PHONE..............408 278-1444
Richard Flores, *CFO*
EMP: 414
SALES (corp-wide): 33MM **Privately Held**
SIC: 7521 Parking garage
PA: Classic Parking, Inc.
3208 Royal St
Los Angeles CA 90007
213 742-1238

(P-17718)
IMPERIAL PARKING (US) LLC
Also Called: City Park
325 5th St, San Francisco (94107-1040)
PHONE..............415 495-3909
Tim Leonoudakis, *Branch Mgr*
Robert Bindel, *Division Mgr*
David Griest, *Info Tech Dir*
Irene Camarena, *Persnl Dir*
Spencer Sechler, *Sales Dir*
EMP: 650
SALES (corp-wide): 448.7MM **Privately Held**
SIC: 7521 Parking lots; parking garage
PA: Imperial Parking (U.S.), Llc
900 Haddon Ave Ste 333
Collingswood NJ 08108
856 854-7111

(P-17719)
IMPERIAL PARKING (US) LLC
195 N Access Rd, South San Francisco (94080-6905)
PHONE..............650 871-5423
David Castagnola, *Branch Mgr*
EMP: 63
SALES (corp-wide): 448.7MM **Privately Held**
SIC: 7521 4724 4111 Automobile parking; travel agencies; airport transportation

7521 - Automobile Parking Lots & Garages County (P-17720)

PA: Imperial Parking (U.S.), Llc
900 Haddon Ave Ste 333
Collingswood NJ 08108
856 854-7111

(P-17720)
IMPERIAL PARKING (US) LLC
Also Called: Sfo Shuttle Bus Company
790 Mcdonnell Rd, San Francisco (94128-3114)
PHONE.................650 877-0430
Dave Gottlieb, *Branch Mgr*
Robert Rooper, *Manager*
EMP: 90
SALES (corp-wide): 448.7MM **Privately Held**
SIC: 7521 Parking lots; parking garage
PA: Imperial Parking (U.S.), Llc
900 Haddon Ave Ste 333
Collingswood NJ 08108
856 854-7111

(P-17721)
IMPERIAL PARKING (US) LLC
Also Called: Sfo Shuttle Bus Company
360 Oak Rd Ste 1, Stanford (94305-4500)
PHONE.................650 724-4309
Dave Gottlieb, *Branch Mgr*
Greg Isenberg, *Office Mgr*
EMP: 50
SALES (corp-wide): 448.7MM **Privately Held**
SIC: 7521 Parking lots; parking garage
PA: Imperial Parking (U.S.), Llc
900 Haddon Ave Ste 333
Collingswood NJ 08108
856 854-7111

(P-17722)
IMPERIAL PARKING (US) LLC
Also Called: Sfo Shuttle Bus Company
7801 Earhart Rd, Oakland (94621-4529)
PHONE.................510 382-2140
Fax: 510 382-2151
Dave Gottlieb, *Manager*
Christina Azila, *Executive*
EMP: 50
SALES (corp-wide): 448.7MM **Privately Held**
SIC: 7521 Parking lots; parking garage
PA: Imperial Parking (U.S.), Llc
900 Haddon Ave Ste 333
Collingswood NJ 08108
856 854-7111

(P-17723)
IMPERIAL PARKING INDUSTRIES (PA)
Also Called: I P I
6404 Wilshire Blvd # 1250, Los Angeles (90048-5501)
PHONE.................323 651-5588
Fax: 323 651-5546
Ali Yeganeh, *President*
James Byrd, *Vice Pres*
Paul Gnasso, *Vice Pres*
Jose Mazariego, *Manager*
EMP: 63
SALES (est): 8.3MM **Privately Held**
SIC: 7521 Automobile parking

(P-17724)
JIM & DOUG CARTERS AUTOMOTIVE
Also Called: Carters Details Plus
2612 N Hollywood Way, Burbank (91505-1020)
PHONE.................818 842-5702
Fax: 818 972-1045
Douglas A Carter, *President*
Joan Carter, *Treasurer*
Derek Sweet, *Vice Pres*
EMP: 50
SQ FT: 10,000
SALES (est): 3.4MM **Privately Held**
SIC: 7521 Automobile parking

(P-17725)
L AND R AUTO PARKS INC
Also Called: Joe's Auto Parks
990 W 8th St Ste 600, Los Angeles (90017-2831)
PHONE.................213 629-3263
Fax: 213 489-1078
Stuart Rubin, *CEO*
Gabriel Rubin, *Corp Secy*
Martha Barranco, *Manager*
Gil Levi, *Supervisor*
EMP: 140
SQ FT: 5,000
SALES (est): 12.1MM **Privately Held**
WEB: www.joesautoparks.com
SIC: 7521 7542 Parking lots; carwashes

(P-17726)
L R INVESTMENT COMPANY
515 S Flower St Ste 3200, Los Angeles (90071-2215)
PHONE.................213 627-8211
Scott Hutchison, *Partner*
Kenneth Oldam, *Partner*
Gary Gower, *CFO*
David Bonaparte, *General Mgr*
Scott Carlson, *Sales Mgr*
EMP: 99
SALES (est): 6.9MM **Privately Held**
SIC: 7521 Automobile parking

(P-17727)
LAZ PARKING LTD
9333 Genesee Ave Ste 220, San Diego (92121-2113)
PHONE.................858 587-8888
Alan Lazowski, *CEO*
Raymond Skoglund, *Treasurer*
Bert Kaplowitz, *Vice Pres*
EMP: 6000 EST: 1981
SQ FT: 30,000
SALES (est): 32.5MM **Privately Held**
SIC: 7521 Parking lots
PA: Laz Karp Associates, Llc
15 Lewis St Fl 5
Hartford CT 06103

(P-17728)
LINDBERGH PARKING INC
3705 N Harbor Dr, San Diego (92101-1021)
PHONE.................619 291-1508
Fax: 619 291-0083
Maurice Gray, *President*
Scott Jones, *Corp Secy*
EMP: 150
SQ FT: 800
SALES (est): 3.2MM **Privately Held**
SIC: 7521 Parking lots

(P-17729)
LRW INVESTMENTS LLC
Also Called: Wally Park
9700 Bellanca Ave, Los Angeles (90045-5510)
PHONE.................310 337-1944
Gilad Lumer, *Branch Mgr*
EMP: 60
SALES (corp-wide): 7.3MM **Privately Held**
WEB: www.wallypark.com
SIC: 7521 Automobile parking
PA: Lrw Investments Llc
990 W 8th St Ste 600
Los Angeles CA 90017
213 629-3263

(P-17730)
MODERN PARKING INC
14110 Palawan Way, Marina Del Rey (90292-6231)
PHONE.................310 821-1081
Arisur Rahnan, *Principal*
EMP: 80
SALES (corp-wide): 55.4MM **Privately Held**
SIC: 7521 Automobile parking
PA: Modern Parking, Inc.
1200 Wilshire Blvd # 300
Los Angeles CA 90017
213 482-8400

(P-17731)
PACIFIC PARK MANAGEMENT (PA)
465 California St Ste 473, San Francisco (94104-1842)
PHONE.................415 434-4400
Fax: 415 434-4455
Robert Stang, *President*
Sam Tadesse, *CEO*
Behailu Mekbib, *COO*
Rob Noiles, *Vice Pres*
▲ EMP: 80

SQ FT: 1,000
SALES (est): 9.8MM **Privately Held**
SIC: 7521 Parking lots

(P-17732)
PARKING CO AMER UNIVERSAL INC
Also Called: Pcamp
11101 Lakewood Blvd, Downey (90241-3810)
PHONE.................562 862-2118
Alex Martin Chaves Jr, *President*
Eric Chaves, *CFO*
Bruce Somerfeld, *Area Mgr*
Shirley Sheum, *Marketing Staff*
EMP: 100 EST: 1990
SQ FT: 4,000
SALES (est): 5.4MM **Privately Held**
SIC: 7521 Parking lots

(P-17733)
PARKING CONCEPTS INC
1036 Broxton Ave, Los Angeles (90024-2824)
PHONE.................310 208-1611
Jorge Lopez, *Manager*
EMP: 50
SALES (corp-wide): 53.2MM **Privately Held**
WEB: www.parkingconcepts.net
SIC: 7521 Parking garage
PA: Parking Concepts, Inc.
12 Mauchly Ste I
Irvine CA 92618
949 753-7525

(P-17734)
PARKING CONCEPTS INC
1801 Georgia St, Los Angeles (90015-3477)
PHONE.................213 746-5764
Fax: 213 746-3654
Bob Hindle, *Manager*
Paul Gnasso, *Vice Pres*
Kermit Kingsbury, *Vice Pres*
Jerry Wasson, *Human Res Dir*
EMP: 50
SALES (corp-wide): 53.2MM **Privately Held**
WEB: www.parkingconcepts.net
SIC: 7521 8748 Automobile parking; traffic consultant
PA: Parking Concepts, Inc.
12 Mauchly Ste I
Irvine CA 92618
949 753-7525

(P-17735)
PARKING CONCEPTS INC
14110 Palawan Way, Venice (90292-6231)
PHONE.................310 821-1081
Fax: 310 821-9855
Frank Vargas, *General Mgr*
Frank Varges, *Manager*
EMP: 180
SALES (corp-wide): 53.2MM **Privately Held**
WEB: www.parkingconcepts.net
SIC: 7521 8741 Parking lots; management services
PA: Parking Concepts, Inc.
12 Mauchly Ste I
Irvine CA 92618
949 753-7525

(P-17736)
PARKING CONCEPTS INC
800 Wilshire Blvd, Los Angeles (90017-2604)
PHONE.................213 623-2661
Fax: 213 614-3300
Juan Cortes, *Branch Mgr*
EMP: 50
SALES (corp-wide): 53.2MM **Privately Held**
WEB: www.parkingconcepts.net
SIC: 7521 Parking garage
PA: Parking Concepts, Inc.
12 Mauchly Ste I
Irvine CA 92618
949 753-7525

(P-17737)
PARKING CONCEPTS INC
12001 Vista Del Mar, Playa Del Rey (90293-8518)
PHONE.................310 322-5008
Zahid Hossian, *Branch Mgr*
EMP: 57
SALES (corp-wide): 53.2MM **Privately Held**
WEB: www.parkingconcepts.net
SIC: 7521 Parking garage
PA: Parking Concepts, Inc.
12 Mauchly Ste I
Irvine CA 92618
949 753-7525

(P-17738)
PREFERRED VALET PARKING LLC
2568 Violet St, San Diego (92105-4567)
PHONE.................619 233-7275
Nick Bernal,
EMP: 50
SALES (est): 2.2MM **Privately Held**
SIC: 7521 7299 Parking lots; valet parking

(P-17739)
PREMIERE VALET SERVICE INC
Also Called: Celebrity Valet
6601 Santa Monica Blvd, Los Angeles (90038-1311)
PHONE.................310 652-4647
Fax: 323 957-4082
David Smith, *President*
EMP: 100
SALES: 1MM **Privately Held**
WEB: www.premierevaletparking.com
SIC: 7521 Automobile parking

(P-17740)
PRG PARKING CENTURY LLC
Also Called: Parking Spot, The
5701 W Century Blvd, Los Angeles (90045-5629)
PHONE.................310 642-0947
Geoffrey Okamoto, *General Mgr*
Chris Simcutter, *General Mgr*
Prg Parking Holding LLC,
Marco Lam, *Manager*
EMP: 100
SQ FT: 620,000
SALES (est): 3MM **Privately Held**
SIC: 7521 Parking garage

(P-17741)
RESORT PARKING SERVICES INC
68364 Commercial Rd A, Cathedral City (92234-7603)
PHONE.................760 328-4041
Fax: 760 770-0091
Mario Gardner, *President*
EMP: 120
SQ FT: 1,100
SALES (est): 4.8MM **Privately Held**
SIC: 7521 7299 Outdoor parking services; indoor parking services; personal item care & storage services

(P-17742)
SAFETYPARK CORPORATION
100 Venice Way, Venice (90291-3674)
PHONE.................310 399-1499
EMP: 137
SALES (corp-wide): 4.7MM **Privately Held**
SIC: 7521 Parking lots
PA: Safetypark Corporation
13420 Beach Ave
Marina Del Rey CA 90292
310 899-0490

(P-17743)
SERVICE PARKING CORPORATION
Also Called: Service Cleaning and Maint
3800 Barham Blvd Ste P1, Los Angeles (90068-3097)
PHONE.................323 851-2416
Fax: 323 874-5658
Aziz Azimi, *CEO*
Aziz Amizi, *CEO*
Philip Chirino, *Vice Pres*
EMP: 65
SQ FT: 1,500

PRODUCTS & SERVICES SECTION
7532 - Top, Body & Upholstery Repair & Paint Shops County (P-17767)

SALES (est): 1.7MM **Privately Held**
SIC: 7521 Parking garage

(P-17744)
TPS PARKING MANAGEMENT LLC
Also Called: Parking Spot, The
9101 S Sepulveda Blvd, Los Angeles (90045-4803)
PHONE..................310 846-4747
Fax: 310 846-4750
Chris Fincutter, *Manager*
Norma Lujan, *Executive*
EMP: 70
SALES (corp-wide): 101.7MM **Privately Held**
SIC: 7521 Parking garage
PA: Tps Parking Management, Llc
200 W Monroe St Ste 1500
Chicago IL 60606
312 781-9396

(P-17745)
UNIPARK LLC
Also Called: Apex Mortgage Solutions
1511 Sycamore Ave Ste 2m, Hercules (94547-1767)
PHONE..................510 724-0811
Robert Cruz,
Ana Hung,
Bill Hung,
Sean Hung,
Charlene Cabural, *Manager*
EMP: 70
SQ FT: 1,000
SALES (est): 4.3MM **Privately Held**
SIC: 7521 7299 Parking lots; valet parking

(P-17746)
VALET PARKING SVC A CAL PARTNR (PA)
6933 Hollywood Blvd, Los Angeles (90028-6146)
PHONE..................323 465-5873
Anthony Policella, *CEO*
Jolene Hayler, *Executive Asst*
EMP: 1268 EST: 1946
SQ FT: 10,000
SALES (est): 22.2MM **Privately Held**
WEB: www.valetparkingservice.com
SIC: 7521 7299 Parking lots; valet parking

7532 Top, Body & Upholstery Repair & Paint Shops

(P-17747)
ANAHEIM HILLS AUTO BODY INC
3500 E La Palma Ave, Anaheim (92806-2116)
PHONE..................714 632-8266
Fax: 714 632-1041
Robert Smith, *President*
Patrick Smith, *Vice Pres*
Bob Eden, *Business Mgr*
EMP: 60
SQ FT: 33,000
SALES (est): 5.8MM **Privately Held**
WEB: www.anaheimhillsautobody.com
SIC: 7532 Body shop, automotive

(P-17748)
AUTO BODY MANAGEMENT INC
Also Called: Precision Auto Body
7654 Tampa Ave, Reseda (91335-1735)
PHONE..................818 888-7654
Fax: 818 349-1561
Audrey Vasquev, *President*
Luis Brlignesi, *Bookkeeper*
Lawyer William, *Manager*
EMP: 50
SALES: 4MM **Privately Held**
SIC: 7532 Body shop, automotive

(P-17749)
CALIBER BODYWORKS INC
1100 Colorado Ave, Santa Monica (90401-3010)
PHONE..................310 392-7662
James Haurd, *Manager*
EMP: 100

SALES (corp-wide): 1.7B **Privately Held**
SIC: 7532 Body shop, automotive
HQ: Caliber Bodyworks Of Texas, Inc.
401 E Corp Dr Ste 150
Lewisville TX 75057
469 948-9500

(P-17750)
CALIBER BODYWORKS INC
1399 Logan Ave, Costa Mesa (92626-4006)
PHONE..................714 436-5010
EMP: 150
SALES (corp-wide): 1.7B **Privately Held**
SIC: 7532 Body shop, automotive
HQ: Caliber Bodyworks Of Texas, Inc.
401 E Corp Dr Ste 150
Lewisville TX 75057
469 948-9500

(P-17751)
CALIBER BODYWORKS INC
20601 Valley Blvd, Walnut (91789-2731)
PHONE..................909 598-1113
Brad Wilson, *Manager*
Cindy Sanders, *Human Res Dir*
EMP: 50
SALES (corp-wide): 1.7B **Privately Held**
SIC: 7532 Body shop, automotive
HQ: Caliber Bodyworks Of Texas, Inc.
401 E Corp Dr Ste 150
Lewisville TX 75057
469 948-9500

(P-17752)
EUGENE N TOWNSEND
Also Called: Gene Townsend's Auto Body
609 S Marshall Ave, El Cajon (92020-4214)
PHONE..................619 442-8807
Eugene N Townsend, *Owner*
EMP: 55
SQ FT: 60,000
SALES (est): 3.4MM **Privately Held**
SIC: 7532 Body shop, automotive; paint shop, automotive

(P-17753)
FAITH QUALITY AUTO BODY INC
41130 Nick Ln, Murrieta (92562-7012)
PHONE..................951 698-8215
Fax: 951 698-6495
Lee Amaradio, *President*
EMP: 60
SALES (est): 6MM **Privately Held**
WEB: www.faithqualityautobody.com
SIC: 7532 Body shop, automotive

(P-17754)
FOUNTAIN VALLEY BODY WORKS M2
Also Called: Fvbw
17481 Newhope St, Fountain Valley (92708-4277)
PHONE..................714 751-8812
Fax: 714 641-9745
David March, *President*
Laurie March, *Vice Pres*
Mike Honrath, *General Mgr*
Sandra Prescott, *Office Mgr*
EMP: 50 EST: 1975
SQ FT: 50,000
SALES: 6MM **Privately Held**
WEB: www.fountainvalleybodyworks.com
SIC: 7532 Body shop, automotive; paint shop, automotive

(P-17755)
GOLDEN STATE COLLISION CENTERS
841 Galleria Blvd, Roseville (95678-1331)
PHONE..................916 772-1666
Fax: 916 772-1803
Dave Finkelstein, *President*
Michelle Finkelstein, *Vice Pres*
Phillip Aliotti, *Manager*
Greg Dias, *Manager*
EMP: 75
SQ FT: 14,000
SALES: 11MM **Privately Held**
WEB: www.goldenstatecollision.com
SIC: 7532 Paint shop, automotive

(P-17756)
GREENWALDS AUTOBODY FRAMEWORKS (PA)
1814 Roosevelt Ave, National City (91950-5537)
PHONE..................619 477-2600
Fax: 619 477-2683
Karen Greenwald, *Owner*
Daniel Greenwald, *Owner*
Lee Fernandez, *CPA*
EMP: 50
SQ FT: 13,325
SALES (est): 3.7MM **Privately Held**
SIC: 7532 Body shop, automotive

(P-17757)
HARRYS AUTO BODY INC
Also Called: Harry's Auto Collision
1013 S La Brea Ave, Los Angeles (90019-6902)
PHONE..................323 933-4600
Fax: 323 935-7054
Harry Barseghian, *President*
Perla Montiel, *Executive Asst*
EMP: 65
SQ FT: 5,000
SALES (est): 8.5MM **Privately Held**
SIC: 7532 Body shop, automotive

(P-17758)
HOLMES BODY SHOP INC (PA)
1095 E Colorado Blvd, Pasadena (91106-1402)
PHONE..................626 795-6447
Fax: 626 795-2123
Thomas V Holmes, *President*
EMP: 64
SQ FT: 300,000
SALES (est): 9.7MM **Privately Held**
WEB: www.holmesbodyshop.com
SIC: 7532 Body shop, automotive; collision shops, automotive

(P-17759)
MARCOS AUTO BODY INC (PA)
1390 E Palm St, Altadena (91001-2042)
PHONE..................626 286-5691
Fax: 626 309-0193
Marco G Maimone, *President*
Mike Gregorian, *President*
Lillian Maimone, *Treasurer*
Carl Canzano, *Vice Pres*
Peter McMullan, *Manager*
EMP: 100
SQ FT: 14,000
SALES (est): 4.8MM **Privately Held**
WEB: www.marcosautobody.com
SIC: 7532 7539 Body shop, automotive; frame & front end repair services

(P-17760)
MARINA AUTO BODY SHOP INC
4095 Redwood Ave, Los Angeles (90066-5101)
PHONE..................310 822-6615
Fax: 310 822-3127
Tom Williamson, *President*
Bill Hubbard, *Assistant*
EMP: 50
SQ FT: 24,000
SALES (est): 2.5MM **Privately Held**
WEB: www.marinaautobody.com
SIC: 7532 Body shop, automotive; paint shop, automotive

(P-17761)
MASS PRECISION INC
Paint Division
2371 Paragon Dr, San Jose (95131-1309)
PHONE..................408 451-0929
Fax: 408 451-0933
Don Mc Duffy, *Branch Mgr*
EMP: 75
SALES (corp-wide): 51.8MM **Privately Held**
WEB: www.massprecision.com
SIC: 7532 Top & body repair & paint shops
PA: Mass Precision, Inc.
2110 Oakland Rd
San Jose CA 95131
408 786-0350

(P-17762)
MIKE ROSES AUTO BODY INC
Also Called: Meks's Auto Body
2001 Fremont St, Concord (94520-2616)
PHONE..................925 686-1739
Michelle Banducci, *Manager*
EMP: 50
SALES (corp-wide): 7.8MM **Privately Held**
SIC: 7532 Upholstery & trim shop, automotive; body shop, trucks
PA: Mike Rose's Auto Body, Inc.
2260 Via De Mercados
Concord CA 94520
925 689-1739

(P-17763)
MULLAHEY CHEVROLET INC
Also Called: Cone Collision Center
11899 Woodruff Ave, Downey (90241-5631)
PHONE..................714 871-2545
Fax: 714 447-3085
Timothy Mullahey, *President*
Larry Valdez, *Controller*
EMP: 50
SQ FT: 11,000
SALES (est): 5.3MM **Privately Held**
WEB: www.mullaheychevrolet.com
SIC: 7532 5511 Top & body repair & paint shops; new & used car dealers

(P-17764)
PAN AMERICAN BODY SHOP INC
555 Burke St, San Jose (95112-4102)
PHONE..................408 289-8745
Fax: 408 289-8301
Melchor Louis Alonso Jr, *President*
Melchor Alonso Sr, *Treasurer*
Gayle Alonso, *Admin Sec*
EMP: 60
SQ FT: 32,000
SALES (est): 10.7MM **Privately Held**
SIC: 7532 Collision shops, automotive

(P-17765)
PK AUTOBODY INC
Also Called: Z J'S Auto Body
361 N Minnewawa Ave, Clovis (93612-0208)
PHONE..................559 298-9691
Fax: 559 323-8690
Pam Hartley, *CEO*
Jay Bruno, *President*
David Rodriguez, *CFO*
Horace Bruno, *Vice Pres*
Kim Torres, *Admin Sec*
EMP: 50
SQ FT: 23,000
SALES (est): 4.5MM **Privately Held**
SIC: 7532 Body shop, automotive

(P-17766)
PLATINUM EQUITY PARTNERS INC
3131 S Standard Ave, Santa Ana (92705-5642)
PHONE..................714 444-3100
Hamid Hojati, *President*
Ingrid Cramer, *Vice Pres*
Elham Hojati, *Vice Pres*
Jose Guzman, *Manager*
Sam Mirabile, *Manager*
EMP: 145
SQ FT: 45,000
SALES (est): 5.1MM **Privately Held**
SIC: 7532 Body shop, automotive

(P-17767)
PRESTIGE AUTO COLLISION INC
23726 Via Fabricante, Mission Viejo (92691-3145)
PHONE..................949 470-6031
Fax: 949 581-7500
Bernie Gates, *President*
Laurie Gates, *Treasurer*
EMP: 65
SQ FT: 10,000
SALES (est): 4.7MM **Privately Held**
WEB: www.prestigeautocollision.com
SIC: 7532 Collision shops, automotive

7532 - Top, Body & Upholstery Repair & Paint Shops County (P-17768)

(P-17768)
PRESTIGE TOO AUTO BODY INC
11899 Woodruff Ave, Downey
(90241-5631)
PHONE.............................310 787-8852
Fax: 310 787-9028
Ben L Guerra, *President*
Carlos Mancera, *Office Mgr*
EMP: 50
SALES (est): 5.2MM **Privately Held**
WEB: www.prestigetooautobody.com
SIC: 7532 Body shop, automotive

(P-17769)
PRIDE COLLISION CENTERS INC (PA)
Also Called: Pride Auto Body
7950 Haskell Ave, Van Nuys (91406-1923)
PHONE.............................818 909-0660
Fax: 818 909-0676
Randy Stabler, *President*
Robert Tirchin, *Vice Pres*
Robert Turchan, *Vice Pres*
Irena Karabin, *Executive*
Emma Concepcion, *Financial Exec*
EMP: 65
SQ FT: 44,000
SALES (est): 9.8MM **Privately Held**
SIC: 7532 Body shop, automotive

(P-17770)
REDLANDS FORD INC
1121 W Colton Ave, Redlands
(92374-2935)
PHONE.............................909 793-3211
Steve Rojas, *CEO*
Tracey Hooper, *Treasurer*
Melinda Overson, *Accountant*
Mike Hauso, *Sales Staff*
Bob Munoz, *Sales Staff*
EMP: 85
SALES (est): 8.8MM **Privately Held**
WEB: www.redlandsford.com
SIC: 7532 5511 Body shop, automotive; automobiles, new & used

(P-17771)
SERVICE KING PAINT & BODY LLC
6080 Dublin Blvd, Dublin (94568-7581)
PHONE.............................925 829-5571
EMP: 150
SALES (corp-wide): 4.6B **Publicly Held**
SIC: 7532 Collision shops, automotive
HQ: Service King Paint & Body, Llc
2600 N Central Expy
Richardson TX 75080
972 960-7595

(P-17772)
SHINAZY ENTERPRISES INC
Also Called: Don's Auto Body
1270 Bush St, San Francisco
(94109-5709)
PHONE.............................415 673-4700
Don Shinazy, *President*
Adam Tritz, *General Mgr*
Phil Hall, *Manager*
Marc Mitchell, *Manager*
EMP: 50
SALES (corp-wide): 3.7MM **Privately Held**
WEB: www.sfcounselingcenter.com
SIC: 7532 Body shop, automotive
PA: Shinazy Enterprises, Inc.
1267 Bush St
San Francisco CA 94109
415 441-2406

(P-17773)
SONSHINE COLLISION SERVICES
Also Called: Sonshine Auto Body
17200 Jasmine St, Victorville (92395-5836)
PHONE.............................760 243-3185
Fax: 760 243-5393
Gary L Cooper, *CEO*
Darlene T Cooper, *Treasurer*
Terry Thomas, *Vice Pres*
Aaron P Cooper, *Admin Sec*
Jeannine Blanchard, *Accountant*
EMP: 60
SALES (est): 5.1MM **Privately Held**
SIC: 7532 Collision shops, automotive

(P-17774)
SONSHINE NORTH AUTOBODY
17200 Jasmine St, Victorville (92395-5836)
PHONE.............................760 245-3183
Fax: 760 245-2289
Gary Cooper, *Owner*
EMP: 60
SALES (est): 1.4MM **Privately Held**
SIC: 7532 Body shop, automotive

(P-17775)
STERLING COLLISION CENTER LLC (PA)
Also Called: Sea Breeze Collision
1111 Bell Ave Ste A, Tustin (92780-6463)
PHONE.............................714 259-1111
Ray Shaai, *General Ptnr*
Christine Moctezuma, *Manager*
EMP: 65
SALES (est): 6.6MM **Privately Held**
SIC: 7532 Body shop, automotive

(P-17776)
WILLIAMSON ENTERPRISES INC
Also Called: Marina Autobody
4095 Redwood Ave, Los Angeles
(90066-5101)
PHONE.............................310 822-6615
Thomas C Williamson, *President*
Abbie Woods, *Executive*
Kathlene R Williamson, *Admin Sec*
Lou Monty, *Manager*
Neil Narido, *Asst Mgr*
EMP: 51
SQ FT: 24,000
SALES (est): 5.9MM **Privately Held**
WEB: www.williamsonenterprises.com
SIC: 7532 Body shop, automotive

(P-17777)
Y & S ENTERPRISES INC (PA)
Also Called: Y & S Auto Body Shop
1441 N Gaffey St, San Pedro (90731-1325)
PHONE.............................310 548-1120
Fax: 310 519-8120
Younan Safar, *CEO*
EMP: 50
SQ FT: 71,000
SALES (est): 5.1MM **Privately Held**
WEB: www.yandsautobody.com
SIC: 7532 Body shop, automotive

7533 Automotive Exhaust System Repair Shops

(P-17778)
FREEMAN INVESTMENTS INC
Also Called: Midas Muffler
2595 Montrose Pl, Santa Barbara
(93105-2141)
PHONE.............................805 687-4327
Michael Freeman, *President*
Janet Freeman, *Admin Sec*
EMP: 60
SQ FT: 3,561
SALES (est): 5.7MM **Privately Held**
SIC: 7533 7538 Muffler shop, sale or repair & installation; general automotive repair shops

7534 Tire Retreading & Repair Shops

(P-17779)
AAA SIGNS INC
Also Called: Total Tire Recycling
2020 Railroad Dr, Sacramento
(95815-3515)
PHONE.............................916 568-3456
Fax: 916 568-3462
Gary Matranga, *President*
Danny L Matranga, *Officer*
Mattie Koppling, *Bookkeeper*
Danny Matranga, *Manager*
Jane Smith, *Receptionist*
EMP: 54
SQ FT: 14,000
SALES (est): 5.2MM **Privately Held**
SIC: 7534 7353 Tire retreading & repair shops; cranes & aerial lift equipment, rental or leasing

(P-17780)
NEW PRIDE CORPORATION
2757 E Del Amo Blvd, Compton
(90221-6005)
PHONE.............................310 631-7000
Edward Eunjong Kim, *President*
Natalie Manning, *Admin Sec*
EMP: 50
SALES (corp-wide): 21.1MM **Privately Held**
SIC: 7534 1799 Rebuilding & retreading tires; antenna installation
PA: New Pride Corporation
333 Hegenberger Rd # 705
Oakland CA 94621
510 567-8800

7536 Automotive Glass Replacement Shops

(P-17781)
ALL STAR GLASS INC (PA)
1845 Morena Blvd, San Diego
(92110-3699)
PHONE.............................619 275-3343
Fax: 619 275-6367
Bob Scharaga, *CEO*
Mark V Doren, *COO*
Hermeen Scharaga, *Treasurer*
Janet Scharaga, *Vice Pres*
▲ EMP: 50
SQ FT: 15,512
SALES (est): 22.4MM **Privately Held**
SIC: 7536 Automotive glass replacement shops

(P-17782)
SAFELITE FULFILLMENT INC
Also Called: Safelite Autoglass
261 Richards Blvd, Sacramento
(95811-0216)
PHONE.............................916 442-4715
Frank Primer, *Manager*
EMP: 80
SALES (corp-wide): 2.9B **Privately Held**
WEB: www.belronus.com
SIC: 7536 4225 Automotive glass replacement shops; general warehousing & storage
HQ: Safelite Fulfillment, Inc.
7400 Safelite Way
Columbus OH 43235
614 210-9747

7538 General Automotive Repair Shop

(P-17783)
AUTO TOWN INC
2150 E Hammer Ln, Stockton
(95210-4122)
P.O. Box 690368 (95269-0368)
PHONE.............................209 473-2513
Paul C Wondries, *President*
EMP: 70 EST: 1947
SQ FT: 40,000
SALES (est): 2.2MM **Privately Held**
SIC: 7538 5511 General automotive repair shops; automobiles, new & used

(P-17784)
AUTOMOBILE CLUB SOUTHERN CAL
Also Called: AAA
3333 Fairview Rd, Costa Mesa
(92626-1698)
PHONE.............................714 850-5111
John Estes, *Manager*
Bethanne Smith, *Bd of Directors*
Anita Lux, *Admin Asst*
Joh Sarnowski, *Systs Prg Mgr*
Chia Yang, *Prgrmr*
EMP: 886
SALES (corp-wide): 4.8B **Privately Held**
WEB: www.aaatexas.com
SIC: 7538 General automotive repair shops
PA: Automobile Club Of Southern California
2601 S Figueroa St
Los Angeles CA 90007
213 741-3686

(P-17785)
BAE SYS SIERRA DETROIT ALLISON (DH)
1755 Adams Ave, San Leandro
(94577-1001)
PHONE.............................510 635-8991
Fax: 510 635-9282
Cindy Bergstrom, *President*
Wade Sperry, *Vice Pres*
EMP: 95
SQ FT: 45,000
SALES (est): 8.4MM
SALES (corp-wide): 2.7B **Privately Held**
SIC: 7538 5084 5085 Diesel engine repair: automotive; engines & parts, diesel; industrial supplies
HQ: Bae Systems Resolution Inc.
1000 La St Ste 4950
Houston TX 77002
713 868-7700

(P-17786)
BREWSTERS AUTOMOTIVE INC
17357 Los Angeles St, Yorba Linda
(92886-1723)
PHONE.............................714 528-4683
John M Brewster, *President*
Karen Brewster, *Treasurer*
EMP: 70 EST: 1973
SALES (est): 4.6MM **Privately Held**
SIC: 7538 7542 General automotive repair shops; carwashes

(P-17787)
BROOKDALE SENIOR LIVING INC
430 N Union Rd, Manteca (95337-4367)
PHONE.............................209 823-0164
EMP: 63
SALES (corp-wide): 4.9B **Publicly Held**
SIC: 7538 General automotive repair shops
PA: Brookdale Senior Living
111 Westwood Pl Ste 400
Brentwood TN 37027
615 221-2250

(P-17788)
CITY OF LONG BEACH
Also Called: Long Beach City Fleet Services
2600 Temple Ave, Long Beach
(90806-2209)
PHONE.............................562 570-2828
Fax: 562 570-5414
Dan Burlenbach, *General Mgr*
EMP: 250 **Privately Held**
WEB: www.polb.com
SIC: 7538 9111 General automotive repair shops; mayors' offices
PA: City Of Long Beach
333 W Ocean Blvd Fl 10
Long Beach CA 90802
562 570-6450

(P-17789)
CRYSTAL CHRYSLER PLYMOUTH DODGE
36444 Auto Park Dr, Cathedral City
(92234-6500)
PHONE.............................760 324-9375
Fax: 760 324-1597
Robert Sherr, *President*
Phyllis Wood, *Business Mgr*
Bill Reynolds, *Sales Mgr*
EMP: 78
SQ FT: 26,000
SALES (est): 9.3MM **Privately Held**
WEB: www.crystalchrysler.com
SIC: 7538 5511 General automotive repair shops; automobiles, new & used

(P-17790)
FLT INC
Also Called: Folsom Lake Toyota
12747 Folsom Blvd, Folsom (95630-8097)
PHONE.............................916 355-1500
Fax: 916 355-1543
Charles G Peterson, *President*
Jeff Bear, *General Mgr*
Pam Peterson, *Admin Sec*

PRODUCTS & SERVICES SECTION

7538 - General Automotive Repair Shop County (P-17812)

Jay Bridgeman, *Manager*
Tim Stockwell, *Manager*
EMP: 125
SALES (est): 9.3MM
SALES (corp-wide): 10.6B **Publicly Held**
WEB: www.folsomlaketoyota.com
SIC: 7538 5511 7532 5531 General automotive repair shops; automobiles, new & used; pickups, new & used; body shop, automotive; automotive parts; automobiles, used cars only
PA: Group 1 Automotive, Inc.
  800 Gessner Rd Ste 500
  Houston TX 77024
  713 647-5700

(P-17791)
FORTRESS RESOURCES LLC (PA)
Also Called: Royal Truck Body
14001 Garfield Ave, Paramount (90723-2137)
PHONE.................562 633-9951
Fax: 323 633-2277
Dudley De Zonia Jr, *President*
Rodney Monroe, *Vice Pres*
Mark Calhoun, *Branch Mgr*
Joe Valdivia, *General Mgr*
Jona Baniqued, *Office Mgr*
EMP: 143
SQ FT: 53,000
SALES: 25MM **Privately Held**
SIC: 7538 General truck repair

(P-17792)
FULLERTON COLLEGE
321 E Chapman Ave, Fullerton (92832-2011)
PHONE.................714 732-5453
Fax: 714 447-4097
Rajen Vurdien, *President*
Melisa Hunt, *Executive Asst*
Melinda Taylor, *Executive Asst*
Sara Blasetti, *Admin Asst*
Etta Dial, *Admin Asst*
EMP: 177
SALES (est): 19.2MM **Privately Held**
SIC: 7538 General automotive repair shops

(P-17793)
GARRICK MOTORS INC
559 S Pine St, Escondido (92025-4021)
PHONE.................760 489-2656
Gary Myers, *Branch Mgr*
EMP: 134
SALES (corp-wide): 100.3MM **Privately Held**
SIC: 7538 7532 General automotive repair shops; body shop, automotive
PA: Garrick Motors, Inc.
  231 E Lincoln Ave
  Escondido CA 92026
  760 746-0601

(P-17794)
GERMAN MOTORS CORPORATION
1140 Harrison St, San Francisco (94103-4525)
PHONE.................415 551-2639
Jeff Burton, *Manager*
EMP: 80
SALES (corp-wide): 101MM **Privately Held**
WEB: www.bmwsf.com
SIC: 7538 General automotive repair shops
PA: German Motors Corporation
  1140 Harrison St
  San Francisco CA 94103
  415 863-9000

(P-17795)
GIBBS INTERNATIONAL INC (PA)
Also Called: Gibbs International Truck Ctrs
2201 E Ventura Blvd, Oxnard (93036-7902)
P.O. Box 5206 (93031-5206)
PHONE.................805 485-0551
Fax: 805 988-1846
Edward A Gibbs, *President*
Ram Pai, *Info Tech Mgr*
Mark Rapin, *Sales Mgr*
John Limoli, *Sales Associate*

Chuck McGowan, *Sales Associate*
EMP: 135
SQ FT: 25,000
SALES: 59MM **Privately Held**
WEB: www.gibbstrucks.com
SIC: 7538 5511 4212 Truck engine repair, except industrial; trucks, tractors & trailers: new & used; local trucking, without storage

(P-17796)
GLENN E THOMAS COMPANY INC
Also Called: Glenn E Thomas Dodge
2100 E Spring St, Long Beach (90755-2115)
PHONE.................562 426-5111
Fax: 562 595-5644
Robert W Davis, *President*
J Allen King, *CFO*
Brad Davis, *Vice Pres*
John Davis, *General Mgr*
Tom Bonnstetter, *Manager*
EMP: 90
SQ FT: 38,000
SALES (est): 13MM **Privately Held**
WEB: www.getdodge.com
SIC: 7538 5511 General automotive repair shops; pickups, new & used; automobiles, new & used

(P-17797)
GRAND AUTO CARE
Also Called: Grand Auto Repair
744 N Grand Ave, Covina (91724-2402)
PHONE.................626 331-8390
Fax: 626 858-9548
Ellie Fingerfield, *Owner*
EMP: 50
SALES (est): 1.1MM **Privately Held**
SIC: 7538 7539 General automotive repair shops; brake repair, automotive

(P-17798)
GRIFFIN MOTORWERKE INC
1146 6th St, Berkeley (94710-1246)
PHONE.................510 524-7447
Fax: 510 524-4946
John Griffin, *President*
▲ **EMP:** 1011
SQ FT: 4,000
SALES (est): 26.4MM **Privately Held**
SIC: 7538 5531 General automotive repair shops; automotive parts

(P-17799)
GRIMMWAY ENTERPRISES INC
2171 W Bannister Rd, Brawley (92227-9653)
PHONE.................760 344-0204
Cheryl Chaney, *Principal*
EMP: 568
SALES (corp-wide): 1.8B **Privately Held**
SIC: 7538 General automotive repair shops
PA: Grimmway Enterprises, Inc.
  14141 Di Giorgio Rd
  Arvin CA 93203
  661 854-6250

(P-17800)
HAMBLINS BDY PNT FRAME SP INC
Also Called: Hamblin's Auto & Body Shop
7590 Cypress Ave, Riverside (92503-1904)
PHONE.................951 689-8440
Fax: 951 689-7363
Rod Perry, *President*
EMP: 70
SALES (est): 7.2MM **Privately Held**
WEB: www.hamblinsbodyandpaint.com
SIC: 7538 7532 General automotive repair shops; body shop, automotive

(P-17801)
HAWTHORNE MACHINERY CO
Also Called: Caterpillar
16945 Camino San Bernardo, San Diego (92127-2499)
PHONE.................858 674-7000
Bob Price, *Manager*
EMP: 100

SALES (corp-wide): 175.7MM **Privately Held**
SIC: 7538 5084 7359 5085 Diesel engine repair: automotive; engines & parts, air-cooled; equipment rental & leasing, industrial supplies; marine crafts & supplies
PA: Hawthorne Machinery Co.
  16945 Camino San Bernardo
  San Diego CA 92127
  858 674-7000

(P-17802)
J&R FLEET SERVICES LLC
18244 Valley Blvd, Bloomington (92316-1736)
PHONE.................909 820-7000
Fax: 909 820-9090
Javier G Rodriguez,
Ricardo Rodriguez,
Roberto Rodriguez,
Jose Solis, *Director*
EMP: 70
SQ FT: 30,000
SALES (est): 8.9MM **Privately Held**
SIC: 7538 General automotive repair shops

(P-17803)
LANCASTER COMM SVCS FNDTN
46008 7th St W, Lancaster (93534-7602)
PHONE.................661 723-6230
Randy Williams, *Manager*
EMP: 70 **Privately Held**
WEB: www.poppyfestival.com
SIC: 7538 9111 General automotive repair shops; mayors' offices
PA: The Lancaster Community Services Foundation Inc
  44933 Fern Ave
  Lancaster CA 93534
  661 723-6000

(P-17804)
LINCOLN WITT MERCURY
Also Called: Auto Collection
728 N Escondido Blvd, Escondido (92025-1704)
PHONE.................760 233-3333
Fax: 760 233-3346
Edward Witt,
George Luna, *Parts Mgr*
EMP: 100
SALES (corp-wide): 43.9MM **Privately Held**
WEB: www.sdautoconnect.com
SIC: 7538 5521 5511 7532 General automotive repair shops; used car dealers; new & used car dealers; top & body repair & paint shops; passenger car leasing; truck rental & leasing, no drivers
PA: Witt Lincoln Mercury
  588 Camino Del Rio N
  San Diego CA 92108
  619 358-5000

(P-17805)
LITHIA MOTORS INC
3077 E Hammer Ln, Stockton (95212-2801)
PHONE.................209 956-1930
David Maldonado, *Branch Mgr*
EMP: 50
SALES (corp-wide): 7.8B **Publicly Held**
SIC: 7538 General automotive repair shops
PA: Lithia Motors, Inc.
  150 N Bartlett St
  Medford OR 97501
  541 776-6401

(P-17806)
MAGNUSSENS DODGE CRYSLER JEEP
1901 Grass Valley Hwy, Auburn (95603-2852)
PHONE.................530 885-2900
Bernie Magnussen, *President*
Larry Carmen, *Owner*
Marci Henry, *Manager*
EMP: 60
SALES (est): 5.6MM **Privately Held**
SIC: 7538 5511 General automotive repair shops; pickups, new & used

(P-17807)
NORMANDINS
Also Called: Normandin Chrysler Jeep
900 Cptl Expy Aut Mall, San Jose (95136-1102)
PHONE.................877 330-0391
Fax: 408 266-1185
Mark Normandin, *CEO*
Paul Normandin, *Exec VP*
Margaret Normandin, *Vice Pres*
Doug Kasch, *Store Mgr*
Ben Zahra, *Finance Mgr*
EMP: 119
SQ FT: 12,000
SALES (est): 18.2MM **Privately Held**
WEB: www.normandinchrysler.com
SIC: 7538 5511 General automotive repair shops; new & used car dealers

(P-17808)
OC IV A CALIFORNIA LP
Also Called: Oil Changers
4511 Willow Rd Ste 1, Pleasanton (94588-2735)
PHONE.................925 734-5800
Lawrence Read, *CEO*
LMC Properties IV, *General Ptnr*
Charles Pass, *CFO*
John Read, *Vice Pres*
EMP: 50
SALES (est): 3.3MM **Privately Held**
SIC: 7538 General automotive repair shops

(P-17809)
PARK PLACE FORD LLC
555 W Foothill Blvd, Upland (91786-3853)
PHONE.................909 946-5555
Timothy Park,
EMP: 83 **EST:** 2012
SQ FT: 15,000
SALES (est): 6.3MM **Privately Held**
SIC: 7538 7532 7549 5561 General automotive repair shops; collision shops, automotive; emissions testing without repairs, automotive; inspection & diagnostic service, automotive; travel trailers: automobile, new & used

(P-17810)
PEP BOYS MANNY MOE JACK OF CAL
11456 Washington Blvd, Whittier (90606-3122)
PHONE.................562 908-4400
Fax: 562 908-4444
Luis Suarez, *Manager*
EMP: 50
SQ FT: 35,341
SALES (corp-wide): 19.1B **Publicly Held**
WEB: www.apdnow.com
SIC: 7538 5531 7549 General automotive repair shops; automotive parts; inspection & diagnostic service, automotive
HQ: The Pep Boys Manny Moe & Jack Of California
  3111 W Allegheny Ave
  Philadelphia PA 19132
  215 430-9095

(P-17811)
PREMIER AUTO W COVINA LLC
298 N Azusa Ave, West Covina (91791-1343)
PHONE.................626 858-7202
Troy Duhon, *Mng Member*
John Chaisson, *Office Mgr*
EMP: 60
SQ FT: 10,000
SALES: 5.7MM **Privately Held**
SIC: 7538 General automotive repair shops

(P-17812)
QUALITY AUTO CRAFT INC
3295 Bernal Ave Ste B, Pleasanton (94566-6298)
PHONE.................925 426-0120
Fax: 925 426-0437
Ivo Soares, *President*
EMP: 1614
SQ FT: 10,000
SALES (est): 30MM **Privately Held**
SIC: 7538 7532 General automotive repair shops; body shop, automotive

7538 - General Automotive Repair Shop County (P-17813) PRODUDUCTS & SERVICES SECTION

(P-17813)
SEIDNER-MILLER AUTOMOTIVE INC
1253 S Lone Hill Ave, Glendora (91740-4507)
PHONE 909 394-3500
Peter Miller, *Vice Pres*
Pierce Caine, *Sales Mgr*
EMP: 50
SALES (est): 1.8MM **Privately Held**
SIC: 7538 General automotive repair shops

(P-17814)
SOUTHERN CALIFORNIA FLEET SVC
6726 Nicolett St, Riverside (92504-1843)
PHONE 951 272-8655
Tom Franchina, *CEO*
Vickie Poff, *Office Spvr*
EMP: 50
SALES (est): 2.4MM **Privately Held**
WEB: www.socalfleet.com
SIC: 7538 General automotive repair shops

(P-17815)
SOUTHERN CALIFORNIA MAR ASSN
3333 Fairview Rd, Costa Mesa (92626-1610)
PHONE 714 850-4004
Fax: 714 850-5444
Betty Chew, *Director*
Jim Doran, *Empl Rel Mgr*
EMP: 73
SALES (est): 10.4MM **Privately Held**
SIC: 7538 General automotive repair shops

(P-17816)
TEAMROSS INC
Also Called: Team Superstores
301 Auto Mall Pkwy, Vallejo (94591-3870)
PHONE 707 643-9000
Kenneth B Ross, *President*
Trish Gress, *Treasurer*
Michael Drinker, *Vice Pres*
Dale Clontz, *Finance Mgr*
Doug Havard, *Sales Mgr*
EMP: 95
SQ FT: 57,000
SALES (est): 7.9MM **Privately Held**
SIC: 7538 5511 General automotive repair shops; automobiles, new & used

(P-17817)
TED FORD JONES INC (PA)
Also Called: Ken Grody Ford
6211 Beach Blvd, Buena Park (90621-2307)
P.O. Box 2154 (90621-0654)
PHONE 714 521-3110
Fax: 714 521-8704
Kenneth B Grody, *President*
Ken Grody, *President*
Curt Maletych, *Vice Pres*
Kurt Maletych, *Vice Pres*
Sandy Salazar, *Administration*
▼ **EMP:** 110
SQ FT: 4,500
SALES (est): 29.1MM **Privately Held**
WEB: www.kengrody.com
SIC: 7538 5511 General automotive repair shops; automobiles, new & used

(P-17818)
TOYOTA-SUNNYVALE INC (PA)
898 W El Camino Real, Sunnyvale (94087-1153)
PHONE 408 245-6640
Fax: 408 730-4485
Adam Simms, *President*
Tom Price, *Vice Pres*
Erika Amin, *Office Mgr*
Albert Macon, *Admin Asst*
Suzanne Allayaud, *Finance Mgr*
EMP: 70 **EST:** 1959
SQ FT: 35,000
SALES (est): 14.3MM **Privately Held**
WEB: www.toyotasunnyvale.com
SIC: 7538 5511 5521 5531 General automotive repair shops; automobiles, new & used; used car dealers; automotive & home supply stores

7539 Automotive Repair Shops, NEC

(P-17819)
ALASKA DIESEL ELECTRIC
425 S Hacienda Blvd, City of Industry (91745-1123)
PHONE 626 934-6211
Peter B Hill Jr, *President*
Robert Humphryes, *CFO*
EMP: 119
SALES (est): 3.8MM
SALES (corp-wide): 193.8MM **Privately Held**
SIC: 7539 Automotive repair shops
PA: Valley Power Systems, Inc.
425 S Hacienda Blvd
City Of Industry CA 91745
626 333-1243

(P-17820)
CALTECK USA INC
33 Goldenrod, Irvine (92614-7923)
PHONE 949 786-4854
David Carmi, *General Mgr*
▲ **EMP:** 50
SALES (est): 2.9MM **Privately Held**
SIC: 7539 Electrical services

(P-17821)
EDF RENEWABLE SERVICES INC (HQ)
Also Called: Enxco
15445 Innovation Dr, San Diego (92128-3432)
PHONE 858 521-3575
Tristan Grimbert, *President*
Deborah Gronvold, *Exec VP*
Ryan Pfaff, *Exec VP*
Jeff Ghilardi, *Vice Pres*
Richard Jigarjian, *Vice Pres*
EMP: 65
SQ FT: 70,000
SALES (est): 85.9MM
SALES (corp-wide): 769.9MM **Privately Held**
SIC: 7539 Alternators & generators, re-building & repair
PA: Edf Renewable Energy, Inc.
15445 Innovation Dr
San Diego CA 92128
858 521-3300

(P-17822)
HIGH SUMMIT LLC
Also Called: Special Events
6909 Las Positas Rd Ste D, Livermore (94551-5113)
PHONE 925 605-2900
Weston Cook,
Danielle Landman, *Manager*
EMP: 50
SALES (est): 3.3MM **Privately Held**
SIC: 7539 Automotive repair shops

(P-17823)
NBCCAT CORP
Also Called: X M G M
1044 Madruga Rd, Lathrop (95330-9779)
PHONE 209 858-0283
Fax: 209 858-9493
Richard Gray, *Manager*
EMP: 51
SALES (corp-wide): 6.3MM **Privately Held**
SIC: 7539 Automotive repair shops
PA: Nbccat Corp
7431 W 90th St
Bridgeview IL 60455
708 793-5191

(P-17824)
SACRAMENTO MUNICPL UTILITY DST
6201 S St, Sacramento (95817-1818)
P.O. Box 15830 (95852-0830)
PHONE 916 452-3211
Jan Shoory, *General Mgr*
Shirley Lewis, *Personnel Exec*
EMP: 2000
SALES (corp-wide): 1.5B **Privately Held**
SIC: 7539 Electrical services
PA: Sacramento Municipal Utility District
6201 S St
Sacramento CA 95817
916 452-3211

(P-17825)
SAN FRANCISCO CITY & COUNTY
1800 Jerrold Ave Ste A, San Francisco (94124-1640)
PHONE 415 550-4600
Peter Aviles, *Manager*
EMP: 110 **Privately Held**
SIC: 7539 9311 7538 Automotive repair shops; finance, taxation & monetary policy; ; ; general automotive repair shops
PA: City & County Of San Francisco
1 Dr Carlton B Goodlett P
San Francisco CA 94102
415 554-7500

(P-17826)
SCL COMPANY INC
Also Called: Discount Tire Center
19545 Parthenia St, Northridge (91324-3414)
PHONE 818 993-4758
Sebouh Donoyan, *CEO*
Sally Reid, *HR Admin*
Steve Donoyan, *Manager*
EMP: 66
SQ FT: 500
SALES (est): 4MM **Privately Held**
SIC: 7539 5531 Automotive repair shops; automotive tires

(P-17827)
VERNON AUTOPARTS INC
1559 W 134th St, Gardena (90249-2215)
PHONE 323 249-7545
Mike Klapper, *President*
Mary Ann Klapper, *Corp Secy*
David Klapper, *Vice Pres*
Paula Robinson, *Bookkeeper*
EMP: 54
SQ FT: 100,000
SALES (est): 520.7K
SALES (corp-wide): 7.6MM **Privately Held**
SIC: 7539 3714 3694 3592 Machine shop, automotive; motor vehicle parts & accessories; engine electrical equipment; carburetors, pistons, rings, valves; power transmission equipment; pumps & pumping equipment
PA: Electrical Rebuilders Sales, Inc.
1559 W 134th St
Gardena CA 90249
323 249-7545

7542 Car Washes

(P-17828)
ALL HNDS CRWASH DTAIL CTR LUBE
22952 Pacific Park Dr, Aliso Viejo (92656-3389)
PHONE 949 716-3600
Fax: 949 916-5749
Raul Valerio, *President*
Carlos Valerio, *CFO*
Ricardo Marquez, *General Mgr*
EMP: 60
SQ FT: 92,000
SALES (est): 1.5MM **Privately Held**
WEB: www.allhandscarwash.com
SIC: 7542 Carwashes; washing & polishing, automotive

(P-17829)
AUTO WORLD CAR WASH LLC
15951 Los Gatos Blvd, Los Gatos (95032-3428)
PHONE 408 345-6532
Jeff Locastro, *CEO*
EMP: 1597
SALES (est): 2.7MM
SALES (corp-wide): 66.5MM **Privately Held**
SIC: 7542 Carwashes
PA: California Secured Investments, Llc
14225 Lora Dr Apt 96
Los Gatos CA

(P-17830)
BEACH AND LA MIRADA CAR WASH
5231 Beach Blvd, Buena Park (90621-1229)
PHONE 714 994-1099
Fax: 714 994-1058
Efrain Garcia, *Manager*
Harry Acebedo, *Systs Prg Mgr*
EMP: 50
SALES (est): 1.4MM **Privately Held**
SIC: 7542 Carwashes

(P-17831)
BOWIE ENTERPRISES
Also Called: Red Carpet Car Wash
1920 S Mooney Blvd, Visalia (93277-4450)
PHONE 559 732-2988
Fax: 559 732-2988
Scott Rotse, *Manager*
Jamie Karr, *Manager*
EMP: 53
SALES (corp-wide): 12.7MM **Privately Held**
WEB: www.redcarpetcarwash.com
SIC: 7542 Washing & polishing, automotive
PA: Bowie Enterprises
4411 N Blackstone Ave
Fresno CA 93726
559 227-6221

(P-17832)
BOWIE ENTERPRISES (PA)
Also Called: Red Carpet Car Wash
4411 N Blackstone Ave, Fresno (93726-1904)
PHONE 559 227-6221
Fax: 559 227-9591
David Bowie, *President*
James M Bowie, *Ch of Bd*
Karen Bowie, *Treasurer*
Kathryn Bowie, *Admin Sec*
EMP: 60 **EST:** 1966
SQ FT: 7,700
SALES (est): 12.7MM **Privately Held**
WEB: www.redcarpetcarwash.com
SIC: 7542 5541 Carwash, automatic; filling stations, gasoline

(P-17833)
BOWIE ENTERPRISES
Also Called: Red Carpet Car Wash
801 W Shaw Ave, Clovis (93612-3218)
PHONE 559 292-6565
Fax: 559 292-0858
Gilbert Allender, *Manager*
Michael Bowi, *Sales Executive*
EMP: 65
SALES (corp-wide): 12.7MM **Privately Held**
WEB: www.redcarpetcarwash.com
SIC: 7542 Carwashes
PA: Bowie Enterprises
4411 N Blackstone Ave
Fresno CA 93726
559 227-6221

(P-17834)
CAR WASH OF AMERICA
120 S Placentia Ave, Placentia (92870-5709)
PHONE 714 528-0833
Fax: 714 528-1170
Howard Jin, *President*
EMP: 50
SALES (est): 1.1MM **Privately Held**
SIC: 7542 Carwashes; washing & polishing, automotive

(P-17835)
CHARLES FENLEY ENTERPRISES
Also Called: Chevron
1109 Oakdale Rd, Modesto (95355-4065)
P.O. Box 577200 (95357-7200)
PHONE 209 523-2832
Fax: 209 523-1042
Gene Rooney, *Manager*
Kristie Olson, *Vice Pres*
EMP: 50

PRODUCTS & SERVICES SECTION

7542 - Car Washes County (P-17861)

SALES (corp-wide): 9MM Privately Held
SIC: 7542 5541 5948 7549 Carwashes; filling stations, gasoline; luggage, except footlockers & trunks; leather goods, except luggage & shoes; lubrication service, automotive
PA: Charles Fenley Enterprises
1121 Oakdale Rd Ste 7
Modesto CA 95355
209 576-0381

(P-17836)
CIRCLE MARINA CAR WASH INC
Also Called: Circle Marina Hand Car Wash
4800 E Pacific Coast Hwy, Long Beach (90804-3243)
PHONE...................................562 494-4698
John C Wang, President
EMP: 50
SALES (est): 1.7MM Privately Held
SIC: 7542 Washing & polishing, automotive

(P-17837)
COAST CARWASH LP
Also Called: Coast Hand Car Wash
5677 E 7th St, Long Beach (90804-4430)
PHONE...................................562 961-5555
Fax: 562 961-5565
James Yang, Partner
Gregory Yang, Partner
Jerry Yang, Partner
Peter Yang, Partner
EMP: 50 EST: 1998
SALES (est): 3MM Privately Held
WEB: www.coastcarwash.com
SIC: 7542 7538 Carwashes; general automotive repair shops

(P-17838)
DUCKYS CAR WASH INC
716 N San Mateo Dr, San Mateo (94401-2224)
PHONE...................................650 375-8100
Fax: 650 375-1882
Stephen Munkdale, President
Jeff Herstik, Area Mgr
Roy Nickolai, Manager
EMP: 60
SALES (est): 1.5MM Privately Held
WEB: www.duckyscarwash.com
SIC: 7542 Carwashes

(P-17839)
DUCKYS OF SAN CARLOS INC
Also Called: Ducky's Car Wash
1301 Old County Rd, San Carlos (94070-5201)
PHONE...................................650 637-1301
Steve Munkdale, President
EMP: 50
SALES (est): 2MM Privately Held
SIC: 7542 Washing & polishing, automotive

(P-17840)
DYNAMIC AUTO IMAGES INC
Also Called: Dynamic Detail
1407 N Batavia St Ste 102, Orange (92867-3525)
PHONE...................................714 981-4367
Tom Miller, President
EMP: 300
SQ FT: 2,500
SALES (est): 13.2MM Privately Held
WEB: www.dynamicautoimages.com
SIC: 7542 7532 Washing & polishing, automotive; collision shops, automotive

(P-17841)
ENCINO CENTER CAR WASH INC
16300 Ventura Blvd, Encino (91436-2116)
PHONE...................................818 788-6300
Bernard Goodman, President
Armando Garcia, Manager
Jeff Goodman, Manager
EMP: 50
SALES (est): 2.2MM Privately Held
SIC: 7542 5541 5947 Carwash, automatic; filling stations, gasoline; gift shop

(P-17842)
GEORGE FASCHING
Also Called: Faschings Car Wash
425 N Santa Anita Ave, Arcadia (91006-2876)
PHONE...................................626 446-0654
George Fasching, Owner
Geri Fasching, Co-Owner
EMP: 50
SQ FT: 60,000
SALES (est): 2MM Privately Held
SIC: 7542 5541 Carwash, automatic; washing & polishing, automotive; filling stations, gasoline

(P-17843)
HLW CORP
Also Called: Shine and Bright Hand Car Wash
11166 Venice Blvd, Culver City (90232-3921)
PHONE...................................310 838-7100
Fax: 310 313-1455
John Watkins, President
Monica Dixon, Manager
Rod Rodriguez, Manager
EMP: 50
SQ FT: 600
SALES (est): 2MM Privately Held
WEB: www.hlwcorp.com
SIC: 7542 Carwashes; washing & polishing, automotive

(P-17844)
IN & OUT CAR WASH INC
Also Called: Spot Free Car Wash
3615 Monte Real, Escondido (92029-7911)
PHONE...................................619 316-8492
Donald Macek, President
Denis McKnight, Vice Pres
EMP: 50
SQ FT: 20,000
SALES (est): 2MM Privately Held
WEB: www.inoutcarwash.com
SIC: 7542 Washing & polishing, automotive

(P-17845)
JEMTOWN INC
Also Called: Five Star Auto Repr & Car Wash
6818 Five Star Blvd, Rocklin (95677-2660)
PHONE...................................916 315-0555
James A Sperlazza, President
Mary Sperlazza, Vice Pres
EMP: 50
SALES (est): 1.8MM Privately Held
SIC: 7542 Carwashes

(P-17846)
JKF AUTO SERVICE INC
Also Called: Five Star Auto Repair and Wash
6818 Five Star Blvd, Rocklin (95677-2660)
PHONE...................................916 315-0555
Fax: 916 315-0550
Jeff Finerman, President
Karen W Finerman, Vice Pres
EMP: 60
SALES (est): 1.3MM Privately Held
SIC: 7542 7549 7539 Carwashes; lubrication service, automotive; automotive repair shops

(P-17847)
LAKEWOOD SOUTH CAR WASH LLC
Also Called: Rossmoor Carwash
11031 Alamitos Ave, Los Alamitos (90720)
PHONE...................................562 430-4975
Fax: 562 596-2595
Foster A Hooper, Principal
EMP: 50
SALES (est): 2.1MM Privately Held
SIC: 7542 Carwashes

(P-17848)
LARK AVENUE CAR WASH
Also Called: Classic Car Washes
5005 Almaden Expy, San Jose (95118-2049)
P.O. Box 5993 (95150-5993)
PHONE...................................408 371-2565
Fax: 408 371-2689
Chuck Mina, Manager
EMP: 72
SQ FT: 7,859
SALES (corp-wide): 11.7MM Privately Held
SIC: 7542 Carwashes
PA: Lark Avenue Car Wash
871 E Hamilton Ave
Campbell CA 95008
408 371-2414

(P-17849)
LITTLE SISTERS TRUCK WASH INC
72189 Varner Rd, Thousand Palms (92276-3364)
PHONE...................................760 343-3448
Fax: 760 343-7434
Bob Crogan, Manager
Tammy Johnson, Sr Corp Ofcr
EMP: 60 Privately Held
SIC: 7542 Carwashes; truck wash
PA: Little Sisters Truck Wash Inc
25 Rolling View Ln
Fallbrook CA 92028

(P-17850)
LITTLE SISTERS TRUCK WASH INC
8899 Three Flags Ave, Oak Hills (92344-0497)
PHONE...................................760 947-4448
Joe McSann, Manager
Joe McFann, Executive
EMP: 65 Privately Held
SIC: 7542 Carwashes; truck wash
PA: Little Sisters Truck Wash Inc
25 Rolling View Ln
Fallbrook CA 92028

(P-17851)
LITTLE SISTERS TRUCK WASH INC
2960 Lenwood Rd, Barstow (92311-9571)
PHONE...................................760 253-2277
Fax: 760 253-2253
B J Elmanza, Manager
EMP: 70
SQ FT: 2,482 Privately Held
SIC: 7542 Carwashes; truck wash
PA: Little Sisters Truck Wash Inc
25 Rolling View Ln
Fallbrook CA 92028

(P-17852)
LITTLE SISTERS TRUCK WASH INC
14264 Valley Blvd, Fontana (92335-5293)
PHONE...................................909 549-1862
Tod Kerns, Manager
EMP: 65 Privately Held
SIC: 7542 Carwashes; truck wash
PA: Little Sisters Truck Wash Inc
25 Rolling View Ln
Fallbrook CA 92028

(P-17853)
LITTLE SISTERS TRUCK WASH INC (PA)
Also Called: Little Sister's Truck Wash
25 Rolling View Ln, Fallbrook (92028-9234)
P.O. Box 1530, Bonsall (92003-1530)
PHONE...................................760 731-3170
Renald J Anelle, President
Cathy Anelle, Corp Secy
William F Wire, Vice Pres
EMP: 69
SALES (est): 8MM Privately Held
SIC: 7542 Carwashes; truck wash

(P-17854)
LOZANO INC
Also Called: Lozano Car Wash
2690 W El Camino Real, Mountain View (94040-1117)
PHONE...................................650 941-0590
Fax: 650 941-1736
Manuel J Lozano, President
Claudia Rozriduez, Manager
EMP: 107
SQ FT: 500
SALES (est): 3.5MM Privately Held
WEB: www.lozano.net
SIC: 7542 Carwash, automatic

(P-17855)
M K H INC
Also Called: Cruisers Carwash & Diner
8870 Tampa Ave, Northridge (91324-3519)
PHONE...................................818 882-9274
Fax: 818 882-9276
Mike Harn, President
Harvey Kampf, General Mgr
EMP: 60
SALES (est): 3.8MM Privately Held
SIC: 7542 5812 Carwashes; diner

(P-17856)
MISSION CAR WASH
Also Called: Mission Car Wash & Quik Lube
59 Mission Cir, Santa Rosa (95409-5304)
PHONE...................................707 537-2040
Fax: 707 537-1467
Tim Mitchell, Owner
EMP: 50
SQ FT: 6,157
SALES (est): 1.2MM Privately Held
SIC: 7542 Carwashes

(P-17857)
NORCO HILLS CAR WASH
Also Called: Norco Auto Wash
18020 Magnolia St, Fountain Valley (92708-5603)
PHONE...................................951 279-4398
Fax: 951 280-9449
Steve Hart, Partner
Robert Keane, Partner
EMP: 50
SALES (est): 2.6MM Privately Held
SIC: 7542 Carwashes

(P-17858)
PLAZA HAND CARWASH INC
Also Called: Prime Stop
23100 Alssndro Blvd Ste B, Moreno Valley (92553-9670)
PHONE...................................951 697-4420
Fax: 951 697-4423
Bob Sherrick, President
EMP: 50
SQ FT: 15,000
SALES (est): 832.2K Privately Held
SIC: 7542 5087 Carwashes; carwash equipment & supplies

(P-17859)
PRECISION AUTO DETAILING LLC
700 Serramonte Blvd, Colma (94014-3220)
PHONE...................................650 992-9775
Anthony Caprini,
James Grasso, Manager
EMP: 80
SALES (est): 1.8MM Privately Held
SIC: 7542 5087 Carwashes; carwash equipment & supplies

(P-17860)
PRESTIGE CAR WASH LAFAYETTE LP
Also Called: Lafayette Car Wash
3319 Mt Diablo Blvd, Lafayette (94549-4011)
PHONE...................................925 283-1190
Fax: 925 284-7243
Jesse Wellen, Partner
Ralph H Sawyer, Agent
EMP: 50
SQ FT: 2,000
SALES (est): 1.7MM Privately Held
WEB: www.lafayettecarwash.com
SIC: 7542 7532 Carwashes; body shop, automotive

(P-17861)
RUSSELL FISHER PARTNERSHIP
Also Called: Bella Terra Carwash
16061 Beach Blvd, Huntington Beach (92647-3802)
PHONE...................................714 842-4453
Fax: 714 842-8113
Ruben Hernandez, Site Mgr
Alphonso Perez, Manager
Juan Rojas, Manager
EMP: 50

7542 - Car Washes County (P-17862)

SALES (corp-wide): 6.5MM Privately Held
SIC: 7542 Carwashes; washing & polishing, automotive
PA: Russell Fisher Partnership
18971 Beach Blvd
Huntington Beach CA 92648
909 930-5420

(P-17862)
SUDS CAR WASH INC
4620 Post St, El Dorado Hills (95762-7102)
PHONE...................................916 673-6300
Jeffery A Lowe, President
Ashley Lowe, Vice Pres
EMP: 50
SALES (est): 1.7MM Privately Held
SIC: 7542 Carwashes

(P-17863)
TEAM DYKSPRA (PA)
2315 California Ave, Corona (92881-6655)
PHONE...................................951 898-6482
Lenny Dykstra, President
Brittany Heath, Accountant
EMP: 60
SALES (est): 3.1MM Privately Held
SIC: 7542 7549 Carwashes; automotive maintenance services

(P-17864)
VERNON TRUCK WASH INC
3308 Bandini Blvd, Vernon (90058-4113)
PHONE...................................323 267-0706
Fax: 323 267-0433
Armen Keshishyan, President
EMP: 105
SQ FT: 800
SALES (est): 5.5MM Privately Held
SIC: 7542 Truck wash

(P-17865)
VLADIGOR INVESTMENT INC
Also Called: Tower Car Wash
1601 Mission St, San Francisco (94103-2413)
PHONE...................................415 558-9274
Fax: 415 558-9308
Igor Paskhover, President
Lisa Syelsky, Vice Pres
EMP: 90
SQ FT: 25,000
SALES (est): 3.2MM Privately Held
SIC: 7542 Carwashes

(P-17866)
WEST LAKE TOUCHLESS CAR WASH
223 87th St, Daly City (94015-1644)
PHONE...................................650 992-5344
Fred Tautenhan, Owner
Dean Tautenhahn, Persnl Dir
EMP: 50
SALES (est): 1.2MM Privately Held
WEB: www.westlaketouchlesscarwash.com
SIC: 7542 5541 Carwashes; gasoline service stations

(P-17867)
WILSHIRE WEST LLC
Also Called: Wilshire West Carwash
9595 Wilshire Blvd # 501, Beverly Hills (90212-2505)
PHONE...................................310 828-2910
Mehdi Soroudi, Mng Member
Limbardo Pirmonces, Manager
EMP: 50
SALES (est): 971.7K Privately Held
SIC: 7542 Carwashes

7549 Automotive Svcs, Except Repair & Car Washes

(P-17868)
AA AUTMTIVE PERSONNEL SVCS INC
2251 Federal Ave, Los Angeles (90064-1403)
PHONE...................................310 914-3012
Alvaro Marcin, President
Pilar Camarena, Office Mgr

EMP: 200
SALES (est): 4.1MM Privately Held
SIC: 7549 Automotive maintenance services

(P-17869)
ABSOLUTE TOWING-HOLLENBECK DIV
4760 Valley Blvd, Los Angeles (90032-3834)
PHONE...................................323 225-9294
Fax: 323 276-6039
Todd Q Smart, President
EMP: 50 EST: 1998
SQ FT: 111,000
SALES (est): 3.9MM Privately Held
SIC: 7549 Towing service, automotive

(P-17870)
ALAMITOS ENTERPRISES LLC (PA)
Also Called: Jiffy Lube
3311 Katella Ave, Los Alamitos (90720-2337)
PHONE...................................562 596-1827
Fax: 562 596-3338
Michael Biddle, Mng Member
Patrick Novak, Administration
Robert Curry,
Steve Ruscack, Manager
EMP: 70
SQ FT: 2,500
SALES (est): 9.3MM Privately Held
SIC: 7549 Lubrication service, automotive

(P-17871)
ALLIED GARDENS TOWING INC (HQ)
9150 Chesapeake Dr # 240, San Diego (92123-1062)
PHONE...................................619 563-4060
Fax: 619 492-5294
Edward S Bischop, President
EMP: 60 EST: 1970
SQ FT: 1,500
SALES (est): 2.6MM
SALES (corp-wide): 540.9MM Publicly Held
SIC: 7549 Towing service, automotive
PA: Miller Industries, Inc.
8503 Hilltop Dr
Ooltewah TN 37363
423 238-4171

(P-17872)
ALLIED LUBE TEXAS LP (PA)
4440 Von Karman Ave # 100, Newport Beach (92660-2011)
PHONE...................................949 486-4008
Anthony Fancicola, Owner
Martin Escobar, Manager
EMP: 71 EST: 2005
SALES (est): 9.8MM Privately Held
SIC: 7549 Automotive maintenance services

(P-17873)
AMERIT FLEET SOLUTIONS INC (PA)
1331 N Calif Blvd Ste 150, Walnut Creek (94596-4535)
PHONE...................................877 512-6374
Gary Herbold, Chairman
Bob Brauer, President
Dan Williams, CEO
Amein Punjani, COO
David Allinson, CFO
EMP: 168 EST: 2012
SALES (est): 40.6MM Privately Held
SIC: 7549 Inspection & diagnostic service, automotive

(P-17874)
ARS WEST LLC
780 W El Norte Pkwy, Escondido (92026-3984)
PHONE...................................760 480-6631
EMP: 75
SALES (corp-wide): 35.6MM Privately Held
SIC: 7549 5499 Automotive maintenance services; dried fruit

PA: Ars West Llc
2204 S El Camino Real # 314
Oceanside CA 92054
760 730-5137

(P-17875)
AUTOMOTIVE TSTG & DEV SVCS INC (PA)
400 Etiwanda Ave, Ontario (91761-8637)
PHONE...................................909 390-1100
Fax: 909 390-9056
Devon Larry Smith, CEO
Kay Smith, Corp Secy
Lin Farmer, Sales Executive
Jason Link, Manager
▲ EMP: 185
SQ FT: 24,000
SALES (est): 15.4MM Privately Held
WEB: www.automotivetesting.com
SIC: 7549 8734 8711 Emissions testing without repairs, automotive; testing laboratories; engineering services

(P-17876)
BOWIE ENTERPRISES
Also Called: Red Carpet Car Wash
4411 N Blackstone Ave, Fresno (93726-1904)
PHONE...................................559 227-3400
EMP: 72
SALES (corp-wide): 12.7MM Privately Held
SIC: 7549 7538 Lubrication service, automotive; general automotive repair shops
PA: Bowie Enterprises
4411 N Blackstone Ave
Fresno CA 93726
559 227-6221

(P-17877)
CA STE ATOM ASSOC INTR-INS BUR
Also Called: AAA
4400 Capitola Rd Ste 100, Capitola (95010-3571)
P.O. Box 250 (95010-0250)
PHONE...................................831 824-9128
Fax: 831 464-1648
Donald Foley, Branch Mgr
Jose Soto, Sales Staff
EMP: 100
SALES (corp-wide): 1.1B Privately Held
WEB: www.viamagazine.com
SIC: 7549 Towing services
HQ: California State Automobile Association Inter-Insurance Bureau
1276 S California Blvd
Walnut Creek CA 94596
925 287-7600

(P-17878)
CAR SPA INC
996 Mountain Ave, Norco (92860-3160)
PHONE...................................951 279-1422
Fax: 951 279-1797
Jesus Medina, Manager
EMP: 50
SALES (corp-wide): 36MM Privately Held
WEB: www.car-spa.com
SIC: 7549 7542 Lubrication service, automotive; washing & polishing, automotive
PA: Car Spa, Inc.
4835 Lyndo B Johns Fwy Ste 650
Dallas TX 75244
469 374-0280

(P-17879)
COMPLETE COACH WORKS
Also Called: John Deere Authorized Dealer
1863 Service Ct, Riverside (92507-2341)
PHONE...................................951 682-2557
Dale E Carson, President
Michael Dominici, CFO
Kleidy Ruiz, Office Mgr
Amber Piccinonno, Admin Asst
Keith Butler, Administration
▲ EMP: 280
SALES (est): 29.2MM
SALES (corp-wide): 60.9MM Privately Held
SIC: 7549 5082 Trailer maintenance; construction & mining machinery

PA: D/T Carson Enterprises, Inc.
42882 Ivy St
Murrieta CA 92562
951 684-9585

(P-17880)
COUNTY OF MADERA
Also Called: Madera County Road Department
200 W 4th St, Madera (93637-3548)
PHONE...................................559 675-7811
Johannes Hoeversz, Manager
Joan Fry, Administration
Richard Cortez, Manager
EMP: 84 Privately Held
WEB: www.madera-county.com
SIC: 7549 Road service, automotive
PA: County Of Madera
209 W Yosemite Ave
Madera CA 93637
559 675-7726

(P-17881)
COVEY AUTO EXPRESS INC (PA)
Also Called: Pacific Towing
1444 El Pinal Dr, Stockton (95205-2642)
PHONE...................................253 826-0461
Michael D Covey, President
Kathy Covey, Vice Pres
EMP: 128
SQ FT: 19,000
SALES (est): 22.6MM Privately Held
SIC: 7549 Towing services

(P-17882)
EZ LUBE LLC (PA)
3540 Howard Way Ste 200, Costa Mesa (92626-1417)
PHONE...................................714 556-1312
Guy Marsala, President
Mark Archer, CFO
Perry Spiroupolous, Executive
Scott Kohn, Info Tech Mgr
Donna Schaefer, Controller
EMP: 60
SQ FT: 2,000
SALES (est): 27.8MM Privately Held
WEB: www.ezlube.com
SIC: 7549 Lubrication service, automotive; inspection & diagnostic service, automotive

(P-17883)
HIGH STREET HAND CAR WASH INC
Also Called: High St Car Wash Lube & Oil
569 High St, Oakland (94601-3905)
PHONE...................................510 536-4333
Fax: 510 536-4299
Chong B Kim, President
EMP: 51
SQ FT: 3,123
SALES (est): 4MM Privately Held
SIC: 7549 7542 Lubrication service, automotive; carwashes

(P-17884)
HONDA PERFORMANCE DEV INC
25145 Anza Dr, Santa Clarita (91355-3416)
PHONE...................................661 294-7300
Eric Berkman, President
Yoko Homma, Admin Asst
Hiroyuki Okubo, Design Engr
Jason Castillo, Engineer
Art S Cyr, Engineer
◆ EMP: 88
SQ FT: 100,000
SALES (est): 15.4MM
SALES (corp-wide): 124.7B Privately Held
SIC: 7549 High performance auto repair & service
HQ: American Honda Motor Co., Inc.
1919 Torrance Blvd
Torrance CA 90501
310 783-2000

(P-17885)
J C TOWING INC
2501 Faivre St, Chula Vista (91911-4603)
PHONE...................................619 429-1492
Gardner J Clark IV, President
Shelly Clarks, Office Mgr

PRODUCTS & SERVICES SECTION
7622 - Radio & TV Repair Shops County (P-17909)

EMP: 52
SQ FT: 2,000
SALES (est): 3.2MM Privately Held
SIC: 7549 Towing services

(P-17886)
JANS TOWING INC (PA)
1045 W Kirkwall Rd, Azusa (91702-5127)
PHONE..................................626 334-1383
Fax: 626 334-1175
Jan Qualkenbush, *President*
Susan Dunken, *Manager*
EMP: 63
SQ FT: 5,896
SALES (est): 8.1MM Privately Held
SIC: 7549 Towing services

(P-17887)
METROPRO ROAD SERVICES INC (PA)
Also Called: A & P Towing-Metropro Rd Svcs
2550 S Garnsey St, Santa Ana (92707-3337)
PHONE..................................714 556-7600
Fax: 714 556-4100
Bradley T Humphreys, *CEO*
Jody Campbell, *President*
Jean Noutary, *General Mgr*
EMP: 85
SQ FT: 85,000
SALES (est): 5.6MM Privately Held
SIC: 7549 Towing service, automotive

(P-17888)
MOC PRODUCTS COMPANY INC
9840 Kitty Ln, Oakland (94603-1070)
PHONE..................................510 635-1230
Fax: 510 635-1282
George Logan, *Branch Mgr*
Mark Deiling, *Sales Dir*
Monty Skinner, *Regl Sales Mgr*
EMP: 68
SALES (corp-wide): 177.4MM Privately Held
WEB: www.mocproducts.com
SIC: 7549 Automotive maintenance services
PA: Moc Products Company, Inc.
12306 Montague St
Pacoima CA 91331
818 794-3500

(P-17889)
POISON SPYDER CUSTOMS INC
Also Called: Transamerican Auto Parts
1177 W Lincoln St Ste 100, Banning (92220-4524)
PHONE..................................951 849-5911
Larry McRae, *President*
Cheri McRae, *CFO*
Garrett Engle, *Mfg Spvr*
EMP: 903
SALES (est): 29.2MM Privately Held
SIC: 7549 Automotive customizing services, non-factory basis
PA: Tap Worldwide, Llc
400 W Artesia Blvd
Compton CA 90220

(P-17890)
REDHILL TOWING & AUTOBODY
428 Irwin St, San Rafael (94901-5113)
PHONE..................................415 456-8943
Joe Paz Jr, *President*
Linda Paz, *Vice Pres*
EMP: 54
SQ FT: 7,000
SALES (est): 4.4MM Privately Held
WEB: www.redhilltowing.com
SIC: 7549 Towing service, automotive

(P-17891)
ROCKET SMOG INC
11413 W Washington Blvd, Los Angeles (90066-6012)
PHONE..................................310 390-7664
Mike Farokh, *Branch Mgr*
EMP: 52
SALES (corp-wide): 1.7MM Privately Held
SIC: 7549 Automotive maintenance services

PA: Rocket Smog Inc
3328 S La Cienega Blvd
Los Angeles CA 90016
323 935-7183

(P-17892)
SEARS ROEBUCK AND CO
40680 Winchester Rd, Temecula (92591-5504)
PHONE..................................951 719-3528
Fax: 951 719-3543
Dan Larue, *Manager*
EMP: 93
SALES (corp-wide): 25.1MM Publicly Held
SIC: 7549 Automotive maintenance services
HQ: Sears, Roebuck And Co.
3333 Beverly Rd
Hoffman Estates IL 60179
847 286-2500

(P-17893)
SEARS ROEBUCK AND CO
Also Called: Sears Auto Center
1235 Colusa Ave, Yuba City (95991-3693)
PHONE..................................530 751-4628
Fax: 530 751-4647
Cathy Nicholls, *Branch Mgr*
EMP: 100
SALES (corp-wide): 25.1MM Publicly Held
SIC: 7549 Automotive maintenance services
HQ: Sears, Roebuck And Co.
3333 Beverly Rd
Hoffman Estates IL 60179
847 286-2500

(P-17894)
STRLNG PATH MEDCL CORP
3030 Old Ranch Pkwy # 430, Seal Beach (90740-2760)
PHONE..................................562 799-8900
Changgao Yang, *President*
EMP: 50
SALES (est): 400.1K Privately Held
SIC: 7549 Inspection & diagnostic service, automotive

(P-17895)
SUNBELT TOWING INC (PA)
Also Called: Western Towing
4370 Pacific Hwy, San Diego (92110-3106)
PHONE..................................619 297-8697
Fax: 619 297-0058
Steven Hendrickson, *President*
Angel Sanchez, *Marketing Staff*
Michelle Martin, *Director*
EMP: 70
SALES: 8.5MM Privately Held
WEB: www.perfectionautobody.net
SIC: 7549 7532 Towing services; top & body repair & paint shops

(P-17896)
TEGSCO LLC
Also Called: Autoreturn
450 7th St, San Francisco (94103-4532)
PHONE..................................415 865-8200
Ray Krouse,
Frank Mecklenburg, *General Mgr*
Crystal Ayot, *Human Resources*
Raymond Krouse,
John Wicker,
EMP: 60
SQ FT: 15,000
SALES (est): 5.2MM Privately Held
SIC: 7549 Towing services

(P-17897)
TOYOTA LOGISTICS SERVICES
1340 Cesar E Chavez Pkwy, San Diego (92113-2133)
PHONE..................................619 531-0157
Antonio Venejas, *Principal*
EMP: 210
SALES (corp-wide): 242.7B Privately Held
SIC: 7549 8999 Automotive maintenance services; artists & artists' studios
HQ: Toyota Logistics Services, Inc
19001 S Western Ave
Torrance CA 90501
310 618-5009

(P-17898)
TOYOTA LOGISTICS SERVICES (DH)
19001 S Western Ave, Torrance (90501-1106)
PHONE..................................310 618-5009
Randy Pflughaupt, *CEO*
Allen Decarr, *President*
Donald Esmond, *Principal*
Cory Deavila, *Administration*
Terry Zercher, *Prgrmr*
◆ EMP: 176
SQ FT: 600
SALES (est): 1.9MM
SALES (corp-wide): 242.7B Privately Held
SIC: 7549 3711 Automotive maintenance services; motor vehicles & car bodies
HQ: Toyota Motor Sales Usa Inc
19001 S Western Ave
Torrance CA 90501
310 468-4000

(P-17899)
TOYOTA LOGISTICS SERVICES
785 Edison Ave, Long Beach (90813-2657)
PHONE..................................562 437-6767
Audie Freeman, *Manager*
Mike Evans, *Manager*
EMP: 289
SALES (corp-wide): 242.7B Privately Held
SIC: 7549 Automotive maintenance services
HQ: Toyota Logistics Services, Inc
19001 S Western Ave
Torrance CA 90501
310 618-5009

(P-17900)
TOYOTA LOGISTICS SERVICES
45250 Fremont Blvd, Fremont (94538-6316)
PHONE..................................510 498-7817
Fax: 510 498-7888
Ron Leutbecher, *Branch Mgr*
EMP: 200
SALES (corp-wide): 242.7B Privately Held
SIC: 7549 Automotive maintenance services
HQ: Toyota Logistics Services, Inc
19001 S Western Ave
Torrance CA 90501
310 618-5009

(P-17901)
UNITED ROAD TOWING INC
Also Called: Bill & Wag's
1516 S Bon View Ave, Ontario (91761-4407)
PHONE..................................909 923-6100
Gabriel Ramirez, *Manager*
Mark Montes, *Manager*
EMP: 56
SALES (corp-wide): 9MM Privately Held
WEB: www.unitedroad.com
SIC: 7549 Towing service, automotive
PA: United Road Towing, Inc.
9550 Bormet Dr Ste 304
Mokena IL 60448
708 390-2200

(P-17902)
UNITED ROAD TOWING INC
Also Called: Bill & Wag's
945 W Brockton Ave, Redlands (92374-2903)
PHONE..................................909 798-4863
Gabriel Ramirez, *Manager*
EMP: 56
SALES (corp-wide): 9MM Privately Held
WEB: www.unitedroad.com
SIC: 7549 Towing service, automotive
PA: United Road Towing, Inc.
9550 Bormet Dr Ste 304
Mokena IL 60448
708 390-2200

(P-17903)
UNITED ROAD TOWING INC
Also Called: Keystone Towing
7817 Woodley Ave, Van Nuys (91406-1703)
PHONE..................................818 782-1996
Fax: 818 782-1992

Jason Kent, *Manager*
EMP: 60
SALES (corp-wide): 9MM Privately Held
SIC: 7549 Towing service, automotive
PA: United Road Towing, Inc.
9550 Bormet Dr Ste 304
Mokena IL 60448
708 390-2200

(P-17904)
UNITED ROAD TOWING INC
Also Called: Quality Towing
1516 S Bon View Ave, Ontario (91761-4407)
PHONE..................................702 649-5711
Clarke Whitney, *Branch Mgr*
Jason Kent, *Executive*
EMP: 56
SALES (corp-wide): 9MM Privately Held
SIC: 7549 4213 Towing service, automotive; automobiles, transport & delivery
PA: United Road Towing, Inc.
9550 Bormet Dr Ste 304
Mokena IL 60448
708 390-2200

(P-17905)
VALVOLINE INTERNATIONAL INC
Also Called: Valvoline Instant Oil Change
9520 John St, Santa Fe Springs (90670-2904)
PHONE..................................562 906-6200
Fax: 562 906-6299
Brian Nichols, *Branch Mgr*
EMP: 50
SALES (corp-wide): 5.3B Publicly Held
SIC: 7549 Automotive maintenance services
HQ: Valvoline International, Inc.
3499 Blazer Pkwy
Lexington KY 40509
800 832-6825

7622 Radio & TV Repair Shops

(P-17906)
BLACK & WHITE TV INC
8756 Dorrington Ave, West Hollywood (90048-1724)
PHONE..................................310 855-1040
Jeffrey Fischgrund, *President*
EMP: 50
SALES (est): 952.8K Privately Held
SIC: 7622 Television repair shop

(P-17907)
CADEN TV
6979 Rockton Pl, San Jose (95119-1331)
PHONE..................................408 275-1908
Kelly Tran, *Office Mgr*
EMP: 50
SALES (est): 635.2K Privately Held
SIC: 7622 Television repair shop

(P-17908)
GROUP 3 TECHNOLOGIES
4888 Ronson Ct Ste O, San Diego (92111-1808)
PHONE..................................858 874-3081
Antonio C Montuya, *President*
EMP: 55
SALES (corp-wide): 1.5MM Privately Held
SIC: 7622 Communication equipment repair
PA: Group 3 Technologies
13353 Alondra Blvd # 115
Santa Fe Springs CA
562 229-1184

(P-17909)
JVC AMERICAS CORP
Also Called: Jvc Company of America
5665 Corporate Ave, Cypress (90630-4727)
PHONE..................................714 527-7500
Fax: 714 952-2361
Ron Serasio, *Manager*
Jack Moran, *Marketing Mgr*
John Banks, *Director*
EMP: 60
SQ FT: 82,000 Privately Held

7622 - Radio & TV Repair Shops

SIC: 7622 Radio & television repair

(P-17910)
JVC AMERICAS CORP
Also Called: Jvc Service & Engineering
11925 Pike St, Santa Fe Springs (90670-2955)
PHONE.................................562 463-8110
EMP: 80 **Privately Held**
SIC: 7622

(P-17911)
MINILEC SERVICE INC
Also Called: Minilec Service-Los Angeles BR
9207 Deering Ave Ste A, Chatsworth (91311-6959)
PHONE.................................818 341-1125
EMP: 50
SQ FT: 7,000
SALES (corp-wide): 6.6MM **Privately Held**
SIC: 7622 4812
PA: Minilec Service Inc.
    9207 Deering Ave Ste A
    Chatsworth CA 91311
    818 773-6300

(P-17912)
PRECISION TELEVISION INC
Also Called: Precision TV
2820 Broadmoor Ave, Concord (94520-4717)
PHONE.................................925 825-5296
Fax: 925 825-5541
Derrick W Behrens, *CEO*
Daryl Behrens, *CFO*
Robert Behrens, *Vice Pres*
EMP: 54
SQ FT: 5,500
SALES (est): 6.8MM **Privately Held**
SIC: 7622 Radio & television repair

(P-17913)
SOHNEN ENTERPRISES INC (PA)
8945 Dice Rd, Santa Fe Springs (90670-2517)
P.O. Box 2884 (90670-0884)
PHONE.................................562 903-4957
Fax: 562 946-3451
Barry Sohnen, *President*
Nathan Balsam, *Vice Pres*
Don Swarts, *General Mgr*
Bryan Chase, *Admin Sec*
Eric Yniguez, *Purch Agent*
▲ EMP: 50
SQ FT: 132,000
SALES (est): 15.3MM **Privately Held**
WEB: www.sohnen.com
SIC: 7622 5065 7629 Radio repair shop; video repair; communication equipment repair; sound equipment, electronic; video equipment, electronic; telephone equipment; communication equipment; electrical repair shops

(P-17914)
SYNTELESYS INC
Also Called: Ytech
2550 Corp Pl Ste C108, Monterey Park (91754)
PHONE.................................323 859-2160
Carey Chrisman, *President*
▼ EMP: 50
SALES (est): 3.2MM **Privately Held**
SIC: 7622 7313 Antenna repair & installation; electronic media advertising representatives

(P-17915)
UCLA SC THEATER FILM & TV EQP
102 East Melnitz, Los Angeles (90095-0001)
PHONE.................................310 825-6165
Bill McDonalds, *CEO*
Harold Shin, *CTO*
Janet Bergstrom, *Professor*
A P Gonzalez, *Professor*
Kathleen McHugh, *Professor*
EMP: 100
SALES (est): 2.9MM **Privately Held**
SIC: 7622 Television repair shop

7623 Refrigeration & Air Conditioning Svc & Repair Shop

(P-17916)
ACCO ENGINEERED SYSTEMS INC
3421 S Malt Ave, Commerce (90040-3127)
PHONE.................................323 727-7765
Fax: 323 727-9577
Eric Porras, *Branch Mgr*
Ryan Hourigan, *Design Engr*
Minh Phan, *Design Engr*
Dave Olivas, *Foreman/Supr*
Peter Santibanez, *Manager*
EMP: 70
SQ FT: 77,399
SALES (corp-wide): 765MM **Privately Held**
WEB: www.accoair.com
SIC: 7623 1711 Air conditioning repair; plumbing, heating, air-conditioning contractors
PA: Acco Engineered Systems, Inc.
    6265 San Fernando Rd
    Glendale CA 91201
    818 244-6571

(P-17917)
BROWER MECHANICAL INC
4060 Alvis Ct, Rocklin (95677-4012)
PHONE.................................530 749-0808
Fax: 916 632-1114
Jeff Brower, *President*
Duane Knickerbocker, *Vice Pres*
Troy Bagwell, *General Mgr*
Debra Dickmeyer, *Controller*
Alex Huey, *Traffic Dir*
EMP: 75
SQ FT: 5,000
SALES (est): 14.9MM **Privately Held**
WEB: www.browermechanical.com
SIC: 7623 7629 Air conditioning repair; electrical household appliance repair

(P-17918)
CARRIER CORPORATION
Also Called: Carrier Commercial Service
1168 National Dr Ste 60, Sacramento (95834-1979)
PHONE.................................916 928-9500
Fax: 916 928-9222
Craig Sweeney, *Branch Mgr*
EMP: 50
SALES (corp-wide): 56.1B **Publicly Held**
WEB: www.carrier.com
SIC: 7623 Air conditioning repair
HQ: Carrier Corporation
    17900 Bee Line Hwy
    Jupiter FL 33478
    561 796-2000

(P-17919)
CLIMA-TECH INC
3610 Placentia Ct, Chino (91710-2978)
PHONE.................................909 613-5513
William C Valenzuela, *CEO*
Ada Roberts, *CFO*
Husein Aziz, *Exec VP*
EMP: 89
SQ FT: 11,500
SALES (est): 15.3MM **Privately Held**
SIC: 7623 1711 Refrigeration service & repair; refrigeration contractor; heating & air conditioning contractors

(P-17920)
CONTROL AIR CONDITIONING CORP
1390 Armorlite Dr, San Marcos (92069-1342)
PHONE.................................760 744-2727
Mike Eepn, *Branch Mgr*
Trish Minutelli, *Administration*
EMP: 190
SALES (corp-wide): 103.2MM **Privately Held**
SIC: 7623 1711 Refrigeration service & repair; heating systems repair & maintenance
PA: Control Air Conditioning Corporation
    5200 E La Palma Ave
    Anaheim CA 92807
    714 777-8600

(P-17921)
GMH INC
Also Called: West Coast Air Conditioning
561 Kinetic Dr Ste A, Oxnard (93030-7947)
PHONE.................................805 485-1410
Fax: 805 981-7189
Michael C Haase, *President*
Gina Haase, *Vice Pres*
Greg Hellmann, *Project Mgr*
Justin Haase, *Controller*
Brian Haase, *Manager*
EMP: 50 EST: 1976
SQ FT: 5,600
SALES (est): 12.2MM **Privately Held**
WEB: www.westcoast-air.com
SIC: 7623 1711 Refrigeration repair service; air conditioning repair; refrigeration contractor; warm air heating & air conditioning contractor

(P-17922)
HUSSMANN SERVICES CORPORATION
Also Called: Ir Hussman
120 Main Ave Ste A1, Sacramento (95838-2043)
PHONE.................................916 920-4993
Fax: 916 920-2417
Manuel Rincon, *General Mgr*
EMP: 110
SALES (corp-wide): 64.5B **Privately Held**
WEB: www.hussmann.com
SIC: 7623 5078 Refrigeration service & repair; refrigeration equipment & supplies
HQ: Hussmann Corporation
    12999 St Charles Rock Rd
    Bridgeton MO 63044
    314 291-2000

(P-17923)
RECURVE INC
220 Montgomery St Ste 820, San Francisco (94104-3439)
PHONE.................................510 540-4860
Andy Leventhal, *CEO*
Matthew Golden, *President*
Joel Truher, *Vice Pres*
Adam Winter, *Vice Pres*
Alison Kampbell, *Admin Asst*
EMP: 52
SQ FT: 8,000
SALES (est): 3.6MM **Privately Held**
SIC: 7623 Air conditioning repair

(P-17924)
SUNBELT CONTROLS INC
4511 Willow Rd Ste 4, Pleasanton (94588-2735)
PHONE.................................925 660-3900
Josh Reding, *Branch Mgr*
EMP: 50
SALES (corp-wide): 765MM **Privately Held**
SIC: 7623 1711 Refrigeration service & repair; septic system construction
HQ: Sunbelt Controls, Inc.
    6265 San Fernando Rd
    Glendale CA 91201
    818 244-6571

(P-17925)
WESTERN ALLIED SERVICE COMPANY
12046 Florence Ave, Santa Fe Springs (90670-4406)
P.O. Box 3628 (90670-1628)
PHONE.................................562 941-3243
Steve Kieve, *CEO*
Mike Taylor, *Engineer*
Laird Anderson, *Controller*
EMP: 300
SQ FT: 15,000
SALES (est): 7.8MM **Privately Held**
SIC: 7623 Air conditioning repair

7629 Electrical & Elex Repair Shop, NEC

(P-17926)
AAR MANUFACTURING INC
AAR Composites
5307 Luce Ave Bldg 243e, McClellan (95652-2440)
PHONE.................................916 830-7011
Eloy Herrera, *Branch Mgr*
David Lund, *Credit Mgr*
Jack Sandes, *Opers Mgr*
EMP: 73
SALES (corp-wide): 1.6B **Publicly Held**
SIC: 7629 Electronic equipment repair
HQ: Aar Manufacturing, Inc.
    1100 N Wood Dale Rd
    Wood Dale IL 60191
    630 227-2000

(P-17927)
AAR MANUFACTURING INC
AAR Mobility Systems
5239 Luce Ave Bldg 243d, McClellan (95652-2427)
PHONE.................................800 422-2213
Lee Krantz, *Branch Mgr*
Eloy Herrera, *Business Dir*
EMP: 73
SALES (corp-wide): 1.6B **Publicly Held**
SIC: 7629 Electronic equipment repair
HQ: Aar Manufacturing, Inc.
    1100 N Wood Dale Rd
    Wood Dale IL 60191
    630 227-2000

(P-17928)
ABLE CABLE INC (PA)
Also Called: A C I Communications
5115 Douglas Fir Rd Ste A, Calabasas (91302-2588)
PHONE.................................818 223-3600
Fax: 818 223-3609
Russell Ramas, *President*
David Gardner, *CFO*
Michael Collette, *Vice Pres*
Curtis Quillin, *Vice Pres*
Dick Lordahl, *Technical Mgr*
EMP: 175
SQ FT: 3,500
SALES (est): 14.4MM **Privately Held**
WEB: www.acicommunications.com
SIC: 7629 1731 4813 Telephone set repair; telephone & telephone equipment installation; telephone communication, except radio

(P-17929)
ADVANTEL INCORPORATED (PA)
Also Called: Advantel Networks
2222 Trade Zone Blvd, San Jose (95131-1845)
PHONE.................................408 954-5100
Fax: 408 435-7928
Dan Ferguson, *President*
George Black, *Shareholder*
Roger Wilson McGibbon, *CEO*
Tom Vignau, *CFO*
Joe Twohy, *Officer*
EMP: 90
SQ FT: 18,000
SALES (est): 31.3MM **Privately Held**
WEB: www.advantel.com
SIC: 7629 5999 Telecommunication equipment repair (except telephones); communication equipment

(P-17930)
BOEING COMPANY
Lemoore Nval Base Hnger 1, Lemoore (93245)
P.O. Box 1160 (93245-1160)
PHONE.................................559 998-8260
George Baldwin, *Manager*
EMP: 50
SALES (corp-wide): 96.1B **Publicly Held**
SIC: 7629 Aircraft electrical equipment repair
PA: The Boeing Company
    100 N Riverside Plz
    Chicago IL 60606
    312 544-2000

▲ = Import ▼ = Export ◆ = Import/Export

PRODUCTS & SERVICES SECTION

7641 - Reupholstery & Furniture Repair County (P-17951)

(P-17931)
CPI ECONCO DIVISION (DH)
Also Called: Econco Broadcast Service
1318 Commerce Ave, Woodland (95776-5908)
PHONE 530 662-7553
Fax: 530 666-7760
David P Elliot, *President*
Joel Littman, *Corp Secy*
Heidi Lindberg, *Info Tech Mgr*
Todd Baker, *Engineer*
Paul Cockern, *Engineer*
▲ **EMP:** 73
SQ FT: 50,000
SALES (est): 9.2MM
SALES (corp-wide): 405.7MM **Privately Held**
SIC: 7629 3671 Electrical repair shops; vacuum tubes

(P-17932)
CUBIC GLOBAL DEFENSE INC (HQ)
9333 Balboa Ave, San Diego (92123-1515)
P.O. Box 85587 (92186-5587)
PHONE 858 277-6780
Fax: 858 505-1502
Jimmie L Balentine, *CEO*
Richard D Koon, *President*
Mark A Harrison, *Treasurer*
James Terry, *Senior VP*
William C Stewart, *Admin Sec*
▲ **EMP:** 50
SALES (est): 346.4MM
SALES (corp-wide): 1.4B **Publicly Held**
SIC: 7629 Electrical repair shops
PA: Cubic Corporation
9333 Balboa Ave
San Diego CA 92123
858 277-6780

(P-17933)
DUTHIE ELECTRIC SERVICE CORP
Also Called: Duthie Power Services
2335 E Cherry Indus Cir, Long Beach (90805-4416)
PHONE 562 790-1772
Fax: 562 790-8230
Christina Duthie, *President*
Richard Duthie, *Corp Secy*
Erik Duthie, *General Mgr*
Fred Sheilds, *Info Tech Mgr*
Kim PHI, *Accountant*
EMP: 50
SQ FT: 17,000
SALES: 13.5MM **Privately Held**
WEB: www.duthiepower.com
SIC: 7629 7359 Generator repair; equipment rental & leasing

(P-17934)
ENCORE REPAIR SERVICES INC
2175 Agate Ct, Simi Valley (93065-1839)
PHONE 805 584-6599
Fax: 805 584-6596
Anthony R Graffia II, *President*
Connie D Dubois, *CFO*
Wayne D Burg, *Vice Pres*
EMP: 170
SALES: 40MM **Privately Held**
SIC: 7629 Electronic equipment repair

(P-17935)
GDSA-LINCOLN INC (PA)
Also Called: Weco Aerospace Systems
1501 Aviation Blvd, Lincoln (95648-9388)
PHONE 916 645-8961
William Weygandt, *President*
Robert Weygandt, *CFO*
Kathleen Weygandt, *Admin Sec*
Elisabeta Bejenariu, *Purchasing*
▲ **EMP:** 55 **EST:** 1971
SQ FT: 7,800
SALES (est): 4.6MM **Privately Held**
SIC: 7629 5088 Aircraft electrical equipment repair; aircraft equipment & supplies

(P-17936)
JJR ENTERPRISES INC (PA)
Also Called: Caltronics Business Systems
10491 Old Placerville Rd # 150, Sacramento (95827-2533)
PHONE 916 363-2666
Fax: 916 361-1829
Daniel F Reilly, *CEO*
Anne Long, *CFO*
John J Reilly, *Chairman*
Dalton Crawford, *Info Tech Dir*
Nazim Shafiq, *Technician*
EMP: 95
SQ FT: 30,000
SALES: 53.7MM **Privately Held**
WEB: www.caltronics.net
SIC: 7629 5044 Business machine repair, electric; office equipment

(P-17937)
MAINLINE EQUIPMENT INC
20917 Higgins Ct, Torrance (90501-1723)
PHONE 800 444-2288
Fax: 310 357-4465
Mark E Lipp, *President*
Chris Hines, *Data Proc Dir*
Jennifer Pegan, *Controller*
David Esposito, *Sales Staff*
EMP: 52
SQ FT: 36,000
SALES (est): 3.5MM **Privately Held**
SIC: 7629 3663 Electrical repair shops; electrical equipment repair services; radio & TV communications equipment

(P-17938)
NSG TECHNOLOGY INC (DH)
Also Called: Foxconn
1705 Junction Ct Ste 200, San Jose (95112-1023)
PHONE 408 547-8700
Ted Dubbs, *CEO*
Ted Jao, *Business Dir*
Joe Chu, *Branch Mgr*
Scott Ho, *Administration*
Eric Chin, *Accountant*
▲ **EMP:** 168 **EST:** 1995
SALES (est): 74.7MM **Privately Held**
SIC: 7629 Electronic equipment repair

(P-17939)
PETERSON MACHINERY CO
Also Called: Peterson Cat
955 Marina Blvd, San Leandro (94577-3440)
P.O. Box 5258 (94577-0610)
PHONE 541 302-9199
Duane S Doyle, *CEO*
Keith Davidge, *CFO*
Ernie Fierro, *Vice Pres*
May Edralin, *Administration*
Bill Nicholson, *Info Tech Dir*
EMP: 1200
SALES (est): 74.5MM **Privately Held**
WEB: www.petersonholding.com
SIC: 7629 Electrical repair shops

(P-17940)
RAYTHEON COMPANY
300 N Lake Ave Ste 1120, Pasadena (91101-4111)
PHONE 626 304-1007
Paul Thompson, *Director*
Craig Trautman, *Program Mgr*
Craig Betts, *Admin Asst*
Joseph Merfalen, *Engineer*
Zena Hart, *Recruiter*
EMP: 100
SALES (corp-wide): 23.2B **Publicly Held**
SIC: 7629 Electrical equipment repair services
PA: Raytheon Company
870 Winter St
Waltham MA 02451
781 522-3000

(P-17941)
RAYTHEON COMPANY
988 Inner Loop Rd, Fort Irwin (92310)
P.O. Box 10079 (92310-0079)
PHONE 760 386-2572
Denise Lapage, *Branch Mgr*
Steve Grossley, *Technology*
Michael Downs, *Manager*
EMP: 500
SALES (corp-wide): 23.2B **Publicly Held**
SIC: 7629 1731 Electrical equipment repair services; electrical work
PA: Raytheon Company
870 Winter St
Waltham MA 02451
781 522-3000

(P-17942)
SCOTTEL VOICE & DATA INC
Also Called: Black Box Network Services
6100 Center Dr Ste 720, Los Angeles (90045-9228)
PHONE 310 737-7300
George Robertson, *General Mgr*
Regan Burns, *General Mgr*
Rachelle Phillips, *Admin Asst*
Stephen Murnane, *Sales Dir*
Evelyn Eisert, *Manager*
EMP: 130
SQ FT: 5,200
SALES (est): 31.8MM
SALES (corp-wide): 912.6MM **Publicly Held**
WEB: www.scottel.com
SIC: 7629 1731 Telecommunication equipment repair (except telephones); telephone & telephone equipment installation
PA: Black Box Corporation
1000 Park Dr
Lawrence PA 15055
724 746-5500

(P-17943)
SERVICE SOLUTIONS GROUP LLC
Also Called: Barkers Food Machinery
5367 2nd St, Irwindale (91706-6608)
PHONE 626 960-9390
Fax: 626 337-4541
Robert Zachary Barasch, *Branch Mgr*
Scott Risley, *Manager*
EMP: 60
SALES (corp-wide): 2.7B **Privately Held**
SIC: 7629 7623 5046 5078 Electrical equipment repair services; refrigeration repair service; restaurant equipment & supplies; commercial refrigeration equipment; plumbing fittings & supplies; electronic parts & equipment
HQ: Service Solutions Group, Llc
800 Aviation Pkwy
Smyrna TN 37167
615 462-4000

(P-17944)
SIEMENS INDUSTRY INC
1585 Parkway Blvd, West Sacramento (95691-5017)
PHONE 916 371-2600
EMP: 68
SALES (corp-wide): 31MM **Privately Held**
SIC: 7629 1731 Electrical repair shops; electrical work
PA: Republic Intelligent Transportation Services, Inc.
371 Bel Marin Blvd Ste 200
Novato CA 94949
415 884-3000

(P-17945)
T-MOBILE USA INC
Also Called: T Mobile Santa Ana
307 E 1st St Ste 1e, Santa Ana (92701-5302)
PHONE 626 261-7359
EMP: 155
SALES (corp-wide): 74.3B **Publicly Held**
SIC: 7629 5999 5065 Electronic equipment repair; communication equipment; mobile telephone equipment
HQ: T-Mobile Usa, Inc.
12920 Se 38th St
Bellevue WA 98006
425 378-4000

(P-17946)
TELENET VOIP INC
850 N Park View Dr, El Segundo (90245-4914)
PHONE 310 253-9000
Asghar Ghassemy, *President*
Nicol Payab, *Vice Pres*
Augie Besa, *Project Mgr*
Emmeline Smilansky, *Project Engr*
Thea Leonardo, *Accountant*
EMP: 65
SQ FT: 11,000
SALES (est): 11.2MM **Privately Held**
WEB: www.telenetusa.net
SIC: 7629 7379 7382 3612 Telephone set repair; computer related consulting services; security systems services; transmission & distribution voltage regulators

(P-17947)
TOSHIBA BUS SOLUTIONS USA INC (DH)
9740 Irvine Blvd, Irvine (92618-1608)
PHONE 949 462-6000
Mark Mathews, *CEO*
EMP: 73
SALES (est): 72.8MM
SALES (corp-wide): 48.4B **Privately Held**
SIC: 7629 5044 5999 Business machine repair, electric; office equipment; business machines & equipment
HQ: Toshiba America Business Solutions, Inc.
9740 Irvine Blvd
Irvine CA 92618
949 462-6000

(P-17948)
USACO SERVICE CORP
Also Called: Kenwood Service Center West
16205 Distribution Way, Cerritos (90703-2329)
PHONE 562 483-8747
Stewart Park, *President*
▲ **EMP:** 150
SALES (est): 7.1MM **Privately Held**
WEB: www.usacoservice.com
SIC: 7629 Electrical repair shops

7631 Watch, Clock & Jewelry Repair

(P-17949)
ADVANCE SERVICES INC
8021 Kern Ave, Gilroy (95020-4051)
PHONE 408 767-2797
Vanessa Valencia, *Manager*
EMP: 3221 **Privately Held**
SIC: 7631 Watch, clock & jewelry repair
PA: Advance Services, Inc.
112 S Birch St
Norfolk NE 68701

(P-17950)
M & G JEWELERS INC
10823 Edison Ct, Rancho Cucamonga (91730-3868)
PHONE 909 989-2929
Juan Guevara, *President*
Michael Insalago, *Vice Pres*
Adolfo Burbano, *Info Tech Mgr*
Tuan Phan, *Info Tech Mgr*
Ryan Tigner, *VP Opers*
EMP: 68
SQ FT: 8,432
SALES (est): 11.5MM **Privately Held**
WEB: www.mandgjewelers.com
SIC: 7631 Watch, clock & jewelry repair

7641 Reupholstery & Furniture Repair

(P-17951)
CORP OF CHURCH OF CHRIST LD ST
Also Called: Los Angeles Deseret Industries
2720 E 11th St, Los Angeles (90023-3404)
PHONE 323 268-7281
Fax: 323 268-6663
Dessin Meyer, *Director*
Terry Hutchens, *Controller*
Lynn Richards, *Sales Mgr*
EMP: 130
SALES (corp-wide): 2.3B **Privately Held**
WEB: www.lds.org
SIC: 7641 5932 7629 8331 Furniture repair & maintenance; furniture, secondhand; household appliances, used; electrical household appliance repair; job training & vocational rehabilitation services

7641 - Reupholstery & Furniture Repair County (P-17952)   PRODUDUCTS & SERVICES SECTION

PA: Corporation Of The President Of The Church Of Jesus Christ Of Latter-Day Saints
50 W North Temple
Salt Lake City UT 84150
801 240-1000

(P-17952)
MOYES CUSTOM FURNITURE INC
3431 E La Palma Ave Ste 3, Anaheim (92806-2022)
P.O. Box 5276 (92806)
PHONE.....................714 729-0234
Brian Moyes, *President*
Jane Moyes, *Corp Secy*
David Moyes, *Administration*
Dawn Moyes, *Manager*
EMP: 50
SQ FT: 59,000
SALES (est): 4MM **Privately Held**
WEB: www.moyesfurniture.com
SIC: 7641 2512 Reupholstery; upholstered household furniture

7692 Welding Repair

(P-17953)
F & B INC
Also Called: Pro Iron Workshop
596 Indian Hill Blvd # 221, Pomona (91767-5302)
PHONE.....................909 203-8436
Toll Free:........................888 -
Robyn Song, *President*
Jin Cha, *Vice Pres*
Young H Song, *Admin Sec*
Jeff Kim, *Manager*
EMP: 50
SALES (est): 4.6MM **Privately Held**
SIC: 7692 Welding repair

(P-17954)
HAYES WELDING INC
Also Called: Valew Welding & Fabrication
12522 Violet Rd, Adelanto (92301-2704)
P.O. Box 310 (92301-0310)
PHONE.....................760 246-4878
Fax: 760 246-4088
Velma D Hayes, *President*
Roger L Hayes, *CEO*
Vernon L Hayes, *Vice Pres*
Gayle Jenkins, *Manager*
▲ EMP: 100
SQ FT: 45,000
SALES (est): 16.4MM **Privately Held**
WEB: www.valew.com
SIC: 7692 3465 3714 3713 Welding repair; automotive stampings; body parts, automobile: stamped metal; fenders, automobile: stamped or pressed metal; fuel systems & parts, motor vehicle; truck & bus bodies; fabricated plate work (boiler shop)

(P-17955)
TIKOS TANKS INC
Also Called: Rte Welding
14561 Hawthorne Ave, Fontana (92335-2508)
PHONE.....................951 757-8014
Fax: 909 350-3147
EMP: 55
SALES (est): 7.5MM **Privately Held**
SIC: 7692 Welding repair

7699 Repair Shop & Related Svcs, NEC

(P-17956)
AER TECHNOLOGIES INC
650 Columbia St, Brea (92821-2912)
PHONE.....................714 871-7357
Fax: 714 446-6105
Kim Quick, *CEO*
Michael McGroarty, *President*
Joe Gorin, *COO*
James Casper, *Executive*
Ingrid Osborne, *Admin Sec*
EMP: 320
SQ FT: 50,000

SALES (est): 37.4MM **Privately Held**
SIC: 7699 Precision instrument repair

(P-17957)
AERO-ENGINES INC
2641 Roseview Ave, Los Angeles (90065-1123)
PHONE.....................323 663-3961
Fax: 323 664-5189
Otis Perera, *President*
William McCan, *Treasurer*
Antonio Ortega, *Vice Pres*
Robert Riveera, *Vice Pres*
William Acosta, *Admin Sec*
▲ EMP: 60
SQ FT: 41,000
SALES (est): 4.6MM **Privately Held**
SIC: 7699 3724 Aircraft & heavy equipment repair services; aircraft engines & engine parts

(P-17958)
ALL AMERICAN SERVICE & SUPS
1776 All American Way, Corona (92879-2070)
P.O. Box 2229 (92878-2229)
PHONE.....................951 736-3880
Daniel D Sisemore, *President*
Thomas Toscas, *Corp Secy*
Mark A Luer, *Principal*
Lean Kitchen, *Office Mgr*
John Garthe, *Controller*
EMP: 90
SALES (est): 7.8MM **Privately Held**
SIC: 7699 Construction equipment repair

(P-17959)
AMERICAN ALLIANCE ALWAYS AVAIL
Also Called: Drain Patrol
503 Bangs Ave Ste H, Modesto (95356-8991)
PHONE.....................209 948-9220
Paul Willenn, *Principal*
EMP: 50
SALES (corp-wide): 9.2MM **Privately Held**
WEB: www.americanalliancels.com
SIC: 7699 7381 Sewer cleaning & rodding; protective services, guard
PA: American Alliance Always Available, Incorporated
2400 Lindbergh St
Auburn CA 95602
916 348-3097

(P-17960)
AMERICAN RESIDENTIAL SVCS LLC
Also Called: Rescue Rooter Bay Area South
2305 Paragon Dr, San Jose (95131-1309)
P.O. Box 640845 (95164-0845)
PHONE.....................408 435-3810
Fax: 408 287-3736
Earnest Bell, *Manager*
James McMahon, *CFO*
Peggy Foreman, *Financial Exec*
Theresa Burke, *Personnel Exec*
Laura Myking, *Personnel Exec*
EMP: 60
SALES (corp-wide): 2.8B **Privately Held**
WEB: www.ars.com
SIC: 7699 1711 Sewer cleaning & rodding; plumbing contractors
PA: American Residential Services Llc
965 Ridge Lake Blvd # 201
Memphis TN 38120
901 271-9700

(P-17961)
AMERICAN VISION WINDOWS INC
2125 N Madera Rd Ste A, Simi Valley (93065-7709)
PHONE.....................805 582-1833
Fax: 805 915-1325
William Herren, *CEO*
Frank Kolesar, *CFO*
Al Alfieri, *Vice Pres*
Monica Estrada, *Vice Pres*
Cybill Pereau, *Office Mgr*
EMP: 215

SALES (est): 27.6MM **Privately Held**
SIC: 7699 1799 5031 Door & window repair; home/office interiors finishing, furnishing & remodeling; metal doors, sash & trim

(P-17962)
ARNIES SUPPLIES SERVICE LTD
1501 N Ditman Ave, Los Angeles (90063-2501)
P.O. Box 26, Philadelphia PA (19105-0026)
PHONE.....................323 263-1696
Arnold Espino, *President*
EMP: 60
SQ FT: 806
SALES (corp-wide): 5MM **Privately Held**
SIC: 7699 Pallet repair
PA: Arnie's Supplies Service Ltd Inc
1541 N Ditman Ave
Los Angeles CA 90063
323 263-1696

(P-17963)
AUTOMATED SYSTEMS AMERICA INC
Also Called: Asai
101 N Brand Blvd Ste 1230, Glendale (91203-2677)
PHONE.....................877 500-0002
Fax: 818 957-5482
John Thomas Steely, *President*
Jackie Steely, *CFO*
Kristen Taylor, *Manager*
Terry King, *Accounts Mgr*
EMP: 52
SQ FT: 1,200
SALES (est): 52.2MM **Privately Held**
WEB: www.asaiatm.com
SIC: 7699 3578 6099 Automated teller machine (ATM) repair; automatic teller machines (ATM); automated teller machine (ATM) network

(P-17964)
CALVIN KLEIN INC
48650 Seminole Dr Ste 182, Cabazon (92230-2156)
PHONE.....................951 849-9538
Shelly Barela, *Manager*
EMP: 50
SALES (corp-wide): 8B **Publicly Held**
SIC: 7699 Cleaning services
HQ: Calvin Klein, Inc.
205 W 39th St Lbby 2
New York NY 10018
212 719-2600

(P-17965)
CALVIN KLEIN INC
8300 Arroyo Cir Ste 260, Gilroy (95020-7335)
PHONE.....................408 842-9132
Brian Gong, *Principal*
EMP: 50
SALES (corp-wide): 8B **Publicly Held**
SIC: 7699 Cleaning services
HQ: Calvin Klein, Inc.
205 W 39th St Lbby 2
New York NY 10018
212 719-2600

(P-17966)
CHROMALLOY SAN DIEGO CORP
7007 Consolidated Way, San Diego (92121-2604)
PHONE.....................858 877-2800
Armand F Lauzon Jr, *CEO*
Carlo Luzzatto, *President*
Bob Shambaugh, *COO*
David G Albert, *Vice Pres*
Michael Beffel, *Vice Pres*
EMP: 120
SQ FT: 120,000
SALES (est): 17.7MM
SALES (corp-wide): 3B **Publicly Held**
WEB: www.chromalloysatx.com
SIC: 7699 3724 Aircraft & heavy equipment repair services; aircraft engines & engine parts
HQ: Chromalloy American Llc
330 Blaisdell Rd
Orangeburg NY 10962
845 230-7355

(P-17967)
COASTAL INDUSTRIAL SVCS INC
2209 Zeus Ct, Bakersfield (93308-6867)
PHONE.....................661 392-0001
Bill Boyd, *Principal*
EMP: 89
SALES (corp-wide): 7.4MM **Privately Held**
SIC: 7699 7349 Tank repair & cleaning services; cleaning service, industrial or commercial
PA: Coastal Industrial Services, Inc.
2209 Zeus Ct
Bakersfield CA 93308
360 912-0108

(P-17968)
COLLECTORS UNIVERSE INC (PA)
1921 E Alton Ave Ste 100, Santa Ana (92705-5845)
P.O. Box 6280, Newport Beach (92658-6280)
PHONE.....................949 567-1234
Fax: 714 833-7955
Robert G Deuster, *CEO*
David G Hall, *President*
Don Willis, *President*
Joseph J Wallace, *CFO*
Stephen H Mayer, *Vice Pres*
EMP: 98
SQ FT: 48,500
SALES: 60.9MM **Publicly Held**
WEB: www.collectors.com
SIC: 7699 Hobby & collectors services

(P-17969)
COMPLETE EQUIPMENT REPAIR
143 Willow Pass Rd, Oroville (95966-8515)
PHONE.....................530 589-1187
Curtis Ensiminger, *Owner*
EMP: 70
SALES (est): 1.6MM **Privately Held**
SIC: 7699 Industrial equipment services

(P-17970)
D S R INC
Also Called: Mr Rooter
3503 Arundell Cir Ste A, Ventura (93003-4916)
PHONE.....................805 275-0039
Richard Svestak, *President*
Richard Svestka, *Manager*
EMP: 70
SQ FT: 6,200
SALES (est): 6.1MM **Privately Held**
SIC: 7699 Sewer cleaning & rodding

(P-17971)
DESIGN MACHINE AND MFG
2491 Simpson St, Kingsburg (93631-9501)
PHONE.....................559 897-7374
Abe Wiabe, *Owner*
John Zweigle, *General Mgr*
EMP: 50
SALES (est): 212.6K **Privately Held**
SIC: 7699 Industrial machinery & equipment repair

(P-17972)
DICALITE MINERALS CORP
36994 Summit Lake Rd, Burney (96013-9636)
PHONE.....................530 335-5451
Fax: 530 335-5348
Raymond Perlman, *President*
Derek J Cusack, *VP Opers*
Rocky Torgrimson, *Opers Mgr*
M B Greenley, *VP Sales*
Doug Witherspoon, *Manager*
▼ EMP: 70
SQ FT: 3,000
SALES (est): 9.6MM **Privately Held**
WEB: www.dicalite-dicaperl.com
SIC: 7699 Filter cleaning

(P-17973)
FLAIR CLEANERS INC
27011 Mcbean Pkwy, Valencia (91355-5166)
PHONE.....................661 753-9900
Fax: 661 799-0035
Gary Futterman, *Branch Mgr*
EMP: 79

PRODUCTS & SERVICES SECTION

7699 - Repair Shop & Related Svcs, NEC County (P-17994)

SALES (corp-wide): 6.4MM **Privately Held**
SIC: 7699 Cleaning services
PA: Flair Cleaners, Inc.
  4060 Laurel Canyon Blvd
  Studio City CA 91604
  818 761-3282

(P-17974)
FOSTER DAIRY FARMS
1472 Hall Rd, Hickman (95323-9615)
PHONE.................................209 874-9605
Ronald Hill, *Manager*
Ted Bracht, *Director*
EMP: 200
SALES (corp-wide): 433.7MM **Privately Held**
SIC: 7699 Farm machinery repair
PA: Foster Dairy Farms
  529 Kansas Ave
  Modesto CA 95351
  209 576-3400

(P-17975)
GENESIS TECH PARTNERS LLC
21540 Plummer St Ste A, Chatsworth (91311-4143)
PHONE.................................800 950-2647
Sandy D Morford,
Dean Devore, *CFO*
Haresh Satiani,
EMP: 175
SQ FT: 3,000
SALES (est): 4.9MM
SALES (corp-wide): 14.3B **Publicly Held**
SIC: 7699 Medical equipment repair, non-electric
HQ: Cohr, Inc.
  10510 Twin Lakes Pkwy
  Charlotte NC 28269
  704 948-5700

(P-17976)
GLOBAL DEV STRATEGIES INC
9985 Businesspark Ave A, San Diego (92131-1132)
P.O. Box 26997 (92196-0997)
PHONE.................................858 408-1173
Marlene Stephens, *President*
Brandon Campbell, *CFO*
EMP: 60
SALES: 14.7MM **Privately Held**
WEB: www.globalstrategy.biz
SIC: 7699 Garage door repair

(P-17977)
GOODRICH CORPORATION
Goodrich Wheel and Brake Svcs
9920 Freeman Ave, Santa Fe Springs (90670-3421)
PHONE.................................562 944-4441
Hosrow Bordbar, *Manager*
Rudy Delarosa, *Officer*
Richard Bentley, *Business Mgr*
Marie Garnica, *Human Res Dir*
Mark Posada, *Purch Dir*
EMP: 55
SALES (corp-wide): 56.1B **Publicly Held**
WEB: www.bfgoodrich.com
SIC: 7699 Tank repair & cleaning services
HQ: Goodrich Corporation
  4 Coliseum Ctr 2730 W
  Charlotte NC 28217
  704 423-7000

(P-17978)
HAWKER PACIFIC AEROSPACE
11240 Sherman Way, Sun Valley (91352-4942)
PHONE.................................818 765-6201
Fax: 818 765-2065
Bernd Riggers, *CEO*
Troy Trower, *CFO*
Blas Maidagan, *Exec VP*
Brian Carr, *Vice Pres*
Valerie Fortner, *Managing Dir*
EMP: 355
SQ FT: 193,000
SALES (est): 60.7MM
SALES (corp-wide): 34.4B **Privately Held**
WEB: www.hawker.com
SIC: 7699 5088 3728 Hydraulic equipment repair; aircraft & parts; aircraft parts & equipment
HQ: Lufthansa Technik Ag
  Weg Beim Jager 193
  Hamburg 22335
  405 070-3667

(P-17979)
HOFFMAN SOUTHWEST CORP
Also Called: Roto-Rooter
1183 N Kraemer Pl, Anaheim (92806-1923)
PHONE.................................714 630-0404
Fax: 714 630-2243
Don Hatcher, *Manager*
David Carpenter, *Production*
Dennis Hoffman, *Contractor*
EMP: 50
SALES (corp-wide): 53.4MM **Privately Held**
SIC: 7699 1711 Sewer cleaning & rodding; plumbing contractors
PA: Hoffman Southwest Corp.
  23311 Madero
  Mission Viejo CA 92691
  949 380-4161

(P-17980)
HOFFMAN SOUTHWEST CORP
Also Called: Roto-Rooter
8930 Center Ave, Rancho Cucamonga (91730-5328)
PHONE.................................909 397-0567
Dan Chavez, *Manager*
Jerry Martinez, *Manager*
EMP: 52
SALES (corp-wide): 53.4MM **Privately Held**
SIC: 7699 Sewer cleaning & rodding
PA: Hoffman Southwest Corp.
  23311 Madero
  Mission Viejo CA 92691
  949 380-4161

(P-17981)
HOFFMAN TEXAS INC
24971 Avenue Stanford, Valencia (91355-1278)
PHONE.................................661 257-9200
Gary Thomas, *Manager*
EMP: 50
SQ FT: 6,936
SALES (corp-wide): 53.4MM **Privately Held**
WEB: www.rw-rotorooter.com
SIC: 7699 Sewer cleaning & rodding
HQ: Hoffman Texas, Inc.
  23311 Madero
  Mission Viejo CA 92691
  949 380-4161

(P-17982)
HRD AERO SYSTEMS INC
Also Called: Hrd Oxygens
25555 Avenue Stanford, Valencia (91355-1101)
PHONE.................................661 295-0670
Tom Salamone, *President*
EMP: 65
SQ FT: 8,000
SALES (est): 1.2MM **Privately Held**
WEB: www.hrd-aerosystems.com
SIC: 7699 Aircraft & heavy equipment repair services; aircraft flight instrument repair; aviation propeller & blade repair

(P-17983)
HRD AERO SYSTEMS INC (PA)
25555 Avenue Stanford, Valencia (91355-1101)
PHONE.................................661 295-0670
Fax: 661 295-0672
Tom Salamone, *President*
Tim McBride, *CFO*
Paul Zapata, *Regional Mgr*
JC Johnson, *General Mgr*
Albert Leon, *MIS Dir*
◆ EMP: 94
SQ FT: 70,000
SALES (est): 14.9MM **Privately Held**
SIC: 7699 8711 Aircraft & heavy equipment repair services; aircraft flight instrument repair; aviation propeller & blade repair; aviation &/or aeronautical engineering

(P-17984)
INDUS LIGHT & MAGIC (VANCO) LL
1110 Gorgas Ave, San Francisco (94129-1406)
PHONE.................................415 292-4671
Steve Condiotti, *CEO*
Barbara Bellanca, *Treasurer*
Chrissie England, *Senior VP*
Lynwen Brennan, *Executive*
Gretchen Libby, *Executive*
▲ EMP: 113
SALES (est): 26.7MM **Publicly Held**
SIC: 7699 Industrial equipment services
HQ: Lucasfilm Ltd. Llc
  1110 Gorgas Ave Bldg C-Hr
  San Francisco CA 94129
  415 623-1000

(P-17985)
INLAND BUSINESS MACHINES INC (DH)
1326 N Market Blvd, Sacramento (95834-1912)
PHONE.................................916 928-0770
Fax: 916 928-0889
Liz Stafford, *President*
John Marlett, *Vice Pres*
Ralph Briggs, *Info Tech Mgr*
Ben Ray, *Purchasing*
Ken Barnes, *Sales Mgr*
EMP: 79
SALES (est): 15.8MM
SALES (corp-wide): 18B **Publicly Held**
WEB: www.ibs-team.com
SIC: 7699 5044 5999 Printing trades machinery & equipment repair; office equipment; photocopy machines
HQ: Global Imaging Systems, Inc.
  3903 Northdale Blvd 200w
  Tampa FL 33624
  813 960-5508

(P-17986)
INNOVATIVE MEDICAL SOLUTIONS
3002 Dow Ave Ste 110, Tustin (92780-7247)
PHONE.................................714 505-7070
Fax: 714 505-7074
James Stevens, *President*
Stephen Ohare, *Officer*
Elizabeth Stevens, *Vice Pres*
Laura Robins, *Systems Staff*
Tom Bennett, *Sales Mgr*
EMP: 58
SALES: 3MM **Privately Held**
SIC: 7699 5047 Hospital equipment repair services; medical & hospital equipment

(P-17987)
KONE INC
9850 Businesspark Ave, San Diego (92131-1121)
PHONE.................................858 578-5100
Fax: 858 679-2410
Jeff Blum, *Manager*
Kevin Wigley, *Program Dir*
EMP: 80
SALES (corp-wide): 583.7MM **Privately Held**
WEB: www.us.kone.com
SIC: 7699 3534 Elevators: inspection, service & repair; elevators & moving stairways
HQ: Kone Inc.
  1 Kone Ct
  Moline IL 61265
  309 764-6771

(P-17988)
LA HYDRO-JET ROOTER SVC INC
Also Called: La Hydrojet
10639 Wixom St, Sun Valley (91352-4603)
PHONE.................................818 768-4225
Daniel Baldwin, *President*
Lori Baldwin, *CFO*
EMP: 68 EST: 1991
SALES (est): 9MM **Privately Held**
SIC: 7699 Sewer cleaning & rodding

(P-17989)
N & S TRACTOR CO (PA)
600 S St 59, Merced (95341-6543)
P.O. Box 910 (95341-0910)
PHONE.................................209 383-5888
Fax: 209 722-2411
Arthur R Nutcher, *CEO*
Mary Wallace, *Corp Secy*
Stephanie Nutcher, *Vice Pres*
▲ EMP: 60
SQ FT: 8,700
SALES (est): 12.1MM **Privately Held**
WEB: www.nstractor.com
SIC: 7699 5083 Farm machinery repair; agricultural machinery & equipment

(P-17990)
NATIONWIDE SEC & BLDG SVCS INC (PA)
9045 Imperial Hwy, Downey (90242-2711)
PHONE.................................800 804-0059
Rhonda Blanchard, *CEO*
Gary Blanchard, *Vice Pres*
Sheryl Bowman Cordero, *Vice Pres*
Bryan Sampson, *Info Tech Mgr*
Dawn Underwood, *Human Res Dir*
EMP: 60
SQ FT: 14,000
SALES: 24.3MM **Privately Held**
WEB: www.nsbs.net
SIC: 7699 7349 1793 Miscellaneous building item repair services; building maintenance services; glass & glazing work

(P-17991)
NIACC-AVITECH TECHNOLOGIES INC (PA)
245 W Dakota Ave, Clovis (93612-5608)
PHONE.................................559 291-2500
Fax: 559 347-6815
Jeff Andrews, *CEO*
Thomas S Irwin, *Treasurer*
Elizabeth R Letendre, *Admin Sec*
Betty Singh, *Admin Asst*
Ben Merlo, *Info Tech Mgr*
EMP: 80
SALES (est): 14.5MM **Privately Held**
WEB: www.niacctech.com
SIC: 7699 3471 Aircraft flight instrument repair; plating of metals or formed products

(P-17992)
NOR-CAL PIPELINE SERVICES
5050 Bus Center Dr 200, Fairfield (94534-6886)
PHONE.................................530 673-3886
David Jaeger, *President*
David L Jaeger, *Vice Pres*
William Jaeger, *Admin Sec*
Larry Lopes, *Opers Mgr*
Roxanne Ohanian, *Manager*
EMP: 70
SALES (est): 9.4MM **Privately Held**
SIC: 7699 Sewer cleaning & rodding

(P-17993)
OTIS ELEVATOR COMPANY
711 E Ball Rd Ste 200, Anaheim (92805-5960)
PHONE.................................714 758-9593
Fax: 714 758-9658
Ricardo Castro, *Manager*
Joe Marquez, *Purchasing*
EMP: 50
SALES (corp-wide): 56.1B **Publicly Held**
WEB: www.otis.com
SIC: 7699 3534 1796 Elevators: inspection, service & repair; elevators & moving stairways; installing building equipment
HQ: Otis Elevator Company
  10 Farm Springs Rd
  Farmington CT 06032
  860 676-6000

(P-17994)
OXYHEAL MEDICAL SYSTEMS INC
3224 Hoover Ave, National City (91950-7224)
PHONE.................................619 336-2022
W Ted Gurnee, *CEO*
Judy Long, *Finance*
Merlyn Baker, *Accounts Mgr*

(PA)=Parent Co (HQ)=Headquarters (DH)=Div Headquarters
✪ = New Business established in last 2 years

7699 - Repair Shop & Related Svcs, NEC County (P-17995)

EMP: 200
SALES: 1.8MM Privately Held
SIC: 7699 Engine repair & replacement, non-automotive; industrial machinery & equipment repair

(P-17995)
PACIFIC ARSPC RSURCES TECH LLC
18200 Phantom W, Victorville (92394-7971)
PHONE.................................760 530-1767
Johan Claasen, *CEO*
Thad Hoffmaster, *President*
Rob Hessong, *COO*
Janet Westhoff, *Technology*
Hongvan Vincent, *Manager*
▲ **EMP:** 62
SALES (est): 10.2MM Privately Held
SIC: 7699 Aircraft & heavy equipment repair services

(P-17996)
PACIFIC CRANE MAINT CO LP (PA)
250 W Wardlow Rd, Long Beach (90807-4429)
PHONE.................................562 432-8066
Fax: 562 432-4828
Steven B McLeod, *Partner*
Joe Gregorio,
EMP: 99
SALES (est): 41.7MM Privately Held
WEB: www.brockwaymoran.com
SIC: 7699 Construction equipment repair

(P-17997)
PACIFIC GAS TURBINE CENTER LLC
7007 Consolidated Way, San Diego (92121-2604)
PHONE.................................858 877-2910
Graham Bell,
Susan Stewart, *Purchasing*
David Brannon, *Facilities Mgr*
John Brumlay, *Manager*
Nat Love, *Manager*
◆ **EMP:** 101
SQ FT: 110,000
SALES (est): 4.5MM Privately Held
SIC: 7699 Industrial equipment services; engine repair & replacement, non-automotive

(P-17998)
PACWEST INSTRUMENT LABS
Also Called: Pacific Southwest Instruments
1721 Railroad St, Corona (92880-2511)
PHONE.................................951 737-0790
Fax: 909 273-7149
Jim Joubert, *President*
Ray McDonald, *Vice Pres*
David Kertz, *Controller*
Dawn Foster, *Bookkeeper*
Rich Lares, *Purchasing*
EMP: 51
SQ FT: 37,000
SALES (est): 9.8MM Privately Held
WEB: www.psilabs.com
SIC: 7699 7629 Aircraft flight instrument repair; aircraft electrical equipment repair

(P-17999)
PEGGS COMPANY INC (PA)
4851 Felspar St, Riverside (92509-3024)
PHONE.................................253 584-9548
Fax: 951 360-9186
Chresten Revelle Nelson, *CEO*
John L Peggs, *President*
Susan Harris, *Manager*
◆ **EMP:** 100
SQ FT: 80,000
SALES (est): 26.9MM Privately Held
WEB: www.thepeggscompany.com
SIC: 7699 3496 5046 7359 Shopping cart repair; miscellaneous fabricated wire products; commercial equipment; equipment rental & leasing

(P-18000)
PKL SERVICES INC
14265 Danielson St C1, Poway (92064-8818)
PHONE.................................858 679-1755
Fax: 858 679-1750
Samuel Flores Jr, *President*
Alex Delacruz, *CFO*
Paul Callan, *Exec VP*
David K Howell, *Vice Pres*
Michael Nisley, *Vice Pres*
EMP: 160
SQ FT: 6,000
SALES (est): 18.6MM Privately Held
WEB: www.pklservices.com
SIC: 7699 Aircraft & heavy equipment repair services

(P-18001)
PROPULSION CONTROLS ENGRG (PA)
1620 Rigel St, San Diego (92113-3832)
P.O. Box 13606 (92170-3606)
PHONE.................................619 235-0961
David P Clapp, *CEO*
John P Reilly III, *Corp Secy*
Ehrich Steinmetz, *General Mgr*
Scott Akau, *Office Mgr*
Eric Higgins, *Opers Mgr*
EMP: 70
SQ FT: 22,000
SALES (est): 26MM Privately Held
WEB: www.pcehawaii.com
SIC: 7699 Boiler repair shop

(P-18002)
RAM-MAR PAINTING INC
11768 Mariposa Rd, Hesperia (92345-1622)
PHONE.................................760 949-4844
Fax: 760 949-7437
Mark Robson, *President*
Nancy Hernandez, *Treasurer*
Ramiro Mejia, *Vice Pres*
Tammi Robson, *Manager*
Judi Sanders, *Manager*
EMP: 100
SQ FT: 2,500
SALES (est): 5.6MM Privately Held
WEB: www.ram-mar.com
SIC: 7699 5231 7359 1721 Industrial equipment services; paint & painting supplies; equipment rental & leasing; exterior residential painting contractor

(P-18003)
RAYMOND HANDLING CONCEPTS CORP (PA)
41400 Boyce Rd, Fremont (94538-3113)
PHONE.................................510 745-7500
Stephen S Raymond, *President*
Ron Curtis, *Vice Pres*
Steven Koel, *Vice Pres*
Al Seiler, *Vice Pres*
EMP: 60
SQ FT: 32,000
SALES (est): 42.3MM Privately Held
WEB: www.raymondhandling.com
SIC: 7699 5084 7359 7629 Industrial equipment services; materials handling machinery; equipment rental & leasing; electrical repair shops

(P-18004)
RENOVO SOLUTIONS LLC
4 Executive Cir Ste 185, Irvine (92614-6791)
PHONE.................................714 599-7969
Sandy Morford, *CEO*
Haresh Saitiani, *COO*
Donald K Carson, *Vice Pres*
Chuck Dille, *District Mgr*
David Momeyer, *District Mgr*
EMP: 270
SQ FT: 5,400
SALES: 57.8MM Privately Held
SIC: 7699 Hospital equipment repair services

(P-18005)
RETRONIX INTERNATIONAL INC
Also Called: Retronix Semiconductors
65 Enterprise, Aliso Viejo (92656-2705)
PHONE.................................949 388-6930
Fax: 949 388-6931
Anthony Boswell, *President*
Mark Diamond, *COO*
Jim Beatty, *Vice Pres*
Stuart Proctor, *Vice Pres*
Stuartor Proct, *Sales Mgr*
EMP: 90
SQ FT: 5,000

SALES: 7.8MM Privately Held
SIC: 7699 Industrial machinery & equipment repair

(P-18006)
ROTO ROOTER PLUMBING & DRAIN S
796 N State St, Hemet (92543-1401)
PHONE.................................951 658-8541
Fax: 951 652-9515
Craig Nunez, *General Mgr*
EMP: 50
SALES (est): 1.4MM Privately Held
SIC: 7699 Sewer cleaning & rodding

(P-18007)
ROTO-ROOTER SERVICES COMPANY
220 Demeter St, East Palo Alto (94303-1303)
PHONE.................................650 322-2366
Cory Feverson, *Branch Mgr*
EMP: 75
SALES (corp-wide): 1.5B Publicly Held
SIC: 7699 Sewer cleaning & rodding
HQ: Roto-Rooter Services Company
2500 Chemed Ctr 255e5th
Cincinnati OH 45202
513 762-6690

(P-18008)
RS CALIBRATION SERVICES INC
1047 Serpentine Ln # 500, Pleasanton (94566-4786)
PHONE.................................925 462-4217
Fax: 925 426-0092
Ralph Sabiel, *President*
Debbie Sabiel, *Treasurer*
Kelly Harris, *Admin Asst*
Sophia Martineau, *Comp Lab Dir*
Christopher Tacotaco, *QA Dir*
EMP: 50
SQ FT: 5,000
SALES (est): 10.8MM Privately Held
WEB: www.rscalibration.com
SIC: 7699 8734 Professional instrument repair services; calibration & certification

(P-18009)
S A CAMP PUMP COMPANY
Also Called: SA Camp Pump and Drilling Co
17876 Zerker Rd, Bakersfield (93308-9221)
P.O. Box 82575 (93380-2575)
PHONE.................................661 399-2976
James S Camp, *President*
John Reiland, *Vice Pres*
MEI Huang, *Controller*
Don Pedersen, *Sales Staff*
EMP: 60
SQ FT: 10,000
SALES (est): 11.4MM
SALES (corp-wide): 19.8MM Privately Held
WEB: www.sacamp.net
SIC: 7699 Agricultural equipment repair services
PA: S A Camp Companies
17876 Zerker Rd
Bakersfield CA 93308
661 399-4451

(P-18010)
SCIENTIFIC CONCEPTS INC
303 Vintage Park Dr # 220, Foster City (94404-1166)
PHONE.................................650 578-1142
Charles Morrison Sr, *President*
Mike Flanagan, *Vice Pres*
Klahn Gboloh Jorbah, *Vice Pres*
Joe Stovall, *Vice Pres*
Carol Morrison, *Admin Sec*
EMP: 350
SQ FT: 23,000
SALES (est): 20.4MM Privately Held
WEB: www.scientificconceptsinc.com
SIC: 7699 Cleaning services

(P-18011)
SEARS ROEBUCK AND CO
100 Brea Mall, Brea (92821-5796)
PHONE.................................714 256-7328
Fax: 714 256-9218
Penny Bishop, *Manager*

EMP: 200
SALES (corp-wide): 25.1MM Publicly Held
SIC: 7699 Household appliance repair services
HQ: Sears, Roebuck And Co.
3333 Beverly Rd
Hoffman Estates IL 60179
847 286-2500

(P-18012)
SEARS ROEBUCK AND CO
Also Called: Direct Delivery Center
5691 E Philadelphia St, Ontario (91761-2805)
PHONE.................................909 390-4210
Fax: 909 390-4215
Rick Ings, *Manager*
Chris Merandas, *Manager*
EMP: 125
SALES (corp-wide): 25.1MM Publicly Held
SIC: 7699 7629 Household appliance repair services; electrical repair shops
HQ: Sears, Roebuck And Co.
3333 Beverly Rd
Hoffman Estates IL 60179
847 286-2500

(P-18013)
SEARS ROEBUCK AND CO
Also Called: Sears Service and Parts Center
3365 W Sussex Way, Fresno (93722-4988)
PHONE.................................559 244-6214
Fax: 559 226-4382
Gary Willis, *Manager*
EMP: 111
SALES (corp-wide): 25.1MM Publicly Held
SIC: 7699 7623 5722 7629 Household appliance repair services; refrigeration service & repair; appliance parts; electrical repair shops
HQ: Sears, Roebuck And Co.
3333 Beverly Rd
Hoffman Estates IL 60179
847 286-2500

(P-18014)
SECURITY CENTRAL INC
Also Called: Reed Brothers Security
4432 Telegraph Ave, Oakland (94609-2018)
PHONE.................................510 652-2477
Fax: 510 652-7081
Ronald Reed, *President*
Randall Reed, *Treasurer*
Michael Salk, *Vice Pres*
Lisa Rose, *Accountant*
Dave Williams, *Buyer*
EMP: 51
SQ FT: 19,000
SALES (est): 10.3MM Privately Held
SIC: 7699 5099 5466 5999 Locksmith shop; locks & lock sets; fences or posts, ornamental iron or steel; electronic parts & equipment

(P-18015)
SIEMENS GOVERNMENT TECH INC
Also Called: Dresser Rand, S
1675 Brandywine Ave Ste F, Chula Vista (91911-6064)
PHONE.................................619 656-4740
Fax: 619 656-4819
Joshua Guedsse, *Manager*
Robert Talamantez, *Foreman/Supr*
Franky Lane, *Manager*
Pearly Ferrer, *Accounts Mgr*
EMP: 50
SALES (corp-wide): 83.5B Privately Held
WEB: www.dresser-rand.com
SIC: 7699 3731 Industrial machinery & equipment repair; shipbuilding & repairing
HQ: Siemens Government Technologies, Inc.
2231 Crystal Dr Ste 700
Arlington VA 22202
703 860-1574

▲ = Import ▼ = Export
◆ = Import/Export

PRODUCTS & SERVICES SECTION
7812 - Motion Picture & Video Tape Production County (P-18036)

(P-18016)
SOUTH BAY SAND BLASTING AND TA
326 W 30th St, National City (91950-7206)
P.O. Box 13009, San Diego (92170-3009)
PHONE................................619 238-8338
Fax: 619 238-8341
Canuto Lopez, *CEO*
Mario Hernandez, *Prdtn Mgr*
Barbara Schilf, *Manager*
Barbara Schilfs, *Accounts Mgr*
EMP: 100
SQ FT: 60,000
SALES (est): 16MM **Privately Held**
SIC: 7699 4212 Ship boiler & tank cleaning & repair, contractors; ship scaling, contractors; hazardous waste transport

(P-18017)
SOUTHBAY SNDBLST & TANK CLG
3589 Dalbergia St, San Diego (92113-3810)
P.O. Box 13009 (92170-3009)
PHONE................................619 238-8338
Adam Juarez, *President*
EMP: 100 EST: 2015
SALES (est): 480.2K **Privately Held**
SIC: 7699 4212 Ship boiler & tank cleaning & repair, contractors; ship scaling, contractors; hazardous waste transport

(P-18018)
SPEEDY LOCKSMITH
429 Avnida De La Estrella, San Clemente (92672)
P.O. Box 5075, Oceanside (92052-5075)
PHONE................................760 439-5000
Micky Abdallah, *Owner*
EMP: 70 EST: 1991
SALES: 320K **Privately Held**
WEB: www.speedylocksmith.com
SIC: 7699 Locksmith shop

(P-18019)
SUPERIOR MARINE SOLUTIONS LLC
2700 Hoover Ave Ste A, National City (91950-6626)
PHONE................................619 773-7800
Robert Laubengayer,
EMP: 99
SALES (est): 3.8MM **Privately Held**
SIC: 7699 Cash register repair

(P-18020)
SURVIVAL SYSTEMS INTL INC (PA)
Also Called: Ssi
34140 Valley Center Rd, Valley Center (92082-6017)
P.O. Box 1855 (92082-1855)
PHONE................................760 749-6800
Fax: 760 749-6804
George Leopold Beatty, *CEO*
Mark Beatty, *Vice Pres*
Colin Hooper, *Vice Pres*
George Teece, *Vice Pres*
Barbara Parker, *Accountant*
▲ EMP: 85
SQ FT: 100,000
SALES: 32.1MM **Privately Held**
WEB: www.survivalsystemsint.net
SIC: 7699 3531 3086 Industrial equipment services; boat repair; life saving & survival equipment, non-medical: repair; winches; plastics foam products

(P-18021)
TARSCO INC (DH)
11905 Regentview Ave, Downey (90241-5515)
PHONE................................562 231-5400
Terrance F Warren, *CEO*
Tracy Cody, *Principal*
Danielle Torres, *Office Mgr*
▼ EMP: 120
SQ FT: 53,000
SALES (est): 16.7MM
SALES (corp-wide): 65.5MM **Privately Held**
WEB: www.tarsco.com
SIC: 7699 Tank repair

HQ: Tarsco Holdings, Llc
11905 Regentview Ave
Downey CA 90241
562 231-5400

(P-18022)
TECH KNOWLEDGE ASSOCIATES LLC
Also Called: Tka
1 Centerpointe Dr Ste 200, La Palma (90623-2529)
PHONE................................714 735-3810
Joe Randolph, *CEO*
Ed Wong, *CFO*
Steve Gilbert, *Exec VP*
Stephen Taylor, *Business Dir*
EMP: 80 EST: 2011
SALES: 45.2MM
SALES (corp-wide): 5.6B **Privately Held**
SIC: 7699 Medical equipment repair, non-electric
HQ: St. Joseph Health System
3345 Michelson Dr Ste 100
Irvine CA 92612
949 381-4000

(P-18023)
TED LEVINE DRUM CO (PA)
1817 Chico Ave, South El Monte (91733-2943)
P.O. Box 3246 (91733-0246)
PHONE................................626 579-1084
Fax: 626 579-9176
Ozzie Levine, *President*
Harvey Kale, *COO*
Guillermo Sandoval, *Business Mgr*
Tess Samoy, *Accountant*
Raymond Ramos, *Opers Mgr*
EMP: 80
SQ FT: 200,000
SALES (est): 13.4MM **Privately Held**
WEB: www.tldrumco.com
SIC: 7699 4959 3412 Industrial equipment services; sanitary services; metal barrels, drums & pails

(P-18024)
THARP TRUCK RENTAL INC (PA)
Also Called: Depot
15243 Road 192, Porterville (93257-8967)
PHONE................................559 782-5800
Morris A Tharp, *CEO*
Carol R Tharp, *Corp Secy*
Casey O Tharp, *Vice Pres*
Bruce Greer, *General Mgr*
◆ EMP: 125
SQ FT: 5,000
SALES (est): 11.2MM **Privately Held**
WEB: www.emtharp.com
SIC: 7699 5013 5511 5012 Agricultural equipment repair services; motor vehicle supplies & new parts; trucks, tractors & trailers: new & used; automobiles & other motor vehicles

(P-18025)
THYSSENKRUPP ELEVATOR CORP
6087 Triangle Dr, Commerce (90040-3642)
PHONE................................323 278-9888
Toll Free:........................877 -
Joe Gonzalles, *Manager*
Curlene Allen, *CFO*
Kirk Vazel, *CFO*
James Riegler, *Exec VP*
Marie Beth Der, *Vice Pres*
EMP: 50
SALES (corp-wide): 47.2B **Privately Held**
WEB: www.thyssenkruppelevator.com
SIC: 7699 1796 Miscellaneous building item repair services; elevator installation & conversion
HQ: Thyssenkrupp Elevator Corporation
11605 Haynes Bridge Rd # 650
Alpharetta GA 30009
678 319-3241

(P-18026)
TURBINE REPAIR SERVICES LLC (PA)
1838 E Cedar St, Ontario (91761-7763)
PHONE................................909 947-2256
Victor M Sanchez, *Mng Member*
Dave Meyer,

Danny Sanchez,
Cesar Siordia,
Michael Dorrel, *Mng Member*
EMP: 59
SQ FT: 12,000
SALES (est): 9.8MM **Privately Held**
WEB: www.steamandgas.com
SIC: 7699 Mechanical instrument repair

(P-18027)
UNICO INDUSTRIAL SERVICE CO (PA)
945 Tyler St, Benicia (94510-2915)
P.O. Box 887 (94510-0887)
PHONE................................707 736-8787
Dean Gordon Potter, *CEO*
D Gordon Potter, *President*
EMP: 50
SQ FT: 10,000
SALES (est): 3.6MM **Privately Held**
WEB: www.unicoservices.com
SIC: 7699 3599 Industrial machinery & equipment repair; machine shop, jobbing & repair

(P-18028)
UNITED CALIFORNIA GLASS & DOOR
745 Cesar Chavez, San Francisco (94124-1211)
PHONE................................415 824-8500
Fax: 415 648-3838
Judith Ticktin, *President*
Jerry Bentsch, *Project Mgr*
David Ticktin, *Controller*
▲ EMP: 70
SQ FT: 31,000
SALES: 10.2MM **Privately Held**
WEB: www.ucgd.com
SIC: 7699 1793 Door & window repair; glass & glazing work

(P-18029)
UNITED SERVICE TECH INC
21801 Cactus Ave Ste A, Riverside (92518-3020)
PHONE................................714 224-1406
Robert J Heidkamp, *CEO*
Sandra Smelcer, *Treasurer*
Rodger Smelcer, *Vice Pres*
Vince Vidales, *Regional Mgr*
Terrie Heidkamp, *Admin Sec*
EMP: 56
SQ FT: 2,400
SALES (est): 8MM **Privately Held**
SIC: 7699 5963 Industrial equipment services; food services, direct sales

(P-18030)
UPWIND BLADE SOLUTIONS INC
4863 Shawline St Ste A, San Diego (92111-1435)
PHONE................................866 927-3142
Marty Crotty, *CEO*
Bo Thisted, *President*
Bryan Coggins, *CFO*
Jenny Belford, *Accountant*
Ben Bruner, *Controller*
EMP: 139
SALES (est): 3.1MM
SALES (corp-wide): 9B **Privately Held**
SIC: 7699 Pumps & pumping equipment repair
HQ: Upwind Solutions, Inc.
4863 Shawline St Ste A
San Diego CA 92111

(P-18031)
VELOCITY AROSPC - BURBANK INC (HQ)
2840 N Ontario St, Burbank (91504-2015)
PHONE................................818 246-8431
Dale Gable, *CEO*
Dennis Suedkamp, *President*
Jeff Black, *Exec VP*
Daniel McDonald, *General Mgr*
Philip Vaillancourt, *General Mgr*
EMP: 56
SALES (est): 7MM
SALES (corp-wide): 27.8MM **Privately Held**
SIC: 7699 Aircraft & heavy equipment repair services

PA: Velocity Aerospace Group, Inc.
2591 Dallas Pkwy Ste 300
Frisco TX 75034
316 847-5606

(P-18032)
VEOLIA ES INDUSTRIAL SVCS INC
Also Called: Brand Precision
4501 California Ct, Benicia (94510-1021)
PHONE................................707 745-1581
Mark Davis, *Manager*
EMP: 60
SALES (corp-wide): 507.8MM **Privately Held**
WEB: www.onyxindustrial.com
SIC: 7699 8748 Waste cleaning services; environmental consultant
HQ: Veolia Es Industrial Services, Inc.
4760 World Houston Pkwy # 100
Houston TX 77032
713 307-2100

(P-18033)
WESTERN PUMP INC (PA)
3235 F St, San Diego (92102-3315)
PHONE................................619 239-9988
Fax: 619 239-9925
Dennis Rethmeier, *CEO*
Ryan Rethmeier, *President*
Janice C Rethmeier, *Corp Secy*
Dejan Ristic, *Mktg Dir*
Stephanie Correia, *Director*
▲ EMP: 55
SQ FT: 10,000
SALES: 13.9MM **Privately Held**
WEB: www.westernpump.com
SIC: 7699 5084 1799 Tank repair & cleaning services; petroleum industry machinery; petroleum storage tanks, pumping & draining

(P-18034)
WEYGANDT & ASSOCIATES
Also Called: Weco Aeorspace Systems
1501 Avi Blvd Ste 100, Lincoln (95648)
PHONE................................916 543-0431
William Weygandt, *President*
Harold Weygandt, *President*
EMP: 50
SQ FT: 7,800
SALES (est): 3.3MM **Privately Held**
SIC: 7699 Aircraft & heavy equipment repair services

7812 Motion Picture & Video Tape Production

(P-18035)
3ALITY DIGITAL LLC (PA)
Also Called: 3ality Technica
55 E Orange Grove Ave, Burbank (91502-1827)
PHONE................................818 759-5551
Fax: 818 759-5553
Steve Schklair, *CEO*
Gari Ann Douglass, *COO*
Sharon Martin, *Senior VP*
Hector Ortega, *Senior VP*
Stephen Pizzo, *Senior VP*
▲ EMP: 54
SQ FT: 25,000
SALES (est): 5.9MM **Privately Held**
WEB: www.3alitydigital.com
SIC: 7812 Motion picture & video production

(P-18036)
ABC FAMILY WORLDWIDE INC (HQ)
500 S Buena Vista St, Burbank (91521-0001)
PHONE................................818 560-1000
Robert A Iger, *President*
Nne Ebong, *Senior VP*
Gary French, *Senior VP*
Tonya Dobine, *Vice Pres*
Irene Lane, *Vice Pres*
EMP: 500
SALES (est): 34.8MM **Publicly Held**
SIC: 7812 4841 Cartoon production, television; cable & other pay television services

7812 - Motion Picture & Video Tape Production County (P-18037)

PRODUDUCTS & SERVICES SECTION

(P-18037)
ABM DISTRIBUTORS INC
811 W 7th St Ste 1040, Los Angeles (90017-3408)
PHONE..................310 401-0434
Alander Pulliam, *CEO*
EMP: 87 **EST:** 2015
SALES (est): 458.7K **Privately Held**
SIC: 7812 Television film production

(P-18038)
ADVANCED DIGITAL SERVICES INC (PA)
Also Called: A D S
948 N Cahuenga Blvd, Los Angeles (90038-2615)
PHONE..................323 962-8585
Fax: 323 468-2211
Thomas Engdahl, *President*
Andrew McIntyre, *Ch of Bd*
Carl Demarco, *President*
Brad Weyl, *COO*
Thayer Jester, *Vice Pres*
▲ **EMP:** 87
SQ FT: 33,000
SALES (est): 9.8MM **Privately Held**
WEB: www.adshollywood.com
SIC: 7812 7819 Video tape production; film processing, editing & titling: motion picture

(P-18039)
ALLDAYEVERYDAY PRODUCTIONS LLC
662 N Crescent Hts Blvd, Los Angeles (90048-2210)
PHONE..................323 556-6200
Arrow Kruse, *Executive*
Ross Vinstein, *CFO*
Michael Karbelnikoff, *Finance*
EMP: 50 **EST:** 2014
SQ FT: 5,000
SALES (est): 751.9K **Privately Held**
SIC: 7812 Motion picture & video production

(P-18040)
ALLIED ENTERTAINMENT GROUP INC (PA)
Also Called: Allied Artists International
273 W Allen Ave, City of Industry (91746)
P.O. Box 2035 (91746-0035)
PHONE..................626 330-0600
Greg Hammond, *President*
Robert Fitzpatrick, *Treasurer*
John Mason, *Vice Pres*
Ashley D Posner, *Vice Pres*
Danny Ramos, *Vice Pres*
◆ **EMP:** 325
SQ FT: 60,000
SALES: 30MM **Privately Held**
SIC: 7812 Motion picture & video production

(P-18041)
AMBLIN/RELIANCE HOLDING CO LLC
Also Called: Story Teller
100 Universal City Plz, Universal City (91608-1002)
PHONE..................818 733-6272
Lindson Harding, *Mng Member*
EMP: 99
SALES (est): 2.5MM **Privately Held**
SIC: 7812 7929 Motion picture production; entertainment group

(P-18042)
AND SYNDICATED PRODUCTIONS INC
3500 W Olive Ste 1000, Burbank (91505-5515)
PHONE..................818 308-5200
▲ **EMP:** 100
SALES (est): 6.2MM **Privately Held**
SIC: 7812

(P-18043)
ANE PRODUCTIONS INC
3500 W Olive Ste 1000, Burbank (91505-5515)
PHONE..................818 972-0777
John Cook, *Manager*
EMP: 60

SALES (est): 3.6MM **Privately Held**
SIC: 7812 Motion picture production & distribution, television

(P-18044)
ANONYMOUS CONTENT LLC (PA)
3532 Hayden Ave, Culver City (90232-2413)
PHONE..................310 558-6000
Steve Golin, *CEO*
Alix Madigan, *Exec VP*
Kim Natier, *Controller*
Melissa Culligan, *Producer*
Dave Morrison, *Producer*
▲ **EMP:** 60 **EST:** 1999
SALES (est): 12.3MM **Privately Held**
WEB: www.anonymouscontent.com
SIC: 7812 Motion picture & video production

(P-18045)
ASSOCIATED ENTRMT RELEASING (PA)
Also Called: Associated Television Intl
4401 Wilshire Blvd, Los Angeles (90010-3703)
P.O. Box 4180 (90078-4180)
PHONE..................323 934-7044
David McKenzie, *President*
Murray Drechsler, *CFO*
Murray Dreschler, *CFO*
Richard Casares, *Exec VP*
Rich Sagehorn, *Vice Pres*
EMP: 50
SQ FT: 35,000
SALES (est): 9.1MM **Privately Held**
WEB: www.associatedtelevision.com
SIC: 7812 Motion picture production & distribution

(P-18046)
ATLAS DIGITAL LLC (PA)
170 S Flower St, Burbank (91502-2122)
P.O. Box 4110 (91503-4110)
PHONE..................323 762-2626
Shawn Sanbar, *Owner*
Steve Sauber, *Software Dev*
Greg Evanski, *Technician*
Dru Goradia, *Engineer*
Allen Theroux, *Senior Engr*
EMP: 75
SQ FT: 13,000
SALES (est): 11.4MM **Privately Held**
SIC: 7812 Motion picture & video production

(P-18047)
ATLAS ENTERTAINMENT INC
9200 W Sunset Blvd Ste 10, West Hollywood (90069-3608)
PHONE..................310 786-4900
Charles V Roven, *President*
Brent Maduro, *Finance*
Patrick Blood, *Legal Staff*
Jake Kurily, *Director*
Melinda Whitaker, *Assistant*
EMP: 50
SALES (est): 3.2MM **Privately Held**
SIC: 7812 Motion picture production & distribution

(P-18048)
AVOCA PRODUCTIONS INC
Also Called: The Newly Wed
10202 Washington Blvd, Culver City (90232-3119)
PHONE..................310 244-4000
Steve Mosko, *President*
Catherine Wozney, *Manager*
EMP: 60
SALES (est): 1.4MM
SALES (corp-wide): 69.2B **Privately Held**
WEB: www.sonypictures.com
SIC: 7812 Television film production
HQ: Sony Pictures Entertainment, Inc.
10202 Washington Blvd
Culver City CA 90232
310 244-4000

(P-18049)
BABY DICA INC
14501 Calvert St, Van Nuys (91411-2806)
PHONE..................818 988-0671
Jay Polan, *President*
Mark Polan, *President*

EMP: 200
SALES (est): 2.2MM **Privately Held**
SIC: 7812 Motion picture production

(P-18050)
BACHELOR PRODUCTIONS INC
2121 Avenue Of The Stars, Los Angeles (90067-5010)
PHONE..................310 567-9249
Desiree Varni, *Accountant*
EMP: 99
SALES (est): 944.5K **Privately Held**
SIC: 7812 Motion picture & video production

(P-18051)
BLAIR TELEVISION INC
Also Called: Blair TV Communication
11111 Santa Monica Blvd # 1900, Los Angeles (90025-3333)
PHONE..................714 537-5923
Fax: 310 444-3666
Nancy Dodson, *Manager*
EMP: 55
SALES (corp-wide): 23.9MM **Privately Held**
SIC: 7812 Motion picture & video production
HQ: Blair Television Inc
200 Park Ave Fl 17
New York NY 10166
212 230-5900

(P-18052)
BRC IMAGINATION ARTS INC
2711 Winona Ave, Burbank (91504-2535)
PHONE..................818 841-8084
Fax: 818 841-4996
Robert Rogers, *President*
Tom McDonald, *CFO*
Carmel Lewis, *Vice Pres*
Brad B Shelton, *Vice Pres*
Rob Wyatt, *Vice Pres*
EMP: 65
SQ FT: 42,000
SALES (est): 11.1MM **Privately Held**
WEB: www.brcweb.com
SIC: 7812 Motion picture production

(P-18053)
BRENTWOOD CMMNCATIONS INTL INC
Also Called: BCII
16135 Roscoe Blvd, North Hills (91343-6226)
PHONE..................818 333-3680
Fax: 818 487-2713
Bud W Brutsman, *President*
Cynthia Whorton, *Opers Staff*
Jill Schneider, *Producer*
EMP: 50
SALES (est): 9.7MM **Privately Held**
SIC: 7812 Television film production

(P-18054)
BRILLSTEIN ENTRMT PARTNERS LLC (PA)
Also Called: Brillstein Grey Entertainment
9150 Wilshire Blvd # 350, Beverly Hills (90212-3427)
PHONE..................310 205-5100
Fax: 310 275-6180
Brad Grey, *President*
Amy Weiss, *Executive*
Teila Blanchfield, *Executive Asst*
Naren Ramanuj, *Controller*
Danny Sussman, *Manager*
EMP: 90
SALES (est): 14.9MM **Privately Held**
SIC: 7812 Television film production

(P-18055)
BUENA VISTA INTERNATIONAL INC (HQ)
350 S Buena Vista St, Burbank (91521-0004)
PHONE..................818 295-5200
Fax: 818 562-3068
David M Hollis, *CEO*
Bob Chapek, *CEO*
Teri Meyer, *Exec VP*
Jerome L Grand, *Senior VP*
Jere R Hausfater, *Principal*
EMP: 98
SQ FT: 40,000

SALES (est): 3.7MM **Publicly Held**
SIC: 7812 3695 Video tape production; video tapes, recorded: wholesale; video recording tape, blank

(P-18056)
BUNIM-MURRAY PRODUCTIONS
Also Called: Bmp
6007 Sepulveda Blvd, Van Nuys (91411-2502)
PHONE..................818 756-5100
Fax: 818 756-5140
Jon Murray, *CEO*
Gil Goldschein, *CEO*
Mark Lebowitz, *CFO*
Bill Shively, *Exec VP*
Erin Cristall, *Vice Pres*
EMP: 150
SQ FT: 20,000
SALES (est): 28MM **Privately Held**
SIC: 7812 Television film production
PA: Banijay Entertainment
5 Rue Francois 1er
Paris Cedex 08 75383

(P-18057)
BVS ENTERTAINMENT INC (DH)
500 S Buena Vista St, Burbank (91521-0001)
PHONE..................818 460-6917
Griffith Foxley, *President*
David K Thompson, *Admin Sec*
EMP: 50
SQ FT: 111,000
SALES (est): 4.7MM **Publicly Held**
SIC: 7812 7822 Cartoon production, television; motion picture distribution; television & video tape distribution
HQ: Abc Family Worldwide, Inc.
500 S Buena Vista St
Burbank CA 91521
818 560-1000

(P-18058)
CAFFEINE PRODUCTIONS
1040 N Las Palmas Ave, Los Angeles (90038-2409)
PHONE..................323 860-8111
Jen Gore, *Director*
Greg Choa, *Owner*
Marc Wolloff, *Exec Dir*
Lars Hansen, *Info Tech Dir*
Marc Wollos, *Director*
EMP: 80
SQ FT: 10,000
SALES (est): 1MM
SALES (corp-wide): 13.2B **Publicly Held**
WEB: www.caffeineproductions.com
SIC: 7812 Television film production
HQ: Comedy Partners
345 Hudson St Fl 9
New York NY 10014
212 767-8600

(P-18059)
CARA COMMUNICATIONS CORP
Also Called: Vin Dibona Productions
12233 W Olympic Blvd # 255, Los Angeles (90064-1034)
PHONE..................310 442-5600
Fax: 310 442-5604
Vincent Dibona, *President*
Sharon Arnett, *Vice Pres*
Janet Ghio, *Office Mgr*
Mike Jordan, *Info Tech Mgr*
Stephanie J Rondeau, *Opers Staff*
EMP: 50
SALES (est): 4.8MM **Privately Held**
SIC: 7812 7819 7922 Television film production; directors, independent: motion picture; television program, including commercial producers

(P-18060)
CBS STUDIOS INC (DH)
Also Called: CBS Paramount Television
6100 Wilshire Blvd # 1000, Los Angeles (90048-5109)
PHONE..................323 634-3519
Leslie Moonves, *President*
Jonathan M Greenberg, *Exec Dir*
EMP: 500

PRODUCTS & SERVICES SECTION
7812 - Motion Picture & Video Tape Production County (P-18083)

SALES (est): 42.4MM
SALES (corp-wide): 13.9B **Publicly Held**
SIC: **7812** Motion picture & video production
HQ: Cbs Corporation
51 W 52nd St Bsmt 1
New York NY 10019
212 975-4321

(P-18061)
CINOVATION INC
6527 San Fernando Rd, Glendale (91201-2108)
P.O. Box 909, Pacific Palisades (90272-0909)
PHONE 818 246-3160
Rick Baker, *President*
EMP: 100
SQ FT: 24,000
SALES (est): 1.9MM **Privately Held**
SIC: **7812** Motion picture production

(P-18062)
CNX MEDIA INC
1 Beach St Ste 300, San Francisco (94133-1228)
PHONE 415 229-8300
James Hornthal, *Ch of Bd*
Allan Horlick, *President*
Angela Pumo Cohen, *Exec VP*
Kimberly Mounter, *Exec VP*
Kimerly Montour, *Senior VP*
EMP: 90
SQ FT: 15,000
SALES (est): 5.1MM **Privately Held**
SIC: **7812** Video tape production

(P-18063)
COLUMBIA PICTURES INDS INC (DH)
10202 Washington Blvd, Culver City (90232-3119)
PHONE 310 244-4000
Fax: 310 244-1363
Michael Lynton, *CEO*
Doug Belgrad, *President*
Andrew Gumpert, *President*
Hannah Minghella, *President*
Matt Tolmach, *President*
EMP: 200
SALES: 86.6MM
SALES (corp-wide): 69.2B **Privately Held**
WEB: www.columbiapictures.com
SIC: **7812** Motion picture production & distribution
HQ: Sony Pictures Entertainment, Inc.
10202 Washington Blvd
Culver City CA 90232
310 244-4000

(P-18064)
COOKIE JAR ENTRMT USA INC
4100 W Alameda Ave # 101, Burbank (91505-4195)
PHONE 818 955-5400
Andy Heyward, *President*
Brad Brooks, *President*
Bob Denton, *CFO*
Scott McCaw, *CFO*
Steve Voleti, *CFO*
EMP: 110
SQ FT: 27,000
SALES (est): 5.1MM
SALES (corp-wide): 7.1MM **Privately Held**
SIC: **7812** Television film production
PA: Dic Entertainment Holdings, Inc.
4100 W Alameda Ave Fl 4
Burbank CA

(P-18065)
CORPORATE PRODUCTION DESIGNS
1427 Goodman Ave, Redondo Beach (90278-4004)
PHONE 310 937-9663
Bill Ganz, *President*
Chelsea Peters, *Development*
Troy Richardson, *Sales Staff*
EMP: 50 **EST:** 1997
SALES (est): 1.7MM **Privately Held**
SIC: **7812** Motion picture & video production

(P-18066)
CYBERNET ENTERTAINMENT LLC
1800 Mission St, San Francisco (94103-3502)
PHONE 415 865-0230
Peter Ackworth, *Mng Member*
Mark Meagher, *Controller*
Adam Boyd, *HR Admin*
EMP: 115
SALES (est): 12MM **Privately Held**
SIC: **7812** Video production

(P-18067)
DALAKLIS MCKEOWN ENTERTAINMENT
2517 Crest Dr, Manhattan Beach (90266-2135)
PHONE 310 545-0120
Charles Dalaklis, *President*
Theresa McKeown, *COO*
EMP: 75
SQ FT: 12,000
SALES (est): 13.5MM **Privately Held**
WEB: www.dmetv.net
SIC: **7812** Television film production

(P-18068)
DCP RIGHTS LLC
2900 Olympic Blvd, Santa Monica (90404-4127)
PHONE 310 255-4600
Allen Shapiro, *President*
Kyla Druckman, *Sales Mgr*
EMP: 50
SQ FT: 45,637
SALES (est): 275.6K **Privately Held**
SIC: **7812** Motion picture & video production

(P-18069)
DELUXE ENTRMT SVCS GROUP INC
Also Called: Deluxe Media Management
29125 Avenue Paine, Valencia (91355-5403)
PHONE 661 702-5000
Michael Alverez Sr, *Branch Mgr*
Michael A Alvarez Jr, *Manager*
EMP: 165
SALES (corp-wide): 5.3B **Privately Held**
SIC: **7812** 7819 Television film production; film processing, editing & titling: motion picture
HQ: Deluxe Entertainment Services Group Inc.
2400 W Empire Ave
Los Angeles CA 90027
323 462-6171

(P-18070)
DELUXE MEDIA SERVICES LLC
1377 N Serrano Ave, Los Angeles (90027-5623)
PHONE 323 462-6171
John Suh, *Principal*
Karen Clifton, *Vice Pres*
Steve Gorman, *Business Dir*
EMP: 900 **EST:** 2012
SALES (est): 51.1MM **Privately Held**
SIC: **7812** Motion picture & video production

(P-18071)
DIGITAL DOMAIN 30 INC (PA)
12641 Beatrice St, Los Angeles (90066-7003)
PHONE 310 314-2800
Fax: 310 314-2990
Daniel Seah, *CEO*
Amit Chopra, *CFO*
Sindy Di Wu, *Vice Pres*
Joseph Gabriel, *Vice Pres*
Heather Jennings, *Executive*
EMP: 300
SALES (est): 75MM **Privately Held**
SIC: **7812** Video production

(P-18072)
DIGITAL KITCHEN LLC
3585 Hayden Ave, Culver City (90232-2412)
PHONE 310 499-9255
Cythia Bimon, *Manager*
Daniel Goldstein, *Info Tech Dir*

EMP: 50
SALES (corp-wide): 10.3B **Privately Held**
SIC: **7812** 7819 Motion picture & video production; services allied to motion pictures
HQ: Digital Kitchen, Llc
314 W Superior St Ste 601
Chicago IL 60654

(P-18073)
DINO BONES PRODUCTIONS INC
4705 Laurel Canyon Blvd, Studio City (91607-5904)
PHONE 818 827-5100
Jack Abernathy, *CEO*
EMP: 80 **EST:** 2013
SALES (est): 361.2K **Privately Held**
SIC: **7812** Motion picture & video production

(P-18074)
DISNEY ENTERPRISES INC (HQ)
500 S Buena Vista St, Burbank (91521-0001)
P.O. Box 3232, Anaheim (92803-3232)
PHONE 818 560-1000
Robert Iger, *President*
Thomas O Staggs, *CFO*
Alan Braverman, *Sr Exec VP*
Mary Parker, *Exec VP*
Anne Sweeney, *Exec VP*
▲ EMP: 6000 **EST:** 1986
SALES (est): 5.2B **Publicly Held**
SIC: **7812** 6794 5331 7996 Motion picture production & distribution; motion picture production & distribution, television; video tape production; television film production; copyright buying & licensing; music royalties, sheet & record; performance rights, publishing & licensing; variety stores; theme park, amusement; ice hockey club

(P-18075)
DISNEY ENTERPRISES INC
3235 S Buena Vista St, Burbank (91521-0001)
PHONE 818 560-3692
EMP: 300 **Publicly Held**
SIC: **7812** Television film production
HQ: Disney Enterprises, Inc.
500 S Buena Vista St
Burbank CA 91521
818 560-1000

(P-18076)
DISNEY INCORPORATED (DH)
500 S Buena Vista St, Burbank (91521-0001)
PHONE 818 560-1000
Matthew L McGinnis, *CEO*
Sanford M Litvack, *President*
Zenia Mucha, *Exec VP*
Mary Parker, *Exec VP*
Tim Klauda, *Vice Pres*
▲ EMP: 150
SALES (est): 32.2MM **Publicly Held**
WEB: www.wdwnews.com
SIC: **7812** Motion picture production & distribution
HQ: Disney Enterprises, Inc.
500 S Buena Vista St
Burbank CA 91521
818 560-1000

(P-18077)
DISNEY WORLDWIDE SERVICES INC (DH)
500 S Buena Vista St, Burbank (91521-0001)
PHONE 818 560-1000
Jeffrey H Smith, *President*
James S Hunt, *Treasurer*
James H Kapenstein, *Vice Pres*
Marsha L Reed, *Admin Sec*
▲ EMP: 5000
SALES (est): 610.8MM **Publicly Held**
SIC: **7812** 5736 Motion picture & video production; cartoon motion picture production; musical instrument stores
HQ: Disney Enterprises, Inc.
500 S Buena Vista St
Burbank CA 91521
818 560-1000

(P-18078)
DUCKPUNK PRODUCTIONS INC
9016 W Olympic Blvd, Beverly Hills (90211-3516)
PHONE 310 836-3818
Fax: 310 944-6466
Mellissa Tong, *President*
EMP: 100
SALES: 202.3K **Privately Held**
SIC: **7812** 7311 7335 7819 Commercials, television: tape or film; advertising agencies; commercial photography; services allied to motion pictures; directors, independent: motion picture

(P-18079)
DWA HOLDINGS LLC (DH)
1000 Flower St, Glendale (91201-3007)
PHONE 818 695-5000
Fax: 818 695-3510
Mellody Hobson, *Ch of Bd*
Ann Daly, *President*
Jeffrey Katzenberg, *CEO*
Fazai Merchant, *CFO*
David Chavez, *Vice Pres*
EMP: 97
SQ FT: 500,000
SALES: 915.8MM
SALES (corp-wide): 74.5B **Publicly Held**
WEB: www.dreamworksanimation.com
SIC: **7812** Cartoon motion picture production
HQ: Nbcuniversal Media, Llc
30 Rockefeller Plz Fl 2
New York NY 10112
212 664-4444

(P-18080)
E P N INC
Screenworks Nep
1580 Magnolia Ave, Corona (92879-2073)
PHONE 951 279-8877
Tom McCracken, *Branch Mgr*
Mike Martinsen, *Info Tech Mgr*
Myron Linde, *Director*
EMP: 50
SALES (corp-wide): 76.5MM **Privately Held**
SIC: **7812** Television film production
PA: Nep Group, Inc.
2 Beta Dr
Pittsburgh PA 15238
412 826-1414

(P-18081)
EARTHBOUND PRODUCTIONS LLC
849 N Occidental Blvd, Los Angeles (90026-2925)
PHONE 504 734-3337
Mandy M Gagliardi,
EMP: 100
SALES (est): 984.1K **Privately Held**
SIC: **7812** Television film production

(P-18082)
EFILM LLC
Also Called: E Film Digital Labratories
1144 N Las Palmas Ave, Los Angeles (90038-1209)
PHONE 323 463-7041
Fax: 323 465-7342
Aria Mehrabi,
Marvin Boonmee, *Software Engr*
Mae Capalla, *Software Engr*
Bob Buckner, *Engineer*
Kit Young, *Engineer*
EMP: 150
SALES (est): 20.4MM
SALES (corp-wide): 5.3B **Privately Held**
WEB: www.efilm.com
SIC: **7812** Motion picture & video production
HQ: Deluxe Laboratories, Inc.
2400 W Empire Ave Ste 200
Burbank CA 91504
323 462-6171

(P-18083)
FILM ROMAN LLC
21600 Oxnard St Ste 1700, Woodland Hills (91367-4972)
PHONE 818 748-4000
Dana Booton, *Manager*
EMP: 200
SQ FT: 87,000

7812 - Motion Picture & Video Tape Production County (P-18084)

SALES (corp-wide): 1.7B **Publicly Held**
SIC: 7812 Cartoon motion picture production; cartoon production, television
HQ: Film Roman, Llc.
8900 Liberty Cir
Englewood CO 80112
720 852-6327

(P-18084)
FILM ROMAN LLC
21600 Oxnard St Ste 1700, Woodland Hills (91367-4972)
PHONE 818 748-4000
Glenn Curtis, *Mng Member*
Carin Davis, *President*
John W Hyde, *President*
Robert Cresci, *Bd of Directors*
James McNamara, *Bd of Directors*
EMP: 200
SQ FT: 81,000
SALES (est): 9.5MM **Privately Held**
SIC: 7812 Television film production

(P-18085)
FILMQUEST PICTURES CORPORATION
15331 Stonewood Ter, Sherman Oaks (91403-4917)
PHONE 818 905-1006
Eric Steven Stahl, *President*
Bonnie Eck, *Executive Asst*
Nana Ishizuka, *Director*
EMP: 175
SALES (est): 3.6MM **Privately Held**
SIC: 7812 Motion picture production & distribution

(P-18086)
FOCUS FEATURES LLC
1540 2nd St Ste 200, Santa Monica (90401-3513)
PHONE 424 214-6360
Fax: 818 866-4577
Peter Schlessel, *CEO*
Scott Stuber, *Vice Chairman*
Howard Meyers, *Exec VP*
Matthew Lipson, *Senior VP*
Stacy Osugi, *Senior VP*
EMP: 121
SQ FT: 30,000
SALES (est): 16.7MM
SALES (corp-wide): 74.5B **Publicly Held**
WEB: www.focusfeatures.net
SIC: 7812 Motion picture production & distribution
HQ: Nbcuniversal Media, Llc
30 Rockefeller Plz Fl 2
New York NY 10112
212 664-4444

(P-18087)
FOX ANIMATION STUDIOS INC
5700 Wilshire Blvd # 325, Los Angeles (90036-3659)
PHONE 323 857-8800
John McKenna, *President*
Jason Pittman, *Info Tech Mgr*
Joe O'Malley, *Systems Mgr*
Joe Malley, *Data Proc Staff*
Helen McDevitt, *Human Res Mgr*
▲ **EMP:** 310
SALES (est): 8.6MM
SALES (corp-wide): 27.3B **Publicly Held**
WEB: www.foxmovies.com
SIC: 7812 Motion picture production & distribution; video tape production; motion picture production & distribution, television; cartoon motion picture production
HQ: Twentieth Century Fox Film Corporation
10201 W Pico Blvd
Los Angeles CA 90064
310 369-1000

(P-18088)
FRIENDS OF MAX ROSE LLC
1639 11th St Ste 260, Santa Monica (90404-3759)
PHONE 424 901-1260
Paul Currie,
EMP: 58 **EST:** 2011
SALES (est): 1MM **Privately Held**
SIC: 7812 Motion picture production

(P-18089)
GLOBAL EAGLE ENTERTAINMENT INC
2941 Alton Pkwy, Irvine (92606-5142)
PHONE 949 608-8700
Rick Warren,
EMP: 140 **Publicly Held**
SIC: 7812 Video production
PA: Global Eagle Entertainment Inc.
4553 Glencoe Ave Ste 200
Marina Del Rey CA 90292

(P-18090)
HARPO PRODUCTIONS INC
Also Called: Harpo Entertainment Group
1041 N Formosa Ave, West Hollywood (90046-6703)
PHONE 312 633-1000
Oprah Winfrey, *Ch of Bd*
Tim Bennett, *President*
Doug Pattison, *CFO*
Bill Becker, *Vice Pres*
James Swick, *Engineer*
EMP: 200
SQ FT: 100,000
SALES (est): 17.2MM **Privately Held**
SIC: 7812 Television film production; video tape production

(P-18091)
HBO INDPENDENT PRODUCTIONS INC (DH)
2500 Broadway Ste 400, Santa Monica (90404-3176)
PHONE 310 382-3000
Christopher P Albrecht, *President*
Kerry Yancheski, *Accountant*
Susan Conradi, *Accounts Mgr*
EMP: 52
SALES (est): 5.2MM
SALES (corp-wide): 28.1B **Publicly Held**
SIC: 7812 Motion picture & video production
HQ: Home Box Office, Inc.
1100 Avenue Of The Americ
New York NY 10036
212 512-1000

(P-18092)
HELINET AVIATION SERVICES LLC (PA)
16303 Waterman Dr, Van Nuys (91406-1222)
PHONE 818 902-0229
Fax: 818 902-9278
Alan D Purwin, *President*
Ron Magocsi, *COO*
Stephanie Snyder, *CFO*
Alex Giuffrida, *Exec VP*
Jack Snyder, *Vice Pres*
EMP: 75
SQ FT: 10,000
SALES (est): 10.2MM **Privately Held**
SIC: 7812 7359 4522 Motion picture & video production; aircraft & industrial truck rental services; helicopter carriers, non-scheduled

(P-18093)
HIGHPOINT PRODUCTIONS INC
13400 Rverside Dr Ste 300, Sherman Oaks (91423)
PHONE 818 728-7600
Gary Benz, *President*
Michael Branton, *Vice Pres*
EMP: 100
SALES (est): 9.4MM **Privately Held**
WEB: www.grbtv.com
SIC: 7812 Television film production

(P-18094)
IGNITION CREATIVE LLC
12959 Coral Tree Pl, Los Angeles (90066-7020)
PHONE 310 315-6300
Fax: 310 315-6399
Ron Moler,
Michael Brittain, *Creative Dir*
Martin Kistler, *Creative Dir*
Mark Wood, *Office Mgr*
Rich Oldfield, *CTO*
EMP: 72

SALES (est): 13.7MM **Privately Held**
WEB: www.ignitionla.com
SIC: 7812 Video production

(P-18095)
INTERDEPENDENT PICTURES LLC
124 S Camden Dr Apt C, Beverly Hills (90212-2322)
PHONE 310 779-2119
Chris Arnil, *Mng Member*
EMP: 100
SALES (est): 598.5K **Privately Held**
SIC: 7812 Motion picture & video production

(P-18096)
JEOPARDY PRODUCTIONS INC
10202 Washington Blvd, Culver City (90232-3119)
PHONE 310 244-8855
Fax: 310 244-1513
Rocky Schmitt, *CEO*
Lisa Dee, *Producer*
Catherine Wozney, *Manager*
EMP: 125 **EST:** 1984
SALES (est): 2.8MM
SALES (corp-wide): 69.2B **Publicly Held**
WEB: www.jeopardy.com
SIC: 7812 Television film production
HQ: Sony Pictures Entertainment, Inc.
10202 Washington Blvd
Culver City CA 90232
310 244-4000

(P-18097)
JIM HENSON COMPANY INC (PA)
Also Called: Henson Recording Studio
1416 N La Brea Ave, Los Angeles (90028-7506)
PHONE 323 856-6680
Fax: 323 802-1825
Lisa Henson, *CEO*
Cheryl Henson, *President*
Peter Schube, *President*
Brian Henson, *CEO*
Laurie Don, *CFO*
EMP: 55 **EST:** 1965
SQ FT: 7,000
SALES (est): 11.3MM **Privately Held**
WEB: www.farscape.com
SIC: 7812 Motion picture production & distribution

(P-18098)
KSBY COMMUNICATIONS INC
1772 Calle Joaquin, San Luis Obispo (93405-7210)
PHONE 805 541-6666
Kathleen Choal, *President*
Lisa Moore, *Sales Mgr*
Tony Cipolla, *Director*
EMP: 80
SALES (est): 7.1MM **Privately Held**
WEB: www.ksby.com
SIC: 7812 Television film production

(P-18099)
LEGEND3D INC
1017 Cole Ave, Los Angeles (90038-2601)
PHONE 858 793-4420
Ian Jessel, *President*
Tom Sinnott, *COO*
Mark Steffler, *CFO*
Steven Wolkenstein, *CFO*
Barry Sandrew, *Ch Credit Ofcr*
EMP: 95
SQ FT: 50,000
SALES (est): 16.7MM **Privately Held**
SIC: 7812 Motion picture & video production

(P-18100)
LIONS GATE ENTERTAINMENT INC (HQ)
2700 Colorado Ave Ste 200, Santa Monica (90404-5502)
PHONE 310 449-9200
Jon Feltheimer, *Ch of Bd*
Michael Burns, *Vice Chairman*
Steven Beeks, *President*
Joseph Drake, *President*
Erik Feig, *President*
EMP: 55

SALES (est): 1.9B
SALES (corp-wide): 2.4B **Publicly Held**
SIC: 7812 Motion picture production & distribution
PA: Lions Gate Entertainment Corp
1055 Hastings St W Suite 2200
Vancouver BC V6E 2
604 669-0011

(P-18101)
LIONS GATE FILMS INC
2700 Colorado Ave Ste 200, Santa Monica (90404-5502)
PHONE 310 449-9200
Jon Feltheimer, *President*
Steve Beeks, *COO*
James Keegan, *CFO*
Phil Strina, *Senior VP*
Joaquin Cormujl, *Vice Pres*
EMP: 147
SQ FT: 30,000
SALES (est): 10.2MM
SALES (corp-wide): 2.4B **Publicly Held**
WEB: www.lionsgatefilms.com
SIC: 7812 Motion picture & video production
HQ: Lions Gate Entertainment Inc.
2700 Colorado Ave Ste 200
Santa Monica CA 90404
310 449-9200

(P-18102)
LMNO PRODUCTIONS INC
Also Called: Lmno Cable Group
15821 Ventura Blvd # 320, Encino (91436-2928)
PHONE 818 995-5555
Fax: 818 995-5544
Eric Schotz, *President*
Ed Horwitz, *Exec VP*
Ned Davis, *Senior VP*
Jeff Rice, *Senior VP*
Andrew Suser, *Senior VP*
EMP: 200
SALES (est): 14.6MM **Privately Held**
SIC: 7812 Television film production

(P-18103)
LOOKOUT PRODUCTIONS LLC
3748 W 9th St Apt 403, Los Angeles (90019-2117)
PHONE 310 408-5687
Gustavo Morales, *Mng Member*
Douglas Wirth,
EMP: 50
SQ FT: 1,500
SALES (est): 2.7MM **Privately Held**
SIC: 7812 Motion picture & video production

(P-18104)
LUCASFILM LTD LLC (HQ)
Also Called: Lucasfilm Coml Productions
1110 Gorgas Ave Bldg C-Hr, San Francisco (94129-1406)
P.O. Box 29901 (94129-0901)
PHONE 415 623-1000
Kathleen Kennedy, *President*
Harriette Helmer, *CFO*
Blaire Chaput, *Top Exec*
Howard Roffman, *Exec VP*
Lori Aultman, *Vice Pres*
▲ **EMP:** 250
SALES (est): 65.6MM **Publicly Held**
WEB: www.lucasfilm.com
SIC: 7812 6794 Motion picture production & distribution; television film production; patent owners & lessors

(P-18105)
LUCASFILM LTD LLC
5858 Lucas Valley Rd, Nicasio (94946-9703)
PHONE 415 662-1800
Micheline Chau, *President*
Dan Dawes, *Vice Pres*
Kevin Parker, *Vice Pres*
Harriette Helmer, *Executive*
Erin Kahn, *Program Mgr*
EMP: 200 **Publicly Held**
WEB: www.lucasfilm.com
SIC: 7812 Motion picture production & distribution; television film production

PRODUCTS & SERVICES SECTION
7812 - Motion Picture & Video Tape Production County (P-18126)

HQ: Lucasfilm Ltd. Llc
1110 Gorgas Ave Bldg C-Hr
San Francisco CA 94129
415 623-1000

(P-18106)
MARK HERZOG & COMPANY INC
4640 Lankershim Blvd, North Hollywood (91602-1841)
PHONE.................................818 762-4640
Fax: 818 762-4648
Mark Herzog, *President*
Joe Lam, *Office Mgr*
EMP: 64 **EST:** 1995
SQ FT: 12,500
SALES (est): 6.3MM **Privately Held**
WEB: www.herzogproductions.com
SIC: 7812 Television film production

(P-18107)
MEDIA VNTURES ENTRMT GROUP LLC
1547 14th St, Santa Monica (90404-3302)
PHONE.................................310 260-3171
Hans Zimmer, *President*
EMP: 50
SALES (est): 1.2MM **Privately Held**
SIC: 7812 Video tape production

(P-18108)
MEDIAPLATFORM INC
Also Called: Vcall
8383 Wilshire Blvd # 460, Beverly Hills (90211-2446)
PHONE.................................310 909-8410
Jim McGovern, *CEO*
Mike Newman, *President*
Steve Coloia, *Vice Pres*
Dena Kendros, *Vice Pres*
Mike Boyle, *Sales Dir*
EMP: 60
SALES (est): 2.7MM
SALES (corp-wide): 11.6MM **Publicly Held**
WEB: www.vodium.com
SIC: 7812 7819 7822 8743 Motion picture & video production; services allied to motion pictures; motion picture & tape distribution; public relations services
HQ: Precisionir Group Inc.
601 Moorefield Park Dr
North Chesterfield VA

(P-18109)
MERLOT FILM PRODUCTIONS INC
Also Called: CBS Network News
7800 Beverly Blvd, Los Angeles (90036-2112)
PHONE.................................323 575-2906
Bruce C Taub, *CEO*
Leslie Moondes, *President*
David Strauss, *CFO*
Claudia E Morf, *Treasurer*
Leo Gorius, *Vice Pres*
EMP: 200
SALES (est): 8.2MM
SALES (corp-wide): 27.1B **Publicly Held**
SIC: 7812 4833 Motion picture & video production; television broadcasting stations
HQ: Cbs Broadcasting Inc.
51 W 52nd St
New York NY 10019
212 975-4321

(P-18110)
METHOD STUDIOS LLC
3401 Exposition Blvd, Santa Monica (90404-5050)
PHONE.................................310 434-6500
Dan Glass, *Creative Dir*
Christine Verzosa, *Tech/Comp Coord*
Robert Owens, *Producer*
Bryan Burger, *Manager*
EMP: 158
SALES (est): 10.8MM
SALES (corp-wide): 34.7MM **Privately Held**
SIC: 7812 Video production

PA: Deluxe Entertainment Services Group Inc.
2400 W Empire Ave Ste 200
Burbank CA 91504
818 565-3600

(P-18111)
METRO-GLDWYN-MAYER STUDIOS INC
Also Called: MGM
245 N Beverly Dr, Beverly Hills (90210-5319)
PHONE.................................310 449-3620
EMP: 200
SALES (corp-wide): 68.3MM **Privately Held**
SIC: 7812 Motion picture production & distribution; television film production
HQ: Metro-Goldwyn-Mayer Studios Inc.
10250 Constellation Blvd
Los Angeles CA 90067
310 449-3590

(P-18112)
METRO-GLDWYN-MAYER STUDIOS INC
Also Called: MGM
245 N Beverly Dr, Beverly Hills (90210-5319)
PHONE.................................310 449-3000
Paul Bischoff, *VP Sales*
Marilyn Bernstein, *Exec Dir*
Alisha Luense, *Administration*
Carol Campbell-Larson, *CIO*
David Giampa, *VP Finance*
EMP: 200
SALES (corp-wide): 68.3MM **Privately Held**
SIC: 7812 Motion picture & video production
HQ: Metro-Goldwyn-Mayer Studios Inc.
10250 Constellation Blvd
Los Angeles CA 90067
310 449-3590

(P-18113)
METRO-GOLDWYN-MAYER INC (DH)
Also Called: MGM
245 N Beverly Dr, Beverly Hills (90210-5319)
PHONE.................................310 449-3000
Gary Barber, *CEO*
Diane Miller, *COO*
Ken Schapiro, *COO*
Doug Finberg, *Treasurer*
Mark McCormick, *Officer*
EMP: 300
SQ FT: 131,400
SALES (est): 61.9MM
SALES (corp-wide): 68.3MM **Privately Held**
WEB: www.mgm.com
SIC: 7812 Motion picture production & distribution; motion picture production & distribution, television; television film production; video production
HQ: Mgm Holdings Ii, Inc.
245 N Beverly Dr
Beverly Hills CA 90210
310 449-3000

(P-18114)
MINDRING PRODUCTIONS LLC
5200 Lankershim Blvd # 200, North Hollywood (91601-3155)
PHONE.................................323 466-9200
Chris Abrego, *Mng Member*
Julie Gordon, *Controller*
Mark Cronin,
EMP: 50
SALES: 15MM **Privately Held**
SIC: 7812 Motion picture & video production

(P-18115)
MIRAMAX FILM NY LLC
2450 Colorado Ave Ste 10, Santa Monica (90404-3575)
PHONE.................................310 409-4321
Steven Schoch, *CEO*
Beth Minehart, *Exec VP*
EMP: 80
SALES (est): 12.5MM **Privately Held**
SIC: 7812 Motion picture & video production

(P-18116)
MPC LA
Also Called: Moving Picture Company
8921 Lindblade St, Culver City (90232-2438)
PHONE.................................310 526-5800
Tim Sarnoff, *President*
Mark Benson, *Managing Dir*
EMP: 60
SALES (est): 1.6MM **Privately Held**
SIC: 7812 Motion picture & video production

(P-18117)
NBC UNIVERSAL INC (HQ)
100 Universal City Plz, Universal City (91608-1002)
PHONE.................................818 777-1000
Katherine Pope, *President*
Russ Randall, *President*
Peter Schade, *President*
Jeffrey Zucker, *CEO*
Salil Mehta, *CFO*
◆ **EMP:** 50 **EST:** 1987
SQ FT: 1,000,000
SALES (est): 126.3MM
SALES (corp-wide): 74.5B **Publicly Held**
WEB: www.nbcuni.com
SIC: 7812 Motion picture production & distribution; motion picture production & distribution, television; non-theatrical motion picture production; non-theatrical motion picture production, television
PA: Comcast Corporation
1701 Jfk Blvd
Philadelphia PA 19103
215 286-1700

(P-18118)
NBCUNIVERSAL MEDIA LLC
Also Called: Access Hollywood
3000 W Alameda Ave, Burbank (91523-0002)
PHONE.................................818 526-7000
Kirk Bowren, *Manager*
EMP: 130
SALES (corp-wide): 74.5B **Publicly Held**
WEB: www.accesshollywood.com
SIC: 7812 Television film production
HQ: Nbcuniversal Media, Llc
30 Rockefeller Plz Fl 2
New York NY 10112
212 664-4444

(P-18119)
NEP GROUP INC
7635 Airport Bus Pkwy, Van Nuys (91406)
PHONE.................................412 423-1354
EMP: 100
SALES (corp-wide): 76.5MM **Privately Held**
SIC: 7812 Television film production
PA: Nep Group, Inc.
2 Beta Dr
Pittsburgh PA 15238
412 826-1414

(P-18120)
NEW PARADIGM PRODUCTIONS INC (PA)
Also Called: Edelman Productions
39 Mesa St Ste 212, San Francisco (94129-1019)
PHONE.................................415 924-8000
Steve Edelman, *President*
Natalie Acevedo, *Office Mgr*
EMP: 100
SQ FT: 8,500
SALES (est): 21.9MM **Privately Held**
WEB: www.edelmanproductions.com
SIC: 7812 Video production

(P-18121)
NEW REGENCY PRODUCTIONS INC (PA)
Also Called: Regency Enterprises
10201 W Pico Blvd Bldg 12, Los Angeles (90064-2606)
PHONE.................................310 369-8300
Fax: 310 969-0470
Yariv Milchan, *President*
Brad Weston, *CEO*
Jonathan Fischer, *COO*
Mimi Mtseng, *CFO*
Stephanie Levine, *Vice Pres*

▼ **EMP:** 60
SQ FT: 13,000
SALES (est): 8.6MM **Privately Held**
WEB: www.newregency.com
SIC: 7812 Motion picture & video production

(P-18122)
NOVASTAR POST INC
23466 Hatteras St, Woodland Hills (91367-3020)
P.O. Box 25724, Miami FL (33102-5724)
PHONE.................................323 467-5020
Fax: 323 957-8707
Greg Geddes, *President*
Bob Sky, *Vice Pres*
Aaron Wilcox, *Manager*
EMP: 52
SQ FT: 7,900
SALES (est): 1.5MM **Privately Held**
WEB: www.novastarpost.com
SIC: 7812 Audio-visual program production

(P-18123)
NW ENTERTAINMENT INC (PA)
Also Called: New Wave Entertainment
2660 W Olive Ave, Burbank (91505-4525)
PHONE.................................818 295-5000
Fax: 818 295-5001
Paul Apel, *CEO*
Brian Volk-Weiss, *President*
Rick Nowak, *COO*
Greg Woertz, *CFO*
Gary Lister, *Senior VP*
▲ **EMP:** 105
SQ FT: 40,000
SALES (est): 19.8MM **Privately Held**
WEB: www.newwaveent.com
SIC: 7812 Motion picture production

(P-18124)
P J VIDEO SERVICES INC
Also Called: Post Factory
200 N Tustin Ave Ste 120, Santa Ana (92705-3817)
PHONE.................................714 705-6088
Fax: 714 705-6090
Todd C Yates, *President*
Johnathan Hicks, *Vice Pres*
George Russell, *Engineer*
EMP: 55 **EST:** 1987
SQ FT: 17,000
SALES (est): 7.1MM **Privately Held**
WEB: www.gearmonkeyrentals.com
SIC: 7812 Video production

(P-18125)
PARAMOUNT PICTURES CORPORATION (HQ)
Also Called: Paramount Studios
5555 Melrose Ave, Los Angeles (90038-3197)
PHONE.................................323 956-5000
Fax: 323 956-0121
Brad Grey, *Ch of Bd*
Rob Moore, *Vice Chairman*
Fred T Gallo, *President*
Adam Goodman, *President*
Shana Levin, *President*
◆ **EMP:** 1700 **EST:** 1912
SALES (est): 306.7MM
SALES (corp-wide): 13.2B **Publicly Held**
WEB: www.paramount.com
SIC: 7812 5099 4833 7829 Motion picture production & distribution, television; motion picture production & distribution; video cassettes, accessories & supplies; television broadcasting stations; motion picture distribution services
PA: Viacom Inc.
1515 Broadway
New York NY 10036
212 258-6000

(P-18126)
PARAMOUNT TELEVISION SERVICE
Also Called: Paramount Pictures
5555 Melrose Ave, Los Angeles (90038-3989)
PHONE.................................323 956-5000
Brad Grey, *CEO*
EMP: 1800

7812 - Motion Picture & Video Tape Production County (P-18127)

PRODUDUCTS & SERVICES SECTION

SALES (est): 14MM
SALES (corp-wide): 13.2B **Publicly Held**
WEB: www.paramount.com
SIC: 7812 Motion picture production & distribution, television
HQ: Paramount Pictures Corporation
5555 Melrose Ave
Los Angeles CA 90038
323 956-5000

(P-18127)
PARTICIPANT MEDIA LLC
331 Foothill Rd Fl 3, Beverly Hills
(90210-3669)
PHONE..................310 550-5100
Jeff Skoll, *CEO*
Jeffrey Ivers, *COO*
Bob Murphy, *CFO*
Chad Boettcher, *Exec VP*
Ann Boyd, *Exec VP*
EMP: 65
SALES (est): 60.5K **Privately Held**
WEB: www.participantproductions.com
SIC: 7812 Motion picture & video production

(P-18128)
PIE TOWN PRODUCTIONS INC
5433 Laurel Canyon Blvd, North Hollywood
(91607-2114)
PHONE..................818 255-9300
Fax: 818 255-9333
Tara Sandler, *President*
Jennifer Davidson, *COO*
Drew Hallmann, *Executive*
Micheal Firestone, *Production*
Lori Gomez, *Producer*
EMP: 160
SALES (est): 9.2MM **Privately Held**
WEB: www.pietownproductions.com
SIC: 7812 Television film production

(P-18129)
PIXAR
Also Called: Pixar Animation Studios
1200 Park Ave, Emeryville (94608-3677)
PHONE..................510 922-3000
Fax: 510 922-3151
James W Morris, *CEO*
Liz Gazzano, *Bd of Directors*
John Lasseter, *Exec VP*
Ann Mather, *Exec VP*
Michael Agulnek, *Vice Pres*
▲ EMP: 850
SQ FT: 247,000
SALES (est): 204.5MM **Publicly Held**
WEB: www.martinreddy.net
SIC: 7812 7372 7371 Cartoon motion picture production; commercials, television: tape or film; prepackaged software; computer software development
PA: The Walt Disney Company
500 S Buena Vista St
Burbank CA 91521
-

(P-18130)
PLAYBOY ENTERPRISES INC (HQ)
Also Called: Playboy Magazine
9346 Civic Center Dr # 200, Beverly Hills
(90210-3604)
PHONE..................310 424-1800
Ben Kohn, *CEO*
David Israel, *President*
Bob Meyers, *President*
Randy A Nicolau, *President*
Alex L Vaickus, *President*
▲ EMP: 155 EST: 1953
SALES (est): 56.5MM **Privately Held**
WEB: www.playboy.com
SIC: 7812 4841 2721 Motion picture production; video production; cable & other pay television services; periodicals

(P-18131)
PLAYBOY ENTRMT GROUP INC (DH)
2300 W Empire Ave, Burbank
(91504-3341)
PHONE..................323 276-4000
Fax: 323 246-4050
Brinda Viloa, *Director*
James Griffiths, *President*
Kendice Briggs, *Vice Pres*
Martha Lindeman, *Vice Pres*

Mark Rubin, *Vice Pres*
EMP: 139
SALES (est): 10.8MM **Privately Held**
SIC: 7812 Video tape production
HQ: Playboy Enterprises, Inc.
9346 Civic Center Dr # 200
Beverly Hills CA 90210
310 424-1800

(P-18132)
POST MODERN EDIT LLC
4551 Glencoe Ave Ste 210, Marina Del Rey
(90292-7930)
PHONE..................310 396-7375
EMP: 70
SALES (corp-wide): 7.6MM **Privately Held**
SIC: 7812 Video production
PA: Post Modern Edit, Llc
2941 Alton Pkwy
Irvine CA 92606
949 608-8700

(P-18133)
POST MODERN EDIT LLC (PA)
2941 Alton Pkwy, Irvine (92606-5142)
PHONE..................949 608-8700
Fax: 949 608-8729
Rick Warren, *Financial Exec*
Amir Samnani, *Managing Prtnr*
John Walker, *Exec VP*
Mike Pearce, *Senior VP*
Rich O'Neill, *Vice Pres*
◆ EMP: 51
SQ FT: 22,000
SALES (est): 7.6MM **Privately Held**
WEB: www.postmoderngroup.com
SIC: 7812 Video production

(P-18134)
POWER STUDIOS INC
Also Called: Digital Domain
300 Rose Ave, Venice (90291-2628)
PHONE..................310 314-2800
Fax: 310 314-2888
Antholy Harri, *CEO*
Michael Bay, *Ch of Bd*
C Bradley Call, *President*
Jody Madden, *COO*
Joseph Gabriel, *Vice Pres*
EMP: 200
SQ FT: 120,000
SALES (est): 25.2MM
SALES (corp-wide): 28.7MM **Privately Held**
SIC: 7812 7819 Motion picture production; video production; services allied to motion pictures; visual effects production
PA: Wyndcrest Holdings Llc
150 Suth U S Hwy 1 St 150
Jupiter FL
772 545-9025

(P-18135)
PRG (CALIFORNIA) INC
Also Called: Fourth Phase Los Angeles
1245 Aviation Pl, San Fernando
(91340-1459)
PHONE..................818 252-2600
Fax: 818 252-2620
Jeremiah Harris, *President*
James Riendeau, *Vice Pres*
Tony Ward, *VP Prdtn*
John Roth, *Director*
Chuck Estrada, *Manager*
▲ EMP: 50
SALES (est): 7.4MM **Privately Held**
SIC: 7812 Motion picture & video production

(P-18136)
PUTTIN ON PRODUCTIONS CORP
Also Called: POPS
2010 N Sepulveda Blvd A, Manhattan Beach (90266-2906)
P.O. Box 397 (90267-0397)
PHONE..................310 546-5544
Julia Mirkovich, *Principal*
EMP: 50
SALES (est): 327.8K **Privately Held**
SIC: 7812 7911 Motion picture & video production; dance studio & school

(P-18137)
QUADRA PRODUCTIONS INC
Also Called: Wheel of Forturne
10202 Washington Blvd, Culver City
(90232-3119)
PHONE..................310 244-1234
Harry Friedman, *President*
Catherine Wozney, *Manager*
EMP: 130
SALES (est): 4.9MM
SALES (corp-wide): 69.2B **Privately Held**
WEB: www.sonypictures.com
SIC: 7812 Television film production
HQ: Sony Pictures Entertainment, Inc.
10202 Washington Blvd
Culver City CA 90232
310 244-4000

(P-18138)
RADLEYS
3780 Wilshire Blvd, Los Angeles
(90010-2805)
PHONE..................310 765-2223
Christian Thompson, *COO*
EMP: 50
SALES (est): 3.9MM **Privately Held**
SIC: 7812 Television film production

(P-18139)
RANCH HAND ENTERTAINMENT INC
11333 Moorpark St Pmb 441, Studio City
(91602-2618)
PHONE..................612 396-2632
Peter Williams, *President*
Jonathan Ward, *Vice Pres*
EMP: 68
SALES (est): 784K **Privately Held**
SIC: 7812 7389 Television film production;

(P-18140)
REEL FX INC
2115 Colorado Ave, Santa Monica
(90404-3503)
PHONE..................310 264-6440
Robin Linn, *Branch Mgr*
EMP: 50
SALES (corp-wide): 31.3MM **Privately Held**
SIC: 7812 Video production
PA: Reel Fx, Inc.
301 N Crowdus St
Dallas TX 75226
214 658-0169

(P-18141)
REGENT WORLDWIDE SALES LLC
10990 Wilshire Blvd, Los Angeles
(90024-3913)
PHONE..................310 806-4288
Fax: 310 806-4268
Stephen P Jarchow,
Stephen Macias, *Senior VP*
Paul Colichman,
Mickey Onuma, *Assistant*
EMP: 50
SALES: 12MM **Privately Held**
SIC: 7812 Motion picture production & distribution

(P-18142)
REILY WORLDWIDE INC
3000 Olympic Blvd, Santa Monica
(90404-5073)
PHONE..................310 449-4065
James M Burnett, *President*
EMP: 50
SALES (est): 1.1MM **Privately Held**
SIC: 7812 Television film production

(P-18143)
RESPOND 2 LLC
Also Called: R2c Group
727 Ansome St, San Francisco (94111)
PHONE..................415 398-4200
Fax: 415 398-1648
Mark Yesayian, *Branch Mgr*
EMP: 68
SALES (corp-wide): 25MM **Privately Held**
SIC: 7812 Video production

PA: Respond 2 Llc
207 Nw Park Ave
Portland OR 97209
503 222-0025

(P-18144)
RHYTHM AND HUES INC (PA)
Also Called: Rhythm & Hues Studios
2100 E Grand Ave Ste A, El Segundo
(90245-5055)
PHONE..................310 448-7500
John Hughes, *President*
Keith Goldfarb, *Shareholder*
Pauline TSO, *Corp Secy*
Keith Nesson, *Administration*
Jay Miya, *Systs Prg Mgr*
EMP: 65
SALES (est): 18.6MM **Privately Held**
WEB: www.floatingmuseum.com
SIC: 7812 Cartoon production, television; commercials, television: tape or film

(P-18145)
ROCK PAPER SCISSORS LLC
2308 Broadway, Santa Monica
(90404-2916)
PHONE..................310 586-0600
Angus Wall,
Arleen Rosenberg, *CFO*
Tommy Asbee, *Engineer*
Gabriel Britz, *Assoc Editor*
David Brodie, *Editor*
EMP: 50
SQ FT: 9,000
SALES (est): 6.6MM **Privately Held**
WEB: www.a52.com
SIC: 7812 8999 Commercials, television: tape or film; editorial service

(P-18146)
ROUNDABOUT ENTERTAINMENT INC
Also Called: Secuto Music
217 S Lake St, Burbank (91502-2111)
PHONE..................818 842-9300
Fax: 818 842-9301
Craig S Clark, *CEO*
Tiffany Price, *Treasurer*
Mike Esfahanian, *Vice Pres*
Randall Lehman, *Vice Pres*
Ross Millard, *Info Tech Mgr*
EMP: 84
SQ FT: 6,000
SALES (est): 9.5MM **Privately Held**
WEB: www.roundabout.com
SIC: 7812 Motion picture & video production

(P-18147)
SCRIPT TO SCREEN INC
200 N Tustin Ave Ste 200, Santa Ana
(92705-3817)
PHONE..................714 558-3287
Fax: 714 558-1759
Barbara L Kerry, *Ch of Bd*
W E Mitchell, *President*
Tony L Kerry, *Senior VP*
Frank Battisti, *Vice Pres*
Kenneth P Kerry, *Vice Pres*
EMP: 75
SQ FT: 6,000
SALES (est): 7.3MM **Privately Held**
WEB: www.scripttoscreen.com
SIC: 7812 Video production; motion picture production

(P-18148)
SENIOR PRDCRS IN RTRMNT TV
Also Called: Senior TV
75895 Altamira Dr, Indian Wells
(92210-8768)
PHONE..................760 773-9525
Janet Underwood, *Director*
EMP: 68
SALES (est): 1.7MM **Privately Held**
WEB: www.seniortv.com
SIC: 7812 Television film production

(P-18149)
SHADOW ANIMATION LLC
940 N Mansfield Ave, Los Angeles
(90038-2312)
PHONE..................323 466-7771
Fax: 323 466-7711
Alex Bulkley, *Owner*
Corey Campodonico,

▲ = Import ▼ = Export
◆ = Import/Export

PRODUCTS & SERVICES SECTION
7812 - Motion Picture & Video Tape Production County (P-18172)

Mike Roberts, *Director*
EMP: 50
SALES (est): 3.3MM **Privately Held**
WEB: www.shadowmachine.com
SIC: 7812 Motion picture & video production

(P-18150)
SMUK INC
3800 Barham Blvd Ste 410, Los Angeles (90068-1042)
PHONE..................323 904-4680
Nick Emmerson, *President*
EMP: 200
SALES (est): 11.4MM **Privately Held**
SIC: 7812 Television film production

(P-18151)
SONY ELECTRONICS INC
Also Called: Urban Sony Service Center
14450 Myford Rd, Irvine (92606-1001)
PHONE..................714 508-7634
Jim Whitehouse, *Principal*
Catherine Wozney, *Manager*
EMP: 101
SALES (corp-wide): 69.2B **Privately Held**
SIC: 7812 7622 5731 Motion picture & video production; video repair; high fidelity stereo equipment
HQ: Sony Electronics Inc.
16535 Via Esprillo Bldg 1
San Diego CA 92127
858 942-2400

(P-18152)
SONY ELECTRONICS INC
835 Howard St, San Francisco (94103-3009)
PHONE..................415 833-4796
Yvonne Miranda, *Principal*
Catherine Wozney, *Manager*
EMP: 300
SALES (corp-wide): 69.2B **Privately Held**
SIC: 7812 7832 Motion picture production & distribution; motion picture distribution, television; motion picture theaters, except drive-in
HQ: Sony Electronics Inc.
16535 Via Esprillo Bldg 1
San Diego CA 92127
858 942-2400

(P-18153)
SONY MEDIA CLOUD SERVICES
10202 Washington Blvd, Culver City (90232-3119)
PHONE..................310 244-4000
Naomi Climer, *President*
EMP: 50
SALES (est): 1.4MM
SALES (corp-wide): 69.2B **Privately Held**
SIC: 7812 7372 Video production; business oriented computer software
PA: Sony Corporation
1-7-1, Konan
Minato-Ku TKY 108-0
367 482-111

(P-18154)
SONY PICTURES ENTRMT INC (DH)
Also Called: Sony Pictures Studios
10202 Washington Blvd, Culver City (90232-3119)
PHONE..................310 244-4000
Fax: 310 244-2626
Michael Lynton, *Ch of Bd*
Doug Belgrad, *President*
Kristine Belson, *President*
David Bishop, *President*
Rory Bruer, *President*
▲ **EMP:** 3000
SALES (est): 503.4MM
SALES (corp-wide): 69.2B **Privately Held**
WEB: www.sonypictures.com
SIC: 7812 7822 7832 Motion picture production & distribution; motion picture production & distribution, television; distribution, exclusive of production: motion picture; distribution for television: motion picture; motion picture theaters, except drive-in
HQ: Sony Corporation Of America
25 Madison Ave Fl 27
New York NY 10010
212 833-8000

(P-18155)
SONY PICTURES STUDIOS INC
1250 S Beverly Glen Blvd # 112, Los Angeles (90024-5204)
PHONE..................310 244-4000
Jack Kindberg, *President*
Steve Burlie, *Vice Pres*
Jared Jussim, *Admin Sec*
Comelli Maurizio, *CIO*
Catherine Wozney, *Manager*
EMP: 380
SALES (est): 9.4MM
SALES (corp-wide): 69.2B **Privately Held**
WEB: www.sonypictures.com
SIC: 7812 Motion picture production
HQ: Sony Pictures Entertainment, Inc.
10202 Washington Blvd
Culver City CA 90232
310 244-4000

(P-18156)
SONY PICTURES TELEVISION INC (DH)
10202 Washington Blvd, Culver City (90232-3119)
PHONE..................310 244-7625
Fax: 310 244-6869
Steve Mosko, *CEO*
Drew Shearer, *CFO*
Glenn Adilman, *Exec VP*
Gregory K Boone, *Exec VP*
Jason Clodfelter, *Exec VP*
▲ **EMP:** 300
SALES: 6MM
SALES (corp-wide): 69.2B **Privately Held**
WEB: www.sonypicturestelevision.com
SIC: 7812 Motion picture production & distribution, television
HQ: Sony Pictures Entertainment, Inc.
10202 Washington Blvd
Culver City CA 90232
310 244-4000

(P-18157)
SPLASH ENTERTAINMENT LLC
21300 Oxnard St Ste 100, Woodland Hills (91367-5016)
PHONE..................818 999-0062
Fax: 818 999-0172
Mike Young, *President*
Steve Rosen, *Exec VP*
Mevelyn Noriega, *Senior VP*
David Di Lorenzo, *Vice Pres*
Tee Chhokar, *Office Mgr*
EMP: 50 **EST:** 2002
SQ FT: 21,000
SALES (est): 5.4MM **Privately Held**
SIC: 7812 Cartoon motion picture production

(P-18158)
SPORTVISION INC
6657 Kaiser Dr, Fremont (94555-3608)
PHONE..................510 736-2925
Fax: 650 961-0102
Rhonda Brewer, *Manager*
Jim McGuffin, *Sr Software Eng*
Steve Zoppi, *CTO*
Dan Thomasson, *QA Dir*
Grant Turner, *Info Tech Mgr*
EMP: 50
SALES (corp-wide): 8.7MM **Privately Held**
SIC: 7812 7371 Commercials, television: tape or film; custom computer programming services
PA: Sportvision, Inc.
4619 N Ravenswood Ave # 304
Chicago IL 60640
773 293-4300

(P-18159)
SPRING BREAK 83 PRODUCTION LLC
650 N Bronson Ave, Los Angeles (90004-1404)
PHONE..................323 871-4466
Mars Callahan, *President*
EMP: 50
SALES (est): 989.9K **Privately Held**
SIC: 7812 Television film production

(P-18160)
STARGATE FILMS INC
Also Called: Stargate Digital
1001 El Centro St, South Pasadena (91030-5206)
PHONE..................626 403-8403
Fax: 626 403-8444
Sam Nicholson, *President*
Linda Nakagawa, *CFO*
Jim Railey, *Exec VP*
Darren Frankel, *Vice Pres*
Al Lopez, *Vice Pres*
EMP: 65
SQ FT: 50,000
SALES (est): 8.2MM **Privately Held**
SIC: 7812 Motion picture production; television film production

(P-18161)
STU SEGALL PRODUCTIONS INC
4705 Ruffin Rd, San Diego (92123-1611)
PHONE..................858 974-8988
Fax: 858 974-8978
Stu Segall, *President*
Joan Etchells, *Vice Pres*
Kevin Waskow, *Vice Pres*
Christopher Burke, *Financial Exec*
Jim Byrnes, *Financial Exec*
EMP: 200
SQ FT: 1,000
SALES (est): 17.6MM **Privately Held**
WEB: www.stusegall.com
SIC: 7812 Motion picture & video production

(P-18162)
STUDY TAPES
Also Called: PINE KNOLL PUBLICATIONS
1341 Pine Knoll Cres, Redlands (92373-6545)
PHONE..................909 792-0111
Dr Gerald A Kirk, *Partner*
Cheryl J Kirk, *Partner*
▲ **EMP:** 52 **EST:** 1972
SALES: 287.5K **Privately Held**
WEB: www.pineknoll.org
SIC: 7812 5735 Video tape production; audio tapes, prerecorded

(P-18163)
SUNNY TV PRODUCTIONS INC
8660 Hayden Pl Fl 2, Culver City (90232-2902)
PHONE..................310 840-7440
Michael Rotenberg, *President*
Shelly Willis, *Accountant*
EMP: 125
SALES (est): 7.5MM **Privately Held**
SIC: 7812 Motion picture & video production

(P-18164)
T25CL ENTERTAINMENT LLC
1074 55th St, Oakland (94608-2746)
PHONE..................951 308-2040
Andre Ward, *CEO*
Ricardo Burgess, *CTO*
Rosalyn Jordan Mills, *Director*
EMP: 229
SQ FT: 8,000
SALES (est): 63MM **Privately Held**
SIC: 7812 7929 Motion picture & video production; entertainment service

(P-18165)
TAFT BROADCASTING COMPANY LLC
23755 Z St, March ARB (92518-2077)
PHONE..................951 413-2337
Robert Dawson, *Branch Mgr*
EMP: 80
SALES (corp-wide): 6.2MM **Privately Held**
WEB: www.taftbroadcasting.com
SIC: 7812 7389 Television film production; video tape production; music & broadcasting services
PA: Taft Broadcasting Company, Llc
1118 Heights Blvd
Houston TX 77008
713 692-2900

(P-18166)
TALL PONY PRODUCTIONS INC
300 Loma Metisse Rd, Malibu (90265-3059)
P.O. Box 1026 (90265-1026)
PHONE..................310 456-7495
Fax: 310 979-5557
Anthony Eaton, *President*
EMP: 150
SQ FT: 2,000
SALES (est): 3.4MM **Privately Held**
WEB: www.tallponyproductions.com
SIC: 7812 Television film production

(P-18167)
TECHNICOLOR NEW MEDIA INC
250 E Olive Ave Ste 300, Burbank (91502-1211)
PHONE..................818 480-5100
Dave Weaphers, *President*
Bill Redmann, *Vice Pres*
Robyn Christensen, *Human Res Mgr*
Barbara Giacomelli, *Buyer*
Gentry Shae, *Transptn Dir*
EMP: 50
SALES (est): 3.4MM **Privately Held**
SIC: 7812 Audio-visual program production

(P-18168)
TIME WARNER CABLE ENTPS LLC
3500 W Olive Ave Ste 1000, Burbank (91505-5515)
PHONE..................818 972-0808
Robert Bordiga, *Legal Staff*
EMP: 75
SALES (corp-wide): 9.7MM **Publicly Held**
SIC: 7812 Motion picture & video production; television film production
HQ: Time Warner Cable Enterprises Llc
60 Columbus Cir Fl 17
New York NY 10023
877 495-9201

(P-18169)
TOUCHSTONE TELEVISION PROD LLC (PA)
500 S Buena Vista St, Burbank (91521-0001)
PHONE..................323 671-5116
Mark Pedowitz, *President*
EMP: 55
SALES (est): 12.4MM **Privately Held**
SIC: 7812 Non-theatrical motion picture production, television

(P-18170)
TRIAGE ENTERTAINMENT INC
6701 Center Dr W Ste 1111, Los Angeles (90045-1552)
PHONE..................310 417-4800
Fax: 310 410-1542
Stuart M Schreiberg, *President*
Pat Shea, *CFO*
Stephen Kroopnick, *Exec VP*
John Bravakis, *Vice Pres*
Mike Liska, *Manager*
EMP: 60
SQ FT: 15,000
SALES (est): 6.7MM **Privately Held**
WEB: www.triageinc.com
SIC: 7812 Motion picture & video production

(P-18171)
TRICOR ENTERTAINMENT INC
Also Called: Chinaamerica Film Distributors
1613 Chelsea Rd, San Marino (91108-2419)
PHONE..................626 282-5184
Craig Darian, *Chairman*
Howard Kazanjian, *Co-COB*
Sally Austin, *Exec VP*
William E Wegner, *General Counsel*
EMP: 240
SQ FT: 350,000
SALES (est): 3.6MM **Privately Held**
SIC: 7812 Motion picture production; television film production

(P-18172)
TTT WEST COAST INC
1840 Victory Blvd, Glendale (91201-2558)
PHONE..................818 972-0500
Mike Darnell, *President*

7812 - Motion Picture & Video Tape Production County (P-18173)

Dave Goldberg, *Vice Pres*
Michael Corbett, *Correspondent*
EMP: 200
SALES (est): 6.2MM
SALES (corp-wide): 3.1B **Publicly Held**
SIC: 7812 Motion picture production; television film production
PA: Time Inc.
  225 Liberty St
  New York NY 10281
  212 522-1212

(P-18173)
TURNER BROADCASTING SYSTEM INC
Also Called: TNT Originals
3500 W Olive Ave Ste 1500, Burbank (91505-4630)
PHONE 818 977-5452
Sandra Dewey, *Vice Pres*
James Robertson, *Vice Pres*
Gary Crotty, *CIO*
David Keehn, *Technical Mgr*
Eric Mortensen, *Web Dvlpr*
EMP: 50
SALES (corp-wide): 28.1B **Publicly Held**
WEB: www.turner.com
SIC: 7812 Television film production
HQ: Turner Broadcasting System, Inc.
  1 Cnn Ctr Nw
  Atlanta GA 30303
  404 827-1700

(P-18174)
TWENTIETH CNTURY FOX FILM CORP (DH)
Also Called: Fox Films Entertainment
10201 W Pico Blvd, Los Angeles (90064-2606)
P.O. Box 900, Beverly Hills (90213-0900)
PHONE 310 369-1000
Fax: 310 203-1558
K Rupert Murdoch, *Ch of Bd*
Robert Harper, *Vice Chairman*
Dean Hallett, *CFO*
Chase Carey, *Sr Corp Ofcr*
Jon Eelbarrio, *Sr Corp Ofcr*
▲ **EMP:** 75
SQ FT: 25,000
SALES (est): 372.2MM
SALES (corp-wide): 27.3B **Publicly Held**
WEB: www.foxmovies.com
SIC: 7812 Motion picture production & distribution; video tape production; motion picture production & distribution, television; television film production
HQ: Fox Entertainment Group, Inc.
  2029 Century Park E # 1400
  Los Angeles CA 90067
  310 369-1000

(P-18175)
TWENTIETH CNTURY FOX FILM CORP
Fox Video International
2121 Avenue Of The Stars, Los Angeles (90067-5010)
P.O. Box 900, Beverly Hills (90213-0900)
PHONE 310 369-2582
Fax: 310 369-5262
Marc Dilorenzo, *President*
Peter Byrne, *Exec VP*
Mary Daily, *Exec VP*
James Finn, *Senior VP*
David Shall, *Senior VP*
EMP: 80
SALES (corp-wide): 27.3B **Publicly Held**
WEB: www.foxmovies.com
SIC: 7812 Television film production
HQ: Twentieth Century Fox Film Corporation
  10201 W Pico Blvd
  Los Angeles CA 90064
  310 369-1000

(P-18176)
UNIVERSAL CITY STUDIOS INC
2220 Colorado Ave, Santa Monica (90404-3506)
PHONE 310 865-5000
Darcey Graver, *Principal*
Chuck Ciongoli, *CFO*
Doug Strain, *Info Tech Dir*
Duncan Chan, *Applctn Conslt*
Ka Cheng, *Technology*
EMP: 100

SALES (corp-wide): 74.5B **Publicly Held**
SIC: 7812 Motion picture production & distribution
HQ: Universal City Studios, Inc.
  100 Universal City Plz
  Universal City CA 91608
  818 622-8477

(P-18177)
UNIVERSAL CITY STUDIOS LLC
Also Called: Universal Studios Hollywood
100 Universal City Plz, Universal City (91608-1085)
PHONE 818 777-1000
Richard Cotton, *Mng Member*
Eliot Sekuler, *President*
Jeffrey M Brauer, *Senior VP*
Hollace Davids, *Senior VP*
Michael Silver, *Senior VP*
EMP: 73
SALES (est): 12.9MM
SALES (corp-wide): 74.5B **Publicly Held**
SIC: 7812 Motion picture production & distribution
HQ: Nbcuniversal Media, Llc
  30 Rockefeller Plz Fl 2
  New York NY 10112
  212 664-4444

(P-18178)
UNIVERSAL STDIOS HM ENTRMT LLC
100 Universal City Plz, Universal City (91608-1002)
PHONE 818 777-1000
Ed Cunningham, *President*
Matt Apice, *Senior VP*
Chris Easley, *Manager*
Eric Martin, *Manager*
Annah Zafrani, *Manager*
EMP: 720
SALES (est): 858.5K
SALES (corp-wide): 74.5B **Publicly Held**
SIC: 7812 Motion picture & video production
HQ: Nbc Universal, Llc
  1221 Avenue Of The Americ
  New York NY 10020
  212 664-4444

(P-18179)
UNIVERSAL STUDIOS INC
Also Called: MCA Music
1000 Univ Studio Blvd 2, Universal City (91608-1008)
PHONE 818 622-4455
James Warren, *Manager*
Kathy Mandato, *Senior VP*
EMP: 400
SALES (corp-wide): 74.5B **Publicly Held**
WEB: www.universalstudios.com
SIC: 7812 Motion picture & video production
HQ: Universal Studios, Inc.
  100 Universal City Plz
  North Hollywood CA 91608
  818 777-1000

(P-18180)
UNIVERSAL STUDIOS INC (DH)
100 Universal City Plz, North Hollywood (91608-1002)
PHONE 818 777-1000
Fax: 818 866-1438
Adam Fogelson, *Chairman*
Ron Meyer, *President*
Zach Horowitz, *COO*
Larry Kurzweil, *COO*
Mike Allen, *CFO*
▲ **EMP:** 141 **EST:** 1924
SQ FT: 100,000
SALES (est): 932.9MM
SALES (corp-wide): 74.5B **Publicly Held**
WEB: www.universalstudios.com
SIC: 7812 3652 2741 5947 Motion picture production & distribution; television film production; phonograph records, prerecorded; magnetic tape (audio): prerecorded; compact laser discs, prerecorded; music, sheet: publishing & printing; gift shop; novelties; jewelry stores; gift items, mail order; novelty merchandise, mail order; jewelry, mail order

HQ: Nbcuniversal Media, Llc
  30 Rockefeller Plz Fl 2
  New York NY 10112
  212 664-4444

(P-18181)
UNIVERSAL STUDIOS INC
MCA Music
100 Universal City Plz # 3, Universal City (91608-1002)
PHONE 818 777-1000
Larry Miller, *Manager*
Frank Soronow, *Sr Ntwrk Engine*
EMP: 155
SALES (corp-wide): 74.5B **Publicly Held**
WEB: www.universalstudios.com
SIC: 7812 Motion picture & video production
HQ: Universal Studios, Inc.
  100 Universal City Plz
  North Hollywood CA 91608
  818 777-1000

(P-18182)
UNIVERSAL STUDIOS INC
1295 Los Angeles St Ste 1, Glendale (91204-2403)
PHONE 818 262-4301
Kate Sullivan, *Branch Mgr*
EMP: 155
SALES (corp-wide): 74.5B **Publicly Held**
WEB: www.universalstudios.com
SIC: 7812 Motion picture & video production
HQ: Universal Studios, Inc.
  100 Universal City Plz
  North Hollywood CA 91608
  818 777-1000

(P-18183)
UNIVERSAL STUDIOS INC
2440 S Sepulveda Blvd # 100, Los Angeles (90064-1784)
PHONE 310 235-4749
David Renzer, *Principal*
Chris Monaco, *Senior VP*
Liz Alvarado, *Vice Pres*
Dan Bess, *Vice Pres*
Alisann Blood, *Vice Pres*
EMP: 125
SALES (corp-wide): 74.5B **Publicly Held**
WEB: www.universalstudios.com
SIC: 7812 Motion picture & video production
HQ: Universal Studios, Inc.
  100 Universal City Plz
  North Hollywood CA 91608
  818 777-1000

(P-18184)
UNIVERSAL STUDIOS INC
MCA Music
4123 Lankershim Blvd, North Hollywood (91602-2828)
PHONE 818 753-0000
George Smith, *Manager*
EMP: 100
SALES (corp-wide): 74.5B **Publicly Held**
WEB: www.universalstudios.com
SIC: 7812 Motion picture & video production
HQ: Universal Studios, Inc.
  100 Universal City Plz
  North Hollywood CA 91608
  818 777-1000

(P-18185)
UNIVERSAL STUDIOS INC
3900 Lankershim Blvd, Studio City (91604)
PHONE 818 777-2351
Edgar Bromfrom Jr, *Manager*
EMP: 155
SALES (corp-wide): 74.5B **Publicly Held**
WEB: www.universalstudios.com
SIC: 7812 Motion picture & video production
HQ: Universal Studios, Inc.
  100 Universal City Plz
  North Hollywood CA 91608
  818 777-1000

(P-18186)
UP STAGE INC
Also Called: Stage Right Production Svcs
30757 Canwood St, Agoura (91301-2022)
PHONE 818 879-8781

Thomas Peachee, *President*
Lisa Peachee, *Admin Sec*
EMP: 50
SALES (est): 899.6K **Privately Held**
SIC: 7812 Commercials, television: tape or film

(P-18187)
VIVID ENTERTAINMENT LLC
3599 Cahuenga Blvd W, Los Angeles (90068-1397)
PHONE 323 845-4557
Steven Hirsch,
Ken Boenish, *President*
Michael H Klein, *President*
Marci Hirsch, *Buyer*
David James,
EMP: 50
SQ FT: 15,000
SALES (est): 6.3MM **Privately Held**
WEB: www.bi-bi.com
SIC: 7812 5099 Video tape production; video & audio equipment

(P-18188)
WAD PRODUCTIONS INC
Also Called: Ellen Degeneres Show, The
3500 W Olive Ave Ste 1000, Burbank (91505-5515)
PHONE 818 260-5673
Greg Gorden, *President*
EMP: 99
SALES (est): 5.4MM **Privately Held**
SIC: 7812 Motion picture & video production

(P-18189)
WALT DISNEY COMPANY
601 Circle Seven Dr, Glendale (91201-2332)
PHONE 818 553-4222
Jan Smith, *Branch Mgr*
Laura Kampo, *Vice Pres*
Howard Safenowitz, *Vice Pres*
Maeis Heshmati, *Research*
Cliff Wong, *Engineer*
EMP: 120 **Publicly Held**
SIC: 7812 Motion picture production & distribution; motion picture production & distribution, television; video tape production; television film production
PA: The Walt Disney Company
  500 S Buena Vista St
  Burbank CA 91521

(P-18190)
WALT DISNEY RECORDS DIRECT (DH)
500 S Buena Vista St, Burbank (91521-0007)
PHONE 818 560-1000
Alan H Bergman, *Senior VP*
Rob Moore, *CFO*
Nick Franklin, *Senior VP*
Marsha Reed, *Admin Sec*
◆ **EMP:** 2990
SQ FT: 600,000
SALES (est): 76.7MM **Publicly Held**
WEB: www.radiodisney.com
SIC: 7812 Motion picture production & distribution; motion picture production & distribution, television; non-theatrical motion picture production; non-theatrical motion picture production, television
HQ: Disney Enterprises, Inc.
  500 S Buena Vista St
  Burbank CA 91521
  818 560-1000

(P-18191)
WARNER BROS ENTERTAINMENT INC
Also Called: Warner Bros. Paint Department
4000 Warner Blvd, Burbank (91522-0002)
PHONE 818 954-1817
Ron Stansberry, *Manager*
EMP: 120
SALES (corp-wide): 28.1B **Publicly Held**
SIC: 7812 7384 Motion picture & video production; home movies, developing & processing
HQ: Warner Bros. Entertainment Inc.
  4000 Warner Blvd
  Burbank CA 91522
  818 954-6000

PRODUCTS & SERVICES SECTION
7819 - Services Allied To Motion Picture Prdtn County (P-18213)

(P-18192)
WARNER BROS ENTERTAINMENT INC
Also Called: Warner Bros. Legal Department
4000 Warner Blvd, Burbank (91522-0002)
PHONE..................818 954-7232
Peter Roch, *President*
Josh Reich, *Vice Pres*
Cheryl Valentine, *Vice Pres*
Deangelo D Jones, *Marketing Staff*
Nona Tallada, *Sales Staff*
EMP: 447
SALES (corp-wide): 28.1B **Publicly Held**
SIC: 7812 8111 Motion picture & video production; specialized legal services
HQ: Warner Bros. Entertainment Inc.
4000 Warner Blvd
Burbank CA 91522
818 954-6000

(P-18193)
WARNER BROS ENTERTAINMENT INC
Also Called: Warner Bros Studio Facilities
4000 Warner Blvd, Burbank (91522-0002)
PHONE..................818 954-3000
David Camp, *Manager*
Janet Grady, *Vice Pres*
EMP: 168
SALES (corp-wide): 28.1B **Publicly Held**
SIC: 7812 Motion picture production; television film production
HQ: Warner Bros. Entertainment Inc.
4000 Warner Blvd
Burbank CA 91522
818 954-6000

(P-18194)
WARNER BROS ENTERTAINMENT INC
Also Called: Warner Bros Domestic TV Dist
4000 Warner Blvd Bldg 118, Burbank (91522-0002)
PHONE..................818 954-5301
Mike Troxler, *Branch Mgr*
EMP: 168
SALES (corp-wide): 28.1B **Publicly Held**
SIC: 7812 Motion picture production & distribution, television
HQ: Warner Bros. Entertainment Inc.
4000 Warner Blvd
Burbank CA 91522
818 954-6000

(P-18195)
WARNER BROS ENTERTAINMENT INC (HQ)
Also Called: Victory Studio
4000 Warner Blvd, Burbank (91522-0002)
PHONE..................818 954-6000
Kevin Tsujihara, *CEO*
Alan Horn, *President*
Kim Williams, *CFO*
Richard J Fox, *Exec VP*
Dee Dee Myers, *Exec VP*
▲ **EMP:** 5000
SALES (est): 538.4MM
SALES (corp-wide): 28.1B **Publicly Held**
SIC: 7812 Motion picture & video production; television film production
PA: Time Warner Inc.
1 Time Warner Ctr Bsmt B
New York NY 10019
212 484-8000

(P-18196)
WARNER BROS ENTERTAINMENT INC
Warner Bros. Animation
4000 Warner Blvd, Burbank (91522-0002)
PHONE..................818 954-3000
Fax: 818 977-0125
Nina Naranja, *Branch Mgr*
EMP: 168
SALES (corp-wide): 28.1B **Publicly Held**
SIC: 7812 Cartoon motion picture production
HQ: Warner Bros. Entertainment Inc.
4000 Warner Blvd
Burbank CA 91522
818 954-6000

(P-18197)
WARNER BROS ENTERTAINMENT INC
Also Called: The War At Home Series
4000 Warner Blvd Bldg 137, Burbank (91522-0002)
PHONE..................818 954-7065
Henry Johnson, *Vice Pres*
EMP: 100
SALES (corp-wide): 28.1B **Publicly Held**
SIC: 7812 Motion picture & video production
HQ: Warner Bros. Entertainment Inc.
4000 Warner Blvd
Burbank CA 91522
818 954-6000

(P-18198)
WARNER BROS ENTERTAINMENT INC
4000 Warner Blvd Bldg 30, Burbank (91522-0002)
PHONE..................818 954-2181
Randy Hoffman, *Branch Mgr*
EMP: 168
SALES (corp-wide): 28.1B **Publicly Held**
SIC: 7812 Motion picture production & distribution, television
HQ: Warner Bros. Entertainment Inc.
4000 Warner Blvd
Burbank CA 91522
818 954-6000

(P-18199)
WARNER BROS ENTERTAINMENT INC
Also Called: Warner Bros Accounting Dept
4000 Warner Blvd B-156, Burbank (91522-0002)
PHONE..................818 954-2187
Cheryl Mathison, *Principal*
EMP: 168
SALES (corp-wide): 28.1B **Publicly Held**
SIC: 7812 8721 Motion picture & video production; accounting, auditing & bookkeeping
HQ: Warner Bros. Entertainment Inc.
4000 Warner Blvd
Burbank CA 91522
818 954-6000

(P-18200)
WARNER BROS ENTERTAINMENT INC
4000 Warner Blvd Bldg 30, Burbank (91522-0002)
PHONE..................818 954-6000
EMP: 168
SALES (corp-wide): 28.1B **Publicly Held**
SIC: 7812 Motion picture & video production
HQ: Warner Bros. Entertainment Inc.
4000 Warner Blvd
Burbank CA 91522
818 954-6000

(P-18201)
WARNER BROS INTL TV DIST INC
4000 Warner Blvd, Burbank (91522-0002)
PHONE..................818 954-6000
Jeffrey R Schlesinger, *President*
Margee Schubert, *Director*
EMP: 99
SALES (est): 2.7MM
SALES (corp-wide): 28.1B **Publicly Held**
SIC: 7812 Motion picture & video production
HQ: Warner Bros. Entertainment Inc.
4000 Warner Blvd
Burbank CA 91522
818 954-6000

(P-18202)
WARNER FILMS LLC
468 N Camden Dr, Beverly Hills (90210-4507)
PHONE..................310 601-3184
Jon Divens, *Mng Member*
EMP: 150
SALES (est): 1.9MM **Privately Held**
WEB: www.warnerfilms.com
SIC: 7812 Motion picture production

(P-18203)
WATCHIT MEDIA INC
655 Montgomery St # 1000, San Francisco (94111-2635)
PHONE..................702 740-1700
James R Lavelle, *Ch of Bd*
John Dong, *CFO*
Jeff Bernardis, *Vice Pres*
Steven C Machiorlette, *Vice Pres*
George P Salerno, *Vice Pres*
EMP: 140
SALES (est): 2.8MM **Privately Held**
WEB: www.cotl.com
SIC: 7812 7822 Motion picture production & distribution, television; film exchange for television; motion picture

(P-18204)
WEINSTEIN COMPANY LLC
9100 Wilshire Blvd 700w, Beverly Hills (90212-3466)
PHONE..................424 204-4800
Harvey Weinstein,
EMP: 60
SALES (corp-wide): 48.8MM **Privately Held**
SIC: 7812 Audio-visual program production
PA: The Weinstein Company Llc
99 Hudson St Fl 4
New York NY 10013
212 845-8600

(P-18205)
WESTWIND MEDIA INC
100 W Alameda Ave, Burbank (91502-2208)
PHONE..................818 972-9000
Fax: 818 953-4065
John A Bidasio, *President*
Dani Pasli, *Office Mgr*
Ben Benedetti, *VP Sales*
EMP: 55
SQ FT: 20,000
SALES (est): 3.3MM **Privately Held**
SIC: 7812 Non-theatrical motion picture production, television

(P-18206)
WESTWIND STUDIOS LLC
Also Called: Westwind Media
100 W Alameda Ave, Burbank (91502-2208)
PHONE..................818 972-9000
John A Bidasio, *Mng Member*
Danny Pasley, *Controller*
Stephen Cannell,
Leland Postil,
EMP: 50
SQ FT: 20,000
SALES: 9MM **Privately Held**
SIC: 7812 Motion picture production; television film production

(P-18207)
YES VIDEOCOM INC (PA)
2805 Bowers Ave Ste 130, Santa Clara (95051-0971)
PHONE..................408 907-7600
Michael Chang, *CEO*
Bill Embleton, *Vice Pres*
Sharleen Reyes, *Executive*
Allison Strouse, *Executive*
Steve Bi, *Sr Software Eng*
▲ **EMP:** 90
SQ FT: 36,000
SALES (est): 28.7MM **Privately Held**
WEB: www.yesvideo.com
SIC: 7812 Motion picture production

(P-18208)
ZEFR INC
Also Called: Movieclips.com
1621 Abbot Kinney Blvd, Venice (90291-3744)
PHONE..................310 392-3555
Rich Raddon, *President*
Jason Kirk, *Exec VP*
Dave Rosner, *Senior VP*
Michael Saperstein, *Senior VP*
Rick Bashkoff, *Vice Pres*
EMP: 200
SALES (est): 17.3MM **Privately Held**
SIC: 7812 Motion picture production

(P-18209)
ZOIC INC
Also Called: Zoic Studios
3582 Eastham Dr, Culver City (90232-2409)
PHONE..................310 838-0770
Fax: 310 838-1169
Loni Peristere, *CEO*
Chris Jones, *President*
Tim McBride, *Treasurer*
Saker Klippsten, *CTO*
Marco Valenzuela, *Technology*
EMP: 125
SQ FT: 15,000
SALES (est): 15.5MM **Privately Held**
WEB: www.zoicstudios.com
SIC: 7812 Motion picture & video production

7819 Services Allied To Motion Picture Prdtn

(P-18210)
525 STUDIOS INC
1632 5th St, Santa Monica (90401-3318)
PHONE..................310 525-1234
Od Welch, *President*
EMP: 70
SQ FT: 19,000
SALES (est): 1.2MM **Privately Held**
SIC: 7819 TV tape services: editing, transfers, etc.

(P-18211)
A FILML INC
Also Called: Film|.a
6255 W Sunset Blvd Fl 12, Los Angeles (90028-7428)
PHONE..................213 977-8600
Fax: 213 977-8610
Paul Audley, *President*
Michael Bennett, *CFO*
Denise Gutches, *CFO*
Art Yoon, *Exec VP*
Wayne Gustafson, *Vice Pres*
EMP: 70
SALES: 11.1MM **Privately Held**
WEB: www.filmla.com
SIC: 7819 Services allied to motion pictures

(P-18212)
ACADEMY FOUNDATION (HQ)
8949 Wilshire Blvd, Beverly Hills (90211-1907)
PHONE..................310 247-3000
Fax: 310 271-3395
Bruce Davis, *Exec Dir*
Andrew Horn, *Comms Dir*
EMP: 50
SQ FT: 35,000
SALES: 21.8MM
SALES (corp-wide): 108.4MM **Privately Held**
WEB: www.academyfoundation.com
SIC: 7819 Services allied to motion pictures
PA: Academy Of Motion Picture Arts & Sciences
8949 Wilshire Blvd
Beverly Hills CA 90211
310 247-3000

(P-18213)
ALOM TECHNOLOGIES CORPORATION (PA)
48105 Warm Springs Blvd, Fremont (94539-7498)
PHONE..................510 360-3600
Fax: 510 226-7617
Hannah Kain, *President*
Kain Hannah, *CFO*
Phil Roloff, *CFO*
Raj Muni, *Exec VP*
Alice Johnson, *Vice Pres*
▲ **EMP:** 95
SQ FT: 150,000
SALES (est): 16.3MM **Privately Held**
WEB: www.alom.com
SIC: 7819 7374 7331 6099 Services allied to motion pictures; data processing & preparation; direct mail advertising services; automated clearinghouses; catalog & mail-order houses; packing & crating

7819 - Services Allied To Motion Picture Prdtn County (P-18214)

(P-18214)
ANT FARM LLC
110 S Fairfax Ave Ste 200, Los Angeles (90036-2174)
PHONE....................323 850-0700
Fax: 323 850-0777
Doug Brandt, *CEO*
Melissa Palazzo, *CFO*
Scott Cookson, *Vice Pres*
Lucas Christman, *Creative Dir*
Lisa Riznikove, *Creative Dir*
EMP: 120
SQ FT: 17,500
SALES (est): 17.7MM **Privately Held**
SIC: 7819 Film processing, editing & titling: motion picture

(P-18215)
AVONGARD PRODUCTS USA LTD
Also Called: Hydraulx
1700 W El Segundo Blvd, Gardena (90249-2012)
PHONE....................310 319-2300
David Strause, *President*
Gregor D Strause, *CEO*
Colin Strause, *Vice Pres*
Shelly Michelson, *General Mgr*
Linda Strause, *Admin Sec*
EMP: 50
SQ FT: 8,000
SALES (est): 8.5MM **Privately Held**
WEB: www.avongard.com
SIC: 7819 Visual effects production

(P-18216)
BAY AREA VIDEO COALITION INC
Also Called: Bavc
2727 Mariposa St Fl 2, San Francisco (94110-1401)
PHONE....................415 861-3282
Fax: 415 861-4316
Ken Ikeda, *Director*
Susan Walters, *Vice Pres*
Mindy Aronoff, *Business Dir*
Zoe Banks, *Exec Dir*
Innesa Goldman, *Accountant*
EMP: 55 EST: 1977
SQ FT: 25,000
SALES: 4.7MM **Privately Held**
WEB: www.bavc.org
SIC: 7819 8249 Video tape or disk reproduction; vocational schools

(P-18217)
CHAPMAN/LEONARD STUDIO EQP INC (PA)
12950 Raymer St, North Hollywood (91605-4211)
PHONE....................323 877-5309
Fax: 818 764-2728
Leonard Chapman, *President*
Charles Huenergardt, *CFO*
Michael Chapman, *Corp Secy*
Michaela Barnes, *Managing Dir*
Jessica Harville, *Admin Asst*
▲ EMP: 145
SQ FT: 300,000
SALES (est): 21.3MM **Privately Held**
WEB: www.chapman-leonard.com
SIC: 7819 Studio property rental, motion picture

(P-18218)
CINELEASE INC (HQ)
5375 W San Fernando Rd, Los Angeles (90039-1013)
PHONE....................855 441-5500
Fax: 818 954-9641
Steven Ortiz, *President*
Brian Macdonald, *President*
Scott Massengill, *Treasurer*
Joseph Ball, *Vice Pres*
Jeffrey Greener, *Office Mgr*
▲ EMP: 50
SALES (est): 10MM
SALES (corp-wide): 13.3B **Publicly Held**
SIC: 7819 Equipment rental, motion picture
PA: Herc Holdings Inc.
27500 Riverview Ctr Blvd
Bonita Springs FL 34134
239 301-1000

(P-18219)
CMS LLNL
7000 East Ave Msl090, Livermore (94550-9698)
PHONE....................925 422-5584
Kim Hallock, *Office Admin*
David Conner, *Administration*
Howard Wright, *Administration*
Teresa Kamakea, *Systems Admin*
Cheryl Collins, *Network Enginr*
EMP: 62
SALES (est): 7.9MM **Privately Held**
SIC: 7819 Laboratory service, motion picture

(P-18220)
COMPANY 3 INC
1661 Lincoln Blvd Ste 400, Santa Monica (90404-3741)
PHONE....................310 255-6600
Fax: 310 255-6602
Stefan Sonnenfeld, *President*
Emily Schaeberle, *Executive Asst*
Douglas Leu, *Administration*
Michael Perl, *Data Proc Staff*
Rich Girardi, *Senior Engr*
EMP: 90
SALES (est): 10MM
SALES (corp-wide): 1.7B **Publicly Held**
SIC: 7819 Services allied to motion pictures
PA: Deluxe Corporation
3680 Victoria St N
Shoreview MN 55126
651 483-7111

(P-18221)
DELUXE DIGITAL DIST INC
2400 W Empire Ave Ste 200, Los Angeles (90027)
PHONE....................818 260-6202
Cyril Drabinsky, *CEO*
Warren Stein, *Exec VP*
Don Gunn, *Manager*
EMP: 50
SALES (est): 4.6MM **Privately Held**
SIC: 7819 Services allied to motion pictures

(P-18222)
DELUXE LABORATORIES INC (DH)
Also Called: Color By Deluxe
2400 W Empire Ave Ste 200, Burbank (91504-3355)
PHONE....................323 462-6171
Fax: 323 461-0608
Cyril Drabinsky, *CEO*
Mike Gunter, *CFO*
Scott Ehrlich, *Exec VP*
Dashiell Morrison, *Exec VP*
Warren Stein, *Exec VP*
EMP: 626 EST: 1990
SQ FT: 150,000
SALES (est): 61.7MM
SALES (corp-wide): 5.3B **Privately Held**
SIC: 7819 Film processing, editing & titling: motion picture
HQ: Deluxe Entertainment Services Group Inc.
2400 W Empire Ave
Los Angeles CA 90027
323 462-6171

(P-18223)
DIRECTORS GUILD AMERICA INC (PA)
Also Called: D G A
7920 W Sunset Blvd # 600, Los Angeles (90046-3334)
PHONE....................310 289-2000
Fax: 310 289-5340
Jay D Roth, *Exec Dir*
Michael Apted, *President*
Brian O'Rourke, *CFO*
Scott Berger, *Treasurer*
Gilbert Cates, *Corp Secy*
EMP: 110
SQ FT: 100,000
SALES: 25.6MM **Privately Held**
WEB: www.directors-guild.com
SIC: 7819 8631 Directors, independent: motion picture; labor unions & similar labor organizations

(P-18224)
DTS INC (PA)
5220 Las Virgenes Rd, Calabasas (91302-1064)
PHONE....................818 436-1000
Fax: 818 879-7668
Jon E Kirchner, *Ch of Bd*
Brian D Towne, *COO*
Melvin L Flanigan, *CFO*
Kevin Doohan, *Exec VP*
Frederick L Kitson, *Exec VP*
▲ EMP: 150
SQ FT: 89,000
SALES: 138.2MM **Publicly Held**
WEB: www.dtsonline.com
SIC: 7819 3651 Services allied to motion pictures; household audio & video equipment

(P-18225)
ENCORE MEDIA SERVICES INC
24853 Avenue Rockefeller, Valencia (91355-3468)
PHONE....................661 705-1323
Steve Kalson, *CFO*
EMP: 86
SALES: 21.5MM **Privately Held**
SIC: 7819 3652 Services allied to motion pictures; compact laser discs, prerecorded

(P-18226)
ESC ENTERTAINMENT INC
4000 Warner Blvd, Burbank (91522-0001)
PHONE....................818 954-1018
Tom Davila, *President*
Ed Jones, *CEO*
Tom Settle, *CFO*
EMP: 250
SQ FT: 61,000
SALES (est): 16.1MM **Privately Held**
SIC: 7819 Visual effects production

(P-18227)
FOTO-KEM INDUSTRIES INC (PA)
Also Called: Foto Kem Film & Video
2801 W Alameda Ave, Burbank (91505-4405)
P.O. Box 7755 (91510-7755)
PHONE....................818 846-3102
Fax: 818 841-2130
William F Brodersen, *CEO*
Robert Semmer, *COO*
Melaine Diego, *Bd of Directors*
Peter Santoro, *Senior VP*
Gerald D Brodersen Jr, *Vice Pres*
▲ EMP: 600
SQ FT: 43,000
SALES (est): 94.9MM **Privately Held**
WEB: www.fotokem.com
SIC: 7819 Laboratory service, motion picture; developing & printing of commercial motion picture film

(P-18228)
FOTO-KEM INDUSTRIES INC
Also Called: Fotokem
2801 W Olive Ave, Burbank (91505-4578)
PHONE....................818 846-3102
Fax: 818 841-7607
William Brodersen, *President*
Ronnie Bordey, *Technical Mgr*
Thomas Ennis, *VP Sales*
James Haley, *Director*
Shawn Leonard, *Supervisor*
EMP: 500
SALES (corp-wide): 94.9MM **Privately Held**
WEB: www.fotokem.com
SIC: 7819 Laboratory service, motion picture; developing & printing of commercial motion picture film
PA: Foto-Kem Industries, Inc.
2801 W Alameda Ave
Burbank CA 91505
818 846-3102

(P-18229)
FUSEFX INC
14823 Califa St, Van Nuys (91411-3108)
PHONE....................661 644-0783
David Altenau, *President*
Jason Fotter, *Principal*
EMP: 140
SQ FT: 12,500
SALES (est): 1.2MM **Privately Held**
SIC: 7819 Visual effects production

(P-18230)
HIGH TECHNOLOGY VIDEO INC
Also Called: H T V
10900 Ventura Blvd, Studio City (91604-3340)
PHONE....................323 969-8822
Fax: 323 969-8860
Jim Hardy, *CEO*
Steve Weiner, *Chairman*
Steve Tannen, *Chief Mktg Ofcr*
Steve Galloway, *Senior VP*
Larry Wyner, *Admin Sec*
EMP: 73
SQ FT: 30,000
SALES (est): 12.3MM **Privately Held**
WEB: www.htvinc.net
SIC: 7819 Video tape or disk reproduction

(P-18231)
HOLLYWOOD RNTALS PROD SVCS LLC (PA)
12800 Foothill Blvd, Sylmar (91342-5315)
PHONE....................818 407-7800
Mark A Rosenthal, *Mng Member*
Godwin Eruaga, *Finance Dir*
Hil Lackey, *Manager*
Jeff Porter, *Manager*
Andres Prieto, *Manager*
▲ EMP: 100
SQ FT: 100,000
SALES (est): 16.5MM **Privately Held**
WEB: www.hollywoodrentals.com
SIC: 7819 Equipment rental, motion picture

(P-18232)
IMAX CORPORATION
12582 Millennium, Los Angeles (90094-2823)
PHONE....................310 255-5500
Fax: 310 255-5501
Richard Gelfond, *CEO*
Greg Foster, *President*
Heather Anthony, *Vice Pres*
Rene Steel, *Executive Asst*
◆ EMP: 71
SALES (est): 16.2MM
SALES (corp-wide): 290.5MM **Privately Held**
WEB: www.imaxcorporation.com
SIC: 7819 Visual effects production
PA: Imax Corporation
2525 Speakman Dr
Mississauga ON L5K 1
905 403-6500

(P-18233)
JACKSON SHRUB SUPPLY INC
11505 Vanowen St, North Hollywood (91605-6232)
PHONE....................818 982-0100
Fax: 818 982-1310
Gary Jackson, *President*
Linda Jackson, *Executive*
Consuelo Vasquez, *Human Resources*
Danny Catalan, *Marketing Staff*
Robert Megge, *Manager*
EMP: 60
SQ FT: 16,000
SALES (est): 4.2MM **Privately Held**
WEB: www.jacksonshrub.com
SIC: 7819 Services allied to motion pictures

(P-18234)
MBS EQUIPMENT COMPANY (PA)
Also Called: Tm Motion Picture Eqp Rentals
4060 Ince Blvd, Culver City (90232-2602)
PHONE....................310 558-3100
Tom May, *President*
Bob Socha, *Exec Dir*
EMP: 76
SALES (est): 20.9MM **Privately Held**
SIC: 7819 Services allied to motion pictures

(P-18235)
MODERN VIDEOFILM (PA)
Also Called: Mvf World Wide Services
2300 W Empire Ave, Burbank (91504-3341)
PHONE....................818 840-1700
Fax: 818 840-1718

PRODUCTS & SERVICES SECTION
7819 - Services Allied To Motion Picture Prdtn County (P-18256)

Scott Avila, *CEO*
Cooper Crouse, *President*
Hugh Miller, *CFO*
Roxanna Sassanian, *CFO*
Alan Hart, *Exec VP*
EMP: 230
SQ FT: 100,000
SALES (est): 42.1MM **Privately Held**
WEB: www.mvfinc.com
SIC: 7819 Video tape or disk reproduction; film processing, editing & titling: motion picture; TV tape services: editing, transfers, etc.

(P-18236)
MODERN VIDEOFILM INC
Also Called: Mod Vid Film
1733 Flower St, Glendale (91201-2022)
PHONE.................................818 637-6800
Fax: 818 637-6866
Mark Smirnoff, *Manager*
EMP: 125
SALES (corp-wide): 42.1MM **Privately Held**
WEB: www.mvfinc.com
SIC: 7819 Video tape or disk reproduction; film processing, editing & titling: motion picture; TV tape services: editing, transfers, etc.
PA: Modern Videofilm
2300 W Empire Ave
Burbank CA 91504
818 840-1700

(P-18237)
MUSIC COLLECTIVE LLC
12711 Ventura Blvd # 110, Studio City (91604-2431)
PHONE.................................818 508-3303
Alan Ett, *Owner*
Alec Puro, *Creative Dir*
Ryan Neill, *VP Prdtn*
Eric Meyers, *Prdtn Mgr*
Scott Liggett, *Producer*
EMP: 50
SALES (est): 2MM **Privately Held**
WEB: www.aemg.com
SIC: 7819 Sound (effects & music production), motion picture

(P-18238)
NATIONAL FILM LABORATORIES
Also Called: Crest Digital
900 Glenneyre St, Laguna Beach (92651-2707)
PHONE.................................323 466-0281
Fax: 323 466-6815
Stephen R Stein, *CEO*
Ronald Stein, *President*
Lorraine Ross, *Corp Secy*
Emily L Hsu, *Controller*
Al Cambrone, *Director*
EMP: 157
SQ FT: 50,000
SALES (est): 7.8MM **Privately Held**
WEB: www.concorddisc.com
SIC: 7819 7812 Film processing, editing & titling: motion picture; reproduction services, motion picture production; motion picture & video production

(P-18239)
NEW DEAL STUDIOS INC
1812 W Burbank Blvd, Burbank (91506-1315)
PHONE.................................310 578-9929
Shannon Gans, *CEO*
Matthew Gratzner, *Vice Pres*
Dave Asling, *Creative Dir*
Ian Hunter, *Admin Sec*
Celeste Masters, *Info Tech Mgr*
EMP: 52
SQ FT: 20,000
SALES (est): 4.2MM **Privately Held**
SIC: 7819 Visual effects production

(P-18240)
NORTHSTAR DUPLICATORS INC
Also Called: North Star Video Duplicators
5198 Colt St Ste B, Ventura (93003-7380)
PHONE.................................805 984-3888
Fax: 805 650-0909
Velimir Jovicic, *President*
Branko Pantelic, *Corp Secy*

Dragan Mijailovic, *Vice Pres*
John Romerus, *Manager*
▲ **EMP:** 60
SQ FT: 32,000
SALES (est): 2.3MM **Privately Held**
SIC: 7819 Video tape or disk reproduction

(P-18241)
NORTHSTAR MEDIA PACKG SVCS LLC
5776 Lindero Canyon Rd D, Westlake Village (91362-6428)
PHONE.................................805 650-0990
Wyman Dunford,
Yvette Plisky, *Office Mgr*
NS Vesko, *Senior Engr*
Emmet Murphy,
EMP: 60
SALES (est): 3.2MM **Privately Held**
SIC: 7819 Services allied to motion pictures

(P-18242)
OMEGA/CINEMA PROPS INC
5857 Santa Monica Blvd, Los Angeles (90038-2001)
PHONE.................................323 466-8201
E Jay Krause, *President*
Cheryl Jordan, *Corp Secy*
Doris Krause, *Vice Pres*
Jack Thai, *Network Mgr*
Barry Pritchard, *Opers Mgr*
▲ **EMP:** 90
SQ FT: 300,000
SALES (est): 10MM **Privately Held**
WEB: www.omegacinemaprops.com
SIC: 7819 Equipment & prop rental, motion picture production

(P-18243)
POINT360
12421 W Olympic Blvd, Los Angeles (90064-1022)
PHONE.................................310 481-7000
David Tuszynski, *General Mgr*
EMP: 60
SALES (corp-wide): 37.5MM **Publicly Held**
WEB: www.vdimultimedia.com
SIC: 7819 Video tape or disk reproduction
PA: Point.360
2701 Media Center Dr
Los Angeles CA 90065
818 565-1400

(P-18244)
POINT360
1133 N Hollywood Way, Burbank (91505-2528)
PHONE.................................818 556-5700
Brian Ehrlich, *Manager*
Fred Springer, *Engineer*
EMP: 100
SALES (corp-wide): 37.5MM **Publicly Held**
WEB: www.vdimultimedia.com
SIC: 7819 Editing services, motion picture production; equipment & prop rental, motion picture production
PA: Point.360
2701 Media Center Dr
Los Angeles CA 90065
818 565-1400

(P-18245)
POINT360 (PA)
2701 Media Center Dr, Los Angeles (90065-1700)
PHONE.................................818 565-1400
Fax: 818 847-2503
Haig S Bagerdjian, *Ch of Bd*
Alan R Steel, *CFO*
EMP: 168
SQ FT: 64,600
SALES: 37.5MM **Publicly Held**
WEB: www.vdimultimedia.com
SIC: 7819 7822 7829 Video tape or disk reproduction; motion picture & tape distribution; television & video tape distribution; motion picture distribution services

(P-18246)
POST GROUP INC (PA)
1415 N Cahuenga Blvd, Los Angeles (90028-8198)
PHONE.................................323 462-2300

Frederic Rheinstein, *Chairman*
Lloyd Guillen, *President*
Vincent Lyons, *President*
Matthew Post, *COO*
Sharra Platt, *General Mgr*
EMP: 110
SQ FT: 40,000
SALES (est): 12.7MM **Privately Held**
WEB: www.postgroup.com
SIC: 7819 7812 Editing services, motion picture production; film processing, editing & titling: motion picture; TV tape services: editing, transfers, etc.; motion picture & video production

(P-18247)
PRIME FOCUS NORTH AMERICA INC (DH)
Also Called: Prime Focus World
5750 Hannum Ave Ste 100, Culver City (90230-6666)
PHONE.................................323 461-7887
Namit Malhotra, *CEO*
Robert Hummel, *CEO*
Marisa Morreale, *COO*
Oliver Welch, *COO*
Massoud Entekhabi, *CFO*
EMP: 85
SQ FT: 50,000
SALES (est): 13.7MM
SALES (corp-wide): 302K **Privately Held**
WEB: www.postlogic.com
SIC: 7819 Sound (effects & music production), motion picture
HQ: Prime Focus London Plc
160 Great Portland Street
London W1W 5
207 268-5086

(P-18248)
QUAD/GRAPHICS INC
Also Called: Vertis Ltc
15342 Graham St, Huntington Beach (92649-1111)
PHONE.................................949 930-5400
Fax: 213 476-0893
Dave Bales, *Manager*
EMP: 110
SALES (corp-wide): 4.6B **Publicly Held**
WEB: www.vertisinc.com
SIC: 7819 Services allied to motion pictures
PA: Quad/Graphics Inc.
N61w23044 Harrys Way
Sussex WI 53089
414 566-6000

(P-18249)
QUIXOTE MM LLC
Also Called: Movie Movers
1011 N Fuller Ave Ste B, West Hollywood (90046-6658)
PHONE.................................323 851-5030
Mikel Elliott, *Mng Member*
EMP: 50
SALES (est): 3.6MM **Privately Held**
SIC: 7819 Equipment rental, motion picture

(P-18250)
RALEIGH ENTERPRISES INC
Also Called: Raleigh Studios
5300 Melrose Ave Fl 3, Los Angeles (90038-5113)
PHONE.................................323 466-3111
Michael Moore, *Branch Mgr*
EMP: 130
SQ FT: 68,388
SALES (corp-wide): 34.2MM **Privately Held**
WEB: www.raleighenterprises.com
SIC: 7819 7359 6512 Services allied to motion pictures; equipment rental & leasing; nonresidential building operators
PA: Raleigh Enterprises, Inc.
5300 Melrose Ave Fl 4
Los Angeles CA 90038
310 899-8900

(P-18251)
RELIANCE MEDIA WORKS VFX INC
1800 Vine St, Los Angeles (90028-5250)
PHONE.................................818 557-7333
Fax: 818 557-7506
Benkatash Roddam, *President*
George Murphy, *Officer*

Ashish R Agarwal, *Admin Sec*
EMP: 50
SQ FT: 25,000
SALES (est): 5.7MM **Privately Held**
SIC: 7819 Visual effects production
PA: Reliance Adae
Fl 7 B Wing, Trade World Senapati
Bapat Marg
Mumbai MH

(P-18252)
SDI MEDIA USA INC (DH)
Also Called: Sdi Media USA
6060 Center Dr Ste 100, Los Angeles (90045-8835)
PHONE.................................323 602-5455
Fax: 310 388-8950
Walter Schonfeld, *CEO*
Rod Peckham, *CFO*
Rick Sanchez, *CFO*
Mary Ann Fialkowski, *Exec VP*
Scott Rose, *Exec VP*
EMP: 66
SQ FT: 13,000
SALES (est): 27.9MM **Privately Held**
WEB: www.sdimediagroup.com
SIC: 7819 TV tape services: editing, transfers, etc.
HQ: Sdi Media Group Limited
1000 Great West Road
Brentford MIDDX TW8 9
208 232-4930

(P-18253)
SIX POINT HARNESS
1759 Glendale Blvd, Los Angeles (90026-1761)
PHONE.................................323 462-3344
Brendan Burch, *Principal*
Walter Santucci, *Director*
EMP: 50
SALES (est): 2.2MM **Privately Held**
SIC: 7819 Services allied to motion pictures

(P-18254)
SKYLAR FILM STUDIOS LLC
13589 Mindanao Way # 11, Marina Del Rey (90292-6950)
PHONE.................................424 653-8902
Jamie Skylar, *CEO*
Dylan Johnson, *Managing Dir*
EMP: 200 **EST:** 2010
SQ FT: 200,000
SALES (est): 3MM **Privately Held**
SIC: 7819 Services allied to motion pictures

(P-18255)
STAN WINSTON INC
Also Called: Stan Winston Studio
340 Parkside Dr, San Fernando (91340-3035)
PHONE.................................818 782-0870
Stan Winston, *President*
Brian Gilbert, *Vice Pres*
EMP: 80
SQ FT: 10,538
SALES (est): 2.1MM **Privately Held**
WEB: www.stanwinston.com
SIC: 7819 Visual effects production

(P-18256)
STEREO D LLC
Also Called: Stereod
3355 W Empire Ave Fl 1, Burbank (91504-3160)
P.O. Box 892164, Temecula (92589-2164)
PHONE.................................818 861-3100
William Sherak, *President*
Aaron Parry, *Exec VP*
Milton Adamou, *Vice Pres*
Prafull Gade, *Vice Pres*
Lindsey Kaiser, *Creative Dir*
EMP: 275
SQ FT: 55,000
SALES (est): 34.1MM
SALES (corp-wide): 5.3B **Privately Held**
SIC: 7819 Editing services, motion picture production
HQ: Deluxe Entertainment Services Group Inc.
2400 W Empire Ave
Los Angeles CA 90027
323 462-6171

(PA)=Parent Co (HQ)=Headquarters (DH)=Div Headquarters
✪ = New Business established in last 2 years

7819 - Services Allied To Motion Picture Prdtn County (P-18257)

PRODUCTS & SERVICES SECTION

(P-18257)
TECHNCLOR CRATIVE SVCS USA INC
6040 W Sunset Blvd, Los Angeles (90028-6402)
PHONE..................818 260-3800
Timothy Sarnoff, *CEO*
Richard Andrews, *President*
Claude Gagnon, *CEO*
John Hancock, *Admin Sec*
EMP: 300
SQ FT: 25,000
SALES (est): 30.7MM
SALES (corp-wide): 64.4MM **Privately Held**
WEB: www.vidfilm.com
SIC: **7819** Video tape or disk reproduction
HQ: Technicolor Thomson Group, Inc
  2233 N Ontario St Ste 300
  Burbank CA 91504
  818 260-3600

(P-18258)
TECHNCLOR CRATIVE SVCS USA INC
Technicolor Complete Post
6040 W Sunset Blvd, Los Angeles (90028-6402)
PHONE..................323 467-1244
Mike Doggett, *Manager*
Heather Sanchez, *Personnel Exec*
Kirsten Mills, *Producer*
John H Oliphant, *Agent*
EMP: 150
SALES (corp-wide): 64.4MM **Privately Held**
WEB: www.vidfilm.com
SIC: **7819** TV tape services: editing, transfers, etc.; sound (effects & music production), motion picture
HQ: Technicolor Creative Services Usa, Inc.
  6040 W Sunset Blvd
  Los Angeles CA 90028
  818 260-3800

(P-18259)
TECHNCLOR VDOCASSETTE MICH INC (DH)
Also Called: Technicolor Video Service
3233 Mission Oaks Blvd, Camarillo (93012-5138)
PHONE..................805 445-1122
Fax: 734 853-3988
Lanni Ormonvo, *President*
John H Oliphant, *Admin Sec*
Pamela Smith, *Administration*
Thu Brodeur, *Engineer*
Jeff Akerlind, *Controller*
▲ EMP: 500
SQ FT: 300,000
SALES (est): 43.5MM
SALES (corp-wide): 64.4MM **Privately Held**
SIC: **7819** Video tape or disk reproduction
HQ: Technicolor Thomson Group, Inc
  2233 N Ontario St Ste 300
  Burbank CA 91504
  818 260-3600

(P-18260)
TECHNICOLOR HM ENTRMT SVCS INC
Also Called: Technicolor - Funimation Ent
1778 Zinetta Rd Ste F, Calexico (92231-9510)
PHONE..................760 357-3372
Heriberto Ramirez, *Manager*
EMP: 268
SALES (corp-wide): 64.4MM **Privately Held**
SIC: **7819** Video tape or disk reproduction
HQ: Technicolor Home Entertainment Services, Inc.
  3233 Mission Oaks Blvd
  Camarillo CA 93012
  805 445-1122

(P-18261)
TECHNICOLOR HM ENTRMT SVCS INC
Also Called: Accounts Payable Department
5491 E Philadelphia St, Ontario (91761-2807)
P.O. Box 2459, Rancho Cucamonga (91729-2459)
PHONE..................909 974-2016
EMP: 301
SALES (corp-wide): 64.4MM **Privately Held**
SIC: **7819** Video tape or disk reproduction
HQ: Technicolor Home Entertainment Services, Inc.
  3233 Mission Oaks Blvd
  Camarillo CA 93012
  805 445-1122

(P-18262)
TECHNICOLOR HM ENTRMT SVCS INC (DH)
Also Called: Technicolor Video Services
3233 Mission Oaks Blvd, Camarillo (93012-5097)
PHONE..................805 445-1122
Fax: 805 445-1111
Lanny Raimondo, *CEO*
Orlando F Raimondo, *President*
Patricia Dave, *CFO*
Elaine Singleton, *Vice Pres*
Catherine Sweeney, *Administration*
▲ EMP: 500
SQ FT: 5,000
SALES (est): 283.4MM
SALES (corp-wide): 64.4MM **Privately Held**
SIC: **7819** Video tape or disk reproduction
HQ: Technicolor Usa, Inc.
  4 Research Way
  Princeton NJ 08540
  317 587-3000

(P-18263)
TECHNICOLOR THOMSON GROUP
Also Called: Technicolor Hollywood
6040 W Sunset Blvd, Los Angeles (90028-6402)
PHONE..................323 817-6600
Michael Doggett, *Manager*
Tom Cotton, *President*
Sandra Carvalho, *Chief Mktg Ofcr*
Jackie Taylor-Boggs, *Exec VP*
Bob Eicholz, *Senior VP*
EMP: 573
SALES (corp-wide): 64.4MM **Privately Held**
SIC: **7819** Video tape or disk reproduction; developing & printing of commercial motion picture film
HQ: Technicolor Thomson Group, Inc
  2233 N Ontario St Ste 300
  Burbank CA 91504
  818 260-3600

(P-18264)
TECHNICOLOR THOMSON GROUP
2255 N Ontario St Ste 100, Burbank (91504-3194)
PHONE..................818 260-3600
Juliana Bacchus, *Branch Mgr*
Michelle Garcia, *Manager*
EMP: 301
SQ FT: 200,000
SALES (corp-wide): 64.4MM **Privately Held**
WEB: www.technicolor.com
SIC: **7822 2759** Film processing, editing & titling: motion picture; TV tape services: editing, transfers, etc.; commercial printing
HQ: Technicolor Thomson Group, Inc
  2233 N Ontario St Ste 300
  Burbank CA 91504
  818 260-3600

(P-18265)
TECHNICOLOR THOMSON GROUP
Technicolor Entertainment Svcs
5491 E Philadelphia St, Ontario (91761-2807)
PHONE..................909 974-2222
Mary Nakagawa, *Manager*
EMP: 300
SALES (corp-wide): 64.4MM **Privately Held**
WEB: www.technicolor.com
SIC: **7819** Video tape or disk reproduction; developing & printing of commercial motion picture film
HQ: Technicolor Thomson Group, Inc
  2233 N Ontario St Ste 300
  Burbank CA 91504
  818 260-3600

(P-18266)
TECHNICOLOR THOMSON GROUP
3301 Mission Oaks Blvd, Camarillo (93012-5048)
PHONE..................805 445-1122
Orlando Raimondo, *CEO*
EMP: 2000
SALES (corp-wide): 64.4MM **Privately Held**
WEB: www.technicolor.com
SIC: **7819** Video tape or disk reproduction; developing & printing of commercial motion picture film
HQ: Technicolor Thomson Group, Inc
  2233 N Ontario St Ste 300
  Burbank CA 91504
  818 260-3600

(P-18267)
WALT DISNEY IMAGINEERING (DH)
1401 Flower St, Glendale (91201-2421)
P.O. Box 25020 (91221-5020)
PHONE..................818 544-6500
Fax: 818 544-4565
Thomas O Staggs, *CEO*
Martin A Sklar, *Vice Ch Bd*
Craig Russell, *Exec VP*
Markus Gross, *Vice Pres*
Jessica Hodgins, *Vice Pres*
EMP: 1011
SQ FT: 100,000
SALES (est): 79.1MM **Publicly Held**
SIC: **7819 8712 1542 8741** Visual effects production; architectural services; custom builders, non-residential; management services; engineering services
HQ: Disney Enterprises, Inc.
  500 S Buena Vista St
  Burbank CA 91521
  818 560-1000

7822 Motion Picture & Video Tape Distribution

(P-18268)
ABC CABLE NETWORKS GROUP
Also Called: Buena Vista Pictures Dist
698 S Buena Vista St, Burbank (91521-0001)
PHONE..................818 560-4365
Cindy Cohen-Hiller, *Vice Pres*
Karen Holm, *Vice Chairman*
Chuch Viane, *President*
Charles Kent, *Vice Pres*
Adina Savin, *Vice Pres*
EMP: 190 **Publicly Held**
WEB: www.breakbar.com
SIC: **7822** Distribution, exclusive of production: motion picture
HQ: Abc Cable Networks Group
  500 S Buena Vista St
  Burbank CA 91521
  818 460-7477

(P-18269)
AEGIS FILM GROUP INC
7510 W Sunset Blvd # 275, Los Angeles (90046-3408)
PHONE..................323 848-7977
Arianna Eisenberg, *President*
Steven Shultz, *Vice Pres*
EMP: 56
SALES: 10.2MM **Privately Held**
SIC: **7822** Film exchange, motion picture

(P-18270)
BLEACHER REPORT INC
153 Kearny St Fl 2, San Francisco (94108-4808)
PHONE..................415 777-5505
Dave Finocchio, *CEO*
Calacci Richard, *Officer*
Josh Abrams, *Vice Pres*
Bill McCandless, *Vice Pres*
Joe Yanarella, *Vice Pres*
EMP: 217
SALES (est): 20.9MM
SALES (corp-wide): 28.1B **Publicly Held**
SIC: **7822 4833 4841 7812** Motion picture distribution; television broadcasting stations; cable television services; motion picture production
HQ: Turner Broadcasting System, Inc.
  1 Cnn Ctr Nw
  Atlanta GA 30303
  404 827-1700

(P-18271)
BUENA VISTA INTERNATIONAL INC (HQ)
500 S Buena Vista St, Burbank (91521-0001)
PHONE..................818 560-1000
Fax: 818 848-7059
David M Hollis, *CEO*
Mark D Zoradi, *President*
David Hughes, *Treasurer*
Marsha Reed, *Manager*
▲ EMP: 50
SALES (est): 5.8MM **Publicly Held**
WEB: www.filmes.net
SIC: **7822** Distribution, exclusive of production: motion picture; distribution for television: motion picture

(P-18272)
DISNEY INTERFINANCE CORP
500 S Buena Vista St, Burbank (91521-0001)
PHONE..................818 560-1000
David K Thompson, *President*
EMP: 360
SALES (est): 2.2MM **Publicly Held**
SIC: **7822** Distribution, exclusive of production: motion picture
HQ: Disney Enterprises, Inc.
  500 S Buena Vista St
  Burbank CA 91521
  818 560-1000

(P-18273)
ERO-TECH CORP
2301 S El Camino Real, San Mateo (94403-2213)
PHONE..................415 468-5600
David Sturman, *President*
▲ EMP: 100
SALES (est): 2.6MM **Privately Held**
SIC: **7822 5192** Video tapes, recorded; wholesale; magazines

(P-18274)
FOX US PRODUCTIONS 27 INC
1600 Rosecrans Ave 200, Manhattan Beach (90266-3708)
PHONE..................310 656-6100
EMP: 231
SALES (est): 736K
SALES (corp-wide): 27.3B **Publicly Held**
SIC: **7822** Motion picture & tape distribution
HQ: Fox Entertainment Group, Inc.
  2029 Century Park E # 1400
  Los Angeles CA 90067
  310 369-1000

(P-18275)
IMAGE ENTERTAINMENT INC (HQ)
6320 Canoga Ave Ste 790, Woodland Hills (91367-2561)
PHONE..................818 407-9100
Fax: 818 407-5775
Miguel Penella, *COO*
Drew Wilson, *CFO*
John Powers, *Vice Pres*
Sylvie Yang, *Vice Pres*
Debbie Wilming, *Executive*
◆ EMP: 56
SQ FT: 30,000

▲ = Import ▼=Export
◆ =Import/Export

PRODUCTS & SERVICES SECTION
7832 - Motion Picture Theaters, Except Drive-In County (P-18296)

SALES (est): 13.2MM
SALES (corp-wide): 124.9MM **Publicly Held**
WEB: www.image-entertainment.com
SIC: 7822 Motion picture & tape distribution
PA: Rlj Entertainment, Inc.
8515 Georgia Ave Ste 650
Silver Spring MD 20910
301 608-2115

(P-18276)
LGH DIGITAL MEDIA INC
Also Called: Larsons Studios
6520 W Sunset Blvd, Los Angeles (90028-7202)
PHONE..................323 469-3986
Richard Larson, *President*
A Richard Larson, *President*
Dave Cottrell, *CFO*
Jim Henderson Jr, *Exec VP*
Nisha Sharma, *Accounting Mgr*
EMP: 50
SALES (est): 7MM **Privately Held**
SIC: 7822 Motion picture distribution

(P-18277)
LIONSGATE PRODUCTIONS
2700 Colorado Ave Ste 200, Santa Monica (90404-5502)
PHONE..................310 255-3937
Jon Feltheimer, *CEO*
Steve Beeks, *COO*
Wayne Levin, *Exec VP*
Kevin Beggs, *Production*
EMP: 95
SALES (est): 14.9MM
SALES (corp-wide): 2.4B **Publicly Held**
SIC: 7822 Motion picture & tape distribution
HQ: Lions Gate Entertainment Inc.
2700 Colorado Ave Ste 200
Santa Monica CA 90404
310 449-9200

(P-18278)
METROLUX THEATRES
Also Called: Metrolux 14 Theatres
8727 W 3rd St, Los Angeles (90048-3843)
PHONE..................310 858-2800
Victoria Uy, *Controller*
EMP: 70
SALES (est): 2.5MM **Privately Held**
SIC: 7822 Motion picture & tape distribution

(P-18279)
TWENTIETH CENTURY FOX (DH)
10201 W Pico Blvd, Los Angeles (90064-2651)
P.O. Box 900, Beverly Hills (90213-0900)
PHONE..................310 369-1000
Pat Wyatt, *Ch of Bd*
Bob Delellis, *President*
Dean Hallett, *CFO*
David Miller, *Treasurer*
Chris Hannan, *Exec VP*
▲ **EMP:** 400
SQ FT: 115,000
SALES (est): 46.8MM
SALES (corp-wide): 27.3B **Publicly Held**
SIC: 7822 7922 Motion picture distribution; television program, including commercial producers
HQ: Twentieth Century Fox Film Corporation
10201 W Pico Blvd
Los Angeles CA 90064
310 369-1000

(P-18280)
UNITED ARTISTS PRODUCTIONS INC
10250 Constellation Blvd # 19, Los Angeles (90067-6200)
PHONE..................310 449-3000
Christopher McGurk, *President*
EMP: 200
SALES (est): 1.3MM
SALES (corp-wide): 68.3MM **Privately Held**
WEB: www.unitedartists.com
SIC: 7822 Distribution, exclusive of production: motion picture; distribution for television: motion picture
HQ: United Artists Pictures Inc
10250 Constellation Blvd
Los Angeles CA 90067
310 449-3000

(P-18281)
VERIZON COMMUNICATIONS INC
201 Flynn Rd, Camarillo (93012-8058)
PHONE..................805 445-8125
Bruce Pickley, *Manager*
Dave De La Rosa, *Project Mgr*
EMP: 170
SALES (corp-wide): 131.6B **Publicly Held**
WEB: www.verizon.com
SIC: 7822 Television & video tape distribution
PA: Verizon Communications Inc.
1095 Ave Of The Americas
New York NY 10036
212 395-1000

(P-18282)
VIACOM NETWORKS
Also Called: Mtv Networks
2600 Colorado Ave, Santa Monica (90404-3519)
PHONE..................310 453-4826
Anthony Disanto, *President*
Jeremy Gonzalez, *President*
Duncan Macdonald, *Senior VP*
Alex Angeledes, *Vice Pres*
Stewart Frey, *Vice Pres*
EMP: 5000
SALES (est): 151.8MM **Privately Held**
SIC: 7822 Motion picture & tape distribution

(P-18283)
VPD IV INC (PA)
Also Called: Video Products Distributors
150 Parkshore Dr, Folsom (95630-4710)
PHONE..................916 605-1500
Fax: 916 605-1760
Tim Shannahan, *President*
David Sein, *CFO*
Russ Frazier, *Senior VP*
Marty Jorgensen, *Senior VP*
Ted Nelson, *Branch Mgr*
▲ **EMP:** 175
SQ FT: 70,000
SALES (est): 31.5MM **Privately Held**
WEB: www.vpdinc.com
SIC: 7822 5092 Video tapes, recorded: wholesale; video games

(P-18284)
VUBIQUITY INC
15301 Ventura Blvd Bldg E, Sherman Oaks (91403-5885)
PHONE..................818 526-5000
Darcy Antonellis, *Branch Mgr*
EMP: 200
SALES (corp-wide): 300MM **Privately Held**
SIC: 7822 Motion picture & tape distribution
HQ: Vubiquity, Inc.
1881 Campus Commons Dr # 101
Reston VA 20191
571 485-2760

(P-18285)
WARNER BROS TRANSATLANTIC INC (DH)
4000 Warner Blvd, Burbank (91522-0002)
PHONE..................818 954-6000
Fax: 818 954-6523
Barry M Meyer, *CEO*
Christina Lee, *CFO*
Ralph Peterson, *Treasurer*
Dean Hale, *Officer*
Richard Fox, *Exec VP*
▲ **EMP:** 1000
SALES (est): 413.8MM
SALES (corp-wide): 28.1B **Publicly Held**
WEB: www.juwannamann.com
SIC: 7822 Distribution, exclusive of production: motion picture

(P-18286)
WARNER BROS TRANSATLANTIC INC
3300 W Olive Ave Unit 200, Burbank (91505-4658)
PHONE..................818 977-6384
Scott Levy, *Branch Mgr*
Dave Hedrick, *Senior VP*
EMP: 515
SALES (corp-wide): 28.1B **Publicly Held**
SIC: 7822 Distribution, exclusive of production: motion picture
HQ: Warner Bros. (Transatlantic), Inc.
4000 Warner Blvd
Burbank CA 91522
818 954-6000

(P-18287)
WARNER BROS TRANSATLANTIC INC
Also Called: Telepictures
3500 W Olive Ave Ste 1000, Burbank (91505-5515)
PHONE..................818 972-0777
Khuyem Phan, *Branch Mgr*
Joshua Barber, *Counsel*
EMP: 515
SALES (corp-wide): 28.1B **Publicly Held**
SIC: 7822 Distribution, exclusive of production: motion picture
HQ: Warner Bros. (Transatlantic), Inc.
4000 Warner Blvd
Burbank CA 91522
818 954-6000

7829 Services Allied To Motion Picture Distribution

(P-18288)
NU IMAGE INC (PA)
Also Called: Nu Image Holdings
6423 Wilshire Blvd, Los Angeles (90048-4907)
PHONE..................310 388-6900
AVI Lerner, *CEO*
Danny Dimbort, *President*
Rick Eyler, *Pharmacy Dir*
Frank Benitez, *Office Mgr*
Tanner Mobley, *Executive Asst*
▲ **EMP:** 60
SQ FT: 16,000
SALES (est): 8.6MM **Privately Held**
WEB: www.nuimage.net
SIC: 7829 Motion picture distribution services

(P-18289)
OUR ALCHEMY LLC
5900 Wilshire Blvd Fl 18, Los Angeles (90036-5013)
PHONE..................310 893-6289
EMP: 80
SQ FT: 30,000
SALES (est): 3.6MM **Privately Held**
SIC: 7829

(P-18290)
PACIFIC THEATERS
Also Called: Northridge Fashion Center 10
9400 Shirley Ave, Northridge (91324-2413)
PHONE..................818 501-5121
Fax: 818 772-9893
Joshua Watts, *Manager*
EMP: 60
SALES (est): 1.1MM **Privately Held**
SIC: 7829 Motion picture distribution services

(P-18291)
SUMMIT ENTERTAINMENT LLC (DH)
2700 Colorado Ave Ste 200, Santa Monica (90404-5502)
PHONE..................310 309-8400
Ronald E Hohauser,
Bob Hayward, *COO*
Eric Kops, *Senior VP*
Brad Kembel, *Vice Pres*
Angela Cruz, *Sales Staff*
EMP: 50
SQ FT: 13,000
SALES (est): 7MM
SALES (corp-wide): 2.4B **Privately Held**
SIC: 7829 Motion picture distribution services
HQ: Lions Gate Entertainment Inc.
2700 Colorado Ave Ste 200
Santa Monica CA 90404
310 449-9200

(P-18292)
WALT DISNEY PICTURES AND TV
500 S Buena Vista St, Burbank (91521-0007)
PHONE..................818 560-1000
Bob Iger, *CEO*
Robert Matschullat, *Vice Chairman*
Alan Bergman, *President*
Sandy Litvack, *COO*
Thomas Staggs, *CFO*
▲ **EMP:** 56
SALES (est): 9.1MM **Publicly Held**
SIC: 7829 Motion picture distribution services
HQ: Disney Enterprises, Inc.
500 S Buena Vista St
Burbank CA 91521
818 560-1000

7832 Motion Picture Theaters, Except Drive-In

(P-18293)
AMC ENTERTAINMENT INC
4549 Mills Cir, Ontario (91764-5220)
PHONE..................909 476-1288
Kristine Saiko, *Manager*
EMP: 50 **Publicly Held**
SIC: 7832 Motion picture theaters, except drive-in
HQ: Amc Entertainment Inc.
11500 Ash St
Leawood KS 66211
913 213-2000

(P-18294)
AMERICAN MULTI-CINEMA INC
Also Called: AMC
125 E Palm Ave, Burbank (91502-1834)
PHONE..................818 953-4020
Breanna Corrigan, *Manager*
EMP: 70 **Publicly Held**
WEB: www.arrowheadtownecenter.com
SIC: 7832 Motion picture theaters, except drive-in
HQ: American Multi-Cinema, Inc.
1 Amc Way
Leawood KS 66211
913 213-2000

(P-18295)
AMERICAN MULTI-CINEMA INC
Also Called: AMC
7037 Friars Rd, San Diego (92108-1129)
PHONE..................619 296-0370
Brian Fuller, *Manager*
Liza Lewis, *Manager*
EMP: 50 **Publicly Held**
WEB: www.arrowheadtownecenter.com
SIC: 7832 Motion picture theaters, except drive-in
HQ: American Multi-Cinema, Inc.
1 Amc Way
Leawood KS 66211
913 213-2000

(P-18296)
AMERICAN MULTI-CINEMA INC
Also Called: AMC
450 N Atlantic Blvd, Monterey Park (91754-1057)
PHONE..................626 407-0240
EMP: 61 **Publicly Held**
SIC: 7832 Motion picture theaters, except drive-in
HQ: American Multi-Cinema, Inc.
1 Amc Way
Leawood KS 66211
913 213-2000

7832 - Motion Picture Theaters, Except Drive-In County (P-18297)

(P-18297)
AMERICAN MULTI-CINEMA INC
Also Called: AMC
1414 N Azusa Ave, Covina (91722-1251)
PHONE....................626 974-8624
Fax: 626 974-8636
John Eisner, *Manager*
EMP: 60 **Publicly Held**
WEB: www.arrowheadtownecenter.com
SIC: 7832 Motion picture theaters, except drive-in
HQ: American Multi-Cinema, Inc.
1 Amc Way
Leawood KS 66211
913 213-2000

(P-18298)
AMERICAN MULTI-CINEMA INC
Also Called: AMC
1000 Van Neca Ave Ste A, San Francisco (94109)
PHONE....................415 674-4630
Shawn Eisern, *Manager*
EMP: 50 **Publicly Held**
SIC: 7832 Motion picture theaters, except drive-in
HQ: American Multi-Cinema, Inc.
1 Amc Way
Leawood KS 66211
913 213-2000

(P-18299)
AMERICAN MULTI-CINEMA INC
Also Called: AMC
2591 Airport Dr, Torrance (90505-6137)
PHONE....................310 326-5011
Craig Adams, *Sales/Mktg Mgr*
Peter Lieu, *Managing Dir*
EMP: 120 **Publicly Held**
WEB: www.arrowheadtownecenter.com
SIC: 7832 Motion picture theaters, except drive-in
HQ: American Multi-Cinema, Inc.
1 Amc Way
Leawood KS 66211
913 213-2000

(P-18300)
AMERICAN MULTI-CINEMA INC
Also Called: AMC
20 City Blvd W Ste E1, Orange (92868-3130)
PHONE....................714 769-4288
Scott Shellenbergar, *Manager*
EMP: 90 **Publicly Held**
WEB: www.arrowheadtownecenter.com
SIC: 7832 Motion picture theaters, except drive-in
HQ: American Multi-Cinema, Inc.
1 Amc Way
Leawood KS 66211
913 213-2000

(P-18301)
AMERICAN MULTI-CINEMA INC
Also Called: AMC
1001 S Lemon St Ste A, Fullerton (92832-3007)
PHONE....................714 992-6961
Fax: 714 992-6979
Brian Lind, *Manager*
Christine Ellis, *Manager*
EMP: 50 **Publicly Held**
WEB: www.arrowheadtownecenter.com
SIC: 7832 Motion picture theaters, except drive-in
HQ: American Multi-Cinema, Inc.
1 Amc Way
Leawood KS 66211
913 213-2000

(P-18302)
AMERICAN MULTI-CINEMA INC
Also Called: AMC
42 Miller Aly, Pasadena (91103-3643)
PHONE....................626 585-8900
Charles Forsgren, *General Mgr*
EMP: 50 **Publicly Held**
WEB: www.arrowheadtownecenter.com
SIC: 7832 Motion picture theaters, except drive-in
HQ: American Multi-Cinema, Inc.
1 Amc Way
Leawood KS 66211
913 213-2000

(P-18303)
AMERICAN MULTI-CINEMA INC
Also Called: AMC
12300 Civic Center Dr, Norwalk (90650-3171)
PHONE....................562 864-6206
Gary Orland, *Executive*
EMP: 50 **Publicly Held**
WEB: www.arrowheadtownecenter.com
SIC: 7832 Motion picture theaters, except drive-in
HQ: American Multi-Cinema, Inc.
1 Amc Way
Leawood KS 66211
913 213-2000

(P-18304)
AMERICAN MULTI-CINEMA INC
Also Called: AMC
10250 Snta Mnca Bld Ste 196, Los Angeles (90067)
PHONE....................310 228-5500
Rick Walsh, *Branch Mgr*
EMP: 50 **Publicly Held**
SIC: 7832 Motion picture theaters, except drive-in
HQ: American Multi-Cinema, Inc.
1 Amc Way
Leawood KS 66211
913 213-2000

(P-18305)
AMERICAN MULTI-CINEMA INC
Also Called: AMC
1640 Cmino Del Rio N 20, San Diego (92108)
PHONE....................619 296-2737
Fax: 619 296-3916
Kathy Dominguez, *Manager*
EMP: 75 **Publicly Held**
WEB: www.arrowheadtownecenter.com
SIC: 7832 Motion picture theaters, except drive-in
HQ: American Multi-Cinema, Inc.
1 Amc Way
Leawood KS 66211
913 213-2000

(P-18306)
AMERICAN MULTI-CINEMA INC
Also Called: AMC
1560 S Azusa Ave, City of Industry (91748-1603)
PHONE....................626 810-7949
Fax: 626 854-2612
Favio Adane, *General Mgr*
EMP: 59 **Publicly Held**
SIC: 7832 Motion picture theaters, except drive-in
HQ: American Multi-Cinema, Inc.
1 Amc Way
Leawood KS 66211
913 213-2000

(P-18307)
AMERICAN MULTI-CINEMA INC
Also Called: AMC
1475 N Montebello Blvd, Montebello (90640-2584)
PHONE....................323 722-4583
Rachell Hatton, *General Mgr*
EMP: 50 **Publicly Held**
WEB: www.arrowheadtownecenter.com
SIC: 7832 Motion picture theaters, except drive-in
HQ: American Multi-Cinema, Inc.
1 Amc Way
Leawood KS 66211
913 213-2000

(P-18308)
ARCLIGHT CINEMA COMPANY
15301 Ventura Blvd Bldg A, Sherman Oaks (91403-3102)
PHONE....................818 501-0753
Christopher S Forman, *Branch Mgr*
EMP: 95
SALES (corp-wide): 14.1MM **Privately Held**
SIC: 7832 Motion picture theaters, except drive-in
PA: Arclight Cinema Company
6360 W Sunset Blvd
Los Angeles CA 90028
323 464-4226

(P-18309)
ARCLIGHT CINEMA COMPANY
120 N Robertson Blvd Fl 3, Los Angeles (90048-3115)
PHONE....................323 464-1465
Christopher S Forman, *Branch Mgr*
EMP: 164
SALES (corp-wide): 14.1MM **Privately Held**
SIC: 7832 Motion picture theaters, except drive-in
PA: Arclight Cinema Company
6360 W Sunset Blvd
Los Angeles CA 90028
323 464-4226

(P-18310)
BRENDEN THEATRE CORPORATION
531 Davis St, Vacaville (95688-4632)
PHONE....................707 469-0180
Tim Kruse, *Branch Mgr*
Brenden Vacavill, *Marketing Staff*
EMP: 70
SALES (corp-wide): 18.1MM **Privately Held**
WEB: www.brendantheaters.com
SIC: 7832 Motion picture theaters, except drive-in
PA: Brenden Theatre Corporation
1985 Willow Pass Rd Ste C
Concord CA 94520
925 677-0462

(P-18311)
BRENDEN THEATRE CORPORATION
1021 10th St Frnt, Modesto (95354-0888)
PHONE....................209 491-7770
Saul Trujllo, *General Mgr*
Jerry Olivarez, *Manager*
EMP: 100
SALES (corp-wide): 18.1MM **Privately Held**
WEB: www.brendantheaters.com
SIC: 7832 Motion picture theaters, except drive-in
PA: Brenden Theatre Corporation
1985 Willow Pass Rd Ste C
Concord CA 94520
925 677-0462

(P-18312)
BRENDEN THEATRE CORPORATION (PA)
1985 Willow Pass Rd Ste C, Concord (94520-2533)
PHONE....................925 677-0462
John Brenden, *President*
Clarence Pelatena, *General Mgr*
Meldoy Graves, *Manager*
EMP: 189
SQ FT: 70,000
SALES (est): 18.1MM **Privately Held**
WEB: www.brendantheaters.com
SIC: 7832 Motion picture theaters, except drive-in

(P-18313)
CAL GRAN THEATRES LLC
Also Called: Valley Drive-In Theatre
3170 Santa Maria Way, Santa Maria (93455-2102)
PHONE....................805 934-1582
Bob Gran, *President*
Diane Gran, *General Mgr*
EMP: 50
SQ FT: 1,200
SALES (est): 1MM **Privately Held**
SIC: 7832 7833 Motion picture theaters, except drive-in; drive-in motion picture theaters

(P-18314)
CALIFRNIA CNEMA INVSTMENTS INC
6941 El Camino Real, Carlsbad (92009-4108)
PHONE....................760 827-6700
Adrian Mijares Elizondo, *CEO*
Maureen Debisaran, *CFO*
Carlos Wellman, *Director*
EMP: 108 **EST:** 2010
SALES (est): 3.1MM **Privately Held**
SIC: 7832 Motion picture theaters, except drive-in

(P-18315)
CINEMA CITY THEATERS
5635 E La Palma Ave, Anaheim (92807-2109)
PHONE....................714 970-0865
Fax: 714 970-0283
Meghan Walsh, *Manager*
EMP: 50
SALES (est): 1.2MM **Privately Held**
WEB: www.cinemacitytheatres.com
SIC: 7832 Motion picture theaters, except drive-in

(P-18316)
CINEMARK 16 BAYFAIR
15555 E 14th St Ste 600, San Leandro (94578-1970)
PHONE....................510 276-9684
Anthony Tan, *Branch Mgr*
EMP: 60
SALES (est): 2.1MM **Privately Held**
SIC: 7832 Motion picture theaters, except drive-in

(P-18317)
CINEMASTAR LUXURY THEATERS
1949 Avenida Del Oro # 100, Oceanside (92056-5829)
PHONE....................760 945-2500
Fax: 760 945-2510
Jack R Crosby, *President*
EMP: 350
SALES (est): 4.1MM **Privately Held**
WEB: www.cinemastar.com
SIC: 7832 Motion picture theaters, except drive-in

(P-18318)
COMMERCE CENTER THEATRES
Also Called: Pacific Thtres Cmmerce Theatre
950 Goodrich Blvd, Commerce (90022-4110)
PHONE....................323 722-5577
Roberta Sanchez, *Manager*
EMP: 60
SALES (est): 585.2K **Privately Held**
SIC: 7832 Motion picture theaters, except drive-in

(P-18319)
DECURION CORPORATION (PA)
120 N Robertson Blvd Fl 3, Los Angeles (90048-3115)
PHONE....................310 659-9432
Michael R Forman, *President*
Bryan Ungard, *COO*
Bill Boersma, *CFO*
Pascal Coustar, *Treasurer*
James Cotter, *Vice Pres*
EMP: 100
SQ FT: 31,000
SALES (est): 200.2MM **Privately Held**
SIC: 7832 7833 Motion picture theaters, except drive-in; drive-in motion picture theaters

(P-18320)
EDWARDS BREA 10 WEST
255 W Birch St, Brea (92821-4965)
PHONE....................714 672-4136
Mike Campbell, *President*
Brea Edwards, *Plant Mgr*
EMP: 50
SALES (est): 780.9K **Privately Held**
SIC: 7832 Motion picture theaters, except drive-in

(P-18321)
EDWARDS THEATRES CIRCUIT INC
Also Called: Jurupa Stadium Cinema 14
8032 Limonite Ave, Riverside (92509-6107)
PHONE....................951 361-1917
EMP: 62
SALES (corp-wide): 3.1B **Publicly Held**
SIC: 7832 Motion picture theaters, except drive-in

PRODUCTS & SERVICES SECTION
7832 - Motion Picture Theaters, Except Drive-In County (P-18343)

HQ: Edwards Theatres Circuit, Inc.
300 Newport Center Dr
Newport Beach CA 92660
949 640-4600

(P-18322)
EDWARDS THEATRES CIRCUIT INC
Also Called: Mesa Pointe Stadium 12
901 S Coast Dr, Costa Mesa (92626-1747)
PHONE.....................714 428-0962
Fax: 714 966-8385
Minh Duong, Branch Mgr
EMP: 62
SALES (corp-wide): 3.1B Publicly Held
SIC: 7832 Motion picture theaters, except drive-in
HQ: Edwards Theatres Circuit, Inc.
300 Newport Center Dr
Newport Beach CA 92660
949 640-4600

(P-18323)
EDWARDS THEATRES CIRCUIT INC
Also Called: Rancho San Diego Cinema 16
2951 Jamacha Rd, El Cajon (92019-4342)
PHONE.....................619 660-3460
EMP: 62
SALES (corp-wide): 3.1B Publicly Held
SIC: 7832 Motion picture theaters, except drive-in
HQ: Edwards Theatres Circuit, Inc.
300 Newport Center Dr
Newport Beach CA 92660
949 640-4600

(P-18324)
EDWARDS THEATRES CIRCUIT INC
Also Called: Kaleidioscope Stadium Cinema
27741 Crown Valley Pkwy # 323, Mission Viejo (92691-6532)
PHONE.....................949 582-4078
EMP: 62
SALES (corp-wide): 3.1B Publicly Held
SIC: 7832 Motion picture theaters, except drive-in
HQ: Edwards Theatres Circuit, Inc.
300 Newport Center Dr
Newport Beach CA 92660
949 640-4600

(P-18325)
EDWARDS THEATRES CIRCUIT INC
Also Called: Mira Mesa Stadium 18
10733 Westview Pkwy, San Diego (92126-2963)
PHONE.....................858 635-7716
Peter Brandon, Branch Mgr
EMP: 62
SALES (corp-wide): 3.1B Publicly Held
SIC: 7832 Motion picture theaters, except drive-in
HQ: Edwards Theatres Circuit, Inc.
300 Newport Center Dr
Newport Beach CA 92660
949 640-4600

(P-18326)
EDWARDS THEATRES CIRCUIT INC
Also Called: South Coast Village
1561 W Sunflower Ave, Santa Ana (92704-7436)
PHONE.....................714 557-5701
EMP: 62
SALES (corp-wide): 3.1B Publicly Held
SIC: 7832 Motion picture theaters, except drive-in
HQ: Edwards Theatres Circuit, Inc.
300 Newport Center Dr
Newport Beach CA 92660
949 640-4600

(P-18327)
EDWARDS THEATRES CIRCUIT INC (DH)
300 Newport Center Dr, Newport Beach (92660-7529)
PHONE.....................949 640-4600
Fax: 949 721-7170
W James Edwards III, Ch of Bd
Steve Coffey, President
Kevin Frabotta, Vice Pres
Joan Randolph, Vice Pres
Marcella Sheldon, Admin Sec
EMP: 118
SQ FT: 30,000
SALES (est): 78.4MM
SALES (corp-wide): 3.1B Publicly Held
SIC: 7832 Motion picture theaters, except drive-in
HQ: Regal Cinemas, Inc.
7132 Regal Ln
Knoxville TN 37918
865 922-1123

(P-18328)
EDWARDS THEATRES CIRCUIT INC
Also Called: Long Beach Stadium Cinemas 26
7501 Carson Blvd, Long Beach (90808-2365)
PHONE.....................562 429-3321
EMP: 62
SALES (corp-wide): 3.1B Publicly Held
SIC: 7832 Motion picture theaters, except drive-in; theater building, ownership & operation
HQ: Edwards Theatres Circuit, Inc.
300 Newport Center Dr
Newport Beach CA 92660
949 640-4600

(P-18329)
EDWARDS THEATRES CIRCUIT INC
Also Called: San Marcos Stadium Cinema 18
1180 W San Marcos Blvd, San Marcos (92078-4009)
PHONE.....................760 471-3734
Jerry Jorgensen, Manager
EMP: 100
SALES (corp-wide): 3.1B Publicly Held
SIC: 7832 Motion picture theaters, except drive-in
HQ: Edwards Theatres Circuit, Inc.
300 Newport Center Dr
Newport Beach CA 92660
949 640-4600

(P-18330)
EDWARDS THEATRES CIRCUIT INC
Also Called: Cerritos Cinemas 10
12761 Towne Center Dr, Artesia (90703-8545)
PHONE.....................562 403-1133
James Edwards III, Branch Mgr
EMP: 60
SALES (corp-wide): 3.1B Publicly Held
SIC: 7832 Motion picture theaters, except drive-in
HQ: Edwards Theatres Circuit, Inc.
300 Newport Center Dr
Newport Beach CA 92660
949 640-4600

(P-18331)
EDWARDS THEATRES CIRCUIT INC
Also Called: Temecula Stadium Cinemas 15
40750 Winchester Rd, Temecula (92591-5524)
PHONE.....................951 296-0144
EMP: 62
SALES (corp-wide): 3.1B Publicly Held
SIC: 7832 Motion picture theaters, except drive-in
HQ: Edwards Theatres Circuit, Inc.
300 Newport Center Dr
Newport Beach CA 92660
949 640-4600

(P-18332)
EDWARDS THEATRES CIRCUIT INC
Also Called: Edwards Theaters
680 Ventura Blvd, Camarillo (93010-5877)
PHONE.....................805 383-8866
J D Powers, Manager
EMP: 62
SALES (corp-wide): 3.1B Publicly Held
SIC: 7832 Motion picture theaters, except drive-in

(P-18333)
EDWARDS THEATRES CIRCUIT INC
Also Called: Edwards Cinemas University
4245 Campus Dr, Irvine (92612-2752)
PHONE.....................949 854-8811
Mike Peterson, Branch Mgr
EMP: 62
SALES (corp-wide): 3.1B Publicly Held
SIC: 7832 Motion picture theaters, except drive-in
HQ: Edwards Theatres Circuit, Inc.
300 Newport Center Dr
Newport Beach CA 92660
949 640-4600

(P-18334)
EDWARDS THEATRES CIRCUIT INC
Also Called: El Monte Cinema 8
10661 Valley Blvd, El Monte (91731-2404)
PHONE.....................626 580-7660
Eduardo Lozaeri, Manager
EMP: 62
SALES (corp-wide): 3.1B Publicly Held
SIC: 7832 Motion picture theaters, except drive-in
HQ: Edwards Theatres Circuit, Inc.
300 Newport Center Dr
Newport Beach CA 92660
949 640-4600

(P-18335)
EDWARDS THEATRES CIRCUIT INC
Also Called: Simi Valley Plaza 10
1457 E Los Angeles Ave, Simi Valley (93065-2807)
PHONE.....................805 526-4329
Dominiqua Lint, Branch Mgr
EMP: 62
SALES (corp-wide): 3.1B Publicly Held
SIC: 7832 Motion picture theaters, except drive-in
HQ: Edwards Theatres Circuit, Inc.
300 Newport Center Dr
Newport Beach CA 92660
949 640-4600

(P-18336)
EDWARDS THEATRES CIRCUIT INC
Also Called: Santa Maria Cinema 10
1521 S Bradley Rd, Santa Maria (93454-8014)
PHONE.....................805 347-1164
Fax: 805 739-0456
Santa Edwards, Manager
EMP: 62
SALES (corp-wide): 3.1B Publicly Held
SIC: 7832 Motion picture theaters, except drive-in
HQ: Edwards Theatres Circuit, Inc.
300 Newport Center Dr
Newport Beach CA 92660
949 640-4600

(P-18337)
KRIKORIAN PREMIERE THEATRE LLC
25 Main St, Vista (92083-5800)
PHONE.....................760 945-7469
EMP: 114
SALES (corp-wide): 62.3MM Privately Held
SIC: 7832 Motion picture theaters, except drive-in
PA: Krikorian Premiere Theatre Llc
2275 W 190th St
Torrance CA 90504
310 856-1270

(P-18338)
METROPLEX THEATRES LLC
2275 W 190th St Ste 201, Torrance (90504-6007)
PHONE.....................310 856-1270
George Krikorian,
Colleen Tubridy, Manager
EMP: 600 EST: 1999
SALES (est): 9.5MM Privately Held
SIC: 7832 Motion picture theaters, except drive-in

(P-18339)
NORTH AMERICAN CINEMAS INC
Also Called: Airport Cinemas 12
409 Aviation Blvd, Santa Rosa (95403-1069)
PHONE.....................707 571-1412
Nicholas Mann, General Mgr
EMP: 365 Privately Held
WEB: www.northamericacinemas.com
SIC: 7832 Motion picture theaters, except drive-in
PA: North American Cinemas, Inc.
917 College Ave
Santa Rosa CA 95404

(P-18340)
PACIFIC THEATERS INC (PA)
120 N Robertson Blvd Fl 3, Los Angeles (90048-3113)
PHONE.....................310 657-8420
Michael Forman, Ch of Bd
Christopher Forman, CEO
Gary Marcotte, CFO
Kevin Elms, Treasurer
Beverly Justice, Exec Sec
EMP: 120 EST: 1950
SQ FT: 25,000
SALES (est): 8.1MM Privately Held
SIC: 7832 7812 Exhibitors, itinerant: motion picture; motion picture production & distribution, television

(P-18341)
PACIFIC THEATERS INC
Also Called: Beach Cities 16 Cinemas
831 S Nash St, El Segundo (90245-4708)
PHONE.....................310 607-0007
Gaye Clemson, Manager
EMP: 55
SALES (corp-wide): 8.1MM Privately Held
SIC: 7832 Motion picture theaters, except drive-in
PA: Pacific Theaters, Inc
120 N Robertson Blvd Fl 3
Los Angeles CA 90048
310 657-8420

(P-18342)
PACIFIC THEATERS INC
4821 Del Amo Blvd, Lakewood (90712-2504)
PHONE.....................562 634-1183
Bill Bayam, Manager
Penny McNamee, Manager
EMP: 80
SALES (corp-wide): 8.1MM Privately Held
SIC: 7832 Exhibitors, itinerant: motion picture
PA: Pacific Theaters, Inc
120 N Robertson Blvd Fl 3
Los Angeles CA 90048
310 657-8420

(P-18343)
READING ENTERTAINMENT INC (HQ)
500 Citadel Dr Ste 300, Commerce (90040-1572)
PHONE.....................213 235-2226
Robert F Smerling, President
Neil Pentecost, COO
Andrzej Matyczynski, CFO
Ellen Cotter, Vice Pres
Charles S Grohon, VP Finance
▲ EMP: 78
SQ FT: 3,300
SALES (est): 3.6MM
SALES (corp-wide): 257.3MM Publicly Held
SIC: 7832 Motion picture theaters, except drive-in
PA: Reading International, Inc.
6100 Center Dr Ste 900
Los Angeles CA 90045
213 235-2240

7832 - Motion Picture Theaters, Except Drive-In County (P-18344)

PRODUCTS & SERVICES SECTION

(P-18344)
READING INTERNATIONAL INC
41090 California Oaks Rd, Murrieta (92562-5749)
PHONE..................................951 696-7045
Dolly Woodland, *General Mgr*
EMP: 50
SALES (corp-wide): 257.3MM **Publicly Held**
SIC: 7832 Motion picture theaters, except drive-in
PA: Reading International, Inc.
6100 Center Dr Ste 900
Los Angeles CA 90045
213 235-2240

(P-18345)
READING INTERNATIONAL INC
Also Called: Angelika Film Center and Cafe
11620 Carmel Mountain Rd, San Diego (92128-4621)
PHONE..................................858 207-2606
Chris Herbert, *General Mgr*
EMP: 60
SALES (corp-wide): 257.3MM **Publicly Held**
SIC: 7832 5812 5182 Motion picture theaters, except drive-in; cafe; wine & distilled beverages
PA: Reading International, Inc.
6100 Center Dr Ste 900
Los Angeles CA 90045
213 235-2240

(P-18346)
READING INTERNATIONAL INC
2508 Land Park Dr, Sacramento (95818-2224)
PHONE..................................916 442-0985
EMP: 1131
SALES (corp-wide): 257.3MM **Publicly Held**
SIC: 7832 Motion picture theaters, except drive-in
PA: Reading International, Inc.
6100 Center Dr Ste 900
Los Angeles CA 90045
213 235-2240

(P-18347)
READING INTERNATIONAL INC (PA)
6100 Center Dr Ste 900, Los Angeles (90045-9207)
PHONE..................................213 235-2240
Ellen M Cotter, *Ch of Bd*
Margaret Cotter, *Vice Chairman*
Robert F Smerling, *President*
Devasis Ghose, *CFO*
Andzei Matyczynski, *CFO*
EMP: 104
SQ FT: 11,700
SALES: 257.3MM **Publicly Held**
SIC: 7832 7922 6512 6531 Motion picture theaters, except drive-in; theatrical producers & services; nonresidential building operators; real estate agents & managers

(P-18348)
REGAL CINEMAS INC
Also Called: Natomas Marketplace 16
3561 Truxel Rd, Sacramento (95834-3641)
PHONE..................................916 419-0205
Ricks Hescock, *Manager*
EMP: 60
SALES (corp-wide): 3.1B **Publicly Held**
WEB: www.regalcinemas.com
SIC: 7832 Motion picture theaters, except drive-in
HQ: Regal Cinemas, Inc.
7132 Regal Ln
Knoxville TN 37918
865 922-1123

(P-18349)
REGAL CINEMAS INC
550 Deep Valley Dr # 339, Rllng HLS Est (90274-7603)
PHONE..................................310 544-3042
Christy Alexander, *Manager*
EMP: 80
SALES (corp-wide): 3.1B **Publicly Held**
WEB: www.regalcinemas.com
SIC: 7832 Motion picture theaters, except drive-in
HQ: Regal Cinemas, Inc.
7132 Regal Ln
Knoxville TN 37918
865 922-1123

(P-18350)
REGENCY THEATRES INC
26901 Agoura Rd Ste 150, Agoura Hills (91301-5114)
PHONE..................................818 224-3825
Lyndon H Golin, *President*
Monica Golin, *CFO*
EMP: 50
SQ FT: 1,000
SALES: 4MM **Privately Held**
WEB: www.regencymovies.com
SIC: 7832 Motion picture theaters, except drive-in

(P-18351)
SANBORN THEATRES INC
41090 Calif Oaks Rd, Murrieta (92562-5749)
PHONE..................................909 296-9728
Arthur Sanborn, *Branch Mgr*
EMP: 70
SALES (corp-wide): 12.3MM **Privately Held**
SIC: 7832 Motion picture theaters, except drive-in
PA: Sanborn Theatres Inc
13 Corporate Plaza Dr # 110
Newport Beach CA 92660
949 640-2370

(P-18352)
SILVER CINEMAS ACQUISITION CO (PA)
Also Called: Landmark Theatres
2222 S Barrington Ave, Los Angeles (90064-1206)
PHONE..................................310 473-6701
Fax: 310 312-2351
Mark Cuban, *President*
George T Mundorff, *CEO*
Todd Wagner, *CEO*
Paul Duchouquette, *Vice Pres*
Richard Lorber, *Vice Pres*
EMP: 52
SALES (est): 75.1MM **Privately Held**
SIC: 7832 Motion picture theaters, except drive-in

(P-18353)
UA GALAXY LOS CERRITOS
Also Called: Ua Galaxy Los Cerritos 33
4900 E 4th St, Ontario (91764-5229)
PHONE..................................562 865-6499
Mike Friextad, *Manager*
Victoria Curtis, *Branch Mgr*
EMP: 70
SALES (est): 939.4K **Privately Held**
SIC: 7832 Motion picture theaters, except drive-in

(P-18354)
WESTSTAR CINEMAS INC
Also Called: Mann's Theatres
6801 Hollywood Blvd # 335, Los Angeles (90028-6136)
PHONE..................................323 461-3331
Laval How, *Manager*
EMP: 95
SALES (corp-wide): 32.7MM **Privately Held**
WEB: www.manntheatres.com
SIC: 7832 Motion picture theaters, except drive-in
PA: Weststar Cinemas, Inc
16530 Ventura Blvd # 500
Encino CA 91436
818 784-6266

(P-18355)
WF CINEMA HOLDINGS LP
Also Called: Village 8
180 Promenade Way Ste R, Westlake Village (91362-3826)
PHONE..................................805 379-8966
Joseph Leptore, *Manager*
Tim Simpson, *Manager*
EMP: 50

SALES (corp-wide): 32.7MM **Privately Held**
WEB: www.manntheatres.com
SIC: 7832 Motion picture theaters, except drive-in
PA: Weststar Cinemas, Inc
16530 Ventura Blvd # 500
Encino CA 91436
818 784-6266

7833 Drive-In Motion Picture Theaters

(P-18356)
CENTURY THEATRES INC
Also Called: Century 14
1555 Eureka Rd, Roseville (95661-3040)
PHONE..................................916 797-3466
Ray Syufy, *President*
EMP: 70
SALES (corp-wide): 2.8B **Publicly Held**
WEB: www.centurytheaters.com
SIC: 7833 7832 Drive-in motion picture theaters; motion picture theaters, except drive-in
HQ: Century Theatres, Inc
3900 Dallas Pkwy Ste 500
Plano TX 75093
972 665-1000

(P-18357)
CENTURY THEATRES INC
3200 Klose Way, Richmond (94806-5792)
PHONE..................................510 758-9626
Makisha Jones, *Manager*
EMP: 90
SALES (corp-wide): 2.8B **Publicly Held**
WEB: www.centurytheaters.com
SIC: 7833 7832 Drive-in motion picture theaters; motion picture theaters, except drive-in
HQ: Century Theatres, Inc
3900 Dallas Pkwy Ste 500
Plano TX 75093
972 665-1000

(P-18358)
CENTURY THEATRES INC
Also Called: Century 8
12827 Victory Blvd, North Hollywood (91606-3012)
PHONE..................................818 508-1943
Terrell Hammack, *Branch Mgr*
Juan Ramirez, *General Mgr*
EMP: 60
SALES (corp-wide): 2.8B **Publicly Held**
WEB: www.centurytheaters.com
SIC: 7833 7832 Drive-in motion picture theaters; motion picture theaters, except drive-in
HQ: Century Theatres, Inc
3900 Dallas Pkwy Ste 500
Plano TX 75093
972 665-1000

(P-18359)
DE ANZA LAND & LEISURE CORP
Also Called: South Bay Drive In Theatre
2170 Coronado Ave, San Diego (92154-2022)
PHONE..................................619 423-2727
Veronica Sarabia, *Branch Mgr*
EMP: 50
SALES (corp-wide): 12.3MM **Privately Held**
SIC: 7833 Drive-in motion picture theaters
PA: De Anza Land & Leisure Corp.
4407 State St
Montclair CA 91763
909 628-0019

(P-18360)
MISSION DRIVE-IN THEATRE CO
Also Called: Los Angeles Dr-In Theatre Co
4407 State St, Montclair (91763-6034)
PHONE..................................909 465-9219
William Oldknow, *Managing Prtnr*
Charles P Skouras III, *Partner*
Charles P Skouras Jr, *Partner*
Diane M Skouras, *Partner*
Christianna Skouras-Marin, *Partner*
EMP: 60
SQ FT: 500

SALES (est): 3.2MM **Privately Held**
WEB: www.missiontiki.com
SIC: 7833 6515 5932 Drive-in motion picture theaters; mobile home site operators; used merchandise stores

(P-18361)
NATIONWIDE THEATRES CORP (HQ)
120 N Robertson Blvd Fl 3, Los Angeles (90048-3115)
PHONE..................................310 657-8420
Christopher Forman, *President*
Nora Dashwood, *COO*
EMP: 75
SQ FT: 25,000
SALES (est): 45.4MM
SALES (corp-wide): 200.2MM **Privately Held**
SIC: 7833 7832 Drive-in motion picture theaters; motion picture theaters, except drive-in
PA: The Decurion Corporation
120 N Robertson Blvd Fl 3
Los Angeles CA 90048
310 659-9432

7911 Dance Studios, Schools & Halls

(P-18362)
CLOVIS UNIFIED SCHOOL DISTRICT
885 Gettysburg Ave, Clovis (93612-3906)
PHONE..................................559 327-3900
Fax: 559 327-3990
EMP: 698 **Privately Held**
SIC: 7911 Dance instructor & school services
PA: Clovis Unified School District
1450 Herndon Ave
Clovis CA 93611
559 327-9000

(P-18363)
GABRIELLA FOUNDATION
639 S Commwl Ave Ste B, Los Angeles (90005)
PHONE..................................213 365-2491
Liza Bercovici, *Exec Dir*
Staci Armao, *Opers Staff*
Missy Mannila, *Director*
EMP: 82
SALES: 1.3MM **Privately Held**
WEB: www.gabriellaaxelradfoundation.org
SIC: 7911 8211 Children's dancing school; elementary & secondary schools

(P-18364)
ODC
3153 17th St, San Francisco (94110-1332)
PHONE..................................415 863-9834
Bartley Deamer, *Branch Mgr*
EMP: 58
SALES (corp-wide): 3.4MM **Privately Held**
SIC: 7911 Dance studios, schools & halls
PA: Odc
351 Shotwell St
San Francisco CA 94110
415 863-6606

7922 Theatrical Producers & Misc Theatrical Svcs

(P-18365)
ADAIR ENTERPRISES
Also Called: American Way Cultural Center
2390 N American Way, Orange (92865-2502)
PHONE..................................714 998-5551
Fax: 714 637-7123
Richard Adair, *Partner*
Marty Adair, *Partner*
EMP: 53
SQ FT: 35,000

PRODUCTS & SERVICES SECTION

7922 - Theatrical Producers & Misc Theatrical Svcs County (P-18386)

SALES (est): 1.1MM **Privately Held**
WEB: www.awccevents.com
SIC: **7922** Performing arts center production

(P-18366)
ADVENTIST MEDIA CENTER INC
Also Called: It Is Written
11291 Pierce St, Riverside (92505-2705)
P.O. Box 101, Simi Valley (93062-0101)
PHONE.................................805 955-7777
Fax: 805 955-7702
Marshall Chase, *President*
Daniel Jackson, *Ch of Bd*
Herbert Swenson, *Treasurer*
Warren Judd, *Vice Pres*
Roy Hunt, *General Mgr*
▲ EMP: 235
SQ FT: 76,000
SALES (est): 14.1MM **Privately Held**
WEB: www.sdamedia.org
SIC: **7922** Theatrical producers & services

(P-18367)
AEG LIVE LLC (DH)
Also Called: Concerts West
425 W 11th St Ste 300, Los Angeles (90015-3461)
PHONE.................................323 930-5700
Randy Phillips,
Ron Chiu, *Senior VP*
Adam Cohen, *Senior VP*
Andrew Bersch, *Vice Pres*
Creighton Burke, *Vice Pres*
▲ EMP: 140
SQ FT: 16,400
SALES (est): 30.3MM
SALES (corp-wide): 110.6MM **Privately Held**
SIC: **7922** Entertainment promotion
HQ: Anschutz Entertainment Group, Inc.
    1100 S Flower St
    Los Angeles CA 90015
    213 763-7700

(P-18368)
AMERICAN CONSERVATORY
415 Geary St, San Francisco (94102-1222)
PHONE.................................415 749-2228
Roger Wahther, *Manager*
Hillary Bray, *Treasurer*
Patsy McCormack, *Master*
Jordan Okano, *Associate*
EMP: 70
SALES (corp-wide): 31.6MM **Privately Held**
WEB: www.acts-at.com
SIC: **7922** Repertory, road or stock companies: theatrical
PA: American Conservatory Theatre Foundation
    30 Grant Ave Fl 7
    San Francisco CA 94108
    415 834-3200

(P-18369)
AMERICAN CONSERVATORY
Also Called: A C T Box Office
405 Geary St, San Francisco (94102-1222)
PHONE.................................415 749-2228
Cheryl Sorokin, *Branch Mgr*
EMP: 70
SALES (corp-wide): 31.6MM **Privately Held**
WEB: www.acts-at.com
SIC: **7922** Repertory, road or stock companies: theatrical
PA: American Conservatory Theatre Foundation
    30 Grant Ave Fl 7
    San Francisco CA 94108
    415 834-3200

(P-18370)
ARMENIAN AMRCN THEA MSICAL SOC
Also Called: Armenian Amercn Thea Musical S
3111 Los Feliz Blvd # 103, Los Angeles (90039-1519)
PHONE.................................323 668-1030
Fax: 323 668-0051
Victor Mardirossi, *Principal*
EMP: 57

SALES (est): 2.6MM **Privately Held**
SIC: **7922** Agent or manager for entertainers

(P-18371)
BEN BOLLINGER PRODUCTIONS INC
Also Called: Bollingers Candelight Pavilion
455 W Foothill Blvd, Claremont (91711-2701)
PHONE.................................909 626-3296
Fax: 909 626-6465
Ben Bollinger, *President*
Isaias Herrada, *Manager*
EMP: 70
SALES (est): 2.8MM **Privately Held**
SIC: **7922** 8999 Theatrical producers; music arranging & composing

(P-18372)
BERKELEY REPERTORY THEATRE (PA)
2025 Addison St, Berkeley (94704-1103)
PHONE.................................510 204-8901
Fax: 510 841-7711
Susan Medak, *Managing Dir*
Karen Racanelli, *General Mgr*
Andrew Susskind, *Executive Asst*
Diana Amezquita, *Information Mgr*
Itzel Ortuno, *Graphic Designe*
▲ EMP: 80
SQ FT: 20,000
SALES: 16.6MM **Privately Held**
WEB: www.berkeleyrep.org
SIC: **7922** Theatrical production services

(P-18373)
BREAK FLOOR PRODUCTIONS LLC
Also Called: Jump Dance Convention
5446 Satsuma Ave, North Hollywood (91601-2837)
PHONE.................................212 247-7277
Gil Stroming, *Mng Member*
George Gregory, *Prdtn Dir*
Nikole Vallins, *Producer*
Jordan Richbart, *Manager*
EMP: 50
SALES: 5MM **Privately Held**
WEB: www.breakthefloor.com
SIC: **7922** Theatrical producers

(P-18374)
BROADWAY BY BAY
1155 Broadway St Ste 206, Redwood City (94063-3127)
PHONE.................................650 579-5565
Waren Doan, *President*
John Blatt, *Treasurer*
EMP: 140
SQ FT: 1,600
SALES: 1.2MM **Privately Held**
WEB: www.bbbay.org
SIC: **7922** Ticket agency, theatrical

(P-18375)
CALIFORNIA REPERTORY COMPANY
Also Called: California University Long Bch
1250 N Bellflower Blvd # 124, Long Beach (90840-0124)
PHONE.................................562 985-7891
Joanne Gordon, *Director*
Pari Kasliwal, *Executive*
Ted Azarmi, *Human Res Mgr*
Howard Burman, *Director*
EMP: 50
SALES: 2.2MM **Privately Held**
SIC: **7922** 6512 Theatrical producers & services; theater building, ownership & operation

(P-18376)
CALIFORNIA SHAKESPEARE THEATER
Also Called: CAL SHAKES
701 Heinz Ave, Berkeley (94710-2732)
PHONE.................................510 548-3422
Fax: 510 843-9921
Jonathan Moscone, *Director*
Derik Cowan, *Office Mgr*
Ilsa Brink, *Webmaster*
Maya R Lawrence, *Benefits Mgr*
Megan Barton, *Marketing Staff*
EMP: 225

SALES: 5.8MM **Privately Held**
WEB: www.calshakes.org
SIC: **7922** Plays, road & stock companies

(P-18377)
CALIFORNIA TICKETSCOM INC
1855 Gateway Blvd Ste 630, Concord (94520-3200)
PHONE.................................925 671-4000
Terry Wojtulewicz, *Branch Mgr*
Shane Miller, *Exec Dir*
Eric Davis, *Executive Asst*
Desre McGraff, *Executive Asst*
Rick Marx, *Info Tech Dir*
EMP: 200
SALES (corp-wide): 271.5MM **Privately Held**
WEB: www.tickets.com
SIC: **7922** 7999 Ticket agency, theatrical; ticket sales office for sporting events, contract
HQ: California Tickets.Com Inc.
    555 Anton Blvd Fl 11
    Costa Mesa CA 92626
    714 327-5400

(P-18378)
CALIFORNIA TICKETSCOM INC (DH)
555 Anton Blvd Fl 11, Costa Mesa (92626-7675)
PHONE.................................714 327-5400
Fax: 714 327-5410
Joe Choti, *President*
Cristine Hurley, *CFO*
Derek Palmer, *Exec VP*
Jennifer Archer, *Vice Pres*
Kamra Gebhardt, *Vice Pres*
▲ EMP: 88
SALES (est): 18.9MM
SALES (corp-wide): 271.5MM **Privately Held**
WEB: www.tickets.com
SIC: **7922** 7999 5961 5045 Ticket agency, theatrical; ticket sales office for sporting events, contract; catalog & mail-order houses; computers, peripherals & software
HQ: Mlb Advanced Media, L.P.
    75 9th Ave Fl 5
    New York NY 10011
    212 485-3444

(P-18379)
CAMERON PACE GROUP LLC
4534 Atoll Ave, Sherman Oaks (91423-3305)
PHONE.................................818 565-0005
Vince Pace,
James Cameron, *Chairman*
Anthony Margulis, *Finance*
EMP: 55
SQ FT: 35,000
SALES (est): 2.3MM **Privately Held**
SIC: **7922** Equipment rental, theatrical

(P-18380)
CENTER THTRE GROUP LOS ANGELES (PA)
601 W Temple St, Los Angeles (90012-2621)
PHONE.................................213 972-7344
Fax: 213 972-8062
Michael Ritchie, *CEO*
William Ahmanson, *Ch of Bd*
Kiki Ramos Gindler, *President*
Cheryl Shepherd, *CFO*
Bruce L Ross, *Treasurer*
▲ EMP: 130
SQ FT: 20,000
SALES: 41.6MM **Privately Held**
WEB: www.ctgla.org
SIC: **7922** Theatrical producers & services

(P-18381)
CITY & COUNTY OF SAN FRANCISCO
Also Called: Zellerbach Rehearsal Hall
401 Van Ness Ave Ste 110, San Francisco (94102-4521)
PHONE.................................415 621-6600
Elizabeth Maury, *Manager*
Elizabeth Murray, *Manager*
EMP: 100 **Privately Held**

SIC: **7922** 9199 Performing arts center production; general government administration;
PA: City & County Of San Francisco
    1 Dr Carlton B Goodlett P
    San Francisco CA 94102
    415 554-7500

(P-18382)
CITY & COUNTY OF SAN FRANCISCO
Also Called: War Memorial Prfrmg Art Ctr
401 Van Ness Ave Ste 110, San Francisco (94102-4521)
PHONE.................................415 621-6600
Fax: 415 621-5091
Elizabeth Murray, *Finance*
Marilou Faro, *Admin Asst*
Stephanie Smith, *Admin Asst*
EMP: 100 **Privately Held**
SIC: **7922** 9199 6512 Performing arts center production; general government administration; ; ; nonresidential building operators
PA: City & County Of San Francisco
    1 Dr Carlton B Goodlett P
    San Francisco CA 94102
    415 554-7500

(P-18383)
CITY OF CONCORD
Also Called: Concord Pavillion
2000 Kirker Pass Rd, Concord (94521-1642)
PHONE.................................925 692-2400
Doug Warrick, *General Mgr*
EMP: 400 **Privately Held**
WEB: www.cpd.ci.concord.ca.us
SIC: **7922** 6512 Theatrical companies; theater building, ownership & operation
PA: City Of Concord
    1950 Parkside Dr
    Concord CA 94519
    925 671-3000

(P-18384)
CITY OF DOWNEY
Also Called: Downey Civic Theatre
8435 Firestone Blvd, Downey (90241-3843)
P.O. Box 607 (90241-0607)
PHONE.................................562 861-8211
Gerald Caton, *Manager*
Amber Vogel, *Manager*
EMP: 97 **Privately Held**
WEB: www.dpoa.org
SIC: **7922** Legitimate live theater producers
PA: City Of Downey
    11111 Brookshire Ave
    Downey CA 90241
    562 869-7331

(P-18385)
CREATING ARTS COMPANY
Also Called: Cac Studios
3110 Pennsylvania Ave, Santa Monica (90404-4216)
PHONE.................................310 804-0223
Shannon Sukovaty, *CEO*
Todd Skinner, *President*
EMP: 50
SALES: 250K **Privately Held**
SIC: **7922** Theatrical companies

(P-18386)
CREATIVE ARTISTS AGENCY LLC (PA)
Also Called: C A A
2000 Avenue Of The Stars # 100, Los Angeles (90067-4705)
PHONE.................................424 288-2000
Rick Nicita, *Chairman*
Kevin Gelbard, *Partner*
Steve Lafferty, *Managing Prtnr*
Michael Rubel, *Managing Prtnr*
Bob Goldman, *CFO*
EMP: 800
SALES (est): 107.1MM **Privately Held**
WEB: www.caa.com
SIC: **7922** Agent or manager for entertainers

7922 - Theatrical Producers & Misc Theatrical Svcs County (P-18387)

(P-18387)
DAVIE BROWN ENTERTAINMENT INC
12777 W Jefferson Blvd # 120, Los Angeles (90066-7038)
PHONE..................................310 979-1980
James Davie, *CEO*
Stephanie Cohen, *President*
Tom Meyer, *President*
Russell Meisels, *CFO*
Adam Smith, *Exec VP*
EMP: 60
SQ FT: 16,100
SALES: 18.5MM
SALES (corp-wide): 15.1B Publicly Held
WEB: www.davie-brown.com
SIC: 7922 Entertainment promotion
HQ: The Marketing Arm Inc
1999 Bryan St Fl 18
Dallas TX 75201

(P-18388)
DELICATE PRODUCTIONS INC (PA)
874 Verdulera St, Camarillo (93010-8371)
PHONE..................................415 484-1174
Fax: 805 388-1037
James Steve Dabbs, *CEO*
Christopher Smyth, *CFO*
Angus Thomson, *Vice Pres*
Gus Thomson, *Vice Pres*
Steven I Gilbard, *Principal*
EMP: 79
SQ FT: 19,937
SALES (est): 7.1MM Privately Held
WEB: www.delicate.com
SIC: 7922 7359 Equipment rental, theatrical; sound & lighting equipment rental

(P-18389)
ELVIS SCHOENBERG PRODUCTION
549 Marie Ave, Los Angeles (90042-1305)
PHONE..................................323 344-1745
Ross Wright, *President*
EMP: 50
SALES (est): 662.1K Privately Held
SIC: 7922 Theatrical producers & services

(P-18390)
ENDEMOL
9255 W Sunset Blvd # 1100, West Hollywood (90069-3308)
PHONE..................................310 860-9914
David Goldberg, *Chairman*
EMP: 70 **EST:** 2012
SALES: 170MM Privately Held
SIC: 7922 Television program, including commercial producers

(P-18391)
EPICENTER LIVE INC
4040 Mahaila Ave Unit A, San Diego (92122-5807)
PHONE..................................424 235-4835
Devon Joseph, *President*
Keith A Joseph, *Exec Dir*
EMP: 150
SALES (est): 2.8MM Privately Held
SIC: 7922 Concert management service

(P-18392)
FAIRGROUNDS
Also Called: Event Center
2198 Riverside Ave, Paso Robles (93446-1330)
P.O. Box 8 (93447-0008)
PHONE..................................805 239-0655
Vivian Robertson, *CEO*
EMP: 56
SALES (est): 669.3K Privately Held
SIC: 7922 Performing arts center production

(P-18393)
FOUNDATION FOR DANCE EDUCATION
Also Called: Inland Pacific Ballet
5050 Arrow Hwy Ste B, Montclair (91763-1311)
PHONE..................................909 482-1590
Fax: 909 482-1589
Victoria Koenig, *Exec Dir*
Ginger Eaton, *Treasurer*
Neal Archer, *Bd of Directors*
George Reeder, *Bd of Directors*
▲ **EMP:** 51
SALES (est): 747.5K Privately Held
SIC: 7922 Theatrical producers & services

(P-18394)
GERSH AGENCY INC (PA)
9465 Wilshire Blvd Fl 6, Beverly Hills (90212-2605)
PHONE..................................310 274-6611
Fax: 310 274-4035
Robert Gersh, *President*
George H Bigelow, *CFO*
Beatrice Gersh, *Vice Pres*
David Gersh, *Vice Pres*
Barbara Halperin, *Vice Pres*
EMP: 100 **EST:** 1949
SQ FT: 15,000
SALES (est): 11.1MM Privately Held
WEB: www.gershagency.com
SIC: 7922 Talent agent, theatrical

(P-18395)
GREENWAY ARTS ALLIANCE INC
544 N Fairfax Ave, Los Angeles (90036-1771)
PHONE..................................323 655-7679
Molly Miles, *Chairman*
D Pierson Blaetz, *Manager*
Whitney Weston, *Manager*
EMP: 79
SALES: 1.7MM Privately Held
SIC: 7922 8299 Theatrical companies; art school, except commercial

(P-18396)
HARPO INC
Also Called: Harpo Studios
1041 N Formosa Ave, West Hollywood (90046-6703)
PHONE..................................312 633-1000
Fax: 312 633-1111
Oprah Winfrey, *President*
Erik Logan, *President*
Sheri Salata, *President*
Douglas J Pattison, *CFO*
Jon Sinclair, *Vice Pres*
EMP: 70
SQ FT: 88,000
SALES (est): 9.2MM Privately Held
SIC: 7922 Television program, including commercial producers

(P-18397)
INNOVATIVE ARTISTS TALENT AGNY (PA)
1505 10th St, Santa Monica (90401-2805)
PHONE..................................310 656-0400
Fax: 310 656-0456
Scott Harris, *President*
EMP: 75
SALES (est): 6MM Privately Held
WEB: www.iany.com
SIC: 7922 7819 Talent agent, theatrical; casting bureau, motion picture

(P-18398)
INTERNATIONAL CREATIVE MGT INC (HQ)
Also Called: I C M
10250 Constellation Blvd, Los Angeles (90067-6200)
PHONE..................................310 550-4000
Fax: 310 550-4108
Jeff Berg, *Ch of Bd*
Michelle Suess, *President*
Robert Murphy, *CFO*
Nancy Josephson, *Co-President*
Ed Limato, *Co-President*
▲ **EMP:** 220
SQ FT: 72,000
SALES (est): 28.5MM Privately Held
WEB: www.icmtalent.com
SIC: 7922 8699 Talent agent, theatrical; literary, film or cultural club
PA: Icm Holdings Inc
40 W 57th St Fl 16
New York NY 10019
212 556-5600

(P-18399)
INTERNATIONAL CREATIVE MGT INC
Also Called: I C M
10250 Constellation Blvd # 1, Los Angeles (90067-6200)
PHONE..................................310 550-4000
Fax: 310 550-4100
Jeff Derg, *Manager*
Steve Stanford, *Vice Pres*
Peter Trinh, *Manager*
EMP: 200
SALES (corp-wide): 28.5MM Privately Held
SIC: 7922 Booking agency, theatrical
HQ: International Creative Management, Inc.
10250 Constellation Blvd
Los Angeles CA 90067
310 550-4000

(P-18400)
J C ENTERTAINMENT LTG SVCS INC
Also Called: E L S
5435 W San Fernando Rd, Los Angeles (90039-1014)
PHONE..................................818 252-7481
Fax: 818 769-2100
John Allen Chuck, *CEO*
Todd Richards, *CFO*
John E Mitchell, *Exec VP*
Kevin Dowling, *Vice Pres*
Derek Smith, *Vice Pres*
EMP: 80
SQ FT: 69,000
SALES (est): 10.7MM Privately Held
WEB: www.elslights.com
SIC: 7922 5719 Equipment rental, theatrical; lighting, lamps & accessories

(P-18401)
JOHN GORE ORGANIZATION INC
255 S B St, San Mateo (94401-4017)
PHONE..................................650 340-0469
EMP: 132
SALES (corp-wide): 473K Privately Held
SIC: 7922 Entertainment promotion
PA: The John Gore Organization Inc
1619 Broadway Fl 9
New York NY 10019
917 421-5400

(P-18402)
KID STOCK INC
1539 Funston Ave, San Francisco (94122-3530)
PHONE..................................415 753-3737
Jane Sullivan, *Deputy Dir*
Noel Donahue, *Deputy Dir*
Noel Donovan, *Director*
EMP: 80
SALES: 311.2K Privately Held
WEB: www.kidstockinc.org
SIC: 7922 Community theater production

(P-18403)
KRIKORIAN PREMIERE THEATRE LLC
8540 Whittier Blvd, Pico Rivera (90660-2520)
PHONE..................................562 205-3456
Todd Cummings, *Branch Mgr*
EMP: 86
SALES (corp-wide): 62.3MM Privately Held
SIC: 7922 Theatrical companies
PA: Krikorian Premiere Theatre Llc
2275 W 190th St
Torrance CA 90504
310 856-1270

(P-18404)
LA LIVE PROPERTIES LLC
800 W Olympic Blvd # 305, Los Angeles (90015-1360)
PHONE..................................213 763-7700
Donna Johnson, *VP Finance*
EMP: 50
SALES (est): 5.3MM
SALES (corp-wide): 110.6MM Privately Held
WEB: www.lalive.com
SIC: 7922 6512 Theatrical producers & services; property operation, auditoriums & theaters
HQ: Anschutz Entertainment Group, Inc.
1100 S Flower St
Los Angeles CA 90015
213 763-7700

(P-18405)
LAGUNA PLAYHOUSE (PA)
606 Laguna Canyon Rd, Laguna Beach (92651-1837)
P.O. Box 1747 (92652-1747)
PHONE..................................949 497-2787
Fax: 949 497-6948
Karen Wood, *CEO*
Bob Crowson, *CFO*
Cynthia Harriss, *Treasurer*
Richard Stein, *Exec Dir*
Louisa Balch, *General Mgr*
EMP: 225
SQ FT: 19,000
SALES: 4.4MM Privately Held
WEB: www.lagunaplayhouse.com
SIC: 7922 Community theater production

(P-18406)
LIGHT & SOUND DESIGN INC
9111 Sunland Blvd, Sun Valley (91352-2053)
PHONE..................................818 260-6260
Nick Jackson, *President*
Tim Murch, *COO*
John Lobel, *Vice Pres*
EMP: 130
SQ FT: 40,000
SALES (est): 1.2MM Privately Held
SIC: 7922 Lighting, theatrical
HQ: Production Resource Group (Europe) Limited
The Cofton Centre
Birmingham W MIDLANDS B31 4
121 766-6400

(P-18407)
LIVE NATION ENTERTAINMENT INC
7060 Hollywood Blvd Ste 2, Los Angeles (90028-6030)
PHONE..................................213 639-6178
Michael Rapino, *Branch Mgr*
ARI Daie, *President*
David Pine, *Vice Pres*
Ken Hudgens, *VP Mktg*
Matt Annerino, *Director*
EMP: 119
SALES (corp-wide): 7.2B Publicly Held
SIC: 7922 Theatrical producers & services
PA: Live Nation Entertainment, Inc.
9348 Civic Center Dr Lbby
Beverly Hills CA 90210
310 867-7000

(P-18408)
LIVE NATION ENTERTAINMENT INC (PA)
9348 Civic Center Dr Lbby, Beverly Hills (90210-3642)
PHONE..................................310 867-7000
Fax: 310 867-7001
Michael Rapino, *President*
Arthur Fogel, *Ch of Bd*
Greg Maffei, *Ch of Bd*
Ron Bension, *President*
Mark Campana, *President*
EMP: 200
SALES: 7.2B Publicly Held
WEB: www.livenation.com
SIC: 7922 7389 7941 Entertainment promotion; theatrical production services; theatrical companies; promoters of shows & exhibitions; sports clubs, managers & promoters

(P-18409)
LIVE NATION WORLDWIDE INC
260 5th St, San Francisco (94103-4116)
P.O. Box 429094 (94142-9094)
PHONE..................................415 371-5500
Lee Smith, *Branch Mgr*
EMP: 78

PRODUCTS & SERVICES SECTION
7922 - Theatrical Producers & Misc Theatrical Svcs County (P-18430)

SALES (corp-wide): 7.2B **Publicly Held**
WEB: www.sfx.com
SIC: 7922 Theatrical producers
HQ: Live Nation Worldwide, Inc.
220 W 42nd St
New York NY 10036
917 421-5100

(P-18410)
LIVE NATION WORLDWIDE INC
6500 Wilshire Blvd # 200, Los Angeles (90048-4920)
PHONE..................................323 966-5066
Fax: 323 658-3890
Terry Dreher, *Principal*
EMP: 130
SALES (corp-wide): 7.2B **Publicly Held**
WEB: www.sfx.com
SIC: 7922 Theatrical producers & services
HQ: Live Nation Worldwide, Inc.
220 W 42nd St
New York NY 10036
917 421-5100

(P-18411)
LIVE NATION WORLDWIDE INC
8808 Irvine Center Dr, Irvine (92618-4201)
PHONE..................................949 860-2070
EMP: 97
SALES (corp-wide): 7.2B **Publicly Held**
SIC: 7922 Theatrical producers & services
HQ: Live Nation Worldwide, Inc.
220 W 42nd St
New York NY 10036
917 421-5100

(P-18412)
LUTHER BURBANK MEM FOUNDATION
50 Mark West Springs Rd, Santa Rosa (95403-1457)
PHONE..................................707 546-3600
Fax: 707 545-0518
Richard Nowlin, *Exec Dir*
Christopher G Costin, *Bd of Directors*
Jennifer Castillo, *Finance*
J David Siembieda, *Director*
Michelle Denham, *Manager*
EMP: 74
SQ FT: 120,000
SALES: 10.9MM **Privately Held**
WEB: www.lbc.net
SIC: 7922 8299 6519 Performing arts center production; music & drama schools; real property lessors

(P-18413)
MAGIC MOUNTAIN LLC
Also Called: Six Flags Magic Mountain
26101 Magic Mountain Pkwy, Valencia (91355-1052)
P.O. Box 5500 (91380-5500)
PHONE..................................661 255-4100
Bonnie Rabjohn,
Sherrie Bang, *Vice Pres*
Tim Tim Burkhart, *Vice Pres*
Del Holland, *General Mgr*
Susan Saturday, *MIS Staff*
▲ EMP: 300
SALES (est): 18.8MM
SALES (corp-wide): 1.2B **Publicly Held**
SIC: 7922 7996 Entertainment promotion; theme park, amusement
PA: Six Flags Entertainment Corp
924 E Avenue J
Grand Prairie TX 75050
972 595-5000

(P-18414)
MCGUIRE TALENT INC
8608 Utica Ave Ste 220, Rancho Cucamonga (91730-4879)
PHONE..................................909 527-7006
EMP: 80
SQ FT: 2,200
SALES: 2MM **Privately Held**
SIC: 7922

(P-18415)
MOUNTAIN PLAY ASSOCIATION
1556 4th St B, San Rafael (94901-2713)
PHONE..................................415 383-1100
Fax: 415 383-4848
Sara Pearson, *Director*
EMP: 50
SQ FT: 650

SALES: 1.1MM **Privately Held**
SIC: 7922 Community theater production

(P-18416)
MUSIC HALL LLC
859 Ofarrell St, San Francisco (94109-7005)
PHONE..................................415 885-0750
Fax: 415 885-5075
Dawn Holiday, *CEO*
EMP: 50
SQ FT: 6,000
SALES (est): 2.5MM **Privately Held**
WEB: www.musichallsf.com
SIC: 7922 5813 Entertainment promotion; cocktail lounge

(P-18417)
NBC STUDIOS INC (DH)
100 Universal City Plz, Universal City (91608-1002)
PHONE..................................818 777-1000
Fax: 818 840-7519
Richard Cotton, *CEO*
Bruce Levinson, *Vice Pres*
Alicen Schneider, *Vice Pres*
Doug Vaughan, *Vice Pres*
Shujaat Ali, *Info Tech Dir*
EMP: 140
SALES (est): 1.1MM
SALES (corp-wide): 74.5B **Publicly Held**
WEB: www.nbcstudios.com
SIC: 7922 Television program, including commercial producers
HQ: Nbc Universal, Llc
1221 Avenue Of The Americ
New York NY 10020
212 664-4444

(P-18418)
NEWPORT TELEVISION LLC
4880 N 1st St, Fresno (93726-0514)
PHONE..................................559 761-0243
EMP: 123
SALES (corp-wide): 48.9MM **Privately Held**
SIC: 7922 Television program, including commercial producers
PA: Newport Television Llc
460 Nichols Rd Ste 250
Kansas City MO 64112
816 751-0200

(P-18419)
NFL PROPERTIES LLC
Also Called: Nfl Network
10950 Wash Blvd Ste 100, Culver City (90232-4032)
PHONE..................................310 840-4635
Steve Bernstein, *Principal*
Lorey Zlotnick, *Senior VP*
Paul Tabor, *Info Tech Dir*
Antoine Boyer, *Software Engr*
Takashi Aoki, *Technology*
EMP: 300
SALES (corp-wide): 62.6MM **Privately Held**
SIC: 7922 Television program, including commercial producers
PA: Nfl Properties Llc
345 Park Ave Bsmt Lc1
New York NY 10154
212 450-2000

(P-18420)
OLD GLOBE THEATRE
1363 Old Globe Way, San Diego (92101-1696)
P.O. Box 122171 (92112-2171)
PHONE..................................619 234-5623
Fax: 619 231-5879
Michael G Murphy, *CEO*
A S Beckhart, *Volunteer Dir*
Louis Spisto, *CEO*
Mark Somers, *CFO*
Eileen Prisby, *Social Dir*
▲ EMP: 500
SALES: 21.6MM **Privately Held**
WEB: www.theoldglobe.org
SIC: 7922 Theatrical production services

(P-18421)
OPERA SAN JOSE INC
2149 Paragon Dr, San Jose (95131-1312)
PHONE..................................408 437-4450
Fax: 408 437-4455

Irene Dalis, *Exec Dir*
George Crow, *President*
Rosa Cohn, *Vice Pres*
Laurie Warner, *Vice Pres*
Bryan Ferraro, *Comms Mgr*
EMP: 100
SQ FT: 25,000
SALES: 4MM **Privately Held**
SIC: 7922 7929 Opera company; entertainers & entertainment groups

(P-18422)
PARADIGM A TLENT LITERARY AGCY (PA)
360 N Crescent Dr, Beverly Hills (90210-4874)
PHONE..................................310 288-8000
Fax: 310 288-2000
Sam Gores, *Ch of Bd*
Lucy Stille, *Partner*
Todd Quinn, *CFO*
Lydia Loizides, *Vice Pres*
Rich Rogers, *VP Bus Dvlpt*
EMP: 70
SALES (est): 9.1MM **Privately Held**
WEB: www.michaelokeefe.com
SIC: 7922 Talent agent, theatrical

(P-18423)
PERFORMING ARTS CENTER OF LA C
Also Called: Music Center
135 N Grand Ave, Los Angeles (90012-3013)
PHONE..................................213 972-7211
Fax: 213 972-3132
John Emerson, *Ch of Bd*
Lisa Specht, *Ch of Bd*
Kent Kresas, *Vice Chairman*
Stephen Rountree, *President*
William Meyerchak, *CFO*
▲ EMP: 250
SQ FT: 24,000
SALES: 51.7MM **Privately Held**
WEB: musiccenter.org
SIC: 7922 Theatrical producers & services; equipment rental, theatrical; concert management service; ticket agency, theatrical

(P-18424)
PLAYWRIGHTS FOUNDATION INC
1616 16th St Ste 350, San Francisco (94103-5164)
PHONE..................................415 626-2176
Amy Mueller, *Director*
Linda Brewer, *President*
Sonia Fernandez, *Admin Asst*
Jericha Senyak, *Business Mgr*
Jill Maclean, *Producer*
EMP: 73
SQ FT: 1,200
SALES: 249.3K **Privately Held**
SIC: 7922 Legitimate live theater producers

(P-18425)
PRDCTIONS N FREMANTLE AMER INC (DH)
Also Called: Fremantle Media
2900 W Alameda Ave 8, Burbank (91505-4220)
PHONE..................................818 748-1100
Thom Beers, *CEO*
Donna Redier Linsk, *COO*
Dan Goldberg, *Exec VP*
Christine Shaw, *Senior VP*
Mark Cordoba, *Vice Pres*
EMP: 100
SALES (est): 14.8MM
SALES (corp-wide): 18.4B **Privately Held**
SIC: 7922 Television program, including commercial producers
HQ: Fremantlemedia Group Limited
1 Stephen Street
London W1T 1
207 691-6000

(P-18426)
PREMIERE RADIO NETWORK INC (DH)
Also Called: Prn Radio Networks
15260 Ventura Blvd # 400, Sherman Oaks (91403-5307)
PHONE..................................818 377-5300

Fax: 818 377-5320
Stephen C Lehman, *CEO*
Kraig T Kitchin, *President*
Timothy M Kelly, *Exec VP*
Alan Korowitz, *Vice Pres*
Rhonda Scheidel, *Exec VP*
EMP: 200
SQ FT: 15,000
SALES (est): 15.1MM
SALES (corp-wide): 6.2B **Publicly Held**
WEB: www.premrad.com
SIC: 7922 7389 4832 Radio producers; advertising, promotional & trade show services; radio broadcasting stations
HQ: Jacor Communications Company
200 E Basse Rd
San Antonio TX 78209
210 822-2828

(P-18427)
PRODUCTION SPECIAL EVENTS SVCS
17326 Devonshire St, Northridge (91325-1543)
PHONE..................................818 831-5326
Wendy Moodie, *President*
Terry Merkle, *Vice Pres*
Don Sheldon, *Finance Dir*
Alan Rosenthal, *CPA*
EMP: 50 EST: 1997
SALES (est): 2.1MM **Privately Held**
SIC: 7922 Entertainment promotion

(P-18428)
RADFORD STUDIO CENTER INC
Also Called: CBS Studio Center
4024 Radford Ave, Studio City (91604-2101)
PHONE..................................818 655-5000
Fax: 818 655-5409
Michael Klausman, *President*
Nina Tassler, *Ch of Bd*
Bill Rimpau, *Top Exec*
Wendi Trilling, *Exec VP*
Barbara Mannina, *Senior VP*
EMP: 300
SALES (est): 33.2MM
SALES (corp-wide): 13.9B **Publicly Held**
WEB: www.cbssc.com
SIC: 7922 6512 7999 Television program, including commercial producers; nonresidential building operators; martial arts school
HQ: Cbs Broadcasting Inc.
51 W 52nd St
New York NY 10019
212 975-4321

(P-18429)
ROSE BRAND WIPERS INC
10616 Lanark St, Sun Valley (91352-4014)
PHONE..................................818 505-6290
Tina Carlin, *Principal*
Jeff Brown, *Manager*
Zoe Paine, *Manager*
EMP: 82
SALES (corp-wide): 103MM **Privately Held**
SIC: 7922 Costume & scenery design services
PA: Rose Brand Wipers, Inc.
4 Emerson Ln
Secaucus NJ 07094
201 809-1730

(P-18430)
SACRAMENTO THEATRICAL LTG LTD
Also Called: S T L
950 Richards Blvd, Sacramento (95811-0333)
PHONE..................................916 447-3258
Fax: 916 447-5012
John W Cox, *CEO*
Kaye Newton, *Vice Pres*
Dianne Jared, *Finance*
Bobbie Odehnal, *Manager*
EMP: 65
SQ FT: 60,000
SALES (est): 6MM **Privately Held**
WEB: www.stl-ltd.com
SIC: 7922 5063 Equipment rental, theatrical; lighting fixtures

7922 - Theatrical Producers & Misc Theatrical Svcs County (P-18431)

PRODUDUCTS & SERVICES SECTION

(P-18431)
SAN DIEGO OPERA ASSOCIATION (PA)
233 A St Ste 500, San Diego (92101-4345)
PHONE..................619 232-7636
Fax: 619 232-5991
Michael Lowry, *Finance*
Michael Lowry, *Officer*
Koko Cattran, *Executive*
Caren Heintzelman, *Office Mgr*
Cindy Bartelli, *Administration*
EMP: 50 EST: 1945
SQ FT: 11,000
SALES: 13.5MM **Privately Held**
SIC: 7922 Opera company

(P-18432)
SAN FRANCISCO BALLET ASSN
455 Franklin St, San Francisco (94102-4471)
PHONE..................415 865-2000
Fax: 415 861-2684
Glenn McCoy, *CEO*
James Marver, *Vice Chairman*
Donald B Paterson, *CFO*
J Stuart Francis, *Treasurer*
Jennifer Peterian, *Treasurer*
▲ EMP: 250 EST: 1933
SQ FT: 70,000
SALES: 24.3MM **Privately Held**
SIC: 7922 7911 Ballet production; dance studio & school

(P-18433)
SAN FRANCISCO OPERA ASSN
301 Van Ness Ave, San Francisco (94102-4509)
PHONE..................415 861-4008
Fax: 415 861-7148
John A Gunn, *Chairman*
Keith B Geeslin, *President*
David Gockley, *CEO*
Michael Simpson, *CFO*
Nancy Reilly, *Bd of Directors*
▲ EMP: 1050 EST: 1932
SALES: 37.4MM **Privately Held**
SIC: 7922 Opera company

(P-18434)
SHOW CALL PRODUCTIONS INC
3605 Hemlock St, San Diego (92113-2749)
P.O. Box 13333, La Jolla (92039-3333)
PHONE..................619 602-0656
Gary Zugel, *CEO*
EMP: 400 EST: 2006
SALES (est): 2.6MM **Privately Held**
SIC: 7922 Concert management service

(P-18435)
SOUTH COAST REPERTORY INC
Also Called: SCR
655 Town Center Dr, Costa Mesa (92626-1918)
P.O. Box 2197 (92628-2197)
PHONE..................714 708-5500
Fax: 714 545-0391
Martin Benson, *Art Dir*
Joan Kaloustian, *Vice Pres*
Kimberly Uhlman, *Executive*
Lauren Hovey, *Social Dir*
Benjamin Horak, *Graphic Designe*
EMP: 60
SQ FT: 40,000
SALES: 11.2MM **Privately Held**
SIC: 7922 Repertory, road or stock companies: theatrical

(P-18436)
STEVE SILVER PRODUCTIONS INC
678 Green St Ste 2, San Francisco (94133-3846)
PHONE..................415 421-4284
EMP: 94
SALES (corp-wide): 3.7MM **Privately Held**
SIC: 7922
PA: Silver Steve Productions Inc
470 Columbus Ave Ste 204
San Francisco CA 94133
415 421-4284

(P-18437)
STORYBOOK PRODUCTIONS INC
6230 W Sunset Blvd, Los Angeles (90028-8701)
PHONE..................323 468-5050
Fax: 323 972-4069
Anthony Orlando, *CEO*
Rocart Corporation, *Principal*
Estrella Capin, *Editor*
Gayle Grech, *Editor*
EMP: 100 EST: 1997
SALES (est): 4MM **Privately Held**
WEB: www.storybookproductions.com
SIC: 7922 Theatrical producers & services

(P-18438)
TENNIS CHANNEL INC (HQ)
2850 Ocean Park Blvd # 150, Santa Monica (90405-6217)
PHONE..................310 392-1920
Ken Solomon, *CEO*
William Simon, *COO*
William S Simon, *COO*
Victoria Quoss, *Exec VP*
Steven Badeau, *Senior VP*
EMP: 70
SALES (est): 13.5MM
SALES (corp-wide): 1.9B **Publicly Held**
WEB: www.thetennischannel.com
SIC: 7922 Television program, including commercial producers
PA: Sinclair Broadcast Group, Inc.
10706 Beaver Dam Rd
Hunt Valley MD 21030
410 568-1500

(P-18439)
THINKWELL GROUP INC
2710 Media Center Dr, Los Angeles (90065-1746)
PHONE..................818 333-3444
Joseph Zenas, *CEO*
Francois Bergeron, *COO*
Craig Hanna, *Ch Credit Ofcr*
Kelly Ryner, *Senior VP*
Aamna Jalal, *Vice Pres*
▲ EMP: 75
SQ FT: 23,000
SALES (est): 11.1MM **Privately Held**
SIC: 7922 7389 Theatrical producers & services; interior design services

(P-18440)
TICKETMASTER ENTERTAINMENT LLC
8800 W Sunset Blvd, West Hollywood (90069-2105)
PHONE..................800 653-8000
Ron Bension, *CEO*
Tejal Gandhi, *Sr Software Eng*
Alan Waldman, *Info Tech Dir*
Joe Ho, *Info Tech Mgr*
Rafi Khardalian, *Info Tech Mgr*
EMP: 4390
SALES (est): 73.1MM
SALES (corp-wide): 7.2B **Publicly Held**
SIC: 7922 Ticket agency, theatrical; agent or manager for entertainers
PA: Live Nation Entertainment, Inc.
9348 Civic Center Dr Lbby
Beverly Hills CA 90210
310 867-7000

(P-18441)
TRISTAR TELEVISION MUSIC INC
10202 Washington Blvd, Culver City (90232-3119)
PHONE..................310 244-4000
Eric Tannenbaum, *President*
Catherine Wozney, *Manager*
EMP: 50
SALES (est): 955.2K
SALES (corp-wide): 69.2B **Privately Held**
WEB: www.paulleydenonline.com
SIC: 7922 Television program, including commercial producers
HQ: Sony Pictures Releasing International Corporation
10202 Washington Blvd
Culver City CA 90232
310 244-4000

(P-18442)
TURNING POINT FOR GOD
Also Called: Turning Point Ministries
10007 Riverford Rd, Lakeside (92040-2772)
PHONE..................619 258-3600
David P Jeremiah, *CEO*
Michael Guzik, *CFO*
Donna Jeremiah, *Admin Sec*
Ian Davies, *Administration*
Jack Gulla, *Engineer*
EMP: 55
SALES: 47.4MM **Privately Held**
SIC: 7922 Radio producers

(P-18443)
WESTWOODONE
Also Called: Metro Networks
5757 Wilshire Blvd # 660, Los Angeles (90036-5810)
PHONE..................323 904-4660
Jennifer Summerville, *Branch Mgr*
Daniel Hart, *Manager*
EMP: 80
SALES (corp-wide): 1.1B **Publicly Held**
WEB: www.westwoodone.com
SIC: 7922 Radio producers
HQ: Westwood One, Inc.
220 W 42nd St Fl 4
New York NY 10036
212 967-2888

(P-18444)
WILLIAM MORRIS ENDEAVOR
Also Called: William Morris Agency
2624 Military Ave, Los Angeles (90064-3132)
PHONE..................310 285-9000
Mark Edkins, *Manager*
EMP: 500
SALES (corp-wide): 49.2MM **Privately Held**
WEB: www.rupaul.com
SIC: 7922 Talent agent, theatrical
PA: William Morris Endeavor Entertainment, Llc
11 Madison Ave Fl 18
New York NY 10010
212 586-5100

(P-18445)
WILLIAM MORRIS ENDEAVOR
Also Called: William Morris Consulting
9601 Wilshire Blvd Fl 3, Beverly Hills (90210-5219)
PHONE..................310 285-9000
Chris Newman, *Vice Pres*
Mark Itkin, *Exec VP*
Aaron Lenzini, *Vice Pres*
Michael J Sheresky, *Vice Pres*
Ilona Jarosiewicz, *Info Tech Mgr*
EMP: 393
SALES (corp-wide): 49.2MM **Privately Held**
WEB: www.rupaul.com
SIC: 7922 Talent agent, theatrical
PA: William Morris Endeavor Entertainment, Llc
11 Madison Ave Fl 18
New York NY 10010
212 586-5100

(P-18446)
WILLIAM MORRIS ENDEAVOR ENTERT (PA)
9601 Wilshire Blvd Fl 3, Beverly Hills (90210-5219)
PHONE..................310 285-9000
Fax: 310 285-9010
Tom Strickler, *Mng Member*
Peter Klein, *CFO*
Dean Georgious, *Info Tech Dir*
Mike Hershfield, *Telecomm Mgr*
Dale Buckman, *Network Mgr*
EMP: 180
SALES (est): 19.4MM **Privately Held**
WEB: www.endeavorla.com
SIC: 7922 Theatrical talent & booking agencies

7929 Bands, Orchestras, Actors & Entertainers

(P-18447)
19 ENTERTAINMENT WORLDWIDE LLC
Also Called: 19 Management
8560 W Sunset Blvd Fl 8, West Hollywood (90069-2340)
PHONE..................310 777-1940
Iain Pirie, *President*
Michele Rosette, *Controller*
Amy Pape, *Manager*
EMP: 60
SALES (est): 3.2MM **Privately Held**
WEB: www.19.co.uk
SIC: 7929 Entertainers & entertainment groups

(P-18448)
42ND STREET MOON
601 Van Ness Ave, San Francisco (94102-3200)
PHONE..................415 255-8207
J Patterson McBaine, *President*
Christine Federici, *Executive*
Joe Mader, *Managing Dir*
Leanna Keyes, *Prdtn Mgr*
Ken Levin, *Director*
EMP: 50
SALES: 790.9K **Privately Held**
SIC: 7929 Musical entertainers

(P-18449)
51 MINDS ENTERTAINMENT LLC
Also Called: Mindless Entertainment
5200 Lankershim Blvd # 200, North Hollywood (91601-3155)
PHONE..................323 466-9200
Fax: 323 466-9202
Mark Cronin,
Ben Samek, *COO*
Melissa Castro, *Vice Pres*
Courtland Cox, *Vice Pres*
Rabih Gholam, *Vice Pres*
▼ EMP: 60
SALES (est): 4.7MM **Privately Held**
WEB: www.51minds.com
SIC: 7929 Entertainers
HQ: Endemol Usa Holding Inc & Subs
9255 W Sunset Blvd # 1100
Los Angeles CA 90069
310 860-9914

(P-18450)
ANSCHUTZ ENTRMT GROUP INC (HQ)
Also Called: AEG Worldwide
1100 S Flower St, Los Angeles (90015-2180)
PHONE..................213 763-7700
Tim Leiweke, *President*
Scott Bosarge, *President*
Todd Goldstein, *President*
Dan Beckerman, *CFO*
Ted Fikre, *Exec VP*
EMP: 78
SALES (est): 54.1MM
SALES (corp-wide): 110.6MM **Privately Held**
SIC: 7929 Entertainment service
PA: The Anschutz Corporation
555 17th St Ste 2400
Denver CO 80202
303 298-1000

(P-18451)
ARAMARK SERVICES INC
800 Asilomar Blvd, Pacific Grove (93950-3704)
P.O. Box 537 (93950-0537)
PHONE..................831 372-8016
Enos Esquivel, *Director*
Maria Enriquez, *Executive*
Mairead Hennessy, *General Mgr*
EMP: 210
SALES (corp-wide): 14.3B **Publicly Held**
SIC: 7929 Entertainment service
HQ: Aramark Services, Inc.
1101 Market St Ste 45
Philadelphia PA 19107
215 238-3000

PRODUCTS & SERVICES SECTION
7929 - Bands, Orchestras, Actors & Entertainers County (P-18476)

(P-18452)
ARAMARK SPT & ENTRMT GROUP LLC
3400 S Figueroa St, Los Angeles (90007-4348)
PHONE..................213 740-1224
EMP: 120
SALES (corp-wide): 14.3B **Publicly Held**
SIC: 7929 Entertainment service
HQ: Aramark Sports And Entertainment Group, Llc
1101 Market St
Philadelphia PA 19107
215 238-3000

(P-18453)
ARAMARK SPT & ENTRMT GROUP LLC
2677 Forty Mile Rd, Marysville (95901)
PHONE..................530 740-4758
Mark Ashrok, *Branch Mgr*
EMP: 400
SALES (corp-wide): 14.3B **Publicly Held**
WEB: www.aramarksports.com
SIC: 7929 Entertainment service
HQ: Aramark Sports And Entertainment Group, Llc
1101 Market St
Philadelphia PA 19107
215 238-3000

(P-18454)
ARAMARK SPT & ENTRMT GROUP LLC
886 Cannery Row, Monterey (93940-1023)
PHONE..................831 648-9809
EMP: 106
SALES (corp-wide): 14.3B **Publicly Held**
SIC: 7929 Entertainers & entertainment groups
HQ: Aramark Sports And Entertainment Group, Llc
1101 Market St
Philadelphia PA 19107
215 238-3000

(P-18455)
ARAMARK SPT & ENTRMT GROUP LLC
5001 Great America Pkwy, Santa Clara (95054-1119)
PHONE..................408 748-7030
Fax: 408 748-7047
Jerry McCarthy, *Manager*
Rick Huking, *Site Mgr*
EMP: 100
SALES (corp-wide): 14.3B **Publicly Held**
WEB: www.aramarksports.com
SIC: 7929 Entertainment service
HQ: Aramark Sports And Entertainment Group, Llc
1101 Market St
Philadelphia PA 19107
215 238-3000

(P-18456)
ARTISTIC ENTRMT SVCS LLC
120 N Aspan Ave, Azusa (91702-4224)
PHONE..................626 334-9388
Craig Bugajski, *Mng Member*
Rick Iiames, *Marketing Staff*
Jeffton Michael, *Manager*
EMP: 60
SALES: 10MM **Privately Held**
SIC: 7929 Entertainers & entertainment groups

(P-18457)
BAKERSFIELD SYMPHONY ORCH
1328 34th St Ste A, Bakersfield (93301-2154)
PHONE..................661 323-7928
Fax: 661 323-7331
M Bryan Burrow, *President*
Suzanne Legrand, *Vice Pres*
Stilian Kirov, *Director*
Kari H Heilman, *Manager*
Mary Moore, *Manager*
EMP: 75
SALES: 904.4K **Privately Held**
WEB: www.bakersfieldsymphony.org
SIC: 7929 Symphony orchestras

(P-18458)
BENTO BOX ENTERTAINMENT LLC
5161 Lankershim Blvd # 1, North Hollywood (91601-4964)
PHONE..................818 333-7900
Scott Greenberg,
Amy Lee, *Executive Asst*
Cherri Accetta, *Human Res Dir*
Carly Berezin, *Prdtn Mgr*
Tony Gennaro, *Prdtn Mgr*
EMP: 300
SALES (est): 8MM **Privately Held**
SIC: 7929 Entertainment service

(P-18459)
BERKELEY SYMPHONY ORCHESTRA
1942 University Ave # 207, Berkeley (94704-1246)
PHONE..................510 841-2800
Fax: 510 841-5422
Gary Ginstling, *Exec Dir*
Janet Maestre, *Vice Pres*
Theresa Gabel, *Exec Dir*
Catherine Henwood, *Exec Dir*
James Kleinmann, *Exec Dir*
EMP: 50
SALES: 1.4MM **Privately Held**
SIC: 7929 Symphony orchestras

(P-18460)
BONANZA PRODUCTIONS INC
4000 Warner Blvd, Burbank (91522-0001)
P.O. Box 1667 (91507-1667)
PHONE..................818 954-4212
John A Rogovin, *CEO*
Jonathan Rosenfeld, *Director*
EMP: 1000 EST: 1991
SALES (est): 12.4MM **Privately Held**
SIC: 7929 Entertainment group

(P-18461)
DANNY MAHAGNA SHAPPRIE
73280 Highway 111, Palm Desert (92260-3915)
PHONE..................760 341-5070
Danny Mahagna Shapprie, *Principal*
EMP: 50
SALES (est): 265.2K **Privately Held**
SIC: 7929 Entertainment service

(P-18462)
DELUXE ENTRMT SVCS GROUP INC (PA)
2400 W Empire Ave Ste 200, Burbank (91504-3355)
PHONE..................818 565-3600
Maria Rubino, *Principal*
Brett Belinsky, *President*
Michael Tomkins, *CEO*
EMP: 56 EST: 2013
SALES (est): 34.7MM **Privately Held**
SIC: 7929 Entertainment service

(P-18463)
DOUBLE G PRODUCTIONS LTD
11301 W Olympic Blvd # 115, Los Angeles (90064-1653)
PHONE..................310 479-0978
Fax: 310 479-1577
Louie Irizarry, *Branch Mgr*
EMP: 74
SALES (corp-wide): 2.1MM **Privately Held**
WEB: www.doubleg.com
SIC: 7929 Disc jockey service
PA: Double G Productions Ltd
1055 Stewart Ave Fl 2
Bethpage NY 11714
516 932-8342

(P-18464)
DREAMWORKS ANIMATION LLC
1000 Flower St, Glendale (91201-3007)
PHONE..................818 695-5000
Lewis Coleman, *Principal*
Evan Smyth, *Technology*
Paul Parmer, *Engineer*
Rick Clifton, *Marketing Staff*
EMP: 313
SALES (est): 25.8MM **Privately Held**
SIC: 7929 Entertainment service

(P-18465)
EDMONDS RECORD GROUP
1635 N Cahuenga Blvd Fl 6, Los Angeles (90028-6201)
PHONE..................323 860-1520
Tracey Edmonds, *President*
Michael McQuarn, *Vice Pres*
EMP: 50
SALES (est): 430.8K **Privately Held**
WEB: www.edmondsent.com
SIC: 7929 Entertainers

(P-18466)
FILLMORE THEATRICAL SERVICES
9348 Civic Center Dr, Beverly Hills (90210-3624)
PHONE..................310 867-7000
EMP: 73
SALES (est): 29K
SALES (corp-wide): 7.2B **Publicly Held**
SIC: 7929 Entertainers & entertainment groups
HQ: Bill Graham Enterprises, Inc.
251 Rhode Island St
San Francisco CA

(P-18467)
FORUM ENTERPRISES INC
333 W Florence Ave, Inglewood (90301-1103)
PHONE..................310 330-7300
Fax: 310 673-6055
Gerard McCallum, *Exec VP*
Ronya Brown, *Executive Asst*
Patrick Malone, *Manager*
EMP: 50
SALES (est): 734.6K **Privately Held**
WEB: www.thelaforum.com
SIC: 7929 4832 Entertainment service; sports

(P-18468)
HATCH ANIMATION & PROD STUDIOS
1171 S Robertson Blvd, Los Angeles (90035-1403)
PHONE..................973 454-8654
SAI Kiran Goud, *Director*
Renick Spencer Chua, *President*
EMP: 75 EST: 2011
SQ FT: 3,000
SALES (est): 1.5MM **Privately Held**
SIC: 7929 Entertainment service

(P-18469)
HOB ENTERTAINMENT LLC
1350 S Disneyland Dr, Anaheim (92802)
PHONE..................714 778-2583
Kristen Kowlminsky, *Branch Mgr*
Tom Furukawa, *Executive*
Patty Leemhuis, *Manager*
Darryl Taketa, *Manager*
EMP: 240
SALES (corp-wide): 7.2B **Publicly Held**
WEB: www.hob.ca
SIC: 7929 Entertainers & entertainment groups
HQ: Hob Entertainment, Llc
7060 Hollywood Blvd
Los Angeles CA 90028
323 769-4600

(P-18470)
HOB ENTERTAINMENT LLC
8430 W Sunset Blvd, West Hollywood (90069-1910)
PHONE..................323 848-5100
Arich Berghammer, *Principal*
Sarah Saltzman, *Marketing Staff*
EMP: 230
SALES (corp-wide): 7.2B **Publicly Held**
WEB: www.hob.ca
SIC: 7929 Entertainers & entertainment groups
HQ: Hob Entertainment, Llc
7060 Hollywood Blvd
Los Angeles CA 90028
323 769-4600

(P-18471)
HOB ENTERTAINMENT LLC
1055 5th Ave, San Diego (92101-5101)
PHONE..................619 299-2583
Jim Biasore, *Manager*
Rob Wooten, *Manager*
John Litz, *Manager*
EMP: 220
SALES (corp-wide): 7.2B **Publicly Held**
WEB: www.hob.ca
SIC: 7929 Entertainers & entertainment groups
HQ: Hob Entertainment, Llc
7060 Hollywood Blvd
Los Angeles CA 90028
323 769-4600

(P-18472)
HOB ENTERTAINMENT LLC (DH)
Also Called: House of Blues
7060 Hollywood Blvd, Los Angeles (90028-6014)
PHONE..................323 769-4600
Fax: 323 769-4787
Michael Rapino, *CEO*
Joseph C Kaczorowski, *President*
Peter Cyffka, *Senior VP*
Todd Miller, *Vice Pres*
Paul Sewell, *Vice Pres*
EMP: 172
SQ FT: 53,000
SALES (est): 78.6MM
SALES (corp-wide): 7.2B **Publicly Held**
WEB: www.hob.ca
SIC: 7929 Entertainers & entertainment groups
HQ: Live Nation Worldwide, Inc.
220 W 42nd St
New York NY 10036
917 421-5100

(P-18473)
HOUSE OF BLUES CONCERTS INC (DH)
6255 W Sunset Blvd Fl 16, Los Angeles (90028-7403)
PHONE..................323 769-4977
Joe Kazoworski, *President*
Joseph Kaczorowsski, *Treasurer*
Adam Friedman, *Exec VP*
John Zeebroeck, *Vice Pres*
Steve Felisan, *Info Tech Mgr*
EMP: 150
SALES (est): 11.8MM
SALES (corp-wide): 7.2B **Publicly Held**
WEB: www.hob.com
SIC: 7929 Entertainers & entertainment groups
HQ: Hob Entertainment, Llc
7060 Hollywood Blvd
Los Angeles CA 90028
323 769-4600

(P-18474)
IMPERIAL PROJECT INC
Also Called: Bare Elegance
4721 Laurel Canyon Blvd # 100, Valley Village (91607-3961)
PHONE..................310 671-3263
Fax: 310 673-8579
Michael Woods, *Treasurer*
David Amos, *President*
Randy Coffee, *Executive*
EMP: 60
SQ FT: 1,500
SALES (est): 735.6K **Privately Held**
WEB: www.bareelegance.com
SIC: 7929 5813 Entertainment service; night clubs

(P-18475)
INSOMNIAC INC
9441 W Olympic Blvd, Beverly Hills (90212-4541)
PHONE..................323 874-7020
Pasquale Rotella, *CEO*
Simon Rust Lamb, *COO*
John Boyle, *Officer*
Betty Tran-Chillino, *Exec VP*
Brian Parisi, *Senior VP*
▲ **EMP:** 86
SALES (est): 6MM **Privately Held**
SIC: 7929 Entertainment service

(P-18476)
ISRAEL POPS ORCHESTRA
4841 Alonzo Ave, Encino (91316-3607)
PHONE..................818 343-6450
Michael Isaacson, *President*

7929 - Bands, Orchestras, Actors & Entertainers County (P-18477)

EMP: 50
SALES (est) 439.4K Privately Held
SIC: 7929 Orchestras or bands

(P-18477)
LIVE MEDIA LLC
1580 Magnolia Ave, Corona (92879-2073)
PHONE..................................951 279-8877
Tom McCracken,
Frank Cuzzo, *General Mgr*
Dave Fediazzlo, *Controller*
EMP: 50
SALES (est): 20MM
SALES (corp-wide): 76.5MM Privately Held
SIC: 7929 Entertainment service
PA: Nep Group, Inc.
  2 Beta Dr
  Pittsburgh PA 15238
  412 826-1414

(P-18478)
LIVE NATION ENTERTAINMENT INC
7083 Hollywood Blvd Fl 2, Los Angeles (90028-8901)
PHONE..................................323 464-1330
Tracey Rid-Bowes, *Branch Mgr*
Shyama Rose, *Vice Pres*
Julie Yoo, *Vice Pres*
EMP: 70
SALES (corp-wide): 7.2B Publicly Held
SIC: 7929 Entertainers
PA: Live Nation Entertainment, Inc.
  9348 Civic Center Dr Lbby
  Beverly Hills CA 90210
  310 867-7000

(P-18479)
LOS ANGELES CHMBER ORCHSTRA
350 S Figueroa St Ste 183, Los Angeles (90071-1117)
PHONE..................................213 622-7001
Andrea Laguni, *Exec Dir*
Thomas Mallen, *CFO*
Bob Attiyeh, *Vice Pres*
Eva Moravcik, *Executive*
Rachel Fine, *Info Tech Mgr*
EMP: 60
SALES: 3MM Privately Held
WEB: www.laco.org
SIC: 7929 Orchestras or bands

(P-18480)
LOS ANGELES PHILHARMONIC ASSN (PA)
Also Called: L A Philharmonic
151 S Grand Ave, Los Angeles (90012-3034)
PHONE..................................213 972-7300
Fax: 213 617-3065
Deborah Borda, *CEO*
David C Bohnett, *Chairman*
Doris Christy, *Bd of Directors*
Rafael G Mendez, *Bd of Directors*
Mona Patel, *Bd of Directors*
EMP: 200
SQ FT: 13,467
SALES: 145.5MM Privately Held
WEB: www.laphil.com
SIC: 7929 Entertainers & entertainment groups

(P-18481)
MAKER STUDIOS INC (HQ)
3562 Eastham Dr, Culver City (90232-2409)
PHONE..................................310 606-2182
Courtney Holt, *CEO*
Tiffanie Petett, *Senior Partner*
Ben Schultz, *Senior Partner*
Lisa Donovan, *CFO*
Amy Finnerty, *Senior VP*
EMP: 250
SQ FT: 20,000
SALES (est): 30.7MM Publicly Held
SIC: 7929 Entertainment service

(P-18482)
MARINE BAND SAN DIEGO
1400 Russell Ave, San Diego (92140-5594)
PHONE..................................619 524-1754
Edward Hayes, *Chief*
EMP: 50
SALES (est): 339.7K Privately Held
WEB: www.marines.mil
SIC: 7929 Entertainers

(P-18483)
NIELSEN COMPANY (US) LLC
6255 W Sunset Blvd Fl 19, Los Angeles (90028-7420)
PHONE..................................323 462-0050
Fax: 323 817-2001
Adam Levy, *Vice Pres*
Tina Teng, *Exec Dir*
Michael Walton, *Exec Dir*
EMP: 80
SALES (corp-wide): 43.6K Privately Held
SIC: 7929 Entertainment service
HQ: The Nielsen Company Us Llc
  85 Broad St
  New York NY 10004
  -

(P-18484)
PACIFIC SYMPHONY
3631 S Harbor Blvd # 100, Santa Ana (92704-8908)
PHONE..................................714 876-2301
Fax: 714 755-5789
Jjohn Forsyte, *President*
John E Forsyte, *CEO*
Anoosheh Oskouian, *Bd of Directors*
Kay Dalton, *Assoc VP*
Gregory Cox, *Vice Pres*
EMP: 60
SQ FT: 5,750
SALES: 21.1MM Privately Held
WEB: www.psyo.org
SIC: 7929 Symphony orchestras

(P-18485)
PALA BAND OF MISSION INDIANS
3478 Sunset Dr, Fallbrook (92028-9579)
PHONE..................................760 207-2603
Ryan McQueen Rusnell, *Branch Mgr*
EMP: 173 Privately Held
SIC: 7929 Entertainers & entertainment groups
PA: Pala Band Of Mission Indians
  12196 Pala Mission Rd
  Pala CA 92059
  760 891-3500

(P-18486)
PHILHARMONIA BAROQUE ORCHESTRA
414 Mason St Ste 606, San Francisco (94102-1719)
PHONE..................................415 252-1288
Fax: 415 252-1488
Robert Birman, *Exec Dir*
Christine Ho, *Volunteer Dir*
Paul Sugarman, *President*
Rachel Fine, *Principal*
George Gelles, *Exec Dir*
EMP: 65
SALES: 3.6MM Privately Held
WEB: www.philharmonia.org
SIC: 7929 Symphony orchestras

(P-18487)
POMONA COLLEGE
150 E 8th St, Claremont (91711-3910)
PHONE..................................909 607-8650
Fax: 909 607-1726
Tzu-Yi Chen, *Branch Mgr*
Mary L Woods, *Manager*
EMP: 204
SALES (corp-wide): 275.5MM Privately Held
SIC: 7929 Entertainers
PA: Pomona College
  550 N College Ave
  Claremont CA 91711
  909 621-8135

(P-18488)
POP MEDIA NETWORKS LLC (DH)
Also Called: TV Guide Networks, LLC
5510 Lincoln Blvd Ste 400, Playa Vista (90094-1900)
PHONE..................................323 856-4000
Allen Shapiro, *Chairman*
Ryan O'Hara, *President*
Brad Schwartz, *President*
Debra Wichser, *CFO*
David Mandell, *Exec VP*
EMP: 70
SALES (est): 9.2MM
SALES (corp-wide): 2.4B Privately Held
SIC: 7929 7313 7379 Entertainment service; electronic media advertising representatives;
HQ: Lions Gate Entertainment Inc.
  2700 Colorado Ave Ste 200
  Santa Monica CA 90404
  310 449-9200

(P-18489)
SAG-AFTRA
5757 Wilshire Blvd Fl 7, Los Angeles (90036-3681)
P.O. Box 7830, Burbank (91510-7830)
PHONE..................................323 954-1600
Fax: 323 549-6656
Christian Rangei, *President*
Arianna Ozzanto, *CFO*
Don Stoller, *Senior VP*
Shane Kunnavatana, *Admin Asst*
Erin Griffin, *CIO*
EMP: 169
SALES (corp-wide): 58.9MM Privately Held
SIC: 7929 Entertainment group
PA: Sag-Aftra
  5757 Wilshire Blvd Fl 7
  Los Angeles CA 90036
  415 391-7510

(P-18490)
SAN BERNARDINO SYMPHONY ASSN
198 N Arrowhead Ave 2b, San Bernardino (92408-1011)
PHONE..................................909 381-5388
Mary Schnepp, *President*
Valerie Peister, *Exec Dir*
EMP: 80
SALES: 754.8K Privately Held
WEB: www.sanbernardinosymphony.org
SIC: 7929 Symphony orchestras

(P-18491)
SAN DIEGO SYMPHONY ORCHESTRA
1245 7th Ave, San Diego (92101-4398)
PHONE..................................619 235-0800
Edward B Gill, *Exec Dir*
Derek Floyd, *Administration*
Anthony Henry, *Opers Staff*
Virginia Tunnell, *Opers Staff*
Michelle Kang,
EMP: 110
SALES: 24.2MM Privately Held
SIC: 7929 Symphony orchestras

(P-18492)
SAN FRANCISCO SYMPHONY INC (PA)
201 Van Ness Ave, San Francisco (94102-4585)
PHONE..................................415 552-8000
Brent Assink, *CEO*
Mark Koenig, *CFO*
John Prunty, *CFO*
Sam Yamada, *Bd of Directors*
Michael Lawrence, *Officer*
▲ **EMP:** 178 EST: 1911
SALES: 91.1MM Privately Held
SIC: 7929 Symphony orchestras

(P-18493)
SANTA CRUZ COUNTY SYMPHONY
307 Church St, Santa Cruz (95060-3811)
PHONE..................................831 462-0553
Mary James, *President*
Scott McAlister, *Treasurer*
Virginia Wright, *Exec Dir*
Jan Derecho, *Director*
EMP: 50
SALES: 1MM Privately Held
WEB: www.santacruzsymphony.com
SIC: 7929 Symphony orchestras

(P-18494)
SANTA ROSA RNCHRIA GAMING COMM
17225 Jersey Ave, Lemoore (93245-9760)
P.O. Box 668 (93245-0668)
PHONE..................................559 924-6948
Fax: 559 924-6571
Abby Ramirez, *Principal*
EMP: 55
SALES (est): 991.6K Privately Held
SIC: 7929 Entertainment service

(P-18495)
SLEEPY GIANT ENTERTAINMENT INC
3501 Jamboree Rd Ste 5000, Newport Beach (92660-2959)
PHONE..................................714 460-4113
Matthew Hannus, *CEO*
David S Lee, *Admin Sec*
▲ **EMP:** 58
SALES: 1.5MM Privately Held
SIC: 7929 Entertainment service

(P-18496)
SOCAL SPORTSNET LLC
100 Park Blvd, San Diego (92101-7405)
PHONE..................................619 795-5000
Ron Fowler,
EMP: 600
SALES (est): 17.5MM Privately Held
SIC: 7929 Entertainment service

(P-18497)
SONY PICTURES ENTRMT INC
Also Called: SONY PICTURES ENTERTAINMENT, INC.
9050 Washington Blvd, Culver City (90232-2518)
PHONE..................................310 840-8000
Olivier Mouroux, *Vice Pres*
Jenny Marchick, *Director*
Catherine Wozney, *Manager*
EMP: 500
SALES (corp-wide): 69.2B Privately Held
WEB: www.sonypictures.com
SIC: 7929 Entertainers
HQ: Sony Pictures Entertainment, Inc.
  10202 Washington Blvd
  Culver City CA 90232
  310 244-4000

(P-18498)
SONY PICTURES ENTRMT INC
9336 Washington Blvd, Culver City (90232-2628)
PHONE..................................310 202-1234
Margi Bertram, *Manager*
Mark Lebowitz, *Senior VP*
Catherine Wozney, *Manager*
EMP: 500
SALES (corp-wide): 69.2B Privately Held
WEB: www.sonypictures.com
SIC: 7929 Entertainers & entertainment groups
HQ: Sony Pictures Entertainment, Inc.
  10202 Washington Blvd
  Culver City CA 90232
  310 244-4000

(P-18499)
SONY PICTURES ENTRMT INC
6527 W 82nd St, Los Angeles (90045-2841)
PHONE..................................310 244-3558
Kriege Janz, *Branch Mgr*
Catherine Wozney, *Manager*
EMP: 500
SALES (corp-wide): 69.2B Privately Held
SIC: 7929 Entertainers & entertainment groups
HQ: Sony Pictures Entertainment, Inc.
  10202 Washington Blvd
  Culver City CA 90232
  310 244-4000

(P-18500)
STREAMRAY INC
Also Called: Hotbox
910 E Hamilton Ave Fl 6, Campbell (95008-0655)
PHONE..................................408 745-5449
Mallorie Burak, *CEO*
Micheal Parot, *Manager*
EMP: 315

PRODUCTS & SERVICES SECTION

7933 - Bowling Centers County (P-18524)

SALES (est): 523.9K **Privately Held**
SIC: 7929 Entertainment group

(P-18501)
UBI SOFT ENTERTAINMENT
625 3rd St Fl 3, San Francisco (94107-1918)
PHONE.................................415 547-4000
Yves Guillemot, *President*
Anne Gleizes, *Chief Mktg Ofcr*
Christian Guillemot, *Exec VP*
Chris Early, *Vice Pres*
Les Fondy, *Vice Pres*
EMP: 78 EST: 2011
SALES (est): 6.9MM
SALES (corp-wide): 854.8MM **Privately Held**
SIC: 7929 Entertainers & entertainment groups
PA: Ubisoft Entertainment
    107 Avenue Henri Freville
    Rennes Cedex 2 35207

(P-18502)
UNIVERSAL MUSIC GROUP INC
Also Called: Verve Music Group
2220 Colorado Ave, Santa Monica (90404-3506)
PHONE.................................310 865-4000
Charles Ciongoli, *Exec VP*
Rob Cromar, *President*
James Bradley, *Exec VP*
Amy Matusek, *Associate Dir*
Nicole Wyskoarko, *Associate Dir*
EMP: 100
SALES (corp-wide): 72.1MM **Privately Held**
SIC: 7929 Entertainment service
HQ: Universal Music Group, Inc.
    2220 Colorado Ave
    Santa Monica CA 90404
    310 865-4000

(P-18503)
US AIRFORCE BAND OF GOLDEN W
551 Waldron St Bldg 240, Travis Afb (94535-2120)
PHONE.................................707 424-2263
Michael Manch, *Principal*
EMP: 50
SALES (est): 625.4K **Privately Held**
SIC: 7929 Orchestras or bands

(P-18504)
WALT DISNEY COMPANY
3900 W Alameda Ave Rm 845, Burbank (91505-4316)
PHONE.................................818 567-5590
Ramona Barnes, *Principal*
EMP: 2002 **Publicly Held**
SIC: 7929 Entertainers & entertainment groups
PA: The Walt Disney Company
    500 S Buena Vista St
    Burbank CA 91521

(P-18505)
WERM INVESTMENTS LLC
Also Called: Exchange La
14242 Ventura Blvd # 212, Sherman Oaks (91423-2771)
PHONE.................................213 627-8070
ADI McBain, *Mng Member*
Viktoriya Khusit, *Accountant*
Camil Sayadeh,
EMP: 50
SALES (est): 1.2MM **Privately Held**
SIC: 7929 Entertainment service

7933 Bowling Centers

(P-18506)
3900 WEST LANE BOWL INC
3900 West Ln, Stockton (95204-2436)
PHONE.................................209 466-6100
Fax: 209 466-0207
Richard Ghio, *President*
Rudy Antonini, *Corp Secy*
Rick Johnson, *Manager*
EMP: 50
SQ FT: 20,000

SALES (est): 2.1MM **Privately Held**
WEB: www.westlanebowl.net
SIC: 7933 5812 5813 Ten pin center; American restaurant; beer garden (drinking places)

(P-18507)
AMF BOWLING CENTERS INC
1201 W Beverly Blvd, Montebello (90640-4142)
PHONE.................................323 728-9161
Fax: 323 887-0339
Norris Runnels, *Manager*
EMP: 50
SALES (corp-wide): 87.1MM **Privately Held**
WEB: www.kidsports.org
SIC: 7933 7999 Ten pin center; tourist attractions, amusement park concessions & rides
HQ: Amf Bowling Centers, Inc.
    7313 Bell Creek Rd
    Mechanicsville VA 23111
    855 263-7278

(P-18508)
AMF BOWLING CENTERS INC
1819 30th St, Bakersfield (93301-1928)
PHONE.................................661 324-4966
Rick Mossman, *Branch Mgr*
EMP: 50
SALES (corp-wide): 87.1MM **Privately Held**
WEB: www.kidsports.org
SIC: 7933 7999 Bowling centers; tourist attractions, amusement park concessions & rides
HQ: Amf Bowling Centers, Inc.
    7313 Bell Creek Rd
    Mechanicsville VA 23111
    855 263-7278

(P-18509)
AMF BOWLING CENTERS INC
22771 Centre Dr, Lake Forest (92630-1747)
PHONE.................................949 770-0055
Fax: 949 770-7839
Darryl Messiah, *Branch Mgr*
EMP: 50
SALES (corp-wide): 87.1MM **Privately Held**
WEB: www.kidsports.org
SIC: 7933 5813 Bowling centers; bar (drinking places)
HQ: Amf Bowling Centers, Inc.
    7313 Bell Creek Rd
    Mechanicsville VA 23111
    855 263-7278

(P-18510)
BDP BOWL INC
Also Called: Classic Bowling Center
900 King Plz, Daly City (94015-4450)
PHONE.................................650 878-0300
Robert Devincenzi, *President*
Richard J Bocci, *Treasurer*
Matthew Devincenzi, *Business Dir*
Steven Devincenzi, *Admin Sec*
Steve Devinchenzi, *Financial Exec*
EMP: 50
SQ FT: 50,000
SALES (est): 1.9MM **Privately Held**
WEB: www.classicbowling.com
SIC: 7933 Bowling centers

(P-18511)
BOWLMOR AMF CORP
Also Called: Brunswick Covino Lanes
1060 W San Bernardino Rd, Covina (91722-4160)
PHONE.................................626 339-1286
Fax: 626 915-8784
Javier Guzman, *Manager*
EMP: 53
SALES (corp-wide): 241.9MM **Privately Held**
SIC: 7933 Bowling centers
PA: Bowlmor Amf Corp.
    222 W 44th St
    New York NY 10036
    212 777-2214

(P-18512)
BOWLMOR AMF CORP
Also Called: West Covina Lanes
675 S Glendora Ave, West Covina (91790-3705)
PHONE.................................626 960-3636
Fax: 626 851-9994
Joe Carridoza, *Manager*
EMP: 55
SQ FT: 57,259
SALES (corp-wide): 241.9MM **Privately Held**
SIC: 7933 Bowling centers
PA: Bowlmor Amf Corp.
    222 W 44th St
    New York NY 10036
    212 777-2214

(P-18513)
BOWLMOR AMF CORP
Also Called: Brunswick Deer Creks Lnes 213
7930 Haven Ave Ste 101, Rancho Cucamonga (91730-3056)
PHONE.................................909 945-9392
Fax: 909 945-9452
Venesa Boudreau, *Assistant VP*
EMP: 50
SALES (corp-wide): 241.9MM **Privately Held**
SIC: 7933 Bowling centers
PA: Bowlmor Amf Corp.
    222 W 44th St
    New York NY 10036
    212 777-2214

(P-18514)
BOWLMOR AMF CORP
Also Called: Brunswick Cal Oaks Bowl
40440 California Oaks Rd, Murrieta (92562-5828)
PHONE.................................951 698-2202
Fax: 951 696-0753
John Tang, *Branch Mgr*
EMP: 50
SALES (corp-wide): 241.9MM **Privately Held**
SIC: 7933 Bowling centers
PA: Bowlmor Amf Corp.
    222 W 44th St
    New York NY 10036
    212 777-2214

(P-18515)
CAL BOWL ENTERPRISES LLC
2500 Carson St, Lakewood (90712-4198)
PHONE.................................562 421-8448
Charles Knistler,
Vincent Rachal, *Manager*
EMP: 50
SALES (est): 836.6K **Privately Held**
SIC: 7933 Bowling centers

(P-18516)
COVINA BOWL INC
1060 W San Bernardino Rd, Covina (91722-4158)
PHONE.................................626 339-1286
Leonard A Brutocao, *President*
Angelo Brutocao, *Treasurer*
Linda Lutz, *Executive*
Don Stetlie, *Manager*
EMP: 80
SQ FT: 60,000
SALES (est): 3.3MM **Privately Held**
SIC: 7933 5812 5813 7999 Ten pin center; American restaurant; drinking places; billiard parlor

(P-18517)
CRENSHAW BOWLING
Also Called: Palos Verdes Bowl
24600 Crenshaw Blvd, Torrance (90505-5307)
PHONE.................................310 326-5120
Fax: 310 539-8021
George Brant, *Vice Pres*
EMP: 50
SQ FT: 40,000
SALES (est): 1.8MM **Privately Held**
SIC: 7933 5812 5813 Ten pin center; snack bar; bar (drinking places)

(P-18518)
FOLSOM RECREATION CORP
Also Called: Lake Bowl
511 E Bidwell St, Folsom (95630-3118)
PHONE.................................916 983-4411
Wally Dreher, *President*
Sue Dreher, *Vice Pres*
Dan Dreher, *General Mgr*
Jeremy Dreher, *General Mgr*
Carly Dreher, *Bookkeeper*
EMP: 70
SQ FT: 18,000
SALES (est): 4.6MM **Privately Held**
SIC: 7933 Bowling centers

(P-18519)
FOURTH STREET BOWL
1441 N 4th St, San Jose (95112-4716)
PHONE.................................408 453-5555
Fax: 408 453-5558
Ken Nakatsu, *President*
MAI Shimizu, *Admin Asst*
EMP: 50
SQ FT: 31,450
SALES (est): 3.1MM **Privately Held**
WEB: www.4thstreetbowl.com
SIC: 7933 5813 5812 Bowling centers; bar (drinking places); coffee shop

(P-18520)
FREMONT SPORTS INC
Also Called: Cloverleaf Bowl
40645 Fremont Blvd Ste 3, Fremont (94538-4368)
PHONE.................................510 656-1955
Fax: 510 651-1204
Donald F Hillman, *President*
EMP: 50
SQ FT: 40,000
SALES (est): 3.2MM **Privately Held**
WEB: www.cloverleafbowl.com
SIC: 7933 5812 5813 Ten pin center; food bars; bar (drinking places)

(P-18521)
GABLE HOUSE INC
Also Called: Gable House Bowl
22501 Hawthorne Blvd, Torrance (90505-2509)
PHONE.................................310 378-2265
Fax: 310 378-6158
Michael Cogan, *President*
EMP: 100
SQ FT: 80,000
SALES (est): 5.2MM **Privately Held**
WEB: www.gablehousebowl.com
SIC: 7933 5813 5812 Ten pin center; bar (drinking places); snack bar

(P-18522)
HARMATZ ENTERTAINMENT CORP
Also Called: Vista Entertainment Center
435 W Vista Way, Vista (92083-5828)
PHONE.................................760 941-1032
William Harmatz, *President*
EMP: 50
SQ FT: 47,000
SALES: 1.5MM **Privately Held**
SIC: 7933 5813 5812 Ten pin center; night clubs; snack bar

(P-18523)
LUCKY STRIKE ENTERTAINMENT LLC
15260 Ventura Blvd # 1110, Sherman Oaks (91403-5346)
PHONE.................................818 933-0872
Mark P'Pool, *Branch Mgr*
EMP: 131
SALES (corp-wide): 241.6MM **Privately Held**
SIC: 7933 Bowling centers
HQ: Lucky Strike Entertainment, Llc
    15260 Ventura Blvd # 1110
    Sherman Oaks CA 91403
    323 467-7776

(P-18524)
LUCKY STRIKE ENTERTAINMENT LLC
Also Called: Lucky Strike Del AMO
3525 W Carson St Ste 77, Torrance (90503-5750)
PHONE.................................310 802-7010

7933 - Bowling Centers County (P-18525)

Daniel Tron, *Branch Mgr*
EMP: 118
SALES (corp-wide): 241.6MM **Privately Held**
SIC: 7933 Bowling centers
HQ: Lucky Strike Entertainment, Llc
15260 Ventura Blvd # 1110
Sherman Oaks CA 91403
323 467-7776

(P-18525)
LUCKY STRIKE ENTERTAINMENT LLC
20 City Blvd W Ste G2, Orange (92868-3131)
PHONE.................................248 374-3420
Fax: 714 937-5250
Ismail Saleem, *Branch Mgr*
Luis Rabo, *Manager*
EMP: 88
SALES (corp-wide): 241.6MM **Privately Held**
SIC: 7933 Bowling centers
HQ: Lucky Strike Entertainment, Llc
15260 Ventura Blvd # 1110
Sherman Oaks CA 91403
323 467-7776

(P-18526)
MCHENRY BOWL INC
3700 Mchenry Ave, Modesto (95356-1597)
PHONE.................................209 571-2695
Fax: 209 571-2701
Garrard Marsh, *President*
Dallas Kadry, *Treasurer*
W Jerry Marsh, *Vice Pres*
Maxine Marsh, *Admin Sec*
EMP: 50
SQ FT: 52,000
SALES (est): 3.2MM **Privately Held**
WEB: www.mchenrybowl.com
SIC: 7933 5813 5941 Bowling centers; bar (drinking places); bowling equipment & supplies

(P-18527)
NATIONWIDE THEATRES CORP
Also Called: Cal Coffee Shop
2500 Carson St, Lakewood (90712-4107)
PHONE.................................562 421-8448
Fax: 562 420-4775
Tom Moeller, *Manager*
Vincent Rachal, *Manager*
EMP: 60
SALES (corp-wide): 200.2MM **Privately Held**
SIC: 7933 5813 5812 Ten pin center; cocktail lounge; coffee shop
HQ: Nationwide Theatres Corp.
120 N Robertson Blvd Fl 3
Los Angeles CA 90048
310 657-8420

(P-18528)
PINSETTERS INC
Also Called: Country Club Lanes
2600 Watt Ave, Sacramento (95821-6296)
PHONE.................................916 488-7545
Fax: 916 483-0732
Greg Kassis, *Ch of Bd*
Dave Haness, *President*
Jim Kassis, *Corp Secy*
Dave Kassis, *Vice Pres*
Kerry Kassis, *Vice Pres*
EMP: 70
SQ FT: 70,000
SALES (est): 3.1MM **Privately Held**
SIC: 7933 5812 5813 Bowling centers; snack bar; bar (drinking places)

(P-18529)
SPARE-TIME INC
429 W Lockeford St, Lodi (95240-2058)
PHONE.................................209 371-0241
Dennis Kaufman, *Principal*
EMP: 314
SALES (corp-wide): 30.7MM **Privately Held**
SIC: 7933 Ten pin center
PA: Spare-Time, Inc.
11344 Coloma Rd Ste 350
Gold River CA 95670
916 859-8910

(P-18530)
STARS RECREATION CENTER LP
155 Browns Valley Pkwy, Vacaville (95688-3011)
PHONE.................................707 455-7827
Ernest E Sousa, *Partner*
Kenneth Sousa, *Partner*
EMP: 50
SQ FT: 65,000
SALES (est): 2.5MM **Privately Held**
SIC: 7933 Bowling centers

(P-18531)
STRIKES UNLIMITED INC
5681 Lonetree Blvd, Rocklin (95765-3735)
PHONE.................................916 626-3600
Kari Pegram, *CEO*
Debbie Haggerty, *General Mgr*
Kathi Miller, *General Mgr*
Prakash Chandra, *Controller*
EMP: 90 **EST:** 2011
SQ FT: 54,000
SALES (est): 4.3MM **Privately Held**
SIC: 7933 5812 Bowling centers; eating places

7941 Professional Sports Clubs & Promoters

(P-18532)
ACE HIGH ENTERTAINNMENT LLC
125 Sconce Way, Sacramento (95838-4744)
PHONE.................................916 243-5515
Rodney Shead, *CEO*
EMP: 50
SALES (est): 303K **Privately Held**
SIC: 7941 5812 7922 Sports field or stadium operator, promoting sports events; Sushi bar; ethnic food restaurants; Chinese restaurant; theatrical talent & booking agencies

(P-18533)
AEG ONTARIO ARENA LLC
Also Called: Citizens Business Bank Arena
4000 E Ontario Ctr Pkwy, Ontario (91764-7966)
PHONE.................................909 244-5500
Kevin Bush, *Finance Dir*
Sandy Lim, *Executive*
Michael Sullivan, *Social Dir*
Therese Everett, *Mktg Dir*
Ben Kirkland, *Sales Staff*
EMP: 100
SALES (est): 3.9MM
SALES (corp-wide): 110.6MM **Privately Held**
SIC: 7941 Boxing & wrestling arena
HQ: Anschutz Entertainment Group, Inc.
1100 S Flower St
Los Angeles CA 90015
213 763-7700

(P-18534)
ANAHEIM ARENA MANAGEMENT LLC
Also Called: AAM
2695 E Katella Ave, Anaheim (92806-5904)
PHONE.................................714 704-2400
Tim Ryan, *President*
Michael Schulman, *Ch of Bd*
Angela Wergechik, *Vice Pres*
Mike Wing, *CIO*
Doug Mullin, *Chief Engr*
EMP: 600
SQ FT: 106,000
SALES (est): 46.8MM **Privately Held**
WEB: www.hondacenter.com
SIC: 7941 Stadium event operator services

(P-18535)
ANGELS BASEBALL LP (PA)
Also Called: Los Angeles Angels of Anaheim
2000 E Gene Autry Way, Anaheim (92806-6143)
PHONE.................................714 940-2000
Fax: 714 940-2205
Dennis Kuhl, *General Ptnr*
Bill Beverage, *Partner*
Molly Jolly, *Partner*
Richard McClemmy, *Partner*
Tim Mead, *Partner*
EMP: 790 **EST:** 1996
SALES (est): 55.2MM **Privately Held**
SIC: 7941 Baseball club, professional & semi-professional

(P-18536)
ANSCHUTZ SO CALIF SPORTS COMPL
Also Called: Stop Hop Center
18400 Avalon Blvd Ste 100, Carson (90746-2180)
PHONE.................................310 630-2000
Kedie Pendolfo,
Anschutz Grp,
EMP: 160
SALES (est): 4.2MM
SALES (corp-wide): 110.6MM **Privately Held**
SIC: 7941 Soccer club
HQ: Anschutz Entertainment Group, Inc.
1100 S Flower St
Los Angeles CA 90015
213 763-7700

(P-18537)
ATHLETICS INVESTMENT GROUP LLC (PA)
Also Called: Oakland Athletics
7000 Coliseum Way, Oakland (94621-1917)
P.O. Box 2220 (94621-0120)
PHONE.................................510 638-4900
Fax: 510 563-2397
Michael Crowley, *Mng Member*
Mike Selleck, *Vice Pres*
Michael Ono, *Creative Dir*
Carolyn Jones, *Executive Asst*
Betty Shinoda, *Executive Asst*
EMP: 151 **EST:** 1901
SALES (est): 18.9MM **Privately Held**
SIC: 7941 Baseball club, professional & semi-professional

(P-18538)
BIG LEAGUE DREAMS JURUPA LLC
10550 Cntu Gllano Rnch Rd, Mira Loma (91752-3261)
PHONE.................................951 685-6900
Fax: 951 685-6548
Scott Parks Letellier, *CEO*
Trey Shipman, *General Mgr*
Gene Lanthorn, *Financial Exec*
Jeffrey Odekirk,
Richard Odekirk,
EMP: 57
SALES (est): 2.9MM **Privately Held**
SIC: 7941 7999 Sports field or stadium operator, promoting sports events; recreation center

(P-18539)
BIG LGUÉ DRAMS CHINO HILLS LLC
16333 Fairfield Ranch Rd, Chino Hills (91709-8816)
PHONE.................................909 287-6900
Rick Odekirk,
Jeff Odekirk,
Mary Porter, *Director*
EMP: 93
SALES (est): 2.2MM **Privately Held**
WEB: www.baseballfirst.com
SIC: 7941 Sports field or stadium operator, promoting sports events

(P-18540)
BIG LGUÉ DREAMS CONSULTING LLC
2155 Trumble Rd, Perris (92571-9211)
PHONE.................................619 846-8855
EMP: 92
SALES (corp-wide): 37.8MM **Privately Held**
SIC: 7941 Stadium event operator services
PA: Big League Dreams Consulting, Llc
16333 Fairfield Ranch Rd
Chino Hills CA 91709
909 287-1700

(P-18541)
CHARGERS FOOTBALL COMPANY LLC (PA)
Also Called: San Diego Chargers
4020 Murphy Canyon Rd, San Diego (92123-4407)
P.O. Box 609609 (92160-9609)
PHONE.................................619 280-2121
Fax: 619 292-2756
Dean A Spanos, *President*
Jeanne Bonk, *CFO*
Alex Spanos, *Chairman*
Alexander G Spanos, *Bd of Directors*
Jeanne M Bonk, *Exec VP*
EMP: 70
SALES (est): 14.2MM **Privately Held**
SIC: 7941 Football club

(P-18542)
CITY OF GLENDALE
541 W Chevy Chase Dr, Glendale (91204-1813)
PHONE.................................818 548-3950
Fax: 818 546-2024
Daniel Hardgrove, *Manager*
EMP: 80 **Privately Held**
WEB: www.glendaleca.com
SIC: 7941 9111 Sports clubs, managers & promoters; mayors' offices
PA: City Of Glendale
141 N Glendale Ave Fl 2
Glendale CA 91206
818 548-2085

(P-18543)
COTO DE CAZA GOLF CLUB INC
25291 Vista Del Verde, Trabuco Canyon (92679-4900)
PHONE.................................949 766-7886
Jack Deal, *Director*
Rick Booth, *Senior Mgr*
Marc Chasman, *Director*
EMP: 135
SALES (est): 2.6MM
SALES (corp-wide): 11.2MM **Privately Held**
WEB: www.coto-de-caza.com
SIC: 7941 5813 7992 7991 Professional & semi-professional sports clubs; drinking places; public golf courses; physical fitness facilities; eating places
PA: Coto De Caza Limited
24800 Chrisanta Dr
Mission Viejo CA

(P-18544)
FORTY NINERS FOOTBALL CO LLC
Also Called: San Francisco 49ers
4949 Mrie P Debartolo Way, Santa Clara (95054-1156)
PHONE.................................408 562-4949
Esther CHI, *Accounting Mgr*
Al Guido, *COO*
Cipora Herman, *CFO*
Jamie Seiff, *Executive Asst*
Lisa Thompson, *Human Res Mgr*
EMP: 99
SALES (est): 14.5MM **Privately Held**
SIC: 7941 Football club

(P-18545)
FOX BASEBALL HOLDINGS INC
1000 Vin Scully Ave, Los Angeles (90090-1112)
PHONE.................................323 224-1500
Frank McCourt, *President*
EMP: 404
SALES (est): 2.5MM
SALES (corp-wide): 27.3B **Publicly Held**
WEB: www.fox.com
SIC: 7941 Baseball club, professional & semi-professional
HQ: Fox Entertainment Group, Inc.
2029 Century Park E # 1400
Los Angeles CA 90067
310 369-1000

(P-18546)
FOX BSB HOLDCO INC
Also Called: Dodger Stadium
1000 Vin Scully Ave, Los Angeles (90090-1112)
PHONE.................................323 224-1500

PRODUCTS & SERVICES SECTION
7948 - Racing & Track Operations County (P-18567)

Fax: 323 224-1269
Steve Soboroff, *Vice Chairman*
Jamie McCourt, *Vice Chairman*
Ron Wheeler, *CEO*
Dannis Mannion, *COO*
Camille Johnston, *Senior VP*
EMP: 3739
SQ FT: 20,000
SALES (est): 152MM
SALES (corp-wide): 1.5B **Privately Held**
WEB: www.ladodgers.com
SIC: 7941 Baseball club, professional & semi-professional
PA: Guggenheim Partners, Llc
330 Madison Ave Rm 201
New York NY 10017
212 739-0700

(P-18547)
GOLDEN STATE WARRIORS LLC
1011 Broadway, Oakland (94607-4027)
PHONE..................510 986-2200
Fax: 510 452-0142
Christopher Cohan, *Mng Member*
Chip Bowers, *Chief Mktg Ofcr*
Tikvah Heller, *Office Admin*
Shari Knight, *Executive Asst*
Ben Draa, *Administration*
EMP: 100 **EST:** 1962
SALES (est): 17.9MM **Privately Held**
WEB: www.gs-warriors.com
SIC: 7941 Basketball club

(P-18548)
HIGH DESERT MAVERICKS INC
Also Called: Minor League Baseball
12000 Stadium Rd, Adelanto (92301-3400)
PHONE..................760 246-6287
Fax: 760 246-3197
Dave Heller, *President*
Ben Hemmen, *General Mgr*
EMP: 100
SALES (est): 2.6MM **Privately Held**
WEB: www.hdmavs.com
SIC: 7941 Baseball club, professional & semi-professional

(P-18549)
HOTROLLERGIRL PRODUCTIONS
11890 Silver Spur St, Ojai (93023-4181)
PHONE..................530 521-2745
Kristin Longstreet, *Owner*
EMP: 100 **EST:** 2015
SALES (est): 360.8K **Privately Held**
SIC: 7941 7231 7221 Stadium event operator services; beauty shops; photographer, still or video

(P-18550)
INLAND EMPRE 66ERS BSEBLL CLB
280 S E St, San Bernardino (92401-2009)
PHONE..................909 888-9922
Fax: 909 888-5251
David Elmore, *CEO*
Donna Tuttle, *President*
Jhon Fonsaker, *CFO*
John Fonseca, *Controller*
John Jensen, *Opers Mgr*
EMP: 110
SQ FT: 600
SALES (est): 5.1MM
SALES (corp-wide): 44.4MM **Privately Held**
WEB: www.ie66ers.com
SIC: 7941 Baseball club, professional & semi-professional
PA: The Elmore Group Ltd
19 N Grant St Ste 2
Hinsdale IL
630 325-6228

(P-18551)
INTERNATIONAL SPEEDWAY INC
3103 S El Camino Real, San Clemente (92672-3439)
P.O. Box 3334 (92674-3334)
PHONE..................949 492-9933
Fax: 949 492-2547
Harry Oxley, *President*
Lauren Oxley, *Manager*
Laurie Oxley, *Manager*
EMP: 53
SQ FT: 2,000
SALES: 550K **Privately Held**
SIC: 7941 7389 Sports promotion; flea market

(P-18552)
KINGS ARENA LTD PARTNERSHIP
Also Called: Maloof Sport Entertainment
1 Sports Pkwy, Sacramento (95834-2300)
PHONE..................916 928-0000
Fax: 916 928-6981
Gavin Maloof, *Managing Prtnr*
John Rinehart, *Partner*
John Thomas, *Partner*
Steve Wille, *Vice Pres*
Troy Hanson, *Director*
EMP: 60 **EST:** 1992
SALES (est): 7.1MM **Privately Held**
SIC: 7941 Boxing & wrestling arena

(P-18553)
LAC BASKETBALL CLUB INC
Also Called: Los Angeles Clippers
1111 S Figueroa St # 1100, Los Angeles (90015-1300)
PHONE..................213 742-7500
Dick Parsons, *CEO*
Ed Lamb, *CFO*
Andrew Roeser, *Exec VP*
Carl Lahr, *Senior VP*
Glenn Rivers, *Senior VP*
EMP: 195
SQ FT: 5,000
SALES (est): 14.8MM **Privately Held**
WEB: www.clippers.com
SIC: 7941 Basketball club

(P-18554)
LOS ANGELES LAKERS INC
555 N Nash St, El Segundo (90245-2818)
PHONE..................310 426-6000
Fax: 310 426-6105
Jerry H Buss, *President*
Jeanie Buss, *Exec VP*
Frank Mariani, *Exec VP*
Joseph McCormack, *Senior VP*
Kim Harris, *Vice Pres*
EMP: 100
SQ FT: 12,000
SALES (est): 904.3K **Privately Held**
WEB: www.lakers.com
SIC: 7941 Basketball club

(P-18555)
LOS ANGELES RAMS LLC (PA)
Also Called: St Louis Rams
29899 Agoura Rd, Agoura Hills (91301-2493)
PHONE..................314 982-7267
Fax: 314 516-8888
E Stanley Kroenke, *General Ptnr*
Lucia Rodriguez, *Owner*
Chip Rosenbloom, *Owner*
Kevin Demoff, *COO*
Les Snead, *General Mgr*
EMP: 100
SALES (est): 26.5MM **Privately Held**
WEB: www.stlouisrams.com
SIC: 7941 Football club

(P-18556)
LOS ANGELES KINGS HOCKEY CLB LP
555 N Nash St, El Segundo (90245-2818)
P.O. Box 912 (90245-0912)
PHONE..................310 535-4502
Dean Lombardi, *General Mgr*
Kelly Cheeseman, *COO*
Rob Blake, *Vice Pres*
Matt Rosenfeld, *Vice Pres*
Tiffany Grommon, *Executive Asst*
EMP: 79
SALES (corp-wide): 11.1MM **Privately Held**
WEB: www.lakings.com
SIC: 7941 Ice hockey club
PA: The Los Angeles Kings Hockey Club L P
300 N Cntntl Blvd Ste 500
Los Angeles CA 90015
888 546-4752

(P-18557)
MANDALAY SPORTS ENTRMT LLC (PA)
Also Called: Mandalay Baseball Properties
4751 Wilshire Blvd Fl 3, Los Angeles (90010-3844)
PHONE..................323 549-4300
Fax: 323 549-4301
Hank Stickney, *CEO*
Peter Guber, *CEO*
Jimmy Bailey, *CFO*
Paul Scheaffer, *Vice Pres*
Brian Hightman, *Technology*
EMP: 80
SALES (est): 7.1MM **Privately Held**
SIC: 7941 Sports clubs, managers & promoters

(P-18558)
MISSION VIEJO PATEADORES INC
7 El Corzo, Rcho STA Marg (92688-3507)
PHONE..................949 350-5590
EMP: 50 **EST:** 2010
SALES (est): 367.2K **Privately Held**
SIC: 7941 Soccer club

(P-18559)
MSG NETWORKS INC
Also Called: Forum, The
333 W Florence Ave, Inglewood (90301-1103)
PHONE..................310 330-7300
Marc Little, *Branch Mgr*
EMP: 57
SALES (corp-wide): 658.2MM **Publicly Held**
SIC: 7941 Stadium event operator services
PA: Msg Networks Inc.
11 Penn Plz
New York NY 10001
212 465-6400

(P-18560)
PADRES LP
Also Called: San Diego Padres
100 Pk Blvd Petco Park Petco Pk, San Diego (92101)
PHONE..................619 795-5000
Fax: 619 795-5315
Mike Dee,
Wayne Partello, *Senior VP*
Jim Kiersnowski, *Exec Dir*
Kevin Towers, *General Mgr*
Virginia Schang, *Executive Asst*
EMP: 1100
SQ FT: 3,000
SALES (est): 247.5K **Privately Held**
SIC: 7941 Baseball club, professional & semi-professional

(P-18561)
SACRAMENTO RIVER CATS BASEBALL
400 Ball Park Dr, West Sacramento (95691-2824)
PHONE..................916 376-4700
Fax: 916 376-4710
Art Savage,
Dan Vistica, *CFO*
Andy Fiske, *Chief Mktg Ofcr*
Darrin Gross, *Vice Pres*
Ripper Hatch, *Vice Pres*
EMP: 50
SALES (est): 6.2MM **Privately Held**
WEB: www.rivercats.net
SIC: 7941 Baseball club, professional & semi-professional
PA: River City Baseball Investment Group Llc
400 Ball Park Dr
West Sacramento CA 95691
916 376-4700

(P-18562)
SAN FRANCISCO FORTY NINERS (PA)
4949 Mrie P Debartolo Way, Santa Clara (95054-1156)
PHONE..................408 562-4949
Fax: 408 727-4937
Denise Debartolo York, *Ch of Bd*
Peter Harris, *President*
Larry Macneil, *CFO*
Jamie Brandt, *Vice Pres*
Edward Goines, *Vice Pres*
EMP: 120
SQ FT: 50,000
SALES (est): 216.8MM **Privately Held**
WEB: www.sf49ers.com
SIC: 7941 Football club

(P-18563)
SAN JOSE SHARKS LLC
Also Called: HP Pavillion At San Jose
525 W Santa Clara St, San Jose (95113-1500)
PHONE..................408 287-6655
Greg Jamison, *President*
Charlie Faas, *CFO*
Mari Quintana, *Prdtn Mgr*
Suzanne Schwartz, *Mktg Dir*
Courtney Jankovich, *Marketing Mgr*
EMP: 170
SALES (est): 16MM **Privately Held**
WEB: www.hppsj.com
SIC: 7941 Ice hockey club

(P-18564)
SHARKS SPORTS & ENTRMT LLC
Also Called: SSE Merchandise
525 W Santa Clara St, San Jose (95113-1520)
PHONE..................408 287-7070
Hasso Plattner, *Mng Member*
Manny Conway, *Human Res Mgr*
Ryan Hilgers, *Sls & Mktg Exec*
Luis Samayoa, *Sls & Mktg Exec*
Kent Russell, *VP Sls/Mktg*
EMP: 800
SALES (est): 38.9MM **Privately Held**
SIC: 7941 Sports clubs, managers & promoters

(P-18565)
UNITED STTES OLYMPIC COMMITTEE
Also Called: Arco Olympic Training Center
2800 Olympic Pkwy, Chula Vista (91915-6002)
PHONE..................619 656-1500
Fax: 619 482-6200
Tracie Lamb, *Director*
EMP: 50
SALES (corp-wide): 270.2MM **Privately Held**
WEB: www.usoc.org
SIC: 7941 Manager of individual professional athletes
PA: United States Olympic Committee Inc
1 Olympic Plz
Colorado Springs CO 80903
719 632-5551

7948 Racing & Track Operations

(P-18566)
BAY MEADOWS RACING ASSOCIATION
2600 S Delaware St, San Mateo (94403-1904)
P.O. Box 1490 (94401-0872)
PHONE..................650 573-4500
Fax: 650 573-4670
F Jack Liebau, *President*
Mike Ziegler, *General Mgr*
Dale Duspila, *Webmaster*
Gina Arellano, *Human Res Dir*
EMP: 200
SALES (est): 4.7MM **Privately Held**
WEB: www.baymeadows.com
SIC: 7948 Horses, racing

(P-18567)
CALIFORNIA SPEEDWAY CORP
Also Called: Auto Club Speedway
9300 Cherry Ave, Fontana (92335-2562)
PHONE..................909 429-5000
Fax: 909 429-5500
William Miller, *President*
Maria Gladowski, *Surgery Dir*
David Talley, *Comms Mgr*
Cal Caldarone, *Executive Asst*
Ray Wilkings, *VP Opers*
EMP: 50

7948 - Racing & Track Operations County (P-18568)

SALES (est): 6MM
SALES (corp-wide): 645.3MM **Publicly Held**
SIC: **7948** Automotive race track operation
HQ: 88 Corporation
1801 W Intl Speedway Blvd
Daytona Beach FL 32114
386 254-2700

(P-18568)
CHURCHILL DOWNS INCORPORATED
800 W El Camino Real, Mountain View (94040-2567)
PHONE.................................502 638-3879
Ted Gay, *President*
Michael Cody, *Vice Pres*
EMP: 900
SALES (corp-wide): 1.2B **Publicly Held**
SIC: **7948 7993** Race track operation; thoroughbred horse racing; gambling machines, coin-operated
PA: Churchill Downs Incorporated
600 N Hurstbourne Pkwy
Louisville KY 40222
502 636-4400

(P-18569)
DEL MAR THOROUGHBRED CLUB
Also Called: Surfside Race Place At Del Mar
2260 Jimmy Durante Blvd, Del Mar (92014-2216)
P.O. Box 700 (92014-0700)
PHONE.................................858 755-1141
Fax: 858 792-1477
Joe Harper, *President*
Mike Ernst, *CFO*
Craig Dado, *Vice Pres*
Craig Fravel, *Vice Pres*
Ann Hall, *Vice Pres*
▲ EMP: 400 EST: 1970
SALES (est): 28MM **Privately Held**
WEB: www.dmtc.com
SIC: **7948** Thoroughbred horse racing

(P-18570)
LOS ANGELES TURF CLUB INC
Also Called: Santa Anita Park
285 W Huntington Dr, Arcadia (91007-3439)
P.O. Box 60014 (91066-6014)
PHONE.................................626 574-6330
Fax: 626 574-5074
Gregory C Avioli, *CEO*
Frank Stronach, *Ch of Bd*
George Haines II, *President*
Frank Demarco Jr, *Vice Pres*
Joyce Buhler, *Admin Sec*
▲ EMP: 450 EST: 1964
SALES (est): 28.3MM
SALES (corp-wide): 32.1B **Privately Held**
WEB: www.santaanita.com
SIC: **7948** Horse race track operation
HQ: Magna Car Top Systems Of America, Inc.
2725 Commerce Pkwy
Auburn Hills MI 48326
248 836-4500

(P-18571)
NATIONAL HOT ROD ASSOCIATION (PA)
Also Called: Nhra
2035 E Financial Way, Glendora (91741-4602)
P.O. Box 5555 (91740-0950)
PHONE.................................626 914-4761
Fax: 626 335-6651
Wally Parks, *Director*
Harvey Palash, *Vice Chairman*
Tom Compton, *President*
Peter Clifford, *CFO*
Kurt Wolfe, *Treasurer*
EMP: 200
SQ FT: 30,000
SALES: 99.2MM **Privately Held**
WEB: www.nhra.com
SIC: **7948 2711 2741** Automotive race track operation; newspapers: publishing only, not printed on site; miscellaneous publishing

(P-18572)
PACIFIC RACING ASSOCIATION
Also Called: Golden Gate Fields
1100 Eastshore Hwy, Albany (94710-1002)
P.O. Box 6027 (94706-0027)
PHONE.................................510 559-7300
Fax: 510 559-7465
Frank Stronach, *President*
Peter W Tunney, *General Mgr*
Robin McHargue, *Sales Mgr*
Bob Hemmer, *Marketing Staff*
Ferdinand Rebusi, *Food Svc Dir*
EMP: 140
SALES: 63MM **Privately Held**
WEB: www.goldengatefields.com
SIC: **7948** Horses, racing

(P-18573)
PHILIP DAMATO RACING LLC
28202 Palmada, Mission Viejo (92692-1422)
PHONE.................................949 830-7027
Philip D'Amato,
EMP: 55 EST: 2014
SALES (est): 206.6K **Privately Held**
SIC: **7948** Horses, racing

(P-18574)
SACRAMENTO HARNESS ASSOCIATION
1600 Exposition Blvd, Sacramento (95815-5104)
PHONE.................................916 239-4040
Ralph Scurfield, *President*
Chris Schick, *Manager*
EMP: 90
SALES (est): 1MM **Privately Held**
WEB: www.sacharness.com
SIC: **7948** Harness horse racing

(P-18575)
SMISC HOLDINGS
Hwy 121, Sonoma (95476)
PHONE.................................707 938-8448
Steve Page, *Manager*
Diana Rose, *Manager*
EMP: 50
SALES (corp-wide): 496.4MM **Publicly Held**
SIC: **7948** Motor vehicle racing & drivers
HQ: Smisc Holdings, Inc.
5401 E Independence Blvd
Charlotte NC 28212
704 455-9453

(P-18576)
SPEEDWAY SONOMA LLC
Also Called: Infineon Raceway
Hwy 37 N, Sonoma (95476)
PHONE.................................707 938-8448
Bruton Smith,
Frank Gullum, *Vice Pres*
Sarah Grasal,
John Cardinale, *Relations*
▲ EMP: 60
SALES (est): 5.3MM
SALES (corp-wide): 496.4MM **Publicly Held**
WEB: www.infineonraceway.com
SIC: **7948** Racing, including track operation
HQ: Speedway Motorsports, Inc.
5555 Concord Pkwy S
Concord NC 28027
704 455-3239

7991 Physical Fitness Facilities

(P-18577)
2 G FITNESS LLC
Also Called: Studio By Clubsport, The
730 Camino Ramon Ste 200, Danville (94526-4263)
PHONE.................................925 838-9200
Patrick J O'Brien, *Mng Member*
Steve Gilmour, *Owner*
Alicia Puoice, *Admin Asst*
Malcolm Pitt, *Finance*
Hien Huynh, *Accounts Mgr*
EMP: 62

SALES (est): 1.2MM
SALES (corp-wide): 213MM **Privately Held**
SIC: **7991** Physical fitness facilities
PA: Leisure Sports, Inc.
4670 Willow Rd Ste 100
Pleasanton CA 94588
925 600-1966

(P-18578)
24 HOUR FITNESS USA INC
Also Called: Folsom Sport Club
1006 Riley St, Folsom (95630-3266)
PHONE.................................916 984-1924
Doug Coelho, *Manager*
Travis Owens, *Manager*
EMP: 50
SALES (corp-wide): 441.6MM **Privately Held**
SIC: **7991** Health club
HQ: 24 Hour Fitness Usa, Inc.
12647 Alcosta Blvd # 500
San Ramon CA 94583
925 543-3100

(P-18579)
24 HOUR FITNESS USA INC
39300 Paseo Padre Pkwy, Fremont (94538-1629)
PHONE.................................510 795-6666
Fax: 510 795-0754
Tammy Egan, *Manager*
EMP: 50
SALES (corp-wide): 441.6MM **Privately Held**
SIC: **7991** Health club
HQ: 24 Hour Fitness Usa, Inc.
12647 Alcosta Blvd # 500
San Ramon CA 94583
925 543-3100

(P-18580)
24 HOUR FITNESS USA INC
Also Called: Boulder Active Club
1265 Laurel Tree Ln # 100, Carlsbad (92011-4221)
PHONE.................................760 602-5001
S Woodard, *Principal*
EMP: 80
SALES (corp-wide): 441.6MM **Privately Held**
SIC: **7991** Health club
HQ: 24 Hour Fitness Usa, Inc.
12647 Alcosta Blvd # 500
San Ramon CA 94583
925 543-3100

(P-18581)
24 HOUR FITNESS USA INC
Also Called: Anaheim Gateway Sport Club
1430 N Lemon St, Anaheim (92801-1200)
PHONE.................................714 525-9924
Fax: 714 446-6508
Dalia Shoham, *Manager*
Otis Jordan, *Manager*
Jared Lee, *Manager*
EMP: 50
SALES (corp-wide): 441.6MM **Privately Held**
SIC: **7991** Health club
HQ: 24 Hour Fitness Usa, Inc.
12647 Alcosta Blvd # 500
San Ramon CA 94583
925 543-3100

(P-18582)
24 HOUR FITNESS USA INC
Also Called: Chula Vista Active Club
1660 Broadway Ste 19, Chula Vista (91911-4857)
PHONE.................................619 425-6600
Louis Carranza, *Manager*
Jeff Demott, *Manager*
EMP: 65
SALES (corp-wide): 441.6MM **Privately Held**
SIC: **7991** Health club
HQ: 24 Hour Fitness Usa, Inc.
12647 Alcosta Blvd # 500
San Ramon CA 94583
925 543-3100

(P-18583)
24 HOUR FITNESS USA INC (HQ)
12647 Alcosta Blvd # 500, San Ramon (94583-4436)
PHONE.................................925 543-3100
Fax: 925 543-3200
Mark Smith, *CEO*
Frank Napolitano, *President*
Patrick Flanagan, *CFO*
Eric McNabb, *Administration*
Kiley Philips, *Administration*
▲ EMP: 183
SALES (est): 441.6MM **Privately Held**
WEB: www.extremephysiques.net
SIC: **7991** Health club
PA: 24 Hour Fitness Worldwide, Inc.
12647 Alcosta Blvd # 500
San Ramon CA 94583
925 543-3100

(P-18584)
24 HOUR FITNESS USA INC
Also Called: Beverly Hills Active Club
9911 W Pico Blvd Ste A, Los Angeles (90035-2708)
PHONE.................................310 553-7600
Fax: 310 553-5636
Julian Jekines, *Manager*
John Raber, *General Mgr*
EMP: 60
SALES (corp-wide): 441.6MM **Privately Held**
SIC: **7991** Health club
HQ: 24 Hour Fitness Usa, Inc.
12647 Alcosta Blvd # 500
San Ramon CA 94583
925 543-3100

(P-18585)
24 HOUR FITNESS USA INC
Also Called: Pasadena Sport Club
525 E Colorado Blvd Bsmt, Pasadena (91101-5229)
PHONE.................................626 795-7121
Fax: 626 795-7565
Mike Priebe, *General Mgr*
EMP: 55
SALES (corp-wide): 441.6MM **Privately Held**
SIC: **7991** Physical fitness facilities
HQ: 24 Hour Fitness Usa, Inc.
12647 Alcosta Blvd # 500
San Ramon CA 94583
925 543-3100

(P-18586)
24 HOUR FITNESS USA INC
Also Called: Rancho Cucamonga Sport Club
11787 Foothill Blvd, Rancho Cucamonga (91730-3907)
PHONE.................................909 944-1000
Bobby Serrano, *Branch Mgr*
Tiffany Harris, *Manager*
EMP: 100
SALES (corp-wide): 441.6MM **Privately Held**
SIC: **7991** Health club
HQ: 24 Hour Fitness Usa, Inc.
12647 Alcosta Blvd # 500
San Ramon CA 94583
925 543-3100

(P-18587)
24 HOUR FITNESS USA INC
Also Called: West Hollywood Sport Club
8612 Santa Monica Blvd, West Hollywood (90069-4110)
PHONE.................................310 652-7440
Robin Morris, *Manager*
John Campbell, *Manager*
Durante Lambert, *Manager*
EMP: 50
SALES (corp-wide): 441.6MM **Privately Held**
SIC: **7991** Health club
HQ: 24 Hour Fitness Usa, Inc.
12647 Alcosta Blvd # 500
San Ramon CA 94583
925 543-3100

(P-18588)
24 HOUR FITNESS USA INC
Also Called: Costa Mesa Sport Club
555 W 19th St, Costa Mesa (92627-2753)
PHONE.................................949 650-3600

PRODUCTS & SERVICES SECTION

7991 - Physical Fitness Facilities County (P-18610)

Fax: 949 650-3633
Andy Breton, Manager
Eric Smith, Sales Executive
EMP: 85
SALES (corp-wide): 441.6MM **Privately Held**
SIC: 7991 Health club
HQ: 24 Hour Fitness Usa, Inc.
12647 Alcosta Blvd # 500
San Ramon CA 94583
925 543-3100

(P-18589)
24 HOUR FITNESS USA INC
Also Called: Citrus Heights Sport Club
12647 Alcostia Blvd # 500, San Ramon (94583-4436)
PHONE.................................916 722-7588
Fax: 916 722-7638
Tom Hatfield, Director
EMP: 70
SALES (corp-wide): 441.6MM **Privately Held**
SIC: 7991 Health club
HQ: 24 Hour Fitness Usa, Inc.
12647 Alcosta Blvd # 500
San Ramon CA 94583
925 543-3100

(P-18590)
24 HOUR FITNESS USA INC
Also Called: Glendale Super-Sport Club
450 N Brand Blvd Ste 100, Glendale (91203-2345)
PHONE.................................818 247-4334
David Crisalli, Branch Mgr
Joel Barios, Executive
Alex Kachanov, CTO
EMP: 100
SALES (corp-wide): 441.6MM **Privately Held**
SIC: 7991 Health club
HQ: 24 Hour Fitness Usa, Inc.
12647 Alcosta Blvd # 500
San Ramon CA 94583
925 543-3100

(P-18591)
24 HOUR FITNESS USA INC
Also Called: Santa Monica Sport Club
2929 31st St, Santa Monica (90405-3036)
PHONE.................................310 450-4464
Fax: 310 450-3965
Tina Rodriguez, Manager
EMP: 98
SALES (corp-wide): 441.6MM **Privately Held**
SIC: 7991 Health club
HQ: 24 Hour Fitness Usa, Inc.
12647 Alcosta Blvd # 500
San Ramon CA 94583
925 543-3100

(P-18592)
24 HOUR FITNESS USA INC
Also Called: Foothill Ranch Sport Club
26781 Rancho Pkwy, Lake Forest (92630-8706)
PHONE.................................949 830-4213
Fax: 949 830-6509
Rick Roe, Manager
Matt Marshall, Manager
EMP: 60
SALES (corp-wide): 441.6MM **Privately Held**
SIC: 7991 Physical fitness facilities
HQ: 24 Hour Fitness Usa, Inc.
12647 Alcosta Blvd # 500
San Ramon CA 94583
925 543-3100

(P-18593)
24 HOUR FITNESS USA INC
Also Called: San Mateo Sport Club
500 El Camino Real, Burlingame (94010-5159)
PHONE.................................650 343-7922
Fax: 650 696-1933
Paul Draubot, Branch Mgr
EMP: 140
SALES (corp-wide): 441.6MM **Privately Held**
SIC: 7991 Health club
HQ: 24 Hour Fitness Usa, Inc.
12647 Alcosta Blvd # 500
San Ramon CA 94583
925 543-3100

(P-18594)
24 HOUR FITNESS USA INC
1640 Camino Del Rio N # 315, San Diego (92108-1525)
PHONE.................................619 294-2424
Fax: 619 491-3014
Denver Warth, Manager
EMP: 50
SALES (corp-wide): 441.6MM **Privately Held**
SIC: 7991 Health club
HQ: 24 Hour Fitness Usa, Inc.
12647 Alcosta Blvd # 500
San Ramon CA 94583
925 543-3100

(P-18595)
24 HOUR FITNESS USA INC
Also Called: Canoga Park/West Hills Club
6653 Fallbrook Ave, Canoga Park (91307-3520)
PHONE.................................818 887-2582
Nichole Lorenz, Branch Mgr
Saeed Musavi, Manager
EMP: 68
SALES (corp-wide): 441.6MM **Privately Held**
SIC: 7991 Health club
HQ: 24 Hour Fitness Usa, Inc.
12647 Alcosta Blvd # 500
San Ramon CA 94583
925 543-3100

(P-18596)
24 HOUR FITNESS USA INC
Also Called: Whittier Active Club
10125 Whittwood Dr, Whittier (90603-2314)
PHONE.................................562 943-3771
Fax: 562 902-4976
Bryan Mirchof, Manager
EMP: 60
SALES (corp-wide): 441.6MM **Privately Held**
SIC: 7991 Health club
HQ: 24 Hour Fitness Usa, Inc.
12647 Alcosta Blvd # 500
San Ramon CA 94583
925 543-3100

(P-18597)
24 HOUR FITNESS USA INC
Also Called: Walnut Creek Active Club
2033 N Main St Ste 110, Walnut Creek (94596-3737)
PHONE.................................925 930-7900
Fax: 925 330-8316
Scott Pendel, General Mgr
EMP: 60
SALES (corp-wide): 441.6MM **Privately Held**
WEB: www.extremephysiques.net
SIC: 7991 Health club
HQ: 24 Hour Fitness Usa, Inc.
12647 Alcosta Blvd # 500
San Ramon CA 94583
925 543-3100

(P-18598)
24 HOUR FITNESS USA INC
Also Called: Mountain View Sport Club
550 Showers Dr Ste 1, Mountain View (94040-1438)
PHONE.................................650 941-2268
Fax: 650 941-2018
Oshkar Gobani, General Mgr
EMP: 50
SALES (corp-wide): 441.6MM **Privately Held**
SIC: 7991 Health club
HQ: 24 Hour Fitness Usa, Inc.
12647 Alcosta Blvd # 500
San Ramon CA 94583
925 543-3100

(P-18599)
24 HOUR FITNESS USA INC
Also Called: Rancho Penasquitos Sport Club
10025 Carmel Mountain Rd, San Diego (92129-3229)
PHONE.................................858 538-4400

Fax: 858 538-9159
Connie Lauda, Manager
Jason Maham, Manager
EMP: 50
SALES (corp-wide): 441.6MM **Privately Held**
SIC: 7991 Health club
HQ: 24 Hour Fitness Usa, Inc.
12647 Alcosta Blvd # 500
San Ramon CA 94583
925 543-3100

(P-18600)
24 HOUR FITNESS USA INC
Also Called: Hayward Active Club
24727 Amador St, Hayward (94544-1801)
PHONE.................................510 264-3275
Fax: 510 264-3282
Stephanie Johnson, Manager
EMP: 75
SALES (corp-wide): 441.6MM **Privately Held**
SIC: 7991 Health club
HQ: 24 Hour Fitness Usa, Inc.
12647 Alcosta Blvd # 500
San Ramon CA 94583
925 543-3100

(P-18601)
24 HOUR FITNESS WORLDWIDE INC (PA)
12647 Alcosta Blvd # 500, San Ramon (94583-4436)
PHONE.................................925 543-3100
Brenden Egen, Sales Staff
David Galvan, Vice Pres
Tim Segneri, Vice Pres
EMP: 100 EST: 2001
SALES (corp-wide): 441.6MM **Privately Held**
WEB: www.24hourfitness.com
SIC: 7991 Health club

(P-18602)
24 HOUR FITNESS WORLDWIDE INC
1601 Pcf Cast Hwy Ste 100, Hermosa Beach (90254)
PHONE.................................310 374-4524
Fax: 310 798-9218
Tommy Cassidy, Manager
EMP: 50
SALES (corp-wide): 441.6MM **Privately Held**
WEB: www.24hourfitness.com
SIC: 7991 Health club
PA: 24 Hour Fitness Worldwide, Inc.
12647 Alcosta Blvd # 500
San Ramon CA 94583
925 543-3100

(P-18603)
A & M GYMS LLC
Also Called: Gold's Gym
5110 Foothills Blvd, Roseville (95747-6581)
PHONE.................................916 788-4241
Fax: 916 788-4272
Pat Accettura,
Tony Accettura,
Marcello Mantagnino,
EMP: 52
SALES (est): 2.4MM **Privately Held**
SIC: 7991 Athletic club & gymnasiums, membership

(P-18604)
ADVENTUREPLEX
1701 Marine Ave, Manhattan Beach (90266-4100)
PHONE.................................310 546-7708
Kate Hurley, Manager
EMP: 50
SALES (est): 1.7MM **Privately Held**
WEB: www.adventureplex.com
SIC: 7991 Physical fitness facilities

(P-18605)
B A M I INC
Also Called: 24 Hour In Motion Fitness
1293 E 1st Ave, Chico (95926-1548)
PHONE.................................530 343-5678
Fax: 530 343-5799
Carleton J Sommer, President
Lance Baxman, Accountant
Adeliz King, Director
Marie Phillips, Director

Lori Pine, Director
EMP: 50
SQ FT: 19,400
SALES (est): 2.1MM **Privately Held**
WEB: www.inmotionfitness.net
SIC: 7991 Physical fitness facilities

(P-18606)
BACK STREET FITNESS INC
Also Called: Health Quest
3175 California Blvd, NAPA (94558-3307)
PHONE.................................707 254-7200
Fax: 707 253-7531
Anthony Giovannoni, President
Tony Giovannoni, Benefits Mgr
Mary A Schaffer, Director
EMP: 50
SALES (est): 1.3MM **Privately Held**
WEB: www.napahealthquest.com
SIC: 7991 Exercise facilities

(P-18607)
BALLY TOTAL FITNESS CORP (HQ)
12440 Imperial Hwy # 300, Norwalk (90650-3178)
PHONE.................................562 484-2000
Marc Tascher, CEO
Lee Hillman, President
John Dwyer, CFO
Cary A Gaan, Senior VP
Ana Vazquez, Manager
▲ EMP: 150
SALES (est): 150.3MM
SALES (corp-wide): 295.8MM **Privately Held**
WEB: www.ballyfitnes.com
SIC: 7991 Health club
PA: Bally Total Fitness Holding Corporation
8700 W Bryn Mawr Ave 620n
Chicago IL 60631
773 380-3000

(P-18608)
BALLY TOTAL FITNESS CORP
3827 Overland Ave Wststdew, Culver City (90232-3306)
PHONE.................................310 204-2030
Ector McClendon, Manager
Maria Alverez, VP Human Res
Dexter McClendon, Sales Executive
Ricky Woods, Manager
EMP: 100
SALES (corp-wide): 295.8MM **Privately Held**
WEB: www.ballyfitnes.com
SIC: 7991 Health club
HQ: Bally Total Fitness Corporation
12440 Imperial Hwy # 300
Norwalk CA 90650
562 484-2000

(P-18609)
BALLY TOTAL FITNESS CORP
28901 S Wstrn 315321, Rancho Palos Verdes (90275)
PHONE.................................310 732-2100
Franvisco Davis, General Mgr
EMP: 50
SALES (corp-wide): 295.8MM **Privately Held**
WEB: www.ballyfitnes.com
SIC: 7991 Health club
HQ: Bally Total Fitness Corporation
12440 Imperial Hwy # 300
Norwalk CA 90650
562 484-2000

(P-18610)
BALLY TOTAL FITNESS CORP
9850 Hibert St, San Diego (92131-1020)
PHONE.................................858 831-0773
Kathy Moore, Principal
EMP: 50
SALES (corp-wide): 295.8MM **Privately Held**
WEB: www.ballyfitnes.com
SIC: 7991 Health club
HQ: Bally Total Fitness Corporation
12440 Imperial Hwy # 300
Norwalk CA 90650
562 484-2000

7991 - Physical Fitness Facilities County (P-18611)

PRODUDUCTS & SERVICES SECTION

(P-18611)
BALLY TOTAL FITNESS CORP
310 S Magnolia Ave, Anaheim
(92804-2116)
PHONE 714 952-3101
Fax: 714 952-0460
Kevin Ambrose, *Manager*
EMP: 50
SALES (corp-wide): 295.8MM **Privately Held**
WEB: www.ballyfitnes.com
SIC: 7991 Health club
HQ: Bally Total Fitness Corporation
12440 Imperial Hwy # 300
Norwalk CA 90650
562 484-2000

(P-18612)
BALLY TOTAL FITNESS CORP
9385 Monte Vista Ave, Montclair
(91763-1924)
PHONE 909 625-2411
Fax: 909 625-1699
Victor Prain, *General Mgr*
EMP: 50
SALES (corp-wide): 295.8MM **Privately Held**
WEB: www.ballyfitnes.com
SIC: 7991 Health club
HQ: Bally Total Fitness Corporation
12440 Imperial Hwy # 300
Norwalk CA 90650
562 484-2000

(P-18613)
BALLY TOTAL FITNESS CORP
2222 W Beverly Blvd, Montebello
(90640-2302)
PHONE 323 722-0994
Fax: 323 724-5987
Joel Hernadez, *Manager*
John Wildman, *COO*
William Fanelli, *Vice Pres*
George Acevedo, *General Mgr*
Jean Puscheck, *Office Admin*
EMP: 50
SALES (corp-wide): 295.8MM **Privately Held**
WEB: www.ballyfitnes.com
SIC: 7991 Health club
HQ: Bally Total Fitness Corporation
12440 Imperial Hwy # 300
Norwalk CA 90650
562 484-2000

(P-18614)
BALLY TOTAL FITNESS CORP
1910 Sweetwater Rd, National City
(91950-7628)
PHONE 619 474-6392
Fax: 619 474-6810
Nathan Ogen, *Manager*
John Luminsky, *Vice Pres*
Ogden Nathan, *Manager*
Nathan Ogden, *Manager*
EMP: 50
SALES (corp-wide): 295.8MM **Privately Held**
WEB: www.ballyfitnes.com
SIC: 7991 Health club
HQ: Bally Total Fitness Corporation
12440 Imperial Hwy # 300
Norwalk CA 90650
562 484-2000

(P-18615)
BAY CLUBS INC (HQ)
1 Lombard St, San Francisco (94111-1132)
PHONE 415 781-1874
Matthew Stevens, *President*
Annie Appel, *Exec VP*
Lisa Graf, *Exec VP*
Victor Woo, *Exec VP*
EMP: 77 **EST:** 2014
SALES: 32.2MM
SALES (corp-wide): 75.2MM **Privately Held**
SIC: 7991 7997 Physical fitness facilities; swimming club, membership; tennis club, membership; racquetball club, membership
PA: York Capital Management (Us) Advisors, L.P.
767 5th Ave Fl 17
New York NY 10153
212 300-1300

(P-18616)
BEING FIT INC
4971 Clairemont Dr Ste A, San Diego
(92117-2785)
PHONE 858 483-9294
Lennie Heck, *President*
EMP: 56
SALES (corp-wide): 700K **Privately Held**
WEB: www.beingfit.net
SIC: 7991 Aerobic dance & exercise classes
PA: Being Fit, Inc
8292 Mira Mesa Blvd
San Diego CA 92126
858 549-3456

(P-18617)
CALIFORNIA FAMILY HEALTH LLC
Also Called: California Family Fitness
8569 Bond Rd Ste 130, Elk Grove
(95624-9522)
PHONE 916 685-3355
Fax: 916 685-1995
Eric Sorenson, *Manager*
Dave Stauffer, *President*
EMP: 50
SALES (corp-wide): 18.2MM **Privately Held**
SIC: 7991 Health club
PA: California Family Health Llc
8680 Greenback Ln Ste 108
Orangevale CA 95662
916 987-2030

(P-18618)
CALISTOGA SPA INC
Also Called: Calistoga Spa Hot Springs
1006 Washington St, Calistoga
(94515-1499)
PHONE 707 942-6269
Fax: 707 942-4214
Bradley L Barrett, *President*
Michael Lennon, *General Mgr*
Diane Barrett, *Admin Sec*
EMP: 65
SQ FT: 50,000
SALES (est): 2.4MM **Privately Held**
WEB: www.calistogaspa.com
SIC: 7991 Spas

(P-18619)
CAPITOL FITNESS NETWORK LLC
Also Called: Gold's Gym
15333 State Highway 88, Jackson
(95642-9733)
PHONE 916 928-4999
Fax: 916 928-4908
Ron A Ask,
Robert Miller, *Controller*
Perry Thomas,
EMP: 96
SALES (est): 3.3MM **Privately Held**
SIC: 7991 Athletic club & gymnasiums, membership

(P-18620)
CASINO MORONGO RESORT SPA
49500 Seminole Dr, Cabazon
(92230-2202)
PHONE 951 846-5100
Angelica Martinez, *Principal*
Debbie Hermann, *Social Dir*
Lee Wolff, *Technician*
Robert Ferrell, *Human Res Dir*
Marlon Ortiz, *Director*
EMP: 58
SALES (est): 4.1MM **Privately Held**
SIC: 7991 Spas

(P-18621)
CLUBSPORT SAN RAMON LLC
Also Called: Oakwood Athletic Club
4000 Mt Diablo Blvd, Lafayette
(94549-3498)
PHONE 925 283-4000
Fax: 925 284-9612
Michael Reardon, *Manager*
Stefanie Balestrieri, *Manager*
EMP: 170
SQ FT: 63,749
SALES (corp-wide): 16.4MM **Privately Held**
WEB: www.clubsportsr.com
SIC: 7991 7997 Athletic club & gymnasiums, membership; membership sports & recreation clubs
PA: Clubsport San Ramon, Llc
350 Bollinger Canyon Ln
San Ramon CA 94582
925 735-1182

(P-18622)
CLUBSPORT SAN RAMON LLC (PA)
Also Called: Spa At Club Sport
350 Bollinger Canyon Ln, San Ramon
(94582-4592)
PHONE 925 735-7916
Fax: 925 735-1182
Dennis Garrison,
John Moore, *Partner*
Al Schaffer, *Partner*
Mike Reardon, *General Mgr*
Kari Gardella, *Admin Asst*
EMP: 170
SQ FT: 70,000
SALES (est): 15.9MM **Privately Held**
WEB: www.clubsportsr.com
SIC: 7991 Athletic club & gymnasiums, membership

(P-18623)
CRUNCH LLC
Also Called: Crunch Fitness
8000 W Sunset Blvd # 220, West Hollywood (90046-2442)
PHONE 323 654-4550
Fax: 323 654-3935
Amita Balla, *Branch Mgr*
Polly Belknap, *Opers Mgr*
James Maclean, *VP Sales*
EMP: 75
SALES (corp-wide): 87MM **Privately Held**
SIC: 7991 Physical fitness facilities
PA: Crunch, Llc
220 W 19th St
New York NY 10011
212 993-0300

(P-18624)
CRUNCH LLC
Also Called: Embarcadero, The
345 Spear St Ste 104, San Francisco
(94105-1659)
PHONE 415 495-1939
Mahogany Lenard, *Branch Mgr*
EMP: 895
SALES (corp-wide): 87MM **Privately Held**
SIC: 7991 Health club
PA: Crunch, Llc
220 W 19th St
New York NY 10011
212 993-0300

(P-18625)
CRUNCH FITNESS
2655 Erringer Rd, Simi Valley
(93065-1107)
PHONE 805 522-5454
Fax: 805 522-1128
Teresa Frost, *General Mgr*
Jen Reed, *Asst Mgr*
EMP: 65
SQ FT: 22,000
SALES (est): 1.7MM **Privately Held**
WEB: www.oakridgefitness.com
SIC: 7991 Athletic club & gymnasiums, membership

(P-18626)
DECATHLON CLUB INC
3250 Central Expy, Santa Clara
(95051-0873)
PHONE 408 738-2582
Fax: 408 738-0320
Kayte Bandcraft, *Manager*
Beverly Trefry, *Marketing Staff*
Wayne Brouchard, *Manager*
Jon Somerville, *Manager*
EMP: 200
SQ FT: 100,000
SALES (est): 5MM **Privately Held**
SIC: 7991 5812 Physical fitness clubs with training equipment; eating places

(P-18627)
DEEPAK CHOPRA LLC
2013 Costa Del Mar Rd, Carlsbad
(92009-6801)
PHONE 760 494-1600
Deepak Chopra,
Valencia Porter, *Director*
EMP: 50
SALES (est): 1.5MM **Privately Held**
WEB: www.chopra.com
SIC: 7991 Health club

(P-18628)
EHARMONY INC (PA)
Also Called: Eharmony.com
10900 Wilshire Blvd, Los Angeles
(90024-6501)
P.O. Box 241810 (90024-9610)
PHONE 424 258-1199
Neil Clark Warren, *CEO*
Greg Steiner, *President*
Cormac Twomey, *President*
Jeremy Verba, *CEO*
John Powers, *CFO*
EMP: 119
SQ FT: 6,000
SALES (est): 20.6MM **Privately Held**
WEB: www.eharmony.com
SIC: 7991 Aerobic dance & exercise classes

(P-18629)
EQUINOX-76TH STREET INC
301 Pine St, San Francisco (94104-3301)
PHONE 415 398-0747
Patrick Ahern, *Manager*
Jonathan Domoleczny, *General Mgr*
Kristina George, *CTO*
Holly Julier, *Teacher*
Delf Enriquez, *Athletic Dir*
EMP: 75
SALES (corp-wide): 10.6B **Privately Held**
SIC: 7991 Physical fitness facilities
HQ: Equinox-76th Street, Inc.
895 Broadway Fl 3
New York NY 10003
212 677-0180

(P-18630)
EXECUTIVE FITNESS MANAGEMENT
Also Called: World Gym Fitness Centers
226 E Palm Ave, Burbank (91502-1227)
P.O. Box 10997 (91510-0997)
PHONE 818 259-6753
Fax: 818 954-9980
Manny Kazanjian, *President*
EMP: 50
SALES (est): 568.9K **Privately Held**
SIC: 7991 Health club

(P-18631)
EXECUTIVES OUTLET INC
Also Called: Decatahalon Club
1 Lombard St Lbby, San Francisco
(94111-1127)
PHONE 415 433-6044
James Gerber, *President*
Sandra Hoeffer, *Vice Pres*
Mindy Steiner, *Vice Pres*
David Smith, *Admin Sec*
EMP: 150
SQ FT: 100,000
SALES: 7.8MM
SALES (corp-wide): 56.2MM **Privately Held**
SIC: 7991 7997 Athletic club & gymnasiums, membership; racquetball club, membership
HQ: W.A. Holding Company
1 Lombard St Lbby
San Francisco CA 94111
415 781-1874

(P-18632)
FITNESS 2000 INC
35145 Newark Blvd, Newark (94560-1219)
PHONE 510 791-2481
Mike Patel, *President*
Sonia Patel, *Principal*
Jay Patel, *Manager*
EMP: 50
SALES (est): 658.3K **Privately Held**
SIC: 7991 Health club

PRODUCTS & SERVICES SECTION

7991 - Physical Fitness Facilities County (P-18656)

(P-18633)
FITNESS INTERNATIONAL LLC
24491 Alicia Pkwy, Mission Viejo (92691-4506)
PHONE....................................949 421-6082
EMP: 50
SALES (corp-wide): 142MM **Privately Held**
SIC: 7991 Physical fitness clubs with training equipment
PA: Fitness International, Llc
3161 Michelson Dr Ste 600
Irvine CA 92612
949 255-7200

(P-18634)
FITNESS INTERNATIONAL LLC
Also Called: L A Fitness Sports Clubs
10535 Heater Ct, San Diego (92121-4111)
PHONE....................................858 550-5912
Fax: 858 550-5966
Joe Torrice, *Manager*
Barbara Cohen, *Manager*
EMP: 50
SALES (corp-wide): 142MM **Privately Held**
WEB: www.proresultsfit.com
SIC: 7991 Physical fitness clubs with training equipment
PA: Fitness International, Llc
3161 Michelson Dr Ste 600
Irvine CA 92612
949 255-7200

(P-18635)
FOCUS UP LLC
Also Called: Gold's Gym
4120 Dale Rd Ste G, Modesto (95356-9239)
PHONE....................................209 545-9055
David Knapp,
Judy Rinauro, *Bookkeeper*
EMP: 70 EST: 2001
SQ FT: 35,000
SALES (est): 3MM **Privately Held**
SIC: 7991 Athletic club & gymnasiums, membership

(P-18636)
GILROY FITNESS INC (PA)
Also Called: Gilroy Health and Fitness
8540 Church St, Gilroy (95020-4231)
PHONE....................................408 848-1234
Fax: 408 848-3400
Joe Gigantino, *President*
Ray Butler, *General Mgr*
Karen Fortino, *Training Spec*
Susie Douglas, *Director*
EMP: 50
SQ FT: 27,000
SALES (est): 1MM **Privately Held**
WEB: www.gilroyfitness.com
SIC: 7991 Health club

(P-18637)
GILROY FITNESS INC
8540 Church St, Gilroy (95020-4231)
PHONE....................................408 848-1234
David Jurevsch, *Manager*
EMP: 50
SALES (corp-wide): 1MM **Privately Held**
WEB: www.gilroyfitness.com
SIC: 7991 Physical fitness facilities
PA: Gilroy Fitness, Inc.
8540 Church St
Gilroy CA 95020
408 848-1234

(P-18638)
GOLDS GYM INTERNATIONAL INC
39 S Altadena Dr, Pasadena (91107-4256)
PHONE....................................626 304-1133
Fax: 626 304-1133
Frank Jordan, *Manager*
EMP: 55
SALES (corp-wide): 1.2B **Privately Held**
SIC: 7991 Physical fitness facilities
HQ: Gold's Gym International, Inc.
125 E J Carpentr Fwy 13
Irving TX 75062
972 444-8527

(P-18639)
HARBOR BAY CLUB INC
200 Packet Landing Rd, Alameda (94502-6599)
P.O. Box 1450 (94501-0158)
PHONE....................................510 521-5414
Fax: 510 521-5535
C Timothy Hoppen, *President*
Timothy Hoppen, *President*
Debbi Douglas, *Bd of Directors*
Lisa Young, *Cust Svc Dir*
Lori Bustos, *Master*
EMP: 83
SQ FT: 30,000
SALES (est): 2.9MM **Privately Held**
WEB: www.harborbayclub.com
SIC: 7991 5813 5941 5812 Athletic club & gymnasiums, membership; aerobic dance & exercise classes; bar (drinking places); golf goods & equipment; eating places
PA: Harbor Bay Club Associates, A California Limited Partnership
1141 Harbor Bay Pkwy Fl 2
Alameda CA 94502
510 769-5151

(P-18640)
HEALTHSPORT LTD A LTD PARTNR (PA)
Also Called: Healthsport-Arcata
300 Dr Martin Luther, Arcata (95521)
PHONE....................................707 822-3488
Susan Johnson, *Partner*
Doug Hartley, *General Mgr*
Stacey Morgan, *Admin Asst*
Jay Lang, *Controller*
Bill Spaeth, *Manager*
EMP: 110
SQ FT: 24,560
SALES (est): 5MM **Privately Held**
WEB: www.healthsport.com
SIC: 7991 Health club

(P-18641)
HERCULES FITNESS
600 Alfred Nobel Dr, Hercules (94547-1834)
PHONE....................................510 724-2900
Steve Buchanan, *Owner*
EMP: 50 EST: 2008
SALES (est): 851.2K **Privately Held**
SIC: 7991 Athletic club & gymnasiums, membership

(P-18642)
HOLLYWOOD SPA INC
Also Called: Hollywood Spa, The
5636 Vineland Ave, North Hollywood (91601-2028)
PHONE....................................323 464-0445
Fax: 323 464-0709
Rosa Klein, *CEO*
Peter D Sykes, *President*
Ricky Leanord, *Manager*
Ricky Lerner, *Manager*
EMP: 50
SQ FT: 20,000
SALES (est): 1.8MM **Privately Held**
WEB: www.hollywoodspa.com
SIC: 7991 Health club

(P-18643)
IN SHAPE MANAGEMENT COMPANY
Also Called: In Shape Health Clubs
6 S El Dorado St, Stockton (95202-2804)
PHONE....................................209 472-2231
Morton Rothbard, *President*
Paul Rothbard, *CEO*
Rob Farrens, *CFO*
EMP: 300
SQ FT: 60,000
SALES: 9MM **Privately Held**
SIC: 7991 Health club

(P-18644)
IN-SHAPE HEALTH CLUBS LLC (PA)
Also Called: In-Shape City
6 S El Dorado St Ste 700, Stockton (95202-2804)
PHONE....................................209 472-2231
Fax: 209 472-2235
Paul Rothbard, *CEO*
Morton Rothbard, *President*
Josh Lyon, *Senior VP*
Ingrid Owen, *Senior VP*
Rob Farrens, *Vice Pres*
EMP: 50
SQ FT: 60,000
SALES (est): 25.6MM **Privately Held**
WEB: www.inshapeclubs.com
SIC: 7991 Health club

(P-18645)
IN-SHAPE HEALTH CLUBS LLC
101 S Tracy Blvd, Tracy (95376-4620)
PHONE....................................209 836-2504
Robin Phillip, *Manager*
EMP: 113
SALES (corp-wide): 25.6MM **Privately Held**
WEB: www.inshapeclubs.com
SIC: 7991 Health club
PA: In-Shape Health Clubs, Llc
6 S El Dorado St Ste 700
Stockton CA 95202
209 472-2231

(P-18646)
INSTITUTE FOR ONE WORLD HEALTH
25 Taylor St 209, San Francisco (94102-3916)
PHONE....................................650 392-2510
Victoria G Hale, *Ch of Bd*
John Graves, *Director*
EMP: 50
SALES (est): 30.6MM **Privately Held**
SIC: 7991 Health club

(P-18647)
JAZZERCISE INC (PA)
2460 Impala Dr, Carlsbad (92010-7226)
PHONE....................................760 476-1750
Fax: 760 476-1788
Judi Sheppard Missett, *CEO*
Sally Baldridge, *CFO*
Shanna Missett Nelson, *Exec VP*
Janet Kreutner, *District Mgr*
Yvonne Wilske, *District Mgr*
EMP: 100
SQ FT: 24,228
SALES (est): 11.2MM **Privately Held**
WEB: www.jazzercise.com
SIC: 7991 6794 5961 Aerobic dance & exercise classes; franchises, selling or licensing; fitness & sporting goods, mail order

(P-18648)
JEFF STOVER INC
Also Called: Chico Sports Club
260 Cohasset Rd Ste 190, Chico (95926-2282)
PHONE....................................530 345-9427
Fax: 530 345-9499
Jeff Stover, *President*
Jimmie Purkey, *General Mgr*
Jason Rooks, *Opers Staff*
Jennifer Jellison, *Director*
EMP: 85
SQ FT: 11,000
SALES (est): 3.6MM **Privately Held**
WEB: www.chicosportsclub.com
SIC: 7991 7997 Health club; membership sports & recreation clubs

(P-18649)
KEISERS HOLDINGS LLC
411 S West Ave, Fresno (93706-1320)
PHONE....................................559 265-4700
Dennis Keiser,
EMP: 80
SALES (est): 622.2K **Privately Held**
SIC: 7991 Physical fitness facilities

(P-18650)
KENNEDY CLUB FITNESS
188 Tank Farm Rd, San Luis Obispo (93401-7528)
PHONE....................................805 781-3488
Fax: 805 781-3491
Brett Weaver,
Barbara Kennedy,
Kevin Kennedy,
EMP: 70
SQ FT: 50,000
SALES (est): 552.7K **Privately Held**
SIC: 7991 Athletic club & gymnasiums, membership

(P-18651)
L & O ALISO VIEJO LLC
Also Called: Renaissnce Clbsport Aliso Vejo
50 Enterprise, Aliso Viejo (92656-6026)
PHONE....................................949 643-6700
Ed Tomlin, *Mng Member*
Chris Collett, *Director*
EMP: 80
SALES (est): 2MM **Privately Held**
SIC: 7991 7011 Spas; hotels

(P-18652)
L A FITNESS INTL LLC
Also Called: L A Fitness Sports Clubs
1760 S Victoria Ave, Ventura (93003-6592)
PHONE....................................805 289-9907
Fax: 805 289-9913
Eric Bjerkens, *Manager*
Tim Belknap, *Manager*
EMP: 60
SALES (corp-wide): 142MM **Privately Held**
WEB: www.proresultsfit.com
SIC: 7991 Physical fitness facilities
PA: Fitness International, Llc
3161 Michelson Dr Ste 600
Irvine CA 92612
949 255-7200

(P-18653)
LA PETITE BALEEN INC
Also Called: La Petite Baleen Swim School
434 San Mateo Ave, San Bruno (94066-4417)
PHONE....................................650 588-7665
Fax: 650 588-7671
John Kolbisen, *Owner*
EMP: 80
SALES (corp-wide): 8.1MM **Privately Held**
WEB: www.swimplb.com
SIC: 7991 7999 Physical fitness facilities; swimming instruction
PA: La Petite Baleen, Inc
775 Main St
Half Moon Bay CA

(P-18654)
LEISURE SPORTS INC
Also Called: Clubsport of Fremont
46650 Landing Pkwy, Fremont (94538-6420)
PHONE....................................510 226-8500
Dan Detrick, *General Mgr*
Steve Volkamer, *Project Mgr*
John Odovanan, *Manager*
EMP: 200
SALES (corp-wide): 213MM **Privately Held**
WEB: www.leisuresportsinc.com
SIC: 7991 Athletic club & gymnasiums, membership
PA: Leisure Sports, Inc.
4670 Willow Rd Ste 100
Pleasanton CA 94588
925 600-1966

(P-18655)
LIVERMORE VALLEY TENNIS CLUB
2000 Arroyo Rd, Livermore (94550-6027)
PHONE....................................925 443-7700
Fax: 925 443-7789
Kim Fuller, *General Ptnr*
Roy Rasmussen, *General Ptnr*
Ann Dekay, *Corp Comm Staff*
Penny Halvorsen, *Manager*
Katherine Kozioziemski, *Manager*
EMP: 100 EST: 1972
SQ FT: 51,758
SALES: 3.1MM **Privately Held**
WEB: www.lvtc.com
SIC: 7991 5941 Athletic club & gymnasiums, membership; sporting goods & bicycle shops; tennis goods & equipment

(P-18656)
LOS ANGELES ATHLETIC CLUB INC
431 W 7th St, Los Angeles (90014-1691)
PHONE....................................213 625-2211

7991 - Physical Fitness Facilities County (P-18657)

PRODUDUCTS & SERVICES SECTION

Karen Hathaway, *President*
Bryan Cusworth, *CFO*
John Hathaway, *Vice Pres*
EMP: 175
SALES (est): 1.9MM
SALES (corp-wide): 18.8MM **Privately Held**
SIC: 7991 Athletic club & gymnasiums, membership
PA: Laaco, Ltd.
 431 W 7th St
 Los Angeles CA 90014
 213 622-1254

(P-18657)
MANUAL ARTS SVC CTR STUDNT BDY
3721 W Washington Blvd, Los Angeles (90018-1160)
PHONE.................323 732-0153
Jameni, *Principal*
EMP: 50
SALES (est): 86.8K **Privately Held**
SIC: 7991 Physical fitness facilities

(P-18658)
MARINER SQUARE ATHLETIC INC
2227 Mariner Square Loop, Alameda (94501-1021)
PHONE.................510 523-8011
Fax: 510 523-6196
Kathy Wagner, *President*
Christian Cornell, *Executive*
Diana Thomas, *General Mgr*
Kevin Truglio, *General Mgr*
Jeff Ray, *Human Res Dir*
EMP: 100 **EST:** 1975
SQ FT: 60,000
SALES (est): 4MM **Privately Held**
WEB: www.marinersq.com
SIC: 7991 7997 Athletic club & gymsiums, membership; membership sports & recreation clubs

(P-18659)
MAXIMUM FITNESS LLC
Also Called: Gold's Gym
135 Dobbins St, Vacaville (95688-3929)
PHONE.................707 447-0606
Fax: 707 447-7684
Richard A Martindale,
Teresa Conner, *General Mgr*
David Conner,
EMP: 50 **EST:** 1997
SQ FT: 27,000
SALES (est): 2.5MM **Privately Held**
SIC: 7991 Athletic club & gymnasiums, membership

(P-18660)
MERITAGE RESORT AND SPA
875 Bordeaux Way, NAPA (94558-7524)
PHONE.................707 259-0633
Fax: 707 254-8274
Timothy R Busch, *Principal*
Gina Blanda, *Executive*
Rosanna Hotchkiss, *Executive*
Evan Harrelson, *Office Mgr*
Pamela Dunn, *Info Tech Mgr*
EMP: 350
SALES (est): 15.8MM **Privately Held**
SIC: 7991 Spas

(P-18661)
MILLENIUM ATHLETIC CLUB LLC
Also Called: Goleta Valley Athletic Club
170 Los Carneros Way, Goleta (93117-3012)
PHONE.................805 562-3845
Fax: 805 685-8890
Jarrod Schwartz,
Rhonda Johnson, *Executive*
Gordon Schwartz,
Sean Yeager-Diamond, *Director*
David Arico, *Manager*
▲ **EMP:** 65 **EST:** 1996
SQ FT: 30,000
SALES (est): 3.1MM **Privately Held**
WEB: www.gvac.com
SIC: 7991 Athletic club & gymnasiums, membership

(P-18662)
MILLENNIUM PARTNERS SPORTS C
Also Called: Sports Club La The
747 Market St, San Francisco (94103-2001)
PHONE.................415 243-0492
Fax: 415 633-3909
Amie Skidmore, *General Mgr*
EMP: 500
SALES (corp-wide): 23.9MM **Privately Held**
SIC: 7991 Health club
PA: Millennium Partners Sports Club Management Llc
 7 Water St Ste 200
 Boston MA 02109
 617 476-8910

(P-18663)
MONIQUE SURACI
Also Called: Murrieta Day Spa
41885 Ivy St, Murrieta (92562-8607)
PHONE.................951 677-8111
Monique Suraci, *Owner*
EMP: 60
SALES: 1.7MM **Privately Held**
SIC: 7991 Spas

(P-18664)
MUSCLE IMPROVEMENT INC
Also Called: Gold's Gym
200 N Harbor Dr, Redondo Beach (90277-2507)
PHONE.................310 374-5522
Fax: 310 372-4741
Abe Tavera, *President*
Joe Coco, *Sales Mgr*
Eddie Gloyne, *Manager*
EMP: 70
SQ FT: 21,000
SALES (est): 3.2MM **Privately Held**
SIC: 7991 Athletic club & gymnasiums, membership

(P-18665)
MUSCLEBOUND INC
Also Called: Golds Gym
197 N Moorpark Rd, Thousand Oaks (91360-4401)
PHONE.................805 496-9331
Bill Holstein, *Manager*
EMP: 338 **Privately Held**
SIC: 7991 Physical fitness facilities
PA: Musclebound, Inc.
 19835 Nordhoff St
 Northridge CA 91324

(P-18666)
MV HOSPITALITY INC
Also Called: Mount View Hotel
1457 Lincoln Ave, Calistoga (94515-1417)
PHONE.................707 942-6877
Fax: 707 942-6904
Steve Carver, *Manager*
Mike Woods, *President*
Rick Howard, *Vice Pres*
Debbie Greene, *General Mgr*
Laurie Jordan, *General Mgr*
EMP: 50
SALES (est): 3.1MM **Privately Held**
WEB: www.mountviewhotel.com
SIC: 7991 7011 Spas; hotels

(P-18667)
PALA CASINO SPA & RESORT
35008 Pala Temecula Rd, Pala (92059-2419)
PHONE.................760 510-5100
Toll Free:..............877 -
Fax: 760 510-5191
Robert Smith, *Ch of Bd*
Garlon Banks, *President*
Bill Bembenek, *CEO*
Shauna Anton, *President*
Michael Crenshaw, *Vice Pres*
EMP: 1800 **EST:** 2000
SQ FT: 140,000
SALES (est): 84MM **Privately Held**
WEB: www.palacasino.com
SIC: 7991 Spas

(P-18668)
PALM CANYON RESORT & SPA
2800 S Palm Canyon Dr, Palm Springs (92264-9337)
PHONE.................760 866-1800
Fax: 760 866-1836
Carl Ellis, *Principal*
Kimberly Schaffe, *Personnel Exec*
Kim Schaeffer, *Manager*
EMP: 56 **EST:** 2004
SALES (est): 2.9MM **Privately Held**
WEB: www.palmcanyonresort.org
SIC: 7991 Spas

(P-18669)
PF WEST LLC
Also Called: Planet Fitness
101 Lucas Valley Rd # 150, San Rafael (94903-1791)
PHONE.................415 479-9600
Roger Bates, *Mng Member*
EMP: 105
SQ FT: 1,500
SALES (est): 2.8MM **Privately Held**
SIC: 7991 Physical fitness facilities

(P-18670)
PISMO BEACH ATHLETIC CLUB
1751 Price St, Pismo Beach (93449-2230)
PHONE.................805 773-3011
Fax: 805 773-3191
Henry F Myers, *President*
Don Wilson, *Administration*
EMP: 50
SALES (est): 1.7MM **Privately Held**
WEB: www.pbac.com
SIC: 7991 Health club

(P-18671)
PRESTON WYNNE SPA INC
14567 Big Basin Way A2, Saratoga (95070-6039)
PHONE.................408 741-1750
Fax: 408 741-5188
Peggy Wynne-Borgman, *President*
Melissa Stevens, *Chief Mktg Ofcr*
Laura Batchelor, *CTO*
Linh Vu, *Accounting Mgr*
Roxanne Cowan, *Controller*
EMP: 56
SQ FT: 4,700
SALES (est): 1.5MM **Privately Held**
WEB: www.prestonwynne.com
SIC: 7991 Spas

(P-18672)
PRIME TIME ATHLETIC CLUB INC
1730 Rollins Rd, Burlingame (94010-2297)
PHONE.................650 204-3662
Fax: 650 697-6003
John Michael, *President*
Ana Catalan, *Finance Mgr*
EMP: 80 **EST:** 1979
SQ FT: 35,000
SALES (est): 3.3MM **Privately Held**
WEB: www.primetimeathleticclub.com
SIC: 7991 Athletic club & gymnasiums, membership

(P-18673)
REACH FITNESS CLUB
1235 Radio Rd Ste 120, Redwood City (94065-1315)
PHONE.................650 327-3224
Darryl Brandon, *Branch Mgr*
Alicia Ambrosini, *Manager*
EMP: 55
SALES (corp-wide): 3.8MM **Privately Held**
WEB: www.reachfitness.com
SIC: 7991 5699 Health club; sports apparel
PA: Reach Fitness Club
 1235 Radio Rd Ste 120
 Redwood City CA 94065
 650 817-9050

(P-18674)
REDWOOD HEALTH CLUB (PA)
3101 S State St, Ukiah (95482-6938)
PHONE.................707 468-0441
Fax: 707 468-1262
Rob Marthe Deomont, *Partner*
Dena Krasts, *Director*
Pat Street, *Manager*
Cathy Toban, *Manager*
Kathy Tobin, *Manager*
EMP: 70
SQ FT: 20,000
SALES (est): 1.7MM **Privately Held**
WEB: www.redwoodhealthclub.com
SIC: 7991 7997 5812 5813 Health club; racquetball club, membership; tennis club, membership; snack bar; drinking places

(P-18675)
ROLLING WILLOW LLC
Also Called: Willow Creek Racquet Club
5555 Mariposa Ave, Citrus Heights (95610-7439)
PHONE.................916 961-6171
Fax: 916 961-1818
Tony Macias, *General Mgr*
EMP: 55
SALES (corp-wide): 2.2MM **Privately Held**
SIC: 7991 Aerobic dance & exercise classes; exercise salon
PA: Rolling Willow Llc
 9373 Winding Oak Dr
 Fair Oaks CA 95628
 916 988-1727

(P-18676)
SALUTARY SPORTS CLUBS INC
Also Called: Sports Club of El Dorado
4242 Sports Club Dr, Shingle Springs (95682-9546)
P.O. Box 659 (95682-0659)
PHONE.................530 677-5705
Fax: 530 677-0809
Don Lynd, *Manager*
EMP: 50
SALES (corp-wide): 8.7MM **Privately Held**
SIC: 7991 Physical fitness facilities
PA: Salutary Sports Clubs, Inc.
 3442 Browns Valley Rd # 100
 Vacaville CA 95688
 707 446-2350

(P-18677)
SALVATION ARMY
6845 University Ave, San Diego (92115-5829)
PHONE.................619 269-1404
Cindy Foley, *Principal*
James Knaggs, *President*
David Hudson, *Vice Pres*
Richard Chalk, *Administration*
Lorraine Pollock, *Accountant*
EMP: 300
SALES (est): 8.6MM **Privately Held**
SIC: 7991 8661 7032 7922 Physical fitness clubs with training equipment; miscellaneous denomination church; sporting & recreational camps; community theater production

(P-18678)
SAN FRANCISCO TENNIS CLUB
645 5th St, San Francisco (94107-1516)
PHONE.................415 777-9000
Fax: 415 777-4325
Jim Hinckley, *President*
Thomas Kanar, *Corp Secy*
Dennis Gibson, *Top Exec*
Jeffrey Jahnke, *Vice Pres*
Jeff Janke, *Vice Pres*
EMP: 100
SQ FT: 300,000
SALES: 209.4K
SALES (corp-wide): 1B **Publicly Held**
WEB: www.sftennis.com
SIC: 7991 7997 5813 Physical fitness facilities; membership sports & recreation clubs; drinking places
HQ: Clubcorp Usa, Inc.
 3030 Lyndon B Johnson Fwy
 Dallas TX 75234
 972 243-6191

(P-18679)
SANTA CLARITA ATHLETIC CLUB
23942 Lyons Ave Ste 106, Newhall (91321-2475)
PHONE.................661 255-3365
Charles Hamilton, *President*
Michelle Marbach, *Vice Pres*

PRODUCTS & SERVICES SECTION

7991 - Physical Fitness Facilities County (P-18702)

Ann Hamilton, *Admin Sec*
EMP: 78
SQ FT: 64,000
SALES: 5MM **Privately Held**
WEB: www.santaclaritaathleticclub.com
SIC: 7991 5812 8699 Physical fitness clubs with training equipment; athletic club & gymnasiums, membership; cafe; athletic organizations

(P-18680)
SANTEE SYSTEMS SERVICES II LL
229 E Gage Ave, Los Angeles (90003-1533)
PHONE 323 445-0044
EMP: 50 **EST:** 2012
SQ FT: 10,000
SALES (est): 1.4MM **Privately Held**
SIC: 7991

(P-18681)
SIM INVESTMENT CORPORATION
Also Called: Right Stuff Health Club, The
1329 Blossom Hill Rd, San Jose (95118-3801)
PHONE 408 445-3310
Fax: 408 445-1091
Enrico Dileonardo, *General Mgr*
EMP: 60
SALES (corp-wide): 8.3MM **Privately Held**
SIC: 7991 Health club
PA: S.I.M. Investment Corporation
1600 W Campbell Ave # 102
Campbell CA 95008
408 874-0610

(P-18682)
SK SANCTUARY DAY SPA SALON LLC
6919 La Jolla Blvd, La Jolla (92037-5427)
PHONE 858 459-2400
Fax: 858 458-4344
Steven Krant, *Mng Member*
Lyn Krant,
Stephen M Krant, *Director*
Sylvia Lopez, *Director*
EMP: 50
SALES (est): 2.4MM **Privately Held**
WEB: www.sk-sanctuary.com
SIC: 7991 Spas

(P-18683)
SOULCYCLE INC
3874 Cross Creek Rd, Malibu (90265-4933)
PHONE 310 973-7685
EMP: 775 **Privately Held**
SIC: 7991 Physical fitness facilities
PA: Soulcycle Inc.
609 Greenwich St Fl Grnd
New York NY 10014

(P-18684)
SPA CAS PALMAS
Also Called: Spa Las Palmas of Marriot Intl
41000 Bob Hope Dr, Rancho Mirage (92270-4416)
PHONE 760 836-3106
Dawn Ferraro, *Exec Dir*
EMP: 50
SALES (est): 848.7K **Privately Held**
SIC: 7991 Spas

(P-18685)
SPA DREAMS
6419 Hesperia Ave, Reseda (91335-6225)
PHONE 818 298-1120
Yvette Vink, *Owner*
EMP: 100
SALES: 350K **Privately Held**
SIC: 7991 Spas

(P-18686)
SPA HAVENS LP
Also Called: Cal-A-Vie
29402 Spa Haven Way, Vista (92084-2234)
PHONE 760 945-2055
John Havens, *Owner*
Gary McGivoney, *Vice Pres*
Curtis Cooke, *Executive*
Ashley Chabaud, *Executive Asst*
Bret Rotheram, *Info Tech Mgr*
▲ **EMP:** 105
SALES (est): 7.8MM **Privately Held**
WEB: www.calavie.com
SIC: 7991 Spas

(P-18687)
SPA PARTNERS INC
Also Called: Mount View Spa
1457 Lincoln Ave, Calistoga (94515-1417)
PHONE 707 942-5789
Fax: 707 942-9165
Thomas M Gottlieb, *President*
EMP: 50
SALES: 4.2MM **Privately Held**
SIC: 7991 Spas

(P-18688)
SPAD HOLDINGS LLC
Also Called: Total Woman - Westlake Village
966 S Westlake Blvd Ste 4, Westlake Village (91361-3153)
PHONE 805 496-9978
Fax: 805 496-4999
Natalie Roberts, *Branch Mgr*
Meghan Temple, *Graphic Designe*
Jill Johnson, *Sales Dir*
Larissa Solomos, *Manager*
Nicole Cole, *Supervisor*
EMP: 70
SALES (corp-wide): 20MM **Privately Held**
WEB: www.totalwomanspa.com
SIC: 7991 Physical fitness clubs with training equipment; spas
HQ: Spad Holdings, Llc
10805 Rnch Bernardo Rd120 Ste 120
San Diego CA 92127
805 449-1005

(P-18689)
SPAD HOLDINGS LLC
24245 Magic Mountain Pkwy, Valencia (91355-3401)
PHONE 661 286-0229
Carol Steen, *Branch Mgr*
EMP: 60
SALES (corp-wide): 20MM **Privately Held**
SIC: 7991 Physical fitness facilities
HQ: Spad Holdings, Llc
10805 Rnch Bernardo Rd120 Ste 120
San Diego CA 92127
805 449-1005

(P-18690)
SPAD HOLDINGS LLC
Also Called: Total Woman - Placentia
860 N Rose Dr, Placentia (92870-7522)
PHONE 714 993-6003
Lori Colagrossi, *Branch Mgr*
EMP: 50
SALES (corp-wide): 20MM **Privately Held**
WEB: www.totalwomanspa.com
SIC: 7991 Physical fitness clubs with training equipment; spas
HQ: Spad Holdings, Llc
10805 Rnch Bernardo Rd120 Ste 120
San Diego CA 92127
805 449-1005

(P-18691)
SPAD HOLDINGS LLC
Also Called: Total Woman - Irvine
14280 Culver Dr Ste B, Irvine (92604-0347)
PHONE 949 733-0473
Mary Gladwill, *Branch Mgr*
Janis Nicholls, *Sales Staff*
Delia Bayna, *Manager*
Jessica Dunn, *Manager*
EMP: 70
SALES (corp-wide): 20MM **Privately Held**
WEB: www.totalwomanspa.com
SIC: 7991 Physical fitness clubs with training equipment; spas
HQ: Spad Holdings, Llc
10805 Rnch Bernardo Rd120 Ste 120
San Diego CA 92127
805 449-1005

(P-18692)
SPAD HOLDINGS LLC
Also Called: Total Woman - Warner Center
6100 Topanga Canyon Blvd # 1310, Woodland Hills (91367-3627)
PHONE 818 710-7606
Gina Licali, *Branch Mgr*
Alexis Rocha, *Supervisor*
EMP: 70
SALES (corp-wide): 20MM **Privately Held**
WEB: www.totalwomanspa.com
SIC: 7991 Physical fitness clubs with training equipment; spas
HQ: Spad Holdings, Llc
10805 Rnch Bernardo Rd120 Ste 120
San Diego CA 92127
805 449-1005

(P-18693)
SPAD HOLDINGS LLC
Also Called: Total Woman - Northridge
19456 Nordhoff St, Northridge (91324-2417)
PHONE 818 772-8900
Floretta Love, *Branch Mgr*
EMP: 70
SALES (corp-wide): 20MM **Privately Held**
WEB: www.totalwomanspa.com
SIC: 7991 Physical fitness clubs with training equipment; spas
HQ: Spad Holdings, Llc
10805 Rnch Bernardo Rd120 Ste 120
San Diego CA 92127
805 449-1005

(P-18694)
SPAD HOLDINGS LLC
Also Called: Total Woman - Glendale
601 N Brand Blvd, Glendale (91203-1211)
PHONE 818 552-2027
Fax: 818 552-2151
Teryn Radvany, *Branch Mgr*
EMP: 70
SALES (corp-wide): 20MM **Privately Held**
WEB: www.totalwomanspa.com
SIC: 7991 Physical fitness clubs with training equipment; spas
HQ: Spad Holdings, Llc
10805 Rnch Bernardo Rd120 Ste 120
San Diego CA 92127
805 449-1005

(P-18695)
SPORT CENTER FITNESS INC
Also Called: King Harbor Sports Center
819 N Harbor Dr, Redondo Beach (90277-2006)
PHONE 310 376-9443
Fax: 310 376-0696
Michael Marinelli, *President*
Melissa Coindreau, *Office Mgr*
EMP: 73
SQ FT: 25,000
SALES (est): 2.6MM **Privately Held**
WEB: www.sportcenterfitness.com
SIC: 7991 7999 Health club; tennis courts, outdoor/indoor: non-membership

(P-18696)
SPORTSMEN OF STANISLAUS INC
Also Called: S O S Club
819 Sunset Ave, Modesto (95351-3756)
P.O. Box 3031 (95353-3031)
PHONE 209 578-5801
Fax: 209 578-1389
Aaron Andrews, *General Mgr*
Bryan Manley, *Ch of Bd*
Mike Eger, *Vice Pres*
Emily Kennerly, *Personnel Exec*
Clive Riddle, *Commissioner*
EMP: 100
SQ FT: 70,000
SALES: 1.1MM **Privately Held**
SIC: 7991 5812 8641 7997 Athletic club & gymnasiums, membership; eating places; civic social & fraternal associations; membership sports & recreation clubs; drinking places

(P-18697)
SWEETWATER GARDENS INC
955 Ukiah, Mendocino (95460)
P.O. Box 337 (95460-0337)
PHONE 707 937-4140
Fax: 707 937-0727
John Carl Fliessbach, *President*
John Fleissbach, *CFO*
EMP: 50
SQ FT: 1,250
SALES (est): 1.2MM **Privately Held**
SIC: 7991 5499 7011 7299 Spas; juices, fruit or vegetable; motels; massage parlor

(P-18698)
TENNIS PRO SHOP
819 Sunset Ave, Modesto (95351-3756)
P.O. Box 3031 (95353-3031)
PHONE 209 529-2446
Daivid Massa, *General Mgr*
EMP: 50 **EST:** 1958
SALES (est): 324.7K **Privately Held**
WEB: www.sosclub.org
SIC: 7991 Physical fitness facilities

(P-18699)
THINK TOGETHER
12016 Telegraph Rd, Santa Fe Springs (90670-3784)
PHONE 562 236-3835
EMP: 877
SALES (corp-wide): 52.4MM **Privately Held**
SIC: 7991 Physical fitness facilities
PA: Think Together
2101 E 4th St Ste 200b
Santa Ana CA 92705
714 543-3807

(P-18700)
TOTAL WOMAN
860 N Rose Dr, Placentia (92870-7522)
PHONE 714 993-6003
Lori Colagrossi, *Manager*
Cheryle Bujarski, *Sales Staff*
EMP: 65
SALES (est): 989.7K **Privately Held**
SIC: 7991 Physical fitness facilities

(P-18701)
VILLAGIO INN & SPA LLC
6481 Washington St, Yountville (94599-1331)
PHONE 707 944-8877
Fax: 707 944-8855
Kerry Egan, *Mng Member*
Caitlyn McPherson, *Admin Asst*
Eric Wallace, *Info Tech Mgr*
Linda Neville, *Controller*
Veronica Castorena, *Human Res Dir*
▲ **EMP:** 200
SALES (est): 13.3MM **Privately Held**
WEB: www.villagio.com
SIC: 7991 Spas

(P-18702)
WESTERN ATHLETIC CLUBS INC (DH)
1 Lombard St Lbby, San Francisco (94111-1127)
PHONE 415 781-1874
Matthew Stevens, *President*
Monica Semolic, *President*
Lisa Graf, *Senior VP*
Victor Woo, *Senior VP*
David D Smith, *Admin Sec*
▲ **EMP:** 116 **EST:** 1978
SQ FT: 10,000
SALES (est): 28.5MM
SALES (corp-wide): 56.2MM **Privately Held**
WEB: www.pacclub.com
SIC: 7991 7997 5812 5699 Physical fitness facilities; swimming club, membership; tennis club, membership; racquetball club, membership; eating places; sports apparel; sporting goods & bicycle shops
HQ: W.A. Holding Company
1 Lombard St Lbby
San Francisco CA 94111
415 781-1874

7991 - Physical Fitness Facilities County (P-18703)

PRODUCTS & SERVICES SECTION

(P-18703)
WESTERN ATHLETIC CLUBS INC
Also Called: Bay Club Marin
220 Corte Madera Town Ctr, Corte Madera (94925-1208)
PHONE.................................415 945-3000
Fax: 415 945-0722
Maegan Devlin, *Manager*
Annie Appel, *Mktg Dir*
Jeff McMullen, *Director*
EMP: 75
SALES (corp-wide): 56.2MM Privately Held
WEB: www.pacclub.com
SIC: 7991 Athletic club & gymnasiums, membership
HQ: Western Athletic Clubs, Inc.
1 Lombard St Lbby
San Francisco CA 94111
415 781-1874

(P-18704)
WESTERN ATHLETIC CLUBS INC
Also Called: Decathlon Club
3250 Central Expy, Santa Clara (95051-0828)
PHONE.................................408 738-2582
Erin Rucker, *Manager*
EMP: 100
SALES (corp-wide): 56.2MM Privately Held
WEB: www.pacclub.com
SIC: 7991 7997 5813 5812 Athletic club & gymnasiums, membership; membership sports & recreation clubs; drinking places; eating places
HQ: Western Athletic Clubs, Inc.
1 Lombard St Lbby
San Francisco CA 94111
415 781-1874

(P-18705)
WESTERN ATHLETIC CLUBS INC
Also Called: Sanctuary, The
200 Redwood Shr Pkwy, Redwood City (94065-1100)
PHONE.................................650 593-1112
Fax: 650 593-3106
Erin Cker, *Manager*
Megan Binkley, *Managing Prtnr*
Terry Romero, *General Mgr*
Frank Schmidt, *Opers Staff*
Charlie Pederson, *Sales Dir*
EMP: 88
SALES (corp-wide): 56.2MM Privately Held
WEB: www.pacclub.com
SIC: 7991 7997 5812 5699 Physical fitness facilities; swimming club, membership; tennis club, membership; racquetball club, membership; eating places; sports apparel; sporting goods & bicycle shops
HQ: Western Athletic Clubs, Inc.
1 Lombard St Lbby
San Francisco CA 94111
415 781-1874

(P-18706)
WESTLAKE NAIL SPA
233 Lake Merced Blvd, Daly City (94015-3113)
PHONE.................................650 994-7777
Loi Duong, *Owner*
EMP: 68
SALES (est): 687.1K Privately Held
SIC: 7991 Spas

(P-18707)
WI SPA LLC
2700 Wilshire Blvd, Los Angeles (90057-3202)
PHONE.................................213 487-2700
Stuart Whang,
Jonathan Suh, *Manager*
EMP: 50
SALES (est): 1.3MM Privately Held
SIC: 7991 Spas

(P-18708)
XI ENTERPRISE INC
2140 E Palmdale Blvd, Palmdale (93550-1202)
PHONE.................................661 266-3200
Shah Roshan, *CEO*
Rene Maldonado, *Controller*
EMP: 75
SALES (est): 1.1MM Privately Held
SIC: 7991 Physical fitness facilities

(P-18709)
YOGA WORKS INC (PA)
Also Called: Yogaworks
2215 Main St, Santa Monica (90405-2217)
PHONE.................................310 664-6470
Fax: 310 656-5892
Phillip Swain, *CEO*
Jay Decoons, *President*
Amber Hazor, *President*
Mike Leonard, *Regional Mgr*
Billy Yost, *Info Tech Mgr*
EMP: 50
SQ FT: 6,000
SALES (est): 10.5MM Privately Held
SIC: 7991 5961 5651 Exercise salon; mail order house; unisex clothing stores

7992 Public Golf Courses

(P-18710)
ALONDRA GOLF COURSE INC
Also Called: Three Rivers Golf Course
16400 Prairie Ave, Lawndale (90260-3037)
PHONE.................................310 217-9915
Steve OH, *President*
Suzette Pascasio, *Accountant*
Bing Longakit, *Controller*
EMP: 52
SQ FT: 12,000
SALES (est): 2.9MM Privately Held
SIC: 7992 5941 5812 Public golf courses; golf goods & equipment; restaurant, family: independent

(P-18711)
AMERICAN GOLF CORPORATION
Also Called: Lakewood Country Club
3101 Carson St, Lakewood (90712-4005)
PHONE.................................562 421-0550
Fax: 562 496-1315
Gary Kossick, *General Mgr*
EMP: 50
SALES (corp-wide): 509.6MM Privately Held
WEB: www.americangolf.com
SIC: 7992 7997 Public golf courses; golf club, membership
PA: American Golf Corporation
6080 Center Dr Ste 500
Los Angeles CA 90045
310 664-4000

(P-18712)
AMERICAN GOLF CORPORATION
Also Called: Wood Ranch Golf Club
301 Wood Ranch Pkwy, Simi Valley (93065-6600)
PHONE.................................805 527-9663
Fax: 805 526-6679
Mark Kelly, *Manager*
Michael Bratcher, *General Mgr*
EMP: 70
SALES (corp-wide): 509.6MM Privately Held
WEB: www.americangolf.com
SIC: 7992 7997 7299 Public golf courses; golf club, membership; banquet hall facilities
PA: American Golf Corporation
6080 Center Dr Ste 500
Los Angeles CA 90045
310 664-4000

(P-18713)
AMERICAN GOLF CORPORATION
Also Called: Coyote Hills Golf Course
1440 E Bastanchury Rd, Fullerton (92835-2822)
PHONE.................................714 672-6800

Fax: 714 672-6808
Brent Boznanski, *Manager*
Mike Shank, *Manager*
Mark Kuramoto, *Asst Mgr*
Josh McDonald, *Asst Mgr*
EMP: 100
SALES (corp-wide): 509.6MM Privately Held
WEB: www.americangolf.com
SIC: 7992 7997 7299 5812 Public golf courses; membership sports & recreation clubs; banquet hall facilities; eating places
PA: American Golf Corporation
6080 Center Dr Ste 500
Los Angeles CA 90045
310 664-4000

(P-18714)
ANTIOCH PUBLIC GOLF CORP
Also Called: LONE TREE GOLF COURSE
4800 Golf Course Rd, Antioch (94531-8012)
P.O. Box 2115 (94531-2115)
PHONE.................................925 706-4220
Fax: 925 706-7709
Ollie Anderson, *President*
Ron Parish, *Exec Dir*
Pat King, *Finance*
Beth Schmidt, *Controller*
EMP: 58
SALES: 3MM Privately Held
SIC: 7992 5941 7999 5812 Public golf courses; golf goods & equipment; golf driving range; restaurant, family: independent

(P-18715)
BARONA CREEK GOLF CLUB
1932 Wildcat Canyon Rd, Lakeside (92040-1553)
PHONE.................................619 387-7018
Fax: 619 390-8931
Clifford Lachappa, *Chairman*
Dean Allen, *CFO*
Mike Murphy, *Info Tech Mgr*
Mary Mackey, *Software Dev*
Dawn Michel, *Project Mgr*
EMP: 60
SALES (est): 3.1MM Privately Held
SIC: 7992 Public golf courses

(P-18716)
BIG SKY COUNTRY CLUB LLC
Also Called: Lost Canyons Golf Course
3301 Lost Canyons Dr, Simi Valley (93063-7168)
PHONE.................................805 522-4653
Fax: 805 522-1389
Jay Collaite,
Liz Leaver, *Controller*
Barbara Glodfelty, *Mktg Dir*
Mike Metz, *Property Mgr*
New Delos Ptnr,
EMP: 100
SQ FT: 30,000
SALES (est): 3.1MM Privately Held
WEB: www.lostcanyons.com
SIC: 7992 5941 5812 Public golf courses; golf, tennis & ski shops; eating places

(P-18717)
BLACK GOLD GOLF CLUB
1 Black Gold Dr, Yorba Linda (92886-2383)
PHONE.................................714 961-0060
Fax: 714 993-9472
Eric Lohman, *General Mgr*
Gustavo Marin, *Executive*
David Bosak, *Controller*
Todd Elder, *Sales Dir*
Elizabeth Mahler, *Sales Mgr*
EMP: 90
SALES (est): 3.1MM Privately Held
SIC: 7992 Public golf courses

(P-18718)
BSL GOLF CORP
Also Called: Bayonet/Blackhorse Golf Course
1 Mcclure Way, Seaside (93955-7100)
PHONE.................................831 899-7271
Fax: 831 899-7169
Joe Priddy, *Manager*
Jennifer Cushman, *Administration*
EMP: 150

SALES (corp-wide): 12.3MM Privately Held
WEB: www.bayonetblackhorse.com
SIC: 7992 Public golf courses
PA: Bsl Golf Corp.
402 Heights Blvd
Houston TX 77007
713 522-4547

(P-18719)
CALIFORNIA FUJI INTERNATIONAL
Also Called: Malibu Country Club
901 Encinal Canyon Rd, Malibu (90265-2405)
P.O. Box 3126, Westlake Village (91359-0126)
PHONE.................................818 889-6680
Fax: 818 889-6683
Norihisa Koda, *General Mgr*
Takashi Nozu, *President*
Motohiro Nozu, *Vice Pres*
EMP: 50
SQ FT: 11,000
SALES: 4MM
SALES (corp-wide): 13.6MM Privately Held
WEB: www.malibucountryclub.net
SIC: 7992 5812 Public golf courses; eating places
PA: Tokyo Leisure Development Co.,Ltd.
10-2, Nihombashikoamicho
Chuo-Ku TKY 103-0
336 692-964

(P-18720)
CHAMPIONSHIP GOLF SERVICES INC
2340 Silver Oak Cir, Corona (92882-6025)
P.O. Box 79156 (92877-0171)
PHONE.................................951 272-4340
Steven Plummer, *President*
EMP: 145
SALES: 5.9MM Privately Held
SIC: 7992 Public golf courses

(P-18721)
CHAPMAN GOLF DEVELOPMENT LLC
Also Called: TRADITION GOLF CLUB
78505 Avenue 52, La Quinta (92253-2802)
PHONE.................................760 564-8723
David Chapman, *Mng Member*
Jose Sanchez, *Executive*
Heidi Risk, *General Mgr*
Kay Larson, *Sales Staff*
Beth Bland, *Hlthcr Dir*
EMP: 100
SALES: 11.3MM Privately Held
SIC: 7992 Public golf courses

(P-18722)
CITY OF CONCORD
4050 Port Chicago Hwy, Concord (94520-1121)
PHONE.................................925 686-6262
Joe Fernandez, *Manager*
Rod Kilcoyne, *VP Mktg*
EMP: 60
SQ FT: 3,200 Privately Held
WEB: www.cpd.ci.concord.ca.us
SIC: 7992 9111 Public golf courses; mayors' offices
PA: City Of Concord
1950 Parkside Dr
Concord CA 94519
925 671-3000

(P-18723)
CITY OF DELANO
Also Called: City Corporation Yard
725 S Lexington St, Delano (93215-3617)
PHONE.................................661 721-3350
Phil Newhouse, *Branch Mgr*
Craig Wilson, *Vice Pres*
EMP: 50
SIC: 7992 Public golf courses
PA: City Of Delano
1015 11th Ave
Delano CA 93215
661 721-3300

PRODUCTS & SERVICES SECTION

7992 - Public Golf Courses County (P-18746)

(P-18724)
CITY OF OXNARD
Also Called: River Ridge Gulf Course
2401 W Vineyard Ave, Oxnard (93036-2218)
PHONE..................805 983-4653
Fax: 805 981-4653
Otto Kenny, *General Mgr*
EMP: 100 **Privately Held**
WEB: www.oxnardtourism.com
SIC: 7992 Public golf courses
PA: City Of Oxnard
300 W 3rd St Uppr Fl4
Oxnard CA 93030
805 385-7803

(P-18725)
CITY OF PASADENA
Also Called: Brookside Golf Course
1133 Rosemont Ave, Pasadena (91103-2401)
PHONE..................626 543-4708
EMP: 60 **Privately Held**
SIC: 7992 9111
PA: City Of Pasadena
100 N Garfield Ave
Pasadena CA 91101
626 744-4386

(P-18726)
CLUBCORP USA INC
Also Called: Turkey Creek Golf Club
1525 Highway 193, Lincoln (95648-9639)
PHONE..................916 434-9100
Fax: 916 434-9477
Brent Cohen, *Manager*
EMP: 50
SALES (corp-wide): 1B **Publicly Held**
WEB: www.remington-gc.com
SIC: 7992 5941 5813 5812 Public golf courses; sporting goods & bicycle shops; drinking places; eating places
HQ: Clubcorp Usa, Inc.
3030 Lyndon B Johnson Fwy
Dallas TX 75234
972 243-6191

(P-18727)
COUNTY OF LOS ANGELES
Also Called: Parks and Recreation Dept
1875 Fairplex Dr, Pomona (91768-1240)
PHONE..................909 629-1166
Chad Hackman, *General Mgr*
EMP: 55 **Privately Held**
WEB: www.co.la.ca.us
SIC: 7992 9512 7299 Public golf courses; recreational program administration, government; ; wedding chapel, privately operated
PA: County Of Los Angeles
500 W Temple St Ste 375
Los Angeles CA 90012
213 974-1101

(P-18728)
COYOTE CREEK GOLF CLUB
1 Coyote Creek Golf Dr, Morgan Hill (95037-9052)
P.O. Box 2527 (95038-2527)
PHONE..................408 463-1400
Fax: 408 463-8318
Stephan Vigiano, *General Mgr*
Erin Horan, *Accountant*
Hae Y Lee, *Director*
Don Leone, *Director*
Kristy Park, *Manager*
EMP: 75
SQ FT: 12,000
SALES (est): 5.5MM **Privately Held**
WEB: www.coyotecreekgolf.com
SIC: 7992 5812 5941 Public golf courses; eating places; sporting goods & bicycle shops

(P-18729)
CROCKETT & COINC
Also Called: Bonita Golf Club
5540 Sweetwater Rd, Bonita (91902-2137)
PHONE..................619 267-1103
Clayton Crockett, *Principal*
Brian Steppe, *Opers Staff*
Marc S Schechter, *Agent*
Norma Maynard, *Relations*
Jesus Murillo, *Asst Supt*
EMP: 56

SALES (corp-wide): 5.2MM **Privately Held**
WEB: www.bonitagolfclub.com
SIC: 7992 5812 Public golf courses; eating places
PA: Crockett & Co.Inc.
5120 Robinwood Rd Ste A22
Bonita CA 91902
619 267-6410

(P-18730)
CRSTB PARTNERS LLC
Also Called: Twelve Bridges Golf Club
3075 Twelve Bridges Dr, Lincoln (95648)
PHONE..................916 645-7200
Fax: 916 645-6729
Chris S Member, *Principal*
EMP: 110
SALES (est): 4.7MM **Privately Held**
SIC: 7992 Public golf courses

(P-18731)
CYPRESS RIDGE GOLF COURSE
780 Cypress Ridge Pkwy, Arroyo Grande (93420-6524)
PHONE..................805 474-7979
Fax: 805 474-7975
Dennis Sullivan, *Owner*
Jodi Sailors, *Relations*
EMP: 50
SALES (est): 1.6MM **Privately Held**
SIC: 7992 6531 Public golf courses; real estate agents & managers

(P-18732)
D C GOLF A CA PARTNERSHIP
Also Called: Eaton Canyon Golf Course
1456 E Mendocino St, Altadena (91001-2600)
PHONE..................626 797-3821
Fax: 626 797-6071
Doug Colliflower, *Managing Prtnr*
EMP: 50
SQ FT: 6,000
SALES (est): 3.4MM **Privately Held**
WEB: www.dcgolf.info
SIC: 7992 5812 Public golf courses; American restaurant

(P-18733)
DAVID CHAPMAN INVESTMENTS LLC
78-505 Old Avenue 52, La Quinta (92253)
PHONE..................760 564-3355
David Chapman,
Julie Harris, *Human Res Mgr*
EMP: 100
SALES (est): 1.3MM **Privately Held**
WEB: www.davidchapman.com
SIC: 7992 Public golf courses

(P-18734)
DIABLO COUNTRY CLUB
Also Called: Golf Pro. Shop
1700 Clubhouse Rd, Diablo (94528)
PHONE..................925 837-9233
Fax: 925 837-4711
Larry Marx, *General Mgr*
Kris Nicholson, *Admin Asst*
Alan Alvistur, *Director*
EMP: 50
SQ FT: 38,199
SALES (est): 1.2MM **Privately Held**
SIC: 7992 Public golf courses

(P-18735)
DONOVAN BROS GOLF LLC
Also Called: Tierra Rejada Golf Course
15187 Tierra Rejada Rd, Moorpark (93021-9756)
PHONE..................805 531-9300
Fax: 805 531-9303
Michael Donovan,
Jerry Crumpler,
Ted Kruger,
Brian Durtschi, *Manager*
Fernando Gonzalez, *Superintendent*
EMP: 60
SALES (est): 3MM **Privately Held**
WEB: www.donovanbrosgolf.com
SIC: 7992 Public golf courses

(P-18736)
DONOVAN GOLF COURSES MGT
Also Called: Western Hills Golf & Cntry CLB
1800 Carbon Canyon Rd, Chino (91708)
PHONE..................714 528-6400
Michael Donovan, *General Mgr*
Kristine Smith, *Assistant*
EMP: 50
SALES (corp-wide): 5.8MM **Privately Held**
WEB: www.willowickgolf.com
SIC: 7992 Public golf courses
PA: Donovan Golf Courses Management, Inc
3017 W 5th St
Santa Ana CA 92703
714 554-0672

(P-18737)
EAGLE GLEN COUNTRY CLUB LLC
Also Called: Eagle Glen Golf Club
1800 Eagle Glen Pkwy, Corona (92883-0620)
PHONE..................951 272-4653
Fax: 909 278-1558
Jim Previty, *Chairman*
Lynn Labella, *Technology*
Lindsay McCarthy, *Controller*
Tiffany Elsner, *Sales Mgr*
EMP: 60
SQ FT: 26,000
SALES (est): 4.4MM **Privately Held**
WEB: www.eaglegiengc.com
SIC: 7992 Public golf courses

(P-18738)
EL PRADO GOLF COURSE LP
6555 Pine Ave, Chino (91708-9192)
PHONE..................909 597-1751
Fax: 909 393-5061
Bruce Jenke, *General Ptnr*
Anthony Foo, *Partner*
G Barton Heuler, *Partner*
Walter Heuler, *Partner*
Kevin Knutson, *Mktg Dir*
EMP: 80
SQ FT: 5,000
SALES (est): 4.9MM **Privately Held**
SIC: 7992 Public golf courses

(P-18739)
EMPIRE GOLF INC (PA)
Also Called: Fairgrounds Golf Center
14670 Cantova Way Ste 228, Rancho Murieta (95683-9009)
P.O. Box 689, Sloughhouse (95683-0689)
PHONE..................916 314-3150
Rod Metzler, *President*
Cliff Rourke, *Senior Mgr*
EMP: 75
SQ FT: 1,500
SALES (est): 5.8MM **Privately Held**
SIC: 7992 8742 Public golf courses; business consultant

(P-18740)
FOUNTAIN GROVE GOLF & ATHC CLB
1525 Fountaingrove Pkwy, Santa Rosa (95403-1778)
PHONE..................707 521-3207
Greg Sabens, *Manager*
Creg Huver, *General Mgr*
Darren Howey, *Athletic Dir*
Margo Zatkovich, *Director*
EMP: 75
SQ FT: 33,000
SALES: 5MM **Privately Held**
WEB: www.fountaingrovegolf.com
SIC: 7992 7299 5941 7997 Public golf courses; banquet hall facilities; golf goods & equipment; golf club, membership

(P-18741)
FOUR SEASONS RESORT AVIARA
Also Called: Aviar Golf Club
7447 Batiquitos Dr, Carlsbad (92011-4732)
PHONE..................760 603-6900
James Bellington, *Manager*
Rick Ransburg, *Executive*
EMP: 74

SALES (corp-wide): 6.9MM **Privately Held**
SIC: 7992 7011 Public golf courses; hotels
HQ: Four Seasons Hotels Limited
1165 Leslie St
North York ON M3C 2
416 449-1750

(P-18742)
GLENROCK GROUP
Also Called: Golf Club At Boulder Ridge
1000 Old Quarry Rd, San Jose (95123-2454)
PHONE..................408 323-9900
Glenda Garcia, *Vice Pres*
Rocke Garcia, *President*
EMP: 75 **EST:** 2001
SALES (est): 1.3MM **Privately Held**
SIC: 7992 Public golf courses

(P-18743)
GREEN RIVER GOLF CORPORATION
Also Called: Green River Golf Course
5215 Green River Rd, Corona (92880-9404)
PHONE..................714 970-8411
Fax: 951 737-7432
Judy Saguchi, *President*
Tom Frost, *General Mgr*
Stephnie Padilla, *Director*
Dave P Kehrli, *Agent*
EMP: 100
SQ FT: 30,000
SALES (est): 6.8MM **Privately Held**
WEB: www.playgreenriver.com
SIC: 7992 5941 5813 5812 Public golf courses; sporting goods & bicycle shops; drinking places; eating places
PA: Courseco, Inc.
1670 Corp Cir Ste 201
Petaluma CA 94954

(P-18744)
HAYWARD AREA RECREATION PKDIST
Also Called: Sky West Golf Course
1401 Golf Course Rd, Hayward (94541-4619)
PHONE..................510 317-2300
Fax: 510 317-2305
Dan Eiamana, *Branch Mgr*
Rick Silva, *Manager*
EMP: 50
SQ FT: 2,400 **Privately Held**
SIC: 7992 Public golf courses
PA: Hayward Area Recreation & Pk.Dist
1099 E St
Hayward CA 94541
510 670-1665

(P-18745)
HERITAGE GOLF GROUP INC
Also Called: Talega Golf Club
990 Avenida Talega, San Clemente (92673-6849)
PHONE..................949 369-6226
Fax: 949 369-6227
David Foster, *Branch Mgr*
Jimmye Curtis, *VP Finance*
Danielle Booker, *Personnel*
EMP: 70
SALES (corp-wide): 567.7MM **Privately Held**
WEB: www.talegagolfclub.com
SIC: 7992 Public golf courses
HQ: Heritage Golf Group, Inc.
12750 High Bluff Dr # 400
San Diego CA 92130
858 720-0694

(P-18746)
HERITAGE GOLF GROUP INC
Also Called: Valencia Country Club
27330 Tourney Rd, Valencia (91355-1806)
PHONE..................661 254-4401
Jim Fitzsimmons, *Manager*
Ken Kikuchi, *Manager*
Ruthann Moore, *Manager*
EMP: 100
SALES (corp-wide): 567.7MM **Privately Held**
WEB: www.talegagolfclub.com
SIC: 7992 Public golf courses

7992 - Public Golf Courses County (P-18747)

HQ: Heritage Golf Group, Inc.
12750 High Bluff Rd # 400
San Diego CA 92130
858 720-0694

(P-18747)
HIGH TIDE AND GREEN GRASS INC
Also Called: River Ridge Golf Club
2401 W Vineyard Ave, Oxnard (93036-2218)
PHONE.................805 981-8722
Carl Kanny, *President*
John Kanny, *Vice Pres*
Otto Kanny, *Vice Pres*
EMP: 84
SQ FT: 27,000
SALES (est): 3.5MM **Privately Held**
SIC: 7992 5812 Public golf courses; snack bar

(P-18748)
INDIAN VALLEY GOLF CLUB INC
3035 Novato Blvd, Novato (94947-1002)
P.O. Box 351 (94948-0351)
PHONE.................415 897-1118
Fax: 415 892-3934
Jeff Mc Andrew, *President*
Fermin Vergara, *Vice Pres*
Jeff McAndrews, *Exec Dir*
EMP: 50
SQ FT: 4,000
SALES (est): 2.6MM **Privately Held**
WEB: www.ivgc.com
SIC: 7992 5941 Public golf courses; golf goods & equipment

(P-18749)
INSTITUTE LLC
14830 Foothill Ave, Morgan Hill (95037-9595)
PHONE.................408 782-7101
Steven Sorenson, *Owner*
EMP: 50
SQ FT: 200
SALES (est): 2.2MM **Privately Held**
SIC: 7992 Public golf courses

(P-18750)
J G GOLFING ENTERPRISES INC
Also Called: San Bernardino Golf Club
1494 S Waterman Ave, San Bernardino (92408-2805)
PHONE.................909 885-2414
Fax: 909 885-1674
Tom Shelf, *President*
EMP: 50
SQ FT: 4,000
SALES (est): 2.8MM **Privately Held**
WEB: www.sanbernardinogolfclub.com
SIC: 7992 Public golf courses

(P-18751)
KOLLWOOD GOLF OPERATING LP
Also Called: Kollstar Golf Company
4343 Von Karman Ave # 150, Newport Beach (92660-2099)
PHONE.................949 833-3025
Joseph Woodard, *Partner*
Donald M Koll, *Partner*
EMP: 400
SALES (est): 4.7MM **Privately Held**
SIC: 7992 Public golf courses

(P-18752)
LAGUNA BCH GOLF BNGLOW VLG LLC
Also Called: Aliso Creek Inn and Golf Crse
31106 Coast Hwy, Laguna Beach (92651-8130)
PHONE.................949 499-2271
Fax: 949 715-1412
Mark Christy, *Mng Member*
Kurt Bjorkman, *General Mgr*
Mark Slymen, *Info Tech Mgr*
Annabel Beltran, *Financial Exec*
Carmen Baarsma, *Human Res Dir*
EMP: 65 **EST:** 1958
SQ FT: 10,000
SALES (est): 6.3MM **Privately Held**
WEB: www.alisocreekinn.com
SIC: 7992 7011 Public golf courses; hotels

(P-18753)
LAGUNA WOODS GOLF CLUB
24112 Moulton Pkwy, Laguna Hills (92637-2781)
PHONE.................949 597-4336
Roger Teel, *Director*
▲ **EMP:** 50
SALES (est): 2.3MM **Privately Held**
SIC: 7992 7997 Public golf courses; membership sports & recreation clubs

(P-18754)
LB HILLS GOLF CLUB LLC
Also Called: Golf Club At Terra Lago, The
84000 Terra Lago Pkwy, Indio (92203-9706)
PHONE.................760 775-2000
Fax: 760 775-1988
Jeff Walser, *Partner*
Jay Glover, *Regl Sales Mgr*
Josh Smith, *Manager*
EMP: 100
SALES (est): 4.1MM **Privately Held**
WEB: www.golfclub-terralago.com
SIC: 7992 7991 7299 Public golf courses; physical fitness facilities; banquet hall facilities

(P-18755)
LINCOLN HILLS GOLF CLUB
1005 Sun City Ln, Lincoln (95648-8443)
PHONE.................916 543-9200
Fax: 916 434-7452
Marker Brian, *President*
Scott Miller, *Manager*
John Reuer, *Manager*
EMP: 50
SALES (est): 2.8MM **Privately Held**
WEB: www.lincolnhillsclub.com
SIC: 7992 7997 Public golf courses; golf club, membership

(P-18756)
LOS SERRANOS GOLF CLUB
Also Called: Los Serranos Golf & Cntry CLB
15656 Yorba Ave, Chino Hills (91709-3129)
PHONE.................909 597-1769
Fax: 909 597-1615
John A Kramer Jr, *CEO*
Gloria Kramer, *Shareholder*
John A Kramer Sr, *President*
Rekha Patel, *CFO*
David Kramer, *Treasurer*
EMP: 135
SQ FT: 41,896
SALES (est): 9.1MM **Privately Held**
WEB: www.losserranoscountryclub.com
SIC: 7992 5812 5813 Public golf courses; American restaurant; snack shop; cocktail lounge

(P-18757)
LOS VERDES MNS GOLF CNTRY CLB
Also Called: Los Verdes Golf Curse
7000 Los Verdes Dr Ste 1, Rancho Palos Verdes (90275-5600)
PHONE.................310 377-7370
Bob Lockhart, *General Mgr*
Fred Weibell, *Principal*
Bradley Davis, *Agent*
EMP: 50
SALES: 87.1K **Privately Held**
SIC: 7992 Public golf courses

(P-18758)
MADISON CLUB OWNERS ASSN
Also Called: Madison Club, The
53035 Meriwether Way, La Quinta (92253-5535)
P.O. Box 1558 (92247-1558)
PHONE.................760 777-9320
Brian Ellis, *CEO*
Doug Siebold, *CFO*
EMP: 125
SQ FT: 70,000
SALES (est): 9.7MM **Privately Held**
SIC: 7992 Public golf courses

(P-18759)
MESA VERDE PARTNERS
Also Called: Costa Mesa Country Club
1701 Golf Course Dr, Costa Mesa (92626-5049)
PHONE.................714 540-7500
Fax: 714 540-1274

Scott Henderson, *Partner*
Joan Uzes, *Manager*
Jim Fetterly, *Superintendent*
EMP: 100
SQ FT: 12,000
SALES (est): 4.1MM
SALES (corp-wide): 5.3MM **Privately Held**
SIC: 7992 7997 5813 5812 Public golf courses; membership sports & recreation clubs; drinking places; eating places
PA: Santa Anita Associates
405 S Santa Anita Ave
Arcadia CA 91006
626 447-2764

(P-18760)
MF DAILY OXNARD RANCH PARTNR
Also Called: Soule Park Golf Course
1033 E Ojai Ave, Ojai (93023-3018)
P.O. Box 758 (93024-0758)
PHONE.................805 646-5633
Fax: 805 646-2675
Don Miller, *General Mgr*
Tim Wolfe, *Officer*
Tyson York, *Manager*
EMP: 50
SQ FT: 13,000
SALES (est): 3.3MM **Privately Held**
SIC: 7992 5941 5812 Public golf courses; golf goods & equipment; eating places

(P-18761)
MILE SQUARE GOLF COURSE
10401 Warner Ave, Fountain Valley (92708-1604)
PHONE.................714 962-5541
Fax: 714 962-3541
David A Rainville, *Partner*
EMP: 109
SQ FT: 12,000
SALES (est): 5.9MM **Privately Held**
WEB: www.milesquaregolfcourse.com
SIC: 7992 7999 5812 Public golf courses; golf driving range; American restaurant

(P-18762)
MONARCH BEACH GOLF LINKS (HQ)
50 Monarch Beach Resort N, Dana Point (92629-4084)
PHONE.................949 240-8247
Hale Kelly, *Director*
Clint Cook, *Manager*
Alan Deck, *Manager*
Collins Tamashiro, *Manager*
Dan Miller, *Superintendent*
EMP: 80
SALES (est): 4.6MM **Privately Held**
WEB: www.monarchbeachgolf.com
SIC: 7992 Public golf courses

(P-18763)
MORTON GOLF LLC
Also Called: Haggin Oaks Golf Shop
3645 Fulton Ave, Sacramento (95821-1808)
PHONE.................916 481-4653
Fax: 916 808-2514
Terry Daubert, *Principal*
Daya Kraemer, *Executive*
Jack Gillette, *Controller*
Kathleen Morton,
Kenneth E Morton,
EMP: 100
SQ FT: 13,800
SALES (est): 11.9MM **Privately Held**
WEB: www.mortongolfsales.com
SIC: 7992 5941 5813 5812 Public golf courses; golf goods & equipment; drinking places; eating places

(P-18764)
MOTHERLODE INVESTORS LLC
Also Called: Greenlaw Grupe Jr Operating Co
711 Mccauley Ranch Rd, Angels Camp (95222-9562)
PHONE.................209 736-8112
Greenlaw Grupe,
EMP: 85
SALES (est): 2.3MM **Privately Held**
SIC: 7992 Public golf courses

(P-18765)
NEW DISCOVERY INC
Also Called: Discovery Bay Golf & Cntry CLB
2600 Cherry Hills Dr, Byron (94505-1430)
P.O. Box 907, Concord (94522-0907)
PHONE.................925 634-0505
Keneth H Hofmann, *President*
EMP: 75
SALES: 18MM **Privately Held**
SIC: 7992 Public golf courses

(P-18766)
OAKMONT GOLF CLUB INC (PA)
7025 Oakmont Dr, Santa Rosa (95409-6301)
PHONE.................707 538-2454
Fax: 707 538-4678
Mike Ash, *General Mgr*
Noel Mechau, *Controller*
Heather Pelleriti, *Sales Dir*
John Theilade, *Director*
Carol Rowland, *Manager*
EMP: 60
SQ FT: 4,000
SALES: 3.8MM **Privately Held**
WEB: www.oakmontgc.com
SIC: 7992 7997 5941 Public golf courses; golf club, membership; golf goods & equipment

(P-18767)
OCEAN LINKS CORPORATION
Also Called: Half Moon Bay Golf Links
2 Miramontes Point Rd, Half Moon Bay (94019-2377)
PHONE.................650 726-1800
Fax: 650 726-5831
Mark Kendall, *President*
▼ **EMP:** 100
SQ FT: 6,000
SALES (est): 4.1MM **Privately Held**
SIC: 7992 Public golf courses

(P-18768)
POPPY HILLS INC
3200 Lopez Rd, Pebble Beach (93953-2900)
PHONE.................831 625-1513
Lyn Nelson, *President*
Erik Chaney, *Systems Dir*
Marshall Greeninger, *Controller*
Tracy Diaz, *Human Resources*
Manny Sousa, *Superintendent*
EMP: 60
SQ FT: 8,000
SALES (est): 1.6MM
SALES (corp-wide): 5.9MM **Privately Held**
SIC: 7992 5941 5812 Public golf courses; golf goods & equipment; eating places
PA: Poppy Holding Inc
3200 Lopez Rd
Pebble Beach CA 93953
831 625-1513

(P-18769)
POPPY RIDGE INC
Also Called: Poppy Ridge Golf Course
4280 Greenville Rd, Livermore (94550-9720)
PHONE.................925 456-8229
Fax: 925 455-2020
Paul Porter, *President*
Raymond Evernham, *Executive*
Leticia Gomez, *Office Mgr*
Jennifer Barbara, *Marketing Mgr*
Chris Bitticks, *Director*
EMP: 75
SALES (est): 4.3MM
SALES (corp-wide): 5.9MM **Privately Held**
SIC: 7992 Public golf courses
PA: Poppy Holding Inc
3200 Lopez Rd
Pebble Beach CA 93953
831 625-1513

(P-18770)
PREMIER GOLF PROPERTIES LP
Also Called: Cottonwood Golf Club
3121 Willow Glen Dr, El Cajon (92019-4604)
PHONE.................619 442-9891
Daryl Idler,
Tom Addis, *General Mgr*

PRODUCTS & SERVICES SECTION

7992 - Public Golf Courses County (P-18794)

Christina Liska, *Manager*
EMP: 90
SALES (est): 4.8MM **Privately Held**
WEB: www.cottonwoodgolf.com
SIC: 7992 Public golf courses

(P-18771)
PRESERVE GOLF CLUB INC
1 Rancho San Carlos Rd, Carmel (93923-7999)
PHONE..................831 620-6871
Fax: 831 626-1849
Thomas Gray, *President*
John Pitero, *General Mgr*
EMP: 50
SQ FT: 20,000
SALES: 4MM **Privately Held**
SIC: 7992 Public golf courses

(P-18772)
PRIMM VALLEY GOLF CLUB
1 Yates Wells Rd, Nipton (92364)
PHONE..................702 679-5509
Keith Flatt, *Director*
Rick Koffler, *Manager*
▲ **EMP:** 70
SALES (est): 2.5MM **Privately Held**
SIC: 7992 Public golf courses

(P-18773)
PYJ V A CALIFORNIA LTD PARTNR
Also Called: Westlake Village Golf Course
4812 Lakeview Canyon Rd, Westlake Village (91361-4030)
PHONE..................805 495-8437
Fax: 818 889-0406
Clinton Airey, *General Mgr*
EMP: 60
SQ FT: 7,131
SALES: 3MM **Privately Held**
SIC: 7992 7999 6531 5091 Public golf courses; golf services & professionals; real estate managers; golf equipment

(P-18774)
QUARRY AT LA QUINTA INC (PA)
41865 Boardwalk Ste 214, Palm Desert (92211-9033)
PHONE..................760 777-1100
William Morrow, *President*
EMP: 60
SALES (est): 5.5MM **Privately Held**
SIC: 7992 Public golf courses

(P-18775)
RANCH GOLF CLUB
4601 Hill Top View Ln, San Jose (95138-2707)
PHONE..................408 270-0557
Fax: 408 270-2099
Mike Higuera Jr, *Superintendent*
Kristy Park, *General Mgr*
Julie Pascua, *Office Mgr*
Tarri Carome, *Controller*
Terri Carome, *Controller*
EMP: 75
SQ FT: 2,880
SALES (est): 5.9MM **Privately Held**
SIC: 7992 Public golf courses

(P-18776)
RAWITSER GOLF SHOP MIKE
Also Called: San Jose Municipal Golf Course
1560 Oakland Rd, San Jose (95131-2430)
PHONE..................408 441-4653
Fax: 408 453-8541
Mike Rawitser, *President*
Berne Finch, *Director*
EMP: 50
SQ FT: 2,500
SALES (est): 2.4MM **Privately Held**
WEB: www.sjmuni.com
SIC: 7992 Public golf courses

(P-18777)
ROBINSON RANCH GOLF LLC
27734 Sand Canyon Rd, Santa Clarita (91387-3639)
PHONE..................818 885-0599
Fax: 661 252-0001
Bill McNair,
David Robinson, *Controller*
Alberto Munoz, *Superintendent*
EMP: 120 **EST:** 1999
SALES (est): 7.4MM **Privately Held**
WEB: www.robinsonranchgolf.com
SIC: 7992 7997 Public golf courses; membership sports & recreation clubs

(P-18778)
ROOSTER RUN GOLF CLUB INC
2301 E Washington St, Petaluma (94954-3897)
PHONE..................707 778-1211
Fax: 707 778-8072
Rob Watson, *President*
John Nice, *Vice Pres*
Lane Morales, *Manager*
EMP: 50
SALES (est): 2.9MM **Privately Held**
WEB: www.roosterrun.com
SIC: 7992 5812 Public golf courses; eating places

(P-18779)
SAN JUAN GOLF INC
Also Called: San Juan Hill Country Club
32120 San Juan Creek Rd, San Juan Capistrano (92675-3840)
PHONE..................949 493-1167
Fax: 949 493-0866
Tony Kato, *President*
Sharon Baker, *Admin Mgr*
John Hendricks, *Director*
EMP: 50
SALES (est): 3.6MM **Privately Held**
SIC: 7992 5812 5941 Public golf courses; eating places; golf goods & equipment

(P-18780)
SAN JUAN OAKS LLC
Also Called: San Juan Oaks Golf Club
3825 Union Rd, Hollister (95023-9135)
PHONE..................831 636-6113
Fax: 831 636-6114
Kenneth Gimelli,
Rachele Giusiana, *Human Resources*
Brandie Brewster, *Sales Staff*
Scott Adams,
Bryant Haneta, *Director*
EMP: 80
SQ FT: 1,800
SALES (est): 7MM **Privately Held**
WEB: www.sanjuanoaks.com
SIC: 7992 5941 5812 5813 Public golf courses; golf goods & equipment; eating places; bar (drinking places); banquet hall facilities

(P-18781)
SAND CANYON LLC
Also Called: Strawberry Farms Golf Club
11 Strawberry Farm Rd, Irvine (92612-2300)
PHONE..................949 551-2560
Doug Decinces, *Partner*
EMP: 80
SALES (est): 4.2MM **Privately Held**
WEB: www.sandcanyon.com
SIC: 7992 Public golf courses

(P-18782)
SANTA ANITA ASSOCIATES (PA)
Also Called: Santa Anita Golf Course
405 S Santa Anita Ave, Arcadia (91006-3509)
PHONE..................626 447-2764
Fax: 626 447-6813
Scott L Henderson, *Managing Prtnr*
Mike Donavan, *Partner*
Anthony Larson, *Agent*
Tony Pinon, *Superintendent*
EMP: 60
SQ FT: 16,000
SALES (est): 5.3MM **Privately Held**
SIC: 7992 5812 7999 7299 Public golf courses; American restaurant; golf cart, power, rental; golf driving range; banquet hall facilities

(P-18783)
SANTA TERESA GOLF CLUB
Also Called: Santa Teresa Golf Center
260 Bernal Rd, San Jose (95119-1809)
PHONE..................408 225-2650
Fax: 408 226-9598
Mike Rawitser, *Partner*
Lawrence Lobue, *General Ptnr*
Victor Lobue, *General Ptnr*
John Mc Enery III, *General Ptnr*

Rudy Steadler, *General Ptnr*
EMP: 70
SQ FT: 5,300
SALES (est): 4.3MM **Privately Held**
WEB: www.all-seasons-golf.com
SIC: 7992 Public golf courses

(P-18784)
SCGA GOLF COURSE MGT INC
39500 Robrt Trnt Jnes Pkw, Murrieta (92563-5849)
PHONE..................951 677-7446
Fax: 951 677-7449
Jon Bilger, *President*
Kevin Heaney, *General Mgr*
Krystal Terry, *Controller*
Brian Wieck, *Manager*
EMP: 72
SQ FT: 4,000
SALES: 2.5MM
SALES (corp-wide): 6.9MM **Privately Held**
WEB: www.scgamembersclub.com
SIC: 7992 5812 5941 7999 Public golf courses; eating places; golf goods & equipment; golf driving range
PA: Southern California Golf Association
3740 Cahuenga Blvd
North Hollywood CA 91604
818 980-3630

(P-18785)
SHAPELL INC
9000 S Gale Ridge Rd, San Ramon (94582-9174)
PHONE..................925 735-4253
Joey Pickavance, *Manager*
EMP: 75
SALES (est): 1MM **Privately Held**
SIC: 7992 Public golf courses

(P-18786)
SIERRA LAKES GOLF CLUB
16600 Clubhouse Dr, Fontana (92336-5138)
PHONE..................909 350-2500
Fax: 909 350-4600
Dave Lewis, *President*
Rick Danruther, *Manager*
Dan Smith, *Manager*
EMP: 60
SALES (est): 3.4MM **Privately Held**
WEB: www.sierralakes.com
SIC: 7992 Public golf courses

(P-18787)
SILVER ROCK RESORT GOLF CLUB
79179 Ahmanson Ln, La Quinta (92253-5715)
PHONE..................760 777-8884
Randy Duncan, *Manager*
Bryan Hamilton, *Asst Mgr*
EMP: 100
SALES (est): 4.5MM **Privately Held**
SIC: 7992 Public golf courses

(P-18788)
SISKIYOU LAKE GOLF RESORT INC
Also Called: Mount Shasta Resort
1000 Siskiyou Lake Blvd, Mount Shasta (96067-9482)
PHONE..................530 926-3030
Fax: 530 926-0333
John Cullison, *President*
Cathy Hodge, *Info Tech Mgr*
Suzanne Bentley, *Human Res Dir*
John Fryer, *Director*
EMP: 80
SALES (est): 6.1MM **Privately Held**
WEB: www.mtshastaresort.com
SIC: 7992 5941 7011 5812 Public golf courses; golf goods & equipment; tourist camps, cabins, cottages & courts; American restaurant

(P-18789)
STEELE CANYON GOLF CLUB CORP
3199 Stonefield Dr, Jamul (91935-1527)
PHONE..................619 441-9000
Fax: 619 441-6909
Lawrence M Taylor, *CEO*
Colin Radchenko, *General Mgr*

Barry Rice, *Food Svc Dir*
Victoria Engan,
Alan Scheer, *Director*
EMP: 67 **EST:** 1991
SALES (est): 4.9MM **Privately Held**
SIC: 7992 Public golf courses

(P-18790)
STEVINSON RANCH-SAVANNAH GP
Also Called: Stevinson Ranch Golf Club
2700 Van Clief Rd, Stevinson (95374-9619)
PHONE..................209 668-8200
Dee Roadman,
George Kelley, *Managing Prtnr*
Doug Colliflower, *General Mgr*
Bob McAlister, *Controller*
Jim Francesconi, *Mktg Dir*
EMP: 80
SALES (est): 5.4MM **Privately Held**
WEB: www.stevinsonranch.com
SIC: 7992 7999 5941 7299 Public golf courses; golf driving range; golf goods & equipment; banquet hall facilities; hotels & motels; eating places

(P-18791)
STONETREE GOLF LLC
Also Called: Stonetree Management
9 Stonetree Ln, Novato (94945-3541)
PHONE..................415 209-6744
Fax: 415 209-6925
Warren Spieker, *Partner*
Bill Bunce, *Partner*
Dennis Singleton, *Partner*
Ken Reinke, *CFO*
Lisa Bell, *Office Mgr*
EMP: 50
SALES (est): 5.1MM **Privately Held**
WEB: www.blackpt.com
SIC: 7992 5941 5812 Public golf courses; golf, tennis & ski shops; family restaurants

(P-18792)
SUN CITY RSVLLE CMNTY ASSN INC (PA)
Also Called: Timber Creek Golf Course
7050 Del Webb Blvd, Roseville (95747-8040)
PHONE..................916 774-3880
Fax: 916 774-3889
Dewolfe Emory, *CEO*
Earl Wiklund, *Exec Dir*
Judy Nicklo, *Admin Sec*
Jean Tracy, *Admin Asst*
Terry Boren, *Info Tech Mgr*
EMP: 180 **EST:** 1994
SALES (est): 10.9MM **Privately Held**
WEB: www.scr-cc.com
SIC: 7992 5812 7991 Public golf courses; eating places; caterers; physical fitness facilities

(P-18793)
SUNOL VLY GOLF & RECREATION CO
Also Called: Sunol Valley Golf Course
6900 Mission Rd, Sunol (94586-9452)
P.O. Box 12198, Pleasanton (94588-2198)
PHONE..................925 862-2404
Fax: 925 862-2250
Ron Ivaldi, *General Ptnr*
Lisa Grannzella, *Partner*
Brian Richardson, *General Mgr*
Carol Richardson, *Office Mgr*
Cindy Kensinger, *Manager*
EMP: 100
SALES (est): 4.5MM **Privately Held**
WEB: www.sunolvalley.com
SIC: 7992 5812 5813 7997 Public golf courses; coffee shop; snack shop; cocktail lounge; membership sports & recreation clubs; sporting goods & bicycle shops

(P-18794)
TAHOE DONNER GOLF COURSE INC
11509 Northwoods Blvd, Truckee (96161-6000)
PHONE..................530 587-9455
Mike Peters, *Director*
EMP: 75

7992 - Public Golf Courses County

SALES: 5MM **Privately Held**
SIC: 7992 5813 5812 Public golf courses; bar (drinking places); American restaurant

(P-18795)
TRADITIONS GOLF LLC
Also Called: Cinnabar Hills Golf Club
23600 Mckean Rd, San Jose (95141-1001)
PHONE..............................408 323-5200
Fax: 408 323-9512
Bill Baron,
D Scott Hoyt, *General Mgr*
Marissa Smith, *Office Mgr*
Scott Giangreco, *Food Svc Dir*
Lee Brandenburg,
EMP: 100
SQ FT: 25,000
SALES (est): 7.5MM **Privately Held**
WEB: www.cinnabarhills.com
SIC: 7992 Public golf courses

(P-18796)
TRILOGY GOLF AT LA QUINTA
60151 Trilogy Pkwy, La Quinta (92253-7640)
PHONE..............................760 771-0707
Fax: 760 771-3355
Tom Williams, *Manager*
Ralph Bernhisel, *General Mgr*
Marge Deschaak, *Office Admin*
Dolan Olson, *Director*
EMP: 64
SALES (est): 2.7MM
SALES (corp-wide): 2B **Privately Held**
WEB: www.jfshea.com
SIC: 7992 Public golf courses
HQ: J.F. Shea Construction, Inc.
655 Brea Canyon Rd
Walnut CA 91789
909 595-4397

(P-18797)
VINTNERS GOLF CLUB
Also Called: Lakeside Grill, The
7901 Solano Ave, Yountville (94599-1453)
PHONE..............................707 944-1992
Fax: 707 944-1993
Mike Stead, *Owner*
Bob Boldt, *Director*
Jason Boldt, *Manager*
EMP: 50
SALES (est): 2.3MM **Privately Held**
WEB: www.vintnersgolfclub.com
SIC: 7992 Public golf courses

(P-18798)
WESTRIDGE GOLF INC
1400 S La Habra Hills Dr, La Habra (90631-6998)
PHONE..............................562 690-4200
Fax: 562 690-0303
J C Song, *General Mgr*
EMP: 75
SQ FT: 15,000
SALES (est): 4.4MM **Privately Held**
WEB: www.westridgegolf.com
SIC: 7992 Public golf courses

(P-18799)
WINDSOR GOLF CLUB INC
1340 19th Hole Dr, Windsor (95492-6829)
PHONE..............................707 838-7888
Fax: 707 838-7800
Charlie Gibson, *General Mgr*
Larry Wasm, *Treasurer*
Brove O'Brien, *Vice Pres*
Alex Wright, *Principal*
Tami Sullberg, *General Mgr*
EMP: 60
SALES (est): 3.5MM **Privately Held**
WEB: www.windsorgolf.com
SIC: 7992 5941 Public golf courses; golf goods & equipment

(P-18800)
WOODLEY LAKES GOLF COURSE
6331 Woodley Ave, Van Nuys (91406-6473)
PHONE..............................818 780-6886
Fax: 818 756-6978
Phil Rigs, *Manager*
EMP: 70
SALES (est): 2.6MM **Privately Held**
SIC: 7992 Public golf courses

7993 Coin-Operated Amusement Devices &

(P-18801)
BROOKDALE SENIOR LIVING INC
7418 Stock Ranch Rd, Citrus Heights (95621-5601)
PHONE..............................916 725-7418
EMP: 79
SALES (corp-wide): 4.9B **Publicly Held**
SIC: 7993 Arcades
PA: Brookdale Senior Living
111 Westwood Pl Ste 400
Brentwood TN 37027
615 221-2250

(P-18802)
CAMPO BAND MISSIONS INDIANS
Also Called: Golden Acorn Casino & Trvl Ctr
1800 Golden Acorn Way, Campo (91906-2301)
PHONE..............................619 938-6000
Fax: 619 938-6100
Don Trimble, *Manager*
June Jones, *Treasurer*
Sandra Burkhimer, *Officer*
Leroy Berg, *Info Tech Mgr*
Katie Wahl, *Accountant*
EMP: 330 **Privately Held**
SIC: 7993 5812 Gambling establishments operating coin-operated machines; American restaurant
PA: Campo Band Of Missions Indians
36190 Church Rd
Campo CA 91906
619 478-9046

(P-18803)
EMOTIV SYSTEMS INC
1770 Post St Ste 350, San Francisco (94115-3606)
PHONE..............................415 503-3601
Tan Le, *President*
Ha Pham, *Director*
EMP: 50
SALES (est): 1.8MM **Privately Held**
SIC: 7993 Game machines

(P-18804)
INDUSTRY EVENTS
25501 Narbonne Ave, Lomita (90717-2511)
PHONE..............................310 834-3422
John Bayouth, *Principal*
EMP: 50
SALES (est): 1.2MM **Privately Held**
SIC: 7993 Amusement arcade

(P-18805)
LOOFS LITE A LINE
2500 Long Beach Blvd, Long Beach (90806-3112)
PHONE..............................562 436-2978
Fax: 562 427-2900
Michael Sincola, *Owner*
Ettamay Errock, *Partner*
EMP: 50
SQ FT: 10,005
SALES (est): 839.8K **Privately Held**
SIC: 7993 Coin-operated amusement devices

(P-18806)
MOORETOWN RANCHERIA
Also Called: Feather Falls Casino
3 Alverda Dr, Oroville (95966-9379)
PHONE..............................530 533-3885
Fax: 530 533-4465
Tom Yarbrough, *General Mgr*
Ronald Bert, *Vice Pres*
Deborah Gutman, *Vice Pres*
Chris Desylva, *Security Dir*
Jerry Morgan, *CTO*
EMP: 340 **Privately Held**
WEB: www.drumvision.com
SIC: 7993 7999 Gambling establishments operating coin-operated machines; gambling establishment
PA: Mooretown Rancheria
1 Alverda Dr
Oroville CA 95966

(P-18807)
PACHINKO WORLD INC
5912 Bolsa Ave Ste 108, Huntington Beach (92649-1105)
PHONE..............................714 895-7772
Shinichi Hirabayashi, *CEO*
Yoneji Hirabayashi, *Ch of Bd*
Akinori Hirabayashi, *COO*
Haruo Miyano, *Corp Secy*
Mark Buck,
EMP: 195
SQ FT: 500
SALES (est): 9MM **Privately Held**
SIC: 7993 7999 5812 5194 Game machines; pinball machines; amusement arcade; game parlor; Japanese restaurant; cigarettes

(P-18808)
PLAYTIKA SANTA MONICA LLC
2120 Colorado Ave Ste 400, Santa Monica (90404-3563)
PHONE..............................310 622-7380
Michael Demartino, *General Mgr*
EMP: 130
SALES (est): 2.4MM **Privately Held**
SIC: 7993 Video game arcade

(P-18809)
SCANDIA RECREATION CENTERS
Also Called: Scandia Amusement Park
1155 S Wanamaker Ave, Ontario (91761-7839)
PHONE..............................909 390-3092
Fax: 909 390-3093
Scott Larson, *President*
Sharilyn Christensen, *Shareholder*
Mark Larson, *Shareholder*
Sara Larson, *Shareholder*
Todd Larson MD, *Shareholder*
EMP: 75
SQ FT: 92,480
SALES (est): 2.1MM **Privately Held**
SIC: 7993 7999 7996 Coin-operated amusement devices; miniature golf course operation; amusement parks

(P-18810)
SEGA ENTERTAINMENT USA INC
Also Called: Gameworks
4541 Mills Cir, Ontario (91764-5220)
PHONE..............................909 987-4263
Fax: 909 481-8174
Jerome Seeney, *General Mgr*
Jim Olson, *General Mgr*
Paul Spada, *General Mgr*
Denise Thompson, *Sales Executive*
EMP: 60
SALES (corp-wide): 2.9B **Privately Held**
SIC: 7993 Mechanical games, coin-operated
HQ: Sega Entertainment Usa Inc
600 N Brand Blvd Fl 5
Glendale CA 91203
310 217-9500

7996 Amusement Parks

(P-18811)
APEX PARKS GROUP LLC (PA)
27061 Aliso Creek Rd, Aliso Viejo (92656-5326)
PHONE..............................949 349-8461
John Malloy, *Mng Member*
David M Tolmie,
EMP: 106 EST: 2014
SALES (est): 27.2MM **Privately Held**
SIC: 7996 Amusement parks

(P-18812)
CASINO MORONGO
49500 Seminole Dr, Cabazon (92230-2202)
P.O. Box 366 (92230-0366)
PHONE..............................951 849-3080
Fax: 951 849-0501
Gene Stachowksi, *Principal*
William Davis, *General Mgr*
Lisa Goad, *HR Admin*
EMP: 56
SALES (est): 5.9MM **Privately Held**
SIC: 7996 Amusement parks

(P-18813)
CEDAR FAIR LP
Great America Theme Park
4701 Great America Pkwy, Santa Clara (95054-1287)
P.O. Box 1776 (95052-1776)
PHONE..............................408 988-1776
Fax: 408 986-5803
David Mannix, *Systems Mgr*
G Ando, *Vice Pres*
David Palmerton, *Systs Prg Mgr*
Gaily Mackie, *VP Human Res*
Lester Aoalin, *Manager*
EMP: 120
SALES (corp-wide): 1.2B **Publicly Held**
WEB: www.cedarfair.com
SIC: 7996 Amusement parks
PA: Cedar Fair, L.P.
1 Cedar Point Dr
Sandusky OH 44870
419 626-0830

(P-18814)
CITY OF OXNARD
Also Called: Streets Street Tree Inquiries
1060 Pacific Ave, Oxnard (93030-7337)
PHONE..............................805 385-7950
Fax: 805 385-7962
Michael Henderson, *Director*
Sergio Cervantes, *Supervisor*
Jim Whiting, *Supervisor*
EMP: 100 **Privately Held**
WEB: www.oxnardtourism.com
SIC: 7996 Amusement parks
PA: City Of Oxnard
300 W 3rd St Uppr Fl4
Oxnard CA 93030
805 385-7803

(P-18815)
CITY OF VALLEJO
Also Called: Marine World/Africa USA
1001 Fairgrounds Dr, Vallejo (94589-4001)
PHONE..............................707 644-4000
Joe Meck, *Vice Pres*
EMP: 350 **Privately Held**
WEB: www.ci.vallejo.ca.us
SIC: 7996 Theme park, amusement
PA: City Of Vallejo
555 Santa Clara St
Vallejo CA 94590
707 648-4575

(P-18816)
COUNTY OF SACRAMENTO
Also Called: Department of Regional Parks
4040 Bradshaw Rd, Sacramento (95827-3804)
PHONE..............................916 363-8383
Ron Suter, *Manager*
Janet Baker, *Principal*
Jill Ritzman, *Manager*
EMP: 82 **Privately Held**
WEB: www.sna.com
SIC: 7996 Amusement parks
PA: County Of Sacramento
700 H St Ste 7650
Sacramento CA 95814
916 874-5544

(P-18817)
DISCOVERY SCNCE CTR ORNGE CNTY
2500 N Main St, Santa Ana (92705-6600)
PHONE..............................714 913-5010
Daniel Bolar, *Ch of Bd*
Joseph Adams, *President*
Jennifer Atkinson, *Vice Pres*
Micheal McGee, *Vice Pres*
Brie Griset Smith, *Vice Pres*
▲ EMP: 135
SALES: 12MM **Privately Held**
WEB: www.discoverycube.org
SIC: 7996 Amusement parks

(P-18818)
DISNEYLAND INTERNATIONAL
105 S Harbor Blvd, Anaheim (92805-3710)
P.O. Box 3232 (92803-3232)
PHONE..............................714 781-4000
Fax: 714 781-3407
James Rasulo, *Manager*
Michael Hayes, *Info Tech Mgr*
Tracy Montoya, *Manager*
Marsha L Reed, *Agent*
EMP: 225 **Publicly Held**

PRODUCTS & SERVICES SECTION
7997 - Membership Sports & Recreation Clubs County (P-18841)

SIC: 7996 Amusement parks
HQ: Disneyland International
770 The Cy Dr S Ste 6000
Orange CA 92868
714 490-3004

(P-18819)
DISNEYLAND INTERNATIONAL INC (DH)
500 S Buena Vista St, Burbank (91521-0001)
Rural Route 2755
PHONE.................818 560-1000
James Thomas, *President*
James Cora, *Ch of Bd*
Robert S Risteen, *Treasurer*
Brent Woodford, *Senior VP*
Michael Eisner, *Principal*
EMP: 200
SALES (est): 179.2MM **Publicly Held**
SIC: 7996 Theme park, amusement
HQ: Disney Enterprises, Inc.
500 S Buena Vista St
Burbank CA 91521
818 560-1000

(P-18820)
FESTIVAL FUN PARKS LLC
3500 Polk St, Riverside (92505-1824)
PHONE.................951 785-3000
EMP: 68
SALES (corp-wide): 145.2MM **Privately Held**
SIC: 7996 Amusement parks
PA: Festival Fun Parks, Llc
4590 Macarthur Blvd # 400
Newport Beach CA 92660
949 261-0404

(P-18821)
FESTIVAL FUN PARKS LLC
Also Called: Malibu Grand Prix 51
4590 Macarthur Blvd # 400, Newport Beach (92660-2027)
PHONE.................949 261-0404
EMP: 50
SALES (corp-wide): 145.2MM **Privately Held**
SIC: 7996 Kiddie park
PA: Festival Fun Parks, Llc
4590 Macarthur Blvd # 400
Newport Beach CA 92660
949 261-0404

(P-18822)
GILROY GARDENS FAMILY THEME PK
3050 Hecker Pass Rd, Gilroy (95020-9411)
PHONE.................408 840-7100
Michael Bonfante, *Director*
Stephanie Anderson, *Office Mgr*
Walter Dunckel, *Opers Staff*
Daniel Martinez, *Marketing Mgr*
Jacquie Sanchez, *Mktg Coord*
EMP: 204
SALES: 9.9MM **Privately Held**
SIC: 7996 Amusement parks

(P-18823)
HARDCORE SKATEPARKS INC
285 N Benson Ave, Upland (91786-5614)
PHONE.................909 949-1601
Joseph M Ciaglia Jr, *CEO*
EMP: 150 EST: 2002
SALES (est): 383K **Privately Held**
SIC: 7996 Amusement parks

(P-18824)
LEGOLAND CALIFORNIA LLC
1 Legoland Dr, Carlsbad (92008-4610)
PHONE.................760 918-5346
Fax: 760 603-0032
John Jakobson,
Clark Kim, *COO*
Paul Geasland, *Executive*
Mercedes Casey, *Social Dir*
Christelle Stubbs, *CIO*
▲ EMP: 400
SALES (est): 42MM **Privately Held**
WEB: www.legoland.com
SIC: 7996 Theme park, amusement

(P-18825)
MALIBU CASTLE
27061 Aliso Creek Rd # 100, Aliso Viejo (92656-5322)
PHONE.................210 341-6663
Ken Vorpaul, *Manager*
EMP: 50
SQ FT: 6,980
SALES: 3.1MM
SALES (corp-wide): 145.2MM **Privately Held**
SIC: 7996 Amusement parks
PA: Festival Fun Parks, Llc
4590 Macarthur Blvd # 400
Newport Beach CA 92660
949 261-0404

(P-18826)
MERLIN ENTERTAINMENTS
Also Called: Legoland Florida
1 Legoland Dr, Carlsbad (92008-4610)
PHONE.................877 350-5346
Adrian Jones,
Keri Gatlin, *Controller*
Todd Andrus, *Sales Staff*
Jason Davies,
John Jakobsen,
▲ EMP: 100
SALES (est): 8.4MM **Privately Held**
SIC: 7996 Amusement parks

(P-18827)
MOUNTASIA FAMILY FUN CENTER
21516 Golden Triangle Rd, Santa Clarita (91350-2612)
PHONE.................661 253-4386
Fax: 661 253-4329
David Fleming, *Partner*
Mike Fleming, *Partner*
Michelle Tambaugh, *General Mgr*
EMP: 60
SQ FT: 22,000
SALES: 2.4MM **Privately Held**
WEB: www.mountasiafuncenter.com
SIC: 7996 Theme park, amusement

(P-18828)
MULLIGAN LTD A CAL LTD PARTNR
Also Called: Mulligan Family Fun Center
24950 Madison Ave, Murrieta (92562-9714)
PHONE.................951 696-9696
Fax: 951 696-9666
Micheal Brooks, *Manager*
Ken Harkness, *General Mgr*
Melissa McKay, *Sales Staff*
EMP: 95
SALES (corp-wide): 5.6MM **Privately Held**
WEB: www.mulliganfun.com
SIC: 7996 7999 Amusement parks; tourist attractions, amusement park concessions & rides
PA: Mulligan Limited, A California Limited Partnership
4281 Katella Ave Ste 215
Los Alamitos CA 90720
714 484-6799

(P-18829)
PARK MANAGEMENT CORP
Also Called: Six Flags Discovery Kingdom
1001 Fairgrounds Dr, Vallejo (94589-4001)
PHONE.................707 643-6722
Dale Kaetzel, *President*
Don McCoy, *President*
Jodi Davenport, *Finance*
EMP: 103
SALES (est): 10.8MM **Privately Held**
SIC: 7996 Amusement parks

(P-18830)
SANTA CRUZ SEASIDE COMPANY (PA)
400 Beach St, Santa Cruz (95060-5416)
PHONE.................831 423-5590
Charles L Canfield, *President*
Jo Anne Dlott, *Vice Pres*
Marq Lipton, *Vice Pres*
Regina Smith, *Managing Dir*
Brigid Fuller, *General Mgr*
▲ EMP: 299
SQ FT: 8,000
SALES: 55.2MM **Privately Held**
WEB: www.scseaside.com
SIC: 7996 7011 7933 6531 Pier, amusement; motels; bowling centers; real estate agents & managers

(P-18831)
SANTA MONICA AMUSEMENTS LLC
Also Called: Pacific Park
380 Santa Monica Pier, Santa Monica (90401-3128)
PHONE.................310 451-9641
Fax: 310 260-8748
Mary Ann Powell, *CEO*
David Gillam, *CFO*
Jeff Klocke, *Vice Pres*
David Gilham, *Finance*
Dorene Goldman, *Controller*
EMP: 325
SQ FT: 70,000
SALES (est): 27MM **Privately Held**
WEB: www.pacpark.com
SIC: 7996 Theme park, amusement

(P-18832)
SEA WORLD LLC
Also Called: Sea World of California
500 Sea World Dr, San Diego (92109-7993)
PHONE.................619 226-3842
James D Atchison, *CEO*
Jim Atchison, *President*
John T Reilly, *President*
Donnie Mills, *COO*
James Heaney, *CFO*
▲ EMP: 1986
SALES (est): 97.7MM
SALES (corp-wide): 1.3B **Publicly Held**
WEB: www.howl-o-scream.com
SIC: 7996 Theme park, amusement
PA: Seaworld Entertainment, Inc.
9205 Southpark Center Loo
Orlando FL 32819
407 226-5011

(P-18833)
SIX FLAGS ENTERTAINMENT CORP
Also Called: Six Flags Discovery Kingdom
2001 Fairgrounds Dr, Vallejo (94589)
PHONE.................707 644-6000
Gavin Grozier, *Sales Mgr*
Ken Gonzales, *Manager*
EMP: 220
SALES (corp-wide): 1.2B **Publicly Held**
WEB: www.sixflags.com
SIC: 7996 Theme park, amusement
PA: Six Flags Entertainment Corp
924 E Avenue J
Grand Prairie TX 75050
972 595-5000

(P-18834)
SIX FLAGS ENTERTAINMENT CORP
Also Called: Waterworld USA
1600 Exposition Blvd, Sacramento (95815-5104)
PHONE.................916 924-3747
Fax: 916 924-1314
Keith Regardons, *Director*
Laura Tooper, *Executive*
Mark Wagner, *Controller*
Diana Bolivar, *Sales Mgr*
EMP: 300
SALES (corp-wide): 1.2B **Publicly Held**
WEB: www.sixflags.com
SIC: 7996 Theme park, amusement
PA: Six Flags Entertainment Corp
924 E Avenue J
Grand Prairie TX 75050
972 595-5000

(P-18835)
SLIDECO RECREATION INC
Also Called: Waterworks Park
151 N Boulder Dr, Redding (96003-4607)
PHONE.................530 246-9550
Fax: 530 246-9554
David Enns, *President*
EMP: 75
SQ FT: 1,000
SALES (est): 2.2MM **Privately Held**
WEB: www.waterworkspark.com
SIC: 7996 5812 Theme park, amusement; snack bar

(P-18836)
WALT DISNEY COMPANY
1133 Flower St, Glendale (91201-2415)
PHONE.................818 544-6500
Grant Crabtree, *Branch Mgr*
Luis Fernandez, *Senior VP*
John Gong, *Vice Pres*
Craig S Russell, *Vice Pres*
Ivan Ruzics, *Vice Pres*
EMP: 714 **Publicly Held**
SIC: 7996 Kiddie park
PA: The Walt Disney Company
500 S Buena Vista St
Burbank CA 91521

(P-18837)
WALT DISNEY COMPANY
650 S Buenavista St, Burbank (91501)
PHONE.................818 553-7333
Sylvian Goessens, *Branch Mgr*
EMP: 250 **Publicly Held**
SIC: 7996 Kiddie park
PA: The Walt Disney Company
500 S Buena Vista St
Burbank CA 91521

(P-18838)
WALT DISNEY COMPANY
501 S State College Blvd, Fullerton (92831-5113)
PHONE.................714 449-6600
Neida Herrera, *Principal*
Ken Kennedy, *Managing Dir*
Nina Walsh, *Info Tech Mgr*
Charmaine Howard, *Project Mgr*
Yee W Fong, *Manager*
EMP: 70 **Publicly Held**
SIC: 7996 Kiddie park
PA: The Walt Disney Company
500 S Buena Vista St
Burbank CA 91521

7997 Membership Sports & Recreation Clubs

(P-18839)
1334 PARTNERS LP
Also Called: Manhattan Country Club
1330 Park View Ave, Manhattan Beach (90266-3704)
PHONE.................310 546-5656
Fax: 310 545-4361
Keith Brackpool, *Partner*
Miles Tucker, *General Mgr*
Summer N Wheaton, *Executive Asst*
Joseph Shurgot, *CTO*
Anne Wharton, *Property Mgr*
EMP: 100
SQ FT: 80,000
SALES (est): 45.3K **Privately Held**
WEB: www.manhattancc.com
SIC: 7997 6512 7991 5813 Country club, membership; commercial & industrial building operation; physical fitness facilities; drinking places; eating places

(P-18840)
16700 ROSCOE ASSOCIATES LLC
Also Called: Maguire Aviation
16700 Roscoe Blvd, Van Nuys (91406-1100)
PHONE.................818 989-2300
Robert F Maguire III, *Mng Member*
Alec Maguire, *President*
Cary Stalding, *CFO*
EMP: 70
SALES: 15MM **Privately Held**
SIC: 7997 Aviation club, membership

(P-18841)
A A A FIVE STAR ADVENTURES
611 S Palm Canyon Dr, Palm Springs (92264-7213)
PHONE.................760 320-1500
Fax: 760 325-4386

7997 - Membership Sports & Recreation Clubs County (P-18842)

A D Kesson, *Principal*
EMP: 50
SALES (est): 619.2K Privately Held
SIC: 7997 Membership sports & recreation clubs

(P-18842)
ADVENTURES IN HOSPITALITY INC
Also Called: Barbara Worth Resort
633 W Canal St, Calexico (92231-3503)
PHONE.................................760 356-2806
Suzanna Esparza, *President*
Manuel Cordova, *Sales Mgr*
Jamie Low, *Manager*
EMP: 65
SQ FT: 15,000
SALES (est): 3.5MM Privately Held
WEB: www.bwresort.com
SIC: 7997 Country club, membership; golf club, membership

(P-18843)
AGI HOLDING CORP (PA)
Also Called: Affinity Group
2575 Vista Del Mar Dr, Ventura (93001-3920)
P.O. Box 6888, Englewood CO (80155-6888)
PHONE.................................805 667-4100
Fax: 805 667-4369
Mr Stephen Adams, *CEO*
Joe McAdams, *President*
Maria Recinos, *COO*
Michael Schneider, *COO*
Mark Boggess, *CFO*
▲ **EMP:** 102
SQ FT: 74,000
SALES (est): 1.4B Privately Held
SIC: 7997 2741 Membership sports & recreation clubs; directories: publishing & printing; newsletter publishing

(P-18844)
AIRPORT CLUB
Also Called: Airport Health Club
432 Aviation Blvd, Santa Rosa (95403-1069)
PHONE.................................707 528-2582
Fax: 707 528-7543
Bob Page, *President*
Vickie Morse, *Corp Secy*
Russell Tow, *Vice Pres*
Theresa Brownley, *Admin Asst*
EMP: 120
SQ FT: 44,000
SALES (est): 6.7MM Privately Held
SIC: 7997 7991 Membership sports & recreation clubs; physical fitness facilities

(P-18845)
ALISO VIEJO GOLF CLUB INC
Also Called: Aliso Viejo Country Club
33 Santa Barbara Dr, Aliso Viejo (92656-1622)
PHONE.................................949 598-9200
Fax: 949 829-8991
Lorraine Grassman, *General Mgr*
Lorraine Gerassman, *General Mgr*
EMP: 110
SQ FT: 8,000
SALES (est): 6.6MM
SALES (corp-wide): 1B Publicly Held
WEB: www.alisogolf.com
SIC: 7997 Golf club, membership
HQ: Clubcorp Usa, Inc.
 3030 Lyndon B Johnson Fwy
 Dallas TX 75234
 972 243-6191

(P-18846)
ALMADEN GOLF & COUNTRY CLUB
6663 Hampton Dr, San Jose (95120-5536)
PHONE.................................408 323-4812
Fax: 408 268-3643
Robert Osshalem, *General Mgr*
Kobi Browwn, *Controller*
Jim Saylor, *Human Resources*
Michael Gardner, *Director*
Robert Sparks, *Manager*
EMP: 60
SQ FT: 26,000

SALES: 17.6MM Privately Held
WEB: www.almadengcc.com
SIC: 7997 Country club, membership; golf club, membership

(P-18847)
ALMADEN VALLEY ATHLETIC CLUB
Also Called: Avac
5400 Camden Ave, San Jose (95124-5897)
PHONE.................................408 445-4900
Fax: 408 267-0264
Joseph Shank, *General Ptnr*
Court Aquatic Sports, *General Ptnr*
Lori Biasca, *Director*
Danielle Griffith, *Manager*
Maria Hurt, *Associate*
EMP: 70
SQ FT: 20,000
SALES (est): 4MM Privately Held
SIC: 7997 Membership sports & recreation clubs

(P-18848)
ALTA SIERRA COUNTRY CLUB INC
11897 Tammy Way, Grass Valley (95949-6626)
PHONE.................................530 273-2041
Fax: 530 273-2207
Del Clement, *President*
Jim Hansen, *Treasurer*
Doug Bulman, *Vice Pres*
Carl Guastaferro, *Admin Sec*
Franca Nielson, *Manager*
EMP: 50
SQ FT: 21,500
SALES (est): 3.4MM Privately Held
WEB: www.altasierracc.com
SIC: 7997 Golf club, membership

(P-18849)
ALTA VISTA COUNTRY CLUB LLC
777 Alta Vista St, Placentia (92870-5101)
PHONE.................................714 524-1591
Karl Reul, *General Mgr*
EMP: 60
SQ FT: 6,751,800
SALES (est): 197.3K Privately Held
SIC: 7997 Membership sports & recreation clubs

(P-18850)
ALTADENA TOWN AND COUNTRY CLUB
2290 Country Club Dr, Altadena (91001-3202)
PHONE.................................626 345-9088
Fax: 626 798-2877
David Edens, *President*
Matthew Zboray, *Executive*
Diane Hough, *Controller*
Craig Sloane, *Opers Mgr*
Sataporn Phermsangngam, *Director*
EMP: 80
SQ FT: 50,000
SALES: 4MM Privately Held
SIC: 7997 Country club, membership

(P-18851)
AMERICAN GOLF CORPORATION
Also Called: Lomas Santa Fe Country Club
Lomas Snta Fe Highland Dr, Solana Beach (92075)
P.O. Box 1007 (92075-1007)
PHONE.................................858 755-6768
Fax: 858 793-0299
Lynn Ferrer, *Sales/Mktg Mgr*
David Duran, *Director*
EMP: 150
SALES (corp-wide): 509.6MM Privately Held
WEB: www.americangolf.com
SIC: 7997 Country club, membership
PA: American Golf Corporation
 6080 Center Dr Ste 500
 Los Angeles CA 90045
 310 664-4000

(P-18852)
AMERICAN GOLF CORPORATION
Also Called: Sunset Hills Country Club
4155 Erbes Rd, Thousand Oaks (91360-6842)
PHONE.................................805 495-5407
Fax: 805 523-7574
Scott Richmond, *Manager*
Charles Steele, *Agent*
EMP: 75
SALES (corp-wide): 509.6MM Privately Held
WEB: www.americangolf.com
SIC: 7997 Country club, membership
PA: American Golf Corporation
 6080 Center Dr Ste 500
 Los Angeles CA 90045
 310 664-4000

(P-18853)
AMERICAN GOLF CORPORATION
Also Called: Rancho San Joaquin Golf Course
1 Ethel Coplen Way, Irvine (92612-1716)
PHONE.................................949 786-1224
Fax: 949 786-2053
Steve Jeffrey, *Manager*
Darren Miyamoto, *Sales Executive*
Alyssa Tavai, *Asst Mgr*
EMP: 125
SALES (corp-wide): 509.6MM Privately Held
WEB: www.americangolf.com
SIC: 7997 7992 Golf club, membership; public golf courses
PA: American Golf Corporation
 6080 Center Dr Ste 500
 Los Angeles CA 90045
 310 664-4000

(P-18854)
AMERICAN GOLF CORPORATION (PA)
6080 Center Dr Ste 500, Los Angeles (90045-9205)
PHONE.................................310 664-4000
Fax: 310 664-6160
Jim Hinckley, *CEO*
Paul Major, *President*
Keith Brown, *COO*
Mike Moecker, *CFO*
Rick Rosen, *CFO*
EMP: 150
SALES (est): 509.6MM Privately Held
WEB: www.americangolf.com
SIC: 7997 7999 5812 5941 Golf club, membership; tennis club, membership; golf services & professionals; eating places; golf goods & equipment; public golf courses

(P-18855)
AMERICAN GOLF CORPORATION
Also Called: Black Lake Golf Course
1490 Golf Course Ln, Nipomo (93444-9307)
PHONE.................................805 343-1214
Fax: 805 343-6317
Bill Burney, *Manager*
Ashlee Hillier, *Manager*
Fran Anacleto, *Supervisor*
EMP: 70
SQ FT: 3,000
SALES (corp-wide): 509.6MM Privately Held
WEB: www.americangolf.com
SIC: 7997 Country club, membership
PA: American Golf Corporation
 6080 Center Dr Ste 500
 Los Angeles CA 90045
 310 664-4000

(P-18856)
AMERICAN GOLF CORPORATION
Also Called: Seacliff Country Club
6501 Palm Ave, Huntington Beach (92648-2611)
PHONE.................................714 536-8866
Fax: 714 536-0239
Mike Cress, *General Mgr*
EMP: 100

SQ FT: 20,000
SALES (corp-wide): 509.6MM Privately Held
WEB: www.americangolf.com
SIC: 7997 Country club, membership
PA: American Golf Corporation
 6080 Center Dr Ste 500
 Los Angeles CA 90045
 310 664-4000

(P-18857)
AMERICAN GOLF CORPORATION
Also Called: Yorba Linda Country Club
19400 Mountain View Ave, Yorba Linda (92886-5530)
PHONE.................................714 779-2461
Fax: 714 779-5667
Scott Lester, *District Mgr*
Shuji Inada, *Buyer*
EMP: 55
SQ FT: 19,800
SALES (corp-wide): 509.6MM Privately Held
WEB: www.americangolf.com
SIC: 7997 Country club, membership
PA: American Golf Corporation
 6080 Center Dr Ste 500
 Los Angeles CA 90045
 310 664-4000

(P-18858)
AMERICAN GOLF CORPORATION
Also Called: Recreation Park Golf Course 18
5001 Deukmejian Dr, Long Beach (90804-4311)
PHONE.................................562 494-4424
Tim Dunlop, *Branch Mgr*
Marisa Breglio, *Manager*
Jay Carvallo, *Manager*
EMP: 50
SQ FT: 2,000
SALES (corp-wide): 509.6MM Privately Held
WEB: www.americangolf.com
SIC: 7997 Golf club, membership
PA: American Golf Corporation
 6080 Center Dr Ste 500
 Los Angeles CA 90045
 310 664-4000

(P-18859)
AMERICAN GOLF CORPORATION
Also Called: Escondido Country Club
17166 Stonerdg Cntry Clb, Poway (92064-1333)
PHONE.................................760 737-9762
Angela Emory, *Manager*
Rose Vossenkemper, *Food Svc Dir*
EMP: 50
SALES (corp-wide): 509.6MM Privately Held
WEB: www.americangolf.com
SIC: 7997 Country club, membership
PA: American Golf Corporation
 6080 Center Dr Ste 500
 Los Angeles CA 90045
 310 664-4000

(P-18860)
AMERICAN GOLF CORPORATION
Also Called: Desert Rose Golf Course
68311 Paseo Real, Cathedral City (92234-6767)
PHONE.................................702 431-2191
Paul Kukida, *Manager*
EMP: 78
SALES (corp-wide): 509.6MM Privately Held
WEB: www.americangolf.com
SIC: 7997 7992 7999 Golf club, membership; golf driving range; public golf courses
PA: American Golf Corporation
 6080 Center Dr Ste 500
 Los Angeles CA 90045
 310 664-4000

PRODUCTS & SERVICES SECTION
7997 - Membership Sports & Recreation Clubs County (P-18881)

(P-18861)
AMERICAN GOLF CORPORATION
Also Called: Reserve At Spanos Park, The
6301 W Eight Mile Rd, Stockton (95219-8702)
P.O. Box 7126 (95267-0126)
PHONE.................................209 477-4653
Fax: 209 477-0169
Barry Ruhl, *Manager*
EMP: 50
SALES (corp-wide): 509.6MM **Privately Held**
WEB: www.americangolf.com
SIC: 7997 7992 Golf club, membership; public golf courses
PA: American Golf Corporation
    6080 Center Dr Ste 500
    Los Angeles CA 90045
    310 664-4000

(P-18862)
AMERICAN GOLF CORPORATION
Also Called: Mountain Gate Country Club
12445 Mountain Gate Dr, Los Angeles (90049-1115)
PHONE.................................310 476-2411
Fax: 310 476-8145
Terry Anglan, *Manager*
Aisa Koh, *Executive*
Jeff Brockman, *Technical Staff*
Mila Komova, *Controller*
Lani Mackay, *Director*
EMP: 140
SQ FT: 20,000
SALES (corp-wide): 509.6MM **Privately Held**
WEB: www.americangolf.com
SIC: 7997 Tennis club, membership; country club, membership; golf club, membership
PA: American Golf Corporation
    6080 Center Dr Ste 500
    Los Angeles CA 90045
    310 664-4000

(P-18863)
AMERICAN GOLF CORPORATION
Also Called: Diamond Bar Golf Course
22751 Golden Springs Dr, Diamond Bar (91765-2218)
PHONE.................................909 861-5757
Fax: 909 396-1635
Andy Melnyk, *Manager*
EMP: 70
SALES (corp-wide): 509.6MM **Privately Held**
WEB: www.americangolf.com
SIC: 7997 7992 Golf club, membership; public golf courses
PA: American Golf Corporation
    6080 Center Dr Ste 500
    Los Angeles CA 90045
    310 664-4000

(P-18864)
AMERICAN GOLF CORPORATION
Also Called: Oakhurst Country Club
1001 Peacock Creek Dr, Clayton (94517-2201)
PHONE.................................925 672-9737
Fax: 925 672-0148
Craig Wong, *General Mgr*
EMP: 100
SALES (corp-wide): 509.6MM **Privately Held**
WEB: www.americangolf.com
SIC: 7997 Membership sports & recreation clubs
PA: American Golf Corporation
    6080 Center Dr Ste 500
    Los Angeles CA 90045
    310 664-4000

(P-18865)
AMERICAN GOLF CORPORATION
Also Called: Summitpointe Golf Club
1500 Country Club Dr, Milpitas (95035-3456)
PHONE.................................408 262-8813
Lance Fong, *General Mgr*
EMP: 50
SALES (corp-wide): 509.6MM **Privately Held**
WEB: www.americangolf.com
SIC: 7997 Membership sports & recreation clubs
PA: American Golf Corporation
    6080 Center Dr Ste 500
    Los Angeles CA 90045
    310 664-4000

(P-18866)
AMERICAN GOLF CORPORATION
Also Called: El Camino Country Club
3202 Vista Way, Oceanside (92056-3607)
PHONE.................................760 757-2100
Fax: 760 966-7117
Ted Axe, *Manager*
Randy Hopton, *Superintendent*
EMP: 75
SALES (corp-wide): 509.6MM **Privately Held**
WEB: www.americangolf.com
SIC: 7997 Golf club, membership
PA: American Golf Corporation
    6080 Center Dr Ste 500
    Los Angeles CA 90045
    310 664-4000

(P-18867)
AMERICAN GOLF CORPORATION
Also Called: Los Verdes Golf Course
7000 Los Verdes Dr Ste 1, Rancho Palos Verdes (90275-5600)
PHONE.................................310 377-7370
Mike Shank, *Branch Mgr*
EMP: 55
SALES (corp-wide): 509.6MM **Privately Held**
WEB: www.americangolf.com
SIC: 7997 Country club, membership
PA: American Golf Corporation
    6080 Center Dr Ste 500
    Los Angeles CA 90045
    310 664-4000

(P-18868)
AMERICAN GOLF CORPORATION
16782 Graham St, Huntington Beach (92649-3754)
PHONE.................................714 846-1364
Brent Boznanski, *Manager*
EMP: 55
SALES (corp-wide): 509.6MM **Privately Held**
WEB: www.americangolf.com
SIC: 7997 Membership sports & recreation clubs
PA: American Golf Corporation
    6080 Center Dr Ste 500
    Los Angeles CA 90045
    310 664-4000

(P-18869)
AMERICAN GOLF CORPORATION
Also Called: Seascape Golf Club
610 Clubhouse Dr Rear, Aptos (95003-4868)
PHONE.................................831 688-3213
Steve Argo, *Manager*
Brian T Prinn, *Agent*
Calvin Brown, *Superintendent*
EMP: 60
SALES (corp-wide): 509.6MM **Privately Held**
WEB: www.americangolf.com
SIC: 7997 5941 5812 Golf club, membership; golf goods & equipment; eating places
PA: American Golf Corporation
    6080 Center Dr Ste 500
    Los Angeles CA 90045
    310 664-4000

(P-18870)
AMERICAN GOLF CORPORATION
Also Called: Monterey Country Club
41500 Monterey Ave, Palm Desert (92260-2173)
PHONE.................................760 568-9311
Fax: 760 341-9785
Rod Winger, *Manager*
Mike Biscotti, *Manager*
Carol Whitlock, *Manager*
EMP: 50
SALES (corp-wide): 509.6MM **Privately Held**
WEB: www.americangolf.com
SIC: 7997 Country club, membership
PA: American Golf Corporation
    6080 Center Dr Ste 500
    Los Angeles CA 90045
    310 664-4000

(P-18871)
AMERICAN GOLF CORPORATION
Also Called: La Mirada Country Club
15501 Alicante Rd, La Mirada (90638-3112)
PHONE.................................562 943-7123
Fax: 562 902-8761
Dill Crawford, *Manager*
EMP: 65
SALES (corp-wide): 509.6MM **Privately Held**
WEB: www.americangolf.com
SIC: 7997 Country club, membership
PA: American Golf Corporation
    6080 Center Dr Ste 500
    Los Angeles CA 90045
    310 664-4000

(P-18872)
AMERICAN GOLF CORPORATION
Also Called: Simi Hills Golf Course
5031 Alamo St, Simi Valley (93063-1949)
PHONE.................................805 522-0803
Fax: 805 520-9379
Brian Reed, *Branch Mgr*
Jackie Cochran, *Director*
Mike Begakis, *Manager*
EMP: 55
SALES (corp-wide): 509.6MM **Privately Held**
WEB: www.americangolf.com
SIC: 7997 5941 7992 Golf club, membership; golf goods & equipment; public golf courses
PA: American Golf Corporation
    6080 Center Dr Ste 500
    Los Angeles CA 90045
    310 664-4000

(P-18873)
ANAHEIM DUCKS HOCKEY CLUB LLC
2695 E Katella Ave, Anaheim (92806-5904)
PHONE.................................714 940-2900
Michel Schulman, *Mng Member*
David McNab, *Senior VP*
Bob Murray, *Vice Pres*
Tim Ryan, *Vice Pres*
Jay Scott, *Vice Pres*
EMP: 150
SALES (est): 21.3MM **Privately Held**
SIC: 7997 Hockey club, except professional & semi-professional

(P-18874)
ANNANDALE GOLF CLUB
1 N San Rafael Ave, Pasadena (91105-1299)
PHONE.................................626 796-6125
Fax: 626 449-2626
Christoff Granger, *General Mgr*
Cliff Bailey, *General Mgr*
Michael Beam, *General Mgr*
Tom Lease, *Controller*
Susy Gorlach, *Human Res Dir*
EMP: 125
SQ FT: 10,000
SALES: 11.9MM **Privately Held**
WEB: www.annandalegolf.com
SIC: 7997 Golf club, membership

(P-18875)
ANTIOCH ROTARY CLUB
324 G St, Antioch (94509-1255)
P.O. Box 692 (94509-0069)
PHONE.................................925 757-1800
EMP: 50 EST: 2010
SALES (est): 1.7MM **Privately Held**
SIC: 7997

(P-18876)
APPLE VALLEY GOLF CLUB
Also Called: Apple Valley Golf Course
15200 Rancherias Rd, Apple Valley (92307-5201)
PHONE.................................760 242-3653
Fax: 760 242-5083
Ned R Curtis, *CEO*
Todd Edwards, *Principal*
Gregg Campbell, *Office Mgr*
Randi Coffman, *Administration*
Nadia Astakhov, *Manager*
EMP: 170
SQ FT: 21,471
SALES (est): 5.2MM **Privately Held**
WEB: www.applevalleycountryclub.net
SIC: 7997 Country club, membership

(P-18877)
ARDEN HILLS COUNTRY CLUB INC
1220 Arden Hills Ln, Sacramento (95864-5378)
PHONE.................................916 482-6111
Fax: 916 483-0372
Jeralyn Favero, *President*
Dara Favero, *Executive*
Brett Favero, *Admin Sec*
Windy Kahana, *Graphic Designe*
Meredith Cassady, *Personnel Exec*
EMP: 70
SALES (est): 5.9MM **Privately Held**
WEB: www.ardenhills.net
SIC: 7997 Country club, membership

(P-18878)
ASSOCIATED KOI CLUBS AMERICA
P.O. Box 10879, Costa Mesa (92627-0272)
PHONE.................................949 650-5225
Robert Finnegan, *Chairman*
EMP: 75
SALES: 13.4K **Privately Held**
SIC: 7997 Membership sports & recreation clubs

(P-18879)
ATSUGI KOKUSAI KANKO USA INC
28095 John F Kennedy Dr, Moreno Valley (92555-6301)
PHONE.................................951 924-4444
Hideo Komuro, *President*
Richard Martin, *Manager*
EMP: 55
SQ FT: 21,000
SALES (est): 1.1MM
SALES (corp-wide): 14.3MM **Privately Held**
WEB: www.hawaiikaigolf.com
SIC: 7997 5812 Membership sports & recreation clubs; eating places
PA: Atsugi Kokusai Kanko Co., Ltd.
    1-12-12, Shintomi
    Chuo-Ku TKY 104-0
    335 533-280

(P-18880)
BAKERSFIELD COUNTRY CLUB
4200 Country Club Dr, Bakersfield (93306-3700)
P.O. Box 6007 (93386-6007)
PHONE.................................661 871-4000
Fax: 661 871-6290
Jon Van Boening, *President*
Dayna Nichols, *Bd of Directors*
Christy Solari, *Controller*
Eric Kuhn, *Manager*
EMP: 75 EST: 1948
SQ FT: 30,000
SALES: 6.3MM **Privately Held**
WEB: www.bakersfieldcountryclub.com
SIC: 7997 5812 5813 Country club, membership; eating places; bar (drinking places)

(P-18881)
BALBOA BAY CLUB INC (HQ)
1221 W Coast Hwy Ste 145, Newport Beach (92663-5092)
PHONE.................................949 645-5000
Fax: 949 630-4215
David Wooten, *President*
W D Ray, *CEO*
Jerry Johnson, *VP Accounting*

7997 - Membership Sports & Recreation Clubs County (P-18882)

Karen Lebrun, *Sales Mgr*
Jirka Batlik, *Director*
EMP: 260
SALES (est): 19.4MM
SALES (corp-wide): 27.7MM **Privately Held**
SIC: 7997 7011 Membership sports & recreation clubs; resort hotel
PA: International Bay Clubs, Llc
1221 W Coast Hwy Ste 145
Newport Beach CA 92663
949 645-5000

(P-18882)
BALBOA YACHT CLUB
1801 Bayside Dr, Corona Del Mar (92625-1898)
PHONE 949 673-3515
Fax: 949 673-8937
Howard Ness, *President*
Israel Castell, *Manager*
EMP: 50 **EST:** 1924
SQ FT: 23,000
SALES: 5.3MM **Privately Held**
WEB: www.balboayachtclub.com
SIC: 7997 Yacht club, membership

(P-18883)
BAY CLUB GOLDEN GATEWAY INC
Also Called: Golden Gtwy Tennis & Swim CLB
370 Drumm St, San Francisco (94111-2010)
PHONE 415 616-8800
Fax: 415 433-5025
Broc Stevens, *General Mgr*
Rachel Ruperto, *President*
David Smith, *Admin Sec*
EMP: 50
SQ FT: 8,000
SALES (est): 1.8MM
SALES (corp-wide): 56.2MM **Privately Held**
WEB: www.ggtsc.com
SIC: 7997 7999 7991 Tennis club, membership; swimming club, membership; swimming instruction; health club
HQ: W.A. Holding Company
1 Lombard St Lbby
San Francisco CA 94111
415 781-1874

(P-18884)
BAY CLUBS INC
Also Called: Racquetball World
22235 Sherman Way, Canoga Park (91303-1058)
PHONE 818 884-5034
Fax: 818 227-8373
Harold Wright, *Branch Mgr*
EMP: 80
SQ FT: 85,294
SALES (corp-wide): 75.2MM **Privately Held**
SIC: 7997 7299 7991 Racquetball club, membership; personal appearance services; physical fitness facilities
HQ: Bay Clubs, Inc.
1 Lombard St
San Francisco CA 94111
415 781-1874

(P-18885)
BEACH CLUB
201 Palisades Beach Rd, Santa Monica (90420-1401)
PHONE 310 395-3254
Gregg Patterson, *Exec Dir*
Kathy Karenko, *Controller*
EMP: 60 **EST:** 1923
SQ FT: 35,000
SALES: 7MM **Privately Held**
WEB: www.beachclub.com
SIC: 7997 5812 5813 Beach club, membership; eating places; bar (drinking places)

(P-18886)
BEAR CREEK GOLF CLUB INC
Also Called: Bear Creek Golf & Country Club
22640 Bear Creek Dr N, Murrieta (92562-3015)
PHONE 951 677-8621
Fax: 951 677-7066
Peter Hanson, *General Mgr*

Rich Gillete, *President*
Kathy Laclair, *Executive*
EMP: 85
SQ FT: 28,000
SALES: 2.9MM **Privately Held**
WEB: www.bearcreekgc.com
SIC: 7997 7992 Golf club, membership; public golf courses

(P-18887)
BEAR CREEK PARTNERS LLC
22640 Bear Creek Dr N, Murrieta (92562-3015)
PHONE 951 677-8621
Fax: 951 677-3805
Richard H Gillette, *Mng Member*
Gary Mineo, *Controller*
Jeffrey Main, *Manager*
EMP: 65
SALES (est): 3.4MM **Privately Held**
SIC: 7997 Membership sports & recreation clubs

(P-18888)
BEL-AIR COUNTRY CLUB
10768 Bellagio Rd, Los Angeles (90077-3799)
PHONE 310 472-9563
Fax: 310 472-7044
Joseph Wagner, *General Mgr*
Peter Best, *CEO*
Pam Quider, *Administration*
Lindy Nielsen, *Controller*
Mayla Moore, *Director*
EMP: 140
SQ FT: 10,000
SALES: 12.1MM **Privately Held**
WEB: www.bel-aircc.com
SIC: 7997 5941 Country club, membership; golf goods & equipment

(P-18889)
BELMONT ATHLETIC CLUB
4918 E 2nd St, Long Beach (90803-5318)
PHONE 562 438-3816
Fax: 562 438-8470
John Doyle, *Partner*
Bill Fraser, *Ltd Ptnr*
Patrick Gormley, *Ltd Ptnr*
Barry Miller, *Ltd Ptnr*
Joyce Pokstaff, *Ltd Ptnr*
EMP: 65 **EST:** 1980
SQ FT: 25,000
SALES (est): 3.2MM **Privately Held**
WEB: www.belmontathleticclub.com
SIC: 7997 7991 Racquetball club, membership; athletic club & gymnasiums, membership

(P-18890)
BERMUDA DUNES COUNTRY CLUB
42765 Adams St, Bermuda Dunes (92203-7937)
PHONE 760 360-2481
Fax: 760 345-8697
Ed Cooney, *CEO*
Steve Hubbard, *President*
George Neidhardt, *Treasurer*
Leon Webrand, *Vice Pres*
Bob Siino, *General Mgr*
EMP: 50
SQ FT: 40,000
SALES: 5.1MM **Privately Held**
WEB: www.bermudanescc.com
SIC: 7997 Country club, membership

(P-18891)
BIG CANYON COUNTRY CLUB
1 Big Canyon Dr, Newport Beach (92660-5299)
PHONE 949 706-5260
Fax: 949 720-9338
Donald Tippett, *CEO*
William Stamply, *President*
Nicholas Corrado, *Executive*
Nick Wynn, *Executive*
David Voorhees, *General Mgr*
EMP: 180
SQ FT: 50,000
SALES: 19.3MM **Privately Held**
WEB: www.bigcanyoncc.com
SIC: 7997 Country club, membership

(P-18892)
BIG LGUE DREAMS CONSULTING LLC
20155 Viking Way, Redding (96003-8293)
PHONE 530 223-1177
Brandi Merkel, *Principal*
EMP: 132
SALES (corp-wide): 37.8MM **Privately Held**
SIC: 7997 Membership sports & recreation clubs
PA: Big League Dreams Consulting, Llc
16333 Fairfield Ranch Rd
Chino Hills CA 91709
909 287-1700

(P-18893)
BIGHORN GOLF CLUB
255 Palowet Dr, Palm Desert (92260-7311)
PHONE 760 773-2468
Fax: 760 776-7125
Carl T Cardinalli, *President*
Joe Curtis, *Treasurer*
Theresa Maggio, *Vice Pres*
Greg Proper, *Executive*
Martin Islas, *Engineer*
EMP: 190
SALES (est): 14.6MM **Privately Held**
SIC: 7997 7992 Membership sports & recreation clubs; public golf courses

(P-18894)
BIRNAM WOOD GOLF CLUB
1941 E Valley Rd, Santa Barbara (93108-1427)
PHONE 805 969-2223
Fax: 805 969-5037
Robert Thornburgh, *President*
Michael-Mc Gardner, *COO*
Lindsay Worden, *Comms Dir*
Robert Trent Jones, *Principal*
Tito Arriaza, *Admin Asst*
EMP: 145
SQ FT: 45,000
SALES (est): 11.1MM **Privately Held**
WEB: www.birnamwoodgolfclub.com
SIC: 7997 7992 5812 Golf club, membership; public golf courses; eating places

(P-18895)
BLACKHAWK COUNTRY CLUB
599 Blackhawk Club Dr, Danville (94506-4522)
PHONE 925 736-6500
Fax: 925 736-6549
Michael G Burton, *CEO*
Larry Marx, *President*
Kevin Dunne, *COO*
Barrett Eiselman, *COO*
Kelly Rothschild, *Executive Asst*
EMP: 230
SQ FT: 35,743
SALES: 15.5MM **Privately Held**
WEB: www.blackhawkcc.org
SIC: 7997 7992 5812 Golf club, membership; tennis club, membership; public golf courses; eating places

(P-18896)
BLADIUM INC (PA)
Also Called: Bladium Sports Clubs
800 W Tower Ave Bldg 40, Alameda (94501-5048)
PHONE 510 814-4999
Fax: 510 814-4990
Brad C Shook, *President*
David Walsh, *CFO*
Adam Loss, *Exec Dir*
Sam Wu, *Accountant*
Diogo Gomes, *Director*
EMP: 60
SQ FT: 115,000
SALES (est): 6MM **Privately Held**
WEB: www.bladium.com
SIC: 7997 Membership sports & recreation clubs

(P-18897)
BORREGO SPRINGS COUNTRY CLUB
1112 Tilting Tee Dr, Borrego Springs (92004)
P.O. Box 981 (92004-0981)
PHONE 760 767-3289
John Cameron, *Owner*

John Yzaguirre, *General Mgr*
Kimberly Daniel, *Marketing Staff*
Michelle Herber, *Director*
Ramon Barroso, *Manager*
EMP: 50
SALES (est): 1.6MM **Privately Held**
SIC: 7997 Membership sports & recreation clubs

(P-18898)
BOYS & GIRLS CLB OF PENINSULA
401 Pierce Rd, Menlo Park (94025-1240)
PHONE 650 322-6255
Fax: 650 322-9042
Peter Fortenbaugh, *Director*
Linda Martinez, *Volunteer Dir*
Jeff Feinman, *Vice Pres*
Sean Hassan, *Vice Pres*
David Cruz, *Executive*
EMP: 60 **EST:** 1975
SQ FT: 2,000
SALES: 7MM **Privately Held**
SIC: 7997 Membership sports & recreation clubs

(P-18899)
BRAEMAR COUNTRY CLUB INC
4001 Reseda Blvd, Tarzana (91356-5530)
P.O. Box 570217 (91357-0217)
PHONE 323 873-6880
Fax: 818 343-0482
Steven Held, *Manager*
Nanor Dekermenjian, *Bd of Directors*
Vicki Johansen, *Bd of Directors*
Teresa Dopps, *Controller*
Eric Prebula, *Opers Staff*
EMP: 199
SQ FT: 20,000
SALES (est): 6.4MM
SALES (corp-wide): 1B **Publicly Held**
WEB: www.braemarclub.com
SIC: 7997 Country club, membership
HQ: Clubcorp Usa, Inc.
3030 Lyndon B Johnson Fwy
Dallas TX 75234
972 243-6191

(P-18900)
BRENTWOOD COUNTRY CLUB
590 S Burlingame Ave, Los Angeles (90049-4896)
PHONE 310 451-8011
Linda Briskman, *President*
Rosemary Bryan, *Director*
David Smith, *Director*
EMP: 120
SALES (est): 355.8K **Privately Held**
SIC: 7997 7999 Country club, membership; golf services & professionals

(P-18901)
BRIDGES AT GALE RANCH LLC
Also Called: Bridges Golf Club, The
9000 S Gale Ridge Rd, San Ramon (94582-9174)
PHONE 925 735-4253
Joey Pickavance, *Manager*
Dean Castelli, *Food Svc Dir*
EMP: 90
SALES (est): 4.9MM **Privately Held**
WEB: www.thebridgesgolf.com
SIC: 7997 Golf club, membership

(P-18902)
BROOKSIDE COUNTRY CLUB
3603 Saint Andrews Dr, Stockton (95219-1868)
PHONE 209 956-6200
Fax: 209 956-8440
Barney Kramer, *CEO*
New England Life, *Partner*
Glenn Leech, *Food Svc Dir*
Gary Olsen, *Manager*
EMP: 70
SQ FT: 5,000
SALES: 3.2MM **Privately Held**
WEB: www.brooksidegolf.net
SIC: 7997 7999 5941 5812 Country club, membership; swimming club, membership; tennis club, membership; golf driving range; golf goods & equipment; eating places

PRODUCTS & SERVICES SECTION
7997 - Membership Sports & Recreation Clubs County (P-18926)

(P-18903)
BURLINGAME COUNTRY CLUB
80 New Place Rd, Hillsborough
(94010-6499)
PHONE..................650 696-8100
Fax: 650 347-3572
Hartmut Hofacker, *Manager*
Jennifer Gatti, *Executive*
EMP: 70 EST: 1893
SALES: 7.3MM **Privately Held**
WEB: www.burlingamecc.org
SIC: 7997 Country club, membership

(P-18904)
BUSINESS AND SUPPORT SERVICES
P.O. Box 6001 (92278-6001)
PHONE..................760 830-6873
EMP: 70 **Publicly Held**
SIC: 7997 Membership sports & recreation clubs
HQ: Business And Support Services
3044 Catlin Ave
Quantico VA 22134
703 432-0109

(P-18905)
CALABASAS COUNTRY CLUB
4515 Park Entrada, Calabasas
(91302-1469)
PHONE..................818 222-8111
Robert W Linn, *General Mgr*
EMP: 74
SALES (est): 411.6K
SALES (corp-wide): 4.8MM **Privately Held**
SIC: 7997 Golf club, membership
PA: Knight-Calabasas Llc
4515 Park Entrada
Calabasas CA 91302
818 222-3200

(P-18906)
CALIFORNIA COUNTRY CLUB
Also Called: S R Mutual Funds
1509 Workman Mill Rd, City of Industry
(90601-1499)
PHONE..................626 333-4571
Fax: 626 336-8260
Will Bayer, *General Mgr*
Duk H Choduplicate, *CFO*
ARA Cho, *Executive*
Ted Parker, *Director*
Olivia Peng, *Manager*
EMP: 60 EST: 1956
SALES (est): 4.9MM **Privately Held**
WEB: www.golfccc.com
SIC: 7997 Country club, membership

(P-18907)
CALIFORNIA GOLF ASSOCIATION
3200 Lopez Rd, Pebble Beach
(93953-2900)
PHONE..................831 625-4653
Bob Scarpitto, *President*
EMP: 55
SALES: 152.2K **Privately Held**
SIC: 7997 Golf club, membership

(P-18908)
CALIFORNIA MOTORCYCLE CLUB
742 45th Ave, Oakland (94601-4429)
PHONE..................510 534-6222
Mark Norris, *Exec Dir*
Larry Steward, *Principal*
Robert Turkletop,
EMP: 75
SQ FT: 2,232
SALES: 88.2K **Privately Held**
WEB: www.oaklandmc.org
SIC: 7997 Membership sports & recreation clubs

(P-18909)
CALIFORNIA OAK VALLEY GOLF
Also Called: Oak Valley Golf Club
1888 Golf Club Dr, Beaumont
(92223-9700)
PHONE..................951 769-9771
Fax: 951 769-1229
Mike Pearson, *Manager*
Lee Curley, *Branch Mgr*
Evlyon Then, *Manager*
EMP: 50
SQ FT: 1,000
SALES (est): 2.1MM **Privately Held**
SIC: 7997 Golf club, membership

(P-18910)
CALIFRNIA GOLF CLB SAN FRNCSCO
844 W Orange Ave, South San Francisco
(94080-3125)
PHONE..................650 588-9021
Fax: 650 588-0206
Jon McGovern, *CEO*
Junaid Sheikh, *Treasurer*
Henry Bullock, *Vice Pres*
Gregory Spencer, *Exec Dir*
Steven Ruwe, *Admin Sec*
EMP: 74
SQ FT: 30,000
SALES: 7.6MM **Privately Held**
SIC: 7997 Golf club, membership

(P-18911)
CAMERON PARK COUNTRY CLUB INC
3201 Royal Dr, Cameron Park
(95682-8559)
PHONE..................530 672-9840
Fax: 530 672-7924
J Poindexter, *Manager*
Jack Mehl, *President*
Mark Carson, *CEO*
Don Seese, *CFO*
Joe William, *Vice Pres*
EMP: 60
SQ FT: 50,000
SALES: 3.6MM **Privately Held**
WEB: www.cameronparkcc.com
SIC: 7997 Country club, membership

(P-18912)
CANYON CREST COUNTRY CLUB INC
Also Called: Golf Pro Shop
975 Country Club Dr, Riverside
(92506-3699)
PHONE..................951 274-7900
Robert H Dedman, *Ch of Bd*
James Maser, *Officer*
Frank Gore, *Exec VP*
Richard S Poole, *Exec VP*
Sidney Simmons, *Exec VP*
EMP: 85
SQ FT: 4,000
SALES (est): 3.7MM
SALES (corp-wide): 1B **Publicly Held**
WEB: www.canyoncrestcc.com
SIC: 7997 5812 5813 Golf club, membership; American restaurant; bar (drinking places)
HQ: Clubcorp Usa, Inc.
3030 Lyndon B Johnson Fwy
Dallas TX 75234
972 243-6191

(P-18913)
CASTLEWOOD COUNTRY CLUB
707 Country Club Cir, Pleasanton
(94566-9743)
PHONE..................925 846-2871
Fax: 925 846-2153
Jerry Olson, *CEO*
Rick Hankins, *President*
Jerry Olsen, *CEO*
Tom Rutherford, *General Mgr*
Desiree Lamerdin, *Finance Mgr*
EMP: 167 EST: 1954
SQ FT: 55,000
SALES: 11.7MM **Privately Held**
WEB: www.castlewoodcc.org
SIC: 7997 Golf club, membership

(P-18914)
CATHEDRAL OAKS TENNIS SWIM ATH
Also Called: Cathedral Oaks Athletic Club
5800 Cathedral Oaks Rd, Goleta
(93117-1898)
PHONE..................805 964-7762
Fax: 805 964-8445
Julie Main, *Exec Dir*
Richard Ortale, *Shareholder*
Charlott Valentine, *Vice Pres*
Dave Bignoe, *Executive*
Monique Morelos, *Manager*
EMP: 75
SQ FT: 8,000
SALES (est): 2.4MM **Privately Held**
SIC: 7997 7991 Swimming club, membership; athletic club & gymnasiums, membership

(P-18915)
CATTA VERDERA COUNTRY CLUB
1111 Catta Verdera, Lincoln (95648-9649)
PHONE..................916 645-7200
Deke Kastner, *Manager*
Robert Delgado, *Director*
Jim Braden, *Manager*
Jeff Wilson, *Manager*
EMP: 90
SQ FT: 196,020
SALES (est): 4.1MM **Privately Held**
SIC: 7997 Golf club, membership

(P-18916)
CHARDONNAY/ CLUB SHAKESPEARE
Also Called: Chardonnay Golf Club
2555 Jamieson Canyon Rd, NAPA (94558)
PHONE..................707 257-1900
Jack Barry, *President*
Trishia Ellison, *Executive Asst*
Todd Brighton, *Admin Sec*
Laura Mena, *Food Svc Dir*
Barbara Crivelli, *Director*
EMP: 100
SQ FT: 24,000
SALES (est): 3.3MM **Privately Held**
WEB: www.chardonnaygolfclub.com
SIC: 7997 Golf club, membership

(P-18917)
CITIZENS DEVELOPMENT CORP (PA)
Also Called: Lake San Marcos Resort
1105 La Bonita Dr, San Marcos
(92078-5296)
PHONE..................760 744-0120
Fax: 760 591-4053
Ronald N Frazar, *President*
Eun Park, *Finance Mgr*
EMP: 59
SALES (est): 3.4MM **Privately Held**
SIC: 7997 Country club, membership

(P-18918)
CLAREMONT COUNTRY CLUB
5295 Broadway Ter, Oakland (94618-1498)
PHONE..................510 653-6789
Fax: 510 653-8469
Harold Peter Smith, *CEO*
Warren Chip Brown, *President*
Richard W Kraber, *Treasurer*
Thomas C Crosby, *Vice Pres*
Alec Churchward, *General Mgr*
EMP: 85
SQ FT: 479,160
SALES: 11.6MM **Privately Held**
WEB: www.claremontcountryclub.org
SIC: 7997 Country club, membership

(P-18919)
CLAREMONT TENNIS CLUB
Also Called: Claremont Club, The
1777 Monte Vista Ave, Claremont
(91711-2916)
PHONE..................909 625-9515
Fax: 909 621-3908
Michael G Alpert, *President*
Geoffrey Clark, *Vice Pres*
Rebecca Wiesenbach, *Admin Asst*
Rose Grasselli, *Director*
Antionette Mara, *Director*
EMP: 200
SQ FT: 40,000
SALES (est): 12.5MM **Privately Held**
SIC: 7997 7991 5812 Membership sports & recreation clubs; health club; eating places

(P-18920)
CLUB AT SHNNDOAH SPRNG VLG INC
32700 Desert Moon Dr, Thousand Palms
(92276-3713)
PHONE..................760 343-3497
Ronald Safren, *President*
Gary Safren, *Treasurer*
Ronald Edwards, *Vice Pres*
Gary Copp, *Controller*
Leonard Colvin, *Director*
EMP: 50 EST: 2006
SALES: 3MM **Privately Held**
SIC: 7997 Country club, membership

(P-18921)
CLUB OF SUNRISE COUNTRY
71601 Country Club Dr, Rancho Mirage
(92270-3546)
PHONE..................760 328-6549
Bill Athan, *General Mgr*
Stacia Kaygill, *Controller*
William Athan, *Agent*
EMP: 64
SQ FT: 15,000
SALES: 3MM **Privately Held**
SIC: 7997 5812 5941 Country club, membership; American restaurant; golf, tennis & ski shops

(P-18922)
CLUB ONE AT PETALUMA
1201 Redwood Way, Petaluma
(94954-6533)
PHONE..................707 766-8080
Yalda Teranchi, *General Mgr*
EMP: 90
SALES (est): 775.7K **Privately Held**
SIC: 7997 Membership sports & recreation clubs

(P-18923)
CLUBCORP USA INC
5690 Cancha De Golf, Rancho Santa Fe
(92091-4408)
PHONE..................858 756-2471
Jim Macdonough, *General Mgr*
EMP: 180
SALES (corp-wide): 1B **Publicly Held**
WEB: www.remington-gc.com
SIC: 7997 Country club, membership
HQ: Clubcorp Usa, Inc.
3030 Lyndon B Johnson Fwy
Dallas TX 75234
972 243-6191

(P-18924)
CONTRA COSTA COUNTRY CLUB
801 Golf Club Rd, Pleasant Hill
(94523-1101)
PHONE..................925 798-7135
Fax: 925 687-8661
Bill Wampler, *Manager*
Suzie Bahary, *Director*
EMP: 69
SQ FT: 20,000
SALES: 5.3MM **Privately Held**
SIC: 7997 5812 5813 Golf club, membership; American restaurant; drinking places

(P-18925)
COPPER RIVER COUNTRY CLUB LP (PA)
2140 E Clubhouse Dr, Fresno
(93730-7020)
P.O. Box 25850 (93729-5850)
PHONE..................559 434-5200
Fax: 559 434-8962
William R Tatham Sr, *Partner*
Renne Antognoli, *Partner*
Michael F Tatham, *Partner*
William T Tatham Jr, *Partner*
Carlos Galvan, *Controller*
EMP: 50
SALES (est): 3.8MM **Privately Held**
SIC: 7997 Golf club, membership

(P-18926)
CORDEVALLE GOLF CLUB LLC
1 Cordevalle Club Dr, San Martin
(95046-9472)
PHONE..................408 695-4500
Earl Wilson,
Luca Rutigliano, *Executive*
Travis Skeesick, *Director*
EMP: 250 EST: 1999
SALES (est): 11.5MM **Privately Held**
WEB: www.cordevalle.com
SIC: 7997 Membership sports & recreation clubs

7997 - Membership Sports & Recreation Clubs County (P-18927)

(P-18927)
CORRAL DE TIERRA COUNTRY CLUB
81 Corral De Tierra Rd, Salinas (93908-9477)
PHONE..................831 484-1325
Fax: 831 484-1003
Mike Oprish, *President*
William Bennett, *Executive*
Dominic Guzzo, *General Mgr*
David Webb, *General Mgr*
Stevie Wagner, *Director*
EMP: 100 EST: 1959
SQ FT: 15,000
SALES: 6.7MM Privately Held
WEB: www.corraldetierracc.com
SIC: 7997 Country club, membership

(P-18928)
CORRAL DEL TIERRA
81 Corral De Tierra Rd, Salinas (93908-9474)
PHONE..................831 372-6244
Dominic Guzzo, *Manager*
EMP: 70
SALES: 40.3K Privately Held
SIC: 7997 Golf club, membership

(P-18929)
COTO DE CAZA GOLF RACQUET CLB
Also Called: Coto De Caza Golf Racquet CLB
25291 Vista Del Verde, Trabuco Canyon (92679-4900)
PHONE..................949 858-4100
Fax: 949 858-2797
John Rosenbluth, *General Mgr*
Kristen Greenough, *Sls & Mktg Exec*
Alice Arimitsu, *Director*
Anne Brooke, *Director*
Matt Gabos, *Director*
EMP: 160
SQ FT: 44,000
SALES (est): 7.2MM
SALES (corp-wide): 1B Publicly Held
WEB: www.remington-gc.com
SIC: 7997 7992 7991 5813 Racquetball club, membership; public golf courses; physical fitness facilities; drinking places; eating places
HQ: Clubcorp Usa, Inc.
  3030 Lyndon B Johnson Fwy
  Dallas TX 75234
  972 243-6191

(P-18930)
COURTSIDE TENNIS CLUB
Also Called: Courtside Club
14675 Winchester Blvd, Los Gatos (95032-1890)
PHONE..................408 395-7111
Fax: 408 354-5854
James Hinckley, *President*
Jim Gerber, *President*
Lisa Graf, *General Mgr*
Dorina Kohler, *Instructor*
Nicole Green, *Director*
EMP: 90
SQ FT: 100,000
SALES (est): 4.8MM
SALES (corp-wide): 1B Publicly Held
WEB: www.courtsideclub.com
SIC: 7997 7991 5812 Membership sports & recreation clubs; physical fitness facilities; eating places
HQ: Clubcorp Usa, Inc.
  3030 Lyndon B Johnson Fwy
  Dallas TX 75234
  972 243-6191

(P-18931)
CROSBY NATIONAL GOLF CLUB LLC
17102 Bing Crosby Blvd, Rancho Santa Fe (92067)
P.O. Box 2504 (92067-2504)
PHONE..................858 756-6310
Fax: 858 759-3840
Rhonda Hill, *Director*
Ron Cropley, *Principal*
Ed Sanabria, *General Mgr*
Ken Halligan, *Manager*
EMP: 70
SALES (est): 4.4MM Privately Held
SIC: 7997 Golf club, membership

(P-18932)
CROW CANYON MANAGEMENT CORP
Also Called: Crow Canyon Country Club
711 Silver Lake Dr, Danville (94526-6241)
PHONE..................925 735-5700
Fax: 925 735-1089
Eric Jacobsen, *President*
John Beckert, *President*
EMP: 50
SQ FT: 55,000
SALES (est): 3.4MM
SALES (corp-wide): 1B Publicly Held
WEB: www.crow-canyon.com
SIC: 7997 7991 5941 5813 Country club, membership; physical fitness facilities; sporting goods & bicycle shops; drinking places; eating places
HQ: Clubcorp Usa, Inc.
  3030 Lyndon B Johnson Fwy
  Dallas TX 75234
  972 243-6191

(P-18933)
CRYSTAL AIRE COUNTRY CLUB GOLF
Also Called: Crystalaire Country Club
15701 Boca Raton Ave, Llano (93544-1211)
PHONE..................661 944-2112
Fax: 661 944-4866
Mike Carpenter, *President*
Jane Reason, *Treasurer*
Dick McDonald, *Vice Pres*
Laura Litten, *Director*
EMP: 50
SALES (est): 2.4MM Privately Held
WEB: www.crystalairecc.com
SIC: 7997 5812 Golf club, membership; American restaurant

(P-18934)
CRYSTAL SPRINGS GOLF PARTNERS
Also Called: Crystal Springs Golf Course
6650 Golf Course Dr, Burlingame (94010-6543)
PHONE..................650 342-4188
Fax: 650 342-1769
Tom Issak, *President*
John Teleshek, *CFO*
Russ Onizuka, *General Mgr*
Jerome Cansino, *Manager*
Mike Leong, *Manager*
EMP: 50
SALES (est): 4.3MM Privately Held
WEB: www.playcrystalsprings.com
SIC: 7997 Country club, membership

(P-18935)
DEL MAR COUNTRY CLUB INC
6001 Clubhouse Dr, Rancho Santa Fe (92067)
P.O. Box 9866 (92067-4866)
PHONE..................858 759-5500
Fax: 858 759-5995
Madeleine Pickens, *President*
Cristy Kielborn, *Purch Mgr*
EMP: 90
SQ FT: 18,000
SALES (est): 7.8MM Privately Held
WEB: www.delmarcountryclub.com
SIC: 7997 Golf club, membership

(P-18936)
DEL PASO COUNTRY CLUB
3333 Marconi Ave, Sacramento (95821-6293)
PHONE..................916 489-3681
Fax: 916 489-4011
Chris Shanks, *Controller*
Eric Hatzenbiler, *CEO*
Bob Kunz, *General Mgr*
EMP: 105
SALES: 6.1MM Privately Held
WEB: www.delpasocountryclub.com
SIC: 7997 5941 5812 Country club, membership; sporting goods & bicycle shops; eating places

(P-18937)
DEL RIO GOLF & COUNTRY CLUB
801 Stewart Rd, Modesto (95356-9639)
PHONE..................209 341-2414
Fax: 209 545-5133
Duncan Reno, *COO*
Larry Keillor, *Treasurer*
Jay Ward, *Admin Sec*
Emmey Paulos, *Controller*
Stephen Smith, *Facilities Mgr*
EMP: 112
SQ FT: 48,000
SALES: 8MM Privately Held
WEB: www.delriocountryclub.com
SIC: 7997 5941 Country club, membership; golf club, membership; tennis club, membership; sporting goods & bicycle shops

(P-18938)
DESERT FALLS COUNTRY CLUB INC
1111 Desert Falls Pkwy, Palm Desert (92211-1709)
PHONE..................760 340-5646
Fax: 760 340-5716
Tim Scogan, *President*
EMP: 90
SALES (est): 4.7MM
SALES (corp-wide): 1B Publicly Held
WEB: www.desert-falls.com
SIC: 7997 5812 7992 7299 Membership sports & recreation clubs; eating places; public golf courses; banquet hall facilities
HQ: Clubcorp Usa, Inc.
  3030 Lyndon B Johnson Fwy
  Dallas TX 75234
  972 243-6191

(P-18939)
DESERT PRINCESS HOME
28555 Landau Blvd, Cathedral City (92234-3508)
PHONE..................760 322-1655
Lynn Gilliam, *President*
John Beachnau, *Food Svc Dir*
Susan McCabe, *Manager*
EMP: 50
SALES (est): 2.8MM Privately Held
WEB: www.desertprincess.com
SIC: 7997 Country club, membership

(P-18940)
DHCCNP
Also Called: DESERT HORIZONS COUNTRY CLUB
44900 Desert Horizons Dr, Indian Wells (92210-7401)
PHONE..................760 340-4646
Fax: 760 341-0356
Jurgen Gross, *Manager*
Mike Shulby, *Executive*
Phyllis Mazur, *Controller*
EMP: 86 EST: 1979
SQ FT: 30,000
SALES: 4.5MM Privately Held
WEB: www.deserthorizonscc.com
SIC: 7997 7992 5812 Country club, membership; public golf courses; eating places

(P-18941)
DIABLO COUNTRY CLUB
1700 Club House Rd, Diablo (94528)
PHONE..................925 837-4221
Tom Gibbons, *CEO*
Steven Buck, *General Mgr*
Katie Hall, *Mktg Dir*
Janelle Lembeck, *Director*
Cameron Neuhauser, *Director*
EMP: 80
SQ FT: 52,000
SALES: 10.3MM Privately Held
WEB: www.diablocc.com
SIC: 7997 5812 5813 5941 Country club, membership; eating places; drinking places; sporting goods & bicycle shops

(P-18942)
EAGLE RIDGE GOLF CNTRY CLB LLC
Also Called: Eagle Ridge Golf Club
2951 Club Dr, Gilroy (95020-3043)
PHONE..................408 846-4531
Mark Gurnow, *Mng Member*
Rick Smith, *General Mgr*
Mike Attara, *Opers Staff*
Jerry Kokes, *Sales Executive*
Scott S Krause, *Manager*
EMP: 125
SALES (est): 3.9MM Privately Held
WEB: www.eagleridgegc.com
SIC: 7997 7992 5812 Country club, membership; public golf courses; eating places

(P-18943)
EAGLE VNES VNYRDS GOLF CLB LLC
580 S Kelly Rd, American Canyon (94503-5600)
P.O. Box 2398, NAPA (94558-0239)
PHONE..................707 257-4470
Tokutaro Umezawa, *President*
Nobu Mizuhara, *Vice Pres*
Ehrin Cadigan, *Director*
John Walsh, *Director*
Ernie Hernandez, *Assistant*
EMP: 70
SALES (est): 3.7MM Privately Held
SIC: 7997 Golf club, membership

(P-18944)
EL CABALLERO COUNTRY CLUB
18300 Tarzana Dr, Tarzana (91356-4216)
PHONE..................818 654-3000
Fax: 818 345-3486
Bary West, *President*
Peter Jimenez, *CFO*
Gary Diamond, *Treasurer*
Thomas H Bernsen, *General Mgr*
Joseph Zarrillo, *Manager*
EMP: 125
SQ FT: 20,000
SALES: 10MM Privately Held
SIC: 7997 7992 5812 Country club, membership; public golf courses; eating places

(P-18945)
EL DORADO COUNTRY CLUB
46000 Fairway Dr, Indian Wells (92210-8631)
PHONE..................760 346-8081
Fax: 760 340-1325
Geoff Hasley, *President*
Neal Hoffman, *CFO*
Richard Jallet, *Executive*
Wade Miller, *General Mgr*
Neil Hartman, *Controller*
EMP: 200
SQ FT: 50,000
SALES: 12.1MM Privately Held
WEB: www.eldoradocountryclub.com
SIC: 7997 5812 Golf club, membership; eating places

(P-18946)
EL MACERO COUNTRY CLUB INC
44571 Clubhouse Dr, El Macero (95618-1073)
PHONE..................530 753-3363
Fax: 530 753-4832
Steven Backman, *General Mgr*
Bruce Summerhays, *Director*
Rachael Levine, *Manager*
Nick Nicoloudis, *Manager*
Kevin Robinson, *Manager*
EMP: 60
SQ FT: 21,000
SALES: 3.5MM Privately Held
SIC: 7997 5941 5812 5813 Golf club, membership; golf goods & equipment; American restaurant; bar (drinking places)

(P-18947)
FAIRBANKS RANCH CNTRY CLB INC
15150 San Dieguito Rd, Rancho Santa Fe (92067)
P.O. Box 8586 (92067-8586)
PHONE..................858 259-8811
Fax: 858 259-8593
Mike Kendall, *CEO*
Brad Forrester, *President*
Robert Macier, *CEO*
Stan Kinsey, *Vice Pres*
Steve Wittert, *General Mgr*
EMP: 180
SQ FT: 35,000
SALES: 12.7MM Privately Held
WEB: www.fairbanksranch.com
SIC: 7997 Country club, membership

PRODUCTS & SERVICES SECTION
7997 - Membership Sports & Recreation Clubs County (P-18970)

(P-18948)
FAMILY MRALE WLFARE RECREATION
Also Called: Fmwr
1317 Normandy Dr, Fort Irwin (92310)
P.O. Box 105094 (92310-5094)
PHONE..................................760 380-3493
Brian Contreras, *Principal*
Marion Taylor, *CFO*
Tricia Berg, *Officer*
Sonia Bonet-Betancourt, *Director*
EMP: 99
SALES (est): 263.2K **Privately Held**
SIC: 7997 5812 8361 8351 Membership sports & recreation clubs; family restaurants; residential care for children; child day care services

(P-18949)
FARMS GOLF CLUB INC
Also Called: Red Tail Golf Assoc
8500 San Andrews Rd, Rancho Santa Fe (92067)
P.O. Box 2769 (92067-2769)
PHONE..................................858 756-5585
Bruce Bennetts, *Manager*
Dennis Kraft, *Manager*
EMP: 63
SALES (est): 2.7MM **Privately Held**
SIC: 7997 Golf club, membership

(P-18950)
FIG GARDEN GOLF COURSE INC
7700 N Van Ness Blvd, Fresno (93711-0499)
PHONE..................................559 439-2928
Fax: 559 439-2129
David Knott, *President*
David T Knott, *President*
Marie D Knott, *Admin Sec*
Jim Connley, *Personnel Exec*
Eric Smith, *Manager*
EMP: 55
SQ FT: 8,000
SALES (est): 3.5MM **Privately Held**
WEB: www.figgardengolf.com
SIC: 7997 5941 5812 Golf club, membership; golf goods & equipment; coffee shop

(P-18951)
FOOTHILL DUPLICATE BRIDGE CLUB
4050 Durock Rd Ste 8, Shingle Springs (95682-8450)
PHONE..................................530 677-3771
Barry Wold, *Manager*
Lori Oliver, *Vice Pres*
Sandy Wold, *Director*
EMP: 50
SALES (est): 759.3K **Privately Held**
SIC: 7997 Bridge club, membership

(P-18952)
FOREST PARK CABANA CLUB
2911 Pruneridge Ave, Santa Clara (95051-5652)
P.O. Box 2151 (95055-2151)
PHONE..................................408 244-1884
Jo Ann Frink, *President*
Marcel Provencher, *Agent*
EMP: 50
SALES: 251.6K **Privately Held**
WEB: www.forestparkcabanaclub.com
SIC: 7997 Membership sports & recreation clubs

(P-18953)
FORT WASH GOLF & CNTRY CLB
Also Called: FORT, THE
10272 N Millbrook Ave, Fresno (93730-3400)
PHONE..................................559 434-1702
Fax: 559 434-1350
Dean Pryor, *President*
Bruce Waltz, *President*
Ali Peyvandi, *Manager*
EMP: 95
SALES: 4.2MM **Privately Held**
SIC: 7997 5813 5812 Golf club, membership; cocktail lounge; American restaurant

(P-18954)
FRIENDLY HILLS COUNTRY CLUB
8500 Villaverde Dr, Whittier (90605-1398)
PHONE..................................562 698-0331
Dave Goodrich, *COO*
Gail Heins, *Controller*
Christine Bobadilla, *Marketing Staff*
Jessica Magdosku, *Marketing Staff*
Chris Banner, *Director*
EMP: 110 **EST:** 1969
SQ FT: 42,000
SALES (est): 3.6MM **Privately Held**
WEB: www.friendlyhillscc.com
SIC: 7997 Country club, membership

(P-18955)
GLENDORA COUNTRY CLUB
2400 Country Club Dr, Glendora (91741)
PHONE..................................626 335-4051
Fax: 626 335-6786
Jack Stoughton, *CEO*
Mike Kerstetter, *President*
Jim Leahy, *CEO*
Bill McKinley, *Treasurer*
EMP: 90
SQ FT: 10,000
SALES: 6MM **Privately Held**
SIC: 7997 5812 5813 Country club, membership; eating places; drinking places

(P-18956)
GRANITE BAY GOLF CLUB
9600 Golf Club Dr, Granite Bay (95746-6721)
PHONE..................................916 791-5379
Fax: 916 791-7515
Bob Kunz, *General Mgr*
Greg Davis, *General Mgr*
EMP: 120
SQ FT: 1,440
SALES (est): 4.8MM
SALES (corp-wide): 1B **Publicly Held**
WEB: www.granitebayclub.com
SIC: 7997 5812 7299 Golf club, membership; eating places; wedding chapel, privately operated
HQ: Clubcorp Usa, Inc.
  3030 Lyndon B Johnson Fwy
  Dallas TX 75234
  972 243-6191

(P-18957)
GREEN VALLEY COUNTRY CLUB
35 Country Club Dr, Fairfield (94534-1305)
PHONE..................................707 864-1101
Fax: 707 864-3501
Tom Snell, *President*
Alisa Azpeitia, *Manager*
Darin Hamner, *Manager*
Don Young, *Manager*
EMP: 75
SALES: 5.1MM **Privately Held**
WEB: www.greenvalleycc.com
SIC: 7997 Country club, membership

(P-18958)
HACIENDA GOLF CLUB
718 East Rd, La Habra Heights (90631-8155)
PHONE..................................562 694-1081
Fax: 562 694-4701
Frank Cordeiro, *General Mgr*
Lane Greenlee, *CFO*
Demetrio Munoz, *Executive*
Cheryl Martenson, *Controller*
Daniel Arsenault, *Director*
EMP: 95
SQ FT: 30,000
SALES: 6.2MM **Privately Held**
WEB: www.haciendagolfclub.com
SIC: 7997 5812 5813 Golf club, membership; American restaurant; bar (drinking places)

(P-18959)
HCC INVESTORS LLC
Also Called: Lennar
18550 Seven Bridges Rd, Rancho Santa Fe (92091-0216)
P.O. Box 1322 (92067-1322)
PHONE..................................858 759-7200
Jon Jaffe,
Patty Aguirre, *Controller*
Joni Stuart, *Sales Mgr*
Mary Lorison, *Director*
EMP: 120
SQ FT: 35,000
SALES (est): 3.9MM **Privately Held**
SIC: 7997 Golf club, membership

(P-18960)
HILLCREST COUNTRY CLUB
10000 W Pico Blvd, Los Angeles (90064-3400)
PHONE..................................310 553-8911
Fax: 310 300-6123
John Jameson, *President*
John Goldsmith, *CEO*
Tom Driefus, *CFO*
Chester Firestien, *Principal*
Leonard Fisher, *Principal*
EMP: 180
SQ FT: 69,081
SALES: 20.9MM **Privately Held**
WEB: www.hcc-la.com
SIC: 7997 Country club, membership

(P-18961)
HUMBOLDT YACHT CLUB
2479 Wrigley Rd, Eureka (95503-9618)
P.O. Box 445 (95502-0445)
PHONE..................................707 443-1469
Tom Elfers, *Principal*
Wayne Sutherland, *Treasurer*
EMP: 75
SALES (est): 2.4MM **Privately Held**
SIC: 7997 Membership sports & recreation clubs

(P-18962)
INTERNATIONAL BAY CLUBS LLC (PA)
Also Called: Balboa Bay Club and Resort
1221 W Coast Hwy Ste 145, Newport Beach (92663-5037)
PHONE..................................949 645-5000
Todd M Pickup, *CEO*
David Wooten, *President*
Phillip Thalstenny, *Accountant*
Dana Lundbald, *Human Resources*
Nickie Rodriguez, *Manager*
EMP: 116
SQ FT: 330,000
SALES: 27.7MM **Privately Held**
WEB: www.balboabayclub.com
SIC: 7997 4493 6552 7011 Membership sports & recreation clubs; beach club, membership; marinas; land subdividers & developers, residential; hotels & motels

(P-18963)
INTERVEC PHOENIX TRAVEL CLUB
1456 Seacoast Dr Unit 4a, Imperial Beach (91932-3198)
PHONE..................................828 728-5287
Donna Weston, *President*
EMP: 130
SALES (est): 5.5MM **Privately Held**
SIC: 7997 Membership sports & recreation clubs

(P-18964)
IW GOLF CLUB INC
Also Called: Indian Wells Country Club
46000 Club Dr, Indian Wells (92210-8870)
PHONE..................................760 345-2561
Fax: 760 360-9492
Garret Kriske, *General Mgr*
James Hinckley, *President*
Jack Lupton, *Treasurer*
Douglas Howe, *Exec VP*
Yvonne Kassler, *Executive*
EMP: 60
SQ FT: 65,000
SALES (est): 3.8MM
SALES (corp-wide): 1B **Publicly Held**
WEB: www.remington-gc.com
SIC: 7997 Country club, membership
HQ: Clubcorp Usa, Inc.
  3030 Lyndon B Johnson Fwy
  Dallas TX 75234
  972 243-6191

(P-18965)
JONATHAN CLUB
Also Called: Jonathan Beach Club
850 Palisades Beach Rd, Santa Monica (90403-1008)
PHONE..................................310 393-9245
Ernie Dunn, *Manager*
Richard Debruijn, *Info Tech Dir*
Fred Dorering, *Manager*
EMP: 150
SQ FT: 12,784
SALES (corp-wide): 38.5MM **Privately Held**
WEB: www.jc.org
SIC: 7997 5812 8641 Beach club, membership; eating places; civic social & fraternal associations
PA: Jonathan Club
  545 S Figueroa St
  Los Angeles CA 90071
  213 624-0881

(P-18966)
KNIGHT-CALABASAS LLC (PA)
Also Called: Calabasas Country Club
4515 Park Entrada, Calabasas (91302-1453)
PHONE..................................818 222-3200
Fax: 818 222-3214
Mike Calabassas,
Robert W Linn, *General Mgr*
Karen Seidman, *Controller*
Veronica Parong, *Human Res Mgr*
Jeff Skolnick, *Marketing Staff*
EMP: 75
SQ FT: 2,000
SALES (est): 4.8MM **Privately Held**
SIC: 7997 Golf club, membership; country club, membership

(P-18967)
KNIGHT-CALABASAS LLC
Also Called: Peacock Gap Golf & Country CLB
333 Biscayne Dr, San Rafael (94901-1577)
PHONE..................................415 453-4940
Bobby Yokito, *Partner*
Val Verhunce, *Director*
Joe Breen, *Manager*
Paul Dunn, *Manager*
Rod Ghilarducci, *Manager*
EMP: 60
SALES (corp-wide): 4.8MM **Privately Held**
SIC: 7997 Country club, membership
PA: Knight-Calabasas Llc
  4515 Park Entrada
  Calabasas CA 91302
  818 222-3200

(P-18968)
LA CANADA FLINTRIDGE CNTRY CLB
5500 Godbey Dr, La Canada (91011-1836)
PHONE..................................818 790-0611
Fax: 818 790-5503
Gilbert Dreyfus, *President*
Shi Wang, *CFO*
Evelyn Dreyfus, *Admin Sec*
Jeanette Martin, *Human Res Dir*
Miki Mootsey, *Director*
EMP: 80 **EST:** 1977
SQ FT: 24,000
SALES (est): 6.5MM **Privately Held**
SIC: 7997 Country club, membership

(P-18969)
LA CUMBRE COUNTRY CLUB
4015 Via Laguna, Santa Barbara (93110-2298)
PHONE..................................805 687-2421
Fax: 805 682-3964
Brian Bahman, *General Mgr*
Deane Wareham, *Controller*
EMP: 100
SQ FT: 8,000
SALES: 7.7MM **Privately Held**
SIC: 7997 Golf club, membership; country club, membership

(P-18970)
LA JOLLA COUNTRY CLUB INC
7301 High Ave, La Jolla (92037-5210)
PHONE..................................858 454-9601
Fax: 858 454-4536
Andrew Gorton, *General Mgr*

7997 - Membership Sports & Recreation Clubs County (P-18971)

PRODUCTS & SERVICES SECTION

Deborah Nixon, *Administration*
Jorge Dominguez, *Facilities Dir*
Rachel Carter, *Director*
Michael Mooney, *Director*
EMP: 122
SQ FT: 39,000
SALES: 10.5MM **Privately Held**
WEB: www.lajollacc.org
SIC: 7997 5812 5941 5813 Golf club, membership; eating places; golf goods & equipment; bar (drinking places); public golf courses

(P-18971)
LA QUINTA COUNTRY CLUB
77750 Avenue 50, La Quinta (92253-2204)
PHONE.................760 564-4151
Fax: 760 564-6393
Ernest Moore, *CFO*
Tana Bustamante,
Kelly O'Day, *Director*
Kelly Wade, *Director*
Tom Emison, *Manager*
EMP: 55
SQ FT: 36,000
SALES: 6MM **Privately Held**
SIC: 7997 Country club, membership

(P-18972)
LA RINCONADA COUNTRY CLUB INC (PA)
Also Called: LA RINCONADA GOLF AND COUNTRY
14595 Clearview Dr, Los Gatos (95032-1799)
PHONE.................408 395-4181
Fax: 408 395-2723
Steve Vindasius, *CEO*
Ernie Andreas, *Executive*
Mac Niven, *General Mgr*
Janett Antle, *Admin Asst*
Brad Streza, *CTO*
EMP: 96
SQ FT: 100,000
SALES: 8MM **Privately Held**
WEB: www.larinconadacc.com
SIC: 7997 5813 5812 Country club, membership; bar (drinking places); eating places

(P-18973)
LAACO LTD
Also Called: California Yacht Club
4469 Admiralty Way, Marina Del Rey (90292-5415)
PHONE.................310 823-4567
Fax: 310 822-3658
Steve Hathaway, *President*
Gus Marks, *Office Admin*
Colleen Cavan, *Director*
Michelle Weston, *Manager*
EMP: 100
SALES (corp-wide): 18.8MM **Privately Held**
SIC: 7997 4493 Yacht club, membership; marinas
PA: Laaco, Ltd.
431 W 7th St
Los Angeles CA 90014
213 622-1254

(P-18974)
LAHONTAN GOLF CLUB
12700 Lodgetrail Dr, Truckee (96161-5125)
PHONE.................530 550-2400
Fax: 530 550-2409
Jon Madonna, *President*
Jeffery Cobain, *General Mgr*
Steve Harris, *Admin Sec*
Kyl Larsen, *Accountant*
Wendy Briggs, *Controller*
EMP: 150 **EST:** 1996
SQ FT: 500,000
SALES (est): 10.4MM **Privately Held**
SIC: 7997 Golf club, membership

(P-18975)
LAKE MERCED GOLF & COUNTRY CLB
2300 Junipero Serra Blvd, Daly City (94015-1630)
PHONE.................650 755-2233
Fax: 650 755-4569
Dale Holub, *CEO*
Doug Morgan, *Bd of Directors*
Donna Lowe, *Manager*

Patricia Llanes, *Director*
EMP: 75
SQ FT: 38,000
SALES: 7MM **Privately Held**
WEB: www.lmgc.org
SIC: 7997 5813 Country club, membership; bars & lounges

(P-18976)
LAKES COUNTRY CLUB ASSN INC (PA)
161 Old Ranch Rd, Palm Desert (92211-3211)
PHONE.................760 568-4321
Fax: 760 773-5142
Gerald Lee Hagood, *President*
Sandy Seddon, *COO*
Ron Phipps, *CFO*
Ruth Crook, *Manager*
Jim Gammon, *Manager*
EMP: 120
SQ FT: 3,600
SALES (est): 7.3MM **Privately Held**
WEB: www.thelakescc.com
SIC: 7997 5941 5812 Country club, membership; sporting goods & bicycle shops; eating places

(P-18977)
LAKESIDE GOLF CLUB
4500 W Lakeside Dr, Burbank (91505-4088)
P.O. Box 2386, Toluca Lake (91610-0386)
PHONE.................818 984-0601
Fax: 818 763-1292
Jerry Fard, *Manager*
Michael E Henry, *CEO*
Isabel Cruz, *Controller*
Lance Subella, *Manager*
EMP: 98 **EST:** 1924
SQ FT: 25,000
SALES: 10.2MM **Privately Held**
WEB: www.lakesidegolfclub.com
SIC: 7997 Golf club, membership

(P-18978)
LANCASTER JETHAWKS
45116 Valley Central Way, Lancaster (93536-1508)
PHONE.................661 726-5400
Fax: 661 726-5406
Peter A Carfagna, *CEO*
Pete Carfagna, *President*
Brad Seymour, *President*
Wendy Richmond, *Treasurer*
Derek Sharp, *General Mgr*
EMP: 80
SALES (est): 2.5MM **Privately Held**
SIC: 7997 Baseball club, except professional & semi-professional

(P-18979)
LAS POSAS CLUB INC
230 Ramona Pl, Camarillo (93010-8406)
P.O. Box 3089 (93011-3089)
PHONE.................805 482-1811
Barbara Stevens, *President*
EMP: 75
SALES: 45.1K **Privately Held**
SIC: 7997 Membership sports & recreation clubs

(P-18980)
LAS POSAS COUNTRY CLUB
Also Called: Lpcc
955 Fairway Dr, Camarillo (93010-8499)
PHONE.................805 482-4518
Fax: 805 389-1378
Sandy McNolty, *Controller*
Charles Burns, *CEO*
Thomas Walling, *CEO*
Alfonso Arechiga, *Executive*
Dena Levy, *Principal*
EMP: 100
SALES: 2.6MM **Privately Held**
SIC: 7997 7992 5812 0781 Country club, membership; tennis club, membership; public golf courses; eating places; landscape counseling & planning

(P-18981)
LONE CYPRESS COMPANY LLC
Also Called: Beach & Tennis Club
1567 Cypress Dr, Pebble Beach (93953)
P.O. Box 1128 (93953-1128)
PHONE.................831 625-8507

Fax: 831 625-8504
Steve Hurst, *Branch Mgr*
Sue Carota, *General Mgr*
EMP: 100
SALES (corp-wide): 111.8MM **Privately Held**
WEB: www.pebblebeach.com
SIC: 7997 7999 5812 7991 Beach club, membership; swimming club, membership; tennis services & professionals; caterers; physical fitness facilities
PA: Lone Cypress Company Llc
2700 17 Mile Dr
Pebble Beach CA 93953
831 647-7500

(P-18982)
LONG BEACH YACHT CLUB
6201 E Appian Way, Long Beach (90803-4199)
PHONE.................562 598-9401
Fax: 562 430-8471
Louis Izurieta, *General Mgr*
Robert Frazer, *Ch of Bd*
Louis Izurieta, *General Mgr*
Amy York, *VP Finance*
Thomas Tan, *Controller*
EMP: 63
SQ FT: 25,000
SALES: 5.3MM **Privately Held**
WEB: www.lbyc.org
SIC: 7997 Yacht club, membership

(P-18983)
LOS ALTOS GOLF AND COUNTRY CLB
1560 Country Club Dr, Los Altos (94024-5907)
PHONE.................650 947-3100
Fax: 650 948-4267
Bill Schneider, *President*
Gary Roth, *Accountant*
Anna Maestrini, *Office Mgr*
Grace Ikan, *Accountant*
Paul Sossaman, *Facilities Mgr*
EMP: 70
SALES: 11.6MM **Privately Held**
WEB: www.lagcc.com
SIC: 7997 Membership sports & recreation clubs

(P-18984)
LOS AMIGOS COUNTRY CLUB INC
Also Called: Los Amigos Golf Course
7295 Quill Dr, Downey (90242-2001)
PHONE.................562 923-9696
Fax: 562 869-3988
Donald Duffin Sr, *President*
Tina Nunez, *Vice Pres*
Mike Shank, *General Mgr*
Anne Hunter, *Admin Sec*
EMP: 65
SALES (est): 3.9MM **Privately Held**
WEB: www.losamigoscountryclub.com
SIC: 7997 Golf club, membership

(P-18985)
LOS ANGELES 2024 EXPLORATORY
10960 Wilshire Blvd, Los Angeles (90024-3702)
PHONE.................310 407-0539
Casey Wasserman, *Chairman*
EMP: 50 **EST:** 2014
SALES (est): 177.7K **Privately Held**
SIC: 7997 Membership sports & recreation clubs

(P-18986)
LOS ANGELES COUNTRY CLUB
10101 Wilshire Blvd, Los Angeles (90024-4703)
PHONE.................310 276-6104
Fax: 310 276-4429
Kirk O Reese, *Principal*
Janet Welsh, *CFO*
Alan Green, *Security Dir*
James H Brewer, *General Mgr*
Nancy Melamad, *Human Res Dir*
EMP: 250 **EST:** 1898
SQ FT: 75,000

SALES: 18.4MM **Privately Held**
WEB: www.thelacc.org
SIC: 7997 Membership sports & recreation clubs; golf club, membership; tennis club, membership

(P-18987)
LOS ANGELES ROYAL VISTA GOLF C
Also Called: Los Angles Ryal Vsta Golf Crse
20055 Colima Rd, Walnut (91789-3502)
PHONE.................909 595-7471
Fax: 909 595-8242
Don Crooker, *Manager*
Yumi Chung, *Director*
EMP: 80
SQ FT: 37,948
SALES (corp-wide): 47.4MM **Privately Held**
SIC: 7997 7299 7992 Golf club, membership; banquet hall facilities; public golf courses
HQ: Los Angeles Royal Vista Golf Courses, Inc.
670 Queen St Ste 200
Honolulu HI 96813
808 592-4800

(P-18988)
MADERAS GOLF CLUB
17750 Old Coach Rd, Poway (92064-6621)
PHONE.................858 451-8100
Fax: 858 613-3897
Bill O'Brien, *General Mgr*
EMP: 80
SALES (est): 3.7MM **Privately Held**
SIC: 7997 Membership sports & recreation clubs

(P-18989)
MARBELLA COUNTRY CLUB
30800 Golf Club Dr, San Juan Capistrano (92675-5415)
PHONE.................949 248-3700
Dan Riker, *Manager*
Ted Clark, *Treasurer*
Jeffrey Krifle, *General Mgr*
Phil Kempler, *Admin Sec*
EMP: 140
SQ FT: 43,000
SALES: 37.6K
SALES (corp-wide): 13.9MM **Privately Held**
WEB: www.marbellacc.net
SIC: 7997 Country club, membership
PA: National Golf Properties Llc
2951 28th St Ste 3000
Santa Monica CA 90405
310 664-4000

(P-18990)
MARBELLA GOLF & COUNTRY CLUB
30800 Golf Club Dr, San Juan Capistrano (92675-5415)
PHONE.................949 248-3700
Fax: 949 248-8246
Rod Hayden, *President*
Gary Lisenbee, *Treasurer*
David Neish, *Vice Pres*
Larry De Pope, *General Mgr*
Robert Hatch, *Admin Sec*
EMP: 114
SQ FT: 43,000
SALES (est): 4MM **Privately Held**
SIC: 7997 Country club, membership

(P-18991)
MARIN COUNTRY CLUB INC
500 Country Club Dr, Novato (94949-5896)
PHONE.................415 382-6700
Fax: 415 382-6703
Richard Pimentel, *CEO*
Marcia Johnson, *Vice Pres*
Ryan Wilson, *General Mgr*
Tiffany Hutchinson, *Admin Asst*
Trisha Bradford, *Administration*
EMP: 75
SQ FT: 5,000
SALES: 6.8MM **Privately Held**
WEB: www.marincountryclub.com
SIC: 7997 5812 Country club, membership; golf club, membership; tennis club, membership; swimming club, membership; eating places

PRODUCTS & SERVICES SECTION
7997 - Membership Sports & Recreation Clubs County (P-19014)

(P-18992)
MARRAKESH GOLF SHOP
Also Called: Marrakesh Management
47000 Marrakesh Dr, Palm Desert (92260-5805)
PHONE.................760 568-2688
Don Lidster, *President*
Carl Buttler, *Manager*
EMP: 70
SQ FT: 5,000
SALES: 394.7K **Privately Held**
SIC: 7997 Golf club, membership

(P-18993)
MAYACAMA GOLF CLUB LLC
1240 Mayacama Club Dr, Santa Rosa (95403-8251)
PHONE.................707 569-2915
Fax: 707 569-2999
Johnathan Wilhelm, *Managing Prtnr*
Scott Pikey, *Executive*
Claire Thomas, *Comms Dir*
Greg Brown, *General Mgr*
Tracy Bell, *Executive Asst*
EMP: 120 **EST:** 1999
SQ FT: 5,000
SALES (est): 13MM **Privately Held**
SIC: 7997 Golf club, membership

(P-18994)
MCAULEY LCX CORPORATION
Also Called: Los Coyotes Pro Shop
8888 Los Coyotes Dr, Buena Park (90621-1030)
PHONE.................714 994-7788
Fax: 714 522-1189
Charles S McAuley, *Ch of Bd*
Charles E Conway, *COO*
Ruth I McAuley, *Vice Pres*
Shirley J Sizemore, *Admin Sec*
EMP: 140
SQ FT: 200
SALES (est): 6MM **Privately Held**
WEB: www.loscoyotescc.com
SIC: 7997 5941 5812 Country club, membership; sporting goods & bicycle shops; eating places

(P-18995)
MEADOW CLUB
1001 Bolinas Rd, Fairfax (94930-2200)
P.O. Box 129 (94978-0129)
PHONE.................415 453-3274
Fax: 415 453-3276
John Grehan, *General Mgr*
Telly Artos, *Finance Mgr*
Delores Narcum, *Human Res Mgr*
EMP: 81
SQ FT: 3,000
SALES: 9.4MM **Privately Held**
WEB: www.meadowclub.com
SIC: 7997 Golf club, membership

(P-18996)
MENIFEE LAKES COUNTRY CLUB
3200 E Guasti Rd Ste 100, Ontario (91761-8661)
PHONE.................951 672-4824
Fax: 951 672-4472
Charles Hou, *President*
EMP: 100
SALES (est): 6.4MM **Privately Held**
SIC: 7997 Country club, membership

(P-18997)
MENLO CIRCUS CLUB
190 Park Ln, Atherton (94027-4194)
PHONE.................650 322-4616
Fax: 650 322-1950
Michael Simonson, *General Mgr*
Christian Thon, *General Mgr*
Robyn Sahleen, *Graphic Designe*
EMP: 70 **EST:** 1923
SQ FT: 14,000
SALES: 12.4MM **Privately Held**
SIC: 7997 Country club, membership

(P-18998)
MESA VERDE COUNTRY CLUB
3000 Club House Rd, Costa Mesa (92626-3599)
PHONE.................714 549-0377
Fax: 714 549-9163
John Hayhoe, *CEO*
Robert Heflin, *President*
Kim Porter, *General Mgr*
Patricia Smith, *Controller*
Diane Burnes, *Director*
EMP: 125
SQ FT: 34,000
SALES: 7.5MM **Privately Held**
WEB: www.mesaverdecc.com
SIC: 7997 Country club, membership

(P-18999)
MID VLLEY RACQUETBALL ATHC CLB
Also Called: Mid-Valley Athletic Club
18420 Hart St, Reseda (91335-4317)
PHONE.................818 705-6500
Fax: 818 705-6269
Ray Haizlip, *President*
Harold Wright, *President*
Jeannie Henning, *Vice Pres*
Christina Hughes, *Admin Sec*
Angel Huitz, *Controller*
EMP: 120
SQ FT: 75,000
SALES (est): 2.2MM **Privately Held**
SIC: 7997 7991 Racquetball club, membership; physical fitness facilities

(P-19000)
MILLBRAE RACQUET CLUB
301 Santa Paula Ave, Millbrae (94030-2026)
P.O. Box 344 (94030-0344)
PHONE.................650 583-4345
Hector Johns, *President*
Olof Flodin, *Agent*
EMP: 82
SALES: 44.3K **Privately Held**
SIC: 7997 Membership sports & recreation clubs

(P-19001)
MIRA VISTA GOLF AND CNTRY CLB
7901 Cutting Blvd, El Cerrito (94530-1877)
PHONE.................510 233-7550
Fax: 510 215-0230
Richard Lee, *President*
Ken Kipp, *Treasurer*
Charles Ibbotson, *Vice Pres*
Patrick Abelman, *Executive*
Ron Svien, *General Mgr*
EMP: 60
SQ FT: 12,000
SALES (est): 4.3MM **Privately Held**
SIC: 7997 Country club, membership

(P-19002)
MISSION HILLS COUNTRY CLUB
34600 Mission Hills Dr, Rancho Mirage (92270-1300)
PHONE.................760 324-9400
Fax: 760 324-9230
Josh Tanner, *General Mgr*
Doug Howe, *Exec VP*
Toby Bills, *Engrg Dir*
Julie Babler, *Director*
Greg Bauer, *Director*
EMP: 130
SQ FT: 75,000
SALES (est): 6.6MM
SALES (corp-wide): 1B **Publicly Held**
WEB: www.remington-gc.com
SIC: 7997 7992 5812 Country club, membership; public golf courses; eating places
HQ: Clubcorp Usa, Inc.
3030 Lyndon B Johnson Fwy
Dallas TX 75234
972 243-6191

(P-19003)
MISSION VIEJO COUNTRY CLUB
26200 Country Club Dr, Mission Viejo (92691-5905)
PHONE.................949 582-1550
Fax: 949 582-3875
Michael Lance Kennedy, *Mng Member*
Enrique Martinez, *President*
Chad Pettit, *Principal*
Veronica Alva Roman, *Accountant*
Joan Grierson, *Manager*
EMP: 103
SALES: 7.2MM **Privately Held**
WEB: www.missionviejocc.com
SIC: 7997 7991 5812 7299 Country club, membership; physical fitness facilities; eating places; banquet hall facilities

(P-19004)
MODESTO COURT ROOM INC
2012 Mchenry Ave, Modesto (95350-3212)
PHONE.................209 577-1060
Fax: 209 577-1812
Lloyd Overholtzer, *President*
Sheri Walker, *Vice Pres*
Sandy Barnett, *Director*
EMP: 90
SQ FT: 43,000
SALES (est): 3.8MM **Privately Held**
WEB: www.modestocourtroom.net
SIC: 7997 5941 Swimming club, membership; racquetball club, membership; handball club, membership; sporting goods & bicycle shops

(P-19005)
MONARCH BAY GOLF RESORT
13800 Monarch Bay Dr, San Leandro (94577-6401)
PHONE.................510 895-2162
Roland Smith, *CEO*
David Price, *President*
EMP: 100
SALES (est): 2.1MM **Privately Held**
SIC: 7997 Golf club, membership

(P-19006)
MONTECITO COUNTRY CLUB INC
920 Summit Rd, Santa Barbara (93108-2326)
P.O. Box 1170 (93102-1170)
PHONE.................805 969-0800
Fax: 805 565-3906
Tai Warner, *President*
Justin Allen, *General Mgr*
Hiro Suzuki, *General Mgr*
Rob Oosterhuis, *Director*
Ernesto Ruiz, *Manager*
EMP: 100
SQ FT: 10,000
SALES (est): 6.2MM
SALES (corp-wide): 210.4MM **Privately Held**
WEB: www.montecitocc.com
SIC: 7997 5812 5813 Country club, membership; eating places; bar (drinking places)
PA: Tsukamoto Corporation Co.,Ltd.
1-6-5, Nihombashihoncho
Chuo-Ku TKY 103-0
332 791-315

(P-19007)
MONTEREY PENINSULA COUNTRY CLB
Also Called: MPCC
3000 Club Rd, Pebble Beach (93953-2542)
PHONE.................831 373-1556
Fax: 831 655-3049
Robert Perry Smith, *CEO*
Michael Bowhay, *Exec Dir*
Janet Wirtz, *Admin Asst*
Gerry Elgart, *Administration*
Brad Spencer, *Asst Controller*
EMP: 130
SQ FT: 70,000
SALES: 22.4MM **Privately Held**
WEB: www.mpccpb.org
SIC: 7997 Country club, membership

(P-19008)
MORAGA CNTRY CLB HMOWNERS ASSN
1600 Saint Andrews Dr, Moraga (94556-1194)
PHONE.................925 376-2200
Fax: 925 376-7835
Frank Meln, *General Mgr*
EMP: 100 **EST:** 1973
SQ FT: 10,000
SALES (est): 6.5MM **Privately Held**
WEB: www.moragacc.com
SIC: 7997 Country club, membership

(P-19009)
NAMASTA INC
Also Called: North American Studio Alliance
2313 Hastings Dr, Belmont (94002-3317)
PHONE.................650 591-3639
Bernard Slede, *President*
Deborah Bos, *Admin Sec*
Trent McEntire, *Director*
EMP: 50
SALES (est): 852K **Privately Held**
WEB: www.namasta.com
SIC: 7997 Membership sports & recreation clubs

(P-19010)
NAPA GOLF ASSOCIATES LLC
2555 Jamieson Canyon Rd, NAPA (94558)
PHONE.................707 257-1900
Kenneth E Laird,
Michelle Waldor, *Controller*
Gus Gianulias,
Jim Gianulias,
EMP: 84
SQ FT: 24,000
SALES: 1.8MM
SALES (corp-wide): 1B **Publicly Held**
WEB: www.remington-gc.com
SIC: 7997 Golf club, membership
HQ: Clubcorp Usa, Inc.
3030 Lyndon B Johnson Fwy
Dallas TX 75234
972 243-6191

(P-19011)
NAPA VALLEY COUNTRY CLUB
3385 Hagen Rd, NAPA (94558-3849)
PHONE.................707 252-1111
Fax: 707 252-1188
Todd Jeffrey Meginness, *CEO*
Todd Meginness, *COO*
Jeorge Hise, *Treasurer*
Mike Wilson, *Vice Pres*
Patrick Smorra, *Admin Sec*
▲ **EMP:** 80
SQ FT: 8,000
SALES: 6.5MM **Privately Held**
WEB: www.napavalleycc.com
SIC: 7997 5813 5812 Country club, membership; bar (drinking places); eating places

(P-19012)
NATIONAL GOLF PROPERTIES INC
Also Called: San Geronimo Golf Course
5800 Sir Francis Drake, San Geronimo (94963)
P.O. Box 130 (94963-0130)
PHONE.................415 488-4030
Fax: 415 488-4385
Heather Loivos, *Manager*
Jennifer Kim, *Exec Dir*
Stephanie Roberts, *Office Mgr*
EMP: 98
SALES (corp-wide): 13.9MM **Privately Held**
WEB: www.nationalgolfproperties.com
SIC: 7997 Golf club, membership
PA: National Golf Properties Llc
2951 28th St Ste 3000
Santa Monica CA 90405
310 664-4000

(P-19013)
NEW DISCOVERY INC
Also Called: Discovery Bay Ctry Club
1475 Clubhouse Dr, Byron (94505-9241)
PHONE.................925 783-6613
Fax: 925 634-0381
Mark Tissot, *Manager*
Janette Patterson,
EMP: 60
SALES (corp-wide): 10.4MM **Privately Held**
SIC: 7997 Golf club, membership
PA: New Discovery Inc
1380 Galaxy Way
Concord CA 94520
925 682-4830

(P-19014)
NEWPORT BEACH COUNTRY CLUB INC
1 Clubhouse Dr, Newport Beach (92660-7107)
PHONE.................949 644-9550
Fax: 949 644-5057
David Wooten, *President*
Gerald Johnson, *CFO*
Jerry Anderson, *Vice Pres*
EMP: 90

7997 - Membership Sports & Recreation Clubs County (P-19015)

SALES (est): 5.5MM
SALES (corp-wide): 27.7MM **Privately Held**
WEB: www.newportbeachcc.com
SIC: 7997 7991 5941 5813 Country club, membership; physical fitness facilities; sporting goods & bicycle shops; drinking places; eating places
PA: International Bay Clubs, Llc
1221 W Coast Hwy Ste 145
Newport Beach CA 92663
949 645-5000

(P-19015)
NORTH RANCH COUNTRY CLUB
4761 Valley Spring Dr, Westlake Village (91362-4399)
PHONE.................................818 889-3531
Fax: 805 373-8343
Mark Bagaaso, *CEO*
Scott London, *Treasurer*
Karl Holst, *Executive*
Carla Torkelson, *Finance*
Karla Torkelson, *Controller*
EMP: 160
SQ FT: 53,000
SALES: 12MM **Privately Held**
SIC: 7997 5812 5941 Country club, membership; eating places; sporting goods & bicycle shops

(P-19016)
NORTH RIDGE COUNTRY CLUB
7600 Madison Ave, Fair Oaks (95628-3400)
PHONE.................................916 967-5716
Fax: 916 967-0346
Rink Sanford, *General Mgr*
Sanford Rink, *General Mgr*
Barbara Kelly, *Manager*
EMP: 75
SQ FT: 5,000
SALES: 5.4MM **Privately Held**
WEB: www.northridgegolf.com
SIC: 7997 Country club, membership; golf club, membership

(P-19017)
OAKDALE GOLF AND COUNTRY CLUB
243 N Stearns Rd, Oakdale (95361-9247)
PHONE.................................209 847-2984
Fax: 209 847-8631
Tom Brennan, *President*
John O'Hearn, *General Mgr*
Rick Schultz, *General Mgr*
Vance Calton, *Assistant*
EMP: 55
SQ FT: 12,000
SALES: 4MM **Privately Held**
WEB: www.oakdalegcc.org
SIC: 7997 Country club, membership

(P-19018)
OAKMONT COUNTRY CLUB
3100 Country Club Dr, Glendale (91208-1799)
PHONE.................................818 542-4260
Fax: 818 248-5157
Pat Dahlson, *CEO*
John Schiller, *President*
Michael Hyler, *COO*
Pierangelo Ramponi, *Executive*
Kemberly Carruthers, *Controller*
EMP: 125
SQ FT: 37,000
SALES: 8.3MM **Privately Held**
SIC: 7997 Country club, membership; golf club, membership; swimming club, membership

(P-19019)
OASIS PALM DSERT HMOWNERS ASSN
Also Called: Oasis Country Club
42330 Casbah Way, Palm Desert (92211-7660)
PHONE.................................760 345-5661
Roy McGowen, *President*
EMP: 52
SALES (est): 2.4MM **Privately Held**
SIC: 7997 Country club, membership

(P-19020)
OLYMPIC CLUB
665 Sutter St, San Francisco (94102-1017)
PHONE.................................415 676-1412
Susan S Morse, *Bd of Directors*
EMP: 97
SALES (corp-wide): 47MM **Privately Held**
SIC: 7997 Membership sports & recreation clubs
PA: The Olympic Club
524 Post St
San Francisco CA 94102
415 345-5100

(P-19021)
OLYMPIC INVESTORS LTD
Also Called: Walnut Creek Spt & Fitnes CLB
1908 Olympic Blvd, Walnut Creek (94596-5023)
PHONE.................................925 322-8996
Fax: 925 932-6404
Linda Hansen, *Partner*
Sam Beler, *General Ptnr*
George Valerio, *General Ptnr*
Robert F Wattles, *General Ptnr*
EMP: 90
SQ FT: 25,000
SALES (est): 4.9MM **Privately Held**
WEB: www.wcsf.net
SIC: 7997 7991 5812 7999 Membership sports & recreation clubs; physical fitness facilities; eating places; physical fitness instruction

(P-19022)
ORINDA COUNTRY CLUB
315 Camino Sobrante, Orinda (94563-1899)
PHONE.................................925 254-4313
Fax: 925 254-0406
Jeff Bause, *President*
John Townsend, *Executive*
Gary Hooks, *Controller*
Dawn Kelly, *Human Res Dir*
Steve Haufler, *Athletic Dir*
EMP: 90
SALES: 11.8MM **Privately Held**
WEB: www.orindacc.org
SIC: 7997 Country club, membership

(P-19023)
PACIFIC CLUB (PA)
4110 Macarthur Blvd, Newport Beach (92660-2012)
PHONE.................................949 955-1123
Fax: 949 724-8926
Douglas M Ammerman, *President*
Richard M Ortwein, *Treasurer*
David Martin, *Executive*
Jon Tice, *Executive*
Brooke B Bentley, *General Mgr*
EMP: 83
SQ FT: 28,000
SALES (est): 6.6MM **Privately Held**
WEB: www.pacificclub.org
SIC: 7997 5812 5813 Membership sports & recreation clubs; eating places; bar (drinking places)

(P-19024)
PACIFIC GOLF & COUNTRY CLUB
200 Avenida La Pata, San Clemente (92673-6301)
PHONE.................................949 498-6604
Fax: 949 498-0517
Tom Frost, *Manager*
Sherri Baker, *Controller*
Paula Olsen, *Director*
EMP: 90
SQ FT: 27,000
SALES (est): 1.8MM
SALES (corp-wide): 3.1MM **Privately Held**
WEB: www.pacificgc.com
SIC: 7997 7992 Golf club, membership; public golf courses
PA: Golf Investment Llc
200 Avenida La Pata
San Clemente CA 92673
949 498-6604

(P-19025)
PALM DSERT RCRTL FCLITIES CORP
Also Called: Pdrfc
38995 Desert Willow Dr, Palm Desert (92260-1674)
P.O. Box 14290 (92255-4290)
PHONE.................................760 346-0015
Richard Mogensen, *General Mgr*
Kathy Anderson, *Controller*
EMP: 100
SQ FT: 10,000
SALES: 2.5MM **Privately Held**
WEB: www.cityofpalmdesert.com
SIC: 7997 Membership sports & recreation clubs
PA: City of Palm Desert
73510 Fred Waring Dr
Palm Desert CA 92260
760 346-0611

(P-19026)
PALOMAR GEM & MINERAL CLUB
2120 Mission Rd Ste 260, Escondido (92029-1014)
P.O. Box 1583 (92033-1583)
PHONE.................................760 743-0809
Mike Nelson, *Principal*
Don Parsley, *Manager*
EMP: 70
SALES (est): 769.5K **Privately Held**
SIC: 7997 Membership sports & recreation clubs

(P-19027)
PALOS VERDES BEACH & ATHC CLB
389 Paseo Del Mar, Palos Verdes Estates (90274-1267)
P.O. Box 158 (90274-0158)
PHONE.................................310 375-8777
Fax: 310 375-8937
Jane Williamson, *Manager*
Chris Manos, *Manager*
EMP: 88
SQ FT: 5,000
SALES: 1.4MM **Privately Held**
SIC: 7997 Swimming club, membership

(P-19028)
PASADENA MODEL RAILROAD CLUB
5458 Alhambra Ave, Los Angeles (90032-3102)
PHONE.................................323 222-1718
Steve Phillips, *President*
William James, *Principal*
Ken Randall, *Manager*
EMP: 55
SQ FT: 6,596
SALES: 26.5K **Privately Held**
SIC: 7997 Membership sports & recreation clubs

(P-19029)
PAUMA VALLEY COUNTRY CLUB
15835 Pauma Valley Dr, Pauma Valley (92061-1612)
P.O. Box 206 (92061-0206)
PHONE.................................760 742-1230
Butt Suze, *President*
EMP: 76
SQ FT: 3,000
SALES: 6.5MM **Privately Held**
SIC: 7997 Country club, membership

(P-19030)
PLANTATION GOLF CLUB INC
50994 Monroe St, Indio (92201-9709)
P.O. Box 1657, La Quinta (92247-1657)
PHONE.................................760 775-3688
Fax: 760 775-3690
Art Schillings, *General Mgr*
Alex Negron, *Executive Asst*
Art Schilling, *Manager*
EMP: 54
SQ FT: 16,000
SALES: 4.3MM **Privately Held**
SIC: 7997 Golf club, membership

(P-19031)
PORTER VALLEY COUNTRY CLUB
Also Called: Porter Valley Catering
19216 Singing Hills Dr, Northridge (91326-1799)
PHONE.................................818 360-1071
Fax: 818 360-1071
Robert H Dedman, *Ch of Bd*
John Beckett, *President*
Doug Howe, *Exec VP*
Johnsie Manlowe, *Financial Exec*
Melanie Brown,
EMP: 110
SQ FT: 18,000
SALES (est): 4.3MM
SALES (corp-wide): 1B **Publicly Held**
WEB: www.remington-gc.com
SIC: 7997 5812 5941 Golf club, membership; steak restaurant; sporting goods & bicycle shops
HQ: Clubcorp Usa, Inc.
3030 Lyndon B Johnson Fwy
Dallas TX 75234
972 243-6191

(P-19032)
RACQUET CLUB OF IRVINE
Also Called: Rci
5 Ethel Coplen Way Ste 5, Irvine (92612-1797)
PHONE.................................949 786-3000
Fax: 949 786-8869
Spearman Industry, *President*
EMP: 54
SQ FT: 15,000
SALES (est): 1.4MM **Privately Held**
SIC: 7997 Tennis club, membership

(P-19033)
RAMS HILL COUNTRY CLUB
1881 Rams Hill Rd, Borrego Springs (92004-5400)
PHONE.................................760 767-4259
Fax: 760 767-3040
Wesley Porter, *President*
Don Davis, *Exec VP*
EMP: 60
SQ FT: 40,000
SALES (est): 2.8MM **Privately Held**
SIC: 7997 Country club, membership

(P-19034)
RANCHO BERNARDO GOLF CLUB
Also Called: County Club of Rancho Bernardo
17550 Bernardo Oaks Dr, San Diego (92128-2112)
PHONE.................................858 487-1134
Fax: 858 487-7595
Robert Schwanhausser, *CEO*
Scott Bentley, *General Mgr*
Ron Cropley, *Office Mgr*
Nancy Flexman, *Controller*
John Kersey,
EMP: 67
SQ FT: 23,000
SALES: 2.6MM **Privately Held**
WEB: www.ccofrb.com
SIC: 7997 Golf club, membership

(P-19035)
RANCHO MURIETA COUNTRY CLUB
7000 Alameda Dr, Rancho Murieta (95683-9148)
PHONE.................................916 354-2400
Fax: 916 354-0916
Robert Wright, *CEO*
Vince Lepera, *President*
Buzz Breedlove, *Treasurer*
Dick Stenstrom, *Vice Pres*
Johnny Frink, *Executive*
EMP: 90
SQ FT: 40,000
SALES (est): 9.4MM **Privately Held**
WEB: www.ranchomurietacc.com
SIC: 7997 Country club, membership; golf club, membership

PRODUCTS & SERVICES SECTION
7997 - Membership Sports & Recreation Clubs County (P-19061)

(P-19036)
RANCHO SANTA FE ASSOCIATION A
Also Called: Rancho Sante Fe Golf Club
5827 Viadelacumere, Rancho Santa Fe (92067)
P.O. Box A (92067-0359)
PHONE..................................858 756-1182
Fax: 858 756-0982
Stephen Nordstrom, *Manager*
Dennis Kraft, *General Mgr*
Peter Smith, *Manager*
EMP: 100
SALES (corp-wide): 16.4MM **Privately Held**
SIC: 7997 Golf club, membership
PA: Rancho Santa Fe Association, A California Non Profit Corporation
17022 Avenida De Acacias
Rancho Santa Fe CA 92067
858 756-1174

(P-19037)
RB ANGLERS CLUB
12578 Cresta Pl, San Diego (92128-2312)
PHONE..................................858 487-6484
Richard Studinka, *President*
EMP: 75
SALES (est): 817.5K **Privately Held**
SIC: 7997 Membership sports & recreation clubs

(P-19038)
RED HILL COUNTRY CLUB
8358 Red Hl Cntry Clb Dr, Rancho Cucamonga (91730-1899)
PHONE..................................909 982-1358
Fax: 909 982-8195
Rob Mocskley, *President*
EMP: 92
SQ FT: 20,000
SALES: 4.7MM **Privately Held**
WEB: www.redhillcc.com
SIC: 7997 5812 Country club, membership; eating places

(P-19039)
REDLANDS COUNTRY CLUB
1749 Garden St, Redlands (92373-7248)
PHONE..................................909 793-2661
Fax: 909 335-1676
Scott Reding, *President*
Pamela Dvorak, *Comms Dir*
Kurt Burmeister, *General Mgr*
Jason Murphy, *General Mgr*
Kathy Knudsen, *Director*
EMP: 80
SQ FT: 22,000
SALES: 5.3MM **Privately Held**
SIC: 7997 5812 5813 Membership sports & recreation clubs; tennis club, membership; golf club, membership; snack shop; diner; bar (drinking places)

(P-19040)
REDWOOD BRIDGE CLUB
3111 6th Ave, San Diego (92103-5836)
PHONE..................................619 296-4274
Warren Edelson, *President*
Evelyn Flowers, *Vice Pres*
Laurie Chranowski, *Manager*
EMP: 80
SALES: 28.3K **Privately Held**
WEB: www.redwoodbridgeclub.com
SIC: 7997 Membership sports & recreation clubs

(P-19041)
RESERVE CLUB
49400 Desert Butte Trl, Indian Wells (92210-7075)
PHONE..................................760 674-2222
Kenneth Novack, *President*
C Ted McCarter, *Treasurer*
Craig Surdy, *General Mgr*
Dan Wylie, *Controller*
Ben Wiley, *Human Resources*
EMP: 80
SQ FT: 10,000
SALES: 9MM **Privately Held**
SIC: 7997 Country club, membership

(P-19042)
RICHMOND COUNTRY CLUB
1 Markovich Ln, Richmond (94806-1825)
PHONE..................................510 231-2241
Fax: 510 232-0209
Mac Niven, *General Mgr*
EMP: 57
SQ FT: 30,000
SALES (est): 4.2MM **Privately Held**
SIC: 7997 Country club, membership

(P-19043)
RIVER ISLAND COUNTRY CLUB INC
31989 River Island Dr, Porterville (93257-9611)
PHONE..................................559 781-2917
Fax: 559 782-1735
Terry Treece, *Director*
Patty Brown, *Manager*
EMP: 52
SQ FT: 13,500
SALES (est): 2.8MM **Privately Held**
SIC: 7997 Golf club, membership; country club, membership

(P-19044)
RIVER RIDGE GOLF CLUB
2401 W Vineyard Ave, Oxnard (93036-2218)
PHONE..................................805 981-8724
Otto Kanny, *General Mgr*
EMP: 92
SALES (est): 1.6MM **Privately Held**
SIC: 7997 Golf club, membership

(P-19045)
RIVERVIEW GOLF AND COUNTRY CLB
4200 Bechelli Ln, Redding (96002-3533)
PHONE..................................530 224-2254
Fax: 530 224-2246
Ralph Stroch, *President*
Ralph Storch, *President*
Lynette Trotter, *Director*
Cliff Hutchinson, *Manager*
Chad Ohmer, *Manager*
EMP: 72
SQ FT: 30,000
SALES: 3MM **Privately Held**
WEB: www.riverviewgolf.net
SIC: 7997 5812 5813 Country club, membership; eating places; bar (drinking places)

(P-19046)
RODDY RANCH PBC LLC
Also Called: Golf Club At Roddy Ranch
1 Tour Way, Antioch (94531-9053)
PHONE..................................925 978-4653
Fax: 925 706-0222
Jack Roddy,
Bernie Holloway, *Administration*
Kevin S Fitzgerald, *Financial Exec*
EMP: 55
SQ FT: 1,400
SALES (est): 5.3MM **Privately Held**
WEB: www.roddyranch.com
SIC: 7997 Golf club, membership

(P-19047)
ROSE BOWL AQUATICS CENTER
360 N Arroyo Blvd, Pasadena (91103-3201)
PHONE..................................626 564-0330
Fax: 626 356-7572
Judy Biggs, *Exec Dir*
Daniel Leyson, *Bd of Directors*
Kurt Knop, *Principal*
Sandra Hiks, *Finance*
Sandra Hilts, *Finance*
EMP: 80
SALES: 6.3MM **Privately Held**
WEB: www.rosebowlpolo.com
SIC: 7997 Boating & swimming clubs

(P-19048)
ROTARY CLUB SAN RAFAEL FUND
851 Irwin St Ste 202, San Rafael (94901-3343)
PHONE..................................415 457-4284
EMP: 54
SALES: 55.9K **Privately Held**
SIC: 7997 Membership sports & recreation clubs

(P-19049)
ROUND HILL COUNTRY CLUB
Also Called: Rh
3169 Roundhill Rd, Alamo (94507-1735)
PHONE..................................925 934-8211
Debby Grauman, *CEO*
Greg Tachiera, *CEO*
Charu Fitzgerald, *Human Res Dir*
John Hattab, *Director*
Steve Mallory, *Director*
EMP: 50 **EST:** 1965
SALES (est): 6.6MM **Privately Held**
SIC: 7997 Membership sports & recreation clubs

(P-19050)
ROUND HILL ENTERPRISES
Also Called: Round Hill Golf & Country Club
3169 Roundhill Rd, Alamo (94507-1735)
PHONE..................................925 934-8211
Arthur Davis, *President*
Jack Mahoney, *COO*
Leonard D'Orazio, *CFO*
Theodore Budach, *Vice Pres*
Lori Primasing, *Admin Sec*
EMP: 180 **EST:** 1959
SQ FT: 20,000
SALES (est): 5.8MM **Privately Held**
WEB: www.rhcountryclub.com
SIC: 7997 5812 5813 Country club, membership; American restaurant; bar (drinking places)

(P-19051)
RUBY HILL GOLF CLUB LLC
3400 W Ruby Hill Dr, Pleasanton (94566-3604)
PHONE..................................925 417-5840
Fax: 925 417-5845
Jim Ghielmetti,
Jeremy Westlake, *CFO*
Carol Sparks, *Treasurer*
Michael Rood, *General Mgr*
Gayle Hansen, *Sales Mgr*
EMP: 100 **EST:** 1994
SALES (est): 10MM **Privately Held**
WEB: www.rubyhill.com
SIC: 7997 Golf club, membership

(P-19052)
RUSSIAN RIVER SPORTSMAN CLUB
25150 Steelhead Blvd, Duncans Mills (95430)
PHONE..................................707 865-9429
Steve Jackson, *President*
EMP: 90
SALES (est): 3.2MM **Privately Held**
SIC: 7997 Membership sports & recreation clubs

(P-19053)
SADDLEBACK VLY
25631 Peter A Hartman Way, Mission Viejo (92691-3142)
PHONE..................................949 586-1234
Fax: 949 586-4378
Don Cuzick, *Principal*
Stephen L McMahon, *Administration*
Alex Bernstein, *Corp Comm Staff*
EMP: 52
SALES (est): 3.7MM **Privately Held**
SIC: 7997 Membership sports & recreation clubs

(P-19054)
SALESIAN BOYS AND GIRLS CLUB
680 Filbert St, San Francisco (94133-2805)
PHONE..................................415 397-3068
Russell Gumina, *Exec Dir*
Randal Demartini, *Asst Director*
EMP: 79
SALES: 3.3MM **Privately Held**
SIC: 7997 Membership sports & recreation clubs

(P-19055)
SAN DIEGO COUNTRY CLUB INC
88 L St, Chula Vista (91911-1499)
PHONE..................................619 422-8895
Fax: 619 425-1142
David Morris, *General Mgr*
Carol Lubin, *Controller*
EMP: 80
SQ FT: 36,140
SALES: 5MM **Privately Held**
WEB: www.sdcc.cc
SIC: 7997 Country club, membership

(P-19056)
SAN DIMAS GOLF INC
Also Called: Via Verde Country Club
1400 Avenida Entrada, San Dimas (91773-4004)
PHONE..................................909 599-8486
Fax: 909 599-0304
Kwan O Lee, *President*
Dal Eun Lee, *Shareholder*
Dal H Lee, *Vice Pres*
Dal K Lee, *Admin Sec*
Lorie Buchanan, *Agent*
EMP: 70 **EST:** 1975
SQ FT: 21,887
SALES (est): 5MM **Privately Held**
WEB: www.viaverdecountryclub.com
SIC: 7997 Country club, membership

(P-19057)
SAN GABRIEL COUNTRY CLUB
350 E Hermosa Dr, San Gabriel (91775-2346)
PHONE..................................626 287-9671
Fax: 626 287-4129
Tom Dukes, *President*
Terry Deasy, *Comms Dir*
Eric Gregory, *General Mgr*
Erika Ortiz, *Admin Asst*
John Sotomonte, *Controller*
EMP: 80 **EST:** 1904
SQ FT: 48,000
SALES: 7.6MM **Privately Held**
WEB: www.sangabrielcc.com
SIC: 7997 Country club, membership

(P-19058)
SAN JOAQUIN COUNTRY CLUB
3484 W Bluff Ave, Fresno (93711-0199)
PHONE..................................559 439-3483
Fax: 559 439-6456
Jeffrey Newman, *President*
Melissa Allen, *Manager*
EMP: 63
SQ FT: 39,615
SALES: 3MM **Privately Held**
SIC: 7997 5812 5813 Country club, membership; American restaurant; bar (drinking places)

(P-19059)
SAN JOSE COUNTRY CLUB
15571 Alum Rock Ave, San Jose (95127-2799)
PHONE..................................408 258-3636
Fax: 408 929-0442
Chris Simpson, *General Mgr*
Jason Green, *General Mgr*
UT Lu, *Asst Controller*
Manny Carillio, *Controller*
Don Allio, *Director*
EMP: 70
SQ FT: 24,000
SALES: 5.7MM **Privately Held**
SIC: 7997 Country club, membership

(P-19060)
SAN LUIS OBISPO GOLF
255 Country Club Dr, San Luis Obispo (93401-8921)
PHONE..................................805 543-3400
Fax: 805 543-3413
David Cole, *President*
Carol Kerwin, *Admin Sec*
Karen Harper, *Programmer Anys*
Christina Kurzi, *Accountant*
Andrew Cook, *Controller*
EMP: 110
SQ FT: 10,000
SALES: 6MM **Privately Held**
SIC: 7997 Country club, membership

(P-19061)
SANTA ANA COUNTRY CLUB
20382 Newport Blvd, Santa Ana (92707-5396)
PHONE..................................714 556-3000
Fax: 714 556-9708
Joseph J Wagner, *CEO*
Sharon Chiaromonte, *Human Res Dir*
EMP: 100

7997 - Membership Sports & Recreation Clubs County (P-19062)

SALES (est): 8MM **Privately Held**
SIC: 7997 Membership sports & recreation clubs

(P-19062)
SANTA BARBARA ATHLETIC CLB INC
520 Castillo St, Santa Barbara (93101-3400)
PHONE 805 966-6147
Fax: 805 963-5796
Gordon Mc Cay, *President*
Eric Geeb, *General Mgr*
Tom Horne, *General Mgr*
Laura Lewis, *Admin Sec*
Valerie Nishimura, *Accounting Mgr*
EMP: 80
SQ FT: 21,600
SALES (est): 2.3MM **Privately Held**
SIC: 7997 Membership sports & recreation clubs

(P-19063)
SANTA CATALINA ISLAND COMPANY
Also Called: Descanso Beach Club
1 Descanso Beach Way, Avalon (90704)
P.O. Box 1 (90704-0001)
PHONE 310 510-7410
Fax: 310 510-3559
EMP: 66
SQ FT: 22,604
SALES (corp-wide): 31.6MM **Privately Held**
SIC: 7997 Beach club, membership
PA: Santa Catalina Island Company
150 Metropole Ave
Avalon CA 90704
310 510-2000

(P-19064)
SANTA CLARA WOMENS CLUB
Also Called: Santa Clara Woman's Club Adobe
3260 The Alameda, Santa Clara (95050-4329)
P.O. Box 367 (95052-0367)
PHONE 408 246-8000
Marlene O'Donnell, *President*
EMP: 92
SALES (est): 1.1MM **Privately Held**
SIC: 7997 Membership sports & recreation clubs

(P-19065)
SANTA LUCIA PRESERVE COMPANY
1 Rancho San Carlos Rd, Carmel (93923-7999)
PHONE 831 620-6760
Tom Gray, *Principal*
Andy Simer, *CFO*
Lisa Guthrie, *Executive*
Jerry Regester, *Executive*
Rich Speciale, *Security Dir*
EMP: 105
SALES (est): 9.4MM **Privately Held**
SIC: 7997 Country club, membership

(P-19066)
SANTA ROSA GOLF & COUNTRY CLUB
333 Country Club Dr, Santa Rosa (95401-5599)
PHONE 707 546-3485
Fax: 707 546-8921
Eric L Affeldt, *CEO*
Kevin Marshall, *General Mgr*
EMP: 100
SQ FT: 40,000
SALES (est): 5.7MM
SALES (corp-wide): 1B **Publicly Held**
WEB: www.santarosagolf.com
SIC: 7997 Country club, membership
PA: Clubcorp Holdings, Inc.
3030 Lbj Fwy Ste 600
Dallas TX 75234
972 243-6191

(P-19067)
SANTALUZ CLUB INC
8170 Caminito Santaluz E, San Diego (92127-2577)
PHONE 858 759-3120
Fax: 858 759-4577
Steve Cowell, *CEO*
Timothy A Kaehr, *CFO*
Timothy A Kehr, *CFO*
Michael Forsum, *Vice Pres*
James Hoselton, *Vice Pres*
EMP: 120
SQ FT: 19,000
SALES (est): 13.7MM **Privately Held**
WEB: www.santaluz.com
SIC: 7997 Country club, membership

(P-19068)
SANYO FOODS CORP AMERICA
Also Called: Tustin Ranch Golf Club
12442 Tustin Ranch Rd, Tustin (92782-1000)
PHONE 714 730-1611
Steve Plummer, *Branch Mgr*
EMP: 130
SALES (corp-wide): 59.1B **Privately Held**
SIC: 7997 Golf club, membership
HQ: Sanyo Foods Corporation Of America
11955 Monarch St
Garden Grove CA 92841
714 891-3671

(P-19069)
SATICOY COUNTRY CLUB
4450 Clubhouse Dr, Somis (93066-9798)
PHONE 805 647-1153
Fax: 805 647-1158
Douglas Taxton, *President*
James R Van Wyck, *CEO*
Jeff Downey, *Executive*
Thomas Swedzinski, *General Mgr*
Amy Hogue, *Accountant*
EMP: 80
SALES: 4.3MM **Privately Held**
WEB: www.saticoycountryclub.com
SIC: 7997 Country club, membership; golf club, membership

(P-19070)
SEBASTOPOL RIFLE & PISTOL CLUB
343 Flynn St, Sebastopol (95472)
P.O. Box 575 (95473-0575)
PHONE 707 824-0184
Greg Bolker, *President*
Greg Bolken, *President*
Garry Goss, *Treasurer*
Barry McLaren, *Vice Pres*
EMP: 72
SALES (est): 1.1MM **Privately Held**
SIC: 7997 Membership sports & recreation clubs

(P-19071)
SEQUOIA WOOD COUNTRY CLUB
1000 Cypress Point Dr, Arnold (95223)
P.O. Box 930 (95223-0930)
PHONE 209 795-1000
Fax: 209 795-5981
Norm Kestner, *President*
EMP: 64
SQ FT: 13,000
SALES (est): 3.5MM **Privately Held**
WEB: www.sequoiawoods.com
SIC: 7997 5812 5813 Golf club, membership; eating places; bar (drinking places)

(P-19072)
SERRANO ASSOCIATES LLC
Also Called: Serrano Country Club
5005 Serrano Pkwy, El Dorado Hills (95762-7511)
PHONE 916 933-5005
Kevitt Sale, *Manager*
EMP: 100
SALES (corp-wide): 8.4MM **Privately Held**
WEB: www.serranoassociates.com
SIC: 7997 5941 5813 5812 Golf club, membership; sporting goods & bicycle shops; drinking places; eating places
PA: Serrano Associates, Llc
4525 Serrano Pkwy
El Dorado Hills CA 95762
916 939-3333

(P-19073)
SERRANO COUNTRY CLUB INC
5005 Serrano Pkwy P, El Dorado Hills (95762-7511)
PHONE 916 933-5005
Fax: 916 933-5761
Dean Cummings, *President*
Bob Stangroom, *General Mgr*
Laura Blaze, *Accounting Mgr*
Tazim Venkataya, *Controller*
EMP: 105
SALES: 7.6MM **Privately Held**
WEB: www.serranocountryclub.com
SIC: 7997 Golf club, membership

(P-19074)
SEVEN LAKES HM ASSN CNTRY CLB
1 Desert Lakes Dr, Palm Springs (92264-5520)
PHONE 760 328-2695
Silas Dreher, *General Mgr*
Diane Hale, *Administration*
EMP: 50
SQ FT: 6,000
SALES (est): 1MM **Privately Held**
SIC: 7997 8641 Country club, membership; homeowners' association

(P-19075)
SEVEN OAKS COUNTRY CLUB
2000 Grand Lakes Ave, Bakersfield (93311-2931)
P.O. Box 11165 (93389-1165)
PHONE 661 664-6404
Fax: 661 664-6472
David H Murdock, *CEO*
Bruce Freeman, *President*
Don Ciota, *General Mgr*
Joslyn Simos, *Accountant*
EMP: 125
SQ FT: 39,000
SALES (est): 7.9MM **Privately Held**
WEB: www.sevenoakscountryclub.com
SIC: 7997 Country club, membership

(P-19076)
SHADY CANYON GOLF CLUB INC
100 Shady Canyon Dr, Irvine (92603-0301)
PHONE 949 856-7000
Fax: 949 856-7001
James T Wood, *CEO*
Thomas Heggi, *President*
Robert Leenhouts, *Principal*
Steve Buck, *General Mgr*
Floridel Sotelo, *Marketing Staff*
EMP: 126
SALES: 186.4K **Privately Held**
WEB: www.shadycanyongolfclub.com
SIC: 7997 Membership sports & recreation clubs

(P-19077)
SHERWOOD COUNTRY CLUB
320 W Stafford Rd, Thousand Oaks (91361-5087)
PHONE 805 496-3036
Fax: 805 495-0146
Lance Fisher, *General Mgr*
Wayne Shearon, *Executive*
Garrett Yokoyama, *Executive*
Melanie Kohagen, *Executive Asst*
Jean Gojkovich, *Human Res Dir*
EMP: 140 **EST:** 1989
SALES: 14.5MM **Privately Held**
SIC: 7997 Membership sports & recreation clubs

(P-19078)
SIERRA LA VERNE CNTRY CLB INC
6300 Country Club Dr, La Verne (91750-1408)
PHONE 909 596-2100
Takaji Kobayashi, *President*
EMP: 100
SQ FT: 8,000
SALES (est): 4.6MM **Privately Held**
WEB: www.sierralavernecc.com
SIC: 7997 5812 7299 Golf club, membership; eating places; banquet hall facilities

(P-19079)
SIERRA VIEW COUNTRY CLUB
105 Alta Vista Ave, Roseville (95678-1647)
P.O. Box Aa (95678)
PHONE 916 782-3741
Fax: 916 783-8455
Barry Macdonald, *CEO*
Steve Rainwater, *President*
Stephen Reynolds, *President*
John Welch, *General Mgr*
Philip King, *Director*
EMP: 75
SQ FT: 5,000
SALES: 4MM **Privately Held**
WEB: www.sierraviewcc.com
SIC: 7997 5812 5813 Golf club, membership; American restaurant; bar (drinking places)

(P-19080)
SILVER CREEK VLY CNTRY CLB INC
5460 Country Club Pkwy, San Jose (95138-2215)
PHONE 408 239-5775
Fax: 408 239-5777
Rene Devos, *General Mgr*
Barrett Eiselman, *General Mgr*
Robert E Lee, *General Mgr*
Stacey Leando, *Administration*
Charlene Hawthorne, *Director*
EMP: 180
SALES (est): 9.9MM **Privately Held**
WEB: www.scvcc.com
SIC: 7997 5941 Country club, membership; sporting goods & bicycle shops

(P-19081)
SILVERADO COUNTRY CLB & RESORT
1303 Jefferson St 300a, NAPA (94559-2442)
PHONE 707 257-0200
Fax: 707 226-8449
Setsuo Okawa, *CEO*
Isao Okawa, *Ch of Bd*
Laurrel Ingram, *Asst Director*
John Vincent, *Director*
EMP: 600
SQ FT: 2,000
SALES: 75.8K
SALES (corp-wide): 1.3MM **Privately Held**
WEB: www.silveradoresort.com
SIC: 7997 Country club, membership
HQ: Silverado Napa Corp
1600 Atlas Peak Rd
Napa CA 94558
707 226-1325

(P-19082)
SNOWBOUNDERS SKI CLUB
5402 Tattershall Ave, Westminster (92683-3447)
PHONE 714 892-4897
Lowe Jacobson, *President*
EMP: 80
SALES: 47.9K **Privately Held**
SIC: 7997 Membership sports & recreation clubs

(P-19083)
SOUTH HILLS COUNTRY CLUB
2655 S Citrus St, West Covina (91791-3405)
PHONE 626 339-1231
Fax: 626 339-1425
James Wendoll, *CEO*
John Espinoza, *Sales Staff*
Candice Allen, *Director*
Alex Godinez, *Manager*
Kailynn Ramos, *Receptionist*
EMP: 78
SQ FT: 34,000
SALES: 5.4MM **Privately Held**
WEB: www.southhillscountryclub.org
SIC: 7997 5813 5812 Country club, membership; golf club, membership; bar (drinking places); American restaurant

(P-19084)
SOUTHWESTERN YACHT CLUB INC
2702 Qualtrough St, San Diego (92106-3415)
PHONE 619 222-0438
Fax: 619 222-8214
Jeff Wheeler, *General Mgr*
Rob Witters, *Treasurer*
Craig Wong, *General Mgr*
Brian Stanford, *Director*
EMP: 50
SQ FT: 10,000

PRODUCTS & SERVICES SECTION
7997 - Membership Sports & Recreation Clubs County (P-19106)

SALES: 3.7MM Privately Held
WEB: www.southwesternyc.org
SIC: 7997 4493 5812 5813 Yacht club, membership; yacht basins; eating places; bar (drinking places)

(P-19085)
SPANISH HILLS COUNTRY CLUB (PA)
999 Crestview Ave, Camarillo (93010-8493)
PHONE...................805 389-1644
Fax: 805 484-7914
Joe Topper, *President*
Steve Thomas, *CEO*
Robin Nishizaki, *Executive*
Michael Orosco, *General Mgr*
Greg Webster, *Controller*
EMP: 150
SQ FT: 42,000
SALES (est): 12.4MM Privately Held
WEB: www.spanishhillscc.com
SIC: 7997 Country club, membership

(P-19086)
SPARE-TIME INC
Also Called: Broadstone Raquet Club
820 Halidon Way, Folsom (95630-8406)
PHONE...................916 983-9180
Fax: 916 984-1288
Gavin Russo, *General Mgr*
EMP: 80
SALES (corp-wide): 30.7MM Privately Held
WEB: www.sparetimeinc.com
SIC: 7997 7991 Racquetball club, membership; health club
PA: Spare-Time, Inc.
   11344 Coloma Rd Ste 350
   Gold River CA 95670
   916 859-5910

(P-19087)
SPARE-TIME INC
11344 Coloma Rd Ste 350, Gold River (95670-6302)
PHONE...................916 859-5910
David Anderson, *Branch Mgr*
EMP: 59
SALES (corp-wide): 30.7MM Privately Held
SIC: 7997 Racquetball club, membership
PA: Spare-Time, Inc.
   11344 Coloma Rd Ste 350
   Gold River CA 95670
   916 859-5910

(P-19088)
SPARE-TIME INC
Also Called: Johnson Ranch Racquet Club
2501 Eureka Rd, Roseville (95661-6400)
PHONE...................916 782-2600
Fax: 916 782-8086
Tim Munson, *General Mgr*
Tim Manson, *General Mgr*
EMP: 60
SQ FT: 21,584
SALES (corp-wide): 30.7MM Privately Held
WEB: www.sparetimeinc.com
SIC: 7997 Racquetball club, membership
PA: Spare-Time, Inc.
   11344 Coloma Rd Ste 350
   Gold River CA 95670
   916 859-5910

(P-19089)
SPARE-TIME INC
Also Called: Gold River Racquet Club
2201 Gold Rush Dr, Gold River (95670-4466)
PHONE...................916 638-7001
Fax: 916 853-1845
Mike Burchett, *General Mgr*
EMP: 50
SALES (corp-wide): 30.7MM Privately Held
WEB: www.sparetimeinc.com
SIC: 7997 Racquetball club, membership
PA: Spare-Time, Inc.
   11344 Coloma Rd Ste 350
   Gold River CA 95670
   916 859-5910

(P-19090)
SPARE-TIME INC
Also Called: Natomas Racquet Club
2450 Natomas Park Dr, Sacramento (95833-2938)
PHONE...................916 649-0909
Fax: 916 649-0828
Joe Rose, *Manager*
EMP: 70
SALES (corp-wide): 30.7MM Privately Held
WEB: www.sparetimeinc.com
SIC: 7997 Racquetball club, membership
PA: Spare-Time, Inc.
   11344 Coloma Rd Ste 350
   Gold River CA 95670
   916 859-5910

(P-19091)
SPARE-TIME INC
Also Called: Laguna Creek Racquet Club
9570 Racquet Ct, Elk Grove (95758-4349)
PHONE...................916 859-5910
Fax: 916 684-8894
Kimberley Miller, *Manager*
Kat Chapel, *Executive*
Carol Wedel, *Manager*
EMP: 59
SALES (corp-wide): 30.7MM Privately Held
WEB: www.sparetimeinc.com
SIC: 7997 7999 7991 Racquetball club, membership; racquetball club, non-membership; health club
PA: Spare-Time, Inc.
   11344 Coloma Rd Ste 350
   Gold River CA 95670
   916 859-5910

(P-19092)
SPE GO HOLDINGS INC
Also Called: Mount Woodson Country Club
16422 N Woodson Dr, Ramona (92065-6800)
PHONE...................858 638-0672
Fax: 760 788-3565
Steve Dawe, *Exec VP*
Amanda Rangel, *General Mgr*
Scott Hardy, *Superintendent*
EMP: 50
SALES (corp-wide): 13.4B Publicly Held
SIC: 7997 Country club, membership
HQ: Spe Go Holdings, Inc.
   11575 Great Oaks Way # 210
   Alpharetta GA 30022
   401 621-4200

(P-19093)
SPRING VALLEY LAKE COUNTRY CLB
13229 Spring Valley Pkwy, Victorville (92395)
P.O. Box 7070 Sbl B
PHONE...................760 245-5356
Fax: 760 245-7597
Erick Affeldt, *CEO*
Steve Postma, *General Mgr*
EMP: 90
SALES (est): 3.2MM
SALES (corp-wide): 1B Publicly Held
WEB: www.remington-gc.com
SIC: 7997 Country club, membership
HQ: Clubcorp Usa, Inc.
   3030 Lyndon B Johnson Fwy
   Dallas TX 75234
   972 243-6191

(P-19094)
SPRINGS CLUB INC
Also Called: Springs Country Club, The
1 Duke Dr, Rancho Mirage (92270-3647)
PHONE...................760 328-0254
Fax: 619 324-7531
Daniel Cooper, *COO*
Matthew Samson, *Executive*
Ronda Allen, *Principal*
Douglas R Hart, *Principal*
Doug Lober, *Principal*
EMP: 65
SQ FT: 36,000
SALES: 5.4MM Privately Held
SIC: 7997 5812 5813 Golf club, membership; tennis club, membership; American restaurant; cocktail lounge

(P-19095)
ST FRANCIS YACHT CLUB
700 Marina Blvd, San Francisco (94123-1044)
PHONE...................415 563-6363
Fax: 415 563-8670
Jim Diepenbrock, *CEO*
Scott Triou, *Treasurer*
Nightingal David, *General Mgr*
Molly Spector, *Admin Sec*
Bruce Munro, *General Counsel*
◆ EMP: 110
SQ FT: 20,000
SALES (est): 13.9MM Privately Held
WEB: www.stfyc.com
SIC: 7997 4493 Yacht club, membership; marinas

(P-19096)
STOCKDALE COUNTRY CLUB
7001 Stockdale Hwy, Bakersfield (93309-1313)
P.O. Box 9727 (93389-9727)
PHONE...................661 832-0310
Fax: 661 832-6590
Sam Monroe, *President*
Michael Davis, *CEO*
Linda Voiland, *Vice Pres*
Susan Greer, *General Mgr*
Linda Turner, *Controller*
EMP: 100
SQ FT: 12,000
SALES: 5.8MM Privately Held
WEB: www.stockdalecountryclub.com
SIC: 7997 Country club, membership

(P-19097)
STONEBRAE LP
Also Called: TPC Stonebrea
222 Country Club Dr, Hayward (94542-7927)
PHONE...................510 728-7878
Fax: 510 728-7897
Lisa Hinman, *General Mgr*
Erin Crawford, *Project Mgr*
EMP: 74
SALES (est): 5.5MM Privately Held
SIC: 7997 Membership sports & recreation clubs

(P-19098)
STONERIDGE COUNTRY CLUB
17166 Stonerdge Cntry, Poway (92064)
PHONE...................858 487-2117
Fax: 858 487-1427
Eric Troll, *General Mgr*
Ron Gorski, *General Mgr*
Hostmaster Ctsnet, *Info Tech Mgr*
Debra Altschuler, *Director*
EMP: 75
SQ FT: 34,000
SALES (est): 5.8MM Privately Held
SIC: 7997 Country club, membership
PA: Milleta (California) Inc
   17166 Stoneridge Ctry Clb
   Poway CA 92064
   858 487-2167

(P-19099)
STRAWBERRY FARMS GOLF CLUB LLC
11 Strawberry Farm Rd, Irvine (92612-2300)
PHONE...................949 551-2560
Doug Decinese,
Kayla Alexander, *Relations*
EMP: 75
SALES (est): 3.7MM Privately Held
WEB: www.strawberryfarmsgolf.com
SIC: 7997 Golf club, membership

(P-19100)
SUN LAKES CNTRY CLUB HMEOWNRS
850 Country Club Dr, Banning (92220-5306)
PHONE...................951 845-2135
Tim Taylor, *Manager*
EMP: 100
SALES: 23.3K Privately Held
SIC: 7997 Country club, membership

(P-19101)
SUNNYSIDE COUNTRY CLUB
Also Called: University Sequoia
5704 E Butler Ave, Fresno (93727-5499)
PHONE...................559 255-8926
Fax: 559 251-3090
Steve Menchinella, *Manager*
Jennifer Leonard, *Mktg Dir*
Tonya Malloch, *Mktg Dir*
EMP: 85
SQ FT: 24,250
SALES (est): 4.4MM Privately Held
WEB: www.sunnyside-cc.com
SIC: 7997 Country club, membership

(P-19102)
SYCAMORE CC INC
Also Called: The Golf Club of California
3742 Flowerwood Ln, Fallbrook (92028-8013)
PHONE...................760 451-3700
Fax: 760 451-3710
William Lyon, *President*
Tom Williams, *General Mgr*
EMP: 60
SQ FT: 4,320
SALES (est): 3MM
SALES (corp-wide): 1.1B Publicly Held
WEB: www.lyonhomes.com
SIC: 7997 Golf club, membership
PA: William Lyon Homes
   4695 Macarthur Ct Ste 800
   Newport Beach CA 92660
   949 833-3600

(P-19103)
TEHAMA GOLF CLUB LLC
4 Tehama, Carmel (93923-9622)
PHONE...................831 622-2200
Roy D Kaufman,
Neal B Morton, *Business Mgr*
Eric Goettsch, *Sales Dir*
Howard M Bernstein,
Gavin Dickson, *Asst Supt*
EMP: 95
SALES (est): 6.2MM Privately Held
WEB: www.tehamagolfclub.com
SIC: 7997 Golf club, membership

(P-19104)
TENNIS EVERYONE INCORPORATED
Also Called: Rolling Hills Club
351 San Andreas Dr, Novato (94945-1206)
PHONE...................415 897-2185
Fax: 415 898-0659
Chuk Trieve, *President*
Anna Levinson, *Exec Dir*
Marybeth Bradley, *General Mgr*
Jolene Graniss, *Human Resources*
Colin Lewis, *Training Spec*
EMP: 85 EST: 1973
SQ FT: 19,000
SALES: 3.4MM Privately Held
WEB: www.rollinghillsclub.com
SIC: 7997 Membership sports & recreation clubs

(P-19105)
THE VALLEY CLUB OF MONTECITO
1901 E Valley Rd, Santa Barbara (93108-1427)
PHONE...................805 969-2215
Fax: 805 969-6174
John S Degroot, *CEO*
Palmer Jackson, *President*
EMP: 50
SQ FT: 3,000
SALES: 6.4MM Privately Held
SIC: 7997 Golf club, membership

(P-19106)
THE WOODBRIDGE GOLF CNTRY CLB
800 E Woodbridge Rd, Woodbridge (95258-9628)
P.O. Box 806 (95258-0806)
PHONE...................209 369-2371
Fax: 209 334-6416
Jerry Leonard, *CEO*
Ernie Micelli, *General Mgr*
Kristine Roberson, *Director*
Courtney Sandison, *Director*
Carrie Sterling, *Manager*

7997 - Membership Sports & Recreation Clubs County (P-19107)

EMP: 79
SQ FT: 20,000
SALES: 3.5MM **Privately Held**
SIC: 7997 Country club, membership

(P-19107)
THERMAL CLUB
86030 62nd Ave, Thermal (92274-9250)
PHONE..................................760 674-0088
John Rogers, *Principal*
EMP: 51
SALES (est): 1.2MM
SALES (corp-wide): 395.3MM **Privately Held**
SIC: 7997 Membership sports & recreation clubs
PA: Tower Energy Group
1983 W 190th St Ste 100
Torrance CA 90504
310 538-8000

(P-19108)
THUNDERBIRD COUNTRY CLUB
70737 Country Club Dr, Rancho Mirage (92270-3500)
P.O. Box 5005 (92270-1065)
PHONE..................................760 328-2161
Fax: 760 321-4940
Brian Rice, *CEO*
Richard Friedman, *COO*
Chris Olson, *Executive*
Michaell Crandall, *General Mgr*
David L Shepler, *General Mgr*
EMP: 60
SQ FT: 30,000
SALES: 8.6MM **Privately Held**
WEB: www.thunderbirdcc.org
SIC: 7997 5812 7011 Country club, membership; eating places; hotels & motels

(P-19109)
TIBURON PENINSULA CLUB INC
1600 Mar West St, Belvedere Tiburon (94920-1830)
P.O. Box 436 (94920-0436)
PHONE..................................415 789-7900
Fax: 415 435-6629
Gerry Pang, *Principal*
Julie Coulston, *General Mgr*
Jerry Pang, *General Mgr*
Keith Pollak, *Administration*
Malcolm Lacey, *Opers Staff*
EMP: 50
SQ FT: 6,674
SALES: 4.9MM **Privately Held**
WEB: www.tiburonpc.org
SIC: 7997 Swimming club, membership; tennis club, membership

(P-19110)
TIERRA OAKS GOLF CLUB INC
19700 La Crescenta Dr, Redding (96003-7474)
PHONE..................................530 275-0795
Fax: 530 275-0895
Shawn Sich, *General Mgr*
Jesse Bullington, *Assistant*
EMP: 90
SALES (est): 3.5MM **Privately Held**
WEB: www.lockefordsprings.com
SIC: 7997 6531 Golf club, membership; real estate agents & managers
PA: Spring Lockeford Golf Course Inc
16360 N Highway 88
Lodi CA 95240
209 333-6275

(P-19111)
TOSCANA COUNTRY CLUB INC
76009 Via Club Villa, Indian Wells (92210-7851)
PHONE..................................760 404-1444
Paul K Levy, *CEO*
Crista Collins, *Director*
Rich Baloga, *Manager*
EMP: 84
SALES: 6.5MM **Privately Held**
SIC: 7997 Membership sports & recreation

(P-19112)
TRADITION GOLF CLUB ASSOCIATES
78505 Avenue 52, La Quinta (92253-2802)
PHONE..................................760 564-3355
David Champman, *General Mgr*

Wendi Park, *Accountant*
Marcy Luna, *Manager*
EMP: 60
SALES (est): 2.3MM **Privately Held**
SIC: 7997 Golf club, membership

(P-19113)
TREASURE ISLAND YACHT CLUB
2333 Lariat Ln, Walnut Creek (94596-6518)
PHONE..................................925 939-0230
Sandra Aberer, *CEO*
George Knies, *Admin Sec*
EMP: 68
SALES (est): 999.7K **Privately Held**
SIC: 7997 Yacht club, membership

(P-19114)
TY INVESTMENT INC
9200 Inwood Dr, Santee (92071-2310)
PHONE..................................619 448-4242
Toru Mise, *President*
Hiromi Carino, *Human Res Mgr*
EMP: 75
SALES (est): 4MM **Privately Held**
WEB: www.carltonoaksgolf.com
SIC: 7997 Country club, membership; golf club, membership

(P-19115)
UC IRVINE RECREATION CENTER
680 California Ave, Irvine (92617-5156)
PHONE..................................949 824-5346
Jio Schingelle, *Director*
Janet Konami, *Director*
Greg Rothberg, *Manager*
EMP: 75
SALES (est): 1.3MM **Privately Held**
SIC: 7997 Membership sports & recreation clubs

(P-19116)
UNITED STATES PONY CLUBS
7010 Hidden Valley Pl, Granite Bay (95746-9456)
PHONE..................................916 791-1223
Linda Gurnee, *Director*
EMP: 82
SALES: 58.2K **Privately Held**
SIC: 7997 Membership sports & recreation clubs

(P-19117)
VALLEY-HI COUNTRY CLUB
9595 Franklin Blvd, Elk Grove (95758-9532)
PHONE..................................916 684-2120
Fax: 916 684-2121
Edgar Gill, *CEO*
Nick West, *Principal*
David Kay, *Controller*
Peggy Thompson, *Controller*
David E Bingham, *Manager*
EMP: 50
SQ FT: 20,000
SALES (est): 3.3MM **Privately Held**
WEB: www.valleyhicc.com
SIC: 7997 Country club, membership

(P-19118)
VILLAGE WEST YACHT CLUB
6633 Embarcadero Dr, Stockton (95219-3329)
PHONE..................................209 478-8992
Fred Von Helf, *President*
Allan Mackey, *Treasurer*
Burt Riisager, *Bd of Directors*
Ray Speetzen, *Director*
EMP: 100
SALES (est): 2MM **Privately Held**
SIC: 7997 7941 Membership sports & recreation clubs; sports clubs, managers & promoters

(P-19119)
VILLAGES GOLF AND COUNTRY CLUB
Also Called: Villages, The
5000 Cribari Ln, San Jose (95135-1397)
PHONE..................................408 274-4400
Fax: 408 223-4635
Virginia Fanelli, *CEO*
Jim White, *Finance Dir*

Carl Starks, *Accountant*
Brad Barncord, *Opers Staff*
Tom Muniz, *Facilities Mgr*
EMP: 170
SALES (est): 17MM **Privately Held**
WEB: www.the-villages.com
SIC: 7997 Country club, membership

(P-19120)
VINTAGE CLUB (PA)
75001 Vintage Club Dr W, Indian Wells (92210)
PHONE..................................760 341-1476
Fax: 760 773-4783
Marc D Ray, *COO*
Jane Richards, *Accountant*
Leeann Patterson, *Controller*
Candice Morgan, *Human Res Dir*
Tom Hart, *Property Mgr*
EMP: 50
SQ FT: 86,000
SALES (est): 21MM **Privately Held**
WEB: www.thevintageclub.com
SIC: 7997 5813 5812 5941 Country club, membership; bar (drinking places); American restaurant; golf goods & equipment

(P-19121)
VIRGINIA CNTRY CLB OF LONG BCH
4602 N Virginia Rd, Long Beach (90807-1999)
PHONE..................................562 427-7994
Fax: 562 424-0924
Jamie Mulligan, *COO*
Francis Adlesh, *General Mgr*
Susan Ledesma, *Controller*
Colleen Carlson, *Manager*
EMP: 110
SQ FT: 15,000
SALES: 5.9MM **Privately Held**
SIC: 7997 Country club, membership; golf club, membership

(P-19122)
VISALIA COUNTRY CLUB
625 N Ranch St, Visalia (93291-4317)
P.O. Box 3410 (93278-3410)
PHONE..................................559 734-3733
Steve Beargeon, *Principal*
Kristen Berry, *Controller*
EMP: 80
SQ FT: 60,000
SALES: 4.4MM **Privately Held**
SIC: 7997 Country club, membership

(P-19123)
VISTA VALLEY COUNTRY CLUB
Also Called: V Vcc Havens
29354 Vista Valley Dr, Vista (92084-2209)
PHONE..................................760 758-5275
Fax: 760 758-3189
John Havens, *President*
Alex Maio, *Executive*
Tanya Bolton, *Business Dir*
John Ledenbach, *General Mgr*
Philip Rodriguez, *General Mgr*
EMP: 70
SQ FT: 15,000
SALES (est): 6.4MM **Privately Held**
WEB: www.vistavalley.com
SIC: 7997 5812 7999 Country club, membership; eating places; golf cart, power, rental

(P-19124)
WEST HILLS GOLF ASSOCIATES
Also Called: Western Hills Country Club
1800 Carbon Canyon Rd, Chino Hills (91709-2300)
PHONE..................................714 528-6400
Fax: 714 528-1513
Michael Donovan, *Partner*
William Donovan, *Ltd Ptnr*
Ron Lane, *Ltd Ptnr*
EMP: 50
SQ FT: 12,000
SALES (est): 2.1MM **Privately Held**
SIC: 7997 7299 Golf club, membership; banquet hall facilities

(P-19125)
WESTGROUP KONA KAI LLC
Also Called: Kona Kai Resort Hotel
1551 Shelter Island Dr, San Diego (92106-3102)
PHONE..................................619 221-8000
Kathy Little,
EMP: 99
SALES (est): 5.3MM **Privately Held**
SIC: 7997 7011 Membership sports & recreation clubs; resort hotel

(P-19126)
WILSHIRE COUNTRY CLUB
301 N Rossmore Ave, Los Angeles (90004-2499)
PHONE..................................323 934-6050
Fax: 323 931-2013
Jeffrey Ornstein, *CEO*
Norman Branchflower, *President*
Mirion Bowers MD, *Vice Pres*
Stephen Farris, *Executive*
Megan Amaya, *Personnel Exec*
EMP: 94
SQ FT: 50,000
SALES: 9.1MM **Privately Held**
WEB: www.wilshirecc.com
SIC: 7997 5941 5812 Country club, membership; sporting goods & bicycle shops; eating places

(P-19127)
WINCHESTER REO LLC
3030 Legends Dr, Meadow Vista (95722-9346)
PHONE..................................530 878-3000
CC Myers,
Cassandra Grauer, *Marketing Mgr*
EMP: 50
SALES (est): 2.1MM **Privately Held**
WEB: www.winchestercountryclub.com
SIC: 7997 Country club, membership; golf club, membership

(P-19128)
YUBA CITY RACQUET CLUB INC
825 Jones Rd, Yuba City (95991-6124)
PHONE..................................530 673-6900
Fax: 530 673-4006
Judie Jacoby, *President*
Pete Bakis, *Exec VP*
▲ EMP: 73
SQ FT: 40,000
SALES: 3.5MM **Privately Held**
WEB: www.ycrc.com
SIC: 7997 7991 Tennis club, membership; health club

7999 Amusement & Recreation Svcs, NEC

(P-19129)
29 PALMS ENTERPRISES CORP
Also Called: Spotlight 29 Casino
46200 Harrison Pl, Coachella (92236-2031)
PHONE..................................760 775-5566
Fax: 760 775-4638
Darrel Mike, *President*
Marcia R Martin, *CFO*
Victor Ortiz, *Executive*
Jim Galvin, *Administration*
Gordon Howe, *Technology*
EMP: 600
SQ FT: 70,000
SALES (est): 39.4MM **Privately Held**
WEB: www.spotlight29.net
SIC: 7999 5812 Gambling establishment; eating places

(P-19130)
ADVENTURE CITY INC
1238 S Beach Blvd, Anaheim (92804-4828)
PHONE..................................714 821-3311
Fax: 714 827-2992
Allan Ansdell Jr, *President*
Yvonne Ansdell, *Treasurer*
Trina Ansdell, *Human Res Mgr*
Sandy Ontiveros, *Purch Agent*
EMP: 100

PRODUCTS & SERVICES SECTION
7999 - Amusement & Recreation Svcs, NEC County (P-19154)

SALES (est): 3MM **Privately Held**
WEB: www.adventurecity.com
SIC: 7999 7996 Tourist attractions, amusement park concessions & rides; amusement parks

(P-19131)
ADVENTURE CONNECTION INC
986 Lotus Rd, Lotus (95651)
P.O. Box 475, Coloma (95613-0475)
PHONE..................530 626-7385
Fax: 530 626-9268
Nathan J Rangel, *President*
EMP: 60
SQ FT: 2,400
SALES (est): 750K **Privately Held**
WEB: www.raftcalifornia.com
SIC: 7999 4725 Rafting tours; tour operators

(P-19132)
ALAMEDA COUNTY AG FAIR ASSN
Also Called: Alameda County Fair
4501 Pleasanton Ave, Pleasanton (94566-7001)
PHONE..................925 426-7600
Fax: 925 426-7599
Rick Pickering, *CEO*
Ted Holder, *CFO*
Randy Maggie, *CFO*
Bill Judd, *Analyst*
EMP: 75
SQ FT: 125,000
SALES: 22.3MM **Privately Held**
WEB: www.alamedacountyfair.com
SIC: 7999 Agricultural fair

(P-19133)
ALPINE CAMP CONFERENCE CTR INC
415 Clubhouse Dr, Blue Jay (92317)
P.O. Box 155 (92317-0155)
PHONE..................909 337-6287
Kim Polson, *Administration*
Anthony Xepolis, *President*
Joel Rude, *Principal*
John Gehring, *Exec Dir*
John Gehrig, *Director*
EMP: 68
SALES (est): 1.3MM **Privately Held**
SIC: 7999 7032 Instruction schools, camps & services; youth camps

(P-19134)
AMBASSADOR GAMING INC
Also Called: Key Largo Casino
660 Newport Center Dr # 1050, Newport Beach (92660-6401)
PHONE..................714 969-8730
Stephen K Bone, *President*
Robert L Mayer Jr, *Treasurer*
EMP: 112
SALES (est): 4.8MM **Privately Held**
WEB: www.keylargocasino.com
SIC: 7999 7993 Gambling machines, operation; gambling establishments operating coin-operated machines; slot machines

(P-19135)
AMBROSE RECREATION & PARK DST
3105 Willow Pass Rd, Bay Point (94565-3149)
PHONE..................925 458-1601
Fax: 925 458-1672
Travis Stombaugh, *General Mgr*
Gloria Magleby, *Ch of Bd*
Doug Long, *General Mgr*
Greg Enholm, *Director*
Eva Garcia, *Director*
EMP: 100 **EST:** 1952
SALES (est): 2.4MM **Privately Held**
SIC: 7999 Recreation services

(P-19136)
ANAHEIM ICE
Also Called: Rinks Anaheim Ice, The
300 W Lincoln Ave, Anaheim (92805-2947)
PHONE..................714 518-3200
Art Trottier, *Vice Pres*
Jill Herzogge, *General Mgr*
Kurt Mallett, *General Mgr*
Cindi Palomarez, *Marketing Staff*
EMP: 70
SALES (est): 2.2MM **Privately Held**
SIC: 7999 Skating rink operation services

(P-19137)
ANGELES LOS EQUESTRIAN CENTER
480 W Riverside Dr, Burbank (91506-3209)
PHONE..................818 840-9063
Fax: 818 333-1465
J Albert Garcia, *President*
George Chatigny, *General Mgr*
Ante Zovich, *Superintendent*
EMP: 120
SALES (est): 3.6MM **Privately Held**
SIC: 7999 Riding stable

(P-19138)
APEX PARKS GROUP LLC
Also Called: Upland Valley Fun Center
1500 W 7th St, Upland (91786-6921)
PHONE..................909 981-5251
Fax: 909 946-1567
Richard Towfiegh, *Manager*
EMP: 70
SALES (corp-wide): 27.2MM **Privately Held**
SIC: 7999 Miniature golf course operation
PA: Apex Parks Group, Llc
27061 Aliso Creek Rd
Aliso Viejo CA 92656
949 349-8461

(P-19139)
APEX PARKS GROUP LLC
Also Called: Malibu Castle
27061 Aliso Creek Rd # 100, Aliso Viejo (92656-5326)
PHONE..................210 341-6663
Debbie Vorpaho, *Branch Mgr*
EMP: 100
SALES (corp-wide): 27.2MM **Privately Held**
SIC: 7999 5599 Baseball batting cage; go-carts
PA: Apex Parks Group, Llc
27061 Aliso Creek Rd
Aliso Viejo CA 92656
949 349-8461

(P-19140)
ARAMARK SERVICES INC
2000 Kirker Pass Rd, Concord (94521-1642)
PHONE..................925 798-3321
Tim Dicker, *Manager*
Tim Dickert, *Manager*
EMP: 250
SALES (corp-wide): 14.3B **Publicly Held**
SIC: 7999 5812 Concession operator; eating places
HQ: Aramark Services, Inc.
1101 Market St Ste 45
Philadelphia PA 19107
215 238-3000

(P-19141)
ARISE LLC
1033 Van Ness Ave, Fresno (93721-2006)
PHONE..................559 485-0881
Darrell Miers, *CEO*
EMP: 60
SALES (est): 1.9MM **Privately Held**
SIC: 7999 Gambling establishment

(P-19142)
AROMA SPA & SPORTS LLC
Also Called: Aroma Wilshire Center
3680 Wilshire Blvd # 301, Los Angeles (90010-2708)
PHONE..................213 387-2111
Fax: 213 387-0730
Byoung G Choi,
Keejune Huh,
EMP: 60
SALES (est): 1.9MM **Privately Held**
SIC: 7999 7991 Recreation center; health club

(P-19143)
ARTICHOKE JOES INC
Also Called: Artichoke Joe's Casino
659 Huntington Ave, San Bruno (94066-3608)
PHONE..................650 589-8812
Fax: 650 872-0101
Dennis J Sammut, *President*
Helen Sammut, *Corp Secy*
EMP: 330
SALES (est): 15.2MM **Privately Held**
WEB: www.artichokejoes.com
SIC: 7999 5812 5813 Game parlor; eating places; tavern (drinking places)

(P-19144)
ARTISTS STUDIO GALLERY
5504 Crestridge Rd, Rancho Palos Verdes (90275-4905)
PHONE..................424 206-9902
EMP: 56
SALES (corp-wide): 97.9K **Privately Held**
SIC: 7999 Art gallery, commercial
PA: Artists Studio Gallery Of The Palos Verdes
550 Deep Valley Dr # 327
Rlling Hls Est CA 90274
310 265-2592

(P-19145)
AUBURN OLD TOWN GALLERY
Also Called: Old Town Gallery of Fine Art
218 Washington St Ste A, Auburn (95603-5048)
PHONE..................530 887-9150
Sonja Hamilton, *President*
Mike Miller,
Marilyn Russell,
EMP: 60
SALES (est): 2.2MM **Privately Held**
WEB: www.auburnoldtowngallery.com
SIC: 7999 5999 Art gallery, commercial; art dealers

(P-19146)
BAY AREA SEATING SERVICE INC
Also Called: Bass Tickets
1855 Gateway Blvd Ste 630, Concord (94520-3200)
PHONE..................925 671-4000
W Thomas Gimple, *President*
Doug Levenson, *Exec VP*
EMP: 300
SQ FT: 18,000
SALES (est): 1.9MM
SALES (corp-wide): 271.5MM **Privately Held**
WEB: www.tickets.com
SIC: 7999 Ticket sales office for sporting events, contract
HQ: California Tickets.Com Inc.
555 Anton Blvd Fl 11
Costa Mesa CA 92626
714 327-5400

(P-19147)
BEAR VALLEY SKI CO
Also Called: Bear Valley Mountain Resort
2280 State Rte 207, Bear Valley (95223)
P.O. Box 5038 (95223-5038)
PHONE..................209 753-2301
Fax: 209 753-6421
Tim Bottomley, *CEO*
Jane Bottomley, *Vice Pres*
Barbara Moreci, *Maintence Staff*
EMP: 325
SQ FT: 70,000
SALES (est): 15.1MM
SALES (corp-wide): 83.5MM **Privately Held**
WEB: www.bearvalley.com
SIC: 7999 5941 Recreation services; ski rental concession; ski instruction; skiing equipment
HQ: Skyline International Development Inc
90 Eglinton Ave E Suite 800
Toronto ON M4P 2
416 368-2565

(P-19148)
BELL GARDENS BICYCLE CLUB INC
Also Called: Bicycle Club Casino
888 Bicycle Casino Dr, Bell Gardens (90201-7617)
PHONE..................562 806-4646
Fax: 562 928-0614
George Hardie, *President*
Jim Griffo, *President*
George G Hardie, *President*
Kelley O'Hara, *Chief Mktg Ofcr*
Joy Harn, *Vice Pres*

EMP: 1300
SQ FT: 110,000
SALES (est): 37.6MM **Privately Held**
WEB: www.thebicyclecasino.com
SIC: 7999 5812 Card rooms; coffee shop

(P-19149)
BIG 5 SPORTING GOODS CORP
11310 Crenshaw Blvd, Inglewood (90303-2807)
PHONE..................323 755-2663
EMP: 1278
SALES (corp-wide): 1B **Publicly Held**
SIC: 7999 5941 5699 5661 Sporting goods rental; sporting goods & bicycle shops; sports apparel; shoe stores
PA: Big 5 Sporting Goods Corp
2525 E El Segundo Blvd
El Segundo CA 90245
310 536-0611

(P-19150)
BIKRAMS YOGA COLLEGE OF INDIA
910 Columbus Ave, San Francisco (94133-2310)
PHONE..................415 346-2480
Bikram Choudhury, *Owner*
James Borsillino, *Principal*
EMP: 50
SALES (est): 484.4K **Privately Held**
SIC: 7999 7299 Yoga instruction; personal appearance services

(P-19151)
BISHOP PAIUTE GAMING CORP
Also Called: Paiute Palace Casino
2742 N Sierra Hwy, Bishop (93514-2218)
PHONE..................760 872-6005
Fax: 760 872-6604
Gloriana Bailey, *President*
Lawrence Sharky, *Security Mgr*
Tim McGlynn, *Mktg Dir*
Deanna Gustie, *Director*
EMP: 150
SALES (est): 7.1MM **Privately Held**
WEB: www.paiutepalace.com
SIC: 7999 Gambling establishment

(P-19152)
BLACK OAK CASINO
19400 Tuolumne Rd N, Tuolumne (95379-9696)
PHONE..................209 928-9300
Fax: 209 928-9301
Ron Patel, *General Mgr*
Daniel Harner, *Officer*
Clint Chapel, *Admin Asst*
Jason Czito, *Technical Mgr*
James Canon, *Technology*
EMP: 99
SQ FT: 168,000
SALES (est): 10.8MM **Privately Held**
WEB: www.blackoakcasino.com
SIC: 7999 Gambling establishment
PA: Tuolumne Me-Wuk Tribal Council
19595 Mi Wu St
Tuolumne CA 95379
209 928-5300

(P-19153)
BLUE BUS TOURS LLC
Also Called: Grayline of San Francisco
50 Quint St, San Francisco (94124-1424)
PHONE..................415 353-5310
Raman Fargoni, *President*
Paul Nakamoto, *Exec VP*
EMP: 120 **EST:** 2011
SQ FT: 4,200
SALES: 350K **Privately Held**
SIC: 7999 Tourist attraction, commercial

(P-19154)
BRIAR GOLF LP
Also Called: Cathedral Cyn Golf Tennis CLB
68311 Paseo Real, Cathedral City (92234-6767)
PHONE..................760 328-6571
Tom Moran, *General Ptnr*
David Flickwir, *General Ptnr*
Michael Winn, *General Mgr*
Mario Mendoza, *Superintendent*
EMP: 70
SALES (est): 1.3MM **Privately Held**
SIC: 7999 Golf services & professionals

7999 - Amusement & Recreation Svcs, NEC County (P-19155)

(P-19155)
BUSINESS AND SUPPORT SERVICES
Also Called: Marine Corps Community Svcs
Mccs Bldg 2273 Elrod Ave, San Diego (92145-0001)
P.O. Box 452008 (92145-2008)
PHONE 858 577-4786
Mary Bradford, *Director*
EMP: 800 **Publicly Held**
WEB: www.mccssc.com
SIC: 7999 9711 Recreation center; Marine Corps;
HQ: Business And Support Services
 3044 Catlin Ave
 Quantico VA 22134
 703 432-0109

(P-19156)
CAHUILLA CREEK REST & CASINO
Also Called: Cahuilla Creek Casino
52702 Us Highway 371, Anza (92539-8707)
PHONE 951 763-1200
Fax: 951 763-2050
Leonardo Pasquarelli, *General Mgr*
Bonnie Clabaugh, *COO*
Jon Gregory, *General Mgr*
Jeremy Leahy, *Finance Mgr*
Leonard Pasquarelli, *Manager*
EMP: 103 **EST:** 1996
SQ FT: 14,000
SALES (est): 8.9MM **Privately Held**
WEB: www.cahuillacreekcasino.com
SIC: 7999 5812 5813 Gambling establishment; American restaurant; bar (drinking places); tavern (drinking places)

(P-19157)
CALIFORNIA CLUB LUCKY LADY
Also Called: Lucky Lady Card Room
5526 El Cajon Blvd, San Diego (92115-3623)
PHONE 619 287-6690
Fax: 619 229-1956
Stanley Penn, *Owner*
EMP: 50
SQ FT: 7,000
SALES: 500K **Privately Held**
WEB: www.calicasinos.net
SIC: 7999 Card rooms

(P-19158)
CAPITOL CASINO
411 N 16th St, Sacramento (95811-0516)
PHONE 916 446-0700
Clarke Rosa, *President*
Gene Clavager, *General Mgr*
EMP: 150
SQ FT: 7,500
SALES (est): 4.6MM **Privately Held**
WEB: www.capitol-casino.com
SIC: 7999 5813 Card rooms; cocktail lounge

(P-19159)
CATALINA BUSINESS ENTPS INC
635 Crescent Ave, Avalon (90704)
P.O. Box 1919 (90704-1919)
PHONE 310 510-1600
Buddy Wilson, *President*
EMP: 50
SALES (corp-wide): 1.4MM **Privately Held**
SIC: 7999 Golf cart, power, rental
PA: Catalina Business Enterprises, Inc.
 800 Cresent Ave
 Avalon CA 90704
 310 510-2550

(P-19160)
CHER-AE HEIGHTS INDIAN CMNTY
Also Called: Cher Ae Heights Casino
27 Scenic Dr, Trinidad (95570-9767)
P.O. Box 610 (95570-0610)
PHONE 707 677-3611
Ron Dadouin, *Manager*
Josh Oshiro, *IT/INT Sup*
EMP: 196 **Privately Held**
WEB: www.trinidadrancheria.com
SIC: 7999 7011 Card rooms; casino hotel
PA: Cher-Ae Heights Indian Community
 1 Cher Ae Ln
 Trinidad CA 95570
 707 677-0211

(P-19161)
CHICKEN RANCH BINGO & CASINO
16929 Chicken Ranch Rd, Jamestown (95327-9779)
P.O. Box 1699 (95327-1699)
PHONE 209 984-3000
Fax: 209 984-4158
Lloyd Matheson, *Owner*
James Beland, *Security Dir*
Coco Raymond, *Controller*
Jamie Lloyd, *Marketing Mgr*
Sam Blackford, *Manager*
EMP: 150
SQ FT: 35,000
SALES: 5.7K **Privately Held**
SIC: 7999 Bingo hall

(P-19162)
CHICO AREA RECREATION & PK DST (PA)
Also Called: Dorothy Johnson Center
545 Vallombrosa Ave, Chico (95926-4037)
PHONE 530 895-4711
Fax: 530 895-4721
Mary Cahill, *General Mgr*
Scott Dowell, *Officer*
Suzanne Bullock, *Executive*
Jennifer Marciales, *Executive Asst*
Olivia Wilson, *Business Mgr*
EMP: 55
SQ FT: 27,000
SALES (est): 5.4MM **Privately Held**
WEB: www.chicorec.com
SIC: 7999 8322 Recreation services; individual & family services

(P-19163)
CHOPRA CNTRE FOR WLL-BEING LLC
Also Called: Chopra Center For Wellbeing
2013 Costa Del Mar Rd, Carlsbad (92009-6801)
PHONE 760 494-1600
Fax: 760 494-1608
Deepak Chopra MD, *Principal*
David Simon MD, *Principal*
Traci Porterfield, *Human Res Dir*
Katy Gallagher, *Marketing Staff*
▲ **EMP:** 51 **EST:** 1996
SALES (est): 4.6MM **Privately Held**
SIC: 7999 8299 7991 Yoga instruction; meditation therapy; spas

(P-19164)
CHRISTIANSEN AMUSEMENTS CORP
1725 S Escondido Blvd E, Escondido (92025-6546)
P.O. Box 997 (92033-0997)
PHONE 760 735-8542
Stacey Brown, *President*
William Jacob, *Vice Pres*
Stacy Brown, *Agent*
EMP: 70
SALES (est): 3.4MM **Privately Held**
WEB: www.carnivalgame.com
SIC: 7999 Carnival operation

(P-19165)
CHUMASH CASINO RESORT
100 Via Juana Rd, Santa Ynez (93460-9669)
PHONE 805 688-7997
Fax: 805 686-2060
Vincent Armenta, *Branch Mgr*
EMP: 821
SALES (corp-wide): 84MM **Privately Held**
SIC: 7999 Gambling establishment
PA: Chumash Casino Resort
 3400 E Highway 246
 Santa Ynez CA 93460
 805 686-0855

(P-19166)
CHUMASH CASINO RESORT (PA)
3400 E Highway 246, Santa Ynez (93460-9405)
PHONE 805 686-0855
Fax: 805 686-3859
Carol Clearwater, *CFO*
John Featherstone, *Executive*
William Peters, *General Mgr*
Michael Armenta, *Planning*
Ed Jara, *Info Tech Dir*
EMP: 99
SQ FT: 29,000
SALES (est): 84MM **Privately Held**
WEB: www.chumashcasino.com
SIC: 7999 7011 Gambling establishment; resort hotel

(P-19167)
CITY OF COMMERCE
Also Called: Parks & Recreation
2535 Commerce Way, Commerce (90040-1410)
PHONE 323 888-6841
Fax: 323 888-6841
Jim Jimenez, *Director*
EMP: 400 **Privately Held**
SIC: 7999 7991 Recreation center; physical fitness facilities
PA: City Of Commerce
 2535 Commerce Way
 Commerce CA 90040
 323 722-4805

(P-19168)
CITY OF COMPTON
Also Called: William Love Swimming Pool
1108 N Oleander Ave, Compton (90222-4041)
PHONE 310 635-3484
Vanessa Little, *Principal*
Marvin Hunt, *Manager*
EMP: 60 **Privately Held**
SIC: 7999 9111 Swimming pool, non-membership; mayors' offices
PA: City Of Compton
 205 S Willowbrook Ave
 Compton CA 90220
 310 605-5500

(P-19169)
CITY OF CORONADO
Also Called: Recreation Dept
1845 Strand Way, Coronado (92118-3005)
PHONE 619 522-7342
Fax: 619 522-7870
Linda Rahn, *Director*
Rahan Linda, *Exec Dir*
Stacy Berman, *Director*
Lori Burke, *Director*
EMP: 100 **Privately Held**
WEB: www.coronadoplayhouse.com
SIC: 7999 7997 Swimming pool, non-membership; membership sports & recreation clubs
PA: City Of Coronado
 1825 Strand Way
 Coronado CA 92118
 619 522-7300

(P-19170)
CITY OF FOLSOM
Also Called: Park and Recreation
50 Natoma St, Folsom (95630-2614)
PHONE 916 355-7285
Robert Goss, *Director*
EMP: 75 **Privately Held**
WEB: www.folsompd.com
SIC: 7999 Recreation services
PA: City Of Folsom
 50 Natoma St
 Folsom CA 95630
 916 355-7200

(P-19171)
CITY OF FOSTER CITY
Parks & Recreation
650 Shell Blvd, Foster City (94404-2501)
PHONE 650 286-3380
Fax: 650 345-1408
Kevin Miller, *Director*
EMP: 50 **Privately Held**
WEB: www.fostercitymothersclub.org
SIC: 7999 9111 Recreation services; mayors' offices
PA: City Of Foster City
 610 Foster City Blvd
 Foster City CA 94404
 650 286-3260

(P-19172)
CITY OF GALT
Also Called: Galt Park Recreation
660 Chabolla Ave, Galt (95632-2033)
PHONE 209 366-7180
Fax: 209 366-7199
Boyce Jeffries, *Director*
EMP: 65 **Privately Held**
WEB: www.ci.galt.ca.us
SIC: 7999 Recreation center
PA: City Of Galt
 380 Civic Dr
 Galt CA 95632
 209 366-7000

(P-19173)
CITY OF INGLEWOOD
Also Called: Edward Vincent Park
700 Warren Ln, Inglewood (90302-3208)
PHONE 310 412-5370
James Henry, *Manager*
EMP: 65 **Privately Held**
SIC: 7999 9111 Recreation services; mayors' offices
PA: City Of Inglewood
 1 W Manchester Blvd
 Inglewood CA 90301
 310 412-5301

(P-19174)
CITY OF IRVINE
Also Called: Parks-Rcreation-Community Svcs
6443 Oak Cyn, Irvine (92618-5202)
PHONE 949 724-7740
EMP: 151 **Privately Held**
SIC: 7999 Recreation services
PA: City Of Irvine
 1 Civic Center Plz
 Irvine CA 92606
 949 724-6000

(P-19175)
CITY OF MILL VALLEY
Also Called: Mill Valley Parks & Recreation
180 Camino Alto, Mill Valley (94941-4603)
PHONE 415 383-1370
Christine Som, *Director*
Kenneth Wachtel,
EMP: 50 **Privately Held**
WEB: www.donnadcuti.com
SIC: 7999 9111 Recreation services; mayors' offices
PA: City Of Mill Valley
 26 Corte Madera Ave
 Mill Valley CA 94941
 415 388-4033

(P-19176)
CITY OF MONTEREY PARK
Also Called: City Mnterey Pk Recreation Ctr
320 W Newmark Ave Fl 1, Monterey Park (91754-2896)
PHONE 626 307-1388
Fax: 626 307-0753
Harry Panagiotes, *Director*
EMP: 100 **Privately Held**
SIC: 7999 9111 Recreation center; mayors' offices
PA: City Of Monterey Park
 320 W Newmark Ave
 Monterey Park CA 91754
 626 307-1255

(P-19177)
CITY OF OAKLAND
Also Called: Sports Office
250 Frank H Ogawa Plz # 6301, Oakland (94612-2035)
PHONE 510 238-3494
Fax: 510 238-2397
Michael Hammock, *Principal*
Victor N Correia, *Human Res Mgr*
Mark T Farley, *Buyer*
Mark Zinn, *Director*
Audree Jones-Taylor, *Manager*
EMP: 50 **Privately Held**
WEB: www.cityofbuellton.com
SIC: 7999 Sports instruction, schools & camps

PRODUCTS & SERVICES SECTION
7999 - Amusement & Recreation Svcs, NEC County (P-19199)

PA: City Of Oakland
150 Frank H Ogawa Plz # 3332
Oakland CA 94612
510 238-3280

(P-19178)
CITY OF OAKLAND
Also Called: Oakland Ice Center
519 18th St, Oakland (94612-1511)
PHONE 510 268-9000
Dave Fies, General Mgr
Peggy Young, Accountant
Lauri Varvais, Director
EMP: 50 Privately Held
WEB: www.cityofbuellton.com
SIC: 7999 Ice skating rink operation
PA: City Of Oakland
150 Frank H Ogawa Plz # 3332
Oakland CA 94612
510 238-3280

(P-19179)
CITY OF ORANGE
Also Called: Parks Recreation Libraries
230 E Chapman Ave, Orange
(92866-1506)
PHONE 714 744-7272
Fax: 714 744-7251
Gary Wann, Director
EMP: 50 Privately Held
WEB: www.cityoforange.org
SIC: 7999 Recreation services
PA: City Of Orange
300 E Chapman Ave
Orange CA 92866
714 744-5500

(P-19180)
CITY OF RICHMOND
Also Called: Convention Center Booking Off
3230 Macdonald Ave Fl 2, Richmond
(94804-3012)
P.O. Box 4046 (94804-0046)
PHONE 510 620-6788
Jesse Washington, Director
Sue Hartman, Director
EMP: 100 Privately Held
WEB: www.kcrt.com
SIC: 7999 Recreation center
PA: City Of Richmond
450 Civic Center Plaza
Richmond CA 94804
510 620-6727

(P-19181)
CITY OF SOUTH LAKE TAHOE
Also Called: Recreation Complex
1180 Rufus Allen Blvd, South Lake Tahoe
(96150-8211)
PHONE 530 542-6056
Fax: 530 542-2981
Gary Moore, Superintendent
Kim George, Engineer
Gregg Ross, Manager
Dennis Churchill, Supervisor
EMP: 78 Privately Held
WEB: www.cityofslt.com
SIC: 7999 Swimming pool, non-membership
PA: City Of South Lake Tahoe
1901 Airport Rd Ste 210
South Lake Tahoe CA 96150
530 541-0480

(P-19182)
CITY OF TORRANCE
Also Called: Park Maintenance
20500 Madrona Ave, Torrance
(90503-3692)
PHONE 310 781-6901
Fax: 310 618-3077
Robert Carson, General Mgr
Kim Turner, Opers Mgr
EMP: 55 Privately Held
SIC: 7999 Recreation center
PA: City Of Torrance
3031 Torrance Blvd
Torrance CA 90503
310 328-5310

(P-19183)
CITY OF VISTA
Wave Water Park
101 Wave Dr, Vista (92083-5824)
PHONE 760 940-9283
Natalie Livingston, Branch Mgr
EMP: 150 Privately Held
WEB: www.cityofvista.com
SIC: 7999 Tourist attractions, amusement park concessions & rides
PA: City Of Vista
200 Civic Center Dr
Vista CA 92084
760 726-1340

(P-19184)
CITY OF WOODLAND
Also Called: Charles Brooks Cmnty Swim Ctr
2001 East St, Woodland (95776-5183)
PHONE 530 661-5878
Dan Gentry, Director
EMP: 200 Privately Held
WEB: www.ci.woodland.ca.us
SIC: 7999 9111 Swimming pool, non-membership; mayors' offices
PA: City Of Woodland
300 1st St
Woodland CA 95695
530 661-5830

(P-19185)
CLUB ONE CASINO INC
1033 Van Ness Ave, Fresno (93721-2006)
PHONE 559 497-3000
Fax: 559 237-2582
Kyle R Kirkland, President
George Sarantos, President
Kirk Atamian, Executive
Miguel Gamboa, Executive
Chee Lee, Info Tech Mgr
EMP: 325
SQ FT: 25,000
SALES (est): 15.7MM Privately Held
WEB: www.clubonecasino.com
SIC: 7999 Card rooms

(P-19186)
CONCESSION MANAGEMENT SVCS INC
Also Called: C M S Hospitality
6033 W Century Blvd # 890, Los Angeles
(90045-6410)
PHONE 310 846-5830
Fax: 310 215-4210
Clarence A Daniels Jr, CEO
Vilma Ong, Admin Asst
Anna Fernandez, Administration
EMP: 150
SQ FT: 800
SALES (est): 12MM Privately Held
SIC: 7999 Concession operator

(P-19187)
CONCESSIONAIRES URBAN PARK (PA)
Also Called: CAMANCHE RECREATION COMPANY
2150 Main St Ste 5, Red Bluff
(96080-2372)
PHONE 530 529-1512
John W Koeberer, CEO
Kris Koeberer, Vice Pres
Pamela Koeberrer Pitts, Vice Pres
Dennis Houchin, CIO
Michele Silva Lane, Controller
EMP: 300
SQ FT: 2,800
SALES: 16.2MM Privately Held
WEB: www.angelisland.com
SIC: 7999 5941 5812 Beach & water sports equipment rental & services; fishing equipment; snack bar

(P-19188)
CONCESSIONAIRES URBAN PARK
Also Called: Camanche Recreation-North
2000 Camanche Rd Ofc Ofc, Ione
(95640-9420)
PHONE 209 763-5121
Fax: 209 763-5789
Terry Willard, Supervisor
EMP: 50
SALES (corp-wide): 16.2MM Privately Held
WEB: www.angelisland.com
SIC: 7999 7032 Beach & water sports equipment rental & services; recreational camps
PA: Urban Park Concessionaires
2150 Main St Ste 5
Red Bluff CA 96080
530 529-1512

(P-19189)
CONCESSIONAIRES URBAN PARK
Also Called: Camanche Northshore Store
2000 Camanche Rd Ofc Ofc, Ione
(95640-9420)
PHONE 209 763-5166
Fax: 209 763-5928
Chris Cantwell, Branch Mgr
EMP: 75
SALES (corp-wide): 16.2MM Privately Held
WEB: www.angelisland.com
SIC: 7999 5941 5812 Beach & water sports equipment rental & services; fishing equipment; snack bar
PA: Urban Park Concessionaires
2150 Main St Ste 5
Red Bluff CA 96080
530 529-1512

(P-19190)
CONCESSIONAIRES URBAN PARK
34600 Ardenwood Blvd, Fremont
(94555-3645)
PHONE 530 529-1596
Michele Silva Lane, Branch Mgr
EMP: 100
SALES (corp-wide): 18.6MM Privately Held
WEB: www.angelisland.com
SIC: 7999 5941 5812 Beach & water sports equipment rental & services; fishing equipment; snack bar
PA: Urban Park Concessionaires
2150 Main St Ste 5
Red Bluff CA 96080
530 529-1512

(P-19191)
CONCESSIONAIRES URBAN PARK
Also Called: Ranch At Little Hills, The
18013 Bollinger Canyon Rd, San Ramon
(94583-1501)
PHONE 530 529-1513
Michele Silva Lane, Manager
EMP: 100
SALES (corp-wide): 18.6MM Privately Held
WEB: www.angelisland.com
SIC: 7999 5941 5812 Beach & water sports equipment rental & services; fishing equipment; snack bar
PA: Urban Park Concessionaires
2150 Main St Ste 5
Red Bluff CA 96080
530 529-1512

(P-19192)
COUNTY OF KERN
Parks & Recreation
500 Cascade Pl, Taft (93268-2641)
P.O. Box 1406 (93268-1406)
PHONE 661 763-4246
Fax: 661 763-4240
Les Clark, Superintendent
Stephanie House, Engineer
Brad White, Foreman/Supr
EMP: 50 Privately Held
WEB: www.kccfc.org
SIC: 7999 Recreation services
PA: County Of Kern
1115 Truxtun Ave Rm 505
Bakersfield CA 93301
661 868-3690

(P-19193)
COUNTY OF RIVERSIDE
Economic Development
82503 Us Highway 111, Indio (92201-5633)
PHONE 760 863-8247
Darrell Shippy, Manager
EMP: 60 Privately Held
SIC: 7999 9611 9512 Fair; economic development agency, government; ; land, mineral & wildlife conservation;
PA: County Of Riverside
4080 Lemon St Fl 11
Riverside CA 92501
951 955-1110

(P-19194)
CRESSE MARK SCHOOL OF BASEBALL
58 Fulmar Ln, Aliso Viejo (92656-1764)
PHONE 714 892-6145
Mark E Cresse, President
Paul Coppes, Bd of Directors
Jeff Courvoisier, Exec Dir
EMP: 80
SALES: 1.4MM Privately Held
SIC: 7999 Baseball instruction school

(P-19195)
DESERT RECREATION DISTRICT (PA)
45305 Oasis St, Indio (92201-4337)
PHONE 760 347-3484
Rudy Acosta, President
Laura McGalliard, Vice Pres
Stan Ford, General Mgr
Mark Amidi, Administration
Mark Amidei, Info Tech Mgr
EMP: 55
SQ FT: 40,000
SALES (est): 4.1MM Privately Held
WEB: www.cvrpd.org
SIC: 7999 Recreation center

(P-19196)
DESERT WILLOW GOLF RESORT INC
Also Called: Desert Willow Golf Course
38995 Desert Willow Dr, Palm Desert
(92260-1674)
PHONE 760 346-0015
Fax: 760 346-7444
Richard Mogensen, General Mgr
Lisa Lozano, Accountant
Derek White, Controller
Debbi Koyama, Purchasing
Jodi Shaver, Marketing Staff
EMP: 150
SQ FT: 33,000
SALES (est): 10.3MM Privately Held
WEB: www.desertwillow.com
SIC: 7999 Golf services & professionals

(P-19197)
DESTINY ARTS CENTER
970 Grace Ave, Oakland (94608-2784)
PHONE 510 597-1619
Cristy Johnson, Exec Dir
Cherryl Williams, Executive
Eden Feil, Office Mgr
Salim Rollins, Director
Ethan Zatko, Manager
EMP: 50
SALES: 1MM Privately Held
WEB: www.destinyarts.org
SIC: 7999 Martial arts school; golf professionals

(P-19198)
DISNEY REGIONAL ENTRMT INC (HQ)
500 S Buena Vista St, Burbank
(91521-0001)
PHONE 818 560-1000
Fax: 818 295-4986
Arthur Levitt, President
Gary Marcotte, CFO
Julie Hodges, Vice Pres
Mike Morrison, Vice Pres
David Auguste, Assoc Editor
EMP: 200
SALES (est): 30.3MM Publicly Held
SIC: 7999 5812 5813 Recreation center; eating places; American restaurant; drinking places; bar (drinking places)

(P-19199)
DOWNTOWN SD VENTURES LLC
Also Called: Bassmnt
20162 Sw Birch St Ste 350, Newport Beach
(92660-0790)
PHONE 619 231-9200
Mike Kinsella, Mng Member
EMP: 60
SQ FT: 1,500

7999 - Amusement & Recreation Svcs, NEC County (P-19200)

SALES (est): 1.1MM **Privately Held**
SIC: 7999 Night club, not serving alcoholic beverages

(P-19200)
EARTHLY DELIGHTS
378 San Pedro Rd, Half Moon Bay (94019-4857)
PHONE 650 726-7227
Fax: 650 726-3155
Fred Tatman, *Owner*
EMP: 90
SALES (est): 2.3MM **Privately Held**
SIC: 7999 Concession operator

(P-19201)
EAST BAY BTNCAL ZOOLOGICAL SOC
Also Called: Oakland Zoo In Knowland Park
9777 Golf Links Rd, Oakland (94605-4925)
P.O. Box 5238 (94605-0238)
PHONE 510 632-9525
Fax: 510 635-5719
Joel J Parrott, *CEO*
Steven E Kane, *Ch of Bd*
Carl Nichols, *CFO*
William L Marchant, *Admin Sec*
Moe Perez, *Merchandising*
EMP: 85
SQ FT: 1,000
SALES: 21.4MM **Privately Held**
SIC: 7999 Zoological garden, commercial

(P-19202)
EAST BAY REGIONAL PARK DST
Also Called: East Bay Regional Park Public
17930 Lake Chabot Rd, Castro Valley (94546-1950)
PHONE 510 881-1833
Fax: 510 538-7743
Timothy Anderson, *Chief*
Heather Gilfillan, *Volunteer Dir*
EMP: 75
SALES (corp-wide): 176MM **Privately Held**
SIC: 7999 Recreation services
PA: East Bay Regional Park District
2950 Peralta Oaks Ct
Oakland CA 94605
888 327-2757

(P-19203)
EAST VALLEY TOURIST DEV AUTH
Also Called: Fantasy Springs Resort Casino
84245 Indio Springs Dr, Indio (92203-3405)
PHONE 760 342-5000
Fax: 760 775-9971
John James, *Ch of Bd*
Angela Roosevelt, *Treasurer*
Angela Roosevelt, *Corp Secy*
Mark Benitez, *Vice Ch Bd*
Brenda Soulliere, *Vice Ch Bd*
EMP: 1200
SQ FT: 94,000
SALES (est): 60.5MM **Privately Held**
WEB: www.fantasyspringsresort.com
SIC: 7999 Gambling establishment; off-track betting

(P-19204)
EASTBIZ CORPORATION (PA)
Also Called: Shipito
3501 Jack Northrop Ave, Hawthorne (90250-4444)
PHONE 310 212-7134
Jan Vanhara, *President*
Anthony Scalise, *Supervisor*
EMP: 54
SALES (est): 8.4MM **Privately Held**
SIC: 7999 5091 Sporting goods rental; sporting & recreation goods

(P-19205)
ELK VALLEY CASINO INC
2500 Howland Hill Rd, Crescent City (95531-9241)
PHONE 707 464-1020
Fax: 707 465-5188
Dale Miller, *Ch of Bd*
Robert Lopez, *Treasurer*
Shirley Hiemstra, *Executive*
John Green, *Software Engr*
Kim Krokodlos, *Human Res Dir*
EMP: 125 **EST:** 1995
SQ FT: 35,000

SALES (est): 6MM **Privately Held**
WEB: www.elkvalleycasino.com
SIC: 7999 Bingo hall

(P-19206)
ENCORE INC
Also Called: Encore Gymnastics Dnce Climbing
999 Bancroft Rd, Concord (94518-3911)
P.O. Box 30113, Walnut Creek (94598-9113)
PHONE 925 932-1033
Fax: 925 932-0610
Tamara Gerlach, *President*
Julie Southern, *Manager*
EMP: 50
SQ FT: 17,000
SALES: 1MM **Privately Held**
SIC: 7999 Gymnastic instruction, non-membership

(P-19207)
FAIRPLEX ENTERPRISES INC
1101 W Mckinley Ave, Pomona (91768-1650)
PHONE 909 623-3111
Fax: 909 629-3374
James Henwood, *President*
Adam Avalos, *General Mgr*
Michelle Demott, *General Mgr*
Marcella Garnica, *Admin Asst*
Vickee McCarty, *Admin Asst*
EMP: 53
SALES (est): 4.6MM **Privately Held**
SIC: 7999 Amusement & recreation

(P-19208)
FESTIVAL FUN PARKS LLC
Also Called: Boomers
4590 Macarthur Blvd # 400, Newport Beach (92660-2027)
PHONE 954 921-1411
Franko Cerrutti, *General Mgr*
EMP: 150
SALES (corp-wide): 145.2MM **Privately Held**
SIC: 7999 Amusement ride
PA: Festival Fun Parks, Llc
4590 Macarthur Blvd # 400
Newport Beach CA 92660
949 261-0404

(P-19209)
FESTIVAL FUN PARKS LLC
Also Called: Camelot Park Santa Maria
2250 Preisker Ln, Santa Maria (93458-9060)
PHONE 805 922-1574
Fax: 805 928-3739
Jesse Ghormley, *Manager*
Karla Azahar, *Manager*
EMP: 160
SALES (corp-wide): 145.2MM **Privately Held**
SIC: 7999 7993 7991 Miniature golf course operation; arcades; physical fitness facilities
PA: Festival Fun Parks, Llc
4590 Macarthur Blvd # 400
Newport Beach CA 92660
949 261-0404

(P-19210)
FESTIVAL FUN PARKS LLC
Also Called: Boomers
1525 W Vista Way, Vista (92083-4001)
PHONE 760 945-9474
Mark Williams, *Manager*
Robert L Eberline, *Manager*
EMP: 85
SALES (corp-wide): 145.2MM **Privately Held**
SIC: 7999 Recreation services
PA: Festival Fun Parks, Llc
4590 Macarthur Blvd # 400
Newport Beach CA 92660
949 261-0404

(P-19211)
FESTIVAL FUN PARKS LLC
Also Called: Palace Park
3405 Michelson Dr, Irvine (92612-1605)
PHONE 949 559-8336
Beth Blifford, *Manager*
EMP: 100

SALES (corp-wide): 145.2MM **Privately Held**
SIC: 7999 7996 Tourist attractions, amusement park concessions & rides; amusement parks
PA: Festival Fun Parks, Llc
4590 Macarthur Blvd # 400
Newport Beach CA 92660
949 261-0404

(P-19212)
FESTIVAL FUNPARKS LLC
Also Called: Family Fun Centers
6999 Clairemont Mesa Blvd, San Diego (92111-1001)
PHONE 858 560-4213
Fax: 858 560-5347
Patrick Beachley, *Principal*
EMP: 50
SALES (corp-wide): 145.2MM **Privately Held**
SIC: 7999 Recreation center
PA: Festival Fun Parks, Llc
4590 Macarthur Blvd # 400
Newport Beach CA 92660
949 261-0404

(P-19213)
FESTIVAL OF ARTS LAGUNA BEACH
650 Laguna Canyon Rd, Laguna Beach (92651-1899)
PHONE 949 494-1145
Fax: 949 494-9387
Fredric Sattler, *CEO*
David Perry, *Vice Pres*
Gary Fowler, *Social Dir*
Pat Kollenda, *Admin Sec*
Alan Kawaratani, *Administration*
EMP: 51
SQ FT: 6,500
SALES: 9MM **Privately Held**
SIC: 7999 Festival operation

(P-19214)
FINLEY SWIM CENTER
Also Called: Ridgway
2060 W College Ave, Santa Rosa (95401-4458)
PHONE 707 543-3760
Fax: 707 543-3768
Don Hicks, *Principal*
EMP: 50
SALES (est): 660.7K **Privately Held**
WEB: www.ridgway.com
SIC: 7999 Swimming pool, non-membership

(P-19215)
FOOD & AGRICULTURE CAL DEPT
Also Called: 32nd District-Orange Cnty Fair
88 Fair Dr, Costa Mesa (92626-6521)
PHONE 714 751-3247
Becky Bailey-Findley, *Branch Mgr*
Sybil Doremus, *General Mgr*
EMP: 70 **Privately Held**
WEB: www.cmab.net
SIC: 7999 9641 6512 Agricultural fair; regulation of agricultural marketing; ; non-residential building operators
HQ: Food & Agriculture, California Dept
1220 N St Ste 365
Sacramento CA 95814
916 654-0462

(P-19216)
GARDEN CITY INC
Also Called: Garden City Casino & Rest
1887 Matrix Blvd, San Jose (95110-2309)
PHONE 408 244-3333
Fax: 408 246-5025
Pete V Lunardi III, *CEO*
Eli Reinhard, *President*
Llene Brandon, *CFO*
Kathy Reiner, *CFO*
Frederick Wyle, *Trustee*
EMP: 569
SQ FT: 22,000
SALES (est): 11.7MM **Privately Held**
SIC: 7999 Card rooms

(P-19217)
GLAD ENTERTAINMENT INC (PA)
Also Called: Blackbeard's Family Fun Center
4055 N Chestnut Ave, Fresno (93726-4701)
PHONE 559 292-9000
Fax: 559 292-6386
Greg Florer, *President*
Don Jackley, *Corp Secy*
EMP: 70
SQ FT: 12,000
SALES (est): 2.8MM **Privately Held**
WEB: www.blackbeardsfresno.com
SIC: 7999 Miniature golf course operation; baseball batting cage; waterslide operation; amusement concession

(P-19218)
GOLF & TENNIS PRO SHOP INC
1751 E Bayshore Rd, East Palo Alto (94303-2523)
PHONE 650 600-5200
Dustin Mahoney, *Branch Mgr*
EMP: 74
SALES (corp-wide): 100.6MM **Privately Held**
SIC: 7999 Tour & guide services
PA: Golf & Tennis Pro Shop, Inc.
1801 Old Alabama Rd # 150
Roswell GA 30076
770 640-0933

(P-19219)
GREATER VALLEJO RECREATION DST
395 Amador St, Vallejo (94590-6320)
PHONE 707 648-4600
Fax: 707 648-4616
William Pendergast III, *Ch of Bd*
Shane McAffee, *Manager*
Anthony Kenaston, *Supervisor*
EMP: 150
SQ FT: 5,000
SALES (est): 7.1MM **Privately Held**
WEB: www.gvrd.org
SIC: 7999 Recreation services

(P-19220)
HAWAIIAN GARDENS CASINO (PA)
21520 Pioneer Blvd # 305, Hawaiian Gardens (90716-2602)
PHONE 562 860-5887
David Moskowitz, *CEO*
Irving Moskowitz, *President*
Jennifer Wright, *CFO*
Sergio Cuevas, *CIO*
Ron M Sarabi, *Manager*
▲ **EMP:** 160
SALES (est): 63.2MM **Privately Held**
WEB: www.hgcasino.com
SIC: 7999 Card & game services

(P-19221)
HAWAIIAN GARDENS CASINO
11871 Carson St, Hawaiian Gardens (90716-1127)
PHONE 562 860-5887
Fax: 562 860-5823
Irving Moskowitz, *Manager*
Peter Lydon, *Info Tech Dir*
Michele Moses, *Accounting Mgr*
Becky Gray, *Human Res Dir*
Nina Rojas, *Human Res Dir*
EMP: 840
SALES (corp-wide): 63.2MM **Privately Held**
SIC: 7999 Card & game services
PA: Hawaiian Gardens Casino
21520 Pioneer Blvd # 305
Hawaiian Gardens CA 90716
562 860-5887

(P-19222)
HIGH DESERT PHOENIX
42980 Staffordshire Dr, Lancaster (93534-6263)
PHONE 661 547-5630
Norma Cook, *Principal*
EMP: 50
SALES (est): 333.9K **Privately Held**
SIC: 7999 Amusement & recreation

PRODUCTS & SERVICES SECTION
7999 - Amusement & Recreation Svcs, NEC County (P-19247)

(P-19223)
HOPLAND BAND POMO INDIANS INC
Also Called: Casino
13101 Nokomis Rd, Hopland (95449-9793)
PHONE......................707 744-1395
Fax: 707 744-8754
John O'Neil, *Manager*
Madeline Bravo, *Personnel Exec*
Aaron Scarioni, *Facilities Mgr*
EMP: 200
SALES (corp-wide): 19.8MM **Privately Held**
WEB: www.hoplandtribe.com
SIC: 7999 7011 5813 5812 Gambling establishment; casino hotel; drinking places; eating places
PA: Hopland Band Of Pomo Indians Inc.
3000 Shanel Rd
Hopland CA 95449
707 472-2100

(P-19224)
HOUSE OF AIR LLC
926 Mason St, San Francisco (94129-1602)
PHONE......................415 345-9675
Paul McGeehan,
David Schaeffer,
EMP: 61 **EST:** 2009
SALES (est): 1.9MM **Privately Held**
SIC: 7999 Recreation center; trampoline operation

(P-19225)
HOWE COMMUNITY CENTER
2201 Cottage Way, Sacramento (95825-1022)
PHONE......................916 927-3802
Jeff Dubchnasky, *General Mgr*
Cathy Spindola, *Manager*
EMP: 50
SALES (est): 375.1K **Privately Held**
SIC: 7999 Recreation center

(P-19226)
ICE CENTER ENTERPRISES LLC
Also Called: Ice Center, The
10123 N Wolfe Rd Ste 1020, Cupertino (95014-2585)
P.O. Box 1433, Alameda (94501-0155)
PHONE......................510 604-8878
Fax: 650 574-4926
Michael Benesh,
Chris Hathaway,
EMP: 75
SQ FT: 28,000
SALES (est): 1.6MM **Privately Held**
WEB: www.icecenter.net
SIC: 7999 Ice skating rink operation

(P-19227)
ICE STATION VALENCIA L L C
27745 Smyth Dr, Valencia (91355-4019)
PHONE......................661 775-8686
Fax: 661 775-8681
Roger Perez, *Principal*
Russell Drinnan, *Facilities Mgr*
EMP: 60
SALES: 277.6K **Privately Held**
SIC: 7999 7299 Ice skating rink operation; party planning service

(P-19228)
IGT GLOBAL SOLUTIONS CORP
Also Called: Gtech
10415 Slusher Dr Ste 1, Santa Fe Springs (90670-7331)
PHONE......................562 946-9922
Fax: 562 946-0975
Lance Gunn, *Branch Mgr*
EMP: 70
SALES (corp-wide): 4.7B **Privately Held**
WEB: www.gtech.com
SIC: 7999 Lottery operation
HQ: Igt Global Solutions Corporation
10 Memorial Blvd
Providence RI 02903
401 392-1000

(P-19229)
JACKSON RANCHERIA CASINO & HT
Also Called: Jackson Rncheria Casino Resort
12222 New York Ranch Rd, Jackson (95642-9407)
PHONE......................209 223-1677
Fax: 209 223-8385
Margaret Dalton, *Ch of Bd*
Michael Turngren, *General Mgr*
Carol Olney, *Info Tech Mgr*
Jim Crow, *Systems Staff*
Shane Liptrap, *Engineer*
EMP: 1000
SQ FT: 24,000
SALES (est): 50.1MM **Privately Held**
WEB: www.jacksoncasino.com
SIC: 7999 5812 7011 5813 Bingo hall; game parlor; eating places; hotels & motels; drinking places

(P-19230)
KAIMANU OUTRIGGER CANOE CLUB
13424 Doolittle Dr, San Leandro (94577-4141)
PHONE......................510 895-0435
Debbie Green, *President*
EMP: 60 **EST:** 1977
SALES (est): 2.2MM **Privately Held**
SIC: 7999 Rowboat & canoe rental

(P-19231)
KATHERINE BOUSSON
1015 Palisade St, Hayward (94542-1025)
PHONE......................510 582-1166
Katherine Bousson, *Owner*
EMP: 85
SQ FT: 1,000
SALES (est): 2.2MM **Privately Held**
WEB: www.palacecardclub.com
SIC: 7999 Card rooms

(P-19232)
KEB KEB MAGIC CLOWN
637 Germaine Dr, Galt (95632-2161)
PHONE......................916 369-6054
Kevin Keller, *Owner*
EMP: 72
SALES: 10MM **Privately Held**
SIC: 7999 Tennis services & professionals

(P-19233)
KERN RIVER TOURS INC
2712 Mayfair Rd, Lake Isabella (93240-9643)
P.O. Box 3444 (93240-3444)
PHONE......................760 379-4616
Fax: 760 379-2103
Kenneth Busheing, *President*
Joseph M Kent, *Corp Secy*
EMP: 70
SQ FT: 2,250
SALES: 500K **Privately Held**
WEB: www.kernrivertours.com
SIC: 7999 Tourist guide

(P-19234)
KINGS CASINO MANAGEMENT CORP
6510 Antelope Rd, Citrus Heights (95621-1077)
PHONE......................916 560-4405
Ryan Stone, *CEO*
Stacy Bierer, *Controller*
EMP: 350 **EST:** 2013
SALES (est): 8.4MM **Privately Held**
SIC: 7999 Card & game services

(P-19235)
LEISURE PLANET
Also Called: Jungle Fun & Adventure
1975 Diamond Blvd, Concord (94520-5792)
PHONE......................925 687-4386
Olivier Sermet, *President*
EMP: 130
SQ FT: 15,000
SALES (est): 2.9MM **Privately Held**
WEB: www.junglefunadventure.com
SIC: 7999 5947 Tourist attractions, amusement park concessions & rides; gifts & novelties

(P-19236)
LEISURE SPORTS INC
Also Called: Club Sport Valley Vista
7090 Johnson Dr, Pleasanton (94588-3328)
PHONE......................925 934-4050
Fax: 925 934-9093
Brian Amador, *Branch Mgr*
EMP: 60
SALES (corp-wide): 213MM **Privately Held**
WEB: www.leisuresportsinc.com
SIC: 7999 7997 7991 Swimming instruction; tennis club, membership; health club
PA: Leisure Sports, Inc.
4670 Willow Rd Ste 100
Pleasanton CA 94588
925 600-1966

(P-19237)
LIVERMORE AREA RCRATION PK DST
71 Trevarno Rd, Livermore (94551-4931)
PHONE......................925 373-5700
Fax: 925 373-5177
Doug Bell, *Branch Mgr*
EMP: 131
SALES (corp-wide): 13.2MM **Privately Held**
SIC: 7999 8211 Recreation services; public elementary & secondary schools
PA: Livermore Area Recreation & Park District
4444 East Ave
Livermore CA 94550
925 373-5700

(P-19238)
LIVERMORE AREA RCRATION PK DST (PA)
4444 East Ave, Livermore (94550-5053)
PHONE......................925 373-5700
Tim Barry, *General Mgr*
Gretchen Sommers, *Admin Asst*
Bob Coomber, *Director*
Maryalice Faltings, *Director*
David Furst, *Director*
EMP: 253 **EST:** 1947
SQ FT: 71,000
SALES (est): 13.2MM **Privately Held**
WEB: www.larpd.dst.ca.us
SIC: 7999 Recreation services

(P-19239)
LOGITECH ICE AT SAN JOSE
Also Called: Shark's Ice
1500 S 10th St, San Jose (95112-6410)
PHONE......................408 279-6000
Jon Gustafson, *Vice Pres*
EMP: 50
SQ FT: 150,000
SALES (est): 2.7MM **Privately Held**
WEB: www.logitechice.com
SIC: 7999 5461 Ice skating rink operation; bakeries

(P-19240)
LOS ANGELES COUNTY FAIR ASSN (PA)
Also Called: Fairplex Rv Park
1101 W Mckinley Ave, Pomona (91768-1639)
PHONE......................909 623-3111
Thelma M De Santa, *Bd of Directors*
Micheal Seder, *Vice Pres*
Iris Kong, *Controller*
Cheryl Rudolph, *Opers Staff*
Mike Driebe,
EMP: 100
SALES (est): 25.4MM **Privately Held**
SIC: 7999 8412 Fair; museums & art galleries

(P-19241)
LUCKY CHANCES INC
Also Called: Lucky Chances Casino
1700 Hillside Blvd, Colma (94014-2801)
PHONE......................650 758-2237
Fax: 650 758-6475
Rommel R Medina, *CEO*
Ruell Medina, *President*
Martin Cruz, *Info Tech Dir*
Larry Oakley, *Info Tech Mgr*
Lori Derenzo, *Human Res Mgr*
EMP: 650
SALES (est): 28.6MM **Privately Held**
SIC: 7999 Card rooms

(P-19242)
LUCKY DERBY CASINO
Also Called: Point-Walker
7433 Greenback Ln Ste C, Citrus Heights (95610-5696)
PHONE......................916 727-2727
Fax: 916 726-6473
Kermit D Schayltz, *Managing Prtnr*
Leo Chu, *Owner*
EMP: 135
SQ FT: 6,500
SALES (est): 4.4MM **Privately Held**
WEB: www.lucky-derby.com
SIC: 7999 7011 Card & game services; casino hotel

(P-19243)
LYTTON RANCHERIA
Also Called: Casino San Pablo
13255 San Pablo Ave, San Pablo (94806-3907)
PHONE......................510 215-7888
Fax: 510 215-5131
Michael Gorczynski, *General Mgr*
Natalie Ferrel, *Executive*
Cathi Hamel, *Principal*
Carole Thomas, *Financial Exec*
Christopher Mavroudis, *Human Res Mgr*
EMP: 547
SALES (est): 20.2MM **Privately Held**
WEB: www.casinosanpablo.com
SIC: 7999 Gambling & lottery services

(P-19244)
MENLO CHARITY HORSE SHOW INC
2470 El Camino Real, Palo Alto (94306-1714)
PHONE......................650 858-0202
Pam Brandon, *Exec Dir*
EMP: 141
SALES (est): 512.5K **Privately Held**
SIC: 7999 Horse shows

(P-19245)
MESQUITE GOLF & COUNTRY CLUB
2700 E Mesquite Ave Ofc, Palm Springs (92264-5009)
PHONE......................760 323-9377
Lee Yoong, *Owner*
Perky Newcomb, *Director*
Kenny Kim, *Manager*
EMP: 50
SALES (est): 922K **Privately Held**
SIC: 7999 5812 Golf driving range; eating places

(P-19246)
MINDFULL BODY
2876 California St, San Francisco (94115-2545)
PHONE......................415 931-2639
Fax: 415 931-8023
Roy N Bergmann, *Owner*
Hillary Bergmann, *Financial Exec*
EMP: 80
SALES (est): 1.6MM **Privately Held**
SIC: 7999 7299 Yoga instruction; massage parlor

(P-19247)
MOORETOWN RANCHERIA (PA)
Also Called: Feather Falls Casino
1 Alverda Dr, Oroville (95966-9379)
PHONE......................530 533-3625
Fax: 530 533-3680
Gary Archuleta, *Ch of Bd*
Kayla Lobo, *Treasurer*
Melvin Jackson, *Vice Pres*
Julie McIntosh, *Principal*
Laura Winner, *Executive Asst*
EMP: 50
SALES (est): 21.4MM **Privately Held**
WEB: www.drumvision.com
SIC: 7999 5993 Gambling establishment; cigar store

7999 - Amusement & Recreation Svcs, NEC County (P-19248)

(P-19248)
MOUNT SAN JCNTO WINTER PK CORP
Also Called: Palm Springs Aerial Tramway
1 Tramway Rd, Palm Springs (92262-1827)
PHONE.................760 325-1449
Fax: 760 325-6682
Rob Parkins, *CEO*
Tera Meinke, *CFO*
Marjorie Dela Cruz, *Vice Pres*
Walt Madison, *VP Opers*
Scott Barrick, *Opers Spvr*
▲ **EMP:** 64 **EST:** 1945
SQ FT: 50,000
SALES (est): 6.3MM **Privately Held**
WEB: www.pstramway.com
SIC: 7999 Aerial tramway or ski lift, amusement or scenic

(P-19249)
MUSEUM OF CHILDRENS ART
Also Called: Mocha
1625 Clay St Ste 100, Oakland (94612-1564)
PHONE.................510 465-8770
Fax: 510 465-0772
Karen Ransom, *Director*
Cisco Devries, *Bd of Directors*
Haldun Morgan, *Marketing Staff*
Katie Sammon, *Program Dir*
Rae Holzman, *Director*
EMP: 50
SQ FT: 4,800
SALES: 844.6K **Privately Held**
WEB: www.mocha.org
SIC: 7999 8412 Art gallery, commercial; instruction schools, camps & services; museum

(P-19250)
NAPA VALLEY WINE TRAIN INC (HQ)
Also Called: NAPA Valley Railroad Co
1275 Mckinstry St, NAPA (94559-1925)
PHONE.................707 253-2160
Fax: 707 253-9264
Anthony J Giaccio, *CEO*
Vincent M De Deminico Jr, *Vice Pres*
Kelly Macdonald, *Executive*
Kayla Giaccio, *Social Dir*
Jaspreet Kaur, *Persnl Mgr*
▲ **EMP:** 125
SQ FT: 20,000
SALES (est): 11.5MM **Privately Held**
WEB: www.winetrain.com
SIC: 7999 5812 4011 4119 Scenic railroads for amusement; eating places; railroads, line-haul operating; local passenger transportation

(P-19251)
NORMANDIE CLUB LP
Also Called: Normandie Casino & Showroom
1045 W Rosecrans Ave, Gardena (90247-2601)
PHONE.................310 352-3486
Fax: 310 515-8340
Lawrence F Miller, *Managing Prtnr*
Russel Miller Jr, *General Ptnr*
Greg Miller, *Partner*
Steve Miller, *Partner*
Marco Casillas, *Purch Dir*
▲ **EMP:** 600
SQ FT: 44,000
SALES (est): 28.6MM **Privately Held**
WEB: www.normandiecasino.com
SIC: 7999 5812 Card & game services; eating places

(P-19252)
O A OUTFITTING INC
Also Called: Kern River Outfitters
6602 Wofford Heights Blvd, Bayside (95524)
P.O. Box 91 (95524-0091)
PHONE.................707 498-2917
James Ritter, *President*
Robert Volpert, *CEO*
EMP: 55
SALES: 1MM **Privately Held**
SIC: 7999 Recreation services

(P-19253)
O C SAILING CLUB INC
Also Called: Olympic Circle Sailing Club
1 Spinnaker Way, Berkeley (94710-1612)
PHONE.................510 843-4200
Fax: 510 843-2155
Anthony P Sandberg, *President*
Richard Jepsen, *CEO*
Alicia Witham, *General Mgr*
Michael Spranger, *Director*
EMP: 65
SQ FT: 5,000
SALES (est): 3.2MM **Privately Held**
WEB: www.ocscsailing.com
SIC: 7999 5651 Sailing instruction; pleasure boat rental; family clothing stores

(P-19254)
OCEANS ELEVEN CASINO
121 Brooks St, Oceanside (92054-3424)
PHONE.................760 439-6988
Fax: 760 439-5099
Mark Kelegian, *Managing Prtnr*
Roy Hoernke, *Administration*
Phr R Holmes, *Human Resources*
Virgina Holmes, *Human Resources*
Carlos Lopez, *Facilities Dir*
EMP: 367 **EST:** 1996
SQ FT: 30,000
SALES (est): 15.3MM **Privately Held**
WEB: www.oceans11.com
SIC: 7999 Gambling establishment

(P-19255)
OCEANSIDE LIFEGUARDS
300 N Coast Hwy, Oceanside (92054-2824)
PHONE.................760 435-4500
Fax: 760 433-6567
Ray Duncan, *Manager*
EMP: 73
SALES (est): 956.6K **Privately Held**
WEB: www.ci.oceanside.ca.us
SIC: 7999 Lifeguard service

(P-19256)
PALACE ENTERTAINMENT INC (DH)
4590 Macarthur Blvd # 400, Newport Beach (92660-2027)
PHONE.................949 261-0404
Alexander Weber Jr, *CEO*
John Cora, *President*
Albert Cabuco, *Vice Pres*
Bill Lentz, *Vice Pres*
A Scherpenzeel, *Vice Pres*
EMP: 50
SQ FT: 8,000
SALES (est): 124.3MM
SALES (corp-wide): 79.8MM **Privately Held**
SIC: 7999 7993 Miniature golf course operation; arcades
HQ: Parque De Atracciones Madrid Sa
Calle Parque Atracciones (Casa De Campo), S/N
Madrid 28011
902 345-001

(P-19257)
PARC MANAGEMENT LLC
Also Called: Waterworld USA
1950 Waterworld Pkwy, Concord (94520-2602)
PHONE.................925 609-1364
Steve Mayer, *Manager*
EMP: 1957
SALES (corp-wide): 143.7MM **Privately Held**
WEB: www.parcmanagement.com
SIC: 7999 Picnic ground operation
PA: Parc Management, Llc
7892 Baymeadows Way
Jacksonville FL 32256
904 732-7272

(P-19258)
PARKS AND RECREATION CAL DEPT
Also Called: Camanche Lake
2000 Camanche Rd Ofc, Ione (95640-9420)
PHONE.................209 763-5121
Mary Mendence, *Manager*
EMP: 50 **Privately Held**

WEB: www.aprpd.org
SIC: 7999 Recreation center; ping pong parlor
HQ: California Department Of Parks And Recreation
1416 9th St Ste 1041
Sacramento CA 95814
800 777-0369

(P-19259)
PAUL MAURER COMPANY
Also Called: Paul Maurer Shows
16081 Warren Ln, Huntington Beach (92649-2433)
PHONE.................714 231-8241
Paul Maurer, *Owner*
EMP: 60
SALES (est): 1.1MM **Privately Held**
SIC: 7999 Amusement ride

(P-19260)
PIT RIVER TRIBAL COUNCIL
Also Called: Pit River Casino
20265 Tamarack Ave, Burney (96013-4064)
PHONE.................530 335-2334
Fax: 530 335-2362
Nathan Schoofield, *Manager*
Helen Myers, *Controller*
Mike Avelar, *Manager*
EMP: 54
SALES (corp-wide): 4.5MM **Privately Held**
WEB: www.pitrivercasino.com
SIC: 7999 Card & game services; bingo hall
PA: Pit River Tribal Council
37960 Park Ave
Burney CA

(P-19261)
PLAYWORKS EDUCATION ENERGIZED (PA)
380 Washington St, Oakland (94607-3800)
PHONE.................510 893-4180
Jill Vialet, *President*
Elizabeth Cushing, *President*
David Carroll, *CFO*
Phillis Carte, *CFO*
Amanda Casey, *CFO*
EMP: 50
SALES: 23MM **Privately Held**
WEB: www.sports4kids.org
SIC: 7999 Recreation services

(P-19262)
PRINCESS CRUISES AND TOURS INC (HQ)
24305 Town Center Dr # 200, Valencia (91355-4999)
PHONE.................206 336-6000
Will Wenholz, *Principal*
Mike Sutton, *Director*
EMP: 5045
SALES (est): 4MM
SALES (corp-wide): 15.7B **Publicly Held**
SIC: 7999 Tour & guide services
PA: Carnival Corporation
3655 Nw 87th Ave
Doral FL 33178
305 599-2600

(P-19263)
PYRAMID ENTERPRISES INC (PA)
Also Called: Lake Piru Marina
28368 Constellation Rd # 380, Valencia (91355-5016)
PHONE.................661 702-1420
Chester Roberts, *President*
Traci Roberts, *Admin Sec*
EMP: 60
SQ FT: 1,300
SALES (est): 3.9MM **Privately Held**
WEB: www.lake-piru.org
SIC: 7999 4493 Beach & water sports equipment rental & services; marinas

(P-19264)
PYRO SPECTACULARS INC
1438 141st Ave, San Leandro (94578-2749)
P.O. Box 6775, Oakland (94603-0775)
PHONE.................510 632-4516

James Souza, *President*
EMP: 50
SALES (est): 317.4K **Privately Held**
SIC: 7999 Fireworks display service

(P-19265)
QUECHAN INDIAN TRIBE
Also Called: Quechan Gaming Commission
350 Picacho Rd, Winterhaven (92283-9769)
P.O. Box 2737, Yuma AZ (85366-2573)
PHONE.................760 572-2413
Mike Jackson, *President*
Charles Montague, *General Mgr*
Juan Gabriel Leyva, *Comp Spec*
EMP: 300 **Privately Held**
SIC: 7999 5812 Gambling establishment; eating places
PA: Quechan Indian Tribe
350 Picacho Rd
Winterhaven CA 92283
760 572-0213

(P-19266)
RAINBOW CAMP INC
26619 Marigold Ct, Calabasas (91302-2945)
PHONE.................310 456-3066
Valerie Ann Woodard, *Director*
EMP: 50
SALES (est): 162K **Privately Held**
WEB: www.rainbowcamp.com
SIC: 7999 Day camp

(P-19267)
RANCHO JURUPA PARK
4800 Crestmore Rd, Riverside (92509-6839)
PHONE.................951 684-7032
Paul Franzen, *President*
John Burns, *Manager*
EMP: 50
SALES (est): 584.9K **Privately Held**
SIC: 7999 Amusement & recreation

(P-19268)
RAZORGATOR INC (PA)
Also Called: Tickco
4094 Glencoe Ave Ste A, Marina Del Rey (90292-5608)
PHONE.................310 481-3400
Nima Moayedi, *CEO*
Mike Harrington, *COO*
Mark Reese, *COO*
Brian Stich, *CFO*
Hamid Saify, *Vice Pres*
EMP: 200 **EST:** 1977
SQ FT: 7,500
SALES (est): 12.7MM **Privately Held**
WEB: www.razorgator.com
SIC: 7999 Ticket sales office for sporting events, contract

(P-19269)
ROCKIN JUMP INC
5875 Arnold Rd Ste 100, Dublin (94568-7310)
PHONE.................925 401-7200
EMP: 57
SALES (corp-wide): 3.6MM **Privately Held**
SIC: 7999 Trampoline operation
PA: Rockin' Jump Inc.
5502 Sunol Blvd
Pleasanton CA 94566
925 828-7676

(P-19270)
ROLLING HILLS CASINO
2655 Everett Freeman Way, Corning (96021-9000)
PHONE.................530 528-3500
Fax: 530 824-2473
Bruce Thomas, *CEO*
Jeff Realander, *COO*
Terry Contreras, *CFO*
Ron Hafey, *Executive*
Joshua Morris, *Technology*
EMP: 489
SQ FT: 70,000
SALES (est): 28MM
SALES (corp-wide): 32.3MM **Privately Held**
WEB: www.paskenta.org
SIC: 7999 Gambling machines, operation; gambling establishment

PA: Paskenta Band Of Nomlaki Indians
2655 Everett Freeman Way
Corning CA 96021
530 528-3500

(P-19271)
ROLLING HLLS ESTTES TENNIS CLB
Also Called: Rolling Hills Estates City of
25851 Hawthorne Blvd, Rllng HLS Est (90275)
PHONE..................310 541-4585
Fax: 310 377-1577
Andy Clark, *Director*
EMP: 50
SALES (est): 424.6K **Privately Held**
WEB: www.ci.rolling-hills-estates.ca.us
SIC: 7999 Tennis courts, outdoor/indoor; non-membership

(P-19272)
ROSEVILLE SPORTWORLD INC
Also Called: Skatetown
1009 Orlando Ave, Roseville (95661-5230)
PHONE..................916 783-8550
Scott Slavensky, *President*
Althea Slavensky, *Shareholder*
Frank Slavensky, *Shareholder*
Kerry Slavensky, *Corp Secy*
Donna Smith, *Director*
EMP: 83
SQ FT: 61,679
SALES (est): 3.1MM **Privately Held**
SIC: 7999 5941 Ice skating rink operation; skating equipment

(P-19273)
SAC RIVER OUTFITTERS
1403 Edgewood Dr, Redding (96003-9227)
PHONE..................530 275-3500
Chris King, *Owner*
EMP: 70
SALES (est): 440.3K **Privately Held**
WEB: www.sacriveroutfitters.com
SIC: 7999 Outfitters, recreation

(P-19274)
SAN FRANCISCO ZOOLOGICAL SOC
1 Zoo Rd, San Francisco (94132-1098)
PHONE..................415 753-7080
Tanya Peterson, *President*
Wayne Reading, *CFO*
Robert Pedrero, *Chairman*
Jean Brennan, *Human Res Mgr*
Gwendolyn Tornatore, *Pub Rel Mgr*
EMP: 160
SQ FT: 2,000
SALES: 21.6MM **Privately Held**
WEB: www.sfzoo.org
SIC: 7999 7389 Concession operator; amusement ride; fund raising organizations

(P-19275)
SAN MANUEL INDIAN BINGO CASINO (PA)
Also Called: San Manuel Indian Bingo Casino
777 San Manuel Blvd, Highland (92346-6713)
P.O. Box 777, Patton (92369-0777)
PHONE..................909 864-5050
Fax: 909 862-0682
James Ramos, *Chairman*
Jody M Fox, *President*
Rebecca Spalding, *CFO*
Andy Marquez, *Vice Pres*
Samira Sayegh, *Vice Pres*
▲ EMP: 2950
SALES (est): 183.2MM **Privately Held**
SIC: 7999 Bingo hall; card & game services

(P-19276)
SAN MATEO CNTY EXPO FAIR ASSN
Also Called: SAN MATEO COUNTY EXPO CENTER
2495 S Delaware St, San Mateo (94403-1902)
PHONE..................650 574-3247
Fax: 650 574-3985
Chris Carpenter, *General Mgr*
Van Beane, *Treasurer*
Kari Foppiano, *Treasurer*
Charlene Andrade, *Office Mgr*
Charlene King, *Manager*
▲ EMP: 50
SQ FT: 225,000
SALES: 8.9MM **Privately Held**
WEB: www.smexpo.com
SIC: 7999 6512 Exhibition operation; exposition operation; fair; nonresidential building operators

(P-19277)
SANTA CLARA COUNTY OF
Parks & Recreation Dept
298 Garden Hill Dr, Los Gatos (95032-7669)
PHONE..................408 355-2200
Lisa Killough, *Branch Mgr*
EMP: 140 **Privately Held**
WEB: www.countyairports.org
SIC: 7999 9512 Recreation services; land, mineral & wildlife conservation;
PA: County Of Santa Clara
3180 Newberry Dr Ste 150
San Jose CA 95118
408 299-5105

(P-19278)
SANTA CLARITA CITY OF
Also Called: Cowboy Poetry
23920 Valencia Blvd # 300, Santa Clarita (91355-2175)
PHONE..................661 284-1423
Ken Pulskamp, *Manager*
Carl Newton,
EMP: 350 **Privately Held**
WEB: www.golfsantaclarita.com
SIC: 7999 Festival operation
PA: Santa Clarita, City Of
23920 Valencia Blvd # 300
Santa Clarita CA 91355
661 259-2489

(P-19279)
SCANDIA SPORTS INC
Also Called: Scandia Family Fun Center
5070 Hillsdale Blvd, Sacramento (95842-3520)
PHONE..................916 331-5757
Fax: 916 331-2515
Paul Wood, *Manager*
EMP: 50
SALES (corp-wide): 2.3MM **Privately Held**
SIC: 7999 Miniature golf course operation; recreation center; trampoline operation
PA: Scandia Sports, Inc
1155 S Wanamaker Ave
Ontario CA 91761
909 390-3092

(P-19280)
SEVEN RESORTS INC (PA)
9771 Irvine Center Dr # 100, Irvine (92618-4344)
PHONE..................949 588-7100
Fax: 949 588-7400
David A Ohanesian, *President*
Anderson Msjacqueline, *CFO*
Jacqueline S Anderson, *Treasurer*
Lynda L Ohanesian-Druan, *Admin Sec*
Rosemary Atalla, *Human Res Mgr*
EMP: 138
SALES (est): 14.7MM **Privately Held**
WEB: www.sevencrown.com
SIC: 7999 Houseboat rentals

(P-19281)
SHASTA LAKE RESORTS LP
Also Called: Jones Valley Resorts
22300 Jones Vly Marina Dr, Redding (96003-7829)
PHONE..................209 785-3300
Fax: 530 275-3523
David M Smith, *Partner*
Steve Woodward, *Partner*
Water Resorts, *Managing Prtnr*
Rich Howe, *Manager*
EMP: 55
SQ FT: 3,500
SALES (est): 3.1MM **Privately Held**
SIC: 7999 4493 5411 Pleasure boat rental; marinas; grocery stores, independent

(P-19282)
SHINGLE SPRNG TRBAL GMING AUTH
Also Called: Red Hawk Casino
1 Red Hawk Pkwy, Placerville (95667-8639)
PHONE..................530 677-7000
Nicholas Fonseca, *Ch of Bd*
Matthew Morgan, *President*
Tyrone Huff, *CFO*
Randall Boynton, *Vice Pres*
Pat Farrington, *Vice Pres*
EMP: 1200
SQ FT: 278,000
SALES (est): 64MM **Privately Held**
WEB: www.shinglespringsrancheria.com
SIC: 7999 Gambling establishment
PA: Shingle Springs Rancheria
5168 Honpie Rd
Placerville CA 95667
530 672-8059

(P-19283)
SKATE ENTERPRISES INC
12356 Central Ave, Chino (91710-2601)
PHONE..................562 924-0911
Jerry Curran, *President*
Robert E Osborne, *Corp Secy*
David O Clark, *Vice Pres*
Robert E Maurer, *Vice Pres*
EMP: 54
SQ FT: 1,200
SALES (est): 2MM **Privately Held**
WEB: www.skateenterprises.com
SIC: 7999 Roller skating rink operation

(P-19284)
SKYGROUP INVESTMENTS LLC
Also Called: Ifly San Diego
2385 Camino Del Rio N, San Diego (92108-1671)
PHONE..................619 432-4359
Alna Metni,
Brendan Nugent, *Director*
EMP: 79
SALES (est): 194.4K **Privately Held**
SIC: 7999 Tourist attractions, amusement park concessions & rides

(P-19285)
SNOW SUMMIT SKI CORPORATION
Also Called: Snow Summit Mountain Resort
43101 Goldmine Dr, Big Bear City (92314)
P.O. Box 77, Big Bear Lake (92315-0077)
PHONE..................909 585-2517
Richard C Kun, *Branch Mgr*
Mark Burnett, *Supervisor*
EMP: 780
SALES (corp-wide): 59MM **Privately Held**
WEB: www.bearmtn.com
SIC: 7999 7011 5941 7992 Aerial tramway or ski lift, amusement or scenic; ski rental concession; ski lodge; skiing equipment; public golf courses
PA: Snow Summit Ski Corporation
880 Summit Blvd
Big Bear Lake CA 92315
909 866-5766

(P-19286)
SPEARMAN CLUBS INC (PA)
Also Called: Laguna Niguel Racquet Club
23500 Clubhouse Dr, Laguna Niguel (92677-2902)
PHONE..................949 496-2070
Fax: 949 240-9203
Cecil E Spearman Jr, *Ch of Bd*
Mark Spearman, *President*
Steven Spearman, *CFO*
Jean Spearman, *Vice Ch Bd*
Scott Spearman, *Vice Pres*
EMP: 50 EST: 1979
SQ FT: 20,000
SALES (est): 5.9MM **Privately Held**
WEB: www.spearmanclubs.com
SIC: 7999 7991 Tennis club, non-membership; physical fitness clubs with training equipment

(P-19287)
SPLASH SWIM SCHOOL INC
2411 Old Crow Canyon Rd, San Ramon (94583-1240)
PHONE..................925 838-7946
Elisabeth Claytor, *President*
Liz Claytor, *Exec Dir*
D Christian Claytor, *Admin Sec*
Debbie Doudikas, *Manager*
EMP: 50
SQ FT: 7,310
SALES (est): 2.3MM **Privately Held**
SIC: 7999 Swimming instruction

(P-19288)
STARLINE TOURS HOLLYWOOD INC
6801 Hollywood Blvd # 221, Los Angeles (90028-6142)
PHONE..................323 463-3333
Tony Cordon, *Manager*
EMP: 60 **Privately Held**
WEB: www.starlinetours.com
SIC: 7999 Tour & guide services
PA: Starline Tours Of Hollywood, Inc.
2130 S Tubeway Ave
Commerce CA 90040

(P-19289)
STARLINE TOURS HOLLYWOOD INC (PA)
2130 S Tubeway Ave, Commerce (90040-1614)
PHONE..................323 262-1114
Fax: 323 463-9601
Kamrouz Farhadi, *CEO*
Noonoosh Farhadi, *Vice Pres*
▲ EMP: 70
SALES (est): 6.9MM **Privately Held**
WEB: www.starlinetours.com
SIC: 7999 Tour & guide services

(P-19290)
SUGAR BOWL CORPORATION
629 Sugar Bowl Rd, Norden (95724)
P.O. Box 5 (95724-0005)
PHONE..................530 426-9000
Fax: 530 426-3723
Nancy Bechtle, *Ch of Bd*
Warren Haellman, *Shareholder*
Robert H Kautz, *President*
Bonny Bavetta, *CFO*
Dan Kingsley, *Treasurer*
▲ EMP: 100
SQ FT: 30,000
SALES (est): 10.8MM **Privately Held**
SIC: 7999 Ski rental concession

(P-19291)
SYCUAN CASINO
Also Called: Sycuan Resort and Casino
5459 Casino Way, El Cajon (92019)
PHONE..................619 445-6002
Fax: 619 445-8305
Sheila Howe, *General Mgr*
Lashunna Davidson, *Treasurer*
Javier Murillo, *Senior VP*
Mitch Bradley, *Exec Dir*
Juan Baca, *Security Dir*
EMP: 2000
SQ FT: 236,000
SALES (est): 79.2MM **Privately Held**
SIC: 7999 7997 Gambling establishment; membership sports & recreation clubs

(P-19292)
TABLE MOUNTAIN CASINO
8184 Table Mountain Rd, Friant (93626)
P.O. Box 445 (93626-0445)
PHONE..................559 822-2485
Frances Dandy, *Senior VP*
Ted Thay, *COO*
Ricardo Nunez, *Executive*
Paul Barlow, *Info Tech Dir*
Phillip C Dana, *Info Tech Mgr*
▲ EMP: 1000
SQ FT: 30,000
SALES (est): 49.9MM **Privately Held**
WEB: www.tmcasino.com
SIC: 7999 Gambling establishment

7999 - Amusement & Recreation Svcs, NEC County (P-19293)

(P-19293)
TICKETWEB LLC
685 Market St Ste 200, San Francisco (94105-4203)
PHONE..............................415 901-0210
Dan Teree, *COO*
Valerie Leclair, *General Mgr*
Todd Kasten, *Director*
EMP: 50
SALES (est): 1.4MM
SALES (corp-wide): 7.2B **Publicly Held**
WEB: www.ticketweb.com
SIC: 7999 Ticket sales office for sporting events, contract
HQ: Ticketmaster L.L.C.
7060 Hollywood Blvd Fl 2
Los Angeles CA 90028
323 441-7336

(P-19294)
TIERRA DEL SOL FOUNDATION
Also Called: Tierra Del Soul
250 W 1st St Ste 120, Claremont (91711-4741)
PHONE..............................909 626-8301
Fax: 909 625-3435
Rebecca Hamm, *Branch Mgr*
EMP: 69
SALES (corp-wide): 11.6MM **Privately Held**
SIC: 7999 5999 Art gallery, commercial; art dealers
PA: Tierra Del Sol Foundation
9919 Sunland Blvd
Sunland CA 91040
818 352-1419

(P-19295)
TOP SEED TENNIS ACADEMY INC
23400 Park Sorrento, Calabasas (91302-1743)
PHONE..............................818 222-2782
Steve McAvoy, *President*
EMP: 65 **EST:** 1996
SALES (est): 1.1MM **Privately Held**
WEB: www.topseed.us
SIC: 7999 Tennis services & professionals

(P-19296)
TOWN OF DANVILLE
420 Front St, Danville (94526-3404)
PHONE..............................925 314-3400
Craig Bowen, *Branch Mgr*
EMP: 185 **Privately Held**
SIC: 7999 Recreation center
PA: Town Of Danville
510 La Gonda Way
Danville CA 94526
925 314-3311

(P-19297)
TRUCKEE DNNER RCREATION PK DST
8924 Donner Pass Rd, Truckee (96161-2996)
PHONE..............................530 582-7720
Fax: 530 582-7724
Steve Randall, *General Mgr*
Peter Werbel, *Chairman*
Kevin Murphy, *Admin Sec*
Debra Alumbaugh, *Controller*
Brandon Perry, *Human Res Mgr*
EMP: 100 **EST:** 1962
SQ FT: 10,000
SALES (est): 4.4MM **Privately Held**
WEB: www.tdrpd.com
SIC: 7999 Recreation services

(P-19298)
TUMBLEWEED EDUCATIONAL ENTPS
Also Called: Tumbleweed Day Camp
1024 Hanley Ave, Los Angeles (90049-1306)
P.O. Box 49291 (90049-0291)
PHONE..............................310 444-3232
Fax: 310 476-7788
Erin Benfield, *President*
John Beitner, *Exec Dir*
Madisen L Siegel, *Exec Dir*
Patrick C Deasy, *Business Mgr*
Mike Sagner, *Maintenance Dir*
EMP: 160
SQ FT: 6,500

SALES: 9.3MM **Privately Held**
SIC: 7999 4151 Day camp; school buses

(P-19299)
UCD RECREATION HALL
1 Shields Ave, Davis (95616-5200)
PHONE..............................530 752-6071
Jim Rodens, *Director*
George Bruening, *Manager*
EMP: 100
SALES (est): 3.9MM **Privately Held**
WEB: www.primal.ucdavis.edu
SIC: 7999 7997 Recreation center; membership sports & recreation clubs

(P-19300)
UCLA MARINA CENTER
111 Deneve Dr, Los Angeles (90095-0001)
PHONE..............................310 825-3671
Steve Tevenajera, *Branch Mgr*
Edgar Torres, *Facilities Mgr*
EMP: 80
SALES (corp-wide): 2.4MM **Privately Held**
SIC: 7999 Recreation services
PA: Marina Ucla Center
14001 Fiji Way
Marina Del Rey CA 90292
310 823-0048

(P-19301)
UNIVERSITY OF PACIFIC
Also Called: Athletic Department
1040 E Stadium Dr, Stockton (95204)
PHONE..............................209 946-2030
Donald Derosa, *President*
EMP: 600
SALES (corp-wide): 444.8MM **Privately Held**
WEB: www.uop.edu
SIC: 7999 8221 Ticket sales office for sporting events, contract; university
PA: University Of The Pacific
3601 Pacific Ave
Stockton CA 95211
209 946-2401

(P-19302)
VALLEY WIDE RECREATION PK DST (PA)
901 W Esplanade Ave, San Jacinto (92582-4501)
P.O. Box 907 (92581-0907)
PHONE..............................951 654-1505
Nick Schouton, *President*
Kenneth Hyatt, *President*
Larry Minor, *Vice Pres*
Sam Goepp, *General Mgr*
Jeff Leatherman, *General Mgr*
EMP: 89
SQ FT: 30,000
SALES: 161.4K **Privately Held**
WEB: www.vwrpd.org/index.cfm
SIC: 7999 7996 Recreation services; amusement parks

(P-19303)
VILLAGE CLUB
429 Broadway, Chula Vista (91910-4320)
PHONE..............................619 425-3333
Fax: 619 476-8368
Harvey Souza, *Owner*
Bridget Fajardo, *Manager*
EMP: 50
SQ FT: 1,200
SALES (est): 1.7MM **Privately Held**
SIC: 7999 Card rooms

(P-19304)
VOLUME SERVICES INC
111 W Harbor Dr, San Diego (92101-7822)
PHONE..............................619 525-5800
EMP: 97
SALES (corp-wide): 1.2B **Privately Held**
WEB: www.volumeservicesamerica.com
SIC: 7999 Concession operator
HQ: Volume Services, Inc.
2187 Atlantic St Ste 6
Stamford CT 06902
203 975-5900

(P-19305)
VOLUME SERVICES INC
Also Called: Centerplate
24 Willie Mays Plz, San Francisco (94107-2134)
PHONE..............................415 972-1500
Angie Perrilliat, *General Mgr*
EMP: 97
SALES (corp-wide): 1.2B **Privately Held**
WEB: www.volumeservicesamerica.com
SIC: 7999 Concession operator
HQ: Volume Services, Inc.
2187 Atlantic St Ste 6
Stamford CT 06902
203 975-5900

(P-19306)
VOLUME SERVICES INC
5333 Zoo Dr, Los Angeles (90027-1451)
PHONE..............................323 644-6038
Greg Edgar, *Manager*
EMP: 97
SALES (corp-wide): 1.2B **Privately Held**
WEB: www.volumeservicesamerica.com
SIC: 7999 Concession operator
HQ: Volume Services, Inc.
2187 Atlantic St Ste 6
Stamford CT 06902
203 975-5900

(P-19307)
VOLUME SERVICES INC
Also Called: Centerplate
500 Diamond Dr, Lake Elsinore (92530-4457)
PHONE..............................951 245-9995
Dan Kreuzer, *Branch Mgr*
EMP: 100
SALES (corp-wide): 1.2B **Privately Held**
WEB: www.volumeservicesamerica.com
SIC: 7999 Concession operator
HQ: Volume Services, Inc.
2187 Atlantic St Ste 6
Stamford CT 06902
203 975-5900

(P-19308)
WEST VALLEY JEWISH CMNTY CTR
22622 Vanowen St, Canoga Park (91307-2646)
PHONE..............................818 348-0048
Fax: 818 464-3390
Anthony Flores, *Director*
Jack Mayer, *Director*
EMP: 60 **EST:** 2000
SALES (est): 2.1MM **Privately Held**
SIC: 7999 Recreation center

(P-19309)
WIN-RIVER RESORT & CASINO
2100 Redding Rancheria Rd, Redding (96001-5530)
PHONE..............................530 243-3377
Fax: 530 246-0188
Redding Rancheria Tribe, *Owner*
Christi Ross, *CFO*
Martin Myers, *Executive*
Jeffery Thorp, *Executive*
Gary Hayward, *General Mgr*
EMP: 310
SQ FT: 3,000
SALES (est): 11MM **Privately Held**
SIC: 7999 Bingo hall

(P-19310)
WINCHESTER MYSTERY HOUSE LLC
525 S Winchester Blvd, San Jose (95128-2588)
PHONE..............................408 247-2000
Fax: 408 247-2090
Ray K Farris II,
Monica Myles, *Office Admin*
Shawn Southorn, *Office Admin*
Damon Blum, *Opers Mgr*
Linda Foerster, *Sales/Mktg Mgr*
EMP: 90
SQ FT: 44,000
SALES (est): 5.9MM **Privately Held**
WEB: www.winchestermysteryhouse.com
SIC: 7999 Tourist attraction, commercial

(P-19311)
XTREME ZONE INC
Also Called: Michelle Alexander
1740 E Shepherd Ave, Fresno (93720-5607)
PHONE..............................559 474-6861
Michelle Alexander, *President*
Charles Alexander, *Treasurer*
Jason Alexander, *Vice Pres*
Patricia Alexander, *Admin Sec*
EMP: 143
SQ FT: 177,000
SALES: 950K **Privately Held**
SIC: 7999 Tourist attractions, amusement park concessions & rides

(P-19312)
YOUNG MENS CHRISTIAN ASSO
Also Called: Simi Valley Family YMCA
3200 Cochran St, Simi Valley (93065-2769)
PHONE..............................805 583-5338
Fax: 805 583-5476
Dan Jaeger, *Director*
Linda Wiggins, *Exec Dir*
EMP: 100
SALES (corp-wide): 20.9MM **Privately Held**
SIC: 7999 8351 8641 7997 Recreation center; child day care services; civic social & fraternal associations; membership sports & recreation clubs
PA: Young Men's Christian Association Of Southeast Ventura County
100 E Thousand Oaks Blvd # 107
Thousand Oaks CA 91360
805 497-3081

(P-19313)
ZEPHYR RIVER EXPEDITIONS INC
Also Called: Zephyr White Water Expeditions
22517 Parrotts Ferry Rd, Columbia (95310-9757)
P.O. Box 510 (95310-0510)
PHONE..............................800 431-3636
Fax: 209 532-4525
Bob Ferguson, *President*
EMP: 60
SQ FT: 2,000
SALES (est): 1.2MM **Privately Held**
WEB: www.zrafting.com
SIC: 7999 Rafting tours

8011 Offices & Clinics Of Doctors Of Medicine

(P-19314)
A & C HEALTH CARE SERVICES INC
Also Called: A & C Convatescent Hospital
33 Mateo Ave, Millbrae (94030-2037)
PHONE..............................650 689-5784
Carlos P Ragudo, *President*
Amparo B Ragudo, *CFO*
EMP: 135
SALES (est): 4.6MM **Privately Held**
SIC: 8011 Clinic, operated by physicians

(P-19315)
ADULT HEALTH CENTER AT SIERRA
3837 N Clark St, Fresno (93726-4806)
PHONE..............................559 459-1550
Mark Felmus MD, *Principal*
EMP: 50
SALES (est): 3.1MM **Privately Held**
SIC: 8011 Offices & clinics of medical doctors

(P-19316)
ADVANCED SURGERY INSTITUTE LLC
1739 4th St, Santa Rosa (95404-3601)
PHONE..............................707 528-6331
Fax: 707 528-6587
Jeff Simmons, *Principal*
Gian Nhan MD,
Heather Morris, *Manager*
Cathy Woodcock, *Manager*
EMP: 176
SALES (est): 35MM
SALES (corp-wide): 5.6B **Privately Held**
SIC: 8011 Surgeon

PRODUCTS & SERVICES SECTION
8011 - Offices & Clinics Of Doctors Of Medicine County (P-19338)

HQ: Santa Rosa Memorial Hospital Inc
1165 Montgomery Dr
Santa Rosa CA 95405
707 546-3210

(P-19317)
ADVANTAGE MEDICAL GROUP INC
Also Called: Take Care Employer Solutions
15035 E 14th St, San Leandro (94578-1901)
PHONE...................510 614-3700
Fax: 510 614-3792
Ed Troy, *President*
Jeane Powers, *Corp Secy*
Dr Tilden Sokoloff, *Vice Pres*
EMP: 72
SQ FT: 11,000
SALES (est): 2.4MM
SALES (corp-wide): 505.9MM **Privately Held**
WEB: www.chdmeridian.com
SIC: 8011 8049 Occupational & industrial specialist, physician/surgeon; physical therapist
HQ: Take Care Employer Solutions, Llc.
5500 Maryland Way Ste 200
Brentwood TN 37027

(P-19318)
ADVENTIST HEALTH SYSTEM/WEST
Also Called: Central Valley Family Heal
2141 High St Ste E, Selma (93662-3065)
PHONE...................559 891-2611
Kirby McKague, *Branch Mgr*
EMP: 115
SALES (corp-wide): 251.4MM **Privately Held**
SIC: 8011 Clinic, operated by physicians
PA: Adventist Health System/West
2100 Douglas Blvd
Roseville CA 95661
916 781-2000

(P-19319)
ADVENTIST HEALTH SYSTEM/WEST
18990 Coyote Valley Rd # 11, Hidden Valley Lake (95467-8337)
PHONE...................707 987-8344
Fax: 707 987-8395
EMP: 75
SALES (corp-wide): 251.4MM **Privately Held**
SIC: 8011 Offices & clinics of medical doctors
PA: Adventist Health System/West
2100 Douglas Blvd
Roseville CA 95661
916 781-2000

(P-19320)
ADVENTIST HEALTH SYSTEM/WEST
1524 W Lacey Blvd Ste 102, Hanford (93230-5966)
PHONE...................559 537-0305
EMP: 75
SALES (corp-wide): 251.4MM **Privately Held**
SIC: 8011 Internal medicine practitioners
PA: Adventist Health System/West
2100 Douglas Blvd
Roseville CA 95661
916 781-2000

(P-19321)
ADVENTIST HEALTH SYSTEM/WEST
14880 Olympic Dr, Clearlake (95422-9521)
P.O. Box 6710 (95422-6710)
PHONE...................707 995-4888
Fax: 707 995-4899
Patricia Van Horn, *Manager*
Julie Garcia, *Manager*
EMP: 115
SALES (corp-wide): 3.2B **Privately Held**
SIC: 8011 Clinic, operated by physicians
PA: Adventist Health System/West
2100 Douglas Blvd
Roseville CA 95661
916 781-2000

(P-19322)
ADVENTIST HEALTH SYSTEM/WEST
1560 E Chevy Chase Dr # 245, Glendale (91206-4197)
PHONE...................818 246-5900
EMP: 121
SALES (corp-wide): 251.4MM **Privately Held**
SIC: 8011 Offices & clinics of medical doctors
PA: Adventist Health System/West
2100 Douglas Blvd
Roseville CA 95661
916 781-2000

(P-19323)
ADVENTIST HEALTH SYSTEM/WEST
Also Called: Adventis Chldren Hlth Care Ctr
1433 N Acacia Ave, Reedley (93654-2102)
PHONE...................559 637-2384
EMP: 91
SALES (corp-wide): 251.4MM **Privately Held**
SIC: 8011 Offices & clinics of medical doctors
PA: Adventist Health System/West
2100 Douglas Blvd
Roseville CA 95661
916 781-2000

(P-19324)
ADVENTIST HEALTH SYSTEM/WEST
Also Called: St Helena Hospital Clearlake
18th Ave Hwy 53, Clearlake (95422)
P.O. Box 6710 (95422-6710)
PHONE...................707 994-6486
Fax: 707 995-5843
Kendall Fults, *CEO*
Dick Hathaway, *COO*
Duane Barnes, *Finance*
Wendy Fox, *Hlthcr Dir*
EMP: 330
SALES (corp-wide): 3.2B **Privately Held**
WEB: www.sthelenahospital.com
SIC: 8011 Surgeon
PA: Adventist Health System/West
2100 Douglas Blvd
Roseville CA 95661
916 781-2000

(P-19325)
AFSHAN BAIG MD
Also Called: Cinicas De Salud Del Pueblo
900 Main St, Brawley (92227-2630)
PHONE...................760 344-6471
Yvonne Bell, *Exec Dir*
Elena Rivas, *Nursing Dir*
Afshan Baig, *Director*
EMP: 50
SALES (est): 1.5MM **Privately Held**
SIC: 8011 Offices & clinics of medical doctors

(P-19326)
AIDS HEALTHCARE FOUNDATION
1669 W Avenue J Ste 301, Lancaster (93534-2870)
PHONE...................661 723-3244
EMP: 225
SALES (corp-wide): 1B **Privately Held**
SIC: 8011 Group health association
PA: Aids Healthcare Foundation
6255 W Sunset Blvd Fl 21
Los Angeles CA 90028
323 860-5200

(P-19327)
AIDS HEALTHCARE FOUNDATION
1300 N Vermont Ave, Los Angeles (90027-6098)
PHONE...................323 662-0492
Fax: 323 662-0196
Gene Nuziard, *Branch Mgr*
Jesse Galan, *Manager*
EMP: 393
SALES (corp-wide): 1B **Privately Held**
WEB: www.aidshealthcarefoundation.com
SIC: 8011 Offices & clinics of medical doctors

PA: Aids Healthcare Foundation
6255 W Sunset Blvd Fl 21
Los Angeles CA 90028
323 860-5200

(P-19328)
AIDS HEALTHCARE FOUNDATION
9200 Colima Rd, Whittier (90605-1814)
PHONE...................562 693-2654
Louis Yen, *Manager*
EMP: 281
SALES (corp-wide): 1B **Privately Held**
SIC: 8011 Offices & clinics of medical doctors
PA: Aids Healthcare Foundation
6255 W Sunset Blvd Fl 21
Los Angeles CA 90028
323 860-5200

(P-19329)
ALL CARE MEDICAL GROUP INC
Also Called: Professional Svcs Med Group
31 Crescent St, Huntington Park (90255)
PHONE...................408 278-3550
Fax: 323 589-4903
Samuel Rotenberg MD, *Director*
Wen Luh, *Info Tech Mgr*
Kelly I Aquino, *Financial Exec*
Burt Fessler, *Purch Mgr*
Mont A Smith, *Surgeon*
EMP: 85
SQ FT: 33,000
SALES (est): 8MM **Privately Held**
WEB: www.allcaremg.com
SIC: 8011 Physicians' office, including specialists

(P-19330)
ALLEN MEDICAL GROUP INC
14416 Victory Blvd # 211, Van Nuys (91401-1441)
PHONE...................818 698-8444
Avionne Petal Allen-Singh, *President*
EMP: 50 EST: 2008
SALES: 11MM **Privately Held**
SIC: 8011 Offices & clinics of medical doctors

(P-19331)
ALLIANCE MEDICAL CENTER INC
1381 University St, Healdsburg (95448-3314)
PHONE...................707 431-8234
Fax: 707 431-8649
Beatrice Bostick, *CEO*
Jack Neureuter, *CEO*
Priscilla Contreras, *Marketing Staff*
Eloisa Nuno,
Mike Dunn, *Manager*
EMP: 99
SALES: 10MM **Privately Held**
WEB: www.alliancemedicalcenter.org
SIC: 8011 Offices & clinics of medical doctors

(P-19332)
ALLIED ANESTHESIA MED GROUP
400 N Tustin Ave, Santa Ana (92705-3813)
P.O. Box 1628, Orange (92856-0628)
PHONE...................951 830-9816
George Kanaly, *CEO*
Kaveh Matin, *President*
Rajesh Bhat, *Anesthesiology*
EMP: 99
SALES (est): 3.3MM **Privately Held**
SIC: 8011 Anesthesiologist

(P-19333)
ALTA VISTA HEALTHCARE AND WELL
9020 Garfield St, Riverside (92503-3903)
PHONE...................951 688-8200
EMP: 105
SALES (est): 5.5MM **Privately Held**
SIC: 8011

(P-19334)
ALTAMED HEALTH SERVICES CORP
5427 Whittier Blvd, Los Angeles (90022-4101)
PHONE...................323 980-4466
Fax: 323 869-5362
Irene Avilar, *Principal*
EMP: 80
SALES (corp-wide): 360.3MM **Privately Held**
WEB: www.altamed.org
SIC: 8011 Offices & clinics of medical doctors
PA: Altamed Health Services Corporation
2040 Camfield Ave
Commerce CA 90040
323 725-8751

(P-19335)
ALTAMED HEALTH SERVICES CORP (PA)
2040 Camfield Ave, Commerce (90040-1574)
PHONE...................323 725-8751
Fax: 323 889-7399
Castulo De La Rocha, *CEO*
Jose U Esparza, *CFO*
Marie S Torres, *Senior VP*
Zoila D Escobar, *Vice Pres*
Elvia Castillodelgado, *Admin Sec*
EMP: 135
SQ FT: 27,345
SALES: 360.3MM **Privately Held**
WEB: www.altamed.org
SIC: 8011 8099 Gynecologist; pediatrician; radiologist; medical services organization

(P-19336)
ALTAMED HEALTH SERVICES CORP
5427 Whittier Blvd, Los Angeles (90022-4101)
PHONE...................323 869-5448
Fax: 323 869-5427
Barsha M Puri, *Pediatrics*
EMP: 91
SALES (corp-wide): 360.3MM **Privately Held**
SIC: 8011 Physicians' office, including specialists
PA: Altamed Health Services Corporation
2040 Camfield Ave
Commerce CA 90040
323 725-8751

(P-19337)
ALTURA CENTERS FOR HEALTH
1201 N Cherry St, Tulare (93274-2233)
PHONE...................559 686-9097
Fax: 559 686-4750
Graciela Soto-Perez, *President*
Nauman Qureshi, *COO*
Victor Gonzalez, *Vice Pres*
Evelyn Benson, *Exec Dir*
Dennis Jungwirth, *Human Res Dir*
EMP: 83
SQ FT: 18,000
SALES: 19.3MM **Privately Held**
WEB: www.tchci.com
SIC: 8011 8021 Clinic, operated by physicians; primary care medical clinic; offices & clinics of dentists

(P-19338)
AMEN CLINICS INC A MED CORP
1000 Marina Blvd Ste 100, Brisbane (94005-1839)
PHONE...................650 416-7830
Daniel G Amen MD, *Owner*
Justin Just, *Administration*
Sylvat Wijangco, *Coordinator*
EMP: 50
SALES (est): 2.5MM **Privately Held**
WEB: www.amenclinic.com
SIC: 8011 Psychiatrist

8011 - Offices & Clinics Of Doctors Of Medicine County (P-19339)

(P-19339)
AMERICAN HEALTH SERVICES LLC
Also Called: Palmdale Med Mental Hlth Svcs
26460 Summit Cir, Santa Clarita (91350-2991)
P.O. Box 801809 (91380-1809)
PHONE.................................661 254-6630
Stan Sharma, CEO
Leni Legaspi, CFO
Hamir Sinha, Treasurer
Sean Sharma, Vice Pres
Sabrina Fendley, Executive
EMP: 110
SALES: 4.9MM Privately Held
SIC: 8011 8361 Offices & clinics of medical doctors; rehabilitation center, residential: health care incidental

(P-19340)
AMIR AHMAD MD
628 California Blvd Ste D, San Luis Obispo (93401-2558)
PHONE.................................805 545-8100
Amir Ahmad, Owner
EMP: 80
SALES (est): 917.5K Privately Held
SIC: 8011 General & family practice, physician/surgeon

(P-19341)
AMN HEALTHCARE INC (HQ)
12400 High Bluff Dr, San Diego (92130-3077)
PHONE.................................858 792-0711
Susan R Nowakowski, CEO
Kim Howard, President
Susan R Salka, President
David C Dreyer, CFO
Jeff Decker, Senior VP
EMP: 168
SALES (est): 191MM
SALES (corp-wide): 1.4B Publicly Held
WEB: www.amnhealthcare.com
SIC: 8011 Primary care medical clinic
PA: Amn Healthcare Services, Inc.
12400 High Bluff Dr
San Diego CA 92130
866 871-8519

(P-19342)
AMPLA HEALTH
Also Called: Chico Family Health Center
680 Cohasset Rd, Chico (95926-2213)
PHONE.................................530 342-4395
Amalia Bejerano, Branch Mgr
Thomas Neuschatz, Internal Med
Ejaz Ahmed, Pediatrics
Yusuf Ali, Med Doctor
Mark Jackson, Med Doctor
EMP: 57
SALES (corp-wide): 43.4MM Privately Held
SIC: 8011 Offices & clinics of medical doctors
PA: Ampla Health
935 Market St
Yuba City CA 95991
530 674-4261

(P-19343)
AMPLA HEALTH
Also Called: Lindhurst Family Health Center
4941 Olivehurst Ave, Olivehurst (95961-4225)
PHONE.................................530 743-4614
Fax: 530 743-5770
Sally Moore, Branch Mgr
Dwayne Vanderberg MD, Med Doctor
EMP: 51
SALES (corp-wide): 43.4MM Privately Held
SIC: 8011 Health maintenance organization
PA: Ampla Health
935 Market St
Yuba City CA 95991
530 674-4261

(P-19344)
ANAHEIM HARBOR MEDICAL GROUP (PA)
Also Called: Family Urgent Care Center
710 N Euclid St, Anaheim (92801-4122)
PHONE.................................714 533-4511
Fax: 714 517-2177
David L Tsoong MD, President
Joseph M Mule MD, Admin Sec
Miguel Estrada, VP Finance
Richard C Razka, Orthopedist
EMP: 50
SQ FT: 10,000
SALES (est): 10MM Privately Held
SIC: 8011 Pediatrician; internal medicine, physician/surgeon; orthopedic physician; obstetrician

(P-19345)
ANAHEIM MEDICAL CENTER
1111 W La Palma Ave, Anaheim (92801-2804)
PHONE.................................714 774-1450
Patrick Petre, Principal
Jeff Deroches, CIO
Sharon Morris, Info Tech Dir
Kathy Doi, Human Res Dir
Cathy Doi, Human Resources
EMP: 62
SALES (est): 6.9MM Privately Held
SIC: 8011 Medical centers

(P-19346)
ANAHEIM REGIONAL MEDICAL CTR
Also Called: Ahmc
1211 W La Palma Ave # 104, Anaheim (92801-2815)
PHONE.................................714 999-3847
Patrick Petre, Branch Mgr
EMP: 127
SALES (corp-wide): 15.7MM Privately Held
SIC: 8011 Offices & clinics of medical doctors
PA: Anaheim Regional Medical Center
1111 W La Palma Ave
Anaheim CA 92801
714 774-1450

(P-19347)
ANDREW M GOLDEN MD
4647 Zion Ave, San Diego (92120-2507)
PHONE.................................619 528-5342
Andrew Golden, Principal
EMP: 51
SALES (est): 4MM Privately Held
SIC: 8011 Physicians' office, including specialists

(P-19348)
ANESTHESIA BUSINESS CONS INC
Also Called: Anesthesia Consultants of Cont
1600 Riviera Ave Ste 420, Walnut Creek (94596-7115)
PHONE.................................925 951-1366
Fax: 925 951-1385
Sepi Azari, Regional Mgr
Ruth Morton, Marketing Staff
Edwin Cheng, Anesthesiology
Kirtikumar Desai, Anesthesiology
Brandon Giniczki, Anesthesiology
EMP: 80
SALES (corp-wide): 8.7MM Privately Held
SIC: 8011 8741 Anesthesiologist; management services
PA: Anesthesia Business Consultants, Inc.
8905 Sw Nimbus Ave # 300
Beaverton OR 97008
503 372-2740

(P-19349)
ANESTHESIA SVC MED GROUP INC
Also Called: Asmg
3626 Ruffin Rd, San Diego (92123-1810)
P.O. Box 82807 (92138-2807)
PHONE.................................858 277-4767
Peter Raudaskoski, President
Thomas R Farrell MD, President
Sandeep K Khanna, Med Doctor
Annie Prochera, Med Doctor
Jeremy Dendle, Manager
EMP: 50
SQ FT: 11,200
SALES (est): 17.4MM Privately Held
WEB: www.asmgmd.com
SIC: 8011 Anesthesiologist

(P-19350)
ANKA BEHAVIORAL HEALTH INC
942 Barbara Ln, Pomona (91767-4118)
PHONE.................................909 622-8217
Tina Bligh, Administration
EMP: 108
SALES (corp-wide): 41.6MM Privately Held
SIC: 8011 Group health association
PA: Anka Behavioral Health, Incorporated
1850 Gateway Blvd Ste 900
Concord CA 94520
925 825-4700

(P-19351)
ANTELOPE VALLEY HOSPITAL AUX
1601 W Avenue J, Lancaster (93534-2824)
PHONE.................................661 949-1550
Pradeep Damle, Branch Mgr
EMP: 86
SALES (corp-wide): 380MM Privately Held
SIC: 8011 General & family practice, physician/surgeon
PA: Antelope Valley Hospital Auxiliary
1600 W Avenue J
Lancaster CA 93534
661 949-5000

(P-19352)
ANTELOPE VALLEY HOSPITAL AUX
Ob Clinic
1600 W Avenue J, Lancaster (93534-2894)
PHONE.................................661 726-6180
Vikki Haley, Principal
D R Rowe, Vice Pres
EMP: 257
SALES (corp-wide): 380MM Privately Held
SIC: 8011 Offices & clinics of medical doctors
PA: Antelope Valley Hospital Auxiliary
1600 W Avenue J
Lancaster CA 93534
661 949-5000

(P-19353)
ANTELOPE VALLEY MEDICAL GROUP
44469 10th St W, Lancaster (93534-3324)
PHONE.................................661 945-2783
Fax: 661 945-8191
Karunyan Arul, Partner
Donna Acosta, Manager
EMP: 50
SALES (est): 1.4MM Privately Held
SIC: 8011 Clinic, operated by physicians

(P-19354)
APLA HEALTH & WELLNESS
611 S Kingsley Dr, Los Angeles (90005-2319)
PHONE.................................213 201-1546
Craig Thompson, CEO
Robyn Goldman, CFO
EMP: 56 EST: 2010
SALES: 5MM
SALES (corp-wide): 20.9MM Privately Held
SIC: 8011 Primary care medical clinic
PA: Aids Project Los Angeles
611 S Kingsley Dr
Los Angeles CA 90005
213 201-1600

(P-19355)
ARIS VISION INS OF CA A MEDCL
11400 W Olympic Blvd # 200, Los Angeles (90064-1550)
PHONE.................................310 914-0150
Paul Daneshrad, President
Bob Quinn, Manager
▲ EMP: 60 EST: 1999
SQ FT: 2,800
SALES (est): 1.4MM Privately Held
SIC: 8011 Ophthalmologist

(P-19356)
ARLENE KELLER MD
Also Called: Pacific Interior Medicine
2100 Webster St Ste 423, San Francisco (94115-2380)
PHONE.................................415 923-3598
Arlene Keller, Principal
EMP: 50
SALES (est): 1.9MM Privately Held
SIC: 8011 General & family practice, physician/surgeon

(P-19357)
ARROYO SECO MEDICAL GROUP (PA)
301 S Fair Oaks Ave # 300, Pasadena (91105-2561)
PHONE.................................626 795-7556
Henry Sideropoulos MD, President
Andrew Muller MD, Vice Pres
EMP: 65
SQ FT: 9,145
SALES (est): 6.5MM Privately Held
WEB: www.arroyoseco.net
SIC: 8011 Internal medicine, physician/surgeon; general & family practice, physician/surgeon

(P-19358)
ASIAN HEALTH SERVICES
270 13th St, Oakland (94612-4801)
PHONE.................................510 986-0601
Sherry Hirota, Branch Mgr
EMP: 58
SALES (corp-wide): 33MM Privately Held
SIC: 8011 Offices & clinics of medical doctors
PA: Asian Health Services
818 Webster St
Oakland CA 94607
510 986-6800

(P-19359)
ASIAN HEALTH SERVICES (PA)
818 Webster St, Oakland (94607-4220)
PHONE.................................510 986-6800
Fax: 510 986-6890
Sherry Hirota, CEO
Grace Fung, Executive
Dong Suh, Associate Dir
Grace Wong, Department Mgr
CHI Le, Pediatrics
EMP: 147
SQ FT: 30,000
SALES: 33MM Privately Held
SIC: 8011 Offices & clinics of medical doctors

(P-19360)
ASSOCIATED INTERNAL MEDICINE (PA)
350 30th St Ste 320, Oakland (94609-3425)
PHONE.................................510 465-6700
Fax: 510 465-6767
Dean J Nickles, President
Scott A Weisenberg, Infectious Dis
Leslie S Tim MD, Med Doctor
▲ EMP: 51
SALES (est): 8.6MM Privately Held
WEB: www.aimmg.com
SIC: 8011 Internal medicine, physician/surgeon

(P-19361)
ASSOCIATED PATHOLOGY MED GROUP
1555 Soquel Dr, Santa Cruz (95065-1705)
PHONE.................................831 462-7625
Fax: 831 462-7607
Steve Mc Carthy, Principal
EMP: 85
SALES (est): 1.5MM Privately Held
SIC: 8011 Offices & clinics of medical doctors

(P-19362)
ASSOCIATED STUDENTS UCLA
Also Called: Ucla Mdcn SC Phrmclgy
650 Chrls Yng S Rm 23 120, Los Angeles (90095-0001)
PHONE.................................310 825-9451
Michael Phelps, Principal
EMP: 800

PRODUCTS & SERVICES SECTION
8011 - Offices & Clinics Of Doctors Of Medicine County (P-19383)

SALES (corp-wide): 40.5MM **Privately Held**
SIC: 8011 General & family practice, physician/surgeon
PA: Associated Students U.C.L.A.
   308 Westwood Plz
   Los Angeles CA 90024
   310 825-4321

(P-19363)
AUDREY ADAMS MD
718 University Ave # 211, Los Gatos (95032-7608)
PHONE................................408 354-2114
Franklin Chow, *Principal*
Anthony Lin, *Anesthesiology*
EMP: 50
SALES (est): 1.4MM **Privately Held**
SIC: 8011 General & family practice, physician/surgeon

(P-19364)
AXMINSTER MEDICAL GROUP INC (PA)
11539 Hawthorne Blvd Fl 6, Hawthorne (90250-2325)
PHONE................................310 670-3255
Fax: 310 338-8695
Raymond Jing MD, *CEO*
Huey-Jer Su MD, *Treasurer*
Spencer H Wenger MD, *Vice Pres*
Stanley E Golden MD, *Admin Sec*
Stanley E Goldn, *Admin Sec*
EMP: 56
SQ FT: 20,000
SALES (est): 15.1MM **Privately Held**
WEB: www.axminstermedicalgroup.com
SIC: 8011 Internal medicine, physician/surgeon; pediatrician; gynecologist

(P-19365)
BARTON MEMORIAL HOSPITAL
Also Called: Barton Ski Clinic At Sierra
1111 Sierra At Tahoe Rd, Twin Bridges (95735-9505)
PHONE................................530 659-7434
EMP: 58
SALES (corp-wide): 114.2MM **Privately Held**
SIC: 8011 Offices & clinics of medical doctors
PA: Barton Memorial Hospital
   2170 South Ave
   South Lake Tahoe CA 96150
   530 541-3420

(P-19366)
BAY AREA SURGICAL MGT LLC
2110 Forest Ave Fl 2, San Jose (95128-1469)
PHONE................................408 297-3432
Stephanie Halls,
EMP: 50
SALES (est): 1.6MM **Privately Held**
SIC: 8011 Offices & clinics of medical doctors

(P-19367)
BAY IMAGING CONS MED GROUP INC (PA)
175 Lennon Ln Ste 100, Walnut Creek (94598-2466)
PHONE................................925 296-7150
Anton C Pogany, *Director*
Lisa Woeffel, *CFO*
Lisa Woelfel, *CFO*
Paula Benone, *Executive*
Angelo Crudale, *Administration*
EMP: 80
SQ FT: 4,500
SALES (est): 8.6MM **Privately Held**
SIC: 8011 Radiologist

(P-19368)
BAY MEDICAL MANAGEMENT LLC
2125 Oak Grove Rd Ste 200, Walnut Creek (94598-2520)
PHONE................................925 296-7150
Fax: 925 296-7170
Mary Gerard, *Mng Member*
Lisa Woelfel, *CFO*
Robert Binder, *Executive*
David Martin, *Admin Asst*
Graciela Paguirigan, *Admin Asst*

EMP: 160
SALES (est): 23.2MM **Privately Held**
WEB: www.bmmi.net
SIC: 8011 Radiologist

(P-19369)
BAY VALLEY MEDICAL GROUP INC (PA)
27212 Calaroga Ave, Hayward (94545-4349)
PHONE................................510 785-5000
Fax: 510 293-5606
Shelley A Horwitz, *CEO*
Roland J Wong, *Ch of Bd*
Eric S Kohleriter, *President*
Kim Ha, *Accountant*
James R Frede, *Director*
EMP: 93
SQ FT: 28,734
SALES (est): 20.3MM **Privately Held**
WEB: www.bvmed.com
SIC: 8011 Clinic, operated by physicians

(P-19370)
BAYSPRING MEDICAL GROUP A PRO
1199 Bush St Ste 500, San Francisco (94109-5976)
PHONE................................415 674-2600
Laurel Dawson, *President*
Marilyn Milkman, *Treasurer*
Susan Rosen, *Vice Pres*
Hannah Wright, *Physician Asst*
EMP: 50
SALES (est): 4.7MM **Privately Held**
SIC: 8011 Offices & clinics of medical doctors; internal medicine practitioners; obstetrician; gynecologist

(P-19371)
BEAVER MEDICAL CLINIC INC (PA)
1615 Orange Tree Ln, Redlands (92374-4501)
P.O. Box 10069, San Bernardino (92423-0069)
PHONE................................909 793-3311
Fax: 909 335-6348
Robert Klein, *President*
Joanne Snowden, *Controller*
Eric R Fox, *Family Practiti*
Norie Sadjadi, *Obstetrician*
Paul S Kim, *Anesthesiology*
EMP: 190
SQ FT: 79,212
SALES (est): 20.6MM **Privately Held**
WEB: www.epiclp.com
SIC: 8011 Clinic, operated by physicians

(P-19372)
BEAVER MEDICAL GROUP LP (HQ)
Also Called: Beaver Medical Clinic
7000 Boulder Ave, Highland (92346-3348)
PHONE................................909 425-3321
Fax: 909 862-2768
John Goodman, *CEO*
James Watson M D, *Partner*
Robert Bourne M D, *Partner*
Robert Rentschler, *Partner*
Stacy Holt, *Administration*
EMP: 67
SALES (est): 16.7MM **Privately Held**
SIC: 8011 Allergist

(P-19373)
BELVILLE ENTERPRISES INC
Also Called: Ron's Pharmacy Services
6225 Nancy Ridge Dr, San Diego (92121-2245)
PHONE................................858 652-6960
Ronald W Belville, *CEO*
Alex Nadzan, *Exec VP*
Sharon Desantis, *Assistant*
Kathy Dunn, *Assistant*
EMP: 100
SQ FT: 27,000
SALES (est): 14.3MM **Privately Held**
SIC: 8011 5912 Offices & clinics of medical doctors; drug stores & proprietary stores

(P-19374)
BIOFUSION LLC
19110 Van Ness Ave, Torrance (90501-1101)
PHONE................................310 803-8100
Fax: 310 320-6446
Dominic Meffe, *CFO*
Dinesh Patel, *President*
Vincent Cook, *CFO*
Bob Rabone, *Exec Dir*
Whai Lim, *Webmaster*
EMP: 80
SQ FT: 9,137
SALES: 85MM
SALES (corp-wide): 109.8B **Publicly Held**
SIC: 8011 Medical centers
HQ: Kroger Specialty Pharmacy Holdings I, Inc.
   6435 Hazeltine National
   Orlando FL 32822
   626 932-1600

(P-19375)
BLOSS MEMORIAL HEALTH CARE DST (PA)
3605 Hospital Rd Ste A, Atwater (95301-5173)
PHONE................................209 381-2000
Fax: 209 722-9020
Ed Lujano, *CEO*
Bill Able, *CFO*
Dawnita Dane, *Accountant*
Debbie Kelley, *Director*
EMP: 55
SQ FT: 168,000
SALES: 1.7MM **Privately Held**
WEB: www.castlefamilyhealth.org
SIC: 8011 Physicians' office, including specialists

(P-19376)
BORREGO CMNTY HLTH FOUNDATION
2721 Washington, Julian (92036)
P.O. Box 969 (92036-0969)
PHONE................................760 765-1223
Gina Glenn, *Branch Mgr*
Jean Merrick, *Administration*
Jan Jones, *Nurse Practr*
EMP: 538
SALES (corp-wide): 64.3MM **Privately Held**
SIC: 8011 Offices & clinics of medical doctors
PA: Borrego Community Health Foundation
   4343 Yaqui Pass Rd
   Borrego Springs CA 92004
   760 767-5051

(P-19377)
BREAST DIAGNOSTIC CENTER
3275 Skypark Dr Ste A, Torrance (90505-5027)
PHONE................................310 517-4709
Fax: 310 530-4488
George Gram, *President*
EMP: 50
SALES (est): 3MM **Privately Held**
SIC: 8011 General & family practice, physician/surgeon

(P-19378)
BRIGHT HEALTH PHYSICIANS (PA)
15725 Whittier Blvd # 500, Whittier (90603-2350)
PHONE................................562 947-8478
Fax: 562 943-5179
William H Stimmler MD, *Ch of Bd*
Keith Miyamoto MD, *President*
Larry Castillo, *Officer*
Shalini Bhargava, *Vice Pres*
Don T Eli, *Principal*
EMP: 140
SQ FT: 50,000
SALES: 120.5MM **Privately Held**
WEB: www.brightmedical.com
SIC: 8011 Physicians' office, including specialists

(P-19379)
BROOKSIDE COMMUNITY HEALTH CTR
1030 Nevin Ave, Richmond (94801-3122)
PHONE................................510 215-5001
Fax: 510 215-1115
Norman L Banks, *Director*
EMP: 50
SALES (corp-wide): 7.9MM **Privately Held**
SIC: 8011 Offices & clinics of medical doctors
PA: Brookside Community Health Center
   2023 Vale Rd
   San Pablo CA 94806
   510 215-9092

(P-19380)
BROWN & TOLAND MEDICAL GROUP (PA)
1221 Broadway Ste 700, Oakland (94612-1898)
P.O. Box 640469, San Francisco (94164-0469)
PHONE................................415 972-4162
Joel Klompus, *President*
Mark Ficker, *CFO*
Michael Gam, *CFO*
Chris Foster, *Exec VP*
Ana Bodendorfer, *Senior VP*
EMP: 240
SQ FT: 8,000
SALES (est): 76.4MM **Privately Held**
WEB: www.brownandtoland.com
SIC: 8011 Offices & clinics of medical doctors

(P-19381)
BROWN & TOLAND MEDICAL GROUP
2100 Webster St Ste 109, San Francisco (94115-2374)
PHONE................................415 923-3015
Lesley Anderson, *Surgeon*
Gregg Jossart, *Surgeon*
Jonathan Leichtling, *Surgeon*
Michael Small, *Surgeon*
Neal S Birnbaum, *Rheumtlgy Spec*
EMP: 200
SALES (corp-wide): 76.4MM **Privately Held**
SIC: 8011 General & family practice, physician/surgeon
PA: Brown & Toland Medical Group Inc
   1221 Broadway Ste 700
   Oakland CA 94612
   415 972-4162

(P-19382)
BUENA PARK MEDICAL GROUP INC (PA)
6301 Beach Blvd Ste 101, Buena Park (90621-4030)
P.O. Box 277 (90621-0277)
PHONE................................714 994-5290
Martin Ahn, *CEO*
Felicia Tran, *Med Doctor*
Joseph Yi,
EMP: 50
SQ FT: 20,000
SALES (est): 5.6MM **Privately Held**
SIC: 8011 General & family practice, physician/surgeon

(P-19383)
BUENAVENTURA MEDICAL GROUP (PA)
888 S Hill Rd, Ventura (93003-8400)
PHONE................................805 477-6000
James Malone, *CEO*
David E Graham, *COO*
David Grahm, *COO*
Kevin Moore, *CFO*
Christopher N White, *Family Practiti*
EMP: 170
SQ FT: 27,000
SALES (est): 12.9MM **Privately Held**
SIC: 8011 Clinic, operated by physicians

8011 - Offices & Clinics Of Doctors Of Medicine County (P-19384)

PRODUDCTS & SERVICES SECTION

(P-19384)
BUENAVENTURA MEDICAL GROUP
2601 E Main St Ste 104, Ventura (93003-2801)
PHONE.................805 477-6220
James Malone, *CEO*
Kevin Moore, *CFO*
Roberta Williams, *Office Spvr*
Susan Graham, *VP Human Res*
William Hill, *Purch Mgr*
EMP: 100
SALES (corp-wide): 12.9MM **Privately Held**
SIC: **8011** Clinic, operated by physicians
PA: Buenaventura Medical Group Inc
    888 S Hill Rd
    Ventura CA 93003
    805 477-6000

(P-19385)
BUTTE PRIMARY CARE MED GROUP
6585 Clark Rd Ste 200, Paradise (95969-3500)
PHONE.................530 877-0762
D L Miller MD, *President*
Thomas Roth MD, *CFO*
Kenneth Logan MD, *Vice Pres*
Donald Smith MD, *Vice Pres*
Richard Gray MD, *Admin Sec*
EMP: 60
SQ FT: 1,150
SALES (est): 3.1MM **Privately Held**
SIC: **8011** Offices & clinics of medical doctors

(P-19386)
BUTTERWICK DR KIMBERLY JANE MD
9339 Genesee Ave Ste 300, San Diego (92121-2122)
PHONE.................858 657-1002
Mitchell Goldman, *Owner*
Kimberly J Butterwick, *Plastic Surgeon*
EMP: 95
SALES (est): 1.9MM **Privately Held**
SIC: **8011** Physicians' office, including specialists

(P-19387)
C E P
400 N Pepper Ave Ste 107, Colton (92324-1801)
PHONE.................909 580-1456
Fax: 909 580-1454
Rodney Burger,
EMP: 60
SALES (est): 1.8MM **Privately Held**
SIC: **8011** Offices & clinics of medical doctors

(P-19388)
C/O UC SAN FRANCISCO
1245 16th St Ste 225, Santa Monica (90404-1240)
PHONE.................310 794-1841
EMP: 87
SALES (corp-wide): 49.8MM **Privately Held**
SIC: **8011** 8221 Specialized medical practitioners, except internal; university
PA: C/O Uc San Francisco
    1111 Franklin St Fl 12
    Oakland CA 94607
    858 534-7323

(P-19389)
CALIFORNIA ANESTHESIA ASSO MED
400 N Tustin Ave Ste 400, Santa Ana (92705-3850)
P.O. Box 10429, Newport Beach (92658-0429)
PHONE.................800 888-2186
Kevin Jones, *President*
Alan Ross, *CEO*
Pam Hunter, *CPA*
EMP: 60
SALES (est): 3.8MM **Privately Held**
SIC: **8011** Anesthesiologist

(P-19390)
CALIFORNIA CANCER ASSCTES
Also Called: Ccare West
7130 N Millbrook Ave, Fresno (93720-3347)
PHONE.................559 447-4949
Fax: 559 447-4925
Marshall Flam, *Med Doctor*
EMP: 80
SALES (corp-wide): 26.4MM **Privately Held**
SIC: **8011** Oncologist; hematologist
PA: California Cancer Associates For Research And Excellence, Inc.
    1791 E Fir Ave
    Fresno CA 93720
    559 326-1222

(P-19391)
CALIFORNIA EYE INSTITUTE
Low Vision Dept St Agnes, Fresno (93720)
PHONE.................559 449-5000
Kathy Ploszaj, *Administration*
Eye Medical Center, *Shareholder*
Gary R Fogg MD, *Shareholder*
Saint Agnes Hospital, *Shareholder*
Larry R Lawrence MD, *Shareholder*
EMP: 180
SQ FT: 59,000
SALES (est): 9.6MM **Privately Held**
SIC: **8011** Ophthalmologist

(P-19392)
CALIFORNIA FORENSIC MED GROUP
1410 Natividad Rd, Salinas (93906-3102)
PHONE.................831 755-3886
EMP: 256
SALES (corp-wide): 29.8MM **Privately Held**
SIC: **8011** Medical centers
PA: California Forensic Medical Group, Inc
    2511 Garden Rd Ste A160
    Monterey CA 93940
    831 649-8994

(P-19393)
CALIFORNIA FORENSIC MED GROUP
200 E Hackett Rd, Modesto (95358-9415)
PHONE.................209 525-5670
L Cottrel, *Principal*
EMP: 102
SALES (corp-wide): 29.8MM **Privately Held**
SIC: **8011** Primary care medical clinic
PA: California Forensic Medical Group, Inc
    2511 Garden Rd Ste A160
    Monterey CA 93940
    831 649-8994

(P-19394)
CALIFORNIA IMAGING INST LLC
6297 N Fresno St, Fresno (93710-5209)
PHONE.................559 447-4000
Mariela Resendes, *Branch Mgr*
EMP: 60
SALES (corp-wide): 9.9MM **Privately Held**
SIC: **8011** Internal medicine, physician/surgeon
PA: California Imaging Institute, Llc
    1867 E Fir Ave Ste 101
    Fresno CA 93720
    559 325-5810

(P-19395)
CALIFORNIA KIDNEY MED GROUP
375 Rolling Oaks Dr # 100, Thousand Oaks (91361-1023)
PHONE.................805 497-7775
Kant Tucker, *President*
Hadyie Hadieman, *Accountant*
Dorothy Schock, *Director*
Margie Manwell, *Manager*
EMP: 130
SALES (est): 4.7MM **Privately Held**
SIC: **8011** Offices & clinics of medical doctors

(P-19396)
CALIFORNIA MEDICAL ASSOCIATION (PA)
Also Called: C M A
1201 J St Ste 200, Sacramento (95814-2949)
PHONE.................916 444-5532
Fax: 916 551-2035
Dustin Corcoren, *CEO*
Lance Lewis, *COO*
Janus Norman, *Senior VP*
Jennifer Williams, *Executive Asst*
Elizabeth McNeil, *Administration*
EMP: 73 EST: 1856
SQ FT: 48,960
SALES: 2MM **Privately Held**
WEB: www.cmanet.org
SIC: **8011** Occupational & industrial specialist, physician/surgeon

(P-19397)
CALIFORNIA PACIFIC CA
2100 Webster St Ste 516, San Francisco (94115-2381)
PHONE.................415 345-0940
Fax: 415 441-3253
Bruce Brent MD, *President*
Elaine Chow, *COO*
Michael Erhard, *COO*
Richard Francoz MD, *Vice Pres*
Anne Thorson, *Research*
EMP: 50
SQ FT: 3,500
SALES (est): 4.1MM **Privately Held**
WEB: www.cpcmg.com
SIC: **8011** Cardiologist & cardio-vascular specialist

(P-19398)
CALIFRNIA PSYCHTRIC TRNSITIONS
9234n Hinton Ave, Delhi (95315-8200)
P.O. Box 339 (95315-0339)
PHONE.................209 667-9304
Fax: 209 669-3978
John T Hackett MD, *President*
Donna M Gowan, *Project Mgr*
Scott A Turpin, *Med Doctor*
Donna McGowan, *Manager*
EMP: 70
SQ FT: 25,000
SALES (est): 4.2MM **Privately Held**
SIC: **8011** Psychiatric clinic

(P-19399)
CANCER FOUNDATION TRTMNT CTR
Also Called: Cancer Center of Santa Barbara
300 W Pueblo St, Santa Barbara (93105-4311)
PHONE.................805 682-7300
Rich Scott, *President*
EMP: 89
SALES (est): 1.2MM
SALES (corp-wide): 223.5MM **Privately Held**
SIC: **8011** Offices & clinics of medical doctors
PA: Sansum Clinic
    470 S Patterson Ave
    Santa Barbara CA 93111
    805 681-7700

(P-19400)
CAPITAL EYE MEDICAL GROUP
6620 Coyle Ave Ste 408, Carmichael (95608-6338)
P.O. Box 279, Roseville (95661-0279)
PHONE.................916 241-9378
Mitra Ayazifar, *President*
EMP: 73
SALES (est): 899.2K
SALES (corp-wide): 4MM **Privately Held**
SIC: **8011** Offices & clinics of medical doctors
PA: Nvision Laser Eye Centers Inc.
    75 Enterprise Ste 200
    Aliso Viejo CA 92656
    877 455-9942

(P-19401)
CARDIC ARITHMIAS
Also Called: Ruder, Michael MD
770 Welch Rd Ste 100, Palo Alto (94304-1505)
PHONE.................650 617-8100
Fax: 650 327-2947
Michael Ruder MD, *Partner*
Edward Anderson, *Med Doctor*
Gregory Engel, *Med Doctor*
Hardwi Mead, *Med Doctor*
Rob Patrawala, *Med Doctor*
EMP: 50
SALES (est): 2.2MM **Privately Held**
SIC: **8011** Cardiologist & cardio-vascular specialist

(P-19402)
CARDIOVASCULAR CONSULTANTS HEA
1207 E Herndon Ave, Fresno (93720-3235)
PHONE.................559 432-4303
Fax: 559 432-4574
Kevin J Boran, *President*
William E Hanks MD, *Treasurer*
Donald Gregory MD, *Admin Sec*
Liana Sheeley, *Business Mgr*
Rohit Sundrani, *Med Doctor*
EMP: 67
SQ FT: 17,000
SALES (est): 14.2MM **Privately Held**
SIC: **8011** Cardiologist & cardio-vascular specialist

(P-19403)
CARDIVSCLR MDCL GRP OF STHRN
Also Called: Harold L Karpman MD
414 N Camden Dr Ste 1100, Beverly Hills (90210-4517)
PHONE.................310 278-3400
Harold L Karpman, *President*
Selvyn B Bleifer MD, *President*
EMP: 50
SALES (est): 4.5MM **Privately Held**
SIC: **8011** Offices & clinics of medical doctors

(P-19404)
CAREMARK RX INC
Also Called: US Family Care
1851 N Riverside Ave, Rialto (92376-8069)
PHONE.................909 822-1164
Fax: 909 874-0826
Steve Heide, *Administration*
Maria A Hutchinson, *Gnrl Med Prac*
Frank Wright, *Manager*
EMP: 70
SALES (corp-wide): 153.2B **Publicly Held**
WEB: www.medpartners.com
SIC: **8011** General & family practice, physician/surgeon; internal medicine, physician/surgeon; obstetrician; gynecologist
HQ: Caremark Rx, Inc.
    445 Great Circle Rd
    Nashville TN 37228
    615 687-7400

(P-19405)
CAREMARK RX LLC
Also Called: US Family Care
15576 Main St, Hesperia (92345-3482)
PHONE.................760 948-6606
Fax: 760 948-1191
Rochelle Steen, *Principal*
EMP: 50
SALES (corp-wide): 153.2B **Publicly Held**
WEB: www.medpartners.com
SIC: **8011** General & family practice, physician/surgeon
HQ: Caremark Rx, Inc.
    445 Great Circle Rd
    Nashville TN 37228
    615 687-7400

(P-19406)
CAREMARK RX LLC
Also Called: Mullikin Medical Center
800 Douglas Rd, Stockton (95207-3607)
PHONE.................209 957-7050
Fax: 209 957-2623
Susan Schofield, *Principal*
EMP: 50

PRODUCTS & SERVICES SECTION
8011 - Offices & Clinics Of Doctors Of Medicine County (P-19429)

SALES (corp-wide): 153.2B **Publicly Held**
WEB: www.medpartners.com
SIC: **8011** Offices & clinics of medical doctors
HQ: Caremark Rx, Inc.
   445 Great Circle Rd
   Nashville TN 37228
   615 687-7400

(P-19407)
CAREMORE HEALTH PLAN (HQ)
Also Called: Caremore Insurance Services
12900 Park Plaza Dr # 150, Cerritos (90703-9329)
PHONE..................562 622-2950
Toll Free:.................888 -
Leeba R Lessin, *President*
Jason Barker, *President*
John KAO, *President*
Allan Hoops, *CEO*
Vish Sankaran, *COO*
EMP: 93
SALES (est): 46.4MM
SALES (corp-wide): 79.1B **Publicly Held**
WEB: www.caremore.com
SIC: **8011** 6411 Offices & clinics of medical doctors; insurance agents, brokers & service
PA: Anthem, Inc.
   120 Monument Cir Ste 200
   Indianapolis IN 46204
   317 488-6000

(P-19408)
CAREMORE MEDICAL GROUP
420 W Central Ave Ste A, Brea (92821-3001)
PHONE..................714 256-1345
Elsy Ybarra, *Office Mgr*
EMP: 146
SALES (corp-wide): 10.1MM **Privately Held**
SIC: **8011** General & family practice, physician/surgeon
PA: Caremore Medical Group
   12898 Towne Center Dr
   Cerritos CA 90703
   562 741-4557

(P-19409)
CAREONSITE INC
1805 Arnold Dr, Martinez (94553-4182)
PHONE..................562 437-0381
EMP: 70
SALES (corp-wide): 12MM **Privately Held**
SIC: **8011** Occupational & industrial specialist, physician/surgeon
PA: Careonsite, Inc.
   1250 Pacific Ave
   Long Beach CA 90813
   562 437-0831

(P-19410)
CAREONSITE INC (PA)
1250 Pacific Ave, Long Beach (90813-3026)
P.O. Box 16149 (90806-0649)
PHONE..................562 437-0831
Helen Tang, *President*
Brian Tang, *Vice Pres*
Bing Cruz, *Manager*
Jennifer Dorosti, *Manager*
EMP: 50
SALES: 12MM **Privately Held**
SIC: **8011** Occupational & industrial specialist, physician/surgeon

(P-19411)
CASSIDY MEDICAL GROUP INC (PA)
145 Thunder Dr, Vista (92083-6010)
PHONE..................760 630-5487
Fax: 760 630-2515
John Bennett, *President*
Judith Krueger, *Administration*
Nona L Hanson, *Med Doctor*
EMP: 50
SQ FT: 14,495
SALES (est): 6.1MM **Privately Held**
SIC: **8011** General & family practice, physician/surgeon

(P-19412)
CATHOLIC CHARITIES
2625 Zanker Rd Ste 200, San Jose (95134-2130)
PHONE..................408 468-0100
Fax: 408 944-0275
Connie D Hobson, *Principal*
EMP: 50 EST: 2009
SALES (est): 6.3MM **Privately Held**
SIC: **8011** 8661 Offices & clinics of medical doctors; Catholic Church

(P-19413)
CEDARS-SINAI MEDICAL CENTER
Also Called: Cardiac Noninvasive Laboratory
127 S San Vicente Blvd # 3417, Los Angeles (90048-3311)
PHONE..................310 423-3849
Robert J Siegel, *Director*
Miklos Peterfy, *Director*
EMP: 174
SALES (corp-wide): 2.7B **Privately Held**
SIC: **8011** Cardiologist & cardio-vascular specialist
PA: Cedars-Sinai Medical Center
   8700 Beverly Blvd
   West Hollywood CA 90048
   310 423-3277

(P-19414)
CEDARS-SINAI MEDICAL CENTER
8631 W 3rd St Ste 730, Los Angeles (90048-5911)
P.O. Box 48955 (90048-0955)
PHONE..................323 866-8483
Graham Woolf, *Principal*
Nancy Nuechterlein, *Human Res Mgr*
Sandy Lohr, *Purchasing*
Stephen Lee, *Pathologist*
Keith L Black, *Surgeon*
EMP: 5079
SALES (corp-wide): 2.7B **Privately Held**
SIC: **8011** Medical centers
PA: Cedars-Sinai Medical Center
   8700 Beverly Blvd
   West Hollywood CA 90048
   310 423-3277

(P-19415)
CENTER FOR AIDS RESEARCH
Also Called: CARES COMMUNITY HEALTH
1500 21st St, Sacramento (95811-5216)
PHONE..................916 443-3299
Fax: 916 325-1984
Bob Kamrath, *CEO*
Bob Styron, *CFO*
Richard Soohoo, *Treasurer*
James Kelleher, *Vice Pres*
Mark Thomas, *Admin Sec*
EMP: 105
SALES: 23MM **Privately Held**
SIC: **8011** 8299 Offices & clinics of medical doctors; educational services

(P-19416)
CENTER MEDICAL COMPANY
12100 Valley Blvd 109a, El Monte (91732-3100)
P.O. Box 6208 (91734-6208)
PHONE..................626 575-7500
Mohammad Rasekhi, *President*
EMP: 50
SALES (est): 602.9K **Privately Held**
SIC: **8011** Offices & clinics of medical doctors

(P-19417)
CENTRAL ANESTHESIA SERVICE
Also Called: Case Medical Group
3315 Watt Ave, Sacramento (95821-3600)
P.O. Box 660910 (95866-0910)
PHONE..................916 481-6800
Fax: 916 481-1881
David Downs MD, *President*
Shaunda Barry, *Executive*
Claudia Halkyer, *Hum Res Coord*
Judi M Cain, *Anesthesiology*
Bea Kandra, *Anesthesiology*
EMP: 80
SALES (est): 17MM **Privately Held**
WEB: www.casemedgroup.com
SIC: **8011** Group health association

(P-19418)
CENTRAL CALIFORNIA EAR NOSE
Also Called: Ent Facial Surgery Center
1351 E Spruce Ave, Fresno (93720-3342)
PHONE..................559 432-3724
Fax: 559 432-0615
Marvin Beil MD, *Partner*
Allan Evans MD, *Partner*
Brent Lanier MD, *Partner*
Jerry Moore MD, *Partner*
Oscar Tamez MD, *Partner*
EMP: 50
SQ FT: 24,000
SALES (est): 11.7MM **Privately Held**
SIC: **8011** 8049 5999 Eyes, ears, nose & throat specialist: physician/surgeon; audiologist; hearing aids

(P-19419)
CENTRAL CALIFORNIA FACULTY MED (PA)
2625 E Divisadero St, Fresno (93721-1431)
PHONE..................559 453-5200
Fax: 559 453-5233
Karl Van Gundy, *CEO*
Robert A Frediani, *COO*
Randall Stern, *Treasurer*
Dean Tsusui, *Executive*
Joyce Fields-Keene, *Exec Dir*
EMP: 100
SQ FT: 19,053
SALES (est): 56.2MM **Privately Held**
WEB: www.ccfmg.org
SIC: **8011** Offices & clinics of medical doctors

(P-19420)
CENTRAL CARDIOLOGY MED CLINIC
2901 Sillect Ave Ste 100, Bakersfield (93308-6372)
P.O. Box 1139 (93302-1139)
PHONE..................661 395-0000
Fax: 661 323-9326
Brijesh Bahmbi, *Partner*
Peter Nalos MD, *Partner*
William Nyitray MD, *Partner*
Daniel Morales, *Financial Exec*
Brijesh K Bhambi, *Cardiovascular*
EMP: 120 EST: 1974
SALES (est): 25.8MM **Privately Held**
WEB: www.heart24.com
SIC: **8011** Cardiologist & cardio-vascular specialist; medical centers

(P-19421)
CENTRAL VALLEY INDIAN HLTH INC (PA)
2740 Herndon Ave, Clovis (93611-6813)
PHONE..................559 299-2578
Fax: 559 299-0245
Chuck Fowler, *CEO*
Pao Yang, *Admin Asst*
Arthur Hugues, *Software Dev*
Gurpal S Bains, *Finance*
Harjinder K Bar, *Nursing Dir*
EMP: 74 EST: 1974
SQ FT: 14,000
SALES: 15.2MM **Privately Held**
WEB: www.cvih.org
SIC: **8011** 8021 8042 8093 Clinic, operated by physicians; dental clinic; offices & clinics of optometrists; substance abuse clinics (outpatient)

(P-19422)
CENTRE CARE MANAGEMENT CO LLC
Also Called: Centre For Health Care
15611 Pomerado Rd Ste 400, Poway (92064-2437)
PHONE..................858 613-6255
Jerome P Brodkin, *Mng Member*
Michael Barker, *Research*
Diana Joyce, *Financial Analy*
David J Carty,
Carol Cornelius,
EMP: 200 EST: 1997
SALES (est): 10.3MM
SALES (corp-wide): 614.2MM **Privately Held**
SIC: **8011** General & family practice, physician/surgeon

HQ: Arch Health Partners, Inc.
   15611 Pomerado Rd Ste 575
   Poway CA 92064
   858 675-3100

(P-19423)
CENTURY CITY PRIMARY CARE
2080 Century Park E # 1605, Los Angeles (90067-2019)
PHONE..................310 553-3189
Jay S Rudin MD, *Principal*
T Kutay, *Vice Pres*
Billie Loftus, *Office Mgr*
Penny Sue, *Administration*
EMP: 50
SALES (est): 6MM **Privately Held**
SIC: **8011** Internal medicine practitioners

(P-19424)
CEP AMERICA LLC
2100 Powell St Ste 900, Emeryville (94608-1844)
PHONE..................510 350-2691
Theo Koury,
Karen Parker, *Emerg Med Spec*
EMP: 90
SALES (est): 2.8MM **Privately Held**
SIC: **8011** Offices & clinics of medical doctors

(P-19425)
CHADWICK CENTER FOR CHILDREN &
3020 Childrens Way, San Diego (92123-4223)
PHONE..................858 966-5814
Charles Wlison, *Principal*
EMP: 50
SALES (est): 2.7MM **Privately Held**
SIC: **8011** Primary care medical clinic

(P-19426)
CHAPA-DE INDIAN HEALTH (PA)
11670 Atwood Rd, Auburn (95603-9522)
PHONE..................530 887-2800
Fax: 530 887-2849
Lisa Davies, *President*
Sierk Haitsma, *CFO*
Debbie Lopez, *Office Mgr*
Ellen M Aoki, *Med Doctor*
James Nichol, *Med Doctor*
EMP: 85
SQ FT: 65,000
SALES: 21.2MM **Privately Held**
SIC: **8011** 8322 8021 8042 Clinic, operated by physicians; outreach program; multi-service center; dentists' office; orthodontist; offices & clinics of optometrists; dietician

(P-19427)
CHARLIE W SHAEFFER JR MD
Also Called: Eisenhower Desert Crdiolgy Ctr
39000 Bob Hope Dr, Rancho Mirage (92270-3221)
PHONE..................760 346-0642
Charlie Schaeffer MD, *Principal*
EMP: 61
SALES (est): 2.8MM **Privately Held**
SIC: **8011** Offices & clinics of medical doctors

(P-19428)
CHICO IMMDATE CARE MED CTR INC (PA)
376 Vallombrosa Ave, Chico (95926-3900)
PHONE..................530 891-1676
Bradley M Smith, *CEO*
Shelly Martinek, *Physician Asst*
EMP: 50
SQ FT: 4,000
SALES (est): 7.8MM **Privately Held**
SIC: **8011** Offices & clinics of medical doctors

(P-19429)
CHILDRENS ASSOC MEDICAL GROUP
Also Called: James Mathewson MD
3020 Chld Way Mc5004 5004 Mc, San Diego (92123)
PHONE..................858 576-1700
Fax: 858 614-7483
James Mathewson, *Principal*
Nancy Booth, *Office Mgr*

8011 - Offices & Clinics Of Doctors Of Medicine County (P-19430)

Betty Hill, *Office Mgr*
Hyunah E Ahn, *Oncology*
Scott Mubarak, *Nursing Dir*
EMP: 50
SALES (est): 7.8MM **Privately Held**
SIC: 8011 Pediatrician

(P-19430)
CHILDRENS CLINIC SERVING CHL
701 E 28th St Ste 200, Long Beach (90806-2784)
PHONE..................562 264-4638
Fax: 562 933-0415
Elisa A Nicholas, *CEO*
Jina Lee Lawler, *COO*
Maria Y Chandler, *CFO*
Albert P Ocampo, *CFO*
Knut P Thune, *CFO*
EMP: 320
SQ FT: 24,000
SALES: 23.6MM **Privately Held**
SIC: 8011 Clinic, operated by physicians

(P-19431)
CHILDRENS HEALTHCARE CAL
Also Called: Pediatric Cancer Research
455 S Main St, Orange (92868-3835)
P.O. Box 5700 (92863-5700)
PHONE..................714 997-3000
Kimberly Crite, *CEO*
EMP: 1600
SALES (corp-wide): 548.7MM **Privately Held**
SIC: 8011 Pediatrician
PA: Children's Healthcare Of California
   455 S Main St
   Orange CA 92868
   714 997-3000

(P-19432)
CHILDRENS HOSPITAL LOS (PA)
Also Called: Childrens Hosp La Med Group
6430 W Sunset Blvd # 600, Los Angeles (90028-7909)
PHONE..................323 361-2336
Robert Adler, *President*
Phoebe Dinsmore, *COO*
Thomas Keens, *Managing Dir*
Teresa Avila, *Executive Asst*
EMP: 60
SQ FT: 10,000
SALES: 111.8MM **Privately Held**
SIC: 8011 Pediatrician

(P-19433)
CHILDRENS HOSPITAL LOS ANGELES
Also Called: Division of Rheumatology
4650 W Sunset Blvd, Los Angeles (90027-6062)
PHONE..................323 361-2119
Fax: 213 668-7926
Andreas O Reiff, *Principal*
Bracha Shaham, *Rheumtlgy Spec*
EMP: 275
SALES (corp-wide): 891.3MM **Privately Held**
SIC: 8011 Offices & clinics of medical doctors
PA: The Childrens Hospital Los Angeles
   4650 W Sunset Blvd
   Los Angeles CA 90027
   323 660-2450

(P-19434)
CHILDRENS HOSPITAL LOS ANGELES
Also Called: Santa Monica Outpatient Center
1301 20th St Ste 460, Santa Monica (90404-2090)
PHONE..................310 820-8608
EMP: 229
SALES (corp-wide): 891.3MM **Privately Held**
SIC: 8011 Pediatrician
PA: The Childrens Hospital Los Angeles
   4650 W Sunset Blvd
   Los Angeles CA 90027
   323 660-2450

(P-19435)
CHILDRENS SPECIALIST OF SAN D (PA)
Also Called: Childrens Associated Med Group
3030 Chld Way Ste 401, San Diego (92123)
PHONE..................858 576-1700
Fax: 858 278-3989
Michael Segall MD, *President*
Tomi Beck, *Executive Asst*
Yvonne Gagen, *Finance*
Wilma A Robb, *Manager*
EMP: 350
SALES: 283.3K **Privately Held**
SIC: 8011 Offices & clinics of medical doctors

(P-19436)
CHINO MEDICAL GROUP INC
5475 Walnut Ave, Chino (91710-2699)
PHONE..................909 591-6446
Fax: 909 591-1309
J A Lira MD, *President*
Fidel F Pinzon MD, *Vice Pres*
Steven Pulverman, *Vice Pres*
Jeffrey R Unger MD, *Vice Pres*
Valerie Guillen, *Office Mgr*
EMP: 100
SQ FT: 36,000
SALES (est): 15.9MM **Privately Held**
WEB: www.chinomedicalgroup.com
SIC: 8011 8031 Medical centers; offices & clinics of osteopathic physicians

(P-19437)
CHRISTIAN COUNSELING CENTERS
3880 S Bascom Ave Ste 202, San Jose (95124-2675)
PHONE..................408 559-1115
Fax: 408 371-9193
Margeret Greig, *Director*
EMP: 56
SALES (corp-wide): 2MM **Privately Held**
SIC: 8011 Psychiatric clinic
PA: Christian Counseling Centers, Inc
   1161 Cherry St Ste P
   San Carlos CA 94070
   650 570-7273

(P-19438)
CIRRUS HEALTH II LP
Also Called: Laguna Hills Surgery Center
24331 El Toro Rd Ste 150, Laguna Hills (92637-8818)
PHONE..................949 855-0562
Kim Wood, *Principal*
Charles Martin, *Executive*
EMP: 113
SALES (corp-wide): 18.4MM **Privately Held**
WEB: www.cirrushealth.com
SIC: 8011 Offices & clinics of medical doctors
PA: Cirrus Health Ii, L.P.
   2800 E Highway 114 # 300
   Trophy Club TX 76262
   214 217-0100

(P-19439)
CITRUS VLY HLTH PARTNERS INC
Also Called: Queen of The Valley Campus
1115 S Sunset Ave, West Covina (91790-3940)
PHONE..................626 962-4011
Debbie Segaram, *Branch Mgr*
Elvia Foulke, *Manager*
EMP: 376
SALES (corp-wide): 58.1MM **Privately Held**
SIC: 8011 Medical centers
PA: Citrus Valley Health Partners, Inc.
   210 W San Bernardino Rd
   Covina CA 91723
   626 331-7331

(P-19440)
CITY OF HOPE
Also Called: City of Hope Medical Group
209 Fair Oaks Ave, South Pasadena (91030-1814)
PHONE..................626 396-2900
Melinda Lane, *Director*
Tushar Patel, *Administration*
Charlie Zhong, *Research*
Fernando Reynoso, *Engineer*
Patty Cardenas, *Analyst*
EMP: 239
SALES (corp-wide): 1.4B **Privately Held**
SIC: 8011 Offices & clinics of medical doctors
PA: City Of Hope
   1500 E Duarte Blvd
   Duarte CA 91010
   626 256-4673

(P-19441)
CLINICA MEDICA FAMILIAR
517 N Main St Ste 100, Santa Ana (92701-4684)
PHONE..................714 541-0870
Fax: 714 647-9465
Ricardo Limon MD, *President*
Jose Cueto, *Exec Dir*
EMP: 100
SALES (est): 8.9MM **Privately Held**
SIC: 8011 Primary care medical clinic

(P-19442)
CLINICA MSR OSCAR A ROMERO (PA)
123 S Alvarado St, Los Angeles (90057-2201)
PHONE..................213 989-7700
Fax: 213 989-0169
Carlos Antonio H Vaquerano, *President*
Harsh Gupta, *CFO*
Pablo F Lopez, *Treasurer*
Marcello Villagomez, *Vice Pres*
Yvonne Bice, *Exec Dir*
EMP: 52
SALES: 10.4MM **Privately Held**
WEB: www.clinicaromero.com
SIC: 8011 Offices & clinics of medical doctors

(P-19443)
CLINICA POPULAR MEDICAL GROUP
101 S Rossmore Ave, Los Angeles (90004-3736)
PHONE..................213 381-7175
Daniel Berdakin MD, *President*
EMP: 50
SQ FT: 7,000
SALES (est): 1.6MM **Privately Held**
SIC: 8011 General & family practice, physician/surgeon

(P-19444)
CLINICA SAGRADO CORAZON
831 S Harbor Blvd, Anaheim (92805-5157)
PHONE..................714 491-7777
Ivone Alfaro, *Principal*
EMP: 50 **EST:** 2011
SALES (est): 792.2K **Privately Held**
SIC: 8011 Offices & clinics of medical doctors

(P-19445)
CLINICA SALUD DEL VALLE SALNS
24285 Lincoln, Chualar (93925)
PHONE..................831 679-0138
EMP: 85
SALES (corp-wide): 23.4MM **Privately Held**
SIC: 8011 8099 Primary care medical clinic; blood related health services
PA: Clinica De Salud Del Valle De Salinas
   440 Airport Blvd
   Salinas CA 93905
   831 757-8689

(P-19446)
CLINICA SIERRA VISTA (PA)
Also Called: KERN RIVER HEALTH CENTER
1430 Truxtun Ave Ste 400, Bakersfield (93301-5220)
P.O. Box 1559 (93302-1559)
PHONE..................661 635-3050
Fax: 661 869-1503
Matthew Clark, *Ch of Bd*
Stephen W Schilling, *CEO*
Christine Goltz, *COO*
Consuelo E Cantu, *CFO*
Consuelo Contu, *CFO*
EMP: 90 **EST:** 1971
SQ FT: 14,599
SALES: 119.8MM **Privately Held**
WEB: www.clinicasierravista.org
SIC: 8011 Clinic, operated by physicians

(P-19447)
CLINICAS DE SLUD DEL PEBLO INC (PA)
1166 K St, Brawley (92227-2737)
P.O. Box 1279 (92227-1279)
PHONE..................760 344-9951
Fax: 760 344-5840
Yvonne Bell, *CEO*
Gloria Santillan, *CFO*
Elizabeth Arriaga, *Office Mgr*
Veronica Abarca, *Admin Asst*
Felix Leon, *Administration*
EMP: 62 **EST:** 1970
SQ FT: 15,251
SALES: 34.5MM **Privately Held**
WEB: www.clinicasdesalud.com
SIC: 8011 8049 Medical centers; gynecologist; nutrition specialist; dental hygienist

(P-19448)
CLINICAS DE SLUD DEL PEBLO INC
Also Called: Betty Jimenez
900 Main St, Brawley (92227-2630)
PHONE..................760 344-6471
Betty Jimenez, *Branch Mgr*
Anita Cardoza, *Office Mgr*
Saima Khan, *Pediatrics*
Nickolas Aguirre, *Nurse Practr*
Leticia Bustamante, *Nurse Practr*
EMP: 55
SALES (corp-wide): 34.5MM **Privately Held**
WEB: www.clinicasdesalud.com
SIC: 8011 8049 Medical centers; gynecologist; nutrition specialist; dental hygienist
PA: Clinicas De Salud Del Pueblo, Inc.
   1166 K St
   Brawley CA 92227
   760 344-9951

(P-19449)
COLORADO RIVER MEDICAL CENTER
1401 Bailey Ave, Needles (92363-3198)
PHONE..................760 326-4531
Fax: 760 326-2744
Steve Lopez, *CEO*
Jennifer Soto, *Office Mgr*
Ron Chiefo, *CIO*
Charlie Parker, *Info Tech Mgr*
Mike Andrews, *Facilities Mgr*
EMP: 100
SQ FT: 46,000
SALES: 8.6MM **Privately Held**
SIC: 8011 8062 Medical centers; general medical & surgical hospitals

(P-19450)
COMMUNICARE HEALTH CENTERS
2051 John Jones Rd, Davis (95616-9701)
P.O. Box 1260 (95617-1260)
PHONE..................530 758-2060
Fax: 530 758-8490
Robin Affrime, *CEO*
Sherry Cauchois, *CFO*
Laudia Ponce, *Opers Mgr*
Deborah L Woolley, *Nurse Midwife*
EMP: 200 **EST:** 1973
SALES: 21.3MM **Privately Held**
SIC: 8011 Medical centers

(P-19451)
COMMUNITY CARE HEALTH CENTERS
Also Called: Indiana Adhc
5425 Pomona Blvd, Los Angeles (90022-1716)
PHONE..................323 980-4000
Irma Wisenberg, *Branch Mgr*
EMP: 50
SALES (corp-wide): 360.3MM **Privately Held**
WEB: www.altamed.org
SIC: 8011 8322 Gynecologist; adult day care center
PA: Altamed Health Services Corporation
   2040 Camfield Ave
   Commerce CA 90040
   323 725-8751

PRODUCTS & SERVICES SECTION   **8011 - Offices & Clinics Of Doctors Of Medicine County (P-19474)**

(P-19452)
COMMUNITY HEALTH CENTERS (PA)
150 Tejas Pl, Nipomo (93444-9123)
P.O. Box 430 (93444-0430)
PHONE..................805 929-3211
Sharon Smith, *CEO*
Denise Stewart, *COO*
Bob Lotwala, *CFO*
Ronald Castle, *Exec Dir*
Ariston Julian, *Regional Mgr*
EMP: 50
SQ FT: 10,000
SALES (est): 25MM **Privately Held**
SIC: 8011 8021 Medical centers; dental clinic

(P-19453)
COMMUNITY HEALTH GROUP
2420 Fenton St 200, Chula Vista (91914-3516)
PHONE..................619 422-0422
Fax: 619 476-3819
Norma A Diaz, *CEO*
Sharon Francis, *CFO*
William Rice, *CFO*
Julian Santoyo, *CFO*
Victor Gonzalez, *Mng Officer*
EMP: 140
SQ FT: 26,000
SALES: 52.1MM **Privately Held**
WEB: www.communityhealthgroup.com
SIC: 8011 Health maintenance organization

(P-19454)
COMMUNITY HEALTH SYSTEMS INC
Also Called: Moreno Valley Family Hlth Ctr
22675 Alessandro Blvd # 1, Moreno Valley (92553-8551)
PHONE..................951 571-2300
Fax: 951 588-1910
Jack E Johns, *CEO*
Lori Holeman, *COO*
Shelly Farrow, *Ch Nursing Ofcr*
Gerardo Gonzalez, *Admin Asst*
Anthony De Boer, *Info Tech Mgr*
EMP: 130
SALES: 14.1MM **Privately Held**
SIC: 8011 Primary care medical clinic

(P-19455)
COMMUNITY MED GROUP OF RVRSIDE
4444 Magnolia Ave, Riverside (92501-4136)
PHONE..................951 274-3414
Thomas W Jackson, *President*
Prabu U Dhalla MD, *Vice Pres*
Larry G Ding, *Vice Pres*
Christophe Fleming MD, *Vice Pres*
Thomas Jackson MD, *Vice Pres*
EMP: 106
SQ FT: 27,000
SALES (est): 12MM **Privately Held**
WEB: www.comgri.com
SIC: 8011 Offices & clinics of medical doctors

(P-19456)
COMMUNITY MEMORIAL HEALTH SYS
2361 E Vineyard Ave, Oxnard (93036-2102)
PHONE..................805 981-3770
Fax: 805 981-3767
EMP: 52
SALES (corp-wide): 353.7MM **Privately Held**
SIC: 8011 Offices & clinics of medical doctors
PA: Community Memorial Health System
147 N Brent St
Ventura CA 93003
805 652-5011

(P-19457)
COMMUNITY MEMORIAL HEALTH SYS
422 Arneill Rd Ste B, Camarillo (93010-6434)
PHONE..................805 482-1282
John Slaght, *Officer*
Samuel D Small, *Officer*
EMP: 52
SALES (corp-wide): 353.7MM **Privately Held**
SIC: 8011 Gynecologist; obstetrician; general & family practice, physician/surgeon
PA: Community Memorial Health System
147 N Brent St
Ventura CA 93003
805 652-5011

(P-19458)
COMMUNITY ORTHOPEDIC MEDICAL
26401 Crown Valley Pkwy # 101, Mission Viejo (92691-6302)
PHONE..................949 348-4000
Fax: 949 348-7466
Kent Adamson, *President*
Sherri Casillas, *Admin Sec*
Edmund Evangelista, *VP Opers*
Kent Maranga, *Surgeon*
Tiva Hanjan, *Physical Med*
EMP: 63
SALES (est): 10.1MM **Privately Held**
WEB: www.comg.com
SIC: 8011 Orthopedic physician

(P-19459)
CONGRESS MED SURGERY CTR LLC
800 S Raymond Ave, Pasadena (91105-3229)
PHONE..................626 396-8100
Veronica Camarena,
EMP: 100
SALES (est): 995.4K **Privately Held**
SIC: 8011 Ambulatory surgical center

(P-19460)
CONRAD A COX
Also Called: Caremore Medical Group
9040 Telegraph Rd, Downey (90240-2393)
PHONE..................562 927-0033
Fax: 562 622-2056
Conrad A Cox, *Owner*
EMP: 50
SALES (est): 3.3MM **Privately Held**
SIC: 8011 Gastronomist

(P-19461)
COPTIC CLINICS
3803 W Mission Blvd, Pomona (91766-6823)
PHONE..................562 900-2692
Henry Kirolos, *Director*
Bishop Serapion, *Exec Dir*
EMP: 99
SALES (est): 1.7MM **Privately Held**
SIC: 8011 8021 Offices & clinics of medical doctors; specialized dental practitioners

(P-19462)
CORIZON HEALTH INC
1125 Third St, NAPA (94559-3015)
PHONE..................707 253-4384
EMP: 55
SALES (corp-wide): 399.6MM **Privately Held**
SIC: 8011 Dispensery, operated by physicians
PA: Corizon Health, Inc.
103 Powell Ct
Brentwood TN 37027
800 729-0069

(P-19463)
CORIZON HEALTH INC
5325 Broder Blvd, Dublin (94568-3309)
PHONE..................925 551-6500
Nomali Toman, *Principal*
Khin Z Tha, *Med Doctor*
EMP: 105
SALES (corp-wide): 399.6MM **Privately Held**
SIC: 8011 Dispensery, operated by physicians
PA: Corizon Health, Inc.
103 Powell Ct
Brentwood TN 37027
800 729-0069

(P-19464)
COUNTY OF ALAMEDA
Also Called: Alameda, County Medical Center
2060 Fairmont Dr, San Leandro (94578-1001)
PHONE..................510 481-4141
Fax: 510 481-4140
Robert Jones, *Director*
Dalys Wright, *Professor*
Anahita Forati, *Acupuncture*
Satira A Dalton, *Director*
EMP: 220 **Privately Held**
WEB: www.co.alameda.ca.us
SIC: 8011 9431 8361 8093 Psychiatric clinic; mental health agency administration, government; ; residential care; specialty outpatient clinics; psychiatric hospitals
PA: County Of Alameda
1221 Oak St Ste 555
Oakland CA 94612
510 272-6691

(P-19465)
COUNTY OF KERN
Also Called: Admin
1721 Westwind Dr, Bakersfield (93301-3026)
PHONE..................661 868-8360
Carol Bowman, *Principal*
EMP: 50 **Privately Held**
WEB: www.kccfc.org
SIC: 8011 9111 Medical centers; county supervisors' & executives' offices
PA: County Of Kern
1115 Truxtun Ave Rm 505
Bakersfield CA 93301
661 868-3690

(P-19466)
COUNTY OF LOS ANGELES
1212 Pico St, San Fernando (91340-3503)
PHONE..................818 837-6969
Fax: 818 837-6028
Gretchen McGinley, *Principal*
EMP: 123 **Privately Held**
WEB: www.co.la.us
SIC: 8011 9111 Clinic, operated by physicians; executive offices
PA: County Of Los Angeles
500 W Temple St Ste 375
Los Angeles CA 90012
213 974-1101

(P-19467)
COUNTY OF LOS ANGELES
Also Called: L A County Hospital
1000 W Carson St, Torrance (90502-2004)
PHONE..................310 222-4220
EMP: 119 **Privately Held**
SIC: 8011 Medical centers
PA: County Of Los Angeles
500 W Temple St Ste 375
Los Angeles CA 90012
213 974-1101

(P-19468)
COUNTY OF LOS ANGELES
Also Called: Health Services, Dept of
1200 N State St, Los Angeles (90033-1029)
PHONE..................323 226-6221
Fax: 323 226-2290
Vernessa Fountin, *Manager*
Philip Ralls, *Med Doctor*
EMP: 300 **Privately Held**
WEB: www.co.la.ca.us
SIC: 8011 9431 Medical centers;
PA: County Of Los Angeles
500 W Temple St Ste 375
Los Angeles CA 90012
213 974-1101

(P-19469)
COUNTY OF LOS ANGELES
Also Called: Hudson, H Claude Cmplte Hlth
2829 S Grand Ave, Los Angeles (90007-3304)
PHONE..................213 744-3677
Fax: 213 746-1498
Michael Mills, *Administration*
EMP: 300 **Privately Held**
WEB: www.co.la.ca.us
SIC: 8011 9431 8093 Medical centers; administration of public health programs; ; specialty outpatient clinics
PA: County Of Los Angeles
500 W Temple St Ste 375
Los Angeles CA 90012
213 974-1101

(P-19470)
COUNTY OF LOS ANGELES
Also Called: HI Desert Hospital
335 E Avenue I, Lancaster (93535-1916)
PHONE..................661 948-8581
Fax: 661 945-8206
Abueg Isagani, *Owner*
Harry Glenchur, *Research*
EMP: 600 **Privately Held**
WEB: www.co.la.ca.us
SIC: 8011 9431 Offices & clinics of medical doctors; administration of public health programs;
PA: County Of Los Angeles
500 W Temple St Ste 375
Los Angeles CA 90012
213 974-1101

(P-19471)
COUNTY OF LOS ANGELES
Also Called: Health Services, Dept of
3834 S Western Ave, Los Angeles (90062-1104)
PHONE..................323 730-3502
Fax: 323 732-1948
Bernard Wilite, *Administration*
Leon Watts, *Vice Pres*
Sylvia Ivie, *Exec Dir*
Patrick Ryan, *Manager*
EMP: 100 **Privately Held**
WEB: www.co.la.ca.us
SIC: 8011 9431 8031 Medical centers; administration of public health programs; ; offices & clinics of osteopathic physicians
PA: County Of Los Angeles
500 W Temple St Ste 375
Los Angeles CA 90012
213 974-1101

(P-19472)
COUNTY OF LOS ANGELES
Also Called: Health Services, Dept of
1325 Broad Ave, Wilmington (90744-2604)
PHONE..................310 518-8800
Fax: 310 835-2970
Dr Jesus Gutierrez, *Director*
Sandra Wuizar, *Office Mgr*
Karen Dong, *Pharmacist*
EMP: 52 **Privately Held**
WEB: www.co.la.ca.us
SIC: 8011 9431 Offices & clinics of medical doctors; administration of public health programs;
PA: County Of Los Angeles
500 W Temple St Ste 375
Los Angeles CA 90012
213 974-1101

(P-19473)
COUNTY OF LOS ANGELES
Also Called: Los Angeles County
13300 Van Nuys Blvd, Pacoima (91331-3004)
PHONE..................818 896-1903
Fax: 818 834-3961
Miriam Sanchez, *Administration*
EMP: 123
SQ FT: 47,532 **Privately Held**
SIC: 8011 Clinic, operated by physicians
PA: County Of Los Angeles
500 W Temple St Ste 375
Los Angeles CA 90012
213 974-1101

(P-19474)
COUNTY OF LOS ANGELES
Also Called: Mental Health Dept of
1975 Long Beach Blvd, Long Beach (90806-5501)
PHONE..................562 599-9200
Margie Pappas, *Chief*
EMP: 123 **Privately Held**
WEB: www.co.la.ca.us
SIC: 8011 9431 Offices & clinics of medical doctors; administration of public health programs;
PA: County Of Los Angeles
500 W Temple St Ste 375
Los Angeles CA 90012
213 974-1101

8011 - Offices & Clinics Of Doctors Of Medicine County (P-19475)

PRODUDUCTS & SERVICES SECTION

(P-19475)
COUNTY OF LOS ANGELES
Also Called: Health Services, Dept of
1900 Zonal Ave Doc1, Los Angeles (90033-1033)
PHONE.................323 226-6056
Toni Lu, *Manager*
EMP: 150 **Privately Held**
WEB: www.co.la.ca.us
SIC: 8011 9431 Medical centers; administration of public health programs;
PA: County Of Los Angeles
500 W Temple St Ste 375
Los Angeles CA 90012
213 974-1101

(P-19476)
COUNTY OF MONTEREY
Also Called: Alisal Health Center
559 E Alisal St Ste 201, Salinas (93905-2516)
PHONE.................831 769-8800
Fax: 831 422-9312
Len Foster, *Director*
Nina Ryan, *Executive*
Tammy Delconte, *Manager*
EMP: 50 **Privately Held**
WEB: www.montereycountyfarmbureau.org
SIC: 8011 Offices & clinics of medical doctors
PA: County Of Monterey
168 W Alisal St Fl 3
Salinas CA 93901
831 755-5040

(P-19477)
COUNTY OF RIVERSIDE
Also Called: Rubidoux Family Care Center
5256 Mission Blvd, Riverside (92509-4624)
PHONE.................951 955-0840
Koen Brown, *Exec Dir*
Myra Palacios, *Office Mgr*
EMP: 84 **Privately Held**
SIC: 8011 Offices & clinics of medical doctors
PA: County Of Riverside
4080 Lemon St Fl 11
Riverside CA 92501
951 955-1110

(P-19478)
COUNTY OF RIVERSIDE
Also Called: Public Social Services
26520 Cactus Ave, Moreno Valley (92555-3927)
PHONE.................951 486-4000
Fax: 951 486-4635
Donna Matney, *Administration*
Afshin Molkara, *Vice Chairman*
Kim Baumgarten, *Nursing Mgr*
Jill Meyer, *Administration*
Rene Ross, *Planning*
EMP: 84 **Privately Held**
SIC: 8011 9431 Medical centers; mental health agency administration, government;
PA: County Of Riverside
4080 Lemon St Fl 11
Riverside CA 92501
951 955-1110

(P-19479)
COUNTY OF RIVERSIDE
Also Called: Community Health Agency
7140 Indiana Ave, Riverside (92504-4544)
PHONE.................951 358-6000
Ibrahim Sumarli, *Med Doctor*
Nomie Atostol, *Manager*
EMP: 84
SQ FT: 1,276 **Privately Held**
SIC: 8011 9431 Clinic, operated by physicians; administration of public health programs;
PA: County Of Riverside
4080 Lemon St Fl 11
Riverside CA 92501
951 955-1110

(P-19480)
COUNTY OF RIVERSIDE
Also Called: Community Health Agency
26520 Cactus Ave, Moreno Valley (92555-3927)
PHONE.................951 486-4000
Fax: 951 486-6747
Jim Watkins, *Principal*

Mark Thomas, *Vice Chairman*
Larry Hinojos, *CFO*
Carol Young, *Admin Sec*
Larry Hinjos, *Controller*
EMP: 300 **Privately Held**
SIC: 8011 9431 Medical centers; public health agency administration, government
PA: County Of Riverside
4080 Lemon St Fl 11
Riverside CA 92501
951 955-1110

(P-19481)
COUNTY OF RIVERSIDE
Also Called: Indio Family Care Center
47923 Oasis St Ste A, Indio (92201-9788)
PHONE.................760 863-8283
Fax: 760 863-8366
Koen Brown, *Exec Dir*
EMP: 84 **Privately Held**
SIC: 8011 Clinic, operated by physicians
PA: County Of Riverside
4080 Lemon St Fl 11
Riverside CA 92501
951 955-1110

(P-19482)
CRIPTS HEALTH CARE
10666 N Torrey Pines Rd, La Jolla (92037-1027)
PHONE.................858 554-8646
Fax: 858 554-6271
Hubert Greenway MD, *Director*
EMP: 50
SALES (est): 914.7K **Privately Held**
SIC: 8011 Offices & clinics of medical doctors

(P-19483)
CYPRESS CTR FOR FMLY MEDICINE
10601 Walker St Ste 250, Cypress (90630-4733)
PHONE.................562 799-4801
Franklin Lowe, *President*
Scott Brunner, *Vice Pres*
Sharon Cooper, *Office Mgr*
Bethany Gray, *Med Doctor*
Steven Maier, *Med Doctor*
EMP: 90
SQ FT: 4,200
SALES (est): 6.1MM **Privately Held**
SIC: 8011 Primary care medical clinic; general & family practice, physician/surgeon

(P-19484)
CYPRESS HALTHCARE PARTNERS LLC (PA)
100 Wilson Rd Ste 100, Monterey (93940-7885)
PHONE.................831 649-1000
Michael K McMillan,
Dan Von Forell, *Analyst*
Siomara Barajas, *Accountant*
Gustavo A Diaz, *Emerg Med Spec*
William Hines,
EMP: 50
SQ FT: 8,500
SALES (est): 21.7MM **Privately Held**
WEB: www.doctorsonduty.com
SIC: 8011 Offices & clinics of medical doctors

(P-19485)
DANIEL O MONGIANO MD A PR
Also Called: AV Occupational Medicine
42220 10th St W Ste 109, Lancaster (93534-7075)
PHONE.................661 951-9195
Daniel Mongiano, *President*
Belle Jarin, *Office Mgr*
Kimberly D Lear, *Radiology*
Janet Medina, *Assistant*
Imelda Rodriguez, *Assistant*
EMP: 50
SALES (est): 3.7MM **Privately Held**
WEB: www.avoccmed.com
SIC: 8011 Offices & clinics of medical doctors

(P-19486)
DAVID CIVALIER MD INC
Also Called: Redding Medical Group
2510 Airpark Dr Ste 104, Redding (96001-2461)
PHONE.................530 244-4034

David Civalier MD, *President*
EMP: 50
SALES (est): 4.1MM **Privately Held**
SIC: 8011 General & family practice, physician/surgeon

(P-19487)
DAVIS COMMUNITY CLINIC (PA)
Also Called: Davis Cmnty Clnic Dntl Program
2040 Sutter Pl, Davis (95616-6201)
P.O. Box 1260 (95617-1260)
PHONE.................530 758-2060
Sherry Cauchois, *Exec Dir*
EMP: 100
SQ FT: 5,000
SALES (est): 5.1MM **Privately Held**
SIC: 8011 Clinic, operated by physicians

(P-19488)
DEL PUERTO HEALTH CARE DST
Also Called: Del Puerto Health Center
875 E St, Patterson (95363-2670)
P.O. Box 187 (95363-0187)
PHONE.................209 892-9100
Fax: 209 892-3755
Margo Arnold, *Administration*
Yumi Edwards, *Admin Asst*
Ursula Schroyer, *Human Res Dir*
EMP: 55
SQ FT: 25,000
SALES (est): 10.4MM **Privately Held**
SIC: 8011 Medical centers

(P-19489)
DESERT CARDIOLOGY CONSULTANTS
Also Called: Desert Cardiology Cons Med G
39000 Bob Hope Dr Ste W30, Rancho Mirage (92270-3221)
PHONE.................760 346-0642
Fax: 760 340-4874
Keenan F Barber MD, *Vice Pres*
Barry Hackshaw, *President*
Merle R Bolton, *Treasurer*
John Nelson, *Officer*
Laura Allen, *Executive Asst*
EMP: 70
SALES (est): 7.8MM **Privately Held**
WEB: www.desertcard.com
SIC: 8011 Internal medicine practitioners; cardiologist & cardio-vascular specialist; surgeon

(P-19490)
DESERT MEDICAL GROUP INC (PA)
Also Called: Desert Oasis Healthcare
275 N El Cielo Rd Ste C, Palm Springs (92262-6972)
PHONE.................760 323-8657
Fax: 760 323-2742
Richard E Merkin MD, *President*
Joe Adams, *Office Mgr*
Irma Ibarra, *Office Mgr*
Scott A Kohnert, *Technology*
Edward Ruiz, *Family Practiti*
EMP: 240
SQ FT: 13,000
SALES (est): 31.3MM **Privately Held**
WEB: www.oasisipa.com
SIC: 8011 General & family practice, physician/surgeon; freestanding emergency medical center

(P-19491)
DESERT MEDICAL GROUP INC
Also Called: Oasis IPA
275 N El Cielo Rd Ste C, Palm Springs (92262-6972)
PHONE.................760 323-8657
Tammy Torres, *Manager*
EMP: 250
SALES (corp-wide): 31.3MM **Privately Held**
WEB: www.oasisipa.com
SIC: 8011 General & family practice, physician/surgeon
PA: Desert Medical Group, Inc.
275 N El Cielo Rd Ste C
Palm Springs CA 92262
760 323-8657

(P-19492)
DESERT ORTHOPDC CENTER A MDCL (PA)
39000 Bob Hope Dr W301, Rancho Mirage (92270-3221)
PHONE.................760 568-2684
Fax: 760 779-7387
Ronald Lamb MD, *President*
Amir Tahernia,
Robert Murphy MD, *Ch of Bd*
Stephen O Connell MD, *CFO*
Jamie Salas, *Officer*
EMP: 78
SQ FT: 23,000
SALES (est): 10.8MM **Privately Held**
SIC: 8011 Orthopedic physician

(P-19493)
DESERT VALLEY MED GROUP INC
12401 Hesperia Rd Ste 9, Victorville (92395-5844)
PHONE.................760 245-2474
Paula Perez, *Manager*
Shrihari Somu, *Info Tech Mgr*
EMP: 68
SALES (corp-wide): 42.7MM **Privately Held**
SIC: 8011 Orthopedic physician
PA: Desert Valley Medical Group, Inc.
16850 Bear Valley Rd
Victorville CA 92395
760 241-8000

(P-19494)
DESERT VALLEY MED GROUP INC (PA)
16850 Bear Valley Rd, Victorville (92395-5794)
PHONE.................760 241-8000
Fax: 760 241-0363
Prem Reddy MD, *CEO*
Lex Reddy, *President*
M Mansukhani, *CFO*
Ginger Buddington, *Vice Pres*
Deirde Lebs, *General Mgr*
EMP: 300
SQ FT: 15,000
SALES (est): 42.7MM **Privately Held**
WEB: www.dvmc.com
SIC: 8011 Physicians' office, including specialists

(P-19495)
DIAGNOSTIC AND INTERVENTIO
13160 Mindanao Way # 150, Marina Del Rey (90292-6358)
PHONE.................310 574-0400
Fax: 310 854-3820
Robert S Bray Jr, *President*
Keren Reiter, *COO*
Gloria Balsley, *Admin Asst*
Peter Drasnin, *Manager*
EMP: 100
SALES: 35MM **Privately Held**
SIC: 8011 Surgeon

(P-19496)
DIGNITY HEALTH
1650 Creekside Dr, Folsom (95630-3400)
PHONE.................916 983-7400
Karl L Silberstein, *Manager*
Amy Mantell, *VP Human Res*
EMP: 193
SALES (corp-wide): 7.1B **Privately Held**
WEB: www.chw.edu
SIC: 8011 Clinic, operated by physicians
PA: Dignity Health
185 Berry St Ste 300
San Francisco CA 94107
415 438-5500

(P-19497)
DIGNITY HEALTH
3400 Data Dr, Rancho Cordova (95670-7956)
PHONE.................916 851-2153
Rick Canning, *Principal*
Marian Bell-Holmes, *Human Res Dir*
David Schnitzer, *Human Resources*
Jill Dryer, *Corp Comm Staff*
Kelley C Evans, *Counsel*
EMP: 193

PRODUCTS & SERVICES SECTION
8011 - Offices & Clinics Of Doctors Of Medicine County (P-19520)

SALES (corp-wide): 7.1B **Privately Held**
WEB: www.chw.edu
SIC: **8011** Offices & clinics of medical doctors
PA: Dignity Health
   185 Berry St Ste 300
   San Francisco CA 94107
   415 438-5500

(P-19498)
DIGNITY HEALTH
8120 Timberlake Way # 201, Sacramento (95823-5412)
PHONE..................916 667-0000
Daniel Yuen, *Principal*
EMP: 193
SALES (corp-wide): 7.1B **Privately Held**
WEB: www.chw.edu
SIC: **8011** Offices & clinics of medical doctors
PA: Dignity Health
   185 Berry St Ste 300
   San Francisco CA 94107
   415 438-5500

(P-19499)
DIGNITY HEALTH
Also Called: Mercy Medical Center Redding
2175 Rosaline Ave Ste A, Redding (96001-2549)
PHONE..................530 225-6345
Scott Foster, *Branch Mgr*
Steve Hosler, *Vice Pres*
Henry Niessink, *Info Tech Dir*
Mark Mitchell, *Prgrmr*
Steve Buhler, *Med Doctor*
EMP: 193
SALES (corp-wide): 7.1B **Privately Held**
SIC: **8011** Medical centers
PA: Dignity Health
   185 Berry St Ste 300
   San Francisco CA 94107
   415 438-5500

(P-19500)
DIGNITY HEALTH
20 N Cottonwood St, Woodland (95695-2585)
PHONE..................530 666-8828
Dawn M Purkey, *Branch Mgr*
Tim Brown, *Info Tech Dir*
Salil Kharat, *Info Tech Dir*
Henry Kano, *Med Doctor*
Eric Mitchel, *Med Doctor*
EMP: 187
SALES (corp-wide): 7.1B **Privately Held**
SIC: **8011** Medical centers
PA: Dignity Health
   185 Berry St Ste 300
   San Francisco CA 94107
   415 438-5500

(P-19501)
DIGNITY HEALTH
1555 Soquel Dr, Santa Cruz (95065-1705)
PHONE..................831 462-7700
Nanette Mickiewicz, *Principal*
Donna Franks, *Admin Asst*
Rita Dean, *Pastor Care Dir*
Camille Clark,
EMP: 1500
SALES (corp-wide): 7.1B **Privately Held**
WEB: www.chw.edu
SIC: **8011** Medical centers
PA: Dignity Health
   185 Berry St Ste 300
   San Francisco CA 94107
   415 438-5500

(P-19502)
DIGNITY HEALTH
Also Called: Mark Twain St Josephs Hospital
768 Mountain Ranch Rd, San Andreas (95249-9707)
PHONE..................209 754-3521
Narlene Cain, *Admin Sec*
Denise Meyer, *Admin Asst*
Robert Pajaro, *Supervisor*
EMP: 193
SALES (corp-wide): 7.1B **Privately Held**
WEB: www.chw.edu
SIC: **8011** Medical centers
PA: Dignity Health
   185 Berry St Ste 300
   San Francisco CA 94107
   415 438-5500

(P-19503)
DIGNITY HEALTH
Also Called: Methodist Hospital Sacramento
7500 Hospital Dr, Sacramento (95823-5403)
PHONE..................916 423-5940
William J Hunt, *Principal*
Robert Morrison, *General Mgr*
Randy Young, *Info Tech Dir*
Steve Hern, *Engineer*
Anita Kennedy, *VP Human Res*
EMP: 193
SALES (corp-wide): 7.1B **Privately Held**
WEB: www.chw.edu
SIC: **8011** Medical centers
PA: Dignity Health
   185 Berry St Ste 300
   San Francisco CA 94107
   415 438-5500

(P-19504)
DIGNITY HEALTH
Also Called: Emergency Physicians Med Group
8350 Auburn Blvd Ste 200, Citrus Heights (95610-0396)
PHONE..................916 536-2420
Art B Wong MD, *Branch Mgr*
EMP: 90
SALES (corp-wide): 7.1B **Privately Held**
WEB: www.chw.edu
SIC: **8011** Offices & clinics of medical doctors
PA: Dignity Health
   185 Berry St Ste 300
   San Francisco CA 94107
   415 438-5500

(P-19505)
DISCOVERY PRACTICE MANAGEMENT
Also Called: Center For Discovery
4136 Ann Arbor Rd, Lakewood (90712-3817)
PHONE..................562 425-6404
Craig M Brown, *President*
Stacy Rusu, *Admin Asst*
Adrianne Altman, *Opers Spvr*
Jennifer Gorman, *Opers Staff*
Heather Truschel, *Psychologist*
EMP: 50
SQ FT: 2,500
SALES (est): 2.2MM **Privately Held**
SIC: **8011** General & family practice, physician/surgeon

(P-19506)
DOCTORS COMPANY
185 Greenwood Rd, NAPA (94558-7540)
PHONE..................707 226-0289
M Puebla, *Owner*
Jeffrey Donaldson, *Vice Pres*
Alice Chen, *Exec Dir*
EMP: 90 EST: 2014
SALES (est): 28.2MM **Privately Held**
SIC: **8011** Offices & clinics of medical doctors

(P-19507)
DOS PALOS MEMORIAL HOSP INC
Also Called: Dos Palos Mem Rur Hlth Clinic
2118 Marguerite St, Dos Palos (93620-2339)
PHONE..................209 392-6121
Fax: 209 392-8872
Margy Barrett, *CEO*
Melinda Vincent, *Director*
Dewayne Jones, *Manager*
Betty H Mitchell, *Agent*
EMP: 60
SQ FT: 16,000
SALES (est): 2.7MM **Privately Held**
SIC: **8011** 8051 Primary care medical clinic; skilled nursing care facilities

(P-19508)
DOUGLAS W JACKSON MD
2760 Atlantic Ave, Long Beach (90806-2755)
PHONE..................562 424-6666
Douglas W Jackson MD, *Owner*
EMP: 60

SALES (est): 817.8K **Privately Held**
SIC: **8011** General & family practice, physician/surgeon

(P-19509)
DRUMMOND MEDICAL GROUP INC
Also Called: Indian Wells Vly Surgery Ctr
900 N Heritage Dr Ste A, Ridgecrest (93555-3196)
PHONE..................760 446-4571
Fax: 760 446-0289
Douglas E Roberts Jr, *President*
Gerry Rodman, *Admin Asst*
EMP: 120 EST: 1958
SQ FT: 30,000
SALES (est): 6.8MM **Privately Held**
WEB: www.drummondmedical.com
SIC: **8011** General & family practice, physician/surgeon

(P-19510)
EBSC LP
Also Called: Surgery Center of Health South
3875 Telegraph Ave, Oakland (94609-2428)
PHONE..................510 547-2244
Fax: 510 547-6637
Judy Rich, *Administration*
EMP: 65
SQ FT: 12,500
SALES (est): 8.7MM **Privately Held**
SIC: **8011** Ambulatory surgical center

(P-19511)
EDEN LABS MED GROUP INC
20103 Lake Chabot Rd, Castro Valley (94546-5305)
PHONE..................510 537-1234
Fax: 510 537-2027
John Carney, *President*
Katherine Thomas, *Admin Sec*
Sharon Daspit, *Research*
David King, *Physician Asst*
EMP: 50
SQ FT: 9,000
SALES (est): 3.7MM **Privately Held**
SIC: **8011** Pathologist

(P-19512)
EDWARDS LIFESCIENCES LLC (HQ)
1 Edwards Way, Irvine (92614-5688)
PHONE..................949 250-2500
Michael A Mussallem, *CEO*
Huimin Wang MD, *President*
Dennis Popovic, *Treasurer*
Thomas Abate, *Vice Pres*
Anita Bessler, *Vice Pres*
▲ EMP: 1700
SALES (est): 369.7MM
SALES (corp-wide): 2.4B **Publicly Held**
SIC: **8011** Cardiologist & cardio-vascular specialist
PA: Edwards Lifesciences Corp
   1 Edwards Way
   Irvine CA 92614
   949 250-2500

(P-19513)
ELDORADO COMMUNITY SERVICE CTR
335 E Manchester Blvd, Inglewood (90301-1814)
PHONE..................424 227-7971
Stan Sharma, *Principal*
Ararat Alex Yarijanian, *Marketing Staff*
EMP: 99
SALES (est): 996.8K **Privately Held**
SIC: **8011** 8049 Physicians' office, including specialists; clinical psychologist

(P-19514)
ELICA HEALTH CENTERS
3701 J St Ste 201, Sacramento (95816-5542)
PHONE..................916 454-2345
Tamara Miroshniehenko, *Branch Mgr*
Tracy Hernandez, *Admin Asst*
Roy Wilson, *Technology*
Charles Wiesen, *Accountant*
Kseniya Golovchenko,
EMP: 80

SALES (corp-wide): 13.6MM **Privately Held**
SIC: **8011** Offices & clinics of medical doctors
PA: Elica Health Centers
   1860 Howe Ave
   Sacramento CA 95825
   916 569-8484

(P-19515)
ENLOE MEDICAL CENTER
Also Called: Payroll Dept.
175 W 5th Ave, Chico (95926)
PHONE..................530 332-7522
Linda Irvine, *Branch Mgr*
EMP: 52
SALES (corp-wide): 505.9MM **Privately Held**
SIC: **8011** Medical centers
PA: Enloe Medical Center
   1531 Esplanade
   Chico CA 95926
   530 332-7300

(P-19516)
ENLOE MEDICAL CENTER
Also Called: Children's Health Center
277 Cohasset Rd, Chico (95926-2242)
PHONE..................530 332-6000
Fax: 530 893-6864
Dorothy Chinnock, *Branch Mgr*
Deanna J McConnell, *Nurse Practr*
EMP: 65
SALES (corp-wide): 505.9MM **Privately Held**
SIC: **8011** Clinic, operated by physicians
PA: Enloe Medical Center
   1531 Esplanade
   Chico CA 95926
   530 332-7300

(P-19517)
ERIC D FELDMAN MD INC
Also Called: Rehab Associates
2760 Atlantic Ave, Long Beach (90806-2755)
PHONE..................562 424-6666
Eric D Feldman MD, *President*
EMP: 50
SALES (est): 1.4MM **Privately Held**
SIC: **8011** General & family practice, physician/surgeon

(P-19518)
EYE MEDICAL CLINIC FRESNO INC
Also Called: Eye Medical Center of Fresno
1360 E Herndon Ave # 301, Fresno (93720-3326)
PHONE..................559 486-5000
Fax: 559 439-7854
Richard H Whitten Jr, *CEO*
George Bertolucci M, *President*
Carolyn Sakauye, *Bd of Directors*
Juanita Esparza, *Office Mgr*
Carmen Mares, *Office Mgr*
EMP: 55
SQ FT: 12,000
SALES (est): 6.8MM **Privately Held**
SIC: **8011** 8042 Ophthalmologist; offices & clinics of optometrists

(P-19519)
EYE Q VISION CARE (PA)
7075 N Sharon Ave, Fresno (93720-3329)
PHONE..................559 486-2000
Fax: 559 256-8504
Scott Bridgeman, *CEO*
Sarah Jaimenez, *Administration*
Rick Holt, *Mktg Dir*
Cody M Pearson, *Ophthalmology*
Thomas Corbett, *Med Doctor*
EMP: 175
SALES (est): 14.5MM **Privately Held**
SIC: **8011** 8042 8031 Offices & clinics of medical doctors; offices & clinics of optometrists; offices & clinics of osteopathic physicians

(P-19520)
FACULTY PHYSCANS SRGEONS LLUSM
11370 Anderson St, Loma Linda (92354-3450)
P.O. Box 945 (92354-0945)
PHONE..................909 558-4000

8011 - Offices & Clinics Of Doctors Of Medicine County (P-19521)

Ricardo Peverini, *President*
EMP: 99
SALES (est): 4.2MM **Privately Held**
SIC: 8011 Offices & clinics of medical doctors

(P-19521)
FAMILY HEALTHCARE NETWORK
33025 159th Rd, Ivanhoe (93235)
PHONE.................559 798-1877
Fax: 559 798-1058
Yterry Abbott, *Manager*
Elizabeth Padilla, *Manager*
EMP: 103
SALES (corp-wide): 82.9MM **Privately Held**
SIC: 8011 8021 Physicians' office, including specialists; offices & clinics of dentists
PA: Family Healthcare Network
305 E Center Ave
Visalia CA 93291
559 737-4700

(P-19522)
FAMILY HLTH CTRS SAN DIEGO INC
1845 Logan Ave, San Diego (92113-2111)
PHONE.................619 515-2526
Fax: 619 239-5178
Gracie Duran, *Branch Mgr*
Mary A Acevedo, *Obstetrician*
Tracie T Davis, *Obstetrician*
Lisa S Lipschitz, *Obstetrician*
Chad Newell, *Allrgy & Immnlg*
EMP: 103
SALES (corp-wide): 125.5MM **Privately Held**
SIC: 8011 Clinic, operated by physicians
PA: Family Health Centers Of San Diego, Inc.
823 Gateway Center Way
San Diego CA 92102
619 515-2303

(P-19523)
FAMILY HLTH CTRS SAN DIEGO INC
2391 Island Ave, San Diego (92102-2941)
PHONE.................619 515-2435
Fax: 619 233-2621
Martha Barba, *Manager*
EMP: 103
SALES (corp-wide): 125.5MM **Privately Held**
SIC: 8011 Clinic, operated by physicians
PA: Family Health Centers Of San Diego, Inc.
823 Gateway Center Way
San Diego CA 92102
619 515-2303

(P-19524)
FAMILY HLTH CTRS SAN DIEGO INC
Also Called: Family Health Center San Diego
8788 Jamacha Rd, Spring Valley (91977-4035)
PHONE.................619 515-2555
Scott Martin, *Office Mgr*
Juanita Salazar, *Pediatrics*
Pat Young, *Nursing Dir*
EMP: 83
SQ FT: 10,970
SALES (corp-wide): 125.5MM **Privately Held**
SIC: 8011 Offices & clinics of medical doctors
PA: Family Health Centers Of San Diego, Inc.
823 Gateway Center Way
San Diego CA 92102
619 515-2303

(P-19525)
FAMILY PLG ASSOC MED GROUP (PA)
3050 E Airport Way, Long Beach (90806-2404)
PHONE.................213 738-7283
Edward C Allred MD, *Principal*
Bob Kreymer, *Info Tech Mgr*
Toni Sloan, *Manager*
EMP: 52
SQ FT: 14,000
SALES (est): 25.6MM **Privately Held**
WEB: www.fpamg.net
SIC: 8011 Clinic, operated by physicians

(P-19526)
FERTILITY & REPRODUCTIVE
Also Called: F R H I
2581 Samaritan Dr Ste 302, San Jose (95124-4112)
PHONE.................408 358-2500
Fax: 408 356-8954
G D Adamson MD, *Director*
Tina Zamora, *VP Mktg*
EMP: 60
SALES (est): 4.3MM
SALES (corp-wide): 11B **Privately Held**
SIC: 8011 Fertility specialist, physician
HQ: Palo Alto Medical Foundation For Health Care, Research And Education (Inc)
795 El Camino Real
Palo Alto CA 94301
650 321-4121

(P-19527)
FRANK D YELIAN MD PC
Also Called: Life Ivf Center
3500 Barranca Pkwy # 300, Irvine (92606-8232)
PHONE.................949 788-1133
EMP: 50 EST: 2010
SALES (est): 8MM **Privately Held**
SIC: 8011 Fertility specialist, physician

(P-19528)
FRED FINCH YOUTH CENTER
3434 Grove St, Lemon Grove (91945-1812)
PHONE.................619 797-1090
Kory Madison, *Branch Mgr*
EMP: 64
SALES (corp-wide): 29.8MM **Privately Held**
SIC: 8011 8211 Psychiatric clinic; private special education school
PA: Fred Finch Youth Center
3800 Coolidge Ave
Oakland CA 94602
510 773-6669

(P-19529)
FREEMONT RIDEOUT HEALTH GROUP
989 Plumas St, Yuba City (95991-4012)
PHONE.................530 751-4000
Fax: 530 751-4226
Kevin Woodward, *Principal*
Cresha Moreland, *Vice Pres*
Tresha Moreland, *VP Human Res*
EMP: 62
SALES (corp-wide): 28.9MM **Privately Held**
SIC: 8011 Medical centers
PA: Freemont Rideout Health Group
989 Plumas St
Yuba City CA 95991
530 751-4010

(P-19530)
FREMONT AMBLTORY SRGERY CTR LP
Also Called: Fremont Surgery Center
39350 Civic Center Dr, Fremont (94538-2343)
PHONE.................510 456-4600
John Mazoros, *General Ptnr*
Ruchelle Cartilla, *Manager*
EMP: 80
SQ FT: 19,000
SALES (est): 13.1MM **Privately Held**
WEB: www.fremontsurgerycenter.com
SIC: 8011 Ambulatory surgical center

(P-19531)
FRIEDMAN PROFESSIONAL MGT CO
Also Called: Post Surgical Recovery Center
17752 Beach Blvd Side, Huntington Beach (92647-6838)
PHONE.................714 842-1426
Fax: 714 847-1503
Kelly Trackman, *President*
Neil Friedman MD, *President*
Madeline Tinkler, *Corp Secy*
Jo Ann Friedman, *Vice Pres*
EMP: 70
SQ FT: 35,500
SALES (est): 4.1MM **Privately Held**
SIC: 8011 Clinic, operated by physicians

(P-19532)
FRITCH EYE CARE MEDICAL CENTER
9000 Ming Ave Ste L2, Bakersfield (93311-1324)
PHONE.................661 665-6020
Fax: 661 665-8820
Donald Bradley, *Partner*
Charles D Fritch, *Partner*
H Mohammadi, *Partner*
EMP: 85
SALES (est): 2.1MM
SALES (corp-wide): 5.8MM **Privately Held**
WEB: www.fritcheyecare.com
SIC: 8011 Eyes, ears, nose & throat specialist: physician/surgeon
PA: Charles D Fritch Md Inc
8501 Brimhall Rd Ste 402
Bakersfield CA 93312
661 665-2020

(P-19533)
GARY LASK
Also Called: U C L A Dermatology
200 Ucla Medical Plz 4, Los Angeles (90095-8344)
PHONE.................310 825-0631
Fax: 310 206-0265
Gary Lask, *Principal*
Bruce Ferrell, *Med Doctor*
Stephanie Smooke, *Med Doctor*
James Bradley, *Senior Mgr*
EMP: 60
SALES (est): 3.4MM **Privately Held**
SIC: 8011 Offices & clinics of medical doctors

(P-19534)
GASTROENTEROLOGY DIVISION
Also Called: San Francisco General Hospital
1001 Potrero Ave Ste 1e21, San Francisco (94110-3518)
PHONE.................415 206-8823
Fax: 415 206-3291
Amy Akbarian, *Administration*
EMP: 50
SALES (est): 33.7MM **Privately Held**
SIC: 8011 Gastronomist

(P-19535)
GEORGE M RAJACICH MD PC
Also Called: Valley Eye Center Group
14914 Sherman Way, Van Nuys (91405-2113)
PHONE.................818 787-2020
George M Rajacich MD, *President*
Dorcas Fikejs, *Office Mgr*
Doreen Fazio-Schwartz, *Surgeon*
Hetty Y Kim,
Rajbir Singh, *Ophthalmic Tech*
EMP: 50
SQ FT: 12,000
SALES (est): 7.2MM **Privately Held**
SIC: 8011 Ophthalmologist

(P-19536)
GLENDALE EYE MEDICAL GROUP
607 N Central Ave Ste 105, Glendale (91203-1851)
PHONE.................818 956-1010
James M Mc Caffery MD, *President*
EMP: 80
SQ FT: 11,000
SALES (est): 4.9MM **Privately Held**
SIC: 8011 Ophthalmologist

(P-19537)
GOLDEN RAIN FOUNDATION
1661 Golden Rain Rd, Seal Beach (90740-4999)
P.O. Box 2685 (90740-1685)
PHONE.................562 493-9581
EMP: 138
SALES (corp-wide): 15MM **Privately Held**
SIC: 8011 Geriatric specialist, physician/surgeon
PA: Rain Golden Foundation
13531 Saint Andrews Dr
Seal Beach CA 90740
562 431-6586

(P-19538)
GOLDEN VALLEY HEALTH CENTERS
1717 Las Vegas St, Modesto (95358-5500)
PHONE.................209 556-5040
Fax: 209 576-4494
Michael Schiffler, *Principal*
Maria Barajas, *Office Mgr*
Maita B Zerda, *Pediatrics*
Delia Y Hernandez, *Physician Asst*
Rachel Balerio, *Manager*
EMP: 69
SALES (corp-wide): 99.7MM **Privately Held**
SIC: 8011 Medical centers
PA: Golden Valley Health Centers
737 W Childs Ave
Merced CA 95341
209 383-1848

(P-19539)
GOLDEN VALLEY HEALTH CENTERS
727 W Childs Ave, Merced (95341-6805)
PHONE.................209 383-7441
Jessie Portillo, *Vice Pres*
Bruce E Atkinson, *Chiropractor*
Maria Obispo, *Nurse Practr*
Katheryn Reid, *Nurse Practr*
EMP: 139
SALES (corp-wide): 99.7MM **Privately Held**
SIC: 8011 Offices & clinics of medical doctors
PA: Golden Valley Health Centers
737 W Childs Ave
Merced CA 95341
209 383-1848

(P-19540)
GOOD SAMARITAN HOSPITAL AUX
1225 Wilshire Blvd, Los Angeles (90017-1901)
PHONE.................213 977-2121
Andrew Leeka, *CEO*
Claus Von Zychlin, *COO*
Donna Nienaber, *Vice Pres*
Mike Gombar, *Radiology Dir*
Laura Norman, *Admin Sec*
EMP: 1500
SALES: 309.6MM **Privately Held**
SIC: 8011 Medical centers

(P-19541)
GOODMAN USA INC
605 W California Ave, Sunnyvale (94086-4831)
PHONE.................408 329-5400
Kiminori Toda, *President*
Vivian Chen, *Finance Dir*
EMP: 66
SALES (est): 1.9MM **Privately Held**
SIC: 8011 Offices & clinics of medical doctors

(P-19542)
GRAYBILL MEDICAL GROUP INC (PA)
225 E 2nd Ave, Escondido (92025-4249)
PHONE.................866 228-2243
Fax: 760 737-7324
Floyd Farley, *CEO*
Marvin V Beddoe, *President*
David Borecky, *CEO*
George A Pleitez, *Vice Pres*
Jackie Craw, *Executive*
EMP: 180
SALES (est): 40.6MM **Privately Held**
SIC: 8011 General & family practice, physician/surgeon

(P-19543)
GROSSMONT FAMILY MEDICAL GROUP
5525 Grossmont Center Dr # 200, La Mesa (91942-3009)
P.O. Box 9012 (91944-9012)
PHONE.................619 644-6500
James Amberg, *President*

Marty Livanos, *Executive*
Carrie Cardenas, *Internal Med*
Rita Farris, *Nurse Practr*
Brad Kesling, *Director*
EMP: 50
SALES (est): 6MM **Privately Held**
WEB: www.gfmg.net
SIC: 8011 Clinic, operated by physicians; general & family practice, physician/surgeon

(P-19544)
HAIDER SPINE CTR MED GROUP INC
6276 River Crest Dr Ste A, Riverside (92507-0754)
PHONE...................951 413-0200
Thomas Haider, *President*
David Siambanes, *Principal*
Todd Ackerman, *Administration*
EMP: 50
SALES (est): 5MM **Privately Held**
SIC: 8011 Surgeon

(P-19545)
HEALTH NET CMNTY SOLUTIONS INC
11971 Foundation Pl, Gold River (95670-4502)
PHONE...................800 675-6110
Woodrow Fennell, *Principal*
EMP: 137 EST: 2013
SALES (est): 1.4MM
SALES (corp-wide): 22.7B **Publicly Held**
SIC: 8011 Health maintenance organization
HQ: Health Net, Inc.
  21650 Oxnard St Fl 25
  Woodland Hills CA 91367
  818 676-6000

(P-19546)
HEALTH POINTE MEDICAL GROUP (PA)
Also Called: Southern Cal Orthopedics
1717 E Lincoln Ave, Anaheim (92805-4345)
PHONE...................714 956-2663
Fax: 714 635-8547
Ismael Silva MD, *President*
Mickie White, *Office Mgr*
Joe O'Neill, *Office Admin*
Ernest Medina, *Mktg Dir*
Silva Ismael, *Med Doctor*
EMP: 52
SQ FT: 10,000
SALES (est): 11.3MM **Privately Held**
SIC: 8011 Orthopedic physician; sports medicine specialist, physician; surgeon

(P-19547)
HEALTHCARE PARTNERS LLC
Also Called: Healthcare Partners Med Group
3932 Long Beach Blvd, Long Beach (90807-2615)
PHONE...................562 304-2100
Kenny Heine, *Branch Mgr*
EMP: 67
SALES (corp-wide): 13.7B **Publicly Held**
SIC: 8011 Group health association
HQ: Healthcare Partners, Llc
  2175 Park Pl
  El Segundo CA 90245

(P-19548)
HEALTHCARE PARTNERS LLC
Harriman Jones Medical
2600 Redondo Ave Ste 405, Long Beach (90806-2330)
PHONE...................562 988-7000
Fax: 562 988-7190
Jill R Cortese, *Principal*
John D Ro, *Family Practiti*
Judson R Schoendorf, *Allrgy & Immnlg*
Raffi Kazazian, *Gnrl Med Prac*
Chrystyne H Tran, *Internal Med*
EMP: 405
SALES (corp-wide): 13.7B **Publicly Held**
WEB: www.davidv.com
SIC: 8011 Clinic, operated by physicians
HQ: Healthcare Partners, Llc
  2175 Park Pl
  El Segundo CA 90245

(P-19549)
HEALTHCARE PARTNERS LLC
Also Called: Healthcare Partners Med Group
3144 Santa Anita Ave # 201, El Monte (91733-1316)
PHONE...................626 444-0333
Fax: 626 582-7990
Joseph Soto, *Branch Mgr*
Sharon Anderson, *Administration*
Edison Houpt, *Med Doctor*
Angelina Espinoza, *Manager*
Paul C Pang, *Agent*
EMP: 60
SALES (corp-wide): 13.7B **Publicly Held**
WEB: www.davidv.com
SIC: 8011 Medical centers
HQ: Healthcare Partners, Llc
  2175 Park Pl
  El Segundo CA 90245

(P-19550)
HEALTHCARE PARTNERS LLC
Also Called: Healthcare Partners Med Group
2601 Via Campo, Montebello (90640-1807)
PHONE...................323 720-1144
Fax: 323 888-2776
Sonia Flores, *Branch Mgr*
Kelly Garcia, *Office Mgr*
Maribeth A Ching, *Family Practiti*
Sean M McLaughlin, *Family Practiti*
Patricia P Ibarra MD, *Med Doctor*
EMP: 100
SALES (corp-wide): 13.7B **Publicly Held**
WEB: www.davidv.com
SIC: 8011 Offices & clinics of medical doctors
HQ: Healthcare Partners, Llc
  2175 Park Pl
  El Segundo CA 90245

(P-19551)
HEALTHCARE PARTNERS LLC (HQ)
Also Called: Healthcare Partners Med Group
2175 Park Pl, El Segundo (90245-4705)
PHONE...................310 354-4200
Robert J Margolis, *CEO*
Marianne Garrity, *President*
Dennis L Kogod, *COO*
Ted Halkias, *CFO*
Gary Standke, *Bd of Directors*
EMP: 600
SQ FT: 38,000
SALES (est): 291.7MM
SALES (corp-wide): 13.7B **Publicly Held**
WEB: www.davidv.com
SIC: 8011 Group health association
PA: Davita Inc.
  2000 16th St
  Denver CO 80202
  303 405-2100

(P-19552)
HEALTHCARE SYSTEM 2000
9191 Westminster Ave, Garden Grove (92844-2751)
PHONE...................714 899-2000
Michael Dao, *Owner*
Linh Bui, *Executive*
Quin Rudin, *Principal*
Dominique Q Tran, *Internal Med*
Peter H Vu, *Pediatrics*
EMP: 65
SALES: 1.6MM **Privately Held**
SIC: 8011 8062 General & family practice, physician/surgeon; general medical & surgical hospitals

(P-19553)
HEALTHY BEGINNINGS FRENCH CAMP
Also Called: Women' S Health
500 W Hospital Rd, French Camp (95231-9693)
P.O. Box 1020, Stockton (95201-3120)
PHONE...................209 468-6147
Fax: 209 468-7177
Michael Smith, *Principal*
EMP: 80
SALES (est): 2.1MM **Privately Held**
SIC: 8011 Offices & clinics of medical doctors

(P-19554)
HENRY MAYO NEWHALL MEM HOSP
23845 Mcbean Pkwy, Valencia (91355-2001)
PHONE...................661 253-8112
EMP: 94 EST: 2013
SALES: 245.5MM **Privately Held**
SIC: 8011

(P-19555)
HERALD CHRISTIAN HEALTH CENTER (PA)
8841 Garvey Ave, Rosemead (91770-3358)
PHONE...................626 286-8700
Fax: 626 286-8650
David Lee, *CEO*
Emily Szeto, *CFO*
EMP: 80
SQ FT: 9,419
SALES (est): 7.2MM **Privately Held**
SIC: 8011 Clinic, operated by physicians

(P-19556)
HERITAGE MEDICAL GROUP (PA)
Also Called: Bakersfield Family Medical Ctr
4580 California Ave, Bakersfield (93309-1104)
P.O. Box 10749 (93389-0749)
PHONE...................661 327-4411
Stanley Wohl, *CEO*
Richard Merkin, *Owner*
EMP: 57
SALES (est): 23.8MM **Privately Held**
SIC: 8011 Offices & clinics of medical doctors

(P-19557)
HIGH DESERT MED CORP A MED GRP (PA)
Also Called: Heritage Health Care
43839 15th St W, Lancaster (93534-4756)
P.O. Box 7007 (93539-7007)
PHONE...................661 945-5984
Fax: 661 947-7625
Richard N Merkin, *CEO*
Brenda Alexander, *Office Mgr*
Rafael Gonzalez, *Administration*
Nathaniel Bautista, *CTO*
Jeanine Straight, *QA Dir*
EMP: 120
SQ FT: 25,000
SALES (est): 20.5MM **Privately Held**
WEB: www.regalmed.com
SIC: 8011 Clinic, operated by physicians

(P-19558)
HIGH DSERT PTENT CARE SVCS LLC
17095 Main St, Hesperia (92345-6004)
PHONE...................760 956-4150
Medhi Izadi,
Chris Atkins, *Finance*
Ziad R El-Hajjaoui,
Zoheir El-Hajjaoui,
EMP: 53
SQ FT: 9,000
SALES: 5MM **Privately Held**
SIC: 8011 Offices & clinics of medical doctors

(P-19559)
HILARY A BRODIE MD PHD
2521 Stockton Blvd 7200, Sacramento (95817-2207)
PHONE...................916 734-3744
Hilary Brodie MD, *Chairman*
EMP: 60
SALES (est): 2.4MM **Privately Held**
SIC: 8011 Ears, nose & throat specialist; physician/surgeon

(P-19560)
HILL PHYSICIANS MED GROUP INC (PA)
2409 Camino Ramon, San Ramon (94583-4285)
P.O. Box 5080 (94583-0980)
PHONE...................800 445-5747
Bruce A Bob D, *Chairman*
Steve McDermott, *President*
Rick Messman, *CFO*
Robert C Feldman, *Treasurer*
Terry Hill, *Vice Pres*
EMP: 412
SQ FT: 36,000
SALES (est): 35.6MM **Privately Held**
SIC: 8011 8031 General & family practice, physician/surgeon; offices & clinics of osteopathic physicians

(P-19561)
HOUSE EAR CLINIC INC (PA)
2100 W 3rd St Ste 111, Los Angeles (90057-1999)
P.O. Box 52001, Phoenix AZ (85072-2001)
PHONE...................213 483-9930
Fax: 213 484-5900
Derald E Brackmann MD, *President*
John W House MD, *Treasurer*
Stephanie Baio, *Executive*
Antonio D La Cruz MD, *Admin Sec*
Victor Go, *IT/INT Sup*
EMP: 55
SQ FT: 25,500
SALES (est): 11.5MM **Privately Held**
WEB: www.houseearclinic.com
SIC: 8011 5999 Ears, nose & throat specialist: physician/surgeon; hearing aids

(P-19562)
HUNTINGTON AMBLTRY SURG CTR
625 S Fair Oaks Ave, Pasadena (91105-2613)
P.O. Box 840189, Los Angeles (90084-0189)
PHONE...................626 229-8999
Harry Bowles, *Mng Member*
Bernadette Molino,
James Noble,
Stephen Ralph,
Michael Chang, *Director*
EMP: 50
SALES (est): 5.4MM **Privately Held**
SIC: 8011 Surgeon

(P-19563)
HUNTINGTON BEACH COMMNTY CLINC
Also Called: Huntington Beach Cmnty Clinic
8041 Newman Ave, Huntington Beach (92647-7034)
PHONE...................714 847-4222
William Borden, *Ch of Bd*
Al Guidotti, *Ch of Bd*
Jacqueline Cherewick, *President*
T Gregory, *Treasurer*
D Harris, *Vice Pres*
▲**EMP:** 120
SQ FT: 3,500
SALES (est): 4.2MM **Privately Held**
WEB: www.cchcoc.org
SIC: 8011 Clinic, operated by physicians

(P-19564)
HUNTINGTON OTPTENT SURGERY CTR
625 S Fair Oaks Ave # 380, Pasadena (91105-2613)
PHONE...................626 535-2434
Fax: 626 397-8003
Sandy Bidlack, *Director*
Beau Thompson, *Accountant*
EMP: 55
SQ FT: 12,030
SALES (est): 4.4MM **Privately Held**
SIC: 8011 Ambulatory surgical center

(P-19565)
HUNTINGTON REPRODCTVE CTR INC (PA)
Also Called: Nelson, Jeffrey Do
333 S Arroyo Pkwy, Pasadena (91105-2515)
PHONE...................626 440-9161
Fax: 626 440-0138
Jeffrey R Nelson, *Vice Pres*
John Wilcox, *Treasurer*
John Wilcon, *Principal*
Robert Boostanfar, *Managing Dir*
Norman Quan, *Controller*
EMP: 50
SQ FT: 22,394
SALES (est): 15.1MM **Privately Held**
WEB: www.havingbabies.com
SIC: 8011 Fertility specialist, physician

(P-19566)
HYPERBARIC MGT SYSTEMS INC
Also Called: H M S
3224 Hoover Ave, National City (91950-7224)
PHONE.................................619 336-2022
W T Gurnee, *President*
Julie Vaickus, *Controller*
Merlyn Baker, *Accounts Mgr*
EMP: 200
SALES (est): 4MM
SALES (corp-wide): 12.8MM **Privately Held**
WEB: www.oxyheal.com
SIC: 8011 Specialized medical practitioners, except internal
PA: Oxyheal Health Group, Inc.
3224 Hoover Ave
National City CA 91950
619 336-2022

(P-19567)
IGO MEDICAL GROUP A MED CORP (PA)
Also Called: Infertility Gynclogy Obstetrics
9339 Genesee Ave Ste 220, San Diego (92121-2196)
PHONE.................................858 455-7520
Fax: 858 554-1312
Benito Villanueva, *President*
Wendy M Buchi, *CEO*
Dr Philip E Young, *CFO*
Steven Hebert, *Bd of Directors*
Dr Stephen Herbert, *Vice Pres*
EMP: 68
SQ FT: 11,500
SALES (est): 9MM **Privately Held**
WEB: www.igomed.com
SIC: 8011 Gynecologist; obstetrician; fertility specialist, physician

(P-19568)
INDEPENDENT PHYSICIAN MGT LLC
1100 E Willow St, Signal Hill (90755-3433)
PHONE.................................562 981-9500
Patricia Page,
Cristine Adams, *Manager*
EMP: 75
SALES (est): 1.8MM
SALES (corp-wide): 157.1B **Publicly Held**
WEB: www.mhipa.com
SIC: 8011 Offices & clinics of medical doctors
HQ: Memorial Healthcare Ipa, A Medical Corporation
11 Technology Dr
Irvine CA 92618
562 981-9500

(P-19569)
INLAND EYE INST MED GROUP INC (PA)
1900 E Washington St, Colton (92324-4698)
P.O. Box 1427 (92324-0836)
PHONE.................................909 825-3425
Loren Denler MD, *President*
Harold P Wallar, *Treasurer*
Wayne B Isaeff, *Vice Pres*
Don Thompson, *Finance*
Linda Gavin, *Human Resources*
EMP: 70
SQ FT: 12,500
SALES (est): 11.1MM **Privately Held**
SIC: 8011 Ophthalmologist

(P-19570)
INLAND HLTH ORG OF SO CAL (HQ)
1980 Orange Tree Ln # 200, Redlands (92374-4534)
P.O. Box 10457, San Bernardino (92423-0457)
PHONE.................................909 335-7171
Jeff Winter, *President*
Paula Lamar, *Vice Pres*
EMP: 50
SQ FT: 12,000
SALES (est): 9.2MM
SALES (corp-wide): 7.1B **Privately Held**
WEB: www.pulliamgroup.com
SIC: 8011 Clinic, operated by physicians

PA: Dignity Health
185 Berry St Ste 300
San Francisco CA 94107
415 438-5500

(P-19571)
INNOVATIVE SLEEP CENTERS INC
Also Called: Mehrdad Razavi
1050 Northgate Dr Ste 250, San Rafael (94903-2511)
PHONE.................................415 927-4990
Mehrdad Razavi, *CEO*
Mary Quenzer, *CFO*
Diane Taylor, *Opers Staff*
EMP: 65 EST: 2014
SQ FT: 2,000
SALES (est): 3MM **Privately Held**
SIC: 8011 Physical medicine, physician/surgeon

(P-19572)
INTREPID HEALTHCARE SVCS INC (HQ)
4605 Lankershim Blvd, North Hollywood (91602-1818)
PHONE.................................888 447-2362
Fax: 818 766-3999
Adam D Singer, *CEO*
R Jeffrey Taylor, *President*
Richard H Kline III, *CFO*
Kerry E Weiner, *Chief Mktg Ofcr*
Richard G Russell, *Exec VP*
EMP: 122
SALES: 693.9MM
SALES (corp-wide): 3.6B **Publicly Held**
WEB: www.ipcm.com
SIC: 8011 Physicians' office, including specialists
PA: Team Health Holdings, Inc.
265 Brookview Centre Way
Knoxville TN 37919
865 693-1000

(P-19573)
JAMES D TATE MD
Also Called: Tate Neurological Surgery
2888 Eureka Way Ste 200, Redding (96001-0210)
PHONE.................................530 225-8710
James D Tate MD, *Owner*
Tracey Lattimore, *Office Mgr*
EMP: 62
SALES (est): 2.4MM **Privately Held**
SIC: 8011 Offices & clinics of medical doctors

(P-19574)
JANET K HARTZLER MD
72057 Dinah Shore Dr D, Rancho Mirage (92270-1791)
PHONE.................................760 340-3937
Janet Hartzler, *Principal*
Bart Ketover, *Manager*
EMP: 60
SALES (est): 1.2MM **Privately Held**
SIC: 8011 Offices & clinics of medical doctors

(P-19575)
JERRY S POWELL MD
4501 X St, Sacramento (95817-2229)
PHONE.................................916 734-5959
Jerry S Powell, *Owner*
Jerry Powell, *Med Doctor*
Chong Pan, *Manager*
EMP: 70
SALES (est): 1.9MM **Privately Held**
SIC: 8011 Oncologist

(P-19576)
JOHN M ADAMS JR MD
1301 20th St Ste 150, Santa Monica (90404-2050)
PHONE.................................310 829-2663
Kevin Airheart MD, *Owner*
Karen Oi, *CTO*
Greg Harrison, *Manager*
EMP: 60
SALES (est): 995.7K **Privately Held**
SIC: 8011 General & family practice, physician/surgeon

(P-19577)
JOHN MUIR PHYSICIAN NETWORK
Also Called: Alamo Medical Group
1505 Saint Alphonsus Way, Alamo (94501-1570)
PHONE.................................925 838-4633
Fax: 925 838-5775
Judy Hicklin, *Manager*
EMP: 50
SALES (corp-wide): 243.9MM **Privately Held**
SIC: 8011 Pediatrician; internal medicine, physician/surgeon
PA: John Muir Physician Network
1450 Treat Blvd
Walnut Creek CA 94597
925 296-9700

(P-19578)
JUDY MADRIGAL & ASSOCIATES INC
Also Called: J M A
2000 Alameda De Las Pulga, San Mateo (94403-1289)
PHONE.................................650 873-3444
Fax: 650 873-2408
Judy Madrigal, *President*
Tammy Attard, *Vice Pres*
Allison Martinez, *Vice Pres*
Sue Plasai, *Director*
Laurie Thornton, *Manager*
EMP: 550
SALES (est): 24.2MM **Privately Held**
WEB: www.judymadrigal.com
SIC: 8011 8742 Offices & clinics of medical doctors; management consulting services

(P-19579)
KAISER FOUNDATION HOSPITALS
Also Called: Lakeview Medical Offices
411 N Lakeview Ave, Anaheim (92807-3028)
PHONE.................................714 279-4675
Suzie Characky, *Manager*
Mark W Gow, *Med Doctor*
Terri Kamaile, *Manager*
EMP: 105
SALES (corp-wide): 27.8B **Privately Held**
SIC: 8011 Offices & clinics of medical doctors
HQ: Kaiser Foundation Hospitals Inc
1 Kaiser Plz
Oakland CA 94612
510 271-6611

(P-19580)
KAISER FOUNDATION HOSPITALS
Also Called: Aliso Viejo Medical Offices
24502 Pacific Park Dr, Aliso Viejo (92656-3033)
PHONE.................................949 425-3150
Bruce Sogioka, *Branch Mgr*
Sepideh Mirfakhraie, *Family Practiti*
Jerry Sueda, *Manager*
EMP: 105
SALES (corp-wide): 27.8B **Privately Held**
SIC: 8011 Offices & clinics of medical doctors
HQ: Kaiser Foundation Hospitals Inc
1 Kaiser Plz
Oakland CA 94612
510 271-6611

(P-19581)
KAISER FOUNDATION HOSPITALS
8889 Rio San Diego Dr, San Diego (92108-1670)
PHONE.................................619 542-7210
Kate Kessler, *Branch Mgr*
Susan Davison, *Financial Exec*
EMP: 55
SALES (corp-wide): 27.8B **Privately Held**
SIC: 8011 Health maintenance organization
HQ: Kaiser Foundation Hospitals Inc
1 Kaiser Plz
Oakland CA 94612
510 271-6611

(P-19582)
KAISER FOUNDATION HOSPITALS
Also Called: Kaiser Permanente Santa
401 Bicentennial Way, Santa Rosa (95403-2149)
PHONE.................................707 393-4000
Fax: 707 571-4234
Susan Janvrin, *Branch Mgr*
Susan Janvrin, *COO*
David Kvancz, *Vice Pres*
Judy Coffey, *Area Mgr*
Peggy Jacobson, *Obstetrician*
EMP: 2000
SALES (corp-wide): 27.8B **Privately Held**
WEB: www.kaiserpermanente.org
SIC: 8011 Medical centers
HQ: Kaiser Foundation Hospitals Inc
1 Kaiser Plz
Oakland CA 94612
510 271-6611

(P-19583)
KAISER FOUNDATION HOSPITALS
Also Called: Kaiser Prmnnte Antioch Med Ctr
4501 Sand Creek Rd, Antioch (94531-8687)
PHONE.................................925 813-6500
Albert L Carver, *Branch Mgr*
Colleen McKeown, *Senior VP*
Barbara D Garcia, *Dermatology*
Naima B Thomas, *Physician Asst*
Abena Dodi, *Director*
EMP: 105
SALES (corp-wide): 27.8B **Privately Held**
SIC: 8011 Internal medicine practitioners
HQ: Kaiser Foundation Hospitals Inc
1 Kaiser Plz
Oakland CA 94612
510 271-6611

(P-19584)
KAISER FOUNDATION HOSPITALS
Also Called: Kaiser Permanente
12100 Euclid St, Garden Grove (92840-3304)
PHONE.................................714 741-3448
Fax: 714 562-3434
Betty Bohner, *Administration*
Trang Nguyen, *Family Practiti*
Paul A Vollucci, *Family Practiti*
Jonathan S Lin, *Pediatrics*
Patrick D Curtin, *Physician Asst*
EMP: 100
SALES (corp-wide): 27.8B **Privately Held**
WEB: www.kaiserpermanente.org
SIC: 8011 Offices & clinics of medical doctors
HQ: Kaiser Foundation Hospitals Inc
1 Kaiser Plz
Oakland CA 94612
510 271-6611

(P-19585)
KAISER FOUNDATION HOSPITALS
Also Called: Oakland Medical Center
3600 Broadway, Oakland (94611-5730)
P.O. Box 12929 (94604-3010)
PHONE.................................510 752-1000
Fax: 510 596-7054
David J Artenburn, *Manager*
Beth Rainsford, *Office Mgr*
Bettie Coles, *Administration*
Kenji Miyaji, *Info Tech Mgr*
Carl Bevan, *IT/INT Sup*
EMP: 2200
SALES (corp-wide): 27.8B **Privately Held**
WEB: www.kaiserpermanente.org
SIC: 8011 8062 Medical centers; general medical & surgical hospitals
HQ: Kaiser Foundation Hospitals Inc
1 Kaiser Plz
Oakland CA 94612
510 271-6611

(P-19586)
KAISER FOUNDATION HOSPITALS
Also Called: Kaiser Permanente San
2425 Geary Blvd, San Francisco (94115-3358)
PHONE.................................415 833-2000

PRODUCTS & SERVICES SECTION
8011 - Offices & Clinics Of Doctors Of Medicine County (P-19606)

Fax: 415 202-2572
Harry Chima, *Branch Mgr*
Debbie Raymond,
Pamela Johnson, *COO*
Bill Wehrle, *Vice Pres*
Leslie King, *Risk Mgmt Dir*
EMP: 750
SALES (corp-wide): 27.8B Privately Held
WEB: www.kaiserpermanente.org
SIC: 8011 8062 Medical centers; general medical & surgical hospitals
HQ: Kaiser Foundation Hospitals Inc
1 Kaiser Plz
Oakland CA 94612
510 271-6611

(P-19587)
KAISER FOUNDATION HOSPITALS
Also Called: Kaiser Permanente
9400 Rosecrans Ave, Bellflower (90706-2246)
PHONE.................................562 461-3000
Fax: 562 461-6054
James T Heidenreich, *Principal*
Christopher C Lin, *President*
Patrick Wirfel, *President*
Gregg Durkee, *Treasurer*
Joyce Sherall, *Vice Pres*
EMP: 2000
SALES (corp-wide): 27.8B Privately Held
WEB: www.kaiserpermanente.org
SIC: 8011 Offices & clinics of medical doctors
HQ: Kaiser Foundation Hospitals Inc
1 Kaiser Plz
Oakland CA 94612
510 271-6611

(P-19588)
KAISER FOUNDATION HOSPITALS
Also Called: Kaiser Permanente
1900 E Lambert Rd, Brea (92821-4371)
PHONE.................................714 672-5100
David Jeng, *Principal*
Dawn Hodges, *Purch Agent*
Lance C Brunner, *Family Practiti*
Sangeeta L Kumar, *Family Practiti*
Cecilia M Chang, *Pediatrics*
EMP: 52
SQ FT: 9,240
SALES (corp-wide): 27.8B Privately Held
WEB: www.kaiserpermanente.org
SIC: 8011 Offices & clinics of medical doctors
HQ: Kaiser Foundation Hospitals Inc
1 Kaiser Plz
Oakland CA 94612
510 271-6611

(P-19589)
KAISER FOUNDATION HOSPITALS
Also Called: Kaiser Permanente
99 Montecillo Rd, San Rafael (94903-3308)
PHONE.................................415 444-2000
Fax: 415 444-2076
Patricia Kendall, *Administration*
Brian Bane,
Aimee Durfee, *Vice Pres*
Lana M Kinney, *Case Mgmt Dir*
Vicki Steffen, *Radiology Dir*
EMP: 1500
SALES (corp-wide): 27.8B Privately Held
WEB: www.kaiserpermanente.org
SIC: 8011 8062 Medical centers; general medical & surgical hospitals
HQ: Kaiser Foundation Hospitals Inc
1 Kaiser Plz
Oakland CA 94612
510 271-6611

(P-19590)
KAISER FOUNDATION HOSPITALS
Also Called: Kaiser Permanente
901 Nevin Ave, Richmond (94801-3143)
PHONE.................................510 307-1500
Fax: 510 307-2409
Debbie Vachau, *Manager*
Tracy Flanigan, *Ch OB/GYN*
Morris Warner, *President*
Linda Marietta, *Office Mgr*

Robert Taylor, *Admin Sec*
EMP: 400
SALES (corp-wide): 27.8B Privately Held
WEB: www.kaiserpermanente.org
SIC: 8011 8062 Medical centers; general medical & surgical hospitals
HQ: Kaiser Foundation Hospitals Inc
1 Kaiser Plz
Oakland CA 94612
510 271-6611

(P-19591)
KAISER FOUNDATION HOSPITALS
Also Called: Kaiser Permanente West
6041 Cadillac Ave, Los Angeles (90034-1700)
PHONE.................................323 857-2000
Fax: 323 857-2107
Howard Fullman, *Admin Director*
Todd Sachs,
Mitch Friedman,
Merrick Schneider, *Ch Radiology*
Ann M Visosky, *Top Exec*
EMP: 2000
SALES (corp-wide): 27.8B Privately Held
WEB: www.kaiserpermanente.org
SIC: 8011 Medical centers
HQ: Kaiser Foundation Hospitals Inc
1 Kaiser Plz
Oakland CA 94612
510 271-6611

(P-19592)
KAISER FOUNDATION HOSPITALS
17284 Slover Ave, Fontana (92337-7584)
PHONE.................................909 609-3800
Gregory Christian, *Branch Mgr*
EMP: 106
SALES (corp-wide): 27.8B Privately Held
SIC: 8011 General & family practice, physician/surgeon
HQ: Kaiser Foundation Hospitals Inc
1 Kaiser Plz
Oakland CA 94612
510 271-6611

(P-19593)
KAISER FOUNDATION HOSPITALS
Also Called: Kaiser Permanente
1301 California St, Redlands (92374-2910)
PHONE.................................888 750-0036
Fax: 909 799-5333
Cindy Wong, *Director*
Kevin Kato, *Internal Med*
Adam S Myers, *Podiatrist*
John M Stutz, *Podiatrist*
EMP: 52
SALES (corp-wide): 27.8B Privately Held
WEB: www.kaiserpermanente.org
SIC: 8011 Offices & clinics of medical doctors
HQ: Kaiser Foundation Hospitals Inc
1 Kaiser Plz
Oakland CA 94612
510 271-6611

(P-19594)
KAISER FOUNDATION HOSPITALS
Also Called: Kaiser Permanente
250 Hospital Pkwy, San Jose (95119-1103)
PHONE.................................408 972-7000
Fax: 408 972-7157
Joann Zimmerman, *Branch Mgr*
Chaya J Prasad, *Ch Pathology*
Valerie Kwai-Ben,
Pravina Sharma,
David Katz, *Ch Radiology*
EMP: 650
SALES (corp-wide): 27.8B Privately Held
WEB: www.kaiserpermanente.org
SIC: 8011 Medical centers
HQ: Kaiser Foundation Hospitals Inc
1 Kaiser Plz
Oakland CA 94612
510 271-6611

(P-19595)
KAISER FOUNDATION HOSPITALS
Also Called: Vacaville Medical Center
1 Quality Dr, Vacaville (95688-9494)
PHONE.................................707 624-4000
EMP: 593
SALES (corp-wide): 27.8B Privately Held
SIC: 8011 Medical centers
HQ: Kaiser Foundation Hospitals Inc
1 Kaiser Plz
Oakland CA 94612
510 271-6611

(P-19596)
KAISER FOUNDATION HOSPITALS
Also Called: Tracy Medical Offices
2185 W Grant Line Rd, Tracy (95377-7309)
PHONE.................................209 839-3200
Anale Cunningham, *Branch Mgr*
EMP: 593
SALES (corp-wide): 27.8B Privately Held
SIC: 8011 Offices & clinics of medical doctors
HQ: Kaiser Foundation Hospitals Inc
1 Kaiser Plz
Oakland CA 94612
510 271-6611

(P-19597)
KAISER FOUNDATION HOSPITALS
Also Called: Union City Medical Offices
3555 Whipple Rd, Union City (94587-1507)
PHONE.................................510 675-4010
EMP: 593
SALES (corp-wide): 27.8B Privately Held
SIC: 8011 Offices & clinics of medical doctors
HQ: Kaiser Foundation Hospitals Inc
1 Kaiser Plz
Oakland CA 94612
510 271-6611

(P-19598)
KAISER FOUNDATION HOSPITALS
Also Called: Rancho Cucamonga Medical Offs
10850 Arrow Rte, Rancho Cucamonga (91730-4833)
PHONE.................................888 750-0036
EMP: 593
SALES (corp-wide): 27.8B Privately Held
SIC: 8011 Offices & clinics of medical doctors
HQ: Kaiser Foundation Hospitals Inc
1 Kaiser Plz
Oakland CA 94612
510 271-6611

(P-19599)
KAISER FOUNDATION HOSPITALS
Also Called: Anaheim Hills Medical Offices
5475 E La Palma Ave, Anaheim (92807-2075)
PHONE.................................888 988-2800
EMP: 593
SALES (corp-wide): 27.8B Privately Held
SIC: 8011 Offices & clinics of medical doctors
HQ: Kaiser Foundation Hospitals Inc
1 Kaiser Plz
Oakland CA 94612
510 271-6611

(P-19600)
KAISER FOUNDATION HOSPITALS
Also Called: Central Medical Offices
3733 San Dimas St, Bakersfield (93301-1407)
PHONE.................................877 524-7373
EMP: 593
SALES (corp-wide): 27.8B Privately Held
SIC: 8011 Offices & clinics of medical doctors
HQ: Kaiser Foundation Hospitals Inc
1 Kaiser Plz
Oakland CA 94612
510 271-6611

(P-19601)
KAISER FOUNDATION HOSPITALS
Also Called: Anaheim Kraemer Medical Offs
3460 E La Palma Ave, Anaheim (92806-2020)
PHONE.................................888 988-2800
EMP: 593
SALES (corp-wide): 27.8B Privately Held
SIC: 8011 Offices & clinics of medical doctors
HQ: Kaiser Foundation Hospitals Inc
1 Kaiser Plz
Oakland CA 94612
510 271-6611

(P-19602)
KAISER FOUNDATION HOSPITALS
Also Called: Chester Avenue Medical Offices
2531 Chester Ave, Bakersfield (93301-2012)
PHONE.................................877 524-7373
EMP: 593
SALES (corp-wide): 27.8B Privately Held
SIC: 8011 Offices & clinics of medical doctors
HQ: Kaiser Foundation Hospitals Inc
1 Kaiser Plz
Oakland CA 94612
510 271-6611

(P-19603)
KAISER FOUNDATION HOSPITALS
Also Called: Chester Avenue Medical Offs II
2620 Chester Ave, Bakersfield (93301-2015)
PHONE.................................661 337-7160
EMP: 593
SALES (corp-wide): 27.8B Privately Held
SIC: 8011 Offices & clinics of medical doctors
HQ: Kaiser Foundation Hospitals Inc
1 Kaiser Plz
Oakland CA 94612
510 271-6611

(P-19604)
KAISER FOUNDATION HOSPITALS
Also Called: Discovery Plz Med & Admin Offs
1200 Discovery Dr, Bakersfield (93309-7032)
PHONE.................................877 524-7373
EMP: 593
SALES (corp-wide): 27.8B Privately Held
SIC: 8011 Offices & clinics of medical doctors
HQ: Kaiser Foundation Hospitals Inc
1 Kaiser Plz
Oakland CA 94612
510 271-6611

(P-19605)
KAISER FOUNDATION HOSPITALS
Also Called: Cerritos Medical Office Bldg
10820 183rd St, Cerritos (90703-8013)
PHONE.................................800 823-4040
EMP: 593
SALES (corp-wide): 27.8B Privately Held
SIC: 8011 Offices & clinics of medical doctors
HQ: Kaiser Foundation Hospitals Inc
1 Kaiser Plz
Oakland CA 94612
510 271-6611

(P-19606)
KAISER FOUNDATION HOSPITALS
Also Called: Las Posas Road Medical Offices
2620 Las Posas Rd, Camarillo (93010-3400)
PHONE.................................888 515-3500
EMP: 593
SALES (corp-wide): 27.8B Privately Held
SIC: 8011 Offices & clinics of medical doctors
HQ: Kaiser Foundation Hospitals Inc
1 Kaiser Plz
Oakland CA 94612
510 271-6611

8011 - Offices & Clinics Of Doctors Of Medicine County (P-19607)

(P-19607)
KAISER FOUNDATION HOSPITALS
Also Called: Ming Medical Offices
8800 Ming Ave, Bakersfield (93311-1308)
PHONE................877 524-7373
EMP: 593
SALES (corp-wide): 27.8B Privately Held
SIC: 8011 Offices & clinics of medical doctors
HQ: Kaiser Foundation Hospitals Inc
1 Kaiser Plz
Oakland CA 94612
510 271-6611

(P-19608)
KAISER FOUNDATION HOSPITALS
Also Called: Crossroads Medical Offices
12801 Crossroads Pkwy S, City of Industry (91746-3502)
PHONE................562 463-4377
EMP: 593
SALES (corp-wide): 27.8B Privately Held
SIC: 8011 Offices & clinics of medical doctors
HQ: Kaiser Foundation Hospitals Inc
1 Kaiser Plz
Oakland CA 94612
510 271-6611

(P-19609)
KAISER FOUNDATION HOSPITALS
Also Called: Orchard Medical Offices
9449 Imperial Hwy, Downey (90242-2814)
PHONE................800 823-4040
Dana G Dumitru, *Osteopathy*
EMP: 593
SALES (corp-wide): 27.8B Privately Held
SIC: 8011 Offices & clinics of medical doctors
HQ: Kaiser Foundation Hospitals Inc
1 Kaiser Plz
Oakland CA 94612
510 271-6611

(P-19610)
KAISER FOUNDATION HOSPITALS
Also Called: Palomar Medical Center
2185 Citracado Pkwy, Escondido (92029-4159)
PHONE................442 281-5000
Sherdan Smith, *Food Svc Dir*
EMP: 593
SALES (corp-wide): 27.8B Privately Held
SIC: 8011 Medical centers
HQ: Kaiser Foundation Hospitals Inc
1 Kaiser Plz
Oakland CA 94612
510 271-6611

(P-19611)
KAISER FOUNDATION HOSPITALS
Also Called: Diamond Bar Medical Offices
1336 Bridgegate Dr, Diamond Bar (91765-3955)
PHONE................800 780-1277
EMP: 593
SALES (corp-wide): 27.8B Privately Held
SIC: 8011 Offices & clinics of medical doctors
HQ: Kaiser Foundation Hospitals Inc
1 Kaiser Plz
Oakland CA 94612
510 271-6611

(P-19612)
KAISER FOUNDATION HOSPITALS
Also Called: Palomar Health Downtown Campus
555 E Valley Pkwy, Escondido (92025-3048)
PHONE................760 739-3000
Fax: 760 739-3283
EMP: 593
SALES (corp-wide): 27.8B Privately Held
SIC: 8011 Medical centers
HQ: Kaiser Foundation Hospitals Inc
1 Kaiser Plz
Oakland CA 94612
510 271-6611

(P-19613)
KAISER FOUNDATION HOSPITALS
Also Called: Garden Medical Offices
9353 Imperial Hwy, Downey (90242-2812)
PHONE................800 823-4040
Michael Y Chen, *Med Doctor*
EMP: 593
SALES (corp-wide): 27.8B Privately Held
SIC: 8011 Offices & clinics of medical doctors
HQ: Kaiser Foundation Hospitals Inc
1 Kaiser Plz
Oakland CA 94612
510 271-6611

(P-19614)
KAISER FOUNDATION HOSPITALS
Also Called: Fairfield Medical Offices
1550 Gateway Blvd, Fairfield (94533-6901)
PHONE................707 427-4000
EMP: 593
SALES (corp-wide): 27.8B Privately Held
SIC: 8011 Offices & clinics of medical doctors
HQ: Kaiser Foundation Hospitals Inc
1 Kaiser Plz
Oakland CA 94612
510 271-6611

(P-19615)
KAISER FOUNDATION HOSPITALS
Also Called: Foothill Ranch Medical Offices
26882 Towne Centre Dr # 1, Foothill Ranch (92610-2862)
PHONE................800 922-2000
EMP: 593
SALES (corp-wide): 27.8B Privately Held
SIC: 8011 Offices & clinics of medical doctors
HQ: Kaiser Foundation Hospitals Inc
1 Kaiser Plz
Oakland CA 94612
510 271-6611

(P-19616)
KAISER FOUNDATION HOSPITALS
Also Called: Fontana Mental Health Offices
9310 Sierra Ave, Fontana (92335-5711)
PHONE................866 205-3595
EMP: 593
SALES (corp-wide): 27.8B Privately Held
SIC: 8011 Psychiatrists & psychoanalysts
HQ: Kaiser Foundation Hospitals Inc
1 Kaiser Plz
Oakland CA 94612
510 271-6611

(P-19617)
KAISER FOUNDATION HOSPITALS
Also Called: Folsom Ambulatory Surgery Ctr
285 Palladio Pkwy, Folsom (95630-8741)
PHONE................916 986-4178
EMP: 593
SALES (corp-wide): 27.8B Privately Held
SIC: 8011 Ambulatory surgical center
HQ: Kaiser Foundation Hospitals Inc
1 Kaiser Plz
Oakland CA 94612
510 271-6611

(P-19618)
KAISER FOUNDATION HOSPITALS
Also Called: Carson Medical Offices
18600 S Figueroa St, Gardena (90248-4505)
PHONE................800 780-1230
EMP: 593
SALES (corp-wide): 27.8B Privately Held
SIC: 8011 Offices & clinics of medical doctors
HQ: Kaiser Foundation Hospitals Inc
1 Kaiser Plz
Oakland CA 94612
510 271-6611

(P-19619)
KAISER FOUNDATION HOSPITALS
Also Called: Balboa Plaza Admin Offices
10605 Balboa Blvd Ste 330, Granada Hills (91344-6358)
PHONE................818 832-7200
EMP: 593
SALES (corp-wide): 27.8B Privately Held
SIC: 8011 Health maintenance organization
HQ: Kaiser Foundation Hospitals Inc
1 Kaiser Plz
Oakland CA 94612
510 271-6611

(P-19620)
KAISER FOUNDATION HOSPITALS
Also Called: Glendale Orange St Med Offs
501 N Orange St, Glendale (91203-1970)
PHONE................800 954-8000
EMP: 593
SALES (corp-wide): 27.8B Privately Held
SIC: 8011 Offices & clinics of medical doctors
HQ: Kaiser Foundation Hospitals Inc
1 Kaiser Plz
Oakland CA 94612
510 271-6611

(P-19621)
KAISER FOUNDATION HOSPITALS
Also Called: Indio Medical Offices
46900 Monroe St, Indio (92201-4827)
PHONE................866 984-7483
EMP: 593
SALES (corp-wide): 27.8B Privately Held
SIC: 8011 Offices & clinics of medical doctors
HQ: Kaiser Foundation Hospitals Inc
1 Kaiser Plz
Oakland CA 94612
510 271-6611

(P-19622)
KAISER FOUNDATION HOSPITALS
Also Called: Rancho San Diego Medical Offs
3875 Avocado Blvd, La Mesa (91941-7303)
PHONE................619 528-5000
EMP: 593
SALES (corp-wide): 27.8B Privately Held
SIC: 8011 Offices & clinics of medical doctors
HQ: Kaiser Foundation Hospitals Inc
1 Kaiser Plz
Oakland CA 94612
510 271-6611

(P-19623)
KAISER FOUNDATION HOSPITALS
Also Called: Lincoln Medical Offices
1900 Dresden Dr, Lincoln (95648-8803)
PHONE................916 543-5153
EMP: 593
SALES (corp-wide): 27.8B Privately Held
SIC: 8011 Offices & clinics of medical doctors
HQ: Kaiser Foundation Hospitals Inc
1 Kaiser Plz
Oakland CA 94612
510 271-6611

(P-19624)
KAISER FOUNDATION HOSPITALS
Also Called: Behavioral Health
44444 20th St W, Lancaster (93534-2714)
PHONE................661 951-0070
Lauren J Waxman, *Psychiatry*
EMP: 593
SALES (corp-wide): 27.8B Privately Held
SIC: 8011 Psychiatrists & psychoanalysts
HQ: Kaiser Foundation Hospitals Inc
1 Kaiser Plz
Oakland CA 94612
510 271-6611

(P-19625)
KAISER FOUNDATION HOSPITALS
Also Called: Lomita Medical Offices
2081 Palos Verdes Dr N, Lomita (90717-3701)
PHONE................310 325-6542
EMP: 593
SALES (corp-wide): 27.8B Privately Held
SIC: 8011 Offices & clinics of medical doctors
HQ: Kaiser Foundation Hospitals Inc
1 Kaiser Plz
Oakland CA 94612
510 271-6611

(P-19626)
KAISER FOUNDATION HOSPITALS
Also Called: Mill Valley Medical Offices
750 Redwood Hwy Frontage # 1206, Mill Valley (94941-2483)
PHONE................415 444-2000
EMP: 593
SALES (corp-wide): 27.8B Privately Held
SIC: 8011 Offices & clinics of medical doctors
HQ: Kaiser Foundation Hospitals Inc
1 Kaiser Plz
Oakland CA 94612
510 271-6611

(P-19627)
KAISER FOUNDATION HOSPITALS
Also Called: Lynwood Medical Offices
3830 Martin Luther King, Lynwood (90262-3625)
PHONE................310 604-5700
Johnny T Wong, *Med Doctor*
EMP: 593
SALES (corp-wide): 27.8B Privately Held
SIC: 8011 Offices & clinics of medical doctors
HQ: Kaiser Foundation Hospitals Inc
1 Kaiser Plz
Oakland CA 94612
510 271-6611

(P-19628)
KAISER FOUNDATION HOSPITALS
Also Called: Modesto Medical Offices
4601 Dale Rd, Modesto (95356-9718)
PHONE................209 735-5000
Dilip Banerjee, *Med Doctor*
Kulwant S Monder, *Med Doctor*
EMP: 593
SALES (corp-wide): 27.8B Privately Held
SIC: 8011 Medical centers
HQ: Kaiser Foundation Hospitals Inc
1 Kaiser Plz
Oakland CA 94612
510 271-6611

(P-19629)
KAISER FOUNDATION HOSPITALS
Also Called: North Hollywood Medical Offs
5250 Lankershim Blvd, North Hollywood (91601-3186)
PHONE................888 778-5000
EMP: 593
SALES (corp-wide): 27.8B Privately Held
SIC: 8011 Offices & clinics of medical doctors
HQ: Kaiser Foundation Hospitals Inc
1 Kaiser Plz
Oakland CA 94612
510 271-6611

(P-19630)
KAISER FOUNDATION HOSPITALS
Also Called: Bangs Avenue Medical Offices
4125 Bangs Ave, Modesto (95356-8713)
PHONE................209 735-5000
EMP: 593
SALES (corp-wide): 27.8B Privately Held
SIC: 8011 Offices & clinics of medical doctors

PRODUCTS & SERVICES SECTION
8011 - Offices & Clinics Of Doctors Of Medicine County (P-19653)

HQ: Kaiser Foundation Hospitals Inc
1 Kaiser Plz
Oakland CA 94612
510 271-6611

(P-19631)
KAISER FOUNDATION HOSPITALS
Also Called: Norwalk Medical Offices
12501 Imperial Hwy, Norwalk (90650-3179)
PHONE.....................562 807-6100
EMP: 593
SALES (corp-wide): 27.8B Privately Held
SIC: 8011 Offices & clinics of medical doctors
HQ: Kaiser Foundation Hospitals Inc
1 Kaiser Plz
Oakland CA 94612
510 271-6611

(P-19632)
KAISER FOUNDATION HOSPITALS
Also Called: Ontario Vineyard Medical Offs
2295 S Vineyard Ave, Ontario (91761-7925)
PHONE.....................909 724-5000
Kent K Miyamoto, Med Doctor
Vivien Choi, Director
EMP: 593
SALES (corp-wide): 27.8B Privately Held
SIC: 8011 Medical centers
HQ: Kaiser Foundation Hospitals Inc
1 Kaiser Plz
Oakland CA 94612
510 271-6611

(P-19633)
KAISER FOUNDATION HOSPITALS
Also Called: Montebello Medical Offices
1550 Town Center Dr, Montebello (90640-2173)
PHONE.....................800 780-1277
EMP: 593
SALES (corp-wide): 27.8B Privately Held
SIC: 8011 Offices & clinics of medical doctors
HQ: Kaiser Foundation Hospitals Inc
1 Kaiser Plz
Oakland CA 94612
510 271-6611

(P-19634)
KAISER FOUNDATION HOSPITALS
Also Called: Oxnard 2200 East Gonzales
2200 E Gonzales Rd, Oxnard (93036-0619)
PHONE.....................888 515-3500
EMP: 593
SALES (corp-wide): 27.8B Privately Held
SIC: 8011 Offices & clinics of medical doctors
HQ: Kaiser Foundation Hospitals Inc
1 Kaiser Plz
Oakland CA 94612
510 271-6611

(P-19635)
KAISER FOUNDATION HOSPITALS
Also Called: Kaiser Permanente Member Svcs
73733 Fred Waring Dr, Palm Desert (92260-2589)
PHONE.....................800 777-1256
EMP: 593
SALES (corp-wide): 27.8B Privately Held
SIC: 8011 Health maintenance organization
HQ: Kaiser Foundation Hospitals Inc
1 Kaiser Plz
Oakland CA 94612
510 271-6611

(P-19636)
KAISER FOUNDATION HOSPITALS
Also Called: Oxnard 2103 East Gonzales Road
2103 E Gonzales Rd, Oxnard (93036-3757)
PHONE.....................805 988-6300
EMP: 593

SALES (corp-wide): 27.8B Privately Held
SIC: 8011 Offices & clinics of medical doctors
HQ: Kaiser Foundation Hospitals Inc
1 Kaiser Plz
Oakland CA 94612
510 271-6611

(P-19637)
KAISER FOUNDATION HOSPITALS
Also Called: Pinole Medical Offices
1301 Pinole Valley Rd, Pinole (94564-1384)
PHONE.....................510 243-4000
EMP: 593
SALES (corp-wide): 27.8B Privately Held
SIC: 8011 Offices & clinics of medical doctors
HQ: Kaiser Foundation Hospitals Inc
1 Kaiser Plz
Oakland CA 94612
510 271-6611

(P-19638)
KAISER FOUNDATION HOSPITALS
Also Called: Palm Desert Medical Offices
University Park Ctr, Palm Desert (92211)
PHONE.....................866 984-7483
EMP: 593
SALES (corp-wide): 19.1B Privately Held
SIC: 8011
PA: Kaiser Foundation Hospitals Inc
1 Kaiser Plz Ste 2600
Oakland CA 94612
510 271-5800

(P-19639)
KAISER FOUNDATION HOSPITALS
Also Called: Canyon Crest Mental Hlth Offs
5225 Canyon Crest Dr, Riverside (92507-6301)
PHONE.....................951 248-4000
EMP: 593
SALES (corp-wide): 27.8B Privately Held
SIC: 8011 Psychiatrists & psychoanalysts
HQ: Kaiser Foundation Hospitals Inc
1 Kaiser Plz
Oakland CA 94612
510 271-6611

(P-19640)
KAISER FOUNDATION HOSPITALS
Also Called: Meridian Medical Offices
14305 Meridian Pkwy, Riverside (92518-3034)
PHONE.....................866 984-7483
David Kvancz, Vice Pres
EMP: 593
SALES (corp-wide): 27.8B Privately Held
SIC: 8011 Offices & clinics of medical doctors
HQ: Kaiser Foundation Hospitals Inc
1 Kaiser Plz
Oakland CA 94612
510 271-6611

(P-19641)
KAISER FOUNDATION HOSPITALS
Also Called: Carmel Valley Medical Offices
3851 Shaw Ridge Rd, San Diego (92130-2807)
PHONE.....................858 847-3500
EMP: 593
SALES (corp-wide): 27.8B Privately Held
SIC: 8011 Offices & clinics of medical doctors
HQ: Kaiser Foundation Hospitals Inc
1 Kaiser Plz
Oakland CA 94612
510 271-6611

(P-19642)
KAISER FOUNDATION HOSPITALS
Also Called: Kaiser Permanente Kearny
4510 Viewridge Ave, San Diego (92123-1637)
PHONE.....................858 502-1350
Patrick A Macapinlac, Nephrology
EMP: 593

SALES (corp-wide): 27.8B Privately Held
SIC: 8011 Specialized medical practitioners, except internal
HQ: Kaiser Foundation Hospitals Inc
1 Kaiser Plz
Oakland CA 94612
510 271-6611

(P-19643)
KAISER FOUNDATION HOSPITALS
Also Called: Kaiser Permanente San
1000 Franklin Pkwy, San Mateo (94403-1922)
PHONE.....................650 358-7000
Thomas E Sipes, Med Doctor
EMP: 593
SALES (corp-wide): 27.8B Privately Held
SIC: 8011 Medical centers
HQ: Kaiser Foundation Hospitals Inc
1 Kaiser Plz
Oakland CA 94612
510 271-6611

(P-19644)
KAISER FOUNDATION HOSPITALS
Also Called: Kaiser Permanente San
2500 Merced St, San Leandro (94577-4201)
PHONE.....................510 454-1000
Thomas S Hanenburg, Senior VP
Renea Allen, Admin Asst
Jay M Goldman, Med Doctor
Melinda J Porter, Nurse Practr
EMP: 593
SALES (corp-wide): 27.8B Privately Held
SIC: 8011 8062 Medical centers; general medical & surgical hospitals
HQ: Kaiser Foundation Hospitals Inc
1 Kaiser Plz
Oakland CA 94612
510 271-6611

(P-19645)
KAISER FOUNDATION HOSPITALS
Also Called: San Ramon Medical Offices
2300 Camino Ramon, San Ramon (94583-1354)
PHONE.....................925 244-7600
EMP: 593
SALES (corp-wide): 27.8B Privately Held
SIC: 8011 Offices & clinics of medical doctors
HQ: Kaiser Foundation Hospitals Inc
1 Kaiser Plz
Oakland CA 94612
510 271-6611

(P-19646)
KAISER FOUNDATION HOSPITALS
Also Called: Harbor Corporate Park
3601 S Harbor Blvd, Santa Ana (92704-7909)
PHONE.....................714 223-2606
EMP: 593
SALES (corp-wide): 27.8B Privately Held
SIC: 8011 Psychiatric clinic
HQ: Kaiser Foundation Hospitals Inc
1 Kaiser Plz
Oakland CA 94612
510 271-6611

(P-19647)
KAISER FOUNDATION HOSPITALS
Also Called: Canyon Country Medical Offices
26415 Carl Boyer Dr, Santa Clarita (91350-5824)
PHONE.....................888 778-5000
EMP: 593
SALES (corp-wide): 27.8B Privately Held
SIC: 8011 Offices & clinics of medical doctors
HQ: Kaiser Foundation Hospitals Inc
1 Kaiser Plz
Oakland CA 94612
510 271-6611

(P-19648)
KAISER FOUNDATION HOSPITALS
Also Called: Thosand Oaks 145 Hodencamp
145 Hodencamp Rd, Thousand Oaks (91360-5810)
PHONE.....................888 515-3500
EMP: 593
SALES (corp-wide): 27.8B Privately Held
SIC: 8011 Offices & clinics of medical doctors
HQ: Kaiser Foundation Hospitals Inc
1 Kaiser Plz
Oakland CA 94612
510 271-6611

(P-19649)
KAISER FOUNDATION HOSPITALS
Also Called: Santa Clara Arques Med Offs
1263 E Arques Ave, Sunnyvale (94085-4701)
PHONE.....................408 851-1000
Todd T Nguyen, Osteopathy
EMP: 593
SALES (corp-wide): 27.8B Privately Held
SIC: 8011 Offices & clinics of medical doctors
HQ: Kaiser Foundation Hospitals Inc
1 Kaiser Plz
Oakland CA 94612
510 271-6611

(P-19650)
KAISER FOUNDATION HOSPITALS
Also Called: Thousand Oaks 322 E Thousand
322 E Thousand Oaks Blvd, Thousand Oaks (91360-5804)
PHONE.....................888 515-3500
EMP: 593
SALES (corp-wide): 27.8B Privately Held
SIC: 8011 Offices & clinics of medical doctors
HQ: Kaiser Foundation Hospitals Inc
1 Kaiser Plz
Oakland CA 94612
510 271-6611

(P-19651)
KAISER FOUNDATION HOSPITALS
Also Called: Tustin Ranch Medical Offices
2521 Michelle Dr, Tustin (92780-7014)
PHONE.....................888 988-2800
EMP: 593
SALES (corp-wide): 27.8B Privately Held
SIC: 8011 Offices & clinics of medical doctors
HQ: Kaiser Foundation Hospitals Inc
1 Kaiser Plz
Oakland CA 94612
510 271-6611

(P-19652)
KAISER FOUNDATION HOSPITALS
Also Called: Kaiser Permanente
9961 Sierra Ave, Fontana (92335-6720)
PHONE.....................909 427-5000
Fax: 909 427-4178
William Meyer, Principal
Lawrence Harms,
Dennis Lindeborg,
Carolyn Yocum, Pharmacy Dir
David Young, CIO
EMP: 1700
SALES (corp-wide): 27.8B Privately Held
WEB: www.kaiserpermanente.org
SIC: 8011 Medical centers
HQ: Kaiser Foundation Hospitals Inc
1 Kaiser Plz
Oakland CA 94612
510 271-6611

(P-19653)
KAISER FOUNDATION HOSPITALS
Also Called: Kaiser Permanente
25825 Vermont Ave, Harbor City (90710-3518)
PHONE.....................310 325-5111
Fax: 310 517-2902
Mary Ann Barnes, Branch Mgr

8011 - Offices & Clinics Of Doctors Of Medicine County (P-19654)

Michael Ward,
Christopher Jenson, *Ch Radiology*
Rebecca KAO, *Bd of Directors*
Michael Kusunoki, *Officer*
EMP: 1700
SALES (corp-wide): 27.8B **Privately Held**
WEB: www.kaiserpermanente.org
SIC: 8011 Medical centers
HQ: Kaiser Foundation Hospitals Inc
1 Kaiser Plz
Oakland CA 94612
510 271-6611

(P-19654)
KAISER FOUNDATION HOSPITALS
Also Called: Kaiser Permanente
1425 S Main St, Walnut Creek
(94596-5318)
PHONE...................925 295-4000
Fax: 925 295-4816
Michael Tully-Cintron, *Branch Mgr*
Jeff Klingman,
Michael Klemm,
John Jacques, *CFO*
Colleen McKeown, *Senior VP*
EMP: 2000
SQ FT: 11,840
SALES (corp-wide): 27.8B **Privately Held**
WEB: www.kaiserpermanente.org
SIC: 8011 Medical centers
HQ: Kaiser Foundation Hospitals Inc
1 Kaiser Plz
Oakland CA 94612
510 271-6611

(P-19655)
KAISER FOUNDATION HOSPITALS
Also Called: Kaiser Permanente
1100 Veterans Blvd, Redwood City
(94063-2037)
PHONE...................650 299-2000
Fax: 650 299-2421
Eric Rasmussen, *Manager*
Derrick Taylor,
Ernest Newkirk,
Todd Osinski, *Ch Radiology*
Tracie Goins, *Office Mgr*
EMP: 1500
SALES (corp-wide): 27.8B **Privately Held**
WEB: www.kaiserpermanente.org
SIC: 8011 8062 Medical centers; general medical & surgical hospitals
HQ: Kaiser Foundation Hospitals Inc
1 Kaiser Plz
Oakland CA 94612
510 271-6611

(P-19656)
KAISER FOUNDATION HOSPITALS
Also Called: Permanentee Medical Group
1001 Riverside Ave, Roseville
(95678-5134)
PHONE...................916 784-4000
Deb Royer, *Manager*
Robert A Lufburrow, *Obstetrician*
Bruce T Ryhal, *Allrgy & Immnlg*
Mihir J Amin, *Internal Med*
Tayyiba Awan, *Internal Med*
EMP: 200
SALES (corp-wide): 27.8B **Privately Held**
WEB: www.kaiserpermanente.org
SIC: 8011 Offices & clinics of medical doctors
HQ: Kaiser Foundation Hospitals Inc
1 Kaiser Plz
Oakland CA 94612
510 271-6611

(P-19657)
KAISER FOUNDATION HOSPITALS
Also Called: La Palma Medical Offices
5 Centerpointe Dr, La Palma (90623-1050)
PHONE...................714 562-3420
Josefina Guzman-Inouye, *Manager*
Wendy Y Leu, *Family Practiti*
Diane V Pham, *Family Practiti*
Anne L Hardebeck, *Obstetrician*
Waldo Luciano, *Med Doctor*
EMP: 50

SALES (corp-wide): 27.8B **Privately Held**
WEB: www.kaiserpermanente.org
SIC: 8011 Offices & clinics of medical doctors
HQ: Kaiser Foundation Hospitals Inc
1 Kaiser Plz
Oakland CA 94612
510 271-6611

(P-19658)
KAISER FOUNDATION HOSPITALS
Also Called: Glendale Medical Offices
444 W Glenoaks Blvd, Glendale
(91202-2917)
PHONE...................818 552-3000
Fax: 818 552-3108
Avetis Tashyan, *Branch Mgr*
Joshua T Fleischman, *Family Practiti*
William I Kaplan, *Family Practiti*
EMP: 50
SALES (corp-wide): 27.8B **Privately Held**
WEB: www.kaiserpermanente.org
SIC: 8011 Offices & clinics of medical doctors
HQ: Kaiser Foundation Hospitals Inc
1 Kaiser Plz
Oakland CA 94612
510 271-6611

(P-19659)
KAISER FOUNDATION HOSPITALS
Also Called: Yorba Linda Medical Offices
22550 Savi Ranch Pkwy, Yorba Linda
(92887-4670)
PHONE...................714 685-3520
Marie Kohl, *Administration*
Silvester R Lim, *Family Practiti*
Mark Shaffer, *Obstetrician*
Lisa Rivera, *Nurse Practr*
Ann Hook, *Manager*
EMP: 50
SALES (corp-wide): 27.8B **Privately Held**
WEB: www.kaiserpermanente.org
SIC: 8011 Offices & clinics of medical doctors
HQ: Kaiser Foundation Hospitals Inc
1 Kaiser Plz
Oakland CA 94612
510 271-6611

(P-19660)
KAISER FOUNDATION HOSPITALS
Also Called: Clairemont Medical Offices
7060 Clairemont Mesa Blvd, San Diego
(92111-1003)
PHONE...................858 573-0299
Fax: 858 573-5475
Michael Mellon MD, *Manager*
Ronald G Ceballos, *Pharmacy Dir*
Michael Hellon, *Research*
Ali Aboutaleb, *Family Practiti*
Mark S Fenster, *Family Practiti*
EMP: 50
SALES (corp-wide): 27.8B **Privately Held**
WEB: www.kaiserpermanente.org
SIC: 8011 Offices & clinics of medical doctors
HQ: Kaiser Foundation Hospitals Inc
1 Kaiser Plz
Oakland CA 94612
510 271-6611

(P-19661)
KAISER FOUNDATION HOSPITALS
Also Called: Escondido Medical Offices
732 N Broadway, Escondido (92025-1897)
PHONE...................619 528-5000
Han Kim, *Manager*
EMP: 50
SALES (corp-wide): 27.8B **Privately Held**
WEB: www.kaiserpermanente.org
SIC: 8011 Offices & clinics of medical doctors
HQ: Kaiser Foundation Hospitals Inc
1 Kaiser Plz
Oakland CA 94612
510 271-6611

(P-19662)
KAISER FOUNDATION HOSPITALS
Also Called: Kaiser Prmnnte Hayward Med Ctr
27400 Hesperian Blvd, Hayward
(94545-4235)
PHONE...................510 678-4000
Fax: 510 784-2076
Cynthia Seay, *Manager*
Robert Heller,
Eve Newton-Gill, *Volunteer Dir*
John Martinez, *Officer*
Kay Rucker, *Executive Asst*
EMP: 1200
SALES (corp-wide): 27.8B **Privately Held**
WEB: www.kaiserpermanente.org
SIC: 8011 Medical centers
HQ: Kaiser Foundation Hospitals Inc
1 Kaiser Plz
Oakland CA 94612
510 271-6611

(P-19663)
KAISER FOUNDATION HOSPITALS
Also Called: Kaiser Prmnnte Psadena Med Off
3280 E Foothill Blvd, Pasadena
(91107-3103)
P.O. Box 7005 (91109-7005)
PHONE...................626 583-2200
Fax: 626 440-5602
Consuelo Casillas, *Family Practiti*
April A Soto, *Family Practiti*
Monica Tantraphol, *Family Practiti*
Mary Ashford, *Med Doctor*
EMP: 50
SALES (corp-wide): 27.8B **Privately Held**
WEB: www.kaiserpermanente.org
SIC: 8011 Offices & clinics of medical doctors
HQ: Kaiser Foundation Hospitals Inc
1 Kaiser Plz
Oakland CA 94612
510 271-6611

(P-19664)
KAISER FOUNDATION HOSPITALS
Also Called: San Bernardino Medical Offices
1717 E Date Pl, San Bernardino
(92404-4428)
PHONE...................909 886-6711
Sinsong Ku, *Manager*
Brian G Bautista, *Family Practiti*
EMP: 50
SALES (corp-wide): 27.8B **Privately Held**
WEB: www.kaiserpermanente.org
SIC: 8011 Offices & clinics of medical doctors
HQ: Kaiser Foundation Hospitals Inc
1 Kaiser Plz
Oakland CA 94612
510 271-6611

(P-19665)
KAISER FOUNDATION HOSPITALS
Also Called: Davis Medical Offices
1955 Cowell Blvd, Davis (95618-6325)
PHONE...................530 757-7100
Fax: 530 757-3929
Robert Talkington, *Manager*
Kim Pawlick, *Psychologist*
Gerald W Upcraft, *Obstetrician*
Peter J Chenaille, *Oncology*
Michael C Kinder, *Director*
EMP: 50
SALES (corp-wide): 27.8B **Privately Held**
WEB: www.kaiserpermanente.org
SIC: 8011 Offices & clinics of medical doctors
HQ: Kaiser Foundation Hospitals Inc
1 Kaiser Plz
Oakland CA 94612
510 271-6611

(P-19666)
KAISER FOUNDATION HOSPITALS
Kaiser Permanente
1950 Franklin St, Oakland (94612-5190)
PHONE...................510 987-1000
Fax: 510 271-5917

Maryanne Williams, *Manager*
Dick Daniels, *Senior VP*
Kathleen A Blackburn, *Vice Pres*
Ray Durkee, *Vice Pres*
Barbara Andrews, *Creative Dir*
EMP: 793
SALES (corp-wide): 27.8B **Privately Held**
WEB: www.kaiserpermanente.org
SIC: 8011 Health maintenance organization
HQ: Kaiser Foundation Hospitals Inc
1 Kaiser Plz
Oakland CA 94612
510 271-6611

(P-19667)
KAISER FOUNDATION HOSPITALS
Also Called: Milpitas Medical Offices
770 E Calaveras Blvd, Milpitas
(95035-5491)
PHONE...................408 945-2900
Fax: 408 945-2001
Ellen Sinclair, *Manager*
Joan Holup, *Research*
Audrey R Ellis, *Internal Med*
Quang D Dao, *Pediatrics*
Harpreet Hansra, *Pediatrics*
EMP: 50
SALES (corp-wide): 27.8B **Privately Held**
WEB: www.kaiserpermanente.org
SIC: 8011 8062 Offices & clinics of medical doctors; general medical & surgical hospitals
HQ: Kaiser Foundation Hospitals Inc
1 Kaiser Plz
Oakland CA 94612
510 271-6611

(P-19668)
KAISER FOUNDATION HOSPITALS
Also Called: Kaiser Permanente
1200 El Camino Real, South San Francisco
(94080-3208)
PHONE...................650 742-2000
Fax: 650 742-2022
Evelyn Chan, *Branch Mgr*
Hamid Motamed,
Serge Teplitsky, *Asst Admin*
Laurel Ullrich, *Info Tech Dir*
Brenda Leonard, *Engineer*
EMP: 1500
SALES (corp-wide): 27.8B **Privately Held**
WEB: www.kaiserpermanente.org
SIC: 8011 8062 Medical centers; general medical & surgical hospitals
HQ: Kaiser Foundation Hospitals Inc
1 Kaiser Plz
Oakland CA 94612
510 271-6611

(P-19669)
KAISER FOUNDATION HOSPITALS
Also Called: Kaiser Permanente South
6600 Bruceville Rd, Sacramento
(95823-4671)
PHONE...................916 688-2000
Fax: 916 688-2943
Sarah Krevans, *Branch Mgr*
Joel Weber,
Robert Alvarez, *President*
Kevin Smith, *Officer*
Marge Geary, *Senior VP*
EMP: 3600
SALES (corp-wide): 27.8B **Privately Held**
WEB: www.kaiserpermanente.org
SIC: 8011 Medical centers
HQ: Kaiser Foundation Hospitals Inc
1 Kaiser Plz
Oakland CA 94612
510 271-6611

(P-19670)
KAISER FOUNDATION HOSPITALS
Also Called: Kaiser Permanente
39400 Paseo Padre Pkwy, Fremont
(94538-2310)
PHONE...................510 248-3000
Fax: 510 795-3442
Calvin Wheeler, *Manager*
David Louie,
Monique Mabey,

PRODUCTS & SERVICES SECTION
8011 - Offices & Clinics Of Doctors Of Medicine County (P-19690)

Debbie Farris, *Office Mgr*
Peter Hendler, *Information Mgr*
EMP: 400
SQ FT: 86,710
SALES (corp-wide): 27.8B **Privately Held**
WEB: www.kaiserpermanente.org
SIC: 8011 8062 Medical centers; general medical & surgical hospitals
HQ: Kaiser Foundation Hospitals Inc
 1 Kaiser Plz
 Oakland CA 94612
 510 271-6611

(P-19671)
KAISER FOUNDATION HOSPITALS
Also Called: Kaiser Perminente
2155 Iron Point Rd, Folsom (95630-8707)
PHONE 916 817-5200
Larry Marini, *Manager*
Thomas A Deeble, *Obstetrician*
Petra Hoette, *Obstetrician*
Anna A Mirzoyan, *Internal Med*
Paul B Sobelman, *Internal Med*
EMP: 200
SALES (corp-wide): 27.8B **Privately Held**
WEB: www.kaiserpermanente.org
SIC: 8011 Health maintenance organization
HQ: Kaiser Foundation Hospitals Inc
 1 Kaiser Plz
 Oakland CA 94612
 510 271-6611

(P-19672)
KAISER FOUNDATION HOSPITALS
Also Called: Kaiser Foundation Health Plan
220 E Hacienda Ave, Campbell (95008-6617)
PHONE 408 871-6500
Fax: 408 871-6502
Joyce Snowbarger, *Manager*
Shan Zhu, *Executive*
Christina Bryant, *Med Doctor*
EMP: 100
SALES (corp-wide): 27.8B **Privately Held**
WEB: www.kaiser.com
SIC: 8011 8062 Medical centers; general medical & surgical hospitals
HQ: Kaiser Foundation Hospitals Inc
 1 Kaiser Plz
 Oakland CA 94612
 510 271-6611

(P-19673)
KAISER FOUNDATION HOSPITALS
Also Called: Kaiser Permanente
27107 Tourney Rd, Santa Clarita (91355-1860)
PHONE 661 222-2323
Pat Kenney, *Principal*
Nina K Shah, *Family Practiti*
Michael V Tran, *Family Practiti*
Scott Steiglitz, *Med Doctor*
Ingrid Schneider, *Pharmacist*
EMP: 52
SQ FT: 70,835
SALES (corp-wide): 27.8B **Privately Held**
WEB: www.kaiserpermanente.org
SIC: 8011 Offices & clinics of medical doctors
HQ: Kaiser Foundation Hospitals Inc
 1 Kaiser Plz
 Oakland CA 94612
 510 271-6611

(P-19674)
KAISER FOUNDATION HOSPITALS
Also Called: Kaiser Permanente
10800 Magnolia Ave, Riverside (92505-3000)
PHONE 951 247-3183
Fax: 909 353-3041
Vita Willett, *Director*
Ashenafi Tedla,
David Kvancz, *Vice Pres*
Tracy Barnes, *Ch Nursing Ofcr*
Larry Morgan, *Security Dir*
EMP: 1000
SALES (corp-wide): 27.8B **Privately Held**
WEB: www.kaiserpermanente.org
SIC: 8011 Medical centers

HQ: Kaiser Foundation Hospitals Inc
 1 Kaiser Plz
 Oakland CA 94612
 510 271-6611

(P-19675)
KAISER FOUNDATION HOSPITALS
Also Called: Kaiser Permanente
250 Hospital Pkwy Bldg D, San Jose (95119-1103)
PHONE 408 972-3000
Fax: 408 972-7178
Greg Schleef, *Principal*
Krammie M Chan, *Radiology Dir*
Patrick W Suen, *Surgeon*
Thomas T Lin, *Obstetrician*
Jerome L Nehemiah, *Obstetrician*
EMP: 105
SQ FT: 5,976
SALES (corp-wide): 27.8B **Privately Held**
WEB: www.kaiserpermanente.org
SIC: 8011 8062 General & family practice, physician/surgeon; general medical & surgical hospitals
HQ: Kaiser Foundation Hospitals Inc
 1 Kaiser Plz
 Oakland CA 94612
 510 271-6611

(P-19676)
KAISER FOUNDATION HOSPITALS
Also Called: Kaiser Permanente Moreno
27300 Iris Ave, Moreno Valley (92555-4802)
PHONE 951 243-0811
Tom Mc Ciltock, *Manager*
Pamela Gibson, *Lab Dir*
Maryann Hishmeh, *Radiology Dir*
Barbara Patton, *Administration*
Alan Mare, *Pathologist*
EMP: 400
SALES (corp-wide): 27.8B **Privately Held**
WEB: www.kaiserpermanente.org
SIC: 8011 Medical centers
HQ: Kaiser Foundation Hospitals Inc
 1 Kaiser Plz
 Oakland CA 94612
 510 271-6611

(P-19677)
KAISER FOUNDATION HOSPITALS
Also Called: Kaiser Permanente
110 N La Brea Ave, Inglewood (90301-1708)
PHONE 310 419-3303
Fax: 310 419-3401
Victor Ahaiwe, *President*
Esteban M Cruz, *Family Practiti*
Pamela T Stitt, *Family Practiti*
Allyson W Allen, *Physician Asst*
Ricky Menor, *Med Doctor*
EMP: 450
SALES (corp-wide): 27.8B **Privately Held**
WEB: www.kaiserpermanente.org
SIC: 8011 Offices & clinics of medical doctors
HQ: Kaiser Foundation Hospitals Inc
 1 Kaiser Plz
 Oakland CA 94612
 510 271-6611

(P-19678)
KAISER FOUNDATION HOSPITALS
Also Called: Kaiser Permanente
1600 Eureka Rd, Roseville (95661-3027)
PHONE 916 784-4000
Fax: 916 784-5424
Douglas Freeman, *Branch Mgr*
Linden Beck, *Officer*
Vince Golla, *Vice Pres*
Jason Goodwin, *Op Rm Dir*
Sripriya Balasubramanian, *Research*
EMP: 2300
SALES (corp-wide): 27.8B **Privately Held**
WEB: www.kaiserpermanente.org
SIC: 8011 Medical centers
HQ: Kaiser Foundation Hospitals Inc
 1 Kaiser Plz
 Oakland CA 94612
 510 271-6611

(P-19679)
KAISER FOUNDATION HOSPITALS
Also Called: Kaiser Permanente
7300 N Fresno St, Fresno (93720-2941)
PHONE 559 448-4500
Susan Ryan, *Senior VP*
David Debutts, *CIO*
Celia Ryan, *QA Dir*
Dan Rodriguez, *Purchasing*
Bernice C Whittle-Randolp, *Anesthesiology*
EMP: 2000
SALES (corp-wide): 27.8B **Privately Held**
WEB: www.kaiserpermanente.org
SIC: 8011 Medical centers
HQ: Kaiser Foundation Hospitals Inc
 1 Kaiser Plz
 Oakland CA 94612
 510 271-6611

(P-19680)
KAISER FOUNDATION HOSPITALS
Also Called: Carlsbad Medical Offices
6860 Avenida Encinas, Carlsbad (92011-3201)
PHONE 760 931-4228
Phong Nguyen, *Manager*
EMP: 105
SALES (corp-wide): 27.8B **Privately Held**
SIC: 8011 Health maintenance organization
HQ: Kaiser Foundation Hospitals Inc
 1 Kaiser Plz
 Oakland CA 94612
 510 271-6611

(P-19681)
KAISER MED CLINIC
555 Castro St, Mountain View (94041-2009)
PHONE 650 903-2103
Fax: 650 903-2752
Patricia Carpenter MGA, *Manager*
Patricia Planchon, *Executive Asst*
EMP: 110
SALES (est): 3.3MM **Privately Held**
SIC: 8011 Clinic, operated by physicians

(P-19682)
KAISER PERMANENTE
Also Called: Nuerology Dept
401 Bicentennial Way, Santa Rosa (95403-2149)
PHONE 707 393-4000
Fax: 707 571-4346
John F Cassidy MD, *Owner*
Al Duffis, *Ch Radiology*
Benjamin K Chu, *Exec VP*
Brian Erickson, *Op Rm Dir*
Patricia Carini, *Risk Mgmt Dir*
EMP: 225
SALES (est): 48.4MM **Privately Held**
SIC: 8011 General & family practice, physician/surgeon

(P-19683)
KAISER PERMENENTS
1830 California Ave, Corona (92881-3378)
PHONE 951 270-1888
Robert Munson, *Director*
Kelley Keele, *Exec Dir*
Brian Middlebrooks, *Admin Asst*
Darryl Duncan, *Technical Mgr*
Kerri Marr, *Business Anlyst*
EMP: 50
SALES (est): 13.7MM **Privately Held**
SIC: 8011 Health maintenance organization

(P-19684)
KAWEAH DLTA HLTH CARE DST GILD
1014 San Juan Ave, Exeter (93221-1312)
PHONE 559 592-7128
Fax: 559 592-9033
Phillip A Myers, *Physician Asst*
EMP: 63
SALES (corp-wide): 475.4MM **Privately Held**
SIC: 8011 Offices & clinics of medical doctors

PA: Kaweah Delta Health Care District Guild
 400 W Mineral King Ave
 Visalia CA 93291
 559 624-2000

(P-19685)
KECK HOSPITAL OF USC
1500 San Pablo St, Los Angeles (90033-5313)
PHONE 800 872-2273
Kamyar Afshar, *CFO*
Mike Fong, *Hlthcr Dir*
Terry Pickering, *Director*
Taileen Soler, *Manager*
▲ **EMP:** 77 **EST:** 2013
SALES: 761.1MM **Privately Held**
SIC: 8011 Health maintenance organization

(P-19686)
KERLAN-JOBE ORTHOPEDIC CLINIC (PA)
6801 Park Ter Ste 500, Los Angeles (90045-9212)
PHONE 310 665-7200
Fax: 310 665-7291
Ralph A Gambardella, *CEO*
Stephen Lombardo, *Admin Sec*
Gary Ito, *Technology*
Joseph Cabaret, *Orthopedist*
Mary Ordaz, *Manager*
EMP: 78
SQ FT: 37,000
SALES (est): 12.7MM **Privately Held**
WEB: www.kerlanjobe.com
SIC: 8011 Orthopedic physician

(P-19687)
KERN HEALTH SYSTEMS INC
Also Called: Kern Family Helathcare
9700 Stockdale Hwy, Bakersfield (93311-3617)
P.O. Box 25003 (93390-5003)
PHONE 661 664-5000
Paul Hensler, *Ch of Bd*
Renae Guerrero, *Purchasing*
Louis Iturriria, *Marketing Staff*
Remington Brooks, *Director*
EMP: 98
SQ FT: 16,000
SALES (est): 22MM **Privately Held**
WEB: www.kernfamilyhealthcare.com
SIC: 8011 Offices & clinics of medical doctors

(P-19688)
LA CLINICA DE LA RAZA INC
243 Georgia St, Vallejo (94590-5905)
PHONE 707 556-8100
Jane Garcia, *Branch Mgr*
Fawn L McCloud, *Nurse Practr*
EMP: 444
SALES (corp-wide): 74.4MM **Privately Held**
SIC: 8011 Clinic, operated by physicians
PA: La Clinica De La Raza, Inc.
 1450 Fruitvale Ave Fl 3
 Oakland CA 94601
 510 535-4000

(P-19689)
LA COUNTY HIGH DESERT HLTH SYS
44900 60th St W, Lancaster (93536-7618)
PHONE 661 945-8461
Fax: 661 723-1906
Beryl Brooks, *Exec Dir*
Camby Smith, *CFO*
Jerry Hooker, *Maintence Staff*
EMP: 400
SALES (est): 11.9MM **Privately Held**
SIC: 8011 8062 8093 Ambulatory surgical center; hospital, AMA approved residency; specialty outpatient clinics

(P-19690)
LA JOLLA ORTHOPAEDIC
4120 La Jolla Village Dr, La Jolla (92037-1406)
PHONE 858 657-0055
Scott Leggett, *Mng Member*
Jenna Pon, *Administration*
Grady Cartwright, *Mfg Dir*
Billy Herman, *Materials Mgr*
EMP: 69

8011 - Offices & Clinics Of Doctors Of Medicine County (P-19691)

SALES (est): 12.4MM Privately Held
WEB: www.osclajolla.com
SIC: 8011 Orthopedic physician

(P-19691)
LA LASER CENTER PC CPMC
10884 Santa Monica Blvd # 300, Los Angeles (90025-7638)
P.O. Box 16297, Beverly Hills (90209-2297)
PHONE 310 446-4400
Mehry Tahery, *Admin Sec*
EMP: 95
SALES (est): 1MM Privately Held
SIC: 8011 Dermatologist

(P-19692)
LA MAESTRA FAMILY CLINIC INC
165 S 1st St, El Cajon (92019-4795)
PHONE 619 280-1105
Marty Straw, *Branch Mgr*
EMP: 100
SALES (corp-wide): 24.2MM Privately Held
SIC: 8011 Clinic, operated by physicians
PA: La Maestra Family Clinic, Inc.
4060 Fairmount Ave
San Diego CA 92105
619 584-1612

(P-19693)
LA MAESTRA FAMILY CLINIC INC
Also Called: La Maestra Community Clinic
4060 Fairmount Ave, San Diego (92105-1608)
PHONE 619 280-4213
Alejanderina Areizaza, *Manager*
EMP: 100
SALES (corp-wide): 24.2MM Privately Held
SIC: 8011 Offices & clinics of medical doctors
PA: La Maestra Family Clinic, Inc.
4060 Fairmount Ave
San Diego CA 92105
619 584-1612

(P-19694)
LA MAESTRA FAMILY CLINIC INC
4305 University Ave # 120, San Diego (92105-1645)
PHONE 619 501-1235
Liv David, *Branch Mgr*
Carlos Hanessian, *Treasurer*
Marty Stroud, *Office Mgr*
EMP: 100
SALES (corp-wide): 24.2MM Privately Held
SIC: 8011 Medical centers
PA: La Maestra Family Clinic, Inc.
4060 Fairmount Ave
San Diego CA 92105
619 584-1612

(P-19695)
LA MESA INTRNL MDC MDCL GR
Also Called: La Mesa Internal Medical Group
5111 Garfield St, La Mesa (91941-5147)
PHONE 619 460-4050
Fax: 619 460-4607
Donald Patterson, *President*
John Dapolito, *Shareholder*
Dr Kenneth Hanson, *Shareholder*
James Malinak, *Shareholder*
Dr Roger English, *President*
EMP: 50
SQ FT: 10,000
SALES (est): 3.2MM Privately Held
SIC: 8011 Internal medicine, physician/surgeon

(P-19696)
LA PEER SURGERY CENTER LLC
Also Called: La Peer Health Systems
8920 Wilshire Blvd # 101, Beverly Hills (90211-2007)
PHONE 310 360-9119
Dr Siamak Tabib, *Mng Member*
Megan Rushall, *Director*
Alpie Ramos, *Manager*
EMP: 78 **EST:** 2000

SQ FT: 2,300
SALES: 28.3MM Privately Held
SIC: 8011 Surgeon

(P-19697)
LA VIDA MLTISPECIALTY MED CTRS
1400 S Grand Ave, Los Angeles (90015-3048)
PHONE 213 765-7500
Chuca Chidi, *President*
Marcy Flowers, *Office Mgr*
EMP: 60
SQ FT: 52,000
SALES: 23MM Privately Held
SIC: 8011 Offices & clinics of medical doctors

(P-19698)
LANCASTER CRDLGY MED GROUP INC (PA)
Also Called: Physicians Referral Service
43847 Heaton Ave Ste B, Lancaster (93534-4936)
PHONE 661 726-3058
Fax: 661 723-6882
Shun K Sunder MD, *President*
E Ekong MD, *Vice Pres*
Kanagarath Sivalingam MD, *Admin Sec*
Mark Agorrilla, *Human Res Mgr*
Harry Chandran, *Manager*
EMP: 80
SQ FT: 30,000
SALES (est): 6.8MM Privately Held
SIC: 8011 Cardiologist & cardio-vascular specialist

(P-19699)
LARCHMONT RADIOLOGY MED GROUP
Also Called: Westcoast Medial Imaging
2010 Wilshire Blvd # 409, Los Angeles (90057-3598)
PHONE 213 483-5953
Fax: 213 484-2984
Stewart A Lapin, *President*
Gabriela Guerra, *Office Mgr*
EMP: 55
SQ FT: 4,500
SALES (est): 3.6MM Privately Held
SIC: 8011 Radiologist

(P-19700)
LAREN D TAN MD
11234 Anderson St, Loma Linda (92354-2804)
PHONE 909 558-4444
Laren Tan, *Principal*
EMP: 78
SALES (est): 2.5MM Privately Held
SIC: 8011 Physicians' office, including specialists

(P-19701)
LAS ISLAS FAMILY MED GROUP PC
325 W Chnnel Islands Blvd, Oxnard (93033-4501)
PHONE 805 385-8662
Fax: 805 385-1848
Miguel Cervantes, *Director*
Julian Todd, *Gnrl Med Prac*
EMP: 65
SALES (est): 6.6MM Privately Held
WEB: www.lasislasfamilymedical.com
SIC: 8011 General & family practice, physician/surgeon

(P-19702)
LASSEN MEDICAL GROUP INC (PA)
Also Called: Mercy Medical
2450 Sster Mary Clumba Dr, Red Bluff (96080-4356)
PHONE 530 527-0414
Fax: 530 527-7090
Kimberli R Frantz, *President*
Dan Mc Daniel MD, *Treasurer*
Richard Wickenheiser, *Bd of Directors*
Richard Caylor, *Executive*
Kim Hake, *Office Mgr*
EMP: 57

SALES (est): 13.5MM Privately Held
SIC: 8011 8099 Physicians' office, including specialists; blood related health services

(P-19703)
LELAND STANFORD JUNIOR UNIV
1201 Welch Rd, Stanford (94305-5102)
PHONE 650 723-7863
Fax: 650 723-8762
William C Mobley, *Principal*
Richard Barth, *Professor*
EMP: 54
SALES (corp-wide): 1.9B Privately Held
SIC: 8011 Radiologist
PA: Leland Stanford Junior University
2575 Sand Hill Rd
Menlo Park CA 94025
650 723-2300

(P-19704)
LELAND STANFORD JUNIOR UNIV
Health Promotion Resource Ctr
211 Quarry Rd N229, Palo Alto (94304-1416)
PHONE 650 725-4416
Wes Alles, *Principal*
Sam Tsai, *Human Res Mgr*
Susan Ayers, *Manager*
EMP: 54
SALES (corp-wide): 1.9B Privately Held
SIC: 8011 8221 Health maintenance organization; university
PA: Leland Stanford Junior University
2575 Sand Hill Rd
Menlo Park CA 94025
650 723-2300

(P-19705)
LELAND STANFORD JUNIOR UNIV
Also Called: Cowell Student Health Service
870 Campus Dr, Stanford (94305-8508)
PHONE 650 723-0821
Dr Ira Friedman, *Director*
EMP: 100
SALES (corp-wide): 1.9B Privately Held
SIC: 8011 8031 8221 Medical centers; offices & clinics of osteopathic physicians; university
PA: Leland Stanford Junior University
2575 Sand Hill Rd
Menlo Park CA 94025
650 723-2300

(P-19706)
LES KELLEY FAMILY HEALTH CTR
1920 Colorado Ave, Santa Monica (90404-3414)
PHONE 310 319-4700
Michele Bholat, *Director*
Eric Chamers, *Administration*
Benjamin Gilmore, *Med Doctor*
Benjamin N Gilmore, *Director*
James P Murray, *Director*
EMP: 60
SALES (est): 2.6MM Privately Held
SIC: 8011 Clinic, operated by physicians

(P-19707)
LIFELONG MEDICAL CARE
Also Called: Over 60 Health Center
3260 Sacramento St, Berkeley (94702-2739)
PHONE 510 981-4100
J I Chen, *Branch Mgr*
Diane E Straus, *Nurse Practr*
EMP: 58
SALES (corp-wide): 59.1MM Privately Held
SIC: 8011 General & family practice, physician/surgeon
PA: Lifelong Medical Care
2344 6th St
Berkeley CA 94710
510 704-6010

(P-19708)
LIFELONG MEDICAL CARE (PA)
Also Called: Over 60 Health Center
2344 6th St, Berkeley (94710-2412)
P.O. Box 11247 (94712-2247)
PHONE 510 704-6010
Fax: 510 841-5437
Marty A Lynch, *CEO*
Brenda Shipp, *COO*
Rick Clark, *CFO*
Philip Klatt, *Info Tech Mgr*
EMP: 50
SQ FT: 4,200
SALES (est): 35.6MM Privately Held
SIC: 8011 General & family practice, physician/surgeon

(P-19709)
LINDA LOMA UNIV HLTH CARE
Also Called: Loma Linda Faculty Med Group
11370 Anderson St # 2100, Loma Linda (92354-3450)
P.O. Box 626 (92354-0626)
PHONE 909 558-2851
Ilene Spencer, *Manager*
Tamara Shankel, *Surgeon*
Aijaz Hashmi, *Cardiology*
Linda Golkar, *Dermatology*
Eba H Hathout, *Endocrinology*
EMP: 250
SALES (corp-wide): 158.3MM Privately Held
SIC: 8011 Offices & clinics of medical doctors
PA: Loma Linda University Health Care
11175 Campus St
Loma Linda CA 92350
909 558-4985

(P-19710)
LINDA LOMA UNIV HLTH CARE (PA)
11175 Campus St, Loma Linda (92350-1700)
PHONE 909 558-4985
Fax: 909 558-4184
Roger Hadley MD, *President*
David B Hinshaw Jr, *Vice Chairman*
James Pappas, *Vice Pres*
Brian Bull MD, *Admin Sec*
Danna Samson, *Administration*
EMP: 850
SQ FT: 70,000
SALES: 158.3MM Privately Held
SIC: 8011 Offices & clinics of medical doctors

(P-19711)
LINDA LOMA UNIV HLTH CARE
Also Called: Llu Center For Fertility
11370 Anderson St # 3950, Loma Linda (92350-1715)
P.O. Box 1009 (92354-1009)
PHONE 909 558-2840
Fax: 909 478-6654
Linda Moore, *Administration*
Mark White, *VP Mktg*
EMP: 153
SALES (corp-wide): 158.3MM Privately Held
SIC: 8011 Fertility specialist, physician
PA: Loma Linda University Health Care
11175 Campus St
Loma Linda CA 92350
909 558-4985

(P-19712)
LINDEN CREST SURGERY CENTER
9735 Wilshire Blvd # 100, Beverly Hills (90212-2114)
PHONE 310 601-3900
Fax: 310 601-3909
Christina Niegos, *Principal*
Garland Perry, *Office Mgr*
Nicholas Karyotakis, *Director*
EMP: 60
SALES (est): 3.2MM Privately Held
WEB: www.lindencrestsurgery.com
SIC: 8011 Surgeon

PRODUCTS & SERVICES SECTION   8011 - Offices & Clinics Of Doctors Of Medicine County (P-19735)

(P-19713)
LIVINGSTON COMMUNITY HEALTH
Also Called: Livingston Health Center
1140 Main St, Livingston (95334-1257)
PHONE..................................209 394-7913
Fax: 209 394-3021
Leslie McGowan, *CEO*
Selina Montoya, *CFO*
Lupe Castaneda, *Executive Asst*
Randall King, *Financial Exec*
Mariela Baeza, *VP Sales*
EMP: 101
SQ FT: 10,623
SALES: 10.5MM **Privately Held**
SIC: **8011** Primary care medical clinic

(P-19714)
LLU ADVNTIST HLTH SCIENCES CTR
Also Called: Risk Management
101 E Redlands Blvd, San Bernardino (92408-3710)
P.O. Box 1770, Loma Linda (92354-0570)
PHONE..................................909 558-4386
Mark Hubbard, *Director*
EMP: 52
SALES (est): 3.8MM **Privately Held**
SIC: **8011** Medical centers

(P-19715)
LODI MEMORIAL HOSP ASSN INC
Also Called: Rehabilitation Center
800 S Lower Sacramento Rd, Lodi (95242-3635)
PHONE..................................209 333-3100
Linda Escobar, *Director*
Sandra Beck-Atwater, *Pharmacy Dir*
Sally Tsunekawa, *Pharmacist*
EMP: 120
SALES (corp-wide): 174.9MM **Privately Held**
SIC: **8011** 8069 Specialized medical practitioners, except internal; specialty hospitals, except psychiatric
PA: Lodi Memorial Hospital Association, Inc.
  975 S Fairmont Ave
  Lodi CA 95240
  209 334-3411

(P-19716)
LOMA LINDA UNIVERSITY
1911 W Park Ave, Redlands (92373-8045)
P.O. Box 1740, Loma Linda (92354-0240)
PHONE..................................909 558-6422
Brian Bull, *President*
Suma Oommen MD, *Med Doctor*
Sandra Adams, *Asst Director*
EMP: 65
SALES: 11.4MM **Privately Held**
SIC: **8011** Pathologist

(P-19717)
LOMPOC VALLEY MEDICAL CENTER
Also Called: Mammography Center
1111 E Ocean Ave Ste 2, Lompoc (93436-2500)
PHONE..................................805 735-9229
Jim Raggio, *Branch Mgr*
EMP: 200
SALES (corp-wide): 85.8MM **Privately Held**
SIC: **8011** Radiologist
PA: Lompoc Valley Medical Center
  1515 E Ocean Ave
  Lompoc CA 93436
  805 737-3300

(P-19718)
LONG BEACH MNTL HLTH SRVCS
Also Called: Long Beach Mental Health Ctr
1975 Long Beach Blvd, Long Beach (90806-5501)
PHONE..................................562 218-4001
Fax: 562 599-3934
Emilia Ramos, *Manager*
Thelma M Angeles, *Psychiatry*
Luzminda C Lachica, *Psychiatry*
Karen A Lee, *Psychiatry*
Marcy Epstein, *Nurse Practr*
EMP: 135

SALES (est): 4.1MM **Privately Held**
SIC: **8011** 8093 Clinic, operated by physicians; mental health clinic, outpatient

(P-19719)
LOS ANGELES CARDIOLOGY ASSOC (PA)
1245 Wilshire Blvd # 703, Los Angeles (90017-4810)
PHONE..................................213 977-0419
Fax: 213 977-0225
David S Cannom MD, *Partner*
Anil K Bhandari MD, *Partner*
Steven Burstein MD, *Partner*
Robert D Lerman MD, *Partner*
Charles Pollick MD, *Partner*
EMP: 65
SQ FT: 12,000
SALES (est): 10.2MM **Privately Held**
SIC: **8011** Cardiologist & cardio-vascular specialist

(P-19720)
LOS ANGELES CHRISTN HLTH CTRS (HQ)
311 Winston St, Los Angeles (90013-1519)
PHONE..................................213 893-1960
Lisa Abdishoo, *CEO*
Bettina Lewis, *Info Tech Mgr*
Cheryl Barnes, *Human Res Dir*
Joseph Mendez, *Manager*
EMP: 50
SALES: 9.3MM
SALES (corp-wide): 11.7MM **Privately Held**
SIC: **8011** Primary care medical clinic
PA: Los Angeles Mission, Inc.
  2403 Dumaine St C
  New Orleans LA 70119
  213 629-1227

(P-19721)
LOS ANGELES COUNTY HEALTH SVC
1108 N Oleander Ave, Compton (90222-4041)
PHONE..................................310 763-2244
Fax: 310 223-0317
Lorraine Madison, *Principal*
EMP: 50
SALES (est): 1.6MM **Privately Held**
SIC: **8011** Clinic, operated by physicians

(P-19722)
LOS ANGELES FREE CLINIC
8405 Beverly Blvd, Los Angeles (90048-3401)
PHONE..................................323 653-8622
Abbe Land, *CEO*
Lisa Gritzner, *Vice Pres*
Neil Romanoff, *Vice Pres*
Rose Saperstein, *Social Dir*
Mary Rainwater, *Exec Dir*
EMP: 99
SALES: 107.2K **Privately Held**
SIC: **8011** General & family practice, physician/surgeon

(P-19723)
LUCILE SALTER PACKARD CHIL
Also Called: Bayside Medical Group
5601 Norris Canyon Rd # 230, San Ramon (94583-5407)
PHONE..................................925 277-7550
K C Campion, *CEO*
EMP: 129
SALES (corp-wide): 1.1B **Privately Held**
SIC: **8011** Pediatrician
PA: Lucile Salter Packard Children's Hospital At Stanford
  725 Welch Rd
  Palo Alto CA 94304
  650 736-7398

(P-19724)
MADERA COMMUNITY HOSPITAL
Also Called: Family Health Services Clinic
1210 E Almond Ave Ste A, Madera (93637-5606)
PHONE..................................559 675-5530
Robert Kelly, *CEO*
Curtis Tanner, *Med Doctor*
EMP: 63

SALES (corp-wide): 75.9MM **Privately Held**
SIC: **8011** Clinic, operated by physicians
PA: Madera Community Hospital
  1250 E Almond Ave
  Madera CA 93637
  559 675-5555

(P-19725)
MAGAN MEDICAL CLINIC INC (PA)
Also Called: M M C
420 W Rowland St, Covina (91723-2943)
PHONE..................................626 331-6411
Fax: 626 859-1394
Bradley J Rosenberg, *President*
Howard Ort MD, *Exec VP*
Miguel Garcia, *Vice Pres*
Tommie Anderson, *Executive*
Kevin Potter, *Info Tech Dir*
EMP: 250
SQ FT: 66,000
SALES (est): 34.3MM **Privately Held**
WEB: www.maganclinic.com
SIC: **8011** Clinic, operated by physicians; urologist; internal medicine, physician/surgeon; ophthalmologist

(P-19726)
MAGAN MEDICAL CLINIC INC
330 W Covina Blvd, San Dimas (91773-2907)
PHONE..................................909 592-9712
Beth Nunn, *Human Resources*
Georgetta McCloud, *CFO*
Bruce Bowne, *Administration*
Doug Loop, *Administration*
Ronald Lane, *MIS Dir*
EMP: 91
SALES (corp-wide): 34.3MM **Privately Held**
WEB: www.maganclinic.com
SIC: **8011** 8071 Offices & clinics of medical doctors; medical laboratories
PA: Magan Medical Clinic, Inc.
  420 W Rowland St
  Covina CA 91723
  626 331-6411

(P-19727)
MANGROVE MEDICAL GROUP
Also Called: Mangrove Lab & X-Ray
1040 Mangrove Ave, Chico (95926-3509)
PHONE..................................530 345-0064
Fax: 530 343-2612
Dewayne E Caviness MD, *Partner*
Randall E Caviness MD, *Partner*
Kurt E Johnson MD, *Partner*
Dean P Smith MD, *Partner*
Randall S Williams MD, *Partner*
EMP: 50
SQ FT: 12,000
SALES (est): 8.5MM **Privately Held**
SIC: **8011** General & family practice, physician/surgeon

(P-19728)
MARIN COMMUNITY CLINIC
Also Called: Marin Community Clinics
1177 Francisco Blvd E B, San Rafael (94901-5403)
PHONE..................................415 448-1500
Linda Tavaszi, *CEO*
Peggy Dracker, *COO*
Arthur Feagles, *CFO*
David Klinetobe, *CFO*
Liz Digan, *Executive*
EMP: 99
SQ FT: 9,000
SALES (est): 31.4MM **Privately Held**
SIC: **8011** Primary care medical clinic

(P-19729)
MARINOW HARRY MD FACS INC
Also Called: Feiwell, Lawrence MD
3742 Katella Ave Ste 401, Los Alamitos (90720-3172)
PHONE..................................562 430-3561
Korinne Walker, *President*
EMP: 50
SALES (est): 2.2MM **Privately Held**
SIC: **8011** Physicians' office, including specialists

(P-19730)
MARK E JACOBSON M D
1260 N Dutton Ave Ste 230, Santa Rosa (95401-7161)
PHONE..................................707 571-4022
Mark Jacobson MD, *President*
EMP: 60
SALES (est): 3.7MM **Privately Held**
SIC: **8011** Offices & clinics of medical doctors

(P-19731)
MARK H LEIBENHAUT MD
Also Called: Ras
2800 L St Ste 110, Sacramento (95816-5616)
PHONE..................................916 454-6600
Mark H Leibenhaut, *Partner*
Jeanine Rust, *Advisor*
EMP: 50
SALES (est): 1.5MM **Privately Held**
SIC: **8011** Offices & clinics of medical doctors

(P-19732)
MARSHALL MEDICAL CENTER
Also Called: Family Intrnal Mdcn-Plcerville
1095 Marshall Way, Placerville (95667-5722)
PHONE..................................530 626-2920
Fax: 530 622-9509
Tracy A Harris, *Nurse Practr*
Maria Rosen, *Nurse Practr*
EMP: 53
SALES (corp-wide): 200.2MM **Privately Held**
SIC: **8011** Offices & clinics of medical doctors
PA: Marshall Medical Center
  1100 Marshall Way
  Placerville CA 95667
  530 622-1441

(P-19733)
MARTECH MEDICAL PRODUCTS INC
565 Clara Nofal Rd, Calexico (92231-9533)
PHONE..................................215 256-8833
EMP: 99
SALES (corp-wide): 37.1MM **Privately Held**
SIC: **8011** Offices & clinics of medical doctors
PA: Martech Medical Products, Inc.
  1500 Delp Dr
  Harleysville PA 19438
  215 256-8833

(P-19734)
MARTIN LTHER KING/DREW MED CTR
1670 E 120th St, Los Angeles (90059-3026)
PHONE..................................310 773-4926
Fax: 310 223-0733
Hank Wells, *CEO*
Kenneth Lewis,
Linda McAuley, *COO*
Anthony Gray, *CFO*
Tony Gray, *CFO*
EMP: 91
SALES (est): 23.4MM **Privately Held**
SIC: **8011** Medical centers

(P-19735)
MCHENRY MEDICAL GROUP INC
1541 Florida Ave Ste 200, Modesto (95350-4438)
PHONE..................................209 577-3388
Fax: 209 523-6720
John Porteous, *President*
Harris M Goodman, *Treasurer*
Sydney Chartrand, *Info Tech Mgr*
Sheila Mansfield, *Bookkeeper*
Ken Scott, *Psychologist*
EMP: 100
SQ FT: 22,000
SALES (est): 9.8MM **Privately Held**
WEB: www.mchenrymedical.com
SIC: **8011** Internal medicine, physician/surgeon; gastronomist; dermatologist; surgeon

8011 - Offices & Clinics Of Doctors Of Medicine County (P-19736)   PRODUDUCTS & SERVICES SECTION

(P-19736)
MD IMAGING INC A PROF MED CORP
Also Called: Women's Imaging Center
2020 Court St, Redding (96001-1822)
PHONE..................530 243-1249
Michael G Davis, *CEO*
Richard J Slepicka, *CFO*
Roxanne Wade, *Business Dir*
Jospeh Hampton, *Technician*
Charlene Cundy, *Human Res Mgr*
EMP: 100
SALES (est): 20MM Privately Held
WEB: www.mdimaging.net
SIC: **8011** Radiologist

(P-19737)
MEDICAL GROUP BVERLY HILLS INC (PA)
Also Called: Cedars Sinai Medical Group
200 N Robertson Blvd, Beverly Hills (90211-1769)
PHONE..................310 385-3200
Fax: 310 385-3556
Thomas D Gordon, *CEO*
Antoinette T Hubenette MD, *President*
Stephen C Deutsch MD, *Treasurer*
James L Caplan MD, *Vice Pres*
Mary Claire Lingel, *Exec Dir*
EMP: 50
SQ FT: 14,500
SALES (est): 11.1MM Privately Held
SIC: **8011** Offices & clinics of medical doctors

(P-19738)
MEDICAL GROUP BVERLY HILLS INC
Also Called: Cedar Sinai Medical Group
250 N Robertson Blvd # 603, Beverly Hills (90211-1788)
PHONE..................310 247-4646
Fax: 310 385-8734
Tom Gordon, *Branch Mgr*
EMP: 50
SALES (corp-wide): 11.1MM Privately Held
SIC: **8011** Offices & clinics of medical doctors
PA: Medical Group Of Beverly Hills, Inc.
  200 N Robertson Blvd
  Beverly Hills CA 90211
  310 385-3200

(P-19739)
MEDICL IMGNG CTR OF SOUTHRN CA
2811 Wilshire Blvd # 100, Santa Monica (90403-4803)
PHONE..................310 829-9788
Fax: 310 264-1649
Bradley Jabour MD, *President*
Nicole Pelissier, *COO*
Ulli Butzke, *Financial Exec*
Ulli Bitcke, *Finance Mgr*
William Cohen, *Med Doctor*
EMP: 65
SQ FT: 22,000
SALES (est): 7.4MM Privately Held
WEB: www.corbyandcorby.com
SIC: **8011** Radiologist

(P-19740)
MEDPOINT MANAGEMENT INC
6400 Canoga Ave Ste 163, Woodland Hills (91367-2435)
PHONE..................818 702-0100
Fax: 818 941-0659
Sheldon Lewenfuff Preident, *Principal*
Sheldon Lewenfuf, *President*
Krin Kuethe, *COO*
Derek Schneider, *CFO*
Sheldon Lewenfus, *Vice Pres*
EMP: 50
SALES (est): 8.5MM Privately Held
WEB: www.medpointmanagement.com
SIC: **8011** Medical insurance associations

(P-19741)
MEMOR ORTHO SURGIC GROUP A M
Also Called: Southern California Cen
2760 Atlantic Ave, Long Beach (90806-2755)
PHONE..................562 424-6666
Fax: 562 427-1235
Peter R Kurzweil, *CEO*
Douglas W Jackson MD, *President*
Curtis W Spencer III, *Vice Pres*
Robert Anderson, *Managing Dir*
David S Morrison MD, *Admin Sec*
▲ EMP: 70
SQ FT: 12,000
SALES (est): 9.3MM Privately Held
SIC: **8011** Orthopedic physician; sports medicine specialist, physician; surgeon; physical medicine, physician/surgeon

(P-19742)
MEMORIAL COUNSELING ASSOC INC
4525 E Atherton St, Long Beach (90815-3700)
PHONE..................562 961-0155
A Sarkis, *President*
Alexanderia Wirga, *Psychiatry*
EMP: 80
SALES (est): 4.2MM Privately Held
WEB: www.mcapsych.com
SIC: **8011** 8322 Offices & clinics of medical doctors; general counseling services

(P-19743)
MEMORIAL PSYCHIATRIC HLTH SVCS
4525 E Atherton St, Long Beach (90815-3700)
PHONE..................562 494-9243
Fax: 562 961-0161
Lee Yoseloff, *President*
Sarkis Gavin MD, *Principal*
Juliette Gabel, *Manager*
EMP: 50
SALES (est): 3MM Privately Held
SIC: **8011** Psychiatrists & psychoanalysts

(P-19744)
MEMORIAL SURGICAL GROUP
2760 Atlantic Ave, Long Beach (90806-2755)
PHONE..................562 424-6666
Edward Southern MD, *Owner*
EMP: 60
SALES (est): 1.1MM Privately Held
SIC: **8011** Surgeon

(P-19745)
MENDOCINO CMNTY HLTH CLNIC INC (PA)
Also Called: McHc
333 Laws Ave, Ukiah (95482-6540)
PHONE..................707 468-1010
Fax: 707 468-0696
John Pavoni, *CEO*
Alicia Gordon, *Office Mgr*
Jeff Wiedenfeld, *Info Tech Dir*
Lisa Schat, *Info Tech Mgr*
Leonilo Yap, *Accountant*
EMP: 130
SQ FT: 24,000
SALES: 28.3MM Privately Held
WEB: www.mchcinc.org
SIC: **8011** Primary care medical clinic

(P-19746)
MENLO MED CLINIC A MED CORP
1300 Crane St, Menlo Park (94025-4260)
PHONE..................650 498-6500
Fax: 650 321-4390
Ed Kelly, *Administration*
Nancy Adelman MD, *Partner*
Gayle S Hunt-Cahan Anp-C, *Partner*
Katherine A Blenko MD, *Partner*
Martin Bronk MD, *Partner*
EMP: 150 EST: 1946
SQ FT: 40,000
SALES (est): 26.5MM Privately Held
WEB: www.ucsfstanford.org
SIC: **8011** Clinic, operated by physicians

(P-19747)
MERCY HM SVCS A CAL LTD PARTNR
Also Called: Administrative Office
2175 Rosaline Ave Ste A, Redding (96001-2549)
PHONE..................530 225-6000
Fax: 530 225-6125
Ronald Cloud, *Branch Mgr*
James N Gonzalez,
Andrea Kofl, *Executive*
Sandra L Le Doux, *Admin Asst*
Carolyn Helfenstein, *Planning*
EMP: 340
SALES (corp-wide): 7.1B Privately Held
SIC: **8011** Medical centers
HQ: Mercy Home Services A California Limited Partnership
  2175 Rosaline Ave Ste A
  Redding CA 96001
  530 225-6000

(P-19748)
MERCY HM SVCS A CAL LTD PARTNR
Also Called: Mercy Medical Center
2740 M St, Merced (95340-2813)
PHONE..................209 564-4200
Fax: 209 722-2902
Lisa Wegley, *Manager*
EMP: 340
SALES (corp-wide): 7.1B Privately Held
WEB: www.mercyhealth.org
SIC: **8011** Medical centers
HQ: Mercy Home Services A California Limited Partnership
  2175 Rosaline Ave Ste A
  Redding CA 96001
  530 225-6000

(P-19749)
MERCY METHODIST HOSPITAL
7601 Hospital Dr Ste 103, Sacramento (95823-5408)
PHONE..................916 681-1600
Fax: 916 681-2671
Amir Sweha MD, *Branch Mgr*
EMP: 50
SALES (corp-wide): 59.2MM Privately Held
SIC: **8011** Offices & clinics of medical doctors
PA: Mercy Methodist Hospital
  7500 Hospital Dr
  Sacramento CA 95823
  916 423-6063

(P-19750)
MERRIDIAN NEURO CARE
18a Journey Ste 200, Aliso Viejo (92656-5342)
PHONE..................949 263-6630
Jim Ashby, *Principal*
EMP: 50
SALES (est): 1.8MM Privately Held
SIC: **8011** Neurologist

(P-19751)
MICHAEL SD NAGATINI
5400 W Hillsdale Ave, Visalia (93291-8222)
PHONE..................559 738-7502
Bill Brower, *CEO*
EMP: 60 EST: 2001
SALES (est): 764.1K Privately Held
SIC: **8011** Offices & clinics of medical doctors

(P-19752)
MISSION INTERNAL MED GROUP INC
Also Called: Arthur Loussararian MD
26800 Crown Valley Pkwy # 103, Mission Viejo (92691-6389)
PHONE..................949 364-3570
Fax: 949 364-3430
Arthur Loussararian, *Principal*
Julia Hayton, *Office Mgr*
Murray L Margolis, *Internal Med*
Amir H Azad, *Nephrology*
Joey R Gee, *Neurology*
EMP: 102
SALES (corp-wide): 20.1MM Privately Held
WEB: www.mimg.com
SIC: **8011** Offices & clinics of medical doctors
PA: Mission Internal Medical Group, Inc.
  26522 La Alameda Ste 120
  Mission Viejo CA 92691
  949 282-1600

(P-19753)
MISSION INTERNAL MED GROUP INC
26800 Crown Valley Pkwy # 103, Mission Viejo (92691-6389)
PHONE..................949 364-6559
Bruce L Nelson, *Manager*
EMP: 200
SALES (corp-wide): 20.1MM Privately Held
WEB: www.mimg.com
SIC: **8011** Internal medicine, physician/surgeon
PA: Mission Internal Medical Group, Inc.
  26522 La Alameda Ste 120
  Mission Viejo CA 92691
  949 282-1600

(P-19754)
MISSION INTERNAL MED GROUP INC
Also Called: West Coast Physical Therapy
27882 Forbes Rd Ste 110, Laguna Niguel (92677-1267)
PHONE..................949 364-3605
Joan Shrum-Brown, *Principal*
EMP: 102
SALES (corp-wide): 20.1MM Privately Held
WEB: www.mimg.com
SIC: **8011** 8049 Cardiologist & cardio-vascular specialist; physical therapist
PA: Mission Internal Medical Group, Inc.
  26522 La Alameda Ste 120
  Mission Viejo CA 92691
  949 282-1600

(P-19755)
MISSION NEIGHBORHOOD HLTH CTR (PA)
240 Shotwell St, San Francisco (94110-1323)
PHONE..................415 552-3870
Fax: 415 431-3178
Brenda Storey, *CEO*
Charles Moser, *President*
Angela Robinson, *CFO*
Brad Kittredge, *Bd of Directors*
Francis Allen, *Vice Pres*
EMP: 110
SQ FT: 21,000
SALES: 16.1MM Privately Held
WEB: www.mnhc.org
SIC: **8011** Primary care medical clinic

(P-19756)
MISSION VALLEY HTS SURGERY CTR
Also Called: Amsurg
7485 Mission Valley Rd # 106, San Diego (92108-4422)
PHONE..................619 291-3737
Fax: 619 291-3738
William S Adsit MD, *Partner*
Drew A Peterson MD, *Partner*
Kevin Smith MD, *Principal*
Jocelyn Day, *Manager*
EMP: 59
SQ FT: 14,000
SALES (est): 7.5MM Privately Held
WEB: www.mvhsc.com
SIC: **8011** Surgeon

(P-19757)
MODERN CONCEPTS MEDICAL GROUP
1217 W Whittier Blvd, Montebello (90640-4642)
PHONE..................323 728-6070
Margaret Herrera, *Branch Mgr*
EMP: 53
SALES (corp-wide): 5.9MM Privately Held
SIC: **8011** Offices & clinics of medical doctors
PA: Modern Concepts Medical Group
  1701 E Cesar E Chavez Ave
  Los Angeles CA 90033
  323 221-5366

(P-19758)
MOLINA HEALTHCARE INC
790 E Foothill Blvd, Rialto (92376-5269)
PHONE..................909 546-7116
EMP: 133

PRODUCTS & SERVICES SECTION
8011 - Offices & Clinics Of Doctors Of Medicine County (P-19781)

SALES (corp-wide): 14.1B **Publicly Held**
SIC: 8011 Offices & clinics of medical doctors
PA: Molina Healthcare, Inc.
200 Oceangate Ste 100
Long Beach CA 90802
562 435-3666

(P-19759)
MOLINA HEALTHCARE INC (PA)
200 Oceangate Ste 100, Long Beach (90802-4317)
P.O. Box 22813 (90801-5813)
PHONE.................................562 435-3666
Fax: 562 437-7235
J Mario Molina, *Ch of Bd*
Craig Bass, *President*
Richard Chambers, *President*
Norman Nichols, *President*
Jesse L Thomas, *President*
EMP: 2800
SQ FT: 460,000
SALES: 14.1B **Publicly Held**
WEB: www.molinahealthcare.com
SIC: 8011 6324 Health maintenance organization; hospital & medical service plans; health maintenance organization (HMO), insurance only

(P-19760)
MOLINA INFORMATION SYSTEMS LLC
200 Oceangate Ste 100, Long Beach (90802-4317)
PHONE.................................562 435-3666
Gary Zeiss, *Administration*
EMP: 1022
SALES (est): 7.2MM **Privately Held**
SIC: 8011 Medical insurance plan

(P-19761)
MONARCH HEALTHCARE A MEDICAL (HQ)
11 Technology Dr, Irvine (92618-2302)
PHONE.................................949 923-3200
Bartley Asner, *CEO*
Marcie Greene, *CEO*
Marvin Gordon MD, *CFO*
Jay J Cohen MD, *Vice Pres*
Steven Rudy MD, *Vice Pres*
EMP: 115
SQ FT: 75,000
SALES (est): 47.9MM
SALES (corp-wide): 157.1B **Publicly Held**
WEB: www.mhealth.com
SIC: 8011 Group health association
PA: Unitedhealth Group Incorporated
9900 Bren Rd E Ste 300w
Minnetonka MN 55343
952 936-1300

(P-19762)
MONROVIA HEALTH CENTER
330 W Maple Ave, Monrovia (91016-3387)
PHONE.................................626 256-1600
Fax: 626 303-2252
Maxine Liggins, *Director*
EMP: 60
SQ FT: 2,400
SALES (est): 3.6MM **Privately Held**
SIC: 8011 Medical centers

(P-19763)
MUIR ORTHOPEDIC SPECIALISTS
2405 Shadelands Dr # 210, Walnut Creek (94598-5905)
PHONE.................................925 939-8585
Fax: 925 933-4932
K C Campion, *CEO*
Ramiro Miranda MD, *President*
Jill Limbacher, *CPA*
Sidney Rocklind, *Controller*
John K Wilhelmy, *Director*
EMP: 177
SALES: 20MM **Privately Held**
SIC: 8011 Orthopedic physician

(P-19764)
NATIVE AMERICAN HEALTH CTR INC (PA)
2950 International Blvd, Oakland (94601-2228)
PHONE.................................510 535-4400
Fax: 510 261-6438
Martin Waukazoo, *CEO*
Kevin Goff, *Executive*
Lucy Nelson, *Admin Dir*
Amadene Castillo, *Office Mgr*
Karen Harrison, *Office Mgr*
EMP: 80 EST: 1971
SQ FT: 16,000
SALES: 22.3MM **Privately Held**
WEB: www.nativehealth.org
SIC: 8011 8021 8093 Clinic, operated by physicians; dentists' office; mental health clinic, outpatient

(P-19765)
NCA PROGRAM
Also Called: Maternal Child Clinic
1000 S Fremont Ave Unit 1, Alhambra (91803-8801)
PHONE.................................323 226-5068
Andrea Kovacs, *Director*
Yolanda Salcedo, *Office Mgr*
Lashonda Y Spencer, *Infectious Dis*
Marie J Eyssallenne, *Physician Asst*
EMP: 70
SALES (est): 4MM **Privately Held**
SIC: 8011 Clinic, operated by physicians

(P-19766)
NEIGHBORHOOD HEALTHCARE (PA)
425 N Date St Ste 203, Escondido (92025-3413)
PHONE.................................760 520-8372
Tracy Ream, *CEO*
Johnny Watson, *President*
Amparo Mahler, *COO*
Lisa Daigle, *CFO*
Stephen P Yerxa, *Treasurer*
EMP: 50
SQ FT: 17,000
SALES: 45.1MM **Privately Held**
SIC: 8011 Clinic, operated by physicians

(P-19767)
NEIGHBORHOOD HEALTHCARE
1001 E Grand Ave, Escondido (92025-4604)
PHONE.................................760 737-7896
Fax: 760 737-7898
Amparo Orozco, *Principal*
EMP: 60
SALES (corp-wide): 45.1MM **Privately Held**
SIC: 8011 General & family practice, physician/surgeon
PA: Neighborhood Healthcare
425 N Date St Ste 203
Escondido CA 92025
760 520-8372

(P-19768)
NEIGHBORHOOD HEALTHCARE
855 E Madison Ave, El Cajon (92020-3819)
PHONE.................................619 440-2751
Alex Nunez, *Director*
Marilyn Jackson, *Nurse*
EMP: 100
SQ FT: 9,198
SALES (corp-wide): 45.1MM **Privately Held**
SIC: 8011 General & family practice, physician/surgeon
PA: Neighborhood Healthcare
425 N Date St Ste 203
Escondido CA 92025
760 520-8372

(P-19769)
NEIGHBORHOOD HEALTHCARE
460 N Elm St, Escondido (92025-3002)
PHONE.................................760 737-2000
Gail Thomsky, *Manager*
Patricia L Christie, *Family Practiti*
Michael Scheffer, *Pharmacist*
EMP: 70
SQ FT: 9,288
SALES (corp-wide): 45.1MM **Privately Held**
SIC: 8011 Clinic, operated by physicians
PA: Neighborhood Healthcare
425 N Date St Ste 203
Escondido CA 92025
760 520-8372

(P-19770)
NEW PORT ORTHOPEDIC INSTITUTE
19582 Beach Blvd Ste 118, Huntington Beach (92648-2996)
PHONE.................................949 722-5071
Alan Beyer MD, *Principal*
Jennifer Lemus, *Admin Sec*
Steven Dennis, *Med Doctor*
Kimberly Safman, *Med Doctor*
EMP: 60
SALES (est): 4.1MM **Privately Held**
SIC: 8011 Orthopedic physician

(P-19771)
NEWPORT BEACH MEDSPA
2131 Westcliff Dr Ste 100, Newport Beach (92660-5549)
PHONE.................................949 631-2800
EMP: 65
SALES (corp-wide): 3MM **Privately Held**
SIC: 8011 Pediatrician
PA: Newport Beach Medspa
4341 Birch St Ste 101
Newport Beach CA 92660
949 756-8633

(P-19772)
NEWPORT BEACH ORTHOPEDIC INST
22 Corporate Plaza Dr, Newport Beach (92660-7985)
P.O. Box 2597 (92659-1597)
PHONE.................................949 722-7038
Alan Beyer MD, *Owner*
EMP: 79
SALES (est): 5.1MM **Privately Held**
SIC: 8011 Orthopedic physician

(P-19773)
NEWPORT BEACH SURGERY CTR LLC
361 Hospital Rd Ste 124, Newport Beach (92663-3521)
PHONE.................................949 631-0988
Fax: 949 631-2504
John McNutt, *Managing Dir*
Eric Reints, *Administration*
Angela Holder, *Nursing Dir*
Bruce Albert,
Robert Anderson,
EMP: 120
SQ FT: 10,000
SALES (est): 16.4MM **Privately Held**
WEB: www.nbbrewco.com
SIC: 8011 Offices & clinics of medical doctors

(P-19774)
NEWPORT FMLY MDCNE/A MED GROUP
Also Called: Campion, Catherine A MD
520 Superior Ave, Newport Beach (92663-3637)
PHONE.................................949 644-1025
Fax: 949 644-7072
Maclyn Somers MD, *Partner*
Catherine A Campion MD, *Partner*
Sheryl L Long MD, *Partner*
William R Somers MD, *Partner*
Benjamin B Wright MD, *Partner*
EMP: 65
SQ FT: 9,000
SALES (est): 6.4MM **Privately Held**
WEB: www.newportfamilymedicine.com
SIC: 8011 General & family practice, physician/surgeon

(P-19775)
NEWPORT HARBOR RADIOLOGY ASSOC
Also Called: Newport Imaging Center
360 San Miguel Dr # 105106, Newport Beach (92660-7853)
PHONE.................................949 721-8191
Hurwitz Robert, *Owner*
Julie Engle, *Executive*
Miles C Chang, *Diag Radio*
Thuan T Tran, *Director*
EMP: 61
SALES (est): 2.7MM **Privately Held**
SIC: 8011 Radiologist

(P-19776)
NORTH BAY EYE ASSOC A MED CORP
Also Called: North Bay Eye Assoc Med Group
50 Professional Center Dr # 210, Rohnert Park (94928-2173)
PHONE.................................707 206-0849
Christian Kim, *Principal*
EMP: 65
SALES (est): 4.1MM **Privately Held**
SIC: 8011 Offices & clinics of medical doctors

(P-19777)
NORTH COUNTY HEALTH PRJ INC (PA)
Also Called: North County Services
150 Valpreda Rd Frnt, San Marcos (92069-2944)
PHONE.................................760 736-6755
Irma Cota, *CEO*
Philip Lenowsky, *CFO*
Kathy Martinez, *CFO*
Diane Slosar, *Vice Pres*
Pamela Simpson, *Quality Imp Dir*
EMP: 221 EST: 1973
SQ FT: 69,880
SALES: 57MM **Privately Held**
SIC: 8011 Clinic, operated by physicians

(P-19778)
NORTH STATE RADIOLOGY
Also Called: North State Imaging
1702 Esplanade, Chico (95926-3315)
PHONE.................................530 898-0504
Scot Woolley, *CEO*
Don Hubbard, *CFO*
Julie D Holochwost, *Admin Asst*
Chris Jones, *Info Tech Mgr*
Thomas Nolan-Gosslin, *Financial Exec*
EMP: 50
SALES (est): 15.1MM **Privately Held**
SIC: 8011 Radiologist

(P-19779)
NORTHCOUNTRY CLINIC
Also Called: Dickinson, Diane MD
785 18th St, Arcata (95521-5683)
PHONE.................................707 822-2481
Fax: 707 822-3656
Herrmann Spetzler, *Administration*
Janelle Bohanan, *Ch of Bd*
Helen Andrews, *Human Res Dir*
Gerald Alston, *Med Doctor*
Maria Spetzler, *Med Doctor*
EMP: 55
SQ FT: 10,000
SALES (est): 3.7MM **Privately Held**
WEB: www.northcoastclinics.org
SIC: 8011 Clinic, operated by physicians

(P-19780)
NORTHEAST VALLEY HEALTH CORP
Also Called: San Fernando Health Center
1600 San Fernando Rd, San Fernando (91340-3115)
PHONE.................................818 365-8086
Fax: 818 898-4826
Beverly Jenkins, *Manager*
Rosie Jadidian, *Pharmacy Dir*
Kim Waldhanz, *Human Res Dir*
Grace S Hardy, *Frmly & Gen Dent*
Norma Casillas, *Manager*
EMP: 85
SALES (corp-wide): 78.3MM **Privately Held**
SIC: 8011 Offices & clinics of medical doctors
PA: Northeast Valley Health Corp
1172 N Maclay Ave
San Fernando CA 91340
818 898-1388

(P-19781)
NORTHEAST VALLEY HEALTH CORP
12756 Van Nuys Blvd, Pacoima (91331-1696)
PHONE.................................818 896-0531
Fax: 818 896-5850
Kathreen Dayanim, *Manager*
Rocio Duque, *Office Mgr*
Beverly Jenkins, *Administration*
Latonya Burnell, *Nurse Practr*

8011 - Offices & Clinics Of Doctors Of Medicine County (P-19782)   PRODUDCTS & SERVICES SECTION

Martha Vargas, *Manager*
EMP: 100
SQ FT: 11,645
SALES (corp-wide): 78.3MM **Privately Held**
SIC: 8011 8071 Clinic, operated by physicians; medical laboratories
PA: Northeast Valley Health Corp
1172 N Maclay Ave
San Fernando CA 91340
818 898-1388

(P-19782)
NORTHEASTERN RUR HLTH CLINICS (PA)
Also Called: Nrhc
1850 Spring Ridge Dr, Susanville (96130-6100)
PHONE.................................530 251-5000
Phil Nowak, *CEO*
Dan Zanine, *CFO*
Richard Hrezo, *Treasurer*
John Dozier, *Bd of Directors*
Albert Geugenburger, *Exec Dir*
EMP: 65 **EST:** 1977
SQ FT: 27,000
SALES: 9.5MM **Privately Held**
WEB: www.northeasternhealth.org
SIC: 8011 Offices & clinics of medical doctors

(P-19783)
NORTHERN CALIFORNIA CARDIOLOGY (PA)
Also Called: Ncca Diagnostics Medical Group
5301 F St Ste 117, Sacramento (95819-3220)
PHONE.................................916 733-1788
Fax: 916 733-8717
David Woodruff, *Partner*
Daniel Flamm, *Partner*
Stanley Henjum, *Partner*
Edmond Lee, *Partner*
Harvey Matlof, *Partner*
EMP: 50
SQ FT: 13,000
SALES (est): 5.3MM **Privately Held**
SIC: 8011 Cardiologist & cardio-vascular specialist

(P-19784)
NORTHWEST MEDICAL GROUP INC
Also Called: Good Neighbor Pharmacy
7355 N Palm Ave Ste 100, Fresno (93711-5770)
PHONE.................................559 271-6302
Fax: 559 271-6322
Cecil Bullard MD, *President*
Diane Hubbard, *Shareholder*
Vivian Hernandez MD, *Admin Sec*
Roman Malley, *Internal Med*
David Pena, *Physician Asst*
EMP: 75
SQ FT: 5,000
SALES (est): 7.9MM **Privately Held**
SIC: 8011 5912 Pediatrician; drug stores

(P-19785)
NORTHWEST PHYSICIANS MED GROUP
Also Called: Northwest Medical Pharmacy
7355 N Palm Ave Ste 100, Fresno (93711-5770)
PHONE.................................559 271-6370
Fax: 559 271-6371
David A Wilcox, *Branch Mgr*
EMP: 82
SALES (corp-wide): 4.3MM **Privately Held**
SIC: 8011 Physicians' office, including specialists
PA: Northwest Physicians Medical Group Inc
7355 N Palm Ave Ste 100
Fresno CA 93711
559 271-6300

(P-19786)
OAK GROVE INST FOUNDATION INC (PA)
Also Called: Oak Grove Center
24275 Jefferson Ave, Murrieta (92562-7285)
PHONE.................................951 677-5599
Fax: 951 698-0461
Tamara L Wilson, *CEO*
Barry Soper, *Ch of Bd*
Fe Santiago, *CFO*
Mark Hollis, *Athletic Dir*
Cathy Glassner, *Case Mgr*
EMP: 88
SQ FT: 39,000
SALES: 16.2MM **Privately Held**
WEB: www.oak-grove.org
SIC: 8011 8211 8361 Psychiatric clinic; specialty education; residential care

(P-19787)
OAKS DIAGNOSTICS INC (PA)
Also Called: California Imaging Nework
6310 San Vicente Blvd, Los Angeles (90048-5426)
PHONE.................................310 855-0035
Fax: 310 289-8412
Ronald Grusd MD, *CEO*
Gonzalo Perez, *Admin Asst*
EMP: 60
SQ FT: 9,000
SALES (est): 7.6MM **Privately Held**
WEB: www.milleniumimaging.com
SIC: 8011 Radiologist

(P-19788)
OCEAN PARK HEALTH CENTER
Also Called: Community Health Netwrk of San
1351 24th Ave, San Francisco (94122-1616)
PHONE.................................415 753-8100
Fax: 415 753-8134
Lisa Golden, *Director*
John Applegarth, *Manager*
Valeria Glover, *Agent*
EMP: 50
SALES (est): 3MM **Privately Held**
SIC: 8011 Offices & clinics of medical doctors

(P-19789)
OCONNOR HOSPITAL
2105 Forest Ave, San Jose (95128-1471)
PHONE.................................408 947-2990
EMP: 177
SALES (corp-wide): 307.1MM **Privately Held**
SIC: 8011 Radiologist
PA: O'connor Hospital
2105 Forest Ave
San Jose CA 95128
408 947-2500

(P-19790)
OCONNOR HOSPITAL RADIOLOGY
Also Called: Oconnor Imaging Medical Group
2105 Forest Ave, San Jose (95128-1471)
PHONE.................................408 947-2992
Charles Griffin MD, *President*
Dr Richard Turner, *Vice Pres*
EMP: 60
SQ FT: 2,000
SALES (est): 3.5MM **Privately Held**
SIC: 8011 Radiologist

(P-19791)
OLE HEALTH
1100 Trancas St Ste 300, NAPA (94558-2921)
PHONE.................................707 254-1770
Beatrice Bostick, *Director*
Audrey Ewig, *Pediatrics*
Sonia S Lee-Ha, *Pediatrics*
Angela E Carreon, *Nurse Practr*
Daniel Bain, *Director*
EMP: 50
SALES: 19.8MM **Privately Held**
WEB: www.clinicole.org
SIC: 8011 General & family practice, physician/surgeon

(P-19792)
OLIVE VIEW-UCLA MEDICAL CENTER (PA)
Also Called: Valley Care Olive View Med Ctr
14445 Olive View Dr, Sylmar (91342-1438)
PHONE.................................818 364-1555
Fax: 818 364-3011
Carolyn Rhee, *CEO*
Cynthia O'Donnell, *Executive*
Kay Selden, *Executive*
Linda Miller, *Admin Sec*
Andrew Marquez, *Admin Asst*
EMP: 70
SALES (est): 47.5K **Privately Held**
WEB: www.uclasfvp.org
SIC: 8011 Medical centers

(P-19793)
OMNI FAMILY HEALTH (PA)
Also Called: COMMUNITY HEALTH CENTER
4900 California Ave 400b, Bakersfield (93309-7024)
P.O. Box 1060, Shafter (93263-1060)
PHONE.................................661 459-1900
Francisco L Castillon, *CEO*
Diego Martinez, *COO*
Novira Irawan, *CFO*
Judy Junkermeier, *CFO*
Simon Jiang, *Technology*
EMP: 80
SQ FT: 14,000
SALES: 47.9MM **Privately Held**
SIC: 8011 Clinic, operated by physicians

(P-19794)
OMNI WOMENS HLTH MED GROUP INC
2550 Merced St, Fresno (93721-1812)
PHONE.................................559 441-4271
Robert Frediani, *Branch Mgr*
EMP: 65
SALES (corp-wide): 13.9MM **Privately Held**
SIC: 8011 Offices & clinics of medical doctors
PA: Omni Women's Health Medical Group, Inc.
3812 N 1st St
Fresno CA 93726
559 495-3120

(P-19795)
ON LOK INC
1333 Bush St, San Francisco (94109-5691)
PHONE.................................415 292-8888
Grace LI, *CEO*
Grace Lee, *COO*
Kelly Walsh, *CFO*
Teveia Barnes, *Bd of Directors*
Jay Luxenberg, *Bd of Directors*
EMP: 99
SALES: 6.7MM **Privately Held**
SIC: 8011 Offices & clinics of medical doctors

(P-19796)
ONE MEDICAL GROUP INC (PA)
130 Sutter St Fl 2, San Francisco (94104-4009)
P.O. Box 779 (94104-0779)
PHONE.................................415 578-3100
Thomas H Lee, *CEO*
Steve Hastings, *President*
Kimber Lockhart, *President*
Andrew Adams, *Bd of Directors*
Sandeep Acharya, *Vice Pres*
EMP: 92
SALES (est): 53MM **Privately Held**
SIC: 8011 Physical medicine, physician/surgeon

(P-19797)
ONE MEDICAL GROUP INC
3885 24th St, San Francisco (94114-3840)
PHONE.................................415 529-4522
Elizabeth Maier, *Administration*
John R Nienow, *Infectious Dis*
EMP: 56
SALES (corp-wide): 53MM **Privately Held**
SIC: 8011 Offices & clinics of medical doctors
PA: One Medical Group, Inc.
130 Sutter St Fl 2
San Francisco CA 94104
415 578-3100

(P-19798)
ONE MEDICAL GROUP INC
130 Sutter St Fl 6, San Francisco (94104-4004)
PHONE.................................415 291-0480
Gurmeet Sran, *Branch Mgr*
EMP: 65
SALES (corp-wide): 53MM **Privately Held**
SIC: 8011 Physical medicine, physician/surgeon
PA: One Medical Group, Inc.
130 Sutter St Fl 2
San Francisco CA 94104
415 578-3100

(P-19799)
OROHEALTH CORPORATION
Also Called: Oroville Hospital
900 Oro Dam Blvd E, Oroville (95965-5832)
PHONE.................................530 534-9183
Fax: 530 532-8668
Mark Heinrich, *Director*
EMP: 1130
SALES (corp-wide): 3.3MM **Privately Held**
WEB: www.orovillehospital.com
SIC: 8011 8062 Offices & clinics of medical doctors; general medical & surgical hospitals
PA: Orohealth Corporation
2767 Olive Hwy
Oroville CA 95966
530 533-8500

(P-19800)
OROVILLE INTERNAL MEDS GROUP
Also Called: Roy C Shannon MD
2721 Olive Hwy Ste 12, Oroville (95966-6115)
PHONE.................................530 538-3171
Fax: 530 533-1145
Roy Shannon, *President*
Lani Walters, *General Mgr*
EMP: 10
SQ FT: 3,600
SALES (est): 3.8MM **Privately Held**
SIC: 8011 Internal medicine, physician/surgeon; physicians' office, including specialists

(P-19801)
ORTHOPEDIC CONSULTANTS (PA)
16311 Ventura Blvd # 800, Encino (91436-2140)
PHONE.................................818 788-7343
Lester Cohn, *President*
EMP: 50
SQ FT: 8,300
SALES (est): 3.3MM **Privately Held**
WEB: www.ocmgortho.com
SIC: 8011 Orthopedic physician

(P-19802)
OUTPATNT EYE SRGRY CTR OF DSRT
Also Called: Milauskas Eye Institute
72057 Dinah Shore Dr D1, Rancho Mirage (92270-1791)
PHONE.................................760 340-3937
Fax: 760 340-1940
Albert T Milauskas, *President*
Heidi Mengel, *Office Mgr*
Tanya Miller,
Leanne Fallone, *Director*
Mary Shields, *Manager*
EMP: 50
SALES (est): 1.4MM **Privately Held**
SIC: 8011 Ambulatory surgical center

(P-19803)
PACIFIC EYE ASSOCIATED INC
2100 Webster St Ste 214, San Francisco (94115-2375)
PHONE.................................415 923-3007
Wayne E Fung MD, *President*
Arthur W Allen Jr, *Vice Pres*
Bea Veeraseati, *Executive*
Bee Veeraseati, *General Mgr*
Roger E Atkins, *Ophthalmology*
EMP: 60
SQ FT: 8,000
SALES (est): 9.1MM **Privately Held**
SIC: 8011 Ophthalmologist

8011 - Offices & Clinics Of Doctors Of Medicine County (P-19826)

(P-19804)
PACIFIC INPTIENT MED GROUP INC
9 Jeffrey Ct, Novato (94945-1739)
P.O. Box 573 (94948-0573)
PHONE..................................415 485-8824
Fabiola Cobarrubias, *President*
Christopher M Valentino, *COO*
EMP: 69
SALES (est): 4.1MM **Privately Held**
SIC: 8011 Offices & clinics of medical doctors

(P-19805)
PACIFIC SHORES MED GROUP INC (PA)
1043 Elm Ave Ste 104, Long Beach (90813-3244)
PHONE..................................562 590-0345
Fax: 562 437-8139
Simon Tchekmedyian, *CEO*
Jonathan Rigutto, *District Mgr*
Joben D Paz, *Technology*
John Liang MD, *Med Doctor*
Concepcion Liberty, *Supervisor*
EMP: 60
SQ FT: 3,300
SALES (est): 12.7MM **Privately Held**
WEB: www.pacshoresoncology.com
SIC: 8011 Medical centers

(P-19806)
PACKARD CHILDRENS HLTH ALIANCE
Also Called: PCHA
725 Welch Rd, Palo Alto (94304-1601)
PHONE..................................650 723-0439
Kim Robert, *CEO*
Lisa Holbrook, *COO*
EMP: 100
SALES: 55.1MM **Privately Held**
SIC: 8011 Pediatrician; obstetrician; cardiologist & cardio-vascular specialist; gynecologist

(P-19807)
PACKARD MEDICAL GROUP INC
770 Welch Rd, Palo Alto (94304-1511)
PHONE..................................650 724-3637
Tika Martin, *Human Resources*
EMP: 85
SALES (est): 3.9MM **Privately Held**
SIC: 8011 Obstetrician; pediatrician

(P-19808)
PAIN MANAGEMENT SPECIALISTS PC
1551 Bishop St Ste 230, San Luis Obispo (93401-4661)
PHONE..................................805 544-7246
Borris Pilch MD, *President*
EMP: 50
SALES (est): 1.4MM **Privately Held**
SIC: 8011 Offices & clinics of medical doctors

(P-19809)
PALMDALE CENTER FOR PAIN MGT
819 Auto Center Dr, Palmdale (93551-4599)
PHONE..................................661 267-6876
Shahin Sadik, *Owner*
EMP: 50
SALES (est): 2.4MM **Privately Held**
SIC: 8011 Offices & clinics of medical doctors

(P-19810)
PALMDALE REGIONAL MEDICAL CTR
38600 Medical Center Dr, Palmdale (93551-4483)
P.O. Box 61558, King of Prussia PA (19406-0958)
PHONE..................................661 382-5000
Richard Allen, *CEO*
Yolanda Douglas, *Op Rm Dir*
Ed Callahan, *Principal*
Suzette Creighton, *QA Dir*
Nawanna Chaidez, *Quality Imp Dir*
EMP: 800
SALES: 159.2MM
SALES (corp-wide): 9B **Publicly Held**
SIC: 8011 Medical centers
PA: Universal Health Services, Inc.
367 S Gulph Rd
King Of Prussia PA 19406
610 768-3300

(P-19811)
PALO ALTO MED FNDTION STA CRUZ
2025 Soquel Ave, Santa Cruz (95062-1323)
PHONE..................................831 458-5670
Larry Beghttaldi, *President*
Glenn Groves, *CFO*
Howard Salvay MD, *Admin Sec*
William Cao, *Family Practiti*
Pia Zoliniak, *Supervisor*
EMP: 2000
SALES (est): 76.8MM **Privately Held**
SIC: 8011 Physical medicine, physician/surgeon

(P-19812)
PALO ALTO MEDICAL CLINIC
795 El Camino Real, Palo Alto (94301-2302)
PHONE..................................650 321-4121
Fax: 650 853-4969
John Cooper, *Principal*
Rita Sohlich, *Radiology Dir*
Recha Winkelman, *Radiology Dir*
Donna Mollenhauer, *Exec Dir*
David S Leibowitz, *Hematology*
EMP: 50
SALES (est): 5.5MM **Privately Held**
SIC: 8011 Primary care medical clinic

(P-19813)
PALO ALTO MEDICAL FOUNDATION
2350 W El Cmino Real Fl 4, Mountain View (94040)
PHONE..................................650 934-3565
Terrigal Burn, *Branch Mgr*
Hala Helm, *Risk Mgmt Dir*
Pam King, *Office Mgr*
Milagros Mitra, *Executive Asst*
Naomi Nasu, *Administration*
EMP: 62
SALES (corp-wide): 11B **Privately Held**
SIC: 8011 8641 Clinic, operated by physicians; civic social & fraternal associations
HQ: Palo Alto Medical Foundation For Health Care, Research And Education (Inc)
795 El Camino Real
Palo Alto CA 94301
650 321-4121

(P-19814)
PALO ALTO MEDICAL FOUNDATION (HQ)
Also Called: Palo Alto Clinic
795 El Camino Real, Palo Alto (94301-2302)
P.O. Box 254738, Sacramento (95865-4738)
PHONE..................................650 321-4121
Fax: 650 853-2930
Jeff Gerard, *CEO*
David Drucker, *President*
James Hereford, *COO*
Christine Kontgas, *Treasurer*
Mark McLaughlin, *Treasurer*
EMP: 700 **EST:** 1948
SQ FT: 200,000
SALES (est): 153.3MM
SALES (corp-wide): 11B **Privately Held**
SIC: 8011 Clinic, operated by physicians
PA: Sutter Health
2200 River Plaza Dr
Sacramento CA 95833
916 733-8800

(P-19815)
PALO ALTO MEDICAL FOUNDATION
Also Called: Los Altos Center
370 Distel Cir, Los Altos (94022-1404)
PHONE..................................650 254-5200
Fax: 650 254-5286
Sandy Greenberg, *Manager*
Monica Rodriguez, *Office Mgr*
Carlos Avalo, *Project Mgr*
Margaret Lo, *Family Practiti*
A Sastri H Sukhdeo, *Obstetrician*
EMP: 60
SQ FT: 32,059
SALES (corp-wide): 11B **Privately Held**
SIC: 8011 Pediatrician
HQ: Palo Alto Medical Foundation For Health Care, Research And Education (Inc)
795 El Camino Real
Palo Alto CA 94301
650 321-4121

(P-19816)
PALO ALTO MEDICAL FOUNDATION
Also Called: Patient Accounting
535 Oakmead Pkwy, Sunnyvale (94085-4023)
PHONE..................................408 730-4321
Lynn Murray, *Branch Mgr*
EMP: 120
SALES (corp-wide): 11B **Privately Held**
SIC: 8011 Medical centers
HQ: Palo Alto Medical Foundation For Health Care, Research And Education (Inc)
795 El Camino Real
Palo Alto CA 94301
650 321-4121

(P-19817)
PALO ALTO MEDICAL FOUNDATION
Also Called: Steven Rubinstein MD
201 Old San Francisco Rd, Sunnyvale (94086-6385)
P.O. Box 3496 (94088-3496)
PHONE..................................408 730-4390
Fax: 408 730-4246
Kam Yung, *Branch Mgr*
Namisha A Chotai, *Med Doctor*
Hung N Ecklund, *Med Doctor*
R J Hess MD, *Med Doctor*
Waymond Jung, *Med Doctor*
EMP: 62
SALES (corp-wide): 11B **Privately Held**
SIC: 8011 Allergist
HQ: Palo Alto Medical Foundation For Health Care, Research And Education (Inc)
795 El Camino Real
Palo Alto CA 94301
650 321-4121

(P-19818)
PALO ALTO MEDICAL FOUNDATION
323 N Mathilda Ave, Sunnyvale (94085-4207)
PHONE..................................408 524-5900
George Stoev, *Technician*
EMP: 62
SALES (corp-wide): 11B **Privately Held**
SIC: 8011 Offices & clinics of medical doctors
HQ: Palo Alto Medical Foundation For Health Care, Research And Education (Inc)
795 El Camino Real
Palo Alto CA 94301
650 321-4121

(P-19819)
PALO ALTO MEDICAL FOUNDATION
701 E El Camino Real, Mountain View (94040-2833)
PHONE..................................408 739-6000
Richard Slavin, *Branch Mgr*
EMP: 62
SALES (corp-wide): 11B **Privately Held**
SIC: 8011 8733 Clinic, operated by physicians; medical research
HQ: Palo Alto Medical Foundation For Health Care, Research And Education (Inc)
795 El Camino Real
Palo Alto CA 94301
650 321-4121

(P-19820)
PAMC LTD
4837 Huntington Dr N, Los Angeles (90032-1981)
PHONE..................................323 343-9460
EMP: 57
SALES (corp-wide): 42.6MM **Privately Held**
SIC: 8011 Medical centers
PA: Pamc, Ltd.
531 W College St
Los Angeles CA 90012
213 624-8411

(P-19821)
PEACH TREE HEALTHCARE
5730 Packard Ave Ste 500, Marysville (95901-7119)
PHONE..................................530 749-3242
Fax: 530 749-3248
Thomas Walther, *President*
Jane Stubbs, *Office Mgr*
Ferhat Indi, *Technology*
Kay Sidhu, *Finance Dir*
Hilla P Irani, *Gnrl Med Prac*
EMP: 97
SALES: 11.8MM **Privately Held**
SIC: 8011 General & family practice, physician/surgeon

(P-19822)
PEACHWOOD MEDICAL GROUP CLOVIS
275 W Herndon Ave, Clovis (93612-0204)
PHONE..................................559 324-6200
Fax: 559 324-6284
Lee Copeland MD, *President*
Jeffrey Hubbard, *Vice Pres*
Sue Marino, *Administration*
Sharon Laird, *Human Res Dir*
Howard L Lichtenstein, *Internal Med*
EMP: 70
SQ FT: 33,595
SALES: 13.7MM **Privately Held**
SIC: 8011 Primary care medical clinic

(P-19823)
PENINSULA WOMENS HEALTH (PA)
1828 El Camino Real Ste 8, Burlingame (94010-3103)
P.O. Box 1509, Millbrae (94030-5509)
PHONE..................................650 692-3818
Andrew Jurow MD, *President*
EMP: 50 **EST:** 1952
SQ FT: 2,800
SALES (est): 5.5MM **Privately Held**
WEB: www.peninsulawomenshealth.com
SIC: 8011 Gynecologist; obstetrician

(P-19824)
PEOPLE CREATING SUCCESS INC
380 Arneill Rd, Camarillo (93010-6406)
PHONE..................................805 644-9480
Marie McManus, *Branch Mgr*
EMP: 122
SALES (corp-wide): 12.4MM **Privately Held**
SIC: 8011 Offices & clinics of medical doctors
PA: People Creating Success, Inc.
2585 Teller Rd
Newbury Park CA 91320
805 375-9222

(P-19825)
PERMANENTE KAISER INTL
6041 Cadillac Ave Fl 4, Los Angeles (90034-1702)
PHONE..................................323 857-2000
Tanisha Dickens, *Manager*
EMP: 598
SALES (corp-wide): 380.5MM **Privately Held**
SIC: 8011 Medical centers
PA: Kaiser Permanente International
1 Kaiser Plz
Oakland CA 94612
510 271-5910

(P-19826)
PERMANENTE KAISER INTL
910 Maple St, Redwood City (94063-2034)
PHONE..................................650 299-3888

8011 - Offices & Clinics Of Doctors Of Medicine County (P-19827)

PRODUCDUCTS & SERVICES SECTION

Raul Perez, *Site Mgr*
Ramon A Quesada, *Med Doctor*
Gerlando F Palaczotto, *Nurse Practr*
EMP: 171
SALES (corp-wide): 380.5MM **Privately Held**
SIC: 8011 Health maintenance organization
PA: Kaiser Permanente International
1 Kaiser Plz
Oakland CA 94612
510 271-5910

(P-19827)
PERMANENTE KAISER INTL
4501 Sand Creek Rd, Antioch (94531-8687)
PHONE.................................925 813-6500
Been Liao, *Top Exec*
Samantha Strong MD, *Med Doctor*
EMP: 854
SALES (corp-wide): 380.5MM **Privately Held**
SIC: 8011 Medical centers
PA: Kaiser Permanente International
1 Kaiser Plz
Oakland CA 94612
510 271-5910

(P-19828)
PERMANENTE KAISER INTL
Also Called: Thousands Oaks Mecial Offices
365 E Hillcrest Dr, Thousand Oaks (91360-5820)
PHONE.................................805 374-7433
EMP: 470
SALES (corp-wide): 380.5MM **Privately Held**
SIC: 8011 Primary care medical clinic
PA: Kaiser Permanente International
1 Kaiser Plz
Oakland CA 94612
510 271-5910

(P-19829)
PERMANENTE KAISER INTL
2829 Watt Ave Ste 150, Sacramento (95821-6245)
PHONE.................................916 979-3531
EMP: 128
SALES (corp-wide): 380.5MM **Privately Held**
SIC: 8011 Offices & clinics of medical doctors
PA: Kaiser Permanente International
1 Kaiser Plz
Oakland CA 94612
510 271-5910

(P-19830)
PERMANENTE KAISER INTL
2500 Merced St, San Leandro (94577-4201)
PHONE.................................510 454-1000
EMP: 213
SALES (corp-wide): 380.5MM **Privately Held**
SIC: 8011 Medical centers
PA: Kaiser Permanente International
1 Kaiser Plz
Oakland CA 94612
510 271-5910

(P-19831)
PERMANENTE KAISER INTL
710 Lawrence Expy, Santa Clara (95051-5173)
PHONE.................................408 236-6400
EMP: 171
SALES (corp-wide): 380.5MM **Privately Held**
SIC: 8011 Physicians' office, including specialists
PA: Kaiser Permanente International
1 Kaiser Plz
Oakland CA 94612
510 271-5910

(P-19832)
PERMANENTE KAISER INTL
1511 W Garvey Ave N, West Covina (91790-2138)
PHONE.................................626 960-4844
Patrick A Casey, *Director*
EMP: 213

SALES (corp-wide): 380.5MM **Privately Held**
SIC: 8011 Psychiatric clinic
PA: Kaiser Permanente International
1 Kaiser Plz
Oakland CA 94612
510 271-5910

(P-19833)
PERMANENTE KAISER INTL
Also Called: Sherman Terrace
18040 Sherman Way, Reseda (91335-4631)
PHONE.................................818 705-5500
EMP: 128
SALES (corp-wide): 380.5MM **Privately Held**
SIC: 8011 General & family practice, physician/surgeon
PA: Kaiser Permanente International
1 Kaiser Plz
Oakland CA 94612
510 271-5910

(P-19834)
PERMANENTE MEDICAL GROUP INC
39400 Paseo Padre Pkwy, Fremont (94538-2310)
PHONE.................................510 248-3000
Fax: 510 795-3375
EMP: 78
SALES (corp-wide): 27.8B **Privately Held**
SIC: 8011 Offices & clinics of medical doctors
HQ: The Permanente Medical Group Inc
1950 Franklin St Fl 18th
Oakland CA 94612
866 858-2226

(P-19835)
PERMANENTE MEDICAL GROUP INC
1150 Veterans Blvd, Redwood City (94063-2037)
PHONE.................................650 299-2000
Arlene McCarthy, *Principal*
Ivan Bernstein, *Physician Asst*
Sandra Canales, *Med Doctor*
William J Chang, *Med Doctor*
Emily Hensarling, *Med Doctor*
EMP: 78
SALES (corp-wide): 27.8B **Privately Held**
SIC: 8011 Offices & clinics of medical doctors
HQ: The Permanente Medical Group Inc
1950 Franklin St Fl 18th
Oakland CA 94612
866 858-2226

(P-19836)
PERMANENTE MEDICAL GROUP INC
1617 Broadway St, Vallejo (94590-2406)
PHONE.................................707 765-3930
Robin E Bjorger, *Branch Mgr*
Honggang Lu, *Pathologist*
Daniel P Chan, *Surgeon*
Toni Lum, *Anesthesiology*
Trupti S Mehta, *Internal Med*
EMP: 58
SALES (corp-wide): 27.8B **Privately Held**
SIC: 8011 Medical centers
HQ: The Permanente Medical Group Inc
1950 Franklin St Fl 18th
Oakland CA 94612
866 858-2226

(P-19837)
PERMANENTE MEDICAL GROUP INC
7300 N Fresno St, Fresno (93720-2941)
PHONE.................................559 448-4500
Irene Ann Heetebry, *Principal*
Christopher T Kuebrich, *Med Doctor*
Donald L Myers, *Med Doctor*
Dana D Determan, *Nurse Practr*
EMP: 63
SALES (corp-wide): 27.8B **Privately Held**
SIC: 8011 Offices & clinics of medical doctors
HQ: The Permanente Medical Group Inc
1950 Franklin St Fl 18th
Oakland CA 94612
866 858-2226

(P-19838)
PERMANENTE MEDICAL GROUP INC
6600 Bruceville Rd, Sacramento (95823-4671)
PHONE.................................916 688-2055
Kevin L Smith, *Branch Mgr*
Hienvu Nguyen, *Podiatrist*
Glenn P Daubert, *Emerg Med Spec*
Monica Balfour, *Med Doctor*
Richard K Bow, *Med Doctor*
EMP: 58
SALES (corp-wide): 27.8B **Privately Held**
WEB: www.permanente.net
SIC: 8011 Gynecologist
HQ: The Permanente Medical Group Inc
1950 Franklin St Fl 18th
Oakland CA 94612
866 858-2226

(P-19839)
PERMANENTE MEDICAL GROUP INC
901 El Camino Real, San Bruno (94066-3009)
PHONE.................................650 742-2100
Cheryl Halcovich, *Manager*
Joe C Wong, *Med Doctor*
EMP: 58
SALES (corp-wide): 27.8B **Privately Held**
SIC: 8011 Offices & clinics of medical doctors
HQ: The Permanente Medical Group Inc
1950 Franklin St Fl 18th
Oakland CA 94612
866 858-2226

(P-19840)
PERMANENTE MEDICAL GROUP INC
3558 Round Barn Blvd, Santa Rosa (95403-1780)
PHONE.................................707 393-4000
Pat Henson, *Principal*
EMP: 58
SALES (corp-wide): 27.8B **Privately Held**
SIC: 8011 Medical centers
HQ: The Permanente Medical Group Inc
1950 Franklin St Fl 18th
Oakland CA 94612
866 858-2226

(P-19841)
PERMANENTE MEDICAL GROUP INC
Also Called: Labratory
2425 Geary Blvd, San Francisco (94115-3358)
PHONE.................................415 833-2000
Harry Chima, *Manager*
Lydia C Alexander, *Med Doctor*
Deborah A Chiarucci, *Med Doctor*
Eve R Maremont, *Med Doctor*
Susie K Chiu,
EMP: 100
SALES (corp-wide): 27.8B **Privately Held**
WEB: www.permanente.net
SIC: 8011 Offices & clinics of medical doctors
HQ: The Permanente Medical Group Inc
1950 Franklin St Fl 18th
Oakland CA 94612
866 858-2226

(P-19842)
PERMANENTE MEDICAL GROUP INC
275 Hospital Pkwy Ste 470, San Jose (95119-1138)
PHONE.................................408 972-6883
Harley A Goldberg, *Osteopathy*
William K Ho, *Med Doctor*
Belinda M Magallanes, *Med Doctor*
James Nguyen, *Med Doctor*
Julie S Shen, *Med Doctor*
EMP: 78
SALES (corp-wide): 27.8B **Privately Held**
SIC: 8011 Offices & clinics of medical doctors
HQ: The Permanente Medical Group Inc
1950 Franklin St Fl 18th
Oakland CA 94612
866 858-2226

(P-19843)
PERMANENTE MEDICAL GROUP INC
200 Muir Rd, Martinez (94553-4614)
PHONE.................................925 372-1000
EMP: 69
SALES (corp-wide): 27.8B **Privately Held**
SIC: 8011 Offices & clinics of medical doctors
HQ: The Permanente Medical Group Inc
1950 Franklin St Fl 18th
Oakland CA 94612
866 858-2226

(P-19844)
PERMANENTE MEDICAL GROUP INC
3779 Piedmont Ave, Oakland (94611-5347)
PHONE.................................510 752-1000
Fax: 510 596-6833
Ellen P Brennan, *Branch Mgr*
Jeanette C Yu, *Oncology*
Gary D Salomon, *Med Doctor*
Tara A Shaw, *Med Doctor*
Kevin H Wang, *Med Doctor*
EMP: 58
SALES (corp-wide): 27.8B **Privately Held**
SIC: 8011 Medical centers
HQ: The Permanente Medical Group Inc
1950 Franklin St Fl 18th
Oakland CA 94612
866 858-2226

(P-19845)
PERMANENTE MEDICAL GROUP INC
235 W Macarthur Blvd, Oakland (94611-5641)
PHONE.................................510 752-1190
Marta Perl, *Branch Mgr*
Katlin A Muscarello, *Physician Asst*
Calvin C Kuo, *Med Doctor*
Paul McDonald, *Med Doctor*
EMP: 58
SALES (corp-wide): 27.8B **Privately Held**
SIC: 8011 Medical centers
HQ: The Permanente Medical Group Inc
1950 Franklin St Fl 18th
Oakland CA 94612
866 858-2226

(P-19846)
PERMANENTE MEDICAL GROUP INC
770 E Calaveras Blvd, Milpitas (95035-5491)
PHONE.................................408 945-2900
Fax: 408 945-2087
Bindu Israni, *Branch Mgr*
Ha Q Le, *Med Doctor*
EMP: 78
SALES (corp-wide): 27.8B **Privately Held**
SIC: 8011 Offices & clinics of medical doctors
HQ: The Permanente Medical Group Inc
1950 Franklin St Fl 18th
Oakland CA 94612
866 858-2226

(P-19847)
PERMANENTE MEDICAL GROUP INC
4501 Sand Creek Rd, Antioch (94531-8687)
PHONE.................................925 813-6149
Kim Daily, *Branch Mgr*
Mary C Klemm, *Osteopathy*
Quoc D Nguyen, *Osteopathy*
Johanna M Richey, *Podiatrist*
Daphne K Solis, *Med Doctor*
EMP: 78
SALES (corp-wide): 27.8B **Privately Held**
SIC: 8011 Offices & clinics of medical doctors
HQ: The Permanente Medical Group Inc
1950 Franklin St Fl 18th
Oakland CA 94612
866 858-2226

PRODUCTS & SERVICES SECTION
8011 - Offices & Clinics Of Doctors Of Medicine County (P-19867)

(P-19848)
PERMANENTE MEDICAL GROUP INC
220 Oyster Point Blvd, South San Francisco (94080-1911)
PHONE...................................650 827-6495
Milan Patel, *Branch Mgr*
Christine E Angeles, *Med Doctor*
Kenneth Lee, *Med Doctor*
Robert E Marshall, *Med Doctor*
Maria H Serwonska, *Med Doctor*
EMP: 70
SALES (corp-wide): 27.8B **Privately Held**
SIC: **8011** Offices & clinics of medical doctors
HQ: The Permanente Medical Group Inc
   1950 Franklin St Fl 18th
   Oakland CA 94612
   866 858-2226

(P-19849)
PERMANENTE MEDICAL GROUP INC
910 Marshall St, Redwood City (94063-2033)
PHONE...................................650 299-2015
Christina Apostolakos, *Director*
Catherine Plevin, *Pediatrics*
EMP: 59
SALES (corp-wide): 27.8B **Privately Held**
SIC: **8011** Medical centers
HQ: The Permanente Medical Group Inc
   1950 Franklin St Fl 18th
   Oakland CA 94612
   866 858-2226

(P-19850)
PERMANENTE MEDICAL GROUP INC
914 Marina Way S, Richmond (94804-3739)
PHONE...................................510 231-5406
C J Bhalla, *Vice Pres*
Nancy Mahoney, *Human Resources*
Linda Hendrickson, *Director*
John Canales, *Manager*
EMP: 70
SALES (corp-wide): 27.8B **Privately Held**
SIC: **8011** Offices & clinics of medical doctors
HQ: The Permanente Medical Group Inc
   1950 Franklin St Fl 18th
   Oakland CA 94612
   866 858-2226

(P-19851)
PERMANENTE MEDICAL GROUP INC
900 Veterans Blvd Ste 400, Redwood City (94063-1742)
PHONE...................................650 598-2852
Diana Patino, *Branch Mgr*
EMP: 70
SALES (corp-wide): 27.8B **Privately Held**
SIC: **8011** Offices & clinics of medical doctors
HQ: The Permanente Medical Group Inc
   1950 Franklin St Fl 18th
   Oakland CA 94612
   866 858-2226

(P-19852)
PERMANENTE MEDICAL GROUP INC
2500 Merced St, San Leandro (94577-4201)
PHONE...................................510 454-1000
Barbara Follestad, *Surgeon*
Pearl Y Hu, *Surgeon*
Michael B Peterson, *Surgeon*
Amanda Schoenberg, *Pediatrics*
Stephen B Shochet, *Pediatrics*
EMP: 63
SALES (corp-wide): 27.8B **Privately Held**
SIC: **8011** Offices & clinics of medical doctors
HQ: The Permanente Medical Group Inc
   1950 Franklin St Fl 18th
   Oakland CA 94612
   866 858-2226

(P-19853)
PERMANENTE MEDICAL GROUP INC
99 Montecillo Rd, San Rafael (94903-3308)
PHONE...................................415 444-2000
Fax: 415 444-2369
Jonathan E Artz, *Med Doctor*
Ingrid K Brennan, *Med Doctor*
Jason W Cunnan, *Med Doctor*
Neeti H Sajnani, *Med Doctor*
Barbara Behrens, *Nurse Practr*
EMP: 63
SALES (corp-wide): 27.8B **Privately Held**
SIC: **8011** Offices & clinics of medical doctors
HQ: The Permanente Medical Group Inc
   1950 Franklin St Fl 18th
   Oakland CA 94612
   866 858-2226

(P-19854)
PERMANENTE MEDICAL GROUP INC
320 Lennon Ln, Walnut Creek (94598-2419)
PHONE...................................925 906-2000
Fax: 925 906-2136
Rochelle Benning, *Director*
David Peterson, *Director*
EMP: 63
SALES (corp-wide): 27.8B **Privately Held**
SIC: **8011** Offices & clinics of medical doctors
HQ: The Permanente Medical Group Inc
   1950 Franklin St Fl 18th
   Oakland CA 94612
   866 858-2226

(P-19855)
PERMANENTE MEDICAL GROUP INC
100 Rowland Way Ste 125, Novato (94945-5012)
PHONE...................................415 209-2444
EMP: 69
SALES (corp-wide): 27.8B **Privately Held**
SIC: **8011** Offices & clinics of medical doctors
HQ: The Permanente Medical Group Inc
   1950 Franklin St Fl 18th
   Oakland CA 94612
   866 858-2226

(P-19856)
PERMANENTE MEDICAL GROUP INC
7373 West Ln, Stockton (95210-3377)
PHONE...................................209 476-3737
Fax: 209 476-3553
Michael Coleman, *Principal*
Blondell A Gage, *Med Doctor*
Golyar Keyhan, *Med Doctor*
Michael J Thornton, *Med Doctor*
Amador Subong, *Director*
EMP: 58
SALES (corp-wide): 27.8B **Privately Held**
SIC: **8011** Medical centers
HQ: The Permanente Medical Group Inc
   1950 Franklin St Fl 18th
   Oakland CA 94612
   866 858-2226

(P-19857)
PERMANENTE MEDICAL GROUP INC
97 San Marin Dr, Novato (94945-1100)
PHONE...................................415 899-7400
Willa Jefferson-Stokes, *Manager*
William Elliott, *Med Doctor*
Robert Lavaysse, *Med Doctor*
Donald Pierce, *Med Doctor*
EMP: 100
SALES (corp-wide): 27.8B **Privately Held**
WEB: www.permanente.net
SIC: **8011** Offices & clinics of medical doctors; internal medicine practitioners
HQ: The Permanente Medical Group Inc
   1950 Franklin St Fl 18th
   Oakland CA 94612
   866 858-2226

(P-19858)
PERMANENTE MEDICAL GROUP INC
1600 Eureka Rd, Roseville (95661-3027)
PHONE...................................916 784-4000
Craig Green MD, *Director*
Michele A De Lorit, *Obstetrician*
Nichole A Zidenberg, *Obstetrician*
Lisa J Van Ert, *OB/GYN*
Jacob Chun, *Surg-Orthopdc*
EMP: 63
SALES (corp-wide): 27.8B **Privately Held**
SIC: **8011** Offices & clinics of medical doctors
HQ: The Permanente Medical Group Inc
   1950 Franklin St Fl 18th
   Oakland CA 94612
   866 858-2226

(P-19859)
PERMANENTE MEDICAL GROUP INC
2238 Geary Blvd, San Francisco (94115-3416)
PHONE...................................415 833-2000
Philip R Madvig MD Physn, *Principal*
Gregory Chang,
Robert Massarotti, *Security Dir*
Alex Lau, *Surgeon*
Jennifer Gunter, *Obstetrician*
EMP: 140
SALES (corp-wide): 27.8B **Privately Held**
WEB: www.permanente.net
SIC: **8011** Offices & clinics of medical doctors
HQ: The Permanente Medical Group Inc
   1950 Franklin St Fl 18th
   Oakland CA 94612
   866 858-2226

(P-19860)
PERMANENTE MEDICAL GROUP INC
1750 2nd St, Berkeley (94710-1705)
PHONE...................................510 559-5338
Dianne Easterwood, *General Mgr*
EMP: 100
SALES (corp-wide): 27.8B **Privately Held**
WEB: www.permanente.net
SIC: **8011** Offices & clinics of medical doctors
HQ: The Permanente Medical Group Inc
   1950 Franklin St Fl 18th
   Oakland CA 94612
   866 858-2226

(P-19861)
PERMANENTE MEDICAL GROUP INC
3900 Lakeville Hwy, Petaluma (94954-5698)
PHONE...................................707 765-3900
Willa Jefferson-Stokes, *Manager*
Maurice Kinsolving, *Med Doctor*
Michael Matsumoto, *Director*
EMP: 75
SALES (corp-wide): 27.8B **Privately Held**
WEB: www.permanente.net
SIC: **8011** Clinic, operated by physicians
HQ: The Permanente Medical Group Inc
   1950 Franklin St Fl 18th
   Oakland CA 94612
   866 858-2226

(P-19862)
PERMANENTE MEDICAL GROUP INC
1305 Tommydon St, Stockton (95210-3364)
PHONE...................................209 476-2000
Fax: 209 476-3009
Jack Gillimand, *Branch Mgr*
Timothy A Dixon, *Anesthesiology*
Elizabeth M Ka, *Dermatology*
Blondell A Gage, *Neurology*
Preetinder K Brar, *Urology*
EMP: 50
SALES (corp-wide): 27.8B **Privately Held**
WEB: www.permanente.net
SIC: **8011** Offices & clinics of medical doctors

(P-19863)
PERMANENTE MEDICAL GROUP INC
3555 Whipple Rd, Union City (94587-1507)
PHONE...................................510 675-4010
Deana Medinas, *Director*
Francine Bashan, *Psychologist*
Cristina A Castagnini, *Psychologist*
Diane Enos, *Psychologist*
Kristine Futa, *Psychologist*
EMP: 100
SALES (corp-wide): 27.8B **Privately Held**
WEB: www.permanente.net
SIC: **8011** Internal medicine practitioners
HQ: The Permanente Medical Group Inc
   1950 Franklin St Fl 18th
   Oakland CA 94612
   866 858-2226

(P-19864)
PERMANENTE MEDICAL GROUP INC
3000 Las Positas Rd, Livermore (94551-9627)
PHONE...................................925 243-2600
Stan Combs, *Manager*
Billy Yee, *Pharmacy Dir*
Damon Koronakos, *Med Doctor*
Iftekhar A Sareshwala, *Med Doctor*
EMP: 55
SALES (corp-wide): 27.8B **Privately Held**
WEB: www.permanente.net
SIC: **8011** Offices & clinics of medical doctors
HQ: The Permanente Medical Group Inc
   1950 Franklin St Fl 18th
   Oakland CA 94612
   866 858-2226

(P-19865)
PERMANENTE MEDICAL GROUP INC
10725 International Dr, Rancho Cordova (95670-7967)
PHONE...................................916 631-3000
Donald Forrester, *Branch Mgr*
Linda E Copeland, *Pediatrics*
Xing F Wang, *Psychiatry*
Linda Baryliuk, *Med Doctor*
Dennis H Nguyen, *Med Doctor*
EMP: 130
SALES (corp-wide): 27.8B **Privately Held**
WEB: www.permanente.net
SIC: **8011** Offices & clinics of medical doctors
HQ: The Permanente Medical Group Inc
   1950 Franklin St Fl 18th
   Oakland CA 94612
   866 858-2226

(P-19866)
PERMANENTE MEDICAL GROUP INC
395 Hickey Blvd Fl 1, Daly City (94015-2770)
PHONE...................................650 301-5860
Jennifer Normoyle, *Branch Mgr*
Betty Lee, *Obstetrician*
Yvonne Ong, *Pediatrics*
Laura Prager, *Pediatrics*
Bertha Saucedo, *Pediatrics*
EMP: 78
SALES (corp-wide): 27.8B **Privately Held**
SIC: **8011** Offices & clinics of medical doctors
HQ: The Permanente Medical Group Inc
   1950 Franklin St Fl 18th
   Oakland CA 94612
   866 858-2226

(P-19867)
PERMANENTE MEDICAL GROUP INC
1000 Franklin Pkwy, San Mateo (94403-1922)
PHONE...................................650 358-7000
George Chuang, *Osteopathy*
EMP: 69
SALES (corp-wide): 27.8B **Privately Held**
SIC: **8011** Offices & clinics of medical doctors
HQ: The Permanente Medical Group Inc
   1950 Franklin St Fl 18th
   Oakland CA 94612
   866 858-2226

8011 - Offices & Clinics Of Doctors Of Medicine County (P-19868)

(P-19868)
PERMANENTE MEDICAL GROUP INC
4601 Dale Rd, Modesto (95356-9718)
PHONE.....................209 735-5000
Jennifer A Beard, *Principal*
Carol Martella, *Op Rm Dir*
Terry Dombroski, *Radiology Dir*
Anita Boronowsky, *Analyst*
Michelle Perez, *Facilities Mgr*
EMP: 63
SALES (corp-wide): 27.8B **Privately Held**
SIC: 8011 Offices & clinics of medical doctors
HQ: The Permanente Medical Group Inc
1950 Franklin St Fl 18th
Oakland CA 94612
866 858-2226

(P-19869)
PETALUMA HEALTH CENTER INC
1179 N Mcdowell Blvd A, Petaluma (94954-1171)
PHONE.....................707 559-7500
Kathryn Powell, *CEO*
Jeanne Zabout, *COO*
Tim Moran, *CFO*
Arthur Feagles, *Principal*
Teresa Tillman, *Principal*
EMP: 100
SALES: 20.4MM **Privately Held**
WEB: www.phealthcenter.org
SIC: 8011 Offices & clinics of medical doctors

(P-19870)
PETER J WOLK MD
2721 Olive Hwy, Oroville (95966-6115)
PHONE.....................530 534-6517
Peter Wolk, *Principal*
EMP: 50 **EST:** 2001
SALES (est): 799.3K **Privately Held**
SIC: 8011 Offices & clinics of medical doctors

(P-19871)
PHYSICIANS PLZ SURGICAL CTR LP
Also Called: HealthSouth Physicians
6000 Physicians Blvd # 205, Bakersfield (93301-1215)
PHONE.....................661 322-4744
Fax: 661 322-2938
Linda Blomquist, *Administration*
EMP: 50
SALES (est): 5.1MM **Privately Held**
SIC: 8011 Surgeon

(P-19872)
PIONEER MEDICAL GROUP INC
11411 Brookshire Ave # 108, Downey (90241-5026)
PHONE.....................562 862-2775
Gergie Salsky, *Manager*
Jamie Rivera, *Office Mgr*
Marisela Bonilla,
EMP: 73
SALES (corp-wide): 39.7MM **Privately Held**
SIC: 8011 5047 Offices & clinics of medical doctors; medical equipment & supplies
PA: Pioneer Medical Group, Inc.
17777 Center Court Dr N # 400
Cerritos CA 90703
562 597-4181

(P-19873)
PIONEER MEDICAL GROUP INC
2220 Clark Ave, Long Beach (90815-2521)
PHONE.....................562 597-4181
Sadalia Sousa, *Manager*
EMP: 73
SALES (corp-wide): 39.7MM **Privately Held**
SIC: 8011 Medical centers
PA: Pioneer Medical Group, Inc.
17777 Center Court Dr N # 400
Cerritos CA 90703
562 597-4181

(P-19874)
PIT RIVER TRIBAL COUNCIL
Also Called: Pit River Health Services
36977 Park Ave, Burney (96013-4067)
PHONE.....................530 335-3651
Keith Ratcliff, *Manager*
Randy Brazelton, *Executive*
EMP: 52
SALES (corp-wide): 4.5MM **Privately Held**
WEB: www.pitrivercasino.com
SIC: 8011 8021 Offices & clinics of medical doctors; offices & clinics of dentists
PA: Pit River Tribal Council
37960 Park Ave
Burney CA

(P-19875)
PLANNED PRNTHOD SHST-DBLO INC
600 Nut Tree Rd Ste 340, Vacaville (95687-4686)
PHONE.....................707 317-2111
EMP: 90
SALES (corp-wide): 22.7MM **Privately Held**
SIC: 8011 Offices & clinics of medical doctors
PA: Planned Parenthood Shasta-Diablo, Inc.
2185 Pacheco St
Concord CA 94520
925 676-0300

(P-19876)
PLUMAS DISTRICT HOSPITAL
Also Called: Quincy Family Medicine
1045 Bucks Lake Rd, Quincy (95971-9507)
PHONE.....................530 283-0650
Fax: 530 283-2116
Dan Brandes, *Director*
Elizabeth McGee, *Nurse Practr*
EMP: 120
SALES (corp-wide): 81K **Privately Held**
SIC: 8011 8062 Offices & clinics of medical doctors; general medical & surgical hospitals
PA: Plumas District Hospital
1065 Bucks Lake Rd
Quincy CA 95971
530 283-2121

(P-19877)
PRIMARY CRITICAL CARE MEDICAL
620 N Brand Blvd Ste 500, Glendale (91203-4218)
P.O. Box 998, North Hollywood (91603-0998)
PHONE.....................818 847-9950
Bruce Gipe MD, *President*
Susan Harris Rn CPA, *CFO*
EMP: 194 **EST:** 1995
SALES (est): 2.5MM
SALES (corp-wide): 3.6B **Publicly Held**
SIC: 8011 Offices & clinics of medical doctors
PA: Team Health Holdings, Inc.
265 Brookview Centre Way
Knoxville TN 37919
865 693-1000

(P-19878)
PRIME HALTHCARE FOUNDATION INC
3300 E Guasti Rd Fl 3, Ontario (91761-8655)
PHONE.....................909 235-4400
Prem Reddy, *CEO*
EMP: 1550
SALES (est): 10.8MM **Privately Held**
SIC: 8011 Health maintenance organization

(P-19879)
PROFESSIONAL HEALTH TECH
Also Called: Cardio Pulmonary Services
8131 Calle Del Cielo, La Jolla (92037-3148)
PHONE.....................858 449-1599
Stanley Pappelbaum MD, *President*
Searle Turner MD, *Corp Secy*
EMP: 77 **EST:** 1976

SALES (est): 7MM **Privately Held**
SIC: 8011 8399 Cardiologist & cardio-vascular specialist; health systems agency

(P-19880)
PROGRESSIVE HEALTH CARE SYSTEM
Also Called: P H S
8510 Balboa Blvd Ste 150, Northridge (91325-5810)
PHONE.....................818 707-9603
Marvin Kanter,
Joan Rose,
EMP: 100 **EST:** 1999
SQ FT: 10,000
SALES (est): 4.4MM **Privately Held**
WEB: www.msophs.com
SIC: 8011 Offices & clinics of medical doctors

(P-19881)
PROMED HLTH CARE ADMINISTRATORS
9302 Pttsbrgh Ave Ste 220, Rancho Cucamonga (91730)
PHONE.....................909 932-1045
Jeereedi Prasad, *President*
Kenneth Brown, *COO*
Brian Wederman, *COO*
Bahram Bahremand, *CFO*
Brian Werderman, *CFO*
EMP: 75
SALES (est): 4.6MM
SALES (corp-wide): 637.4MM **Privately Held**
SIC: 8011 Offices & clinics of medical doctors
PA: Prospect Medical Holdings, Inc.
3415 S Sepulveda Blvd # 9
Los Angeles CA 90034
310 943-4500

(P-19882)
PROSPECT MEDICAL HOLDINGS INC (PA)
3415 S Sepulveda Blvd # 9, Los Angeles (90034-6060)
PHONE.....................310 943-4500
Samuel S Lee, *Ch of Bd*
Steve Aleman, *CFO*
Mike Heather, *CFO*
Linda Hodges, *Exec VP*
Rosa Catalano, *Vice Pres*
EMP: 108
SQ FT: 7,154
SALES (est): 637.4MM **Privately Held**
WEB: www.prospectmedicalholdings.com
SIC: 8011 Health maintenance organization

(P-19883)
PROVIDENCE HEALTH & SERVICES
181 S Buena Vista St # 300, Burbank (91505-4504)
PHONE.....................818 847-4999
Fax: 818 847-4924
Peter Chow, *Radiology*
Edward Jahnke, *Radiology*
Donald Litvak, *Radiology*
EMP: 104
SALES (corp-wide): 10.1B **Privately Held**
SIC: 8011 General & family practice, physician/surgeon
PA: Providence Health & Services
1801 Lind Ave Sw
Renton WA 98057
425 525-3355

(P-19884)
PROVIDENCE HEALTH & SERVICES
18360 Burbank Blvd, Tarzana (91356-2805)
PHONE.....................818 344-3143
Fax: 818 774-9135
EMP: 69
SALES (corp-wide): 10.1B **Privately Held**
SIC: 8011 Primary care medical clinic
PA: Providence Health & Services
1801 Lind Ave Sw
Renton WA 98057
425 525-3355

(P-19885)
PROVIDENCE HEALTH & SERVICES
21311 Madrona Ave Ste D, Torrance (90503-5970)
PHONE.....................310 792-5050
Fax: 310 543-3154
EMP: 87
SALES (corp-wide): 10.1B **Privately Held**
SIC: 8011 Dermatologist
PA: Providence Health & Services
1801 Lind Ave Sw
Renton WA 98057
425 525-3355

(P-19886)
PROVIDENCE HEALTH & SERVICES
1101 N Sepulveda Blvd, Manhattan Beach (90266-5948)
PHONE.....................310 545-6627
Ronald J Ruby, *Branch Mgr*
EMP: 87
SALES (corp-wide): 10.1B **Privately Held**
SIC: 8011 Internal medicine, physician/surgeon
PA: Providence Health & Services
1801 Lind Ave Sw
Renton WA 98057
425 525-3355

(P-19887)
PROVIDENCE HEALTH & SERVICES
1499 W 1st St 2, San Pedro (90732-3255)
PHONE.....................310 831-9482
Olga M Calof, *Endocrinology*
EMP: 104
SALES (corp-wide): 10.1B **Privately Held**
SIC: 8011 General & family practice, physician/surgeon
PA: Providence Health & Services
1801 Lind Ave Sw
Renton WA 98057
425 525-3355

(P-19888)
PROVIDENCE HEALTH & SERVICES
Also Called: Liver and Pancreatic Center
20911 Earl St, Torrance (90503-4352)
PHONE.....................310 793-4263
EMP: 69
SALES (corp-wide): 10.1B **Privately Held**
SIC: 8011 Offices & clinics of medical doctors
PA: Providence Health & Services
1801 Lind Ave Sw
Renton WA 98057
425 525-3355

(P-19889)
PROVIDENCE HEALTH SYSTEM
15031 Rinaldi St, Mission Hills (91345-1207)
PHONE.....................818 898-4530
Terry Carmondy, *Administration*
EMP: 1200
SALES (corp-wide): 10.1B **Privately Held**
SIC: 8011 Offices & clinics of medical doctors
HQ: Providence Health System-Southern California
1801 Lind Ave Sw
Renton WA 98057
425 525-3355

(P-19890)
PROVIDENCE HEALTH SYSTEM
Beach Cties Amblatory Care Ctr
20929 Hawthorne Blvd, Torrance (90503-4611)
PHONE.....................310 376-9474
Andy Hoover, *Owner*
EMP: 1200
SALES (corp-wide): 10.1B **Privately Held**
WEB: www.lcmhs.org
SIC: 8011 Ambulatory surgical center
HQ: Providence Health System-Southern California
1801 Lind Ave Sw
Renton WA 98057
425 525-3355

PRODUCTS & SERVICES SECTION
8011 - Offices & Clinics Of Doctors Of Medicine County (P-19912)

(P-19891)
PROVIDENCE HEALTH SYSTEM
Also Called: Providence Little Co Mary Hosp
4101 Torrance Blvd, Torrance (90503-4607)
PHONE...............................310 540-7676
Fax: 310 540-8213
Michelle Molnar, *Branch Mgr*
Muno Bholat, *Director*
Andrea Flores, *Director*
Kris Ludington, *Director*
EMP: 81
SALES (corp-wide): 10.1B Privately Held
SIC: **8011** 8062 Physical medicine, physician/surgeon; general medical & surgical hospitals
HQ: Providence Health System-Southern California
1801 Lind Ave Sw
Renton WA 98057
425 525-3355

(P-19892)
PROVIDENCE TARZANA MEDICAL CTR
18321 Clark St, Tarzana (91356-3501)
PHONE...............................818 881-0800
Jerry Clute, *CEO*
Phyllis Bushart, *COO*
Nick Lymberopoulos, *CFO*
Connie Lackey, *Director*
EMP: 1300
SQ FT: 524
SALES: 221.2MM Privately Held
SIC: **8011** Offices & clinics of medical doctors

(P-19893)
PSYCHIATRIC CTRS AT SAN DIEGO (PA)
6153 Fairmount Ave # 140, San Diego (92120-3443)
P.O. Box 609001 (92160-9001)
PHONE...............................619 528-4600
Sabah Chammas PHD, *President*
Heather Gude, *CFO*
Dr Sharon McClure, *Treasurer*
Dr Katherine Dixon, *Vice Pres*
Marsha Green, *Gnrl Med Prac*
▲ EMP: 68
SQ FT: 2,000
SALES (est): 9.5MM Privately Held
WEB: www.psychiatriccenters.com
SIC: **8011** Psychiatrist

(P-19894)
PSYCHIATRIC SOLUTIONS INC
Also Called: Sierra Vista Hospital
8001 Bruceville Rd, Sacramento (95823-2329)
PHONE...............................916 288-0300
Fax: 916 689-5517
Mike Zauner, *CEO*
Kimm Dangelius, *Administration*
Sandy Hislop, *Legal Exec*
EMP: 125
SALES (corp-wide): 9B Publicly Held
WEB: www.intermountainhospital.com
SIC: **8011** 8063 Psychiatric clinic; psychiatric hospitals
HQ: Psychiatric Solutions, Inc.
6640 Carothers Pkwy # 500
Franklin TN 37067
615 312-5700

(P-19895)
PSYCHIATRIC SOLUTIONS INC
Heritage Oaks Hospital
4250 Auburn Blvd, Sacramento (95841-4100)
PHONE...............................916 489-3336
Fax: 916 488-9147
Shawn Silva, *Branch Mgr*
Brent Turner, *Exec VP*
Tammy Vanella, *Executive Asst*
Dana Ashcroft, *Human Res Dir*
Ken Dixon, *Director*
EMP: 135
SALES (corp-wide): 9B Publicly Held
WEB: www.intermountainhospital.com
SIC: **8011** 8063 Psychiatric clinic; psychiatric hospitals
HQ: Psychiatric Solutions, Inc.
6640 Carothers Pkwy # 500
Franklin TN 37067
615 312-5700

(P-19896)
PSYCHIATRIC SOLUTIONS INC
Fremont Hospital
39001 Sundale Dr, Fremont (94538-2005)
PHONE...............................510 796-1100
Toll Free:.............................888 -
Fax: 510 574-4801
Joan Bettencourt Newman, *Principal*
John Cooper, *Officer*
Dawn Daniels, *CTO*
Sheila Liboon, *Nursing Dir*
EMP: 150
SALES (corp-wide): 9B Publicly Held
WEB: www.intermountainhospital.com
SIC: **8011** 8093 8361 8069 Psychiatric clinic; specialty outpatient clinics; residential care; specialty hospitals, except psychiatric; psychiatric hospitals
HQ: Psychiatric Solutions, Inc.
6640 Carothers Pkwy # 500
Franklin TN 37067
615 312-5700

(P-19897)
PSYCHIATRIC SOLUTIONS INC
17241 Van Buren Blvd, Riverside (92504-5942)
PHONE...............................951 789-4405
Joseph McCoy, *Branch Mgr*
Terry Bridges, *Co-COO*
Ron Fincher, *Co-COO*
David M Dill, *Bd of Directors*
William M Petrie, *Bd of Directors*
EMP: 137
SALES (corp-wide): 9B Publicly Held
WEB: www.intermountainhospital.com
SIC: **8011** Psychiatric clinic
HQ: Psychiatric Solutions, Inc.
6640 Carothers Pkwy # 500
Franklin TN 37067
615 312-5700

(P-19898)
PUBLIC HEALTH CALIFORNIA DEPT
320 W 4th St Ste 830, Los Angeles (90013-2348)
PHONE...............................213 620-6160
Fax: 213 620-6565
Donna Mc Callum, *Principal*
EMP: 140 Privately Held
SIC: **8011** Clinic, operated by physicians
HQ: California Department Of Public Health
1615 Capitol Ave
Sacramento CA 95814
916 552-8397

(P-19899)
PUBLIC HEALTH CALIFORNIA DEPT
Also Called: Wic
2400 Wible Rd Ste 14, Bakersfield (93304-4734)
PHONE...............................661 835-4668
EMP: 140 Privately Held
SIC: **8011** Offices & clinics of medical doctors
HQ: California Department Of Public Health
1615 Capitol Ave
Sacramento CA 95814
916 552-8397

(P-19900)
PUBLIC HEALTH CALIFORNIA DEPT
Also Called: Genetic Dsase Screening Program
850 Marina Bay Pkwy F175, Richmond (94804-6403)
PHONE...............................510 412-1502
Fax: 510 231-1738
Melissa Huang, *Manager*
Barbara Materna, *Supervisor*
EMP: 140 Privately Held
SIC: **8011** 9431 Offices & clinics of medical doctors; administration of public health programs;
HQ: California Department Of Public Health
1615 Capitol Ave
Sacramento CA 95814
916 552-8397

(P-19901)
PULMONARY MEDICINE ASSOC
2801 K St Ste 500, Sacramento (95816-5119)
PHONE...............................916 733-5040
Geneva Lee, *Manager*
EMP: 54
SALES (corp-wide): 5.9MM Privately Held
SIC: **8011** Clinic, operated by physicians
PA: Pulmonary Medicine Associated Medical Group
1300 Ethan Way Ste 600
Sacramento CA 95825
916 482-7623

(P-19902)
QUEENSCARE HEALTH CENTERS
Also Called: Queenscare Fmly Clinics-Eastsd
4816 E 3rd St, Los Angeles (90022-1602)
PHONE...............................323 780-4510
Evelyn Moody, *Manager*
EMP: 66
SALES (corp-wide): 26.4MM Privately Held
SIC: **8011** Medical centers
PA: Queenscare Health Centers
950 S Grand Ave
Los Angeles CA 90015
323 669-4301

(P-19903)
QUEENSCARE HEALTH CENTERS
4618 Fountain Ave, Los Angeles (90029-1977)
PHONE...............................323 644-6180
Guillermo Diaz, *Branch Mgr*
Cindy Juarez, *Program Dir*
Cynthia Borders, *Director*
EMP: 99
SALES (corp-wide): 26.4MM Privately Held
SIC: **8011** Clinic, operated by physicians
PA: Queenscare Health Centers
950 S Grand Ave
Los Angeles CA 90015
323 669-4301

(P-19904)
RADIOLOGY DEPARTMENT CAL HOSP
1338 S Hope St Fl 4, Los Angeles (90015-2902)
PHONE...............................213 742-5840
Fax: 213 742-6351
Phil Faircharles, *Manager*
EMP: 50
SQ FT: 88,284
SALES (est): 3MM Privately Held
SIC: **8011** Radiologist

(P-19905)
RADNET INC
2708 E Willow St, Signal Hill (90755-2217)
PHONE...............................562 216-5137
Fax: 562 733-5880
EMP: 50
SALES (corp-wide): 809.6MM Publicly Held
SIC: **8011** Offices & clinics of medical doctors
PA: Radnet, Inc.
1510 Cotner Ave
Los Angeles CA 90025
310 445-2800

(P-19906)
RADY CHLD PHYSCN MGT SVCS INC
292 Euclid Ave, San Diego (92114-3643)
PHONE...............................619 262-3415
Cathy Romano, *Branch Mgr*
Sonia Gallegos, *Software Dev*
Leon Kelley, *Pediatrics*
EMP: 145 Privately Held
SIC: **8011** Offices & clinics of medical doctors
PA: Rady Children's Physician Management Services, Inc.
3860 Calle Fortunada # 200
San Diego CA 92123

(P-19907)
REDDING FAMILY MEDICINE ASSOC
2510 Airpark Dr Ste 201, Redding (96001-2461)
PHONE...............................530 244-4907
Fax: 530 244-1821
David Civalier MD, *President*
Vance Harris, *Partner*
Jack Kimple, *Partner*
Richard Maples, *Partner*
David Short, *Partner*
EMP: 50
SALES (est): 4.8MM Privately Held
WEB: www.reddingaquaticcenter.com
SIC: **8011** General & family practice, physician/surgeon

(P-19908)
REDDING PATHOLOGISTS LAB (PA)
1725 Gold St, Redding (96001-1820)
PHONE...............................530 225-8050
Fax: 530 225-8017
Richard Severance MD, *Partner*
Tikoes Blankenberg MD, *Partner*
Richard O Boyd MD, *Partner*
John P Greaves Jr, *Partner*
William Reuss MD, *Partner*
EMP: 115
SQ FT: 8,000
SALES (est): 10.5MM Privately Held
WEB: www.reddingpath.com
SIC: **8011** 8071 Pathologist; medical laboratories

(P-19909)
REDWOOD REGIONAL MEDICAL GROUP
1165 S Dora St Bldg H, Ukiah (95482-8325)
PHONE...............................707 463-3636
Jay Joseph, *Branch Mgr*
EMP: 91
SALES (corp-wide): 13.7MM Privately Held
SIC: **8011** General & family practice, physician/surgeon
PA: Redwood Regional Medical Group Drug Company, Llc
990 Sonoma Ave Ste 15
Santa Rosa CA 95404
707 525-4080

(P-19910)
REGENTS OF UC
4560 Admiralty Way # 100, Marina Del Rey (90292-5423)
PHONE...............................310 827-3700
EMP: 66 EST: 2007
SALES (est): 301.8K
SALES (corp-wide): 49.8MM Privately Held
SIC: **8011** Freestanding emergency medical center
PA: C/O Uc San Francisco
1111 Franklin St Fl 12
Oakland CA 94607
858 534-7323

(P-19911)
REPRODUCTIVE SCIENCE CENTER
Also Called: Reproductive Science Ctr Bay
100 Park Pl Ste 200, San Ramon (94583-4416)
PHONE...............................925 867-1800
Susan Willman, *CEO*
Donald I Galen, *Vice Pres*
Louis Weckstein, *Vice Pres*
Kris Johnson-Ayers, *Exec Dir*
Sheldon Josephs, *Exec Dir*
EMP: 75
SALES (est): 5MM Privately Held
SIC: **8011** Physicians' office, including specialists

(P-19912)
RESPONSELINK LLC
Also Called: Alert One
60 S Market St Ste 1500, San Jose (95113-2358)
P.O. Box 4067, Santa Clara (95056-4067)
PHONE...............................650 864-9801
Russell Poore, *Mng Member*

8011 - Offices & Clinics Of Doctors Of Medicine County (P-19913)

PRODUDUCTS & SERVICES SECTION

Michelle Albertson, *Controller*
Shauna Barker,
Juneen Lee-Mccombs, *Manager*
Katelynn Nguyen, *Manager*
EMP: 80 **EST:** 2006
SALES (est): 12.2MM **Privately Held**
SIC: 8011 5063 Freestanding emergency medical center; alarm systems

(P-19913)
RESPONSIBLE MED SOLUTIONS CORP
Also Called: Temecula 24 Hour Care
41715 Winchester Rd # 101, Temecula (92590-4808)
PHONE..................................951 308-0024
Fax: 951 506-0992
Steven J Schutz, *President*
Paul Schutz, *General Mgr*
Lynn McLain, *Office Mgr*
Kerry Erling, *Physician Asst*
Brian Sharp, *Physician Asst*
EMP: 50 **EST:** 2007
SQ FT: 5,000
SALES (est): 6.5MM **Privately Held**
SIC: 8011 Freestanding emergency medical center

(P-19914)
RETINAL CONSULTANTS INC (PA)
3939 J St Ste 106, Sacramento (95819-3631)
PHONE..................................916 454-4861
Neil E Kelly MD, *President*
Arun C Patel, *Shareholder*
Robert T Wendel, *Shareholder*
James W Wells Jr, *Vice Pres*
Brian Reed, *Executive*
EMP: 55
SALES (est): 11.9MM **Privately Held**
WEB: www.retinamed.com
SIC: 8011 Ophthalmologist

(P-19915)
RIAD ADOUMIE MD
23560 Madison St Ste 110, Torrance (90505-4709)
PHONE..................................310 373-6864
Riad Adoumie MD, *Owner*
EMP: 60
SALES (est): 1.3MM **Privately Held**
SIC: 8011 Offices & clinics of medical doctors

(P-19916)
RICHARD BURNS MD
41637 Margarita Rd # 100, Temecula (92591-2990)
PHONE..................................951 296-9300
Richard Burns, *Principal*
EMP: 70
SALES (est): 1.6MM **Privately Held**
SIC: 8011 Physicians' office, including specialists

(P-19917)
RICHARD FINN
Also Called: Community Family
4444 Magnolia Ave, Riverside (92501-4136)
PHONE..................................951 274-3506
Fax: 909 274-3498
Richard Finn, *Principal*
EMP: 90
SALES (est): 1.2MM **Privately Held**
SIC: 8011 Offices & clinics of medical doctors

(P-19918)
RICHARD J METZ MD INC
2080 Century Park E # 1609, Los Angeles (90067-2019)
PHONE..................................310 553-3189
Richard J Metz MD, *President*
EMP: 50
SALES (est): 2.8MM **Privately Held**
SIC: 8011 Internal medicine practitioners

(P-19919)
RICHARD SHAMES MD
25 Mitchell Blvd Ste 8, San Rafael (94903-2013)
PHONE..................................415 388-0456
Elson Haas, *Director*
Roberta Rossetti, *Manager*

Richard Shames, *Manager*
EMP: 63
SALES (est): 1.4MM **Privately Held**
SIC: 8011 Offices & clinics of medical doctors

(P-19920)
RILEY & POWELL MD
Also Called: Facial Reconstructive Surg &
1900 University Ave 101e, East Palo Alto (94303-2212)
PHONE..................................650 328-0511
Fax: 650 328-3419
Robert W Riley, *Partner*
Nelson B Powell, *Partner*
Carol Oderio, *Business Mgr*
Robert Riley, *Med Doctor*
Mary Lynn Fouche, *Assistant*
EMP: 50
SALES (est): 3.3MM **Privately Held**
WEB: www.sleepsurgery.com
SIC: 8011 Plastic surgeon

(P-19921)
RIVERSIDE MEDICAL CLINIC
6250 Clay, Mira Loma (91752)
PHONE..................................951 360-5260
Naheed Aljilani, *Director*
EMP: 100
SALES (est): 978.9K **Privately Held**
SIC: 8011 Offices & clinics of medical doctors

(P-19922)
RIVERSIDE MEDICAL CLINIC INC
7117 Brockton Ave, Riverside (92506-2658)
PHONE..................................951 683-6370
Judy Carpenter, *Manager*
EMP: 300
SALES (corp-wide): 110MM **Privately Held**
SIC: 8011 Clinic, operated by physicians
PA: Riverside Medical Clinic, Inc.
3660 Arlington Ave
Riverside CA 92506
951 683-6370

(P-19923)
RIVERSIDE MEDICAL CLINIC INC (PA)
Also Called: Riverside Med Clnic Ptient Ctr
3660 Arlington Ave, Riverside (92506-3987)
PHONE..................................951 683-6370
Fax: 951 686-9026
Steven E Larson, *President*
Judy Carpenter, *President*
Susan Marinaro, *COO*
Debbie Church, *Vice Pres*
Tony Lazcano, *Vice Pres*
EMP: 300
SQ FT: 65,000
SALES (est): 110MM **Privately Held**
SIC: 8011 Clinic, operated by physicians

(P-19924)
RIVERSIDE-SAN BERNARDINO
Also Called: Soboba Indian Health Clinic
607 Donna Way, San Jacinto (92583-5517)
PHONE..................................951 654-0803
Maria Adams, *Manager*
Patty Hayner, *Nurse*
Adelaide Presley, *Manager*
EMP: 60
SALES (corp-wide): 35.9MM **Privately Held**
SIC: 8011 Clinic, operated by physicians
PA: Riverside-San Bernardino County Indian Health, Inc.
11555 1/2 Potrero Rd
Banning CA 92220
951 849-4761

(P-19925)
ROBERT C DAVIS MD
400 Estudillo Ave Ste 100, San Leandro (94577-4962)
PHONE..................................510 893-2820
Robert C Davis MD, *Owner*
Ann Floden, *General Mgr*
EMP: 50
SALES (est): 832.6K **Privately Held**
SIC: 8011 Cardiologist & cardio-vascular specialist; surgeon

(P-19926)
ROGER L CRUMLEY MD INC
Also Called: University Head Neck Surgeons
101 City Dr S Bldg 56 5, Orange (92868)
PHONE..................................714 456-5750
Roger L Crumley MD, *President*
Mary A Evans, *Top Exec*
EMP: 50
SALES (est): 3.2MM **Privately Held**
SIC: 8011 Surgeon; plastic surgeon

(P-19927)
ROSTAMI NEJAT MEDICAL GROUP
2007 Wilshire Blvd # 215, Los Angeles (90057-3506)
PHONE..................................213 413-2700
Nejat Rostami, *President*
EMP: 100 **EST:** 1993
SALES (est): 8.9MM **Privately Held**
SIC: 8011 Offices & clinics of medical doctors

(P-19928)
ROUND VALLEY INDIAN HEALTH CTR
Hwy 162 Biggar Ln, Covelo (95428)
P.O. Box 247 (95428-0247)
PHONE..................................707 983-6182
Fax: 707 983-6802
James Russ, *Director*
Barbara Figueroa, *Technician*
EMP: 60 **EST:** 1968
SALES (est): 4.7MM **Privately Held**
SIC: 8011 8021 Clinic, operated by physicians; dental clinic

(P-19929)
RUSSIAN RIVER HEALTH CENTER
16319 3rd St, Guerneville (95446)
PHONE..................................707 869-2849
Fax: 707 869-1477
Mary Szecsey, *Director*
Derek Gong, *Med Doctor*
Surani Hayre-Kwan, *Nurse Practr*
Susan Levelle, *Nurse Practr*
Mary Wyman, *Nurse Practr*
EMP: 50
SALES (est): 11.4MM **Privately Held**
SIC: 8011 8093 8322 Offices & clinics of medical doctors; mental health clinic, outpatient; individual & family services

(P-19930)
SACRAMENTO EAR NOSE & THROAT (PA)
1111 Expo Blvd Ste 700, Sacramento (95815-4314)
PHONE..................................916 736-3399
Fax: 916 736-0203
Ernest E Johnson MD, *President*
Jeff Dudley, *CFO*
Kevin Mc Kennan MD, *Treasurer*
Richard G Areen MD, *Admin Sec*
Eric Salinas, *Info Tech Mgr*
EMP: 55
SQ FT: 12,000
SALES (est): 10.8MM **Privately Held**
SIC: 8011 Ears, nose & throat specialist: physician/surgeon

(P-19931)
SACRAMENTO HEART AND CARDIOVAS (PA)
500 University Ave, Sacramento (95825-6504)
PHONE..................................916 830-2000
Fax: 916 830-2001
Phillip Bach, *Partner*
Drraye L Bellinger, *Partner*
EMP: 55
SQ FT: 45,000
SALES (est): 9MM **Privately Held**
WEB: www.sacheart.com
SIC: 8011 Cardiologist & cardio-vascular specialist

(P-19932)
SACRAMNTO NTIV AMERCN HLTH CTR
2020 J St, Sacramento (95811-3120)
PHONE..................................916 341-0575
Britta Guerrero, *Exec Dir*

Connie Reitman, *President*
D Shane Barnett, *Treasurer*
Earl T Green, *Vice Ch Bd*
Lisa McKay, *Admin Dir*
EMP: 119
SQ FT: 39,573
SALES: 7.6MM **Privately Held**
WEB: www.snahc.org
SIC: 8011 Offices & clinics of medical doctors

(P-19933)
SAINT JHNS HLTH CTR FOUNDATION
Wayne, John Cancer Institute
2200 Santa Monica Blvd, Santa Monica (90404-2312)
PHONE..................................310 315-6111
Fax: 310 449-5259
Donald Mortan, *Director*
Prince Hargrove, *Materials Dir*
Edwin Glass, *Nuclear Medcne*
Richard Essner, *Oncology*
Robert Gray, *Director*
EMP: 125
SQ FT: 7,100
SALES (corp-wide): 2.4B **Privately Held**
SIC: 8011 8731 Primary care medical clinic; commercial physical research
HQ: Saint John's Health Center Foundation.
2121 Santa Monica Blvd
Santa Monica CA 90404
310 829-5511

(P-19934)
SALINAS VALLEY MEMORIAL HLTHCA
440 E Romie Ln, Salinas (93901-4017)
PHONE..................................831 759-3236
EMP: 281
SALES (corp-wide): 344.2MM **Privately Held**
SIC: 8011 Clinic, operated by physicians
PA: Salinas Valley Memorial Healthcare Systems
450 E Romie Ln
Salinas CA 93901
831 757-4333

(P-19935)
SALINAS VALLEY MEMORIAL HLTHCA
5 Lower Ragsdle Dr 102, Monterey (93940)
PHONE..................................831 884-5048
EMP: 280
SALES (corp-wide): 344.2MM **Privately Held**
SIC: 8011 Cardiologist & cardio-vascular specialist
PA: Salinas Valley Memorial Healthcare Systems
450 E Romie Ln
Salinas CA 93901
831 757-4333

(P-19936)
SALINAS VALLEY MEMORIAL HLTHCA
Also Called: Salinas Urgent Care
558 Abbott St, Salinas (93901-4326)
PHONE..................................831 755-7880
Fax: 831 755-7886
Karen Schroeder, *Executive Asst*
Karina A Rusk, *Corp Comm Staff*
Joseph D Zakar, *Pharmacist*
Allen Bernas,
Linda K Roquemore, *Manager*
EMP: 420
SALES (corp-wide): 344.2MM **Privately Held**
WEB: www.salinasurgentcare.com
SIC: 8011 Offices & clinics of medical doctors
PA: Salinas Valley Memorial Healthcare Systems
450 E Romie Ln
Salinas CA 93901
831 757-4333

8011 - Offices & Clinics Of Doctors Of Medicine County (P-19958)

(P-19937)
SALUD PARA LA GENTE
Also Called: Salud Para La Gnte Hlth Clinic
195 Aviation Way Ste 200, Watsonville
(95076-2059)
PHONE...................................831 728-0222
Fax: 831 724-2011
Dori Rose Inda, *CEO*
Tony Balistreri, *CFO*
Dorian Seamster, *Quality Imp Dir*
Jenry Medinilla, *Business Mgr*
Simone Reynaud, *Controller*
EMP: 125
SALES (est): 19MM **Privately Held**
SIC: 8011 Medical centers

(P-19938)
SAN BERNARDINO MED GROUP INC (PA)
1700 N Waterman Ave, San Bernardino
(92404-5115)
PHONE...................................909 883-8611
Fax: 909 881-1632
James Malin, *CEO*
Thomas Hellwig, *President*
James W Malin, *CEO*
Louis Francisco MD, *Treasurer*
Paul G Godfrey MD, *Vice Pres*
EMP: 150
SQ FT: 55,000
SALES (est): 22.2MM **Privately Held**
SIC: 8011 Offices & clinics of medical doctors

(P-19939)
SAN DIEGO FAMILY CARE (PA)
Also Called: LINDA VISTA HEALTH CARE CENTER
6973 Linda Vista Rd, San Diego
(92111-6342)
PHONE...................................858 279-0925
Fax: 858 279-6471
Roberta L Feinberg, *CEO*
Manuel Quintanar, *CFO*
Margarita Caudillo, *Data Proc Staff*
Deborah L Steinberg, *Psychiatry*
Annemarie Selaya, *Med Doctor*
EMP: 93
SALES (est): 17.6MM **Privately Held**
WEB: www.lvhcc.com
SIC: 8011 Offices & clinics of medical doctors

(P-19940)
SAN DIEGO ORTHOPAEDIC ASSOCIAT
Also Called: S D O A
4060 4th Ave Ste 700, San Diego
(92103-2121)
PHONE...................................619 299-8500
Fax: 619 297-1443
Larry Dodge, *President*
William E Bowman MD, *Principal*
Robert M Averill, *Surgeon*
William H Davidson, *Surgeon*
John A Aalbers, *Neurology*
EMP: 52
SQ FT: 11,000
SALES (est): 9.1MM **Privately Held**
SIC: 8011 Orthopedic physician; surgeon

(P-19941)
SAN DIMAS MEDICAL GROUP INC
100 Old River Rd, Bakersfield
(93311-8823)
PHONE...................................661 663-4800
Fax: 661 663-4770
Frank Ynostroza MD, *Ch of Bd*
Ken Knutson, *CFO*
Jackie Hall, *Executive*
Kandi Knudsen, *Executive*
Wendy Crenshaw MD, *Principal*
EMP: 60
SQ FT: 20,000
SALES (est): 13.4MM **Privately Held**
WEB: www.sandimasmedical.com
SIC: 8011 Obstetrician; gynecologist

(P-19942)
SAN FRANCISCO FERTILITY CTRS
55 Francisco St Ste 300, San Francisco
(94133-2113)
PHONE...................................415 834-3000
Fax: 415 834-3099
Carl Herbert, *Med Doctor*
Maryellen Moore, *CEO*
Susan Herbert, *Office Mgr*
John Hamilton, *Controller*
EMP: 74
SALES (est): 6.1MM **Privately Held**
SIC: 8011 Fertility specialist, physician

(P-19943)
SAN FRANCISCO MEDICAL GROUP
1 Shrader St Ste 650, San Francisco
(94117-1036)
PHONE...................................415 221-0665
A Noble MD, *President*
Alan Noble MD, *President*
Dimitriy Kondrashov, *Surgeon*
EMP: 54
SQ FT: 7,000
SALES (est): 1.7MM **Privately Held**
SIC: 8011 Internal medicine, physician/surgeon; pediatrician

(P-19944)
SAN GABRIEL AMBULATORY SUGERY
207 S Santa Anita St G16, San Gabriel
(91776-1147)
PHONE...................................626 300-5300
Brenda Durgin, *Manager*
EMP: 941
SALES (est): 52.6MM **Privately Held**
SIC: 8011 Surgeon
HQ: United Surgical Partners International, Inc.
15305 Dallas Pkwy # 1600
Addison TX 75001
972 713-3500

(P-19945)
SAN JOAQUIN GENERAL HOSPITAL
500 W Hospital Rd, French Camp
(95231-9693)
P.O. Box 1020, Stockton (95201-3120)
PHONE...................................209 468-6000
Fax: 209 468-6246
Sheker Itemi, *Principal*
Ramesh Dharawat,
James Pucelik,
Alan Germany, *CFO*
Ron Kruetner, *CFO*
EMP: 190
SALES (est): 70.3MM **Privately Held**
SIC: 8011 Infectious disease specialist, physician/surgeon

(P-19946)
SAN JOSE FOOTHILL FAMILY COMM
Also Called: Foothill Community Health Ctr
2670 Suite 200, San Jose (95127)
PHONE...................................408 729-4290
Fax: 408 729-1643
Salvador Chavarin, *CEO*
Ramon Pena, *CEO*
Steven Ronquillo, *Human Res Mgr*
EMP: 170
SQ FT: 2,200
SALES (est): 16.8MM **Privately Held**
WEB: www.sjffcc.com
SIC: 8011 Primary care medical clinic

(P-19947)
SAN JOSE MEDICAL CLINIC INC (PA)
Also Called: San Jose Medical Group
400 Race St, San Jose (95126-3518)
PHONE...................................408 278-3000
Fax: 408 278-3292
Ernest Wallerstein, *CEO*
Christine Hoskinson, *CFO*
Kim Salazar, *Branch Mgr*
Mike Patel, *CIO*
Robert Barr, *MIS Mgr*
EMP: 80
SALES (est): 35.5MM **Privately Held**
SIC: 8011 8741 Medical centers; management services

(P-19948)
SAN JOSE MEDICAL CLINIC INC
Also Called: San Jose Medical Group
2585 Samaritan Dr Ste 101, San Jose
(95124-4107)
PHONE...................................408 278-3000
Fax: 408 357-1060
Francis Garcia, *Branch Mgr*
Vladimir Oykhman, *Sr Software Eng*
Lelanya B Kearns, *Obstetrician*
Anca V Neacsu, *Obstetrician*
Mauro B Ruffy, *Plastic Surgeon*
EMP: 320
SALES (corp-wide): 35.5MM **Privately Held**
SIC: 8011 Medical centers
PA: San Jose Medical Clinic, Inc.
400 Race St
San Jose CA 95126
408 278-3000

(P-19949)
SAN JOSE STATE UNIVERSITY
Also Called: Student Health Services
1 Washington Sq, San Jose (95112-3613)
PHONE...................................408 924-1000
Robert J Latta MD, *Director*
John Vo, *Manager*
EMP: 50 **Privately Held**
WEB: www.sjsu.edu
SIC: 8011 9411 8221 Dispensary, operated by physicians; administration of educational programs; ; university
HQ: San Jose State University
1 Washington Sq
San Jose CA 95192
408 924-1000

(P-19950)
SAN JUDAS MEDICAL GROUP INC
2005 Wilshire Blvd # 207, Los Angeles
(90057-3503)
PHONE...................................213 483-1902
Nejat Rostami MD, *President*
EMP: 65
SALES (est): 2.8MM **Privately Held**
SIC: 8011 Clinic, operated by physicians

(P-19951)
SAN LEANDRO SURGERY CENTER LT
15035 E 14th St, San Leandro
(94578-1901)
PHONE...................................510 276-2800
Sheila Cook, *Partner*
David Bates, *Treasurer*
Lena Tam, *City Council*
Fazeela Ferouz, *Anesthesiology*
Gayle R Misle, *Anesthesiology*
EMP: 60
SQ FT: 33,000
SALES (est): 6.6MM **Privately Held**
WEB: www.slsurgery.com
SIC: 8011 Surgeon

(P-19952)
SANSUM CLINIC (PA)
470 S Patterson Ave, Santa Barbara
(93111-2404)
P.O. Box 1200 (93102-1200)
PHONE...................................805 681-7700
Fax: 805 681-7710
Kurt Ransohoff MD, *President*
Chad Hine, *CFO*
Paul Jaconette, *Exec VP*
Joanne Stokes, *General Mgr*
Gerri French, *Executive Asst*
EMP: 60
SQ FT: 10,944
SALES (est): 223.5MM **Privately Held**
WEB: www.sansum.com
SIC: 8011 Clinic, operated by physicians

(P-19953)
SANTA ANA RADIOLOGY CENTER
Also Called: West Coast Radiology Center
1100 N Tustin Ave Ste A, Santa Ana
(92705-3509)
PHONE...................................714 835-6055
Fax: 714 835-7993
Tim Chavez, *CEO*
Matt Albers, *Administration*
Mike Shih, *CIO*
Susan Dalessandro, *Marketing Staff*
Glenda Romero, *Oncology*
EMP: 60
SQ FT: 15,000
SALES (est): 4.8MM **Privately Held**
SIC: 8011 8071 Radiologist; X-ray laboratory, including dental

(P-19954)
SANTA CLARA COUNTY OF
Also Called: Public Health Dept
976 Lenzen Ave Ste 1800, San Jose
(95126-2737)
PHONE...................................408 792-5680
Fax: 408 792-5568
G Dickinson, *Director*
EMP: 75 **Privately Held**
WEB: www.countyairports.org
SIC: 8011 9431 Clinic, operated by physicians; administration of public health programs;
PA: County Of Santa Clara
3180 Newberry Dr Ste 150
San Jose CA 95118
408 299-5105

(P-19955)
SANTA CLARA VALLEY MEDICAL CTR
2400 Moorpark Ave, San Jose
(95128-2631)
PHONE...................................408 885-6300
EMP: 386 **Privately Held**
SIC: 8011 Medical centers
PA: Santa Clara Valley Medical Center
751 S Bascom Ave
San Jose CA 95128

(P-19956)
SANTA CLARA VALLEY MEDICAL CTR
976 Lenzen Ave, San Jose (95126-2737)
PHONE...................................408 792-5586
Fax: 408 792-5544
EMP: 772 **Privately Held**
SIC: 8011 Offices & clinics of medical doctors
PA: Santa Clara Valley Medical Center
751 S Bascom Ave
San Jose CA 95128

(P-19957)
SANTA CLARITA MEDICAL GROUP
25775 Mcbean Pkwy Ste 209, Valencia
(91355-3703)
PHONE...................................661 255-6802
Kurt Olson, *Branch Mgr*
EMP: 50
SALES (corp-wide): 3.3MM **Privately Held**
SIC: 8011 Physicians' office, including specialists
PA: Santa Clarita Medical Group, Inc
1680 S Garfield Ave
Alhambra CA
661 250-0100

(P-19958)
SANTA CRUZ COUNTY OF
Also Called: Watsonville Health Clinic
1430 Freedom Blvd Ste D, Watsonville
(95076-2752)
PHONE...................................831 763-8400
Fax: 831 763-8081
Michelle Violich, *Director*
Marilyn K Marzell, *Physician Asst*
Gerald Landers, *Manager*
Maria Rosillo, *Receptionist Se*
EMP: 50 **Privately Held**
WEB: www.scsheriff.com
SIC: 8011 9111 Clinic, operated by physicians; county supervisors' & executives' offices
PA: County Of Santa Cruz
701 Ocean St Rm 520
Santa Cruz CA 95060
831 454-2100

8011 - Offices & Clinics Of Doctors Of Medicine County (P-19959)

(P-19959)
SANTA CRUZ MEDICAL FOUNDATION (HQ)
2025 Soquel Ave, Santa Cruz (95062-1323)
PHONE..................................831 458-5537
Larry De Ghetaldi, *Director*
Nadder Mirsepassi, *Treasurer*
Blanca Rodriguez, *Office Mgr*
Karl J Christoffersen, *Surgeon*
James D Spiegel, *Surgeon*
EMP: 66
SQ FT: 60,000
SALES (est): 39MM
SALES (corp-wide): 11B **Privately Held**
WEB: www.sutterhealth.org
SIC: 8011 General & family practice, physician/surgeon
PA: Sutter Health
2200 River Plaza Dr
Sacramento CA 95833
916 733-8800

(P-19960)
SANTA MONICA BAY PHYSICIANS
881 Alma Real Dr Ste 214, Pacific Palisades (90272-3750)
PHONE..................................310 459-2363
Fax: 310 395-6313
Mark R Needham, *President*
EMP: 180
SALES (est): 6.8MM **Privately Held**
SIC: 8011 Physical medicine, physician/surgeon

(P-19961)
SANTA MONICA BAY PHYSICIANS HE (PA)
Also Called: Bay Area Community Med Group
5767 W Century Blvd, Los Angeles (90045-5631)
PHONE..................................310 417-5900
Eileen McGrath, *President*
Dr Richard Zachrich, *Treasurer*
Dr Steven Seizer, *Vice Pres*
Dr David Cutler, *Admin Sec*
John Roffi, *Manager*
EMP: 85
SALES (est): 14.9MM **Privately Held**
WEB: www.smbp.com
SIC: 8011 Clinic, operated by physicians

(P-19962)
SANTA MONICA ORTHOPEDIC (PA)
2020 Santa Monica Blvd # 230, Santa Monica (90404-2124)
PHONE..................................310 315-2018
Fax: 310 315-0175
Ramin M Modabber MD, *President*
Kevin M Erhardt MD, *Vice Pres*
John Somerville, *Office Mgr*
Kenton S Horacek MD, *Admin Sec*
Roger Nesbit, *Administration*
EMP: 67
SQ FT: 28,242
SALES: 248.9K **Privately Held**
WEB: www.aclprevent.com
SIC: 8011 Orthopedic physician

(P-19963)
SANTE HEALTH SYSTEM INC
Also Called: Sante Community Physicians
7370 N Palm Ave Ste 101, Fresno (93711-5782)
P.O. Box 1507 (93716-1507)
PHONE..................................559 228-5400
Mateo F Desoto, *CEO*
Scott Wells, *President*
Chris Cheney, *CFO*
Wesley Qualls, *Senior VP*
Debbie Keena, *Vice Pres*
EMP: 125
SQ FT: 20,000
SALES (est): 22.4MM **Privately Held**
SIC: 8011 Physicians' office, including specialists

(P-19964)
SCRIPPS CLINIC
12395 El Camino Real, San Diego (92130-3082)
P.O. Box 2469, La Jolla (92038-2469)
PHONE..................................858 794-1250
Fax: 858 794-1237
Chris Van Gorder, *CEO*
James Collins, *President*
Dr Hubert Greenway, *CEO*
Jess Leano, *Technical Staff*
Claudia Schwartz, *Human Res Dir*
EMP: 129 **EST:** 1999
SALES (est): 22.6MM **Privately Held**
SIC: 8011 Internal medicine practitioners

(P-19965)
SCRIPPS CLINIC CARMEL VALLEY
Also Called: Division Infectious Diseases
10666 N Torrey Pines Rd, La Jolla (92037-1092)
PHONE..................................858 554-8096
EMP: 271
SALES (corp-wide): 21.9MM **Privately Held**
SIC: 8011
PA: Scripps Clinic Carmel Valley
3811 Valley Centre Dr
San Diego CA 92130
858 764-3000

(P-19966)
SCRIPPS CLINIC MEDICAL GROUP
10666 N Torrey Pines Rd, La Jolla (92037-1092)
PHONE..................................858 554-9606
Fax: 858 554-6751
Thomas Waltz, *CEO*
James Collins, *CFO*
Darlene Elias, *Med Doctor*
Kristina M Kjeldsberg, *Med Doctor*
David C Reffield, *Med Doctor*
EMP: 300
SALES (est): 16.6MM **Privately Held**
SIC: 8011 Physicians' office, including specialists

(P-19967)
SCRIPPS DIALASYS INC (PA)
Also Called: Scripps Dialysis Center
9870 Genesee Ave, La Jolla (92037-1205)
PHONE..................................619 453-9070
Fax: 858 457-2554
John Aalbers, *Principal*
Terence Bahr, *Administration*
EMP: 50
SQ FT: 10,000
SALES (est): 2.2MM **Privately Held**
SIC: 8011 8092 Clinic, operated by physicians; kidney dialysis centers

(P-19968)
SCRIPPS HEALTH
Also Called: Scripps Ambulatory Surgery Ctr
320 Santa Fe Dr Ste 310, Encinitas (92024-5140)
PHONE..................................760 753-8413
Donna Danley, *Principal*
John Backman, *Cardiology*
Roy Avalos, *Med Doctor*
EMP: 60
SALES (corp-wide): 1.7B **Privately Held**
SIC: 8011 Surgeon
PA: Scripps Health
4275 Campus Point Ct
San Diego CA 92121
858 678-7000

(P-19969)
SCRIPPS HEALTH
Also Called: Scripps Whttier Dbetes Program
10140 Campus Point Dr, San Diego (92121-1520)
PHONE..................................858 622-9076
Fax: 858 626-5680
Athena Philis-Tsimikas, *Branch Mgr*
Chris Walker, *Admin Dir*
Garay Anna, *Director*
Naomi Bea, *Supervisor*
EMP: 60
SALES (corp-wide): 1.7B **Privately Held**
SIC: 8011 Offices & clinics of medical doctors; diabetes specialist, physician/surgeon
PA: Scripps Health
4275 Campus Point Ct
San Diego CA 92121
858 678-7000

(P-19970)
SCRIPPS HEALTH
237 Church Ave, Chula Vista (91910-2702)
PHONE..................................619 862-6600
EMP: 270
SALES (corp-wide): 1.7B **Privately Held**
SIC: 8011 Primary care medical clinic
PA: Scripps Health
4275 Campus Point Ct
San Diego CA 92121
858 678-7000

(P-19971)
SCRIPPS HEALTH
477 N El Camino Real A208, Encinitas (92024-1328)
PHONE..................................760 479-3900
EMP: 54
SALES (corp-wide): 1.7B **Privately Held**
SIC: 8011 Medical centers
PA: Scripps Health
4275 Campus Point Ct
San Diego CA 92121
858 678-7000

(P-19972)
SCRIPPS HEALTH
4318 Mission Ave, Oceanside (92057-6541)
PHONE..................................760 901-5070
EMP: 216
SALES (corp-wide): 1.7B **Privately Held**
SIC: 8011 Medical centers
PA: Scripps Health
4275 Campus Point Ct
San Diego CA 92121
858 678-7000

(P-19973)
SCRIPPS HEALTH
Also Called: Rancho Clinic Rancho San Diego
10862 Calle Verde, La Mesa (91941-7340)
PHONE..................................619 670-5400
Fax: 619 660-1897
Yvonne Markovitz, *Manager*
Mel M Kurtulus, *OB/GYN*
EMP: 70
SALES (corp-wide): 1.7B **Privately Held**
WEB: www.scripps.org
SIC: 8011 Clinic, operated by physicians
PA: Scripps Health
4275 Campus Point Ct
San Diego CA 92121
858 678-7000

(P-19974)
SCRIPPS HEALTH
7910 Frost St Ste 320, San Diego (92123-2791)
PHONE..................................858 292-4211
Steven F Mosher MD, *Owner*
Silvia Moreno, *Manager*
EMP: 300
SALES (corp-wide): 1.7B **Privately Held**
SIC: 8011 Physicians' office, including specialists
PA: Scripps Health
4275 Campus Point Ct
San Diego CA 92121
858 678-7000

(P-19975)
SCRIPPS HEALTH
Also Called: Scripps Clinic - Encinatas
310 Santa Fe Dr Ste 200, Encinitas (92024-5124)
PHONE..................................760 633-6915
Cheryl Suqua, *Administration*
Scott Musinski, *Obstetrician*
EMP: 60
SQ FT: 38,331
SALES (corp-wide): 1.7B **Privately Held**
WEB: www.scripps.org
SIC: 8011 General & family practice, physician/surgeon
PA: Scripps Health
4275 Campus Point Ct
San Diego CA 92121
858 678-7000

(P-19976)
SCRIPPS HEALTH
488 E Valley Pkwy Ste 411, Escondido (92025-3380)
PHONE..................................760 737-7373
EMP: 270
SALES (corp-wide): 1.7B **Privately Held**
SIC: 8011 Offices & clinics of medical doctors
PA: Scripps Health
4275 Campus Point Ct
San Diego CA 92121
858 678-7000

(P-19977)
SCRIPPS HEALTH
9834 Genesee Ave Ste 311, La Jolla (92037-1221)
PHONE..................................858 458-5100
Marc Effron, *Med Doctor*
EMP: 432
SALES (corp-wide): 1.7B **Privately Held**
SIC: 8011 Plastic surgeon
PA: Scripps Health
4275 Campus Point Ct
San Diego CA 92121
858 678-7000

(P-19978)
SCRIPPS HEALTH
9850 Genesee Ave Ste 620, La Jolla (92037-1217)
PHONE..................................858 626-5200
Matthew Ferguson, *Project Mgr*
EMP: 162
SALES (corp-wide): 1.7B **Privately Held**
SIC: 8011 8059 Offices & clinics of medical doctors; convalescent home
PA: Scripps Health
4275 Campus Point Ct
San Diego CA 92121
858 678-7000

(P-19979)
SCRIPPS HEALTH
10666 N Torrey Pines Rd, La Jolla (92037-1027)
PHONE..................................858 554-8892
Larry Harrison, *President*
Quang Nguyen, *Med Doctor*
EMP: 60
SQ FT: 99,999
SALES (corp-wide): 1.9B **Privately Held**
SIC: 8011 Physicians' office, including specialists
PA: Scripps Health
4275 Campus Point Ct
San Diego CA 92121
858 678-7000

(P-19980)
SCRIPPS HEALTH
10666 N Torrey Pines Rd, La Jolla (92037-1027)
PHONE..................................858 554-9489
Allan Saven MD, *Principal*
EMP: 60
SALES (corp-wide): 1.9B **Privately Held**
WEB: www.scripps.org
SIC: 8011 Physicians' office, including specialists
PA: Scripps Health
4275 Campus Point Ct
San Diego CA 92121
858 678-7000

(P-19981)
SCRIPPS HEALTH
3998 Vista Way Ste E, Oceanside (92056-4514)
PHONE..................................760 901-5200
Karl Steinberg, *Sales Mgr*
John Kroener, *Surgeon*
Maria Murillo, *Obstetrician*
Madeline Rodriguez, *Obstetrician*
EMP: 378
SALES (corp-wide): 1.7B **Privately Held**
SIC: 8011 General & family practice, physician/surgeon
PA: Scripps Health
4275 Campus Point Ct
San Diego CA 92121
858 678-7000

(P-19982)
SCRIPPS HEALTH
Also Called: Clinic Business
10790 Rancho Bernardo Rd, San Diego (92127-5705)
PHONE..................................858 784-5888
Breaux Castleman, *President*

David Kimber, *Manager*
Chuck Korogi, *Manager*
EMP: 100
SALES (corp-wide): 2.3B **Privately Held**
WEB: www.scripps.org
SIC: 8011 Internal medicine practitioners; specialized medical practitioners, except internal
PA: Scripps Health
4275 Campus Point Ct
San Diego CA 92121
858 678-7000

(P-19983)
SD SPORTS MDCNE&FMLY HLTH CNTR
6699 Alvarado Rd Ste 2100, San Diego (92120-5238)
PHONE..................619 229-3910
Fax: 619 287-6132
Jo Baxter, *Manager*
Bill Taylor,
Danny Norrdin, *Director*
EMP: 52
SALES (est): 3.1MM **Privately Held**
WEB: www.sandiegosportsmed.com
SIC: 8011 Offices & clinics of medical doctors

(P-19984)
SEDONA SURGICAL CENTER INC
39700 Bob Hope Dr Ste 301, Rancho Mirage (92270-7129)
PHONE..................760 413-8056
Roland Reinhart, *President*
EMP: 50
SALES (est): 2MM **Privately Held**
SIC: 8011 Ambulatory surgical center

(P-19985)
SENECA HEALTHCARE DISTRICT
130 Brentwood Dr, Chester (96020)
PHONE..................530 258-2151
Larry Blitz, *Manager*
EMP: 78
SALES (corp-wide): 13.2MM **Privately Held**
SIC: 8011 Offices & clinics of medical doctors
PA: Seneca Healthcare District
130 Brentwood Dr
Chester CA 96020
530 258-2151

(P-19986)
SENECA HEALTHCARE DISTRICT
Also Called: Seneca Hospital Almanor Clinic
199 Reynolds Rd, Chester (96020)
PHONE..................530 258-1977
Fax: 530 258-2004
Camille Hovellerdale, *Manager*
EMP: 78
SALES (corp-wide): 13.2MM **Privately Held**
SIC: 8011 Clinic, operated by physicians
PA: Seneca Healthcare District
130 Brentwood Dr
Chester CA 96020
530 258-2151

(P-19987)
SEQUOIA SURGICAL CENTER LP
Also Called: Sequoia Surgical Pavilion
2405 Shadelands Dr # 200, Walnut Creek (94598-5916)
PHONE..................925 935-6700
Debbie Mack, *General Ptnr*
Tina Hadave, *Office Mgr*
EMP: 50
SQ FT: 14,750
SALES (est): 4.9MM
SALES (corp-wide): 291.3MM **Privately Held**
SIC: 8011 Ambulatory surgical center
PA: National Surgical Hospitals, Inc.
250 S Wacker Dr Ste 500
Chicago IL 60606
312 627-8400

(P-19988)
SERRA COMMUNITY MED CLINIC INC
9375 San Fernando Rd, Sun Valley (91352-1418)
PHONE..................818 768-8882
Sadayappa K Durairaj, *CEO*
Adbul Ahmady, *COO*
Karla Pieters, *CFO*
Dr Arnold Jacobs, *Treasurer*
Raffaele Corbisiero, *Executive*
EMP: 163
SQ FT: 60,000
SALES (est): 25.4MM **Privately Held**
SIC: 8011 Medical centers

(P-19989)
SERRA MEDICAL CLINIC INC
9375 San Fernando Rd, Sun Valley (91352-1418)
PHONE..................818 768-3000
Fax: 818 504-4463
S K Durairaj MD, *President*
Bill Magier, *Controller*
EMP: 100 **EST:** 1974
SQ FT: 62,000
SALES (est): 4.3MM **Privately Held**
SIC: 8011 Offices & clinics of medical doctors

(P-19990)
SHARP HEALTHCARE
7910 Frost St Ste 280, San Diego (92123-2752)
PHONE..................619 398-2988
Fax: 619 398-2987
Tim Crowe, *Project Mgr*
Sherry Lipford, *Analyst*
Lan Jacobson, *Purch Agent*
Joanna Adamczak, *Obstetrician*
Barry Uhl, *Oncology*
EMP: 78
SALES (corp-wide): 3.4B **Privately Held**
SIC: 8011 Offices & clinics of medical doctors
PA: Sharp Healthcare
8695 Spectrum Center Blvd
San Diego CA 92123
858 499-4000

(P-19991)
SHARP HEALTHCARE
10670 Wexford St, San Diego (92131-3940)
PHONE..................858 621-4090
Diane Harding, *Surgeon*
Mitzi Albano,
Susan Horton, *Manager*
EMP: 67
SALES (corp-wide): 3.4B **Privately Held**
SIC: 8011 Medical centers
PA: Sharp Healthcare
8695 Spectrum Center Blvd
San Diego CA 92123
858 499-4000

(P-19992)
SHARP HEALTHCARE
Also Called: Sharp Rees-Stealy
8008 Frost St Ste 106, San Diego (92123-4229)
PHONE..................858 939-5434
Julieann Ignacio, *Admin Sec*
Alfred Saleh, *Oncology*
Ruben Felix, *Manager*
Maureen Wallace, *Manager*
EMP: 105
SALES (corp-wide): 3.4B **Privately Held**
SIC: 8011 Medical centers
PA: Sharp Healthcare
8695 Spectrum Center Blvd
San Diego CA 92123
858 499-4000

(P-19993)
SHARP HEALTHCARE
Also Called: Sharp Rees-Stealy Pharmacy
2929 Health Center Dr, San Diego (92123-2762)
PHONE..................619 688-3543
Fax: 858 874-2360
Daniel Gross, *Exec VP*
Nancy Pratt, *Vice Pres*
Judy Bailey, *Office Mgr*
Mary Thrasher, *Office Mgr*
Judy Zunnigan, *Office Mgr*
EMP: 63
SQ FT: 27,810
SALES (corp-wide): 3.4B **Privately Held**
SIC: 8011 5912 Offices & clinics of medical doctors; orthopedic physician; drug stores
PA: Sharp Healthcare
8695 Spectrum Center Blvd
San Diego CA 92123
858 499-4000

(P-19994)
SHARP HEALTHCARE
8901 Activity Rd, San Diego (92126-4427)
PHONE..................858 653-6100
Joy Stewart, *Director*
John M Casey, *Med Doctor*
Michael Keefe, *Manager*
EMP: 100
SALES (corp-wide): 3.4B **Privately Held**
SIC: 8011 Offices & clinics of medical doctors
PA: Sharp Healthcare
8695 Spectrum Center Blvd
San Diego CA 92123
858 499-4000

(P-19995)
SHARP HEALTHCARE
3230 Waring Ct Ste P, Oceanside (92056-4509)
PHONE..................760 901-5100
Maryjo Moimotier, *Manager*
EMP: 63
SALES (corp-wide): 3.4B **Privately Held**
SIC: 8011 Pediatrician
PA: Sharp Healthcare
8695 Spectrum Center Blvd
San Diego CA 92123
858 499-4000

(P-19996)
SHARP HEALTHCARE
2020 Genesee Ave Fl 2, San Diego (92123-4219)
PHONE..................858 616-8411
Leticia Rawls, *Principal*
EMP: 100
SQ FT: 33,244
SALES (corp-wide): 3.4B **Privately Held**
SIC: 8011 Clinic, operated by physicians
PA: Sharp Healthcare
8695 Spectrum Center Blvd
San Diego CA 92123
858 499-4000

(P-19997)
SHARP HEALTHCARE
Also Called: Sharp Reece Stealy Med Group
4510 Viewridge Ave, San Diego (92123-1637)
PHONE..................800 827-4277
Fax: 858 492-3943
Don Balfour, *Manager*
EMP: 70
SALES (corp-wide): 3.4B **Privately Held**
SIC: 8011 Clinic, operated by physicians
PA: Sharp Healthcare
8695 Spectrum Center Blvd
San Diego CA 92123
858 499-4000

(P-19998)
SHARP HEALTHCARE
8860 Center Dr Ste 450, La Mesa (91942-7001)
PHONE..................619 460-6200
Marla Lobenstein, *Manager*
EMP: 72
SALES (corp-wide): 3.4B **Privately Held**
SIC: 8011 General & family practice, physician/surgeon
PA: Sharp Healthcare
8695 Spectrum Center Blvd
San Diego CA 92123
858 499-4000

(P-19999)
SHARP HEALTHCARE
2020 Genesee Ave, San Diego (92123-4219)
PHONE..................858 616-8200
Kathlyn R Ignacio MD, *Med Doctor*
EMP: 111
SALES (corp-wide): 3.4B **Privately Held**
SIC: 8011 Medical centers
PA: Sharp Healthcare
8695 Spectrum Center Blvd
San Diego CA 92123
858 499-4000

(P-20000)
SHARPER FUTURE
Also Called: Social Hbltion Rlpse Prvntion
870 Market St Ste 1265, San Francisco (94102-2917)
PHONE..................415 297-6767
Thomas Tobin, *Partner*
Mary-Perry Miller, *Partner*
Carla Sommers, *Psychologist*
Tony Angelo, *Director*
EMP: 56 **EST:** 1995
SALES (est): 3.5MM **Privately Held**
WEB: www.sharperfuture.com
SIC: 8011 Psychiatric clinic

(P-20001)
SHASTA MEDICAL ASSOCIATES
1555 East St Ste 210, Redding (96001-1153)
PHONE..................530 243-3231
Fax: 530 242-8378
Bruce Kittrick, *President*
Mitchell Akman MD, *CFO*
T Nandakumar MD, *Vice Pres*
Stephen Casey MD, *Admin Sec*
Fernando Alvarez MD, *Director*
EMP: 56
SALES (est): 5.8MM **Privately Held**
SIC: 8011 Internal medicine, physician/surgeon

(P-20002)
SHEPARD EYE CENTER
1418 E Main St Ste 110, Santa Maria (93454-4836)
PHONE..................805 925-2637
Fax: 805 347-0033
Dennis D Shepard MD, *President*
James T Franta, *Principal*
EMP: 50
SQ FT: 10,000
SALES (est): 4.8MM **Privately Held**
SIC: 8011 Ophthalmologist

(P-20003)
SIERRA PACIFIC ORTHO
1630 E Herndon Ave, Fresno (93720-3391)
PHONE..................559 256-5200
Joe Clark, *CEO*
Eric C Hanson, *President*
Annette Hopkins, *Office Mgr*
Jerome Dunklin, *Surgeon*
Timothy Watson, *Surgeon*
EMP: 200 **EST:** 2000
SALES (est): 3.2MM **Privately Held**
WEB: www.spoc-ortho.com
SIC: 8011 Orthopedic physician

(P-20004)
SIERRA VIEW LOCAL HOSPITAL DST (PA)
Also Called: Sierra View District Hospital
465 W Putnam Ave, Porterville (93257-3320)
PHONE..................559 784-1110
Fax: 559 783-0131
Donna Hefner, *President*
Frederick Young,
Thomas Maclennan, *Ch Radiology*
Douglas Dickson, *CFO*
Ruth Gonzalez, *CFO*
◆ **EMP:** 168 **EST:** 1948
SQ FT: 135,000
SALES: 63.6MM **Privately Held**
WEB: www.sierra-view.com
SIC: 8011 8062 Offices & clinics of medical doctors; general medical & surgical hospitals

(P-20005)
SOBOL PHILIP A MD P C INC
8618 S Sepulveda Blvd # 130, Los Angeles (90045-4005)
PHONE..................310 649-5894
Philip A Sobol, *President*
EMP: 50
SALES (est): 2.3MM **Privately Held**
SIC: 8011 Offices & clinics of medical doctors

8011 - Offices & Clinics Of Doctors Of Medicine County (P-20006)

(P-20006)
SOLANO REGIONAL MEDICAL GROUP (PA)
1234 Empire St, Fairfield (94533-5711)
PHONE.................707 426-3911
Edward Levin MD, *President*
George Stock MD, *Treasurer*
George E Stock III, *Treasurer*
Sam Santoro Do, *Vice Pres*
Linnea Lauren, *Business Mgr*
EMP: 250
SQ FT: 40,000
SALES (est): 10.1MM **Privately Held**
SIC: 8011 General & family practice, physician/surgeon

(P-20007)
SOMA SURGICENTER
1580 Valencia St, San Francisco (94110-4423)
PHONE.................415 641-6889
Fax: 415 641-6887
Mary Sherman, *Manager*
EMP: 50
SALES (est): 745.5K **Privately Held**
SIC: 8011 Surgeon

(P-20008)
SONOMA COUNTY INDIAN HEALTH PR (PA)
Also Called: SCIHP
144 Stony Point Rd, Santa Rosa (95401-4122)
PHONE.................707 521-4545
Betty Arterverry, *CEO*
Molin T Malicay, *CEO*
Larry Mackie, *Acting CFO*
Lori Houston, *Planning*
Robert Orr, *CTO*
EMP: 150
SQ FT: 70,000
SALES: 21.8MM **Privately Held**
SIC: 8011 Offices & clinics of medical doctors

(P-20009)
SONOMA WEST MEDICAL CENTER
501 Petaluma Ave, Sebastopol (95472-4215)
PHONE.................707 823-8511
Raymond Hino, *CEO*
Joseph Demont, *CFO*
David Yarbrough, *Ch Nursing Ofcr*
EMP: 100
SQ FT: 60,000
SALES: 33MM **Privately Held**
SIC: 8011 Medical centers

(P-20010)
SOUTH BAY FAMILY MEDICAL GROUP
Also Called: Mellor, Anna B MD
3105 Lomita Blvd, Torrance (90505-5108)
PHONE.................310 378-2234
Fax: 310 378-9795
Glenn M Wishon MD, *Partner*
Nancy Griffith MD, *Partner*
George A Joseph MD, *Partner*
Lee G Kissel MD, *Partner*
Joseph Mansen, *Partner*
EMP: 70
SQ FT: 6,400
SALES (est): 4.6MM **Privately Held**
WEB: www.sbfmg.com
SIC: 8011 General & family practice, physician/surgeon

(P-20011)
SOUTH CENTRAL FAMILY HLTH CTR
4425 S Central Ave, Los Angeles (90011-3629)
PHONE.................323 908-4200
Fax: 323 908-4260
Richard Veloz, *President*
Paul Ramos, *CFO*
Jackie Barton, *Office Mgr*
Temica D Boutte, *Physician Asst*
Alexis Menzies, *Manager*
EMP: 92
SQ FT: 13,000
SALES: 13.7MM **Privately Held**
WEB: www.scfhc.org
SIC: 8011 Clinic, operated by physicians

(P-20012)
SOUTH COUNTY ORTHOPEDIC SPECIA
Also Called: Moskow, Lonnie J MD
24331 El Toro Rd Ste 200, Laguna Hills (92637-3116)
PHONE.................949 586-3200
James Mullen, *President*
Kyle W Coker, *Principal*
Larry M Gursten, *Principal*
Lance R Montgomery, *Principal*
Lonnie J Moskow, *Principal*
EMP: 75
SALES (est): 12.1MM **Privately Held**
WEB: www.scosortho.com
SIC: 8011 Orthopedic physician

(P-20013)
SOUTHERN CA HLTH & RHBLTN PRG
2610 Industry Way Ste A, Lynwood (90262-4028)
PHONE.................310 631-8004
Dr Jack M Barbour, *CEO*
Rita Floyd, *President*
Gary Lu, *Accounts Mgr*
EMP: 165
SQ FT: 6,000
SALES (est): 10.4MM **Privately Held**
SIC: 8011 Psychiatric clinic

(P-20014)
SOUTHERN CAL ORTHPD INST LP
375 Rolling Oaks Dr, Thousand Oaks (91361-1023)
PHONE.................805 497-7015
David M Auerbach, *Branch Mgr*
Mark Getelman, *Sports Medicine*
David Auerbach, *Surgeon*
EMP: 61
SALES (corp-wide): 27.7MM **Privately Held**
SIC: 8011 Primary care medical clinic
PA: Southern California Orthopedic Institute, L.P.
6815 Noble Ave
Van Nuys CA 91405
818 901-6600

(P-20015)
SOUTHERN CAL ORTHPD INST LP
Also Called: Satellite Office
6815 Noble Ave Frnt Frnt, Van Nuys (91405-6515)
PHONE.................818 901-6600
Patricia McKeever, *Partner*
EMP: 150
SALES (corp-wide): 27.7MM **Privately Held**
WEB: www.scoiclasroom.com
SIC: 8011 Orthopedic physician
PA: Southern California Orthopedic Institute, L.P.
6815 Noble Ave
Van Nuys CA 91405
818 901-6600

(P-20016)
SOUTHERN CAL ORTHPD INST LP
6815 Noble Ave Ste 112, Westlake Village (91361)
PHONE.................818 901-6600
Dr Mark Friedman, *Partner*
EMP: 66
SALES (corp-wide): 27.7MM **Privately Held**
WEB: www.scoiclasroom.com
SIC: 8011 Orthopedic physician
PA: Southern California Orthopedic Institute, L.P.
6815 Noble Ave
Van Nuys CA 91405
818 901-6600

(P-20017)
SOUTHERN CAL ORTHPD INST LP (PA)
6815 Noble Ave, Van Nuys (91405-3796)
PHONE.................818 901-6600
Fax: 818 901-6684
Marc J Friedman, *Partner*
Kelly Cowan, *Info Tech Mgr*
Stephen Goodman, *Info Tech Mgr*
Eddie Gandara, *Technology*
Eleanor O'Brien, *Engineer*
EMP: 135
SALES (est): 27.7MM **Privately Held**
WEB: www.scoiclasroom.com
SIC: 8011 8249 Orthopedic physician; medical training services

(P-20018)
SOUTHERN CAL PRMNNTE MED GROUP
6 Willard, Irvine (92604-4694)
PHONE.................949 262-5780
Debra Dannemeyer, *Administration*
Terry Kunysz, *Pharmacy Dir*
EMP: 100
SALES (corp-wide): 3.2B **Privately Held**
WEB: www.permanente.net
SIC: 8011 Clinic, operated by physicians
PA: Southern California Permanente Medical Group
393 Walnut Dr
Pasadena CA 91107
626 405-5704

(P-20019)
SOUTHERN CAL PRMNNTE MED GROUP
13652 Cantara St, Panorama City (91402-5423)
PHONE.................800 272-3500
Fax: 818 375-2145
Arthur Phelps, *Branch Mgr*
EMP: 70
SALES (corp-wide): 3.2B **Privately Held**
SIC: 8011 Offices & clinics of medical doctors
PA: Southern California Permanente Medical Group
393 Walnut Dr
Pasadena CA 91107
626 405-5704

(P-20020)
SOUTHERN CAL PRMNNTE MED GROUP
3501 Stockdale Hwy, Bakersfield (93309-2150)
PHONE.................661 398-5085
Jonathan L Sales, *Surgeon*
Abner M Ward, *Surgeon*
Alfredo C Aparicio, *Urology*
Jeffrey G Nalesnik, *Urology*
EMP: 54
SALES (corp-wide): 3.2B **Privately Held**
SIC: 8011 Offices & clinics of medical doctors
PA: Southern California Permanente Medical Group
393 Walnut Dr
Pasadena CA 91107
626 405-5704

(P-20021)
SOUTHERN CAL PRMNNTE MED GROUP
Also Called: Kaiser Permanente
4647 Zion Ave, San Diego (92120-2507)
PHONE.................619 528-5000
Fax: 619 528-5048
Terry Belmont, *Principal*
Theodore Geer,
Mark Schumacher,
Peter Martin, *Top Exec*
Pamela Reger, *Case Mgmt Dir*
EMP: 53
SALES (corp-wide): 3.2B **Privately Held**
SIC: 8011 Offices & clinics of medical doctors
PA: Southern California Permanente Medical Group
393 Walnut Dr
Pasadena CA 91107
626 405-5704

(P-20022)
SOUTHERN CAL PRMNNTE MED GROUP
3830 Martin L King Jr Blv, Lynwood (90262-3625)
PHONE.................310 604-5700
Johnny K Wong, *Family Practiti*
EMP: 53
SALES (corp-wide): 3.2B **Privately Held**
SIC: 8011 Offices & clinics of medical doctors
PA: Southern California Permanente Medical Group
393 Walnut Dr
Pasadena CA 91107
626 405-5704

(P-20023)
SOUTHERN CAL PRMNNTE MED GROUP
6041 Cadillac Ave, Los Angeles (90034-1702)
PHONE.................323 857-2000
Larry Poston, *Director*
Donald B Shaul, *Med Doctor*
EMP: 58
SALES (corp-wide): 3.2B **Privately Held**
SIC: 8011 Radiologist
PA: Southern California Permanente Medical Group
393 Walnut Dr
Pasadena CA 91107
626 405-5704

(P-20024)
SOUTHERN CAL PRMNNTE MED GROUP
25825 Vermont Ave, Harbor City (90710-3518)
PHONE.................800 780-1230
EMP: 58
SALES (corp-wide): 436MM **Privately Held**
SIC: 8011
PA: Southern California Permanente Medical Group
393 Walnut Dr
Pasadena CA 91107
626 405-5704

(P-20025)
SOUTHERN CAL PRMNNTE MED GROUP
5250 Lankershim Blvd, North Hollywood (91601-3186)
PHONE.................888 778-5000
EMP: 70
SALES (corp-wide): 3.2B **Privately Held**
SIC: 8011 Offices & clinics of medical doctors
PA: Southern California Permanente Medical Group
393 Walnut Dr
Pasadena CA 91107
626 405-5704

(P-20026)
SOUTHERN CAL PRMNNTE MED GROUP
4841 Hollywood Blvd, Los Angeles (90027-5301)
PHONE.................323 783-5455
Alisa Aunskul, *Human Resources*
Kuo Chao, *Med Doctor*
Michael Cheng, *Med Doctor*
Clarence Cole, *Med Doctor*
Sami Jabara, *Med Doctor*
EMP: 70
SALES (corp-wide): 3.2B **Privately Held**
SIC: 8011 Offices & clinics of medical doctors
PA: Southern California Permanente Medical Group
393 Walnut Dr
Pasadena CA 91107
626 405-5704

(P-20027)
SOUTHERN CAL PRMNNTE MED GROUP
1511 W Garvey Ave N, West Covina (91790-2138)
PHONE.................626 960-4844
Fax: 626 856-3010
Jarvis B Ngati, *Psychiatry*
Christine L Um, *Psychiatry*
EMP: 70
SALES (corp-wide): 3.2B **Privately Held**
SIC: 8011 Offices & clinics of medical doctors

PRODUCTS & SERVICES SECTION
8011 - Offices & Clinics Of Doctors Of Medicine County (P-20046)

PA: Southern California Permanente Medical Group
393 Walnut Dr
Pasadena CA 91107
626 405-5704

(P-20028)
SOUTHERN CAL PRMNNTE MED GROUP
17542 17th St Ste 300, Tustin (92780-1960)
PHONE..................714 734-4500
EMP: 70
SALES (corp-wide): 3.2B Privately Held
SIC: 8011 Offices & clinics of medical doctors
PA: Southern California Permanente Medical Group
393 Walnut Dr
Pasadena CA 91107
626 405-5704

(P-20029)
SOUTHERN CAL PRMNNTE MED GROUP
Also Called: Orthopedics Department
4760 W Sunset Blvd, Los Angeles (90027-6063)
PHONE..................323 783-4893
Fax: 323 783-6985
Dolores Cobbarrubias, *Office Mgr*
EMP: 1397
SALES (corp-wide): 3.2B Privately Held
SIC: 8011 Orthopedic physician
PA: Southern California Permanente Medical Group
393 Walnut Dr
Pasadena CA 91107
626 405-5704

(P-20030)
SOUTHERN CAL PRMNNTE MED GROUP
Also Called: S C P M G
789 E Cooley Dr, Colton (92324-4007)
PHONE..................909 370-2501
EMP: 50
SALES (corp-wide): 3.2B Privately Held
WEB: www.permanente.net
SIC: 8011 Offices & clinics of medical doctors
PA: Southern California Permanente Medical Group
393 Walnut Dr
Pasadena CA 91107
626 405-5704

(P-20031)
SOUTHERN CAL PRMNNTE MED GROUP
18081 Beach Blvd, Huntington Beach (92648-1304)
PHONE..................714 841-7293
Kelly Tran, *Admin Sec*
Hemesh M Patel, *Family Practiti*
Sung Chang, *Med Doctor*
Holly Schij, *Manager*
EMP: 50
SALES (corp-wide): 3.2B Privately Held
WEB: www.permanente.net
SIC: 8011 Offices & clinics of medical doctors
PA: Southern California Permanente Medical Group
393 Walnut Dr
Pasadena CA 91107
626 405-5704

(P-20032)
SOUTHERN CAL PRMNNTE MED GROUP
Also Called: S C P M G
1630 E Main St, El Cajon (92021-5204)
PHONE..................619 528-5000
Brenda Scott-Mead, *Manager*
Jennifer M Park, *Psychiatry*
Caroline Paterno, *Psychiatry*
Annette L Pozos, *Psychiatry*
Stephen Tokraks, *Psychiatry*
EMP: 50
SALES (corp-wide): 3.2B Privately Held
WEB: www.permanente.net
SIC: 8011 Offices & clinics of medical doctors

PA: Southern California Permanente Medical Group
393 Walnut Dr
Pasadena CA 91107
626 405-5704

(P-20033)
SOUTHERN CAL PRMNNTE MED GROUP
Also Called: S C P M G
411 N Lakeview Ave, Anaheim (92807-3028)
PHONE..................714 279-4675
Fax: 714 279-4890
Ryan Williams, *Manager*
Young OH, *Top Exec*
Hector Arroyo, *Surgeon*
Mark W Gow, *Surgeon*
Peter S Paik, *Surgeon*
EMP: 50
SALES (corp-wide): 3.2B Privately Held
WEB: www.permanente.net
SIC: 8011 Offices & clinics of medical doctors
PA: Southern California Permanente Medical Group
393 Walnut Dr
Pasadena CA 91107
626 405-5704

(P-20034)
SOUTHERN CAL PRMNNTE MED GROUP
Also Called: S C P M G
30400 Camino Capistrano, San Juan Capistrano (92675-1300)
PHONE..................949 234-2139
David L Haller, *Family Practiti*
Paula M Richter, *Obstetrician*
EMP: 50
SALES (corp-wide): 3.2B Privately Held
WEB: www.permanente.net
SIC: 8011 Offices & clinics of medical doctors
PA: Southern California Permanente Medical Group
393 Walnut Dr
Pasadena CA 91107
626 405-5704

(P-20035)
SOUTHERN CAL PRMNNTE MED GROUP
Also Called: S C P M G
22550 Savi Ranch Pkwy, Yorba Linda (92887-4670)
PHONE..................714 685-3520
Kamil Antonios MD, *Manager*
EMP: 50
SALES (corp-wide): 3.2B Privately Held
WEB: www.permanente.net
SIC: 8011 Offices & clinics of medical doctors
PA: Southern California Permanente Medical Group
393 Walnut Dr
Pasadena CA 91107
626 405-5704

(P-20036)
SOUTHERN CAL PRMNNTE MED GROUP
Also Called: S C P M G
1900 E 4th St, Santa Ana (92705-3962)
PHONE..................714 967-4760
Julie White-Dahlgren, *Branch Mgr*
EMP: 60
SALES (corp-wide): 3.2B Privately Held
WEB: www.permanente.net
SIC: 8011 8049 Obstetrician; psychiatric social worker
PA: Southern California Permanente Medical Group
393 Walnut Dr
Pasadena CA 91107
626 405-5704

(P-20037)
SOUTHERN CAL PRMNNTE MED GROUP
Also Called: S C P M G
4405 Vandever Ave, San Diego (92120-3315)
PHONE..................619 516-6000
Thomas Volle, *Manager*

Susan Lee, *Med Doctor*
EMP: 50
SALES (corp-wide): 3.2B Privately Held
WEB: www.permanente.net
SIC: 8011 Offices & clinics of medical doctors
PA: Southern California Permanente Medical Group
393 Walnut Dr
Pasadena CA 91107
626 405-5704

(P-20038)
SOUTHERN CAL PRMNNTE MED GROUP
Also Called: S C P M G
732 N Broadway, Escondido (92025-1870)
PHONE..................760 839-7200
Alex Anderson, *Manager*
EMP: 50
SALES (corp-wide): 3.2B Privately Held
WEB: www.permanente.net
SIC: 8011 Offices & clinics of medical doctors
PA: Southern California Permanente Medical Group
393 Walnut Dr
Pasadena CA 91107
626 405-5704

(P-20039)
SOUTHERN CAL PRMNNTE MED GROUP
Also Called: S C P M G
7825 Atlantic Ave, Cudahy (90201-5022)
PHONE..................323 562-6459
Maria Gonzalez, *Principal*
Irene Valencia, *Gnrl Med Prac*
EMP: 50
SALES (corp-wide): 3.2B Privately Held
WEB: www.permanente.net
SIC: 8011 Offices & clinics of medical doctors
PA: Southern California Permanente Medical Group
393 Walnut Dr
Pasadena CA 91107
626 405-5704

(P-20040)
SOUTHERN CAL PRMNNTE MED GROUP
Also Called: S C P M G
21263 Erwin St, Woodland Hills (91367-3715)
PHONE..................818 592-3038
Cary Glass, *Branch Mgr*
Anupama S Kalsi, *Psychiatry*
Michael Agress, *Med Doctor*
Matthew Cohen, *Med Doctor*
EMP: 50
SALES (corp-wide): 3.2B Privately Held
WEB: www.permanente.net
SIC: 8011 Offices & clinics of medical doctors
PA: Southern California Permanente Medical Group
393 Walnut Dr
Pasadena CA 91107
626 405-5704

(P-20041)
SOUTHERN CAL PRMNNTE MED GROUP
Also Called: S C P M G
27107 Tourney Rd, Santa Clarita (91355-1860)
PHONE..................661 222-2150
EMP: 50
SALES (corp-wide): 3.2B Privately Held
WEB: www.permanente.net
SIC: 8011 Offices & clinics of medical doctors
PA: Southern California Permanente Medical Group
393 Walnut Dr
Pasadena CA 91107
626 405-5704

(P-20042)
SOUTHERN CAL PRMNNTE MED GROUP
Also Called: S C P M G
17140 Bernardo Center Dr, San Diego (92128-2093)
PHONE..................619 528-5000
Selso Dasco, *Cert Phar Tech*
Mary Nguyen, *Cert Phar Tech*
EMP: 50
SALES (corp-wide): 3.2B Privately Held
WEB: www.permanente.net
SIC: 8011 Offices & clinics of medical doctors
PA: Southern California Permanente Medical Group
393 Walnut Dr
Pasadena CA 91107
626 405-5704

(P-20043)
SOUTHERN CAL PRMNNTE MED GROUP
Also Called: S C P M G
1255 W Arrow Hwy, San Dimas (91773-2340)
PHONE..................909 394-2505
EMP: 50
SALES (corp-wide): 3.2B Privately Held
WEB: www.permanente.net
SIC: 8011 Offices & clinics of medical doctors
PA: Southern California Permanente Medical Group
393 Walnut Dr
Pasadena CA 91107
626 405-5704

(P-20044)
SOUTHERN CAL PRMNNTE MED GROUP
5055 California Ave, Bakersfield (93309-0701)
PHONE..................661 334-2020
Geckeley, *Principal*
EMP: 100
SALES (corp-wide): 2.7B Privately Held
WEB: www.permanente.net
SIC: 8011 Offices & clinics of medical doctors
PA: Southern California Permanente Medical Group
393 Walnut Dr
Pasadena CA 91107
626 405-5704

(P-20045)
SOUTHERN CAL STONE CTR LLC
Also Called: So Calif Stone Center
5400 Balboa Blvd Ste 111, Encino (91316-5206)
PHONE..................818 784-8975
Fax: 818 784-7467
Jerry Garrett MD, *Principal*
James Orecklin MD,
EMP: 56
SALES (est): 4MM Privately Held
SIC: 8011 Medical centers

(P-20046)
SOUTHERN INDIAN HEALTH COUNCIL (PA)
4058 Willows Rd, Alpine (91901-1668)
P.O. Box 2128 (91903-2128)
PHONE..................619 445-1188
Fax: 619 445-4131
Carolina Monsano, *Exec Dir*
Terry King, *CFO*
Steve Martin, *CFO*
Janet Weis, *CFO*
Donna James, *Exec Dir*
EMP: 100
SQ FT: 11,000
SALES: 16.1MM Privately Held
SIC: 8011 8021 Offices & clinics of medical doctors; dental clinic

8011 - Offices & Clinics Of Doctors Of Medicine County (P-20047)

(P-20047)
SOUTHWESTERN ORTHPD MED CORP
Also Called: Downey Orthopedic Med Group
15901 Hawthorne Blvd, Lawndale (90260-2655)
P.O. Box 4489, Montebello (90640-9309)
PHONE.................562 803-0600
Fax: 562 401-4314
Lucy Guttierez, *Branch Mgr*
Nancy Geary, *Surgeon*
EMP: 50
SALES (corp-wide): 3.7MM **Privately Held**
SIC: 8011 Orthopedic physician
PA: Southwestern Orthopedic Medical Corporation
905 S A St
Oxnard CA 93030
805 486-4501

(P-20048)
SPALDING SRGCL CTR OF BVRLY HL
Also Called: S&B Surgery Center II
27520 Hawthorne Blvd # 176, Rlling HLS Est (90274-3539)
PHONE.................310 385-7755
Fax: 310 385-0874
Theordore Goldstrein, *President*
Randy Rosen, *CFO*
Victor F Beederman, *Controller*
Laura D Alexander, *Anesthesiology*
Paul H Chiu, *Anesthesiology*
EMP: 120
SQ FT: 8,000
SALES (est): 13.4MM **Privately Held**
WEB: www.snbsurgery.com
SIC: 8011 Surgeon

(P-20049)
SPECIALTY SURGICAL CENTERS
15825 Laguna Canyon Rd # 200, Irvine (92618-2127)
PHONE.................949 341-3499
Fax: 949 788-0556
Andrew Brooks MD, *President*
Linda Mansfield, *Director*
Terry Weisman, *Director*
EMP: 50
SALES (est): 8.8MM **Privately Held**
SIC: 8011 Physicians' office, including specialists

(P-20050)
SPH-IRVINE LLC
Also Called: Starpoint Surgery Center
18952 Macarthur Blvd # 103, Irvine (92612-1401)
PHONE.................949 833-1432
Eric Friedlander, *Mng Member*
EMP: 50
SALES (est): 244.9K **Privately Held**
SIC: 8011 Ambulatory surgical center

(P-20051)
SPINECARE MEDICAL GROUP INC
455 Hickey Blvd Ste 310, Daly City (94015-2630)
PHONE.................650 985-7500
Arthur H White MD, *Ch of Bd*
James B Reynolds MD, *President*
Noel D Goldthwaite MD, *Treasurer*
Richard Derby MD, *Vice Pres*
Garrett Kine MD, *Vice Pres*
EMP: 57
SQ FT: 82,000
SALES (est): 7.7MM **Privately Held**
WEB: www.spinecare.com
SIC: 8011 Clinic, operated by physicians; surgeon

(P-20052)
ST FRANCIS MEDICAL CE
Also Called: Saint Franceis Fmly Hlth
2700 E Slauson Ave # 200, Huntington Park (90255-3000)
PHONE.................323 588-8558
Fax: 323 581-8793
Arnold J Simoni, *Branch Mgr*
Elizabeth Martinez, *Med Doctor*
Paula McCaplin, *Nurse Practr*
EMP: 84
SQ FT: 12,038
SALES (corp-wide): 72.6MM **Privately Held**
SIC: 8011 Pediatrician
PA: St. Francis Medical Center Of Lynwood Foundation
3630 E Imperial Hwy
Lynwood CA 90262
310 900-8900

(P-20053)
ST FRANCIS MEDICAL CENTER
Also Called: SFMC
3630 E Imperial Hwy, Lynwood (90262-2609)
P.O. Box 1168, San Carlos (94070-1168)
PHONE.................310 900-8900
Fax: 310 603-1879
Gerald Kozai, *CEO*
Nancy Wilson, *CFO*
Anne Schlick, *Telecom Exec*
Shirley Stahl, *Purch Agent*
Bertha Wright, *Facilities Mgr*
EMP: 104
SALES: 407.4MM **Privately Held**
SIC: 8011 Medical centers

(P-20054)
ST JOSEPH HEALTH SYSTEM
Humboldt Medical Speicialists
2280 Harrison Ave Ste B, Eureka (95501-3200)
PHONE.................707 443-9371
William Stiles, *Manager*
EMP: 62
SALES (corp-wide): 5.6B **Privately Held**
SIC: 8011 Internal medicine practitioners; internal medicine, physician/surgeon
HQ: St. Joseph Health System
3345 Michelson Dr Ste 100
Irvine CA 92612
949 381-4000

(P-20055)
ST JOSEPH HERITAGE MED GROUP (PA)
Also Called: Yorba Park Medical Group
2212 E 4th St Ste 201, Santa Ana (92705-3872)
PHONE.................714 633-1011
Fax: 714 997-9411
Charles Foster, *President*
C R Buke, *CFO*
C R Burke, *CFO*
Dennis Long MD, *Treasurer*
Marc Bennette MD, *Vice Pres*
▲ EMP: 134
SQ FT: 58,000
SALES (est): 12.5MM **Privately Held**
WEB: www.sjhmg.org
SIC: 8011 Clinic, operated by physicians

(P-20056)
ST JOSEPH SURGERY CENTER LP
1800 N California St # 1, Stockton (95204-6019)
PHONE.................209 467-6316
Fax: 209 461-6895
Don Wiley, *President*
Annette Aldridge, *Manager*
EMP: 75
SALES (est): 8.7MM **Privately Held**
SIC: 8011 Surgeon

(P-20057)
ST JUDE HERITAGE MEDICAL GROUP
4300 Rose Dr, Yorba Linda (92886-2026)
PHONE.................714 528-4211
Fax: 714 579-6893
Lytton Smith MD, *President*
Richard Kenfield MD, *Treasurer*
R S Hall MD, *Vice Pres*
Lori Porretta, *Office Mgr*
Kenneth Tan MD, *Admin Sec*
EMP: 148
SALES (est): 9.1MM **Privately Held**
SIC: 8011 Clinic, operated by physicians

(P-20058)
ST JUDE HOSPITAL
Also Called: St Jude Medical Ctr Purch Dept
101 E Valencia Mesa Dr, Fullerton (92835-3875)
PHONE.................714 992-3057
David Saffert, *Director*
Elliott C Mercer, *Diag Radio*
Maren R Sowerby, *Diag Radio*
EMP: 2500
SALES (corp-wide): 5.6B **Privately Held**
WEB: www.stjudemedicalcenter.com
SIC: 8011 Medical centers
HQ: St. Jude Hospital
101 E Valencia Mesa Dr
Fullerton CA 92835
714 871-3280

(P-20059)
ST JUDE HOSPITAL YORBA LINDA
Also Called: Bristol Park Medical Group
11420 Warner Ave, Fountain Valley (92708-2529)
PHONE.................714 665-1797
Helena Rivas, *Manager*
Amy Smith, *Executive*
Lynda Kay, *Director*
Tony Whitlinger, *Manager*
EMP: 200
SALES (corp-wide): 5.6B **Privately Held**
SIC: 8011 8071 Offices & clinics of medical doctors; medical laboratories
HQ: St. Jude Hospital Yorba Linda
200 W Ctr St Promenade
Anaheim CA 92805
714 712-3308

(P-20060)
ST JUDE HOSPITAL YORBA LINDA
27800 Medical Center Rd, Mission Viejo (92691-6410)
PHONE.................949 365-2492
Nicki Levitt, *Manager*
Arwa Bedour, *CTO*
EMP: 50
SALES (corp-wide): 5.6B **Privately Held**
SIC: 8011 General & family practice, physician/surgeon
HQ: St. Jude Hospital Yorba Linda
200 W Ctr St Promenade
Anaheim CA 92805
714 712-3308

(P-20061)
ST JUDE HOSPITAL YORBA LINDA
Also Called: Olvera, Robert MD
722 Baker St, Costa Mesa (92626-4320)
PHONE.................714 557-6300
Anh Dinh, *Branch Mgr*
Adam Wuass, *Gnrl Med Prac*
Cindy Beltz, *Manager*
EMP: 60
SALES (corp-wide): 5.6B **Privately Held**
SIC: 8011 8062 Offices & clinics of medical doctors; general medical & surgical hospitals
HQ: St. Jude Hospital Yorba Linda
200 W Ctr St Promenade
Anaheim CA 92805
714 712-3308

(P-20062)
STA CLARA VALLEY MEDICAL CTR
751 S Bascom Ave, San Jose (95128-2604)
PHONE.................408 885-2334
Jeffrey Arnold, *Chief*
EMP: 50
SALES (est): 1.1MM **Privately Held**
SIC: 8011 8062 General & family practice, physician/surgeon; general medical & surgical hospitals

(P-20063)
STANFORD
450 Serra Mall, Stanford (94305-2004)
P.O. Box 13204 (94309-3204)
PHONE.................650 799-3773
Matti Hirpa, *Principal*
Emily Gere, *Office Mgr*
Dianna Ziehm, *Administration*
Vivek Sinha, *Software Dev*
Benjamin Sapp, *Software Engr*
EMP: 65
SALES (est): 4.6MM **Privately Held**
SIC: 8011 Medical centers

(P-20064)
STANFORD FMLY PRCTC-BLAKE WILB
Also Called: Stanford Health Services
211 Quarry Rd Fl 3, Palo Alto (94304-1416)
PHONE.................650 723-6963
Fax: 650 725-8910
Nancy Morioka, *Principal*
Rita Hamad, *Family Practiti*
EMP: 75
SALES (est): 3.2MM **Privately Held**
SIC: 8011 General & family practice, physician/surgeon

(P-20065)
STANLEY M KIRKPATRICK MD
Also Called: Childerns Spec of San Deigo
3020 Childerns Way, San Diego (92123-4223)
PHONE.................858 966-5855
Stanley M Kirkpatrick MD, *Partner*
Lisa Quade, *Office Mgr*
Leanna Klistoff, *Admin Asst*
Linda S Ellis, *Pathologist*
Hart Isaacs, *Pathologist*
▲ EMP: 50
SALES (est): 2.9MM **Privately Held**
SIC: 8011 Pediatrician

(P-20066)
STANLEY R KLEIN MD FACS INC
23451 Madison St Ste 300, Torrance (90505-4737)
PHONE.................310 373-6864
Stanley Klein, *President*
EMP: 50
SALES (est): 3MM **Privately Held**
SIC: 8011 Surgeon

(P-20067)
STEPHEN B MEISEL MD PC
Also Called: Medfocus Radiology Network
2811 Wilshire Blvd # 900, Santa Monica (90403-4803)
PHONE.................310 828-8843
Fax: 310 828-3082
Stephen B Meisel MD, *President*
Karen Byrd, *Opers Staff*
EMP: 50
SQ FT: 20,000
SALES (est): 3MM **Privately Held**
WEB: www.medfocuslogin.net
SIC: 8011 Radiologist

(P-20068)
STEPHEN B MEISEL MD A MED CORP (HQ)
Also Called: Med Focus/California Radiology
2811 Wilshire Blvd # 900, Santa Monica (90403-4803)
PHONE.................310 828-8843
Joseph P Delaney, *President*
Polly Blanchard, *Technology*
Jim Gehres, *Regl Sales Mgr*
Chip Hanley, *Regl Sales Mgr*
Consuela Morales-Streit, *Relations*
EMP: 52
SQ FT: 14,000
SALES (est): 6MM
SALES (corp-wide): 900MM **Privately Held**
WEB: www.medfocus.net
SIC: 8011 Radiologist
PA: One Call Medical Inc.
841 Prudential Dr Ste 900
Jacksonville FL 32207
904 646-0199

(P-20069)
STEVEN G FOGG MD
1360 E Herndon Ave # 401, Fresno (93720-3326)
PHONE.................559 449-5010
Steven G Fogg, *Principal*
EMP: 80
SALES (est): 1.5MM **Privately Held**
SIC: 8011 Offices & clinics of medical doctors

PRODUCTS & SERVICES SECTION
8011 - Offices & Clinics Of Doctors Of Medicine County (P-20092)

(P-20070)
STOCKTON CARDIOLOGY MEDICAL GR
1148 Norman Dr Ste 3, Manteca (95336-5961)
PHONE..................209 824-1555
Fax: 209 832-2515
Gina Callegari, *Manager*
EMP: 60
SALES (corp-wide): 9.8MM **Privately Held**
SIC: 8011 Cardiologist & cardio-vascular specialist
PA: Stockton Cardiology Medical Group Complete Heart Care, Inc
415 E Harding Way Ste D
Stockton CA 95204
209 754-1012

(P-20071)
STOCKTON CARDIOLOGY MEDICAL GR (PA)
415 E Harding Way Ste D, Stockton (95204-6118)
PHONE..................209 754-1012
Fax: 209 467-8271
Surrender Raina, *President*
Tuan A Pham, *Treasurer*
John A Bouteller, *Vice Pres*
George S Charo, *Cardiology*
Leonid Kamenetsky, *Med Doctor*
EMP: 50
SQ FT: 6,500
SALES: 9.8MM **Privately Held**
SIC: 8011 Cardiologist & cardio-vascular specialist

(P-20072)
STOCKTON ORTHPD MED GROUP INC
Also Called: Crooks, Jerry C MD
2545 W Hammer Ln, Stockton (95209-2839)
PHONE..................209 948-1641
Fax: 209 948-0660
Kevin Mikaelian, *Principal*
Scott Bethune, *Treasurer*
Miklein Kevin MD, *Vice Pres*
EMP: 50
SALES (est): 4.3MM **Privately Held**
WEB: www.stocktonortho.com
SIC: 8011 Orthopedic physician; surgeon

(P-20073)
STUART LOVETT
350 30th St Ste 208, Oakland (94609-3425)
PHONE..................510 444-0790
Stuart Lovett, *Owner*
EMP: 51
SALES (est): 492.3K **Privately Held**
SIC: 8011 Obstetrician

(P-20074)
SUCCESS HEALTHCARE 1 LLC
7500 Hellman Ave, Rosemead (91770-2216)
PHONE..................626 288-1160
EMP: 133
SALES (corp-wide): 53.9MM **Privately Held**
SIC: 8011 Offices & clinics of medical doctors
PA: Success Healthcare 1, Llc
1711 W Temple St
Los Angeles CA 90026
213 989-6100

(P-20075)
SUN HEALTHCARE GROUP INC (DH)
18831 Von Karman Ave # 400, Irvine (92612-1533)
PHONE..................949 255-7100
George V Hager, *CEO*
Melissa Craig, *President*
Tracy Chiara, *Officer*
Linda Wiesemann, *Officer*
Richard J Spinello, *Senior VP*
▲ EMP: 300
SALES (est): 484.1MM
SALES (corp-wide): 9.6B **Publicly Held**
WEB: www.sunh.com
SIC: 8011 8322 Medical insurance plan; referral service for personal & social problems
HQ: Genesis Healthcare Corporation
101 E State St
Kennett Square PA 19348
610 444-6350

(P-20076)
SURGERY CENTER OF ALTA BATES
Also Called: Herrick Hospital
2001 Dwight Way, Berkeley (94704-2608)
PHONE..................510 204-4411
Fax: 510 204-5892
Albert Greene, *Branch Mgr*
Mary Cafarella-Aka, *Program Mgr*
Mildred Kawachi, *Research*
Baohoang B Lam, *Hematology*
Alicia Blando, *Manager*
EMP: 50
SQ FT: 6,750
SALES (corp-wide): 11B **Privately Held**
WEB: www.altabates.com
SIC: 8011 8051 Medical centers; skilled nursing care facilities
HQ: The Surgery Center Of Alta Bates Summit Medical Center Llc
2450 Ashby Ave
Berkeley CA 94705
510 204-4444

(P-20077)
SUTTER GOULD MED FOUNDATION (PA)
600 Coffee Rd, Modesto (95355-4201)
PHONE..................209 948-5940
Fax: 209 944-4371
David Bradley, *CEO*
Tim Maurice, *CFO*
E Lewis Cobb, *Obstetrician*
Dan Davidson, *Med Doctor*
Schilling George, *Med Doctor*
EMP: 50
SALES (est): 14.2MM **Privately Held**
SIC: 8011 Obstetrician

(P-20078)
SUTTER HEALTH
2068 John Jones Rd # 100, Davis (95616-9711)
PHONE..................530 747-0389
EMP: 187
SALES (corp-wide): 11B **Privately Held**
SIC: 8011 Internal medicine, physician/surgeon
PA: Sutter Health
2200 River Plaza Dr
Sacramento CA 95833
916 733-8800

(P-20079)
SUTTER HEALTH
1625 Stockton Blvd # 102, Sacramento (95816-7097)
PHONE..................916 733-1025
Michael Burman, *Med Doctor*
William Vetter, *Med Doctor*
EMP: 280
SALES (corp-wide): 11B **Privately Held**
SIC: 8011 Offices & clinics of medical doctors
PA: Sutter Health
2200 River Plaza Dr
Sacramento CA 95833
916 733-8800

(P-20080)
SUTTER HEALTH
Also Called: Mamone James M
3 Medical Plaza Dr # 110, Roseville (95661-3087)
PHONE..................916 797-4725
Fax: 916 781-5187
Dave Gladden, *Branch Mgr*
Nicole A Lopez-Seminario, *Neurology*
Heidi M Lamel, *Physician Asst*
Patricia Fone, *Med Doctor*
David Grattendick, *Med Doctor*
EMP: 93
SALES (corp-wide): 11B **Privately Held**
SIC: 8011 Offices & clinics of medical doctors
PA: Sutter Health
2200 River Plaza Dr
Sacramento CA 95833
916 733-8800

(P-20081)
SUTTER HEALTH
Also Called: Sutter Medical Group
1400 Medical Center Dr, Cotati (94928-2924)
PHONE..................707 586-0440
Fax: 707 586-1444
Sherry S Mill, *Office Mgr*
Lillian Brown, *Buyer*
Roberta Mori, *Manager*
Luz Maruffo, *Assistant*
EMP: 105
SALES (corp-wide): 11B **Privately Held**
WEB: www.suttermedicalgroup.com
SIC: 8011 Offices & clinics of medical doctors
PA: Sutter Health
2200 River Plaza Dr
Sacramento CA 95833
916 733-8800

(P-20082)
SUTTER HEALTH
1020 29th St Ste 600, Sacramento (95816-5126)
PHONE..................916 733-9588
Connie Tam, *Office Mgr*
John Zingheim, *Med Doctor*
EMP: 233
SALES (corp-wide): 11B **Privately Held**
SIC: 8011 Surgeon
PA: Sutter Health
2200 River Plaza Dr
Sacramento CA 95833
916 733-8800

(P-20083)
SUTTER HEALTH
2734 El Camino Real, Santa Clara (95051-3007)
PHONE..................408 524-5952
Irena Matt, *Office Mgr*
EMP: 420
SALES (corp-wide): 11B **Privately Held**
SIC: 8011 Offices & clinics of medical doctors
PA: Sutter Health
2200 River Plaza Dr
Sacramento CA 95833
916 733-8800

(P-20084)
SUTTER HEALTH
2000 Sutter Pl, Davis (95616-6201)
PHONE..................530 757-5111
Fax: 530 757-5128
Lynette Pryor, *Officer*
Angela Lombardi, *Corp Comm Staff*
Deven Merchant, *Med Doctor*
Tom Carlson, *Manager*
EMP: 700
SALES (corp-wide): 11B **Privately Held**
SIC: 8011 Offices & clinics of medical doctors
PA: Sutter Health
2200 River Plaza Dr
Sacramento CA 95833
916 733-8800

(P-20085)
SUTTER HEALTH
3468 California St, San Francisco (94118-1837)
PHONE..................415 345-0100
Fax: 415 345-0107
Steven Goldman, *Med Doctor*
Elizabeth Charney, *Manager*
EMP: 326
SALES (corp-wide): 11B **Privately Held**
SIC: 8011 Endocrinologist
PA: Sutter Health
2200 River Plaza Dr
Sacramento CA 95833
916 733-8800

(P-20086)
SUTTER HEALTH
595 Buckingham Way # 515, San Francisco (94132-1909)
P.O. Box 320427 (94132-0427)
PHONE..................415 731-6300
PA: Sutter Health
2200 River Plaza Dr
Sacramento CA 95833
916 733-8800

EMP: 140
SALES (corp-wide): 11B **Privately Held**
SIC: 8011 Offices & clinics of medical doctors
PA: Sutter Health
2200 River Plaza Dr
Sacramento CA 95833
916 733-8800

(P-20087)
SUTTER HEALTH
100 Mission Blvd, Jackson (95642-2536)
PHONE..................209 223-5445
Melody Eurbe, *Officer*
EMP: 140
SALES (corp-wide): 11B **Privately Held**
SIC: 8011 Cardiologist & cardio-vascular specialist
PA: Sutter Health
2200 River Plaza Dr
Sacramento CA 95833
916 733-8800

(P-20088)
SUTTER HEALTH
Also Called: Sutter Pacific Med Foundation
1375 Sutter St, San Francisco (94109-5438)
PHONE..................415 600-0110
EMP: 187
SALES (corp-wide): 11B **Privately Held**
SIC: 8011 Offices & clinics of medical doctors
PA: Sutter Health
2200 River Plaza Dr
Sacramento CA 95833
916 733-8800

(P-20089)
SUTTER HEALTH
8170 Laguna Blvd Ste 210, Elk Grove (95758-7902)
PHONE..................916 691-5900
Francisco Prieto, *Family Practiti*
EMP: 326
SALES (corp-wide): 11B **Privately Held**
SIC: 8011 General & family practice, physician/surgeon
PA: Sutter Health
2200 River Plaza Dr
Sacramento CA 95833
916 733-8800

(P-20090)
SUTTER HEALTH
Also Called: Sutter Alhambra Surgery Center
1201 Alhambra Blvd # 110, Sacramento (95816-5238)
PHONE..................916 455-8137
John Madigan, *Med Doctor*
Samatha Hovda, *Manager*
EMP: 93
SALES (corp-wide): 11B **Privately Held**
SIC: 8011 Surgeon
PA: Sutter Health
2200 River Plaza Dr
Sacramento CA 95833
916 733-8800

(P-20091)
SUTTER HEALTH
5196 Hill Rd E Ste 300, Lakeport (95453-6374)
PHONE..................707 263-6885
Harneet Bath, *Branch Mgr*
EMP: 200
SALES (corp-wide): 11B **Privately Held**
SIC: 8011 Offices & clinics of medical doctors
PA: Sutter Health
2200 River Plaza Dr
Sacramento CA 95833
916 733-8800

(P-20092)
SUTTER HEALTH
1500 Expo Pkwy, Sacramento (95815-4227)
PHONE..................916 646-8300
EMP: 1000
SALES (corp-wide): 11B **Privately Held**
SIC: 8011 8071
PA: Sutter Health
2200 River Plaza Dr
Sacramento CA 95833
916 286-6670

8011 - Offices & Clinics Of Doctors Of Medicine County (P-20093)

(P-20093)
SUTTER HEALTH
3875 Telegraph Ave, Oakland
(94609-2428)
PHONE.....................510 547-2244
EMP: 606
SALES (corp-wide): 11B **Privately Held**
SIC: **8011** Medical centers
PA: Sutter Health
2200 River Plaza Dr
Sacramento CA 95833
916 733-8800

(P-20094)
SUTTER HEALTH
600 Coffee Rd, Modesto (95355-4201)
PHONE.....................209 524-1211
Laurie Scott, *Principal*
Susan Paez, *Info Tech Dir*
Jean Lei, *Librarian*
Yvonne J Brouard, *Oncology*
Qasim Barra, *Radiology*
EMP: 200
SALES (corp-wide): 11B **Privately Held**
WEB: www.sutterhealth.org
SIC: **8011** Offices & clinics of medical doctors
PA: Sutter Health
2200 River Plaza Dr
Sacramento CA 95833
916 733-8800

(P-20095)
SUTTER HEALTH
475 Pioneer Ave Ste 100, Woodland
(95776-4905)
PHONE.....................530 406-5600
Judi Monday, *Director*
EMP: 200
SALES (corp-wide): 11B **Privately Held**
SIC: **8011** Offices & clinics of medical doctors
PA: Sutter Health
2200 River Plaza Dr
Sacramento CA 95833
916 733-8800

(P-20096)
SUTTER HEALTH
2516 E Whitmore Ave, Ceres (95307-2645)
PHONE.....................209 538-1733
Ying Luo, *Med Doctor*
EMP: 187
SALES (corp-wide): 11B **Privately Held**
SIC: **8011** Offices & clinics of medical doctors
PA: Sutter Health
2200 River Plaza Dr
Sacramento CA 95833
916 733-8800

(P-20097)
SUTTER HEALTH
3612 Dale Rd, Modesto (95356-0500)
PHONE.....................209 522-0146
EMP: 373
SALES (corp-wide): 11B **Privately Held**
SIC: **8011** General & family practice, physician/surgeon
PA: Sutter Health
2200 River Plaza Dr
Sacramento CA 95833
916 733-8800

(P-20098)
SUTTER HEALTH
8170 Laguna Blvd Ste 220, Elk Grove
(95758-7902)
PHONE.....................916 691-5900
Kim Caldwell, *Manager*
EMP: 326
SALES (corp-wide): 11B **Privately Held**
SIC: **8011** General & family practice, physician/surgeon
PA: Sutter Health
2200 River Plaza Dr
Sacramento CA 95833
916 733-8800

(P-20099)
SUTTER HEALTH
50 S San Mateo Dr Ste 470, San Mateo
(94401-3833)
PHONE.....................650 262-4262
Peter Webb, *Dermatology*
EMP: 233
SALES (corp-wide): 11B **Privately Held**
SIC: **8011** Orthopedic physician
PA: Sutter Health
2200 River Plaza Dr
Sacramento CA 95833
916 733-8800

(P-20100)
SUTTER HEALTH
25 W Micheltorena St, Santa Barbara
(93101-2509)
PHONE.....................805 966-1600
Fax: 805 966-6700
EMP: 280
SALES (corp-wide): 11B **Privately Held**
SIC: **8011** Endocrinologist
PA: Sutter Health
2200 River Plaza Dr
Sacramento CA 95833
916 733-8800

(P-20101)
SUTTER HEALTH
Also Called: Nguyen, Myhanh MD
325 N Mathilda Ave, Sunnyvale
(94085-4207)
PHONE.....................408 733-4380
Daniel Florez, *Executive Asst*
Richard Thompson, *Manager*
EMP: 233
SALES (corp-wide): 11B **Privately Held**
SIC: **8011** Occupational & industrial specialist, physician/surgeon
PA: Sutter Health
2200 River Plaza Dr
Sacramento CA 95833
916 733-8800

(P-20102)
SUTTER HEALTH
Also Called: Sutter Pacific Med Foundation
4702 Hoen Ave, Santa Rosa (95405-7824)
PHONE.....................707 545-2255
Ana L Pacheco-Clark, *Family Practiti*
EMP: 187
SALES (corp-wide): 11B **Privately Held**
SIC: **8011** Pediatrician
PA: Sutter Health
2200 River Plaza Dr
Sacramento CA 95833
916 733-8800

(P-20103)
SUTTER HEALTH
Also Called: Sutter Pacific Med Foundation
5196 Hill Rd E Ste 300, Lakeport
(95453-6374)
PHONE.....................707 263-6885
EMP: 121
SALES (corp-wide): 11B **Privately Held**
SIC: **8011**
PA: Sutter Health
2200 River Plaza Dr
Sacramento CA 95833
916 733-8800

(P-20104)
SUTTER HEALTH
Also Called: Palo Alpo Medical Foudation
795 El Camino Real, Palo Alto
(94301-2302)
PHONE.....................650 853-2904
Fax: 650 853-4830
EMP: 187
SALES (corp-wide): 11B **Privately Held**
SIC: **8011** Offices & clinics of medical doctors
PA: Sutter Health
2200 River Plaza Dr
Sacramento CA 95833
916 733-8800

(P-20105)
SUTTER HEALTH
Also Called: Roseville Imaging
1640 E Roseville Pkwy, Roseville
(95661-3902)
PHONE.....................916 784-2277
Jerry Fosselman, *Manager*
David Peredina, *Exec Dir*
EMP: 85
SALES (corp-wide): 11B **Privately Held**
WEB: www.radiological.com
SIC: **8011** 8071 Offices & clinics of medical doctors; medical laboratories
PA: Sutter Health
2200 River Plaza Dr
Sacramento CA 95833
916 733-8800

(P-20106)
SUTTER HEALTH
Also Called: Breast Imaging Center
3161 L St, Sacramento (95816-5234)
PHONE.....................916 451-3344
Jerry Fosselman, *Branch Mgr*
Deborah Stassord, *Office Mgr*
Patrick A Harty, *Med Doctor*
EMP: 100
SALES (corp-wide): 11B **Privately Held**
WEB: www.radiological.com
SIC: **8011** 8071 Offices & clinics of medical doctors; medical laboratories
PA: Sutter Health
2200 River Plaza Dr
Sacramento CA 95833
916 733-8800

(P-20107)
SUTTER HEALTH
1020 29th St Ste 570b, Sacramento
(95816-5173)
PHONE.....................916 453-5955
Fax: 916 733-8250
EMP: 326
SALES (corp-wide): 11B **Privately Held**
SIC: **8011** Physicians' office, including specialists
PA: Sutter Health
2200 River Plaza Dr
Sacramento CA 95833
916 733-8800

(P-20108)
SUTTER HEALTH
3555 Cesar Chavez, San Francisco
(94110-4403)
PHONE.....................415 647-8600
Carol Kunita, *Principal*
Rick Cable, *Accountant*
Michelle Mayfield, *Human Resources*
Janet Lum, *Manager*
Mary Janowitz, *Consultant*
EMP: 109
SALES (corp-wide): 11B **Privately Held**
WEB: www.sutterhealth.org
SIC: **8011** Offices & clinics of medical doctors
PA: Sutter Health
2200 River Plaza Dr
Sacramento CA 95833
916 733-8800

(P-20109)
SUTTER HEALTH
969 Plumas St Ste 103116, Yuba City
(95991-4011)
PHONE.....................530 749-3585
Aparna Kareti, *Branch Mgr*
Harry Wander, *Med Doctor*
EMP: 200
SALES (corp-wide): 11B **Privately Held**
WEB: www.sutterhealth.org
SIC: **8011** Medical centers
PA: Sutter Health
2200 River Plaza Dr
Sacramento CA 95833
916 733-8800

(P-20110)
SUTTER HEALTH
2734 El Camino Real, Santa Clara
(95051-3007)
PHONE.....................408 241-3801
Fax: 408 241-9490
Diana Sanchez, *Executive*
Kenneth Vereschagin, *CTO*
EMP: 233
SALES (corp-wide): 11B **Privately Held**
SIC: **8011** Sports medicine specialist, physician
PA: Sutter Health
2200 River Plaza Dr
Sacramento CA 95833
916 733-8800

(P-20111)
SUTTER HEALTH
Also Called: Shuler, Kurt MD
2030 Sutter Pl Ste 1300, Davis
(95616-6215)
PHONE.....................530 750-5888
EMP: 326
SALES (corp-wide): 11B **Privately Held**
SIC: **8011** Ears, nose & throat specialist: physician/surgeon
PA: Sutter Health
2200 River Plaza Dr
Sacramento CA 95833
916 733-8800

(P-20112)
SUTTER HEALTH
2725 Capitol Ave Dept 404, Sacramento
(95816-6032)
PHONE.....................916 262-9456
EMP: 187
SALES (corp-wide): 11B **Privately Held**
SIC: **8011** Medical centers
PA: Sutter Health
2200 River Plaza Dr
Sacramento CA 95833
916 733-8800

(P-20113)
SUTTER HEALTH AT WORK
Also Called: Sutter Hlth At Work - Natomas
1014 N Market Blvd Ste 20, Sacramento
(95834-1986)
PHONE.....................916 565-8607
Judi Monday, *President*
Sally Greene, *Info Tech Dir*
Coleen Cook, *Bookkeeper*
Michael Cowan, *Med Doctor*
EMP: 75
SALES (est): 2.8MM **Privately Held**
SIC: **8011** Offices & clinics of medical doctors

(P-20114)
SUTTER HLTH SCRMNTO SIERRA REG
Also Called: Sutter West Foundation
2030 Sutter Pl Ste 2000, Davis
(95616-6216)
PHONE.....................530 747-5010
Joel Lubin,
Courtney Wilson, *Marketing Staff*
Jo Lisa Miller, *Radiology*
Meghan Zavod, *Med Doctor*
Karla Lopez, *Assistant*
EMP: 641
SALES (corp-wide): 11B **Privately Held**
SIC: **8011** Offices & clinics of medical doctors
HQ: Sutter Health Sacramento Sierra Region
2200 River Plaza Dr
Sacramento CA 95833
916 733-8800

(P-20115)
SUTTER HLTH SCRMNTO SIERRA REG
Also Called: Sutter Amador Hospital Lab
100 Mission Blvd, Jackson (95642-2536)
PHONE.....................209 223-7540
Margie Souza, *Branch Mgr*
Mindy Epperson,
Robyn Fonbuena, *Manager*
EMP: 1268
SALES (corp-wide): 11B **Privately Held**
SIC: **8011** Radiologist
HQ: Sutter Health Sacramento Sierra Region
2200 River Plaza Dr
Sacramento CA 95833
916 733-8800

(P-20116)
SUTTER HLTH SCRMNTO SIERRA REG
Also Called: Sutter Medical Center
475 Pioneer Ave Ste 100, Woodland
(95776-4905)
PHONE.....................530 406-5616
Leefeldt Randall, *Branch Mgr*
EMP: 641
SALES (corp-wide): 11B **Privately Held**
SIC: **8011** Physicians' office, including specialists

PRODUCTS & SERVICES SECTION
8011 - Offices & Clinics Of Doctors Of Medicine County (P-20137)

HQ: Sutter Health Sacramento Sierra Region
2200 River Plaza Dr
Sacramento CA 95833
916 733-8800

(P-20117)
SUTTER MED GROUP OF REDWOODS
3883 Airway Dr Ste 202, Santa Rosa (95403-1671)
PHONE.................707 546-2788
John Dervin MD, *President*
Steven Levenberg, *President*
Sean Gaskie MD, *Treasurer*
Romayne Farrell Fnp, *Admin Sec*
Hester H Choi, *Gastroenterlgy*
EMP: 62
SALES (est): 7MM
SALES (corp-wide): 11B **Privately Held**
WEB: www.suttersantarosa.com
SIC: **8011** General & family practice, physician/surgeon
HQ: Sutter Santa Rosa Regional Hospital
30 Mark West Springs Rd
Santa Rosa CA 95403
707 576-4000

(P-20118)
SUTTER N MED GROUP A PROF CORP (PA)
969 Plumas St Ste 205, Yuba City (95991-4011)
PHONE.................530 749-3661
Robert H Wright Jr, *President*
Kelly Danna, *CFO*
Lynne Jones, *Office Mgr*
Peter Schwatka, *Technician*
Mandy Baker, *Marketing Staff*
EMP: 82
SQ FT: 30,096
SALES (est): 4.3MM **Privately Held**
SIC: **8011** Offices & clinics of medical doctors

(P-20119)
SUTTER NORTH MED FOUNDATION (PA)
Also Called: Multi Specialty Group Practice
969 Plumas St, Yuba City (95991-4011)
PHONE.................530 741-1300
Fax: 530 741-0182
Bruce Tigner, *CEO*
Tom Walther, *COO*
Kelly Danna, *CFO*
Lisa Osburn, *Executive*
Robert Achtel, *Research*
EMP: 160
SALES (est): 27.5MM **Privately Held**
WEB: www.snmf.com
SIC: **8011** Offices & clinics of medical doctors; clinic, operated by physicians

(P-20120)
SUTTER NORTH MED FOUNDATION
480 Plumas Blvd, Yuba City (95991-5005)
PHONE.................530 749-3635
Fax: 530 749-3618
William G Hoffman MD, *Principal*
Deni Kennedy, *Office Mgr*
David Yamamoto, *Director*
EMP: 100
SALES (corp-wide): 29.7MM **Privately Held**
WEB: www.snmf.com
SIC: **8011** Offices & clinics of medical doctors
PA: North Sutter Medical Foundation
969 Plumas St
Yuba City CA 95991
530 741-1300

(P-20121)
SUTTER NORTH MED FOUNDATION
Also Called: Home Health Brownsville
16911 Willow Glen Rd, Brownsville (95919-9707)
PHONE.................530 675-1245
Fax: 530 675-0943
Cindy White, *Branch Mgr*
EMP: 55

SALES (corp-wide): 27.5MM **Privately Held**
WEB: www.snmf.com
SIC: **8011** Offices & clinics of medical doctors
PA: North Sutter Medical Foundation
969 Plumas St
Yuba City CA 95991
530 741-1300

(P-20122)
SUTTER NORTH MED FOUNDATION
Also Called: Suttter North Home Health
400 Plumas Blvd Ste 115, Yuba City (95991-5081)
PHONE.................530 749-3450
Shelley Sanbury, *Branch Mgr*
Dennis G Bechini, *Family Practiti*
EMP: 55
SALES (corp-wide): 29.7MM **Privately Held**
WEB: www.snmf.com
SIC: **8011** Offices & clinics of medical doctors
PA: North Sutter Medical Foundation
969 Plumas St
Yuba City CA 95991
530 741-1300

(P-20123)
SUTTER REGIONAL MED FOUNDATION
2720 Low Ct, Fairfield (94534-9771)
PHONE.................707 374-6833
Carolyn Appenzeller, *Principal*
Daniel Ferrick, *Med Doctor*
EMP: 326
SALES (corp-wide): 31.7MM **Privately Held**
SIC: **8011** General & family practice, physician/surgeon
PA: Sutter Regional Medical Foundation Inc
2702 Low Ct
Fairfield CA 94534
707 427-4900

(P-20124)
SUTTER REGIONAL MED FOUNDATION
770 Mason St, Vacaville (95688-4646)
PHONE.................707 454-5800
EMP: 93
SALES (corp-wide): 31.7MM **Privately Held**
WEB: www.sutterdavis.org
SIC: **8011** Offices & clinics of medical doctors
PA: Sutter Regional Medical Foundation Inc
2702 Low Ct
Fairfield CA 94534
707 427-4900

(P-20125)
SWAMINATHA MAHADEVAN MD
701 Welch Rd Bldg C, Palo Alto (94304-1713)
PHONE.................650 723-6576
Swaminatha Mahadevan, *Chairman*
EMP: 90
SALES (est): 3.9MM **Privately Held**
SIC: **8011** Freestanding emergency medical center

(P-20126)
SYNERMED
Also Called: Ehs Medical Group
1200 Corp Ctr Dr Ste 200, Monterey Park (91754)
PHONE.................216 406-2845
Fax: 213 830-1800
James Mason, *President*
Eugene Polonsky, *Admin Asst*
Sheryl Reese, *Director*
Tabatha Tate, *Manager*
EMP: 180
SALES (est): 11.1MM **Privately Held**
SIC: **8011** Offices & clinics of medical doctors

(P-20127)
TABAK STEVEN WILLIAM M MD
Also Called: Cardiovascular Medical Group
414 N Camden Dr Ste 1100, Beverly Hills (90210-4517)
PHONE.................310 278-3400
Fax: 310 278-1240
Steven W Tabak MD, *President*
Coni Cosgrove, *Administration*
EMP: 50
SQ FT: 1,400
SALES (est): 8.8MM **Privately Held**
WEB: www.ajdj.com
SIC: **8011** Cardiologist & cardio-vascular specialist

(P-20128)
TAMMI R JAMES MD
7273 14th Ave Ste 120b, Sacramento (95820-3500)
PHONE.................916 383-6783
Tammi James, *Principal*
EMP: 50
SALES (est): 2.8MM **Privately Held**
SIC: **8011** 8093 Pediatrician; mental health clinic, outpatient

(P-20129)
TEAM HEALTH HOLDINGS INC
Also Called: Sharp Grossmont
5555 Grossmont Center Dr, La Mesa (91942-3019)
PHONE.................619 740-4401
EMP: 291
SALES (corp-wide): 3.6B **Publicly Held**
SIC: **8011** Offices & clinics of medical doctors
PA: Team Health Holdings, Inc.
265 Brookview Centre Way
Knoxville TN 37919
865 693-1000

(P-20130)
TENET HEALTHSYSTEM MEDICAL
414 Cliffside Dr, Danville (94526-4810)
PHONE.................925 275-8303
Phillip Gustafson, *Director*
EMP: 500
SALES (corp-wide): 18.7B **Publicly Held**
WEB: www.tenenthealth.com
SIC: **8011** Offices & clinics of medical doctors
HQ: Tenet Healthsystem Medical, Inc
1445 Ross Ave Ste 1400
Dallas TX 75202
469 893-2000

(P-20131)
TENET HEALTHSYSTEM MEDICAL
Also Called: Lakewood Regional Medical Ctr
3700 South St, Lakewood (90712-1419)
PHONE.................562 531-2550
Carol Mammolite, *Branch Mgr*
Sam Soleymani,
Terri Newton, *Ch Nursing Ofcr*
Covina Evans, *Controller*
Sheri Kollerbohm, *Director*
EMP: 700
SALES (corp-wide): 18.7B **Publicly Held**
WEB: www.tenenthealth.com
SIC: **8011** 8062 Medical centers; general medical & surgical hospitals
HQ: Tenet Healthsystem Medical, Inc
1445 Ross Ave Ste 1400
Dallas TX 75202
469 893-2000

(P-20132)
TENET HEALTHSYSTEM MEDICAL
Los Alamitos Med Ctr
3751 Katella Ave, Los Alamitos (90720-3113)
PHONE.................805 546-7698
Michelle Finney, *Principal*
Scott Rifkin, *COO*
Julia Nakano, *Info Tech Dir*
Sally Andrata, *Director*
EMP: 625

SALES (corp-wide): 18.7B **Publicly Held**
WEB: www.tenenthealth.com
SIC: **8011** 8062 Offices & clinics of medical doctors; general medical & surgical hospitals
HQ: Tenet Healthsystem Medical, Inc
1445 Ross Ave Ste 1400
Dallas TX 75202
469 893-2000

(P-20133)
TENET HEALTHSYSTEM MEDICAL
Also Called: Leisure World Pharmacy
1661 Golden Rain Rd, Seal Beach (90740-4907)
P.O. Box 2685 (90740-1685)
PHONE.................562 493-9581
Diana Doyle, *Manager*
Terri Furlow, *Administration*
EMP: 60
SALES (corp-wide): 18.7B **Publicly Held**
WEB: www.tenenthealth.com
SIC: **8011** 5912 Offices & clinics of medical doctors; drug stores
HQ: Tenet Healthsystem Medical, Inc
1445 Ross Ave Ste 1400
Dallas TX 75202
469 893-2000

(P-20134)
TENET HEALTHSYSTEM MEDICAL
1000 S Fremont Ave Unit 1, Alhambra (91803-8801)
PHONE.................626 300-5500
Joy Davis, *Director*
EMP: 200
SALES (corp-wide): 18.7B **Publicly Held**
WEB: www.tenenthealth.com
SIC: **8011** Offices & clinics of medical doctors
HQ: Tenet Healthsystem Medical, Inc
1445 Ross Ave Ste 1400
Dallas TX 75202
469 893-2000

(P-20135)
TENNANT HEALTH SYSTEMS
1000 S Fremont Ave Unit 2, Alhambra (91803-8834)
PHONE.................626 300-3500
Dawn Castro, *Director*
EMP: 120 EST: 1996
SALES (est): 8.1MM **Privately Held**
SIC: **8011** 8721 Offices & clinics of medical doctors; accounting, auditing & bookkeeping

(P-20136)
TIBURCIO VASQUEZ HLTH CTR INC (PA)
33255 9th St, Union City (94587-2137)
PHONE.................510 471-5880
Fax: 510 471-9051
David B Vliet, *CEO*
Yolanda Triana, *President*
Malou Martinez, *CFO*
Jesse Robles, *Treasurer*
Nancy Soto, *Vice Pres*
EMP: 50
SQ FT: 15,000
SALES (est): 25.3MM **Privately Held**
SIC: **8011** Primary care medical clinic

(P-20137)
TIBURCIO VASQUEZ HLTH CTR INC
22331 Mission Blvd, Hayward (94541-3911)
PHONE.................510 471-5907
Malou Martinez, *Branch Mgr*
EMP: 86
SALES (corp-wide): 25.3MM **Privately Held**
SIC: **8011** Primary care medical clinic
PA: Tiburcio Vasquez Health Center Incorporated
33255 9th St
Union City CA 94587
510 471-5880

8011 - Offices & Clinics Of Doctors Of Medicine County (P-20138)

(P-20138)
TORRANCE SURGERY CENTER LP
Also Called: Amsurg
23560 Crenshaw Blvd # 104, Torrance (90505-5233)
PHONE..........................310 784-5880
Fax: 310 325-9675
Nick Silvino MD, *Partner*
Ripu Arora MD, *Partner*
Marc Colman MD, *Partner*
Steve Dinsmore MD, *Partner*
Nelman Low MD, *Partner*
EMP: 1681 EST: 2001
SQ FT: 6,300
SALES (est): 29.3MM
SALES (corp-wide): 2.5B **Publicly Held**
WEB: www.natsurgcare.com
SIC: 8011 Ambulatory surgical center
PA: Amsurg Corp.
   1a Burton Hills Bvld
   Nashville TN 37215
   615 665-1283

(P-20139)
TORRENCE FAMILY PRACTICE
Also Called: McCandless, Harrison MD
20911 Earl St Ste 440, Torrance (90503-4355)
PHONE..........................310 542-0455
John W Annable, *President*
▲EMP: 55
SQ FT: 5,200
SALES (est): 3.5MM **Privately Held**
SIC: 8011 General & family practice, physician/surgeon

(P-20140)
TOWER HEMATOLOGY ONCOLOGY MEDI
9090 Wilshire Blvd # 200, Beverly Hills (90211-1848)
P.O. Box 5624 (90209-5605)
PHONE..........................310 888-8680
Robert W Decker MD, *Partner*
Leland M Green MD, *Partner*
Cheryl Elzinga, *Vice Pres*
Fred Rosenfelt, *Vice Pres*
Fred Rosenfeltmd, *Vice Pres*
EMP: 75
SQ FT: 13,000
SALES (est): 12.3MM **Privately Held**
WEB: www.toweroncology.com
SIC: 8011 Hematologist; oncologist

(P-20141)
TRACY TRUJILLO MD
200 Porter Dr Ste 300, San Ramon (94583-1524)
PHONE..........................925 838-6511
Tracy Trujillo, *Principal*
EMP: 50
SALES (est): 920.3K **Privately Held**
SIC: 8011 Offices & clinics of medical doctors

(P-20142)
TRI CITY ORTHOPEDIC SGY & MDCL
Also Called: Neville Alleyne MD
3905 Waring Rd, Oceanside (92056-4405)
PHONE..........................760 724-9000
Fax: 760 724-3686
James Esch, *President*
Dr Neville Alleyne, *Bd of Directors*
Dr James Helgager, *Bd of Directors*
Dr Norman Kane, *Bd of Directors*
Dr Richard Muir, *Bd of Directors*
▲EMP: 50
SQ FT: 10,000
SALES (est): 8.9MM **Privately Held**
WEB: www.tricityortho.com
SIC: 8011 Orthopedic physician; surgeon

(P-20143)
TRI-CITY HEALTH CENTER (PA)
39500 Liberty St, Fremont (94538-2211)
PHONE..........................510 770-8040
Fax: 510 770-8145
Kathleen Lievre, *CEO*
Michael Ellson, *Manager*
EMP: 104 EST: 1972

SALES: 20.9MM **Privately Held**
WEB: www.tri-cityhealth.org
SIC: 8011 Offices & clinics of medical doctors

(P-20144)
TUOLUMNE ME-WUK INDIAN
Also Called: Tuolumne Mewuk Indian Health
18880 Cherry Valley Blvd, Tuolumne (95379-9506)
PHONE..........................209 928-5400
Fax: 209 928-5412
Christopher Gorsky, *Principal*
Darla Merlin, *Ch of Bd*
Laura E Bailey, *Executive*
Tammy Barker, *Finance Dir*
EMP: 90
SQ FT: 11,000
SALES: 7.8MM **Privately Held**
SIC: 8011 General & family practice, physician/surgeon

(P-20145)
TVDDC EC MURRIETA
25150 Hancock Ave Ste 530, Murrieta (92562-5987)
PHONE..........................951 566-5229
Crystal Sarias, *Principal*
Judy Wiliiam, *Manager*
EMP: 50
SALES (est): 454.6K **Privately Held**
SIC: 8011 Offices & clinics of medical doctors

(P-20146)
TWIN CITIES COMMUNITY HOSP INC
1100 Las Tablas Rd, Templeton (93465-9704)
PHONE..........................805 434-3500
Fax: 805 434-2913
Mark P Lisa, *CEO*
Mark Sada,
Steven Wheeler,
Glen Coopermann, *Ch OB/GYN*
Sue Smith, *COO*
EMP: 450
SQ FT: 120,000
SALES: 27.1K
SALES (corp-wide): 18.7B **Publicly Held**
WEB: www.tenethealth.com
SIC: 8011 8062 Offices & clinics of medical doctors; general medical & surgical hospitals
PA: Tenet Healthcare Corporation
   1445 Ross Ave Ste 1400
   Dallas TX 75202
   469 893-2200

(P-20147)
U C SAN FRANCISCO GYNECOLOGY
2356 Sutter St, San Francisco (94115-3006)
PHONE..........................415 885-7788
Fax: 415 885-7718
EMP: 306
SALES (est): 1.4MM
SALES (corp-wide): 49.8MM **Privately Held**
SIC: 8011 Gynecologist
PA: C/O Uc San Francisco
   1111 Franklin St Fl 12
   Oakland CA 94607
   858 534-7323

(P-20148)
UC DAVIS HEALTH SYSTEM (PA)
4610 X St, Sacramento (95817-2200)
PHONE..........................916 734-1000
Katherine Wesnousky, *Principal*
Jonathan Jeisel, *Vice Pres*
Claire Pomeroy, *Principal*
Jodi Casselman, *Research*
Shang WEI, *HR Admin*
EMP: 73
SALES (est): 16.9MM **Privately Held**
SIC: 8011 Internal medicine practitioners

(P-20149)
UC DAVIS HLTH SYSTM FCLTS DSGN
Also Called: Uc Davis Medical Center
4800 2nd Ave Ste 3010, Sacramento (95817-2216)
PHONE..........................916 734-6570
Eugene Labrie, *Manager*
Thomas E Nordahl, *Professor*
EMP: 50 EST: 2008
SALES (est): 7.7MM **Privately Held**
SIC: 8011 Medical centers

(P-20150)
UC REGENTS
Also Called: Ucla Nrpsychtric Bhvioral Hlth
300 Medical Plaza, Los Angeles (90095-0001)
PHONE..........................310 301-8777
Jody Gaspar, *Principal*
Lavonte Hickman, *Principal*
EMP: 99
SALES (est): 3.5MM **Privately Held**
SIC: 8011 8049 Medical centers; clinical psychologist; speech pathologist; psychiatric social worker; psychotherapist, except M.D.

(P-20151)
UCLA HEALTH SYSTEM
Also Called: Ronald Reagan Building
757 Westwood Plz, Los Angeles (90095-8358)
PHONE..........................310 825-9111
Fax: 310 206-4446
Dr David T Feinberg, *CEO*
Tony Padilla, *Office Mgr*
Kirsten Holguin, *Admin Asst*
Henry Cryer, *Surgeon*
Meena Garg, *Pediatrics*
EMP: 91
SALES (est): 23.7MM **Privately Held**
SIC: 8011 Offices & clinics of medical doctors

(P-20152)
UNITED FAMILY CARE INC
8110 Mango Ave Ste 104, Fontana (92335-3603)
PHONE..........................909 822-1164
Mary Alice Speak, *Manager*
EMP: 60
SQ FT: 1,248
SALES (corp-wide): 5.9MM **Privately Held**
WEB: www.unitedfamilycare.com
SIC: 8011 Medical centers
PA: United Family Care, Inc.
   8110 Mango Ave Ste 104
   Fontana CA 92335
   909 874-1679

(P-20153)
UNITED FAMILY CARE INC (PA)
8110 Mango Ave Ste 104, Fontana (92335-3603)
PHONE..........................909 874-1679
Fax: 909 357-2565
Keith Schauermann, *President*
Raja S Tooma, *Director*
EMP: 60
SALES (est): 5.9MM **Privately Held**
WEB: www.unitedfamilycare.com
SIC: 8011 Offices & clinics of medical doctors

(P-20154)
UNITED INDIAN HEALTH SERVICES (PA)
1600 Weeot Way, Arcata (95521-4734)
PHONE..........................707 825-5000
Fax: 707 825-9166
Robert S Davis III, *CEO*
Mary Hurley, *CFO*
Anthony Titus, *CFO*
Debra Friedenbach, *Pharmacy Dir*
Barbara Bishop, *Ch Nursing Ofcr*
EMP: 125
SQ FT: 46,304
SALES: 20.5MM **Privately Held**
WEB: www.uihs.org
SIC: 8011 8021 8031 Medical centers; primary care medical clinic; dental clinics & offices; offices & clinics of osteopathic physicians

(P-20155)
UNITED MEDICAL IMAGING INC
1762 Westwood Blvd # 230, Los Angeles (90024-5648)
PHONE..........................310 943-8400
Nasser Hiekali, *CEO*
Eddy Simnegar, *Purch Mgr*
EMP: 140
SALES (est): 14MM **Privately Held**
SIC: 8011 Radiologist

(P-20156)
UNITED STATES DEPT OF NAVY
8808 Balboa Ave, San Diego (92123-1592)
PHONE..........................619 532-6397
Mike Clark, *Branch Mgr*
Robin D Moore, *Admin Asst*
EMP: 924 **Publicly Held**
SIC: 8011 Medical centers
HQ: United States Department Of The Navy
   1200 Navy Pentagon
   Washington DC 20350
   703 545-6700

(P-20157)
UNITED STATES DEPT OF NAVY
34800 Bob Wilson Dr # 409, San Diego (92134-1409)
PHONE..........................619 532-8953
Fax: 619 532-8945
Elizabeth Ferrara, *Principal*
EMP: 924 **Publicly Held**
SIC: 8011 Anesthesiologist
HQ: United States Department Of The Navy
   1200 Navy Pentagon
   Washington DC 20350
   703 545-6700

(P-20158)
UNITED STATES DEPT OF NAVY
Also Called: Naval Dental Center
2310 Craven St, San Diego (92136-5596)
PHONE..........................619 556-8210
Fax: 619 556-8559
Pete Seder, *Branch Mgr*
Peter Ruocco, *Director*
EMP: 300 **Publicly Held**
SIC: 8011 9711 Health maintenance organization; Navy;
HQ: United States Department Of The Navy
   1200 Navy Pentagon
   Washington DC 20350
   703 545-6700

(P-20159)
UNITED STATES DEPT OF NAVY
Also Called: US Naval Medical Clinical Lab
162 1st St, Port Hueneme (93043-4316)
PHONE..........................805 982-6392
Sharon West, *Principal*
EMP: 924 **Publicly Held**
SIC: 8011 9711 Primary care medical clinic; Navy;
HQ: United States Department Of The Navy
   1200 Navy Pentagon
   Washington DC 20350
   703 545-6700

(P-20160)
UNITED STATES DEPT OF NAVY
Naval Med Ctr Crdiolgy Clinic
34730 Bob Wilson Dr, San Diego (92134-3098)
PHONE..........................619 532-7400
Ed Doorn, *Manager*
Lucy Rodriguez, *Admin Sec*
Elwood Hopkins, *Research*
Sybil Tasker, *Research*
Christopher W Kocher, *Cardiovascular*
EMP: 924 **Publicly Held**
SIC: 8011 9711 Cardiologist & cardio-vascular specialist; Navy;
HQ: United States Department Of The Navy
   1200 Navy Pentagon
   Washington DC 20350
   703 545-6700

(P-20161)
UNITED STATES DEPT OF NAVY
Also Called: Naval Medical Clinic
162 1st St Bldg 1402, Port Hueneme (93043-4316)
PHONE..........................805 982-6370
J F Murray, *Branch Mgr*
EMP: 924 **Publicly Held**

PRODUCTS & SERVICES SECTION
8011 - Offices & Clinics Of Doctors Of Medicine County (P-20182)

SIC: 8011 9711 Primary care medical clinic; Navy;
HQ: United States Department Of The Navy
1200 Navy Pentagon
Washington DC 20350
703 545-6700

(P-20162)
UNITED STATES DEPT OF NAVY
Also Called: Navmedwest
4170 Norman Scott Rd, San Diego (92136-5501)
PHONE..............................619 767-6592
Cdr M Campbell, Branch Mgr
M Campbell, Branch Mgr
EMP: 924 Publicly Held
SIC: 8011 Offices & clinics of medical doctors
HQ: United States Department Of The Navy
1200 Navy Pentagon
Washington DC 20350
703 545-6700

(P-20163)
UNIVERSITY CAL LOS ANGELES
Also Called: Ucla Primary Care Westlake
1250 Avanta Dr Ste 207, Westlake Village (91361)
PHONE..............................805 494-6920
Dina Sarabia, Branch Mgr
Constance Daino, Admin Asst
Estela Dominguez, Admin Asst
Eugene Acosta, Technology
Wanda Collier, Manager
EMP: 50 Privately Held
SIC: 8011 Primary care medical clinic
HQ: University Of California, Los Angeles
405 Hilgard Ave
Los Angeles CA 90095
310 825-4321

(P-20164)
UNIVERSITY CAL SAN FRANCISCO
Also Called: Ucsf Medical Center
3330 Geary Blvd, San Francisco (94118-3347)
PHONE..............................415 353-3155
Monica Seay, Branch Mgr
Mike Toftely, Project Mgr
Gemma Bernabe, Manager
EMP: 60 Privately Held
SIC: 8011 8221 9411 Medical centers; university; administration of educational programs;
HQ: University Of California, San Francisco
505 Parnassus Ave
San Francisco CA 94143
415 476-9000

(P-20165)
UNIVERSITY CAL SAN FRANCISCO
Also Called: Department of Radiology
505 Parnassus Ave L308, San Francisco (94143-2204)
PHONE..............................415 353-2573
Charles B Higgins MD, Owner
Ruth Goldstein, Professor
Jacqueline Leung, Med Doctor
Steven Polevoi, Med Doctor
Glenn Rosenbluth, Med Doctor
EMP: 300 Privately Held
SIC: 8011 Offices & clinics of medical doctors
HQ: University Of California, San Francisco
505 Parnassus Ave
San Francisco CA 94143
415 476-9000

(P-20166)
UNIVERSITY CAL SAN FRANCISCO
Also Called: Ucsf Mmory Clnic Alzhimers Ctr
1500 Owens St Ste 320, San Francisco (94158-2335)
PHONE..............................415 476-6880
Fax: 415 476-4800
Bruce Miller, Director
Albert Lee, Software Engr
Mary Demay, Research
Caroline Latham, Research
Suzee Lee, Neurology
EMP: 170 Privately Held

SIC: 8011 8221 9411 Medical centers; university; administration of educational programs;
HQ: University Of California, San Francisco
505 Parnassus Ave
San Francisco CA 94143
415 476-9000

(P-20167)
UNIVERSITY CALIFORNIA DAVIS
2315 Stockton Blvd # 6309, Sacramento (95817-2201)
PHONE..............................916 734-2846
Valerie Adame, Branch Mgr
EMP: 50 Privately Held
SIC: 8011 Surgeon
HQ: University Of California, Davis
1 Shields Ave
Davis CA 95616
530 752-1011

(P-20168)
UNIVERSITY CALIFORNIA DAVIS
Also Called: Cowell Student Health Center
Student House Ctr, Davis (95616)
PHONE..............................530 752-2300
Fax: 530 752-2306
Dr Michelle Famula, Director
Debbie Kamber, Executive
Frank Ventimiglia, Lab Dir
Marcy Best, Associate Dir
James Case, Administration
EMP: 150 Privately Held
WEB: www.ucdavis.edu
SIC: 8011 9411 8221 Medical centers; administration of educational programs; ; university
HQ: University Of California, Davis
1 Shields Ave
Davis CA 95616
530 752-1011

(P-20169)
UNIVERSITY CALIFORNIA IRVINE
Also Called: Uc Irvine Hlth Rgonal Burn Ctr
101 The City Dr S Bldg 1a, Orange (92868-3201)
PHONE..............................714 456-6170
Fax: 714 456-7601
Howard Federoff, Vice Chancellor
Pranav Patel,
Ralph Cygan, Exec Dir
Patrick Bird, Administration
Wendy Goldberg, Professor
EMP: 1757 Privately Held
WEB: www.com.uci.edu
SIC: 8011 Medical centers
HQ: University Of California, Irvine
510 Aldrich Hall
Irvine CA 92697
949 824-8343

(P-20170)
UNIVERSITY CALIFORNIA IRVINE
Also Called: UCI Family Health Center
800 N Main St, Santa Ana (92701-3576)
PHONE..............................714 480-2443
Nancy Downey- Hurtado, Manager
Bill Mansour, Manager
EMP: 65
SQ FT: 49,361 Privately Held
WEB: www.com.uci.edu
SIC: 8011 9411 8221 Medical centers; administration of educational programs; ; university
HQ: University Of California, Irvine
510 Aldrich Hall
Irvine CA 92697
949 824-8343

(P-20171)
UNIVERSITY CALIFORNIA BERKELEY
Also Called: University Health Services
2222 Bancroft Way, Berkeley (94720-4301)
PHONE..............................510 642-2000
Fax: 510 642-6428
Diane Liu MD, Principal
Wanda Nieters, Officer
Anna Weidman, Officer
Michelle Chen, Vice Pres

Danny Hellebusch, Vice Pres
EMP: 370 Privately Held
WEB: www.law.berkeley.edu
SIC: 8011 9411 8221 Dispensary, operated by physicians; administration of educational programs; ; university
HQ: The University California Berkeley
200 Clfrnia Hall Spc 1500
Berkeley CA 94720
510 642-6000

(P-20172)
UNIVERSITY CALIFORNIA IRVINE
1640 Newport Blvd Ste 340, Costa Mesa (92627-7730)
PHONE..............................949 646-2267
Olivia Reil, Branch Mgr
EMP: 50 Privately Held
SIC: 8011 9431 Gynecologist; administration of public health programs
HQ: University Of California, Irvine
510 Aldrich Hall
Irvine CA 92697
949 824-8343

(P-20173)
UNIVERSITY SOUTHERN CALIFORNIA
Also Called: Usc Student Health Center
849 W 34th St Ste 208, Los Angeles (90089-0079)
PHONE..............................213 743-5339
Fax: 213 740-0214
Dr Steven Gardner, Principal
Mark D Figatner MD, Med Doctor
Bent Nielsen, Director
EMP: 60
SALES (corp-wide): 4.7B Privately Held
WEB: www.usc.edu
SIC: 8011 8221 Medical centers; university
PA: University Of Southern California
3720 S Flower St Fl 3
Los Angeles CA 90007
213 740-7762

(P-20174)
UROLOGY ASSOC OF CEN CAL
7014 N Whitney Ave Ste A, Fresno (93720-0155)
PHONE..............................559 321-2800
Gilbert Dale MD, President
Artin Jibilian MD, Treasurer
Irwin S Barg MD, Vice Pres
William Schiff MD, Admin Sec
EMP: 90
SQ FT: 28,074
SALES (est): 6.7MM Privately Held
WEB: www.fresnosecurity.us
SIC: 8011 Urologist

(P-20175)
US DEPT OF THE AIR FORCE
Also Called: Sgokc
15301 Warren Shingle Rd, Beale Afb (95903-1907)
PHONE..............................530 634-4738
Melvin Antonio, Branch Mgr
EMP: 90 Publicly Held
WEB: www.af.mil
SIC: 8011 9711 Pediatrician; Air Force;
HQ: United States Department Of The Air Force
1000 Air Force Pentagon
Washington DC 20330
703 545-6700

(P-20176)
US HEALTHWORKS INC (HQ)
Also Called: U.S. Healthworks Medical Group
25124 Springfield Ct, Valencia (91355-1085)
PHONE..............................800 720-2432
Fax: 661 678-2700
Joseph T Mallas, President
Maggy Lange, Shareholder
Cathy Mark, Shareholder
Robert Hutchison, CFO
Sherif Hanna, Senior VP
EMP: 60
SALES (est): 327.1MM
SALES (corp-wide): 7.1B Privately Held
SIC: 8011 Offices & clinics of medical doctors

PA: Dignity Health
185 Berry St Ste 300
San Francisco CA 94107
415 438-5500

(P-20177)
USC EMERGENCY MEDICINE ASSOC
1200 N State St Ste 1011, Los Angeles (90033-1029)
PHONE..............................323 226-6667
Fax: 323 226-6806
Edward Newton, Chairman
Jan M Shoenberger, Emerg Med Spec
EMP: 80
SALES (est): 3.9MM Privately Held
SIC: 8011 Freestanding emergency medical center

(P-20178)
USC INSTITUTE FOR NEUROIMAGING
Also Called: Usc MARk& Mary Steven Neuro
2001 N Soto St Ste 102, Los Angeles (90032-3675)
PHONE..............................323 442-7246
Arthur Toga, Director
EMP: 125
SALES (est): 152.2K Privately Held
SIC: 8011 Offices & clinics of medical doctors

(P-20179)
USC SURGEONS INCORPORATED
Also Called: Usc Srgcal Edcatn RES Fndation
1510 San Pablo St Ste 514, Los Angeles (90033-5324)
PHONE..............................323 442-5910
Fax: 323 442-5735
Tom Demeester MD, President
Eric Alcorn, Exec VP
Albert Yellin MD, Admin Sec
Dennis R Holmes, Surgeon
Douglas Hood, Med Doctor
EMP: 250
SQ FT: 15,000
SALES (est): 11.1MM Privately Held
SIC: 8011 Specialized medical practitioners, except internal

(P-20180)
VALLEY CHILDRENS HEALTHCARE
9300 Valley Childrens Pl, Madera (93636-8761)
PHONE..............................559 353-3000
Todd Suntrapak, CEO
Michele Waldron, CFO
Stephanie Vance, Vice Pres
Wes Segal, Director
EMP: 2800
SALES (est): 44.6K Privately Held
SIC: 8011 8069 Physical medicine, physician/surgeon; physicians' office, including specialists; children's hospital

(P-20181)
VALLEY CHILDRENS HOSPITAL
Also Called: Charlie Mitchell Chld Clinic
9300 Valley Childrens Pl, Madera (93636-8762)
PHONE..............................559 353-6425
Fax: 559 353-5311
Annette Humphrys, Manager
James McCarty, Infectious Dis
Linda Miranda,
EMP: 226
SALES (corp-wide): 575.6MM Privately Held
SIC: 8011 Medical centers
PA: Valley Children's Hospital
9300 Valley Childrens Pl
Madera CA 93636
559 353-3000

(P-20182)
VALLEY COMMUNITY HEALTHCARE
6801 Coldwater Canyon Ave 1b, North Hollywood (91605-5164)
PHONE..............................818 763-8836
Fax: 818 763-7231
Paula Wilson, CEO
Lee Huey, CFO

8011 - Offices & Clinics Of Doctors Of Medicine County (P-20183) — PRODUDUCTS & SERVICES SECTION

Andrea Thomas, *Chairman*
Susan Dion, *Vice Pres*
Michael Bridge, *Sls & Mktg Exec*
EMP: 300
SQ FT: 15,000
SALES: 15.3MM **Privately Held**
WEB: www.valleycommunityclinic.org
SIC: 8011 Clinic, operated by physicians

(P-20183)
VALLEY MEDICAL GROUP OF LOMPOC
Also Called: Bailey, Rollin C MD
136 N 3rd St, Lompoc (93436-7099)
PHONE.................................805 736-1253
Fax: 805 736-5355
William H Gausman Jr, *President*
B J Coughlin MD, *Corp Secy*
Eldon Elam MD, *Vice Pres*
Rollin C Bailey, *Managing Dir*
Thomas E Fritch, *Managing Dir*
EMP: 60 **EST:** 1965
SQ FT: 10,700
SALES (est): 9.3MM **Privately Held**
WEB: www.vmglompoc.com
SIC: 8011 Internal medicine, physician/surgeon; general & family practice, physician/surgeon

(P-20184)
VALLEY OB GYN MEDICAL GROUP
400 N Pepper Ave Fl 6, Colton (92324-1801)
PHONE.................................909 580-6333
Guillermo Valenzuela, *President*
Sharon Kiss, *Office Mgr*
Sue Kunz, *Office Mgr*
Tina Foster, *Obstetrician*
Hugo M Rauld, *Obstetrician*
EMP: 50
SALES (est): 4.3MM **Privately Held**
SIC: 8011 Gynecologist

(P-20185)
VALLEYCARE HOSPITAL CORP (DH)
Also Called: Valleycare Health
1111 E Stanley Blvd, Livermore (94550-4115)
PHONE.................................925 447-7000
Marcelina L Feit, *President*
Robert Quadri, *Project Mgr*
Sherri Graeber, *Accounting Mgr*
Jim Boatman, *Controller*
Arich Henneman, *Manager*
EMP: 103
SALES (est): 94.8MM
SALES (corp-wide): 1.9B **Privately Held**
SIC: 8011 Primary care medical clinic
HQ: The Hospital Committee For The Livermore-Pleasanton Areas
5555 W Las Positas Blvd
Pleasanton CA 94588
925 847-3000

(P-20186)
VAN GROW JACK S MD
1140 W La Veta Ave # 640, Orange (92868-4225)
PHONE.................................714 564-3300
Jack Van Grow, *Partner*
Jack Vangrow, *Partner*
EMP: 50
SALES (est): 893.2K **Privately Held**
WEB: www.ocheart.org
SIC: 8011 Offices & clinics of medical doctors

(P-20187)
VANTAGE ONCOLOGY LLC (HQ)
1500 Rosecrans Ave # 400, Manhattan Beach (90266-3754)
P.O. Box 10033 (90267-7533)
PHONE.................................310 335-4000
Michael Fiore, *CEO*
Dee Delapp, *President*
Marshal Salomon, *COO*
Brian Rizkallah, *CFO*
Leslie E Botnick, *Chief Mktg Ofcr*
EMP: 300
SQ FT: 150,000
SALES (est): 84.7MM
SALES (corp-wide): 190.8B **Publicly Held**
SIC: 8011 Oncologist

PA: Mckesson Corporation
1 Post St Fl 18
San Francisco CA 94104
415 983-8300

(P-20188)
VENICE FAMILY CLINIC
Also Called: Irma Colen Health Center
4700 Inglewood Blvd # 102, Culver City (90230-5896)
PHONE.................................310 392-8636
Ana Gutshall, *Branch Mgr*
Jenny O'Brian, *Director*
EMP: 62
SALES (corp-wide): 31.8MM **Privately Held**
SIC: 8011 Offices & clinics of medical doctors
PA: Venice Family Clinic
604 Rose Ave
Venice CA 90291
310 664-7703

(P-20189)
VENICE FAMILY CLINIC (PA)
604 Rose Ave, Venice (90291-2767)
PHONE.................................310 664-7703
Fax: 310 392-7875
Brian Kan, *President*
Gordon Lee, *Treasurer*
Jeffrey E Sinaiko, *Treasurer*
Elaine Schmidt, *Officer*
Lee Rosenberg, *Vice Pres*
EMP: 70
SALES: 31.8MM **Privately Held**
SIC: 8011 Primary care medical clinic

(P-20190)
VENICE FAMILY CLINIC
2509 Pico Blvd, Santa Monica (90405-1828)
PHONE.................................310 392-8636
Elizabeth B Forer, *Principal*
EMP: 108
SALES (corp-wide): 31.8MM **Privately Held**
SIC: 8011 Clinic, operated by physicians
PA: Venice Family Clinic
604 Rose Ave
Venice CA 90291
310 664-7703

(P-20191)
VENTURA COUNTY MEDICAL CENTER
Also Called: Santa Paula Hospital
845 N 10th St Ste 3, Santa Paula (93060-1348)
PHONE.................................805 933-8600
Fax: 805 525-2955
Minako Watabe, *Obstetrician*
EMP: 87
SALES (corp-wide): 371.8MM **Privately Held**
SIC: 8011 Medical centers
PA: Ventura County Medical Center
3291 Loma Vista Rd
Ventura CA 93003
805 652-6000

(P-20192)
VENTURA COUNTY MEDICAL CENTER (PA)
3291 Loma Vista Rd, Ventura (93003-3099)
PHONE.................................805 652-6000
Fax: 805 652-5992
Ronald O'Halloran, *Principal*
Kate Mills, *Program Mgr*
Veronica Gonzalez, *Executive Asst*
Joel Sanchez, *Admin Asst*
David Lyon, *Technology*
EMP: 160
SALES: 371.8MM **Privately Held**
SIC: 8011 Medical centers

(P-20193)
VENTURA COUNTY MEDICAL CENTER
Also Called: Ana Nacapa Surgical Associates
3291 Loma Vista Rd # 343, Ventura (93003-3099)
PHONE.................................805 652-6201
Thomas K Duncan, *Osteopathy*
Louise E Toutant, *Nurse Practr*

EMP: 99
SALES (corp-wide): 371.8MM **Privately Held**
SIC: 8011 Medical centers
PA: Ventura County Medical Center
3291 Loma Vista Rd
Ventura CA 93003
805 652-6000

(P-20194)
VERDUGO HILLS URGENT CARE MG
Also Called: Verdugo Hills Medical Assoc
544 N Glendale Ave, Glendale (91206-3311)
PHONE.................................818 241-4331
Fax: 818 241-3627
Richard A Foullon, *President*
Cynthia Foullon, *Vice Pres*
Emil Avanes, *Gnrl Med Prac*
EMP: 62
SQ FT: 11,000
SALES (est): 4.8MM **Privately Held**
WEB: www.vhma.com
SIC: 8011 Medical centers

(P-20195)
VETERANS HEALTH ADMINISTRATION
Also Called: Mare Island Outpatient Clinic
Walnut Ave Bldg 201, Vallejo (94589)
PHONE.................................707 562-8200
Debra Nathanson, *Manager*
EMP: 264 **Publicly Held**
WEB: www.veterans-ru.org
SIC: 8011 9451 Clinic, operated by physicians; psychiatric clinic;
HQ: Veterans Health Administration
810 Vermont Ave Nw
Washington DC 20420

(P-20196)
VETERANS HEALTH ADMINISTRATION
Also Called: West Los Angeles V A Med Ctr
11301 Wilshire Blvd, Los Angeles (90073-1003)
PHONE.................................310 478-3711
Fax: 310 268-3646
Donna Beiter, *Director*
Martin Cozyn, *Exec VP*
Vasant Udhoji, *Research*
David Holt, *Facilities Mgr*
Donald S Chang, *Cardiovascular*
EMP: 5400 **Publicly Held**
WEB: www.veterans-ru.org
SIC: 8011 9451 Medical centers; psychiatric clinic;
HQ: Veterans Health Administration
810 Vermont Ave Nw
Washington DC 20420

(P-20197)
VETERANS HEALTH ADMINISTRATION
Also Called: San Luis Obispo VA Cboc
1288 Morro St Ste 200, San Luis Obispo (93401-6302)
PHONE.................................805 543-1233
Mark Donaldson, *Branch Mgr*
EMP: 264 **Publicly Held**
SIC: 8011 9451 Clinic, operated by physicians;
HQ: Veterans Health Administration
810 Vermont Ave Nw
Washington DC 20420

(P-20198)
VETERANS HEALTH ADMINISTRATION
Also Called: Sacramento Mental Hlth Clinic
10535 Hospital Way, Mather (95655-4200)
PHONE.................................916 366-5427
Charles Barnett, *Manager*
Leslie Eaton, *Psychiatry*
Tin Shain, *Psychiatry*
EMP: 264 **Publicly Held**
WEB: www.veterans-ru.org
SIC: 8011 9451 Clinic, operated by physicians; psychiatric clinic;

HQ: Veterans Health Administration
810 Vermont Ave Nw
Washington DC 20420

(P-20199)
VETERANS HEALTH ADMINISTRATION
Also Called: Central Cal Healthcare Sys
2615 E Clinton Ave, Fresno (93703-2223)
PHONE.................................559 225-6100
Al Perry, *Branch Mgr*
Kong P Yap, *Gastroenterlgy*
EMP: 800 **Publicly Held**
WEB: www.veterans-ru.org
SIC: 8011 9451 Medical centers; administration of veterans' affairs;
HQ: Veterans Health Administration
810 Vermont Ave Nw
Washington DC 20420

(P-20200)
VETERANS HEALTH ADMINISTRATION
Also Called: Redding V A Outpatient Clinic
351 Hartnell Ave, Redding (96002-1845)
PHONE.................................530 226-7555
Fax: 530 226-7505
Anthony Pineda, *Branch Mgr*
Pete Privitt, *Site Mgr*
Stephen E Cox, *Internal Med*
Louis M Sherby, *Internal Med*
David L Park, *Chiropractor*
EMP: 264 **Publicly Held**
WEB: www.veterans-ru.org
SIC: 8011 9451 Clinic, operated by physicians; psychiatric clinic;
HQ: Veterans Health Administration
810 Vermont Ave Nw
Washington DC 20420

(P-20201)
VETERANS HEALTH ADMINISTRATION
Also Called: Palo Alto VA Medical Center
3801 Miranda Ave Bldg 101, Palo Alto (94304-1207)
PHONE.................................650 493-5000
Fax: 650 852-3258
Elizabeth Freeman, *Director*
Alice Naqvi, *Admin Director*
Corey Walley, *Web Proj Mgr*
Josefina Ledezma, *Purch Dir*
Kaci J Fairchild, *Professor*
EMP: 3500 **Publicly Held**
WEB: www.veterans-ru.org
SIC: 8011 9451 Medical centers;
HQ: Veterans Health Administration
810 Vermont Ave Nw
Washington DC 20420

(P-20202)
VETERANS HEALTH ADMINISTRATION
Also Called: Oakland V A Outpatient Clinic
2221 Martin Luther King J, Oakland (94612-1318)
PHONE.................................510 267-7820
Dr Elmer Anderson, *Principal*
EMP: 264 **Publicly Held**
WEB: www.veterans-ru.org
SIC: 8011 9451 Clinic, operated by physicians; psychiatric clinic;
HQ: Veterans Health Administration
810 Vermont Ave Nw
Washington DC 20420

(P-20203)
VETERANS HEALTH ADMINISTRATION
Also Called: San Francisco Vamc
4150 Clement St 6205, San Francisco (94121-1545)
PHONE.................................415 750-2009
Brian J Kelly, *Manager*
Linda Penn, *Office Mgr*
Joyce Lam, *Office Admin*
Lawrence Stewart, *Network Mgr*
Eric J Huang, *Pathologist*
EMP: 85 **Publicly Held**
WEB: www.veterans-ru.org

PRODUCTS & SERVICES SECTION

8011 - Offices & Clinics Of Doctors Of Medicine County (P-20224)

SIC: **8011** 9451 Medical centers; psychiatric clinic;
HQ: Veterans Health Administration
810 Vermont Ave Nw
Washington DC 20420

(P-20204)
VETERANS HEALTH ADMINISTRATION
16111 Plummer St, North Hills (91343-2036)
PHONE 818 895-9311
Mike Domres, *Principal*
EMP: 183 **Publicly Held**
WEB: www.veterans-ru.org
SIC: **8011** 9451 Clinic, operated by physicians;
HQ: Veterans Health Administration
810 Vermont Ave Nw
Washington DC 20420

(P-20205)
VETERANS HEALTH ADMINISTRATION
Also Called: Mission Valley V A
8810 Rio San Diego Dr, San Diego (92108-1698)
PHONE 619 400-5000
Brian S Kawaaki, *Ophthalmology*
EMP: 264 **Publicly Held**
WEB: www.veterans-ru.org
SIC: **8011** 9451 Clinic, operated by physicians; psychiatric clinic;
HQ: Veterans Health Administration
810 Vermont Ave Nw
Washington DC 20420

(P-20206)
VETERANS HEALTH ADMINISTRATION
Also Called: Sepulveda Ambulatory Care
16111 Plummer St, North Hills (91343-2036)
PHONE 818 891-7711
Fax: 818 895-9511
Dolly G Whitehead, *Manager*
Eric T Cheng, *Internal Med*
Charles E Marshall, *Internal Med*
Richard H Weisbart, *Internal Med*
Rhonda Caldwell-Willia, *Psychiatry*
EMP: 900 **Publicly Held**
WEB: www.veterans-ru.org
SIC: **8011** 9451 Medical centers; psychiatric clinic;
HQ: Veterans Health Administration
810 Vermont Ave Nw
Washington DC 20420

(P-20207)
VETERANS HEALTH ADMINISTRATION
Also Called: Chico V A Outpatient Clinic
280 Cohasset Rd, Chico (95926-2210)
PHONE 530 879-5000
Sonny Morgan, *Manager*
EMP: 264 **Publicly Held**
WEB: www.veterans-ru.org
SIC: **8011** 9451 Clinic, operated by physicians; psychiatric clinic;
HQ: Veterans Health Administration
810 Vermont Ave Nw
Washington DC 20420

(P-20208)
VETERANS HEALTH ADMINISTRATION
Also Called: Eureka Veterans Clinic
727 E St, Eureka (95501-1854)
PHONE 707 442-5335
Phillip Wagner, *Manager*
EMP: 264 **Publicly Held**
WEB: www.veterans-ru.org
SIC: **8011** 9451 Medical centers; psychiatric clinic;
HQ: Veterans Health Administration
810 Vermont Ave Nw
Washington DC 20420

(P-20209)
VETERANS HEALTH ADMINISTRATION
Also Called: Chula Vista Veterans Center
835 3rd Ave, Chula Vista (91911-1352)
PHONE 619 409-1600
Harvey Souza, *Manager*
EMP: 264 **Publicly Held**
WEB: www.veterans-ru.org
SIC: **8011** 9451 Medical centers; psychiatric clinic;
HQ: Veterans Health Administration
810 Vermont Ave Nw
Washington DC 20420

(P-20210)
VETERANS HEALTH ADMINISTRATION
Also Called: Escondido Veterans Center
815 E Pennsylvania Ave, Escondido (92025-3424)
PHONE 760 745-2000
Jamie Switzer, *Principal*
EMP: 264 **Publicly Held**
WEB: www.veterans-ru.org
SIC: **8011** 9451 Medical centers; psychiatric clinic;
HQ: Veterans Health Administration
810 Vermont Ave Nw
Washington DC 20420

(P-20211)
VETERANS HEALTH ADMINISTRATION
Also Called: Oxnard Veterans Center
250 Citrus Grove Ln # 250, Oxnard (93036-9030)
PHONE 805 983-6384
Josie Esporga, *Manager*
EMP: 263 **Publicly Held**
WEB: www.veterans-ru.org
SIC: **8011** 9451 Medical centers; psychiatric clinic;
HQ: Veterans Health Administration
810 Vermont Ave Nw
Washington DC 20420

(P-20212)
VETERANS HEALTH ADMINISTRATION
Also Called: Santa Rosa Clinic
3315 Chanate Rd, Santa Rosa (95404-1736)
PHONE 707 570-3800
Donald B Dean, *Manager*
EMP: 264 **Publicly Held**
WEB: www.veterans-ru.org
SIC: **8011** 9451 Clinic, operated by physicians; psychiatric clinic;
HQ: Veterans Health Administration
810 Vermont Ave Nw
Washington DC 20420

(P-20213)
VETERANS HEALTH ADMINISTRATION
Also Called: Sacramento V A Medical Center
10535 Hospital Way, Mather (95655-4200)
PHONE 916 843-7000
Lawrence Sandlers, *Director*
John A Mendoza, *COO*
James Wiedeman, *Managing Dir*
EMP: 500 **Publicly Held**
WEB: www.veterans-ru.org
SIC: **8011** 9451 Medical centers; administration of veterans' affairs;
HQ: Veterans Health Administration
810 Vermont Ave Nw
Washington DC 20420

(P-20214)
VETERANS HEALTH ADMINISTRATION
Also Called: Livermore VA Medical Center
4951 Arroyo Rd, Livermore (94550-9650)
PHONE 925 447-2560
Fax: 925 455-7477
C H Nixon, *Director*
Steven Chinn, *Director*

Shakeel Khader, *Director*
Ellen Shibata, *Manager*
EMP: 450 **Publicly Held**
WEB: www.veterans-ru.org
SIC: **8011** 9451 Medical centers;
HQ: Veterans Health Administration
810 Vermont Ave Nw
Washington DC 20420

(P-20215)
VETERANS HEALTH ADMINISTRATION
Also Called: Loma Linda Healthcare Sys 605
11201 Benton St, Loma Linda (92357-1000)
PHONE 909 825-7084
Debbie Romero, *Branch Mgr*
Traian Cojocaru,
Dwight Evans, *Vice Pres*
Dean Stordahl, *Administration*
Lucy Rebuck, *CIO*
EMP: 2000 **Publicly Held**
WEB: www.veterans-ru.org
SIC: **8011** 9451 Medical centers; psychiatric clinic;
HQ: Veterans Health Administration
810 Vermont Ave Nw
Washington DC 20420

(P-20216)
VETERANS HEALTH ADMINISTRATION
Also Called: Menlo Park VA Medical Center
795 Willow Rd, Menlo Park (94025-2539)
PHONE 650 614-9997
Lisa Freeman, *Director*
Peter Rudd, *Research*
Harlan Pinto, *Oncology*
EMP: 3000 **Publicly Held**
WEB: www.veterans-ru.org
SIC: **8011** 9451 Medical centers; psychiatric clinic;
HQ: Veterans Health Administration
810 Vermont Ave Nw
Washington DC 20420

(P-20217)
VETERANS HEALTH ADMINISTRATION
Also Called: VA HSR&d Center of Excellence
16111 Plummer St, North Hills (91343-2036)
PHONE 818 895-9449
Fax: 818 895-5838
Lisa Rubenstein, *Branch Mgr*
Roger Sevrin, *Research*
Sharon Viosca, *Research*
EMP: 99 **Publicly Held**
WEB: www.veterans-ru.org
SIC: **8011** 9451 Medical centers; administration of veterans' affairs;
HQ: Veterans Health Administration
810 Vermont Ave Nw
Washington DC 20420

(P-20218)
VETERANS HEALTH ADMINISTRATION
Also Called: Anaheim V A Clinic
1801 W Romneya Dr Ste 303, Anaheim (92801-1825)
PHONE 714 780-5400
Teresa Carpenter, *Branch Mgr*
Teresa M Carpenter, *Nurse Practr*
EMP: 183 **Publicly Held**
WEB: www.veterans-ru.org
SIC: **8011** 9451 Clinic, operated by physicians; administration of veterans' affairs;
HQ: Veterans Health Administration
810 Vermont Ave Nw
Washington DC 20420

(P-20219)
VETERANS HEALTH ADMINISTRATION
Also Called: Bakersfield Community Based
1801 Westwind Dr, Bakersfield (93301-3028)
PHONE 661 632-1871
Fax: 661 632-1888

Joan Van Horn, *Manager*
Brent H Petersen, *Social Worker*
EMP: 50 **Publicly Held**
WEB: www.veterans-ru.org
SIC: **8011** 9451 Clinic, operated by physicians; psychiatric clinic;
HQ: Veterans Health Administration
810 Vermont Ave Nw
Washington DC 20420

(P-20220)
VETERANS HEALTH ADMINISTRATION
Also Called: Los Angles Ambulatory Care Ctr
351 E Temple St, Los Angeles (90012-3328)
PHONE 213 253-2677
Fax: 213 253-5510
Lane Turzan, *General Mgr*
Elias Paikal, *Managing Dir*
Kitty Koepping, *Administration*
David Woodley, *Med Doctor*
EMP: 190 **Publicly Held**
WEB: www.veterans-ru.org
SIC: **8011** 9451 Medical centers; psychiatric clinic;
HQ: Veterans Health Administration
810 Vermont Ave Nw
Washington DC 20420

(P-20221)
VETERANS HEALTH ADMINISTRATION
Also Called: Bakersfield Vet Center
1110 Golden Valley Fwy, Bakersfield (93301)
PHONE 661 323-8387
Jenney Frank, *Office Mgr*
EMP: 264 **Publicly Held**
SIC: **8011** 9451 Medical centers; psychiatric clinic;
HQ: Veterans Health Administration
810 Vermont Ave Nw
Washington DC 20420

(P-20222)
VETERINARY SURGICAL ASSOCIATES
251 N Amphlett Blvd, San Mateo (94401-1805)
PHONE 650 696-8196
Fax: 650 696-8191
Sharon Ullman, *Manager*
Vanessa Cipriani, *Marketing Staff*
EMP: 60
SALES (corp-wide): 16.7MM **Privately Held**
SIC: **8011** 0742 Freestanding emergency medical center; surgeon; veterinarian, animal specialties
PA: Veterinary Surgical Associates
1410 Monu Blvd Ste 100
Concord CA 94520
925 827-1777

(P-20223)
VIA CARE CMNTY HLTH CTR INC
Also Called: Bienvenidos Community Hlth Ctr
507 S Atlantic Blvd, Los Angeles (90022-2621)
PHONE 323 268-9191
Deborah Villar, *CEO*
Joe Gotsill, *CFO*
EMP: 60
SALES: 2MM **Privately Held**
SIC: **8011** Primary care medical clinic

(P-20224)
VICTOR CORSIGLIA MD
625 Lincoln Ave, San Jose (95126-3785)
PHONE 408 278-3210
Victor Corsiglia MD, *Owner*
EMP: 65
SALES (est): 1.3MM **Privately Held**
SIC: **8011** General & family practice, physician/surgeon

8011 - Offices & Clinics Of Doctors Of Medicine County (P-20225)

(P-20225)
VINOD KUMAR MD
5020 Commerce Dr, Bakersfield (93309-0631)
P.O. Box 1351 (93302-1351)
PHONE..................661 324-4100
Vinod Kumar, *Owner*
EMP: 75
SALES (est): 468.1K **Privately Held**
SIC: 8011 Cardiologist & cardio-vascular specialist

(P-20226)
VISALIA MEDICAL CLINIC INC (PA)
Also Called: Multi Specialty Medical Svc
5400 W Hillsdale Ave, Visalia (93291-5140)
PHONE..................559 733-5222
Fax: 559 625-2581
Richard E Strid, *CEO*
Arthur Desch, *CFO*
Susan Rasmussen, *Executive*
Rebecca Enos, *Office Mgr*
Pico Griffith, *Office Mgr*
EMP: 159
SQ FT: 70,000
SALES (est): 45.7MM **Privately Held**
SIC: 8011 8071 Clinic, operated by physicians; medical laboratories

(P-20227)
VISION CARE CENTER (PA)
Also Called: Vision Care Center Central Cal
7075 N Sharon Ave, Fresno (93720-3329)
PHONE..................559 486-2000
Julie Cleeland, *CEO*
Ralph Hadley Od, *President*
Michael Herman, *CFO*
Lavonne Gordon, *General Mgr*
Kristen Jone, *Persnl Dir*
EMP: 82 EST: 1963
SQ FT: 18,000
SALES (est): 11MM **Privately Held**
WEB: www.eyeqvc.com
SIC: 8011 8042 Ophthalmologist; offices & clinics of optometrists

(P-20228)
WASHINGTON OUTPATIENT
Also Called: Washington Otptent Surgery Ctr
2299 Mowry Ave Fl 1, Fremont (94538-1621)
PHONE..................510 791-5374
Fax: 510 790-8916
Gary Charland, *Partner*
Scott Ashby, *CFO*
Zoe Adams, *Administration*
Kimberly Hartz,
Neil Marks,
EMP: 97
SQ FT: 18,000
SALES (est): 17.2MM **Privately Held**
WEB: www.washosc.com
SIC: 8011 Ambulatory surgical center

(P-20229)
WATTS HEALTHCARE CORPORATION
700 W Imperial Hwy, Los Angeles (90044-4127)
PHONE..................323 241-1780
EMP: 154
SALES (corp-wide): 32.8MM **Privately Held**
SIC: 8011 Medical centers
PA: Watts Healthcare Corporation
10300 Compton Ave
Los Angeles CA 90002
323 568-3059

(P-20230)
WATTS HEALTHCARE CORPORATION (PA)
10300 Compton Ave, Los Angeles (90002-3628)
PHONE..................323 568-3059
William Hobson, *President*
Carroll J McNeely, *CFO*
Hara Yohannes, *Vice Pres*
Roderick N Seamster, *Principal*
Dana Knoll, *Admin Dir*
EMP: 146
SALES: 32.8MM **Privately Held**
WEB: www.wattshealthcare.com
SIC: 8011 Medical centers

(P-20231)
WAVE PLASTIC SURGERY CTR INC
18433 Colima Rd, La Puente (91748-5815)
PHONE..................626 964-7788
Peter Lee, *President*
EMP: 324
SALES (corp-wide): 14.6MM **Privately Held**
SIC: 8011 Surgeon
PA: Wave Plastic Surgery Center Inc.
3680 Wilshire Blvd Fl 2
Los Angeles CA 90010
213 383-4800

(P-20232)
WAYNE R KIDDER
915 Via Los Padres, Santa Barbara (93111-1325)
PHONE..................805 967-6993
Wayne R Kidder, *Owner*
EMP: 80
SALES (est): 3.6MM **Privately Held**
SIC: 8011 Offices & clinics of medical doctors

(P-20233)
WEST COAST CHILDRENS CENTER
545 Ashbury Ave, El Cerrito (94530-3220)
PHONE..................510 269-9030
Fax: 510 527-2013
Dr Stacey Kath, *Exec Dir*
Dr Kenneth Parker, *Exec Dir*
EMP: 50
SALES (est): 11.4MM **Privately Held**
SIC: 8011 8322 8049 Clinic, operated by physicians; social worker; clinical psychologist

(P-20234)
WEST COUNTY HEALTH CENTERS INC
Also Called: Occidental Area Health Center
16312 3rd St, Guerneville (95446)
P.O. Box 1449 (95446-1449)
PHONE..................707 869-2849
Mary Szecsey, *Exec Dir*
John Kornfeld, *President*
Dwight Cary, *Treasurer*
Debra Johnson, *Vice Pres*
Deette M Deville, *Med Doctor*
EMP: 75
SALES (est): 7.7MM **Privately Held**
WEB: www.wchealth.org
SIC: 8011 Primary care medical clinic

(P-20235)
WEST COVINA MEDICAL CLINIC INC (PA)
1500 W Covina Pkwy, West Covina (91790-2708)
PHONE..................626 960-8614
Fax: 626 960-3726
Ziad Dabuni, *President*
Dr Ziad Dabuni, *President*
Dr Suntheetha Ali, *Treasurer*
Ali Suntheetha, *Treasurer*
Dr Shivani Shah, *Exec VP*
EMP: 222 EST: 1950
SQ FT: 50,000
SALES (est): 15.7MM **Privately Held**
SIC: 8011 Clinic, operated by physicians

(P-20236)
WEST VENTURA FAMILY CARE CTR
Also Called: Rocha, Jill B MD
133 W Santa Clara St, Ventura (93001-2543)
PHONE..................805 641-5620
Joan E Baumer MD, *Owner*
EMP: 54
SALES (est): 2.3MM **Privately Held**
SIC: 8011 General & family practice, physician/surgeon

(P-20237)
WESTERN MED ASSOC MED GROUP (PA)
1595 Soquel Dr Ste 330, Santa Cruz (95065-1722)
PHONE..................831 475-1111
Fax: 831 475-0351

Robert D Keet MD, *Principal*
Statish Chandra MD, *Principal*
Vernon Loverde MD, *Principal*
Deedee Riccabona, *Director*
EMP: 60
SALES: 7.5MM **Privately Held**
SIC: 8011 Internal medicine, physician/surgeon

(P-20238)
WHITAKER WELNESS INSTITUTE IN
4321 Birch St Ste 100, Newport Beach (92660-1940)
PHONE..................949 851-1550
Fax: 949 851-9970
Julian Whitaker, *President*
Juliet Gulpo, *Financial Exec*
Rebecca Cawley, *Human Res Mgr*
Erin Nelson, *Marketing Mgr*
Connie Whitaker, *Marketing Staff*
EMP: 60
SQ FT: 8,500
SALES (est): 8.5MM **Privately Held**
WEB: www.whitakerwellness.com
SIC: 8011 Cardiologist & cardio-vascular specialist; diabetes specialist, physician/surgeon

(P-20239)
WHITE MEMORIAL MED GROUP INC (PA)
1701 E Cesar E Chavez Ave # 510, Los Angeles (90033-2464)
P.O. Box 51741 (90051-6041)
PHONE..................323 987-1300
Fax: 323 224-2068
Alan Lau, *President*
Janell Chun, *Administration*
Erlen L Spencer-Smith, *Obstetrician*
Jacob K Jones, *Podiatrist*
James B De Leon, *Physician Asst*
EMP: 71
SQ FT: 20,000
SALES (est): 9.6MM **Privately Held**
SIC: 8011 8742 Medical centers; hospital & health services consultant

(P-20240)
WILLIAM H WARDEN III MD
2760 Atlantic Ave, Long Beach (90806-2755)
PHONE..................562 424-6666
William Warden, *Principal*
EMP: 75
SALES (est): 1.3MM **Privately Held**
SIC: 8011 General & family practice, physician/surgeon

(P-20241)
ZEITER EYE MEDICAL GROUP INC (PA)
255 E Weber Ave, Stockton (95202-2706)
PHONE..................209 366-0446
Fax: 209 466-0535
John H Zeiter MD, *President*
Joseph Zeiter MD, *CFO*
Henry J Zeiter MD, *Vice Pres*
Gennine Gritch, *Executive*
Erin K McCarthy, *Office Mgr*
EMP: 54
SQ FT: 11,500
SALES (est): 10.1MM **Privately Held**
WEB: www.zeitereye.com
SIC: 8011 Ophthalmologist

8021 Offices & Clinics Of Dentists

(P-20242)
ACCESS DENTAL PLAN (PA)
Also Called: Access Dental Centers
8890 Cal Center Dr, Sacramento (95826-3200)
PHONE..................916 922-5000
Reza M Abbaszadeh, *President*
Teri Abbaszadeh, *President*
Hideo Kakiuchi, *CFO*
Charlotte Quider, *Admin Asst*
Miguel Mariona, *Training Spec*
▲ EMP: 70
SQ FT: 4,700
SALES (est): 9.2MM **Privately Held**
SIC: 8021 Dental clinics & offices

(P-20243)
ADVANCED HM HLTH & HOSPICE INC
Also Called: Advanced Home House
4370 Auburn Blvd, Sacramento (95841-4107)
PHONE..................916 978-0744
Angela Sehr, *CEO*
Deb Ryan, *Asst Admin*
EMP: 100
SALES (est): 1.6MM **Privately Held**
SIC: 8021 Group & corporate practice dentists

(P-20244)
AMERICAN DNTL PARTNERS OF CAL
Also Called: Rouche O Edgar DDS
7251 Magnolia Ave, Riverside (92504-3811)
PHONE..................951 689-5031
Greg Serrao, *CEO*
Bill Koffler, *Opers Staff*
Edgar Rouhe, *Manager*
EMP: 165
SQ FT: 9,700
SALES (est): 2.8MM **Privately Held**
SIC: 8021 Dentists' office

(P-20245)
AMPLA HEALTH (PA)
935 Market St, Yuba City (95991-4217)
PHONE..................530 674-4261
Fax: 530 674-4269
Benjamin Flores, *CEO*
Hilton Perez, *COO*
Dale Johnson, *CFO*
Baldev Singh, *Bd of Directors*
Anna Gomez, *Executive Asst*
EMP: 245
SQ FT: 10,200
SALES: 43.4MM **Privately Held**
SIC: 8021 8011 Dental clinic; health maintenance organization; primary care medical clinic; pediatrician

(P-20246)
ANTHONY P GAROFALO A DENTAL
Also Called: Horizon Dental Grp
742 Broadway, El Cajon (92021-4630)
PHONE..................619 440-0071
Fax: 619 440-0719
Anthony P Garofalo, *President*
EMP: 60
SALES (est): 4.8MM **Privately Held**
WEB: www.horizondentalgroup.com
SIC: 8021 Dentists' office

(P-20247)
BUSINESS AND SUPPORT SERVICES
Camp Pendleton Mc Base, Oceanside (92055)
P.O. Box 555221, Camp Pendleton (92055-5221)
PHONE..................760 725-5187
EMP: 320 **Publicly Held**
WEB: www.mccssc.com
SIC: 8021 9711 Offices & clinics of dentists; Marine Corps;
HQ: Business And Support Services
3044 Catlin Ave
Quantico VA 22134
703 432-0109

(P-20248)
CASTLE DENTAL
Also Called: South Gate Dental Group
4433 Tweedy Blvd, South Gate (90280-6303)
PHONE..................323 567-1227
Fax: 323 567-1227
Elliott Schlang DDS, *Manager*
EMP: 50 EST: 1978
SALES (est): 1.6MM **Privately Held**
SIC: 8021 Specialized dental practitioners

(P-20249)
CHILDRENS HOSPITAL LOS ANGELES
7891 Talbert Ave Ste 103, Huntington Beach (92648-8613)
PHONE..................714 841-4990

PRODUCTS & SERVICES SECTION
8021 - Offices & Clinics Of Dentists County (P-20272)

Richard P Mungo DDS, *President*
EMP: 506
SQ FT: 100
SALES (corp-wide): 891.3MM **Privately Held**
SIC: 8021 Dentists' office
PA: The Childrens Hospital Los Angeles
4650 W Sunset Blvd
Los Angeles CA 90027
323 660-2450

(P-20250)
CLINICA SIERRA VISTA
441 Diaz Ave, Delano (93215-4121)
PHONE 661 725-3882
EMP: 102
SALES (corp-wide): 119.8MM **Privately Held**
SIC: 8021 Offices & clinics of dentists
PA: Clinica Sierra Vista
1430 Truxtun Ave Ste 400
Bakersfield CA 93301
661 635-3050

(P-20251)
CUPERTINO DENTAL GROUP
Also Called: Frangadakis, Kenneth DDS
10383 Torre Ave Ste I, Cupertino (95014-3297)
PHONE 408 446-4353
Fax: 408 257-5842
Ken Frangadakis, *Partner*
Gary E Pagonis, *Partner*
Milton J Pagonis, *Partner*
EMP: 53
SQ FT: 4,000
SALES (est): 3.7MM **Privately Held**
SIC: 8021 Dentists' office

(P-20252)
DHS MEMBER SERVICES
3833 Atlantic Ave, Long Beach (90807-3505)
PHONE 562 595-5151
Godfrey Pernell, *Principal*
Robert Tillery, *Vice Pres*
EMP: 50
SALES (est): 833.9K **Privately Held**
SIC: 8021 Dental insurance plan

(P-20253)
ELIAS ELLIOTT LAMPASI FEHN (PA)
7251 Magnolia Ave, Riverside (92504-3811)
PHONE 951 689-5031
Fax: 909 352-2048
Douglass R Gerald, *CEO*
Jay Elliot, *Vice Pres*
Bill Kofler, *Executive*
Dee Elias, *Admin Sec*
Paula D Medlin, *Manager*
EMP: 59
SALES (est): 4MM **Privately Held**
WEB: www.riversidedentalgroup.com
SIC: 8021 Dentists' office

(P-20254)
FAMILY HLTH CTRS SAN DIEGO INC
1809 National Ave, San Diego (92113-2113)
PHONE 619 515-2300
Fax: 619 237-1856
Brian Woolford MD, *Director*
Julia Licea, *COO*
Raul Fortunet, *Program Mgr*
Jamae Marcinko, *Program Mgr*
Thyda Son, *Executive Asst*
EMP: 62
SALES (corp-wide): 125.5MM **Privately Held**
SIC: 8021 Offices & clinics of dentists
PA: Family Health Centers Of San Diego, Inc.
823 Gateway Center Way
San Diego CA 92102
619 515-2303

(P-20255)
GENTLE DENTAL SERVICE CORP (HQ)
9800 S La Cienega Blvd # 800, Inglewood (90301-4440)
PHONE 310 765-2400
Fax: 310 765-2456
Fred Vanerden, *CFO*
Cedric Tuck-Sherman, *VP Mktg*
EMP: 199
SALES (est): 776.8K
SALES (corp-wide): 2.2B **Privately Held**
SIC: 8021 Offices & clinics of dentists
PA: H.I.G. Capital, L.L.C.
1450 Brickell Ave Fl 31
Miami FL 33131
305 379-2322

(P-20256)
INTERDENT INC (HQ)
Also Called: Smile Keepers
9800 S La Cienega Blvd # 800, Inglewood (90301-4442)
PHONE 310 765-2400
Ivar S Chhina, *President*
Scott Bremen, *COO*
Robert W Hill, *CFO*
Scott R McCloud, *CFO*
Karen Feldman, *Vice Pres*
EMP: 55
SQ FT: 10,000
SALES (est): 116.3MM **Privately Held**
SIC: 8021 Dentists' office
PA: H.I.G. Middle Market Llc
1 Market Spear Tower 18f
San Francisco CA 94105
415 439-5500

(P-20257)
INTERDENT SERVICE CORPORATION (DH)
9800 S La Cienega Blvd # 800, Inglewood (90301-4442)
PHONE 310 765-2400
John Stenbrun, *CEO*
Jeff Hertzig, *CFO*
Kevin Webb, *Senior VP*
Michelle Kahan, *Vice Pres*
Traci Klein, *Business Mgr*
EMP: 50
SQ FT: 10,000
SALES (est): 60.6MM
SALES (corp-wide): 116.3MM **Privately Held**
SIC: 8021 Dental clinics & offices
HQ: Interdent, Inc.
9800 S La Cienega Blvd # 800
Inglewood CA 90301
310 765-2400

(P-20258)
JOHN J MAGUIRE DDS
Also Called: Fremont Dental Group
39340 Fremont Blvd, Fremont (94538-1320)
PHONE 213 740-6462
John J Maguire DDS, *Owner*
EMP: 100
SALES (est): 4.6MM **Privately Held**
WEB: www.fremontdentalgroup.com
SIC: 8021 Offices & clinics of dentists

(P-20259)
LA CLINICA DE LA RAZA INC
3050 E 16th St, Oakland (94601-2319)
PHONE 510 535-4700
Magnolia Rios, *Office Mgr*
Edward Rothman,
EMP: 254
SQ FT: 5,208
SALES (corp-wide): 74.4MM **Privately Held**
SIC: 8021 Offices & clinics of dentists
PA: La Clinica De La Raza, Inc.
1450 Fruitvale Ave Fl 3
Oakland CA 94601
510 535-4000

(P-20260)
LA CLINICA DE LA RAZA INC
Also Called: Laclinica
337 E Leland Rd, Pittsburg (94565-4911)
PHONE 925 431-1250
EMP: 444
SALES (corp-wide): 74.4MM **Privately Held**
SIC: 8021 Dental clinic
PA: La Clinica De La Raza, Inc.
1450 Fruitvale Ave Fl 3
Oakland CA 94601
510 535-4000

(P-20261)
LAKE CNTY TRBAL HLTH CNSORTIUM
925 Bevins Ct, Lakeport (95453-9754)
P.O. Box 1950 (95453-1950)
PHONE 707 263-8382
Mike Icay, *President*
Crista Ray, *Ch of Bd*
Tanya Michel, *CFO*
Tina Ramos, *Chairman*
Priscilla Ballente, *Treasurer*
EMP: 80
SQ FT: 10,832
SALES (est): 13.7MM **Privately Held**
WEB: www.lcthc.org
SIC: 8021 Dental clinic

(P-20262)
LAKEWOOD CERRITOS DENTAL CTR
5819 Adenmoor Ave, Lakewood (90713-1067)
PHONE 562 860-0388
Fax: 562 860-8643
Kosmas Pappas DDS, *Owner*
EMP: 100
SQ FT: 5,600
SALES (est): 4.1MM **Privately Held**
WEB: www.doctorlopez.com
SIC: 8021 Dentists' office

(P-20263)
LINDHURST DENTAL CLINIC
4941 Olivehurst Ave, Olivehurst (95961-4225)
PHONE 530 743-4614
Sally Moore, *Manager*
Karen D Aquino, *Internal Med*
EMP: 50
SQ FT: 13,712
SALES (est): 1.5MM **Privately Held**
SIC: 8021 Dental clinic

(P-20264)
MICHAEL P BYKO DDS A PROF CORP (PA)
164 W Hospitality Ln # 14, San Bernardino (92408-3316)
PHONE 909 888-7817
Michael Boyko, *President*
Karen Hatami, *Fmly & Gen Dent*
Karin Johnsen, *Fmly & Gen Dent*
Wesley Okumura, *Fmly & Gen Dent*
Heather Dunham, *Manager*
◆ **EMP:** 60
SQ FT: 3,000
SALES (est): 4.8MM **Privately Held**
SIC: 8021 Dentists' office; orthodontist

(P-20265)
MONTEREY DENTAL GROUP
333 El Dorado St, Monterey (93940-4606)
PHONE 831 373-3068
Rick Baldwin, *Principal*
Mark Bayless, *Partner*
Arthur Benoit, *Partner*
S Bhaskar, *Partner*
P Breuleux, *Partner*
EMP: 55
SQ FT: 13,330
SALES (est): 2.2MM **Privately Held**
WEB: www.quantified.com
SIC: 8021 Dentists' office

(P-20266)
MONTEREY PENINSULA DNTL GROUP
333 El Dorado St, Monterey (93940-4645)
PHONE 831 373-3068
Ronald Faia, *Partner*
J Mark Baliff, *Partner*
S N Bashcor, *Partner*
John Faia III, *Partner*
Mick Falkel, *Partner*
EMP: 60
SQ FT: 13,000
SALES (est): 3.7MM **Privately Held**
WEB: www.mpdg.org
SIC: 8021 Group & corporate practice dentists

(P-20267)
NORTHERN VLY INDIAN HLTH INC
845 W East Ave, Chico (95926-2002)
PHONE 530 896-9400
Fax: 530 896-9407
Maureen Self, *Manager*
Noel Phares, *General Mgr*
Andrew B Miller, *Family Practiti*
Hung Y Wu, *Med Doctor*
Denise L Green, *Fmly & Gen Dent*
EMP: 125
SALES (corp-wide): 29.9MM **Privately Held**
WEB: www.nvih.org
SIC: 8021 8011 Dental clinic; primary care medical clinic
PA: Northern Valley Indian Health, Inc.
207 N Butte St
Willows CA
530 934-9293

(P-20268)
NORTHERN VLY INDIAN HLTH INC
2500 Main St, Red Bluff (96080-2336)
PHONE 530 529-2567
Robin Brownfield, *Manager*
Larissa Tamble, *Director*
EMP: 62
SALES (corp-wide): 29.9MM **Privately Held**
SIC: 8021 Offices & clinics of dentists
PA: Northern Valley Indian Health, Inc.
207 N Butte St
Willows CA
530 934-9293

(P-20269)
PACIFIC DENTAL SERVICES INC (PA)
Also Called: Pds
17000 Red Hill Ave, Irvine (92614-5626)
P.O. Box 19723 (92623-9723)
PHONE 714 845-8500
Stephen E Thorne IV, *CEO*
Brady Ace, *CFO*
Dan Burke, *Senior VP*
Joe Feldsien, *Senior VP*
Jon Thorne, *Senior VP*
EMP: 300
SQ FT: 40,000
SALES (est): 344.2MM **Privately Held**
WEB: www.pacificdentalservices.com
SIC: 8021 6794 Offices & clinics of dentists; franchises, selling or licensing

(P-20270)
PETER WYLAN DDS
Also Called: Bellflower Dental Group
10318 Rosecrans Ave, Bellflower (90706-2702)
PHONE 562 925-3765
Fax: 562 925-2465
Peter Wylan DDS, *Owner*
EMP: 100
SQ FT: 2,000
SALES (est): 4.2MM **Privately Held**
WEB: www.peterwylandds.net
SIC: 8021 8072 Dentists' office; orthodontist; dental laboratories

(P-20271)
PROVIDENCE HEALTH & SERVICES
11570 Indian Hills Rd, Mission Hills (91345-1238)
PHONE 818 898-4445
EMP: 52
SALES (corp-wide): 10.1B **Privately Held**
SIC: 8021 Offices & clinics of dentists
PA: Providence Health & Services
1801 Lind Ave Sw
Renton WA 98057
425 525-3355

(P-20272)
RANCHO NIGUEL DENTAL GROUP
30140 Town Center Dr, Laguna Niguel (92677-2037)
PHONE 949 249-4180
Steve Krieger,
Gina Martin, *Financial Exec*
Gary Mar, *Fmly & Gen Dent*

8021 - Offices & Clinics Of Dentists County (P-20273)

Rodney Boyd,
Hugh Murray,
EMP: 50
SALES (est): 2MM **Privately Held**
SIC: 8021 Dental clinic

(P-20273)
ROISMAN LEON D DMD INC
Also Called: Dental Plus Dental Group
310 S Lake Ave Ste B1, Pasadena (91101-3540)
PHONE 626 795-6855
Fax: 626 432-4260
Leon D Roisman DMD, *President*
Tracy Stallings, *Manager*
EMP: 60
SALES (est): 3.8MM **Privately Held**
SIC: 8021 Dentists' office

(P-20274)
SAC HEALTH SYSTEM (PA)
1455 3rd Ave, San Bernardino (92408-0218)
PHONE 909 382-7100
Fax: 909 382-7101
Richard H Hart MD, *President*
George Cencel, *CFO*
Barry Randolph, *Opers Staff*
Donna S Burgess, *Manager*
EMP: 62
SALES: 14.4MM **Privately Held**
SIC: 8021 8011 8093 Offices & clinics of dentists; offices & clinics of medical doctors; mental health clinic, outpatient

(P-20275)
SANTA ROSA DENTAL GROUP
1820 Sonoma Ave Ste 80, Santa Rosa (95405-6617)
PHONE 707 545-0944
Allen Barbieri, *Partner*
Perry Bingham, *Partner*
Richard L Blechel, *Partner*
James J Bridges, *Partner*
Ted Degolia, *Partner*
EMP: 64
SQ FT: 8,000
SALES (est): 3MM **Privately Held**
SIC: 8021 Dentists' office

(P-20276)
SCHNIEROW DENTAL CARE
Also Called: Piehl, Joel J DDS
13450 Hawthorne Blvd, Hawthorne (90250-5806)
PHONE 310 377-6453
Fax: 310 679-6698
Burton Schnierow DDS, *President*
Rasool Patel, *Fmly & Gen Dent*
EMP: 50
SQ FT: 3,200
SALES (est): 4MM **Privately Held**
SIC: 8021 Dentists' office

(P-20277)
SCOTT JACKS DDS INC
Also Called: Adult & Childrens Dental Group
4444 Tweedy Blvd, South Gate (90280-6392)
PHONE 323 564-2444
Scott Jacks, *CEO*
Marsha Jacks, *Admin Sec*
EMP: 111
SQ FT: 9,375
SALES (est): 7.5MM **Privately Held**
SIC: 8021 Dentists' office

(P-20278)
ST JOHNS WELL CHILD (PA)
Also Called: Saint John's Well Child Center
808 W 58th St, Los Angeles (90037-3632)
PHONE 323 541-1600
Fax: 213 749-7354
James J Mangia, *CEO*
Corazon Alcand, *CFO*
Liz Meisler, *CFO*
Ta'mara Tobin, *Executive*
Betty Horta, *Admin Sec*
EMP: 89
SALES (est): 29.1MM **Privately Held**
WEB: www.wellchild.org
SIC: 8021 8011 Dental clinic; offices & clinics of medical doctors

(P-20279)
THURSTON MARTIN H DDS MS
11616 Iberia Pl, San Diego (92128-2404)
PHONE 858 676-5010
Martin Thurston, *Principal*
EMP: 50
SALES (est): 1.4MM **Privately Held**
SIC: 8021 Orthodontist

(P-20280)
TOIYABE INDIAN HEALTH PRJ INC (PA)
250 N See Vee Ln, Bishop (93514-8130)
PHONE 760 873-8461
Fax: 760 873-3935
David Lent, *CEO*
Libby Watanabe, *COO*
Michael Franks, *CFO*
Monty Bengochia, *Chairman*
Katherine A Huber, *Officer*
EMP: 86
SQ FT: 66,300
SALES: 13.9MM **Privately Held**
WEB: www.toiyabe.us
SIC: 8021 8011 Dental clinic; clinic, operated by physicians; psychiatric clinic

(P-20281)
U C S F SCHOOL OF DENTISTRY
Also Called: Buchanan Dental Center
100 Buchanan St, San Francisco (94102-6147)
PHONE 415 476-5609
Mark Kirkland DDS, *Administration*
Chui Chan,
Avelino Silva,
Jyoti S Singh,
Arthur Nakahara, *Director*
EMP: 50
SALES (est): 2MM **Privately Held**
SIC: 8021 Dental clinics & offices

(P-20282)
VALLEY OAK DENTAL GROUP
1507 W Yosemite Ave, Manteca (95337-5182)
PHONE 209 823-9341
Fax: 209 823-7836
Marvin Bledsoe, *President*
Bonnie Morehead DDS, *Corp Secy*
Mark Hochhalter DDS, *Vice Pres*
Daman Saini, *Fmly & Gen Dent*
EMP: 70
SALES (est): 4.3MM **Privately Held**
SIC: 8021 Offices & clinics of dentists; specialized dental practitioners; periodontist; dentists' office

(P-20283)
VETERANS HEALTH ADMINISTRATION
Also Called: Dental
3350 La Jolla Village Dr, San Diego (92161-0002)
PHONE 858 552-7525
Sharon Webb, *QA Dir*
EMP: 264 **Publicly Held**
WEB: www.veterans-ru.org
SIC: 8021 9451 Dental clinic;
HQ: Veterans Health Administration
810 Vermont Ave Nw
Washington DC 20420

(P-20284)
WESTERN DENTAL SERVICES INC
3880 Chicago Ave, Riverside (92507-5354)
PHONE 951 643-6104
EMP: 50
SALES (corp-wide): 340.2MM **Privately Held**
SIC: 8021 Offices & clinics of dentists
PA: Western Dental Services, Inc.
530 S Main St Ste 600
Orange CA 92868
714 480-3000

(P-20285)
WESTERN DENTAL SERVICES INC
8324 Elk Grove Florin Rd # 100, Sacramento (95829-9546)
PHONE 916 509-3350
EMP: 50

SALES (corp-wide): 340.2MM **Privately Held**
SIC: 8021 Offices & clinics of dentists
PA: Western Dental Services, Inc.
530 S Main St Ste 600
Orange CA 92868
714 480-3000

(P-20286)
WESTERN DENTAL SERVICES INC
921 S Main St Ste A, Salinas (93901-2435)
PHONE 831 998-9427
EMP: 50
SALES (corp-wide): 340.2MM **Privately Held**
SIC: 8021 Offices & clinics of dentists
PA: Western Dental Services, Inc.
530 S Main St Ste 600
Orange CA 92868
714 480-3000

(P-20287)
WESTERN DENTAL SERVICES INC (PA)
530 S Main St Ste 600, Orange (92868-4544)
P.O. Box 14227 (92863-1227)
PHONE 714 480-3000
Thomas W Erickson, *CEO*
Samuel H Gruenbaum, *President*
Stu Gray, *COO*
Stuart Gray, *COO*
David Joe, *CFO*
EMP: 350
SALES (est): 340.2MM **Privately Held**
WEB: www.westerndental.com
SIC: 8021 Dentists' office

(P-20288)
WILSHIRE CENTER DENTAL GROUP
3932 Wilshire Blvd # 102, Los Angeles (90010-3334)
PHONE 213 386-3336
Gregory Kaplan, *Owner*
EMP: 50
SQ FT: 7,000
SALES (est): 1.9MM **Privately Held**
SIC: 8021 Offices & clinics of dentists; dental surgeon; orthodontist; pedodontist

8031 Offices & Clinics Of Doctors Of Osteopathy

(P-20289)
FACEY MEDICAL FOUNDATION
2655 1st St, Simi Valley (93065-1547)
PHONE 805 206-2000
EMP: 168
SALES (corp-wide): 197.1MM **Privately Held**
SIC: 8031 8011 Offices & clinics of osteopathic physicians; offices & clinics of medical doctors
PA: Facey Medical Foundation
15451 San Fernando Msn
Mission Hills CA 91345
818 365-9531

(P-20290)
FACEY MEDICAL FOUNDATION
191 S Buena Vista St, Burbank (91505-4554)
PHONE 818 861-7831
Jennifer Sung MD, *Branch Mgr*
EMP: 168
SALES (corp-wide): 197.1MM **Privately Held**
SIC: 8031 8011 Offices & clinics of osteopathic physicians; offices & clinics of medical doctors
PA: Facey Medical Foundation
15451 San Fernando Msn
Mission Hills CA 91345
818 365-9531

(P-20291)
FCS MEDICAL CORPORATION
1701 E Cesar E Chavez Ave # 230, Los Angeles (90033-2464)
PHONE 323 317-9200
Mimi House, *Manager*

EMP: 93
SALES (corp-wide): 15.6MM **Privately Held**
SIC: 8031 8011 Offices & clinics of osteopathic physicians; offices & clinics of medical doctors
PA: Fcs Medical Corporation
5823 York Blvd Ste 1
Los Angeles CA 90042
323 255-1575

(P-20292)
VISTA COMMUNITY CLINIC (PA)
1000 Vale Terrace Dr, Vista (92084-5218)
PHONE 760 631-5000
Fernando Sanudo, *CEO*
Michele Lambert, *CFO*
Gena Knutson, *Program Mgr*
Jeff Nobis, *CIO*
Karla Segura-Perez, *Information Mgr*
EMP: 280
SQ FT: 60,000
SALES: 41.1MM **Privately Held**
WEB: www.vistacommunityclinic.org
SIC: 8031 8011 Offices & clinics of osteopathic physicians; medical centers

(P-20293)
VISTA COMMUNITY CLINIC
134 Grapevine Rd, Vista (92083-4004)
PHONE 760 631-5030
Sonia Jimenez, *Branch Mgr*
Loretta S Stenzel, *Family Practiti*
EMP: 50
SALES (corp-wide): 37.9MM **Privately Held**
SIC: 8031 8011 Offices & clinics of osteopathic physicians; medical centers
PA: Vista Community Clinic
1000 Vale Terrace Dr
Vista CA 92084
760 631-5000

8041 Offices & Clinics Of Chiropractors

(P-20294)
CORNERSTONE MEDICAL GROUP
1881 Commercenter E # 112, San Bernardino (92408-3442)
PHONE 909 890-4353
Fax: 909 890-0196
Steve Mansker, *CEO*
Michelle Van Dyke, *Treasurer*
Mark C Hamilton DC, *Vice Pres*
EMP: 50
SQ FT: 6,000
SALES (est): 1.8MM **Privately Held**
WEB: www.cornerstonemedical.com
SIC: 8041 Offices & clinics of chiropractors

(P-20295)
HAYWARD AREA RECREATION PKDIST
1099 E St, Hayward (94541-5210)
PHONE 510 881-6700
John Gouveia, *General Mgr*
EMP: 100 **Privately Held**
SIC: 8041 Offices & clinics of chiropractors
PA: Hayward Area Recreation & Pk.Dist
1099 E St
Hayward CA 94541
510 670-1665

(P-20296)
JOINT CORP
3713 S Bristol St, Santa Ana (92704-7303)
PHONE 714 294-2846
EMP: 100
SALES (corp-wide): 13.8MM **Publicly Held**
SIC: 8041 6794 Offices & clinics of chiropractors; franchises, selling or licensing
PA: The Joint Corp
16767 N Perimeter Dr # 240
Scottsdale AZ 85260
480 245-5960

PRODUCTS & SERVICES SECTION
8049 - Offices & Clinics Of Health Practitioners, NEC County (P-20318)

(P-20297)
LANDMARK HEALTHCARE SVCS INC (PA)
1610 Arden Way Ste 280, Sacramento (95815-4050)
PHONE................................800 638-4557
George W Vieth Jr, *President*
Priscilla Stevenson, *CFO*
Carol Hillyard, *Executive Asst*
Veronica McAlister, *Executive Asst*
Arla Hoagland, *Admin Asst*
EMP: 120
SQ FT: 330,215
SALES (est): 8MM **Privately Held**
WEB: www.lmhealthcare.com
SIC: 8041 8049 Offices & clinics of chiropractors; acupuncturist

(P-20298)
S CA UNIVERSITY HLTH SCIENCES
Also Called: Los Angles Cllege Chiropractic
P.O. Box 1166 (90609-1166)
PHONE................................562 947-8755
Fax: 562 902-3349
John Scaringe, *Branch Mgr*
EMP: 50
SALES (corp-wide): 26MM **Privately Held**
SIC: 8041 Offices & clinics of chiropractors
PA: S Ca University Of Health Sciences
  16200 Amber Valley Dr
  Whittier CA 90604
  562 947-8755

8042 Offices & Clinics Of Optometrists

(P-20299)
EYECENTER OPTOMETRIC INC
6809 Five Star Blvd # 100, Rocklin (95677-2687)
PHONE................................916 624-2020
Fax: 916 624-3027
Scott Gittins, *President*
Randall Fuerst, *Partner*
Palm Rid, *Partner*
Lisa Lindner, *Financial Exec*
Brenda Coen, *Manager*
EMP: 50
SALES (est): 1.8MM **Privately Held**
SIC: 8042 Offices & clinics of optometrists

(P-20300)
LINDEN OPTOMETRY A PROF CORP
Also Called: Pasadena Vision
477 E Colorado Blvd, Pasadena (91101-2024)
PHONE................................323 681-5678
Allan Linfat, *President*
William J Linden, *Shareholder*
Maria Dalas, *Manager*
EMP: 100
SALES (est): 8.8MM **Privately Held**
SIC: 8042 Offices & clinics of optometrists

(P-20301)
NATIONAL VISION INC
58501 29 Palms Hwy, Yucca Valley (92284-5765)
PHONE................................760 365-7350
EMP: 73
SALES (corp-wide): 1.2B **Privately Held**
SIC: 8042 Offices & clinics of optometrists
PA: National Vision, Inc.
  2435 Commerce Ave # 2200
  Duluth GA 30096
  770 822-3600

(P-20302)
PACIFIC VISION SERVICES INC
1900 E Washington St, Colton (92324-4614)
PHONE................................909 824-6090
Christopher Blanton, *President*
Linda Georgian, *Administration*
EMP: 90
SQ FT: 5,000
SALES (est): 7.4MM **Privately Held**
WEB: www.visioncarebylaser.com
SIC: 8042 Offices & clinics of optometrists

8049 Offices & Clinics Of Health Practitioners, NEC

(P-20303)
A IS FOR APPLE INC
1485 Saratoga Ave Ste 200, San Jose (95129-4965)
PHONE................................877 991-0009
Marilyn Freeman, *President*
John Freeman, *Vice Pres*
EMP: 113
SALES: 6MM **Privately Held**
SIC: 8049 Speech pathologist

(P-20304)
ADDUS HEALTHCARE INC
926 E Cypress Ave Ste 800, Redding (96002-1040)
PHONE................................530 247-0858
Fax: 530 243-5942
Michele Dugar, *Branch Mgr*
Sharon Kreykes, *Administration*
EMP: 80
SALES (corp-wide): 336.8MM **Publicly Held**
WEB: www.addus.com
SIC: 8049 8011 Nurses & other medical assistants; clinic, operated by physicians
HQ: Addus Healthcare, Inc.
  2300 Warrenville Rd
  Downers Grove IL 60515
  630 296-3400

(P-20305)
ALPHAVISTA SERVICES INC
1290 Kifer Rd Ste 301, Sunnyvale (94086-5323)
PHONE................................408 331-2181
Pradeesh Thomas, *President*
Ganesh Shankar, *CFO*
Bijoy Abraham, *Human Resources*
Melissa Blackwell, *Recruiter*
Manoj Krishnan, *Marketing Staff*
EMP: 60
SQ FT: 1,000
SALES (est): 4.3MM **Privately Held**
SIC: 8049 Speech therapist
PA: Pediatric Therapy Services Inc
  1215 E Orange St
  Lakeland FL 33801
  863 802-3800

(P-20306)
AMN HEALTHCARE SERVICES INC
Also Called: American Mobile Healthcare
12400 High Bluff Dr # 100, San Diego (92130-3077)
PHONE................................858 792-0711
Ralph Henderson, *President*
Mario Melendez, *Admin Asst*
Edwards John, *Info Tech Mgr*
David Asbury, *Software Dev*
Jessica Green, *Finance Mgr*
EMP: 750
SALES (corp-wide): 1.4B **Publicly Held**
WEB: www.amnhealthcare.com
SIC: 8049 Physical therapist; nurses & other medical assistants
PA: Amn Healthcare Services, Inc.
  12400 High Bluff Dr
  San Diego CA 92130
  866 871-8519

(P-20307)
BACCI GLINN PHYSCL THERAPY INC
5533 W Hillsdale Ave A, Visalia (93291-5138)
P.O. Box 7779 (93290-7779)
PHONE................................559 733-2478
Fax: 559 733-2470
Robert Bacci, *President*
James Glinn, *Vice Pres*
Marianne Bacci, *Manager*
EMP: 50
SALES (est): 4MM **Privately Held**
SIC: 8049 Physical therapist

(P-20308)
BURGER PHYSCL THERAPY SVCS INC (HQ)
Also Called: Burger Physcl Thrapy Rhbltion
1301 E Bidwell St Ste 201, Folsom (95630-3565)
PHONE................................916 983-5900
Fax: 916 983-5913
Carol Burger, *President*
Elizabeth Johnson, *Human Resources*
Aaron Abrams, *Manager*
EMP: 200
SALES (est): 7.3MM
SALES (corp-wide): 13.4MM **Privately Held**
SIC: 8049 Physical therapist
PA: Burger Rehabilitation Systems, Inc.
  1301 E Bidwell St Ste 201
  Folsom CA 95630
  800 900-8491

(P-20309)
BURGER PHYSICAL THERAPY
1301 E Bidwell St Ste 101, Folsom (95630-3565)
PHONE................................916 983-5900
Carol K Burger, *President*
EMP: 50
SQ FT: 5,800
SALES (est): 1.1MM
SALES (corp-wide): 13.4MM **Privately Held**
SIC: 8049 8093 Physical therapist; rehabilitation center, outpatient treatment; speech defect clinic
PA: Burger Rehabilitation Systems, Inc.
  1301 E Bidwell St Ste 201
  Folsom CA 95630
  800 900-8491

(P-20310)
BURGER RHBLITATION SYSTEMS INC
2101 Stone Blvd Ste 175, West Sacramento (95691-4055)
PHONE................................916 617-2400
EMP: 71
SALES (corp-wide): 13.4MM **Privately Held**
SIC: 8049 Physical therapist
PA: Burger Rehabilitation Systems, Inc.
  1301 E Bidwell St Ste 201
  Folsom CA 95630
  800 900-8491

(P-20311)
BURGER RHBLITATION SYSTEMS INC
6614 Mercy Ct Ste C, Fair Oaks (95628-3167)
PHONE................................916 863-5785
Fax: 916 863-5787
Carol Burger, *Branch Mgr*
Jack Lomba, *Manager*
EMP: 71
SALES (corp-wide): 13.4MM **Privately Held**
SIC: 8049 Physical therapist
PA: Burger Rehabilitation Systems, Inc.
  1301 E Bidwell St Ste 201
  Folsom CA 95630
  800 900-8491

(P-20312)
BURGER RHBLITATION SYSTEMS INC (PA)
1301 E Bidwell St Ste 201, Folsom (95630-3565)
PHONE................................800 900-8491
Fax: 916 983-5925
Carol K Burger, *President*
Eric Burger, *Business Dir*
Jay Rich, *Technician*
Deena Smith, *Recruiter*
Karen Netherton, *Director*
EMP: 200
SQ FT: 5,000
SALES (est): 13.4MM **Privately Held**
SIC: 8049 Occupational therapist; speech specialist; physical therapist

(P-20313)
CENTER FOR AUTISM & (PA)
21600 Oxnard St Ste 1800, Woodland Hills (91367-7807)
PHONE................................818 345-2345
Doreen Granpeesheh, *Director*
Mark Keller, *CFO*
Katharine Gutshall, *Admin Mgr*
Aubrey Nigoza, *Admin Mgr*
Andrew Blazaitis, *Office Admin*
EMP: 143
SALES (est): 53.6MM **Privately Held**
WEB: www.centerforautism.com
SIC: 8049 Clinical psychologist

(P-20314)
COMPREHENSIVE AUTISM CTR INC
7839 University Ave # 105, La Mesa (91942-0476)
PHONE................................951 813-4035
EMP: 64
SALES (corp-wide): 2.5MM **Privately Held**
SIC: 8049 Physical therapist
PA: Comprehensive Autism Center, Inc.
  40485 Mrreta Hot Sprng Rd
  Murrieta CA 92563
  951 813-4034

(P-20315)
EMPERORS CLG TRDTNL ORNTL MDC
Also Called: Emperor's Clge & Clnc Tradtn
1807 Wilshire Blvd Ste B, Santa Monica (90403-5678)
PHONE................................310 453-8383
Fax: 310 829-3838
Yun Kim, *President*
Bong Dal Kim, *Shareholder*
Alisa Daniels, *COO*
Sylvia Ramirez, *CFO*
Jorn Teutloff, *Bd of Directors*
EMP: 90
SQ FT: 10,000
SALES (est): 4.1MM **Privately Held**
SIC: 8049 Acupuncturist

(P-20316)
ENLOE MEDICAL CENTER
Also Called: E E G and E P
560 Cohasset Rd, Chico (95926-2281)
PHONE................................530 332-4111
Fax: 530 332-5104
Joan Lilly, *Principal*
Lisa Brake, *Office Mgr*
Anne K Dawson, *Oncology*
Steven Wahlen, *Oncology*
Marty Marshall, *Director*
EMP: 53
SALES (corp-wide): 505.9MM **Privately Held**
SIC: 8049 Nutrition specialist
PA: Enloe Medical Center
  1531 Esplanade
  Chico CA 95926
  530 332-7300

(P-20317)
ENLOE MEDICAL CENTER
Also Called: Enloe Rehabilitation Center
340 W East Ave, Chico (95926-7238)
PHONE................................530 332-6138
Fax: 530 389-6874
Diane Jones, *Administration*
Amy Alvarez, *Volunteer Dir*
Cindy Wysong, *Admin Asst*
Les Doll, *Opers Mgr*
Linda Angel, *Director*
EMP: 100
SQ FT: 61,571
SALES (corp-wide): 505.9MM **Privately Held**
SIC: 8049 Physical therapist
PA: Enloe Medical Center
  1531 Esplanade
  Chico CA 95926
  530 332-7300

(P-20318)
EQUINOX-76TH STREET INC
Also Called: Health Fitness America
1980 Main St Fl 4, Irvine (92614-7200)
PHONE................................949 975-8400
Fax: 949 251-1336

8049 - Offices & Clinics Of Health Practitioners, NEC County (P-20319)

Ian McFodden, *Manager*
EMP: 300
SALES (corp-wide): 10.6B **Privately Held**
SIC: 8049 7991 Physical therapist; health club
HQ: Equinox-76th Street, Inc.
895 Broadway Fl 3
New York NY 10003
212 677-0180

(P-20319)
FORTA (PA)
Also Called: Fortanasce & Associates
671 W Naomi Ave, Arcadia (91007-7502)
P.O. Box 661150 (91066-1150)
PHONE...........................626 446-7027
Fax: 626 446-4723
Michael Fortanasce, *President*
Alberto Vallejo, *Research*
Lilian Chen,
EMP: 60
SQ FT: 10,250
SALES (est): 3.9MM **Privately Held**
WEB: www.fortanasce.com
SIC: 8049 Physical therapist

(P-20320)
HOLMAN FAMILY COUNSELING INC (PA)
Also Called: Holman Group, The
9451 Corbin Ave Ste 100, Northridge (91324-1662)
PHONE...........................818 704-1444
Ron Holman PHD, *President*
Marcus Sola, *Senior VP*
Jane Galvin, *Vice Pres*
Linda Holman, *Vice Pres*
Pamela Felten, *Executive Asst*
EMP: 66
SQ FT: 40,000
SALES (est): 8.6MM **Privately Held**
SIC: 8049 Clinical psychologist

(P-20321)
INLAND EMPIRE THERAPY PROVIDER (PA)
Also Called: Life Enchancing Therapies
1150 N Mountain Ave # 214, Upland (91786-3668)
PHONE...........................909 985-7905
Fax: 909 985-5904
James W Milton, *President*
EMP: 65
SALES (est): 2MM **Privately Held**
SIC: 8049 Physical therapist; speech therapist; occupational therapist

(P-20322)
INLAND VALLEY PARTNERS LLC
Also Called: INLAND VALLEY CARE & REHAB CTR
250 W Artesia St, Pomona (91768-1807)
PHONE...........................909 623-7100
Robert Nelson,
Sylvia Johnson, *Records Dir*
Elizabeth Casey,
Phil Chase,
Susan Chase,
EMP: 250
SALES: 23.6MM **Privately Held**
SIC: 8049 Nurses & other medical assistants

(P-20323)
INSTITUTE FOR APPLIED BEHAVIOR (PA)
Also Called: Iaba
5777 W Century Blvd # 675, Los Angeles (90045-5600)
PHONE...........................310 649-0499
Fax: 323 649-3109
Gary W Lavigna PHD, *President*
▲ **EMP:** 140
SQ FT: 3,000
SALES (est): 17.3MM **Privately Held**
WEB: www.iaba.com
SIC: 8049 8741 8093 Clinical psychologist; management services; specialty outpatient clinics

(P-20324)
INSTITUTE FOR APPLIED BEHAVIOR
Also Called: Iaba
2301 E Daily Dr Ste 201, Camarillo (93010-6677)
PHONE...........................805 987-5886
Fax: 805 987-7279
Gary Lavigna, *Director*
EMP: 170
SALES (corp-wide): 17.3MM **Privately Held**
WEB: www.iaba.com
SIC: 8049 8399 Clinical psychologist; community development groups
PA: Institute For Applied Behavior Analysis, A Psychological Corporation
5777 W Century Blvd # 675
Los Angeles CA 90045
310 649-0499

(P-20325)
INSTITUTE FOR APPLIED BEHAVIOR
Also Called: Institute Applied Bhvior Anlis
19510 Ventura Blvd # 204, Tarzana (91356-2969)
PHONE...........................818 881-1933
Fax: 818 881-1835
EMP: 61
SALES (corp-wide): 17.3MM **Privately Held**
SIC: 8049 8322 8093
PA: Institute For Applied Behavior Analysis, A Psychological Corporation
5777 W Century Blvd # 675
Los Angeles CA 90045
310 649-0499

(P-20326)
INSTITUTE FOR HEALTH & HEALING
2300 California St # 101, San Francisco (94115-2754)
P.O. Box 7999 (94120-7999)
PHONE...........................415 600-3503
William B Stewart, *Owner*
Bruce A Roberts, *Med Doctor*
EMP: 60
SALES (est): 1.8MM **Privately Held**
SIC: 8049 Nutrition specialist

(P-20327)
INTERCARE THERAPY INC
4221 Wilshire Blvd 300a, Los Angeles (90010-3537)
PHONE...........................323 866-1880
Fax: 323 866-1881
Naomi Heller, *President*
Eri Heller, *Vice Pres*
EMP: 130
SALES (est): 7.1MM **Privately Held**
SIC: 8049 Psychologist, psychotherapist & hypnotist; occupational therapist; speech specialist

(P-20328)
INTERFACE REHAB INC
774 S Placentia Ave # 200, Placentia (92870-6826)
PHONE...........................714 646-8300
Fax: 714 870-1183
Anant B Desai, *CEO*
Falguni Desai, *Admin Sec*
EMP: 657
SQ FT: 10,000
SALES (est): 35.1MM **Privately Held**
WEB: www.interfacerehab.com
SIC: 8049 Physical therapist; speech specialist

(P-20329)
INTERGRO REHAB SERVICE
1922 N Broadway, Santa Ana (92706-2610)
PHONE...........................714 901-4200
Fax: 714 903-9425
Sherrilyn Tong, *President*
Cheryl Young, *Human Res Mgr*
Katie Jeffery, *Opers Staff*
Alia Wilson, *Manager*
EMP: 80
SQ FT: 2,000
SALES (est): 7.2MM **Privately Held**
WEB: www.intergrorehab.com
SIC: 8049 Physical therapist; speech specialist; occupational therapist

(P-20330)
INTERSTATE RHBLTATION SVCS LLC (PA)
333 E Glenoaks Blvd # 204, Glendale (91207-2074)
PHONE...........................818 244-5656
Fax: 818 244-1102
James Pietsch, *Owner*
Beth C Celo, *Vice Pres*
James Peach, *Executive*
Glenn Dabatos, *Opers Staff*
Beth Cera-Celo,
EMP: 100
SALES (est): 6.3MM **Privately Held**
WEB: www.interstaterehab.com
SIC: 8049 Physical therapist

(P-20331)
LOMA LINDA UNIVERSITY
1686 Barton Rd Ste E, Redlands (92373-1489)
PHONE...........................909 558-4934
Lisa Wolter, *Branch Mgr*
EMP: 63
SALES (corp-wide): 848.5MM **Privately Held**
SIC: 8049 8322 Psychotherapist, except M.D.; family counseling services
PA: Loma Linda University
11060 Anderson St
Loma Linda CA 92350
909 558-4540

(P-20332)
MICHAEL G FORTAANASCE PHYS
920 Lohman Ln, South Pasadena (91030-2906)
PHONE...........................323 254-6000
EMP: 60
SALES (est): 3.9MM **Privately Held**
SIC: 8049 8011 Physical therapist; offices & clinics of medical doctors
PA: Fortanasce, Michael G, Physical Therapy, A Professional Corporation
671 W Naomi Ave
Arcadia CA 91007
626 446-7027

(P-20333)
MOUNTAIN VIEW PHYSICAL THERAPY
Also Called: Inland Hand Therapy & Rehab
299 W Fthill Blvd Ste 200, Upland (91786)
PHONE...........................909 949-6235
Fax: 909 985-4694
Catherine Konn, *President*
EMP: 54
SALES (est): 1MM **Privately Held**
SIC: 8049 Physical therapist

(P-20334)
NUTRICION FUNDAMENTAL INC
Also Called: Primetime Nutrition
811 Grand Ave, Sacramento (95838-3466)
PHONE...........................916 922-0150
EMP: 103 **Privately Held**
SIC: 8049 Nutrition specialist
PA: Nutricion Fundamental, Inc.
19315 San Jose Ave
City Of Industry CA 91748

(P-20335)
NVISION LASER EYE CENTERS
24022 Calle De La Plata, Laguna Hills (92653-3626)
PHONE...........................949 951-1457
Norman Peterson, *Branch Mgr*
EMP: 116
SALES (corp-wide): 4MM **Privately Held**
SIC: 8049 Nutrition specialist
PA: Nvision Laser Eye Centers Inc.
75 Enterprise Ste 200
Aliso Viejo CA 92656
877 455-9942

(P-20336)
OROVILLE HOSPITAL
Also Called: Golden Vly Occpational Therapy
2353 Myers St Ste B, Oroville (95966-5390)
PHONE...........................530 538-8700
Fax: 530 538-8703
Trish Hopps, *Branch Mgr*
EMP: 50
SALES (corp-wide): 236.9MM **Privately Held**
SIC: 8049 Physical therapist
PA: Oroville Hospital
2767 Olive Hwy
Oroville CA 95966
530 533-8500

(P-20337)
P C VERICARE
4715 Vewridge Ave Ste 230, San Diego (92123)
PHONE...........................858 454-3610
Thomas Robbins, *CEO*
Joseph M Casciani, *President*
Bennett O Voit, *CFO*
David Zimmermann, *Senior VP*
Alfred Roebuck, *Admin Asst*
EMP: 250
SALES (est): 15MM **Privately Held**
SIC: 8049 Clinical psychologist

(P-20338)
PERMANENTE KAISER INTL
3285 Claremont Way, NAPA (94558-3313)
PHONE...........................707 258-4541
EMP: 85
SALES (corp-wide): 380.5MM **Privately Held**
SIC: 8049 Physical therapist
PA: Kaiser Permanente International
1 Kaiser Plz
Oakland CA 94612
510 271-5910

(P-20339)
PHYSICAL REHABILITATION NETWRK
2833 Junction Ave Ste 206, San Jose (95134-1920)
P.O. Box 612260 (95161-2260)
PHONE...........................408 570-0510
Fax: 408 570-0516
EMP: 50 **Privately Held**
SIC: 8049 8742
PA: Physical Rehabilitation Network
5962 La Place Ct Ste 170
Carlsbad CA 92008

(P-20340)
PHYSICAL REHABILITATION NETWRK (PA)
5962 La Place Ct Ste 170, Carlsbad (92008-8838)
PHONE...........................760 931-8310
Fax: 760 931-8370
James Ripp, *President*
Tim Varley, *Vice Pres*
Brian Albertson, *Info Tech Dir*
Mark Pin, *Info Tech Mgr*
Ron Cenko, *Supervisor*
EMP: 75
SALES (est): 31.6MM **Privately Held**
SIC: 8049 8742 Physical therapist; hospital & health services consultant

(P-20341)
PHYSICAL THERAPY HAND CTRS INC
Also Called: Valley Physical Theraphy
1815 E Valley Pkwy Ste 5, Escondido (92027-2550)
PHONE...........................760 233-9655
Fax: 760 233-9648
Mike Morasel, *Manager*
EMP: 50
SALES (corp-wide): 3.1MM **Privately Held**
WEB: www.pthc-pt.com
SIC: 8049 Physical therapist
PA: Physical Therapy & Hand Centers, Inc.
540 S Andreasen Dr Ste C
Escondido CA 92029
760 294-9800

PRODUCTS & SERVICES SECTION
8051 - Skilled Nursing Facilities County (P-20364)

(P-20342)
POMONA VALLEY HOSPITAL MED CTR
Also Called: Pamona Valley Physical Therapy
1775 Monte Vista Ave, Claremont (91711-2916)
PHONE..................909 621-7956
Fax: 909 624-7971
Joseph Bomgardner, *Director*
Joe Baumgaertner, *Phys Thrpy Dir*
Melinda Giles, *Manager*
EMP: 70
SALES (corp-wide): 553.9MM **Privately Held**
WEB: www.pvhmc.org
SIC: 8049 Physical therapist
PA: Pomona Valley Hospital Medical Center
  1798 N Garey Ave
  Pomona CA 91767
  909 865-9500

(P-20343)
PROVIDENCE HEALTH & SERVICES
5359 Balboa Blvd, Encino (91316-2803)
PHONE..................818 401-4173
EMP: 52
SALES (corp-wide): 10.1B **Privately Held**
SIC: 8049 Acupuncturist
PA: Providence Health & Services
  1801 Lind Ave Sw
  Renton WA 98057
  425 525-3355

(P-20344)
PROVIDENCE HEALTH & SERVICES
20911 Earl St Ste 380, Torrance (90503-4355)
PHONE..................310 618-8217
Fax: 310 328-4039
Marjan Tavakolian, *Branch Mgr*
EMP: 139
SALES (corp-wide): 10.1B **Privately Held**
SIC: 8049 Physical therapist
PA: Providence Health & Services
  1801 Lind Ave Sw
  Renton WA 98057
  425 525-3355

(P-20345)
R & R PROFESSION
Also Called: R and R Professional Medical
2216 S El Camino Real # 211, Oceanside (92054-6369)
PHONE..................760 754-9020
Fax: 760 754-9070
George Hebeler, *President*
Renee Hebeler, *CFO*
Rachel Sterling, *Vice Pres*
EMP: 150
SQ FT: 900
SALES (est): 3.6MM **Privately Held**
SIC: 8049 7363 7361 Nurses, registered & practical; help supply services; employment agencies

(P-20346)
R DS FOR HEALTHCARE
Also Called: Body Transformations
1420 W Kettleman Ln N5, Lodi (95242-4557)
PHONE..................209 333-2115
Terri Novadinavich, *Owner*
Kim Ishii, *Director*
EMP: 50
SALES (est): 1.2MM **Privately Held**
SIC: 8049 Offices of health practitioner

(P-20347)
RANCHO PHYSICAL THERAPY INC
277 Rancheros Dr, San Marcos (92069-2976)
PHONE..................760 752-1011
James Lin, *Branch Mgr*
EMP: 172
SALES (corp-wide): 15MM **Privately Held**
SIC: 8049 8011 Physical therapist; offices & clinics of medical doctors
PA: Rancho Physical Therapy, Inc.
  24630 Washington Ave # 200
  Murrieta CA 92562
  951 696-9353

(P-20348)
RANCHO PHYSICAL THERAPY INC (PA)
24630 Washington Ave # 200, Murrieta (92562-6177)
PHONE..................951 696-9353
Fax: 951 698-2851
John Waite, *CEO*
Greg Smith, *Principal*
Cindy Knapp, *Exec Dir*
Michael Gunther,
Pete Lorenz,
EMP: 58
SALES: 15MM **Privately Held**
SIC: 8049 8093 Physical therapist; respiratory therapy clinic

(P-20349)
RICHMOND AREA MLT-SERVICES INC
4020 Balboa St, San Francisco (94121-2569)
PHONE..................415 668-5998
Daniel Michael, *Branch Mgr*
Ken Choi, *CFO*
Michael Badolato, *Administration*
Kavoos G Bassiri, *CTO*
Trina De Joya, *Human Res Dir*
EMP: 74
SALES (corp-wide): 16.4MM **Privately Held**
SIC: 8049 Psychologist, psychotherapist & hypnotist
PA: Richmond Area Multi-Services, Inc.
  3626 Balboa St
  San Francisco CA 94121
  415 668-5955

(P-20350)
RIVER OAK CENTER FOR CHILDREN
9412 Big Horn Blvd Ste 6, Elk Grove (95758-1101)
PHONE..................916 226-2800
Laurie Clothier, *Branch Mgr*
Domingo Pena, *Vice Pres*
EMP: 200
SALES (corp-wide): 16.1MM **Privately Held**
SIC: 8049 Psychologist, psychotherapist & hypnotist
PA: River Oak Center For Children
  5445 Laurel Hills Dr
  Sacramento CA 95841
  916 609-5100

(P-20351)
ROBERT BALLARD REHAB HOSPITAL (HQ)
Also Called: Ballard Rehabilitation Hosp
1760 W 16th St, San Bernardino (92411-1160)
PHONE..................909 473-1200
Fax: 909 473-1276
Edward Palacios, *CEO*
Mary Hunt, *Officer*
Barbara Dickerson, *Radiology Dir*
Ravon T McDaniel, *Admin Sec*
Ursula Zeilna, *QA Dir*
▲ EMP: 60
SALES (est): 9.9MM
SALES (corp-wide): 329.7MM **Privately Held**
WEB: www.vibrahealthcare.com
SIC: 8049 8051 8069 Physical therapist; skilled nursing care facilities; specialty hospitals, except psychiatric
PA: Vibra Healthcare, Llc
  4550 Lena Dr
  Mechanicsburg PA 17055
  717 591-5700

(P-20352)
SCRIPPS HEALTH
10670 John J Hopkins Dr, San Diego (92121-1120)
PHONE..................858 554-4100
EMP: 108
SALES (corp-wide): 1.7B **Privately Held**
SIC: 8049 8011 Acupuncturist; offices & clinics of medical doctors
PA: Scripps Health
  4275 Campus Point Ct
  San Diego CA 92121
  858 678-7000

(P-20353)
SIMI VLY HOSP & HLTH CARE SVCS (HQ)
Also Called: ADVENTIST HEALTH
2975 Sycamore Dr, Simi Valley (93065-1201)
P.O. Box 619002 (93065)
PHONE..................805 955-6000
Fax: 805 579-6041
Margaret Peterson, *President*
Eric Cordes, *Ch Radiology*
Caroline Esparza, *President*
Clif Patten, *CFO*
Jenee Potter, *Executive Asst*
EMP: 85
SALES: 139.6MM
SALES (corp-wide): 251.4MM **Privately Held**
SIC: 8049 Physical therapist
PA: Adventist Health System/West
  2100 Douglas Blvd
  Roseville CA 95661
  916 781-2000

(P-20354)
SOUTHERN CAL PRMNNTE MED GROUP
6860 Avenida Encinas, Carlsbad (92011-3201)
PHONE..................619 528-5000
Walter Borschel, *Administration*
Luis Esquenazi, *Family Practiti*
Chitra Minocha, *Family Practiti*
Anais Shannon, *Family Practiti*
EMP: 1746
SALES (corp-wide): 3.2B **Privately Held**
SIC: 8049 Nurses & other medical assistants
PA: Southern California Permanente Medical Group
  393 Walnut Dr
  Pasadena CA 91107
  626 405-5704

(P-20355)
SUTTER HEALTH
965 Orchard Creek Ln, Lincoln (95648-8444)
PHONE..................916 434-1224
Fax: 916 434-1226
Mark Miller, *Director*
Joseph Elmer,
EMP: 200
SALES (corp-wide): 11B **Privately Held**
WEB: www.sutterhealth.org
SIC: 8049 Physical therapist
PA: Sutter Health
  2200 River Plaza Dr
  Sacramento CA 95833
  916 733-8800

(P-20356)
SUTTER MEDICAL FOUNDATION
1014 N Market Blvd Ste 20, Sacramento (95834-1986)
PHONE..................916 924-7764
Fax: 916 565-8601
Judi Monday, *Branch Mgr*
Alex Gonzalez, *Administration*
Thomas Bailey, *Professor*
Alfred Lewy, *Professor*
Barry Scurran, *Professor*
EMP: 505
SALES (corp-wide): 128.4MM **Privately Held**
SIC: 8049 8011 Physical therapist; offices & clinics of medical doctors
PA: Sutter Medical Foundation
  2700 Gateway Oaks Dr
  Sacramento CA 95833
  916 887-7122

(P-20357)
TEXAS HOME HEALTH AMERICA LP (PA)
1455 Auto Center Dr # 200, Ontario (91761-2239)
PHONE..................972 201-3800
Steve Abshire, *Partner*
Judy Bishop, *Partner*
Mark Lamp, *Partner*
Duff Whitaker, *Partner*
Randy Kurtz, *CFO*
EMP: 100
SQ FT: 18,000
SALES (est): 98.6MM **Privately Held**
WEB: www.txhha.com
SIC: 8049 Nurses, registered & practical

(P-20358)
THERAPY FOR KIDS INC
Also Called: Gallagher Pediatric Therapy
233 Orangefair Mall, Fullerton (92832-3038)
PHONE..................714 870-6116
Fax: 714 870-9038
Mary K Gallagher, *President*
Gene Riddle, *CFO*
Todd Anderson, *Vice Pres*
EMP: 50
SALES (est): 2.7MM **Privately Held**
WEB: www.gptkids.com
SIC: 8049 Occupational therapist

(P-20359)
TRI COUNTY REGIONAL CENTER
2220 E Gonzales Rd 210a, Oxnard (93036-8294)
PHONE..................805 485-3177
Gary Feldman, *President*
Sha Azedi, *Director*
Steve Graff, *Director*
EMP: 55
SALES (est): 1.7MM **Privately Held**
WEB: www.garyfeldman.com
SIC: 8049 Psychiatric social worker

(P-20360)
VALLEY NURSES
1450 W 9th St, Pomona (91766-2607)
PHONE..................714 549-2512
Bob Gill, *Owner*
EMP: 65
SALES (est): 2.5MM **Privately Held**
SIC: 8049 7361 Nurses & other medical assistants; nurses' registry

(P-20361)
YOSAN UNIVERSITY
13315 Washington Blvd, Marina Del Rey (90292)
PHONE..................310 301-8115
Dao Shing Ni, *President*
EMP: 50
SALES (est): 863.5K **Privately Held**
SIC: 8049 Acupuncturist

8051 Skilled Nursing Facilities

(P-20362)
1000 EXECUTIVE PARKWAY LLC
Also Called: Oroville Hosp Post Acute Ctr
1000 Executive Pkwy, Oroville (95966-5100)
PHONE..................530 533-7335
Patricia Groth, *Administration*
EMP: 75
SALES (est): 681.4K **Privately Held**
SIC: 8051 Mental retardation hospital

(P-20363)
1130 W LA PALMA AVE INC
Also Called: La Palma Nursing Center
4115 E Broadway, Long Beach (90803-1532)
PHONE..................562 930-0777
Brenda Mandelbaum, *CEO*
Janet Mandelbaum, *Vice Pres*
Joseph Berkowitz, *Administration*
EMP: 90
SALES (est): 3.3MM **Privately Held**
SIC: 8051 Skilled nursing care facilities

(P-20364)
1135 N LEISURE CT INC
Also Called: Leisure Court Nursing Center
1135 N Leisure Ct, Anaheim (92801-2939)
PHONE..................714 772-1353
Fax: 714 563-8058
Patricia Smith, *Director*
Aura Galindo, *Administration*
Fariborz Sham, *Director*
EMP: 130
SQ FT: 15,000
SALES (est): 6.1MM **Privately Held**
SIC: 8051 Skilled nursing care facilities

8051 - Skilled Nursing Facilities County (P-20365)

(P-20365)
3067 ORANGE AVENUE LLC
Also Called: Anaheim Crest Nursing Center
3067 W Orange Ave, Anaheim
(92804-3156)
PHONE..................714 827-2440
Alireza Talebi,
Trudy Strano, *Administration*
Jacob Wintner,
EMP: 120
SALES (est): 3.2MM **Privately Held**
SIC: 8051 Skilled nursing care facilities

(P-20366)
A B C D ASSOCIATES
Also Called: Casa Coloma Health Care Center
10410 Coloma Rd, Rancho Cordova
(95670-2108)
PHONE..................916 363-4843
Fax: 916 363-4316
Deborah Portela, *Administration*
Arden Millermon, *Partner*
Betty Millermon, *Partner*
Terry Fortner, *Food Svc Dir*
Gerson Stauber, *Director*
EMP: 106 **EST:** 1975
SQ FT: 37,000
SALES: 9.4MM **Privately Held**
SIC: 8051 8052 Skilled nursing care facilities; intermediate care facilities

(P-20367)
A F V W HEALTH CENTER
17050 Arnold Dr Ofc, Riverside
(92518-2879)
PHONE..................951 697-2025
James Melin, *President*
Charlie Lamb, *President*
Bruce Cameron, *COO*
Ervin Reed, *CFO*
EMP: 270
SALES (est): 2.1MM **Privately Held**
SIC: 8051 Skilled nursing care facilities

(P-20368)
ACCREDITED NURSING SERVICES
Also Called: Accredited Nursing Care
80 S Lake Ave Ste 630, Pasadena
(91101-4971)
PHONE..................626 573-1234
Teresa Salvino, *Manager*
EMP: 80
SALES (corp-wide): 16.8MM **Privately Held**
WEB: www.accreditednursing.com
SIC: 8051 Skilled nursing care facilities
PA: Accredited Nursing Services
17141 Ventura Blvd # 201
Encino CA
818 986-6017

(P-20369)
ACCREDITED NURSING SERVICES
Also Called: Accredited Nursing Care
950 S Coast Dr Ste 215, Costa Mesa
(92626-7850)
PHONE..................714 973-1234
Fax: 714 430-6804
Meryll Jones, *Manager*
Darrin Carey, *Manager*
Bill Stephens, *Manager*
EMP: 65
SALES (corp-wide): 16.8MM **Privately Held**
WEB: www.accreditednursing.com
SIC: 8051 Skilled nursing care facilities
PA: Accredited Nursing Services
17141 Ventura Blvd # 201
Encino CA
818 986-6017

(P-20370)
AGEMARK CORPORATION (PA)
25 Avenida De Orinda, Orinda
(94563-2305)
PHONE..................925 257-4671
Fax: 510 548-8880
Richard J Westin, *Ch of Bd*
Jesse A Pittore, *CEO*
Martin Hug, *COO*
James P Tolley, *CFO*
Forrest Westin, *Vice Pres*
EMP: 84
SQ FT: 2,100
SALES (est): 13.1MM **Privately Held**
SIC: 8051 Skilled nursing care facilities

(P-20371)
AHMC GARFIELD MEDICAL CTR LP
525 N Garfield Ave, Monterey Park
(91754-1202)
PHONE..................626 573-2222
Fax: 626 571-8972
Philip Cohen, *General Ptnr*
Steve Maekewa, *Partner*
Linda Marsh, *CFO*
Marie Trembath, *Risk Mgmt Dir*
Jane Petre, *Case Mgmt Dir*
EMP: 150
SALES (est): 44.9MM
SALES (corp-wide): 615.4MM **Privately Held**
WEB: www.garfieldmedicalcenter.com
SIC: 8051 8062 Skilled nursing care facilities; general medical & surgical hospitals
PA: Ahmc Healthcare Inc.
1000 S Fremont Ave Unit 6
Alhambra CA 91803
626 943-7526

(P-20372)
AIR FORCE VILLAGE WEST INC
Also Called: Village West Health Center
17050 Arnold Dr Ofc, Riverside
(92518-2879)
PHONE..................951 697-2000
Fax: 951 653-4164
Charles W Lamb, *President*
Ervin Reed, *CFO*
Nancy Valentine, *Bd of Directors*
Charles Dalton, *Vice Pres*
Tim Nalick, *Executive*
EMP: 350
SQ FT: 494,000
SALES: 27.5MM **Privately Held**
WEB: www.afvw.com
SIC: 8051 8052 Convalescent home with continuous nursing care; intermediate care facilities

(P-20373)
ALAMEDA HLTHCARE & WELLNSS CTR
Also Called: Alameda Halthcare Wellness Ctr
430 Willow St, Alameda (94501-6130)
PHONE..................510 523-8857
Sharrod Brooks,
Sol Healthcare LLC,
Sol Majer,
EMP: 99 **EST:** 2010
SALES (est): 4.7MM **Privately Held**
SIC: 8051 Skilled nursing care facilities

(P-20374)
ALHAMBRA CONVALESCENT HOSP LLC
331 Ilene St, Martinez (94553-2631)
PHONE..................925 228-2020
Fax: 925 228-0701
Nina Gilbert, *Administration*
Maria Castillo, *Director*
Walter Peters, *Director*
Amber Lnd, *Manager*
EMP: 60
SALES (est): 2.1MM **Privately Held**
SIC: 8051 8322 Skilled nursing care facilities; rehabilitation services

(P-20375)
ALHAMBRA HEALTHCARE & WELLNESS
415 S Garfield Ave, Alhambra
(91801-3838)
PHONE..................626 282-3151
Sharrod Brooks, *Partner*
EMP: 99 **EST:** 2012
SALES: 9.5MM **Privately Held**
SIC: 8051 Mental retardation hospital

(P-20376)
ALMAVIA OF SAN FRANCISCO
1 Thomas More Way, San Francisco
(94132-2914)
PHONE..................415 337-1339
Janeane Randolph, *Owner*
Phil Altman, *Exec Dir*
EMP: 60
SALES (est): 1.6MM **Privately Held**
SIC: 8051 Convalescent home with continuous nursing care

(P-20377)
AMADA ENTERPRISES INC
Also Called: View Heights Convalescent Hosp
12619 Avalon Blvd, Los Angeles
(90061-2727)
PHONE..................323 757-1881
Fax: 323 757-0601
Shedrick D Jones, *CEO*
John Jones, *Administration*
John Martinez, *MIS Dir*
Ana Chavez, *Facilities Dir*
Melissa Partis, *Education*
EMP: 135
SQ FT: 36,600
SALES (est): 8.9MM **Privately Held**
WEB: www.viewheights.com
SIC: 8051 Skilled nursing care facilities

(P-20378)
APPLE VLY CNVALESCENT HOSP INC
Also Called: Apple Valley Care & Rehab
1035 Gravenstein Hwy N, Sebastopol
(95472-2811)
PHONE..................707 823-7675
Fax: 707 823-1761
Jeff Barbieri, *Administration*
Sharon Conrotto, *Executive*
Sara Reyes, *Office Mgr*
Jonathan Webb, *Administration*
Garrin Obrien, *Hlthcr Dir*
EMP: 120
SQ FT: 20,000
SALES (est): 11.1MM **Privately Held**
WEB: www.applevalleyrehab.com
SIC: 8051 8322 Skilled nursing care facilities; rehabilitation services

(P-20379)
APPLEWOOD CARE CENTER
1090 Rio Ln, Sacramento (95822-1706)
PHONE..................916 446-2506
Fax: 916 446-2029
Bill Drennen, *Administration*
Robert McKenna, *Administration*
EMP: 50
SALES: 2.7MM
SALES (corp-wide): 8.5MM **Privately Held**
SIC: 8051 Skilled nursing care facilities
PA: Riverside Health Care Corporation
1469 Humboldt Rd Ste 175
Chico CA 95928
530 897-5100

(P-20380)
AQUINAS CORPORATION
Also Called: San Tomas Convalescent Hosp
3580 Payne Ave, San Jose (95117-2925)
PHONE..................408 248-7100
Fax: 408 248-1856
Ken Dunton, *Ch of Bd*
Julita Javier, *President*
EMP: 135 **EST:** 1974
SQ FT: 15,000
SALES (est): 9.9MM **Privately Held**
WEB: www.aquinascorp.com
SIC: 8051 8059 Convalescent home with continuous nursing care; convalescent home

(P-20381)
ARPOM INC
Also Called: Camellia Gardens Care Center
1920 N Fair Oaks Ave, Pasadena
(91103-1623)
PHONE..................626 798-6777
Fax: 626 798-7742
Pompeyo Rosales, *President*
Arlene Rosales, *Vice Pres*
Peter Balacuit, *Director*
EMP: 80
SALES (est): 6.4MM **Privately Held**
WEB: www.arpom.org
SIC: 8051 Skilled nursing care facilities

(P-20382)
ARROWHEAD CONVALESCENT HOME
Also Called: Arrowhead Home
4343 N Sierra Way, San Bernardino
(92407-3822)
PHONE..................909 886-4731
Fax: 909 886-3194
Joe Bolton, *President*
Don Popovich, *President*
Thomas Woodbury, *Director*
EMP: 56
SQ FT: 6,000
SALES (est): 3.3MM **Privately Held**
SIC: 8051 Convalescent home with continuous nursing care

(P-20383)
ARTESIA HEALTHCARE INC
Also Called: Alameda Care Center
925 W Alameda Ave, Burbank
(91506-2801)
PHONE..................818 843-1771
Lori De Kruif, *Administration*
EMP: 99
SALES (est): 3MM **Privately Held**
SIC: 8051 Mental retardation hospital

(P-20384)
ASH HOLDINGS LLC
Also Called: Redlands Healthcare Center
1620 W Fern Ave, Redlands (92373-4918)
PHONE..................909 793-2609
Novie Sitanggang, *Administration*
Suzette Banks, *Info Tech Mgr*
Marilyn Ellet, *Nursing Dir*
EMP: 85
SALES (est): 9.2MM **Privately Held**
SIC: 8051 Skilled nursing care facilities

(P-20385)
ASHLEY LTC INC
Also Called: Santa Rosa Convalescent Hosp
446 Arrowood Dr, Santa Rosa
(95407-7503)
PHONE..................707 528-2100
Fax: 707 528-2836
Robert O Benson, *President*
Diana Nelson, *Executive*
Fred Benson, *Administration*
EMP: 60
SQ FT: 18,000
SALES (est): 3.8MM **Privately Held**
WEB: www.santarosaconvalescent.com
SIC: 8051 Skilled nursing care facilities

(P-20386)
ASTORIA CONVALESCENT HOSPITAL
Also Called: Astoria Nursing & Rehab Center
14040 Astoria St, Sylmar (91342-2998)
PHONE..................818 367-5881
Fax: 818 362-1350
Grace Mercado, *Exec Dir*
EMP: 202
SQ FT: 50,000
SALES (est): 5MM **Privately Held**
SIC: 8051 8059 8322 Skilled nursing care facilities; convalescent home; rehabilitation services

(P-20387)
ATHERTON BAPTIST HOMES
214 S Atlantic Blvd, Alhambra
(91801-3298)
PHONE..................626 289-4178
Fax: 626 576-0857
Craig Statton, *President*
Dennis E McFadden, *President*
Jackie Pascual, *CFO*
Dale Torry, *Vice Pres*
Mel Perez, *Executive*
EMP: 200
SQ FT: 42,000
SALES: 17.7MM **Privately Held**
WEB: www.abh.org
SIC: 8051 Convalescent home with continuous nursing care; extended care facility

PRODUCTS & SERVICES SECTION 8051 - Skilled Nursing Facilities County (P-20411)

(P-20388)
ATLANTIC MEM HEALTHCARE ASSOC (PA)
Also Called: Atlantic Mem Healthcare Ctr
2750 Atlantic Ave, Long Beach (90806-2713)
PHONE.................562 424-8101
Jake Rothey, *Administration*
Priscilla Tabu, *Manager*
EMP: 75
SALES (est): 7.9MM **Privately Held**
WEB: www.atlanticmemorial.com
SIC: 8051 Skilled nursing care facilities

(P-20389)
AUBURN OAKS CARE CENTER
3400 Bell Rd, Auburn (95603-9241)
PHONE.................650 949-7777
Ellen Kuykendall, *President*
Kevin Hadfield, *Administration*
Nima Pourfathi, *Pub Rel Dir*
EMP: 99
SALES (est): 3.3MM **Privately Held**
SIC: 8051 Skilled nursing care facilities

(P-20390)
AVALON CARE CENTER - MERCED FR
Also Called: Franciscan Conv. Hospital
3169 M St, Merced (95348-2404)
PHONE.................209 722-6231
Fax: 209 722-6333
Larry Imperial, *Administration*
Mary Imperial, *Manager*
EMP: 74
SALES (est): 3.1MM
SALES (corp-wide): 446.5MM **Privately Held**
SIC: 8051 Skilled nursing care facilities
PA: Avalon Health Care, Inc.
206 N 2100 W Ste 300
Salt Lake City UT 84116
801 596-8844

(P-20391)
AVALON CARE CNTR MERCED HY
Also Called: Hy-Lond Hlth Care Cnter-Merced
3170 Main St, Merced (95340)
PHONE.................209 384-8839
Nancy Williams, *Principal*
John Paiktesch, *Director*
EMP: 76
SALES (est): 2.3MM
SALES (corp-wide): 446.5MM **Privately Held**
SIC: 8051 Skilled nursing care facilities
PA: Avalon Health Care, Inc.
206 N 2100 W Ste 300
Salt Lake City UT 84116
801 596-8844

(P-20392)
AVALON CARE CTR - MADERA LLC
Also Called: Avalon Health Care - Madera
1700 Howard Rd, Madera (93637-5131)
PHONE.................559 673-9278
Fax: 559 673-0753
Jim Lundy, *Exec Dir*
Brian Sierro, *Director*
EMP: 67
SALES (est): 2.5MM **Privately Held**
SIC: 8051 Skilled nursing care facilities

(P-20393)
AVALON CARE CTR - MODESTO LLC
515 E Orangeburg Ave, Modesto (95350-5510)
PHONE.................209 529-0516
Darla Lorenzen, *Exec Dir*
Erma Gutierrez, *Human Resources*
Michael Brodie, *Director*
Stephanie Liebe, *Manager*
EMP: 65
SALES (est): 4.5MM
SALES (corp-wide): 446.5MM **Privately Held**
SIC: 8051 Convalescent home with continuous nursing care
PA: Avalon Health Care, Inc.
206 N 2100 W Ste 300
Salt Lake City UT 84116
801 596-8844

(P-20394)
AVALON CARE CTR - NEWMAN LLC
Also Called: San Luis Care Center
709 N St, Newman (95360-1162)
PHONE.................209 862-2862
David Robinson,
Robin Scesa, *Records Dir*
Liz Gonzalvez, *Office Mgr*
Michael Brodie, *Director*
Liz Gosbalees, *Manager*
EMP: 53
SALES (est): 1.4MM
SALES (corp-wide): 446.5MM **Privately Held**
SIC: 8051 Convalescent home with continuous nursing care
PA: Avalon Health Care, Inc.
206 N 2100 W Ste 300
Salt Lake City UT 84116
801 596-8844

(P-20395)
AVALON HEALTH CARE INC
Also Called: Hy-Lond Hlth Care Cntr-Modesto
1900 Coffee Rd, Modesto (95355-2703)
PHONE.................209 526-1775
Marie Parshall, *Executive*
Michelle Smith, *Administration*
Justin Costa, *Chf Purch Ofc*
Carol Miller, *Chf Purch Ofc*
Sheree Clarke, *Sls & Mktg Exec*
EMP: 86
SALES (est): 2.3MM
SALES (corp-wide): 446.5MM **Privately Held**
SIC: 8051 Skilled nursing care facilities
PA: Avalon Health Care, Inc.
206 N 2100 W Ste 300
Salt Lake City UT 84116
801 596-8844

(P-20396)
AVALON HEALTH CARE INC
Also Called: Healdburg Senior Living Cmnty
725 Grove St, Healdsburg (95448-4756)
PHONE.................707 433-4877
Fax: 707 433-5974
Robert Matthews, *Principal*
Barbara Lillemon, *Manager*
EMP: 69
SQ FT: 8,963
SALES (corp-wide): 446.5MM **Privately Held**
SIC: 8051 Convalescent home with continuous nursing care
PA: Avalon Health Care, Inc.
206 N 2100 W Ste 300
Salt Lake City UT 84116
801 596-8844

(P-20397)
AVALON HEALTH CARE INC
Also Called: Mark Twain Conv. Hospital
900 Mountain Ranch Rd, San Andreas (95249-9713)
PHONE.................209 754-3823
Fax: 209 754-5621
Debra Nelson, *Social Dir*
Larry Washington, *Administration*
Jody Wright, *Hlthcr Dir*
David Giles, *Director*
Dean Kelaita, *Director*
EMP: 109
SALES (est): 3.2MM
SALES (corp-wide): 446.5MM **Privately Held**
SIC: 8051 Skilled nursing care facilities
PA: Avalon Health Care, Inc.
206 N 2100 W Ste 300
Salt Lake City UT 84116
801 596-8844

(P-20398)
AVALON HEALTH CARE INC
Also Called: Chowchilla Conv. Center
1010 Ventura Ave, Chowchilla (93610-2368)
PHONE.................559 665-4826
Ampritpal Pannu, *Director*
EMP: 89
SALES: 4.2MM
SALES (corp-wide): 446.5MM **Privately Held**
PA: Avalon Health Care, Inc.
206 N 2100 W Ste 300
Salt Lake City UT 84116
801 596-8844

(P-20399)
AVALON HEALTH CARE INC
19929 Greenley Rd, Sonora (95370-5996)
PHONE.................209 533-2500
Charlott Beardsley, *Purch Mgr*
Sarah Vickers, *Hlthcr Dir*
EMP: 86
SALES: 9.8MM
SALES (corp-wide): 446.5MM **Privately Held**
SIC: 8051 Skilled nursing care facilities
PA: Avalon Health Care, Inc.
206 N 2100 W Ste 300
Salt Lake City UT 84116
801 596-8844

(P-20400)
AVE MARIA CONVALESCENT HOSP
Also Called: Ave Maria Senior Living
1249 Josselyn Canyon Rd, Monterey (93940-5265)
PHONE.................831 373-1216
Fax: 831 373-2238
Barbara Reid, *Exec Dir*
James Michel, *Director*
Josefina Pimentel, *Director*
EMP: 62
SALES (est): 2.2MM **Privately Held**
SIC: 8051 8361 Skilled nursing care facilities; residential care

(P-20401)
AVENUE H LLC
35253 Avenue H, Yucaipa (92399-5415)
PHONE.................909 795-2476
Carrey Beers, *Principal*
Covey Christensen, *Principal*
EMP: 99
SALES (est): 294.8K **Privately Held**
SIC: 8051 Skilled nursing care facilities

(P-20402)
B-SPRING VALLEY LLC
Also Called: BRIGHTON PLACE SPRING VALLEY
9009 Campo Rd, Spring Valley (91977-1112)
PHONE.................619 797-3991
Fax: 619 460-0451
Sharrod Brooks,
Joellen Zayer, *Administration*
EMP: 91
SALES: 7.1MM **Privately Held**
SIC: 8051 Skilled nursing care facilities

(P-20403)
BAKERSFIELD HEALTHCARE
Also Called: Rehabltion Cntre of Bkrsfield
2211 Mount Vernon Ave, Bakersfield (93306-3309)
PHONE.................661 872-2121
Sharrod Brooks,
EMP: 99 **EST:** 2009
SALES (est): 2.4MM **Privately Held**
SIC: 8051 Mental retardation hospital

(P-20404)
BALBOA ENTERPRISES INC
Also Called: Mountain View Healthcare Ctr
2530 Solace Pl, Mountain View (94040-4309)
PHONE.................650 961-6161
Fax: 650 967-7878
Karl Vitt, *President*
Jessica Delatorre, *Executive*
Desirea Giraldes, *Social Dir*
Ricardo Bautista, *Administration*
Susan Andersen, *Food Svc Dir*
EMP: 130
SQ FT: 30,000
SALES (est): 8.8MM **Privately Held**
WEB: www.mvhealthcare.com
SIC: 8051 Convalescent home with continuous nursing care

(P-20405)
BAY VIEW RHBILITATION HOSP LLC
516 Willow St, Alameda (94501-6127)
PHONE.................510 521-5600
Fax: 510 865-9035
Thomas Chambers, *Mng Member*
EMP: 99
SALES (est): 5.9MM **Privately Held**
SIC: 8051 8062 8361 Skilled nursing care facilities; general medical & surgical hospitals; rehabilitation center, residential: health care incidental

(P-20406)
BAYSHORE HEALTHCARE INC
Also Called: Bella Vsta Trnstional Care Ctr
3033 Augusta St, San Luis Obispo (93401-5820)
PHONE.................805 544-5100
Fax: 805 544-0819
Benjamin Flinders, *CEO*
Paul McLean, *CFO*
Susan Graaff, *Admin Asst*
Johannah Tamba, *Administration*
EMP: 160
SQ FT: 43,000
SALES: 6.4MM **Privately Held**
SIC: 8051 Skilled nursing care facilities

(P-20407)
BEGROUP
Also Called: Kirkwood Assisted Living
1525 E Taft Ave, Orange (92865-4601)
PHONE.................714 282-1409
Fax: 714 282-1465
EMP: 71
SALES (corp-wide): 21.5MM **Privately Held**
SIC: 8051 Skilled nursing care facilities
PA: Be.Group
516 Burchett St
Glendale CA 91203
818 638-4563

(P-20408)
BEGROUP
Also Called: Royal Oaks Manor
1763 Royal Oaks Dr Ofc, Duarte (91010-1989)
PHONE.................626 359-9371
Fax: 626 357-9723
Elizabeth Aragon, *Office Mgr*
Melody Mitchell, *Administration*
Natalie Wood, *Financial Exec*
Debbie Hogan, *Purchasing*
EMP: 79
SALES (corp-wide): 21.5MM **Privately Held**
SIC: 8051 Skilled nursing care facilities
PA: Be.Group
516 Burchett St
Glendale CA 91203
818 638-4563

(P-20409)
BELLA VISTA HEALTHCARE CENTER
Also Called: Kf Bella Vista Health Care
933 E Deodar St, Ontario (91764-1309)
PHONE.................909 985-2731
Fax: 909 946-5713
Doug Ason, *CEO*
EMP: 100
SQ FT: 10,000
SALES (est): 5.1MM **Privately Held**
SIC: 8051 Skilled nursing care facilities

(P-20410)
BENT TREE NURSING CENTER INC
Also Called: Garden Terrace Health Care Ctr
247 E Bobier Dr, Vista (92084-3026)
PHONE.................760 945-3033
Fax: 760 724-3169
Arch B Gilbert, *President*
Candy Rowland, *Administration*
Kristi Barron, *Director*
Mohinderpal Thaper, *Director*
EMP: 200
SQ FT: 57,000
SALES (est): 2.3MM **Privately Held**
SIC: 8051 Skilled nursing care facilities

(P-20411)
BERKLEY VLY CNVLSCENT HOSP INC
6600 Sepulveda Blvd, Van Nuys (91411-1203)
PHONE.................818 786-0020

8051 - Skilled Nursing Facilities County (P-20412)

Sol Galper, *President*
Aileen Duya, *Human Resources*
Suman Patel, *Director*
EMP: 150
SALES: 5.6MM **Privately Held**
SIC: 8051 Skilled nursing care facilities; convalescent home with continuous nursing care

(P-20412)
BEVERLY WEST HEALTH CARE INC
1020 S Fairfax Ave, Los Angeles (90019-4401)
PHONE.................323 938-2451
Fax: 323 938-0361
Louise Koss, *President*
Lydia Cruz, *President*
Josue Morales, *Maintence Staff*
Esther Parades, *Food Svc Dir*
Jimmy Huang, *Director*
EMP: 85
SQ FT: 23,848
SALES (est): 3.6MM **Privately Held**
SIC: 8051 Skilled nursing care facilities

(P-20413)
BITAS
990 W 190th St Ste 120, Torrance (90502-4461)
PHONE.................310 324-2273
Marie Hegerty, *Manager*
EMP: 70
SALES (est): 556.7K **Privately Held**
SIC: 8051 Skilled nursing care facilities

(P-20414)
BLYTHE NURSING CARE CENTER
Also Called: CORPRATE OFFICE
285 W Chanslor Way, Blythe (92225-1246)
PHONE.................760 922-8176
Fax: 760 922-0789
Sandra Blessing, *Owner*
David Shellmann, *Administration*
Adolfo Paglinawan, *Director*
EMP: 64
SQ FT: 12,000
SALES: 3.8MM **Privately Held**
WEB: www.blythenursing.com
SIC: 8051 Convalescent home with continuous nursing care

(P-20415)
BRASWELLS YUCAIPA VALLEY C
35253 Avenue H, Yucaipa (92399-5415)
PHONE.................909 795-2476
Fax: 909 795-3072
James Braswell, *CEO*
Richard Thomas, *Accountant*
EMP: 59
SALES (est): 1MM **Privately Held**
SIC: 8051 Skilled nursing care facilities

(P-20416)
BRIARCREST NURSING CENTER INC
5648 Gotham St, Bell (90201-5413)
PHONE.................562 927-2641
Jack Silverman, *President*
Wilson Park, *CFO*
Jennifer Rodriguez, *Social Dir*
Jesse Liquanan, *Director*
EMP: 110
SALES: 11.4MM **Privately Held**
SIC: 8051 Skilled nursing care facilities

(P-20417)
BRIGHTON GARDENS INC
13101 Hartfield Ave, San Diego (92130-1511)
PHONE.................858 259-2222
Fax: 858 259-2211
Scott Polzin, *Manager*
Karen Worthen, *Lab Dir*
Joyce Ruba, *Social Dir*
Rudy Littlefield, *Exec Dir*
Clare Francisco, *Personnel*
EMP: 100 **EST:** 1999
SALES (est): 2.5MM **Privately Held**
SIC: 8051 8052 Skilled nursing care facilities; intermediate care facilities

(P-20418)
BRIGHTON HEALTH ALLIANCE (PA)
Also Called: Brighton Place of San Diego
8322 Clairemont Mesa Blvd, San Diego (92111-1317)
PHONE.................619 461-0376
Berry T Crow, *President*
EMP: 83
SQ FT: 20,000
SALES (est): 3.3MM **Privately Held**
SIC: 8051 Convalescent home with continuous nursing care

(P-20419)
BRIGHTON PLACE EAST INC
8625 Lamar St, Spring Valley (91977-2518)
PHONE.................619 461-3222
Fax: 619 461-3575
Guy Reggev, *Administration*
EMP: 62
SQ FT: 11,500
SALES: 5.1MM **Privately Held**
SIC: 8051 Skilled nursing care facilities

(P-20420)
BRIGHTON PLACE SAN DIEGO
1350 Euclid Ave, San Diego (92105-5424)
PHONE.................619 263-2166
Fax: 619 263-5413
Cristin Whittaker, *Exec Dir*
Patrick Binarao, *Executive*
Patrick Dinarao, *Accountant*
Kumara Prathipati, *Director*
EMP: 150
SQ FT: 12,000
SALES: 9.6MM **Privately Held**
SIC: 8051 Skilled nursing care facilities

(P-20421)
BROADVIEW INC
Also Called: High Haven
4570 Griffin Ave, Los Angeles (90031-1422)
PHONE.................323 221-9174
Fax: 323 221-7194
Micheal Fisher, *Administration*
Thomas Connor, *Administration*
Harry Gibson, *Manager*
EMP: 50
SQ FT: 24,000
SALES: 4.1MM **Privately Held**
SIC: 8051 Skilled nursing care facilities

(P-20422)
BROOKDALE LVING CMMUNITIES INC
Also Called: Woodside Terrace
485 Woodside Rd Ofc, Redwood City (94061-3890)
PHONE.................650 366-3900
Fax: 650 366-4908
Diane Morton, *Director*
Grace Ndomo, *Nursing Dir*
Shawn Cull, *Director*
Flow Wagner, *Director*
EMP: 64
SALES (corp-wide): 4.9B **Publicly Held**
WEB: www.parkplace-spokane.com
SIC: 8051 Skilled nursing care facilities
HQ: Brookdale Living Communities, Inc.
515 N State St Ste 1750
Chicago IL 60654
-

(P-20423)
BROOKDALE SENIOR LIVING INC
Also Called: Brookdale Folsom
780 Harrington Way, Folsom (95630-3458)
PHONE.................916 983-9300
Rhonda Carter, *Manager*
EMP: 65
SALES (corp-wide): 4.9B **Publicly Held**
SIC: 8051 8059 Skilled nursing care facilities; nursing home, except skilled & intermediate care facility
PA: Brookdale Senior Living
111 Westwood Pl Ste 400
Brentwood TN 37027
615 221-2250

(P-20424)
BUENA VENTURA CARE CENTER INC (PA)
1016 S Record Ave, Los Angeles (90023-2533)
PHONE.................323 268-0106
Vernon Aguirre, *Administration*
Steve Keh, *Vice Pres*
Sophia Seng, *Office Mgr*
Bernadette Cabebe, *Software Dev*
EMP: 75
SQ FT: 15,000
SALES: 6.6MM **Privately Held**
SIC: 8051 Convalescent home with continuous nursing care

(P-20425)
BUENA VISTA CARE CENTER INC
1440 S Euclid St, Anaheim (92802-2156)
PHONE.................714 535-7264
Fax: 714 535-0940
Joann Barantes, *CEO*
Firouzeh Fathi, *Persnl Dir*
EMP: 90
SQ FT: 27,613
SALES (est): 4.2MM **Privately Held**
WEB: www.buenavistacarecenter.com
SIC: 8051 Skilled nursing care facilities

(P-20426)
BURLINGTON CONVALESCENT HOSP (PA)
Also Called: View Park Convalescent Center
845 S Burlington Ave, Los Angeles (90057-4296)
PHONE.................213 381-5585
Fax: 213 384-1710
Jacob Friedman, *President*
Ervin Friedman, *Vice Pres*
Kathleen Becker, *Administration*
Dan Distefano, *Administration*
EMP: 100
SQ FT: 5,000
SALES (est): 6.9MM **Privately Held**
SIC: 8051 8059 8052 Skilled nursing care facilities; convalescent home; intermediate care facilities

(P-20427)
C A C H INC
Also Called: Cypress Acres Cnvalescent Hosp
1633 Cypress Ln, Paradise (95969-2823)
PHONE.................530 877-9316
Jean K Filer, *CEO*
Robert Berndt, *CFO*
Benjamin F S Filer, *Vice Pres*
EMP: 160
SQ FT: 43,000
SALES (est): 4.7MM **Privately Held**
SIC: 8051 Skilled nursing care facilities

(P-20428)
C J HEALTH SERVICES INC
Also Called: Marina Convalescent Center
38650 Mission Blvd, Fremont (94536-4391)
PHONE.................510 793-3000
Catherine Joseph, *President*
Ashwani Bindal, *Director*
EMP: 100
SQ FT: 5,000
SALES (est): 3.3MM **Privately Held**
SIC: 8051 Skilled nursing care facilities

(P-20429)
CAL SOUTHERN PRESBT HOMES (PA)
516 Burchett St, Glendale (91203-1014)
PHONE.................818 247-0420
Fax: 818 247-3871
John H Cochrane, *CEO*
Gerald W Dingivan, *CEO*
Howard Korwes, *CFO*
Ruben Grigorians, *Treasurer*
Dan Hutson, *Bd of Directors*
EMP: 55
SQ FT: 11,000
SALES: 79.2MM **Privately Held**
WEB: www.scths.com
SIC: 8051 Convalescent home with continuous nursing care

(P-20430)
CAL SOUTHERN PRESBT HOMES
Also Called: Buena Vista Manor
802 Buena Vista St, Duarte (91010-1702)
PHONE.................626 359-8141
Fax: 626 359-8144
Judy Phornkein, *Manager*
EMP: 65
SALES (corp-wide): 79.2MM **Privately Held**
WEB: www.scths.com
SIC: 8051 Convalescent home with continuous nursing care
PA: Southern California Presbyterian Homes
516 Burchett St
Glendale CA 91203
818 247-0420

(P-20431)
CAL-COAST HEALTHCARE INC
Also Called: Hillside Care Center
81 Professional Ctr Pkwy, San Rafael (94903-2702)
PHONE.................415 479-5149
Stephen Rodrigues, *Administration*
George Chkhenli, *Administration*
Lasrario Holdare, *Business Mgr*
Janet Valencia, *Nursing Dir*
EMP: 100
SQ FT: 28,000
SALES (est): 4.6MM **Privately Held**
SIC: 8051 Skilled nursing care facilities

(P-20432)
CALDWELL VENTURES LLC
Also Called: Prestige Asstd Lvng in Chico
1351 E Lassen Ave Ofc, Chico (95973-7700)
PHONE.................530 899-0814
Fax: 530 899-0250
Gordon Wiens, *Manager*
EMP: 50
SALES (corp-wide): 4.4MM **Privately Held**
SIC: 8051 Skilled nursing care facilities
PA: Caldwell Ventures, L.L.C.
7700 Ne Parkway Dr # 300
Vancouver WA 98662
360 735-7155

(P-20433)
CALIFORNIA CONVALESCENT HOSPTL
Also Called: Californian-Pasadena
120 Bellefontaine St, Pasadena (91105-3102)
PHONE.................626 793-5114
Luis Pages, *President*
Eva M Casner, *Treasurer*
Clyde L Casner, *Vice Pres*
Nancy Bower, *Administration*
EMP: 100
SQ FT: 30,000
SALES (est): 335.2K **Privately Held**
SIC: 8051 Skilled nursing care facilities

(P-20434)
CALIFORNIA NURSING AND REHAB
Also Called: Califrnia Nrsing Rhblttion Ctr
2299 N Indian Ave, Palm Springs (92262-3098)
PHONE.................760 325-2937
Fax: 619 322-7250
Kennon Shea, *Administration*
Victoria Shea, *Treasurer*
Linda Jackson, *Administration*
Sigrid Irvine, *Controller*
Shlomo Rechnitz,
EMP: 150
SQ FT: 22,000
SALES: 8MM **Privately Held**
SIC: 8051 Skilled nursing care facilities

(P-20435)
CAPISTRANO BEACH EXTENDED
35410 Del Rey, Capistrano Beach (92624-1814)
PHONE.................949 496-5786
Fax: 949 496-0540
Nora Deleon, *Administration*
Maria Alexander, *Personnel*

Jose Ramirez, *Food Svc Dir*
Del Erdman, *Nursing Dir*
Victor Gailica, *Director*
EMP: 60
SALES (est): 1.8MM **Privately Held**
SIC: 8051 Skilled nursing care facilities

(P-20436)
CARE TECH INC
Also Called: Hill Cress Home
4280 Cypress Dr, San Bernardino (92407-2960)
PHONE..................................909 882-2965
Carol Dichman, *Administration*
EMP: 70
SALES (corp-wide): 3.4MM **Privately Held**
SIC: 8051 Skilled nursing care facilities
PA: Care Tech Inc
 401 Ste B N Central Ave
 Upland CA 91786
 909 373-3766

(P-20437)
CARE WITH DIGNITY HEALTHCARE
Also Called: Granite Hills Convalescent Hosp
1340 E Madison Ave, El Cajon (92021-8501)
PHONE..................................619 447-1020
Fax: 619 447-1024
Lynn Festee, *Manager*
EMP: 100
SALES (corp-wide): 4.3MM **Privately Held**
SIC: 8051 Skilled nursing care facilities
PA: Care With Dignity Healthcare, Inc
 8060 Frost St
 San Diego CA 92123
 858 278-4750

(P-20438)
CAREAGE INC
Also Called: Mission De La Casa
2501 Alvin Ave, San Jose (95121-1660)
PHONE..................................408 238-9751
Fax: 408 238-3905
Kim Nguyen, *Branch Mgr*
Yong Kim, *Technology*
EMP: 50
SALES (corp-wide): 12.9MM **Privately Held**
SIC: 8051 Convalescent home with continuous nursing care
PA: Careage, Inc.
 4411 Point Fosdick Dr Nw
 Gig Harbor WA 98335
 253 853-4457

(P-20439)
CARMICHAEL CARE INC
Also Called: Rosewood Rehabilitation
6041 Fair Oaks Blvd, Carmichael (95608-4816)
PHONE..................................916 483-8103
Fax: 916 483-2750
John L Sorensen, *President*
Donald Laws, *Shareholder*
David Sorensen, *Shareholder*
Barabara Hyuck, *Human Res Mgr*
Rose Ullery, *Manager*
EMP: 140
SALES (est): 10.2MM **Privately Held**
SIC: 8051 Extended care facility

(P-20440)
CASAVINA FOUNDATION CORP
2501 Alvin Ave, San Jose (95121-1660)
PHONE..................................408 238-9751
Ngai Nguyen, *President*
CHI Nguyen, *Admin Sec*
Kim Nguyen, *Administration*
EMP: 187
SALES (est): 6MM **Privately Held**
SIC: 8051 Skilled nursing care facilities

(P-20441)
CATHEDRAL PIONEER CHURCH HOMES (PA)
Also Called: PIONEER HOUSE
415 P St Ofc, Sacramento (95814-5300)
PHONE..................................916 442-4906
Fax: 916 442-8665
Calvin Hara, *Administration*
Katie Prozience, *Manager*
EMP: 96

SQ FT: 52,000
SALES: 5.8MM **Privately Held**
SIC: 8051 8699 Skilled nursing care facilities; charitable organization

(P-20442)
CEDAR HOLDINGS LLC
Also Called: HIGHLAND PALMS HEALTHCARE CENT
7534 Palm Ave, Highland (92346-3736)
PHONE..................................909 862-0611
Ryan McCook, *General Mgr*
Julie Smith, *Info Tech Mgr*
Myrna De Guzman,
Paul Hubbard,
Vinod Kaura, *Director*
EMP: 99
SALES: 10.1MM **Privately Held**
SIC: 8051 Skilled nursing care facilities

(P-20443)
CENTINELA SKLLD NRSNG & WLLNSS
1001 S Osage Ave, Inglewood (90301-4116)
PHONE..................................310 674-3216
Chaim Kolodny, *Principal*
EMP: 99
SALES (est): 5.1MM **Privately Held**
SIC: 8051 Skilled nursing care facilities

(P-20444)
CENTRAL GARDENS INC
Also Called: Central Grdns Cnvalescent Hosp
1355 Ellis St, San Francisco (94115-4215)
PHONE..................................415 567-2967
Fax: 415 567-5933
Irene Lieberman, *President*
David P Lieberman, *Treasurer*
Michael Lieberman, *Vice Pres*
Paula Lieberman, *Admin Sec*
BJ Maclelan, *Controller*
EMP: 136 **EST:** 1964
SALES (est): 6.7MM **Privately Held**
WEB: www.centralgardenssf.com
SIC: 8051 Convalescent home with continuous nursing care

(P-20445)
CENTRAL VLY SPECIALTY HOSP INC
730 17th St, Modesto (95354-1209)
PHONE..................................209 248-7700
Gia Smith, *CEO*
Tammy J Thompson, *CFO*
EMP: 103 **EST:** 2012
SALES: 40.7MM **Privately Held**
SIC: 8051 Skilled nursing care facilities

(P-20446)
CF MERCED LA SIERRA LLC
Also Called: Country Villa La Sierra
2424 M St, Merced (95340-2808)
PHONE..................................209 723-4224
Fax: 209 723-0858
Arden Bennett, *President*
Joel Saltzburg, *CFO*
Mathilde Albers, *Treasurer*
Emil Damia, *Vice Pres*
William Gamboa, *Vice Pres*
EMP: 1200
SQ FT: 15,000
SALES (est): 36MM
SALES (corp-wide): 154.7MM **Privately Held**
WEB: www.countryvillahealth.com
SIC: 8051 Skilled nursing care facilities
PA: Country Villa Service Corp.
 2400 E Katella Ave # 800
 Anaheim CA 92806
 310 574-3733

(P-20447)
CF QUINCY LLC
Also Called: COUNTRY VILLA QUINCY HEALTHCAR
50 E Central Ave, Quincy (95971-9718)
PHONE..................................530 283-2110
Fax: 530 283-4983
Joel Saltzburg,
Ira Smedra,
Jacob Wintner,
Ross Morgan, *Director*
EMP: 60

SALES: 3.7MM **Privately Held**
SIC: 8051 Convalescent home with continuous nursing care

(P-20448)
CF SAN RAFAEL LLC
81 Professional Ctr Pkwy, San Rafael (94903-2702)
PHONE..................................415 479-5161
EMP: 99
SALES (est): 4.6MM **Privately Held**
SIC: 8051 Convalescent home with continuous nursing care

(P-20449)
CF WATSONVILLE LLC
Also Called: Watsonville Post Acute Center
525 Auto Center Dr, Watsonville (95076-3745)
PHONE..................................831 724-7505
Doug Easton, *Manager*
EMP: 96
SQ FT: 24,000
SALES (est): 2.2MM **Privately Held**
SIC: 8051 Skilled nursing care facilities

(P-20450)
CF WATSONVILLE EAST LLC
Also Called: Watsonville Nursing Center
535 Auto Center Dr, Watsonville (95076-3745)
PHONE..................................310 574-3733
Fax: 831 763-0141
Joel Saltzburg,
Gordon Buechs, *CFO*
EMP: 99
SALES: 5.1MM **Privately Held**
SIC: 8051 Convalescent home with continuous nursing care

(P-20451)
CF WATSONVILLE WEST LLC
Also Called: Watsonville Post Acute Center
525 Auto Center Dr, Watsonville (95076-3745)
PHONE..................................831 724-4274
Fax: 831 724-7505
Doug Easton, *CEO*
Jacob Wintner, *Manager*
EMP: 96
SQ FT: 24,000
SALES (est): 1.3MM **Privately Held**
SIC: 8051 Skilled nursing care facilities

(P-20452)
CHADLOR ENTERPRISES INC
Also Called: English Oaks Convalescent & RE
2633 W Rumble Rd, Modesto (95350-0154)
PHONE..................................209 577-1001
Fax: 209 577-0366
Terry L Mundy, *President*
Pamela Mundy, *Admin Sec*
Deanna Hill, *Administration*
Kent Hufford, *Director*
EMP: 225
SQ FT: 57,000
SALES (est): 12.2MM **Privately Held**
SIC: 8051 Skilled nursing care facilities

(P-20453)
CHANDLER CONVALESCENT HOSPITAL
525 S Central Ave, Glendale (91204-2099)
PHONE..................................818 240-1610
Fax: 818 240-1662
Richard Statler, *President*
Charles Levine, *President*
Harry Levine, *Vice Pres*
Charles Levin, *Executive*
Marylene Maday, *Food Svc Dir*
EMP: 70
SALES: 4.6MM **Privately Held**
SIC: 8051 Convalescent home with continuous nursing care

(P-20454)
CHAPARRAL FOUNDATION
Also Called: Chaparral House
1309 Allston Way, Berkeley (94702-1920)
PHONE..................................510 848-8774
Fax: 510 848-2438
K J Paige, *Administration*
PA Cooley, *Director*

Walter Peters, *Director*
Page Kj, *Agent*
EMP: 90
SQ FT: 21,000
SALES: 5.2MM **Privately Held**
WEB: www.chaparralhouse.org
SIC: 8051 Skilled nursing care facilities

(P-20455)
CHAPMAN HBR SKLLED NRSING CARE
Also Called: Chapmn-Hrbor Sklled Nrsing Ctr
12232 Chapman Ave, Garden Grove (92840-3717)
PHONE..................................714 971-5517
Fax: 714 748-7851
Lydia Goodell, *President*
Aaron Victor, *President*
Hitesh Patel, *Director*
EMP: 95
SQ FT: 15,000
SALES (est): 3.7MM **Privately Held**
SIC: 8051 Convalescent home with continuous nursing care

(P-20456)
CHINO VALLEY HEALTHCARE CENTER
2351 S Towne Ave, Pomona (91766-6227)
PHONE..................................909 628-1245
Fax: 909 628-0517
Wanita Orkia, *Administration*
Tina Valencia, *Office Mgr*
Gigi Constantino, *Nursing Dir*
EMP: 85 **EST:** 1995
SQ FT: 17,684
SALES: 10.6MM **Privately Held**
SIC: 8051 Convalescent home with continuous nursing care

(P-20457)
CHOWCHILLA MEM HLTH CARE DST (PA)
1104 Ventura Ave, Chowchilla (93610-2244)
PHONE..................................559 665-3781
Cathy Flores, *Administration*
Leland Decker, *Principal*
EMP: 55
SQ FT: 23,000
SALES: 1.9MM **Privately Held**
SIC: 8051 Skilled nursing care facilities

(P-20458)
CITRUS VALLEY HOSPICE
Also Called: Citrus Valley Home Health
820 N Phillips Ave, West Covina (91791-1121)
PHONE..................................626 859-2263
Fax: 626 974-0332
Robert Curry, *CEO*
Felipe Dela Riva, *Records Dir*
Martin Kleinbart, *Vice Pres*
Vicki McGuire, *Accountant*
Gary Pierceall, *Director*
EMP: 100
SQ FT: 16,000
SALES: 7.7MM **Privately Held**
SIC: 8051 8082 Skilled nursing care facilities; home health care services

(P-20459)
CLAIREMONT HEALTHCARE
8060 Frost St, San Diego (92123-2703)
PHONE..................................858 278-4750
Sharrod Brooks,
EMP: 99 **EST:** 2012
SALES: 11MM **Privately Held**
SIC: 8051 Mental retardation hospital

(P-20460)
CLOISTERS OF LA JOLLA INC
7160 Fay Ave, La Jolla (92037-5511)
PHONE..................................858 459-4361
Fax: 858 459-1386
Kennon S Shea, *President*
EMP: 75
SQ FT: 5,000
SALES (est): 4.5MM **Privately Held**
SIC: 8051 Convalescent home with continuous nursing care

8051 - Skilled Nursing Facilities County (P-20461)

(P-20461)
CNRC LLC
Also Called: Califrnia Nrsing Rhblttion Ctr
2299 N Indian Ave, Palm Springs (92262)
PHONE.................................760 325-2937
Fax: 760 322-7250
John Black, *Administration*
EMP: 99 EST: 2000
SALES (est): 3.1MM **Privately Held**
SIC: 8051 Skilled nursing care facilities

(P-20462)
COALINGA DSTNGISHED CMNTY CARE
834 Maple Rd, Coalinga (93210-1348)
PHONE.................................559 935-5939
Fax: 559 935-5944
Richard Carter, *CEO*
Amber Rapp, *Sales Executive*
EMP: 67
SQ FT: 52,000
SALES (est): 1.1MM **Privately Held**
SIC: 8051 Skilled nursing care facilities

(P-20463)
COASTAL HEALTH CARE INC
Also Called: BRENTWOOD HEALTH CARE CENTER
1321 Franklin St, Santa Monica (90404-2603)
PHONE.................................310 828-5596
John Sorensen, *President*
Tim Paulsen, *Exec VP*
Tanner Mitchell, *General Mgr*
EMP: 75
SALES: 8.4MM **Privately Held**
WEB: www.brentwoodnursing.com
SIC: 8051 Skilled nursing care facilities

(P-20464)
COLDWATER CARE CENTER LLC
Also Called: Sherman Village Hlth Care Ctr
12750 Riverside Dr, North Hollywood (91607-3319)
PHONE.................................818 766-6105
Brenan Lowery, *Manager*
Melissa Martinez, *Records Dir*
EMP: 99
SALES: 12.9MM **Privately Held**
SIC: 8051 Skilled nursing care facilities

(P-20465)
COMMUNITY CARE REHAB CTR LLC
Also Called: COMMUNITY CARE & REHABILITATIO
4070 Jurupa Ave, Riverside (92506-2234)
PHONE.................................951 680-6500
Frank Johnson, *CEO*
Irving Bauman, *COO*
Kelly Iasparro, *Vice Pres*
Micah Rhead, *Administration*
EMP: 190
SALES: 12.9MM **Privately Held**
SIC: 8051 Skilled nursing care facilities

(P-20466)
COMMUNITY CONVALESCENT CENTER
9620 Fremont Ave, Montclair (91763-2320)
PHONE.................................909 621-4751
Sim Mndlbum,
EMP: 99
SQ FT: 10,000
SALES (est): 348.7K **Privately Held**
SIC: 8051 Skilled nursing care facilities

(P-20467)
COMMUNITY CONVALESCENT HOSPITA
638 E Colorado Ave, Glendora (91740-4422)
PHONE.................................626 963-6091
Fax: 626 335-4415
Ledmile Gierowitz, *President*
EMP: 80
SQ FT: 10,000
SALES (est): 1.3MM **Privately Held**
SIC: 8051 Convalescent home with continuous nursing care

(P-20468)
COMPASS HEALTH INC
Also Called: Compas Health
290 Heather Ct, Templeton (93465-9738)
PHONE.................................805 434-3035
Mark Woolpert, *President*
Kim Elliott, *Administration*
Sheli Sebo, *Data Proc Staff*
EMP: 73 **Privately Held**
SIC: 8051 Skilled nursing care facilities
PA: Compass Health, Inc.
    200 S 13th St Ste 208
    Grover Beach CA 93433

(P-20469)
COMPASS HEALTH INC
Also Called: Alto Lucero Transitional Care
3880 Via Lucero, Santa Barbara (93110-1605)
PHONE.................................805 687-6651
Kirk Klotthor, *Administration*
Darren Smith, *CEO*
Marie Moya, *Controller*
EMP: 620 **Privately Held**
SIC: 8051 Skilled nursing care facilities
PA: Compass Health, Inc.
    200 S 13th St Ste 208
    Grover Beach CA 93433

(P-20470)
CONVALESCENT MANAGEMENT SVCS
1220 Vienna Dr Spc 573, Sunnyvale (94089-2015)
PHONE.................................408 745-1168
Elayne Groton, *President*
Mary Granvold, *Nursing Dir*
EMP: 120
SALES (est): 1.6MM **Privately Held**
SIC: 8051 Convalescent home with continuous nursing care

(P-20471)
COPPER RIDGE CARE CENTER
Also Called: Applewood Operating
201 Hartnell Ave, Redding (96002-1843)
PHONE.................................530 222-2273
Darrell Thompson, *President*
Miranda Stroud, *Executive*
Dan Gallegos, *Telecom Exec*
Cheryl Spooner, *Marketing Staff*
Loretta Shea, *Social Worker*
EMP: 200
SALES (est): 7.9MM **Privately Held**
SIC: 8051 Skilled nursing care facilities

(P-20472)
CORECARE V A CAL LTD PARTNR
Also Called: Park Vista At Morningside
2525 Brea Blvd, Fullerton (92835-2787)
PHONE.................................714 256-1000
Fax: 714 256-8014
Gary R Stork, *Principal*
Michael Bambrook, *Info Tech Mgr*
Melody Olmstead, *Controller*
Rachel Torres, *Hlthcr Dir*
EMP: 200
SALES: 13.4MM **Privately Held**
SIC: 8051 Skilled nursing care facilities

(P-20473)
COUNTRY HILLS HEALTH CARE INC
1580 Broadway, El Cajon (92021-5124)
PHONE.................................619 441-8745
Fax: 619 442-2553
Glen Larson, *President*
Pat Van, *Administration*
Giovanni Celis, *Human Res Dir*
Nita Hanson, *Human Res Dir*
Robert Knight, *Human Resources*
EMP: 247
SALES (est): 22.9MM **Privately Held**
WEB: www.countryhills.com
SIC: 8051 Skilled nursing care facilities

(P-20474)
COUNTRY OAKS CARE CENTER INC
830 E Chapel St, Santa Maria (93454-4699)
PHONE.................................805 922-6657
Fax: 805 928-9283
John Henning, *President*
Sharon Henning, *Principal*
Mohammad Arain, *Director*
EMP: 70
SQ FT: 14,000
SALES (est): 4.2MM **Privately Held**
SIC: 8051 Skilled nursing care facilities

(P-20475)
COUNTRY OAKS PARTNERS LLC
Also Called: Country Oaks Care Center
215 W Pearl St, Pomona (91768-3114)
PHONE.................................909 622-1067
EMP: 99
SQ FT: 10,601
SALES (est): 294.8K **Privately Held**
SIC: 8051 Skilled nursing care facilities

(P-20476)
COUNTRY VILLA IMPERIAL LLC
Also Called: Country Villa Los Feliz
3002 Rowena Ave, Los Angeles (90039-2005)
PHONE.................................323 666-1544
Stephen E Reissman, *CEO*
Luis Rivas, *Maint Spvr*
EMP: 125
SALES (est): 5.3MM **Privately Held**
SIC: 8051 Skilled nursing care facilities

(P-20477)
COUNTRY VILLA SERVICE CORP
1208 S Central Ave, Glendale (91204-2504)
PHONE.................................818 246-5516
Adam Mitchel, *Administration*
Anna Trejo, *Data Proc Staff*
EMP: 70
SALES (corp-wide): 154.7MM **Privately Held**
SIC: 8051 Skilled nursing care facilities
PA: Country Villa Service Corp.
    2400 E Katella Ave # 800
    Anaheim CA 92806
    310 574-3733

(P-20478)
COUNTRY VILLA SERVICE CORP
400 W Huntington Dr, Arcadia (91007-3470)
PHONE.................................626 445-2421
Fax: 626 821-4916
Shelly Andresen, *Principal*
Sonya Gerberding, *Info Tech Dir*
Levon Gazarian, *Director*
EMP: 70
SALES (corp-wide): 154.7MM **Privately Held**
SIC: 8051 Skilled nursing care facilities
PA: Country Villa Service Corp.
    2400 E Katella Ave # 800
    Anaheim CA 92806
    310 574-3733

(P-20479)
COUNTRY VILLA SERVICE CORP
3611 E Imperial Hwy, Lynwood (90262-2608)
PHONE.................................310 537-2500
Fax: 310 609-0922
Jacob Wintner, *Branch Mgr*
Scott Petterson, *VP Finance*
Beneditta Mordi, *Human Resources*
EMP: 70
SALES (corp-wide): 154.7MM **Privately Held**
SIC: 8051 Skilled nursing care facilities
PA: Country Villa Service Corp.
    2400 E Katella Ave # 800
    Anaheim CA 92806
    310 574-3733

(P-20480)
COUNTY OF MODOC
Also Called: Care Wst-Wrner Mtn Nursing Ctr
228 W Mcdowell Ave, Alturas (96101-3934)
PHONE.................................530 233-3416
Teresa Jacques, *Director*
Joann Campbell, *Vice Pres*
Dick Steyer, *Exec Dir*
Walt Beck, *Branch Mgr*
Jerry Cook, *Info Tech Mgr*
EMP: 161 **Privately Held**
WEB: www.modoccounty.us
SIC: 8051 Skilled nursing care facilities
PA: County Of Modoc
    202 W 4th St Ste A
    Alturas CA 96101
    530 233-6400

(P-20481)
COUNTY OF SACRAMENTO
Also Called: Public Health Nursing Service
9616 Micron Ave Ste 750, Sacramento (95827-2604)
PHONE.................................916 875-0900
Fax: 916 875-0860
Jan Peters, *Director*
EMP: 55 **Privately Held**
WEB: www.sna.com
SIC: 8051 9431 Skilled nursing care facilities; administration of public health programs;
PA: County Of Sacramento
    700 H St Ste 7650
    Sacramento CA 95814
    916 874-5544

(P-20482)
COURTYARD PLAZA
6951 Lennox Ave, Van Nuys (91405-4034)
PHONE.................................818 780-5005
Donahue G Vanderhider, *Principal*
EMP: 50
SALES (est): 2.3MM **Privately Held**
SIC: 8051 Skilled nursing care facilities

(P-20483)
COVENANT CARE LLC
Also Called: Pacific Coast Manor
1935 Wharf Rd, Capitola (95010-2606)
PHONE.................................831 476-0770
Fax: 831 476-0737
Lisa Faraone, *Manager*
Margaret McDaniel, *Manager*
Christine Sims, *Manager*
EMP: 90
SALES (est): 3.2MM
SALES (corp-wide): 188.1MM **Privately Held**
WEB: www.willowtreenursingcenter.com
SIC: 8051 Skilled nursing care facilities
HQ: Covenant Care California, Llc
    27071 Aliso Creek Rd # 100
    Aliso Viejo CA 92656
    949 349-1200

(P-20484)
COVENANT CARE LLC
Also Called: Pacific Hills Manor
370 Noble Ct, Morgan Hill (95037-4134)
PHONE.................................408 779-7347
Fax: 408 779-9435
Lisa Pearson, *Exec Dir*
Jennifer Gonzalez, *CIO*
Lorrie Ann Prado, *Hlthcr Dir*
George Green, *Director*
EMP: 90
SALES (est): 2.9MM
SALES (corp-wide): 188.1MM **Privately Held**
WEB: www.pacifichillsmanor.com
SIC: 8051 Skilled nursing care facilities
HQ: Covenant Care California, Llc
    27071 Aliso Creek Rd # 100
    Aliso Viejo CA 92656
    949 349-1200

(P-20485)
COVENANT CARE CALIFORNIA LLC
Also Called: Downey Care Center
13007 Paramount Blvd, Downey (90242-4329)
PHONE.................................562 923-9301
Fax: 562 862-3126
Marc Brian, *Principal*
EMP: 75
SALES (corp-wide): 188.1MM **Privately Held**
WEB: www.willowtreenursingcenter.com
SIC: 8051 Skilled nursing care facilities
HQ: Covenant Care California, Llc
    27071 Aliso Creek Rd # 100
    Aliso Viejo CA 92656
    949 349-1200

PRODUCTS & SERVICES SECTION
8051 - Skilled Nursing Facilities County (P-20504)

(P-20486)
COVENANT CARE CALIFORNIA LLC
Also Called: Catered Manor
4010 N Virginia Rd, Long Beach (90807-2627)
PHONE..................562 426-0394
Fax: 562 424-1529
Jolene Huren, *Executive*
EMP: 90
SALES (corp-wide): 188.1MM **Privately Held**
WEB: www.willowtreenursingcenter.com
SIC: 8051 Skilled nursing care facilities
HQ: Covenant Care California, Llc
27071 Aliso Creek Rd # 100
Aliso Viejo CA 92656
949 349-1200

(P-20487)
COVENANT CARE CALIFORNIA LLC
Also Called: Palo Alto Nursing Center
911 Bryant St, Palo Alto (94301-2711)
PHONE..................415 327-0511
Roland Gandy, *Branch Mgr*
EMP: 55
SALES (corp-wide): 188.1MM **Privately Held**
WEB: www.willowtreenursingcenter.com
SIC: 8051 8059 Skilled nursing care facilities; personal care home, with health care
HQ: Covenant Care California, Llc
27071 Aliso Creek Rd # 100
Aliso Viejo CA 92656
949 349-1200

(P-20488)
COVENANT CARE CALIFORNIA LLC
Also Called: Mission Skilled Nursing Home
410 N Winchester Blvd, Santa Clara (95050-6325)
PHONE..................408 248-3736
Fax: 408 248-7834
Kathleen Glass, *Manager*
EMP: 75
SALES (corp-wide): 188.1MM **Privately Held**
WEB: www.willowtreenursingcenter.com
SIC: 8051 Skilled nursing care facilities
HQ: Covenant Care California, Llc
27071 Aliso Creek Rd # 100
Aliso Viejo CA 92656
949 349-1200

(P-20489)
COVENANT CARE CALIFORNIA LLC
Also Called: Willow Tree Nursing Center
2124 57th Ave, Oakland (94621-4322)
PHONE..................510 261-2628
Tony Moya, *Manager*
EMP: 90
SALES (corp-wide): 188.1MM **Privately Held**
WEB: www.willowtreenursingcenter.com
SIC: 8051 Skilled nursing care facilities
HQ: Covenant Care California, Llc
27071 Aliso Creek Rd # 100
Aliso Viejo CA 92656
949 349-1200

(P-20490)
COVENANT CARE CALIFORNIA LLC
Also Called: Royal Care Skilled Nursing Ctr
2725 Pacific Ave, Long Beach (90806-2612)
PHONE..................562 427-7493
Fax: 562 424-1833
Nasreen Pervaiz, *Branch Mgr*
Zoraida Ripors, *Assistant*
EMP: 90
SALES (corp-wide): 188.1MM **Privately Held**
WEB: www.willowtreenursingcenter.com
SIC: 8051 Skilled nursing care facilities
HQ: Covenant Care California, Llc
27071 Aliso Creek Rd # 100
Aliso Viejo CA 92656
949 349-1200

(P-20491)
COVENANT CARE CALIFORNIA LLC
Also Called: Shoreline Care Center
5225 S J St, Oxnard (93033-8320)
PHONE..................805 488-3696
Cindy Poulsen, *Exec Dir*
Juanito Joseph, *Maint Spvr*
EMP: 200
SALES (corp-wide): 188.1MM **Privately Held**
WEB: www.willowtreenursingcenter.com
SIC: 8051 Skilled nursing care facilities
HQ: Covenant Care California, Llc
27071 Aliso Creek Rd # 100
Aliso Viejo CA 92656
949 349-1200

(P-20492)
COVENANT CARE CALIFORNIA LLC
Also Called: Huntington Park Nursing Center
6425 Miles Ave, Huntington Park (90255-4348)
PHONE..................323 589-5941
Fax: 323 589-0123
Toni Mazzeo, *Branch Mgr*
Toni L Mazzeo, *Exec Dir*
Toni Mazceo, *Administration*
Nancy Smith, *Data Proc Exec*
Paula Holman, *Purch Agent*
EMP: 140
SALES (corp-wide): 188.1MM **Privately Held**
WEB: www.willowtreenursingcenter.com
SIC: 8051 Skilled nursing care facilities
HQ: Covenant Care California, Llc
27071 Aliso Creek Rd # 100
Aliso Viejo CA 92656
949 349-1200

(P-20493)
COVENANT CARE CALIFORNIA LLC
Also Called: Pacific Gardens Hlth Care Ctr
577 S Peach Ave, Fresno (93727-3952)
PHONE..................559 251-8463
Bart Vanderwal, *Branch Mgr*
EMP: 150
SQ FT: 40,000
SALES (corp-wide): 188.1MM **Privately Held**
WEB: www.willowtreenursingcenter.com
SIC: 8051 Skilled nursing care facilities
HQ: Covenant Care California, Llc
27071 Aliso Creek Rd # 100
Aliso Viejo CA 92656
949 349-1200

(P-20494)
COVENANT CARE CALIFORNIA LLC
Also Called: Capital Transitional Care
6821 24th St, Sacramento (95822-4037)
PHONE..................916 391-6011
Fax: 916 391-4730
Richard Thorp, *Branch Mgr*
Manny Enano, *Social Dir*
Amanda Neasbitt, *Marketing Staff*
Lisa Abelgas, *Hlthcr Dir*
Tess Avenojar, *Director*
EMP: 100
SALES (corp-wide): 188.1MM **Privately Held**
WEB: www.willowtreenursingcenter.com
SIC: 8051 Skilled nursing care facilities
HQ: Covenant Care California, Llc
27071 Aliso Creek Rd # 100
Aliso Viejo CA 92656
949 349-1200

(P-20495)
COVENANT CARE CALIFORNIA LLC
Also Called: Buena Vista Care Center
160 S Patterson Ave, Santa Barbara (93111-2006)
PHONE..................805 964-4871
David Hibarger, *Branch Mgr*
Lance Hassell, *Vice Pres*
Kevin Jeter, *Social Dir*
Cynthia Robles, *Administration*
Michael Malloy, *Analyst*
EMP: 150
SALES (corp-wide): 188.1MM **Privately Held**
WEB: www.willowtreenursingcenter.com
SIC: 8051 Skilled nursing care facilities
HQ: Covenant Care California, Llc
27071 Aliso Creek Rd # 100
Aliso Viejo CA 92656
949 349-1200

(P-20496)
COVENANT CARE CALIFORNIA LLC
Also Called: Turlock Nrsing Rhabilation Ctr
1111 E Tuolumne Rd, Turlock (95382-1541)
PHONE..................209 632-3821
Loris Gielczyk, *Principal*
Alex Chan, *Director*
Gladie Childress, *Director*
Donna Haile, *Director*
EMP: 135
SALES (corp-wide): 188.1MM **Privately Held**
WEB: www.willowtreenursingcenter.com
SIC: 8051 Skilled nursing care facilities
HQ: Covenant Care California, Llc
27071 Aliso Creek Rd # 100
Aliso Viejo CA 92656
949 349-1200

(P-20497)
COVENANT CARE CALIFORNIA LLC
Also Called: Gilroy Health Care
8170 Murray Ave, Gilroy (95020-4605)
PHONE..................408 842-9311
Doreen McGary, *Director*
Suzanne Varnum, *Supervisor*
EMP: 150
SALES (corp-wide): 188.1MM **Privately Held**
WEB: www.willowtreenursingcenter.com
SIC: 8051 Skilled nursing care facilities
HQ: Covenant Care California, Llc
27071 Aliso Creek Rd # 100
Aliso Viejo CA 92656
949 349-1200

(P-20498)
COVENANT CARE CALIFORNIA LLC (HQ)
27071 Aliso Creek Rd # 100, Aliso Viejo (92656-5325)
PHONE..................949 349-1200
Robert Levin, *President*
Mary A Evans, *COO*
Mary Evans, *COO*
Christine Sims, *CFO*
Judy Elmore, *Vice Pres*
EMP: 50
SQ FT: 10,000
SALES (est): 177.2MM
SALES (corp-wide): 188.1MM **Privately Held**
WEB: www.willowtreenursingcenter.com
SIC: 8051 Skilled nursing care facilities
PA: Covenant Care, Llc
27071 Aliso Creek Rd # 100
Aliso Viejo CA 92656
949 349-1200

(P-20499)
COVENANT CARE CALIFORNIA LLC
Also Called: Valle Vista Convalescent Hosp
1025 W 2nd Ave, Escondido (92025-3839)
PHONE..................760 745-1288
Kristina Kuizon, *Branch Mgr*
Sonia Halog, *Executive*
EMP: 50
SQ FT: 15,494
SALES (corp-wide): 188.1MM **Privately Held**
WEB: www.willowtreenursingcenter.com
SIC: 8051 Skilled nursing care facilities
HQ: Covenant Care California, Llc
27071 Aliso Creek Rd # 100
Aliso Viejo CA 92656
949 349-1200

(P-20500)
COVENANT CARE CALIFORNIA LLC
Also Called: St Edna Sbcute Cnvalescent Ctr
1929 N Fairview St, Santa Ana (92706-2205)
PHONE..................714 554-9700
Fax: 714 554-0483
Joshua Torres, *Manager*
Robert Mullaney, *Envir Svcs Dir*
Josh Torres, *Exec Dir*
Carmela Menyhert, *Education*
EMP: 125
SALES (corp-wide): 188.1MM **Privately Held**
WEB: www.willowtreenursingcenter.com
SIC: 8051 Convalescent home with continuous nursing care
HQ: Covenant Care California, Llc
27071 Aliso Creek Rd # 100
Aliso Viejo CA 92656
949 349-1200

(P-20501)
COVENANT CARE CALIFORNIA LLC
Also Called: Los Alts Sub-Acute Rhbltn
809 Fremont Ave, Los Altos (94024-5617)
PHONE..................650 941-5255
Fax: 650 941-2822
Annie Buerhaus, *Branch Mgr*
Alfred Tenoso, *Maintenance Dir*
EMP: 200
SALES (corp-wide): 188.1MM **Privately Held**
WEB: www.willowtreenursingcenter.com
SIC: 8051 8093 Skilled nursing care facilities; rehabilitation center, outpatient treatment
HQ: Covenant Care California, Llc
27071 Aliso Creek Rd # 100
Aliso Viejo CA 92656
949 349-1200

(P-20502)
COVENANT CARE COURTYARD LLC
Also Called: Courtyard Healthcare
1850 E 8th St, Davis (95616-2502)
PHONE..................530 756-1800
Fax: 530 756-1859
Robert Levin, *CEO*
Maria Lira, *Executive*
EMP: 101
SALES (est): 8.9MM
SALES (corp-wide): 188.1MM **Privately Held**
SIC: 8051 Skilled nursing care facilities
HQ: Covenant Care California, Llc
27071 Aliso Creek Rd # 100
Aliso Viejo CA 92656
949 349-1200

(P-20503)
COVENANT CARE LA JOLLA LLC
Also Called: La Jolla Nrsing Rhbltation Ctr
2552 Torrey Pines Rd, La Jolla (92037-3432)
PHONE..................858 453-5810
Carol Tiaadwai, *Administration*
Lorna Miller, *Office Mgr*
Daizel Gasperian, *Administration*
Ezzard McNair, *Administration*
Dan Murray, *Administration*
EMP: 150
SALES (est): 5.9MM
SALES (corp-wide): 188.1MM **Privately Held**
WEB: www.willowtreenursingcenter.com
SIC: 8051 Skilled nursing care facilities
HQ: Covenant Care California, Llc
27071 Aliso Creek Rd # 100
Aliso Viejo CA 92656
949 349-1200

(P-20504)
COVINA REHABILITATION CENTER
Also Called: Regency Health Services
261 W Badillo St, Covina (91723-1907)
PHONE..................626 967-3874
Fax: 626 967-5724
Teresa Dearmond, *Director*
Anil Gupta, *Director*

8051 - Skilled Nursing Facilities County (P-20505)

PRODUDUCTS & SERVICES SECTION

Agnes Maron, *Director*
Vilma Cruz, *Case Mgr*
EMP: 110 **EST:** 1971
SQ FT: 27,800
SALES: 10.7MM **Privately Held**
SIC: 8051 Skilled nursing care facilities

(P-20505)
CREEKSIDE CNVALESCENT HOSP INC
850 Sonoma Ave, Santa Rosa (95404-4715)
PHONE.................707 544-7750
Fax: 707 545-6943
Robert Bates, *Administration*
Lawrence R De Beni, *President*
EMP: 160
SQ FT: 44,000
SALES (est): 4.9MM **Privately Held**
SIC: 8051 Convalescent home with continuous nursing care

(P-20506)
CREEKSIDE REHAB AND BEHAVIORAL
850 Sonoma Ave, Santa Rosa (95404-4715)
PHONE.................707 524-7030
Fax: 707 568-7641
Paul Duranczsk, *Administration*
Prema Thekkek, *President*
EMP: 208 **EST:** 2000
SALES (est): 8MM **Privately Held**
SIC: 8051 Convalescent home with continuous nursing care

(P-20507)
CRESTVIEW CNVALESCENT HOSP INC
1471 S Riverside Ave, Rialto (92376-7703)
PHONE.................909 877-1361
Fax: 909 877-0854
Roy Berglund MD, *President*
Lucia Gonzalez, *Records Dir*
EMP: 220
SQ FT: 44,000
SALES (est): 7MM **Privately Held**
WEB: www.crestviewcarecenter.com
SIC: 8051 Convalescent home with continuous nursing care

(P-20508)
CROCUS HOLDINGS LLC
Also Called: ROSEVILLE CARE CENTER
1161 Cirby Way, Roseville (95661-4421)
PHONE.................916 782-1238
James Huish,
Brittany Qualls, *Info Tech Mgr*
Myrna De Guzman, *Controller*
Jessica Abney, *Food Svc Dir*
Jack Sanofsky, *Manager*
EMP: 99
SALES: 20.8MM **Privately Held**
SIC: 8051 Skilled nursing care facilities

(P-20509)
CUPERTINO HEALTHCARE
Also Called: Cupertino Hlthcare Wllness Ctr
22590 Voss Ave, Cupertino (95014-2627)
PHONE.................408 253-9034
Aaron Robin, *Mng Member*
Kenneth Dunton, *Treasurer*
Gary Vernon, *Administration*
Suzie Mix, *Contract Mgr*
Matthew Gillett, *Director*
EMP: 99
SALES: 15MM **Privately Held**
SIC: 8051 Skilled nursing care facilities

(P-20510)
DANVILLE LONG-TERM CARE INC
Also Called: Danville Post Acute Rehab
336 Diablo Rd, Danville (94526-3417)
PHONE.................925 837-4566
John L Sorensen, *President*
Tim Paulsen, *Vice Pres*
Spencer Brinton, *Executive*
EMP: 80
SALES (est): 2.2MM **Privately Held**
SIC: 8051 Skilled nursing care facilities

(P-20511)
DAVID ROSS INC
Also Called: Rose Garden Convalescent Ctr
1899 N Raymond Ave, Pasadena (91103-1733)
PHONE.................323 684-7673
Fax: 213 797-5824
Arlene Rosales, *Ch of Bd*
Susan Requina, *Nursing Dir*
Jason Boutros, *Director*
Kristina Rivera, *Receptionist*
▲ **EMP:** 100
SQ FT: 27,000
SALES: 7MM **Privately Held**
SIC: 8051 Skilled nursing care facilities

(P-20512)
DAVID-KLEIS INC
Also Called: Beaumont Care Center
9246 Avenida Miravilla, Cherry Valley (92223-3835)
PHONE.................951 845-1166
Jumer Roque, *Administration*
Ariel Foncier, *Executive*
Marisela Carrasco, *Food Svc Dir*
Bernadette Sapalo, *Hlthcr Dir*
Moses Christian, *Director*
EMP: 110
SQ FT: 20,000
SALES (est): 4.3MM **Privately Held**
SIC: 8051 Convalescent home with continuous nursing care

(P-20513)
DEL AMO GRDNS CNVLSCNT HOSP &
Also Called: Del AMO Grdns Cnvalescnt Hosp
22419 Kent Ave, Torrance (90505-2303)
PHONE.................310 378-4233
Fax: 310 378-6801
Morris Weiss, *President*
Barry Weiss, *Vice Pres*
Harumi Takeda, *Risk Mgmt Dir*
Harry Jacobs, *Admin Sec*
Michael Gruenbaum, *Director*
EMP: 92
SQ FT: 21,298
SALES (est): 4.8MM **Privately Held**
WEB: www.delamogardens.com
SIC: 8051 Skilled nursing care facilities

(P-20514)
DEL RIO HEALTH CARE INC
Also Called: Del Rio Convalescent Center
16016 Rio Florida Dr, Whittier (90603-1045)
PHONE.................562 947-5221
Steven Highland, *President*
Mahmood M Moledina, *Treasurer*
EMP: 150
SQ FT: 42,000
SALES (est): 2.4MM **Privately Held**
SIC: 8051 Skilled nursing care facilities

(P-20515)
DEL RIO SANITARIUM INC
Also Called: Del Rio Convalescent
7002 Gage Ave, Bell Gardens (90201-2014)
PHONE.................562 927-6586
Joy Thune, *President*
Maria Perez, *Social Dir*
Jason Kellogg, *Director*
EMP: 150
SALES (est): 9.1MM **Privately Held**
SIC: 8051 Skilled nursing care facilities

(P-20516)
DEL ROSA VILLA INC
2018 Del Rosa Ave, San Bernardino (92404-5642)
PHONE.................909 885-3261
Fax: 909 888-3871
Carol Wagner, *Administration*
Thomas S Plott, *President*
Elizabeth Plott, *Corp Secy*
Angelina Bueshing, *Director*
Thomas Woodbury, *Director*
EMP: 85
SQ FT: 20,000
SALES (est): 4.1MM **Privately Held**
SIC: 8051 Convalescent home with continuous nursing care

(P-20517)
DELANO DST SKLLED NRSING FCLTY
1509 Tokay St, Delano (93215-3603)
PHONE.................661 720-2100
Fax: 661 720-2177
Dennis Karnowski, *Administration*
Brenda Ochoa, *Executive Asst*
Daniel Murray, *Administration*
Janice Calzo, *Director*
EMP: 115
SQ FT: 30,000
SALES: 9.7MM **Privately Held**
SIC: 8051 Skilled nursing care facilities

(P-20518)
DELTA NRSING RHBILITATION HOSP
Also Called: Delta Nrsing Rhabilitation Ctr
420 E Murray Ave, Visalia (93291-5053)
PHONE.................559 625-4003
Fax: 559 732-1082
Mark Fisher, *President*
EMP: 60
SALES (est): 1.2MM **Privately Held**
WEB: www.missioncaregroup.com
SIC: 8051 Skilled nursing care facilities

(P-20519)
DEVELOPMENTAL SVCS CAL DEPT
Also Called: Porterville Developmental Ctr
26501 Avenue 140, Porterville (93257-9109)
P.O. Box 2000 (93258-2000)
PHONE.................559 782-2222
Fax: 559 781-7822
Theresa Villeci, *Principal*
Evone Gibson, *CIO*
Patricia Sutherland, *Director*
EMP: 1800 **Privately Held**
WEB: www.ldc.dds.ca.gov
SIC: 8051 9431 Mental retardation hospital; administration of public health programs;
HQ: California Department Of Developmental Services
1600 9th St
Sacramento CA 95814
916 654-1690

(P-20520)
DIGNITY HEALTH
Also Called: Marian Extended Care Cntr
1530 Cypress Way, Santa Maria (93454-5900)
PHONE.................805 739-3650
Fax: 805 922-9067
Debbie M Young, *Manager*
Bridget Mercadel, *Records Dir*
Sherry Richards, *Nursing Dir*
Kate Sario, *Hlthcr Dir*
Debbie Mockler-Young, *Director*
EMP: 132
SALES (corp-wide): 7.1B **Privately Held**
WEB: www.chw.edu
SIC: 8051 8082 Skilled nursing care facilities; home health care services
PA: Dignity Health
185 Berry St Ste 300
San Francisco CA 94107
415 438-5500

(P-20521)
DOUGLAS FIR HOLDINGS LLC
Also Called: HUNTINGTON VALLEY HEALTHCARE C
8382 Newman Ave, Huntington Beach (92647-7038)
PHONE.................714 842-5551
Brad Truhar, *Administration*
EMP: 145 **EST:** 2000
SALES: 16.6MM **Privately Held**
SIC: 8051 Skilled nursing care facilities

(P-20522)
DOWNEY COMMUNITY HEALTH CENTER
8425 Iowa St, Downey (90241-4929)
P.O. Box 340 (90241-0340)
PHONE.................562 862-6506
Fax: 562 869-1346
Rich Coberly, *Administration*
Stanley Diller, *Partner*
Genevieve Galvin, *Social Dir*

Elsa Custodio, *Office Mgr*
John Nguyen, *Marketing Staff*
EMP: 175
SQ FT: 60,000
SALES: 12.5MM **Privately Held**
SIC: 8051 Skilled nursing care facilities

(P-20523)
E W C H INC
1805 West St, Hayward (94545-1932)
PHONE.................510 783-4811
Ada Lukban, *Administration*
Carmelita Dimaano, *Executive Asst*
Mark Costa, *Sales Executive*
Pam Lewis, *Director*
EMP: 100
SQ FT: 26,000
SALES (est): 1.2MM **Privately Held**
SIC: 8051 8069 Convalescent home with continuous nursing care; specialty hospitals, except psychiatric

(P-20524)
EARLWOOD LLC
Also Called: Earlwood Convalescent Hospital
20820 Earl St, Torrance (90503-4307)
PHONE.................310 371-1228
EMP: 75
SALES (est): 1.1MM
SALES (corp-wide): 9.6B **Publicly Held**
WEB: www.parkviewnursing.net
SIC: 8051 Skilled nursing care facilities
HQ: Skilled Healthcare, Llc
27442 Portola Pkwy # 200
Foothill Ranch CA 92610
949 282-5800

(P-20525)
EASTERN PLUMAS HEALTH CARE
700 3rd St, Loyalton (96118)
PHONE.................530 993-1225
Fax: 530 993-1151
G Koortbojian, *Administration*
Patrick Morgan, *Radiology Dir*
John Evans, *Nurse Practr*
Jim Burson, *Phys Thrpy Dir*
EMP: 85
SQ FT: 20,000
SALES (est): 5.5MM **Privately Held**
SIC: 8051 Skilled nursing care facilities

(P-20526)
EDEN WEST REHABILITATION
1805 West St, Hayward (94545-1932)
PHONE.................510 783-4811
Fax: 510 783-4062
Ruth Gildea, *Administration*
Frank Ryning, *Director*
EMP: 99
SALES (est): 1MM **Privately Held**
SIC: 8051 Skilled nursing care facilities

(P-20527)
EDGEWATER CONVALESCENT HOSP
Also Called: Edgewater Skilled Nursing Ctr
2625 E 4th St, Long Beach (90814-1299)
PHONE.................562 434-0974
Fax: 562 433-1471
Debbie Grani, *President*
Norma Cowles, *Vice Pres*
Ruby Gubay, *Education*
Peter Ferrera, *Director*
Beverley Smith, *Manager*
EMP: 75 **EST:** 1954
SQ FT: 18,000
SALES: 9MM **Privately Held**
SIC: 8051 Skilled nursing care facilities

(P-20528)
EL CAJON VLY CONVALESCENT CTR
510 E Washington Ave, El Cajon (92020-5324)
PHONE.................619 440-1211
Fax: 619 440-2042
Joellen Zayer, *Vice Pres*
Helen Bunn, *President*
EMP: 240
SQ FT: 25,000
SALES (est): 4.8MM **Privately Held**
SIC: 8051 Convalescent home with continuous nursing care

PRODUCTS & SERVICES SECTION
8051 - Skilled Nursing Facilities County (P-20551)

(P-20529)
EL ENCANTO HEALTHCARE & REHAB
Also Called: El Encanto Home Health Care
555 El Encanto Rd, City of Industry (91745-1017)
PHONE..................626 336-1274
Steve Blackwell, *Administration*
EMP: 212
SQ FT: 70,000
SALES (est): 13.7MM **Privately Held**
WEB: www.elencantohealthcare.com
SIC: 8051 Convalescent home with continuous nursing care; mental retardation hospital

(P-20530)
ELDER CARE ALLIANCE SAN RAFAEL
1301 Marina Village Pkwy # 210, Alameda (94501-1082)
PHONE..................510 769-2700
Jesse Janteen, *President*
Janice Washburn, *Controller*
EMP: 75
SALES: 8.7MM **Privately Held**
SIC: 8051 Convalescent home with continuous nursing care

(P-20531)
ELDORADO CARE CENTER LP
510 E Washington Ave, El Cajon (92020-5324)
PHONE..................619 440-1211
Jacob Graff, *Owner*
Gerlyn Ricacho, *Info Tech Mgr*
Ronda Williams, *Info Tech Mgr*
Tony Nguyen, *Director*
EMP: 298
SALES (est): 20.5MM **Privately Held**
WEB: www.eldoradocarecenterllc.com
SIC: 8051 8322 Skilled nursing care facilities; adult day care center

(P-20532)
ELIM ALZHEIMERS & REHAB
668 E Bullard Ave, Fresno (93710-5401)
PHONE..................559 320-2200
Ronald E Howe, *President*
Beverly Montgomery, *Executive*
M K Howe, *Admin Sec*
EMP: 95
SQ FT: 28,000
SALES (est): 1.3MM **Privately Held**
SIC: 8051 Skilled nursing care facilities

(P-20533)
ELMS SANITARIUM INC
Also Called: Elms Convalescent Hospital
212 W Chevy Chase Dr, Glendale (91204-2318)
P.O. Box 251258 (91225-1258)
PHONE..................818 240-6720
Fax: 818 247-3942
Aleck Knell, *President*
Lena Knell, *Treasurer*
William Knell, *Vice Pres*
EMP: 60
SQ FT: 11,000
SALES: 3.8MM **Privately Held**
SIC: 8051 Skilled nursing care facilities

(P-20534)
ELMWOOD LNG TRM& TRAN CARE
Also Called: Shattuck Healthcare
2829 Shattuck Ave, Berkeley (94705-1037)
PHONE..................510 665-2800
Pat Podatorri, *President*
Terry McGregor, *CFO*
Ricku Bauidisty, *Office Mgr*
Jeffrey Mandel, *Director*
EMP: 97
SQ FT: 34,404
SALES (est): 3.6MM **Privately Held**
SIC: 8051 Skilled nursing care facilities

(P-20535)
EMPRES FINANCIAL SERVICES LLC
Also Called: Living Centers
1527 Springs Rd, Vallejo (94591-5448)
PHONE..................707 643-2793
Fax: 707 554-0105
David Hicks, *Manager*

EMP: 61
SALES (corp-wide): 124.2MM **Privately Held**
SIC: 8051 Skilled nursing care facilities
PA: Empres Financial Services, Llc
4601 Ne 77th Ave Ste 300
Vancouver WA 98662
360 892-6628

(P-20536)
ENSIGN CLOVERDALE LLC
Also Called: Cloverdale Healthcare Center
300 Cherry Creek Rd, Cloverdale (95425-3811)
PHONE..................707 894-5201
Jill Browne, *Office Mgr*
Christopher Christensen,
Reyes Rosellah, *Director*
Barbara Seamans, *Director*
Renate Fassbender, *Manager*
EMP: 66
SALES: 5.7MM
SALES (corp-wide): 1.3B **Publicly Held**
SIC: 8051 Skilled nursing care facilities
HQ: Northern Pioneer Healthcare, Inc.
27101 Puerta Real
Mission Viejo CA 92691
949 487-9500

(P-20537)
ENSIGN GROUP INC
340 Victoria St, Costa Mesa (92627-1914)
PHONE..................949 642-0387
EMP: 84
SALES (corp-wide): 1.3B **Publicly Held**
SIC: 8051 Skilled nursing care facilities
PA: The Ensign Group Inc
27101 Puerta Real Ste 450
Mission Viejo CA 92691
949 487-9500

(P-20538)
ENSIGN GROUP INC
Also Called: Panaroma Gardens
9541 Van Nuys Blvd, Panorama City (91402-1315)
PHONE..................818 893-6385
Alicia Gamero, *Administration*
Ludmila Elgourd, *Director*
EMP: 115
SALES (corp-wide): 1.3B **Publicly Held**
WEB: www.theensigngroup.com
SIC: 8051 Skilled nursing care facilities
PA: The Ensign Group Inc
27101 Puerta Real Ste 450
Mission Viejo CA 92691
949 487-9500

(P-20539)
ENSIGN GROUP INC
Also Called: Whittier Hills Health Care Ctr
10426 Bogardus Ave, Whittier (90603-2642)
PHONE..................562 947-7817
Lisa Matarazzo, *Administration*
Matt Flake, *Administration*
Carlos Vazquez, *Bookkeeper*
Roberta Danino, *Education*
Michelle Guerrero, *Nursing Dir*
EMP: 150
SQ FT: 36,316
SALES (corp-wide): 1.3B **Publicly Held**
WEB: www.theensigngroup.com
SIC: 8051 8059 Convalescent home with continuous nursing care; rest home, with health care
PA: The Ensign Group Inc
27101 Puerta Real Ste 450
Mission Viejo CA 92691
949 487-9500

(P-20540)
ENSIGN GROUP INC
Also Called: Park View Gardens
3751 Montgomery Dr, Santa Rosa (95405-5214)
PHONE..................707 525-1250
Fax: 707 525-0159
Eric Moessing, *Director*
Susan Rankin, *Executive*
EMP: 110
SALES (corp-wide): 1.3B **Publicly Held**
WEB: www.theensigngroup.com
SIC: 8051 Convalescent home with continuous nursing care

PA: The Ensign Group Inc
27101 Puerta Real Ste 450
Mission Viejo CA 92691
949 487-9500

(P-20541)
ENSIGN GROUP INC
Also Called: Palomar Vista Healthcare Ctr
201 N Fig St, Escondido (92025-3416)
PHONE..................760 746-0303
William Adams, *Manager*
Bobbi Portillo, *Office Mgr*
Emmett Lee, *Director*
Andrew Rios, *Director*
EMP: 100
SALES (corp-wide): 1.3B **Publicly Held**
SIC: 8051 Skilled nursing care facilities
PA: The Ensign Group Inc
27101 Puerta Real Ste 450
Mission Viejo CA 92691
949 487-9500

(P-20542)
ENSIGN GROUP INC
Also Called: California Mission Inn
8417 Mission Dr, Rosemead (91770-1188)
PHONE..................626 287-0438
David Gatewood, *Owner*
EMP: 96
SALES (corp-wide): 1.3B **Publicly Held**
SIC: 8051 Skilled nursing care facilities
PA: The Ensign Group Inc
27101 Puerta Real Ste 450
Mission Viejo CA 92691
949 487-9500

(P-20543)
ENSIGN GROUP INC
Also Called: Mission Care Center
4800 Delta Ave, Rosemead (91770-1127)
PHONE..................626 607-2400
Fax: 626 607-2490
Tin Nelson, *Director*
EMP: 60
SALES (corp-wide): 1.3B **Publicly Held**
WEB: www.missioncareandrehab.com
SIC: 8051 Skilled nursing care facilities
PA: The Ensign Group Inc
27101 Puerta Real Ste 450
Mission Viejo CA 92691
949 487-9500

(P-20544)
ENSIGN PALM I LLC
Also Called: Premier Care Center For Palm
2990 E Ramon Rd, Palm Springs (92264-7931)
PHONE..................760 323-2638
Fax: 619 323-1723
Soon Burnam, *Treasurer*
Leeron Hever, *Administration*
EMP: 90
SALES (est): 3.5MM **Privately Held**
SIC: 8051 Skilled nursing care facilities

(P-20545)
ENSIGN SERVICES INC
27101 Puerta Real Ste 450, Mission Viejo (92691-8566)
PHONE..................949 487-9500
Christopher Christensen, *CEO*
Beverly B Wittekind, *Treasurer*
Chad Keetch, *Admin Sec*
EMP: 90
SALES (est): 8MM **Privately Held**
SIC: 8051 Skilled nursing care facilities

(P-20546)
ENSIGN SOUTHLAND LLC
Also Called: Southland Care
27101 Puerta Real Ste 450, Mission Viejo (92691-8566)
PHONE..................949 487-9500
Allan Norman,
EMP: 150
SALES (est): 1.5MM
SALES (corp-wide): 1.3B **Publicly Held**
WEB: www.ensigngroup.net
SIC: 8051 Extended care facility
PA: The Ensign Group Inc
27101 Puerta Real Ste 450
Mission Viejo CA 92691
949 487-9500

(P-20547)
EPISCOPAL COMMUNITIES & SERVIC
Also Called: Canterbury, The
5801 Crestridge Rd, Pls Vrds Pnsl (90275-4961)
PHONE..................310 544-2204
Fax: 310 541-9667
Consuelo Haire, *Branch Mgr*
Lois Stroud, *Purchasing*
Inga Liden, *Marketing Staff*
Linda Welmerling, *Director*
EMP: 100
SALES (corp-wide): 35.4MM **Privately Held**
WEB: www.episcopalhome.org
SIC: 8051 8361 8059 Extended care facility; home for the aged; personal care home, with health care
PA: Episcopal Communities & Services For Seniors
1111 S Arroyo Pkwy # 230
Pasadena CA 91105
626 403-5880

(P-20548)
EQUICARE MEDICAL SUPPLY INC
Also Called: Emerald Ter Convalescent Hosp
1154 S Alvarado St, Los Angeles (90006-4110)
PHONE..................213 385-1715
Fax: 213 385-1558
Elena Mendoza-Legaspi, *President*
Elena M Mendoza-Legaspi, *President*
Christina Mendoza, *Administration*
Ronaid Apillo, *Nursing Dir*
EMP: 55
SALES: 3MM **Privately Held**
SIC: 8051 Convalescent home with continuous nursing care

(P-20549)
ESKATON PROPERTIES INC
Also Called: Eskaton Village Care Center
3847 Walnut Ave, Carmichael (95608-2148)
PHONE..................916 974-2060
Fax: 916 974-2106
Larry Bahr, *Manager*
EMP: 1000
SALES (corp-wide): 90.6MM **Privately Held**
SIC: 8051 Skilled nursing care facilities
PA: Eskaton Properties Incorporated
5105 Manzanita Ave Ste A
Carmichael CA 95608
916 334-0810

(P-20550)
ESKATON PROPERTIES INC
Eskaton Manzanita Manor
5318 Manzanita Ave, Carmichael (95608-0512)
PHONE..................916 331-8513
Fax: 916 331-0869
Denie Crum, *Administration*
EMP: 100
SALES (corp-wide): 90.6MM **Privately Held**
SIC: 8051 Extended care facility
PA: Eskaton Properties Incorporated
5105 Manzanita Ave Ste A
Carmichael CA 95608
916 334-0810

(P-20551)
ESKATON PROPERTIES INC
Also Called: Homestead of Fair Oaks
11300 Fair Oaks Blvd, Fair Oaks (95628-5141)
PHONE..................916 965-4663
Fax: 916 961-4347
Tom Coffey, *Manager*
Eric Santiago, *Hlthcr Dir*
Ernesto Quinto, *Director*
Matt Neal, *Manager*
EMP: 160
SALES (corp-wide): 90.6MM **Privately Held**
SIC: 8051 Skilled nursing care facilities
PA: Eskaton Properties Incorporated
5105 Manzanita Ave Ste A
Carmichael CA 95608
916 334-0810

8051 - Skilled Nursing Facilities County (P-20552)

PRODUDUCTS & SERVICES SECTION

(P-20552)
ESKATON PROPERTIES INC
Also Called: Eskaton Center of Greenhaven
455 Florin Rd, Sacramento (95831-2024)
PHONE..................916 393-2550
Heather Craig, *Manager*
Ernesto Quinto, *Director*
Christina Smith, *Director*
EMP: 180
SALES (corp-wide): 90.6MM **Privately Held**
SIC: 8051 Convalescent home with continuous nursing care
PA: Eskaton Properties Incorporated
5105 Manzanita Ave Ste A
Carmichael CA 95608
916 334-0810

(P-20553)
ESTRELLA INC
Also Called: Woodruff Convalescent Center
17836 Woodruff Ave, Bellflower (90706-7029)
PHONE..................562 925-6418
Fax: 562 867-5918
Liberation De Leon MD, *President*
Raelene Ford, *Records Dir*
Edward Chatwin, *Social Dir*
Paul Pinero, *General Mgr*
Jay De De Leon, *VP Finance*
EMP: 110
SQ FT: 32,000
SALES (est): 7.9MM **Privately Held**
SIC: 8051 Skilled nursing care facilities

(P-20554)
EUREKA REHAB & WELLNESS CENTER
Also Called: Eureka Rhbltation Wellness Ctr
2353 23rd St, Eureka (95501-3201)
PHONE..................707 445-3261
Sharrod Brooks, *Partner*
Shlomo Rechnitz, *Partner*
EMP: 98 EST: 2011
SALES: 6.3MM **Privately Held**
SIC: 8051 Skilled nursing care facilities

(P-20555)
EVERGREEN AT LAKEPORT LLC (PA)
Also Called: Evergreen Lkport Hlthcare Ctr
1291 Craig Ave, Lakeport (95453-5704)
PHONE..................707 263-6382
Steve Hendrickson,
Annette A Mott, *Records Dir*
EMP: 100
SQ FT: 36,240
SALES (est): 10.1MM **Privately Held**
SIC: 8051 Skilled nursing care facilities

(P-20556)
EVERGREEN AT LAKEPORT LLC
Also Called: Evergreen Healthcare Center
6212 Tudor Way, Bakersfield (93306-7067)
PHONE..................661 871-3133
Gloria Melliti, *Financial Exec*
EMP: 125
SALES (corp-wide): 10.1MM **Privately Held**
SIC: 8051 Convalescent home with continuous nursing care
PA: Evergreen At Lakeport Llc
1291 Craig Ave
Lakeport CA 95453
707 263-6382

(P-20557)
EVERGREEN AT OROVILLE LLC
Also Called: Olive Ridge Post Acute Care
1000 Executive Pkwy, Oroville (95966-5100)
PHONE..................530 533-7335
Dale Patterson,
Patti Groth, *Admin Sec*
EMP: 99
SALES (est): 2MM **Privately Held**
SIC: 8051 Mental retardation hospital

(P-20558)
EVERGREEN AT PETALUMA LLC
Also Called: Empres Post Acute Rhbilitation
300 Douglas St, Petaluma (94952-2503)
PHONE..................707 763-6887
Connie Smith, *Exec Dir*
Tina Nickolas, *Admin Asst*
Lovette Mayhand, *Director*
EMP: 121
SQ FT: 21,965
SALES (est): 4.5MM
SALES (corp-wide): 538.2K **Privately Held**
SIC: 8051 Skilled nursing care facilities
PA: Empres California Healthcare, Llc
4601 Ne 77th Ave Ste 300
Vancouver WA 98662
360 892-6628

(P-20559)
EVERGREEN GRIDLEY HEALTH CTR
246 Spruce St, Gridley (95948-2216)
PHONE..................530 846-6266
Holly Schmunk, *Exec Dir*
Nikkom Udom, *Director*
EMP: 85
SALES: 4.5MM **Privately Held**
SIC: 8051 Skilled nursing care facilities

(P-20560)
EVERGREEN HEALTH CARE LLC
323 Campus Dr, Arvin (93203-1047)
PHONE..................661 854-4475
C Rasmussen, *Exec Dir*
Cody Rasmussen, *Exec Dir*
Dan Skaggs, *Administration*
Monica Noble, *Nursing Dir*
Monica Noblin, *Nursing Dir*
EMP: 92
SALES: 5.2MM
SALES (corp-wide): 94MM **Privately Held**
SIC: 8051 Skilled nursing care facilities
PA: Evergreen Healthcare Inc
4601 Ne 77th Ave Ste 300
Vancouver WA 98662
360 892-6472

(P-20561)
EVERGREEN HEALTHCARE INC
Also Called: Twin Oaks Nrsing Rhbltion Ctr
1200 Springfield Dr, Chico (95928-6340)
PHONE..................530 342-4885
Fax: 530 342-2847
Barbara Addington, *Manager*
Carla McClintock, *Executive*
Charles Garretson, *Director*
EMP: 150
SALES (corp-wide): 94MM **Privately Held**
SIC: 8051 8069 Convalescent home with continuous nursing care; specialty hospitals, except psychiatric
PA: Evergreen Healthcare Inc
4601 Ne 77th Ave Ste 300
Vancouver WA 98662
360 892-6472

(P-20562)
EXTENDED CARE HOSP WESTMINSTER
206 Hospital Cir, Westminster (92683-3910)
PHONE..................714 891-2769
George Rhodes, *Administration*
Connie Black, *Partner*
Fred Landry, *Partner*
Mark Landry, *Partner*
Arthur Helfat, *Director*
EMP: 115
SALES (est): 6.7MM **Privately Held**
SIC: 8051 8069 Convalescent home with continuous nursing care; specialty hospitals, except psychiatric

(P-20563)
FAIRFIELD NURSING & REHAB CTR
Also Called: Fairfield Healthcare Center
1255 Travis Blvd, Fairfield (94533-4801)
PHONE..................707 425-0623
Fax: 707 425-0704
Steve Hendrickson, *Administration*
Theresa Cadimas, *Administration*
Joan Wandyke, *Administration*
Patti Turner, *Info Tech Mgr*
Gurtreet Dhugga, *Director*
EMP: 90

SALES (est): 6.1MM **Privately Held**
SIC: 8051 Skilled nursing care facilities

(P-20564)
FAITH ENTERPRISES INC
545 W Beverly Pl, Tracy (95376-3012)
PHONE..................209 835-6034
R David Delisle, *President*
Ian Pulliam, *Director*
EMP: 50
SQ FT: 18,159
SALES (est): 3.5MM **Privately Held**
SIC: 8051 Convalescent home with continuous nursing care

(P-20565)
FALLBROOK SKLLED NRSING FCILTY
Also Called: Fallbrook Hospital
325 Potter St, Fallbrook (92028-3068)
PHONE..................760 728-2330
Larry Payton, *CEO*
Douglas Basinger, *Administration*
John Riddell, *Opers Staff*
Victor Lang, *Facilities Dir*
Jennifer Paul, *Director*
EMP: 95 EST: 2001
SALES (est): 4.5MM **Privately Held**
SIC: 8051 7361 Skilled nursing care facilities; nurses' registry

(P-20566)
FAR WEST INC
Also Called: Linwood Grdns Convalescent Ctr
4444 W Meadow Ave, Visalia (93277-1652)
PHONE..................559 627-1241
Fax: 559 627-2809
Robert Barker, *Manager*
Aaron Burrup, *Administration*
Emmy Chavez, *Director*
EMP: 70
SALES (corp-wide): 99MM **Privately Held**
SIC: 8051 8059 Convalescent home with continuous nursing care; convalescent home
HQ: Far West, Inc
4020 Sierra College Blvd
Rocklin CA 95677
916 624-6238

(P-20567)
FAR WEST INC
Also Called: South Gate Care Centers
8455 State St, South Gate (90280-2339)
PHONE..................323 564-7761
Fax: 323 564-4604
James Hagar, *Administration*
Jesicca Paredes, *Office Mgr*
John WEI, *Director*
EMP: 78
SALES (corp-wide): 99MM **Privately Held**
SIC: 8051 8059 Convalescent home with continuous nursing care; convalescent home
HQ: Far West, Inc
4020 Sierra College Blvd
Rocklin CA 95677
916 624-6238

(P-20568)
FAR WEST INC
Also Called: Medical Center
467 E Gilbert St, San Bernardino (92404-5318)
PHONE..................909 884-4781
Fax: 909 381-3162
Frank De Leosa, *Manager*
Anthony Shin, *Director*
EMP: 80
SALES (corp-wide): 99MM **Privately Held**
SIC: 8051 8059 Convalescent home with continuous nursing care; rest home, with health care
HQ: Far West, Inc
4020 Sierra College Blvd
Rocklin CA 95677
916 624-6238

(P-20569)
FERNVIEW CONVALESCENT HOSPITAL
Also Called: Pinegrove Hlthcare Wllness Ctr
126 N San Gabriel Blvd, San Gabriel (91775-2499)
PHONE..................626 285-3131
Fax: 626 286-2391
Benjamin Garret, *President*
Rupa Sharma, *Administration*
Peter MA, *Director*
EMP: 72
SQ FT: 38,000
SALES (est): 2.4MM **Privately Held**
SIC: 8051 8322 8399 Skilled nursing care facilities; rehabilitation services; advocacy group

(P-20570)
FIG HOLDINGS LLC
Also Called: Garden City Healthcare Center
1310 W Granger Ave, Modesto (95350-3911)
PHONE..................209 524-4817
Fax: 209 576-8146
Gary Collins,
Diana Reyes, *Office Mgr*
Mila Parde, *Administration*
Christyn Young, *Hlthcr Dir*
Lee Sorensen,
EMP: 100
SQ FT: 23,000
SALES: 14.6MM
SALES (corp-wide): 40.6MM **Privately Held**
SIC: 8051 Convalescent home with continuous nursing care
PA: Plum Healthcare Group, Llc
100 E San Marcos Blvd
San Marcos CA 92069
760 471-0388

(P-20571)
FIVE STAR QUALITY CARE INC
Also Called: Flagship Health Care Center
466 Flagship Rd, Newport Beach (92663-3635)
PHONE..................949 642-8044
Bonny Christino, *Manager*
Victor Siew, *Director*
EMP: 200
SALES (corp-wide): 1.3B **Publicly Held**
WEB: www.fivestarqualitycare.com
SIC: 8051 Skilled nursing care facilities
PA: Five Star Quality Care, Inc.
400 Centre St
Newton MA 02458
617 796-8387

(P-20572)
FIVE STAR QUALITY CARE INC
Also Called: Lasaltte Hlth Rhbilitation Ctr
537 E Fulton St, Stockton (95204-2227)
PHONE..................209 466-2066
Fax: 209 466-5945
Gus Ropalidis, *Administration*
Chris Fenicle, *Financial Exec*
Claire Sarmiento, *Mktg Dir*
Raymond Metcap, *Manager*
EMP: 150
SALES (corp-wide): 1.3B **Publicly Held**
WEB: www.fivestarqualitycare.com
SIC: 8051 Skilled nursing care facilities
PA: Five Star Quality Care, Inc.
400 Centre St
Newton MA 02458
617 796-8387

(P-20573)
FIVE STAR QUALITY CARE INC
Also Called: Van Nuys Health Care Center
6835 Hazeltine Ave, Van Nuys (91405-3218)
PHONE..................818 997-1841
Fax: 818 997-1844
Grace Alberto, *Administration*
Donald Plance, *Director*
EMP: 65
SALES (corp-wide): 1.3B **Publicly Held**
WEB: www.fivestarqualitycare.com
SIC: 8051 Skilled nursing care facilities
PA: Five Star Quality Care, Inc.
400 Centre St
Newton MA 02458
617 796-8387

PRODUCTS & SERVICES SECTION
8051 - Skilled Nursing Facilities County (P-20595)

(P-20574)
FIVE STAR QUALITY CARE INC
Also Called: Lancaster Health Care Center
1642 W Avenue J, Lancaster (93534-2814)
PHONE..................................661 940-0452
Cathy Bates, *Branch Mgr*
Debra Stella, *Administration*
Young Ko, *Director*
EMP: 115
SQ FT: 7,560
SALES (corp-wide): 1.3B **Publicly Held**
WEB: www.fivestarqualitycare.com
SIC: 8051 Skilled nursing care facilities
PA: Five Star Quality Care, Inc.
  400 Centre St
  Newton MA 02458
  617 796-8387

(P-20575)
FIVE STAR QUALITY CARE INC
Also Called: Thousand Oaks Health Care Ctr
93 W Avnida De Los Arbles, Thousand Oaks (91360)
PHONE..................................805 492-2444
Fax: 805 241-8925
Larisa Machneva, *Administration*
Duc Nguyen, *Director*
Nanci Rodriguez, *Director*
EMP: 130
SALES (corp-wide): 1.3B **Publicly Held**
WEB: www.fivestarqualitycare.com
SIC: 8051 Skilled nursing care facilities
PA: Five Star Quality Care, Inc.
  400 Centre St
  Newton MA 02458
  617 796-8387

(P-20576)
FIVE STAR QUALITY CARE INC
Also Called: Remington Club I & II
16925 Hierba Dr, San Diego (92128-2688)
PHONE..................................858 673-6300
Fax: 858 673-6318
Kristen Crinigan, *Exec Dir*
Angela Takanashi, *Financial Exec*
EMP: 300
SALES (corp-wide): 1.3B **Publicly Held**
WEB: www.fivestarqualitycare.com
SIC: 8051 Skilled nursing care facilities
PA: Five Star Quality Care, Inc.
  400 Centre St
  Newton MA 02458
  617 796-8387

(P-20577)
FIVE STAR QUALITY CARE INC
Also Called: Somerford Place Fresno
6075 N Marks Ave, Fresno (93711-1600)
PHONE..................................559 446-6226
EMP: 220
SALES (corp-wide): 1.3B **Publicly Held**
WEB: www.fivestarqualitycare.com
SIC: 8051 Skilled nursing care facilities
PA: Five Star Quality Care, Inc.
  400 Centre St
  Newton MA 02458
  617 796-8387

(P-20578)
FOOTHILL OAKS CARE CENTER INC
3400 Bell Rd, Auburn (95603-9241)
PHONE..................................530 888-6257
Fax: 530 888-7298
Art Whitney, *CEO*
Ellen Kuykendall, *President*
Chandan Cheema, *Director*
EMP: 90
SALES (est): 2.1MM
SALES (corp-wide): 99MM **Privately Held**
WEB: www.villadelrey.com
SIC: 8051 8093 8062 Convalescent home with continuous nursing care; rehabilitation center, outpatient treatment; general medical & surgical hospitals
HQ: Horizon West Healthcare, Inc.
  4020 Sierra College Blvd # 190
  Rocklin CA 95677
  916 624-6230

(P-20579)
FORUM HEALTHCARE CENTER
23600 Via Esplendor, Cupertino (95014-6571)
PHONE..................................650 944-0200
Fax: 650 903-5946
Lynda Kaser, *Administration*
Nan Boyb, *Financial Exec*
Pam Reed, *Controller*
Ken Fulmore, *Manager*
Dick REA, *Manager*
EMP: 245 **EST:** 1998
SALES (est): 6.8MM **Privately Held**
SIC: 8051 8052 Skilled nursing care facilities; intermediate care facilities

(P-20580)
FOUR SEASONS HEALTHCARE
5335 Laurel Canyon Blvd, North Hollywood (91607-2711)
PHONE..................................818 985-1814
Sharrod Brooks, *Partner*
EMP: 99
SALES (est): 3.3MM **Privately Held**
SIC: 8051 Mental retardation hospital

(P-20581)
FREEDOM VILLAGE HEALTHCARE CTR
Also Called: Rehabworks At Freedom Village
23442 El Toro Rd Bldg 2, Lake Forest (92630-6992)
PHONE..................................949 472-4733
Fax: 949 472-8353
Joel Niblett, *Administration*
Mary Beth Melby, *Records Dir*
Chery Roscamp, *CFO*
Chery Roskamp, *CFO*
Teresa Leleurs, *Administration*
EMP: 100
SALES (est): 5.6MM **Privately Held**
SIC: 8051 8052 Skilled nursing care facilities; intermediate care facilities

(P-20582)
FRENCH PARK CARE CENTER
600 E Washington Ave, Santa Ana (92701-3843)
PHONE..................................714 973-1656
Talmadge Cline, *Administration*
Candise Nomellini, *Marketing Staff*
EMP: 150
SQ FT: 171,000
SALES: 18.6MM
SALES (corp-wide): 18.7B **Publicly Held**
WEB: www.tenethealth.com
SIC: 8051 Convalescent home with continuous nursing care
PA: Tenet Healthcare Corporation
  1445 Ross Ave Ste 1400
  Dallas TX 75202
  469 893-2200

(P-20583)
FRESNO SKILLED NURSING
Also Called: Healthcare Centre of Fresno
1665 M St, Fresno (93721-1121)
PHONE..................................559 268-5361
Sharrod Brooks,
EMP: 99
SALES (est): 7.2MM **Privately Held**
SIC: 8051 Mental retardation hospital

(P-20584)
FRONT PORCH COMMUNITIES
Also Called: Kingsley Manor
1055 N Kingsley Dr, Los Angeles (90029-1207)
PHONE..................................323 661-1128
Fax: 323 660-4091
Cindy Gonzales, *Principal*
Moiz Balkhi, *E-Business*
Azmy Ghaly, *Director*
EMP: 130
SQ FT: 106,521
SALES (corp-wide): 165.1MM **Privately Held**
SIC: 8051 Convalescent home with continuous nursing care
PA: Front Porch Communities And Services - Casa De Manana, Llc
  800 N Brand Blvd Fl 19
  Glendale CA 91203
  818 729-8100

(P-20585)
FRONT PORCH COMMUNITIES & SVCS
Also Called: Apple Valley Care Center
11959 Apple Valley Rd, Apple Valley (92308-7507)
PHONE..................................760 240-5051
Fax: 760 240-8150
Terry Blumer, *Manager*
Bill McDaniel, *Exec Dir*
EMP: 80
SQ FT: 36,151
SALES (corp-wide): 165.1MM **Privately Held**
SIC: 8051 Convalescent home with continuous nursing care
PA: Front Porch Communities And Services - Casa De Manana, Llc
  800 N Brand Blvd Fl 19
  Glendale CA 91203
  818 729-8100

(P-20586)
FRUITVALE LONG TERM CARE LLC
3020 E 15th St, Oakland (94601-2305)
PHONE..................................510 261-5613
Kam McGavock,
EMP: 75
SALES (est): 1MM **Privately Held**
SIC: 8051 Mental retardation hospital

(P-20587)
FULLERTON HEALTHCARE
2222 N Harbor Blvd, Fullerton (92835-2605)
PHONE..................................714 992-5701
Shlomo Rechnitz,
Sharrod Brooks, *Senior VP*
EMP: 125
SALES (est): 4.8MM **Privately Held**
SIC: 8051 Mental retardation hospital

(P-20588)
G AND E HEALTHCARE SVCS LLC
Also Called: Astoria Nursing and Rehab Ctr
14040 Astoria St, Sylmar (91342-2949)
PHONE..................................818 367-5881
Grace Mercado, *Administration*
EMP: 194
SALES (corp-wide): 12MM **Privately Held**
SIC: 8051 Skilled nursing care facilities
PA: G And E Healthcare Services Llc
  445 S Fair Oaks Ave
  Pasadena CA 91105
  818 367-5881

(P-20589)
GARDEN CREST CONVALESCE
Also Called: Garden Crest Rtrment Residence
909 Lucile Ave, Los Angeles (90026-1598)
PHONE..................................323 663-8281
Fax: 323 666-0095
Paul Barron, *CEO*
Vera Barron, *Vice Pres*
Smadar Gal, *Nursing Dir*
EMP: 90
SQ FT: 30,000
SALES (est): 6MM **Privately Held**
WEB: www.gardencrestweb.com
SIC: 8051 8059 8322 Skilled nursing care facilities; convalescent home; old age assistance

(P-20590)
GARDEN GROVE MEDICAL INVESTORS (HQ)
Also Called: Garden Grove Rehabilitation
12332 Garden Grove Blvd, Garden Grove (92843-1804)
PHONE..................................714 534-1041
Fax: 714 534-7921
Nelia Yonzen, *Exec Dir*
Maren Eriksen, *Bd of Directors*
Chance Gilbert, *Chief Mktg Ofcr*
Maria Compose, *Systems Dir*
Gilbert Chan, *Pub Rel Dir*
EMP: 56
SQ FT: 10,000
SALES: 9.1MM
SALES (corp-wide): 10.3MM **Privately Held**
SIC: 8051 8069 Convalescent home with continuous nursing care; specialty hospitals, except psychiatric
PA: Life Care Centers Of America, Inc.
  3570 Keith St Nw
  Cleveland TN 37312
  423 472-9585

(P-20591)
GARDEN VIEW CARE CENTER INC
14475 Garden View Ln, Baldwin Park (91706-6000)
PHONE..................................626 962-7095
Fax: 626 962-2635
John Sorensen, *President*
Jason Roberts, *Administration*
Nikki Holdner, *Accounting Mgr*
Sanjay Khedia, *Director*
EMP: 80
SALES: 12.2MM **Privately Held**
WEB: www.gardenviewcarecenter.com
SIC: 8051 Skilled nursing care facilities

(P-20592)
GARDENA FLORES INC
Also Called: Las Flores Convalescent Hosp
14165 Purche Ave, Gardena (90249-2824)
PHONE..................................310 323-4570
Fax: 310 323-4675
Keith Fortune, *Director*
Diana Fortune, *Treasurer*
Laib Greenspoon, *Administration*
Jeanette Kelly, *Manager*
EMP: 90
SQ FT: 10,000
SALES (est): 5MM **Privately Held**
SIC: 8051 Skilled nursing care facilities

(P-20593)
GARFIELD NURSING HOME INC
Also Called: Morton Bakar Center
1100 Marina Village Pkwy # 100, Alameda (94501-6461)
PHONE..................................510 582-7676
Ann Bakar, *CEO*
Marshall D Langfeld, *CFO*
Ross C Peterson, *Vice Pres*
EMP: 125
SALES (est): 2.3MM
SALES (corp-wide): 126.3MM **Privately Held**
WEB: www.telecarecorp.com
SIC: 8051 Convalescent home with continuous nursing care
PA: Telecare Corporation
  1080 Marina Village Pkwy # 100
  Alameda CA 94501
  510 337-7950

(P-20594)
GEM TRANSITIONAL CARE CENTER
Also Called: Gem Trans Care
716 S Fair Oaks Ave, Pasadena (91105-2618)
PHONE..................................626 737-0560
Rupert Ouano, *Director*
Hermie Faustino, *Records Dir*
Manuel Dellana, *Administration*
Lori Wynstock, *Director*
EMP: 80
SALES (est): 4.6MM **Privately Held**
SIC: 8051 Skilled nursing care facilities

(P-20595)
GENESIS HEALTHCARE CORPORATION
Also Called: Meadowbrook Bhavioral Hlth Ctr
3951 East Blvd, Los Angeles (90066-4605)
PHONE..................................310 391-8266
Fax: 310 390-9878
Michael Mayer, *Branch Mgr*
Richard Edwards, *Treasurer*
Michael Meyer, *Administration*
Lillian Werntz, *Manager*
EMP: 85
SALES (corp-wide): 9.6B **Publicly Held**
SIC: 8051 Skilled nursing care facilities
HQ: Genesis Healthcare Corporation
  101 E State St
  Kennett Square PA 19348
  610 444-6350

8051 - Skilled Nursing Facilities County (P-20596)

(P-20596)
GEORGIA ATKISON SNF LLC
Also Called: Alliance Nrsing Rhbltation Ctr
3825 Durfee Ave, El Monte (91732-2505)
PHONE..................................626 444-2535
Fax: 626 444-6428
Eli Quinones, *Mng Member*
Theresa Dadag, *Data Proc Staff*
Marissa Marquez, *Bookkeeper*
Senena Martinez, *Director*
Teresa Martinez, *Director*
EMP: 125
SQ FT: 30,000
SALES (est): 10MM **Privately Held**
WEB: www.alliancenursingrehab.com
SIC: **8051** Skilled nursing care facilities

(P-20597)
GERI CARE INC
Also Called: Harbor Post Accute Care Center
21521 S Vermont Ave, Torrance (90502-1939)
PHONE..................................310 320-0961
Fax: 310 533-4999
Emmanuel David, *President*
Angie Villanueva, *Admin Sec*
Priscilla Martinez, *QA Dir*
Emil Padre, *Director*
EMP: 100 EST: 1975
SQ FT: 30,000
SALES: 6.6MM **Privately Held**
SIC: **8051** Skilled nursing care facilities

(P-20598)
GHC OF LAKEVIEW TERRACE LLC
Also Called: Lakeview Ter Special Care Ctr
20371 Irvine Ave Ste A210, Newport Beach (92660-0120)
PHONE..................................714 241-5600
Fax: 818 897-4211
Lori Dekruif,
Lois Mastrocola, *Technology*
Tom Olds, *Mng Member*
EMP: 90 EST: 1958
SALES (est): 3.3MM **Privately Held**
SIC: **8051** Skilled nursing care facilities

(P-20599)
GLADIOLUS HOLDINGS LLC
Also Called: Pines At Plcrvlle Hlthcare Ctr
1040 Marshall Way, Placerville (95667-5706)
PHONE..................................530 622-3400
Nick Anderson, *President*
Elisa Misamore, *General Mgr*
Jared Edmunds, *Administration*
EMP: 99
SALES: 950K **Privately Held**
SIC: **8051** Skilled nursing care facilities

(P-20600)
GLENDALE HEALTHCARE CENTER
Also Called: Country Villa Glendale
1208 S Central Ave, Glendale (91204-2504)
PHONE..................................818 246-5516
Adam Mitchel, *Administration*
Christine E Martinez, *Office Mgr*
Nicole Lewis, *Administration*
Tracy Lagasca, *Personnel*
Bernie Lozano, *Chf Purch Ofc*
EMP: 70
SALES (est): 3.8MM **Privately Held**
SIC: **8051** Skilled nursing care facilities

(P-20601)
GLENWOOD GARDENS
Also Called: A E W/Careage Ops
350 Calloway Dr Unit A1, Bakersfield (93312-2966)
PHONE..................................661 587-0221
Cindy Boudreaux, *Business Mgr*
EMP: 260
SALES (est): 9.6MM **Privately Held**
SIC: **8051** Skilled nursing care facilities

(P-20602)
GOLDEN CROSS CARE II INC
Also Called: Golden Cross Hlth Care Fresno
1233 A St, Fresno (93706-3299)
PHONE..................................559 268-3023
Fax: 559 268-5562
Marlene Z Robertson, *President*
EMP: 70
SALES (est): 2.9MM **Privately Held**
SIC: **8051** Skilled nursing care facilities

(P-20603)
GOLDEN LIVING LLC
Also Called: Beverly
1715 S Cedar Ave, Fresno (93702-4331)
PHONE..................................559 237-8377
Fax: 559 237-8106
Ed Johnson, *Exec Dir*
Tona Proxmire, *Executive*
EMP: 93
SALES (corp-wide): 1.6B **Privately Held**
SIC: **8051** 8361 8063 8082 Skilled nursing care facilities; residential care; psychiatric hospitals; home health care services
PA: Golden Living Llc
5220 Tennyson Pkwy # 400
Plano TX 75024
972 372-6300

(P-20604)
GOLDEN LIVING LLC
Also Called: Beverly
1306 E Sumner Ave, Fowler (93625-2627)
PHONE..................................559 834-2542
Christine Clark, *Branch Mgr*
EMP: 60
SALES (corp-wide): 1.6B **Privately Held**
SIC: **8051** 8082 Skilled nursing care facilities; home health care services
PA: Golden Living Llc
5220 Tennyson Pkwy # 400
Plano TX 75024
972 372-6300

(P-20605)
GOLDEN LIVING LLC
Also Called: Beverly Healthcare
340 Victoria St, Costa Mesa (92627-1914)
P.O. Box 1933, San Marcos (92079-1933)
PHONE..................................949 642-0387
David Sedgwick, *Exec Dir*
Tess Villnuvea, *Financial Exec*
Enrique Lemus, *Facilities Dir*
EMP: 100
SALES (corp-wide): 1.6B **Privately Held**
WEB: www.nwbeccorp.com
SIC: **8051** Convalescent home with continuous nursing care
PA: Golden Living Llc
5220 Tennyson Pkwy # 400
Plano TX 75024
972 372-6300

(P-20606)
GOLDEN LIVING LLC
Also Called: Golden Livingcenter - Chateau
1221 Rosemarie Ln, Stockton (95207-6703)
PHONE..................................707 546-0471
Fax: 209 957-7783
Susan Morgan, *Manager*
Sheila Massengale, *Office Mgr*
EMP: 100
SALES (corp-wide): 1.6B **Privately Held**
SIC: **8051** Convalescent home with continuous nursing care
PA: Golden Living Llc
5220 Tennyson Pkwy # 400
Plano TX 75024
972 372-6300

(P-20607)
GOLDEN LIVING LLC
Also Called: Golden Livingctr-Country View
925 N Cornelia Ave, Fresno (93706-1031)
PHONE..................................559 275-4785
Deann Walters, *Manager*
Carol Bojorquez, *Corp Comm Staff*
EMP: 93
SALES (corp-wide): 1.6B **Privately Held**
SIC: **8051** 8059 Skilled nursing care facilities; convalescent home
PA: Golden Living Llc
5220 Tennyson Pkwy # 400
Plano TX 75024
972 372-6300

(P-20608)
GOLDEN LIVING LLC
Also Called: Beverly Healthcare
1477 Grove St, San Francisco (94117-1421)
PHONE..................................415 563-0565
Fax: 415 922-4245
Simon Chen, *Manager*
Jenny Ashley, *Records Dir*
Sean De Ocampo, *Social Dir*
Feven Hu, *Office Mgr*
Rick Issac, *Administration*
EMP: 100
SALES (corp-wide): 1.6B **Privately Held**
WEB: www.nwbeccorp.com
SIC: **8051** Skilled nursing care facilities
PA: Golden Living Llc
5220 Tennyson Pkwy # 400
Plano TX 75024
972 372-6300

(P-20609)
GOLDEN LIVING LLC
Also Called: Golden Lvngcnter - Bakersfield
3601 San Dimas St, Bakersfield (93301-1405)
PHONE..................................661 323-2894
Will Maloney, *Director*
Yolanda Rodriguez, *Financial Exec*
EMP: 70
SALES (corp-wide): 1.6B **Privately Held**
SIC: **8051** Skilled nursing care facilities
PA: Golden Living Llc
5220 Tennyson Pkwy # 400
Plano TX 75024
972 372-6300

(P-20610)
GOLDEN LIVING LLC
Also Called: Golden Livingcenter - Petaluma
217 Lakeville St Apt 3, Petaluma (94952-3166)
PHONE..................................707 763-4109
Monica Choperena, *General Mgr*
Dorothy McReynolds, *Pub Rel Dir*
EMP: 72
SALES (corp-wide): 1.6B **Privately Held**
SIC: **8051** Skilled nursing care facilities
PA: Golden Living Llc
5220 Tennyson Pkwy # 400
Plano TX 75024
972 372-6300

(P-20611)
GOLDEN LIVING LLC
Also Called: Beverly Healthcare
1300 N C St, Oxnard (93030-4006)
PHONE..................................805 983-0305
David Banks, *Ch of Bd*
EMP: 100
SALES (corp-wide): 1.6B **Privately Held**
WEB: www.nwbeccorp.com
SIC: **8051** Skilled nursing care facilities
PA: Golden Living Llc
5220 Tennyson Pkwy # 400
Plano TX 75024
972 372-6300

(P-20612)
GOLDEN LIVING LLC
Also Called: Beverly Healthcare
950 S Fairmont Ave, Lodi (95240-5131)
PHONE..................................209 368-0693
Fax: 209 339-9759
Beverly Mannon, *Principal*
EMP: 70
SALES (corp-wide): 1.6B **Privately Held**
WEB: www.nwbeccorp.com
SIC: **8051** Convalescent home with continuous nursing care
PA: Golden Living Llc
5220 Tennyson Pkwy # 400
Plano TX 75024
972 372-6300

(P-20613)
GOLDEN LIVING LLC
Also Called: Golden Livingcenter - Santa Rosa
4650 Hoen Ave, Santa Rosa (95405-9407)
PHONE..................................707 546-0471
Constance Smith, *Dir Ops-Prd-Mfg*
Mandy Davey, *Executive*
Mary Jensen, *Office Mgr*
Pamela Campbell, *Administration*
Gregg Mitchell, *Maintence Staff*
EMP: 100
SALES (corp-wide): 1.6B **Privately Held**
SIC: **8051** 8069 Skilled nursing care facilities; specialty hospitals, except psychiatric

PA: Golden Living Llc
5220 Tennyson Pkwy # 400
Plano TX 75024
972 372-6300

(P-20614)
GOLDEN LIVING LLC
Also Called: Beverly Healthcare
850 S Sunkist Ave, West Covina (91790-2534)
PHONE..................................626 962-3368
Mary Julienne, *Manager*
EMP: 80
SQ FT: 25,000
SALES (corp-wide): 1.6B **Privately Held**
WEB: www.nwbeccorp.com
SIC: **8051** 8093 Convalescent home with continuous nursing care; rehabilitation center, outpatient treatment
PA: Golden Living Llc
5220 Tennyson Pkwy # 400
Plano TX 75024
972 372-6300

(P-20615)
GOLDEN LIVING LLC
Also Called: Beverly Healthcare
5445 Everglades St, Ventura (93003-6523)
PHONE..................................805 642-1736
Jay Brady, *Branch Mgr*
EMP: 100
SALES (corp-wide): 1.6B **Privately Held**
WEB: www.nwbeccorp.com
SIC: **8051** Skilled nursing care facilities
PA: Golden Living Llc
5220 Tennyson Pkwy # 400
Plano TX 75024
972 372-6300

(P-20616)
GOLDEN LIVING LLC
Also Called: Beverly Healthcare
35410 Del Rey, Capistrano Beach (92624-1814)
PHONE..................................949 496-5786
Nora Saulietis, *Administration*
EMP: 60
SALES (corp-wide): 1.6B **Privately Held**
WEB: www.nwbeccorp.com
SIC: **8051** Extended care facility
PA: Golden Living Llc
5220 Tennyson Pkwy # 400
Plano TX 75024
972 372-6300

(P-20617)
GOLDEN LIVING LLC
Also Called: Golden Livingcenter - Clovis
111 Barstow Ave, Clovis (93612-2225)
PHONE..................................559 299-2591
Michelle Tathem, *Manager*
Harpreet Kaur, *Office Mgr*
EMP: 93
SALES (corp-wide): 1.6B **Privately Held**
SIC: **8051** Convalescent home with continuous nursing care
PA: Golden Living Llc
5220 Tennyson Pkwy # 400
Plano TX 75024
972 372-6300

(P-20618)
GOLDEN LIVING LLC
Also Called: Golden Livingcenter - San Jose
401 Ridge Vista Ave, San Jose (95127-1501)
PHONE..................................408 923-7232
Almaroos Apapira, *Exec Dir*
Michael Darouze, *Exec Dir*
Carlyn Grantham, *Financial Exec*
EMP: 105
SALES (corp-wide): 1.6B **Privately Held**
SIC: **8051** Skilled nursing care facilities
PA: Golden Living Llc
5220 Tennyson Pkwy # 400
Plano TX 75024
972 372-6300

(P-20619)
GOLDEN LIVING LLC
3510 E Shields Ave, Fresno (93726-6909)
PHONE..................................559 222-4807
Kara Pappanduros, *Manager*
Tisha Avilez, *Director*
EMP: 100

PRODUCTS & SERVICES SECTION
8051 - Skilled Nursing Facilities County (P-20642)

SALES (corp-wide): 1.6B **Privately Held**
WEB: www.nwbeccorp.com
SIC: 8051 Skilled nursing care facilities
PA: Golden Living Llc
5220 Tennyson Pkwy # 400
Plano TX 75024
972 372-6300

(P-20620)
GOLDEN LIVING LLC
Also Called: Golden Livingcenter - Reedley
1090 E Dinuba Ave, Reedley (93654-3577)
PHONE.................................559 638-3577
Julie Whiteside, *Manager*
EMP: 93
SALES (corp-wide): 1.6B **Privately Held**
SIC: 8051 8082 Skilled nursing care facilities; home health care services
PA: Golden Living Llc
5220 Tennyson Pkwy # 400
Plano TX 75024
972 372-6300

(P-20621)
GOLDEN LIVING LLC
Also Called: Beverly Healthcare
3672 N 1st St, Fresno (93726-6810)
PHONE.................................559 227-5383
Kristine Clark, *Manager*
Peggy Cantrell, *Social Dir*
Lucille Epperson, *Administration*
EMP: 65
SALES (corp-wide): 1.6B **Privately Held**
WEB: www.nwbeccorp.com
SIC: 8051 Skilled nursing care facilities
PA: Golden Living Llc
5220 Tennyson Pkwy # 400
Plano TX 75024
972 372-6300

(P-20622)
GOLDEN LIVING LLC
Also Called: Beverly Healthcare
1900 Coffee Rd, Modesto (95355-2703)
PHONE.................................209 548-0318
Belinda Guzman, *CEO*
Kim Damale, *Vice Pres*
EMP: 108
SALES (corp-wide): 1.6B **Privately Held**
WEB: www.nwbeccorp.com
SIC: 8051 Skilled nursing care facilities
PA: Golden Living Llc
5220 Tennyson Pkwy # 400
Plano TX 75024
972 372-6300

(P-20623)
GOLDEN LIVING LLC
Also Called: Beverly Healthcare
350 De Soto Dr, Los Gatos (95032-2402)
PHONE.................................408 356-9151
Julie Okada, *Exec Dir*
EMP: 60
SALES (corp-wide): 1.6B **Privately Held**
WEB: www.nwbeccorp.com
SIC: 8051 Convalescent home with continuous nursing care
PA: Golden Living Llc
5220 Tennyson Pkwy # 400
Plano TX 75024
972 372-6300

(P-20624)
GOLDEN LIVING LLC
Also Called: Golden Livingcenter - Portside
2740 N California St, Stockton (95204-5529)
PHONE.................................209 466-3522
Judy Thornhill, *Director*
Michelle Smith, *Exec Dir*
Lilibeth Woo, *Office Mgr*
Michele Smith, *Administration*
Concion Quilenderino, *CTO*
EMP: 100
SALES (corp-wide): 1.6B **Privately Held**
SIC: 8051 Skilled nursing care facilities; convalescent home with continuous nursing care
PA: Golden Living Llc
5220 Tennyson Pkwy # 400
Plano TX 75024
972 372-6300

(P-20625)
GOLDEN LIVING LLC
Also Called: Golden Livingcenter
678 2nd St W, Sonoma (95476-6901)
PHONE.................................707 938-1096
Keith Gold, *Administration*
Jane Gerlock, *Hlthcr Dir*
Walter Prehn, *Director*
EMP: 72
SALES (corp-wide): 1.6B **Privately Held**
SIC: 8051 Skilled nursing care facilities
PA: Golden Living Llc
5220 Tennyson Pkwy # 400
Plano TX 75024
972 372-6300

(P-20626)
GOLDEN LIVING LLC
Also Called: Beverly Healthcare
188 Cohasset Ln, Chico (95926-2206)
PHONE.................................530 343-6084
John Crowley, *Administration*
Deb Hawkins, *Facilities Dir*
Barbara Juede Santos, *Director*
EMP: 80
SALES (corp-wide): 1.6B **Privately Held**
WEB: www.nwbeccorp.com
SIC: 8051 Extended care facility
PA: Golden Living Llc
5220 Tennyson Pkwy # 400
Plano TX 75024
972 372-6300

(P-20627)
GOLDEN LIVING LLC
Also Called: Beverly Healthcare
709 N St, Newman (95360-1162)
PHONE.................................209 862-2862
Fax: 209 862-3250
Darla Larinda, *Exec Dir*
Robinson David, *Administration*
EMP: 69
SALES (corp-wide): 1.6B **Privately Held**
WEB: www.nwbeccorp.com
SIC: 8051 Convalescent home with continuous nursing care
PA: Golden Living Llc
5220 Tennyson Pkwy # 400
Plano TX 75024
972 372-6300

(P-20628)
GOLDEN STATE HABILITATION CONV (PA)
Also Called: Golden State Care Center
1758 Big Dalton Ave, Baldwin Park (91706-5910)
PHONE.................................626 962-3274
Fax: 626 337-2969
Eden Salceda, *President*
Claudio Hernandez, *Vice Pres*
Emmanual David, *Admin Sec*
EMP: 175
SALES (est): 8.5MM **Privately Held**
SIC: 8051 8361 8052 Skilled nursing care facilities; residential care; intermediate care facilities

(P-20629)
GOLDEN STATE HEALTH CTRS INC (PA)
13347 Ventura Blvd, Sherman Oaks (91423-3979)
PHONE.................................818 385-3200
Fax: 818 385-3275
Martin J Weiss, *CEO*
Ronald Mayer, *CFO*
David B Weiss, *Chairman*
Howard Weiss, *Admin Sec*
Danny Reyes, *Controller*
EMP: 95
SQ FT: 2,000
SALES: 62.1MM **Privately Held**
WEB: www.goldenstatehealth.com
SIC: 8051 Skilled nursing care facilities

(P-20630)
GOLDEN STATE WEST VALLEY
7057 Shoup Ave, Canoga Park (91307-2335)
PHONE.................................818 348-8422
Susan Henry, *President*
Rose Kasirer, *Admin Sec*
Maria Rivera, *Personnel*
Freida Campos, *Director*
Ramon Solorzano, *Supervisor*
EMP: 110
SQ FT: 26,937
SALES (est): 3.4MM
SALES (corp-wide): 62.1MM **Privately Held**
WEB: www.goldenstatehealth.com
SIC: 8051 Skilled nursing care facilities
PA: Golden State Health Centers, Inc.
13347 Ventura Blvd
Sherman Oaks CA 91423
818 385-3200

(P-20631)
GOOD SHEPHERD HEALTH CARE CE
1131 Arizona Ave, Santa Monica (90401-2009)
PHONE.................................310 451-4809
Fax: 310 458-3156
Jeong Lee, *CEO*
EMP: 55
SQ FT: 8,136
SALES (est): 2MM **Privately Held**
SIC: 8051 Skilled nursing care facilities

(P-20632)
GRANCARE LLC
Also Called: Vale Healthcare Center
13484 San Pablo Ave, San Pablo (94806-3904)
PHONE.................................510 232-5945
Tim Neal, *Principal*
Remy Rhodes, *President*
Kenneth Tabler, *President*
EMP: 277
SALES (corp-wide): 4.1B **Privately Held**
SIC: 8051 Skilled nursing care facilities
HQ: Grancare Llc
1 Ravinia Dr Ste 1400
Atlanta GA 30346
770 393-0199

(P-20633)
GRAND PARK CONVALESCENT HOSP
2312 W 8th St, Los Angeles (90057-3955)
PHONE.................................213 382-7315
Fax: 213 382-0595
Barry Kohn, *President*
Toby Kohn, *Vice Pres*
Ernie Espino, *Education*
EMP: 135
SQ FT: 60,000
SALES (est): 7MM **Privately Held**
SIC: 8051 8361 Convalescent home with continuous nursing care; rehabilitation center, residential: health care incidental

(P-20634)
GRAND TERRACE CARE CENTER
Also Called: Sunbridge Care Ctr - Grnd Ter
12000 Mount Vernon Ave, Grand Terrace (92313-5174)
PHONE.................................909 825-5221
Darlene Simonias, *Branch Mgr*
EMP: 53
SALES (corp-wide): 8.8MM **Privately Held**
SIC: 8051 Skilled nursing care facilities
PA: Grand Terrace Care Center
12000 Mount Vernon Ave
Grand Terrace CA 92313
909 825-5221

(P-20635)
GRAND VALLEY HEALTH CARE CTR
13524 Sherman Way, Van Nuys (91405-2830)
PHONE.................................818 786-3470
Janet Mandelbaum, *Mng Member*
Brenda Mandelbaum, *Mng Member*
EMP: 108
SALES (est): 4.3MM **Privately Held**
SIC: 8051 Skilled nursing care facilities

(P-20636)
GRANITE HILLS HEALTHCARE
1340 E Madison Ave, El Cajon (92021-8501)
PHONE.................................619 447-1020
Sharrod Brooks,
EMP: 99 EST: 2012
SALES: 9.4MM **Privately Held**
SIC: 8051 Skilled nursing care facilities

(P-20637)
GRIDLEY HLTHCARE & WELLNSS CEN
246 Spruce St, Gridley (95948-2216)
PHONE.................................530 846-6266
Sharrod Brooks,
EMP: 99 EST: 2010
SALES (est): 4.1MM **Privately Held**
SIC: 8051 Mental retardation hospital

(P-20638)
GRIFFITH PK RHBLTATION CTR LLC
Also Called: Griffith Park Healthcare Ctr
201 Allen Ave, Glendale (91201-2803)
PHONE.................................818 845-8507
Crystal Solorzano,
EMP: 75 EST: 2015
SALES (est): 254.4K **Privately Held**
SIC: 8051 Skilled nursing care facilities

(P-20639)
GROSS CONVALESCENT HOSPITAL
321 W Turner Rd, Lodi (95240-0517)
PHONE.................................209 334-3760
Fax: 209 334-1071
Paul Gross, *Vice Pres*
Elsie Gross, *Corp Secy*
Oscar Gross, *Principal*
EMP: 73
SQ FT: 10,000
SALES (est): 3.8MM **Privately Held**
SIC: 8051 Convalescent home with continuous nursing care

(P-20640)
GUARDIANS OF THE LOS ANGELES
10780 Santa Monica Blvd # 225, Los Angeles (90025-7617)
PHONE.................................310 479-2468
Shannon Slater, *Manager*
EMP: 67
SALES: 723.8K **Privately Held**
SIC: 8051 Skilled nursing care facilities

(P-20641)
H C C S INC
Also Called: Sherwood Healthcare Center
4700 Elvas Ave, Sacramento (95819-2250)
PHONE.................................916 454-5752
Fax: 916 453-0863
David Hilburn, *Director*
Bryan Boehrer, *Administration*
Brian Boehrer, *Administration*
John Lund, *Director*
Ernesto Quinto, *Director*
EMP: 70 EST: 1998
SALES (est): 2.7MM **Privately Held**
WEB: www.sherwoods.com
SIC: 8051 Skilled nursing care facilities

(P-20642)
HACIENDA REHABILITATION & HEAL
Also Called: Hacienda Health Care
361 E Grangeville Blvd, Hanford (93230-3054)
PHONE.................................559 582-9221
Fax: 559 582-8955
Rex Moore, *Branch Mgr*
Laura Garcia, *Office Mgr*
Alan Knudson, *Director*
Di R Wimbely, *Director*
EMP: 120
SALES (corp-wide): 10.2MM **Privately Held**
SIC: 8051 8069 Skilled nursing care facilities; specialty hospitals, except psychiatric
PA: Hacienda Rehabilitation & Health Care Center, Inc
1440 S State College Blvd 2a
Anaheim CA 92806
714 778-0221

8051 - Skilled Nursing Facilities County (P-20643)

(P-20643)
HANCOCK PK RHBLITATION CTR LLC
505 N La Brea Ave, Los Angeles (90036-2015)
PHONE...................323 937-4860
Kelly Atkins,
Marilyn Bascar, *Office Mgr*
Midori Breul, *Administration*
Dory Ventura, *Mktg Dir*
Chris Felfe,
EMP: 135
SALES (est): 3.9MM **Privately Held**
SIC: 8051 Skilled nursing care facilities

(P-20644)
HARBOR GLEN CARE CENTER
1033 E Arrow Hwy, Glendora (91740-6110)
PHONE...................626 963-7531
Kevin Thomas, *Principal*
Chris Turney, *Administration*
Longse Vessoua, *Education*
Lorena Medrano, *Food Svc Dir*
Lloyd White, *Hlthcr Dir*
EMP: 100 **EST:** 2000
SALES (est): 2.2MM
SALES (corp-wide): 1.3B **Publicly Held**
WEB: www.theensigngroup.com
SIC: 8051 Convalescent home with continuous nursing care
PA: The Ensign Group Inc
27101 Puerta Real Ste 450
Mission Viejo CA 92691
949 487-9500

(P-20645)
HAWTHORNE HEALTHCARE
11630 Grevillea Ave, Hawthorne (90250-2231)
PHONE...................310 679-9732
Sharrod Brooks, *Managing Prtnr*
EMP: 99 **EST:** 2011
SALES (est): 249.3K **Privately Held**
SIC: 8051 Skilled nursing care facilities

(P-20646)
HB HEALTHCARE ASSOCIATES LLC
Also Called: Sea Cliff Healthcare Center
18811 Florida St, Huntington Beach (92648-1920)
PHONE...................714 887-0144
Mike Williams,
EMP: 90
SALES: 16.2MM **Privately Held**
SIC: 8051 Skilled nursing care facilities

(P-20647)
HCR MANORCARE MED SVCS FLA LLC
Also Called: Manorcare Health Services
1975 Tice Valley Blvd, Walnut Creek (94595-2201)
PHONE...................925 274-1325
Fax: 925 906-0201
Roger Hogan, *Branch Mgr*
Gilbert Castro, *Records Dir*
Jonathan Frank, *Director*
EMP: 125
SQ FT: 53,335
SALES (corp-wide): 3B **Publicly Held**
WEB: www.manorcare.com
SIC: 8051 Skilled nursing care facilities
HQ: Hcr Manorcare Medical Services Of Florida, Llc
333 N Summit St Ste 100
Toledo OH 43604
419 252-5500

(P-20648)
HCR MANORCARE MED SVCS FLA LLC
Also Called: Manorcare Health Services
24962 Calle Aragon, Aliso Viejo (92653)
PHONE...................949 587-9000
Dave Jordan, *Branch Mgr*
EMP: 150
SALES (corp-wide): 3B **Publicly Held**
WEB: www.manorcare.com
SIC: 8051 Skilled nursing care facilities
HQ: Hcr Manorcare Medical Services Of Florida, Llc
333 N Summit St Ste 100
Toledo OH 43604
419 252-5500

(P-20649)
HCR MANORCARE MED SVCS FLA LLC
Also Called: Manor Care
11680 Warner Ave, Fountain Valley (92708-2513)
PHONE...................714 241-9800
Fax: 714 966-1654
Mark Shaffer, *Administration*
Liza Jimenez, *Hlthcr Dir*
Ketan Bhakta, *Director*
EMP: 195
SALES (corp-wide): 3B **Publicly Held**
WEB: www.manorcare.com
SIC: 8051 Skilled nursing care facilities
HQ: Hcr Manorcare Medical Services Of Florida, Llc
333 N Summit St Ste 100
Toledo OH 43604
419 252-5500

(P-20650)
HCR MANORCARE MED SVCS FLA LLC
Also Called: Manor Care
7807 Uplands Way, Citrus Heights (95610-7500)
PHONE...................916 967-2929
Fax: 916 965-8439
Terri Ballesteros, *Principal*
EMP: 180
SALES (corp-wide): 3B **Publicly Held**
WEB: www.manorcare.com
SIC: 8051 Skilled nursing care facilities
HQ: Hcr Manorcare Medical Services Of Florida, Llc
333 N Summit St Ste 100
Toledo OH 43604
419 252-5500

(P-20651)
HCR MANORCARE MED SVCS FLA LLC
Also Called: Manorcare Health Svcs Hemet
1717 W Stetson Ave, Hemet (92545-6882)
PHONE...................951 925-9171
Fax: 951 925-8186
Ron Ellenich, *Branch Mgr*
Marnie Davis, *Purchasing*
Guilherme Carvalho, *Director*
EMP: 180
SALES (corp-wide): 3B **Publicly Held**
WEB: www.manorcare.com
SIC: 8051 Skilled nursing care facilities
HQ: Hcr Manorcare Medical Services Of Florida, Llc
333 N Summit St Ste 100
Toledo OH 43604
419 252-5500

(P-20652)
HCR MANORCARE MED SVCS FLA LLC
Also Called: Manor Care
1150 Tilton Dr, Sunnyvale (94087-2440)
PHONE...................408 735-7200
Fax: 408 736-8619
Arthur Spencer, *Branch Mgr*
Yusra Hussain, *Director*
EMP: 100
SALES (corp-wide): 3B **Publicly Held**
WEB: www.manorcare.com
SIC: 8051 Skilled nursing care facilities
HQ: Hcr Manorcare Medical Services Of Florida, Llc
333 N Summit St Ste 100
Toledo OH 43604
419 252-5500

(P-20653)
HCR MANORCARE MED SVCS FLA LLC
Also Called: Manorcare Health Svcs Rossmoor
1226 Rossmoor Pkwy, Walnut Creek (94595-2538)
PHONE...................925 975-5000
Fax: 925 937-1132
John Gallick, *Manager*
Colleen Kabeary, *Sls & Mktg Exec*
Tina Conner Rn, *Nursing Dir*
Alex Gomez, *Director*
Edgar Kwan, *Director*
EMP: 105
SQ FT: 69,382
SALES (corp-wide): 3B **Publicly Held**
WEB: www.manorcare.com
SIC: 8051 Skilled nursing care facilities
HQ: Hcr Manorcare Medical Services Of Florida, Llc
333 N Summit St Ste 100
Toledo OH 43604
419 252-5500

(P-20654)
HCR MANORCARE MED SVCS FLA LLC
Also Called: Manorcare Hlth Svcs Encinitas
944 Regal Rd, Encinitas (92024-4634)
PHONE...................760 944-0331
Fax: 760 634-1337
James Elton, *Manager*
Andy Pisarik, *Administration*
Dave Sneddon, *Administration*
EMP: 100
SQ FT: 38,890
SALES (corp-wide): 3B **Publicly Held**
SIC: 8051 Skilled nursing care facilities
HQ: Hcr Manorcare Medical Services Of Florida, Llc
333 N Summit St Ste 100
Toledo OH 43604
419 252-5500

(P-20655)
HEALTH & REHABILITATION CENTER
Also Called: Mariner
2065 Los Gatos Almaden Rd, San Jose (95124-5417)
PHONE...................408 377-9275
James Brende, *Administration*
EMP: 50
SALES (est): 2.2MM **Privately Held**
SIC: 8051 Skilled nursing care facilities

(P-20656)
HEALTH CARE INVESTMENTS INC
Also Called: Rosecrans Care Center
1140 W Rosecrans Ave, Gardena (90247-2664)
PHONE...................310 323-3194
Fax: 310 323-8869
Pompeyo Rosales, *President*
Gonzalo Delrosario, *Admin Sec*
Shrikant Tamhane, *Director*
EMP: 106
SALES: 2.8MM **Privately Held**
SIC: 8051 Skilled nursing care facilities

(P-20657)
HEALTHCARE CENTRE OF FRESNO
1665 M St, Fresno (93721-1121)
PHONE...................559 268-5361
Fax: 559 268-8228
Lucille Epperson, *Administration*
Charles J Enoch, *Partner*
Joyce S Lopez, *Partner*
Laverne E Masten, *Partner*
Barbara H Rose, *Partner*
EMP: 163
SQ FT: 87,000
SALES (est): 4.1MM **Privately Held**
SIC: 8051 8069 Skilled nursing care facilities; convalescent home with continuous nursing care; specialty hospitals, except psychiatric

(P-20658)
HEALTHCARE CTR OF DOWNEY LLC
Also Called: Lakewood Healthcare Center
12023 Lakewood Blvd, Downey (90242-2635)
PHONE...................562 869-0978
Vince Hambright, *CEO*
Ken Lehmann,
EMP: 250
SQ FT: 1,076,391
SALES (est): 20.9MM **Privately Held**
SIC: 8051 Mental retardation hospital

(P-20659)
HEALTHCARE MGT SYSTEMS INC (PA)
Also Called: Bradley Court
900 Lane Ave Ste 190, Chula Vista (91914-4558)
PHONE...................619 521-9641
Tanya Pontecorvo, *President*
Kevin Cablayan, *CFO*
Erwin Cablayan, *Vice Pres*
EMP: 90
SALES (est): 6.7MM **Privately Held**
SIC: 8051 Skilled nursing care facilities

(P-20660)
HEALTHCARE MGT SYSTEMS INC
Also Called: Bradley Grdns Convalescent Ctr
980 W 7th St, San Jacinto (92582-3814)
PHONE...................951 654-9347
Fax: 951 654-6106
Dyan Lewis, *Manager*
Tamara Miller, *Exec Dir*
Mike Gomez, *Director*
Jean E Reed, *Agent*
EMP: 55
SALES (corp-wide): 6.7MM **Privately Held**
SIC: 8051 Skilled nursing care facilities
PA: Healthcare Management Systems, Inc.
900 Lane Ave Ste 190
Chula Vista CA 91914
619 521-9641

(P-20661)
HEBREW HOME FOR AGED DISABLED
Also Called: Jewish Home For The Aged
302 Silver Ave, San Francisco (94112-1510)
PHONE...................415 334-2500
Fax: 415 334-4375
Daniel Ruth, *President*
Vic Meinke, *CFO*
Kevin T Potter, *CFO*
Sharon Fried, *Officer*
Ilana Glaun, *Officer*
EMP: 600 **EST:** 1889
SALES: 46.4MM **Privately Held**
WEB: www.jhsf.org
SIC: 8051 Skilled nursing care facilities

(P-20662)
HELIOS HEALTHCARE LLC
Also Called: El Camino Care Center
2540 Carmichael Way, Carmichael (95608-5314)
PHONE...................916 482-0465
Fax: 916 482-7813
Evelyn McGraff, *Administration*
Remy Liong, *Administration*
Stephaney Hadrick, *Food Svc Dir*
Tommy Blaylock, *Supervisor*
EMP: 140
SALES (corp-wide): 23.8MM **Privately Held**
SIC: 8051 Skilled nursing care facilities
PA: Helios Healthcare, Llc
520 Capitol Mall Ste 800
Sacramento CA 95814
916 471-2241

(P-20663)
HELIOS HEALTHCARE LLC
Also Called: Sunridge Care & Rehabilitation
350 Iris Dr, Salinas (93906-3514)
PHONE...................831 449-1515
Rachael Bruton, *Administration*
EMP: 150
SALES (corp-wide): 23.8MM **Privately Held**
SIC: 8051 Skilled nursing care facilities
PA: Helios Healthcare, Llc
520 Capitol Mall Ste 800
Sacramento CA 95814
916 471-2241

(P-20664)
HELIOS HEALTHCARE LLC
Also Called: Rosewood Care Center
1911 Oak Park Blvd, Pleasant Hill (94523-4601)
PHONE...................925 935-6630
Robbie Williams, *General Mgr*
Neil Baldomero, *Administration*

PRODUCTS & SERVICES SECTION

8051 - Skilled Nursing Facilities County (P-20687)

EMP: 110
SALES (corp-wide): 23.8MM Privately Held
SIC: 8051 8093 Skilled nursing care facilities; rehabilitation center, outpatient treatment
PA: Helios Healthcare, Llc
520 Capitol Mall Ste 800
Sacramento CA 95814
916 471-2241

(P-20665)
HELPING HANDS SANCTUARY OF IDA
Also Called: Lacumbre Senior Living
3880 Via Lucero, Santa Barbara (93110-1605)
PHONE 805 687-6651
Lender Warren, *Manager*
Dani Guerrero, *Executive*
EMP: 130
SALES (corp-wide): 54.6MM Privately Held
SIC: 8051 Skilled nursing care facilities
PA: Helping Hands Sanctuary Of Idaho Inc
4978 Rainbow Ln
Pocatello ID

(P-20666)
HELPING HANDS SANCTUARY OF IDA
Also Called: Helping Hands of Westminster
240 Hospital Cir, Westminster (92683-3953)
PHONE 714 892-6686
Jon Peralez, *Administration*
Kimberly Dao, *Social Dir*
Nhi Phan, *Director*
Cristina Saril, *Director*
EMP: 100
SQ FT: 24,214
SALES (est): 4.6MM Privately Held
SIC: 8051 Skilled nursing care facilities

(P-20667)
HERITAGE HEALTH CARE INC
Also Called: Heritage Gardens Hlth Care Ctr
25271 Barton Rd, Loma Linda (92354-3013)
PHONE 909 796-0216
Stephen Flood, *CEO*
Gregory S Goings, *CEO*
Jim Kilian, *CFO*
Lisa Leak, *Psychologist*
Corrie Stevenson, *Director*
EMP: 150
SALES (est): 4.6MM Privately Held
SIC: 8051 8059 Skilled nursing care facilities; rest home, with health care

(P-20668)
HERITAGE MANOR INC
610 N Garfield Ave, Monterey Park (91754-1103)
PHONE 626 573-3141
Fax: 626 571-8461
Janie Campos, *Administration*
Cathriene Mc Dowell, *Financial Exec*
Christie Leadley, *Personnel Exec*
Chung Ng, *Director*
EMP: 80
SALES: 8.4MM Privately Held
SIC: 8051 Skilled nursing care facilities

(P-20669)
HERMAN HEALTH CARE CENTER
2295 Plummer Ave, San Jose (95125-4767)
PHONE 408 269-0701
Jeff Maggard, *Manager*
Susan Kofnovec, *Controller*
Mike Bottarini, *Director*
EMP: 99
SALES (est): 4.3MM Privately Held
SIC: 8051 Skilled nursing care facilities

(P-20670)
HERMAN SANITARIUM
2295 Plummer Ave, San Jose (95125-4767)
PHONE 408 269-0701
Fax: 408 269-2512
Steve Marcus, *Administration*

Robert Sollis, *President*
Marcelina Rivera, *Social Dir*
Sarah Magdelino, *Office Mgr*
Manny Flores, *Food Svc Dir*
EMP: 104
SQ FT: 4,500
SALES (est): 3.8MM Privately Held
SIC: 8051 Skilled nursing care facilities

(P-20671)
HIGHLAND PARK SKILLED NURSING
5125 Monte Vista St, Los Angeles (90042-3931)
PHONE 323 254-6125
Shlomo Rechnitz,
Maria Urbina, *Corp Comm Staff*
Ed Panopio, *Education*
Cristian Urbina, *Food Svc Dir*
Jenny Hwang, *Director*
EMP: 72 EST: 2008
SALES: 6MM Privately Held
SIC: 8051 Skilled nursing care facilities

(P-20672)
HILLVIEW CONVALESCENT HOSPITAL
530 W Dunne Ave, Morgan Hill (95037-4823)
PHONE 408 779-3633
Fax: 408 778-1826
James Ross, *Owner*
Richard Ross, *Co-Owner*
Steve Ross, *Administration*
EMP: 50
SQ FT: 10,000
SALES: 3.7MM Privately Held
SIC: 8051 Skilled nursing care facilities

(P-20673)
HONEYFLOWER HOLDINGS LLC
Also Called: Arlington Gardens Care Center
3688 Nye Ave, Riverside (92505-1818)
PHONE 951 351-2800
Mark Ballif, *Mng Member*
Brett Hill, *Administration*
Shimaree Foster, *Nursing Dir*
Paul Hubbard, *Mng Member*
Marie Hosek, *Director*
EMP: 170
SALES: 15.4MM Privately Held
SIC: 8051 Skilled nursing care facilities

(P-20674)
HORIZON WEST INC
Also Called: Walnut Whtney Convalecent Hosp
3529 Walnut Ave, Carmichael (95608-3049)
PHONE 916 488-8601
Kathy Spake, *Branch Mgr*
EMP: 130
SALES (corp-wide): 99MM Privately Held
SIC: 8051 Convalescent home with continuous nursing care
PA: Horizon West, Inc.
4020 Sierra College Blvd
Rocklin CA 95677
916 624-6230

(P-20675)
HORIZON WEST INC
Also Called: Heritage Conalescent Hospital
5255 Hemlock St, Sacramento (95841-3017)
PHONE 916 331-4590
Fax: 916 331-3048
Randy Balecha, *Manager*
Nicole Vargus, *Executive*
Mary Nollette, *Exec Dir*
Chet Lelio, *Administration*
Myrna Guzman, *Controller*
EMP: 100
SALES (corp-wide): 99MM Privately Held
SIC: 8051 8361 8059 Skilled nursing care facilities; residential care; convalescent home
PA: Horizon West, Inc.
4020 Sierra College Blvd
Rocklin CA 95677
916 624-6230

(P-20676)
HORIZON WEST HEALTHCARE INC (HQ)
4020 Sierra College Blvd # 190, Rocklin (95677-3906)
PHONE 916 624-6230
Martine D Harmon, *CEO*
Jeffrey Graine, *Records Dir*
Mandy Johnson, *Records Dir*
Dennis Roccaforte, *Corp Secy*
Linda Lutz, *Officer*
EMP: 54
SQ FT: 6,000
SALES (corp-wide): 47.8MM Privately Held
WEB: www.villadelrey.com
SIC: 8051 Convalescent home with continuous nursing care
PA: Horizon West, Inc.
4020 Sierra College Blvd
Rocklin CA 95677
916 624-6230

(P-20677)
HORIZON WEST HEALTHCARE INC
Also Called: Valley View Skilled Nursing
1162 S Dora St, Ukiah (95482-6340)
PHONE 707 462-1436
Paul Medlin, *Administration*
EMP: 60
SALES (corp-wide): 99MM Privately Held
WEB: www.villadelrey.com
SIC: 8051 Skilled nursing care facilities
HQ: Horizon West Healthcare, Inc.
4020 Sierra College Blvd # 190
Rocklin CA 95677
916 624-6230

(P-20678)
HOSPICE OF SAN JOAQUIN
3888 Pacific Ave, Stockton (95204-1953)
PHONE 209 957-3888
Fax: 209 957-3986
Stephen L Guasco, *CEO*
Kerrie Biddle, *CFO*
Michael Kiser, *Info Tech Mgr*
Steve Parsons, *Finance*
Patti Reiber, *Human Res Dir*
EMP: 90
SQ FT: 5,000
SALES: 10.8MM Privately Held
WEB: www.hospicesj.org
SIC: 8051 8641 Skilled nursing care facilities; social associations

(P-20679)
HOVLID SKILLED NURSING
240 Spruce St, Gridley (95948-2216)
PHONE 530 846-9065
Fax: 530 846-4217
Juanita Strudt, *Director*
EMP: 50
SALES (est): 2MM Privately Held
SIC: 8051 Skilled nursing care facilities

(P-20680)
HUNTINGTON BCH CNVLESCENT HOSP
Also Called: Sea Cliff Health Care
18811 Florida St, Huntington Beach (92648-1920)
PHONE 714 847-3515
Fax: 714 847-2852
Michael Williams, *Administration*
Evelyn Aranton Rn, *Nursing Dir*
Nicole Llido, *Manager*
EMP: 300
SALES (est): 8.3MM Privately Held
SIC: 8051 Convalescent home with continuous nursing care

(P-20681)
HYDE PARK CONVALESCENT HOSP
6520 West Blvd, Los Angeles (90043-4393)
PHONE 323 753-1354
Fax: 323 753-0509
Jeff Mendell, *President*
Elaine Wiesel, *Admin Sec*
Jesus Villirlo, *Facilities Dir*
Henri Atkinsin, *Director*

EMP: 50
SQ FT: 15,258
SALES: 3.5MM Privately Held
SIC: 8051 Skilled nursing care facilities

(P-20682)
IMAGINATIVE HORIZONS INC
1889 National City Blvd, National City (91950-5517)
PHONE 619 477-1176
Fax: 619 262-1410
Gary Byrnes, *President*
Rosella Byrnes, *Treasurer*
Dan Byrnes, *Info Tech Dir*
Kirstein W Ang, *Bookkeeper*
EMP: 84
SQ FT: 30,000
SALES (est): 6.1MM Privately Held
WEB: www.specialized-care.com
SIC: 8051 Skilled nursing care facilities

(P-20683)
INDIO HLTHCARE WLLNESS CTR LLC
Also Called: Desert Springs Healthcare
82262 Valencia Ave, Indio (92201-3120)
PHONE 760 347-6000
Sharrod Brooks,
EMP: 99 EST: 2010
SALES (est): 3.5MM Privately Held
SIC: 8051 Skilled nursing care facilities

(P-20684)
INFINITY CARE OF EAST LA
101 S Fickett St, Los Angeles (90033-4017)
PHONE 323 261-8108
Fax: 323 261-8213
Dr Bina Kambar, *President*
Rani Magboo, *Financial Exec*
EMP: 98
SALES: 8.1MM Privately Held
SIC: 8051 Skilled nursing care facilities

(P-20685)
INLAND CHRISTIAN HOME INC
1950 S Mountain Ave Ofc, Ontario (91762-6709)
PHONE 909 395-9322
Fax: 909 983-0431
David Stienstra, *President*
Lisa Coots, *Office Mgr*
Ariene Mosqueda, *Data Proc Staff*
Johanna Noppert, *Human Resources*
Joe Whitford, *Opers Staff*
EMP: 114
SQ FT: 100,000
SALES: 10.2MM Privately Held
WEB: www.ichome.org
SIC: 8051 8052 6513 8361 Skilled nursing care facilities; intermediate care facilities; retirement hotel operation; residential care

(P-20686)
INLAND MEDICAL ENTERPRISES
Also Called: Alcott Rehabilitation Hospital
3551 W Olympic Blvd, Los Angeles (90019-3504)
PHONE 323 732-0350
Fax: 323 734-3234
Irving Bauman, *President*
Frank Johnson, *Shareholder*
William Presnell, *Vice Pres*
Mary Allen, *Director*
EMP: 100
SQ FT: 35,000
SALES (est): 5.2MM Privately Held
SIC: 8051 Skilled nursing care facilities

(P-20687)
INTEGRTED CARE COMMUNITIES INC
Also Called: Inegrated Care Communities
11751 Davis St, Moreno Valley (92557-6316)
PHONE 951 243-3837
Carl Rowe, *President*
Meghan O'Connor, *Administration*
Herland Stephen, *Technology*
Sarah Saucedo, *Finance Mgr*
Philip Saucedo, *Finance*
EMP: 50

8051 - Skilled Nursing Facilities County (P-20688)

SALES (est): 3MM Privately Held
WEB: www.icare.bz
SIC: 8051 Skilled nursing care facilities

(P-20688)
INTERCOMMUNITY CARE CENTERS
2626 Grand Ave, Long Beach (90815-1707)
PHONE.....................562 427-8915
Fax: 562 427-2348
Russel Boydston, Branch Mgr
Ronald Philipp, Director
EMP: 120
SQ FT: 32,159
SALES (corp-wide): 7.3MM Privately Held
WEB: www.iccare.org
SIC: 8051 Mental retardation hospital
PA: Intercommunity Care Centers Inc
   2660 Grand Ave
   Long Beach CA
   562 426-1368

(P-20689)
J P H CONSULTING INC (PA)
1101 Crenshaw Blvd, Los Angeles (90019-3112)
PHONE.....................323 934-5660
Jeoung H Lee, President
Greda Bernabe, CFO
Kyle Watanabe, Director
EMP: 50
SALES (est): 21.6MM Privately Held
SIC: 8051 Skilled nursing care facilities

(P-20690)
J P H CONSULTING INC
4515 Huntington Dr S, Los Angeles (90032-1940)
PHONE.....................323 934-5660
EMP: 206
SALES (corp-wide): 21.6MM Privately Held
SIC: 8051 Skilled nursing care facilities
PA: J P H Consulting, Inc.
   1101 Crenshaw Blvd
   Los Angeles CA 90019
   323 934-5660

(P-20691)
JEFFREY PINE HOLDINGS LLC
Also Called: Villa Las Plmas Healthcare Ctr
622 S Anza St, El Cajon (92020-6602)
PHONE.....................619 442-0544
Myrna De Guzman,
Ellen Livingston, Vice Pres
Gavin Brown, Administration
Karlene Winfield, Human Res Dir
Mark Ballif,
EMP: 99
SALES: 17.1MM Privately Held
SIC: 8051 Skilled nursing care facilities

(P-20692)
JOHNRE CARE LLC
461 E Johnston Ave, Hemet (92543-7113)
PHONE.....................951 658-6374
Johnny Sicat, Mng Member
EMP: 60
SALES (est): 2.1MM Privately Held
SIC: 8051 Skilled nursing care facilities

(P-20693)
KARMA INC
Also Called: Manteca Care Rhabilitation Ctr
410 Eastwood Ave, Manteca (95336-3167)
PHONE.....................209 239-1222
Fax: 209 239-4919
Antony Thekkek, President
Prema Thekkek, Vice Pres
Jeff Garrison, General Mgr
Anil Sain, Director
EMP: 165
SQ FT: 29,700
SALES (est): 8.1MM
SALES (corp-wide): 12.1MM Privately Held
WEB: www.paksn.com
SIC: 8051 Skilled nursing care facilities
PA: Paksn, Inc.
   540 W Monte Vista Ave
   Vacaville CA 95688
   707 449-3400

(P-20694)
KATELLA PROPERTIES
Also Called: Alamitos W Convalescent Hosp
3902 Katella Ave, Los Alamitos (90720-3304)
PHONE.....................562 596-5561
Fax: 562 430-8174
Marilyn Gelgincolin, Director
Linda Hardin, Human Res Dir
Gerardo Tapia, Maintenance Dir
EMP: 170
SALES (corp-wide): 4MM Privately Held
WEB: www.katellamanor.com
SIC: 8051 Skilled nursing care facilities
PA: Katella Properties
   3952 Katella Ave
   Los Alamitos CA 90720
   562 596-2773

(P-20695)
KIMBERLY CARE CENTER INC
Also Called: SANTA MARIA CARE CENTER
820 W Cook St, Santa Maria (93458-5414)
PHONE.....................805 925-8877
Fax: 805 349-8371
Walter Matjasic, President
EMP: 75
SQ FT: 20,000
SALES: 3.5MM Privately Held
SIC: 8051 Skilled nursing care facilities

(P-20696)
KINDRED HEALTHCARE OPER INC
Also Called: Kindred Nrsing Hlthcre- Bybrry
1800 Adobe St, Concord (94520-2313)
PHONE.....................925 692-5886
Fax: 925 825-1127
J Seawell, Exec Dir
Sherese Holland, Administration
EMP: 106
SQ FT: 25,780
SALES (corp-wide): 7B Publicly Held
WEB: www.salemhaven.com
SIC: 8051 Skilled nursing care facilities
HQ: Kindred Healthcare Operating, Inc.
   680 S 4th St
   Louisville KY 40202
   502 596-7300

(P-20697)
KINDRED HEALTHCARE OPER INC
4700 Elvas Ave, Sacramento (95819-2250)
PHONE.....................916 454-5752
Gay Anderson, Manager
EMP: 75
SALES (corp-wide): 7B Publicly Held
WEB: www.salemhaven.com
SIC: 8051 Skilled nursing care facilities
HQ: Kindred Healthcare Operating, Inc.
   680 S 4th St
   Louisville KY 40202
   502 596-7300

(P-20698)
KINDRED HEALTHCARE OPER INC
Also Called: Kindred Hospital - Brea
875 N Brea Blvd, Brea (92821-2606)
PHONE.....................714 529-6842
Donna Hoover, Administration
Eva Arnstad, Records Dir
Diana Hanyak, COO
Wendy Ellington, Pharmacy Dir
Darlene Hunt, QA Dir
EMP: 79
SALES (corp-wide): 7B Publicly Held
WEB: www.salemhaven.com
SIC: 8051 Extended care facility
HQ: Kindred Healthcare Operating, Inc.
   680 S 4th St
   Louisville KY 40202
   502 596-7300

(P-20699)
KINDRED HEALTHCARE OPER INC
7534 Palm Ave, Highland (92346-3736)
PHONE.....................909 862-0611
Lance Squire, Administration
EMP: 161

SALES (corp-wide): 7B Publicly Held
WEB: www.salemhaven.com
SIC: 8051 8069 Skilled nursing care facilities; specialty hospitals, except psychiatric
HQ: Kindred Healthcare Operating, Inc.
   680 S 4th St
   Louisville KY 40202
   502 596-7300

(P-20700)
KINDRED HEALTHCARE OPER INC
Also Called: Kindred Nursng & Healthcare
76 Fenton St, Livermore (94550-4144)
PHONE.....................925 443-1800
Canbice Hale, Branch Mgr
Stephanie Kujala, Exec Dir
Margo Nijsure, Exec Dir
Margo Sbatz, Exec Dir
Amina Murtuza, VP Human Res
EMP: 90
SALES (corp-wide): 7B Publicly Held
WEB: www.salemhaven.com
SIC: 8051 Skilled nursing care facilities
HQ: Kindred Healthcare Operating, Inc.
   680 S 4th St
   Louisville KY 40202
   502 596-7300

(P-20701)
KINDRED HEALTHCARE OPER INC
1586 W San Marcos Blvd, San Marcos (92078-4019)
PHONE.....................760 471-2986
Daicel Gasperian, Manager
Susan McDermott, Hlthcr Dir
EMP: 130
SALES (corp-wide): 7B Publicly Held
WEB: www.salemhaven.com
SIC: 8051 Skilled nursing care facilities
HQ: Kindred Healthcare Operating, Inc.
   680 S 4th St
   Louisville KY 40202
   502 596-7300

(P-20702)
KINDRED HEALTHCARE OPER INC
Also Called: Pacific Coast Care Center
720 E Romie Ln, Salinas (93901-4208)
PHONE.....................831 424-8072
Lupe Flores, Manager
Gerald Hunter, Administration
EMP: 165
SALES (corp-wide): 7B Publicly Held
WEB: www.salemhaven.com
SIC: 8051 Skilled nursing care facilities
HQ: Kindred Healthcare Operating, Inc.
   680 S 4th St
   Louisville KY 40202
   502 596-7300

(P-20703)
KINDRED HEALTHCARE OPER INC
Also Called: Kindred Nursing
2121 Pine St, San Francisco (94115-2829)
PHONE.....................415 922-5085
Melissa Jones, Director
EMP: 100
SALES (corp-wide): 7B Publicly Held
WEB: www.salemhaven.com
SIC: 8051 Skilled nursing care facilities
HQ: Kindred Healthcare Operating, Inc.
   680 S 4th St
   Louisville KY 40202
   502 596-7300

(P-20704)
KINDRED HEALTHCARE OPERATING
2211 Mount Vernon Ave, Bakersfield (93306-3309)
PHONE.....................661 872-2121
Lori Hay, Manager
EMP: 200
SALES (corp-wide): 7B Publicly Held
WEB: www.salemhaven.com
SIC: 8051 Skilled nursing care facilities
HQ: Kindred Healthcare Operating, Inc.
   680 S 4th St
   Louisville KY 40202
   502 596-7300

(P-20705)
KINDRED HEALTHCARE OPERATING
223 Fargo Way, Folsom (95630-2961)
PHONE.....................916 351-9151
Meridith Taylor, Administration
Fran U Day, Pat Nrsg Dir
Deborah Stricker, Infect Cntl Dir
Barbara Partridge, Lab Dir
Mark Blum, Radiology Dir
EMP: 150
SALES (corp-wide): 7B Publicly Held
WEB: www.salemhaven.com
SIC: 8051 Skilled nursing care facilities
HQ: Kindred Healthcare Operating, Inc.
   680 S 4th St
   Louisville KY 40202
   502 596-7300

(P-20706)
KINDRED NURSING CENTERS W LLC
Also Called: Kindred Transitional Care
516 Willow St, Alameda (94501-6132)
PHONE.....................510 521-5600
Richard Espinosa, Administration
Tom Wood, Finance Mgr
Norbu Sangpo, Chf Purch Ofc
Frank Rynig, Director
Frank Ryning, Director
EMP: 122
SALES (corp-wide): 7B Publicly Held
WEB: www.salemhaven.com
SIC: 8051 Skilled nursing care facilities
HQ: Kindred Nursing Centers West Llc
   3128 Boxelder Dr
   Cheyenne WY 82001
   307 634-7901

(P-20707)
KINDRED NURSING CENTERS W LLC
Also Called: Kindred Nursing and Reha
1601 5th Ave, San Rafael (94901-1808)
PHONE.....................415 456-7170
Richard Espinoza, Manager
EMP: 65
SALES (corp-wide): 7B Publicly Held
WEB: www.salemhaven.com
SIC: 8051 Convalescent home with continuous nursing care
HQ: Kindred Nursing Centers West Llc
   3128 Boxelder Dr
   Cheyenne WY 82001
   307 634-7901

(P-20708)
KINDRED NURSING CENTERS W LLC
Also Called: Kindred Transitional Care
2120 Benton Dr, Redding (96003-2151)
PHONE.....................530 243-6317
Fax: 530 243-4646
Michael Sowerby, Manager
William Altman, Vice Pres
Barbara Hutchinson, Administration
Lisa Carter, Nursing Dir
Cheryl Akers, Director
EMP: 174
SALES (corp-wide): 7B Publicly Held
WEB: www.salemhaven.com
SIC: 8051 Skilled nursing care facilities
HQ: Kindred Nursing Centers West Llc
   3128 Boxelder Dr
   Cheyenne WY 82001
   307 634-7901

(P-20709)
KINDRED NURSING CENTERS W LLC
Also Called: Kindred Transitional
1517 Knickerbocker Dr, Stockton (95210-3119)
PHONE.....................209 957-4539
Fax: 209 957-5831
Keith Braley, Administration
Dahlia Cano, Records Dir
Joseph Landenwich, Vice Pres
Jeannie Hart, Office Mgr
Mary Sasser, Administration
EMP: 138
SALES (corp-wide): 7B Publicly Held
WEB: www.salemhaven.com
SIC: 8051 Skilled nursing care facilities

PRODUCTS & SERVICES SECTION

8051 - Skilled Nursing Facilities County (P-20731)

HQ: Kindred Nursing Centers West Llc
3128 Boxelder Dr
Cheyenne WY 82001
307 634-7901

(P-20710)
KISSITO HEALTH CASE INC
Also Called: Arbor Vly Nrsing Rhblttion Ctr
1310 W Granger Ave, Modesto
(95350-3911)
PHONE..................................209 524-4817
Al Johnson, *Branch Mgr*
EMP: 127
SALES (corp-wide): 67.9MM **Privately Held**
SIC: **8051** 8361 Convalescent home with continuous nursing care; rehabilitation center, residential: health care incidental
PA: Kissito Health Care, Inc.
5228 Valleypointe Pkwy
Roanoke VA 24019
540 265-0322

(P-20711)
KNOLLS CONVALESCENT HOSPITAL (PA)
Also Called: Desert Knlls Convalescent Hosp
16890 Green Tree Blvd, Victorville
(92395-5618)
PHONE..................................760 245-5361
Fax: 760 245-6247
Gary L Bechtold, *President*
Fred Bechtold, *Vice Pres*
Larry Bechtold, *Vice Pres*
Michelle Schmid, *Administration*
Stacey Sanchez, *Business Mgr*
EMP: 130
SQ FT: 5,421
SALES (est): 10.4MM **Privately Held**
SIC: **8051** 8052 Convalescent home with continuous nursing care; intermediate care facilities

(P-20712)
KNOLLS CONVALESCENT HOSPITAL
Also Called: Desert Knolls Convalescent
14973 Hesperia Rd, Victorville
(92395-3923)
PHONE..................................760 245-6477
Fax: 760 245-7296
Gary Bechtold, *General Mgr*
Jessica Sanchez, *Office Mgr*
Irena Serafin, *Hlthcr Dir*
Victor Sabo, *Director*
EMP: 80
SALES (corp-wide): 10.4MM **Privately Held**
SIC: **8051** 6513 Skilled nursing care facilities; apartment building operators
PA: Knolls Convalescent Hospital Inc
16890 Green Tree Blvd
Victorville CA 92395
760 245-5361

(P-20713)
KNOTT AVENUE CARE CENTER
9021 Knott Ave, Buena Park (90620-4138)
PHONE..................................714 826-2330
Peter Madigan, *President*
Robert Nelson, *President*
Elizabeth Casey, *Executive*
Bob Nelson, *Administration*
Arthur Helfat, *Director*
EMP: 125
SALES (est): 6.1MM **Privately Held**
SIC: **8051** 8059 Skilled nursing care facilities; rest home, with health care

(P-20714)
KSM HEALTHCARE INC
Also Called: DREIER'S NURSING CARE CENTER
1400 W Glenoaks Blvd, Glendale
(91201-1911)
PHONE..................................818 242-1183
John Haedrich, *President*
Ramone Perez, *Facilities Dir*
Beth Montenegro, *Director*
EMP: 76
SQ FT: 40,000
SALES: 4.7MM **Privately Held**
WEB: www.nursing-care.com
SIC: **8051** Skilled nursing care facilities

(P-20715)
KU KYOUNG
Also Called: Eden Villa
19960 Santa Maria Ave, Castro Valley
(94546-4220)
P.O. Box 590428 (94546)
PHONE..................................510 582-2765
Fax: 510 582-9670
Kyoung Ku, *Owner*
EMP: 170
SQ FT: 37,157
SALES (est): 4.3MM **Privately Held**
SIC: **8051** 1522

(P-20716)
LA JOLLA VILLAGE TOWERS 500
8515 Costa Verde Blvd Ofc, San Diego
(92122-1152)
PHONE..................................858 646-7700
Steve Brudnick, *Administration*
Vicki Simpson, *Administration*
EMP: 65
SQ FT: 900,000
SALES (est): 1.3MM **Privately Held**
SIC: **8051** Skilled nursing care facilities

(P-20717)
LA PALMA CARE CENTER
Also Called: La Palma Nursing Center
1130 W La Palma Ave, Anaheim
(92801-2803)
PHONE..................................714 772-7480
Fax: 714 776-1801
Sim Mandelbaum, *President*
Joseph Berkowitc, *Administration*
Soledad Lee, *Director*
EMP: 75
SQ FT: 20,000
SALES (est): 3.5MM **Privately Held**
SIC: **8051** Convalescent home with continuous nursing care

(P-20718)
LAFALTTE RHBILITATION CARE CTR
537 E Fulton St, Stockton (95204-2227)
PHONE..................................209 466-2066
Gus Ropalidas, *Administration*
EMP: 100
SALES (est): 1.3MM **Privately Held**
SIC: **8051** Convalescent home with continuous nursing care

(P-20719)
LAKEWOOD MANOR NORTH INC
831 S Lake St, Los Angeles (90057-4013)
PHONE..................................213 380-9175
Fax: 213 380-1879
Kim C Elliott, *Administration*
EMP: 74
SQ FT: 23,000
SALES (est): 4.6MM **Privately Held**
SIC: **8051** Skilled nursing care facilities

(P-20720)
LAS VILLAS DEL NORTE
Also Called: Healthcare Group
1325 Las Villas Way, Escondido
(92026-1946)
PHONE..................................760 741-1047
Fax: 760 741-0221
John Helpsley, *Director*
Kevin Moriarty, *Vice Pres*
Michael J Presnall, *Vice Pres*
Patricia Salmon, *Vice Pres*
Jared Edmunds, *Exec Dir*
EMP: 100
SALES (corp-wide): 3MM **Privately Held**
SIC: **8051** 8052 Skilled nursing care facilities; intermediate care facilities
PA: Las Villas Del Norte
416 W Spruce St
Junction City KS 66441
760 741-1046

(P-20721)
LAWNDLE HLTHCARE & WELLNSS CEN
15100 Prairie Ave, Lawndale (90260-2209)
PHONE..................................310 679-3344
Sharrod Brooks,
EMP: 99 EST: 2011
SALES: 5.5MM **Privately Held**
SIC: **8051** Mental retardation hospital

(P-20722)
LEXINGTON GROUP INTERNATIONAL (PA)
9200 W Sunset Blvd # 700, West Hollywood (90069-3603)
PHONE..................................310 385-1071
Lee C Samson, *CEO*
Lawrence E Feigen, *COO*
EMP: 53
SALES (est): 67MM **Privately Held**
SIC: **8051** Convalescent home with continuous nursing care

(P-20723)
LIBERTY HEALTHCARE OF OKLAHOMA
Also Called: Regency
4463 San Felipe Rd Ofc, San Jose
(95135-1515)
PHONE..................................408 532-7677
Aliyan Montose, *Manager*
EMP: 80
SALES (corp-wide): 7.3MM **Privately Held**
SIC: **8051** Skilled nursing care facilities
PA: Liberty Healthcare Of Oklahoma Inc
3073 Horseshoe Dr S # 100
Naples FL 34104
239 262-8006

(P-20724)
LIFE CARE CENTERS AMERICA INC
Also Called: Life Care Center of La Habra
1233 W La Habra Blvd, La Habra
(90631-5226)
PHONE..................................562 690-0852
Fax: 562 694-2279
Daniel Husband, *Administration*
Therese Allen, *Office Mgr*
Patty Rosas, *Pub Rel Dir*
EMP: 90
SALES (corp-wide): 10.3MM **Privately Held**
SIC: **8051** Skilled nursing care facilities
PA: Life Care Centers Of America, Inc.
3570 Keith St Nw
Cleveland TN 37312
423 472-9585

(P-20725)
LIFE CARE CENTERS AMERICA INC
Also Called: Mirada Hills Rehb & Conva
12200 La Mirada Blvd, La Mirada
(90638-1306)
PHONE..................................562 947-8691
Selina Stewart, *Exec Dir*
Dolores Estrada, *QC Dir*
EMP: 150
SALES (corp-wide): 10.3MM **Privately Held**
SIC: **8051** Skilled nursing care facilities
PA: Life Care Centers Of America, Inc.
3570 Keith St Nw
Cleveland TN 37312
423 472-9585

(P-20726)
LIFE CARE CENTERS AMERICA INC
11926 La Mirada Blvd, La Mirada
(90638-1303)
PHONE..................................562 943-7156
Chris Stottlemyer, *Manager*
Lili Trejo, *Social Dir*
Dori Vandendries, *Office Mgr*
Khalid Nur, *Director*
EMP: 100
SALES (corp-wide): 10.3MM **Privately Held**
SIC: **8051** Skilled nursing care facilities
PA: Life Care Centers Of America, Inc.
3570 Keith St Nw
Cleveland TN 37312
423 472-9585

(P-20727)
LIFE CARE CENTERS AMERICA INC
Also Called: Life Care Centers of Escondido
1980 Felicita Rd, Escondido (92025-5922)
PHONE..................................760 741-6109
Rodger Groves, *Administration*
Stephanie Bias, *Purchasing*
Andrea Wedderburn, *Teacher Per Dir*
Edgar Coteras, *Hlthcr Dir*
Beverly Liquir, *Hlthcr Dir*
EMP: 200
SALES (corp-wide): 10.3MM **Privately Held**
SIC: **8051** Skilled nursing care facilities
PA: Life Care Centers Of America, Inc.
3570 Keith St Nw
Cleveland TN 37312
423 472-9585

(P-20728)
LIFE CARE CENTERS AMERICA INC
Also Called: Lake Forest Nursing Center
25652 Old Trabuco Rd, Lake Forest
(92630-2776)
PHONE..................................949 380-9380
Kim Le, *Branch Mgr*
Melanie Duzel, *Human Res Dir*
Kim Kelleher, *Director*
EMP: 200
SALES (corp-wide): 10.3MM **Privately Held**
SIC: **8051** Skilled nursing care facilities
PA: Life Care Centers Of America, Inc.
3570 Keith St Nw
Cleveland TN 37312
423 472-9585

(P-20729)
LIFE CARE CENTERS AMERICA INC
Also Called: Imperial Convalescent
11926 La Mirada Blvd, La Mirada
(90638-1303)
PHONE..................................562 943-7156
Fax: 562 947-6084
Ted Stultz, *Manager*
Odette Tawadrous, *Director*
EMP: 150
SALES (corp-wide): 10.3MM **Privately Held**
SIC: **8051** 8741 Skilled nursing care facilities; management services
PA: Life Care Centers Of America, Inc.
3570 Keith St Nw
Cleveland TN 37312
423 472-9585

(P-20730)
LIFE CARE CENTERS AMERICA INC
Also Called: Life Care Center of Bellflower
16910 Woodruff Ave, Bellflower
(90706-6036)
PHONE..................................562 867-1761
Tooren Bel, *Manager*
Mari C Sajise, *Pharmacy Dir*
Ruby Panuncialman, *Administration*
Khrizt Lopez, *Human Res Dir*
Lee Stotts, *Marketing Staff*
EMP: 100
SALES (corp-wide): 10.3MM **Privately Held**
SIC: **8051** Skilled nursing care facilities
PA: Life Care Centers Of America, Inc.
3570 Keith St Nw
Cleveland TN 37312
423 472-9585

(P-20731)
LIFE CARE CENTERS AMERICA INC
Also Called: Life Care Center of Norwalk
12350 Rosecrans Ave, Norwalk
(90650-5064)
PHONE..................................562 921-6624
Steve Ramsdel, *Vice Pres*
Wendy Santos, *Social Dir*
Apple Ang, *Office Mgr*
Jean Paalam, *Chf Purch Ofc*
Pauline Austria, *Hlthcr Dir*
EMP: 60
SALES (corp-wide): 10.3MM **Privately Held**
SIC: **8051** Skilled nursing care facilities
PA: Life Care Centers Of America, Inc.
3570 Keith St Nw
Cleveland TN 37312
423 472-9585

8051 - Skilled Nursing Facilities County (P-20732)

(P-20732)
LIFE CARE CENTERS OF AMERICA
Also Called: Life Care Center San Gabriel
909 W Santa Anita Ave, San Gabriel (91776-1018)
PHONE..................626 289-5365
Fax: 626 458-8612
Eunice Fletcher, *Manager*
Bernie Sauer, *Info Tech Dir*
EMP: 90
SALES (corp-wide): 10.3MM **Privately Held**
SIC: 8051 Skilled nursing care facilities
PA: Life Care Centers Of America, Inc.
3570 Keith St Nw
Cleveland TN 37312
423 472-9585

(P-20733)
LIFE GNERATIONS HEALTHCARE LLC
Also Called: Stanford Court Nursing Center
7800 Parkway Dr, La Mesa (91942-2001)
PHONE..................619 460-2330
Fax: 619 460-5821
James Teddie, *Administration*
Jim Geddie, *Administration*
John Berger, *Director*
Charles Sinclair, *Manager*
EMP: 110
SALES (corp-wide): 68.1MM **Privately Held**
SIC: 8051 Skilled nursing care facilities
PA: Life Generations Healthcare Llc
20371 Irvine Ave Ste 210
Newport Beach CA 92660
714 241-5600

(P-20734)
LIFECARE SYSTEMS INC
Also Called: Medical Inst of Little Co Mary
4101 Torrance Blvd, Torrance (90503-4607)
PHONE..................310 540-7676
Karl Carrier, *President*
Henry G Walker, *President*
EMP: 150
SALES: 17.6MM **Privately Held**
SIC: 8051 Skilled nursing care facilities

(P-20735)
LIGHTHOUSE HEALTHCARE CTR LLC
2222 Santa Ana Blvd, Los Angeles (90059)
PHONE..................323 564-4461
Sharrod Brooks,
David Strother, *Administration*
EMP: 99
SALES (est): 3.1MM **Privately Held**
SIC: 8051 Skilled nursing care facilities

(P-20736)
LILY HOLDINGS LLC
Also Called: Oakwood Gardens Care Center
3510 E Shields Ave, Fresno (93726-6909)
PHONE..................559 222-4807
Ashley Specht,
Richard Martin,
EMP: 99
SALES (est): 2.1MM **Privately Held**
SIC: 8051 Skilled nursing care facilities

(P-20737)
LINDA VISTA MANOR INC
Also Called: Kearny Mesa Convalescent Hosp
7675 Family Cir, San Diego (92111-5304)
PHONE..................858 278-8121
Richard Hebbel, *President*
Jeanette Hebbel, *Vice Pres*
Tamara Chabot, *Personnel*
Nicole Dente, *Food Svc Dir*
Norma Martinez, *Director*
EMP: 109
SQ FT: 30,000
SALES (est): 7.5MM **Privately Held**
WEB: www.kearnymesaconvalescent.com
SIC: 8051 6411 Skilled nursing care facilities; insurance agents, brokers & service

(P-20738)
LITTLE SISTERS THE POOR OF LA
Also Called: Jeanne Jugan, A Residence
2100 S Western Ave, San Pedro (90732-4389)
PHONE..................310 548-0625
Fax: 310 833-6142
Margaret McArthy, *President*
Clotilde Jardim, *Treasurer*
Michael Mugan, *Vice Pres*
Jean Dywan, *Exec Dir*
Julie Martin, *Bookkeeper*
EMP: 100
SQ FT: 145,530
SALES (est): 7.4MM **Privately Held**
SIC: 8051 8361 8052 Extended care facility; residential care; intermediate care facilities

(P-20739)
LONE TREE CONVALESCENT HOSP
4001 Lone Tree Way, Antioch (94509-6232)
PHONE..................925 754-0470
Fax: 925 754-2775
Lowell Callaway, *President*
Mark Callaway, *Corp Secy*
Velda C Pierce, *Vice Pres*
Angelina Camacho, *Social Dir*
Velda C Piere, *VP Sls/Mktg*
EMP: 135 EST: 1968
SQ FT: 10,000
SALES (est): 11.8MM **Privately Held**
SIC: 8051 Skilled nursing care facilities

(P-20740)
LONG BEACH CARE CENTER INC
2615 Grand Ave, Long Beach (90815-1708)
PHONE..................562 426-6141
William A Nelson, *President*
Araceli Flechenstein, *Social Dir*
Francisco Soto, *Purch Agent*
Dennis Bartolome, *Teacher Per Dir*
EMP: 108
SQ FT: 43,962
SALES: 14MM **Privately Held**
WEB: www.longbeachcarecenter.com
SIC: 8051 Convalescent home with continuous nursing care

(P-20741)
LONGWOOD MANAGEMENT CORP
Also Called: Imperial Crest Healthcare Ctr
11834 Inglewood Ave, Hawthorne (90250-0107)
PHONE..................310 679-1461
Fax: 310 679-1237
Robert Villalub, *Administration*
Margie Linder, *Nursing Dir*
EMP: 150
SALES (corp-wide): 169.4MM **Privately Held**
SIC: 8051 Convalescent home with continuous nursing care
PA: Longwood Management Corp.
4032 Wilshire Blvd Fl 6
Los Angeles CA 90010
213 389-6900

(P-20742)
LONGWOOD MANAGEMENT CORP
Also Called: Magnolia Grdns Convalescent HM
17922 San Frnando Msn, Granada Hills (91344-4043)
PHONE..................818 360-1864
Fax: 818 831-0599
Ojijoji Gervacio, *Principal*
Ricky Castro, *Executive*
Tess Ali, *Office Mgr*
Rogerilo Carrera, *Administration*
EMP: 100
SALES (corp-wide): 169.4MM **Privately Held**
SIC: 8051 Skilled nursing care facilities
PA: Longwood Management Corp.
4032 Wilshire Blvd Fl 6
Los Angeles CA 90010
213 389-6900

(P-20743)
LONGWOOD MANAGEMENT CORP
Also Called: Green Acres Lodge
8101 Hill Dr, Rosemead (91770-4169)
PHONE..................626 280-2293
Fax: 626 280-5685
Karen Fugate, *Administration*
Paul Liu, *Director*
EMP: 60
SALES (corp-wide): 169.4MM **Privately Held**
SIC: 8051 Skilled nursing care facilities
PA: Longwood Management Corp.
4032 Wilshire Blvd Fl 6
Los Angeles CA 90010
213 389-6900

(P-20744)
LONGWOOD MANAGEMENT CORP
Also Called: San Gabriel Convalescent Ctr
8035 Hill Dr, Rosemead (91770-4116)
PHONE..................626 280-4820
Fax: 323 280-0227
Gigi Garcia, *Branch Mgr*
Manuel Delallana, *Administration*
Tom Yeh, *Director*
EMP: 150
SALES (corp-wide): 169.4MM **Privately Held**
SIC: 8051 Convalescent home with continuous nursing care
PA: Longwood Management Corp.
4032 Wilshire Blvd Fl 6
Los Angeles CA 90010
213 389-6900

(P-20745)
LONGWOOD MANAGEMENT CORP
Also Called: Crenshaw Nursing
1900 S Longwood Ave, Los Angeles (90016-1408)
PHONE..................323 933-1560
Fax: 323 933-9030
Gilbert Fimbres, *Manager*
EMP: 50
SALES (corp-wide): 169.4MM **Privately Held**
SIC: 8051 8052 Skilled nursing care facilities; intermediate care facilities
PA: Longwood Management Corp.
4032 Wilshire Blvd Fl 6
Los Angeles CA 90010
213 389-6900

(P-20746)
LONGWOOD MANOR
Also Called: Longwood Manor Convalescent HM
4853 W Washington Blvd, Los Angeles (90016-1501)
PHONE..................323 935-1157
Fax: 323 935-3140
Jacob Friedman, *President*
Lea Friedman, *Corp Secy*
Irving Friedman, *Vice Pres*
John Franklin, *Administration*
EMP: 200
SQ FT: 30,000
SALES: 16.3MM **Privately Held**
SIC: 8051 Skilled nursing care facilities

(P-20747)
LOS ANGLES JEWISH HM FOR AGING (PA)
Also Called: Grancell Village
7150 Tampa Ave, Reseda (91335-3700)
PHONE..................818 774-3000
Fax: 818 342-0881
Arthur A Greenberg, *Ch of Bd*
Molly Forrest, *CEO*
John Graham, *COO*
Larissa Stepanians, *COO*
Jeffrey Glassman, *Chairman*
EMP: 400
SQ FT: 35,000
SALES: 22.7MM **Privately Held**
WEB: www.jha.org
SIC: 8051 8361 Skilled nursing care facilities; residential care

(P-20748)
LOS ANGLES JEWISH HM FOR AGING
Also Called: Eisenberg Village
18855 Victory Blvd, Reseda (91335-6445)
PHONE..................818 774-3000
Annette Brinnon, *Manager*
Lianne Coleman, *Administration*
Hadi Pourbeheshtian, *Engineer*
Harriett Zeitlin, *Director*
EMP: 350
SALES (corp-wide): 22.7MM **Privately Held**
WEB: www.jha.org
SIC: 8051 Skilled nursing care facilities
PA: Los Angeles Jewish Home For The Aging
7150 Tampa Ave
Reseda CA 91335
818 774-3000

(P-20749)
LYTTON GARDENS INC (PA)
437 Webster St, Palo Alto (94301-1242)
PHONE..................650 328-3300
Fax: 650 324-6666
Gery Yearout, *CEO*
Jonathan Casey, *CFO*
Jennifer Varno, *Exec Dir*
Jennifer Hong, *Human Resources*
Ron Salvador, *Director*
EMP: 180
SALES: 17.1MM **Privately Held**
WEB: www.lyttongardens.org
SIC: 8051 Skilled nursing care facilities

(P-20750)
LYTTON GARDENS INC
Also Called: Lytton Gardens Health Care Ctr
656 Lytton Ave, Palo Alto (94301-1352)
PHONE..................650 328-3300
Vera Goutille, *Manager*
EMP: 140
SALES (corp-wide): 17.1MM **Privately Held**
WEB: www.lyttongardens.org
SIC: 8051 Skilled nursing care facilities
PA: Lytton Gardens, Inc.
437 Webster St
Palo Alto CA 94301
650 328-3300

(P-20751)
LYTTON GARDENS INC
Also Called: Lyttont Gardens 3
330 Everett Ave, Palo Alto (94301-1456)
PHONE..................650 321-0400
George Hajjar, *Branch Mgr*
EMP: 140
SALES (corp-wide): 17.1MM **Privately Held**
SIC: 8051 Skilled nursing care facilities
PA: Lytton Gardens, Inc.
437 Webster St
Palo Alto CA 94301
650 328-3300

(P-20752)
MADERA CONVALESCENT HOSPITAL (PA)
517 S A St, Madera (93638-3896)
PHONE..................559 673-9228
Fax: 559 673-1245
Arden Bennett, *CEO*
Dennis Albers, *Ch of Bd*
Mathilde Albers, *Corp Secy*
Emile Damia, *Vice Pres*
EMP: 160 EST: 1965
SQ FT: 1,500
SALES (est): 5.9MM **Privately Held**
SIC: 8051 Convalescent home with continuous nursing care

(P-20753)
MADISON CARE CENTER LLC
1391 E Madison Ave, El Cajon (92021-8568)
PHONE..................619 444-1107
Fax: 619 444-1403
Emmanuel David, *President*
Carmelita Ortiz, *Accounting Mgr*
Leo Atanacio, *Director*
EMP: 100
SALES (est): 4.7MM **Privately Held**
SIC: 8051 Skilled nursing care facilities

PRODUCTS & SERVICES SECTION
8051 - Skilled Nursing Facilities County (P-20777)

(P-20754)
MANNING GARDENS CARE CTR INC
2113 E Manning Ave, Fresno (93725-9681)
PHONE.................................559 834-2586
Ronald Kinnersley, *President*
EMP: 82 **EST:** 2011
SALES (est): 1.7MM **Privately Held**
SIC: 8051 Skilled nursing care facilities

(P-20755)
MAQUI HOLDINGS LLC
Also Called: Paradise Ridge Post-Acute
1633 Cypress Ln, Paradise (95969-2823)
PHONE.................................530 877-9316
Howard Brett Hill, *Administration*
EMP: 99
SALES (est): 324.2K **Privately Held**
SIC: 8051 Convalescent home with continuous nursing care

(P-20756)
MARIN CNVLSCENT RHBLTTION HOSP
30 Hacienda Dr, Belvedere Tiburon (94920-1127)
PHONE.................................415 435-4554
Fax: 415 435-6964
Mary Wollam, *President*
Lawrence Posner, *Director*
Debbie Allen, *Manager*
EMP: 60
SQ FT: 5,000
SALES (est): 3.6MM **Privately Held**
WEB: www.marinconvalescent.com
SIC: 8051 Convalescent home with continuous nursing care

(P-20757)
MARINER HEALTH CARE INC
Also Called: Driftwood Health Care Ctr
4109 Emerald St, Torrance (90503-3105)
PHONE.................................310 371-4628
Fax: 310 214-1882
Jennifer Torgrude, *Manager*
EMP: 100
SALES (corp-wide): 4.1B **Privately Held**
WEB: www.marinerhealth.com
SIC: 8051 Extended care facility
HQ: Mariner Health Care, Inc.
1 Ravinia Dr Ste 1500
Atlanta GA 30346
678 443-7000

(P-20758)
MARINER HEALTH CARE INC
Also Called: Freemont Health Care Center
39022 Presidio Way, Fremont (94538-1221)
PHONE.................................510 792-3743
Fax: 510 945-9387
Lisa Chattlow, *Administration*
Mary Grace Abuan, *Chf Purch Ofc*
EMP: 170
SALES (corp-wide): 4.1B **Privately Held**
WEB: www.marinerhealth.com
SIC: 8051 Extended care facility
HQ: Mariner Health Care, Inc.
1 Ravinia Dr Ste 1500
Atlanta GA 30346
678 443-7000

(P-20759)
MARINER HEALTH CARE INC
Also Called: Gilroy Health & Rehab Ctr
8170 Murray Ave, Gilroy (95020-4605)
PHONE.................................408 842-9311
Gerald Hunter, *Administration*
Carla Wyrick, *Office Mgr*
Dalia Velasquez, *Hlthcr Dir*
Hector Yanez, *Director*
EMP: 145
SALES (corp-wide): 4.1B **Privately Held**
WEB: www.marinerhealth.com
SIC: 8051 Extended care facility
HQ: Mariner Health Care, Inc.
1 Ravinia Dr Ste 1500
Atlanta GA 30346
678 443-7000

(P-20760)
MARINER HEALTH CARE INC
7400 24th St, Sacramento (95822-5350)
PHONE.................................916 422-4825
Robert Lorenzo, *Manager*
EMP: 120
SALES (corp-wide): 4.1B **Privately Held**
WEB: www.marinerhealth.com
SIC: 8051 Extended care facility
HQ: Mariner Health Care, Inc.
1 Ravinia Dr Ste 1500
Atlanta GA 30346
678 443-7000

(P-20761)
MARINER HEALTH CARE INC
Also Called: Skyline Health Care Center
2065 Forest Ave, San Jose (95128-4807)
PHONE.................................408 298-3950
Richard Park, *Administration*
Marlene Jones, *Office Mgr*
Nikki Thomas, *Bookkeeper*
EMP: 250
SALES (corp-wide): 4.1B **Privately Held**
SIC: 8051 Extended care facility
HQ: Mariner Health Care, Inc.
1 Ravinia Dr Ste 1500
Atlanta GA 30346
678 443-7000

(P-20762)
MARINER HEALTH CARE INC
Also Called: Skyline Health Care Ctr
3032 Rowena Ave, Los Angeles (90039-2005)
PHONE.................................323 665-1185
Kathleen Glass, *Administration*
Cesar Velez, *Director*
EMP: 100
SALES (corp-wide): 4.1B **Privately Held**
SIC: 8051 Extended care facility
HQ: Mariner Health Care, Inc.
1 Ravinia Dr Ste 1500
Atlanta GA 30346
678 443-7000

(P-20763)
MARINER HEALTH CARE INC
Also Called: Driftwood Convalescent Hosp
1850 E 8th St, Davis (95616-2502)
PHONE.................................530 756-1800
David Ormiston, *Principal*
EMP: 150
SALES (corp-wide): 4.1B **Privately Held**
WEB: www.marinerhealth.com
SIC: 8051 Extended care facility
HQ: Mariner Health Care, Inc.
1 Ravinia Dr Ste 1500
Atlanta GA 30346
678 443-7000

(P-20764)
MARINER HEALTH CARE INC
Also Called: Autumn Hills Convalescent Home
430 N Glendale Ave, Glendale (91206-3309)
PHONE.................................818 246-5677
Fax: 818 546-1213
Jenik Akopian, *Principal*
EMP: 120
SALES (corp-wide): 4.1B **Privately Held**
WEB: www.marinerhealth.com
SIC: 8051 Extended care facility
HQ: Mariner Health Care, Inc.
1 Ravinia Dr Ste 1500
Atlanta GA 30346
678 443-7000

(P-20765)
MARINER HEALTH CARE INC
675 24th Ave, Santa Cruz (95062-4205)
PHONE.................................831 475-6323
EMP: 85
SALES (corp-wide): 4.1B **Privately Held**
WEB: www.marinerhealth.com
SIC: 8051 Extended care facility
HQ: Mariner Health Care, Inc.
1 Ravinia Dr Ste 1500
Atlanta GA 30346
678 443-7000

(P-20766)
MARINER HEALTH CARE INC
Also Called: Hayward Hills Health Care Ctr
1768 B St, Hayward (94541-3102)
PHONE.................................510 538-4424
Annamarie Magna, *Branch Mgr*
EMP: 99
SALES (corp-wide): 4.1B **Privately Held**
WEB: www.marinerhealth.com
SIC: 8051 Extended care facility
HQ: Mariner Health Care, Inc.
1 Ravinia Dr Ste 1500
Atlanta GA 30346
678 443-7000

(P-20767)
MARINER HEALTH CARE INC
Also Called: Driftwood Healthcare Center
19700 Hesperian Blvd, Hayward (94541-4704)
PHONE.................................510 785-2880
Fax: 510 785-6054
Ellen Renner, *Administration*
Jill Despiganovicz, *Administration*
EMP: 135
SALES (corp-wide): 4.1B **Privately Held**
WEB: www.marinerhealth.com
SIC: 8051 Extended care facility
HQ: Mariner Health Care, Inc.
1 Ravinia Dr Ste 1500
Atlanta GA 30346
678 443-7000

(P-20768)
MARINER HEALTH CARE INC
Also Called: El Rancho Vista Hlth Care Ctr
8925 Mines Ave, Pico Rivera (90660-3006)
PHONE.................................562 942-7019
Fax: 562 942-0490
Richard Widerynski, *Sales/Mktg Mgr*
Betty Moreno, *Marketing Staff*
Maneshe Bansal, *Director*
Julie Estrada, *Director*
EMP: 100
SALES (corp-wide): 4.1B **Privately Held**
WEB: www.marinerhealth.com
SIC: 8051 Extended care facility
HQ: Mariner Health Care, Inc.
1 Ravinia Dr Ste 1500
Atlanta GA 30346
678 443-7000

(P-20769)
MARINER HEALTH CARE INC
Also Called: Pinedridge Care Ctr
45 Professional Ctr Pkwy, San Rafael (94903-2702)
PHONE.................................415 479-3610
Fax: 415 479-3618
Louise Kalchek, *Director*
EMP: 70
SALES (corp-wide): 4.1B **Privately Held**
WEB: www.marinerhealth.com
SIC: 8051 Extended care facility
HQ: Mariner Health Care, Inc.
1 Ravinia Dr Ste 1500
Atlanta GA 30346
678 443-7000

(P-20770)
MARINER HEALTH CARE INC
Also Called: Almaden Health & Rehab Ctr
2065 Los Gatos Almaden Rd, San Jose (95124-5417)
PHONE.................................408 377-9275
Fax: 408 377-0140
Yvette Bonnet, *Branch Mgr*
James Brende, *Administration*
Richard Dohn, *Director*
EMP: 100
SALES (corp-wide): 4.1B **Privately Held**
WEB: www.marinerhealth.com
SIC: 8051 Extended care facility
HQ: Mariner Health Care, Inc.
1 Ravinia Dr Ste 1500
Atlanta GA 30346
678 443-7000

(P-20771)
MARINER HEALTH CARE INC
Also Called: Excell Care Ctr
3025 High St, Oakland (94619-1807)
PHONE.................................510 261-5200
Fax: 510 261-1012
Elma Conway, *Administration*
EMP: 100
SALES (corp-wide): 4.1B **Privately Held**
WEB: www.marinerhealth.com
SIC: 8051 Extended care facility
HQ: Mariner Health Care, Inc.
1 Ravinia Dr Ste 1500
Atlanta GA 30346
678 443-7000

(P-20772)
MARINER HEALTH CARE INC
Also Called: La Salette Rehab Convlesc Hos
537 E Fulton St, Stockton (95204-2227)
PHONE.................................209 466-2066
Karol Ford, *Manager*
Anita Finney, *Director*
EMP: 125
SALES (corp-wide): 4.1B **Privately Held**
WEB: www.marinerhealth.com
SIC: 8051 Extended care facility
HQ: Mariner Health Care, Inc.
1 Ravinia Dr Ste 1500
Atlanta GA 30346
678 443-7000

(P-20773)
MARINER HEALTH CARE INC
Also Called: Windsor Gardens Hea
13000 Victory Blvd, North Hollywood (91606-2926)
PHONE.................................818 985-5990
Dolly Piper, *Manager*
Darleen Poe, *Vice Pres*
Melissa Yepez, *Human Res Dir*
Marine Petoyan, *Mktg Dir*
Suman Patel, *Director*
EMP: 100
SALES (corp-wide): 4.1B **Privately Held**
WEB: www.marinerhealth.com
SIC: 8051 Extended care facility
HQ: Mariner Health Care, Inc.
1 Ravinia Dr Ste 1500
Atlanta GA 30346
678 443-7000

(P-20774)
MARINER HEALTH CARE INC
Also Called: Verdugo Vista Healthcare Ctr
3050 Montrose Ave, La Crescenta (91214-3619)
PHONE.................................818 957-0850
Fax: 818 249-2386
Jeri-Enn Shelton, *Administration*
Edmund Lew, *Director*
EMP: 90
SALES (corp-wide): 4.1B **Privately Held**
WEB: www.marinerhealth.com
SIC: 8051 Skilled nursing care facilities
HQ: Mariner Health Care, Inc.
1 Ravinia Dr Ste 1500
Atlanta GA 30346
678 443-7000

(P-20775)
MARINER HEALTH CARE INC
Also Called: Arden Health & Rehab Ctr
3400 Alta Arden Expy, Sacramento (95825-2103)
PHONE.................................916 481-5500
John Pritchard, *Manager*
Bob Bowersox, *Admin Mgr*
Bonnie Gordon, *Administration*
EMP: 150
SALES (corp-wide): 4.1B **Privately Held**
WEB: www.marinerhealth.com
SIC: 8051 8069 Extended care facility; specialty hospitals, except psychiatric
HQ: Mariner Health Care, Inc.
1 Ravinia Dr Ste 1500
Atlanta GA 30346
678 443-7000

(P-20776)
MARLORA INVESTMENTS LLC
Also Called: Marlora Post Accute
3801 E Anaheim St, Long Beach (90804-4004)
PHONE.................................562 494-3311
Marilyn A Hauser,
Cathy Hernandez, *Corp Comm Staff*
Gabriela Patheco, *Manager*
EMP: 100
SQ FT: 22,118
SALES: 8.3MM **Privately Held**
SIC: 8051 Convalescent home with continuous nursing care

(P-20777)
MARY HLTH SCK CNVLSCNT &NRSNG
2929 Theresa Dr, Newbury Park (91320-3136)
PHONE.................................805 498-3644
Fax: 805 498-5112
Jody Rupp, *Administration*

8051 - Skilled Nursing Facilities County (P-20778)

Sister Purificaion Fererro, *CEO*
Diane Zimanski, *Office Mgr*
Mary Rupp, *Administration*
Romy Brubaker, *Nursing Dir*
EMP: 92 **EST:** 1964
SQ FT: 5,000
SALES: 7.2MM **Privately Held**
SIC: 8051 Convalescent home with continuous nursing care

(P-20778)
MARYSVLLE NRSING REHAB CTR LLC
Also Called: Marysville Care Center
1617 Ramirez St, Marysville (95901-4334)
PHONE.................................530 742-7311
Fax: 530 742-2356
Jim Bursey, *Administration*
Cecilia Genella, *Executive*
Joseph Palli,
EMP: 90
SALES (est): 4.7MM **Privately Held**
SIC: 8051 Skilled nursing care facilities

(P-20779)
MAYFLOWER GARDENS HEALTH FACIL
Also Called: Mayflwer Grdns Cnvlescent Hosp
6705 Columbia Way, Lancaster (93536-1233)
PHONE.................................661 943-2832
Fax: 661 943-1303
Billy Culverson, *Manager*
Bertha Ibarra, *Records Dir*
Liza Hopson, *Administration*
EMP: 90
SALES: 3.1MM **Privately Held**
WEB: www.bixbyknollstowers.com
SIC: 8051 Skilled nursing care facilities

(P-20780)
MAYWOOD HALTHCARE WELLNESS CTR
Also Called: Pine Crest
6025 Pine Ave, Maywood (90270-3108)
PHONE.................................323 560-0720
Fax: 323 773-2505
Emmanuel Bernabe, *President*
Jessica Gonzales, *Social Dir*
Judith Hernandez, *Director*
EMP: 50
SALES (est): 4.3MM **Privately Held**
SIC: 8051 Convalescent home with continuous nursing care

(P-20781)
MEADOW VIEW MANOR INC
396 Dorsey Dr, Grass Valley (95945-5368)
PHONE.................................530 272-2273
Fax: 530 272-6085
Jim Bursey, *Administration*
Jim Bersey, *Administration*
Lezley Brown, *Director*
EMP: 100
SQ FT: 22,000
SALES (est): 660K
SALES (corp-wide): 99MM **Privately Held**
WEB: www.villadelrey.com
SIC: 8051 Skilled nursing care facilities
HQ: Horizon West Healthcare, Inc.
4020 Sierra College Blvd # 190
Rocklin CA 95677
916 624-6230

(P-20782)
MEADOWOOD HLTH REHABILITATION
Also Called: Meadowood Care Center
3110 Wagner Heights Rd, Stockton (95209-4848)
PHONE.................................209 956-3444
Fax: 209 956-3454
Keith Berry, *President*
Chard Hardcastle, *President*
Alex Kim, *General Mgr*
Ilona Corpus, *Food Svc Dir*
Susan Morales, *Director*
EMP: 370
SQ FT: 43,800
SALES (est): 5.2MM **Privately Held**
SIC: 8051 Skilled nursing care facilities

(P-20783)
MEDICAL CARE PROFESSIONALS
363 El Cmino Real Ste 215, South San Francisco (94080)
PHONE.................................650 583-9898
Fax: 650 583-9940
Sharon Youngberg, *President*
Gustavo Youngberg, *Mktg Dir*
EMP: 100
SQ FT: 550
SALES (est): 3.2MM **Privately Held**
WEB: www.medicalcareprofessionals.com
SIC: 8051 8082 Skilled nursing care facilities; home health care services

(P-20784)
MEDICREST OF CALIFORNIA 1
Also Called: Montclair Mnor Cnvlescent Hosp
5119 Bandera St, Montclair (91763-4410)
PHONE.................................909 626-1294
Fax: 909 626-4005
Melinda Mabini, *Administration*
Bernie Gunderman, *Branch Mgr*
Betty Benson, *Office Mgr*
Betty Bincent, *Personnel*
Claudia Goodwin, *Food Svc Dir*
EMP: 60
SALES (corp-wide): 99MM **Privately Held**
SIC: 8051 Convalescent home with continuous nursing care
HQ: Medicrest Of California 1, Inc
4020 Sierra College Blvd
Rocklin CA 95677
916 624-6238

(P-20785)
MEK ESCONDIDO LLC
Also Called: Escondido Post Acute Rehab
421 E Mission Ave, Escondido (92025-1909)
PHONE.................................760 747-0430
Frank S Diolosa,
EMP: 99
SALES (est): 2.8MM **Privately Held**
SIC: 8051 Skilled nursing care facilities

(P-20786)
MEK NORWOOD PINES LLC
500 Jessie Ave, Sacramento (95838-2609)
PHONE.................................916 922-7177
Bobby Federico, *Manager*
Angela Kid, *Executive*
Teresa Cedamus, *Purchasing*
Sandra Ewers, *Marketing Staff*
Cheryl Bassard, *Director*
EMP: 99
SALES (est): 4.3MM **Privately Held**
SIC: 8051 Skilled nursing care facilities

(P-20787)
MELON HOLDINGS LLC ◆
Also Called: Marysville Post-Acute
1617 Ramirez St, Marysville (95901-4334)
PHONE.................................530 742-7311
Joseph Cunliffe, *Administration*
Nicklas Anderson, *President*
Matt Jackson, *President*
EMP: 99 **EST:** 2016
SALES (est): 740.5K **Privately Held**
SIC: 8051 Skilled nursing care facilities

(P-20788)
MENTAL HLTH CNVLSCENT SVCS INC
Also Called: Lakewood Park Health Center
12023 Lakewood Blvd, Downey (90242-2635)
PHONE.................................562 869-0978
Daniel C Zilafro, *President*
Regin Laurant, *Controller*
EMP: 300
SQ FT: 60,000
SALES (est): 11.4MM **Privately Held**
SIC: 8051 Skilled nursing care facilities

(P-20789)
MESA VRDE CNVALESCENT HOSP INC
661 Center St, Costa Mesa (92627-2708)
PHONE.................................949 548-5584
Fax: 949 548-1074
Joseph Munoz, *Administration*
Joye Tsuchiyama, *Administration*
Devine Libunao, *VP Finance*
Kelli Herrmann, *Business Mgr*
Greg Katz, *Director*
EMP: 135
SALES (est): 11.6MM **Privately Held**
WEB: www.mesaverdehealthcare.com
SIC: 8051 Skilled nursing care facilities

(P-20790)
MID WILSHIRE HEALTH CARE CTR
676 S Bonnie Brae St, Los Angeles (90057-3710)
PHONE.................................213 483-9921
EMP: 60
SQ FT: 17,469
SALES (est): 4.6MM **Privately Held**
SIC: 8051

(P-20791)
MISSION HILLS HEALTHCARE INC
Also Called: Mission Hills Healthcare Ctr
4033 6th Ave, San Diego (92103-2202)
PHONE.................................619 297-4086
Fax: 619 297-9238
Patrick Higgins, *CEO*
Leah Higgins, *President*
Julian Macias, *Director*
EMP: 92
SQ FT: 25,000
SALES: 5.5MM **Privately Held**
SIC: 8051 Skilled nursing care facilities; convalescent home with continuous nursing care

(P-20792)
MISSION MEDICAL ENTPS INC
Also Called: Hanford Nursing Rehabilitation
1007 W Lacey Blvd, Hanford (93230-4331)
PHONE.................................559 582-2871
Fax: 559 582-5853
Mark Fisher, *General Mgr*
Muriel Migliorini, *Human Res Mgr*
EMP: 120
SALES (corp-wide): 12.4MM **Privately Held**
WEB: www.missioncaregroup.com
SIC: 8051 Skilled nursing care facilities
PA: Mission Medical Enterprises, Inc.
1007 W Lacey Blvd
Hanford CA 93230
559 582-2871

(P-20793)
MISSION MEDICAL ENTPS INC
Also Called: Kings Nrsing Rhabilitation Ctr
851 Leslie Ln, Hanford (93230-5643)
PHONE.................................559 582-4414
Mark Fisher, *Branch Mgr*
EMP: 82
SALES (corp-wide): 12.4MM **Privately Held**
SIC: 8051 Skilled nursing care facilities
PA: Mission Medical Enterprises, Inc.
1007 W Lacey Blvd
Hanford CA 93230
559 582-2871

(P-20794)
MJB PARTNERS LLC
Also Called: Pomona Vista Care Center
651 N Main St, Pomona (91768-3110)
PHONE.................................909 623-2481
EMP: 62
SQ FT: 8,844
SALES (est): 207.3K **Privately Held**
SIC: 8051 Skilled nursing care facilities

(P-20795)
MONTECITO RETIREMENT ASSN
Also Called: Casa Dorinda
300 Hot Springs Rd, Santa Barbara (93108-2037)
PHONE.................................805 969-8011
Robin Drew, *CFO*
Alan Blaver, *Broker*
Jerome Williams, *Human Res Dir*
Domenic Ceaser, *Facilities Dir*
William Koonce, *Director*
EMP: 265
SQ FT: 350,000
SALES: 26.1MM **Privately Held**
WEB: www.casadorinda.com
SIC: 8051 8052 8361 Skilled nursing care facilities; personal care facility; rest home, with health care incidental

(P-20796)
MONTEREY HEALTHCARE & WELLNESS
1267 San Gabriel Blvd, Rosemead (91770-4237)
PHONE.................................626 280-3220
Shlomo Rechnitz, *CEO*
Sharrod Brooks, *Senior VP*
EMP: 90 **EST:** 2013
SALES (est): 2.5MM **Privately Held**
SIC: 8051 Mental retardation hospital

(P-20797)
MONTEREY PINES SKLLD NURSG FAC
Also Called: Horizon West
1501 Skyline Dr, Monterey (93940-4110)
PHONE.................................831 373-3716
Fax: 831 373-8102
Gene Sajcich, *Administration*
Edna Redoble, *Chf Purch Ofc*
Helga Scukes, *Director*
Sacha Warrick, *Director*
EMP: 85 **EST:** 1980
SQ FT: 32,000
SALES (est): 2.2MM
SALES (corp-wide): 99MM **Privately Held**
WEB: www.villadelrey.com
SIC: 8051 Skilled nursing care facilities
HQ: Horizon West Healthcare, Inc.
4020 Sierra College Blvd # 190
Rocklin CA 95677
916 624-6230

(P-20798)
MORNINGSIDE CORECARE ASSOC LP
2180 Sand Hill Rd Ste 200, Menlo Park (94025-6949)
PHONE.................................650 854-5600
Justin Wilson, *Partner*
Carl Wilson, *Director*
EMP: 200
SALES (est): 10.1MM **Privately Held**
SIC: 8051 Skilled nursing care facilities

(P-20799)
MOUNT RBDOUX CONVALESCENT HOSP
Also Called: Plott Family Care Center
6401 33rd St, Riverside (92509-1404)
PHONE.................................951 681-2200
Fax: 951 681-4402
Thomas Plott, *President*
Angelina Parks, *Personnel*
Charles Blaine, *Maintence Staff*
EMP: 150
SALES (est): 6.1MM **Privately Held**
SIC: 8051 8059 Skilled nursing care facilities; convalescent home

(P-20800)
MOUNTAIN VIEW CNVALESCENT HOSP
13333 Fenton Ave, Sylmar (91342-3113)
PHONE.................................818 367-1033
Ray Talebi, *Owner*
EMP: 50
SALES (est): 2.7MM **Privately Held**
SIC: 8051 Convalescent home with continuous nursing care

(P-20801)
MOYLES CENTRAL VLY HLTH CARE (PA)
999 N M St, Tulare (93274-2019)
PHONE.................................559 688-0288
Fax: 559 688-0289
Ken Moyel III, *President*
EMP: 241
SALES (est): 6.9MM **Privately Held**
WEB: www.portervillecon.com
SIC: 8051 Skilled nursing care facilities

PRODUCTS & SERVICES SECTION
8051 - Skilled Nursing Facilities County (P-20824)

(P-20802)
MOYLES CENTRAL VLY HLTH CARE
Also Called: Porterville Convalescent Hosp
1100 W Morton Ave, Porterville (93257-1947)
PHONE..................559 782-1509
Fax: 559 781-5220
James Higbee, *CFO*
Michelle Lawrence, *Administration*
Susan Elston, *Hlthcr Dir*
Rakesh Jindal, *Director*
EMP: 120
SALES (corp-wide): 6.9MM **Privately Held**
WEB: www.portervillecon.com
SIC: **8051** Convalescent home with continuous nursing care
PA: Moyles Central Valley Health Care Inc
999 N M St
Tulare CA 93274
559 688-0288

(P-20803)
NAPA NURSING CENTER INC
3275 Villa Ln, NAPA (94558-3094)
PHONE..................707 257-0931
Fax: 707 257-0936
Martine D Harmon, *CEO*
Tim Motooka, *President*
Georgia Otteросs, *Administration*
Ronald Julis, *Director*
EMP: 130
SQ FT: 48,000
SALES (est): 5.9MM
SALES (corp-wide): 99MM **Privately Held**
WEB: www.napayellowpages.com
SIC: **8051** Skilled nursing care facilities
HQ: Horizon West Healthcare, Inc.
4020 Sierra College Blvd # 190
Rocklin CA 95677
916 624-6230

(P-20804)
NEW COVENANT CARE CAL INC
Also Called: San Mrco Nrsing Rhbltation Ctr
130 Tampico, Walnut Creek (94598-2948)
PHONE..................925 930-7733
Fax: 925 256-1676
Mary Contois, *Branch Mgr*
EMP: 135
SALES (corp-wide): 957.5MM **Privately Held**
SIC: **8051** Skilled nursing care facilities
PA: New Covenant Care Of California, Inc.
2540 Cmino Dieblo Ste 100
Walnut Creek CA
925 937-7400

(P-20805)
NEW COVENANT CARE OF DINUBA
Also Called: NEW COVENANT CARE CENTER OF DI
1730 S College Ave, Dinuba (93618-2812)
PHONE..................559 591-3300
Fax: 559 591-0705
Gary V Guarisco, *President*
EMP: 100
SQ FT: 26,692
SALES: 6.2MM **Privately Held**
SIC: **8051** Skilled nursing care facilities

(P-20806)
NIA HEALTHCARE SERVICES INC
Also Called: Raintree Convalescent Hospital
5265 E Huntington Ave, Fresno (93727-4013)
PHONE..................559 251-1526
Fax: 559 251-5138
Carolyn Norcroff, *Administration*
Alex Sherriffs, *Director*
EMP: 60
SALES (corp-wide): 9.7MM **Privately Held**
SIC: **8051** Skilled nursing care facilities
PA: Nia Healthcare Services, Inc.
8448 E Adams Ave
Fowler CA 93625
559 834-2519

(P-20807)
NICE AVENUE LLC
Also Called: Mill Creek Manor
2278 Nice Ave, Mentone (92359-9655)
PHONE..................909 794-1189
Jason Bell, *Administration*
EMP: 65
SALES (est): 234.3K **Privately Held**
SIC: **8051** Skilled nursing care facilities

(P-20808)
NORTH PT HLTH WELLNESS CTR LLC
Also Called: Northpointe Healthcare Centre
668 E Bullard Ave, Fresno (93710-5401)
PHONE..................559 320-2200
Stephen Reissman,
Janet Bamper,
Cheryl Petterson,
EMP: 99
SALES (est): 3.7MM **Privately Held**
SIC: **8051** Skilled nursing care facilities

(P-20809)
NORTH SHORE INVESTMENT INC
Also Called: Crescent Cy Convalescent Hosp
1280 Marshall St, Crescent City (95531-2217)
PHONE..................707 464-6151
Fax: 707 464-6064
Jeffery Davis, *President*
Crystal Velazquez, *Accountant*
Theresa Payne, *Bookkeeper*
EMP: 100
SQ FT: 35,000
SALES: 5.4MM **Privately Held**
SIC: **8051** Convalescent home with continuous nursing care

(P-20810)
NORTHERN CALIFORNIA PRESBYTERI
Also Called: Sequos-San Frncsco Residential
1400 Geary Blvd, San Francisco (94109-6561)
PHONE..................415 922-9700
Fax: 415 567-2576
Michael Daugherty, *Branch Mgr*
EMP: 117
SALES (corp-wide): 69.3MM **Privately Held**
SIC: **8051** Convalescent home with continuous nursing care
PA: Northern California Presbyterian Homes And Services, Inc.
1525 Post St
San Francisco CA 94109
415 922-0200

(P-20811)
NORWALK MEADOWS NURSING CTR LP
10625 Leffingwell Rd, Norwalk (90650-3434)
PHONE..................562 864-2541
Fax: 562 864-2231
Pnina Graff, *Partner*
Jacob Graff, *Partner*
Lisa Thomashow, *Administration*
Vahram Hakopiannik, *Accountant*
Loretta Mosby, *Director*
EMP: 152
SQ FT: 23,632
SALES (est): 10.1MM **Privately Held**
SIC: **8051** Skilled nursing care facilities

(P-20812)
NOVATO HEALTHCARE CENTER LLC
1565 Hill Rd, Novato (94947-4063)
PHONE..................415 897-6161
Michael J Torgan, *Principal*
Sharrod Brooks,
John Fullerton, *Director*
EMP: 200 **EST**: 2007
SALES: 18MM **Privately Held**
SIC: **8051** Skilled nursing care facilities

(P-20813)
OAK KNOLL CONVALESCENT CENTER
Also Called: Oaks, The
450 Hayes Ln, Petaluma (94952-4010)
PHONE..................707 778-8686
Fax: 707 778-6111
Ann Abbott, *President*
Tony Meyers, *CEO*
Jean Menjivar, *Nursing Dir*
Eran Matalan, *Director*
Shelby Wallace, *Receptionist*
EMP: 72 **EST**: 1980
SQ FT: 36,000
SALES: 4.9MM **Privately Held**
SIC: **8051** Convalescent home with continuous nursing care

(P-20814)
OAK RIVER REHABILITATION
3300 Franklin St, Anderson (96007-3279)
PHONE..................530 365-0025
Andy Tanner, *Manager*
Caprice Gillispie, *Executive*
Cprice Gillespie, *Office Mgr*
Dan Funk, *Administration*
Andy Tenney, *Administration*
EMP: 150
SQ FT: 3,000
SALES: 17.7MM **Privately Held**
SIC: **8051** Convalescent home with continuous nursing care

(P-20815)
OAKDALE HEIGHTS SENIOR LIVING
3209 Brookside Dr, Bakersfield (93311-3459)
PHONE..................661 663-9671
Mike Laudon, *President*
EMP: 50
SALES (est): 1.5MM **Privately Held**
SIC: **8051** Skilled nursing care facilities

(P-20816)
OAKHURST SKILLED NURSING WELLN
Also Called: Oakhurst Healthcare
40131 Highway 49, Oakhurst (93644-9560)
PHONE..................559 683-2244
Stepan Sarmazian, *Administration*
EMP: 99
SALES: 5.4MM **Privately Held**
SIC: **8051** Mental retardation hospital

(P-20817)
OAKLAND HEALTHCARE & WELLNESS
Also Called: Akland Healthcare Wellness Ctr
3030 Webster St, Oakland (94609-3411)
PHONE..................323 330-6572
Sol Majer, *Mng Member*
EMP: 131
SQ FT: 20,000
SALES: 427.9K **Privately Held**
SIC: **8051** Skilled nursing care facilities

(P-20818)
OCADIAN CARE CENTERS LLC
Also Called: Northern Cal Rehabilitation
2801 Eureka Way, Redding (96001-0222)
PHONE..................530 246-9000
Chris Jones, *Exec Dir*
Debbie Wiechman, *Infect Cntl Dir*
Jody Carter, *Radiology Dir*
Tim Linnett, *Pharmacist*
Kevin Rainsford, *Director*
EMP: 250
SALES (corp-wide): 4.8MM **Privately Held**
WEB: www.ocadian.com
SIC: **8051 5912 8069** Skilled nursing care facilities; drug stores & proprietary stores; specialty hospitals, except psychiatric
PA: Ocadian Care Centers, Llc
104 Main St
Belvedere Tiburon CA 94920
415 789-5427

(P-20819)
OCADIAN CARE CENTERS LLC
Also Called: Ygnacio Convalescent Hospital
1449 Ygnacio Valley Rd, Walnut Creek (94598-2932)
PHONE..................925 939-5820
Fax: 925 939-5077
Gary Bernon, *Manager*
EMP: 90
SALES (corp-wide): 4.8MM **Privately Held**
WEB: www.ocadian.com
SIC: **8051** Skilled nursing care facilities
PA: Ocadian Care Centers, Llc
104 Main St
Belvedere Tiburon CA 94920
415 789-5427

(P-20820)
OCADIAN CARE CENTERS LLC
Also Called: Medical Hill Rehabilitation
475 29th St, Oakland (94609-3510)
PHONE..................510 832-3222
Fax: 510 832-5617
Robert G Peirce, *President*
EMP: 100
SALES (corp-wide): 4.8MM **Privately Held**
WEB: www.ocadian.com
SIC: **8051** Convalescent home with continuous nursing care
PA: Ocadian Care Centers, Llc
104 Main St
Belvedere Tiburon CA 94920
415 789-5427

(P-20821)
OCADIAN CARE CENTERS LLC
Also Called: Greenbrea Care Center
1220 S Eliseo Dr, Greenbrae (94904-2006)
PHONE..................415 461-9700
Susan Weaver, *Manager*
EMP: 75
SALES (corp-wide): 4.8MM **Privately Held**
WEB: www.ocadian.com
SIC: **8051 8069 8052** Skilled nursing care facilities; specialty hospitals, except psychiatric; intermediate care facilities
PA: Ocadian Care Centers, Llc
104 Main St
Belvedere Tiburon CA 94920
415 789-5427

(P-20822)
OCADIAN CARE CENTERS LLC
1550 Silveira Pkwy, San Rafael (94903-4879)
PHONE..................415 499-1000
Linda Creekmoore, *Manager*
EMP: 90
SALES (corp-wide): 4.8MM **Privately Held**
WEB: www.ocadian.com
SIC: **8051 8361** Skilled nursing care facilities; residential care
PA: Ocadian Care Centers, Llc
104 Main St
Belvedere Tiburon CA 94920
415 789-5427

(P-20823)
OCADIAN CARE CENTERS LLC
Also Called: Homewood Care Center
75 N 13th St, San Jose (95112-3439)
PHONE..................408 295-2665
Fax: 408 294-4990
David Martinez, *Administration*
EMP: 50
SALES (corp-wide): 4.8MM **Privately Held**
WEB: www.ocadian.com
SIC: **8051** Skilled nursing care facilities
PA: Ocadian Care Centers, Llc
104 Main St
Belvedere Tiburon CA 94920
415 789-5427

(P-20824)
ODYSSEY HEALTHCARE INC
525 Cabrillo Park Dr # 150, Santa Ana (92701-5017)
PHONE..................714 245-7420
Rodney Dirk Allison, *Principal*
EMP: 52
SALES (corp-wide): 7B **Publicly Held**
SIC: **8051** Skilled nursing care facilities
HQ: Odyssey Healthcare, Inc.
7801 Mesquite Bend Dr # 105
Irving TX 75063

8051 - Skilled Nursing Facilities County (P-20825)

(P-20825)
ODYSSEY HEALTHCARE INC
1500 E Hamilton Ave # 212, Campbell (95008-0809)
PHONE...................408 626-4868
Fax: 408 626-4869
Elaine Fritz, *Principal*
EMP: 52
SALES (corp-wide): 7B **Publicly Held**
SIC: 8051 Skilled nursing care facilities
HQ: Odyssey Healthcare, Inc.
7801 Mesquite Bend Dr # 105
Irving TX 75063

(P-20826)
OLEANDER HOLDINGS LLC
Also Called: Sacramento Post-Acute
5255 Hemlock St, Sacramento (95841-3017)
PHONE...................916 331-4590
James Huish,
David Terry, *Administration*
Myrna De Guzman, *Controller*
Nick Anderson,
Toby Tilford,
EMP: 99
SALES (est): 1MM **Privately Held**
SIC: 8051 Skilled nursing care facilities

(P-20827)
OPLV INC
Also Called: Century Skilled Nursing Care
301 Centinela Ave, Inglewood (90302-3231)
PHONE...................310 672-1012
Oscar Parel, *Exec Dir*
Ivy Ferguson, *Records Dir*
Christopher Arias, *Administration*
Armando Yu, *Administration*
Evangeline Estivillo, *Nursing Dir*
EMP: 100
SALES: 5.5MM **Privately Held**
SIC: 8051 Skilled nursing care facilities

(P-20828)
ORANGE HEALTHCARE & WELLNESS
920 W La Veta Ave, Orange (92868-4302)
PHONE...................714 633-3568
Jonathan Weiss,
Sharrod Brooks,
EMP: 110
SALES (est): 6.5MM **Privately Held**
SIC: 8051 Skilled nursing care facilities

(P-20829)
ORCHARD - POST ACUTE CARE CTR
12385 Washington Blvd, Whittier (90606-2502)
PHONE...................562 693-7701
Rich Jorgensen, *Principal*
EMP: 1634
SALES: 15.6MM
SALES (corp-wide): 1.3B **Publicly Held**
SIC: 8051 Convalescent home with continuous nursing care
PA: The Ensign Group Inc
27101 Puerta Real Ste 450
Mission Viejo CA 92691
949 487-9500

(P-20830)
OUR LADY OF FATIMA VILLA INC
20400 Srtoga Los Gatos Rd, Saratoga (95070-5997)
PHONE...................408 741-2950
Fax: 408 741-4930
Bella Mahoney, *Administration*
EMP: 90 **EST:** 1945
SQ FT: 45,123
SALES (est): 11MM **Privately Held**
WEB: www.fatimavilla.org
SIC: 8051 Skilled nursing care facilities

(P-20831)
OXNARD MANOR LP
Also Called: OXNARD MANOR HEALTH-CARE CENTER
1400 W Gonzales Rd, Oxnard (93036-3392)
PHONE...................805 983-0324
Sharrod Brooks, *Partner*

Bertie Krieger, *Partner*
Carlo Oleta, *Hlthcr Dir*
EMP: 99
SALES: 10.3MM **Privately Held**
SIC: 8051 Skilled nursing care facilities

(P-20832)
P R N CONVALESCENT HOSPITAL
Also Called: High Valley Lodge
7912 Topley Ln, Sunland (91040-3336)
PHONE...................818 352-3158
Fax: 818 352-2885
Pauline Albert, *President*
Luis Albert Jr, *Vice Pres*
Ador Bustamante, *Director*
EMP: 54
SQ FT: 11,712
SALES (est): 2.9MM **Privately Held**
SIC: 8051 Skilled nursing care facilities

(P-20833)
PACIFIC REHABILITATION & WEL
2211 Harrison Ave, Eureka (95501-3214)
PHONE...................707 443-9767
Sharrod Brooks, *Senior VP*
EMP: 65 **EST:** 2011
SQ FT: 20,000
SALES: 6.1MM **Privately Held**
SIC: 8051 8322 Mental retardation hospital; rehabilitation services

(P-20834)
PACIFICA CARE CENTER
Also Called: Pacifica Nursing & Rehab Ctr
385 Esplanade Ave, Pacifica (94044-1882)
PHONE...................650 355-5622
Jacob Beaman, *Administration*
Elizabeth De Guzman, *Records Dir*
Brian Ramos, *Administration*
Filipina Atienza, *Director*
Joshua Rassen, *Director*
EMP: 150
SALES: 16.2MM **Privately Held**
WEB: www.pacifica-rehab.com
SIC: 8051 Skilled nursing care facilities

(P-20835)
PACIFICA LINDA MAR INC
Also Called: Linda Mar Care Center
751 San Pedro Terrace Rd, Pacifica (94044-4101)
PHONE...................650 359-4800
Fax: 650 359-8346
David Mahrt, *Administration*
Marylin Carolin, *Business Mgr*
Rosana Levine, *Food Svc Dir*
EMP: 85
SQ FT: 10,000
SALES: 5.8MM **Privately Held**
WEB: www.lawgate.byu.edu
SIC: 8051 Skilled nursing care facilities

(P-20836)
PALM HAVEN NURSING & REHAB LLC
Also Called: Palm Haven Care Center
469 E North St, Manteca (95336-4710)
PHONE...................209 823-2782
Fax: 209 823-9809
Joseph Pallivathicla,
Karen Riggs, *Manager*
EMP: 104
SQ FT: 24,000
SALES (est): 4.5MM **Privately Held**
SIC: 8051 Skilled nursing care facilities

(P-20837)
PALMCREST GRAND CARE CTR INC
3501 Cedar Ave, Long Beach (90807-3809)
PHONE...................562 595-4551
William Nelson, *President*
Amy Delmonda, *Purch Dir*
Ronald Philipp, *Director*
EMP: 99
SALES (est): 5.7MM **Privately Held**
SIC: 8051 Skilled nursing care facilities

(P-20838)
PALMCREST MEDALLION CONVALESC
3355 Pacific Pl, Long Beach (90806-1239)
PHONE...................562 595-4336
Fax: 562 424-6499
Richard Feingold, *Principal*
Sandra Faay, *Administration*
Julian F Feingold, *Agent*
EMP: 85
SQ FT: 30,000
SALES (est): 1.9MM **Privately Held**
SIC: 8051 Skilled nursing care facilities

(P-20839)
PARA & PALLI INC
Also Called: Los Banos Nursing and Rehab
931 Idaho Ave, Los Banos (93635-3405)
PHONE...................209 826-0790
Fax: 209 826-3154
Joseph Palli, *President*
Teresa Palli, *Administration*
Sabrena Flores, *Manager*
▲ **EMP:** 65
SQ FT: 1,000
SALES (est): 4.5MM **Privately Held**
SIC: 8051 Skilled nursing care facilities

(P-20840)
PARADISE VLY HLTH CARE CTR INC
2575 E 8th St, National City (91950-2913)
PHONE...................619 470-6700
Fax: 619 470-0404
Kenneth Michael Funk, *President*
Jason Murray, *CEO*
Mark Hancock, *CFO*
Rosalind Bishop, *Director*
EMP: 66
SALES (est): 6MM **Privately Held**
SIC: 8051 Skilled nursing care facilities

(P-20841)
PARKSIDE SPECIAL CARE CENTER
444 W Lexington Ave, El Cajon (92020-4416)
PHONE...................619 442-7744
Fax: 619 442-1137
Edd Long, *Administration*
Anna Velasco, *Office Mgr*
Michael Nugent, *Administration*
Diego Trevino, *Director*
EMP: 75
SALES (est): 4.7MM **Privately Held**
SIC: 8051 Convalescent home with continuous nursing care

(P-20842)
PARKVIEW JLIAN CNVLESCENT HOSP
1801 Julian Ave, Bakersfield (93304-6419)
PHONE...................661 831-9150
Fax: 661 831-2439
Ligia Denham, *Vice Pres*
Raju Patel, *Director*
EMP: 100
SQ FT: 8,000
SALES: 6.4MM **Privately Held**
WEB: www.parkviewjulian.com
SIC: 8051 Skilled nursing care facilities

(P-20843)
PASADENA HOSPITAL ASSN LTD
Also Called: Huntington Extended Care Ctr
716 S Fair Oaks Ave, Pasadena (91105-2618)
PHONE...................626 397-3322
Fax: 626 397-3752
Ken Hoff, *Manager*
EMP: 75
SALES (corp-wide): 569.3MM **Privately Held**
WEB: www.huntingtonhospital.com
SIC: 8051 Skilled nursing care facilities
PA: Pasadena Hospital Association, Ltd.
100 W California Blvd
Pasadena CA 91105
626 397-5000

(P-20844)
PASADENA MADOWS NURSING CTR LP
150 Bellefontaine St, Pasadena (91105-3102)
PHONE...................626 796-1103
Pnina Graff, *Partner*
EMP: 99
SALES (est): 4.9MM **Privately Held**
SIC: 8051 Skilled nursing care facilities

(P-20845)
PATER DIGNTAS INC
Also Called: Carmel Hills Care Center
23795 Holman Hwy, Monterey (93940-5903)
PHONE...................831 624-1875
Robert Bowersox, *President*
Kim Bowersox, *CFO*
EMP: 90
SQ FT: 30,000
SALES (est): 8.6MM **Privately Held**
WEB: www.carmelhillscarecenter.com
SIC: 8051 Skilled nursing care facilities

(P-20846)
PINE GROVE HEALTHCARE
126 N San Gabriel Blvd, San Gabriel (91775-2427)
PHONE...................626 285-3131
Sharrod Brooks, *Partner*
EMP: 99 **EST:** 2012
SALES (est): 4.3MM **Privately Held**
SIC: 8051 Mental retardation hospital

(P-20847)
PINERS NURSING HOME INC
Also Called: Piner's Medical Supply
1800 Pueblo Ave, NAPA (94558-4751)
PHONE...................707 224-7925
Fax: 707 255-0302
Gary Piner, *President*
Starr Piner, *Treasurer*
Geri Bise, *Controller*
Kathy Hulbert, *VP Sales*
Emily Howe, *Mktg Dir*
EMP: 65
SQ FT: 20,000
SALES (est): 5.7MM **Privately Held**
SIC: 8051 4119 5999 Convalescent home with continuous nursing care; ambulance service; medical apparatus & supplies

(P-20848)
PITTSBURG CARE CENTER LTD
535 School St, Pittsburg (94565-3937)
PHONE...................925 432-3831
Fax: 925 432-1215
Abby Tiller, *Owner*
Purnima Sreenivasan, *Director*
EMP: 50
SQ FT: 20,000
SALES (est): 2.2MM **Privately Held**
SIC: 8051 Extended care facility

(P-20849)
PITTSBURG SKILLED NURSING
535 School St, Pittsburg (94565-3937)
PHONE...................925 808-6540
Allen Leung, *Admin Sec*
EMP: 67
SQ FT: 12,140
SALES (est): 996.5K **Privately Held**
SIC: 8051 Skilled nursing care facilities

(P-20850)
PLEASANT CARE OF VISTA
247 E Bobier Dr, Vista (92084-3026)
PHONE...................760 945-3033
Thomas Delucia, *Administration*
Diane Thibodeau, *Administration*
EMP: 180
SALES (est): 5.1MM **Privately Held**
SIC: 8051 Skilled nursing care facilities

(P-20851)
PLOTT MANAGEMENT CO
Also Called: Plott Family Home Care
264 E 18th St, San Bernardino (92404-4708)
PHONE...................909 883-0288
EMP: 88
SALES (est): 3.6MM **Privately Held**
SIC: 8051

PRODUCTS & SERVICES SECTION
8051 - Skilled Nursing Facilities County (P-20874)

(P-20852)
PLUM HEALTHCARE GROUP LLC
Also Called: White Blossom Care Center
1990 Fruitdale Ave, San Jose (95128-2709)
PHONE 408 998-8447
Mark Lamb, *Manager*
Laura Barrientos, *Administration*
Virend Prasad, *Food Svc Dir*
Kari Bowers, *Director*
Jose Iniguez, *Director*
EMP: 100
SALES (corp-wide): 40.6MM Privately Held
SIC: 8051 Skilled nursing care facilities
PA: Plum Healthcare Group, Llc
100 E San Marcos Blvd
San Marcos CA 92069
760 471-0388

(P-20853)
PLUM HEALTHCARE GROUP LLC (PA)
100 E San Marcos Blvd, San Marcos (92069-2986)
PHONE 760 471-0388
Fax: 760 471-0311
Toby Tilford, *Mng Member*
Will Huish, *Exec VP*
Venus Burnette, *Admin Asst*
Jun Rubio, *Info Tech Mgr*
Stan Anderson, *Technology*
EMP: 100
SALES (est): 40.6MM Privately Held
SIC: 8051 Skilled nursing care facilities

(P-20854)
PLUM HEALTHCARE GROUP LLC
Also Called: Cottonwood Cyn Healthcare Ctr
1391 E Madison Ave, El Cajon (92021-8568)
PHONE 619 873-2500
Leticia Guerrero, *Business Mgr*
Linell Serquina, *Records Dir*
EMP: 120
SALES (corp-wide): 40.6MM Privately Held
SIC: 8051 8059 Skilled nursing care facilities; nursing home, except skilled & intermediate care facility
PA: Plum Healthcare Group, Llc
100 E San Marcos Blvd
San Marcos CA 92069
760 471-0388

(P-20855)
POINT LOMA CONVALESCENT HOSP
3202 Duke St, San Diego (92110-5401)
PHONE 619 224-4141
Fax: 619 224-1328
Samuel Horowitz, *Partner*
Joseph Fisch, *General Ptnr*
Reena Horowitz, *General Ptnr*
J Axelrod, *Ltd Ptnr*
B Crow, *Ltd Ptnr*
EMP: 160
SQ FT: 25,402
SALES (est): 7.1MM Privately Held
WEB: www.pointlomarehab.com
SIC: 8051 Convalescent home with continuous nursing care

(P-20856)
POINT LOMA RHBLITATION CTR LLC
Also Called: Point Loma Post Acute Care Ctr
3202 Duke St, San Diego (92110-5401)
PHONE 619 224-4141
Fax: 619 224-1309
Guy Reggev,
Mac Rodriguez, *Director*
Luchie Diwa, *Manager*
EMP: 130
SQ FT: 30,895
SALES (est): 5MM Privately Held
SIC: 8051 Skilled nursing care facilities

(P-20857)
POMERADO OPERATIONS LLC
Also Called: Boulder Creek Post Acute
12696 Monte Vista Rd, Poway (92064-2500)
PHONE 858 487-6242
Covey Christensen, *CEO*
James Gamett, *President*
Leland Bruce, *COO*
Travis Greenwood, *CFO*
EMP: 99
SALES (est): 757.8K Privately Held
SIC: 8051 Convalescent home with continuous nursing care

(P-20858)
PREFERRED CARE WEST INC
Also Called: Bayside Rhabilitation Care Ctr
3520 4th Ave, San Diego (92103-4913)
PHONE 619 291-5270
Charles Sinclair, *Administration*
EMP: 164
SALES (corp-wide): 91.3MM Privately Held
SIC: 8051 Skilled nursing care facilities
HQ: Preferred Care West, Inc.
5212 Village Creek Dr
Plano TX 75093
972 931-3800

(P-20859)
PROVIDNCE ALL STS SUBACUTE LLC
Also Called: Providence All Saints Subacute
1652 Mono Ave, San Leandro (94578-2020)
PHONE 510 481-3200
Jason Murray, *President*
EMP: 99 EST: 2015
SALES (est): 324.2K Privately Held
SIC: 8051 Skilled nursing care facilities

(P-20860)
QUALITY LONG TERM CARE NEV INC
Also Called: Eineridge Care Center
14122 Hubbard St, Sylmar (91342-4712)
PHONE 818 361-0191
Fax: 818 837-1192
Scott Dale, *Branch Mgr*
Josie Alberto, *Records Dir*
Armand Masongsong, *Director*
EMP: 65
SALES (corp-wide): 4MM Privately Held
SIC: 8051 Skilled nursing care facilities
PA: Quality Long Term Care Of Nevada, Inc.
2800 W Sahara Ave
Las Vegas NV 89102
702 893-8962

(P-20861)
R FELLEN INC
Also Called: Sunnyside Convalescent Hosp
2939 S Peach Ave, Fresno (93725-9302)
PHONE 559 233-6248
Fax: 559 233-3368
Michael Fellen, *President*
Steven Fellen, *Vice Pres*
Steven Grossman, *Director*
EMP: 95
SQ FT: 10,000
SALES (est): 7MM Privately Held
SIC: 8051 Convalescent home with continuous nursing care

(P-20862)
RAMONA CARE CENTER INC
11900 Ramona Blvd, El Monte (91732-2314)
PHONE 626 442-5721
Fax: 626 444-9884
John Sorensen, *Vice Pres*
Jan Stine, *Administration*
Jones D White, *Administration*
Sheila Severo, *Phys Thrpy Dir*
David Gu, *Director*
EMP: 140
SQ FT: 35,000
SALES (est): 15.5MM Privately Held
SIC: 8051 Skilled nursing care facilities

(P-20863)
RAMONA REHABILITATION AND POST
485 W Johnston Ave, Hemet (92543-7012)
PHONE 951 652-0011
Fax: 951 929-5924
Stan Leland, *President*
Heidi Vickers, *Admin Sec*
Patti Salcone Rn, *Nursing Dir*
EMP: 120
SQ FT: 30,000
SALES (est): 9.4MM Privately Held
SIC: 8051 8062 Skilled nursing care facilities; convalescent home with continuous nursing care; general medical & surgical hospitals

(P-20864)
RAZAVI CORPORATION
Also Called: Hilldale Habilitation Center
7979 La Mesa Blvd, La Mesa (91942-5565)
PHONE 619 465-8010
Fax: 619 465-8348
Darius Razavi, *President*
Maria Razavi, *Vice Pres*
▲ **EMP:** 60
SQ FT: 20,080
SALES (est): 2MM Privately Held
SIC: 8051 Convalescent home with continuous nursing care

(P-20865)
REBECCA TERLEY
Also Called: Sunbrdge Care Ctr - Bellflower
9028 Rose St, Bellflower (90706-6418)
PHONE 562 925-4252
Andrew Ashton, *Exec Dir*
Jasmine Valera, *Records Dir*
Mark Muir, *Executive*
Brian Bellantuoni, *Administration*
Carlos Correa, *Maintence Staff*
EMP: 53
SALES (est): 919.7K Privately Held
SIC: 8051 Skilled nursing care facilities

(P-20866)
RECHE CYN RHBLITATION HLTH CTR
Also Called: Reche Cyn Regional Rehab Ctr
1350 Reche Canyon Rd, Colton (92324-9528)
PHONE 909 370-4411
Fred Frank, *Administration*
Benjamin Atkins, *CEO*
Dorthy Pipich, *Office Mgr*
Brian Cain, *Sls & Mktg Exec*
EMP: 350
SALES (est): 25.9MM Privately Held
SIC: 8051 Skilled nursing care facilities

(P-20867)
REGENCY CENTERS LP
40 Main St, Vista (92083-5831)
PHONE 760 724-9795
Darrell Musick, *Principal*
EMP: 506
SALES (est): 52.4K
SALES (corp-wide): 569.7MM Publicly Held
WEB: www.regencycenters.com
SIC: 8051 Skilled nursing care facilities
HQ: Regency Centers Texas Llc
1 Independent Dr Ste 102
Jacksonville FL 32202
904 598-7000

(P-20868)
REGENCY OAKS CARE CENTER
3850 E Esther St, Long Beach (90804-2009)
PHONE 562 498-3368
Fax: 562 494-1786
Vince Hambright, *President*
Jasmine Geary, *Social Dir*
Juliet Pagayatan, *Controller*
Jennifer Gutierrez, *Education*
Kaveh Kashani, *Director*
EMP: 110
SALES (est): 5.3MM Privately Held
SIC: 8051 Convalescent home with continuous nursing care

(P-20869)
REHABLTION CNTRE OF BVRLY HLLS
580 S San Vicente Blvd, Los Angeles (90048-4621)
PHONE 323 782-1500
Fax: 323 782-1500
Eldon Teper, *President*
Fredie Gordillo, *Officer*
Florida Santos, *Office Mgr*
Joyce Tsuchiyama, *Administration*
Jyneth Aguirre, *Human Res Dir*
EMP: 200
SALES (est): 15.9MM Privately Held
SIC: 8051 Skilled nursing care facilities

(P-20870)
REO VISTA HEALTHCARE CENTER
6061 Banbury St, San Diego (92139-3624)
PHONE 619 475-2211
Bryan Brockbank, *Administration*
Lander Ramirez, *Executive*
Curtis White, *Administration*
Stan Anderson, *Info Tech Dir*
Lisa Munoz, *Human Res Dir*
EMP: 52
SALES (est): 16.8MM Privately Held
SIC: 8051 8011 Skilled nursing care facilities; clinic, operated by physicians

(P-20871)
RIDGECREST HEALTHCARE INC (PA)
1131 N China Lake Blvd, Ridgecrest (93555-3131)
PHONE 323 344-0601
Oscar Abaya Parel, *President*
Robert Agiulos, *Administration*
EMP: 52
SALES (est): 6.5MM Privately Held
SIC: 8051 Skilled nursing care facilities

(P-20872)
RIO HNDO SBCUTE NRSING CTR LLC
Also Called: Rio Hondo Convalescent Hosp
273 E Beverly Blvd, Montebello (90640-3775)
PHONE 323 838-5915
Alice Enrique, *Administration*
Jean Aurelio, *Nursing Dir*
EMP: 150
SALES (est): 7.4MM
SALES (corp-wide): 9.6B Publicly Held
WEB: www.parkviewnursing.net
SIC: 8051 Skilled nursing care facilities
PA: Genesis Healthcare, Inc.
101 E State St
Kennett Square PA 19348
610 444-6350

(P-20873)
RIVER BEND NURSING HOME INC
2215 Oakmont Way, West Sacramento (95691-3022)
PHONE 916 371-1890
Nell Stamm, *President*
Pat Zarate, *Asst Admin*
Susan Roberts, *Director*
EMP: 90
SQ FT: 34,000
SALES (est): 3.6MM Privately Held
WEB: www.somersetnursingcenter.com
SIC: 8051 Skilled nursing care facilities

(P-20874)
RIVERA SANITARIUM INC
Also Called: Colonial Gardens Nursing Home
7246 Rosemead Blvd, Pico Rivera (90660-4010)
P.O. Box 2098 (90662-2098)
PHONE 562 949-2591
Fax: 562 949-5268
Elizabeth Stephens, *President*
Kent Stephens, *Administration*
EMP: 86
SQ FT: 30,000
SALES (est): 4.5MM Privately Held
SIC: 8051 Skilled nursing care facilities

8051 - Skilled Nursing Facilities County (P-20875)

(P-20875)
RIVERSIDE CARE INC
Also Called: Valencia Gardens Hlth Care Ctr
4301 Caroline Ct, Riverside (92506-2902)
PHONE..................951 683-7111
Fax: 951 683-6826
Ted Holt, *President*
Spencer E Olsen, *Treasurer*
Jenny Ortiz, *Admin Sec*
EMP: 130
SALES (est): 7.1MM
SALES (corp-wide): 60.3MM **Privately Held**
SIC: **8051** Skilled nursing care facilities
PA: North American Health Care, Inc.
　　32836 Pacific Coast Hwy
　　Dana Point CA 92629
　　949 240-2423

(P-20876)
RIVERSIDE EQUITIES LLC
Also Called: MISSION CARE CENTER
8487 Magnolia Ave, Riverside (92504-3222)
PHONE..................951 688-2222
Fax: 951 688-7659
Frank Johnson, *CEO*
Irving Bauman, *COO*
Carey Van Boxtel, *Administration*
EMP: 93
SALES: 6.8MM **Privately Held**
SIC: **8051** Mental retardation hospital

(P-20877)
RIVERSIDE HEALTH CARE CORP
1090 Rio Ln, Sacramento (95822-1706)
PHONE..................916 446-2506
Larry Meyer, *Administration*
EMP: 65
SALES (corp-wide): 8.9MM **Privately Held**
SIC: **8051** Skilled nursing care facilities
PA: Riverside Health Care Corporation
　　1469 Humboldt Rd Ste 175
　　Chico CA 95928
　　530 897-5100

(P-20878)
RIVERSIDE SANITARIUM LLC
Also Called: Riverside Bhvral Heatharce Ctr
4580 Palm Ave, Riverside (92501-3950)
PHONE..................951 684-7701
Kim Iola, *Principal*
Barbara O'Connor, *Administration*
EMP: 99
SALES (est): 2.8MM **Privately Held**
SIC: **8051** Skilled nursing care facilities

(P-20879)
RIVIERA NURSING & CONVA
Also Called: Riviera Health Care Center
8203 Telegraph Rd, Pico Rivera (90660-4905)
PHONE..................562 806-2576
Fax: 562 806-1496
Morris Weiss, *President*
Harry Jacobs, *Officer*
Bessie Weiss, *Vice Pres*
Rolan Calungsod, *Office Mgr*
Dj Weaver, *Administration*
EMP: 118
SQ FT: 60,000
SALES (est): 7.1MM **Privately Held**
WEB: www.rivierahealthcare.com
SIC: **8051** 8059 Skilled nursing care facilities; convalescent home

(P-20880)
ROBINCROST CARE CORPORATION
Also Called: Pasadena Residential Care Ctr
636 S Plymouth Blvd, Los Angeles (90005-3770)
P.O. Box 76890 (90076-0890)
PHONE..................323 934-3515
Anne Van-Singel, *President*
EMP: 55
SALES (est): 2.6MM **Privately Held**
SIC: **8051** Skilled nursing care facilities

(P-20881)
ROCKPORT ADM SVCS LLC
4585 N Figueroa St, Los Angeles (90065-3026)
PHONE..................323 223-3441
EMP: 87 **Privately Held**
SIC: **8051** Skilled nursing care facilities
PA: Rockport Administrative Services, Llc
　　5900 Wilshire Blvd # 1600
　　Los Angeles CA 90036

(P-20882)
ROWLAND CONVALESCENT HOSP INC
Also Called: Rowland, The
330 W Rowland St, Covina (91723-2941)
PHONE..................626 967-2741
Fax: 626 332-3781
Anthony Kalomas, *President*
Gregg Kiilburn, *Controller*
John Donohoe, *Director*
EMP: 100
SQ FT: 30,000
SALES (est): 7.2MM **Privately Held**
SIC: **8051** Skilled nursing care facilities

(P-20883)
ROYAL TERRACE HEALTHCARE
1340 Highland Ave, Duarte (91010-2520)
PHONE..................626 256-4654
Fax: 626 256-9354
Eloisa Heiser, *Director*
Peter Balacuit, *Director*
Alma Hechanova, *Director*
Anabell Reyes, *Director*
EMP: 60 EST: 2003
SALES (est): 1.7MM **Privately Held**
SIC: **8051** Skilled nursing care facilities

(P-20884)
S L H C C INC
Also Called: Saylor Lane Healthcare Center
3500 Folsom Blvd, Sacramento (95816-6615)
PHONE..................916 457-6521
Fax: 916 457-4652
Dave Hilburn, *President*
Jay Anderson, *Administration*
EMP: 50
SALES (est): 3.1MM **Privately Held**
SIC: **8051** Skilled nursing care facilities

(P-20885)
S&F MANAGEMENT COMPANY INC (PA)
9200 W Sunset Blvd # 700, West Hollywood (90069-3502)
PHONE..................310 385-1090
Lee C Samson, *President*
Harold Walt, *CFO*
Thelma Luna, *Accounting Mgr*
Jesfer Nicdao, *Accountant*
Margy Gunderson, *Manager*
EMP: 100
SALES (est): 13.6MM **Privately Held**
WEB: www.snfmgt.com
SIC: **8051** Convalescent home with continuous nursing care

(P-20886)
SACRAMENTO OPERATING CO LP
Also Called: Double Tree Past Acute
7400 24th St, Sacramento (95822-5350)
PHONE..................916 422-4825
Kenneth Tabler, *Partner*
Cynthia Mitchell,
EMP: 120
SALES (est): 2.4MM **Privately Held**
SIC: **8051** Skilled nursing care facilities

(P-20887)
SAINT CLAIRES NURSING CENTER
6248 66th Ave, Sacramento (95823-2733)
PHONE..................916 392-4440
Fax: 916 392-0111
Kathryn J Hill, *President*
Kathleen Locke, *Social Dir*
Michael Maderas, *Administration*
Judy Peterson, *Bookkeeper*
Daniel Yuen, *Director*
EMP: 100

SALES: 6.4MM **Privately Held**
SIC: **8051** Skilled nursing care facilities

(P-20888)
SAN DIEGO HEBREW HOMES (PA)
Also Called: LEICHTAG ASSISTED LIVING
211 Saxony Rd, Encinitas (92024-2791)
PHONE..................760 942-2695
Fax: 760 942-0894
Yehudi Gaffen, *Chairman*
Pam Ferris, *President*
Robin Weiner, *CFO*
Brad Blose, *Vice Pres*
Kimberly Fuson, *Vice Pres*
EMP: 180
SQ FT: 219,000
SALES: 20.5MM **Privately Held**
WEB: www.seacrestvillage.com
SIC: **8051** 8059 6513 Skilled nursing care facilities; rest home, with health care; retirement hotel operation

(P-20889)
SAN JOSES HEALTHCARE & WELL
Also Called: San Jose Hlthcare Wellness Ctr
75 N 13th St, San Jose (95112-3439)
PHONE..................408 295-2665
Sole Majer, *Mng Member*
Tess Gintu, *Nursing Dir*
Aaron Robins,
Shawna Martinez, *Director*
EMP: 90
SALES (est): 6.7MM **Privately Held**
SIC: **8051** Skilled nursing care facilities

(P-20890)
SAN LEANDRO HEALTHCARE CENTER
368 Juana Ave, San Leandro (94577-4811)
PHONE..................510 357-4015
Fax: 510 357-3466
Pat Poddatoori, *President*
Marissa Ilagan, *Office Mgr*
EMP: 70
SALES (est): 3.1MM **Privately Held**
SIC: **8051** Convalescent home with continuous nursing care

(P-20891)
SAN MARCOS OPERATING CO LP
Also Called: Village Square Healthcare Ctr
1586 W Square Marcos Blvd, San Marcos (92078)
PHONE..................760 471-2986
Kristina Kuizon,
EMP: 85
SALES (est): 248.6K **Privately Held**
SIC: **8051** Skilled nursing care facilities

(P-20892)
SAN MATEO HEALTHCARE & WELLNES
Also Called: Burlingame Long Term Care
1100 Trousdale Dr, Burlingame (94010-3207)
PHONE..................650 692-3758
Sharrod Brooks,
EMP: 99
SALES (est): 7.1MM **Privately Held**
SIC: **8051** Mental retardation hospital

(P-20893)
SAN PEDRO CONVALESCENT HOME
Also Called: Los Palos Convalescent Hosp
1430 W 6th St, San Pedro (90732-3503)
PHONE..................310 519-0359
Fax: 310 514-0291
Celia Valdomar, *President*
Jose Valdomar, *Info Tech Mgr*
EMP: 90
SQ FT: 10,000
SALES (est): 6.6MM **Privately Held**
SIC: **8051** Convalescent home with continuous nursing care

(P-20894)
SANDHURST CONVALES GRP LTD A
Also Called: Windsor Garden Conv Ctr Hwthrn
13922 Cerise Ave, Hawthorne (90250-8688)
PHONE..................310 675-3304
Anne Josafat, *Records Dir*
Paryus Patel, *Director*
EMP: 50
SALES (est): 990K **Privately Held**
SIC: **8051** Convalescent home with continuous nursing care

(P-20895)
SANHYD INC
Also Called: Kyakamena Sklled Nrsing Fcilty
2131 Carleton St, Berkeley (94704-3213)
PHONE..................510 843-2131
Fax: 510 843-2801
Pat Poddatoori, *President*
Tim Motokaa, *Administration*
Emmons Collins, *Director*
EMP: 52
SQ FT: 15,000
SALES (est): 2.5MM **Privately Held**
SIC: **8051** Skilled nursing care facilities; convalescent home with continuous nursing care

(P-20896)
SANTA ROSA MEMORIAL HOSPITAL
1165 Montgomery Dr, Santa Rosa (95405-4897)
PHONE..................707 542-2771
George Perez, *CEO*
Gary Greensweig, *Officer*
Nancy Boostrom, *Risk Mgmt Dir*
Jeanne Steensma, *Legal Exec*
EMP: 200
SALES (corp-wide): 5.6B **Privately Held**
WEB: www.stjosephhealth.org
SIC: **8051** 8062 8063 8011 Skilled nursing care facilities; general medical & surgical hospitals; psychiatric hospitals; psychiatrists & psychoanalysts
HQ: Santa Rosa Memorial Hospital Inc
　　1165 Montgomery Dr
　　Santa Rosa CA 95405
　　707 546-3210

(P-20897)
SCRIPPS HEALTH
Also Called: Scripps Mercy Hospital
4077 5th Ave, San Diego (92103-2105)
PHONE..................619 294-8111
Jacqueline Saucier, *Director*
Michael Tobin, *Ch Radiology*
Richard Rothberger, *Vice Pres*
Chris Nicholson, *Lab Dir*
Tom Gammiere, *Administration*
EMP: 99
SALES (corp-wide): 1.7B **Privately Held**
WEB: www.scripps.org
SIC: **8051** Skilled nursing care facilities
PA: Scripps Health
　　4275 Campus Point Ct
　　San Diego CA 92121
　　858 678-7000

(P-20898)
SCRIPPS HEALTH
Also Called: Scripps Shared Services
10790 Rancho Bernardo Rd, San Diego (92127-5705)
P.O. Box 85105 (92186-5105)
PHONE..................858 657-4218
Vickie Tickel, *Director*
Joel Goehring, *Administration*
Lily Bao, *Programmer Anys*
Winston Carter, *Project Mgr*
Windell Tidwell, *Technology*
EMP: 150
SALES (corp-wide): 1.7B **Privately Held**
WEB: www.scripps.org
SIC: **8051** 8082 Skilled nursing care facilities; home health care services
PA: Scripps Health
　　4275 Campus Point Ct
　　San Diego CA 92121
　　858 678-7000

PRODUCTS & SERVICES SECTION
8051 - Skilled Nursing Facilities County (P-20921)

(P-20899)
SCRIPPS HEALTH (PA)
4275 Campus Point Ct, San Diego (92121-1513)
PHONE.....................858 678-7000
Fax: 858 678-6113
Chris D Van Gorder, *President*
Carrie Cushman, *Volunteer Dir*
Richard K Rothberger, *CFO*
Mary J Anderson, *Trustee*
Westcott W Price, *Trustee*
EMP: 2514
SQ FT: 95,000
SALES (est): 1.7B **Privately Held**
WEB: www.scripps.org
SIC: 8051 8082 8062 8049 Skilled nursing care facilities; home health care services; general medical & surgical hospitals; physical therapist; psychologist, psychotherapist & hypnotist; offices & clinics of optometrists; offices & clinics of podiatrists

(P-20900)
SEA BREEZE HEALTH CARE INC
Also Called: BEACHSIDE NURSING CENTER
7781 Garfield Ave, Huntington Beach (92648-2026)
PHONE.....................714 847-9671
Fax: 714 847-9671
Tim Paulson, *President*
Darlene Barkau, *Administration*
Brian Tanner, *Administration*
May Aquino, *Nursing Dir*
Bobby Lee, *Director*
EMP: 86
SQ FT: 14,895
SALES: 8.9MM **Privately Held**
SIC: 8051 Skilled nursing care facilities

(P-20901)
SEACREST CONVALESCENT HOSP INC
1416 W 6th St, San Pedro (90732-3550)
PHONE.....................310 833-3526
Fax: 310 831-3053
Cecelia Valdomar, *President*
Cecelia D Valdomar, *President*
Joy Nacionales, *Admin Sec*
Abigail Tunque, *Director*
Jose Valdomar, *Director*
EMP: 70
SALES (est): 3.5MM **Privately Held**
SIC: 8051 Convalescent home with continuous nursing care

(P-20902)
SELA HEALTHCARE INC (PA)
Also Called: Holiday Manor Care Center
867 E 11th St, Upland (91786-4867)
PHONE.....................909 985-1981
Philip Weinberger, *CEO*
Marylynn Mahan, *CFO*
Cindy Ebert, *Director*
EMP: 140
SQ FT: 60,000
SALES (est): 9.3MM **Privately Held**
SIC: 8051 Skilled nursing care facilities

(P-20903)
SELA HEALTHCARE INC
Also Called: Holiday Manor
20554 Roscoe Blvd, Canoga Park (91306-1746)
PHONE.....................818 341-9800
Victorio Ocbena Sosing, *Principal*
Jamie Lopez, *Facilities Dir*
Camilo Flores, *Maintence Staff*
Cary Buchman, *Agent*
EMP: 310
SALES (corp-wide): 9.3MM **Privately Held**
SIC: 8051 Skilled nursing care facilities
PA: Sela Healthcare, Inc
  867 E 11th St
  Upland CA 91786
  909 985-1981

(P-20904)
SERRANO COVALESCENT HOSPITAL
5401 Fountain Ave, Los Angeles (90029-1006)
PHONE.....................323 465-2106
Fax: 323 465-3703
Lydia Cruz, *Manager*
EMP: 80
SALES (est): 1.5MM **Privately Held**
SIC: 8051 Skilled nursing care facilities

(P-20905)
SHADOW HLLS CNVLSCENT HOSP INC
10158 Sunland Blvd, Sunland (91040-1651)
PHONE.....................818 352-4438
Fax: 818 951-3780
Orlando Clarizio Jr, *President*
Dino Clarizio, *Treasurer*
Michale Clarizio, *Corp Secy*
EMP: 67
SQ FT: 13,000
SALES: 3.8MM **Privately Held**
SIC: 8051 Skilled nursing care facilities

(P-20906)
SHADOWBROOK HEALTH CARE INC
1 Gilmore Ln, Oroville (95966-5147)
PHONE.....................530 534-1353
Fax: 530 534-0632
Sharon Jennings, *President*
Ron Brown, *Administration*
Christy Johnson, *Education*
EMP: 50
SQ FT: 10,100
SALES: 3.4MM
SALES (corp-wide): 8.5MM **Privately Held**
SIC: 8051 Skilled nursing care facilities
PA: Riverside Health Care Corporation
  1469 Humboldt Rd Ste 175
  Chico CA 95928
  530 897-5100

(P-20907)
SHARON CARE CENTER LLC
8167 W 3rd St, Los Angeles (90048-4314)
PHONE.....................323 655-2023
Fax: 323 651-3302
EMP: 90
SALES (est): 1.2MM
SALES (corp-wide): 9.6B **Publicly Held**
WEB: www.parkviewnursing.net
SIC: 8051 8059 Skilled nursing care facilities; convalescent home
HQ: Skilled Healthcare, Llc
  27442 Portola Pkwy # 200
  Foothill Ranch CA 92610
  949 282-5800

(P-20908)
SHARP HEALTHCARE
Also Called: Sharp Rees-Stealy Div
300 Fir St, San Diego (92101-2327)
PHONE.....................619 446-1575
Donna Mills, *Administration*
Jack Thomas, *Treasurer*
Kalpana Chalasani MD, *Med Doctor*
Kathryn P Nemanich MD, *Med Doctor*
Jennie C Ou MD, *Med Doctor*
EMP: 150
SQ FT: 61,608
SALES (corp-wide): 3.4B **Privately Held**
SIC: 8051 Skilled nursing care facilities
PA: Sharp Healthcare
  8695 Spectrum Center Blvd
  San Diego CA 92123
  858 499-4000

(P-20909)
SHARP HEALTHCARE
Also Called: Birch Ptrick Convalescent Cntr
751 Medical Center Ct, Chula Vista (91911-6617)
PHONE.....................858 499-2000
Fax: 619 482-5835
Lily Reyes, *Director*
Rick King, *CFO*
Monique Santos, *Treasurer*
Laurie Godfrey, *Quality Imp Dir*
Zoe Gardner, *Human Res Mgr*
EMP: 140
SALES (corp-wide): 3.4B **Privately Held**
SIC: 8051 Skilled nursing care facilities
PA: Sharp Healthcare
  8695 Spectrum Center Blvd
  San Diego CA 92123
  858 499-4000

(P-20910)
SHERWOOD OAKS ENTERPRISES
Also Called: Sherwood Oaks Health Center
130 Dana St, Fort Bragg (95437-4506)
PHONE.....................707 964-6333
Fax: 707 964-1596
Melanie Reding, *President*
Joe Reding, *Corp Secy*
John Cottle, *Director*
EMP: 90 **EST:** 1975
SQ FT: 19,000
SALES (est): 5.6MM **Privately Held**
SIC: 8051 Skilled nursing care facilities; convalescent home with continuous nursing care; extended care facility

(P-20911)
SHIELDS NURSING CENTERS INC (PA)
606 Alfred Nobel Dr, Hercules (94547-1834)
PHONE.....................510 724-9911
William Shields Jr, *CEO*
Monique Shields, *COO*
Gregory Shields, *Manager*
Nicole Szilagyi, *Manager*
EMP: 150
SQ FT: 6,100
SALES: 9.8MM **Privately Held**
WEB: www.shieldsnursingcenters.com
SIC: 8051 Skilled nursing care facilities

(P-20912)
SHIELDS NURSING CENTERS INC
3230 Carlson Blvd, El Cerrito (94530-3907)
PHONE.....................510 525-3212
Fax: 510 525-6832
William Shields, *Administration*
Brazelle Carter, *Director*
EMP: 58
SALES (corp-wide): 9.8MM **Privately Held**
WEB: www.shieldsnursingcenters.com
SIC: 8051 Skilled nursing care facilities
PA: Shields Nursing Centers, Inc.
  606 Alfred Nobel Dr
  Hercules CA 94547
  510 724-9911

(P-20913)
SIERRA CARE REHABILITATION CTR
310 Oak Ridge Dr, Roseville (95661-3420)
PHONE.....................916 782-3188
Fax: 916 782-1283
Alice Mills, *Principal*
Rachelle McCoure, *Admin Asst*
EMP: 90
SALES (est): 1MM **Privately Held**
SIC: 8051 Skilled nursing care facilities

(P-20914)
SIERRA VIEW CARE HOLDINGS LLC
Also Called: SIERRA VIEW CARE CENTER
14318 Ohio St, Baldwin Park (91706-2553)
PHONE.....................626 960-1971
Jordan Fishman, *Mng Member*
Irving Bauman, *President*
Kelly Iastarro, *Vice Pres*
Matheson Chambers, *Principal*
David Johnson, *Principal*
EMP: 99
SALES: 8MM **Privately Held**
SIC: 8051 Skilled nursing care facilities

(P-20915)
SIERRA VIEW HOMES
Also Called: SIERRA VIEW HOMES RESIDENTIAL
1155 E Springfield Ave, Reedley (93654-3225)
PHONE.....................559 637-2256
Fax: 559 638-6857
Vito Genna, *Exec Dir*
Janet Habegger, *Director*
Chris Lopez, *Director*
EMP: 140
SQ FT: 63,600
SALES: 7.6MM **Privately Held**
WEB: www.sierraview.org
SIC: 8051 8059 6513 Skilled nursing care facilities; personal care home, with health care; apartment hotel operation

(P-20916)
SILVERADO SENIOR LIVING INC
Also Called: Beach Cities Memory Care Cmnty
514 N Prospect Ave # 120, Redondo Beach (90277-3036)
PHONE.....................424 257-6418
Thomas V Croal, *CFO*
Dawn Usher, *Senior VP*
EMP: 84
SALES (corp-wide): 182.6MM **Privately Held**
SIC: 8051 Skilled nursing care facilities
PA: Senior Silverado Living Inc
  6400 Oak Cyn Ste 200
  Irvine CA 92618
  949 240-7200

(P-20917)
SILVERSCREEN HEALTHCARE INC
Also Called: Golden State Colonial Convales
10830 Oxnard St, North Hollywood (91606-5021)
PHONE.....................818 763-8247
Fax: 818 763-8279
Philip Weinberger, *President*
Marylynn Mahan, *CFO*
Klara Elekes, *Admin Sec*
Rachel Park, *VP Mktg*
EMP: 58
SQ FT: 16,477
SALES (est): 3.2MM **Privately Held**
SIC: 8051 8059 Skilled nursing care facilities; convalescent home

(P-20918)
SKILLED HEALTHCARE LLC
Also Called: Brier Oak On Sunset Rehab
5154 W Sunset Blvd, Los Angeles (90027-5708)
PHONE.....................323 663-3951
Douglas Lehnhoff, *Exec Dir*
EMP: 100
SALES (corp-wide): 9.6B **Publicly Held**
WEB: www.skilledhealthcare.com
SIC: 8051 8049 8059 Skilled nursing care facilities; physical therapist; personal care home, with health care
HQ: Skilled Healthcare, Llc
  27442 Portola Pkwy # 200
  Foothill Ranch CA 92610
  949 282-5800

(P-20919)
SKYLINE HEALTHCARE & WELLNESS
Also Called: Skyline Healthcare Center
3032 Rowena Ave, Los Angeles (90039-2005)
PHONE.....................323 665-1185
Fax: 323 913-0796
Sharrod Brooks,
Doris Moran, *Financial Exec*
EMP: 99
SALES (est): 5.3MM **Privately Held**
SIC: 8051 Mental retardation hospital

(P-20920)
SLCH INC (PA)
Also Called: Sophia Lyn Convalescent Hosp
1920 N Fair Oaks Ave, Pasadena (91103-1623)
PHONE.....................626 798-0558
Fax: 626 798-0140
Phillip Rosales, *President*
Lolita Asero, *Administration*
EMP: 50
SQ FT: 16,757
SALES: 3.2MM **Privately Held**
WEB: www.slch.com
SIC: 8051 Skilled nursing care facilities

(P-20921)
SOLEDAD CMNTY HLTH CARE DST
Also Called: SOLEDAD MEDICAL GROUP
612 Main St, Soledad (93960-2533)
PHONE.....................831 678-2462

8051 - Skilled Nursing Facilities County (P-20922)

Fax: 831 678-1539
Steven Pritt, *CEO*
Ralph Sarmento, *President*
Rosemary Guidotti, *Admin Sec*
Willa Doroy, *Admin Asst*
Debbie Ramirez, *Persnl Dir*
EMP: 80 **EST:** 1948
SALES: 53.3K **Privately Held**
WEB: www.schcd.com
SIC: 8051 Skilled nursing care facilities

(P-20922)
SOUTHERN INYO HEALTHCARE DST
501 E Locust St, Lone Pine (93545)
P.O. Box 1009 (93545-1009)
PHONE...................760 876-5501
Fax: 760 876-2268
Lee Barron, *CEO*
George Lahey, *Lab Dir*
Jaime Franciscus, *Admin Sec*
Mary Gonzales, *Admin Asst*
Donna Donald, *Administration*
EMP: 106
SQ FT: 29,000
SALES (est): 14.4MM **Privately Held**
WEB: www.sihd.org
SIC: 8051 Skilled nursing care facilities

(P-20923)
SPRING VALLEY POST ACUTE LLC
14973 Hesperia Rd, Victorville (92395-3923)
PHONE...................760 245-6477
David Johnson, *Mng Member*
Lizet Ramirez, *Administration*
Matheson Chambers,
Thomas Chambers,
EMP: 200
SALES (est): 3.3MM **Privately Held**
SIC: 8051 Skilled nursing care facilities

(P-20924)
SSC CARMICHAEL OPERATING CO LP
Also Called: Mission Crmchael Healthcare Ctr
3630 Mission Ave, Carmichael (95608-2933)
PHONE...................916 485-4793
Katie Prozicnce, *Office Mgr*
Anne Gilles, *Administration*
Diana Haines, *Administration*
Valerie Toscano, *Education*
Wayne M Sanner,
EMP: 99
SALES: 12.6MM
SALES (corp-wide): 1B **Privately Held**
SIC: 8051 Skilled nursing care facilities
PA: Savaseniorcare, Llc
1 Ravinia Dr Ste 1500
Atlanta GA 30346
770 829-5100

(P-20925)
SSC NEWPORT BEACH OPER CO LP
Also Called: Flagship Healthcare Center
466 Flagship Rd, Newport Beach (92663-3635)
PHONE...................949 642-8044
Fax: 949 642-0102
Scott Harris, *Partner*
Wayne Sanner, *Partner*
Wynn Sims, *Partner*
EMP: 133
SQ FT: 21,903
SALES (est): 4.7MM **Privately Held**
SIC: 8051 Skilled nursing care facilities

(P-20926)
SSC OAKLAND EXCELL OPER CO LP
Also Called: Excell Health Care Center
3025 High St, Oakland (94619-1807)
PHONE...................510 261-5200
Elma Conway, *Manager*
Wayne M Sanner,
EMP: 99
SALES (est): 1.2MM **Privately Held**
SIC: 8051 Skilled nursing care facilities

(P-20927)
SSC SAN JOSE OPERATING CO LP
Also Called: Courtyard Care Center
340 Northlake Dr, San Jose (95117-1251)
PHONE...................408 249-0344
Fax: 408 246-4715
Maxine Niel, *Executive Asst*
Luz Bester, *Personnel Exec*
Wayne M Sanner,
EMP: 94
SALES: 7.7MM
SALES (corp-wide): 1B **Privately Held**
SIC: 8051 Skilled nursing care facilities
PA: Savaseniorcare, Llc
1 Ravinia Dr Ste 1500
Atlanta GA 30346
770 829-5100

(P-20928)
ST LUKE HLTHCR & REHAB CTR LL
2321 Newburg Rd, Fortuna (95540-2815)
PHONE...................707 725-4467
Ted Chigaros,
Donald Baird, *Director*
EMP: 100
SALES: 1,000K **Privately Held**
SIC: 8051 Skilled nursing care facilities

(P-20929)
ST MICHAEL CONVALESCENT HOSP
Also Called: Vintage Estates of Hayward
25919 Gading Rd, Hayward (94544-2798)
PHONE...................510 782-8424
Fax: 510 782-0199
Sally Rapp, *CEO*
Roland Rapp, *Treasurer*
Cheryl A Rapp, *Principal*
Hasmin Koo, *Personnel*
Carmelita Dimaano, *Nursing Dir*
EMP: 99
SQ FT: 6,000
SALES (est): 3.3MM **Privately Held**
WEB: www.vintage-estates.com
SIC: 8051 Skilled nursing care facilities

(P-20930)
STANDARDBEARER INSUR CO LTD
27101 Puerta Real Ste 450, Mission Viejo (92691-8566)
PHONE...................949 487-9500
EMP: 288
SALES (est): 564.4K
SALES (corp-wide): 1.3B **Publicly Held**
SIC: 8051 Skilled nursing care facilities
PA: The Ensign Group Inc
27101 Puerta Real Ste 450
Mission Viejo CA 92691
949 487-9500

(P-20931)
STJOHN GOD RTIREMENT CARE CTR
2468 S St Andrews Pl, Los Angeles (90018-2042)
PHONE...................323 731-0641
Fax: 323 737-1452
Michael Bessimer, *Administration*
Jonathon Harris, *Human Res Dir*
EMP: 200
SQ FT: 99,392
SALES: 13.7MM **Privately Held**
SIC: 8051 8052 Skilled nursing care facilities; intermediate care facilities

(P-20932)
STONEBROOK CONVALESCENT CENTER
Also Called: Stonebrook Health Care Center
4367 Concord Blvd, Concord (94521-1100)
PHONE...................925 689-7457
Fax: 925 689-7473
James D Hightower, *President*
Yvette Roncagliolo, *Asst Admin*
Maribel Reillo, *Admin Asst*
Lori Cooper, *Administration*
Elizabeth Deguzman, *Hlthcr Dir*
EMP: 206
SQ FT: 44,000

SALES (est): 14.1MM
SALES (corp-wide): 14.5MM **Privately Held**
WEB: www.healthmarkservices.com
SIC: 8051 Convalescent home with continuous nursing care
PA: Healthmark Services Inc
217 Lakewood Rd
Van Buren AR 72956
479 471-9797

(P-20933)
SUBACUTE TRTMNT ADOLESCNT REHA (PA)
Also Called: Stars
545 Estudillo Ave, San Leandro (94577-4611)
PHONE...................510 352-9200
Fax: 510 352-3120
Peter Zucker, *President*
John Weller, *CFO*
Kent Dunlap, *Senior VP*
David Young, *Executive Asst*
John Koran, *Info Tech Dir*
EMP: 76
SQ FT: 7,442
SALES: 3.9MM **Privately Held**
SIC: 8051 8093 Skilled nursing care facilities; mental retardation hospital; extended care facility; mental health clinic, outpatient; substance abuse clinics (outpatient); drug clinic, outpatient; rehabilitation center, outpatient treatment

(P-20934)
SUN HAVEN CARE INC
Also Called: Terrace View Care Center
201 E Bastanchury Rd, Fullerton (92835-2604)
PHONE...................714 578-2794
Fax: 714 526-8136
John Sworenson, *CEO*
Brendon Bahl, *Vice Pres*
May Lagman, *Food Svc Dir*
EMP: 60
SALES (est): 3.4MM **Privately Held**
SIC: 8051 Convalescent home with continuous nursing care

(P-20935)
SUN MAR MANAGEMENT SERVICES
8171 Magnolia Ave, Riverside (92504-3409)
PHONE...................951 687-3842
Robert Ginn, *Administration*
Joel Pengson, *Director*
Vernon R Will, *Agent*
EMP: 100
SALES (corp-wide): 59MM **Privately Held**
WEB: www.extendedcarehospital.com
SIC: 8051 Skilled nursing care facilities
PA: Sun Mar Management Services
3050 Saturn St Ste 201
Brea CA 92821
714 577-3880

(P-20936)
SUN VILLA INC
350 N Villa St, Porterville (93257-3211)
PHONE...................559 784-6644
David Green, *Administration*
Salvador Estrada, *Director*
Rakesh Jindal, *Director*
Mark Mann, *Manager*
REO W Jordan, *Agent*
EMP: 120
SQ FT: 50,000
SALES (est): 5.2MM **Privately Held**
SIC: 8051 Skilled nursing care facilities

(P-20937)
SUNBRIDGE BRASWELL ENTPS INC
Also Called: Laurel Park
1425 Laurel Ave, Pomona (91768-2837)
PHONE...................909 622-1069
Fax: 909 622-4319
Gerald Bogard, *Branch Mgr*
Sylvia Roderiguez, *Administration*
Elisabeth Contreas, *Financial Exec*
Lillian Werntz, *Manager*
EMP: 50
SALES (corp-wide): 9.6B **Publicly Held**
SIC: 8051 Skilled nursing care facilities

HQ: Sunbridge Braswell Enterprises, Inc.
5100 Sun Ave Ne
Albuquerque NM

(P-20938)
SUNBRIDGE BRASWELL ENTPS INC
Also Called: Olive Vista, Center
2335 S Towne Ave, Pomona (91766-6227)
PHONE...................909 628-6024
Richard Escontrias, *Branch Mgr*
Lillian Werntz, *Manager*
EMP: 120
SALES (corp-wide): 9.6B **Publicly Held**
SIC: 8051 8361 Convalescent home with continuous nursing care; residential care
HQ: Sunbridge Braswell Enterprises, Inc.
5100 Sun Ave Ne
Albuquerque NM

(P-20939)
SUNBRIDGE BRITTANY REHAB CENTR
Also Called: American River Care
3900 Garfield Ave, Carmichael (95608-6647)
PHONE...................916 484-1393
Fax: 916 481-6489
Andrew Turner, *President*
Summer Olhausen, *Office Mgr*
Anne Butler, *Administration*
Sherry Gray, *MIS Dir*
Roy Copland, *Financial Exec*
EMP: 120
SALES: 4.3MM
SALES (corp-wide): 9.6B **Publicly Held**
SIC: 8051 8069 Skilled nursing care facilities; specialty hospitals, except psychiatric
HQ: Regency Health Services, Inc.
5100 Sun Ave Ne
Albuquerque NM

(P-20940)
SUNBRIDGE CARE ENTPS W INC
Also Called: Kingsburg Center
1101 Stroud Ave, Kingsburg (93631-1016)
PHONE...................559 897-5881
Fax: 559 897-0215
Ron Kennersly, *Manager*
J Richard Edwards, *Treasurer*
EMP: 100
SALES (corp-wide): 9.6B **Publicly Held**
SIC: 8051 Skilled nursing care facilities
HQ: Sunbridge Care Enterprises West, Inc.
101 Sun Ave Ne
Albuquerque NM 87109
925 988-9100

(P-20941)
SUNBRIDGE CARE ENTPS W LLC
Also Called: Kingsburg Center
1101 Stroud Ave, Kingsburg (93631-1016)
PHONE...................559 897-5881
EMP: 3598
SALES (est): 6.5MM
SALES (corp-wide): 9.6B **Publicly Held**
SIC: 8051 Skilled nursing care facilities
HQ: Genesis Healthcare Llc
101 E State St
Kennett Square PA 19348

(P-20942)
SUNBRIDGE HARBOR VIEW
Also Called: Harbor View Rehabilitation Ctr
490 W 14th St, Long Beach (90813-2943)
PHONE...................562 989-9907
Fax: 562 591-0235
Rick Matros, *President*
Marjorie Parez, *Business Mgr*
EMP: 200
SALES (est): 6.3MM
SALES (corp-wide): 9.6B **Publicly Held**
SIC: 8051 8361 Skilled nursing care facilities; residential care
HQ: Regency Health Services, Inc.
5100 Sun Ave Ne
Albuquerque NM

PRODUCTS & SERVICES SECTION
8051 - Skilled Nursing Facilities County (P-20962)

(P-20943)
SUNBRIDGE HEALTHCARE LLC
Also Called: Sunbridge Elmhaven Care Center
6940 Pacific Ave, Stockton (95207-2602)
PHONE..................................209 477-4817
Mike Blaufus, *Administration*
Beth Clark, *Office Mgr*
Karen Smith, *Administration*
Richard Gonzales, *Facilities Dir*
Suzie Vargas, *Director*
EMP: 99
SALES (corp-wide): 9.6B **Publicly Held**
SIC: 8051 Skilled nursing care facilities
HQ: Sunbridge Healthcare, Llc
101 Sun Ave Ne
Albuquerque NM 87109
505 821-3355

(P-20944)
SUNBRIDGE PARADISE RHBLTTN CTR
Also Called: Pine View Center
8777 Skyway, Paradise (95969-2110)
PHONE..................................530 872-3200
Fax: 530 872-5318
Annie Buerhaus, *Branch Mgr*
Maryanne Anderson, *Records Dir*
Lisa Mathews, *Social Dir*
Bene Szczesney, *Office Mgr*
Liz Welch, *Office Mgr*
EMP: 100
SALES (corp-wide): 9.6B **Publicly Held**
SIC: 8051 8049 Skilled nursing care facilities; speech therapist
HQ: Sunbridge Paradise Rehabilitation Center, Inc.
101 Sun Ave Ne
Albuquerque NM

(P-20945)
SUNNYSIDE RHBLTTION NRSING CTR
22617 S Vermont Ave, Torrance (90502-2550)
PHONE..................................310 320-4130
Fax: 310 212-3232
Judy Narloda, *President*
Jaime Deutsch, *Vice Pres*
Stephen Russell, *Research*
Nabil El-Sayad, *Director*
EMP: 220
SQ FT: 35,000
SALES (est): 12.8MM **Privately Held**
SIC: 8051 8361 8069 8052 Skilled nursing care facilities; residential care; specialty hospitals, except psychiatric; intermediate care facilities

(P-20946)
SUNNYVALE HEALTHCARE CENTER
Also Called: Sunnyvale Health Care
1291 S Bernardo Ave, Sunnyvale (94087-2060)
PHONE..................................408 245-8070
Fax: 408 328-0562
Hermina Chavez, *CEO*
Maricel De Guzman, *Records Dir*
John Chavez, *President*
Vanessa Chavez, *Treasurer*
Mario Chavez, *Vice Pres*
EMP: 75
SQ FT: 26,679
SALES (est): 4.9MM **Privately Held**
WEB: www.svhcc.com
SIC: 8051 Skilled nursing care facilities

(P-20947)
SUNRISE SENIOR LIVING INC
Also Called: Sunrise At Alta Loma
9519 Baseline Rd, Rancho Cucamonga (91730-1313)
PHONE..................................909 941-3001
Fax: 909 941-2909
Carol Lininger, *Exec Dir*
Susie Valles, *Social Dir*
Luis Rodriquez, *Exec Dir*
Gloria Tafesh, *Marketing Staff*
Billy Davis, *Food Svc Dir*
EMP: 60
SALES (corp-wide): 3.8B **Publicly Held**
SIC: 8051 8322 Skilled nursing care facilities; senior citizens' center or association
HQ: Sunrise Senior Living, Llc
7902 Westpark Dr
Mc Lean VA 22102

(P-20948)
SUNRISE SENIOR LIVING INC
Also Called: Brighton Gardens of Sunrise
72201 Country Club Dr, Palm Desert (92210)
PHONE..................................760 340-5999
Fax: 760 340-5399
Ernie Schaffer, *Director*
Theresa Ward, *Exec Dir*
EMP: 58
SALES (corp-wide): 3.8B **Publicly Held**
WEB: www.sunrise.com
SIC: 8051 8361 Skilled nursing care facilities; residential care
HQ: Sunrise Senior Living, Llc
7902 Westpark Dr
Mc Lean VA 22102

(P-20949)
SUNRISE SENIOR LIVING INC
Also Called: Sunrise At Wood Ranch
136 Tierra Rejada Rd, Simi Valley (93065-2913)
PHONE..................................805 584-8881
Fax: 805 584-2220
EMP: 62
SALES (corp-wide): 3.8B **Publicly Held**
WEB: www.sunrise.com
SIC: 8051 8361 Skilled nursing care facilities; home for the aged
HQ: Sunrise Senior Living, Llc
7902 Westpark Dr
Mc Lean VA 22102

(P-20950)
SUNRISE SENIOR LIVING INC
Also Called: Sunrise of Oakland Hills
1600 Canyon Rd 103, Moraga (94556-1709)
PHONE..................................510 531-7190
Fax: 510 531-3643
Bill Keck, *Branch Mgr*
Katherine Dunakin, *Exec Dir*
EMP: 65
SQ FT: 64,421
SALES (corp-wide): 3.8B **Publicly Held**
WEB: www.sunrise.com
SIC: 8051 8361 Skilled nursing care facilities; residential care
HQ: Sunrise Senior Living, Llc
7902 Westpark Dr
Mc Lean VA 22102

(P-20951)
SUNRISE SENIOR LIVING INC
Also Called: Sunrise of Petaluma
815 Wood Sorrel Dr, Petaluma (94954-6857)
PHONE..................................707 776-2885
Carla Sanchez, *Exec Dir*
EMP: 62
SALES (corp-wide): 3.8B **Publicly Held**
WEB: www.sunrise.com
SIC: 8051 8361 Skilled nursing care facilities; residential care
HQ: Sunrise Senior Living, Llc
7902 Westpark Dr
Mc Lean VA 22102

(P-20952)
SUNRISE SENIOR LIVING INC
Also Called: Sunrise Asssted Lving San Mteo
955 S El Camino Real, San Mateo (94402-2346)
PHONE..................................650 558-8555
Fax: 650 558-8655
Andrew Smith, *Manager*
Sarah Dillon, *Exec Dir*
Crista Martins, *Director*
EMP: 65

(P-20953)
SUNRISE SENIOR LIVING INC
3840 Lampson Ave, Seal Beach (90740-2797)
PHONE..................................562 594-5788
Bonnie Christie, *Branch Mgr*
Nancy Schlieser, *Mktg Dir*
Carl Johnson, *Director*
EMP: 58
SALES (corp-wide): 3.8B **Publicly Held**
WEB: www.sunrise.com
SIC: 8051 8361 Skilled nursing care facilities; residential care
HQ: Sunrise Senior Living, Llc
7902 Westpark Dr
Mc Lean VA 22102

(P-20954)
SUNRISE SENIOR LIVING INC
Also Called: Sunrise of Woodland Hills
5501 Newcastle Ave # 130, Encino (91316-2147)
PHONE..................................818 346-9046
Fax: 818 346-9146
Tom Colomaria, *Manager*
Lynn Chalk, *Director*
EMP: 50
SALES (corp-wide): 3.8B **Publicly Held**
WEB: www.sunrise.com
SIC: 8051 8361 Skilled nursing care facilities; residential care
HQ: Sunrise Senior Living, Llc
7902 Westpark Dr
Mc Lean VA 22102

(P-20955)
SUNRISE SENIOR LIVING INC
Also Called: Sunrise of Belmont
1010 Almeda De Las Pulgas, Belmont (94002-3508)
PHONE..................................650 508-0400
Fax: 650 508-0600
Janice Rivera, *Exec Dir*
Marilyn Hobson, *Administration*
EMP: 58
SALES (corp-wide): 3.8B **Publicly Held**
WEB: www.sunrise.com
SIC: 8051 8361 Skilled nursing care facilities; residential care
HQ: Sunrise Senior Living, Llc
7902 Westpark Dr
Mc Lean VA 22102

(P-20956)
SUNRISE SENIOR LIVING INC
31741 Rancho Viejo Rd, San Juan Capistrano (92675-6722)
PHONE..................................949 248-8855
Tiffany Calahan, *Manager*
EMP: 58
SALES (corp-wide): 3.8B **Publicly Held**
WEB: www.sunrise.com
SIC: 8051 8361 Skilled nursing care facilities; residential care
HQ: Sunrise Senior Living, Llc
7902 Westpark Dr
Mc Lean VA 22102

(P-20957)
SUNRISE SENIOR LIVING INC
Also Called: Sunrise of Palo Alto
201 N Crescent Dr Apt 503, Beverly Hills (90210-6184)
PHONE..................................650 326-1108
Fax: 650 326-1101
Ken Claire, *Branch Mgr*
Robert Faris, *Manager*
Brandy Velencia, *Manager*
EMP: 65
SALES (corp-wide): 3.8B **Publicly Held**
WEB: www.sunrise.com
SIC: 8051 8361 Skilled nursing care facilities; residential care
HQ: Sunrise Senior Living, Llc
7902 Westpark Dr
Mc Lean VA 22102

(P-20958)
SUNRISE SENIOR LIVING INC
Also Called: Fountains At Sea Bluffs
25421 Sea Bluffs Dr, Dana Point (92629-2196)
PHONE..................................949 234-3000
David Omalley, *Branch Mgr*
EMP: 58
SALES (corp-wide): 3.8B **Publicly Held**
WEB: www.sunrise.com
SIC: 8051 8361 Skilled nursing care facilities; home for the aged
HQ: Sunrise Senior Living, Llc
7902 Westpark Dr
Mc Lean VA 22102

(P-20959)
SUNRISE SENIOR LIVING INC
Also Called: Sunrise of Playa Vista
5555 Playa Vista Dr, Los Angeles (90094-2234)
PHONE..................................310 437-7178
Fax: 310 437-7179
Wendy McIlnay, *Manager*
EMP: 59
SALES (corp-wide): 3.8B **Publicly Held**
WEB: www.sunrise.com
SIC: 8051 8361 Skilled nursing care facilities; home for the aged
HQ: Sunrise Senior Living, Llc
7902 Westpark Dr
Mc Lean VA 22102

(P-20960)
SUNRISE SENIOR LIVING INC
Also Called: Sunrise of Beverly Hills
201 N Crescent Dr, Beverly Hills (90210-4898)
PHONE..................................310 274-4479
Fax: 310 274-4582
Brandy Velencia, *Manager*
EMP: 58
SALES (corp-wide): 3.8B **Publicly Held**
WEB: www.sunrise.com
SIC: 8051 Skilled nursing care facilities
HQ: Sunrise Senior Living, Llc
7902 Westpark Dr
Mc Lean VA 22102

(P-20961)
SUNRISE SENIOR LIVING INC
Also Called: Sunrise At Sterling Canyon
25815 Mcbean Pkwy Ofc, Valencia (91355-2071)
PHONE..................................661 253-3551
Fax: 661 254-1294
Pamela Sellers, *Director*
Dan Cooper, *Exec Dir*
Patrick Delbar, *Office Mgr*
EMP: 65
SALES (corp-wide): 3.8B **Publicly Held**
WEB: www.sunrise.com
SIC: 8051 8361 Skilled nursing care facilities; home for the aged
HQ: Sunrise Senior Living, Llc
7902 Westpark Dr
Mc Lean VA 22102

(P-20962)
SUNRISE SENIOR LIVING INC
1601 19th Ave, San Francisco (94122-3468)
PHONE..................................415 664-6264
Jeannie Hung, *Branch Mgr*
Edie Dascole, *Office Mgr*
Adrienne Fair, *Nursing Dir*
Saima Arnautovic, *Director*
EMP: 58
SALES (corp-wide): 3.8B **Publicly Held**
WEB: www.sunrise.com
SIC: 8051 8361 Skilled nursing care facilities; home for the aged
HQ: Sunrise Senior Living, Llc
7902 Westpark Dr
Mc Lean VA 22102

8051 - Skilled Nursing Facilities County (P-20963)

(P-20963)
SUNRISE SENIOR LIVING INC
Also Called: Vintage Silver Creek
4855 San Felipe Rd, San Jose (95135-1287)
PHONE..................408 223-1312
Fax: 408 223-6581
Rick Qwaza, *Branch Mgr*
EMP: 58
SALES (corp-wide): 3.8B **Publicly Held**
WEB: www.sunrise.com
SIC: 8051 8361 Skilled nursing care facilities; home for the aged
HQ: Sunrise Senior Living, Llc
7902 Westpark Dr
Mc Lean VA 22102

(P-20964)
SUNRISE SENIOR LIVING INC
Also Called: Villa Valencia Health Care Ctr
24552 Paseo De Valencia, Laguna Hills (92653-4236)
PHONE..................949 581-6111
Fax: 949 458-7792
Terry Records, *Chief*
Yanet Vega, *Records Dir*
Jennifer Hall, *Social Dir*
Jennifer Hatch, *Social Dir*
Robin Padilla, *Office Mgr*
EMP: 58
SALES (corp-wide): 3.8B **Publicly Held**
WEB: www.sunrise.com
SIC: 8051 8361 Skilled nursing care facilities; home for the aged
HQ: Sunrise Senior Living, Llc
7902 Westpark Dr
Mc Lean VA 22102

(P-20965)
SUNRISE SENIOR LIVING INC
Also Called: Sunrise of Carmichael
5451 Fair Oaks Blvd, Carmichael (95608-5748)
PHONE..................916 485-4500
Fax: 916 485-4544
EMP: 58
SALES (corp-wide): 3.8B **Publicly Held**
WEB: www.sunrise.com
SIC: 8051 8361 Skilled nursing care facilities; home for the aged
HQ: Sunrise Senior Living, Llc
7902 Westpark Dr
Mc Lean VA 22102

(P-20966)
SUNRISE SENIOR LIVING INC
Also Called: Sunrise of Monterey
1110 Carmelo St, Monterey (93940-4508)
PHONE..................831 643-2400
Fax: 831 643-2401
Susan Sundell, *Branch Mgr*
EMP: 58
SALES (corp-wide): 3.8B **Publicly Held**
WEB: www.sunrise.com
SIC: 8051 8361 Skilled nursing care facilities; home for the aged
HQ: Sunrise Senior Living, Llc
7902 Westpark Dr
Mc Lean VA 22102

(P-20967)
SUNRISE SENIOR LIVING INC
Also Called: Sunrise of Santa Rosa
3250 Chanate Rd Ofc, Santa Rosa (95404-1771)
PHONE..................707 575-7503
Fax: 707 575-5653
Rob Komorowski, *Manager*
Dan Dobar, *Director*
EMP: 50
SALES (corp-wide): 3.8B **Publicly Held**
WEB: www.sunrise.com
SIC: 8051 8361 Skilled nursing care facilities; home for the aged
HQ: Sunrise Senior Living, Llc
7902 Westpark Dr
Mc Lean VA 22102

(P-20968)
SUNRISE SENIOR LIVING LLC
Also Called: Sunrise Assistd Lving of Wlnt
2175 Ygnacio Valley Rd, Walnut Creek (94598-3385)
PHONE..................925 932-3500
Kathlyn McParron, *Manager*
Mallory Broom, *Marketing Staff*
Stephin Jenkins, *Food Svc Dir*
Suzi Giles, *Director*
EMP: 50
SALES (corp-wide): 3.8B **Publicly Held**
WEB: www.sunrise.com
SIC: 8051 Skilled nursing care facilities
HQ: Sunrise Senior Living, Llc
7902 Westpark Dr
Mc Lean VA 22102

(P-20969)
SUNRISE SENIOR LIVING LLC
17650 Devonshire St, Northridge (91325-1445)
PHONE..................818 886-1616
Susan Nasraty, *General Mgr*
Betty Brown, *Food Svc Dir*
EMP: 58
SALES (corp-wide): 3.8B **Publicly Held**
WEB: www.sunrise.com
SIC: 8051 8361 Skilled nursing care facilities; residential care
HQ: Sunrise Senior Living, Llc
7902 Westpark Dr
Mc Lean VA 22102

(P-20970)
SUNRISE SENIOR LIVING LLC
Also Called: Sunrise of Mission Viejo
26151 Country Club Dr, Mission Viejo (92691-5907)
PHONE..................949 582-2010
Fax: 949 582-8146
Lynn Piglao, *Director*
EMP: 60
SALES (corp-wide): 3.8B **Publicly Held**
WEB: www.sunrise.com
SIC: 8051 Skilled nursing care facilities
HQ: Sunrise Senior Living, Llc
7902 Westpark Dr
Mc Lean VA 22102

(P-20971)
SUNRISE SENIOR LIVING LLC
Also Called: Sunrise of Hermosa Beach
1837 Pacific Coast Hwy, Hermosa Beach (90254-3160)
PHONE..................310 937-0959
Fax: 310 937-3989
Josie Hecht, *Manager*
Stephanie Flax, *Director*
EMP: 50
SALES (corp-wide): 3.8B **Publicly Held**
WEB: www.sunrise.com
SIC: 8051 8361 Skilled nursing care facilities; home for the aged
HQ: Sunrise Senior Living, Llc
7902 Westpark Dr
Mc Lean VA 22102

(P-20972)
SUNRISE SENIOR LIVING LLC
Also Called: Sunrise At La Costa
7020 Manzanita St, Carlsbad (92011-5123)
PHONE..................760 930-0060
Fax: 760 930-0072
Euginia Whelch, *Director*
Catherine Carey, *Nursing Dir*
EMP: 100
SALES (corp-wide): 3.8B **Publicly Held**
WEB: www.sunrise.com
SIC: 8051 8361 Skilled nursing care facilities; home for the aged
HQ: Sunrise Senior Living, Llc
7902 Westpark Dr
Mc Lean VA 22102

(P-20973)
SUNRISE SENIOR LIVING LLC
Also Called: Sunrise At Bonita
3302 Bonita Rd, Chula Vista (91910-3207)
PHONE..................619 470-2220
Gwen Krushensky, *Manager*
EMP: 55
SALES (corp-wide): 3.8B **Publicly Held**
WEB: www.sunrise.com
SIC: 8051 8361 Skilled nursing care facilities; residential care
HQ: Sunrise Senior Living, Llc
7902 Westpark Dr
Mc Lean VA 22102

(P-20974)
SUNRISE SENIOR LIVING LLC
Also Called: Sunrise of Sacramento
345 Munroe St, Sacramento (95825-6459)
PHONE..................916 486-0200
Fax: 916 486-0214
Lyndee Whaley, *Manager*
EMP: 50
SALES (corp-wide): 3.8B **Publicly Held**
WEB: www.sunrise.com
SIC: 8051 8361 Skilled nursing care facilities; residential care
HQ: Sunrise Senior Living, Llc
7902 Westpark Dr
Mc Lean VA 22102

(P-20975)
SUNRISE SENIOR LIVING LLC
Also Called: Sunrise of Sunnyvale
633 S Knickerbocker Dr # 263, Sunnyvale (94087-1034)
PHONE..................408 749-8600
Fax: 408 749-8633
Tina Bagheri, *Manager*
Leigh Noniega, *Vice Pres*
J Underwood, *Exec Dir*
Britten Palmer, *Sales Executive*
Ke Lam, *Food Svc Dir*
EMP: 65
SALES (corp-wide): 3.8B **Publicly Held**
WEB: www.sunrise.com
SIC: 8051 8361 Skilled nursing care facilities; home for the aged
HQ: Sunrise Senior Living, Llc
7902 Westpark Dr
Mc Lean VA 22102

(P-20976)
SUNRISE SENIOR LIVING LLC
530 Water St Fl 5, Oakland (94607-3532)
PHONE..................303 410-0500
Shanelle Armas, *Manager*
EMP: 58
SALES (corp-wide): 3.8B **Publicly Held**
WEB: www.sunrise.com
SIC: 8051 Skilled nursing care facilities
HQ: Sunrise Senior Living, Llc
7902 Westpark Dr
Mc Lean VA 22102

(P-20977)
SUNRISE SENIOR LIVING LLC
Also Called: Sunrise of Westlake Village
3101 Townsgate Rd, Westlake Village (91361-5835)
PHONE..................805 557-1100
Fax: 805 557-1599
Angela Ling, *Branch Mgr*
EMP: 58
SALES (corp-wide): 3.8B **Publicly Held**
WEB: www.sunrise.com
SIC: 8051 8361 Skilled nursing care facilities; residential care
HQ: Sunrise Senior Living, Llc
7902 Westpark Dr
Mc Lean VA 22102

(P-20978)
SUNRISE SENIOR LIVING LLC
Also Called: Sunrise of Studio City
4610 Coldwater Canyon Ave, Studio City (91604-1031)
PHONE..................818 505-8484
Fax: 818 505-8884
Jason Malone, *Manager*
Mike Zueg, *Exec Dir*
EMP: 58
SALES (corp-wide): 3.8B **Publicly Held**
WEB: www.sunrise.com
SIC: 8051 8361 Skilled nursing care facilities; residential care
HQ: Sunrise Senior Living, Llc
7902 Westpark Dr
Mc Lean VA 22102

(P-20979)
SUNRISE SENIOR LIVING LLC
Also Called: Sunrise of Fresno
7444 N Cedar Ave, Fresno (93720-3636)
PHONE..................559 325-8170
Fax: 559 325-8430
Jessica Lopez, *Director*
Nancy Cartier, *Office Mgr*
Elaine Ghidelli, *Pub Rel Dir*
Margaret Geir, *Director*
Laurie Johnson, *Director*
EMP: 70
SALES (corp-wide): 3.8B **Publicly Held**
WEB: www.sunrise.com
SIC: 8051 8361 Skilled nursing care facilities; residential care
HQ: Sunrise Senior Living, Llc
7902 Westpark Dr
Mc Lean VA 22102

(P-20980)
SUNRISE SENIOR LIVING LLC
Also Called: Sunrise of Palm Springs
1780 E Baristo Rd, Palm Springs (92262-7114)
PHONE..................760 322-3444
Lisa Kennedy, *Exec Dir*
Hanny Jauwena, *Facilities Dir*
EMP: 80
SALES (corp-wide): 3.8B **Publicly Held**
WEB: www.sunrise.com
SIC: 8051 8361 Skilled nursing care facilities; residential care
HQ: Sunrise Senior Living, Llc
7902 Westpark Dr
Mc Lean VA 22102

(P-20981)
SUNRISE SENIOR LIVING LLC
1301 Ralston Ave Ste A, Belmont (94002-1961)
PHONE..................650 654-9700
Bradford Liebman, *Branch Mgr*
EMP: 58
SALES (corp-wide): 3.8B **Publicly Held**
WEB: www.sunrise.com
SIC: 8051 8361 Skilled nursing care facilities; home for the aged
HQ: Sunrise Senior Living, Llc
7902 Westpark Dr
Mc Lean VA 22102

(P-20982)
SUNRISE SENIOR LIVING LLC
Also Called: Brighton Gardens of Camarillo
6000 Santa Rosa Rd Ofc, Camarillo (93012-7121)
PHONE..................805 388-8086
Fax: 805 388-8450
Stan Main, *Branch Mgr*
EMP: 58
SALES (corp-wide): 3.8B **Publicly Held**
WEB: www.sunrise.com
SIC: 8051 8361 Skilled nursing care facilities; home for the aged
HQ: Sunrise Senior Living, Llc
7902 Westpark Dr
Mc Lean VA 22102

(P-20983)
SUNRISE SENIOR LIVING LLC
Also Called: Sunrise of Hemet
1177 S Palm Ave, Hemet (92543-7817)
PHONE..................951 929-5988
Kent K Goforth, *Branch Mgr*
EMP: 58
SALES (corp-wide): 3.8B **Publicly Held**
WEB: www.sunrise.com
SIC: 8051 Skilled nursing care facilities
HQ: Sunrise Senior Living, Llc
7902 Westpark Dr
Mc Lean VA 22102

PRODUCTS & SERVICES SECTION
8051 - Skilled Nursing Facilities County (P-21005)

(P-20984)
SUNRISE SENIOR LIVING LLC
Also Called: Sunrise of Rocklin
6100 Sierra College Blvd, Rocklin (95677-3505)
PHONE..................916 632-3003
Fax: 916 632-3005
Josh Lancaster, *Branch Mgr*
Angelia Birgance, *Exec Dir*
EMP: 59
SALES (corp-wide): 3.8B **Publicly Held**
WEB: www.sunrise.com
SIC: 8051 Skilled nursing care facilities
HQ: Sunrise Senior Living, Llc
7902 Westpark Dr
Mc Lean VA 22102

(P-20985)
SUNRISE SENIOR LIVING LLC
Also Called: Fountains At The Carlotta
41505 Carlotta Dr, Palm Desert (92211-3279)
PHONE..................760 346-5420
EMP: 58
SALES (corp-wide): 3.8B **Publicly Held**
WEB: www.sunrise.com
SIC: 8051 8361 Skilled nursing care facilities; home for the aged
HQ: Sunrise Senior Living, Llc
7902 Westpark Dr
Mc Lean VA 22102

(P-20986)
SUNRISE SENIOR LIVING LLC
Also Called: Sunrise At Raincross Village
5232 Central Ave, Riverside (92504-1825)
PHONE..................951 785-1200
Christi Steichen, *Branch Mgr*
EMP: 58
SALES (corp-wide): 3.8B **Publicly Held**
WEB: www.sunrise.com
SIC: 8051 8361 Skilled nursing care facilities; home for the aged
HQ: Sunrise Senior Living, Llc
7902 Westpark Dr
Mc Lean VA 22102

(P-20987)
SUTTER HEALTH
3707 Schriever Ave, Mather (95655-4202)
PHONE..................916 454-8200
Sheila Black, *Branch Mgr*
Robert Reed, *CFO*
Chris Jaeger, *Vice Pres*
Rayne McKenzie, *Admin Asst*
Samuel Warnke, *Sr Ntwrk Engine*
EMP: 60
SALES (corp-wide): 11B **Privately Held**
WEB: www.sutterhealth.org
SIC: 8051 8062 Skilled nursing care facilities; general medical & surgical hospitals
PA: Sutter Health
2200 River Plaza Dr
Sacramento CA 95833
916 733-8800

(P-20988)
SUTTER HEALTH
Also Called: Sutter Occupational Hlth Svcs
3 Medical Plaza Dr # 100, Roseville (95661-3087)
PHONE..................916 797-4700
Dave Gladden, *Branch Mgr*
EMP: 60
SALES (corp-wide): 11B **Privately Held**
SIC: 8051 Skilled nursing care facilities
PA: Sutter Health
2200 River Plaza Dr
Sacramento CA 95833
916 733-8800

(P-20989)
SUTTER VSTING NRSE ASSN HSPICE
1651 Alvarado St, San Leandro (94577-2636)
PHONE..................510 618-5277
Fax: 510 347-6866
Rosemarie Avery, *Manager*
EMP: 100

SALES (corp-wide): 11B **Privately Held**
WEB: www.suttervnaandhospice.com
SIC: 8051 8082 Skilled nursing care facilities; home health care services
HQ: Sutter Visiting Nurse Association & Hospice
1900 Powell St Ste 300
Emeryville CA 94608
866 652-9178

(P-20990)
TLC OF BAY AREA INC
Also Called: Valley House Care Center
991 Clyde Ave, Santa Clara (95054-1905)
P.O. Box 607, Indiana PA (15701-0607)
PHONE..................408 988-7667
Marcy Colkitt, *President*
Merlin Davey, *Exec Dir*
Lorna Santillan, *Pub Rel Dir*
EMP: 57
SALES (est): 6.3MM **Privately Held**
SIC: 8051 Skilled nursing care facilities

(P-20991)
TORRANCE CARE CENTER WEST INC
4333 Torrance Blvd, Torrance (90503-4401)
PHONE..................310 370-4561
Fax: 310 371-2365
Vicki P Rollins, *President*
EMP: 180
SALES: 18MM **Privately Held**
SIC: 8051 Skilled nursing care facilities

(P-20992)
TOWN & COUNTRY MANOR OF THE CH
555 E Memory Ln Ofc Ofc, Santa Ana (92706-1708)
PHONE..................714 547-7581
Fax: 714 547-0435
Dirk De Wolfe, *Administration*
Rachel Carramanzana, *Records Dir*
Shauna Stratton, *Chf Purch Ofc*
Marianne Daniels, *Marketing Staff*
Christine Ngyuen, *Education*
EMP: 210 **EST:** 1975
SQ FT: 208,000
SALES: 17.5MM **Privately Held**
SIC: 8051 8059 8052 Skilled nursing care facilities; nursing home, except skilled & intermediate care facility; intermediate care facilities

(P-20993)
TRINITY HEALTH SYSTEMS
Also Called: Villa Maria Care Center
723 E 9th St, Long Beach (90813-4611)
PHONE..................562 437-2797
Fax: 562 437-8688
Jordan Fishman, *Administration*
Edgar Paiz, *Envir Svcs Dir*
Rosemary Griego, *Office Mgr*
Omega Mitchell, *Administration*
Franciosa Concepcion, *Nursing Dir*
EMP: 57
SALES (corp-wide): 10.1MM **Privately Held**
SIC: 8051 8059 Skilled nursing care facilities; nursing home, except skilled & intermediate care facility
PA: Trinity Health Systems
14318 Ohio St
Baldwin Park CA 91706
626 960-1971

(P-20994)
TRINITY HEALTH SYSTEMS (PA)
Also Called: Villa Maria Care Center
14318 Ohio St, Baldwin Park (91706-2553)
PHONE..................626 960-1971
Fax: 626 856-0437
Randal Kleis, *President*
Carol Becerra, *Social Dir*
Gerda Rorong, *Business Mgr*
Aida Hongpuckdee, *Nursing Dir*
Chuck Williams, *Manager*
EMP: 80
SQ FT: 35,000
SALES (est): 10.1MM **Privately Held**
SIC: 8051 Skilled nursing care facilities

(P-20995)
TRINITY HEALTH SYSTEMS
Also Called: Pomona Vista Alzheimers Center
651 N Main St, Pomona (91768-3110)
PHONE..................949 623-2481
Fax: 909 865-0060
Pat Thompson, *Administration*
EMP: 50
SQ FT: 12,834
SALES (corp-wide): 10.1MM **Privately Held**
SIC: 8051 Skilled nursing care facilities
PA: Trinity Health Systems
14318 Ohio St
Baldwin Park CA 91706
626 960-1971

(P-20996)
TULARE NRSING RHBLITATION HOSP
Also Called: Tulare Nrsing Rhbilitation Ctr
680 E Merritt Ave, Tulare (93274-2135)
PHONE..................559 686-8581
Fax: 559 686-5393
Mark Fisher, *President*
Norm Christianson, *CFO*
Sharon A Fisher, *Admin Sec*
EMP: 125
SALES (est): 4.2MM **Privately Held**
WEB: www.missioncaregroup.com
SIC: 8051 Skilled nursing care facilities

(P-20997)
TWILIGHT HAVEN
1717 S Winery Ave, Fresno (93727-5011)
PHONE..................559 251-8417
Fax: 559 251-1103
David Viancourt, *Administration*
Kenneth Karle, *President*
Robert Herman, *Vice Pres*
Sharon Bailey, *Administration*
Patricia A Hickman, *Administration*
EMP: 95
SQ FT: 70,000
SALES: 5.6MM **Privately Held**
WEB: www.twilighthaven.com
SIC: 8051 8052 8361 Convalescent home with continuous nursing care; personal care facility; rest home, with health care incidental

(P-20998)
UNITED COM SERVE
Also Called: FOUNTAINS, THE
1260 Williams Way, Yuba City (95991-2400)
PHONE..................530 790-3000
Fax: 530 751-4894
Tom Hayes, *President*
Chris Parker, *Administration*
EMP: 100
SQ FT: 40,000
SALES: 22.4MM
SALES (corp-wide): 28.9MM **Privately Held**
SIC: 8051 Skilled nursing care facilities
PA: Freemont Rideout Health Group
989 Plumas St
Yuba City CA 95991
530 751-4010

(P-20999)
UNITED HEALTH SYSTEMS INC
Also Called: ALDERSON CONVALESCENT HOSPITAL
124 Walnut St, Woodland (95695-3137)
PHONE..................530 662-9161
Fax: 530 662-8520
Santiago M S Miguel, *CEO*
Thomas E Mullen, *President*
Patrick Forlit, *Executive*
Vince Olvera, *Executive*
Lynn Mullen, *Admin Sec*
EMP: 154
SQ FT: 40,000
SALES: 11.3MM **Privately Held**
WEB: www.unitedhealthsystems.com
SIC: 8051 Skilled nursing care facilities

(P-21000)
US SKILLSERVE INC
Also Called: Community Convlscnt Hosp Mnt-clr
9620 Fremont Ave, Montclair (91763-2320)
PHONE..................909 621-4751
Fax: 909 621-5410

Johannes Simanjuntak, *Manager*
Susan S Cheng, *Personnel*
Alex Castillo, *Marketing Staff*
EMP: 140
SALES (corp-wide): 44.6MM **Privately Held**
SIC: 8051 Convalescent home with continuous nursing care
PA: U.S. Skillserve Inc
4115 E Broadway Ste A
Long Beach CA 90803
562 930-0777

(P-21001)
V S N F INC
Also Called: Valley Skilled Nursing Care
2120 Stockton Blvd, Sacramento (95817-1337)
PHONE..................916 452-6631
Fax: 916 739-0961
John Sorensen, *President*
Ronda Rongo, *Nursing Dir*
Anant Lodhia, *Director*
EMP: 55
SALES (est): 2.2MM **Privately Held**
SIC: 8051 Skilled nursing care facilities

(P-21002)
VALLEY HEALTHCARE CENTER LLC
4840 E Tulare Ave, Fresno (93727-3062)
PHONE..................559 251-7161
George V Hagaer Jr, *CEO*
EMP: 3598 **EST:** 2003
SALES (est): 356.7K
SALES (corp-wide): 9.6B **Publicly Held**
SIC: 8051 Skilled nursing care facilities
HQ: Genesis Healthcare Llc
101 E State St
Kennett Square PA 19348

(P-21003)
VALLEY HEALTHCARE CENTER LLC
4840 E Tulare Ave, Fresno (93727-3062)
P.O. Box 93727 (93727)
PHONE..................559 251-7161
Fax: 559 251-8993
Jiji Cruz, *Nursing Dir*
EMP: 105
SALES (est): 2MM
SALES (corp-wide): 9.6B **Publicly Held**
SIC: 8051 Skilled nursing care facilities
HQ: Skilled Healthcare, Llc
27442 Portola Pkwy # 200
Foothill Ranch CA 92610
949 282-5800

(P-21004)
VALLEY VIEW SKLLED NURSING CTR
1162 S Dora St, Ukiah (95482-6340)
PHONE..................707 462-1436
Rosemary Brown, *Administration*
EMP: 58
SALES (est): 1.2MM
SALES (corp-wide): 99MM **Privately Held**
WEB: www.villadelrey.com
SIC: 8051 Convalescent home with continuous nursing care
HQ: Horizon West Healthcare, Inc.
4020 Sierra College Blvd # 190
Rocklin CA 95677
916 624-6230

(P-21005)
VALLEY WEST HEALTH CARE INC
Also Called: Valley View Care Center
2649 Topeka St, Riverbank (95367-2248)
PHONE..................209 869-2569
Fax: 209 869-1762
Terry Bane, *Principal*
Becky Singleton, *Manager*
EMP: 80
SALES (corp-wide): 5.4MM **Privately Held**
SIC: 8051 8062 Convalescent home with continuous nursing care; general medical & surgical hospitals

8051 - Skilled Nursing Facilities County (P-21006)

PA: Valley West Health Care Inc
1224 E St
Williams CA 95987
530 473-5321

(P-21006)
VETERANS AFFAIRS CAL DEPT
Also Called: Redding Veterans Home, The
3400 Knighton Rd, Redding (96002-9657)
PHONE.................................530 224-3300
Tim Bouseman, *Administration*
EMP: 200 **Privately Held**
SIC: 8051 Skilled nursing care facilities
HQ: California Department Of Veterans Affairs
1227 O St Ste 105
Sacramento CA 95814
800 952-5626

(P-21007)
VETERANS HOME CAL - FRESNO
2811 W California Ave, Fresno (93706-2306)
PHONE.................................559 493-4400
Stanley Jones, *Director*
EMP: 99 **EST:** 2012
SALES (est): 3.8MM **Privately Held**
SIC: 8051 Skilled nursing care facilities

(P-21008)
VIBRA HEALTHCARE LLC
Also Called: Vibra Hospital Northern Cal
2801 Eureka Way, Redding (96001-0222)
PHONE.................................530 246-9000
Christine A Jones, *Administration*
Sharon Neilly, *Administration*
EMP: 84
SALES (corp-wide): 329.7MM **Privately Held**
SIC: 8051 Skilled nursing care facilities
PA: Vibra Healthcare, Llc
4550 Lena Dr
Mechanicsburg PA 17055
717 591-5700

(P-21009)
VICTORIA CARE CENTER
5445 Everglades St, Ventura (93003-6523)
PHONE.................................805 642-1736
Fax: 805 639-3198
Scott Porter, *Exec Dir*
Jay Brady, *President*
Scott Anderson, *Facilities Mgr*
Vinov Valivetti, *Director*
EMP: 100
SQ FT: 85,000
SALES: 16.9MM **Privately Held**
WEB: www.victoriacarecenter.com
SIC: 8051 Skilled nursing care facilities
PA: Beverly Health Care Corporation
5445 Everglades St
Ventura CA 93003
-

(P-21010)
VILLA HEALTH CARE CENTER INC
Also Called: Villa Convalescent Hospital
8965 Magnolia Ave, Riverside (92503-4432)
PHONE.................................951 689-5788
Fax: 951 689-1732
John L Sorensen, *President*
Donald Laws, *Ch of Bd*
David Sorensen, *Treasurer*
Andro Sharobiam, *Director*
EMP: 90 **EST:** 1971
SQ FT: 25,000
SALES: 9.6MM **Privately Held**
WEB: www.villahealthcare.com
SIC: 8051 Skilled nursing care facilities

(P-21011)
VILLA RANCHO BRNO HLTH CR LLC
Also Called: Villa Rancho Bernardo Care Ctr
15720 Bernardo Center Dr, San Diego (92127-5861)
PHONE.................................858 672-3900
Irving Bauman,
Kelly Iastarro, *VP Sales*
Brank Johnson,
EMP: 200

SALES: 22.8MM **Privately Held**
SIC: 8051 Skilled nursing care facilities

(P-21012)
VILLAGE PACIFIC MGT GROUP
Also Called: Village At Sydney Creek
1234 Laurel Ln, San Luis Obispo (93401-5860)
PHONE.................................805 543-2350
Fax: 805 543-1948
Leona Baker, *Manager*
EMP: 55
SALES (corp-wide): 3.4MM **Privately Held**
SIC: 8051 Skilled nursing care facilities
PA: Village Pacific Management Group Inc
55 Broad St
San Luis Obispo CA 93405
805 543-2300

(P-21013)
VILLAGE PACIFIC MGT GROUP (PA)
Also Called: Village At Sydney Creek
55 Broad St, San Luis Obispo (93405-1745)
PHONE.................................805 543-2300
Patrick Smith, *Principal*
EMP: 55
SALES (est): 3.4MM **Privately Held**
SIC: 8051 Skilled nursing care facilities

(P-21014)
VILLAGE SQUARE NURSING CENTER
1586 W San Marcos Blvd, San Marcos (92078-4019)
PHONE.................................760 471-2986
Fax: 760 471-5038
Ron Cadwell, *Manager*
Pam Turner, *Administration*
Sandra Eisenman, *Info Tech Mgr*
Rich Mentze, *Director*
EMP: 140
SALES: 10MM **Privately Held**
SIC: 8051 8093 Skilled nursing care facilities; rehabilitation center, outpatient treatment

(P-21015)
VINDRA INC
Also Called: Meadowood Nursing Center
3805 Dexter Ln, Clearlake (95422-8850)
PHONE.................................707 994-7738
Fax: 707 994-7769
Calvin Baker Jr, *President*
Gloria Ghiringhelli, *Office Mgr*
EMP: 100
SQ FT: 30,250
SALES (est): 7.2MM **Privately Held**
SIC: 8051 8069 Skilled nursing care facilities; specialty hospitals, except psychiatric

(P-21016)
VIRGIL SNTRIUM CNVLESCENT HOSP
Also Called: Virgil Convalescent Hospital
975 N Virgil Ave, Los Angeles (90029-2944)
PHONE.................................323 665-5793
Fax: 323 665-2683
Miriam Weiss, *President*
Lucy Santos, *Records Dir*
Stuart Greenberg, *Administration*
Susan Lopez, *Food Svc Dir*
Adriana Quintero, *Director*
EMP: 150
SALES (est): 7MM
SALES (corp-wide): 62.1MM **Privately Held**
WEB: www.goldenstatehealth.com
SIC: 8051 Skilled nursing care facilities
PA: Golden State Health Centers, Inc.
13347 Ventura Blvd
Sherman Oaks CA 91423
818 385-3200

(P-21017)
VISTA COVE CARE CENTER AT LONG
3401 Cedar Ave, Long Beach (90807-4422)
PHONE.................................562 426-4461
Bonaparte Liu, *Principal*

Sean Brophy, *Principal*
Floyd Rhoades, *Principal*
Marcela Rodriguez, *Principal*
EMP: 99
SALES (est): 5.7MM **Privately Held**
SIC: 8051 Mental retardation hospital

(P-21018)
VISTA COVE CARE CTR - RIALTO
1471 S Riverside Ave, Rialto (92376-7703)
PHONE.................................909 877-1361
Sean William Brophy, *Admin Sec*
EMP: 99
SALES: 10.3MM **Privately Held**
SIC: 8051 Skilled nursing care facilities

(P-21019)
VISTA KNOLL INC
2000 Westwood Rd, Vista (92083-5123)
PHONE.................................760 630-2273
Fax: 760 630-0913
Gary R Byrnes, *President*
Gary Byrnes, *President*
Carol Byrnes, *Officer*
Leo Halpins, *Vice Pres*
EMP: 70
SQ FT: 45,000
SALES (est): 2.3MM **Privately Held**
WEB: www.vistaknoll.com
SIC: 8051 Skilled nursing care facilities

(P-21020)
VISTA PACIFICA ENTERPRISES INC (PA)
Also Called: Vista Pcifica Convalescent Ctr
3674 Pacific Ave, Riverside (92509-1948)
PHONE.................................951 682-4833
Fax: 951 682-1503
Cheryl Jumonville, *CEO*
James Braswell, *Shareholder*
Ruth Braswell, *Shareholder*
A L Braswell Jr, *President*
Adelai Alba-Ortega, *CFO*
EMP: 180
SALES (est): 13.3MM **Privately Held**
SIC: 8051 8059 Skilled nursing care facilities; domiciliary care

(P-21021)
VISTA WOODS HEALTH ASSOC LLC
Also Called: Vista Knoll Spclzed Care Fclty
2000 Westwood Rd, Vista (92083-5123)
PHONE.................................760 630-2273
Ron Cook, *Mng Member*
Clay Gardner, *Exec VP*
Corinne Myer, *VP Finance*
EMP: 130
SALES: 13.9MM
SALES (corp-wide): 1.3B **Publicly Held**
WEB: www.theensigngroup.com
SIC: 8051 Convalescent home with continuous nursing care
PA: The Ensign Group Inc
27101 Puerta Real Ste 450
Mission Viejo CA 92691
949 487-9500

(P-21022)
W H C INC
Also Called: Woodside Healthcare Center
2240 Northrop Ave, Sacramento (95825-7408)
PHONE.................................916 927-9300
Fax: 916 927-3630
John Lund, *CEO*
Jared Leavitt, *Executive*
Judy Cantrell, *Principal*
Jay Anderson, *Administration*
EMP: 75
SALES (est): 4.3MM **Privately Held**
SIC: 8051 Skilled nursing care facilities

(P-21023)
WALNUT WHTNEY CNVALESCENT HOSP
3529 Walnut Ave, Carmichael (95608-3049)
PHONE.................................916 488-8601
Fax: 916 488-3053
Jesse Barrios, *Administration*
Sharon Laidley, *Administration*
EMP: 110

SALES (est): 2.4MM
SALES (corp-wide): 99MM **Privately Held**
WEB: www.villadelrey.com
SIC: 8051 Convalescent home with continuous nursing care
HQ: Horizon West Healthcare, Inc.
4020 Sierra College Blvd # 190
Rocklin CA 95677
916 624-6230

(P-21024)
WASHINGTON ENTERPRISES 3 LLC
Also Called: St Andrews Health Care
2300 W Washington Blvd, Los Angeles (90018-1445)
PHONE.................................323 731-0861
EMP: 68
SQ FT: 5,000
SALES (est): 2MM **Privately Held**
SIC: 8051 Skilled nursing care facilities

(P-21025)
WATERMAN CONVALESCENT HOSPITAL (PA)
Also Called: Mt Rubidoux Convalescent Hosp
1850 N Waterman Ave, San Bernardino (92404-4895)
PHONE.................................909 882-1215
Fax: 909 881-2071
Thomas Plott, *President*
Elizabeth Plott, *Corp Secy*
Thomas Hellwig, *Director*
Angle Borunta, *Manager*
Mr Terry Steege, *Account Dir*
EMP: 109
SQ FT: 13,000
SALES (est): 12.5MM **Privately Held**
SIC: 8051 Convalescent home with continuous nursing care

(P-21026)
WATERMARK RTRMENT CMMNTIES INC
Also Called: Fountains At The Carlotta, The
41505 Carlotta Dr, Palm Desert (92211-3279)
PHONE.................................760 346-5420
Fax: 760 341-7768
EMP: 70
SALES (corp-wide): 127.2MM **Privately Held**
SIC: 8051 8052 Skilled nursing care facilities; intermediate care facilities
HQ: Watermark Retirement Communities, Inc.
2020 W Rudasill Rd
Tucson AZ 85704
520 797-4000

(P-21027)
WELLS HSE HSPICE FUNDATION INC
245 Cherry Ave, Long Beach (90802-3901)
PHONE.................................714 952-3795
Fax: 562 435-9365
Ronald Morgan, *President*
Lorenza Apodaca, *Director*
Ken Lawrence, *Director*
Barbara Woodruff, *Director*
EMP: 60 **EST:** 1997
SALES (est): 1.8MM **Privately Held**
WEB: www.wellshousehospice.com
SIC: 8051 Skilled nursing care facilities

(P-21028)
WESCORDON INCORPORATED (PA)
Also Called: VALLEY CARE CENTER
661 W Poplar Ave, Porterville (93257-5926)
P.O. Box 3566 (93258-3566)
PHONE.................................559 784-8371
Fax: 559 784-8098
Donald C Smith, *President*
EMP: 70 **EST:** 1948
SQ FT: 14,000
SALES (est): 5.9MM **Privately Held**
SIC: 8051 Skilled nursing care facilities

(P-21029) WEST ANAHEIM EXTENDED CARE
Also Called: West Anaheim Care Center
645 S Beach Blvd, Anaheim (92804-3102)
PHONE.................................714 821-1993
Fax: 714 821-0130
Mark Landry, *Managing Prtnr*
Connie Black, *Partner*
George Rodes, *CFO*
Franklin Hanauer, *Director*
EMP: 125
SQ FT: 39,000
SALES (est): 9.7MM Privately Held
SIC: 8051 Skilled nursing care facilities

(P-21030) WEST CNTINELA VLY CARE CTR INC
Also Called: Centinela Skld Nrng Wlns Cntr
950 S Flower St, Inglewood (90301-4186)
PHONE.................................310 674-3216
Koom S Son, *CEO*
EMP: 99
SALES (est): 5.7MM Privately Held
SIC: 8051 Skilled nursing care facilities

(P-21031) WEST ESCONDIDO HEALTHCARE LLC
Also Called: PALOMAR VISTA HEALTHCARE CENTE
201 N Fig St, Escondido (92025-3416)
PHONE.................................760 746-0303
Mike Conrad,
Susan Graaff, *Admin Asst*
Bobbi J Portillo, *Financial Exec*
Soon Burnam,
David Mayo,
EMP: 95
SALES: 6MM Privately Held
SIC: 8051 Skilled nursing care facilities

(P-21032) WESTERN HEALTHCARE MANAGEMENT
Also Called: Western Healthcare Center
1700 E Washington St, Colton (92324-4619)
PHONE.................................909 824-1530
Fax: 909 825-9013
Everett Goings, *Owner*
Tahseen Sharees, *Director*
EMP: 102
SALES (est): 3.9MM Privately Held
SIC: 8051 Skilled nursing care facilities

(P-21033) WESTERN SLOPE HEALTH CENTER
Also Called: WESTERN SLOPE HEALTH CARE
3280 Washington St, Placerville (95667-5838)
PHONE.................................530 622-6842
Fax: 530 622-2361
Jeff Maggard, *Exec Dir*
Laurie Batton, *Administration*
Doug Hawkings, *Administration*
Lorry Randell, *Marketing Staff*
Wagner Tuleu, *Nursing Dir*
EMP: 100
SALES: 12.8MM Privately Held
WEB: www.eldoradocounty.org
SIC: 8051 Convalescent home with continuous nursing care

(P-21034) WESTGATE GARDENS CARE CENTER
4525 W Tulare Ave, Visalia (93277-1560)
PHONE.................................559 733-0901
Eric Tolman, *Administration*
Nadar Peyghambary, *Social Dir*
Heather Marquez, *Office Mgr*
Ralph Agnello, *Administration*
Carmela Arellano, *Personnel*
EMP: 127
SALES (corp-wide): 99MM Privately Held
WEB: www.horizonwest.com
SIC: 8051 Skilled nursing care facilities
HQ: Westgate Gardens Care Center, Inc
4020 Sierra College Blvd # 190
Rocklin CA 95677
916 624-6230

(P-21035) WESTLAKE HEALTH CARE CENTER
1101 Crenshaw Blvd, Los Angeles (90019-3112)
PHONE.................................805 494-1233
Fax: 805 494-1411
Jeoung Lee, *President*
Jackie McMahon, *Executive*
EMP: 250
SALES (est): 9MM
SALES (corp-wide): 21.6MM Privately Held
SIC: 8051 Skilled nursing care facilities
PA: J P H Consulting, Inc.
1101 Crenshaw Blvd
Los Angeles CA 90019
323 934-5660

(P-21036) WESTVIEW HEALH CARE CENTER
Also Called: Kerria
12225 Shale Ridge Ln, Auburn (95602-8870)
PHONE.................................530 885-7511
Edmund Erapt, *Administration*
Todd Pratt, *Administration*
EMP: 222
SALES (est): 6.5MM
SALES (corp-wide): 40.6MM Privately Held
SIC: 8051 Skilled nursing care facilities
PA: Plum Healthcare Group, Llc
100 E San Marcos Blvd
San Marcos CA 92069
760 471-0388

(P-21037) WESTVIEW SERVICES INC
Also Called: Westview Cmnty Arts Program
1701 S Euclid St Ste E, Anaheim (92802-2408)
PHONE.................................714 956-4199
Britain Semain, *Manager*
EMP: 339
SALES (corp-wide): 18.2MM Privately Held
SIC: 8051 8322 Mental retardation hospital; adult day care center
PA: Westview Services, Inc
10522 Katella Ave
Anaheim CA 92804
714 517-6606

(P-21038) WESTWOOD HEALTHCARE CENTER LP
Also Called: Country Villa Westwood Nursing
12121 Santa Monica Blvd, Los Angeles (90025-2515)
PHONE.................................310 826-0821
Fax: 310 207-9311
Stephen Reissman, *General Ptnr*
Hillard Torgan, *Partner*
Althea D Pietro, *Administration*
Rashmi Brila, *Manager*
EMP: 75 EST: 1970
SQ FT: 18,000
SALES (est): 6.1MM Privately Held
SIC: 8051 Skilled nursing care facilities

(P-21039) WHISPERING HOPE CARE CENTER
5320 Carrington Cir, Stockton (95210-3515)
PHONE.................................209 473-3004
Vernon Garren, *Owner*
Keisha Bobo, *Social Dir*
Priscilla Harris, *Envir Svcs Dir*
Melanie Peters, *Office Mgr*
Anabelle Bird, *Food Svc Dir*
EMP: 115
SALES (est): 6.3MM Privately Held
SIC: 8051 Skilled nursing care facilities; convalescent home with continuous nursing care

(P-21040) WILD KARMA INC
Also Called: Divine Home Care
400 Estudillo Ave Ste 100, San Leandro (94577-4962)
PHONE.................................510 639-9088
Robbin R Beebe, *CEO*
EMP: 200 EST: 2007
SQ FT: 2,400
SALES (est): 7.7MM Privately Held
SIC: 8051 Convalescent home with continuous nursing care

(P-21041) WILLOW CREEK HALTHCARE CTR LLC
650 W Alluvial Ave, Clovis (93611-6716)
PHONE.................................559 323-6200
Vivian Toro, *Administration*
Trina Rivera, *Marketing Staff*
EMP: 2474
SALES (est): 7.3MM
SALES (corp-wide): 9.6B Publicly Held
SIC: 8051 Skilled nursing care facilities
HQ: Genesis Healthcare Llc
101 E State St
Kennett Square PA 19348

(P-21042) WILLOW CREEK HALTHCARE CTR LLC
Also Called: Willow Creek Care Center
650 W Alluvial Ave, Clovis (93611-6716)
PHONE.................................559 323-6200
Fax: 559 323-4665
EMP: 99
SALES (est): 1MM
SALES (corp-wide): 9.6B Publicly Held
WEB: www.parkviewnursing.net
SIC: 8051 Skilled nursing care facilities
HQ: Skilled Healthcare, Llc
27442 Portola Pkwy # 200
Foothill Ranch CA 92610
949 282-5800

(P-21043) WILMON CORPORATION
Also Called: Millers Progressive Care
8951 Granite Hill Dr, Riverside (92509-1104)
PHONE.................................951 685-7474
Fax: 951 685-3047
Wilmer W Miller, *President*
Mike Miller, *Marketing Staff*
Thomas Woodbury, *Director*
EMP: 65
SQ FT: 16,000
SALES (est): 4.2MM Privately Held
SIC: 8051 Skilled nursing care facilities

(P-21044) WINDFLOWER HOLDINGS LLC
Also Called: Rocky Point Care Center
625 16th St, Lakeport (95453-3501)
PHONE.................................707 263-6101
Fax: 707 263-6300
Mark Ballif, *Mng Member*
Paul Hubbard,
EMP: 80
SQ FT: 5,000
SALES (est): 4.7MM
SALES (corp-wide): 40.6MM Privately Held
WEB: www.villadelrey.com
SIC: 8051 Skilled nursing care facilities
PA: Plum Healthcare Group, Llc
100 E San Marcos Blvd
San Marcos CA 92069
760 471-0388

(P-21045) WINDSOR CONVALESCENT
Also Called: Windsor Mnor Rhabilitation Ctr
3806 Clayton Rd, Concord (94521-2516)
PHONE.................................925 689-2266
Lee Samson, *Mng Member*
Dee Weaver, *Executive*
Debra Brown, *Social Dir*
Yolanda Thomas, *Human Res Dir*
Melissa Lozano, *Hlthcr Dir*
EMP: 133

SALES: 21.8MM
SALES (corp-wide): 67MM Privately Held
SIC: 8051 Convalescent home with continuous nursing care
PA: Lexington Group International, Inc
9200 W Sunset Blvd # 700
West Hollywood CA 90069
310 385-1071

(P-21046) WINDSOR CONVALESCENT
Also Called: WINDSOR GARDENS REHABILITATION CENTER OF SALINAS
637 E Romie Ln, Salinas (93901-4205)
PHONE.................................831 424-0687
Lee Samson, *Mng Member*
Obila Razo, *Office Mgr*
Mary Robinson, *Administration*
Leslie Foot, *Director*
EMP: 133
SALES: 13.5MM
SALES (corp-wide): 67MM Privately Held
SIC: 8051 Convalescent home with continuous nursing care
PA: Lexington Group International, Inc
9200 W Sunset Blvd # 700
West Hollywood CA 90069
310 385-1071

(P-21047) WINDSOR GARDENS
Also Called: Windsor Gardens of Long Beach
4333 Torrance Blvd, Torrance (90503-4401)
PHONE.................................562 422-9219
Calcin Warren, *Administration*
John Minor, *Vice Pres*
Mike Calderon, *Social Dir*
Raul Renteria, *Purch Dir*
Christina Saril, *Nursing Dir*
EMP: 100
SALES (corp-wide): 13.3MM Privately Held
SIC: 8051 Skilled nursing care facilities
PA: Windsor Gardens
3415 W Ball Rd
Anaheim CA 92804
714 826-8950

(P-21048) WINDSOR GARDENS
Also Called: Southwest Convalesant
13922 Cerise Ave, Hawthorne (90250-8688)
PHONE.................................310 675-3304
Fax: 310 675-4389
Michael Gamet, *Administration*
Magda Villanueva, *Vice Pres*
EMP: 100
SALES (corp-wide): 13.3MM Privately Held
SIC: 8051 Skilled nursing care facilities
PA: Windsor Gardens
3415 W Ball Rd
Anaheim CA 92804
714 826-8950

(P-21049) WINDSOR GARDENS (PA)
Also Called: Windsor Grdns Cnvlescent Ctr A
3415 W Ball Rd, Anaheim (92804-3708)
PHONE.................................714 826-8950
Lee Samson, *President*
Clarita Palaayan, *Records Dir*
Lillian Rastgoo, *Administration*
Arlene Halili, *Education*
Jacinta Lagman, *Nursing Dir*
EMP: 164
SQ FT: 37,245
SALES (est): 13.3MM Privately Held
SIC: 8051 Skilled nursing care facilities

(P-21050) WINDSOR GARDNS HEALTHCARE CNTR
Also Called: WINDSOR GARDENS OF FULLERTON
245 E Wilshire Ave, Fullerton (92832-1935)
PHONE.................................714 871-6020
Lee Samson,
Jorge Garcia, *Envir Svcs Dir*
David Holmberg, *Administration*
Joanna Gomez, *Director*
Magda Villnauva, *Director*

8051 - Skilled Nursing Facilities County (P-21051)   PRODUDUCTS & SERVICES SECTION

EMP: 133
SALES: 10.7MM
SALES (corp-wide): 67MM **Privately Held**
SIC: **8051** Convalescent home with continuous nursing care
PA: Lexington Group International, Inc
9200 W Sunset Blvd # 700
West Hollywood CA 90069
310 385-1071

(P-21051)
WINDSOR GRDNS CNVALESCENT HOSP
915 Crenshaw Blvd, Los Angeles (90019-1938)
PHONE.................................323 937-5466
Fax: 323 936-4795
Nathan Alyeshmerni, *Administration*
Joanne Liwag, *Records Dir*
Lee Samson, *President*
Blaine Lyons, *Exec Dir*
Chris Cangl, *Office Mgr*
EMP: 99
SALES: 11.8MM **Privately Held**
SIC: **8051** 8742 Convalescent home with continuous nursing care; hospital & health services consultant

(P-21052)
WINDSOR HEALTHCARE MANAGEMENT
Also Called: Windsor Gardens Convalescnt
220 E 24th St, National City (91950-6705)
PHONE.................................619 474-6741
Lee Samson, *President*
Faye Baurboue, *Administration*
Faye Bourbeau, *Administration*
Gloria Lopez, *Director*
EMP: 115
SALES: 9.1MM **Privately Held**
SIC: **8051** Convalescent home with continuous nursing care

(P-21053)
WINDSOR REDDING CARE CTR LLC
2490 Court St, Redding (96001-2540)
PHONE.................................530 246-2586
Lawrence E Feigen,
Kandace Quigley, *Office Mgr*
Lee C Samson,
EMP: 99
SALES (est): 6MM **Privately Held**
SIC: **8051** Skilled nursing care facilities

(P-21054)
WINDSOR SKYLINE CARE CTR LLC
348 Iris Dr, Salinas (93906-3514)
PHONE.................................831 449-5496
Lawrence Feigen,
EMP: 91
SALES: 8.1MM
SALES (corp-wide): 13.6MM **Privately Held**
SIC: **8051** Skilled nursing care facilities
PA: S&F Management Company, Inc.
9200 W Sunset Blvd # 700
West Hollywood CA 90069
310 385-1090

(P-21055)
WINDSOR TWIN PALMS HLTHCARE
Also Called: Windsor Palms Care Ctr Artesia
11900 Artesia Blvd, Artesia (90701-4039)
PHONE.................................562 865-0271
John Ryan, *Administration*
Lee Samson, *Partner*
Liza Asis, *Persnl Dir*
Dorothy Garcia, *Corp Comm Staff*
Arnold Ling, *Director*
EMP: 133
SALES (est): 7.6MM
SALES (corp-wide): 67MM **Privately Held**
WEB: www.windsor.com
SIC: **8051** Convalescent home with continuous nursing care
PA: Lexington Group International, Inc
9200 W Sunset Blvd # 700
West Hollywood CA 90069
310 385-1071

(P-21056)
WINE COUNTRY CARE CENTER
321 W Turner Rd, Lodi (95240-0517)
PHONE.................................209 334-3760
Paul Gross, *Administration*
Cedric Gibbons, *Social Dir*
Heather Warmerdam, *Hlthcr Dir*
Robin Kuehne, *Director*
Joseph Nguyen, *Director*
EMP: 50
SALES: 5.2MM **Privately Held**
SIC: **8051** 8062 Skilled nursing care facilities; general medical & surgical hospitals

(P-21057)
WINSOR HOUSE COMPALESSANT
Also Called: Winsor House Convalescent Hosp
101 S Orchard Ave, Vacaville (95688-3635)
PHONE.................................707 448-6458
Fax: 707 448-4403
Prema Thekkek, *President*
Dionne Gunn, *Records Dir*
Ashley Brown, *Office Mgr*
Joe Niccoli, *Administration*
Pam Lopez, *Director*
EMP: 77 EST: 1972
SALES (est): 2.2MM **Privately Held**
SIC: **8051** Convalescent home with continuous nursing care

(P-21058)
WINTER CARE CENTER SACRAMENTO
501 Jessie Ave, Sacramento (95838-2608)
PHONE.................................916 922-8855
Ariane Swick, *Administration*
John Anderson, *Executive*
Melissa Brosas, *Administration*
Stephany Hadrick, *Food Svc Dir*
Kay Conley, *Nursing Dir*
EMP: 120
SQ FT: 25,000
SALES (est): 2.6MM **Privately Held**
SIC: **8051** 8322 Skilled nursing care facilities; rehabilitation services

(P-21059)
WISH I AH CARE CENTER INC
1665 M St, Fresno (93721-1121)
PHONE.................................559 855-2211
Fax: 559 855-6590
Janice Harshman, *President*
John E Harshman II, *Vice Pres*
Barbara Cleason, *CTO*
Steven M Grossman, *Director*
EMP: 118
SQ FT: 60,000
SALES (est): 4.9MM **Privately Held**
WEB: www.fmaaa.org
SIC: **8051** Extended care facility

(P-21060)
WISH-I-AH HLTHCRE & WELLNESS
1665 M St, Fresno (93721-1121)
PHONE.................................559 855-2211
Maceo Garcia, *Principal*
Mandy Scaletta, *Executive*
EMP: 99
SALES (est): 3.7MM **Privately Held**
SIC: **8051** Skilled nursing care facilities

(P-21061)
WISH-I-AH SKILLED NURSING
Also Called: Wish-Ah Skilled
1665 M St, Fresno (93721-1121)
PHONE.................................949 285-8859
Aaron Robin, *COO*
Stetan Sarmazian, *Administration*
EMP: 145 EST: 2008
SALES (est): 2.4MM **Privately Held**
SIC: **8051** Skilled nursing care facilities

(P-21062)
WOODLAND SKLLED NURSING FCILTY
678 3rd St, Woodland (95695-4034)
PHONE.................................530 668-1190
Fax: 530 662-3395
Donald Laws, *President*
Sarah Soto, *Social Dir*
Brett Moore, *Administration*
EMP: 100

SALES (est): 4.7MM **Privately Held**
SIC: **8051** Skilled nursing care facilities

(P-21063)
YORK HLTHCARE WLLNESS CNTRE LP
6071 York Blvd, Los Angeles (90042-3503)
PHONE.................................323 254-3407
Sharrod Brooks, *Partner*
EMP: 99 EST: 2012
SALES (est): 9.4MM **Privately Held**
SIC: **8051** Mental retardation hospital

(P-21064)
YUBA CITY NURSING & REHAB LLC
1220 Plumas St, Yuba City (95991-3411)
PHONE.................................530 671-0550
Fax: 530 671-5316
Joseph Pallivathucal,
Ronald Kwasniewski, *Administration*
Babu Parayil,
James Paul,
EMP: 75
SALES (est): 4.8MM **Privately Held**
SIC: **8051** Skilled nursing care facilities

8052 Intermediate Care Facilities

(P-21065)
834 W ARROW HIGHWAY LP
4032 Wilshire Blvd # 600, Los Angeles (90010-3405)
PHONE.................................213 355-1024
David Friedman, *Vice Pres*
Scott Hayashi, *Finance*
EMP: 99
SALES (est): 839.6K **Privately Held**
SIC: **8052** Intermediate care facilities

(P-21066)
ARCADIA GARDENS MGT CORP
Also Called: Independnt Asstd Lvng & Memory
720 W Camino Real Ave, Arcadia (91007-7839)
PHONE.................................626 574-8571
Julie Chirikian, *President*
David Chirikian, *Vice Pres*
Ramon Curameng, *Controller*
EMP: 100
SQ FT: 120,320
SALES (est): 5.4MM **Privately Held**
SIC: **8052** Intermediate care facilities

(P-21067)
BROOKDALE SENIOR LIVING INC
Also Called: Brookdale Elk Grove
6727 Laguna Park Dr, Elk Grove (95758-5069)
PHONE.................................916 683-1881
Ricky David, *Exec Dir*
EMP: 51
SALES (corp-wide): 4.9B **Publicly Held**
SIC: **8052** Personal care facility
PA: Brookdale Senior Living
111 Westwood Pl Ste 400
Brentwood TN 37027
615 221-2250

(P-21068)
CARE INC
15315 Magnolia Blvd # 306, Sherman Oaks (91403-1173)
PHONE.................................818 232-7940
Yue LI, *Principal*
EMP: 50
SALES (est): 1.3MM **Privately Held**
SIC: **8052** Home for the mentally retarded, with health care

(P-21069)
CC-PALO ALTO INC
Also Called: VI At Palo Alto
620 Sand Hill Rd, Palo Alto (94304-2002)
PHONE.................................650 853-5000
Penny Pritzker, *President*
Joselyn Meli, *Director*
Bree Tran, *Manager*
EMP: 225

SALES (est): 11.2MM **Privately Held**
SIC: **8052** 8322 8361 Personal care facility; adult day care center; rehabilitation center, residential: health care incidental

(P-21070)
CHARTER HOSPICE INC
1012 E Cooley Dr Ste G, Colton (92324-3959)
PHONE.................................909 825-2969
Fax: 909 825-8751
Fred Frank, *President*
Sabina Del Rosario, *Sales Staff*
Yvonne Salgado, *Social Worker*
Susan Chavez, *Manager*
EMP: 120
SALES (est): 16.4MM **Privately Held**
SIC: **8052** Personal care facility

(P-21071)
COMMUNITY HOME PARTNERS LLC
Also Called: Pacific Gardens
2384 Pacific Dr, Santa Clara (95051-1458)
PHONE.................................408 985-5252
Maxine Brookner,
Debra Song, *Admin Asst*
EMP: 85
SQ FT: 56,300
SALES: 4MM **Privately Held**
SIC: **8052** Intermediate care facilities

(P-21072)
COMMUNITY HOSPICE INC (PA)
Also Called: C H I
4368 Spyres Way, Modesto (95356-9259)
PHONE.................................209 578-6300
Harold A Peterson III, *CEO*
Rick Dahlseid, *CFO*
Gary Ervin, *Treasurer*
Lynis Chaffey, *Exec Dir*
Tricia Bond, *Admin Asst*
EMP: 125
SQ FT: 24,000
SALES: 22MM **Privately Held**
SIC: **8052** 8069 Personal care facility; specialty hospitals, except psychiatric

(P-21073)
COMMUNITY HOSPICE INC
2201 Euclid Ave, Hughson (95326-9183)
PHONE.................................209 578-6380
Laura Miller, *Administration*
EMP: 50
SALES (corp-wide): 22MM **Privately Held**
SIC: **8052** Personal care facility
PA: Community Hospice, Inc.
4368 Spyres Way
Modesto CA 95356
209 578-6300

(P-21074)
CORNERSTONE HEALTHCARE INC
143 Triunfo Canyon Rd # 103, Westlake Village (91361-2514)
PHONE.................................805 777-1133
Andre, *Med Doctor*
EMP: 120
SALES (corp-wide): 1.3B **Publicly Held**
SIC: **8052** Personal care facility
HQ: Cornerstone Healthcare, Inc.
420 E State St Ste 135
Eagle ID 83616

(P-21075)
COUNTY OF ORANGE
405 W 5th St Ofc, Santa Ana (92701-4519)
PHONE.................................714 834-6021
David L Riley, *Director*
EMP: 2500 **Privately Held**
SIC: **8052** Intermediate care facilities
PA: County Of Orange
333 W Santa Ana Blvd 3f
Santa Ana CA 92701
714 834-6200

(P-21076)
COUNTY OF SOLANO
Also Called: Adult Mddlhlth Otptient Clinic
2101 Courage Dr, Fairfield (94533-6717)
PHONE.................................707 784-2080
Fax: 707 784-2103
Rod Kennedy, *Manager*

PRODUCTS & SERVICES SECTION

8052 - Intermediate Care Facilities County (P-21100)

EMP: 100 Privately Held
SIC: 8052 5719 Intermediate care facilities; linens
PA: County Of Solano
675 Texas St Ste 2600
Fairfield CA 94533
707 784-6706

(P-21077)
CYPRESS GARDEN AT CITRUS HTS
7375 Stock Ranch Rd, Citrus Heights (95621-5616)
PHONE..................916 729-2722
Pepper Bell, *Exec Dir*
Sondra Campbell, *Deputy Dir*
EMP: 50
SALES (est): 2.1MM Privately Held
SIC: 8052 Personal care facility

(P-21078)
EMERITUS CORPORATION
5219 Clairemont Mesa Blvd, San Diego (92117-2206)
PHONE..................858 292-8044
Lori Tomasello, *Manager*
Bill Lawson, *Exec Dir*
EMP: 50
SALES (corp-wide): 4.9B Publicly Held
SIC: 8052 Personal care facility
HQ: Emeritus Corporation
3131 Elliott Ave Ste 500
Milwaukee WI 53214
206 298-2909

(P-21079)
EMERITUS CORPORATION
800 Oregon St, Sonoma (95476-6445)
PHONE..................707 996-7101
T Andrew Smith, *Branch Mgr*
EMP: 50
SALES (corp-wide): 4.9B Publicly Held
SIC: 8052 8361 Personal care facility; geriatric residential care
HQ: Emeritus Corporation
3131 Elliott Ave Ste 500
Milwaukee WI 53214
206 298-2909

(P-21080)
EMERITUS CORPORATION
2261 Tuolumne St, Vallejo (94589-2560)
PHONE..................707 552-3336
EMP: 50
SALES (corp-wide): 4.9B Publicly Held
SIC: 8052 Personal care facility
HQ: Emeritus Corporation
3131 Elliott Ave Ste 500
Milwaukee WI 53214
206 298-2909

(P-21081)
EMERITUS CORPORATION
Also Called: Emeritus At Villa Colima
19850 Colima Rd, Walnut (91789-3411)
PHONE..................909 544-4871
Wanda Reynolds, *Branch Mgr*
EMP: 50
SALES (corp-wide): 4.9B Publicly Held
SIC: 8052 Personal care facility
HQ: Emeritus Corporation
3131 Elliott Ave Ste 500
Milwaukee WI 53214
206 298-2909

(P-21082)
ESKATON
11390 Coloma Rd Ofc, Gold River (95670-6324)
PHONE..................916 852-7900
Fax: 916 852-9767
Tonae Hasik, *Manager*
David Van Reusen, *Administration*
EMP: 60
SALES (corp-wide): 1.4MM Privately Held
SIC: 8052 Intermediate care facilities
PA: Eskaton
5105 Manzanita Ave Ste D
Carmichael CA 95608
916 334-0296

(P-21083)
GENTIVA HOSPICE
5001 E Commercecenter Dr # 140, Bakersfield (93309-1687)
PHONE..................661 324-1232
EMP: 284
SALES (est): 286.7B
SALES (corp-wide): 7B Publicly Held
SIC: 8052 Personal care facility
PA: Kindred Healthcare, Inc.
680 S 4th St
Louisville KY 40202
502 596-7300

(P-21084)
HILLSIDE HOUSE INC
1235 Veronica Springs Rd, Santa Barbara (93105-4522)
PHONE..................805 687-4818
Fax: 805 563-2867
Pam Flynt, *Administration*
Michael Williams, *CFO*
Chuck Klein, *Principal*
Peter Troesch, *Principal*
Angela Biancone, *Admin Asst*
EMP: 88
SQ FT: 24,000
SALES: 4.4MM Privately Held
WEB: www.hillsidehousesb.org
SIC: 8052 Home for the mentally retarded, with health care

(P-21085)
JONBEC CARE INCORPORATED (PA)
1711 Plum Ln, Redlands (92374-2874)
P.O. Box 10788, San Bernardino (92423-0788)
PHONE..................909 798-4003
Jonathan Joseph, *President*
Cindy Collins, *Treasurer*
Becky Joseph, *Vice Pres*
Oynnie Joseph, *Admin Sec*
EMP: 52
SQ FT: 13,000
SALES: 12.2MM Privately Held
SIC: 8052 Home for the mentally retarded, with health care

(P-21086)
KERN CNTY MNTAL HLTH CHILD SYS
1111 Columbus St Ste 3000, Bakersfield (93305-1939)
P.O. Box 1000 (93302-1000)
PHONE..................661 868-8300
Fax: 661 868-8317
James Waterman, *Director*
EMP: 62
SALES (est): 1.1MM Privately Held
SIC: 8052 Home for the mentally retarded, with health care

(P-21087)
KINDRED HEALTHCARE INC
17290 Jasmine St Ste 104, Victorville (92395-8300)
PHONE..................760 241-7044
EMP: 244
SALES (corp-wide): 7B Publicly Held
SIC: 8052 Personal care facility
PA: Kindred Healthcare, Inc.
680 S 4th St
Louisville KY 40202
502 596-7300

(P-21088)
KINDRED HEALTHCARE INC
2055 Gateway Pl Ste 600, San Jose (95110-1083)
PHONE..................408 297-2078
EMP: 203
SALES (corp-wide): 7B Publicly Held
SIC: 8052 Personal care facility
PA: Kindred Healthcare, Inc.
680 S 4th St
Louisville KY 40202
502 596-7300

(P-21089)
LEISURE CARE LLC
Also Called: Fairwinds-West Hills
8138 Woodlake Ave, Canoga Park (91304-3500)
PHONE..................818 713-0900
Fax: 818 715-6555
Pat Luc, *General Mgr*
Maria Andrade, *Director*
EMP: 60
SALES (corp-wide): 138.2MM Privately Held
WEB: www.leisurecare.com
SIC: 8052 Intermediate care facilities
PA: Leisure Care, Llc
999 3rd Ave Ste 4500
Seattle WA 98104
800 327-3490

(P-21090)
MAGNOLIA SPECIAL CARE CENTER
635 S Magnolia Ave, El Cajon (92020-6012)
PHONE..................619 442-8826
Fax: 619 442-0288
Kennon S Shea, *President*
Monica Ramirez, *Records Dir*
Robert Clark, *Administration*
EMP: 99
SQ FT: 24,088
SALES (est): 5.2MM Privately Held
SIC: 8052 8059 8051 Personal care facility; convalescent home; nursing home, except skilled & intermediate care facility; skilled nursing care facilities

(P-21091)
MARYMOUNT VILLA LLC
345 Davis St Ofc, San Leandro (94577-2795)
PHONE..................510 895-5007
Fax: 510 352-3159
Jasbir Walia, *Mng Member*
Arjun Bhagat, *Mng Member*
Kai Quin, *Asst Director*
EMP: 65
SALES (est): 4.1MM Privately Held
SIC: 8052 8059 Personal care facility; convalescent home

(P-21092)
MILESTONES OF DEVELOPMENT INC
1 Florida St, Vallejo (94590-5000)
PHONE..................707 644-0496
Fax: 707 644-1702
Cynthia Mack, *Purch Dir*
Joan Yates, *Ch of Bd*
Faith Ohara, *Admin Sec*
EMP: 55
SQ FT: 7,564
SALES: 5.8MM Privately Held
SIC: 8052 Home for the mentally retarded, with health care

(P-21093)
MILHOUS CHILDRENS SERVICES INC
24077 State Highway 49, Nevada City (95959-8519)
PHONE..................530 265-9057
Fax: 530 292-3803
Richard Milhous, *CEO*
Teresa Petrie, *Food Svc Dir*
Dan Petrie, *Program Dir*
Mike Stein, *Director*
EMP: 220
SQ FT: 22,000
SALES: 11.8MM Privately Held
SIC: 8052 8361 Intermediate care facilities; residential care

(P-21094)
MOUNTAIN SHADOWS SUPPORT GROUP (PA)
Also Called: Mountain Shadows Cmnty Homes
2067 W El Norte Pkwy, Escondido (92026-1899)
PHONE..................760 743-3714
Richard W Marrs, *President*
Wade Wilde, *Exec Dir*
Stacey Kendalll, *Opers Dir*
Lupe Bryson, *Manager*
EMP: 61
SQ FT: 3,000
SALES (est): 9.3MM Privately Held
WEB: www.mtnshadows.org
SIC: 8052 8059 Personal care facility; rest home, with health care

(P-21095)
MURRIETA GARDENS SENIOR LIVING
18878 E Armstead St, Azusa (91702-4805)
PHONE..................951 600-7676
Michelle Tehlam, *Director*
Linda Boyle, *Executive*
Tammy Barnes, *Manager*
EMP: 60
SALES (est): 3MM Privately Held
SIC: 8052 Intermediate care facilities

(P-21096)
OPTMIAL HOSPICE FOUNDATION
3200 E 19th St, Signal Hill (90755-1244)
PHONE..................562 494-7687
EMP: 52
SALES (corp-wide): 182.7K Privately Held
SIC: 8052 Personal care facility
PA: Optmial Hospice Foundation
1315 Boughton Dr
Bakersfield CA 93308
661 410-3000

(P-21097)
QUAIL PARK
Also Called: Quail Park Retirement Village
4520 W Cypress Ave, Visalia (93277-1577)
PHONE..................559 624-3500
Fax: 559 624-3535
Pat Tyner, *Director*
EMP: 65
SALES (est): 4.1MM Privately Held
WEB: www.quail-park.com
SIC: 8052 6513 Intermediate care facilities; apartment building operators

(P-21098)
RANCHO VISTA HEALTH CENTER
760 E Bobier Dr, Vista (92084-3899)
PHONE..................760 941-1480
Fax: 760 941-5981
Alan Shigley, *Exec Dir*
Neil Levine, *Director*
EMP: 205
SALES (est): 7.3MM
SALES (corp-wide): 33.2MM Privately Held
WEB: www.healthcaregrp.com
SIC: 8052 8051 8361 Intermediate care facilities; skilled nursing care facilities; residential care
PA: Activcare Living, Inc.
9619 Chesapeake Dr # 103
San Diego CA 92123
858 565-4424

(P-21099)
RES-CARE INC
611 S Central Ave, Glendale (91204-2008)
PHONE..................818 637-7727
Michael Sowerby, *Manager*
Matthew Montgomery, *Envir Svcs Dir*
Rodolfo Magfino, *Director*
EMP: 130
SALES (corp-wide): 4.1B Privately Held
WEB: www.rescare.com
SIC: 8052 Home for the mentally retarded, with health care
HQ: Res-Care, Inc.
9901 Linn Station Rd
Louisville KY 40223
502 394-2100

(P-21100)
RES-CARE CALIFORNIA INC
Also Called: Edgewood Center
200 W Paramount St, Azusa (91702-4422)
PHONE..................626 334-7861
Fax: 626 969-4884
Danny Soto, *Branch Mgr*
Steve Kinley, *Branch Mgr*
Rainer Bansuan, *Director*
Dorothy Baker, *Agent*
EMP: 50
SQ FT: 78,991
SALES (corp-wide): 4.1B Privately Held
SIC: 8052 Home for the mentally retarded, with health care

8052 - Intermediate Care Facilities County (P-21101)

HQ: Res-Care California, Inc.
6170 Purple Hills Dr
San Jose CA 95119

(P-21101)
ROSS VALLEY HOMES INC
Also Called: TAMALPAIS
501 Via Casitas, Greenbrae (94904-1901)
PHONE..................................415 461-2300
Fax: 415 461-0241
David Berg, *CEO*
Don Meninga, *CFO*
Belinda Ong, *Controller*
John Koselak, *Director*
EMP: 100
SALES: 21.9MM **Privately Held**
WEB: www.rossvalleyhomes.com
SIC: 8052 Personal care facility

(P-21102)
SCOTT STREET SENIOR HOUSING CO
Also Called: RHODA GOLDMAN PLAZA
2180 Post St, San Francisco (94115-6013)
PHONE..................................415 345-5083
Fax: 415 345-5061
Marrianne Nannesthad, *Director*
Melanie Miguel, *Admin Asst*
Lynn Heath, *Controller*
Nicki Pun, *Controller*
Rhonda Botello, *Human Res Mgr*
EMP: 105
SQ FT: 195,000
SALES: 12MM **Privately Held**
WEB: www.rgplaza.org
SIC: 8052 Personal care facility

(P-21103)
SENIOR CARE INC
3423 Channel Way, San Diego (92110-5104)
PHONE..................................619 817-8855
Fax: 619 224-7301
Floyd C Weathers, *Owner*
Jay Johnson, *Exec Dir*
Erica Kent, *Director*
Amy Salvador, *Director*
EMP: 113
SALES (corp-wide): 147.9MM **Privately Held**
SIC: 8052 Intermediate care facilities
PA: Senior Care, Inc.
700 N Hurstbourne Pkwy # 200
Louisville KY 40222
502 753-6000

(P-21104)
SENIOR CARE INC
4960 Mills St, La Mesa (91942-9310)
PHONE..................................619 928-5644
Rhonda Hernandez, *Corp Comm Staff*
EMP: 113
SALES (corp-wide): 147.9MM **Privately Held**
SIC: 8052 Intermediate care facilities
PA: Senior Care, Inc.
700 N Hurstbourne Pkwy # 200
Louisville KY 40222
502 753-6000

(P-21105)
SENIOR CARE INC
2640 Honolulu Ave, Montrose (91020-1707)
PHONE..................................818 275-9717
EMP: 113
SALES (corp-wide): 147.9MM **Privately Held**
SIC: 8052 Intermediate care facilities
PA: Senior Care, Inc.
700 N Hurstbourne Pkwy # 200
Louisville KY 40222
502 753-6000

(P-21106)
SENIOR LIVING SOLUTIONS LLC
1725 S Bascom Ave Apt 105, Campbell (95008-0676)
PHONE..................................408 385-1835
Daniel P Schneider,
EMP: 120
SALES (est): 2MM **Privately Held**
SIC: 8052 Personal care facility

(P-21107)
SHORELINE S INTERMEDIATE CARE
Also Called: Alameda Care Center
430 Willow St, Alameda (94501-6130)
PHONE..................................510 523-8857
Fax: 510 523-8940
Jack E Easterday, *President*
Elisa MA, *Finance*
EMP: 200
SQ FT: 38,000
SALES (est): 5.2MM **Privately Held**
SIC: 8052 8051 Intermediate care facilities; skilled nursing care facilities

(P-21108)
SIERRA HILLS CARE CENTER INC
1139 Cirby Way, Roseville (95661-4421)
PHONE..................................916 782-7007
Fax: 916 782-1007
Ellen L Kuykendall, *President*
Brad Wilcox, *Treasurer*
EMP: 53
SQ FT: 30,000
SALES (est): 2.1MM
SALES (corp-wide): 99MM **Privately Held**
WEB: www.villadelrey.com
SIC: 8052 Personal care facility
HQ: Horizon West Healthcare, inc.
4020 Sierra College Blvd # 190
Rocklin CA 95677
916 624-6230

(P-21109)
SILVERADO SENIOR LIVING INC
Also Called: Los Angeles Hospice
601 S Glenoaks Blvd # 201, Burbank (91502-1474)
PHONE..................................818 848-4048
Loren Shook, *Branch Mgr*
EMP: 57
SALES (corp-wide): 182.6MM **Privately Held**
SIC: 8052 Personal care facility
PA: Senior Silverado Living Inc
6400 Oak Cyn Ste 200
Irvine CA 92618
949 240-7200

(P-21110)
SNOWLINE HSPC ELDORADO CNTY
3550 Carson Rd, Camino (95709-9330)
PHONE..................................530 647-2703
Melony Bigelow, *Owner*
EMP: 125
SALES (corp-wide): 11MM **Privately Held**
SIC: 8052 Personal care facility
PA: Snowline Hospice Of El Dorado County Inc
6520 Pleasant Valley Rd
Diamond Springs CA 95619
916 817-2338

(P-21111)
SOMERSET SPECIAL CARE CENTER
Also Called: Shea Family Care Somerset
151 Claydelle Ave, El Cajon (92020-4505)
PHONE..................................619 442-0245
Fax: 619 442-3631
Kennon S Shea, *President*
Karey Wideman, *Social Dir*
Diego Trevino, *Envir Svcs Dir*
David Leon, *Telecom Exec*
Polo Carreno, *Food Svc Dir*
EMP: 56
SALES (est): 4.4MM **Privately Held**
SIC: 8052 Intermediate care facilities

(P-21112)
SPECIAL HOME NEEDS
1440 Jackson St, Santa Clara (95050-4210)
PHONE..................................408 985-8666
Fax: 408 985-1566
Vivian Ascusion, *President*
EMP: 51
SALES: 500K **Privately Held**
SIC: 8052 Intermediate care facilities

(P-21113)
STRATGIES TO EMPWER PEOPLE INC (PA)
Also Called: Step
2330 Glendale Ln, Sacramento (95825-2455)
PHONE..................................916 679-1527
Fax: 916 679-1530
Jacquine Difoss, *President*
Tracy Cummins, *Director*
Ayren Gabrielson, *Manager*
Jennifer Johns, *Manager*
Michelle Noschese, *Manager*
EMP: 62
SALES (est): 13.7MM **Privately Held**
SIC: 8052 Personal care facility

(P-21114)
SUNBRIDGE HEALTHCARE LLC
Also Called: Willows Care Rhabilitation Ctr
320 N Crawford St, Willows (95988-2326)
PHONE..................................530 934-2834
Tina Brey, *Manager*
Tina Perry, *Human Res Dir*
Jared Garrison, *Director*
EMP: 99
SALES (corp-wide): 9.6B **Publicly Held**
WEB: www.innoventurehealthcare.com
SIC: 8052 8051 Intermediate care facilities; skilled nursing care facilities
HQ: Sunbridge Healthcare, Llc
101 Sun Ave Ne
Albuquerque NM 87109
505 821-3355

(P-21115)
SUNBRIDGE HEALTHCARE LLC
Also Called: Harbor View Community Svcs Ctr
850 E Wardlow Rd, Long Beach (90807-4628)
PHONE..................................562 981-9392
Dan Thorne, *Branch Mgr*
EMP: 200
SALES (corp-wide): 9.6B **Publicly Held**
WEB: www.innoventurehealthcare.com
SIC: 8052 8051 Intermediate care facilities; skilled nursing care facilities
HQ: Sunbridge Healthcare, Llc
101 Sun Ave Ne
Albuquerque NM 87109
505 821-3355

(P-21116)
SUNBRIDGE HEALTHCARE LLC
Also Called: Sunbridge Care Ctr For Downey
9300 Telegraph Rd, Downey (90240-2425)
PHONE..................................562 869-2567
Wendy Johnson, *Principal*
Gail Conser, *Administration*
Ramon Virina, *Maintence Staff*
EMP: 119
SALES (corp-wide): 9.6B **Publicly Held**
SIC: 8052 8051 Intermediate care facilities; skilled nursing care facilities
HQ: Sunbridge Healthcare, Llc
101 Sun Ave Ne
Albuquerque NM 87109
505 821-3355

(P-21117)
SUNBRIDGE HEALTHCARE LLC
Also Called: San Lndro Care Rhblitation Ctr
14766 Washington Ave, San Leandro (94578-4220)
PHONE..................................510 352-2211
Joe Gengilcore, *Administration*
Teresa Nelson, *Administration*
AMI Medrano, *Nursing Dir*
Flo Mason, *Hlthcr Dir*
EMP: 100
SQ FT: 28,635
SALES (corp-wide): 9.6B **Publicly Held**
WEB: www.innoventurehealthcare.com
SIC: 8052 8093 8051 Intermediate care facilities; rehabilitation center; outpatient treatment; skilled nursing care facilities
HQ: Sunbridge Healthcare, Llc
101 Sun Ave Ne
Albuquerque NM 87109
505 821-3355

(P-21118)
TUSTIN CARE CENTER CORP
1051 Bryan Ave, Tustin (92780-4419)
PHONE..................................714 832-6780
Fax: 714 832-1031
Jeoung H Lee, *President*
Robert Aguilos, *Administration*
Linda Lee, *Nursing Dir*
Chaewon Song, *Director*
EMP: 60
SALES (est): 3.6MM **Privately Held**
SIC: 8052 Intermediate care facilities

(P-21119)
WATTS HEALTH FOUNDATION INC (HQ)
Also Called: Uhp Healthcare
3405 W Imperial Hwy # 304, Inglewood (90303-2219)
PHONE..................................310 424-2220
Dr Clyde W Oden, *President*
Jennifer Stapalding, *CEO*
R S Shean, *CFO*
Frank Stevens, *Vice Pres*
Dr Darryl Leong, *MIS Dir*
EMP: 400
SALES (est): 19.3MM
SALES (corp-wide): 31.9MM **Privately Held**
WEB: www.sonnytran.com
SIC: 8052 8011 8741 Intermediate care facilities; health maintenance organization; management services
PA: Watts Health Systems, Inc
3405 W Imperial Hwy
Inglewood CA
310 424-2220

8059 Nursing & Personal Care Facilities, NEC

(P-21120)
8520 WESTERN AVE INC
Also Called: Buena Park Nursing Center
10811 Kiowa Rd Apt 2a, Apple Valley (92308-7989)
PHONE..................................714 828-8222
Sim Mandelbaum, *President*
Brenda Mandelbaum, *Principal*
Rosalie P Sanchez, *Manager*
EMP: 135
SQ FT: 31,474
SALES (est): 7.4MM **Privately Held**
SIC: 8059 8051 Convalescent home; skilled nursing care facilities

(P-21121)
A T ASSOCIATES INC
Also Called: Berkeley Pines Care Center
2223 Ashby Ave, Berkeley (94705-1907)
PHONE..................................510 649-6670
Fax: 510 843-2711
Natalie Montijo, *Director*
John Chan, *Records Dir*
Eric Smith, *Director*
EMP: 50 **Privately Held**
SIC: 8059 Personal care home, with health care
PA: A T Associates, Inc
535 School St
Pittsburg CA 94565

(P-21122)
A T ASSOCIATES INC
Also Called: Oakridge Care Center
2919 Fruitvale Ave, Oakland (94602-2108)
PHONE..................................510 261-8564
Fax: 510 261-0408
Abby Tiller, *Manager*
Nina Frye, *Administration*
Patricia Scherzi, *Administration*
EMP: 100 **Privately Held**
SIC: 8059 8051 Convalescent home; skilled nursing care facilities
PA: A T Associates, Inc
535 School St
Pittsburg CA 94565

(P-21123)
A T ASSOCIATES INC (PA)
535 School St, Pittsburg (94565-3937)
PHONE..................................925 808-6540
Fax: 925 808-6544
Alba F Tiller, *President*
Stewart Kennon, *Info Tech Mgr*
Wes Capps, *Manager*

PRODUCTS & SERVICES SECTION
8059 - Nursing & Personal Care Facilities, NEC County (P-21143)

EMP: 75
SALES: 2.5MM **Privately Held**
SIC: 8059 8011 Convalescent home; free-standing emergency medical center

(P-21124)
ACCESS INTEGRATED HEALTHCARE
Also Called: A I H
550 N Brand Blvd Fl 20, Glendale (91203-1900)
PHONE..................................866 460-7465
Manel Sweetmore, *CEO*
James Castro, *Exec VP*
Mendy Fry, *Vice Pres*
Sattar Mir, *General Mgr*
Laszlo Kupan, *General Counsel*
EMP: 51
SALES (est): 169.6K **Privately Held**
SIC: 8059 Nursing home, except skilled & intermediate care facility

(P-21125)
AEGIS ASSSTED LIVING PRPTS LLC
Also Called: Aegis of Fremont
3850 Walnut Ave 228, Fremont (94538-2263)
PHONE..................................510 739-1515
Fax: 510 739-1559
Creig R Cooper-Wyble, *Director*
Barb Wilson, *Nurse*
EMP: 50
SALES (corp-wide): 103.6MM **Privately Held**
SIC: 8059 Convalescent home
HQ: Aegis Assisted Living Properties, Llc
220 Concourse Blvd
Santa Rosa CA 95403
707 535-3200

(P-21126)
AG FACILITIES OPERATIONS LLC
6380 Wilshire Blvd # 800, Los Angeles (90048-5017)
PHONE..................................323 651-1808
Jacob Winter,
Leo Krieger, *CFO*
Scott Krieger,
EMP: 1000
SALES (est): 8.5MM **Privately Held**
SIC: 8059 Nursing home, except skilled & intermediate care facility

(P-21127)
AG REDLANDS LLC
Also Called: Highland Care Center Redlands
700 E Highland Ave, Redlands (92374-6233)
PHONE..................................909 793-2678
Tyrus Lefler, *Director*
Doug Easton, *CEO*
EMP: 110
SALES (est): 5.5MM **Privately Held**
SIC: 8059 Nursing home, except skilled & intermediate care facility

(P-21128)
AGE ADVANTAGE HM CARE SVCS
5480 Baltimore Dr Ste 214, La Mesa (91942-2066)
PHONE..................................619 449-5900
Daphne Archer, *President*
Greg Archer, *Co-Owner*
Joyce Porterfield, *Exec VP*
Bert Fox, *Consultant*
EMP: 75
SQ FT: 1,200
SALES (est): 4.2MM **Privately Held**
SIC: 8059 Personal care home, with health care

(P-21129)
ALAIDANDREW CORPORATION
1205 8th St, Bakersfield (93304-2123)
PHONE..................................661 334-2200
Julita A Javier, *President*
Edna Alcober, *Social Dir*
Carolyn Ashlock, *Administration*
Wayne Smith, *Administration*
Jess Cruzate, *Nursing Dir*
EMP: 79

SALES (est): 2.1MM **Privately Held**
SALES (corp-wide): 3.4MM **Privately Held**
SIC: 8059 Convalescent home
PA: Bettec Corporation
3210 W Pico Blvd
Los Angeles CA
323 734-2171

(P-21130)
ALDERWOOD INC
115 Bridge St, San Gabriel (91775-2719)
PHONE..................................626 289-4439
Fax: 626 289-0056
Ben Garrett, *President*
Eva Mae Casner, *Treasurer*
Christin Garret, *Admin Sec*
Louis Pages, *Administration*
Steven Ho, *Director*
EMP: 90
SALES (est): 5.4MM **Privately Held**
SIC: 8059 Convalescent home

(P-21131)
ALEXANDRIA CARE CENTER LLC
1515 N Alexandria Ave, Los Angeles (90027-5203)
PHONE..................................323 660-1800
Fax: 323 660-0023
Robert Snukal, *President*
Edwin Evangelista, *Director*
Julio Guzman, *Director*
EMP: 140
SQ FT: 30,000
SALES (est): 7.3MM
SALES (corp-wide): 9.6B **Publicly Held**
WEB: www.parkviewnursing.net
SIC: 8059 8051 Convalescent home; skilled nursing care facilities
PA: Genesis Healthcare, Inc.
101 E State St
Kennett Square PA 19348
610 444-6350

(P-21132)
ALTA CARE CENTER LLC
13075 Blackbird St, Garden Grove (92843-2902)
PHONE..................................714 530-6322
EMP: 118
SALES (est): 988.4K
SALES (corp-wide): 9.6B **Publicly Held**
WEB: www.parkviewnursing.net
SIC: 8059 8051 Convalescent home; skilled nursing care facilities
HQ: Skilled Healthcare, Llc
27442 Portola Pkwy # 200
Foothill Ranch CA 92610
949 282-5800

(P-21133)
AMDAL IN-HOME CARE INC (PA)
147 N K St, Tulare (93274-4003)
P.O. Box 1318 (93275-1318)
PHONE..................................559 686-6611
Deanne Martin Soares, *CEO*
Julian Mack, *Shareholder*
Charles Mack, *Admin Sec*
EMP: 50
SALES (est): 3.5MM **Privately Held**
WEB: www.amdalinhome.com
SIC: 8059 Personal care home, with health care

(P-21134)
AMDAL IN-HOME CARE INC
4848 N 1st St Ste 104, Fresno (93726-0526)
PHONE..................................559 227-1701
Fax: 559 227-1771
Deanne Martin-Soares, *Manager*
EMP: 55
SALES (corp-wide): 3.5MM **Privately Held**
WEB: www.amdalinhome.com
SIC: 8059 Personal care home, with health care
PA: Amdal In-Home Care, Inc.
147 N K St
Tulare CA 93274
559 686-6611

(P-21135)
AMERICAN BAPTIST HOMES OF WEST
Also Called: Rosewood Retirement Community
1401 New Stine Rd, Bakersfield (93309-3530)
PHONE..................................661 834-0620
Fax: 661 834-0280
Ellen Renner, *Branch Mgr*
Steven Gowan, *Info Tech Mgr*
EMP: 150
SALES (corp-wide): 129.1MM **Privately Held**
WEB: www.abhow.com
SIC: 8059 8052 8051 Rest home, with health care; intermediate care facilities; skilled nursing care facilities
PA: American Baptist Homes Of The West
6120 Stoneridge Mall Rd # 300
Pleasanton CA 94588
925 924-7100

(P-21136)
AMERICAN BAPTIST HOMES OF WEST
Also Called: Plymouth Village
900 Salem Dr, Redlands (92373-6147)
PHONE..................................909 793-1233
Fax: 909 798-5504
Keith Kasin, *Branch Mgr*
EMP: 250
SQ FT: 8,000
SALES (corp-wide): 129.1MM **Privately Held**
WEB: www.abhow.com
SIC: 8059 8051 Rest home, with health care; skilled nursing care facilities
PA: American Baptist Homes Of The West
6120 Stoneridge Mall Rd # 300
Pleasanton CA 94588
925 924-7100

(P-21137)
AMERICAN BAPTIST HOMES OF WEST (PA)
6120 Stoneridge Mall Rd # 300, Pleasanton (94588-3298)
PHONE..................................925 924-7100
Fax: 925 924-7101
David B Ferguson, *CEO*
Bruce Laycook, *Vice Chairman*
Christopher A Vito, *President*
Frank Tsai, *CFO*
Randy Stamper, *Chairman*
EMP: 60 **EST:** 1955
SQ FT: 26,000
SALES: 129.1MM **Privately Held**
WEB: www.abhow.com
SIC: 8059 Rest home, with health care

(P-21138)
AMERICAN BAPTIST HOMES OF WEST
Also Called: Pilgrim Haven Retirement Home
373 Pine Ln, Los Altos (94022-1687)
PHONE..................................650 948-8291
Fax: 650 941-0372
Rae Holt, *Manager*
Sheila Humphries, *Director*
EMP: 120
SQ FT: 95,130
SALES (corp-wide): 129.1MM **Privately Held**
WEB: www.abhow.com
SIC: 8059 8052 8051 Convalescent home; intermediate care facilities; skilled nursing care facilities
PA: American Baptist Homes Of The West
6120 Stoneridge Mall Rd # 300
Pleasanton CA 94588
925 924-7100

(P-21139)
AMERICAN BAPTIST HOMES OF WEST
Also Called: Terraces of Los Gatos Agei
800 Blossom Hill Rd Ofc, Los Gatos (95032-3563)
PHONE..................................408 357-1100
Fax: 408 356-9647
A Candalla, *Exec Dir*
Julie Reyes, *Records Dir*
John Langford, *Maintence Staff*
Wesley Sagumino, *Hlthcr Dir*

EMP: 115
SALES (corp-wide): 129.1MM **Privately Held**
WEB: www.abhow.com
SIC: 8059 8052 8051 6513 Rest home, with health care; intermediate care facilities; skilled nursing care facilities; apartment building operators
PA: American Baptist Homes Of The West
6120 Stoneridge Mall Rd # 300
Pleasanton CA 94588
925 924-7100

(P-21140)
ANTELOPE VLY RETIREMENT HM INC
Also Called: Antelope Vly Convalecent Hosp
44445 15th St W, Lancaster (93534-2801)
PHONE..................................661 948-7501
Fax: 661 949-5498
Marsha Weldon, *Director*
Sue Lin, *Records Dir*
Tony Diaz, *Info Tech Dir*
Marvin Smith, *Info Tech Dir*
Hugo Castellanos, *Technical Staff*
EMP: 400
SALES (corp-wide): 14.3MM **Privately Held**
SIC: 8059 8051 Convalescent home; skilled nursing care facilities
PA: Antelope Valley Retirement Home, Inc.
44523 15th St W
Lancaster CA 93534
661 949-5584

(P-21141)
ANTELOPE VLY RETIREMENT HM INC
Also Called: A V Nursing Care Center
44567 15th St W, Lancaster (93534-2803)
PHONE..................................661 949-5524
Fax: 661 949-5140
Alfred Jones, *Manager*
EMP: 200
SALES (corp-wide): 14.3MM **Privately Held**
SIC: 8059 8051 Convalescent home; skilled nursing care facilities
PA: Antelope Valley Retirement Home, Inc.
44523 15th St W
Lancaster CA 93534
661 949-5584

(P-21142)
ARARAT HOME OF LOS ANGELES
Also Called: Ararat Nursing Facility
15099 Mission Hills Rd, Mission Hills (91345-1102)
PHONE..................................818 837-1800
Fax: 818 898-2224
M Kebhichien, *Administration*
Margarita Kechichian, *Administration*
Evieny Janbazian, *VP Mktg*
EMP: 250
SALES (corp-wide): 25.5MM **Privately Held**
SIC: 8059 8051 Nursing home, except skilled & intermediate care facility; skilled nursing care facilities
PA: Ararat Home Of Los Angeles Inc
15105 Mission Hills Rd
Mission Hills CA 91345
818 365-3000

(P-21143)
ARCADIA CONVALESCENT HOSP INC (PA)
Also Called: Arcadia Health Care Center
1601 S Baldwin Ave, Arcadia (91007-7910)
PHONE..................................323 681-1504
Fax: 626 445-0338
Orlando Clarizio Jr, *CEO*
Carol Ababon, *Business Mgr*
Mario Andrade, *Director*
Dennis Liu, *Director*
EMP: 117 **EST:** 1962
SQ FT: 21,342
SALES (est): 12MM **Privately Held**
SIC: 8059 8051 Convalescent home; skilled nursing care facilities

8059 - Nursing & Personal Care Facilities, NEC County (P-21144)   PRODUDCTS & SERVICES SECTION

(P-21144)
ARIZONA AND 21ST CORP
Also Called: Berkley East Convalescent Hosp
2021 Arizona Ave, Santa Monica
(90404-1335)
PHONE..................310 829-5377
Fax: 310 829-5378
Sol Galper, *President*
Steven Galper, *Corp Secy*
EMP: 60 **EST:** 1968
SALES: 13.2MM **Privately Held**
SIC: 8059 Convalescent home

(P-21145)
ARTESIA CHRISTIAN HOME INC
11614 183rd St, Artesia (90701-5506)
PHONE..................562 865-5218
Fax: 562 865-4153
Elroy Van Derley, *Exec Dir*
Lorna Bomgars, *Executive*
Dianne Shaw, *Receptionist*
Dianne Wise, *Receptionist*
EMP: 140
SQ FT: 43,223
SALES: 8.8MM **Privately Held**
SIC: 8059 8052 8051 Convalescent home; intermediate care facilities; skilled nursing care facilities

(P-21146)
ASBURY PK NRSING RHBLTTION CTR
2257 Fair Oaks Blvd, Sacramento
(95825-5501)
PHONE..................916 649-2000
John Lund, *President*
Davi Moroles, *Executive*
EMP: 130 **EST:** 1997
SQ FT: 30,000
SALES (est): 8.6MM **Privately Held**
SIC: 8059 Nursing home, except skilled & intermediate care facility

(P-21147)
B & E CONVALESCENT CENTER INC (PA)
Also Called: Gardena Convalescent Center
11627 Telg Rd Ste 200, Santa Fe Springs (90670)
PHONE..................562 923-9449
Barry J Weiss, *President*
Esther Weiss, *Treasurer*
EMP: 60
SALES (est): 4.8MM **Privately Held**
WEB: www.gardenaconvalescentcenter.com
SIC: 8059 Convalescent home

(P-21148)
BASSARD CONVALESCENT & MED HM (PA)
Also Called: Bassard Convalscent Home
3269 D St, Hayward (94541-4599)
PHONE..................510 537-6700
Fax: 510 537-1045
Prema Thekkek, *President*
Jill Balloguing, *Records Dir*
Lani Santiago, *Social Dir*
Bobby Singh, *Administration*
Consuelo Castro, *Nursing Dir*
EMP: 65
SQ FT: 25,000
SALES (est): 1.6MM **Privately Held**
SIC: 8059 Convalescent home

(P-21149)
BEGROUP (PA)
516 Burchett St, Glendale (91203-1014)
PHONE..................818 638-4563
John H Cochrane III, *President*
David L Pierce, *CFO*
Daniel S Ogus, *Exec VP*
Michelle Esser, *Vice Pres*
Marc Herrera, *Vice Pres*
EMP: 66
SALES (est): 21.5MM **Privately Held**
SIC: 8059 Nursing home, except skilled & intermediate care facility

(P-21150)
BELMONT VILLAGE LP
Also Called: Belmont Village At Sabre Sprng
13075 Evening Creek Dr S, San Diego (92128-8101)
PHONE..................858 486-5020
Fax: 858 486-3540
Inan Linton, *Manager*
Pat Garner Rn, *Nursing Dir*
Jessica Porter, *Director*
EMP: 85
SALES (corp-wide): 35.2MM **Privately Held**
SIC: 8059 Nursing home, except skilled & intermediate care facility
PA: Belmont Village, L.P.
  8554 Katy Fwy Ste 200
  Houston TX 77024
  713 463-1700

(P-21151)
BEN BENNETT INC (PA)
Also Called: Community Care Rhbltation Ctr
3419 Via Lido 646, Newport Beach (92663-3908)
PHONE..................949 209-9712
Fax: 951 686-1919
Bruce Bennett, *President*
Bill Meert, *Administration*
Dorie Chandler, *Manager*
Dorothy Meza, *Manager*
▲ **EMP:** 200
SQ FT: 50,000
SALES (est): 7.8MM **Privately Held**
WEB: www.commcare.org
SIC: 8059 8069 8051 Convalescent home; specialty hospitals, except psychiatric; skilled nursing care facilities

(P-21152)
BERKELEY E CONVALESCENT HOSP
Also Called: Berkeley E Convalescent Hosp
2021 Arizona Ave, Santa Monica (90404-1335)
PHONE..................310 829-5377
Paul Bartolucce, *President*
Saul Galper, *Corp Secy*
Hernando Artaza, *Controller*
EMP: 150
SQ FT: 10,000
SALES (est): 64.1K **Privately Held**
SIC: 8059 Convalescent home

(P-21153)
BERNARDO HTS HEALTHCARE INC
Also Called: Carmel Mtn Rhab Healthcare Ctr
11895 Avenue Of Industry, San Diego (92128-3423)
PHONE..................858 673-0101
Christopher R Christensen, *CEO*
Covey C Christensen, *President*
Jen Pespano, *Executive*
Glomen Senir, *Executive*
Renee Aquino, *Personnel Exec*
EMP: 99
SALES (est): 4.8MM
SALES (corp-wide): 1.3B **Publicly Held**
SIC: 8059 8051 8011 Nursing home, except skilled & intermediate care facility; skilled nursing care facilities; clinic, operated by physicians
PA: The Ensign Group Inc
  27101 Puerta Real Ste 450
  Mission Viejo CA 92691
  949 487-9500

(P-21154)
BERRYMAN HEALTH INC
Also Called: Ukiah Convalescent Hospital
1349 S Dora St, Ukiah (95482-6512)
PHONE..................707 462-8864
Fax: 707 462-0718
Barbara Jimenez, *Principal*
EMP: 63
SALES (corp-wide): 2.4MM **Privately Held**
WEB: www.ukiahconvalescent.com
SIC: 8059 Convalescent home
PA: Berryman Health Inc
  615 E Chapman Ave Ste 3
  Orange CA

(P-21155)
BETHEL LUTHERAN HOME INC
2280 Dockery Ave, Selma (93662-3898)
PHONE..................559 896-4900
Fax: 559 896-6842
C Kaylene Steele, *Administration*
Kurt Stoner, *Administration*
Lupe Lombera, *Facilities Dir*
Karina Rodriguez, *Food Svc Dir*
EMP: 100
SQ FT: 33,000
SALES (est): 4.4MM **Privately Held**
SIC: 8059 8051 Domiciliary care; extended care facility

(P-21156)
BETHEL RETIREMENT COMMUNITY
2345 Scenic Dr, Modesto (95355-4574)
PHONE..................209 577-1901
Fax: 209 544-1425
Tony Musolino, *General Ptnr*
Kenneth Lemmings DDS, *Partner*
Robert Pirtle, *Partner*
Stephen P Thomas, *Partner*
Jim Hill, *Pastor*
EMP: 100
SQ FT: 120,000
SALES (est): 4.7MM **Privately Held**
WEB: www.bethelretirement.com
SIC: 8059 8361 Nursing home, except skilled & intermediate care facility; home for the aged

(P-21157)
BEVERLY LVING CTR CNTY VW ALZH
925 N Cornelia Ave, Fresno (93706-1031)
PHONE..................559 275-4785
Bill Floyd, *President*
Leslie Cotham, *Exec Dir*
Deann Walters, *Exec Dir*
EMP: 55
SALES (est): 439.3K **Privately Held**
SIC: 8059 Nursing & personal care

(P-21158)
BONNIE BRAE CNVLSCENT HOSP INC (PA)
Also Called: California Convalescent Center
420 S Bonnie Brae St, Los Angeles (90057-3010)
PHONE..................213 483-8144
Fax: 213 483-3658
Elma Cayton, *CEO*
Albert Ballo, *Treasurer*
Michelle Cayton, *Administration*
Evelyn Bonifacio, *Finance*
Divina Matabalan-Billing, *Clerk*
EMP: 60 **EST:** 1960
SALES (est): 5.5MM **Privately Held**
SIC: 8059 8051 Convalescent home; skilled nursing care facilities

(P-21159)
BRASWELL COL CARE REDLANDS CA
1618 Laurel Ave, Redlands (92373-4838)
PHONE..................909 792-6050
Fax: 909 798-8341
James Braswell, *Partner*
EMP: 245 **EST:** 1987
SALES (est): 10.8MM **Privately Held**
SIC: 8059 8051 Rest home, with health care; skilled nursing care facilities

(P-21160)
BRASWELLS VILLA MONTE VISTA
12696 Monte Vista Rd, Poway (92064-2500)
PHONE..................858 487-6242
Fax: 858 487-4282
James Braswell, *Partner*
Adora Ongpin, *Nursing Dir*
Alan Chang, *Director*
Nadine Phelps, *Director*
EMP: 160
SALES (est): 7.3MM **Privately Held**
SIC: 8059 8051 Convalescent home; skilled nursing care facilities

(P-21161)
BRENTWOOD SKILL NURSNG & REHAB
Also Called: Brentwood Sklled Nursng Rhbltn
1795 Walnut St, Red Bluff (96080-3645)
PHONE..................530 527-2046
Fax: 530 527-8737
Phil Sullivan, *Administration*
Daniel McNeal, *Maint Spvr*
Terri Sullivan, *Nursing Dir*
Stephen Datu, *Director*
Becky Taroli, *Receptionist*
EMP: 66
SQ FT: 1,600
SALES (est): 1.8MM **Privately Held**
SIC: 8059 Convalescent home

(P-21162)
BRIARWOOD HEALTH CARE INC
5901 Lemon Hill Ave, Sacramento (95824-3231)
PHONE..................916 383-2741
Fax: 916 383-0243
Sharron Jennings, *President*
Kathy Zaccarias, *Administration*
Ernesto Quinto, *Director*
EMP: 50
SALES: 3.4MM **Privately Held**
SIC: 8059 Convalescent home

(P-21163)
BRIER OAK ON SUNSET LLC
Also Called: Brier Oak On Sunset Rehab Ctr
5154 W Sunset Blvd, Los Angeles (90027-5708)
PHONE..................323 663-3951
Monica Urena, *Exec Dir*
Alex Belisle, *Office Mgr*
Anna Santos, *Human Res Dir*
Zia Siraj, *Facilities Dir*
Efy Macipili, *Nursing Dir*
EMP: 120
SALES: 277.6K
SALES (corp-wide): 9.6B **Publicly Held**
SIC: 8059 8051 Convalescent home; skilled nursing care facilities
HQ: Skilled Healthcare, Llc
  27442 Portola Pkwy # 200
  Foothill Ranch CA 92610
  949 282-5800

(P-21164)
BRIGHTON CONVALESCENT CENTER
1836 N Fair Oaks Ave, Pasadena (91103-1619)
PHONE..................626 798-9124
Fax: 626 794-2964
Alex Makabuhay, *Administration*
Christine Magana, *Records Dir*
Rebecca Ignacio, *Office Mgr*
Pat Capello, *Administration*
Aharon Straks, *Administration*
EMP: 100
SALES: 5.8MM **Privately Held**
SIC: 8059 8051 Convalescent home; skilled nursing care facilities

(P-21165)
BROOKDALE SENIOR LIVING INC
Also Called: Valley View Place Retirement
2050 Gondar Ave, Long Beach (90815-3328)
PHONE..................714 489-8966
Fax: 714 891-3052
EMP: 174
SALES (corp-wide): 4.9B **Publicly Held**
WEB: www.valleyviewplace.com
SIC: 8059 Rest home, with health care
PA: Brookdale Senior Living
  111 Westwood Pl Ste 400
  Brentwood TN 37027
  615 221-2250

(P-21166)
BROOKDALE SENIOR LIVING INC
Also Called: Brookdale Sunwest
1001 N Lyon Ave, Hemet (92545-1753)
PHONE..................951 744-9861
EMP: 65
SALES (corp-wide): 4.9B **Publicly Held**
SIC: 8059 Convalescent home
PA: Brookdale Senior Living
  111 Westwood Pl Ste 400
  Brentwood TN 37027
  615 221-2250

PRODUCTS & SERVICES SECTION **8059 - Nursing & Personal Care Facilities, NEC County (P-21188)**

(P-21167)
BROOKDALE SNIOR LVING CMMNTIES
Also Called: Wynwood At The Palms
25585 Van Leuven St, Loma Linda (92354-2442)
PHONE.....................909 796-5421
David Tamo, *Manager*
EMP: 60
SALES (corp-wide): 4.9B **Publicly Held**
WEB: www.assisted.com
SIC: 8059 Rest home, with health care
HQ: Senior Brookdale Living Communities Inc
6737 W Wa St Ste 2300
Milwaukee WI 53214
414 918-5000

(P-21168)
BUENA VENTURA CARE CENTER INC
Also Called: Leisure Glen Convalescent Ctr
1505 Colby Dr, Glendale (91205-3307)
PHONE.....................818 247-4476
Yolanda Wise, *Administration*
Silvia Hernadez, *Records Dir*
Nick Deleon, *Office Mgr*
Clarissa Dungo, *Hlthcr Dir*
EMP: 80
SALES (corp-wide): 6.6MM **Privately Held**
SIC: 8059 8051 Convalescent home; skilled nursing care facilities
PA: Buena Ventura Care Center Inc
1016 S Record Ave
Los Angeles CA 90023
323 268-0106

(P-21169)
BURLINGAME SENIOR CARE LLC
Also Called: Burlingame Healthcare Center
1100 Trousdale Dr, Burlingame (94010-3207)
PHONE.....................650 692-3758
Fax: 650 692-9674
Timothy B Cassidy, *Mng Member*
Don Doyle, *Admin Asst*
Deana Shannon, *Administration*
Jeffrey Alota, *Facilities Dir*
EMP: 300
SALES (est): 6.1MM **Privately Held**
SIC: 8059 Nursing home, except skilled & intermediate care facility

(P-21170)
BURLINGTON CONVALESCENT HOSP
Also Called: View Park Convalescent Center
3737 Don Felipe Dr, Los Angeles (90008-4210)
PHONE.....................323 295-7737
Fax: 323 294-8453
Joe Voltes, *Manager*
Dolly Piper, *Administration*
Patricia Chavez, *Food Svc Dir*
Leslie Paul, *Director*
EMP: 79
SQ FT: 40,000
SALES (corp-wide): 6.9MM **Privately Held**
SIC: 8059 Nursing home, except skilled & intermediate care facility
PA: Burlington Convalescent Hospital
845 S Burlington Ave
Los Angeles CA 90057
213 381-5585

(P-21171)
BV GENERAL INC
Also Called: Kennedy Care Center
619 N Fairfax Ave, Los Angeles (90036-1714)
PHONE.....................323 651-0043
James Kargol, *Branch Mgr*
EMP: 70
SALES (corp-wide): 13.8MM **Privately Held**
WEB: www.hmscal.com
SIC: 8059 Rest home, with health care
PA: B.V. General, Inc.
1332 S Glendale Ave
Glendale CA 91205
760 747-0430

(P-21172)
C P HOLIDAY MANOR INC
Also Called: Holiday Manor Nursitarium
20554 Roscoe Blvd, Canoga Park (91306-1746)
PHONE.....................818 341-9800
Fax: 818 341-1925
Armand Kain, *President*
Martin Simon, *Vice Pres*
Marylis Villanueva, *Office Mgr*
James Kergol, *Administration*
Camilo Flores, *Maintence Staff*
EMP: 65
SQ FT: 15,000
SALES (est): 804.6K **Privately Held**
SIC: 8059 8051 Nursing home, except skilled & intermediate care; home for the mentally retarded, exc. skilled or intermediate; skilled nursing care facilities

(P-21173)
CALIFORNIA CONVALESCENT HOSP
Also Called: Santa Barbara Convalescent Ctr
2225 De La Vina St, Santa Barbara (93105-3815)
PHONE.....................805 682-1355
Fax: 805 687-1307
Dorothy Shea, *President*
Laurie Shea, *President*
Roger Shea, *Treasurer*
S Laurie Anderson, *Admin Sec*
Kathleen Shea, *Admin Sec*
EMP: 70
SQ FT: 25,000
SALES: 6.2MM **Privately Held**
SIC: 8059 Convalescent home

(P-21174)
CALIFORNIA HM FOR THE AGED INC
Also Called: California Armenian Home
6720 E Kings Canyon Rd, Fresno (93727-3603)
PHONE.....................559 251-8414
Fax: 559 251-5766
Ray Wark, *Administration*
Lucy Grayson, *Vice Pres*
Yuba Radojkovich, *Administration*
Anjelica Rodriguez, *Director*
EMP: 165 **EST:** 1950
SQ FT: 39,000
SALES: 12MM **Privately Held**
SIC: 8059 Convalescent home; nursing home, except skilled & intermediate care facility

(P-21175)
CALIFORNIA VOCATIONS INC
Also Called: CYPRESS CENTER
1620 Cypress Ln, Paradise (95969-2824)
P.O. Box 538 (95967-0538)
PHONE.....................530 877-0937
Fax: 530 877-1170
Bob Irvine, *Exec Dir*
Richard Welsh, *President*
George Dailey, *Treasurer*
Denise Worth, *Vice Pres*
Robert Irvine, *Exec Dir*
EMP: 195
SQ FT: 5,700
SALES: 5.6MM **Privately Held**
WEB: www.calvoc.org
SIC: 8059 Home for the mentally retarded, exc. skilled or intermediate

(P-21176)
CALIFRNIA-NEVADA METHDST HOMES
Also Called: Lake Park Retirement Residence
1850 Alice St Ofc, Oakland (94612-4169)
PHONE.....................510 835-5511
Fax: 510 273-0529
Steve Jacobson, *Manager*
Barbara Conlon, *Executive*
Beverly Garcia, *Office Mgr*
EMP: 100
SALES (corp-wide): 18.9MM **Privately Held**
WEB: www.foresthillmanor.com
SIC: 8059 Rest home, with health care
PA: California-Nevada Methodist Homes
201 19th St Ste 100
Oakland CA 94612
510 893-8989

(P-21177)
CANYON PROPERTIES III LLC
Also Called: Country Manor Health Care
11723 Fenton Ave, Sylmar (91342-6431)
PHONE.....................818 890-0430
Fax: 818 890-5400
Donna Santos, *Administration*
Elizabeth Fernandez, *Records Dir*
EMP: 99
SALES (est): 5.1MM **Privately Held**
WEB: www.countrymanorhealthcare.com
SIC: 8059 Nursing & personal care

(P-21178)
CAPITOLA CARE CENTER INC
Also Called: Capitola Manor
1098 38th Ave, Santa Cruz (95062-4416)
PHONE.....................831 477-0329
Fax: 831 477-0201
Adolfo D Calanoc, *President*
Maria Correa, *Manager*
Vicky Heady, *Manager*
EMP: 70
SQ FT: 10,000
SALES (est): 7.3MM **Privately Held**
SIC: 8059 8051 Convalescent home; skilled nursing care facilities

(P-21179)
CARMEN CASA INC
Also Called: Casa Carmen Guest Home
315 W Dawson Ave, Glendora (91740-5018)
P.O. Box 2236 (91740-2236)
PHONE.....................626 852-9477
Fax: 626 963-4984
Morris Zyskind, *President*
Dena Zyskind, *Treasurer*
EMP: 70
SQ FT: 14,000
SALES (est): 2.7MM **Privately Held**
SIC: 8059 Personal care home, with health care

(P-21180)
CASA DE SANTA FE OF ROCKLIN
3201 Santa Fe Way Apt 1, Rocklin (95765-5582)
PHONE.....................916 435-8800
Fax: 916 435-2001
Joe Donham, *Administration*
Kristine Riley, *Director*
EMP: 80 **EST:** 2001
SALES (est): 3.8MM **Privately Held**
SIC: 8059 Personal care home, with health care

(P-21181)
CASTLE MANOR INC
Also Called: Castle Manor Convalescent Ctr
541 S V Ave, National City (91950-2828)
PHONE.....................619 791-7900
Fax: 619 791-7755
Ruth Cheneweth, *President*
J Edwin Cheneweth, *Treasurer*
Ken Funk, *Administration*
Chris Childers, *Controller*
Vivian Elias, *Bookkeeper*
EMP: 98
SALES: 10.6MM **Privately Held**
SIC: 8059 Convalescent home

(P-21182)
CENTRAL COAST CMNTY HLTH CARE
5 Lower Ragsdale Dr # 102, Monterey (93940-5817)
P.O. Box 2480 (93942-2480)
PHONE.....................831 372-6668
Carol Snow, *President*
Gayle McConnell, *CFO*
Robert Burnett, *CTO*
Angelo Ofrancia, *Technology*
Faith Collins, *Personnel Exec*
EMP: 250
SQ FT: 18,014
SALES (est): 8.9MM **Privately Held**
SIC: 8059 Convalescent home

(P-21183)
CHANCELLOR HLTH CARE CAL I INC (PA)
Also Called: Linda Valley Care Center
25383 Cole St, Loma Linda (92354-3103)
PHONE.....................909 796-0235
Fax: 909 796-6366
Corbin Swafford, *Exec Dir*
Edmond Peters, *Vice Ch Bd*
Hoselito Acuna, *Office Mgr*
Michelle McFeron, *Office Mgr*
Dave Green, *Administration*
EMP: 77
SQ FT: 32,000
SALES (est): 7.6MM **Privately Held**
SIC: 8059 6513 8051 Convalescent home; nursing home, except skilled & intermediate care facility; apartment building operators; skilled nursing care facilities

(P-21184)
CHANNING HOUSE
850 Webster St Ofc, Palo Alto (94301-2859)
PHONE.....................650 327-0950
Fax: 650 324-7585
Melvin Matsumoto, *CEO*
Dr Thomas Fiene, *Trustee*
Carl Braginsky, *Exec Dir*
Carl McBride, *General Mgr*
Ronda Bekkebaho, *Finance*
EMP: 100 **EST:** 1960
SQ FT: 300,000
SALES: 15.9MM **Privately Held**
WEB: www.channinghouse.com
SIC: 8059 Rest home, with health care

(P-21185)
CHASE CARE CENTER INC
1101 Crenshaw Blvd, Los Angeles (90019-3112)
PHONE.....................323 935-8490
Fax: 619 441-7416
Jeoung H Lee, *President*
Pat Marks, *Social Dir*
Veronica Bryan, *Office Mgr*
Nora Saulieties, *Administration*
John Yoo, *Administration*
EMP: 121
SQ FT: 83,000
SALES (est): 7MM **Privately Held**
SIC: 8059 8051 Convalescent home; skilled nursing care facilities

(P-21186)
CLARA BALDWIN STOCKER HOME
527 S Valinda Ave, West Covina (91790-3008)
PHONE.....................626 962-7151
Fax: 626 962-3042
Laura Qualls, *Administration*
Barabara Giesa, *Trustee*
Alfred Giese, *Trustee*
Ann Koecritz, *Trustee*
EMP: 50
SQ FT: 12,218
SALES: 3.6MM **Privately Held**
SIC: 8059 Convalescent home

(P-21187)
COASTAL VIEW HALTHCARE CTR LLC
4904 Telegraph Rd, Ventura (93003-4109)
PHONE.....................805 642-4101
Sim Mandelbaum,
Beverly Bragado, *Administration*
Debbie Smith, *Marketing Staff*
EMP: 96
SALES (est): 3.7MM **Privately Held**
SIC: 8059 Convalescent home

(P-21188)
COLLWOOD TER STELLAR CARE INC
4518 54th St, San Diego (92115-3527)
PHONE.....................619 287-2920
Chris Cho, *President*
EMP: 90
SALES (est): 3.7MM **Privately Held**
SIC: 8059 Personal care home, with health care

8059 - Nursing & Personal Care Facilities, NEC County (P-21189) — PRODUDUCTS & SERVICES SECTION

(P-21189)
COMPASS HEALTH INC
Also Called: Mission View Health Center
1425 Woodside Dr, San Luis Obispo (93401-5936)
PHONE 805 543-0210
Linda Lindsey, *Manager*
EMP: 73 **Privately Held**
SIC: 8059 Nursing home, except skilled & intermediate care facility
PA: Compass Health, Inc.
200 S 13th St Ste 208
Grover Beach CA 93433

(P-21190)
COMPASS HEALTH INC
Also Called: Bayside Care Center
1405 Teresa Dr, Morro Bay (93442-2458)
PHONE 805 772-7372
Fax: 805 772-2536
Harold Carder, *Manager*
Nicole Dauphine, *Director*
Melanie Gutierrez, *Director*
EMP: 109 **Privately Held**
SIC: 8059 Nursing home, except skilled & intermediate care facility
PA: Compass Health, Inc.
200 S 13th St Ste 208
Grover Beach CA 93433

(P-21191)
COMPASS HEALTH INC
Also Called: Arroyo Grande Care Center
1212 Farroll Ave, Arroyo Grande (93420-3718)
PHONE 805 489-8137
Fax: 805 481-1534
Harold Carder, *Administration*
Marcy Woolpert, *Administration*
Joni Nilsby, *Manager*
EMP: 109 **Privately Held**
SIC: 8059 Nursing home, except skilled & intermediate care facility
PA: Compass Health, Inc.
200 S 13th St Ste 208
Grover Beach CA 93433

(P-21192)
COMPASS HEALTH INC
Also Called: Danish Care Center
10805 El Camino Real, Atascadero (93422-8868)
PHONE 805 466-9254
Fax: 805 466-6007
Mark Woolpert, *President*
EMP: 70 **Privately Held**
SIC: 8059 Convalescent home
PA: Compass Health, Inc.
200 S 13th St Ste 208
Grover Beach CA 93433

(P-21193)
COUNTRY VILLA BLMNT HGHT HLTH
Also Called: Belmont Convalescent Hospital
1730 Grand Ave, Long Beach (90804-2011)
PHONE 562 597-8817
Fax: 562 597-0230
Sherry Gradon, *Administration*
Lourdes Contre, *Administration*
Andrew Manos, *Director*
EMP: 70
SALES (est): 9.7MM **Privately Held**
SIC: 8059 Convalescent home

(P-21194)
COUNTRY VILLA EAST LP
Also Called: Country Vlla Nrsing Rhbltation
5916 W Pico Blvd, Los Angeles (90035-2615)
PHONE 323 939-3184
Fax: 323 939-1966
Stephen Reissman, *Partner*
Steve Reissmann, *Partner*
Amy Sacks, *Director*
EMP: 200
SALES (est): 10.2MM **Privately Held**
SIC: 8059 8051 Convalescent home; skilled nursing care facilities

(P-21195)
COUNTRY VILLA TERRACE (PA)
Also Called: Country Vlla Convalescent Hosp
6050 W Pico Blvd, Los Angeles (90035-2647)
PHONE 323 653-3980
Fax: 323 653-2885
Steven Reissman, *President*
Diana Reissman, *Vice Pres*
Stella Yaeough, *Data Proc Staff*
Carlene Para, *Director*
Avery Ramos, *Director*
EMP: 75
SQ FT: 6,000
SALES (est): 5.4MM **Privately Held**
SIC: 8059 8361 Convalescent home; residential care

(P-21196)
COUNTRY VILLA TERRACE
Also Called: Flora Ter Convalescent Hosp
5916 W Pico Blvd, Los Angeles (90035-2615)
PHONE 323 939-3184
Lydia Reyes, *Manager*
Yesnia Trejo, *Executive*
Monique Lee, *Social Dir*
Lydia Cross, *Office Mgr*
Raul Dharwadkar, *Administration*
EMP: 50
SQ FT: 15,240
SALES (corp-wide): 5.4MM **Privately Held**
SIC: 8059 Convalescent home
PA: Country Villa Terrace
6050 W Pico Blvd
Los Angeles CA 90035
323 653-3980

(P-21197)
COVENANT CARE CALIFORNIA LLC
Also Called: Wagner Heights Nursing & Rehab
9289 Branstetter Pl, Stockton (95209-1700)
PHONE 209 477-5252
Janey Hargreaves, *Branch Mgr*
EMP: 160
SALES (corp-wide): 188.1MM **Privately Held**
WEB: www.willowtreenursingcenter.com
SIC: 8059 Convalescent home
HQ: Covenant Care California, Llc
27071 Aliso Creek Rd # 100
Aliso Viejo CA 92656
949 349-1200

(P-21198)
COVENANT CARE CALIFORNIA LLC
Also Called: Vintage Faire Nrsng Rhbltn
3620 Dale Rd Ste B, Modesto (95356-0598)
PHONE 209 521-2094
Fax: 209 521-6180
Julie Abram, *Administration*
Nikki Love, *Social Dir*
Julie Abrahamson, *Administration*
Sophia Costa, *Education*
Micheal Brodie, *Director*
EMP: 105
SALES (corp-wide): 188.1MM **Privately Held**
WEB: www.willowtreenursingcenter.com
SIC: 8059 8051 Convalescent home; skilled nursing care facilities
HQ: Covenant Care California, Llc
27071 Aliso Creek Rd # 100
Aliso Viejo CA 92656
949 349-1200

(P-21199)
COVENANT RTIREMENT COMMUNITIES
325 Kempton St, Spring Valley (91977-5810)
PHONE 619 479-4790
Thad Rothrock, *Branch Mgr*
Jay Caddell, *Admin Asst*
EMP: 193
SALES (corp-wide): 3.3MM **Privately Held**
SIC: 8059 Nursing home, except skilled & intermediate care facility
HQ: Covenant Retirement Communities
5700 Old Orchard Rd # 100
Skokie IL 60077

(P-21200)
CPCC INC
Also Called: Chatsworth Park Hlth Care Ctr
10610 Owensmouth Ave, Chatsworth (91311-2151)
PHONE 818 882-3200
John Sorensen, *President*
Greg Ethington, *Administration*
Leticia Wong, *Director*
Cynthia Cornejo, *Receptionist*
EMP: 99
SALES (est): 5.1MM **Privately Held**
SIC: 8059 8051 Convalescent home; skilled nursing care facilities

(P-21201)
CRESCENT COURT NURSING HOME
1334 S Ham Ln, Lodi (95242-3903)
PHONE 209 367-7400
Fax: 209 368-4491
Kerry Bains, *President*
Jennifer Sanchez, *Records Dir*
Terry Jen, *President*
Sharon Jennings, *President*
Bea Halsell, *Principal*
EMP: 50
SQ FT: 5,000
SALES (est): 2.3MM
SALES (corp-wide): 8.5MM **Privately Held**
SIC: 8059 8052 Convalescent home; intermediate care facilities
PA: Riverside Health Care Corporation
1469 Humboldt Rd Ste 175
Chico CA 95928
530 897-5100

(P-21202)
CULVER WEST HEALTH CENTER LLC
4035 Grand View Blvd, Los Angeles (90066-5211)
PHONE 310 390-9506
Fax: 310 391-1974
Harry Jacobs,
Patti Cook, *Administration*
Byran Melony, *Administration*
Bryon Mooney, *Administration*
EMP: 90
SQ FT: 25,000
SALES (est): 8.1MM **Privately Held**
SIC: 8059 Convalescent home

(P-21203)
CYPRESS GARDENS CONVALESCENT H
9025 Colorado Ave, Riverside (92503-2167)
PHONE 951 688-3643
Fax: 951 688-1507
Stanley Angermeir, *President*
Edward Erzen, *Vice Pres*
EMP: 115
SALES (est): 5MM **Privately Held**
SIC: 8059 8051 Convalescent home; skilled nursing care facilities

(P-21204)
D & C CARE CENTER INC
Also Called: Sunrise Convalescent Hospital
1640 N Fair Oaks Ave, Pasadena (91103-1615)
PHONE 626 798-1175
Fax: 213 798-3810
Felipe T Chu, *CEO*
June Cayabyab, *Administration*
June Ceayabyab, *Administration*
EMP: 75
SALES (est): 5.9MM **Privately Held**
SIC: 8059 Convalescent home

(P-21205)
D K FORTUNE & ASSOCIATES INC
Also Called: Marina Care Center
5240 Sepulveda Blvd, Culver City (90230-5214)
PHONE 310 391-7266
Fax: 310 397-4998
EMP: 130
SALES (est): 9.2MM **Privately Held**
SIC: 8059 8051

(P-21206)
DAVID KING CONVALESCENT HOSP
1340 15th St, Santa Monica (90404-1802)
PHONE 310 451-9706
Miriam Weiss, *President*
EMP: 99
SQ FT: 62,075
SALES (est): 1MM
SALES (corp-wide): 62.1MM **Privately Held**
WEB: www.goldenstatehealth.com
SIC: 8059 Nursing & personal care
PA: Golden State Health Centers, Inc.
13347 Ventura Blvd
Sherman Oaks CA 91423
818 385-3200

(P-21207)
DEVONSHIRE CARE CENTER LLC
1350 E Devonshire Ave, Hemet (92544-8629)
P.O. Box 1405, Riverside (92502-1405)
PHONE 951 925-2571
Jose Lynch, *Mng Member*
Andrea Abbes, *Mng Member*
EMP: 90
SALES (est): 6.6MM **Privately Held**
SIC: 8059 Convalescent home

(P-21208)
EL MONTE CONVALESCENT HOSPITAL
4096 Easy St, El Monte (91731-1054)
PHONE 626 442-1500
Fax: 626 228-0193
Jesse Telles, *CEO*
Nhu Devera, *Nursing Dir*
David Gu, *Director*
Linda Torres, *Receptionist*
EMP: 75
SQ FT: 21,208
SALES: 5.2MM **Privately Held**
WEB: www.elmonteconvalescent.com
SIC: 8059 Convalescent home

(P-21209)
ELENA VILLA HEALTHCARE CENTER
13226 Studebaker Rd, Norwalk (90650-2532)
PHONE 562 868-0591
Fax: 562 929-2185
Floyd Loupot, *President*
Terri Barella, *Records Dir*
Everett E Goings, *Vice Pres*
Judy Escheves, *Social Dir*
Andy Levin, *Administration*
EMP: 90
SQ FT: 24,000
SALES (est): 4.1MM **Privately Held**
SIC: 8059 8051 Convalescent home; skilled nursing care facilities

(P-21210)
EMMANUEL CNVLSCENT HOSP ALMEDA
Also Called: Pleasant Care
508 Westline Dr, Alameda (94501-5847)
PHONE 510 521-5765
Suzanne Valoppi, *Administration*
Laura Lok, *Manager*
EMP: 100
SALES (est): 3.7MM **Privately Held**
SIC: 8059 8051 Convalescent home; skilled nursing care facilities

(P-21211)
EMPRESS CARE CENTER
1299 S Bascom Ave, San Jose (95128-3514)
PHONE 408 287-0616
Ben Laub, *Director*
Kin Mohamed, *Director*
Norman Wood, *Director*
EMP: 65
SALES (est): 3.4MM **Privately Held**
SIC: 8059 Convalescent home

PRODUCTS & SERVICES SECTION **8059 - Nursing & Personal Care Facilities, NEC County (P-21233)**

(P-21212)
ENSIGN WILLITS LLC
Also Called: North Brook Nursing and Rehab
64 Northbrook Way, Willits (95490-3019)
PHONE.................................707 459-5592
Matt Rutter, *Principal*
Shawndee L Gumble, *Administration*
EMP: 60
SALES (est): 1.6MM
SALES (corp-wide): 1.3B **Publicly Held**
SIC: 8059 Nursing & personal care
HQ: Northern Pioneer Healthcare, Inc.
27101 Puerta Real
Mission Viejo CA 92691
949 487-9500

(P-21213)
ESKATON PROPERTIES INC
Also Called: Eskaton Village Charmichael
3939 Walnut Ave Unit 399, Carmichael
(95608-7333)
PHONE.................................916 974-2000
Betsy Donovan, *Exec Dir*
Marylin Kennedy, *Exec Dir*
Charles Here, *Director*
EMP: 200
SALES (corp-wide): 90.6MM **Privately Held**
SIC: 8059 Personal care home, with health care
PA: Eskaton Properties Incorporated
5105 Manzanita Ave
Carmichael CA 95608
916 334-0296

(P-21214)
FAR WEST INC
Also Called: Westgage Grdn Convalescent Ctr
4525 W Tulare Ave, Visalia (93277-1560)
PHONE.................................559 733-0901
Fax: 559 733-8757
Ellen Rioux, *Principal*
EMP: 113
SALES (corp-wide): 99MM **Privately Held**
SIC: 8059 8051 Convalescent home; skilled nursing care facilities
HQ: Far West, Inc
4020 Sierra College Blvd
Rocklin CA 95677
916 624-6238

(P-21215)
FILLMORE CONVALESCENT CTR LLC
118 B St, Fillmore (93015-1763)
PHONE.................................805 524-0083
Fax: 805 524-7260
Ananias E Gonzalez,
Eduardo Gonzales, *Hlthcr Dir*
Kate K Mooney, *Hlthcr Dir*
Eduardo Gonzales,
Milton E Fredricksen, *Agent*
EMP: 80
SQ FT: 13,800
SALES (est): 4.5MM **Privately Held**
WEB: www.fillmoreconvalescentcenter.com
SIC: 8059 8051 Convalescent home; skilled nursing care facilities

(P-21216)
FOWLER CONVALESCENT HOSPITAL
1306 E Sumner Ave, Fowler (93625-2697)
PHONE.................................559 834-2542
Fax: 559 834-5762
Roy Delacerda, *Administration*
Stan Louie, *Director*
EMP: 50
SALES (est): 1MM **Privately Held**
SIC: 8059 8051 Convalescent home; skilled nursing care facilities

(P-21217)
FRAN-JOM INC
Also Called: Temple City Convalescent Hosp
5101 Tyler Ave, Temple City (91780-3682)
PHONE.................................626 443-3028
Fax: 626 443-1988
Gary Elliott, *President*
Bryan Elliott, *Vice Pres*
Frank Elliott, *Vice Pres*
Tess De La Cruz, *Nursing Dir*
Paula Hernandez, *Director*
EMP: 60
SQ FT: 15,000
SALES (est): 1.9MM **Privately Held**
SIC: 8059 Convalescent home

(P-21218)
FRONT PORCH COMMUNITIES
Also Called: Walnut Manor Care Center
1401 W Ball Rd, Anaheim (92802-1711)
PHONE.................................714 776-7150
Fax: 714 239-6297
Sondra Coughlin, *Manager*
EMP: 159
SALES (corp-wide): 165.1MM **Privately Held**
SIC: 8059 8051 Rest home, with health care; skilled nursing care facilities
PA: Front Porch Communities And Services - Casa De Manana, Llc
800 N Brand Blvd Fl 19
Glendale CA 91203
818 729-8100

(P-21219)
FRONT PORCH COMMUNITIES (PA)
Also Called: Fredericka Manor Care Center
800 N Brand Blvd Fl 19, Glendale (91203-1231)
PHONE.................................818 729-8100
Gary Wheeler, *CEO*
Roberta Jacobsen, *President*
Mary Miller, *CFO*
Bonnie Stover, *CTO*
Diane Martinez-Adams, *Human Resources*
EMP: 100
SQ FT: 20,000
SALES: 165.1MM **Privately Held**
SIC: 8059 8051 Rest home, with health care; skilled nursing care facilities

(P-21220)
FRONT PORCH COMMUNITIES
Also Called: Carlsbad By The Sea
2855 Carlsbad Blvd, Carlsbad (92008-2902)
PHONE.................................760 729-4983
Fax: 760 729-0938
Tim Wetzel, *Manager*
EMP: 150
SALES (corp-wide): 165.1MM **Privately Held**
SIC: 8059 Rest home, with health care
PA: Front Porch Communities And Services - Casa De Manana, Llc
800 N Brand Blvd Fl 19
Glendale CA 91203
818 729-8100

(P-21221)
FRONT PORCH COMMUNITIES
Also Called: Claremont Manor
650 Harrison Ave, Claremont (91711-4538)
PHONE.................................909 626-1227
Fax: 909 399-0287
Joseph Peduzzi, *Branch Mgr*
Kari Miner, *President*
Robin Aspinall, *Admin Asst*
EMP: 150
SQ FT: 167,053
SALES (corp-wide): 165.1MM **Privately Held**
SIC: 8059 8052 6513 Convalescent home; intermediate care facilities; apartment building operators
PA: Front Porch Communities And Services - Casa De Manana, Llc
800 N Brand Blvd Fl 19
Glendale CA 91203
818 729-8100

(P-21222)
FRONT PORCH COMMUNITIES
Also Called: Fredericka Manor Care Center
111 3rd Ave, Chula Vista (91910-1822)
PHONE.................................619 427-2777
Fax: 619 420-4295
Loraine Wiencek, *Administration*
Chris Marquand, *General Mgr*
Julia Sink, *Data Proc Staff*
Alvin Emig, *Sales Staff*
Melanie Thompson, *Nursing Dir*
EMP: 178

SALES (corp-wide): 165.1MM **Privately Held**
SIC: 8059 8051 Convalescent home; skilled nursing care facilities
PA: Front Porch Communities And Services - Casa De Manana, Llc
800 N Brand Blvd Fl 19
Glendale CA 91203
818 729-8100

(P-21223)
FRONT PORCH COMMUNITIES & SVCS
Also Called: Wesley Palms
2567 2nd Ave Unit 312, San Diego (92103-6579)
PHONE.................................858 274-4110
Fax: 858 581-6504
Ben Gefke, *Manager*
James Strosberg, *Treasurer*
Gregory Warren, *Analyst*
Amber Pickett, *Marketing Staff*
Joan Stevenson, *Marketing Staff*
EMP: 330
SALES (corp-wide): 165.1MM **Privately Held**
SIC: 8059 Rest home, with health care
PA: Front Porch Communities And Services - Casa De Manana, Llc
800 N Brand Blvd Fl 19
Glendale CA 91203
818 729-8100

(P-21224)
FRONT PORCH COMMUNITIES & SVCS
Also Called: Lutheran Health Facility
303 N Glenoaks Blvd # 1000, Burbank (91502-1116)
PHONE.................................818 729-8100
Fax: 626 570-5289
Bob Moses, *Director*
EMP: 60
SALES (corp-wide): 165.1MM **Privately Held**
SIC: 8059 8011 Rest home, with health care; clinic, operated by physicians
PA: Front Porch Communities And Services - Casa De Manana, Llc
800 N Brand Blvd Fl 19
Glendale CA 91203
818 729-8100

(P-21225)
FRONT PORCH COMMUNITIES & SVCS
Also Called: Lutheran Health Facility, The
2400 S Fremont Ave, Alhambra (91803-4319)
PHONE.................................626 289-6211
Fax: 626 570-5254
Robert Moses, *Exec Dir*
EMP: 200
SALES (corp-wide): 165.1MM **Privately Held**
SIC: 8059 6513 Rest home, with health care; apartment building operators
PA: Front Porch Communities And Services - Casa De Manana, Llc
800 N Brand Blvd Fl 19
Glendale CA 91203
818 729-8100

(P-21226)
FRONT PORCH COMMUNITIES & SVCS
Also Called: Southland Lutheran Home
11701 Studebaker Rd, Norwalk (90650-7544)
PHONE.................................562 868-9761
Fax: 562 863-0336
Covy Christiansen, *Manager*
Ludi Manalo, *Executive*
EMP: 200
SALES (corp-wide): 165.1MM **Privately Held**
SIC: 8059 8011 8052 8051 Rest home, with health care; geriatric specialist, physician/surgeon; intermediate facilities; skilled nursing care facilities
PA: Front Porch Communities And Services - Casa De Manana, Llc
800 N Brand Blvd Fl 19
Glendale CA 91203
818 729-8100

(P-21227)
FRONT PRCH CMMUNITIES/SERVICES
3775 Modoc Rd, Santa Barbara (93105-4474)
PHONE.................................805 687-0793
Roberta Jacobsen, *Branch Mgr*
EMP: 250
SQ FT: 68,000
SALES (corp-wide): 165.1MM **Privately Held**
SIC: 8059 8051 Rest home, with health care; skilled nursing care facilities
PA: Front Porch Communities And Services - Casa De Manana, Llc
800 N Brand Blvd Fl 19
Glendale CA 91203
818 729-8100

(P-21228)
FRONT ST INC
Also Called: Front St Residential Care
2115 7th Ave, Santa Cruz (95062-1663)
PHONE.................................831 420-0120
Fax: 831 420-0136
Anne Butler, *President*
Peggy Butler, *Vice Pres*
EMP: 115
SALES (est): 3.4MM **Privately Held**
WEB: www.frontst.com
SIC: 8059 Personal care home, with health care

(P-21229)
FULLERTON GUEST HOME INC
Also Called: Alzheimer's Center
1510 E Commonwealth Ave, Fullerton (92831-4026)
PHONE.................................714 441-0313
Fax: 714 870-7287
Isaac Neches, *President*
Stella Neches, *Vice Pres*
▲ **EMP:** 60
SQ FT: 22,000
SALES (est): 2.6MM **Privately Held**
SIC: 8059 Domiciliary care

(P-21230)
GAITHERS FAMILY HOME
1408 S Newcomb St, Porterville (93257-9354)
PHONE.................................559 781-0301
Henrietta Gaithers, *President*
EMP: 50
SALES (est): 1.5MM **Privately Held**
SIC: 8059 Home for the mentally retarded, exc. skilled or intermediate

(P-21231)
GARDEN GROVE CONVALES
12882 Shackelford Ln, Garden Grove (92841-5109)
PHONE.................................714 638-9470
Fax: 714 638-4549
Aurea Sarigan, *Administration*
Uri Mandelbaum, *President*
Anh Nguyen, *Director*
EMP: 125
SQ FT: 6,000
SALES (est): 5MM **Privately Held**
SIC: 8059 8051 Convalescent home; skilled nursing care facilities

(P-21232)
GERI-CARE II INC
Also Called: VERMONT CARE CENTER
22035 S Vermont Ave, Torrance (90502-2120)
P.O. Box 6069 (90504-0069)
PHONE.................................310 328-0812
Fax: 310 782-3890
Emmanuel David, *President*
Engelica Vivillanueva, *Vice Pres*
Sohail Davoudian, *Medical Dir*
EMP: 250
SQ FT: 40,000
SALES: 10.7MM **Privately Held**
SIC: 8059 8051 Convalescent home; skilled nursing care facilities

(P-21233)
GHC OF SUNNYVALE LLC
Also Called: Cedar Crest Nrsing & Rehab
797 E Fremont Ave, Sunnyvale (94087-2805)
PHONE.................................408 738-4880

8059 - Nursing & Personal Care Facilities, NEC County (P-21234)

Fax: 408 738-6617
Thomas Olds Jr,
Tracy Murray, *Administration*
Javier Padilla, *Hlthcr Dir*
EMP: 140
SALES (est): 6.4MM
SALES (corp-wide): 68.1MM **Privately Held**
SIC: 8059 8051 Nursing home, except skilled & intermediate care facility; skilled nursing care facilities
PA: Life Generations Healthcare Llc
20371 Irvine Ave Ste 210
Newport Beach CA 92660
714 241-5600

(P-21234)
GIBRALTER CONVALESCENT HOSP
Also Called: Sunset Manor Convalescent Hosp
2720 Nevada Ave, El Monte (91733-2318)
PHONE..................................626 443-9425
Fax: 626 444-3315
Marcel Morales, *Manager*
Ernesto Rodriguez, *Envir Svcs Dir*
Smita Muir, *Administration*
Lorraine Hartford, *Director*
CHI Lam, *Director*
EMP: 100
SALES (corp-wide): 828.1MM **Privately Held**
SIC: 8059 8051 Convalescent home; skilled nursing care facilities
PA: Gibralter Convalescent Hospital
600 E Washington Ave
Santa Ana CA
714 550-5380

(P-21235)
GLENWOOD CORPORATION
Also Called: GLENWOOD CARE CENTER
1300 N C St, Oxnard (93030-4006)
PHONE..................................805 983-0305
Fax: 805 983-2514
Jerry E Wells, *President*
Frank Chung MD, *Treasurer*
Wallace Tamoyose MD, *Vice Pres*
Harvey Wilson, *Admin Sec*
Dave Merkley, *Administration*
EMP: 70
SQ FT: 30,000
SALES: 12.1MM **Privately Held**
SIC: 8059 Convalescent home

(P-21236)
GOLDEN CARE INC
Also Called: Valley Manor Convalescent Hosp
6120 Vineland Ave, North Hollywood (91606-4914)
PHONE..................................818 763-6275
Fax: 323 769-8548
Evelyn Del Rosario, *President*
Gonzalo Del Rosario, *Treasurer*
EMP: 80
SQ FT: 32,000
SALES (est): 4.1MM **Privately Held**
SIC: 8059 8361 Convalescent home; residential care

(P-21237)
GOLDEN CROSS CARE INC
Also Called: Golden Cross Health Care
1450 N Fair Oaks Ave, Pasadena (91103-1801)
PHONE..................................626 791-1948
Fax: 323 791-9282
Marlene Robertson, *President*
Ador Bustamante, *Director*
Noel Aravalo, *Manager*
EMP: 160
SQ FT: 30,000
SALES (est): 9.1MM **Privately Held**
SIC: 8059 Convalescent home

(P-21238)
GOLDEN LIVING LLC
Also Called: Beverly Healthcare
9541 Van Nuys Blvd, Panorama City (91402-1315)
PHONE..................................818 893-6385
Christopher Christenson, *Sales/Mktg Mgr*
EMP: 100
SALES (corp-wide): 1.6B **Privately Held**
WEB: www.nwbeccorp.com
SIC: 8059 8051 Convalescent home; skilled nursing care facilities
PA: Golden Living Llc
5220 Tennyson Pkwy # 400
Plano TX 75024
972 372-6300

(P-21239)
GOLDEN LIVING LLC
Also Called: Beverly Healthcare
2123 Verdugo Blvd, Montrose (91020-1628)
PHONE..................................818 249-3925
Shahid Chaudhry, *Manager*
Devinter Gandhi, *Director*
EMP: 51
SALES (corp-wide): 1.6B **Privately Held**
WEB: www.nwbeccorp.com
SIC: 8059 Convalescent home
PA: Golden Living Llc
5220 Tennyson Pkwy # 400
Plano TX 75024
972 372-6300

(P-21240)
GOLDEN LIVING LLC
Also Called: Golden Livingcenter - NAPA
705 Trancas St, NAPA (94558-3014)
PHONE..................................707 255-6060
Fax: 707 255-7470
Jerry Wells, *Manager*
Brian Adams, *Administration*
Gailyn Dober, *Nursing Dir*
EMP: 55
SALES (corp-wide): 1.6B **Privately Held**
SIC: 8059 8051 Convalescent home; skilled nursing care facilities
PA: Golden Living Llc
5220 Tennyson Pkwy # 400
Plano TX 75024
972 372-6300

(P-21241)
GOLDEN LIVING LLC
Also Called: Beverly Healthcare
515 E Orangeburg Ave, Modesto (95350-5510)
PHONE..................................209 529-0516
Belinda Guzman, *Exec Dir*
EMP: 76
SALES (corp-wide): 1.6B **Privately Held**
WEB: www.nwbeccorp.com
SIC: 8059 Convalescent home
PA: Golden Living Llc
5220 Tennyson Pkwy # 400
Plano TX 75024
972 372-6300

(P-21242)
GOLDEN LIVING LLC
Also Called: Beverly Healthcare
19929 Greenley Rd, Sonora (95370-5996)
PHONE..................................209 533-2500
Fax: 209 533-0728
Michael Ramstead, *Manager*
EMP: 105
SALES (corp-wide): 1.6B **Privately Held**
WEB: www.nwbeccorp.com
SIC: 8059 8051 Convalescent home; skilled nursing care facilities
PA: Golden Living Llc
5220 Tennyson Pkwy # 400
Plano TX 75024
972 372-6300

(P-21243)
GOLDEN LIVING LLC
Also Called: Beverly Healthcare
14966 Terreno De Flores, Los Gatos (95032-2023)
PHONE..................................408 356-8136
Fax: 408 358-3874
Richard Gotmaster, *Branch Mgr*
Sylvia Zaneiger, *Vice Pres*
Tammy Nguyen, *Nursing Dir*
EMP: 70
SALES (corp-wide): 1.6B **Privately Held**
WEB: www.nwbeccorp.com
SIC: 8059 Convalescent home
PA: Golden Living Llc
5220 Tennyson Pkwy # 400
Plano TX 75024
972 372-6300

(P-21244)
GOLDEN LIVING LLC
Also Called: Beverly Healthcare
3000 N Gate Rd, Seal Beach (90740-2535)
PHONE..................................562 598-2477
Lory Heredia, *Director*
Alfredo Cervantes, *Manager*
EMP: 80
SALES (corp-wide): 1.6B **Privately Held**
WEB: www.nwbeccorp.com
SIC: 8059 8051 8721 Convalescent home; skilled nursing care facilities; billing & bookkeeping service
PA: Golden Living Llc
5220 Tennyson Pkwy # 400
Plano TX 75024
972 372-6300

(P-21245)
GOLDEN LIVING LLC
Also Called: Golden Livingcenter - Redding
1836 Gold St, Redding (96001-1817)
PHONE..................................530 241-6756
Fax: 530 241-9077
Pam Eiszele, *Manager*
Janet Stone, *Exec Dir*
Jeanette R Tabbaa, *Exec Dir*
Don Stevens, *Maintence Staff*
EMP: 55
SALES (corp-wide): 1.6B **Privately Held**
SIC: 8059 8051 Convalescent home; skilled nursing care facilities
PA: Golden Living Llc
5220 Tennyson Pkwy # 400
Plano TX 75024
972 372-6300

(P-21246)
GOLDEN LIVING LLC
Also Called: Golden Livingcenter - Fresno
2715 Fresno St, Fresno (93721-1304)
PHONE..................................559 486-4433
Debbie Witt, *Manager*
Lala Mares, *Food Svc Dir*
Sue Downey, *Director*
EMP: 55
SALES (corp-wide): 1.6B **Privately Held**
SIC: 8059 8051 Convalescent home; skilled nursing care facilities
PA: Golden Living Llc
5220 Tennyson Pkwy # 400
Plano TX 75024
972 372-6300

(P-21247)
GOLDEN LIVING LLC
Also Called: Beverly Healthcare
1700 Howard Rd, Madera (93637-5131)
PHONE..................................559 673-9278
Ken Evans, *Principal*
EMP: 65
SALES (corp-wide): 1.6B **Privately Held**
WEB: www.nwbeccorp.com
SIC: 8059 Convalescent home
PA: Golden Living Llc
5220 Tennyson Pkwy # 400
Plano TX 75024
972 372-6300

(P-21248)
GOLDEN LIVING LLC
Also Called: Golden Livingcenter - Hyland
3408 E Shields Ave, Fresno (93726-6907)
PHONE..................................559 227-4063
Michelle Tatham, *Administration*
EMP: 55
SALES (corp-wide): 1.6B **Privately Held**
SIC: 8059 Convalescent home
PA: Golden Living Llc
5220 Tennyson Pkwy # 400
Plano TX 75024
972 372-6300

(P-21249)
GOLDEN LIVING LLC
Also Called: Beverly Healthcare
3169 M St, Merced (95348-2404)
PHONE..................................209 722-6231
Mary Imperial, *Manager*
EMP: 70
SALES (corp-wide): 1.6B **Privately Held**
WEB: www.nwbeccorp.com
SIC: 8059 Convalescent home
PA: Golden Living Llc
5220 Tennyson Pkwy # 400
Plano TX 75024
972 372-6300

(P-21250)
GOLDEN LIVING LLC
Also Called: Golden Livingcenter - Sanger
2550 9th St, Sanger (93657-2716)
PHONE..................................559 875-6501
Leslie Cotham, *Branch Mgr*
Rebecca Xiong, *Hlthcr Dir*
Angel Torres, *Manager*
EMP: 100
SALES (corp-wide): 1.6B **Privately Held**
SIC: 8059 8051 Convalescent home; skilled nursing care facilities
PA: Golden Living Llc
5220 Tennyson Pkwy # 400
Plano TX 75024
972 372-6300

(P-21251)
GOLDEN STATE HEALTH CTRS INC
5522 Gracewood Ave, Temple City (91780)
PHONE..................................626 579-0310
Israel Bastomski, *Manager*
EMP: 153
SALES (corp-wide): 62.1MM **Privately Held**
WEB: www.goldenstatehealth.com
SIC: 8059 8051 Convalescent home; skilled nursing care facilities
PA: Golden State Health Centers, Inc.
13347 Ventura Blvd
Sherman Oaks CA 91423
818 385-3200

(P-21252)
GOLDEN STATE HEALTH CTRS INC
13347 Ventura Blvd # 201, Sherman Oaks (91423-3979)
PHONE..................................818 783-4969
Armand Ongar, *Principal*
EMP: 153
SALES (corp-wide): 62.1MM **Privately Held**
SIC: 8059 Convalescent home
PA: Golden State Health Centers, Inc.
13347 Ventura Blvd
Sherman Oaks CA 91423
818 385-3200

(P-21253)
GOLDEN STATE HEALTH CTRS INC
Also Called: Chatsworth Health & Rehab
21820 Craggy View St, Chatsworth (91311-2909)
P.O. Box 3909 (91313-3909)
PHONE..................................818 882-8233
Fax: 818 882-2269
Emmanuel Ruiz, *Manager*
EMP: 105
SALES (corp-wide): 62.1MM **Privately Held**
WEB: www.goldenstatehealth.com
SIC: 8059 8051 Convalescent home; skilled nursing care facilities
PA: Golden State Health Centers, Inc.
13347 Ventura Blvd
Sherman Oaks CA 91423
818 385-3200

(P-21254)
GOLDSTAR HLTHCR CNTR OF CHTSWR
21820 Craggy View St, Chatsworth (91311-2909)
P.O. Box 3909 (91313-3909)
PHONE..................................818 882-8233
Miriam Weiss, *President*
David Weiss, *Ch of Bd*
Rose Kasirer, *Vice Pres*
Emanuel Ruiz, *Director*
EMP: 147
SQ FT: 26,650
SALES: 7.5MM
SALES (corp-wide): 62.1MM **Privately Held**
WEB: www.goldenstatehealth.com
SIC: 8059 Convalescent home

PRODUCTS & SERVICES SECTION
8059 - Nursing & Personal Care Facilities, NEC County (P-21276)

PA: Golden State Health Centers, Inc.
13347 Ventura Blvd
Sherman Oaks CA 91423
818 385-3200

(P-21255)
GRANADA HEALTHCRE & REHAB CNTR
2885 Harris St, Eureka (95503-4808)
PHONE..................707 443-1627
Maria Coda,
Ted Chigaros,
EMP: 99
SALES (est): 950K **Privately Held**
SIC: 8059 Convalescent home

(P-21256)
GREAT WSTN CNVLESCENT HOSP INC
Also Called: Verdugo Vly Convalescent Hosp
2635 Honolulu Ave, Montrose (91020-1706)
PHONE..................818 248-6856
Fax: 818 248-0925
Ishkhan Khatchadurian, *President*
Barbara Khatchadurian, *Vice Pres*
Phyllis Paver, *Executive*
Teresa Garcia, *Director*
Robert Ladines, *Director*
EMP: 130
SQ FT: 22,000
SALES (est): 3.7MM **Privately Held**
SIC: 8059 8361 8051 Convalescent home; residential care; skilled nursing care facilities

(P-21257)
GUARDIAN REHABILITATION HOSP
533 S Fairfax Ave, Los Angeles (90036-3129)
PHONE..................323 930-4815
Fax: 323 931-1943
Uri Mandelbaum, *President*
EMP: 90
SQ FT: 10,000
SALES (est): 6.3MM **Privately Held**
SIC: 8059 8069 8051 Convalescent home; specialty hospitals, except psychiatric; skilled nursing care facilities

(P-21258)
GVA ENTERPRISES INC (PA)
Also Called: Angels Nursing Center
316 S Westlake Ave, Los Angeles (90057-4500)
PHONE..................213 484-0510
Fax: 213 484-5931
George Rabinowitz, *President*
EMP: 53
SQ FT: 22,578
SALES (est): 5.3MM **Privately Held**
SIC: 8059 Convalescent home

(P-21259)
GVA ENTERPRISES INC
Also Called: Angels Nursing Center
415 S Union Ave, Los Angeles (90017-1007)
PHONE..................213 484-0784
Fax: 213 484-1003
Marco Cortes, *Manager*
Loraine Diego, *Director*
EMP: 52
SALES (corp-wide): 5.3MM **Privately Held**
SIC: 8059 Nursing home, except skilled & intermediate care facility
PA: Gva Enterprises Inc
316 S Westlake Ave
Los Angeles CA 90057
213 484-0510

(P-21260)
HANK FISHER PROPERTIES INC
Also Called: Chateau At River's Edge
641 Feature Dr Apt 233, Sacramento (95825-8331)
PHONE..................916 921-1970
Fax: 916 921-0310
Jeff Hertzig, *Director*
Irene Charnell, *Mktg Dir*
Mike Paular, *Maintenance Dir*
EMP: 92

SALES (est): 3.9MM
SALES (corp-wide): 13.3MM **Privately Held**
SIC: 8059 8052 Convalescent home; intermediate care facilities
PA: Hank Fisher Properties, Inc.
610 Fulton Ave Ste 100
Sacramento CA 95825
916 485-1441

(P-21261)
HARBOR VILLA CARE CENTER
861 S Harbor Blvd, Anaheim (92805-5157)
PHONE..................714 635-8131
Ramon Martinez, *Administration*
EMP: 90
SQ FT: 25,000
SALES (est): 3MM **Privately Held**
SIC: 8059 Convalescent home

(P-21262)
HEALTHCARE BARTON SYSTEM
2170 South Ave, South Lake Tahoe (96150-7026)
PHONE..................530 543-5685
Sharon Bishop, *Branch Mgr*
EMP: 50
SALES (corp-wide): 162.4MM **Privately Held**
SIC: 8059 Convalescent home
PA: Barton Healthcare System
2170 South Ave
South Lake Tahoe CA 96150
530 541-3420

(P-21263)
HELIOS HEALTHCARE LLC
Also Called: Chico Creek Care Rhabilitation
587 Rio Lindo Ave, Chico (95926-1816)
PHONE..................530 345-1306
Fax: 530 342-1353
Carl Lewis, *Manager*
Jackie Baker, *Human Res Dir*
Renee Herrington, *Director*
EMP: 170
SQ FT: 51,457
SALES (corp-wide): 23.8MM **Privately Held**
SIC: 8059 Convalescent home
PA: Helios Healthcare, Llc
520 Capitol Mall Ste 800
Sacramento CA 95814
916 471-2241

(P-21264)
HELIOS HEALTHCARE LLC
Also Called: Windsor Vallejo Care Center
2200 Tuolumne St, Vallejo (94589-2523)
PHONE..................707 644-7401
Laura Curly, *Manager*
Blain Lyons, *Administration*
Erelin Bretulfo, *Manager*
EMP: 180
SALES (corp-wide): 22.7MM **Privately Held**
SIC: 8059 8051 Convalescent home; skilled nursing care facilities
PA: Helios Healthcare, Llc
520 Capitol Mall Ste 800
Sacramento CA 95814
916 471-2241

(P-21265)
HERMITAGE HLTHCR MNKN MNR
400 Circle Dr, Angwin (94508-9806)
PHONE..................410 651-0011
Bonnie Stone,
Montel Wilson, *Chf Purch Ofc*
Kevin Whittington, *Hlthcr Dir*
Jenny Hall, *Director*
EMP: 165
SQ FT: 52,000
SALES (est): 1.6MM **Privately Held**
SIC: 8059 8051 Convalescent home; skilled nursing care facilities

(P-21266)
HILLCREST CARE INC
4280 Cypress Dr, San Bernardino (92407-2960)
PHONE..................909 882-2965
C David Benfield, *President*
Dave Benfield, *Administration*
Thomas Woodbury, *Director*
EMP: 100 **EST:** 1977

SALES (est): 5.5MM **Privately Held**
SIC: 8059 Nursing home, except skilled & intermediate care facility

(P-21267)
HILLCREST CNVALESCENT HOSP INC
3401 Cedar Ave, Long Beach (90807-4422)
PHONE..................323 636-3462
Fax: 562 426-4972
Rosalyn Zisman, *CEO*
Gaby Chacanas, *Treasurer*
Rela Michel, *Bookkeeper*
EMP: 130
SQ FT: 37,500
SALES (est): 4.2MM **Privately Held**
SIC: 8059 Convalescent home

(P-21268)
HILLSDALE GROUP LP
Also Called: Sherman Village Hlth Care Ctr
12750 Riverside Dr, North Hollywood (91607-3319)
PHONE..................818 623-2170
Rich Terrell, *Principal*
EMP: 100
SALES (corp-wide): 13.5MM **Privately Held**
WEB: www.greenhillsretirement.com
SIC: 8059 8051 8093 8011 Convalescent home; skilled nursing care facilities; rehabilitation center, outpatient treatment; clinic, operated by physicians
PA: The Hillsdale Group L P
1199 Howard Ave Ste 200
Burlingame CA 94010
650 348-6783

(P-21269)
HILLSDALE GROUP LP
Also Called: Green Hills Retirement Center
1201 Broadway Ofc, Millbrae (94030-1976)
PHONE..................650 742-9150
Fax: 650 742-9176
Pooja Sadarangani, *Manager*
EMP: 50
SALES (corp-wide): 13.5MM **Privately Held**
WEB: www.greenhillsretirement.com
SIC: 8059 8051 Nursing home, except skilled & intermediate care facility; skilled nursing care facilities
PA: The Hillsdale Group L P
1199 Howard Ave Ste 200
Burlingame CA 94010
650 348-6783

(P-21270)
HILLSDALE GROUP LP
Also Called: Hayward Convalescent Hospital
1832 B St, Hayward (94541-3140)
PHONE..................510 538-3866
Mark Bornta, *Manager*
Terrence Tumbale, *Administration*
Bhutinder Bhandari, *Director*
EMP: 80
SALES (corp-wide): 13.5MM **Privately Held**
WEB: www.greenhillsretirement.com
SIC: 8059 8051 Nursing home, except skilled & intermediate care facility; convalescent home with continuous nursing care
PA: The Hillsdale Group L P
1199 Howard Ave Ste 200
Burlingame CA 94010
650 348-6783

(P-21271)
HOFFMAN HOSPICE OF THE VALLEY
8501 Brimhall Rd Bldg 100, Bakersfield (93312-2327)
PHONE..................661 410-1010
Fax: 661 410-1110
Beth Hosman, *President*
Cindy Tyndall, *Volunteer Dir*
Chris Bergam, *CFO*
Tom Hoffman, *Administration*
Tom Hoffmann, *Administration*
EMP: 67
SQ FT: 8,500
SALES: 15.3MM **Privately Held**
SIC: 8059 Personal care home, with health care

(P-21272)
HORIZON WEST HEALTHCARE INC
Also Called: Hilltop Manor
12225 Shale Ridge Ln, Auburn (95602-8870)
PHONE..................530 885-7511
Sheilia Waddell, *Director*
EMP: 180
SALES (corp-wide): 99MM **Privately Held**
WEB: www.villadelrey.com
SIC: 8059 8051 Convalescent home; skilled nursing care facilities
HQ: Horizon West Healthcare, Inc.
4020 Sierra College Blvd # 190
Rocklin CA 95677
916 624-6230

(P-21273)
INDEPENDENT QUALITY CARE INC
Also Called: Northgate Convalescent Hosp
40 Professional Ctr Pkwy, San Rafael (94903-2703)
PHONE..................415 479-1230
Fax: 415 492-0398
Theresa D Guzman, *Principal*
Zeke Griffin, *Administration*
Dawn Bright, *Director*
Debra Koonce, *Director*
Linda Pearson, *Director*
EMP: 75
SALES (corp-wide): 20.2MM **Privately Held**
WEB: www.iqcare.com
SIC: 8059 Convalescent home
PA: Independent Quality Care, Inc
3 Crow Canyon Ct
San Ramon CA 94583
925 855-0881

(P-21274)
INDEPENDENT QUALITY CARE INC (PA)
Also Called: Woodland Lfytte Cnvlscent Hosp
3 Crow Canyon Ct, San Ramon (94583-1619)
PHONE..................925 855-0881
Daniel W Alger, *President*
Jeremy Grimes, *Vice Pres*
▲ **EMP:** 75
SALES (est): 20.2MM **Privately Held**
WEB: www.iqcare.com
SIC: 8059 Convalescent home

(P-21275)
INDEPENDENT QUALITY CARE INC
Also Called: Woodland Lfyett Sklled Nursing
3721 Mt Diablo Blvd, Lafayette (94549-3538)
PHONE..................925 284-5544
Fax: 925 284-5073
Christine Nacion, *Branch Mgr*
EMP: 75
SALES (corp-wide): 20.2MM **Privately Held**
WEB: www.iqcare.com
SIC: 8059 Convalescent home
PA: Independent Quality Care, Inc
3 Crow Canyon Ct
San Ramon CA 94583
925 855-0881

(P-21276)
INDEPENDENT QUALITY CARE INC
Also Called: Valley Point Nursing Center
2300 Bethards Dr, Santa Rosa (95405-9000)
PHONE..................707 578-3226
L Christopher, *Branch Mgr*
EMP: 75
SALES (corp-wide): 20.2MM **Privately Held**
WEB: www.iqcare.com
SIC: 8059 Convalescent home
PA: Independent Quality Care, Inc
3 Crow Canyon Ct
San Ramon CA 94583
925 855-0881

8059 - Nursing & Personal Care Facilities, NEC County (P-21277)   PRODUDUCTS & SERVICES SECTION

(P-21277)
INNOVATIVE BUS PARTNERSHIPS
17191 Jasmine St, Victorville (92395-7727)
P.O. Box 3339 (92393-3339)
PHONE..................................760 243-2229
Therese Krageness, *President*
EMP: 50
SALES (est): 1MM **Privately Held**
SIC: 8059 Home for the mentally retarded, exc. skilled or intermediate

(P-21278)
KENNEDY CARE CENTER
Also Called: Kennedy Care Ctr Kosher Certif
619 N Fairfax Ave, Los Angeles (90036-1714)
PHONE..................................323 651-0043
Fax: 323 651-3758
Alisa Berdnik, *Administration*
EMP: 98
SQ FT: 25,000
SALES (est): 5.3MM **Privately Held**
SIC: 8059 Convalescent home

(P-21279)
KF COMMUNITY CARE LLC
Also Called: Community Care Center
2335 Mountain Ave, Duarte (91010-3559)
PHONE..................................626 357-3207
Fax: 626 303-1116
Barbara O'Connor, *Administration*
Gordon Buechs, *CFO*
Gina Enriquez, *Human Res Dir*
Consuelo Silva, *Corp Comm Staff*
Riichiro Miwa, *Psychologist*
EMP: 170
SQ FT: 11,000
SALES (est): 9.3MM **Privately Held**
SIC: 8059 Convalescent home

(P-21280)
KF ONTARIO HEALTHCARE LLC
Also Called: Ontario Healthcare Center
1661 S Euclid Ave, Ontario (91762-5826)
PHONE..................................909 984-6713
Jacob Wintner, *CEO*
Patricia Thomas, *Records Dir*
Edward S Shea, *President*
Gordon Buechs, *CFO*
Marcella Allard, *Administration*
EMP: 50
SALES (est): 2.2MM **Privately Held**
SIC: 8059 8051 Convalescent home; nursing home, except skilled & intermediate care facility; skilled nursing care facilities

(P-21281)
KF SUNRAY LLC
Also Called: Sunray Healthcare Center
3210 W Pico Blvd, Los Angeles (90019-3643)
PHONE..................................323 734-2171
Douglas Easton, *Owner*
Daniel Wintner, *General Mgr*
Vandana Desai, *Administration*
EMP: 99
SALES (est): 4.3MM **Privately Held**
SIC: 8059 Convalescent home

(P-21282)
KINDRED HEALTHCARE OPER INC
Also Called: Saylor Lane Healthcare Center
3500 Folsom Blvd, Sacramento (95816-6615)
PHONE..................................916 457-6521
David Hilburn, *Manager*
Justin English, *Director*
EMP: 127
SALES (corp-wide): 7B **Publicly Held**
WEB: www.salemhaven.com
SIC: 8059 Convalescent home
HQ: Kindred Healthcare Operating, Inc.
680 S 4th St
Louisville KY 40202
502 596-7300

(P-21283)
KINDRED HEALTHCARE OPER INC
Also Called: Maywood Acres Health Care Ctr
2641 S C St, Oxnard (93033-4502)
PHONE..................................805 487-7840
Fax: 805 487-6855
Bonnie Velal, *Manager*
Geraldine Rozario, *Administration*
Robert Stauff, *Administration*
Robert Steuff, *Administration*
Peggy Gutierrez, *Director*
EMP: 100
SALES (corp-wide): 7B **Publicly Held**
WEB: www.salemhaven.com
SIC: 8059 8051 Convalescent home; skilled nursing care facilities
HQ: Kindred Healthcare Operating, Inc.
680 S 4th St
Louisville KY 40202
502 596-7300

(P-21284)
KINDRED HEALTHCARE OPERATING
Also Called: Alta Vista Healthcare Center
9020 Garfield St, Riverside (92503-3903)
PHONE..................................951 688-8200
Fax: 909 353-2450
Jeff Henson, *Director*
Carey Vanboxtel, *Administration*
Eloise Castro, *Personnel*
Pam Williams, *Hlthcr Dir*
Mina Dominguez, *Director*
EMP: 100
SALES (corp-wide): 7B **Publicly Held**
WEB: www.salemhaven.com
SIC: 8059 8051 Nursing home, except skilled & intermediate care facility; skilled nursing care facilities
HQ: Kindred Healthcare Operating, Inc.
680 S 4th St
Louisville KY 40202
502 596-7300

(P-21285)
KNOLLS WEST POST ACUTE LLC
16890 Green Tree Blvd, Victorville (92395-5618)
PHONE..................................760 245-5361
David Johnson, *Mng Member*
Thomas Chambers,
Ryan O'Hara,
Maria Zamora, *Supervisor*
EMP: 99
SALES (est): 1.9MM **Privately Held**
SIC: 8059 Nursing home, except skilled & intermediate care facility

(P-21286)
L C C H ASSOCIATES INC
Also Called: Health Care Group
4311 3rd Ave B, San Diego (92103-1407)
PHONE..................................858 565-4424
William M Chance, *President*
Renee Barnard, *COO*
Ronald McElloit, *Exec VP*
Todd Shetter, *Vice Pres*
Randy Padua, *Director*
EMP: 50
SQ FT: 10,000
SALES (est): 2.3MM **Privately Held**
SIC: 8059 Convalescent home

(P-21287)
LA MESA HEALTH CARE CENTER
3780 Massachusetts Ave, La Mesa (91941-7638)
PHONE..................................619 465-1313
Allison Clark, *Administration*
Paul Hubbert, *President*
Novie Sitanggang, *Admin Mgr*
Lovely Magsino, *Office Mgr*
Laurie Lewis, *Executive Asst*
EMP: 130
SQ FT: 22,000
SALES (est): 4.9MM **Privately Held**
SIC: 8059 8051 Convalescent home; skilled nursing care facilities

(P-21288)
LEE JOHNSON
Also Called: Casa Palmera Care Center
14750 El Camino Real, Del Mar (92014-4204)
PHONE..................................858 481-4411
Fax: 858 792-7356
Lee Johnson, *Owner*
Edel Mahdavifar, *Human Res Dir*
Joyce Londono, *Training Spec*
Ernest Georggin, *Marketing Staff*
Roberto Enriquez, *Director*
▲ **EMP:** 132
SQ FT: 36,000
SALES (est): 11.9MM **Privately Held**
SIC: 8059 8051 Convalescent home; skilled nursing care facilities

(P-21289)
LIFE CARE CENTERS AMERICA INC
Also Called: Vista Del Mar Health Centers
304 N Melrose Dr, Vista (92083-4814)
PHONE..................................760 724-8222
Fax: 760 941-4870
Michael Ramstead, *Branch Mgr*
Lucy Moreno, *Vice Pres*
Pinky Quintana, *Exec Dir*
Maureen Quillopo, *Office Mgr*
Donna Tabagan, *Data Proc Staff*
EMP: 170
SALES (corp-wide): 10.3MM **Privately Held**
SIC: 8059 8051 Convalescent home; skilled nursing care facilities
PA: Life Care Centers Of America, Inc.
3570 Keith St Nw
Cleveland TN 37312
423 472-9585

(P-21290)
LIFE GNERATIONS HEALTHCARE LLC
Also Called: Stanford Crt Nrsing Cntr-Sntee
8778 Cuyamaca St, Santee (92071-4255)
PHONE..................................619 449-5555
Andy Ashton, *Administration*
Pam Rhodds, *Finance*
Carolyn Martinez, *Hlthcr Dir*
EMP: 100
SALES (corp-wide): 68.1MM **Privately Held**
SIC: 8059 8051 8049 Convalescent home; skilled nursing care facilities; physical therapist
PA: Life Generations Healthcare Llc
20371 Irvine Ave Ste 210
Newport Beach CA 92660
714 241-5600

(P-21291)
LINCOLN GLEN MANOR
Also Called: LINCOLN GLEN SKILLED NURSING
2671 Plummer Ave Ste A, San Jose (95125-4877)
PHONE..................................408 267-1492
Fax: 408 265-2839
Loren Kroeker, *Exec Dir*
Barbara Filler, *Administration*
Rick Hendrickson, *Plant Mgr*
Raul Lorenzo, *Food Svc Dir*
Daniel TSE, *Director*
EMP: 110
SQ FT: 68,000
SALES: 6.2MM **Privately Held**
WEB: www.lgmanor.org
SIC: 8059 Convalescent home

(P-21292)
LOMA SOLA HOUSE
1291 Loma Sola Ave, Upland (91786-2846)
PHONE..................................909 931-7534
David Huengar, *Principal*
EMP: 50
SALES (est): 452.8K **Privately Held**
SIC: 8059 Nursing & personal care

(P-21293)
LOMITA VERDE INC
Also Called: LOMITA CARE CENTER
1955 Lomita Blvd, Lomita (90717-1807)
PHONE..................................310 325-1970
Fax: 310 325-7566
Donald G Laws, *President*
David E Sorenson, *Treasurer*
Lindon Perez, *Education*
Myrna Sebastian, *Nursing Dir*
Nabil El Sayad, *Director*
EMP: 60
SALES: 8.1MM **Privately Held**
WEB: www.lomitacare.com
SIC: 8059 8322 Convalescent home; individual & family services

(P-21294)
LOMPOC VALLEY MEDICAL CENTER
Also Called: Lompoc Convlsnt Care Ctr
216 N 3rd St, Lompoc (93436-6104)
PHONE..................................805 736-3466
Fax: 805 735-5955
Judy Smith, *Principal*
Susan Russell, *Data Proc Staff*
Deanna Hall, *Facilities Dir*
EMP: 150
SALES (corp-wide): 85.8MM **Privately Held**
SIC: 8059 Convalescent home
PA: Lompoc Valley Medical Center
1515 E Ocean Ave
Lompoc CA 93436
805 737-3300

(P-21295)
LONGWOOD MANAGEMENT CORP
Also Called: Sunny View Care Center
2000 W Washington Blvd, Los Angeles (90018-1637)
PHONE..................................323 735-5146
Fax: 323 734-7261
Amber Gooden, *Administration*
EMP: 80
SALES (corp-wide): 169.4MM **Privately Held**
SIC: 8059 Convalescent home
PA: Longwood Management Corp.
4032 Wilshire Blvd Fl 6
Los Angeles CA 90010
213 389-6900

(P-21296)
LONGWOOD MANAGEMENT CORP
Also Called: Broadway Manor Care Center
605 W Broadway, Glendale (91204-1007)
PHONE..................................818 246-7174
Fax: 818 246-7635
Dolly Piper, *Manager*
Nancy Anda, *Nursing Dir*
Nena Tan,
Michael Habashy, *Director*
EMP: 70
SQ FT: 7,000
SALES (corp-wide): 169.4MM **Privately Held**
SIC: 8059 8051 Convalescent home; skilled nursing care facilities
PA: Longwood Management Corp.
4032 Wilshire Blvd Fl 6
Los Angeles CA 90010
213 389-6900

(P-21297)
LONGWOOD MANAGEMENT CORP
Also Called: Western Convelescence
2190 W Adams Blvd, Los Angeles (90018-2039)
PHONE..................................323 737-7778
Emma Camanag, *Administration*
EMP: 80
SALES (corp-wide): 169.4MM **Privately Held**
SIC: 8059 6512 Convalescent home; commercial & industrial building operation
PA: Longwood Management Corp.
4032 Wilshire Blvd Fl 6
Los Angeles CA 90010
213 389-6900

(P-21298)
LONGWOOD MANAGEMENT CORP
Also Called: Imperial Care Center
11429 Ventura Blvd, Studio City (91604-3143)
PHONE..................................818 980-8200
Fax: 818 762-8339
Emma Dellanuoni, *Manager*
Nelly Akoyan, *Executive*
Danny Farahmadian, *Director*
EMP: 200
SQ FT: 29,525
SALES (corp-wide): 169.4MM **Privately Held**
SIC: 8059 8051 Convalescent home; skilled nursing care facilities

PRODUCTS & SERVICES SECTION
8059 - Nursing & Personal Care Facilities, NEC County (P-21321)

PA: Longwood Management Corp.
4032 Wilshire Blvd Fl 6
Los Angeles CA 90010
213 389-6900

(P-21299)
LONGWOOD MANAGEMENT CORP
Also Called: Aldon Ter Convalsent Hosptial
1240 S Hoover St, Los Angeles (90006-3606)
PHONE..................213 382-8461
Fax: 213 736-5243
John Sicat, *Principal*
Maria Rocha, *Asst Admin*
Ali Haddad, *Director*
EMP: 170
SALES (corp-wide): 169.4MM **Privately Held**
SIC: 8059 8051 Convalescent home; skilled nursing care facilities
PA: Longwood Management Corp.
4032 Wilshire Blvd Fl 6
Los Angeles CA 90010
213 389-6900

(P-21300)
LONGWOOD MANAGEMENT CORP
Also Called: Live Oak Rehab
537 W Live Oak St, San Gabriel (91776-1149)
PHONE..................626 289-3763
Fax: 626 289-2302
Ranita Phan, *Manager*
Camil Estacio, *Records Dir*
Veronica Esparza, *Office Mgr*
Laura Ghazarian, *Administration*
Sarah Lopez, *Education*
EMP: 100
SALES (corp-wide): 169.4MM **Privately Held**
SIC: 8059 8051 Convalescent home; skilled nursing care facilities
PA: Longwood Management Corp.
4032 Wilshire Blvd Fl 6
Los Angeles CA 90010
213 389-6900

(P-21301)
LONGWOOD MANAGEMENT CORP
Also Called: Colonial Care Center
1913 E 5th St, Long Beach (90802-2024)
PHONE..................562 432-5751
Fax: 562 435-0361
Laura McCuphen, *Manager*
EMP: 150
SALES (corp-wide): 169.4MM **Privately Held**
SIC: 8059 8051 Convalescent home; skilled nursing care facilities
PA: Longwood Management Corp.
4032 Wilshire Blvd Fl 6
Los Angeles CA 90010
213 389-6900

(P-21302)
LYNWOOD DEVELOPMENTAL CARE
Also Called: Compton Adult Day Care
14925 S Atlantic Ave, Compton (90221-3005)
PHONE..................310 764-2023
Fax: 310 223-5921
James E Logan, *CEO*
Lavern L Neal, *Treasurer*
EMP: 75
SALES (est): 3MM **Privately Held**
SIC: 8059 Personal care home, with health care

(P-21303)
MADERA CONVALESCENT HOSPITAL
Also Called: Merced Convalescent Hospital
510 W 26th St, Merced (95340-2804)
PHONE..................209 723-2911
Fax: 209 723-1142
Dave Yarborough, *Manager*
EMP: 130
SALES (corp-wide): 5.9MM **Privately Held**
SIC: 8059 8051 Convalescent home; skilled nursing care facilities
PA: Madera Convalescent Hospital, Inc
517 S A St
Madera CA 93638
559 673-9228

(P-21304)
MADERA CONVALESCENT HOSPITAL
Also Called: Auburn Gardens Care Center
260 Racetrack St, Auburn (95603-5422)
PHONE..................530 885-7051
Clayton Green, *Administration*
EMP: 78
SALES (corp-wide): 5.9MM **Privately Held**
SIC: 8059 Convalescent home
PA: Madera Convalescent Hospital, Inc
517 S A St
Madera CA 93638
559 673-9228

(P-21305)
MAGNOLIA RHBLTTION NURSING CTR
Also Called: Magnolia Convalescent Hospital
8133 Magnolia Ave, Riverside (92504-3409)
PHONE..................951 688-4321
Fax: 951 688-0258
Larry Mays, *President*
Grant Edgeson, *Treasurer*
Bennie J Mays, *Vice Pres*
Vanessa Romo, *Executive*
Bobbie N Mays, *Admin Sec*
EMP: 140
SQ FT: 25,000
SALES (est): 10.7MM **Privately Held**
SIC: 8059 8051 Convalescent home; skilled nursing care facilities

(P-21306)
MANCHSTER MNOR CNVLESCENT HOSP
837 W Manchester Ave, Los Angeles (90044-4913)
PHONE..................323 753-1789
Fax: 323 753-0400
Phadra Johnson-Fenton, *Administration*
Susanne Douglas, *Office Mgr*
Phadra Fenton, *Administration*
EMP: 65
SQ FT: 10,000
SALES (est): 3.9MM **Privately Held**
WEB: www.manchestermanorch.com
SIC: 8059 Convalescent home

(P-21307)
MANNING GARDENS INC
Also Called: Manning Grdns Cnvalescent Hosp
2113 E Manning Ave, Fresno (93725-9681)
PHONE..................559 834-2586
Fax: 559 834-2540
Cary Hanson, *Administration*
Jacob Kizirian, *President*
Norman Kizirian, *Vice Pres*
EMP: 50 EST: 1962
SQ FT: 15,000
SALES (est): 2.5MM **Privately Held**
SIC: 8059 Convalescent home

(P-21308)
MARK ONE CORPORATION
Also Called: Ha-Le Aloha Convalescent Hosp
1711 Richland Ave, Ceres (95307-4509)
PHONE..................209 537-4581
Fax: 209 537-0035
EMP: 50
SALES (corp-wide): 12.7MM **Privately Held**
SIC: 8059
PA: Mark One Corporation
812 W Main St
Turlock CA
209 667-2484

(P-21309)
MARLINDA MANAGEMENT INC (PA)
Also Called: Sherwood Guest Home
3351 E Imperial Hwy, Lynwood (90262-3305)
PHONE..................310 638-6691
Fax: 310 763-0993
Martha Lang, *President*

Linda Gassoumis, *CFO*
Gloria Lemus, *Manager*
Billy Compton, *Superintendent*
EMP: 120
SALES (est): 5.9MM **Privately Held**
SIC: 8059 Convalescent home

(P-21310)
MARYCREST MANOR
10664 Saint James Dr, Culver City (90230-5498)
PHONE..................310 838-2778
Fax: 310 838-9647
SIS V Del Carmen, *Administration*
SIS Veronica Del Carmen, *Administration*
Rolando Escamilla, *Administration*
EMP: 86
SQ FT: 43,449
SALES (est): 3.4MM **Privately Held**
SIC: 8059 8051 Convalescent home; skilled nursing care facilities

(P-21311)
MBK SENIOR LIVING LLC
Also Called: Sterling Senior Communities
41780 Btterfield Stage Rd, Temecula (92592-9206)
PHONE..................951 506-5555
Fax: 951 506-2380
Nancy Halleck, *Director*
EMP: 60
SALES (corp-wide): 1.9MM **Privately Held**
SIC: 8059 Rest home, with health care
PA: Senior Mbk Living Llc
895 Dove St Ste 450
Newport Beach CA

(P-21312)
MEDICAL DIAGNOSTIC
Also Called: Bright Caregivers
17682 Beach Blvd Ste 103, Huntington Beach (92647-6812)
PHONE..................714 841-2273
Robert M Soto, *President*
EMP: 62
SQ FT: 1,000
SALES: 2MM **Privately Held**
SIC: 8059 Personal care home, with health care

(P-21313)
MEDICAL INVESTMENT CO
Also Called: Rinaldi Convalescent Hospital
16553 Rinaldi St, Granada Hills (91344-3762)
PHONE..................818 360-1003
Fax: 818 363-8913
Glen Padama, *Principal*
Jemme Mendoza, *Administration*
EMP: 175
SQ FT: 25,000
SALES (est): 6MM **Privately Held**
SIC: 8059 8051 Convalescent home; skilled nursing care facilities

(P-21314)
MERRILL GARDENS LLC
1220 Suey Rd Bldg A, Santa Maria (93454-2687)
PHONE..................805 310-4102
Fax: 805 928-0922
Ole Vonfrausing-Borch,
Mary J Seymour, *Executive*
Laura Cardoza, *Corp Comm Staff*
Stephen Start,
Hershi Ruwanthi, *Director*
EMP: 70
SALES (est): 4MM **Privately Held**
SIC: 8059 Rest home, with health care

(P-21315)
MILLBRAE SERRA SANITARIUM
Also Called: Millbrae Srra Cnvalescent Hosp
150 Serra Ave, Millbrae (94030-2629)
P.O. Box 789 (94030-0789)
PHONE..................650 697-8386
Fax: 650 697-7529
Vincent A Muzzi, *President*
Mary Lou Panganiban, *Office Mgr*
EMP: 125
SQ FT: 10,000

SALES: 4.6MM **Privately Held**
SIC: 8059 8051 Nursing home, except skilled & intermediate care facility; convalescent home; skilled nursing care facilities

(P-21316)
MIRADA HILLS REHABILITATION
12200 La Mirada Blvd, La Mirada (90638-1306)
PHONE..................562 947-8691
Fax: 562 943-9834
Selina Stewart, *Exec Dir*
Becky Davila, *Persnl Dir*
Vic Garcia, *Hlthcr Dir*
EMP: 55
SALES (est): 10.2MM **Privately Held**
SIC: 8059 Nursing home, except skilled & intermediate care facility; convalescent home

(P-21317)
MISSION PROVIDER SERVICES INC
Also Called: M P S
2970 Innsbruck Dr Ste C, Redding (96003-9357)
PHONE..................530 222-5633
Fax: 530 222-5528
Dana Emerson, *President*
Kathleen Emmerson, *Corp Secy*
EMP: 200
SQ FT: 7,500
SALES: 4.5MM **Privately Held**
SIC: 8059 Home for the mentally retarded, exc. skilled or intermediate

(P-21318)
MONROVIA CONVALESCENT HOSPITAL
1220 Huntington Dr, Duarte (91010-2477)
PHONE..................626 359-6618
Fax: 626 301-0330
Lydia Cruz, *President*
EMP: 63
SQ FT: 15,000
SALES (est): 3MM **Privately Held**
SIC: 8059 Convalescent home

(P-21319)
MONTEREY PK CONVALESCENT HOSP
Also Called: Sun Mar Management Service
416 N Garfield Ave, Monterey Park (91754-1203)
PHONE..................626 280-0280
Fax: 626 280-9246
Irving Bauman, *President*
William Presnell, *Treasurer*
Frank Johnson, *Principal*
Eli Marmur, *Principal*
Will Valino, *Office Mgr*
EMP: 85
SQ FT: 22,000
SALES (est): 3.3MM **Privately Held**
SIC: 8059 8051 Convalescent home; skilled nursing care facilities

(P-21320)
MOYLES HEALTH CARE INC
Also Called: Merritt Mnor Convalescent Hosp
604 E Merritt Ave, Tulare (93274-2135)
PHONE..................559 686-1601
Fax: 559 686-8448
Shiriee Zimmerman, *Manager*
Marlene Luiz, *Administration*
Mark Medala, *Maintence Staff*
Lindsey Moyle, *Nursing Dir*
EMP: 100
SALES (corp-wide): 3MM **Privately Held**
SIC: 8059 8051 8062 Convalescent home; convalescent home with continuous nursing care; general medical & surgical hospitals
PA: Moyle's Health Care, Inc.
7323 Sage Ave
Yucca Valley CA

(P-21321)
MOYLES HEALTH CARE INC
Also Called: Browning Mnor Cnvalescent Hosp
729 Browning Rd, Delano (93215-9747)
PHONE..................661 725-2501

8059 - Nursing & Personal Care Facilities, NEC County (P-21322)

PRODUDUCTS & SERVICES SECTION

Fax: 661 725-6739
Rhonda Gale, *Administration*
Hermilinda Menoza, *Food Svc Dir*
Arturo Abalos, *Director*
EMP: 67
SALES (corp-wide): 3MM **Privately Held**
SIC: 8059 8051 Convalescent home; skilled nursing care facilities
PA: Moyle's Health Care, Inc.
7323 Sage Ave
Yucca Valley CA

(P-21322)
MOYLES HEALTH CARE INC
Also Called: Kaweah Manor Convalescent Hosp
37110 W Tulare Ave, Visalia (93277)
PHONE 559 732-2244
Fax: 559 732-0243
Caroline Norcross, *Administration*
EMP: 100
SALES (corp-wide): 3MM **Privately Held**
SIC: 8059 8051 8069 Convalescent home; skilled nursing care facilities; specialty hospitals, except psychiatric
PA: Moyle's Health Care, Inc.
7323 Sage Ave
Yucca Valley CA

(P-21323)
MT MIQUEL COVENANT VILLAGE
325 Kempton St, Spring Valley (91977-5810)
PHONE 619 479-4790
Rich Miller, *Director*
Pat Toth, *Admin Asst*
Laura Brinker, *Accountant*
EMP: 241
SQ FT: 316,465
SALES: 18.4MM
SALES (corp-wide): 3.3MM **Privately Held**
SIC: 8059 Rest home, with health care
PA: Covenant Retirement Communities, Inc.
5700 Old Orchard Rd
Skokie IL 60077
773 878-2294

(P-21324)
NEW VISA HEALTH SERVICES INC
3414 Preakness Ct, Fallbrook (92028-9096)
PHONE 760 723-0053
Robert Craig, *President*
EMP: 500
SALES (est): 4.2MM **Privately Held**
SIC: 8059 Nursing home, except skilled & intermediate care facility

(P-21325)
NEW VISTA HEALTH SERVICES
Also Called: New Vista Pst Act Care Cntr
1516 Sawtelle Blvd, Los Angeles (90025-3207)
PHONE 310 477-5501
Eugene Tipo, *Administration*
Marie Scramneto, *Records Dir*
EMP: 150
SALES (corp-wide): 17.2MM **Privately Held**
WEB: www.newvista.us
SIC: 8059 8051 Nursing home, except skilled & intermediate care facility; skilled nursing care facilities
PA: New Vista Health Services, Inc
1987 Vartikian Ave
Clovis CA 93611
559 298-3236

(P-21326)
NEW VISTA HEALTH SERVICES
Also Called: New Vsta Nrsing Rhbltation Ctr
8647 Fenwick St, Sunland (91040-1957)
PHONE 818 352-1421
Robert Craig, *President*
Alexis Remington-Perez, *Vice Pres*
Joel Waldman, *Administration*
Anoush Oganyuan, *Marketing Staff*
Maria Blanca, *Food Svc Dir*
EMP: 130
SALES (corp-wide): 17.2MM **Privately Held**
WEB: www.newvista.us
SIC: 8059 8361 Nursing home, except skilled & intermediate care facility; rehabilitation center, residential: health care incidental
PA: New Vista Health Services, Inc
1987 Vartikian Ave
Clovis CA 93611
559 298-3236

(P-21327)
NEWPORT SBACUTE HEALTHCARE CTR
Also Called: Milestone Health Care Center
2570 Newport Blvd, Costa Mesa (92627-1331)
PHONE 949 642-1974
Fax: 949 631-8681
Tony Ricci, *President*
Louie Rios, *Administration*
Beth Austria, *Technology*
Dale Ladd, *Finance*
Jennifer Morales, *Director*
EMP: 120
SQ FT: 22,000
SALES (est): 5.7MM **Privately Held**
WEB: www.milestonehealthcare.com
SIC: 8059 Nursing home, except skilled & intermediate care facility

(P-21328)
NORCAL CARE CENTERS INC
Also Called: Antioch Convalescent Hospital
1210 A St, Antioch (94509-2327)
PHONE 925 757-8787
Fax: 925 757-0702
Thaylene Sunga, *Manager*
Mark Callaway, *Manager*
EMP: 80
SALES (corp-wide): 2MM **Privately Held**
SIC: 8059 Convalescent home
PA: Norcal Care Centers Inc
3788 Fairway Dr
Cameron Park CA
530 677-9477

(P-21329)
NORTHERN CA CNGRGTNL RTMT
Also Called: Carmel Valley Manor
8545 Carmel Valley Rd, Carmel (93923-9556)
PHONE 831 624-1281
Fax: 831 625-9827
Roger D Bolgard, *Ch of Bd*
Jane Ipsen, *CEO*
Richard Boluga, *CFO*
Breck Tostevin, *Treasurer*
Lorraine Rivera, *Executive*
EMP: 162 **EST:** 1960
SQ FT: 196,800
SALES: 15MM **Privately Held**
WEB: www.cvmanor.com
SIC: 8059 Convalescent home

(P-21330)
NORTHERN CALIFORNIA PRESBYTERI
Also Called: Tamal Pais
501 Via Casitas Ofc, Greenbrae (94904-1958)
PHONE 415 464-1767
Fax: 415 464-1333
EMP: 100
SALES (corp-wide): 69.3MM **Privately Held**
WEB: www.contracostasbdc.com
SIC: 8059 8062 8051 8052 Rest home, with health care; general medical & surgical hospitals; skilled nursing care facilities; intermediate care facilities
PA: Northern California Presbyterian Homes And Services, Inc.
1525 Post St
San Francisco CA 94109
415 922-0200

(P-21331)
NORTHGATE CARE CENTER
40 Professional Ctr Pkwy, San Rafael (94903-2703)
PHONE 415 479-1230
Jeremy Zrimes, *President*
Ezekiyel Griffin, *Administration*
Mark Hansenn, *Administration*
Nancy Ruiz, *Bookkeeper*
Mel Preimesberger, *Marketing Staff*
EMP: 52 **EST:** 1970
SQ FT: 11,000
SALES (est): 3.7MM
SALES (corp-wide): 20.2MM **Privately Held**
WEB: www.iqcare.com
SIC: 8059 Convalescent home
PA: Independent Quality Care, Inc
3 Crow Canyon Ct
San Ramon CA 94583
925 855-0881

(P-21332)
NOTELLAGE CORPORATION
Also Called: College Vsta Convalescent Hosp
4681 Eagle Rock Blvd, Los Angeles (90041-3036)
PHONE 323 257-8151
Fax: 323 257-4886
Michael Stifere, *Administration*
Marisa Espavillo, *Records Dir*
Shirley Farmer, *Administration*
Jill Place, *Food Svc Dir*
Rudolfo Protacio, *Director*
EMP: 50
SQ FT: 10,000
SALES (est): 2.3MM **Privately Held**
SIC: 8059 Convalescent home

(P-21333)
OAKVIEW CONVALESCENT HOSPITAL
9166 Tujunga Canyon Blvd, Tujunga (91042-3498)
PHONE 818 352-4426
Fax: 818 951-5797
Ben Garrett, *President*
Christen Garrett, *Treasurer*
Clyde Casner, *Vice Pres*
Eva Casner, *Admin Sec*
Luis Phages, *Administration*
EMP: 50
SALES (est): 1.7MM **Privately Held**
SIC: 8059 Convalescent home

(P-21334)
ODYSSEY HEALTHCARE INC
74350 Country Club Dr, Palm Desert (92260-1608)
PHONE 760 674-0066
Fax: 760 674-0796
Candice Heldenbrand, *Manager*
EMP: 50
SALES (corp-wide): 7B **Publicly Held**
SIC: 8059 Convalescent home
HQ: Odyssey Healthcare, Inc.
7801 Mesquite Bend Dr # 105
Irving TX 75063

(P-21335)
OLYMPIA CONVALESCENT HOSPITAL
1100 S Alvarado St, Los Angeles (90006-4110)
PHONE 213 487-3000
Fax: 213 487-1909
Otto Schwartz, *Administration*
Sam Lidell, *Ltd Ptnr*
Andre Pollak, *Ltd Ptnr*
Amargarito Rodriguez, *Facilities Dir*
Aurea Ambrosio, *Director*
EMP: 115
SQ FT: 25,000
SALES (est): 4.2MM **Privately Held**
SIC: 8059 8051 Convalescent home; skilled nursing care facilities

(P-21336)
ORANGE COUNTY ROYALE CONVLSCNT
Also Called: Royale Hlth Care Mission Viejo
23228 Madero, Mission Viejo (92691-2706)
PHONE 949 458-6346
William Arellanes, *Director*
Jenny Forkey, *Manager*
EMP: 100
SQ FT: 54,500
SALES (corp-wide): 22.8MM **Privately Held**
WEB: www.royalehealth.com
SIC: 8059 Convalescent home
PA: Orange County Royale Convalescent Hospital, Inc
1030 W Warner Ave
Santa Ana CA 92707
714 546-6450

(P-21337)
ORANGE COUNTY ROYALE CONVLSCNT (PA)
1030 W Warner Ave, Santa Ana (92707-3147)
PHONE 714 546-6450
Fax: 714 546-8411
Mitchell Kantor, *President*
Donald Connelly, *Administration*
Grace Marqueses, *Info Tech Mgr*
Nellie Hernandez, *Human Resources*
Debra Sanchez, *Food Svc Dir*
EMP: 330
SQ FT: 87,000
SALES (est): 22.8MM **Privately Held**
WEB: www.royalehealth.com
SIC: 8059 8051 Convalescent home; skilled nursing care facilities

(P-21338)
ORINDA CONVALESCENT HOSPITAL
11 Altarinda Rd, Orinda (94563-2602)
PHONE 925 254-6500
Fax: 925 254-9063
David Cronin, *President*
Sue Hawkinson, *Social Dir*
Charles Speers, *Administration*
Jeff Mandel, *Director*
EMP: 52
SQ FT: 5,000
SALES (est): 3.9MM **Privately Held**
SIC: 8059 Convalescent home

(P-21339)
OUR HOUSE RESIDENTIAL CARE CTR
109 E Central Ave, Madera (93638-3109)
PHONE 559 674-8670
Fax: 559 674-5852
Carolyn Pipes, *Owner*
Jan Harold, *Executive*
EMP: 70
SALES (est): 2.5MM **Privately Held**
SIC: 8059 Rest home, with health care

(P-21340)
PACIFIC GROVE CNVALESCNET HOSP
200 Lighthouse Ave, Pacific Grove (93950-3022)
PHONE 831 375-2695
Fax: 831 647-9639
John Lund, *Owner*
Shahid Khan, *Director*
John P Jones, *Manager*
EMP: 60
SALES (est): 1.5MM **Privately Held**
SIC: 8059 Convalescent home

(P-21341)
PACIFIC HAVEN CONVALESCENT HM
Also Called: Pacific Haven Convalescent HM
12072 Trask Ave, Garden Grove (92843-3881)
PHONE 714 534-1942
Fax: 714 534-0967
Mike Uranga, *Administration*
Allan Chou, *Director*
EMP: 100
SALES (est): 9.7MM **Privately Held**
SIC: 8059 8051 Convalescent home; skilled nursing care facilities

(P-21342)
PACIFIC HOMES FOUNDATION
303 N Lennox Glenoaks1000 # 1000, Burbank (91502)
PHONE 818 729-8106
Fax: 818 729-8288
Gary Wheeler, *CEO*
Mort Swales, *CEO*
EMP: 70 **EST:** 2001
SALES: 1.3MM **Privately Held**
SIC: 8059 Nursing home, except skilled & intermediate care facility

PRODUCTS & SERVICES SECTION
8059 - Nursing & Personal Care Facilities, NEC County (P-21364)

(P-21343)
PALM HARBOR RESIDENCY LP
Also Called: Palmcrest North Convalescent
3501 Cedar Ave, Long Beach (90807-3809)
PHONE..................562 595-4551
Fax: 562 426-1099
Leonard Muskin, General Ptnr
EMP: 200 EST: 1971
SQ FT: 120,000
SALES: 2.5MM Privately Held
SIC: 8059 8052 Convalescent home; intermediate care facilities

(P-21344)
PANORAMA MADOWS NURSING CTR LP
Also Called: Sun-Air Convalescent Hospital
14857 Roscoe Blvd, Panorama City (91402-4617)
PHONE..................818 894-5707
Fax: 818 894-8151
Glen Bennett, Administration
Brenda Mandelbaum, Treasurer
Uri Mandelbaum, Vice Pres
Ofelia Rayes, Executive
EMP: 80 EST: 1969
SQ FT: 25,000
SALES (est): 6MM Privately Held
SIC: 8059 Convalescent home

(P-21345)
PARAMOUNT CONVALESCENT GROUP
8558 Rosecrans Ave, Paramount (90723-3644)
PHONE..................562 634-6895
Irving Bauman, President
Grace Yoon, Hlthcr Dir
Zeny Evaldez, Manager
EMP: 65
SQ FT: 12,000
SALES (est): 2.3MM Privately Held
SIC: 8059 Nursing home, except skilled & intermediate care facility

(P-21346)
PARK MARINO CONVALESCENT CTR
2585 E Washington Blvd, Pasadena (91107-1446)
PHONE..................626 463-4105
William Kite, Administration
EMP: 50 EST: 1966
SALES (est): 828K
SALES (corp-wide): 6.8MM Privately Held
SIC: 8059 8051 Convalescent home; skilled nursing care facilities
PA: Diversified Health Services (Del)
    136 Washington Ave
    Richmond CA 94801
    510 231-6200

(P-21347)
PILGRIM PLACE IN CLAREMONT (PA)
625 Mayflower Rd, Claremont (91711-4240)
PHONE..................909 399-5500
Fax: 909 399-5508
William R Cunitz, President
Sue Fairley, Vice Pres
Bernard Valek, Vice Pres
Joyce Yarborough, Vice Pres
Methodist Church, Executive
EMP: 175
SQ FT: 2,000
SALES: 19.5MM Privately Held
WEB: www.pilgrimplace.org
SIC: 8059 8051 8052 Rest home, with health care; skilled nursing care facilities; intermediate care facilities

(P-21348)
PINOLE ASSISTED LIVING CMNTY
Also Called: Pinole Senior Village
2850 Estates Ave, Pinole (94564-1416)
PHONE..................510 758-1122
Fax: 510 669-1649
Tim McDonough, President
Debra Savoie, Exec Dir
EMP: 54

SALES (est): 2.3MM Privately Held
SIC: 8059 Nursing home, except skilled & intermediate care facility

(P-21349)
PLACERVLLE PNES CNVLSCENT HOSP
1040 Marshall Way, Placerville (95667-5706)
PHONE..................530 622-3400
Fax: 530 622-1560
Jared Edmunds, Administration
Laurie Brady, Nursing Dir
Chandan Cheema, Director
EMP: 130
SQ FT: 40,000
SALES (est): 3.5MM
SALES (corp-wide): 99MM Privately Held
WEB: www.villadelrey.com
SIC: 8059 8051 Convalescent home; skilled nursing care facilities
HQ: Horizon West Healthcare, Inc.
    4020 Sierra College Blvd # 190
    Rocklin CA 95677
    916 624-6230

(P-21350)
PLEASANT VIEW CONVALESCENT HOS
22590 Voss Ave, Cupertino (95014-2627)
PHONE..................408 253-9034
Fax: 408 255-9148
Jack Easterday, President
Jet Rupisan, Administration
EMP: 140
SQ FT: 55,000
SALES (est): 4.5MM Privately Held
SIC: 8059 8069 8051 Convalescent home; specialty hospitals, except psychiatric; skilled nursing care facilities

(P-21351)
PORCHLIGHT INC
Also Called: Scan
3800 Kilroy Airport Way, Long Beach (90806-2494)
P.O. Box 22616 (90801-5616)
PHONE..................562 989-5100
Jay Greenberg, President
Jeff Spurrier, COO
Diana Yates, CFO
Michael Lombardi, Chief Mktg Ofcr
Perry Eng, Vice Pres
EMP: 100
SALES (est): 9.4MM
SALES (corp-wide): 302.8MM Privately Held
WEB: www.scanhealthplan.com
SIC: 8059 Personal care home, with health care
PA: Senior Care Action Network Foundation
    3800 Kilroy Airport Way
    Long Beach CA 90806
    562 989-5100

(P-21352)
PROTEAN HEALTH SERVICES INC
Also Called: Clinton Vlg Convalescent Hosp
1833 10th Ave, Oakland (94606-3023)
PHONE..................510 536-6512
Fax: 510 536-1450
Tom Duarte, President
Mary Duarte, Vice Pres
George Lamb, Administration
EMP: 90
SQ FT: 25,009
SALES (est): 3.5MM Privately Held
SIC: 8059 Convalescent home

(P-21353)
PRUITTHEALTH CORPORATION
Also Called: United Care Homes
1982 Camwood Ave, City of Industry (91748-4044)
PHONE..................626 810-5567
Susana Tubianosa, Branch Mgr
EMP: 50
SALES (corp-wide): 234.7MM Privately Held
WEB: www.peachtreechristianhospice.com
SIC: 8059 Convalescent home

PA: Pruitthealth Corporation
    209 E Doyle St
    Toccoa GA 30577
    706 886-8493

(P-21354)
RAFAEL CONVALESCENT HOSPITAL
234 N San Pedro Rd, San Rafael (94903-2858)
PHONE..................415 479-3450
Fax: 415 472-3723
Timothy J Egan, President
Michael Egan, Admin Sec
Shannon Bowman, Personnel
Sandra Carpenter, Education
Filmore Rodich, Medical Dir
EMP: 180
SQ FT: 9,000
SALES (est): 11.8MM Privately Held
SIC: 8059 8051 Convalescent home; skilled nursing care facilities

(P-21355)
RCC FACILITY INCORPORATED
Also Called: Rounseville Rehabilitation Ctr
210 40th Street Way, Oakland (94611-5612)
PHONE..................510 658-2041
Fax: 510 658-6353
Jack Easterday, President
Tyrone Snipes, Director
EMP: 70
SQ FT: 10,000
SALES (est): 6.7MM Privately Held
SIC: 8059 Convalescent home

(P-21356)
RECHE CANYON CONVALESCENT CTR
Also Called: Reche Cyn Rhabilation Hlth Ctr
1350 Reche Canyon Rd, Colton (92324-9528)
PHONE..................909 370-4411
Fax: 909 370-1846
Arch B Gilbert, President
Joseph E Gerahart, Corp Secy
Jean Claude Hage, Director
EMP: 200
SQ FT: 52,000
SALES (est): 6.1MM Privately Held
SIC: 8059 8069 8051 Convalescent home; specialty hospitals, except psychiatric; skilled nursing care facilities
PA: Interwest Medical Corporation
    3221 Hulen St Ste C
    Fort Worth TX 76107
    817 731-2743

(P-21357)
REDLANDS CMNTY HOSP FOUNDATION
Also Called: Asistencia Villa
1875 Barton Rd, Redlands (92373-5308)
PHONE..................909 793-1382
Ron Dahlgren, Manager
EMP: 101
SALES (corp-wide): 2.8MM Privately Held
WEB: www.redlandshospital.com
SIC: 8059 8051 8093 Convalescent home; skilled nursing care facilities; rehabilitation center, outpatient treatment
PA: Redlands Community Hospital Foundation
    350 Terracina Blvd
    Redlands CA 92373
    909 335-5540

(P-21358)
REDWOOD CONVALESCENT HOSPITAL
22103 Redwood Rd, Castro Valley (94546-7173)
PHONE..................510 537-8848
Fax: 510 537-3830
Frank V Kreske MD, President
Elizabeth Kreske, Vice Pres
EMP: 56
SQ FT: 10,000
SALES (est): 4MM Privately Held
SIC: 8059 Convalescent home

(P-21359)
REYNOLDS HEALTH INDUSTRIES
Also Called: Skylight Convalescent Center
1201 Walnut Ave, Long Beach (90813-3822)
PHONE..................562 591-7621
Fax: 562 591-3292
Caul Murayama, President
Vicki Reynolds, Vice Pres
EMP: 70
SQ FT: 21,000
SALES: 2.1MM Privately Held
SIC: 8059 Convalescent home

(P-21360)
RIVER OAK CENTER FOR CHILDREN
5445 Laurel Hills Dr, Sacramento (95841-3105)
PHONE..................916 550-5600
EMP: 94
SALES (corp-wide): 13.5MM Privately Held
SIC: 8059 8063
PA: River Oak Center For Children
    5445 Laurel Hills Dr
    Sacramento CA 95841
    916 609-5100

(P-21361)
RIVERSIDE HEALTH CARE CORP
Also Called: Scenic Circle Care Center
1611 Scenic Dr, Modesto (95355-4907)
PHONE..................209 523-5667
Fax: 209 523-0345
Jim Dickinson, Branch Mgr
EMP: 80
SALES (corp-wide): 8.5MM Privately Held
SIC: 8059 Nursing home, except skilled & intermediate care facility
PA: Riverside Health Care Corporation
    1469 Humboldt Rd Ste 175
    Chico CA 95928
    530 897-5100

(P-21362)
RIVERSIDE HEALTH CARE CORP (PA)
1469 Humboldt Rd Ste 175, Chico (95928-9204)
PHONE..................530 897-5100
Sharon Jennings Kearns, CEO
James Kline, Controller
EMP: 60
SQ FT: 9,000
SALES (est): 8.5MM Privately Held
SIC: 8059 Convalescent home

(P-21363)
ROCK CANYON HEALTHCARE INC
Also Called: Riverwalk PST-Cute Rhblitation
27101 Puerta Real Ste 450, Mission Viejo (92691-8566)
PHONE..................949 487-9500
Dave Jorgensen, President
Soon Burnam, Treasurer
Beverly Wittekind, Admin Sec
EMP: 288 EST: 2014
SALES (est): 1.6MM
SALES (corp-wide): 1.3B Publicly Held
SIC: 8059 Personal care home, with health care
PA: The Ensign Group Inc
    27101 Puerta Real Ste 450
    Mission Viejo CA 92691
    949 487-9500

(P-21364)
SABU ENTERPRISES INC
Also Called: Idle Acres Convalescent Hosp
5044 Buffington Rd, El Monte (91732-1466)
PHONE..................626 443-1351
Solomon Silverberg, President
Uri Mendelbaum, Vice Pres
Gary Schlecter, Director
Barry Silverberg, Director
EMP: 50
SQ FT: 17,000
SALES (est): 2MM Privately Held
SIC: 8059 Convalescent home

8059 - Nursing & Personal Care Facilities, NEC County (P-21365)

(P-21365)
SAN DIEGO CENTER FOR CHILDREN (PA)
3002 Armstrong St, San Diego (92111-5702)
PHONE.................................858 277-9550
Fax: 858 279-2763
Moises Baron, CEO
Erica Gomez-Aranda, Program Mgr
Stewart Holzman, Program Mgr
Carrie Kintz, Program Mgr
Jeff Goodman, Regional Mgr
EMP: 90
SQ FT: 38,000
SALES: 20.9MM Privately Held
WEB: www.centerforchildren.org
SIC: 8059 8361 Personal care home, with health care; residential care

(P-21366)
SAN MARINO MANOR
6812 Oak Ave, San Gabriel (91775-2099)
PHONE.................................626 446-5263
Ruth Jackson, Administration
Solomon Silberberg, Treasurer
Mike Albert, Administration
Mike Elbert, Administration
Barry Silberberg, Administration
EMP: 50
SALES: 3MM Privately Held
SIC: 8059 Convalescent home

(P-21367)
SANTA ANITA CONVALESCENT HOSPI
5522 Gracewood Ave, Temple City (91780)
PHONE.................................626 579-0310
Miriam Weiss, President
Jacob Kasirer, Vice Pres
Lupe Hinojos, Office Mgr
Veronica Gonzales, Education
Norman Chein, Director
EMP: 150
SQ FT: 88,615
SALES (est): 5.2MM
SALES (corp-wide): 62.1MM Privately Held
WEB: www.goldenstatehealth.com
SIC: 8059 Convalescent home
PA: Golden State Health Centers, Inc.
   13347 Ventura Blvd
   Sherman Oaks CA 91423
   818 385-3200

(P-21368)
SECROM INC
Also Called: Carson Senior Assisted Living
345 E Carson St, Carson (90745-2709)
PHONE.................................310 830-4010
Shlomo Rechnitz, CEO
EMP: 55
SALES (est): 536.7K Privately Held
SIC: 8059 Rest home, with health care

(P-21369)
SHASTA CONVALESCENT CENTER
Also Called: Shasta Convalescent Hospital
3550 Churn Creek Rd, Redding (96002-2718)
PHONE.................................530 222-3630
Fax: 530 222-3638
Donald Ostrom, President
Marlene Ostrom, Vice Pres
Karissa King, Director
Nina Perry, Director
EMP: 180
SQ FT: 38,000
SALES (est): 4.6MM Privately Held
SIC: 8059 8051 Convalescent home; nursing home, except skilled & intermediate care facility; skilled nursing care facilities

(P-21370)
SIERRA VALLEY REHAB CENTER
301 W Putnam Ave, Porterville (93257-3429)
PHONE.................................559 784-7375
Steve Brown, Administration
Emmanuel B David, President
Ramona Villaluz, Treasurer
Christopher Avelino, Administration
Steve Browne, Administration
EMP: 170
SQ FT: 26,000
SALES (est): 6.4MM Privately Held
SIC: 8059 8051 Convalescent home; skilled nursing care facilities

(P-21371)
SILVERADO SENIOR LIVING INC (PA)
6400 Oak Cyn Ste 200, Irvine (92618-5233)
PHONE.................................949 240-7200
Fax: 949 240-7270
George L Chapman, CEO
Rick Barker, President
Kathy Greene, President
Loren B Shook, President
Thomas Croal, CFO
EMP: 65 EST: 1996
SQ FT: 65,000
SALES (est): 182.6MM Privately Held
WEB: www.silveradosenior.com
SIC: 8059 Personal care home, with health care

(P-21372)
SILVERADO SENIOR LIVING INC
Also Called: Sierra Vista Memory Care Cmnty
125 W Sierra Madre Ave, Azusa (91702-2023)
P.O. Box 636 (91702-0636)
PHONE.................................626 650-9891
Fax: 626 812-9112
Bida Gwinn, Manager
Maria Torres, Admin Asst
Luis Miranda, Food Svc Dir
Richard Goodman, Hlthcr Dir
EMP: 54
SALES (corp-wide): 182.6MM Privately Held
WEB: www.silveradosenior.com
SIC: 8059 8051 Personal care home, with health care; skilled nursing care facilities
PA: Senior Silverado Living Inc
   6400 Oak Cyn Ste 200
   Irvine CA 92618
   949 240-7200

(P-21373)
SILVERADO SENIOR LIVING INC
Also Called: Newport Mesa Memory Care Cmnty
350 W Bay St, Costa Mesa (92627-2020)
PHONE.................................949 945-0189
Michelle Egrer, Administration
Lee Riggs, COO
Roberta Nelson, Executive
Raul Parra, Opers Mgr
Shannon Ingram, Mktg Dir
EMP: 70
SQ FT: 20,331
SALES (corp-wide): 182.6MM Privately Held
WEB: www.silveradosenior.com
SIC: 8059 Rest home, with health care
PA: Senior Silverado Living Inc
   6400 Oak Cyn Ste 200
   Irvine CA 92618
   949 240-7200

(P-21374)
SILVERADO SENIOR LIVING INC
Also Called: Huntington Memory Care Cmnty
1118 N Stoneman Ave, Alhambra (91801-1007)
PHONE.................................626 872-3941
Fax: 626 281-0777
Vida Gwin, Administration
Tamra Mitchell, Human Res Dir
Heidi Rohland, Recruiter
EMP: 50
SALES (corp-wide): 182.6MM Privately Held
WEB: www.silveradosenior.com
SIC: 8059 Personal care home, with health care
PA: Senior Silverado Living Inc
   6400 Oak Cyn Ste 200
   Irvine CA 92618
   949 240-7200

(P-21375)
SILVERADO SENIOR LIVING INC
Also Called: Escondido Memory Care Cmnty
1500 Borden Rd, Escondido (92026-2373)
PHONE.................................760 456-5137
Fax: 760 737-8184
Jean Busher, Administration
Jolene Farish, Executive
Mark Leestma, Executive
Thomas V Croal, Technology
Neftali Grajales, Director
EMP: 91
SQ FT: 33,000
SALES (corp-wide): 182.6MM Privately Held
WEB: www.silveradosenior.com
SIC: 8059 Rest home, with health care
PA: Senior Silverado Living Inc
   6400 Oak Cyn Ste 200
   Irvine CA 92618
   949 240-7200

(P-21376)
SILVERADO SENIOR LIVING INC
Also Called: Encinitas Memory Care Cmnty
335 Saxony Rd, Encinitas (92024-2723)
PHONE.................................760 270-9917
Dina Trester, Director
Thomas V Croal, CFO
Carol Daluz,
EMP: 70
SALES (corp-wide): 182.6MM Privately Held
WEB: www.silveradosenior.com
SIC: 8059 Personal care home, with health care
PA: Senior Silverado Living Inc
   6400 Oak Cyn Ste 200
   Irvine CA 92618
   949 240-7200

(P-21377)
SILVERADO SENIOR LIVING INC
Also Called: Beverly Pl Memory Care Cmnty
330 N Hayworth Ave, Los Angeles (90048-2702)
PHONE.................................323 984-7313
Beth Medina, Principal
EMP: 80
SALES (corp-wide): 182.6MM Privately Held
SIC: 8059 Personal care home, with health care
PA: Senior Silverado Living Inc
   6400 Oak Cyn Ste 200
   Irvine CA 92618
   949 240-7200

(P-21378)
SILVERSCREEN HEALTHCARE INC
Also Called: Asistencia Villa Rehab & Care
1875 Barton Rd, Redlands (92373-5308)
PHONE.................................909 793-1382
Philip Weinberger, CEO
Marylynn Mahan, CFO
Tracey Johns, Exec Dir
EMP: 135 EST: 2010
SALES (est): 4.9MM Privately Held
SIC: 8059 Convalescent home

(P-21379)
SISTERS OF NAZARETH
Also Called: Nazareth House
245 Nova Albion Way, San Rafael (94903-3539)
PHONE.................................415 479-8282
Fax: 415 479-8824
Sister Rose Hoye, Principal
Sister John Berchmans, Administration
Sloan Vandamme, Info Tech Mgr
Jonnie Manker, Bookkeeper
EMP: 91
SALES (est): 4.7MM Privately Held
SIC: 8059 8051 Rest home, with health care; skilled nursing care facilities

(P-21380)
SPRINGHILL MANOR REHABILITATIO
Also Called: Spring Hl Mnor Cnvlescent Hosp
355 Joerschke Dr, Grass Valley (95945-5288)
PHONE.................................530 273-7247
Fax: 530 273-0506
Clifford E Vixie, President
Patricia Vixie, Treasurer
Gregory Vixie, Vice Pres
Brian Collier, Administration
Lori Fuller, Hlthcr Dir
EMP: 50 EST: 1966
SQ FT: 14,000
SALES: 8.5MM Privately Held
SIC: 8059 Convalescent home

(P-21381)
SSC PITTSBURG OPERATING CO LP
Also Called: Diamond Ridge Healthcare Ctr
2351 Loveridge Rd, Pittsburg (94565-5117)
PHONE.................................925 427-4444
Fax: 925 427-1255
Wayne M Sanner,
Marina Icabalceta, Manager
EMP: 5025
SALES: 14MM
SALES (corp-wide): 1B Privately Held
SIC: 8059 Nursing home, except skilled & intermediate care facility
PA: Savaseniorcare, Llc
   1 Ravinia Dr Ste 1500
   Atlanta GA 30346
   770 829-5100

(P-21382)
ST FRANCIS EXTENDED CARE INC
718 Bartlett Ave, Hayward (94541-3698)
PHONE.................................510 785-3630
Fax: 510 785-5606
Sally Rapp, President
Roland Rapp, Vice Pres
Elizabeth Gonzalez, Accountant
Vickie Baldoza, Personnel
EMP: 67
SQ FT: 13,120
SALES: 5.6MM Privately Held
SIC: 8059 Convalescent home

(P-21383)
ST FRANCIS HEIGHTS CONVALES
35 Escuela Dr, Daly City (94015-4003)
PHONE.................................650 755-9515
Fax: 650 755-2154
Glen Gotter, Director
Michelle Palacana, Executive
Evelyn Goddard, Principal
Kathleen Lovato, Administration
Patrick Cosby, Info Svcs Mgr
EMP: 100 EST: 1967
SQ FT: 12,000
SALES: 5.4MM Privately Held
WEB: www.sfhouseprices.net
SIC: 8059 8051 Convalescent home; skilled nursing care facilities

(P-21384)
ST JOHNS RETIREMENT VILLAGE (PA)
Also Called: STOLLWOOD CONVALESCENT HOSPITA
135 Woodland Ave, Woodland (95695-2701)
PHONE.................................530 662-9674
Fax: 530 662-4639
John Prichard, Administration
Theresa Ely, CFO
Marilyn Mitchell, Treasurer
Charlotte Frank, Social Dir
Siv Winberg, Controller
EMP: 88
SALES: 9.7MM Privately Held
SIC: 8059 8051 8361 Convalescent home; convalescent home with continuous nursing care; geriatric residential care; home for the aged; rest home, with health care incidental

(P-21385)
STOCKTON EDSON HEALTHCARE CORP
Also Called: GOOD SAMARITAN REHAB AND CARE
1630 N Edison St, Stockton (95204-5633)
PHONE.................................209 948-8762
Emanuel Bernabe, President
Gilda Dizon, Corp Secy
Sedy Demesa, Exec VP
EMP: 100
SQ FT: 4,000
SALES: 8.4MM Privately Held
SIC: 8059 8051 Nursing home, except skilled & intermediate care facility; skilled nursing care facilities

PRODUCTS & SERVICES SECTION
8059 - Nursing & Personal Care Facilities, NEC County (P-21407)

(P-21386)
SUN MAR NURSING CENTER INC
Also Called: Sun Mar Management Services
1720 W Orange Ave, Anaheim (92804-2699)
PHONE.................................714 776-1720
Fax: 714 776-1154
Chris William, *Administration*
Blaine Hendrickson, *President*
Bill Presnell, *Corp Secy*
Kent Burkey, *Administration*
Andrew Litchman, *Administration*
EMP: 75
SQ FT: 10,000
SALES: 6.1MM **Privately Held**
SIC: 8059 Nursing home, except skilled & intermediate care facility

(P-21387)
SUNNY RETIREMENT HOME
22445 Cupertino Rd, Cupertino (95014-1052)
PHONE.................................408 454-5600
Fax: 408 255-6015
Sally Plank, *Exec Dir*
Debbie Gonzalez, *Human Resources*
EMP: 140 EST: 1964
SQ FT: 112,000
SALES: 1.7MM **Privately Held**
WEB: www.sunny4care.com
SIC: 8059 Rest home, with health care

(P-21388)
SYCAMORE PARK CARE CENTER LLC
Also Called: SYCAMORE PARK CONVALESCENT HOSPITAL
4585 N Figueroa St, Los Angeles (90065-3026)
PHONE.................................323 223-3441
Fax: 323 223-9568
Robert Snukal, *President*
Consolacion Padama, *Corp Secy*
Manuel Padama, *Vice Pres*
Sheila Snukal, *Vice Pres*
Zenaida Monelar, *Social Dir*
▲ EMP: 80
SQ FT: 20,000
SALES (est): 3.2MM
SALES (corp-wide): 9.6B **Publicly Held**
WEB: www.skilledhealthcare.com
SIC: 8059 8051 Convalescent home; skilled nursing care facilities
PA: Genesis Healthcare, Inc.
101 E State St
Kennett Square PA 19348
610 444-6350

(P-21389)
T C H P INC
Also Called: PALM TERRACE CARE CENTER
11162 Palm Terrace Ln, Riverside (92505-2338)
PHONE.................................951 687-7330
Jeremy Jergensen, *Administration*
Mariela Wilson, *Social Dir*
Jenny Ortiz, *Office Mgr*
David Gunnell, *Administration*
Roxanne Lamas, *Hlthcr Dir*
EMP: 75
SALES: 10.3MM
SALES (corp-wide): 60.3MM **Privately Held**
WEB: www.palmterracecare.com
SIC: 8059 Convalescent home
PA: North American Health Care, Inc.
32836 Pacific Coast Hwy
Dana Point CA 92629
949 240-2423

(P-21390)
TEMPLE PARK CONVALESCENT HOSP
2411 W Temple St, Los Angeles (90026-4899)
PHONE.................................213 380-2035
Fax: 213 380-3283
Barry Kohn, *President*
Gina White, *Records Dir*
Toby Kohn, *Vice Pres*
Rosebell Liong, *Social Dir*
Helene Kohn, *Administration*
EMP: 77
SALES (est): 4.7MM **Privately Held**
SIC: 8059 Convalescent home

(P-21391)
TJD LLC
Also Called: Anberry Rehabilitation Hosp
1685 Shaffer Rd, Atwater (95301-4456)
PHONE.................................209 357-3420
Donald W Gormly Jr,
Becky York, *Executive*
Timothy Johnston, *Medical Dir*
Jerry Holloway,
EMP: 140
SQ FT: 40,000
SALES: 11.9MM **Privately Held**
WEB: www.anberryhospital.com
SIC: 8059 8051 8093 Nursing home, except skilled & intermediate care facility; convalescent home with continuous nursing care; rehabilitation center, outpatient treatment

(P-21392)
TRANQUILITY INCORPORATED
Also Called: SAN MIGUEL VILLA
1050 San Miguel Rd, Concord (94518-2094)
PHONE.................................925 825-4280
Fax: 925 676-1649
Velda Pierce, *CEO*
Gary Miller, *Director*
EMP: 180
SQ FT: 20,000
SALES: 15.7MM **Privately Held**
SIC: 8059 8051 Convalescent home; skilled nursing care facilities

(P-21393)
TRINITY HEALTH SYSTEMS
Also Called: Valley Palms Convalescent Hosp
13400 Sherman Way, North Hollywood (91605-4415)
PHONE.................................818 983-0103
Fax: 818 982-4007
Roland Santos, *Manager*
Cathy Macadam, *Office Mgr*
Danielle Avila, *Food Svc Dir*
Shovek Broyadjian, *Director*
EMP: 100
SALES (corp-wide): 10.1MM **Privately Held**
SIC: 8059 8051 Convalescent home; skilled nursing care facilities
PA: Trinity Health Systems
14318 Ohio St
Baldwin Park CA 91706
626 960-1971

(P-21394)
TWO PALMS NURSING CENTER
150 Bellefontaine St, Pasadena (91105-3102)
PHONE.................................323 681-4615
Marthann Demchuk, *Manager*
EMP: 100
SALES (corp-wide): 10.1MM **Privately Held**
SIC: 8059 8051 Convalescent home; skilled nursing care facilities
PA: Two Palms Nursing Center, Inc.
2637 E Washington Blvd
Pasadena CA 91107
626 798-8991

(P-21395)
TWO PALMS NURSING CENTER INC (PA)
2637 E Washington Blvd, Pasadena (91107-1412)
PHONE.................................626 798-8991
Fax: 626 798-5086
Marthann Demchuk, *CEO*
Peter MA, *Director*
Nidia Evangilias, *Manager*
EMP: 50
SALES (est): 10.1MM **Privately Held**
SIC: 8059 Convalescent home

(P-21396)
TWO PALMS NURSING CENTER INC
Also Called: Marlinda Imperial Hospital
150 Bellefontaine St, Pasadena (91105-3102)
PHONE.................................626 796-1103
Fax: 323 796-0655
Zeny Macalino, *Office Mgr*
Evangeline Molnar, *Administration*
Norman Chien, *Director*
Nancy Pablo, *Director*
EMP: 85
SQ FT: 28,955
SALES (corp-wide): 10.1MM **Privately Held**
SIC: 8059 8051 Convalescent home; skilled nursing care facilities
PA: Two Palms Nursing Center, Inc.
2637 E Washington Blvd
Pasadena CA 91107
626 798-8991

(P-21397)
TZIPPY CARE INC
Also Called: Western Convalescent Hospital
2190 W Adams Blvd, Los Angeles (90018-2039)
PHONE.................................323 737-7778
Fax: 323 735-7825
David Friedman, *President*
Ken Lehman, *Corp Secy*
Aaron Friedman, *Vice Pres*
Susan Scully, *Executive*
Richard Powell, *Director*
EMP: 95
SALES: 10.4MM **Privately Held**
SIC: 8059 Convalescent home

(P-21398)
UNITED CEREBRAL PALSY
Also Called: Ucp Dronfield North
13272 Dronfield Ave, Sylmar (91342-2961)
PHONE.................................818 364-5911
Liz McLaughlin, *Administration*
EMP: 70
SALES (corp-wide): 27.5MM **Privately Held**
SIC: 8059 Home for the mentally retarded, exc. skilled or intermediate
PA: United Cerebral Palsy/Spastic Children's Foundation Of Los Angeles And Ventura Counties
6430 Independence Ave
Woodland Hills CA 91367
818 782-2211

(P-21399)
UNITED CONVALESCENT FACILITIES
Also Called: University Park Healthcare Ctr
230 E Adams Blvd, Los Angeles (90011-1426)
PHONE.................................626 629-6950
Fax: 213 748-3299
Doug Easton, *Owner*
Barbara O'Connor, *Administration*
EMP: 80
SQ FT: 1,300
SALES: 4MM **Privately Held**
SIC: 8059 Nursing home, except skilled & intermediate care facility

(P-21400)
UNITED CP/S CHLDRNS FNDN LA
6430 Independence Ave, Woodland Hills (91367-2607)
PHONE.................................818 782-2211
Mae Stephenson, *General Mgr*
Rudy Galicia, *General Mgr*
EMP: 70
SALES (corp-wide): 27.5MM **Privately Held**
SIC: 8059 Personal care home, with health care
PA: United Cerebral Palsy/Spastic Children's Foundation Of Los Angeles And Ventura Counties
6430 Independence Ave
Woodland Hills CA 91367
818 782-2211

(P-21401)
UNITED MEDICAL MANAGEMENT INC
Also Called: Valley Healthcare
1680 N Waterman Ave, San Bernardino (92404-5113)
PHONE.................................909 886-5291
Alan Hull, *Administration*
Sean Jara, *Administration*
Lisa Dixon, *Nursing Dir*
Magdi Elsaadi, *Director*
EMP: 125
SQ FT: 30,000
SALES (est): 5.9MM **Privately Held**
WEB: www.healthcare-centers.com
SIC: 8059 8051 8322 Convalescent home; skilled nursing care facilities; rehabilitation services

(P-21402)
UNLIMITED FRONTIERS INC
45 N Lincoln St, Redlands (92374-4146)
P.O. Box 7722 (92375-0722)
PHONE.................................909 793-0142
Dennis Jackson, *Manager*
EMP: 70
SALES (corp-wide): 3.3MM **Privately Held**
SIC: 8059 8069 Home for the mentally retarded, exc. skilled or intermediate; specialty hospitals, except psychiatric
PA: Unlimited Frontiers, Inc.
220 Nordina St
Redlands CA
909 793-0142

(P-21403)
UPLAND COMMUNITY CARE INC
Also Called: Upland Rehabilitation Care Ctr
1221 E Arrow Hwy, Upland (91786-4911)
PHONE.................................909 985-1903
Owen Hammond, *CEO*
EMP: 99
SALES (est): 3.4MM
SALES (corp-wide): 1.3B **Publicly Held**
SIC: 8059 Convalescent home
PA: The Ensign Group Inc
27101 Puerta Real Ste 450
Mission Viejo CA 92691
949 487-9500

(P-21404)
US HEALTHCARE PARTNERS INC
Also Called: Health Information Partners
4041 Macarthur Blvd # 360, Newport Beach (92660-2531)
P.O. Box 10129 (92658-0129)
PHONE.................................949 261-5000
Joseph A Farris, *CEO*
EMP: 125
SALES: 7MM **Privately Held**
WEB: www.hip-inc.com
SIC: 8059 Rest home, with health care

(P-21405)
VACAVLLE CNVALESCENT REHAB CTR
585 Nut Tree Ct, Vacaville (95687-3353)
PHONE.................................707 449-8000
Joe Nicolli, *President*
Wendy C Kelly, *Admin Sec*
Nancy Hopp, *Administration*
Lee Morris, *Purchasing*
Aby Hood, *Phys Thrpy Dir*
EMP: 120
SQ FT: 38,000
SALES (est): 6MM **Privately Held**
SIC: 8059 Convalescent home

(P-21406)
VALENCIA HEALTH CARE INC
Also Called: Santa Clarita Convalescent HM
23801 Newhall Ave, Newhall (91321-3126)
PHONE.................................661 254-2425
Fax: 661 255-3709
Ishkhan Khatchadurian, *President*
Armand Masongsong, *Director*
EMP: 75 EST: 1969
SQ FT: 24,000
SALES: 3.9MM **Privately Held**
SIC: 8059 Convalescent home

(P-21407)
VALLE VSTA CNVLESCENT HOSP INC
1025 W 2nd Ave, Escondido (92025-3839)
PHONE.................................760 745-1288
Fax: 760 745-4346
Kristina Kuivon, *CEO*
EMP: 85 EST: 1961
SQ FT: 19,000

8059 - Nursing & Personal Care Facilities, NEC County (P-21408)

SALES (est): 3MM
SALES (corp-wide): 188.1MM Privately Held
SIC: 8059 Convalescent home; nursing home, except skilled & intermediate care facility
PA: Covenant Care, Llc
  27071 Aliso Creek Rd # 100
  Aliso Viejo CA 92656
  949 349-1200

(P-21408)
VALLEY WEST HEALTH CARE INC (PA)
Also Called: Valley West Care Center
1224 E St, Williams (95987-5187)
P.O. Box 1059 (95987-1059)
  PHONE 530 473-5321
  Fax: 530 473-5172
Sharon Jennings, *President*
Gladys Jennings, *CFO*
Jared Garrison, *Director*
EMP: 52
SQ FT: 32,000
SALES (est): 5.4MM Privately Held
SIC: 8059 Convalescent home

(P-21409)
VAN NUYS CARE CENTER INC
Also Called: Lake Balboa Care Center
16955 Vanowen St, Van Nuys (91406-4542)
  PHONE 818 343-0700
Chad Thornton, *President*
John Thornton, *President*
Wayne A Evans, *Vice Pres*
Carina Arceo, *Exec Dir*
Ana Rosa Aguilar, *Director*
EMP: 88
SQ FT: 12,500
SALES (est): 4.1MM Privately Held
SIC: 8059 8051 Convalescent home; skilled nursing care facilities

(P-21410)
VICTORIA POST ACUTE CARE
654 S Anza St, El Cajon (92020-6602)
  PHONE 619 440-5005
Ed Dove, *Administration*
Connie Reyes, *Food Svc Dir*
John Gaidry, *Director*
Michelle Cook, *Manager*
Joan Fehling, *Manager*
EMP: 150
SALES (est): 6.6MM Privately Held
SIC: 8059 8361 Convalescent home; rehabilitation center, residential: health care incidental

(P-21411)
VIENNA CONVALESCENT HOSPITAL
800 S Ham Ln, Lodi (95242-3543)
  PHONE 209 368-7141
  Fax: 209 368-2163
Kenneth Heffel, *President*
Teresa Stocker, *CFO*
Diana Heffel, *Admin Sec*
David Duncan, *Director*
Corey Wright, *Manager*
EMP: 131
SQ FT: 25,000
SALES: 827MM Privately Held
SIC: 8059 Convalescent home

(P-21412)
VILLA DE LA MAR INC
Also Called: Bel Vista Convalescent Hosp
5001 E Anaheim St, Long Beach (90804-3214)
  PHONE 562 494-5001
  Fax: 562 498-0834
Allen Anderson, *Principal*
Sherry Ballance, *Branch Mgr*
Barbara Dana, *Office Mgr*
Clayton Dejong, *Director*
EMP: 50
SALES (corp-wide): 4.2MM Privately Held
WEB: www.villadelafontaine.com
SIC: 8059 Convalescent home
PA: Villa De La Mar, Inc
  3901 E 4th St
  Long Beach CA

(P-21413)
VILLA SIENA
1855 Miramonte Ave 117, Mountain View (94040-4029)
  PHONE 650 961-6484
  Fax: 650 961-6254
Corrine Bernard, *CEO*
Margaret McDonnell, *Treasurer*
Aldijana Kuduzovic, *Office Admin*
Mary Constant, *Admin Asst*
Mary Ellen Barber, *Nursing Dir*
EMP: 60
SQ FT: 40,000
SALES: 1MM Privately Held
WEB: www.villasiena.com
SIC: 8059 Nursing home, except skilled & intermediate care facility

(P-21414)
VINCENT HAYLEY ENTERPRISES
Also Called: St Vincent Health Care
1810 N Fair Oaks Ave, Pasadena (91103-1619)
  PHONE 626 398-8182
  Fax: 626 398-0473
Rob Barrett, *President*
Cipriano Baustista, *Administration*
Janelle Aguerre, *Human Res Dir*
Cecilia Salvador, *Corp Comm Staff*
Ashley McGinty, *Hlthcr Dir*
EMP: 75
SALES (est): 7.2MM Privately Held
SIC: 8059 Nursing home, except skilled & intermediate care facility

(P-21415)
VISTA COVE CARE CENTER
250 March St, Santa Paula (93060-2512)
  PHONE 805 525-7134
Floyd Rhoades, *President*
Bonatarte Liu, *Treasurer*
Sean Brophy, *Admin Sec*
Lupe Barrozo, *Sls & Mktg Exec*
Marcela Rodriguez, *Manager*
EMP: 100
SALES (est): 4.6MM Privately Held
SIC: 8059 Nursing home, except skilled & intermediate care facility

(P-21416)
VISTA DEL SOL HEALTH SERVICES
Also Called: VISTA DEL SOL CARE CENTER
11620 W Washington Blvd, Los Angeles (90066-5916)
  PHONE 310 390-9045
  Fax: 310 398-9667
James R Preimesberger, *CEO*
Shamim Shakibai, *Director*
EMP: 80
SQ FT: 25,000
SALES: 4.4MM Privately Held
SIC: 8059 Convalescent home; personal care home, with health care

(P-21417)
VISTA PACIFICA ENTERPRISES INC
Also Called: Vista Pcifica Convalescent Ctr
3662 Pacific Ave, Riverside (92509-1923)
  PHONE 951 682-4867
  Fax: 909 274-4696
Cheryl Jumonville, *Director*
EMP: 200
SALES (corp-wide): 13.3MM Privately Held
SIC: 8059 Convalescent home
PA: Vista Pacifica Enterprises, Inc.
  3674 Pacific Ave
  Riverside CA 92509
  951 682-4833

(P-21418)
VOCH INC
Also Called: Villa Oaks Convalescent Homes
1920 N Fair Oaks Ave, Pasadena (91103-1623)
  PHONE 626 798-1111
  Fax: 626 345-1901
Pompeyo Rosales, *Owner*
Lotia Arsero, *Executive*
Rose Rodriguez, *Human Res Dir*
Robert Yujuico, *Facilities Dir*
Donald Plance, *Director*

EMP: 60
SQ FT: 16,000
SALES (est): 2.5MM
SALES (corp-wide): 3.2MM Privately Held
WEB: www.slch.com
SIC: 8059 Convalescent home
PA: Slch, Inc
  1920 N Fair Oaks Ave
  Pasadena CA 91103
  626 798-0558

(P-21419)
WEST COAST HOSPITALS INC
Also Called: Valley Convalescent Hospital
919 Freedom Blvd, Watsonville (95076-3804)
P.O. Box 1242 (95077-1242)
  PHONE 831 722-3581
  Fax: 831 722-4805
Richard Murphy, *Principal*
Frank Ravago, *Director*
EMP: 65
SQ FT: 20,000
SALES (est): 6.5MM Privately Held
SIC: 8059 Convalescent home

(P-21420)
WESTMINSTER GARDENS
1420 Santo Domingo Ave, Duarte (91010-2698)
  PHONE 626 359-2571
  Fax: 626 358-7566
Judy Thorndyke, *Exec Dir*
Mimi Brown, *Director*
Mary Anderson, *Manager*
EMP: 54
SQ FT: 1,306,800
SALES (est): 6.3MM Privately Held
WEB: www.westgardens.org
SIC: 8059 Rest home, with health care; nursing home, except skilled & intermediate care facility

(P-21421)
WICORO INC (HQ)
Also Called: COLONIAL MANOR CONVALESCENT HOSPITAL
919 N Sunset Ave, West Covina (91790-1244)
  PHONE 626 962-4489
  Fax: 626 337-4044
C David Benfield, *President*
Cherish Maldanado, *Executive*
Ralph Diokno, *Personnel*
Ivan Breed, *Director*
George Duallan, *Director*
EMP: 50
SQ FT: 15,000
SALES: 3.3MM
SALES (corp-wide): 3.4MM Privately Held
SIC: 8059 Convalescent home
PA: Care Tech Inc
  401 Ste B N Central Ave
  Upland CA 91786
  909 373-3766

(P-21422)
WILLOW TREE NURSING CENTER
Also Called: Willow Tree Convalescent Hosp
2124 57th Ave, Oakland (94621-4322)
  PHONE 510 261-2628
  Fax: 510 261-9581
Breta Conroy, *Director*
Wanda Solis, *MIS Mgr*
Marina Wilson, *Bookkeeper*
Maria Lew, *Nursing Dir*
Regina Smith, *Nursing Dir*
EMP: 90 EST: 1976
SQ FT: 18,000
SALES (est): 3.8MM Privately Held
SIC: 8059 8052 Convalescent home; intermediate care facilities

(P-21423)
WILSHIRE HEALTH AND CMNTY SVCS
Also Called: Wilshire Nursing & Rehab
290 Heather Ct, Templeton (93465-9738)
  PHONE 805 434-3035
  Fax: 805 434-3065
Jack Doria, *Manager*
EMP: 100

SALES (corp-wide): 13MM Privately Held
SIC: 8059 8051 Convalescent home; skilled nursing care facilities
PA: Wilshire Health And Community Services, Inc.
  285 South St Ste J
  San Luis Obispo CA 93401
  805 547-7025

(P-21424)
WILSHIRE HLTH & CMNTY SVCS INC
Also Called: Hawthorne Convalescent Center
11630 Grevillea Ave, Hawthorne (90250-2231)
  PHONE 310 679-9732
  Fax: 310 679-3672
Bill Kite, *Director*
EMP: 100
SALES (corp-wide): 13MM Privately Held
SIC: 8059 8051 Convalescent home; skilled nursing care facilities
PA: Wilshire Health And Community Services, Inc.
  285 South St Ste J
  San Luis Obispo CA 93401
  805 547-7025

(P-21425)
WILSHIRE HLTH & CMNTY SVCS INC
Also Called: Kings Nrsing Rhabilitaion Hosp
851 Leslie Ln, Hanford (93230-5643)
  PHONE 559 582-4414
Mark Fisher, *Owner*
EMP: 74
SALES (corp-wide): 13MM Privately Held
SIC: 8059 Convalescent home
PA: Wilshire Health And Community Services, Inc.
  285 South St Ste J
  San Luis Obispo CA 93401
  805 547-7025

(P-21426)
WINDSOR GARDENS HEALTHCARE C
1628 B St, Hayward (94541-3020)
  PHONE 510 582-4636
Lee Samson, *CEO*
Richard Taylor, *Administration*
Yalonda Deguzman, *Human Res Dir*
Celina Tercias, *Chf Purch Ofc*
Rene Huezo, *Maintence Staff*
EMP: 133
SQ FT: 5,000
SALES: 8.8MM
SALES (corp-wide): 67MM Privately Held
SIC: 8059 Convalescent home
PA: Lexington Group International, Inc
  9200 W Sunset Blvd # 700
  West Hollywood CA 90069
  310 385-1071

(P-21427)
WINDSOR MONTEREY CARE CTR LLC
1575 Skyline Dr, Monterey (93940-4110)
  PHONE 831 373-2731
  Fax: 831 373-3162
Lawrence Feigen,
Brenda Lopez, *Social Dir*
Patsy Gillespie, *Contract Mgr*
Sushila Singh, *Chf Purch Ofc*
Alice Martin, *Purchasing*
EMP: 95
SALES (est): 5.4MM Privately Held
SIC: 8059 Nursing home, except skilled & intermediate care facility

(P-21428)
WING LAM HA
615 Las Tunas Dr Ste J, Arcadia (91007-8470)
  PHONE 626 462-0048
Wing Lam Ha, *CEO*
EMP: 50
SALES (est): 403.3K Privately Held
SIC: 8059 Personal care home, with health care

PRODUCTS & SERVICES SECTION

8062 - General Medical & Surgical Hospitals County (P-21448)

(P-21429)
WOODLAND CARE CENTER LLC
7120 Corbin Ave, Reseda (91335-3618)
PHONE.................................818 881-4540
Fax: 818 881-0039
Brian Bellantuoni, *Administration*
EMP: 100
SALES (est): 1.5MM
SALES (corp-wide): 9.6B **Publicly Held**
WEB: www.parkviewnursing.net
SIC: **8059** 8051 Convalescent home; skilled nursing care facilities
HQ: Skilled Healthcare, Llc
27442 Portola Pkwy # 200
Foothill Ranch CA 92610
949 282-5800

8062 General Medical & Surgical Hospitals

(P-21430)
ADVENTIST HEALTH CLEARLAKE (HQ)
Also Called: Saint Helena Hosp Clearlake
15630 18th Ave, Clearlake (95422-9336)
P.O. Box 6710 (95422-6710)
PHONE.................................707 994-6486
David Santos, *CEO*
Jeniffer Swenson, *Senior VP*
Terry Newmyer, *Principal*
Denise Love, *Exec Dir*
Denise Orpustanlove, *Exec Dir*
EMP: 287
SQ FT: 41,750
SALES: 82.5MM
SALES (corp-wide): 251.4MM **Privately Held**
SIC: **8062** 8011 General medical & surgical hospitals; medical centers
PA: Adventist Health System/West
2100 Douglas Blvd
Roseville CA 95661
916 781-2000

(P-21431)
ADVENTIST HEALTH SYSTEM/WEST (PA)
2100 Douglas Blvd, Roseville (95661-3898)
P.O. Box 619002 (95661-9002)
PHONE.................................916 781-2000
Fax: 916 783-9146
Robert Carmen, *President*
Carrie Bannister, *President*
Roland Fargo, *President*
Dag Jakobsen, *COO*
Raymond Holm, *CFO*
EMP: 350
SQ FT: 55,000
SALES: 251.4MM **Privately Held**
SIC: **8062** General medical & surgical hospitals

(P-21432)
ADVENTIST HEALTH SYSTEM/WEST
Also Called: Adventist Hlth Med Foundation
381 Merrill Ave, Glendale (91206-4178)
PHONE.................................818 409-8540
Fax: 818 546-5694
Iris Weil, *CEO*
Diane Beers, *Director*
Nellie Zaldivia, *Manager*
EMP: 50
SALES (corp-wide): 3.2B **Privately Held**
SIC: **8062** General medical & surgical hospitals
PA: Adventist Health System/West
2100 Douglas Blvd
Roseville CA 95661
916 781-2000

(P-21433)
ADVENTIST HEALTH SYSTEM/WEST
Also Called: Clearlake Family Health Center
15230 Lakeshore Dr, Clearlake (95422-8107)
PHONE.................................707 995-4500
Ilona Horton, *Director*
EMP: 50

SALES (corp-wide): 3.2B **Privately Held**
SIC: **8062** General medical & surgical hospitals
PA: Adventist Health System/West
2100 Douglas Blvd
Roseville CA 95661
916 781-2000

(P-21434)
ADVENTIST MED CENTER-REEDLEY
372 W Cypress Ave, Reedley (93654-2113)
PHONE.................................559 638-8155
Wayne Ferch, *President*
Amy Simm, *Accounts Mgr*
EMP: 75 EST: 2011
SALES: 54.1MM **Privately Held**
SIC: **8062** General medical & surgical hospitals

(P-21435)
ADVENTIST HLTH CLEARLAKE HOSP
Also Called: St Helana Hospital Clearlake
18th Ave & Hwy 53, Clearlake (95422)
PHONE.................................707 994-6486
Terry Newmeyer, *CEO*
Jeniffer Swenson, *Vice Pres*
Duane Barnes, *Finance Dir*
Claudia Helmes,
Barbara Peremski, *Nursing Dir*
EMP: 340
SQ FT: 62,000
SALES: 65.9MM **Privately Held**
WEB: www.rchea.org
SIC: **8062** General medical & surgical hospitals

(P-21436)
AHM GEMCH INC
Also Called: Greater El Monte Cmnty Hosp
1701 Santa Anita Ave, El Monte (91733-3411)
PHONE.................................626 579-7777
Fax: 626 350-0368
Jeffrey Flocken, *CEO*
Patrick Steinhauser, *COO*
Gary Louis, *CFO*
Pasha Dourseau, *Op Rm Dir*
George Thorimbert, *Lab Dir*
EMP: 180
SQ FT: 71,500
SALES (est): 34.4MM
SALES (corp-wide): 615.4MM **Privately Held**
WEB: www.greaterelmonte.com
SIC: **8062** General medical & surgical hospitals
PA: Ahmc Healthcare Inc.
1000 S Fremont Ave Unit 6
Alhambra CA 91803
626 943-7526

(P-21437)
AHMC HEALTHCARE
55 S Raymond Ave Ste 105, Alhambra (91801-7101)
PHONE.................................626 570-0612
Jonathan Wu, *Ch of Bd*
Judy Saito, *Vice Pres*
Paz Battung, *Case Mgmt Dir*
Corrine Pichardo, *Executive Asst*
Sharon Morris, *Analyst*
EMP: 150
SALES (est): 15.7MM **Privately Held**
SIC: **8062** General medical & surgical hospitals

(P-21438)
AHMC HEALTHCARE INC (PA)
1000 S Fremont Ave Unit 6, Alhambra (91803-8836)
PHONE.................................626 943-7526
Fax: 626 457-7455
Jonathan Wu MD, *CEO*
Jose Ortega, *COO*
Daniel Song, *CFO*
Linda Marsh, *Senior VP*
Judy Saito, *Vice Pres*
EMP: 150
SALES (est): 615.4MM **Privately Held**
SIC: **8062** 8641 General medical & surgical hospitals; civic social & fraternal associations

(P-21439)
AHMC HEALTHCARE INC
1701 Santa Anita Ave, South El Monte (91733-3411)
PHONE.................................626 579-7777
Gary Hu, *Admin Asst*
Linda Du, *Controller*
Mark Underwood, *Materials Dir*
Pacita Diaz, *Manager*
Erik Jiang, *Manager*
EMP: 346
SALES (corp-wide): 615.4MM **Privately Held**
SIC: **8062** General medical & surgical hospitals
PA: Ahmc Healthcare Inc.
1000 S Fremont Ave Unit 6
Alhambra CA 91803
626 943-7526

(P-21440)
AHMC WHITTIER HOSP MED CTR LP
9080 Colima Rd, Whittier (90605-1600)
PHONE.................................562 945-3561
Richard Castro, *CEO*
Lee Panton, *Lab Dir*
Ernie Matsuo, *Radiology Dir*
Abegail Camus, *Controller*
Norma Bridger, *Purch Mgr*
EMP: 850
SQ FT: 16,782
SALES (est): 54.1MM
SALES (corp-wide): 615.4MM **Privately Held**
WEB: www.ahmchealth.com
SIC: **8062** General medical & surgical hospitals
PA: Ahmc Healthcare Inc.
1000 S Fremont Ave Unit 6
Alhambra CA 91803
626 943-7526

(P-21441)
ALAKOR HEALTHCARE LLC
Also Called: Monrovia Memorial Hospital
323 S Heliotrope Ave, Monrovia (91016-2914)
PHONE.................................626 408-9800
Fax: 626 408-9809
Kevin Smith,
Jon Woods, *General Counsel*
Ron Kupferstein,
EMP: 126
SQ FT: 10,000
SALES: 47.2MM **Privately Held**
SIC: **8062** General medical & surgical hospitals

(P-21442)
ALECTO HEALTHCARE SERVICES LLC (PA)
16310 Bake Pkwy Ste 200, Irvine (92618-4684)
P.O. Box 351209, Los Angeles (90035-9609)
PHONE.................................323 938-3161
Fax: 323 932-5049
John A Calderone, *CEO*
Babur Ozkan, *CFO*
Natalie Tran, *Program Mgr*
Yeza Ortiz, *Admin Asst*
John Fonacier, *Data Proc Staff*
EMP: 900
SALES (est): 1B **Privately Held**
WEB: www.olympiamc.com
SIC: **8062** General medical & surgical hospitals

(P-21443)
ALHAMBRA HOSPITAL MED CTR LP
Also Called: Alhambra Hospital Medical Ctr
100 S Raymond Ave, Alhambra (91801-3166)
PHONE.................................626 570-1606
Fax: 626 458-4728
Iris Lai, *Marketing Staff*
Geraldine Thaung,
Sarah Lemayers, *Administration*
Ed Mercado, *Comp Lab Dir*
Juan Rodriguez, *Business Mgr*
EMP: 160 EST: 1920
SQ FT: 200,000

SALES (est): 40.9MM
SALES (corp-wide): 615.4MM **Privately Held**
SIC: **8062** General medical & surgical hospitals
PA: Ahmc Healthcare Inc.
1000 S Fremont Ave Unit 6
Alhambra CA 91803
626 943-7526

(P-21444)
ALPHA ENTRPRNEUR HLTH FNDATION
3655 Ruthelen St, Los Angeles (90018-4417)
PHONE.................................323 735-0873
Greg Witman, *CEO*
Dexter Love, *CFO*
EMP: 200
SALES (est): 3.6MM **Privately Held**
SIC: **8062** General medical & surgical hospitals

(P-21445)
ALTA HOSPITALS SYSTEM LLC
Also Called: Los Angeles Community Hospital
4081 E Olympic Blvd, Los Angeles (90023-3330)
PHONE.................................323 267-0477
Remy Hart, *Branch Mgr*
Patti James, *Records Dir*
Grant Clarke, *Social Dir*
Clive Negatani, *Radiology Dir*
Jim Trowbridge, *Quality Imp Dir*
EMP: 250
SQ FT: 64,024
SALES (corp-wide): 637.4MM **Privately Held**
SIC: **8062** General medical & surgical hospitals
HQ: Alta Hospitals System, Llc
10780 Santa Monica Blvd # 400
Los Angeles CA 90025
310 943-4500

(P-21446)
ALTA HOSPITALS SYSTEM LLC (HQ)
10780 Santa Monica Blvd # 400, Los Angeles (90025-7616)
PHONE.................................310 943-4500
Fax: 310 943-4501
Samuel S Lee, *Mng Member*
Jeremy Redin, *CFO*
Bruce Grimshaw, *Senior VP*
Cathleen Navejas, *Vice Pres*
Elizabeth Aguilera, *Admin Asst*
EMP: 143
SALES (est): 69.7MM
SALES (corp-wide): 637.4MM **Privately Held**
SIC: **8062** General medical & surgical hospitals
PA: Prospect Medical Holdings, Inc.
3415 S Sepulveda Blvd # 9
Los Angeles CA 90034
310 943-4500

(P-21447)
ALTA LOS ANGELES HOSPITALS INC
4081 E Olympic Blvd, Los Angeles (90023-3330)
PHONE.................................323 267-0477
David R Topper, *President*
EMP: 54
SQ FT: 19,739
SALES (est): 8.5MM **Privately Held**
SIC: **8062** General medical & surgical hospitals

(P-21448)
AMERICAN HOSPITAL MGT CORP (PA)
Also Called: Mad River Community Hospital
3800 Janes Rd, Arcata (95521-4742)
P.O. Box 1115 (95518-1115)
PHONE.................................707 822-3621
Fax: 707 822-6311
Allen E Shaw, *President*
Vicky Sleight, *Vice Chairman*
Michael Young, *CFO*
Steve Engle, *Officer*
Doug A Shaw, *Vice Pres*
EMP: 500

8062 - General Medical & Surgical Hospitals County (P-21449)

SQ FT: 60,000
SALES (est): 53.2MM **Privately Held**
WEB: www.madriverhospital.com
SIC: **8062** General medical & surgical hospitals

(P-21449)
AMI-HTI TARZANA ENCINO JOINT V
Also Called: A M I Encn-Trzana Rgnal Med Ce
18321 Clark St, Tarzana (91356-3501)
PHONE..................................818 881-0800
Dale Surowitz, *Managing Prtnr*
Gregg Olsen, *Research*
Cari Erickson, *Controller*
Jo Ann Lewis, *Director*
EMP: 1800
SQ FT: 180,000
SALES: 14.6MM **Privately Held**
SIC: **8062** General medical & surgical hospitals

(P-21450)
AMISUB (IRVINE REGIONAL HOSPI)
1400 S Douglass Rd # 250, Anaheim (92806-6904)
PHONE..................................949 916-7556
Fax: 949 753-2131
Dan F Ausman, *CEO*
Mark Stein, *Ch Radiology*
Dr Jack Campion, *Ch of Bd*
Richard Robinson, *Principal*
Jill Hall, *Office Mgr*
EMP: 590
SQ FT: 244,000
SALES (est): 17.9MM **Privately Held**
SIC: **8062** 5912 General medical & surgical hospitals; drug stores

(P-21451)
AMISUB OF CALIFORNIA INC (DH)
Also Called: TENET
18321 Clark St, Tarzana (91356-3501)
PHONE..................................818 881-0800
Fax: 818 708-5382
Dale Surowitz, *CEO*
Don Kreitz, *COO*
Nick Lymberopolous, *CFO*
Edward Gong, *Vice Pres*
Nancy Sheftel, *Manager*
EMP: 900
SQ FT: 180,000
SALES: 480K
SALES (corp-wide): 18.7B **Publicly Held**
SIC: **8062** General medical & surgical hospitals
HQ: Tenet Healthsystem Medical, Inc
1445 Ross Ave Ste 1400
Dallas TX 75202
469 893-2000

(P-21452)
ANAHEIM GLOBAL MEDICAL CENTER
Also Called: Western Medical Center-Anaheim
1025 S Anaheim Blvd, Anaheim (92805-5806)
PHONE..................................714 533-6220
Fax: 714 502-2678
Marven E Howard, *CEO*
Michael Poh, *Ch Radiology*
Robert Heinemeier, *CFO*
Maxine Hatten, *Op Rm Dir*
Jason Liu, *Principal*
EMP: 500
SALES (est): 10.5MM
SALES (corp-wide): 449.3MM **Privately Held**
SIC: **8062** General medical & surgical hospitals
PA: Kpc Healthcare, Inc.
1301 N Tustin Ave
Santa Ana CA 92705
714 953-3652

(P-21453)
ANTELOPE VALLEY HOSPITAL AUX (PA)
Also Called: ANTELOPE VALLEY HLTH CARE DST
1600 W Avenue J, Lancaster (93534-2894)
P.O. Box 7001 (93539-7001)
PHONE..................................661 949-5000
Fax: 661 949-5510
Harriet Lee, *CEO*
Anil Kumar,
Alon Antebi,
Patalappa Chandrashekar,
Jennifer Hill, *Ch Radiology*
EMP: 1660
SQ FT: 300,000
SALES: 380MM **Privately Held**
WEB: www.avhospital.com
SIC: **8062** General medical & surgical hospitals

(P-21454)
ARROWHEAD REGIONAL MEDICAL CTR
Also Called: ARMC
400 N Pepper Ave, Colton (92324-1819)
PHONE..................................909 580-1000
Fax: 909 580-1363
Patrick Petre, *Director*
Theodore Friedman, *Lab Dir*
Claire Ciresa, *Nursing Mgr*
Laurie Robinson, *Nursing Mgr*
Eva Hoggan, *Executive Asst*
EMP: 2500 EST: 1952
SQ FT: 950,000
SALES: 468.9MM **Privately Held**
SIC: **8062** General medical & surgical hospitals
PA: County Of San Bernardino
385 N Arrowhead Ave
San Bernardino CA 92415
909 387-3841

(P-21455)
AURORA HEALTHCARE INC
Also Called: Aurora Behavioral Hlth Care
11878 Avenue Of Industry, San Diego (92128-3423)
PHONE..................................858 487-3200
Fax: 858 675-9241
James S Plummer, *CEO*
Peggy McGowan, *Nursing Dir*
Heather Bennion, *Health Info Dir*
Andrea Niestas, *Director*
EMP: 50
SALES (est): 4.2MM **Privately Held**
SIC: **8062** General medical & surgical hospitals

(P-21456)
AUXILIARY OF MISSION
27700 Medical Center Rd, Mission Viejo (92691-6426)
PHONE..................................949 364-1400
Fax: 949 365-2376
Eduardo Jordan, *Ch of Bd*
Kenn McFarland, *President*
Vicki J Veal, *CEO*
EMP: 54 EST: 2011
SALES: 501.8K
SALES (corp-wide): 511.1MM **Privately Held**
SIC: **8062** General medical & surgical hospitals
PA: Mission Hospital Regional Medical Center Inc
27700 Medical Center Rd
Mission Viejo CA 92691
949 364-1400

(P-21457)
AVANTI HOSPITALS LLC
1145 W Redondo Beach Blvd, Gardena (90247-3511)
PHONE..................................310 532-4200
EMP: 165
SALES (corp-wide): 139.1MM **Privately Held**
SIC: **8062** General medical & surgical hospitals
PA: Avanti Hospitals, Llc
222 N Splvd Blvd Ste 950
El Segundo CA 90245
310 356-0550

(P-21458)
AVANTI HOSPITALS LLC
13100 Studebaker Rd, Norwalk (90650-2531)
PHONE..................................562 868-3751
Joel Freedman, *Branch Mgr*
EMP: 660
SALES (corp-wide): 139.1MM **Privately Held**
SIC: **8062** General medical & surgical hospitals
PA: Avanti Hospitals, Llc
222 N Splvd Blvd Ste 950
El Segundo CA 90245
310 356-0550

(P-21459)
BAKERSFIELD MEMORIAL HOSPITAL
Also Called: C H W
420 34th St, Bakersfield (93301-2237)
P.O. Box 1888 (93303-1888)
PHONE..................................661 327-1792
Fax: 661 326-0706
Jon Van Boening, *CEO*
Ron Clyde,
Gordon K Foster, *Ch of Bd*
R Mark R Root, *Vice Pres*
Sheri Comaianni, *VP Human Res*
EMP: 1100
SQ FT: 364,000
SALES: 373MM
SALES (corp-wide): 7.1B **Privately Held**
SIC: **8062** General medical & surgical hospitals
PA: Dignity Health
185 Berry St Ste 300
San Francisco CA 94107
415 438-5500

(P-21460)
BANNER HEALTH
1800 Spring Ridge Dr, Susanville (96130-6100)
PHONE..................................530 251-3147
Peter S Fine, *Branch Mgr*
Teena Carver, *Officer*
Bonnie B Olsen, *Officer*
Dan Bandy, *Radiology*
Kewei Chen, *Radiology*
EMP: 165
SALES (corp-wide): 5.4B **Privately Held**
WEB: www.bannerhealth.com
SIC: **8062** General medical & surgical hospitals
PA: Banner Health
2901 N Central Ave # 160
Phoenix AZ 85012
602 747-4000

(P-21461)
BANNER LASSEN MEDICAL CENTER
1800 Spring Ridge Dr, Susanville (96130-6100)
PHONE..................................530 252-2000
Bob Edwards, *CEO*
Shelby Diede, *CFO*
Debbie Ingle, *Accountant*
Hal Brown, *Purchasing*
Michelle Williams, *Mktg Dir*
EMP: 200
SALES: 40.2MM **Privately Held**
SIC: **8062** 8051 General medical & surgical hospitals; skilled nursing care facilities

(P-21462)
BARTON HOSPITAL
2170 South Ave, South Lake Tahoe (96150-7026)
P.O. Box 9578 (96158-9578)
PHONE..................................530 543-5685
Clint Purvance, *CEO*
Darcy Wallace, *Vice Pres*
EMP: 1200
SALES (est): 80.4K **Privately Held**
SIC: **8062** General medical & surgical hospitals

(P-21463)
BEAR VLY CMNTY HEALTHCARE DST (PA)
41870 Garstin Dr, Big Bear Lake (92315)
P.O. Box 1649 (92315-1649)
PHONE..................................909 866-6501

Raymond Hino, *CEO*
Barbara Espinoza, *Vice Pres*
Donna Nicely, *Vice Pres*
Shelly Egerer, *General Mgr*
Christopher Fagan, *Admin Sec*
EMP: 150
SQ FT: 25,000
SALES: 26.2K **Privately Held**
SIC: **8062** General medical & surgical hospitals

(P-21464)
BEVERLY COMMUNITY HOSP ASSN
101 E Beverly Blvd # 104, Montebello (90640-4300)
PHONE..................................323 889-2452
Norma Valdez, *Principal*
EMP: 297
SALES (corp-wide): 176.9MM **Privately Held**
SIC: **8062** 8011 General medical & surgical hospitals; clinic, operated by physicians
PA: Beverly Community Hospital Association
309 W Beverly Blvd
Montebello CA 90640
323 726-1222

(P-21465)
BEVERLY COMMUNITY HOSP ASSN (PA)
Also Called: BEVERLY HOSPITAL
309 W Beverly Blvd, Montebello (90640-4308)
PHONE..................................323 726-1222
Fax: 323 725-4263
Gary Kiff, *CEO*
Kristian Narayanan,
Karen Ragland, *Ch Radiology*
Luis Sanchez, *President*
Narci Egan, *CFO*
EMP: 103
SQ FT: 274,000
SALES: 176.9MM **Privately Held**
WEB: www.beverly.org
SIC: **8062** General medical & surgical hospitals

(P-21466)
BEVERLY COMMUNITY HOSP ASSN
Also Called: Kelpien Health Care
1920 W Whittier Blvd, Montebello (90640-4009)
PHONE..................................323 725-1519
Wendy Torres, *Manager*
EMP: 595
SALES (corp-wide): 176.9MM **Privately Held**
WEB: www.beverly.org
SIC: **8062** General medical & surgical hospitals
PA: Beverly Community Hospital Association
309 W Beverly Blvd
Montebello CA 90640
323 726-1222

(P-21467)
C H W MERCY HEALTHCARE
Also Called: Mercy General Hospital Bus Off
4001 J St, Sacramento (95819-3626)
P.O. Box 3008, Rancho Cordova (95741-3008)
PHONE..................................916 453-4545
Thomas Peterson, *Director*
EMP: 1600
SALES (corp-wide): 7.1B **Privately Held**
WEB: www.mercycare.net
SIC: **8062** General medical & surgical hospitals
HQ: Mercy Healthcare Sacramento
3400 Data Dr
Rancho Cordova CA 95670
916 379-2871

(P-21468)
C H W MERCY HEALTHCARE
Methodist Hospital Sacramento
7500 Hospital Dr, Sacramento (95823-5403)
PHONE..................................916 423-3000
Fax: 916 423-6034
Timothy Moran, *President*

PRODUCTS & SERVICES SECTION
8062 - General Medical & Surgical Hospitals County (P-21486)

Michael Earn, *CEO*
Caroline Fraser, *Lab Dir*
Derek Garner, *Envir Svcs Dir*
Stanley C Oppegard, *Administration*
EMP: 990
SQ FT: 1,000
SALES (corp-wide): 7.1B **Privately Held**
WEB: www.mercycare.net
SIC: 8062 8011 General medical & surgical hospitals; clinic, operated by physicians
HQ: Mercy Healthcare Sacramento
3400 Data Dr
Rancho Cordova CA 95670
916 379-2871

(P-21469)
CALIFORNIA PACIFIC MEDICAL CTR
2100 Webster St Ste 115, San Francisco (94115-2374)
PHONE 415 600-1378
Fax: 415 923-6546
Matthew Poland, *Principal*
Kathy Blankenship, *Vice Pres*
Michael Erhard, *Branch Mgr*
Barbara H Swor, *Administration*
Michelle Haynes Do, *Osteopathy*
EMP: 99
SALES (est): 7.6MM **Privately Held**
SIC: 8062 General medical & surgical hospitals

(P-21470)
CALIFRNIA HOSP MED CTR FNDTION
1401 S Grand Ave, Los Angeles (90015-3010)
PHONE 213 748-2411
Phillip C Hill, *Ch of Bd*
Nathan R Nusbaum, *President*
Margaret R Peterson, *President*
Harold Newton, *COO*
Clark Underwood, *CFO*
▲ **EMP:** 1500
SQ FT: 800,000
SALES (est): 123MM
SALES (corp-wide): 7.1B **Privately Held**
WEB: www.chw.edu
SIC: 8062 Hospital, medical school affiliated with nursing & residency
PA: Dignity Health
185 Berry St Ste 300
San Francisco CA 94107
415 438-5500

(P-21471)
CASA COLINA HOSPITAL AND CENTE (HQ)
Also Called: Casa Clina Ctrs For Rhbltation
255 E Bonita Ave, Pomona (91767-1933)
P.O. Box 6001 (91769-6001)
PHONE 909 596-7733
Felice Loverso, *CEO*
David Morony, *CFO*
Steve Norin, *Chairman*
Stephen Graeber, *Treasurer*
Stephanie Bradhurst, *Chief Mktg Ofcr*
▲ **EMP:** 500
SQ FT: 90,000
SALES: 80.9MM **Privately Held**
WEB: www.casacolina.org
SIC: 8062 General medical & surgical hospitals
PA: Casa Colina, Inc.
255 E Bonita Ave
Pomona CA 91767
909 596-7733

(P-21472)
CATHOLIC HLTHCARE W STHERN CAL (HQ)
1050 Linden Ave, Long Beach (90813-3321)
PHONE 562 491-9000
Jeff Winter, *COO*
Gary Conner, *CFO*
Kim Bradley, *Project Mgr*
Sharon McNally, *Finance Dir*
EMP: 125
SALES (est): 42.8MM
SALES (corp-wide): 7.1B **Privately Held**
SIC: 8062 General medical & surgical hospitals

PA: Dignity Health
185 Berry St Ste 300
San Francisco CA 94107
415 438-5500

(P-21473)
CEDARS-SINAI MEDICAL CENTER
Also Called: Health System Medical Network
250 N Robertson Blvd # 101, Beverly Hills (90211-1788)
PHONE 310 385-3400
Tom Gordon, *CEO*
Josie Sapien, *Admin Asst*
Clement Yang, *Med Doctor*
Diane McWhorter, *Nurse Practr*
EMP: 200
SALES (corp-wide): 2.7B **Privately Held**
SIC: 8062 8011 General medical & surgical hospitals; offices & clinics of medical doctors
PA: Cedars-Sinai Medical Center
8700 Beverly Blvd
West Hollywood CA 90048
310 423-3277

(P-21474)
CENTINELA SKILLED NURSING AND
950 S Flower St, Inglewood (90301-4186)
PHONE 310 674-3216
Nichole Tons, *Vice Pres*
EMP: 99
SQ FT: 6,000
SALES (est): 442K **Privately Held**
SIC: 8062 General medical & surgical hospitals

(P-21475)
CENTRAL VALLEY GENERAL HOSP (HQ)
Also Called: ADVENTIST HEALTH
1025 N Douty St, Hanford (93230-3722)
P.O. Box 619002 (93230)
PHONE 559 583-2100
Fax: 559 583-2212
Wayne Ferch, *CEO*
Thomas Enloe, *Ch OB/GYN*
Douglas Lafferty, *COO*
Eric Martisen, *CFO*
Michele Waldrin, *CFO*
EMP: 400
SQ FT: 96,000
SALES: 109MM
SALES (corp-wide): 251.4MM **Privately Held**
SIC: 8062 General medical & surgical hospitals
PA: Adventist Health System/West
2100 Douglas Blvd
Roseville CA 95661
916 781-2000

(P-21476)
CFHS HOLDINGS INC
Also Called: Centinela Frman Rgonal Med Ctr
4650 Lincoln Blvd, Marina Del Rey (90292-6306)
PHONE 310 823-8911
Jeannie Fisher, *Bd of Directors*
Steve Hopkins, *Admin Asst*
Stephen Packwood, *Administration*
Waldo Romero, *Engrg Dir*
Kristine Peterson, *Human Res Mgr*
EMP: 650
SQ FT: 150,000
SALES (corp-wide): 341.5MM **Privately Held**
SIC: 8062 General medical & surgical hospitals
PA: Cfhs Holdings, Inc.
4650 Lincoln Blvd
Marina Del Rey CA 90292
310 823-8911

(P-21477)
CFHS HOLDINGS INC
Also Called: Centinela Frman Rgonal Med Ctr
4640 Admiralty Way # 650, Marina Del Rey (90292-6667)
PHONE 310 448-7800
Bob Bokern, *Principal*
Kevin Hubbard, *Vice Pres*
Regina C Salazar, *Vice Pres*
Peggy Dickey, *MIS Dir*
John Jant, *MIS Dir*

EMP: 1940
SALES (corp-wide): 341.5MM **Privately Held**
SIC: 8062 General medical & surgical hospitals
PA: Cfhs Holdings, Inc.
4650 Lincoln Blvd
Marina Del Rey CA 90292
310 823-8911

(P-21478)
CFHS HOLDINGS INC
Also Called: Centinela Frman Rgonal Med Ctr
555 E Hardy St, Inglewood (90301-4011)
PHONE 310 673-4660
Michael Rembis, *Branch Mgr*
Kim Bowtlin, *Pharmacy Dir*
Joanne Lamb, *MIS Dir*
Ken Poyer, *Info Tech Mgr*
Granville Thomas, *Analyst*
EMP: 1200
SALES (corp-wide): 341.5MM **Privately Held**
SIC: 8062 General medical & surgical hospitals
PA: Cfhs Holdings, Inc.
4650 Lincoln Blvd
Marina Del Rey CA 90292
310 823-8911

(P-21479)
CHA HOLLYWOOD MEDICAL CTR LP (PA)
Also Called: HOLLYWOOD PRESBYTERIAN MEDICAL
1300 N Vermont Ave, Los Angeles (90027-6098)
PHONE 213 413-3000
Fax: 323 644-9503
Jeff A Nelson, *CEO*
Romeo Velasco, *CFO*
Galen Gorman, *CFO*
Ryan Reichert, *Vice Pres*
Sofia Gezalyan, *Pharmacy Dir*
▲ **EMP:** 101
SQ FT: 900,000
SALES: 260.5MM **Privately Held**
WEB: www.hollywoodpresbyterian.com
SIC: 8062 8351 General medical & surgical hospitals; child day care services

(P-21480)
CHAPMAN GLOBAL MEDICAL CENTER
Also Called: Chapman Medical Center Inc.
2601 E Chapman Ave, Orange (92869-3206)
PHONE 714 633-0011
Don Kreitz, *CEO*
Kelvin Nguyen, *CEO*
Lori Firman, *President*
Kenneth K Westbrook, *CEO*
Robert Heinemeier, *CFO*
EMP: 425
SQ FT: 96,000
SALES: 46.3MM
SALES (corp-wide): 449.3MM **Privately Held**
WEB: www.chapmanmedicalcenter.com
SIC: 8062 General medical & surgical hospitals
PA: Kpc Healthcare, Inc.
1301 N Tustin Ave
Santa Ana CA 92705
714 953-3652

(P-21481)
CHHP HOLDINGS II LLC (PA)
2623 E Slauson Ave, Huntington Park (90255-2926)
P.O. Box 2729 (90255-8129)
PHONE 323 583-1931
Fax: 323 587-0892
Hector Hernandez, *CEO*
Elizabeth Bustamonte, *Opers Staff*
Yolanda Vasquez, *Exec Sec*
EMP: 65
SQ FT: 6,000
SALES: 42.1MM **Privately Held**
SIC: 8062 General medical & surgical hospitals

(P-21482)
CHHP MANAGEMENT LLC
Also Called: Community Hosp Huntington Pk
2623 E Slauson Ave, Huntington Park (90255-2926)
PHONE 323 583-1931
Fax: 323 582-8179
Joel Freedman, *Principal*
Terry McAbe, *Lab Dir*
Mark Bell, *Principal*
Jamie Macpherson, *Principal*
Yolanda Vasquez, *Executive Asst*
EMP: 99 **EST:** 2010
SALES (est): 12MM
SALES (corp-wide): 42.1MM **Privately Held**
SIC: 8062 General medical & surgical hospitals
PA: Chhp Holdings Ii, Llc
2623 E Slauson Ave
Huntington Park CA 90255
323 583-1931

(P-21483)
CHILDRENS HOSPITAL LOS ANGELES
468 E Santa Clara St, Arcadia (91006-7228)
PHONE 626 795-7177
Anahit Petrosyan, *Nurse*
EMP: 275
SALES (corp-wide): 891.3MM **Privately Held**
SIC: 8062 General medical & surgical hospitals
PA: The Childrens Hospital Los Angeles
4650 W Sunset Blvd
Los Angeles CA 90027
323 660-2450

(P-21484)
CHILDRENS HOSPITAL LOS ANGELES
Foundation Division
4650 W Sunset Blvd, Los Angeles (90027-6062)
PHONE 323 660-2450
Claudia Looney, *Vice Pres*
Susan B Turkel, *Psychiatry*
EMP: 80
SALES (corp-wide): 891.3MM **Privately Held**
SIC: 8062 8641 General medical & surgical hospitals; civic social & fraternal associations
PA: The Childrens Hospital Los Angeles
4650 W Sunset Blvd
Los Angeles CA 90027
323 660-2450

(P-21485)
CHILDRENS HOSPOTAL & RESEARCH (PA)
Also Called: UCSF BENIOFF CHILDREN'S HOSPIT
747 52nd St, Oakland (94609-1809)
PHONE 510 428-3000
Fax: 510 654-8474
Bertram Lubin, *President*
Ziad Saba,
Richard Rowe,
Kenneth Henderson, *Records Dir*
Harold Davis, *Ch of Bd*
EMP: 1900
SQ FT: 160,000
SALES: 178.6MM **Privately Held**
SIC: 8062 Hospital, AMA approved residency

(P-21486)
CHINESE HOSPITAL ASSOCIATION (PA)
845 Jackson St, San Francisco (94133-4899)
PHONE 415 982-2400
Fax: 415 217-4188
Brenda Yee, *CEO*
Linda Schumacher, *COO*
Thomas Bolger, *CFO*
Stuart Fong, *Risk Mgmt Dir*
Peggy Cmiel, *Ch Nursing Ofcr*
EMP: 279
SQ FT: 54,000

8062 - General Medical & Surgical Hospitals County (P-21487)

SALES: 130.5MM **Privately Held**
WEB: www.cchphmo.com
SIC: 8062 Hospital, affiliated with AMA residency

(P-21487)
CHINO RDOLOGICAL REGISTRY CORP
6719 Eagle Dr, Chino (91710-6283)
PHONE..................................909 591-6688
Robert A Esquibel, *President*
EMP: 99
SALES: 950K **Privately Held**
SIC: 8062 7361 General medical & surgical hospitals; employment agencies

(P-21488)
CITRUS VALLEY MEDICAL CTR INC (PA)
1115 S Sunset Ave, West Covina (91790-3940)
P.O. Box 6108, Covina (91722-5108)
PHONE..................................626 962-4011
Robert Curry, *President*
Elvia Foulke, *COO*
Roger Sharma, *CFO*
Jill Jacobs, *Risk Mgmt Dir*
Todd Smith, *Admin Sec*
EMP: 1229 **EST:** 1959
SQ FT: 285,000
SALES: 397.2MM **Privately Held**
WEB: www.cvpg.org
SIC: 8062 General medical & surgical hospitals

(P-21489)
CITRUS VALLEY MEDICAL CTR INC
Also Called: Human Resources Department
140 W College St, Covina (91723-2007)
PHONE..................................626 858-8515
EMP: 746
SALES (corp-wide): 397.2MM **Privately Held**
SIC: 8062 General medical & surgical hospitals
PA: Citrus Valley Medical Center, Inc.
   1115 S Sunset Ave
   West Covina CA 91790
   626 962-4011

(P-21490)
CITRUS VALLEY MEDICAL CTR INC
Also Called: Queen of The Valley Hospital
1115 S Sunset Ave, West Covina (91790-3940)
PHONE..................................626 963-8411
Robert Curry, *President*
Karen Dean, *Comp Spec*
EMP: 2000
SALES (corp-wide): 397.2MM **Privately Held**
WEB: www.cvpg.org
SIC: 8062 General medical & surgical hospitals
PA: Citrus Valley Medical Center, Inc.
   1115 S Sunset Ave
   West Covina CA 91790
   626 962-4011

(P-21491)
CITRUS VALLEY MEDICAL CTR INC
Also Called: Inter Community Hospital
210 W San Bernardino Rd, Covina (91723-1515)
PHONE..................................626 331-7331
Toll Free:..................................877 -
Jim Yoshioka, *President*
Anna Leung, *Ch OB/GYN*
Jody Galli, *Vice Pres*
Annette Mickelson, *Vice Pres*
Kent Martyn, *Pharmacy Dir*
EMP: 1000
SALES (corp-wide): 397.2MM **Privately Held**
WEB: www.cvpg.org
SIC: 8062 General medical & surgical hospitals
PA: Citrus Valley Medical Center, Inc.
   1115 S Sunset Ave
   West Covina CA 91790
   626 962-4011

(P-21492)
CITY & COUNTY OF SAN FRANCISCO
Also Called: San Francisco General Hospital
1001 Potrero Ave, San Francisco (94110-3518)
PHONE..................................415 206-8000
Fax: 415 206-5153
Susan Currin, *CEO*
Ronald Pickens, *COO*
Linda Lee, *Risk Mgmt Dir*
Michael Gotway, *Radiology Dir*
Richard Hollingsworth, *Radiology Dir*
EMP: 5000 **Privately Held**
SIC: 8062 General medical & surgical hospitals
PA: City & County Of San Francisco
   1 Dr Carlton B Goodlett P
   San Francisco CA 94102
   415 554-7500

(P-21493)
CITY & COUNTY OF SAN FRANCISCO
Also Called: Public Health Dept
375 Laguna Honda Blvd, San Francisco (94116-1411)
PHONE..................................415 759-2300
Fax: 415 759-2374
Larry Funk, *Exec Dir*
Verwina Roble, *Comms Mgr*
John Lam, *CIO*
Dennis Sato, *MIS Staff*
Mary Funk, *Systems Staff*
EMP: 5000 **Privately Held**
SIC: 8062 9431 8069 8051 General medical & surgical hospitals; administration of public health programs; ; ; specialty hospitals, except psychiatric; skilled nursing care facilities; rehabilitation center, outpatient treatment
PA: City & County Of San Francisco
   1 Dr Carlton B Goodlett P
   San Francisco CA 94102
   415 554-7500

(P-21494)
CITY ALAMEDA HEALTH CARE CORP (PA)
Also Called: Alameda Hospital
2070 Clinton Ave, Alameda (94501-4399)
PHONE..................................510 522-3700
Fax: 510 814-4005
Deborah E Stebbins, *CEO*
Elliott Gorelick, *Treasurer*
Michael J McCormick, *Treasurer*
Roger Rieger, *Executive*
Karmella Borashan, *Lab Dir*
EMP: 63
SQ FT: 150,000
SALES: 0 **Privately Held**
WEB: www.alamedahospital.com
SIC: 8062 8051 General medical & surgical hospitals; skilled nursing care facilities

(P-21495)
CITY HOPE NATIONAL MEDICAL CTR
1500 Duarte Rd, Duarte (91010-3012)
PHONE..................................626 256-4673
Fax: 626 301-8233
Michael A Friedman, *CEO*
Robert Stone, *CEO*
Jill Olausson, *Bd of Directors*
William Davis, *Assoc VP*
Cynthia Garcia, *Executive*
EMP: 1900
SALES: 860.5MM **Privately Held**
SIC: 8062 General medical & surgical hospitals

(P-21496)
COALINGA REGIONAL MEDICAL CTR
Also Called: Crmc
1191 Phelps Ave, Coalinga (93210-9609)
PHONE..................................559 935-6400
Fax: 559 935-6596
Sharon A Spurgen, *CEO*
Freddie Whitworth, *Records Dir*
Sandy Beach, *President*
Sandra Earls, *CFO*
Mark Gritton, *Vice Pres*
EMP: 230 **EST:** 1947
SQ FT: 60,000

SALES (est): 39.3MM **Privately Held**
WEB: www.coalingamedical.com
SIC: 8062 8051 General medical & surgical hospitals; skilled nursing care facilities

(P-21497)
COMMUNITY HLTH ALANCE PASADENA (PA)
Also Called: Chap
1855 N Fair Oaks Ave # 200, Pasadena (91103-1620)
P.O. Box 94873 (91109-4873)
PHONE..................................626 398-6300
Fax: 626 398-5948
Margaret Martinez, *CEO*
Sergio Bautista, *COO*
Marcy Chavez, *Office Mgr*
EMP: 70
SALES: 9.9MM **Privately Held**
SIC: 8062 General medical & surgical hospitals

(P-21498)
COMMUNITY HOSP SAN BERNARDINO (HQ)
1805 Medical Center Dr, San Bernardino (92411-1217)
PHONE..................................909 887-6333
Fax: 909 887-6468
June Collisone, *President*
Ed Sorenson, *CFO*
Denice Findlay, *Executive*
Dave Evans, *General Mgr*
Sharon Kerns, *Info Tech Mgr*
EMP: 350
SALES: 185.4MM
SALES (corp-wide): 7.1B **Privately Held**
SIC: 8062 Hospital, affiliated with AMA residency
PA: Dignity Health
   185 Berry St Ste 300
   San Francisco CA 94107
   415 438-5500

(P-21499)
COMMUNITY HOSPITAL LONG BEACH
1720 Termino Ave, Long Beach (90804-2104)
PHONE..................................562 494-0600
Fax: 562 498-4429
John Bishop, *CEO*
Denise Brown,
Krikor Jansian, *President*
Kevin Peterson, *CEO*
Dana Plat, *Risk Mgmt Dir*
EMP: 570
SALES: 329.2K
SALES (corp-wide): 2B **Privately Held**
SIC: 8062 General medical & surgical hospitals
PA: Memorial Health Services
   17360 Brookhurst St # 160
   Fountain Valley CA 92708
   714 377-6748

(P-21500)
COMMUNITY MEDICAL CENTER (PA)
Also Called: Community Health System
2823 Fresno St, Fresno (93721-1324)
P.O. Box 1232 (93715-1232)
PHONE..................................559 459-6000
Fax: 559 459-0261
Tim A Joslin, *CEO*
Al French,
Gordon Webster Jr, *Vice Chairman*
Jan Coon, *COO*
Mike McGinnis, *COO*
EMP: 3400
SQ FT: 200,000
SALES (est): 1.4B **Privately Held**
SIC: 8062 8011 8051 General medical & surgical hospitals; ambulatory surgical center; clinic, operated by physicians; extended care facility

(P-21501)
COMMUNITY MEDICAL CENTERS
Also Called: Information Services Dept
1140 T St, Fresno (93721-1413)
P.O. Box 9732 (93794-9732)
PHONE..................................559 459-2916
Terri Lutz, *Branch Mgr*

Sargis Oshana, *Executive*
Darlene Wetto, *Ch Nursing Ofcr*
Ron Lyster, *Network Enginr*
Joshua Powell, *Programmer Anys*
EMP: 150
SALES (corp-wide): 1.4B **Privately Held**
SIC: 8062 7374 8741 General medical & surgical hospitals; hospital, AMA approved residency; data processing & preparation; hospital management
PA: Community Medical Center
   2823 Fresno St
   Fresno CA 93721
   559 459-6000

(P-21502)
COMMUNITY MEDICAL CENTERS
Also Called: Community Medical Ctr Clovis
2755 Herndon Ave, Clovis (93611-6800)
PHONE..................................559 324-4000
Fax: 559 323-4098
Phyllis Baltz, *Manager*
Brent Cope, *COO*
Joseph Boado, *Lab Dir*
John Hall, *Security Dir*
Mason Mathews, *Office Mgr*
EMP: 95
SQ FT: 36,000
SALES (corp-wide): 1.4B **Privately Held**
SIC: 8062 General medical & surgical hospitals
PA: Community Medical Center
   2823 Fresno St
   Fresno CA 93721
   559 459-6000

(P-21503)
COMMUNITY MEDICAL CENTERS
Also Called: Clovis Community Living
3003 N Mariposa St, Fresno (93703-1127)
PHONE..................................559 222-7416
Lesi McQuone, *Manager*
EMP: 150
SALES (corp-wide): 1.4B **Privately Held**
SIC: 8062 8051 General medical & surgical hospitals; skilled nursing care facilities
PA: Community Medical Center
   2823 Fresno St
   Fresno CA 93721
   559 459-6000

(P-21504)
COMMUNITY MEDICAL CENTERS
Also Called: Alzheimer's Living Center
668 E Bullard Ave, Fresno (93710-5401)
PHONE..................................559 320-2200
Fax: 559 439-8024
Patrick Uribe, *Manager*
Harvey L Edmonds, *Neurology*
EMP: 110
SQ FT: 28,845
SALES (corp-wide): 1.4B **Privately Held**
SIC: 8062 8051 General medical & surgical hospitals; skilled nursing care facilities
PA: Community Medical Center
   2823 Fresno St
   Fresno CA 93721
   559 459-6000

(P-21505)
COMMUNITY MEDICAL CENTERS
Also Called: California Cancer Center
7257 N Fresno St, Fresno (93720-2950)
PHONE..................................559 447-4050
Fax: 559 447-4086
Maria Schaffer, *Manager*
Paul Nugent, *Surgeon*
Ujagger S Dhillon, *Gastroenterlgy*
Alec Beach, *Manager*
EMP: 75
SQ FT: 25,044
SALES (corp-wide): 1.4B **Privately Held**
SIC: 8062 8069 General medical & surgical hospitals; cancer hospital
PA: Community Medical Center
   2823 Fresno St
   Fresno CA 93721
   559 459-6000

PRODUCTS & SERVICES SECTION
8062 - General Medical & Surgical Hospitals County (P-21525)

(P-21506)
COMMUNITY MEDICAL CENTERS
Also Called: Advanced Medical Imaging
6297 N Fresno St, Fresno (93710-5209)
PHONE 559 447-4000
Donna Moora, *Director*
Hans Hildebrandt, *Med Doctor*
EMP: 70
SALES (corp-wide): 1.4B **Privately Held**
SIC: 8062 8011 8093 General medical & surgical hospitals; radiologist; specialty outpatient clinics
PA: Community Medical Center
 2823 Fresno St
 Fresno CA 93721
 559 459-6000

(P-21507)
COMMUNITY MEDICAL CENTERS INC
Also Called: Channel Medical Center
701 E Channel St, Stockton (95202-2628)
P.O. Box 779 (95201-0779)
PHONE 209 944-4700
Fax: 209 463-2171
Alice Souligen, *Manager*
June Koenig, *Personnel Exec*
Dawnell Moody, *Pediatrics*
EMP: 100
SALES (corp-wide): 36.8MM **Privately Held**
SIC: 8062 General medical & surgical hospitals
PA: Community Medical Centers Inc
 7210 Murray Dr
 Stockton CA 95210
 209 373-2800

(P-21508)
COMMUNITY MEM HSP/SN BENUA
Also Called: Purchasing Department
147 N Brent St, Ventura (93003-2809)
PHONE 805 652-5072
Chuck Gray, *Manager*
David Glyar, *Vice Pres*
Adam Thunell, *Vice Pres*
Michael Bakst, *Exec Dir*
Helen Bagley, *Manager*
▲ **EMP:** 99
SALES: 285MM **Privately Held**
WEB: www.cmhhospital.org
SIC: 8062 General medical & surgical hospitals

(P-21509)
COMMUNITY MEMORIAL HEALTH SYS
120 N Ashwood Ave, Ventura (93003-1810)
PHONE 805 658-5800
EMP: 52
SALES (corp-wide): 353.7MM **Privately Held**
SIC: 8062 General medical & surgical hospitals
PA: Community Memorial Health System
 147 N Brent St
 Ventura CA 93003
 805 652-5011

(P-21510)
CONCORDE CAREER COLLEGES INC
12951 Euclid St Ste 101, Garden Grove (92840-9201)
PHONE 714 620-1000
Chris Vaulker, *Principal*
Martha Ayala, *CTO*
EMP: 60
SALES (corp-wide): 47.4MM **Privately Held**
WEB: www.concordcollege.com
SIC: 8062 Hospital, medical school affiliation
PA: Concorde Career Colleges, Inc.
 5800 Foxridge Dr Ste 500
 Shawnee Mission KS 66202
 816 531-5223

(P-21511)
CORCORAN DISTRICT HOSPITAL
1310 Hanna Ave, Corcoran (93212-2314)
P.O. Box 758 (93212-0758)
PHONE 559 992-3300
Fax: 559 992-3972
Mike Graville, *CEO*
Jonathan Brain, *CEO*
Debbie Bach, *CFO*
Alan Macphee, *CFO*
Ronnie Bico, *Lab Dir*
EMP: 100
SQ FT: 35,000
SALES (est): 10.7MM **Privately Held**
SIC: 8062 General medical & surgical hospitals

(P-21512)
CORRECTONS RHBLTATION CAL DEPT
Also Called: Cdcr Cal Instn For Men Hosp
14901 Central Ave, Chino (91710-9500)
P.O. Box 128 (91708-0128)
PHONE 909 597-1821
Fax: 909 597-4983
ME Poulls, *Warden*
Victor Buere, *COO*
Jorge Gomez, *Executive*
Ella Youngblood, *Executive*
Jill Knacke, *Admin Sec*
EMP: 179 **Privately Held**
SIC: 8062 9223 General medical & surgical hospitals; house of correction, government;
HQ: California Department Of Corrections & Rehabilitation
 1515 S St
 Sacramento CA 95811
 916 341-7066

(P-21513)
COTTAGE CARE CENTER
Also Called: Santa Barbara Cottage Care Ctr
2415 De La Vina St, Santa Barbara (93105-3819)
P.O. Box 689 (93102-0689)
PHONE 805 682-7111
Dr Peter Macdougall, *Ch of Bd*
James L Ash, *President*
Reece Duca, *CFO*
EMP: 160
SQ FT: 45,000
SALES: 7.8MM **Privately Held**
SIC: 8062 General medical & surgical hospitals

(P-21514)
COUNTY OF CONTRA COSTA
Also Called: Department of Health Services
2500 Alhambra Ave, Martinez (94553-3156)
PHONE 925 370-5000
Fax: 925 370-5138
Jeff Smith, *CEO*
Peter Won, *Ch Radiology*
Anna Roth, *Officer*
Art Webb, *Office Mgr*
Sharon L Hiner, *Oncology*
EMP: 200 **Privately Held**
WEB: www.cccounty.us
SIC: 8062 9431 General medical & surgical hospitals; administration of public health programs;
PA: County Of Contra Costa
 625 Court St Ste 100
 Martinez CA 94553
 925 957-5280

(P-21515)
COUNTY OF KERN
Public Health Dept
1700 Mount Vernon Ave, Bakersfield (93306-4018)
PHONE 661 326-2054
Fax: 661 873-0931
Peter Bryan, *CEO*
David Weinstein, *Associate Dir*
Liz Bouchama, *Office Mgr*
Bill Fawns, *Info Tech Mgr*
Eric Mansfield, *Info Tech Mgr*
EMP: 800 **Privately Held**
WEB: www.kccfc.org
SIC: 8062 9431 General medical & surgical hospitals; administration of public health programs;
PA: County Of Kern
 1115 Truxtun Ave Rm 505
 Bakersfield CA 93301
 661 868-3690

(P-21516)
COUNTY OF LOS ANGELES
Health Services, Dept of
14445 Olive View Dr 2b, Sylmar (91342-1437)
PHONE 818 364-1555
Melinda Anderson, *CEO*
Niloo Shahi, *COO*
Steevio Bardakijan, *Manager*
Andy Trinidad, *Supervisor*
Richard Tennant, *Associate*
EMP: 200 **Privately Held**
WEB: www.co.la.ca.us
SIC: 8062 9431 General medical & surgical hospitals;
PA: County Of Los Angeles
 500 W Temple St Ste 375
 Los Angeles CA 90012
 213 974-1101

(P-21517)
COUNTY OF LOS ANGELES
Also Called: Health Services Dept
1000 W Carson St Fl 8, Palos Verdes Peninsu (90274)
PHONE 310 222-2401
Miguel Ortiz Marroquin, *CEO*
EMP: 300 **Privately Held**
WEB: www.co.la.ca.us
SIC: 8062 9431 General medical & surgical hospitals; administration of public health programs
PA: County Of Los Angeles
 500 W Temple St Ste 375
 Los Angeles CA 90012
 213 974-1101

(P-21518)
COUNTY OF LOS ANGELES
Health Services, Dept of
12025 Wilmington Ave, Los Angeles (90059-3019)
PHONE 310 668-4545
Willie T May, *Exec Dir*
EMP: 197 **Privately Held**
WEB: www.co.la.ca.us
SIC: 8062 9431 General medical & surgical hospitals; administration of public health programs
PA: County Of Los Angeles
 500 W Temple St Ste 375
 Los Angeles CA 90012
 213 974-1101

(P-21519)
COUNTY OF LOS ANGELES
Also Called: Health Services Dept
1100 N Mission Rd Rm 236, Los Angeles (90033-1017)
PHONE 323 226-6021
Scott Drewgan, *Director*
EMP: 200 **Privately Held**
WEB: www.co.la.ca.us
SIC: 8062 9431 General medical & surgical hospitals; administration of public health programs
PA: County Of Los Angeles
 500 W Temple St Ste 375
 Los Angeles CA 90012
 213 974-1101

(P-21520)
COUNTY OF LOS ANGELES
Also Called: Los Angles Cnty Cntl Jail Hosp
450 Bauchet St, Los Angeles (90012-2907)
PHONE 213 473-6100
Don Knable, *Ch of Bd*
Julia Huang, *Pharmacist*
Neil Putra, *Pharmacist*
EMP: 278 **Privately Held**
WEB: www.co.la.ca.us
SIC: 8062 9431 General medical & surgical hospitals;
PA: County Of Los Angeles
 500 W Temple St Ste 375
 Los Angeles CA 90012
 213 974-1101

(P-21521)
COUNTY OF MONTEREY
Also Called: Residncy Prgram Natividad Hosp
1441 Constitution Blvd # 100, Salinas (93906-3136)
P.O. Box 81611 (93912-1611)
PHONE 831 755-4201
Dr Gary Gray, *Director*
EMP: 600 **Privately Held**
WEB: www.montereycountyfarmbureau.org
SIC: 8062 General medical & surgical hospitals
PA: County Of Monterey
 168 W Alisal St Fl 3
 Salinas CA 93901
 831 755-5040

(P-21522)
COUNTY OF MONTEREY
Also Called: Natividad Medical Center
1441 Constitution Blvd # 100, Salinas (93906-3136)
PHONE 831 647-7611
Serena Sy, *Director*
Chris Glenn, *Ch Radiology*
Rosenberg Andren, *COO*
Ashok Khanchandani, *CFO*
Mary A Leffel, *Trustee*
EMP: 700 **Privately Held**
WEB: www.montereycountyfarmbureau.org
SIC: 8062 General medical & surgical hospitals
PA: County Of Monterey
 168 W Alisal St Fl 3
 Salinas CA 93901
 831 755-5040

(P-21523)
COUNTY OF SAN LUIS OBISPO
Also Called: County General Hospital
2180 Johnson Ave, San Luis Obispo (93401-4513)
PHONE 805 781-4800
Fax: 805 781-1096
Nancy Rosen, *Manager*
Larry Hood, *Human Res Dir*
Beverly Heaton, *Persnl Mgr*
EMP: 275
SQ FT: 4,500 **Privately Held**
SIC: 8062 8721 General medical & surgical hospitals; accounting, auditing & bookkeeping
PA: County Of San Luis Obispo
 Government Center Rm. 300
 San Luis Obispo CA 93408
 805 781-5040

(P-21524)
COUNTY OF SONOMA
Also Called: Palm Drive Healthcare District
501 Petaluma Ave, Sebastopol (95472-4215)
PHONE 707 823-8511
Shawndra Nimtz, *CEO*
EMP: 200
SQ FT: 3,684 **Privately Held**
WEB: www.sonomacompost.com
SIC: 8062 8051 General medical & surgical hospitals; skilled nursing care facilities
PA: County Of Sonoma
 585 Fiscal Dr 100
 Santa Rosa CA 95403
 707 565-2431

(P-21525)
COUNTY OF STANISLAUS
Also Called: Stanislaus Medical Center
830 Scenic Dr, Modesto (95350-6131)
P.O. Box 3271 (95353-3271)
PHONE 209 525-7000
Fax: 209 558-7262
Beverly M Finley, *Manager*
Donna Meyer, *Technology*
Thomas R Wenstrup, *Director*
EMP: 600
SQ FT: 1,866 **Privately Held**
WEB: www.co.stanislaus.ca.us
SIC: 8062 General medical & surgical hospitals
PA: County Of Stanislaus
 1010 10th St Ste 5100
 Modesto CA 95354
 209 525-6398

8062 - General Medical & Surgical Hospitals County (P-21526)   PRODUUCTS & SERVICES SECTION

(P-21526)
COVENANT CARE CALIFORNIA LLC
Also Called: Grant-Cuesta Nursing Center
1949 Grant Rd, Mountain View (94040-3217)
PHONE..................650 964-0543
Fax: 650 964-0956
Cheryl Cartney, *Branch Mgr*
Roger Mason, *Envir Svcs Dir*
Juana Castaneda, *Personnel*
EMP: 100
SALES (corp-wide): 188.1MM **Privately Held**
WEB: www.willowtreenursingcenter.com
SIC: **8062** 8051 8069 General medical & surgical hospitals; skilled nursing care facilities; specialty hospitals, except psychiatric
HQ: Covenant Care California, Llc
   27071 Aliso Creek Rd # 100
   Aliso Viejo CA 92656
   949 349-1200

(P-21527)
DAMERON HOSPITAL ASSOCIATION (PA)
525 W Acacia St, Stockton (95203-2484)
PHONE..................209 944-5550
Fax: 209 461-3130
Lorraine Auerbach, *CEO*
Melanie Parker,
Debbie Grooms, *Volunteer Dir*
Michael Glasberg, *COO*
David Kerrins, *CFO*
EMP: 987
SQ FT: 136,061
SALES: 190.4MM **Privately Held**
WEB: www.dameronhospital.org
SIC: **8062** General medical & surgical hospitals

(P-21528)
DEL MAR CONVALESCENT HOSPITAL
3136 Del Mar Ave, Rosemead (91770-2326)
PHONE..................626 288-8353
Fax: 626 571-7782
Walter Chameides, *Principal*
Channon Balanay, *Administration*
Kent Berkey, *Administration*
Zenaida Bonsol, *Hlthcr Dir*
EMP: 60
SALES: 4.7MM **Privately Held**
SIC: **8062** 8051 8322 General medical & surgical hospitals; skilled nursing care facilities; rehabilitation services

(P-21529)
DESERT REGIONAL MED CTR INC (HQ)
Also Called: Tenet Healthsystem Desert Inc
1150 N Indian Canyon Dr, Palm Springs (92262-4872)
P.O. Box 2739 (92263-2739)
PHONE..................760 323-6374
Toll Free:..................888 -
Fax: 760 323-6772
Carolyn Caldwell, *CEO*
Robert Rosser, *Ch Pathology*
David Duffner,
Lisa Wilson, *President*
Ken Wheat, *CFO*
EMP: 1200
SQ FT: 400,000
SALES (est): 206.5MM
SALES (corp-wide): 18.7B **Publicly Held**
SIC: **8062** General medical & surgical hospitals
PA: Tenet Healthcare Corporation
   1445 Ross Ave Ste 1400
   Dallas TX 75202
   469 893-2200

(P-21530)
DESERT VALLEY HOSPITAL INC (HQ)
16850 Bear Valley Rd, Victorville (92395-5794)
PHONE..................760 241-8000
Fax: 760 241-4840
Margaret R Peterson, *CEO*
Prem Reddy MD, *Shareholder*
Panch Jeyakumar, *COO*
Roger Krissman, *CFO*
Richard Hayes, *Exec VP*
▲ EMP: 65
SQ FT: 63,000
SALES (est): 36.4MM
SALES (corp-wide): 2.6B **Privately Held**
SIC: **8062** General medical & surgical hospitals
PA: Prime Healthcare Services Inc
   3300 E Guasti Rd Ste 300
   Ontario CA 91761
   909 235-4400

(P-21531)
DIGNITY HEALTH
3215 Prospect Park Dr, Rancho Cordova (95670-6017)
PHONE..................916 861-1100
Diane Brack, *Branch Mgr*
Julie Chang, *Manager*
Norman Chapman, *Manager*
EMP: 140
SALES (corp-wide): 7.1B **Privately Held**
WEB: www.chw.edu
SIC: **8062** General medical & surgical hospitals
PA: Dignity Health
   185 Berry St Ste 300
   San Francisco CA 94107
   415 438-5500

(P-21532)
DIGNITY HEALTH
2131 W 3rd St, Los Angeles (90057-1901)
PHONE..................213 484-7111
William Parente, *President*
Connie Rangel, *Supervisor*
EMP: 500
SALES (corp-wide): 7.1B **Privately Held**
WEB: www.chw.edu
SIC: **8062** General medical & surgical hospitals
PA: Dignity Health
   185 Berry St Ste 300
   San Francisco CA 94107
   415 438-5500

(P-21533)
DIGNITY HEALTH
Also Called: Marian Regional Medical Center
1400 E Church St, Santa Maria (93454-5906)
PHONE..................805 739-3000
Charles Cova, *President*
Pius Fahlstrom, *Controller*
Nancy McGough, *Manager*
EMP: 400
SALES (corp-wide): 7.1B **Privately Held**
WEB: www.chw.edu
SIC: **8062** 8011 General medical & surgical hospitals; offices & clinics of medical doctors
PA: Dignity Health
   185 Berry St Ste 300
   San Francisco CA 94107
   415 438-5500

(P-21534)
DIGNITY HEALTH
5051 Verdugo Way Ste 100, Camarillo (93012-8681)
PHONE..................805 384-8071
Tom Lowry, *Branch Mgr*
Jason Newmark, *Mktg Dir*
Borge Riis-Vestgaard, *Sales Dir*
Cynthia Fiacco, *Nurse Practr*
EMP: 452
SALES (corp-wide): 7.1B **Privately Held**
SIC: **8062** General medical & surgical hospitals
PA: Dignity Health
   185 Berry St Ste 300
   San Francisco CA 94107
   415 438-5500

(P-21535)
DIGNITY HEALTH
Also Called: Arroyo Grande Community Hosp
345 S Halcyon Rd, Arroyo Grande (93420-3817)
PHONE..................805 473-7626
Fax: 805 473-7603
Sue Anderson, *CFO*
Cheri Dematteo, *Materials Mgr*
Sean Porcher, *Opers Staff*
Ray Davis, *Director*
Villa Infanto, *Director*
EMP: 400
SALES (corp-wide): 7.1B **Privately Held**
SIC: **8062** General medical & surgical hospitals
PA: Dignity Health
   185 Berry St Ste 300
   San Francisco CA 94107
   415 438-5500

(P-21536)
DIGNITY HEALTH
Also Called: Saint Mary Medical Center
1050 Linden Ave, Long Beach (90813-3321)
PHONE..................562 491-9000
Fax: 562 590-8652
Chris Diccio, *Principal*
Pamela Fair,
Steven Scheuer,
Bertram Sohl, *Ch OB/GYN*
Ann Marie Levan, *Ch Radiology*
EMP: 1450
SALES (corp-wide): 7.1B **Privately Held**
WEB: www.chw.edu
SIC: **8062** General medical & surgical hospitals
PA: Dignity Health
   185 Berry St Ste 300
   San Francisco CA 94107
   415 438-5500

(P-21537)
DIGNITY HEALTH (PA)
185 Berry St Ste 300, San Francisco (94107-1773)
PHONE..................415 438-5500
Lloyd Dean, *President*
Michael Erne, *COO*
Marvin O'Quinn, *COO*
Michael Blaszyk, *CFO*
Michael Blazysk, *CFO*
▲ EMP: 120
SALES (est): 7.1B **Privately Held**
WEB: www.chw.edu
SIC: **8062** General medical & surgical hospitals

(P-21538)
DIGNITY HEALTH
1700 Montgomery St # 300, San Francisco (94111-1021)
PHONE..................415 438-5500
Fax: 415 438-5724
Parmod Garg, *Finance*
Doreen Hartmann, *CFO*
Rodney Winegarner, *CFO*
Ken Harrison, *Manager*
Elizabeth Steckline, *Manager*
EMP: 474
SALES (corp-wide): 7.1B **Privately Held**
WEB: www.chw.edu
SIC: **8062** General medical & surgical hospitals
PA: Dignity Health
   185 Berry St Ste 300
   San Francisco CA 94107
   415 438-5500

(P-21539)
DIGNITY HEALTH
Also Called: California Hospital Med Ctr
1401 S Grand Ave, Los Angeles (90015-3010)
PHONE..................213 748-2411
Fax: 213 742-5416
Mark A Meyers, *President*
Bruce Swartz, *Senior VP*
Nicole Kerns, *Administration*
Nina Chokshi, *Technology*
Lydia F De Pano, *Analyst*
EMP: 1500
SALES (corp-wide): 7.1B **Privately Held*
WEB: www.chw.edu
SIC: **8062** 8741 General medical & surgical hospitals; management services
PA: Dignity Health
   185 Berry St Ste 300
   San Francisco CA 94107
   415 438-5500

(P-21540)
DIGNITY HEALTH
Also Called: St. Johns Pleasant Valley Hosp
2309 Antonio Ave, Camarillo (93010-1414)
PHONE..................805 389-5800
Fax: 805 383-7450
Daniel Herlinger, *Branch Mgr*
Ivan Hayward, *Ch Radiology*
William J Theurer, *Ch Radiology*
M Eugene Fussell, *Vice Pres*
Rich Carvotta, *Pharmacy Dir*
EMP: 250
SALES (corp-wide): 7.1B **Privately Held**
WEB: www.chw.edu
SIC: **8062** General medical & surgical hospitals
PA: Dignity Health
   185 Berry St Ste 300
   San Francisco CA 94107
   415 438-5500

(P-21541)
DIGNITY HEALTH
Also Called: St Johns Regional Medical Ctr
1600 N Rose Ave, Oxnard (93030-3722)
PHONE..................805 988-2500
Fax: 805 483-4572
George West, *Branch Mgr*
Chris Champlin, *Business Dir*
Amy Carrillo, *Executive Asst*
Kim Spencer, *Admin Asst*
Jeff Perry, *Info Tech Dir*
EMP: 1900
SALES (corp-wide): 7.1B **Privately Held**
SIC: **8062** General medical & surgical hospitals
PA: Dignity Health
   185 Berry St Ste 300
   San Francisco CA 94107
   415 438-5500

(P-21542)
DIGNITY HEALTH
Also Called: Pedi Center
400 Old River Rd, Bakersfield (93311-9781)
P.O. Box 119 (93302-0119)
PHONE..................661 632-5279
Fax: 661 663-6570
Kirk Douglas, *Branch Mgr*
Karen Karnot, *Op Rm Dir*
Jeanette Smart, *Materials Mgr*
Kim Horton, *Nursing Dir*
Mark Gilbert, *Pharmacist*
EMP: 120
SALES (corp-wide): 7.1B **Privately Held**
WEB: www.chw.edu
SIC: **8062** 8099 8011 General medical & surgical hospitals; childbirth preparation clinic; offices & clinics of medical doctors
PA: Dignity Health
   185 Berry St Ste 300
   San Francisco CA 94107
   415 438-5500

(P-21543)
DIGNITY HEALTH
Also Called: Mercy Hospital
2215 Truxtun Ave, Bakersfield (93301-3602)
PHONE..................661 632-5000
Rodney B Winegarner, *Branch Mgr*
Andy Cantu, *Human Res Dir*
Jason Helton,
Lynn Godat, *Director*
Debbie Hull, *Director*
EMP: 474
SALES (corp-wide): 7.1B **Privately Held**
SIC: **8062** General medical & surgical hospitals
PA: Dignity Health
   185 Berry St Ste 300
   San Francisco CA 94107
   415 438-5500

(P-21544)
DOCTORS HOSPITAL W COVINA INC
Also Called: West Covina Physical Therapy
725 S Orange Ave, West Covina (91790-2614)
PHONE..................626 338-8481
Fax: 626 960-9178
Pareed Mohamed, *CEO*
Richard Makamura, *CFO*
Jong Kim MD, *Treasurer*
Akbar Omar MD, *Vice Pres*
Pareed Aliyar MD, *Admin Sec*
EMP: 155
SQ FT: 50,000

▲ = Import ▼=Export
◆ =Import/Export

PRODUCTS & SERVICES SECTION

8062 - General Medical & Surgical Hospitals County (P-21564)

SALES: 10.6MM **Privately Held**
SIC: **8062** 8049 General medical & surgical hospitals; physical therapist

(P-21545)
DOCTORS MEDICAL CENTER LLC (HQ)
2000 Vale Rd, San Pablo (94806-3808)
P.O. Box 20760, El Sobrante (94820-0760)
PHONE 510 970-5000
Fax: 510 970-5728
Jo Stuart, *President*
Candy Markwith, *COO*
Lonnie Cantu, *Admin Sec*
Adele Margrave, *Human Res Dir*
Lita Ramos, *Purchasing*
EMP: 71
SQ FT: 276,000
SALES (est): 100.8MM **Privately Held**
SIC: **8062** General medical & surgical hospitals
PA: West Contra Costa Healthcare District
2000 Vale Rd
San Pablo CA 94806
510 970-5102

(P-21546)
DOMINICAN HOSPITAL FOUNDATION (HQ)
Also Called: C H W
1555 Soquel Dr, Santa Cruz (95065-1794)
PHONE 831 462-7700
Fax: 831 462-7769
Beverly Grova, *CEO*
Chuck Maffia, *President*
Jon Sisk, *President*
Sam Leask, *CEO*
Ted Burke, *Vice Pres*
EMP: 168
SQ FT: 110,000
SALES: 4.4MM
SALES (corp-wide): 7.1B **Privately Held**
SIC: **8062** 8051 General medical & surgical hospitals; skilled nursing care facilities
PA: Dignity Health
185 Berry St Ste 300
San Francisco CA 94107
415 438-5500

(P-21547)
DOWNEY REGIONAL MEDICAL
Also Called: PIH HOME HEALTH SERVICES
11500 Brookshire Ave, Downey (90241-4990)
PHONE 562 698-0811
Fax: 562 904-5102
James R West, *President*
Parakrama T Chandrasoma, *Ch Pathology*
Paul H Yoshino,
David G Aguilar, *Ch OB/GYN*
Bryan Smolskis, *COO*
EMP: 1150
SQ FT: 225,000
SALES: 126.8MM
SALES (corp-wide): 555.9MM **Privately Held**
SIC: **8062** General medical & surgical hospitals
PA: Presbyterian Intercommunity Hospital, Inc.
12401 Washington Blvd
Whittier CA 90602
562 698-0811

(P-21548)
EAST LOS ANGELES DOCTORS
4060 Whittier Blvd, Los Angeles (90023-2526)
PHONE 323 268-5514
Fax: 323 266-1145
Hector Hernandez, *CEO*
Antonette Scott, *Records Dir*
Steve Lopez, *CFO*
Carmelo James, *Ch Nursing Ofcr*
Nadine Mariotti, *Ch Nursing Ofcr*
EMP: 350
SQ FT: 25,000
SALES: 71.2MM **Privately Held**
WEB: www.elalax.com
SIC: **8062** Hospital, affiliated with AMA residency

(P-21549)
EAST VALLEY GLENDORA HOSP LP
Also Called: East Valley Hospital Med Ctr
150 W Route 66, Glendora (91740-6207)
PHONE 626 335-0231
Fax: 626 335-5082
C Joseph Chang, *Ch of Bd*
Cerna Atil,
Linda Reitz, *CFO*
Keith Scholl, *Technician*
Maryann Bennett, *Nursing Dir*
EMP: 300
SQ FT: 60,592
SALES: 59.4MM **Privately Held**
WEB: www.evhmc.org
SIC: **8062** General medical & surgical hospitals

(P-21550)
EDEN TOWNSHIP HOSPITAL DST
Also Called: SUTTER C H S
20103 Lake Chabot Rd, Castro Valley (94546-5305)
PHONE 510 537-1234
Terry Glubka, *President*
Nadder Mirsepassi, *Treasurer*
Deborah Henderson, *Risk Mgmt Dir*
Jan Hoang, *Pharmacy Dir*
Julie Clayton, *Asst Admin*
EMP: 968
SQ FT: 190,000
SALES: 378K
SALES (corp-wide): 11B **Privately Held**
WEB: www.edenmedcenter.org
SIC: **8062** 8011 General medical & surgical hospitals; offices & clinics of medical doctors
PA: Sutter Health
2200 River Plaza Dr
Sacramento CA 95833
916 733-8800

(P-21551)
EISENHOWER MEDICAL CENTER (PA)
39000 Bob Hope Dr, Rancho Mirage (92270-3221)
PHONE 760 340-3911
Fax: 760 346-8857
G Aubrey Serfling, *CEO*
Barbara Comess, *Ch Pathology*
Alfred Shen,
Martin Massielo, *COO*
Kimberly Osborne, *CFO*
▲ EMP: 2000 EST: 1971
SQ FT: 240,000
SALES: 571.7MM **Privately Held**
SIC: **8062** 8082 General medical & surgical hospitals; home health care services

(P-21552)
EL CAMINO SURGERY CENTER LLC
2480 Grant Rd Fl 1, Mountain View (94040-4334)
PHONE 650 961-1200
Fax: 650 960-7041
Lisa Cooper, *Mng Member*
Ann Fyfe, *Vice Pres*
Sandy Keating, *Administration*
Greg Walton, *CTO*
Judy Twitchell, *Info Tech Mgr*
EMP: 70
SALES (est): 10.6MM **Privately Held**
WEB: www.ecsc.com
SIC: **8062** General medical & surgical hospitals

(P-21553)
EL CENTRO REGIONAL MEDICAL CTR (PA)
Also Called: E C R M C
1415 Ross Ave, El Centro (92243-4306)
PHONE 760 339-7100
Fax: 760 339-7345
Robert R Frantz, *President*
Barbara Blevins, *President*
Claudia Dubbe, *President*
Kathy Farmer, *CFO*
Amanda Brooke, *Trustee*
EMP: 603
SQ FT: 187,044

SALES: 127.8MM **Privately Held**
WEB: www.ecrmc.org
SIC: **8062** General medical & surgical hospitals

(P-21554)
ELADH LP
Also Called: East Los Angeles Doctors Hosp
4060 Whittier Blvd, Los Angeles (90023-2526)
PHONE 323 268-5514
Hector Hernandez, *Managing Prtnr*
EMP: 99
SALES (est): 6.8MM
SALES (corp-wide): 105.9MM **Privately Held**
SIC: **8062** General medical & surgical hospitals
PA: Avanti Health System, Llc
222 N Sepulveda Blvd # 950
El Segundo CA 90245
310 356-0550

(P-21555)
EMANUEL MEDICAL CENTER INC
Also Called: Brandel Manor
1801 N Olive Ave, Turlock (95382-2568)
PHONE 209 667-5600
Fax: 209 669-2366
Dawn Sughruel, *Director*
EMP: 160
SQ FT: 58,282
SALES (corp-wide): 18.7B **Publicly Held**
WEB: www.emanuelmedicalcenter.com
SIC: **8062** 8051 General medical & surgical hospitals; convalescent home with continuous nursing care
HQ: Emanuel Medical Center, Inc.
825 Delbon Ave
Turlock CA 95382
209 667-4200

(P-21556)
EMANUEL MEDICAL CENTER INC (DH)
825 Delbon Ave, Turlock (95382-2016)
PHONE 209 667-4200
Fax: 209 669-2372
Susan Micheletti, *CEO*
Huy Dao,
Ronald Arakelian MD,
Judy Walters,
Joseph L Higgins, *Ch Radiology*
EMP: 850
SQ FT: 200,000
SALES: 236.2MM
SALES (corp-wide): 18.7B **Publicly Held**
WEB: www.emanuelmedicalcenter.com
SIC: **8062** General medical & surgical hospitals
HQ: Doctors Medical Center Of Modesto, Inc.
1441 Florida Ave
Modesto CA 95350
209 578-1211

(P-21557)
EMANUEL MEDICAL CENTER INC
Also Called: Turlock Diagnostic Center
2121 Colorado Ave Ste A, Turlock (95382-2012)
PHONE 209 664-2520
Fax: 209 656-5510
Michael Iltis, *Manager*
EMP: 103
SALES (corp-wide): 18.7B **Publicly Held**
WEB: www.emanuelmedicalcenter.com
SIC: **8062** 8011 General medical & surgical hospitals; medical centers
HQ: Emanuel Medical Center, Inc.
825 Delbon Ave
Turlock CA 95382
209 667-4200

(P-21558)
EMERGENCY MEDICINE SPECIALIST
Also Called: Emsoc
1010 W La Veta Ave # 755, Orange (92868-4306)
PHONE 714 543-8911
Fax: 714 744-8527
James E Pierog, *Chairman*

Linda J Pierog, *Office Mgr*
David Merin, *Emerg Med Spec*
EMP: 90
SALES (est): 6.5MM **Privately Held**
SIC: **8062** General medical & surgical hospitals

(P-21559)
ENCINO HOSPITAL MEDICAL CENTER
16237 Ventura Blvd, Encino (91436-2272)
PHONE 818 995-5000
Fax: 818 907-5382
Bockhi Park, *CEO*
Prem Reddy, *President*
Sherry Yeom, *Buyer*
EMP: 400
SALES (est): 52.9MM
SALES (corp-wide): 2.6B **Privately Held**
SIC: **8062** General medical & surgical hospitals
PA: Prime Healthcare Services Inc
3300 E Guasti Rd Ste 300
Ontario CA 91761
909 235-4400

(P-21560)
ENCINO TRZANA REGIONAL MED CTR
16237 Ventura Blvd, Encino (91436-2201)
PHONE 818 995-5000
EMP: 450
SALES: 41.7MM **Privately Held**
SIC: **8062**

(P-21561)
ENLOE HOSPT-PHYS THRPY
1444 Magnolia Ave, Chico (95926-3227)
PHONE 530 891-7300
Brenda Logan, *Director*
EMP: 141
SALES (corp-wide): 3.6MM **Privately Held**
SIC: **8062** General medical & surgical hospitals
PA: Enloe Hospital - Physical Therapy Dept
1600 Esplanade
Chico CA 95926
530 891-7300

(P-21562)
ENLOE MEDICAL CENTER
1448 Esplanade, Chico (95926-3309)
PHONE 530 332-6745
Fax: 530 891-5609
Robert Adams, *Branch Mgr*
EMP: 75
SALES (corp-wide): 505.9MM **Privately Held**
SIC: **8062** General medical & surgical hospitals
PA: Enloe Medical Center
1531 Esplanade
Chico CA 95926
530 332-7300

(P-21563)
ENLOE MEDICAL CENTER
Also Called: Enloe Outpatient Center
888 Lakeside Vlg Cmns, Chico (95928-3979)
PHONE 530 332-6400
Fax: 530 899-2061
Joleen Nixon, *Director*
Kathy Buck, *Director*
EMP: 130
SQ FT: 44,171
SALES (corp-wide): 505.9MM **Privately Held**
SIC: **8062** 8093 General medical & surgical hospitals; specialty outpatient clinics
PA: Enloe Medical Center
1531 Esplanade
Chico CA 95926
530 332-7300

(P-21564)
FAMILY MDCINE RSIDENCY PROGRAM
155 N Fresno St Ste 326, Fresno (93701-2302)
PHONE 559 499-6450
Ivan Gomez MD, *Director*
EMP: 60

8062 - General Medical & Surgical Hospitals County (P-21565)

SALES (est): 968.2K Privately Held
SIC: 8062 Hospital, AMA approved residency

(P-21565)
FEATHER RIVER HOSPITAL (PA)
5974 Pentz Rd, Paradise (95969-5593)
PHONE.................530 877-9361
Fax: 530 876-2160
Wayne Ferch, CEO
Tim Gleason,
Dan Gordon, CFO
Patricia Sangl, Treasurer
James P Lacey, Top Exec
EMP: 620
SQ FT: 30,000
SALES: 207MM Privately Held
SIC: 8062 8051 General medical & surgical hospitals; convalescent home with continuous nursing care

(P-21566)
FEATHER RIVER HOSPITAL
Also Called: Feather River Home Health
6626 Clark Rd Ste P, Paradise (95969-3523)
PHONE.................530 872-3378
Fax: 530 872-2064
Gregg Quattlevaum, Manager
Lisa Shaffer, Sales Executive
EMP: 60
SALES (corp-wide): 207MM Privately Held
SIC: 8062 8082 General medical & surgical hospitals; home health care services
PA: Feather River Hospital
5974 Pentz Rd
Paradise CA 95969
530 877-9361

(P-21567)
FOOTHILL HOSPITAL-MORRIS L JO (PA)
Also Called: Foothill Presbyterian Hospital
250 S Grand Ave, Glendora (91741-4218)
PHONE.................626 857-3145
Fax: 626 857-3138
Robert Curry, President
Nadia Koelliker, Lab Dir
Casey Vitalez, Admin Asst
Melissa Howard, Administration
Diana Zenner, Administration
EMP: 127
SQ FT: 104,371
SALES: 82.7MM Privately Held
SIC: 8062 General medical & surgical hospitals

(P-21568)
FOUNTAIN VALLEY REGL HOSPL
Also Called: TENET
17100 Euclid St, Fountain Valley (92708-4043)
P.O. Box 8010 (92728-8010)
PHONE.................714 966-7200
Fax: 714 966-7204
Joseph Badalian, Principal
Surinder Thind,
Jennifer Kramer,
Debra Derda,
Kay Woinarowicz, Records Dir
EMP: 1200
SALES: 351.3MM
SALES (corp-wide): 18.7B Publicly Held
WEB: www.tenenthealth.com
SIC: 8062 General medical & surgical hospitals
HQ: Tenet Healthsystem Medical, Inc
1445 Ross Ave Ste 1400
Dallas TX 75202
469 893-2000

(P-21569)
FREEMONT RIDEOUT HEALTH GROUP
Also Called: Freemont Rideout Hospice
939 Live Oak Blvd Ste A4, Yuba City (95991-4002)
PHONE.................530 749-4386
Fax: 530 751-4896
Tina Wilson, Branch Mgr
EMP: 50

SALES (corp-wide): 28.9MM Privately Held
SIC: 8062 8361 General medical & surgical hospitals; residential care
PA: Freemont Rideout Health Group
989 Plumas St
Yuba City CA 95991
530 751-4010

(P-21570)
FREMONT HOSPITAL
Also Called: Fremont Medical Center
620 J St, Marysville (95901-5413)
PHONE.................530 751-4000
Thomas P Hayes, CEO
Jeanne Martin, Admin Sec
EMP: 598
SQ FT: 121,000
SALES: 24.5MM
SALES (corp-wide): 28.9MM Privately Held
SIC: 8062 General medical & surgical hospitals
PA: Freemont Rideout Health Group
989 Plumas St
Yuba City CA 95991
530 751-4010

(P-21571)
FRENCH HOSP MED CTR FOUNDATION (HQ)
1911 Johnson Ave, San Luis Obispo (93401-4131)
PHONE.................805 543-5353
Fax: 805 543-5708
Jim Copeland, Chairman
Allan Iftiniuk, CEO
Sue Anderson, CFO
Patricia Gomez, Admin Sec
Lori Shield, Admin Sec
EMP: 480
SQ FT: 80,000
SALES (est): 53.8MM
SALES (corp-wide): 7.1B Privately Held
SIC: 8062 General medical & surgical hospitals
PA: Dignity Health
185 Berry St Ste 300
San Francisco CA 94107
415 438-5500

(P-21572)
FRESNO CMNTY HOSP & MED CTR (HQ)
2823 Fresno St, Fresno (93721-1324)
P.O. Box 1232 (93715-1232)
PHONE.................559 459-6000
Fax: 559 442-6470
Phillip Hinton, President
Tim A Joslin, CEO
Maria Garcia, CFO
William Grigg, CFO
Roger Fretwell, Treasurer
EMP: 3000
SQ FT: 2,469
SALES: 1.3B
SALES (corp-wide): 1.4B Privately Held
SIC: 8062 General medical & surgical hospitals
PA: Community Medical Center
2823 Fresno St
Fresno CA 93721
559 459-6000

(P-21573)
FRESNO SURGERY CENTER LP (PA)
Also Called: Fresno Surgical Hospital
6125 N Fresno St, Fresno (93710-5207)
PHONE.................559 431-8000
Kristine Kassahn, CEO
Robin Ryder,
Roberta Holguin, Records Dir
Bruce Cecil, CFO
Barry Smith, CFO
EMP: 91
SQ FT: 32,000
SALES: 64.2MM Privately Held
WEB: www.fresnosurgerycenter.com
SIC: 8062 8011 General medical & surgical hospitals; orthopedic physician; gynecologist; surgeon

(P-21574)
GARDENA HOSPITAL LP
Also Called: Memorial Hospital of Gardena
1145 W Redondo Beach Blvd, Gardena (90247-3511)
PHONE.................310 532-4200
Kathy Wojno, CEO
John N Loizeaux-Witte, Partner
EMP: 760
SALES: 124.6MM Privately Held
SIC: 8062 General medical & surgical hospitals; rehabilitation services; freestanding emergency medical center

(P-21575)
GARDENS RGNAL HOSP MED CTR INC
Also Called: Gardens Regional Hosp Med Ctr
21530 Pioneer Blvd, Hawaiian Gardens (90716-2608)
PHONE.................877 877-1104
Gregory Padilla, CEO
Terri Davis, CFO
Brian Walton, Chairman
Daisy Schneidman, Officer
Manuela Ochoa, Business Dir
EMP: 350
SQ FT: 66,000
SALES: 48.5MM Privately Held
SIC: 8062 General medical & surgical hospitals

(P-21576)
GLENDALE ADVENTIST MEDICAL CTR (HQ)
Also Called: ADVENTIST HEALTH
1509 Wilson Ter, Glendale (91206-4007)
P.O. Box 619002 (91206)
PHONE.................818 409-8000
Fax: 818 409-5600
Warren L Tetz, CEO
Igor Fineman,
Robert McKay, Ch Radiology
Frank Dupper, Ch of Bd
Fred Manchur, President
EMP: 2550
SQ FT: 700,000
SALES: 408.3MM
SALES (corp-wide): 251.4MM Privately Held
WEB: www.glendaleadventist.com
SIC: 8062 8093 8011 General medical & surgical hospitals; mental health clinic, outpatient; freestanding emergency medical center
PA: Adventist Health System/West
2100 Douglas Blvd
Roseville CA 95661
916 781-2000

(P-21577)
GLENDALE MEMORIAL HEALTH CORP
Also Called: Glendale Memorial Breast Ctr
222 W Eulalia St, Glendale (91204-2849)
PHONE.................818 502-2323
Fax: 818 502-4747
Mark Meyers, President
EMP: 1000
SALES (corp-wide): 7.1B Privately Held
SIC: 8062 8099 General medical & surgical hospitals; medical services organization
HQ: Glendale Memorial Health Corporation
1420 S Central Ave
Glendale CA 91204
818 502-1900

(P-21578)
GLENN MEDICAL CENTER INC
1133 W Sycamore St, Willows (95988-2601)
PHONE.................530 934-4681
Fax: 530 934-1815
William Casey, CEO
Kate Lewis, Records Dir
Gary Pea, CFO
Deborah McMillan, Executive
Norma Pieper, Infect Cntl Dir
EMP: 99
SQ FT: 62,000
SALES: 13.8MM Privately Held
SIC: 8062 General medical & surgical hospitals

(P-21579)
GLENOAKS CONVALESCENT HOSP LP
409 W Glenoaks Blvd, Glendale (91202-2916)
PHONE.................818 240-4300
Fax: 818 247-0949
Elaine Levine, Partner
Rudolfo Protatio, Director
EMP: 85
SQ FT: 22,306
SALES: 473.1MM Privately Held
SIC: 8062 General medical & surgical hospitals

(P-21580)
GOLDEN EMPIRE CONVALESCENT HOS
121 Dorsey Dr, Grass Valley (95945-5201)
PHONE.................530 273-1316
Fax: 530 273-4809
Vicki Young, Partner
Chan Sinsaeng, Social Dir
Nicki Talman, Office Mgr
Claire Enright, Nursing Dir
Christopher Claydon, Director
EMP: 180
SALES (est): 14.4MM Privately Held
WEB: www.goldenempiresnf.com
SIC: 8062 General medical & surgical hospitals

(P-21581)
GOLETA VALLEY COTTAGE HOSPITAL
Also Called: Cottage Health System
351 S Patterson Ave, Santa Barbara (93111-2403)
P.O. Box 689 (93102-0689)
PHONE.................805 681-6468
Fax: 805 681-6488
Ronald C Werft, President
Robert Knight, Ch of Bd
Joan Bricher, President
Jeff Allen, Vice Pres
Diane Wisby, Vice Pres
EMP: 275
SQ FT: 92,273
SALES: 76.1MM Privately Held
SIC: 8062 General medical & surgical hospitals

(P-21582)
GOOD SAMARITAN HOSPITAL (PA)
901 Olive Dr, Bakersfield (93308-4144)
P.O. Box 85002 (93380-5002)
PHONE.................661 399-4461
Fax: 661 399-4224
Andrew B Leeka, CEO
David Huff, Partner
Sakrepatna Manohara, President
Anand Manohara, CEO
Canesh Acharya, CFO
EMP: 203
SQ FT: 49,001
SALES (est): 56.3MM Privately Held
SIC: 8062 8063 8069 General medical & surgical hospitals; psychiatric hospitals; specialty hospitals, except psychiatric

(P-21583)
GOOD SAMARITAN HOSPITAL (PA)
1225 Wilshire Blvd, Los Angeles (90017-1901)
PHONE.................213 977-2121
Fax: 213 977-2309
Andrew B Leeka, CEO
Marcia Stein, Records Dir
Charles Munger, Ch of Bd
Dan McLaughlin, COO
Lynne Whaley-Welty, COO
▲ EMP: 76
SQ FT: 350,000
SALES: 351.9MM Privately Held
SIC: 8062 General medical & surgical hospitals

PRODUCTS & SERVICES SECTION
8062 - General Medical & Surgical Hospitals County (P-21602)

(P-21584)
GOOD SAMARITAN HOSPITAL LP (DH)
2425 Samaritan Dr, San Jose (95124-3985)
P.O. Box 240002 (95154-2402)
PHONE..............................408 559-2011
Fax: 408 559-2499
Paul Beaupre, *CEO*
Jordan Herget, *COO*
Lana Arad, *CFO*
Darrel Neuenschwander, *CFO*
Paul Deaupre, *Officer*
EMP: 1200
SALES (est): 209.6MM **Publicly Held**
WEB: www.goodsamsj.org
SIC: **8062** General medical & surgical hospitals
HQ: Hca Inc.
1 Park Plz
Nashville TN 37203
615 344-9551

(P-21585)
GOOD SAMARITAN HOSPITAL LP
Also Called: Mission Oaks Hospital
15891 Los Gtos Almaden Rd, Los Gatos (95032-3742)
PHONE..............................408 356-4111
Fax: 408 358-5685
Brian Knecht, *COO*
Betsy Collins, *QA Dir*
Elaine Retzer, *Manager*
EMP: 200 **Publicly Held**
WEB: www.goodsamsj.org
SIC: **8062** General medical & surgical hospitals
HQ: Good Samaritan Hospital, L.P.
2425 Samaritan Dr
San Jose CA 95124
408 559-2011

(P-21586)
GORDON LANE CONVALESCENT HOSP
1821 E Chapman Ave, Fullerton (92831-4102)
PHONE..............................714 879-7301
Fax: 714 224-3320
Lee Shannon, *President*
Grace Rivera, *Nursing Dir*
EMP: 65 EST: 1971
SQ FT: 24,180
SALES (est): 5.5MM **Privately Held**
SIC: **8062** 8051 General medical & surgical hospitals; skilled nursing care facilities

(P-21587)
GROSSMONT HOSPITAL CORPORATION (HQ)
5555 Grossmont Center Dr, La Mesa (91942-3077)
PHONE..............................619 740-6000
Fax: 619 461-7191
Dan Gross, *CEO*
Tere Trout, *Ch Radiology*
Susan Olsen, *Administration*
Branko Vasich, *Engineer*
Daniel Kindron, *Finance*
EMP: 1740
SQ FT: 494,000
SALES: 712.6MM
SALES (corp-wide): 3.4B **Privately Held**
WEB: www.grossmonthealthcare.com
SIC: **8062** General medical & surgical hospitals
PA: Sharp Healthcare
8695 Spectrum Center Blvd
San Diego CA 92123
858 499-4000

(P-21588)
GROSSMONT HOSPITAL CORPORATION
Also Called: Grossmont Home Hlth & Hospice
8881 Fletcher Pkwy # 105, La Mesa (91942-3134)
PHONE..............................619 667-1900
Jean Cruise, *Manager*
Lorraine Banawa,
EMP: 150

SALES (corp-wide): 3.4B **Privately Held**
WEB: www.grossmonthealthcare.com
SIC: **8062** 8082 General medical & surgical hospitals; home health care services
HQ: Grossmont Hospital Corporation
5555 Grossmont Center Dr
La Mesa CA 91942
619 740-6000

(P-21589)
HANFORD COMMUNITY HOSPITAL (HQ)
Also Called: ADVENTIST HEALTH
450 Greenfield Ave, Hanford (93230-3513)
P.O. Box 619002, Roseville (95661-9002)
PHONE..............................559 582-9000
Fax: 559 584-7401
Scott Reiner, *Chairman*
Eric Martinson, *CFO*
Kurby McKague, *Senior VP*
Carrie Luyster, *Vice Pres*
Michael Aubrey, *Info Tech Dir*
EMP: 640
SQ FT: 52,060
SALES: 230.4MM
SALES (corp-wide): 251.4MM **Privately Held**
WEB: www.hanford.ah.org
SIC: **8062** General medical & surgical hospitals
PA: Adventist Health System/West
2100 Douglas Blvd
Roseville CA 95661
916 781-2000

(P-21590)
HARBOR-CLA MED CTR DEPT SRGERY
1000 W Carson St 25, Torrance (90502-2004)
PHONE..............................310 222-2700
Christian De Virgillo, *Principal*
Steven Lee, *Principal*
Kyle Mock, *Principal*
Alexander Schwed, *Principal*
Monica Sifuentes, *Director*
EMP: 99
SALES (est): 588.3K **Privately Held**

(P-21591)
HARBOR-UCLA MEDICAL CENTER
1000 W Carson St 2, Torrance (90502-2059)
PHONE..............................310 222-2345
Fax: 310 222-5658
Miguel Ortiz, *CEO*
Esmeralda Guillen, *Analyst*
Raimund Hirschberg, *Nephrology*
Karl Burgoyne, *Director*
Darrell Harrington, *Director*
EMP: 3000
SALES (est): 184MM **Privately Held**
SIC: **8062** General medical & surgical hospitals

(P-21592)
HAYWARD SISTERS HOSPITAL (HQ)
Also Called: ST ROSE HOSPITAL
27200 Calaroga Ave, Hayward (94545-4339)
P.O. Box 351209 (94545)
PHONE..............................510 264-4000
Fax: 510 264-4007
Michael Mahoney, *President*
Robert Heath, *President*
Roger Krissman, *CFO*
Aman Dhuper, *Exec Dir*
Rene Macias, *Program Mgr*
EMP: 842
SQ FT: 173,000
SALES: 112.9MM
SALES (corp-wide): 1B **Privately Held**
WEB: www.aboutinfectioncontrol.com
SIC: **8062** General medical & surgical hospitals
PA: Alecto Healthcare Services Llc
16310 Bake Pkwy Ste 200
Irvine CA 92618
323 938-3161

(P-21593)
HCA INC
Also Called: Main Hospital
225 N Jackson Ave, San Jose (95116-1603)
PHONE..............................408 729-2801
Trey Abshier, *COO*
Cathy Parker,
Darina Kavanagh, *Ch Nursing Ofcr*
Rosalie Bryant, *CTO*
Gary Goeringer, *CTO*
EMP: 115 **Publicly Held**
SIC: **8062** General medical & surgical hospitals
HQ: Hca Inc.
1 Park Plz
Nashville TN 37203
615 344-9551

(P-21594)
HCA INC
Also Called: West Hills Hospital & Med Ctr
7300 Medical Center Dr, West Hills (91307-1902)
PHONE..............................818 676-4000
Beverly Gilmore, *CEO*
Robert Howard, *Ch Radiology*
Lisa Nagy, *Volunteer Dir*
Patricia Gautreau, *Op Rm Dir*
Gail Geyer, *Risk Mgmt Dir*
EMP: 195 **Publicly Held**
SIC: **8062** General medical & surgical hospitals
HQ: Hca Inc.
1 Park Plz
Nashville TN 37203
615 344-9551

(P-21595)
HCA INC
Also Called: Columbia San Clemente Hospital
654 Camino De Los Mares, San Clemente (92673-2827)
PHONE..............................949 496-1122
Patricia Wolfram, *CEO*
Jamie Coate, *Info Tech Mgr*
Deanne Moran, *Human Res Dir*
EMP: 250 **Publicly Held**
SIC: **8062** General medical & surgical hospitals
HQ: Hca Inc.
1 Park Plz
Nashville TN 37203
615 344-9551

(P-21596)
HEALTH RESOURCES CORP
Also Called: Coastal Community Hospital
2701 S Bristol St, Santa Ana (92704-6201)
PHONE..............................714 754-5454
Trevor Fetter, *President*
Susan Houraney, *Executive Asst*
EMP: 400
SALES (est): 12MM
SALES (corp-wide): 449.3MM **Privately Held**
WEB: www.ihhioc.com
SIC: **8062** General medical & surgical hospitals
PA: Kpc Healthcare, Inc.
1301 N Tustin Ave
Santa Ana CA 92705
714 953-3652

(P-21597)
HEALTHCARE BARTON SYSTEM (PA)
2170 South Ave, South Lake Tahoe (96150-7026)
P.O. Box 9578 (96158-9578)
PHONE..............................530 541-3420
John Williams, *CEO*
Dick Derby, *CFO*
Richard Derby, *CFO*
Gary F Willen, *Executive*
Barry Keil, *Business Dir*
EMP: 554
SQ FT: 112,190
SALES: 162.4MM **Privately Held**
SIC: **8062** General medical & surgical hospitals

(P-21598)
HEALTHSMART PACIFIC INC (PA)
Also Called: Long Beach Pain Center
20377 Sw Acacia St # 110, Newport Beach (92660-0781)
P.O. Box 513565, Los Angeles (90051-3565)
PHONE..............................562 595-1911
Fax: 562 492-1363
Michael Ddrobot, *CEO*
Jay M Jazayeri,
Michael D Drobot, *CEO*
Jim Canedo, *Vice Pres*
Patricia Bussey, *Case Mgmt Dir*
EMP: 610
SQ FT: 150,000
SALES (est): 148.3MM **Privately Held**
SIC: **8062** General medical & surgical hospitals

(P-21599)
HEMET VLY MED CENTER-EDUCATION
1117 E Devonshire Ave, Hemet (92543-3083)
PHONE..............................951 652-2811
Fax: 951 766-6470
Kali Chaudhuri, *CEO*
Mildred Ramos, *Ch Pathology*
Syed Rizvi, *Ch OB/GYN*
Frederick E Whit, *Ch Radiology*
Kathy Cain, *CFO*
EMP: 1200
SQ FT: 300,000
SALES (est): 98MM **Privately Held**
SIC: **8062** General medical & surgical hospitals

(P-21600)
HENRY MAYO NEWHALL HOSPITAL (PA)
23845 Mcbean Pkwy, Valencia (91355-2083)
PHONE..............................661 253-8000
Fax: 661 253-8142
Roger E Seaver, *President*
Elizabeth Hopp, *Ch of Bd*
Cathy Richardson, *CFO*
James Hickens, *Treasurer*
Sheron Mitchell, *Chief Mktg Ofcr*
EMP: 54
SQ FT: 210,000
SALES: 307.4MM **Privately Held**
WEB: www.henrymayo.com
SIC: **8062** General medical & surgical hospitals

(P-21601)
HENRY MAYO NEWHALL MEM HLTH
Also Called: Henrymayo Newhall Mem Hosp
23845 Mcbean Pkwy, Valencia (91355-2001)
P.O. Box 55279 (91385-0279)
PHONE..............................661 253-8000
Fax: 661 253-7031
Roger Seaver, *President*
Adrian Thompson, *Administration*
Maria Strmsek, *Facilities Mgr*
Nicholas J Tuso, *Obstetrician*
Weston Anderson, *Manager*
EMP: 1500
SALES: 251.8MM **Privately Held**
SIC: **8062** General medical & surgical hospitals

(P-21602)
HI-DESERT MEM HLTH CARE DST (PA)
Also Called: Hi-Desert Medical Center
6601 White Feather Rd, Joshua Tree (92252-6607)
PHONE..............................760 366-3711
Fax: 619 366-6251
Keith Mesmer, *CEO*
Sharon Kulch, *Records Dir*
Thoma Duda, *CFO*
Robert Petrina, *CFO*
Herman Galicia, *Pharmacy Dir*
EMP: 480 EST: 1964
SQ FT: 100,000

8062 - General Medical & Surgical Hospitals County (P-21603)

SALES (est): 69.5MM **Privately Held**
WEB: www.carolyager.com
SIC: 8062 Hospital, affiliated with AMA residency

(P-21603)
HOAG MEMORIAL HOSPITAL PRESBT (PA)
1 Hoag Dr, Newport Beach (92663-4162)
P.O. Box 6100 (92658-6100)
PHONE 949 764-4624
Fax: 949 760-2083
Robert Braithwaite, *CEO*
William Vandalsem, *Ch Radiology*
Tim Paulson, *CFO*
Michael Ricks, *Exec VP*
Flynn A Andrizzi, *Senior VP*
EMP: 3600
SALES: 822.4MM **Privately Held**
SIC: 8062 General medical & surgical hospitals

(P-21604)
HOAG MEMORIAL HOSPITAL PRESBT
16200 Sand Canyon Ave, Irvine (92618-3714)
PHONE 949 764-4624
EMP: 1818
SALES (corp-wide): 822.4MM **Privately Held**
SIC: 8062 General medical & surgical hospitals
PA: Hoag Memorial Hospital Presbyterian
1 Hoag Dr
Newport Beach CA 92663
949 764-4624

(P-21605)
HOLLYWOOD COMMUNITY HOSPITAL M
Also Called: Hollywood Cmnty Hosp Hollywood
6245 De Longpre Ave, Los Angeles (90028-8253)
PHONE 323 462-2271
Fax: 323 461-9278
Robert Starling, *CEO*
Ron Messenger, *President*
Manfred Krukemeyer, *Vice Ch Bd*
Cecilia Militante, *Lab Dir*
Clive Nagatani, *Radiology Dir*
EMP: 220
SQ FT: 100,000
SALES (est): 75.2MM **Privately Held**
WEB: www.clarenthospital.com
SIC: 8062 General medical & surgical hospitals

(P-21606)
HOLLYWOOD MEDICAL CENTER LP
Also Called: Hollywood Presbyterian Med Ctr
1300 N Vermont Ave, Los Angeles (90027-6098)
PHONE 213 413-3000
Jeff Nelson, *Partner*
Micheal Almanzor, *Controller*
EMP: 1250
SALES: 281.2MM **Privately Held**
WEB: www.qahpmc.com
SIC: 8062 General medical & surgical hospitals
PA: Cha Health Systems, Inc
3731 Wilshire Blvd # 850
Los Angeles CA 90010
213 487-3211

(P-21607)
HOSPITAL OF BARSTOW INC
Also Called: Barstow Community Hospital
820 E Mountain View St, Barstow (92311-3004)
P.O. Box 1120 (92312-1120)
PHONE 760 256-1761
Fax: 619 256-3490
Sean Fowler, *CEO*
Michelle Brooks, *President*
Michael T Portacci, *President*
Richard D Staggs, *Nurse Practr*
Sheryl Curry, *Director*
EMP: 215
SQ FT: 54,000
SALES (est): 68.3MM
SALES (corp-wide): 22.5B **Publicly Held**
WEB: www.barstowhospital.com
SIC: 8062 Hospital, affiliated with AMA residency
PA: Community Health Systems, Inc.
4000 Meridian Blvd
Franklin TN 37067
615 465-7000

(P-21608)
HUNTINGTON HOSPITAL
100 W California Blvd, Pasadena (91105-3010)
PHONE 626 397-5000
Peter W Corrigan, *Principal*
Gail Cinexi,
William Caton,
Linda Jackson, *President*
Bernadette Merlino, *Vice Pres*
EMP: 237 **EST:** 2011
SALES: 513.4MM **Privately Held**
SIC: 8062 General medical & surgical hospitals

(P-21609)
INDIAN HEALTH SERVICE
1 Indian Hill Rd, Winterhaven (92283)
PHONE 760 572-0217
EMP: 81 **Publicly Held**
SIC: 8062 General medical & surgical hospitals
HQ: Indian Health Service
5600 Fishers Ln
Rockville MD 20852

(P-21610)
INDIAN VALLEY HEALTH CARE DIST
Also Called: Indian Valley Hospital
184 Hot Springs Rd, Greenville (95947-9747)
PHONE 530 284-7191
Fax: 530 284-6696
Sue Neer, *CEO*
Sheila Grothe, *Administration*
Wick Viswell, *Administration*
Robert Robertson, *Finance Dir*
Sharla Satterfield, *Librarian*
EMP: 80
SQ FT: 20,000
SALES (est): 3.2MM **Privately Held**
WEB: www.ivhcd.com
SIC: 8062 General medical & surgical hospitals

(P-21611)
INLAND FAMILY HEALTH WELLNESS
Also Called: Sierra Family Health Center
400 N Pepper Ave Fl 6, Colton (92324-1801)
PHONE 909 475-2300
Guillermo Valenzuela, *President*
EMP: 50
SALES (est): 2.8MM **Privately Held**
SIC: 8062 General medical & surgical hospitals

(P-21612)
INLAND VLY RGIONAL MED CTR INC (HQ)
36485 Inland Valley Dr, Wildomar (92595-9681)
PHONE 951 677-1111
Fax: 951 677-0056
Alan B Miller, *CEO*
Diane Moon, *CFO*
Barry Thorfinnson, *CFO*
Derek Shiba, *Infect Cntl Dir*
Teri Ransbury, *Risk Mgmt Dir*
EMP: 50
SQ FT: 77,000
SALES (est): 49.5MM
SALES (corp-wide): 9B **Publicly Held**
SIC: 8062 8011 General medical & surgical hospitals; clinic, operated by physicians
PA: Universal Health Services, Inc.
367 S Gulph Rd
King Of Prussia PA 19406
610 768-3300

(P-21613)
INTERHEALTH CORPORATION (PA)
Also Called: Pih Health
12401 Washington Blvd, Whittier (90602-1006)
PHONE 562 698-0811
Richard Casford, *Ch of Bd*
Daniel F Adams, *President*
Gary Koger, *CFO*
Ronald Yoshihara, *Vice Pres*
Peggy Chulack, *Admin Sec*
EMP: 1100
SQ FT: 500,000
SALES: 15MM **Privately Held**
SIC: 8062 8011 General medical & surgical hospitals; offices & clinics of medical doctors

(P-21614)
JOHN C FREMONT HEALTHCARE DST
Also Called: FREMONT HOSPITAL
5189 Hospital Rd, Mariposa (95338-9524)
P.O. Box 216 (95338-0216)
PHONE 209 966-3631
Fax: 209 742-6749
Alan Macphee, *CEO*
Matthew Matthiessen, *CFO*
Tish Miller, *CFO*
John C Fremont, *Bd of Directors*
Dana Oster, *Bd of Directors*
EMP: 250
SQ FT: 59,112
SALES: 17.7MM **Privately Held**
SIC: 8062 General medical & surgical hospitals

(P-21615)
JOHN F KENNEDY MEMORIAL HOSP
Also Called: John F Knedy Mem Hosp Emrgncy
47111 Monroe St, Indio (92201-6799)
PHONE 760 347-6191
Fax: 760 775-8178
Gary Honts, *CEO*
Matt Keating, *CFO*
Bruce Gottlieb, *Pharmacy Dir*
Joyce Preston, *Program Mgr*
Sue Smothers, *Admin Sec*
EMP: 650
SALES: 695.4K
SALES (corp-wide): 18.7B **Publicly Held**
WEB: www.jfkfoundation.org
SIC: 8062 General medical & surgical hospitals
HQ: Des Peres Hospital, Inc.
2345 Dougherty Ferry Rd
Saint Louis MO 63122
314 966-9100

(P-21616)
JOHN MUIR HEALTH
5003 Commercial Cir, Concord (94520-1268)
PHONE 925 692-5600
Cynthia Liedstrand, *Branch Mgr*
Barbara Brunell, *Manager*
EMP: 775
SALES (corp-wide): 1.2B **Privately Held**
SIC: 8062 General medical & surgical hospitals
PA: John Muir Health
1601 Ygnacio Valley Rd
Walnut Creek CA 94598
925 939-3000

(P-21617)
JOHN MUIR HEALTH
380 Civic Dr Ste. 100, Pleasant Hill (94523-1946)
PHONE 925 952-2887
Fax: 925 676-1792
EMP: 940
SALES (corp-wide): 1.2B **Privately Held**
SIC: 8062 General medical & surgical hospitals
PA: John Muir Health
1601 Ygnacio Valley Rd
Walnut Creek CA 94598
925 939-3000

(P-21618)
JOHN MUIR HEALTH (PA)
1601 Ygnacio Valley Rd, Walnut Creek (94598-3122)
P.O. Box 9023 (94596-9023)
PHONE 925 939-3000
Fax: 925 947-2989
Calvin Knight, *CEO*
David L Goldsmith, *Vice Chairman*
Michael S Thomas, *President*
Jane A Willemsen, *President*
Lee Huskins, *COO*
EMP: 1600
SQ FT: 5,500
SALES: 1.2B **Privately Held**
WEB: www.johnmuirmtdiablo.com
SIC: 8062 General medical & surgical hospitals

(P-21619)
JOHN MUIR HEALTH
Also Called: Outpatient Rehabilitation Svcs
1981 N Broadway Ste 180, Walnut Creek (94596-3817)
PHONE 925 947-5300
Fax: 925 947-3262
Sid Hsu, *Manager*
Wendy Hull, *Site Mgr*
Joseph F Barakeh, *Ophthalmology*
Vandana D Sharma, *Rheumtlgy Spec*
Rhonda Young, *Pharmacist*
EMP: 50
SALES: 1.2B **Privately Held**
WEB: www.johnmuirmtdiablo.com
SIC: 8062 8049 8093 General medical & surgical hospitals; clinical psychologist; rehabilitation center; outpatient treatment
PA: John Muir Health
1601 Ygnacio Valley Rd
Walnut Creek CA 94598
925 939-3000

(P-21620)
JOHN MUIR HEALTH
Also Called: John Muir Medical Center
1601 Ygnacio Valley Rd, Walnut Creek (94598-3122)
PHONE 925 939-3000
Fax: 925 947-4414
Vicki C Lee, *Administration*
Lawrence Gluckstein,
Sharon Capece, *Officer*
Ken Meehan, *Exec VP*
Donna Brackley, *Senior VP*
EMP: 775
SALES (corp-wide): 1.2B **Privately Held**
SIC: 8062 General medical & surgical hospitals
PA: John Muir Health
1601 Ygnacio Valley Rd
Walnut Creek CA 94598
925 939-3000

(P-21621)
JOHN MUIR HEALTH
Also Called: John Muir Med Ctr Cncord Cmpus
2540 East St, Concord (94520-1906)
PHONE 925 682-8200
Tish Murphy, *Director*
Bernard Larner, *Ch Pathology*
Nancy Boren, *President*
Elizebeth Stallings, *COO*
Ran Kim, *Vice Pres*
EMP: 1500
SALES (corp-wide): 1.2B **Privately Held**
SIC: 8062 General medical & surgical hospitals
PA: John Muir Health
1601 Ygnacio Valley Rd
Walnut Creek CA 94598
925 939-3000

(P-21622)
JOHN MUIR PHYSICIAN NETWORK
112 La Casa Via Ste 300, Walnut Creek (94598-3059)
PHONE 925 952-2701
EMP: 634
SALES (corp-wide): 243.9MM **Privately Held**
SIC: 8062 General medical & surgical hospitals

PRODUCTS & SERVICES SECTION
8062 - General Medical & Surgical Hospitals County (P-21639)

PA: John Muir Physician Network
1450 Treat Blvd
Walnut Creek CA 94597
925 296-9700

(P-21623)
JOHN MUIR PHYSICIAN NETWORK
91 Gregory Ln Ste 15, Pleasant Hill (94523-4927)
PHONE.................................925 685-0843
Fax: 925 685-1899
Aileen Mirabel, *Branch Mgr*
EMP: 634
SALES (corp-wide): 243.9MM **Privately Held**
SIC: 8062 General medical & surgical hospitals
PA: John Muir Physician Network
1450 Treat Blvd
Walnut Creek CA 94597
925 296-9700

(P-21624)
JOHN MUIR PHYSICIAN NETWORK
Also Called: Mount Diablo Medical Center
2540 East St, Concord (94520-1906)
PHONE.................................925 682-8200
Deborah Kolhede, *Vice Pres*
Sue Ellen Thompson, *Cardiology*
Terrence Chen, *Neurology*
Michaela Straznicka, *Thoracic Surgeo*
Deborah Arce, *Director*
EMP: 1500
SALES (corp-wide): 243.9MM **Privately Held**
SIC: 8062 8011 General medical & surgical hospitals; offices & clinics of medical doctors
PA: John Muir Physician Network
1450 Treat Blvd
Walnut Creek CA 94597
925 296-9700

(P-21625)
JOHN MUIR PHYSICIAN NETWORK
Also Called: Mt Diablo Medical Center
1601 Ygnacio Valley Rd, Walnut Creek (94598-3122)
PHONE.................................925 939-3000
J Kendall Anderson, *President*
Masanna Loui, *Financial Analy*
Angela Weberski, *Analyst*
EMP: 399
SALES (corp-wide): 243.9MM **Privately Held**
SIC: 8062 General medical & surgical hospitals
PA: John Muir Physician Network
1450 Treat Blvd
Walnut Creek CA 94597
925 296-9700

(P-21626)
JOHN MUIR PHYSICIAN NETWORK (PA)
Also Called: John Muir Medical Center
1450 Treat Blvd, Walnut Creek (94597-2168)
PHONE.................................925 296-9700
Fax: 925 941-2026
Lynn Baskett, *Vice Pres*
Mitchell Zack, *Vice Pres*
Laura Kazaglis, *Admin Asst*
Ted Spaete, *Analyst*
Alice Villanueva, *VP Human Res*
EMP: 1601
SQ FT: 83,579
SALES (est): 243.9MM **Privately Held**
SIC: 8062 8069 8093 7363 General medical & surgical hospitals; substance abuse hospitals; substance abuse clinics (outpatient); medical help service

(P-21627)
JOHN MUIR PHYSICIAN NETWORK
Also Called: Mt Diablo Heart Health Center
2720 Grant St, Concord (94520-2294)
PHONE.................................925 674-2200
Fax: 707 674-2201
Elizabeth Stalling, *Branch Mgr*
Jerome Klusky, *CFO*
Heather Kenward, *Personnel Assit*
Pat Sehielie, *Sales Executive*
Marty Tarnowski, *Marketing Staff*
EMP: 634
SALES (corp-wide): 243.9MM **Privately Held**
SIC: 8062 General medical & surgical hospitals
PA: John Muir Physician Network
1450 Treat Blvd
Walnut Creek CA 94597
925 296-9700

(P-21628)
KAISER FOUNDATION HOSPITALS
Also Called: Kaiser Permanente Medical Cen
400 Craven Rd, San Marcos (92078-4201)
PHONE.................................760 591-4276
Fax: 619 641-4195
Sally Friedman, *Manager*
Bryan J Fort, *Security Dir*
Kimberlee Haddock, *Information Mgr*
Betty Cox, *Technology*
Diana McRae, *Analyst*
EMP: 105
SALES (corp-wide): 27.8B **Privately Held**
SIC: 8062 General medical & surgical hospitals
HQ: Kaiser Foundation Hospitals Inc
1 Kaiser Plz
Oakland CA 94612
510 271-6611

(P-21629)
KAISER FOUNDATION HOSPITALS
Also Called: Barranca Medical Offices
6 Willard, Irvine (92604-4694)
PHONE.................................949 262-5780
Fax: 949 262-5716
George Disalvo, *Owner*
Ani A Atoian, *Family Practiti*
Bradford W Edgerton, *Dermatology*
Roy Benedetti, *Med Doctor*
Ashok Chopra, *Med Doctor*
EMP: 105
SQ FT: 51,080
SALES (corp-wide): 27.8B **Privately Held**
SIC: 8062 General medical & surgical hospitals
HQ: Kaiser Foundation Hospitals Inc
1 Kaiser Plz
Oakland CA 94612
510 271-6611

(P-21630)
KAISER FOUNDATION HOSPITALS
Also Called: Kaiser Permanente Eye
1680 E Roseville Pkwy, Roseville (95661-3988)
PHONE.................................916 746-3937
Daniel Rule, *Branch Mgr*
Michael E Hanlon, *Psychologist*
Don R Robinson, *Psychiatry*
EMP: 105
SALES (corp-wide): 27.8B **Privately Held**
SIC: 8062 General medical & surgical hospitals
HQ: Kaiser Foundation Hospitals Inc
1 Kaiser Plz
Oakland CA 94612
510 271-6611

(P-21631)
KAISER FOUNDATION HOSPITALS
Also Called: Kaiser Permanente
5601 De Soto Ave, Woodland Hills (91367-6701)
PHONE.................................818 719-2000
Fax: 805 719-3291
Cathy Casas, *Administration*
Diane S Scott, *Lab Dir*
Lisa Jimenez, *Executive Asst*
Belen Rocha, *Executive Asst*
Daniel Torres, *Administration*
EMP: 1200
SALES (corp-wide): 27.8B **Privately Held**
WEB: www.kaiserpermanente.org
SIC: 8062 General medical & surgical hospitals

HQ: Kaiser Foundation Hospitals Inc
1 Kaiser Plz
Oakland CA 94612
510 271-6611

(P-21632)
KAISER FOUNDATION HOSPITALS
Also Called: Kaiser Permanente
43112 15th St W, Lancaster (93534-6219)
PHONE.................................661 726-2500
Fax: 661 726-2359
Barbara Fordice, *General Mgr*
Joseph E Anekwe, *Family Practiti*
Rana S Shenoy, *Infectious Dis*
Florcita S Alvarez-Galoosi, *Internal Med*
Anne Chen, *Internal Med*
EMP: 175
SALES (corp-wide): 27.8B **Privately Held**
WEB: www.kaiserpermanente.org
SIC: 8062 General medical & surgical hospitals; hospital, affiliated with AMA residency
HQ: Kaiser Foundation Hospitals Inc
1 Kaiser Plz
Oakland CA 94612
510 271-6611

(P-21633)
KAISER FOUNDATION HOSPITALS
Also Called: Kaiser Permanente
4867 W Sunset Blvd, Los Angeles (90027-5969)
PHONE.................................323 783-4011
Fax: 323 667-4787
Vicken Aharonian, *Director*
Yu Lee,
Roy Braganza,
Sima Hartounian, *Officer*
Barry Wolfman, *Vice Pres*
EMP: 60
SALES (corp-wide): 27.8B **Privately Held**
WEB: www.kaiserpermanente.org
SIC: 8062 8099 6321 6324 General medical & surgical hospitals; physical examination service, insurance; health insurance carriers; hospital & medical service plans
HQ: Kaiser Foundation Hospitals Inc
1 Kaiser Plz
Oakland CA 94612
510 271-6611

(P-21634)
KAISER FOUNDATION HOSPITALS
Also Called: Park Shadelands Medical Offs
320 Lennon Ln, Walnut Creek (94598-2419)
PHONE.................................925 906-2380
David Nievr, *President*
Robbie Robinson, *Technology*
Susan Chuang, *Family Practiti*
Larry L Dotson, *Med Doctor*
EMP: 52
SALES (corp-wide): 27.8B **Privately Held**
WEB: www.kaiserpermanente.org
SIC: 8062 8011 General medical & surgical hospitals; general & family practice, physician/surgeon
HQ: Kaiser Foundation Hospitals Inc
1 Kaiser Plz
Oakland CA 94612
510 271-6611

(P-21635)
KAISER FOUNDATION HOSPITALS
Also Called: Kaiser Permanente
1011 Baldwin Park Blvd, Baldwin Park (91706-5806)
PHONE.................................626 851-1011
Fax: 626 851-5433
Linda Margarita Gutierrez, *Principal*
Diana Laplaze,
Linda Salazar, *Officer*
Harold Chow, *Top Exec*
Paula J Rodgers, *Top Exec*
EMP: 793
SALES (corp-wide): 27.8B **Privately Held**
WEB: www.kaiserpermanente.org
SIC: 8062 General medical & surgical hospitals

HQ: Kaiser Foundation Hospitals Inc
1 Kaiser Plz
Oakland CA 94612
510 271-6611

(P-21636)
KAISER FOUNDATION HOSPITALS
Also Called: Kaiser Prmnente Downey Med Ctr
9333 Imperial Hwy, Downey (90242-2812)
PHONE.................................562 657-9000
Gemma Abad, *Branch Mgr*
Rafael Franco, *Executive*
Kevin Godfrey, *Pathologist*
Julie Wu, *Pathologist*
David Chiu, *Med Doctor*
EMP: 410
SALES (corp-wide): 27.8B **Privately Held**
SIC: 8062 General medical & surgical hospitals
HQ: Kaiser Foundation Hospitals Inc
1 Kaiser Plz
Oakland CA 94612
510 271-6611

(P-21637)
KAISER FOUNDATION HOSPITALS (HQ)
Also Called: Kaiser Permanente
1 Kaiser Plz, Oakland (94612-3610)
P.O. Box 12929 (94604-3010)
PHONE.................................510 271-6611
Fax: 510 271-6642
Bernard J Tyson, *President*
Janet Liang, *President*
Kathy Lancaster, *CFO*
Patrick Courneya, *Exec VP*
Thomas Curtin, *Senior VP*
▲ **EMP:** 250
SQ FT: 90,000
SALES (corp-wide): 27.8B **Privately Held**
WEB: www.kaiserpermanente.org
SIC: 8062 8011 General medical & surgical hospitals; medical centers
PA: Kaiser Foundation Health Plan, Inc.
1 Kaiser Plz
Oakland CA 94612
510 271-5800

(P-21638)
KAISER FOUNDATION HOSPITALS
Also Called: Kaiser Permanente
280 W Macarthur Blvd, Oakland (94611-5642)
PHONE.................................510 752-1000
Fax: 510 596-6431
Bettie Coles, *Manager*
Garwood Gee,
Michael Moore,
Erica D Hansen, *Family Practiti*
Ireneo B Lazo, *Family Practiti*
EMP: 708
SALES (corp-wide): 27.8B **Privately Held**
SIC: 8062 General medical & surgical hospitals
HQ: Kaiser Foundation Hospitals Inc
1 Kaiser Plz
Oakland CA 94612
510 271-6611

(P-21639)
KAISER FOUNDATION HOSPITALS
Also Called: Kaiser Permanente
1255 W Arrow Hwy, San Dimas (91773-2340)
PHONE.................................909 394-2530
Will Tatum, *Manager*
Jennie J Chang, *Obstetrician*
EMP: 52
SQ FT: 23,801
SALES (corp-wide): 27.8B **Privately Held**
WEB: www.kaiserpermanente.org
SIC: 8062 8011 General medical & surgical hospitals; general & family practice, physician/surgeon
HQ: Kaiser Foundation Hospitals Inc
1 Kaiser Plz
Oakland CA 94612
510 271-6611

8062 - General Medical & Surgical Hospitals County (P-21640)

(P-21640)
KAISER FOUNDATION HOSPITALS
Also Called: Kaiser Permanente
4405 Vandever Ave Fl 5, San Diego (92120-3315)
PHONE.................................619 528-2583
Fax: 619 516-6145
David Mandler, *Manager*
Suzanne E Afflalo, *Family Practiti*
Sara Fassihi, *Family Practiti*
Mark E Nunes, *Pediatrics*
Rita Feghali, *Med Doctor*
EMP: 52
SALES (corp-wide): 27.8B **Privately Held**
WEB: www.kaiserpermanente.org
SIC: 8062 General medical & surgical hospitals
HQ: Kaiser Foundation Hospitals Inc
1 Kaiser Plz
Oakland CA 94612
510 271-6611

(P-21641)
KAISER FOUNDATION HOSPITALS
Also Called: Kaiser Permanente
13651 Willard St, Panorama City (91402)
PHONE.................................818 375-2000
Fax: 818 375-3480
Dev Mahadevan, *Principal*
Mayann Fodran, *Lab Dir*
Harry Monson, *Radiology Dir*
Ralph Bowman, *Admin Sec*
Eugene Kenigsberg, *Engineer*
EMP: 3000
SALES (corp-wide): 27.8B **Privately Held**
WEB: www.kaiserpermanente.org
SIC: 8062 General medical & surgical hospitals
HQ: Kaiser Foundation Hospitals Inc
1 Kaiser Plz
Oakland CA 94612
510 271-6611

(P-21642)
KAISER FOUNDATION HOSPITALS
280 Hospital Pkwy, San Jose (95119-1103)
PHONE.................................408 972-6010
Fax: 408 972-6054
Rajan Bhandari, *Branch Mgr*
Cristina Celaya, *Phys Thrpy Dir*
John Justice, *Phys Thrpy Dir*
EMP: 267
SALES (corp-wide): 27.8B **Privately Held**
SIC: 8062 General medical & surgical hospitals
HQ: Kaiser Foundation Hospitals Inc
1 Kaiser Plz
Oakland CA 94612
510 271-6611

(P-21643)
KAISER FOUNDATION HOSPITALS
Also Called: San Joaquin Community Hospital
2615 Chester Ave, Bakersfield (93301-2014)
PHONE.................................661 395-3000
EMP: 267
SALES (corp-wide): 27.8B **Privately Held**
SIC: 8062 General medical & surgical hospitals
HQ: Kaiser Foundation Hospitals Inc
1 Kaiser Plz
Oakland CA 94612
510 271-6611

(P-21644)
KAISER FOUNDATION HOSPITALS
Also Called: Antelope Valley Hospital
1600 W Avenue␣J, Lancaster (93534-2814)
PHONE.................................661 949-5000
EMP: 267
SALES (corp-wide): 27.8B **Privately Held**
SIC: 8062 General medical & surgical hospitals
HQ: Kaiser Foundation Hospitals Inc
1 Kaiser Plz
Oakland CA 94612
510 271-6611

(P-21645)
KAISER FOUNDATION HOSPITALS
Also Called: Kaiser Prmanente Internet Svcs
5820 Owens Dr Bldg E-2, Pleasanton (94588-3900)
PHONE.................................925 598-2799
Andy Wells, *Vice Pres*
Amy Hughes, *Comms Mgr*
John Burger, *Info Tech Dir*
Simon TSE, *IT/INT Sup*
Lindsay R Beigle, *Project Mgr*
EMP: 267
SALES (corp-wide): 27.8B **Privately Held**
SIC: 8062 General medical & surgical hospitals
HQ: Kaiser Foundation Hospitals Inc
1 Kaiser Plz
Oakland CA 94612
510 271-6611

(P-21646)
KAISER FOUNDATION HOSPITALS
Also Called: Kaiser Permanente
1650 Response Rd, Sacramento (95815-4807)
PHONE.................................916 973-5000
Fax: 916 614-4145
Sandra Lee Panora, *Branch Mgr*
Alex Llanera, *Info Tech Mgr*
Courtney Tran, *Project Mgr*
Roderick V Vitangcol, *Family Practiti*
Monica Balfour, *Obstetrician*
EMP: 52
SALES (corp-wide): 27.8B **Privately Held**
WEB: www.kaiserpermanente.org
SIC: 8062 General medical & surgical hospitals
HQ: Kaiser Foundation Hospitals Inc
1 Kaiser Plz
Oakland CA 94612
510 271-6611

(P-21647)
KAISER FOUNDATION HOSPITALS
Also Called: Permanente Medical Group
555 Castro St Fl 3, Mountain View (94041-2009)
PHONE.................................650 903-3000
Patricia Carpenter, *Director*
Steven N Shpall, *Dermatology*
Arlene Chang, *Internal Med*
John G Poochigian, *Internal Med*
Sandy Chun, *Med Doctor*
EMP: 200
SALES (corp-wide): 27.8B **Privately Held**
WEB: www.kaiserpermanente.org
SIC: 8062 General medical & surgical hospitals; hospital, affiliated with AMA residency
HQ: Kaiser Foundation Hospitals Inc
1 Kaiser Plz
Oakland CA 94612
510 271-6611

(P-21648)
KAISER FOUNDATION HOSPITALS
Also Called: Kaiser Permanente
501 Lennon Ln, Walnut Creek (94598-2414)
PHONE.................................925 906-2000
Christina Robinson, *Principal*
Martha Realivasquez, *Admin Asst*
Scott Dambrauckas, *Info Tech Mgr*
Susan Jaffe, *Applctn Conslt*
Heather Pfeifer, *Business Anlyst*
EMP: 1000
SALES (corp-wide): 27.8B **Privately Held**
WEB: www.kaiserpermanente.org
SIC: 8062 General medical & surgical hospitals
HQ: Kaiser Foundation Hospitals Inc
1 Kaiser Plz
Oakland CA 94612
510 271-6611

(P-21649)
KAISER FOUNDATION HOSPITALS
Also Called: Kaiser Permanente
7601 Stoneridge Dr, Pleasanton (94588-4501)
PHONE.................................925 847-5000
Fax: 925 847-5232
Linsey Dicks, *Admin Director*
Arthur Southam, *Exec VP*
Carl Haupt, *Info Tech Mgr*
Irena Sepaher, *Psychologist*
Monica K Cheong, *Obstetrician*
EMP: 350
SALES (corp-wide): 27.8B **Privately Held**
WEB: www.kaiserpermanente.org
SIC: 8062 General medical & surgical hospitals
HQ: Kaiser Foundation Hospitals Inc
1 Kaiser Plz
Oakland CA 94612
510 271-6611

(P-21650)
KAISER FOUNDATION HOSPITALS
Also Called: Wildomar Medical Offices
36450 Inland Valley Dr # 204, Wildomar (92595-9583)
PHONE.................................951 353-2000
Geoffrey Gomez, *Principal*
Anh T Dinh, *Family Practiti*
EMP: 50
SALES (corp-wide): 27.8B **Privately Held**
WEB: www.kaiserpermanente.org
SIC: 8062 General medical & surgical hospitals
HQ: Kaiser Foundation Hospitals Inc
1 Kaiser Plz
Oakland CA 94612
510 271-6611

(P-21651)
KAISER FOUNDATION HOSPITALS
Also Called: Bostonia Medical Offices
1630 E Main St, El Cajon (92021-5204)
PHONE.................................619 528-5000
Jon Pinter, *Executive*
Noha Jackson, *Pharmacy Dir*
Jennifer Park, *Med Doctor*
EMP: 50
SALES (corp-wide): 27.8B **Privately Held**
WEB: www.kaiserpermanente.org
SIC: 8062 General medical & surgical hospitals
HQ: Kaiser Foundation Hospitals Inc
1 Kaiser Plz
Oakland CA 94612
510 271-6611

(P-21652)
KAISER FOUNDATION HOSPITALS
Also Called: Cudahy Medical Offices
7825 Atlantic Ave, Cudahy (90201-5022)
PHONE.................................323 562-6400
Fax: 323 562-6419
Karen Warren, *Manager*
Robert L Escalera, *Family Practiti*
Milagro D Ramos, *Family Practiti*
Vicki L Cordts, *Obstetrician*
Juan C Ruiz, *Pediatrics*
EMP: 100
SALES (corp-wide): 27.8B **Privately Held**
WEB: www.kaiserpermanente.org
SIC: 8062 General medical & surgical hospitals
HQ: Kaiser Foundation Hospitals Inc
1 Kaiser Plz
Oakland CA 94612
510 271-6611

(P-21653)
KAISER FOUNDATION HOSPITALS
Also Called: El Cajon Medical Offices
250 Travelodge Dr, El Cajon (92020-4126)
PHONE.................................619 528-5000
Fax: 619 441-3168
Carolyn Bonner, *Administration*
Katherine A Hartzell, *Obstetrician*
Jeffrey D Korn, *Podiatrist*
Donald Fithian, *Med Doctor*
EMP: 50
SQ FT: 47,486
SALES (corp-wide): 27.8B **Privately Held**
WEB: www.kaiserpermanente.org
SIC: 8062 General medical & surgical hospitals
HQ: Kaiser Foundation Hospitals Inc
1 Kaiser Plz
Oakland CA 94612
510 271-6611

(P-21654)
KAISER FOUNDATION HOSPITALS
Also Called: Kaiser Permanente
1249 S Sunset Ave, West Covina (91790-3960)
PHONE.................................866 319-4269
Jane Lau, *General Mgr*
Chan Kiet Wong, *Pharmacist*
EMP: 50
SALES (corp-wide): 27.8B **Privately Held**
WEB: www.kaiserpermanente.org
SIC: 8062 General medical & surgical hospitals
HQ: Kaiser Foundation Hospitals Inc
1 Kaiser Plz
Oakland CA 94612
510 271-6611

(P-21655)
KAISER FOUNDATION HOSPITALS
Also Called: Long Beach Medical Offices
3900 E Pacific Coast Hwy, Long Beach (90804-2000)
PHONE.................................310 325-5111
Fax: 562 986-2203
Richard Schaar, *Branch Mgr*
Anne L Sever, *Administration*
Albert J Lin, *Family Practiti*
Milan Vora, *Physician Asst*
Vanessa Gavin-Headen, *Med Doctor*
EMP: 50
SALES (corp-wide): 27.8B **Privately Held**
WEB: www.kaiserpermanente.org
SIC: 8062 General medical & surgical hospitals
HQ: Kaiser Foundation Hospitals Inc
1 Kaiser Plz
Oakland CA 94612
510 271-6611

(P-21656)
KAISER FOUNDATION HOSPITALS
Also Called: Gardena Medical Offices
15446 S Western Ave, Gardena (90249-4319)
PHONE.................................310 517-2956
Fax: 310 217-5346
Mary Mauch, *Manager*
Agnes E Chen, *Family Practiti*
Esther S Min, *Family Practiti*
Cristina Y Amaya, *Obstetrician*
Douglas Carman, *Med Doctor*
EMP: 50
SQ FT: 114,575
SALES (corp-wide): 27.8B **Privately Held**
WEB: www.kaiserpermanente.org
SIC: 8062 General medical & surgical hospitals
HQ: Kaiser Foundation Hospitals Inc
1 Kaiser Plz
Oakland CA 94612
510 271-6611

(P-21657)
KAISER FOUNDATION HOSPITALS
Also Called: Erwin Street Medical Offices
21263 Erwin St, Woodland Hills (91367-3715)
PHONE.................................818 592-3100
Karen Kim, *Executive*
Clifford A Gimenez, *Psychiatry*
Michael Agress, *Med Doctor*
EMP: 50
SQ FT: 28,398
SALES (corp-wide): 27.8B **Privately Held**
WEB: www.kaiserpermanente.org
SIC: 8062 General medical & surgical hospitals

PRODUCTS & SERVICES SECTION　　　　　　　　　　**8062 - General Medical & Surgical Hospitals County (P-21674)**

HQ: Kaiser Foundation Hospitals Inc
　1 Kaiser Plz
　Oakland CA 94612
　510 271-6611

(P-21658)
KAISER FOUNDATION HOSPITALS
Also Called: Rancho Cordova Medical Offices
10725 International Dr, Rancho Cordova (95670-7967)
PHONE..................916 631-3088
Fax: 916 614-4301
David Haddad, *Principal*
Wil Neria, *Engineer*
Sara L Koehler, *Obstetrician*
Aisha R Taylor, *Obstetrician*
Elbert H Chen, *Dermatology*
EMP: 50
SALES (corp-wide): 27.8B **Privately Held**
WEB: www.kaiserpermanente.org
SIC: 8062 General medical & surgical hospitals
HQ: Kaiser Foundation Hospitals Inc
　1 Kaiser Plz
　Oakland CA 94612
　510 271-6611

(P-21659)
KAISER FOUNDATION HOSPITALS
Also Called: Petaluma Medical Offices
3900 Lakeville Hwy, Petaluma (94954-5698)
PHONE..................707 765-3900
Fax: 707 765-3475
Claudia Renate Viazzoli, *Principal*
David Kvancz, *Vice Pres*
Sean O Calandrella, *Family Practiti*
Helene M Spivak, *Obstetrician*
Donald S Hensley, *Pediatrics*
EMP: 50
SQ FT: 39,000
SALES (corp-wide): 27.8B **Privately Held**
WEB: www.kaiserpermanente.org
SIC: 8062 General medical & surgical hospitals
HQ: Kaiser Foundation Hospitals Inc
　1 Kaiser Plz
　Oakland CA 94612
　510 271-6611

(P-21660)
KAISER FOUNDATION HOSPITALS
Also Called: Novato Medical Offices
97 San Marin Dr, Novato (94945-1100)
PHONE..................415 899-7400
Margaret R Hill, *Principal*
Patricia Burkett, *Executive*
Vicki C Darrow, *Obstetrician*
Dennis S Moribe, *Pediatrics*
EMP: 50
SALES (corp-wide): 27.8B **Privately Held**
WEB: www.kaiserpermanente.org
SIC: 8062 General medical & surgical hospitals
HQ: Kaiser Foundation Hospitals Inc
　1 Kaiser Plz
　Oakland CA 94612
　510 271-6611

(P-21661)
KAISER FOUNDATION HOSPITALS
10990 San Dego Mission Rd, San Diego (92108-2417)
PHONE..................619 641-4663
Fax: 619 641-4343
Caroline Bonner, *Director*
Michelle Knapp, *Executive Asst*
Claudia F De Carvalho, *Pharmacist*
Inga X Garmanyan, *Pharmacist*
Christina T Nguyen, *Pharmacist*
EMP: 410
SALES (corp-wide): 27.8B **Privately Held**
WEB: www.kaiserpermanente.org
SIC: 8062 General medical & surgical hospitals
HQ: Kaiser Foundation Hospitals Inc
　1 Kaiser Plz
　Oakland CA 94612
　510 271-6611

(P-21662)
KAISER FOUNDATION HOSPITALS
Also Called: La Mesa Medical Offices
8080 Parkway Dr, La Mesa (91942-2104)
PHONE..................619 528-5000
Caroline Wu, *Principal*
David McIntosh, *Chief Engr*
Sandy Cadruvi, *Human Resources*
Brian Kleker, *Med Doctor*
John Tran, *Med Doctor*
EMP: 50
SALES (corp-wide): 27.8B **Privately Held**
WEB: www.kaiserpermanente.org
SIC: 8062 General medical & surgical hospitals
HQ: Kaiser Foundation Hospitals Inc
　1 Kaiser Plz
　Oakland CA 94612
　510 271-6611

(P-21663)
KAISER FOUNDATION HOSPITALS
Also Called: Stockdale Medical Offices
3501 Stockdale Hwy, Bakersfield (93309-2150)
PHONE..................661 398-5011
KY P Ho, *Principal*
Nooshin Jahangiri, *Family Practiti*
Tiffany M Pierce, *Family Practiti*
Linda R Kahega, *Pediatrics*
Armando Gonzalez, *Cardiovascular*
EMP: 50
SALES (corp-wide): 27.8B **Privately Held**
WEB: www.kaiserpermanente.org
SIC: 8062 General medical & surgical hospitals
HQ: Kaiser Foundation Hospitals Inc
　1 Kaiser Plz
　Oakland CA 94612
　510 271-6611

(P-21664)
KAISER FOUNDATION HOSPITALS
Also Called: Kaiser Permanente Division RES
2000 Brdwy, Oakland (94612)
PHONE..................510 891-3400
Joe Shelby MD, *Director*
Leslie M Litton, *Vice Pres*
Lawrence H Kushi, *Associate Dir*
Hemant Karnik, *Admin Asst*
Karen Lacy, *Admin Asst*
EMP: 400
SQ FT: 86,875
SALES (corp-wide): 27.8B **Privately Held**
WEB: www.kaiserpermanente.org
SIC: 8062 General medical & surgical hospitals
HQ: Kaiser Foundation Hospitals Inc
　1 Kaiser Plz
　Oakland CA 94612
　510 271-6611

(P-21665)
KAISER FOUNDATION HOSPITALS
Also Called: Kaiser Permanente
5055 California Ave # 110, Bakersfield (93309-0701)
P.O. Box 12099 (93389-2099)
PHONE..................661 334-2020
Fax: 661 631-3983
Abdul Siddiqui, *Info Tech Dir*
Amy Trammell, *Analyst*
M Robert MD, *Med Doctor*
Leslie Golich, *Director*
Audra Kessler, *Director*
EMP: 105
SALES (corp-wide): 27.8B **Privately Held**
SIC: 8062 General medical & surgical hospitals
HQ: Kaiser Foundation Hospitals Inc
　1 Kaiser Plz
　Oakland CA 94612
　510 271-6611

(P-21666)
KAISER FOUNDATION HOSPITALS
Also Called: Kaiser Prmnnte Vallejo Med Ctr
975 Sereno Dr, Vallejo (94589-2441)
PHONE..................707 651-1000
Fax: 707 651-3313
Katie Rickleff, *Principal*
Jayson Santiago, *Op Rm Dir*
Nam P Nguyen, *Pharmacy Dir*
Carolyn Doyle, *Admin Asst*
Monieca Jones, *Info Tech Mgr*
EMP: 2700
SALES (corp-wide): 27.8B **Privately Held**
WEB: www.kaiserpermanente.org
SIC: 8062 General medical & surgical hospitals
HQ: Kaiser Foundation Hospitals Inc
　1 Kaiser Plz
　Oakland CA 94612
　510 271-6611

(P-21667)
KAISER FOUNDATION HOSPITALS
Also Called: Kaiser Permanente
12470 Whittier Blvd, Whittier (90602-1017)
PHONE..................562 907-3510
Beth Lopez, *Principal*
Rocio Perez, *Pediatrics*
Carmen Gutierrez, *Med Doctor*
Zoltan Katona, *Med Doctor*
Michael Lee, *Med Doctor*
EMP: 50
SALES (corp-wide): 27.8B **Privately Held**
WEB: www.kaiserpermanente.org
SIC: 8062 General medical & surgical hospitals
HQ: Kaiser Foundation Hospitals Inc
　1 Kaiser Plz
　Oakland CA 94612
　510 271-6611

(P-21668)
KAISER FOUNDATION HOSPITALS
Also Called: Kaiser Prmnnte Manteca Med Ctr
1777 W Yosemite Ave, Manteca (95337-5187)
PHONE..................209 825-3700
Anita Kennedy, *COO*
Debra Brown, *Office Mgr*
Cathy Ohlinger, *Administration*
Lisa Dasko, *Controller*
Phu T Vu, *Family Practiti*
EMP: 593
SALES (corp-wide): 27.8B **Privately Held**
SIC: 8062 General medical & surgical hospitals
HQ: Kaiser Foundation Hospitals Inc
　1 Kaiser Plz
　Oakland CA 94612
　510 271-6611

(P-21669)
KAISER FOUNDATION HOSPITALS
Also Called: Bonita Medical Offices
3955 Bonita Rd, Bonita (91902-1230)
PHONE..................619 409-6405
James Lentz, *Principal*
EMP: 72
SQ FT: 67,760
SALES (corp-wide): 27.8B **Privately Held**
WEB: www.kaiser.com
SIC: 8062 General medical & surgical hospitals
HQ: Kaiser Foundation Hospitals Inc
　1 Kaiser Plz
　Oakland CA 94612
　510 271-6611

(P-21670)
KAISER FOUNDATION HOSPITALS
Also Called: Kaiser Foundation Health Plan
11666 Sherman Way, North Hollywood (91605-5831)
PHONE..................818 503-7082
Fax: 818 503-6995
Charles Ford, *Manager*
Al Zimmerman, *Lab Dir*
Kent Cox, *Director*
Zaffar Hassain, *Manager*
Pushpa Ramachandran, *Manager*
EMP: 53
SALES (corp-wide): 27.8B **Privately Held**
WEB: www.kaiser.com
SIC: 8062 General medical & surgical hospitals

HQ: Kaiser Foundation Hospitals Inc
　1 Kaiser Plz
　Oakland CA 94612
　510 271-6611

(P-21671)
KAISER FOUNDATION HOSPITALS
Also Called: Kaiser Permanente San
275 Hospital Pkwy 765a, San Jose (95119-1106)
PHONE..................408 972-6700
Diana Ochoa, *Branch Mgr*
Genny Castaneda, *General Mgr*
Faezeh M Ghaffari, *Med Doctor*
Nayanatara RAO, *Med Doctor*
EMP: 105
SALES (corp-wide): 27.8B **Privately Held**
WEB: www.kaiserpermanente.org
SIC: 8062 8021 General medical & surgical hospitals; offices & clinics of dentists
HQ: Kaiser Foundation Hospitals Inc
　1 Kaiser Plz
　Oakland CA 94612
　510 271-6611

(P-21672)
KAISER FOUNDATION HOSPITALS
Also Called: Kaiser Permanente
1055 E Colo Blvd Ste 100, Pasadena (91106)
PHONE..................626 440-5659
Fax: 626 405-2583
Jeanine Boudakian, *Branch Mgr*
George Di Salvo, *CFO*
George D Saleo, *CFO*
Patti Harvey, *Senior VP*
Laurel Junk, *Senior VP*
EMP: 500
SALES (corp-wide): 27.8B **Privately Held**
WEB: www.kaiserpermanente.org
SIC: 8062 General medical & surgical hospitals
HQ: Kaiser Foundation Hospitals Inc
　1 Kaiser Plz
　Oakland CA 94612
　510 271-6611

(P-21673)
KAISER FOUNDATION HOSPITALS
Also Called: Kaiser Foundation Health Plan
4867 W Sunset Blvd, Los Angeles (90027-5969)
PHONE..................800 954-8000
Joseph Hummel, *Manager*
Karla Bates, *Director*
EMP: 50
SALES (corp-wide): 27.8B **Privately Held**
WEB: www.kaiser.com
SIC: 8062 6324 General medical & surgical hospitals; hospital & medical service plans
HQ: Kaiser Foundation Hospitals Inc
　1 Kaiser Plz
　Oakland CA 94612
　510 271-6611

(P-21674)
KAISER FOUNDATION HOSPITALS
Also Called: Kaiser Foundation Health Plan
7300 N Fresno St, Fresno (93720-2941)
PHONE..................559 448-4500
Fax: 559 448-4201
Jeffrey Collins, *Manager*
Adolfo Alvarez,
David Kvancz, *Vice Pres*
Diana Chun, *Pharmacy Dir*
Jeff Owens, *General Mgr*
EMP: 2300
SALES (corp-wide): 27.8B **Privately Held**
WEB: www.kaiser.com
SIC: 8062 General medical & surgical hospitals
HQ: Kaiser Foundation Hospitals Inc
　1 Kaiser Plz
　Oakland CA 94612
　510 271-6611

8062 - General Medical & Surgical Hospitals County (P-21675)
PRODUDUCTS & SERVICES SECTION

(P-21675)
KAISER FOUNDATION HOSPITALS
Also Called: Kaiser Permanente
250 W San Jose Ave, Claremont (91711-5295)
PHONE.................................888 750-0036
Fax: 909 398-2173
Bell Pacific, *Manager*
Frances P Burke, *Family Practiti*
Richard Hom, *Physician Asst*
EMP: 267
SQ FT: 17,908
SALES (corp-wide): 27.8B **Privately Held**
WEB: www.kaiserpermanente.org
SIC: 8062 General medical & surgical hospitals
HQ: Kaiser Foundation Hospitals Inc
1 Kaiser Plz
Oakland CA 94612
510 271-6611

(P-21676)
KAISER FOUNDATION HOSPITALS
Also Called: Kaiser Permanente Advice
7300 Wyndham Dr, Sacramento (95823-4913)
PHONE.................................916 525-6300
Tony Le, *Manager*
Susan C Doi, *Psychologist*
Arlene R Burton, *Psychiatry*
Kimberly J Davis, *Psychiatry*
Alison W Newman, *Psychiatry*
EMP: 105
SALES (corp-wide): 27.8B **Privately Held**
SIC: 8062 General medical & surgical hospitals
HQ: Kaiser Foundation Hospitals Inc
1 Kaiser Plz
Oakland CA 94612
510 271-6611

(P-21677)
KAISER FOUNDATION HOSPITALS
Also Called: Kaiser Permanente
7373 West Ln, Stockton (95210-3377)
PHONE.................................209 476-3101
Gene Long, *Branch Mgr*
Edward Rocha, *Chief Engr*
Carlos Ramirez Jr, *Surgeon*
Joanne Chao, *Surg-Orthopdc*
Troy Hamilton, *Otolaryngology*
EMP: 175
SALES (corp-wide): 27.8B **Privately Held**
WEB: www.kaiserpermanente.org
SIC: 8062 General medical & surgical hospitals
HQ: Kaiser Foundation Hospitals Inc
1 Kaiser Plz
Oakland CA 94612
510 271-6611

(P-21678)
KAISER FOUNDATION HOSPITALS
Also Called: Kaiser Permanente Santa
710 Lawrence Expy, Santa Clara (95051-5173)
PHONE.................................408 851-1000
Ana Herdocia, *Executive Asst*
Esther Kimm, *Pharmacy Dir*
Sean McElligott, *Pharmacy Dir*
Kurt Lieber, *Exec Dir*
Janet McCalmont, *Engineer*
EMP: 593
SALES (corp-wide): 27.8B **Privately Held**
SIC: 8062 General medical & surgical hospitals
HQ: Kaiser Foundation Hospitals Inc
1 Kaiser Plz
Oakland CA 94612
510 271-6611

(P-21679)
KAISER FOUNDATION HOSPITALS
Also Called: Kaiser Permanente
1900 E 4th St, Santa Ana (92705-3962)
PHONE.................................714 967-4700
Fax: 714 967-4575
Martha Bieser, *Principal*
Nora E Canty, *Radiology Dir*
Thomas T Kang, *Family Practiti*

Carrie A Nelson-Vasquez, *Family Practiti*
Dorothy L Siddall, *Family Practiti*
EMP: 50
SALES (corp-wide): 27.8B **Privately Held**
WEB: www.kaiserpermanente.org
SIC: 8062 General medical & surgical hospitals
HQ: Kaiser Foundation Hospitals Inc
1 Kaiser Plz
Oakland CA 94612
510 271-6611

(P-21680)
KAISER PERMANENTE
9985 Sierra Ave, Fontana (92335-6720)
PHONE.................................909 427-3910
Fax: 909 427-4285
Terry Bellmonte, *Principal*
Thao Tran, *Pharmacy Dir*
Valerie Hammel, *Office Mgr*
Heather Jimenez, *Admin Asst*
Javier M Sanchez, *Family Practiti*
EMP: 127
SALES (est): 10MM **Privately Held**
SIC: 8062 General medical & surgical hospitals

(P-21681)
KAWEAH DLTA HLTH CARE DST GILD (PA)
Also Called: KAWEAH DELTA DISTRICT HOSPITAL
400 W Mineral King Ave, Visalia (93291-6237)
PHONE.................................559 624-2000
Fax: 559 627-9153
Donna Archer, *CEO*
Lindsay K Mann, *CEO*
Gary Herbst, *CFO*
May Stevens, *Treasurer*
Thomas Rayner, *Senior VP*
EMP: 1800
SQ FT: 250,255
SALES: 475.4MM **Privately Held**
SIC: 8062 Hospital, AMA approved residency

(P-21682)
KENNETH CORP
Also Called: Garden Grove Hospital
12601 Garden Grove Blvd, Garden Grove (92843-1908)
PHONE.................................714 537-5160
Fax: 714 741-3322
Edward Mirzabegian, *CEO*
Hassan Alkhouli, *Ch of Bd*
Mary B Formy, *CFO*
Carla Glaze, *Vice Pres*
Jacinto Panes, *Risk Mgmt Dir*
EMP: 615
SQ FT: 133,083
SALES (est): 63.7MM **Privately Held**
SIC: 8062 General medical & surgical hospitals

(P-21683)
KERN VALLEY HOSP FOUNDATION (PA)
6412 Laurel Ave, Lake Isabella (93240-9529)
P.O. Box 1628 (93240-1628)
PHONE.................................760 379-2681
Fax: 619 379-3133
Clarence Semonious, *President*
Bruce Swinyer, *Ch Pathology*
Chet Beadle, *CFO*
Mary Completo, *Treasurer*
Anne Litz, *Vice Pres*
EMP: 300
SQ FT: 65,000
SALES (est): 40.9MM **Privately Held**
SIC: 8062 8051 General medical & surgical hospitals; extended care facility

(P-21684)
KINDRED HEALTHCARE INC
2224 Medical Center Dr, Perris (92571-2638)
PHONE.................................951 436-3535
EMP: 81
SALES (corp-wide): 7B **Publicly Held**
SIC: 8062 General medical & surgical hospitals

PA: Kindred Healthcare, Inc.
680 S 4th St
Louisville KY 40202
502 596-7300

(P-21685)
KINDRED HEALTHCARE INC
1503 30th St, San Diego (92102-1503)
PHONE.................................619 546-9653
EMP: 284
SALES (corp-wide): 7B **Publicly Held**
SIC: 8062 General medical & surgical hospitals
PA: Kindred Healthcare, Inc.
680 S 4th St
Louisville KY 40202
502 596-7300

(P-21686)
KINDRED HEALTHCARE OPER INC
145 E Dana St, Mountain View (94041-1507)
PHONE.................................650 962-6000
Fax: 650 335-1200
Rod Wong, *Branch Mgr*
EMP: 219
SALES (corp-wide): 7B **Publicly Held**
WEB: www.salemhaven.com
SIC: 8062 General medical & surgical hospitals
HQ: Kindred Healthcare Operating, Inc.
680 S 4th St
Louisville KY 40202
502 596-7300

(P-21687)
KINDRED HEALTHCARE OPER INC
Also Called: Kindred Hospital
2800 Benedict Dr, San Leandro (94577-6840)
PHONE.................................510 357-8300
Wendy Mamoon, *CEO*
Virgil Williams, *Ch Radiology*
Ruth Anne, *COO*
Jack Boggess, *COO*
Ciba Aflack, *CFO*
EMP: 450
SALES (corp-wide): 7B **Publicly Held**
WEB: www.salemhaven.com
SIC: 8062 General medical & surgical hospitals
HQ: Kindred Healthcare Operating, Inc.
680 S 4th St
Louisville KY 40202
502 596-7300

(P-21688)
KINDRED HEALTHCARE OPER INC
1575 7th Ave, San Francisco (94122-3704)
PHONE.................................415 566-1200
Melissa Jones, *Administration*
Estella Cachuela, *Records Dir*
Bo Andres, *Data Proc Staff*
EMP: 218
SALES (corp-wide): 7B **Publicly Held**
SIC: 8062 General medical & surgical hospitals
HQ: Kindred Healthcare Operating, Inc.
680 S 4th St
Louisville KY 40202
502 596-7300

(P-21689)
KINDRED HEALTHCARE OPER INC
Also Called: Ontario Community Hospital
550 N Monterey Ave, Ontario (91764-3318)
PHONE.................................909 391-0333
Peter Adamo, *CEO*
Curtis Powell, *COO*
Joseph Landenwich, *Vice Pres*
Guillermo Santa, *Lab Dir*
Wanka Wilke, *Pharmacy Dir*
EMP: 275
SALES (corp-wide): 7B **Publicly Held**
WEB: www.salemhaven.com
SIC: 8062 General medical & surgical hospitals
HQ: Kindred Healthcare Operating, Inc.
680 S 4th St
Louisville KY 40202
502 596-7300

(P-21690)
KINDRED HEALTHCARE OPERATING
5525 W Slauson Ave, Los Angeles (90056-1047)
PHONE.................................310 642-0325
Adam Darvish, *Manager*
Nancy Sagaral, *President*
Michael Gonzales, *CFO*
Cathrine Rodriguez, *CFO*
Roger Ellison, *CIO*
EMP: 280
SALES (corp-wide): 7B **Publicly Held**
WEB: www.salemhaven.com
SIC: 8062 General medical & surgical hospitals
HQ: Kindred Healthcare Operating, Inc.
680 S 4th St
Louisville KY 40202
502 596-7300

(P-21691)
KINDRED HOSPITAL-WESTMINSTER
200 Hospital Cir, Westminster (92683-3910)
PHONE.................................714 372-3014
Virg Narbutas, *CEO*
Jack Boggess, *COO*
Julie Myers, *Admin Sec*
Jack Boggess, *Administration*
David McConnell, *Quality Imp Dir*
EMP: 400
SQ FT: 107,000
SALES (est): 42MM
SALES (corp-wide): 7B **Publicly Held**
WEB: www.khwestminster.com
SIC: 8062 General medical & surgical hospitals
PA: Kindred Healthcare, Inc.
680 S 4th St
Louisville KY 40202
502 596-7300

(P-21692)
KINGSBURG HOSPITAL DISTRICT BD
Also Called: Kingsburg Medical Center
1200 Smith St, Kingsburg (93631-2216)
P.O. Box 563 (93631-0563)
PHONE.................................559 897-5841
Fax: 559 897-5579
Pilo Chavez, *Ch of Bd*
Luis Sierra, *CFO*
Richie Hernandez, *Radiology*
Michael L Farley, *Agent*
EMP: 120 **EST:** 1961
SQ FT: 16,000
SALES (est): 8.5MM **Privately Held**
SIC: 8062 General medical & surgical hospitals

(P-21693)
KND DEVELOPMENT 55 LLC
Also Called: Kindred Hospital - Rancho
10841 White Oak Ave, Rancho Cucamonga (91730-3817)
PHONE.................................909 581-6400
Miller Debroah, *Director*
Tessie Mancilla, *Human Res Mgr*
Julian Burke, *Director*
EMP: 68
SALES: 45.1MM **Privately Held**
SIC: 8062 General medical & surgical hospitals

(P-21694)
KPC HEALTHCARE INC
2701 S Bristol St, Santa Ana (92704-6201)
PHONE.................................714 800-1919
EMP: 150
SALES (corp-wide): 449.3MM **Privately Held**
SIC: 8062 General medical & surgical hospitals
PA: Kpc Healthcare, Inc.
1301 N Tustin Ave
Santa Ana CA 92705
714 953-3652

▲ = Import ▼ =Export
◆ =Import/Export

8062 - General Medical & Surgical Hospitals County (P-21712)

(P-21695)
LA METROPOLITAN MEDICAL CTR
2231 Southwest Dr, Los Angeles (90043-4523)
PHONE..................323 730-7300
John Fenton, *CEO*
James W Young, *President*
Audrey O'Donnell, *COO*
Ron Stinett, *COO*
Michael Grubb, *CFO*
EMP: 600
SQ FT: 140,000
SALES (est): 39.4MM
SALES (corp-wide): 136.2MM **Privately Held**
SIC: 8062 General medical & surgical hospitals
HQ: Pacific Health Corporation
14642 Newport Ave
Tustin CA 92780
714 838-9600

(P-21696)
LA PALMA HOSPITAL MEDICAL CTR
Also Called: La Palma Intercommunity Hosp
7901 Walker St, La Palma (90623-1764)
PHONE..................714 670-7400
Fax: 714 523-4580
Virg Narbutas, *CEO*
Allen Spefanek, *CFO*
Sami Shoukair, *Chairman*
Marlene Pritchard, *Vice Pres*
Diane Wolf, *Administration*
EMP: 400
SQ FT: 94,000
SALES (est): 59.3MM
SALES (corp-wide): 2.6B **Privately Held**
SIC: 8062 General medical & surgical hospitals
PA: Prime Healthcare Services Inc
3300 E Guasti Rd Ste 300
Ontario CA 91761
909 235-4400

(P-21697)
LAC USC MEDICAL CENTER
Also Called: Los Angeles County Hospital
1200 N State St Rm 5250, Los Angeles (90033-1083)
P.O. Box 63 (90078-0063)
PHONE..................323 226-7858
Fax: 323 226-5760
Robert Henderson, *Director*
Hung Jeff, *CFO*
Carol Salminen, *Infect Cntl Dir*
Phillip Valdez, *Associate Dir*
Michael Siegel, *Principal*
EMP: 180
SALES (est): 65.9MM **Privately Held**
SIC: 8062 6324 General medical & surgical hospitals; hospital & medical service plans

(P-21698)
LAST FRONTIER HEALTHCARE DST
Also Called: Modoc Medical Center
228 W Mcdowell Ave, Alturas (96101-3934)
PHONE..................530 233-7036
Fax: 530 233-4310
Kevin Kramer, *CEO*
Duwine Matthew, *Ch Radiology*
Jo Knoch, *CFO*
Camila Lopez'pasos, *Social Dir*
Lorie Fogerty, *Human Res Dir*
EMP: 161
SQ FT: 56,094
SALES (est): 33.4MM **Privately Held**
WEB: www.modoccounty.us
SIC: 8062 General medical & surgical hospitals

(P-21699)
LELAND STANFORD JUNIOR UNIV
Also Called: Cantor Art Ctr Stanford Univ
328 Lomita Dr, Palo Alto (94305-5006)
PHONE..................650 723-2997
Jesse Cool, *Manager*
Simon Clopton, *Info Tech Mgr*
Sara Larsen, *Manager*
EMP: 50

SALES (corp-wide): 1.9B **Privately Held**
SIC: 8062 8069 8221 General medical & surgical hospitals; children's hospital; university
PA: Leland Stanford Junior University
2575 Sand Hill Rd
Menlo Park CA 94025
650 723-2300

(P-21700)
LELAND STANFORD JUNIOR UNIV
Also Called: Stanford Hospitals and Clinics
820 Quarry Rd, Palo Alto (94304-2202)
PHONE..................650 725-2377
Roy King, *Branch Mgr*
Antonios Issa, *Med Doctor*
Norman H Silverman, *Med Doctor*
EMP: 2285
SALES (corp-wide): 1.9B **Privately Held**
SIC: 8062 8221 General medical & surgical hospitals; university
PA: Leland Stanford Junior University
2575 Sand Hill Rd
Menlo Park CA 94025
650 723-2300

(P-21701)
LELAND STANFORD JUNIOR UNIV
Also Called: Stanford Medical Center
2680 Hanover St, Palo Alto (94304-1117)
PHONE..................650 723-4000
Elizabeth Eilers, *Director*
Negin Behzadian, *Research*
Thuylinh Nguyen, *Research*
Bruce Lusignan, *Professor*
Eugene Roh, *Professor*
EMP: 2285
SALES (corp-wide): 1.9B **Privately Held**
SIC: 8062 8221 General medical & surgical hospitals; university
PA: Leland Stanford Junior University
2575 Sand Hill Rd
Menlo Park CA 94025
650 723-2300

(P-21702)
LELAND STANFORD JUNIOR UNIV
Also Called: Stanford University Med Ctr
1000 Welch Rd, Palo Alto (94304-1811)
PHONE..................650 725-4617
Fax: 650 725-6798
Kate Lorig, *Principal*
Ann Wiersma, *Office Mgr*
Clifford Chin, *Assoc Prof*
Matias Bruzoni, *Surgeon*
Mary T Jacobson, *Obstetrician*
EMP: 2285
SALES (corp-wide): 1.9B **Privately Held**
SIC: 8062 8221 Hospital, medical school affiliation; university
PA: Leland Stanford Junior University
2575 Sand Hill Rd
Menlo Park CA 94025
650 723-2300

(P-21703)
LELAND STANFORD JUNIOR UNIV
Also Called: Stanford University
473 Via Ortega, Stanford (94305-4121)
PHONE..................650 725-2386
Richard Luthy, *Branch Mgr*
Roger Trippel, *Associate Dir*
Susan Carter, *Admin Asst*
Grace Fontanilla, *Admin Asst*
Mark Jacobson, *Professor*
EMP: 2285
SALES (corp-wide): 1.9B **Privately Held**
SIC: 8062 8069 8221 General medical & surgical hospitals; children's hospital; university
PA: Leland Stanford Junior University
2575 Sand Hill Rd
Menlo Park CA 94025
650 723-2300

(P-21704)
LELAND STANFORD JUNIOR UNIV
Also Called: Stanford University
243 Panama St, Stanford (94305-4102)
PHONE..................650 725-6127

Phil Reese, *Branch Mgr*
Prescilla Young, *Executive*
Eryn Mills, *Program Mgr*
Michelle Collette, *Technical Mgr*
Philip Lavori, *Professor*
EMP: 2285
SALES (corp-wide): 1.9B **Privately Held**
SIC: 8062 8069 8221 General medical & surgical hospitals; children's hospital; university
PA: Leland Stanford Junior University
2575 Sand Hill Rd
Menlo Park CA 94025
650 723-2300

(P-21705)
LELAND STANFORD JUNIOR UNIV
Also Called: Stanford University Medical
300 Pasteur Dr, Stanford (94305-2200)
PHONE..................650 723-4000
Martha Marsh, *Administration*
Jenni Vargas, *President*
Margaret Vosburgh, *COO*
Daniel J Morissette, *CFO*
Jill Buathier, *Vice Pres*
EMP: 6800
SQ FT: 33,503
SALES (corp-wide): 1.9B **Privately Held**
SIC: 8062 8011 8221 General medical & surgical hospitals; offices & clinics of medical doctors; university
PA: Leland Stanford Junior University
2575 Sand Hill Rd
Menlo Park CA 94025
650 723-2300

(P-21706)
LINDA LOMA UNIV HLTH CARE (HQ)
11370 Anderson St # 3900, Loma Linda (92350-1715)
P.O. Box 2000 (92354-0200)
PHONE..................909 558-2806
Fax: 909 478-6177
Richard Hart, *President*
Robert Martin,
Rosita Fike, *CEO*
Maxine Ullery, *Associate Dir*
Rhodes Rigsby, *Exec Dir*
EMP: 56
SALES (est): 846.2MM
SALES (corp-wide): 848.5MM **Privately Held**
SIC: 8062 8011 8051 5999 Hospital, medical school affiliated with residency; medical centers; extended care facility; convalescent equipment & supplies
PA: Loma Linda University
11060 Anderson St
Loma Linda CA 92350
909 558-4540

(P-21707)
LITTLE COMPANY MARY HOSPITAL
Also Called: Leader Drug Store
4101 Torrance Blvd, Torrance (90503-4664)
PHONE..................310 540-7676
Fax: 310 303-5738
Joseph Zanetta, *CEO*
Francesca Wachs, *COO*
Elizabeth Zuanich, *CFO*
Mary Reyes, *Vice Pres*
Jody Molloy, *Admin Sec*
▲ **EMP:** 1200
SQ FT: 300,000
SALES: 8.5MM
SALES (corp-wide): 10.1B **Privately Held**
WEB: www.lcmhs.org
SIC: 8062 8051 General medical & surgical hospitals; skilled nursing care facilities
HQ: Providence Health System-Southern California
1801 Lind Ave Sw
Renton WA 98057
425 525-3355

(P-21708)
LODI MEMORIAL HOSP ASSN INC (PA)
975 S Fairmont Ave, Lodi, (95240-5118)
P.O. Box 3004 (95241-1908)
PHONE..................209 334-3411

Fax: 209 334-0386
Joseph P Harrington, *CEO*
Willis Marzolf,
Roland Simeon,
Nagui N Sorour,
Michael Catz,
EMP: 700
SQ FT: 97,057
SALES: 120.3MM **Privately Held**
SIC: 8062 General medical & surgical hospitals

(P-21709)
LODI MEMORIAL HOSP ASSN INC
Also Called: Conrad Lab, The
1200 W Vine St, Lodi (95240-5136)
PHONE..................209 339-7583
Dave Mack, *Director*
Sue Anderson, *Manager*
Karel Cole, *Manager*
Cindy Billups, *Supervisor*
Jackie Vollmer, *Supervisor*
EMP: 50
SALES (corp-wide): 174.9MM **Privately Held**
SIC: 8062 General medical & surgical hospitals
PA: Lodi Memorial Hospital Association, Inc.
975 S Fairmont Ave
Lodi CA 95240
209 334-3411

(P-21710)
LOMA LINDA - INLAND EMPIRE C
Also Called: Llieche
11175 Campus St Csp 11006 11006 Csp, Loma Linda (92354)
PHONE..................909 651-5832
Daniel Giang, *President*
EMP: 141 **EST:** 2013
SALES (est): 1.6MM **Privately Held**
SIC: 8062 Hospital, medical school affiliated with residency

(P-21711)
LOMA LINDA UNIVERSITY MED CTR
Also Called: Craniofacial Department
11370 Anderson St 2100, Loma Linda (92350-1715)
P.O. Box 982 (92354-0982)
PHONE..................909 558-2100
Leonard Bailey MD, *Principal*
Sandy Wilson, *MIS Mgr*
Duane Baldwin, *Urology*
Charles E Stewart Sr, *Otolaryngology*
Helen X Xiao-Ou, *Otolaryngology*
EMP: 105
SALES (corp-wide): 848.5MM **Privately Held**
WEB: www.llumc.com
SIC: 8062 8221 Hospital, medical school affiliation; university
HQ: Loma Linda University Medical Center
11234 Anderson St
Loma Linda CA 92354
909 558-4000

(P-21712)
LOMA LINDA UNIVERSITY MED CTR (DH)
Also Called: LLUMC
11234 Anderson St, Loma Linda (92354-2871)
P.O. Box 2000 (92354-0200)
PHONE..................909 558-4000
Fax: 909 558-0337
Richard H Hart, *CEO*
Austin Colohan,
Brenda Taylor, *Records Dir*
James Jesse, *President*
Noni Patchett, *Treasurer*
EMP: 4600
SQ FT: 630,000
SALES: 846.2MM
SALES (corp-wide): 848.5MM **Privately Held**
WEB: www.llumc.com
SIC: 8062 8011 8051 5999 Hospital, medical school affiliated with residency; medical centers; extended care facility; medical apparatus & supplies

8062 - General Medical & Surgical Hospitals County (P-21713)

HQ: Loma Linda University Health Care
11370 Anderson St # 3900
Loma Linda CA 92350
909 558-2806

(P-21713)
LOMA LINDA UNIVERSITY MED CTR
Also Called: Loma Linda Catering Center
11175 Campus St, Loma Linda (92350-1700)
PHONE 909 558-8244
Fax: 909 558-0236
Najwa Medina, *Manager*
Janelle Pyke, *Records Dir*
Barbara Sharp, *Exec Dir*
Brent Boyko, *Technology*
Douglas Deming, *Professor*
EMP: 100
SALES (corp-wide): 848.5MM **Privately Held**
WEB: www.llumc.com
SIC: 8062 Hospital, medical school affiliation
HQ: Loma Linda University Medical Center
11234 Anderson St
Loma Linda CA 92354
909 558-4000

(P-21714)
LOMA LINDA UNIVERSITY MED CTR
Also Called: Behavioral Medicine Center
1710 Barton Rd, Redlands (92373-5304)
PHONE 909 558-9275
Fax: 909 335-4262
Ruthita Fike, *Manager*
Steven Mohr, *Senior VP*
Edward L Field, *Exec Dir*
Art Earll, *Admin Sec*
Cherry Zhuang, *Food Svc Dir*
EMP: 310
SQ FT: 62,476
SALES (corp-wide): 848.5MM **Privately Held**
WEB: www.llumc.com
SIC: 8062 8221 Hospital, medical school affiliation; university
HQ: Loma Linda University Medical Center
11234 Anderson St
Loma Linda CA 92354
909 558-4000

(P-21715)
LOMA LINDA UNIVERSITY MED CTR
Also Called: Loma Linda Community Hospital
25333 Barton Rd, Loma Linda (92350-0210)
PHONE 909 796-0167
Fax: 909 558-0438
Todd Nelson, *Manager*
Carlos Garberoglio,
Ron Swensen, *Ch OB/GYN*
Denise Winters, *Volunteer Dir*
Mark Hubbard, *Vice Pres*
EMP: 172
SQ FT: 79,580
SALES (corp-wide): 848.5MM **Privately Held**
WEB: www.llumc.com
SIC: 8062 General medical & surgical hospitals
HQ: Loma Linda University Medical Center
11234 Anderson St
Loma Linda CA 92354
909 558-4000

(P-21716)
LOMPOC VALLEY MEDICAL CENTER (PA)
Also Called: Lompoc Skilled Care Center
1515 E Ocean Ave, Lompoc (93436-7092)
P.O. Box 1058 (93438-1058)
PHONE 805 737-3300
Fax: 805 735-7491
Jim Raggio, *CEO*
Khawar Gal,
Naishadh Buch, *COO*
Roger McConnell, *Bd of Directors*
Jayne Scalise, *Principal*
EMP: 325
SQ FT: 150,000
SALES (est): 85.8MM **Privately Held**
SIC: 8062 8051 General medical & surgical hospitals; skilled nursing care facilities

(P-21717)
LONG BEACH MEMORIAL MED CTR (HQ)
Also Called: MEMORIAL CARE MEDICAL CENTERS
2801 Atlantic Ave Fl 2, Long Beach (90806-1701)
P.O. Box 20894 (90801-3894)
PHONE 562 933-2000
Fax: 562 492-6089
John Bishop, *CEO*
Barry Arbuckle PHD, *President*
Tamra Kaplan, *COO*
Suize Reinsvold, *COO*
Susie Reinsvold, *COO*
EMP: 2000
SQ FT: 1,100,000
SALES: 624MM
SALES (corp-wide): 2B **Privately Held**
WEB: www.longbeachstate.com
SIC: 8062 General medical & surgical hospitals
PA: Memorial Health Services
17360 Brookhurst St # 160
Fountain Valley CA 92708
714 377-6748

(P-21718)
LONGWOOD MANAGEMENT CORP
Also Called: Northridge Nursing Center
7836 Reseda Blvd, Reseda (91335-1902)
PHONE 818 881-7414
Deffie Biczi, *General Mgr*
Maria Flores, *Director*
Mehran Okhovat, *Director*
EMP: 80
SALES (corp-wide): 169.4MM **Privately Held**
SIC: 8062 General medical & surgical hospitals
PA: Longwood Management Corp.
4032 Wilshire Blvd Fl 6
Los Angeles CA 90010
213 389-6900

(P-21719)
LONGWOOD MANAGEMENT CORP
Also Called: Shea Convalescent Hospital
7716 Pickering Ave, Whittier (90602-2001)
PHONE 562 693-5240
Fax: 562 698-5270
Richard Esconrias, *Manager*
Michael Gray, *Administration*
EMP: 100
SALES (corp-wide): 169.4MM **Privately Held**
SIC: 8062 8051 8011 General medical & surgical hospitals; skilled nursing care facilities; offices & clinics of medical doctors
PA: Longwood Management Corp.
4032 Wilshire Blvd Fl 6
Los Angeles CA 90010
213 389-6900

(P-21720)
LOS ALAMITOS MEDICAL CTR INC (HQ)
3751 Katella Ave, Los Alamitos (90720-3113)
P.O. Box 533 (90720-0533)
PHONE 714 826-6400
Fax: 562 493-2812
Michele Finney, *CEO*
Alice Livingood, *President*
Margaret Watkins, *President*
Sherrie Fernandez, *Radiology Dir*
Kristy Ballard, *Admin Asst*
EMP: 1100
SQ FT: 900
SALES: 25.4K
SALES (corp-wide): 18.7B **Publicly Held**
SIC: 8062 General medical & surgical hospitals
PA: Tenet Healthcare Corporation
1445 Ross Ave Ste 1400
Dallas TX 75202
469 893-2200

(P-21721)
MADERA COMMUNITY HOSPITAL
Also Called: Chowchilla Medical Center
285 Hospital Dr, Chowchilla (93610-2041)
PHONE 559 665-3768
Mark J Foote, *CEO*
EMP: 89
SALES (corp-wide): 75.9MM **Privately Held**
SIC: 8062 General medical & surgical hospitals
PA: Madera Community Hospital
1250 E Almond Ave
Madera CA 93637
559 675-5555

(P-21722)
MADERA COMMUNITY HOSPITAL (PA)
Also Called: Mch
1250 E Almond Ave, Madera (93637-5696)
P.O. Box 1328 (93639-1328)
PHONE 559 675-5555
Fax: 559 675-5467
Evan J Rayner, *CEO*
Peter Nassar,
Mary Aguirre, *President*
Donna Tooley, *CFO*
Steve Jones, *Lab Dir*
EMP: 720
SQ FT: 66,300
SALES: 75.9MM **Privately Held**
SIC: 8062 General medical & surgical hospitals

(P-21723)
MAIN STREET SPECIALTY SURGERY
280 S Mn St Ste 100, Orange (92868)
PHONE 714 704-1900
Fax: 714 704-1912
Betty Hoogenban, *Director*
Tammy Tanner, *Manager*
EMP: 102
SALES (est): 14.6MM **Privately Held**
WEB: www.msssc.com
SIC: 8062 General medical & surgical hospitals

(P-21724)
MARIN GENERAL HOSPITAL
250 Bon Air Rd, Greenbrae (94904-1784)
P.O. Box 8010, San Rafael (94912-8010)
PHONE 415 925-7000
Fax: 415 925-7108
Lee Domanico, *CEO*
Peter Allen,
David Bradley, *CEO*
David Cox, *CFO*
Theresa Daughton, *CFO*
EMP: 1100 **EST:** 1947
SQ FT: 125,000
SALES: 342.3MM **Privately Held**
WEB: www.sutterhealth.org
SIC: 8062 8011 General medical & surgical hospitals; offices & clinics of medical doctors
PA: Marin Healthcare District
100b Drakes Landing Rd
Greenbrae CA 94904
415 464-2090

(P-21725)
MARINA DEL REY HOSPITAL
4650 Lincoln Blvd, Marina Del Rey (90292-6306)
PHONE 310 823-8911
Sean Fowler, *CEO*
James Keefe, *Ch Pathology*
Jose Gomez, *Office Mgr*
Farshad Nosratian, *Cardiology*
Van Scott, *Manager*
EMP: 601
SQ FT: 117,640
SALES (est): 16.9MM **Privately Held**
SIC: 8062 General medical & surgical hospitals

(P-21726)
MARK TWAIN MEDICAL CENTER (HQ)
Also Called: Mark Twain St Josephs Hospital
768 Mountain Ranch Rd, San Andreas (95249-9707)
PHONE 209 754-3521
Fax: 209 754-2626
Craig J Marks, *CEO*
Rick R Baier, *Ch Pathology*
Keri Caligiure,
Ruth Huffman, *Records Dir*
Greg Jordan, *President*
EMP: 225
SQ FT: 40,000
SALES: 56MM
SALES (corp-wide): 7.1B **Privately Held**
SIC: 8062 General medical & surgical hospitals
PA: Dignity Health
185 Berry St Ste 300
San Francisco CA 94107
415 438-5500

(P-21727)
MARK TWAIN MEDICAL CENTER
Also Called: Silver Service
768 Mountain Ranch Rd, San Andreas (95249-9707)
PHONE 209 754-1487
Mike Lawson, *President*
EMP: 300
SALES (corp-wide): 7.1B **Privately Held**
SIC: 8062 8322 General medical & surgical hospitals; geriatric social service
HQ: Mark Twain Medical Center
768 Mountain Ranch Rd
San Andreas CA 95249
209 754-3521

(P-21728)
MARSHALL MEDICAL CENTER
1100 Marshall Way, El Dorado Hills (95762)
PHONE 916 933-2273
EMP: 221
SALES (corp-wide): 200.2MM **Privately Held**
PA: Marshall Medical Center
1100 Marshall Way
Placerville CA 95667
530 622-1441

(P-21729)
MARSHALL MEDICAL CENTER (PA)
Also Called: Marshall Hospital
1100 Marshall Way, Placerville (95667-6533)
P.O. Box 872 (95667-0872)
PHONE 530 622-1441
Fax: 530 622-7853
James Whipple, *CEO*
Jennifer Fiterre, *Volunteer Dir*
Shannon Truesdell, *COO*
Laurie Eldridge, *CFO*
Marlene Markowich, *General Mgr*
EMP: 1000
SQ FT: 124,000
SALES: 200.2MM **Privately Held**
SIC: 8062 8071 8082 General medical & surgical hospitals; medical laboratories; X-ray laboratory, including dental; home health care services

(P-21730)
MATER MISERICORDIAE HOSPITAL (PA)
Also Called: Mercy Medical Center Merced
333 Mercy Ave, Merced (95340-8319)
PHONE 209 564-5000
Fax: 209 564-4272
David Dunham, *CEO*
Chuck Kassis, *COO*
Terry Bohlke, *CFO*
Doreen Hartmann, *CFO*
Michael Strasser, *CFO*
EMP: 668
SQ FT: 60,000
SALES (est): 70.8MM **Privately Held**
SIC: 8062 General medical & surgical hospitals

PRODUCTS & SERVICES SECTION

8062 - General Medical & Surgical Hospitals County (P-21749)

(P-21731)
MCKINLEY PARK CARE CENTER
3700 H St, Sacramento (95816-4611)
PHONE.....................................916 452-3592
Fax: 916 451-7854
Radio Shey, *Administration*
Gary Weemers, *Administration*
EMP: 85
SALES (est): 5.3MM **Privately Held**
SIC: 8062 General medical & surgical hospitals

(P-21732)
MEMORIAL HOSPITAL OF GARDENA
4060 Woody Blvd, Los Angeles (90023)
PHONE.....................................323 268-5514
Fax: 310 532-7561
Araceli Lonergan, *CEO*
Daniel Heckathorne, *CFO*
Hector Hernandez, *Vice Pres*
Pat Hess, *Lab Dir*
Moises Nunez, *Administration*
EMP: 400
SQ FT: 111,000
SALES (est): 99.1MM
SALES (corp-wide): 105.9MM **Privately Held**
WEB: www.mhglax.com
SIC: 8062 General medical & surgical hospitals
PA: Avanti Health System, Llc
 222 N Sepulveda Blvd # 950
 El Segundo CA 90245
 310 356-0550

(P-21733)
MENDOCINO COAST DISTRICT HOSP (PA)
700 River Dr, Fort Bragg (95437-5403)
PHONE.....................................707 961-1234
Fax: 707 961-5916
Jonathan Baker, *CEO*
Jacob Lewis, *CFO*
Mark Smith, *CFO*
Patricia Jauregui Darland, *Chairman*
Tom Birdsell, *Treasurer*
▲ **EMP:** 300 **EST:** 1971
SQ FT: 71,500
SALES: 46.8MM **Privately Held**
SIC: 8062 General medical & surgical hospitals

(P-21734)
MENDOCINO COAST DISTRICT HOSP
Also Called: Mendicino Cast Otptent Surgery
700 River Dr, Fort Bragg (95437-5403)
PHONE.....................................707 961-4736
Jonathan Baker, *Branch Mgr*
EMP: 167
SALES (corp-wide): 46.8MM **Privately Held**
SIC: 8062 8011 General medical & surgical hospitals; surgeon
PA: Mendocino Coast District Hospital
 700 River Dr
 Fort Bragg CA 95437
 707 961-1234

(P-21735)
MERCY HEALTHCARE SACRAMENTO
Also Called: Mercy San Juan Hospital
6501 Coyle Ave Fl 6, Carmichael (95608-0306)
PHONE.....................................916 537-5151
Fax: 916 537-1111
Donna Utley, *Director*
Ed Oliveras, *Exec VP*
Linda Ubaldi, *Risk Mgmt Dir*
Kathy Yeager, *Security Dir*
Herman Kensky, *Research*
EMP: 1700
SALES (corp-wide): 7.1B **Privately Held**
WEB: www.mercycare.net
SIC: 8062 General medical & surgical hospitals
HQ: Mercy Healthcare Sacramento
 3400 Data Dr
 Rancho Cordova CA 95670
 916 379-2871

(P-21736)
MERCY HEALTHCARE SACRAMENTO
Also Called: Mercy San Juan Medical Center
6501 Coyle Ave, Carmichael (95608-0306)
PHONE.....................................916 537-5000
Rian Ivie, *Branch Mgr*
Rick Canning, *CFO*
Clay Taft, *Vice Pres*
Theresa A Demrco, *Radiology Dir*
Roland D Emarco, *Radiology Dir*
EMP: 1500
SALES (corp-wide): 7.1B **Privately Held**
WEB: www.mercycare.net
SIC: 8062 8011 General medical & surgical hospitals; offices & clinics of medical doctors
HQ: Mercy Healthcare Sacramento
 3400 Data Dr
 Rancho Cordova CA 95670
 916 379-2871

(P-21737)
MERCY HEALTHCARE SACRAMENTO (HQ)
Also Called: Mercy San Juan Hospital
3400 Data Dr, Rancho Cordova (95670-7956)
PHONE.....................................916 379-2871
Fax: 916 851-2727
Michael Erne, *President*
William Hunt, *COO*
Richard Rothberger, *CFO*
Dan Ferguson, *Chief Mktg Ofcr*
John Chambers, *Senior VP*
EMP: 450
SQ FT: 92,000
SALES (est): 442.2MM
SALES (corp-wide): 7.1B **Privately Held**
WEB: www.mercycare.net
SIC: 8062 General medical & surgical hospitals
PA: Dignity Health
 185 Berry St Ste 300
 San Francisco CA 94107
 415 438-5500

(P-21738)
MERCY HEALTHCARE SACRAMENTO
Mercy Hospital of Folsom
1650 Creekside Dr, Folsom (95630-3400)
PHONE.....................................916 983-7400
Fax: 916 983-7406
Donald Hudson, *President*
Nancy Shilts, *Bd of Directors*
Sue Miller, *Asst Admin*
Kathleen Noble, *Human Res Dir*
James Majewski, *Security Mgr*
EMP: 400
SALES (corp-wide): 7.1B **Privately Held**
WEB: www.mercycare.net
SIC: 8062 4119 General medical & surgical hospitals; ambulance service
HQ: Mercy Healthcare Sacramento
 3400 Data Dr
 Rancho Cordova CA 95670
 916 379-2871

(P-21739)
MERCY HM SVCS A CAL LTD PARTNR
2215 Truxtun Ave, Bakersfield (93301-3602)
PHONE.....................................661 632-5234
Russel Judd, *President*
EMP: 200
SALES (corp-wide): 7.1B **Privately Held**
WEB: www.mercyhealth.org
SIC: 8062 General medical & surgical hospitals
HQ: Mercy Home Services A California Limited Partnership
 2175 Rosaline Ave Ste A
 Redding CA 96001
 530 225-6000

(P-21740)
MERCY HM SVCS A CAL LTD PARTNR (HQ)
Also Called: Mercy Medical Center - Redding
2175 Rosaline Ave Ste A, Redding (96001-2549)
P.O. Box 496009 (96049-6009)
PHONE.....................................530 225-6000
Fax: 530 225-7297
George A Govier, *CEO*
Jill Belk, *CFO*
Robert Folden, *Lab Dir*
Steve Buhler, *Radiology Dir*
Wendy Scott, *Info Tech Mgr*
EMP: 700
SQ FT: 250,000
SALES (est): 172.7MM
SALES (corp-wide): 7.1B **Privately Held**
WEB: www.mercyhealth.org
SIC: 8062 General medical & surgical hospitals
PA: Dignity Health
 185 Berry St Ste 300
 San Francisco CA 94107
 415 438-5500

(P-21741)
MERCY HM SVCS A CAL LTD PARTNR
914 Pine St, Mount Shasta (96067-2143)
PHONE.....................................530 926-6111
Fax: 530 926-0517
Kenneth Platou, *CEO*
Steven Scharpf, *Vice Pres*
Gail Schwagerl, *Records Dir*
Sherie Ambrose, *Vice Pres*
Sandy Eastman, *Recruiter*
EMP: 340
SALES (corp-wide): 7.1B **Privately Held**
WEB: www.mercyhealth.org
SIC: 8062 General medical & surgical hospitals
HQ: Mercy Home Services A California Limited Partnership
 2175 Rosaline Ave Ste A
 Redding CA 96001
 530 225-6000

(P-21742)
MERCY HM SVCS A CAL LTD PARTNR
Also Called: Mercy General Hospital
4001 J St, Sacramento (95819-3626)
PHONE.....................................916 453-4545
Fax: 916 453-4379
Edmundo Castaneda, *President*
Conrad Megia, *Vice Pres*
Cynthia Kirch, *VP Human Res*
Jane Crable, *Maintence Staff*
Robert Quadro, *Oncology*
EMP: 1000
SALES (corp-wide): 7.1B **Privately Held**
WEB: www.mercyhealth.org
SIC: 8062 General medical & surgical hospitals
HQ: Mercy Home Services A California Limited Partnership
 2175 Rosaline Ave Ste A
 Redding CA 96001
 530 225-6000

(P-21743)
MERCY MEDICAL CENTER NAMPA
315 Merced Mall, Merced (95348-2410)
PHONE.....................................209 485-1380
EMP: 101 **Privately Held**
SIC: 8062 General medical & surgical hospitals
HQ: Saint Alphonsus Medical Center - Nampa Health Foundation, Inc.
 1512 12th Ave Rd
 Nampa ID 83686
 208 467-1171

(P-21744)
MERCY METHODIST HOSPITAL (PA)
7500 Hospital Dr, Sacramento (95823-5403)
PHONE.....................................916 423-6063
Carla Moznett, *Principal*
Steven J Barad, *Orthopedist*
EMP: 57
SALES (est): 59.2MM **Privately Held**
WEB: www.methodistsacramento.com
SIC: 8062 General medical & surgical hospitals

(P-21745)
MERCY METHODIST HOSPITAL
3400 Data Dr, Rancho Cordova (95670-7956)
PHONE.....................................916 379-2996
Susan Carson, *Principal*
EMP: 936
SALES (corp-wide): 59.2MM **Privately Held**
SIC: 8062 General medical & surgical hospitals
PA: Mercy Methodist Hospital
 7500 Hospital Dr
 Sacramento CA 95823
 916 423-6063

(P-21746)
METHODIST HOSP SOUTHERN CAL (PA)
300 W Huntington Dr, Arcadia (91007-3402)
PHONE.....................................626 898-8000
Dan F Ausman, *CEO*
Gary Moscarello,
Bridgett Didier, *Records Dir*
Donald Deshotels, *CFO*
Clifford R Daniels, *Senior VP*
EMP: 933
SQ FT: 100,000
SALES: 279.4MM **Privately Held**
SIC: 8062 General medical & surgical hospitals

(P-21747)
METHODIST HOSPITAL OF S CA
300 W Huntington Dr, Arcadia (91007-3402)
P.O. Box 60016 (91066-6016)
PHONE.....................................626 574-3755
Fax: 626 446-1709
Dennis Lee, *Principal*
Jason Aranda, *Manager*
Joe Lussier, *Manager*
EMP: 66
SALES (est): 8MM **Privately Held**
SIC: 8062 General medical & surgical hospitals

(P-21748)
MILLS-PENINSULA HEALTH SVCS (HQ)
Also Called: Mills-Peninsula Hospitals
1501 Trousdale Dr, Burlingame (94010-4506)
PHONE.....................................650 696-5400
Fax: 650 696-5487
Robert W Merwin, *President*
Evelyn Khoo, *Vice Chairman*
Iftikhar Hussaon, *CFO*
James Cody, *Treasurer*
Lorraine Massa, *Treasurer*
EMP: 939 **EST:** 1906
SALES: 609.8MM
SALES (corp-wide): 11B **Privately Held**
WEB: www.mills-peninsula.org
SIC: 8062 General medical & surgical hospitals
PA: Sutter Health
 2200 River Plaza Dr
 Sacramento CA 95833
 916 733-8800

(P-21749)
MISSION HOSP REGIONAL MED CTR (PA)
27700 Medical Center Rd, Mission Viejo (92691-6426)
PHONE.....................................949 364-1400
Fax: 949 364-2056
Kenn Nicfaralnd, *CEO*
Don White, *Lab Dir*
Connie Gagliardo, *Exec Dir*
Joe Galiardo, *Exec Dir*
Scott Odonnell, *Security Dir*
EMP: 1349
SQ FT: 750,000
SALES: 511.1MM **Privately Held**
WEB: www.drvonmaur.com
SIC: 8062 General medical & surgical hospitals

8062 - General Medical & Surgical Hospitals County (P-21750)

(P-21750)
MOFFITT H C HOSPITAL
505 Parnassus Ave, San Francisco (94143-2204)
PHONE.................................415 476-1000
Mark Lourette, *CEO*
EMP: 90 **EST:** 2008
SALES (est): 234.1K **Privately Held**
SIC: 8062 General medical & surgical hospitals
HQ: University Of California, San Francisco
505 Parnassus Ave
San Francisco CA 94143
415 476-9000

(P-21751)
MONTEREY PARK HOSPITAL
Also Called: Monterey Park Hospital
900 S Atlantic Blvd, Monterey Park (91754-4780)
PHONE.................................626 570-9000
Fax: 626 281-4719
Philip A Cohen, *CEO*
Robert M Dubbs, *President*
Robert W Fleming Jr, *Senior VP*
Tom Nakatuchi, *Pharmacy Dir*
Robin Houston, *Personnel*
EMP: 150
SQ FT: 90,575
SALES (est): 38.4MM
SALES (corp-wide): 615.4MM **Privately Held**
WEB: www.montereyparkhosp.com
SIC: 8062 General medical & surgical hospitals
PA: Ahmc Healthcare Inc.
1000 S Fremont Ave Unit 6
Alhambra CA 91803
626 943-7526

(P-21752)
MONTEREY PENINSULA HOSPITAL
Also Called: Community Hosp Recovery Ctr
576 Hartnell St Ste 260, Monterey (93940-2887)
PHONE.................................831 373-0924
EMP: 50
SALES (est): 2.8MM
SALES (corp-wide): 4.7MM **Privately Held**
SIC: 8062
PA: Community Hospital Foundation Inc
23625 Holman Hwy
Monterey CA 93940
831 625-4830

(P-21753)
MOTION PICTURE AND TV FUND (PA)
Also Called: BOB HOPE HEALTH CENTER
23388 Mulholland Dr # 200, Woodland Hills (91364-2733)
P.O. Box 51151, Los Angeles (90051-5451)
PHONE.................................818 876-1777
Fax: 818 225-1359
Robert Beitcher, *CEO*
Bob Pisano, *Ch of Bd*
Jay Roth, *Treasurer*
Juan Acosta, *Executive*
Sue Schubert, *Executive*
EMP: 688
SQ FT: 50,000
SALES: 23.5MM **Privately Held**
WEB: www.mptvfund.org
SIC: 8062 8051 8011 8351 General medical & surgical hospitals; convalescent home with continuous nursing care; medical centers; child day care services; individual & family services; retirement hotel operation

(P-21754)
MOTION PICTURE AND TV FUND
Also Called: Westside Health Center
1950 Sawtelle Blvd # 130, Los Angeles (90025-7072)
PHONE.................................310 231-3000
Fax: 310 231-3016
Micheal West, *Manager*
Arlene Glassner, *Marketing Mgr*
Donald Legg, *Director*
Norman Solomon, *Director*
EMP: 66
SALES (corp-wide): 23.5MM **Privately Held**
SIC: 8062 8011 General medical & surgical hospitals; offices & clinics of medical doctors
PA: Motion Picture And Television Fund
23388 Mulholland Dr # 200
Woodland Hills CA 91364
818 876-1777

(P-21755)
MOUNTAIN COMM HLTH CRE DIST
Also Called: Trinity Hospital
410 N Taylor St, Weaverville (96093)
P.O. Box 1229 (96093-1229)
PHONE.................................530 623-5541
David Yarbrough, *Director*
Diane Rieke, *Pat Nrsg Dir*
Ed Hsu, *Finance*
Tamara Harris, *Human Res Dir*
Donna Petersen, *Director*
EMP: 130
SALES (corp-wide): 12.1MM **Privately Held**
SIC: 8062 General medical & surgical hospitals
PA: Mountain Communities Health Care District
60 Easter Ave
Weaverville CA 96093
530 623-5541

(P-21756)
MOUNTAIN COMM HLTH CRE DIST (PA)
Also Called: Trinity Hospital
60 Easter Ave, Weaverville (96093)
P.O. Box 1229 (96093-1229)
PHONE.................................530 623-5541
Fax: 530 623-3073
Aaron Rogers, *CEO*
Ed Hsu, *CFO*
Tom Piper, *CFO*
Judy Nordlund, *Infect Cntl Dir*
Doug McLaskey, *Pharmacy Dir*
EMP: 90
SALES: 12.1MM **Privately Held**
WEB: www.mcmedical.org
SIC: 8062 General medical & surgical hospitals

(P-21757)
MOUNTAIN VIEW CHILD CARE INC (PA)
Also Called: Totally Kids Rhbilitation Hosp
1720 Mountain View Ave, Loma Linda (92354-1799)
PHONE.................................909 796-6915
Fax: 909 796-8580
Doug Pagett, *CEO*
Cynthia Capetillo, *CFO*
Donald Nydam, *Vice Pres*
Loma Linda, *Principal*
Sun Valley, *Principal*
EMP: 275
SALES (est): 60.9MM **Privately Held**
SIC: 8062 8052 8051 General medical & surgical hospitals; intermediate care facilities; skilled nursing care facilities

(P-21758)
MOUNTAINS COMMU
29101 Hospital Rd, Lake Arrowhead (92352-9706)
P.O. Box 70 (92352-0070)
PHONE.................................909 336-3651
Fax: 909 336-4730
Don Willerth, *CEO*
Terry Pena, *COO*
Tandi Orangetree, *Officer*
April Ramirez, *Accounting Mgr*
Sheila Craft, *Corp Comm Staff*
EMP: 180
SQ FT: 18,500
SALES: 452.1K **Privately Held**
WEB: www.mchcares.com
SIC: 8062 8051 General medical & surgical hospitals; skilled nursing care facilities

(P-21759)
NATIVIDAD HOSPITAL INC
Also Called: Occupational Medicine
1441 Constitution Blvd, Salinas (93906-3100)
PHONE.................................831 755-4111
Wiiliam Foley, *President*
EMP: 659
SALES (est): 33.3MM **Privately Held**
WEB: www.natividad.com
SIC: 8062 8011 8093 General medical & surgical hospitals; offices & clinics of medical doctors; specialty outpatient clinics

(P-21760)
NORTH SONOMA COUNTY HOSP DST
Also Called: Healdsburg District Hospital
1375 University St, Healdsburg (95448-3382)
PHONE.................................707 431-6500
Fax: 707 431-6525
Evan J Rayner, *CEO*
Regina Novello, *COO*
Dan Hull, *CFO*
Thomas Warr, *Officer*
Johnny Hargrove, *Vice Pres*
EMP: 171 **EST:** 2001
SALES (est): 34.1MM **Privately Held**
SIC: 8062 General medical & surgical hospitals

(P-21761)
NORTHBAY HEALTHCARE CORP (PA)
Also Called: Northbay Healthcare System
1200 B Gale Wilson Blvd, Fairfield (94533-3552)
PHONE.................................707 646-5000
Gary J Passama, *President*
Judy Winters,
Linda Hill,
Jane Schilling, *Volunteer Dir*
Denio Art, *CFO*
EMP: 114
SQ FT: 24,000
SALES (est): 63.6MM **Privately Held**
SIC: 8062 8011 General medical & surgical hospitals; offices & clinics of medical doctors

(P-21762)
NORTHBAY HEALTHCARE GROUP (PA)
Also Called: NORTHBAY MEDICAL CENTER
1200 B Gale Wilson Blvd, Fairfield (94533-3552)
PHONE.................................707 646-5000
Toll Free:.................................888 -
Fax: 707 426-5287
Deborah Sugiyama, *CEO*
Gallen Gorman, *CFO*
George Stock, *CFO*
Susan Gornall, *Op Rm Dir*
Colleen Knight, *Executive Asst*
EMP: 900
SQ FT: 125,000
SALES: 460.5MM **Privately Held**
SIC: 8062 General medical & surgical hospitals

(P-21763)
NORTHERN CALIFORNIA REHAB
2801 Eureka Way, Redding (96001-0222)
PHONE.................................530 246-9000
Brad Hollinger, *Mng Member*
Chris Jones, *Business Dir*
Penny Booth, *Info Tech Dir*
Kristy Thompson, *Accountant*
Mark Cardenas, *Plant Mgr*
EMP: 250
SALES: 39.2MM
SALES (corp-wide): 329.7MM **Privately Held**
SIC: 8062 General medical & surgical hospitals
PA: Vibra Healthcare, Llc
4550 Lena Dr
Mechanicsburg PA 17055
717 591-5700

(P-21764)
NORTHERN INYO CTY HOSPITAL DST
Also Called: Northern Inyo Hospital
150 Pioneer Ln, Bishop (93514-2556)
PHONE.................................760 873-5811
Fax: 760 872-2768
Victoria Alexander-Lane, *CEO*
Kelli Huntsinger, *Records Dir*
Ann Rusk, *Records Dir*
Marie Boyd, *Vice Chairman*
M C Hubbard, *President*
EMP: 402
SQ FT: 55,000
SALES: 72.9MM **Privately Held**
WEB: www.nih.org
SIC: 8062 General medical & surgical hospitals

(P-21765)
NORWALK COMMUNITY HOSPITAL
13222 Bloomfield Ave, Norwalk (90650-3200)
PHONE.................................562 863-4763
Fax: 562 207-9721
David Topper, *President*
David Herrera, *Vice Pres*
Ted Estrado, *Manager*
EMP: 100
SQ FT: 18,935
SALES (est): 9.3MM
SALES (corp-wide): 637.4MM **Privately Held**
SIC: 8062 General medical & surgical hospitals
HQ: Alta Healthcare System Llc
4081 E Olympic Blvd
Los Angeles CA 90023
323 267-0477

(P-21766)
OAK VALLEY HOSPITAL DISTRICT (HQ)
350 S Oak Ave, Oakdale (95361-3519)
PHONE.................................209 847-3011
Fax: 209 848-4110
John McCormick, *CEO*
Bob Wikoff, *Ch of Bd*
Gail McCarthy, *Chairman*
Gail Sward, *Vice Ch Bd*
Edward Sarno, *Pharmacy Dir*
EMP: 325
SQ FT: 55,000
SALES: 67.6MM
SALES (corp-wide): 7.1B **Privately Held**
WEB: www.ovhd.com
SIC: 8062 8051 General medical & surgical hospitals; skilled nursing care facilities
PA: Dignity Health
185 Berry St Ste 300
San Francisco CA 94107
415 438-5500

(P-21767)
OCONNOR HOSPITAL (PA)
Also Called: O'Connor Wound Care Clinic
2105 Forest Ave, San Jose (95128-1471)
PHONE.................................408 947-2500
Fax: 408 947-2819
James F Dover, *CEO*
Ron Galonsky, *COO*
David W Carroll, *Senior VP*
David Carroll, *Senior VP*
Craig Rucker, *Vice Pres*
EMP: 1000
SQ FT: 750,000
SALES: 307.1MM **Privately Held**
SIC: 8062 General medical & surgical hospitals

(P-21768)
OJAI VALLEY COMMUNITY HOSPITAL
1306 Maricopa Hwy, Ojai (93023-3131)
PHONE.................................805 646-1401
Fax: 805 640-1051
Jim Van Duzer, *Exec Dir*
Gary Wilde, *CEO*
Adam Thunell, *COO*
Norm Bergman, *CFO*
Cynthia Demotte, *Vice Pres*
EMP: 120
SALES: 24.9MM **Privately Held**
WEB: www.brimhealthcare.com
SIC: 8062 General medical & surgical hospitals
HQ: Healthtech Management Services Inc
5110 Maryland Way Ste 200
Brentwood TN 37027
615 309-6053

(P-21769)
OLYMPIA HEALTH CARE LLC
5900 W Olympic Blvd, Los Angeles (90036-4671)
PHONE..................................323 938-3161
John A Calderone, *CEO*
Babur Ozkan, *CFO*
Karen Knueven,
William Smith, *Director*
EMP: 875 **EST:** 2004
SQ FT: 500,000
SALES (est): 46.6MM
SALES (corp-wide): 1B **Privately Held**
SIC: 8062 Hospital, affiliated with AMA residency
PA: Alecto Healthcare Services Llc
   16310 Bake Pkwy Ste 200
   Irvine CA 92618
   323 938-3161

(P-21770)
ORANGE COST CNTR FOR SURG CARE
18111 Brookhurst St # 3200, Fountain Valley (92708-6728)
PHONE..................................714 369-1070
Cheryl Jacob, *Principal*
John Fenger, *Manager*
EMP: 65
SALES (est): 8.8MM **Privately Held**
SIC: 8062 General medical & surgical hospitals

(P-21771)
ORANGE COUNTY GLOBAL MED CTR
1001 N Tustin Ave, Santa Ana (92705-3502)
PHONE..................................714 953-3500
Fax: 714 560-7318
Susan Richards, *CEO*
Martha Guerra, *Comp Lab Dir*
Greg Olson, *Info Tech Dir*
Michael Price, *Supervisor*
EMP: 55 **EST:** 1972
SALES: 324.9K **Privately Held**
SIC: 8062 General medical & surgical hospitals

(P-21772)
ORANGETREE CONVALESCENT HOSP
Also Called: Plott Family Care Centers
4000 Harrison St, Riverside (92503-3599)
PHONE..................................951 785-6060
Fax: 951 785-6710
Elizabeth Plott, *President*
Sue Johnson, *Asst Admin*
Sampate Saste, *Director*
EMP: 120
SALES (est): 9.6MM **Privately Held**
SIC: 8062 8051 General medical & surgical hospitals; skilled nursing care facilities

(P-21773)
ORCHARD HOSPITAL
240 Spruce St, Gridley (95948-2216)
P.O. Box 97 (95948-0097)
PHONE..................................530 846-5671
Fax: 530 846-6406
Wade Sturgeon, *CEO*
Steve Stark, *CEO*
Tracy Atkins, *COO*
Kristina Hessong, *CFO*
Clark Redfield, *Bd of Directors*
EMP: 235
SQ FT: 12,000
SALES: 24.3MM **Privately Held**
SIC: 8062 General medical & surgical hospitals

(P-21774)
OROVILLE HOSPITAL (PA)
2767 Olive Hwy, Oroville (95966-6118)
PHONE..................................530 533-8500
Fax: 530 532-8177
Robert J Wentz, *CEO*
Scott Chapple, *COO*
Ashok Khanchandani, *CFO*
Matthew Fine, *Chief Mktg Ofcr*
David Bryning, *Officer*
EMP: 1170
SQ FT: 68,133

SALES: 236.9MM **Privately Held**
SIC: 8062 General medical & surgical hospitals

(P-21775)
ORTHOPAEDIC HOSPITAL (PA)
Also Called: Orthopaedic Inst For Children
403 W Adams Blvd, Los Angeles (90007-2664)
P.O. Box 60132 (90060-0132)
PHONE..................................213 742-1000
Fax: 213 742-1137
Anthony A Scaduto, *President*
Dennis Strum, *COO*
Jeff Goldberg, *CFO*
Joseph Luevanos, *CFO*
Diane Moon, *CFO*
EMP: 159
SQ FT: 105,000
SALES: 44.4MM **Privately Held**
SIC: 8062 General medical & surgical hospitals

(P-21776)
PACIFIC OCCPTNAL MEDICINE SVCS
2776 Pacific Ave, Long Beach (90806-2613)
PHONE..................................562 997-2290
Fax: 562 427-4478
Michael PH, *Principal*
David Wueste, *Vice Pres*
Kathy Gerard, *Principal*
EMP: 50
SALES (est): 930K **Privately Held**
SIC: 8062 General medical & surgical hospitals

(P-21777)
PACIFICA OF VALLEY CORPORATION
Also Called: Pacifica Hospital of Valley
9449 San Fernando Rd, Sun Valley (91352-1421)
PHONE..................................818 767-3310
Fax: 818 252-2439
Paul Tuft, *Ch of Bd*
Andro Sarmac,
Krishnaswamy Narayanan,
Ayman Mousa, *CEO*
Kathryn Calafato, *CFO*
EMP: 525
SQ FT: 148,020
SALES (est): 82MM **Privately Held**
WEB: www.pacificahospital.com
SIC: 8062 General medical & surgical hospitals

(P-21778)
PALO VERDE HEALTH CARE DST
Also Called: Palo Verde Hospital
250 N 1st St, Blythe (92225-1702)
PHONE..................................760 922-4115
Peter Klune, *CEO*
Dennis Rutherford, *CFO*
Lilly Lopez, *Human Res Mgr*
Samuel Burton, *Director*
Jim Carney, *Director*
EMP: 180 **EST:** 1938
SALES (est): 12.1MM **Privately Held**
WEB: www.paloverdehospital.com
SIC: 8062 8069 General medical & surgical hospitals; specialty hospitals, except psychiatric

(P-21779)
PALOMAR HEALTH (PA)
Also Called: Palomar Medical Center
456 E Grand Ave, Escondido (92025-3319)
PHONE..................................442 281-5000
Fax: 858 675-5132
Diane Hansen, *Exec VP*
Kimberly Jackson, *Records Dir*
Linda Greer, *Vice Chairman*
Robert A Hemker, *CEO*
Robert Trifunovic MD, *Officer*
EMP: 180
SQ FT: 66,000
SALES: 614.2MM **Privately Held**
WEB: www.sunbridge.com
SIC: 8062 8059 General medical & surgical hospitals; convalescent home

(P-21780)
PALOMAR HEALTH
Also Called: Palomar Medical Center
2185 Citracado Pkwy, Escondido (92029-4159)
PHONE..................................760 739-3000
Fax: 760 739-3108
Michael Covert, *CEO*
Jerry Kolins, *Ch Pathology*
Barbara Batterman, *Officer*
Gerald Bracht, *Officer*
Martha Knutson, *Officer*
EMP: 1200
SALES (corp-wide): 614.2MM **Privately Held**
WEB: www.sunbridge.com
SIC: 8062 General medical & surgical hospitals
PA: Palomar Health
   456 E Grand Ave
   Escondido CA 92025
   442 281-5000

(P-21781)
PALOMAR HEALTH
Also Called: Pomerado Hospital
15615 Pomerado Rd, Poway (92064-2405)
PHONE..................................858 613-4000
Fax: 858 485-4690
Jim Flinn, *Administration*
Gary Spoto, *Ch Radiology*
Della Shaw, *Exec VP*
Craig Parrish, *Telecomm Dir*
William Turner, *Pharmacy Dir*
EMP: 300
SALES (corp-wide): 614.2MM **Privately Held**
WEB: www.sunbridge.com
SIC: 8062 General medical & surgical hospitals
PA: Palomar Health
   456 E Grand Ave
   Escondido CA 92025
   442 281-5000

(P-21782)
PAMC LTD (PA)
Also Called: Pamc Health Foundation
531 W College St, Los Angeles (90012-2315)
PHONE..................................213 624-8411
John Edwards, *CEO*
Allan Shubin, *Senior VP*
Yi Siu, *Lab Dir*
Natalie Kast, *Admin Asst*
Tsai Selena, *Admin Asst*
EMP: 530
SQ FT: 75,600
SALES (est): 42.6MM **Privately Held**
SIC: 8062 General medical & surgical hospitals

(P-21783)
PANORAMA COMMUNITY HOSPITAL
14850 Roscoe Blvd, Panorama City (91402-4618)
PHONE..................................818 787-2222
Fax: 818 904-3529
David Green, *CEO*
Rick Velagarza, *Vice Pres*
EMP: 50
SALES (est): 3.3MM **Privately Held**
SIC: 8062 General medical & surgical hospitals

(P-21784)
PARACELSUS LOS ANGELES COMM
4081 E Olympic Blvd, Los Angeles (90023-3330)
PHONE..................................323 267-0477
Fax: 323 269-4079
Lou Rubino, *Acting CEO*
Omar Ramirez, *COO*
Rick Monroe, *CFO*
Keith Levy, *Analyst*
Lillian Brach, *Human Res Dir*
EMP: 250
SALES: 141.6MM **Privately Held**
SIC: 8062 General medical & surgical hospitals

(P-21785)
PARADISE VALLEY HOSPITAL (PA)
2400 E 4th St, National City (91950-2098)
PHONE..................................619 470-4100
Fax: 619 470-4124
Alan Soderblom, *CEO*
Robert Carmen, *Ch of Bd*
Prem Reddy, *Ch of Bd*
Luin Leon, *CEO*
Sally Shaw, *COO*
EMP: 925 **EST:** 1904
SQ FT: 230,000
SALES (est): 159.3MM **Privately Held**
WEB: www.paradisevalleyhospital.org
SIC: 8062 General medical & surgical hospitals

(P-21786)
PARKVIEW CMNTY HOSP MED CTR
3865 Jackson St, Riverside (92503-3919)
PHONE..................................951 354-7404
Norm Martin, *President*
Doug Drumwright, *CEO*
Cheryl Daniels, *Officer*
Carol Parker, *Radiology Dir*
Ken Culver, *Pharmacy Dir*
EMP: 1149
SQ FT: 132,651
SALES: 159.7MM **Privately Held**
SIC: 8062 8011 General medical & surgical hospitals; offices & clinics of medical doctors

(P-21787)
PASADENA HOSPITAL ASSN LTD (PA)
Also Called: HUNTINGTON MEMORIAL HOSPITAL
100 W California Blvd, Pasadena (91105-3010)
P.O. Box 7013 (91109-7013)
PHONE..................................626 397-5000
Fax: 626 397-2914
Lois Matthews, *Chairman*
Gail Cinexi,
Sharon Muenchow,
Paul Ouyang, *Ch of Bd*
Stephen A Ralph, *President*
EMP: 2100
SQ FT: 928,000
SALES: 569.3MM **Privately Held**
WEB: www.huntingtonhospital.com
SIC: 8062 8051 8063 General medical & surgical hospitals; skilled nursing care facilities; psychiatric hospitals

(P-21788)
PATIENTS HOSPITAL
2900 Eureka Way, Redding (96001-0220)
PHONE..................................530 225-8700
Fax: 530 225-8718
James D Tate MD, *President*
Kim Needles, *Office Mgr*
Brett Banwagner, *Administration*
Shari Lejsek, *Administration*
Brett Vanwagner, *Engineer*
EMP: 80
SALES: 5.5MM **Privately Held**
WEB: www.patientshospital.com
SIC: 8062 General medical & surgical hospitals

(P-21789)
PERMANENTE KAISER INTL
3955 Bonita Rd Bldg B, Bonita (91902-1230)
PHONE..................................619 409-6050
Fax: 619 409-6310
David Parra, *Med Doctor*
EMP: 512
SALES (corp-wide): 380.5MM **Privately Held**
SIC: 8062 General medical & surgical hospitals
PA: Kaiser Permanente International
   1 Kaiser Plz
   Oakland CA 94612
   510 271-5910

(P-21790)
PERMANENTE KAISER INTL
9961 Sierra Ave, Fontana (92335-6720)
PHONE..................................909 427-5000

8062 - General Medical & Surgical Hospitals County (P-21791)

PRODUDUCTS & SERVICES SECTION

Fax: 909 427-4096
Jeff Jobe, *Radiology Dir*
Lee Ward, *Engineer*
Vivien Choi, *Food Svc Dir*
Gary L McLarty, *Emerg Med Spec*
Julie Chae, *Pharmacist*
EMP: 1281
SALES (corp-wide): 380.5MM **Privately Held**
SIC: 8062 General medical & surgical hospitals
PA: Kaiser Permanente International
1 Kaiser Plz
Oakland CA 94612
510 271-5910

(P-21791)
PERMANENTE KAISER INTL
25965 Normandie Ave Fl 3, Harbor City (90710-3416)
PHONE..................310 517-2645
Fax: 310 517-2482
Evan Bass, *Med Doctor*
EMP: 683
SALES (corp-wide): 380.5MM **Privately Held**
SIC: 8062 General medical & surgical hospitals
PA: Kaiser Permanente International
1 Kaiser Plz
Oakland CA 94612
510 271-5910

(P-21792)
PERMANENTE KAISER INTL
555 E Valley Pkwy, Escondido (92025-3048)
P.O. Box 523, Rancho Santa Fe (92067-0523)
PHONE..................760 739-3000
William Tench, *Pathologist*
EMP: 1580
SALES (corp-wide): 380.5MM **Privately Held**
SIC: 8062 General medical & surgical hospitals
PA: Kaiser Permanente International
1 Kaiser Plz
Oakland CA 94612
510 271-5910

(P-21793)
PERMANENTE KAISER INTL
Also Called: Playa Vista Medical Offices
5620 Mesmer Ave, Culver City (90230-6315)
PHONE..................310 737-4800
Fax: 310 737-4880
Christine A Shaw, *Family Practiti*
Karen Warren, *Manager*
EMP: 555
SALES (corp-wide): 380.5MM **Privately Held**
SIC: 8062 General medical & surgical hospitals
PA: Kaiser Permanente International
1 Kaiser Plz
Oakland CA 94612
510 271-5910

(P-21794)
PERMANENTE KAISER INTL
3700 New Horizons Way, Vacaville (95688-9477)
PHONE..................707 453-5197
EMP: 256
SALES (corp-wide): 380.5MM **Privately Held**
SIC: 8062 General medical & surgical hospitals
PA: Kaiser Permanente International
1 Kaiser Plz
Oakland CA 94612
510 271-5910

(P-21795)
PERMANENTE MEDICAL GROUP INC
1725 Eastshore Hwy, Berkeley (94710-1703)
PHONE..................510 559-5119
Susan Yee, *Administration*
Xiaoyuan Liu, *Med Doctor*
EMP: 58

SALES (corp-wide): 27.8B **Privately Held**
WEB: www.permanente.net
SIC: 8062 General medical & surgical hospitals
HQ: The Permanente Medical Group Inc
1950 Franklin St Fl 18th
Oakland CA 94612
866 858-2226

(P-21796)
PERMANENTE MEDICAL GROUP INC
1550 Gateway Blvd, Fairfield (94533-6901)
PHONE..................707 427-4000
Fax: 707 427-4380
Laura Coffman, *Branch Mgr*
David J Danzeisen, *Family Practiti*
Isaac Tam, *Pharmacist*
Pat Van Nordstrom, *Manager*
EMP: 50
SALES (corp-wide): 27.8B **Privately Held**
WEB: www.permanente.net
SIC: 8062 General medical & surgical hospitals
HQ: The Permanente Medical Group Inc
1950 Franklin St Fl 18th
Oakland CA 94612
866 858-2226

(P-21797)
PERRIS VALLEY CMNTY HOSP LLC
Also Called: Vista Hospital Riverside
10841 White Oak Ave, Rancho Cucamonga (91730-3817)
PHONE..................909 581-6400
Edward L Kuntz, *CEO*
EMP: 234
SALES (corp-wide): 12.7MM **Privately Held**
SIC: 8062 General medical & surgical hospitals
PA: Perris Valley Community Hospital, Llc
2224 Medical Center Dr
Perris CA 92571
951 436-5000

(P-21798)
PHYSICIANS FOR HEALTHY HOSPITA
Also Called: Menifee Valley Hospital Center
28400 Mccall Blvd, Sun City (92585-9658)
PHONE..................951 679-8888
Fax: 951 672-7050
Jeffrey Lang, *CEO*
Larry Menestrina, *Ch Radiology*
Debbie Elmore, *Vice Pres*
Thomas Mathiesen, *Pharmacy Dir*
Fred Meyer, *Exec Dir*
EMP: 300
SALES (corp-wide): 150.8MM **Privately Held**
SIC: 8062 General medical & surgical hospitals
PA: Physicians For Healthy Hospitals, Inc.
1117 E Devonshire Ave
Hemet CA 92543
951 652-2811

(P-21799)
PHYSICIANS FOR HEALTHY HOSPITA
1280 S Buena Vista St, San Jacinto (92583-4604)
PHONE..................951 652-2811
Tim Murray, *Manager*
EMP: 180
SALES (corp-wide): 150.8MM **Privately Held**
SIC: 8062 General medical & surgical hospitals
PA: Physicians For Healthy Hospitals, Inc.
1117 E Devonshire Ave
Hemet CA 92543
951 652-2811

(P-21800)
PIONEERS MEM HEALTHCARE DST (PA)
Also Called: Pioneers Memorial Hospital
207 W Legion Rd, Brawley (92227-7780)
PHONE..................760 351-3333
Fax: 760 344-4401
Richard L Mendoza, *CEO*
Christopher Lai,

Devendra Kapoor,
David F Hagen, *Ch OB/GYN*
Steven Campbell, *COO*
EMP: 571
SQ FT: 171,445
SALES (est): 82.7MM **Privately Held**
WEB: www.pioneersmemorialhospital.com
SIC: 8062 General medical & surgical hospitals

(P-21801)
PLUMAS DISTRICT HOSPITAL (PA)
1065 Bucks Lake Rd, Quincy (95971-9599)
PHONE..................530 283-2121
Fax: 530 283-0674
Doug Lafferty, *President*
Stephen Johnson, *COO*
Brenda Compton, *Info Tech Mgr*
Marion Gonzalez, *Controller*
Melissa Klundby, *Personnel Assit*
▲ **EMP:** 180 **EST:** 1959
SQ FT: 30,000
SALES: 81K **Privately Held**
SIC: 8062 General medical & surgical hospitals

(P-21802)
POMONA VALLEY HOSPITAL MED CTR (PA)
Also Called: Pvhmc
1798 N Garey Ave, Pomona (91767-2918)
PHONE..................909 865-9500
Fax: 909 620-7462
Richard E Yochum, *CEO*
Elmer Pineda,
Mona Limm,
Jasvir Sandhu,
Kurt Weinmeister, *COO*
EMP: 2121
SQ FT: 362,000
SALES: 553.9MM **Privately Held**
WEB: www.pvhmc.org
SIC: 8062 Hospital, medical school affiliated with residency

(P-21803)
POMONA VALLEY HOSPITAL MED CTR
Also Called: Claremont Outpatient Clinic
1601 Monte Vista Ave, Claremont (91711-2962)
PHONE..................909 865-9104
Joan Harper, *Manager*
EMP: 728
SALES (corp-wide): 553.9MM **Privately Held**
SIC: 8062 Hospital, medical school affiliated with residency
PA: Pomona Valley Hospital Medical Center
1798 N Garey Ave
Pomona CA 91767
909 865-9500

(P-21804)
POMONA VALLEY HOSPITAL MED CTR
Also Called: Montclair Physical Therapy
1601 Monte Vista Ave # 270, Claremont (91711-2962)
PHONE..................909 865-9977
Antoinette Fernandez, *Director*
EMP: 728
SALES (corp-wide): 553.9MM **Privately Held**
WEB: www.montclairphysicaltherapy.com
SIC: 8062 Hospital, medical school affiliated with residency
PA: Pomona Valley Hospital Medical Center
1798 N Garey Ave
Pomona CA 91767
909 865-9500

(P-21805)
PRESBYTERIAN INTRCMMNTY HOSPTL (PA)
Also Called: PIH HOME HEALTH SERVICES
12401 Washington Blvd, Whittier (90602-1006)
PHONE..................562 698-0811
Fax: 562 698-1728
James R West, *CEO*
Haig Minassian,
Kennith Thompson,
Brian Smolskis, *COO*

Mitchell Thomas, *CFO*
EMP: 1900
SQ FT: 500,000
SALES: 555.9MM **Privately Held**
SIC: 8062 General medical & surgical hospitals

(P-21806)
PRESBYTERIAN INTRCMMNTY HOSPTL
Also Called: Downey Regional Medical Center
11500 Brookshire Ave, Downey (90241-4917)
PHONE..................562 904-5482
James R West, *CEO*
Brick Bunch, *Officer*
Kathy Foster, *Vice Pres*
Marjorie Parsons, *Radiology Dir*
Daphnie Nguyen, *Pharmacy Dir*
EMP: 1150
SALES (corp-wide): 555.9MM **Privately Held**
SIC: 8062 8071 General medical & surgical hospitals; medical laboratories
PA: Presbyterian Intercommunity Hospital, Inc.
12401 Washington Blvd
Whittier CA 90602
562 698-0811

(P-21807)
PRESIDIO SURGERYCENTER
1635 Divisadero St # 200, San Francisco (94115-3036)
PHONE..................415 346-1218
Cynthia Cleveland, *Principal*
Jessie Scott, *Manager*
EMP: 53 **EST:** 2007
SALES (est): 5.8MM **Privately Held**
SIC: 8062 8011 General medical & surgical hospitals; clinic, operated by physicians

(P-21808)
PRIME HEALTH CARE SVCS GRDN GR
Also Called: Garden Grove Hospital Med Ctr
12601 Garden Grove Blvd, Garden Grove (92843-1908)
PHONE..................714 537-5160
Mike Sarian, *President*
Kevan Metcalfe, *CEO*
Alan Smith, *CFO*
Sofia Abrina, *Administration*
Martin Wieler, *Chief*
EMP: 500
SALES (est): 16.4MM **Privately Held**
SIC: 8062 General medical & surgical hospitals

(P-21809)
PRIME HEALTHCARE ANAHEIM LLC
Also Called: West Anaheim Medical Center
3033 W Orange Ave, Anaheim (92804-3156)
PHONE..................714 827-3000
Fax: 714 229-4052
Virg Narbutas, *CEO*
Kora Guoyavatin, *CFO*
Stephanie Sioson, *Human Res Dir*
Vivian Cheng, *Pharmacist*
EMP: 800 **EST:** 1963
SQ FT: 180,000
SALES (est): 120MM
SALES (corp-wide): 2.6B **Privately Held**
SIC: 8062 Hospital, affiliated with AMA residency
PA: Prime Healthcare Services Inc
3300 E Guasti Rd Ste 300
Ontario CA 91761
909 235-4400

(P-21810)
PRIME HEALTHCARE CENTINELA LLC
Also Called: Centinela Hospital Medical Ctr
555 E Hardy St, Inglewood (90301-4011)
PHONE..................310 673-4660
Fax: 310 674-7064
Linda Bradley, *CEO*
Adrien Christianson, *Co-COB*
Kimberly Saxon, *Admin Asst*
Kristina Nguyen, *Controller*

PRODUCTS & SERVICES SECTION

8062 - General Medical & Surgical Hospitals County (P-21829)

Barbara Kokolowski, *Director*
EMP: 1500 **EST:** 1952
SALES: 260MM
SALES (corp-wide): 2.6B **Privately Held**
SIC: 8062 General medical & surgical hospitals
PA: Prime Healthcare Services Inc
3300 E Guasti Rd Ste 300
Ontario CA 91761
909 235-4400

(P-21811)
PRIME HEALTHCARE SERVICES
Also Called: Shasta Regional Med Ctr Srmc
1100 Butte St, Redding (96001-0852)
PHONE 530 244-5400
Cyndy Gordon, *CEO*
Richard Bergstrom,
Marcia McCampbell, *Ch of Bd*
Randall Hempling, *CEO*
Linda Leaell, *COO*
EMP: 1500
SALES (est): 145.7MM
SALES (corp-wide): 2.6B **Privately Held**
SIC: 8062 8011 General medical & surgical hospitals; offices & clinics of medical doctors
PA: Prime Healthcare Services Inc
3300 E Guasti Rd Ste 300
Ontario CA 91761
909 235-4400

(P-21812)
PRIME HEALTHCARE SERVS SH
1450 Liberty St, Redding (96001-0838)
P.O. Box 491810 (96049-1810)
PHONE 530 244-5458
Cindy Gordon, *CEO*
EMP: 902
SALES: 50MM **Privately Held**
SIC: 8062 General medical & surgical hospitals

(P-21813)
PRIME HEALTHCARE SVCS II LLC
Also Called: Sherman Oaks Hospital
4929 Van Nuys Blvd, Sherman Oaks (91403-1702)
PHONE 818 981-7111
Fax: 818 907-4527
Prem Reddy, *CEO*
John Deady, *CFO*
Sue Eichenberger, *Lab Dir*
Leslie Wolder, *Pharmacy Dir*
David Chou, *MIS Dir*
EMP: 500
SQ FT: 36,000
SALES: 62.4MM
SALES (corp-wide): 2.6B **Privately Held**
SIC: 8062 General medical & surgical hospitals
PA: Prime Healthcare Services Inc
3300 E Guasti Rd Ste 300
Ontario CA 91761
909 235-4400

(P-21814)
PRIME HEALTHCARE SVCS III LLC (HQ)
Also Called: Montclair Hospital Medical Ctr
5000 San Bernardino St, Montclair (91763-2326)
PHONE 909 625-5411
Jennifer Ramirez, *Exec Sec*
Greg Bentano, *CFO*
Prem Reddy, *Chairman*
EMP: 64
SALES: 42.3MM
SALES (corp-wide): 2.6B **Privately Held**
WEB: www.dhmcm.com
SIC: 8062 General medical & surgical hospitals
PA: Prime Healthcare Services Inc
3300 E Guasti Rd Ste 300
Ontario CA 91761
909 235-4400

(P-21815)
PRIME HEALTHCARE-SAN DIMAS LLC
Also Called: San Dimas Community Hospital
1350 W Covina Blvd, San Dimas (91773-3245)
P.O. Box 330, Ontario (91762-8330)
PHONE 909 599-6811
Fax: 909 599-0629
Gregory Brentano, *CEO*
Dan Galles, *CFO*
Dora Noriega, *Risk Mgmt Dir*
Gerry Martin, *CIO*
Douglas Blayney, *Research*
EMP: 350
SQ FT: 90,000
SALES: 56.9MM
SALES (corp-wide): 2.6B **Privately Held**
SIC: 8062 General medical & surgical hospitals
PA: Prime Healthcare Services Inc
3300 E Guasti Rd Ste 300
Ontario CA 91761
909 235-4400

(P-21816)
PRIME HLTHCARE HNTNGTON BCH
Also Called: Huntington Beach Hospital
17772 Beach Blvd, Huntington Beach (92647-6819)
PHONE 714 843-5000
Fax: 714 843-5033
Prem Reddy, *CEO*
Eileen Fisler, *CFO*
Ravi Alla, *Vice Pres*
David Devalk, *Vice Pres*
Uma Mahesh, *Info Tech Dir*
EMP: 480 **EST:** 1957
SQ FT: 100,000
SALES (est): 77MM
SALES (corp-wide): 2.6B **Privately Held**
WEB: www.hbhospital.com
SIC: 8062 General medical & surgical hospitals
PA: Prime Healthcare Services Inc
3300 E Guasti Rd Ste 300
Ontario CA 91761
909 235-4400

(P-21817)
PROMISE HOSP E LOS ANGELES LP
16453 Colorado Ave, Paramount (90723-5011)
PHONE 323 261-0432
Fax: 562 531-4699
Michael Kerr, *CEO*
Howard Yonet, *Ch Radiology*
Brian Weise, *CFO*
Robert Balagot, *Lab Dir*
Guillermo Torres, *Radiology Dir*
EMP: 242
SALES (est): 20.5MM
SALES (corp-wide): 656.9MM **Privately Held**
SIC: 8062 General medical & surgical hospitals
PA: Promise Healthcare, Inc.
999 Yamato Rd Ste 300
Boca Raton FL 33431
561 869-3100

(P-21818)
PROVIDENCE HEALTH & SERVICES S
Also Called: Providence Little Company of M
1300 W 7th St, San Pedro (90732-3505)
PHONE 310 832-3311
EMP: 99
SALES (est): 4.7MM **Privately Held**
SIC: 8062

(P-21819)
PROVIDENCE HEALTH & SVCS - ORE
540 23rd St, Oakland (94612-1724)
PHONE 510 444-0839
Tim Zaricznyj, *Director*
EMP: 360
SALES (corp-wide): 10.1B **Privately Held**
WEB: www.providence.org
SIC: 8062 General medical & surgical hospitals
HQ: Providence Health & Services - Oregon
1801 Lind Ave Sw
Renton WA 98057
425 525-3355

(P-21820)
PROVIDENCE HEALTH & SVCS - ORE
Also Called: Providence Holy Cross Med Ctr
15031 Rinaldi St, Mission Hills (91345-1207)
PHONE 818 365-8051
David Mast, *Branch Mgr*
Jeff Butcher, *Finance*
Tanya McGee, *Opers Staff*
Natasha Shows, *Mktg Dir*
EMP: 350
SALES (corp-wide): 10.1B **Privately Held**
SIC: 8062 General medical & surgical hospitals
HQ: Providence Health & Services - Oregon
1801 Lind Ave Sw
Renton WA 98057
425 525-3355

(P-21821)
PROVIDENCE HEALTH SYSTEM
Also Called: Providence Holy Cross Med Ctr
15031 Rinaldi St, Mission Hills (91345-1207)
PHONE 818 898-4561
Kerry Carmody, *Administration*
EMP: 1000
SALES (corp-wide): 10.1B **Privately Held**
SIC: 8062 8661 General medical & surgical hospitals; Catholic Church
HQ: Providence Health System-Southern California
1801 Lind Ave Sw
Renton WA 98057
425 525-3355

(P-21822)
PROVIDENCE HEALTH SYSTEM
Providence St Joseph Med Ctr
501 S Buena Vista St, Burbank (91505-4809)
PHONE 818 843-5111
Georgianne Johnson, *COO*
Arnie Schaffer, *CEO*
Doug Jones, *Info Tech Mgr*
Kimberly Hernandez, *Director*
EMP: 2000
SALES (corp-wide): 10.1B **Privately Held**
SIC: 8062 General medical & surgical hospitals
HQ: Providence Health System-Southern California
1801 Lind Ave Sw
Renton WA 98057
425 525-3355

(P-21823)
PROVIDENCE HEALTH SYSTEM
2601 Airport Dr Ste 230, Torrance (90505-6142)
PHONE 310 530-3800
Catherine Pearlman, *Branch Mgr*
Michael Kawada, *Opers Staff*
EMP: 760
SALES (corp-wide): 10.1B **Privately Held**
SIC: 8062 General medical & surgical hospitals
HQ: Providence Health System-Southern California
1801 Lind Ave Sw
Renton WA 98057
425 525-3355

(P-21824)
PROVIDENCE HOLY CROSS (PA)
15031 Rinaldi St, Mission Hills (91345-1207)
PHONE 818 365-8051
Fax: 818 496-4125
Lee Kanon Alpert, *Chairman*
June E Drake, *CEO*
Michael White, *COO*
Chet Taylor, *CFO*
Valerie Sullivan, *Practice Mgr*
▲ **EMP:** 64 **EST:** 1960
SALES (est): 257.9MM **Privately Held**
SIC: 8062 General medical & surgical hospitals

(P-21825)
QUANTUM PROPERTIES LP
Also Called: Promise Hospital of San Diego
5550 University Ave, San Diego (92105-2307)
PHONE 619 582-3800
Bill Mitchell, *CEO*
Mohamed Bari, *President*
Tim Patten, *CEO*
Saleem Ishaque, *Corp Secy*
David Capuno, *Lab Dir*
EMP: 300
SQ FT: 68,000
SALES (est): 60.1MM **Privately Held**
SIC: 8062 General medical & surgical hospitals

(P-21826)
QUEEN OF ANGELS HOLLYWOOD PRES
1300 N Vermont Ave, Los Angeles (90027-6300)
PHONE 213 413-3000
Fax: 213 644-7613
John Fenton, *President*
Judith Maass, *Ch Nursing Ofcr*
H D Mesrobian MD, *Med Doctor*
EMP: 1200
SALES: 23.7MM **Privately Held**
SIC: 8062 Hospital, affiliated with AMA residency

(P-21827)
QUEEN OF VALLEY MEDICAL CENTER (DH)
Also Called: NAPA VALLEY MEDICAL CENTER
1000 Trancas St, NAPA (94558-2906)
PHONE 707 252-4411
Fax: 707 257-4169
Walt Mickens, *President*
Vincent Morgese, *COO*
Bob Diehl, *CFO*
Don Miller, *COO*
Mich Riccioni, *CFO*
EMP: 653
SQ FT: 278,500
SALES: 243.6MM
SALES (corp-wide): 5.6B **Privately Held**
SIC: 8062 General medical & surgical hospitals
HQ: St. Joseph Health System
3345 Michelson Dr Ste 100
Irvine CA 92612
949 381-4000

(P-21828)
RANCHO CCAMONGA CMNTY HOSP LLC
Also Called: Rancho Speciality Hospital
10841 White Oak Ave, Rancho Cucamonga (91730-3817)
PHONE 909 581-6400
Marc C Ferrell,
Victoria Selby, *COO*
Debeorah Miller, *Business Dir*
Arlene Abraham,
Mark Ferrell,
EMP: 110
SQ FT: 100,000
SALES (est): 10.5MM **Privately Held**
SIC: 8062 General medical & surgical hospitals

(P-21829)
REDWOOD MEMORIAL HOSPITAL INC (PA)
3300 Renner Dr, Fortuna (95540-3198)
PHONE 707 725-7327
Fax: 707 725-7212
Thomas McConnell, *CEO*
Bob Branigan, *COO*
Joe Rogers, *COO*
Kevin Clouder, *CFO*
Lisa Shirk, *Vice Pres*
EMP: 150
SQ FT: 65,000
SALES: 43.8MM **Privately Held**
SIC: 8062 General medical & surgical hospitals

8062 - General Medical & Surgical Hospitals County (P-21830)

(P-21830)
REGENTS OF THE UNIVERSITY CAL
Also Called: Nevada Cancer Institute
1111 Franklin St, Oakland (94607-5201)
PHONE..................619 543-3713
Tom McAsee, *Principal*
Margarita Baggett, *CEO*
Duncan Campbell, *COO*
Angela Sciao, *Chief Mktg Ofcr*
EMP: 1000
SALES (est): 11.7MM **Privately Held**
SIC: **8062** General medical & surgical hospitals

(P-21831)
RIDEOUT MEMORIAL HOSPITAL (HQ)
726 4th St, Marysville (95901-5656)
P.O. Box 2128 (95901-0075)
PHONE..................530 749-4416
Fax: 530 749-4543
Ronald M Sweeney, *Chairman*
Theresa Hamilton, *CEO*
John Cary, *Treasurer*
Lisa Del Pero, *Admin Sec*
Carl Plantholt, *MIS Staff*
EMP: 700
SQ FT: 100,000
SALES: 324.1MM
SALES (corp-wide): 28.9MM **Privately Held**
SIC: **8062** 8082 General medical & surgical hospitals; home health care services
PA: Freemont Rideout Health Group
989 Plumas St
Yuba City CA 95991
530 751-4010

(P-21832)
RIDGECREST REGIONAL HOSPITAL
Also Called: SOUTHERN SIERRA MEDICAL CLINIC
1081 N China Lake Blvd, Ridgecrest (93555-3130)
PHONE..................760 446-3551
James A Suver, *CEO*
Donna Kiser, *CFO*
Charles Pietrangelo, *Bd of Directors*
Darrell Eddins, *Vice Pres*
Scott Davis, *Lab Dir*
EMP: 500
SQ FT: 80,000
SALES: 86MM **Privately Held**
WEB: www.rrh.org
SIC: **8062** General medical & surgical hospitals

(P-21833)
RIVER SIDE CMNTY HOSP FD SVCS
4445 Magnolia Ave, Riverside (92501-4135)
PHONE..................951 788-3121
David Daniel, *Director*
Brian Eagleton, *Pharmacy Dir*
Elise Nguyen, *Pharmacist*
EMP: 70
SALES (est): 3.5MM **Privately Held**
SIC: **8062** General medical & surgical hospitals

(P-21834)
RIVERSIDE CMNTY HLTH SYSTEMS (DH)
Also Called: COLUMBIA HCA
4445 Magnolia Ave Fl 6, Riverside (92501-4135)
P.O. Box 550, Nashville TN (37202-0550)
PHONE..................951 788-3000
Fax: 951 788-3201
Partrick Brilliant, *President*
Doug Long, *COO*
Tracey Fernandez, *CFO*
May Kim, *Lab Dir*
Diane Elkhoury, *Admin Asst*
EMP: 56
SQ FT: 386,100
SALES: 435.8MM **Publicly Held**
WEB: www.rchc.org
SIC: **8062** 8011 General medical & surgical hospitals; offices & clinics of medical doctors

HQ: Hca Inc.
1 Park Plz
Nashville TN 37203
615 344-9551

(P-21835)
RIVERSIDE HEALTHCARE SYSTEM LP
Also Called: Riverside Community Hospital
4445 Magnolia Ave, Riverside (92501-4135)
PHONE..................951 788-3000
Patrick Brilliant, *Managing Prtnr*
EMP: 1600
SALES (est): 36.8MM **Publicly Held**
SIC: **8062** General medical & surgical hospitals
HQ: Hca Inc.
1 Park Plz
Nashville TN 37203
615 344-9551

(P-21836)
SADDLEBACK MEMORIAL MED CTR (HQ)
Also Called: MEMORIAL CARE MEDICAL CENTERS
24451 Health Center Dr, Laguna Hills (92653-3689)
P.O. Box 20894 (92653)
PHONE..................949 837-4500
Fax: 949 452-3276
Steve Geidt, *CEO*
Daniel Lamont,
Kathleen Sullivan,
Barry Arbuckle, *President*
Adolfo Chanez, *CFO*
EMP: 1020
SQ FT: 195,000
SALES: 337.2MM
SALES (corp-wide): 2B **Privately Held**
SIC: **8062** 8011 8093 8099 General medical & surgical hospitals; medical centers; diabetes specialist, physician/surgeon; cardiologist & cardio-vascular specialist; pediatrician; rehabilitation center, outpatient treatment; blood related health services; medical laboratories; cancer hospital; maternity hospital; orthopedic hospital
PA: Memorial Health Services
17360 Brookhurst St # 160
Fountain Valley CA 92708
714 377-6748

(P-21837)
SAINT AGNES MEDICAL CENTER (HQ)
1303 E Herndon Ave, Fresno (93720-3309)
PHONE..................559 450-3000
Fax: 559 449-3368
Nancy R Hollingsworth, *CEO*
Tai-PO Tschang, *Ch Pathology*
Charles Sohn,
Harold Groom, *Ch OB/GYN*
Michael Martinez, *Vice Chairman*
EMP: 1688
SQ FT: 200,000
SALES: 503.7MM
SALES (corp-wide): 1B **Privately Held**
SIC: **8062** General medical & surgical hospitals
PA: Trinity Health Corporation
20555 Victor Pkwy
Livonia MI 48152
734 343-1000

(P-21838)
SAINT FRANCIS MEMORIAL HOSP (HQ)
900 Hyde St, San Francisco (94109-4899)
PHONE..................415 353-6000
Fax: 415 353-6631
Thomas G Hennessy, *CEO*
John G Williams, *President*
Cheryl A Fama Rn, *COO*
Craig Rucker, *CFO*
Ray Miller, *Pharmacy Dir*
EMP: 800
SQ FT: 300,000
SALES: 222.4MM
SALES (corp-wide): 7.1B **Privately Held**
SIC: **8062** General medical & surgical hospitals

PA: Dignity Health
185 Berry St Ste 300
San Francisco CA 94107
415 438-5500

(P-21839)
SAINT JHNS HLTH CTR FOUNDATION
Also Called: St John's Health Centre
2020 Santa Monica Blvd 3rdfl3, Santa Monica (90404-2023)
PHONE..................310 829-8970
Lou Laztin, *CEO*
Barbara Mooney, *Buyer*
Patrick Schulte, *Director*
EMP: 297
SALES (corp-wide): 2.4B **Privately Held**
SIC: **8062** General medical & surgical hospitals
HQ: Saint John's Health Center Foundation.
2121 Santa Monica Blvd
Santa Monica CA 90404
310 829-5511

(P-21840)
SAINT LOUISE HOSPITAL
9400 N Name Uno, Gilroy (95020-3528)
PHONE..................408 848-2000
Fax: 408 848-4920
Jim Dober, *CEO*
Terry Curley, *Vice Pres*
Ernest Spencer, *Lab Dir*
Joanne Allan, *Principal*
Ben Nguyen, *Facilities Mgr*
EMP: 500
SALES: 101.9MM **Privately Held**
SIC: **8062** General medical & surgical hospitals

(P-21841)
SALINAS VALLEY MEMORIAL HLTHCA (PA)
Also Called: SALINAS VALLEY MEMORIAL HOSPIT
450 E Romie Ln, Salinas (93901-4029)
P.O. Box 3827 (93912-3827)
PHONE..................831 757-4333
Fax: 831 754-2638
Sam Downing, *CEO*
Timothy Albert,
Khanh Ngo,
Paul Steinberg,
Beverly Ranzenberger, *COOoo*
▲ EMP: 80
SQ FT: 187,942
SALES: 344.2MM **Privately Held**
SIC: **8062** General medical & surgical hospitals

(P-21842)
SAN ANTONIO COMMUNITY HOSPITAL (PA)
999 San Bernardino Rd, Upland (91786-4920)
PHONE..................909 985-2811
Fax: 909 920-4732
Jim Milhiser, *Chairman*
Carlos Canizales,
Ian F Sandy,
Regina Millard,
Carl Schultz, *Ch Radiology*
▲ EMP: 1900 EST: 1906
SQ FT: 349,000
SALES: 290.5MM **Privately Held**
WEB: www.sach.com
SIC: **8062** 5912 General medical & surgical hospitals; drug stores & proprietary stores

(P-21843)
SAN ANTONIO COMMUNITY HOSPITAL
Also Called: Rancho San Antonio Medical Ctr
7777 Milliken Ave Ste A, Rancho Cucamonga (91730-7489)
PHONE..................909 948-8000
Fax: 909 948-8082
Jullian Doxon, *Director*
EMP: 50
SALES (corp-wide): 290.5MM **Privately Held**
WEB: www.sach.com
SIC: **8062** General medical & surgical hospitals

PA: San Antonio Community Hospital
999 San Bernardino Rd
Upland CA 91786
909 985-2811

(P-21844)
SAN BENITO HEALTH CARE DST (PA)
Also Called: Hazel Hawkins Memorial Hosp
911 Sunset Dr Ste A, Hollister (95023-5608)
PHONE..................831 637-5711
Fax: 831 636-2668
Ken Underwood, *CEO*
Beth Ivy, *President*
Mark Robinson, *CFO*
Lois Owens, *Vice Pres*
Denette Perrien, *Op Rm Dir*
▲ EMP: 270
SQ FT: 42,000
SALES (est): 66.7MM **Privately Held**
WEB: www.hazelhawkins.com
SIC: **8062** 8051 8059 General medical & surgical hospitals; skilled nursing care facilities; convalescent home

(P-21845)
SAN CLEMENTE MEDICAL CTR LLC
Also Called: Saddleback Memorial Hospital
654 Camino De Los Mares, San Clemente (92673-2827)
PHONE..................949 496-1122
Fax: 949 489-4558
Ronald McGee,
Arturo Fontanes,
Gus Galamas,
William Van Derreis,
Robert Pompei, *Ch Radiology*
EMP: 300
SQ FT: 65,000
SALES (est): 27.7MM **Privately Held**
SIC: **8062** 8011 General medical & surgical hospitals; offices & clinics of medical doctors

(P-21846)
SAN FRANCISCO CITY & COUNTY
Also Called: Assembly Member Ammiano
455 Golden Gate Ave Fl 1, San Francisco (94102-3667)
PHONE..................415 557-3013
EMP: 5000 **Privately Held**
SIC: **8062** General medical & surgical hospitals
PA: City & County Of San Francisco
1 Dr Carlton B Goodlett P
San Francisco CA 94102
415 554-7500

(P-21847)
SAN GBRIEL VLY MED CTR FNDTION
438 W Las Tunas Dr, San Gabriel (91776-1216)
P.O. Box 1507 (91778-1507)
PHONE..................626 289-5454
Thomas Mone, *CEO*
Paula Lamar, *CFO*
Harold Way, *CFO*
Richard Polver, *Treasurer*
Paz Battung, *Case Mgmt Dir*
EMP: 850
SQ FT: 42,000
SALES: 2.5K
SALES (corp-wide): 7.1B **Privately Held**
WEB: www.sgvmc.com
SIC: **8062** General medical & surgical hospitals
PA: Dignity Health
185 Berry St Ste 300
San Francisco CA 94107
415 438-5500

(P-21848)
SAN GORGONIO MEMORIAL HOSPITAL (PA)
600 N Highland Sprng Ave, Banning (92220-3046)
PHONE..................951 845-1121
Fax: 951 845-2836
Mark Turner, *CEO*
Thuan Dang, *Ch Radiology*
Hillary Falconer, *President*

Dave Recoupero, *CFO*
Dorothy Ellis, *Chairman*
EMP: 183
SQ FT: 76,000
SALES: 54.7MM **Privately Held**
WEB: www.sgmh.org
SIC: 8062 General medical & surgical hospitals

(P-21849)
SAN JOAQUIN COMMUNITY HOSPITAL (PA)
2615 Chester Ave, Bakersfield (93301-2014)
P.O. Box 2615 (93303-2615)
PHONE.................................661 395-3000
Fax: 661 321-3703
Doug Duffield, *CEO*
Bob Beehler, *President*
Greg McGovern, *Officer*
Tracey S Stewart, *Top Exec*
Kelly Barber, *Op Rm Dir*
EMP: 850 **EST:** 1910
SQ FT: 137,000
SALES: 367.1MM **Privately Held**
SIC: 8062 8011 General medical & surgical hospitals; offices & clinics of medical doctors

(P-21850)
SAN JOAQUIN HOSPITAL
Also Called: Healthcare Services
500 W Hospital Rd, French Camp (95231-9693)
PHONE.................................209 468-6000
Fax: 209 468-6046
David Colberson, *CEO*
Ronald Kruetner, *CFO*
Laverne Self, *Finance*
Usman Ali, *Director*
EMP: 1300
SALES (est): 43.9MM **Privately Held**
SIC: 8062 General medical & surgical hospitals

(P-21851)
SAN LEANDRO HOSPITAL LP
13855 E 14th St, San Leandro (94578-2600)
PHONE.................................510 357-6500
Fax: 510 351-6372
Ronnie Bayduza, *CEO*
Kathleen Cain, *CFO*
Dale Blake, *Admin Asst*
Janay Defer, *Administration*
Michelle Luckett, *Human Res Dir*
EMP: 475
SALES: 13.7K **Privately Held**
WEB: www.triadhospitals.com
SIC: 8062 8361 General medical & surgical hospitals; residential care

(P-21852)
SAN MIGUEL HOSPITAL ASSN
Also Called: Hillside Hospital
1940 El Cajon Blvd, San Diego (92104-1005)
PHONE.................................619 297-2251
Fax: 619 294-2979
Kenneth R Dillard, *President*
Rupert Graves MD, *Ch of Bd*
Edwin Yorbe MD, *Corp Secy*
John Ingersoll, *Vice Ch Bd*
EMP: 248
SQ FT: 100,000
SALES: 31.8MM **Privately Held**
SIC: 8062 General medical & surgical hospitals

(P-21853)
SAN PEDRO PENINSULA HOSPITAL (PA)
Also Called: Little Co Mary- San Pedro Hosp
1300 W 7th St, San Pedro (90732-3593)
PHONE.................................310 832-3311
Fax: 310 514-5213
Garry Olney, *COO*
Nancy Carlson, *CEO*
Tim Kirk, *COO*
Carol Carrier, *CFO*
Dale Johnson, *Executive Asst*
EMP: 556
SQ FT: 200,000
SALES (est): 65.5MM **Privately Held**
SIC: 8062 8051 5912 General medical & surgical hospitals; skilled nursing care facilities; drug stores

(P-21854)
SAN PEDRO PENINSULA HOSPITAL
Also Called: San Pedro Hospital Pavilion
1322 W 6th St, San Pedro (90732-3501)
PHONE.................................310 514-5270
Fax: 310 514-5253
Julie Theiring, *Branch Mgr*
EMP: 100
SALES (corp-wide): 65.5MM **Privately Held**
SIC: 8062 8051 General medical & surgical hospitals; convalescent home with continuous nursing care
PA: San Pedro Peninsula Hospital
1300 W 7th St
San Pedro CA 90732
310 832-3311

(P-21855)
SAN RAMON REGIONAL MED CTR INC
6001 Norris Canyon Rd, San Ramon (94583-5400)
PHONE.................................925 275-0634
Fax: 925 275-0107
Gary J Sloan, *CEO*
Kimi Miyamura, *Volunteer Dir*
Susan Micheletti, *COO*
Vera Foster, *Lab Dir*
Tim Jefferson, *Radiology Dir*
EMP: 600
SALES: 203.2K
SALES (corp-wide): 18.7B **Publicly Held**
WEB: www.tenethealth.com
SIC: 8062 8093 General medical & surgical hospitals; rehabilitation center, outpatient treatment
PA: Tenet Healthcare Corporation
1445 Ross Ave Ste 1400
Dallas TX 75202
469 893-2200

(P-21856)
SAN VICENTE HOSPITAL
6000 San Vicente Blvd, Los Angeles (90036-4404)
PHONE.................................323 930-1040
Fax: 323 934-9137
Gill Tepper, *President*
John Fenton, *CEO*
EMP: 100
SALES: 699.4K **Privately Held**
SIC: 8062 General medical & surgical hospitals

(P-21857)
SANTA BARBARA COTTAGE HOSPITAL (PA)
Also Called: COTTAGE HOSPITAL CHILDREN'S CE
400 W Pueblo St, Santa Barbara (93105-4353)
P.O. Box 689 (93102-0689)
PHONE.................................805 682-7111
Gretchen Milligan, *Chairman*
Ronald C Werft, *President*
Steven Fellows, *Exec VP*
Karen Jones Grandidier, *Principal*
Gary Gill, *Info Tech Dir*
EMP: 152
SQ FT: 485,874
SALES: 610.4MM **Privately Held**
SIC: 8062 General medical & surgical hospitals; hospital, AMA approved residency

(P-21858)
SANTA BARBRA CTTGE HSPTL
Also Called: Santa Barbara Cnty Social Svcs
2125 Centerpointe Pkwy, Santa Maria (93455-1337)
PHONE.................................805 346-7135
Fax: 805 346-7197
Charlene Chase, *Director*
Linda Rodriguez, *Info Tech Mgr*
EMP: 210
SALES (corp-wide): 610.4MM **Privately Held**
SIC: 8062 General medical & surgical hospitals
PA: Santa Barbara Cottage Hospital
400 W Pueblo St
Santa Barbara CA 93105
805 682-7111

(P-21859)
SANTA CLARA COUNTY OF
Also Called: Santa Clara Valley Health & Ho
2325 Enborg Ln Ste 380, San Jose (95128-2649)
PHONE.................................408 885-6818
Kim Roberts, *Finance*
EMP: 50 **Privately Held**
WEB: www.countyairports.org
SIC: 8062 9431 9311 Hospital, medical school affiliated with nursing & residency; administration of public health programs; ; finance, taxation & monetary policy;
PA: County Of Santa Clara
3180 Newberry Dr Ste 150
San Jose CA 95118
408 299-5105

(P-21860)
SANTA CLARA VALLEY MEDICAL CTR (PA)
Also Called: Scvmc
751 S Bascom Ave, San Jose (95128-2699)
PHONE.................................408 885-5000
Fax: 408 885-3361
Paul E Lorenz, *CEO*
Kim Roberts, *CFO*
Cheryl Bernard-Shaw, *Officer*
Tom Bush, *Vice Pres*
Narinder Singh, *Pharmacy Dir*
EMP: 357
SALES (est): 103.1MM **Privately Held**
SIC: 8062 6324 General medical & surgical hospitals; hospital & medical service plans

(P-21861)
SANTA ROSA MEMORIAL HOSPITAL (DH)
Also Called: SJHS SONOMA COUNTY
1165 Montgomery Dr, Santa Rosa (95405-4897)
P.O. Box 522 (95402-0522)
PHONE.................................707 546-3210
Fax: 707 525-5250
Todd Salnas, *CEO*
Kathy Exelby, *Volunteer Dir*
Mich Riccioni, *CFO*
Gary Greensweig, *Vice Pres*
Lorri Martinez, *Op Rm Dir*
EMP: 1500
SQ FT: 163,692
SALES: 489.4MM
SALES (corp-wide): 5.6B **Privately Held**
WEB: www.stjosephhealth.org
SIC: 8062 General medical & surgical hospitals
HQ: St. Joseph Health System
3345 Michelson Dr Ste 100
Irvine CA 92612
949 381-4000

(P-21862)
SANTA ROSA SURGERY CENTER LP
Also Called: Sutter Health
1111 Sonoma Ave Ste 308, Santa Rosa (95405-4820)
PHONE.................................707 578-4100
Dan Peterson, *Administration*
Jiries Mogannam, *Principal*
Donice Parsegian, *Purchasing*
Wanda Godsey, *Nurse*
Tom Blechel, *Manager*
EMP: 75
SQ FT: 8,000
SALES (est): 7.7MM **Privately Held**
WEB: www.srsurgerycenter.com
SIC: 8062 Hospital, affiliated with AMA residency

(P-21863)
SANTA TERESA CONV HOSPITAL
9140 Verner St, Pico Rivera (90660-2741)
PHONE.................................562 948-1961
Fax: 562 949-5998
Nick Cardenas, *Director*
EMP: 85

SALES (est): 1.6MM **Privately Held**
SIC: 8062 5912 General medical & surgical hospitals; drug stores & proprietary stores

(P-21864)
SANTA TERESITA INC (PA)
Also Called: MANOR AT SANTA TERESITA HOSPIT
819 Buena Vista St, Duarte (91010-1703)
PHONE.................................626 359-3243
Sister Mary Clare Mancini, *CEO*
Mamie Hao, *Vice Pres*
Michael Stevesn, *Radiology Dir*
Esther Cisneros, *Envir Svcs Dir*
Margaret Mary, *Controller*
EMP: 101
SQ FT: 232,165
SALES: 11.5MM **Privately Held**
WEB: www.santa-teresita.org
SIC: 8062 8051 General medical & surgical hospitals; skilled nursing care facilities

(P-21865)
SANTA YNEZ VALLEY COTTAGE HOSP
2050 Viborg Rd, Solvang (93463-2220)
P.O. Box 689, Santa Barbara (93102-0689)
PHONE.................................805 688-6431
Fax: 805 686-1224
Ron Werft, *President*
Wende Cappeta, *Vice Pres*
Wende Cappeta, *Vice Pres*
Madeline Lozono, *Lab Dir*
June Martin, *Administration*
EMP: 75 **EST:** 1962
SQ FT: 30,000
SALES: 15.2MM **Privately Held**
WEB: www.cottagehealthsystem.org
SIC: 8062 General medical & surgical hospitals

(P-21866)
SCHMIDT PHYLLIS MD CORPORATION
711 W College St, Los Angeles (90012-1163)
PHONE.................................213 613-1163
Phyllis Schmidt MD, *President*
EMP: 600
SALES (est): 4.5MM **Privately Held**
SIC: 8062 General medical & surgical hospitals

(P-21867)
SCRIPPS HEALTH
Also Called: Scripps Mem Hosp - Encinatas
354 Santa Fe Dr, Encinitas (92024-5142)
P.O. Box 230817 (92023-0817)
PHONE.................................760 753-6501
Fax: 760 633-7356
Rebecca Ropchan, *Branch Mgr*
Rajgopal Ujwala,
Alice Dang, *Bd of Directors*
Lisa Blair, *Officer*
Randall Goskowicz, *Executive*
EMP: 250
SALES (corp-wide): 1.7B **Privately Held**
WEB: www.scripps.org
SIC: 8062 5912 General medical & surgical hospitals; drug stores
PA: Scripps Health
4275 Campus Point Ct
San Diego CA 92121
858 678-7000

(P-21868)
SCRIPPS HEALTH
Also Called: Scripps Mercy Hospitals
435 H St, Chula Vista (91910-4307)
PHONE.................................619 691-7000
Pott Hoff, *COO*
Edgardo Gracia,
Kris Vanlom, *Ch Radiology*
Juan Tovar MD, *Vice Chairman*
Wilbur Moore, *President*
EMP: 1000
SALES (corp-wide): 1.7B **Privately Held**
WEB: www.scripps.org
SIC: 8062 General medical & surgical hospitals
PA: Scripps Health
4275 Campus Point Ct
San Diego CA 92121
858 678-7000

8062 - General Medical & Surgical Hospitals County (P-21869)

(P-21869)
SCRIPPS HEALTH
Also Called: Scripps Green Hospital
10666 N Torrey Pines Rd, La Jolla (92037-1027)
PHONE..................................858 455-9100
Fax: 858 554-6014
Robin Brown, *Branch Mgr*
James Heywood,
Alison Edinger, *Bd of Directors*
Christopher Harris, *Pharmacy Dir*
Ed Turk, *CIO*
EMP: 326
SALES (corp-wide): 1.7B Privately Held
WEB: www.scripps.org
SIC: 8062 General medical & surgical hospitals
PA: Scripps Health
4275 Campus Point Ct
San Diego CA 92121
858 678-7000

(P-21870)
SCRIPPS HEALTH
Also Called: Scripps Mercy Hospital
4077 Fifth Ave, San Diego (92103-2105)
PHONE..................................619 294-8111
Medical Records, *Manager*
Margaret Mayer, *Finance*
Alexandra Salazar, *Analyst*
Kristy Jaques, *QC Mgr*
Margaret Brannigan, *Anesthesiology*
EMP: 300
SQ FT: 3,062
SALES (corp-wide): 1.7B Privately Held
WEB: www.scripps.org
SIC: 8062 General medical & surgical hospitals
PA: Scripps Health
4275 Campus Point Ct
San Diego CA 92121
858 678-7000

(P-21871)
SCRIPPS HEALTH
Also Called: Scripps Torrey Pines
10666 N Torrey Pines Rd, La Jolla (92037-1027)
PHONE..................................800 727-4777
Fax: 858 554-2261
Larry Harrison, *Manager*
Corrine Yarbrough, *Project Mgr*
E Sakas, *Pathologist*
Kimberly Harper, *Nephrology*
Andrew J King, *Nephrology*
EMP: 200
SALES (corp-wide): 1.9B Privately Held
WEB: www.scripps.org
SIC: 8062 General medical & surgical hospitals
PA: Scripps Health
4275 Campus Point Ct
San Diego CA 92121
858 678-7000

(P-21872)
SCRIPPS HEALTH
Also Called: Scripps Mem Hospital-La Jolla
9888 Genesee Ave, La Jolla (92037-1205)
PHONE..................................858 626-6150
James Bruffey, *Branch Mgr*
Kenneth Ott,
Anil Keswani, *Vice Pres*
Cheryl Gann, *Risk Mgmt Dir*
Sharon Baldwin, *Case Mgmt Dir*
EMP: 326
SALES (corp-wide): 1.9B Privately Held
SIC: 8062 General medical & surgical hospitals
PA: Scripps Health
4275 Campus Point Ct
San Diego CA 92121
858 678-7000

(P-21873)
SCRIPPS HEALTH
Also Called: Scripps Mem Hosp - La Jolla
9888 Genesee Ave, La Jolla (92037-1205)
PHONE..................................858 626-4123
Fax: 858 457-6122
Gary Fybel, *CEO*
Martin Griglak, *Vice Pres*
Darrell Dewindt, *Lab Dir*
Donald Ritt, *Research*
Johan Otter, *Phys Thrpy Dir*
EMP: 200

SALES (corp-wide): 2.3B Privately Held
WEB: www.scripps.org
SIC: 8062 General medical & surgical hospitals
PA: Scripps Health
4275 Campus Point Ct
San Diego CA 92121
858 678-7000

(P-21874)
SCRIPPS MEMORIAL HOSPITALS
9834 Genesee Ave Ste 328, La Jolla (92037-1216)
PHONE..................................858 450-4481
Fax: 858 450-4485
Kathleen A Bulley, *Principal*
Terence Webb, *Pharmacy Dir*
Janet Kruse, *Executive Asst*
Gale Keel, *Admin Sec*
Paul Loflin, *Administration*
EMP: 54
SALES (est): 7.7MM Privately Held
SIC: 8062 General medical & surgical hospitals

(P-21875)
SCRIPPS MERCY HOSPITAL
4077 5th Ave Mer35, San Diego (92103-2105)
PHONE..................................619 294-8111
Andrew C Ping, *Principal*
David Shaw, *Vice Pres*
George Ochoa, *Radiology Dir*
Steve Cornelius, *Info Tech Mgr*
Veronica Esparza, *Human Res Dir*
EMP: 77
SALES: 750.4MM Privately Held
SIC: 8062 General medical & surgical hospitals

(P-21876)
SEEPEEDEE INC (PA)
13100 Studebaker Rd, Norwalk (90650-2531)
PHONE..................................562 868-3751
Fax: 562 868-3198
John Ferrelli, *CEO*
Craig B Garner, *CEO*
Mihi Lee, *CFO*
Joel Freedman, *Principal*
Janan Pitta, *Office Mgr*
EMP: 74
SQ FT: 58,000
SALES (est): 41MM Privately Held
WEB: www.coastplazahospital.com
SIC: 8062 General medical & surgical hospitals

(P-21877)
SELMA COMMUNITY HOSPITAL INC
Also Called: Urgent Care-Selma Dst Hosp
1141 Rose Ave, Selma (93662-3241)
PHONE..................................559 891-1000
Fax: 559 891-6212
Richard L Rawson, *President*
Scott Cleveland, *CFO*
Kreby McKague, *CFO*
Douglas Lafferty, *Vice Pres*
Mario Rosario, *Radiology Dir*
EMP: 339 EST: 1962
SQ FT: 67,000
SALES (est): 39.3MM Privately Held
SIC: 8062 8051 General medical & surgical hospitals; skilled nursing care facilities

(P-21878)
SENECA HEALTHCARE DISTRICT (PA)
Also Called: Lake Almanor Clinic
130 Brentwood Dr, Chester (96020)
P.O. Box 737 (96020-0737)
PHONE..................................530 258-2151
Fax: 530 258-2068
Linda Wagner, *CEO*
Hector Medellin, *Ch Radiology*
David Slusher Jr, *President*
Cheryl Darnell, *CFO*
William Howe, *Treasurer*
EMP: 105
SQ FT: 12,417
SALES (est): 13.2MM Privately Held
SIC: 8062 General medical & surgical hospitals

(P-21879)
SEQUOIA HEALTH SERVICES (HQ)
Also Called: Sequoia Hospital
170 Alameda De Las Pulgas, Redwood City (94062-2751)
PHONE..................................650 369-5811
Fax: 650 367-5288
Glenna Vaskelas, *Administration*
Kim Griffin, *Bd of Directors*
Malcolm Macnaughton, *Bd of Directors*
Michael D Hollett, *Radiology Dir*
Eile Barsi, *Project Mgr*
EMP: 63
SQ FT: 350,000
SALES (est): 119.9MM
SALES (corp-wide): 7.1B Privately Held
WEB: www.sequoiahealthcaredistrict.com
SIC: 8062 General medical & surgical hospitals
PA: Dignity Health
185 Berry St Ste 300
San Francisco CA 94107
415 438-5500

(P-21880)
SETON MEDICAL CENTER (HQ)
1900 Sullivan Ave, Daly City (94015-2229)
PHONE..................................650 992-4000
Fax: 650 991-6024
John Ferrelli, *President*
Christopher Yoo, *Ch Radiology*
Patricia White, *Exec VP*
John Thomas, *Vice Pres*
Vida A Campbell, *Radiology Dir*
EMP: 1099
SQ FT: 400,000
SALES: 246.5MM
SALES (corp-wide): 225.4MM Privately Held
WEB: www.sportsmedshop.com
SIC: 8062 8051 General medical & surgical hospitals; skilled nursing care facilities
PA: Verity Health System Of California, Inc.
203 Redwood Shores Pkwy
Redwood City CA 94065
650 551-6650

(P-21881)
SETON MEDICAL CENTER
Also Called: Seton Medical Center Coastside
600 Marine Blvd, Moss Beach (94038-9641)
PHONE..................................650 728-5521
Fax: 650 728-5314
Judy Cook, *Director*
Ron Viray, *Analyst*
Rong W Zeng, *OB/GYN*
Richard Gravina MD, *Med Doctor*
Robert Telfer MD, *Med Doctor*
EMP: 160
SALES (corp-wide): 225.4MM Privately Held
WEB: www.sportsmedshop.com
SIC: 8062 5812 8051 General medical & surgical hospitals; eating places; skilled nursing care facilities
HQ: Seton Medical Center
1900 Sullivan Ave
Daly City CA 94015
650 992-4000

(P-21882)
SETON MEDICAL CENTER
West Bay HM Hlth & Cmnty Svcs
1784 Sullivan Ave Ste 200, Daly City (94015-2067)
PHONE..................................650 992-4000
Fax: 650 991-4146
Alice Alexander, *Director*
EMP: 60
SALES (corp-wide): 225.4MM Privately Held
WEB: www.sportsmedshop.com
SIC: 8062 7361 8082 General medical & surgical hospitals; nurses' registry; home health care services
HQ: Seton Medical Center
1900 Sullivan Ave
Daly City CA 94015
650 992-4000

(P-21883)
SHARP CHULA VISTA MEDICAL CTR
Also Called: Sharp Chula Vista Medical Ctr
751 Medical Center Ct, Chula Vista (91911-6617)
PHONE..................................619 502-5800
Fax: 619 482-5833
Chris Boyd, *CEO*
Richard Prutow,
Michael Murphy, *President*
Rick King, *CFO*
Phung Caldwell, *Admin Asst*
EMP: 1600
SQ FT: 270,205
SALES: 367.2MM
SALES (corp-wide): 3.4B Privately Held
SIC: 8062 General medical & surgical hospitals
PA: Sharp Healthcare
8695 Spectrum Center Blvd
San Diego CA 92123
858 499-4000

(P-21884)
SHARP CHULA VISTA MEDICAL CTR
8695 Spectrum Center Blvd, San Diego (92123-1489)
PHONE..................................858 499-5150
Chris Boyd, *CEO*
Lori Moody, *Recruiter*
Karen Simpson, *Hlthcr Dir*
Susan Ressmeyer, *Director*
EMP: 99
SALES: 315.6MM Privately Held
SIC: 8062 General medical & surgical hospitals

(P-21885)
SHARP HEALTHCARE (PA)
Also Called: Sharp Rees-Stealy Pharmacy
8695 Spectrum Center Blvd, San Diego (92123-1489)
PHONE..................................858 499-4000
Fax: 858 541-4030
Michael Murphy, *President*
Lance Altenau,
Teri Featheringill, *Vice Chairman*
Ann Pumpian, *CFO*
Joanne Boyle, *Treasurer*
EMP: 760
SQ FT: 15,700
SALES: 3.4B Privately Held
SIC: 8062 8741 6324 General medical & surgical hospitals; hospital management; nursing & personal care facility management; hospital & medical service plans

(P-21886)
SHARP HEALTHCARE
Also Called: Sharp Health Care
3554 Ruffin Rd Ste Soca, San Diego (92123-2596)
PHONE..................................858 627-5152
Alison Fleury, *Finance Other*
Michael Murphy, *Director*
Terry Kalfayan, *Agent*
Robert Kelly, *Agent*
EMP: 150
SALES (corp-wide): 3.4B Privately Held
SIC: 8062 General medical & surgical hospitals
PA: Sharp Healthcare
8695 Spectrum Center Blvd
San Diego CA 92123
858 499-4000

(P-21887)
SHARP HEALTHCARE
Also Called: Sharp Mission Park Medical Ctr
130 Cedar Rd, Vista (92083-5102)
PHONE..................................760 806-5600
Fax: 760 631-3274
Meredith Acosta, *Branch Mgr*
Adam Waterbury, *Analyst*
EMP: 59
SALES (corp-wide): 3.4B Privately Held
SIC: 8062 General medical & surgical hospitals
PA: Sharp Healthcare
8695 Spectrum Center Blvd
San Diego CA 92123
858 499-4000

PRODUCTS & SERVICES SECTION 8062 - General Medical & Surgical Hospitals County (P-21907)

(P-21888)
SHARP HEALTHCARE
10670 Wexford St, San Diego (92131-3940)
PHONE..............................858 621-4010
Susan Horton, *Branch Mgr*
EMP: 59
SALES (corp-wide): 3.4B **Privately Held**
SIC: 8062 General medical & surgical hospitals
PA: Sharp Healthcare
8695 Spectrum Center Blvd
San Diego CA 92123
858 499-4000

(P-21889)
SHARP MARY BIRCH H
3003 Health Center Dr, San Diego (92123-2700)
PHONE..............................858 939-3400
Trisha Khaleghi, *CEO*
Elizabeth Chan, *Administration*
Karen Friedrichs, *Training Spec*
John S Lee, *Pathologist*
Henrik Manassarians, *Neurology*
EMP: 73
SALES (est): 13.8MM **Privately Held**
SIC: 8062 General medical & surgical hospitals

(P-21890)
SHARP MEMORIAL HOSPITAL (HQ)
7901 Frost St, San Diego (92123-2701)
PHONE..............................858 939-3636
Fax: 858 541-3220
Tim Smith, *CEO*
Kathryn Hanna, *Vice Pres*
Cheryl Balderas, *Lab Dir*
Ann Arcelona-Manuel, *Admin Sec*
Tim Beaulieu, *Administration*
EMP: 3000
SALES: 1.2B
SALES (corp-wide): 3.4B **Privately Held**
SIC: 8062 General medical & surgical hospitals
PA: Sharp Healthcare
8695 Spectrum Center Blvd
San Diego CA 92123
858 499-4000

(P-21891)
SHERMAN OAKS HEALTH SYSTEM
4929 Van Nuys Blvd, Sherman Oaks (91403-1702)
PHONE..............................818 981-7111
Fax: 818 907-2873
David Levinsohn, *CEO*
EMP: 51
SALES: 341.2K **Privately Held**
SIC: 8062 General medical & surgical hospitals

(P-21892)
SIERRA VIEW LOCAL HOSPITAL DST
Also Called: Sierra View District Hospital
283 Pearson Dr, Porterville (93257-3353)
PHONE..............................559 781-7877
Fax: 559 781-7156
Dennis Coleman, *Branch Mgr*
John A Hodge, *Director*
EMP: 432
SALES (corp-wide): 63.6MM **Privately Held**
SIC: 8062 General medical & surgical hospitals
PA: Sierra View Local Hospital District
465 W Putnam Ave
Porterville CA 93257
559 784-1110

(P-21893)
SIERRA VISTA HOSPITAL INC (HQ)
Also Called: Sierra Vista Regional Med Ctr
1010 Murray Ave, San Luis Obispo (93405-8801)
P.O. Box 1367 (93406-1367)
PHONE..............................805 546-7600
Fax: 805 546-7710
Joseph Deschryver, *CEO*
Virginia Bargas,
Joseph R Kuntze,
Kurt L Haupt, *Ch OB/GYN*
Candace Markwith, *President*
EMP: 575
SQ FT: 138,690
SALES (est): 87.9MM
SALES (corp-wide): 18.7B **Publicly Held**
WEB: www.rasloweb.com
SIC: 8062 General medical & surgical hospitals
PA: Tenet Healthcare Corporation
1445 Ross Ave Ste 1400
Dallas TX 75202
469 893-2200

(P-21894)
SISKIYOU HOSPITAL INC
Also Called: FAIRCHILD MEDICAL CENTER
444 Bruce St, Yreka (96097-3450)
PHONE..............................530 842-4121
Fax: 530 841-0913
Dwayne Jones, *CEO*
Marcus Issoglio, *President*
Jonathon C Andrus, *CEO*
Kelly Martin, *CFO*
Liz Pimentel, *Infect Cntl Dir*
EMP: 450
SALES: 72MM **Privately Held**
WEB: www.fairchildmed.org
SIC: 8062 General medical & surgical hospitals

(P-21895)
SONOMA VALLEY HEALTH CARE DST (PA)
Also Called: SONOMA VALLEY HOSPITAL
347 Andrieux St, Sonoma (95476-6811)
PHONE..............................707 935-5000
Fax: 707 938-1632
Carl Gerlach, *CEO*
James Price,
Stephen Likata,
Madolyn Agrimonti, *Vice Chairman*
Peter Hohorst, *Vice Chairman*
EMP: 445
SQ FT: 115,000
SALES: 48.2MM **Privately Held**
WEB: www.svh.com
SIC: 8062 General medical & surgical hospitals

(P-21896)
SONOMA WEST MEDICAL CENTER
501 Petaluma Ave, Sebastopol (95472-4215)
PHONE..............................707 823-8511
Lori Austin, *CEO*
David Glassburn, *CFO*
David Glassman, *CFO*
Glenn Minervini-Zick, *CFO*
Joy Sherman, *Mng Officer*
EMP: 250
SQ FT: 2,492
SALES (est): 35.3MM **Privately Held**
SIC: 8062 8051 General medical & surgical hospitals; skilled nursing care facilities

(P-21897)
SONORA REGIONAL MEDICAL CENTER (HQ)
1000 Greenley Rd, Sonora (95370-5200)
PHONE..............................209 532-5000
Larry Davis, *President*
Felix A Conte, *Ch OB/GYN*
David Larsen, *CFO*
Jeff Eler, *Principal*
Tracey Barnes, *Admin Asst*
EMP: 712
SQ FT: 60,000
SALES: 249.4MM
SALES (corp-wide): 251.4MM **Privately Held**
SIC: 8062 8051 General medical & surgical hospitals; skilled nursing care facilities
PA: Adventist Health System/West
2100 Douglas Blvd
Roseville CA 95661
916 781-2000

(P-21898)
SOUTH COAST MEDICAL CENTER (PA)
2100 Douglas Blvd, Roseville (95661-3804)
PHONE..............................949 364-1770

Bruce Christian, *President*
Andrea Kofl, *COO*
Nancy Boerner, *Vice Pres*
Teri Garza, *Administration*
Gary Irish, *Info Tech Dir*
EMP: 690
SQ FT: 220,000
SALES (est): 27.6MM **Privately Held**
SIC: 8062 General medical & surgical hospitals

(P-21899)
SOUTHERN CAL HALTHCARE SYS INC
3415 S Sepulveda Blvd # 9, Los Angeles (90034-6060)
PHONE..............................310 943-4500
David R Topper, *CEO*
Brice Keyser, *Director*
EMP: 1000
SALES (est): 32.6MM **Privately Held**
SIC: 8062 General medical & surgical hospitals

(P-21900)
SOUTHERN CAL HOSP AT CULVER CY (HQ)
Also Called: Brotman Medical Partners
3828 Delmas Ter, Culver City (90232-2713)
PHONE..............................310 836-7000
Fax: 310 202-4141
Barbara Schneider, *CEO*
Peter Pop, *Ch Radiology*
Howard H Levine, *President*
Elayne Brown, *Executive Asst*
Stanley Otake, *Administration*
EMP: 87
SQ FT: 183,000
SALES (est): 157.2MM
SALES (corp-wide): 637.4MM **Privately Held**
WEB: www.brotmanmedicalcenter.com
SIC: 8062 General medical & surgical hospitals
PA: Prospect Medical Holdings, Inc.
3415 S Sepulveda Blvd # 9
Los Angeles CA 90034
310 943-4500

(P-21901)
SOUTHERN CAL PRMNNTE MED GROUP
26415 Carl Boyer Dr, Santa Clarita (91350-5824)
PHONE..............................661 290-3100
EMP: 78
SALES (corp-wide): 3.2B **Privately Held**
SIC: 8062 General medical & surgical hospitals
PA: Southern California Permanente Medical Group
393 Walnut Dr
Pasadena CA 91107
626 405-5704

(P-21902)
SOUTHERN CAL PRMNNTE MED GROUP
Also Called: S C P M G
9961 Sierra Ave, Fontana (92335-6720)
PHONE..............................909 427-5000
Fax: 909 427-4249
Gerald McCall, *Branch Mgr*
Vincent Roger, *Research*
David K Denkers, *Physician Asst*
Robert Carie, *Health Info Dir*
George Kable, *Director*
EMP: 50
SALES (corp-wide): 3.2B **Privately Held**
WEB: www.permanente.net
SIC: 8062 General medical & surgical hospitals
PA: Southern California Permanente Medical Group
393 Walnut Dr
Pasadena CA 91107
626 405-5704

(P-21903)
SOUTHERN CAL SPCIALTY CARE INC
Also Called: Kindred Hospital La Mirata
845 N Lark Ellen Ave, West Covina (91791-1069)
PHONE..............................626 339-5451

Nenda Estudillo, *Director*
Robert Benson, *Ch Radiology*
Norm Andrews, *Administration*
Susan Myers, *Administration*
Fernando Cortez, *Persnl Mgr*
EMP: 100
SQ FT: 34,082
SALES (corp-wide): 7B **Publicly Held**
SIC: 8062 General medical & surgical hospitals
HQ: Southern California Specialty Care, Inc.
14900 Imperial Hwy
La Mirada CA 90638
562 944-1900

(P-21904)
SOUTHERN CAL SPCIALTY CARE INC
Also Called: Kindred Hospital Orange County
1901 College Ave, Santa Ana (92706-2334)
PHONE..............................714 564-7800
Fax: 714 564-7815
Birg Narbetus, *Principal*
Robert Koo, *CFO*
Adam Darvish, *Exec Dir*
Diana Hanyak, *Administration*
Mark Winters, *Engineer*
EMP: 200
SALES (corp-wide): 7B **Publicly Held**
SIC: 8062 8051 General medical & surgical hospitals; skilled nursing care facilities
HQ: Southern California Specialty Care, Inc.
14900 Imperial Hwy
La Mirada CA 90638
562 944-1900

(P-21905)
SOUTHERN HMBLDT CMNTY DST HOSP
Also Called: Southern Humboldt Cmnty Clinic
733 Cedar St, Garberville (95542-3201)
PHONE..............................707 923-3921
Fax: 707 923-9352
Deborah Scaife, *President*
Guy Vitello, *Opers Staff*
Marie Brown, *Supervisor*
EMP: 95
SQ FT: 17,000
SALES (est): 5.7MM **Privately Held**
SIC: 8062 General medical & surgical hospitals

(P-21906)
SOUTHERN MNTEREY CNTY MEM HOSP (PA)
Also Called: GEORGE L MEE MEMORIAL HOSPITAL
300 Canal St, King City (93930-3431)
PHONE..............................831 385-7100
Fax: 831 385-0636
Lex T Smith, *CEO*
Susan Childers, *CFO*
Denise Miller, *Officer*
Jim Keller, *Vice Pres*
Christina Zaro, *Vice Pres*
EMP: 495
SQ FT: 5,000
SALES: 65.3MM **Privately Held**
WEB: www.meememorial.com
SIC: 8062 General medical & surgical hospitals

(P-21907)
SOUTHERN MNTEREY CNTY MEM HOSP
467 El Camino Real, Greenfield (93927-4915)
PHONE..............................831 674-0112
Fax: 831 674-4199
Camille Sanz, *Director*
EMP: 146
SALES (corp-wide): 65.3MM **Privately Held**
SIC: 8062 General medical & surgical hospitals
PA: Southern Monterey County Memorial Hospital Inc
300 Canal St
King City CA 93930
831 385-7100

8062 - General Medical & Surgical Hospitals County (P-21908)

PRODUDUCTS & SERVICES SECTION

(P-21908)
SOUTHERN MONO HEALTHCARE DST
Also Called: Mammoth Hospital
85 Sierra Park Rd, Mammoth Lakes (93546-2073)
P.O. Box 660 (93546-0660)
PHONE.................................760 934-3311
Fax: 760 924-4006
Gary Myers, *CEO*
Joseph Bottom, *COO*
James Smith, *CFO*
Tabby Manneter, *Executive Asst*
Mark Lind, *VP Opers*
EMP: 350
SQ FT: 20,000
SALES: 59MM **Privately Held**
SIC: 8062 General medical & surgical hospitals

(P-21909)
SOUTHWEST HEALTHCARE SYS AUX
Also Called: Business Department
38977 Sky Canyon Dr # 200, Murrieta (92563-2681)
PHONE.................................800 404-6627
Paula Dalbeck, *Controller*
EMP: 50
SALES (corp-wide): 9B **Publicly Held**
SIC: 8062 General medical & surgical hospitals
HQ: Southwest Healthcare System Auxiliary
   25500 Medical Center Dr
   Murrieta CA 92562
   951 696-6000

(P-21910)
SOUTHWEST HEALTHCARE SYS AUX (HQ)
Also Called: Rancho Springs Medical Center
25500 Medical Center Dr, Murrieta (92562-5965)
PHONE.................................951 696-6000
Brad Neet, *CEO*
Brian Klebash,
Diane Moon, *CFO*
Barry Thorfenson, *CFO*
Anne Marie Watkins, *Ch Nursing Ofcr*
▲ **EMP:** 450
SALES: 60.6K
SALES (corp-wide): 9B **Publicly Held**
SIC: 8062 8051 8059 4119 General medical & surgical hospitals; skilled nursing care facilities; convalescent home; ambulance service
PA: Universal Health Services, Inc.
   367 S Gulph Rd
   King Of Prussia PA 19406
   610 768-3300

(P-21911)
SOUTHWEST HOSPITAL DEV GROUP
Also Called: Valley Plaza Doctors Hospital
2224 Medical Center Dr, Perris (92571-2638)
P.O. Box 100 (92572-0100)
PHONE.................................951 943-4555
Ismael Silva Jr, *President*
EMP: 120
SQ FT: 24,000
SALES (est): 11.2MM **Privately Held**
SIC: 8062 General medical & surgical hospitals

(P-21912)
SRM ALLIANCE HOSPITAL SERVICES (PA)
Also Called: Petaluma Valley Hospital
400 N Mcdowell Blvd, Petaluma (94954-2339)
PHONE.................................707 778-1111
Fax: 707 778-1425
Deborah A Proctor, *President*
Todd Salnas, *COO*
Jane Reed, *Vice Pres*
Cooleen Torrento, *Social Dir*
Ryan Ackerman, *Admin Asst*
EMP: 400
SQ FT: 50,000
SALES: 79.7MM **Privately Held**
SIC: 8062 General medical & surgical hospitals

(P-21913)
ST ELIZABETH COMMUNITY HOSP (HQ)
2550 Sster Mary Clumba Dr, Red Bluff (96080-4327)
PHONE.................................530 529-7760
Fax: 530 529-8019
Todd Smith, *CEO*
John Halfhide, *President*
Sally Guiney, *Lab Dir*
John Halfide, *Administration*
John Halshide, *Administration*
EMP: 61
SQ FT: 98,000
SALES (est): 37MM
SALES (corp-wide): 7.1B **Privately Held**
SIC: 8062 6513 General medical & surgical hospitals; retirement hotel operation
PA: Dignity Health
   185 Berry St Ste 300
   San Francisco CA 94107
   415 438-5500

(P-21914)
ST FRANCIS MEDICAL CENTER OF (PA)
3630 E Imperial Hwy, Lynwood (90262-2609)
PHONE.................................310 900-8900
Mary Eileen Drees, *CEO*
Gerald T Kozai, *President*
Arnold J Simoni, *CEO*
Dien Ton, *Pharmacist*
Vivek Mehta, *Director*
EMP: 1570
SALES (est): 72.6MM **Privately Held**
SIC: 8062 General medical & surgical hospitals

(P-21915)
ST HELENA HOSPITAL (PA)
Also Called: DEER PARK PHARMACY
10 Woodland Rd, Saint Helena (94574-9554)
PHONE.................................707 963-1882
Steven Herber, *CEO*
Timothy Lyons,
Edward Buck McDonald, *Senior VP*
Tricia Williams, *Vice Pres*
Jay Whitcomb, *Executive*
EMP: 750
SQ FT: 200,000
SALES: 208.2MM **Privately Held**
WEB: www.sthelenahospital.com
SIC: 8062 8063 General medical & surgical hospitals; psychiatric hospitals

(P-21916)
ST JOHNS RETIREMENT VILLAGE
Also Called: Stollwood Convalescent Hosp
135 Woodland Ave, Woodland (95695-2701)
PHONE.................................530 662-9674
John Pripchard, *Exec Dir*
Jeffrey Yee, *Director*
EMP: 54
SALES (corp-wide): 9.7MM **Privately Held**
SIC: 8062 General medical & surgical hospitals
PA: St John's Retirement Village
   135 Woodland Ave
   Woodland CA 95695
   530 662-9674

(P-21917)
ST JOSEPH HEALTH SYSTEM
101 E Valencia Mesa Dr, Fullerton (92835-3809)
PHONE.................................714 992-3000
Fax: 714 447-6415
Deborah Proctor, *Principal*
Robert Morten, *Ch Radiology*
John Bennett, *COO*
Teresa Frey, *Vice Pres*
Karen Mihelic, *Exec Dir*
EMP: 82
SALES (est): 3.8MM **Privately Held**
SIC: 8062 General medical & surgical hospitals

(P-21918)
ST JOSEPH HEALTH SYSTEM
Also Called: Petaluma Valley Hospital
400 N Mcdowell Blvd Fl 1, Petaluma (94954-2339)
PHONE.................................707 778-2505
Hollis Belwaey, *Manager*
June Lang, *Director*
Brenda McMillin, *Director*
Brett Shinn, *Associate*
EMP: 50
SALES (corp-wide): 5.6B **Privately Held**
SIC: 8062 General medical & surgical hospitals
HQ: St. Joseph Health System
   3345 Michelson Dr Ste 100
   Irvine CA 92612
   949 381-4000

(P-21919)
ST JOSEPH HOSPITAL (PA)
2700 Dolbeer St, Eureka (95501-4799)
PHONE.................................707 445-8121
Toll Free:............................888 -
Fax: 707 269-3849
Joseph Mark, *CEO*
Terry Conrad, *CFO*
Andrew Rybolt, *CFO*
John Bennett, *Vice Pres*
Laurie W Stone, *Vice Pres*
▲ **EMP:** 54 **EST:** 1920
SQ FT: 125,000
SALES: 248.2MM **Privately Held**
WEB: www.meyerinsure.com
SIC: 8062 General medical & surgical hospitals

(P-21920)
ST JOSEPH HOSPITAL OF EUREKA
2700 Dolbeer St, Eureka (95501-4736)
PHONE.................................707 445-8121
EMP: 970
SALES (est): 768K
SALES (corp-wide): 5.6B **Privately Held**
SIC: 8062 General medical & surgical hospitals
HQ: St. Joseph Hospital Of Orange
   1100 W Stewart Dr
   Orange CA 92868
   714 633-9111

(P-21921)
ST JOSEPH HOSPITAL OF ORANGE (DH)
1100 W Stewart Dr, Orange (92868-3891)
P.O. Box 5600 (92863-5600)
PHONE.................................714 633-9111
Fax: 714 744-8505
Larry K Ainsworth, *President*
Tina Nycroft, *CFO*
Jim Cora, *Chairman*
Warren D Johnson, *Vice Ch Bd*
Cory Rayyes, *Vice Pres*
EMP: 2100 **EST:** 1929
SQ FT: 448,000
SALES: 567.4MM
SALES (corp-wide): 5.6B **Privately Held**
SIC: 8062 General medical & surgical hospitals
HQ: St. Joseph Health System
   3345 Michelson Dr Ste 100
   Irvine CA 92612
   949 381-4000

(P-21922)
ST JOSEPH HOSPITAL OF ORANGE
Also Called: Renal Center
1100 W Stewart Dr, Orange (92868-3891)
P.O. Box 5600 (92863-5600)
PHONE.................................714 771-8037
Mary McKenzie, *Director*
EMP: 100
SALES (corp-wide): 5.6B **Privately Held**
SIC: 8062 General medical & surgical hospitals
HQ: St. Joseph Hospital Of Orange
   1100 W Stewart Dr
   Orange CA 92868
   714 633-9111

(P-21923)
ST JOSEPHS MED CTR STOCKTON
1800 N California St, Stockton (95204-6019)
P.O. Box 213008 (95213-9008)
PHONE.................................209 943-2000
Fax: 209 461-3299
Donald J Wiley, *President*
Teresa Bryant, *Lab Dir*
Randy Gamino, *Info Tech Dir*
Nicki O Choa, *Controller*
EMP: 2366
SALES: 4.2MM
SALES (corp-wide): 7.1B **Privately Held**
WEB: www.chw.edu
SIC: 8062 General medical & surgical hospitals
PA: Dignity Health
   185 Berry St Ste 300
   San Francisco CA 94107
   415 438-5500

(P-21924)
ST JOSEPHS MEDICAL CENTER
1800 N California St, Stockton (95204-6019)
P.O. Box 213008 (95213-9008)
PHONE.................................209 943-2000
Fax: 209 461-3462
Donald J Wiley, *President*
George S Charos,
Charles S Johnson,
John Hiltibidal,
Kevin E Rine, *Ch OB/GYN*
EMP: 150
SQ FT: 18,000
SALES (est): 51.6MM
SALES (corp-wide): 7.1B **Privately Held**
WEB: www.chw.edu
SIC: 8062 General medical & surgical hospitals
PA: Dignity Health
   185 Berry St Ste 300
   San Francisco CA 94107
   415 438-5500

(P-21925)
ST JUDE HOSPITAL (DH)
Also Called: St Jude Medical Center
101 E Valencia Mesa Dr, Fullerton (92835-3875)
PHONE.................................714 871-3280
Fax: 714 738-3057
Robert Fraschetti, *President*
Patrick L Fitzgibbons, *Ch Pathology*
Michael Lillie,
Pamela Frey, *Records Dir*
Doreen Dann, *CEO*
▲ **EMP:** 2582
SQ FT: 190,000
SALES: 477.4MM
SALES (corp-wide): 5.6B **Privately Held**
WEB: www.stjudemedicalcenter.com
SIC: 8062 General medical & surgical hospitals
HQ: St. Joseph Health System
   3345 Michelson Dr Ste 100
   Irvine CA 92612
   949 381-4000

(P-21926)
ST JUDE HOSPITAL
Also Called: Administration
279 Imperial Hwy Ste 770, Fullerton (92835-1059)
PHONE.................................714 578-8500
Claudette Desforges, *Principal*
EMP: 120
SALES (corp-wide): 5.6B **Privately Held**
WEB: www.stjudemedicalcenter.com
SIC: 8062 General medical & surgical hospitals
HQ: St. Jude Hospital
   101 E Valencia Mesa Dr
   Fullerton CA 92835
   714 871-3280

(P-21927)
ST LUKES HOSPITAL (HQ)
2351 Clay St, San Francisco (94115-1931)
PHONE.................................415 600-3959
Michael Holdsworth, *President*
Ed Kersh,
Richard A Anderson, *COO*
Nadder Mirsepassi, *Treasurer*

▲ = Import ▼ = Export
◆ = Import/Export

PRODUCTS & SERVICES SECTION
8062 - General Medical & Surgical Hospitals County (P-21945)

Carol Kuplen, *Vice Pres*
EMP: 802
SQ FT: 500,000
SALES (est): 63.6MM
SALES (corp-wide): 11B **Privately Held**
SIC: 8062 General medical & surgical hospitals
PA: Sutter Health
2200 River Plaza Dr
Sacramento CA 95833
916 733-8800

(P-21928)
ST MARY MEDICAL CENTER (HQ)
Also Called: St Mary's School of Nursing
1050 Linden Ave, Long Beach (90813-3321)
P.O. Box 887 (90801-0887)
PHONE 562 491-9000
Fax: 562 491-9146
Trammie McMann, *CEO*
Ronald Fields,
Alan Garrett, *CEO*
Tammie McMann, *CEO*
Joel Yuhaf, *COO*
EMP: 1929
SQ FT: 700,000
SALES (est): 122.4MM
SALES (corp-wide): 7.1B **Privately Held**
SIC: 8062 Hospital, medical school affiliated with nursing & residency
PA: Dignity Health
185 Berry St Ste 300
San Francisco CA 94107
415 438-5500

(P-21929)
ST MARYS MED CTR FOUNDATION
Also Called: C H W
450 Stanyan St, San Francisco (94117-1019)
PHONE 415 668-1000
Ken Steele, *President*
James Wentz, *CFO*
Diane Brack, *Finance*
EMP: 1067 **EST:** 1983
SALES: 6.7MM
SALES (corp-wide): 7.1B **Privately Held**
WEB: www.chw.edu
SIC: 8062 Hospital, professional nursing school
PA: Dignity Health
185 Berry St Ste 300
San Francisco CA 94107
415 438-5500

(P-21930)
ST VINCENT MEDICAL CENTER
2131 W 3rd St, Los Angeles (90057-1901)
P.O. Box 57992 (90057-0992)
PHONE 213 484-7111
Fax: 213 484-7092
Michael McMongle, *Ch Radiology*
Michael Garko, *CFO*
Joan Simon, *Ch Nursing Ofcr*
Joan Simons, *Ch Nursing Ofcr*
Steven Keller, *Executive Asst*
EMP: 1200 **EST:** 1856
SALES: 237.2MM
SALES (corp-wide): 225.4MM **Privately Held**
SIC: 8062 General medical & surgical hospitals
PA: Verity Health System Of California, Inc.
203 Redwood Shores Pkwy
Redwood City CA 94065
650 551-6650

(P-21931)
STANFORD HEALTH CARE
Also Called: Quality Management
300 Pasteur Dr, Stanford (94305-2200)
PHONE 650 723-4000
Vicki O'Malley, *Senior Buyer*
EMP: 2523
SALES (corp-wide): 1.9B **Privately Held**
SIC: 8062 8099 Hospital, medical school affiliated with residency; childbirth preparation clinic
HQ: Stanford Health Care
300 Pasteur Dr
Stanford CA 94305
650 723-4000

(P-21932)
STANFORD HEALTH CARE
Also Called: Stanford Cancer Center S Bay
2589 Samaritan Dr, San Jose (95124-4102)
PHONE 408 426-4900
Patrick Swift, *Med Doctor*
EMP: 2523
SALES (corp-wide): 1.9B **Privately Held**
SIC: 8062 Hospital, medical school affiliated with residency
HQ: Stanford Health Care
300 Pasteur Dr
Stanford CA 94305
650 723-4000

(P-21933)
STANFORD HEALTH CARE (HQ)
Also Called: Stanford Medical Center
300 Pasteur Dr, Stanford (94305-2200)
PHONE 650 723-4000
Amir Dan Rubin, *CEO*
Barbara Clemons, *President*
Betsy Williams, *COO*
Raksha Patel, *Bd of Directors*
Ying-Ying Goh, *Trustee*
▲ **EMP:** 5000
SALES (est): 1.9B
SALES (corp-wide): 1.9B **Privately Held**
WEB: www.stanfordmedicalcenter.com
SIC: 8062 Hospital, medical school affiliated with residency
PA: Leland Stanford Junior University
2575 Sand Hill Rd
Menlo Park CA 94025
650 723-2300

(P-21934)
STANFORD HEALTH CARE
Also Called: Shc Reference Laboratory
3375 Hillview Ave, Palo Alto (94304-1204)
PHONE 650 736-7844
Karen Hoexter, *Admin Asst*
Lynda Wolfe, *Planning*
Glenda Cruz, *Analyst*
Martha Aragon, *Director*
Sharon Bird, *Manager*
EMP: 2523
SALES (corp-wide): 1.9B **Privately Held**
SIC: 8062 General medical & surgical hospitals
HQ: Stanford Health Care
300 Pasteur Dr
Stanford CA 94305
650 723-4000

(P-21935)
STANFORD HOSPITAL AND CLINICS
1510 Page Mill Rd Ste 2, Palo Alto (94304-1133)
PHONE 650 213-8360
Martha Marsh, *President*
Mike Mucha, *Info Tech Dir*
Katie Lipovsky, *Corp Comm Staff*
Bassam Kadry, *Anesthesiology*
EMP: 2523
SALES (corp-wide): 1.9B **Privately Held**
SIC: 8062 Hospital, medical school affiliated with residency
HQ: Stanford Health Care
300 Pasteur Dr
Stanford CA 94305
650 723-4000

(P-21936)
STANISLAUS SURGICAL HOSP LLC (PA)
Also Called: Stanislaus Surgical Center
1421 Oakdale Rd, Modesto (95355-3356)
PHONE 209 572-2700
Fax: 209 572-0151
Douglas V Johnson, *CEO*
Kerry Darnell, *Vice Pres*
Denise Portillo, *Executive Asst*
Kelsey Holder, *Admin Asst*
Greta Tiffin, *Admin Asst*
EMP: 140
SQ FT: 50,000
SALES (est): 39.6MM **Privately Held**
WEB: www.stanislaussurgical.com
SIC: 8062 General medical & surgical hospitals

(P-21937)
SURGERY CENTER OF ALTA BATES (HQ)
Also Called: Alta Bates Summit Medical Ctr
2450 Ashby Ave, Berkeley (94705-2067)
PHONE 510 204-4444
Fax: 510 548-0318
Warren Kirk, *President*
Robert Petrina, *CFO*
Steve Austin, *Officer*
William Green, *Associate Dir*
Adam Husney, *Associate Dir*
EMP: 653
SQ FT: 749,000
SALES (est): 365.1MM
SALES (corp-wide): 11B **Privately Held**
WEB: www.altabates.com
SIC: 8062 General medical & surgical hospitals
PA: Sutter Health
2200 River Plaza Dr
Sacramento CA 95833
916 733-8800

(P-21938)
SURPRISE VALLEY HLTH CARE DST
741 N Main St, Cedarville (96104)
P.O. Box 246 (96104-0246)
PHONE 530 279-6111
Fax: 530 279-2680
Wanda Grove, *CEO*
Jason Diven, *President*
Cindy Linker, *Treasurer*
Carl Quigley, *Vice Pres*
Bunne Hartmann, *Admin Sec*
EMP: 72
SQ FT: 13,330
SALES (est): 4.7MM **Privately Held**
SIC: 8062 General medical & surgical hospitals

(P-21939)
SUTTER AMADOR HOSPITAL (HQ)
200 Mission Blvd, Jackson (95642-2564)
PHONE 209 223-7500
Fax: 209 223-7454
Anne Platt, *CEO*
Nadder Mirsepassi, *Treasurer*
Thomas Bowhay, *Chief Mktg Ofcr*
Denise Sammons, *Officer*
Sherry Paterson, *Risk Mgmt Dir*
EMP: 385
SALES: 72.3MM
SALES (corp-wide): 11B **Privately Held**
WEB: www.sutteramador.com
SIC: 8062 General medical & surgical hospitals
PA: Sutter Health
2200 River Plaza Dr
Sacramento CA 95833
916 733-8800

(P-21940)
SUTTER BAY HOSPITALS (HQ)
Also Called: California Pacific Medical Ctr
633 Folsom St Fl 7, San Francisco (94107-3618)
P.O. Box 7999 (94120-7999)
PHONE 415 600-6000
Fax: 415 474-9583
Martin Brotman MD, *President*
Edward A Eisler,
Warren Browner, *CEO*
John F Forbes, *Bd of Directors*
Judy Garber, *Bd of Directors*
EMP: 2578
SALES: 1.5B
SALES (corp-wide): 11B **Privately Held**
WEB: www.cpmc.org
SIC: 8062 8733 General medical & surgical hospitals; research institute
PA: Sutter Health
2200 River Plaza Dr
Sacramento CA 95833
916 733-8800

(P-21941)
SUTTER CENTRAL VLY HOSPITALS (HQ)
Also Called: Memorial Medical Center
1700 Coffee Rd, Modesto (95355-2803)
P.O. Box 942 (95353-0942)
PHONE 209 526-4500
Fax: 209 526-1946
James Conforti, *CEO*
Todd Smith, *Ch of Bd*
Tom V Groningen, *Vice Chairman*
David P Benn, *CFO*
Sutter Pat Fry, *CEO*
EMP: 112 **EST:** 1947
SQ FT: 180,000
SALES (est): 392.7MM
SALES (corp-wide): 11B **Privately Held**
WEB: www.memorialmedicalcenter.org
SIC: 8062 General medical & surgical hospitals
PA: Sutter Health
2200 River Plaza Dr
Sacramento CA 95833
916 733-8800

(P-21942)
SUTTER COAST HOSPITAL (HQ)
Also Called: SUTTER C H S
800 E Washington Blvd, Crescent City (95531-8359)
PHONE 707 464-8511
Fax: 707 464-8941
Eugene Suksi, *President*
Jim Strong, *CFO*
Nadder Mirsepassi, *Systems Dir*
Debra Faulk, *Systems Mgr*
Lynn M Szabo, *Med Doctor*
▲ **EMP:** 250
SQ FT: 70,000
SALES: 69.9MM
SALES (corp-wide): 11B **Privately Held**
WEB: www.suttercoast.com
SIC: 8062 General medical & surgical hospitals
PA: Sutter Health
2200 River Plaza Dr
Sacramento CA 95833
916 733-8800

(P-21943)
SUTTER DELTA MEDICAL CTR AUX
3901 Lone Tree Way, Antioch (94509-6200)
P.O. Box 3225 (94531-3225)
PHONE 925 779-7200
Linda Lee Rovai, *President*
Ken Hammer, *COO*
Carol Jurccak, *Executive Asst*
Linda Horn, *Administration*
Janice Falzano, *Finance*
EMP: 53
SQ FT: 150,000
SALES (est): 11MM **Privately Held**
WEB: www.sutterdelta.com
SIC: 8062 8082 8093 8069 General medical & surgical hospitals; home health care services; specialty outpatient clinics; orthopedic hospital

(P-21944)
SUTTER EAST BAY HOSPITALS
Also Called: Alta Bates Summit Medical Ctr
2420 Ashby Ave, Berkeley (94705-2002)
PHONE 510 204-1609
Jeff Gerard, *CEO*
Anthony Wagner, *Ch of Bd*
John Gates, *CFO*
Sarah Love, *Director*
EMP: 99
SALES (est): 486.2K **Privately Held**
SIC: 8062 General medical & surgical hospitals

(P-21945)
SUTTER HEALTH (PA)
Also Called: SUTTER C H S
2200 River Plaza Dr, Sacramento (95833-4134)
PHONE 916 733-8800
Patrick Fry, *President*
Richard Porzio, *Ch Radiology*
Randy Ross, *COO*
William Anderson, *CFO*
Siri Nelson, *CFO*
EMP: 900
SALES: 11B **Privately Held**
WEB: www.sutterhealth.org
SIC: 8062 8051 8011 6513 General medical & surgical hospitals; skilled nursing care facilities; offices & clinics of medical doctors; retirement hotel operation

8062 - General Medical & Surgical Hospitals County (P-21946)

(P-21946)
SUTTER HEALTH
2880 Soquel Ave Ste 10, Santa Cruz (95062-1423)
PHONE..................................831 477-3600
Kathleen McNupp, *Manager*
Katherine Manual, *COO*
Terri S Sterrett, *Executive Asst*
Michelle Mathieu, *Analyst*
EMP: 50
SALES (corp-wide): 11B **Privately Held**
WEB: www.sutterhealth.org
SIC: 8062 General medical & surgical hospitals
PA: Sutter Health
2200 River Plaza Dr
Sacramento CA 95833
916 733-8800

(P-21947)
SUTTER HLTH SCRMNTO SIERRA REG (HQ)
Also Called: Sutter Memorial Hospital
2200 River Plaza Dr, Sacramento (95833-4134)
P.O. Box 160727 (95816-0727)
PHONE..................................916 733-8800
Patrick E Fry, *CEO*
Darling Lones, *President*
Kristi Bradley, *Nursing Mgr*
Mark McDaniel, *Engineer*
Lynnann Maryatt, *Business Mgr*
▲ **EMP:** 300
SQ FT: 20,000
SALES: 1.8B
SALES (corp-wide): 11B **Privately Held**
SIC: 8062 8063 8052 General medical & surgical hospitals; psychiatric hospitals; intermediate care facilities
PA: Sutter Health
2200 River Plaza Dr
Sacramento CA 95833
916 733-8800

(P-21948)
SUTTER HLTH SCRMNTO SIERRA REG
Also Called: Sutter Davis Hospital
2000 Sutter Pl, Davis (95616-6201)
P.O. Box 1617 (95617-1617)
PHONE..................................530 756-6440
Fax: 530 757-5127
Janet Wagner, *Branch Mgr*
David Rosas, *President*
Stella Henthorn, *Nursing Mgr*
Isha Nagi, *Analyst*
George Lenzi, *Controller*
EMP: 350
SALES (corp-wide): 11B **Privately Held**
SIC: 8062 8011 General medical & surgical hospitals; offices & clinics of medical doctors
HQ: Sutter Health Sacramento Sierra Region
2200 River Plaza Dr
Sacramento CA 95833
916 733-8800

(P-21949)
SUTTER HLTH SCRMNTO SIERRA REG
Also Called: Sutter Roseville Medical Ctr
1 Medical Plaza Dr, Roseville (95661-3037)
PHONE..................................916 781-1000
Patrick Grady, *Manager*
Pat Hamm, *Infect Cntl Dir*
Karen Farewell, *Social Dir*
Robert Royer, *Radiology Dir*
Marcia Hansen, *Executive Asst*
EMP: 1180
SALES (corp-wide): 11B **Privately Held**
SIC: 8062 General medical & surgical hospitals
HQ: Sutter Health Sacramento Sierra Region
2200 River Plaza Dr
Sacramento CA 95833
916 733-8800

(P-21950)
SUTTER LAKESIDE HOSPITAL (HQ)
5176 Hill Rd E, Lakeport (95453-6357)
PHONE..................................707 262-5000
Fax: 707 262-5003
Siri Nelson, *CEO*
Bob Anderson, *CFO*
Robert Anderson, *CFO*
Kelly Mather, *Administration*
Richard Eagar, *Network Mgr*
EMP: 340 **EST:** 1945
SQ FT: 26,000
SALES: 33.1MM
SALES (corp-wide): 11B **Privately Held**
SIC: 8062 General medical & surgical hospitals
PA: Sutter Health
2200 River Plaza Dr
Sacramento CA 95833
916 733-8800

(P-21951)
SUTTER MATERNITY & SURGERY CTR
2900 Chanticleer Ave, Santa Cruz (95065-1816)
PHONE..................................831 477-2200
Larry De Ghetaldi, *CEO*
William Berg, *Ch Radiology*
Glen Groves, *CFO*
Richard Nichols, *Administration*
Mark S Isaacson, *Anesthesiology*
EMP: 225
SALES (est): 53.2MM **Privately Held**
SIC: 8062 General medical & surgical hospitals

(P-21952)
SUTTER ROSEVILLE MEDICAL CTR
1 Medical Plaza Dr, Roseville (95661-3037)
PHONE..................................916 781-1000
Fax: 916 781-1802
Patrick Brady, *CEO*
Gary Hubschman, *CFO*
Bob Smith, *Info Tech Dir*
Julie Fralick, *Hum Res Coord*
Julie Hussey, *Human Resources*
EMP: 1700
SALES: 484MM **Privately Held**
SIC: 8062 General medical & surgical hospitals

(P-21953)
SUTTER RSVLLE MED CTR FNDATION
1 Medical Plaza Dr, Roseville (95661-3037)
PHONE..................................916 781-1000
Patricia Marquez, *President*
Lance Rossi, *Physician Asst*
EMP: 2000
SALES: 2.6MM **Privately Held**
SIC: 8062 General medical & surgical hospitals

(P-21954)
SUTTER SOLANO MEDICAL CENTER (HQ)
Also Called: SSMC
300 Hospital Dr, Vallejo (94589-2594)
PHONE..................................707 554-4444
Fax: 707 648-3227
Laybon Jones,
Brett Moore, *CFO*
Jim Barringham, *Info Tech Dir*
Tamra Pahl, *IT/INT Sup*
Forest Latendresse, *Chief Engr*
EMP: 542
SQ FT: 94,000
SALES: 121.5MM
SALES (corp-wide): 11B **Privately Held**
WEB: www.suttersolano.org
SIC: 8062 General medical & surgical hospitals
PA: Sutter Health
2200 River Plaza Dr
Sacramento CA 95833
916 733-8800

(P-21955)
SUTTER SURGICAL HOSPITAL N VLY
455 Plumas Blvd, Yuba City (95991-5074)
PHONE..................................530 749-5700
Toni Morris, *Principal*
EMP: 125 **EST:** 2010
SALES (est): 15.5MM
SALES (corp-wide): 291.3MM **Privately Held**
SIC: 8062 General medical & surgical hospitals
PA: National Surgical Hospitals, Inc.
250 S Wacker Dr Ste 500
Chicago IL 60606
312 627-8400

(P-21956)
SUTTER WEST BAY HOSPITALS (HQ)
Also Called: Novato Community Hospital
180 Rowland Way, Novato (94945-5009)
P.O. Box 1108 (94948-1108)
PHONE..................................415 209-1300
Fax: 415 209-1321
Brian Alexander, *CEO*
Cooper Chao,
David Bradley, *President*
Cheryl Harless, *Ch Nursing Ofcr*
Patricia Mosser, *Admin Sec*
▲ **EMP:** 329
SQ FT: 50,000
SALES: 60.1MM
SALES (corp-wide): 11B **Privately Held**
WEB: www.sutterhealth.org
SIC: 8062 General medical & surgical hospitals
PA: Sutter Health
2200 River Plaza Dr
Sacramento CA 95833
916 733-8800

(P-21957)
TAHOE FOREST HOSPITAL DISTRICT
Also Called: Tahoe Workx
10956 Donner Paca Rd Ste 230, Truckee (96161)
PHONE..................................530 582-3277
Fax: 530 550-0544
Christine Spencer, *Director*
Patricia Barrett, *Admin Asst*
Elizabeth Henasey, *Research*
Ted Owens, *Pub Rel Dir*
Deborah Brown, *Pediatrics*
EMP: 111
SALES (corp-wide): 93.4MM **Privately Held**
SIC: 8062 8071 General medical & surgical hospitals; X-ray laboratory, including dental
PA: Tahoe Forest Hospital District
10121 Pine Ave
Truckee CA 96161
530 587-6011

(P-21958)
TAHOE FOREST HOSPITAL DISTRICT (PA)
10121 Pine Ave, Truckee (96161-4856)
P.O. Box 759 (96160-0759)
PHONE..................................530 587-6011
Fax: 530 582-1864
Robert Schapper, *CEO*
Timothy J Lombard,
Jeff Dodd,
Thomas Specht,
Tad Laird, *Ch Radiology*
EMP: 302
SQ FT: 120,000
SALES (est): 93.4MM **Privately Held**
WEB: www.tfhd.com
SIC: 8062 General medical & surgical hospitals

(P-21959)
TEHACHAPI VLY HOSP HLTHCRE DIS (PA)
115 W E St, Tehachapi (93561-1607)
P.O. Box 1900 (93581-1900)
PHONE..................................661 823-3000
Eugene Suksi, *CEO*
Juliana Kirby, *COO*
William Vannoy, *CFO*
Gary Olsen, *Vice Pres*
Allen Burgess, *Principal*
EMP: 93
SQ FT: 18,000
SALES (est): 224.7K **Privately Held**
SIC: 8062 General medical & surgical hospitals

(P-21960)
TEMPLE HOSPITAL CORPORATION
Also Called: Temple Community Hospital
242 N Hoover St, Los Angeles (90004-3628)
PHONE..................................213 355-3200
Fax: 213 381-6410
Herbert G Needman, *CEO*
Michael Camras, *Vice Pres*
Saul Burakoff, *Director*
EMP: 350 **EST:** 1927
SQ FT: 100,000
SALES (est): 50.8MM **Privately Held**
SIC: 8062 General medical & surgical hospitals

(P-21961)
TENET HEALTHSYSTEM MEDICAL
13032 Earlham St, Santa Ana (92705-2113)
PHONE..................................714 966-8191
Tim Smith, *CEO*
EMP: 1500
SALES (corp-wide): 18.7B **Publicly Held**
WEB: www.tenenthealth.com
SIC: 8062 General medical & surgical hospitals
HQ: Tenet Healthsystem Medical, Inc
1445 Ross Ave Ste 1400
Dallas TX 75202
469 893-2000

(P-21962)
TENET HEALTHSYSTEM MEDICAL
16331 Arthur St, Cerritos (90703-2128)
PHONE..................................562 531-2550
John R Nickens, *Principal*
EMP: 509
SALES (corp-wide): 18.7B **Publicly Held**
WEB: www.tenenthealth.com
SIC: 8062 8011 General medical & surgical hospitals; offices & clinics of medical doctors
HQ: Tenet Healthsystem Medical, Inc
1445 Ross Ave Ste 1400
Dallas TX 75202
469 893-2000

(P-21963)
TENET HEALTHSYSTEM MEDICAL
Also Called: Tenet Health System Hospital
1205 E North St, Manteca (95336-4932)
PHONE..................................209 823-3111
Brenden Panzarello, *Branch Mgr*
Carmen Silva, *COO*
Gary Modlin, *Security Dir*
Michele Bava, *Human Res Dir*
Debra Garcia, *Hlthcr Dir*
EMP: 474
SALES (corp-wide): 18.7B **Publicly Held**
SIC: 8062 General medical & surgical hospitals
HQ: Tenet Healthsystem Medical, Inc
1445 Ross Ave Ste 1400
Dallas TX 75202
469 893-2000

(P-21964)
TENET HEALTHSYSTEM MEDICAL
Also Called: Irvine Regional Hospital
1400 S Duglaca Rd Ste 250, Anaheim (92680)
PHONE..................................714 428-6800
Donald Lorack, *CEO*
Michael Vargas,
Eric Degado, *CFO*
Dennis Gutierrez,
Edward Pillar, *Director*
EMP: 509
SALES (corp-wide): 18.7B **Publicly Held**
WEB: www.tenenthealth.com
SIC: 8062 General medical & surgical hospitals
HQ: Tenet Healthsystem Medical, Inc
1445 Ross Ave Ste 1400
Dallas TX 75202
469 893-2000

PRODUCTS & SERVICES SECTION
8062 - General Medical & Surgical Hospitals County (P-21984)

(P-21965)
TENET HEALTHSYSTEM MEDICAL
Cnty HSP/Rhb Ctr/Ls GTS-Srtg
815 Pollard Rd, Los Gatos (95032-1438)
PHONE...................................408 378-6131
Toll Free:...888 -
Fax: 408 866-4006
Gary Honts, CEO
Cecilia Jazier, Lab Dir
Rebecca Cheng, VP Finance
Lindell Bradley, Human Res Dir
Cindy Harmer, Manager
EMP: 750
SALES (corp-wide): 18.7B Publicly Held
WEB: www.tenenthealth.com
SIC: 8062 8011 General medical & surgical hospitals; offices & clinics of medical doctors
HQ: Tenet Healthsystem Medical, Inc
1445 Ross Ave Ste 1400
Dallas TX 75202
469 893-2000

(P-21966)
THE FOR HOSPITAL COMMITTEE (DH)
Also Called: Valley Care Health System, The
5555 W Las Positas Blvd, Pleasanton (94588-4000)
PHONE....................................925 847-3000
Fax: 925 373-4164
Scott Gregerson, CEO
Michael Ranahan, Managing Prtnr
Doug Gunderson, COO
Ryan Chance, Trustee
Felicia Ziomek, Officer
EMP: 500
SALES (est): 155.8MM
SALES (corp-wide): 1.9B Privately Held
WEB: www.valleycare.com
SIC: 8062 8741 General medical & surgical hospitals; hospital management
HQ: Stanford Health Care
300 Pasteur Dr
Stanford CA 94305
650 723-4000

(P-21967)
THOUSAND OAKS SURGICAL HOSP LP
401 Rolling Oaks Dr, Thousand Oaks (91361-1050)
PHONE....................................805 777-7750
Fax: 805 418-1381
Micheal Bass, Partner
Marissa Mc Arthur, Exec Sec
EMP: 100
SQ FT: 50,000
SALES (est): 15.5MM Privately Held
WEB: www.toshospital.com
SIC: 8062 General medical & surgical hospitals

(P-21968)
TORRANCE HEALTH ASSN INC (PA)
Also Called: Physician Office Support Svcs
23550 Hawthorne Blvd, Torrance (90505-4731)
P.O. Box 13717 (90503-0717)
PHONE...................................310 325-9110
Craig Leach, CEO
Doug Klebe, CFO
Peggy Berwald, Senior VP
Sally Eberhard, Senior VP
John McNamara, Senior VP
EMP: 3000
SQ FT: 180,000
SALES: 554.5MM Privately Held
SIC: 8062 General medical & surgical hospitals

(P-21969)
TORRANCE HOSPITAL IPA
23600 Telo Ave, Torrance (90505-4035)
PHONE...................................310 784-0800
John Panitch, President
Alex Cluge, Financial Exec
EMP: 50
SALES (est): 2.6MM Privately Held
SIC: 8062 General medical & surgical hospitals

(P-21970)
TORRANCE MEMORIAL MEDICAL CTR (HQ)
3330 Lomita Blvd, Torrance (90505-5002)
PHONE...................................310 325-9110
Fax: 310 517-4745
Craig Leach, President
Bill Larson, CFO
Dennis Fitzgerald, Treasurer
Peggy Berwald, Senior VP
John McNamara, Senior VP
EMP: 1500
SALES: 303.1MM
SALES (corp-wide): 554.5MM Privately Held
WEB: www.torrancememorial.org
SIC: 8062 Hospital, affiliated with AMA residency
PA: Torrance Health Association, Inc.
23550 Hawthorne Blvd
Torrance CA 90505
310 325-9110

(P-21971)
TRACY SUTTER COMMUNITY HOSP
1420 N Tracy Blvd, Tracy (95376-3451)
PHONE...................................209 835-1500
Fax: 209 832-6024
David Thompson, President
Tom Lowry, CFO
Mina Whyte, Vice Pres
Robert Green, Exec Dir
Susan Duarte, Admin Sec
▲ EMP: 400
SQ FT: 80,000
SALES (est): 67.8MM
SALES (corp-wide): 11B Privately Held
WEB: www.suttertracy.org
SIC: 8062 8051 8011 General medical & surgical hospitals; skilled nursing care facilities; offices & clinics of medical doctors
PA: Sutter Health
2200 River Plaza Dr
Sacramento CA 95833
916 733-8800

(P-21972)
TRI-CITY HOSPITAL DISTRICT (PA)
Also Called: TRI-CITY MEDICAL CENTER
4002 Vista Way, Oceanside (92056-4506)
PHONE...................................760 724-8411
Fax: 760 724-1010
Larry Schallock, Chairman
Stephen Schmitter, Ch Radiology
Chris Bass, President
Casey Fatch, CEO
Robert Wardwell, CFO
EMP: 2100
SQ FT: 50,000
SALES: 321.8MM Privately Held
WEB: www.tcmccareers.com
SIC: 8062 General medical & surgical hospitals

(P-21973)
TULARE LOCAL HEALTH CARE DST
Also Called: Tulare Home Care
869 N Cherry St, Tulare (93274-2207)
PHONE...................................559 685-3462
Fax: 559 685-9345
Shawn Bolouki, CEO
Sherrie Bell, President
Fred Capozello, CFO
Steven Debuskey, Vice Pres
Prem Camboj, Admin Sec
EMP: 700
SQ FT: 140,000
SALES (est): 88MM Privately Held
SIC: 8062 General medical & surgical hospitals

(P-21974)
TUSTIN HOSPITAL AND MED CTR
Also Called: Newport Specialty Hospital
3699 Wilshire Blvd # 540, Los Angeles (90010-2723)
PHONE...................................714 619-7700
Fax: 714 669-2014
Gary Lewis, CEO
EMP: 360
SALES (est): 42.1MM
SALES (corp-wide): 136.2MM Privately Held
SIC: 8062 General medical & surgical hospitals
HQ: Pacific Health Corporation
14642 Newport Ave
Tustin CA 92780
714 838-9600

(P-21975)
TY FIVE STAR CORPORATION
Also Called: ALL SAINTS SUBACUTE REHABILITA
27285 Sleepy Hollow Ave S # 204, Hayward (94545-4321)
PHONE...................................510 317-7360
James Preimesberger, President
Jennifer Mata, Infect Cntl Dir
Daniel Whitman, Administration
Cathy Del Rosario, Nursing Dir
Tobias Yeh, Manager
EMP: 150
SALES: 10MM Privately Held
WEB: www.allsaints-subacute.com
SIC: 8062 General medical & surgical hospitals

(P-21976)
U C MED HUMN RSRCES APLCAT SVC
Also Called: U C Health Systems
2730 Stockton Blvd # 21002500, Sacramento (95817-2217)
PHONE...................................916 734-5916
Fax: 916 734-0210
Gloria Alvardo, Director
John Gubbels, Manager
EMP: 75
SALES (est): 2.1MM Privately Held
SIC: 8062 General medical & surgical hospitals

(P-21977)
UCLA HEALTHCARE
1821 Wilshire Blvd Fl 6, Santa Monica (90403-5618)
PHONE...................................310 319-4560
Ted Braun, Principal
Ted Brown, Principal
EMP: 77
SALES (est): 15.3MM Privately Held
SIC: 8062 General medical & surgical hospitals
HQ: University Of California, Los Angeles
405 Hilgard Ave
Los Angeles CA 90095
310 825-4321

(P-21978)
UHS-CORONA INC (HQ)
Also Called: Corona Regional Med Ctr Hosp
800 S Main St, Corona (92882-3420)
PHONE...................................951 737-4343
Fax: 909 736-6310
Marvin Pember, CEO
Alaa Afifi,
Alan B Miller, President
Ken Rivers, CEO
Nancy Jangaon, CFO
▲ EMP: 900
SALES: 140.9MM
SALES (corp-wide): 9B Publicly Held
SIC: 8062 General medical & surgical hospitals
PA: Universal Health Services, Inc.
367 S Gulph Rd
King Of Prussia PA 19406
610 768-3300

(P-21979)
UKIAH ADVENTIST HOSPITAL (PA)
Also Called: UKIAH VALLEY MEDICAL CENTER
275 Hospital Dr, Ukiah (95482-4531)
PHONE...................................707 463-7346
Fax: 707 463-7384
Terry Burns, President
David Debooy,
Rod Granger, CFO
Jeremy Mann, Bd of Directors
Beverly Schmunk, Vice Pres
EMP: 500
SQ FT: 50,000
SALES: 148MM Privately Held
SIC: 8062 General medical & surgical hospitals

(P-21980)
UKIAH ADVENTIST HOSPITAL
1120 S Dora St, Ukiah (95482-6340)
PHONE...................................707 462-3111
Val Gene Devitt, Branch Mgr
EMP: 150
SQ FT: 43,500
SALES (corp-wide): 148MM Privately Held
SIC: 8062 General medical & surgical hospitals
PA: Ukiah Adventist Hospital
275 Hospital Dr
Ukiah CA 95482
707 463-7346

(P-21981)
UNITED STATES DEPT OF NAVY
Also Called: Navy Hospital
937 Vista Pl, Lemoore (93245-9019)
PHONE...................................559 998-4201
Clinton Butler, Exec Dir
Thomas Bui, CFO
R Casey, Radiology Dir
Eileen Chaney, Info Tech Dir
R Barbour, Director
EMP: 711 Publicly Held
SIC: 8062 9711 General medical & surgical hospitals; Navy;
HQ: United States Department Of The Navy
1200 Navy Pentagon
Washington DC 20350
703 545-6700

(P-21982)
UNITED STATES DEPT OF NAVY
Also Called: Naval Hospital Lemoore
Bldg 937 Franklin Ave, Lemoore (93246-0001)
PHONE...................................559 998-4481
Fax: 559 998-4438
Stephen Mandia, Director
Sylvia Henning, Human Res Dir
Mike Spieth, Safety Mgr
Gerard Kennedy, Director
David Shiveley, Manager
EMP: 600 Publicly Held
SIC: 8062 9711 General medical & surgical hospitals; Navy;
HQ: United States Department Of The Navy
1200 Navy Pentagon
Washington DC 20350
703 545-6700

(P-21983)
UNITED STATES DEPT OF NAVY
Us Naval Hosp Bldg 1145, Twentynine Palms (92278)
P.O. Box 788250 (92278-8250)
PHONE...................................760 830-2190
Vanda Stanley, Officer
EMP: 500 Publicly Held
SIC: 8062 9711 General medical & surgical hospitals; Navy;
HQ: United States Department Of The Navy
1200 Navy Pentagon
Washington DC 20350
703 545-6700

(P-21984)
UNITED STATES DEPT OF NAVY
Also Called: Naval Medical Center
34800 Bob Wilson Dr, San Diego (92134-1098)
PHONE...................................619 532-6400
Fax: 619 532-5500
Esther Lynn, Branch Mgr
Marilyn Hundley, Officer
Ronald Moody, Officer
Neil Delossantos, Top Exec
Marc Perez, Executive
EMP: 4250 Publicly Held
SIC: 8062 9711 General medical & surgical hospitals; Navy;
HQ: United States Department Of The Navy
1200 Navy Pentagon
Washington DC 20350
703 545-6700

8062 - General Medical & Surgical Hospitals County (P-21985) — PRODUDCTS & SERVICES SECTION

(P-21985)
UNITED STATES DEPT OF NAVY
Also Called: Daps Naval Hosp
937 Franklin Blvd, Lemoore (93246-4700)
PHONE.................................559 998-2894
Maryalice Morro, *Principal*
EMP: 400 Publicly Held
SIC: 8062 General medical & surgical hospitals
HQ: United States Department Of The Navy
1200 Navy Pentagon
Washington DC 20350
703 545-6700

(P-21986)
UNIVERS OF CALIF SAN DIEGO HS
200 W Arbor Dr 8201, San Diego (92103-1911)
PHONE.................................619 543-3713
Tom McAsee, *Principal*
Margarita Baggett, *CEO*
Duncan Campbell, *COO*
Angela Sciao, *Chief Mktg Ofcr*
EMP: 5000
SALES (est): 205.7MM Privately Held
SIC: 8062 General medical & surgical hospitals

(P-21987)
UNIVERSITY CAL LOS ANGELES
Also Called: Ucla Radiation Oncology
200 Medical Pl Ste B265, Los Angeles (90095-0001)
PHONE.................................310 825-9771
Travis Gilchrist, *CEO*
Michael Steinberg, *Principal*
Monica A Rocha, *Admin Asst*
Julia Melkonian, *Administration*
Jenny Seaver, *Administration*
EMP: 90
SALES (est): 364.8K Privately Held
SIC: 8062 Hospital, medical school affiliated with residency

(P-21988)
UNIVERSITY CAL LOS ANGELES
Also Called: Ucla Medical Center
200 Ucla Medical Plz, Los Angeles (90095-8344)
PHONE.................................310 825-0640
Fax: 310 267-0189
Evelyn Cederbaum, *Branch Mgr*
Cheryl Abraham, *Office Mgr*
Lisa Reyes, *Administration*
Risa M Hoffman, *Infectious Dis*
William J Martin, *Surgeon*
EMP: 2056 Privately Held
WEB: www.ucla.edu
SIC: 8062 9411 8221 General medical & surgical hospitals; administration of educational programs; ; university
HQ: University Of California, Los Angeles
405 Hilgard Ave
Los Angeles CA 90095
310 825-4321

(P-21989)
UNIVERSITY CAL LOS ANGELES
Also Called: Ucla Medical Center
14445 Olive View Dr, Sylmar (91342-1437)
PHONE.................................818 364-1555
Dr Dennis Cope, *Branch Mgr*
Soma Wali, *Internal Med*
Rebecca Dudovitz, *Med Doctor*
Richard Hu, *Med Doctor*
Miriam Parsa, *Med Doctor*
EMP: 3000 Privately Held
WEB: www.ucla.edu
SIC: 8062 9411 8221 General medical & surgical hospitals; administration of educational programs; ; university
HQ: University Of California, Los Angeles
405 Hilgard Ave
Los Angeles CA 90095
310 825-4321

(P-21990)
UNIVERSITY CAL LOS ANGELES
Also Called: Santa Monica Ucla Medical Ctr
1225 15th St, Santa Monica (90404-1101)
PHONE.................................310 319-4000
Susan Colley, *Principal*
Jeffrey Eckardt,
Chester Griffith,
Brenda Kuhn, *COO*
Paul A Staton, *CFO*
EMP: 1111
SQ FT: 7,350 Privately Held
WEB: www.ucla.edu
SIC: 8062 9411 8221 General medical & surgical hospitals; administration of educational programs; ; university
HQ: University Of California, Los Angeles
405 Hilgard Ave
Los Angeles CA 90095
310 825-4321

(P-21991)
UNIVERSITY CAL LOS ANGELES
Also Called: Ronald Reagan Ucla Medical Ctr
757 Westwood Plz, Los Angeles (90095-8358)
PHONE.................................310 825-9111
Tatiana Orloff, *Branch Mgr*
Cecilia Lucero, *Human Res Mgr*
Drew Winston, *Infectious Dis*
Lamya Jarjour, *Obstetrician*
Jennifer Correa, *Cardiology*
EMP: 2056 Privately Held
SIC: 8062 General medical & surgical hospitals
HQ: University Of California, Los Angeles
405 Hilgard Ave
Los Angeles CA 90095
310 825-4321

(P-21992)
UNIVERSITY CAL SAN DIEGO
Also Called: Medical Center
200 W Arbor Dr Frnt, San Diego (92103-9000)
PHONE.................................619 543-6654
Fax: 619 543-3305
Richard Likeweg, *Manager*
Jennifer Atkins, *Officer*
Kristover Fitzsimmons, *Officer*
Grace Guarin, *Program Mgr*
Kirsten L Allen, *Admin Asst*
EMP: 4000 Privately Held
WEB: www.medicine.ucsd.edu
SIC: 8062 9411 8221 General medical & surgical hospitals; administration of educational programs; ; university
HQ: University Of California, San Diego
9500 Gilman Dr
La Jolla CA 92093
858 534-2230

(P-21993)
UNIVERSITY CAL SAN DIEGO
Also Called: Ucsd Thornton Hospital
9300 Campus Point Dr, La Jolla (92037-1300)
PHONE.................................858 657-7000
Fax: 858 657-6939
Paul Hensler, *Director*
Chuck Daniels, *Pharmacy Dir*
Gary Hagney, *Pharmacy Dir*
Mark Wallace, *Research*
Brian Whisenant, *Research*
EMP: 500 Privately Held
WEB: www.medicine.ucsd.edu
SIC: 8062 9411 8221 General medical & surgical hospitals; administration of educational programs; ; university
HQ: University Of California, San Diego
9500 Gilman Dr
La Jolla CA 92093
858 534-2230

(P-21994)
UNIVERSITY CAL SAN FRANCISCO
Also Called: Ucsf Medical Center
185 Berry St Ste 2000, San Francisco (94107-1704)
PHONE.................................415 476-1000
Fax: 415 476-2317
Sheree Garcia, *Manager*
Tony Hang, *Comp Lab Dir*
Paul Garcia, *Director*
Roshilla Lal, *Manager*
EMP: 200 Privately Held
WEB: www.uchastings.edu
SIC: 8062 9411 8221 General medical & surgical hospitals; administration of educational programs; ; university
HQ: University Of California, San Francisco
505 Parnassus Ave
San Francisco CA 94143
415 476-9000

(P-21995)
UNIVERSITY CAL SAN FRANCISCO
Also Called: Ucsf Vascular Laboratories
505 Parnassus Ave, San Francisco (94143-2204)
P.O. Box 816 (94104-0816)
PHONE.................................415 476-1000
Fax: 415 476-1734
Mark Laret, *Director*
Cyrus Buhari,
Francesca Byrne,
Michael Crawford,
Marc Vincent,
EMP: 1200 Privately Held
WEB: www.uchastings.edu
SIC: 8062 9411 8221 General medical & surgical hospitals; administration of educational programs; ; university
HQ: University Of California, San Francisco
505 Parnassus Ave
San Francisco CA 94143
415 476-9000

(P-21996)
UNIVERSITY CAL SAN FRANCISCO
Ucsf Langley Porter
401 Parnassus Ave, San Francisco (94143-2211)
PHONE.................................415 476-7000
Fax: 415 476-7722
Craig Van Dyke, *Manager*
Kim Terry, *Office Mgr*
Ann Saggio, *Data Proc Dir*
Tula Gourdin, *Analyst*
Laurence Tecott, *Professor*
EMP: 1000 Privately Held
WEB: www.uchastings.edu
SIC: 8062 9411 General medical & surgical hospitals; administration of educational programs;
HQ: University Of California, San Francisco
505 Parnassus Ave
San Francisco CA 94143
415 476-9000

(P-21997)
UNIVERSITY CAL SAN FRANCISCO
Also Called: Ucsf Medical Center At Mt Zion
1600 Divisadero St, San Francisco (94143-3010)
PHONE.................................415 567-6600
Fax: 415 885-7395
Mark Laret, *Manager*
Roger Baxter, *Research*
Rodger Liddle, *Research*
Art Wong, *Research*
EMP: 360 Privately Held
WEB: www.uchastings.edu
SIC: 8062 8221 9411 General medical & surgical hospitals; university;
HQ: University Of California, San Francisco
505 Parnassus Ave
San Francisco CA 94143
415 476-9000

(P-21998)
UNIVERSITY CALIFORNIA DAVIS
Also Called: Uc Davis Medical Center
2315 Stockton Blvd, Sacramento (95817-2201)
PHONE.................................916 734-2011
Fax: 916 452-2739
Ann Madden Rice, *CEO*
Ray Dougherty, *Ch Radiology*
Alexander Soshnikov, *Vice Chairman*
Amie Smith, *Executive Asst*
Marguerite Cosens, *Admin Asst*
EMP: 7000 Privately Held
WEB: www.ucdavis.edu
SIC: 8062 9411 8221 General medical & surgical hospitals; administration of educational programs; ; university
HQ: University Of California, Davis
1 Shields Ave
Davis CA 95616
530 752-1011

(P-21999)
UNIVERSITY CALIFORNIA DAVIS
Also Called: Medical Centre
4400 V St, Sacramento (95817-1445)
PHONE.................................916 734-3141
Dr William Ellis, *Principal*
Sarah Barnhard, *Pathologist*
Claudia Greco, *Pathologist*
Jason Rockwood, *Manager*
EMP: 3575 Privately Held
WEB: www.ucdavis.edu
SIC: 8062 9411 8221 General medical & surgical hospitals; administration of educational programs; ; university
HQ: University Of California, Davis
1 Shields Ave
Davis CA 95616
530 752-1011

(P-22000)
UNIVERSITY CALIFORNIA DAVIS
Also Called: Uc Davis Medical Center
2450 48th St Ste 2401, Sacramento (95817-1538)
PHONE.................................916 734-2011
Fax: 916 734-7001
Mauda Butte, *Principal*
Madeleine Silva, *Project Mgr*
Mark Carroll, *Asst Director*
Monte Ratzlaff, *Manager*
EMP: 3575 Privately Held
SIC: 8062 General medical & surgical hospitals
HQ: University Of California, Davis
1 Shields Ave
Davis CA 95616
530 752-1011

(P-22001)
UNIVERSITY CALIFORNIA DAVIS
Also Called: Department of Ane
4150 V St Ste 1200, Sacramento (95817-1460)
PHONE.................................916 734-5113
Karen Anderson, *Manager*
Pia Anette Hof, *Anesthesiology*
Anna Kowslczyk, *Anesthesiology*
Brian L Pitts, *Anesthesiology*
Anna K Kowalczyk, *Med Doctor*
EMP: 3575 Privately Held
SIC: 8062 General medical & surgical hospitals
HQ: University Of California, Davis
1 Shields Ave
Davis CA 95616
530 752-1011

(P-22002)
UNIVERSITY CALIFORNIA IRVINE
Also Called: Uc Irvine Medical Center
101 The City Dr S, Orange (92868-3201)
PHONE.................................714 456-6011
Fax: 714 456-5690
Mary Piccione, *Exec Dir*
Karen Smith, *Office Mgr*
Keith Beaulieu, *Opers Staff*
Jeffrey Bonadio, *Pathologist*
Doreen Myers, *Physician Asst*
EMP: 3000 Privately Held
WEB: www.com.uci.edu
SIC: 8062 8221 9431 General medical & surgical hospitals; university;
HQ: University Of California, Irvine
510 Aldrich Hall
Irvine CA 92697
949 824-8343

(P-22003)
UNIVERSITY CALIFORNIA IRVINE
Also Called: Irvine Medical Center
200 S Manchester Ave # 400, Orange (92868-3220)
PHONE.................................714 456-5558
Joy Grosse, *Director*
Mike Tran, *Programmer Anys*
EMP: 4000 Privately Held
WEB: www.com.uci.edu
SIC: 8062 9411 8221 General medical & surgical hospitals; administration of educational programs; ; university

HQ: University Of California, Irvine
510 Aldrich Hall
Irvine CA 92697
949 824-8343

(P-22004)
UNIVERSITY SOUTHERN CALIFORNIA
Also Called: Intergraded Media Systems Ctr
3737 Watt Way Fl 3, Los Angeles (90089-0096)
PHONE..................213 740-9790
Adam Powell, *Branch Mgr*
Lev Vaikhanski, *Professor*
Nune K Abraamyan, *Nurse Practr*
EMP: 200
SALES (corp-wide): 4.7B **Privately Held**
WEB: www.usc.edu
SIC: **8062** 8221 Hospital, medical school affiliation; university
PA: University Of Southern California
3720 S Flower St Fl 3
Los Angeles CA 90007
213 740-7762

(P-22005)
UNIVERSITY SOUTHERN CALIFORNIA
Also Called: Usc University Hospital
1500 San Pablo St, Los Angeles (90033-5313)
PHONE..................323 442-8500
Fax: 323 442-8909
Paul Vivano, *Director*
Leslie A Saxon,
Joy Smith,
Claire L Templeman, *Ch OB/GYN*
Edward G Grant, *Ch Radiology*
EMP: 875
SALES (corp-wide): 4.7B **Privately Held**
WEB: www.tenenthealth.com
SIC: **8062** 8011 General medical & surgical hospitals; offices & clinics of medical doctors
PA: University Of Southern California
3720 S Flower St Fl 3
Los Angeles CA 90007
213 740-7762

(P-22006)
US DEPT OF THE AIR FORCE
Also Called: 9th Medical Group
15301 Warren Shingle Rd, Marysville (95903-1907)
PHONE..................530 634-4839
Fax: 530 634-4836
Melvin Antonio, *Branch Mgr*
EMP: 400 **Publicly Held**
WEB: www.af.mil
SIC: **8062** 9711 General medical & surgical hospitals; Air Force;
HQ: United States Department Of The Air Force
1000 Air Force Pentagon
Washington DC 20330
703 545-6700

(P-22007)
USC CARE MEDICAL GROUP INC
Also Called: Cardiology Department
1510 San Pablo St Ste 649, Los Angeles (90033-5404)
PHONE..................323 442-5100
Varma Rohit, *President*
Vivian MO, *CEO*
Angel Padilla, *Office Mgr*
Glenn Ehresmann, *Rheumtlgy Spec*
Nahid Hamoui, *Med Doctor*
EMP: 80 **EST**: 1995
SALES (est): 6.5MM **Privately Held**
SIC: **8062** Hospital, medical school affiliated with nursing & residency

(P-22008)
USC VERDUGO HILLS HOSPITAL LLC
1812 Verdugo Blvd, Glendale (91208-1407)
PHONE..................818 790-7100
Paul Craig, *CEO*
Hack Lash, *CFO*
Thomas Jackiewicz,
Cynthia Trousdale,
Debbie Walsh,
EMP: 750
SQ FT: 45,000
SALES (est): 61.4MM
SALES (corp-wide): 4.7B **Privately Held**
SIC: **8062** Hospital, affiliated with AMA residency
PA: University Of Southern California
3720 S Flower St Fl 3
Los Angeles CA 90007
213 740-7762

(P-22009)
VALLEY HOSPITAL MEDICAL CENTER (HQ)
Also Called: Calex
18300 Roscoe Blvd, Northridge (91325-4105)
PHONE..................818 885-8500
Fax: 818 349-6366
Patrick Hawthorne, *President*
John E Glassco, *Ch Pathology*
Stephen Farnum,
Peggy Diller, *Executive*
Linda Tigert, *Risk Mgmt Dir*
EMP: 400
SQ FT: 300,000
SALES (est): 86.7MM
SALES (corp-wide): 7.1B **Privately Held**
WEB: www.northridgemg.com
SIC: **8062** General medical & surgical hospitals
PA: Dignity Health
185 Berry St Ste 300
San Francisco CA 94107
415 438-5500

(P-22010)
VALLEY PRESBYTERIAN HOSPITAL
Also Called: V P H
15107 Vanowen St, Van Nuys (91405-4597)
PHONE..................818 782-6600
Fax: 818 902-3949
Gustavo Valdespino, *CEO*
Tony Desai,
Virginia Napoles, *Sr Corp Ofcr*
Robert C Bills, *Bd of Directors*
Jose Claudio, *Officer*
EMP: 1600
SQ FT: 400,000
SALES: 389.4MM **Privately Held**
SIC: **8062** General medical & surgical hospitals

(P-22011)
VERDUGO HILLS HOSP FOUNDATION (PA)
1812 Verdugo Blvd, Glendale (91208-1407)
PHONE..................818 790-7100
Paul Craig, *CEO*
Edward Hahn,
Ron Reed, *President*
Debbie L Walsh, *President*
Jennifer Berger, *Admin Sec*
EMP: 446
SQ FT: 225,000
SALES (est): 83.4MM **Privately Held**
SIC: **8062** General medical & surgical hospitals

(P-22012)
VERITAS HEALTH SERVICES INC
Also Called: Chino Valley Medical Center
5451 Walnut Ave, Chino (91710-2609)
PHONE..................909 464-8600
Fax: 909 627-1870
Prem Reddy, *CEO*
Irv E Edwards, *President*
Jackie Dominquez, *Admin Asst*
Allan Tucker, *CTO*
Pilar E Guzman, *Controller*
EMP: 600 **EST**: 2000
SALES: 90MM
SALES (corp-wide): 2.6B **Privately Held**
WEB: www.cvmc.com
SIC: **8062** General medical & surgical hospitals
PA: Prime Healthcare Services Inc
3300 E Guasti Rd Ste 300
Ontario CA 91761
909 235-4400

(P-22013)
VERITY HEALTH SYSTEM CAL INC
Also Called: St Francis Medical Center
203 Redwood Shores Pkwy, Redwood City (94065-1198)
PHONE..................310 900-8900
Fax: 626 744-3686
Gerald Kozai, *CEO*
Wj Budai, *Admin Asst*
Matt Liston, *Buyer*
Reid Mecon, *Materials Mgr*
Albert H Hicks, *Director*
EMP: 300
SALES (corp-wide): 225.4MM **Privately Held**
SIC: **8062** General medical & surgical hospitals
PA: Verity Health System Of California, Inc.
203 Redwood Shores Pkwy
Redwood City CA 94065
650 551-6650

(P-22014)
VERITY HEALTH SYSTEM CAL INC
Also Called: Daughter of Charity
2105 Forest Ave, San Jose (95128-1425)
PHONE..................408 947-2762
Robert Curry, *CEO*
Ron Nagata, *Pharmacy Dir*
Lisa Golkar, *Info Tech Dir*
Keegan Duchicela, *Family Practiti*
Amy Watson, *Family Practiti*
EMP: 200
SALES (corp-wide): 225.4MM **Privately Held**
SIC: **8062** General medical & surgical hospitals
PA: Verity Health System Of California, Inc.
203 Redwood Shores Pkwy
Redwood City CA 94065
650 551-6650

(P-22015)
VERITY HEALTH SYSTEM CAL INC
Also Called: Parryroll Department
203 Redwood Shores Pkwy # 700, Redwood City (94065-1198)
PHONE..................650 551-6507
Mark Golan, *Manager*
EMP: 200
SALES (corp-wide): 225.4MM **Privately Held**
SIC: **8062** 8721 General medical & surgical hospitals; payroll accounting service
PA: Verity Health System Of California, Inc.
203 Redwood Shores Pkwy
Redwood City CA 94065
650 551-6650

(P-22016)
VERITY HEALTH SYSTEM CAL INC
9400 N Name Uno, Gilroy (95020-3528)
PHONE..................408 848-2000
Mark Laguna, *Purch Agent*
Amanda Graca, *Director*
EMP: 996
SALES (corp-wide): 225.4MM **Privately Held**
SIC: **8062** General medical & surgical hospitals
PA: Verity Health System Of California, Inc.
203 Redwood Shores Pkwy
Redwood City CA 94065
650 551-6650

(P-22017)
VERITY HEALTH SYSTEM CAL INC
3680 E Imperial Hwy # 306, Lynwood (90262-2659)
PHONE..................310 900-2000
Joan Rollin, *Director*
Trish Baesemann, *Senior VP*
Larry Stahl, *Vice Pres*
Jerry Boden, *Pharmacy Dir*
Carmelita Ybera, *Nursing Mgr*
EMP: 100

SALES (corp-wide): 225.4MM **Privately Held**
WEB: www.chw.edu
SIC: **8062** General medical & surgical hospitals
PA: Verity Health System Of California, Inc.
203 Redwood Shores Pkwy
Redwood City CA 94065
650 551-6650

(P-22018)
VERITY HEALTH SYSTEM CAL INC
Also Called: St. Francis Medical Center
3630 E Imperial Hwy, Lynwood (90262-2609)
PHONE..................650 917-4500
Gerald Kozai, *Branch Mgr*
Laura Kato, *Vice Pres*
Kaushal Tamboli, *CIO*
Benjamin Monroe, *Obstetrician*
Donna Locurto, *Director*
EMP: 760
SALES (corp-wide): 225.4MM **Privately Held**
SIC: **8062** 8011 General medical & surgical hospitals; medical centers
PA: Verity Health System Of California, Inc.
203 Redwood Shores Pkwy
Redwood City CA 94065
650 551-6650

(P-22019)
VETERANS HEALTH ADMINISTRATION
Also Called: VA Hospital
2615 E Clinton Ave, Fresno (93703-2223)
PHONE..................559 225-6100
Fax: 559 228-5369
Rhonda Aday, *CFO*
Jack Shantz, *President*
Patty Almond, *Officer*
Cynthia M Aguilar, *Pharmacy Dir*
Al Perry, *Branch Mgr*
EMP: 961 **Publicly Held**
SIC: **8062** 9451 General medical & surgical hospitals;
HQ: Veterans Health Administration
810 Vermont Ave Nw
Washington DC 20420

(P-22020)
VIBRA HEALTHCARE LLC
1315 Shaw Ave Ste 102, Clovis (93612-3963)
PHONE..................559 325-5601
Scott Mooneyham, *Branch Mgr*
EMP: 71
SALES (corp-wide): 329.7MM **Privately Held**
SIC: **8062** General medical & surgical hospitals
PA: Vibra Healthcare, Llc
4550 Lena Dr
Mechanicsburg PA 17055
717 591-5700

(P-22021)
VIBRA HEALTHCARE LLC
7173 N Sharon Ave, Fresno (93720-3329)
PHONE..................559 436-3600
Mary Jacobson, *Principal*
EMP: 71
SALES (corp-wide): 329.7MM **Privately Held**
SIC: **8062** General medical & surgical hospitals
PA: Vibra Healthcare, Llc
4550 Lena Dr
Mechanicsburg PA 17055
717 591-5700

(P-22022)
VIBRA HEALTHCARE LLC
Also Called: Vibra Hospital of San Diego
555 Washington St, San Diego (92103-2289)
PHONE..................619 260-8300
Meeta Jones, *CEO*
Emily Emmons, *Case Mgmt Dir*
Vic Gajipara, *Pharmacy Dir*
EMP: 141

8062 - General Medical & Surgical Hospitals County (P-22023)

PRODUDUCTS & SERVICES SECTION

SALES (corp-wide): 329.7MM **Privately Held**
WEB: www.vibrahealthcare.com
SIC: **8062** 8069 8322 General medical & surgical hospitals; specialty hospitals, except psychiatric; rehabilitation services
PA: Vibra Healthcare, Llc
4550 Lena Dr
Mechanicsburg PA 17055
717 591-5700

(P-22023)
VIBRA HOSP SAN BERNARDINO LLC
Also Called: Ballard Rehabilitation Hosp
1760 W 16th St, San Bernardino (92411-1160)
PHONE...................909 473-1233
Brad Hollinger, *Mng Member*
Clint Fegan, *CFO*
Jonathan Silver, *Controller*
EMP: 185
SQ FT: 55,000
SALES: 22MM **Privately Held**
SIC: **8062** General medical & surgical hospitals

(P-22024)
VIBRA HOSPITAL SAN DIEGO LLC
555 Washington St, San Diego (92103-2289)
PHONE...................619 260-8300
Martha Heubach, *CEO*
Mike Gonzales, *CFO*
Brian Deitz, *Pharmacy Dir*
Allison Moreno, *Human Resources*
Allison Moreno-Suares, *Human Resources*
EMP: 57
SALES (est): 9.7MM **Privately Held**
SIC: **8062** General medical & surgical hospitals

(P-22025)
VISTA SPECIALTY HOSP CAL LP
Also Called: Vista Hospital San Gabriel Vly
14148 Francisquito Ave, Baldwin Park (91706-6120)
PHONE...................626 388-2700
Marc C Ferrell, *Partner*
Vartan J Hovsepian, *Senior VP*
Ron Kupsertein, *Administration*
EMP: 200
SQ FT: 44,400
SALES (est): 9.2MM **Privately Held**
WEB: www.vistahealthcare.net
SIC: **8062** General medical & surgical hospitals

(P-22026)
WARRACK CORPORATION
Also Called: Warrack Hospital
3033 Cleveland Ave, Santa Rosa (95403-2126)
PHONE...................707 523-7271
Fax: 707 523-7106
Dale Iversen, *CEO*
Stephen Pinks, *Ch Pathology*
Jerome Morgan,
Scott Lomax MD, *Ch of Bd*
Robert Huntington, *Treasurer*
EMP: 265
SQ FT: 42,000
SALES (est): 8.1MM
SALES (corp-wide): 11B **Privately Held**
WEB: www.sutterhealth.org
SIC: **8062** 8011 General medical & surgical hospitals; offices & clinics of medical doctors
PA: Sutter Health
2200 River Plaza Dr
Sacramento CA 95833
916 733-8800

(P-22027)
WASHINGTON HOSP HEALTHCARE SYS
2000 Mowry Ave, Fremont (94538-1716)
PHONE...................510 797-3342
Fax: 510 745-6407
Nancy Farber, *CEO*
Chris Henry, *CFO*
Cathy Messman, *Treasurer*
Macaria C Meyer, *Bd of Directors*
Minh-Thu Dennen, *Pharmacy Dir*
EMP: 1600

SQ FT: 250,000
SALES (est): 205.1MM **Privately Held**
SIC: **8062** General medical & surgical hospitals

(P-22028)
WATSONVILLE COMMUNITY HOSPITAL
75 Neilson St, Watsonville (95076-2468)
PHONE...................831 724-4741
Fax: 831 761-1524
Jeff Borenstein, *CEO*
John Nacol, *VP Finance*
Matko Vranjes, *Facilities Mgr*
Inga Quillama, *Nurse*
Ellen Jones,
EMP: 650
SALES (est): 97.7MM
SALES (corp-wide): 22.5B **Publicly Held**
WEB: www.chs.net
SIC: **8062** General medical & surgical hospitals
PA: Community Health Systems, Inc.
4000 Meridian Blvd
Franklin TN 37067
615 465-7000

(P-22029)
WEST SIDE DISTRICT HOSPITAL
Also Called: Skilled Nursing Facility
110 E North St, Taft (93268-3606)
PHONE...................805 763-4211
Fax: 661 763-5641
Morgan Clayton, *Ch of Bd*
John Ruffner, *Administration*
EMP: 130
SQ FT: 30,000
SALES: 7.2MM **Privately Held**
WEB: www.chw.com
SIC: **8062** 8051 8011 General medical & surgical hospitals; skilled nursing care facilities; offices & clinics of medical doctors

(P-22030)
WESTERN MEDICAL CENTER AUX (HQ)
Also Called: Western Med Center-Santa Ana
1301 N Tustin Ave, Santa Ana (92705-8619)
PHONE...................714 835-3555
Fax: 714 953-4599
Dan Brothman, *CEO*
Patricia Stites, *CEO*
Luci Miller, *Administration*
Janet Haynes, *Food Svc Dir*
EMP: 200
SALES (est): 137.9MM
SALES (corp-wide): 449.3MM **Privately Held**
WEB: www.westernmedanaheim.com
SIC: **8062** General medical & surgical hospitals
PA: Kpc Healthcare, Inc.
1301 N Tustin Ave
Santa Ana CA 92705
714 953-3652

(P-22031)
WHITE MEMORIAL MEDICAL CENTER (HQ)
Also Called: ADVENTIST HEALTH SYSTEM
1720 E Cesar E Chavez Ave, Los Angeles (90033-2414)
PHONE...................323 268-5000
Fax: 213 881-8601
Beth D Zachary, *CEO*
Mark J Newmyer, *President*
John G Raffoul, *CEO*
Bill Wing, *COO*
Terri Day, *CFO*
EMP: 1200
SQ FT: 454,000
SALES: 417.6MM
SALES (corp-wide): 251.4MM **Privately Held**
WEB: www.whitememorial.com
SIC: **8062** General medical & surgical hospitals
PA: Adventist Health System/West
2100 Douglas Blvd
Roseville CA 95661
916 781-2000

(P-22032)
WHITTIER HOSPITAL MED CTR INC
9080 Colima Rd, Whittier (90605-1600)
PHONE...................562 945-3561
Richard Castro, *CEO*
Tedd Kim, *Business Dir*
Thomas J Phillips, *Orthopedist*
Bay Ngo, *Radiology*
Jeffrey W Kronson, *Vascular Srgry*
EMP: 180
SQ FT: 144,000
SALES (est): 37.2MM
SALES (corp-wide): 615.4MM **Privately Held**
SIC: **8062** General medical & surgical hospitals
PA: Ahmc Healthcare Inc.
1000 S Fremont Ave Unit 6
Alhambra CA 91803
626 943-7526

(P-22033)
WILLITS HOSPITAL INC
Also Called: HOWARD, FRANK R MEMORIAL HOSPI
1 Madrone St, Willits (95490-4225)
PHONE...................707 459-6801
Fax: 707 459-9486
Rich Bockmann, *CEO*
Richard Nessif,
Carlton Jacobsen, *CFO*
Karen Scott, *Vice Pres*
Karen Scott Vpres, *Vice Pres*
EMP: 283
SQ FT: 27,000
SALES: 50.7MM **Privately Held**
WEB: www.howardhospital.com
SIC: **8062** General medical & surgical hospitals

(P-22034)
WOODLAND HEALTHCARE
2660 W Covell Blvd, Davis (95616-5645)
PHONE...................530 756-2364
Fax: 530 756-5817
Kevin Mould, *Branch Mgr*
Philip M Laughlin MD, *Med Doctor*
Philip Laughlin, *Med Doctor*
Kevin S Mould MD, *Med Doctor*
EMP: 63
SALES (corp-wide): 7.1B **Privately Held**
SIC: **8062** 8011 General medical & surgical hospitals; offices & clinics of medical doctors
HQ: Woodland Healthcare
1325 Cottonwood St
Woodland CA 95695
530 662-3961

(P-22035)
WOODLAND HEALTHCARE
1207 Fairchild Ct, Woodland (95695-4321)
PHONE...................530 668-2600
Fax: 530 661-0880
Bill Hunt, *Principal*
Eduardo O Zapata Do, *Osteopathy*
Mark P Ewens MD, *Med Doctor*
George W Jordan, *Med Doctor*
Pamela O Petersen MD, *Med Doctor*
EMP: 150
SALES (corp-wide): 7.1B **Privately Held**
WEB: www.woodlandhealthcare.com
SIC: **8062** 8011 General medical & surgical hospitals; offices & clinics of medical doctors
HQ: Woodland Healthcare
1325 Cottonwood St
Woodland CA 95695
530 662-3961

8063 Psychiatric Hospitals

(P-22036)
7TH AVENUE CENTER LLC
1171 7th Ave, Santa Cruz (95062-2714)
PHONE...................831 476-1700
Fax: 831 476-1582
Ann Butler,
Donald Moody, *Exec Dir*
Tami Toop, *Office Mgr*
Kathy Curtin, *Technology*
Diana Cornell, *Bookkeeper*
EMP: 92

SALES: 4.3MM **Privately Held**
WEB: www.insuranceneighborhood.com
SIC: **8063** 8361 8011 Psychiatric hospitals; residential care; offices & clinics of medical doctors

(P-22037)
ALTA HOLLYWOOD COMMUNITY HSPTL
14433 Emelita St, Van Nuys (91401-4213)
PHONE...................818 787-1511
Irving Loube, *President*
Claude Lowen, *Corp Secy*
EMP: 115
SQ FT: 34,192
SALES (est): 5.4MM **Privately Held**
SIC: **8063** Psychiatric hospitals

(P-22038)
AURORA BEHAVIORAL HEALTH
1287 Fulton Rd, Santa Rosa (95401-4923)
PHONE...................707 800-7700
Kenneth Meibert, *CEO*
EMP: 75 **EST**: 2000
SQ FT: 50,000
SALES (est): 4.7MM
SALES (corp-wide): 3.5B **Publicly Held**
SIC: **8063** Psychiatric hospitals
HQ: Aurora Behavioral Healthcare Llc
4238 Green River Rd
Corona CA 92880
951 549-8032

(P-22039)
AURORA BEHAVIORAL HEALTH CARE
Also Called: Aurora San Diego
11878 Avenue Of Industry, San Diego (92128-3423)
PHONE...................858 487-3200
Fax: 858 674-4491
Jim Plummer, *CEO*
Jane Jones, *CFO*
John Phillips, *CFO*
Veronica Herrera, *Executive*
Michael Ross, *Pharmacy Dir*
EMP: 150
SQ FT: 50,000
SALES (est): 18.9MM
SALES (corp-wide): 3.5B **Publicly Held**
WEB: www.aurorabehavioral.com
SIC: **8063** 8069 Psychiatric hospitals; drug addiction rehabilitation hospital
PA: Magellan Health, Inc.
4800 N Scottsdale Rd
Scottsdale AZ 85251
602 572-6050

(P-22040)
AURORA LAS ENCINAS LLC
Also Called: Aurora Las Encinas Hospital
2900 E Del Mar Blvd, Pasadena (91107-4375)
PHONE...................626 356-2500
Fax: 626 356-2776
James Wilcox,
Pual Smith, *CFO*
Ariane Loera, *Admin Asst*
Joyce Vega, *Administration*
Marie Sweetman, *Accountant*
EMP: 236
SQ FT: 132,000
SALES (est): 28.2MM **Publicly Held**
WEB: www.lasencinashospital.com
SIC: **8063** 8069 Hospital for the mentally ill; alcoholism rehabilitation hospital
HQ: Hca Inc.
1 Park Plz
Nashville TN 37203
615 344-9551

(P-22041)
BAYVIEW HOSPITAL AND MENTAL
330 Moss St, Chula Vista (91911-2005)
PHONE...................619 426-6311
Fax: 619 585-4525
Robert Bourseau, *Principal*
Janet Caceres, *CFO*
David Clingo, *CFO*
Sherilyn Fagan, *Infect Cntl Dir*
Gemma Rama-Banaag, *Ch Nursing Ofcr*
EMP: 250
SALES (est): 16.3MM **Privately Held**
SIC: **8063** Psychiatric hospitals

PRODUCTS & SERVICES SECTION
8063 - Psychiatric Hospitals County (P-22062)

(P-22042)
BEACON HEALTHCARE SERVICES
Also Called: Newport Bay Hospital
1501 E 16th St, Newport Beach (92663-5924)
PHONE....................949 650-9750
James E Parkhurst, *President*
EMP: 60
SALES: 10.3MM **Privately Held**
WEB: www.newportbayhospital.com
SIC: 8063 Psychiatric hospitals

(P-22043)
BEHAVIORAL H BAKERSFIELD
5201 White Ln, Bakersfield (93309-6200)
PHONE....................661 398-1800
Ganesh Acharya, *CEO*
EMP: 235
SALES (est): 726.7K **Privately Held**
SIC: 8063 8011 Psychiatric hospitals; medical centers

(P-22044)
BEHAVIORAL HEALTH RESOURCES
Also Called: KNOLLWOOD PSYCHIATRIC CENTER
5900 Brockton Ave, Riverside (92506-1862)
PHONE....................951 275-8400
Fax: 951 275-8411
Robert B Summerour, *President*
Craig Pulsipher, *Food Svc Dir*
Mercedese Estrada, *Director*
Edwin Peng, *Director*
EMP: 175
SALES: 7MM **Privately Held**
SIC: 8063 Psychiatric hospitals

(P-22045)
BH-SD OPCO LLC
7050 Parkway Dr, La Mesa (91942-1535)
PHONE....................619 465-4411
Patrick Ziemer, *CEO*
Chad Engbrecht, *CFO*
James Adamson,
EMP: 99 EST: 2014
SALES (est): 1.4MM **Privately Held**
SIC: 8063 Psychiatric hospitals

(P-22046)
CALIFRNIA DEPT STATE HOSPITALS
Also Called: Coalinga State Hospital
24511 W Jayne Ave, Coalinga (93210-9503)
P.O. Box 5000 (93210-5000)
PHONE....................559 935-4300
Tom Voss, *Director*
EMP: 300 **Privately Held**
SIC: 8063 9431 Psychiatric hospitals; mental health agency administration, government;
HQ: California Department Of State Hospitals
1600 9th St Ste 120
Sacramento CA 95814
916 654-3890

(P-22047)
CALIFRNIA DEPT STATE HOSPITALS
Also Called: Fairview Developmental Center
2501 Harbor Blvd, Costa Mesa (92626-6143)
PHONE....................714 957-5000
Fax: 714 668-7685
Michael Hatton, *Principal*
Robin Lemonds, *Info Tech Mgr*
Lilia Tan-Figueroa, *Plant Mgr*
EMP: 1500 **Privately Held**
SIC: 8063 9431 Hospital for the mentally ill; mental health agency administration, government;
HQ: California Department Of State Hospitals
1600 9th St Ste 120
Sacramento CA 95814
916 654-3890

(P-22048)
CALIFORNIA DEPT STATE HOSPITALS
Also Called: NAPA State Hospital
2100 Napa Vallejo Hwy, NAPA (94558-6234)
PHONE....................707 253-5000
Fax: 707 253-5315
Sidney Herndon, *Branch Mgr*
Tanya Cinq-Mars, *Office Admin*
Cindy Black, *Admin Asst*
Melkamu Habtemariam, *Info Tech Mgr*
Thomas Nordahl, *Engineer*
EMP: 2500 **Privately Held**
SIC: 8063 9431 8361 Hospital for the mentally ill; mental health agency administration, government; ; residential care
HQ: California Department Of State Hospitals
1600 9th St Ste 120
Sacramento CA 95814
916 654-3890

(P-22049)
CALIFRNIA DEPT STATE HOSPITALS
Also Called: Patton State Hospital
3102 E Highland Ave, Patton (92369-7813)
PHONE....................909 425-7000
Fax: 909 425-7151
Bruce Parks, *Director*
Janine Merlo, *Info Tech Mgr*
Winston Offil, *Opers Mgr*
Huy La, *Pharmacist*
Hong Nguyen, *Pharmacist*
EMP: 2000 **Privately Held**
SIC: 8063 9431 Hospital for the mentally ill; mental health agency administration, government;
HQ: California Department Of State Hospitals
1600 9th St Ste 120
Sacramento CA 95814
916 654-3890

(P-22050)
CALIFRNIA DEPT STATE HOSPITALS
Also Called: Atascadero State Hospital
10333 El Camino Real, Atascadero (93422-5808)
P.O. Box 7001 (93423-7001)
PHONE....................805 468-2000
Fax: 805 466-6011
John De Morales, *Branch Mgr*
Phil Grauer, *Lab Dir*
Susan Cahill, *Office Mgr*
John J Consoli, *Office Mgr*
Linda Summers, *Administration*
EMP: 1600 **Privately Held**
SIC: 8063 9431 8062 Hospital for the mentally ill; mental health agency administration, government; ; general medical & surgical hospitals
HQ: California Department Of State Hospitals
1600 9th St Ste 120
Sacramento CA 95814
916 654-3890

(P-22051)
CALIFRONIA DEPARTMENT OF STATE
10333 El Camino Real, Atascadero (93422-5808)
PHONE....................805 468-2501
Peter Sotello,
Christopher Stuiber, *Partner*
Faith Jewell,
EMP: 1953 EST: 1954
SALES (est): 42.4MM **Privately Held**
SIC: 8063 Psychiatric hospitals

(P-22052)
CANYON RIDGE HOSPITAL INC
Also Called: UHS
5353 G St, Chino (91710-5250)
PHONE....................909 590-3700
Fax: 909 590-4019
Peggy Minnick, *CEO*
Joseph Catalano, *Pharmacy Dir*
Laura Fredlow, *Personnel Exec*
Kim McGinty, *Director*
Ed Nodler, *Director*
EMP: 150
SALES (est): 23.5MM
SALES (corp-wide): 9B **Publicly Held**
WEB: www.intermountainhospital.com
SIC: 8063 8093 Hospital for the mentally ill; mental health clinic, outpatient
HQ: Psychiatric Solutions, Inc.
6640 Carothers Pkwy # 500
Franklin TN 37067
615 312-5700

(P-22053)
CHARTER BEHAVIORAL HEALTH SYST
Also Called: Charter Oak Hospital
1161 E Covina Blvd, Covina (91724-1523)
PHONE....................626 966-1632
Fax: 626 915-5902
Todd Smith, *CEO*
Sheila Cordova, *COO*
Janet Ray Perkins, *Officer*
Erin Boyd, *Business Dir*
Kristal Morales, *Asst Admin*
EMP: 100
SALES (est): 8.6MM **Privately Held**
SIC: 8063 Psychiatric hospitals

(P-22054)
CHLB LLC
Also Called: College Medical Center
2776 Pacific Ave, Long Beach (90806-2613)
PHONE....................562 997-2000
Joe Avelino, *CEO*
Roderick Bell, *CFO*
EMP: 84
SALES (est): 15.2MM **Privately Held**
SIC: 8063 Psychiatric hospitals
PA: College Health Enterprises
11627 Telg Rd Ste 200
Santa Fe Springs CA 90670
562 923-9449

(P-22055)
COLLEGE HOSPITAL INC (PA)
Also Called: College Hospital Cerritos
10802 College Pl, Cerritos (90703-1579)
PHONE....................562 924-9581
Fax: 562 865-1624
Stephen A Witt, *President*
Bessie Weiss, *Corp Secy*
Theresa Berkin, *Ch Nursing Ofcr*
Martha Leija, *Administration*
Aida Estrada, *CIO*
EMP: 300
SQ FT: 60,000
SALES: 71.1MM **Privately Held**
WEB: www.collegehospitals.com
SIC: 8063 Hospital for the mentally ill

(P-22056)
COUNTY OF EL DORADO
Also Called: Psychiatric Health Facility
935b Spring St, Placerville (95667-4523)
PHONE....................530 621-6210
Kathlen Burne, *Branch Mgr*
Suzanne Cochran, *Patnt Acct Dir*
Rob Evans, *Program Mgr*
Cheree Haffner, *Social Worker*
Donald Ashton, *Director*
EMP: 76 **Privately Held**
WEB: www.filmtahoe.com
SIC: 8063 9111 Psychiatric hospitals; executive offices
PA: County Of El Dorado
330 Fair Ln
Placerville CA 95667
530 621-5830

(P-22057)
COUNTY OF SAN DIEGO
Also Called: Health & Human Services
3853 Rosecrans St, San Diego (92110-3115)
PHONE....................619 692-8200
Karen Hogan, *CEO*
Patt Zamary, *Executive*
Michael Drake, *Webmaster*
Pat Espejo, *Human Res Dir*
Ronald Higley, *Purchasing*
EMP: 350 **Privately Held**
WEB: www.sdicc.org
SIC: 8063 9431 Psychiatric hospitals; administration of public health programs;
PA: County Of San Diego
1600 Pacific Hwy Ste 209
San Diego CA 92101
619 531-5880

(P-22058)
COUNTY OF SONOMA
Department Mental Health Svcs
3322 Chanate Rd, Santa Rosa (95404-1708)
PHONE....................707 565-4850
Marcus Crosdowny, *Director*
Nathan Thuma, *Med Doctor*
Steve Parsons, *Director*
EMP: 63 **Privately Held**
WEB: www.sonomacompost.com
SIC: 8063 Hospital for the mentally ill
PA: County Of Sonoma
585 Fiscal Dr 100
Santa Rosa CA 95403
707 565-2431

(P-22059)
CRESTWOOD BEHAVIORAL HLTH INC
Also Called: 112 Modesto Snf
1400 Celeste Dr, Modesto (95355-5041)
PHONE....................209 526-8050
Fax: 209 526-0652
Lauri Blaufus, *Branch Mgr*
Linda Trokey, *Financial Exec*
Michael Brodie, *Director*
EMP: 200
SQ FT: 56,538
SALES (corp-wide): 148MM **Privately Held**
WEB: www.dreamcatch.us
SIC: 8063 Psychiatric hospitals
PA: Crestwood Behavioral Health, Inc.
520 Capitol Mall Ste 800
Sacramento CA 95814
510 651-1244

(P-22060)
CRESTWOOD BEHAVIORAL HLTH INC
Also Called: 106 Sacramento Mhrc
2600 Stockton Blvd, Sacramento (95817-2210)
PHONE....................916 452-1431
Fax: 916 457-9263
Cindy Mataraso, *Administration*
B Rowlett, *Manager*
EMP: 120
SALES (corp-wide): 148MM **Privately Held**
WEB: www.dreamcatch.us
SIC: 8063 8361 Hospital for the mentally ill; residential care
PA: Crestwood Behavioral Health, Inc.
520 Capitol Mall Ste 800
Sacramento CA 95814
510 651-1244

(P-22061)
CRESTWOOD BEHAVIORAL HLTH INC
Also Called: 115 Bakersfield Mhrc
6700 Eucalyptus Dr Ste A, Bakersfield (93306-6076)
PHONE....................661 363-8127
Fax: 661 363-9124
Martha Crawford, *Director*
Deleon Delphina, *Exec Dir*
EMP: 75
SALES (corp-wide): 148MM **Privately Held**
WEB: www.crestwoodbehavioralhealth.com
SIC: 8063 8011 Psychiatric hospitals; psychiatric clinic
PA: Crestwood Behavioral Health, Inc.
520 Capitol Mall Ste 800
Sacramento CA 95814
510 651-1244

(P-22062)
CRESTWOOD BEHAVIORAL HLTH INC
Also Called: 145 Fresno Bridge
153 N U St, Fresno (93701-2438)
PHONE....................559 445-9094
Giang T Nguyen, *Principal*
Patricia Blum, *Vice Pres*
EMP: 89

SALES (corp-wide): 135.6MM **Privately Held**
SIC: **8063** Psychiatric hospitals
PA: Crestwood Behavioral Health, Inc.
520 Capitol Mall Ste 800
Sacramento CA 95814
510 651-1244

(P-22063)
CRESTWOOD BEHAVIORAL HLTH INC
Also Called: Our House
2201 Tuolumne St, Vallejo (94589-2524)
PHONE..........................707 558-1777
Fax: 707 558-1770
Gail McDonald, *Branch Mgr*
Angel Casanova, *VP Finance*
Susan Kachuck, *Mktg Dir*
Carleton Gillenwater, *Marketing Mgr*
EMP: 55
SALES (corp-wide): 135.6MM **Privately Held**
SIC: **8063** 8011 Psychiatric hospitals; offices & clinics of medical doctors
PA: Crestwood Behavioral Health, Inc.
520 Capitol Mall Ste 800
Sacramento CA 95814
510 651-1244

(P-22064)
CRESTWOOD BEHAVIORAL HLTH INC
Also Called: 111 Vallejo IMD
115 Oddstad Dr, Vallejo (94589-2520)
PHONE..........................707 552-0215
Fax: 707 553-2161
Minda Bunggay, *Administration*
EMP: 89
SALES (corp-wide): 135.6MM **Privately Held**
SIC: **8063** Psychiatric hospitals
PA: Crestwood Behavioral Health, Inc.
520 Capitol Mall Ste 800
Sacramento CA 95814
510 651-1244

(P-22065)
CRESTWOOD BEHAVIORAL HLTH INC
Also Called: 153 American River PHF
4741 Engle Rd, Carmichael, (95608-2223)
PHONE..........................916 977-0949
Betsy Donovan, *Administration*
EMP: 89
SALES (corp-wide): 135.6MM **Privately Held**
SIC: **8063** Psychiatric hospitals
PA: Crestwood Behavioral Health, Inc.
520 Capitol Mall Ste 800
Sacramento CA 95814
510 651-1244

(P-22066)
CRESTWOOD BEHAVIORAL HLTH INC
Also Called: 144 Pleasant Hill The Pathway
550 Patterson Blvd, Pleasant Hill (94523-4155)
PHONE..........................925 938-8050
Fax: 925 938-8040
Cynthia Mathraso, *Branch Mgr*
EMP: 89
SALES (corp-wide): 135.6MM **Privately Held**
SIC: **8063** Psychiatric hospitals
PA: Crestwood Behavioral Health, Inc.
520 Capitol Mall Ste 800
Sacramento CA 95814
510 651-1244

(P-22067)
DEANCO HEALTHCARE LLC
Also Called: Mission Community Hospital
14850 Roscoe Blvd, Panorama City (91402-4618)
PHONE..........................818 787-2222
James Theiring,
Joe Magpantay, *Lab Dir*
Chelan Maierhoffer, *Executive Asst*
Erick Rivers, *Info Tech Dir*
Ishmael Silla, *Info Tech Mgr*
EMP: 700
SALES (est): 103.4MM **Privately Held**
SIC: **8063** Psychiatric hospitals

(P-22068)
DEL AMO HOSPITAL INC
23700 Camino Del Sol, Torrance (90505-5000)
PHONE..........................310 530-1151
Fax: 310 539-5061
Lisa Moncen, *CEO*
Alan B Miller, *Ch of Bd*
Kirk E Gorman, *Treasurer*
Sidney Miller, *Exec VP*
Jane Tinio, *Administration*
EMP: 300
SQ FT: 88,000
SALES: 37.7MM
SALES (corp-wide): 9B **Publicly Held**
WEB: www.uhsinc.com
SIC: **8063** Psychiatric hospitals
PA: Universal Health Services, Inc.
367 S Gulph Rd
King Of Prussia PA 19406
610 768-3300

(P-22069)
GATEWAYS HOSP MENTAL HLTH CTR
340 N Madison Ave, Los Angeles (90004-3504)
PHONE..........................323 644-2026
Mara Pelsman, *Branch Mgr*
EMP: 92
SALES (corp-wide): 27.4MM **Privately Held**
SIC: **8063** Hospital for the mentally ill
PA: Gateway's Hospital And Mental Health Center Inc
1891 Effie St
Los Angeles CA 90026
323 644-2000

(P-22070)
GATEWAYS HOSP MENTAL HLTH CTR (PA)
1891 Effie St, Los Angeles (90026-1711)
PHONE..........................323 644-2000
Fax: 323 666-1417
Mara Pelsman, *CEO*
Jeff Emery, *CFO*
Hal Espinosa, *Treasurer*
Anil Churana, *Lab Dir*
Brett Morana, *Branch Mgr*
EMP: 150 EST: 1953
SQ FT: 40,000
SALES: 27.4MM **Privately Held**
WEB: www.gatewayshospital.org
SIC: **8063** 8093 Hospital for the mentally ill; mental health clinic, outpatient

(P-22071)
GOLDEN STATE HEALTH CTRS INC
Also Called: Sylmar Hlth Rehabilitation Ctr
12220 Foothill Blvd, Sylmar (91342-6001)
PHONE..........................818 834-5082
Cherlyn Hawkins, *Manager*
Jorge Hernandez, *Executive*
Michael Freeman, *Manager*
EMP: 250
SALES (corp-wide): 62.1MM **Privately Held**
WEB: www.goldenstatehealth.com
SIC: **8063** 8069 Psychiatric hospitals; specialty hospitals, except psychiatric
PA: Golden State Health Centers, Inc.
13347 Ventura Blvd
Sherman Oaks CA 91423
818 385-3200

(P-22072)
GOOD SAMARITAN HOSPITAL
Also Called: Good Samaritan Hosp Southwest
5201 White Ln, Bakersfield (93309-6200)
PHONE..........................661 398-1800
Deirdre Terlaski, *Branch Mgr*
EMP: 134
SALES (corp-wide): 56.3MM **Privately Held**
SIC: **8063** Psychiatric hospitals
PA: Good Samaritan Hospital
901 Olive Dr
Bakersfield CA 93308
661 399-4461

(P-22073)
HELIX HEALTHCARE INC
Also Called: Alvarado Parkway Institute
7050 Parkway Dr, La Mesa (91942-1535)
PHONE..........................619 465-4411
Fax: 619 465-8614
Roy Rodriguez, *CEO*
Robert Sanders, *Shareholder*
Megan Monrgomery -West, *COO*
Chad Engbrecht, *CFO*
Mohammed Bari, *Vice Pres*
EMP: 310
SQ FT: 37,354
SALES (est): 54.9MM **Privately Held**
WEB: www.alvaradoparkwayinstitute.com
SIC: **8063** Psychiatric hospitals

(P-22074)
HILLVIEW MENTAL HEALTH CENTER
12450 Van Nuys Blvd # 200, Pacoima (91331-1391)
PHONE..........................818 363-7813
Fax: 818 896-5069
Eva S McCraven, *President*
Beth Meltzer, *COO*
Carl C Mc Craven, *Treasurer*
Julie E Jones, *Vice Pres*
Beth K Meltzer, *Vice Pres*
EMP: 80
SQ FT: 17,600
SALES: 10.8MM **Privately Held**
SIC: **8063** Hospital for the mentally ill

(P-22075)
JOHN MUIR BEHAVIORAL HLTH CTR
2740 Grant St, Concord (94520-2265)
PHONE..........................925 674-4100
Fax: 925 686-2476
Elizabeth Stallings, *COO*
Arman Danielyan, *Executive*
Donny Deleon, *Engineer*
Nabil Abudayeh, *Cardiology*
Peter D Tamulevich, *Psychiatry*
EMP: 165
SQ FT: 40,000
SALES (est): 17.6MM **Privately Held**
SIC: **8063** 8051 Psychiatric hospitals; skilled nursing care facilities

(P-22076)
KAISER FOUNDATION HOSPITALS
Also Called: Kaiser Mental Health Center
765 W College St, Los Angeles (90012-1181)
PHONE..........................213 580-7200
Fax: 213 580-7220
Kurt Hastings, *Manager*
Margaret Tishler, *Administration*
Eugene Wong, *Pharmacist*
EMP: 200
SQ FT: 66,697
SALES (corp-wide): 27.8B **Privately Held**
WEB: www.kaiserpermanente.org
SIC: **8063** Psychiatric hospitals
HQ: Kaiser Foundation Hospitals Inc
1 Kaiser Plz
Oakland CA 94612
510 271-6611

(P-22077)
KEDREN COMMUNITY HLTH CTR INC (PA)
Also Called: Kedren Acute Psychia Hospit An
4211 Avalon Blvd, Los Angeles (90011-5622)
PHONE..........................323 233-0425
Fax: 323 233-5015
John Griffith, *President*
Robert Lawson, *Treasurer*
Lupe Ross, *Admin Sec*
Maria Dia, *Administration*
Wakelin McNeel, *Research*
EMP: 400
SQ FT: 144,000
SALES: 55.3MM **Privately Held**
WEB: www.kedren.com
SIC: **8063** 8093 Hospital for the mentally ill; specialty outpatient clinics

(P-22078)
KNOLLWOOD PSYCHIATRIC AND CHEM
Also Called: Knollwood Center
5900 Brockton Ave, Riverside (92506-1862)
PHONE..........................951 275-8400
Robert B Summerour, *President*
Byron Defour, *Shareholder*
Raymond Cooper, *CFO*
Rance Leth, *Sls & Mktg Exec*
EMP: 100
SQ FT: 50,000
SALES (est): 6.3MM **Privately Held**
SIC: **8063** Psychiatric hospitals

(P-22079)
LANDMARK MEDICAL SERVICES INC
Also Called: Landmark Medical Center
2030 N Garey Ave, Pomona (91767-2722)
PHONE..........................909 593-2585
Fax: 909 593-4120
Rose Horsman, *President*
Andy Stinton, *Materials Mgr*
EMP: 100
SQ FT: 27,500
SALES (est): 7.6MM **Privately Held**
SIC: **8063** Hospital for the mentally ill

(P-22080)
LINDEN CENTER
Also Called: LINDEN CENTER BUSINESS OFC
812 N Fairfax Ave, Los Angeles (90046-7208)
P.O. Box 57366 (90057-0366)
PHONE..........................213 251-8226
Fax: 213 251-8238
Ronald Ricker, *Exec Dir*
Zoom Bui, *Office Mgr*
Lachaundra Bolton, *Human Res Dir*
EMP: 80
SQ FT: 6,000
SALES: 236.8K **Privately Held**
WEB: www.lindencenter.com
SIC: **8063** Psychiatric hospitals

(P-22081)
MADERA CONVALESCENT HOSPITAL
1255 B St, Merced (95341-6345)
PHONE..........................209 723-8814
Jerry Allgood, *Principal*
EMP: 80
SALES (corp-wide): 5.9MM **Privately Held**
SIC: **8063** Psychiatric hospitals
PA: Madera Convalescent Hospital, Inc
517 S A St
Madera CA 93638
559 673-9228

(P-22082)
MARIN COUNTY SART PROGRAM
Also Called: Canyon Manor Residential Treat
655 Canyon Rd, Novato (94947-4331)
P.O. Box 865 (94948-0865)
PHONE..........................415 892-1628
Donald Harris, *President*
Ben Lan, *Corp Secy*
EMP: 100
SQ FT: 15,000
SALES (est): 3MM **Privately Held**
SIC: **8063** 8361 8069 Hospital for the mentally ill; residential care; specialty hospitals, except psychiatric

(P-22083)
MELISSA SWEITZER PHD INC
Also Called: Behavioral Support Partnership
17853 Santiago Blvd, Villa Park (92861-4113)
PHONE..........................714 974-8727
Melissa Sweitzer, *President*
Richard Sherman, *COO*
EMP: 78
SQ FT: 4,900
SALES: 5MM **Privately Held**
SIC: **8063** Psychiatric hospitals

PRODUCTS & SERVICES SECTION

8063 - Psychiatric Hospitals County (P-22105)

(P-22084)
MENTAL HEALTH CALIFORNIA DEPT
Also Called: Vacaville Psychiatric Program
1600 California Dr, Vacaville (95696)
P.O. Box 2297 (95696-8297)
PHONE.................................707 449-6504
Victor Brewer, Director
EMP: 283 Privately Held
SIC: 8063 9431 Hospital for the mentally ill; mental health agency administration, government;
HQ: California Department Of State Hospitals
1600 9th St Ste 120
Sacramento CA 95814
916 654-3890

(P-22085)
OASIS MENTAL HEALTH TRTMNT CTR
47915 Oasis St, Indio (92201-6950)
PHONE.................................760 863-8609
Mary Jane Gross, President
EMP: 103 EST: 1995
SALES (est): 2.7MM Privately Held
SIC: 8063 Hospital for the mentally ill

(P-22086)
REGENTS OF THE UNIV OF CAL
Also Called: Mount Zion Hospital & Med Ctr
1600 Divisadero St, San Francisco (94143-3010)
PHONE.................................415 476-9000
Fax: 415 476-6800
Martin Diamond, Administration
Sarah Zins, Executive
Daniel Anderson, Lab Dir
Isgard S Hueck, Lab Dir
Ann Rosenthal, Lab Dir
EMP: 64 Privately Held
SIC: 8063 Psychiatric hospitals
HQ: The Regents Of The University Of California
1111 Franklin St Fl 12
Oakland CA 94607
510 987-0700

(P-22087)
RICHMOND AREA MLT-SERVICES INC (PA)
3626 Balboa St, San Francisco (94121-2604)
PHONE.................................415 668-5955
Fax: 415 668-0246
Kavoos Bassiri, CEO
Natalie Quan, Admin Asst
Michael Leyva, Psychologist
Liz Ren, Nurse Practr
Mike Silva, Nurse Practr
EMP: 76
SQ FT: 8,400
SALES: 16.4MM Privately Held
WEB: www.ramsinc.org
SIC: 8063 Hospital for the mentally ill

(P-22088)
RIVER OAK CENTER FOR CHILDREN (PA)
5445 Laurel Hills Dr, Sacramento (95841-3105)
PHONE.................................916 609-5100
Fax: 916 344-3303
Laurie Clothier, CEO
Bonnie Ferreira, Exec Dir
Bruce Kuban, Program Mgr
Alex Melendez, Technology
Terri Wolford, Controller
EMP: 140
SQ FT: 26,000
SALES: 16.1MM Privately Held
SIC: 8063 Psychiatric hospitals

(P-22089)
SAGE BEHAVIOR SERVICES INC
505 E Commonwealth Ave, Fullerton (92832-4009)
P.O. Box 1435n (92836-8435)
PHONE.................................714 773-0077
Tammy Heo, Director
Hazel Tongco, Opers Mgr
Cindy Hebert, Director
Kareem A Khouri, Director
EMP: 60

SQ FT: 6,000
SALES (est): 3MM Privately Held
SIC: 8063 Psychiatric hospitals

(P-22090)
SAN GBRIEL VLY CNVLESCENT HOSP
Also Called: Pennmar
3938 Cogswell Rd, El Monte (91732-2404)
PHONE.................................626 401-1557
Fax: 626 401-0024
Dori Dimla, Administration
Mitchel Kantor, President
Pedro Florescio, Director
Andrew Minyard, Manager
EMP: 65
SALES: 5MM Privately Held
WEB: www.pennmar.com
SIC: 8063 Psychiatric hospitals

(P-22091)
SHARP MEMORIAL HOSPITAL
Also Called: Sharp Mesa Vista Hospital
7850 Vista Hill Ave, San Diego (92123-2717)
PHONE.................................858 278-4110
Fax: 858 278-5920
Carolyn Mason, Director
Perry Jensen, Ch Pathology
Joel Berger,
Philip Diamond, Ch OB/GYN
James Lyon, Ch Radiology
EMP: 190
SALES (corp-wide): 3.4B Privately Held
SIC: 8063 8069 8093 Psychiatric hospitals; substance abuse hospitals; specialty outpatient clinics
HQ: Sharp Memorial Hospital
7901 Frost St
San Diego CA 92123
858 939-3636

(P-22092)
STAR VIEW ADOLESCENT CENTER
4025 W 226th St, Torrance (90505-2340)
PHONE.................................310 373-4556
Fax: 310 373-2826
Mary Jane Gross, President
Barbara O'Connor, Administration
Dana Wyss, Safety Dir
Deidra Kearns, Manager
Joel Nagler, Manager
EMP: 80 EST: 1996
SALES (est): 6MM Privately Held
SIC: 8063 Psychiatric hospitals

(P-22093)
SYLMAR HLTH REHABILITATION CTR
Also Called: Sylmar Hlth Rehabilitation Ctr
12220 Foothill Blvd, Sylmar (91342-6001)
PHONE.................................818 834-5082
Fax: 818 834-5981
Marty Weiss, President
Cherlyn Brintnell, Administration
Michael Freeman, Business Mgr
EMP: 200
SALES (est): 9MM
SALES (corp-wide): 62.1MM Privately Held
WEB: www.goldenstatehealth.com
SIC: 8063 Psychiatric hospitals
PA: Golden State Health Centers, Inc.
13347 Ventura Blvd
Sherman Oaks CA 91423
818 385-3200

(P-22094)
TELECARE CORPORATION
275 Baker St E, Costa Mesa (92626-4566)
PHONE.................................714 361-6760
Anne Bakar, Branch Mgr
EMP: 61
SALES (corp-wide): 126.3MM Privately Held
SIC: 8063 Psychiatric hospitals
PA: Telecare Corporation
1080 Marina Village Pkwy # 100
Alameda CA 94501
510 337-7950

(P-22095)
TELECARE CORPORATION
Also Called: Willow Rock Center
2050 Fairmont Dr, San Leandro (94578-1001)
PHONE.................................510 895-5502
Peter Zucker, Branch Mgr
EMP: 60
SALES (corp-wide): 126.3MM Privately Held
SIC: 8063 Psychiatric hospitals
PA: Telecare Corporation
1080 Marina Village Pkwy # 100
Alameda CA 94501
510 337-7950

(P-22096)
TELECARE CORPORATION
16460 Victor St, Victorville (92395-3918)
PHONE.................................760 245-8837
Clarissa Dodd, Branch Mgr
EMP: 60
SALES (corp-wide): 126.3MM Privately Held
SIC: 8063 8093 Psychiatric hospitals; mental health clinic, outpatient
PA: Telecare Corporation
1080 Marina Village Pkwy # 100
Alameda CA 94501
510 337-7950

(P-22097)
TELECARE CORPORATION
1675 Morena Blvd Ste 100, San Diego (92110-3703)
PHONE.................................619 275-8000
Tara Booth, Administration
EMP: 60
SALES (corp-wide): 126.3MM Privately Held
SIC: 8063 Psychiatric hospitals
PA: Telecare Corporation
1080 Marina Village Pkwy # 100
Alameda CA 94501
510 337-7950

(P-22098)
TELECARE CORPORATION
Also Called: La Casa Mhrc
6060 N Paramount Blvd, Long Beach (90805-3711)
PHONE.................................562 630-8672
Anne Bakar, CEO
Anna Beal,
Philip Lewis, Manager
EMP: 99
SALES (est): 5.8MM
SALES (corp-wide): 126.3MM Privately Held
SIC: 8063 Psychiatric hospitals
PA: Telecare Corporation
1080 Marina Village Pkwy # 100
Alameda CA 94501
510 337-7950

(P-22099)
TELECARE CORPORATION
Also Called: La Casa Mental Health Center
6060 N Paramount Blvd, Long Beach (90805-3711)
PHONE.................................562 634-9534
Fax: 562 634-8354
David Effron, Branch Mgr
Rigo Rosales, Envir Svcs Dir
EMP: 230
SALES (corp-wide): 126.3MM Privately Held
WEB: www.telecarecorp.com
SIC: 8063 8011 Psychiatric hospitals; health maintenance organization
PA: Telecare Corporation
1080 Marina Village Pkwy # 100
Alameda CA 94501
510 337-7950

(P-22100)
TELECARE CORPORATION
Also Called: Garfield Nuerobehavioral Ctr
1451 28th Ave, Oakland (94601-1632)
PHONE.................................510 261-9191
Alonzo Clemens, Director
EMP: 110
SQ FT: 2,117

SALES (corp-wide): 126.3MM Privately Held
WEB: www.telecarecorp.com
SIC: 8063 8011 Psychiatric hospitals; health maintenance organization
PA: Telecare Corporation
1080 Marina Village Pkwy # 100
Alameda CA 94501
510 337-7950

(P-22101)
TELECARE CORPORATION
Also Called: Morton Bakar Center
494 Blossom Way, Hayward (94541-1948)
PHONE.................................510 582-7676
Fax: 510 582-9080
Mary Thrower, Branch Mgr
Raj Prasad, Office Mgr
Kishor Kumar, Director
EMP: 125
SALES (corp-wide): 126.3MM Privately Held
WEB: www.telecarecorp.com
SIC: 8063 8011 Psychiatric hospitals; health maintenance organization
PA: Telecare Corporation
1080 Marina Village Pkwy # 100
Alameda CA 94501
510 337-7950

(P-22102)
TELECARE CORPORATION
Also Called: Villa Fairmont Mental Hlth Ctr
15200 Foothill Blvd, San Leandro (94578-1013)
PHONE.................................510 352-9690
Fax: 510 352-9008
Regina Scott, Manager
Karin Powlen, Director
EMP: 132
SALES (corp-wide): 126.3MM Privately Held
WEB: www.telecarecorp.com
SIC: 8063 8011 Psychiatric hospitals; health maintenance organization
PA: Telecare Corporation
1080 Marina Village Pkwy # 100
Alameda CA 94501
510 337-7950

(P-22103)
TELECARE CORPORATION
Also Called: San Diego Choices
3851 Rosecrans St, San Diego (92110-3115)
PHONE.................................619 692-8225
Scherry Messic, Branch Mgr
EMP: 58
SALES (corp-wide): 126.3MM Privately Held
WEB: www.telecarecorp.com
SIC: 8063 8011 Psychiatric hospitals; health maintenance organization
PA: Telecare Corporation
1080 Marina Village Pkwy # 100
Alameda CA 94501
510 337-7950

(P-22104)
TELECARE CORPORATION
Also Called: Los Posadas Service Center
1756 S Lewis Rd, Camarillo (93012-8520)
PHONE.................................805 383-3669
Tim Kuehnel, Manager
EMP: 55
SALES (corp-wide): 126.3MM Privately Held
WEB: www.telecarecorp.com
SIC: 8063 8011 Psychiatric hospitals; health maintenance organization
PA: Telecare Corporation
1080 Marina Village Pkwy # 100
Alameda CA 94501
510 337-7950

(P-22105)
TELECARE CORPORATION
Also Called: Cordilleras Mental Health Ctr
200 Edmonds Rd, Redwood City (94062-3813)
PHONE.................................650 367-1890
Fax: 650 369-6465
Bill Kruse, Sales & Mktg St
Tien Hsu, Business Mgr
Andy Gossett, Director
Diane Montgomery, Director

8063 - Psychiatric Hospitals County (P-22106)

(P-22106) continued
Robert Mele, *Manager*
EMP: 123
SALES (corp-wide): 126.3MM **Privately Held**
WEB: www.telecarecorp.com
SIC: **8063** 8011 Psychiatric hospitals; health maintenance organization
PA: Telecare Corporation
1080 Marina Village Pkwy # 100
Alameda CA 94501
510 337-7950

(P-22106)
TELECARE CORPORATION
Also Called: Cresta Loma
1080 Marina Village Pkwy # 100, Alameda (94501-1078)
PHONE..................510 337-7950
Becky Clark, *Branch Mgr*
EMP: 101
SQ FT: 44,000
SALES (corp-wide): 126.3MM **Privately Held**
WEB: www.telecarecorp.com
SIC: **8063** 8011 Psychiatric hospitals; health maintenance organization
PA: Telecare Corporation
1080 Marina Village Pkwy # 100
Alameda CA 94501
510 337-7950

(P-22107)
TELECARE CORPORATION
Also Called: La Paz Geropsychiatric Center
8835 Vans St, Paramount (90723-4656)
PHONE..................562 633-5111
Fax: 562 633-1510
Rich Widerynski, *Administration*
Richard Widerynski, *Officer*
David Heffron, *Administration*
Diana Jones, *Data Proc Staff*
Kiana Moten, *Director*
EMP: 150
SALES (corp-wide): 126.3MM **Privately Held**
WEB: www.telecarecorp.com
SIC: **8063** 8011 Psychiatric hospitals; health maintenance organization
PA: Telecare Corporation
1080 Marina Village Pkwy # 100
Alameda CA 94501
510 337-7950

(P-22108)
TELECARE CORPORATION
300 Harbor Blvd E, Belmont (94002-4018)
PHONE..................650 817-9070
Dick Enck, *Manager*
EMP: 60
SALES (corp-wide): 126.3MM **Privately Held**
SIC: **8063** 8621 Psychiatric hospitals; health association
PA: Telecare Corporation
1080 Marina Village Pkwy # 100
Alameda CA 94501
510 337-7950

(P-22109)
TELECARE CORPORATION
Also Called: Heritage Psychiatric Health
2633 E 27th St, Oakland (94601-1912)
PHONE..................510 535-5115
Fax: 510 534-5202
Patty Espeseth, *Branch Mgr*
Stacy Calhoun, *Senior VP*
Robert Quintana, *Manager*
EMP: 120
SALES (corp-wide): 126.3MM **Privately Held**
WEB: www.telecarecorp.com
SIC: **8063** 8011 Psychiatric hospitals; health maintenance organization
PA: Telecare Corporation
1080 Marina Village Pkwy # 100
Alameda CA 94501
510 337-7950

(P-22110)
TENET HEALTHSYSTEM MEDICAL
330 Moss St, Chula Vista (91911-2005)
PHONE..................619 426-6310
EMP: 150
SALES (corp-wide): 11.1B **Publicly Held**
SIC: **8063**

HQ: Tenet Healthsystem Medical, Inc
1445 Ross Ave Ste 1400
Dallas TX 75202
469 893-2000

(P-22111)
VISTA BEHAVIORAL HEALTH INC
Also Called: Pacific Grove Hospital
5900 Brockton Ave, Riverside (92506-1862)
PHONE..................800 992-0901
Elizabeth Homiston, *Bd of Directors*
EMP: 67 EST: 2015
SALES (est): 1.5MM **Publicly Held**
SIC: **8063** Psychiatric hospitals
PA: Acadia Healthcare Company, Inc.
6100 Tower Cir Ste 1000
Franklin TN 37067

8069 Specialty Hospitals, Except Psychiatric

(P-22112)
1125 SIR FRANCIS DRAKE BOULEVA
Also Called: Kentfield Rehabilation Hosp
1125 Sir Francis Drake Bl, Kentfield (94904-1418)
PHONE..................415 456-9680
Fax: 415 485-3507
Brad Hollinger,
Deborah Doherty, *Executive*
Denise Mace, *Radiology Dir*
Osas Nosa-Idahosa, *Pharmacy Dir*
Chris Yarnovich, *Office Mgr*
EMP: 250
SALES (est): 23.4MM **Privately Held**
WEB: www.kentfieldrehab.com
SIC: **8069** Specialty hospitals, except psychiatric

(P-22113)
ALAMITOS-BELMONT REHAB INC
Also Called: Alamitos Blmont Rhbltton Hosp
3901 E 4th St, Long Beach (90814-1632)
PHONE..................562 434-8421
Fax: 562 433-6732
Darian Dahl, *Administration*
Arlene Donato, *Human Res Dir*
Raquel Quijano, *Hlthcr Dir*
Nancy Plichta, *Director*
EMP: 150 EST: 1969
SQ FT: 30,000
SALES: 10.5MM **Privately Held**
WEB: www.alamitosbelmont.com
SIC: **8069** Specialty hospitals, except psychiatric

(P-22114)
ASIAN AMERCN RECOVERY SVCS INC
Also Called: Place Asian Amrcn Rcovery Svcs
1340 Tully Rd Ste 304, San Jose (95122-3055)
PHONE..................408 271-3900
Fax: 408 271-3909
Jeff Mori, *Exec Dir*
Nelson Kobayashi, *Bd of Directors*
Mary Cheung, *Human Res Dir*
Huong Ly, *Case Mgr*
David Mineta, *Manager*
EMP: 125
SALES (corp-wide): 9.7MM **Privately Held**
WEB: www.aars-inc.org
SIC: **8069** Drug addiction rehabilitation hospital
PA: Asian American Recovery Services, Inc.
1115 Mission Rd 2
South San Francisco CA 94080
650 243-4888

(P-22115)
BARLOW GROUP (PA)
Also Called: Barlow Respirtory Hospital
2000 Stadium Way, Los Angeles (90026-2606)
PHONE..................213 250-4200
EMP: 250

SALES: 4.2MM **Privately Held**
SIC: **8069** 7389 8733 Specialty hospitals, except psychiatric; fund raising organizations; medical research

(P-22116)
BARLOW RESPIRATORY HOSPITAL (PA)
2000 Stadium Way, Los Angeles (90026-2606)
PHONE..................213 250-4200
Fax: 213 250-3274
Margaret W Crane, *CEO*
Edward Engesser, *CFO*
Kirk Watson, *Vice Pres*
Shirley Moore, *Admin Asst*
Pao Prasarttong, *Admin Asst*
EMP: 250 EST: 1902
SQ FT: 80,000
SALES: 50.9MM **Privately Held**
SIC: **8069** Specialty hospitals, except psychiatric

(P-22117)
BETTY FORD CENTER (HQ)
39000 Bob Hope Dr, Rancho Mirage (92270-3297)
P.O. Box 1560 (92270-1056)
PHONE..................760 773-4100
Fax: 760 773-4141
Mark Mishek, *President*
James Blaha, *CFO*
Catherine McLeod, *CFO*
Mat Durkan, *Officer*
Betsy Farver, *Officer*
EMP: 250
SALES: 38.3MM
SALES (corp-wide): 164.4MM **Privately Held**
SIC: **8069** Substance abuse hospitals
PA: Hazelden Betty Ford Foundation
15251 Pleasant Valley Rd
Center City MN 55012
651 213-4000

(P-22118)
CALIFORNIA HISPANIC COM
9033 Washington Blvd, Pico Rivera (90660-3839)
PHONE..................562 942-9625
Samuel Campbell, *Director*
EMP: 123
SALES (corp-wide): 11.5MM **Privately Held**
SIC: **8069** Substance abuse hospitals
PA: California Hispanic Commission On Alcohol And Drug Abuse Inc
9942 13th St
Garden Grove CA 92844
916 443-5473

(P-22119)
CAMP RECOVERY CENTERS LP
Also Called: Azure Acres
2264 Green Hill Rd, Sebastopol (95472-9034)
PHONE..................707 823-3385
Fax: 415 823-8972
Shannon Clay, *Human Res Dir*
Kathleen Sylvia, *Exec Dir*
Irenne Magoulas, *Director*
Audrey Mello, *Accounts Mgr*
EMP: 4046 **Privately Held**
WEB: www.azureacres.com
SIC: **8069** 8361 Substance abuse hospitals; rehabilitation center, residential: health care incidental
PA: The Camp Recovery Centers L P
6100 Tower Cir Ste 1000
Franklin TN 37067

(P-22120)
CBEST INC
11620 Wilshire Blvd # 450, Los Angeles (90025-1779)
PHONE..................310 445-2378
Bahador, *President*
EMP: 80
SALES (est): 728K **Privately Held**
SIC: **8069** Children's hospital

(P-22121)
CENTER FOR DSCOVERY ADOLESCENT
4136 Ann Arbor Rd, Lakewood (90712-3817)
PHONE..................562 425-6404
Craig Brown, *Director*
Greg Corbin, *COO*
Jenni Scharf, *Senior VP*
EMP: 50
SALES (est): 790.7K **Privately Held**
SIC: **8069** Drug addiction rehabilitation hospital

(P-22122)
CHILDRENS HEALTHCARE CAL (PA)
455 S Main St, Orange (92868-3835)
PHONE..................714 997-3000
Kimberly C Cripe, *President*
Thomas Brotherton, *COO*
Kerri Ruppert, *CFO*
Maria Minon MD, *Vice Pres*
Cheryl Arnold, *Executive*
EMP: 1500
SALES: 548.7MM **Privately Held**
SIC: **8069** Children's hospital

(P-22123)
CHILDRENS HOSPITAL LOS ANGELES
5000 W Sunset Blvd # 400, Los Angeles (90027-5865)
PHONE..................323 361-2153
Fax: 323 663-1645
Mohammed Bari, *CTO*
EMP: 184
SALES (corp-wide): 891.3MM **Privately Held**
SIC: **8069** Children's hospital
PA: The Childrens Hospital Los Angeles
4650 W Sunset Blvd
Los Angeles CA 90027
323 660-2450

(P-22124)
CHILDRENS HOSPITAL LOS ANGELES (PA)
4650 W Sunset Blvd, Los Angeles (90027-6062)
PHONE..................323 660-2450
Richard Cordova, *President*
Lannie Tonnu, *CFO*
Robert Adler, *Trustee*
Otis Booth, *Trustee*
Thomas E Larkin, *Trustee*
▲ EMP: 88 EST: 1901
SQ FT: 750,000
SALES: 891.3MM **Privately Held**
SIC: **8069** 8062 Children's hospital; general medical & surgical hospitals

(P-22125)
CHILDRENS HOSPITAL LOS ANGELES
800 N Brand Blvd, Glendale (91203-1245)
PHONE..................323 361-2215
EMP: 367
SALES (corp-wide): 891.3MM **Privately Held**
SIC: **8069** 8093 Children's hospital; specialty outpatient clinics
PA: The Childrens Hospital Los Angeles
4650 W Sunset Blvd
Los Angeles CA 90027
323 660-2450

(P-22126)
CHILDRENS HOSPITAL LOS ANGELES
Also Called: Chidren's Hospital Center
4661 W Sunset Blvd, Los Angeles (90027-6042)
PHONE..................323 361-5702
Nikita Tripuraneni, *Principal*
EMP: 92
SALES (corp-wide): 891.3MM **Privately Held**
SIC: **8069** Children's hospital
PA: The Childrens Hospital Los Angeles
4650 W Sunset Blvd
Los Angeles CA 90027
323 660-2450

PRODUCTS & SERVICES SECTION

8069 - Specialty Hospitals, Except Psychiatric County (P-22148)

(P-22127)
CHILDRENS HOSPITAL ORANGE CNTY (PA)
Also Called: CHOC
1201 W La Veta Ave, Orange (92868-4203)
PHONE..................................714 997-3000
Fax: 714 289-4010
Kimberly Cripe, *President*
Nick G Anas,
L Kenneth Heuler DDS, *Ch of Bd*
Patricia Faiman, *President*
Sally Gallagher, *President*
EMP: 82
SQ FT: 328,200
SALES: 518.8MM **Privately Held**
SIC: 8069 Children's hospital

(P-22128)
CHILDRENS HOSPITAL ORANGE CNTY
Also Called: Choc Mission
455 S Main St, Orange (92868-3835)
PHONE..................................949 365-2416
Kerri Ruppert Schiller, *Principal*
Janne M Gish, *Exec Dir*
Stacy Rios, *Information Mgr*
Bernard Javier, *Technology*
Timothy K Flannery, *Endocrinology*
EMP: 1037
SALES (corp-wide): 518.8MM **Privately Held**
SIC: 8069 Children's hospital
PA: Children's Hospital Of Orange County
1201 W La Veta Ave
Orange CA 92868
714 997-3000

(P-22129)
CITY OF SAN DIEGO
Also Called: Park and Recreation
202 C St Ms37c, San Diego (92101-3860)
PHONE..................................619 533-6518
Albert Cuevas, *Administration*
EMP: 99
SALES (est): 442K **Privately Held**
SIC: 8069 Specialty hospitals, except psychiatric

(P-22130)
COMMUNITY HOSPITALS CENTL CAL
Also Called: COMMUNITY REGIONAL MEDICAL CEN
2823 Fresno St, Fresno (93721-1324)
PHONE..................................559 459-6000
Tim Joslin, *President*
Sarah Rowe, *Info Tech Mgr*
Quentin Phillips, *Materials Dir*
Dalpinder Sandhu, *Med Doctor*
Richard Brescione, *Nursing Dir*
EMP: 6000
SALES: 127.4MM **Privately Held**
SIC: 8069 Specialty hospitals, except psychiatric

(P-22131)
COUNTY OF LOS ANGELES
Also Called: Health Services, Dept of
30500 Arrastre Canyon Rd, Acton (93510-2160)
P.O. Box 25 (93510-0025)
PHONE..................................661 223-8700
Fax: 661 269-0427
Suzanna Kassinger, *Administration*
EMP: 100 **Privately Held**
WEB: www.co.la.ca.us
SIC: 8069 9431 8361 Alcoholism rehabilitation hospital; administration of public health programs; ; residential care
PA: County Of Los Angeles
500 W Temple St Ste 375
Los Angeles CA 90012
213 974-1101

(P-22132)
COUNTY OF LOS ANGELES
515 E 6th St, Los Angeles (90021-1009)
PHONE..................................213 974-7284
Maria Lopez, *Manager*
EMP: 1000 **Privately Held**
WEB: www.co.la.ca.us
SIC: 8069 9111 Tuberculosis hospital; executive offices

PA: County Of Los Angeles
500 W Temple St Ste 375
Los Angeles CA 90012
213 974-1101

(P-22133)
COUNTY OF LOS ANGELES
Also Called: Department of Health Services
1240 N Mission Rd, Los Angeles (90033-1019)
PHONE..................................323 226-3468
Fax: 323 226-3161
Barbara Oliver, *Exec Dir*
Murphy T Goodwin, *Director*
EMP: 1000 **Privately Held**
WEB: www.co.la.ca.us
SIC: 8069 9431 8062 Specialty hospitals, except psychiatric; administration of public health programs; ; general medical & surgical hospitals
PA: County Of Los Angeles
500 W Temple St Ste 375
Los Angeles CA 90012
213 974-1101

(P-22134)
CRC HEALTH CORPORATION (DH)
20400 Stevens Creek Blvd, Cupertino (95014-2296)
PHONE..................................877 272-8668
Jerome E Rhodes, *CEO*
R Andrew Eckert, *Ch of Bd*
Leanne M Stewart, *CFO*
Philip L Herschman, *Officer*
Pamela B Burke, *Senior VP*
EMP: 80
SALES: 452.2MM **Publicly Held**
WEB: www.crchealth.com
SIC: 8069 8099 8322 8093 Drug addiction rehabilitation hospital; medical services organization; general counseling services; substance abuse clinics (outpatient)
HQ: Crc Health Group, Inc.
20400 Stev Creek Blvd 6
Cupertino CA 95014
877 272-8668

(P-22135)
CRESTWOOD BEHAVIORAL HLTH INC
Also Called: 137 Bakersfield Bridge
6744 Eucalyptus Dr, Bakersfield (93306-6053)
PHONE..................................661 363-6711
Lori Blackburn, *Branch Mgr*
EMP: 200
SALES (corp-wide): 135.6MM **Privately Held**
SIC: 8069 Specialty hospitals, except psychiatric
PA: Crestwood Behavioral Health, Inc.
520 Capitol Mall Ste 800
Sacramento CA 95814
510 651-1244

(P-22136)
DANIEL LORIA NOVARTIS
4560 Horton St, Emeryville (94608-2916)
PHONE..................................510 655-8729
Daniel Loria Novartis, *Principal*
Shari Annes, *Vice Pres*
Stephen D Rubino, *Vice Pres*
Scott Latimer, *Executive*
Barbara C Boner, *Associate Dir*
EMP: 129
SALES (est): 13MM **Privately Held**
SIC: 8069 Eye, ear, nose & throat hospital

(P-22137)
DESERT REGIONAL MED CTR INC
Also Called: Tenet
1695 N Sunrise Way, Palm Springs (92262-3701)
PHONE..................................760 323-6640
Truman Gates, *Manager*
EMP: 190
SALES (corp-wide): 18.7B **Publicly Held**
SIC: 8069 8082 Specialty hospitals, except psychiatric; home health care services

HQ: Desert Regional Medical Center, Inc.
1150 N Indian Canyon Dr
Palm Springs CA 92262
760 323-6374

(P-22138)
DOCTORS HOSPITAL MANTECA INC
1205 E North St, Manteca (95336-4900)
PHONE..................................209 823-3111
Fax: 209 239-8329
Nicholas Tejeda, *CEO*
Mark Lisa, *President*
Katherine Medeiros, *President*
Carmen Silva, *COO*
Tracy Roman, *CFO*
EMP: 400 **EST:** 2001
SALES (est): 68.2MM
SALES (corp-wide): 18.7B **Publicly Held**
SIC: 8069 Specialty hospitals, except psychiatric
PA: Tenet Healthcare Corporation
1445 Ross Ave Ste 1400
Dallas TX 75202
469 893-2200

(P-22139)
EDGEMOOR HOSPITAL
655 Park Center Dr, Santee (92071-3094)
PHONE..................................619 956-2880
EMP: 350
SALES: 26MM **Privately Held**
SIC: 8069

(P-22140)
EL CAMINO HOSPITAL
Also Called: Occupational Health Services
625 Ellis St Ste 100, Mountain View (94043-2225)
PHONE..................................650 988-4825
Todd Blancept, *Manager*
Brian Dennis, *Anesthesiology*
Deborah K Derek, *Anesthesiology*
Derek W Liau, *Anesthesiology*
Huy M Nguyen, *Anesthesiology*
EMP: 246
SALES (corp-wide): 776.4MM **Privately Held**
SIC: 8069 Alcoholism rehabilitation hospital
PA: El Camino Hospital
2500 Grant Rd
Mountain View CA 94040
408 224-6660

(P-22141)
EXODUS RECOVERY CTR AT BROTMAN (PA)
3828 Delmas Ter, Culver City (90232-2713)
PHONE..................................310 253-9494
Luana Murphy, *Principal*
Richard Davis, *Education*
Patrick Hooks, *Manager*
EMP: 59
SALES (est): 2.8MM **Privately Held**
SIC: 8069 Drug addiction rehabilitation hospital

(P-22142)
FRESNO HEART HOSPITAL LLC
15 E Audubon Dr, Fresno (93720-1542)
PHONE..................................559 433-8000
Fax: 559 433-8125
Wanda Holderman, *Mng Member*
Tim A Joslin, *CEO*
Roger Fretwell, *Treasurer*
Patrick Rafferty, *Exec VP*
Peg Breen, *Senior VP*
EMP: 330
SQ FT: 140,000
SALES (est): 54.6MM
SALES (corp-wide): 1.4B **Privately Held**
WEB: www.fresnoheart.com
SIC: 8069 Specialty hospitals, except psychiatric
PA: Community Medical Center
2823 Fresno St
Fresno CA 93721
559 459-6000

(P-22143)
HEALTHSOUTH CORPORATION
3875 Telegraph Ave, Oakland (94609-2428)
PHONE..................................510 547-2244
Ann Banchero, *Branch Mgr*

EMP: 55
SALES (corp-wide): 3.1B **Publicly Held**
WEB: www.healthsouth.com
SIC: 8069 Orthopedic hospital
PA: Healthsouth Corporation
3660 Grandview Pkwy # 200
Birmingham AL 35243
205 967-7116

(P-22144)
HERMITAGE HEALTH CARE
Also Called: Fircrest Convalescent
7025 Corline Ct, Sebastopol (95472-4520)
PHONE..................................707 823-1238
April Trask, *Administration*
Leslie Breckenridge, *President*
Robert Bates, *Administration*
Ahmed El Ghoneimy, *Director*
EMP: 65
SQ FT: 18,000
SALES (est): 3.4MM **Privately Held**
SIC: 8069 Specialty hospitals, except psychiatric

(P-22145)
HORIZON WEST HEALTHCARE INC
Also Called: Roseville Convalescent Hosp
1161 Cirby Way, Roseville (95661-4421)
PHONE..................................916 782-1238
Fax: 916 786-3597
James Paul, *Manager*
EMP: 150
SALES (corp-wide): 99MM **Privately Held**
WEB: www.villadelrey.com
SIC: 8069 8051 Specialty hospitals, except psychiatric; skilled nursing care facilities
HQ: Horizon West Healthcare, Inc.
4020 Sierra College Blvd # 190
Rocklin CA 95677
916 624-6230

(P-22146)
HOSPITAL OF COMMUNITY (HQ)
23625 Holman Hwy, Monterey (93940-5902)
P.O. Box Hh (93942-6032)
PHONE..................................831 624-5311
Fax: 831 333-0245
Steven J Packer, *President*
Mike Barber,
Heinrich Brinks,
Laura Zehm, *CFO*
George W Couch, *Treasurer*
EMP: 1500
SQ FT: 550,000
SALES: 483.4MM
SALES (corp-wide): 200MM **Privately Held**
SIC: 8069 8011 Geriatric hospital; hematologist
PA: Community Hospital Foundation Inc
23625 Holman Hwy
Monterey CA 93940
831 625-4830

(P-22147)
KAISER FOUNDATION HOSPITALS
Also Called: Kaiser Permanente Post Acute
1440 168th Ave, San Leandro (94578-2409)
PHONE..................................510 481-8575
Fax: 510 481-6310
Bob Bustretsky, *Manager*
EMP: 300
SALES (corp-wide): 27.8B **Privately Held**
WEB: www.kaiserpermanente.org
SIC: 8069 Specialty hospitals, except psychiatric
HQ: Kaiser Foundation Hospitals Inc
1 Kaiser Plz
Oakland CA 94612
510 271-6611

(P-22148)
KINDRED HEALTHCARE OPER INC
1940 El Cajon Blvd, San Diego (92104-1005)
PHONE..................................502 596-7300
Susan Baley, *CEO*
Thomas Sullivan,
Linda Seale, *Executive*

8069 - Specialty Hospitals, Except Psychiatric County (P-22149)

Carol Wilson, *Op Rm Dir*
Leo Galan, *Radiology Dir*
EMP: 222
SALES (corp-wide): 7B **Publicly Held**
WEB: www.salemhaven.com
SIC: 8069 Specialty hospitals, except psychiatric
HQ: Kindred Healthcare Operating, Inc.
  680 S 4th St
  Louisville KY 40202
  502 596-7300

(P-22149)
KINDRED HEALTHCARE OPERATING
Also Called: Hillhaven Convalescent Hosp
1609 Trousdale Dr, Burlingame (94010-4520)
PHONE 650 697-1865
Fax: 650 697-4310
Jan Clemons, *Administration*
EMP: 500
SALES (corp-wide): 7B **Publicly Held**
WEB: www.salemhaven.com
SIC: 8069 Specialty hospitals, except psychiatric
HQ: Kindred Healthcare Operating, Inc.
  680 S 4th St
  Louisville KY 40202
  502 596-7300

(P-22150)
KND DEVELOPMENT 53 LLC
Also Called: KINDRED HOSPITAL- SOUTH BAY
1246 W 155th St, Gardena (90247-4011)
PHONE 310 323-5330
Kevin Chavez,
Christina Mada, *Office Mgr*
EMP: 54
SALES (est): 10.5MM **Privately Held**
SIC: 8069 Specialty hospitals, except psychiatric

(P-22151)
LELAND STANFORD JUNIOR UNIV
Also Called: Lucile Packard Childrens Hosp
725 Welch Rd, Palo Alto (94304-1601)
PHONE 650 497-8000
Fax: 650 497-8870
Mary Spangler, *Director*
Lawrence Rinsky,
Daniel Ginsburg, *COO*
Anne McCune, *COO*
David Ebel, *CFO*
EMP: 150
SALES (corp-wide): 1.9B **Privately Held**
SIC: 8069 8082 5912 8221 Children's hospital; home health care services; drug stores & proprietary stores; university
PA: Leland Stanford Junior University
  2575 Sand Hill Rd
  Menlo Park CA 94025
  650 723-2300

(P-22152)
LIGHTBRIDGE HOSPICE LLC
Also Called: Lightbrdge Hspice Plltive Care
6155 Cornerstone Ct E, San Diego (92121-4736)
PHONE 858 458-2992
Fax: 858 458-3655
Jill Mendlen, *CEO*
Pamela Hough, *Senior VP*
Cindy Zacharyasz, *Senior VP*
Cindy Hutchinson, *Vice Pres*
Nan Johnson, *Vice Pres*
EMP: 90
SALES: 130.2K **Privately Held**
WEB: www.lightbridgehospice.com
SIC: 8069 Specialty hospitals, except psychiatric

(P-22153)
LUCILE PACKARD CHILDRENS HOSP
1520 Page Mill Rd, Palo Alto (94304-1125)
PHONE 650 736-4089
Anita Brewer, *Director*
Christopher Longhurst, *Officer*
Harinder Singh, *Info Tech Mgr*
Kathy Schneider, *Controller*
Dan Dickenson, *Manager*
EMP: 56

SALES (est): 9.1MM **Privately Held**
SIC: 8069 Children's hospital

(P-22154)
LUCILE SALTER PACKARD CHIL
4100 Bohannon Dr, Menlo Park (94025-1013)
PHONE 650 724-0503
EMP: 104
SALES (corp-wide): 1.1B **Privately Held**
SIC: 8069 Children's hospital
PA: Lucile Salter Packard Children's Hospital At Stanford
  725 Welch Rd
  Palo Alto CA 94304
  650 736-7398

(P-22155)
LUCILE SALTER PACKARD CHIL (PA)
725 Welch Rd, Palo Alto (94304-1601)
PHONE 650 736-7398
Fax: 650 497-8837
Christopher Dawes, *President*
Timothy W Carmack, *CFO*
Gary May, *Vice Pres*
Paul Shuttleworth, *Ch Nursing Ofcr*
Laurie Jones, *Office Mgr*
▲ **EMP:** 168
SALES: 1.1B **Privately Held**
SIC: 8069 8082 5912 Children's hospital; home health care services; drug stores & proprietary stores

(P-22156)
LUCILE SALTER PACKARD CHIL
300 Pasteur Dr, Stanford (94305-2200)
PHONE 650 723-5791
Jeff Driver, *Principal*
Craig Albanese, *Vice Pres*
EMP: 181
SALES (corp-wide): 1.1B **Privately Held**
SIC: 8069 Children's hospital
PA: Lucile Salter Packard Children's Hospital At Stanford
  725 Welch Rd
  Palo Alto CA 94304
  650 736-7398

(P-22157)
MARINE CORPS UNITED STATES
Also Called: Camp Pendleton Hospital
Camp Pendleton, Oceanside (92055)
P.O. Box 555191, Camp Pendleton (92055-5191)
PHONE 760 725-1304
Fax: 760 725-1101
Richard R Jeffries, *Manager*
EMP: 1000 **Publicly Held**
WEB: www.usmc.mil
SIC: 8069 9711 Specialty hospitals, except psychiatric; Marine Corps;
HQ: United States Marine Corps
  Pentagon Rm 4b544
  Washington DC 20380
  816 394-7628

(P-22158)
MEDCATH INCORPORATED
Also Called: Bakersfield Heart Hospital
3001 Sillect Ave, Bakersfield (93308-6337)
PHONE 704 815-7700
Fax: 661 616-5431
Rod Vieira, *Controller*
Marvin Derrick,
Anita Tripp, *President*
Ken Jordan, *CFO*
Kenneth Jordan, *CFO*
EMP: 360
SALES (corp-wide): 318.8MM **Privately Held**
WEB: www.bakersfieldhearthospital.com
SIC: 8069 Specialty hospitals, except psychiatric
HQ: Medcath Incorporated
  10800 Sikes Pl Ste 200
  Charlotte NC 28277
  704 815-7700

(P-22159)
MEDMARK SERVICES INC
1310 M St, Fresno (93721-1808)
PHONE 559 264-2700
William Gecsey, *Branch Mgr*
EMP: 50

SALES (corp-wide): 52.1MM **Privately Held**
SIC: 8069 Drug addiction rehabilitation hospital
PA: Medmark Services, Inc.
  401 E Corp Dr Ste 220
  Lewisville TX 75057
  214 379-3300

(P-22160)
NEW BRIDGE FOUNDATION INC
1820 Scenic Ave, Berkeley (94709-1395)
PHONE 510 548-7270
Fax: 510 548-1060
Kosta Markakis, *Exec Dir*
Marsha Jones, *Finance*
Georgette Cobbs, *Manager*
EMP: 73
SQ FT: 3,000
SALES: 6.2MM **Privately Held**
SIC: 8069 Drug addiction rehabilitation hospital

(P-22161)
POMONA VALLEY HOSPITAL MED CTR
Also Called: Pamona Vallley Hospital
1798 N Garey Ave, Pomona (91767-2918)
PHONE 909 865-9700
Fax: 909 865-9938
Dee Ann Gibs, *Director*
EMP: 200
SALES (corp-wide): 553.9MM **Privately Held**
WEB: www.pvhmc.org
SIC: 8069 Maternity hospital
PA: Pomona Valley Hospital Medical Center
  1798 N Garey Ave
  Pomona CA 91767
  909 865-9500

(P-22162)
PROGRESSIVE SUB-ACUTE CARE
Also Called: Sub-Acute Saratoga Hospital
13425 Sousa Ln, Saratoga (95070-4637)
PHONE 408 378-8875
Michael Zarcone, *President*
Kathy Nguyen, *Office Mgr*
Steve Chao, *Finance*
Ann Kwansey, *Phys Thrpy Dir*
Anne Kwansey, *Occ Therapy Dir*
EMP: 130
SQ FT: 10,000
SALES (est): 19.8MM **Privately Held**
WEB: www.subacutesaratoga.com
SIC: 8069 Specialty hospitals, except psychiatric

(P-22163)
RADY CHILDRENS HOSP & HLTH CTR (PA)
3020 Childrens Way, San Diego (92123-4223)
PHONE 858 576-1700
Fax: 858 571-3372
Donald B Kearns, *President*
Nicholas Holmes, *COO*
Roger G Roux, *CFO*
Irvin A Kaufman, *Chief Mktg Ofcr*
Margareta E Norton, *Exec VP*
EMP: 1700
SALES: 3.3MM **Privately Held**
SIC: 8069 Children's hospital

(P-22164)
RADY CHLD HOSPITAL-SAN DIEGO
8001 Frost St, San Diego (92123-2746)
PHONE 858 966-6795
Fax: 858 492-9375
Lynn M Dubenko, *Principal*
Rachel Abramson, *Med Doctor*
EMP: 1025
SALES (corp-wide): 838.7MM **Privately Held**
SIC: 8069 Children's hospital
PA: Rady Children's Hospital-San Diego
  3020 Childrens Way
  San Diego CA 92123
  858 576-1700

(P-22165)
RADY CHLD HOSPITAL-SAN DIEGO (PA)
3020 Childrens Way, San Diego (92123-4223)
PHONE 858 576-1700
Fax: 858 966-8535
Donald Kearns, *CEO*
Diania Felix,
Christopher E Dory, *Ch Radiology*
Dorothy O'Hagan, *Records Dir*
Nicholas Holmes, *COO*
EMP: 2000 **EST:** 1952
SQ FT: 276,000
SALES: 838.7MM **Privately Held**
SIC: 8069 Children's hospital

(P-22166)
RADY CHLD HOSPITAL-SAN DIEGO
Also Called: Center For Children Protection
3020 Childrens Way, San Diego (92123-4223)
PHONE 858 576-5803
Fax: 858 495-7709
Barbara Ryan, *Manager*
EMP: 50
SALES (corp-wide): 838.7MM **Privately Held**
SIC: 8069 Specialty hospitals, except psychiatric
PA: Rady Children's Hospital-San Diego
  3020 Childrens Way
  San Diego CA 92123
  858 576-1700

(P-22167)
RECOVERY PLACE INC
5000 E Spring St Ste 650, Long Beach (90815-5205)
PHONE 954 200-8308
John Cates, *President*
Jonathan Sobelman, *COO*
Marianne Coy, *Administration*
EMP: 100
SALES (est): 8.5MM **Privately Held**
SIC: 8069 Substance abuse hospitals

(P-22168)
REDLANDS COMMUNITY HOSPITAL (PA)
350 Terracina Blvd, Redlands (92373-4897)
PHONE 909 335-5500
Fax: 909 335-6497
James R Holmes, *CEO*
Kathi Sankey-Robinson, *President*
Sabi A Dadabhai, *CFO*
Harvey Hansen, *Vice Pres*
Richard Ocello, *Risk Mgmt Dir*
EMP: 61
SALES: 174.1MM **Privately Held**
SIC: 8069 Specialty hospitals, except psychiatric

(P-22169)
ROSS HOSPITAL
1111 Sir Francis Dr, Kentfield (94904-1418)
PHONE 415 258-6900
Judy House, *President*
Wahid Choudhury, *CFO*
EMP: 175 **EST:** 1917
SQ FT: 30,000
SALES (est): 3.5MM **Privately Held**
SIC: 8069 8063 Alcoholism rehabilitation hospital; psychiatric hospitals

(P-22170)
SALVATION ARMY
809 E 5th St, Los Angeles (90013-2112)
PHONE 323 254-9015
Fax: 213 626-0717
Conrad Watson, *Exec Dir*
EMP: 59
SQ FT: 60,064
SALES (corp-wide): 4.3B **Privately Held**
WEB: www.salvationarmy.usawest.org
SIC: 8069 Alcoholism rehabilitation hospital
HQ: The Salvation Army
  180 E Ocean Blvd Fl 2
  Long Beach CA 90802
  562 491-8464

PRODUCTS & SERVICES SECTION
8071 - Medical Laboratories County (P-22191)

(P-22171)
SEQUOIA REGIONAL CANCER CENTER
602 W Willow Ave, Visalia (93291-6102)
PHONE...................559 624-3000
Fax: 559 635-4747
Toni M Boniske, *Admin Dir*
EMP: 63
SALES (est): 6.1MM
SALES (corp-wide): 475.4MM **Privately Held**
SIC: 8069 Cancer hospital
PA: Kaweah Delta Health Care District Guild
  400 W Mineral King Ave
  Visalia CA 93291
  559 624-2000

(P-22172)
SHIELDS FOR FAMILIES (PA)
11601 S Western Ave, Los Angeles (90047-5006)
P.O. Box 59129 (90059-0129)
PHONE...................323 242-5000
Kathryn S Icenhower, *CEO*
Xylina Bean, *President*
Norma Mtume, *CFO*
Gerald Phillips, *Chairman*
Susan Haynes, *Treasurer*
EMP: 82
SALES (est): 20.3MM **Privately Held**
SIC: 8069 Drug addiction rehabilitation hospital

(P-22173)
SHRINERS HSPITALS FOR CHILDREN
Also Called: Shriner's Hospital
3160 Geneva St, Los Angeles (90020-1117)
PHONE...................213 388-3151
Fax: 213 368-3304
Terence Cunningham, *Principal*
Beverly Wood, *Ch Radiology*
Jason Banks, *Admin Asst*
G Frank Labonte, *Administration*
Janet Sanders, *Administration*
EMP: 300 **Privately Held**
SIC: 8069 8062 Children's hospital; general medical & surgical hospitals
HQ: Shriners Hospitals For Children
  12502 Usf Pine Dr
  Tampa FL 33612
  813 972-2250

(P-22174)
SHRINERS HSPITALS FOR CHILDREN
2425 Stockton Blvd, Sacramento (95817-2215)
PHONE...................916 453-2050
Margaret Bryan, *Administration*
Jenny Wong, *Pharmacy Dir*
Deborah Rubens, *Human Res Dir*
Cynthia Clayton, *Train & Dev Mgr*
Andrew A Hader, *Buyer*
EMP: 500 **Privately Held**
SIC: 8069 Children's hospital
HQ: Shriners Hospitals For Children
  12502 Usf Pine Dr
  Tampa FL 33612
  813 972-2250

(P-22175)
SHRINERS HSPITALS FOR CHILDREN
2425 Stockton Blvd, Sacramento (95817-2215)
PHONE...................916 453-2000
Fax: 916 453-2388
Margaret B Brian, *Director*
James Barone, *Radiology Dir*
Erick Sencil, *Radiology Dir*
Margaret Bryan, *Administration*
Star Deppe, *Administration*
EMP: 400 **Privately Held**
SIC: 8069 8062 Specialty hospitals, except psychiatric; general medical & surgical hospitals
HQ: Shriners Hospitals For Children
  12502 Usf Pine Dr
  Tampa FL 33612
  813 972-2250

(P-22176)
SOCIAL SCIENCE SERVICE CENTER
Also Called: Cedar House Rehabilitation Ctr
18612 Santa Ana Ave, Bloomington (92316-2636)
PHONE...................909 421-7120
Fax: 909 421-7128
Daniel Gakgolla, *CEO*
Jennifer Arkin, *Admin Sec*
Allen Eisenman, *Admin Sec*
Jamie Vergilio, *Human Res Mgr*
Michelle Shutters, *Manager*
EMP: 63
SQ FT: 29,000
SALES (est): 3.2MM **Privately Held**
WEB: www.cedarhouse.org
SIC: 8069 8322 Substance abuse hospitals; individual & family services

(P-22177)
SOUTHERN CAL SPCIALTY CARE INC (DH)
Also Called: Kindred Hospital La Mirada
14900 Imperial Hwy, La Mirada (90638-2172)
PHONE...................562 944-1900
Fax: 714 906-3455
Ty Richardson, *President*
George Burkley, *COO*
Robin Rapp, *COO*
George Koutsakos, *CFO*
Judie Sheldon, *Ch Credit Ofcr*
EMP: 100
SQ FT: 74,074
SALES (est): 20.8MM
SALES (corp-wide): 7B **Publicly Held**
SIC: 8069 Specialty hospitals, except psychiatric
HQ: Specialty Healthcare Services, Inc
  680 S 4th St
  Louisville KY 40202
  502 596-7300

(P-22178)
SPECIAL NEEDS NETWORK
4401 Crenshaw Blvd # 215, Los Angeles (90043-1200)
PHONE...................323 291-7100
Julia Djeke, *President*
Shamya Ullah, *Bd of Directors*
EMP: 50 **EST:** 2013
SALES: 489.4K **Privately Held**
SIC: 8069 Children's hospital

(P-22179)
SUBACUTE CHILDRENS HOSP OF CAL
Also Called: Childrens Rcvery Ctr Nthrn Cal
3777 S Bascom Ave, Campbell (95008-7320)
PHONE...................408 558-3644
Fax: 408 377-1139
Micahel Zarcone, *CEO*
Julie Harris, *Director*
Scott Yamikoshi, *Director*
Doug Stephens, *Manager*
EMP: 80
SQ FT: 17,000
SALES (est): 9.2MM **Privately Held**
SIC: 8069 Children's hospital

(P-22180)
SURE HAVEN
Also Called: Sure Haven Addic
2900 Bristol St Ste B300, Costa Mesa (92626-5948)
PHONE...................949 467-9213
Steve Fennelly, *CEO*
Tanisha Porreca, *COO*
Elizabeth Perry, *Vice Pres*
Mark Shandrow, *Vice Pres*
EMP: 550 **EST:** 2010
SQ FT: 7,500
SALES (est): 60.1MM **Privately Held**
SIC: 8069 Alcoholism rehabilitation hospital

(P-22181)
TENET HEALTH SYSTEMS NORRIS
Also Called: Kenneth Norris Cancer Hospital
1441 Eastlake Ave, Los Angeles (90089-0112)
PHONE...................323 865-3000
Fax: 323 342-2442
Scott Evans, *CEO*
Earl Strum,
Strawn Steele, *CFO*
William Oehlenschlager, *Radiology Dir*
Josie De La Torre, *Admin Sec*
EMP: 352
SQ FT: 175,000
SALES: 179.2MM **Privately Held**
SIC: 8069 Cancer hospital

(P-22182)
TENET HEALTHSYSTEM MEDICAL
Also Called: Placentia Linda Hospital
1301 N Rose Dr, Placentia (92870-3802)
PHONE...................714 993-2000
Fax: 714 524-4818
Kent Clayton, *CEO*
John P Lake, *Ch Pathology*
Michael P Rubinstein,
Joyce Titus, *Op Rm Dir*
Lena Laroco, *Infect Cntl Dir*
EMP: 400
SALES (corp-wide): 18.7B **Publicly Held**
WEB: www.tenethealth.com
SIC: 8069 8011 8062 Specialty hospitals, except psychiatric; offices & clinics of medical doctors; general medical & surgical hospitals
HQ: Tenet Healthsystem Medical, Inc
  1445 Ross Ave Ste 1400
  Dallas TX 75202
  469 893-2000

(P-22183)
UNITED CEREBRAL PALSY ASSOCIAT
Also Called: United Cerebral Palsy Assn San
333 W Benjamin Holt Dr # 1, Stockton (95207-3906)
PHONE...................209 956-0295
Ray Call, *CEO*
Leslie Heier, *COO*
Lillian Callangan, *Finance*
EMP: 137
SALES: 3.5MM **Privately Held**
SIC: 8069 8322 Chronic disease hospital; individual & family services

(P-22184)
VALLEY CHILDRENS HOSPITAL (PA)
9300 Valley Childrens Pl, Madera (93636-8762)
PHONE...................559 353-3000
Fax: 559 353-8225
Todd Sunterapak, *President*
Timothy Hansen, *President*
Gordon Alexander, *President*
Jessie Hudgins, *COO*
Michele Waldrin, *CFO*
EMP: 1500
SQ FT: 300,000
SALES: 575.6MM **Privately Held**
SIC: 8069 Children's hospital

(P-22185)
VIBRA HOSPITAL SACRAMENTO LLC
330 Montrose Dr, Folsom (95630-2720)
PHONE...................916 351-9151
Janet Biedrone, *CEO*
Brad E Hollinger, *Mng Member*
EMP: 246
SQ FT: 22,000
SALES (est): 22.2MM
SALES (corp-wide): 329.7MM **Privately Held**
SIC: 8069 Specialty hospitals, except psychiatric
PA: Vibra Healthcare, Llc
  4550 Lena Dr
  Mechanicsburg PA 17055
  717 591-5700

(P-22186)
WATERMAN CONVALESCENT HOSPITAL
Mt Rubidoux Convalescent Hosp
6401 33rd St, Riverside (92509-1404)
PHONE...................951 681-2200
Magda Williams, *Director*
EMP: 130
SALES (corp-wide): 12.5MM **Privately Held**
SIC: 8069 8051 Specialty hospitals, except psychiatric; skilled nursing care facilities
PA: Waterman Convalescent Hospital, Inc
  1850 N Waterman Ave
  San Bernardino CA 92404
  909 882-1215

(P-22187)
WESTSIDE COUNSELING CENTER
Also Called: Inland Behaviour and Hlth Svcs
1963 N E St, San Bernardino (92405-3919)
PHONE...................909 881-2425
Lindsey Temetry, *Owner*
EMP: 75 **EST:** 1972
SALES (est): 8.7MM **Privately Held**
WEB: www.westsidecounselingcenter.com
SIC: 8069 Drug addiction rehabilitation hospital

8071 Medical Laboratories

(P-22188)
ALLIANCE HEALTHCARE SVCS INC (PA)
100 Bayview Cir Ste 400, Newport Beach (92660-2984)
PHONE...................949 242-5300
Fax: 949 242-5372
Percy C Tomlinson, *CEO*
Qisen Huang, *Ch of Bd*
Richard A Jones, *President*
Steven M Siwek, *President*
Gregory E Spurlock, *President*
EMP: 250
SQ FT: 40,596
SALES: 473MM **Publicly Held**
WEB: www.mvhs.org
SIC: 8071 Medical laboratories; ultrasound laboratory

(P-22189)
AMEN CLINICS INC A MED CORP (PA)
Also Called: Mindworks Press
3150 Bristol St Ste 400, Costa Mesa (92626-3054)
PHONE...................888 564-2700
Daniel Amen, *President*
Catherine J Hanlon, *Administration*
Amy Hernandez, *Controller*
Nicole Miller, *Controller*
Todd Elwynn, *Psychiatry*
▲ EMP: 50
SALES (est): 8.1MM **Privately Held**
WEB: www.amenclinics.com
SIC: 8071 Neurological laboratory

(P-22190)
BIO-DIAGNOSTICS LABORATORIES (PA)
Also Called: Bdl
19951 Mariner Ave Ste 150, Torrance (90503-1738)
PHONE...................818 780-3300
Alfred Lui, *President*
Jerree A Stroh, *CFO*
Richard Ellis, *Vice Pres*
EMP: 194
SQ FT: 20,000
SALES (est): 2.6MM **Privately Held**
SIC: 8071 Medical laboratories

(P-22191)
BIO-REFERENCE LABORATORIES INC
2605 Winchester Blvd, Campbell (95008-5320)
PHONE...................408 341-8600
Fax: 408 341-8610
EMP: 150
SALES (corp-wide): 491.7MM **Publicly Held**
SIC: 8071 Medical laboratories
HQ: Bio-Reference Laboratories, Inc.
  481 Edward H Ross Dr
  Elmwood Park NJ 07407
  201 791-2600

8071 - Medical Laboratories County (P-22192)

(P-22192)
BIOCEPT INC
5810 Nancy Ridge Dr # 150, San Diego (92121-2840)
PHONE...................................858 320-8200
Fax: 858 320-8225
Michael W Nall, *President*
David F Hale, *Ch of Bd*
Mark G Foletta, *CFO*
Timothy C Kennedy, *CFO*
David Hale, *Chairman*
EMP: 53
SQ FT: 48,000
SALES: 609.9K **Privately Held**
WEB: www.biocept.com
SIC: 8071 Pathological laboratory

(P-22193)
BIOIMAGENE INC
919 Hermosa Ct, Sunnyvale (94085-4103)
PHONE...................................408 207-4200
Ajit Singh, *CEO*
G Steven Burrill, *Ch of Bd*
EMP: 50
SALES (est): 2.4MM **Privately Held**
WEB: www.bioimagene.com
SIC: 8071 Pathological laboratory

(P-22194)
BIONANO GENOMICS INC (PA)
9640 Twne Cntre Dr 100, San Diego (92121)
PHONE...................................858 888-7600
Fax: 858 888-7601
Erik Holmlin, *President*
David Barker, *Ch of Bd*
Joel Jung, *CFO*
Han Cao, *Officer*
Terry Salyer, *Officer*
EMP: 80
SQ FT: 700
SALES (est): 14.2MM **Privately Held**
WEB: www.bionanogenomics.com
SIC: 8071 Biological laboratory

(P-22195)
BIOTHERANOSTICS INC (DH)
9640 Towne Centre Dr # 200, San Diego (92121-1987)
P.O. Box 749249, Los Angeles (90074-9249)
PHONE...................................858 678-0940
Fax: 858 587-5871
Nicolas Barthelemy, *President*
Richard Ding, *Ch of Bd*
Gail Sloan, *CFO*
Michael C Dugan, *Officer*
Isaac Bright, *Vice Pres*
EMP: 55
SALES (est): 10.1MM **Privately Held**
WEB: www.aviaradx.com
SIC: 8071 Medical laboratories
HQ: Biomerieux Sa
376 Chemin De L Orme
Marcy L Etoile 69280
478 872-000

(P-22196)
CARDIODX INC
600 Saginaw Dr, Redwood City (94063-4751)
PHONE...................................650 475-2788
Khush Mehta, *President*
Timothy Henn, *CFO*
Mark Monane, *Chief Mktg Ofcr*
Pamela Forbes, *Program Mgr*
Cynthia Lee, *Software Dev*
EMP: 146
SQ FT: 33,000
SALES: 7.9MM **Privately Held**
WEB: www.cardiodx.com
SIC: 8071 2834 Medical laboratories; drugs acting on the cardiovascular system, except diagnostic

(P-22197)
CAREDX INC (PA)
3260 Bayshore Blvd, Brisbane (94005-1021)
PHONE...................................415 287-2300
Peter Maag, *President*
Michael D Goldberg, *Ch of Bd*
Mitchell J Nelles, *COO*
Charles Constanti, *CFO*
James P Yee, *Chief Mktg Ofcr*
EMP: 126

SQ FT: 46,000
SALES: 28.1MM **Publicly Held**
SIC: 8071 8733 8011 Medical laboratories; research institute; offices & clinics of medical doctors

(P-22198)
CENTRAL REFERENCE LAB INC (PA)
Also Called: Diamond Reference Laboratory
1470 Valley Vista Dr # 100, Pomona (91765-3903)
PHONE...................................909 861-6966
Fax: 909 861-5487
Morteza Rajaee, *Vice Pres*
Abbas Rajaee, *President*
Kareena Renteria, *Assistant*
EMP: 70
SQ FT: 6,000
SALES: 15MM **Privately Held**
SIC: 8071 Medical laboratories

(P-22199)
CHILDRENS HOSPITAL LOS ANGELES
Also Called: Childrens Laboratory
5353 Balboa Blvd Ste 100, Encino (91316-2857)
PHONE...................................818 728-4930
Fax: 818 728-4932
Paul Pattengale, *Director*
EMP: 184
SALES (corp-wide): 891.3MM **Privately Held**
SIC: 8071 Medical laboratories
PA: The Childrens Hospital Los Angeles
4650 W Sunset Blvd
Los Angeles CA 90027
323 660-2450

(P-22200)
CLARIENT DIAGNOSTIC SVCS INC
31 Columbia, Aliso Viejo (92656-1460)
PHONE...................................888 443-3310
Cindy Collins, *CEO*
Renika Seghal, *CFO*
Michael Brown, *Vice Pres*
Mark Machulcz, *Vice Pres*
Brian Montgomery, *General Mgr*
EMP: 313
SALES (est): 1.9MM
SALES (corp-wide): 99.8MM **Privately Held**
SIC: 8071 Testing laboratories
HQ: Clarient Diagnostic Services Inc
31 Columbia
Aliso Viejo CA 92656
949 425-5700

(P-22201)
COMMUNITY MBL DIAGNOSTICS LLC
10948 Bigge St, San Leandro (94577-1121)
PHONE...................................925 516-6851
William McDonald, *Mng Member*
Joseph Cleberg,
Joe Cleberg, *Manager*
Fipe Mose, *Manager*
EMP: 72
SALES (est): 2.5MM **Privately Held**
SIC: 8071 X-ray laboratory, including dental

(P-22202)
CONSOLDTED MED BO-ANALYSIS INC (PA)
Also Called: Cmb Laboratory
10700 Walker St, Cypress (90630-4703)
P.O. Box 2369 (90630-1869)
PHONE...................................714 657-7369
Fax: 714 657-7555
Chin Kuo Fan, *President*
Gloria Fan, *Shareholder*
CAM Chinh Fan, *Senior VP*
Michelle Fan, *Vice Pres*
EMP: 100
SQ FT: 11,000
SALES: 12MM **Privately Held**
SIC: 8071 Medical laboratories

(P-22203)
CONSOLDTED MED BO-ANALYSIS INC
7631 Wyoming St Ste 105a, Westminster (92683-3904)
PHONE...................................714 657-7389
Fax: 714 657-7388
Chin Kuo Fan, *President*
David Tran, *Manager*
EMP: 51
SALES (corp-wide): 12MM **Privately Held**
SIC: 8071 Medical laboratories
PA: Consolidated Medical Bio-Analysis, Inc.
10700 Walker St
Cypress CA 90630
714 657-7369

(P-22204)
CONSOLDTED MED BO-ANALYSIS INC
12665 Garden Grove Blvd, Garden Grove (92843-1901)
PHONE...................................714 467-0240
Fax: 714 636-7252
Chin Kuo Fan, *Owner*
EMP: 51
SALES (corp-wide): 12MM **Privately Held**
SIC: 8071 Medical laboratories
PA: Consolidated Medical Bio-Analysis, Inc.
10700 Walker St
Cypress CA 90630
714 657-7369

(P-22205)
CONSOLDTED MED BO-ANALYSIS INC
12980 Frederick St Ste E, Moreno Valley (92553-5263)
PHONE...................................951 243-2600
Chin Kuo Fan, *President*
EMP: 51
SALES (corp-wide): 12MM **Privately Held**
SIC: 8071 Medical laboratories
PA: Consolidated Medical Bio-Analysis, Inc.
10700 Walker St
Cypress CA 90630
714 657-7369

(P-22206)
COUNTY OF ORANGE
Also Called: Health Care Agency
1729 W 17th St, Santa Ana (92706-2316)
PHONE...................................714 834-8385
Fax: 714 834-7960
Richard Alexander, *Lab Dir*
Lydia Mikhail, *Lab Dir*
Douglas Moore, *Exec Dir*
Paul Hannah, *Comp Lab Dir*
EMP: 50 **Privately Held**
SIC: 8071 9431 Medical laboratories; administration of public health programs;
PA: County Of Orange
333 W Santa Ana Blvd 3f
Santa Ana CA 92701
714 834-6200

(P-22207)
COUNTY OF SAN BERNARDINO
Arrowhead Regional Medical Ctr
400 N Pepper Ave, Colton (92324-1801)
PHONE...................................909 580-1000
Toll Free:...................................877 -
June Griffith, *CEO*
Patrick Petre, *CEO*
Joseph Davis, *Osteopathy*
Gary Guyton, *Director*
EMP: 210 **Privately Held**
SIC: 8071 9431 Medical laboratories; administration of public health programs;
PA: County Of San Bernardino
385 N Arrowhead Ave
San Bernardino CA 92415
909 387-3841

(P-22208)
DEPARTMENT HEALTH CARE SVCS
Also Called: Microbial Diseases Laboratory
850 Marina Bay Pkwy, Richmond (94804-6403)
PHONE...................................510 412-3700
Michael Janda, *Branch Mgr*

Anita Flynn, *E-Business*
EMP: 70 **Privately Held**
WEB: www.calsurv.org
SIC: 8071 9431 Medical laboratories; administration of public health programs;
HQ: Department Of Health Care Services
1501 Capitol Ave
Sacramento CA 95814
916 445-4171

(P-22209)
DIGNITY HEALTH
Health Care Lab
2102 N California St, Stockton (95204-6031)
PHONE...................................209 467-6430
Terry Bryan, *Director*
EMP: 115
SQ FT: 2,944
SALES (corp-wide): 7.1B **Privately Held**
WEB: www.chw.edu
SIC: 8071 Testing laboratories
PA: Dignity Health
185 Berry St Ste 300
San Francisco CA 94107
415 438-5500

(P-22210)
DR SYSTEMS INC
Also Called: Dominator Radiology Systems
10140 Mesa Rim Rd, San Diego (92121-2914)
PHONE...................................858 625-3344
Fax: 858 625-3335
Justin Dearborn, *President*
Charles Zuckerman, *CFO*
Joe Longa, *Vice Pres*
Florent Saint-Clair, *Vice Pres*
Thomas Wrightson, *Vice Pres*
EMP: 205
SQ FT: 42,250
SALES (est): 26.4MM
SALES (corp-wide): 81.7B **Publicly Held**
WEB: www.dominator.com
SIC: 8071 Testing laboratories
HQ: Merge Healthcare Incorporated
71 S Wacker Dr Ste 2
Chicago IL 60606
312 565-6868

(P-22211)
DUAL DIAGNOSIS TRTMNT CTR INC
Also Called: Sovereign Health of California
12832 Short Ave, Los Angeles (90066-6421)
PHONE...................................424 289-9031
EMP: 192
SALES (corp-wide): 74.5MM **Privately Held**
SIC: 8071 Medical laboratories
PA: Dual Diagnosis Treatment Center, Inc.
1211 Puerta Del Sol # 270
San Clemente CA 92673
949 276-5553

(P-22212)
EL CAMINO HOSPITAL
Evergreen Dialisist
2240 Tully Rd, San Jose (95122-1347)
PHONE...................................650 940-7000
Fax: 408 223-4037
Chu Nuyen, *Manager*
Lisa N Yue, *Admin Asst*
Alicia Antonia, *Manager*
EMP: 246
SALES (corp-wide): 776.4MM **Privately Held**
SIC: 8071 Medical laboratories
PA: El Camino Hospital
2500 Grant Rd
Mountain View CA 94040
408 224-6660

(P-22213)
ELLIOTT LABORATORIES INC
41039 Boyce Rd, Fremont (94538-2434)
PHONE...................................510 440-9500
Conrad Chu, *Principal*
EMP: 50
SALES (est): 2.8MM **Privately Held**
SIC: 8071 Testing laboratories

PRODUCTS & SERVICES SECTION 8071 - Medical Laboratories County (P-22235)

(P-22214)
ENDOCRINE SCIENCES INC
Also Called: Esoterix Ctr For Clncal Trails
4301 Lost Hills Rd, Calabasas
(91301-5358)
PHONE..................818 880-8040
Fax: 818 880-8541
Darrel Mayes, CEO
Dennis Griffin, President
Teri French, Executive
Victoria Gillispie, Lab Dir
Morgan Herle, Lab Dir
EMP: 125
SQ FT: 35,000
SALES (est): 8.2MM
SALES (corp-wide): 8.6B Publicly Held
WEB: www.esoterix.com
SIC: 8071 2869 Medical laboratories; industrial organic chemicals
HQ: Esoterix Inc
    4509 Freidrich Ln Ste 100
    Austin TX 78744
    512 225-1100

(P-22215)
EXQUISITE DENTAL TECHNOLOGY
4816 Temple City Blvd, Temple City
(91780-4235)
PHONE..................626 237-0107
Ron Tsai, President
EMP: 70
SQ FT: 920
SALES (est): 1MM Privately Held
SIC: 8071 Medical laboratories

(P-22216)
FOCUS DIAGNOSTICS INC
11331 Valley View St # 150, Cypress
(90630-5366)
PHONE..................714 220-1900
Fax: 714 220-1820
John Hurrell PHD, President
Sandy Cruz, Vice Pres
Wally Narajowski, Vice Pres
Anders Sjoholm, Vice Pres
Michelle Tabb, Vice Pres
EMP: 400
SQ FT: 36,000
SALES (est): 2.2MM
SALES (corp-wide): 7.4B Publicly Held
WEB: www.focusdx.com
SIC: 8071 Testing laboratories
PA: Quest Diagnostics Incorporated
    3 Giralda Farms
    Madison NJ 07940
    973 520-2700

(P-22217)
FOCUS TECHNOLOGIES HOLDING CO
10703 Progress Way, Cypress
(90630-4714)
PHONE..................800 838-4548
Fax: 714 821-4353
Charles C Harwood, President
Edward Caffrey, Vice Pres
Wayne Hogrefe, Vice Pres
Don Mooney, Vice Pres
Brynne Pettiford, Admin Asst
EMP: 454
SQ FT: 28,000
SALES (est): 7.7MM Privately Held
WEB: www.focustechnologies.com
SIC: 8071 3826 Testing laboratories; analytical instruments

(P-22218)
GARDEN GROVE ADVANCED IMAGING
1510 Cotner Ave, Los Angeles
(90025-3303)
PHONE..................310 445-2800
EMP: 115
SALES (est): 863.4K
SALES (corp-wide): 809.6MM Publicly Held
SIC: 8071 Medical laboratories
HQ: Radnet Management, Inc.
    1510 Cotner Ave
    Los Angeles CA 90025
    310 445-2800

(P-22219)
GENOMEDX BIOSCIENCES CORP
10355 Science Center Dr # 240, San Diego
(92121-1158)
PHONE..................888 975-4540
Doug Dolginow, CEO
Andy Katz, COO
EMP: 100 EST: 2012
SQ FT: 15,000
SALES: 7.3MM
SALES (corp-wide): 2.1MM Privately Held
SIC: 8071 Biological laboratory
PA: Genomedx Biosciences Inc
    1038 Homer St
    Vancouver BC V6B 2
    888 975-4540

(P-22220)
GENOMIC HEALTH INC (PA)
301 Penobscot Dr, Redwood City
(94063-4700)
PHONE..................650 556-9300
Kimberly J Popovits, Ch of Bd
G Bradley Cole, COO
Phillip Febbo, Chief Mktg Ofcr
Jason W Radford,
Laura Leber Kammeyer, Officer
EMP: 85
SQ FT: 180,700
SALES: 287.4MM Publicly Held
WEB: www.genomichealth.com
SIC: 8071 8731 Medical laboratories; biotechnical research, commercial

(P-22221)
GENOMIC HEALTH INC
101 Galveston Dr, Redwood City
(94063-4734)
PHONE..................650 556-9300
Kathy Haller, Human Res Mgr
Kim Akers, Purch Mgr
Jon Cassel, VP Opers
Kelly McClellan, Corp Counsel
June Liu, Manager
EMP: 717
SALES (corp-wide): 287.4MM Publicly Held
SIC: 8071 8731 Medical laboratories; commercial physical research
PA: Genomic Health, Inc.
    301 Penobscot Dr
    Redwood City CA 94063
    650 556-9300

(P-22222)
GENOPTIX INC (DH)
Also Called: Genoptix Medical Laboratory
1811 Aston Ave Ste 100, Carlsbad
(92008-7396)
PHONE..................760 268-6200
Fax: 760 268-6201
Tina S Nova PHD, President
Samuel D Riccitelli, COO
Douglas A Schuling, CFO
Christian V Kuhlen MD, Vice Pres
Jonathan Lawson, Lab Dir
EMP: 151
SQ FT: 116,000
SALES (est): 1.4MM
SALES (corp-wide): 49.4B Privately Held
WEB: www.genoptix.com
SIC: 8071 Medical laboratories
HQ: Novartis Finance Corporation
    230 Park Ave Fl 21
    New York NY 10169
    212 307-1122

(P-22223)
GENZYME CORPORATION
Also Called: Genzyme Genetics
655 E Huntington Dr, Monrovia
(91016-3636)
PHONE..................800 255-1616
Fax: 714 245-9259
Jane Willis, Branch Mgr
Gary Corn, Lab Dir
Edward R Wassman, Director
EMP: 80
SALES (corp-wide): 421.5MM Privately Held
WEB: www.genzyme.com
SIC: 8071 Testing laboratories
HQ: Genzyme Corporation
    500 Kendall St
    Cambridge MA 02142
    617 252-7500

(P-22224)
GRIFOLS DIAGNSTC SOLUTIONS INC (HQ)
4560 Horton St, Emeryville (94608-2916)
PHONE..................323 225-2221
David Bell, Exec VP
David Dew, Marketing Staff
Jennifer Katz, Cust Mgr
EMP: 168
SALES (est): 35.2MM
SALES (corp-wide): 464.6MM Privately Held
SIC: 8071 Testing laboratories; biological laboratory; blood analysis laboratory; pathological laboratory
PA: Grifols Sa
    Calle Jesus I Maria 6
    Barcelona 08022
    935 710-196

(P-22225)
IDEXX REFERENCE LABS INC
1370 Reynolds Ave Ste 109, Irvine
(92614-5546)
PHONE..................949 477-2840
Carlos Vasquez, Manager
Carlos Basquez, QC Mgr
EMP: 50
SALES (corp-wide): 1.6B Publicly Held
SIC: 8071 Testing laboratories
HQ: Idexx Reference Laboratories, Inc.
    1 Idexx Dr
    Westbrook ME 04092
    207 856-0300

(P-22226)
IDEXX REFERENCE LABS INC
2825 Kovr Dr, West Sacramento
(95605-1600)
PHONE..................916 372-4200
Fax: 916 267-2413
Lewis Knight, Branch Mgr
William Flaherty, Opers Mgr
Kerry Bennett, Director
Vera Yang, Manager
EMP: 175
SALES (corp-wide): 1.6B Publicly Held
SIC: 8071 Testing laboratories
HQ: Idexx Reference Laboratories, Inc.
    1 Idexx Dr
    Westbrook ME 04092
    207 856-0300

(P-22227)
KAISER MANTECA MEDICAL OFFICE
1721 W Yosemite Ave, Manteca
(95337-5130)
PHONE..................209 825-3700
Melanie Hatchel, Owner
Nadine Neswick, Hlthcr Dir
EMP: 115 EST: 1998
SALES (est): 5.2MM Privately Held
SIC: 8071 Medical laboratories

(P-22228)
KAISER RADIOLOGY
7300 N Fresno St, Fresno (93720-2941)
PHONE..................559 448-5541
Quemars Ahmadi, Manager
Linda Monte, Technical Staff
Mary Cooper, Manager
EMP: 80
SALES (est): 4.6MM Privately Held
SIC: 8071 X-ray laboratory, including dental

(P-22229)
KAN-DI-KI LLC
Also Called: Diagnostic Labs & Rdlgy
2820 N Ontario St, Burbank (91504-2015)
PHONE..................818 549-1880
Fax: 818 333-7239
Kelly McCullum,
Brian Tees, Vice Pres
Nedd Sherbanee, Area Mgr
Oscar Castro, Administration
James Harland, Administration
EMP: 1500
SQ FT: 7,000
SALES (est): 74.5MM Privately Held
SIC: 8071 Testing laboratories; X-ray laboratory, including dental

(P-22230)
KERN RDLGY IMAGING SYSTEMS INC (PA)
2301 Bahamas Dr, Bakersfield
(93309-0663)
PHONE..................661 326-9600
Fax: 661 283-4288
David P Schale, CEO
Jeff Child MD, Treasurer
John Gundzik MD, Vice Pres
Karen Jett, Executive
Penny Bloching, Accounts Mgr
EMP: 65
SQ FT: 20,000
SALES (est): 21.1MM Privately Held
SIC: 8071 X-ray laboratory, including dental

(P-22231)
LABORATORY CORP AMER HOLDINGS
14901 Rinaldi St Ste 203, Mission Hills
(91345-1251)
PHONE..................818 361-7089
Paul Rodriguez, Manager
EMP: 84
SALES (corp-wide): 8.6B Publicly Held
SIC: 8071 Medical laboratories
PA: Laboratory Corporation Of America Holdings
    358 S Main St
    Burlington NC 27215
    336 229-1127

(P-22232)
LABORATORY CORP AMER HOLDINGS
19951 Mariner Ave Ste 150, Torrance
(90503-1738)
PHONE..................818 908-3600
EMP: 80
SALES (corp-wide): 8.6B Publicly Held
SIC: 8071 Medical laboratories
PA: Laboratory Corporation Of America Holdings
    358 S Main St
    Burlington NC 27215
    336 229-1127

(P-22233)
LABORATORY CORP AMER HOLDINGS
10930 Bigge St, San Leandro
(94577-1121)
PHONE..................510 635-4555
Kimberly Williams, Branch Mgr
EMP: 84
SALES (corp-wide): 8.6B Publicly Held
SIC: 8071 Testing laboratories
PA: Laboratory Corporation Of America Holdings
    358 S Main St
    Burlington NC 27215
    336 229-1127

(P-22234)
LATARA ENTERPRISE INC (PA)
Also Called: Foundation Laboratory
1716 W Holt Ave, Pomona (91768-3333)
PHONE..................909 623-9301
Stepan Vartanian, CEO
Taleen Vartanian, CFO
ARA Vartanian, Treasurer
Linda Vartanian, Vice Pres
Lala Vartanian, Admin Sec
EMP: 120 EST: 1966
SQ FT: 19,000
SALES (est): 10.2MM Privately Held
WEB: www.foundationlaboratory.com
SIC: 8071 Testing laboratories

(P-22235)
LATARA ENTERPRISE INC
9610 Stockdale Hwy, Bakersfield
(93311-3625)
PHONE..................661 665-9780
Rosie Chavez, Manager
EMP: 62
SALES (corp-wide): 10.2MM Privately Held
SIC: 8071 Medical laboratories

8071 - Medical Laboratories County (P-22236)
PRODUDUCTS & SERVICES SECTION

PA: Latara Enterprise, Inc.
1716 W Holt Ave
Pomona CA 91768
909 623-9301

(P-22236)
LATARA ENTERPRISE INC
705 E Virginia Way Ste D, Barstow (92311-3955)
PHONE.................760 256-3450
Susan Reese, Manager
EMP: 62
SALES (corp-wide): 10.2MM **Privately Held**
SIC: 8071 Medical laboratories
PA: Latara Enterprise, Inc.
1716 W Holt Ave
Pomona CA 91768
909 623-9301

(P-22237)
LATARA ENTERPRISE INC
817 S Main St, Corona (92882-3406)
PHONE.................951 272-9420
EMP: 62
SALES (corp-wide): 10.2MM **Privately Held**
SIC: 8071 Medical laboratories
PA: Latara Enterprise, Inc.
1716 W Holt Ave
Pomona CA 91768
909 623-9301

(P-22238)
LAWRENCE BERKELEY NATIONAL LAB
1 Cyclotron Rd, Berkeley (94720-8099)
PHONE.................510 486-6792
Fax: 510 486-4000
Paul Alivisatos, Director
Glenn D Kubiak, COO
Deborah Wendt, COO
Kim Williams, CFO
Jim Garbe, Vice Pres
▲ **EMP:** 6000
SALES (est): 206.1MM **Privately Held**
SIC: 8071 Medical laboratories; biological laboratory; testing laboratories

(P-22239)
MADISON RADIOLOGY MED GROUP
65 N Madison Ave Ste M250, Pasadena (91101-2000)
PHONE.................626 793-8189
Terry S Becker, President
Eric Becker, Info Tech Dir
Jeanette Velasco, Manager
EMP: 55
SALES (est): 3.4MM **Privately Held**
SIC: 8071 X-ray laboratory, including dental

(P-22240)
MAGNETIC IMAGING AFFILATES
5730 Telegraph Ave, Oakland (94609-1710)
PHONE.................510 204-1820
Stefan Arnold, Director
Ray Nakashima, Administration
EMP: 55
SQ FT: 3,500
SALES (est): 2.4MM **Privately Held**
SIC: 8071 Medical laboratories

(P-22241)
MAX/MR IMAGING INC
17530 Ventura Blvd # 105, Encino (91316-3883)
PHONE.................818 382-2220
Javad Ahmadian, President
Rafi Hedvat, CFO
Majid Ahmadian, Vice Pres
Cecilia Saldana, Manager
EMP: 100
SALES (est): 2.8MM **Privately Held**
SIC: 8071 X-ray laboratory, including dental

(P-22242)
MERCY HEALTHCARE SACRAMENTO
Also Called: Mercy General Hospital
4001 J St, Sacramento (95819-3626)
PHONE.................916 453-4453

Tom Peterson, President
Ron Kroll, CFO
Linda Gregory, Human Res Dir
Bob Rhodda, Materials Mgr
Virginia Sullivan, Pub Rel Mgr
EMP: 2000
SALES (corp-wide): 7.1B **Privately Held**
WEB: www.mercycare.net
SIC: 8071 X-ray laboratory, including dental
HQ: Mercy Healthcare Sacramento
3400 Data Dr
Rancho Cordova CA 95670
916 379-2871

(P-22243)
MOSS LANDING MARINE LABS
8272 Moss Landing Rd, Moss Landing (95039-9647)
PHONE.................831 771-4400
Fax: 831 632-4403
James Harvey, Director
Sandy Yarbrough, Admin Asst
Toni Fitzwater, Financial Exec
Maria Kaanapu, Analyst
Gary Adams, Facilities Mgr
EMP: 150
SALES (est): 13.6MM **Privately Held**
WEB: www.mlml.calstate.edu
SIC: 8071 Biological laboratory

(P-22244)
MUIR LABS
Also Called: Muirlab
1601 Ygnacio Valley Rd, Walnut Creek (94598-3122)
PHONE.................925 947-3335
Fax: 925 947-4497
Pat Morgan, Director
Christine Moore, Manager
EMP: 400
SALES (est): 5MM **Privately Held**
SIC: 8071 Medical laboratories

(P-22245)
NATERA INC (PA)
201 Industrial Rd Ste 410, San Carlos (94070-2396)
PHONE.................650 249-9090
Fax: 650 533-7999
Matthew Rabinowitz, Ch of Bd
Herm Rosenman, CFO
Robert Pelham, Associate Dir
Jonathan Sheena, CTO
Alma Hurley, Project Mgr
EMP: 215
SQ FT: 88,000
SALES: 190.3MM **Publicly Held**
SIC: 8071 2835 Testing laboratories; in vitro diagnostics

(P-22246)
NATIONAL GENETICS INSTITUTE
2440 S Sepulveda Blvd # 235, Los Angeles (90064-1748)
PHONE.................310 996-6610
Mike Aicher, CEO
EMP: 169
SALES (corp-wide): 8.6B **Publicly Held**
SIC: 8071 Testing laboratories
HQ: National Genetics Institute
2440 S Sepulveda Blvd # 235
Los Angeles CA 90064
310 996-6610

(P-22247)
NEWPORT DIAGNOSTIC CENTER INC (PA)
Also Called: Newport Radio Surgery Center
1605 Avocado Ave, Newport Beach (92660-7725)
PHONE.................949 760-3025
Fax: 949 720-3944
Hazem H Chehabi, President
Nader Morcos, Vice Pres
Brian Olson, Exec Dir
Kathy Wortham, Exec Dir
Gregg Stempson, Info Tech Dir
EMP: 60
SQ FT: 26,000
SALES (est): 7.7MM **Privately Held**
SIC: 8071 Testing laboratories

(P-22248)
NICHOLS INST REFERENCE LABS (DH)
33608 Ortega Hwy, San Juan Capistrano (92675-2042)
PHONE.................949 728-4000
Douglas Harrington, President
Charles Olson, CFO
Jolene Kahn, Treasurer
Michael O'Gorman, Vice Pres
Murugan R Pandian, Vice Pres
EMP: 525
SQ FT: 240,000
SALES (est): 13.3MM
SALES (corp-wide): 7.4B **Publicly Held**
SIC: 8071 Testing laboratories
HQ: Quest Diagnostics Nichols Institute
33608 Ortega Hwy
San Juan Capistrano CA 92675
949 728-4000

(P-22249)
OPTICS LABORATORY INC
9480 Telstar Ave Ste 3, El Monte (91731-2988)
PHONE.................626 350-1926
Fax: 626 350-1906
Patricia Chiu, CEO
Shawn Ko, Chairman
Sweety Wijaya, Assistant VP
▲ **EMP:** 60
SQ FT: 7,500
SALES (est): 4.8MM **Privately Held**
WEB: www.opticslab.com
SIC: 8071 Medical laboratories

(P-22250)
PACIFIC DIAGNOSTIC LABS LLC
64 N Brent St, Ventura (93003-2808)
PHONE.................805 653-5443
EMP: 56
SALES (corp-wide): 7.3MM **Privately Held**
SIC: 8071 Medical laboratories
PA: Pacific Diagnostic Laboratories, Llc
454 S Patterson Ave
Santa Barbara CA 93111
805 879-8100

(P-22251)
PACIFIC TOXICOLOGY LABS
Also Called: Forensic Toxicology Associates
9348 De Soto Ave, Chatsworth (91311-4926)
PHONE.................818 598-3110
Jeff Lanzolatta, CEO
Sue Barbosa, COO
Greg Carroll, CFO
Neil Patel Carroll, CFO
Neil Patel, CFO
EMP: 75
SQ FT: 19,000
SALES (est): 9.5MM **Privately Held**
WEB: www.pactox.com
SIC: 8071 Medical laboratories

(P-22252)
PASADENA CYTO PATHOLOGY LAB
Also Called: Huntington Med Pathology Group
100 W Calif Blvd Fl 3, Pasadena (91105-3010)
PHONE.................626 397-8616
Fax: 626 397-2187
Susan Murakami MD, President
Henry Slosser MD, Vice Pres
Steve Ralph, Director
EMP: 300
SALES (est): 8.1MM **Privately Held**
SIC: 8071 Pathological laboratory

(P-22253)
PENNISULA PTHLOGISTS MED GROUP
Also Called: Peninsula Pathology Associates
393 E Grand Ave Ste I, South San Francisco (94080-6233)
PHONE.................650 616-2940
Leonard A Valentino MD, President
Judy Alonzo, President
Carolyn Katzen MD, Treasurer
Jay A Guichard MD, Vice Pres
Martha S Hales, Admin Sec
EMP: 60

SALES (est): 3.7MM **Privately Held**
SIC: 8071 Pathological laboratory

(P-22254)
PENTRON CLINICAL TECH LLC
1717 W Collins Ave, Orange (92867-5422)
PHONE.................203 265-7397
Gordon Cohen,
Robin Bavin, President
Scott T Willey, CFO
Sean Perkins, Marketing Staff
Bruce Albert,
EMP: 85
SALES (est): 2.5MM
SALES (corp-wide): 16.1MM **Privately Held**
SIC: 8071 Medical laboratories
PA: Pentron Corporation
53 N Plains Industrial Rd
Wallingford CT 06492
203 265-7397

(P-22255)
PHIFACTOR TECHNOLOGIES LLC
6415 Surfside Way, Malibu (90265-3627)
PHONE.................424 234-9494
EMP: 60
SQ FT: 2,700
SALES: 6.5MM **Privately Held**
SIC: 8071 3841 8731 Medical laboratories; diagnostic apparatus, medical; biotechnical research, commercial

(P-22256)
PHYSICIANS AUTOMATED LAB INC (PA)
Also Called: Central Coast Pathology Lab
820 34th St Ste 102, Bakersfield (93301-1933)
P.O. Box 1500 (93302-1500)
PHONE.................661 325-0744
Fax: 661 327-9163
Ken Botta, CEO
William R Schmalhorst MD, President
Bruce Smith, CEO
Joyce Hulen, Admin Sec
Mimi Breslin, Finance Dir
EMP: 69
SQ FT: 63,000
SALES (est): 25MM **Privately Held**
SIC: 8071 Medical laboratories

(P-22257)
POLYPEPTIDE LABORATORIES INC (DH)
365 Maple Ave, Torrance (90503-2602)
PHONE.................310 782-3569
Fax: 310 782-3645
Jane Salik, President
Tim Culbreth, Vice Pres
Nagana Goud, Vice Pres
Michael Verlander, Vice Pres
Mark Miles, QA Dir
▲ **EMP:** 90
SQ FT: 19,200
SALES: 12.8MM **Privately Held**
WEB: www.polypeptide.com
SIC: 8071 8731 Medical laboratories; biotechnical research, commercial
HQ: Polypeptide Laboratories B.V.
Siriusdreef 22
Hoofddorp 2132
235 560-460

(P-22258)
PRECISION TOXICOLOGY LLC
3030 Bunker Hill St, San Diego (92109-5754)
PHONE.................858 274-4813
Jason Hansen, CEO
Miguel Gallego, COO
Kenton Whitfield, CFO
EMP: 60
SALES (est): 6.2MM
SALES (corp-wide): 17.7MM **Privately Held**
SIC: 8071 Medical laboratories
PA: Belhealth Investment Partners, Llc
126 E 56th St Fl 10r
New York NY 10022
347 308-7011

PRODUCTS & SERVICES SECTION

8071 - Medical Laboratories County (P-22280)

(P-22259)
PRIMEX CLINICAL LABS INC (PA)
16742 Stagg St Ste 120, Van Nuys (91406-1641)
PHONE.....................818 779-0496
Fax: 818 779-1067
Oshin Hartoonian, *President*
Erik Avaniss-Aghajano, *Vice Pres*
ARA Hartoonian, *Vice Pres*
Andre Aslanian, *Info Tech Dir*
Bianca Gharimian, *Director*
EMP: 80
SQ FT: 3,000
SALES (est): 11.4MM **Privately Held**
WEB: www.primexlab.com
SIC: 8071 Blood analysis laboratory

(P-22260)
PROGENITY INC (PA)
Also Called: Amdx Laboratory Sciences
4330 La Jolla Village Dr # 200, San Diego (92122-6206)
PHONE.....................855 293-2639
Harry Stylli, *CEO*
Eric Fox, *Vice Pres*
Michael Weindel, *Director*
EMP: 125 **EST:** 2012
SALES (est): 27MM **Privately Held**
WEB: www.amdxlabs.com
SIC: 8071 8731 Blood analysis laboratory; biotechnical research, commercial

(P-22261)
PROOVE MEDICAL LABS INC
15326 Elton Pkwy, Irvine (92618)
PHONE.....................949 427-5303
Brian Meshkin, *CEO*
Sean Roddi, *COO*
Russell Skibsted, *CFO*
EMP: 175
SQ FT: 71,000
SALES: 201MM **Privately Held**
SIC: 8071 Biological laboratory

(P-22262)
PROVIDENCE HEALTH & SERVICES
1360 W 6th St Ste 100, San Pedro (90732-3528)
PHONE.....................310 831-0371
EMP: 87
SALES (corp-wide): 10.1B **Privately Held**
SIC: 8071 Testing laboratories
PA: Providence Health & Services
1801 Lind Ave Sw
Renton WA 98057
425 525-3355

(P-22263)
PSYCHEMEDICS CORPORATION
5832 Uplander Way, Culver City (90230-6608)
PHONE.....................310 216-7776
Fax: 310 216-6662
Michael Schaffer, *Manager*
Allison Arms, *Vice Pres*
Virginia Hill, *Lab Dir*
Paul Matsui, *QA Dir*
Oscar Chao, *Research*
EMP: 75
SALES (corp-wide): 26.9MM **Publicly Held**
WEB: www.psychemedics.com
SIC: 8071 Testing laboratories
PA: Psychemedics Corporation
125 Nagog Park Ste 200
Acton MA 01720
978 206-8220

(P-22264)
QUEST DGNSTICS CLNCAL LABS INC
2369 Bering Dr, San Jose (95131-1125)
PHONE.....................408 975-1015
Dennis Hogle, *Manager*
Leslie Ingram, *Facilities Mgr*
EMP: 320
SALES (corp-wide): 7.4B **Publicly Held**
WEB: www.questcentralab.com
SIC: 8071 Testing laboratories
HQ: Quest Diagnostics Clinical Laboratories, Inc.
1201 S Collegeville Rd
Collegeville PA 19426
610 454-6000

(P-22265)
QUEST DGNSTICS CLNCAL LABS INC
26081 Avenue Hall 150, Valencia (91355-1241)
PHONE.....................661 964-6582
Dennis Hogle, *Branch Mgr*
EMP: 350
SQ FT: 40,000
SALES (corp-wide): 7.4B **Publicly Held**
WEB: www.questcentralab.com
SIC: 8071 Medical laboratories
HQ: Quest Diagnostics Clinical Laboratories, Inc.
1201 S Collegeville Rd
Collegeville PA 19426
610 454-6000

(P-22266)
QUEST DIAGNOSTICS INCORPORATED
401 Gregory Ln Ste 146, Pleasant Hill (94523-2836)
PHONE.....................925 687-2514
Claire McCrossen, *Manager*
EMP: 450
SALES (corp-wide): 7.4B **Publicly Held**
WEB: www.questdiagnostics.com
SIC: 8071 Medical laboratories
PA: Quest Diagnostics Incorporated
3 Giralda Farms
Madison NJ 07940
973 520-2700

(P-22267)
QUEST DIAGNOSTICS INCORPORATED
33608 Ortega Hwy, Mission Viejo (92675-2042)
PHONE.....................949 728-4235
Fax: 949 728-4984
Jon Nakamoto, *Manager*
EMP: 500
SALES (corp-wide): 7.4B **Publicly Held**
WEB: www.questdiagnostics.com
SIC: 8071 Medical laboratories
PA: Quest Diagnostics Incorporated
3 Giralda Farms
Madison NJ 07940
973 520-2700

(P-22268)
QUEST DIAGNOSTICS INCORPORATED
1275 E Spruce Ave Ste 102, Fresno (93720-3372)
PHONE.....................559 438-2893
EMP: 60
SALES (corp-wide): 7.1B **Publicly Held**
SIC: 8071
PA: Quest Diagnostics Incorporated
3 Giralda Farms
Madison NJ 07940
973 520-2700

(P-22269)
RADNET INC (PA)
1510 Cotner Ave, Los Angeles (90025-3303)
PHONE.....................310 445-2800
Howard G Berger, *Ch of Bd*
Stephen M Forthuber, *COO*
Mark D Stolper, *CFO*
Norman R Hames, *Exec VP*
Jeffrey Inden, *Exec VP*
EMP: 150
SQ FT: 21,500
SALES: 809.6MM **Publicly Held**
WEB: www.radnetonline.com
SIC: 8071 Medical laboratories; ultrasound laboratory; neurological laboratory; X-ray laboratory, including dental

(P-22270)
REDDING PATHOLOGISTS LAB
2036 Railroad Ave, Redding (96001-1801)
PHONE.....................530 225-8050
Richard Severance, *Manager*
EMP: 55
SALES (corp-wide): 11.6MM **Privately Held**
WEB: www.reddingpath.com
SIC: 8071 Pathological laboratory
PA: Redding Pathologists Laboratory
1725 Gold St
Redding CA 96001
530 225-8050

(P-22271)
REDWOOD REGIONAL MEDICAL GROUP
3555 Round Barn Cir, Santa Rosa (95403-1757)
PHONE.....................707 546-4062
Sharon Debennedetti, *Exec Dir*
EMP: 50
SALES (corp-wide): 13.7MM **Privately Held**
WEB: www.rrmginc.com
SIC: 8071 X-ray laboratory, including dental
PA: Redwood Regional Medical Group Drug Company, Llc
990 Sonoma Ave Ste 15
Santa Rosa CA 95404
707 525-4080

(P-22272)
REDWOOD REGIONAL MEDICAL GROUP (PA)
Also Called: Redwood Regional Oncology Ctr
990 Sonoma Ave Ste 15, Santa Rosa (95404-4813)
PHONE.....................707 525-4080
Mike Smith, *CFO*
Rachael Codding, *Oncology*
Julius M Jaffe MD, *Med Doctor*
Allan P Fishbein,
David A Keefer,
EMP: 70
SQ FT: 20,000
SALES (est): 13.7MM **Privately Held**
WEB: www.rrmginc.com
SIC: 8071 8011 X-ray laboratory, including dental; radiologist

(P-22273)
REDWOOD TOXICOLOGY LAB INC
3650 Westwind Blvd, Santa Rosa (95403-1066)
P.O. Box 5680 (95402-5680)
PHONE.....................707 577-7958
Fax: 707 577-0365
Albert Berger, *CEO*
Wayne Ross, *Shareholder*
Alber Berger, *CEO*
Barry Chapman, *CFO*
Robert Mount, *Vice Pres*
▲ **EMP:** 120
SQ FT: 23,000
SALES (est): 16MM
SALES (corp-wide): 2.4B **Publicly Held**
WEB: www.redwoodtoxicology.com
SIC: 8071 8734 Medical laboratories; testing laboratories
PA: Alere Inc.
51 Sawyer Rd Ste 200
Waltham MA 02453
781 647-3900

(P-22274)
RHEUMATOLOGY DIAGNOSTICS LAB
Also Called: Rdl Reference Laboratory
10755 Venice Blvd, Los Angeles (90034-6214)
P.O. Box 34020 (90034-0020)
PHONE.....................310 253-5455
Fax: 310 253-5466
Morris Robert I, *President*
Laura Lehrhoff, *COO*
Allan Metzger MD, *Vice Pres*
Barbara Morris, *Exec Dir*
Jhoon Whang, *Info Tech Mgr*
EMP: 60
SQ FT: 33,000
SALES (est): 7.3MM **Privately Held**
WEB: www.rdlinc.com
SIC: 8071 Testing laboratories

(P-22275)
SAN DIEGO IMAGING - CHULA VIST (PA)
8745 Aero Dr Ste 200, San Diego (92123-1774)
PHONE.....................858 565-0950
Keth Prince, *Principal*
Jamie Hanfen, *Manager*
Lucinda Martinez, *Manager*
▲ **EMP:** 50
SALES (est): 5.5MM **Privately Held**
WEB: www.sandiegoimaging.com
SIC: 8071 X-ray laboratory, including dental

(P-22276)
SANTA BARBRA CTTGE HSPTL
Pathology Department
400 W Pueblo St, Santa Barbara (93105-4353)
P.O. Box 689 (93102-0689)
PHONE.....................805 569-7367
Fax: 805 569-8223
Ron Werdt, *President*
Joseph Ilvento, *Research*
EMP: 160
SALES (corp-wide): 610.4MM **Privately Held**
WEB: www.santabarbaracottagehospital.com
SIC: 8071 Pathological laboratory
PA: Santa Barbara Cottage Hospital
400 W Pueblo St
Santa Barbara CA 93105
805 682-7111

(P-22277)
SANTA BARBRA CTTGE HSPTL
Respiratory Care
400 W Pueblo St, Santa Barbara (93105-4353)
PHONE.....................805 569-7224
Dr Phillip Michael, *Director*
Lisa Dominguez, *Manager*
EMP: 960
SALES (corp-wide): 610.4MM **Privately Held**
SIC: 8071 Medical laboratories
PA: Santa Barbara Cottage Hospital
400 W Pueblo St
Santa Barbara CA 93105
805 682-7111

(P-22278)
SANTA MNICA WLSHIRE IMGING LLC
Also Called: Tower St John Imaging
5455 Wilshire Blvd, Los Angeles (90036-4201)
PHONE.....................323 549-3055
Fax: 310 264-9004
Gerald Roth MD,
Arnold L Vinstein, *Exec Dir*
Rafael Ramirez, *Finance*
Sachiko Carpenter, *Bookkeeper*
Tammy Kim, *Mktg Dir*
EMP: 50
SALES (est): 5MM **Privately Held**
SIC: 8071 X-ray laboratory, including dental

(P-22279)
SANTA ROSA RADIOLOGY MED GROUP (PA)
121 Sotoyome St, Santa Rosa (95405-4871)
PHONE.....................707 546-4062
Fax: 707 525-4095
Kim Miranda, *CFO*
Shahab Dadjou, *Exec Dir*
Noreen Griffin, *Executive Asst*
EMP: 50
SQ FT: 20,000
SALES (est): 5.4MM **Privately Held**
WEB: www.wyominglobbyist.com
SIC: 8071 8011 X-ray laboratory, including dental; radiologist

(P-22280)
SCANTIBODIES CLINICAL LAB INC
9236 Abraham Way, Santee (92071-5611)
PHONE.....................866 249-1212
Thomas L Cantor, *President*
Marisol Reynoso, *Admin Asst*

8071 - Medical Laboratories County (P-22281)

Lisa Shouse, *Manager*
Natalie Steward, *Supervisor*
EMP: 50
SALES (est): 2MM
SALES (corp-wide): 97.8MM **Privately Held**
SIC: 8071 Medical laboratories
PA: Scantibodies Laboratory, Inc.
9336 Abraham Way
Santee CA 92071
619 258-9300

(P-22281)
SCHRYVER MED SLS & MKTG LLC
526 Mccormick St, San Leandro (94577-1108)
PHONE..................303 371-0073
Todd Hubbard, *Manager*
EMP: 120
SALES (corp-wide): 59.2MM **Privately Held**
SIC: 8071 Medical laboratories
PA: Schryver Medical Sales And Marketing, Llc
12075 E 45th Ave Ste 600
Denver CO 80239
303 371-0073

(P-22282)
SCHRYVER MED SLS & MKTG LLC
8545 Arjons Dr, San Diego (92126-4361)
PHONE..................303 459-8160
Jose Silva, *Branch Mgr*
EMP: 91
SALES (corp-wide): 59.2MM **Privately Held**
SIC: 8071 Ultrasound laboratory; X-ray laboratory, including dental
PA: Schryver Medical Sales And Marketing, Llc
12075 E 45th Ave Ste 600
Denver CO 80239
303 371-0073

(P-22283)
SCHRYVER MED SLS & MKTG LLC
1845 N Case St, Orange (92865-4234)
PHONE..................303 459-8160
Jose Silva, *Branch Mgr*
EMP: 91
SALES (corp-wide): 59.2MM **Privately Held**
SIC: 8071 Ultrasound laboratory; X-ray laboratory, including dental
PA: Schryver Medical Sales And Marketing, Llc
12075 E 45th Ave Ste 600
Denver CO 80239
303 371-0073

(P-22284)
SCHRYVER MED SLS & MKTG LLC
310 N Cluff Ave Ste 212, Lodi (95240-0764)
PHONE..................303 459-8150
Marc Martin, *Branch Mgr*
EMP: 91
SALES (corp-wide): 59.2MM **Privately Held**
SIC: 8071 Ultrasound laboratory; X-ray laboratory, including dental
PA: Schryver Medical Sales And Marketing, Llc
12075 E 45th Ave Ste 600
Denver CO 80239
303 371-0073

(P-22285)
SEQUENOM CENTER FOR MOLECULAR
Also Called: Sequenom Laboratories
3595 John Hopkins Ct, San Diego (92121-1121)
PHONE..................858 202-9051
Jeffrey D Linton, *Admin Sec*
Carolyn D Beaver, *Treasurer*
Daniel Grosu, *Vice Pres*
Ryan Blitz, *Info Tech Dir*
Selena Kruse, *Research*
◆ **EMP:** 400

SALES: 89.7MM
SALES (corp-wide): 8.6B **Publicly Held**
WEB: www.sequenom.com
SIC: 8071 Medical laboratories
HQ: Sequenom, Inc.
3595 John Hopkins Ct
San Diego CA 92121

(P-22286)
SPECIALTY LABORATORIES INC (DH)
Also Called: Quest Diagn Nichols Inst Valen
27027 Tourney Rd, Valencia (91355-5386)
PHONE..................661 799-6543
Fax: 310 799-6634
R Keith Laughman, *President*
Bart E Thielen, *Treasurer*
Dan R Angress, *Vice Pres*
Vicki Difrancesco, *Vice Pres*
Cheryl G Gallarda, *Vice Pres*
▲ **EMP:** 633 **EST:** 1975
SALES (est): 28MM
SALES (corp-wide): 7.4B **Publicly Held**
WEB: www.specialtylabs.com
SIC: 8071 Testing laboratories
HQ: Ameripath, Inc.
7111 Fairway Dr Ste 101
Palm Beach Gardens FL 33418
561 712-6200

(P-22287)
SUTTER HEALTH
3000 Telegraph Ave, Oakland (94609-3218)
PHONE..................510 869-8777
EMP: 326
SALES (corp-wide): 11B **Privately Held**
SIC: 8071 Medical laboratories
PA: Sutter Health
2200 River Plaza Dr
Sacramento CA 95833
916 733-8800

(P-22288)
SUTTER HEALTH
2001 Dwight Way, Berkeley (94704-2608)
PHONE..................510 204-1591
Veronica Corprew, *Human Resources*
EMP: 187
SALES (corp-wide): 11B **Privately Held**
SIC: 8071 Medical laboratories
PA: Sutter Health
2200 River Plaza Dr
Sacramento CA 95833
916 733-8800

(P-22289)
TAURUS WEST INC (DH)
Also Called: Health Line Clinical Lab
1903 W Empire Ave, Burbank (91504-3433)
PHONE..................818 954-0202
Fax: 818 954-8695
Gary Burkhartsmeier, *CEO*
Natella Lalabekyan, *President*
Sokrates Karimian, *CFO*
Joe Barnes, *Exec VP*
EMP: 212
SQ FT: 66,000
SALES (est): 8.2MM
SALES (corp-wide): 228.6MM **Privately Held**
SIC: 8071 Medical laboratories

(P-22290)
TRUXTUN RADIOLOGY MED GROUP LP
3940 San Dimas St, Bakersfield (93301-1458)
PHONE..................661 325-6200
Fax: 661 325-4941
Girish Patel, *General Ptnr*
EMP: 150
SALES (est): 2MM **Privately Held**
SIC: 8071 X-ray laboratory, including dental

(P-22291)
UNILAB CORPORATION
3714 Northgate Blvd, Sacramento (95834-1617)
P.O. Box 515002 (95851-5002)
PHONE..................916 927-9900
Fax: 916 927-1492
David Weavil, *President*

Brian Urban, *CFO*
Mark Bibi, *Vice Pres*
Gary Hall, *Executive*
Chad Arnold, *Human Res Mgr*
EMP: 250
SQ FT: 660
SALES (est): 5.1MM **Privately Held**
SIC: 8071 Medical laboratories

(P-22292)
UNILAB CORPORATION (HQ)
Also Called: Quest Diagnostics
8401 Fallbrook Ave, West Hills (91304-3226)
PHONE..................818 737-6000
Surya Mohapatra, *CEO*
Delbert Fisher, *Vice Pres*
Michael Hughes, *Vice Pres*
Ed Norris, *Vice Pres*
Christopher Hoagland, *Executive*
EMP: 400
SALES (est): 407.1MM
SALES (corp-wide): 7.4B **Publicly Held**
WEB: www.unilab.com
SIC: 8071 Testing laboratories
PA: Quest Diagnostics Incorporated
3 Giralda Farms
Madison NJ 07940
973 520-2700

(P-22293)
UNILAB CORPORATION
6475 Camden Ave Ste 104, San Jose (95120-2847)
PHONE..................408 927-8331
Ian Brotchie, *President*
David Garcia, *Bd of Directors*
Valerie P Oceguera, *Bd of Directors*
Steve Stanley, *Bd of Directors*
EMP: 300
SALES (corp-wide): 7.4B **Publicly Held**
WEB: www.unilab.com
SIC: 8071 Testing laboratories
HQ: Unilab Corporation
8401 Fallbrook Ave
West Hills CA 91304
818 737-6000

(P-22294)
UNITED WESTLABS INC
25751 Mcbean Pkwy Ste 200, Santa Clarita (91355-3701)
PHONE..................661 254-0801
EMP: 66
SALES (corp-wide): 9.3MM **Privately Held**
SIC: 8071 Medical laboratories
PA: United Westlabs, Inc.
801 Parkcenter Dr Ste 202
Santa Ana CA 92705
714 560-8429

(P-22295)
VALLEY RADIOLOGY CONSULTANTS (PA)
6185 Paseo Del Norte # 110, Carlsbad (92011-1152)
PHONE..................619 797-8248
Allen Nalbandian, *President*
Raymond Sung, *Treasurer*
Dmitri Segal, *Branch Mgr*
Tana Jackson, *Office Mgr*
Marcus Van Demetrie, *Admin Sec*
EMP: 54
SALES (est): 10.7MM **Privately Held**
WEB: www.valleyrad.com
SIC: 8071 8011 X-ray laboratory, including dental; radiologist

(P-22296)
VALLEY TOXICOLOGY SERVICE INC
Also Called: Valtox Laboratories
2401 Port St, West Sacramento (95691-3501)
P.O. Box 427 (95691-0427)
PHONE..................916 371-5440
Fax: 916 371-8660
Jon Knapp, *President*
Carol Knapp, *Admin Sec*
EMP: 70
SQ FT: 7,000
SALES (est): 2MM **Privately Held**
WEB: www.valtox.com
SIC: 8071 3826 Bacteriological laboratory; analytical instruments

(P-22297)
VERACYTE INC
6000 Shoreline Ct Ste 300, South San Francisco (94080-7606)
PHONE..................650 243-6200
Bonnie H Anderson, *President*
Brian G Atwood, *Ch of Bd*
Christopher M Hall, *COO*
Shelly D Guyer, *CFO*
Neil M Barth, *Chief Mktg Ofcr*
EMP: 192
SQ FT: 59,000
SALES: 49.5MM **Privately Held**
SIC: 8071 8733 Medical laboratories; medical research

(P-22298)
VERGENCE LABS INC
333 Wshington Blvd Ste 50, Marina Del Rey (90292)
PHONE..................650 691-3009
Cory Grenier, *Director*
EMP: 362
SALES (est): 192.4K
SALES (corp-wide): 7.4MM **Privately Held**
SIC: 8071 Medical laboratories
PA: Snap Inc.
63 Market St
Venice CA 90291
310 399-3339

(P-22299)
WHITEFIELD MEDICAL LAB INC (PA)
Also Called: Whitefield Medical Lab & Rdlgy
764 Indigo Ct Ste A, Pomona (91767-2269)
PHONE..................909 625-2114
Fax: 909 625-7735
Jatin Laxpati, *President*
Shaila Laxpati, *Corp Secy*
EMP: 50
SQ FT: 7,000
SALES (est): 6.6MM **Privately Held**
SIC: 8071 Medical laboratories

8072 Dental Laboratories

(P-22300)
ADVANCED DENTAL IMAGING LLC
4028 Via Laguna, Santa Barbara (93110-2116)
PHONE..................805 687-5571
Kathleen S Cox,
Barbara Cone, *Research*
EMP: 50
SALES (est): 3.5MM **Privately Held**
WEB: www.adisb.com
SIC: 8072 Dental laboratories

(P-22301)
CALIFORNIA DENTAL ARTS LLC
20421 Pacifica Dr, Cupertino (95014-3013)
PHONE..................408 255-1020
Leon Frangadakis, *Principal*
Matt Froess, *Vice Pres*
Lonnie Fountain, *Marketing Mgr*
Lan Khuc, *Frmly & Gen Dent*
Steve Pavlidakis, *Manager*
EMP: 58
SQ FT: 4,000
SALES (est): 6MM **Privately Held**
WEB: www.caldentalarts.com
SIC: 8072 Dental laboratories; crown & bridge production; denture production

(P-22302)
CANEW INC
22135 Roscoe Blvd, Canoga Park (91304-3885)
PHONE..................818 703-5100
Dan Materdomini, *President*
EMP: 120
SQ FT: 22,000
SALES (est): 13.9MM **Privately Held**
WEB: www.davincilab.com
SIC: 8072 5047 Dental laboratories; dental equipment & supplies

PRODUCTS & SERVICES SECTION
8082 - Home Health Care Svcs County (P-22326)

(P-22303)
CONTINENTAL DNTL CERAMICS INC
1873 Western Way, Torrance (90501-1124)
PHONE...................310 618-8821
Fax: 310 618-1238
Jerry Doviack, *President*
Krystina Doviack, *Corp Secy*
Terri Kump, *Technician*
Robert Gonzalez, *Manager*
Janine Poche, *Manager*
EMP: 50
SQ FT: 12,000
SALES (est): 5.1MM **Privately Held**
SIC: 8072 Dental laboratories

(P-22304)
DLH DAVINCI LLC
22135 Roscoe Blvd, West Hills (91304-3885)
PHONE...................818 703-5100
Thomas Rochefort, *Vice Pres*
EMP: 65
SALES (est): 268K **Privately Held**
SIC: 8072 Dental laboratories

(P-22305)
DURA METRICS INC (PA)
816 Piner Rd, Santa Rosa (95403-2019)
P.O. Box 873 (95402-0873)
PHONE...................707 546-5138
Fax: 707 523-3143
Michael Kulwiec, *President*
EMP: 68 EST: 1968
SQ FT: 7,500
SALES (est): 4.9MM **Privately Held**
SIC: 8072 Dental laboratories

(P-22306)
EURODENT INC
9310 Topanga Canyon Blvd, Chatsworth (91311-5713)
PHONE...................818 832-1325
Fax: 818 832-7075
Adam Adamonis, *President*
V J Lyons, *Vice Pres*
Simon Avanessian, *Manager*
Amira Rucker, *Manager*
EMP: 60
SQ FT: 1,800
SALES (est): 4.1MM **Privately Held**
WEB: www.eurodentlab.com
SIC: 8072 Crown & bridge production

(P-22307)
G & H DENTAL ARTS INC (PA)
Also Called: G&H Dental Arts Cushman Dental
4212 Artesia Blvd, Torrance (90504-3106)
PHONE...................310 214-8007
Fax: 310 214-9137
Glen Yamamoto, *President*
Kiichi Yamamoto, *Vice Pres*
Emiko Onda, *Accountant*
Ino Yoshitaka, *Purch Mgr*
Brian Smith, *Sales Staff*
▲ EMP: 79
SQ FT: 4,500
SALES: 10MM **Privately Held**
WEB: www.gandhdental.com
SIC: 8072 Dental laboratories

(P-22308)
JAMES R GLIDEWELL DENTAL
Also Called: Bdl Prosthetics
2181 Dupont Dr, Irvine (92612-1301)
PHONE...................800 411-9723
Fax: 949 863-5599
Robert Rosen, *Branch Mgr*
Hitesh Hansalia, *Info Tech Mgr*
Matthieu Ennis, *Research*
Robert Manwell, *Manager*
EMP: 1000
SALES (corp-wide): 177.9MM **Privately Held**
SIC: 8072 Dental laboratories
PA: James R. Glidewell, Dental Ceramics, Inc.
4141 Macarthur Blvd
Newport Beach CA 92660
949 440-2600

(P-22309)
JAMES R GLIDEWELL DENTAL (PA)
Also Called: Glidewell Laboratories
4141 Macarthur Blvd, Newport Beach (92660-2015)
PHONE...................949 440-2600
Fax: 949 440-2784
James R Glidewell, *CEO*
Greg Minzenmayer, *COO*
Rob Grice, *CFO*
Glenn Sasaki, *CFO*
Glenn Sasaki, *CFO*
▲ EMP: 1100 EST: 1969
SQ FT: 72,000
SALES (est): 177.9MM **Privately Held**
WEB: www.glidewelldental.com
SIC: 8072 Dental laboratories

(P-22310)
KEATING DENTAL ARTS INC
16881 Hale Ave Ste A, Irvine (92606-5068)
PHONE...................949 955-2100
Shaun Keating, *President*
Shannon Keating, *Vice Pres*
EMP: 115
SQ FT: 8,000
SALES: 13MM **Privately Held**
WEB: www.keatingdentalarts.com
SIC: 8072 Dental laboratories

(P-22311)
MICRO DENTAL LABORATORIES (HQ)
Also Called: A Dti Company
5601 Arnold Rd Fl 100, Dublin (94568-7726)
PHONE...................925 829-3611
Fax: 925 829-0685
Kimberley Bradshaw, *President*
Bill Johnson, *CFO*
Jeffrey Zellmer, *CFO*
Laing Rikkers, *Senior VP*
Randall Leininger, *Vice Pres*
EMP: 168
SQ FT: 90,000
SALES (est): 23.3MM
SALES (corp-wide): 24.4MM **Privately Held**
WEB: www.microdental.com
SIC: 8072 Dental laboratories; artificial teeth production; denture production; orthodontic appliance production
PA: Healthpoint Capital, Llc
505 Park Ave Fl 12
New York NY 10022
212 935-7780

(P-22312)
PALOMAR HEALTH
Also Called: Pomerado Hospital
15615 Pomerado Rd, Poway (92064-2405)
PHONE...................858 613-4000
Fax: 760 739-2109
David Parrot, *Administration*
Steve Gold, *Administration*
Howard N Kaye, *Rheumtlgy Spec*
Maryam Zarei, *Immunologist*
Archana Narayan, *Director*
EMP: 100
SALES (corp-wide): 614.2MM **Privately Held**
WEB: www.sunbridge.com
SIC: 8072 Dental laboratories
PA: Palomar Health
456 E Grand Ave
Escondido CA 92025
442 281-5000

(P-22313)
TRIDENT LABS INC
Also Called: Trident Dental Laboratories
12000 Aviation Blvd, Hawthorne (90250-3438)
PHONE...................310 915-9121
Laurence K Fishman, *CEO*
Richard B Mc Donald, *CFO*
Veronica Fitzgerald, *Executive Asst*
Conhuelo Wilson, *Administration*
Earl Gales, *Technology*
▲ EMP: 125
SQ FT: 16,000
SALES (est): 16.1MM **Privately Held**
WEB: www.tridentlab.com
SIC: 8072 Dental laboratories

8082 Home Health Care

(P-22314)
A & A HOME CARE SERVICES
7756 Cntry Clb Dr Bldg A, Palm Springs (92263)
PHONE...................760 416-6769
Suzanne O Armstrong, *Owner*
EMP: 60
SALES (est): 588.7K **Privately Held**
SIC: 8082 7299 Home health care services; personal financial services; personal shopping service

(P-22315)
A BETTER SOLUTION IN HOME CARE
1409 N 2nd St, El Cajon (92021-3436)
PHONE...................619 447-1528
Lillia Smith Pratt, *Branch Mgr*
EMP: 183
SALES (corp-wide): 8.1MM **Privately Held**
SIC: 8082 Home health care services
PA: A Better Solution In Home Care, Inc
3636 Camino Del Rio N
San Diego CA 92108
619 585-9011

(P-22316)
A CAOS MEDICAL CORPORATION
2655 Camino Del R Ste 330, San Diego (92108)
PHONE...................800 362-2731
Angel Iscovich, *President*
Lynne Liko, *Office Mgr*
EMP: 99
SALES (est): 307K **Privately Held**
SIC: 8082 Home health care services

(P-22317)
A CAREGIVER LLC
31520 Rr Cyn Rd Ste A, Canyon Lake (92587-9499)
PHONE...................951 676-4190
EMP: 50
SALES (est): 841.8K **Privately Held**
SIC: 8082

(P-22318)
ABLE HANDS INC
18780 Amar Rd Ste 207, Walnut (91789-4559)
PHONE...................626 965-2233
Salvador L Abiera, *President*
Cynthia Magtoto, *CFO*
EMP: 100
SALES (est): 1.7MM **Privately Held**
SIC: 8082 Home health care services

(P-22319)
ABOVE HLTH HM CARE SLTIONS LLC
960 S Peregrine Pl, Anaheim (92806-4727)
PHONE...................714 585-2185
Jesselie Macis,
EMP: 53
SALES (est): 425.4K **Privately Held**
SIC: 8082 Home health care services

(P-22320)
ACCENTCARE INC
1301 Redwood Way, Petaluma (94954-1107)
PHONE...................707 792-2211
EMP: 91
SALES (corp-wide): 316.1MM **Privately Held**
SIC: 8082 Home health care services
PA: Accentcare, Inc.
17855 Dallas Pkwy
Dallas TX 75287
800 834-3059

(P-22321)
ACCENTCARE INC
5050 Mrphy Knyan Rd St200 Ste 200, San Diego (92123)
PHONE...................858 576-7410
Fax: 858 576-9695
EMP: 821
SALES (corp-wide): 316.1MM **Privately Held**
SIC: 8082 7389 Home health care services
PA: Accentcare, Inc.
17855 Dallas Pkwy
Dallas TX 75287
800 834-3059

(P-22322)
ACCENTCARE HM HLTH SCRMNTO INC
2880 Sunrise Blvd Ste 218, Rancho Cordova (95742-6101)
PHONE...................916 852-5888
Fax: 916 852-5889
Karin Stark, *President*
Rochelle Ward, *Vice Pres*
Debra Henry, *Office Mgr*
EMP: 55
SQ FT: 10,000
SALES (est): 1.6MM
SALES (corp-wide): 316.1MM **Privately Held**
SIC: 8082 Visiting nurse service
HQ: Accentcare Home Health, Inc.
135 Technology Dr Ste 150
Irvine CA 92618
949 623-1500

(P-22323)
ACCENTCARE HOME HEALTH
2344 S 2nd St Ste A, El Centro (92243-5606)
PHONE...................760 352-4022
Melanie Ihler, *CEO*
EMP: 50
SALES (est): 1.1MM
SALES (corp-wide): 316.1MM **Privately Held**
WEB: www.accentcare.com
SIC: 8082 Home health care services
HQ: Accentcare Home Health, Inc.
135 Technology Dr Ste 150
Irvine CA 92618
949 623-1500

(P-22324)
ACCENTCARE HOME HEALTH CAL INC
Also Called: Sunplus HM Care - Pleasant Hl
2300 Contra Costa Blvd # 125, Pleasant Hill (94523-3918)
PHONE...................925 356-6066
Fax: 925 676-2587
Francine Cummings, *Administration*
Sumiko Greene, *Exec Dir*
EMP: 84
SALES (corp-wide): 316.1MM **Privately Held**
WEB: www.dhsi.com
SIC: 8082 Home health care services
HQ: Accentcare Home Health Of California, Inc.
17855 Dallas Pkwy
Dallas TX 75287
949 623-1500

(P-22325)
ACCENTCARE HOME HEALTH CAL INC
16461 Sherman Way Ste 178, Van Nuys (91406-3879)
PHONE...................818 528-8855
Patricia Haynes, *Administration*
Annette Van As, *Administration*
EMP: 50
SALES (corp-wide): 316.1MM **Privately Held**
WEB: www.dhsi.com
SIC: 8082 8051 Home health care services; skilled nursing care facilities
HQ: Accentcare Home Health Of California, Inc.
17855 Dallas Pkwy
Dallas TX 75287
949 623-1500

(P-22326)
ACCENTCARE HOME HEALTH CAL INC
Also Called: Sunplus Home Care - Ontario
1455 Auto Center Dr # 200, Ontario (91761-2239)
PHONE...................909 605-7000

8082 - Home Health Care Svcs County (P-22327) — PRODUDUCTS & SERVICES SECTION

Sharon Guller, *Branch Mgr*
EMP: 58
SALES (corp-wide): 316.1MM **Privately Held**
WEB: www.dhsi.com
SIC: **8082** 8051 Home health care services; skilled nursing care facilities
HQ: Accentcare Home Health Of California, Inc.
   17855 Dallas Pkwy
   Dallas TX 75287
   949 623-1500

(P-22327)
ACCENTCARE HOME HEALTH CAL INC
Also Called: Sunplus Home Hlth - San Marino
2549 Huntington Dr, San Marino (91108-2603)
PHONE..............................626 568-9478
Nancy Flanders, *Manager*
EMP: 50
SALES (corp-wide): 316.1MM **Privately Held**
WEB: www.dhsi.com
SIC: **8082** 8051 Home health care services; skilled nursing care facilities
HQ: Accentcare Home Health Of California, Inc.
   17855 Dallas Pkwy
   Dallas TX 75287
   949 623-1500

(P-22328)
ACCENTCARE HOME HEALTH CAL INC
Also Called: Sunplus Home Care - San Diego
5050 Murphy Canyon Rd # 200, San Diego (92123-4441)
PHONE..............................858 576-7410
Joan Laforteza, *Manager*
EMP: 184
SQ FT: 4,000
SALES (corp-wide): 316.1MM **Privately Held**
WEB: www.dhsi.com
SIC: **8082** Home health care services
HQ: Accentcare Home Health Of California, Inc.
   17855 Dallas Pkwy
   Dallas TX 75287
   949 623-1500

(P-22329)
ACCENTCARE HOME HEALTH CAL INC
Also Called: Sunplus Home Care - W Covina
750 Terrado Plz Ste 221, Covina (91723-3449)
PHONE..............................626 869-0250
Isabella Barrans, *General Mgr*
EMP: 81
SALES (corp-wide): 316.1MM **Privately Held**
WEB: www.dhsi.com
SIC: **8082** Home health care services
HQ: Accentcare Home Health Of California, Inc.
   17855 Dallas Pkwy
   Dallas TX 75287
   949 623-1500

(P-22330)
ACCENTCARE HOME HEALTH CAL INC
Also Called: Sunplus HM Hlth - Newport Bch
3636 Birch St Ste 195, Newport Beach (92660-2644)
PHONE..............................949 250-0133
Mary Lynn, *Manager*
Kurt Yoder, *Administration*
EMP: 56
SALES (corp-wide): 316.1MM **Privately Held**
WEB: www.dhsi.com
SIC: **8082** 8051 Home health care services; skilled nursing care facilities
HQ: Accentcare Home Health Of California, Inc.
   17855 Dallas Pkwy
   Dallas TX 75287
   949 623-1500

(P-22331)
ACCUMEN INC (PA)
9246 Lightwave Ave # 320, San Diego (92123-6411)
PHONE..............................858 777-8160
Jeff Osborne, *President*
Jim Bredy, *COO*
John Adams, *CFO*
Xaver Douwes, *Vice Pres*
Mary Kopp, *Vice Pres*
EMP: 63
SALES (est): 9.1MM **Privately Held**
SIC: **8082** Home health care services

(P-22332)
ACT HOME HEALTH INC
12431 Lewis St Ste 101, Garden Grove (92840-4653)
PHONE..............................714 560-0800
Fax: 714 560-9836
Catherine Johnston, *President*
EMP: 60
SQ FT: 2,500
SALES (est): 3.1MM **Privately Held**
WEB: www.acthh.com
SIC: **8082** Home health care services; visiting nurse service

(P-22333)
ACTION HOME NURSING SERVICES
1190 Suncast Ln Ste 6, El Dorado Hills (95762-9329)
PHONE..............................530 756-2600
Fax: 916 939-1959
J Karen Hahn, *President*
Steven Weishaar, *Vice Pres*
EMP: 70
SALES (est): 3.1MM **Privately Held**
WEB: www.actionhomenursing.com
SIC: **8082** Home health care services

(P-22334)
ADDUS HEALTHCARE INC
936 Mangrove Ave, Chico (95926-3950)
PHONE..............................530 566-0405
Fax: 530 566-0114
Mary Gorman, *Manager*
Valencia Thorpe, *Office Admin*
EMP: 50
SALES (corp-wide): 336.8MM **Publicly Held**
WEB: www.addus.com
SIC: **8082** Home health care services
HQ: Addus Healthcare, Inc.
   2300 Warrenville Rd
   Downers Grove IL 60515
   630 296-3400

(P-22335)
ADDUS HEALTHCARE INC
1730 S Amphlett Blvd, San Mateo (94402-2707)
PHONE..............................650 638-7943
Nancy Kline, *Manager*
EMP: 495
SALES (corp-wide): 336.8MM **Publicly Held**
WEB: www.addus.com
SIC: **8082** Home health care services
HQ: Addus Healthcare, Inc.
   2300 Warrenville Rd
   Downers Grove IL 60515
   630 296-3400

(P-22336)
ADIA LLC
3625 Del Amo Blvd Ste 225, Torrance (90503-1696)
PHONE..............................310 370-0555
Pamela Penson, *Mng Member*
EMP: 70
SALES (est): 2.3MM **Privately Held**
SIC: **8082** Home health care services

(P-22337)
ADMIRAL HOME HEALTH INC
4010 Watson Plaza Dr # 140, Lakewood (90712-4047)
PHONE..............................562 421-0777
Fax: 562 461-2038
Josie Jones, *President*
Danilo Bautista, *Vice Pres*
Ruben Cagan, *Controller*
EMP: 70
SQ FT: 5,900
SALES (est): 3.2MM **Privately Held**
WEB: www.admiralhomehealth.com
SIC: **8082** Home health care services

(P-22338)
ADVANCE HEALTH SOLUTIONS LLC
7825 Fay Ave Ste 200, La Jolla (92037-4270)
PHONE..............................858 876-0136
F Chubak,
Maryam Navaie,
EMP: 60
SALES (est): 729.6K **Privately Held**
SIC: **8082** Home health care services

(P-22339)
ADVANCED HOME HEALTH INC
4370 Auburn Blvd, Sacramento (95841-4107)
PHONE..............................916 978-0744
Fax: 916 978-0745
Angela Sehr, *President*
Angie Macadangdang, *Principal*
Thelma Finch, *Admin Asst*
Deb Ryan, *Administration*
Linda Tromblay, *Bookkeeper*
EMP: 75
SQ FT: 4,000
SALES (est): 4.8MM **Privately Held**
SIC: **8082** 8621 Home health care services; nursing association

(P-22340)
ADVENTIST HEALTH SYSTEM/WEST
460 Kings County Dr # 105, Hanford (93230-5953)
PHONE..............................559 537-2860
Rhonda Dwyer, *Branch Mgr*
EMP: 121
SALES (corp-wide): 251.4MM **Privately Held**
SIC: **8082** Home health care services
PA: Adventist Health System/West
   2100 Douglas Blvd
   Roseville CA 95661
   916 781-2000

(P-22341)
ADVENTIST HEALTH SYSTEM/WEST
Also Called: Phoenix Hospice
100 San Hedrin Cir, Willits (95490-8753)
PHONE..............................707 459-1818
Fax: 707 459-9298
Trudy Miller, *Director*
EMP: 136
SALES (corp-wide): 251.4MM **Privately Held**
SIC: **8082** Home health care services
PA: Adventist Health System/West
   2100 Douglas Blvd
   Roseville CA 95661
   916 781-2000

(P-22342)
ADVISORY BOARD COMPANY
23 Geary St, San Francisco (94108-5701)
PHONE..............................415 671-7750
Fax: 415 671-7761
R W Musslewhite, *CEO*
EMP: 85
SALES (corp-wide): 768.3MM **Publicly Held**
SIC: **8082** Home health care services
PA: The Advisory Board Company
   2445 M St Nw Ste 500
   Washington DC 20037
   202 266-5600

(P-22343)
AEGIS SENIOR COMMUNITIES LLC
Also Called: Aegis of Corte Madera
5555 Paradise Dr, Corte Madera (94925-1861)
PHONE..............................415 483-1399
Fax: 415 927-4244
Bill Phelts, *Branch Mgr*
Stuti Bali, *Human Res Dir*
Dan Allen, *Maintence Staff*
EMP: 80
SALES (corp-wide): 103.6MM **Privately Held**
WEB: www.aegisal.com
SIC: **8082** 8361 8322 Home health care services; residential homes; emergency social services
PA: Senior Aegis Communities Llc
   17602 Ne Union Hill Rd
   Redmond WA 98052
   866 688-5829

(P-22344)
AEGIS SENIOR COMMUNITIES LLC
Also Called: Aegis Gardens
36281 Fremont Blvd, Fremont (94536-3509)
PHONE..............................510 739-0909
Fax: 510 739-0946
Emily Poon, *Manager*
EMP: 50
SALES (corp-wide): 103.6MM **Privately Held**
WEB: www.aegisal.com
SIC: **8082** 8051 Home health care services; skilled nursing care facilities
PA: Senior Aegis Communities Llc
   17602 Ne Union Hill Rd
   Redmond WA 98052
   866 688-5829

(P-22345)
AEGIS SENIOR COMMUNITIES LLC
Also Called: Aegis Living
1660 Oak Park Blvd, Pleasant Hill (94523-4422)
PHONE..............................925 588-7030
Fax: 925 939-2785
Duane Clark, *Partner*
EMP: 70
SALES (corp-wide): 103.6MM **Privately Held**
WEB: www.aegisal.com
SIC: **8082** 8051 Home health care services; skilled nursing care facilities
PA: Senior Aegis Communities Llc
   17602 Ne Union Hill Rd
   Redmond WA 98052
   866 688-5829

(P-22346)
AEGIS SENIOR COMMUNITIES LLC
Also Called: Aegis Assisted Living
125 Heather Ter, Aptos (95003-3825)
PHONE..............................831 684-2700
Fax: 831 684-2719
Janice Ibaio, *Manager*
Victor Langer, *Exec Dir*
Claudia Anaya, *Director*
Matt Judd, *Director*
EMP: 50
SALES (corp-wide): 103.6MM **Privately Held**
WEB: www.aegisal.com
SIC: **8082** 8051 Home health care services; skilled nursing care facilities
PA: Senior Aegis Communities Llc
   17602 Ne Union Hill Rd
   Redmond WA 98052
   866 688-5829

(P-22347)
AEGIS SENIOR COMMUNITIES LLC
Also Called: Aegis of Laguna Niguel
32170 Niguel Rd, Laguna Niguel (92677-4264)
PHONE..............................949 496-8080
Fax: 949 496-8181
Pamela Kerr, *Exec Dir*
Becky Spencer, *Info Tech Mgr*
Amber Digangi, *Benefits Mgr*
Brendon Mill, *Food Svc Dir*
EMP: 50
SALES (corp-wide): 103.6MM **Privately Held**
WEB: www.aegisal.com
SIC: **8082** Home health care services
PA: Senior Aegis Communities Llc
   17602 Ne Union Hill Rd
   Redmond WA 98052
   866 688-5829

PRODUCTS & SERVICES SECTION

8082 - Home Health Care Svcs County (P-22374)

(P-22348)
AEGIS SENIOR COMMUNITIES LLC
Also Called: Aegis of Granada Hills
10801 Lindley Ave, Granada Hills (91344-4441)
PHONE 818 363-3373
Fax: 818 363-1933
Steve Kregel, *Manager*
EMP: 80
SALES (corp-wide): 103.6MM **Privately Held**
WEB: www.aegisal.com
SIC: 8082 8052 8051 8361 Home health care services; intermediate care facilities; skilled nursing care facilities; residential care
PA: Senior Aegis Communities Llc
17602 Ne Union Hill Rd
Redmond WA 98052
866 688-5829

(P-22349)
AGAPE IN HOME CARE INC
4800 District Blvd Ste A, Bakersfield (93313-2325)
PHONE 661 835-0364
Sandra Oxford, *President*
EMP: 50
SALES (est): 1.2MM **Privately Held**
SIC: 8082 Home health care services

(P-22350)
ALLIANCE HOSPITAL SERVICES
Also Called: Mills-Peninsula Health HM Care
100 S San Mateo Dr, San Mateo (94401-3805)
PHONE 650 697-6900
Fax: 650 696-4636
Sheila Schubert, *Branch Mgr*
Rick Navarro, *Bd of Directors*
Holly Vafi, *Pathologist*
EMP: 50
SALES (corp-wide): 7.5MM **Privately Held**
WEB: www.hospitalconsort.org
SIC: 8082 Home health care services
PA: Alliance Hospital Services, Inc
309 Lennon Ln Ste 200
Walnut Creek CA 94598
925 304-1107

(P-22351)
ALLIED PHYSICIANS
Also Called: Allied Physicians, IPA
1680 S Garfield Ave, Alhambra (91801-5413)
PHONE 626 282-2116
Fax: 626 282-8006
Samuel K Zia, *CEO*
James Chang, *COO*
Thomas Hwee, *Treasurer*
Thomas Lam, *Admin Sec*
EMP: 60
SALES (est): 2.2MM **Privately Held**
SIC: 8082 Home health care services

(P-22352)
ALLIED PROF NURSING CARE
2345 W Fthlls Blvd Ste 14, Upland (91786)
PHONE 909 949-1066
Fax: 909 949-1066
Michael Gutierrez, *President*
Karen Gutierrez, *Administration*
EMP: 80 EST: 1996
SALES (est): 1MM **Privately Held**
SIC: 8082 Visiting nurse service

(P-22353)
ALTA HOME CARE INC
1059 N Palm Canyon Dr, Palm Springs (92262-4419)
PHONE 760 778-3443
EMP: 126
SALES (corp-wide): 9.2MM **Privately Held**
SIC: 8082 Home health care services
PA: Alta Home Care Inc.
1315 Crona Pinte Ct 201
Corona CA 92879
714 744-8191

(P-22354)
ALWAYS HOME NURSING SVC INC
7777 Greenback Ln Ste 208, Citrus Heights (95610-5800)
PHONE 916 989-6420
Nancy Giachino, *President*
Janice Simcoe, *Business Mgr*
EMP: 200
SALES (est): 7.1MM **Privately Held**
SIC: 8082 Home health care services

(P-22355)
ALWAYS THERE LIVE IN CARE LLC
7121 Magnolia Ave, Riverside (92504-3805)
PHONE 888 606-8880
Anntwonette Howard, *President*
Anntwonette Bonner, *President*
EMP: 72
SALES (est): 190K **Privately Held**
SIC: 8082 7389 Home health care services;

(P-22356)
ALZHEIMERS CARE SINCE 1983
Also Called: Garden, The
3730 S Greenville St, Santa Ana (92704-7092)
PHONE 714 641-0959
Violet Lazarescu, *Administration*
EMP: 50
SALES (est): 1.9MM **Privately Held**
SIC: 8082 Home health care services

(P-22357)
AMBIENTE ENTERPRISES INC
Also Called: Home Instead Senior Care
73726 Alessandro Dr # 203, Palm Desert (92260-3640)
PHONE 760 674-1905
Fax: 760 328-3067
Rob Costello, *President*
EMP: 120 EST: 1996
SQ FT: 2,600
SALES: 1.5MM **Privately Held**
SIC: 8082 Home health care services

(P-22358)
AMERICAN CAREQUEST INC
3921 Geary Blvd, San Francisco (94118-3218)
PHONE 415 752-9100
Maragret Riskin, *Branch Mgr*
EMP: 52
SALES (corp-wide): 3.7MM **Privately Held**
SIC: 8082 Home health care services
PA: American Carequest, Inc.
1426 Fillmore St Ste 210
San Francisco CA 94115
415 885-3324

(P-22359)
AMERICAN PRIVATE DUTY INC
Also Called: American Untd HM Care Crp-Priv
13111 Ventura Blvd # 100, Studio City (91604-2218)
PHONE 818 386-6358
Fax: 818 377-6207
Ann Koshy, *President*
EMP: 80
SALES (est): 4.2MM **Privately Held**
WEB: www.americanprivateduty.com
SIC: 8082 Visiting nurse service

(P-22360)
AMERICAN SPCLTY HLTH GROUP INC (HQ)
10221 Wateridge Cir # 201, San Diego (92121-2702)
PHONE 858 754-2000
George T Devries, *CEO*
Robert White, *COO*
William M Comer Jr, *CFO*
Kevin E Kujawa, *Exec VP*
R Douglas Metz, *Exec VP*
▲ EMP: 378
SQ FT: 148,000
SALES (est): 160.6MM
SALES (corp-wide): 919.9MM **Privately Held**
WEB: www.ashbenefits.com
SIC: 8082 Home health care services
PA: American Specialty Health Incorporated
10221 Wateridge Cir # 201
San Diego CA 92121
858 754-2000

(P-22361)
AN COMPANION HOSPICE
150 E Colorado Blvd # 100, Pasadena (91105-3831)
PHONE 877 303-0692
Eleanor Phillips, *Manager*
EMP: 75 EST: 2015
SALES (est): 215K **Privately Held**
SIC: 8082 Home health care services

(P-22362)
ANGEL CARE HOME HEALTH INC
850 Colorado Blvd Ste 103, Los Angeles (90041-1733)
PHONE 818 248-8811
Vivian A Kono, *President*
EMP: 50
SQ FT: 1,700
SALES: 3MM **Privately Held**
SIC: 8082 Home health care services

(P-22363)
ANGELES HOME HEALTH CARE INC
3701 Wilshire Blvd # 900, Los Angeles (90010-2871)
PHONE 213 487-5131
Fax: 213 387-8733
Rita L Doll, *CEO*
EMP: 125
SALES (est): 3.4MM
SALES (corp-wide): 1.3B **Publicly Held**
SIC: 8082 Visiting nurse service
HQ: Cornerstone Healthcare, Inc.
420 E State St Ste 135
Eagle ID 83616

(P-22364)
ANGELS EVERYDAY INC
Also Called: Visiting Angels
330 Sixth St Ste 201, Redlands (92374-3337)
PHONE 909 793-7788
Brandon Hector, *President*
Sara Hector, *Principal*
EMP: 95
SQ FT: 1,400
SALES (est): 1MM **Privately Held**
SIC: 8082 Home health care services

(P-22365)
ANGELS IN MOTION LLC
Also Called: Visiting Angels
4091 Riverside Dr Ste 111, Chino (91710-3195)
PHONE 909 590-9102
Dominique Alvarez, *Mng Member*
Mariecele Mercado, *Office Mgr*
EMP: 70
SALES (est): 2.9MM **Privately Held**
SIC: 8082 Home health care services

(P-22366)
ANGELS OF VLY HOSPICE CARE LLC
2600 Foothill Blvd # 202, La Crescenta (91214-4578)
PHONE 818 542-3070
Fax: 818 542-3071
Rowena I Argonza,
Rowena Argonza, *CFO*
EMP: 55
SALES: 950K **Privately Held**
SIC: 8082 Home health care services

(P-22367)
APRIA HEALTHCARE LLC
1565 Eastwood Ct, Riverside (92507-2411)
PHONE 951 320-1100
Fax: 951 320-1132
Diana Castro, *Manager*
Elisa Hodge, *Office Mgr*
EMP: 83
SALES (corp-wide): 2.4B **Privately Held**
WEB: www.apria.com
SIC: 8082 Home health care services
HQ: Apria Healthcare Llc
26220 Enterprise Ct
Lake Forest CA 92630
949 616-2606

(P-22368)
APRIA HEALTHCARE LLC
2476 Verna Ct, San Leandro (94577-4223)
PHONE 510 346-4000
Carl Caldwell, *Branch Mgr*
EMP: 66
SALES (corp-wide): 2.4B **Privately Held**
WEB: www.apria.com
SIC: 8082 Home health care services
HQ: Apria Healthcare Llc
26220 Enterprise Ct
Lake Forest CA 92630
949 616-2606

(P-22369)
ARCADIA HEALTH CARE INC
4340 Redwood Hwy Ste 123, San Rafael (94903-2104)
PHONE 415 472-2273
Charles Seins, *President*
Linda Leary, *President*
EMP: 200
SQ FT: 1,200
SALES (est): 3.5MM **Privately Held**
SIC: 8082 8049 Visiting nurse service; nurses, registered & practical

(P-22370)
ARCADIA HEALTH SERVICES INC
1400 Florida Ave Ste 206, Modesto (95350-4445)
PHONE 209 572-7650
Corie Moyers, *Manager*
Sheli Watson, *Manager*
EMP: 100
SALES (corp-wide): 168.8MM **Privately Held**
SIC: 8082 Home health care services
HQ: Arcadia Health Services, Inc.
20750 Civic Center Dr # 100
Southfield MI 48076
248 352-7530

(P-22371)
AT HOME NURSING
2227 Capricorn Way # 105, Santa Rosa (95407-5478)
PHONE 707 546-8773
Fax: 707 546-8788
Dianna Brabetz, *President*
EMP: 100
SALES (est): 2.1MM **Privately Held**
WEB: www.athomenursing.com
SIC: 8082 Home health care services

(P-22372)
ATTENDANT CARE REFERRALS INC
2801 Ocean Park Blvd # 192, Santa Monica (90405-2905)
PHONE 310 399-2904
Fax: 310 390-4405
Gail Shaffer, *President*
EMP: 85
SALES (est): 2.8MM **Privately Held**
WEB: www.tlcacr.com
SIC: 8082 Home health care services

(P-22373)
AVIDA CAREGIVERS INC
11500 W Olympic Blvd # 400, Los Angeles (90064-1525)
PHONE 323 498-1500
Chanel N Devlin, *CEO*
Nicholas Kuluva, *Vice Chairman*
Samuel Bradley, *President*
EMP: 855
SALES (est): 266.2K **Privately Held**
SIC: 8082 Home health care services

(P-22374)
BAYWOOD COURT (PA)
Also Called: Baywood Court Retirement Ctr
21966 Dolores St Apt 279, Castro Valley (94546-6973)
PHONE 510 733-2102

8082 - Home Health Care Svcs County (P-22375)

PRODUDUCTS & SERVICES SECTION

Fax: 510 733-2480
Kelly Wiest, *Exec Dir*
Mike Murphy, *Branch Mgr*
Todd Peterson, *Data Proc Staff*
Kim Konig, *Human Res Dir*
Jody Holdsworth, *Pub Rel Dir*
EMP: 107
SALES: 17.7MM Privately Held
WEB: www.baywoodcourt.org
SIC: 8082 8051 6513 Home health care services; skilled nursing care facilities; retirement hotel operation

(P-22375)
BBT HEALTH LLC
5105 E Dakota Ave, Fresno (93727-7443)
PHONE 559 222-0007
Christopher Dery, *CEO*
EMP: 52
SALES (est): 158.3K Privately Held
SIC: 8082 Home health care services

(P-22376)
BEACH CITIES ELDERCARE INC (PA)
Also Called: Home Instead Senior Care
5500 E Atherton St # 204, Long Beach (90815-4017)
PHONE 562 596-4884
Fax: 562 596-7334
Debra Teofilo, *President*
Tom Teofilo, *General Mgr*
EMP: 78
SQ FT: 750
SALES (est): 4.3MM Privately Held
SIC: 8082 Home health care services

(P-22377)
BEAR FLAG MARKETING CORP
Also Called: At Home Caregivers
7599 Redwood Blvd Ste 200, Novato (94945-7706)
PHONE 415 899-8466
Peter L Rubens, *CEO*
EMP: 117
SQ FT: 1,200
SALES (est): 3.4MM Privately Held
WEB: www.bearflagmarketing.com
SIC: 8082 Home health care services

(P-22378)
BLIZE HEALTHCARE CAL INC
828 San Pablo Ave Ste 105, Albany (94706-1678)
PHONE 800 343-2549
Ukeje Elendu, *President*
Blessing Elendu, *COO*
EMP: 100
SQ FT: 3,700
SALES: 7MM Privately Held
SIC: 8082 Home health care services

(P-22379)
BRADEN PARTNERS LP A CALIF (DH)
Also Called: Pacific Pulmonary Services Co
773 San Marin Dr Ste 2230, Novato (94945-1366)
PHONE 415 893-1518
Fax: 415 893-1522
Jane Thomas, *CEO*
Tsutomu Igawa, *Ch of Bd*
Chris Kane, *COO*
Alan Winters, *Senior VP*
Jon Alsterlind, *Vice Pres*
▲ **EMP:** 65
SALES (est): 102.4MM
SALES (corp-wide): 6.7B Privately Held
SIC: 8082 Home health care services

(P-22380)
BRANLYN PROMINENCE INC (PA)
Also Called: Home Instead Senior Care
9213 Archibald Ave, Rancho Cucamonga (91730-5207)
PHONE 909 476-9030
Fax: 909 476-9130
Brandi Johnson, *CEO*
Lynda Patriquin, *Vice Pres*
EMP: 100
SALES (est): 8.1MM Privately Held
SIC: 8082 Home health care services

(P-22381)
BRIGHT EXPECTATIONS
8175 Limonite Ave Ste C, Riverside (92509-6121)
PHONE 951 360-2070
Fax: 951 727-4304
Charley Cox, *President*
EMP: 50
SQ FT: 1,000
SALES (est): 1.9MM Privately Held
SIC: 8082 Home health care services

(P-22382)
BRITTNEY HOUSE
5401 E Centralia St, Long Beach (90808-1494)
PHONE 562 421-4717
Major Chief, *Owner*
EMP: 72
SALES (est): 299.4K Privately Held
SIC: 8082 8051 Home health care services; skilled nursing care facilities

(P-22383)
BROOKDALE SENIOR LIVING INC
355 W Grant Line Rd Ofc, Tracy (95376-2586)
PHONE 209 839-6623
EMP: 190
SALES (corp-wide): 4.9B Publicly Held
SIC: 8082 Home health care services
PA: Brookdale Senior Living
111 Westwood Pl Ste 400
Brentwood TN 37027
615 221-2250

(P-22384)
BURDETTE DE COCK INC
Also Called: Home Instead Senior Care
3625 Del Amo Blvd Ste 105, Torrance (90503-1698)
PHONE 310 542-0563
Fax: 310 542-1534
Denise De Cock, *President*
EMP: 110
SALES (est): 4.4MM Privately Held
SIC: 8082 Home health care services

(P-22385)
BUTTE HOME HEALTH INC
Also Called: Butte Home Health & Hospice
10 Constitution Dr, Chico (95973-4903)
P.O. Box 5171 (95927-5171)
PHONE 530 895-0462
Fax: 530 896-8327
Brooke Quilici, *President*
Mike Quilici, *Vice Pres*
Isabella Stewart, *Asst Admin*
EMP: 105
SQ FT: 7,100
SALES: 8.1MM Privately Held
WEB: www.buttehomehealth.com
SIC: 8082 Home health care services

(P-22386)
CALIFORNIA HOME CARE INC
3078 El Cajon Blvd, San Diego (92104-1322)
PHONE 619 521-5858
Fax: 619 521-5866
Margarette Borg, *President*
EMP: 350
SALES (est): 10.3MM Privately Held
WEB: www.cahomecare.com
SIC: 8082 Home health care services

(P-22387)
CAMBRIAN HOMECARE INC
27994 Bradley Rd Ste A, Sun City (92586-2240)
PHONE 951 301-4300
Rhiannon Acree, *Owner*
EMP: 105 Privately Held
SIC: 8082 Home health care services
PA: Cambrian Homecare Inc
5199 E Pacific Coast Hwy
Long Beach CA 90804

(P-22388)
CARE HEALTH SERVICES OF FLA
Also Called: Pacific Nursing Services
2223 Avenida Delaplya 103, La Jolla (92037)
PHONE 619 692-1020
Brittney Salerano, *Manager*
EMP: 150
SALES (corp-wide): 6.5MM Privately Held
WEB: www.carehealth.com
SIC: 8082 Home health care services
HQ: Care Health Services Of Florida Inc
2290 10th Ave N Ste 304
Lake Worth FL 33461
561 433-8700

(P-22389)
CARE OPTIONS MANAGEMENT PLANS
7000 Village Pkwy Ste A, Dublin (94568-2413)
PHONE 925 551-3227
Joanne McCarley, *Branch Mgr*
Rhonda McGlasham, *Personnel Exec*
EMP: 76 Privately Held
SIC: 8082 Home health care services
PA: Care Options Management Plans And Supportive Services, Llc
475 Knollcrest Dr
Redding CA 96002

(P-22390)
CARE OPTIONS MANAGEMENT PLANS (PA)
Also Called: C.O.M.P.A.S.S.
475 Knollcrest Dr, Redding (96002-0101)
P.O. Box 993753 (96099-3753)
PHONE 530 242-8580
Fax: 530 242-8585
Sadie Hess, *Exec Dir*
Laurie Meyers, *Purchasing*
Eric Hess,
Joanne McCarley, *Mng Member*
Erica L Goldman, *Asst Director*
▲ **EMP:** 64
SALES (est): 8MM Privately Held
WEB: www.compasscares.com
SIC: 8082 Home health care services

(P-22391)
CARE PLUS HOME CARE INC
22931 Triton Way Ste 133, Laguna Hills (92653-1237)
PHONE 949 716-2273
Carl Buffa, *President*
Maria Buffa, *Admin Sec*
EMP: 250
SALES (est): 5.6MM Privately Held
SIC: 8082 Home health care services

(P-22392)
CARE PLUS NURSING SERVICES INC
Also Called: Care Plus Home Health
22931 Triton Way Ste 236, Laguna Hills (92653-1237)
PHONE 949 600-7194
Carl Buffa, *President*
Maria Buffa, *Marketing Staff*
EMP: 160
SALES (est): 4MM Privately Held
SIC: 8082 8051 Visiting nurse service; skilled nursing care facilities

(P-22393)
CARE SOLUTION ASSOCIATES LLC
179 Contractors Ave, Livermore (94551-8856)
PHONE 925 443-1000
Keith Beck, *Exec Dir*
EMP: 100
SALES (est): 250K Privately Held
SIC: 8082 Home health care services

(P-22394)
CARE UNLIMITED HEALTH SYSTEMS
1025 W Arrow Hwy Ste 105, Glendora (91740-5407)
PHONE 626 332-3767
Fax: 626 332-9979
Carol Weatherburns, *Owner*
EMP: 75 **EST:** 1999
SALES (est): 1.9MM Privately Held
SIC: 8082 Home health care services

(P-22395)
CAREABILITY HEALTH SVCS CORP
Also Called: All For You Home Care
1321 Howe Ave Ste 111, Sacramento (95825-3365)
PHONE 916 479-8554
Daniel Gourley, *Director*
Jane Anderson, *Manager*
EMP: 65
SALES: 950K Privately Held
SIC: 8082 Home health care services

(P-22396)
CARESOUTH HOME HEALTH SVCS LLC
815 Pollard Rd, Los Gatos (95032-1438)
PHONE 408 378-6131
Carol Parker, *Branch Mgr*
EMP: 50
SALES (corp-wide): 127.1MM Privately Held
SIC: 8082 Home health care services
HQ: Caresouth Home Health Services, Llc
1 10th St Ste 500
Augusta GA 30901

(P-22397)
CARING COMPANIONS HOME
Also Called: Caring Cmpanions Referral Agcy
116 Las Lunas St, Hemet (92543-4028)
PHONE 951 765-1441
Deanna Hosick, *President*
EMP: 80
SQ FT: 700
SALES (est): 3.7MM Privately Held
SIC: 8082 Home health care services

(P-22398)
CARLTON SENIOR LIVING
Also Called: Senior Assisted Living Comm Ch
175 Cleaveland Rd, Pleasant Hill (94523-3875)
PHONE 925 935-1001
Fax: 925 935-1511
Jeffrey Dillon, *Manager*
EMP: 65
SALES (corp-wide): 31.1MM Privately Held
SIC: 8082 Home health care services
PA: Senior Carlton Living Inc
4005 Port Chicago Hwy
Concord CA 94520
925 338-2434

(P-22399)
CASTRO VALLEY HEALTH INC
Also Called: Cvh Home Health Services
2410 Camino Ramon Ste 331, San Ramon (94583-4324)
PHONE 510 690-1930
Mark R Parinas, *CEO*
Isobel Parinas, *CFO*
Mandy Chu,
Jessica Lee, *Author*
Selina Castaneda, *Director*
EMP: 200
SALES: 3MM Privately Held
WEB: www.parinashouse.com
SIC: 8082 Home health care services

(P-22400)
CASWELL BAY INC
Also Called: Hillendale Home Care
1777 N Calif Blvd Ste 210, Walnut Creek (94596-4150)
PHONE 925 933-8181
Bridget Waller, *President*
Weldon Waller, *Corp Secy*
EMP: 60
SQ FT: 1,100
SALES (est): 2.3MM Privately Held
WEB: www.hillendale.net
SIC: 8082 Home health care services

▲ = Import ▼ = Export
◆ = Import/Export

PRODUCTS & SERVICES SECTION

8082 - Home Health Care Svcs County (P-22424)

(P-22401)
CENTRAL COAST VNA & HOSPICE (PA)
5 Lower Ragsdle Dr 102, Monterey (93940)
P.O. Box 2480 (93942-2480)
PHONE...................831 372-6668
Carol Snow, *CEO*
Gayle McConnell, *President*
Steven A Johnson, *CEO*
James Graber, *CFO*
Jeff KAO, *CFO*
EMP: 55
SALES: 26.7MM **Privately Held**
SIC: 8082 Home health care services

(P-22402)
CENTRAL COAST VNA & HOSPICE
6 Quail Run Cir Ste 101, Salinas (93907-2345)
PHONE...................831 758-8243
Raul Perez, *Manager*
EMP: 75
SALES (corp-wide): 26.7MM **Privately Held**
SIC: 8082 Visiting nurse service
PA: Central Coast Vna & Hospice, Inc
   5 Lower Ragsdle Dr 102
   Monterey CA 93940
   831 372-6668

(P-22403)
CENTRAL HEALTH PLAN CAL INC
1055 Park View Dr Ste 355, Covina (91724-3745)
PHONE...................626 938-7120
Sam Kam, *President*
EMP: 3638
SQ FT: 16,144
SALES (est): 20.7MM
SALES (corp-wide): 615.4MM **Privately Held**
SIC: 8082 Home health care services
PA: Ahmc Healthcare Inc.
   1000 S Fremont Ave Unit 6
   Alhambra CA 91803
   626 943-7526

(P-22404)
CHAROLAIS CARE V INC
Also Called: San Francisco Bay
1426 Fillmore St Ste 207, San Francisco (94115-4164)
PHONE...................415 921-5038
Jim Everton, *CEO*
Matthew Phillips, *Vice Pres*
EMP: 100 **EST:** 2008
SALES (est): 964.9K
SALES (corp-wide): 27MM **Privately Held**
SIC: 8082 Home health care services
PA: B.R.P. Health Management Systems, Inc.
   275 S 5th Ave Lowr Level
   Pocatello ID 83201
   208 233-4673

(P-22405)
COLLABRIA CARE
414 S Jefferson St, NAPA (94559-4515)
PHONE...................707 258-9080
Fax: 707 258-9090
Linda Gibson, *President*
Celine Regalia, *Executive*
Debra Dommen, *Exec Dir*
Mark Maltun, *Finance*
Bonni Lesser, *Director*
EMP: 90
SALES: 10.3MM **Privately Held**
WEB: www.hospiceofnapa.org
SIC: 8082 Home health care services

(P-22406)
COMMUNITY HEALTH NETWORK LLC
27922 Tamrack Way, Murrieta (92563-7028)
PHONE...................951 265-8281
Greg Maasberg, *Mng Member*
EMP: 55
SALES (est): 1.6MM **Privately Held**
SIC: 8082 Home health care services

(P-22407)
COMMUNITY HOME CARE
Also Called: Community HM Care & HM Support
259 S Randolph Ave # 180, Brea (92821-5739)
PHONE...................714 671-6877
Fax: 626 574-1981
Jeannine Fitzgerald, *Partner*
EMP: 150
SQ FT: 4,500
SALES (est): 2.9MM **Privately Held**
SIC: 8082 Home health care services

(P-22408)
COMPANION HOME HLTH & HOSPICE
Also Called: Companion Hospice
2041 W Orangewood Ave, Orange (92868-1944)
PHONE...................714 560-8177
Michael Uranga, *President*
Chris Vallandigham, *COO*
Norma Arce, *Human Resources*
Eleonor Phillips, *Manager*
EMP: 95
SALES (est): 12.3MM **Privately Held**
WEB: www.companionhospice.com
SIC: 8082 Home health care services

(P-22409)
COMPANION HOSPICE AND
6133 Bristol Parkday 11 # 110, Culver City (90230)
PHONE...................310 338-1257
Elo Sahagian,
Eleonor Phillips, *Manager*
EMP: 99
SQ FT: 2,000
SALES (est): 229.3K **Privately Held**
SIC: 8082 Home health care services

(P-22410)
COMPANION HOSPICE CARE LLC
8130 Florence Ave Ste 200, Downey (90240-3977)
PHONE...................562 944-2711
Michael A Uranga, *CEO*
Chris Vallandigham, *COO*
Terry Ferencik, *Manager*
Eleonor Phillips, *Manager*
EMP: 125
SQ FT: 5,000
SALES (est): 5MM **Privately Held**
SIC: 8082 Home health care services

(P-22411)
COMPANION HOSPICE LLC
8130 Florence Ave Ste 200, Downey (90240-3977)
PHONE...................562 944-2711
Eleonor Phillips, *Manager*
EMP: 99
SALES (est): 229.3K **Privately Held**
SIC: 8082 Home health care services

(P-22412)
COMPETENT CARE INC
Also Called: Competent Care HM Hlth Nursing
2900 Bristol St Ste D107, Costa Mesa (92626-5940)
PHONE...................714 545-4818
Fax: 714 545-8830
Lynett Laroche, *President*
Lynette L Roche, *Administration*
Debbie Wilson, *Manager*
EMP: 70
SALES: 1.2MM **Privately Held**
WEB: www.competentcare.com
SIC: 8082 7299 Home health care services; information services, consumer

(P-22413)
COMPPARTNERS INC
333 City Blvd W Ste 1500, Orange (92868-5913)
PHONE...................949 253-3111
Fax: 949 253-3099
Bruce Carlin, *CEO*
Bernard J Mansheim, *Chief Mktg Ofcr*
Long Doan, *Vice Pres*
Eleanor Marciniak, *CTO*
Jonathan Mujica, *Info Tech Dir*
EMP: 70
SQ FT: 15,000
SALES (est): 2.9MM
SALES (corp-wide): 10.1MM **Privately Held**
WEB: www.comppartners.com
SIC: 8082 Home health care services
PA: Mcrs Holdings, Inc
   300 Crown Colony Dr # 203
   Quincy MA 02169
   617 375-7700

(P-22414)
COMPREHENSIVE CMNTY HLTH CTRS
801 S Chevy Chase Dr, Glendale (91205-4431)
PHONE...................818 265-2210
Grace Javellana, *CFO*
EMP: 50
SALES: 20.7MM **Privately Held**
SIC: 8082 Home health care services

(P-22415)
CORAM ALTERNATE SITE SVCS INC
Also Called: Coram Specialty Infusion
12310 World Trade Dr # 100, San Diego (92128-3793)
PHONE...................858 576-6969
Fax: 858 974-6606
Myone Fernadez, *Branch Mgr*
Robert Allen, *President*
Michael Dell, *Vice Pres*
Erik Heikkenen, *Director*
EMP: 60
SALES (corp-wide): 153.2B **Publicly Held**
SIC: 8082 Home health care services
HQ: Coram Alternate Site Services, Inc.
   555 17th St Ste 1500
   Denver CO 80202

(P-22416)
CORNERSTONE HOSPICE CAL LLC
1461 E Cooley Dr Ste 220, Colton (92324-3921)
PHONE...................909 872-8100
Fax: 909 872-8106
Blaine Whitson, *President*
Chris Felfe, *Officer*
Erick Kerner, *Vice Pres*
Gayelyn Smith, *Administration*
EMP: 60
SALES (est): 2MM
SALES (corp-wide): 9.6B **Publicly Held**
WEB: www.cornerstonehospice.net
SIC: 8082 Visiting nurse service
PA: Genesis Healthcare, Inc.
   101 E State St
   Kennett Square PA 19348
   610 444-6350

(P-22417)
COSMOPRO WEST INC
15773 Gateway Cir, Tustin (92780-6470)
PHONE...................714 258-8301
Fax: 714 597-9944
Antoine Macoule, *President*
Sylvie Hennessy, *Vice Pres*
Lora Scalzo, *Manager*
◆ **EMP:** 50
SALES (est): 1.4MM **Privately Held**
SIC: 8082 Home health care services

(P-22418)
COUNTY OF LOS ANGELES
Also Called: Health Services, Dept of
245 S Fetterly Ave, Los Angeles (90022-1605)
PHONE...................323 780-2373
Fax: 323 364-3771
Harry Furuya, *Manager*
Vivian C Branchick, *Ch Nursing Ofcr*
EMP: 250 **Privately Held**
WEB: www.co.la.ca.us
SIC: 8082 9431 8011 Home health care services; administration of public health programs; ; offices & clinics of medical doctors
PA: County Of Los Angeles
   500 W Temple St Ste 375
   Los Angeles CA 90012
   213 974-1101

(P-22419)
COURTYARDS AT PINE CREEK INC
1081 Mohr Ln, Concord (94518-3757)
PHONE...................925 798-3900
Patricia Mead, *Executive*
Kirt Hamburg, *President*
Susan McLauglin, *Marketing Staff*
Juan Marical, *Maintence Staff*
Jose Covabarus, *Food Svc Dir*
EMP: 50
SALES (est): 2.1MM **Privately Held**
SIC: 8082 Home health care services

(P-22420)
CRESCENT HEALTHCARE INC (DH)
11980 Telg Rd Ste 100, Santa Fe Springs (90670)
PHONE...................714 520-6300
Fax: 562 941-1170
Paul Mastrapa, *CEO*
Virginia Havai, *President*
David Zelaskowski, *President*
William P Forster, *CFO*
Bob Edwards, *Vice Pres*
EMP: 150
SQ FT: 26,000
SALES (est): 27.4MM
SALES (corp-wide): 117.3B **Publicly Held**
WEB: www.crescenthealthcare.com
SIC: 8082 Home health care services
HQ: Walgreen Co.
   200 Wilmot Rd
   Deerfield IL 60015
   847 315-2500

(P-22421)
CUSTOMCARE HOME HLTH SVCS INC
9826 Bond Rd Ste A, Elk Grove (95624-9419)
PHONE...................916 714-1155
EMP: 70
SALES (est): 3.2MM **Privately Held**
SIC: 8082 7361

(P-22422)
DELTA-T GROUP INC
4420 Hotel Circle Ct # 205, San Diego (92108-3423)
PHONE...................619 543-0556
EMP: 521
SALES (corp-wide): 88.4MM **Privately Held**
SIC: 8082 Home health care services
PA: Delta-T Group, Inc.
   950 E Haverford Rd # 200
   Bryn Mawr PA 19010
   610 527-0830

(P-22423)
DIGNITY HEALTH
Also Called: Marian Hospital Homecare
1054 E Grand Ave Ste A, Arroyo Grande (93420-2527)
PHONE...................805 489-4261
Mike Cornaire, *Manager*
Ray Davis, *Director*
Elva Nava, *Director*
EMP: 73
SALES (corp-wide): 7.1B **Privately Held**
WEB: www.chw.edu
SIC: 8082 Home health care services
PA: Dignity Health
   185 Berry St Ste 300
   San Francisco CA 94107
   415 438-5500

(P-22424)
DIGNITY HEALTH
Also Called: Marian Home Care and Hospice
124 S College Dr, Santa Maria (93454-5325)
PHONE...................805 739-3830
Toll Free:...................877 -
Fax: 805 739-3838
Cathy Sullivan, *Administration*
Kathleen Sullivan, *Administration*
EMP: 120
SALES (corp-wide): 7.1B **Privately Held**
WEB: www.chw.edu
SIC: 8082 Home health care services

8082 - Home Health Care Svcs County (P-22425) — PRODUDCTS & SERVICES SECTION

PA: Dignity Health
185 Berry St Ste 300
San Francisco CA 94107
415 438-5500

(P-22425)
DIGNITY HEALTH
551 Shanley Ct, Bakersfield (93311-1306)
PHONE.................................661 663-6767
Mike Depetro, Manager
EMP: 50
SALES (corp-wide): 7.1B Privately Held
WEB: www.chw.edu
SIC: 8082 Home health care services
PA: Dignity Health
185 Berry St Ste 300
San Francisco CA 94107
415 438-5500

(P-22426)
DIGNITY HEALTH
Home Health Dept of St Joseph
2333 W March Ln Ste B, Stockton (95207-5272)
PHONE.................................209 943-4663
EMP: 50
SALES (corp-wide): 10.4B Privately Held
SIC: 8082
PA: Dignity Health
185 Berry St Ste 300
San Francisco CA 94107
415 438-5500

(P-22427)
DUNN & BERGER INC
Also Called: Accredited Nursing Care
5955 De Soto Ave Ste 160, Woodland Hills (91367-5101)
PHONE.................................818 986-1234
Fax: 818 808-0629
Barry Berger, President
Steve Arredondo, Finance
Leena Patel, Director
James Field III, Manager
EMP: 500
SALES (est): 13MM Privately Held
SIC: 8082 Home health care services

(P-22428)
DYNAMIC HOME CARE SERVICE INC (PA)
14260 Ventura Blvd # 301, Sherman Oaks (91423-2734)
PHONE.................................818 981-4446
Nissan Pardo, CEO
Carol Silver, President
Monica Kaplan, Opers Staff
Jeff Friedman, Sales Staff
EMP: 100
SALES (est): 10MM Privately Held
WEB: www.dynamicnursing.com
SIC: 8082 Home health care services

(P-22429)
E R G HOME HEALTH PROVIDER
11700 South St Ste 200, Artesia (90701-6619)
PHONE.................................562 403-1070
Fax: 562 403-1068
Esma Grecia, Administration
EMP: 60
SALES (est): 2.2MM Privately Held
SIC: 8082 Home health care services

(P-22430)
EL CAMINO HOSPITAL AUXILIARY
2500 Grant Rd, Mountain View (94040-4378)
P.O. Box 7025 (94039-7025)
PHONE.................................650 940-7214
Linda Heider, President
Frank Diamatia, Vice Pres
EMP: 600
SQ FT: 2,000
SALES: 105K
SALES (corp-wide): 776.4MM Privately Held
SIC: 8082 Home health care services
PA: El Camino Hospital
2500 Grant Rd
Mountain View CA 94040
408 224-6660

(P-22431)
EMINENCE HOME HEALTH CARE INC
16921 Parthenia St # 301, Northridge (91343-4559)
PHONE.................................818 830-7113
Fax: 818 830-1633
Oscar Parel, CEO
EMP: 50
SALES (est): 2.6MM Privately Held
SIC: 8082 Home health care services

(P-22432)
ENLOE MEDICAL CENTER
Also Called: Enloe Homecare Services
1390 E Lassen Ave, Chico (95973-7823)
PHONE.................................530 332-6050
Fax: 530 893-6840
Leslie Gunghl, Director
Mari Flynn, VP Human Res
Micah Browning, Marketing Staff
Carissa Fanucchi, Marketing Staff
Laura Bradanini, Manager
EMP: 300
SALES (corp-wide): 505.9MM Privately Held
SIC: 8082 Home health care services
PA: Enloe Medical Center
1531 Esplanade
Chico CA 95926
530 332-7300

(P-22433)
ESKATON
9722 Fair Oaks Blvd Ste A, Fair Oaks (95628-7039)
PHONE.................................916 536-3750
Fax: 916 536-3749
Marilyn Swick, Branch Mgr
Teri Tift, QC Dir
EMP: 595
SALES (corp-wide): 1.4MM Privately Held
SIC: 8082 Home health care services
PA: Eskaton
5105 Manzanita Ave Ste D
Carmichael CA 95608
916 334-0296

(P-22434)
EXCEL HOME HEALTH INC
5575 Lake Park Way # 220, La Mesa (91942-1664)
PHONE.................................619 460-6622
Fax: 619 460-6873
SRI Gopal, President
Anidta Krishnan, Vice Pres
Sonia Silva, Sls & Mktg Exec
EMP: 50
SALES: 600K Privately Held
WEB: www.excelhomehealth.com
SIC: 8082 Home health care services

(P-22435)
EXPERIENCED HOME CARE REGISTRY
110 Civic Center Dr # 206, Vista (92084-6039)
PHONE.................................760 724-0880
Fax: 760 724-4390
Deborah W Dahlin, Owner
EMP: 60
SALES (est): 1.3MM Privately Held
SIC: 8082 Home health care services

(P-22436)
FAITH JONES & ASSOCIATES INC (PA)
Also Called: Aall Care In Home Services
7801 Mission Center Ct # 106, San Diego (92108-1314)
PHONE.................................619 297-9601
Fax: 619 297-4225
Faith Jones, President
Norman Jones, CFO
EMP: 90
SQ FT: 1,200
SALES (est): 5.2MM Privately Held
WEB: www.aallcare.com
SIC: 8082 Home health care services

(P-22437)
FAR EAST HOME CARE INC
3407 W 6th St Ste 710, Los Angeles (90020-2554)
PHONE.................................949 673-3100
Fax: 213 386-8298
Rosendo Labadlabad, President
Emma Obut, Manager
EMP: 110
SALES (est): 2.5MM Privately Held
WEB: www.fareasthomecare.com
SIC: 8082 8322 Home health care services; individual & family services

(P-22438)
FIRSTAT NURSING SERVICES INC
411 Camino Del Rio S # 100, San Diego (92108-3508)
PHONE.................................619 220-7600
Linnea Goodrich, Owner
Kathleen Tickle, President
EMP: 105
SQ FT: 1,800
SALES (est): 3.2MM Privately Held
SIC: 8082 Home health care services

(P-22439)
FIVE STAR QUALITY CARE INC
Also Called: Somerford Place Stockton
3530 Deer Park Dr, Stockton (95219-2350)
PHONE.................................209 951-6500
Fax: 209 951-9968
Leslie Anderson, Manager
EMP: 50
SALES (corp-wide): 1.3B Publicly Held
WEB: www.fivestarqualitycare.com
SIC: 8082 Home health care services
PA: Five Star Quality Care, Inc.
400 Centre St
Newton MA 02458
617 796-8387

(P-22440)
FOUNDERS HEALTHCARE LLC
Also Called: Lifecare Solutions
170 N Daisy Ave, Pasadena (91107-3465)
PHONE.................................626 683-5401
Fax: 626 683-5428
Rene Moreno, Principal
Jorge Barajas, Manager
EMP: 57
SALES (corp-wide): 129.6MM Privately Held
SIC: 8082 Home health care services
HQ: Founders Healthcare, L.L.C.
4601 E Hilton Ave Ste 100
Phoenix AZ 85034
800 636-2123

(P-22441)
GLOBAL MED SERVICES INC
Also Called: East West
11818 South St Ste 201a, Cerritos (90703-6831)
PHONE.................................562 207-6970
Kwang Chang, President
Janet Chang, Officer
▲ EMP: 600
SQ FT: 22,250
SALES (est): 10MM Privately Held
SIC: 8082 Home health care services

(P-22442)
GOLDEN LIVING LLC
Also Called: Golden Livingcenter - Galt
144 F St, Galt (95632-1833)
PHONE.................................209 745-1537
Fax: 209 745-2405
Brigitte Coleman, Administration
EMP: 90
SALES (corp-wide): 1.6B Privately Held
SIC: 8082 8051 Home health care services; skilled nursing care facilities
PA: Golden Living Llc
5220 Tennyson Pkwy # 400
Plano TX 75024
972 372-6300

(P-22443)
GOLDEN LIVING LLC
Also Called: California Healthcare
6700 Sepulveda Blvd, Van Nuys (91411-1248)
PHONE.................................805 494-4949
Jerry Catama, Exec Dir

Suman Patel, Director
EMP: 100
SALES (corp-wide): 1.6B Privately Held
WEB: www.nwbeccorp.com
SIC: 8082 Home health care services
PA: Golden Living Llc
5220 Tennyson Pkwy # 400
Plano TX 75024
972 372-6300

(P-22444)
GOLDEN LIVING LLC
Also Called: Beverly Healthcare
23795 Holman Hwy, Big Sur (93920)
PHONE.................................831 624-1875
Fax: 831 624-7138
John Maraino, Manager
EMP: 75
SALES (corp-wide): 1.6B Privately Held
WEB: www.nwbeccorp.com
SIC: 8082 Home health care services
PA: Golden Living Llc
5220 Tennyson Pkwy # 400
Plano TX 75024
972 372-6300

(P-22445)
GOLDEN LIVING LLC
Also Called: Beverly
1131 N China Lake Blvd, Ridgecrest (93555-3131)
PHONE.................................760 446-3591
Fax: 760 446-2452
Steven Rodriguez, Exec Dir
EMP: 100
SALES (corp-wide): 1.6B Privately Held
WEB: www.nwbeccorp.com
SIC: 8082 8051 Home health care services; skilled nursing care facilities
PA: Golden Living Llc
5220 Tennyson Pkwy # 400
Plano TX 75024
972 372-6300

(P-22446)
GOOD WORKS LLC
Also Called: Right At Home
1250 E Walnut St Ste 220, Pasadena (91106-5118)
PHONE.................................626 584-8130
Fax: 626 584-8132
Diane M Fortner, President
Robert Hingston, Treasurer
EMP: 65
SQ FT: 1,300
SALES (est): 2.5MM Privately Held
SIC: 8082 Home health care services

(P-22447)
GRANDCARE HEALTH SERVICES LLC (PA)
2555 E Colorado Blvd Fl 4, Pasadena (91107-6620)
PHONE.................................866 554-2447
EMP: 150
SALES (est): 3.5MM Privately Held
SIC: 8082 Home health care services

(P-22448)
GREATER SOUTH BAY AREA HM HLTH
Also Called: Greater South Bay Home Health
18726 S Wstn Ave Ste 409, Gardena (90248)
PHONE.................................310 329-4835
Lilia Ramos, President
EMP: 50
SALES (est): 2.6MM Privately Held
WEB: www.gsbhh.com
SIC: 8082 Home health care services

(P-22449)
H & K ABOUAF CORPORATION
9100 S Sepulveda Blvd # 1, Los Angeles (90045-4814)
PHONE.................................310 393-1282
Hadas Abouaf, CEO
Jeffrey Taylor, CFO
EMP: 65
SALES: 950K Privately Held
SIC: 8082 Home health care services

PRODUCTS & SERVICES SECTION

8082 - Home Health Care Svcs County (P-22478)

(P-22450)
HARMONY HOME HEALTH LLC
Also Called: Harmony Homecare
2500 Ranch Rd Ste 104, Placerville (95667-9181)
PHONE..........................916 933-9777
Jennifer Jarrett, *Mng Member*
Patrick Philbrick, *Mng Member*
EMP: 70
SALES: 500K **Privately Held**
SIC: 8082 Home health care services

(P-22451)
HEALTH BY DESIGN
2636 Fulton Ave Ste 100, Sacramento (95821-5731)
PHONE..........................916 974-3322
Fax: 916 974-3323
Peg Cannon, *President*
▲ EMP: 50
SQ FT: 1,200
SALES (est): 1.6MM **Privately Held**
WEB: www.healthbydesign.net
SIC: 8082 Home health care services; visiting nurse service

(P-22452)
HEALTH ENTPS LF LONG PLAN
Also Called: Health Entps Life-Long Plans
5805 Sepulveda Blvd, Van Nuys (91411-2546)
PHONE..........................818 654-0330
Johnathan Istrin, *President*
EMP: 500
SQ FT: 4,000
SALES (est): 6MM **Privately Held**
SIC: 8082 Home health care services

(P-22453)
HEALTH SOURCE STAFFING INC
438 Camino Ste 101, San Diego (92108)
PHONE..........................619 220-8044
Lloyd Enke, *CEO*
Renee Freitas, *Vice Pres*
EMP: 60
SQ FT: 1,000
SALES (est): 2.1MM **Privately Held**
SIC: 8082 Oxygen tent service

(P-22454)
HEALTHCARE CALIFORNIA
5709 N West Ave, Fresno (93711-2366)
PHONE..........................559 243-9990
Harry G Harris, *President*
Bevan S Nugent, *COO*
Dawn Bolf, *Director*
June Webb, *Director*
EMP: 70
SALES (est): 3.1MM **Privately Held**
SIC: 8082 Home health care services

(P-22455)
HEALTHCARE PATHWAYS MANAGEMENT
5 Mandeville Ct, Monterey (93940-5745)
PHONE..........................831 373-1111
Duncan McCarter, *President*
Elizabeth Johnson Rn, *COO*
Maribeth Long, *Director*
Bruce Foster, *Manager*
EMP: 99
SQ FT: 250
SALES (est): 1.2MM **Privately Held**
WEB: www.advantacarehpm.com
SIC: 8082 Home health care services

(P-22456)
HELP UNLMTED PERSONNEL SVC INC
319 E Carrillo St Ste 102, Santa Barbara (93101-7453)
PHONE..........................805 962-4646
Fax: 805 963-7690
Leanna McNealy, *Manager*
Anna Barajas, *Director*
EMP: 150
SALES (corp-wide): 21.6MM **Privately Held**
SIC: 8082 7363 Home health care services; medical help service
PA: Help Unlimited Personnel Service, Inc.
1767 Goodyear Ave Ste 104
Ventura CA 93003
805 654-6990

(P-22457)
HINDS HOSPICE (PA)
Also Called: Hinds Hospice Home
2490 W Shaw Ave Ste 100a, Fresno (93711-3305)
PHONE..........................559 248-8579
Fax: 559 226-1028
Amy Tobin, *President*
Nancy Hinds, *Principal*
Lynne Pietz, *Admin Dir*
Pam Pytlak, *Admin Dir*
Denny Viloria, *Admin Dir*
EMP: 170
SQ FT: 9,000
SALES: 15.4MM **Privately Held**
SIC: 8082 8051 Home health care services; skilled nursing care facilities

(P-22458)
HIRED HAND
2901 Cleveland Ave # 203, Santa Rosa (95403-2785)
PHONE..........................707 575-4700
Lynn Winter, *Owner*
EMP: 200 EST: 2007
SALES (est): 1.2MM **Privately Held**
SIC: 8082 Home health care services

(P-22459)
HIS PASSION INC
Also Called: Senior Helpers South Coast
17195 Newhope St Ste 201, Fountain Valley (92708-4211)
PHONE..........................800 760-6389
George Miller, *President*
Dawn Miller, *Vice Pres*
EMP: 50
SALES: 896.4K **Privately Held**
SIC: 8082 Home health care services

(P-22460)
HOLLYWOOD HEALTH SYSTEM INC
Also Called: Hollywood Home Health Services
4640 Lankershim Blvd # 100, North Hollywood (91602-1845)
PHONE..........................323 662-3731
Siranush Manukyan, *CEO*
EMP: 99
SALES (est): 3.6MM **Privately Held**
SIC: 8082 Home health care services

(P-22461)
HOME CARE OF AMERICA INC
Also Called: Home Care America-San Marino
750 E Green St Ste 303, Pasadena (91101-2134)
PHONE..........................626 309-7696
Fax: 626 309-1419
Nymia Cucueco, *President*
Michael Cucueco, *Manager*
Offelia Tilares, *Manager*
EMP: 75
SQ FT: 1,600
SALES (est): 3.5MM **Privately Held**
WEB: www.americani.org
SIC: 8082 Visiting nurse service

(P-22462)
HOME HEALTH CARE MANAGEMENT
1398 Ridgewood Dr, Chico (95973-7801)
PHONE..........................530 226-0120
Barbara Hanna, *Principal*
EMP: 60
SALES (corp-wide): 5.5MM **Privately Held**
SIC: 8082 Home health care services
PA: Home Health Care Management
1398 Ridgewood Dr
Chico CA 95973
530 343-0727

(P-22463)
HOME HELPERS SAN MATEO COUNTY
655 Miramontes St, Half Moon Bay (94019-1945)
PHONE..........................650 532-3122
Peggy Milne, *Owner*
EMP: 60
SALES (est): 311.7K **Privately Held**
SIC: 8082 Home health care services

(P-22464)
HOME INSTEAD SENIOR CARE
9665 Gran Rdge Dr Ste 250, San Diego (92123)
PHONE..........................858 277-3722
Fax: 619 330-4568
Robert Perez, *President*
Jessica Perez, *Vice Pres*
EMP: 60
SQ FT: 900
SALES (est): 3.1MM **Privately Held**
SIC: 8082 Home health care services

(P-22465)
HOME INSTEAD SENIOR CARE
11160 Sun Center Dr, Rancho Cordova (95670-6121)
PHONE..........................916 920-2273
Fax: 916 922-8260
Scott Shaw, *Owner*
Rosemary Dance, *Admin Sec*
Mary Alexander, *Director*
EMP: 60
SALES (est): 1.5MM **Privately Held**
WEB: www.scottshaw.com
SIC: 8082 Home health care services

(P-22466)
HOME INSTEAD SENIOR CARE
1720 E Los Angeles Ave H, Simi Valley (93065-2080)
PHONE..........................805 577-0926
Fax: 805 577-0258
Don Reed, *Owner*
EMP: 175 EST: 1997
SALES (est): 5.1MM **Privately Held**
SIC: 8082 Home health care services

(P-22467)
HOME INSTEAD SENIOR CARE
5360 Jackson Dr Ste 120, La Mesa (91942-6003)
PHONE..........................619 460-6222
Fax: 619 460-2395
Leslie Bojorquez, *President*
Steve Bojorquez, *CFO*
EMP: 50
SQ FT: 1,500
SALES (est): 1.3MM **Privately Held**
SIC: 8082 Home health care services

(P-22468)
HOME INSTEAD SENIOR CARE
405 Court St, Woodland (95695-3421)
PHONE..........................707 678-2005
Fax: 530 666-0283
Thomas Suharik, *President*
EMP: 50
SALES (est): 1.1MM **Privately Held**
SIC: 8082 Home health care services

(P-22469)
HOME INSTEAD SENIOR CARE
303 W Joaquin Ave Ste 230, San Leandro (94577-3666)
PHONE..........................510 686-9940
Fax: 510 541-1551
Ron Macarthur, *President*
Renee Macarthur, *CFO*
EMP: 100
SALES (est): 2.2MM **Privately Held**
SIC: 8082 Home health care services

(P-22470)
HOME INSTEAD SENIOR CARE
28570 Marguerite Pkwy # 221, Mission Viejo (92692-3733)
PHONE..........................949 347-6767
Jim Efzlinger, *Managing Prtnr*
Fred Wollman, *Managing Prtnr*
Joe Sanders, *Principal*
EMP: 50
SALES (est): 1.9MM **Privately Held**
SIC: 8082 8322 Home health care services; senior citizens' center or association

(P-22471)
HOMECARE PROFESSIONALS INC
1849 Willow Pass Rd # 305, Concord (94520-2524)
PHONE..........................925 215-1214
Andrew Howard, *Principal*
Juliana Williams, *Director*
EMP: 80 EST: 2005
SQ FT: 1,200
SALES: 223.2K **Privately Held**
SIC: 8082 Home health care services

(P-22472)
HOSPICE & HOME HEALTH OF E BAY
Also Called: Pathways
333 Hegenberger Rd # 700, Oakland (94621-1420)
PHONE..........................510 632-4390
Fax: 510 632-3334
Barbara Burgess, *President*
Donna Lopez, *Vice Pres*
EMP: 200
SQ FT: 10,000
SALES (est): 3.3MM **Privately Held**
WEB: www.pathwayshealth.org
SIC: 8082 Home health care services

(P-22473)
HOSPICE BY BAY (PA)
Also Called: HOSPICE OF MARIN
17 E Sir Francis Drake Bl, Larkspur (94939-1708)
PHONE..........................415 927-2273
Fax: 415 927-1369
Kitty Whitaker, *CEO*
Mary Taverna, *President*
Denis Viscek, *CFO*
Dennis A Gilardi, *Chairman*
Michael R Dailey, *Treasurer*
EMP: 220
SQ FT: 8,000
SALES: 41MM **Privately Held**
SIC: 8082 Home health care services

(P-22474)
HOSPICE CARING PROJECT OF SANT
940 Disc Dr, Scotts Valley (95066-4544)
PHONE..........................831 430-3000
Ann Pomper, *Director*
Michelle Smagacz, *COO*
Nancy Houseman, *Financial Exec*
EMP: 85
SQ FT: 2,300
SALES: 14.6MM **Privately Held**
WEB: www.hospicesantacruz.org
SIC: 8082 Home health care services

(P-22475)
HOSPICE CHEERS
625 Fair Oaks Ave Ste 229, South Pasadena (91030-2697)
PHONE..........................626 799-2727
Fax: 213 403-0330
David Friedman, *President*
Vivian Allen, *Opers Staff*
EMP: 95
SALES (est): 1.2MM **Privately Held**
SIC: 8082 Home health care services

(P-22476)
HOSPICE OF FOOTHILLS (PA)
11270 Rough And Ready Hwy, Grass Valley (95945-8530)
PHONE..........................530 272-5739
Fax: 530 477-6683
Vanessa Bengston, *Director*
Sue Hodge, *Exec Dir*
EMP: 55
SQ FT: 5,000
SALES: 7.7MM **Privately Held**
WEB: www.hospiceofthefoothills.org
SIC: 8082 Visiting nurse service

(P-22477)
HOSPICE OF OWENS VALLEY
162 E Line St Ste C, Bishop (93514-3557)
PHONE..........................760 872-4663
Janie Carrington, *Director*
Tammy McDermith, *Director*
EMP: 50
SQ FT: 2,250
SALES (est): 511.6K **Privately Held**
SIC: 8082 Home health care services

(P-22478)
HOSPICE TOUCH INC
3401 W Sunflower Ave # 100, Santa Ana (92704-7961)
PHONE..........................310 574-5750
Troy Smith, *Branch Mgr*
EMP: 51

8082 - Home Health Care Svcs County (P-22479) PRODUDUCTS & SERVICES SECTION

SALES (corp-wide): 5.8MM **Privately Held**
SIC: **8082** 8069 Home health care services; specialty hospitals, except psychiatric
PA: Hospice Touch, Inc.
3401 W Sunflower Ave # 100
Santa Ana CA 92704
714 327-1936

(P-22479)
HUMAN TOUCH HOME HEALTH
3629 N Sepulveda Blvd, Manhattan Beach (90266-3632)
PHONE..................424 247-8165
Kameria Ahmed Ibrahim, *Principal*
Sada Kelisa, *Financial Exec*
EMP: 120
SALES: 950K **Privately Held**
SIC: **8082** Home health care services

(P-22480)
HUNTINGTON CARE LLC
Also Called: Huntington Care, Inc.
2555 E Colo Blvd Ste 400h, Pasadena (91107)
PHONE..................877 405-6990
Carlo Stepanians, *CEO*
Sergio Varela, *President*
EMP: 350
SALES (est): 3.5MM **Privately Held**
SIC: **8082** Home health care services
PA: Grandcare Health Services Llc
2555 E Colorado Blvd Fl 4
Pasadena CA 91107
866 554-2447

(P-22481)
IN HOME HEALTH INC
Also Called: Home Health Plus
2005 De La Cruz Blvd # 271, Santa Clara (95050-3031)
PHONE..................408 986-8160
Fax: 408 986-0354
Cheryl Bartin, *Manager*
Hernando Lucero, *Office Mgr*
Dolton Goddwin, *Administration*
EMP: 132
SALES (corp-wide): 29.2MM **Privately Held**
SIC: **8082** Home health care services; visiting nurse service
PA: In Home Health, Inc.
333 N Summit St
Toledo OH
419 252-5500

(P-22482)
IN HOME HEALTH INC
Also Called: Home Health Plus
1000 Lakes Dr Ste 200, West Covina (91790-2927)
PHONE..................419 254-7841
Fax: 626 918-6018
Wendy Myers, *Director*
EMP: 60
SALES (corp-wide): 29.2MM **Privately Held**
SIC: **8082** Home health care services
PA: In Home Health, Inc.
333 N Summit St
Toledo OH
419 252-5500

(P-22483)
INFINITE HOME HEALTH INC
22151 Ventura Blvd # 102, Woodland Hills (91364-1587)
PHONE..................818 888-7772
Taimoor Bidari, *President*
Reza Bidari, *Administration*
EMP: 60
SQ FT: 4,000
SALES: 4.5MM **Privately Held**
SIC: **8082** Home health care services

(P-22484)
INTEGRITY HLTHCARE SLTIONS INC (PA)
Also Called: Interim Hlthcare San Dego Cnty
5625 Ruffin Rd Ste 225, San Diego (92123-6396)
PHONE..................858 576-9501
Wendy Olayvar, *President*
EMP: 80

SALES (est): 3.3MM **Privately Held**
SIC: **8082** Home health care services

(P-22485)
INTEGRITY HLTHCARE SLTIONS INC
425 W 5th Ave Ste 101, Escondido (92025-4843)
PHONE..................760 432-9811
Wendy Olayvar, *President*
EMP: 99
SALES: 950K **Privately Held**
SIC: **8082** Home health care services

(P-22486)
INTERHEALTH SERVICES INC (HQ)
Also Called: Presbyterian Inter Cmnty Hosp
12401 Washington Blvd, Whittier (90602-1006)
PHONE..................562 698-0811
Daniel F Adams, *President*
Jim West, *President*
Gary Koger, *CFO*
Peggy Chulack, *Admin Sec*
Bobby Olivas, *Purchasing*
EMP: 53
SQ FT: 1,000
SALES (est): 7.6MM
SALES (corp-wide): 15MM **Privately Held**
SIC: **8082** 8062 Home health care services; general medical & surgical hospitals
PA: Interhealth Corporation
12401 Washington Blvd
Whittier CA 90602
562 698-0811

(P-22487)
INTERIM ASSISITED CARE OF NORT
Also Called: Interim Services
373 Smile Pl, Redding (96001-3637)
PHONE..................530 722-1530
Robert Seawright, *President*
EMP: 99
SALES (est): 1.4MM **Privately Held**
SIC: **8082** Home health care services

(P-22488)
KAISER FOUNDATION HOSPITAL
4501 Broadway, Oakland (94611-4615)
PHONE..................510 752-6295
Kirs Holm, *Director*
EMP: 50 EST: 2013
SALES (est): 192.7K **Privately Held**

(P-22489)
KAISER FOUNDATION HOSPITALS
Also Called: Kaiser Permanente
50 Great Oaks Blvd, San Jose (95119-1381)
PHONE..................408 361-2100
John C OH, *Med Doctor*
EMP: 793
SALES (corp-wide): 27.8B **Privately Held**
SIC: **8082** 8011 Home health care services; health maintenance organization
HQ: Kaiser Foundation Hospitals Inc
1 Kaiser Plz
Oakland CA 94612
510 271-6611

(P-22490)
KEARN ALTERNATIVE CARE INC (PA)
2029 21st St, Bakersfield (93301-4219)
PHONE..................661 631-2036
Fax: 661 631-2104
Jean Schamblin, *President*
J R Doty, *Admin Sec*
EMP: 300
SALES (est): 5.5MM **Privately Held**
SIC: **8082** Home health care services

(P-22491)
KERN ALTERNATIVE CARE INC
2029 21st St, Bakersfield (93301-4219)
PHONE..................661 631-2036
Jeanne Schamblin, *President*
Leo Schamblin, *Vice Pres*

EMP: 160
SQ FT: 1,800
SALES (est): 6.3MM **Privately Held**
SIC: **8082** Visiting nurse service

(P-22492)
KIDS OVERCOMING LLC
40029 St Ste 204, Oakland (94609)
PHONE..................415 748-8052
Anne Swinney, *Mng Member*
Matt McAlear
EMP: 75 EST: 2013
SALES (est): 1.3MM **Privately Held**
SIC: **8082** Home health care services

(P-22493)
KIM WILSON
Also Called: A Better Life Together
3322 Sweetwater Spg, Spring Valley (91977-3162)
PHONE..................619 741-1548
Kim Wilson, *Principal*
Kimberly Mills, *Owner*
EMP: 90
SALES (est): 1.9MM **Privately Held**
SIC: **8082** Home health care services

(P-22494)
KINDRED HEALTHCARE INC
5095 Murphy Canyon Rd # 240, San Diego (92123-4346)
PHONE..................858 380-4491
EMP: 162
SALES (corp-wide): 7B **Publicly Held**
SIC: **8082** Home health care services
PA: Kindred Healthcare, Inc.
680 S 4th St
Louisville KY 40202
502 596-7300

(P-22495)
KISSITO HEALTH CARE INC
Also Called: Bay Point Healthcare Center
442 Sunset Blvd, Hayward (94541-3832)
PHONE..................510 582-8311
Fax: 510 582-0723
Bob Ewing, *Manager*
EMP: 100
SALES (corp-wide): 67.9MM **Privately Held**
SIC: **8082** 8051 8052 Home health care services; skilled nursing care facilities; intermediate care facilities
PA: Kissito Health Care, Inc.
5228 Valleypointe Pkwy
Roanoke VA 24019
540 265-0322

(P-22496)
KISSITO HEALTH CASE INC
Also Called: Willow Pass Healthcare Center
3318 Willow Pass Rd, Concord (94519-2316)
PHONE..................925 689-9222
Fax: 925 689-3412
EMP: 100
SALES (corp-wide): 62.4MM **Privately Held**
SIC: **8082** 8051
PA: Kissito Health Care, Inc.
5228 Valleypointe Pkwy
Roanoke VA 24019
540 265-0322

(P-22497)
KISSITO HEALTH CASE INC
Also Called: San Leandro Healthcare Center
368 Juana Ave, San Leandro (94577-4811)
PHONE..................510 357-4015
Vinny Poddapoori, *Administration*
EMP: 80
SALES (corp-wide): 67.9MM **Privately Held**
SIC: **8082** 8051 Home health care services; skilled nursing care facilities
PA: Kissito Health Care, Inc.
5228 Valleypointe Pkwy
Roanoke VA 24019
540 265-0322

(P-22498)
KRISTINE NICKEL
721 E St, Eureka (95501-1854)
PHONE..................707 443-9332
Kristy Nickels, *Director*
Kristy Nickols, *Sales Staff*

EMP: 73
SALES (est): 604K **Privately Held**
WEB: www.sje.stjoe.org
SIC: **8082** Home health care services

(P-22499)
LANCASTER COMMUNITY HOSPITAL
520 W Palmdale Blvd Ste Q, Palmdale (93551-4231)
PHONE..................661 947-3300
Ken Clayton, *Branch Mgr*
EMP: 294
SALES (corp-wide): 10.5MM **Privately Held**
SIC: **8082** Home health care services
PA: Lancaster Community Hospital
38600 Medical Center Dr
Palmdale CA 93551
661 940-1321

(P-22500)
LOMA LINDA UNIVERSITY MED CTR
Loma Linda Home Health Care
11265 Mountain View Ave E, Loma Linda (92354-3863)
P.O. Box 2000 (92354-0200)
PHONE..................909 558-3096
Fax: 909 558-3082
Jan Huckins, *Director*
Steve Mohr, *Senior VP*
Terence D Lewis, *Assoc Prof*
EMP: 120
SALES (corp-wide): 848.5MM **Privately Held**
WEB: www.llumc.com
SIC: **8082** 7361 Home health care services; nurses' registry
HQ: Loma Linda University Medical Center
11234 Anderson St
Loma Linda CA 92354
909 558-4000

(P-22501)
LOVELY LIVING HOMECARE
112 Harvard Ave, Claremont (91711-4716)
PHONE..................909 625-7999
Lee Rodriguez, *President*
EMP: 65
SALES (est): 632.2K **Privately Held**
SIC: **8082** Home health care services

(P-22502)
LUMINA HEALTHCARE LLC (PA)
Also Called: Lumina At Home
5220 Pacific Concourse Dr, Los Angeles (90045-6277)
PHONE..................888 958-6462
Mary Ellen Hardin, *President*
Robert C Mathuny, *Vice Pres*
EMP: 55
SALES: 8MM **Privately Held**
SIC: **8082** Home health care services

(P-22503)
MANAGED HOMECARE INC
2520 Redhill Ave, Santa Ana (92705-5542)
PHONE..................951 341-0782
Fax: 951 274-3638
David Ross, *Administration*
EMP: 50
SQ FT: 1,910
SALES (est): 1.9MM **Privately Held**
SIC: **8082** Home health care services

(P-22504)
MATCHED CAREGIVERS INC
Also Called: Matched Care Gvrs Cntns Care
1800 El Camino Real Ste B, Atherton (94027-4103)
PHONE..................408 560-2382
Fax: 650 321-2352
Kathryn Janz, *President*
EMP: 130
SQ FT: 2,000
SALES (est): 2.3MM **Privately Held**
SIC: **8082** Home health care services

PRODUCTS & SERVICES SECTION

8082 - Home Health Care Svcs County (P-22530)

(P-22505)
MAXIM HEALTHCARE SERVICES INC
Also Called: Los Angles Homecare Pediatrics
4221 Wilshire Blvd # 394, Los Angeles (90010-3561)
PHONE.................323 937-9410
Jeff Poitras, *Manager*
Stephen Walsh, *Administration*
David Coats, *Manager*
EMP: 250
SALES (corp-wide): 1.2B **Privately Held**
WEB: www.maximstaffing.com
SIC: 8082 Home health care services
PA: Maxim Healthcare Services, Inc.
7227 Lee Deforest Dr
Columbia MD 21046
410 910-1500

(P-22506)
MAXIMUS INC
3130 Kilgore Rd Ste 100, Rancho Cordova (95670-6298)
PHONE.................916 364-6610
Bob Britton, *Principal*
Harry Gill, *Telecom Exec*
Greg Hanzelka, *Technology*
Brian Morgan, *Technology*
Ankur Jaswal, *Analyst*
EMP: 80
SALES (corp-wide): 2.1B **Publicly Held**
SIC: 8082 Home health care services
PA: Maximus, Inc.
1891 Metro Center Dr
Reston VA 20190
703 251-8500

(P-22507)
MERCY HM SVCS A CAL LTD PARTNR
1544 Market St, Redding (96001-1023)
P.O. Box 496009 (96049-6009)
PHONE.................530 245-4070
Fax: 530 245-4060
Ginger White, *Director*
EMP: 80
SALES (corp-wide): 7.1B **Privately Held**
WEB: www.mercyhealth.org
SIC: 8082 Home health care services
HQ: Mercy Home Services A California Limited Partnership
2175 Rosaline Ave Ste A
Redding CA 96001
530 225-6000

(P-22508)
MIRACLE HOME HEALTH AGENCY
13146 Mungo Ct, Rancho Cucamonga (91739-9157)
PHONE.................562 653-0668
Fax: 562 653-0687
Bernice Osunwa, *President*
EMP: 50
SALES (est): 898.2K **Privately Held**
SIC: 8082 Home health care services

(P-22509)
MOMS ORANGE COUNTY
1128 W Santa Ana Blvd, Santa Ana (92703-3833)
PHONE.................714 972-2610
Pamela Pimentel Rn, *Exec Dir*
Mary Fox, *Office Mgr*
EMP: 50
SALES (est): 4.1MM **Privately Held**
WEB: www.oc-moms.org
SIC: 8082 Home health care services

(P-22510)
MSJ HEALTHCARE LLC
Also Called: Grandcare Home Health Services
2555 E Colorado Blvd Fl 4, Pasadena (91107-6620)
PHONE.................818 244-8446
Sergio Varela, *President*
Jay Pamintuan, *Vice Pres*
Douglas Saylor, *Marketing Staff*
Nurmina Banaag, *Director*
Dr David Bell, *Director*
EMP: 50
SQ FT: 4,800
SALES (est): 2.3MM **Privately Held**
SIC: 8082 Home health care services

(P-22511)
MY CHOICE INHOME CARE LLC
31610 Rr Cyn Rd Ste 4, Canyon Lake (92587-9454)
PHONE.................951 244-8770
Julie Zimmerer,
EMP: 87
SALES: 480K **Privately Held**
SIC: 8082 Home health care services

(P-22512)
NEW HORIZONS WORLDWIDE INC
15917 Chase St, North Hills (91343-6305)
PHONE.................818 894-9301
Carlos Arvizu, *Branch Mgr*
Leilani Downer, *Comms Mgr*
Cameron Lee, *Manager*
EMP: 512
SALES (corp-wide): 795.8MM **Privately Held**
SIC: 8082 Home health care services
PA: New Horizons Worldwide, Inc.
100 4 Falls Corporate Ctr # 408
Conshohocken PA 19428
888 236-3625

(P-22513)
NO ORDINARY MOMENTS INC
16742 Gothard St Ste 115, Huntington Beach (92647-4564)
PHONE.................714 848-3800
Fax: 714 848-3075
Luis Pena, *President*
EMP: 250
SALES (est): 5MM **Privately Held**
SIC: 8082 8322 Home health care services; emergency social services

(P-22514)
NORTH COAST HOME CARE INC
Also Called: Homewatch Caregivers
5845 Avenida Encinas S129, Carlsbad (92008-4432)
PHONE.................760 260-8700
Tanya Finnerty, *President*
Michael Finnerty, *Admin Sec*
EMP: 70
SQ FT: 1,000
SALES: 1MM **Privately Held**
SIC: 8082 Home health care services

(P-22515)
NORTHERN CALIFORNIA HLTH CARE
Also Called: Arcadia Healthcare
16201 Plateau Cir, Redding (96001-9720)
PHONE.................530 223-2332
Fax: 530 223-4721
Tim Araiza, *President*
Timothy Araiza, *Administration*
EMP: 60
SALES (est): 1.2MM **Privately Held**
WEB: www.norcalarcadia.com
SIC: 8082 Home health care services

(P-22516)
NURSES TUCH HM HLTH PRVDER INC
135 S Jackson St Ste 100, Glendale (91205-4917)
PHONE.................818 500-4877
Evangeline Ursua, *President*
Mike Astro, *Nurse*
EMP: 50
SALES (est): 483.7K **Privately Held**
SIC: 8082 Home health care services

(P-22517)
NURSING & REHAB AT HOME
1660 S Amphlett Blvd # 112, San Mateo (94402-2507)
PHONE.................650 286-4272
Lorna Beukema, *President*
EMP: 54
SQ FT: 3,000
SALES (est): 3MM **Privately Held**
WEB: www.rehabathome.org
SIC: 8082 Home health care services

(P-22518)
OAK HILL CAPITAL PARTNERS LP
2775 Sand Hill Rd Ste 220, Menlo Park (94025-7085)
PHONE.................650 234-0500
Steven B Gruber, *President*
EMP: 868
SALES (corp-wide): 173.7MM **Privately Held**
SIC: 8082 Home health care services
PA: Oak Hill Capital Partners, L.P.
65 E 55th St Fl 32
New York NY 10022
212 527-8400

(P-22519)
ODYSSEY HEALTHCARE INC
9444 Balboa Ave Ste 290, San Diego (92123-4901)
PHONE.................858 565-2499
Diana Thompson, *Manager*
Patty Kincade, *Executive*
EMP: 70
SALES (corp-wide): 7B **Publicly Held**
SIC: 8082 Home health care services
HQ: Odyssey Healthcare, Inc.
7801 Mesquite Bend Dr # 105
Irving TX 75063

(P-22520)
ODYSSEY HEALTHCARE INC
17290 Jasmine St Ste 104, Victorville (92395-8300)
PHONE.................760 241-7044
Jodi Schmidt, *Branch Mgr*
EMP: 53
SALES (corp-wide): 7B **Publicly Held**
SIC: 8082 Home health care services
HQ: Odyssey Healthcare, Inc.
7801 Mesquite Bend Dr # 105
Irving TX 75063

(P-22521)
ONEBODY INC
Also Called: Consensus Health
2000 Powell St Ste 555, Emeryville (94608-1804)
P.O. Box 6219, Moraga (94570-6219)
PHONE.................510 285-2000
Fax: 510 285-2000
Kendall Lockhart, *Ch of Bd*
Susan M Rowe, *CFO*
David Hansen, *Vice Pres*
Gene Ruda, *CTO*
EMP: 60 **EST:** 1996
SALES (est): 2.2MM **Privately Held**
SIC: 8082 Home health care services

(P-22522)
ONTARIO HEALTH EDUCATN CO INC
3130 Sedona Ct, Ontario (91764-6554)
PHONE.................951 817-8553
David Pyle, *President*
Will Tu, *Controller*
EMP: 50 **EST:** 2008
SALES (est): 510.6K **Privately Held**
SIC: 8082 Home health care services

(P-22523)
OPTIMAL HEALTH SERVICES INC
1315 Boughton Dr, Bakersfield (93308-1613)
PHONE.................661 393-4483
Fax: 661 387-7140
Doug Clary, *President*
Sarah Shelbourne, *CFO*
Shelly Hutsell,
EMP: 90 **EST:** 1992
SALES (est): 8.2MM **Privately Held**
SIC: 8082 Home health care services

(P-22524)
OPTMIAL HOSPICE FOUNDATION
Also Called: Optimal Hospice Care
1675 Chester Ave Ste 401, Bakersfield (93301-5225)
PHONE.................661 716-4000
Doug Clary, *CEO*
EMP: 112
SALES (corp-wide): 182.7K **Privately Held**
SIC: 8082 Home health care services
PA: Optmial Hospice Foundation
1315 Boughton Dr
Bakersfield CA 93308
661 410-3000

(P-22525)
OPTMIAL HOSPICE FOUNDATION
Also Called: Optimal Hospice Care
3375 Scott Blvd Ste 410, Santa Clara (95054-3114)
PHONE.................408 207-9222
Doug Clary, *CEO*
EMP: 60
SALES (corp-wide): 182.7K **Privately Held**
SIC: 8082 Home health care services
PA: Optmial Hospice Foundation
1315 Boughton Dr
Bakersfield CA 93308
661 410-3000

(P-22526)
OUR WATCH
Also Called: Assistance In Home Care
12832 Valley View St # 211, Garden Grove (92845-2524)
PHONE.................714 897-1022
Fax: 714 897-1088
Ramona Streit, *Principal*
EMP: 52
SALES (est): 1.6MM **Privately Held**
SIC: 8082 Home health care services

(P-22527)
OWENS HEALTH CARE
2247 Court St, Redding (96001-2529)
PHONE.................530 246-1075
Jon Friefen, *President*
Mike Edginton, *Manager*
EMP: 160 **EST:** 2001
SALES (est): 5.4MM **Privately Held**
SIC: 8082 Home health care services

(P-22528)
PACIFIC CARE INC
Also Called: Pro Care 2000 Home Health Care
1903 Redondo Ave, Long Beach (90755-1226)
PHONE.................562 494-6500
Fax: 562 494-8834
Michael Siller, *President*
Steve Liss, *Vice Pres*
Mike Bladuka MD, *Medical Dir*
EMP: 60
SALES: 1.2MM **Privately Held**
SIC: 8082 Home health care services

(P-22529)
PACIFIC COAST SERVICES INC
Also Called: Pacific Homecare Services
1919 Grand Canal Blvd C3, Stockton (95207-8114)
PHONE.................209 956-2532
Leticia Robles, *President*
Jose Cabral, *Controller*
EMP: 145
SQ FT: 2,000
SALES (est): 4.3MM **Privately Held**
SIC: 8082 Home health care services

(P-22530)
PACIFIC PALMS HEALTHCARE LLC
Empress Rehabilitation Center
1020 Termino Ave, Long Beach (90804-4123)
PHONE.................562 433-6791
Fax: 562 433-9801
Emmanuel B David, *Branch Mgr*
EMP: 57
SALES (corp-wide): 4.1MM **Privately Held**
SIC: 8082 Home health care services
PA: Pacific Palms Healthcare, Llc
1020 Termino Ave
Long Beach CA 90804
562 433-6791

8082 - Home Health Care Svcs County (P-22531) — PRODUCTS & SERVICES SECTION

(P-22531)
PARADISE VALLEY HOSPITAL INC
Also Called: West Health Care
180 Otay Lakes Rd Ste 100, Bonita (91902-2464)
PHONE.................................619 472-7500
Fax: 619 472-1534
EMP: 80
SALES (corp-wide): 159.3MM **Privately Held**
SIC: 8082
PA: Paradise Valley Hospital
2400 E 4th St
National City CA 91950
619 470-4100

(P-22532)
PATHFINDER HEALTH INC
10051 Lampson Ave, Garden Grove (92840-4716)
PHONE.................................714 636-5649
Fax: 714 636-5973
Avelina Cumbis, *President*
EMP: 150
SALES (est): 3.8MM **Privately Held**
SIC: 8082 Home health care services

(P-22533)
PEACEFUL HEARTS HOME CARE INC
387 Magnolia Ave Ste 103, Corona (92879-3308)
PHONE.................................951 541-9343
Brian McKee, *President*
EMP: 55
SALES (est): 980.6K **Privately Held**
SIC: 8082 Home health care services

(P-22534)
PEGASUS HOME HEALTH CARE A CA
Also Called: Pegasus Home Health Services
132 N Maryland Ave, Glendale (91206-4235)
PHONE.................................818 551-1932
Fax: 818 551-1936
Pamela Spiszman, *President*
Caroline Agagon, *Bookkeeper*
Kishore Mandyam, *Manager*
▼ EMP: 80
SQ FT: 2,800
SALES (est): 4.7MM **Privately Held**
SIC: 8082 Home health care services

(P-22535)
PEOPLES CARE INC
13901 Amargosa Rd Ste 101, Victorville (92392-2409)
PHONE.................................760 962-1900
Stacey Minwalla, *Owner*
Cristina Cordeiro, *Director*
EMP: 202
SALES (corp-wide): 32.9MM **Privately Held**
SIC: 8082 Home health care services
PA: People's Care Inc.
13920 City Center Dr # 290
Chino Hills CA 91709
855 773-6753

(P-22536)
PERMANENTE KAISER INTL
10917 Magnolia Ave, Riverside (92505-3044)
PHONE.................................951 358-2600
Fax: 909 358-2632
EMP: 299
SALES (corp-wide): 380.5MM **Privately Held**
SIC: 8082 Home health care services
PA: Kaiser Permanente International
1 Kaiser Plz
Oakland CA 94612
510 271-5910

(P-22537)
PERSONLZED HMCARE HMMAKER AGCY
4700 Northgate Blvd, Sacramento (95834-1128)
PHONE.................................916 979-4975
Celso Avaricio II, *CEO*
EMP: 100
SQ FT: 900
SALES (est): 302.8K **Privately Held**
SIC: 8082 Home health care services

(P-22538)
PREMIER MANAGEMENT COMPANY
Also Called: Jacob Health Care Center
4075 54th St, San Diego (92105-2301)
PHONE.................................619 582-5168
Guy Reggeb, *Manager*
EMP: 50
SALES (corp-wide): 6.1MM **Privately Held**
SIC: 8082 8051 Home health care services; skilled nursing care facilities
PA: Premier Management Company
9615 Knox Ave
Skokie IL

(P-22539)
PROFESSIONAL HEALTHCARE AT HM
395 Taylor Blvd Ste 118, Pleasant Hill (94523-2276)
PHONE.................................925 363-7876
Fax: 925 246-6004
Tanya Abrea, *Principal*
Erin Brutlag,
Brooks Anderson, *Manager*
Yvonne Enriquez, *Manager*
Jennifer Wallace, *Manager*
EMP: 82
SALES (corp-wide): 8.9MM **Privately Held**
SIC: 8082 Home health care services
PA: Professional Healthcare At Home, Inc
395 Taylor Blvd Ste 118
Pleasant Hill CA 94523
925 849-1160

(P-22540)
PROVIDENCE HEALTH & SERVICES
5315 Torrance Blvd, Torrance (90503-4011)
PHONE.................................310 370-5895
EMP: 191
SALES (corp-wide): 10.1B **Privately Held**
SIC: 8082 Home health care services
PA: Providence Health & Services
1801 Lind Ave Sw
Renton WA 98057
425 525-3355

(P-22541)
PROVIDENCE HEALTH & SERVICES
17315 Studebaker Rd # 310, Cerritos (90703-2563)
PHONE.................................562 865-4600
EMP: 174
SALES (corp-wide): 10.1B **Privately Held**
SIC: 8082 Home health care services
PA: Providence Health & Services
1801 Lind Ave Sw
Renton WA 98057
425 525-3355

(P-22542)
PROVIDENT CARE INC
100 Sycamore Ave Ste 100, Modesto (95354-0575)
P.O. Box 3558 (95352-3558)
PHONE.................................209 526-5160
Fax: 209 543-1697
Robin Conley, *President*
▲ EMP: 167
SQ FT: 4,571
SALES (est): 2.2MM **Privately Held**
SIC: 8082 Home health care services

(P-22543)
PW JADE LLC
Also Called: Right At Home
1111 Sonoma Ave Ste 324, Santa Rosa (95405-4820)
PHONE.................................707 843-5192
Robert Brohmer, *Principal*
EMP: 60
SALES (est): 548.8K **Privately Held**
SIC: 8082 Home health care services

(P-22544)
QUALITY IN-HMECARE SPECIALISTS
1166 Broadway Ste T, Placerville (95667-5745)
PHONE.................................530 303-3477
Fax: 530 622-8428
Pete Messimore, *CEO*
Arlene Secondo, *Treasurer*
Gloria Tingley, *Principal*
EMP: 99
SQ FT: 597
SALES (est): 3.1MM **Privately Held**
WEB: www.qualityinhomecare.com
SIC: 8082 Home health care services

(P-22545)
RAINBOW HOME CARE SERVICES
202 Fashion Ln Ste 118, Tustin (92780-3319)
PHONE.................................714 544-8070
Fax: 714 583-6991
Barbara Hedges, *CEO*
Beverly Dilday, *Office Mgr*
EMP: 55
SALES (est): 3MM **Privately Held**
WEB: www.rainbowhomecareservices.com
SIC: 8082 Home health care services

(P-22546)
RAMONA COMMUNITY SERVICES CORP (HQ)
Also Called: Ramona Vna & Hospice
890 W Stetson Ave Ste A, Hemet (92543-7311)
PHONE.................................951 658-9288
Fax: 951 765-6229
Patricia McBe, *Branch Mgr*
Patrick Searl, *Ch of Bd*
Kenn Hyatt, *Vice Chairman*
Carol Wood, *CEO*
Lauien Mahieu, *COO*
EMP: 150
SQ FT: 14,000
SALES (corp-wide): 20.7MM **Privately Held**
WEB: www.ramonavna.org
SIC: 8082 Visiting nurse service
PA: Kpc Group Llc
6800 Indiana Ave Ste 130
Riverside CA 92506
951 782-8812

(P-22547)
RELIABLE CAREGIVERS INC
1700 California St # 400, San Francisco (94109-0429)
PHONE.................................415 436-0100
Linda Leary, *President*
Bobbie Joe Keating, *Finance Dir*
Everett Moland, *Human Res Mgr*
Talya Onorato, *Manager*
EMP: 120
SALES: 3MM **Privately Held**
WEB: www.reliablecaregivers.net
SIC: 8082 Home health care services

(P-22548)
RES-CARE INC
Also Called: Socal Home Care-Givers Svcs
17291 Irvine Blvd Ste 150, Tustin (92780-2900)
PHONE.................................800 707-8781
Fax: 949 474-8377
Babli Dusttrama, *Branch Mgr*
EMP: 100
SALES (corp-wide): 4.1B **Privately Held**
SIC: 8082 Home health care services
HQ: Res-Care, Inc.
9901 Linn Station Rd
Louisville KY 40223
502 394-2100

(P-22549)
RIGHT AT HOME
Also Called: Sierra West Home Care
3435 Ocean Park Blvd # 110, Santa Monica (90405-3318)
PHONE.................................310 313-0600
Timothy Petlin, *Principal*
EMP: 75
SALES: 1.2MM **Privately Held**
SIC: 8082 Home health care services

(P-22550)
RIGHT CHOICE IN-HOME CARE INC
7104 Owensmouth Ave, Canoga Park (91303-2007)
PHONE.................................818 836-6001
Don Lucas, *Director*
Linda Weinberg, *President*
EMP: 680
SQ FT: 1,800
SALES (est): 10MM **Privately Held**
SIC: 8082 Home health care services

(P-22551)
ROBERTS & ASSOCIATES INC
Also Called: Visiting Angels Riverside Cnty
8175 Limonite Ave Ste A1, Riverside (92509-6121)
PHONE.................................951 727-4357
Joan Roberts, *President*
Robert Roberts, *Treasurer*
Benita Roberts, *Vice Pres*
EMP: 55
SQ FT: 400
SALES (est): 1.9MM **Privately Held**
SIC: 8082 Home health care services

(P-22552)
S B C SENIOR CARE INC
Also Called: Home Instead Senior Care
101 W Anapamu St Ste C, Santa Barbara (93101-3140)
PHONE.................................805 560-6995
Fax: 805 560-6994
Susan Johnson, *Owner*
EMP: 75
SALES (est): 1.5MM **Privately Held**
SIC: 8082 Home health care services

(P-22553)
SAN DIEGO HOMECARE
6181 Arnoldson Pl, San Diego (92122-2116)
PHONE.................................858 457-1520
Harry Quinn, *CEO*
EMP: 100
SQ FT: 500
SALES (est): 3.9MM **Privately Held**
SIC: 8082 Home health care services

(P-22554)
SAN DIEGO HOSPICE
Also Called: San Diego Hospice & Institute
2400 Historic Decatur Rd # 107, San Diego (92106-6158)
PHONE.................................619 688-1600
Fax: 619 688-1599
EMP: 600
SALES (corp-wide): 9.8MM **Privately Held**
SIC: 8082
PA: San Diego Hospice & Palliative Care Corporation
4311 3rd Ave
San Diego CA 92103
619 688-1600

(P-22555)
SAN PEDRO PENINSULA HOSPITAL
Also Called: Trinity Home Care
4101 Torrance Blvd, Torrance (90503-4607)
PHONE.................................310 370-5895
Linda Smith, *Exec VP*
Bill Kemp, *Security Dir*
Evie Trinidad, *Info Tech Mgr*
Glen Komatsu, *Director*
EMP: 200
SALES (corp-wide): 65.5MM **Privately Held**
SIC: 8082 8051 Home health care services; skilled nursing care facilities
PA: San Pedro Peninsula Hospital
1300 W 7th St
San Pedro CA 90732
310 832-3311

(P-22556)
SANSUM CLINIC
Also Called: Community Home Health Agency
509 E Montecito St # 200, Santa Barbara (93103-3259)
PHONE.................................805 682-6507
Melanie Thompson, *Director*

PRODUCTS & SERVICES SECTION

8082 - Home Health Care Svcs County (P-22579)

EMP: 50
SALES (corp-wide): 223.5MM Privately Held
WEB: www.sansum.com
SIC: 8082 Home health care services
PA: Sansum Clinic
    470 S Patterson Ave
    Santa Barbara CA 93111
    805 681-7700

(P-22557)
SCRIPPS HEALTH
3811 Valley Centre Dr, San Diego (92130-3318)
PHONE..................................858 764-3000
Chris Allen, *Office Mgr*
Lauren Alden, *Opers Spvr*
Charles Edwards, *Obstetrician*
Kris Ghosh, *Obstetrician*
Ronald Salzetti, *Obstetrician*
EMP: 378
SALES (corp-wide): 1.7B Privately Held
SIC: 8082 Home health care services
PA: Scripps Health
    4275 Campus Point Ct
    San Diego CA 92121
    858 678-7000

(P-22558)
SELECT HOME CARE
660 Hampshire Rd Ste 100, Westlake Village (91361-2549)
PHONE..................................805 777-3855
Dylan Hull, *CEO*
EMP: 100
SALES (est): 3.2MM Privately Held
SIC: 8082 Home health care services

(P-22559)
SERACADA
Also Called: Home Instead Senior Care
709 E Lavender Way, Azusa (91702-6294)
PHONE..................................626 486-0800
Fax: 626 486-0802
Ada Wong, *President*
EMP: 50
SALES: 350K Privately Held
SIC: 8082 Home health care services

(P-22560)
SERVING SENIORS LLC
2764 Rogue River Cir, West Sacramento (95691-4922)
PHONE..................................916 372-9640
Priyanka Bansal, *Mng Member*
EMP: 70
SALES (est): 482.5K Privately Held
SIC: 8082 Home health care services

(P-22561)
SHARP HEALTHCARE
Also Called: Sharp Home Care
8080 Dagget St Ste 200, San Diego (92111-2333)
PHONE..................................858 541-4850
Fax: 858 541-4804
Dan Gross, *Manager*
Marlene Gerendash, *Human Res Mgr*
Ray Kelley, *Purchasing*
Shirley Drescher, *Nurse*
Lyleen Pricor, *Director*
EMP: 66
SALES (corp-wide): 3.4B Privately Held
SIC: 8082 Home health care services
PA: Sharp Healthcare
    8695 Spectrum Center Blvd
    San Diego CA 92123
    858 499-4000

(P-22562)
SHARP HEALTHCARE
Also Called: Sharp Home Health
9765 Clairemont Mesa Blvd, San Diego (92124-1334)
PHONE..................................858 541-4896
Fax: 858 541-4843
Chirs Jenkins, *Director*
EMP: 122
SALES (corp-wide): 3.4B Privately Held
SIC: 8082 Home health care services
PA: Sharp Healthcare
    8695 Spectrum Center Blvd
    San Diego CA 92123
    858 499-4000

(P-22563)
SHERPAUL CORPORATION
Also Called: Home Instead Senior Care
901 Hacienda Dr B, Vista (92081-6401)
PHONE..................................760 639-6472
Fax: 760 639-6473
Sherry Dziuban, *President*
Paul Dziuban, *Vice Pres*
EMP: 54
SQ FT: 951
SALES (est): 2.8MM Privately Held
SIC: 8082 Home health care services

(P-22564)
SIERRA NEVADA MEMORIAL HM CARE
Also Called: Sierra Nevada Home Care
1020 Mccourtney Rd Ste A, Grass Valley (95949-7453)
P.O. Box 1029 (95945-1029)
PHONE..................................530 274-6350
Fax: 530 274-9023
Sharon Turner, *Director*
Jean Wootan, *Admin Sec*
Sandy Beck, *Administration*
Carolyn Canady, *Marketing Staff*
Brook Surber, *Nursing Dir*
EMP: 90
SQ FT: 6,200
SALES: 3.7MM
SALES (corp-wide): 7.1B Privately Held
WEB: www.snhc.org
SIC: 8082 7361 Home health care services; nurses' registry
PA: Dignity Health
    185 Berry St Ste 300
    San Francisco CA 94107
    415 438-5500

(P-22565)
SISTERS OF ST JOSEPH ORANGE
980 Trancas St Ste 9, NAPA (94558-2933)
PHONE..................................707 257-4124
Judy White, *QC Mgr*
EMP: 224
SALES (corp-wide): 5.6B Privately Held
SIC: 8082 Home health care services
PA: Sisters Of St. Joseph Of Orange
    480 S Batavia St
    Orange CA 92868
    714 633-8121

(P-22566)
SMITH RESIDENTIAL CARE FCILTY (PA)
318 E 4th St, Hanford (93230-5125)
P.O. Box 1093 (93232-1093)
PHONE..................................559 584-8451
Fax: 559 584-8674
Catherine Smith, *Owner*
EMP: 60
SALES (est): 2.2MM Privately Held
SIC: 8082 Home health care services

(P-22567)
SOUTH BAY SENIOR SERVICES INC
Also Called: Homewatch Caregivers
8939 S Sepulveda Blvd # 330, Los Angeles (90045-3647)
PHONE..................................310 338-7558
Fax: 310 496-2083
Richard Williams, *President*
Patricia Greaney, *Admin Sec*
EMP: 77
SQ FT: 700
SALES (est): 1.9MM Privately Held
WEB: www.homewatchcaregivers.com/los-angeles
SIC: 8082 Home health care services

(P-22568)
SOUTH BAY SENIOR SOLUTIONS INC
Also Called: Home Instead Senior Care
1660 Hamilton Ave Ste 204, San Jose (95125-5434)
PHONE..................................408 370-6360
Fax: 408 370-6408
Brian Jackson, *President*
EMP: 65 EST: 1996
SQ FT: 1,500
SALES (est): 2.7MM Privately Held
SIC: 8082 Home health care services

(P-22569)
ST JOSEPH COMMUNITY HOME CARE
7400 Shoreline Dr Ste 4, Stockton (95219-5498)
PHONE..................................209 478-9547
Fax: 209 478-9549
Carol Harpman, *Director*
EMP: 75
SALES (est): 2.5MM Privately Held
SIC: 8082 Home health care services

(P-22570)
ST JOSEPH HEALTH SYSTEM (HQ)
3345 Michelson Dr Ste 100, Irvine (92612-0693)
PHONE..................................949 381-4000
Fax: 714 347-7501
Annette Walker, *President*
Sandy Barber, *Records Dir*
Daniel Pothen, *Records Dir*
Jeff Allport, *President*
Wesley Okamoto, *President*
▲ EMP: 900
SALES (est): 5.6B Privately Held
WEB: www.stjhs.org
SIC: 8082 8741 Home health care services; hospital management
PA: Sisters Of St. Joseph Of Orange
    480 S Batavia St
    Orange CA 92868
    714 633-8121

(P-22571)
ST JOSEPH HOME HEALTH NETWORK (DH)
200 W Center St Promenade, Anaheim (92805-3960)
PHONE..................................714 712-9500
Linda Glomp, *Director*
Vincent Castaldo, *CFO*
Clara Seal, *Supervisor*
EMP: 92
SQ FT: 25,000
SALES (est): 28.1MM
SALES (corp-wide): 5.6B Privately Held
SIC: 8082 Home health care services
HQ: St. Joseph Health System
    3345 Michelson Dr Ste 100
    Irvine CA 92612
    949 381-4000

(P-22572)
ST JOSEPH HOME HEALTH NETWORK
Also Called: Saint Joseph Hlth Sys HM Hlth
200 W Center St Promenade, Anaheim (92805-3960)
PHONE..................................714 712-9559
Fax: 714 712-7157
Kris Kowlaski, *Director*
EMP: 50
SALES (corp-wide): 5.6B Privately Held
SIC: 8082 Visiting nurse service
HQ: St Joseph Home Health Network
    200 W Center St Promenade
    Anaheim CA 92805
    714 712-9500

(P-22573)
STAFFING SPECIALISTS INTL
Also Called: Staffing Home Care
2598 Olympic Dr, San Bruno (94066-1251)
PHONE..................................650 737-0777
Fax: 650 589-5909
Tina Desuasido, *Owner*
EMP: 50
SALES (est): 1.5MM Privately Held
SIC: 8082 Home health care services

(P-22574)
SUCCESS HEALTHCARE 1 LLC (PA)
Also Called: Silver Lake Medical Center
1711 W Temple St, Los Angeles (90026-5421)
PHONE..................................213 989-6100
Brent A Cope, *CEO*
George Watkins, *CFO*
Peter R Baronoff, *Principal*
Howard B Koslow, *Principal*
Lawrence Leder, *Principal*
EMP: 567

SALES (est): 53.9MM Privately Held
SIC: 8082 Home health care services

(P-22575)
SUTTER VSTING NRSE ASSN HSPICE
1625 Van Ness Ave, San Francisco (94109-3370)
PHONE..................................415 600-6200
Fax: 415 600-7592
Cindy Brown, *Manager*
EMP: 80
SALES (corp-wide): 11B Privately Held
SIC: 8082 8049 7361 Visiting nurse service; nurses & other medical assistants; nurses' registry
HQ: Sutter Visiting Nurse Association & Hospice
    1900 Powell St Ste 300
    Emeryville CA 94608
    866 652-9178

(P-22576)
SUTTER VSTING NRSE ASSN HSPICE (HQ)
Also Called: Vnahnc
1900 Powell St Ste 300, Emeryville (94608-1815)
P.O. Box 22250, Salt Lake City UT (84122-0250)
PHONE..................................866 652-9178
Fax: 510 450-8532
Marcia Reissig, *CEO*
Maryellen Rota, *COO*
Greg Davis, *CFO*
Gregg Davis, *CFO*
Maurita Kessler, *Project Mgr*
EMP: 50
SQ FT: 24,000
SALES: 171MM
SALES (corp-wide): 11B Privately Held
WEB: www.suttervnaandhospice.com
SIC: 8082 Visiting nurse service
PA: Sutter Health
    2200 River Plaza Dr
    Sacramento CA 95833
    916 733-8800

(P-22577)
SUTTER VSTING NRSE ASSN HSPICE
Also Called: Sutter Vsiting Nurse Assn Hosp
1900 Bates Ave Ste A, Concord (94520-1263)
PHONE..................................925 677-4250
Fax: 925 687-4261
Windi Heaton, *Manager*
Nancy Werdmann, *Manager*
EMP: 100
SALES (corp-wide): 11B Privately Held
SIC: 8082 Visiting nurse service
HQ: Sutter Visiting Nurse Association & Hospice
    1900 Powell St Ste 300
    Emeryville CA 94608
    866 652-9178

(P-22578)
TA-KAI HOME CARE INC
22343 La Palma Ave # 128, Yorba Linda (92887-3821)
PHONE..................................714 393-4586
Brian Nakamura, *Principal*
EMP: 69
SALES (est): 1.8MM Privately Held
SIC: 8082 Home health care services

(P-22579)
TENET HEALTHSYSTEM MEDICAL
Also Called: Redding Medical Home Care
475 Knollcrest Dr, Redding (96002-0101)
P.O. Box 494130 (96049-4130)
PHONE..................................530 222-1992
Fax: 530 222-1540
Judith Moroney, *Manager*
EMP: 60
SALES (corp-wide): 18.7B Publicly Held
WEB: www.tenenthealth.com
SIC: 8082 Home health care services
HQ: Tenet Healthsystem Medical, Inc
    1445 Ross Ave Ste 1400
    Dallas TX 75202
    469 893-2000

8082 - Home Health Care Svcs County (P-22580)

PRODUDUCTS & SERVICES SECTION

(P-22580)
THERAPY IN YOUR HOME O TP TS
147 Vista Del Monte, Los Gatos (95030-6335)
PHONE.....................408 358-0201
Fax: 408 358-0201
Julie Groves, *Owner*
EMP: 51
SALES (est): 1.4MM **Privately Held**
WEB: www.therapyinyourhome.net
SIC: 8082 Home health care services

(P-22581)
THOM SHARON & G ENTERPRISES
Also Called: Home Helpers
2620 Larkspur Ln Ste N, Redding (96002-1043)
PHONE.....................530 226-8350
Fax: 530 226-8375
Sharon Clark, *President*
EMP: 50
SQ FT: 750
SALES (est): 1.4MM **Privately Held**
SIC: 8082 Home health care services

(P-22582)
TRI-CITY HOME CARE SERVICES
2095 W Vista Way Ste 220, Vista (92083-6029)
PHONE.....................760 940-5800
Vernon Petelle, *Director*
Barbara Beckman, *Exec Dir*
Jim Parra, *Materials Dir*
EMP: 140
SALES (est): 4.1MM **Privately Held**
SIC: 8082 Home health care services

(P-22583)
TRINITY HOME HEALTH SVCS INC
Also Called: Saint Agnes HM Hlth & Hospice
6729 N Willow Ave Ste 103, Fresno (93710-5952)
PHONE.....................559 450-5112
Fax: 559 450-5190
B Smart, *Exec Dir*
Erin Denholm, *President*
Barbara Sears, *Principal*
EMP: 90
SALES (corp-wide): 64.6MM **Privately Held**
SIC: 8082 8093 Home health care services; rehabilitation center, outpatient treatment
PA: Trinity Home Health Services, Inc.
17410 College Pkwy # 150
Livonia MI 48152
734 542-8200

(P-22584)
TRINITYCARE LLC (PA)
Also Called: Trinity Care & Nutria
13030 Alondra Blvd, Cerritos (90703-2246)
PHONE.....................818 709-4221
Fax: 562 921-3459
Peggy Chris,
EMP: 50
SALES (est): 1.5MM **Privately Held**
SIC: 8082 Home health care services

(P-22585)
UCLA HEALTH SYSTEM AUXILIARY
10920 Wilshire Blvd # 1700, Los Angeles (90024-6502)
PHONE.....................310 794-0500
David T Feinberg, *President*
Patricia Kapur, *Exec VP*
Patty Cuen, *Exec Dir*
Tania Kaprealian, *Oncology*
Khiem Lam, *Manager*
EMP: 17000
SALES (est): 206.1MM **Privately Held**
SIC: 8082 Home health care services

(P-22586)
UNIVERSAL HOME CARE INC
151 N San Vicente Blvd, Beverly Hills (90211-2323)
PHONE.....................323 653-9222
Fax: 323 852-6768

Marina Greenberg, *CEO*
Stephen Shapiro MD, *Vice Pres*
EMP: 200
SALES (est): 5.5MM **Privately Held**
SIC: 8082 Home health care services

(P-22587)
UNIVERSITY HEALTHCARE ALLIANCE
7999 Gateway Blvd Ste 200, Newark (94560-1197)
PHONE.....................510 974-8281
Bruce Harrison, *CEO*
Brian Bohman, *President*
Quin Ngo, *Manager*
EMP: 97
SALES (est): 187.4MM **Privately Held**
SIC: 8082 Home health care services

(P-22588)
VERDUGO HLLS VSTING NURSE ASSN
Also Called: Vna Care
2826 E Foothill Blvd # 101, Pasadena (91107-3400)
PHONE.....................949 263-4704
Marie Reynolds, *Exec Dir*
EMP: 150
SALES (est): 6.4MM **Privately Held**
SIC: 8082 Visiting nurse service

(P-22589)
VINA HOLDINGS INC
13800 Arizona St, Westminster (92683-3951)
PHONE.....................714 622-5334
Cuong Nguyen, *President*
EMP: 80 EST: 2015
SALES (est): 297.1K **Privately Held**
SIC: 8082 Home health care services

(P-22590)
VISITING CARE & COMPANIONS INC
509 E Montecito St # 200, Santa Barbara (93103-3259)
PHONE.....................805 690-6202
Lynda Panner, *CEO*
Gail Rink, *Exec Dir*
John Dougherty, *Info Tech Dir*
Marion Schoneberger, *Manager*
Paul Huelar, *Accounts Mgr*
EMP: 84
SALES: 3MM **Privately Held**
SIC: 8082 Visiting nurse service

(P-22591)
VISITING NRSE ASSN ORANGE CNTY (PA)
Also Called: Vna Home Health Systems
2520 Redhill Ave, Santa Ana (92705-5542)
PHONE.....................949 263-4700
Fax: 949 263-4750
Jeneane A Brian, *President*
Joan Randall, *COO*
▼ EMP: 55
SQ FT: 30,000
SALES (est): 2MM **Privately Held**
WEB: www.vnahhs.com
SIC: 8082 Home health care services

(P-22592)
VISITING NURSE ASSOCI
Also Called: Vna Private Duty Care
150 W 1st St Ste 176, Claremont (91711-4739)
P.O. Box 1208 (91711-1208)
PHONE.....................909 621-3961
Fax: 909 625-1621
Marsha Fox, *Director*
Laura Meyer-Lee, *Human Res Mgr*
Matt Postiy, *Purchasing*
EMP: 100 EST: 1984
SALES (est): 2.8MM **Privately Held**
SIC: 8082 Visiting nurse service

(P-22593)
VISITING NURSE ASSOCIATION
Also Called: Center Coast Home Help Care
5 Lower Ragsdle Dr 102, Monterey (93940)
P.O. Box 2480 (93942-2480)
PHONE.....................831 385-1014
Fax: 831 648-7734
Carol Snow, *President*

Gayle McConnell, *CFO*
Mark Burnet, *IT/INT Sup*
Gena Gett, *Director*
Margie McCurry, *Director*
EMP: 80
SALES (est): 823.2K **Privately Held**
SIC: 8082 Visiting nurse service

(P-22594)
VISITING NURSE ASSOCIATION OF
20100 Cedar Rd N Ste C, Sonora (95370-5925)
PHONE.....................209 736-2338
Sara Herrin, *Director*
EMP: 55
SALES (est): 654.9K **Privately Held**
SIC: 8082 Home health care services

(P-22595)
VISITING NURSE ASSOCIATION OF (DH)
2880 Soquel Ave Ste 10, Santa Cruz (95062-1423)
PHONE.....................831 477-2600
Fax: 831 688-1146
Bella Hughes, *Exec Dir*
EMP: 100
SQ FT: 19,000
SALES (est): 8.3MM
SALES (corp-wide): 11B **Privately Held**
SIC: 8082 Home health care services
HQ: Palo Alto Medical Foundation For Health Care, Research And Education (Inc)
795 El Camino Real
Palo Alto CA 94301
650 321-4121

(P-22596)
VISITNG NURSE ASSN INLND CNT (PA)
Also Called: Vnaic
6235 River Crest Dr Ste L, Riverside (92507-0758)
P.O. Box 1649 (92502-1649)
PHONE.....................951 413-1200
Fax: 951 656-4257
Mike A Rusnak, *President*
Greg Del Gado, *General Mgr*
Anna Spencer, *Administration*
Carol Bromley, *Info Tech Mgr*
Mary Reed, *Info Tech Mgr*
EMP: 720
SQ FT: 12,000
SALES: 56.8MM **Privately Held**
SIC: 8082 Visiting nurse service

(P-22597)
VISITNG NURSE ASSN INLND CNT
42600 Cook St Ste 202, Palm Desert (92211-5143)
PHONE.....................760 346-3982
Anne Tyer, *Director*
Doug Morin, *Director*
John Prekeces, *Director*
EMP: 130
SALES (corp-wide): 56.8MM **Privately Held**
SIC: 8082 8621 Visiting nurse service; nursing association
PA: Visiting Nurse Association Of The Inland Counties
6235 River Crest Dr Ste L
Riverside CA 92507
951 413-1200

(P-22598)
VISITNG NURSE ASSN INLND CNT
12421 Hesperia Rd Ste 11, Victorville (92395-5870)
PHONE.....................760 962-1966
Fax: 760 241-7055
Pam Wood, *Manager*
Cindy Roy, *Manager*
EMP: 75
SALES (corp-wide): 56.8MM **Privately Held**
SIC: 8082 8051 Visiting nurse service; skilled nursing, care facilities

PA: Visiting Nurse Association Of The Inland Counties
6235 River Crest Dr Ste L
Riverside CA 92507
951 413-1200

(P-22599)
VITAS HEALTHCARE CORP CAL (DH)
7888 Mission Grove Pkwy S, Riverside (92508-5089)
PHONE.....................305 374-4143
David A Wester, *President*
Peggy Pettit, *COO*
Barry M Kinzbrunner, *Chief Mktg Ofcr*
Kal Mistry, *Senior VP*
EMP: 300 EST: 1993
SALES (est): 38.6K
SALES (corp-wide): 1.5B **Publicly Held**
SIC: 8082 8011 Home health care services; physical medicine, physician/surgeon
HQ: Vitas Healthcare Corporation
100 S Biscayne Blvd # 1600
Miami FL 33131
305 374-4143

(P-22600)
VITAS HEALTHCARE CORP CAL
Also Called: Vitas Innovative Hospice Care
670 N Mccarthy Blcvd 220, Milpitas (95035)
PHONE.....................408 964-6800
Fax: 510 360-4816
Roslyn Stenson, *Branch Mgr*
Dawn M Gross, *Hematology*
EMP: 80
SALES (corp-wide): 1.5B **Publicly Held**
WEB: www.vitasinnovativehospicecare.com
SIC: 8082 Home health care services
HQ: Vitas Healthcare Corporation Of California
7888 Mission Grove Pkwy S
Riverside CA 92508
305 374-4143

(P-22601)
VITAS HEALTHCARE CORP CAL
2710 Gateway Oaks Dr # 100, Sacramento (95833-3505)
PHONE.....................916 925-7010
Fax: 916 566-2250
Sharon Rostoker, *Principal*
Sheila Clark, *General Mgr*
Shannon Peacock, *Office Mgr*
Noemi Howell, *Administration*
EMP: 95
SALES (corp-wide): 1.5B **Publicly Held**
WEB: www.vitasinnovativehospicecare.com
SIC: 8082 Home health care services
HQ: Vitas Healthcare Corporation Of California
7888 Mission Grove Pkwy S
Riverside CA 92508
305 374-4143

(P-22602)
VITAS HEALTHCARE CORP CAL
365 Lennon Ln Ste 140, Walnut Creek (94598-5911)
PHONE.....................925 930-9373
Fax: 925 945-3850
Shirley Blethen, *Branch Mgr*
EMP: 95
SALES (corp-wide): 1.5B **Publicly Held**
WEB: www.vitasinnovativehospicecare.com
SIC: 8082 Home health care services
HQ: Vitas Healthcare Corporation Of California
7888 Mission Grove Pkwy S
Riverside CA 92508
305 374-4143

(P-22603)
VITAS HEALTHCARE CORP CAL
1343 N Grand Ave Ste 100, Covina (91724-4043)
PHONE.....................626 918-2273
Thomas E Combs, *Owner*
Darren Le, *Personnel*
Susan Patterson, *Manager*
EMP: 80
SALES (corp-wide): 1.5B **Publicly Held**
WEB: www.vitasinnovativehospicecare.com
SIC: 8082 Home health care services

PRODUCTS & SERVICES SECTION

8092 - Kidney Dialysis Centers County (P-22625)

HQ: Vitas Healthcare Corporation Of California
7888 Mission Grove Pkwy S
Riverside CA 92508
305 374-4143

(P-22604)
VITAS HEALTHCARE CORP CAL
990 W 190th St Ste 550, Torrance
(90502-1046)
PHONE.................310 324-2273
Fax: 310 225-5959
Marie Hagerty, *Principal*
Peggy Murray, *Executive*
Marie Haggerty, *General Mgr*
EMP: 70
SALES (corp-wide): 1.5B **Publicly Held**
WEB: www.vitasinnovativehospicecare.com
SIC: 8082 Home health care services
HQ: Vitas Healthcare Corporation Of California
7888 Mission Grove Pkwy S
Riverside CA 92508
305 374-4143

(P-22605)
VITAS HEALTHCARE CORP CAL
Also Called: Vitas Innovative Hospice Care
7888 Mission Grove Pkwy S, Riverside
(92508-5089)
PHONE.................909 386-6000
Fax: 909 386-6004
Karen Bennett, *Manager*
Wesley Rogers, *General Mgr*
Noemi Howell, *Administration*
Steve Girod,
Leticia Goodwin, *Representative*
EMP: 170
SALES (corp-wide): 1.5B **Publicly Held**
WEB: www.vitasinnovativehospicecare.com
SIC: 8082 8011 Home health care services; physical medicine, physician/surgeon
HQ: Vitas Healthcare Corporation Of California
7888 Mission Grove Pkwy S
Riverside CA 92508
305 374-4143

(P-22606)
VITAS HEALTHCARE CORP CAL
Also Called: Vitas Innovative Hospice Care
16830 Ventura Blvd # 315, Encino
(91436-1723)
PHONE.................818 760-0290
Fax: 818 385-0291
Susie Fishenfeld, *Branch Mgr*
Albert Hoston, *Technology*
Ashkan Imanzahrai, *Med Doctor*
EMP: 60
SALES (corp-wide): 1.5B **Publicly Held**
WEB: www.vitasinnovativehospicecare.com
SIC: 8082 Home health care services
HQ: Vitas Healthcare Corporation Of California
7888 Mission Grove Pkwy S
Riverside CA 92508
305 374-4143

(P-22607)
VITAS HEALTHCARE CORP CAL
Also Called: Vitas Innovative Hospice Care
9655 Gran Rdge Dr Ste 300, San Diego
(92123)
PHONE.................619 680-4400
Fax: 619 503-4785
Judy Brenton, *Branch Mgr*
EMP: 95
SALES (corp-wide): 1.5B **Publicly Held**
WEB: www.vitasinnovativehospicecare.com
SIC: 8082 Home health care services
HQ: Vitas Healthcare Corporation Of California
7888 Mission Grove Pkwy S
Riverside CA 92508
305 374-4143

(P-22608)
VITAS HEALTHCARE CORPORATION
333 N Lantana St Ste 124, Camarillo
(93010-9007)
PHONE.................805 437-2100
Rita Peddycoart, *Manager*
EMP: 95

SALES (corp-wide): 1.5B **Publicly Held**
WEB: www.vitasinnovativehospicecare.com
SIC: 8082 Home health care services
HQ: Vitas Healthcare Corporation
100 S Biscayne Blvd # 1600
Miami FL 33131
305 374-4143

(P-22609)
VN HOME HEALTH CARE LP
2528 Qume Dr Ste 7, San Jose
(95131-1836)
PHONE.................408 998-0550
Fax: 408 998-8984
Ngai Nguyen, *Principal*
EMP: 62
SALES (est): 1.6MM **Privately Held**
SIC: 8082 Home health care services

(P-22610)
VNA HOSPICE & PLLATVE CRE S CA
Also Called: V N A & Hospice Southern Calif
412 E Vanderbilt Way, San Bernardino
(92408-3552)
PHONE.................909 384-0737
Toll Free:................888 -
Fax: 909 384-1628
Marsha Fox, *President*
Carol Dorris, *Manager*
EMP: 150
SQ FT: 3,230
SALES (corp-wide): 40.1MM **Privately Held**
WEB: www.vnasocal.org
SIC: 8082 Visiting nurse service
PA: Vna Hospice And Palliative Care Of Southern California
150 W 1st St Ste 270
Claremont CA 91711
909 624-3574

(P-22611)
VNA HOSPICE & PLLATVE CRE S CA (PA)
Also Called: Vna Private Duty Care
150 W 1st St Ste 270, Claremont
(91711-4756)
P.O. Box 908 (91711-0908)
PHONE.................909 624-3574
Marsha Fox, *President*
Gayle Wilson, *Vice Pres*
Bak Bakayoko, *Software Dev*
Patty Meinhardt, *Business Mgr*
Sergio Recio, *Analyst*
EMP: 101
SALES: 40.1MM **Privately Held**
SIC: 8082 Visiting nurse service

(P-22612)
WALGREENS HOME CARE INC
9401 Chivers Ave, Sun Valley
(91352-2655)
PHONE.................818 351-3000
Jon Pyshny, *Branch Mgr*
EMP: 55
SALES (corp-wide): 117.3B **Publicly Held**
SIC: 8082 Home health care services
HQ: Walgreens Home Care, Inc.
1417 Lake Cook Rd Ste 100
Deerfield IL 60015
847 940-2500

(P-22613)
WALGREENS HOME CARE INC
975 Industrial Rd Ste E, San Carlos
(94070-4138)
PHONE.................650 551-7020
Lucinda Chan, *Manager*
EMP: 123
SALES (corp-wide): 117.3B **Publicly Held**
SIC: 8082 Home health care services
HQ: Walgreens Home Care, Inc.
1417 Lake Cook Rd Ste 100
Deerfield IL 60015
847 940-2500

(P-22614)
WAY COOL HOMECARE INC
Also Called: Comfort Keepers
450 Fletcher Pkwy Ste 216, El Cajon
(92020-2520)
PHONE.................619 444-3200
Fax: 619 588-0448

Moura A Everhart, *President*
Benjamin Everhart, *Treasurer*
EMP: 50
SQ FT: 1,650
SALES: 1.4MM **Privately Held**
SIC: 8082 Home health care services

(P-22615)
WELL BEING GROUP INC
7075 N Howard St Ste 102, Fresno
(93720-2922)
PHONE.................559 432-3737
Mark Dyson, *President*
EMP: 80
SALES (est): 1.3MM **Privately Held**
SIC: 8082 Home health care services

(P-22616)
YOLO HOSPICE INC (PA)
1909 Galileo Ct Ste A, Davis (95618-4890)
P.O. Box 1014 (95617-1014)
PHONE.................530 758-5566
Fax: 530 758-9017
Doug Jena, *Exec Dir*
Janene Ramos, *Exec Dir*
Laura Reyes, *Admin Sec*
Laura Reys, *Admin Sec*
EMP: 60
SALES: 5.6MM **Privately Held**
WEB: www.yolohospice.org
SIC: 8082 8322 Home health care services; individual & family services

---

8092 Kidney Dialysis Centers

(P-22617)
BAKERSFIELD DIALYSIS CENTER
5143 Office Park Dr, Bakersfield
(93309-0660)
PHONE.................661 325-4741
Robert Kopelman MD, *President*
Harold Baer MD, *Vice Pres*
EMP: 100
SQ FT: 1,200
SALES (est): 6MM **Privately Held**
WEB: www.bdcn.com
SIC: 8092 Kidney dialysis centers

(P-22618)
BIO MDCAL APPLICATIONS FLA INC
Also Called: San Joaquin Vly Dialysis Ctr
3636 N 1st St Ste 144, Fresno
(93726-6818)
PHONE.................559 221-6311
Monique Hartell, *Manager*
Cathy Greene, *Exec Dir*
EMP: 53
SALES (corp-wide): 16.6B **Privately Held**
SIC: 8092 Kidney dialysis centers
HQ: Bio Medical Applications Of Florida, Inc.
920 Winter St Ste A
Waltham MA 02451
781 699-9000

(P-22619)
BIO-MDCAL APPLICATIONS CAL INC
Also Called: FMC Dialysis Svcs Bellflower
10116 Rosecrans Ave, Bellflower
(90706-2564)
PHONE.................562 920-2070
Fax: 562 920-2190
Nelly McPhail, *Administration*
Rowena Padua, *Manager*
EMP: 52
SALES (corp-wide): 16.6B **Privately Held**
WEB: www.fresenius.org
SIC: 8092 Kidney dialysis centers
HQ: Bio-Medical Applications Of California, Inc.
920 Winter St
Waltham MA 02451
781 699-4404

(P-22620)
BIO-MDCAL APPLICATIONS CAL INC
Also Called: BMA San Gabriel
1801 W Valley Blvd # 102, Alhambra
(91803-2300)
PHONE.................626 457-9002
Monique Hartell, *Manager*
EMP: 50
SALES (corp-wide): 16.6B **Privately Held**
SIC: 8092 Kidney dialysis centers
HQ: Bio-Medical Applications Of California, Inc.
920 Winter St
Waltham MA 02451
781 699-4404

(P-22621)
BIO-MDCAL APPLICATIONS CAL INC
Also Called: FMC Dialysis Svcs Riverside
3470 La Sierra Ave Ste E, Riverside
(92503-5223)
PHONE.................951 343-7700
Fax: 951 343-7718
Monique Hartell, *Manager*
EMP: 52
SALES (corp-wide): 16.6B **Privately Held**
SIC: 8092 Kidney dialysis centers
HQ: Bio-Medical Applications Of California, Inc.
920 Winter St
Waltham MA 02451
781 699-4404

(P-22622)
DAVITA INC
15271 Laguna Canyon Rd, Irvine
(92618-3146)
PHONE.................949 930-4400
Viki Anderson, *Branch Mgr*
Terry Lindsey, *Vice Pres*
David Kolojay, *Regional Mgr*
Clark Herrman, *IT/INT Sup*
Edward Flash, *Finance*
EMP: 270
SALES (corp-wide): 13.7B **Publicly Held**
WEB: www.davita.com
SIC: 8092 Kidney dialysis centers
PA: Davita Inc.
2000 16th St
Denver CO 80202
303 405-2100

(P-22623)
DIALYSIS CENTERS VENTURA CNTY
4567 Telephone Rd Ste 101, Ventura
(93003-5665)
PHONE.................805 658-9211
Fax: 805 658-9920
Laura Norkinson, *Manager*
EMP: 67
SQ FT: 6,000
SALES (est): 1.4MM **Privately Held**
SIC: 8092 Kidney dialysis centers

(P-22624)
DIALYSIS CLINIC INC
1771 Stockton Blvd # 200, Sacramento
(95816-7040)
PHONE.................916 453-0803
Cecelia Cronk, *Manager*
EMP: 50
SALES (corp-wide): 712.6MM **Privately Held**
WEB: www.dciinc.org
SIC: 8092 Kidney dialysis centers
PA: Dialysis Clinic, Inc.
1633 Church St Ste 500
Nashville TN 37203
615 327-3061

(P-22625)
DVA RENAL HEALTHCARE INC
Also Called: Saddleback Dialysis
23141 Plaza Pointe Dr, Laguna Hills
(92653-1425)
PHONE.................949 588-9211
Remy Obrt, *Branch Mgr*
EMP: 75
SALES (corp-wide): 13.7B **Publicly Held**
WEB: www.us.gambro.com
SIC: 8092 Kidney dialysis centers

8092 - Kidney Dialysis Centers County (P-22626)

HQ: Dva Renal Healthcare, Inc.
5200 Virginia Way
Brentwood TN 37027
615 320-4200

(P-22626)
EL CAMINO HOSPITAL
Also Called: Camino Dialysis Svcs Oak 110
2505 Hospital Dr Ste 1, Mountain View (94040-4127)
PHONE..................................650 940-7310
George Ting MD, *Director*
Cristina Byerly, *Sales Associate*
David F Chang, *Ophthalmology*
Kimberly Cockerham, *Ophthalmology*
Rahul Khurana, *Ophthalmology*
EMP: 75
SALES (corp-wide): 776.4MM **Privately Held**
SIC: 8092 Kidney dialysis centers
PA: El Camino Hospital
2500 Grant Rd
Mountain View CA 94040
408 224-6660

(P-22627)
FRESENIUS MED CARE LONG BEACH
Also Called: BMA Long Beach
440 W Ocean Blvd, Long Beach (90802-4518)
PHONE..................................562 432-4444
Fax: 562 435-5764
Monique Hartell, *Manager*
EMP: 50
SALES (corp-wide): 16.6B **Privately Held**
WEB: www.fresenius.org
SIC: 8092 Kidney dialysis centers
HQ: Fresenius Medical Care Long Beach, Llc
920 Winter St
Waltham MA 02451
781 699-9000

(P-22628)
HEMODIALYSIS INC (PA)
Also Called: Glentrans
710 W Wilson Ave, Glendale (91203-2409)
PHONE..................................818 500-8736
Fax: 818 500-7662
John R Depalma, *President*
James Calder, *Systems Admin*
Evelyn Amador, *Manager*
EMP: 50
SQ FT: 1,500
SALES (est): 8.7MM **Privately Held**
SIC: 8092 Kidney dialysis centers

(P-22629)
HEMODIALYSIS INC
14901 Rinaldi St Ste 100, Mission Hills (91345-1253)
PHONE..................................818 365-6961
Fax: 818 365-3061
John R Depalma, *Branch Mgr*
EMP: 50
SALES (corp-wide): 8.7MM **Privately Held**
SIC: 8092 Kidney dialysis centers
PA: Hemodialysis, Inc.
710 W Wilson Ave
Glendale CA 91203
818 500-8736

(P-22630)
INTERCOMMUNITY DIALYSIS SVCS
Also Called: Intercommunity Dialysis Center
12291 Washington Blvd # 410, Whittier (90606-3815)
P.O. Box 11065 (90603-0065)
PHONE..................................562 696-1841
Fax: 562 696-9953
Riad Darwish, *Administration*
Evelyn Sandoval, *Principal*
Dr John Shaib, *Principal*
Maritess Cabel, *Admin Sec*
EMP: 50
SQ FT: 7,400
SALES (est): 3.7MM **Privately Held**
SIC: 8092 8011 Kidney dialysis centers; clinic, operated by physicians

(P-22631)
JAMBOOR MEDICAL CORPORATION
Also Called: Desert Cities Dialysis
12675 Hesperia Rd, Victorville (92395-5878)
PHONE..................................760 241-8063
Fax: 760 241-5037
Jay Shankar, *President*
Saguna Jayashankar, *Admin Sec*
Leann Groff, *Controller*
EMP: 65
SQ FT: 7,000
SALES (est): 5.8MM **Privately Held**
SIC: 8092 Kidney dialysis centers

(P-22632)
KIDNEY CENTER INC
Also Called: Kidney Dialysis Center Verdugo
50 Moreland Rd, Simi Valley (93065-1659)
P.O. Box 940838 (93094-0838)
PHONE..................................805 433-7777
Kant Tucker MD, *CEO*
Ushakant Thakkar, *President*
Sandip Thakkar, *Exec VP*
Raj Thakkar, *Vice Pres*
Leena Thakkar, *Director*
EMP: 200
SQ FT: 10,000
SALES (est): 14.6MM **Privately Held**
SIC: 8092 Kidney dialysis centers

(P-22633)
LOS ALMTOS HMODIALYSIS CTR INC
Also Called: Los Alamitos Hemo Dialysis Ctr
3810 Katella Ave, Los Alamitos (90720-3302)
PHONE..................................562 426-8881
Fax: 562 594-8085
Maher A Azer, *President*
EMP: 60
SQ FT: 15,000
SALES (est): 4.6MM **Privately Held**
WEB: www.dialysisflorence.com
SIC: 8092 Kidney dialysis centers

(P-22634)
MOHAN DIALYSIS CENTER INDUSTRY
15757 E Valley Blvd, City of Industry (91744-3900)
PHONE..................................626 333-3801
Fax: 626 336-1303
Krishna Mohan, *Director*
Ana Mohan, *Admin Sec*
Eva Avila, *Administration*
EMP: 70
SALES (est): 5MM **Privately Held**
SIC: 8092 Kidney dialysis centers

(P-22635)
MOHAN DIALYSIS CTR OF COVINA
Also Called: Mdcc
158 W College St, Covina (91723-2007)
PHONE..................................626 859-2522
Fax: 626 967-3849
Dr Krishna Mohan, *Director*
▲ EMP: 70
SQ FT: 5,500
SALES (est): 5MM **Privately Held**
WEB: www.mdcc.com
SIC: 8092 Kidney dialysis centers

(P-22636)
RAI CARE CTRS NTHRN CAL II LLC
Also Called: Rai Csar Chvez St-San Frncisco
1750 Cesar Chavez Ste A, San Francisco (94124-1140)
PHONE..................................415 206-9775
Monique Hartell, *Branch Mgr*
Vicki Yarcia, *Office Mgr*
Lyas Ilyla, *Nephrology*
Mark Kasselik, *Nephrology*
EMP: 50
SALES (corp-wide): 16.6B **Privately Held**
SIC: 8092 Kidney dialysis centers
HQ: Rai Care Centers Of Northern California Ii, Llc
920 Winter St
Waltham MA 02451
781 699-9000

(P-22637)
RENAL TREATMENT CTRS - CAL INC
Also Called: Davita Dialysis
15271 Laguna Canyon Rd, Irvine (92618-3146)
PHONE..................................949 930-6882
Kent Thiry, *CEO*
Edna McCoy, *Manager*
EMP: 99
SALES (est): 3.1MM **Privately Held**
SIC: 8092 Kidney dialysis centers

(P-22638)
RENAL TRTMNT CNTRS-CLFRNIA INC
Also Called: RTC Brea
595 Tamarack Ave Ste A, Brea (92821-3125)
PHONE..................................714 990-0110
Agnes Henry, *Branch Mgr*
Nathan Ramani, *Nephrology*
Tyler Bloom, *Manager*
EMP: 70
SALES (corp-wide): 13.7B **Publicly Held**
WEB: www.davita.com
SIC: 8092 Kidney dialysis centers
HQ: Renal Treatment Centers-California, Inc.
941 Merchant St
Vacaville CA 95688
707 447-8191

(P-22639)
RIVERSIDE DIALYSIS CENTER
4361 Latham St Ste 100, Riverside (92501-1767)
PHONE..................................951 682-2700
Linda Sherman, *Principal*
Hisham Zurnai, *Executive*
▲ EMP: 50
SALES (est): 1.2MM **Privately Held**
SIC: 8092 Kidney dialysis centers

(P-22640)
SATELLITE HEALTHCARE INC
Also Called: Satellite Dialysis
3500 Coffee Rd Ste 21, Modesto (95355-1315)
PHONE..................................209 578-0691
Susie Phillips, *Manager*
EMP: 60
SALES (corp-wide): 188.9MM **Privately Held**
WEB: www.satellitehealth.com
SIC: 8092 8011 Kidney dialysis centers; offices & clinics of medical doctors
PA: Satellite Healthcare, Inc.
300 Santana Row Ste 300
San Jose CA 95128
650 404-3600

(P-22641)
SATELLITE HEALTHCARE INC (PA)
Also Called: Satellite Dialysis Centers
300 Santana Row Ste 300, San Jose (95128-2424)
PHONE..................................650 404-3600
Rick J Barnett, *President*
Kathy Hoyer, *Shareholder*
Norman S Coplon, *Ch of Bd*
Dave Carter, *COO*
Rosemary Fox, *COO*
EMP: 75
SQ FT: 12,000
SALES: 188.9MM **Privately Held**
WEB: www.satellitehealth.com
SIC: 8092 Kidney dialysis centers

(P-22642)
SATELLITE HEALTHCARE INC
2121 Alexian Dr Ste 118, San Jose (95116-1905)
PHONE..................................408 258-8720
Mark Carlston, *Manager*
Ken Membreve, *Executive*
Ashraf Noorani, *Nephrology*
EMP: 80
SALES (corp-wide): 188.9MM **Privately Held**
WEB: www.satellitehealth.com
SIC: 8092 8011 Kidney dialysis centers; clinic, operated by physicians
PA: Satellite Healthcare, Inc.
300 Santana Row Ste 300
San Jose CA 95128
650 404-3600

(P-22643)
TOTAL RENAL CARE INC
Also Called: TRC Pleasanton Dialysis Cntr
5720 Stoneridge Mall Rd # 160, Pleasanton (94588-2828)
PHONE..................................925 737-0120
Fax: 925 737-0155
Connie Edwards, *Administration*
Kari Everson, *Administration*
EMP: 50
SALES (corp-wide): 13.7B **Publicly Held**
WEB: www.davita.com
SIC: 8092 Kidney dialysis centers
HQ: Total Renal Care, Inc.
2000 16th St
Denver CO 80202
253 280-9501

(P-22644)
TOTAL RENAL CARE INC
15253 Bake Pkwy, Irvine (92618-2502)
PHONE..................................949 930-6882
Kent Thiry, *President*
Jennifer Werner, *Info Tech Mgr*
EMP: 99
SALES (est): 1.9MM **Privately Held**
SIC: 8092 Kidney dialysis centers

(P-22645)
TOTAL RENAL CARE INC
Also Called: Carquinez Dialysis
125 Corporate Pl Ste C, Vallejo (94590-6968)
PHONE..................................707 556-3637
Agnes Brabek, *CEO*
Tyler Broom, *Manager*
EMP: 600
SALES (corp-wide): 13.7B **Publicly Held**
WEB: www.davita.com
SIC: 8092 Kidney dialysis centers
HQ: Total Renal Care, Inc.
2000 16th St
Denver CO 80202
253 280-9501

(P-22646)
TOTAL RENAL CARE INC
Also Called: Davita Hesperia Dialysis Ctr
14135 Main St Ste 501, Hesperia (92345-8097)
PHONE..................................760 947-7405
EMP: 60
SALES (corp-wide): 12.8B **Publicly Held**
SIC: 8092
HQ: Total Renal Care, Inc.
601 Hawaii St
El Segundo CA 80202
310 536-2400

8093 Specialty Outpatient Facilities, NEC

(P-22647)
21ST CENTURY HEALTH CLUB (PA)
680a E Cotati Ave, Cotati (94931-4092)
PHONE..................................707 795-0400
John Ford, *President*
Dr Robert Gardner, *Treasurer*
Frank Ford, *Vice Pres*
Elizabeth Gardner, *Admin Sec*
David Chasin, *Manager*
▲ EMP: 70
SQ FT: 20,000
SALES (est): 3.1MM **Privately Held**
SIC: 8093 7991 Rehabilitation center, outpatient treatment; health club

(P-22648)
ADDICTION RES & TRTMNT INC
433 Turk St, San Francisco (94102-3329)
PHONE..................................415 928-7800
Teresa Fleming, *Branch Mgr*
EMP: 56 **Privately Held**
SIC: 8093 Drug clinic, outpatient

PRODUCTS & SERVICES SECTION
8093 - Specialty Outpatient Facilities, NEC County (P-22671)

PA: Addiction Research And Treatment, Inc.
1145 Market St Fl 10
San Francisco CA 94103

(P-22649)
ADVENTIST HEALTH SYSTEM/WEST
Also Called: Handford Community Center
470 Greenfield Ave, Hanford (93230-3576)
PHONE..................................559 537-2510
Fax: 559 585-5705
Matthew Beehler, *Business Dir*
Kenny MAI, *Surgeon*
Aleksandr Reznichenko, *Surgeon*
Frank Buchanan, *Med Doctor*
EMP: 106
SALES (corp-wide): 251.4MM **Privately Held**
SIC: 8093 Specialty outpatient clinics
PA: Adventist Health System/West
2100 Douglas Blvd
Roseville CA 95661
916 781-2000

(P-22650)
AEGIS TREATMENT CENTERS LLC (PA)
7246 Remmet Ave, Canoga Park (91303-1531)
PHONE..................................818 206-0360
Alex Dodd, *CEO*
David Devine, *Controller*
EMP: 63
SALES (est): 10.3MM **Privately Held**
SIC: 8093 Rehabilitation center, outpatient treatment

(P-22651)
AGENDIA INC
22 Morgan, Irvine (92618-2022)
PHONE..................................949 540-6300
Mark R Straley, *CEO*
Glen Fredenberg, *CFO*
Kurt Schmidt, *CFO*
Peter C Wulff, *CFO*
M William Audeh, *Chief Mktg Ofcr*
EMP: 107 EST: 2008
SALES: 18.7MM
SALES (corp-wide): 23.2MM **Privately Held**
SIC: 8093 Specialty outpatient clinics
PA: Agendia N.V.
Science Park 406
Amsterdam
204 621-500

(P-22652)
ALCOHOL DRG PROGRAM YOLO CNTY
137 N Cottonwood St Ste 1, Woodland (95695-6646)
PHONE..................................530 666-8650
Karen Gerbasi, *Exec Dir*
Eileen Florento, *Psychiatry*
George Graman, *Psychiatry*
Thacharawut Kanchananakhin, *Psychiatry*
Harry Tullin, *Psychiatry*
EMP: 50 EST: 2001
SALES (est): 1.6MM **Privately Held**
SIC: 8093 Specialty outpatient clinics

(P-22653)
ALGOS INC A MEDICAL CORP (PA)
Also Called: Pasadena Rehabilitation Inst
224 N Fair Oaks Ave, Pasadena (91103-3618)
PHONE..................................626 696-1400
Fax: 626 403-2580
Clayton Varga, *President*
Robert Castaneda, *CFO*
Gerri Summe, *CFO*
Andrea Ferreiro, *Vice Pres*
Damian Dyer, *CIO*
EMP: 60
SQ FT: 8,000
SALES (est): 7MM **Privately Held**
WEB: www.thebigmd.com
SIC: 8093 8049 8011 Rehabilitation center, outpatient treatment; physical therapist; specialized medical practitioners, except internal

(P-22654)
ALLIANT EDUCATIONAL FOUNDATION
5130 E Clinton Way, Fresno (93727-2014)
PHONE..................................559 456-2777
Jennifer Wilson, *Branch Mgr*
EMP: 200
SALES (corp-wide): 71.7MM **Privately Held**
SIC: 8093 8221 Mental health clinic, outpatient; university
PA: Alliant International University, Inc.
10455 Pomerado Rd
San Diego CA 92131
415 955-2000

(P-22655)
ALPINE CONVALESCENT CENTER
Also Called: Alpine Special Treatment Ctr
2120 Alpine Blvd, Alpine (91901-2113)
PHONE..................................619 659-3120
Fax: 619 445-0444
Michael E Doyle, *Partner*
Victoria Klein, *Administration*
EMP: 90
SQ FT: 15,000
SALES (est): 9MM **Privately Held**
WEB: www.astci.com
SIC: 8093 Rehabilitation center, outpatient treatment

(P-22656)
AMANECER CMNTY COUNSELING SVC
1200 Wilshire Blvd # 510, Los Angeles (90017-1908)
PHONE..................................213 481-7464
Tim Ryder, *Exec Dir*
Frank Chargualaf, *CFO*
Laura Gonzalez, *Executive Asst*
Luis Montenegro, *Accountant*
Dawn Wallace, *Human Res Dir*
EMP: 100
SALES: 8MM **Privately Held**
WEB: www.ccsla.org
SIC: 8093 Mental health clinic, outpatient

(P-22657)
ANKA BEHAVIORAL HEALTH INC (PA)
1850 Gateway Blvd Ste 900, Concord (94520-8418)
PHONE..................................925 825-4700
Chris Withrow, *CEO*
Yolanda Braxton, *President*
Naja W Boyd, *COO*
Janice Washburn, *CFO*
Marty Giffin, *Senior VP*
EMP: 168
SALES: 41.6MM **Privately Held**
SIC: 8093 Specialty outpatient clinics

(P-22658)
ARC - IMPERIAL VALLEY
340 E 1st St, Calexico (92231-2732)
PHONE..................................760 768-1944
Fax: 760 768-1944
Alex King, *Branch Mgr*
EMP: 58
SALES (corp-wide): 10.6MM **Privately Held**
SIC: 8093 4783 2051 5812 Rehabilitation center, outpatient treatment; packing goods for shipping; bakery; wholesale or wholesale/retail combined; delicatessen (eating places); caterers
PA: Arc - Imperial Valley
298 E Ross Ave
El Centro CA 92243
760 352-0180

(P-22659)
ARC OF VENTURA COUNTY INC
Also Called: ARC Community Enrichment
210 Canada St, Ojai (93023-2523)
PHONE..................................805 650-8611
Fax: 805 646-5879
Lisa Emery, *Manager*
Penny Balicki, *Manager*
EMP: 60
SALES (corp-wide): 11.8MM **Privately Held**
SIC: 8093 8322 Rehabilitation center, outpatient treatment; social services for the handicapped
PA: The Arc Of Ventura County Inc
5103 Walker St
Ventura CA 93003
805 650-8611

(P-22660)
ARC OF VENTURA COUNTY INC
4277 Transport St Ste D, Ventura (93003-5657)
PHONE..................................805 644-0880
Alisa Mahrer, *Manager*
EMP: 192
SALES (corp-wide): 11.8MM **Privately Held**
SIC: 8093 8361 8322 8331 Rehabilitation center, outpatient treatment; residential care; individual & family services; sheltered workshop
PA: The Arc Of Ventura County Inc
5103 Walker St
Ventura CA 93003
805 650-8611

(P-22661)
ASIAN COMMUNITY MENTAL HLTH BD
Also Called: Asian Cmnty Mental Hlth Svcs
310 8th St Ste 201, Oakland (94607-6527)
PHONE..................................510 625-1650
Lawrence Fong, *President*
John Fong, *Treasurer*
Betty Hong, *Vice Pres*
Lily L Stearns, *Exec Dir*
Sharon Sue, *Admin Sec*
EMP: 95
SALES: 6.5MM **Privately Held**
WEB: www.acmhs.org
SIC: 8093 Mental health clinic, outpatient

(P-22662)
AXIS COMMUNITY HEALTH INC
4361 Railroad Ave, Pleasanton (94566-6611)
PHONE..................................925 462-1755
Sue Compton, *CEO*
Christina McFadden, *COO*
Joe Flarity, *CFO*
Kanwar Singh, *CFO*
Sonia Cross, *Officer*
EMP: 99 EST: 1972
SALES: 12.2MM **Privately Held**
WEB: www.axishealth.org
SIC: 8093 Specialty outpatient clinics

(P-22663)
BAART BEHAVIORAL HLTH SVCS INC
433 Turk St, San Francisco (94102-3329)
PHONE..................................415 928-7800
Teresa Fleming, *Branch Mgr*
EMP: 56
SALES (corp-wide): 3.1MM **Privately Held**
SIC: 8093 Substance abuse clinics (outpatient)
PA: Baart Behavioral Health Services, Inc.
1145 Market St Fl 10
San Francisco CA 94103
415 552-7914

(P-22664)
BAART BEHAVIORAL HLTH SVCS INC (PA)
Also Called: Bbhs
1145 Market St Fl 10, San Francisco (94103-1566)
PHONE..................................415 552-7914
Fax: 415 863-7434
Jason Kletter, *President*
Evan Kletter, *CFO*
Stephen Rosen, *Vice Pres*
Israel Amrani, *Opers Spvr*
Don Cooper, *Psychologist*
EMP: 54
SALES (est): 3.1MM **Privately Held**
SIC: 8093 Substance abuse clinics (outpatient)

(P-22665)
BAART COMMUNITY HEALTHCARE
433 Turk St, San Francisco (94102-3329)
PHONE..................................415 928-7800
Teresa Fleming, *Branch Mgr*
EMP: 56
SALES (corp-wide): 3.9MM **Privately Held**
SIC: 8093 Drug clinic, outpatient
PA: Baart Community Healthcare
1145 Market St Fl 10
San Francisco CA 94103
415 863-3883

(P-22666)
BAKER PLACES INC
101 Gough St, San Francisco (94102-5903)
PHONE..................................415 503-3137
EMP: 116
SALES (corp-wide): 13.2MM **Privately Held**
SIC: 8093 Substance abuse clinics (outpatient)
PA: Baker Places, Inc.
1000 Brannan St Ste 401
San Francisco CA 94103
415 864-4655

(P-22667)
BASQUEZ TIBURCIO HEALTH CENTER
33255 9th St, Union City (94587-2137)
PHONE..................................510 471-5907
Jose J Garcia, *CEO*
Jesse Robles, *Bd of Directors*
Carlos Londo, *Program Dir*
EMP: 160
SALES (est): 8.5MM **Privately Held**
SIC: 8093 Specialty outpatient clinics

(P-22668)
BODY CONQUEROR INC
Also Called: Body Balance
4570 Van Nuys Blvd B, Sherman Oaks (91403-2913)
PHONE..................................310 651-0387
Gregory Gunn, *President*
EMP: 120
SALES (est): 5.5MM **Privately Held**
SIC: 8093 Weight loss clinic, with medical staff

(P-22669)
BRIDGES AT SN PDRO PNNSLA HSPT
1300 W 7th St Fl 4, San Pedro (90732-3505)
PHONE..................................310 514-5359
Fax: 310 514-5432
Vivian Harvey, *Director*
EMP: 55
SALES (est): 894K **Privately Held**
SIC: 8093 Mental health clinic, outpatient

(P-22670)
CAMINAR
Also Called: Jobs Plus
376 Rio Lindo Ave, Chico (95926-1914)
PHONE..................................530 343-4472
Colleen Egan, *Branch Mgr*
Charles Huggins, *CEO*
Taylor Dial, *CFO*
EMP: 65
SALES (corp-wide): 17.4MM **Privately Held**
SIC: 8093 Mental health clinic, outpatient
PA: Caminar
2600 S El Camino Real # 200
San Mateo CA 94403
650 372-4080

(P-22671)
CAMP RECOVERY CENTERS LLP
3192 Glen Canyon Rd, Santa Cruz (95066-4916)
P.O. Box 66569, Scotts Valley (95067-6569)
PHONE..................................831 438-1868
Page Bottom, *Exec Dir*
Steve Hanusa, *Director*
EMP: 100

8093 - Specialty Outpatient Facilities, NEC County (P-22672)   PRODUCTS & SERVICES SECTION

SALES (est): 6.7MM Privately Held
WEB: www.camprecovery.com
SIC: 8093 Rehabilitation center, outpatient treatment

(P-22672)
CARLSBAD SURGERY CENTER LLC
6121 Paseo Del Norte # 100, Carlsbad (92011-1161)
PHONE..............................760 448-2488
David W Douglas, *Mng Member*
Tom Jung, *Administration*
Heather Goland, *Opers Mgr*
David Douglas, *Director*
EMP: 50
SALES (est): 5.4MM Privately Held
SIC: 8093 Specialty outpatient clinics

(P-22673)
CARNAHAN OCCUPATIONAL THERAPY
116 E College Ave Ste G, Lompoc (93436-5331)
PHONE..............................805 737-1604
Juanita Carnahan, *Owner*
EMP: 50
SALES (est): 785.2K Privately Held
WEB: www.carnahantherapy.com
SIC: 8093 Rehabilitation center, outpatient treatment

(P-22674)
CASA COLIN COMPREHENSIVE
255 E Bonita Ave, Pomona (91767-1923)
PHONE..............................909 596-7733
Felice Loverso, *CEO*
Ross Lessons, *MIS Dir*
Ross Lesins, *Telecomm Mgr*
EMP: 150
SQ FT: 35,000
SALES: 2.6MM Privately Held
SIC: 8093 Rehabilitation center, outpatient treatment

(P-22675)
CASTLE FAMILY HEALTH CTRS INC (PA)
3605 Hospital Rd Ste H, Atwater (95301-5173)
PHONE..............................209 381-2000
Edward H Lujano, *CEO*
Bill Able, *CFO*
Sabrina Cooksey, *Executive*
Donita Dame, *Executive*
David Thompson, *Info Tech Dir*
EMP: 99
SALES: 16.3MM Privately Held
SIC: 8093 Specialty outpatient clinics

(P-22676)
CENTER FOR AUTSM RSRCH EVLTN
Also Called: Cares
10065 Old Grove Rd # 200, San Diego (92131-1664)
PHONE..............................858 444-8823
Fax: 858 444-8827
Olanderia Brown, *Manager*
EMP: 140 EST: 2007
SALES (est): 3.8MM
SALES (corp-wide): 75.4MM Privately Held
SIC: 8093 Specialty outpatient clinics
HQ: Novata Behavioral Health
10065 Old Grove Rd
San Diego CA

(P-22677)
CENTRAL VALLEY CLINIC INC
Also Called: Sants Clair Alcohol Meth Prog
2425 Enborg Ln, San Jose (95128-2648)
PHONE..............................408 885-5400
Robert Garner, *Director*
EMP: 50 EST: 1985
SALES (est): 1.2MM Privately Held
SIC: 8093 Drug clinic, outpatient

(P-22678)
CENTRAL VLY REGIONAL CTR INC
5441 W Cypress Ave, Visalia (93277-8341)
PHONE..............................559 738-2200
Fax: 559 738-2265
Lorraine Bortes, *General Mgr*
EMP: 120
SALES (corp-wide): 222.1MM Privately Held
SIC: 8093 8399 Specialty outpatient clinics; social service information exchange
PA: Central Valley Regional Center, Inc.
4615 N Marty Ave
Fresno CA
559 276-4300

(P-22679)
CENTRE FOR NEURO SKILLS (PA)
5215 Ashe Rd, Bakersfield (93313-2069)
PHONE..............................661 872-3408
Fax: 661 872-5150
Mark J Ashley, *CEO*
Susan Ashley, *Vice Pres*
Steve Katomski, *Regional Mgr*
Susan Swanfeldt, *Admin Asst*
Susan Trihey, *Human Res Dir*
EMP: 153
SQ FT: 14,000
SALES (est): 39.1MM Privately Held
SIC: 8093 Rehabilitation center, outpatient treatment

(P-22680)
CENTRO DE SALUD DE LA (PA)
Also Called: San Ysidro Health Center
4004 Beyer Blvd, San Ysidro (92173-2007)
PHONE..............................619 428-4463
Fax: 619 428-2625
Kevin Mattson, *CEO*
M Gutierrez, *President*
Matthew Weeks, *Vice Pres*
Ed Martinez, *Principal*
Patricia Mejia, *Executive Asst*
EMP: 80
SQ FT: 2,000
SALES: 87.1MM Privately Held
SIC: 8093 8011 Specialty outpatient clinics; offices & clinics of medical doctors

(P-22681)
CHILD AND FAMILY GUIDANCE CTR
Also Called: Valley Child Guidance Clinic
310 E Plmdle Blvd G, Palmdale (93550)
PHONE..............................661 265-8627
Fax: 661 265-7936
Joelle Hunnewell, *Director*
Rocio Cabrales, *Director*
Nancy Cline, *Manager*
EMP: 72
SALES (corp-wide): 25.8MM Privately Held
WEB: www.childguidance.org
SIC: 8093 Mental health clinic, outpatient
PA: Child And Family Guidance Center
9650 Zelzah Ave
Northridge CA 91325
818 739-5140

(P-22682)
CHILD AND FAMILY GUIDANCE CTR (PA)
Also Called: Northpoint Day Treatment Sch
9650 Zelzah Ave, Northridge (91325-2003)
PHONE..............................818 739-5140
Fax: 818 739-5393
Roy Marshall, *Exec Dir*
Russell Jones, *Ch of Bd*
Robert Garcia, *President*
Ronald Call, *Treasurer*
Stephen J Howard PHD, *Vice Pres*
EMP: 200
SQ FT: 35,000
SALES: 25.8MM Privately Held
WEB: www.childguidance.org
SIC: 8093 Mental health clinic, outpatient

(P-22683)
CHILD AND FAMILY GUIDANCE CTR
Also Called: Family Stress Center
8550 Balboa Blvd Ste 150, Northridge (91325-3579)
PHONE..............................818 830-0200
Fax: 818 830-0206
Jessica Card, *Director*
Alpa A Patel, *Director*
EMP: 50

SALES (corp-wide): 25.8MM Privately Held
WEB: www.childguidance.org
SIC: 8093 8322 Mental health clinic, outpatient; general counseling services
PA: Child And Family Guidance Center
9650 Zelzah Ave
Northridge CA 91325
818 739-5140

(P-22684)
CHILDRENS HOSPITAL LOS ANGELES
3440 Torrance Blvd # 100, Torrance (90503-5805)
PHONE..............................310 303-3890
EMP: 184
SALES (corp-wide): 891.3MM Privately Held
SIC: 8093 Alcohol clinic, outpatient
PA: The Childrens Hospital Los Angeles
4650 W Sunset Blvd
Los Angeles CA 90027
323 660-2450

(P-22685)
CHOICE MEDICAL GROUP INC
2322 Butano Dr Ste 205, Sacramento (95825-0657)
PHONE..............................916 483-2885
Fax: 916 483-4036
Lisa Vaughn, *General Mgr*
Laurie Luiza, *Treasurer*
EMP: 70
SALES (est): 1.4MM Privately Held
SIC: 8093 Abortion clinic

(P-22686)
CLEAR VIEW TREATMENT CENTER
1131 N Dearborn St, Redlands (92374-4947)
PHONE..............................909 794-6688
Robert Decker, *CEO*
Daniel Tapanes, *Exec Dir*
EMP: 55 EST: 1998
SALES: 2.2MM Privately Held
SIC: 8093 Mental health clinic, outpatient

(P-22687)
CLINIC INC (PA)
3834 S Western Ave, Los Angeles (90062-1104)
PHONE..............................323 730-1920
Fax: 323 731-8805
Jamesina E Henderson, *Exec Dir*
Tatyana Klochko, *Vice Pres*
Sylvia D Ivie, *Exec Dir*
Shahriar Gharavi, *Technology*
Rise K Phillips, *Technology*
EMP: 63
SQ FT: 26,000
SALES: 11.1MM Privately Held
WEB: www.theclinicinc.org
SIC: 8093 Specialty outpatient clinics

(P-22688)
CLINICAS DEL CAMINO REAL INC
Also Called: Dental Office
650 Meta St, Oxnard (93030-7182)
PHONE..............................805 487-5351
Fax: 805 487-2599
Patricia Andrade, *General Mgr*
Aimee R Brecht-Doscher MD, *Med Doctor*
Shilpa Jindani MD, *Med Doctor*
Prantee P Sak, *Manager*
EMP: 73
SALES (corp-wide): 67.9MM Privately Held
SIC: 8093 8011 Specialty outpatient clinics; ambulatory surgical center
PA: Clinicas Del Camino Real, Inc.
200 S Wells Rd Ste 200
Ventura CA 93004
805 647-6322

(P-22689)
COMMUNITY ACTION MARIN
Also Called: Community Action Marine
1108 Tamalpais Ave, San Rafael (94901-3247)
PHONE..............................415 459-6330
Michael Payne, *President*
EMP: 203

SALES (corp-wide): 14.8MM Privately Held
SIC: 8093 Mental health clinic, outpatient
PA: Community Action Marin
29 Mary St
San Rafael CA 94901
415 485-1489

(P-22690)
COMMUNITY MEDICAL CENTERS INC (PA)
7210 Murray Dr, Stockton (95210-3339)
P.O. Box 779 (95201-0779)
PHONE..............................209 373-2800
Fax: 209 373-2878
Kathleen Marshall, *CEO*
Art Feagles, *CFO*
Maria Flores, *Executive*
Pamela Koltun, *Admin Asst*
Karen Rowley, *Project Mgr*
EMP: 90 EST: 1978
SQ FT: 14,000
SALES: 36.8MM Privately Held
SIC: 8093 8011 Specialty outpatient clinics; offices & clinics of medical doctors

(P-22691)
CONSOLIDATED TRIBAL HEALTH PRJ
6991 N State St, Redwood Valley (95470-9629)
P.O. Box 387, Calpella (95418-0387)
PHONE..............................707 485-5115
Fax: 707 485-5199
Michael Knight, *Chairman*
George Provencher, *Treasurer*
Debra Ramirez, *Principal*
Donna Schuler, *Admin Sec*
Thomas Madden, *CIO*
EMP: 65
SALES: 11.1MM Privately Held
WEB: www.cthp.org
SIC: 8093 Specialty outpatient clinics

(P-22692)
CORRECTONS RHBLTATION CAL DEPT
Also Called: Cdcr - California Men's Colony
Hwy 1 N, San Luis Obispo (93409-0001)
P.O. Box 8101 (93403-8101)
PHONE..............................805 547-7900
Fax: 805 543-3856
John Marshall, *Warden*
Michael Day, *Administration*
William Duncan, *Administration*
Galen Kirn, *Administration*
Ron York, *Engineer*
EMP: 2000 Privately Held
SIC: 8093 9223 Specialty outpatient clinics;
HQ: California Department Of Corrections & Rehabilitation
1515 S St
Sacramento CA 95811
916 341-7066

(P-22693)
COUNTY OF BUTTE
Also Called: Butte County Mental Hlth Svcs
107 Parmac Rd Ste 4, Chico (95926-2298)
PHONE..............................530 891-2850
Bradford Luz PHD, *Director*
Jack Joiner, *Exec Dir*
Michelle Berry, *Human Res Mgr*
Anne Robin, *Director*
EMP: 400 Privately Held
WEB: www.bcihsspa.org
SIC: 8093 9111 Substance abuse clinics (outpatient); county supervisors' & executives' offices
PA: County Of Butte
25 County Center Dr # 218
Oroville CA 95965
530 538-7701

(P-22694)
COUNTY OF CONTRA COSTA
Also Called: Department of Health Services
1420 Willow Pass Rd # 140, Concord (94520-5823)
PHONE..............................925 646-5480
John Allen, *Director*
EMP: 50 Privately Held
WEB: www.cccounty.us

PRODUCTS & SERVICES SECTION
8093 - Specialty Outpatient Facilities, NEC County (P-22715)

SIC: **8093** 9431 Mental health clinic, outpatient; administration of public health programs;
PA: County Of Contra Costa
625 Court St Ste 100
Martinez CA 94553
925 957-5280

(P-22695)
COUNTY OF FRESNO
Also Called: Department Behavioral Health
4417 E Inyo St Bldg 333, Fresno (93702-2977)
PHONE..................................559 600-4600
Sean Patterson, *Business Mgr*
EMP: 99
SQ FT: 4,000
SALES (est): 317.4K **Privately Held**
SIC: **8093** Mental health clinic, outpatient

(P-22696)
COUNTY OF GLENN
Also Called: Department of Mental Health
242 N Villa Ave, Willows (95988-2641)
PHONE..................................530 934-6582
Fax: 530 934-6592
Scott Gruentl, *Director*
Parker Hunt, *Accounting Mgr*
Robert L Zadra, *Med Doctor*
Maureen Hernandez, *Director*
Cecilia Hutsell, *Manager*
EMP: 75 **Privately Held**
WEB: www.countyofglen.net
SIC: **8093** 9111 Mental health clinic, outpatient; county supervisors' & executives' offices
PA: County Of Glenn
516 W Sycamore St Fl 2
Willows CA 95988
530 934-6410

(P-22697)
COUNTY OF HUMBOLDT
Also Called: Humboldt County Mental Health
720 Wood St, Eureka (95501-4413)
PHONE..................................707 476-4054
Fax: 707 445-7287
Cindy Moore, *Manager*
Gale Beer, *Admin Sec*
Jennifer Albrecht, *Nurse Practr*
John Kafel, *Supervisor*
EMP: 120 **Privately Held**
SIC: **8093** 9111 8063 Mental health clinic, outpatient; county supervisors' & executives' offices; psychiatric hospitals
PA: County Of Humboldt
825 5th St
Eureka CA 95501
707 268-2543

(P-22698)
COUNTY OF IMPERIAL
Also Called: Imperial County Mental Health
202 N 8th St, El Centro (92243-2302)
PHONE..................................760 482-4120
Fax: 760 337-9040
Rudy Lopez, *Director*
Patti Berber, *Executive*
Anna Welzein, *Human Res Dir*
Marcy Sesma, *Superintendent*
EMP: 100 **Privately Held**
WEB: www.imperialcounty.net
SIC: **8093** 9111 Mental health clinic, outpatient; county supervisors' & executives' offices
PA: County Of Imperial
940 W Main St Ste 208
El Centro CA 92243
760 482-4556

(P-22699)
COUNTY OF LOS ANGELES
Also Called: Health Services, Dept of
7601 Imperial Hwy, Downey (90242-3456)
PHONE..................................562 401-7088
Fax: 562 401-6570
Valeria Orange, *Director*
EMP: 1400 **Privately Held**
WEB: www.co.la.ca.us
SIC: **8093** 9431 Rehabilitation center, outpatient treatment;
PA: County Of Los Angeles
500 W Temple St Ste 375
Los Angeles CA 90012
213 974-1101

(P-22700)
COUNTY OF LOS ANGELES
Also Called: Health Dept
5850 S Main St, Los Angeles (90003-1215)
PHONE..................................323 846-4122
Fax: 323 234-6518
Floretta Taylor, *Admin Director*
Lakshmi D Makam, *Med Doctor*
Harry Lamotte, *Director*
Stephen Puentes, *Director*
EMP: 120 **Privately Held**
WEB: www.co.la.ca.us
SIC: **8093** 9431 8011 Specialty outpatient clinics; administration of public health programs; ; offices & clinics of medical doctors
PA: County Of Los Angeles
500 W Temple St Ste 375
Los Angeles CA 90012
213 974-1101

(P-22701)
COUNTY OF LOS ANGELES
Also Called: Health Services, Dept of
5205 Melrose Ave, Los Angeles (90038-3144)
PHONE..................................323 769-7800
Fax: 323 962-9484
Rosa Pinon, *Branch Mgr*
Joon Yoon, *Research*
EMP: 100 **Privately Held**
WEB: www.co.la.ca.us
SIC: **8093** 9431 Family planning & birth control clinics; administration of public health programs.
PA: County Of Los Angeles
500 W Temple St Ste 375
Los Angeles CA 90012
213 974-1101

(P-22702)
COUNTY OF LOS ANGELES
Also Called: Mental Health Dept
17707 Studebaker Rd, Artesia (90703-2640)
PHONE..................................562 402-0688
Fax: 562 809-0185
Latisha Guvman, *Manager*
EMP: 50 **Privately Held**
WEB: www.co.la.ca.us
SIC: **8093** Specialty outpatient clinics; administration of public health programs;
PA: County Of Los Angeles
500 W Temple St Ste 375
Los Angeles CA 90012
213 974-1101

(P-22703)
COUNTY OF LOS ANGELES
Also Called: Antelope Valley Health Center
335 E Avenue K6 Ste B, Lancaster (93535-4645)
PHONE..................................661 524-2005
Mary Nolan, *Manager*
EMP: 59 **Privately Held**
SIC: **8093** Family planning clinic
PA: County Of Los Angeles
500 W Temple St Ste 375
Los Angeles CA 90012
213 974-1101

(P-22704)
COUNTY OF MARIN
Also Called: Community Mental Health Clinic
250 Bon Air Rd, Greenbrae (94904-1702)
P.O. Box 2728, San Rafael (94912-2728)
PHONE..................................415 448-1500
Fax: 415 461-7334
Bruce Gurganus, *Director*
Tara Clark, *Volunteer Dir*
Chris Kughn, *Program Mgr*
Jean Maki, *Office Mgr*
Jack Liebster, *Planning Mgr*
EMP: 100 **Privately Held**
SIC: **8093** 9111 Mental health clinic, outpatient; county supervisors' & executives' offices
PA: County Of Marin
1600 Los Gamos Dr Ste 200
San Rafael CA 94903
415 473-6358

(P-22705)
COUNTY OF MENDOCINO
Also Called: County of Medocina Dept of Mnt
860a N Bush St, Ukiah (95482-3919)
PHONE..................................707 463-4396
Anna Mahoney, *Manager*
EMP: 200 **Privately Held**
WEB: www.mcdss.org
SIC: **8093** 9111 Mental health clinic, outpatient; county supervisors' & executives' offices
PA: County Of Mendocino
501 Low Gap Rd Rm 1010
Ukiah CA 95482
707 463-4441

(P-22706)
COUNTY OF NAPA
Also Called: Health Department
2261 Elm St, NAPA (94559-3721)
PHONE..................................707 253-4461
Bruce Heid, *Manager*
Richard J Forde, *Psychiatry*
EMP: 260 **Privately Held**
WEB: www.billkeller.com
SIC: **8093** 9111 Specialty outpatient clinics; county supervisors' & executives' offices
PA: County Of Napa
1195 Third St Ste 310
Napa CA 94559
707 253-4421

(P-22707)
COUNTY OF PLACER
Also Called: Health & Human Services
11583 C Ave, Auburn (95603-2703)
PHONE..................................530 889-7215
Fax: 530 889-7276
Robert Long, *Systems Mgr*
Jo McCormack, *Branch Mgr*
Terri M Friedman, *Physician Asst*
Mark Rideout, *Architect*
Mitchel Ruffman, *Manager*
EMP: 75
SQ FT: 1,100 **Privately Held**
WEB: www.ssvems.com
SIC: **8093** 9431 Specialty outpatient clinics; administration of public health programs;
PA: County Of Placer
2968 Richardson Dr
Auburn CA 95603
530 889-4200

(P-22708)
COUNTY OF SAN JOAQUIN
Also Called: Mental Health Services
1212 N California St, Stockton (95202-1552)
PHONE..................................209 468-8750
Fax: 209 468-3741
Bruce Hopperstead, *Principal*
John Hamilton, *Programmer Anys*
Tosh Saruwatari, *Manager*
EMP: 300 **Privately Held**
WEB: www.sjclawlib.org
SIC: **8093** 9111 8361 Mental health clinic, outpatient; county supervisors' & executives' offices; residential care
PA: County Of San Joaquin
44 N San Joaquin St # 640
Stockton CA 95202
209 468-3203

(P-22709)
COUNTY OF SAN LUIS OBISPO
Also Called: Community Mental Health Svcs
2178 Johnson Ave, San Luis Obispo (93401-4535)
PHONE..................................805 781-4700
Tom Omalley, *Principal*
Jim Scarletta, *Prgrmr*
Karen Baylor, *Manager*
EMP: 250 **Privately Held**
SIC: **8093** Mental health clinic, outpatient
PA: County Of San Luis Obispo
Government Center Rm. 300
San Luis Obispo CA 93408
805 781-5040

(P-22710)
COUNTY OF SAN MATEO
Also Called: Health System
150 W 20th Ave, San Mateo (94403-1341)
PHONE..................................650 372-8540
Sonia Celmira Lucana, *Principal*
EMP: 100 **Privately Held**
WEB: www.ci.sanmateo.ca.us
SIC: **8093** 9431 Mental health clinic, outpatient;
PA: County Of San Mateo
400 County Ctr
Redwood City CA 94063
650 363-4123

(P-22711)
COUNTY OF SANTA BARBARA ALCOHO
Also Called: Admhs
300 N San Antonio Rd, Santa Barbara (93110-1316)
PHONE..................................805 681-4093
Fax: 805 681-5413
Al Rodriguez, *Principal*
Dana Fahey, *Info Tech Mgr*
Nancy Gottlied, *Manager*
EMP: 90
SALES (est): 2.2MM **Privately Held**
SIC: **8093** Alcohol clinic, outpatient

(P-22712)
COUNTY OF SISKIYOU
Also Called: Behavioral Health Services
1107 Ream Ave, Mount Shasta (96067-9768)
PHONE..................................530 918-7200
Fax: 530 918-7216
Hap Stemm, *Manager*
Arden Carr, *Hlthcr Dir*
EMP: 60 **Privately Held**
WEB: www.siskiyoucounty.org
SIC: **8093** 9111 Specialty outpatient clinics; county supervisors' & executives' offices
PA: County Of Siskiyou
311 4th St Rm 108
Yreka CA 96097
530 841-4100

(P-22713)
COUNTY OF STANISLAUS
Also Called: Stanisluas County Mental Hlth
800 Scenic Dr Bldg B, Modesto (95350-6131)
PHONE..................................209 525-7423
Fax: 209 525-6291
Dennise Han, *Director*
Dennis Louis, *Manager*
Larry Poster, *Manager*
EMP: 200 **Privately Held**
WEB: www.co.stanislaus.ca.us
SIC: **8093** Specialty outpatient clinics
PA: County Of Stanislaus
1010 10th St Ste 5100
Modesto CA 95354
209 525-6398

(P-22714)
COUNTY OF SUTTER
Also Called: Sutter Yuba Mental Health Svcs
1965 Live Oak Blvd, Yuba City (95991-8850)
P.O. Box 1520 (95992-1520)
PHONE..................................530 822-7250
Fax: 530 822-3261
Joann Hoss, *Director*
Tom Sherry, *Comms Dir*
Stephen Marshall, *General Mgr*
Patrick Larrigan, *Info Tech Mgr*
Rolando Carramanzana, *Accountant*
EMP: 200 **Privately Held**
WEB: www.co.yuba.ca.us
SIC: **8093** 9431 Mental health clinic, outpatient; mental health agency administration, government;
PA: County Of Sutter
1160 Civic Center Blvd A
Yuba City CA 95993
530 822-7100

(P-22715)
COUNTY OF YOLO
Also Called: Dept of Mental Health
292 W Beamer St, Woodland (95695-2511)
PHONE..................................530 666-8630
Fax: 530 666-8294
Kim Suderman, *Director*
Leslie Lindbo, *Director*
EMP: 80 **Privately Held**
WEB: www.yctd.org

8093 - Specialty Outpatient Facilities, NEC County (P-22716)

PRODUCDUCTS & SERVICES SECTION

SIC: 8093 9111 Mental health clinic, outpatient; county supervisors' & executives' offices
PA: County Of Yolo
625 Court St Ste 102
Woodland CA 95695
530 666-8114

(P-22716)
CRASH INC SHORT TERM I
4161 Marlborough Ave, San Diego (92105-1412)
PHONE..............................619 282-7274
Fax: 619 282-7496
Sue Dolby, *Exec Dir*
EMP: 50
SALES (est): 1MM Privately Held
SIC: 8093 Substance abuse clinics (outpatient)

(P-22717)
CRC HEALTH CORPORATE
Also Called: Recovery Solutions Santa Ana
2101 E 1st St, Santa Ana (92705-4007)
PHONE..............................714 542-3581
Tfu Bach Tran, *Manager*
Mariaelena Rebolledo, *Executive*
EMP: 60 Publicly Held
SIC: 8093 Drug clinic, outpatient
HQ: Crc Health Corporate
20400 Stevens
Cupertino CA 95014
408 367-0044

(P-22718)
CRC HEALTH CORPORATE (DH)
Also Called: Willamette Valley Trtmnt Ctr
20400 Stevens, Cupertino (95014)
PHONE..............................408 367-0044
R Andrew Eckert, *CEO*
Kevin Hogge, *CFO*
Sandra J Tullis, *Treasurer*
Gary Fisher, *Chief Mktg Ofcr*
Pamela B Burke, *Vice Pres*
EMP: 60
SALES (est): 56.9MM Publicly Held
SIC: 8093 Substance abuse clinics (outpatient)
HQ: Crc Health Corporation
20400 Stevens Creek Blvd
Cupertino CA 95014
877 272-8668

(P-22719)
DEL AMO DIAGNOSTIC CENTER
Also Called: Little Mary Amblatory Care Ctr
3531 Fashion Way, Torrance (90503-4807)
PHONE..............................310 316-2424
Fax: 310 316-6038
Steve Magennis, *Director*
Garth A Green MD, *Med Doctor*
Janella Carresco, *Manager*
EMP: 50
SQ FT: 25,000
SALES (est): 2.8MM Privately Held
SIC: 8093 8011 Specialty outpatient clinics; clinic, operated by physicians

(P-22720)
DIGNITY HEALTH
Also Called: Marian West
505 Plaza Dr, Santa Maria (93454-6907)
PHONE..............................805 739-3100
Kathleen Sullivan, *Manager*
Carlton Haley, *Manager*
EMP: 1400
SALES (corp-wide): 7.1B Privately Held
WEB: www.chw.edu
SIC: 8093 Rehabilitation center, outpatient treatment
PA: Dignity Health
185 Berry St Ste 300
San Francisco CA 94107
415 438-5500

(P-22721)
DRUG & ALCOHOL SERVICES OF
2180 Johnson Ave Ste A, San Luis Obispo (93401-4542)
PHONE..............................805 781-4275
Fax: 805 781-1227
Paul Hyman, *Director*
Jeff Hamm, *Director*
EMP: 80

SALES (est): 1.6MM Privately Held
SIC: 8093 Rehabilitation center, outpatient treatment

(P-22722)
DRUG ABUSE ALTERNATIVES CENTER
Also Called: Redwood Empire Addctons Prgram
2403 Prof Dr Ste 103, Santa Rosa (95403)
PHONE..............................707 571-2233
Fax: 707 526-0527
Sushana Taylor, *President*
EMP: 50
SALES (corp-wide): 6MM Privately Held
WEB: www.daacinfo.org
SIC: 8093 Drug clinic, outpatient
PA: Drug Abuse Alternatives Center
2403 Prof Dr Ste 102
Santa Rosa CA 95403
707 544-3295

(P-22723)
DUAL DIAGNOSIS TRTMNT CTR INC (PA)
Also Called: Sovereign Health of California
1211 Puerta Del Sol # 270, San Clemente (92673-6342)
PHONE..............................949 276-5553
Fax: 949 276-5183
Tonmoy Sharma, *CEO*
Rishi Barkataki, *President*
Vicki Hartman, *Hlthcr Dir*
Barry L Aaronson, *Director*
Michael Frye, *Manager*
EMP: 168
SALES (est): 74.5MM Privately Held
SIC: 8093 Mental health clinic, outpatient

(P-22724)
DUAL DIAGNOSIS TRTMNT CTR INC
6167 Bristol Pkwy, Culver City (90230-6610)
PHONE..............................424 207-2220
Marissa Maldonado, *Branch Mgr*
EMP: 240
SALES (corp-wide): 74.5MM Privately Held
SIC: 8093 Mental health clinic, outpatient
PA: Dual Diagnosis Treatment Center, Inc.
1211 Puerta Del Sol # 270
San Clemente CA 92673
949 276-5553

(P-22725)
EAST LOS ANGELES MENTAL HLTH
1436 Goodrich Blvd, Commerce (90022-5111)
PHONE..............................323 725-1337
Fax: 323 278-5344
Alfredo Lavios, *President*
EMP: 60
SALES (est): 3MM Privately Held
SIC: 8093 Mental health clinic, outpatient

(P-22726)
EAST VALLEY CMNTY HLTH CTR INC (PA)
420 S Glendora Ave, West Covina (91790-3001)
PHONE..............................626 919-3402
Fax: 626 919-6972
Alicia Mardini, *CEO*
Sophia Shavira, *Ch of Bd*
Alicia Thomas, *CEO*
Cheryl Petersen, *CFO*
Clara Potes-Fellow, *Comms Dir*
EMP: 65
SQ FT: 24,000
SALES (est): 17.4MM Privately Held
SIC: 8093 Specialty outpatient clinics; family planning clinic; mental health clinic, outpatient

(P-22727)
ELEMENTS BEHAVIORAL HEALTH INC (HQ)
5000 E Spring St Ste 650, Long Beach (90815-5205)
PHONE..............................562 741-6470
David Sack, *CEO*
James Adams, *CFO*
Rob Mahan, *CFO*

Vera Appleyard, *Vice Pres*
Keith Arnold, *Vice Pres*
EMP: 96 EST: 2010
SALES (est): 16.6MM
SALES (corp-wide): 300K Privately Held
SIC: 8093 8049 Substance abuse clinics (outpatient); nutrition specialist
PA: The Sexual Recovery Institute
1964 Westwood Blvd # 400
Los Angeles CA 90025
310 360-0130

(P-22728)
ENKY HEALTH
1436 Goodrich Blvd, Commerce (90022-5111)
PHONE..............................323 725-1337
Alfredo Lavios, *Principal*
EMP: 50
SALES (est): 2.5MM Privately Held
SIC: 8093 Mental health clinic, outpatient

(P-22729)
EXODUS RECOVERY INC (PA)
9808 Venice Blvd Ste 700, Culver City (90232-6824)
PHONE..............................310 945-3350
Luana Murphy, *President*
Leeann Skorohod, *President*
Lezlie Murch, *Senior VP*
Grace Lee, *Vice Pres*
Kathy Shoemaker, *Vice Pres*
EMP: 93
SALES (est): 4MM Privately Held
SIC: 8093 Mental health clinic, outpatient

(P-22730)
FAMILY HLTH CTRS SAN DIEGO INC (PA)
823 Gateway Center Way, San Diego (92102-4541)
PHONE..............................619 515-2303
Fran Butler-Cohen, *President*
Ibrahim Sawaya, *CTO*
Barbara Greer, *QA Dir*
Flavia Gastelum, *Comp Spec*
Brian L Tisher, *Project Mgr*
EMP: 65 EST: 1972
SQ FT: 32,000
SALES: 125.5MM Privately Held
SIC: 8093 Specialty outpatient clinics

(P-22731)
GARDNER FAMILY CARE CORP
160 E Virginia St Ste 280, San Jose (95112-5817)
PHONE..............................408 935-3906
Reymundo Estinoza, *CEO*
Frania Coria, *COO*
Ignacio Perez, *CFO*
EMP: 190
SALES (est): 20.1MM Privately Held
SIC: 8093 Mental health clinic, outpatient

(P-22732)
GARDNER FAMILY HLTH NETWRK INC (PA)
160 E Virginia St Ste 100, San Jose (95112-5865)
PHONE..............................408 918-2682
Fax: 408 278-7799
Reymundo C Espinoza, *CEO*
Efrain Coria, *Vice Pres*
Amalia Chavez, *Manager*
EMP: 50 EST: 1968
SALES (est): 26.3MM Privately Held
SIC: 8093 Specialty outpatient clinics

(P-22733)
GENESIS HEALTHCARE PARTNERS PC
Also Called: Integrated Medical Specialists
2466 1st Ave Ste B, San Diego (92101-1408)
P.O. Box 33865 (92163-3865)
PHONE..............................619 230-0400
Edward S Cohen, *CEO*
EMP: 113
SALES (corp-wide): 16.8MM Privately Held
SIC: 8093 Specialty outpatient clinics
PA: Genesis Healthcare Partners, P.C.
9333 Genesee Ave Ste 300
San Diego CA 92121
858 888-7700

(P-22734)
GHC OF LOMPOC LLC
Also Called: Lompoc Skilled Nrsng & Rehab
1428 W North Ave, Lompoc (93436-3961)
PHONE..............................805 735-4010
Fax: 805 736-4010
Thomas Olds,
Lisa Baker, *Office Mgr*
Lois Mastrocola,
EMP: 250
SALES (est): 9MM
SALES (corp-wide): 68.1MM Privately Held
SIC: 8093 Rehabilitation center, outpatient treatment
PA: Life Generations Healthcare Llc
20371 Irvine Ave Ste 210
Newport Beach CA 92660
714 241-5600

(P-22735)
GOLDEN VALLEY HEALTH CENTERS (PA)
737 W Childs Ave, Merced (95341-6805)
PHONE..............................209 383-1848
Fax: 209 383-0136
Tony Weber, *CEO*
Mark A Millan, *COO*
Lue Thao, *CFO*
Crystal Andersen, *Executive*
Michael Buda, *Executive*
EMP: 250
SQ FT: 23,000
SALES: 99.7MM Privately Held
SIC: 8093 Specialty outpatient clinics

(P-22736)
GOLDEN VALLEY HEALTH CENTERS
Also Called: Women's Health Center
797 W Childs Ave, Merced (95341-6805)
PHONE..............................209 383-5871
Fax: 209 383-1402
Pierre Scales, *Branch Mgr*
EMP: 100
SALES (corp-wide): 99.7MM Privately Held
SIC: 8093 8011 Specialty outpatient clinics; clinic, operated by physicians
PA: Golden Valley Health Centers
737 W Childs Ave
Merced CA 95341
209 383-1848

(P-22737)
GOODWILL INDS S CENTL CAL
1832 E Tulare Ave, Tulare (93274-3216)
PHONE..............................559 366-1030
EMP: 54
SALES (corp-wide): 16MM Privately Held
SIC: 8093 Rehabilitation center, outpatient treatment
PA: Goodwill Industries Of South Central California
4901 Stine Rd
Bakersfield CA 93313
661 837-0595

(P-22738)
GRASSHOPPER HOUSE LLC
Also Called: Passages
6428 Meadows Ct, Malibu (90265-4492)
PHONE..............................310 589-2880
Fax: 310 589-2858
Chris Prentiss,
Pax Prentiss,
EMP: 105
SQ FT: 16,000
SALES (est): 7.9MM Privately Held
WEB: www.passagesmalibu.com
SIC: 8093 Substance abuse clinics (outpatient)

(P-22739)
GREATER SACRAMENTO SUR
Also Called: Greater Sacramento Surgery Ctr
2288 Auburn Blvd Ste 201, Sacramento (95821-1620)
PHONE..............................916 929-7229
Fax: 916 929-2590
Marvin Kamras, *Partner*
Nancy Nissen, *Officer*
Sheryl Kaley, *Admin Asst*
Susan Brunone, *Administration*

PRODUCTS & SERVICES SECTION
8093 - Specialty Outpatient Facilities, NEC County (P-22763)

Denise Dempsey, *Accounting Mgr*
EMP: 60
SQ FT: 15,000
SALES (est): 8.4MM **Privately Held**
SIC: 8093 8011 Specialty outpatient clinics; ambulatory surgical center

(P-22740)
GREATER VALLEY MEDICAL GROUP (PA)
11600 Indian Hills Rd # 300, Mission Hills (91345-1225)
PHONE................................818 838-4500
Fax: 818 838-7509
Don Rebhun MD, *President*
Howard Sawyer MD, *Corp Secy*
Mohyi Soleiman MD, *Vice Pres*
Lubna Alayed, *Accounting Mgr*
Melayne Yokum, *Obstetrician*
EMP: 75
SALES (est): 8.4MM **Privately Held**
SIC: 8093 Specialty outpatient clinics

(P-22741)
HEALTHRIGHT 360
1340 Tully Rd Ste 304, San Jose (95122-3055)
PHONE................................408 934-1110
Vitka Eisen, *Principal*
EMP: 181
SALES (corp-wide): 77.9MM **Privately Held**
SIC: 8093 Detoxification center, outpatient
PA: Healthright 360
1735 Mission St Ste 2050
San Francisco CA 94103
415 762-3700

(P-22742)
HEALTHRIGHT 360
2515 Camino Del Rio S, San Diego (92108-3792)
PHONE................................213 216-0484
EMP: 181
SALES (corp-wide): 77.9MM **Privately Held**
SIC: 8093 Detoxification center, outpatient
PA: Healthright 360
1735 Mission St Ste 2050
San Francisco CA 94103
415 762-3700

(P-22743)
HEALTHSOUTH CORPORATION
14851 Yorba St, Tustin (92780-2925)
PHONE................................714 832-9200
Fax: 714 508-4550
Cathline Smith, *Branch Mgr*
Lee Fallon, *Mktg Dir*
Marcella Bejinez, *Facilities Dir*
Glenn Barrera, *Food Svc Dir*
EMP: 200
SALES (corp-wide): 3.1B **Publicly Held**
WEB: www.healthsouth.com
SIC: 8093 Rehabilitation center, outpatient treatment
PA: Healthsouth Corporation
3660 Grandview Pkwy # 200
Birmingham AL 35243
205 967-7116

(P-22744)
HEALTHSOUTH CORPORATION
75 Scripps Dr, Sacramento (95825-6320)
PHONE................................916 929-9431
Fax: 916 929-0132
Deanne Conner, *Administration*
EMP: 60
SALES (corp-wide): 3.1B **Publicly Held**
WEB: www.healthsouth.com
SIC: 8093 Rehabilitation center, outpatient treatment
PA: Healthsouth Corporation
3660 Grandview Pkwy # 200
Birmingham AL 35243
205 967-7116

(P-22745)
HELP GROUP WEST (PA)
13130 Burbank Blvd, Sherman Oaks (91401-6000)
PHONE................................818 781-0360
Barbara Firestone, *President*
Michael Love, *CFO*
Susan Berman PH, *Exec VP*
Brian Silverman, *Teacher*
EMP: 200
SQ FT: 100,000
SALES: 15.5MM **Privately Held**
SIC: 8093 Speech defect clinic

(P-22746)
HOLLYWOOD MENTAL HEALTH CENTER
1224 Vine St, Los Angeles (90038-1612)
PHONE................................323 769-6100
Fax: 323 467-0297
Barbara Engleman, *President*
EMP: 65
SALES (est): 3.3MM **Privately Held**
SIC: 8093 Mental health clinic, outpatient

(P-22747)
HOPE OF VALLEY MISSION
19379 Soledad Canyon Rd, Santa Clarita (91351-2630)
PHONE................................661 673-5951
EMP: 50
SALES (est): 350.4K **Privately Held**
SIC: 8093 Rehabilitation center, outpatient treatment

(P-22748)
I P S SERVICES INC
627 E Foothill Blvd, San Dimas (91773-1208)
PHONE................................909 305-0250
Robert Hernandez, *CEO*
David Nickel, *Shareholder*
Elizabeth Cruz, *Treasurer*
Travis Holland, *Admin Sec*
EMP: 60
SALES (est): 4.3MM **Privately Held**
SIC: 8093 Mental health clinic, outpatient

(P-22749)
IMPERIAL COUNTY BEHAVIORAL HLT
2695 S 4th St, El Centro (92243-6012)
PHONE................................760 482-2149
Michael Horn, *Director*
Mary Esquer, *Program Mgr*
Franciso Ortiz, *Senior Mgr*
EMP: 50
SALES (est): 911.9K **Privately Held**
SIC: 8093 Substance abuse clinics (outpatient); mental health clinic, outpatient

(P-22750)
JUDIANNE CHEW LCSW
Also Called: Uc Davies Caare Center
3671 Business Dr Ste 100, Sacramento (95820-2165)
PHONE................................916 734-6629
Anthony Urquiza, *Director*
EMP: 60
SALES (est): 695.2K **Privately Held**
SIC: 8093 Mental health clinic, outpatient

(P-22751)
KAISER FOUNDATION HOSPITALS
Also Called: Kaiser Permanente
710 S Broadway, Walnut Creek (94596-5294)
PHONE................................925 295-4145
Fax: 925 295-4927
Vikki Antonelli, *Manager*
Maisie S Mok, *Osteopathy*
Kelvin K Shiu, *Osteopathy*
Richard W King, *Physician Asst*
Deborah Tresch, *Director*
EMP: 793
SALES (corp-wide): 27.8B **Privately Held**
WEB: www.kaiserpermanente.org
SIC: 8093 Mental health clinic, outpatient
HQ: Kaiser Foundation Hospitals Inc
1 Kaiser Plz
Oakland CA 94612
510 271-6611

(P-22752)
KAISER FOUNDATION HOSPITALS
Also Called: Oak Street Physical Therapy
2040 Pacific Coast Hwy, Lomita (90717-2660)
PHONE................................424 251-7000
EMP: 192

SALES (corp-wide): 27.8B **Privately Held**
SIC: 8093 Rehabilitation center, outpatient treatment
HQ: Kaiser Foundation Hospitals Inc
1 Kaiser Plz
Oakland CA 94612
510 271-6611

(P-22753)
KAISER FOUNDATION HOSPITALS
Also Called: Positive Choice Wellness Ctr
7035 Convoy Ct, San Diego (92111-1016)
PHONE................................858 573-0090
Caryl Polk, *Training Dir*
Albert Ray, *Family Practiti*
EMP: 192
SALES (corp-wide): 27.8B **Privately Held**
SIC: 8093 Weight loss clinic, with medical staff
HQ: Kaiser Foundation Hospitals Inc
1 Kaiser Plz
Oakland CA 94612
510 271-6611

(P-22754)
KAISER FOUNDATION HOSPITALS
Also Called: Santa Clarita Executive Plaza
27201 Tourney Rd, Santa Clarita (91355-1854)
PHONE................................661 222-2000
EMP: 192
SALES (corp-wide): 27.8B **Privately Held**
SIC: 8093 Specialty outpatient clinics
HQ: Kaiser Foundation Hospitals Inc
1 Kaiser Plz
Oakland CA 94612
510 271-6611

(P-22755)
KAISER FOUNDATION HOSPITALS
Also Called: Health Educatn Psychiatry Offs
5105 W Goldleaf Cir, Los Angeles (90056-1269)
PHONE................................323 298-3300
Natasha Elliott, *Branch Mgr*
Felicia K Wong, *Med Doctor*
EMP: 200
SALES (corp-wide): 27.8B **Privately Held**
SIC: 8093 Specialty outpatient clinics
HQ: Kaiser Foundation Hospitals Inc
1 Kaiser Plz
Oakland CA 94612
510 271-6611

(P-22756)
KAISER FOUNDATION HOSPITALS
Also Called: Kaiser Permanente
3400 Delta Fair Blvd, Antioch (94509-4004)
PHONE................................925 779-5000
Fax: 925 779-5357
Dan Sonnier, *Manager*
John Rosa, *Administration*
Eric Tepper, *Research*
Kara O King, *Obstetrician*
Mary A Klemm, *Obstetrician*
EMP: 200
SQ FT: 47,307
SALES (corp-wide): 27.8B **Privately Held**
WEB: www.kaiserpermanente.org
SIC: 8093 8011 8062 Specialty outpatient clinics; general & family practice, physician/surgeon; general medical & surgical hospitals
HQ: Kaiser Foundation Hospitals Inc
1 Kaiser Plz
Oakland CA 94612
510 271-6611

(P-22757)
KAISER FOUNDATION HOSPITALS
Also Called: Kaiser Permanente
23621 Main St, Carson (90745-5743)
PHONE................................310 513-6707
Fax: 310 816-5312
Lora Griffin, *Branch Mgr*
Ann La Fever, *Executive*
Donna Menecola, *Branch Mgr*
Ann Lafever, *Administration*
Michael Meyers, *Psychiatry*
EMP: 60

SALES (corp-wide): 27.8B **Privately Held**
WEB: www.kaiserpermanente.org
SIC: 8093 8062 Specialty outpatient clinics; general medical & surgical hospitals
HQ: Kaiser Foundation Hospitals Inc
1 Kaiser Plz
Oakland CA 94612
510 271-6611

(P-22758)
KEITH T KUSUNIS MD
Also Called: Family Health Center
91767 N Orange Grv Ave Ste 101, Pomona (91767)
PHONE................................909 469-9494
Keith T Kusunas, *Principal*
Keith T Kusunis, *President*
EMP: 65
SALES (est): 697.4K **Privately Held**
SIC: 8093 Family planning clinic

(P-22759)
KIMA W MEDICAL CENTER
1200 Airport Rd, Hoopa (95546)
P.O. Box 1288 (95546-1288)
PHONE................................530 625-4114
Emmit Chase, *CEO*
Dennis Jones, *COO*
EMP: 80
SQ FT: 11,000
SALES: 6.5MM **Privately Held**
SIC: 8093 8399 Specialty outpatient clinics; health systems agency

(P-22760)
KINDRED HOSPITAL SAN DIEGO
1940 El Cajon Blvd, San Diego (92104-1096)
PHONE................................619 543-4500
William Mitchell, *Principal*
Thomas Sullivan,
Geoff Blomeley, *CFO*
Judy Vincent, *Chief Mktg Ofcr*
Javid Javdani, *Pharmacy Dir*
EMP: 52
SALES (est): 5.6MM **Privately Held**
SIC: 8093 Rehabilitation center, outpatient treatment

(P-22761)
KINDRED NURSING CENTERS W LLC
Also Called: Kindred Transitional Care
1359 Pine St, San Francisco (94109-4807)
PHONE................................415 673-8405
Joseph L Landenwich,
Yuri Angert, *Records Dir*
Rosa Bray, *Office Mgr*
Ruslan Nechay, *Admin Sec*
David Stacy, *Opers Staff*
EMP: 200
SALES (est): 184K
SALES (corp-wide): 7B **Publicly Held**
SIC: 8093 Rehabilitation center, outpatient treatment
HQ: Kindred Healthcare Operating, Inc.
680 S 4th St
Louisville KY 40202
502 596-7300

(P-22762)
KINGS VIEW
Also Called: Mental Hlth Svcs For Kngs Cnty
289 E 8th St, Hanford (93230-3935)
PHONE................................559 582-9307
Brenda Johnson Hill, *Principal*
Maria Abina, *Executive*
Yolanda Estrada, *Administration*
Brenda Johnsonhill, *Manager*
Lucy Mendoza, *Manager*
EMP: 100
SALES (corp-wide): 23.3MM **Privately Held**
SIC: 8093 Mental health clinic, outpatient
PA: Kings View
7170 N Fincl Dr Ste 110
Fresno CA 93720
559 256-0100

(P-22763)
KINGSVIEW CORP
Also Called: Tuolomne Cnty Bhvrl Hlth
2 S Green St, Sonora (95370-4618)
PHONE................................209 533-6245
Jack Tanebaum, *Exec Dir*
Sheila Mortier, *Administration*

8093 - Specialty Outpatient Facilities, NEC County (P-22764)

PRODUDUCTS & SERVICES SECTION

Anne Robin, *Director*
EMP: 63
SALES (est): 862.3K **Privately Held**
SIC: 8093 Mental health clinic, outpatient

(P-22764)
LA CLINICA DE LA RAZA INC
Also Called: Mental Health Department
1601 Fruitvale Ave, Oakland (94601-2418)
PHONE.................510 535-6200
Melissa Jenkins, *Planning*
Debbie Giron, *Purchasing*
Stephanie Vielman, *Nutritionist*
Jon Froyd, *Med Doctor*
Monica M Pearson, *Fmly & Gen Dent*
EMP: 127
SALES (corp-wide): 74.4MM **Privately Held**
SIC: 8093 Mental health clinic, outpatient
PA: La Clinica De La Raza, Inc.
1450 Fruitvale Ave Fl 3
Oakland CA 94601
510 535-4000

(P-22765)
LATINO COMMISSION
301 Grand Ave Ste 301, South San Francisco (94080-3641)
PHONE.................650 244-0304
Fax: 650 244-1447
Debra Camarillo, *Principal*
Doren Martin, *Principal*
Marivel Leiva, *Manager*
EMP: 50
SALES (est): 1.7MM **Privately Held**
SIC: 8093 8361 Mental health clinic, outpatient; home for the mentally retarded

(P-22766)
LEARNING SERVICES CORPORATION
Also Called: Learning Services Northern Cal
10855 De Bruin Way, Gilroy (95020-9315)
PHONE.................408 848-4379
Fax: 408 848-6509
Kayree Fhreeve, *Director*
Kayree Shreeve, *Exec Dir*
EMP: 50
SALES (corp-wide): 19.9MM **Privately Held**
WEB: www.learningservices.com
SIC: 8093 Rehabilitation center, outpatient treatment
PA: Learning Services Corporation
131 Langley Dr Ste B
Lawrenceville GA 30046
470 235-4700

(P-22767)
LEARNING SERVICES CORPORATION
2335 Bear Valley Pkwy, Escondido (92027-3854)
PHONE.................760 746-3223
Fax: 760 432-6834
Sharon Brown, *Manager*
EMP: 50
SALES (corp-wide): 19.9MM **Privately Held**
WEB: www.learningservices.com
SIC: 8093 Rehabilitation center, outpatient treatment
PA: Learning Services Corporation
131 Langley Dr Ste B
Lawrenceville GA 30046
470 235-4700

(P-22768)
LINCOLN CHILD CENTER INC (PA)
1266 14th St, Oakland (94607-2205)
PHONE.................510 273-4700
Fax: 510 530-8083
Christine Stoner-Mertz, *CEO*
Nancy L Oakley, *COO*
Enrico Hernandez, *CFO*
Allison Becwar, *Principal*
Eric Handy, *Program Mgr*
EMP: 80
SQ FT: 40,000
SALES: 17.3MM **Privately Held**
WEB: www.lincolncc.org
SIC: 8093 8361 Mental health clinic, outpatient; orphanage

(P-22769)
LINDAMOOD-BELL LRNG PROCESSES (PA)
406 Higuera St Ste 120, San Luis Obispo (93401-6131)
PHONE.................805 541-3836
Fax: 805 541-8756
Nanci Bell, *President*
Patricia Lindamood, *Treasurer*
Erika Blackwell, *Associate Dir*
Melissa Garner, *Associate Dir*
Erin Bell, *Comms Dir*
EMP: 200
SQ FT: 8,000
SALES (est): 45.3MM **Privately Held**
WEB: www.lblp.com
SIC: 8093 Specialty outpatient clinics

(P-22770)
LOS ANGELES UNIFIED SCHOOL DST
Also Called: Mental Health Dept
6651 Balboa Blvd, Van Nuys (91406-5529)
PHONE.................818 997-2640
Gil Palacio, *Director*
Ernesto Garcia, *Analyst*
EMP: 300
SALES (corp-wide): 4.4B **Privately Held**
WEB: www.lausd.k12.ca.us
SIC: 8093 Mental health clinic, outpatient
PA: Los Angeles Unified School District
333 S Beaudry Ave Ste 209
Los Angeles CA 90017
213 241-1000

(P-22771)
MADERA CNTY BHVIORAL HLTH SVCS
209 E 7th St, Madera (93638-3780)
P.O. Box 1288 (93639-1288)
PHONE.................559 673-3508
Fax: 559 661-2818
Dennis Koch, *President*
Janet Mesiah, *Manager*
EMP: 126 **EST:** 2010
SQ FT: 25,000
SALES: 17MM **Privately Held**
SIC: 8093 Specialty outpatient clinics

(P-22772)
MCALISTER INSTITUTE FOR TREAT
3923 Waring Rd, Oceanside (92056-4457)
PHONE.................760 726-4451
EMP: 69
SALES (corp-wide): 10.7MM **Privately Held**
SIC: 8093 Drug clinic, outpatient
PA: Mcalister Institute For Treatment & Education, Inc.
1400 N Johnson Ave # 101
El Cajon CA 92020
619 442-0277

(P-22773)
MENDOCINO COAST CLINICS INC
205 South St, Fort Bragg (95437-5540)
PHONE.................707 964-1251
Fax: 707 961-2722
Paula Cohen, *Exec Dir*
Jeff Warner, *Chairman*
Richard Moon, *Treasurer*
Claudia Boudreau, *Admin Sec*
Beth Pine, *Admin Asst*
▲ **EMP:** 93
SQ FT: 5,000
SALES: 9.7MM **Privately Held**
WEB: www.mendocinocoastclinics.org
SIC: 8093 Family planning & birth control clinics

(P-22774)
MENTAL HEALTH SYSTEMS INC (PA)
Also Called: Joshua Tree Center For Change
9465 Farnham St, San Diego (92123-1308)
PHONE.................858 573-2600
Fax: 858 573-2602
Kimberly Bond, *CEO*
Wendy Broughton, *COO*
Kathryn Wage, *Bd of Directors*
Michael Hawkey, *Senior VP*
Delrena Swaggerty, *Vice Pres*
EMP: 70
SQ FT: 18,000
SALES (est): 75.4MM **Privately Held**
WEB: www.mhsinc.org
SIC: 8093 Specialty outpatient clinics

(P-22775)
MHM SERVICES INC
230 Station Way, Arroyo Grande (93420-3358)
PHONE.................805 904-6678
EMP: 234
SALES (corp-wide): 91.6MM **Privately Held**
SIC: 8093 Mental health clinic, outpatient
PA: Mhm Services, Inc.
1593 Spring Hill Rd # 600
Vienna VA 22182
703 749-4600

(P-22776)
MHM SERVICES INC
350 Brannan St, San Francisco (94107-1879)
PHONE.................415 416-6992
EMP: 175
SALES (corp-wide): 91.6MM **Privately Held**
SIC: 8093 Mental health clinic, outpatient
PA: Mhm Services, Inc.
1593 Spring Hill Rd # 600
Vienna VA 22182
703 749-4600

(P-22777)
MHM SERVICES INC
2380 Professional Dr, Santa Rosa (95403-3016)
PHONE.................707 623-9080
EMP: 175
SALES (corp-wide): 91.6MM **Privately Held**
SIC: 8093 Mental health clinic, outpatient
PA: Mhm Services, Inc.
1593 Spring Hill Rd # 600
Vienna VA 22182
703 749-4600

(P-22778)
NATIONAL THERAPEUTIC SVCS INC (PA)
Also Called: Joshua House
4343 Von Karman Ave # 100, Newport Beach (92660-2099)
PHONE.................949 650-4334
Fax: 714 432-1928
Michael Neatherton, *President*
Paul Alexander, *COO*
Ray Pacini, *CFO*
David Tessers, *CFO*
Sally Pahl, *Controller*
EMP: 69
SALES (est): 12.5MM **Privately Held**
SIC: 8093 Alcohol clinic, outpatient

(P-22779)
NATIONL MEDCL ASSN COMP HEALTH
3177 Ocean View Blvd, San Diego (92113-1432)
PHONE.................619 231-9300
Shirleen Freeman, *Director*
Myrna Inocencio, *Lab Dir*
Rose Gallegos, *Exec Dir*
Anne D Kaufhold, *Family Practiti*
Yalitza Ortiz, *Manager*
EMP: 60
SALES (corp-wide): 3.7MM **Privately Held**
WEB: www.nmasandiego.org
SIC: 8093 Specialty outpatient clinics
PA: National Medical Association Comprehensive Health Center
1275 30th St
San Diego CA 92154
619 231-3200

(P-22780)
NEVADA COUNTY BEHAVIORAL HLTH
500 Crown Point Cir # 120, Grass Valley (95945-9561)
PHONE.................530 265-1450
Fax: 530 265-9820

Michael Heggarty, *Director*
Cathy Brown, *Supervisor*
EMP: 50
SQ FT: 22,168
SALES (est): 2.5MM **Privately Held**
SIC: 8093 Mental health clinic, outpatient

(P-22781)
NORTH COAST SURGERY CENTER
3903 Waring Rd, Oceanside (92056-4405)
PHONE.................760 940-0997
Fax: 760 940-0407
Dr Bruce Hochman, *Partner*
Gary Philips, *CFO*
Arlene Shatzer, *Office Mgr*
Donna Danley, *Administration*
EMP: 79
SQ FT: 11,000
SALES (est): 6.2MM **Privately Held**
SIC: 8093 Specialty outpatient clinics

(P-22782)
NORTHWEST CORRECTNL MED GRP
Also Called: Correctionl Med Grp Co, Inc.
2511 Garden Rd Ste A160, Monterey (93940-5377)
PHONE.................831 649-8994
Kip Hallman, *CEO*
Elaine Hustedt, *COO*
Don Myll, *CFO*
Ray Herr, *Chief Mktg Ofcr*
Alexis Wing, *Administration*
EMP: 50
SQ FT: 4,075
SALES (est): 1.8MM
SALES (corp-wide): 9.7MM **Privately Held**
SIC: 8093 Specialty outpatient clinics
PA: Correctional Medical Group Companies, Inc.
1 Market St
San Francisco CA 94105
831 649-8994

(P-22783)
OPEN DOOR COMMUNITY HLTH CTRS
Also Called: Humboldt Open Door Clinic
770 10th St, Arcata (95521-6210)
PHONE.................707 826-8610
Hermann Spetzler, *Branch Mgr*
Stacy Watkins, *Administration*
EMP: 72
SALES (corp-wide): 22.4MM **Privately Held**
WEB: www.opendoorhealth.com
SIC: 8093 8011 Smoking clinic; offices & clinics of medical doctors
PA: Open Door Community Health Centers
670 9th St Ste 203cfo
Arcata CA 95521
707 826-8642

(P-22784)
OPEN DOOR COMMUNITY HLTH CTRS (PA)
670 9th St Ste 203cfo, Arcata (95521-6248)
PHONE.................707 826-8642
Sydney Fisher Larsen, *CEO*
Stacy Watkins, *Assistant*
EMP: 70
SQ FT: 18,000
SALES (est): 22.4MM **Privately Held**
WEB: www.opendoorhealth.com
SIC: 8093 Smoking clinic

(P-22785)
OPTIONS FAMILY OF SERVICES
5755 Valentina Ave, Atascadero (93422-3532)
PHONE.................805 462-8544
EMP: 50
SQ FT: 576
SALES (corp-wide): 5.6MM **Privately Held**
SIC: 8093
PA: Options Family Of Services, Inc
800 Quintana Rd Ste 2c
Morro Bay CA 93442
805 772-6066

PRODUCTS & SERVICES SECTION

8093 - Specialty Outpatient Facilities, NEC County (P-22809)

(P-22786)
ORANGE COUNTY ASSOCIATION (PA)
Also Called: Mental Health Assn Orange Cnty
822 W Town And Country Rd, Orange (92868-4712)
PHONE..................714 547-7559
Fax: 714 543-4431
Margaret Riley, *President*
Jeff Thrash, *Exec Dir*
EMP: 56
SQ FT: 3,000
SALES: 5.4MM **Privately Held**
WEB: www.mhaoc.org
SIC: 8093 Mental health clinic, outpatient

(P-22787)
PACIFIC CLINICS
11741 Telegraph Rd Ste G, Santa Fe Springs (90670-3687)
PHONE..................562 942-8256
Fax: 562 942-9789
EMP: 93
SALES (corp-wide): 97.4MM **Privately Held**
SIC: 8093 Specialty outpatient clinics
PA: Pacific Clinics
   800 S Santa Anita Ave
   Arcadia CA 91006
   626 254-5000

(P-22788)
PACIFIC CLINICS
11721 Telegraph Rd Ste A, Santa Fe Springs (90670-6835)
PHONE..................562 949-8455
Fax: 562 949-4807
Sharon Corey, *Director*
EMP: 65
SALES (corp-wide): 96.7MM **Privately Held**
SIC: 8093 Mental health clinic, outpatient
PA: Pacific Clinics
   800 S Santa Anita Ave
   Arcadia CA 91006
   626 254-5000

(P-22789)
PACIFIC FRNSIC PSYCHLOGY ASSOC
9261 Folsom Blvd Ste 300, Sacramento (95826-2559)
PHONE..................925 253-3111
Tom Tobin, *CEO*
EMP: 75
SALES (est): 604.7K **Privately Held**
SIC: 8093 Mental health clinic, outpatient

(P-22790)
PARAGON HEALTH & REHAB CT
1090 E Dinuba Ave, Reedley (93654-3577)
PHONE..................559 638-3578
EMP: 50 **EST:** 2005
SALES (est): 2.3MM **Privately Held**
SIC: 8093

(P-22791)
PARENTHOOD OF PLANNED (PA)
1075 Camino Del Rio S # 100, San Diego (92108-3539)
PHONE..................619 881-4500
Darrah Johnson, *CEO*
Bob Coles, *CFO*
Len Dodson, *CFO*
Rebecca Karpinski, *Vice Pres*
Cita Walsh, *Vice Pres*
EMP: 100
SQ FT: 24,000
SALES: 29.6MM **Privately Held**
WEB: www.planned.org
SIC: 8093 Family planning clinic

(P-22792)
PARENTHOOD OF PLANNED (PA)
518 Garden St, Santa Barbara (93101-1606)
PHONE..................805 963-2445
Cheryl Rollings, *Exec Dir*
Emma Mayer, *CFO*
Ruben Grigorians, *Vice Pres*
Pam Sutherland, *Vice Pres*
Carla Berkowitz, *Technology*
EMP: 54
SQ FT: 9,000
SALES: 15.2MM **Privately Held**
SIC: 8093 Birth control clinic

(P-22793)
PARENTHOOD OF PLANNED
12900 Frederick St Ste C, Moreno Valley (92553-5266)
PHONE..................951 222-3101
EMP: 88
SALES (corp-wide): 29.6MM **Privately Held**
SIC: 8093 Specialty outpatient clinics
PA: Planned Parenthood Of San Diego And Riverside Counties
   1075 Camino Del Rio S # 100
   San Diego CA 92108
   619 881-4500

(P-22794)
PASADENA CHILD DEV ASSOC INC
620 N Lake Ave, Pasadena (91101-1220)
PHONE..................626 793-7350
Fax: 626 793-7341
Diane Cullinane MD, *Principal*
Brandy Bell, *Comms Mgr*
Cambria Piersol, *Office Mgr*
Barb Bobier,
Diane A Cullinne, *Manager*
EMP: 80
SALES: 3.9MM **Privately Held**
SIC: 8093 Specialty outpatient clinics

(P-22795)
PATHWAY SOCIETY
102 S 11th St, San Jose (95112-2132)
PHONE..................408 244-1834
Joanne Buckley, *Exec Dir*
EMP: 50
SALES (corp-wide): 5.9MM **Privately Held**
WEB: www.pathwayinc.com
SIC: 8093 Drug clinic, outpatient; rehabilitation center, outpatient treatment
PA: Pathway Society
   1659 Scott Blvd Ste 30
   Santa Clara CA 95050
   408 244-1834

(P-22796)
PEDIATRIC & FAMILY MEDICAL CTR
Also Called: Eisner Pediatric Fmly Med Ctr
1530 S Olive St, Los Angeles (90015-3023)
PHONE..................213 342-3325
Carl Coan, *CEO*
Kevin Rossi, *Ch of Bd*
Herb Schultz, *President*
Carl Edward Coan, *CEO*
Chona De Leon, *COO*
EMP: 160
SQ FT: 21,000
SALES: 25.4MM **Privately Held**
SIC: 8093 Specialty outpatient clinics

(P-22797)
PEDIATRIC PHYSICAL REHAB CLNC
Also Called: Physical/Occupational Therapy
9300 Valley Childrens Pl, Madera (93636-8761)
PHONE..................559 353-6130
Fax: 559 353-8030
Carol Kurushima, *Manager*
Shirlene Fowler, *Manager*
EMP: 50 **EST:** 1999
SALES (est): 2.3MM **Privately Held**
SIC: 8093 Rehabilitation center, outpatient treatment

(P-22798)
PEDIATRIC THERAPY NETWORK
1815 W 213th St Ste 100, Torrance (90501-2852)
PHONE..................310 328-0275
Fax: 310 328-7058
Zoe Mailloux, *Exec Dir*
Tom Gosney, *CFO*
Heather McGuire, *Comms Mgr*
Gina Coleman, *Exec Dir*
Terri Nishimura, *Exec Dir*
EMP: 100
SQ FT: 20,000
SALES: 6.8MM **Privately Held**
WEB: www.pediatrictherapy.com
SIC: 8093 Rehabilitation center, outpatient treatment

(P-22799)
PLACER COUNTY- ADULT SYS CARE
11533 C Ave, Auburn (95603-2703)
PHONE..................530 886-2974
Maureen F Bauman, *Director*
EMP: 99
SALES (est): 1.1MM **Privately Held**
SIC: 8093 Specialty outpatient clinics

(P-22800)
PLANNED PARENTHOOD
1873 Commercenter W, San Bernardino (92408-3303)
PHONE..................909 890-5511
EMP: 99
SQ FT: 6,540
SALES (corp-wide): 38.6MM **Privately Held**
SIC: 8093 Abortion clinic
PA: Planned Parenthood/Orange And San Bernardino Counties, Inc.
   700 S Tustin St Fl 1
   Orange CA 92866
   714 633-6373

(P-22801)
PLANNED PARENTHOOD FEDERATION
601 W 19th St Ste B, Costa Mesa (92627-5060)
PHONE..................949 548-8830
EMP: 73
SALES (corp-wide): 196.8MM **Privately Held**
SIC: 8093 8011 Family planning clinic; clinic, operated by physicians
PA: Planned Parenthood Federation Of America, Inc.
   123 William St Fl 10
   New York NY 10038
   212 541-7800

(P-22802)
PLANNED PARENTHOOD FEDERATION
220 Euclid Ave Ste 40, San Diego (92114-3617)
PHONE..................619 262-3941
EMP: 73
SALES (corp-wide): 196.8MM **Privately Held**
SIC: 8093 Family planning & birth control clinics
PA: Planned Parenthood Federation Of America, Inc.
   123 William St Fl 10
   New York NY 10038
   212 541-7800

(P-22803)
PLANNED PARENTHOOD FEDERATION
555 Capitol Mall Ste 510, Sacramento (95814-4581)
PHONE..................916 446-5247
Fax: 916 441-0632
Ana Sandoval, *Director*
Stephanie Goodner, *Personnel Assit*
EMP: 63
SALES (corp-wide): 196.8MM **Privately Held**
SIC: 8093 Family planning & birth control clinics
PA: Planned Parenthood Federation Of America, Inc.
   123 William St Fl 10
   New York NY 10038
   212 541-7800

(P-22804)
PLANNED PARENTHOOD LOS ANGELES (PA)
400 W 30th St, Los Angeles (90007-3320)
PHONE..................213 284-3200
Sue Dunlap, *President*
Mark Kimura, *CFO*
Adrianne Black, *Vice Pres*
Sid Lorenzana, *Network Enginr*
Francisco Soto, *Technology*
EMP: 80
SQ FT: 30,000
SALES: 59.7MM **Privately Held**
WEB: www.plannedparenthood.org
SIC: 8093 Family planning clinic; birth control clinic

(P-22805)
PLANNED PRNTHOD SHST-DBLO INC (PA)
Also Called: Planned Parenthood Shasta-Paci
2185 Pacheco St, Concord (94520-2309)
PHONE..................925 676-0300
Fax: 925 676-2650
Heather Estes, *President*
Cecile Richards, *President*
Jeff Novick, *Administration*
Gene Boyett, *Info Tech Dir*
Tiffany Trueman, *Info Tech Mgr*
EMP: 50
SQ FT: 5,500
SALES (est): 22.7MM **Privately Held**
SIC: 8093 Family planning & birth control clinics

(P-22806)
PLANNED PRNTHOOD MAR MONTE INC
1691 The Alameda, San Jose (95126-2203)
PHONE..................408 287-7529
Linda Williams, *CEO*
EMP: 150
SALES (corp-wide): 95.9MM **Privately Held**
SIC: 8093 Family planning clinic
PA: Planned Parenthood Mar Monte, Inc.
   1691 The Alameda
   San Jose CA 95126
   408 287-7532

(P-22807)
PLANNED PRNTHOOD MAR MONTE INC (PA)
1691 The Alameda, San Jose (95126-2203)
PHONE..................408 287-7532
Fax: 408 971-6935
Linda T Williams, *President*
Adelina Garcia, *COO*
John Giambruno, *CFO*
Jeanne Ewy, *Vice Pres*
Alison Gaulden, *Vice Pres*
EMP: 79
SQ FT: 41,000
SALES: 95.9MM **Privately Held**
SIC: 8093 Family planning clinic

(P-22808)
PLANNED PRNTHOOD MAR MONTE INC
26302 La Paz Rd 200, Mission Viejo (92691-5313)
PHONE..................949 768-3643
Fax: 949 768-5660
EMP: 50
SALES (corp-wide): 95.9MM **Privately Held**
SIC: 8093 8011 Family planning & birth control clinics; clinic, operated by physicians
PA: Planned Parenthood Mar Monte, Inc.
   1691 The Alameda
   San Jose CA 95126
   408 287-7532

(P-22809)
PLEASANTVIEW INDUSTRIES INC
27921 Urbandale Ave, Saugus (91350-1916)
PHONE..................661 296-6700
Fax: 661 296-4761
Gerald Howard, *Director*
Del Duyer, *President*
EMP: 77
SQ FT: 5,500
SALES: 696.2K **Privately Held**
WEB: www.pleasantviewindustries.org
SIC: 8093 Rehabilitation center, outpatient treatment

8093 - Specialty Outpatient Facilities, NEC County (P-22810)   PRODUDUCTS & SERVICES SECTION

(P-22810)
PRINCIPLES INC (PA)
Also Called: IMPACT DRUG & ALCOHOL TREATMEN
1680 N Fair Oaks Ave, Pasadena (91103-1642)
P.O. Box 93607 (91109-3607)
PHONE..................323 681-2575
Fax: 323 798-6970
James M Stillwell, *CEO*
Ray Quiroz, *Patnt Acct Dir*
Lois Gonzales, *Controller*
Louise Gonzalez, *Controller*
Debbie Stillwell, *Human Resources*
EMP: 51 EST: 1971
SQ FT: 40,000
SALES: 10.7MM Privately Held
WEB: www.mcdpartners.com
SIC: 8093 8049 Rehabilitation center, outpatient treatment

(P-22811)
PROVIDENCE HEALTH & SERVICES
21135 Hawthorne Blvd, Torrance (90503-4615)
PHONE..................310 792-3440
Fax: 310 316-8027
EMP: 69
SALES (corp-wide): 10.1B Privately Held
SIC: 8093 Rehabilitation center, outpatient treatment; acupuncturist
PA: Providence Health & Services
    1801 Lind Ave Sw
    Renton WA 98057
    425 525-3355

(P-22812)
PROVIDENCE SPEECH HEARING CTR
Also Called: Word and Brown Hearing Ctr
1301 W Providence Ave, Orange (92868-3892)
PHONE..................714 639-4990
Fax: 714 744-3841
Linda Smith, *CEO*
Bill Ross, *President*
Jack Shradder, *Treasurer*
Margaret A Inman PH, *Founder*
Jerry O'Connor, *Exec VP*
EMP: 50
SQ FT: 15,000
SALES: 11.3MM Privately Held
WEB: www.pshc.org
SIC: 8093 Speech defect clinic

(P-22813)
PSYCHIATRIC SOLUTIONS INC
Also Called: B H C Alhambra Hospital
4619 Rosemead Blvd, Rosemead (91770-1478)
P.O. Box 369 (91770-0369)
PHONE..................626 286-1191
Fax: 626 286-2489
Margaret Minnick, *Manager*
Ali Allahyar, *Engineer*
Wakelin McNeel, *Persnl Dir*
Carlos Figueroa, *Director*
Ashley Bullock, *Advisor*
EMP: 200
SALES (corp-wide): 9B Publicly Held
WEB: www.intermountainhospital.com
SIC: 8093 8011 8361 8063 Specialty outpatient clinics; psychiatric clinic; residential care; hospital for the mentally ill
HQ: Psychiatric Solutions, Inc.
    6640 Carothers Pkwy # 500
    Franklin TN 37067
    615 312-5700

(P-22814)
RICHMOND AREA MLT-SERVICES INC
720 Sacramento St, San Francisco (94108-2535)
PHONE..................415 392-4453
Kavoos Bassiri, *CEO*
Ken Choi, *CFO*
EMP: 99
SALES (est): 4.9MM Privately Held
SIC: 8093 Mental health clinic, outpatient

(P-22815)
RICHMOND AREA MLT-SERVICES INC
3120 Mission St, San Francisco (94110-4504)
PHONE..................415 800-0699
Kavoos Bassiri, *CEO*
Ken Choi, *CFO*
EMP: 99
SALES (est): 4.9MM Privately Held
SIC: 8093 Mental health clinic, outpatient

(P-22816)
RICHMOND AREA MLT-SERVICES INC
Also Called: Rams
639 14th Ave, San Francisco (94118-3502)
PHONE..................415 800-0699
Kavoos Bassiri, *CEO*
Kenneth Choi, *CFO*
Helena Chan, *Director*
Janny Wong, *Consultant*
EMP: 72
SALES (est): 9.7MM Privately Held
SIC: 8093 Mental health clinic, outpatient

(P-22817)
RICHMOND AREA MLT-SERVICES INC
1375 Mission St, San Francisco (94103-2621)
PHONE..................415 689-5662
Kavoos Bassiri, *CEO*
Kenneth Choi, *CFO*
EMP: 99
SALES (est): 662.5K Privately Held
SIC: 8093 Mental health clinic, outpatient

(P-22818)
RIVERSIDE-SAN BERNARDINO (PA)
11555 1/2 Potrero Rd, Banning (92220-6946)
PHONE..................951 849-4761
Fax: 951 849-3651
Jackie Wisespirit, *President*
Bill Thomsen, *COO*
Brandie Miranda, *Treasurer*
Charles Castelio, *Vice Pres*
Faith Morreo, *Admin Sec*
EMP: 100
SQ FT: 5,200
SALES: 35.9MM Privately Held
SIC: 8093 8011 Specialty outpatient clinics; offices & clinics of medical doctors

(P-22819)
SAFE HARBOR TREATMENT CEN
1966 Maple Ave, Costa Mesa (92627-2660)
PHONE..................949 645-1026
Fax: 714 242-6775
Maggie Grisham, *Director*
Monique Edwards, *Bookkeeper*
Christine Aubele, *Opers Mgr*
Heather Henretig, *Marketing Mgr*
EMP: 50
SALES (est): 1.3MM Privately Held
SIC: 8093 Alcohol clinic, outpatient

(P-22820)
SALVATION ARMY
200 19th St, Bakersfield (93301-4904)
PHONE..................661 325-8626
Fax: 661 631-2815
Michael Gomes, *Branch Mgr*
EMP: 79
SALES (corp-wide): 4.3B Privately Held
WEB: www.salvationarmy.usawest.org
SIC: 8093 Substance abuse clinics (outpatient)
HQ: The Salvation Army
    180 E Ocean Blvd Fl 2
    Long Beach CA 90802
    562 491-8464

(P-22821)
SALVATION ARMY
1247 S Wilson Way, Stockton (95205-7096)
PHONE..................209 466-3871
Fax: 209 466-9347
Dale Brockelman, *Manager*
Judith Rockey, *Persnl Mgr*
EMP: 82
SALES (corp-wide): 4.3B Privately Held
WEB: www.salvationarmy.usawest.org
SIC: 8093 Rehabilitation center, outpatient treatment
HQ: The Salvation Army
    180 E Ocean Blvd Fl 2
    Long Beach CA 90802
    562 491-8464

(P-22822)
SALVATION ARMY
363 S Doolittle Ave, San Bernardino (92408-1623)
PHONE..................909 889-9604
Fax: 909 889-0378
Jack Smith, *Principal*
EMP: 80
SQ FT: 49,540
SALES (corp-wide): 4.3B Privately Held
WEB: www.salvationarmy-usaeast.org
SIC: 8093 8331 4225 Rehabilitation center, outpatient treatment; job training & vocational rehabilitation services; general warehousing & storage
HQ: The Salvation Army
    180 E Ocean Blvd Fl 2
    Long Beach CA 90802
    562 491-8464

(P-22823)
SAN FERNANDO CITY OF INC
10605 Balboa Blvd Ste 100, Granada Hills (91344-6367)
PHONE..................818 832-2400
Fax: 818 832-6197
Wendi Tovey, *Branch Mgr*
EMP: 100 Privately Held
SIC: 8093 9111 Mental health clinic, outpatient; county supervisors' & executives' offices
PA: San Fernando, City Of Inc
    117 N Macneil St
    San Fernando CA 91340
    818 898-1201

(P-22824)
SAN FERNANDO VALLEY COMMUNITY (PA)
16360 Roscoe Blvd Ste 210, Van Nuys (91406-1213)
PHONE..................818 901-4830
Ian Hunter PHD, *President*
Emily Chen, *CFO*
Nancy Gussin, *Program Mgr*
Denise Richman, *Admin Sec*
Connie Early, *Admin Asst*
EMP: 55
SQ FT: 13,000
SALES: 38.8MM Privately Held
SIC: 8093 Substance abuse clinics (outpatient); mental health clinic, outpatient

(P-22825)
SAN FRANCISCO CITY CLINIC
356 7th St, San Francisco (94103-4030)
PHONE..................415 487-5500
Fax: 415 495-6463
Jeffrey Klausner, *Director*
Wendy Wolf, *Deputy Dir*
Susan Philip, *Director*
Gail Bolan, *Manager*
EMP: 80
SQ FT: 2,500
SALES (est): 4MM Privately Held
WEB: www.cityclinic.net
SIC: 8093 Birth control clinic

(P-22826)
SAN JOAQUIN VALLEY REHABILI (HQ)
7173 N Sharon Ave, Fresno (93720-3329)
PHONE..................559 436-3600
Fax: 559 436-3606
Edward C Palacios, *Partner*
Joyce Burnett, *Admin Asst*
Diane Kisling, *Accountant*
Ruby De Leon, *Hlthcr Dir*
Ralph Renteria, *Hlthcr Dir*
EMP: 275
SALES: 35MM
SALES (corp-wide): 329.7MM Privately Held
WEB: www.sjvrehab.com
SIC: 8093 Rehabilitation center, outpatient treatment
PA: Vibra Healthcare, Llc
    4550 Lena Dr
    Mechanicsburg PA 17055
    717 591-5700

(P-22827)
SAN MATEO CNTY PUB HLTH CLINIC
380 90th St, Daly City (94015-1807)
PHONE..................650 301-8600
Cathy Lehmkuhl, *Director*
EMP: 50
SALES (est): 1.6MM Privately Held
WEB: www.sanmateolafco.org
SIC: 8093 Birth control clinic

(P-22828)
SARAH ELIZABETH TREUSDELL
921 W Avenue J Ste C, Lancaster (93534-3443)
PHONE..................661 949-0131
S E Treusdell, *Principal*
Sarah Elizabeth Treusdell, *Principal*
EMP: 50
SALES (est): 124.3K Privately Held
SIC: 8093 Mental health clinic, outpatient

(P-22829)
SCRIPPS HEALTH
Also Called: Scripps Rancho Bernardo
15004 Innovation Dr, San Diego (92128-3491)
PHONE..................858 271-9770
Melody Stewart, *Administration*
Joseph Weiss, *Research*
Donald Stevenson, *Allrgy & Immnlg*
Juliet L Bleha, *Pediatrics*
Erik Hogen, *Pediatrics*
EMP: 259
SALES (corp-wide): 1.7B Privately Held
WEB: www.scripps.org
SIC: 8093 Specialty outpatient clinics
PA: Scripps Health
    4275 Campus Point Ct
    San Diego CA 92121
    858 678-7000

(P-22830)
SCRIPPS HEALTH
Also Called: Scripps Del Mar
3811 Valley Centre Dr, San Diego (92130-3318)
PHONE..................858 794-0160
Fax: 858 764-3264
Melody Stewart, *Manager*
Kenneth Vanwieren, *Pediatrics*
Leland Housman MD, *Med Doctor*
EMP: 250
SALES (corp-wide): 2.3B Privately Held
WEB: www.scripps.org
SIC: 8093 Specialty outpatient clinics
PA: Scripps Health
    4275 Campus Point Ct
    San Diego CA 92121
    858 678-7000

(P-22831)
SHEA FAMILY CARE MISSION HLTH
Also Called: Cloisters Mssion Hills Hosp HM
3680 Reynard Way, San Diego (92103-3847)
PHONE..................619 297-4484
Fax: 619 297-4490
Kennon S Shea, *President*
Sandra Comstock, *Records Dir*
Angel Peoples, *Administration*
Daniel Bressler, *Director*
Cindy Martinez, *Director*
EMP: 92
SQ FT: 16,920
SALES (est): 7.2MM Privately Held
SIC: 8093 8051 Rehabilitation center, outpatient treatment; skilled nursing care facilities

2017 Directory of California Wholesalers and Service Companies

▲ = Import ▼ = Export
◆ = Import/Export

PRODUCTS & SERVICES SECTION
8093 - Specialty Outpatient Facilities, NEC County (P-22853)

(P-22832)
SKIN HEALTH EXPERTS MEDIC
Also Called: Kate Summerville
144 S Beverly Dr Ste 500, Beverly Hills (90212-3023)
PHONE.................................310 623-6869
Michelle Taylor, *CEO*
Laura Shaff, *CFO*
EMP: 70
SALES (est): 869.9K **Privately Held**
SIC: 8093 Specialty outpatient clinics

(P-22833)
SMILE HOUSING CORPORATION
800 Quintana Rd Ste 2c, Morro Bay (93442-2300)
P.O. Box 877 (93443-0877)
PHONE.................................805 772-6066
Debbie Bertrando, *CEO*
Jennifer Gaalswyk, *CFO*
EMP: 99 **EST:** 2008
SALES: 77.2K **Privately Held**
SIC: 8093 Specialty outpatient clinics

(P-22834)
SOCIAL VOCATIONAL SERVICES INC
8550 Balboa Blvd Ste 218, Northridge (91325-5805)
PHONE.................................818 831-1321
Fax: 818 831-1322
Leticia Campbell, *Regional Mgr*
Cassaundra Flores, *Director*
Henry Tharpe, *Manager*
EMP: 56
SALES (corp-wide): 80.6MM **Privately Held**
SIC: 8093 Rehabilitation center, outpatient treatment
PA: Social Vocational Services, Inc.
3555 Torrance Blvd
Torrance CA 90503
310 944-3303

(P-22835)
SOUTH BAYLO UNIVERSITY
Also Called: South Baylo Acupuncture Clinic
2727 W 6th St, Los Angeles (90057-3111)
PHONE.................................213 387-2414
Fax: 213 480-1332
David J Park, *President*
Hong Feng, *Dean*
EMP: 136
SALES (corp-wide): 6.6MM **Privately Held**
SIC: 8093 8221 8049 Specialty outpatient clinics; university; acupuncturist
PA: South Baylo University
1126 N Brookhurst St
Anaheim CA 92801
714 533-1495

(P-22836)
SOUTH CNTL HEATLH & REHAB PROG
Also Called: Barbour & Floyd Medical Assoc
2620 Industry Way, Lynwood (90262-4024)
PHONE.................................310 667-4070
Jack M Barbour, *Principal*
EMP: 53
SALES (corp-wide): 2MM **Privately Held**
SIC: 8093 Rehabilitation center, outpatient treatment
PA: South Central Health & Rehabilitation Program
2610 Industry Way Ste A
Lynwood CA 90262
310 631-8004

(P-22837)
SOUTH CNTL HEATLH & REHAB PROG
Also Called: Scharp's Oasis House
5201 S Vermont Ave, Los Angeles (90037-3527)
PHONE.................................323 751-2677
Jack Barbour, *Director*
EMP: 100
SALES (corp-wide): 2MM **Privately Held**
SIC: 8093 Mental health clinic, outpatient
PA: South Central Health & Rehabilitation Program
2610 Industry Way Ste A
Lynwood CA 90262
310 631-8004

(P-22838)
SOUTHERN CALIFORNIA ALCOHOL AN (PA)
11500 Paramount Blvd, Downey (90241-4530)
PHONE.................................562 923-4545
Lynne Appel, *CEO*
Gary Munger, *Ch of Bd*
Marsie Alford, *CFO*
Judith Edwards, *Treasurer*
Leon Emerson, *Treasurer*
EMP: 60 **EST:** 1972
SALES: 7.8MM **Privately Held**
SIC: 8093 Specialty outpatient clinics

(P-22839)
SOUTHWEST CORRECTIONAL MEDICAL
Also Called: Correctional Medical Grp
2511 Garden Rd Ste A160, Monterey (93940-5377)
PHONE.................................831 641-3298
Kip Hallman, *CEO*
Elaine Hustedt, *COO*
Don Myll, *CFO*
Dan Hustedt,
EMP: 60 **EST:** 2014
SQ FT: 12,000
SALES: 1.1MM
SALES (corp-wide): 9.7MM **Privately Held**
SIC: 8093 Mental health clinic, outpatient
PA: Correctional Medical Group Companies, Inc.
1 Market St
San Francisco CA 94105
831 649-8994

(P-22840)
SPIRIT OF WOMAN OF CALIFORNIA
327 W Belmont Ave, Fresno (93728-2801)
PHONE.................................559 233-4353
Fax: 559 233-4344
Candis Bazley, *Administration*
James Betts, *Chairman*
Dallas Nuemann, *Treasurer*
Audrey Riley, *Principal*
Jennette Williams, *Principal*
EMP: 52
SALES: 1.6MM **Privately Held**
WEB: www.spiritofwomanunlimited.com
SIC: 8093 Substance abuse clinics (outpatient)

(P-22841)
STANISLAUS RECOVERY CENTER
Also Called: Behavioral Health and Recovery
1904 Richland Ave, Ceres (95307-4562)
PHONE.................................209 541-2121
Fax: 209 541-2083
Dawn Dertelli, *Administration*
Bernardo J Mora, *Psychiatry*
Dan Middleton, *Manager*
EMP: 65
SALES (est): 1.2MM **Privately Held**
SIC: 8093 Rehabilitation center, outpatient treatment

(P-22842)
SURGERY CENTER OF ALTA BATES
Also Called: Alta Btes Cmprhnsive Cncer Ctr
2001 Dwight Way, Berkeley (94704-2608)
PHONE.................................510 204-1591
Fax: 510 204-6440
Peter H Jessup, *CEO*
Beth Tapen, *Research*
Rajesh Behl, *Oncology*
Michael J Cassidy, *Oncology*
Gary R Cecchi, *Oncology*
EMP: 82
SALES (corp-wide): 11B **Privately Held**
SIC: 8093 Specialty outpatient clinics
HQ: The Surgery Center Of Alta Bates Summit Medical Center Llc
2450 Ashby Ave
Berkeley CA 94705
510 204-4444

(P-22843)
SUTTER HEALTH
Also Called: Biomedical Engineering Center
5151 F St, Sacramento (95819-3223)
PHONE.................................916 733-8133
Fax: 916 733-8445
Jon Rice, *Engrg Dir*
Melanie Harper, *Associate Dir*
Christine Aasen, *Office Mgr*
Joanne Ikerd, *Admin Sec*
Danielle Conner, *Admin Asst*
EMP: 60
SALES (corp-wide): 11B **Privately Held**
WEB: www.sutterhealth.org
SIC: 8093 Specialty outpatient clinics
PA: Sutter Health
2200 River Plaza Dr
Sacramento CA 95833
916 733-8800

(P-22844)
SUTTER HEALTH
Also Called: Sutter Auburn Faith Hospital
11815 Education St, Auburn (95602-2410)
PHONE.................................530 888-4500
Fax: 530 889-6054
Mitch Hanna, *CEO*
Kathy Smith, *Lab Dir*
Bob Brearley, *Radiology Dir*
Lori Lange, *Regional Mgr*
Cindy Chan, *Admin Asst*
EMP: 650
SQ FT: 7,584
SALES (corp-wide): 11B **Privately Held**
WEB: www.sutterhealth.org
SIC: 8093 8062 8011 Rehabilitation center, outpatient treatment; general hospitals; hospital, medical school affiliated with nursing & residency; freestanding emergency medical center
PA: Sutter Health
2200 River Plaza Dr
Sacramento CA 95833
916 733-8800

(P-22845)
TARZANA TREATMENT CENTERS INC
422 W Rancho Vista Blvd C280, Palmdale (93551-3720)
PHONE.................................818 654-3815
Albert Senella, *President*
Moises Luna, *Professor*
EMP: 84
SALES (corp-wide): 29.3MM **Privately Held**
SIC: 8093 Substance abuse clinics (outpatient)
PA: Tarzana Treatment Centers, Inc.
18646 Oxnard St
Tarzana CA 91356
818 996-1051

(P-22846)
TARZANA TREATMENT CENTERS INC (PA)
18646 Oxnard St, Tarzana (91356-1411)
PHONE.................................818 996-1051
Fax: 818 345-3778
Albert Senella, *President*
Jim Sorg, *Records Dir*
Sylvia Cadena, *CFO*
Bobbi Sloan, *Corp Secy*
Veronica Esparza, *Office Mgr*
EMP: 160
SQ FT: 14,000
SALES (est): 29.3MM **Privately Held**
WEB: www.tarzanatc.com
SIC: 8093 8322 8063 Mental health clinic, outpatient; individual & family services; psychiatric hospitals

(P-22847)
TARZANA TREATMENT CENTERS INC
Also Called: Tarzana Trtmnt Ctrs LNG Bch O
5190 Atlantic Ave, Lakewood (90805-6510)
PHONE.................................562 428-4111
Fax: 562 984-5610
Muhammad Arisah, *Exec Dir*
Veronica Moya, *Manager*
EMP: 169
SALES (corp-wide): 29.3MM **Privately Held**
SIC: 8093 8299 Substance abuse clinics (outpatient); airline training
PA: Tarzana Treatment Centers, Inc.
18646 Oxnard St
Tarzana CA 91356
818 996-1051

(P-22848)
TARZANA TREATMENT CENTERS INC
2101 Magnolia Ave, Long Beach (90806-4521)
PHONE.................................562 218-1868
Fax: 562 591-0346
Angela Knox, *Branch Mgr*
Susan Avakian, *Human Resources*
Stephanie Morris, *Human Resources*
April Castleman, *Case Mgr*
EMP: 50
SQ FT: 11,482
SALES (corp-wide): 29.3MM **Privately Held**
WEB: www.tarzanatc.com
SIC: 8093 Drug clinic, outpatient
PA: Tarzana Treatment Centers, Inc.
18646 Oxnard St
Tarzana CA 91356
818 996-1051

(P-22849)
TARZANA TREATMENT CENTERS INC
Also Called: Tarzana Treatment Ctr
44447 10th St W, Lancaster (93534-3324)
PHONE.................................661 726-2630
Theresa Scott, *Director*
Stan Sorenson, *Manager*
EMP: 70
SALES (corp-wide): 29.3MM **Privately Held**
WEB: www.tarzanatc.com
SIC: 8093 8069 8011 Drug clinic, outpatient; drug addiction rehabilitation hospital; clinic, operated by physicians
PA: Tarzana Treatment Centers, Inc.
18646 Oxnard St
Tarzana CA 91356
818 996-1051

(P-22850)
TELECARE LA STEP DOWN
4335 Atlantic Ave, Long Beach (90807-2803)
PHONE.................................562 216-4900
Mariela Gorosito, *Branch Mgr*
EMP: 50
SALES (est): 439.4K **Privately Held**
SIC: 8093 Mental health clinic, outpatient

(P-22851)
TELECARE LAS POSADAS
1756 S Lewis Rd, Camarillo (93012-8520)
PHONE.................................805 383-3669
Fax: 805 383-3692
Larry Berent, *Principal*
EMP: 60
SALES (est): 99.4K **Privately Held**
SIC: 8093 8082 Mental health clinic, outpatient; home health care services

(P-22852)
TRANSITIONS - MENTAL HLTH ASSN
117 W Tunnell St, Santa Maria (93458-4096)
PHONE.................................805 614-4940
Frank Ricceri, *Principal*
EMP: 104 **Privately Held**
SIC: 8093 8049 Mental health clinic, outpatient; psychologist, psychotherapist & hypnotist
PA: Transitions - Mental Health Association
784 High St
San Luis Obispo CA 93401

(P-22853)
TRI CITY MENTAL HEALTH CENTER
1900 Royalty Dr, Pomona (91767-3032)
PHONE.................................909 784-3200
Debbie Johnson, *Branch Mgr*
Mark Bellegia, *Technician*

8093 - Specialty Outpatient Facilities, NEC County (P-22854)

EMP: 60
SALES (corp-wide): 5.9MM Privately Held
SIC: 8093 8322 Mental health clinic, outpatient; individual & family services
PA: Tri City Mental Health Center
2008 N Garey Ave Ste 2c
Pomona CA 91767
909 623-6131

(P-22854)
TULE RIVER INDIAN HLTH CTR INC
380 N Reservation Rd, Porterville (93257-9673)
P.O. Box 768 (93258-0768)
PHONE....................559 784-2316
Fax: 559 625-1476
Zahid Sheikh, CEO
Casey Carrillo, CFO
Jan L Trigleth, Physician Asst
Don Hanson, Agent
EMP: 65
SQ FT: 15,000
SALES: 5.9MM Privately Held
SIC: 8093 Specialty outpatient clinics

(P-22855)
UHS-CORONA INC
Also Called: Corona Regional Medical Center
730 Magnolia Ave, Corona (92879-3117)
PHONE....................951 736-7200
Fax: 909 736-7220
Pat Sanders, Director
Dana Vonallmen, CIO
David Aguirre, Marketing Staff
John Calderone, Manager
Pat Maldonaldo, Manager
EMP: 200
SALES (corp-wide): 9B Publicly Held
SIC: 8093 8062 8069 8051 Rehabilitation center, outpatient treatment; general medical & surgical hospitals; specialty hospitals, except psychiatric; skilled nursing care facilities
HQ: Uhs-Corona, Inc.
800 S Main St
Corona CA 92882
951 737-4343

(P-22856)
UNITED HEALTH CTRS SAN JOAQUIN (PA)
650 S Zediker Ave Bldg 3, Parlier (93648-2667)
P.O. Box 790 (93648-0790)
PHONE....................559 646-6618
Colleen Curtis, CEO
Justin Preas, COO
Robert Shankerman, Principal
Peter Lopez, Personnel
Mark Maurer, Purchasing
EMP: 70
SQ FT: 7,500
SALES: 38.6MM Privately Held
WEB: www.unitedhealthcenters.org
SIC: 8093 Specialty outpatient clinics

(P-22857)
UNITED HEALTH CTRS SAN JOAQUIN
Also Called: Orange Cove Health Center
445 11th St, Orange Cove (93646-2211)
P.O. Box 427 (93646-0427)
PHONE....................559 626-4031
Fax: 559 626-4963
Lynee Wilder, Manager
Lorena Valdez, Marketing Staff
Matthew J Easton Do, Osteopathy
EMP: 51
SQ FT: 14,623
SALES (corp-wide): 38.6MM Privately Held
SIC: 8093 Family planning clinic
PA: United Health Centers Of The San Joaquin Valley
650 S Zediker Ave Bldg 3
Parlier CA 93648
559 646-6198

(P-22858)
UNIVERSAL CARE INC (PA)
Also Called: Smile Wide Dental
19762 Macarthur Blvd # 100, Irvine (92612-2425)
PHONE....................562 424-6200

Fax: 562 424-4095
Howard E Davis, CEO
Mark Gunter, CFO
Jay Davis, Vice Pres
Jeffrey Davis, Admin Sec
Romeo Santos, Telecomm Mgr
EMP: 350
SQ FT: 73,000
SALES (est): 26.2MM Privately Held
WEB: www.universalcare.com
SIC: 8093 Specialty outpatient clinics

(P-22859)
UNIVERSAL CARE INC
Also Called: Medical and Dental Clinics
17660 Lakewood Blvd, Bellflower (90706-6410)
PHONE....................562 461-1179
Fax: 562 804-0862
Howard Davis, Branch Mgr
Dorey Montoya, Office Mgr
John Adams, Director
Penelope Leon, Director
EMP: 50
SALES (corp-wide): 26.2MM Privately Held
WEB: www.universalcare.com
SIC: 8093 Specialty outpatient clinics
PA: Universal Care, Inc.
19762 Macarthur Blvd # 100
Irvine CA 92612
562 424-6200

(P-22860)
UPLIFT FAMILY SERVICES
Also Called: Emq Familiesfirst
499 Loma Alta Ave, Los Gatos (95030-6227)
PHONE....................408 379-3790
Cynthia Goodman, Branch Mgr
E Sorensen, Administration
Cynthia L Goodman, Agent
EMP: 100
SALES (corp-wide): 82.8MM Privately Held
SIC: 8093 8063 8011 Mental health clinic, outpatient; hospital for the mentally ill; offices & clinics of medical doctors
PA: Uplift Family Services
251 Llewellyn Ave
Campbell CA 95008
408 379-3790

(P-22861)
VERDUGO MENTAL HEALTH
1540 E Colorado St, Glendale (91205-1514)
PHONE....................818 244-7257
Fax: 818 243-5431
Jeff Smith, Exec Dir
Karo Povolitis, Vice Ch Bd
David Igler, Vice Ch Bd
Lois Neil, Vice Pres
J Buckley, Executive Asst
EMP: 64
SALES (est): 2.4MM Privately Held
WEB: www.vmhc.org
SIC: 8093 Mental health clinic, outpatient

(P-22862)
VILLAGE FAMILY SERVICES (PA)
6736 Laurel Canyon Blvd # 200, North Hollywood (91606-1576)
PHONE....................818 755-8786
Fax: 818 755-8789
Hugo C Villa, CEO
Irma Seilicovich, COO
Krista Brown, Vice Pres
Charles Robbins, Vice Pres
Ivonne Wolovich, Vice Pres
EMP: 64
SQ FT: 1,000
SALES: 13MM Privately Held
SIC: 8093 8322 Mental health clinic, outpatient; family counseling services

(P-22863)
VISIONS UNLIMITED (PA)
6833 Stockton Blvd # 485, Sacramento (95823-2372)
PHONE....................916 394-0800
Fax: 916 429-7824
Roleda Bates, CEO
Nicole Wofford, Program Mgr
EMP: 82
SQ FT: 20,000

SALES: 3.6MM Privately Held
WEB: www.vuinc.org
SIC: 8093 Mental health clinic, outpatient

(P-22864)
WELLSPACE HEALTH (PA)
Also Called: Effort, The
1820 J St, Sacramento (95811-3010)
PHONE....................916 325-5556
Fax: 916 444-5620
Robert Caulk, CEO
Jonathan Porteus, President
Valerie Peterson, Exec Dir
Richard D Keegan, Nurse Practr
Yolanda Torris, Supervisor
EMP: 56
SQ FT: 12,500
SALES (est): 10.1MM Privately Held
WEB: www.theeffort.org
SIC: 8093 Specialty outpatient clinics; alcohol clinic, outpatient; rehabilitation center, outpatient treatment

(P-22865)
WEST OAKLAND HEALTH COUNCIL (PA)
Also Called: West Oakland Health Center
700 Adeline St, Oakland (94607-2608)
PHONE....................510 465-1800
Fax: 510 272-0209
Robert R Cooper, CEO
Maribeth Ugalde, Officer
Ola Bennett, Exec Dir
Pei Huang, Comp Spec
Mike Lee, Engineer
EMP: 138
SQ FT: 26,000
SALES (est): 17.3MM Privately Held
SIC: 8093 8021 8011 Mental health clinic, outpatient; drug clinic, outpatient; dental clinic; offices & clinics of medical doctors

(P-22866)
WESTCOAST CHILDRENS CLINIC
3301 E 12th St Ste 259, Oakland (94601-2940)
PHONE....................510 269-9030
Stacy Anne Katz, Exec Dir
Melek Totah, CFO
Jodie Langs, Associate Dir
Tom Peters, Admin Asst
Michael Schrecker, Network Mgr
EMP: 104
SALES: 13.2MM Privately Held
SIC: 8093 Mental health clinic, outpatient

(P-22867)
WINDSOR RDGE RHBLTTION CTR LLC
350 Iris Dr, Salinas (93906-3514)
PHONE....................831 449-1515
Lee C Samson,
Rachyl Bruton, Admin Asst
Lawrence E Feigen,
Jim Thornton, Director
EMP: 99
SALES: 13.4MM Privately Held
SIC: 8093 Rehabilitation center, outpatient treatment

(P-22868)
WORKING WITH AUTISM
16530 Ventura Blvd # 310, Encino (91436-4598)
PHONE....................818 501-4240
Fax: 818 501-0470
Jennifer Sabin, Director
Paul Craig, Administration
Jill Reder, Opers Spvr
Hilya Delband, Director
Traci Oberg, Supervisor
EMP: 100
SALES (est): 5.1MM Privately Held
WEB: www.workingwithautism.com
SIC: 8093 Specialty outpatient clinics

8099 Health & Allied Svcs, NEC

(P-22869)
1LIFE HEALTHCARE INC
Also Called: One Medical Group
130 Sutter St Fl 2, San Francisco (94104-4009)
P.O. Box 779 (94104-0779)
PHONE....................415 644-5265
Thomas H Lee MD, President
Sharon Knight, COO
Paul Kirincich, CFO
Michael Swartzburg, Vice Pres
Melissa Costa, Admin Asst
EMP: 98
SQ FT: 11,500
SALES (est): 9.6MM Privately Held
WEB: www.1life.com
SIC: 8099 Medical services organization

(P-22870)
24 HOUR FITNESS USA INC
6345 Commerce Blvd, Rohnert Park (94928-2403)
PHONE....................707 536-0048
John-Paul Scirica, Manager
EMP: 50
SALES (corp-wide): 441.6MM Privately Held
SIC: 8099 7991 Nutrition services; health club
HQ: 24 Hour Fitness Usa, Inc.
12647 Alcosta Blvd # 500
San Ramon CA 94583
925 543-3100

(P-22871)
24 HOUR FITNESS USA INC
1903 W Empire Ave, Burbank (91504-3433)
PHONE....................818 531-0257
EMP: 50
SALES (corp-wide): 441.6MM Privately Held
SIC: 8099 7991 Nutrition services; physical fitness clubs with training equipment
HQ: 24 Hour Fitness Usa, Inc.
12647 Alcosta Blvd # 500
San Ramon CA 94583
925 543-3100

(P-22872)
24 HOUR FITNESS USA INC
1870 Harbor Blvd Ste 124, Costa Mesa (92627-5023)
PHONE....................949 610-0651
EMP: 50
SALES (corp-wide): 441.6MM Privately Held
SIC: 8099 7991 Nutrition services; physical fitness clubs with training equipment
HQ: 24 Hour Fitness Usa, Inc.
12647 Alcosta Blvd # 500
San Ramon CA 94583
925 543-3100

(P-22873)
ACUTUS MEDICAL INC
2210 Faraday Ave Ste 100, Carlsbad (92008-7225)
PHONE....................858 673-1621
Randy Werneth, CEO
Tim Corvi, Vice Pres
John Schultz, Vice Pres
Rob Walsh, Info Tech Mgr
Derrick Chou, Research
EMP: 68
SALES (est): 7.7MM Privately Held
SIC: 8099 Blood related health services

(P-22874)
ADVENTIST HEALTH SYSTEM/WEST
3191 Casitas Ave Ste 216, Los Angeles (90039-2470)
PHONE....................323 454-4481
Adventist Network, Branch Mgr
EMP: 121
SALES (corp-wide): 251.4MM Privately Held
SIC: 8099 Blood related health services

PRODUCTS & SERVICES SECTION 8099 - Health & Allied Svcs, NEC County (P-22896)

PA: Adventist Health System/West
  2100 Douglas Blvd
  Roseville CA 95661
  916 781-2000

(P-22875)
ADVENTIST HEALTH SYSTEM/WEST
Also Called: Adventist Hlth Cmnty Care-Taft
501 6th St, Taft (93268-2704)
PHONE..................................661 763-5131
Alan Ferch, *Branch Mgr*
EMP: 60
SALES (corp-wide): 251.4MM **Privately Held**
SIC: **8099** Blood related health services
PA: Adventist Health System/West
  2100 Douglas Blvd
  Roseville CA 95661
  916 781-2000

(P-22876)
ADVENTIST HEALTH SYSTEM/WEST
125 Mall Dr, Hanford (93230-5787)
PHONE..................................559 537-2299
EMP: 60
SALES (corp-wide): 251.4MM **Privately Held**
SIC: **8099** Childbirth preparation clinic
PA: Adventist Health System/West
  2100 Douglas Blvd
  Roseville CA 95661
  916 781-2000

(P-22877)
ADVENTIST HEALTH SYSTEM/WEST
1025 N Douty St, Hanford (93230-3722)
PHONE..................................888 443-2273
Janie Neal, *Info Tech Dir*
Javier Amu, *Pediatrics*
Omar A Araim, *Vascular Srgry*
Razan Ammari, *Emerg Med Spec*
Wynn J Allen, *Nurse*
EMP: 60
SALES (corp-wide): 251.4MM **Privately Held**
SIC: **8099** Childbirth preparation clinic
PA: Adventist Health System/West
  2100 Douglas Blvd
  Roseville CA 95661
  916 781-2000

(P-22878)
ADVENTIST HEALTH SYSTEM/WEST
Also Called: Dventist Health Community
372 W Cypress Ave, Reedley (93654-2113)
PHONE..................................559 638-8155
EMP: 121
SALES (corp-wide): 251.4MM **Privately Held**
SIC: **8099** Childbirth preparation clinic
PA: Adventist Health System/West
  2100 Douglas Blvd
  Roseville CA 95661
  916 781-2000

(P-22879)
ADVENTIST HEALTH SYSTEM/WEST
20100 Cedar Rd N, Sonora (95370-5925)
PHONE..................................209 536-5700
EMP: 60
SALES (corp-wide): 251.4MM **Privately Held**
SIC: **8099** Childbirth preparation clinic
PA: Adventist Health System/West
  2100 Douglas Blvd
  Roseville CA 95661
  916 781-2000

(P-22880)
AHMC HEALTHCARE INC
500 E Main St, Alhambra (91801-3961)
PHONE..................................626 248-3452
Cheryl Sanchez, *Admin Asst*
Joyce Cervantes, *CTO*
Peggy Yeung, *Facilities Mgr*
Jeromy Lian, *Med Doctor*
Claudia Ang, *Nurse*
EMP: 693

SALES (corp-wide): 615.4MM **Privately Held**
SIC: **8099** 8062 Blood bank; general medical & surgical hospitals
PA: Ahmc Healthcare Inc.
  1000 S Fremont Ave Unit 6
  Alhambra CA 91803
  626 943-7526

(P-22881)
ALL VALLEY HOME HLTH CARE INC
Also Called: All Valley Home Care
3665 Ruffin Rd Ste 103, San Diego (92123-1871)
PHONE..................................619 276-8001
EMP: 100
SQ FT: 2,500
SALES (est): 1.7MM **Privately Held**
SIC: **8099** Health & allied services

(P-22882)
ALTAMED HEALTH SERVICES CORP
Also Called: Slauson Plaza Med Group
9436 Slauson Ave, Pico Rivera (90660-4748)
PHONE..................................562 949-8717
Fax: 562 949-9094
Alfredo Nunez, *Branch Mgr*
Michelle Jaramillo, *Office Mgr*
Dana Primo, *Surgeon*
Anh Le, *Gnrl Med Prac*
William P Dunne, *Internal Med*
EMP: 60
SALES (corp-wide): 360.3MM **Privately Held**
WEB: www.altamed.org
SIC: **8099** 8011 Medical services organization; clinic, operated by physicians
PA: Altamed Health Services Corporation
  2040 Camfield Ave
  Commerce CA 90040
  323 725-8751

(P-22883)
AMERICAN HLTHCARE ADM SVCS INC
Also Called: American Health Care
3850 Atherton Rd, Rocklin (95765-3700)
PHONE..................................916 773-7227
Lance Aizen, *CEO*
Christine Lee, *Ch Credit Ofcr*
John W Weaver, *Vice Pres*
Rachana K Patel, *Pharmacy Dir*
Christian Reid, *Exec Dir*
EMP: 490
SQ FT: 8,000
SALES (est): 20.2MM **Privately Held**
WEB: www.americanhealthcare.com
SIC: **8099** Medical services organization

(P-22884)
AMERICAN INDIAN HEALTH & SVCS
4141 State St Ste B11, Santa Barbara (93110-1898)
PHONE..................................805 681-7356
Fax: 805 681-7358
Scott Black, *Exec Dir*
Andrea Carnaghe, *Accountant*
Hollanda A Leon, *Family Practiti*
Kevin N Teehee, *Family Practiti*
EMP: 50
SQ FT: 4,000
SALES: 4.9MM **Privately Held**
SIC: **8099** Health screening service

(P-22885)
AMERICAN NATIONAL RED CROSS
6230 Claremont Ave, Oakland (94618-1324)
PHONE..................................510 594-5100
Jay Winkenbach, *CEO*
Conrad Anderson, *Admin Sec*
Patricia Lari, *Personnel Exec*
Theresa Evangelista, *Marketing Mgr*
EMP: 165
SQ FT: 42,714
SALES (corp-wide): 2.6B **Privately Held**
WEB: www.redcross.org
SIC: **8099** Blood related health services

PA: American Red Cross
  431 18th St Nw
  Washington DC 20006
  202 737-8300

(P-22886)
AMERICAN NATIONAL RED CROSS
100 Red Cross Cir, Pomona (91768-2580)
PHONE..................................909 859-7006
Joan Manning, *General Mgr*
Leeann Olson, *Admin Asst*
Janelle Brown, *Administration*
Marcela Martinez, *Manager*
Ann Tunick, *Manager*
EMP: 1200
SALES (corp-wide): 2.6B **Privately Held**
WEB: www.redcross.org
SIC: **8099** Blood donor station
PA: American Red Cross
  431 18th St Nw
  Washington DC 20006
  202 737-8300

(P-22887)
ANKA BEHAVIORAL HEALTH INC
458 Almond Dr, Lodi (95240-7823)
PHONE..................................209 982-4697
EMP: 69
SALES (corp-wide): 41.6MM **Privately Held**
SIC: **8099** Childbirth preparation clinic
PA: Anka Behavioral Health, Incorporated
  1850 Gateway Blvd Ste 900
  Concord CA 94520
  925 825-4700

(P-22888)
ANKA BEHAVIORAL HEALTH INC
7515 Willow Way, Citrus Heights (95610-2936)
PHONE..................................916 722-3700
EMP: 92
SALES (corp-wide): 41.6MM **Privately Held**
SIC: **8099** Childbirth preparation clinic
PA: Anka Behavioral Health, Incorporated
  1850 Gateway Blvd Ste 900
  Concord CA 94520
  925 825-4700

(P-22889)
ANKA BEHAVIORAL HEALTH INC
Also Called: Casa Fremont
5149 Winston Ct, Fremont (94536-6523)
PHONE..................................510 494-1567
Wayne Thurston, *Director*
EMP: 92
SALES (corp-wide): 41.6MM **Privately Held**
SIC: **8099** Childbirth preparation clinic
PA: Anka Behavioral Health, Incorporated
  1850 Gateway Blvd Ste 900
  Concord CA 94520
  925 825-4700

(P-22890)
APRIA HEALTHCARE LLC
Also Called: Distribution Warehouse
1680 Tide Ct Ste B, Woodland (95776-6237)
PHONE..................................530 669-6441
Dan Starck, *Branch Mgr*
EMP: 60
SALES (corp-wide): 2.4B **Privately Held**
WEB: www.respimed.com
SIC: **8099** Blood related health services
HQ: Apria Healthcare Llc
  26220 Enterprise Ct
  Lake Forest CA 92630
  949 616-2606

(P-22891)
APRIA HEALTHCARE LLC
220 Scttsvlle Blvd Bldg A, Jackson (95642)
PHONE..................................209 223-7727
Fax: 209 223-7717
Lawrence Mastrovich, *Principal*
EMP: 180
SALES (corp-wide): 2.4B **Privately Held**
WEB: www.respimed.com
SIC: **8099** Blood related health services

HQ: Apria Healthcare Llc
  26220 Enterprise Ct
  Lake Forest CA 92630
  949 616-2606

(P-22892)
ARBORMED INC (PA)
725 W Town And Country Rd, Orange (92868-4703)
PHONE..................................714 689-1500
Fax: 714 918-0222
Charles Morf, *President*
William Shaw, *CFO*
Scott Everson, *Vice Pres*
Ellen Baker, *Administration*
Tom Hare, *Technology*
EMP: 123
SQ FT: 11,000
SALES (est): 4.7MM **Privately Held**
WEB: www.arbormed.com
SIC: **8099** 8742 Medical services organization; management consulting services

(P-22893)
BIO-MED SERVICES INC
Also Called: Prime Healthcare Services
3300 E Guasti Rd, Ontario (91761-8655)
PHONE..................................909 235-4400
Prem Reddy, *CEO*
EMP: 85
SALES (est): 653.1K
SALES (corp-wide): 2.6B **Privately Held**
SIC: **8099** Medical services organization
PA: Prime Healthcare Services Inc
  3300 E Guasti Rd Ste 300
  Ontario CA 91761
  909 235-4400

(P-22894)
BIOMAT USA INC
2410 Lillyvale Ave, Los Angeles (90032-3514)
PHONE..................................310 772-7777
Barry Plost, *Manager*
Tomas Daga, *Director*
Victor Grifols, *Director*
Juan Ignacio, *Director*
Javier Jorba, *Director*
EMP: 975
SALES (corp-wide): 464.6MM **Privately Held**
SIC: **8099** Plasmapherous center
HQ: Biomat Usa, Inc.
  2410 Lillyvale Ave
  Los Angeles CA 90032
  323 225-2221

(P-22895)
BIOMAT USA INC (DH)
2410 Lillyvale Ave, Los Angeles (90032-3514)
PHONE..................................323 225-2221
Gregory Rich, *CEO*
Jerry L Burdick, *CFO*
Max Debrouwer, *CFO*
Javier Chagoyen, *Treasurer*
Shinji Wada, *Exec VP*
▲ EMP: 50
SQ FT: 20,000
SALES (est): 147.3MM
SALES (corp-wide): 464.6MM **Privately Held**
SIC: **8099** Plasmapherous center
HQ: Grifols Shared Services North America, Inc.
  2410 Lillyvale Ave
  Los Angeles CA 90032
  323 225-2221

(P-22896)
BIOMAT USA INC
246 Bernard St, Bakersfield (93305-3541)
PHONE..................................661 863-0621
Gustavo Castellanos, *Manager*
EMP: 62
SALES (corp-wide): 464.6MM **Privately Held**
SIC: **8099** Blood related health services
HQ: Biomat Usa, Inc.
  2410 Lillyvale Ave
  Los Angeles CA 90032
  323 225-2221

8099 - Health & Allied Svcs, NEC County (P-22897)

PRODUDUCTS & SERVICES SECTION

(P-22897)
BLOOD BANK OF SAN BERNARDINO A (PA)
Also Called: Lifestream
384 W Orange Show Rd, San Bernardino (92408-2028)
P.O. Box 1429 (92402-1429)
PHONE...................909 885-6503
Fax: 909 381-2036
Frederick B Axelrod, CEO
Robert Albee, Vice Pres
Joseph Dunn, Vice Pres
Susan Marquez, Vice Pres
Gary Thorn, Vice Pres
EMP: 240
SQ FT: 50,000
SALES: 54.5MM Privately Held
WEB: www.bbsbrc.org
SIC: 8099 Blood bank; blood donor station

(P-22898)
BLOOD CENTERS OF PACIFIC (PA)
Also Called: SHASTA BLOOD CENTER
270 Masonic Ave, San Francisco (94118-4496)
PHONE...................415 567-6400
Fax: 415 921-6184
Nora Hirschler, President
Mary Sjostrom, CFO
Lage Anderson, Treasurer
Phyllis Weber, Bd of Directors
Steve Hinman, Vice Pres
EMP: 120
SQ FT: 67,000
SALES: 59.7MM Privately Held
SIC: 8099 Blood bank

(P-22899)
BLOOD CENTERS OF PACIFIC
Also Called: NAPA Solano Cmnty Blood Ctr
1325 Gateway Blvd Ste C1, Fairfield (94533-6919)
PHONE...................707 428-6001
Fax: 707 428-1804
Lana Dyson, Manager
EMP: 50
SALES (corp-wide): 59.7MM Privately Held
SIC: 8099 Blood bank
PA: Blood Centers Of The Pacific
270 Masonic Ave
San Francisco CA 94118
415 567-6400

(P-22900)
BLOOD SYSTEMS INC
Also Called: United Blood Services Ventura
4119 Broad St Ste 100, San Luis Obispo (93401-7965)
PHONE...................805 543-1077
Vicki Finson, Exec Dir
Michael Hayward, Branch Mgr
EMP: 90
SALES (corp-wide): 966.8MM Privately Held
SIC: 8099 Blood bank
PA: Blood Systems, Inc.
6210 E Oak St
Scottsdale AZ 85257
480 946-4201

(P-22901)
BLOOD SYSTEMS INC
Also Called: Tri-Counties Blood Bank
4119 Broad St Ste 100, San Luis Obispo (93401-7965)
PHONE...................831 751-1993
Vicky Finson, Director
EMP: 80
SALES (corp-wide): 966.8MM Privately Held
SIC: 8099 Blood bank
PA: Blood Systems, Inc.
6210 E Oak St
Scottsdale AZ 85257
480 946-4201

(P-22902)
BLOODSOURCE INC (PA)
10536 Peter A Mccuen Blvd, Mather (95655-4128)
PHONE...................916 456-1500
Michael J Fuller, CEO
Jim Eldridge, CFO
Dirk Johnson, Vice Pres
Theresa Hoover, Admin Asst
Cindy Enloe, Info Tech Dir
EMP: 325
SQ FT: 105,000
SALES: 88.1MM Privately Held
WEB: www.bloodsource.org
SIC: 8099 Blood bank

(P-22903)
BLOODSOURCE INC
382 E Yosemite Ave, Merced (95340-9100)
PHONE...................209 724-0428
Fax: 209 722-8461
Jaime Suarez, Manager
EMP: 54
SALES (corp-wide): 88.1MM Privately Held
SIC: 8099 Blood bank
PA: Bloodsource, Inc.
10536 Peter A Mccuen Blvd
Mather CA 95655
916 456-1500

(P-22904)
BLOODSOURCE INC
3099 Fair Oaks Blvd, Sacramento (95864-5613)
PHONE...................916 488-1701
Whitney Karen, Branch Mgr
EMP: 50
SALES (corp-wide): 88.1MM Privately Held
SIC: 8099 Blood donor station
PA: Bloodsource, Inc.
10536 Peter A Mccuen Blvd
Mather CA 95655
916 456-1500

(P-22905)
CALIFORNIA CRYOBANK INC (PA)
11915 La Grange Ave, Los Angeles (90025-5213)
PHONE...................310 443-5244
Charles A Sims MD, CEO
Pamela Richardson, President
Don Fish, Lab Dir
Eddie Jacildo, Lab Dir
Lora Turovsky, Lab Dir
EMP: 75
SQ FT: 21,300
SALES (est): 19.7MM Privately Held
WEB: www.cryobank.com
SIC: 8099 Sperm bank

(P-22906)
CALIFORNIA FORENSIC MED GROUP
2801 Meadow Lark Dr, San Diego (92123-2709)
PHONE...................858 694-4690
Penny Looper, General Mgr
EMP: 55
SALES (corp-wide): 29.8MM Privately Held
WEB: www.cfmg.com
SIC: 8099 8322 Medical services organization; probation office
PA: California Forensic Medical Group, Inc
2511 Garden Rd Ste A160
Monterey CA 93940
831 649-8994

(P-22907)
CALIFORNIA FORENSIC MED GROUP
800 S Victoria Ave, Ventura (93009-0001)
PHONE...................805 654-3343
Elaine Hustedt, Vice Pres
EMP: 100
SALES (corp-wide): 29.8MM Privately Held
WEB: www.cfmg.com
SIC: 8099 Medical services organization
PA: California Forensic Medical Group, Inc
2511 Garden Rd Ste A160
Monterey CA 93940
831 649-8994

(P-22908)
CALIFRNIA DSSTER MED SVCS ASSN
101 Dale Ave, San Carlos (94070-2940)
P.O. Box 1265 (94070-1265)
PHONE...................408 970-9202
David Lipin, President
Eileen Burwell, Treasurer
EMP: 120
SQ FT: 1,500
SALES: 21.1K Privately Held
SIC: 8099 Medical rescue squad

(P-22909)
CARE 1ST HEALTH PLAN (PA)
601 Potrero Grande Dr # 2, Monterey Park (91755-7444)
PHONE...................323 889-6638
Maureen Tyson, President
Anna Tran, CEO
Janet Jan, CFO
Brooks Jones, Officer
Michael Rowan, Vice Pres
EMP: 165
SALES (est): 28.9MM Privately Held
WEB: www.care1st.com
SIC: 8099 Blood related health services

(P-22910)
CARE 1ST HEALTH PLAN
1000 S Fremont Ave Unit 4, Alhambra (91803-8859)
PHONE...................626 299-4299
Fax: 626 458-0415
Anna Tran, CEO
David Yu, Prgrmr
Jade Bulante, Manager
Stefany Ramos, Manager
EMP: 84
SALES (corp-wide): 28.9MM Privately Held
SIC: 8099 Blood related health services
PA: Care 1st Health Plan
601 Potrero Grande Dr # 2
Monterey Park CA 91755
323 889-6638

(P-22911)
CAREFUSION CORPORATION
22745 Savi Ranch Pkwy, Yorba Linda (92887-4668)
PHONE...................800 231-2466
Bill Ross, Branch Mgr
Claudio Arugay, QA Dir
Dody Dunquez, QA Dir
Katherine Hosford, Comp Spec
Matthew Quach, Engng Exec
EMP: 55
SALES (corp-wide): 10.2B Publicly Held
SIC: 8099 Medical services organization
HQ: Carefusion Corporation
3750 Torrey View Ct
San Diego CA 92130
858 617-2000

(P-22912)
CBR SYSTEMS INC (HQ)
1200 Bayhill Dr Fl 3, San Bruno (94066-3006)
PHONE...................650 635-1420
Geoff Crouse, President
Mike Johnson, CFO
Patricia Ferrin Loucks, Vice Pres
Tia Newcomer, Vice Pres
Angel Stephens, Vice Pres
EMP: 80
SALES (est): 36.1MM
SALES (corp-wide): 418.2MM Publicly Held
WEB: www.cordblood.com
SIC: 8099 Blood related health services
PA: Amag Pharmaceuticals, Inc.
1100 Winter St Fl 3
Waltham MA 02451
617 498-3300

(P-22913)
CENTER FOR BETTER HEALTH AND
1520 Nutmeg Pl Ste 220, Costa Mesa (92626-2597)
PHONE...................714 751-8110
Jeff Catanzarite, Exec Dir
Jennifer Gross, Office Mgr
Sonia Ortiz, Office Mgr

Clark Canedy, Financial Exec
Jacky Le, Accountant
EMP: 59
SALES (est): 7.2MM Privately Held
SIC: 8099 8011 5734 Health screening service; medical centers; computer software & accessories

(P-22914)
CENTER TO PROMOTE HEALTHCARE A (PA)
Also Called: ONE EAPP
1333 Broadway Ste 604, Oakland (94612-1906)
PHONE...................510 834-1300
John Caterham, President
Lucy Streett, General Mgr
CHI Huynh, Info Tech Mgr
John Weiss, Technology
Vera Ramirez, Accountant
EMP: 50
SQ FT: 3,225
SALES: 42.7MM Privately Held
SIC: 8099 Medical services organization

(P-22915)
CENTRAL CALIFORNIA BLOOD CTR
Also Called: Ccbc Reference Lab
4343 W Herndon Ave, Fresno (93722-3794)
PHONE...................559 389-5433
Kenneth Benell, Branch Mgr
EMP: 98
SALES (corp-wide): 20.1MM Privately Held
SIC: 8099 8071 Blood bank; medical laboratories
PA: Central California Blood Center
4343 W Herndon Ave
Fresno CA 93722
559 389-5433

(P-22916)
CENTRAL CALIFORNIA BLOOD CTR
8094 N Cedar Ave, Fresno (93720-1817)
PHONE...................559 324-1211
Fax: 559 324-1741
Dean Eller, Branch Mgr
EMP: 98
SALES (corp-wide): 20.1MM Privately Held
SIC: 8099 Blood bank
PA: Central California Blood Center
4343 W Herndon Ave
Fresno CA 93722
559 389-5433

(P-22917)
CENTRAL CALIFORNIA BLOOD CTR (PA)
4343 W Herndon Ave, Fresno (93722-3794)
PHONE...................559 389-5433
Dean Eller, President
Jerry Harder, CFO
Monica Rivera, General Mgr
Latravana Tasker, Admin Asst
Betzabel Gonzalez, QA Dir
EMP: 180
SQ FT: 53,000
SALES: 20.1MM Privately Held
WEB: www.cencalblood.org
SIC: 8099 Blood bank

(P-22918)
CENTRAL CALIFORNIA FACULTY MED
1085 W Minnesota Ave, Turlock (95382-0827)
PHONE...................209 620-6937
Jason Elliot, Branch Mgr
EMP: 262
SALES (corp-wide): 56.2MM Privately Held
SIC: 8099 Blood related health services
PA: Central California Faculty Medical Group, Inc.
2625 E Divisadero St
Fresno CA 93721
559 453-5200

PRODUCTS & SERVICES SECTION
8099 - Health & Allied Svcs, NEC County (P-22942)

(P-22919)
CENTRAL COAST CMNTY HLTH CARE
Also Called: Central Cast Vsting Nurse Assn
40 Ragsdale Dr Ste 150, Monterey (93940-5790)
P.O. Box 2480 (93942-2480)
PHONE 831 648-4200
Norma J Harlacher, *President*
Mose Thomas, *Treasurer*
Nida Bautista, *Vice Pres*
Carol Snow, *Exec Dir*
Steven A Godfrey, *Admin Sec*
EMP: 350
SALES (est): 8MM **Privately Held**
SIC: 8099 Medical services organization

(P-22920)
CITRUS VLY HLTH PARTNERS INC
1325 N Grand Ave Ste 300, Covina (91724-4046)
PHONE 626 732-3100
Carol Eaton, *Principal*
EMP: 1127
SALES (corp-wide): 58.1MM **Privately Held**
SIC: 8099 Blood related health services
PA: Citrus Valley Health Partners, Inc.
210 W San Bernardino Rd
Covina CA 91723
626 331-7331

(P-22921)
CLINICA SIERRA VISTA
1430 Truxtun Ave Ste 300, Bakersfield (93301-5220)
PHONE 661 326-6490
Steve Shilling, *Director*
Tony Carbone, *CIO*
EMP: 50
SALES (corp-wide): 119.8MM **Privately Held**
SIC: 8099 Childbirth preparation clinic
PA: Clinica Sierra Vista
1430 Truxtun Ave Ste 400
Bakersfield CA 93301
661 635-3050

(P-22922)
COMMUNITY BLOOD BANK INC
70025 Highway 111 Ste 101, Rancho Mirage (92270-2935)
PHONE 760 773-4190
Fax: 760 773-4188
Robert E Albee, *President*
Barbara Maurits, *Officer*
Michelle Shanahan,
Roberto Thais, *Human Res Mgr*
James Larson, *Agent*
EMP: 61 **EST:** 1972
SQ FT: 8,000
SALES: 80.9K **Privately Held**
SIC: 8099 Blood bank

(P-22923)
COMMUNITY RECOVERY
6708 Melrose Ave, Los Angeles (90038-3412)
PHONE 323 525-0961
EMP: 50
SALES (est): 667.9K **Privately Held**
SIC: 8099 Health & allied services

(P-22924)
COUNTY LAKE HEALTH SERVICES
Also Called: Lake County Public Health Svcs
922 Bevins Ct, Lakeport (95453-9754)
PHONE 707 263-1090
Fax: 707 262-4280
Jim Brown, *Director*
Jessie Wiser, *Admin Sec*
Jane McClean, *Nurse*
Karen Tait, *Director*
Val Kuhn, *Manager*
EMP: 90
SALES (est): 2.3MM **Privately Held**
SIC: 8099 Medical services organization

(P-22925)
COUNTY OF GLENN
Also Called: Glenn County Health Svcs Agcy
247 N Villa Ave, Willows (95988-2607)
PHONE 530 934-6582
Scott Gruendl, *Director*
Parker Hunt, *Accounting Mgr*
Grinnell Norton, *Manager*
EMP: 100 **Privately Held**
WEB: www.countyofglen.net
SIC: 8099 9111 Medical services organization; county supervisors' & executives' offices
PA: County Of Glenn
516 W Sycamore St Fl 2
Willows CA 95988
530 934-6410

(P-22926)
COUNTY OF IMPERIAL
Also Called: Public Health Department
935 Broadway Ave, El Centro (92243-2349)
PHONE 760 482-4441
Evon Smith, *Director*
Josephine Marcial, *Executive*
Kathleen Lang, *Mktg Dir*
Danila Vargas, *Director*
Carlos Trujillo, *Manager*
EMP: 134 **Privately Held**
WEB: www.imperialcounty.net
SIC: 8099 9111 Health screening service; county supervisors' & executives' offices
PA: County Of Imperial
940 W Main St Ste 208
El Centro CA 92243
760 482-4556

(P-22927)
COUNTY OF LOS ANGELES
Also Called: Countywide Childrens Case MGT
600 S Commwl Ave Fl 2, Los Angeles (90005)
PHONE 213 739-2360
Bryan Mershon, *Branch Mgr*
EMP: 85 **Privately Held**
SIC: 8099 Blood related health services
PA: County Of Los Angeles
500 W Temple St Ste 375
Los Angeles CA 90012
213 974-1101

(P-22928)
COUNTY OF LOS ANGELES
Also Called: Compton Family Mhc Fsp
546 W Compton Blvd, Compton (90220-3011)
PHONE 310 885-2100
Phillip Mobley, *Manager*
EMP: 85 **Privately Held**
SIC: 8099 Blood related health services
PA: County Of Los Angeles
500 W Temple St Ste 375
Los Angeles CA 90012
213 974-1101

(P-22929)
COUNTY OF LOS ANGELES
921 E Compton Blvd, Compton (90221-3303)
PHONE 310 668-6845
Marvin Southard, *Branch Mgr*
EMP: 85 **Privately Held**
SIC: 8099 Blood related health services
PA: County Of Los Angeles
500 W Temple St Ste 375
Los Angeles CA 90012
213 974-1101

(P-22930)
COUNTY OF LOS ANGELES
Also Called: Specilzed Foster Care Pasadena
532 E Colorado Blvd Fl 8, Pasadena (91101-2044)
PHONE 626 229-3825
Angela Parkspyles, *Executive*
EMP: 85 **Privately Held**
SIC: 8099 Blood related health services
PA: County Of Los Angeles
500 W Temple St Ste 375
Los Angeles CA 90012
213 974-1101

(P-22931)
COUNTY OF LOS ANGELES
2829 S Grand Ave Rm 116, Los Angeles (90007-3304)
PHONE 213 744-3922
C Clark, *CEO*
EMP: 85 **Privately Held**

SIC: 8099 Health screening service
PA: County Of Los Angeles
500 W Temple St Ste 375
Los Angeles CA 90012
213 974-1101

(P-22932)
COUNTY OF LOS ANGELES
Also Called: Department of Health
3530 Wilshire Blvd Fl 9, Los Angeles (90010-2344)
PHONE 213 351-7800
Michelle Parra PHD, *Manager*
Eloisa Gonzalez, *Info Tech Dir*
Karina Flores, *Manager*
EMP: 70 **Privately Held**
WEB: www.co.la.ca.us
SIC: 8099 9431 Medical services organization; administration of public health programs;
PA: County Of Los Angeles
500 W Temple St Ste 375
Los Angeles CA 90012
213 974-1101

(P-22933)
COUNTY OF LOS ANGELES
Also Called: Los Angeles County Pub Works
5525 Imperial Hwy, South Gate (90280-7417)
PHONE 562 861-0316
Fax: 562 861-3957
Phil Doudar, *Manager*
EMP: 100 **Privately Held**
WEB: www.co.la.ca.us
SIC: 8099 9111 Blood related health services; executive offices
PA: County Of Los Angeles
500 W Temple St Ste 375
Los Angeles CA 90012
213 974-1101

(P-22934)
COUNTY OF LOS ANGELES
313 N Figueroa St, Los Angeles (90012-2602)
PHONE 213 240-7780
Fax: 213 250-3909
Valerie Orange, *Branch Mgr*
EMP: 85 **Privately Held**
WEB: www.co.la.ca.us
SIC: 8099 9431 Physical examination & testing services; health statistics center, government
PA: County Of Los Angeles
500 W Temple St Ste 375
Los Angeles CA 90012
213 974-1101

(P-22935)
COUNTY OF RIVERSIDE DEPARTMENT
554 S Paseo Dorotea, Palm Springs (92264-1445)
PHONE 760 320-1048
Fax: 760 320-1470
EMP: 76
SALES (corp-wide): 7.7MM **Privately Held**
SIC: 8099 Childbirth preparation clinic
PA: The County Of Riverside Department Of Public Health Auxialiary
4065 County Circle Dr
Riverside CA 92503
951 358-5000

(P-22936)
COUNTY OF SAN DIEGO
Also Called: Medical Examiner Forensic Ctr
5570 Overland Ave Ste 101, San Diego (92123-1215)
PHONE 619 531-4521
Glenn Wagner, *Chief Mktg Ofcr*
EMP: 60 **Privately Held**
WEB: www.sdlcc.org
SIC: 8099 Medical services organization
PA: County Of San Diego
1600 Pacific Hwy Ste 209
San Diego CA 92101
619 531-5880

(P-22937)
DANVILLE VILLAGE SKILLED NURSN
Also Called: DANVILLE REHSBILITATION
336 Diablo Rd, Danville (94526-3417)
PHONE 925 837-4566
Spencer Brinton, *Administration*
Susan Devine, *Administration*
EMP: 65
SQ FT: 13,760
SALES: 8.3MM **Privately Held**
SIC: 8099 Medical services organization

(P-22938)
DELTA BLOOD BANK
1900 W Orangeburg Ave, Modesto (95350-3740)
PHONE 209 943-3830
Fax: 209 549-8485
Dr Benjamin Spindler, *Principal*
EMP: 100
SQ FT: 6,239
SALES (corp-wide): 2.6B **Privately Held**
SIC: 8099 7389 Blood bank; personal service agents, brokers & bureaus
HQ: Delta Blood Bank
65 N Commerce St
Stockton CA 95202
800 244-6794

(P-22939)
DELTA BLOOD BANK (HQ)
65 N Commerce St, Stockton (95202-2318)
P.O. Box 800 (95201-0800)
PHONE 800 244-6794
Fax: 209 462-0221
Benjamin Spindler, *CEO*
Robert Lawrence, *Ch of Bd*
Alfonso Figueroa, *CFO*
Joan Barker, *Lab Dir*
Rita Pinto, *Lab Dir*
◆ **EMP:** 85
SQ FT: 30,000
SALES: 3.1MM
SALES (corp-wide): 2.6B **Privately Held**
SIC: 8099 Blood bank
PA: American Red Cross
431 18th St Nw
Washington DC 20006
202 737-8300

(P-22940)
DIGNITY HEALTH MED FOUNDATION
Also Called: Dignity Hlth Med Grp-Dominican
9515 Soquel Dr Ste 100, Aptos (95003-4136)
PHONE 831 535-1560
EMP: 95
SALES (corp-wide): 570.1MM **Privately Held**
SIC: 8099 Medical services organization
PA: Dignity Health Medical Foundation
3400 Data Dr
Rancho Cordova CA 95670
916 379-2840

(P-22941)
DIGNITY HEALTH MED FOUNDATION
Also Called: Dignity Health Medical Grp
1667 Dominican Way # 134, Santa Cruz (95065-1518)
PHONE 831 475-8834
George Lenzi, *CFO*
EMP: 95
SALES (corp-wide): 570.1MM **Privately Held**
SIC: 8099 Medical rescue squad
PA: Dignity Health Medical Foundation
3400 Data Dr
Rancho Cordova CA 95670
916 379-2840

(P-22942)
DIGNITY HEALTH MED FOUNDATION
Also Called: Dignity Hlth Med Grp-Dominican
3400 Data Dr, Rancho Cordova (95670-7956)
PHONE 916 379-2840
Laurie Schwarctz, *President*
EMP: 1000
SQ FT: 45,000

SALES (corp-wide): 570.1MM **Privately Held**
SIC: 8099 Medical services organization
PA: Dignity Health Medical Foundation
3400 Data Dr
Rancho Cordova CA 95670
916 379-2840

(P-22943)
DIGNITY HEALTH MED FOUNDATION
2110 Prfcional Dr Ste 120, Roseville (95661)
PHONE.....................916 787-0404
A Alan White, *Principal*
Miguel A Nieves, *Diag Radio*
EMP: 76
SALES (corp-wide): 570.1MM **Privately Held**
SIC: 8099 8071 8011 Medical services organization; medical laboratories; radiologist
PA: Dignity Health Medical Foundation
3400 Data Dr
Rancho Cordova CA 95670
916 379-2840

(P-22944)
DIGNITY HEALTH MED FOUNDATION (PA)
Also Called: Dignity Hlth Med Grp-Dominican
3400 Data Dr, Rancho Cordova (95670-7956)
PHONE.....................916 379-2840
Laurie Schwarctz, *President*
Sue Haddad, *CFO*
Jennean Rogers, *Admin Asst*
Steve Bell, *Info Tech Dir*
Katie Boehm-Padgett, *Recruiter*
EMP: 200
SQ FT: 45,000
SALES: 570.1MM **Privately Held**
WEB: www.chwmedicalfoundation.com
SIC: 8099 Medical services organization

(P-22945)
DIRECT FLOW MEDICAL INC (PA)
451 Aviation Blvd 107a, Santa Rosa (95403-1055)
PHONE.....................707 576-0420
Fax: 707 576-0430
Daniel Lemaitre, *President*
David R Elizondo, *COO*
David Boyle, *CFO*
Holly Pagels, *Executive Asst*
Mary Huebner, *QA Dir*
EMP: 121
SALES (est): 22.7MM **Privately Held**
WEB: www.directflowmedical.com
SIC: 8099 Medical services organization

(P-22946)
DIVERSIFIED CLINICAL SERVICES
4225 E La Palma Ave, Anaheim (92807-1815)
PHONE.....................714 579-8400
James R Sechrist, *Ch of Bd*
Dan Nguyen, *CFO*
Judy Chandler, *Admin Mgr*
Ruth Gordon,
Veronica Lau, *Program Dir*
EMP: 85
SQ FT: 74,000
SALES (est): 1.1MM **Privately Held**
SIC: 8099 Medical services organization

(P-22947)
DONOR NETWORK WEST (PA)
12667 Alcosta Blvd # 500, San Ramon (94583-4427)
PHONE.....................925 480-3100
Fax: 510 444-8501
Cynthia D Siljestrom, *CEO*
Sandra Mejia, *CFO*
Jt Mason, *Senior VP*
Mark Borer, *Vice Pres*
Vivian Curd, *Nursing Mgr*
EMP: 121
SQ FT: 41,039
SALES: 64.4MM **Privately Held**
SIC: 8099 Medical services organization

(P-22948)
DONOR NETWORK WEST
Also Called: Ctdn - Redding
5800 Airport Rd Ste B, Redding (96002-9359)
PHONE.....................510 418-0336
EMP: 78
SALES (corp-wide): 64.4MM **Privately Held**
SIC: 8099 Medical services organization
PA: Donor Network West
12667 Alcosta Blvd # 500
San Ramon CA 94583
925 480-3100

(P-22949)
DRX LLC
Also Called: Ancillary Medical Solutions
330 A St Ste 80, San Diego (92101-4213)
PHONE.....................888 315-1519
Michael J Berg, *President*
EMP: 60
SALES (est): 7.2K **Privately Held**
SIC: 8099 5999 Childbirth preparation clinic; hospital equipment & supplies

(P-22950)
EAST BAY FOUNDATION GRAD MED
1411 E 31st St, Oakland (94602-1018)
P.O. Box 309, Concord (94522-0309)
PHONE.....................510 437-4197
Theresa Azevedo, *Exec Dir*
Alden Harken, *Ch of Bd*
EMP: 54
SALES: 3.5MM **Privately Held**
SIC: 8099 Medical services organization

(P-22951)
EASTER SEAL SOC SUPERIOR CAL (PA)
Also Called: EASTER SEALS MAIN OFFICE
3205 Hurley Way, Sacramento (95864-3853)
PHONE.....................916 485-6711
Fax: 916 485-2653
Gary T Kasai, *President*
Joanne Budge, *CFO*
Teresa Muth, *MIS Dir*
Mary Schachten, *Program Dir*
EMP: 100
SQ FT: 28,500
SALES: 10.7MM **Privately Held**
WEB: www.essuperior.org
SIC: 8099 8093 Medical services organization; rehabilitation center, outpatient treatment

(P-22952)
EASTERN PLUMAS HEALTH CARE (PA)
Also Called: Eastern Plumas Hospital
500 1st Ave, Portola (96122-9406)
PHONE.....................530 832-4277
Fax: 530 832-0160
Charles Guenther, *CEO*
Anton Dahlman,
Virginia Luhring, *President*
Jeri Nelson, *CFO*
Cathy Conant, *Info Tech Mgr*
EMP: 161 EST: 1992
SQ FT: 18,500
SALES: 52.8K **Privately Held**
SIC: 8099 8011 8322 Medical services organization; primary care medical clinic; rehabilitation services

(P-22953)
EHEALTHWIRECOM INC
2450 Venture Oaks Way # 100, Sacramento (95833-3292)
PHONE.....................916 924-8092
Fax: 916 924-8209
Yousry Mekhamer, *Chairman*
John Mactavish, *Manager*
EMP: 250
SQ FT: 17,000
SALES (est): 3MM **Privately Held**
WEB: www.ehealthline.com
SIC: 8099 Health screening service

(P-22954)
ELIZABETH GLASER PEDIA
16130 Ventura Blvd # 250, Encino (91436-2529)
PHONE.....................310 231-0400
Charles Lyons, *Branch Mgr*
EMP: 875
SALES (corp-wide): 126MM **Privately Held**
SIC: 8099 Medical services organization
PA: Elizabeth Glaser Pediatric Aids Foundation
1140 Conn Ave Nw Ste 200
Washington DC 20036
310 314-1459

(P-22955)
EPOCRATES INC (HQ)
50 Hawthorne St, San Francisco (94105-3902)
PHONE.....................650 227-1700
Fax: 650 227-2770
Rob Cosinuke, *President*
Meredith Aucker, *President*
Murat Erdem, *President*
Patti Paczkowski, *President*
Howard Schargel, *President*
EMP: 54
SQ FT: 59,000
SALES (est): 24.5MM
SALES (corp-wide): 924.7MM **Publicly Held**
WEB: www.epocrates.com
SIC: 8099 Health screening service
PA: Athenahealth, Inc.
311 Arsenal St Ste 14
Watertown MA 02472
617 402-1000

(P-22956)
EVOLENT HEALTH INC
1 Kearny St Ste 300, San Francisco (94108-5560)
PHONE.....................571 389-6000
EMP: 408
SALES (corp-wide): 96.8MM **Publicly Held**
SIC: 8099 Medical services organization
PA: Evolent Health, Inc.
800 N Glebe Rd Ste 500
Arlington VA 22203
571 389-6000

(P-22957)
FACEY MEDICAL FOUNDATION (PA)
15451 San Fernando Msn, Mission Hills (91345-1368)
P.O. Box 9601 (91346-9601)
PHONE.....................818 365-9531
Bill Gill, *CEO*
Teresa David, *COO*
Jim Corwin, *CFO*
Abraham Rakelian, *Comms Mgr*
Pat Mahony, *Office Mgr*
EMP: 170
SQ FT: 306,000
SALES: 197.1MM **Privately Held**
WEB: www.facey.com
SIC: 8099 Medical services organization

(P-22958)
FACEY MEDICAL FOUNDATION
11211 Sepulveda Blvd, Mission Hills (91345-1115)
PHONE.....................818 837-5677
Cathy Hawes, *Branch Mgr*
Margie Melby, *Executive*
Michael Wilson, *Info Tech Dir*
Rusty Wilmes, *Technology*
Anna Ventura, *Financial Exec*
EMP: 200
SALES (corp-wide): 197.1MM **Privately Held**
SIC: 8099 8042 8011 Medical services organization; offices & clinics of optometrists; offices & clinics of medical doctors
PA: Facey Medical Foundation
15451 San Fernando Msn
Mission Hills CA 91345
818 365-9531

(P-22959)
FACEY MEDICAL FOUNDATION
Also Called: Facey Medical Group
17909 Soledad Canyon Rd, Santa Clarita (91387-3210)
PHONE.....................661 250-5225
Fax: 661 250-5210
Leslie Holland, *Branch Mgr*
Ana Lopes, *Family Practiti*
Erik E Davydov, *Internal Med*
Michael Dalali MD, *Med Doctor*
Atul Sharma, *Med Doctor*
EMP: 60
SALES (corp-wide): 197.1MM **Privately Held**
SIC: 8099 8011 Medical services organization; offices & clinics of medical doctors
PA: Facey Medical Foundation
15451 San Fernando Msn
Mission Hills CA 91345
818 365-9531

(P-22960)
FACEY MEDICAL FOUNDATION
27924 Seco Canyon Rd, Santa Clarita (91350-3870)
PHONE.....................661 513-2100
Joan Rhee, *Manager*
EMP: 86
SALES (corp-wide): 197.1MM **Privately Held**
SIC: 8099 Blood related health services
PA: Facey Medical Foundation
15451 San Fernando Msn
Mission Hills CA 91345
818 365-9531

(P-22961)
FACEY MEDICAL FOUNDATION
Also Called: Marshall, Spector MD
1237 E Main St, San Gabriel (91776)
PHONE.....................626 576-0800
Ana Ventura, *Manager*
France Adamson MD, *Med Doctor*
John Herziger MD, *Med Doctor*
EMP: 86
SALES (corp-wide): 197.1MM **Privately Held**
SIC: 8099 8011 Medical services organization; pediatrician
PA: Facey Medical Foundation
15451 San Fernando Msn
Mission Hills CA 91345
818 365-9531

(P-22962)
FACEY MEDICAL FOUNDATION
Also Called: Facey Medical Group
18460 Roscoe Blvd, Northridge (91325-4107)
PHONE.....................818 734-3600
Fax: 818 734-3616
Stella Shroyer, *Branch Mgr*
Jaytee Narvaez, *Technology*
Chris Gushi, *Financial Exec*
Mary Dickens, *Gnrl Med Prac*
Jayvee R Regala, *Med Doctor*
EMP: 80
SALES (corp-wide): 197.1MM **Privately Held**
SIC: 8099 8011 Medical services organization; offices & clinics of medical doctors
PA: Facey Medical Foundation
15451 San Fernando Msn
Mission Hills CA 91345
818 365-9531

(P-22963)
FAMILY HLTH CTRS SAN DIEGO INC
7592 Broadway, Lemon Grove (91945-1604)
PHONE.....................619 515-2550
EMP: 103
SALES (corp-wide): 125.5MM **Privately Held**
SIC: 8099 Blood related health services
PA: Family Health Centers Of San Diego, Inc.
823 Gateway Center Way
San Diego CA 92102
619 515-2303

PRODUCTS & SERVICES SECTION
8099 - Health & Allied Svcs, NEC County (P-22987)

(P-22964)
GLENVIEW ASSISTED LIVING LLP
1950 Calle Barcelona, Carlsbad (92009-8401)
PHONE..................760 704-6800
Fax: 760 704-6806
Justin Wilson, *Partner*
EMP: 50
SALES (est): 1MM **Privately Held**
SIC: 8099 8361 8052 Health & allied services; residential care; intermediate care facilities

(P-22965)
GLOBAL MEDDATA INC
1725 E Byshore Rd Ste 103, Redwood City (94063)
PHONE..................650 369-9734
Raj Patel, *CEO*
Naina Khatri, *Director*
EMP: 62
SQ FT: 3,200
SALES (est): 1.3MM **Privately Held**
WEB: www.globalmeddata.net
SIC: 8099 7374 Medical services organization; data processing & preparation

(P-22966)
HALO UNLIMTED INC
Also Called: Infant Hring Scrning Spcalists
1867 California Ave # 101, Corona (92881-7281)
P.O. Box 77010 (92877-0100)
PHONE..................714 692-2270
Martha Hawkins, *President*
Harriet Brown, *Opers Mgr*
EMP: 54
SQ FT: 7,500
SALES (est): 5.6MM **Privately Held**
SIC: 8099 Hearing testing service

(P-22967)
HALYARD HEALTH INC
Also Called: Halyard Irvine
43 Discovery Ste 100, Irvine (92618-3773)
PHONE..................800 448-3569
Diana Kramer, *Director*
EMP: 2298
SALES (corp-wide): 1.5B **Publicly Held**
SIC: 8099 Childbirth preparation clinic
PA: Halyard Health, Inc.
5405 Windward Pkwy
Alpharetta GA 30004
678 425-9273

(P-22968)
HARBOR HEALTH SYSTEMS LLC
3501 Jamboree Rd Ste 3000, Newport Beach (92660-2904)
PHONE..................949 273-7020
Gregory Moore, *CEO*
James W Dolan, *CEO*
EMP: 180 **EST:** 2001
SALES (est): 3.7MM
SALES (corp-wide): 900MM **Privately Held**
SIC: 8099 7372 Blood related health services; business oriented computer software
PA: One Call Medical Inc.
841 Prudential Dr Ste 900
Jacksonville FL 32207
904 646-0199

(P-22969)
HEALTH SERVICES ADVISORY GROUP
700 N Brand Blvd Fl 1, Glendale (91203-3236)
PHONE..................818 409-9220
Lawrence Shapiro, *Principal*
EMP: 54
SALES (est): 939.8K
SALES (corp-wide): 41.9MM **Privately Held**
SIC: 8099 Health & allied services
PA: Health Services Holdings, Inc.
3133 E Camelback Rd # 300
Phoenix AZ 85016
602 264-6382

(P-22970)
HEALTHCARE PARTNERS LLC
1236 N Magnolia Ave, Anaheim (92801-2607)
PHONE..................714 995-1000
Fax: 714 827-3620
Kathy Porter, *Admin Asst*
Jenny S Young Lee, *Obstetrician*
Bruce W Chow Do, *Osteopathy*
Frederick A Mayer, *Podiatrist*
Dustin Chea, *Physician Asst*
EMP: 60
SALES (corp-wide): 13.7B **Publicly Held**
SIC: 8099 8011 Medical services organization; offices & clinics of medical doctors
HQ: Healthcare Partners, Llc
2175 Park Pl
El Segundo CA 90245

(P-22971)
HEALTHCARE PARTNERS LLC
Also Called: Family Health Program
4910 Airport Plaza Dr, Long Beach (90815-1264)
PHONE..................562 429-2473
Fax: 562 429-7503
Rhonda Luster, *Director*
Lisa T Marie Worsch, *OB/GYN*
Mahnaz Behboodikhah, *Cardiovascular*
Jennifer D Armstrong MD, *Med Doctor*
Joseph L Abijay, *Director*
EMP: 100
SALES (corp-wide): 13.7B **Publicly Held**
SIC: 8099 8011 Medical services organization; clinic, operated by physicians
HQ: Healthcare Partners, Llc
2175 Park Pl
El Segundo CA 90245

(P-22972)
HEALTHCARE PARTNERS LLC
3501 S Harbor Blvd # 100, Santa Ana (92704-6919)
PHONE..................714 964-6229
Fax: 714 378-6569
Francis Gale, *Manager*
Fernando H Austin, *Med Doctor*
John Buckman, *Med Doctor*
Karen Frei, *Med Doctor*
Anhtuan Tong MD, *Med Doctor*
EMP: 50
SALES (corp-wide): 13.7B **Publicly Held**
SIC: 8099 Blood related health services
HQ: Healthcare Partners, Llc
2175 Park Pl
El Segundo CA 90245

(P-22973)
HEMACARE CORPORATION (PA)
15350 Sherman Way, Van Nuys (91406-4203)
PHONE..................818 986-3883
Pete Van Der Wal, *President*
Anna Stock, *COO*
Lisa Bacerra, *CFO*
Robert Chilton, *CFO*
Viktor Mohacsy, *CFO*
EMP: 120 **EST:** 1978
SQ FT: 19,600
SALES (est): 14.1MM **Publicly Held**
WEB: www.hemacare.com
SIC: 8099 5122 Blood related health services; blood bank; blood donor station; blood plasma

(P-22974)
HENRY MAYO NEWHALL MEM HOSP
Also Called: Santa Clarita Health Care Ctr
23845 Mcbean Pkwy, Santa Clarita (91355-2001)
PHONE..................661 253-8227
David R Tumilty, *Principal*
EMP: 468
SALES (corp-wide): 307.4MM **Privately Held**
WEB: www.henrymayo.com
SIC: 8099 Childbirth preparation clinic
PA: Henry Mayo Newhall Hospital
23845 Mcbean Pkwy
Valencia CA 91355
661 253-8000

(P-22975)
HERITAGE MEDICAL GROUP
12370 Hesperia Rd Ste 6, Victorville (92395-4787)
PHONE..................760 956-1286
Fax: 760 241-7793
Stanley Wohl, *Branch Mgr*
EMP: 231 **Privately Held**
SIC: 8099 Blood related health services
PA: Heritage Medical Group
4580 California Ave
Bakersfield CA 93309

(P-22976)
HOAG FAMILY CANCER INSTITUTE
1190 Baker St Ste 103, Costa Mesa (92626-4105)
PHONE..................949 764-7777
Fax: 714 668-2530
Inga Barillas, *Branch Mgr*
Philip Grossman, *Project Mgr*
Vivek Srinivasan, *Portfolio Mgr*
Peri Gunay, *Emerg Med Spec*
Van Haynie, *Counsel*
EMP: 748
SALES (corp-wide): 40.1MM **Privately Held**
SIC: 8099 Blood related health services
PA: Hoag Family Cancer Institute
1 Hoag Dr Bldg 41
Newport Beach CA 92663
949 722-6237

(P-22977)
HORIZONS ADULT DAY HEALTH CARE
1035 Harbison Ave, National City (91950-3919)
PHONE..................619 474-1822
Fax: 619 474-1826
Marina Murashova, *President*
Russ Kraus, *CFO*
EMP: 75
SALES (est): 2.9MM **Privately Held**
SIC: 8099 Blood related health services

(P-22978)
HOUCHIN BLOOD SERVICES
11515 Bolthouse Dr, Bakersfield (93311-8822)
PHONE..................661 327-8541
Fax: 661 327-0509
Greg Gallion, *Branch Mgr*
EMP: 60
SALES (corp-wide): 8.6MM **Privately Held**
WEB: www.hcbb.com
SIC: 8099 Blood bank
PA: Houchin Blood Services
11515 Bolthouse Dr
Bakersfield CA 93311
661 323-4222

(P-22979)
IN SHAPE HEALTH CLUB
14601 Valley Center Dr, Victorville (92395-4216)
PHONE..................760 381-1200
Derrick Johnson, *General Mgr*
EMP: 50
SALES (est): 172.5K **Privately Held**
SIC: 8099 7991 Health & allied services; health club

(P-22980)
INCARE DME
15446 Sherman Way Apt 319, Van Nuys (91406-4254)
PHONE..................818 582-1016
Natasha Larson, *Owner*
EMP: 99
SALES (est): 801.9K **Privately Held**
SIC: 8099 Health & allied services

(P-22981)
INLAND BHAVIORAL HLTH SVCS INC (PA)
1963 N E St, San Bernardino (92405-3919)
PHONE..................909 881-6146
Fax: 909 881-0111
Temetry Ann Lindsey, *President*
Vernon Bragg Jr, *Ch of Bd*
John Wilson, *COO*
Peter Demel, *CFO*
Christina Sarabia, *Accountant*
EMP: 68
SQ FT: 13,500
SALES: 8.8MM **Privately Held**
WEB: www.ibhealth.org
SIC: 8099 8093 Medical services organization; drug clinic, outpatient; alcohol clinic, outpatient

(P-22982)
JWCH INSTITUTE INC
14371 Clark Ave, Bellflower (90706-2901)
PHONE..................562 867-7999
Alvaro Ballesteros, *Branch Mgr*
EMP: 72
SALES (corp-wide): 27.6MM **Privately Held**
SIC: 8099 Blood related health services
PA: Jwch Institute, Inc.
5650 Jillson St
Commerce CA 90040
323 477-1171

(P-22983)
KAISER FOUNDATION HOSPITALS
Also Called: Kaiser Foundation Health Plan
2055 Kellogg Ave, Corona (92879-3111)
PHONE..................866 984-7483
Ruth Jasse, *Administration*
Gana M Mody, *Med Doctor*
Janet Tang, *Pharmacist*
Rina Williams, *Pharmacist*
EMP: 99
SALES (corp-wide): 27.8B **Privately Held**
WEB: www.kaiser.com
SIC: 8099 Childbirth preparation clinic
HQ: Kaiser Foundation Hospitals Inc
1 Kaiser Plz
Oakland CA 94612
510 271-6611

(P-22984)
KAWEAH DLTA HLTH CARE DST GILD
4945 W Cypress Ave, Visalia (93277-1592)
PHONE..................559 624-3100
EMP: 114
SALES (corp-wide): 475.4MM **Privately Held**
SIC: 8099 Childbirth preparation clinic
PA: Kaweah Delta Health Care District Guild
400 W Mineral King Ave
Visalia CA 93291
559 624-2000

(P-22985)
KAWEAH DLTA HLTH CARE DST GILD
1014 San Juan Ave Ste A, Exeter (93221-1312)
PHONE..................559 592-7300
Blanca Bedolla, *Assistant*
EMP: 63
SALES (corp-wide): 475.4MM **Privately Held**
SIC: 8099 Childbirth preparation clinic
PA: Kaweah Delta Health Care District Guild
400 W Mineral King Ave
Visalia CA 93291
559 624-2000

(P-22986)
KIDANGO INC
730 Empey Way, San Jose (95128-4705)
PHONE..................408 297-9044
Stacey Gray, *Manager*
EMP: 161
SALES (corp-wide): 26MM **Privately Held**
SIC: 8099 Blood related health services
PA: Kidango, Inc.
44000 Old Warm Sprng Blvd
Fremont CA 94538
510 897-6900

(P-22987)
KIMCO STAFFING SERVICES INC
1801 Oakland Blvd Ste 220, Walnut Creek (94596-7033)
PHONE..................925 256-3132

8099 - Health & Allied Svcs, NEC County (P-22988)

EMP: 2767
SALES (corp-wide): 177.3MM **Privately Held**
SIC: 8099 Medical services organization
PA: Kimco Staffing Services, Inc.
 17872 Cowan
 Irvine CA 92614
 949 331-1199

(P-22988)
KINDRED HEALTHCARE INC
Also Called: Odyssey Healthcare Bakersfield
5001 E Commercecenter Dr, Bakersfield (93309-1659)
PHONE.................................661 324-1232
Fax: 661 391-8868
EMP: 203
SALES (corp-wide): 7B **Publicly Held**
SIC: 8099 Childbirth preparation clinic
PA: Kindred Healthcare, Inc.
 680 S 4th St
 Louisville KY 40202
 502 596-7300

(P-22989)
KINDRED HEALTHCARE INC
Also Called: Professional Healthcare At HM
901 Campisi Way Ste 205, Campbell (95008-2348)
PHONE.................................408 871-9860
EMP: 81
SALES (corp-wide): 7B **Publicly Held**
SIC: 8099 Childbirth preparation clinic
PA: Kindred Healthcare, Inc.
 680 S 4th St
 Louisville KY 40202
 502 596-7300

(P-22990)
KINDRED HEALTHCARE INC
1805 Medical Center Dr, San Bernardino (92411-1217)
PHONE.................................909 887-6391
Fax: 909 806-1059
Darryl Vandenbosch, *Vice Pres*
EMP: 122
SALES (corp-wide): 7B **Publicly Held**
SIC: 8099 Childbirth preparation clinic
PA: Kindred Healthcare, Inc.
 680 S 4th St
 Louisville KY 40202
 502 596-7300

(P-22991)
KPC HEALTHCARE INC
1800 30th St Ste 340, Bakersfield (93301-1937)
PHONE.................................661 229-4009
EMP: 199
SALES (corp-wide): 449.3MM **Privately Held**
SIC: 8099 Blood related health services
PA: Kpc Healthcare, Inc.
 1301 N Tustin Ave
 Santa Ana CA 92705
 714 953-3652

(P-22992)
LELAND STANFORD JUNIOR UNIV
Stanford Blood Center
3373 Hillview Ave, Palo Alto (94304-1204)
PHONE.................................650 723-5548
Fax: 650 725-9925
Edgar Engleman, *Director*
Steven Foung, *Pathologist*
Morvarid Moayeri, *Pathologist*
Deba Hiraki, *Med Doctor*
EMP: 200
SALES (corp-wide): 1.9B **Privately Held**
SIC: 8099 8221 Blood bank; university
PA: Leland Stanford Junior University
 2575 Sand Hill Rd
 Menlo Park CA 94025
 650 723-2300

(P-22993)
LODI MEMORIAL HOSP ASSN INC
1235 W Vine St Ste 22, Lodi (95240-5144)
PHONE.................................209 334-8520
EMP: 62
SALES (corp-wide): 120.3MM **Privately Held**
SIC: 8099 Childbirth preparation clinic

PA: Lodi Memorial Hospital Association, Inc.
 975 S Fairmont Ave
 Lodi CA 95240
 209 334-3411

(P-22994)
LODI MEMORIAL HOSP ASSN INC
Also Called: Loda Mem Hosp Occpational Hlth
975 S Fairmont Ave Ste 8, Lodi (95240-5118)
PHONE.................................209 339-7441
EMP: 77
SALES (corp-wide): 120.3MM **Privately Held**
SIC: 8099 Childbirth preparation clinic
PA: Lodi Memorial Hospital Association, Inc.
 975 S Fairmont Ave
 Lodi CA 95240
 209 334-3411

(P-22995)
LOS ANGELES CNTY DEV SVC FNDTN
Also Called: FRANK D LANTERMAN REGIONAL CEN
3303 Wilshire Blvd # 700, Los Angeles (90010-4000)
PHONE.................................213 383-1300
Fax: 213 383-6526
Dianne Anand, *Exec Dir*
Maureen Wilson, *COO*
Frank Lanterman, *Bd of Directors*
Marjorie Heller, *Vice Pres*
John Walker, *Branch Mgr*
EMP: 180
SQ FT: 80,000
SALES: 135.4MM **Privately Held**
SIC: 8099 8322 8093 Medical services organization; individual & family services; mental health clinic, outpatient

(P-22996)
MARNA HEALTH SERVICES INC
Also Called: Sillcrest Nursing Home
4280 Cypress Dr, San Bernardino (92407-2960)
PHONE.................................909 882-2965
Fax: 909 886-2895
Maria Barrios, *CEO*
Napoleon Garcia, *Vice Pres*
EMP: 70
SQ FT: 120
SALES (est): 3.3MM **Privately Held**
SIC: 8099 7389 Blood related health services;

(P-22997)
MEDASEND BIOMEDICAL INC (PA)
1402 Daisy Ave, Long Beach (90813-1521)
PHONE.................................800 200-3581
Steve Grand, *CEO*
Stephanie Harrison, *Vice Pres*
EMP: 150
SQ FT: 10,000
SALES: 5MM **Privately Held**
SIC: 8099 4953 Health screening service; hazardous waste collection & disposal

(P-22998)
MEDISCAN DIAGNOSTIC SVCS LLC
Also Called: Mediscan Diagnostic Svcs Inc
21050 Califa St Ste 100, Woodland Hills (91367-5103)
PHONE.................................818 758-4224
Val Serebryany, *President*
EMP: 100
SALES (est): 4.4MM
SALES (corp-wide): 767.4MM **Publicly Held**
WEB: www.mediscan.net
SIC: 8099 Medical services organization
HQ: Mediscan Nursing Staffing, Llc
 21050 Califa Ste 100
 Woodland Hills CA 91367
 818 758-8680

(P-22999)
MERCY FOUNDATION NORTH
2625 Edith Ave Ste E, Redding (96001-3040)
PHONE.................................530 247-3424
Fax: 530 247-3418
Jeanine Hedman, *President*
Maggie Redmon, *General Mgr*
Sandy Dole, *Admin Sec*
Alisa Johnson, *Director*
EMP: 60
SALES: 2.4MM **Privately Held**
SIC: 8099 Medical services organization

(P-23000)
MILESTONE HOSPICE
1500 Crenshaw Blvd # 200, Torrance (90501-2400)
PHONE.................................310 782-1177
Fax: 310 782-1171
Harry Mc Namra, *CEO*
Minda Mc Namra, *Administration*
Ivette Carrillo, *Human Res Dir*
Minda McNamara, *Manager*
EMP: 120
SQ FT: 3,800
SALES: 14MM **Privately Held**
SIC: 8099 Medical services organization

(P-23001)
MOLINA HEALTHCARE INC
9275 Sky Park Ct Ste 400, San Diego (92123-4386)
PHONE.................................858 614-1580
Lisa Ferrari, *Manager*
Linda Dixon, *Engineer*
EMP: 129
SALES (corp-wide): 14.1B **Publicly Held**
SIC: 8099 Blood related health services
PA: Molina Healthcare, Inc.
 200 Oceangate Ste 100
 Long Beach CA 90802
 562 435-3666

(P-23002)
MORRISON MGT SPECIALISTS INC
Also Called: Morrison MGT Specialists
2823 Fresno St, Fresno (93721-1324)
PHONE.................................559 459-6449
EMP: 200
SALES (corp-wide): 27.3B **Privately Held**
SIC: 8099
HQ: Morrison Management Specialists, Inc.
 5801 Pachtree Dunwoody Rd
 Atlanta GA 30342

(P-23003)
NATIONAL ORGANIZATION OF
18663 Ventura Blvd, Tarzana (91356-4162)
PHONE.................................800 489-0210
Amonra Elohim, *President*
EMP: 150 EST: 1999
SALES (est): 9.3MM **Privately Held**
SIC: 8099 Blood related health services

(P-23004)
NEIGHBORHOOD HEALTHCARE
41840 Enterprise Cir N, Temecula (92590-5654)
PHONE.................................951 225-6400
Fax: 951 735-2842
EMP: 80
SALES (corp-wide): 45.1MM **Privately Held**
SIC: 8099 Childbirth preparation clinic
PA: Neighborhood Healthcare
 425 N Date St Ste 203
 Escondido CA 92025
 760 520-8372

(P-23005)
NEIGHBORHOOD HEALTHCARE
10039 Vine St Ste A, Lakeside (92040-3122)
PHONE.................................619 390-9975
Tracy Ream, *Branch Mgr*
EMP: 80
SALES (corp-wide): 45.1MM **Privately Held**
SIC: 8099 8011 Health screening service; clinic, operated by physicians

PA: Neighborhood Healthcare
 425 N Date St Ste 203
 Escondido CA 92025
 760 520-8372

(P-23006)
NEW MEDISCAN II LLC
Also Called: Mediscan, Inc.
21050 Califa St 100, Woodland Hills (91367-5103)
PHONE.................................818 462-0000
Val Serebryany, *President*
Jeff Geller, *Accountant*
EMP: 100
SQ FT: 7,500
SALES (est): 4.7MM
SALES (corp-wide): 767.4MM **Publicly Held**
WEB: www.mediscan.net
SIC: 8099 Medical services organization
HQ: Mediscan Nursing Staffing, Llc
 21050 Califa St Ste 100
 Woodland Hills CA 91367
 818 758-8680

(P-23007)
NORTHEAST VALLEY HEALTH CORP
7107 Remmet Ave, Canoga Park (91303-2016)
PHONE.................................818 340-3570
Gary Morris, *Branch Mgr*
EMP: 106
SALES (corp-wide): 78.3MM **Privately Held**
SIC: 8099 Blood related health services
PA: Northeast Valley Health Corp
 1172 N Maclay Ave
 San Fernando CA 91340
 818 898-1388

(P-23008)
NORTHEAST VALLEY HEALTH CORP
26974 Rainbow Glen Dr, Canyon Country (91351-4875)
PHONE.................................661 673-8888
EMP: 71
SALES (corp-wide): 78.3MM **Privately Held**
SIC: 8099 Childbirth preparation clinic
PA: Northeast Valley Health Corp
 1172 N Maclay Ave
 San Fernando CA 91340
 818 898-1388

(P-23009)
NORTHEAST VALLEY HEALTH CORP
7223 Fair Ave, Sun Valley (91352-4964)
PHONE.................................818 432-4400
Erin Wyner, *Family Practiti*
Veronica Yee, *Family Practiti*
EMP: 106
SALES (corp-wide): 78.3MM **Privately Held**
SIC: 8099 Childbirth preparation clinic
PA: Northeast Valley Health Corp
 1172 N Maclay Ave
 San Fernando CA 91340
 818 898-1388

(P-23010)
OCCUPNL URGNT CARE HLTH SYST
Also Called: Ouch Systems
750 Riverpoint Dr, West Sacramento (95605-1625)
PHONE.................................916 374-4600
James C Smith, *President*
Joseph Whitters, *CFO*
Dan Brunner, *Exec VP*
Melissa Cadwell, *Webmaster*
EMP: 380
SALES (est): 4.9MM **Privately Held**
WEB: www.ouchsystems.com
SIC: 8099 Medical services organization

(P-23011)
OCEANSIDE HLTHCARE STFFING INC
Also Called: R and R Prof Hlthcare Staffing
2216 El Camino Rela 211, Santa Clarita (91350)
PHONE.................................213 503-5649

PRODUCTS & SERVICES SECTION

8099 - Health & Allied Svcs, NEC County (P-23035)

Andy Gibbs, *President*
EMP: 140
SALES: 2.2MM **Privately Held**
SIC: 8099 Childbirth preparation clinic

(P-23012)
OMNI FAMILY HEALTH
277 E Front St, Buttonwillow (93206)
PHONE..................661 764-5211
Fax: 661 764-6311
Jagdeep Garewal, *Branch Mgr*
EMP: 59
SALES (corp-wide): 47.9MM **Privately Held**
SIC: 8099 Blood related health services
PA: Omni Family Health
4900 California Ave 400b
Bakersfield CA 93309
661 459-1900

(P-23013)
ONELEGACY (PA)
221 S Figueroa St Ste 500, Los Angeles (90012-2526)
PHONE..................213 625-0665
Thomas D Mone, *CEO*
Robert Mendez, *President*
Anita Corliss, *COO*
David Graft, *CFO*
Alan Cochran, *Vice Pres*
EMP: 60
SALES: 75.5MM **Privately Held**
SIC: 8099 Organ bank

(P-23014)
ONTARIO MONTCLAR SCH DIST FOOD
1525 S Bon View Ave, Ontario (91761-4408)
PHONE..................909 930-6360
James Hammon, *Principal*
Sara Maragni, *Director*
EMP: 120
SALES (est): 3.6MM **Privately Held**
SIC: 8099 Nutrition services

(P-23015)
PALOMAR HEALTH
Also Called: Patient Business Services
555 E Valley Pkwy 6, Escondido (92025-3048)
PHONE..................858 675-5360
Laurie Rose, *Manager*
Steven Tolliver, *Admin Asst*
Dennis Dechant, *Administration*
Nancy Ventura, *MIS Dir*
Tammy Chung, *Marketing Staff*
EMP: 300
SALES (corp-wide): 614.2MM **Privately Held**
WEB: www.sunbridge.com
SIC: 8099 Blood related health services
PA: Palomar Health
456 E Grand Ave
Escondido CA 92025
442 281-5000

(P-23016)
PANCREATIC CANCR ACTN NETWRK I (PA)
Also Called: Pancan
1500 Rosecrans Ave # 200, Manhattan Beach (90266-3763)
PHONE..................310 725-0025
Fax: 310 725-0029
Julie Fleshman, *President*
Jeanne Weaver Ruesch, *Ch of Bd*
Abigail Winston, *CFO*
Megan Gordon Don, *Vice Pres*
Tak Fujii, *Vice Pres*
EMP: 90
SALES: 22MM **Privately Held**
WEB: www.pancan.com
SIC: 8099 8399 Medical services organization; social service information exchange

(P-23017)
PATHWAYS HOME HEALTH
395 Oyster Point Blvd # 128, South San Francisco (94080-1928)
PHONE..................650 634-0133
Fax: 650 871-0991
Mary Dias, *Manager*
EMP: 50

SALES (est): 264.7K **Privately Held**
SIC: 8099 Health & allied services

(P-23018)
PERMANENTE KAISER INTL
10990 San Dego Mission Rd, San Diego (92108-2417)
PHONE..................619 641-4300
EMP: 342
SALES (corp-wide): 380.5MM **Privately Held**
SIC: 8099 Childbirth preparation clinic
PA: Kaiser Permanente International
1 Kaiser Plz
Oakland CA 94612
510 271-5910

(P-23019)
PERMANENTE MEDICAL GROUP INC (DH)
1950 Franklin St Fl 18th, Oakland (94612-5118)
PHONE..................866 858-2226
Robert M Pearl, *CEO*
Gerard C Bajada, *CFO*
Christopher J Palkowski, *Chairman*
Judy D Lively, *Treasurer*
Pat Conolly, *Exec Dir*
EMP: 500
SQ FT: 10,000
SALES (est): 692.8MM
SALES (corp-wide): 27.8B **Privately Held**
WEB: www.permanente.net
SIC: 8099 Medical services organization
HQ: Kaiser Foundation Hospitals Inc
1 Kaiser Plz
Oakland CA 94612
510 271-6611

(P-23020)
PIONEER MEDICAL GROUP INC
16510 Bloomfield Ave, Cerritos (90703-2115)
PHONE..................562 229-0902
Tanya Lee-Jordan, *Manager*
Marilyn Kamerer, *Human Res Mgr*
EMP: 84
SALES (corp-wide): 39.7MM **Privately Held**
SIC: 8099 Blood related health services
PA: Pioneer Medical Group, Inc.
17777 Center Court Dr N # 400
Cerritos CA 90703
562 597-4181

(P-23021)
PIT RIVER HEALTH SERVICE INC (PA)
36977 Park Ave, Burney (96013-4067)
PHONE..................530 335-5090
Fax: 530 335-5241
Inder Wadhwa, *Administration*
Jeremy Wheeler, *General Mgr*
Randy Brazelton, *Administration*
Diane Jordan, *Manager*
EMP: 51
SALES: 5.6MM **Privately Held**
SIC: 8099 Medical services organization

(P-23022)
PLASMA COLLECTION CENTERS INC
2410 Lillyvale Ave, Los Angeles (90032-3514)
PHONE..................323 441-7720
David Bell, *Ch of Bd*
Shinji Wada, *President*
Harry Knapp, *Asst Treas*
EMP: 200
SALES (est): 16.6MM **Privately Held**
SIC: 8099 Blood related health services

(P-23023)
PPONEXT INC
1501 Hughes Way Ste 400, Long Beach (90810-1881)
PHONE..................888 446-6098
Barbara E Rodin PHD, *President*
EMP: 300 **EST:** 1999
SALES (est): 2.6MM
SALES (corp-wide): 3.7B **Publicly Held**
WEB: www.pponext.com
SIC: 8099 Medical services organization

HQ: Beech Street Corporation
25500 Commercentre Dr # 100
Lake Forest CA 92630
949 672-1000

(P-23024)
PROVIDENCE HEALTH & SERVICES
Also Called: Diabetes Care Center
18321 Clark St, Tarzana (91356-3501)
PHONE..................818 881-0800
EMP: 52
SALES (corp-wide): 10.1B **Privately Held**
SIC: 8099 8011 Medical services organization; clinic, operated by physicians
PA: Providence Health & Services
1801 Lind Ave Sw
Renton WA 98057
425 525-3355

(P-23025)
PROVIDENCE HEALTH & SERVICES
13355 Hawthorne Blvd, Hawthorne (90250-5802)
PHONE..................310 355-0100
Fax: 310 355-0110
EMP: 87
SALES (corp-wide): 10.1B **Privately Held**
SIC: 8099 Childbirth preparation clinic
PA: Providence Health & Services
1801 Lind Ave Sw
Renton WA 98057
425 525-3355

(P-23026)
PROVIDENCE HEALTH & SERVICES
2601 W Alameda Ave # 212, Burbank (91505-4800)
PHONE..................818 841-0112
EMP: 156
SALES (corp-wide): 10.1B **Privately Held**
SIC: 8099 Childbirth preparation clinic
PA: Providence Health & Services
1801 Lind Ave Sw
Renton WA 98057
425 525-3355

(P-23027)
PROVIDENCE HEALTH & SERVICES
21501 Avalon Blvd, Carson (90745-2201)
PHONE..................310 835-6627
EMP: 52
SALES (corp-wide): 10.1B **Privately Held**
SIC: 8099 Childbirth preparation clinic
PA: Providence Health & Services
1801 Lind Ave Sw
Renton WA 98057
425 525-3355

(P-23028)
PROVIDENCE HEALTH & SERVICES
21311 Madrona Ave, Torrance (90503-5970)
PHONE..................310 540-1334
EMP: 156
SALES (corp-wide): 10.1B **Privately Held**
SIC: 8099 Childbirth preparation clinic
PA: Providence Health & Services
1801 Lind Ave Sw
Renton WA 98057
425 525-3355

(P-23029)
PROVIDENCE HEALTH & SERVICES
4314 W Slauson Ave, Los Angeles (90043-2808)
PHONE..................323 298-2530
EMP: 139
SALES (corp-wide): 10.1B **Privately Held**
SIC: 8099 Blood related health services
PA: Providence Health & Services
1801 Lind Ave Sw
Renton WA 98057
425 525-3355

(P-23030)
PROVIDENCE HEALTH & SERVICES
Also Called: Little Company of Mary
20929 Hawthorne Blvd, Torrance (90503-4611)
PHONE..................310 937-1980
Christine Vandoren, *Purchasing*
Lucas I Nishioka, *Radiology*
Andy Hoover, *Manager*
EMP: 243
SALES (corp-wide): 10.1B **Privately Held**
SIC: 8099 Childbirth preparation clinic
PA: Providence Health & Services
1801 Lind Ave Sw
Renton WA 98057
425 525-3355

(P-23031)
PUBLIC HEALTH INSTITUTE
1825 Bell St Ste 203, Sacramento (95825-1020)
PHONE..................916 285-1231
Arti Parikhpatel, *Branch Mgr*
EMP: 210
SALES (corp-wide): 106.7MM **Privately Held**
SIC: 8099 Blood related health services
PA: Public Health Institute
555 12th St Ste 1050
Oakland CA 94607
510 285-5500

(P-23032)
PUBLIC HLTH FNDATION ENTPS INC
12781 Schabarum Ave, Irwindale (91706-6807)
PHONE..................626 856-6600
Fax: 626 856-6631
Eloise Jenks, *Branch Mgr*
Kiran Saluja, *Principal*
Joseph Tessier, *Admin Asst*
Mike Whaley, *Info Tech Dir*
Claudia Bustillos, *Purch Agent*
EMP: 129
SALES (corp-wide): 97.5MM **Privately Held**
SIC: 8099 Blood related health services
PA: Public Health Foundation Enterprises, Inc.
12801 Crossrds Pkwy S 200
City Of Industry CA 91746
562 692-4643

(P-23033)
PUBLIC HLTH FNDATION ENTPS INC
3648 E Olympic Blvd, Los Angeles (90023-3129)
PHONE..................323 261-6388
EMP: 172
SALES (corp-wide): 97.5MM **Privately Held**
SIC: 8099 Blood related health services
PA: Public Health Foundation Enterprises, Inc.
12801 Crossrds Pkwy S 200
City Of Industry CA 91746
562 692-4643

(P-23034)
PUBLIC HLTH FNDATION ENTPS INC
8666 Whittier Blvd, Pico Rivera (90660-2655)
PHONE..................562 801-2323
Nicolle Fevere, *Principal*
EMP: 129
SALES (corp-wide): 97.5MM **Privately Held**
SIC: 8099 Blood related health services
PA: Public Health Foundation Enterprises, Inc.
12801 Crossrds Pkwy S 200
City Of Industry CA 91746
562 692-4643

(P-23035)
PUBLIC HLTH FNDATION ENTPS INC
1649 W Washington Blvd, Los Angeles (90007-1116)
PHONE..................323 733-9381
Eloise Jenks, *President*

EMP: 172
SALES (corp-wide): 97.5MM Privately Held
SIC: 8099 Blood related health services
PA: Public Health Foundation Enterprises, Inc.
    12801 Crossrds Pkwy S 200
    City Of Industry CA 91746
    562 692-4643

(P-23036)
PUBLIC HLTH FNDATION ENTPS INC
125 E Anaheim St, Wilmington (90744-4590)
PHONE.....................310 518-2835
EMP: 86
SALES (corp-wide): 97.5MM Privately Held
SIC: 8099 Blood related health services
PA: Public Health Foundation Enterprises, Inc.
    12801 Crossrds Pkwy S 200
    City Of Industry CA 91746
    562 692-4643

(P-23037)
PUBLIC HLTH FNDATION ENTPS INC
Also Called: Wic
12781 Shama Rd, El Monte (91732)
PHONE.....................626 856-6618
Juan Chong, Branch Mgr
EMP: 215
SALES (corp-wide): 97.5MM Privately Held
SIC: 8099 Blood related health services
PA: Public Health Foundation Enterprises, Inc.
    12801 Crossrds Pkwy S 200
    City Of Industry CA 91746
    562 692-4643

(P-23038)
QTC MANAGEMENT INC (HQ)
Also Called: Q T C
21700 Copley Dr Ste 200, Diamond Bar (91765-2219)
P.O. Box 5679 (91765-7679)
PHONE.....................909 396-6902
Stephanie Hill, CEO
Darryl Pegram, Office Mgr
Francisco Vasquez, QA Dir
Chris Mu, Engineer
Gordon Burgess, Manager
▼ EMP: 160
SQ FT: 20,000
SALES (est): 215.2K
SALES (corp-wide): 5B Publicly Held
SIC: 8099 Medical services organization
PA: Leidos Holdings, Inc.
    11951 Freedom Dr Ste 500
    Reston VA 20190
    571 526-6000

(P-23039)
REDDING RANCHERIA
Also Called: Ihs
1441 Liberty St, Redding (96001-0811)
PHONE.....................530 224-2700
Fax: 530 224-2738
Ron Sissan, Director
Doug Dawson, Pharmacist
Francine Hutchins, Pharmacist
Davis Radley, Manager
EMP: 65
SALES (corp-wide): 40MM Privately Held
WEB: www.redding-rancheria.com
SIC: 8099 Medical services organization
PA: Redding Rancheria
    2000 Redding Rancheria Rd
    Redding CA 96001
    530 225-8979

(P-23040)
RELIANT IMMEDIATE CARE
9601 S Sepulveda Blvd, Los Angeles (90045-5203)
PHONE.....................310 215-6020
Max Franklin Lebow, President
Gene Howell, Exec Dir
EMP: 55
SQ FT: 24,000
SALES (est): 4.6MM Privately Held
SIC: 8099 Medical services organization

(P-23041)
RESCUE MISSION ALLIANCE
125 S Harrison Ave, Oxnard (93030-6038)
PHONE.....................805 201-4341
Carol Roberg, Principal
Dave Chittenden, Vice Pres
Joe Thomas, Info Tech Mgr
Kathy Button, Project Mgr
Cassie Sorenson, Director
EMP: 56
SALES (est): 1.4MM
SALES (corp-wide): 24.8MM Privately Held
WEB: www.erescuemission.com
SIC: 8099 Health & allied services
PA: Rescue Mission Alliance
    315 N A St
    Oxnard CA 93030
    805 487-1234

(P-23042)
SAINT AGNES MED PROVIDERS INC
1105 E Spruce Ave Ste 201, Fresno (93720-3313)
PHONE.....................559 450-7200
Stephen Soldo, CEO
EMP: 100
SALES (est): 5.6MM Privately Held
SIC: 8099 8011 Childbirth preparation clinic

(P-23043)
SAINT-JOSEPH HOME HEALTH
1525 Mccarthy Blvd # 208, Milpitas (95035-7452)
PHONE.....................408 244-5488
Daryl Velasco, Principal
EMP: 50
SALES (est): 1.6MM Privately Held
SIC: 8099 Medical services organization

(P-23044)
SALINAS MED MNGT SRVCS ORG INC
Also Called: Salinas Valley Prime Care Med
355 Abbott St Ste 100, Salinas (93901-4484)
PHONE.....................831 751-7070
Gerald W Oehler, President
Glen Yoneda, Treasurer
Robert Patton, Vice Pres
Warren S Nishimoto, Family Practiti
Joanna T Oppenheim, Family Practiti
EMP: 70 EST: 1997
SQ FT: 6,612
SALES (est): 3.3MM Privately Held
SIC: 8099 Medical services organization

(P-23045)
SAN BERNARDINO CITY UNF SCHOOL
Also Called: Child Nutrition Center
1257 Northpark Blvd, San Bernardino (92407-2946)
PHONE.....................909 881-8000
Fax: 909 881-8016
Adrian Robles, Branch Mgr
EMP: 65
SALES (corp-wide): 331.5MM Privately Held
WEB: www.sbcusd.k12.ca.us
SIC: 8099 8211 Nutrition services; elementary school
PA: San Bernardino City Unified School District
    777 N F St
    San Bernardino CA 92410
    909 381-1100

(P-23046)
SAN DIEGO BLOOD BANK (PA)
Also Called: San Diego Blood Bnk Foundation
3636 Gtwy Ctr Ave Ste 100, San Diego (92102-4508)
PHONE.....................619 296-6393
Fax: 619 220-8416
Ramona Walker, CEO
Doug Morton, COO
Mark Insley, CFO
Jennifer Long, CFO
Marge Lorang, Bd of Directors
▲ EMP: 160
SQ FT: 132,000
SALES: 39MM Privately Held
SIC: 8099 8071 Blood bank; medical laboratories

(P-23047)
SAN DIEGO BLOOD BANK
776 Arnele Ave, El Cajon (92020-2502)
PHONE.....................619 441-1804
Ramona Walker, Branch Mgr
Barbara Davies, Manager
EMP: 205
SALES (corp-wide): 39MM Privately Held
SIC: 8099 Blood bank
PA: San Diego Blood Bank
    3636 Gtwy Ctr Ave Ste 100
    San Diego CA 92102
    619 296-6393

(P-23048)
SAN DIEGO COASTL MED GROUP INC
2201 Mission Ave, Oceanside (92058-2313)
PHONE.....................760 901-5259
Meredith Acosta, Principal
Mary Beth Casement, Pediatrics
Barry H Goldberg, Pediatrics
David C Herz, Pediatrics
Trieva K Scanlan, Pediatrics
EMP: 216
SALES (est): 1.4MM
SALES (corp-wide): 1.7B Privately Held
SIC: 8099 Health & allied services
PA: Scripps Health
    4275 Campus Point Ct
    San Diego CA 92121
    858 678-7000

(P-23049)
SAN FRNCSCO CONSERVATION CORPS
102 Fort Mason, San Francisco (94123-1306)
PHONE.....................415 928-7417
EMP: 263
SALES (corp-wide): 5.1MM Privately Held
SIC: 8099 Childbirth preparation clinic
PA: San Francisco Conservation Corps Inc
    5 Thomas Mellon Cir # 248
    San Francisco CA 94134
    415 928-7322

(P-23050)
SAN MATEO HEALTH COMMISSION
Also Called: Health Plan of San Mateo
701 Gateway Blvd, South San Francisco (94080-7009)
PHONE.....................650 616-0050
Fax: 650 616-0060
Maya Altman, CEO
Craig Kellar, COO
Ron Robinson, CFO
Barrie Cheung, Pharmacy Dir
Khoa Nguyen, Business Dir
EMP: 211
SQ FT: 58,758
SALES (est): 21.2MM Privately Held
WEB: www.hpsm.org
SIC: 8099 Physical examination service, insurance

(P-23051)
SAN PBLO HLTHCARE WELLNESS CTR
13328 San Pablo Ave, San Pablo (94806-3902)
PHONE.....................510 235-3720
Suzette Cheatham, Principal
EMP: 130
SALES (est): 7.5MM Privately Held
SIC: 8099 Health screening service

(P-23052)
SANTA ANA UNIFIED SCHOOL DST
Also Called: Nutririon Services
1749 Carnegie Ave, Santa Ana (92705-5525)
PHONE.....................714 431-1900
Fax: 714 431-1999
Mark Chavez, Director
EMP: 100

SQ FT: 30,295
SALES (corp-wide): 9.6MM Privately Held
WEB: www.santaanaeducation.com
SIC: 8099 Nutrition services
PA: Santa Ana Unified School District
    1601 E Chestnut Ave
    Santa Ana CA 92701
    714 558-5501

(P-23053)
SANTA BARBARA COUNTY OF
Also Called: Public Health Dept
345 Camino Del Remedio, Santa Barbara (93110-1332)
PHONE.....................805 681-5100
Tekashi Wada, Director
EMP: 60 Privately Held
WEB: www.sbcountyhr.org
SIC: 8099 9431 Medical services organization; administration of public health programs;
PA: County Of Santa Barbara
    105 E Anapamu St Rm 406
    Santa Barbara CA 93101
    805 568-3400

(P-23054)
SANTA CLARA VALLEY MEDICAL CTR
2220 Moorpark Ave, San Jose (95128-2613)
PHONE.....................408 885-5730
EMP: 772 Privately Held
SIC: 8099 Childbirth preparation clinic
PA: Santa Clara Valley Medical Center
    751 S Bascom Ave
    San Jose CA 95128

(P-23055)
SCRIPPS HEALTH
7565 Mission Valley Rd # 200, San Diego (92108-4431)
PHONE.....................619 245-2350
Fax: 619 245-2353
Sevil Brahme, Branch Mgr
EMP: 378
SALES (corp-wide): 1.7B Privately Held
SIC: 8099 Blood related health services
PA: Scripps Health
    4275 Campus Point Ct
    San Diego CA 92121
    858 678-7000

(P-23056)
SEA VIEW MEDICAL GROUP INC
1901 Solar Dr Ste 265, Oxnard (93036-2692)
PHONE.....................805 373-5781
Fax: 805 988-2284
Dr Gary Prossfett, Director
Dr Yacoob Mall, Treasurer
Dr Richard Brand, Admin Sec
Robin Granholm, Accountant
EMP: 80
SQ FT: 6,000
SALES (est): 1.7MM
SALES (corp-wide): 190.8B Publicly Held
WEB: www.hserve.com
SIC: 8099 Medical services organization
HQ: Med3000 Group, Inc.
    680 Andersen Dr Foster Pl
    Pittsburgh PA 15220
    412 937-8887

(P-23057)
SIERRA VISTA FAMILY MEDICAL
1227 E Los Angeles Ave, Simi Valley (93065-2871)
PHONE.....................805 582-4000
EMP: 80 EST: 2009
SALES (est): 2.6MM Privately Held
SIC: 8099

(P-23058)
SIGNET ARMORLITE INC (DH)
5803 Newton Dr Ste A, Carlsbad (92008-7380)
P.O. Box 3309, Carol Stream IL (60132-3309)
PHONE.....................760 744-4000
Fax: 760 471-1405
Brad Staley, President

PRODUCTS & SERVICES SECTION

8111 - Legal Svcs County (P-23081)

Bruno Salvadori, *Ch of Bd*
Lauri Crawford, *Exec VP*
Edward P Derosa, *Exec VP*
M Kathryn Bernard, *Vice Pres*
▲ **EMP:** 400 **EST:** 1969
SQ FT: 138,000
SALES: 76MM
SALES (corp-wide): 88.1MM Privately Held
WEB: www.signetarmorlite.com
SIC: 8099 Eye banks
HQ: Essilor Of America, Inc.
13555 N Stemmons Fwy
Dallas TX 75234
214 496-4000

(P-23059)
SOBALIVING LLC
22669 Pacific Coast Hwy, Malibu (90265-5036)
PHONE 800 595-3803
Gregory Hannley, *President*
EMP: 50
SALES (est): 3.7MM Privately Held
SIC: 8099 Health & allied services

(P-23060)
SOUTH CNTY CMNTY HLTH CTR INC (PA)
Also Called: Ravenswood Family Health
1885 Bay Rd, East Palo Alto (94303-1312)
PHONE 650 330-7407
Wayne Yost, *CFO*
Lisa Chamberlain, *Bd of Directors*
Kathleen Alexander, *Comms Dir*
Luisa Buada, *Exec Dir*
Rhonda McClinton-Brown, *Exec Dir*
EMP: 70
SALES: 31.4MM Privately Held
SIC: 8099 Medical services organization

(P-23061)
SOUTHERN CAL PRMNNTE MED GROUP
Also Called: Kaiser Permanente
9353 Imperial Hwy, Downey (90242-2812)
PHONE 562 657-2200
Jim Branchick, *COO*
Swayne A Cofield, *Family Practiti*
Kymberly M Franklin, *Family Practiti*
Jose L Goncalves, *Family Practiti*
Melody R Padilla, *Family Practiti*
EMP: 1397
SALES (corp-wide): 3.2B Privately Held
SIC: 8099 Blood related health services
PA: Southern California Permanente Medical Group
393 Walnut Dr
Pasadena CA 91107
626 405-5704

(P-23062)
SOUTHERN CAL PRMNNTE MED GROUP
23781 Maquina, Mission Viejo (92691-2716)
PHONE 949 376-8619
EMP: 1397
SALES (corp-wide): 3.2B Privately Held
SIC: 8099 Blood related health services
PA: Southern California Permanente Medical Group
393 Walnut Dr
Pasadena CA 91107
626 405-5704

(P-23063)
ST JOHNS HEALTH CENTER
2121 Santa Monica Blvd, Santa Monica (90404-2303)
P.O. Box 34562, Los Angeles (90034-0562)
PHONE 310 829-5511
Fax: 310 449-5229
A A Cumming, *Principal*
Bob O Klein, *Vice Pres*
Tseten Phanucharas, *Lab Dir*
Martha Ponce, *CIO*
Eduardo A Verruno, *Anesthesiology*
EMP: 75
SALES (est): 12.1MM Privately Held
SIC: 8099 Health screening service

(P-23064)
STAR OF CALIFORNIA
299 W Hillcrest Dr, Thousand Oaks (91360-4264)
PHONE 805 379-1401
Doug Moes, *Branch Mgr*
Keegan Tangeman, *Director*
Kristina Utecht, *Manager*
EMP: 56
SALES (corp-wide): 4.8MM Privately Held
SIC: 8099 Medical services organization
PA: Star Of California, A Professional Psychological Corporation
4880 Market St
Ventura CA 93003
805 644-7823

(P-23065)
STAR OF CALIFORNIA (PA)
4880 Market St, Ventura (93003-7783)
PHONE 805 644-7823
Doug Moes, *President*
Doug Wright, *CFO*
Jodi Turner, *Opers Mgr*
EMP: 110
SQ FT: 6,640
SALES (est): 4.8MM Privately Held
SIC: 8099 Medical services organization

(P-23066)
SUPERIOR MOBILE MEDICS INC
7480 Mission Valley Rd # 101, San Diego (92108-4433)
P.O. Box 639014 (92163-9014)
PHONE 619 299-3926
Joseph Gaudio, *CEO*
Kevin Sanders, *President*
Georgia K Allen, *Vice Pres*
Christina Paterniti, *Vice Pres*
Meg Rose, *Vice Pres*
EMP: 100
SQ FT: 1,800
SALES (est): 12MM Privately Held
WEB: www.supermedics.com
SIC: 8099 Physical examination service, insurance

(P-23067)
SUTTER HEALTH
Also Called: Sutter Med Group of Redwoods
510 Doyle Park Dr, Santa Rosa (95405-4570)
PHONE 707 526-1800
Norma Driscoll Johns, *Branch Mgr*
EMP: 280
SALES (corp-wide): 11B Privately Held
SIC: 8099 Blood related health services
PA: Sutter Health
2200 River Plaza Dr
Sacramento CA 95833
916 733-8800

(P-23068)
SUTTER HEALTH
1335 S Fairmont Ave, Lodi (95240-5520)
PHONE 209 366-2007
EMP: 93
SALES (corp-wide): 11B Privately Held
SIC: 8099 Childbirth preparation clinic
PA: Sutter Health
2200 River Plaza Dr
Sacramento CA 95833
916 733-8800

(P-23069)
SUTTER HEALTH
3 Medical Plaza Dr, Roseville (95661-3087)
PHONE 916 797-4715
David Sox, *Med Doctor*
EMP: 140
SALES (corp-wide): 11B Privately Held
SIC: 8099 Childbirth preparation clinic
PA: Sutter Health
2200 River Plaza Dr
Sacramento CA 95833
916 733-8800

(P-23070)
SUTTER HEALTH
2880 Gateway Oaks Dr # 220, Sacramento (95833-4332)
PHONE 916 566-4819
Vicki Flemming, *Branch Mgr*
Kristin Maxim, *Project Mgr*
Kristi Ford, *Sales Staff*
Amanda Peterson, *Sr Project Mgr*
Troy Franklin, *Manager*
EMP: 233
SALES (corp-wide): 11B Privately Held
SIC: 8099 Blood related health services
PA: Sutter Health
2200 River Plaza Dr
Sacramento CA 95833
916 733-8800

(P-23071)
SUTTER HEALTH
100 Rowland Way Ste 210, Novato (94945-5041)
PHONE 415 897-8495
Vicki Del, *Branch Mgr*
Eric Siegel, *Nurse*
EMP: 93
SALES (corp-wide): 11B Privately Held
SIC: 8099 Blood related health services
PA: Sutter Health
2200 River Plaza Dr
Sacramento CA 95833
916 733-8800

(P-23072)
SUTTER HLTH SCRMNTO SIERRA REG
701 Howe Ave Ste F20, Sacramento (95825-4681)
PHONE 916 733-7080
Mary Ashuckian, *Branch Mgr*
Samuel Warnke, *Admin Asst*
Barbara Berry, *Manager*
EMP: 1265
SALES (corp-wide): 11B Privately Held
SIC: 8099 Blood related health services
HQ: Sutter Health Sacramento Sierra Region
2200 River Plaza Dr
Sacramento CA 95833
916 733-8800

(P-23073)
SUTTER HLTH SCRMNTO SIERRA REG
Also Called: Sutter Medical Center
2800 L St, Sacramento (95816-5616)
P.O. Box 160727 (95816-0727)
PHONE 916 733-3095
Sarah Krevans, *Branch Mgr*
Gary Zufelt, *COO*
Sandra Hansen, *Info Tech Mgr*
Mike Boyce, *Chief Engr*
Darryl Fenley, *Accounting Mgr*
EMP: 2500
SALES (corp-wide): 11B Privately Held
SIC: 8099 Health screening service
HQ: Sutter Health Sacramento Sierra Region
2200 River Plaza Dr
Sacramento CA 95833
916 733-8800

(P-23074)
TENDERLOIN HOUSING CLINIC INC
472 Turk St, San Francisco (94102-3330)
PHONE 415 771-2427
Fax: 415 921-8691
Randall Shaw, *Branch Mgr*
Colleen Carrigan, *Sales Dir*
EMP: 226
SALES (corp-wide): 28.3MM Privately Held
SIC: 8099 Blood related health services
PA: Tenderloin Housing Clinic, Inc.
126 Hyde St
San Francisco CA 94102
415 771-9850

(P-23075)
TRIANIM HEALTH SERVICES INC
27201 Tourney Rd Ste 115, Valencia (91355-1801)
PHONE 818 362-6882
Fax: 818 362-8681
Gary Winkler, *Buyer*
Tom Sampson, *Vice Pres*
Kelly Hoey, *Credit Staff*
Karen Hickman, *Buyer*
Todd Anderson, *Regl Sales Mgr*
EMP: 58

SALES (est): 4.1MM Privately Held
SIC: 8099 Health & allied services

(P-23076)
UCSD HEALTHCARE
355 Dickinson St 340, San Diego (92103-2075)
P.O. Box 33268 (92163-3268)
PHONE 858 657-7105
Stephen Crawford, *Principal*
EMP: 92
SALES (est): 11.4MM Privately Held
SIC: 8099 Health & allied services

(P-23077)
UNIFIED INV PROGRAMS INC (PA)
Also Called: Palm Grove Health Care
2368 Torrance Blvd # 200, Torrance (90501-2500)
PHONE 310 782-1878
Cynthia Schein, *Owner*
Emmanuel B David, *President*
EMP: 50
SALES (est): 3.1MM Privately Held
SIC: 8099 8051 Medical services organization; skilled nursing care facilities

(P-23078)
UNIVERSITY CAL IRVINE MED CENT
208 Giotto, Irvine (92614-8573)
PHONE 714 456-5678
Glenn Levine, *Principal*
Toshi Nakamura, *Administration*
Hans Wunsch, *Administration*
William McIlvaine, *Database Admin*
Jamie Anand, *Project Mgr*
EMP: 269
SALES (est): 11.8MM Privately Held
SIC: 8099 Health & allied services

8111 Legal Svcs

(P-23079)
AARON DOWLING INCORPORATED
8080 N Palm Ave Ste 300, Fresno (93711-5797)
P.O. Box 28902 (93729-8902)
PHONE 559 432-4500
Fax: 559 432-4590
Larry B Lindenau, *CEO*
Stephanie Borchers, *Shareholder*
Donald Fischbach, *Shareholder*
Kevin Grant, *Shareholder*
Kenton J Klassen, *Shareholder*
EMP: 80
SQ FT: 16,000
SALES (est): 14.7MM Privately Held
SIC: 8111 Corporate, partnership & business law

(P-23080)
ABRAMS KAZAN MCCLAIN
171 12th St Ste 300, Oakland (94607-4911)
PHONE 510 465-7728
Fax: 510 835-4913
Steven Kazan, *President*
Denise Abrams, *Vice Pres*
Victoria Edises, *Vice Pres*
Simona A Farrise, *Vice Pres*
Frank Fernandez, *Vice Pres*
EMP: 108
SQ FT: 13,500
SALES (est): 11.3MM Privately Held
SIC: 8111 General practice law office

(P-23081)
ADELSON TESTAN BRUNDO NOVEL (PA)
31330 Oak Crest Dr, Westlake Village (91361-4632)
PHONE 805 367-5663
Steven Testan, *President*
Christine King, *President*
Lilly Shyu, *CFO*
Judy Robertson, *Executive Asst*
Bryan Montalbon, *Info Tech Dir*
EMP: 50
SQ FT: 17,900

8111 - Legal Svcs County (P-23082)   PRODUDUCTS & SERVICES SECTION

SALES (est): 65.2MM Privately Held
SIC: 8111 Legal services

(P-23082)
ADVANCED DISCOVERY INC
350 Sansome St Ste 510, San Francisco
(94104-1349)
PHONE...................................866 342-3282
Cortney Johnson, *Sales Mgr*
Meggan Capps, *President*
Alex Borosage, *Vice Pres*
Andrew Stone, *Vice Pres*
Barry Boudinot, *Manager*
EMP: 150 EST: 2008
SALES (est): 33MM
SALES (corp-wide): 42.2MM Privately Held
SIC: 8111 Legal services
PA: Advanced Discovery Inc.
　　13915 N Mo Pac Expy # 210
　　Austin TX 78728
　　512 828-6558

(P-23083)
AKIN GUMP STRAUSS
2029 Century Park E # 2400, Los Angeles
(90067-3010)
PHONE...................................310 229-1000
Fax: 310 728-2209
David Allen, *Managing Prtnr*
Sharon Parker, *CFO*
Eric Kurtz, *Info Tech Mgr*
Lorna Vartanian, *VP Finance*
Joyce Chambless, *Accounting Mgr*
EMP: 100
SALES (corp-wide): 343.9MM Privately Held
WEB: www.akingump.com
SIC: 8111 General practice law office
PA: Akin, Gump, Strauss, Hauer, & Feld Llp
　　1333 New Hampshire Ave Nw
　　Washington DC 20036
　　202 887-4000

(P-23084)
AKIN GUMP STRAUSS
580 California St # 1500, San Francisco
(94104-1036)
PHONE...................................415 765-9500
Karen Kubin, *Branch Mgr*
EMP: 131
SALES (corp-wide): 343.9MM Privately Held
WEB: www.akingump.net
SIC: 8111 Administrative & government law
PA: Akin, Gump, Strauss, Hauer, & Feld Llp
　　1333 New Hampshire Ave Nw
　　Washington DC 20036
　　202 887-4000

(P-23085)
ALDRIDGE PITE LLP
4375 Jutland Dr Ste 200, San Diego
(92117-3600)
P.O. Box 17935 (92177-7923)
PHONE...................................858 750-7700
Greg Boumpani, *Administration*
Arnold Graff, *Associate*
EMP: 145
SALES (corp-wide): 46.4MM Privately Held
SIC: 8111 Real estate law
PA: Aldridge Pite Llp
　　3575 Piedmont Rd Ne 15-500
　　Atlanta GA 30305
　　404 994-7400

(P-23086)
ALLEN MATKINS LECK GMBLE
3 Embarcadero Ctr Fl 12, San Francisco
(94111-4015)
PHONE...................................415 837-1515
Fax: 415 837-1516
Richard C Mallory, *Partner*
Jerry Neuman, *Partner*
Mary Cain, *Associate*
Bryan Hawkins, *Associate*
EMP: 80
SALES (corp-wide): 77.6MM Privately Held
WEB: www.allenmatkins.com
SIC: 8111 Real estate law
PA: Allen Matkins Leck Gamble Mallory & Natsis Llp
　　515 S Figueroa St Fl 9
　　Los Angeles CA 90071
　　213 622-5555

(P-23087)
ALLEN MATKINS LECK GMBLE
1900 Main St Fl 5, Irvine (92614-7321)
PHONE...................................949 553-1313
Fax: 714 553-8354
Drew Emmel, *Senior Partner*
Erin Murphy, *Receiver*
Gabrielle Fischer, *Office Admin*
Frank Gillman, *CTO*
Eileen Nottoli, *Instructor*
EMP: 100
SALES (corp-wide): 77.6MM Privately Held
WEB: www.allenmatkins.com
SIC: 8111 Legal services
PA: Allen Matkins Leck Gamble Mallory & Natsis Llp
　　515 S Figueroa St Fl 9
　　Los Angeles CA 90071
　　213 622-5555

(P-23088)
ALLEN MATKINS LECK GMBLE (PA)
515 S Figueroa St Fl 9, Los Angeles
(90071-3301)
PHONE...................................213 622-5555
Fax: 213 620-8816
Frederick L Allen, *Partner*
Keith Paul Bishop, *Partner*
Raymond M Buddie, *Partner*
Jeffrey Chine, *Partner*
John C Condas, *Partner*
EMP: 130
SQ FT: 40,000
SALES (est): 77.6MM Privately Held
WEB: www.allenmatkins.com
SIC: 8111 Legal services; labor & employment law; corporate, partnership & business law; real estate law

(P-23089)
ALSTON & BIRD LLP
333 S Hope St Ste 1600, Los Angeles
(90071-1410)
PHONE...................................213 626-8830
Wayne Mitchell, *Branch Mgr*
Kathleen Hill, *Plan/Corp Dev D*
Cynthia Ambriz, *Admin Sec*
Charles Ostrowski, *Info Tech Mgr*
William B Anaya, *Counsel*
EMP: 165
SALES (corp-wide): 324.5MM Privately Held
SIC: 8111 General practice attorney, lawyer
PA: Alston & Bird Llp
　　1201 W Peachtree St Ne # 4000
　　Atlanta GA 30309
　　404 881-7654

(P-23090)
ALSTON & BIRD LLP
2815 Townsgate Rd Ste 200, Westlake Village (91361-3091)
PHONE...................................202 239-3673
Michael D Bradbury, *Principal*
EMP: 294
SALES (corp-wide): 324.5MM Privately Held
SIC: 8111 General practice attorney, lawyer
PA: Alston & Bird Llp
　　1201 W Peachtree St Ne # 4000
　　Atlanta GA 30309
　　404 881-7654

(P-23091)
ANDATHA INTERNATIONAL INC (PA)
Also Called: Evolve Discovery
611 Mission St Fl 4, San Francisco
(94105-3535)
PHONE...................................415 398-8600
Andrew Jimenez, *CEO*
Tony Dinh, *COO*
David Wilner, *COO*
Sam CHI, *Senior VP*
Marlena Fejerang, *Senior VP*
EMP: 87

SQ FT: 3,500
SALES (est): 37.2MM Privately Held
SIC: 8111 Legal services

(P-23092)
ANDERSON MCPHARLIN CONNERS LLP (PA)
Also Called: AMC&
707 Wilshire Blvd # 4000, Los Angeles
(90017-3623)
PHONE...................................213 688-0080
Fax: 213 622-7594
David T Dibiase, *Partner*
Mark E Aronson, *Partner*
Carleton R Burch, *Partner*
Colleen A Dziel, *Partner*
Jesse S Hernandez, *Partner*
EMP: 57 EST: 1947
SQ FT: 23,000
SALES (est): 12.2MM Privately Held
WEB: www.amclaw.com
SIC: 8111 General practice attorney, lawyer

(P-23093)
ARCHER NORRIS A PROF LAW CORP (PA)
2033 N Main St Ste 800, Walnut Creek
(94596-3759)
P.O. Box 8035 (94596-8035)
PHONE...................................925 930-6600
Fax: 925 222-5992
Eugene C Blackard Jr, *Partner*
W Eric Blumhardt, *Partner*
Richard Norris, *Partner*
Ric Blumhardt, *Vice Pres*
Richard E Norris, *Admin Sec*
EMP: 138
SQ FT: 43,254
SALES: 46.5MM Privately Held
SIC: 8111 General practice law office

(P-23094)
ARENT FOX LLP
555 W 5th St Ste 4800, Los Angeles
(90013-1065)
PHONE...................................213 629-7400
Robert O'Brien, *Partner*
Charles P Rullman, *Associate*
EMP: 115
SALES (corp-wide): 116.9MM Privately Held
SIC: 8111 Legal services
PA: Arent Fox Llp
　　1717 K St Nw Ste B1
　　Washington DC 20006
　　202 857-6000

(P-23095)
ARNOLD & PORTER PC
3 Embarcadero Ctr Fl 7, San Francisco
(94111-4078)
PHONE...................................415 434-1600
Fax: 415 217-5910
Lawrence Rabkin, *Ch of Bd*
Jill Hernandez, *President*
Judy Lord, *President*
Richard Holdrup, *CFO*
Michelle Johnson, *Exec Dir*
EMP: 350
SQ FT: 70,000
SALES (est): 26MM Privately Held
WEB: www.hrice.com
SIC: 8111 Corporate, partnership & business law

(P-23096)
ATKINSON AND LY RD & RM LW (PA)
Also Called: Atkinson Andelson Loya
12800 Center Court Dr S # 300, Cerritos
(90703-9363)
PHONE...................................562 653-3200
James C Romo, *CEO*
Edward Ho, *Partner*
Gerald A Conradi, *Managing Prtnr*
Terry Filliman, *Managing Prtnr*
Sherry G Gordon, *Managing Prtnr*
EMP: 150
SALES (est): 40.6MM Privately Held
SIC: 8111 General practice attorney, lawyer

(P-23097)
BAKER KEENER & NAHRA
Also Called: Baker Keener & Nahra
633 W 5th St Fl 49, Los Angeles
(90071-2005)
PHONE...................................213 241-0900
Robert Baker, *Partner*
Mitchell Mulbarger,
Kenneth F Spencer, *Associate*
EMP: 50
SQ FT: 18,000
SALES (est): 9.9MM Privately Held
WEB: www.bknlawyers.com
SIC: 8111 Malpractice & negligence law

(P-23098)
BAKER & HOSTETLER LLP
11601 Wilshire Blvd Fl 14, Los Angeles
(90025-1750)
PHONE...................................310 820-8800
Fax: 310 975-1740
John F Cermak Jr, *Partner*
Cathryn Rowley, *Partner*
Bob Lofton,
Teresa R Tracy,
Thomas Roberts, *Counsel*
EMP: 76
SALES (corp-wide): 333.2MM Privately Held
SIC: 8111 Legal services; bankruptcy law; labor & employment law; real estate law
PA: Baker & Hostetler Llp
　　127 Public Sq Ste 2000
　　Cleveland OH 44114
　　216 621-0200

(P-23099)
BAKER & MCKENZIE LLP
2 Embarcadero Ctr Fl 11, San Francisco
(94111-3802)
PHONE...................................415 576-3000
Fax: 415 576-3099
Peter Engstrom, *Manager*
Bartley Baer, *Partner*
Robin Chesler, *Partner*
Peter Denwood, *Partner*
Tyrrell Prosser, *Partner*
EMP: 120
SALES (corp-wide): 1.1B Privately Held
SIC: 8111 Administrative & government law; corporate, partnership & business law
PA: Baker & Mckenzie Llp
　　300 E Randolph St # 5000
　　Chicago IL 60601
　　312 861-8000

(P-23100)
BAKER & MCKENZIE LLP
660 Hansen Way Ste 1, Palo Alto
(94304-1045)
PHONE...................................650 856-2400
Fax: 650 856-9299
Peter Engstrom, *Branch Mgr*
Jon Appleton, *Partner*
Bartley Baer, *Partner*
Michael Bumbaca, *Partner*
Robin Chesler, *Partner*
EMP: 60
SALES (corp-wide): 1.1B Privately Held
SIC: 8111 8011 General practice law office; medical centers
PA: Baker & Mckenzie Llp
　　300 E Randolph St # 5000
　　Chicago IL 60601
　　312 861-8000

(P-23101)
BAKER MNOCK JENSEN A PROF CORP
Also Called: Baker Mnock Jnsen Attys At Law
5260 N Palm Ave Ste 421, Fresno
(93704-2217)
PHONE...................................559 432-5400
Bob Smittcamp, *CEO*
Donald P Fishbach, *Senior Partner*
Douglas B Jensen, *Senior Partner*
Kendall Manock, *Senior Partner*
David Camenson, *Vice Pres*
EMP: 110 EST: 1904
SQ FT: 30,000
SALES (est): 12.5MM Privately Held
WEB: www.bmj-law.com
SIC: 8111 General practice law office

PRODUCTS & SERVICES SECTION
8111 - Legal Svcs County (P-23123)

(P-23102)
BALLARD SPAHR LLP
2029 Century Park E # 800, Los Angeles (90067-2909)
PHONE..................................424 204-4400
Fax: 424 204-4350
Alan Petlak, *Branch Mgr*
Irma Williams, *Marketing Mgr*
Anne Stowell, *Accounts Exec*
EMP: 76
SALES (corp-wide): 231MM **Privately Held**
SIC: 8111 Legal services
PA: Ballard Spahr Llp
   1735 Market St Fl 51
   Philadelphia PA 19103
   215 665-8500

(P-23103)
BALLARD SPAHR LLP
655 W Broadway Ste 1600, San Diego (92101-8494)
PHONE..................................619 696-9200
Charles La Bella, *Branch Mgr*
EMP: 76
SALES (corp-wide): 214.7MM **Privately Held**
SIC: 8111 Legal services
PA: Ballard Spahr Llp
   1735 Market St Fl 51
   Philadelphia PA 19103
   215 665-8500

(P-23104)
BANKRUPTCY MGT SOLUTIONS INC
Also Called: B M S
5 Peters Canyon Rd # 200, Irvine (92606-1404)
PHONE..................................949 222-1212
Steve Moore, *CEO*
David S Watkins, *Ch of Bd*
Rod Ennico, *COO*
Brian Soper, *Vice Pres*
Melinda Teter, *Vice Pres*
EMP: 120
SALES (est): 22.1MM **Privately Held**
SIC: 8111 Bankruptcy referee

(P-23105)
BARGER & WOLEN LLP
275 Battery St Ste 480, San Francisco (94111-3309)
PHONE..................................415 434-2800
Fax: 415 434-2533
Linda Kiel, *Branch Mgr*
Yvette A Margolis, *Legal Staff*
EMP: 50
SALES (corp-wide): 19.3MM **Privately Held**
WEB: www.bargerwolen.com
SIC: 8111 General practice attorney, lawyer
PA: Barger & Wolen Llp
   633 W 5th St Ste 5000
   Los Angeles CA
   213 680-2800

(P-23106)
BARNES & THORNBURG LLP
2029 Century Park E # 300, Los Angeles (90067-2904)
PHONE..................................310 284-3880
Amanda Taber, *Legal Staff*
Jonathan J Boustani, *Associate*
EMP: 113
SALES (corp-wide): 150.2MM **Privately Held**
SIC: 8111 Legal services
PA: Barnes & Thornburg Llp
   11 S Meridian St Ste 1313
   Indianapolis IN 46204
   317 236-1313

(P-23107)
BARTHOLOMEW BARRY & ASSOCIATES
701 N Brand Blvd Ste 800, Glendale (91203-3179)
PHONE..................................818 543-4000
EMP: 73
SALES (est): 3.7MM **Privately Held**
SIC: 8111

(P-23108)
BARTKO ZANKEL TARRANT & MIL
1 Embarcadero Ctr Ste 800, San Francisco (94111-3629)
PHONE..................................415 956-1900
Fax: 415 956-1152
Richard T Tarrant, *President*
Martin I Zankel, *Chairman*
Charles Miller, *Vice Pres*
John Bartko, *Principal*
Susan Stevenson, *Admin Asst*
EMP: 80 EST: 1975
SQ FT: 18,000
SALES (est): 12.5MM **Privately Held**
WEB: www.bztm.com
SIC: 8111 Corporate, partnership & business law; real estate law; bankruptcy law

(P-23109)
BERDING & WEIL LLP (PA)
2175 N Calif Blvd Ste 500, Walnut Creek (94596-7336)
PHONE..................................925 838-2090
Fax: 925 820-5592
Tyler Berding, *Partner*
Roanne Jolicoeur, *Chief Mktg Ofcr*
Roderic Oswald, *Creative Dir*
Julianne Spence, *Admin Asst*
Rochelle Ceballos, *Mktg Dir*
EMP: 75
SQ FT: 20,000
SALES (est): 21MM **Privately Held**
WEB: www.bwclassaction.com
SIC: 8111 General practice law office

(P-23110)
BERGER KAHN (PA)
Also Called: Simon and Gladstone A Prof
4551 Glencoe Ave Ste 245, Marina Del Rey (90292-7925)
PHONE..................................310 578-6800
Fax: 310 578-6178
Craig Simon, *Owner*
Ron Alberts, *Partner*
Jason Wallach, *Partner*
Allen L Miche, *Managing Prtnr*
Mike Aiken, *Principal*
EMP: 70 EST: 1928
SQ FT: 22,250
SALES (est): 18MM **Privately Held**
WEB: www.bergerkahn.com
SIC: 8111 General practice attorney, lawyer

(P-23111)
BERGER KAHN
2 Park Plz Ste 650, Irvine (92614-2519)
P.O. Box 19694 (92623-9694)
PHONE..................................310 821-9000
Fax: 949 474-7265
Craig S Simon, *Manager*
Andrew Immerman, *Info Tech Dir*
Jess Block, *Mktg Dir*
Julia Mouser,
Carol Schaner,
EMP: 50
SALES (corp-wide): 18MM **Privately Held**
WEB: www.bergerkahn.com
SIC: 8111 General practice attorney, lawyer
PA: Berger Kahn
   4551 Glencoe Ave Ste 245
   Marina Del Rey CA 90292
   310 578-6800

(P-23112)
BERRY & BERRY LAW FIRM
475 14th St Ste 550, Oakland (94612-1938)
PHONE..................................510 250-0200
Phillip S Berry, *President*
Ben Acosta, *Info Tech Dir*
Rich Steine, *Human Res Dir*
Carla G Berry, *Supervisor*
EMP: 75
SALES (est): 8.7MM **Privately Held**
SIC: 8111 General practice attorney, lawyer

(P-23113)
BEST BEST & KRIEGER LLP (PA)
Also Called: BB&k
3390 University Ave # 500, Riverside (92501-3369)
P.O. Box 1028 (92502-1028)
PHONE..................................951 686-1450
Fax: 951 686-3083
Eric L Garner, *Managing Prtnr*
Jason M Ackerman, *Partner*
Franklin C Adams, *Partner*
Franklin Adams, *Partner*
Clark Alsop, *Partner*
EMP: 188 EST: 1891
SQ FT: 57,000
SALES (est): 62.8MM **Privately Held**
WEB: www.bbklaw.com
SIC: 8111 General practice attorney, lawyer

(P-23114)
BET TZEDEK
3250 Wilshire Blvd Fl 13, Los Angeles (90010-1601)
PHONE..................................323 939-0506
Fax: 323 939-1040
Jessie Kornberg, *President*
Zachary Lebovits, *Volunteer Dir*
Stanley Kandel, *Partner*
David Lash, *President*
Jen Petrovich, *CFO*
EMP: 51
SALES: 7.4MM **Privately Held**
SIC: 8111 Legal aid service

(P-23115)
BIRD MRLLA BXER WLPERT A PROF
1875 Century Park E Fl 23, Los Angeles (90067-2337)
PHONE..................................310 201-2100
Fax: 310 201-2110
Vincent Marella, *Partner*
Terry Bird, *Partner*
Joel Boxer, *Partner*
Dorothy Wolpert, *Partner*
Sandy Palmieri, *President*
EMP: 60
SALES: 6MM **Privately Held**
WEB: www.bmbwlaw.com
SIC: 8111 General practice law office

(P-23116)
BISHOP BARRY HOWE HANEY & RYDE
6001 Shellmound St # 875, Emeryville (94608-1968)
PHONE..................................510 596-0888
Fax: 415 596-0899
Nelson C Barry Sr, *President*
Carol Healey, *Shareholder*
Nelson C Barry III, *Vice Pres*
Jeffrey N Haney, *Vice Pres*
Fredric W Trester, *Vice Pres*
EMP: 60 EST: 1917
SQ FT: 14,000
SALES (est): 7.3MM **Privately Held**
WEB: www.bbhhr.com
SIC: 8111 General practice law office

(P-23117)
BLAKELY SKLOFF TYLOR ZFMAN LLP (PA)
Also Called: Bstz
12400 Wilshire Blvd # 700, Los Angeles (90025-1019)
PHONE..................................310 207-3800
Fax: 310 820-5270
Farzad E Amini, *Partner*
Dax Alvarez, *Partner*
W Thomas Babbitt, *Partner*
Thomas Babitt, *Partner*
Jordon Becker, *Partner*
EMP: 80
SQ FT: 30,000
SALES (est): 44.4MM **Privately Held**
WEB: www.bstz.com
SIC: 8111 Specialized law offices, attorneys

(P-23118)
BLAKELY SKLOFF TYLOR ZFMAN LLP
1279 Oakmead Pkwy, Sunnyvale (94085-4040)
PHONE..................................408 720-8300
Fax: 408 720-9397
Karen Wilson, *Director*
Roger Blakely, *Managing Prtnr*
Gregory Caldwell, *Managing Prtnr*
Michael Desanctis, *Managing Prtnr*
Tarek N Fahmi, *Managing Prtnr*
EMP: 120
SALES (corp-wide): 44.4MM **Privately Held**
WEB: www.bstz.com
SIC: 8111 General practice law office
PA: Blakely, Sokoloff, Taylor & Zafman Llp
   12400 Wilshire Blvd # 700
   Los Angeles CA 90025
   310 207-3800

(P-23119)
BLANK ROME LLP
2029 Century Park E Fl 6, Los Angeles (90067-2901)
PHONE..................................424 239-3400
William Small, *Branch Mgr*
Todd Boock, *Counsel*
Danielle Garcia, *Counsel*
Cheryl Chang, *Associate*
EMP: 91
SALES (corp-wide): 168.2MM **Privately Held**
SIC: 8111 Legal services
PA: Blank Rome Llp
   1 Logan Sq
   Philadelphia PA 19103
   215 569-5500

(P-23120)
BLANK ROME LLP
2049 Century Park E # 700, Los Angeles (90067-3101)
PHONE..................................650 690-9500
Dror Nemirovsky, *Branch Mgr*
EMP: 100
SALES (corp-wide): 168.2MM **Privately Held**
SIC: 8111 General practice attorney, lawyer
PA: Blank Rome Llp
   1 Logan Sq
   Philadelphia PA 19103
   215 569-5500

(P-23121)
BLANK ROME LLP
2049 Century Park E # 700, Los Angeles (90067-3101)
PHONE..................................310 772-8300
Kirk Pasich, *Partner*
EMP: 50
SALES (corp-wide): 168.2MM **Privately Held**
SIC: 8111 Legal services
PA: Blank Rome Llp
   1 Logan Sq
   Philadelphia PA 19103
   215 569-5500

(P-23122)
BLOOM DAVID LAW OFFICES OF
3699 Wilshire Blvd Fl 10, Los Angeles (90010-2766)
PHONE..................................323 938-5248
Fax: 213 385-2009
David Bloom, *Owner*
Cheri Munger, *Financial Exec*
EMP: 50
SALES (est): 3MM **Privately Held**
SIC: 8111 General practice law office

(P-23123)
BLOOM HERGOTT DIEMER COOK LLC
Also Called: Bloom, Jacob A
150 S Rodeo Dr Fl 3, Beverly Hills (90212-2410)
PHONE..................................310 859-6800
Jacob A Bloom, *Partner*
Lawrence H Graves, *Partner*
Candice S Hansen, *Partner*
Allen Hergott, *Partner*

Tina J Kahn, *Partner*
EMP: 52
SALES (est): 7MM **Privately Held**
SIC: 8111 General practice law office

(P-23124)
BMC GROUP INC
Also Called: Bankruptcy Management Cons
300 N Cntntl Blvd Ste 570, El Segundo (90245)
PHONE.....................310 321-5555
Shawn Allen, *President*
Jeff Kalina, *Senior VP*
Mathew Satuloff, *Info Tech Dir*
Igor Braude, *Manager*
Yuliya Neporent, *Manager*
EMP: 100
SALES (corp-wide): 17.2MM **Privately Held**
SIC: 8111 Bankruptcy referee
PA: The Bmc Group Inc
220 3rd Ave Fl 23
Seattle WA 98104
206 516-3300

(P-23125)
BONNE BRIDGE MUELL OKEEF & (PA)
3699 Wilsh Boule Fl 10, Los Angeles (90010)
PHONE.....................213 480-1900
Fax: 213 738-5888
David J O'Keefe, *President*
William Johnson, *Shareholder*
Carolyn Lindholm, *Shareholder*
George Peterson, *Corp Secy*
James D Nichols, *Vice Pres*
EMP: 100
SQ FT: 48,000
SALES (est): 21.3MM **Privately Held**
SIC: 8111 General practice attorney, lawyer

(P-23126)
BOORNAZIAN JENSEN & GARTHE A
555 12th St, Oakland (94607-4046)
PHONE.....................510 834-4350
Fax: 510 839-1897
David Garthe, *Principal*
Joanne M Perri, *President*
Charles Eisner, *CFO*
Bill Mulvihill, *Treasurer*
Thomas Borbely, *Bd of Directors*
EMP: 60
SQ FT: 18,500
SALES (est): 6.7MM **Privately Held**
WEB: www.bjg.com
SIC: 8111 General practice attorney, lawyer

(P-23127)
BOWLES & VERNA
2121 N Calif Blvd Ste 875, Walnut Creek (94596-7335)
PHONE.....................925 935-3300
Fax: 925 935-0371
Richard Bowles, *Partner*
Richard Ergo, *Partner*
Kp Dean Harper, *Partner*
Mary Sullivan, *Partner*
Michael Verna, *Partner*
EMP: 50
SQ FT: 15,000
SALES (est): 6.8MM **Privately Held**
WEB: www.bv-law.com
SIC: 8111 Corporate, partnership & business law

(P-23128)
BOWMAN AND BROOKE LLP
Also Called: Bowman & Brooke-Attys
970 W 190th St Ste 700, Torrance (90502-1091)
PHONE.....................310 768-3068
Fax: 310 719-1019
Mark Berry, *Manager*
Anthony Thomas, *COO*
Chris Rose, *Network Enginr*
Ann Wixted, *Legal Staff*
Anthony Parascandola, *Counsel*
EMP: 84
SALES (corp-wide): 63.8MM **Privately Held**
WEB: www.bowmanandbrooke.com
SIC: 8111 Legal services

PA: Bowman And Brooke Llp
150 S 5th St Ste 3000
Minneapolis MN 55402
612 339-8682

(P-23129)
BRADFORD & BARTHEL LLP (PA)
2518 River Plaza Dr, Sacramento (95833-3673)
PHONE.....................916 569-0790
Fax: 916 569-0799
Donald R Barthel, *Partner*
Tom Bradford, *Partner*
Dana Anderson, *President*
Yolanda Cordero, *President*
Melissa Gorski, *President*
EMP: 50
SALES (est): 35.2MM **Privately Held**
SIC: 8111 Legal services

(P-23130)
BRADY VORWERCK RYDR & CSPNO (PA)
19200 Von Karman Ave, Irvine (92612-8553)
PHONE.....................480 456-9888
Fax: 714 703-2121
James Brady, *CEO*
Robert Ryder, *Principal*
Gregg Vorwerck, *Principal*
Damian Galindo, *Info Tech Dir*
EMP: 75
SALES (est): 11.2MM **Privately Held**
SIC: 8111 Legal services

(P-23131)
BRAYTON PURCELL APC (PA)
222 Rush Landing Rd, Novato (94945-2469)
P.O. Box 6169 (94948-6169)
PHONE.....................415 898-1555
Alan Richard Brayton, *CEO*
Matthew Fleumer, *CFO*
Jennifer Harwood, *Executive*
Mike Molakides, *Administration*
Mel Sibayan, *Administration*
EMP: 107
SQ FT: 40,000
SALES (est): 31MM **Privately Held**
WEB: www.asbestosnetwork.com
SIC: 8111 General practice attorney, lawyer

(P-23132)
BREMER & WHYTE LLP (PA)
Also Called: Bremer Whyte Brown Omeara
20320 Sw Birch St Ste 200, Newport Beach (92660-1791)
PHONE.....................949 221-1000
Fax: 949 221-1001
Keith Bremer, *Partner*
Nicole Whyte, *Partner*
Arash Arabi, *Managing Prtnr*
John Belanger, *Managing Prtnr*
John O'Meara, *Managing Prtnr*
EMP: 50
SQ FT: 6,000
SALES (est): 16.7MM **Privately Held**
SIC: 8111 Specialized legal services

(P-23133)
BRYAN CAVE LLP
333 Market St Fl 25, San Francisco (94105-2126)
PHONE.....................415 675-3400
Alicia Kuhn, *Manager*
Danielle B Mangogna, *Counsel*
Derek Rose, *Counsel*
David M Unseth, *Counsel*
Donald A Cole, *Associate*
EMP: 50
SALES (corp-wide): 435.5MM **Privately Held**
SIC: 8111 General practice attorney, lawyer
PA: Bryan Cave Llp
1 Metropolitan Sq
Saint Louis MO 63102
314 259-2000

(P-23134)
BRYAN CAVE LLP
3161 Michelson Dr # 1500, Irvine (92612-4414)
PHONE.....................949 223-7000

Fax: 949 223-7100
Ren Hayhurst, *Manager*
Ren Hayhurft, *Partner*
Steven Sunshine, *Info Tech Dir*
Megan E Meyers, *Technical Staff*
Amit S Parekh, *Technical Staff*
EMP: 56
SALES (corp-wide): 435.5MM **Privately Held**
SIC: 8111 General practice attorney, lawyer
PA: Bryan Cave Llp
1 Metropolitan Sq
Saint Louis MO 63102
314 259-2000

(P-23135)
BRYAN CAVE LLP
120 Broadway Ste 300, Santa Monica (90401-2386)
PHONE.....................310 576-2100
Fax: 310 576-2200
Louise Caplan, *Manager*
Jeffrey Modistt, *Managing Prtnr*
Toni Palomares, *Office Mgr*
Ronald N Jacobi, *Technical Staff*
Christopher J Kunke, *Technical Staff*
EMP: 130
SALES (corp-wide): 359.9MM **Privately Held**
SIC: 8111 General practice attorney, lawyer
PA: Bryan Cave Llp
1 Metropolitan Sq
Saint Louis MO 63102
314 259-2000

(P-23136)
BUCHALTER NEMER A PROF CORP (PA)
1000 Wilshire Blvd # 1500, Los Angeles (90017-1730)
PHONE.....................213 891-0700
Adam Bass, *CEO*
Paul Weiser, *Managing Prtnr*
Mia S Blackler, *Shareholder*
Alicia Guerra, *Shareholder*
James Rose, *Shareholder*
EMP: 209
SQ FT: 84,000
SALES (est): 55.8MM **Privately Held**
SIC: 8111 General practice law office

(P-23137)
BUCHALTER NEMER A PROF CORP
18400 Von Karman Ave # 800, Irvine (92612-0514)
PHONE.....................714 549-5150
Tammy Curtis, *Manager*
Mitchell Olejko, *Shareholder*
Philip Schroeder, *Shareholder*
Paul Rigdon, *Info Tech Mgr*
Thomas Wagstaff, *Info Tech Mgr*
EMP: 60
SALES (corp-wide): 55.8MM **Privately Held**
SIC: 8111 Legal services
PA: Buchalter Nemer, A Professional Corporation
1000 Wilshire Blvd # 1500
Los Angeles CA 90017
213 891-0700

(P-23138)
BURKE WILLIAMS & SORENSEN LLP (PA)
444 S Flower St Ste 2400, Los Angeles (90071-2953)
PHONE.....................213 236-0600
Fax: 213 236-2700
John J Welsh, *Managing Prtnr*
James T Bradshaw Jr, *Partner*
Harold Bridges, *Partner*
Steven J Dawson, *Partner*
Leland C Dolley, *Partner*
EMP: 90
SQ FT: 51,000
SALES (est): 30.8MM **Privately Held**
WEB: www.bwslaw.com
SIC: 8111 General practice law office

(P-23139)
BURNHAM BROWN A PROF CORP
Also Called: Burnham & Brown
1901 Harrison St Ste 1100, Oakland (94612-3648)
P.O. Box 119 (94604-0119)
PHONE.....................510 444-6800
Fax: 510 835-6666
Gregory D Brown, *President*
Cathy Arias, *Partner*
Thomas Downey, *Partner*
Michael Johnson, *Partner*
John Verber, *Managing Prtnr*
EMP: 120
SQ FT: 50,000
SALES (est): 20.5MM **Privately Held**
WEB: www.burnhambrown.com
SIC: 8111 General practice law office

(P-23140)
C T CORPORATION SYSTEM
1350 Treat Blvd Ste 350, Walnut Creek (94597-2151)
PHONE.....................925 287-9801
Fax: 925 287-9801
Despina Shields, *Regional Mgr*
EMP: 60
SALES (corp-wide): 4.5B **Privately Held**
WEB: www.ctadvantage.com
SIC: 8111 5999 7375 Legal services; telephone equipment & systems; information retrieval services
HQ: C T Corporation System
111 8th Ave Fl 13
New York NY 10011
212 894-8940

(P-23141)
CALL & JENSEN APC
610 Nwport Ctr Dr Ste 700, Newport Beach (92660)
PHONE.....................949 717-3000
Fax: 714 717-3100
Wayne W Call, *Principal*
Jon Jensen, *Administration*
Vanessa Turner, *Counsel*
Tatiana Berger, *Associate*
J Boyer, *Associate*
EMP: 50
SALES (est): 7.7MM **Privately Held**
SIC: 8111 General practice attorney, lawyer

(P-23142)
CARR & FERRELL
120 Constitution Dr, Menlo Park (94025-1107)
PHONE.....................650 812-3400
Fax: 650 812-3444
Wininger Aaron, *Principal*
Dale Withers, *Admin Asst*
Jennifer Cardin, *Human Res Mgr*
Stuart Clark, *Marketing Staff*
Bryan Boyle, *Associate*
EMP: 72
SALES (est): 3.4MM **Privately Held**
SIC: 8111 Legal services

(P-23143)
CARR & FERRELL LLP (PA)
120 Constitution Dr, Menlo Park (94025-1107)
PHONE.....................650 812-3400
Barry Carr, *Partner*
John S Ferrell, *General Ptnr*
Stuart Clark, *Partner*
Jill E Fishbein, *Partner*
Jefferson F Scher, *Partner*
EMP: 53
SALES (est): 9.8MM **Privately Held**
WEB: www.carr-ferrell.com
SIC: 8111 Legal services; corporate, partnership & business law; patent, trademark & copyright law; labor & employment law

(P-23144)
CARR MC CLELLAN INGERSOLL THOM (PA)
Also Called: Carr, McClellan
216 Park Rd, Burlingame (94010-4200)
P.O. Box 513 (94011-0513)
PHONE.....................650 342-9600
Fax: 650 342-7685
Mark A Cassanego, *President*

PRODUCTS & SERVICES SECTION

8111 - Legal Svcs County (P-23165)

Tracy Francis, *President*
Steven D Anderson, *CFO*
Edward J Willig, *Admin Sec*
Edward Willig, *Admin Sec*
EMP: 65
SQ FT: 19,000
SALES (est): 11.7MM **Privately Held**
WEB: www.cmithlaw.com
SIC: 8111 General practice attorney, lawyer

(P-23145)
CARROLL BURDICK MC DONOUGH LLP (PA)
275 Battery St Ste 2600, San Francisco (94111-3356)
PHONE...............................415 989-5900
Fax: 415 989-0932
Angela Bradstreet, *Partner*
Doris Alexander, *Exec Dir*
Soua Vue, *IT/INT Sup*
Marcelino Nogueiro, *Analyst*
Mary Holland, *Human Res Dir*
EMP: 142
SQ FT: 50,000
SALES (est): 21.9MM **Privately Held**
WEB: www.cbmlaw.com
SIC: 8111 General practice attorney, lawyer

(P-23146)
CARSON KURTZMAN CONSULTANTS (DH)
Also Called: K C C
2335 Alaska Ave, El Segundo (90245-4808)
PHONE...............................310 823-9000
Jon A Orr,
James Le, *COO*
Michael Frishberg, *Exec VP*
James Le Transitions, *Exec VP*
Evan Gershbein, *Senior VP*
EMP: 180
SQ FT: 46,000
SALES (est): 28.2MM
SALES (corp-wide): 1.4B **Privately Held**
WEB: www.kccllc.com
SIC: 8111 Specialized legal services

(P-23147)
CHILDRENS LAW CENTER CAL
Also Called: Childrens Law Ctr - Sacramento
8950 Cal Center Dr # 101, Sacramento (95826-3259)
PHONE...............................916 520-2000
Starr Leslie, *Branch Mgr*
Rachel Raymond, *Director*
EMP: 67
SALES (corp-wide): 21.8MM **Privately Held**
SIC: 8111 Legal services
PA: Children's Law Center Of California
201 Centre Plaza Dr Ste 8
Monterey Park CA 91754
323 980-8700

(P-23148)
CHILDRENS LAW CENTER CAL (PA)
201 Centre Plaza Dr Ste 8, Monterey Park (91754-2179)
PHONE...............................323 980-8700
Leslie Starr Heimov, *CEO*
Esther Wu, *Officer*
Lisa Romero, *Executive Asst*
Jessica Wilde, *Executive Asst*
Lesa Lomero, *Controller*
EMP: 55
SALES (est): 21.8MM **Privately Held**
SIC: 8111 Legal aid service

(P-23149)
CHODOROW DE CASTRO WEST
10960 Wilshire Blvd # 1400, Los Angeles (90024-3717)
PHONE...............................310 478-2541
Fax: 310 473-0123
Hugo Decastro, *President*
Mark Share, *Shareholder*
Jonathan Reich, *Bd of Directors*
Merna Figoten, *Info Tech Mgr*
Dyan Traynor, *Info Tech Mgr*
EMP: 65
SQ FT: 19,400
SALES (est): 9.7MM **Privately Held**
WEB: www.dwclaw.com
SIC: 8111 General practice law office

(P-23150)
CITY & COUNTY OF SAN FRANCISCO
Also Called: City Attorney
1 Carlton B Goodlett Pl # 234, San Francisco (94102-4604)
PHONE...............................415 554-4700
Fax: 415 554-4755
Dennis Herrera, *Principal*
Dale Riley, *Manager*
EMP: 250 **Privately Held**
SIC: 8111 9222 General practice attorney, lawyer; legal counsel & prosecution; ;
PA: City & County Of San Francisco
1 Dr Carlton B Goodlett P
San Francisco CA 94102
415 554-7500

(P-23151)
CITY & COUNTY OF SAN FRANCISCO
Also Called: District Attorney's Office
850 Bryant St Ste 600, San Francisco (94103-4613)
PHONE...............................415 553-1752
Kamala Harris, *Manager*
EMP: 130 **Privately Held**
SIC: 8111 9222 Legal services; legal counsel & prosecution; ;
PA: City & County Of San Francisco
1 Dr Carlton B Goodlett P
San Francisco CA 94102
415 554-7500

(P-23152)
CITY OF LONG BEACH
Also Called: Long Beach Cty Flt Svc Ofc
2600 Temple Ave, Long Beach (90806-2209)
PHONE...............................562 570-5423
Dennis Hill, *Principal*
EMP: 67 **Privately Held**
WEB: www.polb.com
SIC: 8111 Legal services
PA: City Of Long Beach
333 W Ocean Blvd Fl 10
Long Beach CA 90802
562 570-6450

(P-23153)
CITY OF LONG BEACH
Also Called: City Attorneys Office
333 W Ocean Blvd Lbby, Long Beach (90802-4664)
PHONE...............................562 570-6919
Karen Brandt, *Manager*
EMP: 67 **Privately Held**
WEB: www.polb.com
SIC: 8111 9111 General practice attorney, lawyer; mayors' offices
PA: City Of Long Beach
333 W Ocean Blvd Fl 10
Long Beach CA 90802
562 570-6450

(P-23154)
CITY OF LOS ANGELES
Also Called: City Los Angeles General Svcs
111 E 1st St Ste 401, Los Angeles (90012-3678)
PHONE...............................213 978-4049
Len Appledaum, *Chief Acct*
Victor Yee, *Administration*
Gail Brown, *Info Tech Mgr*
Charles Huang, *Analyst*
David Bloomberg, *Accountant*
EMP: 200 **Privately Held**
WEB: www.lacity.org
SIC: 8111 Legal services
PA: City Of Los Angeles
200 N Spring St Ste 303
Los Angeles CA 90012
213 978-0600

(P-23155)
CITY OF LOS ANGELES
Also Called: City Attorney
200 N Main St Ste 800, Los Angeles (90012-4133)
PHONE...............................213 978-8100
Fax: 213 978-8212
Mike Feuer, *General Mgr*
Mary C Higgins, *Analyst*
Gordon B Lawler, *Analyst*
Henry Lee, *Manager*
EMP: 800 **Privately Held**
WEB: www.lacity.org
SIC: 8111 9222 Legal services; legal counsel & prosecution;
PA: City Of Los Angeles
200 N Spring St Ste 303
Los Angeles CA 90012
213 978-0600

(P-23156)
CLIFFORD & BROWN A PROF CORP
1430 Truxtun Ave Ste 900, Bakersfield (93301-5226)
PHONE...............................661 322-6023
Fax: 661 322-3508
Steven Clifford, *President*
Arnold Anchordoquy, *Treasurer*
Jim Brown, *Principal*
Kathy Smith, *Office Mgr*
Bob Harding, *Admin Sec*
EMP: 51
SQ FT: 100,000
SALES (est): 2.5MM **Privately Held**
WEB: www.clifford-law.com
SIC: 8111 Legal services

(P-23157)
CLYDE & CO US LLP
101 2nd St Fl 24, San Francisco (94105-3672)
PHONE...............................415 365-9800
Rhonda Jenkins, *Principal*
Rhonda Jenkin, *Administration*
Jeremy Leblanc, *Info Tech Dir*
Douglas Maag, *Counsel*
Carolyn Babula, *Director*
EMP: 55
SALES (corp-wide): 584.7MM **Privately Held**
SIC: 8111 Legal services
HQ: Clyde & Co Us Llp
The Chrysler Bldg
New York NY 10174
212 710-3900

(P-23158)
COBLENTZ PATCH DUFFY BASS LLP
1 Ferry Building Ste 200, San Francisco (94111-4213)
PHONE...............................510 655-4598
Michael Meyers, *Partner*
William Coblentz, *Senior Partner*
Paul Escobosa, *Partner*
Susan Jamison, *Partner*
Jeffrey B Knowles, *Partner*
EMP: 100
SQ FT: 30,000
SALES (est): 23MM **Privately Held**
WEB: www.cpdb.com
SIC: 8111 General practice attorney, lawyer

(P-23159)
COLLINS CLLINS MUIR STWART LLP
1100 El Centro St Frnt, South Pasadena (91030-5213)
PHONE...............................626 243-1100
John Collins, *Partner*
Samuel J Muir, *Partner*
Brian Stewart, *Partner*
Robert H Stellwagen, *Manager*
Michael B McDonald, *Associate*
EMP: 50
SQ FT: 20,000
SALES (est): 7MM **Privately Held**
SIC: 8111 General practice attorney, lawyer

(P-23160)
COMMUNITY ACTION PARTNERSHIP
1152 E Grand Ave, Arroyo Grande (93420-2583)
PHONE...............................805 489-4026
Raye Flemming, *Branch Mgr*
EMP: 587
SALES (corp-wide): 57.3MM **Privately Held**
SIC: 8111 General practice law office
PA: Community Action Partnership Of San Luis Obispo County, Inc.
1030 Southwood Dr
San Luis Obispo CA 93401
805 544-4355

(P-23161)
COMPEX LEGAL SERVICES INC (PA)
325 Maple Ave, Torrance (90503-2602)
PHONE...............................310 782-1801
Fax: 310 781-9717
Arvind Korde, *CEO*
Nitin Mehta, *Chairman*
Anthony Bazurto, *Senior VP*
Humildad Pasimio, *Vice Pres*
Rajesh Rangaswamy, *Vice Pres*
EMP: 120
SQ FT: 47,740
SALES (est): 92.3MM **Privately Held**
WEB: www.compexlegal.com
SIC: 8111 7338 7334 Specialized legal services; secretarial & court reporting; photocopying & duplicating services

(P-23162)
COOKSEY TOOLEN GAGE DUFFY (PA)
535 Anton Blvd Fl 10, Costa Mesa (92626-1947)
PHONE...............................714 431-1100
Fax: 714 431-1119
David Cooksey, *President*
Robert L Toolen, *Vice Pres*
Dawson Byrd, *Info Tech Mgr*
Charlene Clemente, *Info Tech Mgr*
Stephanie Korper, *Info Tech Mgr*
EMP: 58
SALES (est): 14.8MM **Privately Held**
WEB: www.cookseylaw.com
SIC: 8111 General practice law office

(P-23163)
COOLEY GODWARD KRONISH LLP
3000 El Camino Real 5-400, Palo Alto (94306-2197)
PHONE...............................650 842-7201
Kenneth J Adelson, *Principal*
Bob Eisenbach, *Managing Prtnr*
Elizabeth Baldwin, *President*
Andrea Behrend, *President*
Jami Biwer, *President*
EMP: 70
SALES (est): 4.7MM **Privately Held**
SIC: 8111 Legal services

(P-23164)
COOLEY LLP
Also Called: Cooley Godward Kronish
101 California St Fl 5, San Francisco (94111-5800)
PHONE...............................415 693-2000
Fax: 415 951-3795
Lee Benton, *Partner*
Charlie Cameron, *Senior VP*
Joseph Perna, *Office Admin*
Christina Salinas, *Accounting Mgr*
Steven Przesmicki, *General Counsel*
EMP: 100
SALES (corp-wide): 174.8MM **Privately Held**
WEB: www.cooley.com
SIC: 8111 Legal services
PA: Cooley Llp
3175 Hanover St
Palo Alto CA 94304
650 843-5000

(P-23165)
COOLEY LLP (PA)
3175 Hanover St, Palo Alto (94304-1130)
PHONE...............................650 843-5000
Fax: 415 981-4027
Joe Conroy, *Mng Member*
Tom Reicher -, *Partner*
Kenneth J Adelson, *Partner*
Mike Attanasio, *Partner*
Andrew Basile, *Partner*
EMP: 300
SQ FT: 59,100
SALES (est): 174.8MM **Privately Held**
WEB: www.cooley.com
SIC: 8111 Specialized law offices, attorneys; corporate, partnership & business law

8111 - Legal Svcs County (P-23166)

PRODUDUCTS & SERVICES SECTION

(P-23166)
COOLEY LLP
4 Palo Alto Sq, Palo Alto (94306-2122)
PHONE..................................650 843-5124
Chris Johnston, *Branch Mgr*
Ariana Amparan, *President*
Mercedes Milana, *President*
Laurie Wilson, *Executive Asst*
MEI Lee, *Financial Analy*
EMP: 143
SALES (corp-wide): 174.8MM **Privately Held**
SIC: 8111 General practice attorney, lawyer
PA: Cooley Llp
3175 Hanover St
Palo Alto CA 94304
650 843-5000

(P-23167)
COOLEY LLP
4401 Eastgate Mall, San Diego (92121-1909)
PHONE..................................858 550-6000
Fred Muto, *Partner*
Christopher J Kearns, *Partner*
Lisa St John, *Personnel Exec*
Bill Fong, *Director*
Jennifer Detrani, *Manager*
EMP: 150
SALES (corp-wide): 174.8MM **Privately Held**
WEB: www.cooley.com
SIC: 8111 General practice law office
PA: Cooley Llp
3175 Hanover St
Palo Alto CA 94304
650 843-5000

(P-23168)
COOPER WHITE & COOPER LLP (PA)
201 California St Fl 17, San Francisco (94111-5019)
PHONE..................................415 433-1900
Fax: 415 433-5530
Mark P Schreiber, *Partner*
Walter Hansell, *Partner*
Keith Howard, *Partner*
Peter Sibley, *Partner*
Jed Solomon, *Partner*
EMP: 120
SQ FT: 44,000
SALES (est): 24.4MM **Privately Held**
WEB: www.cwclaw.com
SIC: 8111 General practice law office

(P-23169)
COUNTY OF FRESNO
Also Called: Superior Court Unit
1130 O St, Fresno (93724-2201)
PHONE..................................559 600-3420
Fax: 559 457-2035
Rick Chavez, *Manager*
Sharon Borbon, *Director*
EMP: 96 **Privately Held**
WEB: www.first5fresno.org
SIC: 8111 9199 Divorce & family law;
PA: County Of Fresno
2420 Mariposa St
Fresno CA 93721
559 600-1710

(P-23170)
COUNTY OF FRESNO
Also Called: Public Defender's Office
2220 Tulare St Ste 300, Fresno (93721-2130)
PHONE..................................559 600-3546
Fax: 559 262-4104
Kenneth Taniguchi, *Branch Mgr*
EMP: 96 **Privately Held**
WEB: www.first5fresno.org
SIC: 8111 9222 Specialized law offices, attorneys; public defenders' offices;
PA: County Of Fresno
2420 Mariposa St
Fresno CA 93721
559 600-1710

(P-23171)
COUNTY OF KERN
1215 Truxtun Ave Fl 4, Bakersfield (93301-4619)
PHONE..................................661 868-2000
William Fawns, *Branch Mgr*
EMP: 95 **Privately Held**
SIC: 8111 Legal services
PA: County Of Kern
1115 Truxtun Ave Rm 505
Bakersfield CA 93301
661 868-3690

(P-23172)
COUNTY OF LOS ANGELES
Also Called: Public Defenders Office
1601 Eastlake Ave Ste 4, Los Angeles (90033-1009)
PHONE..................................323 226-8998
Fax: 323 226-8553
Ron Brown, *Principal*
EMP: 214 **Privately Held**
SIC: 8111 Legal services
PA: County Of Los Angeles
500 W Temple St Ste 375
Los Angeles CA 90012
213 974-1101

(P-23173)
COUNTY OF LOS ANGELES
300 S Park Ave Ste 770, Pomona (91766-1557)
PHONE..................................909 620-3330
Steven Hobson, *Manager*
EMP: 214 **Privately Held**
SIC: 8111 General practice attorney, lawyer
PA: County Of Los Angeles
500 W Temple St Ste 375
Los Angeles CA 90012
213 974-1101

(P-23174)
COUNTY OF LOS ANGELES
Also Called: District Attorney
200 W Compton Blvd # 700, Compton (90220-6676)
PHONE..................................310 603-7483
Julie Sulman, *Manager*
EMP: 110 **Privately Held**
WEB: www.co.la.ca.us
SIC: 8111 9222 Legal services; District Attorneys' offices;
PA: County Of Los Angeles
500 W Temple St Ste 375
Los Angeles CA 90012
213 974-1101

(P-23175)
COUNTY OF LOS ANGELES
Also Called: Public Defender Administration
210 W Temple St Fl 19, Los Angeles (90012-3231)
PHONE..................................213 974-2811
Fax: 213 625-5031
Ronald Brown, *Branch Mgr*
Ernesto Diaz, *Agent*
EMP: 200 **Privately Held**
WEB: www.co.la.ca.us
SIC: 8111 9222 Legal services; public defenders' offices;
PA: County Of Los Angeles
500 W Temple St Ste 375
Los Angeles CA 90012
213 974-1101

(P-23176)
COUNTY OF LOS ANGELES
Also Called: Public Defender
200 W Compton Blvd Fl 8, Compton (90220-6676)
PHONE..................................310 603-7271
Fax: 310 604-9436
John Brock, *Manager*
EMP: 214 **Privately Held**
WEB: www.co.la.ca.us
SIC: 8111 9222 Legal services; public defenders' offices;
PA: County Of Los Angeles
500 W Temple St Ste 375
Los Angeles CA 90012
213 974-1101

(P-23177)
COUNTY OF LOS ANGELES
Also Called: Court House
20221 Hamilton Ave, Torrance (90502-1321)
PHONE..................................310 222-3552
Charles Mandel, *Branch Mgr*
EMP: 214 **Privately Held**
SIC: 8111 General practice attorney, lawyer
PA: County Of Los Angeles
500 W Temple St Ste 375
Los Angeles CA 90012
213 974-1101

(P-23178)
COUNTY OF LOS ANGELES
Also Called: District Attorney
6230 Sylmar Ave Ste 201, Van Nuys (91401-2731)
PHONE..................................818 374-2406
Nancy Lidamore, *Director*
EMP: 60 **Privately Held**
WEB: www.co.la.ca.us
SIC: 8111 9222 General practice attorney, lawyer; District Attorneys' offices;
PA: County Of Los Angeles
500 W Temple St Ste 375
Los Angeles CA 90012
213 974-1101

(P-23179)
COUNTY OF ORANGE
Also Called: Public Defender
1440 N Harbor Blvd # 400, Fullerton (92835-4127)
PHONE..................................714 626-3700
Fax: 714 626-3749
Sharon Petrosino, *Manager*
Brooks Talley, *Branch Mgr*
Araceli Martinez, *Admin Asst*
Christine Young, *Accountant*
Paula Kielich, *Manager*
EMP: 50 **Privately Held**
SIC: 8111 9222 Legal services; public defenders' offices;
PA: County Of Orange
333 W Santa Ana Blvd 3f
Santa Ana CA 92701
714 834-6200

(P-23180)
COUNTY OF RIVERSIDE
Also Called: Public Defender- Main Office
4200 Orange St, Riverside (92501-3827)
PHONE..................................951 955-6000
Fax: 951 955-6114
Gary Windom, *Administration*
Evelyn Betancur, *Admin Sec*
Ron Mallari, *Manager*
EMP: 200 **Privately Held**
SIC: 8111 9222 Legal services; public defenders' offices;
PA: County Of Riverside
4080 Lemon St Fl 11
Riverside CA 92501
951 955-1110

(P-23181)
COUNTY OF SACRAMENTO
Also Called: Public Defender's Office
700 H St Ste 270, Sacramento (95814-1289)
PHONE..................................916 874-5411
Paulino G Duran, *Director*
EMP: 170 **Privately Held**
WEB: www.sna.com
SIC: 8111 9222 Legal services; public defenders' offices;
PA: County Of Sacramento
700 H St Ste 7650
Sacramento CA 95814
916 874-5544

(P-23182)
COUNTY OF SAN DIEGO
District Attorney
330 W Broadway Ste 1020, San Diego (92101-3827)
PHONE..................................619 531-4040
Steven Silva, *Admin Sec*
Desiree Gonzalez, *Admin Asst*
Mike Franco, *Info Tech Mgr*
Wilson Tang, *Technology*
Arvin Viernes, *Technology*
EMP: 93 **Privately Held**
WEB: www.sdlcc.org
SIC: 8111 9222 Specialized legal services; District Attorneys' offices
PA: County Of San Diego
1600 Pacific Hwy Ste 209
San Diego CA 92101
619 531-5880

(P-23183)
COUNTY OF SHASTA
Also Called: Dist Attorney's Office
1355 West St, Redding (96001-1652)
PHONE..................................530 245-6300
Gerald Benito, *Principal*
EMP: 85 **Privately Held**
WEB: www.rsdnmp.org
SIC: 8111 Legal services
PA: County Of Shasta
1450 Court St Ste 308a
Redding CA 96001
530 225-5561

(P-23184)
COUNTY OF SONOMA
Also Called: District Attorney
600 Administration Dr 212j, Santa Rosa (95403-2825)
PHONE..................................707 565-2209
Jill R Ravitch, *Branch Mgr*
EMP: 120 **Privately Held**
WEB: www.sonomacompost.com
SIC: 8111 9111 Legal services; county supervisors' & executives' offices
PA: County Of Sonoma
585 Fiscal Dr 100
Santa Rosa CA 95403
707 565-2431

(P-23185)
COVINGTON & BURLING LLP
333 Twin Dolphin Dr # 700, Redwood City (94065-1418)
PHONE..................................650 632-4700
Kurt G Calia, *Manager*
EMP: 115
SALES (corp-wide): 275.8MM **Privately Held**
SIC: 8111 Legal services
PA: Covington & Burling Llp
1 Citycente # 850
Washington DC 20001
202 662-6000

(P-23186)
COVINGTON & BURLING LLP
1 Front St Fl 35, San Francisco (94111-5323)
PHONE..................................415 591-6000
Fax: 415 591-6091
Jim Snipes, *Partner*
George M Chester Jr, *Partner*
Jason Smith, *Info Tech Mgr*
Stephen Humenik, *Counsel*
Thomas Isaacson, *Counsel*
EMP: 50
SALES (corp-wide): 275.8MM **Privately Held**
SIC: 8111 General practice law office
PA: Covington & Burling Llp
1 Citycente # 850
Washington DC 20001
202 662-6000

(P-23187)
COVINGTON & BURLING LLP
2029 Century Park E # 3100, Los Angeles (90067-3044)
PHONE..................................424 332-4800
EMP: 311
SALES (corp-wide): 275.8MM **Privately Held**
SIC: 8111 General practice law office
PA: Covington & Burling Llp
1 Citycente # 850
Washington DC 20001
202 662-6000

(P-23188)
COX CASTLE & NICHOLSON LLP (PA)
Also Called: Cox Castle
2029 Cntury Nicholson Llp, Los Angeles (90067)
PHONE..................................310 284-2200
Fax: 310 277-7889
Gary A Glick, *Partner*
Lindsey H Barr, *Partner*
Robin L Bennett, *Partner*
Kenneth B Bley, *Partner*
Erica A Bose, *Partner*
EMP: 165
SQ FT: 60,000

PRODUCTS & SERVICES SECTION
8111 - Legal Svcs County (P-23210)

SALES: 98MM **Privately Held**
SIC: 8111 General practice attorney, lawyer

(P-23189)
CROWELL & MORING LLP
275 Battery St Ste 2200, San Francisco (94111-3337)
PHONE 415 986-2800
Dawn Tonya, *Branch Mgr*
Joanne Richardson, *President*
Cristina Solorio, *President*
Anita Stephen, *Admin Asst*
Sumeena Birdi, *Legal Staff*
EMP: 60
SALES (corp-wide): 191.9MM **Privately Held**
SIC: 8111 General practice attorney, lawyer
PA: Crowell & Moring Llp
1001 Penn Ave Nw Fl 10
Washington DC 20004
202 624-2500

(P-23190)
CROWELL & MORING LLP
3 Park Plz Ste 2000, Irvine (92614-2591)
PHONE 949 263-8400
Fax: 949 263-8414
Daniel Sasse, *Manager*
Karen A Gibbs, *Partner*
John Oliverio, *CFO*
Randall Erickson, *Admin Asst*
Van D Nguyen, *Counsel*
EMP: 50
SALES (corp-wide): 191.9MM **Privately Held**
WEB: www.crowell.com
SIC: 8111 General practice law office
PA: Crowell & Moring Llp
1001 Penn Ave Nw Fl 10
Washington DC 20004
202 624-2500

(P-23191)
CUNEO BLACK WARD MISSLER A LAW
Also Called: Cuneo, Black, Ward & Missler
700 University Ave # 110, Sacramento (95825-6722)
P.O. Box 276650 (95827-6650)
PHONE 916 363-8822
Fax: 916 363-8821
John Black, *President*
Jim Cuneo, *Partner*
Jim Missler, *Partner*
Alan Jong, *CFO*
Gretchen Tilden, *Human Res Dir*
EMP: 50
SQ FT: 13,000
SALES (est): 5.8MM **Privately Held**
WEB: www.cbwmlaw.com
SIC: 8111 General practice law office

(P-23192)
CURTIS LEGAL GROUP A PROFESSI
1300 K St Fl 2, Modesto (95354-0928)
P.O. Box 3030 (95353-3030)
PHONE 209 521-1800
Ralph S Curtis, *President*
Maria Jaime, *Associate*
EMP: 50
SQ FT: 18,000
SALES (est): 7.7MM **Privately Held**
SIC: 8111 General practice attorney, lawyer

(P-23193)
DALEY & HEFT ATTORNEYS
462 Stevens Ave Ste 201, Solana Beach (92075-2099)
PHONE 858 755-5666
Fax: 858 755-7870
Dennis W Daley, *Partner*
Robert Brockman Jr, *Partner*
Mitchell D Dean, *Partner*
Robert Heft, *Partner*
Neal Meyers, *Partner*
EMP: 50
SALES (est): 7.7MM **Privately Held**
WEB: www.daleyheft.com
SIC: 8111 General practice law office

(P-23194)
DAMRELL NELSON SCHRIMP PALL
Also Called: Schrimp, Roger Attorney
703 W F St, Oakdale (95361-3736)
PHONE 209 848-3500
Fax: 209 848-3400
Roger Schrimp, *Branch Mgr*
EMP: 50
SALES (corp-wide): 4.7MM **Privately Held**
SIC: 8111 General practice law office
PA: Damrell, Nelson, Schrimp, Pallios, Pacher, Silva Pc
1601 I St Ste 500
Modesto CA 95354
209 526-3500

(P-23195)
DANIEL ROBERT KNOWLTON
68368 Madrid Rd, Cathedral City (92234-4836)
PHONE 760 265-5293
Daniel Robert Knowlton, *Owner*
EMP: 73 EST: 2010
SALES (est): 137.1K **Privately Held**
SIC: 8111 Legal services

(P-23196)
DANNING GILL DAMND KOLLITZ LLP
1900 Avenue Of The Stars # 1100, Los Angeles (90067-4301)
PHONE 310 277-0077
Fax: 310 277-5735
David A Gill, *Partner*
Richard K Diamond, *Partner*
Howard Kollitz, *Partner*
David M Poitras, *Partner*
Eric P Israel PC, *Partner*
EMP: 70
SALES (est): 8.6MM **Privately Held**
WEB: www.dgdk.com
SIC: 8111 General practice law office

(P-23197)
DANNIS WLVER KLLEY A PROF CORP (PA)
71 Stevenson St Fl 19, San Francisco (94105-2939)
PHONE 415 543-4111
Gregory Dannis, *President*
Janet Mueller, *Shareholder*
Lawrence Schoenke, *Shareholder*
Sandra Woliver, *Shareholder*
David Miller, *Vice Pres*
EMP: 70
SQ FT: 14,000
SALES (est): 8.5MM **Privately Held**
WEB: www.mbdlaw.com
SIC: 8111 General practice attorney, lawyer

(P-23198)
DAVID E BLAND
2049 Century Park E # 3400, Los Angeles (90067-3101)
PHONE 310 552-0130
Roman Silverfeld, *Managing Prtnr*
EMP: 70
SALES (est): 1.8MM **Privately Held**
SIC: 8111 Legal services

(P-23199)
DAVIS WRIGHT TREMAINE LLP
505 Montgomery St Ste 800, San Francisco (94111-6533)
PHONE 415 276-6500
Fax: 415 276-6599
Jeff Gray, *Partner*
Gerald Hinkley, *Partner*
Michael Labianca, *Partner*
Paul Leboffe, *Partner*
Gregory Miller, *Partner*
EMP: 75
SALES (corp-wide): 136MM **Privately Held**
WEB: www.dwt.com
SIC: 8111 Legal services
PA: Davis Wright Tremaine Llp
1201 3rd Ave Ste 2200
Seattle WA 98101
206 622-3150

(P-23200)
DAVIS WRIGHT TREMAINE LLP
865 S Figueroa St # 2400, Los Angeles (90017-2566)
PHONE 213 633-6800
Fax: 213 627-4874
Mary Haas, *Partner*
EMP: 90
SALES (corp-wide): 136MM **Privately Held**
WEB: www.dwt.com
SIC: 8111 General practice law office
PA: Davis Wright Tremaine Llp
1201 3rd Ave Ste 2200
Seattle WA 98101
206 622-3150

(P-23201)
DECHERT LLP
2010 Main St Ste 500, Irvine (92614-7269)
PHONE 949 442-6000
Christian Gehman, *Manager*
Joshua Strathman, *Administration*
EMP: 210
SALES (corp-wide): 328.9MM **Privately Held**
SIC: 8111 Legal services
PA: Dechert Llp
2929 Arch St Ste 400
Philadelphia PA 19104
202 261-3300

(P-23202)
DECHERT LLP
633 W 5th St Ste 3700, Los Angeles (90071-2013)
PHONE 213 489-1357
EMP: 210
SALES (corp-wide): 328.9MM **Privately Held**
SIC: 8111 Legal services
PA: Dechert Llp
2929 Arch St Ste 400
Philadelphia PA 19104
202 261-3300

(P-23203)
DECHERT LLP
1 Bush St Ste 1600, San Francisco (94104-4422)
PHONE 415 262-4500
John Randal, *Office Mgr*
Charlene Benjamin, *President*
Laura Melendez, *President*
Susan Spencer, *President*
Patricia Walsh, *President*
EMP: 50
SALES (corp-wide): 328.9MM **Privately Held**
SIC: 8111 8748 General practice law office; business consulting
PA: Dechert Llp
2929 Arch St Ste 400
Philadelphia PA 19104
202 261-3300

(P-23204)
DEMLER ARMSTRONG & ROWLAND LLP
4500 E Pacific Cst Hwy # 400, Long Beach (90804-3293)
PHONE 562 498-8979
Fax: 562 494-3958
Robert Armstrong, *Partner*
Sean Beatty, *Partner*
Edison Demler, *Partner*
Terry Rowland, *Partner*
Linda Rowland, *Accountant*
EMP: 50
SQ FT: 13,500
SALES (est): 6.1MM **Privately Held**
WEB: www.darlaw.com
SIC: 8111 General practice law office

(P-23205)
DENTONS US LLP
1530 Page Mill Rd Ste 200, Palo Alto (94304-1140)
PHONE 650 798-0300
Joe Borski, *Director*
Ginevra Saylor, *Director*
EMP: 65
SALES (corp-wide): 515.7MM **Privately Held**
SIC: 8111 General practice attorney, lawyer

PA: Dentons Us Llp
233 S Wacker Dr Ste 5900
Chicago IL 60606
312 876-8000

(P-23206)
DENTONS US LLP
2030 Main St Ste 1000, Irvine (92614-7239)
PHONE 949 732-3700
Roger Rushing, *Owner*
Jennifer E Bigelow, *Human Res Dir*
EMP: 104
SALES (corp-wide): 515.7MM **Privately Held**
SIC: 8111 Legal services
PA: Dentons Us Llp
233 S Wacker Dr Ste 5900
Chicago IL 60606
312 876-8000

(P-23207)
DENTONS US LLP
750 B St Ste 3300, San Diego (92101-8188)
PHONE 619 595-5400
Douglas Farry, *Director*
Elsa Gonzales, *Office Admin*
Christian Humphreys, *Manager*
Barbara Ippolito, *Manager*
EMP: 51
SALES (corp-wide): 515.7MM **Privately Held**
WEB: www.mckennalong.com
SIC: 8111 Legal services
PA: Dentons Us Llp
233 S Wacker Dr Ste 5900
Chicago IL 60606
312 876-8000

(P-23208)
DENTONS US LLP
4655 Executive Dr Ste 700, San Diego (92121-3128)
PHONE 619 236-1414
F Vandeveer, *Executive*
Kathy Caudillo, *Manager*
James Turner, *Associate*
EMP: 350
SALES (corp-wide): 515.7MM **Privately Held**
SIC: 8111 General practice law office
PA: Dentons Us Llp
233 S Wacker Dr Ste 5900
Chicago IL 60606
312 876-8000

(P-23209)
DENTONS US LLP
1 Market Plz Fl 24, San Francisco (94105-1102)
PHONE 415 882-5000
Paul Glad, *Branch Mgr*
D W Kallstrom,
Mark Mackler,
Obie Moore, *Counsel*
Mengmeng Zhang, *Associate*
EMP: 120
SALES (corp-wide): 515.7MM **Privately Held**
WEB: www.sonnenschein.com
SIC: 8111 General practice law office
PA: Dentons Us Llp
233 S Wacker Dr Ste 5900
Chicago IL 60606
312 876-8000

(P-23210)
DENTONS US LLP
601 S Figueroa St # 2500, Los Angeles (90017-5704)
PHONE 213 623-9300
Edwin Reeser, *General Mgr*
Michael Lubic, *Partner*
John Walker, *Partner*
Sharon Atkinson, *Officer*
Paterson Lee,
EMP: 150
SALES (corp-wide): 515.7MM **Privately Held**
WEB: www.sonnenschein.com
SIC: 8111 General practice attorney, lawyer

8111 - Legal Svcs County (P-23211)

PRODUDUCTS & SERVICES SECTION

PA: Dentons Us Llp
233 S Wacker Dr Ste 5900
Chicago IL 60606
312 876-8000

(P-23211)
DENTONS US LLP
300 S Grand Ave Fl 14, Los Angeles
(90071-3124)
PHONE...................213 688-1000
Janice Moor, *Administration*
Mark Flanagan, *Managing Prtnr*
Charles E Wilson III, *Officer*
Ned Black, *Technology*
Geraldine Chua, *Legal Staff*
EMP: 104
SALES (corp-wide): 515.7MM **Privately Held**
SIC: 8111 General practice attorney, lawyer
PA: Dentons Us Llp
233 S Wacker Dr Ste 5900
Chicago IL 60606
312 876-8000

(P-23212)
DICKENSON PEATMAN & FOGARTY A (PA)
1455 1st St Ste 301, NAPA (94559-2822)
PHONE...................707 252-7122
Fax: 707 255-6876
Rodeo Ocampo, *Office Mgr*
Jaymie Kilgore, *President*
Joanne Frazier, *Office Admin*
Mark Phillips, *Planning*
Melvin Cheah, *Network Mgr*
EMP: 50
SQ FT: 3,000
SALES (est): 6.4MM **Privately Held**
WEB: www.dpfnapa.com
SIC: 8111 General practice attorney, lawyer

(P-23213)
DIEPENBROCK ELKIN LLP
500 Capitol Mall Ste 650, Sacramento
(95814-4739)
PHONE...................916 492-5000
Bradley Elkin, *President*
Gary Bradus, *Managing Prtnr*
Michael V Brady, *Shareholder*
John Diepenbrock, *Shareholder*
Karen Diepenbrock, *Shareholder*
EMP: 56
SQ FT: 20,000
SALES: 15MM **Privately Held**
WEB: www.diepenbrock.com
SIC: 8111 General practice law office

(P-23214)
DIETZ GLMOR CHAZEN A PROF CORP (PA)
7071 Convoy Ct Ste 300, San Diego
(92111-1023)
PHONE...................858 565-0269
Fax: 619 236-9028
William Dietz, *Principal*
Avery G Chazen, *Principal*
Michael Dofflemyre, *Principal*
Mark R Gilmor, *Principal*
EMP: 61
SALES (est): 13.7MM **Privately Held**
SIC: 8111 Legal services

(P-23215)
DISABILITY GROUP INC
604 Arizona Ave, Santa Monica
(90401-1610)
PHONE...................310 829-5100
Ronald D Miller, *President*
Susan Wherle, *Administration*
EMP: 258
SALES (est): 16.9MM **Privately Held**
SIC: 8111 Specialized law offices, attorneys

(P-23216)
DISABILITY RIGHTS CALIFORNIA (PA)
Also Called: D R C
1831 K St, Sacramento (95811-4114)
PHONE...................916 488-9950
Izetta Jackson, *President*
Herb Anderson, *CFO*
Diana Lynn Nelson, *CFO*

Catherine Blakemore, *Exec Dir*
Griselda Alvarez, *Office Mgr*
EMP: 55
SQ FT: 8,500
SALES: 21.2MM **Privately Held**
SIC: 8111 Legal services

(P-23217)
DISCOVERREADY LLC
27200 Tourney Rd Ste 450, Valencia
(91355-4992)
PHONE...................661 284-6401
Phil Richard, *Branch Mgr*
EMP: 70
SALES (corp-wide): 28.9MM **Privately Held**
SIC: 8111 Legal services
PA: Discoverready Llc
200 S College St Fl 10
Charlotte NC 28202
980 939-7516

(P-23218)
DLA PIPER LLP (US)
550 S Hope St Ste 2300, Los Angeles
(90071-2678)
PHONE...................213 330-7700
Betty Shumener, *Principal*
Nancy Bizzini, *Office Mgr*
Jerry Berndsen, *Credit Mgr*
Paul Wallis, *Controller*
Stephanie Cooley, *Marketing Mgr*
EMP: 305
SALES (corp-wide): 5.1MM **Privately Held**
SIC: 8111 Legal services
PA: Dla Piper Llp (Us)
6225 Smith Ave Ste 200
Baltimore MD 21209
410 580-3000

(P-23219)
DLA PIPER LLP (US)
2000 University Ave # 100, East Palo Alto
(94303-2215)
PHONE...................650 833-2000
Francis Burch Jr, *CEO*
Carol Buss,
Elisabeth Eisner,
Michelle Harbottle,
Stacy Snowman,
EMP: 300
SALES (corp-wide): 5.1MM **Privately Held**
SIC: 8111 General practice attorney, lawyer
PA: Dla Piper Llp (Us)
6225 Smith Ave Ste 200
Baltimore MD 21209
410 580-3000

(P-23220)
DLA PIPER LLP (US)
2000 Avenue Of The Stars 400n, Los Angeles (90067-4735)
PHONE...................310 595-3000
Erin Walsh, *Branch Mgr*
Richard Friedman, *Counsel*
Patrick Hunnius, *Counsel*
Susan N Acquista, *Associate*
Joshua D Arisohn, *Associate*
EMP: 100
SALES (corp-wide): 5.1MM **Privately Held**
SIC: 8111 General practice attorney, lawyer
PA: Dla Piper Llp (Us)
6225 Smith Ave Ste 200
Baltimore MD 21209
410 580-3000

(P-23221)
DLA PIPER LLP (US)
2000 University Ave # 100, East Palo Alto
(94303-2215)
PHONE...................650 833-2000
Rusty Conner, *Partner*
Ruth Dickinson, *President*
Danica Joseph-Boxill, *President*
Arlene Parry, *President*
Tomika Thomas, *President*
EMP: 400
SALES (corp-wide): 5.1MM **Privately Held**
SIC: 8111 General practice law office

PA: Dla Piper Llp (Us)
6225 Smith Ave Ste 200
Baltimore MD 21209
410 580-3000

(P-23222)
DLA PIPER LLP (US)
401 B St Ste 1700, San Diego
(92101-4297)
PHONE...................619 699-2700
Steven Draeger, *Branch Mgr*
Penny Huber, *Director*
Mike Reese, *Director*
EMP: 250
SALES (corp-wide): 5.1MM **Privately Held**
SIC: 8111 General practice attorney, lawyer
PA: Dla Piper Llp (Us)
6225 Smith Ave Ste 200
Baltimore MD 21209
410 580-3000

(P-23223)
DLA PIPER LLP (US)
4365 Executive Dr # 1100, San Diego
(92121-2123)
PHONE...................858 677-1400
Gary O'Malley, *Partner*
Jeffrey Baglio, *COO*
Carla Hoffman, *Office Admin*
David M Clark, *Counsel*
Joyce Hulbert, *Manager*
EMP: 100
SALES (corp-wide): 5.1MM **Privately Held**
SIC: 8111 General practice attorney, lawyer
PA: Dla Piper Llp (Us)
6225 Smith Ave Ste 200
Baltimore MD 21209
410 580-3000

(P-23224)
DONAHUE GALLAGER WOODS LLP (PA)
1999 Harrison St Ste 2500, Oakland
(94612-4705)
PHONE...................415 381-4161
Lawrence K Rockwell, *Partner*
George J Barron, *Partner*
John J Coppinger, *Partner*
Michael J Dalton, *Partner*
Eric W Doney, *Partner*
EMP: 75 EST: 1918
SQ FT: 20,827
SALES (est): 6.3MM **Privately Held**
WEB: www.donahue.com
SIC: 8111 General practice attorney, lawyer

(P-23225)
DOWNEY BRAND LLP (PA)
621 Capitol Mall Fl 18, Sacramento
(95814-4731)
PHONE...................916 444-1000
Dale A Stern, *Managing Prtnr*
David R E Aladjem, *Partner*
Rhonda Cate Canby, *Partner*
Julie A Carter, *Partner*
Thomas N Cooper, *Partner*
EMP: 207 EST: 1926
SALES (est): 33.2MM **Privately Held**
WEB: www.dbsr.com
SIC: 8111 Legal services

(P-23226)
DREYER BBICH BCCOLA CLLHAM LLP
20 Bicentennial Cir, Sacramento
(95826-2802)
PHONE...................916 379-3500
Roger A Dreyer, *Managing Prtnr*
Joseph J Babich, *Partner*
Robert A Buccola, *Partner*
William Callaham, *Partner*
Stephen Davids,
EMP: 70
SQ FT: 5,000
SALES (est): 7.4MM **Privately Held**
WEB: www.dbbc.com
SIC: 8111 General practice attorney, lawyer

(P-23227)
DRINKER BIDDLE & REATH LLP
1800 Century Park E # 1400, Los Angeles
(90067-1517)
PHONE...................310 229-1282
Heather Abrigo,
Summer Conley, *Counsel*
Joseph Faucher, *Counsel*
Ryan Tzeng, *Associate*
EMP: 170
SALES (corp-wide): 269.3MM **Privately Held**
SIC: 8111 Legal services
PA: Drinker, Biddle & Reath Llp
1 Logan Sq Ste 2000
Philadelphia PA 19103
215 988-2700

(P-23228)
DRINKER BIDDLE & REATH LLP
50 Fremont St Fl 20, San Francisco
(94105-2235)
PHONE...................415 591-7500
Debra Krueger, *Principal*
Gail Guglielmo, *Personnel Assit*
Steven Dwyer, *Manager*
Amy Frenzen, *Associate*
Matthew Smith, *Associate*
EMP: 170
SALES (corp-wide): 269.3MM **Privately Held**
SIC: 8111 Legal services
PA: Drinker, Biddle & Reath Llp
1 Logan Sq Ste 2000
Philadelphia PA 19103
215 988-2700

(P-23229)
DUANE MORRIS LLP
1 Market Plz Ste 2000, San Francisco
(94105-1104)
PHONE...................415 957-3000
Leslye Olson, *Manager*
Glenn Manishin, *Partner*
Steven Packer, *Accountant*
Victor Keen, *Counsel*
Sallie Kim, *Counsel*
EMP: 150
SALES (corp-wide): 318.9MM **Privately Held**
WEB: www.duanemorris.com
SIC: 8111 Legal services
PA: Duane Morris Llp
30 S 17th St Fl 5
Philadelphia PA 19103
215 979-1000

(P-23230)
DUCKOR SPRADLING METZGER
3043 4th Ave, San Diego (92103-5801)
PHONE...................619 209-3000
Michael J Duckor, *President*
Laura Van Story, *President*
Gary J Spradling, *Vice Ch Bd*
Sarah O'Brien, *Executive*
Scott Metzger, *Admin Sec*
EMP: 70
SQ FT: 25,000
SALES (est): 8.5MM **Privately Held**
WEB: www.dsm-law.com
SIC: 8111 Legal services

(P-23231)
DYKEMA GOSSETT PLLC
333 S Grand Ave Ste 2100, Los Angeles
(90071-1525)
PHONE...................213 457-1800
Caroline Acossano, *Manager*
David Newman, *Technology*
Nancy Adams, *Sales Executive*
E L Horton, *Counsel*
Brian Newman, *Counsel*
EMP: 60
SALES (corp-wide): 102.9MM **Privately Held**
SIC: 8111 General practice law office
PA: Dykema Gossett P.L.L.C.
400 Renaissance Ctr
Detroit MI 48243
313 568-6800

PRODUCTS & SERVICES SECTION

8111 - Legal Svcs County (P-23252)

(P-23232)
EILEEN NOTTOLI
Also Called: Allen Matkins
3 Embarcadero Ctr # 1200, San Francisco (94111-4003)
PHONE 415 837-1515
EMP: 75 EST: 2013
SALES (est): 1.7MM **Privately Held**
SIC: 8111

(P-23233)
ENGSTROM LIPSCOMB AND LACK A (PA)
10100 Santa Monica Blvd # 1200, Los Angeles (90067-4113)
PHONE 310 552-3800
Fax: 310 552-9434
Paul Engstrom, *President*
Lee G Lipscomb, *Vice Pres*
Walter J Lack, *Admin Sec*
Joseph J Segui Jr, *Admin Sec*
Eric Greshler, *Analyst*
EMP: 70 EST: 1974
SQ FT: 22,000
SALES (est): 15.1MM **Privately Held**
WEB: www.elllaw.com
SIC: 8111 General practice law office

(P-23234)
EPSTEIN BECKER & GREEN PC
1875 Century Park E # 500, Los Angeles (90067-2337)
PHONE 310 556-8861
Sandy Siciliano, *Manager*
Alan B Dickson,
Ted Gehring, *Associate*
Rhea Mariano, *Associate*
EMP: 60
SALES (corp-wide): 57.8MM **Privately Held**
SIC: 8111 Legal services
PA: Epstein Becker & Green P.C.
250 Park Ave Fl 12
New York NY 10177
212 351-4500

(P-23235)
EVOLVE DISCOVERY LA LLC
811 Wilshire Blvd # 1400, Los Angeles (90017-2606)
PHONE 213 802-1260
Andrew Jimenez, *CEO*
Greg Tam, *Associate Dir*
Laura Tsang, *Administration*
EMP: 99
SALES (est): 4.9MM **Privately Held**
SIC: 8111 Legal services

(P-23236)
FALLBROOK PUBLIC UTILITY DST
990 E Mission Rd, Fallbrook (92028-2232)
P.O. Box 2290 (92088-2290)
PHONE 760 728-1125
Bryan Bradry, *General Mgr*
Nick Hoskot, *President*
Marcie Eilers, *Treasurer*
Mary McNeil, *Vice Pres*
Brian J Brady, *General Mgr*
EMP: 67
SQ FT: 12,000
SALES (est): 27.4MM **Privately Held**
WEB: www.fpud.com
SIC: 8111 Administrative & government law

(P-23237)
FENWICK & WEST LLP (PA)
801 California St, Mountain View (94041-1990)
PHONE 650 988-8500
Fax: 650 938-5200
Gordon K Davidson, *General Ptnr*
Michael R Blum, *Partner*
Darren E Donnelly, *Partner*
Dan Dorosin, *Partner*
Stephen D Gillespie, *Partner*
EMP: 375 EST: 1971
SALES (est): 104.5MM **Privately Held**
SIC: 8111 Legal services; patent, trademark & copyright law; taxation law

(P-23238)
FENWICK & WEST LLP
555 California St Fl 12, San Francisco (94104-1515)
PHONE 415 875-2300
Kacey Leonis, *Office Mgr*
Kevin Moore, *CTO*
Karla Cardona, *Librarian*
Chris Howland, *Legal Staff*
Daniel Brownstone, *Associate*
EMP: 120
SALES (corp-wide): 104.5MM **Privately Held**
SIC: 8111 Legal services; patent, trademark & copyright law; taxation law
PA: Fenwick & West Llp
801 California St
Mountain View CA 94041
650 988-8500

(P-23239)
FIRM A CHUGH PROFESSIONAL CORP
15925 Carmenita Rd, Cerritos (90703-2206)
PHONE 562 229-1220
Fax: 562 229-1221
Navneet Singh Chugh, *Principal*
Kathryn Uy, *Office Mgr*
Guneet Singh, *Administration*
Shilpa Mehta, *CPA*
Francesca Echavarria, *Marketing Staff*
EMP: 73
SALES (est): 10.5MM **Privately Held**
SIC: 8111 General practice law office

(P-23240)
FIRM A CHUGH PROFESSIONAL CORP
4800 Great America Pkwy # 310, Santa Clara (95054-1227)
PHONE 408 970-0100
Navneet Chugh, *Manager*
EMP: 50
SALES (corp-wide): 17.3MM **Privately Held**
WEB: www.chugh.com
SIC: 8111 General practice law office
PA: Chugh Firm, The A Professional Corporation
15925 Carmenita Rd
Cerritos CA 90703
562 229-1220

(P-23241)
FIRST LEGAL SUPPORT SVCS LLC (PA)
1517 Beverly Blvd, Los Angeles (90026-5704)
PHONE 213 250-1111
Fax: 213 481-3771
Elisha Gilboa, *Mng Member*
Aida Lopez, *Area Mgr*
Yvonne Thompson, *Area Mgr*
Pablo Rios, *Office Mgr*
Don Hoefnagel, *Sales Dir*
EMP: 54
SQ FT: 3,000
SALES (est): 14.3MM **Privately Held**
WEB: www.firstlegalsupport.com
SIC: 8111 Legal aid service

(P-23242)
FISH & RICHARDSON PC
500 Arguello St Ste 500, Redwood City (94063-1568)
PHONE 650 839-5070
Fax: 650 839-5071
Peter Devlin, *President*
Leeanne Martin, *Executive*
Wayne Wilde, *CTO*
Yvonne Mills, *Financial Exec*
Sherry Hunt, *Legal Staff*
EMP: 100
SALES (corp-wide): 106.1MM **Privately Held**
WEB: www.fr.com
SIC: 8111 General practice attorney, lawyer
PA: Fish & Richardson P.C.
1 Marina Park Dr Ste 1700
Boston MA 02210
617 542-5070

(P-23243)
FISH & RICHARDSON PC
12390 El Camino Real, San Diego (92130-3162)
PHONE 858 678-5070
Fax: 858 678-5099
Cindy Winters, *Manager*
Neil Hansuvadha, *Software Engr*
Jenifer Potter, *Project Mgr*
Rudy Cobian, *Technology*
Deborah Pollinger, *Human Res Dir*
EMP: 150
SALES (corp-wide): 96.4MM **Privately Held**
WEB: www.fr.com
SIC: 8111 Legal services
PA: Fish & Richardson P.C.
1 Marina Park Dr Ste 1700
Boston MA 02210
617 542-5070

(P-23244)
FISHER & PHILLIPS LLP
2050 Main St Ste 1000, Irvine (92614-8240)
PHONE 949 851-2424
Connie Jedrzejewski, *Admin Asst*
Donna Cosky, *Network Mgr*
Mark J Jacobs, *Associate*
Bruce A Lrson, *Associate*
Danielle Moore, *Associate*
EMP: 53
SALES (corp-wide): 128.6MM **Privately Held**
WEB: www.laborlawyers.com
SIC: 8111 General practice attorney, lawyer
PA: Fisher & Phillips Llp
1075 Peachtree St Ne # 3500
Atlanta GA 30309
404 231-1400

(P-23245)
FITZGRALD ABBOTT BEARDSLEY LLP
1221 Broadway Fl 21, Oakland (94612-1837)
P.O. Box 12867 (94604-2867)
PHONE 510 451-3300
Fax: 510 451-1527
Michael S Word, *Managing Prtnr*
Lawrence Shepp, *Chief Mktg Ofcr*
Robert Carstensen, *Admin Sec*
Kathi Kling, *Accounting Mgr*
Susan Von,
EMP: 71
SQ FT: 20,000
SALES (est): 9MM **Privately Held**
WEB: www.fablaw.com
SIC: 8111 General practice law office

(P-23246)
FLIESLER DUBB MYER LOVEJOY LLP
4 Embarcadero Ctr Ste 400, San Francisco (94111-4156)
PHONE 415 362-3800
Fax: 415 362-2928
Martin C Fliesler, *Partner*
David E Lovejoy, *Partner*
Sheldon R Meyer, *Partner*
Mark E Miller, *Partner*
Gerald B Rosenberg, *Partner*
EMP: 54
SQ FT: 19,674
SALES (est): 4MM **Privately Held**
SIC: 8111 Patent, trademark & copyright law

(P-23247)
FLOYD SKEREN & KELLY LLP (PA)
Also Called: FS&k
101 Moody Ct Ste 200, Thousand Oaks (91360-6068)
PHONE 818 206-9222
Fax: 818 591-3572
Thomas M Skeren Jr, *President*
Todd Kelly, *Principal*
Thomas Skeren, *Principal*
Artur Karsanov, *Info Tech Dir*
Patty S Salomon, *Legal Staff*
EMP: 93
SALES (est): 20.9MM **Privately Held**
SIC: 8111 General practice law office

(P-23248)
FOLEY & LARDNER LLP
975 Page Mill Rd, Palo Alto (94304-1013)
PHONE 650 856-3700
Susan Lamont, *Manager*
Monique Blakey, *President*
Deborah Collins, *President*
Christine Escavaille, *President*
Karen Fay, *President*
EMP: 121
SALES (corp-wide): 383.5MM **Privately Held**
SIC: 8111 General practice attorney, lawyer
PA: Foley & Lardner Llp
777 E Wisconsin Ave # 3800
Milwaukee WI 53202
414 271-2400

(P-23249)
FOLEY & LARDNER LLP
555 California St # 1700, San Francisco (94104-1503)
PHONE 415 434-4484
Eileen Ridley, *Managing Prtnr*
Nancy Geenen, *Partner*
Jina Goldenberg, *Administration*
Deborah Feliciano, *Manager*
EMP: 80
SQ FT: 3,000
SALES (corp-wide): 383.5MM **Privately Held**
WEB: www.foley.com
SIC: 8111 General practice attorney, lawyer
PA: Foley & Lardner Llp
777 E Wisconsin Ave # 3800
Milwaukee WI 53202
414 271-2400

(P-23250)
FOLEY & LARDNER LLP
555 S Flower St Ste 3500, Los Angeles (90071-2411)
PHONE 213 972-4500
Sergiy Sivochek, *Branch Mgr*
Richard Torres, *Technical Staff*
Jeff Atkin, *Counsel*
Daniel Danny, *Manager*
Justin Sobaje, *Associate*
EMP: 125
SALES (corp-wide): 383.5MM **Privately Held**
SIC: 8111 Specialized law offices, attorneys
PA: Foley & Lardner Llp
777 E Wisconsin Ave # 3800
Milwaukee WI 53202
414 271-2400

(P-23251)
FOLEY & LARDNER LLP
3579 Vly Cntre Dr Ste 300, San Diego (92130)
PHONE 858 847-6700
Greg Moser, *Partner*
Steven Millendorf, *Associate*
EMP: 70
SALES (corp-wide): 383.5MM **Privately Held**
WEB: www.foley.com
SIC: 8111 Legal services
PA: Foley & Lardner Llp
777 E Wisconsin Ave # 3800
Milwaukee WI 53202
414 271-2400

(P-23252)
FORD MOTOR COMPANY
3 Glen Bell Way Ste 200, Irvine (92618-3392)
PHONE 949 341-5800
Fax: 949 341-6151
Michael O'Driscoll, *President*
Ulrich John, *Sales Staff*
Tony Varlesi, *Manager*
EMP: 450
SALES (corp-wide): 149.5B **Publicly Held**
WEB: www.ford.com
SIC: 8111 7549 Corporate, partnership & business law; automotive customizing services, non-factory basis

8111 - Legal Svcs County (P-23253)

PA: Ford Motor Company
1 American Rd
Dearborn MI 48126
313 322-3000

(P-23253)
FOX ROTHSCHILD LLP
1800 Century Park E # 300, Los Angeles (90067-1501)
PHONE..................213 624-6560
Anne Fisher, *Branch Mgr*
EMP: 63
SALES (corp-wide): 169.9MM **Privately Held**
SIC: 8111 Legal services
PA: Fox Rothschild Llp
2000 Market St Fl 20
Philadelphia PA 19103
215 299-2000

(P-23254)
FRAGOMEN DEL REY BERNSE
11238 El Camino Real # 100, San Diego (92130-2653)
PHONE..................858 793-1600
Gary Perl, *Partner*
Nicole M Richard, *Assistant*
EMP: 60
SALES (corp-wide): 285.9MM **Privately Held**
SIC: 8111 Legal services
PA: Fragomen, Del Rey, Bernsen & Loewy, Llp
7 Hanover Sq Ste 800
New York NY 10004
732 862-5000

(P-23255)
FRAGOMEN DEL REY BERNSE
11150 W Olympic Blvd # 1000, Los Angeles (90064-1827)
PHONE..................310 820-3322
Fax: 310 820-2702
Peter Loewy, *Principal*
Thomas O'Neil, *General Mgr*
EMP: 50
SALES (corp-wide): 285.9MM **Privately Held**
SIC: 8111 General practice law office
PA: Fragomen, Del Rey, Bernsen & Loewy, Llp
7 Hanover Sq Ste 800
New York NY 10004
732 862-5000

(P-23256)
FRAGOMEN DEL REY BERNSE
18401 Von Karman Ave # 255, Irvine (92612-1596)
PHONE..................949 660-3504
Michael Boshnaick, *Manager*
Tonia Cheong, *Human Res Mgr*
Maria Fajatin, *Legal Staff*
EMP: 81
SALES (corp-wide): 285.9MM **Privately Held**
SIC: 8111 General practice attorney, lawyer
PA: Fragomen, Del Rey, Bernsen & Loewy, Llp
7 Hanover Sq Ste 800
New York NY 10004
732 862-5000

(P-23257)
FRAGOMEN DEL REY BERNSE
2121 Tasman Dr, Santa Clara (95054-1027)
PHONE..................408 919-0600
Cynthia Lang, *Branch Mgr*
Tonia Cheong, *Human Resources*
Lynne Hansen, *Human Resources*
EMP: 81
SALES (corp-wide): 259.9MM **Privately Held**
SIC: 8111 General practice attorney, lawyer
PA: Fragomen, Del Rey, Bernsen & Loewy, Llp
7 Hanover Sq Ste 800
New York NY 10004
732 862-5000

(P-23258)
FRANCISCO EMILIO ASSOC LAW OFF
17532 Von Karman Ave, Irvine (92614-6208)
PHONE..................949 474-2222
Fax: 949 622-1038
Emilio Francisco, *President*
EMP: 100
SALES (est): 3.9MM **Privately Held**
SIC: 8111 General practice attorney, lawyer

(P-23259)
FRANDZEL SHARE ROBINS BLOOM LC
1000 Wilshire Blvd # 1900, Los Angeles (90017-2427)
PHONE..................323 852-1000
Steve N Bloom, *President*
Lawrence Grosberg, *Shareholder*
Thomas Robins, *Vice Pres*
Albert Moon,
EMP: 55
SQ FT: 40,000
SALES (est): 7.7MM **Privately Held**
WEB: www.frandzel.com
SIC: 8111 General practice attorney, lawyer; general practice law office

(P-23260)
FREEMAN FREEMAN & SMILEY LLP (PA)
1888 Century Park E Fl 19, Los Angeles (90067-1723)
PHONE..................310 398-6227
Fax: 310 391-4042
Douglas K Freeman, *Partner*
Jill Draffin, *Partner*
Richard D Freeman, *Partner*
Fred J Marcus, *Partner*
Glenn T Sherman, *Partner*
EMP: 78
SQ FT: 25,000
SALES (est): 17.6MM **Privately Held**
WEB: www.ffslaw.com
SIC: 8111 General practice law office

(P-23261)
FULBRIGHT & JAWORSKI LLP
555 S Flower St Ste 4100, Los Angeles (90071-2417)
PHONE..................213 244-9941
Harry Hathaway, *Managing Prtnr*
Mark A McLean, *Partner*
Stevens Lynne, *Administration*
Scott Preston, *MIS Mgr*
Maryann Goodkind, *Counsel*
EMP: 200
SALES (corp-wide): 386.3MM **Privately Held**
WEB: www.fulbright.com
SIC: 8111 General practice attorney, lawyer
PA: Norton Rose Fulbright Us Llp
1301 Mckinney St Ste 5100
Houston TX 77010
713 651-5151

(P-23262)
FULWIDER AND PATTON LLP
6100 Center Dr Ste 1200, Los Angeles (90045-9203)
PHONE..................310 824-5555
Fax: 310 824-9696
Richard A Bardin, *Managing Prtnr*
Morley Drucker, *Senior Partner*
Scott Hansen, *Partner*
Katherine McDaniel, *Partner*
David Pitman, *Partner*
EMP: 100
SQ FT: 48,000
SALES (est): 12.5MM **Privately Held**
SIC: 8111 General practice attorney, lawyer

(P-23263)
GALLOWAY LUCCHESE EVERSON
2300 Contra Costa Blvd Ste 350, Walnut Creek (94596)
PHONE..................925 930-9090
Fax: 925 943-7542
G Patrick Galloway, *President*
David R Lucchese, *Vice Pres*
Connie Werschem, *Office Mgr*
Joseph S Picchi,
Martin J Everson, *Director*
EMP: 50
SQ FT: 13,700
SALES (est): 5.5MM **Privately Held**
WEB: www.glattys.com
SIC: 8111 General practice law office

(P-23264)
GAW VAN MALE SMITH MYERS
1411 Oliver Rd Ste 300, Fairfield (94534-3433)
PHONE..................707 425-1250
Fax: 707 425-1255
Scott Reynolds, *Manager*
EMP: 62
SALES (corp-wide): 10.8MM **Privately Held**
WEB: www.gvmsmm.com
SIC: 8111 General practice attorney, lawyer
PA: Gaw, Van Male, Smith, Myers & Miroglio A Professional Corp
1000 Main St Ste 300
Napa CA 94559
707 469-7100

(P-23265)
GIBBS GIDEN LOCHER
1880 Century Park E # 1200, Los Angeles (90067-1621)
PHONE..................310 552-3400
Fax: 310 552-0805
Richard J Wittbrodt, *Principal*
Lannette M Pabon, *Chief Mktg Ofcr*
Lisa Tores, *Executive*
Kenneth C Gibbs, *Principal*
Joseph M Giden, *Principal*
EMP: 70
SQ FT: 27,000
SALES (est): 10.8MM **Privately Held**
WEB: www.ggt.com
SIC: 8111 General practice attorney, lawyer

(P-23266)
GIBSON DUNN & CRUTCHER LLP
Also Called: Gibson Dun Law Firm
1881 Page Mill Rd, Palo Alto (94304-1146)
PHONE..................650 849-5300
Fax: 650 849-5333
Russel Hansel, *Managing Prtnr*
Paul J Collins, *Partner*
H Mark Lyon, *Partner*
Dave Goodell, *Info Tech Mgr*
Katherine Edwards, *Human Res Mgr*
EMP: 60
SALES (corp-wide): 360.8MM **Privately Held**
WEB: www.gibsondunn.com
SIC: 8111 Legal services
PA: Gibson, Dunn & Crutcher Llp
333 S Grand Ave Ste 4400
Los Angeles CA 90071
213 229-8063

(P-23267)
GIBSON DUNN & CRUTCHER LLP
3161 Michelson Dr # 1200, Irvine (92612-4412)
PHONE..................949 451-3800
Karen Kubani, *Branch Mgr*
Alba Cabriales, *President*
Candie Trainor, *President*
Roger Smiley, *Telecomm Dir*
Misty Lenahan, *Admin Asst*
EMP: 200
SALES (corp-wide): 360.8MM **Privately Held**
WEB: www.gibsondunn.com
SIC: 8111 General practice law office
PA: Gibson, Dunn & Crutcher Llp
333 S Grand Ave Ste 4400
Los Angeles CA 90071
213 229-8063

(P-23268)
GIBSON DUNN & CRUTCHER LLP (PA)
Also Called: Gibson Dunn
333 S Grand Ave Ste 4400, Los Angeles (90071-3197)
PHONE..................213 229-8063
Fax: 213 621-0272
Ken Doran, *Managing Prtnr*
Nicholas Aleksander, *Partner*
Peter Alexiadis, *Partner*
Lisa A Alfaro, *Partner*
Terrence R Allen, *Partner*
EMP: 500
SQ FT: 250,000
SALES (est): 360.8MM **Privately Held**
WEB: www.gibsondunn.com
SIC: 8111 General practice law office

(P-23269)
GIBSON DUNN & CRUTCHER LLP
2029 Century Park E # 4000, Los Angeles (90067-3026)
PHONE..................310 552-8500
Fax: 213 229-7180
Julie Denton, *General Mgr*
William Stinehart Jr, *Partner*
EMP: 65
SALES (corp-wide): 360.8MM **Privately Held**
WEB: www.gibsondunn.com
SIC: 8111 General practice law office
PA: Gibson, Dunn & Crutcher Llp
333 S Grand Ave Ste 4400
Los Angeles CA 90071
213 229-8063

(P-23270)
GIBSON DUNN & CRUTCHER LLP
555 Mission St Ste 3000, San Francisco (94105-0921)
PHONE..................415 393-8200
Fax: 415 393-8306
Mike Saad, *Manager*
Kathrin Sears, *Partner*
Brian O'Shea, *Software Engr*
Aileen Y MO, *Criminal Law*
Sarah E Pipmir, *Criminal Law*
EMP: 101
SALES (corp-wide): 360.8MM **Privately Held**
WEB: www.gibsondunn.com
SIC: 8111 General practice attorney, lawyer
PA: Gibson, Dunn & Crutcher Llp
333 S Grand Ave Ste 4400
Los Angeles CA 90071
213 229-8063

(P-23271)
GILBERT KLLY CRWLEY JNNETT LLP (PA)
550 S Hope St Ste 2200, Los Angeles (90071-2631)
PHONE..................213 615-7000
Fax: 213 615-7101
Jon H Tisdale, *Managing Prtnr*
Paul Bigley, *Partner*
Timothy Kenna, *Partner*
Arthur J Mc Keon III, *Partner*
Lisa Braham, *President*
EMP: 75
SQ FT: 30,000
SALES (est): 16.8MM **Privately Held**
WEB: www.gilbertkelly.com
SIC: 8111 General practice law office

(P-23272)
GIPSON HOFFMAN & PANCIONE A
1901 Avenue Of The Stars # 1100, Los Angeles (90067-6002)
PHONE..................310 556-4660
Lawrence R Barnett, *President*
Richard P Solomon, *Partner*
Kenneth I Sidle, *President*
J R Zeeck, *COO*
Robert E Gipson, *Vice Pres*
EMP: 70
SQ FT: 27,000
SALES (est): 9.8MM **Privately Held**
WEB: www.ghplaw.com
SIC: 8111 General practice attorney, lawyer; corporate, partnership & business law; bankruptcy law

PRODUCTS & SERVICES SECTION

8111 - Legal Svcs County (P-23294)

(P-23273)
GIRARDI & KEESE (PA)
1126 Wilshire Blvd, Los Angeles (90017-1904)
PHONE....................213 977-0211
Fax: 213 481-1554
Thomas V Girardi, *Partner*
Robert M Keese, *Partner*
Grace Fujioka, *President*
Rachel Nelson, *President*
Shirleen Fujimoto, *Admin Asst*
EMP: 95
SQ FT: 5,000
SALES (est): 13.4MM Privately Held
WEB: www.girardikeese.com
SIC: 8111 General practice attorney, lawyer

(P-23274)
GLASER WEIL FINK JACOBS (PA)
10250 Constellation Blvd # 1900, Los Angeles (90067-6229)
PHONE....................310 553-3000
Terry Christensen, *Managing Prtnr*
Barry E Fink, *Partner*
Patricia L Glaser, *Partner*
John Mason, *Partner*
Peter Weil, *Partner*
EMP: 160
SQ FT: 76,000
SALES (est): 29.6MM Privately Held
SIC: 8111 General practice law office

(P-23275)
GLASPY & GLASPY A PROF CORP
100 Pringle Ave Ste 750, Walnut Creek (94596-7330)
P.O. Box 8104 (94596-8104)
PHONE....................408 279-8844
Fax: 408 279-6941
David M Glaspy, *President*
Thomas C Glaspy, *Vice Pres*
Sheri Rollo, *Office Mgr*
▲ EMP: 50
SALES (est): 4.5MM Privately Held
WEB: www.glaspy.com
SIC: 8111 Specialized law offices, attorneys

(P-23276)
GLOBAL USA GREEN CARD ✪
201 Spear St Ste 1100, San Francisco (94105-6164)
PHONE....................415 915-4151
Eran Druker, *VP Opers*
EMP: 60 EST: 2016
SALES (est): 881.5K Privately Held
SIC: 8111 Immigration & naturalization law

(P-23277)
GOLD VALLEY PROPERTIES
Also Called: Nolan Hamerly Etienne & Hoss
333 Salinas St, Salinas (93901-2751)
P.O. Box 2510 (93902-2510)
PHONE....................831 424-1414
Myron Ettienne Jr, *Partner*
Lloyd Lowry Jr, *Partner*
Stephen Pearson, *Partner*
James Schwefel, *Partner*
Leslie Finnegan,
EMP: 70
SALES (est): 4.3MM Privately Held
SIC: 8111 General practice attorney, lawyer

(P-23278)
GOODWIN PROCTER LLP
601 S Figueroa St # 4100, Los Angeles (90017-5710)
PHONE....................213 426-2500
Dean Pappas, *Managing Prtnr*
Lee Sherman, *Associate*
Jennifer Sung, *Associate*
EMP: 60
SALES (corp-wide): 284.5MM Privately Held
SIC: 8111 General practice attorney, lawyer
PA: Goodwin Procter Llp
   100 Northern Ave
   Boston MA 02210
   617 570-1000

(P-23279)
GORDON EDELSTEIN KREPACK
3580 Wilshire Blvd # 1800, Los Angeles (90010-2530)
PHONE....................213 739-7000
Fax: 213 386-1671
Roger L Gordon, *Partner*
Mark Edelstein, *Partner*
Richard Felton, *Partner*
Irwin Goldstein, *Partner*
Larry Goldstein, *Partner*
EMP: 50
SALES (est): 9.9MM Privately Held
WEB: www.geklaw.com
SIC: 8111 Legal services

(P-23280)
GORDON R LEVINSON A PROF CORP
Also Called: Levinson Law Group
2768 Loker Ave W Ste 101, Carlsbad (92010-6681)
PHONE....................760 692-2260
Gordon Levinson, *President*
EMP: 99
SALES (est): 5.4MM Privately Held
SIC: 8111 Legal services

(P-23281)
GORDON REES SCLLY MNSKHANI LLP
655 University Ave # 200, Sacramento (95825-6707)
PHONE....................916 830-6900
Kathleen M Rhoads, *Managing Prtnr*
Marquis Gardner, *Marketing Staff*
Julie Vernon, *Legal Staff*
EMP: 94
SALES (corp-wide): 111.6MM Privately Held
SIC: 8111 Legal services
PA: Rees Gordon Scully Mansukhani Llp
   275 Battery St Ste 2000
   San Francisco CA 94111
   415 986-5900

(P-23282)
GORDON REES SCLLY MNSKHANI LLP
2211 Michelson Dr Ste 400, Irvine (92612-1390)
PHONE....................949 255-6950
Douglas Smith, *Office Mgr*
Steve Holub, *Financial Exec*
EMP: 80
SALES (corp-wide): 111.6MM Privately Held
SIC: 8111 Legal services
PA: Rees Gordon Scully Mansukhani Llp
   275 Battery St Ste 2000
   San Francisco CA 94111
   415 986-5900

(P-23283)
GORDON REES SCLLY MNSKHANI LLP (PA)
275 Battery St Ste 2000, San Francisco (94111-3361)
PHONE....................415 677-9673
Fax: 415 677-9673
Dion N Cominos, *Managing Prtnr*
Jewel K Basse, *Senior Partner*
Jorge J Perez, *Partner*
David C Capell, *Managing Prtnr*
Thomas Chairs, *Managing Prtnr*
EMP: 325
SQ FT: 57,500
SALES (est): 111.6MM Privately Held
WEB: www.gordonrees.com
SIC: 8111 Specialized law offices, attorneys; corporate, partnership & business law; product liability law

(P-23284)
GORDON REES SCLLY MNSKHANI LLP
633 W 5th St Fl 52, Los Angeles (90071-2086)
PHONE....................213 576-5000
Fax: 213 680-4470
Scott Sirlin, *Owner*
Mila Owen, *President*
Allison M Andrews, *Legal Staff*
Michael Brown, *Legal Staff*
Randall Stubblefield, *Legal Staff*

(P-23285)
GORDON REES SCLLY MNSKHANI LLP
101 W Broadway Ste 1600, San Diego (92101-8217)
PHONE....................619 696-6700
Fax: 619 696-7124
Gary Zacher, *Managing Prtnr*
Roger Mansukhani, *COO*
Suzanna Canales, *Admin Asst*
Sharee Gill, *Legal Staff*
Annette Berrio, *Counsel*
EMP: 100
SQ FT: 7,000
SALES (corp-wide): 111.6MM Privately Held
WEB: www.gordonrees.com
SIC: 8111 General practice law office
PA: Rees Gordon Scully Mansukhani Llp
   275 Battery St Ste 2000
   San Francisco CA 94111
   415 986-5900

(P-23286)
GORDON REES SCLLY MNSKHANI LLP
101 W Broadway Ste 2000, San Diego (92101-8221)
PHONE....................415 986-5900
Craig Hill, *Manager*
EMP: 90
SALES (corp-wide): 111.6MM Privately Held
WEB: www.gordonrees.com
SIC: 8111 Legal services
PA: Rees Gordon Scully Mansukhani Llp
   275 Battery St Ste 2000
   San Francisco CA 94111
   415 986-5900

(P-23287)
GREEN GLUSK FIELD CLAMA & MACH
1900 Avenue Of The Stars 21f, Los Angeles (90067-4301)
PHONE....................310 553-3610
Fax: 212 553-0687
Jonathan R Fitzgerrald, *Principal*
ARI B Brumer, *Partner*
Ricardo P Cestero, *Partner*
Stephen Claman, *Partner*
Bert Fields, *Partner*
EMP: 200
SQ FT: 80,000
SALES (est): 37.1MM Privately Held
SIC: 8111 General practice attorney, lawyer

(P-23288)
GREENBERG TRAURIG LLP
4 Embarcadero Ctr # 3000, San Francisco (94111-5983)
PHONE....................415 655-1300
Evan S Nadel, *Branch Mgr*
Michele Thomas, *Marketing Staff*
Andrew Bell, *Manager*
EMP: 98
SALES (corp-wide): 457.3MM Privately Held
SIC: 8111 Legal services
HQ: Greenberg Traurig, Llp
   200 Park Ave Fl 39
   New York NY 10166

(P-23289)
GREENBERG TRAURIG LLP
1840 Century Park E # 1900, Los Angeles (90067-2121)
PHONE....................310 586-7708
Fax: 310 586-7800
Richard Rowan, *Branch Mgr*
Edward Schultz, *Shareholder*
Pamela Sims, *President*
Jim Burns, *Administration*
Coral-Mary Southam, *Marketing Mgr*
EMP: 76

SALES (corp-wide): 111.6MM Privately Held
SIC: 8111 General practice law office
PA: Rees Gordon Scully Mansukhani Llp
   275 Battery St Ste 2000
   San Francisco CA 94111
   415 986-5900

(P-23290)
GREENBERG TRAURIG LLP
1900 University Ave Fl 5, East Palo Alto (94303-2283)
PHONE....................650 328-8500
Lance Joseph, *Branch Mgr*
Charles Birenbaum, *Shareholder*
Vivek Chavan, *Shareholder*
Shirley Taylor, *Branch Mgr*
Gail Case, *Legal Staff*
EMP: 73
SALES (corp-wide): 457.3MM Privately Held
SIC: 8111 General practice law office
HQ: Greenberg Traurig, Llp
   200 Park Ave Fl 39
   New York NY 10166

(P-23291)
GREENBERG TRAURIG LLP
3161 Michelson Dr # 1000, Irvine (92612-4410)
PHONE....................949 732-6500
Ray Lee, *Managing Prtnr*
Bruce Fischer, *Shareholder*
Jeffrey Joy, *Shareholder*
EMP: 70
SALES (corp-wide): 457.3MM Privately Held
SIC: 8111 Legal services
HQ: Greenberg Traurig, Llp
   200 Park Ave Fl 39
   New York NY 10166

(P-23292)
GREENE RDVSKY MALONEY SHARE LP
4 Embarcadero Ctr # 4000, San Francisco (94111-4106)
PHONE....................415 981-1400
Fax: 415 777-4961
Mark Hennigh, *Managing Prtnr*
Richard Green, *Senior Partner*
James Abrams, *Partner*
Thomas Feldstein, *Partner*
James Fotenos, *Partner*
EMP: 69
SQ FT: 18,800
SALES (est): 8.2MM Privately Held
WEB: www.grmslaw.com
SIC: 8111 Specialized law offices, attorneys; corporate, partnership & business law; real estate law; taxation law

(P-23293)
GRESHAM SAVAGE NOLAN & TILDEN (PA)
550 E Hospitality Ln # 300, San Bernardino (92408-4205)
PHONE....................619 794-0050
Mark A Ostoich, *President*
Bob Ritter, *Partner*
Tom Jacobsen, *COO*
Robert Ritter, *CFO*
Mario Alfaro, *Treasurer*
EMP: 53
SQ FT: 16,500
SALES (est): 11.8MM Privately Held
SIC: 8111 General practice law office

(P-23294)
GUNDERSON DETTMER STOUGH VILLE (PA)
1200 Seaport Blvd, Redwood City (94063-5537)
PHONE....................650 321-2400
Robert Gunderson, *Partner*
Darrin Brown, *Partner*
Colin Chapman, *Partner*
Dan O Connor, *Partner*
Joshua Cook, *Partner*
▲ EMP: 125
SALES (est): 35.5MM Privately Held
WEB: www.gdsvfh.com
SIC: 8111 General practice law office

8111 - Legal Svcs County (P-23295)

PRODUDUCTS & SERVICES SECTION

(P-23295)
H & R BLOCK INC
1745 Van Ness Ave, San Francisco (94109-3620)
PHONE.................................415 441-2666
Sharon Williams, *Manager*
Michelle Beacham, *Manager*
Kate Quillman, *Manager*
EMP: 50
SALES (corp-wide): 3B **Publicly Held**
WEB: www.hrblock.com
SIC: 8111 Legal services
PA: H&R Block, Inc.
1 H&R Block Way
Kansas City MO 64105
816 854-3000

(P-23296)
HAHN & HAHN LLP
301 E Colo Blvd Ste 900, Pasadena (91101)
PHONE.................................626 796-9123
Fax: 626 449-7357
Karl Swaidan, *Managing Prtnr*
Gene E Gregg Jr, *Partner*
R Scott Jenkins, *Partner*
Kristianne Kerns, *Partner*
Natasha Zaharov, *Partner*
EMP: 80
SQ FT: 15,175
SALES (est): 12.3MM **Privately Held**
WEB: www.hahnlawyers.com
SIC: 8111 General practice attorney, lawyer

(P-23297)
HAIGHT BROWN & BONESTEEL LLP (PA)
555 S Flower St Ste 4500, Los Angeles (90071-2441)
PHONE.................................213 542-8000
Fax: 310 215-7300
S Christian Stouder, *Managing Prtnr*
Kenneth Anderson, *Senior Partner*
Michael Bonesteel, *Senior Partner*
Carolyn Harper, *CFO*
Sharon Barnes, *Human Res Mgr*
EMP: 80
SQ FT: 36,265
SALES (est): 29MM **Privately Held**
WEB: www.hbblaw.com
SIC: 8111 General practice law office

(P-23298)
HANNA BROPHY MAC LEAN MC ALE (PA)
1956 Webster St Ste 450, Oakland (94612-2930)
PHONE.................................510 839-1180
Fax: 510 839-4804
Leslie Tuxhorn, *Managing Prtnr*
Joseph Nisim, *Partner*
Barbara Wood, *Partner*
Wendy Harnett, *Executive*
Meding Malone, *Administration*
EMP: 50
SQ FT: 10,000
SALES (est): 39.9MM **Privately Held**
WEB: www.hannabrophy.com
SIC: 8111 General practice law office

(P-23299)
HANSON BRIDGETT LLP
500 Capitol Mall Ste 1500, Sacramento (95814-4740)
PHONE.................................916 442-3333
Terrie Rasica, *Branch Mgr*
EMP: 50
SALES (corp-wide): 59.2MM **Privately Held**
SIC: 8111 General practice attorney, lawyer
PA: Hanson Bridgett Llp
425 Market St Fl 26
San Francisco CA 94105
415 543-2055

(P-23300)
HANSON BRIDGETT LLP (PA)
425 Market St Fl 26, San Francisco (94105-5401)
PHONE.................................415 543-2055
Fax: 415 541-9366
Andrew G Giacomini,
Alexander J Berline, *Senior Partner*

Lawrence Cirelli, *Partner*
Frank Lopez, *Partner*
Mary McEachron, *Partner*
EMP: 263
SQ FT: 79,120
SALES (est): 59.2MM **Privately Held**
WEB: www.hansonbridgett.com
SIC: 8111 General practice attorney, lawyer

(P-23301)
HARRIS STOCKWELL (PA)
3580 Wilshire Blvd Fl 19, Los Angeles (90010-2532)
PHONE.................................310 277-6669
Fax: 323 935-0198
Steven I Harris, *CEO*
Joanne Igyarto, *President*
Christine McKenna, *President*
Kimberly Hansen, *Vice Pres*
Richard M Widom, *Vice Pres*
EMP: 50 **EST:** 1970
SALES (est): 18.9MM **Privately Held**
SIC: 8111 General practice attorney, lawyer

(P-23302)
HART KING COLDREN A PROF CORP
4 Hutton Cntre Dr Ste 900, Santa Ana (92707)
PHONE.................................714 432-8700
Fax: 714 546-7457
Robert S Coldren, *President*
Gary R King, *Treasurer*
William R Hart, *Admin Sec*
Robin Offerdahl, *MIS Dir*
Travis Kiger, *Info Tech Mgr*
EMP: 60
SQ FT: 20,000
SALES (est): 9.2MM **Privately Held**
WEB: www.hkclaw.com
SIC: 8111 General practice attorney, lawyer

(P-23303)
HASSARD BONNINGTON LLP (PA)
Also Called: H B
275 Battery St Ste 1600, San Francisco (94111-3993)
PHONE.................................415 288-9800
Fax: 415 288-9801
James M Goodman, *General Ptnr*
Phillip F Ward, *Partner*
Eliana Paoletti, *Finance Mgr*
Marylou Miller, *Human Res Mgr*
Marcell P Neri, *Associate*
EMP: 59
SALES (est): 12.3MM **Privately Held**
WEB: www.hassard.com
SIC: 8111 General practice law office

(P-23304)
HAYNES AND BOONE LLP
525 University Ave # 400, Palo Alto (94301-1918)
PHONE.................................650 687-8800
Laurie Armstrong, *Manager*
Robert Baden, *Vice Pres*
Brian Duffy, *Vice Pres*
Tom Ho, *Vice Pres*
Dante Billups, *Office Spvr*
EMP: 91
SALES (corp-wide): 192.6MM **Privately Held**
SIC: 8111 Legal services
PA: Haynes And Boone, Llp
2323 Victory Ave Ste 700
Dallas TX 75219
214 651-5000

(P-23305)
HEIGHT BROWN AND BONESTEEL
555 S Flower St Ste 4500, Los Angeles (90071-2441)
PHONE.................................213 241-0900
Christian Stouder, *Managing Prtnr*
EMP: 60
SALES (est): 1.9MM **Privately Held**
SIC: 8111 Legal services

(P-23306)
HEMAR ROUSSO & HEALD L L P
Also Called: Hemar & Rousso Attys At Law
15910 Ventura Blvd # 1201, Encino (91436-2829)
PHONE.................................818 501-3800
Fax: 818 501-2985
Richard P Hemar, *Managing Prtnr*
Daniel E Heald, *Partner*
Martin J Rousso, *Partner*
Kelly Dreher, *COO*
Susan Breen, *Executive*
EMP: 50
SQ FT: 10,000
SALES (est): 6.6MM **Privately Held**
WEB: www.hemar-rousso.com
SIC: 8111 General practice law office

(P-23307)
HIGGS FLETCHER & MACK LLP
401 W A St Ste 2600, San Diego (92101-7913)
PHONE.................................619 236-1551
Fax: 619 696-1410
John Morrell, *General Ptnr*
Anna F Roppo, *Partner*
Phillip C Samouis, *Partner*
Therese P Ketteringham, *Vice Pres*
Martin Eliopulos, *Dept Chairman*
EMP: 150
SQ FT: 45,000
SALES (est): 23.6MM **Privately Held**
WEB: www.higgslaw.com
SIC: 8111 General practice attorney, lawyer

(P-23308)
HILL FARRER & BURRILL
Also Called: One California Plaza
300 S Grand Ave Fl 37, Los Angeles (90071-3147)
PHONE.................................213 620-0460
Fax: 213 624-4840
Scott Gilmore, *Chairman*
Leon S Anguire, *Partner*
Steven W Bacon, *Partner*
Julia L Birkel, *Partner*
William M Bitting, *Partner*
EMP: 100
SQ FT: 32,000
SALES (est): 17.4MM **Privately Held**
WEB: www.hillfarrer.com
SIC: 8111 General practice law office

(P-23309)
HOLLAND & KNIGHT LLP
400 S Hope St Ste 800, Los Angeles (90071-2809)
PHONE.................................213 896-2400
Maita Prout, *Manager*
Arlene Martin, *Administration*
Dean Leung, *CIO*
J L Morrison, *Technology*
Lauren Zielke, *Technology*
EMP: 100
SALES (corp-wide): 531.9MM **Privately Held**
WEB: www.hollandandknight.com
SIC: 8111 General practice law office
PA: Holland & Knight Llp
524 Grand Regency Blvd
Brandon FL 33510
813 901-4200

(P-23310)
HOLLAND & KNIGHT LLP
Also Called: Haight Gdnr Holland & Knight
50 California St Ste 2800, San Francisco (94111-4726)
PHONE.................................415 743-6900
Erik Dale, *Manager*
Scott Abrams, *Partner*
Matthew Vafidis, *Partner*
Erik Scales, *Business Mgr*
Linda Decker, *Legal Staff*
EMP: 50
SALES (corp-wide): 531.9MM **Privately Held**
WEB: www.hollandandknight.com
SIC: 8111 General practice law office
PA: Holland & Knight Llp
524 Grand Regency Blvd
Brandon FL 33510
813 901-4200

(P-23311)
HOLLINS SCHECHTER A PROF CORP
1851 E 1st St Ste 600, Santa Ana (92705-4049)
PHONE.................................714 558-9119
Andrew S Hollins, *President*
Bruce L Schechter, *Vice Pres*
Richard Hubbard, *Info Tech Mgr*
Jennifer Tusko, *Finance*
Stephen H Doorlag, *Manager*
EMP: 60 **EST:** 1978
SQ FT: 15,000
SALES (est): 4.8MM **Privately Held**
WEB: www.hollins-law.com
SIC: 8111 General practice attorney, lawyer

(P-23312)
HOPKINS & CARLEY A LAW CORP (PA)
70 S 1st St, San Jose (95113-2406)
P.O. Box 1469 (95109-1469)
PHONE.................................408 286-9800
William S Klein, *Principal*
Garth E Pickett, *Shareholder*
Daniel F Pyne, *Shareholder*
Candice Allen, *President*
Toni Antonio, *President*
EMP: 80
SQ FT: 33,000
SALES (est): 16.7MM **Privately Held**
WEB: www.hopkinscarley.com
SIC: 8111 Corporate, partnership & business law; divorce & family law; environmental law; real estate law

(P-23313)
HOWREY LLP
1950 University Ave # 400, East Palo Alto (94303-2295)
PHONE.................................650 798-3300
Jeanni McBride, *Manager*
Jim Valentine, *Managing Prtnr*
Nikki Habershon, *IT/INT Sup*
Nicholas Bauz, *Corp Counsel*
Eva Almirantearena,
EMP: 65
SALES (corp-wide): 53.9MM **Privately Held**
SIC: 8111 Legal services
PA: Howrey Llp
1299 Pennsylvania Ave Nw
Washington DC 20004
202 783-0800

(P-23314)
HUNT ORTMANN PALFFY NIEVES
301 N Lake Ave Fl 7, Pasadena (91101-5118)
PHONE.................................626 440-5200
Fax: 626 796-0107
Dale A Ortmann, *Co-Founder*
Thomas Palffy, *Treasurer*
Laurence Lubka, *Principal*
Omel Nieves, *Principal*
Barbara Gamboa, *Office Mgr*
EMP: 50
SQ FT: 18,000
SALES (est): 7.9MM **Privately Held**
SIC: 8111 General practice law office

(P-23315)
HUNTON & WILLIAMS LLP
575 Market St Ste 3700, San Francisco (94105-5827)
PHONE.................................415 975-3700
Fraser McAlpine, *Partner*
H Elmore, *Associate*
EMP: 94
SALES (corp-wide): 374.6MM **Privately Held**
SIC: 8111 Legal services
PA: Hunton & Williams Llp
Riverfront Plz E Towe 951
Richmond VA 23219
804 788-8200

(P-23316)
HUNTON & WILLIAMS LLP
550 S Hope St Ste 2000, Los Angeles (90071-2631)
PHONE.................................213 532-2000
Wally Martinez, *Managing Prtnr*

PRODUCTS & SERVICES SECTION
8111 - Legal Svcs County (P-23336)

Ann M Mortimer, *Managing Prtnr*
Becky MA, *Office Admin*
Julio Matamoros, *Info Tech Mgr*
Stephanie Der, *Associate*
EMP: 91
SALES (corp-wide): 374.6MM **Privately Held**
SIC: 8111 General practice law office
PA: Hunton & Williams Llp
Riverfront Plz E Towe 951
Richmond VA 23219
804 788-8200

(P-23317)
IMMERSION MEDICAL INC
50 Rio Robles, San Jose (95134-1806)
PHONE 408 467-1900
Victor Viegas, *President*
Shum Mukherjee, *CFO*
Alicia Avala, *Executive Asst*
Erick Baker, *IT Executive*
Marybeth Sabol, *Purchasing*
EMP: 85 **EST:** 1995
SALES (est): 5.3MM
SALES (corp-wide): 63.3MM **Publicly Held**
WEB: www.immersion.com
SIC: 8111 5047 Patent, trademark & copyright law; instruments, surgical & medical
PA: Immersion Corporation
50 Rio Robles
San Jose CA 95134
408 467-1900

(P-23318)
IRELL & MANELLA LLP (PA)
1800 Avenue Of The Stars # 900, Los Angeles (90067-4276)
PHONE 310 277-1010
Fax: 213 203-7199
Elliot Brown, *Managing Prtnr*
Gregory Klein, *Partner*
David Siegel, *Partner*
Morgan Chu, *Managing Prtnr*
Andra Barmash Greene, *Managing Prtnr*
EMP: 400
SQ FT: 154,000
SALES: 34.6K **Privately Held**
WEB: www.irell.com
SIC: 8111 General practice law office

(P-23319)
IRELL & MANELLA LLP
840 Nwport Ctr Dr Ste 400, Newport Beach (92660)
PHONE 949 760-0991
Nancy Adams, *Manager*
Daniel Lefler, *Partner*
Sherman Richard,
Robert W Stedman,
EMP: 100
SALES (corp-wide): 34.6K **Privately Held**
WEB: www.irell.com
SIC: 8111 General practice attorney, lawyer
PA: Irell & Manella Llp
1800 Avenue Of The Stars # 900
Los Angeles CA 90067
310 277-1010

(P-23320)
IRELL & MANELLA LLP
1800 Avenue Of The Stars # 900, Los Angeles (90067-4276)
PHONE 213 620-1555
Fax: 213 229-0514
Ed Cauffman, *Partner*
EMP: 500
SALES (corp-wide): 34.6K **Privately Held**
WEB: www.irell.com
SIC: 8111 General practice law office
PA: Irell & Manella Llp
1800 Avenue Of The Stars # 900
Los Angeles CA 90067
310 277-1010

(P-23321)
IRON LAW INC (PA)
663 S Rancho Santa Fe Rd, San Marcos (92078-3973)
PHONE 844 476-6529
Jesse Wagner, *CEO*
EMP: 50 **EST:** 2015
SQ FT: 500
SALES (est): 2.2MM **Privately Held**
SIC: 8111 Legal services

(P-23322)
IVIE MCNEILL WYATT A PROF LAW
444 S Flower St Ste 1800, Los Angeles (90071-2919)
PHONE 213 489-0028
Robert H Mc Neill Jr, *President*
Rickey Ivie, *Vice Pres*
Keith Wyatt, *Admin Sec*
Robert H McNeill, *Agent*
Lilia Duchrow, *Associate*
EMP: 50
SALES (est): 7.1MM **Privately Held**
WEB: www.imwlaw.com
SIC: 8111 General practice attorney, lawyer

(P-23323)
JACKOWAY TYREMAN WERTHEIMER AU
1925 Century Park E # 1500, Los Angeles (90067-2701)
PHONE 310 553-0305
Fax: 310 553-5036
Barry Hirsch, *President*
Leonard Cox, *CFO*
Mary E Doyle, *Admin Asst*
Maryeloen Dlyela, *Administration*
EMP: 100
SQ FT: 3,000
SALES (est): 14.8MM **Privately Held**
SIC: 8111 General practice law office

(P-23324)
JACKSON DEMARCO TIDUS PETER (PA)
2030 Main St Ste 1200, Irvine (92614-7256)
P.O. Box 19703 (92623-9703)
PHONE 949 752-8585
Fax: 714 752-0597
M Alim Malik, *CEO*
James Demarco, *President*
Thomas D Peckenpaugh, *President*
Ruth Mijuskovic, *CEO*
Andrew V Leitch,
EMP: 70
SQ FT: 23,000
SALES (est): 12.9MM **Privately Held**
SIC: 8111 General practice law office

(P-23325)
JEFFER MNGELS BTLR MTCHELL LLP (PA)
Also Called: Jmbm
1900 Avenue Of The Stars, Los Angeles (90067-4301)
PHONE 310 203-8080
Fax: 310 203-0567
Bruce P Jeffer, *Managing Prtnr*
Jonathan Bloch, *Partner*
James R Butler Jr, *Partner*
Dan E Chambers, *Partner*
Jennifer A Irrgang, *Partner*
EMP: 190
SALES (est): 39.9MM **Privately Held**
WEB: www.jmbm.com
SIC: 8111 General practice attorney, lawyer

(P-23326)
JEFFER MNGELS BTLR MTCHELL LLP
2 Embarcadero Ctr Fl 5, San Francisco (94111-3813)
PHONE 415 398-8080
Richard Rogan, *Manager*
Scott Castro, *Partner*
Nicolas De Lancie, *Partner*
Nicolas Delancie, *Partner*
Michael Hassen, *Partner*
EMP: 65
SALES (corp-wide): 39.9MM **Privately Held**
WEB: www.jmbm.com
SIC: 8111 Legal services
PA: Jeffer, Mangels, Butler & Mitchell, Llp
1900 Avenue Of The Stars
Los Angeles CA 90067
310 203-8080

(P-23327)
JOHN STEWART COMPANY
Also Called: Stewart, John Attorney At Law
642 S 2nd Ave, Covina (91723-3521)
PHONE 626 967-3734
John Stewart, *Branch Mgr*
Kathy Mulligan, *Manager*
EMP: 71
SALES (corp-wide): 107.7MM **Privately Held**
SIC: 8111 Legal services
PA: John Stewart Company
1388 Sutter St Ste 1100
San Francisco CA 94109
213 833-1860

(P-23328)
JOHNSON LA FOLLETTE
2677 N Main St Ste 901, Santa Ana (92705-6632)
PHONE 714 558-7008
Fax: 714 558-7008
Dennis Ames, *Managing Prtnr*
Odell Steven,
Kimberly D Snow, *Manager*
EMP: 65
SALES (corp-wide): 16.3MM **Privately Held**
WEB: www.ljdfa.com
SIC: 8111 General practice law office
PA: La Follette, Johnson, De Haas,
865 S Figueroa St # 3200
Los Angeles CA 90017
213 426-3600

(P-23329)
JONES DAY LIMITED PARTNERSHIP
12265 El Cmino Real 200, San Diego (92130)
PHONE 858 314-1200
Gerga Dow Lamaire, *Mng Member*
Irina Britva, *CTO*
Jordan B Arakawa, *Associate*
EMP: 60
SALES (corp-wide): 992.1MM **Privately Held**
SIC: 8111 Legal services
PA: Jones Day Limited Partnership
901 Lakeside Ave E Ste 2
Cleveland OH 44114
216 586-3939

(P-23330)
JONES DAY LIMITED PARTNERSHIP
1755 Embarcadero Rd # 101, Palo Alto (94303-3309)
PHONE 650 320-8412
Fax: 650 739-3900
Shawn Farrell, *Manager*
Behrooz Shariati, *Partner*
Bob Clarkson, *Managing Prtnr*
Brian Selden,
Laura E Alanis, *Associate*
EMP: 100
SALES (corp-wide): 992.1MM **Privately Held**
SIC: 8111 General practice attorney, lawyer
PA: Jones Day Limited Partnership
901 Lakeside Ave E Ste 2
Cleveland OH 44114
216 586-3939

(P-23331)
JONES DAY LIMITED PARTNERSHIP
3161 Michelson Dr Ste 800, Irvine (92612-4408)
PHONE 949 851-3939
Fax: 949 553-7539
R J Grabowski, *General Mgr*
Michelle Blum, *Executive*
Jeffrey Kirzner,
Steven Zadravecz,
Dulcie D Brand, *Manager*
EMP: 85
SQ FT: 22,500
SALES (corp-wide): 992.1MM **Privately Held**
SIC: 8111 General practice law office
PA: Jones Day Limited Partnership
901 Lakeside Ave E Ste 2
Cleveland OH 44114
216 586-3939

(P-23332)
JOSEPH C SANSONE COMPANY (PA)
Also Called: Tobin Lucks
21300 Victory Blvd # 300, Woodland Hills (91367-2525)
P.O. Box 4502 (91365-4502)
PHONE 818 226-3400
Fax: 818 226-3401
Irvin Lucks, *Managing Prtnr*
Edwin Lucks, *Partner*
Donald Tobin, *Partner*
Lynn Caprarelli, *Data Proc Exec*
EMP: 97
SALES (est): 19.4MM **Privately Held**
SIC: 8111 General practice law office

(P-23333)
K&L GATES LLP
55 2nd St Ste 1700, San Francisco (94105-3493)
PHONE 415 882-8200
Bob Schweda, *Manager*
Polly A Dinkel, *Partner*
Robert Mora, *Librarian*
Holly Hogan, *Associate*
EMP: 70
SALES (corp-wide): 507.3MM **Privately Held**
WEB: www.klxtra.com
SIC: 8111 General practice attorney, lawyer
PA: K&L Gates Llp
210 6th Ave Ste 1100
Pittsburgh PA 15222
412 355-6500

(P-23334)
K&L GATES LLP
10100 Santa Monica Blvd # 700, Los Angeles (90067-4003)
PHONE 310 552-5000
Fax: 310 552-5001
Karen Doyle, *Manager*
Jeryl A Bowers, *Partner*
Frederick J Ufkes, *Partner*
Paul Sweeney, *Admin Asst*
Alex Korotkevich, *Administration*
EMP: 50
SALES (corp-wide): 507.3MM **Privately Held**
WEB: www.klxtra.com
SIC: 8111 General practice law office
PA: K&L Gates Llp
210 6th Ave Ste 1100
Pittsburgh PA 15222
412 355-6500

(P-23335)
K&L GATES LLP
1 Park Plz Ste 1200, Irvine (92614-8509)
PHONE 949 756-0210
Fax: 949 253-0902
David Perry, *Manager*
Raymond Veldman, *Partner*
Fiona Oboussier-Lowe, *Administration*
Christine Dart, *Legal Staff*
Dean G Stathakis, *Director*
EMP: 50
SALES (corp-wide): 507.3MM **Privately Held**
WEB: www.klxtra.com
SIC: 8111 General practice attorney, lawyer
PA: K&L Gates Llp
210 6th Ave Ste 1100
Pittsburgh PA 15222
412 355-6500

(P-23336)
K&L GATES LLP
4 Embarcadero Ctr Fl 10, San Francisco (94111-4168)
PHONE 415 249-1000
Fax: 415 249-1001
Patsy Pressley, *Administration*
Laurence A Goldberg, *Partner*
Mark D Perlow, *Partner*
Peter S Heinecke, *Counsel*
Sharoni Finkelstein, *Associate*
EMP: 100

8111 - Legal Svcs County (P-23337)

SALES (corp-wide): 507.3MM **Privately Held**
SIC: 8111 Corporate, partnership & business law
PA: K&L Gates Llp
  210 6th Ave Ste 1100
  Pittsburgh PA 15222
  412 355-6500

(P-23337)
KASDAN SMNDS RILEY VAUGHAN LLP (PA)
19900 Macarthur Blvd # 850, Irvine (92612-8422)
PHONE 949 851-9000
Fax: 714 833-9455
Kenneth Kasdan, *Partner*
Cristi Paris, *President*
Eva Tripoett, *Admin Sec*
Devonne Sauceda, *Admin Asst*
Eric Mitchell, *Technology*
EMP: 56
SQ FT: 20,000
SALES (est): 10.4MM **Privately Held**
SIC: 8111 General practice law office

(P-23338)
KATTEN MUCHIN ROSENMAN LLP
100 Spectrum Center Dr # 1050, Irvine (92618-4977)
PHONE 714 386-5708
Austin Beardsley, *Branch Mgr*
Elizabeth Dominguez, *Associate*
Peter Wilson, *Associate*
EMP: 175
SALES (corp-wide): 263.3MM **Privately Held**
SIC: 8111 General practice law office
PA: Katten Muchin Rosenman Llp
  525 W Monroe St Ste 1900
  Chicago IL 60661
  312 902-5200

(P-23339)
KATTEN MUCHIN ROSENMAN LLP
515 S Flower St, Los Angeles (90071-2201)
PHONE 310 788-4498
Susan Taylor, *Branch Mgr*
Jennifer K Brooks, *Associate*
EMP: 175
SALES (corp-wide): 263.3MM **Privately Held**
SIC: 8111 General practice law office
PA: Katten Muchin Rosenman Llp
  525 W Monroe St Ste 1900
  Chicago IL 60661
  312 902-5200

(P-23340)
KATTEN MUCHIN ROSENMAN LLP
1999 Harrison St Ste 700, Oakland (94612-4704)
PHONE 415 360-5444
Shannon Broome, *Branch Mgr*
Thelma Patterson, *Manager*
Brian Poronsky, *Associate*
EMP: 175
SALES (corp-wide): 263.3MM **Privately Held**
SIC: 8111 General practice law office
PA: Katten Muchin Rosenman Llp
  525 W Monroe St Ste 1900
  Chicago IL 60661
  312 902-5200

(P-23341)
KATTEN MUCHIN ROSENMAN LLP
2029 Century Park E # 2600, Los Angeles (90067-3012)
PHONE 310 788-4400
Tanya Russell, *Branch Mgr*
Bruce G Vanyo, *Managing Prtnr*
Travis Mogren, *Technology*
Kathryn Gepner, *Marketing Mgr*
Alberto Magana, *Facilities Asst*
EMP: 150
SALES (corp-wide): 263.3MM **Privately Held**
WEB: www.kattenlaw.com
SIC: 8111 General practice law office

PA: Katten Muchin Rosenman Llp
  525 W Monroe St Ste 1900
  Chicago IL 60661
  312 902-5200

(P-23342)
KAWELA ONE LLC
3000 El Camino Real, Palo Alto (94306-2100)
PHONE 650 843-5000
Cooley Godward, *Principal*
Craig Dauchy, *CPA*
Gregg Kleiner, *CPA*
EMP: 98
SALES (est): 9.2MM **Privately Held**
SIC: 8111 Legal services

(P-23343)
KAYE SCHOLER LLP
3000 El Camino Real 2-400, Palo Alto (94306-2112)
PHONE 650 319-4500
Aurel Iderstine, *Manager*
EMP: 68
SALES (corp-wide): 265.4MM **Privately Held**
SIC: 8111 General practice law office
PA: Kaye Scholer Llp
  250 W 55th St Fl 4
  New York NY 10019
  212 836-8000

(P-23344)
KAYE SCHOLER LLP
1999 Ave Of Stars # 1500, Los Angeles (90067-6112)
PHONE 310 788-1000
Fax: 310 788-1200
Aurel Van Iderstine, *Branch Mgr*
Barry Lawrence, *Managing Prtnr*
Larry R Feldman, *CPA*
Cindy Fortune, *Persnl Dir*
Ruth Vega,
EMP: 128
SALES (corp-wide): 265.4MM **Privately Held**
SIC: 8111 General practice law office
PA: Kaye Scholer Llp
  250 W 55th St Fl 4
  New York NY 10019
  212 836-8000

(P-23345)
KEESAL YOUNG LOGAN A PROF CORP (PA)
400 Oceangate Ste 1400, Long Beach (90802-4325)
PHONE 562 436-2000
Fax: 562 436-7416
Samuel A Keesal Jr, *CEO*
Lisa Beazley, *Shareholder*
Robert J Stemler, *Shareholder*
Robert Stemler, *Shareholder*
Racquel Sullivan, *President*
EMP: 90
SQ FT: 65,000
SALES (est): 636.2K **Privately Held**
WEB: www.kyl.com
SIC: 8111 General practice law office

(P-23346)
KEKER AND VAN NEST LLP
633 Battery St Bsmt 91, San Francisco (94111-1899)
PHONE 415 391-5400
John W Keker,
Bryant Cavers, *President*
DOT D Fox, *President*
Laure Mandin, *President*
Diane Miller, *President*
EMP: 100
SQ FT: 70,000
SALES (est): 18.6MM **Privately Held**
WEB: www.kvn.com
SIC: 8111 Criminal law; specialized law offices, attorneys

(P-23347)
KELLEY DRYE & WARREN LLP
10100 Santa Monica Blvd, Los Angeles (90067-4003)
PHONE 310 712-6100
Ken Kow, *Branch Mgr*
EMP: 210

PA: Katten Muchin Rosenman Llp
  525 W Monroe St Ste 1900
  Chicago IL 60661
  312 902-5200

SALES (corp-wide): 150.3MM **Privately Held**
SIC: 8111 General practice law office
PA: Kelley Drye & Warren Llp
  101 Park Ave Fl 30
  New York NY 10178
  212 808-7800

(P-23348)
KHORRAMI SHAWN LAW OFFICE
14550 Haynes St, Van Nuys (91411-1613)
PHONE 818 947-5111
Fax: 818 947-5121
Shawn Khorrami, *Partner*
Danny Abir, *Partner*
Dyln Hollard, *Partner*
EMP: 50
SALES (est): 3.1MM **Privately Held**
WEB: www.kpalawyers.com
SIC: 8111 Legal services

(P-23349)
KILPATRICK TWNSEND STCKTON LLP
2175 N California Blvd, Walnut Creek (94596-3579)
PHONE 925 472-5000
Harold Williams, *Branch Mgr*
Houtan Amanat, *Agent*
Nisha Agarwal, *Associate*
Lisa Flanagan, *Associate*
EMP: 103
SALES (corp-wide): 246.6MM **Privately Held**
SIC: 8111 General practice attorney, lawyer
PA: Kilpatrick Townsend & Stockton Llp
  1100 Peachtree St Ne
  Atlanta GA 30309
  404 815-6500

(P-23350)
KILPATRICK TWNSEND STCKTON LLP
Also Called: Townsend and Townsend
1080 Marshall Rd, Menlo Park (94025)
PHONE 650 326-2595
Fax: 650 326-2422
Jim Karkas, *Manager*
Fredricka Gatewood, *President*
Lauren Week, *Admin Sec*
Aaron Hokamura, *Admin Asst*
Ted Dunning, *CTO*
EMP: 140
SQ FT: 1,500
SALES (corp-wide): 246.6MM **Privately Held**
SIC: 8111 Patent, trademark & copyright law
PA: Kilpatrick Townsend & Stockton Llp
  1100 Peachtree St Ne
  Atlanta GA 30309
  404 815-6500

(P-23351)
KIMBALL TIREY & ST JOHN LLP (PA)
7676 Hazard Center Dr # 900, San Diego (92108-4515)
PHONE 619 234-1690
Fax: 619 237-0457
Theodore C Kimball, *Partner*
Steven Mehlman, *Managing Prtnr*
Patrick O'Laughlin, *Managing Prtnr*
Machelle Lozano, *Vice Pres*
Marlene Rios, *Vice Pres*
EMP: 70
SQ FT: 6,000
SALES (est): 21.2MM **Privately Held**
SIC: 8111 General practice attorney, lawyer

(P-23352)
KING & SPALDING LLP
101 2nd St Ste 2300, San Francisco (94105-3664)
PHONE 415 318-1200
Donald Zimmer, *Partner*
Gracy Alexander, *President*
Sharon Jackson, *Executive Asst*
Micheal Gibson, *Admin Asst*
Diane Miller, *Director*
EMP: 296

SALES (corp-wide): 374MM **Privately Held**
SIC: 8111 General practice law office
PA: King & Spalding Llp
  1180 Peachtree St
  Atlanta GA 30309
  404 572-4600

(P-23353)
KIRKLAND & ELLIS LLP
3330 Hillview Ave, Palo Alto (94304-1059)
PHONE 650 852-9131
Alex Kaufman, *Branch Mgr*
Maria Vito, *Office Mgr*
Stephen G Tomlinson, *Manager*
Sean O Christofferson, *Associate*
Emily Hill, *Associate*
EMP: 510
SALES (corp-wide): 539.6MM **Privately Held**
SIC: 8111 Specialized law offices, attorneys
PA: Kirkland & Ellis Llp
  300 N La Salle Dr # 2400
  Chicago IL 60654
  312 862-2000

(P-23354)
KIRKLAND & ELLIS LLP
555 California St # 2700, San Francisco (94104-1603)
PHONE 415 439-1400
Caroline Recht, *Manager*
Bao Nguyen, *Executive*
Janaya Guerrero, *Admin Sec*
Jared Hansen, *Financial Exec*
Gregory Low, *Human Res Dir*
EMP: 200
SALES (corp-wide): 539.6MM **Privately Held**
WEB: www.kirkland.com
SIC: 8111 Legal services
PA: Kirkland & Ellis Llp
  300 N La Salle Dr # 2400
  Chicago IL 60654
  312 862-2000

(P-23355)
KIRKLAND & ELLIS LLP
333 S Hope St Ste 3000, Los Angeles (90071-3039)
PHONE 213 680-7480
Cynthia Barnes, *Office Mgr*
Douglas Dawson, *President*
Shellye R Pruitt, *Associate Dir*
June Han, *Info Tech Mgr*
Julie Perez, *Personnel Assit*
EMP: 250
SALES (corp-wide): 539.6MM **Privately Held**
WEB: www.kirkland.com
SIC: 8111 General practice law office
PA: Kirkland & Ellis Llp
  300 N La Salle Dr # 2400
  Chicago IL 60654
  312 862-2000

(P-23356)
KLEIN DENATALE GOLDNER ET AL (PA)
Also Called: Klein Denatale Goldner Cooper
4550 California Ave Fl 2, Bakersfield (93309-7012)
P.O. Box 11172 (93389-1172)
PHONE 661 401-7755
Fax: 661 326-0418
Anthony J Klein, *Partner*
Jennifer A Adams, *Partner*
Hagop T Bedoyan, *Partner*
David J Cooper, *Partner*
Thomas V Denatale Jr, *Partner*
EMP: 92
SQ FT: 25,000
SALES (est): 23.8MM **Privately Held**
SIC: 8111 General practice law office

(P-23357)
KLEIN-TESTAN-BRUNDO
1851 E 1st St Ste 100, Santa Ana (92705-4036)
PHONE 714 245-8888
Jeffrey Adelson, *Partner*
EMP: 50
SALES (est): 192.7K **Privately Held**
SIC: 8111 Labor & employment law

PRODUCTS & SERVICES SECTION
8111 - Legal Svcs County (P-23379)

(P-23358)
KNOBBE MARTENS OLSON BEAR LLP (PA)
2040 Main St Fl 14, Irvine (92614-8214)
PHONE.....................949 760-0404
Steven J Nataupsky, *Managing Prtnr*
William B Bunker, *Partner*
Drew S Hamilton, *Partner*
Ned Israelsen, *Partner*
Steven Nataupsky, *Partner*
EMP: 350
SQ FT: 120,000
SALES (est): 91MM **Privately Held**
WEB: www.knobbe.com
SIC: 8111 General practice law office

(P-23359)
KOELLER NBKER CRLSON HLUCK LLP (PA)
3 Park Plz Ste 1500, Irvine (92614-8558)
PHONE.....................949 864-3400
Keith Koeller, *Managing Prtnr*
Bob Carlson, *Managing Prtnr*
William Haluck, *Managing Prtnr*
Bill Nebeker, *Managing Prtnr*
Dale Langley, *Office Mgr*
EMP: 56
SALES (est): 15.2MM **Privately Held**
SIC: 8111 General practice law office

(P-23360)
KRONICK MOSKOVITZ TIEDEMANN (PA)
400 Capitol Mall Fl 27, Sacramento (95814-4416)
PHONE.....................916 321-4500
Fax: 916 321-4555
Robert Murphy, *Chairman*
Frederick G Girard, *Shareholder*
Michael A Grob, *President*
Bruce A Scheidt, *CEO*
Rick Fowler, *COO*
EMP: 98
SQ FT: 35,781
SALES (est): 19.1MM **Privately Held**
WEB: www.kmtg.com
SIC: 8111 General practice law office

(P-23361)
LA FOLLETTE JOHNSON DE HAAS (PA)
865 S Figueroa St # 3200, Los Angeles (90017-5431)
PHONE.....................213 426-3600
Fax: 213 426-3650
Daren T Johnson, *President*
Mark Stewart, *Shareholder*
Dennis Ames, *Treasurer*
Alfred Gerisch Jr, *Treasurer*
Louis De Haas Jr, *Vice Pres*
EMP: 105
SALES (est): 16.3MM **Privately Held**
WEB: www.ljdfa.com
SIC: 8111 General practice law office

(P-23362)
LADAS & PARRY LLP
5670 Wilshire Blvd # 2100, Los Angeles (90036-5606)
PHONE.....................323 934-2300
Fax: 323 934-0202
Richard P Berg, *Partner*
Jay Peitzer, *Admin Asst*
Lawrence Brown, *Info Tech Mgr*
Louis Pezzullo, *Financial Exec*
Maria H Barrera, *Associate*
EMP: 50
SALES (corp-wide): 26.2MM **Privately Held**
WEB: www.ladas.com
SIC: 8111 General practice law office
PA: Ladas & Parry Llp
    1040 Ave Of The Amrcs 5
    New York NY 10018
    212 246-8959

(P-23363)
LANAHAN & REILLEY LLP (PA)
600 Bicentennial Way # 300, Santa Rosa (95403-7427)
P.O. Box 5227 (95402-5227)
PHONE.....................415 856-4700
Daniel Lanahan, *Managing Prtnr*
Martin Reilley, *Partner*
Terri Marquering, *Finance*
Michael A Shiffman,
Robert Anderson, *Manager*
EMP: 74
SQ FT: 18,030
SALES (est): 6.7MM **Privately Held**
WEB: www.lanahan.com
SIC: 8111 General practice attorney, lawyer

(P-23364)
LANG RICHERT & PATCH
Also Called: Attorneys At Law
5200 N Palm Ave Ste 401, Fresno (93704-2227)
P.O. Box 40012 (93755-4012)
PHONE.....................559 228-6700
Fax: 559 228-6727
Val W Saldana, *President*
Robert Patch, *President*
Douglas Griffin, *CFO*
Tamara Lyles, *Bd of Directors*
Rene La Streto II, *Vice Pres*
EMP: 50
SQ FT: 17,500
SALES (est): 7.9MM **Privately Held**
WEB: www.lrplaw.net
SIC: 8111 General practice law office

(P-23365)
LATHAM & WATKINS LLP
140 Scott Dr, Menlo Park (94025-1008)
PHONE.....................650 328-4600
Fax: 650 463-2600
Ora Fisher, *Branch Mgr*
Kathy Henry, *Administration*
Pat Civiletti, *Legal Staff*
Matthew Aichele, *Associate*
Mark M Bekheit, *Associate*
EMP: 180
SALES (corp-wide): 861.2MM **Privately Held**
WEB: www.lw.com
SIC: 8111 Corporate, partnership & business law
PA: Latham & Watkins Llp
    355 S Grand Ave Ste 1000
    Los Angeles CA 90071
    213 485-1234

(P-23366)
LATHAM & WATKINS LLP
1722 Skyhill Way, Santa Ana (92705-2585)
PHONE.....................714 755-8288
Perry Viscouty, *Partner*
EMP: 323
SALES (corp-wide): 861.2MM **Privately Held**
SIC: 8111 Legal services
PA: Latham & Watkins Llp
    355 S Grand Ave Ste 1000
    Los Angeles CA 90071
    213 485-1234

(P-23367)
LATHAM & WATKINS LLP
12670 High Bluff Dr # 100, San Diego (92130-3086)
PHONE.....................619 236-1234
Fax: 619 236-3624
Bruce Shepard, *Partner*
Cynthia H Cwik-Martin, *Partner*
Wendy Wilkins, *Office Admin*
Charles Matzner, *Software Dev*
Phuoc Le, *Project Mgr*
EMP: 180
SALES (corp-wide): 861.2MM **Privately Held**
WEB: www.lw.com
SIC: 8111 General practice attorney, lawyer
PA: Latham & Watkins Llp
    355 S Grand Ave Ste 1000
    Los Angeles CA 90071
    213 485-1234

(P-23368)
LATHAM & WATKINS LLP
111 Univrsl Hllywd 257, Universal City (91608-1054)
PHONE.....................818 753-5000
Fax: 818 753-5657
EMP: 323
SALES (corp-wide): 861.2MM **Privately Held**
SIC: 8111 Legal services
PA: Latham & Watkins Llp
    355 S Grand Ave Ste 1000
    Los Angeles CA 90071
    213 485-1234

(P-23369)
LATHAM & WATKINS LLP (PA)
355 S Grand Ave Ste 1000, Los Angeles (90071-3419)
PHONE.....................213 485-1234
Fax: 213 614-8763
Robert Dell, *Managing Prtnr*
Christopher J Allen, *Partner*
James P Beaubien, *Partner*
Joseph A Bevash, *Partner*
Jos Luis Blanco, *Partner*
EMP: 570 **EST:** 1934
SALES (est): 861.2MM **Privately Held**
WEB: www.lw.com
SIC: 8111 Legal services

(P-23370)
LATHAM & WATKINS LLP
555 W 5th St Ste 800, Los Angeles (90013-1021)
PHONE.....................213 891-7108
Wayne Gustafson, *Risk Mgmt Dir*
Joe Pantera, *Admin Asst*
Corwin Wills, *Admin Asst*
John Kane, *Info Tech Mgr*
Cindy Chick, *Information Mgr*
EMP: 63
SALES (corp-wide): 861.2MM **Privately Held**
SIC: 8111 Legal services
PA: Latham & Watkins Llp
    355 S Grand Ave Ste 1000
    Los Angeles CA 90071
    213 485-1234

(P-23371)
LATHAM & WATKINS LLP
650 Town Center Dr # 2000, Costa Mesa (92626-7135)
PHONE.....................714 540-1235
Fax: 714 755-8290
R Scott Shean, *Managing Prtnr*
Scott Shean, *Managing Prtnr*
Nancy Eberhart, *Administration*
Bror Andringa, *Info Tech Mgr*
Tauhid R Rahman, *Info Tech Mgr*
EMP: 175
SALES (corp-wide): 861.2MM **Privately Held**
WEB: www.lw.com
SIC: 8111 General practice law office
PA: Latham & Watkins Llp
    355 S Grand Ave Ste 1000
    Los Angeles CA 90071
    213 485-1234

(P-23372)
LATHAM & WATKINS LLP
505 Montgomery St # 1900, San Francisco (94111-2562)
PHONE.....................415 391-0600
Fax: 415 395-8095
Scott Haber, *Managing Prtnr*
Kenneth Blohm, *Partner*
Parker Yates, *Vice Pres*
Lisa Loef, *Office Admin*
Sean McGlamery, *Admin Asst*
EMP: 240
SALES (corp-wide): 861.2MM **Privately Held**
WEB: www.lw.com
SIC: 8111 General practice law office
PA: Latham & Watkins Llp
    355 S Grand Ave Ste 1000
    Los Angeles CA 90071
    213 485-1234

(P-23373)
LATHAM & WATKINS LLP
520 S Grand Ave Ste 200, Los Angeles (90071-2655)
PHONE.....................213 891-1200
Leanne Black, *Director*
Lourdes C Lopez, *Admin Asst*
Rene Mendoza, *Admin Asst*
Anthony Ojeda, *Administration*
Kenneth L Heaps, *CIO*
EMP: 200
SALES (corp-wide): 861.2MM **Privately Held**
SIC: 8111 Specialized legal services

PA: Latham & Watkins Llp
    355 S Grand Ave Ste 1000
    Los Angeles CA 90071
    213 485-1234

(P-23374)
LATHROP & GAGE LLP
1888 Century Park E # 1000, Los Angeles (90067-1714)
PHONE.....................310 789-4600
John Schaffer, *Branch Mgr*
EMP: 70
SALES (corp-wide): 117.7MM **Privately Held**
SIC: 8111 General practice law office
PA: Lathrop & Gage Llp
    2345 Grand Blvd Ste 2200
    Kansas City MO 64108
    816 292-2000

(P-23375)
LAUGHLIN FALBO LEVY MORESI LLP (PA)
555 12th St Ste 1900, Oakland (94607-4098)
PHONE.....................510 628-0496
James Pettibone, *Managing Prtnr*
John Bennett Jr, *Partner*
Phillip J Klein, *Partner*
James Wesolowski, *Partner*
Kevin Calegari, *Managing Prtnr*
EMP: 76
SQ FT: 25,000
SALES (est): 37.2MM **Privately Held**
SIC: 8111 Specialized law offices, attorneys; labor & employment law

(P-23376)
LAW OFFICE OF CURTIS O BARNES
390 W Cerritos Ave, Anaheim (92805-6550)
P.O. Box 1390 (92815-1390)
PHONE.....................866 477-8222
Curtis Barnes, *President*
Connie Keblis, *Administration*
Gregory Barnes, *CIO*
Robert Barnes, *Counsel*
EMP: 60
SALES (est): 5.1MM **Privately Held**
SIC: 8111 Legal services

(P-23377)
LAW OFFICES BERGLUND & JOHNSON (PA)
Also Called: Berglund & Johnson Law Office
21550 Oxnard St Ste 900, Woodland Hills (91367-7144)
PHONE.....................951 276-4783
Fax: 818 992-1541
David W Berglund, *Partner*
Daniel W Johnson, *Partner*
EMP: 56
SALES (est): 4MM **Privately Held**
WEB: www.bjslawfirm.com
SIC: 8111 General practice law office

(P-23378)
LAW OFFICES OF THOMAS W
14286 Danielson St # 103, Poway (92064-8819)
P.O. Box 503230, San Diego (92150-3230)
PHONE.....................858 883-2000
Thomas W Rutledge, *President*
Allison R Rutledge, *Exec VP*
Laurie Neill, *Accounting Mgr*
Ace Blackburn, *General Counsel*
EMP: 135
SQ FT: 6,000
SALES (est): 12.8MM **Privately Held**
SIC: 8111 Legal services

(P-23379)
LEE HONG DEGERMAN KANG
3501 Jamboree Rd Ste 6000, Newport Beach (92660-2960)
PHONE.....................949 250-9954
Melissa Well, *Principal*
EMP: 60
SALES (corp-wide): 7.5MM **Privately Held**
SIC: 8111 Legal services

8111 - Legal Svcs County (P-23380)

PA: Lee, Hong, Degerman, Kang & Waimey, A Professional Corporation
660 S Figueroa St # 2300
Los Angeles CA 90017
213 623-2221

(P-23380)
LEGAL RECOVERY LAW OFFICES INC
5030 Camino De La Siesta, San Diego (92108-3116)
P.O. Box 84060 (92138-4060)
PHONE.................................619 275-4001
Mark Walsh, *President*
Rick Moses, *Vice Pres*
Andrew Rundquist, *Admin Sec*
David Barajas, *Credit Mgr*
Stu Jameson, *Manager*
EMP: 70
SQ FT: 2,500
SALES (est): 10.1MM **Privately Held**
WEB: www.lrlo.com
SIC: 8111 Legal services

(P-23381)
LEGAL SOLUTIONS HOLDINGS INC
Also Called: Getmedlegal
955 Overland Ct Ste 200, San Dimas (91773-1747)
P.O. Box 955 (91773-0955)
PHONE.................................800 244-3495
Greg Webber, *CEO*
Kenneth Gleockler, *CFO*
Keahi Kakugawa, *Principal*
EMP: 237
SALES (est): 29.3MM **Privately Held**
SIC: 8111 Legal services

(P-23382)
LEGALLY YOURS LLC
750 N Diamond Bar Blvd # 224, Diamond Bar (91765-1023)
PHONE.................................909 396-7200
Andrea Dubois, *Mng Member*
John Dickson,
EMP: 123
SQ FT: 2,200
SALES (est): 9.9MM **Privately Held**
SIC: 8111 Legal services

(P-23383)
LEGALMATCHCOM
395 Oyster Point Blvd, South San Francisco (94080-1928)
PHONE.................................415 946-0800
Randy Wells, *CEO*
Neal Carmichael, *Vice Pres*
Donald Keane, *Vice Pres*
Laurie Ziffrin, *Vice Pres*
Joseph Rara, *Technology*
EMP: 50
SQ FT: 25,000
SALES (est): 5.1MM **Privately Held**
WEB: www.legalmatch.com
SIC: 8111 Legal services

(P-23384)
LEVIN AND SIMES
353 Sacramento St Fl 20, San Francisco (94111-3675)
PHONE.................................415 426-3000
William A Levin, *Mng Member*
Martha-Alice Berman, *Principal*
Marcia Rey, *Human Res Dir*
EMP: 50
SQ FT: 10,000
SALES (est): 5MM **Privately Held**
SIC: 8111 Specialized law offices, attorneys

(P-23385)
LEWIS BRSBOIS BSGARD SMITH LLP
633 W 5th St Ste 4000, Los Angeles (90071-2074)
PHONE.................................213 250-1800
EMP: 97
SALES (corp-wide): 227.1MM **Privately Held**
SIC: 8111 General practice law office
PA: Lewis Brisbois Bisgaard & Smith Llp
633 W 5th St Ste 4000
Los Angeles CA 90071
213 250-1800

(P-23386)
LEWIS BRSBOIS BSGARD SMITH LLP
28765 Single Oak Dr Ste 1, Temecula (92590-3661)
PHONE.................................951 252-6150
Robert F Lewis, *Managing Prtnr*
EMP: 97
SALES (corp-wide): 227.1MM **Privately Held**
SIC: 8111 General practice law office
PA: Lewis Brisbois Bisgaard & Smith Llp
633 W 5th St Ste 4000
Los Angeles CA 90071
213 250-1800

(P-23387)
LEWIS BRSBOIS BSGARD SMITH LLP (PA)
633 W 5th St Ste 4000, Los Angeles (90071-2074)
PHONE.................................213 250-1800
Fax: 213 250-7900
Robert F Lewis, *Managing Prtnr*
Christopher P Bisgaard, *Partner*
Roy M Brisbois, *Partner*
Michael Yu, *Info Svcs Mgr*
Chris Fletcher, *Technology*
EMP: 650
SQ FT: 80,000
SALES (est): 227.1MM **Privately Held**
WEB: www.lbbslaw.com
SIC: 8111 General practice law office

(P-23388)
LEWIS BRSBOIS BSGARD SMITH LLP
701 B St Ste 1900, San Diego (92101-8198)
PHONE.................................619 233-1006
Fax: 619 233-8627
Susan O' Brien, *Systems Mgr*
Robert G Bernstein, *Principal*
Tim Botsko, *Technician*
Bryany Bergstrom, *Legal Staff*
Nan Garcia, *Legal Staff*
EMP: 100
SALES (corp-wide): 227.1MM **Privately Held**
WEB: www.lbbslaw.com
SIC: 8111 General practice law office
PA: Lewis Brisbois Bisgaard & Smith Llp
633 W 5th St Ste 4000
Los Angeles CA 90071
213 250-1800

(P-23389)
LEWIS BRSBOIS BSGARD SMITH LLP
650 Town Center Dr # 1400, Costa Mesa (92626-1989)
PHONE.................................714 545-6015
Fax: 714 850-1030
Shawn Derfer, *Manager*
Lee A Wood, *Partner*
Charles Harris, *Managing Prtnr*
Dana Trevers, *Office Mgr*
Steve T Gubner,
EMP: 60
SALES (corp-wide): 227.1MM **Privately Held**
WEB: www.lbbslaw.com
SIC: 8111 General practice law office
PA: Lewis Brisbois Bisgaard & Smith Llp
633 W 5th St Ste 4000
Los Angeles CA 90071
213 250-1800

(P-23390)
LEWIS BRSBOIS BSGARD SMITH LLP
333 Bush St, San Francisco (94104-2806)
PHONE.................................415 362-2580
Cindy Aiello, *Manager*
Kathryn L Anderson, *Partner*
Jeffrey Bairey, *Partner*
Donald E Brier, *Partner*
Peter Dixon, *Partner*
EMP: 150
SALES (corp-wide): 227.1MM **Privately Held**
WEB: www.lbbslaw.com
SIC: 8111 General practice law office

(P-23391)
LEWIS BRSBOIS BSGARD SMITH LLP
650 E Hospitality Ln # 600, San Bernardino (92408-3535)
PHONE.................................909 387-1130
Fax: 909 387-1138
John Lowenthal, *Manager*
Ralph Juarez, *Personnel*
William Jeffrion, *Associate*
Roxanne Reyna, *Associate*
EMP: 50
SQ FT: 6,203
SALES (corp-wide): 227.1MM **Privately Held**
WEB: www.lbbslaw.com
SIC: 8111 General practice attorney, lawyer
PA: Lewis Brisbois Bisgaard & Smith Llp
633 W 5th St Ste 4000
Los Angeles CA 90071
213 250-1800

(P-23392)
LEWIS MARENSTEIN WICKE SHERWIN
20750 Ventura Blvd # 400, Woodland Hills (91364-2390)
PHONE.................................818 703-6000
Fax: 818 703-0200
Michael B Lewis, *Partner*
Alan B Marenstein, *Partner*
Robert Sherwin, *Partner*
Thomas Wicke, *Partner*
Kal Borisov, *Info Tech Mgr*
EMP: 50
SQ FT: 15,000
SALES (est): 5.9MM **Privately Held**
WEB: www.lmwslaw.com
SIC: 8111 General practice law office

(P-23393)
LEWIS P C JACKSON
50 California St Fl 9, San Francisco (94111-4615)
PHONE.................................415 394-9400
Gloria Kennard, *Administration*
Robert Pattison, *Managing Prtnr*
Wolfgang Timm, *MIS Dir*
John Bartkowiak, *Legal Staff*
Shane Anderies, *Associate*
EMP: 50
SALES (corp-wide): 323.1MM **Privately Held**
WEB: www.jacksonlewis.com
SIC: 8111 Legal services
PA: Lewis P C Jackson
1133 Weschester Ave
White Plains NY 10604
914 872-8060

(P-23394)
LEWIS P C JACKSON
725 S Figueroa St # 2500, Los Angeles (90017-5408)
PHONE.................................213 689-0404
Wendy Sweet, *Manager*
Valerie Barnard, *CFO*
Marjorie Sasseen, *Admin Sec*
Josh Sable,
Talya Friedman, *Associate*
EMP: 50
SQ FT: 2,000
SALES (corp-wide): 323.1MM **Privately Held**
WEB: www.jacksonlewis.com
SIC: 8111 General practice law office
PA: Lewis P C Jackson
1133 Weschester Ave
White Plains NY 10604
914 872-8060

(P-23395)
LIEFF CABRASER HEIMANN & (PA)
275 Battery St Fl 29, San Francisco (94111-3339)
PHONE.................................415 788-0245
Robert L Lieff, *Partner*
William Bernstein, *Partner*
Elizabeth J Cabraser, *Partner*
James M Finberg, *Partner*
Richard M Heimann, *Partner*
EMP: 120
SQ FT: 42,592
SALES (est): 22.5MM **Privately Held**
SIC: 8111 Antitrust & trade regulation law; environmental law; labor & employment law; securities law

(P-23396)
LINER LLP (PA)
1100 Glendon Ave Fl 14, Los Angeles (90024-3518)
PHONE.................................310 500-3500
Heather H Gilhooly, *Partner*
Gerald Scott Janoffl, *Partner*
Mitchell C Regenstreif, *Partner*
Randall J Sunshine, *Partner*
Cody Cluff, *CFO*
EMP: 74 **EST:** 1996
SQ FT: 21,000
SALES (est): 20.6MM **Privately Held**
SIC: 8111 Legal services

(P-23397)
LITTLER MENDELSON PC (PA)
333 Bush St Fl 34, San Francisco (94104-2874)
P.O. Box 45547 (94145-0547)
PHONE.................................415 433-1940
Fax: 415 399-8490
Thomas J Bender, *CEO*
Brian R Dixon, *Shareholder*
L T Duffie, *Shareholder*
Todd Nierman, *Shareholder*
Michael Royal, *Shareholder*
EMP: 500
SQ FT: 85,000
SALES (est): 397.1MM **Privately Held**
SIC: 8111 General practice law office

(P-23398)
LLP LOCKE LORD
44 Montgomery St Ste 4100, San Francisco (94104-4815)
PHONE.................................415 318-8800
Matthew Blackburn, *Branch Mgr*
Regina J McClendon, *Counsel*
Krista Dunzweiler, *Associate*
EMP: 161
SALES (corp-wide): 402.8MM **Privately Held**
SIC: 8111 General practice attorney, lawyer
PA: Locke Lord Llp
2200 Ross Ave Ste 2800
Dallas TX 75201
214 740-8000

(P-23399)
LLP LOCKE LORD
300 S Grand Ave Ste 2600, Los Angeles (90071-3194)
PHONE.................................213 485-1500
Marilyn Loreta, *Administration*
Curtis Chubbuck, *Info Tech Mgr*
Norris Clark, *Consultant*
EMP: 161
SALES (corp-wide): 402.8MM **Privately Held**
SIC: 8111 Specialized law offices, attorneys
PA: Locke Lord Llp
2200 Ross Ave Ste 2800
Dallas TX 75201
214 740-8000

(P-23400)
LLP LOCKE LORD
660 Nwport Ctr Dr Ste 900, Newport Beach (92660)
PHONE.................................949 423-2100
Jon-Paul Lapointe, *Branch Mgr*
EMP: 87
SALES (corp-wide): 402.8MM **Privately Held**
SIC: 8111 General practice law office
PA: Locke Lord Llp
2200 Ross Ave Ste 2800
Dallas TX 75201
214 740-8000

PRODUCTS & SERVICES SECTION

8111 - Legal Svcs County (P-23421)

(P-23401)
LLP LOCKE LORD
1901 Avenue Of The Stars, Los Angeles (90067-6001)
PHONE...................................310 860-8700
Edward Schultz, *Branch Mgr*
EMP: 142
SALES (corp-wide): 321.1MM **Privately Held**
SIC: 8111 Legal services
PA: Locke Lord Llp
2200 Ross Ave Ste 2200
Dallas TX 75201
214 740-8000

(P-23402)
LLP MAYER BROWN
2 Palo Alto Sq Ste 300, Palo Alto (94306-2112)
PHONE...................................650 331-2000
Martin Collins, *Branch Mgr*
EMP: 679
SALES (corp-wide): 594.3MM **Privately Held**
SIC: 8111 General practice attorney, lawyer
PA: Mayer Brown Llp
71 S Wacker Dr Ste 1000
Chicago IL 60606
312 782-0600

(P-23403)
LLP MAYER BROWN
Also Called: Mayer Brown & Platt
350 S Grand Ave Ste 2500, Los Angeles (90071-3486)
PHONE...................................213 229-9500
Fax: 213 625-0248
Jim Tancula, *Manager*
David B Bolstad, *Partner*
Pierre Vogelenzang, *Partner*
Connie Yu, *CTO*
L Eatman,
EMP: 130
SALES (corp-wide): 594.3MM **Privately Held**
SIC: 8111 General practice law office
PA: Mayer Brown Llp
71 S Wacker Dr Ste 1000
Chicago IL 60606
312 782-0600

(P-23404)
LLP ROBINS KAPLAN
2049 Century Park E # 3400, Los Angeles (90067-3208)
PHONE...................................310 552-0130
Fax: 310 229-5800
Roman Silberfeld, *Manager*
Carl Noel, *Technical Staff*
David Martinez, *Associate*
EMP: 78
SALES (corp-wide): 109.5MM **Privately Held**
WEB: www.rkmc.com
SIC: 8111 General practice attorney, lawyer
PA: Llp Robins Kaplan
800 Lasalle Ave Ste 2800
Minneapolis MN 55402
612 349-8500

(P-23405)
LOEB & LOEB LLP (PA)
10100 Santa Monica Blvd # 2200, Los Angeles (90067-4120)
PHONE...................................310 282-2000
Fax: 310 282-2192
Barry I Slotnick, *Chairman*
Kenneth B Anderson, *Partner*
Craig A Emanuel, *Partner*
Daniel D Frohling, *Partner*
Douglas N Masters, *Partner*
EMP: 134
SALES (est): 46.9MM **Privately Held**
WEB: www.loeb.com
SIC: 8111 General practice law office

(P-23406)
LOEWS CORPORATION
4000 Coronado Bay Rd, Coronado (92118-3290)
PHONE...................................619 424-4000
Kathleen Cochran, *General Mgr*
Zanna Liedike, *Info Tech Mgr*
Carlos Murillo, *Sales Staff*
Hillary Rath, *Sales Staff*
Kurt Johnson, *Manager*
EMP: 400
SALES (corp-wide): 13.4B **Publicly Held**
WEB: www.loews.com
SIC: 8111 General practice law office
PA: Loews Corporation
667 Madison Ave Fl 7
New York NY 10065
212 521-2000

(P-23407)
LONG & LEVIT LLP
465 California St Ste 500, San Francisco (94104-1814)
PHONE...................................415 397-2222
Fax: 415 397-6392
Joseph McMonigle, *Managing Prtnr*
Jessica R Macgregor, *Partner*
Robert Kwong, *Info Tech Dir*
Diana Hadley, *Finance Mgr*
Shane Cahill, *Sr Associate*
EMP: 50
SQ FT: 48,500
SALES (est): 9.1MM **Privately Held**
WEB: www.longlevit.com
SIC: 8111 Specialized law offices, attorneys; taxation law; environmental law

(P-23408)
LORBER GREENFIELD & POLITO LLP (PA)
13985 Stowe Dr, Poway (92064-6887)
PHONE...................................858 486-6757
Bruce Lorber, *Partner*
Joyia Greenfield, *Partner*
Jill Ann Herman, *Partner*
Steven Polito, *Partner*
Debbie S Hamilton, *President*
EMP: 62 **EST:** 1980
SQ FT: 20,000
SALES (est): 18MM **Privately Held**
SIC: 8111 General practice law office

(P-23409)
LOUIE ALMEIDA & SETTLER (PA)
303 N Glenoaks Blvd Fl 4, Burbank (91502-1169)
PHONE...................................818 461-9559
Peter Louie, *CIO*
David Stettler, *Senior Partner*
Donald Leiber, *Partner*
Mark Koenig, *Controller*
EMP: 54
SALES (est): 6.1MM **Privately Held**
SIC: 8111 General practice law office

(P-23410)
LOW BALL & LYNCH A PROF CORP
2 Lower Ragsdale Dr # 120, Monterey (93940-7810)
PHONE...................................831 655-8822
Fax: 831 665-8822
David Lynch, *President*
Murlie Hanson, *Associate*
EMP: 50
SALES (corp-wide): 10MM **Privately Held**
SIC: 8111 Legal services
PA: Low, Ball & Lynch, A Professional Corporation
505 Montgomery St Fl 7
San Francisco CA 94111
415 981-6630

(P-23411)
LOW BALL & LYNCH A PROF CORP (PA)
505 Montgomery St Fl 7, San Francisco (94111-6522)
PHONE...................................415 981-6630
Fax: 415 982-1634
Steven D Werth, *President*
Christine Reed, *Shareholder*
Mark Hazelwood, *Treasurer*
Raymont Coates, *Principal*
Linda Meyer, *Admin Sec*
EMP: 72
SQ FT: 20,000
SALES (est): 10MM **Privately Held**
SIC: 8111 General practice law office

(P-23412)
LOWENSTEIN SANDLER LLP
390 Lytton Ave, Palo Alto (94301-1432)
PHONE...................................650 433-5800
Joan Arbolante, *Administration*
Mary Hildebrand, *Shareholder*
Joe Mignone, *Legal Staff*
Darrin E Burnham, *Associate*
Rahul Shekher, *Associate*
EMP: 50
SALES (corp-wide): 140.4MM **Privately Held**
SIC: 8111 General practice law office
PA: Lowenstein Sandler Llp
65 Livingston Ave Ste 2
Roseland NJ 07068
973 597-2500

(P-23413)
LOZANO SMITH A PROF CORP (PA)
7404 N Spalding Ave, Fresno (93720-3370)
PHONE...................................559 431-5600
Fax: 559 261-9366
Gregory A Wedner, *CEO*
Tina Cobabe, *President*
Jennifer Ha, *President*
Lou Lozano, *President*
Krista Steiner, *President*
EMP: 54
SALES (est): 21.7MM **Privately Held**
SIC: 8111 Specialized law offices, attorneys

(P-23414)
LRN CORPORATION (PA)
1100 Glendon Ave Ste 800, Los Angeles (90024-3512)
PHONE...................................310 209-5400
Fax: 310 209-5401
Dov Seidman, *CEO*
Sue Darow, *Partner*
Carla Schoonderbeek, *Partner*
Jean-Marc Levy, *President*
Ron Charow, *CFO*
EMP: 100
SALES (est): 43.4MM **Privately Held**
WEB: www.lrn.com
SIC: 8111 Corporate, partnership & business law

(P-23415)
LYNBERG & WATKINS A PROF CORP (PA)
Also Called: Lynberg & Watkins Attys At Law
888 S Figueroa St # 1600, Los Angeles (90017-5465)
PHONE...................................213 624-8700
Fax: 213 627-3732
Norman J Watkins, *President*
Charles A Lynberg, *President*
Randall J Peters, *CEO*
Aracely Estrada, *Admin Asst*
Michael Mason, *Accountant*
EMP: 50
SQ FT: 32,108
SALES (est): 10.4MM **Privately Held**
WEB: www.lynberg.com
SIC: 8111 General practice law office

(P-23416)
LYNCH GILARDI & GRUMMER LLP
170 Columbus Ave Fl 5, San Francisco (94133-5128)
PHONE...................................415 397-2800
Robert Lynch, *Managing Prtnr*
Dwane Grummer, *Managing Prtnr*
William A Bogdan,
James E Sell,
Kenneth F Vierra Jr,
EMP: 50
SQ FT: 4,000
SALES (est): 6MM **Privately Held**
WEB: www.lgglaw.com
SIC: 8111 Malpractice & negligence law; product liability law; corporate, partnership & business law

(P-23417)
MALCOLM & CISNEROS A LAW CORP
Also Called: Malcolm Cisneros
2112 Business Center Dr # 200, Irvine (92612-7137)
PHONE...................................949 252-1039
Fax: 949 252-1032
William Malcolm, *CEO*
Roman Cisneros, *COO*
Arturo Cisneros, *CFO*
Ashley Malcolm, *Marketing Staff*
Stacy Kim, *Director*
EMP: 110
SALES (est): 16MM **Privately Held**
WEB: www.malcolmcisneros.com
SIC: 8111 General practice law office

(P-23418)
MANATT PHELPS & PHILLIPS LLP
11355 W Olympic Blvd Fl 2, Los Angeles (90064-1656)
PHONE...................................310 312-4249
Ronald Turovsky, *Manager*
John Ray, *Partner*
Larry Blake, *Counsel*
Andrea Cohen, *Counsel*
Robert Eller,
EMP: 50
SALES (corp-wide): 175.1MM **Privately Held**
WEB: www.manatt.com
SIC: 8111 Legal services
PA: Manatt, Phelps & Phillips, Llp
11355 W Olympic Blvd Fl 2
Los Angeles CA 90064
310 312-4000

(P-23419)
MANATT PHELPS & PHILLIPS LLP
695 Town Center Dr # 1400, Costa Mesa (92626-7223)
PHONE...................................714 371-2500
Shierley Hands, *Manager*
John Grosvenor, *Partner*
Tracey Dunn, *President*
Stella D'Agostino, *Accounting Mgr*
William Connelly III, *Associate*
EMP: 50
SALES (corp-wide): 175.1MM **Privately Held**
WEB: www.manatt.com
SIC: 8111 General practice attorney, lawyer
PA: Manatt, Phelps & Phillips, Llp
11355 W Olympic Blvd Fl 2
Los Angeles CA 90064
310 312-4000

(P-23420)
MANNING KASS ELLROD RAM TRESTR (PA)
801 S Figueroa St Fl 15, Los Angeles (90017-5504)
PHONE...................................213 624-6900
Fax: 213 624-6999
Steven D Manning, *Managing Prtnr*
Robert Zelms, *Managing Prtnr*
Tess Maguire, *Chief Mktg Ofcr*
Alice Napier, *Data Proc Exec*
Rose McCormack, *Accounting Mgr*
EMP: 150
SALES (est): 32MM **Privately Held**
WEB: www.mmker.com
SIC: 8111 General practice attorney, lawyer

(P-23421)
MATHENY SARS LINKERT JAIME LLP
3638 American River Dr, Sacramento (95864-5901)
PHONE...................................916 978-3434
Fax: 916 978-3430
Richard S Linkert, *Partner*
Matthew C Jamie, *Partner*
Douglas A Sears, *Partner*
Jerry Brewer, *Controller*
Mary Palmer, *Manager*
EMP: 52
SQ FT: 12,000

8111 - Legal Svcs County (P-23422) — PRODUDUCTS & SERVICES SECTION

SALES (est): 5.9MM **Privately Held**
WEB: www.msll.com
SIC: **8111** General practice law office

(P-23422)
MAYNARD COOPER & GALE PC
600 Montgomery St # 2600, San Francisco (94111-2728)
PHONE 415 704-7433
EMP: 117
SALES (corp-wide): 53.2MM **Privately Held**
SIC: **8111** Specialized law offices, attorneys; general practice attorney, lawyer
PA: Maynard, Cooper & Gale, P.C.
1901 6th Ave N Ste 2400
Birmingham AL 35203
205 254-1000

(P-23423)
MC NAMARA DODGE NEY BEATT (PA)
1211 Newell Ave, Walnut Creek (94596-5238)
PHONE 925 939-5330
Fax: 925 939-0203
Richard Dodge, *General Ptnr*
Thomas G Beatty, *Partner*
Guy Borges, *Partner*
Roger Brothers, *Partner*
Michael J Ney, *Partner*
EMP: 70 EST: 1965
SQ FT: 9,500
SALES (est): 6.8MM **Privately Held**
WEB: www.mcnamaralaw.com
SIC: **8111** Specialized law offices, attorneys; malpractice & negligence law

(P-23424)
MCCORMICK BARSTOW SHEPPRD WAYT (PA)
Also Called: McCormick Barstow
7647 N Fresno St, Fresno (93720-2578)
P.O. Box 28912 (93729-8912)
PHONE 559 433-1300
Jeffrey M Reid, *Managing Prtnr*
Kenneth A Baldwin, *Partner*
Michael F Ball, *Partner*
Todd W Baxter, *Partner*
Mario L Beltramo Jr, *Partner*
EMP: 137
SQ FT: 67,000
SALES (est): 34.7MM **Privately Held**
WEB: www.mbswc.com
SIC: **8111** Antitrust & trade regulation law; corporate, partnership & business law; bankruptcy law

(P-23425)
MCDERMOTT WILL & EMERY LLP INC
2049 Century Park E Fl 38, Los Angeles (90067-3101)
PHONE 310 277-4110
Fax: 310 277-4730
Jeff Lemkin, *Partner*
Robert Mallory, *Managing Prtnr*
Alison Silverstein, *Managing Dir*
Margaret Dalmada, *Admin Sec*
Mark Avis, *Info Tech Mgr*
EMP: 140
SALES (corp-wide): 1.5B **Privately Held**
WEB: www.europe.mwe.com
SIC: **8111** General practice law office
PA: Mcdermott Will & Emery Llp Inc.
227 W Monroe St Ste 4400
Chicago IL 60606
312 372-2000

(P-23426)
MCDERMOTT WILL & EMERY LLP INC
4 Park Plz Ste 1700, Irvine (92614-2559)
PHONE 949 757-7165
Vicki Lowenstein, *Systems Mgr*
Todd Mobley,
Kenneth Cheney, *Associate*
William Li, *Associate*
EMP: 70
SALES (corp-wide): 1.5B **Privately Held**
WEB: www.europe.mwe.com
SIC: **8111** General practice law office

PA: Mcdermott Will & Emery Llp Inc.
227 W Monroe St Ste 4400
Chicago IL 60606
312 372-2000

(P-23427)
MCGUIREWOODS LLP
1800 Century Park E Fl 8, Los Angeles (90067-1501)
PHONE 310 315-8200
Richard Grant, *Managing Prtnr*
Amina Cooper, *President*
Phyllis Julius, *President*
Marc Goldsmith, *Counsel*
Leslie M Werlin Jr, *Manager*
EMP: 92
SALES (corp-wide): 396.6MM **Privately Held**
SIC: **8111** General practice attorney, lawyer
PA: Mcguirewoods Llp
800 E Canal St
Richmond VA 23219
804 775-1000

(P-23428)
MCKOOL SMITH HENNIGAN
300 S Grand Ave Ste 2900, Los Angeles (90071-3139)
PHONE 213 694-1200
Fax: 213 694-1234
J Michael Hennigan, *Partner*
Bruce Bennett, *Partner*
James W Mercer, *Partner*
Robert Palmer, *Managing Prtnr*
Jaime Nolasco, *Info Tech Dir*
EMP: 90
SQ FT: 35,000
SALES (est): 11.4MM **Privately Held**
WEB: www.hbdlawyers.com
SIC: **8111** Legal services

(P-23429)
MCMANIS FAULKNER A PROF CORP
50 W San Fernando St # 1000, San Jose (95113-2415)
PHONE 408 279-8700
Fax: 408 279-3244
James McManis, *President*
Sharon Kirsch, *President*
Saba Shakoori, *President*
Jamie Smith, *Executive*
William Faulkner, *Admin Sec*
EMP: 50
SALES (est): 7.6MM **Privately Held**
WEB: www.mfmlaw.com
SIC: **8111** General practice attorney, lawyer

(P-23430)
MELMET STEVEN J LAW OFC
2912 Daimler St, Santa Ana (92705-5811)
PHONE 949 263-1000
Fax: 949 660-1800
Steven J Melmet, *President*
Nancy Salzman,
EMP: 70
SALES: 10MM **Privately Held**
WEB: www.melmetlaw.com
SIC: **8111** 6531 General practice law office; debt collection law; escrow agent, real estate

(P-23431)
MEYERS NAVE RIBACK SILVER & (PA)
555 12th St Ste 1500, Oakland (94607-4095)
PHONE 510 351-4300
Fax: 510 444-1108
David W Skinner, *CEO*
Jo Barrington, *Partner*
Anabelle Cotapos, *President*
Patricia McNulty, *President*
Steven R Meyers, *President*
EMP: 100
SQ FT: 28,678
SALES (est): 24.2MM **Privately Held**
WEB: www.meyersnave.com
SIC: **8111** Legal services

(P-23432)
MILBANK TWEED HDLEY MCCLOY LLP
Also Called: Milbank Global Securities
2029 Century Park E # 3300, Los Angeles (90067-3019)
PHONE 213 892-4000
Fax: 213 629-5063
David C Frauman, *Director*
Thomas Hurd, *MIS Mgr*
Annabelle Abundo, *Accounting Mgr*
Dino T Barajas, *Principal*
Allan Marks, *Associate*
EMP: 120
SQ FT: 40,000
SALES (corp-wide): 138.2MM **Privately Held**
WEB: www.mthm.net
SIC: **8111** General practice law office
PA: Milbank Tweed Hadley & Mccloy, Llp
28 Liberty St Fl 47
New York NY 10005
212 530-5000

(P-23433)
MILLER STARR & REGALIA A PRO (PA)
1331 N Calif Blvd Ste 500, Walnut Creek (94596-4599)
P.O. Box 8177 (94596-8177)
PHONE 925 935-9400
Fax: 925 933-4126
Anthony M Leones, *CEO*
Scott A Sommer, *Shareholder*
Richard Carlson, *Principal*
Eugene Miller, *Admin Mgr*
Albert Dacasin, *Info Tech Mgr*
EMP: 90
SQ FT: 30,000
SALES (est): 15.3MM **Privately Held**
WEB: www.msandr.com
SIC: **8111** General practice law office

(P-23434)
MILLER & ASSOCIATES LLP
2530 Wilshire Blvd Fl 1, Santa Monica (90403-4664)
PHONE 310 315-1100
Fax: 310 315-1152
Ronald Miller, *Partner*
Randall Mainor, *Senior Partner*
Derek Sells, *Managing Prtnr*
Hezekiah Sistrunk, *Managing Prtnr*
Sheldon Miller, *Vice Pres*
EMP: 60
SALES (est): 11.1MM **Privately Held**
WEB: www.criminallawyer.net
SIC: **8111** General practice attorney, lawyer

(P-23435)
MINAMI TAMAKI LLP
360 Post St Fl 8, San Francisco (94108-4911)
PHONE 415 788-9000
Fax: 415 398-3887
Dale Minami, *Partner*
Minette Kwok, *Partner*
Jack Lee, *Partner*
Donald K Tamaki, *Partner*
Brad Yamauchi, *Partner*
EMP: 50
SQ FT: 4,500
SALES: 10MM **Privately Held**
WEB: www.mltsf.com
SIC: **8111** General practice attorney, lawyer

(P-23436)
MINTZ LEVIN COHN FERRIS GL
3580 Carmel Mountain Rd # 300, San Diego (92130-6768)
PHONE 858 314-1500
Howard Wisnia, *Branch Mgr*
EMP: 239
SALES (corp-wide): 190.6MM **Privately Held**
SIC: **8111** General practice law office
PA: Mintz, Levin, Cohn, Ferris, Glovsky And Popeo, P.C.
1 Financial Ctr Fl 39
Boston MA 02111
617 348-4951

(P-23437)
MITCHELL SILBERBERG KNUPP LLP (PA)
11377 W Olympic Blvd Fl 2, Los Angeles (90064-1683)
PHONE 310 312-2000
Fax: 310 231-8381
Thomas P Lambert, *Managing Prtnr*
Constance Haft, *President*
Kevin E Gaut, *COO*
Jerry Kaufman, *Exec Dir*
Rebecca Sattin, *Admin Asst*
EMP: 121
SALES: 27.7K **Privately Held**
WEB: www.msk.com
SIC: **8111** General practice law office; real estate law; taxation law; labor & employment law

(P-23438)
ML PRIOR INC
955 Berrand Ct Ste 200, San Dimas (91773)
PHONE 626 653-5160
Stephen Schneider, *President*
Warren Schneider, *CEO*
Lisa Magana, *Administration*
EMP: 135
SQ FT: 31,770
SALES (est): 13.1MM **Privately Held**
SIC: **8111** Legal services

(P-23439)
MOORE LAW GROUP A PROF CORP
3710 S Susan St Ste 210, Santa Ana (92704-6956)
PHONE 714 431-2000
Harvey Moore, *President*
Angela Dawson, *Info Tech Mgr*
Connie Kopp, *Manager*
EMP: 65 EST: 2008
SALES (est): 8.3MM **Privately Held**
SIC: **8111** General practice law office

(P-23440)
MORGAN LEWIS & BOCKIUS LLP
1 Market St Ste 500, San Francisco (94105-1306)
PHONE 415 393-2000
Donn Pickett, *Partner*
Dale Barnes, *Partner*
Michael Begert, *Partner*
Charles Crompton, *Partner*
Anne Deibert, *Partner*
EMP: 696
SALES (est): 92.7MM
SALES (corp-wide): 771.4MM **Privately Held**
SIC: **8111** General practice law office
PA: Morgan, Lewis & Bockius Llp
1701 Market St Ste Con
Philadelphia PA 19103
215 963-5000

(P-23441)
MORGAN LEWIS & BOCKIUS LLP
1400 Page Mill Rd, Palo Alto (94304-1124)
PHONE 650 843-4000
Fax: 650 843-4001
Thomas Kellerman, *Managing Prtnr*
Rekha Chudasama, *President*
Teresa Hillstrom, *Facilities Mgr*
Lee Neugebauer, *Librarian*
Frank E Morris,
EMP: 75
SALES (corp-wide): 771.4MM **Privately Held**
WEB: www.envinfo.com
SIC: **8111** General practice law office
PA: Morgan, Lewis & Bockius Llp
1701 Market St Ste Con
Philadelphia PA 19103
215 963-5000

(P-23442)
MORGAN LEWIS & BOCKIUS LLP
600 Anton Blvd Ste 1800, Costa Mesa (92626-7653)
PHONE 949 399-7000
Anne M Brafford, *Branch Mgr*
Shawn Beem, *President*

PRODUCTS & SERVICES SECTION
8111 - Legal Svcs County (P-23461)

Christopher M Robertson, *Counsel*
Christopher Robertson, *Counsel*
Jennifer E White, *Counsel*
EMP: 181
SALES (corp-wide): 771.4MM **Privately Held**
SIC: 8111 General practice attorney, lawyer
PA: Morgan, Lewis & Bockius Llp
1701 Market St Ste Con
Philadelphia PA 19103
215 963-5000

(P-23443)
MORGAN LEWIS & BOCKIUS LLP
1117 S California Ave, Palo Alto (94304-1106)
PHONE...................650 858-2400
Christopher Chang, *Administration*
EMP: 189
SALES (corp-wide): 771.4MM **Privately Held**
SIC: 8111 Legal services
PA: Morgan, Lewis & Bockius Llp
1701 Market St Ste Con
Philadelphia PA 19103
215 963-5000

(P-23444)
MORGAN LEWIS & BOCKIUS LLP
300 S Grand Ave Ste 2200, Los Angeles (90071-3132)
PHONE...................213 612-2500
Fax: 213 612-2501
John F Hartigan, *Managing Prtnr*
Michael Jack, *Partner*
Gary C Moss, *Partner*
Cecilia Ambrose, *President*
Vivian Dohi, *President*
EMP: 200
SALES (corp-wide): 771.4MM **Privately Held**
WEB: www.envinfo.com
SIC: 8111 General practice law office
PA: Morgan, Lewis & Bockius Llp
1701 Market St Ste Con
Philadelphia PA 19103
215 963-5000

(P-23445)
MORGAN LEWIS & BOCKIUS LLP
1 Market Plz Lbby 1, San Francisco (94105-1002)
PHONE...................415 442-1000
Erika Smith, *Officer*
Gerardo Murillo, *Analyst*
Elena Perez, *Human Res Mgr*
EMP: 300
SALES (corp-wide): 771.4MM **Privately Held**
WEB: www.envinfo.com
SIC: 8111 General practice law office
PA: Morgan, Lewis & Bockius Llp
1701 Market St Ste Con
Philadelphia PA 19103
215 963-5000

(P-23446)
MORGAN LEWIS & BOCKIUS LLP
Also Called: Burton P Scott
355 S Grand Ave Fl 44, Los Angeles (90071-1560)
PHONE...................213 680-6400
Fax: 213 680-6499
John Morrissey, *Manager*
Christopher Wells, *Vice Chairman*
Diana Deorio, *Admin Asst*
Colleen Doyle, *Systems Analyst*
Theresa Dressler, *Systems Analyst*
EMP: 110
SALES (corp-wide): 637.5MM **Privately Held**
SIC: 8111 General practice law office
PA: Morgan, Lewis & Bockius Llp
1701 Market St Ste Con
Philadelphia PA 19103
215 963-5000

(P-23447)
MORRIS POLICH & PURDY LLP (PA)
1055 W 7th St Ste 2400, Los Angeles (90017-2550)
PHONE...................213 891-9100
Fax: 213 488-1178
Theodore D Levin, *Partner*
Jeff Barron, *Partner*
William M Betley, *Partner*
Anthony Brazil, *Partner*
James Chantland, *Partner*
EMP: 100
SQ FT: 40,000
SALES (est): 24.3MM **Privately Held**
WEB: www.mplaw.com
SIC: 8111 General practice attorney, lawyer

(P-23448)
MORRISON & FOERSTER LLP
707 Wilshire Blvd # 6000, Los Angeles (90017-3543)
PHONE...................213 892-5200
Fax: 213 892-5303
Gregory Koltun, *Managing Prtnr*
John W Alden Jr, *Partner*
Mark T Gillett, *Partner*
Dan Marmalefsky, *Partner*
A Max Olson, *Partner*
EMP: 250
SALES (corp-wide): 440.8MM **Privately Held**
SIC: 8111 General practice law office
PA: Morrison & Foerster, Llp
425 Market St Fl 30
San Francisco CA 94105
415 268-7000

(P-23449)
MORRISON & FOERSTER LLP
12531 High Bluff Dr # 100, San Diego (92130-3014)
PHONE...................858 720-5100
Fax: 858 720-5125
Mark Zebrowski, *Managing Prtnr*
James J Mullen, *Managing Prtnr*
Jenkin Clark, *President*
Rajka K Hayden, *Regional Mgr*
Jean Horrall, *Technician*
EMP: 125
SALES (corp-wide): 440.8MM **Privately Held**
SIC: 8111 General practice law office
PA: Morrison & Foerster, Llp
425 Market St Fl 30
San Francisco CA 94105
415 268-7000

(P-23450)
MORRISON & FOERSTER LLP (PA)
Also Called: Mofo
425 Market St Fl 30, San Francisco (94105-2482)
PHONE...................415 268-7000
Fax: 415 268-7432
Philip T Besirof, *Managing Prtnr*
Gladys H Monroy, *Senior Partner*
Jay Baris, *Partner*
Eric J Coffill, *Managing Prtnr*
Charles C Comey, *Managing Prtnr*
EMP: 400 **EST:** 1883
SALES (est): 440.8MM **Privately Held**
SIC: 8111 Specialized law offices, attorneys

(P-23451)
MORRISON & FOERSTER LLP
Also Called: Marketing Department
425 Market St Fl 32, San Francisco (94105-2467)
PHONE...................415 268-7178
Roland Brandel, *Branch Mgr*
Kathy Skinner, *Manager*
EMP: 143
SALES (corp-wide): 440.8MM **Privately Held**
SIC: 8111 Legal services
PA: Morrison & Foerster, Llp
425 Market St Fl 30
San Francisco CA 94105
415 268-7000

(P-23452)
MORRISON & FOERSTER LLP
Also Called: Morrison & Foerster - Library
755 Page Mill Rd Ste A100, Palo Alto (94304-1061)
PHONE...................650 813-5600
Fax: 650 494-0792
Alan Cope Johnston, *Managing Prtnr*
Michael Carlson, *Partner*
Gerald Dodson, *Partner*
Tyler M Dylan, *Partner*
Suzanne S Graeser, *Partner*
EMP: 277
SALES (corp-wide): 440.8MM **Privately Held**
SIC: 8111 General practice law office
PA: Morrison & Foerster, Llp
425 Market St Fl 30
San Francisco CA 94105
415 268-7000

(P-23453)
MORRISON & FOERSTER LLP
425 Market St Fl 32, San Francisco (94105-2467)
P.O. Box 8130, Walnut Creek (94596-8130)
PHONE...................925 295-3300
Fax: 925 946-9912
David A Gold, *Managing Prtnr*
R Clark Morrison, *Partner*
Kris Saad, *Office Mgr*
Neeraj Rajpal, *CIO*
Eric Murriguez, *Web Dvlpr*
EMP: 50
SALES (corp-wide): 440.8MM **Privately Held**
SIC: 8111 General practice law office
PA: Morrison & Foerster, Llp
425 Market St Fl 30
San Francisco CA 94105
415 268-7000

(P-23454)
MULLEN & HENZELL LLP
112 E Victoria St, Santa Barbara (93101-2068)
P.O. Box 789 (93102-0789)
PHONE...................805 966-1501
Fax: 805 966-9204
Dennis W Reilly, *Mng Member*
Brittany Boon, *President*
Erin Costigan, *President*
Samantha Curnow, *President*
Lea Hanna, *President*
EMP: 50 **EST:** 1931
SQ FT: 15,000
SALES (est): 7.3MM **Privately Held**
WEB: www.mullenlaw.com
SIC: 8111 Real estate law; will, estate & trust law; general practice attorney, lawyer

(P-23455)
MUNGER TOLLES & OLSON LLP
355 S Grand Ave Fl 35, Los Angeles (90071-3161)
PHONE...................213 683-9100
Fax: 213 687-3792
Sandra Seville-Jones, *Partner*
Thomas B Edwards, *Exec Dir*
Ted Dane, *Info Tech Mgr*
Kimberly A CHI, *Associate*
EMP: 116
SALES (est): 31.8MM **Privately Held**
SIC: 8111 Specialized law offices, attorneys

(P-23456)
MUNGER TOLLES OLSON FOUNDATION (PA)
355 S Grand Ave Ste 3500, Los Angeles (90071-3161)
PHONE...................213 683-9100
O'Malley M Miller, *CEO*
Robert Johnson, *President*
Larry Kleinberg, *CFO*
Mark Helm, *Vice Pres*
Steven B Weisburd, *Vice Pres*
EMP: 420
SQ FT: 100,000
SALES (est): 28.5MM **Privately Held**
WEB: www.mto.com
SIC: 8111 General practice attorney, lawyer

(P-23457)
MUNGER TOLLES OLSON FOUNDATION
560 Mission St Fl 27, San Francisco (94105-3089)
PHONE...................415 512-4000
Fax: 415 512-4077
Kim Coates, *Branch Mgr*
EMP: 50
SALES (corp-wide): 28.5MM **Privately Held**
WEB: www.mto.com
SIC: 8111 General practice law office
PA: Munger Tolles & Olson Foundation
355 S Grand Ave Ste 3500
Los Angeles CA 90071
213 683-9100

(P-23458)
MURCHISON & CUMMING LLP (PA)
Also Called: M & C
801 S Grand Ave Ste 900, Los Angeles (90017-4624)
PHONE...................213 623-7400
Fax: 213 623-6336
Friedrich W Seitz, *Partner*
Edmund G Farrell, *Senior Partner*
Edmund Farrell, *Senior Partner*
Guy R Gruppie, *Senior Partner*
Guy Gruppie, *Senior Partner*
EMP: 100
SQ FT: 30,000
SALES (est): 20.1MM **Privately Held**
WEB: www.murchison-cumming.com
SIC: 8111 General practice law office

(P-23459)
MURPHY (PA)
88 Kearny St Fl 10, San Francisco (94108-5524)
PHONE...................415 788-1900
Fax: 415 393-8087
Michael P Bradley, *President*
Gregory A Bastian, *Vice Pres*
John H Feeney, *Vice Pres*
Timothy J Halloran, *Vice Pres*
James A Murphy, *Vice Pres*
EMP: 53
SALES (est): 17.2MM **Privately Held**
WEB: www.mpbf.com
SIC: 8111 General practice law office

(P-23460)
MURTAUGH MYER NLSON TRGLIA LLP
2603 Main St, Irvine (92614-6232)
P.O. Box 19627 (92623-9627)
PHONE...................949 794-4000
Fax: 909 794-4099
Michael J Nelson, *Managing Prtnr*
Harry A Halkowich, *Partner*
Mark S Himmelstein, *Partner*
Robert T Lemen, *Partner*
James A Murphy IV, *Partner*
EMP: 60
SALES (est): 7.8MM **Privately Held**
WEB: www.mmnt.com
SIC: 8111 General practice law office

(P-23461)
MUSICK PEELER & GARRETT LLP (PA)
624 S Grand Ave Ste 2000, Los Angeles (90017-3321)
PHONE...................213 629-7600
Fax: 213 624-1376
R Joseph De Briyn, *Managing Prtnr*
Peter J Diedrich, *Partner*
Edward Landrey, *Partner*
Wayne Littlefied, *Partner*
Gary Overstreet, *Partner*
EMP: 168
SQ FT: 100,000
SALES (est): 32.3MM **Privately Held**
WEB: www.mpgweb.com
SIC: 8111 General practice law office; taxation law; corporate, partnership & business law; labor & employment law

8111 - Legal Svcs County (P-23462)

(P-23462)
NATIONWIDE LEGAL LLC
Also Called: Sacramento
716 10th St Ste 102, Sacramento (95814-1807)
PHONE..................916 443-4400
Fax: 916 443-8692
Alex Cain, *Branch Mgr*
EMP: 57
SALES (corp-wide): 36.3MM **Privately Held**
SIC: 8111 Legal services
PA: Nationwide Legal, Llc
1609 James M Wood Blvd
Los Angeles CA 90015
213 249-9999

(P-23463)
NATIONWIDE LEGAL LLC (PA)
Also Called: Headquarters
1609 James M Wood Blvd, Los Angeles (90015-1005)
PHONE..................213 249-9999
Tony Davoodi, *CEO*
Joe Caamal, *COO*
Louis Nelson, *Exec VP*
Michael Lazcano, *Senior VP*
Hector Velazquez, *Branch Mgr*
EMP: 67
SALES (est): 36.3MM **Privately Held**
SIC: 8111 Legal services

(P-23464)
NED E DUNPHY
4550 California Ave Fl 2, Bakersfield (93309-7012)
P.O. Box 11172 (93389-1172)
PHONE..................661 395-1000
Ned E Dunphy, *Partner*
EMP: 56
SALES (est): 2.1MM **Privately Held**
SIC: 8111 General practice attorney, lawyer

(P-23465)
NEIGHBORHOOD LEGAL SVCS LLC
9354 Telstar Ave, El Monte (91731-2816)
PHONE..................626 572-9330
Sandra Daza, *Branch Mgr*
EMP: 52
SALES (corp-wide): 12.4MM **Privately Held**
SIC: 8111 7389 Legal services; paralegal service
PA: Neighborhood Legal Services, Llc
1102 E Chevy Chase Dr
Glendale CA 91205
818 291-1760

(P-23466)
NEIL DYMOTT FRANK MCFALL
Also Called: Neil Dymott Perkins Brown
1010 2nd Ave Ste 2500, San Diego (92101-4959)
PHONE..................619 238-1712
Michael I Neil, *President*
Hannah Dubois, *President*
Mona McKee, *President*
Sheila Trexler, *Bd of Directors*
Robert Frank, *Vice Pres*
EMP: 108
SQ FT: 15,000
SALES (est): 9.2MM **Privately Held**
WEB: www.neil-dymott.com
SIC: 8111 Legal services; general practice law office

(P-23467)
NEWMEYER & DILLION LLP (PA)
895 Dove St Fl 5, Newport Beach (92660-2999)
PHONE..................949 854-7000
Fax: 714 854-7099
Gregory L Dillion, *Partner*
Michael S Cucchissi, *Partner*
Joseph A Ferrentino, *Partner*
John A O Hara, *Partner*
Jon J Janecek, *Partner*
EMP: 115
SQ FT: 52,000
SALES: 35.7MM **Privately Held**
WEB: www.newmeyeranddillion.com
SIC: 8111 General practice law office

(P-23468)
NICOLAIDES FINK THO
601 California St Fl 3, San Francisco (94108-2808)
PHONE..................415 745-3778
Sarah Thorpe, *Mng Member*
EMP: 60 EST: 2014
SALES (est): 3.6MM **Privately Held**
SIC: 8111 Legal services

(P-23469)
NICOLE PTTRSON CRT RPRTING LLC
545 E Alluvial Ave # 109, Fresno (93720-2826)
PHONE..................559 400-2407
Nicole Patterso, *President*
Nicole Patterson, *President*
EMP: 50
SALES (est): 1.5MM **Privately Held**
SIC: 8111 7338 Legal services; court reporting service

(P-23470)
NIXON PEABODY LLP
1 Embarcadero Ctr # 1800, San Francisco (94111-3667)
PHONE..................415 984-8200
Gina Hrens, *Manager*
Rosie Mangin, *President*
Janice Newland, *Manager*
Domenico C Perrella, *Manager*
Shady E Joulani, *Associate*
EMP: 150
SALES (corp-wide): 233.7MM **Privately Held**
SIC: 8111 Specialized law offices, attorneys; antitrust & trade regulation law; environmental law; labor & employment law
PA: Nixon Peabody Llp
1300 Clinton Sq
Rochester NY 14604
585 263-1000

(P-23471)
NIXON PEABODY LLP
555 W 5th St Fl 30, Los Angeles (90013-1048)
PHONE..................213 629-6000
Steph Levy, *Managing Prtnr*
Kate M Ferrara, *Associate*
EMP: 85
SALES (corp-wide): 233.7MM **Privately Held**
SIC: 8111 General practice law office
PA: Nixon Peabody Llp
1300 Clinton Sq
Rochester NY 14604
585 263-1000

(P-23472)
NORDMAN CORMANY HAIR & COMPTON
1000 Town Center Dr Fl 6, Oxnard (93036-1132)
P.O. Box 9100 (93031-9100)
PHONE..................805 485-1000
Fax: 805 988-8387
Tammian Cook, *CEO*
Meghan Clark, *Senior Partner*
Marc L Charney, *Partner*
Robert L Compton, *Partner*
Glenn J Dickinson, *Partner*
EMP: 115
SQ FT: 35,000
SALES (est): 10.6MM **Privately Held**
WEB: www.nchc.com
SIC: 8111 General practice law office

(P-23473)
NOSSAMAN LLP (PA)
777 S Figueroa St # 3400, Los Angeles (90017-5834)
PHONE..................213 612-7800
Fax: 213 612-7801
E George Joseph, *Managing Prtnr*
Lasjon Blacksher, *President*
Leanne Boucher, *President*
Kelly Pepper, *COO*
Teri Ceterson, *CFO*
EMP: 74 EST: 1944
SQ FT: 20,000
SALES (est): 50.6MM **Privately Held**
WEB: www.nossaman.com
SIC: 8111 General practice attorney, lawyer

(P-23474)
NOSSAMAN LLP
Also Called: Bagley, William T
50 California St Ste 3400, San Francisco (94111-4799)
PHONE..................415 398-3600
Susan Eres, *Manager*
Patrick Moore, *Admin Mgr*
Barney Allison,
Martin A Mattes,
Keysha Alexander, *Legal Staff*
EMP: 50
SALES (corp-wide): 50.6MM **Privately Held**
WEB: www.nossaman.com
SIC: 8111 General practice law office
PA: Nossaman Llp
777 S Figueroa St # 3400
Los Angeles CA 90017
213 612-7800

(P-23475)
NOSSAMAN LLP
18101 Von Karman Ave # 1800, Irvine (92612-0177)
PHONE..................949 833-7800
Fax: 714 833-7878
Howard Harrison, *Partner*
Patricia Cooper, *Admin Asst*
Nancy Neptune, *Admin Asst*
Katherine Contreras, *Corp Comm Staff*
Gregory W Sanders,
EMP: 50
SALES (corp-wide): 50.6MM **Privately Held**
WEB: www.nossaman.com
SIC: 8111 General practice attorney, lawyer
PA: Nossaman Llp
777 S Figueroa St # 3400
Los Angeles CA 90017
213 612-7800

(P-23476)
ODONNELL & SHAEFFER LLP
550 S Hope St Ste 2000, Los Angeles (90071-2631)
PHONE..................213 627-3769
Fax: 213 532-2020
Pierce O'Donnell, *Partner*
John J Shaeffer, *Partner*
EMP: 55
SQ FT: 10,000
SALES (est): 3.2MM **Privately Held**
WEB: www.oslaw.com
SIC: 8111 Legal services

(P-23477)
OMELVENY & MYERS LLP (PA)
400 S Hope St Fl 19, Los Angeles (90071-2831)
PHONE..................213 430-6000
Fax: 323 669-7857
Arthur B Culvahouse Jr, *Mng Member*
Kurt J Berney, *Managing Prtnr*
Riccardo Celli, *Managing Prtnr*
John Daghlian, *Managing Prtnr*
Elizabeth L McKeen, *Managing Prtnr*
EMP: 850
SQ FT: 250,000
SALES (est): 331.9MM **Privately Held**
SIC: 8111 General practice law office

(P-23478)
OMELVENY & MYERS LLP
610 Nwport Ctr Dr Fl 17, Newport Beach (92660)
PHONE..................949 760-9600
Fax: 714 823-6994
Elizabeth L McKeen, *Manager*
Terrence R Allen, *Partner*
Philip Grayson, *Info Tech Mgr*
Richard Jones,
Hana Chen, *Legal Staff*
EMP: 130
SALES (corp-wide): 331.9MM **Privately Held**
SIC: 8111 General practice law office
PA: O'melveny & Myers Llp
400 S Hope St Fl 19
Los Angeles CA 90071
213 430-6000

(P-23479)
OMELVENY & MYERS LLP
1999 Avenue Of The Stars # 600, Los Angeles (90067-6035)
PHONE..................310 553-6700
Fax: 310 246-6779
Jodi Yamada, *Manager*
Evelyn Harris, *Administration*
Cindy Brown, *Human Res Mgr*
Martin Checov, *General Counsel*
Linda Gray, *Legal Staff*
EMP: 225
SALES (corp-wide): 331.9MM **Privately Held**
SIC: 8111 General practice attorney, lawyer; general practice law office
PA: O'melveny & Myers Llp
400 S Hope St Fl 19
Los Angeles CA 90071
213 430-6000

(P-23480)
OMELVENY & MYERS LLP
2765 Sand Hill Rd, Menlo Park (94025-7019)
PHONE..................650 473-2600
Fax: 650 473-2601
Tina Schinick, *Branch Mgr*
Todd Bell, *Vice Pres*
Natalie Beacroft, *Executive*
Ellen Sandel, *Admin Asst*
Susie Sarkissian, *Info Tech Mgr*
EMP: 201
SALES (corp-wide): 331.9MM **Privately Held**
SIC: 8111 General practice law office
PA: O'melveny & Myers Llp
400 S Hope St Fl 19
Los Angeles CA 90071
213 430-6000

(P-23481)
OMELVENY & MYERS LLP
2 Embarcadero Ctr Fl 28, San Francisco (94111-3903)
PHONE..................415 984-8700
Luann Simmons, *Manager*
Debra Belaga, *Partner*
William Franklin Birchfield, *Partner*
Cristina Shinnick, *Office Admin*
Deeksha Prabhakar, *Web Dvlpr*
EMP: 175
SALES (corp-wide): 331.9MM **Privately Held**
SIC: 8111 General practice law office
PA: O'melveny & Myers Llp
400 S Hope St Fl 19
Los Angeles CA 90071
213 430-6000

(P-23482)
ORRICK HRRINGTON SUTCLIFFE LLP (PA)
405 Howard St, San Francisco (94105-2625)
PHONE..................415 773-5700
Ralph H Baxter Jr, *CEO*
Martin Bartlam, *Partner*
Neel Chatterjee, *Partner*
Luigi Colombo, *Partner*
Cameron L Cowan, *Partner*
EMP: 148
SQ FT: 146,000
SALES (est): 391.9MM **Privately Held**
WEB: www.orrick.com
SIC: 8111 General practice law office

(P-23483)
ORRICK HRRINGTON SUTCLIFFE LLP
1020 Marsh Rd, Menlo Park (94025-1015)
PHONE..................650 614-7454
Fax: 650 614-7401
Barbara Whiteley, *Branch Mgr*
Peter Cohen, *Partner*
Christopher R Ottenweller,
EMP: 152
SALES (corp-wide): 391.9MM **Privately Held**
WEB: www.orrick.com
SIC: 8111 Legal services

PRODUCTS & SERVICES SECTION
8111 - Legal Svcs County (P-23504)

PA: Orrick, Herrington & Sutcliffe, Llp
405 Howard St
San Francisco CA 94105
415 773-5700

(P-23484)
ORRICK HRRINGTON SUTCLIFFE LLP
1000 Marsh Rd, Menlo Park (94025-1015)
PHONE..................650 614-7400
Gary WEI, *Branch Mgr*
Stacey Donlon, *Executive*
Marjorie Kenneally, *Executive*
Barbara Whiteley, *Office Mgr*
Lynne C Hermle,
EMP: 95
SALES (corp-wide): 391.9MM **Privately Held**
SIC: 8111 General practice attorney, lawyer
PA: Orrick, Herrington & Sutcliffe, Llp
405 Howard St
San Francisco CA 94105
415 773-5700

(P-23485)
ORRICK HRRINGTON SUTCLIFFE LLP
777 S Figueroa St # 3200, Los Angeles (90017-5830)
PHONE..................213 629-2020
Fax: 213 612-2499
Delores Hamilton, *Branch Mgr*
William Oxley, *Partner*
Daniel Tyukody Jr, *Partner*
Jerry J Walsh, *Partner*
Nanci Kawa, *Administration*
EMP: 118
SALES (corp-wide): 391.9MM **Privately Held**
WEB: www.orrick.com
SIC: 8111 General practice attorney, lawyer
PA: Orrick, Herrington & Sutcliffe, Llp
405 Howard St
San Francisco CA 94105
415 773-5700

(P-23486)
ORRICK HRRINGTON SUTCLIFFE LLP
400 Capitol Mall Ste 3000, Sacramento (95814-4497)
PHONE..................916 447-9200
Betty Neal,
Virginia Magan, *Partner*
Jeff Cox, *Exec Dir*
John Myers,
EMP: 67
SQ FT: 19,336
SALES (corp-wide): 391.9MM **Privately Held**
WEB: www.orrick.com
SIC: 8111 General practice attorney, lawyer
PA: Orrick, Herrington & Sutcliffe, Llp
405 Howard St
San Francisco CA 94105
415 773-5700

(P-23487)
PACHULSKI STANG ZEHL JONES LLP (PA)
Also Called: Pszyjw
10100 Santa Monica Blvd # 1100, Los Angeles (90067-4003)
PHONE..................310 277-6910
Richard M Pachulski, *President*
Melisa Desjardien, *President*
Olga Ginsburg, *President*
Diane Potts, *President*
Dean A Ziehl, *Vice Pres*
EMP: 90
SQ FT: 21,000
SALES (est): 29.3MM **Privately Held**
WEB: www.pszyj.com
SIC: 8111 General practice law office

(P-23488)
PACIFIC LEGAL FOUNDATION (PA)
930 G St, Sacramento (95814-1802)
PHONE..................916 419-7111
Robert K Best, *President*
John C Harris, *Ch of Bd*

Robin L Rivett, *President*
Paula Puccio, *Office Mgr*
Kim Devincenvi, *Finance Dir*
EMP: 50
SQ FT: 14,000
SALES: 10.6MM **Privately Held**
SIC: 8111 Legal services

(P-23489)
PARASEC INCORPORATED (PA)
2804 Gateway Oaks Dr # 200, Sacramento (95833-4346)
P.O. Box 160568 (95816-0568)
PHONE..................916 576-7000
Fax: 916 576-7010
Matthew Marzucco, *CEO*
Barbara Geiger, *Vice Pres*
Rose Tran, *Technician*
Theresa Robinson, *Manager*
Ramona Gagnon, *Representative*
EMP: 53
SQ FT: 24,000
SALES (est): 15.3MM **Privately Held**
WEB: www.parasec.com
SIC: 8111 Legal services

(P-23490)
PARKER MILLIKEN CLARK OHAR
555 S Flower St Fl 30, Los Angeles (90071-2440)
PHONE..................818 784-8087
Fax: 213 683-6669
Larry Ivanjack, *President*
Gary Ganchrow, *Shareholder*
Richard D Robbins, *President*
William M Reid, *CFO*
David Eldan, *Executive*
EMP: 70 **EST:** 1914
SQ FT: 25,000
SALES (est): 8.3MM **Privately Held**
WEB: www.pmcos.com
SIC: 8111 General practice law office

(P-23491)
PARKER STANBURY LLP (PA)
444 S Flower St Ste 1900, Los Angeles (90071-2909)
PHONE..................619 528-1259
Robert Lo Presti, *Partner*
Graham J Baldwin, *Partner*
John D Barrett Jr, *Partner*
John W Dannhausen, *Partner*
Douglas M Degrade, *Partner*
EMP: 60
SQ FT: 17,152
SALES (est): 11.6MM **Privately Held**
WEB: www.parkstan.com
SIC: 8111 General practice law office

(P-23492)
PATENAUDE & FELIX A PROF CORP (PA)
4545 Murphy Canyon Rd # 3, San Diego (92123-4363)
PHONE..................702 952-2031
Fax: 858 232-2674
Raymond Patenaude, *Partner*
Patrick Felix, *Partner*
Neal Prasad, *COO*
Jeff Dillon, *CFO*
Roseann Blevins, *Executive*
EMP: 60
SQ FT: 30,000
SALES (est): 19.9MM **Privately Held**
WEB: www.pandf.us
SIC: 8111 General practice attorney, lawyer

(P-23493)
PATTERSON RITNER LOCKWOOD (PA)
620 N Brand Blvd Fl 3, Glendale (91203-4221)
PHONE..................818 241-8001
William F Ritner, *Partner*
Harold H Gartner III, *Partner*
John A Jurich, *Partner*
Clyde E Lockwood, *Partner*
James McGahan, *Partner*
EMP: 50
SQ FT: 16,000
SALES (est): 4.9MM **Privately Held**
WEB: www.pattersonritner.com
SIC: 8111 General practice law office

(P-23494)
PAUL HASTINGS LLP
4747 Executive Dr # 1200, San Diego (92121-3095)
PHONE..................858 458-3000
Carl R Sanchez, *Branch Mgr*
Lauren Bonnes, *Admin Asst*
Lisa Vermeulen, *Legal Staff*
Steven Moseley, *Associate*
EMP: 168
SALES (corp-wide): 441.2MM **Privately Held**
SIC: 8111 General practice law office
PA: Paul Hastings Llp
515 S Flower St Fl 25
Los Angeles CA 90071
213 683-6000

(P-23495)
PAUL HASTINGS LLP
695 Town Center Dr # 120, Costa Mesa (92626-7216)
PHONE..................714 668-6200
Fax: 714 929-1921
Marilyn Radley, *Managing Prtnr*
Douglas A Schaaf, *Partner*
Peter J Tennyson, *Partner*
Jon Montgomery, *E-Business*
Stephen D Coke,
EMP: 200
SALES (corp-wide): 441.2MM **Privately Held**
SIC: 8111 General practice law office
PA: Paul Hastings Llp
515 S Flower St Fl 25
Los Angeles CA 90071
213 683-6000

(P-23496)
PAUL HASTINGS LLP (PA)
515 S Flower St Fl 25, Los Angeles (90071-2228)
PHONE..................213 683-6000
Fax: 213 627-0705
Greg Nitzkowski, *Managing Prtnr*
George W Abele, *Partner*
Jesse H Austin, *Partner*
Elena R Baca, *Partner*
Dino T Barajas, *Partner*
EMP: 148
SQ FT: 209,000
SALES (est): 441.2MM **Privately Held**
SIC: 8111 General practice law office

(P-23497)
PAUL HASTINGS LLP
55 2nd St Fl 24, San Francisco (94105-3492)
PHONE..................415 856-7000
Dennis Dehrens, *Administration*
Eric Roth, *Human Res Mgr*
Lane D Barrasso, *Associate*
Kelly R Winslow, *Associate*
EMP: 168
SALES (corp-wide): 441.2MM **Privately Held**
SIC: 8111 General practice law office
PA: Paul Hastings Llp
515 S Flower St Fl 25
Los Angeles CA 90071
213 683-6000

(P-23498)
PAUL HASTINGS LLP
1117 S California Ave, Palo Alto (94304-1106)
PHONE..................650 320-1800
Paul Janofsky, *Owner*
Tom Wisialowski, *Manager*
EMP: 179
SALES (corp-wide): 441.2MM **Privately Held**
SIC: 8111 Legal services
PA: Paul Hastings Llp
515 S Flower St Fl 25
Los Angeles CA 90071
213 683-6000

(P-23499)
PAYNE & FEARS LLP (PA)
4 Park Plz Ste 1100, Irvine (92614-8550)
PHONE..................949 851-1101
Fax: 714 851-1212
James L Payne, *Partner*
Jeffrey Brown, *Partner*
Daniel Fears, *Partner*

Eric Fohlgren, *Partner*
Karen Frankudakis, *Partner*
EMP: 62
SQ FT: 22,000
SALES (est): 13.2MM **Privately Held**
SIC: 8111 Corporate, partnership & business law; labor & employment law

(P-23500)
PEARLMAN BORSKA & WAX LLP (PA)
15910 Ventura Blvd Fl 18, Encino (91436-2819)
PHONE..................818 501-4343
Fax: 818 386-5700
Barry S Pearlman, *Partner*
Elliot F Borska, *Partner*
Dean Brown, *Partner*
Steven H Wax, *Partner*
Carol Ellison, *CFO*
EMP: 60
SQ FT: 4,000
SALES: 13.3MM **Privately Held**
WEB: www.4pbw.com
SIC: 8111 General practice law office

(P-23501)
PERKINS COIE LLP
3150 Porter Dr, Palo Alto (94304-1212)
PHONE..................415 725-1313
Edward West, *Manager*
Colin M Fowler, *Associate*
Daniel Lassen, *Associate*
Christian Lee, *Associate*
EMP: 70
SALES (corp-wide): 311.6MM **Privately Held**
WEB: www.perkinscoie.com
SIC: 8111 Legal services
PA: Perkins Coie Llp
1201 3rd Ave Ste 4900
Seattle WA 98101
206 359-8000

(P-23502)
PERKINS COIE LLP
1620 26th St Ste 600s, Santa Monica (90404-4013)
PHONE..................310 788-9900
Sally Cano, *Manager*
Mark E Birnbaum, *Partner*
Donald E Karl,
EMP: 75
SALES (corp-wide): 292.4MM **Privately Held**
WEB: www.perkinscoie.com
SIC: 8111 General practice law office
PA: Perkins Coie Llp
1201 3rd Ave Ste 4900
Seattle WA 98101
206 359-8000

(P-23503)
PERKINS COIE LLP
505 Howard St Ste 1000, San Francisco (94105-3222)
PHONE..................415 344-7000
Fax: 415 344-7050
John Rossiter, *Principal*
Zachary Jones, *CFO*
Catherine Simonsen, *Bd of Directors*
John Page, *Admin Asst*
Duston Barton, *Counsel*
EMP: 50
SALES (corp-wide): 292.4MM **Privately Held**
WEB: www.perkinscoie.com
SIC: 8111 Legal services
PA: Perkins Coie Llp
1201 3rd Ave Ste 4900
Seattle WA 98101
206 359-8000

(P-23504)
PERONA LANGER BECK A PROF CORP
300 E San Antonio Dr, Long Beach (90807-2002)
PHONE..................562 426-6155
Fax: 562 490-9823
James T Perona, *President*
Major A Langer, *CFO*
Ronald Beck, *Admin Sec*
Richard Fugio, *Web Proj Mgr*
Stephanie Grant, *Human Resources*
EMP: 100 **EST:** 1966

8111 - Legal Svcs County (P-23505)

SQ FT: 18,000
SALES (est): 13.9MM **Privately Held**
WEB: www.fightforyou.com
SIC: 8111 General practice attorney, lawyer

(P-23505)
PETTI KOHN INGRASSIA & L PR CO
11622 El Camino Real, San Diego (92130-2049)
PHONE...................310 649-5772
Andrew N Kohn, *President*
Kelly Douglas, *Shareholder*
Jeff Miyamoto, *Shareholder*
Grant Waterkotte, *COO*
Thomas S Ingrassia, *CFO*
EMP: 66
SALES (est): 11.1MM **Privately Held**
SIC: 8111 General practice law office

(P-23506)
PHILLIPS & ASSOC LAW OFFS PC
1300 Clay St Ste 600, Oakland (94612-1427)
PHONE...................510 464-8040
P Knudsen, *Branch Mgr*
EMP: 76
SALES (corp-wide): 16.2MM **Privately Held**
SIC: 8111 Legal services
PA: Phillips & Associates Law Offices Pc
3101 N Central Ave # 1500
Phoenix AZ 85012
602 258-8888

(P-23507)
PILLSBURY WINTHROP SHAW
4 Embarcadero Ctr Fl 22, San Francisco (94111-5998)
PHONE...................415 983-1000
Jeffrey M Vesely, *General Ptnr*
Terri Chytrowski, *Comms Dir*
Maria Stanfield, *Administration*
Lisa McMahon, *Legal Staff*
EMP: 194
SALES (corp-wide): 355.7MM **Privately Held**
SIC: 8111 Legal services
PA: Pillsbury Winthrop Shaw Pittman Llp
1540 Broadway Fl 9
New York NY 10036
212 858-1000

(P-23508)
PILLSBURY WINTHROP SHAW
725 S Figueroa St # 2800, Los Angeles (90017-5524)
PHONE...................213 488-7100
Melissa Burton, *Administration*
Catherine D Meyer,
Bradley E Wolf, *Counsel*
Kimberly Theragood, *Manager*
EMP: 150
SALES (corp-wide): 355.7MM **Privately Held**
SIC: 8111 General practice law office
PA: Pillsbury Winthrop Shaw Pittman Llp
1540 Broadway Fl 9
New York NY 10036
212 858-1000

(P-23509)
PILLSBURY WINTHROP SHAW
29 Eucalyptus Rd, Berkeley (94705-2801)
PHONE...................415 983-1865
Thomas Loran, *Branch Mgr*
EMP: 143
SALES (corp-wide): 355.7MM **Privately Held**
SIC: 8111 Legal services
PA: Pillsbury Winthrop Shaw Pittman Llp
1540 Broadway Fl 9
New York NY 10036
212 858-1000

(P-23510)
PILLSBURY WINTHROP SHAW
50 Fremont St Ste 522, San Francisco (94105-2232)
P.O. Box 7880 (94120-7880)
PHONE...................415 983-1075
Jeffrey M Vesely, *Partner*
Stephen Wurzburg, *Managing Prtnr*
Emily Jamison, *President*

Catherine Schmitz, *President*
Lisa Onomoto, *Officer*
EMP: 300
SALES (corp-wide): 355.7MM **Privately Held**
SIC: 8111 General practice law office
PA: Pillsbury Winthrop Shaw Pittman Llp
1540 Broadway Fl 9
New York NY 10036
212 858-1000

(P-23511)
PILLSBURY WINTHROP SHAW
2550 Hanover St, Palo Alto (94304-1115)
PHONE...................650 233-4500
Kathie Pieri, *Manager*
Scott Smith, *Managing Prtnr*
Faruq Ahmad, *Vice Pres*
Ashar Aziz, *Vice Pres*
Robert Corace, *Vice Pres*
EMP: 200
SALES (corp-wide): 355.7MM **Privately Held**
SIC: 8111 General practice law office
PA: Pillsbury Winthrop Shaw Pittman Llp
1540 Broadway Fl 9
New York NY 10036
212 858-1000

(P-23512)
PIRCHER NICHOLS & MEEKS (PA)
1925 Century Park E # 1700, Los Angeles (90067-2740)
PHONE...................310 201-0132
Gary Laughlin, *Senior Partner*
Stevens Carey, *Partner*
Eugene Leone, *Partner*
Leo Pircher, *Partner*
Helen Brooks, *President*
EMP: 95
SQ FT: 35,000
SALES (est): 17.7MM **Privately Held**
WEB: www.pircher.com
SIC: 8111 General practice law office

(P-23513)
POLLARD CRNERT CRWFORD STEVENS
35 N Lake Ave Ste 500, Pasadena (91101-4195)
PHONE...................626 793-4440
Fax: 626 793-1556
Michael Pollard, *Principal*
EMP: 50
SALES (est): 4MM **Privately Held**
SIC: 8111 General practice attorney, lawyer

(P-23514)
POLSINELLI PC
2049 Century Park E, Los Angeles (90067-3101)
PHONE...................310 556-1801
Paula Kane, *Owner*
EMP: 64
SALES (corp-wide): 354MM **Privately Held**
SIC: 8111 General practice attorney, lawyer
PA: Polsinelli Pc
900 W 48th Pl Ste 900
Kansas City MO 64112
816 753-1000

(P-23515)
PRICE LAW GROUP A PROF CORP (PA)
15760 Ventura Blvd # 800, Encino (91436-3000)
PHONE...................818 995-4540
Fax: 818 995-9277
Stuart M Price, *President*
Steven A Alpert, *Manager*
EMP: 115
SQ FT: 15,000
SALES (est): 11.9MM **Privately Held**
SIC: 8111 Bankruptcy law; debt collection law

(P-23516)
PRICE POSTEL AND PARMA LLP
200 E Carrillo St Ste 400, Santa Barbara (93101-2190)
P.O. Box 99 (93102-0099)
PHONE...................805 962-0011
Fax: 805 965-3978
Terry J Schwartz, *Partner*
Lonni Meanley Collins, *Partner*
James H Hurley Jr, *Partner*
Gerald S Thede, *Partner*
David W Van Horne, *Partner*
EMP: 60
SQ FT: 5,000
SALES (est): 8.2MM **Privately Held**
WEB: www.ppplaw.com
SIC: 8111 General practice law office

(P-23517)
PRINDLE DECKER & AMARO LLP (PA)
310 Golden Shore Fl 4, Long Beach (90802-4232)
PHONE...................562 436-3946
Fax: 562 495-0564
Michael Amaro, *Partner*
R Joseph Decker, *Partner*
Kenneth Prindle, *Partner*
Sonia Baskins, *Admin Asst*
Greg Fox, *Technology*
EMP: 85
SALES (est): 8.8MM **Privately Held**
SIC: 8111 General practice attorney, lawyer

(P-23518)
PRISON INDUSTRY AUTHORITY-PIA
1 Kings Way, Avenal (93204-9708)
PHONE...................559 386-6060
Kemy Boyce, *Technician*
Dan Leroy, *Manager*
EMP: 60
SALES (est): 8.9MM **Privately Held**
SIC: 8111 Legal services

(P-23519)
PROBER & RAPHAEL A LAW CORP
Also Called: Prober & Raphael, ALC
20750 Ventura Blvd # 100, Woodland Hills (91364-2338)
P.O. Box 4365 (91365-4365)
PHONE...................818 227-0100
Dean R Prober, *President*
Lee S Raphael, *Principal*
Dean Prober, *General Mgr*
Philip Haro, *Admin Asst*
Franz Wise, *Info Tech Mgr*
EMP: 70
SALES (est): 7.7MM **Privately Held**
SIC: 8111 General practice law office

(P-23520)
PROSKAUER ROSE LLP
Also Called: Scott J Witlin Atty
2049 Century Park E # 3200, Los Angeles (90067-3206)
PHONE...................310 557-2900
Alan Jaffe, *President*
EMP: 60
SALES (corp-wide): 238MM **Privately Held**
SIC: 8111 General practice attorney, lawyer
PA: Proskauer Rose Llp
11 Times Sq Fl 17
New York NY 10036
212 969-3000

(P-23521)
PRYOR CASHMAN LLP
1801 Century Park E # 2419, Los Angeles (90067-2302)
PHONE...................310 556-9608
Ronald H Shechtman, *Branch Mgr*
EMP: 107
SALES (corp-wide): 30.5MM **Privately Held**
SIC: 8111 Legal services
PA: Pryor Cashman Llp
7 Times Sq Fl 3
New York NY 10036
212 421-4100

(P-23522)
PUBLIC COUNSEL
610 S Ardmore Ave, Los Angeles (90005-2322)
PHONE...................213 385-2977
Fax: 213 385-9089
Hernan D Vera, *President*
Madaline Kleiner, *Ch of Bd*
Paul Freese Jr, *Vice Pres*
Lewis Mills, *Branch Mgr*
EMP: 94 EST: 1970
SQ FT: 12,000
SALES (est): 11.6MM **Privately Held**
SIC: 8111 Legal services

(P-23523)
QUINN EMANUEL URQUHART
50 California St Fl 22, San Francisco (94111-4788)
PHONE...................415 875-6600
Fax: 415 875-6700
Charles K Verhoeven, *Managing Prtnr*
Norman Madden, *Admin Sec*
Eric Gebhardt, *Administration*
Leonard Tingin, *Technology*
Kate Bearman, *Associate*
EMP: 50
SALES (corp-wide): 144.8MM **Privately Held**
SIC: 8111 General practice attorney, lawyer
PA: Quinn Emanuel Urquhart & Sullivan, Llp
865 S Figueroa St Fl 10
Los Angeles CA 90017
213 443-3000

(P-23524)
QUINN EMANUEL URQUHART
555 Twin Dolphin Dr Fl 5, Redwood City (94065-2129)
PHONE...................650 801-5000
Claude M Stern, *Managing Prtnr*
Chad Okada, *Technology*
Tracy Anderson, *Recruiter*
Maryann Bramhall, *Recruiter*
Robin A Ramirez, *Legal Staff*
EMP: 80
SALES (corp-wide): 144.8MM **Privately Held**
SIC: 8111 Specialized law offices, attorneys
PA: Quinn Emanuel Urquhart & Sullivan, Llp
865 S Figueroa St Fl 10
Los Angeles CA 90017
213 443-3000

(P-23525)
QUINN EMANUEL URQUHART (PA)
865 S Figueroa St Fl 10, Los Angeles (90017-5003)
PHONE...................213 443-3000
Fax: 213 624-0643
John B Quinn, *Managing Prtnr*
Adam Abensohn, *Partner*
Anthony Alden, *Partner*
Wayne Alexander, *Partner*
Steven Anderson, *Partner*
EMP: 366
SALES (est): 144.8MM **Privately Held**
SIC: 8111 General practice law office

(P-23526)
RAINES LAW GROUP LLP
9720 Wilshire Blvd Fl 5, Beverly Hills (90212-2014)
PHONE...................310 440-4100
Andrew Raines, *General Ptnr*
Robert Pardo, *Partner*
Stephanie Segovia, *Administration*
Brenda Orayo, *Manager*
EMP: 50
SALES (est): 1MM **Privately Held**
SIC: 8111 General practice law office

(P-23527)
REED SMITH LLP
2 Embarcadero Ctr Fl 20, San Francisco (94111-3922)
PHONE...................415 659-5964
Janette Davis, *Manager*
Carl Krasik, *Officer*
Aaron W Harris, *Technology*
Devin Hemraj, *Technology*

PRODUCTS & SERVICES SECTION

8111 - Legal Svcs County (P-23548)

Rachel E Steckel, *Hum Res Coord*
EMP: 70
SALES (corp-wide): 431.9MM **Privately Held**
SIC: 8111 General practice law office
PA: Reed Smith Llp
225 5th Ave Ste 1200
Pittsburgh PA 15222
412 288-3131

(P-23528)
REED SMITH LLP
355 S Grand Ave Ste 2900, Los Angeles (90071-1514)
PHONE...................213 457-8000
Peter Kennedy, *Partner*
Aaron Hritz, *Network Analyst*
Lynn Laguardia, *Human Res Mgr*
Stefania Hoffstetter, *Human Resources*
Evy Wild, *Counsel*
EMP: 158
SALES (corp-wide): 431.9MM **Privately Held**
WEB: www.reedsmith.com
SIC: 8111 General practice attorney, lawyer
PA: Reed Smith Llp
225 5th Ave Ste 1200
Pittsburgh PA 15222
412 288-3131

(P-23529)
REED SMITH LLP
101 2nd St Ste 1800, San Francisco (94105-3659)
PHONE...................415 543-8700
Fax: 415 391-8269
Bettie B Epstein, *Partner*
Nancy Schulein, *President*
Patricia Pritchett, *Technician*
Byron Barrett, *Analyst*
James Schad, *Analyst*
EMP: 158
SALES (corp-wide): 431.9MM **Privately Held**
WEB: www.reedsmith.com
SIC: 8111 Legal services
PA: Reed Smith Llp
225 5th Ave Ste 1200
Pittsburgh PA 15222
412 288-3131

(P-23530)
REED SMITH LLP
2 Embarcadero Ctr Fl 21, San Francisco (94111-3995)
PHONE...................415 543-8700
David A Thompson, *Partner*
Gloria Sandoval, *President*
Amy Hathaway, *Human Resources*
Cristina Shea, *Counsel*
Paul Pitts, *Associate*
EMP: 143
SALES (corp-wide): 431.9MM **Privately Held**
WEB: www.reedsmith.com
SIC: 8111 Legal services
PA: Reed Smith Llp
225 5th Ave Ste 1200
Pittsburgh PA 15222
412 288-3131

(P-23531)
REID & HELLY
3880 Lemon St Fl 5, Riverside (92501-3667)
P.O. Box 1300 (92502-1300)
PHONE...................951 682-1771
Michael Kerbs, *Partner*
Manning James,
EMP: 60
SALES (est): 3.5MM **Privately Held**
SIC: 8111 Legal services

(P-23532)
RICHARDS WATSON & GERSHON PC (PA)
Also Called: RW&g
355 S Grand Ave Fl 40, Los Angeles (90071-1560)
PHONE...................213 626-8484
Fax: 213 626-0078
Laurence S Wiener, *CEO*
Terence Boga, *Shareholder*
Robert Ceccon, *Shareholder*
Diana Chuang, *Shareholder*
Regina Danner, *Shareholder*
EMP: 120
SQ FT: 45,000
SALES (est): 21.2MM **Privately Held**
WEB: www.rwglaw.com
SIC: 8111 General practice law office

(P-23533)
ROBBINS GELLER RUDMAN DOWD LLP (PA)
655 W Broadway Ste 1900, San Diego (92101-8498)
PHONE...................619 231-1058
Michael J Dowd, *Partner*
Jonathan E Behar, *Partner*
Christopher M Burke, *Partner*
James Deguelle, *Partner*
Amber L Eck, *Partner*
EMP: 300
SQ FT: 135,000
SALES (est): 59.6MM **Privately Held**
WEB: www.lcsr.com
SIC: 8111 Specialized law offices, attorneys

(P-23534)
ROBINSN CLGNE RSN SHPR DVS INC
620 Nwport Ctr Dr Ste 700, San Diego (92101)
PHONE...................619 338-4060
Mark P Robinson, *Principal*
Allan F Davis,
EMP: 60
SALES (corp-wide): 10.5MM **Privately Held**
SIC: 8111 Legal services
PA: Robinson Calcagnie Robinson Shapiro Davis, Inc.
19 Corporate Plaza Dr
Newport Beach CA 92660
949 720-1288

(P-23535)
ROBINSON AND WOOD INC
Also Called: Bautista, Jennifer L
227 N 1st St, San Jose (95113-1000)
PHONE...................408 298-7120
Fax: 408 298-0477
Archie Robinson, *President*
Hugh Lennon, *Corp Secy*
Joseph Balestrieri, *Vice Pres*
Arthur Casey, *Vice Pres*
Thomas Fellows, *Vice Pres*
EMP: 60
SQ FT: 23,000
SALES (est): 7.1MM **Privately Held**
WEB: www.robinsonwood.com
SIC: 8111 General practice law office

(P-23536)
ROGERS JOSEPH ODONNELL A PRO (PA)
311 California St Fl 10, San Francisco (94104-2695)
PHONE...................415 956-2828
Neil H O' Donnell, *President*
Allan J Joseph, *Corp Secy*
Joseph W Rogers Jr, *Executive*
Yuvan Wallace, *Asst Sec*
Jeffery Chiow, *Associate*
EMP: 54
SQ FT: 22,000
SALES (est): 8.5MM **Privately Held**
WEB: www.rjo.com
SIC: 8111 General practice attorney, lawyer

(P-23537)
RONALD J LEMIEUX ASSOC LAW OFF
4195 N Viking Way Ste E, Long Beach (90808-1470)
PHONE...................562 375-0095
Ronald J Lemieux, *President*
EMP: 60
SALES (est): 5.1MM **Privately Held**
SIC: 8111 Specialized law offices, attorneys

(P-23538)
ROPERS MAJESKI KOHN BENTLEY (PA)
Also Called: Ropers Majeski Kohn & Bentley
1001 Marshall St Fl 3, Redwood City (94063-2054)
PHONE...................650 364-8200
Fax: 650 367-0997
Jesshill E Love, *CEO*
Stephan Barber, *Senior Partner*
Anthony CHI-Hung, *Partner*
Anthony Grande, *Partner*
Geoffrey Heineman, *Partner*
EMP: 81
SQ FT: 69,000
SALES (est): 46.1MM **Privately Held**
WEB: www.ropers.com
SIC: 8111 General practice law office

(P-23539)
ROPES & GRAY LLP
3 Embarcadero Ctr Ste 300, San Francisco (94111-4006)
PHONE...................415 315-6300
Adam Trott, *Branch Mgr*
Jeff Murray, *Network Enginr*
Colleen Bathen, *Associate*
Joshua Cronin, *Associate*
Alice Ho, *Associate*
EMP: 410
SALES (corp-wide): 318.1MM **Privately Held**
SIC: 8111 General practice law office
PA: Ropes & Gray Llp
800 Prudential Tower # 3600
Boston MA 02199
617 951-7000

(P-23540)
ROPES & GRAY LLP
1900 University Ave # 600, East Palo Alto (94303-2299)
PHONE...................650 617-4000
Kitty Dowgert, *Branch Mgr*
Eric Wright, *Partner*
Alisa Vogel, *Marketing Mgr*
Robert Goldman,
Mark Rowland,
EMP: 63
SALES (corp-wide): 318.1MM **Privately Held**
SIC: 8111 General practice attorney, lawyer
PA: Ropes & Gray Llp
800 Prudential Tower # 3600
Boston MA 02199
617 951-7000

(P-23541)
ROSSI HAMERSLOUGH REISHCHL &
Also Called: Susan S Reishchl
1960 The Alameda Ste 200, San Jose (95126-1451)
PHONE...................408 244-4570
Sam Chuck, *President*
Stan Chuck, *President*
Craig Needham, *President*
EMP: 54
SALES (est): 4.7MM **Privately Held**
SIC: 8111 General practice law office

(P-23542)
RUTAN & TUCKER LLP (PA)
611 Anton Blvd Ste 1400, Costa Mesa (92626-1931)
P.O. Box 1950 (92628-1950)
PHONE...................714 641-5100
Fax: 714 546-9035
Paul F Marx, *Mng Member*
Donna Hiatt, *President*
Tony Malkani, *CFO*
Josette Cann, *Managing Dir*
David Crunkleton, *MIS Dir*
EMP: 141
SQ FT: 90,000
SALES: 82MM **Privately Held**
WEB: www.rutan.com
SIC: 8111 General practice law office

(P-23543)
SALTZBURG RAY & BERGMAN LLP
12121 Wilshire Blvd # 600, Los Angeles (90025-1188)
PHONE...................310 481-6700
Fax: 213 481-6720
David Ray, *Partner*
Alan Bergman, *Partner*
Genise Reiter, *Partner*
Henley Saltzburg, *Partner*
Linda Hariton, *Managing Prtnr*
EMP: 124
SQ FT: 15,000
SALES (est): 13.8MM **Privately Held**
WEB: www.srblaw.com
SIC: 8111 7389 General practice attorney, lawyer; courier or messenger service

(P-23544)
SANTA BARBARA COUNTY OF
Also Called: District Attorney
312 E Cook St Ste D, Santa Maria (93454-5162)
PHONE...................805 346-7540
Fax: 805 346-7588
Joyce Bedley, *Principal*
EMP: 50 **Privately Held**
WEB: www.sbcountyhr.org
SIC: 8111 9222 General practice attorney, lawyer; District Attorneys' offices;
PA: County Of Santa Barbara
105 E Anapamu St Rm 406
Santa Barbara CA 93101
805 568-3400

(P-23545)
SANTA CLARA COUNTY OF
Also Called: District Attorney's Office
3180 Newberry Dr Ste 150, San Jose (95118-1566)
PHONE...................408 792-2704
George Doorley, *Manager*
Louisa Wong, *Admin Sec*
EMP: 600 **Privately Held**
WEB: www.countyairports.org
SIC: 8111 Legal services
PA: County Of Santa Clara
3180 Newberry Dr Ste 150
San Jose CA 95118
408 299-5105

(P-23546)
SANTA ROSA CITY OF
100 Santa Rosa Ave, Santa Rosa (95404-4959)
P.O. Box 1678 (95402-1678)
PHONE...................707 543-3040
Fax: 707 543-3055
Sean McGlynn, *Branch Mgr*
EMP: 90 **Privately Held**
SIC: 8111 Specialized law offices, attorneys
PA: Santa Rosa, City Of
100 Santa Rosa Ave
Santa Rosa CA 95404
707 543-3010

(P-23547)
SCOTT A PORTER PROF CORP
350 University Ave # 200, Sacramento (95825-6581)
P.O. Box 255428 (95865-5428)
PHONE...................916 929-1481
Fax: 916 927-3706
Russell G Porter, *Partner*
Tom Bailey, *Partner*
Tim Blaine, *Partner*
Craig Caldwell, *Partner*
Carl Calnero, *Partner*
EMP: 85
SQ FT: 22,000
SALES (est): 12.1MM **Privately Held**
WEB: www.pswdlaw.com
SIC: 8111 General practice attorney, lawyer

(P-23548)
SEAN P OCONNOR
Also Called: D'Angelo, Michael L
1900 Main St Ste 700, Irvine (92614-7328)
PHONE...................949 851-7323
Michael L D'Angelo, *Principal*
EMP: 80

SALES (est): 2.4MM **Privately Held**
SIC: 8111 General practice attorney, lawyer

(P-23549)
SECOND IMAGE NATIONAL LLC (PA)
170 E Arrow Hwy, San Dimas (91773-3336)
P.O. Box 809 (91773-0809)
PHONE.................................800 229-7477
Fax: 909 305-0839
Norman Fogwell, *CEO*
EMP: 145
SQ FT: 25,500
SALES (est): 23.2MM **Privately Held**
WEB: www.secondimage.net
SIC: 8111 Legal aid service

(P-23550)
SEDGWICK LLP (PA)
333 Bush St Fl 30, San Francisco (94104-2834)
PHONE.................................415 781-7900
Fax: 415 781-2635
Michael F Healy, *Managing Prtnr*
Michael H Bernstein, *Partner*
Bruce D Celebrezze, *Partner*
Earl L Hagstrm, *Partner*
Tristan C Hall, *Partner*
EMP: 208 EST: 1932
SQ FT: 115,000
SALES (est): 179.1MM **Privately Held**
WEB: www.sdma.com
SIC: 8111 Specialized law offices, attorneys

(P-23551)
SEDGWICK LLP
801 S Figueroa St # 1800, Los Angeles (90017-5509)
PHONE.................................213 426-6900
Fax: 213 426-6921
Craig Barnes, *Managing Prtnr*
Marlene Adelman, *President*
Trish Marwedel, *President*
Yvonne Navarro, *President*
Rosemary Pereda, *President*
EMP: 115
SALES (corp-wide): 179.1MM **Privately Held**
WEB: www.sdma.com
SIC: 8111 Legal services
PA: Sedgwick Llp
 333 Bush St Fl 30
 San Francisco CA 94104
 415 781-7900

(P-23552)
SEDGWICK LLP
2020 Main St Ste 1100, Irvine (92614-8234)
PHONE.................................949 852-8200
Fax: 949 852-8282
Ralph Duirgis, *Manager*
Sean Simpson, *Associate*
EMP: 50
SALES (corp-wide): 179.1MM **Privately Held**
WEB: www.sdma.com
SIC: 8111 Legal services
PA: Sedgwick Llp
 333 Bush St Fl 30
 San Francisco CA 94104
 415 781-7900

(P-23553)
SEDGWICK LLP
135 Main St Fl 14, San Francisco (94105-1812)
PHONE.................................415 537-3000
Dale Strang, *Branch Mgr*
Jim Nations, *Info Tech Dir*
Kathy Kubat, *Info Tech Mgr*
Bernadette Lawson, *Marketing Mgr*
David Mesa, *Associate*
EMP: 59
SALES (corp-wide): 179.1MM **Privately Held**
WEB: www.sdma.com
SIC: 8111 Specialized law offices, attorneys
PA: Sedgwick Llp
 333 Bush St Fl 30
 San Francisco CA 94104
 415 781-7900

(P-23554)
SELTZER CAPLAN MCMAHON (PA)
750 B St Ste 2100, San Diego (92101-8177)
PHONE.................................619 685-3003
Robert Caplan, *President*
Michael Leone, *Shareholder*
Brian Seltzer, *COO*
James Dawe, *CFO*
Neal P Panish, *Treasurer*
EMP: 78
SQ FT: 78,000
SALES (est): 19.5MM **Privately Held**
WEB: www.scmv.com
SIC: 8111 General practice law office

(P-23555)
SEVERSON & WERSON A PROF CORP
1 Embarcadero Ctr Fl 26, San Francisco (94111-3745)
PHONE.................................415 283-4911
Fax: 415 956-0439
James B Werson, *Ch of Bd*
Veronica Appleberry, *President*
Emily Rhea, *President*
Oleg Berlan, *CFO*
Robert L Lofts, *CFO*
EMP: 100
SQ FT: 40,000
SALES (est): 19.5MM **Privately Held**
WEB: www.severson.com
SIC: 8111 Specialized law offices, attorneys; corporate, partnership & business law

(P-23556)
SEYFARTH SHAW LLP
333 S Hope St Ste 3900, Los Angeles (90071-3043)
PHONE.................................213 270-9600
Arthur Wood IV, *Branch Mgr*
Hilary White, *Office Mgr*
Christopher D Bordenave, *Associate*
Christine Kim, *Associate*
Linnea Miron, *Associate*
EMP: 125
SALES (corp-wide): 328.5MM **Privately Held**
SIC: 8111 General practice attorney, lawyer
PA: Seyfarth Shaw Llp
 131 S Dearborn St # 2400
 Chicago IL 60603
 312 460-5000

(P-23557)
SEYFARTH SHAW LLP
2029 Century Park E # 3400, Los Angeles (90067-3020)
PHONE.................................310 277-7200
Fax: 310 201-5219
Sandy Abrahamian, *Branch Mgr*
Fern Jenkins, *President*
Jennifer Malcho, *Office Admin*
James Aguilera, *Admin Sec*
Karen Shepardson, *Admin Sec*
EMP: 200
SALES (corp-wide): 328.5MM **Privately Held**
WEB: www.seyfarth.com
SIC: 8111 General practice law office
PA: Seyfarth Shaw Llp
 131 S Dearborn St # 2400
 Chicago IL 60603
 312 460-5000

(P-23558)
SEYFARTH SHAW LLP
560 Mission St Fl 31, San Francisco (94105-2930)
PHONE.................................415 397-2823
Fax: 415 397-8549
William Dritsas, *Principal*
Constance Hughes, *Admin Asst*
Bryan R Thomas, *Administration*
Patricia H Cullison,
Nicole Bolson, *Counsel*
EMP: 100
SALES (corp-wide): 328.5MM **Privately Held**
WEB: www.seyfarth.com
SIC: 8111 General practice law office

PA: Seyfarth Shaw Llp
 131 S Dearborn St # 2400
 Chicago IL 60603
 312 460-5000

(P-23559)
SHARTSIS FRIESE LLP
1 Maritime Plz Fl 18, San Francisco (94111-3508)
PHONE.................................415 421-6500
Fax: 415 421-2922
Arthur J Shartsis, *Partner*
Derek Boswell, *Partner*
Zesara Chan, *Partner*
Frank Cialone, *Partner*
Paul Feasby, *Partner*
EMP: 120
SQ FT: 47,709
SALES (est): 23MM **Privately Held**
WEB: www.sflaw.com
SIC: 8111 Patent, trademark & copyright law; taxation law; will, estate & trust law; real estate law

(P-23560)
SHEKINAH INC
7755 Center Ave Ste 1000, Huntington Beach (92647-3090)
PHONE.................................714 475-5460
Cecilia Trent, *President*
James Trent, *CFO*
David Vasquez Sr, *Vice Pres*
Scott Cass, *Director*
Dana Kowprowski, *Director*
EMP: 50
SQ FT: 2,400
SALES (est): 2.4MM **Privately Held**
SIC: 8111 Debt collection law

(P-23561)
SHEPPARD MULLIN RICHTER (PA)
Also Called: Sheppard Mullin
333 S Hope St Fl 43, Los Angeles (90071-1422)
PHONE.................................213 620-1780
Guy N Halgren, *Partner*
Charles Barker, *Partner*
Robert Beall, *Partner*
Lawrence Braun, *Partner*
Justine M Casey, *Partner*
EMP: 370
SQ FT: 52,820
SALES (est): 239.7MM **Privately Held**
WEB: www.smrh.com
SIC: 8111 General practice law office

(P-23562)
SHEPPARD MULLIN RICHTER
12275 El Camino R Ste 200, San Diego (92130)
PHONE.................................619 338-6500
EMP: 84
SALES (corp-wide): 200.4MM **Privately Held**
SIC: 8111
PA: Sheppard, Mullin, Richter & Hampton, Llp
 333 S Hope St Fl 43
 Los Angeles CA 90071
 202 218-0000

(P-23563)
SHEPPARD MULLIN RICHTER
4 Embarcadero Ctr # 1700, San Francisco (94111-4158)
PHONE.................................415 434-9100
Fax: 415 434-3947
Aline Pearl, *Executive*
Phipp Atkins-Pattensen, *Partner*
Julie Ebert, *Partner*
Douglas R Hart, *Partner*
Betsey McDaniel, *Partner*
EMP: 62
SALES (corp-wide): 239.7MM **Privately Held**
SIC: 8111 Corporate, partnership & business law
PA: Sheppard, Mullin, Richter & Hampton, Llp
 333 S Hope St Fl 43
 Los Angeles CA 90071
 213 620-1780

(P-23564)
SHEPPARD MULLIN RICHTER
1901 Avenue Of The Stars # 1600, Los Angeles (90067-6055)
PHONE.................................310 228-3700
Sherry Wilson, *Administration*
David Garcia, *Partner*
Pravin Jha, *Engineer*
Vivian Katapodis, *Legal Staff*
Cristina Ongsing, *Legal Staff*
EMP: 61
SALES (corp-wide): 239.7MM **Privately Held**
SIC: 8111 Legal services
PA: Sheppard, Mullin, Richter & Hampton, Llp
 333 S Hope St Fl 43
 Los Angeles CA 90071
 213 620-1780

(P-23565)
SHEPPARD MULLIN RICHTER
650 Town Center Dr Fl 4, Costa Mesa (92626-1993)
PHONE.................................714 513-5100
Fax: 714 513-5130
Sheila Cantrell, *Office Admin*
Finley Taylor, *Partner*
Carole Dubienny, *President*
Tina Hammer, *President*
Alice Luciano, *Admin Asst*
EMP: 100
SALES (corp-wide): 239.7MM **Privately Held**
SIC: 8111 General practice law office
PA: Sheppard, Mullin, Richter & Hampton, Llp
 333 S Hope St Fl 43
 Los Angeles CA 90071
 213 620-1780

(P-23566)
SHERIFFS OFFICES
Also Called: Inyo Sheriff Office
550 S Clay St, Independence (93526)
PHONE.................................760 878-0383
Fax: 760 878-0402
Dan Lucas, *Principal*
William Lutze, *Principal*
EMP: 60 EST: 2001
SALES (est): 2.5MM **Privately Held**
SIC: 8111 General practice law office

(P-23567)
SHOOK HARDY & BACON LLP
1 Montgomery St Ste 2700, San Francisco (94104-5527)
PHONE.................................415 544-1900
Fax: 415 391-0281
Shannon Spangler, *Managing Prtnr*
Denise Elliott, *Manager*
Randall Haimovici, *Associate*
Matthew Vanis, *Associate*
EMP: 60
SALES (corp-wide): 310MM **Privately Held**
WEB: www.shb.com
SIC: 8111 General practice law office
PA: Shook, Hardy & Bacon L.L.P.
 2555 Grand Blvd
 Kansas City MO 64108
 816 474-6550

(P-23568)
SIDEMAN & BANCROFT LLP
1 Embarcadero Ctr Fl 22, San Francisco (94111-3711)
PHONE.................................415 392-1960
Fax: 415 392-0827
Jeffrey Hallam, *General Ptnr*
Kelly P McCarthy, *Partner*
Janice Graves, *President*
Robert Cozzolina, *CTO*
Jovanie Cuago, *Info Tech Dir*
EMP: 95
SALES (est): 15MM **Privately Held**
SIC: 8111 Legal services

(P-23569)
SIDLEY AUSTIN LLP
1001 Page Mill Rd Bldg 1, Palo Alto (94304-1006)
PHONE.................................650 565-7000
Bryan K Anderson, *Branch Mgr*
Matthew J Dolan, *Associate*
Ilan Goldbard, *Associate*

PRODUCTS & SERVICES SECTION

8111 - Legal Svcs County (P-23590)

Nathan A Greenblatt, *Associate*
Ilan B Hornstein, *Associate*
EMP: 85
SALES (corp-wide): 811.1MM **Privately Held**
SIC: 8111 Legal services
PA: Sidley Austin Llp
1 S Dearborn St Ste 900
Chicago IL 60603
312 853-7000

(P-23570)
SIDLEY AUSTIN LLP
555 California St Fl 20, San Francisco (94104-1522)
PHONE..........................415 772-1200
Fax: 415 772-7400
Paul C Pringle, *Managing Prtnr*
William Johnson, *IT/INT Sup*
Yvonne Millette, *Financial Exec*
Elpidio Benitag, *Personnel*
Yvonne Babb, *Facilities Mgr*
EMP: 70
SALES (corp-wide): 811.1MM **Privately Held**
WEB: www.cyberlawatsidley.com
SIC: 8111 General practice law office
PA: Sidley Austin Llp
1 S Dearborn St Ste 900
Chicago IL 60603
312 853-7000

(P-23571)
SILVER FREDMAN A PROF LAW CORP
2029 Century Park E # 1900, Los Angeles (90067-2901)
PHONE..........................310 556-2356
Perry Silver, *President*
Andrew B Kaplan, *Partner*
Neil Freedman, *Admin Sec*
Maria Poltorak, *Finance*
Adreena Thomas, *Marketing Mgr*
EMP: 50
SQ FT: 21,500
SALES (est): 3.6MM **Privately Held**
WEB: www.silver-freedman.com
SIC: 8111 General practice attorney, lawyer

(P-23572)
SIMPSON DELMORE AND GREENE LLP (PA)
600 W Broadway Ste 400, San Diego (92101-3352)
PHONE..........................619 515-1194
Paul Delmore, *Partner*
Terence Greene, *Partner*
John Simpson, *Partner*
Kris Boggis, *President*
Carla Sanderson, *Associate*
EMP: 50
SQ FT: 20,000
SALES (est): 5.8MM **Privately Held**
WEB: www.sdgllp.com
SIC: 8111 General practice law office

(P-23573)
SIMPSON THACHER & BARTLETT LLP
2475 Hanover St, Palo Alto (94304-1155)
PHONE..........................650 251-5000
Fax: 650 251-5002
Richard Capelouto, *Manager*
Rachel Goodman, *President*
Teresa Firoozye, *Admin Asst*
Misael Amador, *Technology*
Jonathan Lindabury, *Counsel*
EMP: 120
SALES (corp-wide): 825.5K **Privately Held**
WEB: www.stblaw.com
SIC: 8111 Corporate, partnership & business law
PA: Simpson Thacher & Bartlett Llp
425 Lexington Ave Fl 15
New York NY 10017
212 455-2000

(P-23574)
SKADDEN ARPS SLATE MEAGHER & F
300 S Grand Ave Ste 3400, Los Angeles (90071-3137)
PHONE..........................213 687-5000
Rand S April, *Partner*
Michael Beinus, *Partner*
Kenneth J Betts, *Partner*
Brian J McCarthy, *Partner*
Wahida Khan, *Human Res Mgr*
EMP: 250
SALES (corp-wide): 629.6MM **Privately Held**
SIC: 8111 General practice law office
PA: Skadden, Arps, Slate, Meagher & Flom Llp
4 Times Sq Fl 24
New York NY 10036
212 735-3000

(P-23575)
SMS TRANSPORTATION
18516 S Broadway, Gardena (90248-4615)
PHONE..........................310 527-9200
Fax: 310 527-9206
John W Harris, *Principal*
Jennifer Wiltz, *Manager*
EMP: 100
SALES (est): 8MM **Privately Held**
SIC: 8111 Legal services

(P-23576)
SNELL & WILMER LLP
600 Anton Blvd Ste 1400, Costa Mesa (92626-7689)
PHONE..........................714 427-7000
Fax: 714 427-7799
Andrea Bryant, *Principal*
Alexander L Conti, *Partner*
Frank Cronin, *Partner*
Christy D Joseph, *Partner*
William S O'Hare, *Officer*
EMP: 160
SQ FT: 3,000
SALES (corp-wide): 105.9MM **Privately Held**
SIC: 8111 Legal services; specialized law offices, attorneys
PA: Snell & Wilmer L.L.P.
400 E Van Buren St Fl 10
Phoenix AZ 85004
602 382-6000

(P-23577)
SOBEL ROSS H LAW OFFICES
Also Called: Sobel, Ross Howell
1875 Century Park E, Los Angeles (90067-2337)
PHONE..........................310 788-8995
Fax: 310 552-8047
Ross H Sobel, *Owner*
EMP: 50
SALES (est): 2.6MM **Privately Held**
SIC: 8111 Legal services

(P-23578)
SOLOMON WARD SDNWURM SMITH LLP
401 B St Ste 1200, San Diego (92101-4295)
PHONE..........................619 231-0303
Fax: 619 231-4755
Herbert Solomon, *Partner*
Lawrence Kaplan, *Partner*
Richard E McCarthy, *Partner*
Richard L Seidenwurm, *Partner*
Jeffrey H Silberman, *Partner*
EMP: 60
SQ FT: 17,000
SALES (est): 10.1MM **Privately Held**
WEB: www.swsslaw.com
SIC: 8111 General practice attorney, lawyer

(P-23579)
SQUIRE PATTON BOGGS (US) LLP
275 Battery St Ste 2600, San Francisco (94111-3356)
PHONE..........................415 954-0334
Thomas H Woofter, *Manager*
Thomas Woofter, *Managing Prtnr*
Andrew Armer, *President*
Mary Padilla, *Executive*
Carolyn Winter, *Executive*
EMP: 120
SALES (corp-wide): 442.5MM **Privately Held**
WEB: www.squiresandersdempsey.com
SIC: 8111 General practice law office
PA: Squire Patton Boggs (Us) Llp
4900 Key Tower 127 Pub Sq
Cleveland OH 44114
216 479-8500

(P-23580)
SQUIRE SANDERS (US) LLP
555 S Flower St Fl 31, Los Angeles (90071-2300)
PHONE..........................213 624-2500
Chris M Amantea, *Managing Prtnr*
Andrea C Townsend, *Counsel*
Gabriel Colwell, *Sr Associate*
Anne C Goodwin, *Sr Associate*
Stacie Yee, *Sr Associate*
EMP: 60
SALES (corp-wide): 442.5MM **Privately Held**
WEB: www.squiresandersdempsey.com
SIC: 8111 General practice law office
PA: Squire Patton Boggs (Us) Llp
4900 Key Tower 127 Pub Sq
Cleveland OH 44114
216 479-8500

(P-23581)
ST JOSEPH PROF SVCS ENTPS INC
Also Called: Humboldt Home Health Services
440 S Batavia St, Orange (92868-3907)
PHONE..........................714 347-7500
Rich Stuatuto, *President*
EMP: 70
SALES (est): 2.8MM
SALES (corp-wide): 5.6B **Privately Held**
WEB: www.stjhs.org
SIC: 8111 Legal services
HQ: St. Joseph Health System
3345 Michelson Dr Ste 100
Irvine CA 92612
949 381-4000

(P-23582)
STEELE CIS INC
1 Sansome St Ste 3500, San Francisco (94104-4436)
PHONE..........................415 692-5000
Ken Kurtz, *President*
EMP: 350
SALES (est): 23.8MM **Privately Held**
SIC: 8111 Legal services

(P-23583)
STEIN & LUBIN LLP
600 Montgomery St Fl 14, San Francisco (94111-2716)
PHONE..........................415 981-0550
Fax: 415 981-4343
Mark Lubin, *Partner*
Robert S Stein, *Partner*
Tina Chissell, *President*
Helen Colombo, *President*
Catherine Montoya, *President*
EMP: 50
SALES (est): 9.4MM **Privately Held**
WEB: www.steinlubin.com
SIC: 8111 General practice law office

(P-23584)
STEINHART & FALCONER LLP
153 Townsend St Ste 800, San Francisco (94107-1957)
PHONE..........................415 836-2500
Robb Scott, *Managing Prtnr*
John Cusack, *Partner*
Karen Dow, *Partner*
Browning Marean, *Partner*
Gina Zawitoski, *Partner*
EMP: 85
SALES (est): 3.8MM **Privately Held**
SIC: 8111 General practice law office

(P-23585)
STEPTOE & JOHNSON LLP
633 W 5th St Fl 7, Los Angeles (90071-3503)
PHONE..........................213 439-9400
Fax: 213 439-9599
Leslie Graine, *Administration*
Marsha Kendall, *Admin Asst*
Leslie Green, *Technology*
Michael Lin, *Technology*
Lesley A Reisinger, *Sales Executive*
EMP: 50
SALES (corp-wide): 92.6MM **Privately Held**
WEB: www.steptoe.com
SIC: 8111 Legal services; general practice law office
PA: Steptoe & Johnson Llp
1330 Connecticut Ave Nw
Washington DC 20036
202 429-3000

(P-23586)
STRADLING YOCCA CARLSON & RAUT (PA)
660 Newport Center Dr # 1600, Newport Beach (92660-6458)
PHONE..........................949 725-4000
Fax: 949 725-4100
Fritz Stradling, *Ch of Bd*
Benedict Kwon, *Shareholder*
Shahzad Malik, *Shareholder*
Kathleen Marcus, *Shareholder*
Carol Lew, *Vice Chairman*
EMP: 200
SQ FT: 64,000
SALES (est): 36.9MM **Privately Held**
WEB: www.sycr.com
SIC: 8111 General practice law office

(P-23587)
STRADLING YOCCA CARLSON & RAUT
500 Capitol Mall Ste 1120, Sacramento (95814-4742)
PHONE..........................916 449-2350
Kevin Civale, *Manager*
EMP: 108
SALES (corp-wide): 36.9MM **Privately Held**
SIC: 8111 General practice law office
PA: Stradling Yocca Carlson & Rauth A Professional Corp
660 Newport Center Dr # 1600
Newport Beach CA 92660
949 725-4000

(P-23588)
STROOCK & STROOCK & LAVAN LLP
2029 Century Park E # 1800, Los Angeles (90067-3086)
PHONE..........................310 556-5800
Fax: 310 556-5959
Judy Ciasulli, *Branch Mgr*
Howard Lavin, *Partner*
Arlene Drexler, *Office Admin*
Terri Oppelt, *Administration*
Anika Lira, *Info Tech Mgr*
EMP: 150
SALES (corp-wide): 91.1MM **Privately Held**
SIC: 8111 General practice law office
PA: Stroock & Stroock & Lavan Llp
180 Maiden Ln Fl 17
New York NY 10038
212 806-5400

(P-23589)
SULLIVAN & CROMWELL LLP
1888 Century Park E # 2100, Los Angeles (90067-1725)
PHONE..........................310 712-6600
Fax: 310 712-8800
Laura Henry, *Manager*
Hollie A Paul, *CFO*
M N Inosi, *Senior VP*
Perske Jacquelynn, *Admin Sec*
William Huelbig, *Administration*
EMP: 65
SALES (corp-wide): 370.6MM **Privately Held**
SIC: 8111 Legal services
PA: Sullivan & Cromwell Llp
125 Broad St Fl 35
New York NY 10004
212 558-4000

(P-23590)
SUTHERLAND ASBILL BRENNAN LLP
500 Capitol Mall Ste 2500, Sacramento (95814-4741)
PHONE..........................916 241-0500
Carley A Roberts, *Branch Mgr*
Alistair McMaster, *Legal Staff*
Chris Drymalla, *Counsel*

8111 - Legal Svcs County (P-23591) — PRODUDUCTS & SERVICES SECTION

Joshua Belcher, *Associate*
Daniel Levisohn, *Associate*
EMP: 171
SALES (corp-wide): 130.1MM **Privately Held**
SIC: 8111 Corporate, partnership & business law
PA: Sutherland, Asbill & Brennan L.L.P.
700 6th St Nw Ste 700
Washington DC 20001
202 383-0100

(P-23591)
SYNNEXXUS LLC
20251 Sw Acacia St # 200, Newport Beach (92660-0768)
PHONE.................................714 933-4500
Frank Nese, *Mng Member*
EMP: 50
SALES (est): 3MM **Privately Held**
SIC: 8111 Legal services

(P-23592)
TERIS-BAY AREA LLC
2455 Faber Pl Ste 200, Palo Alto (94303-3316)
PHONE.................................650 213-9922
Stefan Wikstrom, *CEO*
Kip Hauser, *COO*
Darisa Hill, *Controller*
EMP: 99
SALES (est): 3.8MM **Privately Held**
SIC: 8111 Legal services

(P-23593)
THARPE & HOWELL (PA)
15250 Ventura Blvd Fl 9, Sherman Oaks (91403-3221)
PHONE.................................714 437-4900
Fax: 818 205-9944
John Maile, *Managing Prtnr*
Todd R Howell, *Partner*
Timothy D Lake, *Partner*
Christopher S Maile, *Partner*
Christopher P Ruiz, *Partner*
EMP: 78
SQ FT: 13,500
SALES (est): 12.1MM **Privately Held**
WEB: www.tharpe-howell.com
SIC: 8111 General practice law office

(P-23594)
THOMPSON & COLEGATE LLP
3610 14th St Lowr, Riverside (92501-3852)
P.O. Box 1299 (92502-1299)
PHONE.................................951 682-5550
Fax: 951 781-4012
John W Marshall, *Partner*
John A Boyd, *Partner*
Donald G Grant, *Partner*
J E Holmes III, *Partner*
Michael J Marlatt, *Partner*
EMP: 50 **EST:** 1920
SQ FT: 28,500
SALES (est): 4.9MM **Privately Held**
WEB: www.tclaw.net
SIC: 8111 General practice attorney, lawyer

(P-23595)
THOMPSON COBURN LLP
2029 Century Park E # 1900, Los Angeles (90067-2901)
PHONE.................................310 282-2500
EMP: 304
SALES (corp-wide): 155.8MM **Privately Held**
SIC: 8111 General practice law office
PA: Thompson Coburn Llp
505 N 7th St Ste 2700
Saint Louis MO 63101
314 552-6000

(P-23596)
THORSNES BARTOLOTTA & MCGUIRE
2550 5th Ave Ste 1100, San Diego (92103-6694)
PHONE.................................619 236-9363
Fax: 619 236-9653
Mickey McGuire, *Partner*
Vincent Bartolotta, *Partner*
Mitchell Golub, *Partner*
Darel Mazzerlla, *Partner*
Kevin Quinn, *Partner*
EMP: 67

SQ FT: 20,000
SALES (est): 10.6MM **Privately Held**
WEB: www.tbmlawyers.com
SIC: 8111 General practice law office

(P-23597)
TRESSLER LLP
2 Park Plz Ste 1050, Irvine (92614-8521)
PHONE.................................949 336-1200
Katherine Liner, *Owner*
Ryan Luther, *Associate*
EMP: 69
SALES (corp-wide): 46.4MM **Privately Held**
SIC: 8111 Specialized law offices, attorneys
PA: Tressler Llp
233 S Wacker Dr Fl 22
Chicago IL 60606
312 627-4000

(P-23598)
TROPE AND TROPE LLP
Also Called: Trope & Trope
12121 Wilshire Blvd # 801, Los Angeles (90025-1164)
PHONE.................................323 879-2726
Fax: 310 826-1122
Sorrell Trope, *Partner*
Ashley Peterson, *Legal Staff*
EMP: 57
SALES (est): 8.5MM **Privately Held**
SIC: 8111 Divorce & family law

(P-23599)
TROUTMAN SANDERS LLP
11682 El Camino Real # 400, San Diego (92130-2092)
PHONE.................................858 509-6000
Michael J Whitton, *Branch Mgr*
Roy Bell, *Counsel*
Erik M Ideta, *Associate*
Andrew K Puls, *Associate*
EMP: 88
SALES (corp-wide): 323.4MM **Privately Held**
SIC: 8111 General practice law office
PA: Troutman Sanders Llp
600 Peachtree St Ne # 5200
Atlanta GA 30308
404 885-3000

(P-23600)
TROUTMAN SANDERS LLP
580 California St # 1100, San Francisco (94104-1000)
PHONE.................................415 477-5700
EMP: 82
SALES (corp-wide): 323.4MM **Privately Held**
SIC: 8111 Legal services
PA: Troutman Sanders Llp
600 Peachtree St Ne # 5200
Atlanta GA 30308
404 885-3000

(P-23601)
TROYGOULD PC
1801 Century Park E # 1600, Los Angeles (90067-2367)
PHONE.................................310 553-4441
Fax: 310 201-4746
Sanford J Hillsberg, *Principal*
Lawrence Schnapp, *Bd of Directors*
Diane Gordon, *Exec Dir*
Susan Takata, *Admin Sec*
Keith Brownley, *Admin Asst*
EMP: 80
SQ FT: 24,000
SALES (est): 11.5MM **Privately Held**
WEB: www.troygould.com
SIC: 8111 General practice law office

(P-23602)
TRUCK UNDERWRITERS ASSOCIATION (DH)
4680 Wilshire Blvd, Los Angeles (90010-3807)
P.O. Box 2478 (90051-0478)
PHONE.................................323 932-3200
Fax: 323 964-8092
Leonard H Gelfand, *President*
Gerald Faulwell, *Vice Pres*
Martin Feinstein, *Vice Pres*
Jason Katz, *Vice Pres*
John Lynch, *Vice Pres*

EMP: 1767
SALES (est): 45.9MM
SALES (corp-wide): 62B **Privately Held**
SIC: 8111 Legal services
HQ: Farmers Group, Inc.
6301 Owensmouth Ave
Woodland Hills CA 91367
323 932-3200

(P-23603)
TUCKER ELLIS LLP
1000 Wilshire Blvd # 1800, Los Angeles (90017-2457)
PHONE.................................213 430-3400
William Weech, *Administration*
Nicole Lewis, *Vice Pres*
Bill Weech, *Executive*
Alec Boyd, *Counsel*
Larry Donovan, *Counsel*
EMP: 54
SALES (corp-wide): 44.6MM **Privately Held**
WEB: www.tuckerellis.com
SIC: 8111 General practice attorney, lawyer
PA: Tucker Ellis Llp
950 Main Ave Ste 1100
Cleveland OH 44113
216 592-5000

(P-23604)
TYLER PALMIERI WIENER
1900 Main St Ste 700, Irvine (92614-7328)
P.O. Box 19712 (92623-9712)
PHONE.................................949 851-9400
James E Wilhelm, *Partner*
Mike Greene, *Partner*
Robert Ihrke, *Partner*
David Parr, *Partner*
L Richard Rawls, *Partner*
EMP: 100
SQ FT: 34,000
SALES (est): 19.3MM **Privately Held**
SIC: 8111 General practice law office

(P-23605)
VEATCH CARLSON GROGAN & NELSON
700 S Flower St Ste 2200, Los Angeles (90017-4209)
PHONE.................................213 381-2861
Fax: 213 383-6370
Jim Galloway, *Partner*
David Failer, *Partner*
Anna Sepulveda, *Officer*
Cyril Czajkowskyj, *Executive*
Phillip M Borini, *Exec Dir*
EMP: 50
SALES (est): 7MM **Privately Held**
WEB: www.veatchfirm.com
SIC: 8111 General practice law office

(P-23606)
VINSON & ELKINS LLP
1841 Page Mill Rd Fl 2, Palo Alto (94304-1255)
PHONE.................................650 617-8400
EMP: 198
SALES (corp-wide): 347.7MM **Privately Held**
SIC: 8111 General practice attorney, lawyer
PA: Vinson & Elkins L.L.P.
1001 Fannin St Ste 2500
Houston TX 77002
713 758-2222

(P-23607)
VINSON & ELKINS LLP
555 Mission St Ste 2000, San Francisco (94105-0923)
PHONE.................................415 979-6900
EMP: 198
SALES (corp-wide): 347.7MM **Privately Held**
SIC: 8111 Legal services
PA: Vinson & Elkins L.L.P.
1001 Fannin St Ste 2500
Houston TX 77002
713 758-2222

(P-23608)
WALKUP MLDIA KLLY SCHOENBERGER
650 California St Fl 26, San Francisco (94108-2615)
PHONE.................................415 981-7210
Fax: 415 391-6965
Paul W Melodia, *President*
Heather Ehmke, *President*
Kevin Domecus, *Treasurer*
Matthew Davis, *Bd of Directors*
Jefferey Holl, *Vice Pres*
EMP: 50
SQ FT: 30,000
SALES (est): 7.1MM **Privately Held**
WEB: www.walkuplawoffice.com
SIC: 8111 Specialized law offices, attorneys; malpractice & negligence law

(P-23609)
WALSWRTH FRNKLIN BEVINS MCCALL (PA)
Also Called: Walsworth Franklin & Bevins
1 City Blvd W Ste 500, Orange (92868-3677)
PHONE.................................714 634-2522
Fax: 714 634-0686
Jeffrey P Walsworth, *Partner*
Ronald H Bevins Jr, *Partner*
Ian P Dillon, *Partner*
Ferdie F Franklin, *Partner*
Daniel R Jacobs, *Partner*
EMP: 55
SQ FT: 2,800
SALES (est): 15.8MM **Privately Held**
SIC: 8111 General practice law office

(P-23610)
WARREN DRYE KELLEY
10100 Santa Monica Blvd # 1050, Los Angeles (90067-4003)
PHONE.................................310 712-6100
Andrew White, *Managing Prtnr*
Michael O'Connor, *Managing Prtnr*
Marilyn Legayada, *Executive*
Jean Jewel, *Office Mgr*
Gean Jewell, *Sales Executive*
EMP: 60
SALES (est): 5.1MM **Privately Held**
SIC: 8111 Legal services

(P-23611)
WARTNICK CHABER HAROWITZ
Also Called: Wartnick Law Firm
100 1st St Ste 2500, San Francisco (94105-3082)
PHONE.................................415 986-5566
Fax: 415 986-5896
Harry F Wartnick, *Partner*
Madelyn J Chaber, *Partner*
Steven M Harowitz, *Partner*
Audrey A Smith, *Partner*
Stephen M Tigerman, *Partner*
EMP: 76
SALES (est): 5.7MM **Privately Held**
WEB: www.wartnicklaw.com
SIC: 8111 Legal services

(P-23612)
WASSERMAN COMDEN & CASSELMAN (PA)
5567 Reseda Blvd Ste 330, Tarzana (91356-2699)
P.O. Box 7033 (91357-7033)
PHONE.................................323 872-0995
Fax: 818 345-0162
Steve Wasserman, *Partner*
David B Casselman, *Partner*
Leonard J Comden, *Partner*
Clifford H Pearson, *Partner*
Donald I Wessman, *Asbestos Litgtn*
EMP: 88
SQ FT: 15,000
SALES (est): 11.6MM **Privately Held**
WEB: www.wcclaw.com
SIC: 8111 General practice law office

(P-23613)
WEIL GOTSHAL & MANGES LLP
201 Redwood Shors Pkwy Ste 400, Redwood City (94065)
PHONE.................................650 802-3000
Craig Adas, *Managing Prtnr*
Rod J Howard, *Partner*
Curtis L MO, *Partner*

PRODUCTS & SERVICES SECTION

8111 - Legal Svcs County (P-23633)

Tricia Dresel, *President*
Mahra Fields, *President*
EMP: 180
SALES (corp-wide): 358.3MM **Privately Held**
WEB: www.weil.com
SIC: 8111 Legal services
PA: Weil, Gotshal & Manges Llp
767 5th Ave Fl Conc1
New York NY 10153
212 310-8000

(P-23614)
WEINBERG ROGER & RESENFELD (PA)
1001 Marina Village Pkwy # 200, Alameda (94501-6480)
PHONE 510 337-1001
Stewart Weinberg, *President*
Kristina Hillman, *Shareholder*
David Rosenfeld, *Shareholder*
Antonio Ruiz, *Shareholder*
Laurie Arnold, *President*
EMP: 69 **EST:** 1964
SQ FT: 12,000
SALES (est): 11.4MM **Privately Held**
WEB: www.unioncounsel.net
SIC: 8111 General practice law office

(P-23615)
WEINTRAUB TOBIN CHEDIAK
201 Santa Monica Blvd # 300, Santa Monica (90401-2214)
PHONE 310 393-9500
Laurence Berman, *Branch Mgr*
EMP: 50
SALES (corp-wide): 23.2MM **Privately Held**
SIC: 8111 Legal services
PA: Weintraub Tobin Chediak Coleman Grodin Law Corporation
400 Capitol Mall Fl 11
Sacramento CA 95814
916 558-6000

(P-23616)
WEINTRAUB TOBIN CHEDIAK
9665 Wilshire Blvd # 900, Beverly Hills (90212-2315)
PHONE 310 858-7888
Marvin Gelfand, *Partner*
John Christian, *Shareholder*
Vida Thomas, *Counsel*
Kristen Bewley, *Associate*
Lukas Clary, *Associate*
EMP: 50
SALES (corp-wide): 23.2MM **Privately Held**
SIC: 8111 General practice law office
PA: Weintraub Tobin Chediak Coleman Grodin Law Corporation
400 Capitol Mall Fl 11
Sacramento CA 95814
916 558-6000

(P-23617)
WEINTRAUB TOBIN CHEDIAK (PA)
400 Capitol Mall Fl 11, Sacramento (95814-4434)
PHONE 916 558-6000
Fax: 916 498-0822
Michael Kvarme, *CEO*
Thadd A Blizzard, *Partner*
Karen L Boon, *Partner*
Kelly L Borelli, *Partner*
Gary L Bradus, *Partner*
EMP: 50
SQ FT: 44,900
SALES (est): 23.2MM **Privately Held**
WEB: www.weintraub.com
SIC: 8111 General practice law office

(P-23618)
WEITZ & LUXENBERG PC
1880 Century Park E # 700, Los Angeles (90067-1618)
PHONE 310 247-0921
Perry Weitz, *Branch Mgr*
EMP: 68
SALES (corp-wide): 73.3MM **Privately Held**
SIC: 8111 General practice attorney, lawyer
PA: Weitz & Luxenberg, P.C.
700 Broadway Lbby A
New York NY 10003
212 558-5500

(P-23619)
WENDEL ROSEN BLACK & DEAN LLP (PA)
1111 Broadway Ste 24, Oakland (94607-4139)
PHONE 510 834-6600
Fax: 510 834-1928
Howard Lance, *Managing Prtnr*
C Gregg Ankenman, *Partner*
Mark S Bostic, *Partner*
Elizabeth Burke-Dreyfuss, *Partner*
Joan M Cambray, *Partner*
EMP: 84
SQ FT: 40,000
SALES (est): 20.4MM **Privately Held**
WEB: www.wendel.com
SIC: 8111 General practice attorney, lawyer

(P-23620)
WESTON BNSHF RCHFRT RUBLCV & M
333 S Hope St Fl 16, Los Angeles (90071-1410)
PHONE 213 576-1000
Fax: 213 576-1100
John M Rochefort, *Partner*
Ward L Benshoof, *Partner*
N V Carlsen, *Partner*
E J Casey, *Partner*
C W Cohen, *Partner*
EMP: 140
SQ FT: 60,000
SALES (est): 9.4MM **Privately Held**
WEB: www.wbcounsel.com
SIC: 8111 General practice attorney, lawyer

(P-23621)
WHITE & CASE LLP
555 S Flower St Ste 2700, Los Angeles (90071-2433)
PHONE 213 687-9655
Fax: 213 452-2329
Betty Archer, *Manager*
Richard K Smith Jr, *Managing Prtnr*
Christopher Rieck, *Pub Rel Mgr*
Brian Arnold, *Counsel*
John Anderson Jr, *Associate*
EMP: 115
SALES (corp-wide): 729.2MM **Privately Held**
SIC: 8111 General practice attorney, lawyer
PA: White & Case Llp
1155 Ave Of The Flr 9
New York NY 10036
212 819-8200

(P-23622)
WILMER CUTLER PICK HALE DORR
350 S Grand Ave Ste 2100, Los Angeles (90071-3409)
PHONE 213 443-5300
Mark Flanagan, *Partner*
Andrew Margolis, *Office Admin*
EMP: 247
SALES (corp-wide): 334.3MM **Privately Held**
SIC: 8111 Specialized law offices, attorneys
PA: Wilmer Cutler Pickering Hale And Dorr Llp
1875 Pennsylvania Ave Nw
Washington DC 20006
202 663-6000

(P-23623)
WILNER KLEIN SIEGEL
9601 Wilshire Blvd # 700, Beverly Hills (90210-5213)
PHONE 310 550-4595
Fax: 310 275-3509
Sam Wilner, *Partner*
Walter Klein, *Partner*
Lynn Siegel, *Partner*
EMP: 50
SALES (est): 2.1MM **Privately Held**
SIC: 8111 Legal services

(P-23624)
WILSON ELSER MOSKOWITZ
555 S Flower St Ste 2900, Los Angeles (90071-2407)
PHONE 213 443-5100
Fax: 213 443-5101
Patrick M Kelly, *Manager*
Richean Martin, *Admin Asst*
Annette Johnson, *Legal Staff*
Ruben Silva, *Director*
Daniel Braude, *Associate*
EMP: 62
SALES (corp-wide): 351.4MM **Privately Held**
SIC: 8111 General practice attorney, lawyer
PA: Wilson, Elser, Moskowitz, Edelman & Dicker Llp
150 E 42nd St Fl 23
New York NY 10017
212 490-3000

(P-23625)
WILSON SONSINI GOODRICH & ROSA
12235 El Camino Real # 200, San Diego (92130-3002)
PHONE 858 350-2300
Fax: 858 350-2399
Tina Drews, *Office Mgr*
Monica Huettl, *President*
Matthew Grumbling, *Associate*
EMP: 120
SALES (corp-wide): 184.4MM **Privately Held**
SIC: 8111 General practice attorney, lawyer
PA: Wilson Sonsini Goodrich & Rosati, Professional Corporation
650 Page Mill Rd
Palo Alto CA 94304
650 493-9300

(P-23626)
WILSON SONSINI GOODRICH & ROSA (PA)
650 Page Mill Rd, Palo Alto (94304-1001)
PHONE 650 493-9300
Steven E Bochner, *CEO*
James A Diboise, *Partner*
Jack Sheridan, *Partner*
Effie Toshav, *Partner*
Douglas Clark, *Managing Prtnr*
EMP: 1100 **EST:** 1961
SQ FT: 184,000
SALES (est): 184.4MM **Privately Held**
WEB: www.rsklaw.com
SIC: 8111 Corporate, partnership & business law

(P-23627)
WILSON SONSINI GOODRICH & ROSA
1 Market Plz Fl 33, San Francisco (94105-1196)
PHONE 415 947-2000
Fax: 415 947-2099
Peter Mostow, *Partner*
Debra Jones, *Admin Asst*
Anthony Lee, *Network Analyst*
Usha Smerdon,
Eric C Little, *Manager*
EMP: 60
SALES (corp-wide): 184.4MM **Privately Held**
WEB: www.rsklaw.com
SIC: 8111 Corporate, partnership & business law
PA: Wilson Sonsini Goodrich & Rosati, Professional Corporation
650 Page Mill Rd
Palo Alto CA 94304
650 493-9300

(P-23628)
WILSON TURNER KOSMO LLP
550 W C St Ste 1050, San Diego (92101-3532)
PHONE 619 236-9600
Claudette G Wilson, *Partner*
Frederick W Kosmo Jr, *Partner*
Joe Devos, *Administration*
Barbara Boxer,
Wilson Kosmo,
EMP: 54
SQ FT: 13,000
SALES (est): 11.4MM **Privately Held**
WEB: www.wilsonturnerkosmo.com/
SIC: 8111 General practice law office

(P-23629)
WINGERT GREBING BRUBAKER & JUS
600 W Broadway Ste 1200, San Diego (92101-3314)
PHONE 619 232-8151
Fax: 619 232-4665
Stephen Grebing, *Partner*
Michael Anello, *Partner*
Alan Brubaker, *Partner*
James Goodwin, *Partner*
Charles Grebing, *Partner*
EMP: 100
SALES (est): 11.2MM **Privately Held**
WEB: www.wingertlaw.com
SIC: 8111 General practice attorney, lawyer

(P-23630)
WINSTON & STRAWN LLP
Also Called: Silicon Valley Office
275 Middlefield Rd # 205, Menlo Park (94025-3597)
PHONE 650 858-6500
Tom Fitzgerald, *Partner*
EMP: 411
SALES (corp-wide): 311.6MM **Privately Held**
SIC: 8111 Patent, trademark & copyright law
PA: Winston & Strawn Llp
35 W Wacker Dr Ste 4200
Chicago IL 60601
312 558-5600

(P-23631)
WOLF FIRM A LAW CORPORATION
2955 Main St Ste 200, Irvine (92614-2528)
PHONE 949 720-9200
Alan S Wolf, *President*
Scott Jackson, *Exec VP*
Ann Thompson, *Accounting Dir*
Kacy Ford, *Accounting Mgr*
Brenda Britten, *Sales Staff*
EMP: 60
SALES (est): 10.4MM **Privately Held**
WEB: www.wolffirm.com
SIC: 8111 Legal services; specialized law offices, attorneys

(P-23632)
WOOD SMITH HENNING BERMAN LLP (PA)
Also Called: WSH&b
10960 Wilshire Blvd Fl 18, Los Angeles (90024-3804)
PHONE 310 481-7600
David Wood, *Partner*
Daniel Berman, *Partner*
Steven Henning, *Partner*
Kevin Smith, *Partner*
Jason Gless, *Managing Prtnr*
EMP: 50
SQ FT: 24,500
SALES (est): 46.1MM **Privately Held**
WEB: www.wshblaw.com
SIC: 8111 Legal services

(P-23633)
WOODRUFF SPRADLIN & SMART
555 Anton Blvd Ste 1200, Costa Mesa (92626-7670)
PHONE 714 558-7000
Ken Smart, *President*
Thomas L Woodruff, *Treasurer*
Lois E Jeffrey, *Vice Pres*
Daniel K Spradlin, *Vice Pres*
Toni Vigil, *Office Mgr*
EMP: 62
SALES (est): 10MM **Privately Held**
WEB: www.wss-law.com
SIC: 8111 General practice attorney, lawyer

8111 - Legal Svcs County (P-23634)

PRODUDUCTS & SERVICES SECTION

(P-23634)
WRIGHT FINLEY & ZAK LLP
4665 Macarthur Ct Ste 200, Newport Beach (92660-1811)
PHONE 949 477-5050
Robin P Wright, *Managing Prtnr*
Robert Finley, *Partner*
Jonathan Zak, *Partner*
Brian Stewart, *Vice Pres*
Taylor Hubbard, *Legal Staff*
EMP: 60
SALES (est): 9.5MM **Privately Held**
WEB: www.wrightlegal.net
SIC: 8111 Specialized law offices, attorneys

(P-23635)
WULFSBERG REESE COLVING AND
300 Lakeside Dr Ste 2400, Oakland (94612-3539)
PHONE 510 835-9100
Fax: 510 451-2170
H James Wulfsberg, *Ch of Bd*
Charles W Reese, *President*
Wulfsberg Colvig, *Producer*
EMP: 60
SQ FT: 34,000
SALES (est): 6MM **Privately Held**
WEB: www.wulfslaw.com
SIC: 8111 General practice attorney, lawyer

(P-23636)
ZELLE HOFMANN VOELBEL MASN LLP
44 Montgomery St Ste 3400, San Francisco (94104-4807)
PHONE 415 693-0700
Fax: 415 693-0770
Dan Mason, *Manager*
David CHI, *Office Admin*
Angelo Alano, *Technology*
Elizabeth Kniffen, *Associate*
EMP: 50
SALES (corp-wide): 18.4MM **Privately Held**
WEB: www.zelle.com
SIC: 8111 General practice law office
PA: Zelle Llp
500 Washington Ave S # 4000
Minneapolis MN 55415
612 339-2020

(P-23637)
ZIFFREN B B F G-L S&C FND
1801 Century Park W, Los Angeles (90067-6409)
PHONE 310 552-3388
Fax: 310 553-7068
Kenneth Ziffren, *Owner*
Nora Encinas, *President*
John G Branca, *Principal*
Harry M Brittenham, *Principal*
Steven Burkow, *Principal*
EMP: 103
SQ FT: 33,000
SALES (est): 14.9MM **Privately Held**
WEB: www.ziffrenlaw.com
SIC: 8111 General practice law office

(P-23638)
ZWICKER & ASSOCIATES PC
1320 Willow Paca Rd 730, Concord (94520)
PHONE 925 689-7070
Dawn Valverde, *Human Res Mgr*
Jonathan Espinola, *VP Opers*
EMP: 225
SALES (corp-wide): 80MM **Privately Held**
SIC: 8111 General practice attorney, lawyer
PA: Zwicker & Associates, P.C.
80 Minuteman Rd
Andover MA 01810
978 686-2255

8322 Individual & Family Social Svcs

(P-23639)
A TOUCH OF KINDNESS
353 1/2 N La Brea Ave, Los Angeles (90036-2517)
P.O. Box 481270 (90048-9761)
PHONE 323 997-6500
Yona Landau, *Director*
EMP: 75
SALES (est): 1.1MM **Privately Held**
WEB: www.atouchofkindness.com
SIC: 8322 Public welfare center

(P-23640)
ABILITYFIRST
Also Called: LL Frank Work Center
3812 S Grand Ave, Los Angeles (90037-1336)
PHONE 213 748-7309
Fennie Washington, *Director*
EMP: 80
SQ FT: 15,854
SALES (corp-wide): 19.8MM **Privately Held**
WEB: www.abilityfirst.com
SIC: 8322 8093 Association for the handicapped; rehabilitation center, outpatient treatment
PA: Abilityfirst
1300 E Green St
Pasadena CA 91106
626 396-1010

(P-23641)
ABODE SERVICES (PA)
40849 Fremont Blvd, Fremont (94538-4306)
PHONE 510 657-7409
Louis Chicoine, *Exec Dir*
Katie Derrig, *Comms Mgr*
Minling Chung, *Executive Asst*
Dario Loeb, *Info Tech Mgr*
Catherine Vu, *Accountant*
EMP: 70
SALES: 24.6MM **Privately Held**
WEB: www.tricityhomeless.org
SIC: 8322 Individual & family services

(P-23642)
ABRAZAR INC
Also Called: ABRAZAR ELDERLY ASSISTANCE
7101 Wyoming St, Westminster (92683-3811)
PHONE 714 893-3581
Fax: 714 893-4819
Gloria Reyes, *CEO*
Mario Ortega, *COO*
Hoang Than, *Executive*
EMP: 80
SALES: 5.1MM **Privately Held**
WEB: www.abrazarinc.com
SIC: 8322 Individual & family services

(P-23643)
ADMINSTRTIVE OFFICE OF US CRTS
Also Called: United States Fdral Prbatn
280 S 1st St, San Jose (95113-3002)
PHONE 408 535-5200
Sue Rossi, *Office Mgr*
EMP: 69 **Publicly Held**
WEB: www.ao.uscourts.gov
SIC: 8322 Probation office
HQ: The United States Courts Administrative Office Of
1 Columbus Cir Ne
Washington DC 20544
202 502-3800

(P-23644)
ADMINSTRTIVE OFFICE OF US CRTS
Also Called: United States Probation Office
101 W Broadway Ste 700, San Diego (92101-8208)
PHONE 619 557-6650
Fax: 619 557-6138
Kenneth O Young, *Director*
Frank Domurad, *Vice Pres*
Lisa Quintanar, *Administration*
EMP: 200 **Publicly Held**
WEB: www.ao.uscourts.gov
SIC: 8322 9211 Individual & family services; courts
HQ: The United States Courts Administrative Office Of
1 Columbus Cir Ne
Washington DC 20544
202 502-3800

(P-23645)
AFRICAN AMERICAN UNITY CENTER
Also Called: A A U C
944 W 53rd St, Los Angeles (90037-3643)
PHONE 323 789-7300
Charisse Bermond, *Exec Dir*
Will Harris, *Principal*
Elondra Jackson, *Principal*
Charisse Bremond, *Exec Dir*
EMP: 62
SALES: 175.2K **Privately Held**
SIC: 8322 8331 Individual & family services; job training & vocational rehabilitation services

(P-23646)
AGE CONCERNS INC
2650 Camino Del Rio N # 203, San Diego (92108-1621)
PHONE 619 544-1622
Ed Petrivelli, *Exec Dir*
Laura Spitler-Hansen, *President*
Joan Kallin, *Comp Spec*
Reese A Jrrett, *Manager*
EMP: 295
SQ FT: 2,700
SALES (est): 1.9MM
SALES (corp-wide): 64MM **Privately Held**
SIC: 8322 8082 7361 Geriatric social service; home health care services; nurses' registry
PA: Livhome, Inc.
5670 Wilshire Blvd # 500
Los Angeles CA 90036
800 807-5854

(P-23647)
AIDS PROJECT LOS ANGELES (PA)
Also Called: Aids Project La
611 S Kingsley Dr, Los Angeles (90005-2319)
PHONE 213 201-1600
Fax: 323 201-1598
Craig E Thompson, *CEO*
Robyn Goldman, *CFO*
Jerry Levinson, *Controller*
EMP: 90
SALES: 20.9MM **Privately Held**
SIC: 8322 Individual & family services

(P-23648)
AIDS SVCS FNDATION ORANGE CNTY
Also Called: AIDS WALK ORANGE COUNTY
17982 Sky Park Cir Ste J, Irvine (92614-6482)
PHONE 949 809-5700
Fax: 949 809-5779
Alan Witchey, *Exec Dir*
Adele Kellick, *Executive Asst*
Stewat Hale, *IT/INT Sup*
Willie Ingkapattanakul, *Finance Dir*
David Aremendariz, *Director*
EMP: 66
SQ FT: 16,051
SALES: 4.4MM **Privately Held**
SIC: 8322 8011 Individual & family services; clinic, operated by physicians

(P-23649)
ALAMEDA CNTY CMNTY FD BNK INC
7900 Edgewater Dr, Oakland (94621-2004)
P.O. Box 2599 (94614-0599)
PHONE 510 635-3663
Suzan Bateson, *President*
Barbara D Blake, *Marketing Staff*
Justine Kaplan, *Director*
EMP: 70
SQ FT: 118,000
SALES: 14.4MM **Privately Held**
WEB: www.accfb.org
SIC: 8322 Individual & family services

(P-23650)
ALAMEDA COUNTY
Also Called: Behavioral Health Care Svcs
2000 Embarcadero Ste 101, Oakland (94606-5300)
PHONE 510 383-1556
Fax: 510 532-7561
Marye Thomas, *Director*
Jason Pokorny, *Volunteer Dir*
Keith Lewis, *Exec Dir*
Scott Haggerty, *Branch Mgr*
Diana Cruz, *General Mgr*
EMP: 550
SQ FT: 45,000
SALES (est): 23.5MM **Privately Held**
WEB: www.alamedacounty.com
SIC: 8322 Rehabilitation services

(P-23651)
ALL CARE SERVICES INC
17671 Irvine Blvd Ste 110, Tustin (92780-3128)
PHONE 714 669-1148
Fax: 714 669-1380
Lynn Stevens, *Director*
Kenneth E Stevens, *Administration*
Babli Sarma, *Client Mgr*
EMP: 100
SALES: 2.5MM **Privately Held**
WEB: www.allcareservices.com
SIC: 8322 Old age assistance

(P-23652)
ALTA CAL REGIONAL CTR INC
950 Tharp Rd Ste 202, Yuba City (95993-8345)
PHONE 530 674-3070
Fax: 530 674-7228
Terry Rhoades, *Manager*
EMP: 300
SALES (corp-wide): 322.2MM **Privately Held**
WEB: www.altaregional.org
SIC: 8322 8699 General counseling services; charitable organization
PA: Alta California Regional Center, Inc.
2241 Harvard St Ste 100
Sacramento CA 95815
916 978-6400

(P-23653)
ALTA LOMA ASSISTED LIVING LLC
Also Called: Sunlit Gardens
9428 19th St, Murrieta (92562)
PHONE 909 481-2600
Ernest Hix, *Mng Member*
Sharon Hix,
EMP: 66
SALES (est): 1.5MM **Privately Held**
SIC: 8322 Old age assistance

(P-23654)
ALZHEIMERS FAMILY SERVICES CTR
9451 Indianapolis Ave, Huntington Beach (92646-5955)
PHONE 714 593-9630
Guita Sharifi, *Administration*
Lisa Guerrero, *Info Tech Mgr*
Lisa Huanosto, *Info Tech Mgr*
Cindy Howe, *Education*
Karen Freeman, *Asst Director*
EMP: 67
SALES: 5MM **Privately Held**
SIC: 8322 Adult day care center

(P-23655)
ALZHEIMERS GREATER LOS ANGELES
4221 Wilshire Blvd # 400, Los Angeles (90010-3512)
PHONE 323 938-3379
Fax: 323 938-1036
Susan Galeas, *CEO*
Thomas J Winkel, *Treasurer*
Debra Cherry, *Exec VP*
John Seiber, *Vice Pres*
Peter Braun, *Exec Dir*
EMP: 58

PRODUCTS & SERVICES SECTION **8322 - Individual & Family Social Svcs County (P-23678)**

SALES: 6.3MM **Privately Held**
SIC: 8322 Geriatric social service

(P-23656)
AMERICAN CARE GIVERS WESTWOOD
947 Tiverton Ave Ste 533, Los Angeles (90024-3012)
PHONE...............310 208-8005
Vicky London, *President*
Denise London, *CFO*
David London, *Vice Pres*
EMP: 60
SALES (est): 1.2MM **Privately Held**
WEB: www.americancaregivers.com
SIC: 8322 Geriatric social service

(P-23657)
AMERICAN CORRECTIVE COUNSELING
Also Called: Accs
180 Avenida La Pata # 200, San Clemente (92673-6300)
PHONE...............949 369-6210
Michael C Schreck, *President*
F Galton, *Incorporator*
Mike Wilhelms, *CFO*
Brett Stohlton, *Exec VP*
Don Mealing, *Admin Sec*
EMP: 297
SQ FT: 2,000
SALES (est): 4.8MM
SALES (corp-wide): 18MM **Privately Held**
SIC: 8322 General counseling services
PA: Accs Corp
  180 Avenida La Pata # 200
  San Clemente CA 92673
  949 369-6210

(P-23658)
AMERICAN NATIONAL RED CROSS
1663 Market St, San Francisco (94103-1238)
PHONE...............415 427-8134
Harold Brooks, *Manager*
Rita Chick, *Executive*
Harriet Lehmann, *Database Admin*
Darren Lee, *Manager*
Aaron Litwin, *Manager*
EMP: 120
SALES (corp-wide): 2.6B **Privately Held**
WEB: www.redcross.org
SIC: 8322 Individual & family services
PA: American Red Cross
  431 18th St Nw
  Washington DC 20006
  202 737-8300

(P-23659)
AMERICAN NATIONAL RED CROSS
Also Called: American Red Cross
1300 Alberta Way, Concord (94521-3705)
PHONE...............925 603-7400
Harold Brooks, *Principal*
Barbara Wright, *Sales Staff*
EMP: 50
SQ FT: 4,765
SALES (corp-wide): 2.6B **Privately Held**
SIC: 8322 Individual & family services
HQ: The American National Red Cross
  8550 Arlington Blvd # 100
  Fairfax VA 22031
  703 584-8400

(P-23660)
AMERICAN NATIONAL RED CROSS
3950 Calle Fortunada, San Diego (92123-1827)
PHONE...............858 309-1200
Dodie Rotherham, *CEO*
Melinda McDonald, *Executive*
James Sweet, *Branch Mgr*
Neil Myers, *Manager*
EMP: 90
SALES (corp-wide): 2.6B **Privately Held**
WEB: www.redcross.org
SIC: 8322 Social service center
PA: American Red Cross
  431 18th St Nw
  Washington DC 20006
  202 737-8300

(P-23661)
AMERICAN RED CROSS
11355 Ohio Ave, Los Angeles (90025-3266)
PHONE...............310 445-9900
Enrique Rivera, *Office Mgr*
Brian Kilb, *Partner*
Paul Holman, *Director*
EMP: 100
SALES (corp-wide): 2.6B **Privately Held**
WEB: www.redcross.org
SIC: 8322 Individual & family services
PA: American Red Cross
  431 18th St Nw
  Washington DC 20006
  202 737-8300

(P-23662)
AMERICAN WHT MSSN IN STHRN
7212 Orangethorpe Ave 7a, Buena Park (90621-3341)
P.O. Box 1400, Cypress (90630-6400)
PHONE...............714 522-4599
Young Lee, *Owner*
Adam Brown, *Executive*
EMP: 100
SALES (est): 1.1MM **Privately Held**
SIC: 8322 Temporary relief service

(P-23663)
ANTELOPE VALLEY FOUNDATION
Also Called: Daystar Foundation
646 W Lancaster Blvd # 109, Lancaster (93534-3154)
PHONE...............661 945-7290
Fax: 661 945-7294
Steven Sultan, *President*
Dorothy Edgar, *CEO*
EMP: 50
SQ FT: 11,000
SALES: 2.4MM **Privately Held**
SIC: 8322 5999 Individual & family services; technical aids for the handicapped

(P-23664)
ARC - IMPERIAL VALLEY (PA)
298 E Ross Ave, El Centro (92243-9303)
P.O. Box 1828 (92244-1828)
PHONE...............760 352-0180
Arturo Santos, *CEO*
Poli Flores, *President*
Lorie Weaver, *Human Res Dir*
Randy Harman, *Opers Mgr*
Tina Snyder, *Director*
EMP: 60
SQ FT: 22,000
SALES: 10.6MM **Privately Held**
SIC: 8322 4729 8361 Adult day care center; carpool/vanpool arrangement; home for the mentally handicapped

(P-23665)
ARC OF BUTTE COUNTY (PA)
2030 Park Ave, Chico (95928-6701)
P.O. Box 3697 (95927-3697)
PHONE...............530 891-5865
Courtney Casey, *CEO*
Jean Campbell, *Treasurer*
Nelson Corwin, *Associate Dir*
Tom Leonardi, *Associate Dir*
Michael McGinnis, *Associate Dir*
EMP: 200
SQ FT: 12,268
SALES: 6MM **Privately Held**
WEB: www.arcbutte.org
SIC: 8322 Individual & family services

(P-23666)
ARC SAN FRANCISCO
6644 Mission St, Daly City (94014-2014)
PHONE...............650 756-1304
Timothy Hornbecker, *Branch Mgr*
EMP: 151
SALES (corp-wide): 10.3MM **Privately Held**
SIC: 8322 Individual & family services
PA: The Arc San Francisco
  1500 Howard St
  San Francisco CA 94103
  415 255-7200

(P-23667)
ARC STARLIGHT CENTER
Also Called: ARC of San Diego
1280 Nolan Ave, Chula Vista (91911-3738)
PHONE...............619 427-7524
Terri Thorn, *Director*
EMP: 70
SALES (est): 1.6MM **Privately Held**
SIC: 8322 Individual & family services

(P-23668)
ARGONAUT KENSINGTON ASSOCIATES
Also Called: Kensington Place
1580 Geary Rd Ofc, Walnut Creek (94597-2786)
PHONE...............925 943-1121
Fax: 925 943-6705
Richard Fordiani, *Partner*
James Houston, *Partner*
Jane Graham, *Facilities Dir*
EMP: 60
SALES (est): 2.9MM **Privately Held**
SIC: 8322 Senior citizens' center or association

(P-23669)
ARMENIAN AMRCN CUNCIL ON AGING
Also Called: ARMENIAN-AMERICAN COUNCIL ON A
407 E Colorado St, Glendale (91205-1604)
PHONE...............818 241-8690
Mardiros Edgarian, *Director*
Minas Dersarkissian, *Treasurer*
EMP: 50
SQ FT: 5,600
SALES: 50K **Privately Held**
SIC: 8322 Individual & family services

(P-23670)
ARROYO DEVELOPMENTAL SERVICES
1839 Potrero Grande Dr, Monterey Park (91755-5847)
PHONE...............626 307-2240
Fax: 626 307-2244
Robert Wark, *President*
Federico Nicoletti, *Human Res Mgr*
EMP: 60
SQ FT: 1,232
SALES (est): 4.1MM **Privately Held**
SIC: 8322 Individual & family services

(P-23671)
ASANA INTEGRATED MEDICAL GROUP
26135 Mureau Rd Ste 101, Calabasas (91302-3125)
PHONE...............888 212-7545
Nitin Nanda, *Principal*
EMP: 76
SALES (est): 2.1MM
SALES (corp-wide): 3.6B **Publicly Held**
SIC: 8322 General counseling services
HQ: Intrepid Healthcare Services, Inc.
  4605 Lankershim Blvd
  North Hollywood CA 91602
  888 447-2362

(P-23672)
ASPIRANET
Also Called: Excell Center, The
2513 Youngstown Rd, Turlock (95380-9707)
PHONE...............209 667-0327
Fax: 209 667-7339
Christopher Essary, *Principal*
EMP: 60
SALES (corp-wide): 52.7MM **Privately Held**
WEB: www.verosantes.com
SIC: 8322 8361 Individual & family services; residential care
PA: Aspiranet
  400 Oyster Point Blvd # 501
  South San Francisco CA 94080
  650 866-4080

(P-23673)
ASSOCIATED STUDENTS INC (PA)
Also Called: ASSICIATED STUDENTS
University Un Bldg 65, San Luis Obispo (93407)
PHONE...............805 756-1281
Richard Johnson, *Director*
Dwayne Brummett, *Business Mgr*
EMP: 70
SQ FT: 110,000
SALES: 12.7MM **Privately Held**
SIC: 8322 8221 Multi-service center; colleges universities & professional schools

(P-23674)
ATKINSON YOUTH SERVICES INC
4253 Balsam St, Sacramento (95838-2801)
PHONE...............916 927-1863
Jim Atkinson, *Branch Mgr*
EMP: 64 **Privately Held**
SIC: 8322 Youth center
PA: Atkinson Youth Services Inc.
  1906 El Camino Ave
  Sacramento CA 95815

(P-23675)
AVALON A CERRITOS
11000 New Falcon Way Ofc # 177, Cerritos (90703-1553)
PHONE...............562 865-9500
Fax: 562 865-9509
Laura Trujillo, *Exec Dir*
EMP: 50
SALES (est): 2.6MM **Privately Held**
SIC: 8322 Senior citizens' center or association

(P-23676)
BAY AREA COMMUNITY SVCS INC (PA)
Also Called: East Bay Transitional Homes
629 Oakland Ave, Oakland (94611-4567)
PHONE...............510 613-0330
Fax: 510 986-8920
Jamie Almanza, *CEO*
Howard CHI, *COO*
David Stoloff, *Chairman*
Rita Stuckey, *Exec Dir*
Ben Koerner, *Program Mgr*
EMP: 50
SQ FT: 1,000
SALES: 12.2MM **Privately Held**
WEB: www.bayareacs.org
SIC: 8322 Individual & family services

(P-23677)
BAY AREA SENIOR SERVICES INC
Also Called: Peninsula Regent, The
1 Baldwin Ave Ofc, San Mateo (94401-3837)
PHONE...............650 579-5500
Fax: 650 579-0446
M Mannstab, *Exec Dir*
Patty Avena, *Human Res Dir*
EMP: 140
SALES (corp-wide): 20.5MM **Privately Held**
WEB: www.peninsularegent.com
SIC: 8322 Senior citizens' center or association
HQ: Bay Area Senior Services Inc
  1 Hawthorne St Ste 400
  San Francisco CA 94105
  415 989-1111

(P-23678)
BEACON HEALTH OPTIONS INC
10805 Holder St Ste 300, Cypress (90630-5147)
PHONE...............714 763-2405
Steve Rockowitz, *Principal*
EMP: 111
SALES (corp-wide): 431.2MM **Privately Held**
SIC: 8322 Individual & family services
HQ: Beacon Health Options, Inc.
  240 Corporate Blvd # 100
  Norfolk VA 23502
  757 459-5100

8322 - Individual & Family Social Svcs County (P-23679)

(P-23679)
BEHAVIORAL HEALTH SERVICES INC (PA)
15519 Crenshaw Blvd, Gardena (90249-4525)
PHONE...................310 679-9031
Fax: 310 679-2920
Henry Van Oudheudsen, *CEO*
Lawrence T Gentile, *President*
Candy Cargill, *COO*
Shirley Summers, *COO*
Andy Worrell, *CFO*
EMP: 50
SQ FT: 35,000
SALES: 19.8MM **Privately Held**
SIC: 8322 Substance abuse counseling

(P-23680)
BEHAVIORAL HEALTH SERVICES INC
Also Called: Redgate Memorial Hospital
1775 Chestnut Ave, Long Beach (90813-1674)
PHONE...................562 599-4194
Fax: 562 591-6134
Robert Worrell, *Director*
Wendy Swavedra, *Admin Asst*
Mike Ladre, *Engineer*
Elaine Yard, *Human Res Dir*
Gloria Riese, *Teacher*
EMP: 65
SQ FT: 21,780
SALES (corp-wide): 19.8MM **Privately Held**
SIC: 8322 8069 Substance abuse counseling; alcoholism rehabilitation hospital
PA: Behavioral Health Services, Inc.
15519 Crenshaw Blvd
Gardena CA 90249
310 679-9031

(P-23681)
BEHAVIORAL HEALTH SERVICES INC
Also Called: American Recovery Center
2180 Valley Blvd, Pomona (91768-3325)
PHONE...................909 865-2336
Fax: 909 865-1831
Booker Blebsoe, *Administration*
Debra Priestly, *Ch Nursing Ofcr*
Rory Moore, *Hlthcr Dir*
Son Hong J Le, *Director*
Debbie Bledsoe, *Supervisor*
EMP: 100
SQ FT: 40,868
SALES (corp-wide): 19.8MM **Privately Held**
SIC: 8322 8093 8361 Drug abuse counselor, nontreatment; specialty outpatient clinics; residential care
PA: Behavioral Health Services, Inc.
15519 Crenshaw Blvd
Gardena CA 90249
310 679-9031

(P-23682)
BERNARD OSHER MARIN JEWISH COM
Also Called: J C C
200 N San Pedro Rd, San Rafael (94903-4213)
PHONE...................415 444-8000
Marty Friedman, *President*
Penny Wallace, *Volunteer Dir*
Michael Baumstein, *COO*
Mark Goodman, *Treasurer*
Martin Brownstein, *Bd of Directors*
EMP: 200
SQ FT: 90,000
SALES: 11.2MM **Privately Held**
SIC: 8322 Community center

(P-23683)
BETTER WAY SERVICES
5329 Office Center Ct # 100, Bakersfield (93309-7425)
PHONE...................661 326-6444
Fax: 661 326-6446
Jim Kirkendole, *President*
EMP: 100 **EST:** 2000
SQ FT: 4,000
SALES (est): 3MM **Privately Held**
SIC: 8322 Individual & family services

(P-23684)
BILL WILSON CENTER (PA)
3490 The Alameda, Santa Clara (95050-4333)
PHONE...................408 243-0222
Sparky Harlan, *CEO*
Kirsten Mc Keraghan, *Program Mgr*
Nishtha Jolly, *Technology*
Judy Whittier, *Commissioner*
Jessica Paz-Cedillos, *Manager*
EMP: 105
SQ FT: 19,000
SALES: 16.4MM **Privately Held**
SIC: 8322 Individual & family services

(P-23685)
BIRTH CHOICE OF SAN MARCO
277 S Rancho Santa Fe Rd, San Marcos (92078-2341)
PHONE...................760 744-1313
Fax: 760 744-1393
Rose Mary Brown, *Director*
EMP: 60
SALES: 290.8K **Privately Held**
SIC: 8322 Individual & family services

(P-23686)
BIRTH FAMILY SERVICES INC
1968 W Adams Blvd Apt 1, Los Angeles (90018-3515)
PHONE...................310 323-8181
Glenda Lang, *Exec Dir*
EMP: 50
SALES (est): 1.8MM **Privately Held**
SIC: 8322 Individual & family services

(P-23687)
BONITA HOUSE INC
6333 Telg Ave Ste 102, Oakland (94609)
PHONE...................510 923-0180
Fax: 510 923-0894
Rick Crispino, *Exec Dir*
Lorna Jones, *General Mgr*
Marisa Angeles, *Office Mgr*
Lori Magistrado, *Administration*
Allegra Count, *Opers Mgr*
EMP: 76
SQ FT: 4,000
SALES: 6.4MM **Privately Held**
SIC: 8322 Association for the handicapped

(P-23688)
BOYS & GIRLS CLUB SILICON VLY
518 Valley Way, Milpitas (95035-4106)
PHONE...................408 957-9685
Dana Fraticelli, *Director*
Steven Tedesco, *Exec Dir*
Lynne Hall, *Program Dir*
EMP: 51
SALES: 2.9MM **Privately Held**
WEB: www.bgclub.org
SIC: 8322 Youth center

(P-23689)
BOYS GIRLS CLB HUNTINGTON VLY (PA)
16582 Brookhurst St, Fountain Valley (92708-2353)
PHONE...................714 531-2582
Fax: 714 531-7850
Tanya Hoxsie, *President*
Sharanjit Dhaliwal, *Program Dir*
Diana Martinez, *Program Dir*
Rebecca Sanchez, *Program Dir*
Danielle Tobias, *Program Dir*
EMP: 89
SALES: 7.3MM **Privately Held**
SIC: 8322 Youth center

(P-23690)
BOYS GRLS CLB DSERT HOT SPRNG
42600 Cook St Ste 120, Palm Desert (92211-5143)
PHONE...................760 329-1312
Fax: 760 329-8995
Jack Burke, *Exec Dir*
Dan Gibbons, *Bd of Directors*
Chris Mega, *Director*
EMP: 55
SALES: 438.3K **Privately Held**
SIC: 8322 8641 Youth center; civic social & fraternal associations

(P-23691)
BOYS GRLS CLUBS OF SQUOIAS INC
1003 San Juan Ave, Exeter (93221-1342)
PHONE...................559 592-4074
Joe Engelbrecht, *Exec Dir*
Galen Quenzer, *COO*
Mat Keel, *Director*
Jim Maxfield, *Director*
EMP: 62
SQ FT: 1,800
SALES (est): 2.4MM **Privately Held**
SIC: 8322 Child related social services

(P-23692)
BRAILLE INSTITUTE AMERICA INC (PA)
741 N Vermont Ave, Los Angeles (90029-3594)
PHONE...................323 663-1111
Fax: 323 663-0867
Lester M Sussman, *Ch of Bd*
Barbara Hoffmann, *Volunteer Dir*
Peter Mindnich, *President*
Les Stocker, *President*
John F Llewellyn, *Bd of Directors*
EMP: 208 **EST:** 1919
SQ FT: 167,079
SALES: 21MM **Privately Held**
SIC: 8322 8231 2731 2759 Individual & family services; specialized libraries; textbooks: publishing & printing; commercial printing

(P-23693)
BRANLYN PROMINENCE INC
Also Called: Home Instead Senior Care
13334 Amargosa Rd, Victorville (92392-8504)
PHONE...................760 843-5655
Chris Parmelee, *General Mgr*
EMP: 130
SQ FT: 1,800
SALES (corp-wide): 8.1MM **Privately Held**
SIC: 8322 Homemakers' service
PA: Branlyn Prominence, Inc.
9213 Archibald Ave
Rancho Cucamonga CA 91730
909 476-9030

(P-23694)
BREAKOUT PRISON OUTREACH
Also Called: California Youth Outreach
1560 Berger Dr, San Jose (95112-2703)
P.O. Box 8671, Fresno (93747-8671)
PHONE...................408 702-2405
Fax: 408 280-0144
Anthony Ortiz, *President*
Kurt Foreman, *Treasurer*
Ron Soto, *Exec Dir*
Sandra Martinez, *Admin Sec*
Christina Yee, *Administration*
EMP: 72
SQ FT: 1,800
SALES (est): 4.5MM **Privately Held**
SIC: 8322 Youth center

(P-23695)
BRIGHTER BEGINNINGS (PA)
3478 Buskirk Ave Ste 105, Pleasant Hill (94523-4345)
PHONE...................510 903-7503
Barbara B McCullough, *CEO*
Muang Saephan, *Program Mgr*
Yuan Huang, *Controller*
Claudia Cesena, *Personnel Assit*
Sandra Schueling, *Psychologist*
EMP: 50
SALES: 5.2MM **Privately Held**
WEB: www.brighter-beginnings.org
SIC: 8322 8011 8093 Individual & family services; primary care medical clinic; mental health clinic, outpatient

(P-23696)
BROOKDALE SENIOR LIVING INC
285 W Central Ave, Brea (92821-3374)
PHONE...................714 671-7898
Steve Ilten, *Sls & Mktg Exec*
EMP: 127
SALES (corp-wide): 4.9B **Publicly Held**
SIC: 8322 Old age assistance
PA: Brookdale Senior Living
111 Westmoreland Pl Ste 400
Brentwood TN 37027
615 221-2250

(P-23697)
BUCKELEW PROGRAMS (PA)
555 Northgate Dr Ste 200, San Rafael (94903-3696)
PHONE...................415 457-6964
Fax: 415 721-0281
Steve Eckert, *CEO*
Ed Walsh, *CFO*
Dian Allen, *Exec Dir*
Lori Albertson, *Admin Asst*
Mia Grigg, *CTO*
EMP: 86
SQ FT: 3,000
SALES: 14.5MM **Privately Held**
WEB: www.buckelew.org
SIC: 8322 Individual & family services

(P-23698)
CALIFORNIA CHILD CARE RESOURC
Also Called: Infant/Toddler Consort
5232 Claremont Ave, Oakland (94618-1033)
PHONE...................510 658-0381
Betty Cohen, *Exec Dir*
EMP: 50
SALES (corp-wide): 2.5MM **Privately Held**
WEB: www.rrnetwork.org
SIC: 8322 Referral service for personal & social problems
PA: California Child Care Resource And Referral Network
111 New Montgomery St # 7
San Francisco CA 94105
415 882-0234

(P-23699)
CALIFORNIA PEDIATRIC FMLY SVCS
Also Called: ABLE
326 E Foothill Blvd, Azusa (91702-2515)
PHONE...................626 812-0055
Fax: 626 334-1227
Louise Vanzee PHD, *President*
Kelly Prieto, *Vice Chairman*
Faviola Acevedo, *Manager*
EMP: 75
SQ FT: 2,417
SALES: 386.1K **Privately Held**
WEB: www.cal-peds.com
SIC: 8322 Family counseling services

(P-23700)
CAMP FIRE USA LONG BEACH CNCL
7070 E Carson St, Long Beach (90808-2353)
PHONE...................562 421-2725
Fax: 562 421-4056
Shirlee Jackert, *Administration*
Paul Rodriguez, *Vice Pres*
Angela Olsen, *Sales Executive*
Georgia Stewart, *Director*
EMP: 50
SALES: 1.7MM **Privately Held**
WEB: www.campfirelb.org
SIC: 8322 Youth center

(P-23701)
CAN-DO
Also Called: Compass Actn Netwk Dirct Outcm
578 Washington Blvd 39o, Marina Del Rey (90292-5442)
PHONE...................646 228-7049
Eric Klein, *Director*
Erica Leahy, *Project Mgr*
EMP: 60
SALES (est): 2.7MM **Privately Held**
SIC: 8322 Disaster service

(P-23702)
CARE 4 U LLC
22726 Eccles St, West Hills (91304-3324)
P.O. Box 10297, Canoga Park (91309-1297)
PHONE...................818 593-7911
Ralph Stokes,
Orli Almog,

PRODUCTS & SERVICES SECTION

8322 - Individual & Family Social Svcs County (P-23725)

EMP: 56
SALES: 225K Privately Held
SIC: 8322 Social service center

(P-23703)
CARESCOPE LLC
1455 Response Rd Ste 115, Sacramento (95815-4848)
P.O. Box 2121 (95812-2121)
PHONE.................................916 780-1384
Okja Sim,
Frank Sim, *General Mgr*
EMP: 60
SALES (est): 672.9K Privately Held
SIC: 8322 Senior citizens' center or association

(P-23704)
CARMICHAEL RECREATION & PK DST
5750 Grant Ave, Carmichael (95608-3779)
PHONE.................................916 485-5322
Fax: 916 485-0805
Ronald D Cuppy, *Administration*
Jerry Eppler, *Maint Spvr*
EMP: 170
SALES (est): 6.4MM Privately Held
WEB: www.carmichaelpark.com
SIC: 8322 Community center

(P-23705)
CASA COLINA INC (PA)
255 E Bonita Ave, Pomona (91767-1933)
PHONE.................................909 596-7733
Felice L Loverso, *CEO*
EMP: 500 EST: 1981
SALES: 80.9MM Privately Held
SIC: 8322 Rehabilitation services

(P-23706)
CASA PACIFICA CENTERS (PA)
1722 S Lewis Rd, Camarillo (93012-8520)
PHONE.................................805 482-3260
Fax: 805 987-7237
Steven E Elson, *CEO*
Felice Ginsberg, *CFO*
Michael Redard, *CFO*
Michelle Maye, *Bd of Directors*
Valerie Machain, *Exec Dir*
EMP: 175
SQ FT: 63,000
SALES: 28.7MM Privately Held
WEB: www.casapacifica.org
SIC: 8322 8361 8211 Child related social services; residential care for children; specialty education

(P-23707)
CASPAR COMMUNITY
15051 Caspar Rd, Caspar (95420-0114)
P.O. Box 84 (95420)
PHONE.................................707 964-4997
Judy Parbell, *President*
Rochelle Elkan, *Treasurer*
Maryflannery Kaurt, *Treasurer*
Dalen Anderson, *Admin Sec*
EMP: 50
SALES: 202K Privately Held
SIC: 8322 Community center

(P-23708)
CATHOLIC CHARITIES DIOCESE SAN
6360 El Cajon Blvd, San Diego (92115-2643)
PHONE.................................619 286-1100
Roxana Ramirez, *Principal*
EMP: 124
SALES (corp-wide): 15MM Privately Held
SIC: 8322 Individual & family services
PA: Catholic Charities Of The Diocese Of San Diego
349 Cedar St
San Diego CA 92101
619 231-2828

(P-23709)
CATHOLIC CHARITIES DIOCESE SAN
Also Called: Refugee Resettlement
4575 Mission Gorge Pl A, San Diego (92120-4106)
PHONE.................................619 287-9454
Robert Moser, *Director*

Alberto Deleon, *Business Mgr*
EMP: 50
SALES (corp-wide): 15MM Privately Held
SIC: 8322 Refugee service
PA: Catholic Charities Of The Diocese Of San Diego
349 Cedar St
San Diego CA 92101
619 231-2828

(P-23710)
CATHOLIC CHARITIES OF LA INC
21600 Hart St, Canoga Park (91303)
PHONE.................................818 883-6015
EMP: 50
SALES (corp-wide): 29MM Privately Held
SIC: 8322
PA: Catholic Charities Of Los Angeles, Inc.
1531 James M Wood Blvd
Los Angeles CA 90015
213 251-3400

(P-23711)
CATHOLIC CHARITIES OF LA INC
1400 James M Wood Blvd, Los Angeles (90015-1210)
P.O. Box 15095 (90015-0095)
PHONE.................................213 251-3400
James E Bathker, *Branch Mgr*
EMP: 58
SALES (corp-wide): 29MM Privately Held
SIC: 8322 Individual & family services
PA: Catholic Charities Of Los Angeles, Inc.
1531 James M Wood Blvd
Los Angeles CA 90015
213 251-3400

(P-23712)
CATHOLIC CHARITIES OF SANTA CL (PA)
2625 Zanker Rd Ste 200, San Jose (95134-2130)
PHONE.................................408 468-0100
Gregory Kepferle, *CEO*
Tom Kemnitz, *Program Mgr*
Marvin Neu, *Executive Asst*
Sachi Mizuno, *Administration*
Don Ngo, *Info Tech Mgr*
EMP: 200
SQ FT: 50,000
SALES: 34MM Privately Held
SIC: 8322 Individual & family services; social service center

(P-23713)
CATHOLIC CHARITIES OF SANTA CL
303 N Ventura Ave Ste A, Ventura (93001-1961)
PHONE.................................805 643-4694
Fax: 805 643-4781
Robert Batdazian, *Director*
EMP: 60
SALES (corp-wide): 34MM Privately Held
SIC: 8322 Family counseling services
PA: Catholic Charities Of Santa Clara County
2625 Zanker Rd Ste 200
San Jose CA 95134
408 468-0100

(P-23714)
CATHOLIC CHARITIES OF THE DIOC (PA)
Also Called: Catholic Charities of East Bay
433 Jefferson St, Oakland (94607-3592)
PHONE.................................510 768-3100
Chuck Fernandez, *Exec Dir*
Ida Tolentino, *Executive*
Solomon Belette, *Exec Dir*
Elizabeth Brown, *Office Mgr*
Elena Drozdova, *Accounting Mgr*
EMP: 83
SQ FT: 10,376
SALES: 5.5MM Privately Held
SIC: 8322 8661 Social service center; religious organizations

(P-23715)
CATHOLIC CHRTS CYO ARCHDIOCS
810 Avenue D, San Francisco (94130-2002)
PHONE.................................415 743-0017
Nella Goncalves, *Principal*
EMP: 61
SALES (corp-wide): 39.6MM Privately Held
SIC: 8322 Individual & family services
PA: Catholic Charities Cyo Of The Archdiocese Of San Francisco
990 Eddy St
San Francisco CA 94109
415 972-1200

(P-23716)
CATHOLIC CHRTS CYO ARCHDIOCS
Also Called: Leland House
141 Leland Ave, San Francisco (94134-2847)
PHONE.................................415 405-2000
Fax: 415 337-1137
Paul Raia, *Exec Dir*
Jose Cartagena, *Program Mgr*
Kevin Cunz, *Business Mgr*
Tammy Carrow, *Assistant*
EMP: 61
SALES (corp-wide): 39.6MM Privately Held
SIC: 8322 Child guidance agency
PA: Catholic Charities Cyo Of The Archdiocese Of San Francisco
990 Eddy St
San Francisco CA 94109
415 972-1200

(P-23717)
CATHOLIC CHRTS CYO ARCHDIOCS
1111 Junipero Serra Blvd, San Francisco (94132-2653)
PHONE.................................415 334-5550
Jeffrey Bialik V, *Principal*
EMP: 61
SALES (corp-wide): 39.6MM Privately Held
SIC: 8322 Individual & family services
PA: Catholic Charities Cyo Of The Archdiocese Of San Francisco
990 Eddy St
San Francisco CA 94109
415 972-1200

(P-23718)
CATHOLIC CHRTS CYO ARCHDIOCS (PA)
990 Eddy St, San Francisco (94109-7713)
PHONE.................................415 972-1200
Fax: 415 972-1201
Jeffrey V Bialik, *Exec Dir*
Keith Spindle, *CFO*
Nanette Miller, *Treasurer*
Lauren Muszynski, *Program Mgr*
Liz Sparks, *Office Mgr*
EMP: 56 EST: 1907
SALES: 39.6MM Privately Held
SIC: 8322 Child guidance agency; senior citizens' center or association; family service agency; rehabilitation services

(P-23719)
CATHOLIC CHRTS CYO ARCHDIOCS
Also Called: Derek Silva Community
20 Franklin St, San Francisco (94102-6000)
PHONE.................................415 553-8700
Theresa Flores, *Principal*
Erwin Barrios, *Case Mgr*
EMP: 61
SALES (corp-wide): 39.6MM Privately Held
SIC: 8322 Child guidance agency
PA: Catholic Charities Cyo Of The Archdiocese Of San Francisco
990 Eddy St
San Francisco CA 94109
415 972-1200

(P-23720)
CATHOLIC CHRTS CYO ARCHDIOCS
1 Saint Vincents Dr, San Rafael (94903-1504)
PHONE.................................415 507-2000
Chuck Fernandez, *Branch Mgr*
EMP: 300
SALES (corp-wide): 39.6MM Privately Held
SIC: 8322 8641 Child related social services; civic social & fraternal associations
PA: Catholic Charities Cyo Of The Archdiocese Of San Francisco
990 Eddy St
San Francisco CA 94109
415 972-1200

(P-23721)
CENTER CNSLNG EDCTN & CRISIS
Also Called: Valley Community Health Center
4361 Railroad Ave, Pleasanton (94566-6611)
PHONE.................................925 462-1755
Ronald Greenspane, *Exec Dir*
Brian Castro, *Info Tech Dir*
EMP: 73
SALES (est): 3.3MM Privately Held
SIC: 8322 General counseling services

(P-23722)
CENTER FOR HUMAN SERVICES (PA)
2000 W Briggsmore Ave I, Modesto (95350-3839)
PHONE.................................209 526-1476
Fax: 209 525-0908
Linda Kovacs, *Exec Dir*
Fiona Macpherson, *Bd of Directors*
Joyce Ayres, *Associate Dir*
Rosemary McFadden, *Associate Dir*
Taryn Muralt, *Associate Dir*
EMP: 68
SQ FT: 8,000
SALES: 10.3MM Privately Held
SIC: 8322 8331 Child guidance agency; job training services

(P-23723)
CENTER FOR INDVDUAL AND FAM TH
840 W Town And Country Rd, Orange (92868-4712)
PHONE.................................714 558-9266
Jim Masteller, *Director*
EMP: 55
SALES (est): 700.7K Privately Held
SIC: 8322 Family counseling services

(P-23724)
CENTER POINT INC (PA)
135 Paul Dr, San Rafael (94903-2023)
PHONE.................................415 492-4444
Sushma D Taylor PHD, *Exec Dir*
Terrell Anderson, *Treasurer*
Patti Trail, *Vice Pres*
Angelito Kemp, *CTO*
Miquel Garibay, *Manager*
EMP: 103
SQ FT: 7,750
SALES: 20.2MM Privately Held
SIC: 8322 Social service center

(P-23725)
CENTRAL CAL NIKKEI FOUNDATION
Also Called: VINTAGE GARDENS
540 S Peach Ave, Fresno (93727-3957)
PHONE.................................559 237-4006
Melvin K Renge, *President*
Joyce Contreras, *Admin Dir*
Louis Gebbia, *Exec Dir*
Susan Martinez, *Admin Asst*
Floyd Green, *Director*
EMP: 52
SALES: 2.5MM Privately Held
SIC: 8322 Old age assistance

8322 - Individual & Family Social Svcs County (P-23726)

(P-23726)
CENTRAL VALLEY AUTISM PROJECT
3425 Coffee Rd Ste C2, Modesto (95355-1582)
PHONE 209 521-4791
Gina Pallotta, *Director*
Julie Gradford, *Admin Asst*
Donna Pearson, *Project Mgr*
Khadijah Al-Faraj, *Supervisor*
Angela Castro, *Supervisor*
EMP: 80 EST: 2000
SALES (est): 4MM **Privately Held**
SIC: 8322 Individual & family services

(P-23727)
CENTRAL VLY CHLD SVCS NETWRK
1911 N Helm Ave, Fresno (93727-1614)
PHONE 559 456-1100
Jane Martin, *Exec Dir*
Gayle L Duffy, *Exec Dir*
Irene Alvarado, *Admin Asst*
Esperanza Napoles, *Project Mgr*
Ofelia Gonzalez, *Pub Rel Dir*
EMP: 60
SQ FT: 15,000
SALES: 12.1MM **Privately Held**
WEB: www.cvcsn.org
SIC: 8322 Individual & family services

(P-23728)
CENTRL TERRITRL SALVATION ARMY
10200 Pioneer Rd, Tustin (92782-1417)
PHONE 714 832-7100
Fax: 714 832-2361
Nigel Cross, *Director*
Praise Byun, *Hum Res Coord*
Bruce Freeman, *Director*
EMP: 60
SALES (corp-wide): 4.3B **Privately Held**
WEB: www.salarmychicago.org
SIC: 8322 8661 8699 Individual & family services; religious organizations; charitable organization
HQ: Central Territorial Of The Salvation Army
5550 Prairie Stone Pkwy # 130
Hoffman Estates IL 60192
847 294-2000

(P-23729)
CENTRO DE SALUD DE LA
1420 E Plaza Blvd Ste E4, National City (91950-3636)
PHONE 619 477-0165
Fax: 619 477-7049
Marie Mulhall, *Principal*
EMP: 57
SALES (corp-wide): 87.1MM **Privately Held**
SIC: 8322 Individual & family services
PA: Centro De Salud De La Comunidad De San Ysidro, Inc.
4004 Beyer Blvd
San Ysidro CA 92173
619 428-4463

(P-23730)
CHILD ABUSE LSTENING MEDIATION
Also Called: C A L M
1236 Chapala St, Santa Barbara (93101-3116)
PHONE 805 965-2376
Fax: 805 963-6707
Anna M Kokotovic, *Exec Dir*
Janet Ames, *Exec Dir*
M Kokotovic, *Exec Dir*
Alana Walczak, *General Mgr*
Sarah Rettinger, *Info Tech Mgr*
EMP: 50 EST: 1971
SALES: 6.1MM **Privately Held**
WEB: www.calm4kids.org
SIC: 8322 Crisis intervention center

(P-23731)
CHILD CARE COORDINATING COUNSL
330 Twin Dolphin Dr # 119, Redwood City (94065-1455)
PHONE 650 517-1400
Fax: 650 655-6776
Jan Stokley, *Exec Dir*

Milan Havel, *Executive*
Bruce Lyau, *CTO*
Julie Baldocchi, *Manager*
Linda Eskridge, *Manager*
EMP: 50
SALES: 8.7MM **Privately Held**
WEB: www.thecouncil.net
SIC: 8322 Referral service for personal & social problems

(P-23732)
CHILD CARE RESOURCE CENTER INC (PA)
20001 Prairie St, Chatsworth (91311-6508)
PHONE 818 717-1000
Michael Olenick, *CEO*
Casey Quinn, *CFO*
Denise Trinh, *CFO*
Ellen Cervantes, *Vice Pres*
Rick Robertss, *Vice Pres*
EMP: 130
SALES: 111.3MM **Privately Held**
SIC: 8322 Child related social services

(P-23733)
CHILD CARE RESOURCE CENTER INC
20001 Prairie St, Chatsworth (91311-6508)
PHONE 661 255-2474
Michael Olenick, *CEO*
EMP: 500
SALES (corp-wide): 111.3MM **Privately Held**
SIC: 8322 Child related social services
PA: Child Care Resource Center, Inc.
20001 Prairie St
Chatsworth CA 91311
818 717-1000

(P-23734)
CHILD CARE RESOURCE CENTER INC
250 Grand Cypress Ave # 601, Palmdale (93551-3675)
PHONE 661 723-3246
Ann Bubont, *Principal*
Elizabeth Chiaro, *Director*
Jopie Smith, *Director*
Janice Alfaro, *Manager*
Larry Ellis, *Manager*
EMP: 50
SALES (corp-wide): 111.3MM **Privately Held**
SIC: 8322 Child related social services
PA: Child Care Resource Center, Inc.
20001 Prairie St
Chatsworth CA 91311
818 717-1000

(P-23735)
CHILD DEVELOPMENT INSTITUTE
Also Called: CDI
6340 Variel Ave Ste A, Woodland Hills (91367-2514)
PHONE 818 888-4559
Fax: 818 888-4005
Joan Samaltese, *Exec Dir*
William Powers Jr, *Vice Chairman*
Peter Bowers, *CFO*
Dana Kalek, *Program Mgr*
Laura Counts, *Comp Spec*
EMP: 50
SALES: 3.3MM **Privately Held**
WEB: www.childdevelopmentinstitute.org
SIC: 8322 Child related social services

(P-23736)
CHILD DEVELOPMENT RESOURCES OF (PA)
Also Called: C D R
221 E Ventura Blvd, Oxnard (93036-0277)
PHONE 805 485-7878
Dana Johnson, *Exec Dir*
Kent Kellegrew, *Vice Pres*
Rocio Llamas-Leyva, *Executive*
Sara O'Colon, *Executive*
Alicia Ramirez, *Executive*
EMP: 200
SQ FT: 67,007
SALES: 33MM **Privately Held**
SIC: 8322 Child guidance agency

(P-23737)
CHILD SUPPORT SVCS CAL DEPT (DH)
11120 International Dr, Rancho Cordova (95670-6096)
P.O. Box 419064 (95741-9064)
PHONE 916 464-5000
Jan Sturla, *Director*
EMP: 62
SALES (est): 30MM **Privately Held**
SIC: 8322 9441 Individual & family services; administration of social & manpower programs;
HQ: California Health & Human Servcs Agency
1600 9th St Ste 460
Sacramento CA 95814
916 654-3454

(P-23738)
CHILDRENS ANGELCARE AID INTL
6457 Elmhurst Dr, San Diego (92120-3959)
P.O. Box 600370 (92160-0370)
PHONE 619 795-6234
Michael Challgren, *Chairman*
T P Grosser, *President*
Wayne Peimann, *Vice Pres*
EMP: 200
SQ FT: 2,500
SALES: 5.5MM **Privately Held**
SIC: 8322 Individual & family services

(P-23739)
CHILDRENS CRISIS CNTR STANISLS
1244 Fiori Ave, Modesto (95350-5503)
P.O. Box 1062 (95353-1062)
PHONE 209 577-4413
Fax: 209 577-4337
Colleen Garcia, *Director*
EMP: 100 EST: 1980
SALES: 2.8MM **Privately Held**
SIC: 8322 Social service center; crisis center

(P-23740)
CHILDRENS HUNGER FUND (PA)
13931 Balboa Blvd, Sylmar (91342-1084)
PHONE 818 979-7100
Dav Phillips, *President*
Christopher Sue, *CFO*
Fred Martin, *Comms Dir*
Michael Richards, *Exec Dir*
Carol McDonald, *Executive Asst*
EMP: 59
SQ FT: 60,000
SALES (est): 1.1MM **Privately Held**
SIC: 8322 Individual & family services

(P-23741)
CHILDRENS INST LOS ANGELES
679 S New Hampshire Ave, Los Angeles (90005-1355)
PHONE 213 383-2765
Mary Emmons, *Branch Mgr*
EMP: 650
SALES (corp-wide): 915.5K **Privately Held**
SIC: 8322 Social service center
PA: Children's Institute Of Los Angeles
2121 W Temple St
Los Angeles CA 90026
213 385-5100

(P-23742)
CHILDRENS INSTITUTE INC (PA)
2121 W Temple St, Los Angeles (90026-4915)
PHONE 213 385-5100
Fax: 213 383-1820
Mary Emmons, *President*
Nina Revoyr, *Exec VP*
Dr Steve Ambrose, *Senior VP*
Manny Castellanos, *Vice Pres*
Yivette O Dell, *Vice Pres*
EMP: 190 EST: 1906
SQ FT: 18,000
SALES: 66.1MM **Privately Held**
SIC: 8322 Child related social services

(P-23743)
CHILDRENS INSTITUTE INC
Also Called: Childrens Inst Intrntnal-Burto
21810 Normandie Ave, Torrance (90502-2047)
PHONE 310 783-4677
Fax: 310 783-4676
Marta Rodriguez, *Director*
EMP: 80
SALES (corp-wide): 66.1MM **Privately Held**
SIC: 8322 Individual & family services
PA: Childrens Institute, Inc.
2121 W Temple St
Los Angeles CA 90026
213 385-5100

(P-23744)
CHILDRENS PROTECTIVE SERVICES
5730 Packard Ave, Marysville (95901-7118)
P.O. Box 2320 (95901-0082)
PHONE 530 749-6311
Suzanne Noble, *Director*
EMP: 60
SALES (est): 492.9K **Privately Held**
WEB: www.childrensprotectiveservices.com
SIC: 8322 Children's aid society

(P-23745)
CHILDRENS SERVICES
Also Called: Colusa City Office Education
345 5th St Ste A, Colusa (95932-2445)
PHONE 530 458-0300
Rick Perym, *Director*
Bonjie Immoos, *Superintendent*
EMP: 90
SALES (est): 4.1MM **Privately Held**
SIC: 8322 Children's aid society

(P-23746)
CHURCH OF SCIENTOLOGY
Also Called: Dianetics
3226 Scott Blvd, Santa Clara (95054-3007)
PHONE 650 969-5262
Fax: 650 969-2033
Adriana Morse, *Director*
EMP: 85
SALES (est): 3.1MM **Privately Held**
SIC: 8322 Self-help organization

(P-23747)
CITY & COUNTY OF SAN FRANCISCO
Also Called: Adult Probation Department
850 Bryant St Ste 200, San Francisco (94103-4614)
PHONE 415 553-1706
Fax: 415 553-1771
Arturo Faro, *Manager*
Norvella Brooks, *Officer*
Steve Martinez, *Executive*
Armando Cervantes, *Manager*
Wendy Still, *Manager*
EMP: 150 **Privately Held**
SIC: 8322 9221 Probation office; ;
PA: City & County Of San Francisco
1 Dr Carlton B Goodlett P
San Francisco CA 94102
415 554-7500

(P-23748)
CITY & COUNTY OF SAN FRANCISCO
Also Called: Sheriff's Dept
375 Woodside Ave 1, San Francisco (94127-1221)
PHONE 415 753-7561
Janete Shalwitz, *Branch Mgr*
EMP: 93 **Privately Held**
SIC: 8322 9441 Child related social services; administration of social & manpower programs;
PA: City & County Of San Francisco
1 Dr Carlton B Goodlett P
San Francisco CA 94102
415 554-7500

(P-23749)
CITY IMPACT INC
829 N A St, Oxnard (93030-4310)
P.O. Box 5678 (93031-5678)
PHONE 805 983-3636

PRODUCTS & SERVICES SECTION
8322 - Individual & Family Social Svcs County (P-23772)

Fax: 805 988-2240
Betty Alvarez Ham, *President*
Pam Stewart, *Vice Pres*
Griselda Hernandez, *Admin Mgr*
Carma Bryan, *Admin Asst*
Adriana Juarez, *Admin Asst*
EMP: 55
SALES: 2.3MM **Privately Held**
WEB: www.cityimpact.com
SIC: 8322 Family (marriage) counseling

(P-23750)
CITY OF BAKERSFIELD
Rabobank Arena Theater & Conve
1001 Truxtun Ave, Bakersfield
(93301-4714)
PHONE..................661 852-7300
Fax: 661 861-9904
John Dorman, *General Mgr*
Amber Logsdon, *Store Mgr*
Ariel Roberts, *Executive Asst*
Deslund Grimes, *Opers Mgr*
Sam Williams, *Sales Mgr*
EMP: 110 **Privately Held**
WEB: www.bakersfieldfire.us
SIC: 8322 9111 6512 Community center; mayors' offices; nonresidential building operators
PA: City Of Bakersfield
1600 Truxtun Ave Fl 5th
Bakersfield CA 93301
661 326-3000

(P-23751)
CITY OF BELL
Also Called: Dept of Community Services
6330 Pine Ave, Bell (90201-1221)
PHONE..................323 773-1596
Fax: 323 560-8192
Annett Peretz, *Director*
Carlos Alvarado, *Director*
Lourdes Garcia, *Director*
EMP: 100 **Privately Held**
SIC: 8322 9111 Community center; mayors' offices
PA: City Of Bell
6330 Pine Ave
Bell CA 90201
323 588-6211

(P-23752)
CITY OF CARSON
Also Called: Carson Community Center
3 Civic Plaza Dr, Carson (90745-2231)
PHONE..................310 835-0212
Fax: 310 835-0160
Zenora Bellard, *Director*
Duane Munson, *Executive*
EMP: 53 **Privately Held**
SIC: 8322 9111 7299 5812 Community center; mayors' offices; banquet hall facilities; caterers
PA: City Of Carson
701 E Carson St
Carson CA 90745
310 830-7600

(P-23753)
CITY OF LA HABRA
Also Called: Community Services Department
101 W La Habra Blvd, La Habra (90631-5401)
P.O. Box 337 (90633-0337)
PHONE..................562 905-9708
Sal Failla, *Director*
EMP: 50 **Privately Held**
SIC: 8322 Community center
PA: City Of La Habra
201 E La Habra Blvd
La Habra CA 90631
562 383-4000

(P-23754)
CITY OF LOS ANGELES
Also Called: Parks & Recreation Dept
1762 S La Cienega Blvd, Los Angeles (90035-4602)
PHONE..................310 204-6707
Barbara Bonner-Snead, *Manager*
EMP: 81 **Privately Held**
WEB: www.lacity.org
SIC: 8322 9441 Individual & family services; administration of social & manpower programs;
PA: City Of Los Angeles
200 N Spring St Ste 303
Los Angeles CA 90012
213 978-0600

(P-23755)
CITY OF MOORPARK
Also Called: Moorpark Active Adult Center
799 Moorpark Ave, Moorpark (93021-1155)
PHONE..................805 517-6261
Steven Kueny, *CEO*
Peggy Rothschild, *Manager*
EMP: 60 **Privately Held**
SIC: 8322 Senior citizens' center or association
PA: City Of Moorpark
799 Moorpark Ave
Moorpark CA 93021
805 517-6200

(P-23756)
CITY OF OAKLAND
Also Called: Human Services Dept
150 Frank H Ogawa Plz # 3332, Oakland (94612-2021)
PHONE..................510 238-6796
Andrea Youngdahl, *Director*
Sean Gascie, *Opers Staff*
Enrique Padilla, *Opers Staff*
EMP: 300 **Privately Held**
WEB: www.cityofbuellton.com
SIC: 8322 9441 Individual & family services; administration of social & manpower programs;
PA: City Of Oakland
150 Frank H Ogawa Plz # 3332
Oakland CA 94612
510 238-3280

(P-23757)
CITY OF ORANGE
230 E Chapman Ave, Orange (92866-1506)
PHONE..................714 744-7264
Bonnie Hagen, *Director*
Virginia Miscione, *Admin Sec*
Barbara Messick, *Project Mgr*
Megan M Hanley, *Manager*
Rachael Gomez, *Supervisor*
EMP: 75 **Privately Held**
WEB: www.cityoforange.org
SIC: 8322 9111 Community center; mayors' offices
PA: City Of Orange
300 E Chapman Ave
Orange CA 92866
714 744-5500

(P-23758)
CITY OF OXNARD
Also Called: Senior Services
350 N C St, Oxnard (93030-4646)
PHONE..................805 385-8019
Fax: 805 385-7494
Jocelyn Peterson, *Director*
Eddie Sanchez, *Vice Pres*
EMP: 99 **Privately Held**
WEB: www.oxnardtourism.com
SIC: 8322 9111 Senior citizens' center or association; mayors' offices
PA: City Of Oxnard
300 W 3rd St Uppr Fl4
Oxnard CA 93030
805 385-7803

(P-23759)
CITY OF VACAVILLE
1100 Alamo Dr, Vacaville (95687-5606)
PHONE..................707 449-6122
Carry Walker, *Manager*
EMP: 80 **Privately Held**
WEB: www.lenaugustine.com
SIC: 8322 Community center
PA: City Of Vacaville
650 Merchant St
Vacaville CA 95688
707 449-5100

(P-23760)
CITY OF WHITTIER
Also Called: Whittier City Community Svcs
7630 Washington Ave, Whittier (90602-1733)
PHONE..................562 567-9446
Fran Shields, *Director*
EMP: 100 **Privately Held**
WEB: www.whittierpd.org
SIC: 8322 Community center
PA: City Of Whittier
13230 Penn St
Whittier CA 90602
562 567-9999

(P-23761)
CLARE FOUNDATION INC (PA)
909 Pico Blvd, Santa Monica (90405-1326)
PHONE..................310 314-6200
Nicholas Vrataric, *Exec Dir*
William Blatt, *President*
Cindy Davis, *Officer*
Cathy Walter, *Executive Asst*
EMP: 65
SQ FT: 1,162
SALES: 6.9MM **Privately Held**
SIC: 8322 Self-help organization

(P-23762)
CLARE FOUNDATION INC
Also Called: Dui Program
1871 9th St, Santa Monica (90404-4501)
PHONE..................310 314-6200
Fax: 310 396-6974
Nicholas Vrataric, *Exec Dir*
EMP: 60
SALES (corp-wide): 6.9MM **Privately Held**
SIC: 8322 Substance abuse counseling
PA: Clare Foundation, Inc.
909 Pico Blvd
Santa Monica CA 90405
310 314-6200

(P-23763)
CLINICA SIERRA VISTA
3727 N 1st St Ste 106, Fresno (93726-5628)
PHONE..................559 457-6900
Enas F Attia, *Pediatrics*
EMP: 239
SALES (corp-wide): 119.8MM **Privately Held**
SIC: 8322 Community center
PA: Clinica Sierra Vista
1430 Truxtun Ave Ste 400
Bakersfield CA 93301
661 635-3050

(P-23764)
COACHELLA VLY RESCUE MISSION
Also Called: CVRM
82873 Via Venecia, Indio (92201-6971)
PHONE..................760 347-3512
Fax: 760 347-8073
Floyd Rhoades, *Ch of Bd*
Pete Del Rio, *Vice Chairman*
Joseph Hayes, *Treasurer*
Jim Parrish, *Vice Ch Bd*
Linda Garland, *Executive*
EMP: 50
SQ FT: 43,000
SALES: 5.3MM **Privately Held**
WEB: www.cvrm.org
SIC: 8322 8661 Individual & family services; non-church religious organizations

(P-23765)
COALITION FOR FAMILY HARMONY
1030 N Ventura Rd, Oxnard (93030-3855)
PHONE..................805 983-6014
Cherie Douval, *President*
EMP: 75
SQ FT: 20,000
SALES: 1.7MM **Privately Held**
SIC: 8322 Emergency shelters

(P-23766)
COASTAL CMNTY SENIOR CARE LLC
Also Called: Home Instead Senior Care
5500 E Atherton St # 216, Long Beach (90815-4016)
PHONE..................562 596-4884
Donald Pierce, *CEO*
EMP: 130
SQ FT: 2,300
SALES (est): 655.6K **Privately Held**
SIC: 8322 Individual & family services

(P-23767)
COLUSA CNTY SBSTNCE ABUSE SVCS
Also Called: Colusa County Behavioral Hlth
162 E Carson St Ste A, Colusa (95932-2880)
PHONE..................530 458-0520
Terrance Rooney, *Director*
Jack Joiner, *Deputy Dir*
Gerardo S Toribio, *Director*
EMP: 52
SALES (est): 1.8MM **Privately Held**
SIC: 8322 Substance abuse counseling

(P-23768)
COMMUNITY ACCESS NETWORK
2275 S Main St Ste 201, Corona (92882-5303)
PHONE..................951 279-1333
Fax: 951 279-5222
Rafik Philobos, *President*
Karen Shah, *Vice Pres*
Magaly Sevillano, *Admin Sec*
Darin Plott, *Accountant*
EMP: 60
SQ FT: 10,000
SALES: 4.9MM **Privately Held**
WEB: www.canffa.org
SIC: 8322 8361 Individual & family services; family counseling services; residential care

(P-23769)
COMMUNITY ACTION PARTNERSHI
11870 Monarch St, Garden Grove (92841-2113)
PHONE..................714 897-6670
Alberta Christy, *Principal*
EMP: 79
SALES (corp-wide): 20.4MM **Privately Held**
SIC: 8322 Social service center
PA: Community Action Partnership Of Orange County
11870 Monarch St
Garden Grove CA 92841
714 897-6670

(P-23770)
COMMUNITY ACTION PARTNERSHIP (PA)
1030 Southwood Dr, San Luis Obispo (93401-5813)
PHONE..................805 544-4355
Anita Robinson, *Ch of Bd*
Frances I Coughlin, *President*
Jim Famalette, *COO*
Rob Garcia, *Treasurer*
Missey Hobson, *Corp Secy*
EMP: 72
SQ FT: 20,000
SALES: 57.3MM **Privately Held**
SIC: 8322 Individual & family services

(P-23771)
COMMUNITY ACTION PARTNR KERN (PA)
5005 Business Park N, Bakersfield (93309-1651)
PHONE..................661 336-5236
Jeremy Tobias, *Exec Dir*
Loretta Andrews, *Program Mgr*
Diana Morrison, *Program Mgr*
Sandi Truman, *Program Mgr*
Ken White, *Program Mgr*
EMP: 50
SQ FT: 14,500
SALES: 63.1MM **Privately Held**
WEB: www.capk.org
SIC: 8322 Individual & family services; senior citizens' center or association; child guidance agency; public welfare center

(P-23772)
COMMUNITY CARE ADHC INC
Also Called: Consultants For Adhc
9917 Las Tunas Dr, Temple City (91780-2211)
PHONE..................626 614-8999
Fax: 626 614-8095
Behrooz Sumekh, *President*
EMP: 60 **EST:** 2001

8322 - Individual & Family Social Svcs County (P-23773)

SALES (est): 1.8MM **Privately Held**
SIC: 8322 Adult day care center

(P-23773)
COMMUNITY GATEPATH
Also Called: Impact Business Service
350 Twin Dolphin Dr # 123, Redwood City (94065-1457)
PHONE.................................650 259-8500
Fax: 650 697-5010
Sheryl Young, *CEO*
Kenneth Jones, *Chief Mktg Ofcr*
Tracey Fecher, *Vice Pres*
Anne Jarchow, *Vice Pres*
Gabrielle Karampelas, *Vice Pres*
EMP: 120
SQ FT: 25,000
SALES: 13.3MM **Privately Held**
WEB: www.communitygatepath.com
SIC: 8322 Social services for the handicapped

(P-23774)
COMMUNITY HOUSING OPTIONS
Also Called: CHOICESS
348 E Foothill Blvd, Arcadia (91006-2542)
PHONE.................................626 359-3300
Fax: 626 447-5855
Joseph Donofrio, *Director*
Lydia Del Rio, *Office Mgr*
Lynn Basso, *Accountant*
EMP: 100
SQ FT: 850
SALES: 1.9MM **Privately Held**
WEB: www.choicess.com
SIC: 8322 Social services for the handicapped

(P-23775)
COMMUNITY INTERFACE SERVICES
2621 Roosevelt St Ste 100, Carlsbad (92008-1660)
PHONE.................................760 729-3866
Fax: 760 729-8526
Rose M Hanson, *President*
Rojane Lindkvist, *Treasurer*
Cheryl Carman, *Accountant*
Pamela Oakes, *Director*
EMP: 100
SALES: 6.6MM **Privately Held**
WEB: www.communityinterfaceservices.org
SIC: 8322 Individual & family services

(P-23776)
COMMUNITY PARTNERS
Also Called: Inner City Struggle
530 S Boyle Ave, Los Angeles (90033-3817)
PHONE.................................323 780-7605
Maria Brenes, *Director*
Maryann Aguirre, *Administration*
Lydia Avila, *Director*
Hector Flores, *Director*
EMP: 112
SALES (corp-wide): 30.5MM **Privately Held**
WEB: www.communitypartners.org
SIC: 8322 Community center
PA: Community Partners
  1000 N Alameda St Ste 240
  Los Angeles CA 90012
  213 346-3200

(P-23777)
COMMUNITY SERVICE PROGRAMS INC (PA)
Also Called: C S P
1221 E Dyer Rd Ste 120, Santa Ana (92705-5634)
PHONE.................................714 492-1010
Fax: 949 975-0250
Margot R Carlson, *Exec Dir*
John Griffin, *Bd of Directors*
Thomas Coad, *Executive*
Heather Stoerck, *Admin Asst*
Penny Hose, *Info Tech Dir*
EMP: 60
SQ FT: 16,000
SALES: 15.3MM **Privately Held**
SIC: 8322 Individual & family services

(P-23778)
COMMUNITY SUPPORT OPTIONS INC
1401 Poso Dr, Wasco (93280-2584)
P.O. Box 8018 (93280-8108)
PHONE.................................661 758-5331
John Stockton, *CEO*
Anna Poggi, *President*
Ben Goosen, *Treasurer*
Jose Hernandez, *Vice Pres*
Violet Ratzlass, *Admin Sec*
EMP: 102
SQ FT: 9,000
SALES: 5.9MM **Privately Held**
SIC: 8322 Association for the handicapped

(P-23779)
COMMUNITY YOUTH MINISTRIES
Also Called: FRESH START CAFE
1592 11th St Ste E, Reedley (93654-2939)
P.O. Box 816 (93654-0816)
PHONE.................................559 638-6585
Sheri Wiedenhoefer, *CEO*
Regina Garza, *Ch of Bd*
Don Reimer, *COO*
Frank Duerksen, *CFO*
EMP: 100
SALES: 2.1MM **Privately Held**
WEB: www.cymreedley.org
SIC: 8322 Outreach program

(P-23780)
COMMUNTY SLNS FOR CHLDRN FMLS (PA)
9015 Murray Ave Ste 100, Gilroy (95020-3617)
P.O. Box 546, Morgan Hill (95038-0546)
PHONE.................................408 779-2113
Fax: 408 842-0757
Erin O'Brien, *CEO*
Linda Jordon, *Office Mgr*
Lynn Magruder, *Administration*
Susan Peng, *Controller*
EMP: 120
SALES: 17.7MM **Privately Held**
SIC: 8322 General counseling services; family counseling services

(P-23781)
COMPASS FAMILY SERVICES
Also Called: Compass Connecting Point
995 Market St Fl 6, San Francisco (94103-1732)
PHONE.................................415 644-0504
Fax: 415 442-5138
Erica Kisch, *Exec Dir*
Charles Slocumb, *Human Res Dir*
Leslie Hammann, *Marketing Staff*
Charleen Casey-Lerma, *Program Dir*
Rachel Del Rossi, *Program Dir*
EMP: 109
SALES: 8MM **Privately Held**
SIC: 8322 Individual & family services

(P-23782)
COMPASS FAMILY SERVICES
626 Polk St, San Francisco (94102-3328)
PHONE.................................415 644-0504
Erica Kisch, *Exec Dir*
EMP: 87
SALES: 950K **Privately Held**
SIC: 8322 Individual & family services

(P-23783)
COMPASS FAMILY SERVICES
Also Called: Compass Clara House
111 Page St, San Francisco (94102-5892)
PHONE.................................415 644-0504
Erica Kisch, *Exec Dir*
Jane Schisgal, *Manager*
EMP: 87
SALES: 950K **Privately Held**
SIC: 8322 Individual & family services

(P-23784)
COMPREHENSIVE YOUTH SER
Also Called: C Y S
4545 N West Ave Ste 101, Fresno (93705-0946)
PHONE.................................559 229-3561
Fax: 559 229-3681
Captain Mike Reid, *President*
Sylvia Kim, *Treasurer*
Kevin Torosian, *Vice Pres*
Sheryl Noel, *Admin Sec*
Anna Silva, *Finance Mgr*
EMP: 90
SQ FT: 9,000
SALES: 4.4MM **Privately Held**
WEB: www.cys.com
SIC: 8322 Child related social services

(P-23785)
CONCERTO HEALTHCARE INC
2030 Main St Ste 600, Irvine (92614-7235)
PHONE.................................949 537-3400
Alec Cunningham, *CEO*
Dawn Gilbert, *CFO*
Dave Goltz, *CFO*
Toby Thomas, *Exec VP*
EMP: 200 **EST:** 2004
SALES (est): 3.6MM **Privately Held**
SIC: 8322 Adult day care center

(P-23786)
CORNELL CORRECTIONS CAL INC (DH)
1811 Knoll Dr, Ventura (93003-7321)
PHONE.................................805 644-8700
Fax: 805 654-1792
David M Cornell, *Ch of Bd*
Tom Jenkens, *President*
Steven W Logan, *President*
Bill Schoeffield, *COO*
Brian E Bergeron, *CFO*
EMP: 255
SQ FT: 4,100
SALES (est): 6.4MM
SALES (corp-wide): 1.8B **Privately Held**
SIC: 8322 Rehabilitation services
HQ: Geo Reentry, Inc.
  621 Nw 53rd St Ste 700
  Boca Raton FL 33487
  561 893-0101

(P-23787)
CORNERSTONE AFFILIATES INC
6120 Stoneridge, Pleasanton (94588)
PHONE.................................925 924-7100
David B Ferguson, *President*
Andrew McDonald, *Vice Pres*
EMP: 2000
SQ FT: 60
SALES: 207MM **Privately Held**
SIC: 8322 Old age assistance

(P-23788)
CORRECTONS RHBLTATION CAL DEPT
Also Called: Parole Unit Office
930 3rd St Ste 100, Eureka (95501-0554)
PHONE.................................707 445-6520
Fax: 707 445-6620
Ray Hilburn, *Manager*
EMP: 73 **Privately Held**
SIC: 8322 Parole office; offender self-help agency
HQ: California Department Of Corrections & Rehabilitation
  1515 S St
  Sacramento CA 95811
  916 341-7066

(P-23789)
CORRECTONS RHBLTATION CAL DEPT
Also Called: San Bernardino Parole Unit 14
303 W 5th St, San Bernardino (92401-1306)
PHONE.................................909 806-3516
Michael Passmore, *Administration*
Ellie Chambers, *Treasurer*
EMP: 60 **Privately Held**
SIC: 8322 9223 Parole office; offender self-help agency; correctional institutions;
HQ: California Department Of Corrections & Rehabilitation
  1515 S St
  Sacramento CA 95811
  916 341-7066

(P-23790)
COUNTRY VILLA SERVICE CORP
3000 N Gate Rd, Seal Beach (90740-2535)
PHONE.................................562 598-2477
Jennifer Rose, *Branch Mgr*
William Lee, *Records Dir*
Maria Cody, *Office Mgr*
Jaime Garcia, *Administration*
Emma Loza, *Director*
EMP: 82
SALES (corp-wide): 154.7MM **Privately Held**
SIC: 8322 8011 Rehabilitation services; medical centers
PA: Country Villa Service Corp.
  2400 E Katella Ave # 800
  Anaheim CA 92806
  310 574-3733

(P-23791)
COUNTRY VILLA SERVICE CORP
Also Called: Cntry Vlla Merced Hlthcre Cntr
510 W 26th St, Merced (95340-2804)
PHONE.................................209 723-2911
Joel Saltzburg, *CEO*
EMP: 82
SALES (corp-wide): 154.7MM **Privately Held**
SIC: 8322 8051 Rehabilitation services; skilled nursing care facilities
PA: Country Villa Service Corp.
  2400 E Katella Ave # 800
  Anaheim CA 92806
  310 574-3733

(P-23792)
COUNTY MONTEREY SOCIAL SVCS
Also Called: County of Monterey Social Svcs
1281 Broadway Ave, Seaside (93955-4925)
PHONE.................................831 899-8001
Loma Livernois, *Manager*
EMP: 65
SALES (est): 3.1MM **Privately Held**
SIC: 8322 Social service center

(P-23793)
COUNTY OF ALAMEDA
Also Called: Health Care Services Agency
1000 San Leandro Blvd # 200, San Leandro (94577-1598)
PHONE.................................510 618-3452
David J Kears, *Director*
Alex Driscoe, *Deputy Dir*
David Kears, *Director*
EMP: 55 **Privately Held**
WEB: www.co.alameda.ca.us
SIC: 8322 9431 Individual & family services; administration of public health programs;
PA: County Of Alameda
  1221 Oak St Ste 555
  Oakland CA 94612
  510 272-6691

(P-23794)
COUNTY OF BUTTE
Also Called: Butte County Probation
25 County Center Dr # 218, Oroville (95965-3365)
PHONE.................................530 538-7661
Fax: 530 538-6826
John Wardell, *Chief*
Scott Kennelly, *Asst Director*
EMP: 130 **Privately Held**
WEB: www.bcihsspa.org
SIC: 8322 Probation office
PA: County Of Butte
  25 County Center Dr # 218
  Oroville CA 95965
  530 538-7701

(P-23795)
COUNTY OF BUTTE
25 County Center Dr # 110, Oroville (95965-3366)
PHONE.................................530 538-7721
Ken Rimmers, *Branch Mgr*
EMP: 300 **Privately Held**
SIC: 8322 Probation office
PA: County Of Butte
  25 County Center Dr # 110
  Oroville CA 95965
  530 538-7701

(P-23796)
COUNTY OF BUTTE
5910 Clark Rd Ste W, Paradise (95969-4860)
PHONE.................................530 872-6328
Mac McAll, *Manager*
EMP: 300 **Privately Held**

PRODUCTS & SERVICES SECTION
8322 - Individual & Family Social Svcs County (P-23817)

WEB: www.bcihsspa.org
SIC: 8322 Children's aid society
PA: County Of Butte
25 County Center Dr # 218
Oroville CA 95965
530 538-7701

(P-23797)
COUNTY OF BUTTE
Also Called: Welfare Administration
202 Mira Loma Dr, Oroville (95965-3500)
P.O. Box 1649 (95965-1649)
PHONE.................................530 538-7572
Fax: 530 534-5745
Cathy Grams, *Director*
Art Robison, *Info Tech Mgr*
Allen Jennings, *IT/INT Sup*
Connie Meahan, *Analyst*
Wendy Castillo, *Manager*
EMP: 570 Privately Held
WEB: www.bcihsspa.org
SIC: 8322 9111 Individual & family services; county supervisors' & executives' offices
PA: County Of Butte
25 County Center Dr # 218
Oroville CA 95965
530 538-7701

(P-23798)
COUNTY OF BUTTE
Also Called: Welfare Dept Warehouse
205 Mira Loma Dr, Oroville (95965-3582)
P.O. Box 1649 (95965-1649)
PHONE.................................530 538-6802
Art Howe, *Superintendent*
EMP: 500 Privately Held
WEB: www.bcihsspa.org
SIC: 8322 9111 Individual & family services; county supervisors' & executives' offices
PA: County Of Butte
25 County Center Dr # 218
Oroville CA 95965
530 538-7701

(P-23799)
COUNTY OF BUTTE
Also Called: Butte County Employment Center
78 Table Mountain Blvd, Oroville (95965-3578)
P.O. Box 1649 (95965-1649)
PHONE.................................530 538-7711
Fax: 530 538-2036
Cathy Grams, *Branch Mgr*
EMP: 570 Privately Held
WEB: www.bcihsspa.org
SIC: 8322 9111 Public welfare center; county supervisors' & executives' offices
PA: County Of Butte
25 County Center Dr # 218
Oroville CA 95965
530 538-7701

(P-23800)
COUNTY OF CALAVERAS
Also Called: Road Dept
891 Mountain Ranch Rd, San Andreas (95249-9713)
PHONE.................................209 754-6402
Fax: 209 754-6664
Rob Houghton, *Director*
EMP: 80 Privately Held
WEB: www.ccsolidwaste.org
SIC: 8322 Public welfare center
PA: County Of Calaveras
891 Mountain Ranch Rd
San Andreas CA 95249
209 754-6303

(P-23801)
COUNTY OF CONTRA COSTA
50 Douglas Dr Ste 200, Martinez (94553-8500)
PHONE.................................925 313-4000
Fax: 925 313-4191
Lionel Chatman, *Chief*
David Roffi, *COO*
Lionel Chapman, *Manager*
Yvette McCollum, *Manager*
EMP: 150 Privately Held
SIC: 8322 9441 Probation office; parole office; administration of social & manpower programs

PA: County Of Contra Costa
625 Court St Ste 100
Martinez CA 94553
925 957-5280

(P-23802)
COUNTY OF CONTRA COSTA
Also Called: Employment & Human Services
40 Douglas Dr, Martinez (94553-4068)
PHONE.................................925 313-1500
Fax: 925 313-1575
Danna Fabella, *Director*
EMP: 200 Privately Held
SIC: 8322 9441 Individual & family services; administration of social & manpower programs;
PA: County Of Contra Costa
625 Court St Ste 100
Martinez CA 94553
925 957-5280

(P-23803)
COUNTY OF EL DORADO
Also Called: Edc Probation
3974 Durock Rd Ste 205, Shingle Springs (95682-8568)
PHONE.................................530 621-5625
Joseph Warchol, *Chief*
Stephanie Clark, *Officer*
Deborah Dill, *Admin Asst*
Brian Richart, *Manager*
EMP: 109 Privately Held
WEB: www.filmtahoe.com
SIC: 8322 Probation office
PA: County Of El Dorado
330 Fair Ln
Placerville CA 95667
530 621-5830

(P-23804)
COUNTY OF EL DORADO
Also Called: Department of Social Services
3057 Briw Rd Ste A, Placerville (95667-5335)
PHONE.................................530 642-7130
Glen Helland, *Director*
EMP: 85 Privately Held
WEB: www.filmtahoe.com
SIC: 8322 9111 Individual & family services; executive offices
PA: County Of El Dorado
330 Fair Ln
Placerville CA 95667
530 621-5830

(P-23805)
COUNTY OF FRESNO
Also Called: Probation Department
2212 N Winery Ave Ste 122, Fresno (93703-2896)
PHONE.................................559 600-3800
Fax: 559 452-2848
Rick Chavez, *Manager*
Norm Baird, *Manager*
EMP: 59 Privately Held
SIC: 8322 9441 Probation office;
PA: County Of Fresno
2420 Mariposa St
Fresno CA 93721
559 600-1710

(P-23806)
COUNTY OF FRESNO
Also Called: Probation Department
890 S 10th St, Fresno (93702-3506)
PHONE.................................559 600-5127
Fax: 559 455-5187
Rick Chavez, *Manager*
Linda Penner, *Executive*
Daniel Moore, *Info Tech Mgr*
Joy Thompson, *Director*
EMP: 100 Privately Held
WEB: www.first5fresno.org
SIC: 8322 9441 Probation office;
PA: County Of Fresno
2420 Mariposa St
Fresno CA 93721
559 600-1710

(P-23807)
COUNTY OF FRESNO
Behavioral Health
4441 E Kings Canyon Rd, Fresno (93702-3604)
P.O. Box 1912 (93718-1912)
PHONE.................................559 453-4099

Fax: 559 253-9144
Giang T Nguyen, *Director*
Sandra Seely, *Admin Sec*
Joseph Rangel, *Analyst*
Annie Lee, *Persnl Mgr*
Heather Stevens, *Purch Agent*
EMP: 175 Privately Held
WEB: www.first5fresno.org
SIC: 8322 9441 Individual & family services; administration of social & manpower programs;
PA: County Of Fresno
2420 Mariposa St
Fresno CA 93721
559 600-1710

(P-23808)
COUNTY OF FRESNO
Probation Department
3333 E American Ave Ste B, Fresno (93725-9248)
PHONE.................................559 600-3996
Rick Chavez, *Manager*
Vicki Passmore, *Persnl Mgr*
EMP: 130 Privately Held
WEB: www.first5fresno.org
SIC: 8322 9441 Probation office; administration of social & manpower programs;
PA: County Of Fresno
2420 Mariposa St
Fresno CA 93721
559 600-1710

(P-23809)
COUNTY OF FRESNO
P.O. Box 352 (93708-0352)
PHONE.................................559 488-3275
Robyn Esraelian, *Manager*
EMP: 168 Privately Held
SIC: 8322 9199 Probation office
PA: County Of Fresno
2420 Mariposa St
Fresno CA 93721
559 600-1710

(P-23810)
COUNTY OF GLENN
525 W Sycamore St Ste A1, Willows (95988-2748)
P.O. Box 366 (95988-0366)
PHONE.................................530 934-6453
Fax: 530 934-6576
Robert Chittenden, *Branch Mgr*
Dennis Michum, *Treasurer*
Scott Gruendl, *Info Tech Dir*
Parker Hunt, *Accounting Mgr*
Chrissy Millen, *Financial Analy*
EMP: 97 Privately Held
SIC: 8322 Social service center
PA: County Of Glenn
516 W Sycamore St Fl 2
Willows CA 95988
530 934-6410

(P-23811)
COUNTY OF GLENN
Also Called: Glenn County Humn Resorce Agcy
420 E Laurel St, Willows (95988-3115)
P.O. Box 611 (95988-0611)
PHONE.................................530 934-6514
Fax: 530 934-6499
Kim Gaghagen, *Principal*
Suzi Kochems, *Info Tech Mgr*
Parker Hunt, *Accounting Mgr*
Ernest Peters, *Manager*
EMP: 250 Privately Held
WEB: www.countyofglen.net
SIC: 8322 9111 Individual & family services; county supervisors' & executives' offices
PA: County Of Glenn
516 W Sycamore St Fl 2
Willows CA 95988
530 934-6410

(P-23812)
COUNTY OF HUMBOLDT
Also Called: Dept of Social Services
929 Koster St, Eureka (95501-0106)
PHONE.................................707 445-6180
Fax: 707 445-6254
John Frank, *Branch Mgr*
EMP: 300 Privately Held

SIC: 8322 9441 Social service center; administration of social & manpower programs;
PA: County Of Humboldt
825 5th St
Eureka CA 95501
707 268-2543

(P-23813)
COUNTY OF IMPERIAL
Also Called: Imperial County Probation Off
324 Applestille Rd, El Centro (92243-9661)
PHONE.................................760 336-3581
Fax: 760 339-6241
Micheal Kelly, *Director*
Elizabeth Castro, *Info Tech Mgr*
Debbie Angulo, *Sales Executive*
EMP: 150 Privately Held
WEB: www.imperialcounty.net
SIC: 8322 9111 Individual & family services; county supervisors' & executives' offices
PA: County Of Imperial
940 W Main St Ste 208
El Centro CA 92243
760 482-4556

(P-23814)
COUNTY OF KERN
Also Called: Probation Dept-Juvenile
2005 Ridge Rd, Bakersfield (93305-4123)
P.O. Box 3309 (93385-3309)
PHONE.................................661 868-4100
Fax: 661 868-4199
John R Roberts, *Chief*
Art Davis, *General Mgr*
Cathy Lemon, *Manager*
Raymon Yocum, *Manager*
EMP: 600 Privately Held
WEB: www.kccfc.org
SIC: 8322 9111 Probation office; county supervisors' & executives' offices;
PA: County Of Kern
1115 Truxtun Ave Rm 505
Bakersfield CA 93301
661 868-3690

(P-23815)
COUNTY OF KERN
Also Called: Aging & Adult Services
2014 Calloway Dr, Bakersfield (93312-2729)
PHONE.................................661 392-2010
Grace Bradbury, *Manager*
Kathy Gibbs, *Manager*
EMP: 61 Privately Held
WEB: www.kccfc.org
SIC: 8322 9441 Community center; administration of social & manpower programs;
PA: County Of Kern
1115 Truxtun Ave Rm 505
Bakersfield CA 93301
661 868-3690

(P-23816)
COUNTY OF KERN
2001 28th St Ste C, Bakersfield (93301-1924)
PHONE.................................661 336-6800
Fax: 661 336-6801
Lewis Verna, *Exec Dir*
Verna Lewis, *Exec Dir*
Sandra Chester, *Human Res Dir*
Shirley Treadwell, *Purch Agent*
Renita Nunn, *Director*
EMP: 61 Privately Held
SIC: 8322 Probation office
PA: County Of Kern
1115 Truxtun Ave Rm 505
Bakersfield CA 93301
661 868-3690

(P-23817)
COUNTY OF KERN
Also Called: Aging & Adult Services
401 Harrison St, Taft (93268-1707)
P.O. Box 1534 (93268-0834)
PHONE.................................661 763-1535
Fax: 661 763-5355
Connie Redfield, *Director*
EMP: 61 Privately Held
WEB: www.kccfc.org
SIC: 8322 9441 Geriatric social service; administration of social & manpower programs;

8322 - Individual & Family Social Svcs County (P-23818)

PA: County Of Kern
1115 Truxtun Ave Rm 505
Bakersfield CA 93301
661 868-3690

(P-23818)
COUNTY OF KERN
Also Called: Human Services Dept
1816 Cecil Ave, Delano (93215-1520)
P.O. Box 339 (93216-0339)
PHONE.................................661 721-5134
Fax: 661 721-5162
Donalda Salsbery, *Director*
Collins Dennis, *Supervisor*
EMP: 60 **Privately Held**
WEB: www.kccfc.org
SIC: **8322** 9441 Public welfare center; administration of social & manpower programs;
PA: County Of Kern
1115 Truxtun Ave Rm 505
Bakersfield CA 93301
661 868-3690

(P-23819)
COUNTY OF KERN
Also Called: Aging & Adult Services
6601 Niles Senior St, Bakersfield (93306)
PHONE.................................661 363-8910
Lavita Greenly, *Branch Mgr*
EMP: 61 **Privately Held**
WEB: www.kccfc.org
SIC: **8322** 9441 Individual & family services; administration of social & manpower programs;
PA: County Of Kern
1115 Truxtun Ave Rm 505
Bakersfield CA 93301
661 868-3690

(P-23820)
COUNTY OF KINGS
Also Called: Kings County Probation Dept.
1424 Forum Dr, Hanford (93230-5900)
PHONE.................................559 852-4316
Dorothy Van Den Berg, *Chief*
EMP: 160 **Privately Held**
WEB: www.countyofkings.com
SIC: **8322** Probation office
PA: County Of Kings
1400 W Lacey Blvd
Hanford CA 93230
559 582-0326

(P-23821)
COUNTY OF LOS ANGELES
Also Called: Probation Department
300 E Walnut St Dept 200, Pasadena
(91101-1584)
PHONE.................................626 356-5281
Diana Cunningham, *Principal*
EMP: 135 **Privately Held**
WEB: www.co.la.ca.us
SIC: **8322** 9199 Probation office;
PA: County Of Los Angeles
500 W Temple St Ste 375
Los Angeles CA 90012
213 974-1101

(P-23822)
COUNTY OF LOS ANGELES
Also Called: Probation Office
350 W Mcaion Blvd Ste 109, Pomona
(91766)
PHONE.................................909 620-3189
EMP: 138 **Privately Held**
SIC: **8322** Probation office
PA: County Of Los Angeles
500 W Temple St Ste 375
Los Angeles CA 90012
213 974-1101

(P-23823)
COUNTY OF LOS ANGELES
Also Called: County Probation
11234 Valley Blvd Ste 103, El Monte
(91731-3239)
PHONE.................................626 575-4059
Fax: 626 443-1040
Kwadwo Akosah, *Principal*
EMP: 140 **Privately Held**
SIC: **8322** Probation office
PA: County Of Los Angeles
500 W Temple St Ste 375
Los Angeles CA 90012
213 974-1101

(P-23824)
COUNTY OF LOS ANGELES
Also Called: Probation Department
5300 W Avenue I, Lancaster (93536-8312)
PHONE.................................661 940-4181
Willie Doyle, *Director*
EMP: 300 **Privately Held**
WEB: www.co.la.ca.us
SIC: **8322** 9223 Probation office; correctional institutions;
PA: County Of Los Angeles
500 W Temple St Ste 375
Los Angeles CA 90012
213 974-1101

(P-23825)
COUNTY OF LOS ANGELES
7601 Imperial Hwy, Downey (90242-3456)
PHONE.................................562 401-9413
Lily Atalla, *Branch Mgr*
EMP: 137 **Privately Held**
SIC: **8322** Individual & family services
PA: County Of Los Angeles
500 W Temple St Ste 375
Los Angeles CA 90012
213 974-1101

(P-23826)
COUNTY OF LOS ANGELES
Also Called: Child Support Services
5770 S Eastern Ave Fl 4th, Commerce
(90040-2948)
PHONE.................................323 889-3405
Philip Browning, *Manager*
EMP: 300 **Privately Held**
WEB: www.co.la.ca.us
SIC: **8322** 9441 Child related social services; administration of social & manpower programs;
PA: County Of Los Angeles
500 W Temple St Ste 375
Los Angeles CA 90012
213 974-1101

(P-23827)
COUNTY OF LOS ANGELES
Also Called: Social Services, Dept of
349 E Avenue K6 Ste B, Lancaster
(93535-4546)
PHONE.................................661 723-4051
Joyce Ward, *Principal*
EMP: 175 **Privately Held**
WEB: www.co.la.ca.us
SIC: **8322** 9441 Individual & family services; parole office; administration of social & manpower programs
PA: County Of Los Angeles
500 W Temple St Ste 375
Los Angeles CA 90012
213 974-1101

(P-23828)
COUNTY OF LOS ANGELES
Also Called: Children & Family Svcs Dept
10355 Slusher Dr, Santa Fe Springs
(90670-7353)
PHONE.................................562 903-5000
Fax: 562 906-3400
Barbara Betlem, *Director*
Larry Gasco, *Manager*
EMP: 350 **Privately Held**
WEB: www.co.la.ca.us
SIC: **8322** 9441 Individual & family services;
PA: County Of Los Angeles
500 W Temple St Ste 375
Los Angeles CA 90012
213 974-1101

(P-23829)
COUNTY OF LOS ANGELES
Also Called: Dept Children and Family Svcs
4060 Watson Plaza Dr, Lakewood
(90712-4033)
PHONE.................................562 497-3500
Fax: 562 421-5218
Joy Russell, *Administration*
EMP: 500 **Privately Held**
WEB: www.co.la.ca.us
SIC: **8322** 9111 Children's aid society; executive offices
PA: County Of Los Angeles
500 W Temple St Ste 375
Los Angeles CA 90012
213 974-1101

(P-23830)
COUNTY OF LOS ANGELES
1000 Corp Ctr Dr Ste 200b, Monterey Park
(91754)
PHONE.................................323 265-1804
Renee Watkinson, *Branch Mgr*
EMP: 137 **Privately Held**
SIC: **8322** Individual & family services
PA: County Of Los Angeles
500 W Temple St Ste 375
Los Angeles CA 90012
213 974-1101

(P-23831)
COUNTY OF LOS ANGELES
Also Called: Community & Senior Svcs
777 W Jackman St, Lancaster
(93534-2419)
PHONE.................................661 948-2320
Nusun Muhamad, *Manager*
EMP: 135 **Privately Held**
WEB: www.co.la.ca.us
SIC: **8322** 9441 Senior citizens' center or association; administration of social & manpower programs;
PA: County Of Los Angeles
500 W Temple St Ste 375
Los Angeles CA 90012
213 974-1101

(P-23832)
COUNTY OF LOS ANGELES
210 W Temple St Fl 18, Los Angeles
(90012-3229)
PHONE.................................818 374-2161
EMP: 140 **Privately Held**
SIC: **8322** Probation office
PA: County Of Los Angeles
500 W Temple St Ste 375
Los Angeles CA 90012
213 974-1101

(P-23833)
COUNTY OF LOS ANGELES
2707 S Grand Dwntwn S Ave, Los Angeles
(90007)
PHONE.................................213 744-5730
EMP: 135 **Privately Held**
WEB: www.co.la.ca.us
SIC: **8322** 9441 Individual & family services; administration of social & human resources
PA: County Of Los Angeles
500 W Temple St Ste 375
Los Angeles CA 90012
213 974-1101

(P-23834)
COUNTY OF LOS ANGELES
Also Called: Florence Office
1740 E Gage Ave, Los Angeles
(90001-1814)
PHONE.................................323 586-7263
Olga Miranda, *Director*
EMP: 255 **Privately Held**
WEB: www.co.la.ca.us
SIC: **8322** 9441 Aid to families with dependent children (AFDC); administration of social & manpower programs;
PA: County Of Los Angeles
500 W Temple St Ste 375
Los Angeles CA 90012
213 974-1101

(P-23835)
COUNTY OF LOS ANGELES
600 S Commwl Ave Ste 700, Los Angeles
(90005)
PHONE.................................213 351-8739
Mike Judge, *Branch Mgr*
Michelle Walker, *Facilities Mgr*
EMP: 135 **Privately Held**
WEB: www.co.la.ca.us
SIC: **8322** 9111 Child related social services; county supervisors' & executives' offices
PA: County Of Los Angeles
500 W Temple St Ste 375
Los Angeles CA 90012
213 974-1101

(P-23836)
COUNTY OF LOS ANGELES
Also Called: Probation Department
1601 Eastlake Ave, Los Angeles
(90033-1009)
PHONE.................................323 226-8511
Fax: 323 342-9540
Taula Heath, *Director*
EMP: 135 **Privately Held**
WEB: www.co.la.ca.us
SIC: **8322** Probation office; parole office
PA: County Of Los Angeles
500 W Temple St Ste 375
Los Angeles CA 90012
213 974-1101

(P-23837)
COUNTY OF LOS ANGELES
Also Called: Children & Family Svcs Dept
425 Shatto Pl, Los Angeles (90020-1712)
PHONE.................................213 351-5600
Jackie Contreras, *Director*
Onnie Williams III, *General Mgr*
Elizabeth Becerra, *Director*
David Samders, *Director*
EMP: 100 **Privately Held**
WEB: www.co.la.ca.us
SIC: **8322** 9441 Child related social services; administration of social & manpower programs;
PA: County Of Los Angeles
500 W Temple St Ste 375
Los Angeles CA 90012
213 974-1101

(P-23838)
COUNTY OF LOS ANGELES
Also Called: La County Probation
8240 Broadway Ave, Whittier (90606-3120)
PHONE.................................562 908-3119
Fax: 562 695-5919
Donna Rose, *Manager*
Daniel M Ramirez, *Officer*
EMP: 102 **Privately Held**
WEB: www.co.la.ca.us
SIC: **8322** 9111 Probation office; county supervisors' & executives' offices
PA: County Of Los Angeles
500 W Temple St Ste 375
Los Angeles CA 90012
213 974-1101

(P-23839)
COUNTY OF LOS ANGELES
Also Called: Probation Dept
320 W Temple St Ste 1101, Los Angeles
(90012-3289)
PHONE.................................213 974-9331
Fax: 213 485-0102
Mike Verilla, *Director*
Terry Clark, *Exec Dir*
Marie Montanez, *Admin Sec*
EMP: 170 **Privately Held**
WEB: www.co.la.ca.us
SIC: **8322** 9223 8093 Probation office; correctional institutions; ; mental health clinic, outpatient
PA: County Of Los Angeles
500 W Temple St Ste 375
Los Angeles CA 90012
213 974-1101

(P-23840)
COUNTY OF LOS ANGELES
530 12th St Fl 1, Paso Robles
(93446-2201)
PHONE.................................805 237-3110
Fax: 805 237-3115
Michelle Chambers, *Manager*
EMP: 140 **Privately Held**
SIC: **8322** Social service center
PA: County Of Los Angeles
500 W Temple St Ste 375
Los Angeles CA 90012
213 974-1101

(P-23841)
COUNTY OF LOS ANGELES
Also Called: Public Social Services
2707 S Grand Ave, Los Angeles
(90007-3300)
PHONE.................................213 744-5601
Fax: 213 729-2924
Petra Gonzalez, *Director*
Rosa Orozco, *Manager*
EMP: 430 **Privately Held**

PRODUCTS & SERVICES SECTION
8322 - Individual & Family Social Svcs County (P-23863)

WEB: www.co.la.ca.us
SIC: **8322** 9441 Individual & family services; administration of social & manpower programs;
PA: County Of Los Angeles
500 W Temple St Ste 375
Los Angeles CA 90012
213 974-1101

(P-23842)
COUNTY OF LOS ANGELES
5445 Whittier Blvd Fl 400, Los Angeles (90022-4125)
PHONE......................................323 727-1639
Fax: 323 728-5926
Minhha Ngyuen, *Branch Mgr*
EMP: 140 **Privately Held**
SIC: **8322** Individual & family services
PA: County Of Los Angeles
500 W Temple St Ste 375
Los Angeles CA 90012
213 974-1101

(P-23843)
COUNTY OF LOS ANGELES
Also Called: San Fernando Valley Interfaith
14555 Osborne St Ofc, Van Nuys (91402-1821)
PHONE......................................818 362-6437
Estella Lyons, *Chairman*
Berta Acebes, *Branch Mgr*
EMP: 135 **Privately Held**
WEB: www.co.la.ca.us
SIC: **8322** 9441 Geriatric social service; administration of social & manpower programs;
PA: County Of Los Angeles
500 W Temple St Ste 375
Los Angeles CA 90012
213 974-1101

(P-23844)
COUNTY OF LOS ANGELES
Also Called: Health Services, Dept of
17171 Gale Ave, City of Industry (91745-1822)
PHONE......................................626 854-4987
Fax: 626 913-1896
Althea Shirley, *Director*
Jeanette McClinton, *Manager*
EMP: 200 **Privately Held**
WEB: www.co.la.ca.us
SIC: **8322** 9431 Public welfare center; administration of public health programs;
PA: County Of Los Angeles
500 W Temple St Ste 375
Los Angeles CA 90012
213 974-1101

(P-23845)
COUNTY OF LOS ANGELES
Also Called: Probation Dept
12310 Lower Azusa Rd, Arcadia (91006-5872)
PHONE......................................626 350-4566
Deborah F Weathersby, *Director*
EMP: 80 **Privately Held**
WEB: www.co.la.ca.us
SIC: **8322** 9223 Probation office; correctional institutions;
PA: County Of Los Angeles
500 W Temple St Ste 375
Los Angeles CA 90012
213 974-1101

(P-23846)
COUNTY OF LOS ANGELES
Also Called: County Los Angles Prbtion Dept
1660 W Mission Blvd, Pomona (91766-1200)
PHONE......................................909 469-4500
Lorraine Hubbard-Johns, *Manager*
Michael Jimenez, *Technology*
EMP: 100 **Privately Held**
WEB: www.co.la.ca.us
SIC: **8322** 9223 Probation office; correctional institutions;
PA: County Of Los Angeles
500 W Temple St Ste 375
Los Angeles CA 90012
213 974-1101

(P-23847)
COUNTY OF LOS ANGELES
Also Called: Probation Dept
14414 Delano St, Van Nuys (91401-2703)
PHONE......................................818 374-2000
Fax: 818 781-7044
Ed Johnson, *Director*
John E Edwards Jr, *Director*
EMP: 100 **Privately Held**
WEB: www.co.la.ca.us
SIC: **8322** 9223 Probation office; correctional institutions;
PA: County Of Los Angeles
500 W Temple St Ste 375
Los Angeles CA 90012
213 974-1101

(P-23848)
COUNTY OF LOS ANGELES
Also Called: Mental Health Dept of
330 E Live Oak Ave, Arcadia (91006-5617)
PHONE......................................626 821-5858
Fax: 626 821-0858
Len Tower, *Director*
Diana D Carlo, *Psychiatry*
John S Wells, *Psychiatry*
Len Symonds, *Director*
EMP: 50 **Privately Held**
WEB: www.co.la.ca.us
SIC: **8322** 9431 Crisis center; mental health agency administration, government;
PA: County Of Los Angeles
500 W Temple St Ste 375
Los Angeles CA 90012
213 974-1101

(P-23849)
COUNTY OF LOS ANGELES
Also Called: Probation Dept
1725 Main St Rm 125, Santa Monica (90401-3267)
PHONE......................................310 266-3711
Fax: 310 395-7971
Ernest P Gonzalez, *Branch Mgr*
Curtis McClendon, *Exec Dir*
Glenda Dunn, *Sales Executive*
EMP: 65 **Privately Held**
WEB: www.co.la.ca.us
SIC: **8322** 9223 Probation office; correctional institutions;
PA: County Of Los Angeles
500 W Temple St Ste 375
Los Angeles CA 90012
213 974-1101

(P-23850)
COUNTY OF LOS ANGELES
Also Called: Probation Dept
4849 Civic Center Way, Los Angeles (90022-1679)
PHONE......................................323 780-2185
Fax: 323 262-8418
Debbie Nelson, *Director*
Michael W Agopian, *Agent*
EMP: 80 **Privately Held**
WEB: www.co.la.ca.us
SIC: **8322** 9223 Probation office; correctional institutions;
PA: County Of Los Angeles
500 W Temple St Ste 375
Los Angeles CA 90012
213 974-1101

(P-23851)
COUNTY OF LOS ANGELES
Also Called: Public Social Services
12727 Norwalk Blvd, Norwalk (90650-3145)
PHONE......................................562 807-7860
Fax: 562 864-9621
Tony Iniguez, *Director*
EMP: 250 **Privately Held**
WEB: www.co.la.ca.us
SIC: **8322** 9441 Individual & family services; administration of social & manpower programs;
PA: County Of Los Angeles
500 W Temple St Ste 375
Los Angeles CA 90012
213 974-1101

(P-23852)
COUNTY OF LOS ANGELES
Also Called: Department Children Fmly Svcs
501 Shatto Pl Ste 301, Los Angeles (90020-1749)
PHONE......................................213 351-7257
Bill Browning, *Director*
EMP: 700 **Privately Held**
WEB: www.co.la.ca.us
SIC: **8322** 9111 Individual & family services; executive offices
PA: County Of Los Angeles
500 W Temple St Ste 375
Los Angeles CA 90012
213 974-1101

(P-23853)
COUNTY OF LOS ANGELES
Also Called: Probation Dept
8526 Grape St, Los Angeles (90001-4134)
PHONE......................................323 586-6469
Mark Garcia, *Director*
EMP: 60 **Privately Held**
WEB: www.co.la.ca.us
SIC: **8322** 9223 Probation office; correctional institutions;
PA: County Of Los Angeles
500 W Temple St Ste 375
Los Angeles CA 90012
213 974-1101

(P-23854)
COUNTY OF LOS ANGELES
Also Called: Probation Dept
200 W Compton Blvd # 300, Compton (90220-6676)
PHONE......................................310 603-7311
Fax: 310 638-1755
Peggy May, *Director*
Trudy Ballard, *Admin Sec*
EMP: 140 **Privately Held**
WEB: www.co.la.ca.us
SIC: **8322** 9223 Probation office; correctional institutions;
PA: County Of Los Angeles
500 W Temple St Ste 375
Los Angeles CA 90012
213 974-1101

(P-23855)
COUNTY OF LOS ANGELES
Also Called: Probation Dept
199 N Euclid Ave, Pasadena (91101-1757)
PHONE......................................626 356-5281
Fax: 626 568-9461
Steve Yoder, *Director*
EMP: 71 **Privately Held**
WEB: www.co.la.ca.us
SIC: **8322** 9223 Probation office; correctional institutions;
PA: County Of Los Angeles
500 W Temple St Ste 375
Los Angeles CA 90012
213 974-1101

(P-23856)
COUNTY OF LOS ANGELES
Also Called: Probation Department
9150 Imperial Hwy, Downey (90242-2835)
PHONE......................................562 940-2476
Robert Taedler, *Chief*
Michael Jimenez, *Technology*
Rumi Salihue, *Technology*
Robert Aragon, *Manager*
EMP: 500 **Privately Held**
WEB: www.co.la.ca.us
SIC: **8322** 9223 Probation office; correctional institutions;
PA: County Of Los Angeles
500 W Temple St Ste 375
Los Angeles CA 90012
213 974-1101

(P-23857)
COUNTY OF LOS ANGELES
Also Called: Probation Department
9150 Imperial Hwy, Downey (90242-2835)
PHONE......................................562 803-6682
Fax: 562 803-6341
Richard Shumsky, *Owner*
Debbie Migliaro, *Division Mgr*
Francesca Jones, *CIO*
Jim Wilkinson, *Info Tech Mgr*
Bruce Drury, *Technology*
EMP: 135 **Privately Held**
SIC: **8322** Probation office

(P-23858)
COUNTY OF LOS ANGELES
Also Called: Dpss
3307 N Glenoaks Blvd, Burbank (91504-2011)
PHONE......................................818 557-4164
Pamar Amirian, *Manager*
EMP: 135 **Privately Held**
WEB: www.co.la.ca.us
SIC: **8322** Emergency social services
PA: County Of Los Angeles
500 W Temple St Ste 375
Los Angeles CA 90012
213 974-1101

(P-23859)
COUNTY OF LOS ANGELES
200 W Woodward Ave, Alhambra (91801-3459)
PHONE......................................626 308-5542
Roger Fernandez, *Branch Mgr*
Marina Rojas, *Manager*
EMP: 135 **Privately Held**
WEB: www.co.la.ca.us
SIC: **8322** 9111 Probation office; county supervisors' & executives' offices
PA: County Of Los Angeles
500 W Temple St Ste 375
Los Angeles CA 90012
213 974-1101

(P-23860)
COUNTY OF LOS ANGELES
427 Encinal Canyon Rd, Malibu (90265-2404)
PHONE......................................818 889-1353
Greg Levy, *Manager*
EMP: 140 **Privately Held**
WEB: www.co.la.ca.us
SIC: **8322** 9111 Probation office; county supervisors' & executives' offices
PA: County Of Los Angeles
500 W Temple St Ste 375
Los Angeles CA 90012
213 974-1101

(P-23861)
COUNTY OF LOS ANGELES
Also Called: Madera County Probation Dept
209 W Yosemite Ave, Madera (93637-3534)
PHONE......................................559 675-7739
Fax: 559 673-0521
Linda Nash, *Manager*
Shelley Stinnett, *Technology*
EMP: 140 **Privately Held**
SIC: **8322** Individual & family services
PA: County Of Los Angeles
500 W Temple St Ste 375
Los Angeles CA 90012
213 974-1101

(P-23862)
COUNTY OF MARIN
164 Donahue St, Sausalito (94965-1250)
PHONE......................................415 332-6158
EMP: 300 **Privately Held**
SIC: **8322** Community center
PA: County Of Marin
1600 Los Gamos Dr Ste 200
San Rafael CA 94903
415 473-6358

(P-23863)
COUNTY OF MARIN
Also Called: Marin County Welfare Dept
120 N Redwood Dr, San Rafael (94903-1941)
P.O. Box 4160 (94913-4160)
PHONE......................................415 499-6970
Jane Chopson, *Director*
Lyda Beardsley, *Exec Dir*
Cecilia Zamora, *Exec Dir*
Susan Catalano, *Analyst*
Lori Fromm, *Manager*
EMP: 300 **Privately Held**
SIC: **8322** 9441 Public welfare center; administration of social & manpower programs;

8322 - Individual & Family Social Svcs County (P-23864)

PA: County Of Marin
1600 Los Gamos Dr Ste 200
San Rafael CA 94903
415 473-6358

(P-23864)
COUNTY OF MENDOCINO
Also Called: Social Services, Department of
737 S State St, Ukiah (95482-5815)
P.O. Box 8508 (95482-8508)
PHONE.................................707 463-2437
Fax: 707 463-5404
Alison Glassey, Administration
Doug Gherkin, Administration
Steve Prochter, Asst Director
Bonita Brady, Assistant
EMP: 300 Privately Held
WEB: www.mcdss.org
SIC: 8322 Individual & family services
PA: County Of Mendocino
501 Low Gap Rd Rm 1010
Ukiah CA 95482
707 463-4441

(P-23865)
COUNTY OF MODOC
Also Called: Department of Social Services
120 N Main St, Alturas (96101-4045)
PHONE.................................530 233-6501
Pauline Cravens, Branch Mgr
Sarah K Holshouser, Exec Dir
EMP: 52 Privately Held
SIC: 8322 Social service center
PA: County Of Modoc
202 W 4th St Ste A
Alturas CA 96101
530 233-6400

(P-23866)
COUNTY OF MODOC
Also Called: Modoc County ADM Svcs
204 S Court St Ste 6, Alturas (96101-4138)
PHONE.................................530 233-6400
Michael Maxwell, Branch Mgr
EMP: 99 Privately Held
WEB: www.modoccounty.us
SIC: 8322 9111 Individual & family services; county supervisors' & executives' offices
PA: County Of Modoc
202 W 4th St Ste A
Alturas CA 96101
530 233-6400

(P-23867)
COUNTY OF MONTEREY
Department Social & Employment
1000 S Main St Ste 216, Salinas (93901-2390)
PHONE.................................831 755-8500
Fax: 831 755-8404
Elliot Robinson, Director
Casey Castillo, Officer
Andrew Heald, Officer
Salvador M Castillo, Exec Dir
Frances Perez, Admin Asst
EMP: 600 Privately Held
WEB: www.montereycountyfarmbureau.org
SIC: 8322 9111 Social service center; county supervisors' & executives' offices
PA: County Of Monterey
168 W Alisal St Fl 3
Salinas CA 93901
831 755-5040

(P-23868)
COUNTY OF NAPA
Also Called: NAPA Auto Parts
650 Imperial Way Ste 101, NAPA (94559-1344)
PHONE.................................707 253-4625
Fax: 707 253-6117
Randy Snowden, Director
Jose Pelayo, Technology
Dan Glasscot, Manager
EMP: 450 Privately Held
WEB: www.billkeller.com
SIC: 8322 Geriatric social service
PA: County Of Napa
1195 Third St Ste 310
Napa CA 94559
707 253-4421

(P-23869)
COUNTY OF NAPA
Also Called: NAPA County Juvenile Probation
212 Walnut St, NAPA (94559-3703)
PHONE.................................707 253-4361
Mary Butler, Director
EMP: 50
SQ FT: 122,839 Privately Held
WEB: www.billkeller.com
SIC: 8322 9111 Probation office; county supervisors' & executives' offices
PA: County Of Napa
1195 Third St Ste 310
Napa CA 94559
707 253-4421

(P-23870)
COUNTY OF ORANGE
Also Called: District Attorney
8141 13th St, Westminster (92683-4576)
PHONE.................................714 896-7188
Gary Tackett, Branch Mgr
EMP: 56 Privately Held
SIC: 8322 9211 Substance abuse counseling; courts
PA: County Of Orange
333 W Santa Ana Blvd 3f
Santa Ana CA 92701
714 834-6200

(P-23871)
COUNTY OF ORANGE
Also Called: Probation Dept
1535 E Orangewood Ave, Anaheim (92805-6824)
PHONE.................................714 937-4500
Fax: 714 937-4555
Lalaw Reagan, Manager
Steve Sentman, Manager
EMP: 100 Privately Held
SIC: 8322 9111 Probation office; executive offices
PA: County Of Orange
333 W Santa Ana Blvd 3f
Santa Ana CA 92701
714 834-6200

(P-23872)
COUNTY OF ORANGE
Also Called: Probation Dept
14180 Beach Blvd Ste 120, Westminster (92683-4452)
PHONE.................................714 896-7500
Fax: 714 894-5779
Mac Jenkins, Director
EMP: 58 Privately Held
SIC: 8322 9223 Probation office; correctional institutions;
PA: County Of Orange
333 W Santa Ana Blvd 3f
Santa Ana CA 92701
714 834-6200

(P-23873)
COUNTY OF ORANGE
Also Called: Probation Dept
301 City Dr S, Orange (92868)
P.O. Box 10260, Santa Ana (92711-0260)
PHONE.................................714 935-7411
EMP: 56 Privately Held
SIC: 8322 9223 Probation office; correctional institutions;
PA: County Of Orange
333 W Santa Ana Blvd 3f
Santa Ana CA 92701
714 834-6200

(P-23874)
COUNTY OF ORANGE
Also Called: Children & Family Serivces
800 N Eckhoff St Bldg 121, Orange (92868-1008)
P.O. Box 14101 (92863-1501)
PHONE.................................714 704-8000
Michael Riley, Director
EMP: 150 Privately Held
SIC: 8322 9441 Children's aid society; administration of social & manpower programs;
PA: County Of Orange
333 W Santa Ana Blvd 3f
Santa Ana CA 92701
714 834-6200

(P-23875)
COUNTY OF ORANGE
Also Called: Social Services Agency
2020 W Walnut St, Santa Ana (92703-4315)
P.O. Box 1943 (92702-1943)
PHONE.................................714 834-8899
Fax: 714 567-7906
Terry Row, Branch Mgr
EMP: 56 Privately Held
SIC: 8322 9441 Individual & family services; public welfare administration: non-operating, government;
PA: County Of Orange
333 W Santa Ana Blvd 3f
Santa Ana CA 92701
714 834-6200

(P-23876)
COUNTY OF ORANGE
Also Called: Social Services Agency
341 The City Dr S, Orange (92868-3205)
PHONE.................................714 935-6435
Fax: 714 935-6284
Linda Perring, Director
EMP: 56 Privately Held
SIC: 8322 9441 Social service center; administration of social & manpower programs;
PA: County Of Orange
333 W Santa Ana Blvd 3f
Santa Ana CA 92701
714 834-6200

(P-23877)
COUNTY OF PLACER
Also Called: Health & Human Services
379 Nevada St, Auburn (95603-3722)
PHONE.................................530 886-1870
Fax: 530 886-3606
Don Ferretti, Manager
Larry Risser, MIS Dir
John Barnett, Info Tech Mgr
EMP: 58 Privately Held
WEB: www.ssvems.com
SIC: 8322 9441 8231 Senior citizens' center or association; administration of social & manpower programs; ; public library
PA: County Of Placer
2968 Richardson Dr
Auburn CA 95603
530 889-4200

(P-23878)
COUNTY OF PLACER
Also Called: Probation Department Roseville
2929 Richardson Dr Ste B, Auburn (95603-2615)
PHONE.................................530 889-7900
Steve Pecor, Chief
Judy Laporte, Admin Asst
Virginia Valenzuela, Admin Asst
Erik Carlson, Info Tech Mgr
EMP: 100 Privately Held
WEB: www.ssvems.com
SIC: 8322 9223 Probation office; correctional institutions;
PA: County Of Placer
2968 Richardson Dr
Auburn CA 95603
530 889-4200

(P-23879)
COUNTY OF PLACER
Also Called: Mental Hlth Sbstnce Abuse Svcs
11512 B Ave, Auburn (95603-2605)
PHONE.................................530 823-4300
Fax: 530 889-7275
Maureen Bauman, Director
EMP: 150 Privately Held
WEB: www.ssvems.com
SIC: 8322 9431 Substance abuse counseling; mental health agency administration, government;
PA: County Of Placer
2968 Richardson Dr
Auburn CA 95603
530 889-4200

(P-23880)
COUNTY OF PLACER
Also Called: Probation Dept
2929 Richardson Dr Ste B, Auburn (95603-2615)
PHONE.................................530 889-7900
Fax: 530 889-7950
Stephen G Pecor, Principal
EMP: 120 Privately Held
WEB: www.ssvems.com
SIC: 8322 9221 Probation office; parole office; police protection
PA: County Of Placer
2968 Richardson Dr
Auburn CA 95603
530 889-4200

(P-23881)
COUNTY OF RIVERSIDE
Also Called: Public Social Service
3178 Hamner Ave, Norco (92860-1936)
PHONE.................................951 272-5400
Fax: 909 272-5482
Sherri Feldt, Manager
EMP: 50 Privately Held
SIC: 8322 9441 Individual & family services; public welfare administration: non-operating, government;
PA: County Of Riverside
4080 Lemon St Fl 11
Riverside CA 92501
951 955-1110

(P-23882)
COUNTY OF RIVERSIDE
2560 N Perris Blvd Ste N1, Perris (92571-3251)
PHONE.................................951 443-2262
Kevin Jeffries, Branch Mgr
EMP: 99 Privately Held
SIC: 8322 Probation office
PA: County Of Riverside
4080 Lemon St Fl 11
Riverside CA 92501
951 955-1110

(P-23883)
COUNTY OF RIVERSIDE
Also Called: Public Social Services
1400 W Minthorn St, Lake Elsinore (92530-2808)
PHONE.................................951 245-3060
Mary Thoman, Principal
EMP: 99 Privately Held
SIC: 8322 9441 Individual & family services; administration of social & manpower programs;
PA: County Of Riverside
4080 Lemon St Fl 11
Riverside CA 92501
951 955-1110

(P-23884)
COUNTY OF RIVERSIDE
Also Called: Public Social Services
1400 W Minthorn St, Lake Elsinore (92530-2808)
PHONE.................................951 245-3100
Tom Barnidge, Manager
EMP: 100 Privately Held
SIC: 8322 9199 Individual & family services; general government administration;
PA: County Of Riverside
4080 Lemon St Fl 11
Riverside CA 92501
951 955-1110

(P-23885)
COUNTY OF RIVERSIDE
Also Called: Economic Development Dept
1025 N State St, Hemet (92543-1474)
PHONE.................................951 791-3500
Virginia Irvin, Manager
EMP: 106 Privately Held
SIC: 8322 9441 Individual & family services; administration of social & manpower programs;
PA: County Of Riverside
4080 Lemon St Fl 11
Riverside CA 92501
951 955-1110

(P-23886)
COUNTY OF RIVERSIDE
43264 Business Park Dr # 102, Temecula (92590-3646)
PHONE.................................951 600-6500
Fax: 951 694-5110
Virginia Hedberg, Branch Mgr
EMP: 99 Privately Held
SIC: 8322 Public welfare center

PRODUCTS & SERVICES SECTION
8322 - Individual & Family Social Svcs County (P-23908)

PA: County Of Riverside
4080 Lemon St Fl 11
Riverside CA 92501
951 955-1110

(P-23887)
COUNTY OF RIVERSIDE
4168 12th St, Riverside (92501-3409)
PHONE.....................................951 275-8783
Yab Cordinator, *Principal*
EMP: 99 Privately Held
SIC: 8322 Youth center
PA: County Of Riverside
4080 Lemon St Fl 11
Riverside CA 92501
951 955-1110

(P-23888)
COUNTY OF RIVERSIDE
Also Called: Office On Aging, ADRC Of River
6296 River Crest Dr Ste K, Riverside (92507-0738)
PHONE.....................................951 697-4699
Edward Walsh, *Director*
Becky Foreman, *Exec Dir*
Dan Tanase, *Business Anlyst*
Jerry Licayan, *Technology*
Stanley Cox, *Analyst*
EMP: 80 Privately Held
SIC: 8322 9441 Geriatric social service; administration of social & manpower programs;
PA: County Of Riverside
4080 Lemon St Fl 11
Riverside CA 92501
951 955-1110

(P-23889)
COUNTY OF RIVERSIDE
Also Called: Riverside Cnty Probation Dept
3960 Orange St Ste 500, Riverside (92501-3644)
P.O. Box 833 (92502-0833)
PHONE.....................................951 955-0905
Michelina Iybar, *Supervisor*
Julie Terrell, *Manager*
EMP: 875 Privately Held
SIC: 8322 Probation office
PA: County Of Riverside
4080 Lemon St Fl 11
Riverside CA 92501
951 955-1110

(P-23890)
COUNTY OF RIVERSIDE
Also Called: Van Horn Youth Center
10000 County Farm Rd, Riverside (92503-3508)
PHONE.....................................951 358-4415
Fax: 909 358-4420
Pam Cronk, *Principal*
Mike Malone, *Manager*
EMP: 99 Privately Held
SIC: 8322 9223 Youth center; correctional institutions;
PA: County Of Riverside
4080 Lemon St Fl 11
Riverside CA 92501
951 955-1110

(P-23891)
COUNTY OF SACRAMENTO
Also Called: Health and Human Services
9750 Bus Park Dr Ste 104, Sacramento (95827-1716)
P.O. Box 5140 (95817-0140)
PHONE.....................................916 875-4467
Mindy Yamasaki, *Branch Mgr*
EMP: 135 Privately Held
WEB: www.sna.com
SIC: 8322 9441 Old age assistance; administration of social & human resources;
PA: County Of Sacramento
700 H St Ste 7650
Sacramento CA 95814
916 874-5544

(P-23892)
COUNTY OF SAN BERNARDINO
Also Called: Human Services Systems
412 W Hospitality Ln Fl 2, San Bernardino (92415-0913)
PHONE.....................................909 891-3300
Fax: 909 891-3399
Mae Harns-Oglesby, *Director*
Hernaldo Sequeira, *Technology*
Katherine Giles, *Social Worker*
EMP: 70 Privately Held
SIC: 8322 9441 Adoption services; administration of social & manpower programs;
PA: County Of San Bernardino
385 N Arrowhead Ave
San Bernardino CA 92415
909 387-3841

(P-23893)
COUNTY OF SAN BERNARDINO
Also Called: Probation Dept
8303 Haven Ave, Rancho Cucamonga (91730-3848)
PHONE.....................................909 945-4000
Fax: 909 945-4017
Wes Krause, *Branch Mgr*
Evelyn McCorkle, *Officer*
Doreen Boxer, *Director*
EMP: 70 Privately Held
SIC: 8322 9441 Probation office; administration of social & manpower programs;
PA: County Of San Bernardino
385 N Arrowhead Ave
San Bernardino CA 92415
909 387-3841

(P-23894)
COUNTY OF SAN BERNARDINO
Also Called: Aging & Adult Services
17270 Bear Valley Rd # 108, Victorville (92395-7751)
PHONE.....................................760 843-5100
EMP: 51 Privately Held
SIC: 8322 9441
PA: County Of San Bernardino
385 N Arrowhead Ave
San Bernardino CA 92415
909 387-5455

(P-23895)
COUNTY OF SAN BERNARDINO
Also Called: Transitional Assistance Dept
56357 Pima Trl, Yucca Valley (92284-3607)
PHONE.....................................760 228-5234
Fax: 760 228-5289
John Michealson, *Director*
EMP: 70 Privately Held
SIC: 8322 9441 Individual & family services; administration of social & manpower programs
PA: County Of San Bernardino
385 N Arrowhead Ave
San Bernardino CA 92415
909 387-3841

(P-23896)
COUNTY OF SAN DIEGO
Also Called: Health & Human Services
6950 Levant St, San Diego (92111-6010)
PHONE.....................................858 694-5141
Fax: 858 694-5240
Debra Zanders-Willis, *Director*
Valesha Bullock, *Manager*
EMP: 82 Privately Held
WEB: www.sdlcc.org
SIC: 8322 9441 Adoption services; administration of social & manpower programs;
PA: County Of San Diego
1600 Pacific Hwy Ste 209
San Diego CA 92101
619 531-5880

(P-23897)
COUNTY OF SAN DIEGO
Also Called: Health & Human Services
130 E Alvarado St, Fallbrook (92028-2048)
PHONE.....................................866 262-9881
Fax: 760 723-7608
Carol Schier, *Branch Mgr*
EMP: 82 Privately Held
WEB: www.sdlcc.org
SIC: 8322 Individual & family services; parole office
PA: County Of San Diego
1600 Pacific Hwy Ste 209
San Diego CA 92101
619 531-5880

(P-23898)
COUNTY OF SAN DIEGO
Also Called: Health and Human Service Agcy
5560 Overland Ave Ste 310, San Diego (92123-1204)
PHONE.....................................858 495-5537
Pamela B Smith, *Manager*
Ellen Schmeding, *Principal*
David Steele, *Admin Asst*
Kristen Smith, *Administration*
Katherine Baker, *MIS Mgr*
EMP: 70 Privately Held
WEB: www.sdlcc.org
SIC: 8322 9441 Individual & family services; administration of social & manpower programs;
PA: County Of San Diego
1600 Pacific Hwy Ste 209
San Diego CA 92101
619 531-5880

(P-23899)
COUNTY OF SAN DIEGO
Also Called: Probation Dept
330 W Broadway Ste 1100, San Diego (92101-3827)
P.O. Box 23596 (92193-3596)
PHONE.....................................619 515-8202
Fax: 619 515-8696
Don Blevins, *Director*
Celeste Schwartz, *COO*
Marcella McLaughlin, *Bd of Directors*
Julie Martin-Sexauer, *General Mgr*
Rob Bird, *Technology*
EMP: 82 Privately Held
WEB: www.sdlcc.org
SIC: 8322 9431 Probation office; parole office; administration of public health programs
PA: County Of San Diego
1600 Pacific Hwy Ste 209
San Diego CA 92101
619 531-5880

(P-23900)
COUNTY OF SAN DIEGO
Also Called: Health & Human Services
3851 Rosecrans St, San Diego (92110-3115)
P.O. Box 85222 (92186-5222)
PHONE.....................................619 692-8202
Fax: 619 236-3884
Golnaz Agahi, *Principal*
Tia Anzelotti, *Bd of Directors*
EMP: 82 Privately Held
WEB: www.sdlcc.org
SIC: 8322 9441 Individual & family services; administration of social & manpower programs;
PA: County Of San Diego
1600 Pacific Hwy Ste 209
San Diego CA 92101
619 531-5880

(P-23901)
COUNTY OF SAN DIEGO
Also Called: Parks & Recreation Dept
8735 Jamacha Blvd, Spring Valley (91977-5632)
PHONE.....................................619 479-1832
Fax: 619 479-1883
Renell Nailon, *Director*
EMP: 75 Privately Held
WEB: www.sdlcc.org
SIC: 8322 9512 Individual & family services; recreational program administration, government;
PA: County Of San Diego
1600 Pacific Hwy Ste 209
San Diego CA 92101
619 531-5880

(P-23902)
COUNTY OF SAN DIEGO
Also Called: Health and Human Services Agcy
3255 Camino Del Rio S, San Diego (92108-3806)
PHONE.....................................619 563-2765
Fax: 619 563-2775
Delia Mateo, *Principal*
David Steele, *Admin Asst*
Alfredo Aguirre, *Director*
EMP: 74 Privately Held
SIC: 8322 Individual & family services
PA: County Of San Diego
1600 Pacific Hwy Ste 209
San Diego CA 92101
619 531-5880

(P-23903)
COUNTY OF SAN DIEGO
Also Called: Health and Human Services
4588 Market St, San Diego (92102-4764)
PHONE.....................................619 236-8725
Fax: 619 266-3877
Deborah Lester, *Branch Mgr*
Pat Lopez, *Manager*
EMP: 150 Privately Held
WEB: www.sdlcc.org
SIC: 8322 9431 Individual & family services; administration of public health programs
PA: County Of San Diego
1600 Pacific Hwy Ste 209
San Diego CA 92101
619 531-5880

(P-23904)
COUNTY OF SAN DIEGO DEPT CHIL
225 Broadway Ste 1200, San Diego (92101-5028)
PHONE.....................................619 578-6660
Jeff Grissom, *Director*
Julie Gamboa, *Admin Asst*
EMP: 500
SALES (est): 124.9K Privately Held
SIC: 8322 Individual & family services

(P-23905)
COUNTY OF SAN JOAQUIN
Also Called: Dept of Child Support
826 N California St, Stockton (95202-1820)
PHONE.....................................209 468-2601
Judy Grimes, *Branch Mgr*
EMP: 400
SQ FT: 1,005 Privately Held
WEB: www.sjclawlib.org
SIC: 8322 9441 Child related social services; public welfare administration: non-operating, government
PA: County Of San Joaquin
44 N San Joaquin St # 640
Stockton CA 95202
209 468-3203

(P-23906)
COUNTY OF SAN JOAQUIN
Also Called: San Joaquin County Adult Svcs
24 S Hunter St Ste 201, Stockton (95202-3231)
PHONE.....................................209 468-4100
Fax: 209 468-8094
Dave Newaj, *CEO*
Paul Rinaldo, *Officer*
Mike Martinez, *Manager*
EMP: 78 Privately Held
SIC: 8322 Probation office
PA: County Of San Joaquin
44 N San Joaquin St # 640
Stockton CA 95202
209 468-3203

(P-23907)
COUNTY OF SAN JOAQUIN
Also Called: Mary Grahams Childrens Shelter
500 W Hospital Rd, French Camp (95231-9693)
P.O. Box 201056, Stockton (95201-3006)
PHONE.....................................209 468-6966
Fax: 209 468-6999
Brian Woods, *Director*
EMP: 75 Privately Held
WEB: www.sjclawlib.org
SIC: 8322 9512 Child related social services; land conservation agencies
PA: County Of San Joaquin
44 N San Joaquin St # 640
Stockton CA 95202
209 468-3203

(P-23908)
COUNTY OF SAN LUIS OBISPO
Also Called: Department of Social Services
3433 S Higuera St, San Luis Obispo (93401-7301)
PHONE.....................................805 781-5437
Fax: 805 781-1701
Lee Collins, *Director*
Tracy Schiro, *Asst Director*
EMP: 108 Privately Held
SIC: 8322 Child related social services

8322 - Individual & Family Social Svcs County (P-23909)

PRODUDUCTS & SERVICES SECTION

PA: County Of San Luis Obispo
Government Center Rm. 300
San Luis Obispo CA 93408
805 781-5040

(P-23909)
COUNTY OF SAN LUIS OBISPO
Also Called: Dept of Social Services Dss
3433 S Higuera St, San Luis Obispo (93401-7301)
P.O. Box 8119 (93403-8119)
PHONE.....................805 781-1864
Leland Collins, Director
Kim Wooten, Program Mgr
EMP: 450 Privately Held
SIC: 8322 Individual & family services
PA: County Of San Luis Obispo
Government Center Rm. 300
San Luis Obispo CA 93408
805 781-5040

(P-23910)
COUNTY OF SAN MATEO
Also Called: Probation Department
680 Warren St, Redwood City (94063-1522)
PHONE.....................650 599-7336
Michael J Stauffer, Manager
EMP: 130 Privately Held
WEB: www.ci.sanmateo.ca.us
SIC: 8322 9223 Probation office;
PA: County Of San Mateo
400 County Ctr
Redwood City CA 94063
650 363-4123

(P-23911)
COUNTY OF SAN MATEO
Also Called: Probation Department
222 Paul Scannell Dr, San Mateo (94402-4061)
PHONE.....................650 312-5327
Fax: 650 312-5354
Stuart Forrest, Chief
EMP: 250 Privately Held
WEB: www.ci.sanmateo.ca.us
SIC: 8322 9223 Probation office; parole office;
PA: County Of San Mateo
400 County Ctr
Redwood City CA 94063
650 363-4123

(P-23912)
COUNTY OF SAN MATEO
Also Called: Probation Department
222 Paul Scannell Dr Fl 2, San Mateo (94402-4061)
PHONE.....................650 312-8887
Stewart Forest, Manager
Felice Smith, Admin Sec
EMP: 400 Privately Held
WEB: www.ci.sanmateo.ca.us
SIC: 8322 9199 Probation office; general government administration;
PA: County Of San Mateo
400 County Ctr
Redwood City CA 94063
650 363-4123

(P-23913)
COUNTY OF SAN MATEO
Also Called: Probation Department
2277 University Ave, East Palo Alto (94303-1717)
PHONE.....................650 853-3139
Fax: 650 325-5327
Robert Hoover, Manager
EMP: 51 Privately Held
WEB: www.ci.sanmateo.ca.us
SIC: 8322 9223 Probation office; parole office;
PA: County Of San Mateo
400 County Ctr
Redwood City CA 94063
650 363-4123

(P-23914)
COUNTY OF SAN MATEO
Child Support Services Dept
555 County Ctr Fl 2, Redwood City (94063-1665)
PHONE.....................650 363-1910
Kim Cagno, Director
Sandy Wong, Deputy Dir
EMP: 80 Privately Held

WEB: www.ci.sanmateo.ca.us
SIC: 8322 9441 Child related social services;
PA: County Of San Mateo
400 County Ctr
Redwood City CA 94063
650 363-4123

(P-23915)
COUNTY OF SAN MATEO
Also Called: Human Services Agency
400 Harbor Blvd Bldg B, Belmont (94002-4047)
PHONE.....................650 802-6470
Fax: 650 595-7516
Beverly Beasley Johnson, Manager
Dan Laden, Vice Pres
Daniel Gee, Technician
Ricardo Villarin, Network Analyst
Diana Gomez, Analyst
EMP: 150 Privately Held
WEB: www.ci.sanmateo.ca.us
SIC: 8322 9441 Adoption services; administration of social & manpower programs;
PA: County Of San Mateo
400 County Ctr
Redwood City CA 94063
650 363-4123

(P-23916)
COUNTY OF SAN MATEO
Also Called: Probation Department
222 Paul Scannell Dr, San Mateo (94402-4061)
PHONE.....................650 312-8803
Loren Buddress, Chief
EMP: 200 Privately Held
WEB: www.ci.sanmateo.ca.us
SIC: 8322 9199 Probation office; general government administration;
PA: County Of San Mateo
400 County Ctr
Redwood City CA 94063
650 363-4123

(P-23917)
COUNTY OF SAN MATEO
Also Called: Probation Department
400 County Ctr Fl 5, Redwood City (94063-1662)
P.O. Box 441 (94064-0441)
PHONE.....................650 312-8803
John Keene,
EMP: 143 Privately Held
SIC: 8322 9223 Probation office;
PA: County Of San Mateo
400 County Ctr
Redwood City CA 94063
650 363-4123

(P-23918)
COUNTY OF SHASTA
Also Called: Children's Protective Services
1313 Yuba St, Redding (96001-1012)
PHONE.....................530 225-5554
Fax: 530 225-5150
Nancy Bolen, Branch Mgr
EMP: 75 Privately Held
WEB: www.rsdnmp.org
SIC: 8322 Children's aid society
PA: County Of Shasta
1450 Court St Ste 308a
Redding CA 96001
530 225-5561

(P-23919)
COUNTY OF SISKIYOU
Also Called: Human Services Department
818 S Main St, Yreka (96097-3321)
PHONE.....................530 841-2700
Fax: 530 841-2700
Nadine Dellabitta, Director
Frank J Mecca, Exec Dir
EMP: 60 Privately Held
WEB: www.siskiyoucounty.org
SIC: 8322 Individual & family services
PA: County Of Siskiyou
311 4th St Rm 108
Yreka CA 96097
530 841-4100

(P-23920)
COUNTY OF SOLANO
Also Called: Health and Social Services
275 Beck Ave, Fairfield (94533-6804)
PHONE.....................707 784-8400

Fax: 707 421-3207
Patrick Dulerte, Director
Esther Alberg, Accountant
Gerald Huber, Director
EMP: 56 Privately Held
SIC: 8322 Individual & family services
PA: County Of Solano
675 Texas St Ste 2600
Fairfield CA 94533
707 784-6706

(P-23921)
COUNTY OF SOLANO
Also Called: Solano County Probation Dept
475 Union Ave, Fairfield (94533-6319)
PHONE.....................707 784-7600
Isabelle Voight, Principal
Donna Vestal, Analyst
EMP: 237 Privately Held
SIC: 8322 Rehabilitation services
PA: County Of Solano
675 Texas St Ste 2600
Fairfield CA 94533
707 784-6706

(P-23922)
COUNTY OF SONOMA
2300 County Center Dr B100, Santa Rosa (95403-3013)
PHONE.....................707 527-2641
Peter Boomer, Branch Mgr
Robert Kambak, Architect
EMP: 60 Privately Held
WEB: www.sonomacompost.com
SIC: 8322 Child related social services
PA: County Of Sonoma
585 Fiscal Dr 100
Santa Rosa CA 95403
707 565-2431

(P-23923)
COUNTY OF STANISLAUS
Also Called: Community Services
830 Scenic Dr, Modesto (95350-6131)
PHONE.....................209 558-8828
Nancy Fisher, Superintendent
EMP: 75 Privately Held
WEB: www.co.stanislaus.ca.us
SIC: 8322 Youth self-help agency
PA: County Of Stanislaus
1010 10th St Ste 5100
Modesto CA 95354
209 525-6398

(P-23924)
COUNTY OF STANISLAUS
801 11th St Ste 4000, Modesto (95354-2355)
PHONE.....................209 567-4120
Delia Basquez, Branch Mgr
EMP: 110 Privately Held
SIC: 8322 Probation office
PA: County Of Stanislaus
1010 10th St Ste 5100
Modesto CA 95354
209 525-6398

(P-23925)
COUNTY OF STANISLAUS
108 Campus Way, Modesto (95350-5803)
PHONE.....................209 558-7377
Fax: 209 558-7508
Elaine Emory, Manager
EMP: 110 Privately Held
SIC: 8322 Individual & family services
PA: County Of Stanislaus
1010 10th St Ste 5100
Modesto CA 95354
209 525-6398

(P-23926)
COUNTY OF STANISLAUS
Also Called: Dcss
251 E Hackett Rd, Modesto (95358-9800)
P.O. Box 4189 (95352-4189)
PHONE.....................209 558-9675
Tamara Thomas, Branch Mgr
David Ingersoll, Branch Mgr
Rhonda Brown, Manager
EMP: 223 Privately Held
WEB: www.modairport.com
SIC: 8322 Family counseling services
PA: County Of Stanislaus
1010 10th St Ste 5100
Modesto CA 95354
209 525-6398

(P-23927)
COUNTY OF STANISLAUS
Also Called: Family Support Division
108 Campus Way, Modesto (95350-5803)
P.O. Box 4189 (95352-4189)
PHONE.....................209 558-2500
Joan Kingman, Branch Mgr
EMP: 95 Privately Held
WEB: www.co.stanislaus.ca.us
SIC: 8322 Child related social services
PA: County Of Stanislaus
1010 10th St Ste 5100
Modesto CA 95354
209 525-6398

(P-23928)
COUNTY OF TEHAMA
Also Called: Mental Health Services
1860 Walnut St, Red Bluff (96080-3611)
P.O. Box 400 (96080-0400)
PHONE.....................530 527-5631
Fax: 530 527-0240
Valerie Lucero, Director
Jayme Bottke, Info Tech Mgr
Richard Harig, Director
EMP: 200 Privately Held
SIC: 8322 9111 Individual & family services; county supervisors' & executives' offices
PA: The County Of Tehama
20639 Walnut St
Red Bluff CA 96080
530 527-4655

(P-23929)
COUNTY OF TEHAMA
Also Called: Probation
1840 Walnut St, Red Bluff (96080-3611)
P.O. Box 99 (96080-0099)
PHONE.....................530 527-4052
Fax: 530 527-1579
David Finch, Branch Mgr
Ashley Jennings, Admin Sec
Peggy Murphy, Admin Sec
Jackie Douglas, Admin Asst
Larry Champion, Superintendent
EMP: 70 Privately Held
SIC: 8322 9111 Probation office; county supervisors' & executives' offices
PA: The County Of Tehama
20639 Walnut St
Red Bluff CA 96080
530 527-4655

(P-23930)
COUNTY OF TUOLUMNE
Also Called: Welfare Department
20075 Cedar Rd N, Sonora (95370-5900)
PHONE.....................209 533-5711
Fax: 209 533-5726
Kent Skellenger, Director
Ann Connolly, Director
EMP: 110 Privately Held
WEB: www.tuolumne.courts.ca.gov
SIC: 8322 Individual & family services
PA: County Of Tuolumne
2 S Green St
Sonora CA 95370
209 533-5521

(P-23931)
COUNTY OF VENTURA
Also Called: County Ventura Human Resources
800 S Victoria Ave, Ventura (93009-0003)
PHONE.....................805 654-2561
Jodi Lee Prior, Branch Mgr
George Boghassian, Pharmacy Dir
John Nicoll, Administration
Mark Schneider, Technology
Maria Moreno, Buyer
EMP: 104 Privately Held
WEB: www.vcoe.org
SIC: 8322 9441 Individual & family services; administration of social & human resources
PA: County Of Ventura
800 S Victoria Ave
Ventura CA 93009
805 654-2551

PRODUCTS & SERVICES SECTION **8322 - Individual & Family Social Svcs County (P-23954)**

(P-23932)
COUNTY OF VENTURA
Also Called: Foster Care Licensing & Svc
4651 Telephone Rd Ste 300, Ventura (93003-8779)
PHONE.................805 654-3456
Fax: 805 654-3454
Ellen Mastright, *Branch Mgr*
Jenny Medrano, *Admin Asst*
Ken Sewell, *Deputy Dir*
EMP: 90 **Privately Held**
WEB: www.vcoe.org
SIC: 8322 9111 Hotline; executive offices
PA: County Of Ventura
 800 S Victoria Ave
 Ventura CA 93009
 805 654-2551

(P-23933)
COUNTY OF VENTURA
1400 Vanguard Dr Fl 2nd, Oxnard (93033-2402)
PHONE.................805 385-8654
Fax: 805 385-8504
Bonita Kraft, *Branch Mgr*
EMP: 104 **Privately Held**
SIC: 8322 Probation office
PA: County Of Ventura
 800 S Victoria Ave
 Ventura CA 93009
 805 654-2551

(P-23934)
COUNTY OF VENTURA
Also Called: Medical Center
3291 Loma Vista Rd, Ventura (93003-3099)
PHONE.................805 652-6000
Michael Powers, *Manager*
Jeana Miller, *Office Mgr*
Jerry Conway, *Opers Mgr*
EMP: 600 **Privately Held**
WEB: www.vcoe.org
SIC: 8322 9431 Individual & family services; administration of public health programs;
PA: County Of Ventura
 800 S Victoria Ave
 Ventura CA 93009
 805 654-2551

(P-23935)
COUNTY OF VENTURA
Also Called: Department Child Support Svcs
5171 Verdugo Way, Camarillo (93012-8603)
PHONE.................805 654-5529
Stanley Trom, *Director*
EMP: 273 **Privately Held**
WEB: www.vcoe.org
SIC: 8322 9431 Individual & family services; child health program administration, government
PA: County Of Ventura
 800 S Victoria Ave
 Ventura CA 93009
 805 654-2551

(P-23936)
COUNTY OF YUBA
Also Called: Yuba County Probation Dept
215 5th St Ste 154, Marysville (95901-5737)
PHONE.................530 749-7550
Fax: 530 634-7649
Jim Arnold, *Director*
Monica Lara, *Officer*
Kelly Purdom, *Director*
EMP: 183 **Privately Held**
SIC: 8322 9199 Probation office;
PA: County Of Yuba
 915 8th St Ste 109
 Marysville CA 95901
 530 749-7575

(P-23937)
CRUCIBLE
1260 7th St, Oakland (94607-2150)
PHONE.................510 444-0919
Fax: 510 444-0918
Steven Young, *President*
Janet Hiebert, *Top Exec*
Autumn King, *Comms Dir*
Michael Sturtz, *Exec Dir*
Joey Gottbrath, *Opers Staff*
EMP: 100

SQ FT: 46,980
SALES: 2.5MM **Privately Held**
WEB: www.thecrucible.com
SIC: 8322 8331 Outreach program; skill training center

(P-23938)
CRYSTAL STAIRS INC (PA)
5110 W Goldleaf Cir # 150, Los Angeles (90056-1287)
PHONE.................323 299-8998
Jackie B Majors, *CEO*
Dianna Torres, *Ch of Bd*
Dr Karen Hill-Scott, *President*
Javier La Fianza, *COO*
Robert Trujillo, *Treasurer*
EMP: 330
SQ FT: 83,000
SALES: 107.6MM **Privately Held**
WEB: www.crystalstairs.com
SIC: 8322 Individual & family services

(P-23939)
DAVIS STREET COMMUNITY CENTER (PA)
Also Called: Davis Street Fmly Resource Ctr
3081 Teagarden St, San Leandro (94577-5720)
PHONE.................510 347-4620
Rose Johnson, *Exec Dir*
Silan Stahlhut, *CFO*
Terri Wrigley, *Office Admin*
Denise Kaplan, *Info Tech Mgr*
Collin Cirese, *Technology*
EMP: 53
SQ FT: 7,000
SALES: 7.6MM **Privately Held**
SIC: 8322 8021 8011 8093 Individual & family services; dental clinic; primary care medical clinic; mental health clinic, outpatient

(P-23940)
DESERT AIDS PROJECT (PA)
Also Called: REVIVALS THRIFT STORES
1695 N Sunrise Way Bldg 1, Palm Springs (92262-3702)
P.O. Box 2890 (92263-2890)
PHONE.................760 323-2118
Fax: 760 323-9865
David Brinkman, *CEO*
Mary Park, *CFO*
Steve Lachs, *Vice Pres*
Alex Christianson, *Administration*
Keith Cornell, *Accountant*
EMP: 65
SQ FT: 46,050
SALES: 25.4MM **Privately Held**
WEB: www.desertaidsproject.org
SIC: 8322 5932 8011 General counseling services; used merchandise stores; clinic, operated by physicians

(P-23941)
DESERTARC (PA)
Also Called: DESERT VALLEY INDUSTRIES
73255 Country Club Dr, Palm Desert (92260-2309)
PHONE.................760 346-1611
Lori Serfling, *Treasurer*
Robert Anzalone, *President*
Robin Keagen, *CFO*
Robin Keegan, *CFO*
Jay Chesterton, *Treasurer*
EMP: 230 EST: 1959
SQ FT: 12,000
SALES: 12.3MM **Privately Held**
WEB: www.desertarc.org
SIC: 8322 Association for the handicapped

(P-23942)
DEVELOP DISABILITIES SVC ORG
Also Called: Community Integration Program
2331 Saint Marks Way G1, Sacramento (95864-0626)
PHONE.................916 973-1953
Yvonne Soto, *CEO*
Amy Nishimura, *CEO*
Susan Burger, *Deputy Dir*
EMP: 75
SALES (est): 826.7K **Privately Held**
SIC: 8322 Social services for the handicapped

(P-23943)
DIAMOND LEARNING CENTER INC
1620 W Fairmont Ave, Fresno (93705-0323)
PHONE.................559 241-0580
Fax: 559 241-0585
Jamie Delacerda, *President*
Daniel F Delacerda, *Vice Pres*
Isaac Jimenez, *Transptn Dir*
Daniel D Cerda, *Director*
Bridgette Franco, *Director*
EMP: 53
SALES: 151.3K **Privately Held**
SIC: 8322 Adult day care center

(P-23944)
DIDI HIRSCH PSYCHIATRIC SVC (PA)
Also Called: Didi Hirsch Community Mental
4760 Sepulveda Blvd, Culver City (90230-4820)
PHONE.................310 390-6612
Michael Wierwille, *Chairman*
Kita S Curry, *President*
Martin Frank, *Treasurer*
Peter Golio, *Vice Pres*
Andrew Rubin, *Admin Sec*
EMP: 150 EST: 1944
SQ FT: 35,000
SALES: 44.4MM **Privately Held**
SIC: 8322 8093 Individual & family services; mental health clinic, outpatient

(P-23945)
DIGNITY HEALTH
Also Called: Older Adult Health Services
1720 Termino Ave, Long Beach (90804-2104)
PHONE.................562 494-0576
Fax: 562 498-4434
Charlene Young, *Director*
EMP: 50
SALES (corp-wide): 7.1B **Privately Held**
WEB: www.chw.edu
SIC: 8322 Senior citizens' center or association
PA: Dignity Health
 185 Berry St Ste 300
 San Francisco CA 94107
 415 438-5500

(P-23946)
DISTRICT COUNCIL DC (PA)
Also Called: St Vincent De Paul
9235 San Leandro St, Oakland (94603-1237)
PHONE.................510 638-7600
Fax: 510 638-8354
EMP: 100
SQ FT: 40,000
SALES: 7.4MM **Privately Held**
SIC: 8322 5932 Individual & family services; used merchandise stores

(P-23947)
DIVERSE JOURNEYS INC (PA)
525 S Douglas St Ste 210, El Segundo (90245-4827)
PHONE.................310 643-7403
Amanda Gerhart, *President*
Laura Broderick, *Director*
Wynnette Jones, *Manager*
EMP: 78
SQ FT: 2,000
SALES (est): 2.8MM **Privately Held**
SIC: 8322 Social services for the handicapped

(P-23948)
DREW CHILD DEV CORP INC (PA)
1770 E 118th St, Los Angeles (90059-2518)
PHONE.................323 249-2950
Fax: 323 249-2970
Michael Jackson, *President*
James Hays, *CEO*
Stephanie Cole, *Branch Mgr*
Jackie Clarke, *General Mgr*
Carol Gillard, *Human Res Dir*
EMP: 102
SALES: 18.8MM **Privately Held**
SIC: 8322 Individual & family services; child guidance agency

(P-23949)
EAST BAY ASIAN YOUTH CENTER
2025 E 12th St, Oakland (94606-4925)
PHONE.................510 533-1092
Gianna Tran, *President*
Colin Jiang, *Manager*
Mae Saeteurn, *Manager*
EMP: 50
SALES (corp-wide): 5.7MM **Privately Held**
WEB: www.ebayc.org
SIC: 8322 Youth center
PA: East Bay Asian Youth Center
 2025 E 12th St
 Oakland CA 94606
 510 533-1092

(P-23950)
EASTER SEAL SOC SUPERIOR CAL
1670 Sierra Ave Ste 601, Yuba City (95993-9411)
PHONE.................530 673-4585
Foster Campbell-Mcman, *Branch Mgr*
Tony Kildare, *Manager*
EMP: 60
SALES (corp-wide): 10.7MM **Privately Held**
SIC: 8322 Adult day care center
PA: Easter Seal Society Of Superior California
 3205 Hurley Way
 Sacramento CA 95864
 916 485-6711

(P-23951)
EASTER SEALS CENTRAL CAL
9010 Soquel Dr, Aptos (95003-4082)
PHONE.................831 684-2166
Bruce Hinman, *President*
Maryann Porter, *Manager*
EMP: 300
SALES: 3.7MM **Privately Held**
SIC: 8322 Social service center

(P-23952)
EASTERN LOS ANGELES RE (PA)
1000 S Fremont Ave # 23, Alhambra (91803-8800)
P.O. Box 7916 (91802-7916)
PHONE.................626 299-4700
Fax: 626 281-1163
Gloria Wong, *Exec Dir*
Theresa Chen, *Bd of Directors*
Ana Young, *Admin Sec*
Sophia Tang Hao, *Controller*
Heike I Ballmaier, *Psychologist*
EMP: 242
SQ FT: 31,704
SALES: 184MM **Privately Held**
WEB: www.elarc.org
SIC: 8322 Association for the handicapped

(P-23953)
EASTERN STAR HOMES CALIFORNIA (PA)
Also Called: EASTERN STAR PROFESSIONAL BUIL
16850 Bastanchury Rd, Yorba Linda (92886-1608)
PHONE.................714 986-2380
Norma Stillwell, *President*
Danna Willoughby, *President*
EMP: 56
SQ FT: 15,604
SALES: 4.4MM **Privately Held**
SIC: 8322 Geriatric social service

(P-23954)
EDGEWOOD CTR FOR CHILDRENS
Also Called: Edgewood Family Center
101 15th St, San Francisco (94103-5103)
PHONE.................415 865-3000
Jenny McTackett, *Regional Mgr*
Sheryl Matteo, *Controller*
EMP: 60
SALES (corp-wide): 19MM **Privately Held**
WEB: www.edgewoodcenter.org
SIC: 8322 8742 Individual & family services; management consulting services

8322 - Individual & Family Social Svcs County (P-23955)

PA: Edgewood Center For Children And Families
1801 Vicente St
San Francisco CA 94116
415 681-3211

(P-23955) EGGLESTON YOUTH CENTERS INC (PA)
13001 Ramona Blvd Ste E, Irwindale (91706-3752)
P.O. Box 638, Baldwin Park (91706-0638)
PHONE..................................626 480-8107
Fax: 626 851-9789
Clarence Brown, *Exec Dir*
April Mitchell, *President*
Cassandra Gibson-Judkins, *Exec VP*
Don Gutierrez, *Administration*
Michael Ograham, *Agent*
EMP: 90
SQ FT: 7,616
SALES: 8MM **Privately Held**
SIC: 8322 Social service center; youth center

(P-23956) EL CAMINO CHILDREN & FMLY SVCS
9900 Lakewood Blvd # 104, Downey (90240-4038)
PHONE..................................562 364-1258
Fax: 562 286-5154
Jorge Gutierrez, *CEO*
Robert Donin, *Chairman*
John Rojas, *Vice Pres*
David Sanchez, *Admin Sec*
EMP: 50
SQ FT: 3,000
SALES: 55.1K **Privately Held**
WEB: www.eccafs.com
SIC: 8322 Family counseling services

(P-23957) EL CAMINO HOSPITAL
1503 Grant Rd Ste 120, Mountain View (94040-3293)
PHONE..................................650 988-7444
Vicki Chryssos, *Exec Dir*
Charles Neff, *Vice Pres*
Jan Peach, *Director*
Jennifer S Borrelli, *Manager*
Mirella Nguyen, *Manager*
EMP: 246
SALES (corp-wide): 776.4MM **Privately Held**
SIC: 8322 Social worker
PA: El Camino Hospital
2500 Grant Rd
Mountain View CA 94040
408 224-6660

(P-23958) EL CONCILIO SAN MATEO CNTY INC
1419 Burlingame Ave Ste N, Burlingame (94010-4123)
PHONE..................................650 373-1080
Fax: 650 373-1090
Ortensia Lopez, *President*
EMP: 50
SALES: 2.7MM **Privately Held**
WEB: www.el-concilio.com
SIC: 8322 Individual & family services

(P-23959) EL NIDO FAMILY CENTERS (PA)
10200 Sepulveda Blvd # 350, Mission Hills (91345-3318)
PHONE..................................818 830-3646
Fax: 818 830-3654
Liz Herrera, *Director*
Patricia Alba, *Program Mgr*
Ana C Burgos, *Case Mgr*
Liza Bernstein, *Manager*
Margie Guzman, *Manager*
EMP: 130
SQ FT: 3,650
SALES: 9MM **Privately Held**
WEB: www.elnidofamilycenters.org
SIC: 8322 Individual & family services

(P-23960) ENCOMPASS COMMUNITY SERVICES
Also Called: Headstart
225 Westridge Dr, Watsonville (95076-4168)
P.O. Box 927 (95077-0927)
PHONE..................................831 724-3885
Fax: 831 724-3534
Gloria Martinez, *Branch Mgr*
EMP: 300
SALES (corp-wide): 26.9MM **Privately Held**
SIC: 8322 8351 Individual & family services; head start center, except in conjunction with school
PA: Encompass Community Services
380 Encinal St Ste 200
Santa Cruz CA 95060
831 427-9670

(P-23961) ENKI HEALTH AND RES SYSTEMS
3208 Rosemead Blvd, El Monte (91731-2830)
PHONE..................................626 227-0341
Veronikue Warner, *Branch Mgr*
EMP: 126
SALES (corp-wide): 23.9MM **Privately Held**
SIC: 8322 Individual & family services
PA: Enki Health And Research Systems
150 E Olive Ave Ste 203
Burbank CA 91502
818 973-4899

(P-23962) ESKATON PROPERTIES INC
Also Called: Senior Connection, The
5105 Manzanita Ave, Carmichael (95608-0523)
PHONE..................................916 334-1072
Fax: 916 331-2986
Todd Murch, *Manager*
Stuart Greenbaum, *Vice Pres*
Lawrence Dawes, *Manager*
EMP: 100
SALES (corp-wide): 90.6MM **Privately Held**
SIC: 8322 Adult day care center
PA: Eskaton Properties Incorporated
5105 Manzanita Ave Ste A
Carmichael CA 95608
916 334-0810

(P-23963) ETNA POLICE ACTIVITIES LEAGUE
448 Main St, Etna (96027-9781)
PHONE..................................530 467-3400
Josh Short, *President*
Autumn Kistler, *Director*
EMP: 200
SALES: 12.9K **Privately Held**
SIC: 8322 Community center

(P-23964) EXCEPTNAL PRENTS UNLIMITED INC
Also Called: E P U
4440 N 1st St, Fresno (93726-2304)
PHONE..................................559 229-2000
Fax: 559 229-2956
Marion Karian, *Exec Dir*
Suzanne Ellis, *Exec Dir*
Reva Guimont, *Program Mgr*
Cindy Stoops, *Program Mgr*
Barbara Swan, *Program Mgr*
EMP: 100
SQ FT: 24,000
SALES: 6.6MM **Privately Held**
WEB: www.exceptionalparents.org
SIC: 8322 Family counseling services

(P-23965) EXTEND A HAND INC
24551 Raymond Way Ste 230, Lake Forest (92630-4486)
PHONE..................................949 586-5142
Gilbert Williams, *CEO*
EMP: 80
SALES (est): 1.2MM **Privately Held**
SIC: 8322 Social service center

(P-23966) FAMILY ASSESSMENT CNSLNG EDCTN
1651 E 4th St Ste 128, Santa Ana (92701-5141)
PHONE..................................714 547-7345
Fax: 714 835-6098
Mary O Harris, *Branch Mgr*
Chris Simon, *Exec Dir*
EMP: 50
SALES (corp-wide): 392.9K **Privately Held**
SIC: 8322 Family counseling services
PA: Family Assessment Counseling Education Services
505 E Commwl Ave Ste 200
Fullerton CA 92832
714 447-9024

(P-23967) FAMILY BRIDGES INC
168 11th St, Oakland (94607-4841)
PHONE..................................510 839-2270
Fax: 510 839-2435
Corinne Jan, *Exec Dir*
Susanna Ng-Lee, *Vice Pres*
Jennifer Tu, *Executive Asst*
Mary Marshall, *Admin Sec*
Vienna Gao, *Admin Asst*
EMP: 126
SQ FT: 5,000
SALES: 6.3MM **Privately Held**
WEB: www.familybridges.net
SIC: 8322 8641 Social service center; civic social & fraternal associations

(P-23968) FAMILY CIRCLE INC
Also Called: Oxnard Family Circle Adhc
2100 Outlet Center Dr # 380, Oxnard (93036-0612)
PHONE..................................805 385-4180
Fax: 805 385-4170
Inna Berger, *CEO*
Katy Krul, *CFO*
EMP: 56
SQ FT: 12,000
SALES: 3.3MM **Privately Held**
WEB: www.familycircle.com
SIC: 8322 Adult day care center

(P-23969) FAMILY RESOURCE & REFERRAL CTR
509 W Weber Ave Ste 101, Stockton (95203-3107)
PHONE..................................209 948-1553
Fax: 209 948-3554
Kay Ruhstaller, *Director*
Pearl Agas, *Info Tech Mgr*
EMP: 100
SALES (est): 31.8MM **Privately Held**
SIC: 8322 Individual & family services; child related social services

(P-23970) FAMILY RESOURCE CENTER
6249 Skyway, Paradise (95969-4534)
PHONE..................................530 872-4015
Wendy Martinez, *Exec Dir*
Melody D Giles, *Psychologist*
Diane Kellegrew, *Director*
Kathleen Shenk, *Director*
EMP: 50 EST: 2001
SALES (est): 449.8K **Privately Held**
WEB: www.familyresourcecenters.net
SIC: 8322 Individual & family services

(P-23971) FAMILY SERVICE AGENCY
Also Called: FSA
110 S C St Ste A, Lompoc (93436-7340)
PHONE..................................805 735-4376
Fax: 805 737-3261
Stephanie Wilson, *Co-President*
Lisa Brabo, *Exec Dir*
Sarah Rudd-Lawlor, *Program Mgr*
EMP: 50
SALES (est): 706.6K **Privately Held**
SIC: 8322 8011 General counseling services; health maintenance organization

(P-23972) FAMILY SERVICES TULARE COUNTY
815 W Oak Ave, Visalia (93291-6033)
PHONE..................................559 732-1970
Fax: 559 732-6404
Caity Meader, *Exec Dir*
Pam Pulford, *Treasurer*
John Blyleven, *Executive*
Evelyn F Lessing, *Analyst*
EMP: 85
SQ FT: 2,000
SALES: 3.9MM **Privately Held**
SIC: 8322 Individual & family services; family counseling services; social service center

(P-23973) FAMILY SVC AGCY SANTA BARBARA
123 W Gutierrez St, Santa Barbara (93101-3424)
PHONE..................................805 965-1001
Denise Cicourel, *Administration*
EMP: 100
SALES: 3.8MM **Privately Held**
WEB: www.fsacares.org
SIC: 8322 Family (marriage) counseling

(P-23974) FAMILY SVCS AGCY MARIN CNTY (PA)
Also Called: Family Service Agency
555 Northgate Dr, San Rafael (94903-3680)
PHONE..................................415 491-5700
Margret Hallett, *Director*
Thompson Argo, *Exec Dir*
Roger Crawford, *Deputy Dir*
Chris Grogan, *Manager*
EMP: 82
SALES: 1.8MM **Privately Held**
SIC: 8322 Family (marriage) counseling

(P-23975) FAMILY YMCA OF DESERT
42575 Valley Dr, Palm Desert (92210)
PHONE..................................760 423-5860
Rosemary Wagner, *Branch Mgr*
EMP: 57
SALES (corp-wide): 7.3MM **Privately Held**
SIC: 8322 Individual & family services
PA: Family Ymca Of The Desert
43930 San Pablo Ave
Palm Desert CA 92260
760 469-4521

(P-23976) FAR NORTHERN COORDINATING COUN
Also Called: Regional Center
1377 E Lassen Ave, Chico (95973-7824)
PHONE..................................530 895-8633
Fax: 530 895-1501
Laura Larson, *Director*
Ivor Thomas, *Analyst*
EMP: 75
SALES (corp-wide): 121MM **Privately Held**
SIC: 8322 8399 Social services for the handicapped; health & welfare council
PA: Far Northern Coordinating Council On Developmental Disabilities
1900 Churn Creek Rd # 31
Redding CA 96002
530 222-4791

(P-23977) FAR NORTHERN COORDINATING COUN (PA)
Also Called: Far Northern Regional Center
1900 Churn Creek Rd # 31, Redding (96002-0292)
P.O. Box 492418 (96049-2418)
PHONE..................................530 222-4791
Fax: 530 222-8908
Laura L Larson, *Exec Dir*
Cynthia Presidio, *COO*
Michael Mintline, *CFO*
Diane Abraham, *Office Mgr*
Lauren Leisz, *Admin Asst*
EMP: 100

PRODUCTS & SERVICES SECTION
8322 - Individual & Family Social Svcs County (P-24002)

SALES: 121MM **Privately Held**
SIC: **8322** Social services for the handicapped

(P-23978)
FHAR FMLY HSING ADULT RSOURCES
205 W 20th Ave, San Mateo (94403-1302)
PHONE.................................650 573-3341
Dave Carson, *President*
Phil Surdel, *Director*
Evelynda Villarosa, *Manager*
Dave Curson, *Agent*
EMP: 90
SALES (est): 3.9MM **Privately Held**
WEB: www.fhar.org
SIC: **8322** Individual & family services

(P-23979)
FIREFIGHTER CANCER SUPPORT NTW
3460 Fletcher Ave, El Monte (91731-3002)
PHONE.................................866 994-3276
Dan Crow, *President*
Jeffrey Howe, *Treasurer*
Bryan Frieders, *Comms Dir*
EMP: 50
SALES: 411.4K **Privately Held**
SIC: **8322** Individual & family services

(P-23980)
FIRST PLACE FOR YOUTH (PA)
426 17th St Ste 100, Oakland (94612-2814)
PHONE.................................510 272-0979
Sam Cobbs, *Exec Dir*
Wen Lee, *Comms Mgr*
Amber Nave, *Program Mgr*
Alan Palm, *Program Mgr*
Melinda Robinson, *Program Mgr*
EMP: 50 EST: 1999
SALES: 15.9MM **Privately Held**
SIC: **8322** Child related social services

(P-23981)
FOUNDATION FOR EARLY CHILDHOOD (PA)
3360 Flair Dr Ste 100, El Monte (91731-2833)
PHONE.................................626 572-5107
Fax: 626 572-7663
Sharyn Muhammad-Beeker, *CEO*
Cindy Nishi, *General Mgr*
Jaleh Hazian, *Administration*
EMP: 80
SALES: 14.8MM **Privately Held**
SIC: **8322** Child guidance agency

(P-23982)
FRESHLUNCHES INC
19431 Business Center Dr # 24, Northridge (91324-6450)
PHONE.................................310 478-5705
Alan Razzaghi, *CEO*
EMP: 50 EST: 2006
SALES (est): 2.2MM **Privately Held**
SIC: **8322** Meal delivery program

(P-23983)
FRESNO CNTY ECONOMIC OPPORTUNT
Also Called: Fresno Eoc
1900 Mariposa Mall # 300, Fresno (93721-2514)
PHONE.................................559 263-1000
Fax: 559 263-1072
Bryan Angus, *CEO*
EMP: 1200
SALES (corp-wide): 108.8MM **Privately Held**
SIC: **8322** Individual & family services
PA: Fresno County Economic Opportunities Commission
1920 Mariposa Mall # 300
Fresno CA 93721
559 263-1010

(P-23984)
FRESNO CNTY ECONOMIC OPPORTUNT (PA)
Also Called: Fresno Eoc
1920 Mariposa Mall # 300, Fresno (93721-2504)
PHONE.................................559 263-1010
Brian Angus, *CEO*

Vongsavanh Mouanoutoua, *President*
Salam Nalia, *CFO*
Marina Magdaleno, *Treasurer*
Celiese Kai, *Executive*
EMP: 600 EST: 1965
SQ FT: 115,312
SALES: 108.8MM **Privately Held**
SIC: **8322** **8399** Individual & family services; community development groups

(P-23985)
FRESNO RESCUE MISSION INC (PA)
310 G St, Fresno (93706-3421)
P.O. Box 470, West Yellowstone MT (59758-0470)
PHONE.................................559 268-0839
Fax: 559 268-1317
Larry Arce, *CEO*
Bob Brown, *COO*
Emil Rusconi, *Treasurer*
John Avila, *Bd of Directors*
Diane Cantando, *Bd of Directors*
EMP: 50
SQ FT: 29,000
SALES: 5.3MM **Privately Held**
WEB: www.fresnorescuemission.org
SIC: **8322** Emergency shelters; child related social services

(P-23986)
FRIENDLY VALLEY RECRTL ASSN
Also Called: FRIENDLY VILLAGE COMMUNITY ASS
19345 Avenue Of The Oaks, Santa Clarita (91321-1406)
PHONE.................................661 252-3223
Fax: 661 252-7501
Debbie Makaryk, *Manager*
Ruth Gauthier, *President*
Joan Ring, *Manager*
Carol Arnold, *Agent*
EMP: 50
SQ FT: 1,500
SALES: 1.9MM **Privately Held**
SIC: **8322** Senior citizens' center or association

(P-23987)
FRIENDS OF FAMILY
16861 Parthenia St, Northridge (91343-4539)
PHONE.................................818 988-4430
Fax: 818 988-4633
Susan Kaplan, *Exec Dir*
Margie Abel, *Agent*
EMP: 50
SQ FT: 5,500
SALES: 2.2MM **Privately Held**
WEB: www.fofca.org
SIC: **8322** Family counseling services

(P-23988)
FRIENDS OUTSIDE
7272 Murray Dr, Stockton (95210-3339)
P.O. Box 4085 (95204-0085)
PHONE.................................209 955-0701
Gretchen Newby, *Exec Dir*
Melissa Hafoka, *Controller*
EMP: 130
SQ FT: 7,800
SALES: 4.2MM **Privately Held**
WEB: www.friendsoutside.org
SIC: **8322** Individual & family services

(P-23989)
FULL SPECTRUM SERVICES INC
Also Called: Community Actv Rhbltn & Emplym
1570 S Railroad Ave, Crescent City (95531-6821)
P.O. Box 592 (95531-0592)
PHONE.................................707 465-1460
Michael Roach, *President*
EMP: 50
SALES: 31.8K **Privately Held**
SIC: **8322** Individual & family services

(P-23990)
FUTURES EXPLORED INC
Also Called: NIFTY THRIFT
3547 Wilkinson Ln, Lafayette (94549-4322)
PHONE.................................925 284-3240
Fax: 925 284-3291
Will Stanford, *Director*

Robert Bass, *Human Resources*
Christine Imrie, *Director*
EMP: 60
SQ FT: 1,740
SALES: 10MM **Privately Held**
WEB: www.futures-explored.org
SIC: **8322** Association for the handicapped

(P-23991)
FUTURO INFANTIL HISPANO FFA
2227 E Garvey Ave N, West Covina (91791-1500)
PHONE.................................626 339-1824
Fax: 626 277-5517
Oma Velasco-Rodrigues, *President*
Lily Olan, *Administration*
Jose Tejeda, *Finance Mgr*
Robert Quintana, *Supervisor*
EMP: 50
SALES: 6.6MM **Privately Held**
SIC: **8322** Individual & family services

(P-23992)
G & L PENASQUITOS INC
Also Called: Arbors, The
10584 Rancho Carmel Dr, San Diego (92128-3629)
PHONE.................................858 538-0802
Gary Penovich, *Exec Dir*
Geralyn Tacloban, *Executive*
EMP: 65
SQ FT: 48,685
SALES (est): 2.5MM
SALES (corp-wide): 266.6MM **Privately Held**
WEB: www.glrealty.com
SIC: **8322** Individual & family services
PA: G&L Realty Corp, Llc
439 N Bedford Dr
Beverly Hills CA 90210
310 273-9930

(P-23993)
GIARRETTO INSTITUTE
Also Called: Parents United
232 E Gish Rd, San Jose (95112-4706)
PHONE.................................408 453-7616
Fax: 408 453-9064
Jerry Doyle, *CEO*
EMP: 50
SALES (est): 2.5MM **Privately Held**
SIC: **8322** Individual & family services

(P-23994)
GOLDEN GATE REGIONAL CTR INC (PA)
1355 Market St Ste 220, San Francisco (94103-1314)
PHONE.................................415 546-9222
Ron Fell, *CEO*
Chris Rognier, *CFO*
Robert Ramirez, *Treasurer*
Judy Leonard, *Executive Asst*
Rudy Barroco, *Info Tech Mgr*
EMP: 120 EST: 1966
SQ FT: 16,901
SALES: 228.6MM **Privately Held**
SIC: **8322** Referral service for personal & social problems; outreach program

(P-23995)
GOLDEN GATE REGIONAL CTR INC
3130 La Selva St Ste 202, San Mateo (94403-2191)
PHONE.................................650 574-9232
Fax: 650 345-2361
David Beuerman, *General Mgr*
EMP: 65
SALES (corp-wide): 228.6MM **Privately Held**
SIC: **8322** Social services for the handicapped
PA: Golden Gate Regional Center, Inc.
1355 Market St Ste 220
San Francisco CA 94103
415 546-9222

(P-23996)
GOLDEN LIVING LLC
Also Called: Beverly Healthcare
24100 Monroe Ave, Murrieta (92562-9507)
PHONE.................................951 600-4640
Fax: 951 600-4738
Doug Lendoff, *Manager*
Catherine Broyles, *Administration*

Elia Lopez, *Personnel*
Roseanna D Rosario, *Teacher Per Dir*
Fenita Nieto, *Nursing Dir*
EMP: 100
SALES (corp-wide): 1.6B **Privately Held**
WEB: www.nwbeccorp.com
SIC: **8322** Rehabilitation services
PA: Golden Living Llc
5220 Tennyson Pkwy # 400
Plano TX 75024
972 372-6300

(P-23997)
GOOD SAMARITAN SHELTER
245 Inger Dr Ste 103, Santa Maria (93454-8670)
PHONE.................................805 346-8185
Fax: 805 346-8656
Sylvia Barnard, *Director*
EMP: 60
SQ FT: 2,400
SALES: 4MM **Privately Held**
SIC: **8322** Emergency shelters

(P-23998)
GREATER LOS ANGELES AGENCY
2239 Norwalk Ave, Los Angeles (90041-2901)
PHONE.................................323 478-8000
Patricia Hughes, *CEO*
EMP: 70
SALES: 7.1MM **Privately Held**
SIC: **8322** Individual & family services

(P-23999)
H E L P INC
53 S 6th St, Banning (92220-4809)
PHONE.................................951 922-2305
Al Silva, *President*
Nancy Guthrie, *Admin Sec*
EMP: 85
SQ FT: 3,000
SALES (est): 186.6K **Privately Held**
SIC: **8322** Individual & family services

(P-24000)
HALLMARK REHABILITATION GP LLC
27442 Portola Pkwy # 200, El Toro (92610-2822)
PHONE.................................949 282-5900
Fax: 949 282-5859
Jose Lynch,
Jimmy Sims,
Mark Whartley,
Laurie Thomas, *Mng Member*
Greg Tallarida, *Director*
EMP: 1200
SQ FT: 10,000
SALES (est): 21.9MM **Privately Held**
WEB: www.hallmarkrehabinc.com
SIC: **8322** Rehabilitation services

(P-24001)
HAMILTON FAMILIES
1631 Hayes St, San Francisco (94117-1326)
PHONE.................................415 409-2100
Rosa Caspaneda, *Director*
Jaime Aragon, *Vice Chairman*
Jane Chamblee, *Executive*
Jeff Kositsky, *Exec Dir*
Patricia Babiraz, *Administration*
EMP: 65
SALES: 8.8MM **Privately Held**
WEB: www.hamiltonfamilycenter.org
SIC: **8322** Emergency shelters

(P-24002)
HANFORD JOINT UN HIGH SCHL DST
Also Called: Hanford Adult School
905 Campus Dr, Hanford (93230-3552)
PHONE.................................559 583-5905
Fax: 559 589-9564
Heather Keran, *Principal*
Irma Castillo, *Admin Asst*
Judy Willett, *Assistant*
EMP: 56
SALES (corp-wide): 26.8MM **Privately Held**
SIC: **8322** Adult day care center

8322 - Individual & Family Social Svcs County (P-24003)

PA: Hanford Joint Union High School District
823 W Lacey Blvd
Hanford CA 93230
559 583-5901

(P-24003)
HATHAWAY RESOURCE CENTER
5701 S Eastrn Ave Ste 550, Los Angeles (90040)
PHONE...................323 837-0838
Many Galledos, *Branch Mgr*
EMP: 50
SALES (corp-wide): 3.1MM **Privately Held**
SIC: 8322 Family counseling services
PA: Hathaway Resource Center
840 N Avenue 66
Los Angeles CA 90042
323 257-9600

(P-24004)
HELP AT HOME INC
4535 Mcuri Flat Rd Ste 2h, Placerville (95667)
PHONE...................916 933-9050
Fax: 530 622-4055
Marie Harlow, *Director*
EMP: 65
SALES: 1.2MM **Privately Held**
WEB: www.milner-fenwick.com
SIC: 8322 8082 Senior citizens' center or association; home health care services

(P-24005)
HELP FOR THE HURTING INC
Also Called: Helping Hands Pantry
2205 S Artesia St, San Bernardino (92408-3906)
P.O. Box 1224, Redlands (92373-0401)
PHONE...................909 796-4222
Paul Dickau, *Exec Dir*
EMP: 90 **EST:** 2009
SALES: 1.6MM **Privately Held**
SIC: 8322 Individual & family services

(P-24006)
HELP HOSPITALIZED VETERANS II
36585 Penfield Ln, Winchester (92596-9672)
PHONE...................951 926-4500
Mike Lynch, *Exec Dir*
EMP: 65 **EST:** 1971
SQ FT: 25,000
SALES: 31MM **Privately Held**
WEB: www.hhv.org
SIC: 8322 Individual & family services

(P-24007)
HELPLINE YOUTH COUNSELING (PA)
14181 Telegraph Rd, Whittier (90604-2554)
PHONE...................562 273-0722
Fax: 562 864-4596
Jeff Farber, *Exec Dir*
Deepak Nanda, *Ch of Bd*
Jeffrey Fleischer, *Executive*
Laurie Pieper, *Finance*
Debbie J MA, *Program Dir*
EMP: 50
SQ FT: 9,000
SALES: 3.4MM **Privately Held**
WEB: www.vfnet.com
SIC: 8322 Family (marriage) counseling; social service center

(P-24008)
HOME FOR JEWISH PARENTS
Also Called: Reutlinger Community
4000 Camino Tassajara, Danville (94506-4711)
PHONE...................925 964-2062
Fax: 925 648-2801
Jay Zimmer, *CEO*
Janice Corran, *Exec Dir*
Rhoda Verzosa, *Admin Asst*
Bev Harms, *Nursing Dir*
Judy Greif,
EMP: 160
SALES: 15.2MM **Privately Held**
WEB: www.rcjl.org
SIC: 8322 Individual & family services

(P-24009)
HOMEBOY INDUSTRIES (PA)
Also Called: HOMEBOY BAKERY
130 Bruno St, Los Angeles (90012-1815)
PHONE...................323 526-1254
Fax: 323 526-1257
Greg Boyle, *Exec Dir*
John Brady, *Ch of Bd*
Jack Faherty, *CFO*
Carrie Bollwinkle, *Exec Dir*
James Horton, *Admin Asst*
EMP: 270
SQ FT: 3,690
SALES: 13.3MM **Privately Held**
SIC: 8322 Rehabilitation services; social service center

(P-24010)
HOMEBRIDGE INC
Also Called: IHSS Consortium, The
1035 Market St Ste L1, San Francisco (94103-1666)
PHONE...................415 255-2079
Fax: 415 255-0679
Gay Kaplan, *CEO*
Margaret Baran, *Principal*
Mark Burns, *Principal*
Debra J Dolch, *Principal*
Donna Calame, *Exec Dir*
EMP: 500
SALES: 20.5MM **Privately Held**
SIC: 8322 Individual & family services; homemakers' service

(P-24011)
HOMEFRST SVCS SANTA CLARA CNTY
Also Called: EHC LIFEBUILDERS
507 Valley Way, Milpitas (95035-4105)
PHONE...................408 539-2100
Jennifer Niklaus, *CEO*
Daniel Mount, *Treasurer*
Philip Gregory, *Exec Dir*
Byron Scordelis, *Exec Dir*
Tonya Clarke, *Program Mgr*
EMP: 115
SALES: 10.6MM **Privately Held**
SIC: 8322 Individual & family services

(P-24012)
HOMELESS PRENATAL PROGRAM
33 Middle Point Rd, San Francisco (94124-4439)
PHONE...................415 546-6756
Martha Ryan, *Director*
Sharon Bechtol, *Volunteer Dir*
Beverly Ashworth, *General Mgr*
Carol Brennan, *Office Mgr*
Susie Mattos, *Project Mgr*
EMP: 50
SALES: 7.1MM **Privately Held**
WEB: www.homelessprenatal.org
SIC: 8322 Individual & family services

(P-24013)
HOPE OF VALLEY RESCUE MISSION
8165 San Fernando Rd, Sun Valley (91352-4063)
P.O. Box 7609, Mission Hills (91346-7609)
PHONE...................818 392-0020
Ken Craft, *President*
Michael Klausman, *Ch of Bd*
David Faustina, *COO*
Chris Delaplane, *Treasurer*
Jin Pak, *Bd of Directors*
EMP: 54
SQ FT: 22,000
SALES: 3.2MM **Privately Held**
SIC: 8322 Individual & family services

(P-24014)
HUMAN OPTIONS INC
1901 Newport Blvd Ste 240, Costa Mesa (92627-2294)
PHONE...................949 757-3635
Maricela Rios, *Branch Mgr*
EMP: 50
SALES (corp-wide): 3.6MM **Privately Held**
SIC: 8322 Individual & family services

PA: Human Options, Inc
5540 Trabuco Rd Ste 100
Irvine CA 92620
949 737-5242

(P-24015)
HUMAN SERVICES ASSOCIATION (PA)
6800 Florence Ave, Bell (90201-4957)
PHONE...................562 806-5400
Fax: 562 806-5394
Susanne Sundberg, *Principal*
Darren Dunaway, *Associate Dir*
Celia Marquez, *VP Mktg*
Rosie Ramos, *Senior Mgr*
Maria Velasquez, *Senior Mgr*
EMP: 75
SQ FT: 10,000
SALES: 15.9MM **Privately Held**
WEB: www.hsala.org
SIC: 8322 Community center; senior citizens' center or association

(P-24016)
HUMBOLDT COMMNTY ACCSS RESRC
Also Called: Baybridge Employment Services
415 7th St, Eureka (95501-1802)
PHONE...................707 444-9631
Fax: 707 443-2836
Ross Jantz, *Principal*
EMP: 56
SALES (corp-wide): 4.2MM **Privately Held**
WEB: www.thestudioonline.org
SIC: 8322 Referral service for personal & social problems
PA: Humboldt Community Access And Resource Center
1707 E St Ste 2
Eureka CA 95501
707 443-7077

(P-24017)
HUMBOLDT SENIOR RESOURCE CTR (PA)
1910 California St, Eureka (95501-2899)
PHONE...................707 443-9747
Joyce Hayes, *Exec Dir*
Monique Belanger, *Finance*
Tina Taylor, *Food Svc Dir*
EMP: 60
SQ FT: 14,000
SALES: 5.4MM **Privately Held**
SIC: 8322 8741 Senior citizens' center or association; management services

(P-24018)
HUNTINGTON PK POLICE LEAGUE
Also Called: HUNTINGTON PARK POLICE DEPARTM
6542 Miles Ave, Huntington Park (90255-4318)
PHONE...................323 584-6254
Fax: 323 584-1137
Paul Wadley, *President*
Jorge Cisneros, *President*
Lily Garcia, *Administration*
EMP: 75
SALES: 11.9K **Privately Held**
SIC: 8322 Outreach program

(P-24019)
IN-ROADS CREATIVE PROGRAMS
9057 Arrow Rte Ste 120, Rancho Cucamonga (91730-4452)
PHONE...................909 989-9944
Sharon Barton, *Branch Mgr*
EMP: 370
SALES (corp-wide): 13.4MM **Privately Held**
SIC: 8322 Individual & family services
PA: In-Roads Creative Programs, Inc
7955 Webster St Ste 7
Highland CA 92346
909 864-1551

(P-24020)
IN-ROADS CREATIVE PROGRAMS
1951 E Saint Andrews Dr, Ontario (91761-6447)
PHONE...................909 947-9142
Sharon Barton, *Branch Mgr*
EMP: 278
SALES (corp-wide): 13.4MM **Privately Held**
SIC: 8322 Individual & family services
PA: In-Roads Creative Programs, Inc
7955 Webster St Ste 7
Highland CA 92346
909 864-1551

(P-24021)
IN-ROADS CREATIVE PROGRAMS
26890 Cherry Hills Blvd, Sun City (92586-2574)
PHONE...................951 672-1800
EMP: 93
SALES (corp-wide): 13.4MM **Privately Held**
SIC: 8322 Individual & family services
PA: In-Roads Creative Programs, Inc
7955 Webster St Ste 7
Highland CA 92346
909 864-1551

(P-24022)
IN2VISION PROGRAMS LLC
13601 Whittier Blvd, Whittier (90605-1902)
PHONE...................562 789-8888
Maria Del Carmen Torres, *Mng Member*
Cesar Torres, *Mng Member*
EMP: 51 **EST:** 2009
SALES (est): 2.1MM **Privately Held**
SIC: 8322 Social services for the handicapped

(P-24023)
INCLUSION SERVICES LLC
13225 Philadelphia St E, Whittier (90601-4321)
PHONE...................562 945-2000
Cesar Torres, *Mng Member*
Erica Huerta, *Admin Asst*
Flor Ulloa, *Human Res Mgr*
Israel Ibenez, *Mng Member*
EMP: 103
SQ FT: 1,200
SALES (est): 5.8MM **Privately Held**
SIC: 8322 8331 Social services for the handicapped; skill training center

(P-24024)
INDEPENDENT OPTIONS
Also Called: Harbor Village II
2532 Santa Catalina Dr # 104, Costa Mesa (92626-6880)
PHONE...................714 434-1175
Dennis Mattson, *Owner*
EMP: 100
SALES (est): 1.8MM **Privately Held**
SIC: 8322 8361 Social services for the handicapped; residential care

(P-24025)
INDIVIDUALS NOW
Also Called: Social Advocates For Youth
2447 Summerfield Rd, Santa Rosa (95405-7815)
PHONE...................707 544-3299
Fax: 707 544-6837
Matt Martin, *CEO*
Katrina Thurman, *COO*
Dave Koressel, *CFO*
Cat Cvengros, *Officer*
Frances Caballo, *Exec Dir*
EMP: 55
SALES: 7.5MM **Privately Held**
SIC: 8322 Child guidance agency; youth center

(P-24026)
INLAND VALLEY DRUG & ALCOHOL (PA)
916 N Mountain Ave Ste A, Upland (91786-3658)
PHONE...................909 932-1069
Fax: 909 868-1432
Stacy Smith, *CEO*
Sandra Romero, *Principal*
Laurie Figueroa, *Finance*
EMP: 51
SALES: 4.5MM **Privately Held**
WEB: www.ivdars.org
SIC: 8322 Alcoholism counseling, nontreatment

PRODUCTS & SERVICES SECTION
8322 - Individual & Family Social Svcs County (P-24050)

(P-24027)
INSIDE OUTDOORS FOUNDATION
8755 Santiago Canyon Rd, Silverado (92676-9758)
P.O. Box 9050, Costa Mesa (92628-9050)
PHONE..................714 708-3885
Manny Kiesser, *President*
Kimberely Casey, *Development*
Lori Kiesser, *Manager*
Stephanie Smith, *Manager*
EMP: 200
SQ FT: 3,000
SALES: 910.2K **Privately Held**
SIC: 8322 Outreach program

(P-24028)
INSTITUTE ON AGING
Also Called: Irene Swindell's Adult Day Car
3698 California St, San Francisco (94118-1702)
PHONE..................415 600-2690
Cindy Kauffman, *Administration*
EMP: 250
SALES (corp-wide): 30.1MM **Privately Held**
SIC: 8322 Individual & family services
PA: Institute On Aging
3575 Geary Blvd
San Francisco CA 94118
415 750-4101

(P-24029)
INSTITUTE ON AGING (PA)
Also Called: Mssp
3575 Geary Blvd, San Francisco (94118-3212)
PHONE..................415 750-4101
Fax: 415 750-4179
J Thomas Briody, *President*
Cindy Kaufmann, *COO*
Roxana Blades, *CFO*
Roxana Tsougarakis, *CFO*
Ruth Kasle, *Chief Mktg Ofcr*
EMP: 100
SQ FT: 10,000
SALES: 30.1MM **Privately Held**
SIC: 8322 Geriatric social service

(P-24030)
INTERCOMMUNITY CHILD
10155 Colima Rd, Whittier (90603-2042)
PHONE..................562 692-0383
Charlene Dimas, *CEO*
EMP: 70
SALES (est): 655.1K **Privately Held**
SIC: 8322 Child related social services

(P-24031)
INTERFACE COMMUNITY (PA)
Also Called: INTERFACE CHILDREN FAMILY SERV
4001 Mission Oaks Blvd I, Camarillo (93012-5121)
PHONE..................805 485-6114
Fax: 805 389-0789
Charles T Watson, *President*
Dale Stoeber, *CFO*
Terryl Miller,
Erik Sternad, *Exec Dir*
Fernando Salguero, *General Mgr*
EMP: 86
SQ FT: 3,000
SALES: 7.7MM **Privately Held**
WEB: www.icfs.org
SIC: 8322 Family service agency

(P-24032)
INTERNATIONAL INST LOS ANGELES (PA)
3845 Selig Pl, Los Angeles (90031-3143)
PHONE..................323 224-3800
E Stephen Voss, *President*
Stephen J Holt, *Vice Chairman*
Susan Eckert, *VP Admin*
Sandra Rosas, *VP Finance*
Robert Foss, *Director*
EMP: 52 **EST:** 1935
SQ FT: 18,000
SALES: 14.6MM **Privately Held**
WEB: www.iilosangeles.org
SIC: 8322 Family service agency

(P-24033)
INTERNATIONAL MEDICAL CORPS (PA)
12400 Wilshire Blvd # 1500, Los Angeles (90025-1030)
PHONE..................310 826-7800
Fax: 310 442-6622
Robert Simon, *Chairman*
Nancy Aossey, *President*
Sarah Ahrens, *Trustee*
Elizabeth Apopo, *Officer*
John Gayflor, *Officer*
EMP: 63
SALES: 232.6MM **Privately Held**
WEB: www.imc-la.com
SIC: 8322 Disaster service

(P-24034)
INTERNTNAL RSCUE COMMITTEE INC
5348 University Ave # 205, San Diego (92105-8025)
PHONE..................619 641-7510
Fax: 619 641-7520
Roisin Wisneski, *Branch Mgr*
Lucy Carrigan, *Officer*
Joseph Jok, *Case Mgr*
Kasra Movahedi, *Manager*
EMP: 63
SALES (corp-wide): 688.9MM **Privately Held**
SIC: 8322 Social service center
PA: International Rescue Committee, Inc.
122 E 42nd St Fl 12
New York NY 10168
212 551-3000

(P-24035)
INTERPRSNAL DVLPMNTAL FCLTTORS
Also Called: IDS
891 Worcester Ave Apt 3, Pasadena (91104-4258)
PHONE..................626 793-8967
Dorothea A Bradley, *CEO*
EMP: 71
SALES (est): 630.9K **Privately Held**
SIC: 8322 Association for the handicapped; meal delivery program

(P-24036)
INVENTUS POWER INC
Also Called: ICC-NEXERGY, INC.
17672 Armstrong Ave, Irvine (92614-5728)
PHONE..................949 553-0097
Chris Turner, *Vice Pres*
EMP: 213 **Privately Held**
SIC: 8322 Community center
PA: Inventus Power, Inc.
1200 Internationale Pkwy
Woodridge IL 60517

(P-24037)
ISLAMIC RELIEF USA
6131 Orangethorpe Ave # 450, Buena Park (90620-4903)
PHONE..................714 676-1300
Abed Ayoub, *Branch Mgr*
Mohammad Abdelmagd, *Principal*
Ahmed El-Bendary, *Principal*
Almas Talib, *Principal*
Pinky Talib, *Controller*
EMP: 70
SALES (corp-wide): 65.2MM **Privately Held**
SIC: 8322 Individual & family services
PA: Islamic Relief Usa
3655 Wheeler Ave
Alexandria VA 22304
703 370-7202

(P-24038)
J GELT CORPORATION
Also Called: Casa Pacifica Adult Day H
1424 30th St Ste C, San Diego (92154-3417)
PHONE..................619 424-8181
Luba Vaisman, *President*
Mark Woodruff, *Director*
Tatyana Cohen, *Assistant VP*
EMP: 50
SQ FT: 15,000
SALES (est): 2MM **Privately Held**
SIC: 8322 Adult day care center

(P-24039)
JACOBS CSHMAN SAN DIEGO FD BNK
9850 Distribution Ave, San Diego (92121-2320)
PHONE..................858 527-1419
James Floros, *President*
Casey Castillo, *CFO*
Stephen M Brigandi, *Bd of Directors*
Marc Farrar, *Vice Pres*
Liz Sheahan, *Vice Pres*
EMP: 50
SALES: 33.2MM **Privately Held**
SIC: 8322 Individual & family services

(P-24040)
JAMISON CHILDRENS HOME
1010 Shalimar Dr, Bakersfield (93306-5633)
P.O. Box 511 (93302-0511)
PHONE..................661 334-3500
Carl Guilford, *Director*
EMP: 60
SALES (est): 738K **Privately Held**
SIC: 8322 Individual & family services

(P-24041)
JANUS OF SANTA CRUZ
200 7th Ave Ste 150, Santa Cruz (95062-4669)
PHONE..................831 462-1060
Fax: 831 462-4970
Rod Libbey, *Exec Dir*
Shelley Hull, *Admin Asst*
Guillermo Rodriguez, *Project Mgr*
Scott Barnes, *Psychologist*
Robin Oakey, *Psychologist*
EMP: 100
SALES: 5.5MM **Privately Held**
WEB: www.janussc.org
SIC: 8322 Rehabilitation services

(P-24042)
JELANI HOUSE INC
1601 Quesada Ave, San Francisco (94124-2334)
PHONE..................415 822-5977
Fax: 415 822-5943
Margaret Gold, *Director*
EMP: 50
SQ FT: 10,000
SALES: 2.2MM **Privately Held**
SIC: 8322 Individual & family services

(P-24043)
JEWISH COMMUNITY CTR LONG BCH
Also Called: ALPERT JEWISH COMMUNITY CENTRE
3801 E Willow St, Long Beach (90815-1734)
PHONE..................562 426-7601
Gordon Lentzner, *President*
Michael Witenstin, *Exec Dir*
Katie Clowdus, *Admin Asst*
Lindsey Weaver, *Admin Asst*
Jarred Xavier, *Admin Asst*
EMP: 150
SQ FT: 90,000
SALES: 5.5MM **Privately Held**
SIC: 8322 Community center

(P-24044)
JEWISH FAMILY AND CHLD SVCS (PA)
Also Called: CLEANERIFIC
2150 Post St, San Francisco (94115-3508)
P.O. Box 159004 (94115-9004)
PHONE..................415 449-1200
Fax: 415 820-7234
Anita Friedman, *Exec Dir*
Michael R Zent, *CEO*
Marga Dusedau, *CFO*
Javier Favela, *CFO*
Frank Jacobson, *Vice Pres*
EMP: 80
SALES: 30.5MM **Privately Held**
SIC: 8322 Family service agency

(P-24045)
JEWISH FAMILY AND CHLD SVCS
Also Called: Parents Place
200 Channing Ave, Palo Alto (94301-2720)
PHONE..................650 688-3030
Fax: 650 330-0866
EMP: 337
SALES (corp-wide): 30.5MM **Privately Held**
SIC: 8322 Family counseling services
PA: Jewish Family And Children's Services
2150 Post St
San Francisco CA 94115
415 449-1200

(P-24046)
JEWISH FAMILY SVC LOS ANGELES (PA)
Also Called: Jewish Free Loan Association
6505 Wilshire Blvd # 715, Los Angeles (90048-4906)
PHONE..................323 761-8800
Fax: 323 651-1332
Paul Castro, *CEO*
Tran Maggard, *CFO*
Todd Sosna, *Senior VP*
Jennifer Levitt, *Comms Dir*
Karen Leaf, *Exec Dir*
EMP: 50
SQ FT: 7,600
SALES: 33MM **Privately Held**
WEB: www.jewishla.com
SIC: 8322 Social service center

(P-24047)
JEWISH FAMILY SVC LOS ANGELES
Also Called: Valley Stre Frnt Jwsh Fmly Svc
12821 Victory Blvd, North Hollywood (91606-3012)
PHONE..................818 984-0276
Fax: 323 766-3926
Karen Leaf, *Director*
EMP: 72
SALES (corp-wide): 33MM **Privately Held**
WEB: www.jewishla.com
SIC: 8322 5331 Individual & family services; variety stores
PA: Jewish Family Service Of Los Angeles
6505 Wilshire Blvd # 715
Los Angeles CA 90048
323 761-8800

(P-24048)
JEWISH FAMILY SVC LOS ANGELES
Senior Citizens Center
330 N Fairfax Ave, Los Angeles (90036-2109)
PHONE..................323 937-5900
Doreen Klee, *Owner*
EMP: 50
SALES (corp-wide): 33MM **Privately Held**
WEB: www.jewishla.com
SIC: 8322 Old age assistance
PA: Jewish Family Service Of Los Angeles
6505 Wilshire Blvd # 715
Los Angeles CA 90048
323 761-8800

(P-24049)
JEWISH STUDENT UNION
9831 W Pico Blvd Ste 101, Los Angeles (90035-4712)
PHONE..................310 229-9006
Jason Ciment, *President*
Craig Ackreman, *Treasurer*
EMP: 100
SQ FT: 6,088
SALES: 966.9K **Privately Held**
WEB: www.jewishinlosangeles.com
SIC: 8322 Public welfare center

(P-24050)
JON K TAKATA CORPORATION (PA)
Also Called: Restoration Management Company
4142 Point Eden Way, Hayward (94545-3703)
PHONE..................510 315-5400
Jon Takata, *President*
Tyler Hampton, *Exec VP*
Alicia Arias, *Project Mgr*
Matt Stimson, *Accounting Mgr*
Rodney Day, *Manager*
EMP: 70
SQ FT: 100,000

8322 - Individual & Family Social Svcs County (P-24051)

SALES (est): 31.4MM **Privately Held**
WEB: www.restorationmanagement.com
SIC: **8322** 1799 4959 Disaster service; asbestos removal & encapsulation; environmental cleanup services

(P-24051)
JONI AND FRIENDS (PA)
30009 Ladyface Ct, Agoura (91301-2583)
PHONE..................................818 707-5664
Fax: 818 707-2391
Joni E Tada, *CEO*
Chuck Musfeldt, *Bd of Directors*
George Panga, *Bd of Directors*
Colin Reeves, *Bd of Directors*
Terry Winkler, *Bd of Directors*
EMP: 84
SQ FT: 30,000
SALES: 21.2MM **Privately Held**
SIC: **8322** Association for the handicapped

(P-24052)
KAINOS HOME & TRAINING CTR
Also Called: Kainos Work Activity Ctr
2761 Fair Oaks Ave Ste A, Redwood City (94063-3540)
PHONE..................................650 361-1355
Fax: 650 361-1616
Christen Rodgers, *Manager*
Kristen Uthman, *Program Mgr*
EMP: 50
SALES (corp-wide): 5.2MM **Privately Held**
WEB: www.kainosusa.org
SIC: **8322** Individual & family services
PA: Kainos Home & Training Center For Developmentally Disabled Adults
3631 Jefferson Ave
Redwood City CA
650 363-2423

(P-24053)
KEDREN COMMUNITY HLTH CTR INC
231 W Vernon Ave, Los Angeles (90037-2700)
PHONE..................................562 335-9601
EMP: 120
SALES (corp-wide): 55.3MM **Privately Held**
SIC: **8322** Community center
PA: Kedren Community Health Center, Inc.
4211 Avalon Blvd
Los Angeles CA 90011
323 233-0425

(P-24054)
KEDREN COMMUNITY HLTH CTR INC
3800 S Figueroa St, Los Angeles (90037-1206)
PHONE..................................323 524-0634
John Griffith, *President*
Kathy Acosta-Smith, *Human Res Dir*
EMP: 199
SALES (corp-wide): 55.3MM **Privately Held**
SIC: **8322** Community center
PA: Kedren Community Health Center, Inc.
4211 Avalon Blvd
Los Angeles CA 90011
323 233-0425

(P-24055)
KERN REGIONAL CENTER (PA)
3200 N Sillect Ave, Bakersfield (93308-6333)
P.O. Box 2536 (93303-2536)
PHONE..................................661 327-8531
Michal Clark, *Exec Dir*
Duane Law, *CEO*
Jerry Bowman, *CFO*
Diane Macchi, *Human Res Mgr*
Tom Moore, *Maintenance Dir*
EMP: 147 EST: 1971
SQ FT: 33,000
SALES: 147.9MM **Privately Held**
SIC: **8322** Association for the handicapped

(P-24056)
KINGS COMMUNITY ACTION O (PA)
1130 N 11th Ave, Hanford (93230-3608)
PHONE..................................559 582-4386
Fax: 559 582-1536

David Droker, *Exec Dir*
Mona Andres, *Info Tech Mgr*
David Lozano, *Finance Dir*
Janet Gordon, *Accountant*
Saul Leal, *Opers Staff*
EMP: 100
SQ FT: 15,000
SALES: 16.5MM **Privately Held**
SIC: **8322** 8399 Individual & family services; antipoverty board

(P-24057)
KINGS REHABILITATION CENTER (PA)
490 E Hanford Armona Rd, Hanford (93230-6129)
P.O. Box 719 (93232-0719)
PHONE..................................559 582-9234
Fax: 559 582-9234
Carol Rogers, *Marketing Staff*
Sherrie Martin, *Executive*
Steve Mendoza, *Exec Dir*
Veronica Chavarin, *MIS Dir*
Carol Ropers, *Agent*
EMP: 57
SQ FT: 13,000
SALES: 5.2MM **Privately Held**
WEB: www.kingsrehab.com
SIC: **8322** 8361 Rehabilitation services; rehabilitation center, residential: health care incidental

(P-24058)
KINSHIP CENTER
18302 Irvine Blvd Ste 300, Tustin (92780-3437)
PHONE..................................714 979-2365
Josie Romehiod, *Director*
Sharon Kaplanroszia, *Exec Dir*
Sully Thamu, *Sales Executive*
EMP: 100
SALES (corp-wide): 6.7MM **Privately Held**
SIC: **8322** 8093 Adoption services; mental health clinic, outpatient
PA: Kinship Center
124 River Rd
Salinas CA 93908
831 455-9965

(P-24059)
KOREAN COMMUNITY SERVICES INC
Also Called: Kc Services
8633 Knott Ave, Buena Park (90620-3852)
PHONE..................................714 527-6561
Ellen Ahn, *Exec Dir*
Kay Ahn, *CFO*
EMP: 50
SALES: 2.7MM **Privately Held**
SIC: **8322** 8069 Social service center; drug addiction rehabilitation hospital

(P-24060)
KOREAN HEALTH EDUCATION (PA)
Also Called: KHEIR
3727 W 6th St Ste 210, Los Angeles (90020-5108)
PHONE..................................213 427-4000
Erin K Pak, *CEO*
Jenny Paik, *Executive*
Laura Jeon, *Exec Dir*
Laura Dellacruz, *Opers Staff*
EMP: 59
SQ FT: 800
SALES: 5.6MM **Privately Held**
SIC: **8322** 8011 Individual & family services; offices & clinics of medical doctors

(P-24061)
LA ASOCIACION NACIONAL PRO PER
Also Called: National Assn For Hispanic
1452 W Temple St Ste 100, Los Angeles (90026-5649)
PHONE..................................213 202-5900
Fax: 213 202-5905
Zecia Soto, *Principal*
EMP: 350
SALES (corp-wide): 12.7MM **Privately Held**
SIC: **8322** 7361 8611 Social service center; employment agencies; business associations

PA: La Asociacion Nacional Pro Personas Mayores
234 E Colo Blvd Ste 300
Pasadena CA 91101
626 564-1988

(P-24062)
LA FAMILIA COUNSELING CENTER
5523 34th St, Sacramento (95820-4725)
PHONE..................................916 452-3601
Fax: 916 452-7628
Rachell R Rios, *Exec Dir*
Phylis Rodriquez, *Office Mgr*
Nick Willow, *Info Tech Mgr*
Orelia Bermudez, *Director*
Lynnaia Keune, *Manager*
EMP: 60
SALES: 3.4MM **Privately Held**
WEB: www.lafcc.com
SIC: **8322** General counseling services

(P-24063)
LA MAESTRA FAMILY CLINIC INC (PA)
Also Called: La Maestra Community Hlth Ctrs
4060 Fairmount Ave, San Diego (92105-1608)
PHONE..................................619 584-1612
Zara Marselian, *CEO*
Carlos Hanessian, *Ch of Bd*
Alejandrina Areizaga, *COO*
Mary David, *CFO*
Alex Pantoja, *CFO*
EMP: 115
SQ FT: 5,000
SALES: 24.2MM **Privately Held**
SIC: **8322** Individual & family services

(P-24064)
LAURAS HOUSE
999 Corporate Dr Ste 225, Mission Viejo (92694-2156)
PHONE..................................949 361-3775
Margaret Bayston, *Exec Dir*
Sandra Condello, *Principal*
EMP: 56
SALES: 4MM **Privately Held**
WEB: www.laurashouse.net
SIC: **8322** Crisis center

(P-24065)
LIFE STEPS FOUNDATION INC
500 E 4th St, Long Beach (90802-2501)
PHONE..................................562 436-0751
Fax: 562 437-0901
Kristine Engels, *Director*
Sharon Jones, *Exec Dir*
Dave Nelson, *Manager*
Robert Turner, *Manager*
EMP: 70
SALES (corp-wide): 3.9MM **Privately Held**
WEB: www.lifestepsfoundation.org
SIC: **8322** 8399 Individual & family services; community development groups
PA: Life Steps Foundation, Inc.
5839 Green Valley Cir # 204
Culver City CA 90230
310 306-4746

(P-24066)
LIFEMOVES (PA)
181 Constitution Dr, Menlo Park (94025-1106)
PHONE..................................650 685-5880
Bruce Ives, *CEO*
Brian Greenberg, *Vice Pres*
Katherine Finnigan, *Principal*
Marie Chiesa, *Accounting Mgr*
Carolyn Hooper, *Marketing Staff*
EMP: 50
SALES: 18.8MM **Privately Held**
SIC: **8322** Individual & family services

(P-24067)
LIFESTYLES SENIOR HOUSING MAN
Also Called: Meadows Senior Living, The
9325 E Stockton Blvd, Elk Grove (95624-1282)
PHONE..................................916 714-3755
Fax: 916 686-4389
Dan Carsel, *Manager*
Kelly Kolodziejz, *Exec Dir*

EMP: 60 **Privately Held**
SIC: **8322** 8052 Geriatric social service; intermediate care facilities
PA: Lifestyles Senior Housing Managers Llc
7600 Ne 41st St Ste 330
Vancouver WA 98662

(P-24068)
LIONS CLUB HOUSE
417 Lincoln Ave, Woodland (95695-3926)
PHONE..................................530 661-3104
Norm Campbell, *Principal*
EMP: 50
SALES (est): 728.8K **Privately Held**
SIC: **8322** Individual & family services

(P-24069)
LIVHOME INC (PA)
5670 Wilshire Blvd # 500, Los Angeles (90036-5679)
PHONE..................................800 807-5854
Toll Free:..................................877 -
Fax: 323 933-5126
Mike Nicholson, *Ch of Bd*
Danny Gampe, *CFO*
Cody D Legler, *Officer*
Maureen Kehan, *Vice Pres*
Chris Foster, *Exec Dir*
EMP: 1299
SQ FT: 7,454
SALES (est): 64MM **Privately Held**
SIC: **8322** Geriatric social service

(P-24070)
LOS ANGELES REGIONAL FOOD BANK
1734 E 41st St, Vernon (90058-1502)
PHONE..................................323 234-3030
Fax: 323 234-0943
Michael Flood, *President*
May Duong, *Volunteer Dir*
Jeff McIlvain, *Volunteer Dir*
Anna Raguindin, *Volunteer Dir*
Czarina Luna, *CFO*
EMP: 120
SQ FT: 100,000
SALES: 79.4MM **Privately Held**
SIC: **8322** Meal delivery program

(P-24071)
LOS ANGELES UNIFIED SCHOOL DST
1157 S Berendo St, Los Angeles (90006-3301)
PHONE..................................213 739-5600
Mary Argandona, *Tech/Comp Coord*
Susan Diamond, *Librarian*
Marcia Aldana, *Assistant*
EMP: 130
SALES (corp-wide): 4.4B **Privately Held**
SIC: **8322** Individual & family services
PA: Los Angeles Unified School District
333 S Beaudry Ave Ste 209
Los Angeles CA 90017
213 241-1000

(P-24072)
LOS ANGELES UNIFIED SCHOOL DST
Also Called: Westchester Emerson Cmnty
8810 Emerson Ave, Los Angeles (90045-3609)
PHONE..................................310 258-2000
Patricia Colby, *Principal*
Ray Millette, *Assistant*
EMP: 150
SALES (corp-wide): 4.4B **Privately Held**
WEB: www.lausd.k12.ca.us
SIC: **8322** Adult day care center
PA: Los Angeles Unified School District
333 S Beaudry Ave Ste 209
Los Angeles CA 90017
213 241-1000

(P-24073)
LOS ANGELES UNIFIED SCHOOL DST
Also Called: Marine Avenue Adult Center
1468 N Marine Ave, Wilmington (90744-2046)
PHONE..................................310 518-1128
Lanny Nelms, *Principal*
EMP: 109

PRODUCTS & SERVICES SECTION
8322 - Individual & Family Social Svcs County (P-24097)

SALES (corp-wide): 4.4B **Privately Held**
WEB: www.lausd.k12.ca.us
SIC: **8322** Adult day care center
PA: Los Angeles Unified School District
333 S Beaudry Ave Ste 209
Los Angeles CA 90017
213 241-1000

(P-24074)
LOS ANGLES CHILD GDANCE CLINIC (PA)
3031 S Vermont Ave, Los Angeles (90007-3033)
PHONE.................................323 766-2360
Fax: 323 766-3636
Elizabeth Pfromm, *President*
John R Liebman, *Treasurer*
Peter Nylund, *Treasurer*
Teresa Leingang, *Vice Pres*
Tiffany T Rodriguez, *Vice Pres*
EMP: 110
SALES: 19.5MM **Privately Held**
WEB: www.lacgc.net
SIC: **8322** Child guidance agency

(P-24075)
LYDIA C GONZALEZ
1400 Veterans Blvd, Redwood City (94063-2612)
PHONE.................................650 299-4707
EMP: 50
SALES (est): 1.9MM **Privately Held**
SIC: **8322**

(P-24076)
MANCHESTER BAND POMO INDIANS
Also Called: Manchester Point Arena
24 Mamie Laiwa Dr, Point Arena (95468)
P.O. Box 623 (95468-0623)
PHONE.................................707 882-2788
Fax: 707 882-3417
Christina Dukatz, *CEO*
Nelson Pinola, *Chairman*
EMP: 96
SALES: 1.6MM **Privately Held**
SIC: **8322** Individual & family services

(P-24077)
MARTHAS VILLAGE & KITCHEN
83791 Date Ave, Indio (92201-4737)
PHONE.................................760 347-4741
Fax: 760 347-9551
Joe Carol, *President*
Matthew Packard, *Vice Pres*
Ron Christian, *Info Tech Dir*
Claudia Castorena, *Director*
Gloria Gomez, *Director*
EMP: 65
SALES: 3.9MM **Privately Held**
SIC: **8322** Social service center

(P-24078)
MBK SENIOR LIVING LLC (PA)
4 Park Plz Ste 400, Irvine (92614-2507)
PHONE.................................949 242-1400
Terry Howard, *President*
Nicole Tucker,
EMP: 61
SALES (est): 62.4MM **Privately Held**
WEB: www.mbk.com
SIC: **8322** Old age assistance

(P-24079)
MD P FOUNDATION INC
Also Called: Martin De Porres House
225 Potrero Ave, San Francisco (94103-4814)
PHONE.................................415 552-0240
Charles Engelstein, *President*
EMP: 200
SQ FT: 7,000
SALES: 203.4K **Privately Held**
WEB: www.mdpfoundation.com
SIC: **8322** Individual & family services

(P-24080)
MEADOWBROOK SENIOR LIVING
5217 Chesebro Rd, Agoura Hills (91301-2212)
PHONE.................................818 991-3544
Isaac Chernoesky, *Director*
Isaac Chernotsky, *Exec Dir*
EMP: 80 EST: 2013

SALES (est): 1MM **Privately Held**
SIC: **8322** Old age assistance

(P-24081)
MEALS ON WHEELS-THE HEALTH TR
1400 Parkmoor Ave Ste 230, San Jose (95126-3798)
PHONE.................................408 961-9870
Gary Allen, *President*
EMP: 50
SALES (est): 997.6K **Privately Held**
SIC: **8322** Meal delivery program

(P-24082)
MEALS ON WHELS SAN FRNCSCO INC
1375 Fairfax Ave, San Francisco (94124-1735)
PHONE.................................415 920-1111
Fax: 415 920-1110
Ashley McCumber, *Exec Dir*
Patrick Smith, *Bd of Directors*
Vivien Thorp, *Comms Mgr*
Sami Dahi, *Principal*
Anne Quaintance, *Principal*
EMP: 50
SQ FT: 19,330
SALES: 10MM **Privately Held**
WEB: www.mowsf.org
SIC: **8322** Meal delivery program

(P-24083)
MENTAL HEALTH AMER LOS ANGELES
Also Called: Village Integrated Svc Agcy
456 Elm Ave, Long Beach (90802-2426)
PHONE.................................562 437-6717
Leslie Giambone, *Exec Dir*
Mark R D, *Psychiatry*
Stan Sorensen, *Manager*
EMP: 74
SQ FT: 25,129
SALES (corp-wide): 13.4MM **Privately Held**
WEB: www.myfrontdoor.org
SIC: **8322** Social service center
PA: Mental Health America Of Los Angeles
100 W Broadway Ste 5010
Long Beach CA 90802
562 285-1330

(P-24084)
MEXICAN AMRCN ALCOHOLISM PROGR (PA)
Also Called: Maap
4241 Florin Rd Ste 110, Sacramento (95823-2535)
PHONE.................................916 394-2320
Fax: 916 394-2453
Paul Cruz, *President*
Sergio Beltran, *Admin Asst*
Min Davis, *Technology*
Tressa Dorsey, *Program Dir*
EMP: 62
SALES: 2.7MM **Privately Held**
WEB: www.maap.com
SIC: **8322** Alcoholism counseling, nontreatment

(P-24085)
MEXICAN AMRCN OPRTNTY FNDATION (PA)
Also Called: MAOF
401 N Garfield Ave, Montebello (90640-2901)
P.O. Box 4602 (90640-9311)
PHONE.................................323 890-9600
Fax: 323 890-9636
Martin Vasquez Castro, *President*
Orlando M Sayson, *CFO*
Vidal Pedro, *Vice Pres*
Carlos J Viramontes, *Principal*
Fernando D Necochea, *Admin Sec*
EMP: 100
SQ FT: 25,000
SALES: 63.8MM **Privately Held**
SIC: **8322** Social service center

(P-24086)
MEXICAN AMRCN OPRTNTY FNDATION
Also Called: M A O F
5657 E Washington Blvd, Commerce (90040-1405)
PHONE.................................323 890-1555
Fax: 323 890-1558
Martin Castro, *President*
EMP: 60
SALES (corp-wide): 63.8MM **Privately Held**
SIC: **8322** Individual & family services
PA: Mexican American Opportunity Foundation
401 N Garfield Ave
Montebello CA 90640
323 890-9600

(P-24087)
MHN GOVERNMENT SERVICES INC
2370 Kerner Blvd, San Rafael (94901-5546)
PHONE.................................916 294-4941
Juanell Hefner, *President*
Lynette Orme, *CFO*
Joseph Klinger, *Admin Sec*
Lisa Ostergren, *Info Tech Mgr*
John Crocker, *Director*
EMP: 189
SQ FT: 67,000
SALES (est): 5.8MM
SALES (corp-wide): 22.7B **Publicly Held**
WEB: www.mhn.com
SIC: **8322** Individual & family services
HQ: Health Net, Inc.
21650 Oxnard St Fl 25
Woodland Hills CA 91367
818 676-6000

(P-24088)
MILESTONES ADULT DEV CTR
1 Florida St, Vallejo (94590-5000)
PHONE.................................707 644-0464
Terry Rowland, *General Mgr*
Steve Mack, *Administration*
John Yates, *Administration*
EMP: 90
SALES (est): 1.3MM **Privately Held**
SIC: **8322** Adult day care center

(P-24089)
MILKEN FAMILY FOUNDATION
1250 4th St Fl 1, Santa Monica (90401-1418)
PHONE.................................310 570-4800
Fax: 310 998-2828
Lowell J Milken, *President*
Susan Fox, *CFO*
Joni Noah, *Bd of Directors*
Mariano Guzm N, *Trustee*
C Crain, *Vice Pres*
EMP: 200
SALES: 38.1MM **Privately Held**
WEB: www.mff.org
SIC: **8322** Individual & family services

(P-24090)
MINORITY AIDS PROJECT INC
5147 W Jefferson Blvd, Los Angeles (90016-3836)
PHONE.................................323 936-4949
Fax: 323 936-4973
Victor McKamie, *Exec Dir*
Ogechi Mbaneu, *Manager*
Riki Smith, *Manager*
EMP: 55
SQ FT: 3,500
SALES: 1.6MM **Privately Held**
WEB: www.map-usa.org
SIC: **8322** Individual & family services

(P-24091)
MONO NATION
58288 Road 225, North Fork (93643-9428)
P.O. Box 1377 (93643-1377)
PHONE.................................559 877-2450
Kendrick Sherman, *Principal*
Leora Beihn, *Manager*
EMP: 65
SALES: 40.2K **Privately Held**
SIC: **8322** Individual & family services

(P-24092)
MUIR SENIOR CARE
1790 Muir Rd, Martinez (94553-4718)
PHONE.................................925 228-8383
Linda Joseph, *Administration*
Thomas Joseph, *Principal*
Burnadett Joseph, *Admin Asst*
Sherry Jansen, *Director*
EMP: 90
SALES (est): 3.8MM **Privately Held**
SIC: **8322** Senior citizens' center or association

(P-24093)
MV TRANSPORTATION INC
705 Tully Rd, San Jose (95111-1035)
PHONE.................................408 292-3600
Fax: 408 278-9370
Tony Mercado, *General Mgr*
Jack Fellman, *General Mgr*
Harley Kempter, *General Mgr*
EMP: 218
SALES (corp-wide): 2.7B **Privately Held**
WEB: www.mvtransit.com
SIC: **8322** Social services for the handicapped
PA: Mv Transportation, Inc
5910 N Cntrl Expy # 1145
Dallas TX 75206
707 474-7784

(P-24094)
NATIONAL CENTER ON DEAFNESS
18111 Nordhoff St, Northridge (91330-0001)
PHONE.................................818 677-2054
Fax: 818 677-4899
Meri C Pearson, *Director*
Dean Meri C Pearson, *Pastor*
EMP: 80 EST: 2001
SALES (est): 3.3MM **Privately Held**
SIC: **8322** Social services for the handicapped

(P-24095)
NEIGHBORHOOD HOUSE ASSOCIATION (PA)
Also Called: N H A
5660 Copley Dr, San Diego (92111-7902)
PHONE.................................858 715-2642
Rudolph A Johnson III, *CEO*
Michael Kemp, *COO*
Kim Peck, *CFO*
Derek Brown, *Treasurer*
Norma Johnson, *Vice Pres*
EMP: 500
SQ FT: 60,000
SALES (est): 40.9MM **Privately Held**
WEB: www.sandiegofoodbank.org
SIC: **8322** Neighborhood center

(P-24096)
NEIGHBORHOOD HOUSE ASSOCIATION
Also Called: Naht Care At
4425 Federal Blvd Ste 24, San Diego (92102-2500)
PHONE.................................619 527-1287
Frank Andrews, *Principal*
EMP: 50
SALES (corp-wide): 40.9MM **Privately Held**
WEB: www.sandiegofoodbank.org
SIC: **8322** Neighborhood center
PA: The Neighborhood House Association
5660 Copley Dr
San Diego CA 92111
858 715-2642

(P-24097)
NEIGHBORHOOD HOUSE ASSOCIATION
Also Called: Neighborhood Hse Assoc Fmily
841 S 41st St, San Diego (92113-1899)
PHONE.................................619 263-7761
Fax: 619 263-6398
Ellen Brown, *Manager*
Jean Smith, *Office Spvr*
Elizabeth Hernandez, *Manager*
EMP: 100

SALES (corp-wide): 40.9MM **Privately Held**
WEB: www.sandiegofoodbank.org
SIC: **8322** 8399 Neighborhood center; community development groups
PA: The Neighborhood House Association
5660 Copley Dr
San Diego CA 92111
858 715-2642

(P-24098)
NEW BRIDGE FOUNDATION INC
2323 Hearst Ave, Berkeley (94709-1319)
PHONE.....................510 548-7270
Fax: 510 526-1507
Kosta Markakis, *CEO*
Jenny Knowles, *CFO*
Victoria Leff, *Executive*
Georgette L Cobbs, *Advisor*
EMP: 65
SALES: 5.4MM **Privately Held**
WEB: www.newbridgefoundation.org
SIC: **8322** Rehabilitation services

(P-24099)
NEW DIRECTIONS INC (PA)
Also Called: New Directions For Veterans
1529 E 1st St 12, Long Beach (90802-5997)
P.O. Box 25536 11420 San, Los Angeles (90025)
PHONE.....................310 914-4045
Fax: 310 914-5495
Edgar H Howell, *CEO*
Usha Murthy, *CFO*
Mary Macgyver, *Plan/Corp Dev D*
Tony Reinis, *Exec Dir*
Anthony Belcher, *Program Mgr*
EMP: 80
SQ FT: 60,000
SALES: 6.6MM **Privately Held**
SIC: **8322** Substance abuse counseling

(P-24100)
NEW ECONOMICS FOR WOMEN (PA)
303 Loma Dr, Los Angeles (90017-1103)
PHONE.....................213 483-2060
Maggie Cervantes, *Exec Dir*
Edith Martinez, *Project Mgr*
Michelle Reyes, *Personnel Assit*
Alicia Matricardi, *Director*
Andrea Osorio, *Director*
EMP: 70
SQ FT: 25,000
SALES: 10.7MM **Privately Held**
WEB: www.neweconomicsforwomen.org
SIC: **8322** Settlement house

(P-24101)
NEW HAVEN YOUTH FMLY SVCS INC
P.O. Box 1199 (92085-1199)
PHONE.....................760 630-4060
Doreen Quinn, *Manager*
EMP: 108
SALES (corp-wide): 8.2MM **Privately Held**
SIC: **8322** Family counseling services
PA: New Haven Youth And Family Services, Inc.
216 W Los Angeles Dr
Vista CA

(P-24102)
NEW START HOME HEALTH CARE INC
21515 Vanowen St Ste 205, Canoga Park (91303-2715)
PHONE.....................818 665-7898
Mary Williams, *CEO*
Martha Fonseca, *Administration*
John Eckels, *Manager*
EMP: 200
SQ FT: 2,000
SALES (est): 6.5MM **Privately Held**
SIC: **8322** 8082 Social services for the handicapped; home health care services

(P-24103)
NEXCARE COLLABORATIVE (PA)
15477 Ventura Blvd, Sherman Oaks (91403-3006)
PHONE.....................818 907-0322
Pejman Salimpour, *President*
Ralph Salimpour MD, *Corp Secy*
Pedram Salimpour MD, *Exec VP*
EMP: 50
SQ FT: 15,000
SALES (est): 6.7MM **Privately Held**
WEB: www.carenex.com
SIC: **8322** Child related social services

(P-24104)
NO BARRIERS
479 Mason St Ste 325, Vacaville (95688-4592)
PHONE.....................707 451-1947
Fax: 707 451-1947
Joe Zavala, *President*
EMP: 75
SALES (est): 619.1K **Privately Held**
SIC: **8322** Social services for the handicapped

(P-24105)
NORRISE INSTITUTE OF TRAINING
5938 Clement Ave, San Pablo (94806-4123)
PHONE.....................510 229-6545
Ameena Latifa Norrise, *Owner*
EMP: 99
SALES: 1,000K **Privately Held**
SIC: **8322** Individual & family services

(P-24106)
NORTHCOAST CHILDRENS SERVICES
730 Hwy 96, Willow Creek (95573)
P.O. Box 149 (95573-0149)
PHONE.....................530 629-2283
Jamie Mackenzie, *Director*
EMP: 52
SALES (corp-wide): 8.9MM **Privately Held**
SIC: **8322** Individual & family services
PA: Northcoast Children's Services Inc
1266 9th St
Arcata CA 95521
707 822-7206

(P-24107)
NORTHEAST VALLEY HEALTH CORP (PA)
1172 N Maclay Ave, San Fernando (91340-1328)
PHONE.....................818 898-1388
Fax: 818 365-4031
Kimberly Wyard, *CEO*
Missy Nitescu, *COO*
Patricia Moraga, *CFO*
Nelson Wong, *Chairman*
Antonio Lugo, *Treasurer*
EMP: 75
SALES: 78.3MM **Privately Held**
SIC: **8322** Community center

(P-24108)
NORTHERN VALLEY CATHOLIC SOCIA
2400 Washington Ave, Redding (96001-2802)
PHONE.....................530 241-0552
Jan Maurer Watkins, *CEO*
Don C Chapman, *CEO*
Dan Johnson, *Financial Exec*
EMP: 151
SALES: 9.9MM **Privately Held**
SIC: **8322** Outreach program

(P-24109)
NOVAEON INC
9665 Chesapeake Dr # 430, San Diego (92123-1367)
PHONE.....................858 503-1588
William McBride, *Ch of Bd*
Patrick J Sullivan, *President*
Craig Bissell, *Vice Pres*
Colleen Carney, *Vice Pres*
Richard Morgan, *Vice Pres*
EMP: 330

SALES (est): 2.2MM **Privately Held**
SIC: **8322** Individual & family services

(P-24110)
OCEAN PARK COMMUNITY CENTER
Daybreak
1751 Cloverfield Blvd, Santa Monica (90404-4007)
PHONE.....................310 450-0650
Anya Booker, *Director*
Andrew Nicholas, *Officer*
Kevin Goins, *Program Mgr*
Amy Tuck, *Director*
Emily Creecy, *Manager*
EMP: 60
SALES (corp-wide): 12.1MM **Privately Held**
SIC: **8322** Community center
PA: Ocean Park Community Center
1453 16th St
Santa Monica CA 90404
310 264-6646

(P-24111)
OFJCC
Also Called: Oshman Family Jewish Cmnty Ctr
3921 Fabian Way, Palo Alto (94303-4606)
PHONE.....................650 223-8600
Zachary Bodner, *CEO*
EMP: 50
SALES (est): 690.9K **Privately Held**
SIC: **8322** Community center

(P-24112)
OLDER ADULTS CARE MANAGEMENT (PA)
881 Fremont Ave Ste A2, Los Altos (94024-5637)
PHONE.....................650 329-1411
Fax: 650 329-8854
Cherry Jackson, *Director*
Jim Wilde, *Supervisor*
EMP: 180
SQ FT: 2,000
SALES (est): 4.4MM **Privately Held**
SIC: **8322** 8741 8082 Geriatric social service; general counseling services; management services; home health care services

(P-24113)
OLDTIMERS HOUSING DEV CORP III
18750 Clarkdale Ave, Artesia (90701-5817)
PHONE.....................562 924-6509
Betty Ormonde, *Manager*
EMP: 71
SALES (corp-wide): 5.8MM **Privately Held**
SIC: **8322** Senior citizens' center or association
PA: Oldtimers Housing Development Corporation Iii
9161 Sierra Ave Ste 213
Fontana CA

(P-24114)
OMEGA WALNUT INC
7233 County Road 24, Orland (95963-9777)
PHONE.....................530 865-0136
Todd J Southam, *CEO*
Marsha Squier, *Office Mgr*
Rachel McGowan, *Opers Mgr*
Tim L Merril, *Manager*
EMP: 50
SALES (est): 4.3MM **Privately Held**
SIC: **8322** 8611 Individual & family services; growers' marketing advisory service

(P-24115)
ONE GENERATION (PA)
17400 Victory Blvd, Van Nuys (91406-5349)
PHONE.....................818 708-6625
Lawrence Gordon, *Exec Dir*
Angela Pennacchio, *Executive Asst*
Judy Hamilton, *Director*
Anna Swift, *Director*
EMP: 73

SALES: 4.4MM **Privately Held**
WEB: www.onegeneration.net
SIC: **8322** Senior citizens' center or association

(P-24116)
OPARC
355 S Lemon Ave Ste J, Walnut (91789-2739)
PHONE.....................909 598-8055
Tom Randall, *Branch Mgr*
EMP: 53
SALES (corp-wide): 11.7MM **Privately Held**
SIC: **8322** 8051 8049 Association for the handicapped; mental retardation hospital; psychologist, psychotherapist or hypnotist
PA: Oparc
9029 Vernon Ave
Montclair CA 91763
909 982-4090

(P-24117)
ORANGE COUNTY CHILD ABUSE
Also Called: Welcome Baby
2390 E Orangewood Ave # 300, Anaheim (92806-6138)
PHONE.....................714 543-4333
Scott Trotter, *Exec Dir*
Stephanie Enano, *Principal*
EMP: 99
SALES: 7MM **Privately Held**
SIC: **8322** Individual & family services; child related social services; family counseling services; general counseling services

(P-24118)
OSHMAN FAMILY JEWISH CMNTY CTR
3921 Fabian Way, Palo Alto (94303-4606)
PHONE.....................650 223-8700
Alan Sataloff, *Exec Dir*
Haim Hovav, *CFO*
Paul Raczynski, *Info Tech Dir*
EMP: 200
SALES: 21.3MM **Privately Held**
SIC: **8322** Community center

(P-24119)
PACIFIC ASIAN CONSORTM EMPLYMN
Also Called: Pace Administrator To Work
1055 Wilshire Blvd # 1475, Los Angeles (90017-2431)
PHONE.....................213 989-3228
Kerry Doi, *Branch Mgr*
Tana Veazthuyarn, *Admin Sec*
EMP: 100
SALES (corp-wide): 13.8MM **Privately Held**
SIC: **8322** Individual & family services
PA: Pacific Asian Consortium In Employment
1055 Wilshire Blvd Ste 14
Los Angeles CA 90017
213 353-3982

(P-24120)
PAJARO VALLEY PREVNTN & STUDEN
335 E Lake Ave, Watsonville (95076-4826)
PHONE.....................831 728-6445
Fax: 831 761-6011
Jenny Sarmiento, *CEO*
Linda Perez, *Exec Dir*
Doreen Diego, *Program Mgr*
Esmeralda Sanchez, *Opers Mgr*
Ellen Garfield, *Psychologist*
EMP: 65
SALES: 2.1MM **Privately Held**
SIC: **8322** Alcoholism counseling, nontreatment; drug abuse counselor, nontreatment

(P-24121)
PARADISE OAKS YOUTH SERVICES
Also Called: Hoffmann House
7806 Uplands Way A, Citrus Heights (95610-7567)
PHONE.....................916 725-7182
EMP: 65

PRODUCTS & SERVICES SECTION
8322 - Individual & Family Social Svcs County (P-24145)

SALES (corp-wide): 3.1MM **Privately Held**
WEB: www.hoffmannhouse.com
SIC: **8322** Youth center
PA: Paradise Oaks Youth Services, Inc
7806 Uplands Way Ste A
Citrus Heights CA 95610
916 967-6253

(P-24122)
PARTNERS FOR COMMUNITY ACCESS
708 Gilman St, Berkeley (94710-1333)
PHONE..................................510 558-6700
Rosalee Shubert, *Principal*
EMP: 60 EST: 2011
SALES (est): 802.9K **Privately Held**
SIC: **8322** Social service center

(P-24123)
PASADENA CHILD DEVELOPMENT ASS
620 N Lake Ave, Pasadena (91101-1220)
PHONE..................................626 793-7350
Diane Cullinane, *Owner*
Mimi Winer, *Co-Owner*
EMP: 70 EST: 1997
SALES (est): 981.6K **Privately Held**
WEB: www.pasadenachilddevelopment.org
SIC: **8322** Individual & family services

(P-24124)
PATHWAY INC
287 W Orange Show Ln, San Bernardino (92408-2037)
PHONE..................................909 890-1070
Fax: 909 890-1072
Robert McGuire, *President*
Joyce Hampton, *President*
EMP: 100
SQ FT: 2,300
SALES (est): 2.8MM **Privately Held**
SIC: **8322** 5999 Social services for the handicapped; technical aids for the handicapped

(P-24125)
PATHWAY TO CHOICES INC
751 Belmont Way, Pinole (94564-2661)
PHONE..................................510 724-9044
Juan Velasquez, *President*
Gover Dixon, *Sales Staff*
Priscilla Silva, *Director*
EMP: 52
SALES (est): 2MM **Privately Held**
SIC: **8322** Individual & family services

(P-24126)
PATHWAYS LA (PA)
3325 Wilshire Blvd # 1100, Los Angeles (90010-1703)
PHONE..................................213 427-2700
Fax: 213 427-2701
Karen Park, *President*
Carla Buck, *Vice Pres*
Les Guttman, *Principal*
Duane Dennis, *Exec Dir*
Ruth Gribin, *Exec Dir*
EMP: 50
SQ FT: 24,000
SALES: 17.6MM **Privately Held**
WEB: www.pathwaysla.org
SIC: **8322** Individual & family services; child related social services

(P-24127)
PENINSULA ASSOC FOR RETARDED
Also Called: Parca
800 Airport Blvd Ste 320, Burlingame (94010-1919)
PHONE..................................650 312-0730
Diana Conti, *Exec Dir*
Cathy Schiffer, *Executive Asst*
Suzanne Hinton, *Human Res Dir*
Brad Pence, *Sales Mgr*
Lori B Milburn, *Corp Comm Staff*
EMP: 86 EST: 1952
SALES: 2.6MM **Privately Held**
WEB: www.parca.org
SIC: **8322** Association for the handicapped

(P-24128)
PENINSULA FAMILY SERVICE
260 Van Buren Rd, Menlo Park (94025-1745)
PHONE..................................650 325-8719
Stephanie Wong, *Manager*
EMP: 83
SALES (corp-wide): 10.6MM **Privately Held**
SIC: **8322** Individual & family services
PA: Peninsula Family Service
24 2nd Ave
San Mateo CA 94401
650 403-4300

(P-24129)
PENINSULA FAMILY SERVICE (PA)
Also Called: Community Infant Tddler Prgram
24 2nd Ave, San Mateo (94401-3828)
PHONE..................................650 403-4300
Judy Swanson, *CEO*
Laurie Wishard, *President*
Arne Croce, *CEO*
Heather Cleary, *CFO*
Helen Calhoun, *Vice Pres*
EMP: 100 EST: 1950
SALES: 10.6MM **Privately Held**
WEB: www.familyserviceagency.org
SIC: **8322** 8351 Family (marriage) counseling; group day care center

(P-24130)
PENINSULA FAMILY SERVICE
Also Called: Leo J Ryan Child Care Ctr
1200 Miller Ave, South San Francisco (94080-1221)
PHONE..................................650 952-6848
Fax: 650 877-5285
Liliya Sergiyemko, *Branch Mgr*
EMP: 55
SALES (corp-wide): 10.6MM **Privately Held**
WEB: www.familyserviceagency.org
SIC: **8322** 8351 Family (marriage) counseling; child day care services
PA: Peninsula Family Service
24 2nd Ave
San Mateo CA 94401
650 403-4300

(P-24131)
PENINSULA JEWISH COMMUNITY CTR
800 Foster City Blvd, Foster City (94404-2228)
PHONE..................................650 212-7522
Paul Gedulig, *CEO*
Fred Weiner, *CFO*
Lisa Gurwitch, *Exec Dir*
Lisa Tabak, *Exec Dir*
Cynthia Gradwohl, *Human Res Dir*
EMP: 200
SALES: 17.9MM **Privately Held**
SIC: **8322** Community center

(P-24132)
PEOPLE ASSISTING HOMELESS
Also Called: P A T H
340 N Madison Ave, Los Angeles (90004-3504)
PHONE..................................323 644-2216
Joel John Roberts, *President*
Jonathan CHI, *Associate Dir*
Sandy McQueen, *Associate Dir*
Matthew Rayburn, *Associate Dir*
Michuan Fleming, *Managing Dir*
EMP: 167
SALES: 15.7MM **Privately Held**
WEB: www.epath.org
SIC: **8322** Individual & family services

(P-24133)
PEOPLE CREATING SUCCESS INC
1607 E Palmdale Blvd H, Palmdale (93550-7801)
PHONE..................................661 225-9700
Robert Donery, *Branch Mgr*
EMP: 91
SALES (corp-wide): 12.4MM **Privately Held**
SIC: **8322** Individual & family services

PA: People Creating Success, Inc.
2585 Teller Rd
Newbury Park CA 91320
805 375-9222

(P-24134)
PEOPLE CREATING SUCCESS INC
5350 Hollister Ave Ste I, Santa Barbara (93111-2326)
PHONE..................................805 692-5290
Brian Fay, *Manager*
EMP: 91
SALES (corp-wide): 12.4MM **Privately Held**
SIC: **8322** Individual & family services
PA: People Creating Success, Inc.
2585 Teller Rd
Newbury Park CA 91320
805 375-9222

(P-24135)
PHFE WIC PROGRAM
12871 Schabarum Ave, Irwindale (91706-6808)
PHONE..................................626 856-6650
Eloise Jenks, *Director*
EMP: 120
SALES (est): 3.6MM **Privately Held**
SIC: **8322** Individual & family services

(P-24136)
PINOLE SENIOR CENTER
2500 Charles St, Pinole (94564-1301)
PHONE..................................510 724-9800
Janette Bilbas, *Director*
Jonathan Torres, *Administration*
EMP: 58
SALES (est): 864.3K **Privately Held**
SIC: **8322** Senior citizens' center or association
PA: City Of Pinole
2131 Pear St
Pinole CA 94564
510 724-9000

(P-24137)
PLAN-IT LIFE INC
5729 Vista Del Caballero, Riverside (92509-6423)
P.O. Box 2994, Corona (92878-2994)
PHONE..................................951 742-7561
Sheila McLean, *CEO*
Nyron McLean, *CFO*
Carl Sampson MD, *Vice Pres*
EMP: 56
SQ FT: 2,800
SALES: 2.3MM **Privately Held**
SIC: **8322** Substance abuse counseling

(P-24138)
PLUMAS RURAL SERVICES
711 E Main St, Quincy (95971-9722)
PHONE..................................530 283-2725
Fax: 530 283-5652
Michele Pillar, *Exec Dir*
Leslie Wall, *Exec VP*
Jim McCulloch, *Vice Pres*
Paula Johnston, *General Mgr*
Michele Piller, *General Mgr*
EMP: 90
SQ FT: 6,000
SALES: 3.9MM **Privately Held**
WEB: www.plumasruralservices.org
SIC: **8322** Drug abuse counselor, nontreatment

(P-24139)
POMEROY RCRTION RHBLTATION CTR (PA)
Also Called: R C H
207 Skyline Blvd, San Francisco (94132-1025)
PHONE..................................415 665-4100
Fax: 415 665-7543
John McCue, *Exec Dir*
Henry Woo, *Exec Dir*
Laurie Petronis, *Administration*
Terry Twitchell, *Administration*
Ted Magbitang, *Finance*
EMP: 178
SQ FT: 22,000
SALES: 6.1MM **Privately Held**
WEB: www.janetpomeroy.org
SIC: **8322** Social services for the handicapped

(P-24140)
PROJECT OPEN HAND (PA)
730 Polk St Fl 3, San Francisco (94109-7813)
PHONE..................................415 292-3400
Fax: 415 447-2490
Mark Ryle, *CEO*
Simon Pitchford, *CEO*
Kevin Davidson, *Executive*
Jay Owens, *Associate Dir*
Maria Stokes, *Comms Dir*
EMP: 96
SQ FT: 50,000
SALES: 9.4MM **Privately Held**
WEB: www.openhand.org
SIC: **8322** Meal delivery program

(P-24141)
PROTEUS INC
1816 Cecil Ave, Delano (93215-1520)
PHONE..................................661 721-5800
Luis Conde, *Manager*
EMP: 127
SALES (corp-wide): 28.6MM **Privately Held**
SIC: **8322** Individual & family services
PA: Proteus, Inc.
1830 N Dinuba Blvd
Visalia CA 93291
559 733-5423

(P-24142)
PROTOTYPES CENTERS FOR INNOV
Also Called: Prototypes Women's Center
845 E Arrow Hwy, Pomona (91767-2535)
PHONE..................................909 624-1233
Fax: 909 621-5999
April Wilson, *Vice Pres*
EMP: 100
SALES (corp-wide): 20.1MM **Privately Held**
SIC: **8322** 8069 Individual & family services; drug addiction rehabilitation hospital
PA: Prototypes, Centers For Innovation In Health, Mental Health And Social Services
1000 N Alameda St Ste 390
Los Angeles CA 90012
213 542-3838

(P-24143)
R L SAFETY INC
2157 Cherrystone Dr, San Jose (95128-1217)
PHONE..................................408 557-0887
Brent Rapport, *President*
Loisa Rapport, *Vice Pres*
EMP: 50
SALES (est): 669.9K **Privately Held**
SIC: **8322** 8099 7389 Emergency social services; blood related health services;

(P-24144)
RANCHO LOS AMIGOS NATIONA
Also Called: Information Management Svcs
7601 Imperial Hwy, Downey (90242-3456)
PHONE..................................562 401-7111
EMP: 425 **Privately Held**
SIC: **8322** Individual & family services
PA: Rancho Los Amigos National Rehabilatation Center
7601 Imperial Hwy
Downey CA 90242

(P-24145)
RANCHO LOS AMIGOS NATIONA
Also Called: Professional Staffing Associat
7601 Imperial Hwy, Downey (90242-3456)
PHONE..................................562 401-7111
Fax: 562 803-5623
Consuelo Diaz, *CEO*
Michelle Sterling, *Ch Nursing Ofcr*
Cheryl Williams, *Admin Asst*
Steve Hamberger, *QA Dir*
Yolanda Youseff, *Human Res Dir*
EMP: 850 **Privately Held**
WEB: www.co.la.ca.us
SIC: **8322** Individual & family services
PA: Rancho Los Amigos National Rehabilatation Center
7601 Imperial Hwy
Downey CA 90242

8322 - Individual & Family Social Svcs County (P-24146)

(P-24146)
RANCHO LOS AMIGOS NATIONA
12852 Erickson Ave, Downey (90242-4004)
PHONE...............................310 940-7266
Sydney Pearson, *Supervisor*
EMP: 106 **Privately Held**
SIC: 8322 Individual & family services
PA: Rancho Los Amigos National Rehabilitation Center
7601 Imperial Hwy
Downey CA 90242
-

(P-24147)
RANCHO LOS AMIGOS NATIONA (PA)
7601 Imperial Hwy, Downey (90242-3456)
PHONE...............................562 401-7111
Fax: 562 803-5693
Jorge R Orozco, *CEO*
Benjamin Ovando Sr, *COO*
Robin Bayus, *CFO*
Michelle Sterling, *Ch Nursing Ofcr*
Aries Limbaga, *Principal*
EMP: 69
SALES (est): 61.6MM **Privately Held**
SIC: 8322 Rehabilitation services

(P-24148)
RAY STONE INCORPORATED
Also Called: Hilltop Commons Senior Living
131 Eureka St, Grass Valley (95945-6355)
PHONE...............................530 272-5274
Nancy Stadel, *Owner*
EMP: 60
SALES (corp-wide): 25.1MM **Privately Held**
SIC: 8322 Senior citizens' center or association
PA: Ray Stone Incorporated
550 Howe Ave Ste 200
Sacramento CA 95825
916 649-7500

(P-24149)
READING PARTNERS
600 Valley Way, Milpitas (95035-4138)
PHONE...............................408 945-5720
Michael Lombardo, *Exec Dir*
Diana Martin, *Program Mgr*
EMP: 80
SALES (corp-wide): 23.5MM **Privately Held**
SIC: 8322 Individual & family services
PA: Reading Partners
180 Grand Ave Ste 800
Oakland CA 94612
510 444-9800

(P-24150)
REDWOOD COAST REGIONAL
Also Called: Redwood Coast Regional Center
525 2nd St Ste 300, Eureka (95501-0488)
PHONE...............................707 445-0893
Fax: 707 444-3409
Clay Jones, *Director*
Jeanine Ross, *Opers Staff*
Mary Block, *Director*
Cindy Claus-John, *Manager*
Sylvia Lodge, *Manager*
EMP: 50
SALES (corp-wide): 81.1MM **Privately Held**
WEB: www.redwoodcoastrc.org
SIC: 8322 8699 Individual & family services; personal interest organization
PA: Redwood Coast Developmental Services Corporation
1116 Airport Park Blvd
Ukiah CA 95482
707 462-3832

(P-24151)
REDWOOD COAST SENIORS INC
Also Called: SENIOR NUTRITION
490 N Harold St, Fort Bragg (95437-3331)
PHONE...............................707 964-0443
Joseph Curren, *Exec Dir*
EMP: 60
SALES: 993.8K **Privately Held**
SIC: 8322 Senior citizens' center or association

(P-24152)
REGIONAL CENTER OF E BAY INC (PA)
7677 Oakport St Ste 300, Oakland (94621-1933)
PHONE...............................510 383-1200
Fax: 510 633-5020
Jim Burton, *Director*
Nancy Kubota, *CFO*
Maria Garcia-Puig, *Executive*
Patricia Saugar, *Admin Sec*
Carol Bohnsack, *Administration*
EMP: 150 **EST:** 1975
SQ FT: 26,000
SALES: 311.1MM **Privately Held**
SIC: 8322 Social services for the handicapped

(P-24153)
REHABILITATION CALIFORNIA DEPT
Also Called: Los Angeles South Bay Dst Off
4300 Long Beach Blvd # 200, Long Beach (90807-2011)
PHONE...............................562 422-8325
Fax: 562 428-8565
Brenda Brent, *Manager*
EMP: 50 **Privately Held**
WEB: www.carehab.org
SIC: 8322 9431 Rehabilitation services; administration of public health programs
HQ: California Department Of Rehabilitation
721 Capitol Mall Fl 6
Sacramento CA 95814
916 558-5683

(P-24154)
RESCUE CHILDREN INC
Also Called: CRAYCROFT YOUTH CENTER
335 G St, Fresno (93706-3422)
P.O. Box 1422 (93716-1422)
PHONE...............................559 268-1123
Fax: 559 268-3465
Larry Arce, *CEO*
Larry Gray, *Administration*
Francis Brannan, *Manager*
EMP: 50
SALES: 1.3MM **Privately Held**
SIC: 8322 Youth center

(P-24155)
RESOURCE CONNECTION OF AMADOR
Also Called: W I C
430 Sutter Hill Rd, Sutter Creek (95685-4149)
PHONE...............................209 223-7685
Fax: 209 223-7687
Damian Wolin, *President*
EMP: 68
SALES (corp-wide): 6.8MM **Privately Held**
SIC: 8322 Individual & family services
PA: The Resource Connection Of Amador And Calaveras Counties Incorporated
444 E Saint Charles St
San Andreas CA 95249
209 754-3114

(P-24156)
RESOURCE RFRRAL CHILD CARE DEV
1225 Gill Ave, Madera (93637-5234)
PHONE...............................559 673-9173
Mary Jane Nabors, *Director*
Velvet Rhoads, *Treasurer*
Irene Yang, *Human Res Dir*
EMP: 50
SALES (est): 392.2K **Privately Held**
SIC: 8322 Individual & family services

(P-24157)
RICHMOND DST NEIGHBORHOOD CTR
Also Called: Richmond Village Beacon
600 32nd Ave T3, San Francisco (94121-2733)
PHONE...............................415 750-8554
Fax: 415 754-8572
Pat Kaussen, *Branch Mgr*
EMP: 58

(P-24158)
RICHMOND RESCUE MISSION (PA)
Also Called: Bay Area Rescue Mission
2114 Macdonald Ave, Richmond (94801-3311)
P.O. Box 1112 (94802-0112)
PHONE...............................510 215-4555
Fax: 510 215-4555
John M Anderson, *President*
David Bradley, *Volunteer Dir*
Harry Parks, *Treasurer*
Tim Hammack, *Vice Pres*
Gary Kingbury, *Vice Pres*
EMP: 51
SQ FT: 80,000
SALES (est): 9.9MM **Privately Held**
SIC: 8322 Individual & family services

(P-24159)
RIO HONDO EDUCATION CONSORTIUM
Also Called: Learn
7200 Greenleaf Ave # 300, Whittier (90602-1383)
PHONE...............................562 945-0150
Fax: 562 945-0191
Robert Arellanes, *CEO*
Brenda Carrillo, *COO*
Carolina Arce, *Principal*
Robert Bell, *Principal*
Linda Contreras, *Principal*
EMP: 150
SALES: 3.6MM **Privately Held**
WEB: www.riohondoec.org
SIC: 8322 Individual & family services

(P-24160)
ROCK CANCER CARE INC
5402 Ruffin Rd Ste 205, San Diego (92123-1306)
P.O. Box 17716 (92177-7716)
PHONE...............................888 251-0620
Tamela Reed, *CEO*
EMP: 250
SALES: 44.4K **Privately Held**
SIC: 8322 Individual & family services

(P-24161)
RURAL CMNTY ASSISTANCE CORP (PA)
Also Called: Rcac
3120 Freeboard Dr Ste 201, West Sacramento (95691-5039)
PHONE...............................916 447-2854
Stan Keasling, *CEO*
Kevin McCumber, *CFO*
David Ebenezer, *Controller*
Michael Flanagan, *Director*
George Schelender, *Director*
EMP: 60
SALES: 15.4MM **Privately Held**
SIC: 8322 6111 Individual & family services; federal & federally sponsored credit agencies

(P-24162)
RUTH BARAJAS
Also Called: Bacr
965 Mission St Ste 520, San Francisco (94103-2959)
PHONE...............................415 977-6949
Fax: 415 977-6950
Ruth Barajas, *Administration*
Andrea Juarez, *Associate Dir*
EMP: 50
SALES (est): 754K **Privately Held**
WEB: www.chalk.org
SIC: 8322 Youth center

(P-24163)
SACRAMENTO CHINESE COMMUNITY S
420 I St Ste 5, Sacramento (95814-2319)
PHONE...............................916 442-4228

SALES (corp-wide): 3.2MM **Privately Held**
WEB: www.rdnc.org
SIC: 8322 Individual & family services
PA: Richmond District Neighborhood Center
741 30th Ave
San Francisco CA 94121
415 751-6600

(P-24164)
SACRAMENTO COUNTY OFF EDUCATN
Also Called: Probation Department
9750 Bus Park Dr Ste 220, Sacramento (95827-1716)
PHONE...............................916 875-0312
Lee Seale, *Director*
EMP: 50
SALES (corp-wide): 50.6MM **Privately Held**
WEB: www.sna.com
SIC: 8322 9199 Probation office;
PA: Sacramento County Office Of Education
10474 Mather Blvd
Mather CA 95655
916 228-2500

(P-24165)
SACRAMENTO LOAVES & FISHES (PA)
1351 N C St Ste 22, Sacramento (95811-0608)
P.O. Box 2161 (95812-2161)
PHONE...............................916 446-0874
Libby Hernandez, *Director*
Rebecca Brasser, *Teacher*
EMP: 55
SALES: 5.9MM **Privately Held**
SIC: 8322 Individual & family services

(P-24166)
SALINAS VALLEY MEMORIAL HLTHCA
120 Wilgart Way, Salinas (93901-4013)
PHONE...............................831 759-1995
Fax: 831 771-8805
Harry Wardwell, *Principal*
EMP: 422
SALES (corp-wide): 344.2MM **Privately Held**
SIC: 8322 Rehabilitation services
PA: Salinas Valley Memorial Healthcare Systems
450 E Romie Ln
Salinas CA 93901
831 757-4333

(P-24167)
SALVATION ARMY
2737 W Sunset Blvd, Los Angeles (90026-2181)
PHONE...............................213 484-0772
Fax: 213 454-4226
Ana Aguirre, *Director*
EMP: 50
SALES (corp-wide): 4.3B **Privately Held**
WEB: www.salvationarmy.usawest.org
SIC: 8322 Refugee services
HQ: The Salvation Army
180 E Ocean Blvd Fl 2
Long Beach CA 90802
562 491-8464

(P-24168)
SALVATION ARMY GLDEN STATE DIV (PA)
832 Folsom St Fl 6, San Francisco (94107-1142)
P.O. Box 193465 (94119-3465)
PHONE...............................415 553-3500
Fax: 415 495-5849
Steve Smith, *Principal*
Jessica Sibbernsen, *Controller*
Eric Hansen, *Human Res Dir*
Cindy Sutter-Tkeo, *Consultant*
EMP: 80
SALES (est): 6.6MM **Privately Held**
SIC: 8322 8741 Individual & family services; administrative management

Fax: 916 442-1089
Henry Kloczkowski, *Director*
Mario Garcia, *Associate Dir*
Shawn Baker, *Program Mgr*
Oscar Bermudez, *Program Mgr*
Rian Carroll, *Program Mgr*
EMP: 200
SQ FT: 2,000
SALES: 4.9MM **Privately Held**
SIC: 8322 8699 8611 Social service center; charitable organization; community affairs & services

8322 - Individual & Family Social Svcs County (P-24190)

(P-24169)
SALVATION ARMY RESIDENCES INC
900 James M Wood Blvd, Los Angeles (90015-1356)
PHONE...................213 553-3273
Paul Bollwahn, *Director*
Alen Davtian, *Sales Mgr*
Joseph Wambugu, *Director*
EMP: 100
SALES (corp-wide): 4.3B **Privately Held**
WEB: www.salvationarmy.usawest.org
SIC: 8322 Individual & family services
HQ: The Salvation Army
180 E Ocean Blvd Fl 2
Long Beach CA 90802
562 491-8464

(P-24170)
SAMARITAN VILLAGE INC
7700 Fox Rd, Hughson (95326-9100)
P.O. Box 444, Yuba City (95992-0444)
PHONE...................209 883-3212
Fax: 209 883-3001
Daniel Aguilar, *CEO*
Victor Savage, *CEO*
EMP: 115
SALES: 43K **Privately Held**
SIC: 8322 Adult day care center

(P-24171)
SAN ANDREAS REGIONAL CENTER (PA)
300 Orchard Cy Dr Ste 170, Campbell (95008)
P.O. Box 50002, San Jose (95150-0002)
PHONE...................408 374-9960
Fax: 408 376-0586
Mary Lu Gonzalez, *CEO*
Yoshiharu Kuroiwa, *CFO*
Lisa Lopez, *Vice Pres*
Troy Hernandez, *Admin Sec*
Lilbeth Calara, *Finance*
EMP: 174
SQ FT: 29,000
SALES: 310.1MM **Privately Held**
SIC: 8322 Association for the handicapped

(P-24172)
SAN DEGO STATE UNIV FOUNDATION
Also Called: Wic Prgram Admnstrative Office
9210 Sky Park Ct Ste 150, San Diego (92123-4479)
PHONE...................888 999-6897
Sarah Larson, *Director*
EMP: 90 **Privately Held**
SIC: 8322 Individual & family services
HQ: San Diego State University Foundation
5250 Campanile Dr Mc1947
San Diego CA 92182
619 594-1900

(P-24173)
SAN DIEGO COUNTY ADULT SUPPORT
Also Called: In Home Supportive Services
780 Bay Blvd Ste 200, Chula Vista (91910-5260)
PHONE...................619 476-6300
Fax: 619 422-2622
Shirley Downs, *Manager*
EMP: 99
SALES (est): 2.5MM **Privately Held**
SIC: 8322 Social services for the handicapped

(P-24174)
SAN DIEGO CREATIVE COMMUNITY S
1501 Front St Unit 509, San Diego (92101-2978)
PHONE...................619 250-3394
Mia Hall, *Director*
EMP: 50
SALES (est): 2.1MM **Privately Held**
SIC: 8322 Individual & family services

(P-24175)
SAN DIEGO LESBIAN GAY BISEXU
Also Called: CENTER, THE
3909 Centre St, San Diego (92103-3410)
P.O. Box 3357 (92163-1357)
PHONE...................619 692-2077
Fax: 619 260-3092
Delores Jacobs, *Exec Dir*
Vaneessa Peek, *Accountant*
Connor Maddocks, *Facilities Mgr*
Patricia E Celaya, *Psychologist*
Dean Rosenstein, *Agent*
EMP: 50
SQ FT: 15,490
SALES: 4.4MM **Privately Held**
WEB: www.thecentersd.org
SIC: 8322 Individual & family services

(P-24176)
SAN DIEGO YOUTH SERVICES INC (PA)
Also Called: S D Y S
3255 Wing St Ste 550, San Diego (92110-4641)
P.O. Box 80756 (92138-0756)
PHONE...................619 221-8600
Walter Philips, *Exec Dir*
Angie Tran, *CFO*
Jan Stankus, *Exec Dir*
Tamara Bandak, *Analyst*
Don Makeever, *Human Res Dir*
EMP: 55
SQ FT: 5,634
SALES: 16.6MM **Privately Held**
SIC: 8322 Individual & family services; senior citizens' center or association; youth center

(P-24177)
SAN DIEGO-IMPERIAL
Also Called: Developmentally Research Ctr
1370 W Sn Mrcos Blvd # 100, San Marcos (92078-1601)
PHONE...................760 736-1200
Nina Garrett, *Director*
EMP: 70
SALES (corp-wide): 288.8MM **Privately Held**
WEB: www.sdrc.org
SIC: 8322 Social services for the handicapped
PA: San Diego-Imperial Counties Developmental Services, Inc.
4355 Ruffin Rd Ste 110
San Diego CA 92123
858 576-2996

(P-24178)
SAN DIEGO-IMPERIAL
Also Called: San Diego Regional Ctr For Dev
2727 Hoover Ave, National City (91950-6602)
PHONE...................619 336-6600
Fax: 619 477-6248
Judy Borchert, *Manager*
Sue Cavanagh, *Program Mgr*
Michael Rath, *Program Mgr*
Alicia Bautista, *Social Worker*
Leigh Harms, *Social Worker*
EMP: 54
SALES (corp-wide): 288.8MM **Privately Held**
WEB: www.sdrc.org
SIC: 8322 Social service center
PA: San Diego-Imperial Counties Developmental Services, Inc.
4355 Ruffin Rd Ste 110
San Diego CA 92123
858 576-2996

(P-24179)
SAN DIEGO-IMPERIAL COUNTIES DE (PA)
4355 Ruffin Rd Ste 110, San Diego (92123-4307)
PHONE...................858 576-2996
Carlos Flores, *Exec Dir*
Edward Kenney, *CFO*
Judy Wallace Patton, *Treasurer*
Myrtle Mark, *Office Mgr*
Robin Alter Haas, *Executive Asst*
EMP: 286
SQ FT: 62,000
SALES: 288.8MM **Privately Held**
WEB: www.sdrc.org
SIC: 8322 Social services for the handicapped

(P-24180)
SAN FRANCISCO CITY & COUNTY
Also Called: San Francisco Public Schools
1520 Oakdale Ave, San Francisco (94124-2323)
PHONE...................415 695-5660
David Hollands, *Branch Mgr*
EMP: 93 **Privately Held**
SIC: 8322 Child related social services
PA: City & County Of San Francisco
1 Dr Carlton B Goodlett P
San Francisco CA 94102
415 554-7500

(P-24181)
SAN FRANCISCO CITY & COUNTY
Also Called: Youth Treatment & Educatn Crt
2400 Hillcrest Dr, NAPA (94558-1555)
PHONE...................415 753-4439
Carol Taniguchi, *Branch Mgr*
Elizabeth Fairbanks, *Bd of Directors*
Michael Pritchard, *Bd of Directors*
Elizabeth Siggins, *Bd of Directors*
Caitlin Walsh, *Bd of Directors*
EMP: 93 **Privately Held**
SIC: 8322 9199 Youth self-help agency;
PA: City & County Of San Francisco
1 Dr Carlton B Goodlett P
San Francisco CA 94102
415 554-7500

(P-24182)
SAN FRANCISCO AIDS FOUNDATION (PA)
1035 Market St Ste 400, San Francisco (94103-1665)
PHONE...................415 487-3000
Fax: 415 487-3009
Neil Giuliano, *CEO*
Jody Schaffer, *Volunteer Dir*
Irene Wysocki, *Volunteer Dir*
Liz Pesch, *CFO*
John Zimman, *CFO*
EMP: 78
SQ FT: 40,000
SALES: 27.9MM **Privately Held**
WEB: www.sfaf.org
SIC: 8322 Individual & family services

(P-24183)
SAN FRANCISCO CITY & COUNTY
Also Called: Child Support Services
617 Mission St, San Francisco (94105-3503)
PHONE...................415 356-2700
Christine Anderson, *Manager*
Mitzi Ramirez, *Officer*
EMP: 93 **Privately Held**
SIC: 8322 9441 Individual & family services; administration of social & manpower programs; ;
PA: City & County Of San Francisco
1 Dr Carlton B Goodlett P
San Francisco CA 94102
415 554-7500

(P-24184)
SAN FRANCISCO CITY & COUNTY
Also Called: Family Support Bureau
617 Mission St, San Francisco (94105-3503)
PHONE...................415 356-2700
EMP: 93 **Privately Held**
SIC: 8322 9441 Individual & family services; administration of social & manpower programs; ;
PA: City & County Of San Francisco
1 Dr Carlton B Goodlett P
San Francisco CA 94102
415 554-7500

(P-24185)
SAN FRANCISCO FOOD BANK
Also Called: Sf-Marin Food Bank
900 Pennsylvania Ave, San Francisco (94107-3498)
PHONE...................415 286-3614
Fax: 415 282-1909
Paul Ash, *Exec Dir*
Leslie Bacho, *COO*
Michael Braude, *CFO*
Sheila Kopf, *Program Mgr*
Karen Diamond, *Accounting Mgr*
EMP: 80
SQ FT: 55,000
SALES: 90.4MM **Privately Held**
WEB: www.sffb.org
SIC: 8322 Individual & family services

(P-24186)
SAN GABRIEL/POMONA VALLEYS
Also Called: SAN GABRIEL/POMONA REGIONAL CE
75 Rancho Camino Dr, Pomona (91766-4728)
PHONE...................909 620-7722
Fax: 909 622-1873
R Keith Penman, *Exec Dir*
John Hunt, *CFO*
Floria Garcia, *Admin Asst*
Edith Aburto, *Administration*
Cristina Luceno, *Accountant*
EMP: 323
SQ FT: 100,000
SALES: 196.2MM **Privately Held**
SIC: 8322 Social service center

(P-24187)
SANTA BARBARA COUNTY OF
Also Called: Probation Dept
117 E Carrillo St, Santa Barbara (93101-2110)
PHONE...................805 882-3700
Beverly Taylor, *Chief*
EMP: 400 **Privately Held**
WEB: www.sbcountyhr.org
SIC: 8322 Probation office; parole office
PA: County Of Santa Barbara
105 E Anapamu St Rm 406
Santa Barbara CA 93101
805 568-3400

(P-24188)
SANTA BARBARA COUNTY OF
Also Called: Probation Dept
1410 S Broadway Ste L, Santa Maria (93454-6971)
PHONE...................805 614-1550
Brian Carroll, *Branch Mgr*
EMP: 122 **Privately Held**
WEB: www.sbcountyhr.org
SIC: 8322 9223 Child related social services; parole office; correctional institutions;
PA: County Of Santa Barbara
105 E Anapamu St Rm 406
Santa Barbara CA 93101
805 568-3400

(P-24189)
SANTA BARBARA COUNTY OF
Also Called: Social Services Dept
1100 W Laurel Ave, Lompoc (93436-5155)
PHONE...................805 737-7080
Fax: 805 737-7089
Beverly Littlejohn, *Director*
EMP: 122 **Privately Held**
WEB: www.sbcountyhr.org
SIC: 8322 9441 Public welfare center; administration of social & manpower programs;
PA: County Of Santa Barbara
105 E Anapamu St Rm 406
Santa Barbara CA 93101
805 568-3400

(P-24190)
SANTA BARBARA COUNTY OF
Also Called: Probation Dept
429 N San Antonio Rd, Santa Barbara (93110-1399)
PHONE...................805 884-1600
Fax: 805 884-1602
Scott Whiteley, *Manager*
EMP: 70 **Privately Held**
WEB: www.sbcountyhr.org

8322 - Individual & Family Social Svcs County (P-24191)

SIC: 8322 9223 Child related social services; correctional institutions;
PA: County Of Santa Barbara
105 E Anapamu St Rm 406
Santa Barbara CA 93101
805 568-3400

(P-24191)
SANTA BARBARA COUNTY OF
Also Called: Human Resources
4 E Carrillo St, Santa Barbara (93101-2707)
PHONE..................................866 901-3212
Karin Roser, *Branch Mgr*
EMP: 122 **Privately Held**
WEB: www.sbcountyhr.org
SIC: 8322 9441 Individual & family services; administration of social & manpower programs;
PA: County Of Santa Barbara
105 E Anapamu St Rm 406
Santa Barbara CA 93101
805 568-3400

(P-24192)
SANTA CLARA COUNTY OF
Also Called: Adult Probation Department
2314 N 1st St, San Jose (95131-1011)
PHONE..................................408 435-2000
Fax: 408 456-0527
Karen Fletcher, *Chief*
Carlos Austin, *General Mgr*
Adam Perez, *Manager*
EMP: 100 **Privately Held**
SIC: 8322 Probation office
PA: County Of Santa Clara
3180 Newberry Dr Ste 150
San Jose CA 95118
408 299-5105

(P-24193)
SANTA CLARA COUNTY OF
Also Called: Probation Dept
2314 N 1st St, San Jose (95131-1011)
PHONE..................................408 435-2111
Sheila Mitchel, *Director*
EMP: 200 **Privately Held**
WEB: www.countyairports.org
SIC: 8322 9441 Probation office; parole office; administration of social & manpower programs
PA: County Of Santa Clara
3180 Newberry Dr Ste 150
San Jose CA 95118
408 299-5105

(P-24194)
SANTA CLARITA VLLY CMMTT AGING
Also Called: SANTA CLARITA VALLEY SENIOR CE
22900 Market St, Santa Clarita (91321-3608)
PHONE..................................661 259-9444
Brad Berens, *Director*
Jeff Pollard, *President*
Greg Kory, *CFO*
Don Kimball, *Vice Pres*
Rachelle Dardeau, *Exec Dir*
EMP: 65
SQ FT: 10,000
SALES: 2.5MM **Privately Held**
WEB: www.scvseniorcenter.org
SIC: 8322 Senior citizens' center or association

(P-24195)
SANTA ROSA COMMUNITY HLTH CTRS (PA)
3569 Round Barn Cir, Santa Rosa (95403-5781)
PHONE..................................707 547-2222
Fax: 707 547-2230
Naomi Fuchs, *CEO*
Steve Strands, *Info Tech Dir*
Paulomi Shah, *Osteopathy*
EMP: 76 **EST:** 1996
SALES: 51.1MM **Privately Held**
WEB: www.swhealthcenter.org
SIC: 8322 Individual & family services

(P-24196)
SANTEE SYSTEMS SERVICES II
229 E Gage Ave, Los Angeles (90003-1533)
PHONE..................................323 445-0044
Veronica Santee, *CEO*
EMP: 99
SALES (est): 636K **Privately Held**
SIC: 8322 Child related social services

(P-24197)
SECOND HARVEST FOOD
8014 Marine Way, Irvine (92618-2235)
PHONE..................................949 653-2900
Joe Schoeningh, *Owner*
Steven Knight, *Opers Mgr*
EMP: 56 **EST:** 2008
SALES: 43.1MM **Privately Held**
SIC: 8322 Individual & family services

(P-24198)
SECOND HARVEST FOOD BANK (PA)
750 Curtner Ave, San Jose (95125-2118)
PHONE..................................408 266-8866
Fax: 408 266-9042
Kathryn Jackson, *CEO*
Bruno Pillet, *Vice Pres*
Keith Flager, *Exec Dir*
Larry Diskin, *General Mgr*
Emily Donoho, *Office Admin*
EMP: 50 **EST:** 1974
SQ FT: 65,000
SALES: 124.2MM **Privately Held**
SIC: 8322 Meal delivery program

(P-24199)
SEIU LOCAL 721
1545 Wilshire Blvd # 100, Los Angeles (90017-4510)
PHONE..................................213 368-8660
Annelle Grajeda, *Owner*
Roslyn Jones, *Admin Asst*
EMP: 58
SALES (est): 4.8MM **Privately Held**
SIC: 8322 Social service center

(P-24200)
SELF-HELP FOR ELDERLY
777 Stockton St Ste 110, San Francisco (94108-2372)
PHONE..................................415 391-3843
EMP: 57
SALES (corp-wide): 18.5MM **Privately Held**
SIC: 8322 Senior citizens' center or association
PA: Self-Help For The Elderly
731 Sansome St Ste 100
San Francisco CA 94111
415 677-7600

(P-24201)
SELF-HELP FOR ELDERLY (PA)
Also Called: San Francisco Residential Care
731 Sansome St Ste 100, San Francisco (94111-1735)
PHONE..................................415 677-7600
Fax: 415 296-0313
Anni Chung, *President*
Andy Bryant, *Vice Chairman*
Janie Kaung, *Vice Chairman*
Anthony Tam, *CFO*
William Schulte, *Chairman*
EMP: 145
SALES: 18.5MM **Privately Held**
WEB: www.selfhelpelderly.org
SIC: 8322 8361 8082 Geriatric social service; residential care; home health care services

(P-24202)
SELF-HELP FOR ELDERLY
940 S Stelling Rd, Cupertino (95014-4269)
PHONE..................................408 873-1183
Nhi Hua, *Branch Mgr*
EMP: 57
SALES (corp-wide): 18.5MM **Privately Held**
SIC: 8322 Senior citizens' center or association
PA: Self-Help For The Elderly
731 Sansome St Ste 100
San Francisco CA 94111
415 677-7600

(P-24203)
SELMA PORTUGUESE AZORIAN ASSN
1245 Nebraska Ave, Selma (93662-9738)
P.O. Box 734 (93662-0734)
PHONE..................................559 896-2508
Louis Cardoza, *President*
EMP: 50
SALES: 60.1K **Privately Held**
SIC: 8322 5813 Community center; drinking places

(P-24204)
SENECA FAMILY OF AGENCIES
Also Called: Seneca Center
40950 Chapel Way, Fremont (94538-4236)
PHONE..................................510 226-6180
Fax: 510 226-6352
Jessica Stryczek, *Principal*
Matt Camann, *Assistant*
EMP: 100
SALES (corp-wide): 88.8MM **Privately Held**
WEB: www.senecacenter.org
SIC: 8322 8211 8361 Social service center; elementary & secondary schools; home for the emotionally disturbed
PA: Seneca Family Of Agencies
15942 Foothill Blvd
San Leandro CA 94578
510 317-1444

(P-24205)
SENIOR ASSIST OF PENINSULA LLC
1720 Marco Polo Way Ste E, Burlingame (94010-4513)
P.O. Box 117190 (94011-7190)
PHONE..................................650 652-9791
John E Neill Jr,
Gina Demartini,
Terri Neill,
EMP: 71
SALES (est): 457.2K **Privately Held**
SIC: 8322 Old age assistance

(P-24206)
SENIOR COMPANIONS AT HOME
650 El Camino Real Ste E, Redwood City (94063-1345)
P.O. Box 795 (94064-0795)
PHONE..................................650 364-1265
Jovie Magbanua, *Director*
EMP: 50
SALES (est): 1.2MM **Privately Held**
SIC: 8322 Senior citizens' center or association

(P-24207)
SEQUOIA ADRC LP
Also Called: Sequoia Alchol DRG Rcovery Ctr
650 Main St, Redwood City (94063-1922)
PHONE..................................650 364-5504
Fax: 510 261-3977
Barry Rosan, *Exec Dir*
EMP: 60
SALES (est): 4.1MM **Privately Held**
SIC: 8322 Rehabilitation services

(P-24208)
SEQUOIA SENIOR SOLUTIONS INC
1372 N Mcdowell Blvd S, Petaluma (94954-7102)
PHONE..................................707 763-6600
Fax: 707 763-6607
Gabriella Ambrosi, *CEO*
Stanton Lawson, *CFO*
EMP: 200
SALES (est): 8.7MM **Privately Held**
WEB: www.sequoiaseniorsolutions.com
SIC: 8322 Adult day care center

(P-24209)
SER JOBS FOR PROGRESS INC SAN
255 N Fulton St Ste 106, Fresno (93701-1600)
PHONE..................................559 452-0881
Fax: 559 452-8038
Rebecca Mendibles, *Exec Dir*
Michael Jimenez, *President*
Ofelia Gamez, *Chairman*
Dee Munguia, *Hum Res Coord*
EMP: 67

SQ FT: 1,500
SALES: 2.8MM **Privately Held**
SIC: 8322 Social service center

(P-24210)
SIERRA FOREVER FAMILIES
Also Called: SFF
8928 Volunteer Ln Ste 100, Sacramento (95826-3238)
PHONE..................................916 368-5114
Bob Herne, *Exec Dir*
Pamela Camino, *Opers Spvr*
Jennifer Highley, *Social Worker*
Shahni Smith, *Social Worker*
Jeanne Reaves, *Director*
EMP: 68
SALES: 5.9MM **Privately Held**
SIC: 8322 Adoption services

(P-24211)
SOCIAL ADVOCATES FOR YOUTH
87550 Drive, San Diego (92117)
PHONE..................................858 974-3603
EMP: 152
SALES (corp-wide): 16.8MM **Privately Held**
SIC: 8322 Individual & family services
PA: Social Advocates For Youth, San Diego, Inc.
8755 Aero Dr Ste 100
San Diego CA 92123
858 565-4148

(P-24212)
SOCIAL ADVOCATES FOR YOUTH
4275 El Cajon Blvd # 101, San Diego (92105-1293)
PHONE..................................619 283-9624
Fax: 619 582-9057
Laurie Rennie, *Exec Dir*
EMP: 202
SALES (corp-wide): 16.8MM **Privately Held**
SIC: 8322 Social worker
PA: Social Advocates For Youth, San Diego, Inc.
8755 Aero Dr Ste 100
San Diego CA 92123
858 565-4148

(P-24213)
SOCIAL VOCATIONAL SERVICES INC
2772 Artesia Blvd Ste 204, Redondo Beach (90278-3370)
PHONE..................................310 793-9600
Trisha Castro, *General Mgr*
Cesar Daproza, *Director*
EMP: 56
SALES (corp-wide): 80.6MM **Privately Held**
SIC: 8322 7363 Individual & family services; temporary help service
PA: Social Vocational Services, Inc.
3555 Torrance Blvd
Torrance CA 90503
310 944-3303

(P-24214)
SOCIE OF SAINT VINCE DE PA
Also Called: SVDPLA
210 N Avenue 21, Los Angeles (90031-1713)
PHONE..................................323 224-6280
Fax: 323 225-4997
David Fields, *Exec Dir*
EMP: 132 **EST:** 1908
SQ FT: 10,000
SALES: 12MM **Privately Held**
SIC: 8322 Child related social services

(P-24215)
SOCIETY OF ST VINCENT DE PAUL
344 Grand Ave, South San Francisco (94080-3605)
PHONE..................................650 589-9039
Carolyn Ghiorso, *Branch Mgr*
EMP: 70 **Privately Held**
SIC: 8322 Individual & family services

PRODUCTS & SERVICES SECTION
8322 - Individual & Family Social Svcs County (P-24239)

PA: Society Of St Vincent De Paul Particular Council Of San Mateo Inc
50 N B St
San Mateo CA 94401

(P-24216)
SOLANO COUNTY MENTAL HEALTH
Also Called: Exodus Recovery
2101 Courage Dr, Fairfield (94533-6717)
PHONE................................707 428-1131
Fax: 707 435-2103
Camille Dullathan, *Director*
David A Godwin, *Psychiatry*
EMP: 50
SALES (est): 1.5MM **Privately Held**
SIC: 8322 Emergency social services

(P-24217)
SOURCEWISE
2115 The Alameda, San Jose (95126-1141)
PHONE................................408 350-3200
Stephen M Schmoll, *Director*
Manuel Altamirano, *COO*
Altamirano Manuel, *COO*
Kimberly Marlar, *CFO*
Kimberly R Marlar, *CFO*
EMP: 100
SQ FT: 10,000
SALES: 10.6MM **Privately Held**
WEB: www.sccoa.org
SIC: 8322 Individual & family services; old age assistance

(P-24218)
SOUTH ASIAN HELP REFERRAL AGCY
Also Called: Sahara
17100 Pioneer Blvd # 260, Artesia (90701-2776)
PHONE................................562 402-4132
EMP: 50
SALES: 914.4K **Privately Held**
SIC: 8322

(P-24219)
SOUTH BAY COMMUNITY SERVICES
430 F St, Chula Vista (91910-3711)
PHONE................................619 420-3620
Kathryn Lembo, *Exec Dir*
Ismena Valdez, *Human Res Dir*
Carolyn Mitrovich, *Purchasing*
EMP: 200
SQ FT: 2,900
SALES: 24.9MM **Privately Held**
WEB: www.southbaycommunityservices.org
SIC: 8322 Social service center

(P-24220)
SOUTH BAY CTR FOR COUNSELING
540 N Marine Ave, Wilmington (90744-5528)
PHONE................................310 414-2090
Fax: 310 414-2096
Colleen Mooney, *Exec Dir*
Cathy Cesarz, *Division Mgr*
Elisea Ramirez, *Admin Sec*
Gina Lomibao-Budnick, *Info Tech Mgr*
Gaby Ramirez, *Legal Staff*
EMP: 80
SALES: 6.5MM **Privately Held**
WEB: www.sbaycenter.com
SIC: 8322 General counseling services

(P-24221)
SOUTH COAST CHILDRENS SOC INC
Also Called: South Coast Community Services
27261 Las Ramblas Ste 220, Mission Viejo (92691-6468)
PHONE................................714 966-8650
R Scott McGuirk, *CEO*
Alice M Blair, *CFO*
Kathleen Rasmussen, *Executive Asst*
Mayra Armas, *CIO*
Nancy Huang, *Controller*
EMP: 315
SQ FT: 2,000
SALES: 18.7MM **Privately Held**
SIC: 8322 Individual & family services; rehabilitation services; community center

(P-24222)
SOUTHEAST AREA SOCIAL SERVICES
10400 Pioneer Blvd Ste 8, Santa Fe Springs (90670-3728)
PHONE................................562 946-2237
Kirk Kain, *Director*
EMP: 50
SALES (est): 2MM **Privately Held**
SIC: 8322 Individual & family services

(P-24223)
SOUTHGATE RECREATION & PK DST
Also Called: Rizal Community Center
7320 Florin Mall Dr, Sacramento (95823-3255)
PHONE................................916 421-7275
Fax: 916 395-3934
Jeremy Yee, *Manager*
Phyllis Evans, *Director*
Christine Thompson, *Director*
EMP: 50 **Privately Held**
SIC: 8322 Community center
PA: Southgate Recreation & Park District
6000 Orange Ave
Sacramento CA 95823
916 428-1171

(P-24224)
SPANISH TRLS GIRL SCOUT CNCIL
5007 Center St, Chino (91710-3409)
PHONE................................909 627-2609
Bervely Fowler, *Owner*
EMP: 50
SALES (est): 412.1K **Privately Held**
SIC: 8322 Youth center

(P-24225)
SPIRITUAL DIRECTION
164 San Luis Ave, San Bruno (94066-5507)
P.O. Box 1454, Millbrae (94030-5454)
PHONE................................650 952-9456
Ariosto Coelho, *Owner*
EMP: 50
SALES (est): 489.7K **Privately Held**
WEB: www.spiritualdirection.com
SIC: 8322 Individual & family services

(P-24226)
ST ANTHONY FOUNDATION (PA)
150 Golden Gate Ave, San Francisco (94102-3810)
PHONE................................415 241-2600
Fax: 415 252-7764
John Hardin, *Exec Dir*
Barry J Stenger, *Exec Dir*
Phillip Cunliffe, *Finance*
Raisa Shmukler, *Purchasing*
Paula Lewis, *Opers Staff*
EMP: 50
SQ FT: 45,000
SALES (est): 14.9MM **Privately Held**
WEB: www.stanthonysf.org
SIC: 8322 Individual & family services

(P-24227)
ST BARNABAS SENIOR CENTER OF L
Also Called: SAINT BARNABAS SENIOR SERVICES
675 S Carondelet St, Los Angeles (90057-3309)
PHONE................................213 388-4444
Fax: 213 388-6228
Rigo Sabareo, *President*
Nick Dumicreseu, *Treasurer*
Carmen Torres, *Executive*
Jina Provencio, *Admin Asst*
Corazon Velazco, *Controller*
EMP: 61
SQ FT: 27,000
SALES: 5.1MM **Privately Held**
SIC: 8322 Senior citizens' center or association

(P-24228)
ST JOSEPH CENTER
Also Called: Saint Joseph Center Volunteer
204 Hampton Dr, Venice (90291-8633)
PHONE................................310 396-6468
Fax: 310 392-8402
Felecia Adams, *Vice Pres*
Lonnie Herring, *CFO*
John McGann, *CFO*
Laura Porter, *Vice Pres*
VA Lecia Adams Kellum, *Exec Dir*
EMP: 85
SQ FT: 32,000
SALES: 11.6MM **Privately Held**
SIC: 8322 8331 8351 Individual & family services; child related social services; temporary relief service; job training services; vocational rehabilitation agency; child day care services

(P-24229)
ST JOSEPH HOSPICE
Also Called: Saint Joseph Hlth Sys Hospice
200 W Center St Promenade, Anaheim (92805-3960)
PHONE................................714 712-7100
Linda Glomp, *Director*
Ron Nagano, *CFO*
Maire Blaistell, *Director*
Stan Karczynski, *Manager*
EMP: 80 **EST:** 1994
SQ FT: 3,000
SALES (est): 2.6MM
SALES (corp-wide): 5.6B **Privately Held**
WEB: www.stjosephhospice.com
SIC: 8322 8063 Geriatric social service; psychiatric hospitals
HQ: St Joseph Home Health Network
200 W Center St Promenade
Anaheim CA 92805
714 712-9500

(P-24230)
ST VINCENT DE PAUL SOCIETY
3100 Norris Ave, Sacramento (95821-4023)
PHONE................................916 485-3482
EMP: 147
SALES (corp-wide): 18.6MM **Privately Held**
SIC: 8322 Individual & family services
PA: St. Vincent De Paul Of Baltimore, Inc.
2305 N Charles St Ste 300
Baltimore MD 21218
410 662-0500

(P-24231)
STANFORD UNIV MED CTR AUX
Also Called: STANFORD LINEAR ACCELERATOR CE
300 Pasteur Dr, Stanford (94305-2200)
P.O. Box 20410, Palo Alto (94309-0410)
PHONE................................650 723-6636
Fax: 650 723-7917
Mary Dahlquist, *CEO*
Sarah Clark, *President*
Scott Butler, *Administration*
Glenda Cruz, *Business Anlyst*
Christine Hopkins, *Project Dir*
EMP: 400
SALES: 21.4K
SALES (corp-wide): 1.9B **Privately Held**
SIC: 8322 Adult day care center
PA: Leland Stanford Junior University
2575 Sand Hill Rd
Menlo Park CA 94025
650 723-2300

(P-24232)
STANISLAUS COUNTY POLICE
1325 Beverly Dr, Modesto (95351-2313)
PHONE................................209 529-9121
Fax: 209 529-8794
Alfredo Guerra, *Exec Dir*
Vicki Bauman, *President*
Carla Teas, *Vice Pres*
Julio Madrigal, *Supervisor*
EMP: 144
SALES: 1.6MM **Privately Held**
SIC: 8322 Social service center

(P-24233)
STAR INC
Also Called: Enrichment Program
4145 Delmar Ave Ste 1, Rocklin (95677-4041)
PHONE................................916 632-8407
Fax: 916 632-8427
Cindy Daniels, *Administration*
Sharron Cosker, *Controller*
Erick Bozzi II,
EMP: 150 **EST:** 1999
SALES (est): 3.7MM **Privately Held**
WEB: www.starsacramento.org
SIC: 8322 Individual & family services

(P-24234)
STAR VIEW CHLDRN FMLY SRVCS
1085 W Victoria St, Compton (90220-5817)
PHONE................................310 868-5379
Fax: 310 868-5397
Paul Stansbury, *CEO*
Kent Dunlap, *Vice Pres*
Maryjane Gross, *Admin Sec*
Ontson Placide, *Director*
EMP: 99
SALES (est): 2.6MM **Privately Held**
SIC: 8322 Individual & family services

(P-24235)
STARVISTA
610 Elm St Ste 212, San Carlos (94070-3070)
PHONE................................650 591-9623
Michael GRB, *CEO*
Rahael Solomon, *Volunteer Dir*
Elayne Pace, *Bd of Directors*
Roger Toguchi, *Bd of Directors*
Sarah Dobkin, *Program Mgr*
EMP: 118
SQ FT: 7,200
SALES (est): 5.8MM **Privately Held**
SIC: 8322 Individual & family services; substance abuse counseling; child related social services

(P-24236)
STEELWRKERS OLD TMERS FNDATION
3355 E Gage Ave, Huntington Park (90255-5530)
PHONE................................323 582-6090
Fax: 323 582-5957
George Cole, *CEO*
Patricia Topete, *Manager*
EMP: 90
SALES: 6.9MM **Privately Held**
SIC: 8322 Individual & family services

(P-24237)
STEPHOUSE RECOVERY CENTER
Also Called: Step House Recovery
10529 Slater Ave, Fountain Valley (92708-4841)
PHONE................................714 394-3494
George J Vilagut, *CEO*
EMP: 70
SALES: 8MM **Privately Held**
SIC: 8322 General counseling services

(P-24238)
SUMMITVIEW CHILD TREATMENT
670 Placerville Dr Ste 1b, Placerville (95667-4200)
PHONE................................530 621-9800
Carla Well, *Principal*
Carla Wills, *Exec Dir*
EMP: 80
SALES (est): 3.8MM **Privately Held**
SIC: 8322 8093 Individual & family services; mental health clinic, outpatient

(P-24239)
SUNNY CAL ADHC INC
8450 Valley Blvd Ste 121b, Rosemead (91770-1681)
PHONE................................626 307-7772
Fax: 626 307-7776
Tony Leung, *President*
EMP: 60
SALES (est): 1MM **Privately Held**
SIC: 8322 Adult day care center

8322 - Individual & Family Social Svcs County (P-24240)

(P-24240)
SUNRISE FOOD MINISTRY
5901 San Juan Ave, Citrus Heights (95610-6508)
PHONE..................916 965-5431
Fred Chirstensen, *President*
EMP: 60
SALES: 89K **Privately Held**
SIC: 8322 Individual & family services

(P-24241)
SUNRISE SENIOR LIVING LLC
Also Called: Sunrise of Danville
1027 Diablo Rd, Danville (94526-1923)
PHONE..................925 309-4178
Fax: 925 831-1713
Sol Spencer, *Director*
Gina McGaha, *Director*
Renee Sproles, *Director*
EMP: 80
SALES (corp-wide): 3.8B **Publicly Held**
WEB: www.sunrise.com
SIC: 8322 Old age assistance
HQ: Sunrise Senior Living, Llc
7902 Westpark Dr
Mc Lean VA 22102

(P-24242)
SUPREME COURT UNITED STATES
Also Called: US Probation
101 W Broadway Ste 700, San Diego (92101-8208)
PHONE..................619 557-7149
Kenneth Young, *Chief*
EMP: 157 **Publicly Held**
WEB: www.supremecourtus.gov
SIC: 8322 Probation office; offender rehabilitation agency
HQ: Supreme Court, United States
1 1st St Ne
Washington DC 20543
202 479-3000

(P-24243)
SUTTER HEALTH
475 Pioneer Ave Ste 400, Woodland (95776-4905)
PHONE..................530 406-5600
Rigoberto Barba, *Med Doctor*
EMP: 420
SALES (corp-wide): 11B **Privately Held**
SIC: 8322 Individual & family services
PA: Sutter Health
2200 River Plaza Dr
Sacramento CA 95833
916 733-8800

(P-24244)
SUTTER HLTH RHABILITATION SVCS
Also Called: Sutter Medical Ctr Sacramento
2801 L St Fl 3, Sacramento (95816-5615)
P.O. Box 160727 (95816-0727)
PHONE..................916 733-3040
Fax: 916 733-8336
Lisa Drewslucero, *Manager*
Yuhwan Hong, *Surgeon*
Lawrence Tkach, *Surgeon*
Tim Way, *Cardiovascular*
Nellie Nanda, *Med Doctor*
EMP: 70
SALES (est): 7.5MM **Privately Held**
SIC: 8322

(P-24245)
SUTTER HLTH SCRMNTO SIERRA REG
Also Called: Sutter Senior Care
1234 U St, Sacramento (95818-1433)
PHONE..................916 446-3100
Fax: 916 446-3699
Janet Tedesco, *Branch Mgr*
EMP: 57
SALES (corp-wide): 11B **Privately Held**
SIC: 8322 Senior citizens' center or association
HQ: Sutter Health Sacramento Sierra Region
2200 River Plaza Dr
Sacramento CA 95833
916 733-8800

(P-24246)
TEEN CHALLENGE NORWESTCAL NEV
Also Called: Southbay Teen Challenge
390 Mathew St, Santa Clara (95050-3114)
P.O. Box 24309, San Jose (95154-4309)
PHONE..................408 703-2001
Dana Rowe, *Director*
Jay Patterson, *Director*
EMP: 100
SALES: 1.3MM **Privately Held**
SIC: 8322 Individual & family services

(P-24247)
TENET HEALTHSYSTEM MEDICAL
Also Called: Redding Specialty Hospital
2801 Eureka Way, Redding (96001-0222)
PHONE..................530 246-9000
Fax: 530 244-1812
Christine Jones, *Manager*
EMP: 250
SALES (corp-wide): 18.7B **Publicly Held**
WEB: www.tenenthealth.com
SIC: 8322 Rehabilitation services
HQ: Tenet Healthsystem Medical, Inc
1445 Ross Ave Ste 1400
Dallas TX 75202
469 893-2000

(P-24248)
TERKENSHA ASSOCIATES INC
Also Called: North Area Cmmnty Mntl Hlth CN
811 Grand Ave Ste D, Sacramento (95838-3466)
PHONE..................916 922-9868
Fax: 916 922-7342
William Benda, *Director*
William Moss, *President*
EMP: 52 **EST:** 1980
SALES (est): 2.8MM **Privately Held**
SIC: 8322 General counseling services

(P-24249)
TERRA NOVA COUNSELING (PA)
5750 Sunrise Blvd Ste 100, Citrus Heights (95610-7639)
PHONE..................916 344-0249
Mary Stroube, *Exec Dir*
Juliet Hakopain, *Info Tech Mgr*
Robert Ellis, *Business Mgr*
Fran Reilly, *Finance*
EMP: 80
SQ FT: 4,789
SALES: 4.5MM **Privately Held**
WEB: www.after.com
SIC: 8322 Alcoholism counseling, nontreatment; drug abuse counselor, nontreatment; family (marriage) counseling; family counseling services

(P-24250)
TESSIE CLVLAND CMNTY SVCS CORP
Also Called: Tccsc
8019 Compton Ave Ste 219, Los Angeles (90001-3409)
PHONE..................323 586-7333
Forescee Hogan-Rowles, *CEO*
Tyrone Ingram, *President*
Carolyn Chadwick, *CFO*
Moses Chadwick, *Exec Dir*
Sylvia Ramirez, *General Mgr*
EMP: 100
SALES: 12MM **Privately Held**
WEB: www.tccsc.org
SIC: 8322 Child related social services

(P-24251)
TLCS INC
650 Howe Ave Ste 400, Sacramento (95825-4732)
PHONE..................916 441-0123
Michael Lazar, *Exec Dir*
Leslie Mitchell, *Vice Pres*
EMP: 100
SQ FT: 1,868
SALES: 9MM **Privately Held**
SIC: 8322 Individual & family services

(P-24252)
TOOLWORKS INC
3075 Adeline St Ste 230, Berkeley (94703-2578)
PHONE..................510 649-1322
Steve Crabiel, *Branch Mgr*
EMP: 407
SALES (corp-wide): 12.9MM **Privately Held**
SIC: 8322 Individual & family services
PA: Toolworks Inc
25 Kearny St Ste 400
San Francisco CA 94108
415 733-0990

(P-24253)
TOWARD MAXIMUM INDEPENDENCE (PA)
Also Called: T M I
4740 Murphy Canyon Rd # 300, San Diego (92123-4385)
PHONE..................858 467-0600
Fax: 858 467-9059
Kerby Wohlander, *Director*
Rachel Harris, *Exec Dir*
Cathena Ferrero, *Division Mgr*
Deana Sanchez, *Division Mgr*
David Cross, *Office Mgr*
EMP: 125
SQ FT: 5,700
SALES: 10.2MM **Privately Held**
SIC: 8322 Individual & family services

(P-24254)
TPD DELL DIOS
1817 Avenida Del Diablo, Escondido (92029-3112)
PHONE..................760 741-2888
D Williams, *Exec Dir*
Donald Williams, *Exec Dir*
EMP: 50
SALES (est): 590.9K **Privately Held**
SIC: 8322 Old age assistance

(P-24255)
TRACY INTERFAITH MINISTRIES
311 W Grant Line Rd, Tracy (95376-2547)
P.O. Box 404 (95378-0404)
PHONE..................209 836-5424
Darlene Quinn, *Director*
Lamar Stephenson, *Chairman*
Robert Weinberg, *Treasurer*
EMP: 65
SALES: 309.4K **Privately Held**
SIC: 8322 Social service center

(P-24256)
TRAINING TOWARD SELF RELIANCE
Also Called: TTSR
620 Bercut Dr, Sacramento (95811-0131)
PHONE..................916 442-8877
Fax: 916 442-8824
Nancy Chance, *Director*
EMP: 56
SALES: 1.4MM **Privately Held**
WEB: www.ttsr.org
SIC: 8322 Social services for the handicapped

(P-24257)
TRANSITIONS - MENTAL HLTH ASSN (PA)
Also Called: SLO TRANSITIONS
784 High St, San Luis Obispo (93401-5243)
P.O. Box 15408 (93406-5408)
PHONE..................805 540-6500
Jill B White, *Exec Dir*
Kim Banks, *Human Res Dir*
EMP: 60
SQ FT: 8,000
SALES: 10.7MM **Privately Held**
WEB: www.t-mha.org
SIC: 8322 Social services for the handicapped

(P-24258)
TRI COUNTY RESPITE CARE SVC
Also Called: RESPITE SERVICE
1215 Plumas St Ste 1600, Yuba City (95991-3456)
P.O. Box 1296 (95992-1296)
PHONE..................530 755-3500
Diane Rose, *Director*
Joy Scott, *Principal*
EMP: 56
SALES: 1.1MM **Privately Held**
SIC: 8322 Individual & family services

(P-24259)
TRI-COUNTIES ASSOCIATION F (PA)
Also Called: TRI-COUNTIES REGIONAL CENTER
520 E Montecito St, Santa Barbara (93103-3278)
PHONE..................805 962-7881
Fax: 805 884-7229
Bob Cobbs, *President*
Omar Noorzad, *Exec Dir*
Phil Stucky, *Controller*
Luzmaria Espinosa, *Director*
EMP: 60
SQ FT: 16,000
SALES: 229.2MM **Privately Held**
SIC: 8322 Association for the handicapped

(P-24260)
TULARE YOUTH SERVICE BUREAU (PA)
Also Called: Tulare Yth Sxl ABS Trtmnt Prgr
327 S K St, Tulare (93274-5416)
PHONE..................559 685-8547
Fax: 559 688-1304
C Lnn-Armas, *Exec Dir*
Anna Ferreira, *CFO*
Cheryl Lennon-Armas, *Exec Dir*
Timothy Zavala, *Social Worker*
Dejuan Singletary, *Manager*
EMP: 50
SQ FT: 18,000
SALES (est): 4.7MM **Privately Held**
WEB: www.tysb.org
SIC: 8322 Youth self-help agency

(P-24261)
TURNING POINT CENTRAL CAL INC
117 N R St, Madera (93637-4465)
PHONE..................559 664-9021
EMP: 52
SALES (corp-wide): 54.5MM **Privately Held**
SIC: 8322 Individual & family services
PA: Turning Point Of Central California, Inc.
615 S Atwood St
Visalia CA 93277
559 732-8086

(P-24262)
TURNING POINT CENTRAL CAL INC
Also Called: Visalia Youth Services
711 N Court St, Visalia (93291-3638)
PHONE..................559 627-1490
Fax: 559 627-0607
Jose Ochoa, *Branch Mgr*
Shirley Kluver, *Director*
Dale Rowden, *Manager*
EMP: 50
SALES (corp-wide): 54.8MM **Privately Held**
SIC: 8322 8093 Individual & family services; mental health clinic, outpatient
PA: Turning Point Of Central California, Inc.
615 S Atwood St
Visalia CA 93277
559 732-8086

(P-24263)
UCSF AIDS HEALTH PROJECT
1930 Market St, San Francisco (94102-6228)
PHONE..................415 476-3902
Fax: 415 476-3655
Jim Dilley, *President*
Audrey Dayauon, *Financial Exec*
Joanna Rinaldi, *Director*
Sherrill Arms, *Manager*
Crawford Carrel, *Manager*
EMP: 80 **EST:** 1985
SALES (est): 2.9MM **Privately Held**
SIC: 8322 Individual & family services

(P-24264)
UNION PAN ASIAN COMMUNITIES (PA)
Also Called: UPAC
1031 25th St, San Diego (92102-2194)
PHONE..................619 232-6454
Fax: 619 235-4607
Margaret Iwanaga-Penrose, *Director*
Koji Fukumura, *Vice Chairman*
Sunnyo Tak, *Exec Dir*

PRODUCTS & SERVICES SECTION
8322 - Individual & Family Social Svcs County (P-24286)

Margaret Penrose, *Webmaster*
Annette Phan, *Controller*
EMP: 58
SQ FT: 14,000
SALES: 6.9MM **Privately Held**
WEB: www.upacsd.com
SIC: 8322 Individual & family services

(P-24265)
UNION STATION HOMELESS SVCS
825 E Orange Grove Blvd, Pasadena (91104-4554)
PHONE.................626 240-4550
Marvin Gross, *CEO*
Rabbi Marvin Gross, *CEO*
Terry Krupczak, *Treasurer*
Linda Jahnke, *Vice Pres*
Bradley Schwartz, *Admin Sec*
EMP: 73
SQ FT: 6,500
SALES: 5.8MM **Privately Held**
SIC: 8322 Emergency social services

(P-24266)
UNITED CEREBRAL PALSY ASSOC
980 Roosevelt Ste 100, Irvine (92620-3670)
PHONE.................949 333-6400
Deborah Levy, *President*
Barbara Jones, *Administration*
Francesca Costilla,
Yvette Salcedo, *Manager*
EMP: 130
SQ FT: 5,000
SALES: 3.8MM **Privately Held**
SIC: 8322 Association for the handicapped

(P-24267)
UNITED CEREBRAL PALSY ASSOC (PA)
333 W Benjamin Holt Dr # 1, Stockton (95207-3906)
PHONE.................209 956-0290
Ray All, *Exec Dir*
EMP: 110
SQ FT: 15,000
SALES: 5.6MM **Privately Held**
WEB: www.ucpsj.org
SIC: 8322 Association for the handicapped

(P-24268)
UNITED CP/S CHLDRNS FNDN LA
2170 N Westlake Blvd 22, Westlake Village (91362-5122)
PHONE.................805 494-1141
Fax: 805 496-5823
Steve Bird, *Administration*
EMP: 50
SALES (corp-wide): 27.5MM **Privately Held**
SIC: 8322 Individual & family services
PA: United Cerebral Palsy/Spastic Children's Foundation Of Los Angeles And Ventura Counties
6430 Independence Ave
Woodland Hills CA 91367
818 782-2211

(P-24269)
UNITED CP/S CHLDRNS FNDN LA
2628 Brighton Ave, Los Angeles (90018-2752)
PHONE.................323 737-0303
Nicole Seaton, *Director*
EMP: 71
SALES (corp-wide): 27.5MM **Privately Held**
SIC: 8322 Individual & family services
PA: United Cerebral Palsy/Spastic Children's Foundation Of Los Angeles And Ventura Counties
6430 Independence Ave
Woodland Hills CA 91367
818 782-2211

(P-24270)
UNITED CRBRL PLSY OF CNTRL CA (PA)
Also Called: U C P-UNITED CEREBAL PALSY ASS
4224 N Cedar Ave, Fresno (93726-3731)
PHONE.................559 221-8272
Fax: 559 221-9347
Mark Lanier, *President*
Carol Kloninger, *Vice Pres*
Lynn Cundick, *Exec Dir*
Jamie Marrash, *Exec Dir*
Bonnie Peterson, *Admin Sec*
EMP: 50
SQ FT: 15,000
SALES: 4MM **Privately Held**
WEB: www.mcvalleycup.com
SIC: 8322 Association for the handicapped

(P-24271)
UNITED WAY OF BAY AREA (PA)
Also Called: United Way, The
550 Kearny St Ste 1000, San Francisco (94108-2524)
PHONE.................415 808-4300
Fax: 415 808-4243
Anne Wilson, *CEO*
Michael Scanlon, *Chairman*
Moses Awe, *Treasurer*
Ronald Caton, *Exec VP*
John Schaver, *Vice Pres*
EMP: 85 **EST:** 1923
SQ FT: 40,000
SALES: 12.5MM **Privately Held**
WEB: www.uwba.org
SIC: 8322 8399 Individual & family services; fund raising organization, non-fee basis

(P-24272)
UPLIFT FAMILY SERVICES
9343 Tech Center Dr # 200, Sacramento (95826-2592)
PHONE.................916 366-6820
Demetra Carter-Whitted, *Manager*
Harriet Wasserstrum, *Exec Dir*
EMP: 100
SALES (corp-wide): 82.8MM **Privately Held**
SIC: 8322 Individual & family services
PA: Uplift Family Services
251 Llewellyn Ave
Campbell CA 95008
408 379-3790

(P-24273)
US CONTROL GROUP INC
9157 W Sunset Blvd # 212, West Hollywood (90069-3167)
P.O. Box 1630, Beverly Hills (90213-1630)
PHONE.................888 500-7090
Monte Caplan, *President*
Mary Keeler, *Info Tech Mgr*
Dave Montgomery, *Manager*
EMP: 66
SALES (est): 5.4MM **Privately Held**
SIC: 8322 Disaster service

(P-24274)
VALLEY HEALTH CARE SYSTEMS INC
1401 El Cmino Ave Ste 510, Sacramento (95815)
PHONE.................916 669-0508
Steven Swan, *CEO*
Tim Coxen, *President*
Jon Wright, *Vice Pres*
Lisa Baker, *Manager*
EMP: 200
SQ FT: 5,000
SALES (est): 4.5MM **Privately Held**
SIC: 8322 7361 Travelers' aid; nurses' registry

(P-24275)
VALLEY MTN REGIONAL CTR INC (PA)
702 N Aurora St, Stockton (95202-2200)
P.O. Box 692290 (95269-2290)
PHONE.................209 473-0951
Fax: 209 473-0719
Paul Billodeau, *CEO*
Evonne Lucero, *COO*
Debra Roth, *CFO*
Robert Bianco, *Bd of Directors*
Terri Miniaci, *Vice Pres*
EMP: 160
SQ FT: 63,000
SALES: 150MM **Privately Held**
SIC: 8322 Multi-service center

(P-24276)
VALLEY OAKS RESIDENTIAL
10623 E Highway 120, Manteca (95336-9715)
P.O. Box 1358 (95336-1146)
PHONE.................209 239-3244
Mario Duenas, *President*
Gregg Potts, *Director*
EMP: 60
SQ FT: 1,700
SALES: 2.7MM **Privately Held**
SIC: 8322 Individual & family services

(P-24277)
VENTURA CNTY COUNCIL ON AGING
4917 S Rose Ave, Oxnard (93033-7803)
P.O. Box 2429 (93034-2429)
PHONE.................805 986-1424
Tom Carlisle, *CEO*
EMP: 60
SQ FT: 15,000
SALES: 50K **Privately Held**
SIC: 8322 Senior citizens' center or association

(P-24278)
VINTAGE SENIOR MANAGEMENT INC
2721 W Willow St, Burbank (91505-4544)
PHONE.................818 954-9500
Brian Flornes, *Branch Mgr*
EMP: 517
SALES (corp-wide): 69.9MM **Privately Held**
SIC: 8322 Geriatric social service
PA: Senior Vintage Management Inc
23 Corporate Plaza Dr # 190
Newport Beach CA 92660
949 719-4080

(P-24279)
VISALIA UNIFIED SCHOOL DST
Also Called: Office of Nutritional Services
801 N Mooney Blvd, Visalia (93291-3230)
PHONE.................559 730-7871
Fax: 559 730-7858
Regina Ocampo, *Director*
Angela Sanchez, *Administration*
Steve Harrell, *Teacher*
EMP: 180
SALES (corp-wide): 275MM **Privately Held**
SIC: 8322 8621 Individual & family services; health association
PA: Visalia Unified School District
5000 W Cypress Ave
Visalia CA 93277
559 730-7529

(P-24280)
VISTA CARE GROUP LLC (PA)
Also Called: Vista Gardens
1863 Devon Pl, Vista (92084-7624)
PHONE.................760 295-3900
Harry Crowell, *Chairman*
Joe Balbas,
EMP: 80
SALES (est): 4.2MM **Privately Held**
SIC: 8322 Senior citizens' center or association

(P-24281)
VOLUNTEER CENTER LOS ANGELES
Also Called: Volunteer Center of La Alsc
1375 N St Andrews Pl, Los Angeles (90028-8530)
PHONE.................818 908-5151
Fax: 818 908-5147
Nancy Onsen, *Director*
Maria Sedano, *Regional Mgr*
Gilbert Gonzales, *Manager*
EMP: 50
SALES (est): 1.7MM **Privately Held**
SIC: 8322 Senior citizens' center or association

(P-24282)
VOLUNTEERS OF AMER LOS ANGELES
Also Called: Maud Booth Family Center
11243 Kittridge St, North Hollywood (91606-2605)
PHONE.................818 506-0597
Fax: 818 980-7634
Felix Cruz, *Manager*
EMP: 50
SALES (corp-wide): 41.6K **Privately Held**
WEB: www.voala.org
SIC: 8322 8351 Social service center; child day care services
HQ: Volunteers Of America Of Los Angeles
3600 Wilshire Blvd # 1500
Los Angeles CA 90010
213 389-1500

(P-24283)
VOLUNTEERS OF AMERICA
2100 N Broadway Ste 300, Santa Ana (92706-2624)
PHONE.................714 426-9834
Bob Pratt, *Exec Dir*
EMP: 150
SQ FT: 7,000
SALES (est): 2.4MM
SALES (corp-wide): 41.6K **Privately Held**
SIC: 8322 7361 9531 Individual & family services; employment agencies; building standards agency, government
HQ: Volunteers Of America Of Los Angeles
3600 Wilshire Blvd # 1500
Los Angeles CA 90010
213 389-1500

(P-24284)
VOLUNTEERS OF AMERICA GREATER
3434 Marconi Ave Ste A, Sacramento (95821-6242)
PHONE.................916 265-3400
Fax: 916 442-1861
Leo McFarland, *CEO*
Amani Sawires, *Vice Pres*
Monique Mendyke, *Associate Dir*
Rachelle Pellissier, *Exec Dir*
Joanna Michaels, *Admin Asst*
EMP: 350
SALES (est): 24.3MM
SALES (corp-wide): 41.6K **Privately Held**
WEB: www.voa.org
SIC: 8322 Social service center
PA: Volunteers Of America, Inc.
1660 Duke St Ste 100
Alexandria VA 22314
703 341-5000

(P-24285)
WATCH RESOURCES INC (PA)
Also Called: T.C.A.H
12801 Cabezut Rd, Sonora (95370-5938)
PHONE.................209 533-0510
Christine Daily, *Exec Dir*
Jeff Rains, *President*
Eric Carlson, *Treasurer*
Bruce Chan, *Treasurer*
Jason Land, *Vice Pres*
EMP: 50
SQ FT: 7,200
SALES: 3.2MM **Privately Held**
SIC: 8322 0782 7349 4783 Association for the handicapped; landscape contractors; janitorial service, contract basis; packing & crating; mailing & messenger services

(P-24286)
WEINGART CENTER ASSOCIATION
Also Called: Weingart Center For Homeless
566 S San Pedro St, Los Angeles (90013-2102)
PHONE.................213 622-6359
Fax: 213 488-3419
Kevin Murray, *President*
David Furman, *Ch of Bd*
Sonny Santa Ines, *CFO*
Jeffrey Catania, *Vice Pres*
Deborah Villar, *Vice Pres*
EMP: 150
SQ FT: 175,000

8322 - Individual & Family Social Svcs County (P-24287)

PRODUDUCTS & SERVICES SECTION

SALES: 12.9MM **Privately Held**
SIC: 8322 Individual & family services; emergency social services; general counseling services

(P-24287)
WEST COUNTRA COSTA YOUTH SVCS (PA)
263 S 20th St, Richmond (94804-2709)
PHONE.................510 412-5647
Fax: 510 215-9713
John Ziesenhenne, *President*
Kristie Johnson, *Exec Dir*
Robert Wilkins, *Exec Dir*
Merlin Cases, *Admin Asst*
Becca Glass, *Training Spec*
EMP: 53
SALES: 3.2MM **Privately Held**
SIC: 8322 Child related social services

(P-24288)
WESTERN MED RHBLTTION ASSOC LP
14851 Yorba St, Tustin (92780-2925)
PHONE.................714 832-9200
Paula Redman, *Controller*
Ben Zavala, *Engineer*
Paula Redmond, *Controller*
Alana Gilbert, *Hlthcr Dir*
Lisa Henton, *Director*
EMP: 140
SQ FT: 90,000
SALES (est): 2.3MM
SALES (corp-wide): 3.1B **Publicly Held**
WEB: www.healthsouth.com
SIC: 8322 8069 Rehabilitation services; specialty hospitals, except psychiatric
PA: Healthsouth Corporation
3660 Grandview Pkwy # 200
Birmingham AL 35243
205 967-7116

(P-24289)
WESTERN YOUTH SERVICES
26137 La Paz Rd Ste 230, Mission Viejo (92691-5337)
PHONE.................949 595-8610
Muhammad I Rajput, *Psychiatry*
David Sthwartz, *Manager*
EMP: 52
SALES (corp-wide): 12.7MM **Privately Held**
SIC: 8322 Individual & family services
PA: Western Youth Services
23461 S Pointe Dr Ste 220
Laguna Hills CA 92653
949 855-1556

(P-24290)
WHOLE CHILD
10155 Colima Rd, Whittier (90603-2042)
PHONE.................562 692-0383
Charlene Dinas Peinado, *CEO*
EMP: 90
SALES (est): 3.4MM **Privately Held**
SIC: 8322 General counseling services

(P-24291)
WILLITS SENIORS INC
1501 Baechtel Rd, Willits (95490-4516)
PHONE.................707 459-8826
Fax: 707 459-1772
Allyn Noneman, *Director*
Allyn Nonneman, *Exec Dir*
John Bredehoft, *Agent*
EMP: 57
SQ FT: 4,000
SALES: 954.9K **Privately Held**
SIC: 8322 Individual & family services

(P-24292)
WOMANS ALLIANCE WOMA
234 E Gish Rd Ste 200, San Jose (95112-4724)
PHONE.................408 279-2962
Kathleen Krenek, *Principal*
EMP: 52
SALES (est): 2.1MM **Privately Held**
SIC: 8322 Individual & family services

(P-24293)
WOMEN INFANT & CHILDREN
Also Called: Nutrition Service Division
2525 Grand Ave, Long Beach (90815-1765)
PHONE.................562 570-4228
Fax: 562 570-1754
Judy Ogunji, *Director*
EMP: 55
SALES (est): 663.3K **Privately Held**
SIC: 8322 Individual & family services

(P-24294)
WOMENS LAW CENTER
950 W 17th St Ste D, Santa Ana (92706-3573)
PHONE.................714 667-1038
Richard C Gilbert, *Owner*
EMP: 100
SALES (est): 1.1MM **Privately Held**
SIC: 8322 Adoption services

(P-24295)
YOUNG MENS CHRSTN ASSN OF LA
Also Called: Downey YMCA
11531 Downey Ave, Downey (90241-4936)
PHONE.................562 862-4201
Fax: 562 861-1700
George Saikali, *Exec Dir*
Beth Crawford, *Exec Dir*
EMP: 150
SALES (corp-wide): 103.1MM **Privately Held**
SIC: 8322 7997 Social service center; membership sports & recreation clubs
PA: Young Men's Christian Association Of Metropolitan Los Angeles
625 S New Hampshire Ave
Los Angeles CA 90005
213 351-2256

(P-24296)
YOUNG MENS CHRSTN ASSN OF LA
Also Called: National Fitness Testing
1553 N Shrader Blvd, Los Angeles (90028)
PHONE.................323 467-4161
Fax: 323 467-3026
Rosa Najera, *Branch Mgr*
Jenny Chiu, *Vice Pres*
Karen Carey, *Admin Asst*
Lipmin Wong, *Comp Spec*
Jim Jablonski, *Business Mgr*
EMP: 150
SALES (corp-wide): 103.1MM **Privately Held**
SIC: 8322 Individual & family services
PA: Young Men's Christian Association Of Metropolitan Los Angeles
625 S New Hampshire Ave
Los Angeles CA 90005
213 351-2256

(P-24297)
YOUNG MN CHRSTN ASSC (PA)
Also Called: YMCA
401 Corto St, Alhambra (91801-4553)
PHONE.................626 576-0226
Fax: 626 576-1351
Valarie Gomez, *CEO*
Art Narvaez, *Manager*
EMP: 70
SQ FT: 17,000
SALES: 1.2MM **Privately Held**
WEB: www.wsgymca.org
SIC: 8322 8661 Individual & family services; youth center; community center; religious organizations

(P-24298)
YOUTH FOR CHANGE
2400 Washington Ave, Redding (96001-2802)
PHONE.................530 605-1520
EMP: 68
SALES (corp-wide): 11.1MM **Privately Held**
SIC: 8322 Youth center
PA: Youth For Change
7200 Skyway
Paradise CA 95969
530 877-1965

(P-24299)
YOUTH FOR CHANGE (PA)
Also Called: PARADISE RIDGE FAMILY RESOURCE
7200 Skyway, Paradise (95969-3280)
P.O. Box 1476 (95967-1476)
PHONE.................530 877-1965
Fax: 530 872-7784

Keith Robbins, *President*
Andy Martinez, *CFO*
Mike Efford, *Chairman*
Michele Peterson, *Chairman*
Alan White, *Chairman*
EMP: 115
SQ FT: 5,000
SALES: 11.1MM **Privately Held**
SIC: 8322 Child related social services

(P-24300)
YOUTH FOR CHANGE
2185 Baldwin Ave, Oroville (95966-5312)
PHONE.................530 538-8347
Bobby Jones, *Branch Mgr*
EMP: 68
SALES (corp-wide): 11.1MM **Privately Held**
SIC: 8322 Youth center
PA: Youth For Change
7200 Skyway
Paradise CA 95969
530 877-1965

(P-24301)
YWCA CONTRA COSTA/SACRAMENTO (PA)
1320 Arnold Dr Ste 170, Martinez (94553-6537)
PHONE.................925 372-4213
Fax: 925 372-4216
Nancy Atkinson, *CEO*
Pamela Mitchell, *Controller*
Monica Garcia, *Program Dir*
Annette Hee Jimenez, *Director*
EMP: 60
SQ FT: 8,000
SALES: 2.4MM **Privately Held**
SIC: 8322 8641 8351 Individual & family services; community membership club; child day care services

---

8331 Job Training & Vocational Rehabilitation Svcs

(P-24302)
ABILITY COUNTS INC (PA)
775 Trademark Cir Ste 101, Corona (92879-2084)
PHONE.................951 734-6595
Fax: 951 734-5574
Joyce Hearn, *CEO*
Jeannie Roak, *Software Dev*
EMP: 57
SQ FT: 28,000
SALES: 7.6MM **Privately Held**
WEB: www.abilitycounts.org
SIC: 8331 Sheltered workshop

(P-24303)
APPRENTICE & JOURNEYMEN TRN TR
Also Called: Compton Training Center
7850 Haskell Ave, Van Nuys (91406-1907)
PHONE.................323 636-9871
Micheal Hazard, *Exec Dir*
Milt Edwards, *Manager*
EMP: 99
SALES: 16.1MM **Privately Held**
SIC: 8331 Job training & vocational rehabilitation services

(P-24304)
ARC FRESNO/MADERA COUNTIES (PA)
4490 E Ashlan Ave, Fresno (93726-2647)
PHONE.................559 226-6268
Fax: 559 226-6269
Lori Rmirez, *CEO*
Carolyn Wallace, *President*
Mike Takechi, *Treasurer*
Peter Mersino, *Vice Pres*
Alan Lagunoff, *Admin Sec*
EMP: 85
SALES: 9.7MM **Privately Held**
SIC: 8331 Job training & vocational rehabilitation services; job training services

(P-24305)
ARC MID-CITIES INC
14208 Towne Ave, Los Angeles (90061-2653)
PHONE.................310 329-9272
Lena Cole Dennis, *President*
John Wagner, *Exec Dir*
Bedsog Jugo, *Human Res Mgr*
EMP: 160
SALES (est): 6.6MM **Privately Held**
WEB: www.arcmidcities.org
SIC: 8331 8322 Job training services; individual & family services

(P-24306)
ARC OF ALAMEDA COUNTY
Also Called: Walpert Center
1101 Walpert St, Hayward (94541-6705)
PHONE.................510 582-8151
Fax: 510 582-0506
Renee Tuddel, *Manager*
EMP: 110
SQ FT: 2,000
SALES (corp-wide): 4.7MM **Privately Held**
WEB: www.tiw-alameda.com
SIC: 8331 Sheltered workshop
PA: The Arc Of Alameda County
14700 Doolittle Dr
San Leandro CA 94577
310 357-3569

(P-24307)
ASIAN REHABILITATION SVC INC (PA)
4322 Wilshire Blvd # 310, Los Angeles (90010-3794)
PHONE.................213 743-9242
Fax: 213 743-9266
Brad Bagasao, *CEO*
Cherry Habacon, *Executive*
Howard Yin, *Accountant*
EMP: 62
SQ FT: 28,000
SALES: 3.4MM **Privately Held**
WEB: www.asianrehab.org
SIC: 8331 Vocational rehabilitation agency

(P-24308)
ASIAN REHABILITATION SVC INC
Also Called: ARS
312 N Spring St Ste B30, Los Angeles (90012-3152)
PHONE.................213 680-3790
George Allen, *Manager*
EMP: 120
SALES (corp-wide): 3.4MM **Privately Held**
WEB: www.asianrehab.org
SIC: 8331 Vocational rehabilitation agency
PA: Asian Rehabilitation Service, Inc.
4322 Wilshire Blvd # 310
Los Angeles CA 90010
213 743-9242

(P-24309)
ASSOC FOR RETARDED CITIZENS
Also Called: School of Hope
796 E 6th St, San Bernardino (92410-4532)
PHONE.................909 884-6484
Fax: 909 885-3111
Kris Oxnevad, *Director*
EMP: 55 **EST:** 1952
SALES: 984.6K **Privately Held**
WEB: www.schoolofhope.com
SIC: 8331 5399 Job training & vocational rehabilitation services; surplus & salvage goods

(P-24310)
ASSOCIATION FOR RETARDED (PA)
Also Called: Hillside Enterprises
4519 E Stearns St, Long Beach (90815-2540)
PHONE.................562 597-7716
Fax: 562 494-8152
Harry A Van Loon, *Director*
EMP: 81
SQ FT: 35,000
SALES: 4.8MM **Privately Held**
SIC: 8331 Sheltered workshop

PRODUCTS & SERVICES SECTION
8331 - Job Training & Vocational Rehabilitation Svcs County (P-24333)

(P-24311)
ASSOCIATION FOR RETARDED CITZN (PA)
Also Called: SOUTHEAST INDUSTRIES
12049 Woodruff Ave, Downey (90241-5669)
PHONE.................................562 803-1556
Fax: 562 803-4080
Kevin Mac Donald, *Exec Dir*
EMP: 75
SQ FT: 9,800
SALES: 3.7MM **Privately Held**
SIC: 8331 5932 Skill training center; vocational training agency; used merchandise stores

(P-24312)
BAKERSFIELD ASSC RRTD CTZNS
2240 S Union Ave, Bakersfield (93307-4158)
PHONE.................................661 834-2272
Jim Baldwin, *President*
Bill Frowning, *CFO*
Mike Grover, *Vice Pres*
EMP: 210
SQ FT: 30,000
SALES: 10.8MM **Privately Held**
SIC: 8331 Sheltered workshop; skill training center; work experience center

(P-24313)
BENEFITVISION INC
5550 Topanga Canyon Blvd # 180, Woodland Hills (91367-6478)
PHONE.................................818 348-3100
Terry Fuzue, *Branch Mgr*
EMP: 58
SALES (corp-wide): 20MM **Privately Held**
SIC: 8331 Job training & vocational rehabilitation services
PA: Benefitvision, Inc.
4522 Rfd
Long Grove IL 60047
847 438-8796

(P-24314)
BLANCHARDCOACHINGCOM INC
125 State Pl, Escondido (92029-1323)
PHONE.................................760 489-5005
Kenneth S Blanchard, *President*
Tom McKee, *CEO*
Randy Redwitz, *CFO*
EMP: 300 EST: 1979
SALES (est): 7MM **Privately Held**
SIC: 8331 Job training & vocational rehabilitation services

(P-24315)
BUFFINI & COMPANY (PA)
6349 Palomar Oaks Ct, Carlsbad (92011-1428)
PHONE.................................760 827-2100
Brian Buffini, *Ch of Bd*
Jim Polzin, *CFO*
Beverly Buffini, *Treasurer*
Brian Wildermuth, *Vice Pres*
Derek Jones, *Social Dir*
EMP: 182
SALES (est): 18.4MM **Privately Held**
WEB: www.buffiniandcompany.com
SIC: 8331 Job training services

(P-24316)
CALIDAD INDUSTRIES INC
1301 30th Ave, Oakland (94601-2208)
PHONE.................................510 534-6666
Robert Taylor, *CEO*
James Caponigro, *CEO*
Patrick Schmalz, *CFO*
EMP: 52
SQ FT: 35,000
SALES: 6.3MM
SALES (corp-wide): 25.6MM **Privately Held**
WEB: www.eastbaygoodwill.org
SIC: 8331 Vocational training agency
PA: Goodwill Industries Of The Greater East Bay, Inc.
1301 30th Ave
Oakland CA 94601
510 698-7200

(P-24317)
CALIFORNIA COMMUNITY COLLEGES
1102 Q St Fl 4, Sacramento (95811-6549)
PHONE.................................916 445-8752
Brice Harris, *Chancellor*
Alice Vanommeren, *Prgrmr*
James Walker, *Technician*
Debra Jones, *Dean*
Faye James, *Assistant*
EMP: 150
SALES: 50MM **Privately Held**
SIC: 8331 Job training & vocational rehabilitation services

(P-24318)
CALIFORNIA HUMAN DEV CORP (PA)
Also Called: Anthony Soto Emplyment Trining
3315 Airway Dr, Santa Rosa (95403-2005)
PHONE.................................707 523-1155
Fax: 707 523-3776
Christopher Paige, *CEO*
Lucy Vigil, *Human Res Mgr*
Hannah Rubin, *Manager*
EMP: 140
SQ FT: 15,000
SALES: 12.6MM **Privately Held**
SIC: 8331 7361 8399 7374 Job training services; placement agencies; community development groups; calculating service (computer)

(P-24319)
CAMBLE CENTER
Also Called: Self-Aid Workshop
6512 San Fernando Rd, Glendale (91201-2109)
PHONE.................................818 242-2434
Fax: 818 242-3010
Wendy Jacoby, *President*
Sandy Doughty, *Executive*
Carole Jourgan, *Manager*
EMP: 100 EST: 1958
SQ FT: 8,000
SALES: 2.1MM **Privately Held**
SIC: 8331 5947 8322 7389 Job training & vocational rehabilitation services; gift, novelty & souvenir shop; individual & family services; packaging & labeling services; mailing service; recycling, waste materials

(P-24320)
CAREER TRANSITION CENTER
Also Called: Workforce Development Bureau
3447 Atlantic Ave Ste 100, Long Beach (90807-4513)
PHONE.................................562 570-9675
Fax: 562 570-3657
Brian Rogers, *Director*
EMP: 135
SALES (est): 3MM **Privately Held**
SIC: 8331 Job training services

(P-24321)
CENTER FOR EMPLOYMENT TRAINING (PA)
Also Called: C E T
701 Vine St, San Jose (95110-2940)
PHONE.................................408 287-7924
Fax: 408 294-7849
Hermelinda Sapien, *CEO*
Mohammad Aryanpour, *CFO*
Amy Lawrence, *Executive Asst*
Claudia Pilios, *Admin Asst*
Ryan Nelson, *Administration*
EMP: 70
SQ FT: 120,000
SALES: 33.2MM **Privately Held**
SIC: 8331 9721 Vocational training agency; immigration services, government

(P-24322)
CENTRAL VALLEY OPRTNTY CTR INC (PA)
Also Called: Cvoc
6838 W Bridgett Ct, Winton (95388)
P.O. Box 1389 (95388-1389)
PHONE.................................209 357-0062
Fax: 559 673-8556
Ernie Flores, *Exec Dir*
Don Curiel-Ruth, *Info Tech Mgr*
Ofelia Reynoso, *Persnl Dir*
EMP: 63
SQ FT: 27,000
SALES (est): 7.6MM **Privately Held**
SIC: 8331 Vocational training agency

(P-24323)
CHINATOWN SERVICE CENTER
320 S Grfield Ave Ste 118, Alhambra (91801)
PHONE.................................213 808-1700
Roy Jasso, *Branch Mgr*
EMP: 111
SALES (corp-wide): 6.3MM **Privately Held**
SIC: 8331 Job counseling
PA: Chinatown Service Center
767 N Hill St Ste 400
Los Angeles CA 90012
213 808-1700

(P-24324)
COMMUNITY INTEGRATED WORK PROG
Also Called: Cwip
4623 W Jacquelyn Ave, Fresno (93722-6413)
PHONE.................................559 276-8564
Fax: 559 276-8565
Louis Leon, *Director*
EMP: 50
SALES (corp-wide): 49.9MM **Privately Held**
SIC: 8331 Vocational training agency
PA: Community Integrated Work Program, Inc.
2219 Buchanan Rd Ste 3
Antioch CA 94509
925 776-1040

(P-24325)
COMMUNITY INTEGRATED WORK PROG
Also Called: Community Intgrted Work Prgram
1875 Whipple Rd, Hayward (94544-7834)
PHONE.................................510 487-9768
Fax: 510 487-9769
Cathi Vaughns, *Manager*
EMP: 50
SALES (corp-wide): 49.9MM **Privately Held**
SIC: 8331 Vocational training agency
PA: Community Integrated Work Program, Inc.
2219 Buchanan Rd Ste 3
Antioch CA 94509
925 776-1040

(P-24326)
CONSERVATION CORPS LONG BEACH
340 Nieto Ave, Long Beach (90814-1845)
PHONE.................................562 986-1249
Fax: 562 986-9390
Samara Ashley, *Principal*
Mike Bassett, *CEO*
Melvyn Bell, *Treasurer*
Mario R Beas, *Admin Sec*
John Dunay, *Finance*
EMP: 165
SQ FT: 10,000
SALES: 2.7MM **Privately Held**
WEB: www.cclb-corps.org
SIC: 8331 8322 Community service employment training program; individual & family services

(P-24327)
CONTRA COSTA ARC
Also Called: Commercial Spport Svcs Antioch
2505 W 10th St, Antioch (94509-1374)
PHONE.................................925 755-4925
Fax: 925 755-4915
David Duart, *Manager*
EMP: 70
SQ FT: 7,992
SALES (corp-wide): 19.5MM **Privately Held**
WEB: www.ccarealtors.com
SIC: 8331 7389 Skill training center; packaging & labeling services
PA: Contra Costa Arc
1340 Arnold Dr Ste 127
Martinez CA 94553
925 646-4690

(P-24328)
CORPORATION OF THE PRESIDENT
Also Called: Deseret Industries
3000 Auburn Blvd Ste B, Sacramento (95821-1831)
PHONE.................................916 482-1480
Fax: 916 482-0151
Jack P McKinney, *Manager*
EMP: 100
SALES (corp-wide): 2.3B **Privately Held**
WEB: www.lds.org
SIC: 8331 5932 Sheltered workshop; used merchandise stores
PA: Corporation Of The President Of The Church Of Jesus Christ Of Latter-Day Saints
50 W North Temple
Salt Lake City UT 84150
801 240-1000

(P-24329)
COUNTY OF ALAMEDA
Private Industry Council
24100 Amador St Ste 130, Hayward (94544-1287)
PHONE.................................510 670-5700
Fax: 510 670-5706
Kirill Elistratov, *Manager*
EMP: 50 **Privately Held**
WEB: www.co.alameda.ca.us
SIC: 8331 9411 Job training services; administration of educational programs;
PA: County Of Alameda
1221 Oak St Ste 555
Oakland CA 94612
510 272-6691

(P-24330)
COUNTY OF MERCED
Also Called: Workforce Investment- Admin
1880 Wardrobe Ave, Merced (95341-6407)
PHONE.................................209 724-2000
Fax: 209 725-3592
Andrea P Baker, *Director*
EMP: 110 **Privately Held**
WEB: www.mercedncp-hcp.net
SIC: 8331 9441 Job training services; administration of social & manpower programs;
PA: County Of Merced
2222 M St
Merced CA 95340
209 385-7511

(P-24331)
COUNTY OF RIVERSIDE
Also Called: Economic Development
3403 10th St Ste 500, Riverside (92501-3658)
P.O. Box 553 (92502-0553)
PHONE.................................951 955-3100
Selicia Slournoy, *Director*
Melissa Reid, *Manager*
EMP: 97 **Privately Held**
SIC: 8331 9441 Skill training center; administration of social & manpower programs;
PA: County Of Riverside
4080 Lemon St Fl 11
Riverside CA 92501
951 955-1110

(P-24332)
COUNTY OF SAN JOAQUIN
San Joaquin County
56 S Lincoln St, Stockton (95203-3100)
PHONE.................................209 468-3500
EMP: 200 **Privately Held**
SIC: 8331 9111
PA: County Of San Joaquin
44 N San Joaquin St # 640
Stockton CA 95202
209 468-3203

(P-24333)
COUNTY OF STANISLAUS
Also Called: Alliance Work Net
251 E Hackett Rd Ste 2, Modesto (95358-9800)
P.O. Box 3389 (95353-3389)
PHONE.................................209 558-2100
Fax: 209 558-2164
Khristy Santos, *Director*
Alisha Cruz, *Pub Rel Mgr*
EMP: 150 **Privately Held**

8331 - Job Training & Vocational Rehabilitation Svcs County (P-24334)

WEB: www.co.stanislaus.ca.us
SIC: 8331 Job training & vocational rehabilitation services
PA: County Of Stanislaus
1010 10th St Ste 5100
Modesto CA 95354
209 525-6398

(P-24334)
DENC SERVICES INC
1024 Iron Point Rd, Folsom (95630-8013)
PHONE 916 351-1720
Dennis Cavender, *Principal*
EMP: 50
SALES (est): 874.5K **Privately Held**
SIC: 8331 Skill training center

(P-24335)
DEVELOPMENTAL SVCS CAL DEPT
Also Called: Fairview Developmental Center
2501 Harbor Blvd, Costa Mesa (92626-6143)
PHONE 714 957-5151
Bill Wilson, *Exec Dir*
Dilia Vega, *Office Mgr*
Sheila Buckingham, *Admin Sec*
Becky Manning, *Administration*
Robin Lemons, *Info Tech Dir*
EMP: 1500 **Privately Held**
WEB: www.ldc.dds.ca.gov
SIC: 8331 9431 8361 Job training & vocational rehabilitation services; administration of public health programs; ; residential care
HQ: California Department Of Developmental Services
1600 9th St
Sacramento CA 95814
916 654-1690

(P-24336)
EDEN AREA REGNL OCCUPATIONAL P
Also Called: Eden Area Rop School
26316 Hesperian Blvd, Hayward (94545-2458)
PHONE 510 293-2900
Fax: 510 783-2955
Cyril Bonanno, *Exec Dir*
David Espinoza, *Technology*
Linda Granger, *Superintendent*
EMP: 90
SQ FT: 74,000
SALES (est): 5.8MM **Privately Held**
WEB: www.edenrop.org
SIC: 8331 8249 Vocational training agency; skill training center; vocational schools

(P-24337)
EMPLOYMENT & COMMUNITY OPTIONS
9370 Sky Park Ct Ste 210, San Diego (92123-5303)
PHONE 858 565-9870
Nancy Batterman, *President*
Richard Gutierrez, *CFO*
Rick Clarke, *Program Mgr*
Lisha Erez, *Program Mgr*
Sharon Grinnell, *Program Mgr*
EMP: 250
SQ FT: 6,000
SALES: 10.6MM **Privately Held**
SIC: 8331 Job training & vocational rehabilitation services

(P-24338)
EXCEPTIONAL CHLD FOUNDATION (PA)
Also Called: Par Services
5350 Machado Ln, Culver City (90230-8800)
PHONE 310 204-3300
Fax: 310 204-4878
Scott Bowling, *President*
Emily Lloyd, *Vice Pres*
Debbi Winter, *Vice Pres*
Shirley Bianca, *Exec Dir*
Eric Myles, *Program Mgr*
EMP: 120
SQ FT: 45,000
SALES: 23MM **Privately Held**
WEB: www.ecf-la.org
SIC: 8331 Vocational training agency; vocational rehabilitation agency

(P-24339)
EXCEPTIONAL CHLD FOUNDATION
Also Called: Par Services
5350 Machado Ln, Culver City (90230-8800)
PHONE 323 870-2000
Scott Bowling, *President*
EMP: 55
SALES (corp-wide): 23MM **Privately Held**
WEB: www.ecf-la.org
SIC: 8331 7363 Vocational training agency; employee leasing service
PA: Exceptional Children's Foundation
5350 Machado Ln
Culver City CA 90230
310 204-3300

(P-24340)
EXCEPTIONAL CHLD FOUNDATION
Also Called: Par Services
5350 Machado Ln, Culver City (90230-8800)
PHONE 310 204-3300
Scott Bowling, *President*
EMP: 240
SALES (corp-wide): 23MM **Privately Held**
WEB: www.ecf-la.org
SIC: 8331 8351 8699 8322 Vocational training agency; child day care services; charitable organization; individual & family services
PA: Exceptional Children's Foundation
5350 Machado Ln
Culver City CA 90230
310 204-3300

(P-24341)
FONTANA RESOURCES AT WORK
Also Called: Industrial Support Systems
8608 Live Oak Ave, Fontana (92335-3172)
P.O. Box 848 (92334-0848)
PHONE 909 428-3833
Fax: 909 428-3835
Ulric Jones, *CFO*
Carole Graham, *Vice Pres*
Sylvia Anderson, *Exec Dir*
Danny Cervera, *Production*
Sylvia E Anderson, *Manager*
EMP: 135
SQ FT: 22,600
SALES: 3.6MM **Privately Held**
SIC: 8331 3444 Vocational rehabilitation agency; sheet metalwork

(P-24342)
GLENN CNTY HUMN RESOURCE AGCY
Also Called: Colusa, Glenn, Trinity Communt
420 E Laurel St, Willows (95988-3115)
PHONE 530 934-6510
Fax: 530 934-6521
Kim W Gaghagen, *Director*
Betty Skala, *Deputy Dir*
EMP: 130
SALES (est): 2.9MM **Privately Held**
SIC: 8331 8322 Job training services; emergency social services

(P-24343)
GLOBAL UNDERSTANDING INC
1190 Encinitas Blvd 237i, Encinitas (92024-2829)
PHONE 760 812-9650
Hosai Wasimi, *President*
Meena Wasimi, *Vice Pres*
EMP: 99 **EST:** 2012
SALES (est): 869.5K **Privately Held**
SIC: 8331 Skill training center

(P-24344)
GOODWILL INDS S CENTL CAL
1115 Olive Dr, Bakersfield (93308-4141)
PHONE 661 377-0191
Debbie Stwart, *Principal*
EMP: 54
SALES (corp-wide): 16MM **Privately Held**
SIC: 8331 Job training & vocational rehabilitation services
PA: Goodwill Industries Of South Central California
4901 Stine Rd
Bakersfield CA 93313
661 837-0595

(P-24345)
GOODWILL INDS SAN DIEGO CNTY
6386 Del Cerro Blvd, San Diego (92120-4703)
PHONE 619 955-5626
EMP: 144
SALES (corp-wide): 75.9MM **Privately Held**
SIC: 8331 Job training & vocational rehabilitation services
PA: Goodwill Industries Of San Diego County
3663 Rosecrans St
San Diego CA 92110
619 225-2200

(P-24346)
GOODWILL INDS SAN FRNCISCO INC
1270 Oddstad Dr, Redwood City (94063-2606)
PHONE 650 556-9709
EMP: 86
SALES (corp-wide): 62MM **Privately Held**
SIC: 8331 Job training & vocational rehabilitation services
PA: Goodwill Industries Of San Francisco, San Mateo, And Marin Counties, Inc.
1500 Mission St
San Francisco CA 94103
415 575-2101

(P-24347)
GOODWILL INDUSTRS OF SAN FRANC
1669 Fillmore St, San Francisco (94115-3517)
PHONE 415 354-8570
EMP: 69
SALES (corp-wide): 62MM **Privately Held**
SIC: 8331 Job training & vocational rehabilitation services
PA: Goodwill Industries Of San Francisco, San Mateo, And Marin Counties, Inc.
1500 Mission St
San Francisco CA 94103
415 575-2101

(P-24348)
HOPE SERVICES
19055 Portola Dr, Salinas (93908-1212)
PHONE 831 455-4940
Greg Dinsmore, *Manager*
Alisa Harrington, *Admin Asst*
Sheila Davison, *Athletic Dir*
EMP: 65
SALES (corp-wide): 38.5MM **Privately Held**
SIC: 8331 Vocational rehabilitation agency
PA: Hope Services
30 Las Colinas Ln
San Jose CA 95119
408 284-2850

(P-24349)
HOPE SERVICES (PA)
30 Las Colinas Ln, San Jose (95119-1212)
PHONE 408 284-2850
John C Christensen, *CEO*
Fred Gawlick, *President*
Ray Abe, *CFO*
Ric Lnd, *CFO*
Rex Zimmerman, *Vice Pres*
EMP: 50 **EST:** 1952
SQ FT: 29,400
SALES: 38.5MM **Privately Held**
SIC: 8331 Vocational rehabilitation agency

(P-24350)
HOWARD TRAINING CENTER (PA)
1424 Stonum Rd, Modesto (95351-5197)
PHONE 209 538-2431
Fax: 209 538-6406
Claudia K Miller, *Exec Dir*
Tony Thornton, *President*
Lance Hatcher, *Executive*
Carla Strong, *Exec Dir*
Marisol Moreno, *Program Mgr*
EMP: 50
SQ FT: 10,000
SALES: 6MM **Privately Held**
SIC: 8331 Skill training center

(P-24351)
ICI ENTERPRISES INC
790 E Willow St Ste 150, Long Beach (90806-2719)
PHONE 562 989-7715
Robert Nelson, *Principal*
EMP: 100
SALES: 8MM **Privately Held**
SIC: 8331 Job training & vocational rehabilitation services

(P-24352)
INCLUSIVE CMNTY RESOURCES LLC
2855 Telegraph Ave Ste LI, Berkeley (94705-1168)
PHONE 510 981-8115
Julie Steinbaugh,
Michael Steinbaugh,
EMP: 120
SQ FT: 4,800
SALES (est): 4.1MM **Privately Held**
SIC: 8331 Community service employment training program

(P-24353)
INSTITUTE FOR EDUCTL THERAPY
1007 University Ave, Berkeley (94710-2113)
PHONE 831 457-1207
Marlina Eckel, *Associate Dir*
Karen Rotstein, *Exec Dir*
Melanie Wu, *Admin Asst*
Vicko Cesko, *Tech/Comp Coord*
Lori Cottrell, *Teacher*
EMP: 50
SALES (corp-wide): 3.3MM **Privately Held**
WEB: www.baumancollege.com
SIC: 8331 8249 Vocational training agency; vocational schools
PA: Institute For Educational Therapy
10151 Main St Ste 128
Penngrove CA

(P-24354)
JAY NOLAN COMMUNITY SVCS INC
3699 Wilshire Blvd # 530, Los Angeles (90010-2718)
PHONE 323 937-0094
Fax: 323 937-4780
Angie Argote, *Principal*
EMP: 314
SALES (corp-wide): 14.9MM **Privately Held**
SIC: 8331 8361 8322 Job training & vocational rehabilitation services; residential care; social services for the handicapped
PA: Jay Nolan Community Services, Inc.
15501 San Fernando Missio
Mission Hills CA 91345
818 361-6400

(P-24355)
JEWIS VOCATIONAL & COUNSELING
225 Bush St Ste 400, San Francisco (94104-4252)
PHONE 415 391-3600
Abby Snay, *Exec Dir*
Jennifer Isfan, *Mktg Coord*
Stephanie Colosi, *Asst Director*
Lisa Countryman, *Manager*
Melanie Derynck, *Manager*
EMP: 70
SQ FT: 8,000

SALES: 6.8MM **Privately Held**
WEB: www.jvs.org
SIC: **8331** Job counseling; job training services

(P-24356)
JEWISH VOCATIONAL SERVICES (PA)
Also Called: JVSLA
6505 Wilshire Blvd # 200, Los Angeles (90048-4957)
PHONE........................323 761-8888
Fax: 323 761-8581
Vivian B Seigel, *CEO*
Claudia Finkel, *COO*
Olwen Brown, *CFO*
Zoya Kavutskaya, *Info Tech Dir*
Karen Schneider, *Project Mgr*
EMP: 50
SQ FT: 11,000
SALES: 16.7MM **Privately Held**
SIC: **8331** Vocational rehabilitation agency

(P-24357)
KINGS VIEW
100 Airpark Rd, Atwater (95301-9535)
P.O. Box 774 (95301-0774)
PHONE........................209 357-0321
Fax: 209 357-0398
Sam Kalember, *Branch Mgr*
EMP: 50
SALES (corp-wide): 23.7MM **Privately Held**
SIC: **8331** Sheltered workshop; work experience center
PA: Kings View
7170 N Fincl Dr Ste 110
Fresno CA 93720
559 256-0100

(P-24358)
LINCOLN TRAININ
2643 Loma Ave, South El Monte (91733-1419)
PHONE........................626 442-0621
Fax: 626 442-0177
Judith Angelo, *CEO*
David Nelson, *Vice Chairman*
Eric Brown, *Chairman*
Judy Angelo, *Admin Sec*
Kim Neal, *Human Res Mgr*
EMP: 85
SQ FT: 30,000
SALES: 14.3MM **Privately Held**
WEB: www.lincolntc.com
SIC: **8331** Vocational rehabilitation agency

(P-24359)
LOS ANGELES JOB CORPS
1020 S Olive St, Los Angeles (90015-1602)
PHONE........................213 748-0135
Fax: 213 741-5359
Fred Williams, *Director*
Francaesca Jones, *Personnel Exec*
Irma Casas, *Manager*
Barbara Harper, *Manager*
EMP: 197
SALES (est): 3.8MM **Privately Held**
SIC: **8331** Job training & vocational rehabilitation services

(P-24360)
LOS ANGELES UNIFIED SCHOOL DST
Also Called: North Valley Occupational Ctr
11450 Sharp Ave, Mission Hills (91345-1232)
PHONE........................818 365-9645
Fax: 818 365-2695
Rosario Galvan, *Principal*
Donald Gaskin, *Principal*
Gloria Martinez, *Principal*
Sonia Nava, *Finance Mgr*
Jerry Dandurand, *Instructor*
EMP: 250
SALES (corp-wide): 4.4B **Privately Held**
WEB: www.lausd.k12.ca.us
SIC: **8331** 8211 Job training & vocational rehabilitation services; elementary & secondary schools
PA: Los Angeles Unified School District
333 S Beaudry Ave Ste 209
Los Angeles CA 90017
213 241-1000

(P-24361)
MARINE CORPS UNITED STATES
Also Called: US Fhotc
Bldg 632044, Camp Pendleton (92055)
PHONE........................760 725-7144
Elizabeth Breza, *Manager*
EMP: 50 **Publicly Held**
WEB: www.usmc.mil
SIC: **8331** 9711 Job training & vocational rehabilitation services; Marine Corps;
HQ: United States Marine Corps
Pentagon Rm 4b544
Washington DC 20380
816 394-7628

(P-24362)
MARRIOTT FOUNDATION FOR PEOPLE
Also Called: Bridges From School To Work
1970 Broadway Ste 1000, Oakland (94612-2222)
PHONE........................510 834-4700
Anthea Charles, *Director*
Linda Bender, *Director*
EMP: 80
SALES: 20K **Privately Held**
SIC: **8331** Job training & vocational rehabilitation services

(P-24363)
METROPOLITAN AREA ADVISORY COM (PA)
Also Called: M A A C Project
1355 3rd Ave, Chula Vista (91911-4302)
PHONE........................619 426-3595
Arnulfo Manriquez, *CEO*
Antonio Pizano, *President*
Austin Foye, *CFO*
Richard Gonzalez, *Info Tech Dir*
Penny Molina, *Accountant*
EMP: 100
SQ FT: 820,000
SALES (est): 20.6MM **Privately Held**
SIC: **8331** 8351 8748 Job training services; head start center, except in conjunction with school; energy conservation consultant

(P-24364)
METROPOLITAN AREA ADVISORY COM
Also Called: Maac Project Cwbh
1102 Cesar E Chavez Pkwy, San Diego (92113-2108)
PHONE........................619 255-7284
Vicky Rodriguez, *Branch Mgr*
EMP: 350
SALES (corp-wide): 20.6MM **Privately Held**
SIC: **8331** Job training & vocational rehabilitation services
PA: Metropolitan Area Advisory Committee On Anti-Poverty Of San Diego County, Inc.
1355 3rd Ave
Chula Vista CA 91911
619 426-3595

(P-24365)
METROPOLITAN AREA ADVISORY COM
Also Called: Maac Project
1355 3rd Ave, Chula Vista (91911-4302)
PHONE........................619 420-8981
Michael Finneran, *Manager*
EMP: 122
SALES (corp-wide): 20.6MM **Privately Held**
SIC: **8331** 8011 Job training services; offices & clinics of medical doctors
PA: Metropolitan Area Advisory Committee On Anti-Poverty Of San Diego County, Inc.
1355 3rd Ave
Chula Vista CA 91911
619 426-3595

(P-24366)
MID CITIES ASSN RETARDED CTZNS (PA)
Also Called: HUB-LIMITED WORKSHOP
14208 Towne Ave, Los Angeles (90061-2653)
PHONE........................310 537-4510
John Wagoner, *Exec Dir*
EMP: 60
SALES: 7.2MM **Privately Held**
SIC: **8331** Sheltered workshop

(P-24367)
NAPA VALLEY PSI INC
651 Trabajo Ln, NAPA (94559-4258)
P.O. Box 600 (94559-0600)
PHONE........................707 255-0177
Fax: 707 255-0802
Jeanne Fauquet, *President*
Tim Cooney, *Vice Pres*
Leona Egeland, *Vice Pres*
Nancy Guiterrez, *General Mgr*
Lea Ronald, *General Mgr*
EMP: 80
SQ FT: 43,800
SALES: 674.5K **Privately Held**
SIC: **8331** 2521 2511 Vocational rehabilitation agency; filing cabinets (boxes), office: wood; wood household furniture

(P-24368)
NATIONAL MENTOR INC
Also Called: First Step Ind Living Program
9166 Anaheim Pl Ste 200, Rancho Cucamonga (91730-8547)
PHONE........................909 483-2505
Gregory Torres, *President*
EMP: 80
SALES (corp-wide): 1.2B **Privately Held**
SIC: **8331** Job training & vocational rehabilitation services
HQ: National Mentor, Inc.
313 Congress St Fl 5
Boston MA 02210
617 790-4800

(P-24369)
NINTH HOUSE INC
Also Called: Ninth House Network
1 Montgomery St Ste 2200, San Francisco (94104-5501)
PHONE........................612 339-0927
Fax: 415 277-8203
Robert J Heckman, *Director*
Connie S Chan, *Bd of Directors*
Susan D Cochran, *Bd of Directors*
Jack Drescher, *Bd of Directors*
Oliva Espin, *Bd of Directors*
EMP: 50 EST: 1996
SQ FT: 6,000
SALES (est): 2.2MM
SALES (corp-wide): 1.3B **Publicly Held**
WEB: www.9h.net
SIC: **8331** Job training & vocational rehabilitation services
HQ: Korn Ferry Hay Group, Inc.
33 S 6th St Ste 4900
Minneapolis MN 55402
612 339-0927

(P-24370)
NORTH BAY DEVELOPMENTAL (PA)
Also Called: North Bay Regional Center
10 Executive Ct Ste A, NAPA (94558-6267)
P.O. Box 3360 (94558-0295)
PHONE........................707 256-1224
Toll Free:........................888 -
Fax: 707 256-1112
Nancy Gardner, *Exec Dir*
David Johnson, *CFO*
Kathy Newman, *Admin Sec*
EMP: 100 EST: 1972
SALES: 157.1MM **Privately Held**
WEB: www.nbrc.net
SIC: **8331** 8322 Job training services; individual & family services

(P-24371)
NORTHERN CALIFORNIA INALLIANCE (PA)
6950 21st Ave, Sacramento (95820-5948)
PHONE........................916 381-1300
Richard Royse, *Exec Dir*
Ruby Alcartado, *CFO*
Vanessa Simonich, *Bd of Directors*
Jennifer Reuther, *Business Dir*
William King, *Psychologist*
EMP: 190
SQ FT: 20,000
SALES: 15.7MM **Privately Held**
WEB: www.inallianceinc.com
SIC: **8331** Vocational rehabilitation agency

(P-24372)
OAKLAND PRIVATE INDUSTRY COUNC
1212 Broadway Ste 300, Oakland (94612-1809)
PHONE........................510 768-4400
Gay Plair Cobb, *President*
Robin Raveneau, *Admin Asst*
Thelma Simmons, *Admin Asst*
West Oakland, *Project Dir*
Victor Chumbe, *Manager*
EMP: 64 EST: 1980
SALES: 7.1MM **Privately Held**
SIC: **8331** Job training services

(P-24373)
OPARC (PA)
Also Called: DIVERSIFIED INDUSTRIES
9029 Vernon Ave, Montclair (91763-2000)
PHONE........................909 982-4090
Fax: 909 982-5180
Ronald P Wolff, *President*
Sonia Borja, *Vice Pres*
Jennifer Senee, *Opers Mgr*
Barbara Chavez, *Manager*
EMP: 50
SQ FT: 350,000
SALES: 11.7MM **Privately Held**
WEB: www.oparc.org
SIC: **8331** 8322 Job training & vocational rehabilitation services; individual & family services

(P-24374)
ORANGE CNTY CONSERVATION CORPS
1853 N Raymond Ave, Anaheim (92801-1117)
PHONE........................714 451-1301
Dick Dittmar, *President*
Peggy Dougherty, *Treasurer*
Max Carter, *Exec Dir*
Jeff Hosenfeld, *Opers Staff*
George Patino, *Manager*
EMP: 100
SQ FT: 10,000
SALES: 5.1MM **Privately Held**
SIC: **8331** Job training & vocational rehabilitation services

(P-24375)
OWL EDUCATION AND TRAINING
2465 Campus Dr, Irvine (92612-1502)
PHONE........................949 797-2000
Gregory J Burden, *President*
Stephen E Sastrom, *Treasurer*
Stephen Seastrom, *Corp Secy*
Silvia Golstien, *Manager*
EMP: 1380
SQ FT: 22,800
SALES (est): 5.3MM
SALES (corp-wide): 108.5MM **Privately Held**
WEB: www.owlcompanies.com
SIC: **8331** Job training & vocational rehabilitation services
PA: Owl Companies
4695 Macarthur Ct Ste 950
Newport Beach CA 92660
949 797-2000

(P-24376)
OXNARD CITY CORPS
555 S A St Ste 200, Oxnard (93030-8105)
PHONE........................805 385-8081
Efren Gorre, *Director*
EMP: 89 EST: 1995
SALES (est): 840.1K **Privately Held**
SIC: **8331** Job training & vocational rehabilitation services; community service employment training program

8331 - Job Training & Vocational Rehabilitation Svcs County (P-24377) — PRODUDCTS & SERVICES SECTION

(P-24377)
PACIFIC ASIAN CONSORTM EMPLYMN (PA)
Also Called: P A C E
1055 Wilshire Blvd Ste 14, Los Angeles (90017-2431)
PHONE..................213 353-3982
Kerry N Doi, *Exec Dir*
Yusa Chang, *COO*
Tim Maschler, *Exec Dir*
Lin Vong, *Program Mgr*
Derrick Mains, *VP Sales*
EMP: 130 EST: 1976
SQ FT: 20,000
SALES (est): 13.8MM **Privately Held**
SIC: 8331 8322 7361 1521 Community service employment training program; individual & family services; labor contractors (employment agency); new construction, single-family houses

(P-24378)
PATHPOINT
11491 Los Osos Valley Rd, San Luis Obispo (93405-6428)
P.O. Box 1451 (93406-1451)
PHONE..................805 782-8890
Aline Graham, *Director*
EMP: 100
SALES (corp-wide): 21.8MM **Privately Held**
SIC: 8331 Skill training center; vocational rehabilitation agency
PA: Pathpoint
    315 W Haley St Ste 102
    Santa Barbara CA 93101
    805 966-3310

(P-24379)
PERALTA SERVICE CORPORATION
1900 Fruitvale Ave Ste 2a, Oakland (94601-2468)
PHONE..................510 535-5027
Chris Iglesias, *CEO*
Harold Dees, *General Mgr*
Peter Leahey, *Administration*
EMP: 60
SQ FT: 250
SALES: 1.4MM **Privately Held**
SIC: 8331 Community service employment training program

(P-24380)
PRIDE INDUSTRIES
Also Called: Auburn Pride
13080 Earhart Ave, Auburn (95602-9536)
PHONE..................530 888-0331
Fax: 530 888-9083
Vic Wursten, *Branch Mgr*
Becky Wood, *Executive Asst*
Don Phelps, *Engineer*
Christina Schlieter, *Buyer*
Ryan Herrera, *Psychologist*
EMP: 180
SQ FT: 5,000
SALES (corp-wide): 279.8MM **Privately Held**
SIC: 8331 Sheltered workshop
PA: Pride Industries
    10030 Foothills Blvd
    Roseville CA 95747
    916 788-2100

(P-24381)
PRIDE INDUSTRIES
12451 Loma Rica Dr, Grass Valley (95945-9059)
PHONE..................530 477-1832
Fax: 530 477-8038
Kimberly Jones, *Branch Mgr*
Kathryn Gardinier, *Manager*
EMP: 72
SQ FT: 16,290
SALES (corp-wide): 279.8MM **Privately Held**
SIC: 8331 7389 7331 Sheltered workshop; packaging & labeling services; mailing service
PA: Pride Industries
    10030 Foothills Blvd
    Roseville CA 95747
    916 788-2100

(P-24382)
PRIDE INDUSTRIES
3608 Madison Ave Ste 43, North Highlands (95660-5002)
PHONE..................916 334-5415
Vicki Coyle, *Branch Mgr*
Ralph Mendez, *Planning*
Sarah Hudson, *Case Mgr*
EMP: 57
SQ FT: 2,500
SALES (corp-wide): 279.8MM **Privately Held**
SIC: 8331 Sheltered workshop
PA: Pride Industries
    10030 Foothills Blvd
    Roseville CA 95747
    916 788-2100

(P-24383)
SACRAMENTO EMPLOYEMENT & TRAIN
Also Called: Set A Head Start Westside
925 Del Paso Blvd Ste 100, Sacramento (95815-3568)
PHONE..................916 263-3800
Kathy Kossick, *Exec Dir*
Roger Bartlett, *Manager*
EMP: 250 **Privately Held**
SIC: 8331 8351 Job training services; head start center, except in conjunction with school
PA: Sacramento Employment & Training Agency
    925 Del Paso Blvd Ste 100
    Sacramento CA 95815

(P-24384)
SACRAMENTO EMPLOYEMENT & TRAIN (PA)
Also Called: Seta
925 Del Paso Blvd Ste 100, Sacramento (95815-3568)
PHONE..................916 263-3800
Kathy Kossick, *Exec Dir*
Donna Hubbs, *Exec Dir*
Nathaniel Brown, *Admin Asst*
Stephanie Murphy, *Administration*
Ed Proctor, *Telecom Exec*
EMP: 250
SQ FT: 30,000
SALES (est): 17.9MM **Privately Held**
WEB: www.seta.net
SIC: 8331 7361 8351 Job training services; employment agencies; child day care services

(P-24385)
SAN JOSE CONSERVATION CORPS
2650 Senter Rd, San Jose (95111-1121)
PHONE..................408 283-7171
Fax: 408 288-6521
Bob Hennessy, *CEO*
Scott Curtis, *Teacher*
Erin Krueger, *Director*
Marjorie Matthews, *Director*
Kim Nguyen, *Director*
EMP: 150
SQ FT: 1,800
SALES: 7.2MM **Privately Held**
WEB: www.sjcccharterschool.org
SIC: 8331 Community service employment training program; job counseling

(P-24386)
SANTA ANITA FAMILY YOUNG
501 S Mountain Ave, Monrovia (91016-3655)
PHONE..................626 359-9244
Patrice Reinhard, *Ch of Bd*
Damian Colaluca, *CEO*
EMP: 60 EST: 1999
SALES: 1.8MM **Privately Held**
WEB: www.safymca.org
SIC: 8331 Community service employment training program

(P-24387)
SISKIYOU OPPORTUNITY CENTER (PA)
Also Called: Yreka Employment Services
1516 S Mount Shasta Blvd, Mount Shasta (96067-2700)
PHONE..................530 926-4698
Fax: 530 926-0689
Stephen Rogers, *Director*
EMP: 60
SQ FT: 4,820
SALES: 1.7MM **Privately Held**
WEB: www.siskiyouopportunitycenter.org
SIC: 8331 Job counseling

(P-24388)
SOUTH BAY REGL PUBLIC SAFETY T
Also Called: Sbrpstc
3095 Yerba Buena Rd, San Jose (95135-1513)
PHONE..................408 270-6494
Steve Cushing, *President*
Gregg Giusiana, *Vice Pres*
Mike Lombardo, *Vice Pres*
Mable Rodeo, *Executive*
Michael Manning, *Comp Spec*
EMP: 50
SALES (est): 3.5MM **Privately Held**
WEB: www.theacademy.ca.gov
SIC: 8331 Job training services

(P-24389)
SOUTH BAY VOCATIONAL CENTER
Also Called: SOUTH BAY PACKAGING & ASSEMBLY
20706 Main St, Carson (90745-1117)
PHONE..................310 784-2032
Fax: 310 784-2034
Corey Sylve, *President*
Celia Bennett, *CFO*
Clare Gray, *Vice Pres*
Clare Grey, *Vice Pres*
Santiago Lindo, *Technology*
EMP: 50
SQ FT: 19,000
SALES: 1.8MM **Privately Held**
WEB: www.sbvc1.com
SIC: 8331 Work experience center

(P-24390)
SOUTHERN OREGON GOODWILL INDS
1202 S Main St, Yreka (96097-3411)
PHONE..................530 842-6627
Shae Johns, *Branch Mgr*
EMP: 54
SALES (corp-wide): 16.9MM **Privately Held**
SIC: 8331 Job training & vocational rehabilitation services
PA: Southern Oregon Goodwill Industries Inc
    11 W Jackson St
    Medford OR 97501
    541 772-3300

(P-24391)
SPECIAL SERVICE FOR GROUPS INC (PA)
Also Called: SSG ADMINISTRATIVE OFFICES
905 E 8th St Unit 1, Los Angeles (90021-1853)
PHONE..................213 368-1888
Herbert K Hatanaka, *CEO*
Harmony Frederick, *Officer*
Antonio Gutierrez, *Officer*
Stephanie Bonjack, *Top Exec*
Donna Wong, *Vice Pres*
EMP: 100
SALES: 57.9MM **Privately Held**
WEB: www.ssgmain.org
SIC: 8331 8093 8399 Vocational rehabiltation agency; mental health clinic, outpatient; advocacy group

(P-24392)
ST MADELEINE SOPHIES CENTER
2119 E Madison Ave, El Cajon (92019-1111)
PHONE..................619 442-5129
Fax: 619 442-2590
Debra Turner, *Director*
Debra Emerson, *Exec Dir*
Martin Breceda, *Program Mgr*
David Butler, *Info Tech Dir*
Gale Schaffroth, *Financial Exec*
EMP: 70
SQ FT: 13,092
SALES: 7.6MM **Privately Held**
WEB: www.stmsc.org
SIC: 8331 Vocational training agency

(P-24393)
STEPPING STN GRWTH CTR FR CHLD
Also Called: Boatworks
311 Macarthur Blvd, San Leandro (94577-2110)
PHONE..................510 568-3331
Paula Champagne, *President*
Monte Cohen, *Director*
EMP: 85
SALES: 2.5MM **Privately Held**
WEB: www.steppingstonesgrowth.org
SIC: 8331 8211 8351 Skill training center; private special education school; child day care services

(P-24394)
SUCCESS STRATEGIES INST INC
Also Called: Tom Ferry Your Coach
6 Executive Cir Ste 250, Irvine (92614-6732)
PHONE..................888 866-3377
Thomas Ferry, *President*
Mark Le, *Info Tech Mgr*
Landsey Florence, *Accountant*
Eddie Ho, *Marketing Staff*
EMP: 70
SALES (est): 6.3MM **Privately Held**
WEB: www.yourcoach.com
SIC: 8331 Job training & vocational rehabilitation services

(P-24395)
THE FOR WORK TRAINING CENTER
1811 Kusel Rd, Oroville (95966-9528)
PHONE..................530 534-1112
Dave Ennes, *Manager*
Michelle Ely, *Director*
EMP: 50
SALES (corp-wide): 10.8MM **Privately Held**
WEB: www.wtcinc.org
SIC: 8331 Job training & vocational rehabilitation services
PA: Work Training Center For The Handicapped, Inc.
    2255 Fair St
    Chico CA 95928
    530 343-7994

(P-24396)
TOOLWORKS INC (PA)
25 Kearny St Ste 400, San Francisco (94108-5518)
PHONE..................415 733-0990
Fax: 415 733-0991
Steve Crabiel, *Exec Dir*
Gail Chu, *COO*
Mike Oxley, *Project Mgr*
Joe Abrams, *Analyst*
Daniel Woody, *Human Res Dir*
EMP: 70
SQ FT: 3,500
SALES: 12.9MM **Privately Held**
WEB: www.toolworks.org
SIC: 8331 Vocational rehabilitation agency

(P-24397)
TULARE CTY TRNG CTR HNDCPD
Also Called: Able Industries
8929 W Goshen Ave, Visalia (93291-7969)
PHONE..................559 651-3683
Fax: 559 651-0357
Wende Ayers, *Exec Dir*
Bill Wittell, *Controller*
Sheree Hooper, *Production*
Brandi Miller, *Marketing Staff*
Gerald Ormonde, *Mktg Coord*
EMP: 52
SQ FT: 75,000
SALES: 5.9MM **Privately Held**
WEB: www.ableindustries.org
SIC: 8331 Community service employment training program; job counseling

PRODUCTS & SERVICES SECTION
8351 - Child Day Care Svcs County (P-24421)

(P-24398)
UCP WORK INC (PA)
Also Called: W O R K
5464 Carpinteria Ave B, Carpinteria (93013-1483)
PHONE...............................805 566-9000
Fax: 805 566-9070
Kathy Webb, *Exec Dir*
EMP: 60
SQ FT: 2,000
SALES: 8.5MM **Privately Held**
SIC: 8331 Vocational rehabilitation agency; vocational training agency

(P-24399)
UNYEWAY INC
11440 Riverside Dr Ste D, Lakeside (92040-2731)
PHONE...............................619 562-6330
Fax: 619 562-6547
Carrie Hancock, *Branch Mgr*
EMP: 52
SALES (corp-wide): 5.1MM **Privately Held**
SIC: 8331 8322 Skill training center; family counseling services
PA: Unyeway, Inc
2330 Main St Ste E
Ramona CA 92065
760 789-5960

(P-24400)
URBAN CORPS OF SAN DIEGO
3127 Jefferson St, San Diego (92110-4422)
P.O. Box 80156 (92138-0156)
PHONE...............................619 235-6884
Fax: 619 235-5425
Sam Duran, *CEO*
Michael Sterns, *Chairman*
Yolanda Maeder, *Officer*
Leah Healy, *Info Tech Mgr*
Joy Hochstein, *Info Tech Mgr*
EMP: 132
SQ FT: 25,000
SALES: 7.4MM **Privately Held**
WEB: www.urbancorpssd.org
SIC: 8331 Work experience center

(P-24401)
VALLEY LIGHT INDUSTRIES INC
5360 Irwindale Ave, Baldwin Park (91706-2086)
PHONE...............................626 337-6200
Fax: 626 337-0220
Andrew M Altman, *CEO*
Pamela Hayes, *President*
Julie Garcia, *Finance Mgr*
Penny Wiegand, *Director*
Johnny Camacho, *Manager*
EMP: 250
SQ FT: 14,220
SALES: 4MM **Privately Held**
WEB: www.valleylightind.org
SIC: 8331 Job training & vocational rehabilitation services

(P-24402)
VALLEY RESOURCE CENTER FOR TH (PA)
1285 N Santa Fe St, Hemet (92543-1823)
PHONE...............................951 657-0609
Lee Trisler, *Exec Dir*
Quinn Hawley, *Vice Pres*
Valerie Patterson, *Accounting Mgr*
Stephanie Pfaff, *Accounting Mgr*
Mary Morse, *Director*
EMP: 50
SQ FT: 80,000
SALES: 8.4MM **Privately Held**
SIC: 8331 Job training & vocational rehabilitation services

(P-24403)
VOCATIONAL IMPRV PROGRAM INC (PA)
8675 Boston Pl, Rancho Cucamonga (91730-4940)
PHONE...............................909 483-5924
Fax: 909 483-5927
Wendy A Rogina, *CEO*
Christopher J McArdle, *Treasurer*
Rick Rogina, *Vice Pres*
M Stephen Cho, *Admin Sec*
Kenny Solano, *Marketing Staff*
EMP: 90
SQ FT: 23,000
SALES: 10.4MM **Privately Held**
WEB: www.vipsolutions.com
SIC: 8331 Vocational rehabilitation agency

(P-24404)
VOCATIONAL VISIONS
26041 Pala, Mission Viejo (92691-2705)
PHONE...............................949 837-7280
Joan McKinney, *CEO*
Kathryn Hebel, *Exec Dir*
Ted Donoho, *Mktg Dir*
Rosemary White, *Director*
EMP: 170 EST: 1975
SQ FT: 17,000
SALES: 7.5MM **Privately Held**
WEB: www.vocationalvisions.org
SIC: 8331 Sheltered workshop

(P-24405)
VTC ENTERPRISES (PA)
2445 A St, Santa Maria (93455-1401)
P.O. Box 1187 (93456-1187)
PHONE...............................805 928-5000
Fax: 805 922-9359
Jason Telander, *CEO*
Dr Mark Malangko, *President*
Lisa Walker, *CFO*
Henry M Grennan, *Treasurer*
Tanya Astroskey, *Executive*
EMP: 96 EST: 1962
SQ FT: 21,093
SALES: 11.4MM **Privately Held**
WEB: www.vtc-sm.org
SIC: 8331 Vocational rehabilitation agency

(P-24406)
WESTVIEW SERVICES INC
Also Called: Starlight Educational Center
9421 Edinger Ave, Westminster (92683-7426)
PHONE...............................714 418-2090
Fax: 714 418-2093
Lourdis Painter, *Principal*
EMP: 70
SQ FT: 3,775
SALES (corp-wide): 18.2MM **Privately Held**
SIC: 8331 8244 Job training & vocational rehabilitation services; business & secretarial schools
PA: Westview Services, Inc
10522 Katella Ave
Anaheim CA 92804
714 517-6606

(P-24407)
XQAWESOME INC
20 Mason Ln, Ladera Ranch (92694-0325)
PHONE...............................949 929-9622
Bonnie Jean Bradley, *CEO*
EMP: 183
SALES (est): 6.6MM **Privately Held**
SIC: 8331 8742 7389 Job training services; marketing consulting services;

8351 Child Day Care Svcs

(P-24408)
4 CS COUNCIL
2515 N 1st St, San Jose (95131-1003)
PHONE...............................408 487-0747
Alfredo Villasenor, *Principal*
Fred Villasenor, *Exec Dir*
Batool Yazdanpanahi, *Payroll Mgr*
EMP: 110
SQ FT: 6,100
SALES (est): 4.9MM **Privately Held**
SIC: 8351 Child day care services

(P-24409)
ABRAHAM JSHA HSCHL DY SCHL WST
27400 Canwood St, Agoura (91301-2462)
PHONE...............................818 707-2365
Bruce Friedman, *CEO*
Suzan Huntington, *Director*
EMP: 62
SALES: 2MM **Privately Held**
SIC: 8351 Group day care center

(P-24410)
ACHIEVER CHRISTIAN PRE-SCHL &
540 Sands Dr, San Jose (95125-6233)
PHONE...............................408 264-2345
Julie Brown, *Principal*
EMP: 50
SALES (est): 677.6K **Privately Held**
SIC: 8351 8211 Montessori child development center; private elementary & secondary schools; private elementary school

(P-24411)
ACTION DAY NRSERIES PRMRY PLUS
18720 Bucknall Rd, Saratoga (95070-4106)
PHONE...............................408 370-0350
Fax: 408 378-9081
Tracy Sarge, *Director*
Dawna Dow, *Director*
Dawna Esquibel, *Manager*
Carol Freitas, *Manager*
EMP: 51
SALES (corp-wide): 5.5MM **Privately Held**
WEB: www.actiondayprimaryplus.com
SIC: 8351 Child day care services
PA: Action Day Nurseries & Primary Plus, Inc
3030 Moorpark Ave Bldg D
San Jose CA 95128
408 247-6972

(P-24412)
ACTION DAY NRSERIES PRMRY PLUS
2148 Lincoln Ave, San Jose (95125-3540)
PHONE...............................408 266-8952
Fax: 408 266-5054
Carol Freitas, *Manager*
EMP: 50
SALES (corp-wide): 5.5MM **Privately Held**
WEB: www.actiondayprimaryplus.com
SIC: 8351 Child day care services
PA: Action Day Nurseries & Primary Plus, Inc
3030 Moorpark Ave Bldg D
San Jose CA 95128
408 247-6972

(P-24413)
ADESTE PROGRAM COMPANY
1531 James M Wood Blvd, Los Angeles (90015-1112)
PHONE...............................213 251-3551
Gregory Cox, *Exec Dir*
James E Bathker, *CFO*
Ronald G Lopez, *Officer*
Elvia Martinez, *Administration*
Patricia Graves, *Controller*
EMP: 400
SALES (est): 2.8MM **Privately Held**
SIC: 8351 Child day care services

(P-24414)
ALAMEDA FAMILY SERVICES
2325 Clement Ave, Alameda (94501-7063)
PHONE...............................510 629-6300
Irene Kudarauskas, *Exec Dir*
Bruce Kariya, *VP Finance*
Marianne Boudreau, *Human Res Mgr*
Susan Ono, *Opers Spvr*
Marjorie Ball, *Facilities Mgr*
EMP: 100 EST: 1970
SALES: 6MM **Privately Held**
WEB: www.alamedafs.org
SIC: 8351 8322 Head start center, except in conjunction with school; youth self-help agency; offender rehabilitation agency; child guidance agency; general counseling services

(P-24415)
ASSOCIATED STUDENTS CDC
460 S 8th St, San Jose (95112-3835)
PHONE...............................408 924-6988
Maria Davis, *Director*
Sheryl Vargas, *Exec Dir*
EMP: 60
SALES (est): 628K **Privately Held**
SIC: 8351 Child day care services

(P-24416)
BELMONT OAKS ACADEMY
2200 Carlmont Dr, Belmont (94002-3310)
PHONE...............................650 593-6175
Fax: 650 593-7937
Pamela Clarke, *President*
Janet Graetz, *Ch of Bd*
Joanna Reams, *Maintence Staff*
Joanna Reames, *Director*
EMP: 63
SALES (est): 2MM **Privately Held**
SIC: 8351 8211 Preschool center; private elementary school

(P-24417)
BERMUDA DUNES LEARNING CTR INC
42115 Yucca Ln, Bermuda Dunes (92203-8111)
PHONE...............................760 772-7127
Gayle Clark, *President*
EMP: 50
SALES (est): 1.3MM **Privately Held**
SIC: 8351 Preschool center

(P-24418)
BRIGHT HORIZONS CHLD CTRS LLC
Also Called: Sisco Family Connection
800 Barber Ln, Milpitas (95035-7926)
PHONE...............................408 853-2196
Janice Inman, *Exec Dir*
Monica McCarthy, *Executive*
Janice Inaman, *Administration*
EMP: 120
SALES (corp-wide): 1.4B **Publicly Held**
WEB: www.atlantaga.ncr.com
SIC: 8351 Child day care services
HQ: Bright Horizons Children's Centers Llc
200 Talcott Ave
Watertown MA 02472
617 673-8000

(P-24419)
BRIGHT HORIZONS CHLD CTRS LLC
Also Called: Camp Amgen
1 Amgen Center Dr, Thousand Oaks (91320-1730)
PHONE...............................805 447-6793
Kelly Travis, *Director*
EMP: 170
SALES (corp-wide): 1.4B **Publicly Held**
WEB: www.atlantaga.ncr.com
SIC: 8351 Child day care services
HQ: Bright Horizons Children's Centers Llc
200 Talcott Ave
Watertown MA 02472
617 673-8000

(P-24420)
BUSINESS AND SUPPORT SERVICES
Also Called: Browne Child Development Ctr
Santa Jancinto Rd 20286 Bldg 202860, Oceanside (92054)
PHONE...............................760 725-2817
Maria Langlie, *Director*
EMP: 50 **Publicly Held**
WEB: www.mccssc.com
SIC: 8351 9711 Child day care services; Marine Corps;
HQ: Business And Support Services
3044 Catlin Ave
Quantico VA 22134
703 432-0109

(P-24421)
CABRILLO COLLEGE CHILDREN CTR
6500 Soquel Dr, Aptos (95003-3198)
PHONE...............................831 479-6352
Erick Hoffman, *CEO*
EMP: 70
SALES (est): 2.6MM **Privately Held**
SIC: 8351 8221 Child day care services; colleges universities & professional schools

8351 - Child Day Care Svcs County (P-24422)

(P-24422)
CALVARY BAPTIST CH LOS GATOS
Also Called: Calvary Infant Care Center
16330 Los Gatos Blvd, Los Gatos (95032-4520)
PHONE..................408 356-5126
Bob Thomas, *Principal*
McKenna Raasch, *Director*
EMP: 80
SALES (corp-wide): 3.9MM **Privately Held**
WEB: www.calvarylosgatos.org
SIC: 8351 Child day care services
PA: Calvary Baptist Church Of Los Gatos
16330 Los Gatos Blvd # 408
Los Gatos CA 95032
408 358-8871

(P-24423)
CALVARY CHURCH SANTA ANA INC
1010 N Tustin Ave, Santa Ana (92705-3598)
PHONE..................714 973-4800
Fax: 714 285-0286
Michael Welles, *Pastor*
Pat Prichard, *Administration*
Jane Taylor, *Controller*
Dr D J Mitchell, *Sr Pastor*
Louise Chandler, *Manager*
EMP: 160
SQ FT: 133,000
SALES: 10.9MM **Privately Held**
SIC: 8351 8661 Nursery school; miscellaneous denomination church

(P-24424)
CAROLYN E WYLIE CENTER
4164 Brockton Ave Ste A, Riverside (92501-3400)
PHONE..................951 683-5193
Melody Amaral, *CEO*
Jj Johnston, *Program Dir*
EMP: 100
SQ FT: 3,000
SALES: 3.5MM **Privately Held**
SIC: 8351 Child day care services

(P-24425)
CENTRAL STATE PRE-SCHOOL
2310 Aldergrove Ave, Escondido (92029-1935)
PHONE..................760 432-2499
Susan Chambers, *Principal*
Eric Fisher, *Vice Pres*
Lee Molini, *Executive*
Jane Zelasko, *Managing Dir*
Dan Johnoson, *MIS Dir*
EMP: 50
SALES (est): 693.5K **Privately Held**
SIC: 8351 Child day care services

(P-24426)
CHALLENGER SCHOOLS
4949 Harwood Rd, San Jose (95124-5209)
PHONE..................408 266-7073
Edward Gonzalez, *Principal*
EMP: 50
SALES (corp-wide): 109.8MM **Privately Held**
SIC: 8351 Preschool center
PA: Challenger Schools
9424 S 300 W
Sandy UT 84070
801 569-2700

(P-24427)
CHARLES DREW UNIV MDCINE SCNCE
Also Called: Head Start Program
135 W Victoria St, Long Beach (90805-2162)
PHONE..................310 605-0164
Linda Rahman, *Director*
EMP: 210
SALES (corp-wide): 61.1MM **Privately Held**
WEB: www.cdrewu.edu
SIC: 8351 8221 Preschool center; university

PA: Charles Drew University Of Medicine And Science
1731 E 120th St
Los Angeles CA 90059
323 563-4800

(P-24428)
CHILD & YOUTH SERVICES
841 Sherman Ct, Marina (93933-5043)
PHONE..................831 583-1050
Lela Casillo, *Director*
EMP: 60
SALES (est): 309K **Privately Held**
SIC: 8351 Child day care services

(P-24429)
CHILD DEVELOPMENT ASSOC INC (PA)
180 Otay Lakes Rd Ste 310, Bonita (91902-2442)
PHONE..................619 427-4411
Richard Richardson, *President*
Jorge Hernandez, *Treasurer*
Jane Masters, *CTO*
Vinh Dang, *Info Tech Mgr*
Rosalva Mendoza, *Info Tech Mgr*
EMP: 50
SQ FT: 6,000
SALES: 36MM **Privately Held**
WEB: www.cdasandiego.com
SIC: 8351 8322 Preschool center; child related social services

(P-24430)
CHILD DEVELOPMENT CENTER
309 N Rios Ave, Solana Beach (92075-1241)
PHONE..................858 794-7160
Fax: 858 794-7165
Susan Blackwood, *Director*
EMP: 50 EST: 1980
SALES (est): 1.9MM **Privately Held**
SIC: 8351 Child day care services

(P-24431)
CHILD DEVELOPMENT INCORPORATED (PA)
Also Called: Child Development Centers
20 Great Oaks Blvd # 200, San Jose (95119-1399)
PHONE..................408 556-7300
Vernon A Plaskett, *CEO*
Jennifer Stone, *Sales Executive*
EMP: 50
SALES: 28MM **Privately Held**
SIC: 8351 Child day care services

(P-24432)
CHILD DEVELOPMENT INCORPORATED
Also Called: Turtle Rock Cdc
5151 Amalfi Dr, Irvine (92603-3443)
PHONE..................949 854-5060
Mindy Ho, *Director*
EMP: 363
SALES (corp-wide): 28MM **Privately Held**
SIC: 8351 Child day care services
PA: Child Development Incorporated
20 Great Oaks Blvd # 200
San Jose CA 95119
408 556-7300

(P-24433)
CHILD EDUCATIONAL CENTER
Also Called: Cec
140 Foothill Blvd, La Canada (91011-3727)
PHONE..................818 354-3418
Fax: 818 393-4243
Elyssa Nelson, *Director*
Lisa Chang, *Program Dir*
Sahar Farmanesh, *Director*
EMP: 100
SALES (est): 6.5MM **Privately Held**
SIC: 8351 Child day care services

(P-24434)
CHILD FAMILY & CMNTY SVCS INC
32980 Alvarado Niles Rd # 846, Union City (94587-8104)
PHONE..................510 796-9512
Fax: 510 675-0631
Karen Deshayes, *Exec Dir*
Tina Terry, *Office Admin*

John Anthony Borsella, *Finance Dir*
Catherine Clennen Seymour, *Business Mgr*
Cynthia Esquivel-Delgado, *Human Res Mgr*
EMP: 140
SQ FT: 20,000
SALES: 14.8MM **Privately Held**
SIC: 8351 Preschool center

(P-24435)
CHILDREN OF RAINBOW INC (PA)
4890 Logan Ave, San Diego (92113-3004)
PHONE..................619 615-0652
Fax: 619 615-0653
Gale R Walker, *President*
Shirley Pauley, *Office Mgr*
Nicoo Evans, *Manager*
EMP: 64
SQ FT: 8,500
SALES (est): 3.6MM **Privately Held**
WEB: www.childrenoftherainbow.com
SIC: 8351 Child day care services

(P-24436)
CHILDREN OF THE RAINBOW HEAD
4890 Logan Ave, San Diego (92113-3004)
PHONE..................619 266-7311
Gale Walker, *Mng Member*
Kursat Misrlioglu,
EMP: 185
SALES: 6.8MM **Privately Held**
SIC: 8351 Child day care services

(P-24437)
CHILDRENS DAY SCHOOL
333 Dolores St, San Francisco (94110-1006)
PHONE..................415 861-5432
Fax: 415 861-5419
Rick Ackerly, *Director*
Jake Fishman, *Executive*
Diane Larrabee, *Associate Dir*
Mary Denardo, *Comms Dir*
Laura Delafuente, *Planning*
EMP: 50
SQ FT: 22,050
SALES: 13.7MM **Privately Held**
WEB: www.cds-sf.org
SIC: 8351 8211 Preschool center; elementary & secondary schools

(P-24438)
CHILDRENS HOSPITAL ORANGE CNTY
500 Superior Ave, Newport Beach (92663-3657)
PHONE..................949 631-2062
EMP: 2073
SALES (corp-wide): 518.8MM **Privately Held**
SIC: 8351 Child day care services
PA: Children's Hospital Of Orange County
1201 W La Veta Ave
Orange CA 92868
714 997-3000

(P-24439)
CITY OF PACIFICA-VALLEMAR
170 Santa Maria Ave, Pacifica (94044-2506)
PHONE..................650 738-7466
Scott Leslie, *Director*
Steven Rhodes, *Manager*
EMP: 55
SALES (est): 459.5K **Privately Held**
SIC: 8351 Child day care services; preschool center

(P-24440)
COLLEGE OPERATIONS LLC
1730 S College Ave, Dinuba (93618-2812)
PHONE..................559 353-0576
Travis Greenwood, *CFO*
EMP: 50
SALES (est): 451.7K **Privately Held**
SIC: 8351 Nursery school

(P-24441)
COLTON JOINT UNIFIED SCHL DST
Also Called: San Salvador Pre-School
471 Agua Mansa Rd, Colton (92324-3325)
PHONE..................909 876-4240
Fax: 909 824-7406

Karen Gladue, *Principal*
EMP: 100
SALES (corp-wide): 132.8MM **Privately Held**
WEB: www.colton.k12.ca.us
SIC: 8351 8211 Child day care services; public elementary school
PA: Colton Joint Unified School District
1212 Valencia Dr
Colton CA 92324
909 580-5000

(P-24442)
COMMUNITY ACTION PARTNR KERN
Also Called: Sunrise Villa Ctr Head Start
1600 Poplar Ave, Wasco (93280-3405)
PHONE..................661 758-0129
Yolanda Gonzales, *Director*
EMP: 143
SALES (corp-wide): 63.1MM **Privately Held**
SIC: 8351 Child day care services
PA: Community Action Partnership Of Kern
5005 Business Park N
Bakersfield CA 93309
661 336-5236

(P-24443)
COMMUNITY ACTION PARTNR KERN
4404 Pioneer Dr, Bakersfield (93306-5730)
PHONE..................661 366-5953
Marie Galaviz, *Branch Mgr*
EMP: 86
SALES (corp-wide): 63.1MM **Privately Held**
SIC: 8351 Child day care services
PA: Community Action Partnership Of Kern
5005 Business Park N
Bakersfield CA 93309
661 336-5236

(P-24444)
COMMUNITY ACTION PRTNRSHP (PA)
1225 Gill Ave, Madera (93637-5234)
PHONE..................559 673-9173
Mattie Mendez, *Exec Dir*
Linda L Wright, *CEO*
Donna Tooley, *CFO*
Jane Nabors, *Exec Dir*
Adaluz Ramirez, *Director*
EMP: 200
SQ FT: 18,000
SALES: 19.9MM **Privately Held**
WEB: www.maderacap.org
SIC: 8351 Head start center, except in conjunction with school

(P-24445)
COMMUNITY CHLD CRE CNCL SONOMA (PA)
Also Called: 4 C'S
131 Stony Cir Ste 300, Santa Rosa (95401-9594)
PHONE..................707 522-1413
Fax: 707 544-2625
Mary Ann Doan, *Exec Dir*
EMP: 60
SALES (est): 10.9MM **Privately Held**
WEB: www.sonoma4cs.org
SIC: 8351 Child day care services

(P-24446)
COMMUNITY DEV INST HEAD START
12988 Bowron Rd, Poway (92064-5790)
PHONE..................858 668-2985
EMP: 60
SALES (corp-wide): 150.5MM **Privately Held**
SIC: 8351 Head start center, except in conjunction with school
PA: Community Development Institute Head Start
10065 E Harvard Ave # 700
Denver CO 80231
720 747-5100

(P-24447)
COMPASS FAMILY SERVICES
49 Powell St Fl 3, San Francisco (94102-2853)
PHONE..................415 644-0504

PRODUCTS & SERVICES SECTION

8351 - Child Day Care Svcs County (P-24472)

Eirca Kisch, *Director*
Carrie Hook, *CFO*
Brian McInerney, *Bd of Directors*
Beth Mitchell, *Program Dir*
EMP: 85
SALES: 9.2MM **Privately Held**
SIC: 8351 Child day care services

(P-24448)
COMPASS FAMILY SERVICES
Also Called: Compass Children's Center
144 Leavenworth St, San Francisco (94102-3806)
PHONE.................................415 644-0504
Mary McNamara, *Director*
Erica Kisch, *Exec Dir*
Helen Meier, *Director*
EMP: 87
SQ FT: 12,143
SALES: 950K **Privately Held**
SIC: 8351 Child day care services

(P-24449)
COUNTY OF SAN BERNARDINO
Also Called: Preschool Service
385 N Arrowhead Ave, San Bernardino (92415-0103)
PHONE.................................909 387-5455
Robyn Johnson, *Branch Mgr*
EMP: 100 **Privately Held**
SIC: 8351 Head start center, except in conjunction with school
PA: County Of San Bernardino
385 N Arrowhead Ave
San Bernardino CA 92415
909 387-3841

(P-24450)
COUNTY OF SAN BERNARDINO
Also Called: Human Services Systems
250 S Lena Rd, San Bernardino (92415-0461)
PHONE.................................909 387-2363
Ron Griffin, *Director*
Roberta York, *Mng Officer*
EMP: 67
SQ FT: 934 **Privately Held**
SIC: 8351 9411 8741 Head start center, except in conjunction with school; preschool center; administration of educational programs; ; management services
PA: County Of San Bernardino
385 N Arrowhead Ave
San Bernardino CA 92415
909 387-3841

(P-24451)
COUNTY OF SAN BERNARDINO
Also Called: Highland Head Start
26887 5th St, Highland (92346-4178)
PHONE.................................909 425-0785
Fax: 909 425-0210
Lisa Simmons, *Branch Mgr*
EMP: 50 **Privately Held**
SIC: 8351 Head start center, except in conjunction with school
PA: County Of San Bernardino
385 N Arrowhead Ave
San Bernardino CA 92415
909 387-3841

(P-24452)
COUNTY OF SHASTA
Also Called: Monte Vista School
43 Hilltop Dr, Redding (96003-2807)
PHONE.................................530 225-2999
Fax: 530 224-3241
Sharon Simpson, *Principal*
EMP: 50 **Privately Held**
WEB: www.rsdnmp.org
SIC: 8351 Preschool center
PA: County Of Shasta
1450 Court St Ste 308a
Redding CA 96001
530 225-5561

(P-24453)
COUNTY OF VENTURA
Also Called: Ventura Cnty Human Srvce
300 W 9th St, Oxnard (93030-7014)
PHONE.................................805 240-2701
David Weinreich, *Manager*
EMP: 50 **Privately Held**
WEB: www.vcoe.org

SIC: 8351 9431 Child day care services; child health program administration, government
PA: County of Ventura
800 S Victoria Ave
Ventura CA 93009
805 654-2551

(P-24454)
DESER SANDS UNIFI SCHOO DISTR
Also Called: Early Childhood Education
47950 Dune Palms Rd, La Quinta (92253-4000)
PHONE.................................760 777-4200
Debra Loukatos, *Principal*
EMP: 74
SALES (corp-wide): 178.2MM **Privately Held**
SIC: 8351 Preschool center
PA: Desert Sands Unified School District
School Building Corporation
47950 Dune Palms Rd
La Quinta CA 92253
760 771-8567

(P-24455)
DIANNE ADAIR DAY CARE CENTERS (PA)
1862 Bailey Rd, Concord (94521-1349)
PHONE.................................925 429-3232
Todd Porter, *CEO*
Brian Carbine, *CFO*
EMP: 100
SALES (est): 3.7MM **Privately Held**
SIC: 8351 Group day care center

(P-24456)
DIGNITY HEALTH
2301 Ashe Rd, Bakersfield (93309-4301)
P.O. Box 119 (93302-0119)
PHONE.................................661 832-8300
Sharon Brown, *Director*
EMP: 60
SALES (corp-wide): 7.1B **Privately Held**
WEB: www.chw.edu
SIC: 8351 Child day care services
PA: Dignity Health
185 Berry St Ste 300
San Francisco CA 94107
415 438-5500

(P-24457)
E CENTER
1506 Starr Dr, Yuba City (95993-2602)
PHONE.................................530 634-1200
Fax: 530 741-8347
Kulraj Samra, *CEO*
Amanda Rhyne, *Administration*
Cerie Johnson, *Human Resources*
EMP: 150 **EST:** 1973
SQ FT: 4,000
SALES: 21.5MM **Privately Held**
SIC: 8351 Head start center, except in conjunction with school

(P-24458)
ENRICHMENT EDUCTL EXPERIENCES
4400 Coldwater Canyon Ave # 300, Studio City (91604-5053)
PHONE.................................818 989-7509
Nancy Simpson, *President*
EMP: 55
SALES (est): 844.4K **Privately Held**
SIC: 8351 Child day care services

(P-24459)
ENVIRONMENTS FOR LEARNING INC (PA)
Also Called: Montessori On The Lake
24291 Muirlands Blvd, Lake Forest (92630-3001)
PHONE.................................949 855-5630
Fax: 949 855-5633
Sara Smith, *President*
EMP: 65
SALES (est): 2.3MM **Privately Held**
SIC: 8351 8211 Child day care services; preparatory school; private combined elementary & secondary school

(P-24460)
EPISCOPAL COMMUNITY
Also Called: Ecs South Bay Head Start
1261 3rd Ave Ste B, Chula Vista (91911-3262)
PHONE.................................619 422-1642
Fax: 619 409-9465
Gene Merlino, *Director*
EMP: 60
SALES (est): 844.7K **Privately Held**
SIC: 8351 8741 Head start center, except in conjunction with school; management services

(P-24461)
FAIRPLEX CHILD DEVELOPMENT CTR
1101 W Mckinley Ave, Pomona (91768-1650)
PHONE.................................909 623-3899
Jim Henwood, *CEO*
Stephen Morgan, *Bd of Directors*
Margie Johnson, *Office Mgr*
John Ly, *IT/INT Sup*
Don Thay, *Technology*
EMP: 65 **EST:** 1980
SQ FT: 5,000
SALES: 1.8MM **Privately Held**
SIC: 8351 Child day care services

(P-24462)
FAMILY CARE NETWORK INC (PA)
1255 Kendall Rd, San Luis Obispo (93401-8750)
PHONE.................................805 503-6240
Fax: 805 201-3535
James Robert, *CEO*
Megan Yoder, *Volunteer Dir*
Jonathan Nibbio, *COO*
Bobbie Boyer, *CFO*
Shay Peck, *Bd of Directors*
EMP: 71
SQ FT: 2,600
SALES: 14.3MM **Privately Held**
SIC: 8351 Child day care services

(P-24463)
FIRST BAPTIST HEAD START
3890 Railroad Ave, Pittsburg (94565-6540)
PHONE.................................925 473-2000
Fax: 925 526-8600
Arika Spencer-Brown, *Exec Dir*
Brenda P Battle, *Exec Dir*
EMP: 87
SALES (est): 2.3MM **Privately Held**
WEB: www.firstbaptistheadstart.org
SIC: 8351 Child day care services; head start center, except in conjunction with school

(P-24464)
FIRST EVANG LUTHERAN CH & SCHL
2900 W Carson St, Torrance (90503-6005)
PHONE.................................310 320-9920
Fax: 310 320-1963
Elizabeth Kebschull, *Principal*
Kristine Olson, *Principal*
Nick Zagorin, *Comp Lab Dir*
Glenna Shelton, *Librarian*
EMP: 100
SQ FT: 50,232
SALES (est): 4.8MM **Privately Held**
SIC: 8351 Child day care services

(P-24465)
GLENN COUNTY OFFICE EDUCATION
Also Called: Child & Family Services
676 E Walker St Fl 2, Orland (95963-2203)
PHONE.................................530 865-1145
Tracey Quarne, *Superintendent*
EMP: 81
SALES: 4.4MM **Privately Held**
SIC: 8351 8322 Child day care services; family counseling services

(P-24466)
HARMONIUM INC (PA)
Also Called: CITY ARTS ACADEMY
9245 Activity Rd Ste 200, San Diego (92126-2383)
PHONE.................................858 684-3080
Rosa Ana Lozada, *CEO*

Doug Reiss, *COO*
Melinda Mallie, *CFO*
Miguel Ortega, *Admin Asst*
Owen Williams, *Tech/Comp Coord*
EMP: 150
SALES: 9.7MM **Privately Held**
SIC: 8351 Child day care services

(P-24467)
IMMANUEL BAPTIST CRUCH
Also Called: Immanuel Baptist Day School
28355 Baseline St, Highland (92346-5008)
PHONE.................................909 862-6641
Fax: 909 862-6677
Rob Zinn, *Pastor*
Kimberly Drake, *Exec Dir*
Ruthie Barker, *Executive Asst*
EMP: 65
SALES (est): 2.7MM **Privately Held**
WEB: www.ibchighland.org
SIC: 8351 8661 Preschool center; Baptist Church

(P-24468)
INGLEWOOD UNIFIED SCHOOL DST
Also Called: Inglewood Child Dev Ctr
401 S Inglewood Ave, Inglewood (90301-2599)
PHONE.................................310 419-2691
Fax: 310 419-2808
Linda Anderson, *Principal*
EMP: 80
SALES (corp-wide): 6.8MM **Privately Held**
WEB: www.payne.inglewood.k12.ca.us
SIC: 8351 8211 Child day care services; public elementary school
PA: Inglewood Unified School District
401 S Inglewood Ave
Inglewood CA 90301
310 419-2500

(P-24469)
INSTITUTE FOR HUMN SOCIAL DEV (PA)
Also Called: SAN MATEO HEAD START PROGRAM
155 Bovet Rd Ste 300, San Mateo (94402-3142)
PHONE.................................650 871-5613
Fax: 650 589-5710
Amy Liew, *Director*
Vaneges Silvia, *Admin Asst*
Amy Lieu, *Finance Mgr*
EMP: 69
SQ FT: 6,000
SALES: 9.9MM **Privately Held**
SIC: 8351 Head start center, except in conjunction with school

(P-24470)
IXL LEARNING INC
777 Mariners Island Blvd # 600, San Mateo (94404-5008)
PHONE.................................650 357-6976
Paul Mishkin, *CEO*
EMP: 51
SALES (est): 4.3MM **Privately Held**
SIC: 8351 Child day care services

(P-24471)
KID IQ 24 HR CHILDCARE
Also Called: Child Care
4451 E Sierra Madre Ave, Fresno (93726-1158)
PHONE.................................310 492-3037
Jotasha Taylor, *Exec VP*
EMP: 99
SALES (est): 480.5K **Privately Held**
SIC: 8351 Child day care services

(P-24472)
KIDS KLUB CARE CENTERS INC (PA)
Also Called: Kids Klub Pasadena
380 S Raymond Ave, Pasadena (91105-2608)
PHONE.................................626 795-2501
Michael Wojciechowski, *President*
Bambi Wojciechowski, *Chairman*
Grant Bruemmer, *Asst Director*
Michelle Lomeli, *Asst Director*
EMP: 60
SQ FT: 7,800

8351 - Child Day Care Svcs County (P-24473)

PRODUDUCTS & SERVICES SECTION

SALES (est): 4.7MM **Privately Held**
SIC: **8351** Child day care services

(P-24473)
KINDERCARE EDUCATION LLC
3280 Crow Canyon Rd, San Ramon (94583-1304)
PHONE.....................925 824-0267
Thomas Jamison, *Manager*
EMP: 85
SALES (corp-wide): 1.2B **Privately Held**
WEB: www.knowledgelearning.com
SIC: **8351** Child day care services
PA: Kindercare Education Llc
  650 Ne Holladay St # 1400
  Portland OR 97232
  503 872-1300

(P-24474)
KINDERCARE LEARNING CTRS LLC
Also Called: Belmont Shores Kindercare
5251 E Las Lomas St, Long Beach (90815-4206)
PHONE.....................562 961-8882
Fax: 562 961-8784
Bernice Gonzalez, *Director*
Alicia Syfers, *Exec Dir*
Theresa Kappermeyer, *Director*
Tanea Robinson, *Manager*
Vangie Robles, *Manager*
EMP: 80
SALES (corp-wide): 1.2B **Privately Held**
WEB: www.kindercare.com
SIC: **8351** Group day care center
HQ: Kindercare Learning Centers, Llc
  650 Ne Holladay St # 1400
  Portland OR 97232
  503 872-1300

(P-24475)
LINDA BEACH COOP PRE-SCHOOL
400 Highland Ave, Piedmont (94611-4043)
PHONE.....................510 547-4332
Barbara Ulbrich, *Director*
Parents Co-Op, *Principal*
EMP: 50
SALES: 144.1K **Privately Held**
SIC: **8351** Preschool center

(P-24476)
LITTLE CITIZENS SCHOOLS INC
4256 S Western Ave, Los Angeles (90062-1645)
PHONE.....................323 732-1212
Fax: 323 732-6142
Doris Evans, *President*
Roy Evans, *Corp Secy*
Lauren Matsuyama, *Administration*
EMP: 100
SQ FT: 5,000
SALES (est): 1.8MM **Privately Held**
SIC: **8351** 8211 Preschool center; elementary school

(P-24477)
LONG BEACH DAY NURSERY
3965 N Bellflower Blvd, Long Beach (90808-1902)
PHONE.....................562 421-1488
Fax: 562 429-0492
Amy Bigolow, *Director*
Shannon Deeter, *Exec Dir*
EMP: 50
SALES (corp-wide): 2.9MM **Privately Held**
WEB: www.lbdn.org
SIC: **8351** Group day care center
PA: Long Beach Day Nursery
  1548 Chestnut Ave
  Long Beach CA 90813
  562 421-1488

(P-24478)
LOS ANGELES UNIFIED SCHOOL DST
Also Called: Queen Anne Early Education Ctr
1212 Queen Anne Pl, Los Angeles (90019-6819)
PHONE.....................323 939-7322
Fax: 323 934-8694
Salvador Rodriguez, *Principal*
Sidney Thompson, *Superintendent*
EMP: 60

SALES (corp-wide): 4.4B **Privately Held**
WEB: www.lausd.k12.ca.us
SIC: **8351** Preschool center
PA: Los Angeles Unified School District
  333 S Beaudry Ave Ste 209
  Los Angeles CA 90017
  213 241-1000

(P-24479)
LOS ANGLES UNIVERSAL PRESCHOOL
888 S Figueroa St Ste 800, Los Angeles (90017-5306)
PHONE.....................213 416-1200
Celia C Ayala, *CEO*
Elsa Luna, *CFO*
Clare Shephard, *Officer*
Dawn Kurtz, *Senior VP*
Fernando Almodovar, *Vice Pres*
EMP: 200
SQ FT: 12,000
SALES: 73.6MM **Privately Held**
WEB: www.laup.net
SIC: **8351** Preschool center

(P-24480)
MARIN HORIZON SCHOOL INC
305 Montford Ave, Mill Valley (94941-3370)
PHONE.....................415 388-8408
Fax: 415 388-7831
Rosalind Hamar, *Exec Dir*
Claire Lennon, *Info Tech Mgr*
Kristen Commesso, *Tech/Comp Coord*
Anna Shubeau, *Finance*
Catherine Hills, *Safety Dir*
EMP: 50
SQ FT: 20,000
SALES: 8MM **Privately Held**
WEB: www.marinhorizon.org
SIC: **8351** 8211 Montessori child development center; private elementary school

(P-24481)
MARYVALE DAY CARE CENTER
Also Called: Maryvale Edcatn Fmly Rsrce Ctr
2502 Huntington Dr, Duarte (91010-2221)
PHONE.....................626 357-1514
Fax: 626 357-1514
Steve Gunther, *Director*
EMP: 191
SALES (corp-wide): 14.6MM **Privately Held**
SIC: **8351** Child day care services
PA: Maryvale Day Care Center
  7600 Graves Ave
  Rosemead CA 91770
  626 280-6511

(P-24482)
MCCUSKER ENTERPRISES INC
Also Called: Kids World Preschool
29879 Santiago Rd, Temecula (92592-3004)
PHONE.....................951 676-5445
Fax: 951 699-1509
John McCusker, *President*
Kris Dean McCusker, *Vice Pres*
EMP: 70 EST: 1976
SQ FT: 6,000
SALES (est): 3.8MM **Privately Held**
SIC: **8351** 8211 Preschool center; private elementary school

(P-24483)
MEXICAN AMRCN OPRTNTY FNDATION
2650 Zoe Ave Fl 3, Huntington Park (90255-4198)
PHONE.....................323 588-7320
Lisa Viveros, *Branch Mgr*
EMP: 50
SALES (corp-wide): 63.8MM **Privately Held**
SIC: **8351** Head start center, except in conjunction with school
PA: Mexican American Opportunity Foundation
  401 N Garfield Ave
  Montebello CA 90640
  323 890-9500

(P-24484)
MOUNTAIN VIEW CHILD CARE INC
Also Called: Totally Kids Spcalty Hlth Care
10716 La Tuna Canyon Rd, Sun Valley (91352-2130)
PHONE.....................818 252-5863
Michelle Nydam, *Branch Mgr*
EMP: 150
SALES (corp-wide): 60.9MM **Privately Held**
SIC: **8351** Child day care services
PA: Mountain View Child Care, Inc.
  1720 Mountain View Ave
  Loma Linda CA 92354
  909 796-6915

(P-24485)
NAWS CHILDREN CENTER
Also Called: Part Time Day Care Center
1 Administration Cir, Ridgecrest (93555-6104)
PHONE.....................760 939-2653
Debra Schmidt, *Director*
EMP: 55
SALES (est): 1.1MM **Privately Held**
SIC: **8351** Child day care services

(P-24486)
NORTH COAST PRESBYTERIAN CH
1831 S El Camino Real, Encinitas (92024-4913)
PHONE.....................760 753-2535
Fax: 760 753-2998
Daniel Foley, *Business Mgr*
Donald Seltzer, *Pastor*
Earl Joss, *Agent*
EMP: 70
SALES (est): 1.9MM **Privately Held**
WEB: www.ncpcinfo.com
SIC: **8351** 8661 Preschool center; Presbyterian Church

(P-24487)
NORTH WEST LEARNING CENTER
3542 W Gettysburg Ave, Fresno (93722-4198)
PHONE.....................559 228-3057
Rosemary Avalos, *Director*
Alvis Bytel, *Exec Dir*
EMP: 50
SALES (est): 604.3K **Privately Held**
SIC: **8351** Child day care services

(P-24488)
OFFICE OF CHILD DEVELOPMENT
10800 Farragut Dr, Culver City (90230-4107)
PHONE.....................310 842-4230
Audrey Stephens, *Director*
Audrey Jones, *Director*
Audrey Stevens, *Director*
EMP: 80
SALES (est): 561.6K **Privately Held**
SIC: **8351** Preschool center

(P-24489)
OLIVE KNOLLS CHRISTIAN SCHOOL
6201 Fruitvale Ave, Bakersfield (93308-2706)
PHONE.....................661 393-3566
Fax: 661 393-3467
Shirley Friberg, *Director*
Cory Marcoux, *Comp Lab Dir*
Theron Friberg, *Director*
EMP: 60
SALES (est): 3.6MM **Privately Held**
WEB: www.okcs.org
SIC: **8351** 8661 Child day care services; religious organizations

(P-24490)
OLYMPUS ADHC INC
Also Called: Olympus Adult Day Hlthcare Ctr
11613 Washington Pl, Los Angeles (90066-5013)
PHONE.....................310 572-7272
Boris Frigman, *President*
EMP: 50

SALES (est): 1MM **Privately Held**
SIC: **8351** Group day care center

(P-24491)
OPTIONS FOR LEARNING
Also Called: State Preschool
2001 Elm St, Alhambra (91803-2905)
PHONE.....................626 308-2411
EMP: 75
SALES (corp-wide): 64.6MM **Privately Held**
SIC: **8351** Group day care center
PA: Options For Learning
  885 S Village Oaks Dr # 12
  Covina CA 91724
  626 967-7848

(P-24492)
ORANGE CHILDREN & PARENTS
Also Called: O C P T
1063 N Glassell St, Orange (92867-5602)
PHONE.....................714 639-4000
Fax: 714 639-3408
Robyn Class, *Exec Dir*
Stephanie Ignatius, *Finance*
Maria Encalada, *Accountant*
Tracy Reyes, *Director*
Rosalinda Orellana, *Manager*
EMP: 58
SALES: 3.4MM **Privately Held**
SIC: **8351** Preschool center

(P-24493)
ORANGE CNTY SPRNTNDENT SCHOOLS
Also Called: Lindburgh Child Development
220 23rd St, Costa Mesa (92627-1810)
PHONE.....................949 650-2506
Fax: 949 548-3015
Elivira Frescas, *Director*
EMP: 60
SALES (corp-wide): 111.8MM **Privately Held**
WEB: www.ocprob.com
SIC: **8351** Child day care services
PA: Orange County Superintendent Of Schools
  200 Kalmus Dr
  Costa Mesa CA 92626
  714 966-4000

(P-24494)
ORANGE COUNTY HEAD START (PA)
2501 Pullman St Ste 100, Santa Ana (92705-5515)
P.O. Box 9269, Fountain Valley (92728-9269)
PHONE.....................714 241-8920
Colleen Versteeg, *Exec Dir*
Diane Maldonaldo, *Admin Sec*
Loyal Sharp, *Finance Dir*
Monica Portan, *Human Res Mgr*
Doris Wood, *Pub Rel Dir*
EMP: 75
SQ FT: 20,000
SALES: 34.9MM **Privately Held**
SIC: **8351** Preschool center

(P-24495)
ORANGE COUNTY HEAD START
9200 W Pacific Pl, Anaheim (92804-6387)
PHONE.....................714 761-4967
Colleen Versteeg, *Director*
EMP: 136
SALES (corp-wide): 34.9MM **Privately Held**
SIC: **8351** Head start center, except in conjunction with school
PA: Orange County Head Start
  2501 Pullman St Ste 100
  Santa Ana CA 92705
  714 241-8920

(P-24496)
PALCARE INC
945 California Dr, Burlingame (94010-3605)
PHONE.....................650 340-1289
Fax: 650 340-1315
Pettis Perry, *Exec Dir*
Lisa Kiesselbach, *Exec Dir*
Camella Mumm, *Admin Sec*
Diane Yvonne, *Business Mgr*
Tina Hardley, *Asst Director*
EMP: 50

PRODUCTS & SERVICES SECTION
8351 - Child Day Care Svcs County (P-24522)

SQ FT: 12,000
SALES: 3.2MM **Privately Held**
WEB: www.palcare.org
SIC: 8351 Child day care services

(P-24497)
PALO ALTO COMMUNITY CHILD CARE
890 Escondido Rd, Stanford (94305-7101)
PHONE.................................650 855-9828
Gary Prehn, *Principal*
EMP: 66
SALES (corp-wide): 9.2MM **Privately Held**
SIC: 8351 Child day care services
PA: Palo Alto Community Child Care Inc
   3990 Ventura Ct
   Palo Alto CA
   650 493-5990

(P-24498)
PARA LOS NINOS
845 E 6th St, Los Angeles (90021-1026)
PHONE.................................213 623-3942
EMP: 113
SALES (corp-wide): 22MM **Privately Held**
SIC: 8351 Child day care services
PA: Para Los Ninos
   500 Lucas Ave
   Los Angeles CA 90017
   213 250-4800

(P-24499)
PARENT CHILD DEVELOPMENT CTR (PA)
690 18th St, Oakland (94612-1339)
PHONE.................................510 452-0492
Fax: 510 452-0508
Adella Gaston, *Director*
Lyda Gfernandez, *Director*
EMP: 50
SQ FT: 2,162
SALES: 1MM **Privately Held**
SIC: 8351 Child day care services

(P-24500)
PEOPLES CARE INC
7355 Greenleaf Ave, Whittier (90602-1621)
PHONE.................................562 320-0174
Conrado Nilo, *Controller*
Frank Fernandez, *Manager*
EMP: 145
SALES (corp-wide): 32.9MM **Privately Held**
SIC: 8351 Child day care services
PA: People's Care Inc.
   13920 City Center Dr # 290
   Chino Hills CA 91709
   855 773-6753

(P-24501)
PITTSBURG PRE-SCHOOL & C
Also Called: Pittsburg Pre School
1760 Chester Dr, Pittsburg (94565-3920)
PHONE.................................925 439-2061
Francis Green, *Exec Dir*
John D Coker, *Agent*
EMP: 68
SQ FT: 9,600
SALES: 908.4K **Privately Held**
SIC: 8351 Group day care center; pre-school center

(P-24502)
PLAZA DE LA RAZA CHILD DEVELOP
225 N Avenue 25, Los Angeles (90031-1794)
PHONE.................................323 224-1788
EMP: 93
SALES (corp-wide): 17.1MM **Privately Held**
SIC: 8351 Preschool center
PA: Plaza De La Raza Child Development Services, Inc.
   8337 Telegraph Rd Ste 300
   Pico Rivera CA 90660
   562 776-1301

(P-24503)
PLAZA DE LA RAZA CHILD DEVELOP
6411 Norwalk Blvd, Whittier (90606-1502)
PHONE.................................562 695-1070
EMP: 93
SALES (corp-wide): 17.1MM **Privately Held**
SIC: 8351 Head start center, except in conjunction with school
PA: Plaza De La Raza Child Development Services, Inc.
   8337 Telegraph Rd Ste 300
   Pico Rivera CA 90660
   562 776-1301

(P-24504)
PLAZA DE LA RAZA CHILD DEVELOP (PA)
8337 Telegraph Rd Ste 300, Pico Rivera (90660-4957)
PHONE.................................562 776-1301
Anthony Rendon, *Exec Dir*
Virginia Villarruel, *Admin Sec*
Rosalina Fine, *Director*
EMP: 72
SALES: 17.1MM **Privately Held**
SIC: 8351 Head start center, except in conjunction with school

(P-24505)
PTSA 31ST DST CREATIVE KIDS
17445 Cantlay St, Van Nuys (91406-2455)
PHONE.................................818 996-2668
Linda Ross, *President*
Linda Loss, *President*
Deborah Velarde, *Treasurer*
EMP: 60
SALES (est): 542.8K **Privately Held**
SIC: 8351 Child day care services

(P-24506)
QUALITY CHILDRENS SERVICES
Also Called: Quality Childrens Services
710 S Stage Coach Ln, Fallbrook (92028-3649)
PHONE.................................760 723-3228
Lupita Flores Alatorr, *Director*
EMP: 74 **Privately Held**
SIC: 8351 Child day care services
PA: Quality Children's Services
   6108 Innovation Way
   Carlsbad CA 92009

(P-24507)
RAINBOW CHILDRENS ACADEMY INC
1213 Centinela Ave, Inglewood (90302-1137)
PHONE.................................310 672-2400
Turunz T Paesachov, *President*
EMP: 50
SQ FT: 12,000
SALES (est): 2.5MM **Privately Held**
SIC: 8351 Child day care services

(P-24508)
SAINT JHNS HLTH CTR FOUNDATION
Also Called: Saint Johns Child Fmly Dev Ctr
1339 20th St, Santa Monica (90404-2033)
PHONE.................................310 829-8921
Fax: 310 829-8455
Laura Osorio, *Director*
Barbara Mooney, *Buyer*
EMP: 70
SQ FT: 26,032
SALES (corp-wide): 2.4B **Privately Held**
SIC: 8351 Child day care services
HQ: Saint John's Health Center Foundation
   2121 Santa Monica Blvd
   Santa Monica CA 90404
   310 829-5511

(P-24509)
SAN BERNARDINO CITY UNF SCHOOL
Also Called: Allred Child Developement Ctr
303 S K St, San Bernardino (92410-2416)
PHONE.................................909 388-6307
Latashia Kelly, *Director*
Rosa Tubbs, *Administration*
EMP: 100
SALES (corp-wide): 331.5MM **Privately Held**
WEB: www.sbcusd.k12.ca.us
SIC: 8351 Child day care services
PA: San Bernardino City Unified School District
   777 N F St
   San Bernardino CA 92410
   909 381-1100

(P-24510)
SAN MARCOS UNIFIED SCHOOL DST
255 Pico Ave Ste 250, San Marcos (92069-3712)
PHONE.................................760 752-1252
Pamella Mc Coy, *Manager*
Marti Gray, *Network Mgr*
Micah Boggs, *Technology*
EMP: 100
SALES (corp-wide): 177MM **Privately Held**
WEB: www.smusd.k12.ca.us
SIC: 8351 Child day care services
PA: San Marcos Unified School District
   255 Pico Ave Ste 250
   San Marcos CA 92069
   760 744-4776

(P-24511)
SANTA CRUZ MONTESSORI SCHOOL
Also Called: SCMS
6230 Soquel Dr, Aptos (95003-3118)
PHONE.................................831 476-1646
Fax: 831 476-2073
Kathleen Ann Rideout, *CEO*
Norma Capus, *Office Mgr*
Carol Spivey, *Bookkeeper*
EMP: 50
SALES: 4.4MM **Privately Held**
WEB: www.savmait.com
SIC: 8351 8211 Preschool center; private elementary & secondary schools; private elementary school; private junior high school

(P-24512)
SANTA MONICA CITY OF
Also Called: Child Development Office, The
2802 4th St, Santa Monica (90405-4308)
PHONE.................................310 399-5865
Alice Chung, *Director*
Judy Abdp, *Exec Dir*
Stuart Sam, *Admin Asst*
Nancy Cohen, *Manager*
EMP: 60 **Privately Held**
WEB: www.santamonicapd.org
SIC: 8351 Child day care services
PA: City Of Santa Monica
   1685 Main St
   Santa Monica CA 90401
   310 458-8281

(P-24513)
SCOTTS MONTESSORI VALLEY INC
123 S Navarra Dr, Scotts Valley (95066-3618)
PHONE.................................831 439-9313
Fax: 831 439-9075
Bill Tershy, *President*
EMP: 50
SALES (est): 2.4MM **Privately Held**
WEB: www.montessorisv.com
SIC: 8351 Montessori child development center

(P-24514)
SHASTA COUNTY HEAD START CHILD (PA)
375 Lake Blvd Ste 100, Redding (96003-2557)
PHONE.................................530 241-1036
Fax: 530 241-2703
Carla Clark, *Exec Dir*
Nancy Dover, *Sales Executive*
Tanya Jones, *Director*
Gordon Chatham, *Manager*
EMP: 50
SQ FT: 5,000
SALES: 11.3MM **Privately Held**
SIC: 8351 Head start center, except in conjunction with school

(P-24515)
SIERRA CSCADE FMLY OPPRTNITIES (PA)
Also Called: HEAD START
424 N Mill Creek Rd, Quincy (95971-9678)
PHONE.................................530 283-1242
Fax: 530 283-1024
Brenda Poteete, *Director*
EMP: 65
SQ FT: 2,600
SALES: 3.2MM **Privately Held**
SIC: 8351 Head start center, except in conjunction with school

(P-24516)
SOLANO FAMILY & CHLD COUNCIL
421 Executive Ct N, Fairfield (94534-4019)
PHONE.................................707 863-3950
Fax: 707 784-1345
Kurt Galvez, *Exec Dir*
EMP: 74
SALES: 17.1MM **Privately Held**
WEB: www.solanosfcs.org
SIC: 8351 Child day care services

(P-24517)
SOUTH OF MARKET CHILD CARE
790 Folsom St, San Francisco (94107-1276)
PHONE.................................415 820-3500
Noushin Mofakham, *Director*
EMP: 54
SALES (est): 184.2K **Privately Held**
SIC: 8351 Montessori child development center

(P-24518)
ST ANDREWS CHILDREN CENTER
4400 Barranca Pkwy, Irvine (92604-4739)
PHONE.................................949 651-0198
Sue Ko, *Director*
EMP: 50
SALES (est): 1.3MM **Privately Held**
SIC: 8351 Child day care services

(P-24519)
STATE PRESCHOOL
831 E Avenue K2, Lancaster (93535-4788)
PHONE.................................661 940-4535
Fax: 661 945-4498
Stephanie Lester, *Manager*
EMP: 50 EST: 2010
SALES (est): 281.1K **Privately Held**
SIC: 8351 Preschool center

(P-24520)
STATE PRESCHOOL
Also Called: Martin Lthr Kng Chldr Ctr
950 El Pueblo Ave, Pittsburg (94565-4116)
PHONE.................................925 473-4380
Fax: 925 473-4371
Karan Latimer, *Director*
EMP: 50
SALES (est): 389.9K **Privately Held**
SIC: 8351 Preschool center

(P-24521)
STRATFORD SCHOOL INC
220 Kensington Way, Los Gatos (95032-4028)
PHONE.................................408 371-3020
Fax: 408 371-3250
Esperanza Hernandez, *Principal*
Sherry Adams, *Exec Dir*
EMP: 53
SALES (corp-wide): 8.3MM **Privately Held**
SIC: 8351 8211 Preschool center; preparatory school
PA: Stratford School, Inc.
   870 N California Ave
   Palo Alto CA 94303
   650 493-1151

(P-24522)
STUDENTS OF ASSOCIATED
Also Called: Csus Children's Center
6000 J St, Sacramento (95819-2605)
PHONE.................................916 278-6216
Denise Wessels, *Director*
Larry Gilbert, *Telecom Exec*
EMP: 80

8351 - Child Day Care Svcs County (P-24523)

SALES (corp-wide): 8.1MM **Privately Held**
SIC: 8351 Child day care services
PA: Associated Students Of California State University, Sacramento
6000 J St
Sacramento CA
916 278-7917

(P-24523)
SUNSHINE DAY CAMP INC
Also Called: Sunshine Child Care & Lrng Ctr
23720 Wiley Canyon Rd, Valencia (91355-2900)
PHONE.................................661 254-6855
Timothy W Borruel, *President*
EMP: 150
SALES (est): 7.3MM **Privately Held**
SIC: 8351 8211 Group day care center; kindergarten

(P-24524)
TAFT COLLEGE CHILDREN CENTER
29 Emmons Park Dr, Taft (93268-2317)
PHONE.................................661 763-7850
Genevieve Garcia, *Director*
Leslie Braggo, *Director*
Dennis McCall, *Director*
EMP: 50
SALES (est): 853.4K **Privately Held**
SIC: 8351 Child day care services

(P-24525)
THINK TOGETHER
1730 W Cameron Ave, West Covina (91790-2722)
PHONE.................................626 373-2311
Tom Lopez, *Branch Mgr*
Tiffany Alva, *Director*
EMP: 1536
SALES (corp-wide): 52.4MM **Privately Held**
SIC: 8351 Child day care services
PA: Think Together
2101 E 4th St Ste 200b
Santa Ana CA 92705
714 543-3807

(P-24526)
TOM SAWYER CAMPS INC
Also Called: T.S.c
707 W Woodbury Rd Ste F, Altadena (91001-5386)
PHONE.................................626 794-1156
Fax: 626 794-1401
Sarah Horner Fish, *CEO*
Michael H Horner, *President*
Sally Horner, *Vice Pres*
Katie Enney, *Program Dir*
Kevin Austin, *Director*
EMP: 120
SQ FT: 4,000
SALES (est): 5.4MM **Privately Held**
WEB: www.daycampjobs.com
SIC: 8351 Child day care services

(P-24527)
TULARE CNTY CHLD CARE HOME EDU
7000 N Doe Ave Ste C, Visalia (93291-8623)
PHONE.................................559 651-0247
Fax: 559 651-2465
Senaida Garcia, *Director*
EMP: 68
SALES (est): 2.6MM **Privately Held**
SIC: 8351 Head start center, except in conjunction with school

(P-24528)
VANDENBERG AFB CHILD CARE
Summersill Bldg 11613, Lompoc (93437)
PHONE.................................805 606-1555
Verna D Brown, *Director*
EMP: 50
SALES (est): 1.2MM **Privately Held**
SIC: 8351 Child day care services

(P-24529)
WALNUT VALLEY UNIFIED SCHL DST
Also Called: Castle Rock Enrichment Program
2975 Castle Rock Rd, Diamond Bar (91765-3420)
PHONE.................................909 444-3460
Susan Peter, *Director*
EMP: 78
SALES (corp-wide): 146.8MM **Privately Held**
SIC: 8351 Child day care services
PA: Walnut Valley Unified School District
880 S Lemon Ave
Walnut CA 91789
909 595-1261

(P-24530)
WE CARE DAY CARE & PRE SCHOOL
Also Called: West Valley Christian Academy
1790 Sequoia Blvd, Tracy (95376-4329)
PHONE.................................209 832-4072
Fax: 209 832-4073
Tim Smith, *Administration*
EMP: 60 **EST:** 1996
SALES (est): 2.2MM **Privately Held**
SIC: 8351 Child day care services

(P-24531)
WEST VALLEY FAMILY YMCA
Also Called: Vanalden Ave School
18810 Vanowen St, Reseda (91335-5213)
PHONE.................................818 774-2840
Greg Koubek, *Director*
Ralph Drengson, *Vice Pres*
Stacy Childress, *Principal*
Shane Ruffin, *Principal*
Tim Oconnor, *Director*
EMP: 125
SALES (est): 2.4MM **Privately Held**
SIC: 8351 8322 Child day care services; youth center

(P-24532)
WESTMINSTER PRESBYTERIAN CH
Also Called: Westmnster Prsbt Preschool Ctr
32111 Watergate Rd, Westlake Village (91361-3602)
PHONE.................................818 889-1491
Fax: 818 889-7132
Dick Thompson, *Pastor*
Steve Miller, *Principal*
Jennifer Kates Witten, *Principal*
Richard H Thompson, *Pastor*
Judy Hightower, *Director*
EMP: 50
SQ FT: 33,093
SALES (est): 1.5MM **Privately Held**
SIC: 8351 Preschool center

(P-24533)
WESTSIDE CHILDRENS CENTER INC
5721 W Slauson Ave # 140, Culver City (90230-6554)
PHONE.................................310 846-4100
Fax: 310 578-6831
Heather Carrigan, *CEO*
Richard Klein, *CFO*
Gil Ciensuegos, *Info Tech Mgr*
Jolie Laurent, *Opers Staff*
Samuel Kirk, *Education*
EMP: 92
SQ FT: 18,000
SALES (est): 7.8MM **Privately Held**
SIC: 8351 8322 Child day care services; child related social services

(P-24534)
WU YEE CHILDRENS SERVICES
880 Clay St, San Francisco (94108-1611)
PHONE.................................415 677-0100
Alyson Suzeuki, *Program Dir*
Winnie Kwei, *Manager*
EMP: 68
SALES (corp-wide): 20.4MM **Privately Held**
WEB: www.wuyee.org
SIC: 8351 8322 Group day care center; individual & family services

PA: Wu Yee Children's Services
827 Broadway
San Francisco CA 94133
415 230-7504

(P-24535)
YESHIVA RAU ISACSOHN ACADEMY
Also Called: Yeshivath Torath Emeth Academy
540 N La Brea Ave, Los Angeles (90036-2016)
PHONE.................................323 549-3170
Fax: 323 934-3907
Charles Abbott, *Ch of Bd*
Morris Weiss, *President*
Rabbi Berish Goldenberg, *Corp Secy*
EMP: 120
SALES (est): 4.4MM **Privately Held**
SIC: 8351 8211 Preschool center; nursery school; elementary school

(P-24536)
YOUNG MENS CHRSTN ASSN OF LA
Also Called: East Valley Family YMCA Dcc
5142 Tujunga Ave, North Hollywood (91601-3742)
PHONE.................................818 763-5126
Fax: 818 763-0393
Debbie Lozano, *Director*
EMP: 90
SQ FT: 11,260
SALES (corp-wide): 103.1MM **Privately Held**
SIC: 8351 8322 Group day care center; youth center
PA: Young Men's Christian Association Of Metropolitan Los Angeles
625 S New Hampshire Ave
Los Angeles CA 90005
213 351-2256

8361 Residential Care

(P-24537)
24HR HOMECARE LLC
300 N Sepulveda Blvd # 1065, El Segundo (90245-4490)
PHONE.................................310 906-3683
Sonia Aouriri, *Principal*
Jenny Lien, *Admin Asst*
Joseph Zimmer, *Regl Sales Mgr*
Amanda Brady,
EMP: 62
SALES (est): 7.7MM **Privately Held**
SIC: 8361 Residential care

(P-24538)
5 ACRS-THE BYS GRLS AID SOC LA
Also Called: Five Acres
760 Mountain View St, Altadena (91001-4925)
PHONE.................................626 798-6793
Fax: 626 797-7722
Chanel W Boutakidis, *CEO*
Regina Bette, *COO*
Daniel Braun, *CFO*
Robert A Ketch, *Exec Dir*
Kim Hutchigs, *Admin Sec*
EMP: 419
SQ FT: 70,000
SALES (est): 34MM **Privately Held**
SIC: 8361 8322 8211 Children's home; public welfare center; public combined elementary & secondary school

(P-24539)
ABILTY FIRST
3770 E Willow St, Long Beach (90815-1731)
PHONE.................................562 426-6161
Lori Ganbmi, *President*
EMP: 60
SALES (est): 571.1K **Privately Held**
SIC: 8361 Residential care

(P-24540)
ACTS FOR CHILDREN (PA)
Also Called: A C T S
18136 Jurupa Ave, Bloomington (92316-3009)
P.O. Box 848, Colton (92324-0848)
PHONE.................................909 877-5499
Fax: 909 877-1343
Ike Kerhulas, *President*
Bobbie Bundy, *Manager*
EMP: 55
SALES: 608.9K **Privately Held**
SIC: 8361 Residential care

(P-24541)
ADVENT GROUP MINISTRIES INC
90 Great Oaks Blvd # 108, San Jose (95119-1314)
PHONE.................................408 281-0708
Fax: 408 281-2658
Jeff Davis, *Ch of Bd*
Jeff Blythe, *COO*
Mark Miller, *Exec Dir*
EMP: 63
SQ FT: 4,400
SALES: 2.8MM **Privately Held**
WEB: www.adventgm.com
SIC: 8361 Children's home

(P-24542)
AEGIS ASSSTED LIVING PRPTS LLC
Also Called: Aegis At Shadowridge
1440 S Melrose Dr, Oceanside (92056-5394)
PHONE.................................760 806-3600
Fax: 760 806-9508
Sam Bergstron, *Manager*
EMP: 65
SALES (corp-wide): 103.6MM **Privately Held**
SIC: 8361 Home for the aged
HQ: Aegis Assisted Living Properties, Llc
220 Concourse Blvd
Santa Rosa CA 95403
707 535-3200

(P-24543)
AEGIS OF CARMICHAEL
4050 Walnut Ave, Carmichael (95608-1600)
PHONE.................................916 972-1313
Fax: 916 972-1060
Dwane Clark, *President*
Jerry Myer, *COO*
Layla Seiler, *Exec Dir*
Danelle Houle, *Finance*
EMP: 60 **EST:** 1999
SALES (est): 2.9MM **Privately Held**
SIC: 8361 Residential care

(P-24544)
ALLEN SPEES FAMILY HOMES
524 W Roberts Ave, Fresno (93704-1832)
PHONE.................................559 432-3664
Fax: 559 438-0647
Sue Allen, *Partner*
Terry Spees, *Partner*
EMP: 50
SALES (est): 2.2MM **Privately Held**
SIC: 8361 Residential care

(P-24545)
ALTCARE CEDAR CREEK LLC
Also Called: Cedar Creek Alzhimers Dementia
868 Ensenada Ave, Berkeley (94707-1850)
PHONE.................................510 527-7282
Terry Carson, *CEO*
Cole Smith,
EMP: 55
SALES (est): 975.3K **Privately Held**
SIC: 8361 Residential care

(P-24546)
AMERICAN BAPTIST HOMES OF WEST
Also Called: San Joaquin Gardens
5555 N Fresno St, Fresno (93710-6006)
PHONE.................................559 439-4770
Fax: 559 439-2457
Keli Swales, *Branch Mgr*
EMP: 203

PRODUCTS & SERVICES SECTION

8361 - Residential Care County (P-24568)

SALES (corp-wide): 129.1MM **Privately Held**
WEB: www.abhow.com
SIC: **8361** 8051 Home for the aged; skilled nursing care facilities
PA: American Baptist Homes Of The West
6120 Stoneridge Mall Rd # 300
Pleasanton CA 94588
925 924-7100

(P-24547)
AMERICAN BAPTIST HOMES OF WEST
Also Called: Piedmont Gardens
110 41st St Ofc, Oakland (94611-5219)
PHONE.................................510 654-7172
Reginald Nyles, *Branch Mgr*
EMP: 220
SALES (corp-wide): 129.1MM **Privately Held**
WEB: www.abhow.com
SIC: **8361** Residential care
PA: American Baptist Homes Of The West
6120 Stoneridge Mall Rd # 300
Pleasanton CA 94588
925 924-7100

(P-24548)
AMERICAN RETIREMENT CORP
2107 Ocean Ave, Santa Monica (90405-2299)
PHONE.................................310 399-3227
EMP: 112
SALES (corp-wide): 4.9B **Publicly Held**
SIC: **8361** Home for the aged
HQ: American Retirement Corporation
111 Westwood Pl Ste 200
Brentwood TN 37027
615 221-2250

(P-24549)
ANGEL VIEW INC
Also Called: Angel View Resale Store
454 N Indian Canyon Dr, Palm Springs (92262-6018)
PHONE.................................760 322-2440
Tracy Powers, *General Mgr*
EMP: 50
SALES (corp-wide): 24.9MM **Privately Held**
SIC: **8361** Rehabilitation center, residential: health care incidental
PA: Angel View, Inc.
12379 Miracle Hill Rd
Desert Hot Springs CA 92240
760 329-6471

(P-24550)
ARC INDUSTRIES
5143 Cochran St Ste 93063, Simi Valley (93063-3064)
PHONE.................................805 520-0399
Fax: 805 520-4723
Larry Rice, *Manager*
Lisa Emery, *Manager*
EMP: 57
SALES (est): 753.6K **Privately Held**
SIC: **8361** 8999 Rehabilitation center, residential: health care incidental; services

(P-24551)
ARDCORE SENIOR LIVING
Also Called: Canyon Hills Club
525 S Anaheim Hills Rd, Anaheim (92807-4721)
PHONE.................................714 974-2226
Fax: 714 637-7421
J Bert Sprenger, *Manager*
Vicki Markley, *Administration*
EMP: 70
SALES (corp-wide): 15.1B **Privately Held**
SIC: **8361** 6513 Home for the aged; apartment building operators
PA: Obayashi Corporation
2-15-2, Konan
Minato-Ku TKY 108-0
357 691-111

(P-24552)
ASIAN COMMUNITY CENTER OF SAC
7801 Rush River Dr, Sacramento (95831-4602)
PHONE.................................916 393-9020
Fax: 916 393-9128
Darren Trisel, *Branch Mgr*

Raymond Gee, *Technology*
EMP: 101
SALES (corp-wide): 21.9MM **Privately Held**
SIC: **8361** Residential care
PA: Asian Community Center Of Sacramento Valley, Inc.
7334 Park City Dr
Sacramento CA 95831
916 394-6399

(P-24553)
ASPEN RANCH LLC
20400 Stevens Creek Blvd, Cupertino (95014-2217)
PHONE.................................435 836-2080
Kevin Knutson, *Director*
Matt Alexander, *Director*
EMP: 131
SALES (est): 1.7MM **Publicly Held**
WEB: www.aspenranch.com
SIC: **8361** 8322 Residential care; individual & family services
HQ: Aspen Education Group, Inc.
17777 Center Court Dr N # 300
Cerritos CA 90703
562 467-5500

(P-24554)
ASPIRANET
Also Called: Sunset Neighborhood Beacon Ctr
3925 Noriega St, San Francisco (94122-3935)
PHONE.................................415 759-3690
Fax: 415 759-0883
Ruby LI, *Manager*
Sean Chen, *Vice Pres*
Jennifer Ho, *Admin Asst*
Eunice Nichols, *Director*
Janet OH, *Director*
EMP: 67
SALES (corp-wide): 52.7MM **Privately Held**
WEB: www.verosantes.com
SIC: **8361** 8322 Residential care; individual & family services
PA: Aspiranet
400 Oyster Point Blvd # 501
South San Francisco CA 94080
650 866-4080

(P-24555)
ASPIRANET
151 E Canal Dr, Turlock (95380-3901)
PHONE.................................209 669-2582
Fax: 209 669-2593
Sharon Salaiz, *Administration*
EMP: 55
SALES (corp-wide): 52.7MM **Privately Held**
SIC: **8361** Residential care
PA: Aspiranet
400 Oyster Point Blvd # 501
South San Francisco CA 94080
650 866-4080

(P-24556)
ATRIA SENIOR LIVING INC
Also Called: Atria Grand Oaks
2177 E Thousand Oaks Blvd, Thousand Oaks (91362-2904)
PHONE.................................805 370-5400
Evan Granucci, *Branch Mgr*
Karla Nelson, *Business Dir*
EMP: 70
SALES (corp-wide): 3.2B **Publicly Held**
SIC: **8361** Residential care
HQ: Senior Atria Living Inc
300 E Market St Ste 100
Louisville KY 40202

(P-24557)
ATRIA SENIOR LIVING GROUP INC
Also Called: Villa Las Posas
24 Las Posas Rd, Camarillo (93010-2780)
PHONE.................................805 482-9771
Fax: 805 987-9899
Cyntia Drachenberg, *Director*
Tabitha McCoy, *Administration*
Janice Hodgdon, *Marketing Staff*
Doug Paschen, *Food Svc Dir*
EMP: 63

SALES (corp-wide): 3.2B **Publicly Held**
WEB: www.atriacom.com
SIC: **8361** Residential care
HQ: Atria Senior Living Group Inc
300 E Market St Ste 100
Louisville KY 40202

(P-24558)
ATRIA SENIOR LIVING GROUP INC
Also Called: Chateau San Juan
32353 San Juan Creek Rd, San Juan Capistrano (92675-4254)
PHONE.................................949 661-1220
Fax: 949 661-3855
Del Woytek, *Manager*
EMP: 109
SALES (corp-wide): 3.2B **Publicly Held**
WEB: www.atriacom.com
SIC: **8361** Residential care
HQ: Atria Senior Living Group Inc
300 E Market St Ste 100
Louisville KY 40202

(P-24559)
ATRIA SENIOR LIVING GROUP INC
Also Called: Tamalpais Creek
853 Tamalpais Ave Ofc, Novato (94947-3052)
PHONE.................................415 892-0944
Fax: 415 898-0272
Jason Englehorn, *Exec Dir*
CJ Kory, *Office Mgr*
Lauren Harms, *Financial Exec*
Tammy Cherry, *Marketing Staff*
Kalia Norris, *Nursing Dir*
EMP: 50
SALES (corp-wide): 3.2B **Publicly Held**
WEB: www.atriacom.com
SIC: **8361** Residential care
HQ: Atria Senior Living Group Inc
300 E Market St Ste 100
Louisville KY 40202

(P-24560)
ATRIA SENIOR LIVING GROUP INC
Also Called: Hacienda De Monterey
44600 Monterey Ave Ofc, Palm Desert (92260-3328)
PHONE.................................760 341-0890
Fax: 760 773-5163
Tim Mattson, *Exec Dir*
Susan Maderick, *Social Dir*
EMP: 75
SALES (corp-wide): 3.2B **Publicly Held**
WEB: www.atriacom.com
SIC: **8361** Residential care
HQ: Atria Senior Living Group Inc
300 E Market St Ste 100
Louisville KY 40202

(P-24561)
AVALON AT NEWPORT LLC
Also Called: Avalon At Newport Beach
393 Hospital Rd, Newport Beach (92663-3501)
PHONE.................................949 631-3555
Fran Lacas, *Administration*
Lauren Soules, *Director*
EMP: 93
SQ FT: 4,562
SALES (corp-wide): 5.8MM **Privately Held**
SIC: **8361** Residential care
PA: Avalon At Newport, Llc
23 Corporate Plaza Dr # 190
Newport Beach CA 92660
949 719-4082

(P-24562)
AVALON GOLDEN GATE LLC
Also Called: Vintage Golden Gate
1601 19th Ave Apt 122, San Francisco (94122-3469)
PHONE.................................415 664-6264
Eric K Davidson, *Principal*
Cynthia Langas, *Nursing Dir*
Vicki R Clark,
Brian J Flornes,
EMP: 77

SALES (est): 4.3MM **Privately Held**
SIC: **8361** Geriatric residential care

(P-24563)
BARTON MEMORIAL HOSPITAL
Also Called: Barton Home Health and Hospice
2092 Lake Tahoe Blvd # 500, South Lake Tahoe (96150-6422)
PHONE.................................530 543-5581
Kindle Craig, *Exec Dir*
EMP: 462
SALES (corp-wide): 114.2MM **Privately Held**
SIC: **8361** Residential care
PA: Barton Memorial Hospital
2170 South Ave
South Lake Tahoe CA 96150
530 541-3420

(P-24564)
BETHESDA LTHRAN CMMUNITIES INC
5440 W Wren Ave, Visalia (93291-9142)
PHONE.................................559 636-6300
EMP: 83
SALES (corp-wide): 126.5MM **Privately Held**
SIC: **8361** Home for destitute men & women
PA: Bethesda Lutheran Communities, Inc.
600 Hoffmann Dr
Watertown WI 53094
920 261-3050

(P-24565)
BEYER PARK VILLAS LLC
3529 Forest Glenn Dr, Modesto (95355-1360)
PHONE.................................209 236-1900
Bill Schilz,
Sue Keith, *Human Res Dir*
Clarence Becker,
Donald Cefaloni,
Harold Johnson,
EMP: 75
SQ FT: 59,000
SALES (est): 3.7MM **Privately Held**
SIC: **8361** Residential care

(P-24566)
BHO LLC
5801 Sun Lakes Blvd, Banning (92220-6507)
PHONE.................................951 845-2220
Terry Raisio,
EMP: 50
SALES (est): 1MM **Privately Held**
SIC: **8361** Geriatric residential care

(P-24567)
BOYS REPUBLIC (PA)
Also Called: Girls Republic
1907 Boys Republic Dr, Chino Hills (91709-5447)
PHONE.................................909 902-6690
Dennis Slattery, *CEO*
Timothy J Kay, *President*
Robert Carter, *Vice Pres*
Robert Key, *Vice Pres*
Jeff Seymour, *Vice Pres*
EMP: 150
SQ FT: 173,000
SALES: 20.5MM **Privately Held**
SIC: **8361** Group foster home

(P-24568)
BRETHREN HILLCREST HOMES
2705 Mountain View Dr Ofc, La Verne (91750-4398)
PHONE.................................909 593-4917
Fax: 909 596-5538
Matthew Neeley, *President*
Barbara Feliciano, *CFO*
Margaret Marquez, *Social Dir*
Vince Schnabel, *Info Tech Mgr*
Valerie Rennie, *Accountant*
EMP: 230
SQ FT: 34,000
SALES: 21.7MM **Privately Held**
WEB: www.livingathillcrest.org
SIC: **8361** 8059 8051 Rest home, with health care incidental; nursing home, except skilled & intermediate care facility; extended care facility

8361 - Residential Care County (P-24569)

(P-24569)
BRITTANY HOUSE LLC
5401 E Centralia St, Long Beach (90808-1452)
PHONE..................562 421-4717
Fax: 562 421-3746
Colleen Rosatti, *Exec Dir*
Ricardo Lopez, *Manager*
EMP: 100
SQ FT: 43,018
SALES (est): 3.3MM
SALES (corp-wide): 33.2MM Privately Held
WEB: www.healthcaregrp.com
SIC: 8361 Geriatric residential care
PA: Activcare Living, Inc.
  9619 Chesapeake Dr # 103
  San Diego CA 92123
  858 565-4424

(P-24570)
BROOKDALE LVING CMMUNITIES INC
Also Called: Atrium of San Jose
1009 Blossom River Way, San Jose (95123-6304)
PHONE..................408 445-7770
Fax: 408 267-1069
Michele Merritt, *Exec Dir*
Jim Buchta, *Exec Dir*
Cynthia King, *VP Sales*
EMP: 110
SALES (corp-wide): 4.9B Publicly Held
WEB: www.parkplace-spokane.com
SIC: 8361 Geriatric residential care
HQ: Brookdale Living Communities, Inc.
  515 N State St Ste 1750
  Chicago IL 60654

(P-24571)
BROOKDALE SENIOR LIVING INC
1177 S Palm Ave, Hemet (92543-7817)
PHONE..................951 929-5988
EMP: 79
SALES (corp-wide): 4.9B Publicly Held
SIC: 8361 Home for destitute men & women
PA: Brookdale Senior Living
  111 Westwood Pl Ste 400
  Brentwood TN 37027
  615 221-2250

(P-24572)
BROOKDALE SENIOR LIVING INC
72750 Country Club Dr, Rancho Mirage (92270-4083)
PHONE..................760 346-7772
EMP: 87
SALES (corp-wide): 4.9B Publicly Held
SIC: 8361 6513 Residential care; retirement hotel operation
PA: Brookdale Senior Living
  111 Westwood Pl Ste 400
  Brentwood TN 37027
  615 221-2250

(P-24573)
BROOKDALE SENIOR LIVING INC
2005 Kellogg Ave, Corona (92879-3111)
PHONE..................951 808-9387
EMP: 174
SALES (corp-wide): 4.9B Publicly Held
SIC: 8361 8093 8059 Home for the aged; mental health clinic, outpatient; convalescent home
PA: Brookdale Senior Living
  111 Westwood Pl Ste 400
  Brentwood TN 37027
  615 221-2250

(P-24574)
CAL SOUTHERN PRESBT HOMES
Also Called: White Sands of La Jolla Clinic
7450 Olivetas Ave Ofc, La Jolla (92037-4900)
PHONE..................858 454-4201
Fax: 858 450-5298
Wendy Matalon, *Branch Mgr*
Mike Coates, *Project Mgr*
Maggy Kwee, *Human Resources*
Rochelle Balaban, *Director*
Leonard Lazarus, *Director*
EMP: 165
SALES (corp-wide): 79.2MM Privately Held
WEB: www.scths.com
SIC: 8361 Home for the aged; skilled nursing care facilities
PA: Southern California Presbyterian Homes
  516 Burchett St
  Glendale CA 91203
  818 247-0420

(P-24575)
CAL SOUTHERN PRESBT HOMES
Also Called: Redwood Senior Homes & Svcs
710 W 13th Ave, Escondido (92025-5511)
PHONE..................760 747-4306
Fax: 760 480-2759
Gary Boriero, *Manager*
Don Smith, *Administration*
Elizabeth Salada, *Director*
EMP: 161
SQ FT: 8,552
SALES (corp-wide): 74.7MM Privately Held
WEB: www.scths.com
SIC: 8361 Residential care
PA: Southern California Presbyterian Homes
  516 Burchett St
  Glendale CA 91203
  818 247-0420

(P-24576)
CAL SOUTHERN PRESBT HOMES
Also Called: Redwood Town Court
500 E Valley Pkwy Ofc, Escondido (92025-3073)
PHONE..................760 737-5110
Fax: 760 737-2439
Les Curtis, *Manager*
EMP: 89
SALES (corp-wide): 74.7MM Privately Held
WEB: www.scths.com
SIC: 8361 Residential care
PA: Southern California Presbyterian Homes
  516 Burchett St
  Glendale CA 91203
  818 247-0420

(P-24577)
CALIFORNIA FRIENDS HOMES
Also Called: QUAKER GARDENS
12151 Dale Ave, Stanton (90680-3889)
PHONE..................714 530-9100
Randy Brown, *CEO*
Gina Kolb, *Exec Dir*
Dixie Mathers, *Exec Dir*
Glenda Hementiza, *Managing Dir*
Zina Quigley, *Marketing Staff*
EMP: 315
SQ FT: 10,000
SALES: 15.2MM Privately Held
WEB: www.quakergardens.com
SIC: 8361 8051 Home for the aged; convalescent home with continuous nursing care

(P-24578)
CALIFORNIA PEO HOME
Also Called: Marguerite Gardens
700 N Stoneman Ave, Alhambra (91801-1408)
PHONE..................626 300-0400
Fax: 626 299-4235
EMP: 95
SQ FT: 77,343
SALES: 4.3MM Privately Held
SIC: 8361

(P-24579)
CARE ASSOCIATES INC
Also Called: Helen Evans Home For Children
15125 Gale Ave, Hacienda Heights (91745-1407)
PHONE..................626 330-4048
Paula De Lisio, *President*
EMP: 60 EST: 1998
SQ FT: 9,698
SALES: 2.7MM Privately Held
SIC: 8361 Children's home; home for the mentally retarded

(P-24580)
CARLTON SENIOR LIVING INC
1075 Fulton Ave, Sacramento (95825-4275)
PHONE..................916 971-4800
EMP: 155
SALES (corp-wide): 31.1MM Privately Held
SIC: 8361 8052 8051 Residential care; intermediate care facilities; skilled nursing care facilities
PA: Senior Carlton Living Inc
  4005 Port Chicago Hwy
  Concord CA 94520
  925 338-2434

(P-24581)
CARSON SENIOR ASSISTED LIVING
345 E Carson St, Carson (90745-2709)
PHONE..................310 830-4010
Fax: 310 830-0264
EMP: 75
SALES (est): 3.3MM Privately Held
SIC: 8361

(P-24582)
CASA DE AMPARO (PA)
325 Buena Creek Rd, San Marcos (92069-9679)
PHONE..................760 754-5500
Fax: 760 757-0792
Sharon Delphenich, *Exec Dir*
Annette Garrison, *Treasurer*
Debbie Slattery, *Treasurer*
Tamara Fleck-Myers, *Exec Dir*
Kisha Caldwell, *Info Tech Mgr*
EMP: 74
SQ FT: 25,000
SALES: 7.4MM Privately Held
WEB: www.casadeamparo.org
SIC: 8361 8351 Residential care; child day care services

(P-24583)
CASA DE LAS CAMPANAS INC
24317 Del Amo Rd, Ramona (92065-4075)
PHONE..................760 789-4746
Susan Freemire, *Principal*
EMP: 227
SALES (corp-wide): 38.3MM Privately Held
SIC: 8361 Residential care
PA: Casa De Las Campanas, Inc.
  18655 W Bernardo Dr # 489
  San Diego CA 92127
  858 451-9152

(P-24584)
CASA DE LAS CAMPANAS INC (PA)
18655 W Bernardo Dr # 489, San Diego (92127-3099)
PHONE..................858 451-9152
Fax: 858 451-8660
Jill Sorenson, *Exec Dir*
David Johnson, *CFO*
Robert L Reeves, *Chairman*
Maria Rivera, *Officer*
Marge Pronovost, *Exec Dir*
EMP: 123
SQ FT: 709,627
SALES: 38.3MM Privately Held
SIC: 8361 8052 8051 6513 Home for the aged; intermediate care facilities; skilled nursing care facilities; apartment building operators

(P-24585)
CASA-PACIFICA INC
Also Called: Freedom Properties
2200 W Acacia Ave Ofc, Hemet (92545-3737)
PHONE..................951 658-3369
Mary Ann Casino, *Director*
EMP: 300
SALES (corp-wide): 17.6MM Privately Held
WEB: www.fmcwest.com
SIC: 8361 8059 Geriatric residential care; rest home, with health care
PA: Casa-Pacifica, Inc
  27130a Paseo Espada A
  San Juan Capistrano CA 92675
  949 489-0430

(P-24586)
CASA-PACIFICA INC
Also Called: Freedom Village
23442 El Toro Rd, Lake Forest (92630-6979)
PHONE..................949 586-4466
Mary Ann Casino, *Manager*
EMP: 200
SQ FT: 37,974
SALES (corp-wide): 17.6MM Privately Held
WEB: www.fmcwest.com
SIC: 8361 8059 8052 Geriatric residential care; rest home, with health care; intermediate care facilities
PA: Casa-Pacifica, Inc
  27130a Paseo Espada A
  San Juan Capistrano CA 92675
  949 489-0430

(P-24587)
CASA-PACIFICA INC
Also Called: Freedom Properties Village
2400 W Acacia Ave, Hemet (92545-3743)
PHONE..................951 766-5116
Fax: 951 766-5316
Valeria Machain, *General Mgr*
Dorothy Nelson, *Executive*
EMP: 100
SALES (corp-wide): 17.6MM Privately Held
WEB: www.fmcwest.com
SIC: 8361 8052 8051 6513 Geriatric residential care; intermediate care facilities; skilled nursing care facilities; apartment building operators
PA: Casa-Pacifica, Inc
  27130a Paseo Espada A
  San Juan Capistrano CA 92675
  949 489-0430

(P-24588)
CASABLANCA ALZHEIMERS RESID
Also Called: Casablanca Alzheimer's Care
158 Rockaway Rd, Oak View (93022-9306)
PHONE..................805 649-5143
Nilson Froula, *President*
Laurie Froula, *Partner*
EMP: 60
SQ FT: 12,000
SALES (est): 2.8MM Privately Held
SIC: 8361 Rest home, with health care incidental

(P-24589)
CENTINELA VALLEY CARE CENTER
950 S Flower St, Inglewood (90301-4186)
PHONE..................310 674-3216
Fax: 310 674-3219
William A Nelson, *President*
EMP: 200
SALES (est): 5.6MM Privately Held
SIC: 8361 8059 Home for the aged; convalescent home

(P-24590)
CHAMBERLAINS CHILDREN CTR INC
1850 Cienega Rd, Hollister (95023-5516)
P.O. Box 1269 (95024-1269)
PHONE..................831 636-2121
Robert Freiri, *Exec Dir*
Rosemary Cardinalli, *Food Svc Dir*
EMP: 60
SALES (est): 2.8MM Privately Held
WEB: www.chamberlaincc.org
SIC: 8361 Residential care for children

(P-24591)
CHARLEE FAMILY CARE
136 E 6th St, Beaumont (92223-2146)
PHONE..................951 845-3588
Richard E Rios, *Principal*
Diane Eldred, *CFO*
EMP: 79
SALES: 3.4MM Privately Held
SIC: 8361 Residential care

PRODUCTS & SERVICES SECTION   8361 - Residential Care County (P-24614)

(P-24592)
CHILDHELP INC
Also Called: Child Help Head Start Center
14700 Manzanita Rd, Beaumont
(92223-3026)
P.O. Box 247 (92223-0247)
PHONE.................................951 845-6737
Klara Pakozdi, *Manager*
Amelia Murillo, *Treasurer*
Diana Correa, *Exec Dir*
Jack Belcher, *Administration*
Duff Wenz, *Human Res Dir*
EMP: 165
SALES (corp-wide): 33.8MM **Privately Held**
WEB: www.childhelpusa.com
SIC: 8361 Children's home
PA: Childhelp, Inc.
    4350 E Camelback Rd F250
    Phoenix AZ 85018
    480 922-8212

(P-24593)
CHILDNET YOUTH & FMLY SVCS INC
Also Called: Behavioral Health Svcs Dept
5150 E Pacific Cst Hwy # 100, Long Beach
(90804-3312)
PHONE.................................562 492-9983
Cathy Hughes, *CEO*
EMP: 65
SALES (corp-wide): 24.3MM **Privately Held**
WEB: www.childnet.net
SIC: 8361 8322 Juvenile correctional facilities; family counseling services
PA: Childnet Youth And Family Services, Inc.
    4155 Outer Traffic Cir
    Long Beach CA 90804
    562 498-5500

(P-24594)
CHILDRENS BUREAU SOUTHERN CAL (PA)
1910 Magnolia Ave, Los Angeles
(90007-1220)
PHONE.................................213 342-0100
Alex Morales, *President*
Sona Chandwani, *CFO*
Laura Bachman, *Executive*
Richard Ledwin, *Executive*
Ann Winkle, *Executive*
EMP: 107 EST: 1904
SQ FT: 43,000
SALES: 31.2MM **Privately Held**
SIC: 8361 Residential care for children

(P-24595)
CHILDRENS HOME OF STOCKTON
430 N Pilgrim St, Stockton (95205-4428)
PHONE.................................209 466-0853
Fax: 209 466-1770
Michael Dutra, *Principal*
Russ Backman, *Comp Lab Dir*
Linden Howe, *Assistant*
EMP: 90
SQ FT: 10,000
SALES: 6.8MM **Privately Held**
WEB: www.chsstk.com
SIC: 8361 8211 Children's home; private combined elementary & secondary school

(P-24596)
CHILDRENS RECVG HM SACRAMENTO
3555 Auburn Blvd, Sacramento
(95821-2005)
PHONE.................................916 482-2370
Fax: 916 482-1539
David Ballard, *CEO*
Rich Bryan, *CFO*
Nick Maloof, *Vice Pres*
Robert Roth, *Vice Pres*
Rob Kerth, *Exec Dir*
EMP: 160
SQ FT: 26,000
SALES: 9.2MM **Privately Held**
WEB: www.crhkids.org
SIC: 8361 Children's home

(P-24597)
CHILDRENS THERAPUTIC COMMUNITY
17675 Van Buren Blvd A, Riverside
(92504-6084)
P.O. Box 2277 (92516-2277)
PHONE.................................951 789-4410
Donald J Bosic, *President*
Blayne Cohn, *Admin Sec*
EMP: 100
SALES: 2.2MM **Privately Held**
SIC: 8361 Home for the emotionally disturbed

(P-24598)
CHILDRENS VLG OF SONOMA CNTY
1321 Lia Ln, Santa Rosa (95404-8087)
P.O. Box 2025 (95405-0025)
PHONE.................................707 566-7044
Fax: 707 566-7105
A Utarid, *Exec Dir*
Lynne Carpenter, *Senior VP*
Anjana Utarid, *Principal*
Dena Peacock, *Admin Asst*
Kris Lamping, *Social Worker*
EMP: 50
SALES: 2MM **Privately Held**
SIC: 8361 Group foster home

(P-24599)
CHURCH OF VLY RTRMENT HMES INC
Also Called: Valley Village
390 N Winchester Blvd Ofc, Santa Clara
(95050-6570)
PHONE.................................408 241-7750
Fax: 408 241-4237
Martha Ayala, *President*
EMP: 52
SALES: 4.2MM **Privately Held**
SIC: 8361 Home for the aged

(P-24600)
CLAREMONT HOUSE INCORPORATED
Also Called: Claremont Retirement MGT
4500 Gilbert St, Oakland (94611-4657)
PHONE.................................510 658-9266
Fax: 510 658-9407
Douglas R Gill, *President*
Justin Gill, *Exec Dir*
Karen Midlo, *Exec Dir*
Elena Cazares, *Personnel Exec*
EMP: 75
SALES: 6MM **Privately Held**
SIC: 8361 Home for the aged

(P-24601)
CLIFF VIEW TERRACE INC
Also Called: Mission Terrace
623 W Junipero St, Santa Barbara
(93105-4213)
PHONE.................................805 682-7443
Fax: 805 966-9611
Eve Murphy, *Manager*
Michelle Armet, *Director*
EMP: 100
SALES (corp-wide): 14.5MM **Privately Held**
SIC: 8361 8051 Home for the aged; convalescent home with continuous nursing care
PA: Cliff View Terrace Inc
    1020 Cliff Dr
    Santa Barbara CA 93109
    805 963-7556

(P-24602)
CLIFTON TATUM CENTER
4333 E Vineyard Ave, Oxnard
(93036-1013)
PHONE.................................805 652-5727
Chris Weidenhermer, *Director*
EMP: 60
SALES (est): 2.9MM **Privately Held**
SIC: 8361 Juvenile correctional facilities

(P-24603)
COMMUNITY HOUSING INC
Also Called: LYTTON GARDEN I
437 Webster St, Palo Alto (94301-1242)
PHONE.................................650 328-3300
Gery Yearout, *President*
Jonathan Casey, *Vice Pres*
Linda Hibbs, *Manager*
EMP: 50
SALES: 7.3MM **Privately Held**
SIC: 8361 Home for the aged

(P-24604)
CONGREGATION OF POOR SISTERS
Also Called: Nazareth House
2121 N 1st St, Fresno (93703-2301)
PHONE.................................559 237-3444
Fax: 559 237-1958
Sister Rose, *Director*
Rosemary O'Neill, *Exec Dir*
Cecilia Pistacchio, *Asst Admin*
Antionette Farrell, *Administration*
Leah D Santos, *Personnel*
EMP: 84
SQ FT: 58,644
SALES (corp-wide): 5MM **Privately Held**
SIC: 8361 Geriatric residential care
PA: Nazareth House
    Nazareth House
    London W6 8D
    208 748-3549

(P-24605)
CONTRA COSTA ARC
Also Called: Commercial Support Services
1420 Regatta Blvd, Richmond
(94804-4579)
PHONE.................................510 233-7303
Betty Jo Dubois, *Director*
EMP: 90
SALES (corp-wide): 19.5MM **Privately Held**
WEB: www.ccarealtors.com
SIC: 8361 Home for the mentally retarded
PA: Contra Costa Arc
    1340 Arnold Dr Ste 127
    Martinez CA 94553
    925 646-4690

(P-24606)
CORECARE III
Also Called: Morningside of Fullerton
800 Morningside Dr, Fullerton
(92835-3597)
PHONE.................................714 256-8000
Fax: 714 256-2469
Carl Wilkins, *Administration*
Ron Marott, *Controller*
EMP: 130
SQ FT: 24,000
SALES (est): 7.7MM **Privately Held**
WEB: www.msfpv.com
SIC: 8361 8052 Geriatric residential care; intermediate care facilities

(P-24607)
COUNSELING AND RESEARCH ASSOC (PA)
Also Called: Masada Homes
108 W Victoria St, Gardena (90248-3523)
P.O. Box 47001 (90247-6801)
PHONE.................................310 715-2020
Fax: 310 323-5565
George Igi, *Exec Dir*
Bernard Smith, *COO*
Denise Brady, *Opers Spvr*
Kristin Mischou, *Opers Spvr*
Richard Coleman, *Sls & Mktg Exec*
EMP: 125
SQ FT: 2,500
SALES: 18MM **Privately Held**
SIC: 8361 Children's home

(P-24608)
COUNSELING AND RESEARCH ASSOC
Also Called: Masada Homes Foster Fmly Agcy
314 E Avenue K4, Lancaster (93535-4689)
PHONE.................................661 726-5500
Rick Colman, *Branch Mgr*
EMP: 74
SALES (corp-wide): 18MM **Privately Held**
SIC: 8361 Children's home
PA: Counseling And Research Associates
    108 W Victoria St
    Gardena CA 90248
    310 715-2020

(P-24609)
COUNTY OF LOS ANGELES
Also Called: Probation Dept
12653 N Little Tjng Cyn, Sylmar
(91342-6311)
PHONE.................................818 896-0571
Fax: 818 896-9239
Sheryn Flanagan, *Manager*
Rick Stutley, *IT/INT Sup*
EMP: 54 **Privately Held**
WEB: www.co.la.us
SIC: 8361 9111 Juvenile correctional home; rest home, with health care incidental; executive offices
PA: County Of Los Angeles
    500 W Temple St Ste 375
    Los Angeles CA 90012
    213 974-1101

(P-24610)
COUNTY OF LOS ANGELES
1605 Eastlake Ave, Los Angeles
(90033-1009)
PHONE.................................323 226-8611
Fax: 323 227-0862
Richard Shumsky, *Manager*
EMP: 62 **Privately Held**
WEB: www.co.la.ca.us
SIC: 8361 9111 Juvenile correctional facilities; executive offices
PA: County Of Los Angeles
    500 W Temple St Ste 375
    Los Angeles CA 90012
    213 974-1101

(P-24611)
COUNTY OF LOS ANGELES
Also Called: San Fernando Juvenile Hall
16350 Filbert St, Sylmar (91342-1002)
PHONE.................................818 364-2011
Dan Torres, *Superintendent*
Dan Feldstern, *Plant Mgr*
EMP: 69 **Privately Held**
WEB: www.co.la.ca.us
SIC: 8361 9223 8093 Juvenile correctional home; correctional institutions; ; mental health clinic, outpatient
PA: County Of Los Angeles
    500 W Temple St Ste 375
    Los Angeles CA 90012
    213 974-1101

(P-24612)
COUNTY OF LOS ANGELES
Also Called: Camps Fred Miller
433 Encinal Canyon Rd, Malibu
(90265-2404)
PHONE.................................818 889-0260
Fax: 818 707-0364
Jerry Powers, *Chief*
EMP: 57 **Privately Held**
WEB: www.co.la.ca.us
SIC: 8361 9111 Juvenile correctional home; county supervisors' & executives' offices
PA: County Of Los Angeles
    500 W Temple St Ste 375
    Los Angeles CA 90012
    213 974-1101

(P-24613)
COUNTY OF LOS ANGELES
4024 Durfee Ave Rm 225, El Monte
(91732-2510)
PHONE.................................626 455-4700
Michael Mills, *Manager*
EMP: 62 **Privately Held**
WEB: www.co.la.ca.us
SIC: 8361 9111 Juvenile correctional home; county supervisors' & executives' offices
PA: County Of Los Angeles
    500 W Temple St Ste 375
    Los Angeles CA 90012
    213 974-1101

(P-24614)
COUNTY OF RIVERSIDE
Also Called: Juvenile Hall
47 665 Oasis St, Indio (92201)
PHONE.................................760 863-7600
Fax: 760 863-7615
Rick Quinata, *Director*
EMP: 100 **Privately Held**

8361 - Residential Care County (P-24615)

SIC: 8361 9441 Juvenile correctional home; administration of social & manpower programs;
PA: County Of Riverside
4080 Lemon St Fl 11
Riverside CA 92501
951 955-1110

(P-24615)
COUNTY OF SAN BERNARDINO
Also Called: Children Services
860 E Gilbert St, San Bernardino (92415-0002)
PHONE.................................909 387-0535
Allyson Williams, *Manager*
EMP: 60 **Privately Held**
SIC: 8361 9441 Juvenile correctional facilities; rest home, with health care incidental; administration of social & manpower programs
PA: County Of San Bernardino
385 N Arrowhead Ave
San Bernardino CA 92415
909 387-3841

(P-24616)
COVENANT HOUSE CALIFORNIA
Also Called: Chc
1325 N Western Ave, Los Angeles (90027-5615)
PHONE.................................323 461-3131
Fax: 323 957-2464
Luz Juan, *CEO*
Luz Buan, *CFO*
AMI Rowland, *Associate Dir*
George Lozano, *Principal*
Patrick S McCabe, *Exec Dir*
EMP: 150
SQ FT: 16,000
SALES: 7.3MM **Privately Held**
WEB: www.covenanthousecalifornia.net
SIC: 8361 Children's home

(P-24617)
COVENANT RTIREMENT COMMUNITIES
Also Called: Covenant Village of Turlock
2125 N Olive Ave Ofc, Turlock (95382-1947)
PHONE.................................209 632-9976
Fax: 209 632-7885
Dwayne Gabrielson, *Administration*
Linda Lundquist, *CFO*
Karen Boehme, *CPA*
Robert W Anderson, *Pastor*
Ginger Taylor,
EMP: 130
SALES (corp-wide): 3.3MM **Privately Held**
SIC: 8361 8052 8051 Rest home, with health care incidental; intermediate care facilities; skilled nursing care facilities
HQ: Covenant Retirement Communities
5700 Old Orchard Rd # 100
Skokie IL 60077

(P-24618)
CREATIVE ALTERNATIVES
2855 Geer Rd Ste A, Turlock (95382-1133)
PHONE.................................209 668-9361
Fax: 209 634-9738
Stephanie Biddle, *CEO*
Janice Husman,
Joy Biddle, *Asst Director*
Janice Tovar, *Manager*
Lisa Jacobs, *Supervisor*
EMP: 220
SQ FT: 40,000
SALES: 15.3MM **Privately Held**
SIC: 8361 8211 8322 Children's home; private special education school; child related social services

(P-24619)
CREATIVE LIVING OPTIONS INC
2945 Ramco St Ste 120, West Sacramento (95691-5998)
PHONE.................................916 372-2102
Joan Schmidt, *CEO*
Mary Anne Delaney, *Finance Dir*
Andy Rowntree, *Manager*
EMP: 115

SALES: 3.4MM **Privately Held**
WEB: www.creativelivingoptions.com
SIC: 8361 Home for the physically handicapped

(P-24620)
CRESTWOOD BEHAVIORAL HLTH INC
Also Called: 120 Fremont Snf
3062 Churn Creek Rd, Redding (96002-2124)
PHONE.................................530 221-0976
Fax: 530 223-3923
Nicoletta Groff, *Administration*
EMP: 80
SQ FT: 15,000
SALES (corp-wide): 148MM **Privately Held**
WEB: www.dreamcatch.us
SIC: 8361 8051 Halfway group home, persons with social or personal problems; skilled nursing care facilities
PA: Crestwood Behavioral Health, Inc.
520 Capitol Mall Ste 800
Sacramento CA 95814
510 651-1244

(P-24621)
CRESTWOOD BEHAVIORAL HLTH INC
Also Called: 107 San Jose Mhrc
1425 Fruitdale Ave, San Jose (95128-3234)
PHONE.................................408 275-1067
Fax: 408 275-1066
John Suggs, *Branch Mgr*
Dancey Conger, *VP Finance*
EMP: 85
SALES (corp-wide): 148MM **Privately Held**
WEB: www.dreamcatch.us
SIC: 8361 8063 7389 Halfway group home, persons with social or personal problems; psychiatric hospitals; personal service agents, brokers & bureaus
PA: Crestwood Behavioral Health, Inc.
520 Capitol Mall Ste 800
Sacramento CA 95814
510 651-1244

(P-24622)
CRESTWOOD BEHAVIORAL HLTH INC
Also Called: 152 Vallejo Rcfe
115 Oddstad Dr, Vallejo (94589-2520)
PHONE.................................707 552-0215
Minda Bunnggay, *Manager*
Rebecca Best, *Director*
EMP: 150
SALES (corp-wide): 148MM **Privately Held**
WEB: www.dreamcatch.us
SIC: 8361 8063 8051 Halfway group home, persons with social or personal problems; psychiatric hospitals; skilled nursing care facilities
PA: Crestwood Behavioral Health, Inc.
520 Capitol Mall Ste 800
Sacramento CA 95814
510 651-1244

(P-24623)
CRESTWOOD BEHAVIORAL HLTH INC
Also Called: 134 Alameda Snf
4303 Stevenson Blvd, Fremont (94538-2645)
PHONE.................................510 651-1244
Fax: 510 651-1543
Leeann Labrie, *Administration*
EMP: 150
SQ FT: 33,790
SALES (corp-wide): 148MM **Privately Held**
WEB: www.dreamcatch.us
SIC: 8361 8069 Halfway group home, persons with social or personal problems; specialty hospitals, except psychiatric
PA: Crestwood Behavioral Health, Inc.
520 Capitol Mall Ste 800
Sacramento CA 95814
510 651-1244

(P-24624)
CRESTWOOD BEHAVIORAL HLTH INC
Also Called: 120 Fremont Snf
2171 Mowry Ave, Fremont (94538-1717)
PHONE.................................510 793-8383
Fax: 510 793-3384
Janet Timble, *Superintendent*
Leann Labrie, *Nursing Dir*
Madeline Zaragova, *Director*
EMP: 100
SQ FT: 10,000
SALES (corp-wide): 148MM **Privately Held**
WEB: www.dreamcatch.us
SIC: 8361 8063 8052 8069 Halfway group home, persons with social or personal problems; psychiatric hospitals; intermediate care facilities; specialty hospitals, except psychiatric
PA: Crestwood Behavioral Health, Inc.
520 Capitol Mall Ste 800
Sacramento CA 95814
510 651-1244

(P-24625)
CRI-HELP INC (PA)
Also Called: Cri Help Drug Rehabilitation
11027 Burbank Blvd, North Hollywood (91601-2431)
P.O. Box 899 (91603-0899)
PHONE.................................818 985-8323
Fax: 818 985-4297
Jack Bernstein, *President*
Markus Sola, *Ch of Bd*
Anthony Edmonson, *Corp Secy*
Kim Long, *Program Mgr*
Oscar Morales, *Info Tech Dir*
EMP: 71 EST: 1971
SQ FT: 40,000
SALES: 7.3MM **Privately Held**
WEB: www.cri-help.org
SIC: 8361 8069 Rehabilitation center, residential: health care incidental; drug addiction rehabilitation hospital

(P-24626)
CROWN COVE SENIOR CARE CMNTY
3901 E Coast Hwy Ofc, Corona Del Mar (92625-5504)
PHONE.................................949 760-2800
Fax: 949 760-2839
Sanford Fleschman, *Exec Dir*
Patti Watters, *Business Mgr*
Vicki Kaiser, *Manager*
EMP: 70
SALES (est): 2.8MM **Privately Held**
SIC: 8361 Residential care

(P-24627)
DAVID AND MARGARET HOME INC
Also Called: David Margaret Youth Fmly Svcs
1350 3rd St, La Verne (91750-5299)
PHONE.................................909 596-5921
Fax: 909 596-3954
Arun Tolia, *President*
Cindy Walkenbach, *President*
Timothy Evans, *Treasurer*
Betty Jackson, *Vice Pres*
Sabina Sullivan, *Vice Pres*
EMP: 240
SQ FT: 40,000
SALES: 12.9MM **Privately Held**
WEB: www.dmhome.org
SIC: 8361 8322 Home for the emotionally disturbed; individual & family services

(P-24628)
DAYBREAK CARE CENTER (PA)
9040 Sunland Blvd, Sun Valley (91352-2049)
PHONE.................................818 504-6154
Fax: 818 504-6156
Robert Nydam, *President*
Linda Nydam, *CFO*
Bobby Fernandez, *Manager*
EMP: 61
SALES (est): 5.6MM **Privately Held**
SIC: 8361 Residential care for the handicapped

(P-24629)
DELANCEY STREET FOUNDATION (PA)
Also Called: Delancey Street Coach Service
600 The Embarcadero, San Francisco (94107-2116)
PHONE.................................415 957-9800
Fax: 415 512-5186
Mimi Silbert, *President*
Jerry Raymond, *Treasurer*
Sylvia Piatt, *Exec Sec*
EMP: 400
SQ FT: 325,000
SALES (est): 46.4MM **Privately Held**
SIC: 8361 5199 8322 4212 Rehabilitation center, residential: health care incidental; advertising specialties; individual & family services; moving services; eating places; caterers

(P-24630)
DESERT MANOR CARE CENTER LP
8515 Cholla Ave, Yucca Valley (92284-4247)
PHONE.................................760 365-0717
Fax: 760 365-7127
Rich Thomas, *CFO*
Sylvia Sanchez-Figueroa, *Administration*
Veva Dyer, *Food Svc Dir*
Lori Meadows, *Nursing Dir*
Eldene Smith, *Director*
EMP: 70
SALES (est): 447.5K **Privately Held**
SIC: 8361 8059 Geriatric residential care; nursing home, except skilled & intermediate care facility; skilled nursing care facilities

(P-24631)
DEVELOPMENTAL SVCS CONTINUUM
7944 Golden Ave, Lemon Grove (91945-1810)
PHONE.................................619 460-7333
Elaine Lewis, *President*
EMP: 75
SALES: 2.9MM **Privately Held**
SIC: 8361 Group foster home

(P-24632)
DIVERSIFIED HEALTH SVCS DEL
Also Called: Terraces At Par Marino
2585 E Washington Blvd, Pasadena (91107-1446)
PHONE.................................626 798-6753
Maru Cohen, *Director*
Christina Watanabe, *Exec Dir*
Brett Cleveland, *Manager*
EMP: 50
SALES (corp-wide): 6.8MM **Privately Held**
SIC: 8361 8059 Home for the aged; convalescent home
PA: Diversified Health Services (Del)
136 Washington Ave
Richmond CA 94801
510 231-6200

(P-24633)
DOMINICAN HOSPITAL FOUNDATION
Also Called: Dominican Rehab Services
610 Frederick St, Santa Cruz (95062-2203)
PHONE.................................831 457-7057
Fax: 831 457-7044
Debbie Hite, *Branch Mgr*
Kate Kenny, *Social Dir*
Lisa Akey, *Administration*
Gaspar Barros, *Director*
Christian Snegard, *Director*
EMP: 200
SALES (corp-wide): 7.1B **Privately Held**
SIC: 8361 8093 Rehabilitation center, residential: health care incidental; rehabilitation center, outpatient treatment
HQ: Dominican Hospital Foundation
1555 Soquel Dr
Santa Cruz CA 95065
831 462-7700

PRODUCTS & SERVICES SECTION
8361 - Residential Care County (P-24654)

(P-24634)
DREAM HOME CARE INC
4150 Locust Ave, Long Beach (90807-2605)
PHONE..................................562 595-9021
Coral Manalang, *President*
Cora Manalang, *CEO*
Reynaldo David, *COO*
Hazel Manalang, *CFO*
EMP: 60
SALES: 2.8MM **Privately Held**
SIC: 8361 Group foster home

(P-24635)
DREAMCTCHERS EMPWERMENT NETWRK
Also Called: Rosewood Convalescent Hospital
1911 Oak Park Blvd, Pleasant Hill (94523-4601)
PHONE..................................925 935-6630
Fax: 925 933-3863
Maggie Youssess, *Administration*
Maggie Youssef, *Executive*
Neall Baldomero, *Purch Agent*
EMP: 111
SALES (corp-wide): 1.3MM **Privately Held**
WEB: www.dreamcatch.us
SIC: 8361 8051 8059 Halfway group home, persons with social or personal problems; skilled nursing care facilities; convalescent home
PA: Dreamcatchers Empowerment Network
7590 Shoreline Dr Ste B
Stockton CA 95219
209 478-5291

(P-24636)
DREAMCTCHERS EMPWERMENT NETWRK
Elmhaven Convelescent Hospital
6940 Pacific Ave, Stockton (95207-2602)
PHONE..................................209 477-4817
Fax: 209 477-0522
Mike Blaufus, *Principal*
Ella Adams, *Executive*
Henry Yrlas, *Food Svc Dir*
Fabio Lando, *Nursing Dir*
EMP: 100
SALES (corp-wide): 1.3MM **Privately Held**
WEB: www.dreamcatch.us
SIC: 8361 8051 8052 Halfway group home, persons with social or personal problems; skilled nursing care facilities; intermediate care facilities
PA: Dreamcatchers Empowerment Network
7590 Shoreline Dr Ste B
Stockton CA 95219
209 478-5291

(P-24637)
E & S RSIDENTIAL CARE SVCS LLC
6083 N Marks Ave, Fresno (93711-1600)
PHONE..................................559 275-3555
Fax: 559 275-3666
Stephanie Hendricks, *Mng Member*
Eddie Gilbert, *Mng Member*
EMP: 100
SALES (est): 6.8MM **Privately Held**
SIC: 8361 Residential care for the handicapped

(P-24638)
E R I T INC (PA)
251 Airport Rd, Oceanside (92058-1201)
PHONE..................................760 433-6024
Cheryl Kilmer, *Exec Dir*
Joe Michalowski, *CFO*
Nora Estrada, *Finance*
Charity Kardol, *Finance*
William Hopkins, *Instructor*
EMP: 85
SQ FT: 15,000
SALES: 16.4MM **Privately Held**
WEB: www.teriinc.org
SIC: 8361 Home for the mentally retarded

(P-24639)
E R I T INC
Also Called: Our Way
251 Airport Rd, Oceanside (92058-1201)
PHONE..................................760 721-1706
Cheryl Kilmer, *Principal*
Laura Kauffman, *Human Res Dir*
EMP: 250
SALES (corp-wide): 15.4MM **Privately Held**
WEB: www.teriinc.org
SIC: 8361 Home for the mentally retarded
PA: E R I T Inc
251 Airport Rd
Oceanside CA 92058
760 433-6024

(P-24640)
EDGEWOOD CTR FOR CHILDRENS (PA)
1801 Vicente St, San Francisco (94116-2923)
PHONE..................................415 681-3211
Nancy Rubin, *CEO*
Ken Auletta, *Executive*
Jeffery Davis, *Exec Dir*
Lori Kandels, *Exec Dir*
William Brimmer, *Program Mgr*
EMP: 224 **EST:** 1850
SQ FT: 100,000
SALES (est): 19MM **Privately Held**
WEB: www.edgewoodcenter.org
SIC: 8361 8211 8322 8361 Home for the emotionally disturbed; specialty education; child related social services; specialty outpatient clinics

(P-24641)
EES RESIDENTIAL GROUP HOMES
5369 Camden Ave Ste 280, San Jose (95124-5856)
PHONE..................................408 265-8780
Richard Shanley, *Exec Dir*
Edward Eldefonso, *Ch of Bd*
Jennifer Mihojevich, *Program Mgr*
EMP: 55
SALES: 1.2MM **Privately Held**
SIC: 8361 8322 Juvenile correctional facilities; child related social services

(P-24642)
ELDER CARE ALLIANCE CAMARILLO
Also Called: ALMA VIA OF CAMARILLO
1301 Marina Village Pkwy # 210, Alameda (94501-1049)
PHONE..................................510 769-2700
Jesse Jantzen, *CEO*
EMP: 60
SALES: 5MM **Privately Held**
SIC: 8361 Residential care

(P-24643)
ENCORE SENIOR LIVING III LLC
Also Called: Encore Senior Vlg At Riverside
6280 Clay St, Riverside (92509-6005)
PHONE..................................951 360-1616
Fax: 951 360-7789
Barbara Reece, *Director*
Brenda Jackson, *Social Dir*
Alicia Padilla, *Office Mgr*
Rose Calabrese, *Marketing Staff*
Gabriela Hernandez, *Nursing Dir*
EMP: 50 **Privately Held**
WEB: www.retirementnn.com
SIC: 8361 Rest home, with health care incidental
PA: Encore Senior Living Iii, Llc
400 Locust St Ste 820
Des Moines IA 50309

(P-24644)
ENSIGN GROUP INC
1405 E Main St, Santa Maria (93454-4801)
PHONE..................................805 925-8713
Shawn Taylor, *Branch Mgr*
EMP: 96
SALES (corp-wide): 1.3B **Publicly Held**
SIC: 8361 6513 Geriatric residential care; retirement hotel operation
PA: The Ensign Group Inc
27101 Puerta Real Ste 450
Mission Viejo CA 92691
949 487-9500

(P-24645)
EPISCOPAL SENIOR COMMUNITIES
Also Called: St Paul's Towers
100 Bay Pl Ofc, Oakland (94610-4422)
PHONE..................................510 835-4700
Fax: 510 891-8110
Christopher Iechien, *Exec Dir*
Ladi Markham, *Executive*
Michael Kim, *Director*
EMP: 180
SALES (corp-wide): 106.3MM **Privately Held**
SIC: 8361 8052 8051 Home for the aged; intermediate care facilities; skilled nursing care facilities
PA: Episcopal Senior Communities
2185 N Calif Blvd Ste 575
Walnut Creek CA 94596
925 956-7400

(P-24646)
EPISCOPAL SENIOR COMMUNITIES
Also Called: Los Gatos Meadows
110 Wood Rd Ofc, Los Gatos (95030-6799)
PHONE..................................408 354-0211
Fax: 408 354-4193
Tina Heany, *Exec Dir*
Nancy Cutforth, *Office Mgr*
Elsa Tedros, *QC Dir*
Jyl Campana, *Pub Rel Dir*
Judy Haley, *Sales Staff*
EMP: 120
SALES (corp-wide): 106.3MM **Privately Held**
SIC: 8361 Geriatric residential care
PA: Episcopal Senior Communities
2185 N Calif Blvd Ste 575
Walnut Creek CA 94596
925 956-7400

(P-24647)
EPISCOPAL SENIOR COMMUNITIES
Also Called: Canterbury Woods
651 Sinex Ave, Pacific Grove (93950-4253)
PHONE..................................831 373-3111
Fax: 831 373-2140
Norma Brenbella, *Director*
EMP: 90
SALES (corp-wide): 106.3MM **Privately Held**
SIC: 8361 Home for the aged
PA: Episcopal Senior Communities
2185 N Calif Blvd Ste 575
Walnut Creek CA 94596
925 956-7400

(P-24648)
EPISCOPAL SENIOR COMMUNITIES
Also Called: Spring Lake Village
5555 Montgomery Dr, Santa Rosa (95409-8846)
P.O. Box 1105, Boyes Hot Springs (95416-1105)
PHONE..................................707 538-8400
Fax: 707 579-6997
Sharon York, *Exec Dir*
Linda Goldman, *Social Dir*
Dennis McLean, *Maintenance Dir*
Diana Neely, *Receptionist*
EMP: 300
SALES (corp-wide): 106.3MM **Privately Held**
SIC: 8361 6531 8052 8051 Home for the aged; real estate managers; intermediate care facilities; skilled nursing care facilities
PA: Episcopal Senior Communities
2185 N Calif Blvd Ste 575
Walnut Creek CA 94596
925 956-7400

(P-24649)
EPISCOPAL SENIOR COMMUNITIES
Also Called: San Francisco Towers
1661 Pine St Apt 911, San Francisco (94109-0410)
PHONE..................................415 776-0500
Fax: 415 776-5192
Donna Teandler, *Branch Mgr*
EMP: 139
SALES (corp-wide): 106.3MM **Privately Held**
SIC: 8361 8052 8051 Residential care; intermediate care facilities; skilled nursing care facilities
PA: Episcopal Senior Communities
2185 N Calif Blvd Ste 575
Walnut Creek CA 94596
925 956-7400

(P-24650)
ESKATON LODGE
8550 Barton Rd, Granite Bay (95746-8843)
PHONE..................................916 789-0326
Fax: 916 789-0598
Vicky Cross, *Director*
Stephanie Watson, *Principal*
David Keaton, *Director*
EMP: 50
SALES (est): 1.9MM **Privately Held**
SIC: 8361 Residential care

(P-24651)
ESKATON PROPERTIES INC
Also Called: Eskaton Village-Grass Valley
625 Eskaton Cir Apt 213, Grass Valley (95945-5730)
PHONE..................................530 265-2699
Mary Eaton Campbell, *Manager*
EMP: 78
SALES (corp-wide): 90.6MM **Privately Held**
SIC: 8361 Residential care
PA: Eskaton Properties Incorporated
5105 Manzanita Ave Ste A
Carmichael CA 95608
916 334-0810

(P-24652)
ESKATON PROPERTIES INC
Also Called: Eskaton Village Roseville
1650 Eskaton Loop, Roseville (95747-5180)
PHONE..................................916 334-0810
Vicki Cross, *Manager*
EMP: 60
SALES (corp-wide): 90.6MM **Privately Held**
SIC: 8361 Residential care
PA: Eskaton Properties Incorporated
5105 Manzanita Ave Ste A
Carmichael CA 95608
916 334-0810

(P-24653)
ESKATON PROPERTIES INC (PA)
Also Called: 0epi
5105 Manzanita Ave Ste A, Carmichael (95608-0523)
PHONE..................................916 334-0810
Fax: 916 348-6715
Todd Murch, *President*
Betsy Donovan, *Senior VP*
Bill Pace, *Senior VP*
Sheri Peifer, *Senior VP*
Charles Garcia, *Vice Pres*
EMP: 60
SQ FT: 27,000
SALES: 90.6MM **Privately Held**
SIC: 8361 Home for the aged

(P-24654)
EVANGELICAL COVENANT CHURCH
Also Called: Mount Miguel Covenant Village
325 Kempton St, Spring Valley (91977-5810)
PHONE..................................619 931-1114
Fax: 619 479-2337
Thad Rothrock, *Administration*
Robert Clough, *COO*
Geoffrey Perley, *Executive*
Dan Brant, *CTO*
Lynn Brownwood, *Mktg Dir*
EMP: 100
SALES (corp-wide): 88MM **Privately Held**
WEB: www.npcts.edu
SIC: 8361 Rest home, with health care incidental
PA: The Evangelical Covenant Church
8303 W Higgins Rd Fl 1
Chicago IL 60631
773 907-3303

8361 - Residential Care County (P-24655)

(P-24655)
EVANGELICAL COVENANT CHURCH
Also Called: Samarkand Retirement Community
2550 Treasure Dr, Santa Barbara (93105-4148)
PHONE.................................805 687-0701
Fax: 805 687-3386
Kenneth D Noreen, *Administration*
Dave Johnson, *Bookkeeper*
EMP: 200
SALES (corp-wide): 88MM **Privately Held**
WEB: www.npcts.edu
SIC: 8361 8059 Home for the aged; rest home, with health care
PA: The Evangelical Covenant Church
  8303 W Higgins Rd Fl 1
  Chicago IL 60631
  773 907-3303

(P-24656)
EVOLVE GROWTH INITIATIVES LLC
Also Called: Evolve Treatment Centers
9301 Wilshire Blvd # 516, Beverly Hills (90210-5424)
PHONE.................................424 281-5000
Menachem Baron, *CEO*
EMP: 50
SQ FT: 1,700
SALES (est): 1.9MM **Privately Held**
SIC: 8361 8093 Rehabilitation center, residential: health care incidental; mental health clinic, outpatient

(P-24657)
FERREES GROUP HOME INC
878 Highland Home Rd, Banning (92220-1244)
PHONE.................................951 849-1927
Philip Anthony Ferrees, *Director*
EMP: 60
SALES: 1.3MM **Privately Held**
SIC: 8361 Group foster home

(P-24658)
FIVE STAR QUALITY CARE INC
Also Called: Somerford Place Encinitas
1350 S El Camino Real, Encinitas (92024-4904)
PHONE.................................760 479-1818
Fax: 760 436-8072
Terry Records, *Manager*
Andrea Taylor, *Executive*
EMP: 50
SALES (corp-wide): 1.3B **Publicly Held**
WEB: www.fivestarqualitycare.com
SIC: 8361 Residential care
PA: Five Star Quality Care, Inc.
  400 Centre St
  Newton MA 02458
  617 796-8387

(P-24659)
FLORENCE CRITTENTON SERVICES
Also Called: CRITTENTON SERVICES FOR CHILDR
801 E Chapman Ave Ste 203, Fullerton (92831-3846)
P.O. Box 9 (92836-0009)
PHONE.................................714 680-9000
Fax: 714 680-8207
Joyce Capelle, *CEO*
Judy Parsons, *Executive*
Becky Nelson, *Program Mgr*
Susan Emerson, *General Mgr*
Juliana Hoyos, *Psychologist*
EMP: 320
SALES: 31.2MM **Privately Held**
SIC: 8361 Residential care for children; home for the emotionally disturbed

(P-24660)
FORD STREET PROJECT INC
139 Ford St, Ukiah (95482-4011)
PHONE.................................707 462-1934
Fax: 707 468-9860
Jacque Williams, *President*
Jacqueline Williams, *Info Tech Mgr*
Prilla Gorforth, *Director*
Veronica I Moynahan, *Director*
EMP: 50
SALES: 1.7MM **Privately Held**
WEB: www.fordstreet.org
SIC: 8361 Rehabilitation center, residential: health care incidental

(P-24661)
FOREMOST OPERATIONS LLC
Also Called: Foremost Terrace Room
17581 Sultana St, Hesperia (92345-6552)
PHONE.................................760 244-5579
Ben Vangala, *Owner*
Leonard M Crites, *President*
Dana Ramirez, *Vice Pres*
Maria Nunez, *Marketing Staff*
EMP: 50
SALES (est): 1.7MM **Privately Held**
SIC: 8361 6531 Residential care; rental agent, real estate

(P-24662)
FOUNTAINWOOD RESIDENTIAL CARE
8773 Oak Ave, Orangevale (95662-2410)
PHONE.................................916 988-2200
Fax: 916 988-2219
Robert Spince, *President*
Mary Eaton, *Administration*
EMP: 80
SALES (est): 3.6MM **Privately Held**
WEB: www.fountainwood.org
SIC: 8361 8059 Residential care; convalescent home

(P-24663)
FRED FINCH YOUTH CENTER
Contra Costa Services
2523 El Portal Dr Ste 103, San Pablo (94806-3305)
PHONE.................................510 439-3130
John F Steinfirst, *Principal*
EMP: 64
SALES (corp-wide): 29.8MM **Privately Held**
SIC: 8361 Children's home
PA: Fred Finch Youth Center
  3800 Coolidge Ave
  Oakland CA 94602
  510 773-6669

(P-24664)
FREDERICKA MANOR
183 3rd Ave, Chula Vista (91910-1894)
PHONE.................................619 422-9271
Fax: 619 422-2686
Robert Anderson, *Principal*
Betsy Keller, *Mktg Coord*
Kathi Lenig, *Nursing Dir*
EMP: 77
SALES (est): 5.8MM **Privately Held**
SIC: 8361 6513 Residential care; apartment building operators

(P-24665)
FRESNO HERITAGE PARTNERS
Also Called: Somerford Place
6075 N Marks Ave, Fresno (93711-1600)
PHONE.................................559 446-6226
Fax: 559 449-7351
Sharol Hutchison, *Exec Dir*
Fresno Surgery Center, *General Ptnr*
EMP: 50
SQ FT: 26,166
SALES (est): 1.8MM **Privately Held**
SIC: 8361 Residential care

(P-24666)
FRONT PORCH COMMUNITIES & SVCS
Also Called: Villa Gardens
842 E Villa St, Pasadena (91101-1259)
PHONE.................................626 796-8162
Jeff Sianko, *CEO*
Craig Sumner, *Sales Mgr*
EMP: 192
SALES (corp-wide): 165.1MM **Privately Held**
SIC: 8361 Geriatric residential care
PA: Front Porch Communities And Services - Casa De Manana, Llc
  800 N Brand Blvd Fl 19
  Glendale CA 91203
  818 729-8100

(P-24667)
GATE THREE HEALTHCARE LLC
Also Called: Palm Ter Hlth Care Rhblitation
24962 Calle Aragon, Laguna Hills (92637-3883)
PHONE.................................949 770-3348
Fax: 949 859-0673
Soon Burnam,
Dave Jorgensen, *Administration*
EMP: 120
SALES: 13.4MM **Privately Held**
SIC: 8361 Rehabilitation center, residential: health care incidental

(P-24668)
GATEWAY CTR OF MONTEREY CNTY (PA)
850 Congress Ave, Pacific Grove (93950-4811)
PHONE.................................831 372-8002
Fax: 831 372-2411
Kathleen Adanson, *President*
Cathy Lindstrom, *Treasurer*
W Parham, *Bd of Directors*
Duane Burnell, *Exec Dir*
Stephanie Lyon, *Exec Dir*
EMP: 57
SQ FT: 33,000
SALES: 3.9MM **Privately Held**
WEB: www.gatewaycenter.org
SIC: 8361 Residential care for the handicapped

(P-24669)
GOLDEN LIVING LLC
Also Called: Beverly Healthcare
5555 Prospect Rd Ofc, San Jose (95129-4897)
PHONE.................................408 255-5555
Ron Anderson, *Manager*
EMP: 50
SALES (corp-wide): 1.6B **Privately Held**
WEB: www.nwbeccorp.com
SIC: 8361 Geriatric residential care
PA: Golden Living Llc
  5220 Tennyson Pkwy # 400
  Plano TX 75024
  972 372-6300

(P-24670)
GOLDEN LIVING LLC
Also Called: Chowchilla Convalescent
1010 Ventura Ave, Chowchilla (93610-2368)
PHONE.................................559 665-3745
Branden Biglow, *Administration*
Jeri Morris, *Administration*
Enrique Delmerro, *Maintenance Dir*
EMP: 60
SALES (corp-wide): 1.6B **Privately Held**
WEB: www.nwbeccorp.com
SIC: 8361 Rest home, with health care incidental
PA: Golden Living Llc
  5220 Tennyson Pkwy # 400
  Plano TX 75024
  972 372-6300

(P-24671)
GOLDEN POND LP
Also Called: Golden Pond Retirement Cmnty
3415 Mayhew Rd Ofc, Sacramento (95827-3107)
PHONE.................................916 369-8967
Fax: 916 369-1603
Doug Gill, *Partner*
Paul Mason, *Partner*
Dana McManus, *Partner*
Brian Walgenbach, *Partner*
EMP: 50
SALES (est): 3.2MM **Privately Held**
SIC: 8361 6513 Home for the aged; apartment building operators

(P-24672)
GOOD SHEPHERD LUTHERAN HM OF W (PA)
Also Called: Good Shepherd Communities
119 N Main St, Porterville (93257-3713)
PHONE.................................559 791-2000
Fax: 559 791-2011
David Geske, *CEO*
Ricki Hawell, *Manager*
EMP: 67
SQ FT: 6,000
SALES (est): 15.6MM **Privately Held**
SIC: 8361 Residential care for the handicapped

(P-24673)
GRASS VALLEY LLC
Also Called: Quail Ridge Senior Living
150 Sutton Way Ofc, Grass Valley (95945-4104)
PHONE.................................530 272-1055
Fax: 530 272-1092
Mark E Nicol,
Pari Manouchehri, *Exec Dir*
Leslie Hernandez, *Manager*
EMP: 60
SALES (est): 2.5MM **Privately Held**
WEB: www.quailridgeseniorliving.com
SIC: 8361 Geriatric residential care

(P-24674)
GREENRIDGE SENIOR CARE
2150 Pyramid Dr, El Sobrante (94803-3220)
PHONE.................................510 758-9600
Fax: 510 758-9685
Linda Joseph, *Owner*
EMP: 110
SALES (est): 3.4MM **Privately Held**
SIC: 8361 Geriatric residential care; home for the aged

(P-24675)
HALL WINDSOR
1415 James M Wood Blvd, Los Angeles (90015-1209)
PHONE.................................213 383-1547
Fax: 213 387-4429
Michael Bolong, *Owner*
Windsor Hall, *Owner*
EMP: 80
SALES (est): 1.4MM **Privately Held**
WEB: www.windsorhall.com
SIC: 8361 Residential care

(P-24676)
HAMBURGER HOME (PA)
Also Called: Aviva Center
7120 Franklin Ave, Los Angeles (90046-3002)
PHONE.................................323 876-0550
Fax: 323 386-6952
Regina Bette, *President*
Thomas Bernal, *CFO*
Michelle Cordero, *Vice Pres*
EMP: 90
SQ FT: 25,000
SALES: 19MM **Privately Held**
SIC: 8361 Residential care for children

(P-24677)
HANK FISHER PROPERTIES INC
Also Called: Chateau On Capitol Avenue, The
2701 Capitol Ave, Sacramento (95816-6036)
PHONE.................................916 447-4444
Nancy Fisher, *Branch Mgr*
Jim Dunning, *Exec Dir*
Nancy L Hopp, *Financial Exec*
EMP: 112
SALES (corp-wide): 13.3MM **Privately Held**
SIC: 8361 Geriatric residential care
PA: Hank Fisher Properties, Inc.
  610 Fulton Ave Ste 100
  Sacramento CA 95825
  916 485-1441

(P-24678)
HARBOR HEALTH CARE INC
16917 Clark Ave, Bellflower (90706-5703)
PHONE.................................562 866-7054
Cheryl Hutchins, *President*
EMP: 200
SALES (est): 10.2MM **Privately Held**
WEB: www.harborhealthcare.org
SIC: 8361 Residential care for the handicapped

(P-24679)
HARVEST MANAGEMENT SUB LLC
Also Called: Las Brisas
1299 Briarwood Dr, San Luis Obispo (93401-5965)
PHONE.................................805 543-0187
David Dolan, *Branch Mgr*

EMP: 3735
SALES (corp-wide): 399MM Privately Held
SIC: 8361 Rest home, with health care incidental
PA: Harvest Management Sub Llc
5885 Meadows Rd Ste 500
Lake Oswego OR 97035
503 370-7070

(P-24680)
HATHAWAY-SYCAMORES CHLD FAM SV
Also Called: Hathaway Children and Family
12502 Van Nuys Blvd # 120, Pacoima (91331-1321)
PHONE..................................818 897-1766
Muriel Gaudin, *Manager*
EMP: 60
SALES (corp-wide): 51.8MM Privately Held
SIC: 8361 Residential care
PA: Hathaway-Sycamores Child And Family Services
210 S De Lacey Ave # 110
Pasadena CA 91105
626 844-1677

(P-24681)
HATHAWAY-SYCAMORES CHLD FAM SV
840 N Avenue 66, Los Angeles (90042-1508)
PHONE..................................323 257-9600
Jim Cheney, *President*
EMP: 54
SALES (corp-wide): 51.8MM Privately Held
SIC: 8361 8093 Home for the emotionally disturbed; mental health clinic, outpatient
PA: Hathaway-Sycamores Child And Family Services
210 S De Lacey Ave # 110
Pasadena CA 91105
626 844-1677

(P-24682)
HATHAWAY-SYCAMORES CHLD FAM SV
44738 Sierra Hwy, Lancaster (93534-3225)
PHONE..................................661 942-5749
Debbie Manners, *Exec VP*
EMP: 421
SALES (corp-wide): 51.8MM Privately Held
SIC: 8361 Home for the mentally handicapped
PA: Hathaway-Sycamores Child And Family Services
210 S De Lacey Ave # 110
Pasadena CA 91105
626 844-1677

(P-24683)
HATHAWAY-SYCAMORES CHLD FAM SV
1968 W Adams Blvd, Los Angeles (90018-3515)
PHONE..................................323 733-0322
Debbie Manners, *Branch Mgr*
EMP: 60
SALES (corp-wide): 51.8MM Privately Held
SIC: 8361 Home for the emotionally disturbed
PA: Hathaway-Sycamores Child And Family Services
210 S De Lacey Ave # 110
Pasadena CA 91105
626 844-1677

(P-24684)
HATHAWAY-SYCAMORES CHLD FAM SV (PA)
210 S De Lacey Ave # 110, Pasadena (91105-2048)
PHONE..................................626 844-1677
Michael Galper, *Ch of Bd*
William Martone, *President*
Jim Huser, *CFO*
Samuel Heinrichs, *Exec VP*
Steven Shaw, *Exec VP*
EMP: 65
SQ FT: 75,175

SALES: 51.8MM Privately Held
SIC: 8361 8093 Home for the emotionally disturbed; mental health clinic, outpatient

(P-24685)
HAYNES FAMILY PROGRAMS INC
Also Called: Leroy Haynes Center
233 Baseline Rd, La Verne (91750-2353)
P.O. Box 400 (91750-0400)
PHONE..................................909 593-2581
Fax: 909 596-3567
Daniel Maydeck, *President*
Tony Williams, *CFO*
Frank Linebaugh, *Senior VP*
Kristine Gutierrez, *Human Res Mgr*
Jane Woods, *Professor*
EMP: 225
SQ FT: 72,466
SALES: 15.3MM Privately Held
WEB: www.leroyhaynes.org
SIC: 8361 8211 8099 Boys' Towns; specialty education; medical services organization

(P-24686)
HEALTHCARE GROUP
Also Called: Grossmont Grdns Rtrement Cmnty
5480 Marengo Ave Ste 619, La Mesa (91942-2408)
PHONE..................................619 463-0281
Fax: 619 461-7736
Mary Shepherd, *Exec Dir*
EMP: 235
SQ FT: 5,000
SALES (est): 9.3MM Privately Held
SIC: 8361 8052 8051 Residential care; intermediate care facilities; skilled nursing care facilities

(P-24687)
HEALTHSOUTH CORPORATION
5001 Commerce Dr, Bakersfield (93309-0648)
PHONE..................................661 323-5500
Rosa Arriola, *Manager*
Robert Mosesian, *Controller*
Faye Bergeron, *Director*
Kathleen Mershon, *Director*
Yolanda Watson, *Director*
EMP: 200
SALES (corp-wide): 3.1B Publicly Held
WEB: www.healthsouth.com
SIC: 8361 8069 Rehabilitation center, residential; health care incidental; specialty hospitals, except psychiatric
PA: Healthsouth Corporation
3660 Grandview Pkwy # 200
Birmingham AL 35243
205 967-7116

(P-24688)
HEALTHVIEW INC (PA)
Also Called: Harbor View House
921 S Beacon St, San Pedro (90731-3740)
P.O. Box 1860 (90733-1860)
PHONE..................................310 547-3341
Fax: 310 547-9933
Jeff Smith, *CEO*
Ronna Lindner, *Vice Pres*
Susan Major, *Principal*
Brenda Navarro, *Personnel*
Michael Fitzgerald, *Program Dir*
EMP: 135
SQ FT: 110,000
SALES: 5.2MM Privately Held
WEB: www.hvi.com
SIC: 8361 8052 Home for the mentally handicapped; rehabilitation center, residential: health care incidental; home for the mentally retarded, with health care

(P-24689)
HEALTHVIEW INC
Also Called: Lifecare Health
12750 Center Court Dr S # 410, Cerritos (90703-8581)
PHONE..................................562 468-0136
Fax: 562 468-0835
Denise Stanton, *Branch Mgr*
EMP: 50

SALES (corp-wide): 5.2MM Privately Held
WEB: www.hvi.com
SIC: 8361 8082 Home for the mentally handicapped; home health care services
PA: Healthview, Inc.
921 S Beacon St
San Pedro CA 90731
310 547-3341

(P-24690)
HELPING HEARTS FOUNDATION INC
3050 Fite Cir Ste 205, Sacramento (95827-1807)
PHONE..................................916 368-7200
James Borgmeyer, *President*
EMP: 55
SALES (est): 3MM Privately Held
SIC: 8361 Residential care

(P-24691)
HILLSIDES
940 Avenue 64, Pasadena (91105-2711)
PHONE..................................323 254-2274
Fax: 323 257-1742
Joseph M Costa, *CEO*
Ryan Herren, *CFO*
John Sterner, *CFO*
Margaret Campbell, *Bd of Directors*
Marisol Barrios, *Comms Dir*
EMP: 460 EST: 1913
SQ FT: 18,217
SALES: 33.9MM Privately Held
SIC: 8361 Home for the emotionally disturbed

(P-24692)
HILLVIEW ACRES
Also Called: Hillview Acres Childrens Home
23091 Mill Creek Dr, Laguna Hills (92653-1258)
PHONE..................................714 694-2828
Fax: 909 627-1906
Noah McMahon, *Chairman*
Ronald Storm, *President*
Eric Carter, *Corp Secy*
EMP: 75 EST: 1929
SQ FT: 39,989
SALES: 3.5MM Privately Held
WEB: www.hillview.org
SIC: 8361 Children's home

(P-24693)
HOLLENBECK PALMS
Also Called: HOLLENBECK HOME FOR THE AGED
24431 Lyons Ave Apt 336, Newhall (91321-2360)
PHONE..................................323 263-6195
Fax: 323 264-6955
William G Heideman Jr, *President*
Morris Shockley, *Vice Pres*
Johnny Young, *Controller*
Joseph Meza, *Human Resources*
Peggy Heideman, *Pub Rel Dir*
EMP: 170
SALES: 17.7MM Privately Held
WEB: www.hollenbeckhome.com
SIC: 8361 Halfway group home, persons with social or personal problems

(P-24694)
HOME GUIDING HANDS CORPORATION (PA)
1825 Gillespie Way # 200, El Cajon (92020-0501)
PHONE..................................619 938-2850
Mark Klaus, *CEO*
Jan Adams, *CFO*
Karen Lanning, *Treasurer*
Carol A Fitzgibbons, *Exec Dir*
Rene Doehrer, *Administration*
EMP: 266
SALES: 17.4MM Privately Held
WEB: www.guidinghands.org
SIC: 8361 8052 Residential care for the handicapped; intermediate care facilities

(P-24695)
HOPE HSE FOR MLTPL-HANDICAPPED (PA)
4215 Peck Rd, El Monte (91732-2198)
PHONE..................................626 443-1313
Fax: 626 443-1134

David Bernstein, *Exec Dir*
Dorothy Gonzalez, *Exec Dir*
Mary Guardado, *Admin Sec*
Jason Smallwood, *Admin Asst*
Jason Swift, *Admin Asst*
EMP: 100
SQ FT: 15,000
SALES: 4.8MM Privately Held
SIC: 8361 Residential care for the handicapped; rest home, with health care incidental

(P-24696)
HR MISSION COMMONS FC 5183
10 Terracina Blvd, Redlands (92373-4808)
PHONE..................................909 793-8691
Patty Van Dyk, *Principal*
Mark Stanley, *Manager*
Pam Stanley, *Manager*
EMP: 88
SALES (est): 3.1MM Privately Held
SIC: 8361 Residential care

(P-24697)
HUMAN SERVICES PROJECTS INC
Also Called: TEEN TRIUMPH
5361 N Pershing Ave Ste H, Stockton (95207-5450)
P.O. Box 77908 (95267-1208)
PHONE..................................209 951-9625
Fax: 209 477-4667
Marti Fredericks, *CEO*
Craig Fredericks, *CFO*
Tamela Jones, *Office Mgr*
Penny Frasier, *Admin Sec*
EMP: 120
SQ FT: 6,800
SALES: 3.1MM Privately Held
WEB: www.hsp1980.org
SIC: 8361 Residential care for children

(P-24698)
JEWISH HOME FOR THE AGED OF OR
Also Called: Heritage Pointe
27356 Bellogente Apt 221, Mission Viejo (92691-6344)
PHONE..................................949 364-0010
Fax: 949 582-8957
Rena Loveless, *Administration*
Brad Plose, *President*
Gary Kramer, *Vice Pres*
Ira Victer, *Vice Pres*
Bernadett Riley, *Administration*
EMP: 120
SQ FT: 88,928
SALES: 9.5MM Privately Held
SIC: 8361 Geriatric residential care

(P-24699)
KIDS FIRST FOUNDATION
1025 Service Pl Ste 103, Vista (92084-7271)
PHONE..................................760 631-7550
Ihab Shahawi, *CEO*
EMP: 165
SALES: 6.7MM Privately Held
SIC: 8361 Residential care

(P-24700)
KIDS FIRST FOUNDATION
993 S Santa Fe Ave Ste C, Vista (92083-6995)
PHONE..................................760 631-7550
Ihab Shahawi, *CEO*
EMP: 99
SALES (est): 2.1MM Privately Held
SIC: 8361 Residential care

(P-24701)
KNOLLS WEST ENTERPRISE
Also Called: Knolls West Residential Care
16890 Green Tree Blvd, Victorville (92395-5618)
PHONE..................................760 245-0107
Fax: 760 843-1861
Larry Bechtold, *Partner*
Fred Bechtold, *Partner*
Gary Bechtold, *Partner*
EMP: 100
SQ FT: 44,000

8361 - Residential Care County (P-24702)

SALES (est): 4MM
SALES (corp-wide): 10.2MM **Privately Held**
WEB: www.desertknollsconvhospital.com
SIC: **8361** Geriatric residential care
PA: Knolls Convalescent Hospital Inc
16890 Green Tree Blvd
Victorville CA 92395
760 245-5361

(P-24702)
L A FAMILY HOUSING CORP
Also Called: Valley Shelter
7843 Lankershim Blvd, North Hollywood (91605-2523)
PHONE.................................818 503-3908
Stephanie Klasky-Gamer, *CEO*
EMP: 95 **Privately Held**
SIC: **8361** Home for destitute men & women
PA: L. A. Family Housing Corporation
7843 Lankershim Blvd
North Hollywood CA 91605
818 982-4091

(P-24703)
L A U S D PROGRAM
Also Called: Visually Handicapped
5210 Clinton St, Los Angeles (90004-1506)
PHONE.................................323 962-9560
Shirley Kirk, *Director*
EMP: 50 EST: 1998
SALES (est): 948.5K **Privately Held**
SIC: **8361** Home for the physically handicapped

(P-24704)
LA HABRA VILLA
220 Newport Center Dr # 11, Newport Beach (92660-7506)
PHONE.................................714 529-1697
Fax: 562 267-0362
David Tsoong, *Partner*
Herbert Tarlow MD, *Partner*
EMP: 54
SQ FT: 100,000
SALES (est): 3.3MM **Privately Held**
SIC: **8361** Residential care

(P-24705)
LABELLE FMLY RTREAT ORGNZATION
Also Called: Community Retreat Center
269 S Beverly Dr 1257, Beverly Hills (90212-3851)
PHONE.................................310 527-1883
Kettly Jules, *Principal*
EMP: 50
SALES (est): 950K **Privately Held**
SIC: **8361** Residential care

(P-24706)
LAKE OROVILLE COUNTRY RETIREME
Also Called: Country Crest Health Center
55 Concordia Ln Apt 309, Oroville (95966-6352)
PHONE.................................530 533-7857
Fax: 530 533-7887
Larry Bradley, *Exec Dir*
EMP: 75
SALES: 20K **Privately Held**
WEB: www.countrycrest.org
SIC: **8361** Residential care

(P-24707)
LASSEN HSE ASSISTED LIVING LLC
705 Luther Rd, Red Bluff (96080-4265)
PHONE.................................530 529-2900
Fax: 530 529-2979
Eric Jacobsen,
EMP: 50
SALES: 1.2MM **Privately Held**
SIC: **8361** Residential care

(P-24708)
LE BLEU CHATEAU INC
Also Called: Bleu Chateau Assisted Living
1900 Grismer Ave, Burbank (91504-4405)
PHONE.................................818 843-3141
Madeline Rosenberg, *President*
Ramon Parado, *President*
Robert Rosenberg, *Vice Pres*
EMP: 50

SALES (est): 1.3MM **Privately Held**
WEB: www.lebleuchateau.com
SIC: **8361** Home for the aged

(P-24709)
LEISURE CARE LLC
Also Called: Nohl Ranch Inn
380 S Anaheim Hills Rd, Anaheim (92807-4026)
PHONE.................................714 974-1616
Fax: 714 974-1414
Wanda Reynolds, *Branch Mgr*
EMP: 50
SQ FT: 82,222
SALES (corp-wide): 138.2MM **Privately Held**
WEB: www.leisurecare.com
SIC: **8361** 8051 Residential care; skilled nursing care facilities
PA: Leisure Care, Llc
999 3rd Ave Ste 4500
Seattle WA 98104
800 327-3490

(P-24710)
LEISURE CARE LLC
Also Called: Fairwinds Woodward Park
9525 N Fort Washington Rd, Fresno (93730-0662)
PHONE.................................559 434-1237
Fax: 559 434-0234
Coint Folwer, *Branch Mgr*
Alice Quijano, *Financial Exec*
EMP: 100
SALES (corp-wide): 138.2MM **Privately Held**
WEB: www.leisurecare.com
SIC: **8361** Residential care
PA: Leisure Care, Llc
999 3rd Ave Ste 4500
Seattle WA 98104
800 327-3490

(P-24711)
LINCOLN CHILD CENTER INC
Also Called: Hope Contra Costa
51 Marina Blvd, Pittsburg (94565-2068)
PHONE.................................925 521-1270
Allison Staulcup, *Principal*
EMP: 72
SALES (corp-wide): 17.3MM **Privately Held**
SIC: **8361** Home for the mentally handicapped
PA: Lincoln Child Center, Inc.
1266 14th St
Oakland CA 94607
510 273-4700

(P-24712)
LITTLE PEOPLES
39514 Brookside Ave, Cherry Valley (92223-4602)
P.O. Box 248, Beaumont (92223-0248)
PHONE.................................951 849-1959
C S Jay Kidogo, *President*
EMP: 60
SALES: 2.8MM **Privately Held**
WEB: www.littlepeoples.com
SIC: **8361** Residential care

(P-24713)
LITTLE PEOPLES WORLD INC
39514 Brookside Ave, Cherry Valley (92223-4602)
PHONE.................................951 845-8367
C S J Kidogo, *Exec Dir*
EMP: 50
SALES: 2.5MM **Privately Held**
SIC: **8361** Residential care for children

(P-24714)
LITTLE SISTERS OF POOR
Also Called: ST ANNE'S HOME
300 Lake St, San Francisco (94118-1397)
PHONE.................................415 751-6510
Fax: 415 751-1423
Patricia Metzgar, *President*
Alla Novak, *Accountant*
Steve Lewey, *Human Res Dir*
Andrew Millan, *Training Spec*
Esther Laguda, *Nursing Dir*
EMP: 107
SQ FT: 110,000

SALES: 7.4MM **Privately Held**
SIC: **8361** 8661 Home for the aged; religious organizations

(P-24715)
LONGWOOD MANAGEMENT CORP
Also Called: Parkers Retirement Residence
9925 La Alameda Ave, Fountain Valley (92708-3548)
PHONE.................................714 962-5531
Fax: 714 962-9875
Stephanie Radu, *Manager*
EMP: 65
SALES (corp-wide): 169.4MM **Privately Held**
SIC: **8361** 8059 Residential care; rest home, with health care
PA: Longwood Management Corp.
4032 Wilshire Blvd Fl 6
Los Angeles CA 90010
213 389-6900

(P-24716)
LONGWOOD MANAGEMENT INC
Also Called: Huntington Rsdntial Rtrment Ht
20920 Earl St Ofc, Torrance (90503-4357)
PHONE.................................310 370-5828
Fax: 310 442-1961
Heather Argeta, *Administration*
Chiqui Olalia, *Administration*
EMP: 65
SALES (est): 1.3MM **Privately Held**
WEB: www.longwoodmanagement.com
SIC: **8361** Home for the aged

(P-24717)
LOS ANGELES ORPHAN ASYLUM INC
7600 Graves Ave, Rosemead (91770-3414)
PHONE.................................323 283-9311
Sister Linda A Cahill, *Director*
Michael Giron, *Manager*
EMP: 122
SQ FT: 25,000
SALES: 10.7MM **Privately Held**
SIC: **8361** Orphanage

(P-24718)
LOS ANGELES ORPHANS HOME SOC (HQ)
815 N El Centro Ave, Los Angeles (90038-3805)
PHONE.................................323 463-2119
Darrell Evora, *President*
Gordon Freitas, *COO*
Jeanne Barry, *Vice Pres*
Scott Staub, *Vice Pres*
EMP: 192
SQ FT: 45,000
SALES (est): 3.3MM
SALES (corp-wide): 82.8MM **Privately Held**
SIC: **8361** Residential care for children
PA: Uplift Family Services
251 Llewellyn Ave
Campbell CA 95008
408 379-3790

(P-24719)
LOS ANGELES RESDNTL CMMNTY FDN
Also Called: LARC RANCH
29890 Bouquet Canyon Rd, Santa Clarita (91390-5111)
PHONE.................................661 296-8636
Fax: 661 296-8653
Christine Bratzel, *CEO*
Larry Sallows, *CFO*
Kathleen Sturkey, *Exec Dir*
Kym Strong, *Purch Mgr*
Sal Villasenor, *Opers Spvr*
EMP: 80
SALES: 5.9MM **Privately Held**
SIC: **8361** Home for the mentally retarded

(P-24720)
LOS ANGELES RESIDENTIAL COMM F
29890 Bouquet Canyon Rd, Santa Clarita (91390-5111)
PHONE.................................661 296-8636
Kathy Sturky, *Exec Dir*
Larry Sallows, *CFO*

Maureen Medeiros, *Office Mgr*
Arleen Almsted, *Admin Asst*
Peggy Sallows, *HR Admin*
EMP: 85
SQ FT: 5,000
SALES (est): 2.7MM **Privately Held**
WEB: www.larcfoundation.org
SIC: **8361** 8322 8051 Residential care for the handicapped; individual & family services; skilled nursing care facilities

(P-24721)
LOS PRIETOS BOYS CAMP
3900 Paradise Rd, Santa Barbara (93105-9734)
PHONE.................................805 692-1750
Fax: 805 692-1772
Patricia Stewart, *Director*
EMP: 60
SALES (est): 1MM **Privately Held**
SIC: **8361** Juvenile correctional facilities

(P-24722)
LOYALTON AT RANCHO SOLANO
3350 Cherry Hills Ct Ofc, Fairfield (94534-7885)
PHONE.................................707 425-3588
Kimberly Kent, *Exec Dir*
Pat Jensen, *Office Mgr*
Dorothy King, *Manager*
EMP: 60
SALES (est): 2MM **Privately Held**
SIC: **8361** Residential care

(P-24723)
MAGNOLIA OF MILLBRAE INC
201 Chadbourne Ave, Millbrae (94030-2570)
PHONE.................................650 697-7700
Fax: 650 697-1734
Vincent Muzzi, *President*
EMP: 93 EST: 1986
SALES (est): 5.8MM **Privately Held**
WEB: www.themagnolia.com
SIC: **8361** Residential care

(P-24724)
MARTINS ACHIEVEMENT PLACE
5240 Jackson St, North Highlands (95660-5003)
PHONE.................................916 338-1001
Fax: 916 338-1044
Daniel Martin, *Exec Dir*
James Martin, *Director*
EMP: 80
SALES: 5.2MM **Privately Held**
SIC: **8361** Residential care for children

(P-24725)
MARY AND FRIENDS
1101 Farrington Dr, La Habra (90631-2510)
PHONE.................................562 691-1575
Eric Rico, *CEO*
Christine Rico, *President*
EMP: 120
SALES (est): 3MM **Privately Held**
SIC: **8361** Residential care for the handicapped

(P-24726)
MARYVALE
7600 Graves Ave, Rosemead (91770-3414)
P.O. Box 1039 (91770-1000)
PHONE.................................626 280-6510
Steve Gunter, *CEO*
EMP: 66 EST: 2011
SALES: 19.1MM **Privately Held**
SIC: **8361** 8322 Residential care for children; public welfare center

(P-24727)
MASONIC HOMES OF CALIFORNIA (PA)
1111 California St, San Francisco (94108-2252)
PHONE.................................415 776-7000
David R Doan, *President*
Timothy A Wood, *CFO*
Andrew Uehling, *Vice Pres*
Allan L Casalou, *Admin Sec*
Norman M Schultz, *Master*
EMP: 375
SQ FT: 8,000

PRODUCTS & SERVICES SECTION
8361 - Residential Care County (P-24751)

SALES: 82.8MM Privately Held
WEB: www.mhcuc.org
SIC: 8361 Children's home

(P-24728)
MASONIC HOMES OF CALIFORNIA
Also Called: Masonic Home For Adults
34400 Mission Blvd, Union City (94587-3604)
PHONE..............................510 441-3700
Fax: 510 429-9206
Gilbert Smart, *Branch Mgr*
Chuck Major, *Exec VP*
Pam Friedman, *Vice Pres*
Manny Gallardo, *Executive*
Dixie U Reeve, *Administration*
EMP: 350
SALES (corp-wide): 20.5MM Privately Held
WEB: www.mhcuc.org
SIC: 8361 8051 Rest home, with health care incidental; skilled nursing care facilities
PA: Masonic Homes Of California Inc
    1111 California St
    San Francisco CA 94108
    415 776-7000

(P-24729)
MASONIC HOMES OF CALIFORNIA
1650 E Old Badillo St, Covina (91724-3163)
PHONE..............................626 251-2200
Fax: 626 332-0538
John Howle, *Manager*
Christina Drislane, *CTO*
Rick Quinn, *Facilities Dir*
EMP: 100
SALES (corp-wide): 20.5MM Privately Held
WEB: www.mhcuc.org
SIC: 8361 Children's home
PA: Masonic Homes Of California Inc
    1111 California St
    San Francisco CA 94108
    415 776-7000

(P-24730)
MCKINLEY CHILDRENS CENTER INC (PA)
762 Cypress St, San Dimas (91773-3505)
PHONE..............................909 599-1227
Fax: 909 592-3841
Anil Vadatary, *CEO*
Mike Fraser, *CFO*
Michael Frazer, *CFO*
Kurt Brungardt, *Pharmacy Dir*
Anil Vadaparty, *Administration*
EMP: 190
SQ FT: 8,055
SALES (est): 13.6MM Privately Held
WEB: www.mckinleycc.org
SIC: 8361 8211 Boys' Towns; private elementary & secondary schools

(P-24731)
MEADOWBROOK CONVALESCENT HOSP
461 E Johnston Ave, Hemet (92543-7195)
PHONE..............................951 658-2293
Bridgette Grimaldi, *President*
Lisa Lima, *Social Dir*
Richard Chang, *Nursing Dir*
EMP: 78 EST: 1955
SALES: 2.8MM Privately Held
SIC: 8361 8051 Rest home, with health care incidental; convalescent home with continuous nursing care

(P-24732)
MERCY RETIREMENT AND CARE CTR
3431 Foothill Blvd, Oakland (94601-3199)
PHONE..............................510 534-8540
Fax: 510 261-2276
Jesse Jantzen, *CEO*
Asha Kooliyadan, *Hlthcr Dir*
Janet Thompson, *Hlthcr Dir*
Jana Gesinger, *Director*
Jonathan Serbellon, *Director*
EMP: 160 EST: 1872
SQ FT: 125,000

SALES: 23.9MM Privately Held
SIC: 8361 8051 Home for the aged; skilled nursing care facilities

(P-24733)
MERRILL GARDENS LLC
800 Oregon St, Sonoma (95476-6445)
PHONE..............................707 996-7101
Sunny Notimoh, *Manager*
EMP: 63
SALES (corp-wide): 85.5MM Privately Held
SIC: 8361 Geriatric residential care
PA: Merrill Gardens L.L.C.
    1938 Frview Ave E Ste 300
    Seattle WA 98102
    206 676-5300

(P-24734)
MERRILL GARDENS LLC
430 N Union Rd, Manteca (95337-4367)
PHONE..............................209 823-0164
Travis Barnett, *Manager*
EMP: 63
SALES (corp-wide): 85.5MM Privately Held
SIC: 8361 Geriatric residential care
PA: Merrill Gardens L.L.C.
    1938 Frview Ave E Ste 300
    Seattle WA 98102
    206 676-5300

(P-24735)
MERRILL GARDENS LLC
Also Called: Merrill Gardns At Chateau Whit
13250 Philadelphia St Ofc, Whittier (90601-4319)
PHONE..............................562 693-0505
Suzie Magpayo, *Manager*
EMP: 60
SALES (corp-wide): 85.5MM Privately Held
SIC: 8361 Geriatric residential care
PA: Merrill Gardens L.L.C.
    1938 Frview Ave E Ste 300
    Seattle WA 98102
    206 676-5300

(P-24736)
MGH CORPORATION
Also Called: Mitchells Group Home
1202 W 101st St, Los Angeles (90044-1802)
PHONE..............................323 754-1408
Hazel Mitchell, *President*
Stephnie Weathersby, *Vice Pres*
EMP: 50
SALES (est): 3.4MM Privately Held
SIC: 8361 Geriatric residential care

(P-24737)
MISSION VILLA LLC
995 E Market St, Daly City (94014-2168)
PHONE..............................650 756-1995
Fax: 650 756-3995
Jeannie Lawler, *Director*
Julianna Kaitting, *Administration*
Jay Catiz, *Manager*
EMP: 50
SALES (est): 2.7MM Privately Held
WEB: www.missionvillage.org
SIC: 8361 Residential care

(P-24738)
MISSION VLLA ALZHMERS RSIDENCE
3333 S Bascom Ave, Campbell (95008-7005)
PHONE..............................408 559-8301
Fax: 408 559-7089
Jeanie Lalor, *Administration*
EMP: 50
SQ FT: 14,535
SALES (est): 1.1MM Privately Held
SIC: 8361 Residential care

(P-24739)
MONARCH PLACE PIEDMONT LLC
4500 Gilbert St, Oakland (94611-4657)
PHONE..............................510 658-9266
Frank J Haffner II, *Mng Member*
EMP: 125
SALES (est): 3.7MM Privately Held
SIC: 8361 Home for the aged

(P-24740)
MONTE VISTA GROVE HOMES
2889 San Pasqual St, Pasadena (91107-5364)
PHONE..............................626 796-6135
Fax: 626 796-9753
M Helen Baatz, *Exec Dir*
Nancy Lain, *Admin Asst*
Barbara Stevens, *Accountant*
Jacqueline Choi, *Human Res Dir*
Marlene Hinton, *Human Resources*
EMP: 85
SQ FT: 12,000
SALES: 4.5MM Privately Held
SIC: 8361 Geriatric residential care

(P-24741)
MOTHER LODE REHABILIT
Also Called: MORE WORKSHOP
399 Placerville Dr, Placerville (95667-3912)
PHONE..............................530 622-4848
Susie Davies, *Exec Dir*
David Eggerton, *Exec Dir*
Carol Keates, *Director*
Chris Bailey, *Manager*
EMP: 150
SQ FT: 20,000
SALES: 2.8MM Privately Held
SIC: 8361 8322 Rehabilitation center, residential; health care incidental; individual & family services

(P-24742)
NATIONAL MENTOR HOLDINGS INC
Also Called: Horrigan Cole Enterprises
30033 Technology Dr, Murrieta (92563-3520)
PHONE..............................951 677-1453
EMP: 266
SALES (corp-wide): 1.2B Privately Held
SIC: 8361 Residential care
PA: National Mentor Holdings, Inc.
    313 Congress St Fl 5
    Boston MA 02210
    617 790-4800

(P-24743)
NATIONAL MENTOR HOLDINGS INC
19640 Bermuda St, Chatsworth (91311-1908)
PHONE..............................818 366-8389
Crystal D Immerman, *Admin Mgr*
EMP: 2129
SALES (corp-wide): 1.2B Privately Held
SIC: 8361 6513 Residential care; retirement hotel operation
PA: National Mentor Holdings, Inc.
    313 Congress St Fl 5
    Boston MA 02210
    617 790-4800

(P-24744)
NEW BTHNY RSDNTL CRE&SKLLD
1441 Berkeley Dr, Los Banos (93635-9599)
PHONE..............................209 827-8933
Fax: 209 827-8989
Lucinda Fonseca, *Exec Dir*
Lucinda Fonscca, *Exec Dir*
EMP: 80
SALES (est): 2.7MM Privately Held
SIC: 8361 Residential care

(P-24745)
NEW WAY LLC
1130 Burnett Ave Ste G, Concord (94520-5610)
PHONE..............................925 688-1520
Fax: 925 688-1525
Lupe Henry, *Mng Member*
Steve Zolno, *Mng Member*
EMP: 80
SALES (est): 3.3MM Privately Held
SIC: 8361 Residential care for the handicapped

(P-24746)
NINOS LATINO UNIDOS FSA
10016 Pioneer Blvd # 123, Santa Fe Springs (90670-3245)
PHONE..............................562 801-5454
Fax: 562 942-8955

Fahir Milian, *President*
Gurith Torres, *Corp Secy*
Luis I Mendes, *Administration*
Heidi Lopez, *Manager*
EMP: 60
SALES: 6.8MM Privately Held
WEB: www.nlu.org
SIC: 8361 8322 Residential care; individual & family services

(P-24747)
NORTH COUNTY SERENITY HSE INC (PA)
240 S Hickory St Ste 210, Escondido (92025-4357)
PHONE..............................760 233-4533
Kathy Valenzuela, *Director*
Wes Jay Oindquist, *Treasurer*
Janelle Devera, *Principal*
James Jackson Jr, *Principal*
Denise Bradley, *Office Mgr*
EMP: 54 EST: 1949
SQ FT: 8,050
SALES: 624.2K Privately Held
SIC: 8361 Home for destitute men & women

(P-24748)
NORTHERN CA RETIREDD OFCRS
Also Called: Paradise Valley Estates
2600 Estates Dr, Fairfield (94533-9711)
PHONE..............................707 432-1200
Fax: 707 426-1130
James G Mertz, *CEO*
Debra Murphy, *CFO*
Janet Olson, *Vice Pres*
Rick Hust, *Risk Mgmt Dir*
Karen Whiteman, *Controller*
EMP: 225
SALES: 33MM Privately Held
WEB: www.pvestates.com
SIC: 8361 Residential care

(P-24749)
NUEVO AMNECER LATINO CHLD SVCS (PA)
5400 Pomona Blvd, Los Angeles (90022-1717)
PHONE..............................323 720-9951
Fax: 323 720-9953
Norma Duque-Acosta, *President*
Omar Palao, *Manager*
EMP: 61
SQ FT: 2,600
SALES: 10.3MM Privately Held
SIC: 8361 Residential care

(P-24750)
NURSECORE MANAGEMENT SVCS
1010 S Broadway, Santa Maria (93454-6600)
PHONE..............................805 938-7660
EMP: 251 Privately Held
SIC: 8361 8082 8049 7361 Residential care; home health care services; nurses & other medical assistants; nurses' registry
PA: Nursecore Management Services, Llc
    2201 Brookhollow Plaza Dr # 450
    Arlington TX 76006

(P-24751)
ODD FELLOW-REBEKAH CHLD HM CAL (PA)
Also Called: Rebekah Children's Services
290 I O O F Ave, Gilroy (95020-5204)
PHONE..............................408 846-2100
Fax: 408 842-1989
Nancy Johnson, *CEO*
Christophe Rebboah, *CEO*
Charmian Hadlock, *Bd of Directors*
Alejandra Arreola, *Program Mgr*
Lisa Apodaca, *Executive Asst*
EMP: 101
SQ FT: 46,000
SALES: 17.3MM Privately Held
SIC: 8361 8093 Home for the emotionally disturbed; mental health clinic, outpatient

8361 - Residential Care County (P-24752)

(P-24752)
ODD FELLOW-REBEKAH CHLD HM CAL
Also Called: Rebekah Children's Services
1260 S Main St Ste 101, Salinas (93901-2292)
PHONE.................................831 775-0348
Jorge Montes, *Branch Mgr*
Rachel Talavera, *Program Mgr*
Karen Lerma, *Human Resources*
EMP: 72
SALES (corp-wide): 17.3MM **Privately Held**
SIC: 8361 8093 Home for the emotionally disturbed; mental health clinic, outpatient
PA: Odd Fellow-Rebekah Children's Home Of California
290 I O O F Ave
Gilroy CA 95020
408 846-2100

(P-24753)
ODD FELLOWS HOME CALIFORNIA
Also Called: Saratoga Retirement Community
14500 Fruitvale Ave # 3000, Saratoga (95070-6169)
PHONE.................................408 741-7100
Fax: 408 867-7629
Cathy Schumacher, *Administration*
Kathy Maida, *Administration*
Ingrid Jones, *Human Res Dir*
Jennifer Martinez, *Director*
Christina Rosseau, *Director*
EMP: 275 EST: 1853
SALES: 48.7MM **Privately Held**
SIC: 8361 8051 Residential care; skilled nursing care facilities

(P-24754)
OLIVE CREST
73700 Dinah Shore Dr # 101, Palm Desert (92211-0815)
PHONE.................................760 341-8507
EMP: 77
SALES (corp-wide): 6.6K **Privately Held**
SIC: 8361 Group foster home
PA: Olive Crest
2130 E 4th St Ste 200
Santa Ana CA 92705
714 543-5437

(P-24755)
OLIVE CREST (PA)
2130 E 4th St Ste 200, Santa Ana (92705-3818)
PHONE.................................714 543-5437
Fax: 714 543-5463
Donald A Verleur, *CEO*
Edward Becker, *CFO*
Ed Beker, *CFO*
Lois Verleur, *Vice Pres*
Tim Bauer, *VP Admin*
EMP: 300
SQ FT: 40,000
SALES: 6.6K **Privately Held**
WEB: www.olivecrest.net
SIC: 8361 8322 Home for the emotionally disturbed; individual & family services

(P-24756)
OLIVE CREST
Also Called: Olive Crest Op
917 Pine Ave, Long Beach (90813-4325)
PHONE.................................562 216-8841
Donald Verleur, *Branch Mgr*
EMP: 77
SALES (corp-wide): 6.6K **Privately Held**
SIC: 8361 Home for the emotionally disturbed
PA: Olive Crest
2130 E 4th St Ste 200
Santa Ana CA 92705
714 543-5437

(P-24757)
OMNITRANS
Also Called: Omnitrans Access
234 S I St, San Bernardino (92410-2408)
PHONE.................................909 383-1680
Fax: 909 381-9620
Brian Niemann, *Principal*
EMP: 400

SALES (corp-wide): 15.6MM **Privately Held**
SIC: 8361 Home for the physically handicapped
PA: Omnitrans
1700 W 5th St
San Bernardino CA 92411
909 379-7100

(P-24758)
P MONTEREY LP
Also Called: Park Lane, The
200 Glenwood Cir Ste A50, Monterey (93940-6748)
PHONE.................................831 250-6159
Deepak Israni, *Principal*
EMP: 70
SALES (est): 3.1MM **Privately Held**
SIC: 8361 Residential care

(P-24759)
PACIFIC LODGE YOUTH SERVICES
Also Called: Pacific Lodge Boy's Home
4900 Serrania Ave, Woodland Hills (91364-3301)
P.O. Box 308 (91365-0308)
PHONE.................................818 347-1577
Fax: 818 883-5452
Lisa Alegria, *CEO*
Ashlei Sullivan, *QA Dir*
Gabrielle Tungate, *Accountant*
Bruce West, *Human Res Dir*
Jackeline Gonzalez, *Psychologist*
EMP: 110
SQ FT: 22,634
SALES (est): 7.9MM **Privately Held**
WEB: www.plys.org
SIC: 8361 Residential care

(P-24760)
PACIFIC RETIREMENT SVCS INC
Also Called: University Retirement Cmnty
1515 Shasta Dr Ofc, Davis (95616-6695)
PHONE.................................530 753-1450
Fax: 530 747-7007
Mark Blazer, *Exec Dir*
Michael Morris, *Administration*
Kimberly Carston, *Marketing Staff*
Judi Del Ponte, *Marketing Staff*
EMP: 170
SALES (corp-wide): 15.9MM **Privately Held**
WEB: www.prsmedia.com
SIC: 8361 Home for the aged
PA: Pacific Retirement Services, Inc.
1 W Main St Ste 303
Medford OR 97501
541 857-7777

(P-24761)
PALADIN EASTSIDE SERVICES INC
111 S Grfield Ave Ste 101, Montebello (90640)
PHONE.................................323 890-0180
Fax: 657 622-0379
Octavio Delgado, *President*
Raquel Zepeda, *Finance*
EMP: 100
SQ FT: 1,800
SALES (est): 3.6MM **Privately Held**
SIC: 8361 Residential care

(P-24762)
PALM GRDNS RSDNTIAL CARE FCLTY
240 Palm Ave, Woodland (95695-2844)
PHONE.................................530 661-0574
Fax: 530 661-0774
Sue Farrow, *President*
Jane Bair, *Exec Dir*
EMP: 50
SALES (est): 2.5MM **Privately Held**
SIC: 8361 8322 Residential care; individual & family services

(P-24763)
PALMS ASSISTD LVNG & MMRY CRE
Also Called: The Palms
100 Sterling Ct Ofc, Roseville (95661-3753)
PHONE.................................916 786-7200
Fax: 916 786-5562

J M Harder, *Mng Member*
Leslie Elowson, *Administration*
EMP: 74
SQ FT: 70,213
SALES: 631.6K
SALES (corp-wide): 4.9B **Publicly Held**
WEB: www.thepalmsalf.com
SIC: 8361 Geriatric residential care
HQ: Emeritus Corporation
3131 Elliott Ave Ste 500
Milwaukee WI 53214
206 298-2909

(P-24764)
PALO ALTO COMMONS
4075 El Camino Way, Palo Alto (94306-4005)
PHONE.................................650 494-0760
Fax: 650 494-0942
William Reller, *Partner*
Carolyn Reller, *Partner*
Sue Jordan, *Exec Dir*
Mary L Marshall, *Mktg Dir*
EMP: 85
SQ FT: 80,000
SALES (est): 6.7MM **Privately Held**
WEB: www.paloaltocommons.com
SIC: 8361 8052 Geriatric residential care; intermediate care facilities

(P-24765)
PARK CNTL CARE RHBLITATION CTR
2100 Parkside Dr, Fremont (94536-5326)
PHONE.................................510 797-5300
Fax: 510 797-3767
Anthony P Thekkek, *President*
Prema Thekkek, *Vice Pres*
EMP: 100
SALES (est): 4.6MM **Privately Held**
SIC: 8361 Rehabilitation center, residential: health care incidental

(P-24766)
PASADENA CHLD TRAINING SOC
Also Called: Sycamores School
2933 El Nido Dr, Altadena (91001-4529)
PHONE.................................626 798-0853
Fax: 626 798-4531
William P Martone, *Exec Dir*
Robert Martin, *Officer*
P Martone, *Exec Dir*
Frank Tran, *Sr Ntwrk Engine*
Julie Farino, *Director*
EMP: 192
SQ FT: 24,658
SALES (corp-wide): 12.8MM **Privately Held**
WEB: www.sycamores.com
SIC: 8361 8322 Home for the emotionally disturbed; individual & family services
PA: Pasadena Children's Training Society
210 S De Lacey Ave # 110
Pasadena CA 91105
626 395-7100

(P-24767)
PEPPERMINT RIDGE (PA)
825 Magnolia Ave, Corona (92879-3129)
PHONE.................................951 273-7320
Fax: 951 737-0726
Betsy Mullen, *Exec Dir*
Susan Glenn, *Treasurer*
Amy E Allemann, *Agent*
Elizabeth Muller, *Agent*
EMP: 83
SQ FT: 25,000
SALES: 6.3MM **Privately Held**
WEB: www.peppermintridge.org
SIC: 8361 8322 Residential care for the handicapped; individual & family services

(P-24768)
PHOENIX HOUSE ORANGE COUNTY
1207 E Fruit St, Santa Ana (92701-4296)
PHONE.................................714 953-9373
Pouria Abbassi, *CEO*
Elena Ksendzov, *CFO*
Stephen Donowitz, *Vice Pres*
EMP: 67

SALES (est): 2.8MM
SALES (corp-wide): 112.5MM **Privately Held**
SIC: 8361 Rehabilitation center, residential: health care incidental
HQ: Phoenix Houses Of California, Inc
11600 Eldridge Ave
Sylmar CA 91342
818 896-1121

(P-24769)
PHOENIX HOUSES LOS ANGELES INC
Also Called: PHOENIX HSE FNDTN, INC. & AF
11600 Eldridge Ave, Lake View Terrace (91342-6506)
PHONE.................................818 686-3000
Winifred Wechsler, *President*
Aracely Mayoral, *Controller*
EMP: 99
SALES: 13.7MM
SALES (corp-wide): 112.5MM **Privately Held**
SIC: 8361 Rehabilitation center, residential: health care incidental
HQ: Phoenix Houses Of California, Inc
11600 Eldridge Ave
Sylmar CA 91342
818 896-1121

(P-24770)
POOR SISTERS OF NAZARETH OF SA
Also Called: Nazareth House
6333 Rancho Mission Rd, San Diego (92108-2001)
PHONE.................................619 563-0480
Fax: 619 283-7829
Sister Margaret Spence, *Administration*
EMP: 75
SALES (est): 5.6MM **Privately Held**
WEB: www.nazarethhouse.org
SIC: 8361 8051 Geriatric residential care; skilled nursing care facilities

(P-24771)
PRIMROSE ALZHEIMERS LIVING (PA)
726 College Ave, Santa Rosa (95404-4107)
PHONE.................................707 568-4355
John Wotring, *President*
EMP: 50
SALES (est): 5.5MM **Privately Held**
WEB: www.primrosealz.com
SIC: 8361 Home for the aged

(P-24772)
PRIMROSE ALZHEIMERS LIVING
2080 Guerneville Rd, Santa Rosa (95403-4117)
PHONE.................................707 578-8360
Fax: 707 578-3110
John J Wortring, *Manager*
Jack Burton, *Food Svc Dir*
Graziella Rego, *Director*
Ericka Wotring, *Manager*
EMP: 50
SALES (corp-wide): 5.5MM **Privately Held**
WEB: www.primrosealz.com
SIC: 8361 Residential care
PA: Primrose Alzheimer's Living Inc
726 College Ave
Santa Rosa CA 95404
707 568-4355

(P-24773)
PRIMROSE ALZHEIMERS LIVING
Also Called: Primrose Sacramento
7707 Rush River Dr, Sacramento (95831-5229)
PHONE.................................916 392-3510
Fax: 916 392-3511
John Wotring, *Exec Dir*
John Wortring, *Exec Dir*
EMP: 65
SALES (corp-wide): 5.5MM **Privately Held**
WEB: www.primrosealz.com
SIC: 8361 8099 Home for the aged; medical services organization

PRODUCTS & SERVICES SECTION
8361 - Residential Care County (P-24796)

PA: Primrose Alzheimer's Living Inc
726 College Ave
Santa Rosa CA 95404
707 568-4355

(P-24774)
PROMESA BEHAVIORAL HEALTH
2815 G St, Merced (95340-2133)
PHONE.....................209 725-3114
Lisa Weigant, *Branch Mgr*
EMP: 63
SALES (corp-wide): 8.6MM **Privately Held**
SIC: 8361 Group foster home
PA: Promesa Behavioral Health
7120 N Marks Ave
Fresno CA 93711
559 439-5437

(P-24775)
PSYNERGY PROGRAMS INC
18225 Hale Ave, Morgan Hill (95037-3547)
PHONE.....................408 776-0422
Fax: 408 465-8281
Christopher Zubaite, *President*
Arturo Uribe, *COO*
Michael S Weinstein, *CFO*
L Jean Edwards, *Ch Credit Ofcr*
Lynda Kaufmann, *Government*
EMP: 55
SALES (est): 5.3MM **Privately Held**
SIC: 8361 Residential care

(P-24776)
RAISER SENIOR SERVICES LLC
Also Called: Stratford
601 Laurel Ave Apt 903, San Mateo (94401-4164)
PHONE.....................650 342-4106
Fax: 650 375-1392
Jennifer Raiser, *President*
Russell McClure, *Officer*
Phillip Raiser, *Vice Pres*
Lisa Kennedy, *Exec Dir*
Krystle Carter, *Professor*
EMP: 75
SQ FT: 184,000
SALES (est): 2.8MM **Privately Held**
SIC: 8361 Residential care; rest home, with health care incidental

(P-24777)
RANCHO DE SUS NINOS INC
Also Called: HIS KIDS RANCH
P.O. Box 360 (91963-0360)
PHONE.....................619 661-9232
Fax: 559 641-5704
Steve Horner, *Director*
EMP: 60
SALES: 2MM **Privately Held**
SIC: 8361 Orphanage

(P-24778)
RANCHO SAN ANTONIO BOYS HM INC (PA)
21000 Plummer St, Chatsworth (91311-4996)
PHONE.....................818 882-6400
Brother John Crowe, *CEO*
Nicholas Rizzo, *Finance Dir*
EMP: 100 **EST:** 1933
SALES: 2.1MM **Privately Held**
SIC: 8361 Boys' Towns

(P-24779)
RANCHO SAN ANTONIO RETIREMENT
Also Called: Forum At Rancho San Antonio
23500 Cristo Rey Dr, Cupertino (95014-6503)
PHONE.....................650 265-2637
Fax: 650 903-5920
Ken Fullmore, *Exec Dir*
Nan Boyd, *Finance Dir*
EMP: 302
SALES (est): 17.9MM **Privately Held**
SIC: 8361 8051 Rest home, with health care incidental; skilled nursing care facilities

(P-24780)
REDWOOD ELDERLINK SCPH
Also Called: Redwood Elderlink & Homelink
710 W 13th Ave, Escondido (92025-5511)
PHONE.....................760 480-1030
Fax: 760 737-0170
Kurt Norden, *Director*
Dan Johnson, *President*
Tom Vedvick, *Chairman*
Fran Hillebrecht, *Treasurer*
Doug Best, *Admin Sec*
EMP: 450
SQ FT: 200,000
SALES (est): 7.2MM
SALES (corp-wide): 79.2MM **Privately Held**
WEB: www.redwoodelderlink.com
SIC: 8361 8742 Home for the aged; compensation & benefits planning consultant
PA: Southern California Presbyterian Homes
516 Burchett St
Glendale CA 91203
818 247-0420

(P-24781)
REGENCY PARK SENIOR LIVING INC
Also Called: Regency Park Oak Knoll
255 S Oak Knoll Ave, Pasadena (91101-2992)
PHONE.....................626 396-4911
Fax: 626 584-5719
EMP: 62
SALES (corp-wide): 10.6MM **Privately Held**
SIC: 8361
PA: Regency Park Senior Living, Inc.
150 S Los Robles Ave # 480
Pasadena CA 91101
626 773-8800

(P-24782)
REGENT ASSISTED LIVING INC
Also Called: Regent Senior Living W Covina
150 S Grand Ave Ofc, West Covina (91791-2355)
PHONE.....................626 332-3344
Fax: 626 332-3364
Lorena Arechiga, *Manager*
EMP: 60
SALES (corp-wide): 27.4MM **Privately Held**
WEB: www.regentassistedliving.com
SIC: 8361 Residential care
PA: Regent Assisted Living, Inc.
121 Sw Morrison St # 950
Portland OR 97204
503 227-4000

(P-24783)
REGENT ASSISTED LIVING INC
Also Called: Regent At Laurel Springs
8100 Westwold Dr Ofc, Bakersfield (93311-3471)
PHONE.....................661 663-8400
Fax: 661 663-8196
Janice Calco, *Manager*
EMP: 50
SALES (corp-wide): 27.4MM **Privately Held**
WEB: www.regentassistedliving.com
SIC: 8361 Residential care
PA: Regent Assisted Living, Inc.
121 Sw Morrison St # 950
Portland OR 97204
503 227-4000

(P-24784)
REGENT ASSISTED LIVING INC
Also Called: Sunshine Villa Assisted Living
80 Front St, Santa Cruz (95060-5098)
PHONE.....................831 459-8400
Fax: 831 459-9588
Deann Daniel, *Manager*
Bob Niethold, *Maintence Staff*
EMP: 80
SALES (corp-wide): 24.9MM **Privately Held**
WEB: www.regentassistedliving.com
SIC: 8361 8052 Residential care; intermediate care facilities
PA: Regent Assisted Living, Inc.
121 Sw Morrison St # 950
Portland OR 97204
503 227-4000

(P-24785)
REGENT ASSISTED LIVING INC
Also Called: Orchard Park
675 W Alluvial Ave Ofc, Clovis (93611-4403)
PHONE.....................559 325-8400
Fax: 559 325-9660
Debbie Aramian, *Manager*
Pat Holhan, *Manager*
EMP: 80
SALES (corp-wide): 24.9MM **Privately Held**
WEB: www.regentassistedliving.com
SIC: 8361 8052 Residential care; intermediate care facilities
PA: Regent Assisted Living, Inc.
121 Sw Morrison St # 950
Portland OR 97204
503 227-4000

(P-24786)
RETIREMENT HOUSING FOUNDATION
Also Called: Auburn Ravine Terrace
750 Auburn Ravine Rd, Auburn (95603-3820)
PHONE.....................530 823-6131
Robert Mauer, *General Mgr*
EMP: 104
SQ FT: 9,756
SALES (corp-wide): 32.1MM **Privately Held**
WEB: www.bixbyknollstowers.com
SIC: 8361 Residential care
PA: Retirement Housing Foundation Inc
911 N Studebaker Rd # 100
Long Beach CA 90815
562 257-5100

(P-24787)
RETIREMENT LF CARE COMMUNITIES
Also Called: Carlton Plaza of Fremont
3800 Walnut Ave Apt 401, Fremont (94538-2273)
PHONE.....................510 505-0555
Fax: 510 505-0639
Stephanie Brice, *Exec Dir*
Susan Hughes, *Marketing Staff*
EMP: 64
SQ FT: 104,000
SALES (est): 2.7MM **Privately Held**
SIC: 8361 6513 Home for the aged; retirement hotel operation

(P-24788)
RHF PLYMOUTH TOWER
3401 Lemon St Ofc, Riverside (92501-2817)
PHONE.....................951 248-0456
Fax: 951 784-1508
Wes Jones, *Administration*
EMP: 65
SALES (est): 2.4MM **Privately Held**
WEB: www.bixbyknollstowers.com
SIC: 8361 Residential care

(P-24789)
RITE OF PASS ATHLETIC TRNG CTR
10400 Fricot City Rd, San Andreas (95249-9642)
PHONE.....................209 736-4500
Fax: 209 736-1800
Ken Dukek, *Manager*
Natalie Pearson, *Human Res Dir*
EMP: 103
SALES (corp-wide): 16.7MM **Privately Held**
SIC: 8361 Residential care
PA: Rite Of Passage Adolescent Treatment Centers And Schools, Inc.
2560 Business Pkwy Ste B
Minden NV 89423
775 267-9411

(P-24790)
ROBERT C HAMILTON
Also Called: Bel Vista Convalescent Hosp
1760 N Fair Oaks Ave, Pasadena (91103-1617)
PHONE.....................626 794-4103
Robert C Hamilton, *Owner*
Ann Hamilton, *Owner*
EMP: 70
SQ FT: 2,230
SALES: 767.5K **Privately Held**
SIC: 8361 Children's boarding home

(P-24791)
ROSEMARY CHILDRENS SERVICES (PA)
36 S Kinneloa Ave 200, Pasadena (91107-3853)
PHONE.....................626 844-3033
Fax: 626 844-3034
Greg Wessels, *Exec Dir*
Sungo Wang, *President*
Lynn Lu, *Vice Pres*
Veronica Fuentes, *Admin Sec*
Ian Shaw, *IT/INT Sup*
EMP: 101
SQ FT: 9,000
SALES: 9.4MM **Privately Held**
WEB: www.rosemarychildren.org
SIC: 8361 Home for the emotionally disturbed

(P-24792)
SACRAMENTO CHILDRENS HOME
1217 Del Paso Blvd Ste B, Sacramento (95815-3660)
PHONE.....................916 927-5059
EMP: 62
SALES (corp-wide): 13.6MM **Privately Held**
SIC: 8361 Residential care for children
PA: Sacramento Childrens Home
2750 Sutterville Rd
Sacramento CA 95820
916 452-3981

(P-24793)
SACRAMENTO CHILDRENS HOME (PA)
2750 Sutterville Rd, Sacramento (95820-1093)
PHONE.....................916 452-3981
Fax: 916 454-5031
Roy Alexander, *CEO*
David Baker, *COO*
Julia Chubb, *CFO*
Julie Chubb, *CFO*
Tammy Davis Sr, *Senior VP*
EMP: 125 **EST:** 1867
SQ FT: 15,500
SALES: 13.6MM **Privately Held**
WEB: www.donatetocharity.com
SIC: 8361 Children's home

(P-24794)
SAFE REFUGE
Also Called: Sobriety House
1041 Redondo Ave, Long Beach (90804-3928)
PHONE.....................562 987-5722
Fax: 562 438-6891
Kathryn Romo, *Exec Dir*
Debrah Mgaune, *Managing Dir*
EMP: 80
SQ FT: 2,300
SALES (est): 4.5MM **Privately Held**
WEB: www.safinc.org
SIC: 8361 Rehabilitation center, residential: health care incidental

(P-24795)
SAINT JOSEPH HOME CARE NETWORK
1165 Montgomery Dr, Santa Rosa (95405-4801)
PHONE.....................707 206-9124
Fax: 707 206-9420
Shirley Sleeker, *Administration*
Cynthia Dorfman, *Executive*
Linda Glomp, *Administration*
Robert Stanley, *Manager*
EMP: 80
SALES: 11.3MM **Privately Held**
SIC: 8361 Home for the aged

(P-24796)
SALEM LUTHERAN HOME ASSOCIATIO
Also Called: ELDER CARE ALLIANCE
1301 Marina Vil Pkwy 21 # 210, Alameda (94501)
PHONE.....................510 769-2700
Fax: 510 434-2806

8361 - Residential Care County (P-24797)

Glen Goddard, *Exec Dir*
Patty Creedon, *COO*
Marjorie Bailey, *CFO*
Janise Washburn, *CFO*
Carl Arnoult, *Vice Pres*
EMP: 135
SALES: 10MM **Privately Held**
SIC: 8361 8059 8051 Rest home, with health care incidental; convalescent home; personal care home, with health care; skilled nursing care facilities

(P-24797)
SALVATION ARMY
2799 Health Center Dr, San Diego (92123-2708)
PHONE....................858 279-1100
Susan Rothman, *Administration*
Lynn Sharpe, *Administration*
EMP: 80
SQ FT: 30,972
SALES (corp-wide): 4.3B **Privately Held**
WEB: www.salvationarmy.usawest.org
SIC: 8361 Halfway group home, persons with social or personal problems
HQ: The Salvation Army
180 E Ocean Blvd Fl 2
Long Beach CA 90802
562 491-8464

(P-24798)
SALVATION ARMY
2799 Health Center Dr, San Diego (92123-2708)
PHONE....................858 279-1100
Fax: 858 279-1100
James Knaggs, *President*
David Hudson, *Vice Pres*
Michael Woodruff, *Admin Sec*
Richard Chalk, *Administration*
EMP: 79
SALES (est): 2.2MM **Privately Held**
SIC: 8361 8322 Self-help group home; emergency shelters

(P-24799)
SALVATION ARMY
1500 Valencia St, San Francisco (94110-4489)
PHONE....................415 643-8000
Larry Nakashima, *Principal*
EMP: 100
SALES (corp-wide): 4.3B **Privately Held**
WEB: www.salvationarmy.usawest.org
SIC: 8361 Rehabilitation center, residential: health care incidental
HQ: Western Territorial Of The Salvation Army
180 E Ocean Blvd Fl 2
Long Beach CA 90802
562 264-3600

(P-24800)
SALVATION ARMY RESIDENCES INC
200 Lytton Springs Rd, Healdsburg (95448-7068)
P.O. Box 668 (95448-0668)
PHONE....................707 433-3334
Raltch Gimenez, *Branch Mgr*
Elizabeth Try, *Manager*
EMP: 100
SALES (corp-wide): 4.3B **Privately Held**
WEB: www.salvationarmy.usawest.org
SIC: 8361 8331 5521 Rehabilitation center, residential: health care incidental; job training & vocational rehabilitation services; used car dealers
HQ: Western Territorial Of The Salvation Army
180 E Ocean Blvd Fl 2
Long Beach CA 90802
562 264-3600

(P-24801)
SAN CLEMENTE VILLAS BY SEA
660 Camino De Los Mares, San Clemente (92673-1800)
PHONE....................949 489-3400
Fax: 949 234-0081
Paul J Brazeau, *Principal*
Maria Nemeth, *Sales Executive*
Stephanie Alter, *Mktg Dir*
EMP: 80
SALES (est): 6.2MM **Privately Held**
SIC: 8361 Residential care

(P-24802)
SAN FRANCISCO LADIES PROTECTI
Also Called: HERITAGE, THE
3400 Laguna St, San Francisco (94123-2271)
PHONE....................415 931-3136
Fax: 415 292-7080
Marla Hastings, *Administration*
Connie Tiret, *Executive*
Cindy Johnson, *Controller*
David Eberhardt, *Food Svc Dir*
Raygenia Stewart, *Nursing Dir*
EMP: 100 **EST:** 1853
SQ FT: 15,000
SALES: 16MM **Privately Held**
SIC: 8361 Home for the aged

(P-24803)
SAN GABRIEL CHILDRENS CTR INC
4740 N Grand Ave, Covina (91724-2005)
PHONE....................626 859-2089
Peter Rincon, *Manager*
Tracy Wilson, *QA Dir*
EMP: 70
SALES (corp-wide): 7.5MM **Privately Held**
WEB: www.sangabrielchild.com
SIC: 8361 8322 Children's home; crisis intervention center
PA: San Gabriel Children's Center, Inc.
2200 E Route 66 Ste 100
Glendora CA 91740
626 859-2089

(P-24804)
SANTA CLARA COUNTY OF
Also Called: Probation Dept-Juvenile Div
19050 Malaguerra Ave, Morgan Hill (95037-9032)
PHONE....................408 201-7600
Fax: 408 779-4393
Nick Berchard, *Manager*
Edward Titus, *Manager*
EMP: 70 **Privately Held**
WEB: www.countyairports.org
SIC: 8361 9223 Juvenile correctional home; correctional institutions;
PA: County Of Santa Clara
3180 Newberry Dr Ste 150
San Jose CA 95118
408 299-5105

(P-24805)
SEASONS
200 W Whittier Blvd, La Habra (90631-3877)
PHONE....................562 691-1200
Phil Smith, *Director*
Sherry Burmmer, *Director*
EMP: 80
SALES (est): 3.1MM **Privately Held**
SIC: 8361 Residential care

(P-24806)
SEAVIEW HLTHCRE & REHAB CTR LL
6400 Purdue Dr, Eureka (95503-7095)
PHONE....................707 443-5668
Fax: 707 441-8448
Ted Chigaros, *Vice Pres*
Chris Crowl, *Office Mgr*
Kirk Deverteuil, *Administration*
Christa Fitzgerald, *Purchasing*
Joseph Reis, *Marketing Staff*
EMP: 99
SALES (est): 3.2MM **Privately Held**
WEB: www.seaviewfoundation.org
SIC: 8361 Rehabilitation center, residential: health care incidental

(P-24807)
SEIU ULTCW
2910 Beverly Blvd, Los Angeles (90057-1012)
PHONE....................213 985-0463
Tyrone Freeman, *Principal*
Deborah Vargas, *Director*
EMP: 53
SALES (est): 4MM **Privately Held**
SIC: 8361 Residential care

(P-24808)
SENIOR KEIRO HEALTH CARE
Also Called: Japanese Retirement Home
325 S Boyle Ave, Los Angeles (90033-3812)
PHONE....................323 263-9651
Fax: 323 263-2163
Shawn Miyake, *CEO*
George Aratani, *President*
Rev David Shigekawa, *Treasurer*
Janie Teshima, *Administration*
Kenji Mada, *Comp Spec*
EMP: 90
SQ FT: 50,000
SALES: 7.7MM **Privately Held**
SIC: 8361 Home for the aged

(P-24809)
SHALEV SENIOR LIVING
6245 Matilija Ave, Van Nuys (91401-2923)
PHONE....................818 780-4808
Fax: 818 994-0041
Mia Levi, *Principal*
EMP: 50
SALES (est): 1.3MM **Privately Held**
SIC: 8361 Residential care

(P-24810)
SIERRA OAKS SENIOR LIVING
1520 Collyer Dr, Redding (96003-9535)
PHONE....................530 241-5100
Fax: 530 247-7350
Sue Becker, *Director*
Carla Jones, *Food Svc Dir*
EMP: 60
SALES (est): 2.8MM **Privately Held**
SIC: 8361 Residential care

(P-24811)
SILVERADO SENIOR LIVING INC
Also Called: Tustin Hcnda Memory Care Cmnty
240 E 3rd St, Tustin (92780-3623)
PHONE....................657 888-5752
Pamela Jones, *Director*
EMP: 71
SALES (corp-wide): 182.6MM **Privately Held**
SIC: 8361 Home for the aged
PA: Senior Silverado Living Inc
6400 Oak Cyn Ste 200
Irvine CA 92618
949 240-7200

(P-24812)
SIPPI ANNE RIVERSIDE RANCH LLP
Also Called: Anne Sppi Clnic Riverside Rnch
18200 Highway 178, Bakersfield (93306-9510)
PHONE....................661 871-9697
Fax: 661 871-1270
Michael Rosberg, *Owner*
Suzaane Rajlal, *Administration*
EMP: 50
SALES: 2MM **Privately Held**
SIC: 8361 Residential care

(P-24813)
SISTERS OF NZARETH LOS ANGELES
3333 Manning Ave, Los Angeles (90064-4804)
PHONE....................310 839-2361
Fax: 310 839-4204
Margarette Brody, *Administration*
Denise Thibault, *Exec Dir*
Kevin Chamas, *Director*
EMP: 100
SQ FT: 62,558
SALES (est): 14.3MM **Privately Held**
WEB: www.nazarethhousela.org
SIC: 8361 Geriatric residential care

(P-24814)
SKY PARK GARDENS ASSISTED
5510 Sky Pkwy Ofc, Sacramento (95823-2282)
PHONE....................916 422-5650
Habib Bokhari, *Owner*
Dorothy Ting, *Administration*
Sonia Johnson, *Manager*
Craig Wich, *Manager*
EMP: 55
SALES (est): 1.2MM **Privately Held**
SIC: 8361 Residential care

(P-24815)
SOLHEIM LUTHERAN HOME
2236 Merton Ave, Los Angeles (90041-1915)
PHONE....................323 257-7518
Fax: 323 255-3544
James Graunke, *Principal*
Antonio Davila, *CFO*
Norma Heaton, *Exec Dir*
Joyce Dohlin, *Administration*
Sarah Keever, *Human Res Dir*
EMP: 185
SQ FT: 82,591
SALES: 11.7MM **Privately Held**
WEB: www.solheimlh.org
SIC: 8361 Home for the aged

(P-24816)
SONOMA CNTY IND LIVING SKILLS
Also Called: Scils
1799 Pepper Rd, Petaluma (94952-9616)
PHONE....................707 765-8444
Fax: 707 765-8445
Sean Dirworth, *Director*
EMP: 60 **EST:** 1958
SQ FT: 1,100
SALES: 969.3K **Privately Held**
SIC: 8361 8322 Home for the mentally handicapped; individual & family services

(P-24817)
SONORA RETIREMENT CENTER INC
Also Called: Skyline Place
12877 Sylva Ln Ofc, Sonora (95370-6965)
PHONE....................209 588-0373
Fax: 209 588-0736
Mark Weisner, *President*
Kelly Grounds, *Administration*
EMP: 50
SQ FT: 56,000
SALES (est): 3.2MM **Privately Held**
SIC: 8361 Residential care

(P-24818)
SPRINGHUSE MANOR CARE HLTH SVC
285 W Central Ave Ofc, Brea (92821-7518)
PHONE....................714 671-7898
Fax: 714 671-1714
Larry Roseth, *Exec Dir*
EMP: 60
SALES (est): 1.1MM **Privately Held**
SIC: 8361 Residential care

(P-24819)
ST ANNES MATERNITY HOME
155 N Occidental Blvd, Los Angeles (90026-4641)
PHONE....................213 381-2931
Fax: 213 381-7804
Tony Walker, *President*
Carlos Tobar, *QA Dir*
Mellissa Wu, *Finance*
Judy Ng, *Human Resources*
Veronica Garcia, *Director*
EMP: 158
SQ FT: 100,000
SALES: 14.5MM **Privately Held**
SIC: 8361 Rehabilitation center, residential: health care incidental

(P-24820)
ST PAULS EPISCOPAL HOME INC
Saint Pauls Health Care Center
235 Nutmeg St, San Diego (92103-6201)
PHONE....................619 239-8687
Fax: 619 239-1201
Ben Geske, *Manager*
EMP: 65
SQ FT: 1,100
SALES (corp-wide): 19.1MM **Privately Held**
SIC: 8361 8051 Rest home, with health care incidental; skilled nursing care facilities
PA: St. Paul's Episcopal Home, Inc.
328 Maple St
San Diego CA 92103
619 239-6900

PRODUCTS & SERVICES SECTION
8361 - Residential Care County (P-24843)

(P-24821)
ST PAULS EPISCOPAL HOME INC
2635 2nd Ave Ofc, San Diego (92103-6597)
PHONE..................619 239-2097
Fax: 619 236-0034
EMP: 53
SALES (corp-wide): 19.1MM **Privately Held**
SIC: 8361 Residential care
PA: St. Paul's Episcopal Home, Inc.
328 Maple St
San Diego CA 92103
619 239-6900

(P-24822)
ST PAULS EPISCOPAL HOME INC
Also Called: St Paul's Villa
2700 E 4th St, National City (91950-3006)
PHONE..................619 232-2996
Cheryl Wilson, *Director*
Kay Fitzgerald, *Director*
EMP: 65
SALES (corp-wide): 19.1MM **Privately Held**
SIC: 8361 Home for the aged
PA: St. Paul's Episcopal Home, Inc.
328 Maple St
San Diego CA 92103
619 239-6900

(P-24823)
STOCKTON CONGREGATIONAL HOME
Also Called: Plymouth Square
1319 N Madison St Ofc, Stockton (95202-1001)
PHONE..................209 466-4341
Fax: 209 466-6853
Peter Peabody, *President*
Stuart Hartman, *Principal*
Gary Wiemers, *Administration*
Wendy Riley, *Mktg Dir*
EMP: 84
SALES: 3.3MM **Privately Held**
SIC: 8361 Residential care

(P-24824)
SUMMERVILLE AT HAZEL CREEK LLC
Also Called: Hazel Creek Assisted Living
6125 Hazel Ave, Orangevale (95662-4558)
PHONE..................916 988-7901
Fax: 916 988-9223
Lonnie Irvine, *Owner*
Hazel Creek, *Minister*
EMP: 3394
SALES (est): 22.2MM
SALES (corp-wide): 4.9B **Publicly Held**
SIC: 8361 Home for the aged
HQ: Emeritus Corporation
3131 Elliott Ave Ste 500
Milwaukee WI 53214
206 298-2909

(P-24825)
SUMMERVILLE SENIOR LIVING INC
10615 Jordan Rd, Whittier (90603-2932)
PHONE..................562 943-3724
Granger Cobb, *CEO*
Phyllis Ricard, *Exec Dir*
Lynnett Smith, *Exec Dir*
Debbie Marcado, *Director*
EMP: 51
SALES (corp-wide): 4.9B **Publicly Held**
SIC: 8361 Residential care
HQ: Senior Summerville Living Inc
3131 Elliott Ave Ste 500
Seattle WA 98121
206 298-2909

(P-24826)
SUMMERVILLE SENIOR LIVING INC
20801 Devonshire St, Chatsworth (91311-3216)
PHONE..................818 341-2552
Ram Nemani, *Owner*
EMP: 51
SALES (corp-wide): 4.9B **Publicly Held**
SIC: 8361 Residential care

HQ: Senior Summerville Living Inc
3131 Elliott Ave Ste 500
Seattle WA 98121
206 298-2909

(P-24827)
SUMMITVIEW CHILD TREATMENT CTR
5036 Sunrey Rd, Placerville (95667-9529)
PHONE..................530 644-2412
Carla Wills, *Exec Dir*
Paul Sunseri, *Director*
EMP: 50
SALES: 5.2MM **Privately Held**
SIC: 8361 Halfway group home, persons with social or personal problems

(P-24828)
SUN CITY RHF HOUSING INC
Also Called: Sun City Gardens
28500 Bradley Rd, Sun City (92586-3029)
PHONE..................951 679-2391
Fax: 909 679-8002
Trudi Hendrix, *Administration*
Jean Walker, *Executive*
Kalilah Muhammad, *Director*
EMP: 69
SALES: 4.3MM **Privately Held**
WEB: www.bixbyknollstowers.com
SIC: 8361 Residential care

(P-24829)
SUNHARBOR MANAGEMENT LLC
Also Called: The Valley Inn
708 E 5th St, Holtville (92250-1514)
PHONE..................760 356-1262
Fax: 760 356-2503
Gary Rust,
Rene Baylon, *Executive*
Fred Harder,
John Harder,
Elaine Rust,
EMP: 50
SALES (est): 2.9MM **Privately Held**
SIC: 8361 Residential care

(P-24830)
SUNNYSIDE GARDENS
1025 Carson Dr, Sunnyvale (94086-5800)
PHONE..................408 730-4070
Anna Ready, *Director*
Toni Adame, *Case Mgr*
Jann Acevedo, *Manager*
EMP: 72
SALES (est): 2.9MM **Privately Held**
SIC: 8361 Residential care

(P-24831)
SUNRISE OF PETALUMA
815 Wood Sorrel Dr, Petaluma (94954-6857)
PHONE..................707 776-2885
Fax: 707 776-0956
Erin Carlson, *Director*
EMP: 70
SALES (est): 1.4MM **Privately Held**
SIC: 8361 Residential care

(P-24832)
SUNRISE SENIOR LIVING LLC
Also Called: Sunrise of La Palma
5321 La Palma Ave Fl 2, La Palma (90623-1703)
PHONE..................714 739-8111
Fax: 714 739-8112
Jennifer Munoz, *Mayor*
Brandon Roemer, *Marketing Staff*
EMP: 60
SALES (corp-wide): 3.8B **Publicly Held**
WEB: www.sunrise.com
SIC: 8361 Home for the aged
HQ: Sunrise Senior Living, Llc
7902 Westpark Dr
Mc Lean VA 22102

(P-24833)
TEMPLE GARDEN HOMES INC
5746 Loma Ave, Temple City (91780-2452)
PHONE..................626 286-6408
Florencia Pilpa, *President*
EMP: 50

SALES (est): 2.3MM **Privately Held**
SIC: 8361 Home for the mentally handicapped

(P-24834)
TERRACES RETIREMENT COMMUNITY
Also Called: Lodge Inn and Health Center
2850 Sierra Sunrise Ter, Chico (95928-8401)
PHONE..................530 894-1010
Fax: 530 894-0147
Cheryl Haury, *CEO*
Cerel Havority, *President*
Heidi Hukill, *CFO*
Leo McKinley, *CFO*
Grace Mejia, *Principal*
EMP: 166
SQ FT: 1,000
SALES (est): 3.3MM **Privately Held**
WEB: www.theterraceschico.com
SIC: 8361 8051 Geriatric residential care; skilled nursing care facilities

(P-24835)
THE REDWOODS A CMNTY SENIORS
Also Called: Redwoods, The
40 Camino Alto Ofc, Mill Valley (94941-2997)
PHONE..................415 383-2741
Barbara Solomon, *CEO*
Susan Badger, *COO*
Alan Kern, *CFO*
Ron Bruno, *Human Resources*
Lorna Wilson, *Opers Mgr*
EMP: 140
SQ FT: 140,000
SALES: 4.3MM **Privately Held**
WEB: www.redwoodsoft.com
SIC: 8361 Geriatric residential care

(P-24836)
TIERRA DEL SOL FOUNDATION (PA)
9919 Sunland Blvd, Sunland (91040-1599)
PHONE..................818 352-1419
Fax: 818 353-0777
Steve Miller, *Exec Dir*
Kevin Lehmann, *Program Mgr*
Ingrid Mares, *Program Mgr*
Sergio Uribe, *Program Mgr*
Mirlo Tello, *Executive Asst*
EMP: 95
SQ FT: 20,000
SALES: 11.6MM **Privately Held**
WEB: www.tierradelsol.org
SIC: 8361 8211 8322 Home for the mentally handicapped; home for the physically handicapped; public special education school; individual & family services

(P-24837)
TRINITY YOUTH SERVICES (PA)
201 N Indian Hill Blvd # 201, Claremont (91711-4668)
P.O. Box 1210 (91711-1210)
PHONE..................909 825-5588
John Neiuber, *CEO*
Aris Alexandre, *President*
Nathan Mitakides, *President*
Leonard Bryan, *CFO*
Fr Paul O'Callaghan, *Treasurer*
EMP: 60
SQ FT: 7,600
SALES: 26.6MM **Privately Held**
WEB: www.trinitycfs.org
SIC: 8361 Halfway home for delinquents & offenders

(P-24838)
TUTERA GROUP INC
Also Called: Kit Carson Nursing & Rehab
811 Court St, Jackson (95642-2131)
PHONE..................209 223-2231
Shawn Moody, *Manager*
EMP: 100
SALES (corp-wide): 74.5MM **Privately Held**
WEB: www.tutera.com
SIC: 8361 Rest home, with health care incidental
PA: Tutera Group Inc.
7611 State Line Rd # 301
Kansas City MO 64114
816 444-0900

(P-24839)
UNITED CP/S CHLDRNS FNDN LA
11051 Old Snta Susna Pass, Chatsworth (91311-1206)
PHONE..................818 998-8755
Fax: 818 998-1263
Rick Macdonough, *Administration*
Norma De Haan, *Administration*
EMP: 135
SQ FT: 20,019
SALES (corp-wide): 27.5MM **Privately Held**
SIC: 8361 8322 Rehabilitation center, residential: health care incidental; individual & family services
PA: United Cerebral Palsy/Spastic Children's Foundation Of Los Angeles And Ventura Counties
6430 Independence Ave
Woodland Hills CA 91367
818 782-2211

(P-24840)
UPLIFT FAMILY SERVICES (PA)
Also Called: Emq Familiesfirst
251 Llewellyn Ave, Campbell (95008-1940)
PHONE..................408 379-3790
Fax: 530 753-3390
Darrell Evora, *CEO*
R Donald McNeil, *Ch of Bd*
Jason D Gurahoo, *CFO*
Kathy McCarthy,
Craig Wolfe, *Officer*
EMP: 60
SQ FT: 65,000
SALES: 82.8MM **Privately Held**
SIC: 8361 Home for the emotionally disturbed

(P-24841)
VALLEY MTN REGIONAL CTR INC
1620 Cummins Dr, Modesto (95358-6414)
PHONE..................209 529-2626
Fax: 209 526-5763
Richard Jacobs, *Branch Mgr*
EMP: 70
SALES (corp-wide): 150MM **Privately Held**
SIC: 8361 Residential care for the handicapped
PA: Valley Mountain Regional Center, Inc.
702 N Aurora St
Stockton CA 95202
209 473-0951

(P-24842)
VALLEY PINTE NURSING REHAB CTR
20090 Stanton Ave, Castro Valley (94546-5203)
PHONE..................510 538-8464
Daniel Wittman, *Administration*
Cali Phan, *Office Mgr*
Carol Janow, *Food Svc Dir*
Oyama Wesley, *Director*
EMP: 50
SQ FT: 7,500
SALES (est): 5MM **Privately Held**
SIC: 8361 Rehabilitation center, residential: health care incidental

(P-24843)
VALLEY TEEN RANCH
2610 W Shaw Ln Ste 105, Fresno (93711-2775)
PHONE..................559 437-1144
Fax: 559 438-5004
Connie Clendenan, *Exec Dir*
Legion Escobar, *Tech/Comp Coord*
Kathy Hilton, *Finance*
Jennifer Moore, *Social Worker*
David Flores, *Supervisor*
EMP: 76
SQ FT: 9,996
SALES: 4.1MM **Privately Held**
WEB: www.valleyteenranch.org
SIC: 8361 8322 Residential care for children; individual & family services

8361 - Residential Care County (P-24844)

(P-24844)
VASINDAS AROUND THE CLOCK CARE
Also Called: Around The Clock Home Care
5251 Office Park Dr # 403, Bakersfield (93309-0695)
PHONE..................661 395-5820
Mary Vasinda, *President*
John Vasinda, *Vice Pres*
Cassandra Ortiz, *Program Dir*
EMP: 50
SALES: 1.5MM Privately Held
SIC: 8361 Geriatric residential care

(P-24845)
VENTAGE SENIOR HOUSING
Also Called: Avalon At Newport
4000 Hilaria Way, Newport Beach (92663-3610)
PHONE..................949 631-3555
Mary Heilgeist, *Exec Dir*
Barbara Briscoe, *Exec Dir*
EMP: 50
SQ FT: 41,704
SALES (est): 2.2MM Privately Held
SIC: 8361 Residential care

(P-24846)
VICTOR TREATMENT CENTERS INC
Also Called: Regional Youth Svcs N Vly Schl
9150 E Hwy 12, Victor (95253)
P.O. Box 680 (95253-0680)
PHONE..................209 340-7900
Fax: 209 340-7950
David Baker, *President*
EMP: 127
SALES (corp-wide): 25.7MM Privately Held
WEB: www.victor.org
SIC: 8361 Residential care
PA: Victor Treatment Centers, Inc.
1360 E Lassen Ave
Chico CA 95973
530 893-0758

(P-24847)
VICTOR TREATMENT CENTERS INC
Also Called: Willow Creek Treatment Center
341 Irwin Ln, Santa Rosa (95401-5603)
PHONE..................707 576-0171
Fax: 707 576-7243
Gala Goodwin, *Branch Mgr*
EMP: 130
SQ FT: 3,060
SALES (corp-wide): 25.7MM Privately Held
WEB: www.victor.org
SIC: 8361 Home for the emotionally disturbed
PA: Victor Treatment Centers, Inc.
1360 E Lassen Ave
Chico CA 95973
530 893-0758

(P-24848)
VILLAGE AT GRANITE BAY
8550 Barton Rd, Granite Bay (95746-8843)
PHONE..................916 789-0326
Vicky Krauss, *Administration*
Vicky Cross, *Administration*
EMP: 68
SALES (est): 579K Privately Held
SIC: 8361 Residential care

(P-24849)
VILLAGE AT NORTHRIDGE
9222 Corbin Ave, Northridge (91324-2409)
PHONE..................818 514-4497
EMP: 144
SALES (est): 1MM
SALES (corp-wide): 70.7MM Privately Held
SIC: 8361 Home for the aged
PA: Senior Resource Group, Llc
500 Stevens Ave Ste 100
Solana Beach CA 92075
858 792-9300

(P-24850)
VILLAS DE CARLSBAD LTD A CALI
Also Called: Las Villas De Carlsbad
1088 Laguna Dr, Carlsbad (92008-1858)
PHONE..................760 434-7116
Fax: 760 434-9261
Jack Rowe, *Owner*
Karl Steinberg, *Medical Dir*
Robert Yuhaf, *Medical Dir*
Carina Lopez, *Manager*
EMP: 50
SALES (corp-wide): 4.3MM Privately Held
SIC: 8361 Home for the aged
PA: Villas De Carlsbad Ltd, A California Limited Partnership
9619 Chesapeake Dr # 103
San Diego CA 92123
858 565-4424

(P-24851)
VISTA DEL MAR CHILD FMLY SVCS
1533 Euclid St, Santa Monica (90404-3306)
PHONE..................310 836-1223
Louis Josephson, *Branch Mgr*
EMP: 428
SALES (corp-wide): 40.4MM Privately Held
SIC: 8361 Home for the mentally handicapped
PA: Vista Del Mar Child And Family Services
3200 Motor Ave
Los Angeles CA 90034
310 202-0669

(P-24852)
WARNER MOUNTAIN GROUP HOM
250 Cnty Rd 82, Canby (96015)
P.O. Box 347 (96015-0347)
PHONE..................530 233-5200
Fax: 530 233-5847
Larry Trotter, *Administration*
EMP: 57
SALES (est): 711.1K Privately Held
SIC: 8361 Self-help group home

(P-24853)
WATERS EDGE LODGE
801 Island Dr Apt 267, Alameda (94502-6765)
PHONE..................510 769-6264
Fax: 510 748-4277
Christian Zimmerman, *Partner*
John Zimmerman, *Partner*
EMP: 50
SALES (est): 3.5MM Privately Held
WEB: www.watersedgelodge.com
SIC: 8361 Geriatric residential care

(P-24854)
WESTMONT LIVING INC
Also Called: Terraces of Roseville, The
707 Sunrise Ave, Roseville (95661-4524)
PHONE..................916 786-3277
Eileen Bonomo, *Pub Rel Dir*
EMP: 321
SALES (corp-wide): 38.7MM Privately Held
SIC: 8361 Home for the aged
PA: Westmont Living, Inc.
7660 Fay Ave Ste N
La Jolla CA 92037
858 456-1233

(P-24855)
WESTMONT LIVING INC (PA)
7660 Fay Ave Ste N, La Jolla (92037-4875)
PHONE..................858 456-1233
Michael O Rourke, *CEO*
Susie Stangroom, *Shareholder*
Andrew Plant, *President*
Leo McKinley, *CFO*
Jackie Budrovic, *Vice Pres*
EMP: 149
SALES (est): 38.7MM Privately Held
SIC: 8361 Residential care

(P-24856)
WHITE RABBIT PARTNERS INC
9000 W Sunset Blvd # 1500, West Hollywood (90069-5815)
PHONE..................310 975-1450
Andrew William Spanswick, *CEO*
EMP: 150 EST: 2009
SALES (est): 3.2MM Privately Held
SIC: 8361 Residential care

(P-24857)
WILLOW SPRNGS ALZHMRS SPCL CR
191 Churn Creek Rd, Redding (96003-3044)
PHONE..................530 242-0654
Fax: 530 242-0655
Jerry Erwin, *Partner*
EMP: 50
SALES (est): 2.1MM Privately Held
SIC: 8361 8099 Rehabilitation center, residential: health care incidental; blood related health services

(P-24858)
WILSHIRE HEALTH AND CMNTY SVCS
Also Called: Heritage House
903 Carmen Dr, Camarillo (93010-4527)
PHONE..................805 484-2777
Fax: 805 388-7837
Heather Frankel, *Director*
EMP: 60
SALES (corp-wide): 13MM Privately Held
SIC: 8361 Home for the aged
PA: Wilshire Health And Community Services, Inc.
285 South St Ste J
San Luis Obispo CA 93401
805 547-7025

(P-24859)
YOUTH HOMES INCORPORATED
Also Called: Anderson House
1159 Everett Ct, Concord (94518-1714)
P.O. Box 5759, Walnut Creek (94596-1759)
PHONE..................925 933-2627
Stuart McCoullough, *Exec Dir*
Laura Stark, *Administration*
Yuliya Korentsvit, *Manager*
EMP: 55
SALES (corp-wide): 11.2MM Privately Held
WEB: www.youthhomes.org
SIC: 8361 Home for the emotionally disturbed
PA: Youth Homes Incorporated
3480 Buskirk Ave Ste 210
Pleasant Hill CA 94523
925 933-2627

8399 Social Services, NEC

(P-24860)
A COMMUNITY FOR PEACE
6060 Sunrise Vista Dr, Citrus Heights (95610-7053)
PHONE..................916 728-5613
Carole Ching, *President*
Nancy O'Neill, *Administration*
Robin Basinger, *Program Dir*
EMP: 51
SALES: 611.5K Privately Held
SIC: 8399 Advocacy group

(P-24861)
ADVANCED MEDICAL PLACEMENT
18401 Burbank Blvd # 201, Tarzana (91356-6601)
PHONE..................818 996-9812
Labanyendu Pattanaik, *President*
Chris Speer, *Info Tech Dir*
EMP: 120
SQ FT: 1,400
SALES: 2MM Privately Held
SIC: 8399 Health systems agency

(P-24862)
ALTA HEALTHCARE SYSTEM LLC
Also Called: Van Nuys Community Hospital
14433 Emelita St, Van Nuys (91401-4213)
PHONE..................818 787-1511
Fax: 818 530-0519
Tony Lozano, *Branch Mgr*
Gigi Kim, *Pharmacy Dir*
Fawzu Basta, *Director*
EMP: 250
SALES (corp-wide): 637.4MM Privately Held
SIC: 8399 8063 Health systems agency; psychiatric hospitals
HQ: Alta Healthcare System Llc
4081 E Olympic Blvd
Los Angeles CA 90023
323 267-0477

(P-24863)
ALTA HEALTHCARE SYSTEM LLC (HQ)
4081 E Olympic Blvd, Los Angeles (90023-3330)
PHONE..................323 267-0477
David Topper, *Mng Member*
Elizabeth Aguilera, *Administration*
Mellisa Ramirez, *Human Res Mgr*
Melisa Bolanos, *Human Resources*
Sam Lee,
EMP: 250 EST: 1998
SALES (est): 28MM
SALES (corp-wide): 637.4MM Privately Held
SIC: 8399 Health systems agency
PA: Prospect Medical Holdings, Inc.
3415 S Sepulveda Blvd # 9
Los Angeles CA 90034
310 943-4500

(P-24864)
AMADOR TLMNE CMNTY ACTION AGCY (PA)
Also Called: Atcaa
935 S State Highway 49, Jackson (95642-2673)
PHONE..................209 296-2785
Fax: 209 223-4178
Shelly Hance, *Exec Dir*
Patty Cunningham, *Deputy Dir*
Marianne Jim, *Assistant*
EMP: 68
SALES (est): 12.8MM Privately Held
SIC: 8399 Community action agency

(P-24865)
AMADOR TLMNE CMNTY ACTION AGCY
Also Called: Aatcaa Headstart
427 Highway 49, Sonora (95370-5666)
PHONE..................209 533-1397
Fax: 209 533-1034
Shelly Hance, *Exec Dir*
Shana Monaco, *Director*
EMP: 50
SALES (corp-wide): 12.8MM Privately Held
SIC: 8399 Community action agency
PA: Amador Tuolumne Community Action Agency
935 S State Highway 49
Jackson CA 95642
209 296-2785

(P-24866)
AMADOR-TOLUMNE CMNTY RESOURCES
Also Called: Atcr
935 S State Highway 49, Jackson (95642-2673)
PHONE..................209 223-1485
Shelly Hance, *Exec Dir*
EMP: 99
SALES: 188.9K Privately Held
SIC: 8399 Social services

(P-24867)
AMERICAN CANCER SOC CAL DIV
Also Called: Discovery Shop
1103 Branham Ln, San Jose (95118-3702)
PHONE..................408 265-5535
Fax: 408 265-5570

Lucy Derkatch, *Manager*
Lucy Derkach, *Manager*
EMP: 50
SALES (corp-wide): 36.7MM **Privately Held**
SIC: 8399 Social service information exchange
PA: American Cancer Society California Division, Inc
1001 Marina Village Pkwy
Alameda CA 94501
510 893-7900

(P-24868)
AMERICAN HEART ASSOCIATION INC
Also Called: Western States Affiliate
816 S Figueroa St, Los Angeles (90017-2516)
PHONE 213 291-7000
Cass Wheeler, *Branch Mgr*
Lisa J Barker, *Senior VP*
Jason J Lustina, *Business Dir*
Cindy Noboa, *Business Dir*
EMP: 50
SALES (corp-wide): 780.2MM **Privately Held**
WEB: www.americanheart.org
SIC: 8399 Health systems agency
PA: American Heart Association, Inc.
7272 Greenville Ave
Dallas TX 75231
214 373-6300

(P-24869)
AMERICAN RED CROSS LA CHAPTER (PA)
11355 Ohio Ave, Los Angeles (90025-3266)
PHONE 310 445-9900
Fax: 213 445-9959
Roger Dixon, *CEO*
Kirk Richard Hyde, *Ch of Bd*
Michelle McCarthy, *CFO*
Thomas E Stephenson, *CFO*
Joann Cuyle, *Human Res Dir*
EMP: 150
SQ FT: 5,000
SALES (est): 20.5MM **Privately Held**
SIC: 8399 Community development groups

(P-24870)
AMERICAN RED CROSS SAN DIEGO (PA)
3950 Calle Fortunada, San Diego (92123-1827)
PHONE 858 309-1200
Fax: 858 298-0649
Joe Craver, *CEO*
Melinda McDonald, *CFO*
Tanya Linsdau, *Executive*
Sabina Cizmic, *Human Res Mgr*
Savina Cizmic, *Human Res Mgr*
EMP: 90
SALES (est): 9.2MM **Privately Held**
SIC: 8399 Council for social agency

(P-24871)
ARC OF SAN DIEGO (PA)
Also Called: ARC Enterprises
3030 Market St, San Diego (92102-3230)
PHONE 619 685-1175
David W Schneider, *CEO*
Anthony J Desalis, *COO*
Victoria Cendreda, *CFO*
Chad Lyle, *CFO*
Jennifer Bates Navarra, *Vice Pres*
EMP: 200
SQ FT: 55,093
SALES: 34.2MM **Privately Held**
WEB: www.arc-sd.com
SIC: 8399 8351 8361 8322 Advocacy group; child day care services; home for the mentally retarded; individual & family services

(P-24872)
ARC OF SAN DIEGO
Also Called: ARC - SD E Cnty Training Ctrs
1855 John Towers Ave, El Cajon (92020-1116)
PHONE 619 448-2415
Fax: 619 449-7853
Millie Oveross, *Manager*
EMP: 175

SALES (corp-wide): 34.2MM **Privately Held**
WEB: www.arc-sd.com
SIC: 8399 8361 Advocacy group; home for the physically handicapped
PA: The Arc Of San Diego
3030 Market St
San Diego CA 92102
619 685-1175

(P-24873)
ASIAN PCF HLTH CARE VENTR INC (PA)
4216 Fountain Ave, Los Angeles (90029-2256)
PHONE 323 644-3880
Fax: 323 644-3892
Kazue Shibata, *CEO*
Elizabeth Wang, *COO*
Nardo Beltran, *CFO*
Betty Bjors, *Vice Pres*
Peggy Schatz, *Vice Pres*
EMP: 130
SQ FT: 1,800
SALES (est): 14.2MM **Privately Held**
WEB: www.realyc.com
SIC: 8399 Health systems agency

(P-24874)
ASSISTANCE LEAGUE COVINA VLY
Also Called: NATIONAL LEAGUE
636 E San Bernardino Rd, Covina (91723-1735)
PHONE 626 966-7550
Fax: 626 966-3546
Karen Cocordan, *CEO*
Patsy Gorrell, *Treasurer*
EMP: 150
SQ FT: 10,000
SALES: 341.3K **Privately Held**
SIC: 8399 5932 Community development groups; used merchandise stores

(P-24875)
ASSISTANCE LEAGUE FOOTHILL COM
Also Called: San Antnio Cmnty Hosp Dntl Ctr
8555 Archibald Ave 8593, Rancho Cucamonga (91730-4633)
P.O. Box 927, Upland (91785-0927)
PHONE 909 987-2813
Fax: 909 484-0504
Esther Mott, *Treasurer*
Sandy Kimball, *Treasurer*
Linda Melmeth, *Director*
EMP: 167
SQ FT: 10,000
SALES: 396.4K **Privately Held**
SIC: 8399 Fund raising organization, non-fee basis

(P-24876)
ASSISTANCE LEAGUE OF REDLANDS
Also Called: ASSISTANCE LEAGUE THRIFT SHOP
506 W Colton Ave, Redlands (92374-3054)
PHONE 909 792-2675
Fax: 909 798-0436
Madelene Handy, *President*
Sandy Arsenault, *Treasurer*
Beth Goodrich, *Manager*
EMP: 150
SALES: 402.4K **Privately Held**
WEB: www.assistanceleague.org
SIC: 8399 5932 Advocacy group; clothing, secondhand

(P-24877)
ASSOCIATED STUDENTS UCLA (PA)
Also Called: Ucla Bookstore
308 Westwood Plz, Los Angeles (90024-5657)
PHONE 310 825-4321
Robert Williams,
Rich Delia, *CFO*
Moises Roman, *Bd of Directors*
Rik Pedersen, *Officer*
Kelly Ryan, *Executive*
EMP: 500
SQ FT: 200,000

SALES: 40.5MM **Privately Held**
SIC: 8399 5942 Council for social agency; book stores

(P-24878)
ASSOCIATED STUDENTS UCLA
924 Westwood Blvd, Los Angeles (90024-2910)
PHONE 310 794-0242
Roseanna P Malone, *Branch Mgr*
Nicole Durden, *Program Mgr*
EMP: 108
SALES (corp-wide): 40.5MM **Privately Held**
SIC: 8399 Council for social agency
PA: Associated Students U.C.L.A.
308 Westwood Plz
Los Angeles CA 90024
310 825-4321

(P-24879)
BASIC OCCPATIONAL TRAINING CTR
Also Called: Basic Occpational Training Ctr
1323 Jet Way, Perris (92571-7466)
PHONE 951 657-8028
Richard Yodites, *President*
Mitzies Yodites, *Exec Dir*
EMP: 154 EST: 1994
SQ FT: 12,000
SALES: 6.5MM **Privately Held**
SIC: 8399 Community development groups

(P-24880)
BEACH CITIES HEALTH DISTRICT
514 N Prospect Ave Fl 3, Redondo Beach (90277-3039)
PHONE 310 318-7939
Fax: 310 376-4738
Susan Burden, *CEO*
Steve Groom, *CFO*
Joanne Edgerton, *Sr Corp Ofcr*
Sunny Robilotta, *Controller*
Michelle Bholat, *Site Mgr*
EMP: 108
SQ FT: 3,156
SALES (est): 9.9MM **Privately Held**
SIC: 8399 Health systems agency

(P-24881)
BOYS & GIRLS CLUBS OF MARIN A
203 Maria Dr, Petaluma (94954-2301)
PHONE 707 769-5322
David Solo, *President*
Michael Fishman, *General Mgr*
Danny Alvarez, *Athletic Dir*
Chris Bell, *Athletic Dir*
Jim Duel, *Program Dir*
EMP: 56
SQ FT: 11,000
SALES: 1.9MM **Privately Held**
WEB: www.petalumabgc.org
SIC: 8399 Community development groups

(P-24882)
CALIFORNIA ENDOWMENT (PA)
1000 N Alameda St, Los Angeles (90012-1804)
PHONE 800 449-4149
Fax: 213 703-4193
Robert K Ross, *President*
Robert Alaniz, *President*
Julie Tugend, *COO*
Dan C Deleon, *CFO*
Marion Standish, *Bd of Directors*
EMP: 80
SQ FT: 110,000
SALES: 159.6MM **Privately Held**
SIC: 8399 Fund raising organization, non-fee basis

(P-24883)
CALIFORNIA RURAL INDIAN HEALTH
4400 Auburn Blvd Fl 2, Sacramento (95841-4145)
PHONE 916 437-0104
Fax: 916 929-7246
James Crouch, *Exec Dir*
Jason C Lopez, *CFO*
Richard S Moran, *CFO*
Laura Rambeau-Lawson, *Treasurer*
Susan Dahl, *Officer*

EMP: 80
SQ FT: 18,627
SALES: 47MM **Privately Held**
WEB: www.crihb.org
SIC: 8399 Health systems agency

(P-24884)
CALIFRNIA FMLY HLTH CUNCIL INC (PA)
Also Called: CFHC
3600 Wilshire Blvd # 600, Los Angeles (90010-2603)
PHONE 213 386-5614
Fax: 213 292-0659
Julie Rabinovitz, *CEO*
Margie Fites Seigle, *CEO*
Diane Chamberlain, *COO*
Brenda Flores, *Vice Pres*
Ron Frezieres, *Vice Pres*
EMP: 81
SQ FT: 18,000
SALES: 25.1MM **Privately Held**
SIC: 8399 8011 8099 Fund raising organization, non-fee basis; primary care medical clinic; medical services organization

(P-24885)
CALIFRNIA HLTH CARE FOUNDATION (PA)
1438 Webster St Ste 400, Oakland (94612-3228)
PHONE 510 891-3963
Fax: 510 238-1388
Mark D Smith, *President*
Craig Ziegler, *CFO*
EMP: 60
SALES: 54.7MM **Privately Held**
WEB: www.chcf.org
SIC: 8399 Fund raising organization, non-fee basis

(P-24886)
CAPC INC
Also Called: COMMUNITY ADVOCATE FOR PEOPLE'
7200 Greenleaf Ave # 170, Whittier (90602-1391)
PHONE 562 693-8826
Carolyn Reggio, *Exec Dir*
Paul Velasco, *President*
Cheryl Turner, *Treasurer*
Maria Segovia, *Admin Sec*
Trish Garcia, *Finance*
EMP: 150
SALES: 5.4MM **Privately Held**
SIC: 8399 Advocacy group

(P-24887)
CEMENT MASON HEALTH & WELFARE
220 Campus Ln, Suisun City (94534-1497)
PHONE 707 864-3300
Marvin Johnson, *Manager*
EMP: 100
SQ FT: 43,000
SALES: 25.7MM **Privately Held**
WEB: www.norcalcementmasons.org
SIC: 8399 6282 Fund raising organization, non-fee basis; investment advice

(P-24888)
CHILDNET YOUTH & FMLY SVCS INC (PA)
4155 Outer Traffic Cir, Long Beach (90804-2111)
P.O. Box 4550 (90804-0550)
PHONE 562 498-5500
Fax: 562 498-5501
Kathy L Hughes, *CEO*
Monica Quinones, *COO*
Allan Greenberg, *CFO*
Tami Bender, *Executive Asst*
Amy Wilson, *Accountant*
EMP: 177
SQ FT: 16,073
SALES: 24.3MM **Privately Held**
WEB: www.childnet.net
SIC: 8399 Health & welfare council

(P-24889)
CITY OF HOPE
Also Called: City Hope Development Center
1500 Duarte Rd, Duarte (91010-3012)
PHONE 213 202-5735
Fax: 213 241-7190

8399 - Social Services, NEC County (P-24890)

Kathleen Cane, *Vice Pres*
Rowelle Enriquez, *Officer*
Stephanie Hsieh, *Officer*
Gloria Preciado, *Assoc VP*
Kathleen L Kane, *Exec VP*
EMP: 200
SALES (corp-wide): 1.4B **Privately Held**
WEB: www.cityofhope.com
SIC: 8399 9532 Fund raising organization, non-fee basis; urban & community development;
PA: City Of Hope
1500 E Duarte Blvd
Duarte CA 91010
626 256-4673

(P-24890)
CITY OF POMONA
Also Called: Welfare Dept
2040 W Holt Ave Fl 2, Pomona (91768-3307)
PHONE...............................909 397-5506
John Minato, *Director*
EMP: 400
SQ FT: 3,455 **Privately Held**
SIC: 8399 Social service information exchange
PA: Pomona, City Of (Inc)
585 E Holt Ave
Pomona CA 91767
909 620-2051

(P-24891)
COLUSA INDIAN CMNTY COUNCIL
Also Called: Colusa Casino
3740 Highway 45, Colusa (95932-4030)
PHONE...............................530 458-6572
Laurie Costa, *Director*
Tammy Harris, *Human Res Mgr*
EMP: 650 **Privately Held**
WEB: www.colusacasino.com
SIC: 8399 7991 Community development groups; health club
PA: Colusa Indian Community Council
3730 State Highway 45 B
Colusa CA 95932
530 458-8231

(P-24892)
COMMUNICATION SVC FOR DEAF INC
Also Called: Community Services For Deaf
81 W March Ln, Stockton (95207-5723)
PHONE...............................209 475-5000
Rhasan Waser, *Manager*
EMP: 50
SALES (corp-wide): 27MM **Privately Held**
WEB: www.relaysd.com
SIC: 8399 Social service information exchange
PA: Communication Service For The Deaf, Inc.
200 W C Chavez St 650
Austin TX 78701
844 222-0002

(P-24893)
COMMUNITY ACTION COMMSN SANTA
4545 10th St, Guadalupe (93434-1421)
PHONE...............................805 343-0615
Fran Forman, *Exec Dir*
EMP: 122
SALES (corp-wide): 22.1MM **Privately Held**
SIC: 8399 Community action agency
PA: Community Action Commission Of
Santa Barbara County
5638 Hollister Ave # 230
Goleta CA 93117
805 964-8857

(P-24894)
COMMUNITY ACTION COMMSN SANTA
1890 Sandalwood Dr, Santa Maria (93455-2846)
PHONE...............................805 614-0786
Fax: 805 928-0198
Mary Flores, *Branch Mgr*
EMP: 400

SALES (corp-wide): 22.1MM **Privately Held**
WEB: www.cacsb.com
SIC: 8399 8322 Community action agency; individual & family services
PA: Community Action Commission Of
Santa Barbara County
5638 Hollister Ave # 230
Goleta CA 93117
805 964-8857

(P-24895)
COMMUNITY ACTION COMMSN SANTA (PA)
Also Called: C A C
5638 Hollister Ave # 230, Goleta (93117-3474)
PHONE...............................805 964-8857
Fran Forman, *President*
Cassandra Hart, *Exec Dir*
Cesar Arroyo, *Program Mgr*
Linda Wilkes, *Regional Mgr*
Jackie Nix, *Office Mgr*
EMP: 50
SALES: 22.1MM **Privately Held**
WEB: www.cacsb.com
SIC: 8399 Community action agency

(P-24896)
COMMUNITY ACTION COMMSN SANTA
201 W Chapel St, Santa Maria (93458-4303)
PHONE...............................805 922-2243
Fax: 805 349-8165
Maggie Espinosa, *Manager*
Maggie Espinoza, *Manager*
EMP: 60
SALES (corp-wide): 22.1MM **Privately Held**
WEB: www.cacsb.com
SIC: 8399 Community development groups
PA: Community Action Commission Of
Santa Barbara County
5638 Hollister Ave # 230
Goleta CA 93117
805 964-8857

(P-24897)
COMMUNITY ACTION PARTNERSHIP O
141 Stony Cir Ste 210, Santa Rosa (95401-4142)
PHONE...............................707 544-0120
Oscar Chavez, *President*
Karen Erickson, *Vice Pres*
Autumn Buss, *Program Mgr*
Joan Michler, *Administration*
Teri McClanahan, *Info Tech Mgr*
EMP: 226
SQ FT: 18,000
SALES: 9.4MM **Privately Held**
WEB: www.fhosc.org
SIC: 8399 Antipoverty board; community action agency

(P-24898)
COMMUNITY ACTION PARTNR KERN
2400 Truxtun Ave, Bakersfield (93301-3405)
PHONE...............................661 336-0317
EMP: 86
SALES (corp-wide): 63.1MM **Privately Held**
SIC: 8399 8351 Community action agency; preschool center
PA: Community Action Partnership Of Kern
5005 Business Park N
Bakersfield CA 93309
661 336-5236

(P-24899)
COMMUNITY ACTION PARTNR KERN
814 N Norma St, Ridgecrest (93555-3509)
PHONE...............................760 371-1469
Maria Harley, *Branch Mgr*
EMP: 143
SALES (corp-wide): 63.1MM **Privately Held**
SIC: 8399 8351 Community action agency; child day care services

PA: Community Action Partnership Of Kern
5005 Business Park N
Bakersfield CA 93309
661 336-5236

(P-24900)
COMMUNITY PARTNERS (PA)
1000 N Alameda St Ste 240, Los Angeles (90012-1804)
PHONE...............................213 346-3200
Fax: 213 439-9650
Paul Vandeventer, *President*
Gary Erickson, *Ch of Bd*
Bill Babiez, *CFO*
Janet Elliot, *CFO*
Janet Elliott, *CFO*
EMP: 86
SALES: 30.5MM **Privately Held**
WEB: www.communitypartners.org
SIC: 8399 Social service information exchange

(P-24901)
CONGRGTNAL CH RETIREMENT CMNTY
Also Called: Auburn Ravine Terrace
750 Auburn Ravine Rd, Auburn (95603-3820)
PHONE...............................530 823-6131
Fax: 530 823-9510
Deborah Stouff, *Admin Sec*
Robert Mauer, *General Mgr*
Lynn Wilson-Hilliard, *Office Mgr*
EMP: 85
SALES: 6.9MM **Privately Held**
SIC: 8399 Advocacy group

(P-24902)
CONTRA CSTA CHILD CARE COUNCIL (PA)
1035 Detroit Ave Ste 200, Concord (94518-2478)
PHONE...............................925 676-5442
Catherine Ertz-Berger, *Director*
Rowena Hernandez, *Senior VP*
Deedee Carson, *Admin Sec*
Susan Santiago, *Admin Asst*
William S Ingram, *Technology*
EMP: 50 EST: 1976
SALES: 20MM **Privately Held**
WEB: www.cocokids.org
SIC: 8399 8351 Community action agency; child day care services

(P-24903)
CONTRA CSTA CHILD CARE COUNCIL
2280 Diamond Blvd Ste 500, Concord (94520-5719)
PHONE...............................925 676-5437
Fax: 925 676-6283
June Harrison, *Manager*
EMP: 100
SALES (corp-wide): 20MM **Privately Held**
WEB: www.cocokids.org
SIC: 8399 8351 Community action agency; child day care services
PA: Contra Costa Child Care Council
1035 Detroit Ave Ste 200
Concord CA 94518
925 676-5442

(P-24904)
COUNTY OF DEL NORTE
Also Called: Health and Human Service
880 Northcrest Dr, Crescent City (95531-2313)
PHONE...............................707 464-3191
Fax: 707 465-1783
Gary Blatnick, *Director*
Jeanne M Riecke, *Manager*
Jocelyn Woodral, *Supervisor*
EMP: 120 **Privately Held**
SIC: 8399 Health systems agency
PA: County Of Del Norte
981 H St Ste 200
Crescent City CA 95531
707 464-7204

(P-24905)
COUNTY OF KERN
Also Called: Human Services Dept
100 E California Ave, Bakersfield (93307-1031)
P.O. Box 511 (93302-0511)
PHONE...............................661 631-6346
Kathleen Irvine, *Director*
Devron Kidwell, *Manager*
EMP: 800 **Privately Held**
WEB: www.kccfc.org
SIC: 8399 9199 Health & welfare council; general government administration
PA: County Of Kern
1115 Truxtun Ave Rm 505
Bakersfield CA 93301
661 868-3690

(P-24906)
COUNTY OF LOS ANGELES
Also Called: Health Services, Dept of
5555 Ferguson Dr, Commerce (90022-5164)
PHONE...............................323 869-7063
Angie Toyota, *Manager*
EMP: 75 **Privately Held**
WEB: www.co.la.ca.us
SIC: 8399 9431 Health systems agency; administration of public health programs;
PA: County Of Los Angeles
500 W Temple Ste 375
Los Angeles CA 90012
213 974-1101

(P-24907)
COUNTY OF LOS ANGELES
Also Called: Department Public Social Svcs
8130 Atlantic Ave, Cudahy (90201-5804)
PHONE...............................323 560-5001
Fax: 323 560-0575
Lilia Erviti, *Director*
EMP: 220 **Privately Held**
SIC: 8399 Community development groups
PA: County Of Los Angeles
500 W Temple Ste 375
Los Angeles CA 90012
213 974-1101

(P-24908)
COUNTY OF MONTEREY
Also Called: Health Department
1270 Natividad Rd, Salinas (93906-3122)
PHONE...............................831 755-4500
Len Foster, *Manager*
David Mesa, *Finance Mgr*
John Ramirez, *Manager*
EMP: 50 **Privately Held**
WEB: www.montereycountyfarmbureau.org
SIC: 8399 9111 Health & welfare council; county supervisors' & executives' offices
PA: County Of Monterey
168 W Alisal St Fl 3
Salinas CA 93901
831 755-5040

(P-24909)
COUNTY OF RIVERSIDE
Also Called: Community Health Agency
4065 County Circle Dr, Riverside (92503-3410)
P.O. Box 7600 (92513-7600)
PHONE...............................951 358-5306
Gary Feldman, *Director*
EMP: 400 **Privately Held**
SIC: 8399 9511 Health systems agency;
PA: County Of Riverside
4080 Lemon St Fl 11
Riverside CA 92501
951 955-1110

(P-24910)
COUNTY OF SAN JOAQUIN
Also Called: Neighborhood Preservation Div
1810 E Hazelton Ave, Stockton (95205-6232)
PHONE...............................209 468-3021
Carrie Sullivan, *Director*
EMP: 60 **Privately Held**
WEB: www.sjclawlib.org
SIC: 8399 9441 Community development groups; public welfare administration: non-operating, government
PA: County Of San Joaquin
44 N San Joaquin St # 640
Stockton CA 95202
209 468-3203

(P-24911)
COUNTY OF STANISLAUS
Also Called: Behavioral Hlth Recovery Svcs
800 Scenic Dr, Modesto (95350-6131)
PHONE....................................209 525-6225
Denise C Hunt, *Director*
EMP: 99 **Privately Held**
WEB: www.co.stanislaus.ca.us
SIC: 8399 Health & welfare council
PA: County Of Stanislaus
1010 10th St Ste 5100
Modesto CA 95354
209 525-6398

(P-24912)
DESERT AREA RESOURCES TRAINING
Also Called: Early Childhood Services
201 E Ridgecrest Blvd, Ridgecrest (93555-3919)
PHONE....................................760 375-8494
Fax: 760 375-1288
EMP: 70
SALES (est): 619.4K **Privately Held**
SIC: 8399

(P-24913)
DEVEREUX FOUNDATION
Also Called: Devereux California Center
7055 Seaway Dr, Goleta (93117-4358)
P.O. Box 6784, Santa Barbara (93160-6784)
PHONE....................................805 968-2525
Fax: 805 968-8575
Amy Evans, *Principal*
Shawna Johnson, *Assistant*
EMP: 400
SALES (corp-wide): 391.5MM **Privately Held**
SIC: 8399 Social change association
PA: Devereux Foundation
444 Devereux Dr
Villanova PA 19085
610 520-3000

(P-24914)
DREW HEALTH FOUNDATION
1191 Runnymede St, East Palo Alto (94303-1331)
P.O. Box 50997, Palo Alto (94303-0678)
PHONE....................................650 328-1619
Myrtle Walker, *President*
Ora Johnson, *Manager*
EMP: 50
SQ FT: 84,000
SALES: 53K **Privately Held**
SIC: 8399 Health & welfare council; health systems agency

(P-24915)
EAST BAY COMMUNITY FOUNDATION
Also Called: E B C F
200 Frank H Ogawa Plz, Oakland (94612-2005)
PHONE....................................510 836-3223
Fax: 510 836-3287
Nichole Taylor, *President*
Robert R Davenport III, *Managing Prtnr*
Karen Stevenson, *President*
Ted Liebst, *CFO*
Ernest S Leopold, *Treasurer*
EMP: 55
SQ FT: 15,500
SALES: 21.5MM **Privately Held**
WEB: www.eastbaycf.org
SIC: 8399 Community development groups

(P-24916)
EASTER SEALS SOUTHERN CAL INC
710 W Broadway, Glendale (91204-1010)
PHONE....................................818 551-0128
Fax: 818 551-9846
Gloria Acosta, *Director*
Mary Hoskin, *Executive*
EMP: 80
SALES (corp-wide): 108.9MM **Privately Held**
WEB: www.essc.org
SIC: 8399 8322 Fund raising organization, non-fee basis; individual & family services
PA: Easter Seals Southern California, Inc.
1570 E 17th St
Santa Ana CA 92705
714 834-1111

(P-24917)
EASTER SEALS SOUTHERN CAL INC
Also Called: Easter Seal Society
340 E Avenue I Ste 101, Lancaster (93535-1941)
PHONE....................................661 723-3414
Fax: 661 729-3318
Paula Pompa-Craven, *Director*
EMP: 50
SALES (corp-wide): 108.9MM **Privately Held**
WEB: www.essc.org
SIC: 8399 8322 Fund raising organization, non-fee basis; individual & family services
PA: Easter Seals Southern California, Inc.
1570 E 17th St
Santa Ana CA 92705
714 834-1111

(P-24918)
EDUCATION PROGRAM ASSOCIATES
1 W Campbell Ave 45e, Campbell (95008-1004)
PHONE....................................408 374-3720
Margie Fites-Siegel, *CEO*
EMP: 55
SALES (est): 649.9K
SALES (corp-wide): 25.1MM **Privately Held**
SIC: 8399 Health & welfare council
PA: California Family Health Council, Inc.
3600 Wilshire Blvd # 600
Los Angeles CA 90010
213 386-5614

(P-24919)
EL SEGUNDO EDUCTL FOUNDATION
641 Sheldon St, El Segundo (90245-3036)
P.O. Box 591 (90245)
PHONE....................................310 615-2650
Duane Conover, *President*
Alex Abad, *Vice Chairman*
Geoff Yantz, *Superintendent*
EMP: 300
SALES: 1.6MM **Privately Held**
SIC: 8399 Fund raising organization, non-fee basis

(P-24920)
ETHIOPIAN WORLD FEDERATION
422 E 41st St, Los Angeles (90011-2906)
PHONE....................................323 844-1826
Enoch Nack, *Principal*
EMP: 50
SALES (est): 3.7MM **Privately Held**
SIC: 8399 Social services

(P-24921)
FRIENDS FITZGERALD MAR RESERVE
Also Called: F F M L R
200 Nevada Ave, Moss Beach (94038-9615)
P.O. Box 669 (94038-0669)
PHONE....................................650 728-3584
Mary Wolfe, *Admin Sec*
Mary Delong, *President*
EMP: 70
SALES (est): 3.3MM **Privately Held**
WEB: www.fitzgeraldreserve.org
SIC: 8399 Social service information exchange

(P-24922)
FRIENDS OF THE LOS ANGELES
8405 Beverly Blvd, Los Angeles (90048-3401)
PHONE....................................323 653-0440
Stanley Toy, *President*
Daniel Beasley, *Treasurer*
Lisa Gritzner, *Vice Pres*
Meredith Weiss, *Admin Sec*
Jeffrey Bujer, *Agent*
EMP: 200

SALES: 2.4MM **Privately Held**
SIC: 8399 Fund raising organization, non-fee basis

(P-24923)
GOLD COUNTRY HEALTH CENTER INC (PA)
4301 Golden Center Dr, Placerville (95667-6260)
PHONE....................................530 621-1100
Fax: 530 621-1104
Suzanne Valoppi, *Administration*
EMP: 130
SQ FT: 57,000
SALES (est): 8.2MM **Privately Held**
SIC: 8399 Health & welfare council

(P-24924)
GREATER LOS ANGELES ZOO ASSN
Also Called: Glaza
5333 Zoo Dr, Los Angeles (90027-1451)
PHONE....................................323 644-4200
Connie M Morgan, *President*
Jeb Bonner, *CFO*
Robert N Ruth, *Treasurer*
Eugenia Vasels, *Vice Pres*
Genie Vasels, *Vice Pres*
EMP: 100
SQ FT: 8,200
SALES: 13.2MM **Privately Held**
SIC: 8399 7999 Fund raising organization, non-fee basis; concession operator

(P-24925)
HABITAT FOR HUMANITY OF GREATE
8739 Artesia Blvd, Bellflower (90706-6330)
PHONE....................................310 323-4663
Fax: 310 323-0789
Erin Garrity Rank, *President*
Mark Van Lue, *COO*
Gia Stokes, *CFO*
Veronica Garcia, *Vice Pres*
Alison Treleaven J, *Vice Pres*
EMP: 50
SALES: 33.2MM **Privately Held**
WEB: www.habitatla.org
SIC: 8399 Fund raising organization, non-fee basis

(P-24926)
HARBOR DEVELOPMENTAL DISABILIT
Also Called: Harbor Regional Center
21231 Hawthorne Blvd, Torrance (90503-5501)
P.O. Box 2930 (90509-2930)
PHONE....................................310 540-1711
Fax: 310 540-9538
Patricia Del Monico, *Principal*
Judy Wada, *CFO*
Audrey Clurfeld, *Program Mgr*
Liz Cohen-Zeboulon, *Program Mgr*
Steve Hankow, *Program Mgr*
EMP: 225
SQ FT: 60,000
SALES: 152.2MM **Privately Held**
SIC: 8399 Council for social agency

(P-24927)
HEALTH ADVOCATES LLC
14721 Califa St, Van Nuys (91411-3107)
PHONE....................................818 995-9500
Al Leibovic, *Mng Member*
AVI Leibovic, *Info Tech Mgr*
Aaron Leibovic, *Mng Member*
EMP: 371
SQ FT: 40,900
SALES (est): 20MM **Privately Held**
SIC: 8399 Advocacy group

(P-24928)
HOSPITAL ASSN SOUTHERN CAL (PA)
Also Called: Hasc
515 S Figueroa St # 1300, Los Angeles (90071-3301)
PHONE....................................213 347-2002
Fax: 213 629-4272
Jim Barber, *CEO*
Roger Seaver, *Ch of Bd*
Scott Toomey, *CFO*
Martin Gallegos, *Senior VP*
Jennifer Bayer, *Vice Pres*

EMP: 58
SQ FT: 30,000
SALES (est): 7.8MM **Privately Held**
WEB: www.reddinet.com
SIC: 8399 Advocacy group

(P-24929)
IAS ADMINISTRATIONS INC
1311 N New Hampshire Ave, Los Angeles (90027-6001)
PHONE....................................323 953-3490
Deborah Fraser, *President*
Mislav Raos, *Treasurer*
Terence Macmahon, *Admin Sec*
EMP: 65
SALES (est): 4.4MM **Privately Held**
SIC: 8399 7997 8999 8743 Fund raising organization, non-fee basis; country club; membership; writing for publication; promotion service

(P-24930)
JAPANESE CMNTY YOUTH COUNCIL (PA)
Also Called: CHIBI CHAN PRESCHOOL
2012 Pine St, San Francisco (94115-2899)
PHONE....................................415 202-7905
John Osaki, *Exec Dir*
Ayumi Sohn, *Bd of Directors*
David Ujita, *Bd of Directors*
Idries Aziz-Pearson, *Associate Dir*
Derrick Lee, *Office Admin*
EMP: 60
SQ FT: 4,000
SALES: 10.7MM **Privately Held**
SIC: 8399 Community development groups

(P-24931)
JEWISH COMMUNITY FEDRTN SAN FR (PA)
121 Steuart St Fl 7, San Francisco (94105-1280)
PHONE....................................415 777-0411
Fax: 415 495-6635
Jennifer Gorvitz, *CEO*
Bill Powers, *CFO*
Carol Weitz, *Vice Pres*
Bab Freiberg, *Associate Dir*
Kevin Ho, *Info Tech Mgr*
EMP: 70
SQ FT: 50,000
SALES: 136MM **Privately Held**
SIC: 8399 Fund raising organization, non-fee basis

(P-24932)
KCRW FOUNDATION INC
Also Called: Kcrw FM Radio
1900 Pico Blvd, Santa Monica (90405-1628)
PHONE....................................310 450-5183
Fax: 310 450-7172
Jennifer Ferro, *CEO*
Herbert Roney, *Treasurer*
Tom Wertheimer, *Treasurer*
Warren Olney, *Social Dir*
Kaitlin Parker, *Producer*
EMP: 51
SQ FT: 4,000
SALES: 16.8MM **Privately Held**
SIC: 8399 Fund raising organization, non-fee basis

(P-24933)
KEVIN HOLUBOWSKI LLC
7462 Denrock Ave, Los Angeles (90045-1022)
PHONE....................................310 908-6542
Kevin Holubowski,
EMP: 103
SALES (est): 423.7K **Privately Held**
SIC: 8399 Social services

(P-24934)
KEYSTONE NPS LLC (DH)
Also Called: Keystone Schools-Ramona
11980 Mount Vernon Ave, Grand Terrace (92313-5172)
PHONE....................................909 633-6354
Alfredo Alvarado, *Principal*
Don Whitfield, *CFO*
Martha Petrey, *Exec VP*
EMP: 100
SALES (est): 18.3MM
SALES (corp-wide): 9B **Publicly Held**
SIC: 8399 Advocacy group

8399 - Social Services, NEC County (P-24935)

HQ: Children's Comprehensive Services, Inc.
3401 West End Ave Ste 400
Nashville TN 37203
615 250-0000

(P-24935)
KIPP FOUNDATION
135 Main St Ste 1700, San Francisco (94105-1850)
PHONE..............................415 399-1556
Richard Barth, *CEO*
Tarun Bhatia, *CFO*
Jack Chorowsky, *CFO*
Tina Sachs, *CFO*
Anne Patterson, *Exec Dir*
EMP: 110
SQ FT: 10,000
SALES: 64.8MM Privately Held
SIC: 8399 Fund raising organization, non-fee basis

(P-24936)
LAKE ARROWHEAD CMNTY SVCS DST
6727 Arrowhead Lake Rd, Hesperia (92345-9343)
P.O. Box 700, Lake Arrowhead (92352-0700)
PHONE..............................909 337-6395
Bob Bobki, *Branch Mgr*
Francisco Izeta, *Foreman/Supr*
Scott Schroder, *Manager*
EMP: 50
SALES (corp-wide): 12.5MM Privately Held
WEB: www.lakearrowheadcsd.com
SIC: 8399 Advocacy group
PA: Lake Arrowhead Community Services District
28200 Highway 189
Lake Arrowhead CA 92352
909 336-1359

(P-24937)
LAWRENCE FAMILY JEWISH COMMU (PA)
4126 Executive Dr, La Jolla (92037-1348)
PHONE..............................858 362-1144
Fax: 858 457-2422
Craig Schluss, *President*
David Wax, *President*
Nancy Johnson, *CFO*
Susan Villeria, *Executive*
Laura Strafaci, *Asst Controller*
EMP: 150 **EST:** 1945
SALES: 9.4MM Privately Held
WEB: www.lfjcc.com
SIC: 8399 8351 Community development groups; child day care services

(P-24938)
LIFESPAN INC
Also Called: Lifespan Care Management Agcy
600 Frederick St, Santa Cruz (95062-2203)
PHONE..............................831 469-4900
Fax: 831 469-4950
Pamela Goodman, *President*
Pam Goodman, *President*
Monica Pielage, *Office Mgr*
Kirstie Kew, *Financial Exec*
Becky Peters, *Sales Associate*
EMP: 90
SALES (est): 3.6MM Privately Held
WEB: www.lifespancare.com
SIC: 8399 8082 Health systems agency; home health care services

(P-24939)
LONG BEACH CMNTY ACTION PARTNR
Also Called: LONG BEACH CAP
117 W Victoria St, Long Beach (90805-2162)
PHONE..............................562 216-4600
Darrick Simpson, *Exec Dir*
Janet McCarthy, *Ch of Bd*
Mary Sramek, *Treasurer*
Baty Amit, *Principal*
Stacey Lewis, *Admin Sec*
EMP: 110
SQ FT: 10,000
SALES: 7MM Privately Held
WEB: www.lbcaa.org
SIC: 8399 Antipoverty board

(P-24940)
LOS ANGELES LGBT CENTER (PA)
Also Called: L.A. Gay & Lesbian Center
1625 Schrader Blvd, Los Angeles (90028-6213)
P.O. Box 2988 (90078-2988)
PHONE..............................323 993-7618
Fax: 323 308-4449
Lorri L Jean, *CEO*
Randy Hogan, *CFO*
Michael Holtzman, *CFO*
Mike Holtzman, *CFO*
Darrel Cummings, *Officer*
EMP: 148
SQ FT: 45,000
SALES: 81MM Privately Held
WEB: www.lagaycenter.org
SIC: 8399 Community development groups

(P-24941)
MCKINLEY HOME FOUNDATION
762 Cypress St, San Dimas (91773-3505)
PHONE..............................909 599-1227
Victor Liotta, *President*
Joanne Gilby, *Controller*
EMP: 100
SQ FT: 8,055
SALES: 2.1MM Privately Held
SIC: 8399 6519 Fund raising organization, non-fee basis; landholding office

(P-24942)
MIRAMNTE HIGH SCHL PARENTS CLB
750 Moraga Way, Orinda (94563-4330)
PHONE..............................925 280-3965
Raul Zamora, *Principal*
Catherine Corn, *President*
Peter Clauson, *Chairman*
Dr Craig Dennis, *Treasurer*
Dixie Mohan, *Vice Pres*
EMP: 130
SALES: 450K Privately Held
SIC: 8399 Fund raising organization, non-fee basis

(P-24943)
MOMENTUM FOR MENTAL HEALTH
Also Called: Maccarthy House
2001 The Alameda, San Jose (95126-1136)
PHONE..............................408 261-7777
Paul S Taylor, *CEO*
Flo Laflamme, *Info Tech Mgr*
Ross Luntayao, *Technician*
Jackson Rowland, *Psychiatry*
EMP: 100
SALES (corp-wide): 33.6MM Privately Held
WEB: www.alliance4care.org
SIC: 8399 8093 8322 Health systems agency; specialty outpatient clinics; individual & family services
PA: Momentum For Mental Health
438 N White Rd
San Jose CA 95127
408 254-6828

(P-24944)
MORALE WELFARE RECREATION FUND
4260 Gigling Rd, Seaside (93955-6300)
PHONE..............................831 242-6631
Bob Emanuel, *President*
EMP: 200
SALES (est): 9.1MM Privately Held
SIC: 8399 Fund raising organization, non-fee basis

(P-24945)
NEVER IGNORE KIDS EDUCATION
2785 Pacific Coast Hwy # 356, Torrance (90505-7066)
PHONE..............................310 984-6847
Rashaad Lassiter, *CEO*
EMP: 68
SALES: 950K Privately Held
SIC: 8399 Social services

(P-24946)
NEW ADVANCES FOR PEOPLE DISABI
Also Called: Center For Achievement Center
1120 21st St, Bakersfield (93301-4613)
PHONE..............................661 327-0188
Fax: 661 325-8229
Linda Waninger, *Manager*
Deran Smith, *Director*
EMP: 60
SALES (corp-wide): 7MM Privately Held
SIC: 8399 Community development groups
PA: New Advances For People With Disabilities
2601 F St
Bakersfield CA 93301
661 395-1361

(P-24947)
NEXT DOOR SLTONS TO DOM VLENCE
234 E Gish Rd Ste 200, San Jose (95112-4724)
PHONE..............................408 279-2962
Fax: 408 441-7562
Kathleen Krenek, *Exec Dir*
Wayne Mascia, *President*
Margarita R Alcantar, *Exec Dir*
Joe Strizich, *Software Engr*
Susan McInnis, *Finance*
EMP: 80
SQ FT: 4,100
SALES: 2.8MM Privately Held
WEB: www.nextdoor.org
SIC: 8399 8322 Advocacy group; social change association; individual & family services

(P-24948)
NEXTDOORCOM INC
760 Market St Ste 300, San Francisco (94102-2404)
PHONE..............................415 236-0000
Nirav Tolia, *CEO*
Prakash Janakiraman, *Vice Pres*
Minna King, *Vice Pres*
Sarah Leary, *Vice Pres*
Kip Kaehler, *Software Engr*
EMP: 100
SALES (est): 9.2MM Privately Held
SIC: 8399 2741 7371 Social service information exchange; miscellaneous publishing; computer software development & applications

(P-24949)
NORTHERN CALIFORNIA INSTITUTE
Also Called: Ncire
4150 Clement St, San Francisco (94121-1545)
PHONE..............................415 750-6954
Fax: 415 750-9358
Robert Obana, *Exec Dir*
Judy Yee, *Ch Radiology*
Stephen Morange, *CFO*
Renee Binder, *Bd of Directors*
Lilly Bourguignon, *Bd of Directors*
EMP: 300
SQ FT: 1,650
SALES: 44.3MM Privately Held
SIC: 8399 8741 Fund raising organization, non-fee basis; management services

(P-24950)
ON THE MOVE
780 Lincoln Ave, NAPA (94558-5110)
PHONE..............................707 251-9432
Leslie Medine, *Exec Dir*
Diana Gordon, *CFO*
EMP: 50
SALES: 3.3MM Privately Held
SIC: 8399 Social services

(P-24951)
ORENDA CENTER
1430 Neotomas Ave, Santa Rosa (95405-7575)
PHONE..............................707 565-7450
Gino Giannavio, *Director*
Gino Ginannavioa, *Director*
EMP: 60
SALES (est): 970.6K Privately Held
SIC: 8399 Health systems agency

(P-24952)
PENNY LANE CENTERS (PA)
15305 Rayen St, North Hills (91343-5117)
P.O. Box 2548 (91393-2548)
PHONE..............................818 892-3423
Arthur Barr, *President*
Ivelise Markovits, *Exec Dir*
Patricia Robles, *QA Dir*
Lee Overson, *Technology*
Cindy Sanchez, *Recruiter*
EMP: 275
SQ FT: 7,000
SALES (est): 53MM Privately Held
WEB: www.pennylane.org
SIC: 8399 Social service information exchange

(P-24953)
PENNY LANE CENTERS
15317 Rayen St, North Hills (91343-5198)
PHONE..............................818 892-3423
Ivelise Markovits, *Branch Mgr*
Theresa Chavez, *Human Resources*
Peter Padin, *Hlthcr Dir*
EMP: 166
SALES (corp-wide): 53MM Privately Held
SIC: 8399 Social service information exchange
PA: Penny Lane Centers
15305 Rayen St
North Hills CA 91343
818 892-3423

(P-24954)
PENNY LANE CENTERS
Valley High School
15317 Rayen St, North Hills (91343-5198)
PHONE..............................818 892-3423
Shawn Welch, *Principal*
EMP: 170
SALES (corp-wide): 53MM Privately Held
WEB: www.pennylane.org
SIC: 8399 Social service information exchange
PA: Penny Lane Centers
15305 Rayen St
North Hills CA 91343
818 892-3423

(P-24955)
PENNY LANE CENTERS
10330 Pioneer Blvd # 290, Santa Fe Springs (90670-8279)
PHONE..............................562 903-4135
Fax: 562 941-6984
Lily Amezqua, *Manager*
EMP: 170
SALES (corp-wide): 53MM Privately Held
SIC: 8399 Social service information exchange
PA: Penny Lane Centers
15305 Rayen St
North Hills CA 91343
818 892-3423

(P-24956)
PENNY LANE CENTERS
15331 Rayen St, North Hills (91343-5117)
PHONE..............................818 892-3423
Ivelise Markovits, *Branch Mgr*
EMP: 170
SALES (corp-wide): 53MM Privately Held
WEB: www.pennylane.org
SIC: 8399 Social service information exchange
PA: Penny Lane Centers
15305 Rayen St
North Hills CA 91343
818 892-3423

(P-24957)
PENNY LANE CENTERS
15305 Ranch St, North Hills (91343)
PHONE..............................818 894-9162
Ive Maikovits, *President*
EMP: 170
SALES (corp-wide): 53MM Privately Held
SIC: 8399 Social service information exchange

PA: Penny Lane Centers
15305 Rayen St
North Hills CA 91343
818 892-3423

(P-24958)
PENNY LANE CENTERS
15302 Rayen St, North Hills (91343-5118)
PHONE.................................818 892-1112
Fax: 818 892-9723
Evy Markovits, *Manager*
EMP: 170
SALES (corp-wide): 53MM **Privately Held**
SIC: 8399 Social service information exchange
PA: Penny Lane Centers
15305 Rayen St
North Hills CA 91343
818 892-3423

(P-24959)
PENNY LANE CENTERS
15256 Acre St, North Hills (91343-5256)
PHONE.................................818 892-3423
EMP: 170
SALES (corp-wide): 53MM **Privately Held**
SIC: 8399 Social service information exchange
PA: Penny Lane Centers
15305 Rayen St
North Hills CA 91343
818 892-3423

(P-24960)
PENNY LANE CENTERS
1020 E Palmdale Blvd, Palmdale (93550-4756)
PHONE.................................818 892-3423
EMP: 170
SALES (corp-wide): 53MM **Privately Held**
SIC: 8399 Social service information exchange
PA: Penny Lane Centers
15305 Rayen St
North Hills CA 91343
818 892-3423

(P-24961)
PENNY LANE CENTERS
2450 S Atl Blvd Ste 101, Commerce (90040)
PHONE.................................323 318-9960
Rosana La Fianza, *Branch Mgr*
EMP: 170
SALES (corp-wide): 53MM **Privately Held**
SIC: 8399 Health & welfare council
PA: Penny Lane Centers
15305 Rayen St
North Hills CA 91343
818 892-3423

(P-24962)
PENNY LANE CENTERS
43520 Division St, Lancaster (93535-4089)
PHONE.................................661 274-0770
Elizabeth Bedoya, *Branch Mgr*
Rosana La Fianza, *Director*
EMP: 170
SALES (corp-wide): 53MM **Privately Held**
SIC: 8399 Social service information exchange
PA: Penny Lane Centers
15305 Rayen St
North Hills CA 91343
818 892-3423

(P-24963)
PENNY LANE CENTERS
44248 44258 Cedar Ave, Lancaster (93534)
PHONE.................................818 892-3423
EMP: 170
SALES (corp-wide): 53MM **Privately Held**
SIC: 8399 Social service information exchange
PA: Penny Lane Centers
15305 Rayen St
North Hills CA 91343
818 892-3423

(P-24964)
PERMANENTE KAISER INTL
156 Acacia Glen Dr, Riverside (92506-6202)
PHONE.................................951 662-8194
EMP: 128
SALES (corp-wide): 380.5MM **Privately Held**
SIC: 8399 7389 Community development groups;
PA: Kaiser Permanente International
1 Kaiser Plz
Oakland CA 94612
510 271-5910

(P-24965)
PROVIDENCE HEALTH & SERVICES F
Also Called: PROVIDENCE HOLY CROSS FOUNDATI
501 S Buena Vista St, Burbank (91505-4809)
PHONE.................................818 843-5111
Patricia Modrzejewski, *CEO*
Julie Sprengel, *COO*
James Reiner, *CFO*
Lee Kanon Alpert, *Chairman*
Debbie Burton, *Vice Pres*
EMP: 2000
SALES: 21.4MM **Privately Held**
SIC: 8399 Fund raising organization, non-fee basis

(P-24966)
REACHING FOR INDEPENDENCE INC
609 14th St, Fortuna (95540-2464)
PHONE.................................707 725-9010
Jeffrey Pockett, *Exec Dir*
EMP: 66 EST: 2008
SALES: 1.2MM **Privately Held**
SIC: 8399 Community development groups

(P-24967)
RESOURCE CONNECTION OF AMADOR (PA)
Also Called: RESOURCE CONNECTION, THE
444 E Saint Charles St, San Andreas (95249-9658)
P.O. Box 919 (95249-0919)
PHONE.................................209 754-3114
Linda Foster, *Ch of Bd*
Misty Clayton, *Bd of Directors*
Amber Shelton, *Principal*
Kelli Fraguero, *Admin Dir*
Arleen Garland, *Program Dir*
EMP: 52
SALES: 6.8MM **Privately Held**
WEB: www.theresourceconnection.net
SIC: 8399 Health & welfare council

(P-24968)
RIO HONDO COMMUNITY DEV CORP
11706 Ramona Blvd Ste 107, El Monte (91732-2300)
PHONE.................................626 401-2784
Donna L Duncan, *President*
Tom Morgan, *Director*
EMP: 57
SALES: 306K **Privately Held**
SIC: 8399 Community development groups

(P-24969)
ROMAN CTHLIC BSHP OF SNTA ROSA
987 Airway Ct, Santa Rosa (95403-2048)
P.O. Box 4900 (95402-4900)
PHONE.................................707 528-8712
Len Marabella, *Branch Mgr*
Marla A Gullickson CP, *Treasurer*
Angie Moeller, *Principal*
Maureen E Shaw, *Exec Dir*
Michelle Sawyer, *General Mgr*
EMP: 110
SALES (corp-wide): 8.1MM **Privately Held**
SIC: 8399 Social service information exchange
PA: Roman Catholic Bishop Of Santa Rosa, The
985 Airway Ct
Santa Rosa CA 95403
707 545-7610

(P-24970)
ROSE & KINDEL GRAYLING
1414 K St Ste 220, Sacramento (95814-3967)
PHONE.................................916 441-1034
Fax: 916 444-9362
Carl London, *CEO*
Peter Harris, *Senior Mgr*
EMP: 200
SQ FT: 4,000
SALES (est): 2.7MM **Privately Held**
SIC: 8399 Advocacy group

(P-24971)
SAFE HARBOR INTL RELIEF
30615 Avnida De Las Flres, Rancho Santa Margari (92688)
P.O. Box 80820, Rcho STA Marg (92688-0820)
PHONE.................................949 858-6786
Gary Kusunoki, *CEO*
David Kruckenberg, *Principal*
Annette Namatovu, *Nursing Dir*
EMP: 50
SALES: 110.9K **Privately Held**
SIC: 8399 Social services

(P-24972)
SAINT JUSTIN EDUCATION FU
Also Called: IN TOUCH LEADERSHIP PROJECT
2415 Shoredale Ave, Los Angeles (90031-1120)
P.O. Box 27790 (90027-0790)
PHONE.................................323 221-3400
Gary Krauss, *CEO*
EMP: 51 EST: 1992
SALES: 444.2K **Privately Held**
SIC: 8399 Fund raising organization, non-fee basis

(P-24973)
SALVATION ARMY
3755 N Freeway Blvd, Sacramento (95834-1926)
P.O. Box 348000 (95834-8000)
PHONE.................................916 563-3700
Fax: 916 648-0535
Mjr Frank Brown, *Principal*
Steven T Rice, *Commissioner*
David Bentley, *Director*
Sarah Bentley, *Director*
Tim Rodriguera, *Director*
EMP: 75
SALES (corp-wide): 4.3B **Privately Held**
WEB: www.salvationarmy.usawest.org
SIC: 8399 Advocacy group
HQ: Western Territorial Of The Salvation Army
180 E Ocean Blvd Fl 2
Long Beach CA 90802
562 264-3600

(P-24974)
SAN DIEGO RESCUE MISSION INC (PA)
Also Called: City Rescue Mission
120 Elm St, San Diego (92101-2602)
P.O. Box 80427 (92138-0427)
PHONE.................................619 819-1880
Herb Johnson, *CEO*
Deborah Krakauer, *Volunteer Dir*
Glen Brush, *Treasurer*
Kimberly K Elliott, *Bd of Directors*
Jeff Fisher, *Bd of Directors*
EMP: 93
SQ FT: 98,000
SALES: 19.7MM **Privately Held**
WEB: www.sdrescue.org
SIC: 8399 5932 8322 Social change association; used merchandise stores; emergency shelters

(P-24975)
SAN FRNCSCO ECON OPRTNTY CNCIL
1426 Fillmore St Ste 301, San Francisco (94115-4164)
PHONE.................................415 749-3798
Nathaniel Mason, *Exec Dir*
EMP: 110 EST: 1964
SALES: 6MM **Privately Held**
SIC: 8399 Health & welfare council

(P-24976)
SAN FRNNDO VLY INTRFITH CUNCIL
8956 Vanalden Ave, Northridge (91324-3753)
PHONE.................................818 885-5220
EMP: 102
SALES (corp-wide): 4.1MM **Privately Held**
SIC: 8399 Council for social agency
PA: San Fernando Valley Interfaith Council, Inc
4505 Las Virgenes Rd
Calabasas CA 91302
818 880-4842

(P-24977)
SILICON VLY EDUCATN FOUNDATION
1400 Parkmoor Ave Ste 200, San Jose (95126-3798)
PHONE.................................408 790-9400
Muhammed Chaudhry, *CEO*
Joanne Chin, *Purch Dir*
Rosemary Kamei, *Director*
EMP: 1000 EST: 1958
SALES: 2.6MM **Privately Held**
WEB: www.fmsd.k12.ca.us
SIC: 8399 Fund raising organization, non-fee basis

(P-24978)
SIX RIVERS PLANNED PARENTHOOD
3225 Timber Fall Ct, Eureka (95503-4892)
P.O. Box 97, Cutten (95534-0097)
PHONE.................................707 442-5700
Denise Danden Boss, *CEO*
EMP: 75
SQ FT: 3,900
SALES: 3.6MM **Privately Held**
SIC: 8399 8322 Community development groups; individual & family services

(P-24979)
SNOWLINE HSPICE EL DORADO CNTY
6520 Pleasant Valley Rd, Diamond Springs (95619-9512)
PHONE.................................530 621-7820
Michael Sehmidt, *Exec Dir*
Richard B Esposito, *President*
William Fisher, *Treasurer*
Jon Lehrman, *Vice Pres*
Leah Hall, *Admin Sec*
EMP: 140
SQ FT: 8,900
SALES: 6.6MM **Privately Held**
SIC: 8399 Health systems agency

(P-24980)
SOUTH CENTRAL LOS (PA)
Also Called: Sclarc
2500 S Western Ave, Los Angeles (90018-2609)
PHONE.................................213 744-7000
Fax: 213 744-8494
Dexter Henderson, *CEO*
Roy Doronila, *COO*
Irma Escobar, *Admin Asst*
Maribel Aguilar, *Accountant*
Robert Johnson, *Controller*
EMP: 52
SQ FT: 110,470
SALES: 160.5MM **Privately Held**
WEB: www.sclarc.org
SIC: 8399 Health & welfare council

(P-24981)
SPECIAL SERVICE FOR GROUPS INC
Also Called: Occupational Therapy Training
19401 S Vt Ave Ste A200, Torrance (90502-4418)
PHONE.................................310 323-6887
Fax: 310 323-1570
Sarah Bream, *Branch Mgr*
EMP: 60
SALES (corp-wide): 57.9MM **Privately Held**
SIC: 8399 8322 Community action agency; individual & family services

8399 - Social Services, NEC County (P-24982) — PRODUCTS & SERVICES SECTION

PA: Special Service For Groups, Inc.
905 E 8th St Unit 1
Los Angeles CA 90021
213 368-1888

(P-24982)
SPECIAL SERVICE FOR GROUPS INC
470 E 3rd St Ste D, Los Angeles (90013-1630)
PHONE..................213 620-5713
EMP: 65
SALES (corp-wide): 57.9MM Privately Held
SIC: 8399 Community action agency
PA: Special Service For Groups, Inc.
905 E 8th St Unit 1
Los Angeles CA 90021
213 368-1888

(P-24983)
STANFORD YOUTH SOLUTIONS (PA)
Also Called: STANFORD & LATHROP MEMORIAL HO
8912 Volunteer Ln, Sacramento (95826-3221)
PHONE..................916 344-0199
Jovina Neves, CFO
Laura Heintz, Principal
Holly Hoppman, Admin Asst
Jennifer Shebesta, Director
Susan Davini, Manager
EMP: 84
SQ FT: 30,000
SALES: 10.4MM Privately Held
SIC: 8399 Community development groups

(P-24984)
TEMPLO CALVARIO CMNTY DEV CORP
2501 W 5th St, Santa Ana (92703-1816)
PHONE..................714 543-3711
Eleazar De Leon, President
Beatriz Santana, Treasurer
Linda Decker, Admin Sec
Armando Arellano, Admin Asst
EMP: 60
SQ FT: 9,000
SALES: 2.9MM Privately Held
SIC: 8399 Community action agency

(P-24985)
THE MUSIC CTR OF LA CTY INC
Also Called: Music Center Unified Fund
135 N Grand Ave Ste 201, Los Angeles (90012-3017)
PHONE..................213 972-8007
Fax: 213 687-3490
Andrea Van De Kamp, Ch of Bd
Maria D Hammer, Admin Sec
Shreve Stanwood, Controller
Luisa Cariaga, Manager
EMP: 150 EST: 1964
SALES (est): 5.7MM Privately Held
SIC: 8399 Fund raising organization, non-fee basis

(P-24986)
TIDES INC (PA)
Also Called: TIDES SHARED SPACES
1014 Torney Ave Ste 1, San Francisco (94129-1756)
P.O. Box 29198 (94129-0198)
PHONE..................415 561-6400
Melissa Bradley, CEO
Nick Hodges, COO
Brian Byrnes, Senior VP
Carla Dartis, Senior VP
China Brotsky, Vice Pres
EMP: 90
SQ FT: 180,000
SALES: 2.9MM Privately Held
SIC: 8399 Community development groups

(P-24987)
TIDES CENTER
520 Jones St, San Francisco (94102-2008)
PHONE..................415 673-0234
EMP: 67 Privately Held
SIC: 8399 Community development groups
PA: The Tides Center
The Prsdio 1014 Trney Ave
San Francisco CA 94129
-

(P-24988)
TIDES NETWORK
The Prsdio 1014 Trney Ave, San Francisco (94129)
P.O. Box 29198 (94129-0198)
PHONE..................415 561-6400
Gary Schwartz, CEO
Judith Hill, CFO
Pauline Vela, Purchasing
Kim Sarnecki, Director
EMP: 80
SALES: 11.8MM Privately Held
SIC: 8399 Community development groups

(P-24989)
TRI-COUNTIES ASSOCIATION F
1234 Fairway Dr A, Santa Maria (93455-1406)
PHONE..................805 922-4640
EMP: 136
SALES (corp-wide): 229.2MM Privately Held
SIC: 8399 Community development groups
PA: Tri-Counties Association For The Developmentally Disabled, Inc.
520 E Montecito St
Santa Barbara CA 93103
805 962-7881

(P-24990)
UNITED CEREBRAL PALSY ASSOC OF
Also Called: RIDE ON TRANSPORTATION
3620 Sacramento Dr # 201, San Luis Obispo (93401-7215)
PHONE..................805 543-2039
Fax: 805 543-2045
Mark Shaffer, Exec Dir
Mark Shafer, Exec Dir
Ira Glick, Info Tech Dir
EMP: 100
SQ FT: 1,600
SALES: 6.9MM Privately Held
WEB: www.ucp-oc.org
SIC: 8399 Fund raising organization, non-fee basis

(P-24991)
UNITED WAY INC
44907 10th St W, Lancaster (93534-2313)
PHONE..................661 874-4288
EMP: 120
SALES (corp-wide): 28.9MM Privately Held
SIC: 8399 Fund raising organization, non-fee basis
PA: United Way, Inc.
1150 S Olive St Ste T500
Los Angeles CA 90015
213 808-6220

(P-24992)
UNITED WAY INC (PA)
Also Called: United Way Greater Los Angeles
1150 S Olive St Ste T500, Los Angeles (90015-2482)
PHONE..................213 808-6220
Fax: 213 630-2389
Caroline W Nahas, Ch of Bd
Elise Buik, President
Rebecca Edwards, Officer
Evelyn Garcia, Officer
Les Brockhurst, Vice Pres
EMP: 95
SQ FT: 40,000
SALES (est): 28.9MM Privately Held
WEB: www.unitedwayla.org
SIC: 8399 Fund raising organization, non-fee basis; United Fund councils; health & welfare council

(P-24993)
VALLEY CAN
921 11th St Ste 220, Sacramento (95814-2842)
PHONE..................916 273-4890
Carla Musser, President
EMP: 50
SALES: 5.5MM Privately Held
SIC: 8399 Advocacy group

(P-24994)
VALLEY RSRCE CTR FOR RETARDED
Also Called: Exceed
1285 N Santa Fe St, Hemet (92543-1823)
PHONE..................951 766-8659
Lee Trisler, Exec Dir
EMP: 99
SALES (est): 4.7MM Privately Held
SIC: 8399 Community development groups

(P-24995)
VIETNAMESE CMNTY ORANGE CNTY (PA)
Also Called: Southland Health Center
1618 W 1st St, Santa Ana (92703-3614)
PHONE..................714 558-6009
Tricia Nguyen, CEO
EMP: 68
SALES: 4MM Privately Held
WEB: www.vietnam-minnesota.org
SIC: 8399 8322 8351 8011 Community development groups; senior citizens' center or association; social service center; preschool center; primary care medical clinic; mental health clinic, outpatient

(P-24996)
WATSON CARTON
4178 Ross Ave, San Jose (95124-3728)
PHONE..................408 979-9618
Peter Frietman, CEO
EMP: 63
SALES (est): 3.4MM Privately Held
SIC: 8399 Community development groups

(P-24997)
WEST VALLEY AREA SQUAD CLUB
Also Called: Highway Patrol
5825 De Soto Ave, Woodland Hills (91367-5202)
PHONE..................818 888-1034
Fax: 818 888-0980
Brian Denike, President
Orrin Heitmann, Vice Pres
EMP: 104
SALES (est): 1.8MM Privately Held
SIC: 8399 Fund raising organization, non-fee basis

(P-24998)
WESTSIDE JEWISH CMNTY CTR INC (PA)
5870 W Olympic Blvd, Los Angeles (90036-4657)
PHONE..................323 938-2531
Brian Greene, Exec Dir
Jackie Armistead, Opers Staff
Oscar Yglesias, Facilities Dir
Deborah Kaplan, Director
EMP: 200
SQ FT: 150,000
SALES: 3.4MM Privately Held
SIC: 8399 8641 8322 Community development groups; civic social & fraternal associations; individual & family services

(P-24999)
WESTSIDE LODGE
120 Page St, San Francisco (94102-5811)
PHONE..................415 864-1515
Jonanthan Dernick, President
Stephanie Nickelrather, Exec Dir
EMP: 50
SALES (est): 456.1K Privately Held
SIC: 8399 Social services

(P-25000)
X PRIZE FOUNDATION INC
800 Crprate Pinte Ste 350, Culver City (90230)
PHONE..................310 741-4880
Fax: 310 741-4974
Robert Weiss, President
Paul Rappoport, COO
David Donell, CFO
Richard Garriott, Bd of Directors
Jeremy Rosner, Senior VP
EMP: 50
SQ FT: 17,705
SALES: 39.4MM Privately Held
SIC: 8399 Fund raising organization, non-fee basis

8412 Museums & Art Galleries

(P-25001)
ANAHEIM ARTS COUNCIL
P.O. Box 1364 (92815-1364)
PHONE..................714 868-6094
Charlotte Brady, Owner
Sallie Vravis, Executive
June Travers, Representative
EMP: 200 EST: 1977
SALES: 52.5K Privately Held
WEB: www.anaheimartscouncil.com
SIC: 8412 Museums & art galleries

(P-25002)
ARMAND HAMMER MUSEUM
10899 Wilshire Blvd, Los Angeles (90024-4343)
PHONE..................310 443-7000
Ann Philbin, Director
Samuel Young, Sales Executive
Mitch Marr, Senior Mgr
Maggie Sarkissian, Manager
Maryann Sears, Manager
▲ EMP: 101
SQ FT: 20,000
SALES: 24.3MM Privately Held
SIC: 8412 Museum

(P-25003)
ASIAN ART MUSEUM FOUND SAN FRA
Also Called: Asian Art Meuseum of SF
200 Larkin St, San Francisco (94102-4734)
PHONE..................415 581-3701
Fax: 415 581-4700
Anthony Sun, CEO
Akiko Yamazaki, President
Timothy F Kahn, Treasurer
Robert L Duffy, Vice Pres
Jay Xu, Principal
▲ EMP: 140
SALES (est): 7.2MM Privately Held
SIC: 8412 Arts or science center

(P-25004)
AUTRY MUSEUM OF AMERICAN WEST
Also Called: Autry National Centre
4700 Western Heritage Way, Los Angeles (90027-1462)
PHONE..................323 667-2000
Luke J Swetland, CEO
John Gray, President
Shelby Tisdale, Vice Pres
Carl Cornils, Finance Dir
Lois Hauser, Manager
EMP: 140
SQ FT: 144,000
SALES: 31.6MM Privately Held
SIC: 8412 5947 5812 6512 Museum; gift shop; cafeteria; theater building, ownership & operation

(P-25005)
CALIFRNIA SCNCE CTR FOUNDATION
700 Exposition Park Dr, Los Angeles (90037-1254)
PHONE..................213 744-2545
Jeffrey N Rudolph, President
Cynthia Pygin, CFO
Dennis R Spurgeon, Bd of Directors
Jill Demicis, Vice Pres
Erica Guzman, Accountant
EMP: 260
SALES: 37.6MM Privately Held
WEB: www.casciencectr.com
SIC: 8412 7832 5947 Museum; motion picture theaters, except drive-in; gifts & novelties

(P-25006)
CHARLES W BOWERS MUSEUM CORP
2002 N Main St, Santa Ana (92706-2731)
PHONE..................714 567-3600
Fax: 714 567-3603
Peter C Keller, President
Megan Birkenhauer, CIO
Laura Belani, Credit Mgr
Jennifer Peterson, Mktg Dir

PRODUCTS & SERVICES SECTION
8412 - Museums & Art Galleries County (P-25029)

Jennifer Alvarado, *Director*
▲ **EMP:** 72
SALES: 6.3MM **Privately Held**
SIC: 8412 Museum

(P-25007)
CHILDRENS CREATIVITY MUSEUM
221 4th St, San Francisco (94103-3116)
PHONE.....................415 820-3320
Adrienne Pon, *CEO*
Laney Whitcanack, *Ch of Bd*
MAI MAI Wythes, *Chairman*
John Gonzalez, *Treasurer*
Michael Nobleza, *Exec Dir*
EMP: 65
SALES: 1.8MM **Privately Held**
WEB: www.zeum.com
SIC: 8412 5947 Museums & art galleries; gift shop

(P-25008)
CHILDRENS MUSEUM OF DESERT
Also Called: Children's Discovery Museum
71701 Gerald Ford Dr, Rancho Mirage (92270-1934)
PHONE.....................760 321-0602
Fax: 760 321-1605
Betty Barker, *Chairman*
Wes Oliphant, *Vice Pres*
Carey Morales, *Admin Mgr*
Lee Vanderbeck, *Director*
EMP: 50
SQ FT: 18,000
SALES: 846.9K **Privately Held**
WEB: www.cdmod.org
SIC: 8412 Museum

(P-25009)
CITY & COUNTY OF SAN FRANCISCO
Also Called: Asian Art Museum
200 Larkin St, San Francisco (94102-4734)
PHONE.....................415 581-3500
Emily Sano, *Director*
Indra Mungal, *Officer*
David Hill, *Creative Dir*
Peri Danton, *Exec Dir*
Calen McEldowney, *Security Dir*
EMP: 60 **Privately Held**
SIC: 8412 9199 Museum; general government administration; ;
PA: City & County Of San Francisco
1 Dr Carlton B Goodlett P
San Francisco CA 94102
415 554-7500

(P-25010)
CITY OF FREMONT
Also Called: Ardenwood Farm
34600 Ardenwood Blvd, Fremont (94555-3645)
P.O. Box 5006 (94537-5006)
PHONE.....................510 791-4196
Fax: 510 635-3478
Randy Hees, *Manager*
EMP: 105
SQ FT: 72,576 **Privately Held**
WEB: www.ci.fremont.ca.us
SIC: 8412 9111 Historical society; mayors' offices
PA: City Of Fremont
3300 Capitol Ave
Fremont CA 94538
510 284-4000

(P-25011)
CITY OF LOS ANGELES
Also Called: Parks & Recreation Dept
2800 E Observatory Ave, Los Angeles (90027-1255)
PHONE.....................213 473-0800
Fax: 323 663-4323
Edwin C Krupp, *Director*
Anthony Cook, *Director*
EMP: 200 **Privately Held**
WEB: www.lacity.org
SIC: 8412 9532 Museum; urban & community development
PA: City Of Los Angeles
200 N Spring St Ste 303
Los Angeles CA 90012
213 978-0600

(P-25012)
COMPUTER HISTORY MUSEUM
1401 N Shoreline Blvd, Mountain View (94043-1311)
PHONE.....................650 810-1010
Fax: 650 810-1055
John C Hollar, *President*
Lori K Crawford, *CFO*
Leonard Shustek, *Bd of Directors*
Eileen Gill, *Vice Pres*
George Holmes, *Vice Pres*
▲ **EMP:** 52
SQ FT: 111,670
SALES (est): 3.2MM **Privately Held**
SIC: 8412 Museum

(P-25013)
COPIA THE AMERICAN C
500 1st St, NAPA (94559-2642)
PHONE.....................707 259-1600
Peggy Loar, *President*
Kurt Nystrom, *COO*
Sudhir Aggarwal, *Managing Dir*
Maryanne Reat, *Executive Asst*
Lynn Macdonald, *Controller*
▼ **EMP:** 90
SQ FT: 80,000
SALES (est): 2MM **Privately Held**
SIC: 8412 Museums & art galleries

(P-25014)
CORPORTION OF FINE ARTS MSEUMS
Also Called: Palace of The Legion Honor
50 Hagiwara Tea Garden Dr, San Francisco (94118-4502)
PHONE.....................415 750-3600
John Duchanan, *Manager*
EMP: 200
SALES (corp-wide): 35.4MM **Privately Held**
SIC: 8412 Museum
PA: Corporation Of The Fine Arts Museums
50 Hagiwara Tea Garden Dr
San Francisco CA 94118
415 750-3600

(P-25015)
CORPORTION OF FINE ARTS MSEUMS
Also Called: M H Deyoung Memorial
50 Golden Gate Pk Hgiwara, San Francisco (94118)
PHONE.....................415 750-3600
Debbie Albuquerque, *Branch Mgr*
EMP: 125
SALES (corp-wide): 35.4MM **Privately Held**
SIC: 8412 Museums & art galleries
PA: Corporation Of The Fine Arts Museums
50 Hagiwara Tea Garden Dr
San Francisco CA 94118
415 750-3600

(P-25016)
CORPORTION OF FINE ARTS MSEUMS (PA)
Also Called: Deyoung Museum
50 Hagiwara Tea Garden Dr, San Francisco (94118-4502)
PHONE.....................415 750-3600
Fax: 415 750-7686
Michelle Gutierrez, *CFO*
Laura Amador, *Volunteer Dir*
Steve Dykes, *Treasurer*
Suzy Varadi, *Associate Dir*
Ken Garcia, *Comms Dir*
▲ **EMP:** 168
SQ FT: 300,000
SALES: 40.5MM **Privately Held**
SIC: 8412 Museums & art galleries

(P-25017)
COUNTY OF LOS ANGELES
Also Called: Administration
5905 Wilshire Blvd, Los Angeles (90036-4504)
PHONE.....................323 857-6000
Andrea L Rich, *President*
EMP: 100 **Privately Held**
WEB: www.co.la.ca.us
SIC: 8412 9411 Art gallery, noncommercial; administration of educational programs;
PA: County Of Los Angeles
500 W Temple St Ste 375
Los Angeles CA 90012
213 974-1101

(P-25018)
COUNTY OF SAN BERNARDINO
Also Called: San Bernardino County Museum
2024 Orange Tree Ln, Redlands (92374-2850)
PHONE.....................909 307-2669
Robert L McKernan, *Manager*
EMP: 63 **Privately Held**
SIC: 8412 9512 Museum; recreational program administration, government;
PA: County Of San Bernardino
385 N Arrowhead Ave
San Bernardino CA 92415
909 387-3841

(P-25019)
DESERT ARTS CENTER
Also Called: DAC
550 N Palm Canyon Dr, Palm Springs (92262-5526)
P.O. Box 2813 (92263-2813)
PHONE.....................760 323-7973
Adele Hill, *President*
EMP: 90
SALES: 142.7K **Privately Held**
SIC: 8412 Art gallery, noncommercial

(P-25020)
ETIWANDA HISTORICAL SOCIETY
7150 Etiwanda Ave, Rancho Cucamonga (91739-9758)
P.O. Box 63 (91739-0063)
PHONE.....................909 899-8432
Jan Sutton, *President*
EMP: 99
SALES (est): 3.9MM **Privately Held**
SIC: 8412 Historical society

(P-25021)
EXPLORATORIUM (PA)
17 Pier Ste 100, San Francisco (94111-1455)
PHONE.....................415 528-4462
Fax: 415 561-0307
Dennis Bartels, *Exec Dir*
Debra Menaker, *CFO*
Supriya Batra, *Treasurer*
Patricia Ayite, *Bd of Directors*
Aaron Vermut, *Bd of Directors*
▲ **EMP:** 163
SQ FT: 200,000
SALES: 65.1MM **Privately Held**
WEB: www.exploratorium.org
SIC: 8412 Museum

(P-25022)
HISTORICAL SOC CENTINELA VLY
7634 Midfield Ave, Los Angeles (90045-3234)
PHONE.....................310 649-6272
Leonard Utter, *President*
Claydine Burt, *Vice Pres*
EMP: 300
SALES (est): 2MM **Privately Held**
SIC: 8412 Historical society

(P-25023)
KIDSPACE A PRTICIPATORY MUSEUM
480 N Arroyo Blvd, Pasadena (91103-3269)
PHONE.....................626 449-9144
Jane Popovich, *President*
Mark McKinley, *Treasurer*
Chris Morphy, *Vice Pres*
Stephen H Baumann, *Exec Dir*
Tracy Bechtold, *Exec Dir*
EMP: 83
SALES: 4.2MM **Privately Held**
WEB: www.kidspacemuseum.org
SIC: 8412 Museum

(P-25024)
LINDSAY WILDLIFE MUSEUM
1931 1st Ave, Walnut Creek (94597-2540)
PHONE.....................925 935-1978
Fax: 925 935-8015
Kramer Klabau, *President*
John Kikuchi, *President*
Lizzie Coyle, *Officer*
Lizzie Phelps, *Officer*
Teresa Herrera, *Vice Pres*
EMP: 90
SQ FT: 28,000
SALES: 2.4MM **Privately Held**
WEB: www.wildlife-museum.org
SIC: 8412 Museum

(P-25025)
LONG BCH MUSEUM ART FOUNDATION
2300 E Ocean Blvd, Long Beach (90803-2442)
PHONE.....................562 439-2119
Fax: 562 439-3587
Ronald B Nelson, *Director*
Suzanne Poulsen, *Trustee*
Rody N Lopez, *Executive Asst*
Jillian Taylor, *Executive Asst*
Margery Butler-Hilo, *Admin Sec*
▲ **EMP:** 62
SQ FT: 24,000
SALES: 1.3MM **Privately Held**
WEB: www.lbma.org
SIC: 8412 Museum

(P-25026)
LOS ANGELES CNTY MSEUM OF ART
Also Called: Lacma
5905 Wilshire Blvd, Los Angeles (90036-4504)
PHONE.....................323 857-6000
Fax: 323 931-7347
Michael Govan, *CEO*
Ann Rowland, *CFO*
Alison Edelstein, *Officer*
Rachel Zelaya, *Officer*
Melissa Bomes, *Assoc VP*
▲ **EMP:** 104
SALES (est): 10MM **Privately Held**
SIC: 8412 Museum

(P-25027)
MUSEUM ASSOCIATES
Also Called: LA COUNTY MUSEUM OF ART
5905 Wilshire Blvd, Los Angeles (90036-4504)
PHONE.....................323 857-6172
Fax: 323 936-5755
Michael Gavin, *CEO*
Diana Vesga, *Officer*
CHI-Young Kim, *Info Tech Mgr*
Stephanie Odenheimer, *Research*
Lawrence Webster, *Controller*
EMP: 400
SALES: 111.6MM **Privately Held**
SIC: 8412 Museum

(P-25028)
MUSEUM CNTMPRARY ART SAN DIEGO
Also Called: MCASD
700 Prospect St, La Jolla (92037-4228)
PHONE.....................858 454-3541
Fax: 858 454-6985
Hugh M Davies, *CEO*
Kathlene J Gusel, *Admin Asst*
Javier Martinez, *Admin Asst*
Jocelyn Saucedo, *Admin Asst*
Jini Bernstein, *CTO*
▼ **EMP:** 70
SQ FT: 45,200
SALES: 8.7MM **Privately Held**
SIC: 8412 Museum

(P-25029)
MUSEUM OF CONTEMPORARY ART (PA)
250 S Grand Ave, Los Angeles (90012-3021)
PHONE.....................213 626-6222
Fax: 213 620-8674
Charles Young, *CEO*
Jeffrey Deitch, *CEO*
Michael Harrison, *CFO*
Matti Allison, *Store Mgr*
Monica Roache, *Admin Asst*
▲ **EMP:** 150
SQ FT: 100,000
SALES: 91.5MM **Privately Held**
SIC: 8412 Museums & art galleries

8412 - Museums & Art Galleries County (P-25030)

(P-25030)
MUSEUM OF LATIN AMERICAN ART
628 Alamitos Ave, Long Beach (90802-1513)
PHONE..................562 437-1689
Fax: 562 437-7043
Robert M Gumbiner, *Chairman*
Jessica Salazar, *President*
Mike Deovlet, *Corp Secy*
Lee Gumbiner, *Vice Pres*
Alia Brown, *Social Dir*
▲ EMP: 50
SQ FT: 30,000
SALES: 2.7MM **Privately Held**
SIC: 8412 Arts or science center

(P-25031)
NATIONAL CENTER FOR THE PRES
369 E 1st St, Los Angeles (90012-3901)
PHONE..................213 625-0414
Irene Hirano, *President*
EMP: 90
SQ FT: 33,000
SALES: 5.7MM **Privately Held**
SIC: 8412 5947 Museum; gift shop

(P-25032)
NATURAL HISTORY MUSEUM OF LOS
900 Exposition Blvd, Los Angeles (90007-4057)
PHONE..................213 763-3442
EMP: 300
SALES: 54MM **Privately Held**
SIC: 8412

(P-25033)
NORTON SIMON MUSEUM
411 W Colorado Blvd, Pasadena (91105-1825)
PHONE..................626 449-6840
Fax: 626 796-4978
Ronald H Dykhuizen, *Principal*
Jennifer J Simon, *Ch of Bd*
Walter W Timoshuk, *Treasurer*
Harry Savage, *Vice Pres*
Robert Walker, *Vice Pres*
▲ EMP: 100
SQ FT: 70,000
SALES: 7.9MM **Privately Held**
WEB: www.nortonsimon.org
SIC: 8412 Museum

(P-25034)
OAKLAND MUSEUM OF CALIFORNIA
1000 Oak St, Oakland (94607-4892)
PHONE..................510 318-8519
Lori Fogarty, *CEO*
Lori G Fogarty, *CEO*
Steven Anderson, *Exec VP*
Francis Pingatore, *Vice Pres*
Michael Silverman, *Associate Dir*
EMP: 100
SQ FT: 150,000
SALES: 16MM **Privately Held**
SIC: 8412 Historical society; museum

(P-25035)
PALM SPRINGS ART MUSEUM INC
101 N Museum Dr, Palm Springs (92262-5659)
P.O. Box 2310 (92263-2310)
PHONE..................760 322-4800
Fax: 619 327-5069
Donna Macmillan, *Ch of Bd*
Joseph E Bonner, *CFO*
Elizabeth Armstrong, *Exec Dir*
Greg Polzin, *General Mgr*
Darcy Carozza, *Administration*
▲ EMP: 96
SQ FT: 75,000
SALES: 18.4MM **Privately Held**
WEB: www.psmuseum.org
SIC: 8412 Museum

(P-25036)
PARKS AND RECREATION CAL DEPT
Also Called: Malibu Lagoon Museum
23200 Pacific Coast Hwy, Malibu (90265-4937)
P.O. Box 291 (90265-0291)
PHONE..................310 456-8432
Sandra Mitchell, *Branch Mgr*
EMP: 80 **Privately Held**
WEB: www.californiastatepark.com
SIC: 8412 9512 Museum; land, mineral & wildlife conservation;
HQ: California Department Of Parks And Recreation
1416 9th St Ste 1041
Sacramento CA 95814
800 777-0369

(P-25037)
PETERSEN AUTO MSEUM FOUNDATION
6060 Wilshire Blvd, Los Angeles (90036-3605)
PHONE..................323 930-2277
Fax: 323 930-6642
Buddy Pepp, *Exec Dir*
Eitan Ginsburg, *CFO*
Joe Wickham, *CFO*
Adam Langsbard, *Chief Mktg Ofcr*
Mandy Hanlon, *Social Dir*
▲ EMP: 50
SALES (est): 4.6MM **Privately Held**
SIC: 8412 Museum

(P-25038)
REUBEN H FLEET SCIENCE CENTER
1875 El Prado, San Diego (92101-1625)
P.O. Box 33303 (92163-3303)
PHONE..................619 238-1233
Fax: 619 685-5771
Gary Thomas Phillips, *CEO*
Craig A Blower, *COO*
Tom Fetter, *Treasurer*
Jeffrey Kirsch, *Exec Dir*
Julie Schardin, *Info Tech Mgr*
EMP: 105
SQ FT: 93,500
SALES: 6.1MM **Privately Held**
WEB: www.rhfleet.org
SIC: 8412 Museum

(P-25039)
SAN DEGO SOC OF NTURAL HISTORY
Also Called: San Dego Ntural History Museum
1788 El Prado, San Diego (92101-1624)
P.O. Box 121390 (92112-1390)
PHONE..................619 232-3821
Fax: 619 232-0248
Michael W Hager, *CEO*
George Gonyer, *COO*
Susan Loveall, *Vice Pres*
Chena Popper, *Executive Asst*
Jennifer Muller, *Controller*
▲ EMP: 70 EST: 1874
SQ FT: 60,000
SALES: 33.6MM **Privately Held**
WEB: www.sdnhm.org
SIC: 8412 5047 Museum; dental equipment & supplies

(P-25040)
SAN DIEGO AEROSPACE MUSEUM
335 Kenney St, El Cajon (92020-1249)
PHONE..................619 258-1221
Fax: 619 448-6411
Jeff Eads, *Manager*
EMP: 60
SALES (est): 587.3K **Privately Held**
WEB: www.sdasm.org
SIC: 8412 Museums & art galleries

(P-25041)
SAN DIEGO ARCFT CARIER MUSEUM
910 N Harbor Dr, San Diego (92101-5811)
PHONE..................619 544-9600
Fax: 619 238-1200
Theresa Randall, *President*
Jon Lynch, *Pub Rel Mgr*
EMP: 150
SALES: 21.9MM **Privately Held**
WEB: www.midway.org
SIC: 8412 Museum

(P-25042)
SAN DIEGO MUSEUM OF ART
1450 El Prado, San Diego (92101-1618)
P.O. Box 122107 (92112-2107)
PHONE..................619 696-1971
Fax: 619 232-9367
Philip Tom Gildred, *CEO*
Katy Dessent, *Trustee*
Jill Larson, *Trustee*
Jacquelyn Littlefield, *Trustee*
John McNeece, *Trustee*
▲ EMP: 82
SQ FT: 96,278
SALES: 11.2MM **Privately Held**
WEB: www.sdmart.org
SIC: 8412 Museum

(P-25043)
SAN FRANCISCO MERITIME N H P
Fort Myson Ctr Bldg E265, San Francisco (94123)
PHONE..................415 561-7000
Craig Kenkel, *Superintendent*
EMP: 80
SALES (est): 540.4K **Privately Held**
SIC: 8412 Museum

(P-25044)
SAN FRANCISCO MUSEUM MODRN ART (PA)
Also Called: Sfmoma Museum Store
151 3rd St, San Francisco (94103-3107)
PHONE..................415 357-4035
Fax: 415 357-4037
Robert J Fisher, *President*
Charles R Schwab, *Chairman*
Dennis J Wong, *Treasurer*
Katherine Abbey, *Bd of Directors*
Elizabeth Waller, *Associate Dir*
▲ EMP: 168
SQ FT: 225,000
SALES: 97MM **Privately Held**
WEB: www.sfmoma.org
SIC: 8412 5942 Museum; book stores

(P-25045)
SAN JOSE CHLD DISCOVERY MUSEUM
180 Woz Way, San Jose (95110-2722)
PHONE..................408 298-5437
Fax: 408 298-6826
William Sullivan, *CEO*
Patience Davidson, *Executive*
Patience Davidson-Lutz, *Executive*
Marilee Gennings, *Exec Dir*
Marilee Jennings, *General Mgr*
EMP: 85
SQ FT: 52,000
SALES: 7.8MM **Privately Held**
SIC: 8412 Museums & art galleries

(P-25046)
SAN JOSE MUSEUM OF ART ASSN
110 S Market St, San Jose (95113-2383)
PHONE..................408 271-6840
Fax: 408 288-6884
Daniel Keegan, *Director*
Karen Rapp, *Officer*
Hannah Cahalan, *Bookkeeper*
John Renzel, *Facilities Mgr*
Denise Liberi, *Manager*
▲ EMP: 70 EST: 1969
SQ FT: 80,000
SALES: 3.6MM **Privately Held**
WEB: www.sjmusart.org
SIC: 8412 5942 5947 Museum; book stores; gift shop

(P-25047)
SANTA BARBARA MUSEUM
2559 Puesta Del Sol, Santa Barbara (93105-2936)
PHONE..................805 682-4711
Fax: 805 569-3170
Luke Swetland, *CEO*
Palmer Jackson Jr, *President*
Jenny Kearns, *COO*
Diane Wondowloski, *CFO*
Carolyn Chandler, *Vice Pres*
EMP: 95 EST: 1916
SALES: 13.4MM **Privately Held**
WEB: www.sbnature.org
SIC: 8412 Museum

(P-25048)
SANTA BARBARA MUSEUM OF ART (PA)
Also Called: Fine Arts Museum
1130 State St, Santa Barbara (93101-2746)
PHONE..................805 963-4364
Fax: 805 966-6840
Larry J Feinberg, *CEO*
James Owen, *President*
Larry Feinberg, *CEO*
James Hutchinson, *CFO*
Carl Mottek, *CFO*
▲ EMP: 60
SQ FT: 50,000
SALES: 3.1MM **Privately Held**
WEB: www.sbmuseart.org
SIC: 8412 Art gallery, noncommercial

(P-25049)
SOUTHWESTERN ARTISTS ASSN
1770 Vlg Pl Gallery 23 23 Gallery, San Diego (92101)
PHONE..................619 232-3522
Geln White, *President*
John Davis,
EMP: 50
SALES (est): 386.3K **Privately Held**
SIC: 8412 Art gallery

(P-25050)
STANSBURY HM PRESERVATION ASSN
307 W 5th St, Chico (95928-5505)
P.O. Box 3262 (95927-3262)
PHONE..................530 895-3848
Dino Corbin, *President*
EMP: 50
SQ FT: 3,500
SALES (est): 2.1MM **Privately Held**
SIC: 8412 Museums & art galleries

(P-25051)
TECH MUSEUM OF INNOVATION (PA)
201 S Market St, San Jose (95113-2008)
PHONE..................408 795-6116
Peter Friess, *CEO*
Christopher Digiorgio, *Ch of Bd*
Tim Ritchie, *President*
Jonathan Camacho, *CFO*
Daniel Cunningham, *CFO*
◆ EMP: 153
SQ FT: 130,000
SALES: 15.7MM **Privately Held**
SIC: 8412 Arts or science center; museum

(P-25052)
THE FOR CALIFO CENTE
340 N Escondido Blvd, Escondido (92025-2600)
PHONE..................760 839-4138
Fax: 760 739-0205
Vicky Basehore, *President*
Nicole Patton, *Accountant*
Julie Riggert, *Marketing Staff*
Kirsten Vega, *Education*
Jennifer Nichols, *Manager*
EMP: 185
SALES: 9.9MM **Privately Held**
WEB: www.artcenter.org
SIC: 8412 5999 Arts or science center; art dealers

(P-25053)
TURTLE BAY EXPLORATION PARK
1335 Arboretum Dr Ste A, Redding (96003-3628)
PHONE..................530 243-4282
John C Peterson, *President*
Maggie Redmon, *COO*
Stephen Gaston, *Chairman*
Mike Warren, *Bd of Directors*
Judy Lalouche, *Vice Pres*
EMP: 50
SALES: 3.9MM **Privately Held**
SIC: 8412 Museum

PRODUCTS & SERVICES SECTION
8611 - Business Associations County (P-25076)

(P-25054)
WALT DISNEY FAMILY MUSEUM
104 Montgomery St, San Francisco (94129-1718)
PHONE..............................415 345-6800
Ronald W Miller, *President*
Jennifer Miller-Goff, *Corp Secy*
Joanna Miller, *Vice Pres*
Kirsten Komoroske, *Exec Dir*
Robert Moseley, *Systems Mgr*
EMP: 60
SALES (est): 1.4MM **Privately Held**
SIC: 8412 Museum

(P-25055)
WEST ANTLOPE VLY HSTORICAL SOC
45026 11th St W, Lancaster (93534-2206)
PHONE..............................661 945-5369
Milt Stark, *Vice Pres*
David Earl, *President*
EMP: 98
SALES (est): 628.2K **Privately Held**
SIC: 8412 Historical society

8422 Arboreta, Botanical & Zoological Gardens

(P-25056)
AQUARIUM OF PACIFIC
310 Golden Shore Ste 300, Long Beach (90802-4240)
PHONE..............................562 590-3100
Fax: 562 590-3109
Jerry R Schubel, *Branch Mgr*
EMP: 56 **Privately Held**
SIC: 8422 Aquarium
PA: Aquarium Of The Pacific
   100 Aquarium Way
   Long Beach CA 90802

(P-25057)
AQUARIUM OF PACIFIC (PA)
100 Aquarium Way, Long Beach (90802-8126)
PHONE..............................562 590-3100
Fax: 562 951-1629
Jerry R Schubel, *President*
Anthony Brown, *CFO*
Cecile Fisher, *Vice Pres*
Perry Hampton, *Vice Pres*
Kathryn Nirschl, *Vice Pres*
▲ **EMP:** 220
SQ FT: 10,000
SALES: 34.6MM **Privately Held**
SIC: 8422 Aquariums & zoological gardens

(P-25058)
BAYORG
Also Called: Aquarium of The Bay, The Embarcadero At Beach St, San Francisco (94133)
PHONE..............................415 623-5300
John Frawley, *President*
Bobbi Evans, *CFO*
EMP: 99
SALES: 10.2MM **Privately Held**
SIC: 8422 Aquarium

(P-25059)
BIRCH AQUARIUM AT SCRIPPS
Also Called: Scripps Aquarium
2300 Expedition Way, La Jolla (92037)
PHONE..............................858 534-4109
Nigella Hillgarth, *Director*
Ken Steitz, *VP Finance*
Karen Olmos, *Purchasing*
Patrick Helbling, *Opers Dir*
EMP: 50
SALES (est): 3MM **Privately Held**
SIC: 8422 8412 Aquarium; museum

(P-25060)
CALIFORNIA ACADEMY SCIENCES (PA)
55 Music Concourse Dr, San Francisco (94118-4503)
PHONE..............................415 379-8000
John Hafernik, *President*
Scott Moran, *COO*
Alison Brown, *CFO*
Kris Pettersen, *Bd of Directors*

Stephanie Stone, *Officer*
EMP: 635 **EST:** 1853
SQ FT: 410,000
SALES: 67.4MM **Privately Held**
SIC: 8422 2721 8412 Aquarium; periodicals: publishing only; museums & art galleries

(P-25061)
CITY OF SAN JOSE
Also Called: Visitor Services & Facilities
1300 Senter Rd, San Jose (95112-2520)
PHONE..............................408 794-6400
Fax: 408 975-9369
Randy Adams, *Supervisor*
Carol Reed, *Manager*
EMP: 60 **Privately Held**
WEB: www.csjfinance.org
SIC: 8422 9512 Zoological garden, noncommercial; recreational program administration, government;
PA: City Of San Jose
   200 E Santa Clara St
   San Jose CA 95113
   408 535-3500

(P-25062)
FILOLI CENTER
Also Called: Filoli Garden Shop
86 Canada Rd, Woodside (94062-4144)
PHONE..............................650 364-8300
Fax: 650 367-0724
Cynthia D'Agosta, *CEO*
Pamela Smith, *President*
Robert Walker, *Principal*
Cathy Rampley, *Admin Asst*
Ryan Patterson, *Info Tech Mgr*
EMP: 60
SQ FT: 1,000
SALES: 6.8MM **Privately Held**
SIC: 8422 Botanical garden

(P-25063)
FRESNOS CHAFFEE ZOO CORP
894 W Belmont Ave, Fresno (93728-2807)
PHONE..............................559 498-5910
Scott Barton, *CEO*
Brian Goldman, *CFO*
Pam Wheelen, *Social Dir*
Lisa Condoian, *Executive Asst*
Heather Davis, *Graphic Designe*
◆ **EMP:** 121
SALES: 41.6MM **Privately Held**
WEB: www.fresnochaffeezoo.com
SIC: 8422 Animal & reptile exhibit

(P-25064)
LIVING DESERT
47900 Portola Ave, Palm Desert (92260-6156)
PHONE..............................760 346-5694
Allen Monroe, *CEO*
Terrie Correll, *COO*
Bill Powers, *Bd of Directors*
Tom Laliberte, *Social Dir*
Wendy Enright, *Admin Asst*
EMP: 124
SQ FT: 1,700
SALES: 15MM **Privately Held**
WEB: www.livingdesert.org
SIC: 8422 5947 Aquariums & zoological gardens; botanical garden; gift shop

(P-25065)
LOS ANGLES ARBRETUM FOUNDATION
301 N Baldwin Ave, Arcadia (91007-2697)
PHONE..............................626 821-3222
Fax: 626 821-4642
Richard Schulhof, *CEO*
Jennifer Williams, *Principal*
Kathy Kwans, *Manager*
EMP: 65
SALES: 1.7MM **Privately Held**
SIC: 8422 Arboretum

(P-25066)
MONTALVO ASSOCIATION
Also Called: VILLA MONTALVO
15400 Montalvo Rd, Saratoga (95070-6327)
P.O. Box 158 (95071-0158)
PHONE..............................408 961-5800
Fax: 408 961-5850
Sonny Bazan, *Director*
Neal Dempsey, *Managing Prtnr*

Lonnie Cedillo, *Principal*
Elisbeth Challener, *Exec Dir*
Robert Sain, *Exec Dir*
EMP: 65
SQ FT: 13,000
SALES: 5.5MM **Privately Held**
WEB: www.villamontalvo.org
SIC: 8422 8412 Arboretum; art gallery, noncommercial

(P-25067)
MONTEREY BAY AQAR FOUNDATION (PA)
886 Cannery Row, Monterey (93940-1023)
PHONE..............................831 648-4800
Fax: 831 648-4810
Peter Bing, *Ch of Bd*
Julie E Packard, *CEO*
Edward Prohaska, *CFO*
Johnnie Ivey, *Officer*
Andrew Marchese, *Officer*
EMP: 142
SQ FT: 326,000
SALES (est): 100.8MM **Privately Held**
WEB: www.montereyaquarium.org
SIC: 8422 Aquarium

(P-25068)
RANCHO SANTA ANA BOTANIC GRDN
1500 N College Ave, Claremont (91711-3157)
PHONE..............................909 625-8767
Fax: 909 626-7670
Clement Hamilton, *Exec Dir*
Richard Grant, *Chairman*
Liliana Derewnicka, *Officer*
Sonja Evensen, *Vice Pres*
Deborah Szekely, *Creative Dir*
EMP: 52
SQ FT: 30,000
SALES: 3.5MM **Privately Held**
WEB: www.rsabg.org
SIC: 8422 Botanical garden

(P-25069)
SACRAMENTO ZOOLOGICAL SOCIETY
3930 W Land Park Dr, Sacramento (95822-1123)
PHONE..............................916 808-5888
Fax: 916 264-5887
Mary Healy, *Exec Dir*
Delta Mello, *Vice Pres*
Charlie Weiss, *Manager*
Tonja Swank, *Relations*
EMP: 50
SALES: 7MM **Privately Held**
WEB: www.saczoo.com
SIC: 8422 Arboreta & botanical or zoological gardens

(P-25070)
SANTA BRBARA ZLGCAL FOUNDATION
500 Ninos Dr, Santa Barbara (93103-3759)
PHONE..............................805 962-1673
Fax: 805 962-1673
Yul Vanek, *CEO*
Fred Clough, *President*
Nancy McToldridge, *COO*
Carol Bedford, *CFO*
Eldon Shiffman, *Treasurer*
▲ **EMP:** 130
SQ FT: 1,200
SALES: 10.1MM **Privately Held**
WEB: www.santabarbarazoo.org
SIC: 8422 Zoological garden, noncommercial

(P-25071)
ZOOLOGICAL SOCIETY SAN DIEGO (PA)
Also Called: SAN DIEGO WILD ANIMAL PARK
2920 Zoo Dr, San Diego (92101-1646)
P.O. Box 120551 (92112-0551)
PHONE..............................619 231-1515
Fax: 619 231-0249
Berit Durler, *Principal*
Richard B Gulley, *President*
Paula S Brock, *CFO*
Frank Alexander, *Treasurer*
Paula Beck, *Vice Pres*
◆ **EMP:** 1500

SALES: 294.9MM **Privately Held**
WEB: www.sdzoo.com
SIC: 8422 5812 5947 Arboreta & botanical or zoological gardens; eating places; gift shop

(P-25072)
ZOOLOGICAL SOCIETY SAN DIEGO
Also Called: San Diego Wild Animal Park
15500 San Pasqual Vly Rd, Escondido (92027-7017)
PHONE..............................760 747-8702
Fax: 760 746-7081
Robert McClure, *Manager*
Douglas Myers, *Bd of Directors*
Stan Thompson, *Personnel*
Susan Licon, *Food Svc Dir*
Tracy Bareno, *Director*
EMP: 800
SALES (corp-wide): 294.9MM **Privately Held**
WEB: www.sdzoo.com
SIC: 8422 7999 Animal & reptile exhibit; tourist attraction, commercial
PA: Zoological Society Of San Diego
   2920 Zoo Dr
   San Diego CA 92101
   619 231-1515

(P-25073)
ZOOLOGICAL SOCIETY SAN DIEGO
Also Called: San Diego Zoo
2920 Zoo Dr, San Diego (92101-1646)
P.O. Box 120551 (92112-0551)
PHONE..............................619 744-3325
Richard Farrar, *Director*
Karen Beck, *Associate Dir*
Deirdre Ballou, *Director*
Jennifer Dunlap, *Manager*
EMP: 1200
SALES (corp-wide): 294.9MM **Privately Held**
WEB: www.sdzoo.com
SIC: 8422 Arboreta & botanical or zoological gardens
PA: Zoological Society Of San Diego
   2920 Zoo Dr
   San Diego CA 92101
   619 231-1515

8611 Business Associations

(P-25074)
AEROVIRONMENT INC
900 Innovators Way, Simi Valley (93065)
PHONE..............................805 581-2187
Fax: 805 581-4512
John Grabowsky, *Branch Mgr*
Jennifer L Klobus, *President*
Daniel Stone, *Vice Pres*
Calvin Au, *Program Mgr*
Natalie Halvorson, *Program Mgr*
EMP: 150
SALES (corp-wide): 264.1MM **Publicly Held**
WEB: www.avinc.com
SIC: 8611 Manufacturers' institute
PA: Aerovironment, Inc.
   800 Royal Oaks Dr Ste 210
   Monrovia CA 91016
   626 357-9983

(P-25075)
ASOCIACON DE BOMBEROS DEL ESTA
1100 Calle Del Cerro 52d, San Clemente (92672-6022)
PHONE..............................949 355-4249
Marco Olmos, *Principal*
EMP: 99
SALES (est): 902.6K **Privately Held**
SIC: 8611 Business associations

(P-25076)
BERES CONSULTING
Also Called: PCA
470 S Bentley Ave, Los Angeles (90049-3513)
P.O. Box 252008 (90025-8908)
PHONE..............................310 476-9941
Fax: 310 479-5515
John Gleason, *President*

8611 - Business Associations County (P-25077)

Attila Beres, *Manager*
EMP: 80
SALES (est): 1.3MM **Privately Held**
SIC: 8611 Trade associations

(P-25077)
BUSINESS FOR SOCIAL RESPONSIBI (PA)
Also Called: B S R
88 Kearny St Fl 12, San Francisco (94108-5539)
PHONE..................415 984-3200
Robert H Dunn, *CEO*
Dan Luscher, *CFO*
Geir Westgaard, *Vice Pres*
Mike Wilkinson, *Vice Pres*
Ted Rose, *Controller*
EMP: 50
SQ FT: 20,000
SALES: 20.6MM **Privately Held**
WEB: www.bsr.org
SIC: 8611 8742 Business associations; management consulting services

(P-25078)
C A H H S
1215 K St Ste 800, Sacramento (95814-3946)
PHONE..................916 552-7507
Duane Dauner, *President*
EMP: 65
SALES (est): 4.9MM **Privately Held**
WEB: www.calhospital.org
SIC: 8611 Trade associations

(P-25079)
CALIFORNIA ASSN REALTORS INC (PA)
525 S Virgil Ave, Los Angeles (90020-1403)
PHONE..................213 739-8200
Fax: 213 480-7724
Joel S Singer, *CEO*
Lefrancis Arnold, *CEO*
Joel S Singer, *CEO*
Don Flyn, *CFO*
Don Faught, *Treasurer*
EMP: 110 **EST:** 1907
SQ FT: 52,000
SALES: 33.4MM **Privately Held**
SIC: 8611 8742 Real Estate Board; real estate consultant

(P-25080)
CALIFORNIA CERTIFIED ORGANIC
Also Called: CCOF CERTIFICATION SERVICES
2155 Delaware Ave Ste 150, Santa Cruz (95060-5732)
PHONE..................831 423-2263
Fax: 831 423-4528
Cathy Calfo, *Exec Dir*
Read Jake, *COO*
Phil Larocca, *Principal*
Rachel Witte, *General Mgr*
Jesse Cowan, *Accounting Mgr*
EMP: 58
SALES (est): 2.4MM **Privately Held**
SIC: 8611 Trade associations

(P-25081)
CALIFORNIA CHAMBER COMMERCE (PA)
Also Called: Cal Chamber
1215 K St Ste 1400, Sacramento (95814-3953)
P.O. Box 1736 (95812-1736)
PHONE..................916 444-6670
Fax: 916 325-1272
Allan Zaremberg, *President*
Lawrence M Dicke, *CFO*
Oliver Hauck, *Bd of Directors*
John W Koeberer, *Bd of Directors*
Anthony Sabatino, *Bd of Directors*
EMP: 65 **EST:** 1890
SQ FT: 26,000
SALES: 23MM **Privately Held**
WEB: www.calchamber.com
SIC: 8611 Chamber of Commerce

(P-25082)
CALIFORNIA CHAMBER COMMERCE
920 Riverside Pkwy Ste 30, West Sacramento (95605-1529)
PHONE..................916 928-2124
Fax: 916 928-2136
EMP: 65
SALES (corp-wide): 23MM **Privately Held**
SIC: 8611
PA: California Chamber Of Commerce
1215 K St Ste 1400
Sacramento CA 95814
916 444-6670

(P-25083)
DOWNTOWN SAN DIEGO PARTNR INC
1111 6th Ave Ste 101, San Diego (92101-5230)
PHONE..................619 234-8900
Fax: 619 234-2303
Ryan Loofbourrow, *Manager*
Lindsay Kirkman, *Vice Pres*
Daniel Reeves, *Vice Pres*
John Hanley, *VP Finance*
Kaitlin Phillips, *Manager*
EMP: 55
SQ FT: 10,480
SALES (corp-wide): 7MM **Privately Held**
WEB: www.downtown-digital.com
SIC: 8611 Business associations
PA: Downtown San Diego Partnership, Inc.
401 B St Ste 100
San Diego CA 92101
619 234-0201

(P-25084)
ELECTRA OWNERS ASSOC
700 W E St, San Diego (92101-5984)
PHONE..................619 236-3310
J E Martin, *Principal*
EMP: 196
SALES (est): 7.4MM
SALES (corp-wide): 76.5MM **Privately Held**
SIC: 8611 Business associations
PA: Action Property Management, Inc.
2603 Main St Ste 500
Irvine CA 92614
949 450-0202

(P-25085)
ELK GROVE ADULT CMNTY TRAINING
8810 Elk Grove Blvd, Elk Grove (95624-1811)
PHONE..................916 431-3162
Fax: 916 685-4657
Larry Sherrill, *CEO*
Gary Lawson, *Exec Dir*
Rebecca Brubaker, *Director*
EMP: 54
SALES: 3.2MM **Privately Held**
WEB: www.egact.org
SIC: 8611 Community affairs & services

(P-25086)
FIRE AND POLICE
4645 E Anaheim St, Long Beach (90804-3122)
PHONE..................562 961-0066
Patrick Ahern, *CEO*
Kevin Davis, *Director*
EMP: 50
SALES (est): 3MM **Privately Held**
SIC: 8611 Community affairs & services

(P-25087)
FRIENDS ABROAD
2173 La Salle Dr, Walnut Creek (94598-1138)
PHONE..................925 939-9420
Pat Delaney, *President*
Bill Landis,
EMP: 70
SALES (est): 4MM **Privately Held**
WEB: www.friendsabroad.com
SIC: 8611 Community affairs & services

(P-25088)
GOLDEN BEAR REST ASSN LLC
760 2nd St, San Francisco (94107-2012)
PHONE..................415 227-8660
Peter W Osborne, *Mng Member*
EMP: 50
SALES (est): 1.2MM **Privately Held**
SIC: 8611 Merchants' association

(P-25089)
HAPPY CAMP CHAMBER COMMERCE
35 Davis Rd, Happy Camp (96039)
P.O. Box 1188 (96039-1188)
PHONE..................530 493-2900
James Buchner, *President*
Rosemary Boren, *Treasurer*
Carly Manley, *Treasurer*
Roberta Cullum, *Vice Pres*
EMP: 50
SALES (est): 2.8MM **Privately Held**
SIC: 8611 Chamber of Commerce

(P-25090)
IAPMO RESEARCH AND TESTING INC (PA)
Also Called: INTERNATIONAL ASSOCIATION OF P
5001 E Philadelphia St, Ontario (91761-2816)
PHONE..................909 472-4100
G P Russ Chaney, *Exec Dir*
Russ Chaney, *Executive*
Shahin Moinian, *Surgery Dir*
Pariyada Bunyasai, *Accountant*
Neil Bogatz, *General Counsel*
EMP: 57
SALES (est): 32.8MM **Privately Held**
SIC: 8611 Contractors' association

(P-25091)
INDIAN HEALTH COUNCIL
50100 Golsh Rd, Valley Center (92082-5338)
P.O. Box 406, Pauma Valley (92061-0406)
PHONE..................760 749-1410
Fax: 760 749-2376
Romelle Majelmccauley, *Director*
Orvin Hanson, *COO*
Bill Gallagher, *CFO*
Robert Schostag, *Pharmacy Dir*
Connie Kirk, *Exec Dir*
EMP: 99
SALES (est): 21.2MM **Privately Held**
SIC: 8611 Business associations

(P-25092)
LOS ANGLES AREA CHMBER CMMERCE
350 S Bixel St, Los Angeles (90017-1418)
PHONE..................213 580-7500
Fax: 213 580-7511
Gary Toebben, *President*
David Eads, *COO*
Benjamin Stilp, *CFO*
Natalie Pitman, *Office Admin*
Amy Cortina, *Manager*
EMP: 85
SALES (est): 6.9MM **Privately Held**
SIC: 8611 Business associations

(P-25093)
MENS APPAREL GUILD IN CAL INC
Also Called: Magic International
2901 28th St Ste 100, Santa Monica (90405-2975)
PHONE..................310 857-7500
Fax: 818 513-8816
Joe Loggia, *President*
Theodore Alpert, *Exec VP*
Anthony Calanca, *Exec VP*
Georgiann Decenzo, *Exec VP*
Chris Demoulin, *Exec VP*
EMP: 100 **EST:** 1932
SALES (est): 3.2MM
SALES (corp-wide): 1.1B **Privately Held**
WEB: www.magiconline.com
SIC: 8611 Manufacturers' institute
HQ: Advanstar Communications Inc.
2501 Colorado Ave Ste 280
Santa Monica CA 90404
310 857-7500

(P-25094)
MOTION PICTURE ASSN AMER INC
Also Called: Motion Picture Assn Amer In
15301 Ventura Blvd Bldg E, Sherman Oaks (91403-5885)
PHONE..................818 995-6600
Fax: 818 285-4403
Kathy Grant, *Manager*
Stewart McLaurin, *Exec VP*
Cristina Giroux, *Manager*
Kori Bernards, *Relations*
EMP: 100
SALES (corp-wide): 29.9MM **Privately Held**
SIC: 8611 Trade associations
PA: Motion Picture Association Of America, Inc.
1600 I St Nw
Washington DC 20006
202 293-1966

(P-25095)
NATIONAL ASSN MUS MRCHANTS INC
Also Called: Namm
5790 Armada Dr, Carlsbad (92008-4608)
PHONE..................760 438-8001
Fax: 760 438-7327
Joe Lamond, *President*
Pat Martin, *COO*
Neil Lilien, *CFO*
Larry Manley, *CFO*
Larry Morton, *Treasurer*
EMP: 62
SQ FT: 38,000
SALES: 21.1MM **Privately Held**
WEB: www.namm.com
SIC: 8611 Trade associations

(P-25096)
NORTHERN MONO CHAMBER COMMERCE
115281 Us Highway 395, Topaz (96133-9127)
PHONE..................530 208-6078
Pam Hamick, *President*
Dianne Evans, *Corp Secy*
Mary Dayhoff, *Vice Pres*
Susan Robbins, *Admin Sec*
EMP: 50
SALES (est): 1.6MM **Privately Held**
SIC: 8611 Chamber of Commerce

(P-25097)
OWENS VALLEY INTER AGENCY
351 Pacu Ln, Bishop (93514-3101)
PHONE..................760 873-2405
Tammy Longest, *Manager*
EMP: 50
SALES (est): 654.2K **Privately Held**
SIC: 8611 Business associations

(P-25098)
PGANDE
10901 E Highway 120, Manteca (95336-8920)
PHONE..................209 942-1745
R Nick Jordan, *Principal*
EMP: 50 **EST:** 2010
SALES (est): 569K **Privately Held**
SIC: 8611 Public utility association

(P-25099)
PRINTING INDS ASSN SUTHERN CAL
5800 S Eastrn Ave Ste 400, Commerce (90040)
P.O. Box 910936, Los Angeles (90091-0936)
PHONE..................323 728-9500
Fax: 323 724-2327
Robert Lindgren, *President*
Lina Lindgren, *Office Mgr*
Jerry Bonetto, *Technology*
Raul Mendrano, *Controller*
Gerry Bonetto, *Manager*
EMP: 75
SQ FT: 14,000
SALES: 8.5MM **Privately Held**
SIC: 8611 Trade associations

PRODUCTS & SERVICES SECTION
8621 - Professional Membership Organizations County (P-25120)

(P-25100)
PROJECT CONCERN INTERNATIONAL (PA)
Also Called: PCI
5151 Murphy Canyon Rd # 320, San Diego (92123-4339)
PHONE.................858 279-9690
Fax: 858 694-0294
George Guimaraes, *CEO*
Mark O Donnell, *COO*
Kote Lomidze, *CFO*
Janine Schooley, *Senior VP*
Chistopher A Lee, *Vice Pres*
EMP: 112
SQ FT: 12,000
SALES: 59.5MM **Privately Held**
WEB: www.projectconcern.org
SIC: 8611 Business associations

(P-25101)
PUBLIC POLICY INSTITUTE CAL (PA)
Also Called: Ppic
500 Washington St Ste 600, San Francisco (94111-2907)
PHONE.................415 291-4400
Fax: 415 291-4401
David Lyon, *President*
Robert E Obana, *CFO*
Andy Grose, *Principal*
Emily Loeschinger, *Executive Asst*
Alexia Cortez, *Admin Asst*
EMP: 72
SQ FT: 105,044
SALES (est): 9.7MM **Privately Held**
WEB: www.ppic.org
SIC: 8611 8732 Business associations; commercial nonphysical research

(P-25102)
SAN JOSE SILICON VALLEY CHAM
Also Called: Chamberpac
101 W Santa Clara St, San Jose (95113-1760)
PHONE.................408 291-5250
Patricia Dando, *President*
Todd Grafley, *CFO*
Barabara Wigderson, *CFO*
Terry Austen, *Treasurer*
J Baldwin, *Sr Corp Ofcr*
EMP: 61
SALES: 2.4MM **Privately Held**
SIC: 8611 Chamber of Commerce

(P-25103)
SEMICONDUCTOR EQP & MTLS INTL (PA)
3081 Zanker Rd, San Jose (95134-2127)
PHONE.................408 943-6900
Fax: 408 428-9600
Dennis P McGuirk, *President*
Eric Tien, *President*
Richard Salsman, *CFO*
Douglas Neugold, *Chairman*
Lubab L Sheet, *Surgery Dir*
EMP: 133 **EST:** 1970
SALES: 41.7MM **Privately Held**
WEB: www.semi.org
SIC: 8611 Trade associations

(P-25104)
SOUTHERN CALIFORNIA GOLF ASSN (PA)
3740 Cahuenga Blvd, North Hollywood (91604-3502)
P.O. Box 7186 (91615-0186)
PHONE.................818 980-3630
Ken Bien, *President*
Keenan Barber, *Treasurer*
Al Frank, *Vice Pres*
Bianca Avina, *Executive*
Tom Lindgren, *Principal*
EMP: 63
SQ FT: 15,000
SALES: 7MM **Privately Held**
WEB: www.scga.org
SIC: 8611 7992 Business associations; public golf courses

(P-25105)
SPECIALTY EQUIPMENT MKT ASSN (PA)
Also Called: SEMA
1575 Valley Vista Dr, Diamond Bar (91765-3914)
PHONE.................909 396-0289
Fax: 909 860-0184
Christopher J Kersting, *President*
Joel Ayres, *Bd of Directors*
Jim Cozzie, *Bd of Directors*
Dennis Gage, *Bd of Directors*
Tim Watts, *Bd of Directors*
EMP: 70
SQ FT: 23,000
SALES: 40.5MM **Privately Held**
WEB: www.enjoythedrive.com
SIC: 8611 Trade associations

(P-25106)
SURPLUS LINE ASSOCIATION CAL
50 California St Fl 18, San Francisco (94111-4602)
PHONE.................415 434-4900
Fax: 415 434-3716
Ted Pierce, *Exec Dir*
Philip Ballinger Jr, *Exec Dir*
Coleen Davey, *Executive Asst*
Amanda Archuleta, *Admin Asst*
Dave Taylor, *Webmaster*
EMP: 65
SQ FT: 8,400
SALES: 11.9MM **Privately Held**
SIC: 8611 Business associations

(P-25107)
UNITED AGRIBUSINESS LEAGUE (PA)
Also Called: UNITED AGRICULTURAL BENEFIT TR
54 Corporate Park, Irvine (92606-5105)
PHONE.................949 975-1424
Fax: 949 975-1671
William C Goodrich, *President*
Kirti Mutatkar, *CFO*
Clare M Einsmann, *Exec VP*
Donna Baresvp, *Vice Pres*
Jodi Martin, *Vice Pres*
EMP: 50
SQ FT: 14,099
SALES: 45.2MM **Privately Held**
WEB: www.ual.org
SIC: 8611 Growers' associations

(P-25108)
US LINES LLC (HQ)
3501 Jamboree Rd Ste 300, Newport Beach (92660-2936)
PHONE.................714 751-3333
Fax: 714 751-3323
Ed Aldridge, *President*
Timothy Dillon, *Vice Pres*
Shirley Wang, *Human Res Mgr*
Anthony Aulisio, *Regl Sales Mgr*
Todd Bring, *Regl Sales Mgr*
EMP: 75
SALES (est): 28.2MM **Privately Held**
WEB: www.uslines.com
SIC: 8611 Shipping & steamship company association
PA: Cma Cgm
Tour Cma Cgm
Marseille Cedex 02 13304
488 919-000

(P-25109)
WATER RESOURCES CONTROL BD CAL
Also Called: San Diego Region
2375 Northside Dr Ste 100, San Diego (92108-2700)
PHONE.................619 521-3010
David Gibson, *Exec Dir*
EMP: 90 **Privately Held**
WEB: www.rb3.swrcb.ca.gov
SIC: 8611 Regulatory associations
HQ: Water Resources Control Board, California
1001 I St
Sacramento CA 95814
916 341-5250

(P-25110)
WESTERN GROWERS ASSOCIATION (PA)
Also Called: W G A
15525 Sand Canyon Ave, Irvine (92618-3114)
P.O. Box 57089 (92619-7089)
PHONE.................949 863-1000
Fax: 949 863-9028
Tom A Nassif, *CEO*
Steve Patricio, *Ch of Bd*
Lori Duquette, *Officer*
Matt McInerney, *Exec VP*
Dave Puglia, *Senior VP*
EMP: 150
SQ FT: 35,000
SALES: 7.7MM **Privately Held**
WEB: www.wga.com
SIC: 8611 8111 Growers' associations; legal services

(P-25111)
WORKING SOLUTIONS INC
19360 Rinaldi St Ste 450, Northridge (91326-1607)
PHONE.................818 366-5009
Jane Lowenthal, *President*
EMP: 50
SALES (est): 681.3K **Privately Held**
SIC: 8611 Community affairs & services

8621 Professional Membership Organizations

(P-25112)
ACADEMY MPIC ARTS & SCIENCES (PA)
8949 Wilshire Blvd, Beverly Hills (90211-1907)
PHONE.................310 247-3000
Fax: 310 550-5034
Dawn Hudson, *CEO*
Andy Horn, *CFO*
Clay Crutchfield, *Chief Mktg Ofcr*
Bruce Davis, *Exec Dir*
Lorenza Munoz, *Managing Dir*
EMP: 100
SQ FT: 35,000
SALES: 108.4MM **Privately Held**
SIC: 8621 7819 8611 Professional membership organizations; services allied to motion pictures; business associations

(P-25113)
ACADEMY TV ARTS & SCIENCES
Also Called: Television Academy
5220 Lankershim Blvd, North Hollywood (91601-3141)
PHONE.................818 754-2800
Maury McIntyre, *President*
EMP: 60
SALES: 2.9MM **Privately Held**
SIC: 8621 Professional membership organizations

(P-25114)
AMERICAN ACADEMY OF OPTHALMLGY (PA)
655 Beach St Fl 1, San Francisco (94109-1346)
P.O. Box 7424 (94120-7424)
PHONE.................415 561-8500
Fax: 415 561-8576
David W Parke II, *CEO*
William L Rich III, *President*
Gregory L Skuta, *President*
Paul Sternberg Jr, *President*
Jill Boyett, *CFO*
EMP: 160 **EST:** 1896
SQ FT: 66,000
SALES: 61.7MM **Privately Held**
WEB: www.aao.org
SIC: 8621 Medical field-related associations

(P-25115)
AMERICAN COLLEGE PHLEBOLOGY
101 Callan Ave Ste 210, San Leandro (94577-4558)
PHONE.................510 346-6800
Bruce Sanders, *Exec Dir*
John Mauriello, *President*
Christopher Freed, *Exec Dir*
Keith Darby, *Finance*
Marlin Schul, *Med Doctor*
EMP: 70
SQ FT: 4,927
SALES: 4.4MM **Privately Held**
WEB: www.phlebology.org
SIC: 8621 Medical field-related associations

(P-25116)
ARMED FORCES OFFICIALS ASSN
14532 Penasquitos Dr, San Diego (92129-1606)
PHONE.................858 672-1438
Paul Bardsley, *Treasurer*
Robert Cauffman, *President*
Robery Kauffman, *President*
Clarence Langston, *Vice Pres*
Donald Robinson, *Admin Sec*
EMP: 50
SALES (est): 4.1MM **Privately Held**
SIC: 8621 Professional membership organizations

(P-25117)
ARTISTS OF RIVER TOWN
56 Highlands Blvd, Oroville (95966-3643)
PHONE.................530 534-7690
Dawn Bozine, *President*
Carmen Hironimus, *President*
Bee Boyd, *Treasurer*
Karen Comvey, *Admin Sec*
EMP: 76
SALES (est): 4.5MM **Privately Held**
WEB: www.global411.net
SIC: 8621 Professional membership organizations

(P-25118)
BAR ASSCATION OF SAN FRANCISCO (PA)
301 Battery St Fl 3, San Francisco (94111-3237)
PHONE.................415 982-1600
James Donato, *President*
Jonathan Bond, *CFO*
Dan Burkhardt, *Exec Dir*
Kelly Cohen, *Admin Asst*
Eric White, *Info Tech Dir*
EMP: 85
SQ FT: 23,600
SALES: 6.8MM **Privately Held**
SIC: 8621 Bar association

(P-25119)
CALIFORNIA ASSOCIATION O (PA)
Also Called: California Hospital Assn Cha
1215 K St Ste 800, Sacramento (95814-3946)
PHONE.................916 443-7401
Fax: 916 552-7588
C Duane Dauner, *President*
Jennifer Davenport, *President*
Lois M Suder, *COO*
Bill Emmerson, *Senior VP*
Dietmar Grellmann, *Senior VP*
EMP: 74
SQ FT: 30,000
SALES: 20.1MM **Privately Held**
SIC: 8621 8011 Health association; group health association

(P-25120)
CALIFORNIA CANCER SPECIALISTS (PA)
1333 S Mayflower Ave # 200, Monrovia (91016-5266)
PHONE.................626 775-3200
Lawrence Weiss, *CEO*
Patricia Gallardo, *Bus Dvlpt Dir*
Denise Bills, *Manager*
EMP: 300
SALES (est): 16.9MM **Privately Held**
SIC: 8621 7389 Medical field-related associations; financial services

8621 - Professional Membership Organizations County (P-25121)

PRODUDUCTS & SERVICES SECTION

(P-25121)
CALIFORNIA DENTAL ASSOCIATION (PA)
1201 K St Fl 14, Sacramento (95814-3925)
P.O. Box 13749 (95853-3749)
PHONE...............916 443-0505
Fax: 916 443-2943
Peter A Dubois, *CEO*
Dennis Kalebjian, *President*
Carol Summerhayes, *President*
Cynthia Schneider, *CFO*
Mark Soeth, *CFO*
EMP: 120
SQ FT: 28,932
SALES: 21.4MM **Privately Held**
WEB: www.sbvcds.org
SIC: 8621 Dental association

(P-25122)
CALIFORNIA NURSES ASSOCIATION (PA)
Also Called: National Nurses United
155 Grand Ave, Oakland (94612-3758)
PHONE...............510 273-2200
Fax: 510 663-1625
Rose Anne Demoro, *CEO*
Deborah Burger, *President*
Nikki Dones, *Admin Sec*
Ifeoma Adams, *Controller*
Mike Griffing, *Director*
EMP: 100
SQ FT: 36,000
SALES: 27.9MM **Privately Held**
WEB: www.calnurse.org
SIC: 8621 Nursing association

(P-25123)
CALIFORNIA SCHOOL BOARDS ASSN
Also Called: Csba
3251 Beacon Blvd, West Sacramento (95691-3531)
PHONE...............916 371-4691
Vernon M Billy, *CEO*
Cindy Marks, *President*
Stephen Pogemiller, *CFO*
Lynne Craig, *Bd of Directors*
Jesus Holguin, *Vice Pres*
EMP: 100
SQ FT: 15,000 **Privately Held**
WEB: www.csba.org
SIC: 8621 Education & teacher association

(P-25124)
CALIFORNIA TEACHERS ASSN
222 Judy Dr, Kelsey (95667-3325)
PHONE...............530 622-8013
George Sabato, *Admin Sec*
EMP: 65
SALES (corp-wide): 72.9MM **Privately Held**
WEB: www.cntaonline.org
SIC: 8621 Education & teacher association
PA: California Teachers Association
1705 Murchison Dr
Burlingame CA 94010
650 697-1400

(P-25125)
CALIFORNIA TEACHERS ASSN (PA)
1705 Murchison Dr, Burlingame (94010-4583)
P.O. Box 921 (94011-0921)
PHONE...............650 697-1400
Fax: 650 552-5002
Carolyn Doggett, *Exec Dir*
Linda Virden, *CFO*
Laura Murphy, *Executive Asst*
Nancy Stinson, *Admin Asst*
Terry Ng, *Database Admin*
EMP: 210
SALES: 187.1MM **Privately Held**
WEB: www.cntaonline.org
SIC: 8621 8631 Education & teacher association; labor unions & similar labor organizations

(P-25126)
CALIFRNIA CPA EDCATN FUNDATION
1800 Gateway Dr Ste 200, San Mateo (94404-4072)
PHONE...............800 922-5272
Loretta Doon, *CEO*
Tori Dean, *Finance*
EMP: 60 **EST:** 1966
SQ FT: 8,071
SALES: 12.5MM **Privately Held**
SIC: 8621 Professional membership organizations

(P-25127)
CAPITAL INVSTMNTS VNTURES CORP (PA)
Also Called: Civco
30151 Tomas, Rcho STA Marg (92688-2125)
PHONE...............949 858-0647
Drew Richardson, *President*
Brian Cronin, *Ch of Bd*
Gary Prenovost, *CFO*
Joy Obade, *Telecom Exec*
Marjorie Kelso, *Human Resources*
EMP: 195
SQ FT: 95,000
SALES (est): 49.3MM **Privately Held**
SIC: 8621 4724 Professional membership organizations; travel agencies

(P-25128)
CITY & COUNTY OF SAN FRANCISCO
Public Works Dept Bureau Arch
30 Van Ness Ave Ste 4100, San Francisco (94102-6034)
PHONE...............415 557-4713
Fax: 415 557-4701
Gary Hoy, *Principal*
Judi Soto, *Network Enginr*
Albert Ko, *Engineer*
Natalie Sierra, *Engineer*
Narinder Sood, *Engineer*
EMP: 75 **Privately Held**
SIC: 8621 9199 Architect association; general government administration; ;
PA: City & County Of San Francisco
1 Dr Carlton B Goodlett P
San Francisco CA 94102
415 554-7500

(P-25129)
CITY OF IRVINE
Also Called: Irvine Police Department
1 Civic Center Plz, Irvine (92606-5208)
PHONE...............949 724-7101
Fax: 949 724-7114
David Maggard, *President*
Michael Berkow, *CTO*
EMP: 76 **Privately Held**
SIC: 8621 Professional membership organizations
PA: City Of Irvine
1 Civic Center Plz
Irvine CA 92606
949 724-6000

(P-25130)
COMMUNITY CLINICS HLTH NETWRK
Also Called: Hqp
7535 Metropolitan Dr, San Diego (92108-4402)
PHONE...............619 542-4300
Henry Tuttle, *CEO*
Michael Beyer, *Executive*
Rasaun Robinson, *Regional Mgr*
Linda Johnson, *Administration*
Rich Swassort, *CTO*
EMP: 50
SALES: 8.2MM
SALES (corp-wide): 2.4MM **Privately Held**
SIC: 8621 Medical field-related associations
PA: Council Of Community Clinics
7535 Metropolitan Dr
San Diego CA 92108
619 542-4300

(P-25131)
COOPERTIVE AMRCN PHYSICIANS INC (PA)
Also Called: Cap-Mpt
333 S Hope St Fl 8, Los Angeles (90071-3001)
PHONE...............213 473-3600
Fax: 213 473-8773
James Weidner, *CEO*
Cindy Belcher, *COO*
John Donaldson, *CFO*
Hammon P Acuna, *Senior VP*
Nancy Brusegaard Johnson, *Senior VP*
EMP: 100
SALES (est): 19.7MM **Privately Held**
WEB: www.cap-mpt.com
SIC: 8621 Medical field-related associations

(P-25132)
COUNTY OF FRESNO
Also Called: Assessor-Recorder's Office
2281 Tulare St Ste 201, Fresno (93721-2139)
P.O. Box 1146 (93715-1146)
PHONE...............559 600-3534
Paul Dictos, *Manager*
EMP: 166 **Privately Held**
WEB: www.first5fresno.org
SIC: 8621 9441 Accounting association;
PA: County Of Fresno
2420 Mariposa St
Fresno CA 93721
559 600-1710

(P-25133)
COUNTY OF LOS ANGELES
313 N Figueroa St Fl 9, Los Angeles (90012-2602)
PHONE...............213 240-8412
Fax: 213 481-9853
Thomas L Garthwaite, *Branch Mgr*
Hal Yee, *Chief Mktg Ofcr*
Day Al, *Manager*
Kathleen Dinsmore, *Manager*
EMP: 863 **Privately Held**
WEB: www.co.la.ca.us
SIC: 8621 9431 Professional membership organizations; prenatal (maternity) health program administration, govt.
PA: County Of Los Angeles
500 W Temple St Ste 375
Los Angeles CA 90012
213 974-1101

(P-25134)
EMPLOYEE HEALTH SYSTEM MEDICAL
Also Called: Ehsmd
3131 Santa Anita Ave # 104, El Monte (91733-1369)
P.O. Box 2002, Monterey Park (91754-0952)
PHONE...............866 430-4288
Howard P Rosenberg MD, *President*
EMP: 75
SALES (est): 3.2MM **Privately Held**
SIC: 8621 8742 Health association; hospital & health services consultant

(P-25135)
GLOBAL TECH MGT RESOURCES INC
Also Called: Gtmr
7100 Moanache Mtn Ave, Inyokern (93527)
PHONE...............760 377-5522
EMP: 99
SALES (est): 490.5K **Privately Held**
SIC: 8621 Engineering association

(P-25136)
HEALTH TRUST (PA)
3180 Newberry Dr Ste 200, San Jose (95118-1566)
PHONE...............408 513-8700
Fax: 408 961-9856
Frederick J Ferrer, *CEO*
Robert Humphreys, *Partner*
Gary Allen, *President*
Todd Hansen J D, *COO*
Ira Holtzman, *CFO*
EMP: 100
SALES: 14.1MM **Privately Held**
SIC: 8621 8299 Health association; educational services

(P-25137)
HISPANIC BUSINESS STUDENT ASSN
5245 N Bcker Ave M/S Pd 7, Fresno (93740-0001)
PHONE...............209 769-7279
Norma Reyes, *President*
EMP: 51
SALES: 13K **Privately Held**
SIC: 8621 Education & teacher association

(P-25138)
INDYNE
300 W Point Ave, El Granada (94018)
PHONE...............805 606-0664
C Donald Bishop, *President*
Bob Miller, *CFO*
EMP: 99
SALES: 950K **Privately Held**
SIC: 8621 Professional membership organizations

(P-25139)
INTERNAL MDCINE RSDNCY AFFAIRS
Also Called: EC Davis Health Services
4150 V St Ste 3116, Sacramento (95817-1460)
PHONE...............916 734-7080
Kristi Threlkeld, *Manager*
Mark Henderson, *Director*
EMP: 85
SALES (est): 5.8MM **Privately Held**
SIC: 8621 Health association

(P-25140)
INTERNATIONAL CODE COUNCIL
Also Called: Los Angeles Regional Office
3060 Saturn St Ste 100, Brea (92821-1732)
PHONE...............562 699-0541
Mark Johnson, *Branch Mgr*
Steve Daggers, *President*
Thomas Frost, *Senior VP*
Karla Higgs, *Vice Pres*
Esmeralda Martinez, *Vice Pres*
EMP: 315
SALES (corp-wide): 53.4MM **Privately Held**
WEB: www.icccampus.com
SIC: 8621 Professional membership organizations
PA: International Code Council Inc
500 New Jersey Ave Nw # 6
Washington DC 20001
202 370-1800

(P-25141)
J M J ENTERPRISES INTL
10759 Magnolia Ave Ste F, Riverside (92505-3053)
PHONE...............951 343-2323
Alex Vista, *President*
Gerald Mujemulta, *Corp Secy*
Antonia Dumagas, *Vice Pres*
EMP: 60
SALES: 1MM **Privately Held**
SIC: 8621 Professional membership organizations

(P-25142)
LEIGHTON GROUP INC
75450 Gerald Ford Dr, Palm Desert (92211-6022)
PHONE...............760 776-4192
Fax: 760 776-4080
EMP: 105
SALES (corp-wide): 26.8MM **Privately Held**
SIC: 8621 Professional membership organizations
PA: Leighton Group, Inc.
17781 Cowan
Irvine CA 92614
949 477-4040

(P-25143)
LEXISNEXIS COURTLINK INC
2101 K St, Sacramento (95816-4920)
PHONE...............425 974-5000
Michele Vivona, *President*
Brian Hanson, *Info Tech Dir*
Al Cushon, *Production*
Connor O'Mara, *Accounts Exec*
EMP: 160
SQ FT: 40,000
SALES (est): 6.5MM
SALES (corp-wide): 9B **Privately Held**
SIC: 8621 Professional membership organizations

PRODUCTS & SERVICES SECTION

8631 - Labor Unions & Similar Organizations County (P-25164)

HQ: Relx Inc.
230 Park Ave
New York NY 10169
212 309-8100

(P-25144)
LOS ANGELES COUNTY BAR ASSN (PA)
Also Called: Los Angeles Lawyer Magazine
1055 W 7th St Ste 2700, Los Angeles (90017-2553)
P.O. Box 55020 (90055-2020)
PHONE....................213 627-2727
Fax: 213 623-4328
Paul R Kiesel, President
Brian K Condon, Bd of Directors
Katessa C Davis, Bd of Directors
Erin M Donovan, Bd of Directors
James P Drummy, Bd of Directors
EMP: 85
SQ FT: 25,000 Privately Held
WEB: www.lacba.org
SIC: 8621 Bar association

(P-25145)
MARIANNE FROSTIG CENTER (PA)
971 N Altadena Dr, Pasadena (91107-1870)
PHONE....................626 791-1255
Fax: 626 798-1801
Bennett Ross PHD, CEO
Dean Conklin, Exec Dir
Rick Benavides, Admin Asst
Kathleen Birk, Admin Asst
Rita Zobayan, Planning
EMP: 50 EST: 1948
SQ FT: 33,000
SALES: 4.9MM Privately Held
WEB: www.frostig.org
SIC: 8621 Education & teacher association

(P-25146)
MEDIMPACT HLTHCARE SYSTEMS INC (HQ)
10181 Scripps Gateway Ct, San Diego (92131-5152)
PHONE....................858 566-2727
Fax: 858 549-5348
Frederick Howe, Ch of Bd
James Gollaher, CFO
David Wheeler, CFO
Jerry Parker, Senior VP
John Treiman, Senior VP
EMP: 595
SQ FT: 100,000
SALES: 16MM Privately Held
WEB: www.medegram.com
SIC: 8621 Medical field-related associations

(P-25147)
NATIONAL NOTARY ASSOCIATION
Also Called: Nna Services
9350 De Soto Ave, Chatsworth (91311-4926)
PHONE....................818 739-4071
Fax: 818 700-1942
Milton G Valera, Chairman
Thomas A Heymann, CEO
Robert Clarke, CFO
Deborah M Thaw, Exec VP
Patrizia Dimolfetta, Controller
EMP: 204
SQ FT: 55,000
SALES (est): 43.9MM Privately Held
SIC: 8621 Professional membership organizations

(P-25148)
ORANGE COUNTY HEALTH AUTH
505 City Pkwy W, Orange (92868-2924)
PHONE....................714 246-8500
Richard Chambers, CEO
Michael Schracer, CEO
William Jones, COO
Novella Quesada, CFO
Chet Uma, CFO
EMP: 422
SALES (est): 113.8MM Privately Held
SIC: 8621 8011 Professional membership organizations; offices & clinics of medical doctors

(P-25149)
PADI AMERICAS INC
30151 Tomas, Rcho STA Marg (92688-2125)
P.O. Box 7005 (92688-7005)
PHONE....................949 858-7234
Fax: 949 267-1267
Kimberly Gould, Sr Corp Ofcr
Dana Stewart, Exec VP
Al Hornsby, Senior VP
David Espinosa, Executive
Nick Jenny, Executive
EMP: 200
SQ FT: 96,000
SALES (est): 47.7MM
SALES (corp-wide): 49.3MM Privately Held
WEB: www.padi.com
SIC: 8621 Professional membership organizations
HQ: Padi Worldwide Corp.
30151 Tomas
Rcho Sta Marg CA 92688
949 858-7234

(P-25150)
PADI WORLDWIDE CORP (HQ)
30151 Tomas, Rcho STA Marg (92688-2125)
PHONE....................949 858-7234
Drew Richardson, President
Gary Prenovost, Vice Pres
Debbi Tromley, Admin Sec
Bill Lindsey, Web Dvlpr
EMP: 180
SQ FT: 95,000
SALES (est): 47.7MM
SALES (corp-wide): 49.3MM Privately Held
SIC: 8621 Professional membership organizations
PA: Capital Investments & Ventures Corp.
30151 Tomas
Rcho Sta Marg CA 92688
949 858-0647

(P-25151)
PALO VERDE HOSPITAL ASSN
250 N 1st St, Blythe (92225-1702)
PHONE....................760 922-4115
Fax: 760 922-2050
Larry Blitz, CEO
Jim Carney, President
Richard Gianello, CFO
Samuel Burton, Treasurer
Beatrice Pinon, Vice Pres
EMP: 135
SQ FT: 44,000
SALES (est): 20.4MM Privately Held
SIC: 8621 Medical field-related associations

(P-25152)
QUEEN OF VALLEY HOSPITAL
1115 S Sunset Ave, West Covina (91790-3940)
PHONE....................626 962-4011
Fax: 626 814-2428
Louis Conyers, CFO
Robert Curry, CEO
Elvia Foulke, COO
Gilbert Furman, Med Doctor
Norman Owashi, Med Doctor
EMP: 900
SALES (est): 43.2MM Privately Held
SIC: 8621 Health association

(P-25153)
REGAL MEDICAL GROUP INC (PA)
Also Called: Heritage California Aco
8510 Balboa Blvd Ste 275, Northridge (91325-5809)
PHONE....................818 654-3400
Fax: 818 357-5039
Richard N Merkin, CEO
Rich Lipeles, Exec Dir
Dianna Cardenas, Administration
Manuel Corona, Info Tech Mgr
Marc Milnes, Engineer
EMP: 136
SALES (est): 32.3MM Privately Held
SIC: 8621 Medical field-related associations

(P-25154)
SALU BEAUTY INC
Also Called: Salu.net
11344 Coloma Rd Ste 725, Gold River (95670-4464)
PHONE....................916 475-1400
Jim O Steeb, President
Steve Brown, COO
John V Crisan, CFO
Jeff Askenas, Vice Pres
Marc Cawdrey, Vice Pres
EMP: 55
SALES (est): 11MM
SALES (corp-wide): 52.8B Publicly Held
SIC: 8621 Health association; general merchandise, mail order
HQ: Drugstore.Com, Inc.
411 108th Ave Ne Ste 1600
Bellevue WA 98004
425 372-3200

(P-25155)
SAN FRANCISCO HEALTH AUTHORITY (PA)
Also Called: Hsf Programme
50 Beale St Fl 12, San Francisco (94105-1813)
P.O. Box 194247 (94119-4247)
PHONE....................415 615-4407
Fax: 415 547-7824
John Grgurina Jr, CEO
Philip Hartman, President
Deena Louie, COO
Jacquelyn Oliveri, CFO
Robert S Yturria, CFO
EMP: 99
SQ FT: 26,000
SALES (est): 27.7MM Privately Held
WEB: www.sfhp.org
SIC: 8621 Health association

(P-25156)
SHARP COMMUNITY MEDICAL GROUP
Also Called: Scmg
8695 Spectrum Center Blvd, San Diego (92123-1489)
PHONE....................858 499-4525
Kenneth Roth, President
Lynn Briscoe, Executive Asst
Kelli Huff, Admin Asst
Eden Keh, Business Mgr
Manuel Deleon, Analyst
EMP: 200
SALES (est): 14.7MM
SALES (corp-wide): 3.4B Privately Held
WEB: www.scmg.com
SIC: 8621 Professional membership organizations
PA: Sharp Healthcare
8695 Spectrum Center Blvd
San Diego CA 92123
858 499-4000

(P-25157)
ST BALDRICKS FOUNDATION INC (PA)
1333 S Mayflower Ave, Monrovia (91016-4066)
PHONE....................626 792-8247
Charles M Chamness, Ch of Bd
Kathleen Ruddy, Exec Dir
Becky Weaver, Chief
Paolina Milana Dir Comm, Director
Liz Jackson, Director
EMP: 60
SALES: 37.7MM Privately Held
SIC: 8621 Health association

(P-25158)
ST VINCENT SENIOR CITIZN NUTR (PA)
2131 W 3rd St, Los Angeles (90057-1901)
PHONE....................213 484-7775
Sister A Marie Quinn, President
Alice Marie Quinn, President
Marie Fazio, Business Dir
EMP: 88
SALES: 8.2MM Privately Held
SIC: 8621 Professional membership organizations

(P-25159)
STATE BAR OF CALIFORNIA (PA)
180 Howard St Fl Grnd, San Francisco (94105-6155)
PHONE....................415 538-2000
Fax: 415 538-2247
Bill Hebert, President
Peggy Van Horn, CFO
Dina Diloreto, Managing Dir
Lorna Choy, Admin Asst
Scott Drexel, Admin Asst
EMP: 296
SQ FT: 72,000
SALES (est): 69.6MM Privately Held
SIC: 8621 Bar association

(P-25160)
STATE BAR OF CALIFORNIA
845 S Figueroa St, Los Angeles (90017-2515)
PHONE....................213 765-1000
Fax: 213 765-1109
Judy Johnson, Director
Louis Buchhold, Case Mgr
Gene Yoo, Manager
Kathleen Beitiks, Editor
EMP: 277
SALES (corp-wide): 69.6MM Privately Held
SIC: 8621 Bar association
PA: State Bar Of California
180 Howard St Fl Grnd
San Francisco CA 94105
415 538-2000

(P-25161)
UCLA FACULTY CENTER ASSN INC
480 Charles E Young Dr S, Los Angeles (90095-8363)
PHONE....................310 825-0877
Ali Tabrizi, Manager
EMP: 70
SQ FT: 30,000
SALES: 3.1MM Privately Held
SIC: 8621 Education & teacher association

(P-25162)
VISITING NURSE & HOSPICE CARE (PA)
Also Called: Visiting Nurse & Hospice Care
509 E Montecito St # 200, Santa Barbara (93103-3293)
PHONE....................805 965-5555
Lynda Tanner, CEO
Michelle Martinich, Chairman
Mary Pritchard, Treasurer
Michael Bordofsky, Bd of Directors
Rick Keith, Exec Dir
EMP: 80
SQ FT: 13,765
SALES: 23.5MM Privately Held
WEB: www.sbvna.org
SIC: 8621 Nursing association

(P-25163)
VISTA HILL FOUNDATION (PA)
8910 Clairemont Mesa Blvd, San Diego (92123-1104)
PHONE....................585 514-5100
Robert Dean, President
Belle Nunley, Vice Pres
Karen Giannini, Program Mgr
Melinda Katahara, Program Mgr
Mariel Bridges, Admin Asst
EMP: 50
SQ FT: 16,802
SALES: 22.6MM Privately Held
SIC: 8621 8741 Medical field-related associations; management services

---

8631 Labor Unions & Similar Organizations

(P-25164)
ALPHA CONNECTION GROUP HOME
Also Called: ALPHA CONNECTION YOUTH FAMILY
22675 Anoka Rd, Apple Valley (92308-5436)
PHONE....................760 247-6370

(PA)=Parent Co (HQ)=Headquarters (DH)=Div Headquarters
✪ = New Business established in last 2 years

8631 - Labor Unions & Similar Organizations County (P-25165)

Fax: 760 247-8920
Juanita Wilson, *President*
Barron Wilson, *Vice Pres*
EMP: 70
SALES: 2.3MM **Privately Held**
SIC: 8631 Labor unions & similar labor organizations

(P-25165)
AMERICAN POSTAL WORKERS UNION
28201 Franklin Pkwy, Santa Clarita (91383-8900)
PHONE..................661 775-8174
Edwardo Ruiz, *Principal*
EMP: 67
SALES (corp-wide): 133.4MM **Privately Held**
WEB: www.denverapwu.com
SIC: 8631 Labor unions & similar labor organizations
PA: American Postal Workers Union
   1300 L St Nw Ste 200
   Washington DC 20005
   202 842-4200

(P-25166)
ASSOCIATIONS OF UNITED NURSES (PA)
Also Called: UNAC/UHCP
955 Overland Ct Ste 150, San Dimas (91773-1740)
PHONE..................909 599-8622
Fax: 909 620-9119
Ken Deitz, *President*
Jettie Deden-Castillo, *Treasurer*
Denise Duncan, *Vice Pres*
Charmaine Morales, *Admin Sec*
EMP: 63
SALES: 3.5MM **Privately Held**
SIC: 8631 Employees' association

(P-25167)
BUENA PARK POLICE ASSOCIATION
6650 Beach Blvd, Buena Park (90621-2905)
PHONE..................714 562-3901
Fax: 714 523-2911
Sgt Steven Martinez, *President*
Tom Monson, *COO*
Thomas Carney, *Officer*
Joseph Davenport, *Officer*
Ryan Dieringer, *Officer*
EMP: 90
SALES: 107.9K **Privately Held**
SIC: 8631 Employees' association

(P-25168)
CALIFORNIA CORRECTNL PEACE OFC (PA)
Also Called: CCPOA
755 Riverpoint Dr, West Sacramento (95605-1673)
PHONE..................916 372-6060
Fax: 916 372-6623
Chuck Alexander, *President*
James Martin, *Treasurer*
Sandra Caraway, *Sr Corp Ofcr*
Perry Speth, *Admin Sec*
Amber Hollingsworth, *Admin Asst*
EMP: 60 **EST:** 1957
SQ FT: 32,000
SALES: 28.6MM **Privately Held**
WEB: www.ccpoa.org
SIC: 8631 8111 Labor union; legal services

(P-25169)
CALIFORNIA SCHL EMPLOYEES ASSN (PA)
Also Called: Csea
2045 Lundy Ave, San Jose (95131-1865)
PHONE..................408 473-1000
Fax: 408 954-0948
Allan Clark, *President*
Rob Freckner, *Sr Corp Ofcr*
Hortensia Benner, *Bd of Directors*
Al Martinez, *Bd of Directors*
Michael Mazzanti, *Bd of Directors*
EMP: 180
SQ FT: 65,000
SALES: 65.6MM **Privately Held**
WEB: www.csea.com
SIC: 8631 Labor union

(P-25170)
CALIFRNIA STATE EMPLOYEES ASSN (PA)
Also Called: Csea
1108 O St Ste 405, Sacramento (95814-5746)
PHONE..................916 444-8134
Fax: 916 623-4215
Dave Hart, *President*
Dave Okunura, *Treasurer*
Lee King, *General Mgr*
Debbie Cotton, *Admin Sec*
Mike Carr, *Controller*
EMP: 80
SQ FT: 30,000
SALES: 7.4MM **Privately Held**
SIC: 8631 Labor unions & similar labor organizations

(P-25171)
COUNTY OF LOS ANGELES
Also Called: Carson Gang Diversion Team
21356 Avalon Blvd, Carson (90745-2213)
PHONE..................310 847-4018
EMP: 226 **Privately Held**
SIC: 8631
PA: County Of Los Angeles
   500 W Temple St Ste 375
   Los Angeles CA 90012
   213 974-1101

(P-25172)
HAYWARD POLICE OFFICERS ASSN
300 W Winton Ave, Hayward (94544-1137)
PHONE..................510 293-7207
Fax: 510 293-7208
Julie Kirkland, *Principal*
EMP: 75
SALES: 432.9K **Privately Held**
SIC: 8631 Labor union

(P-25173)
INTERNATIONAL ALLIANCE THEA
Also Called: Local 442
P.O. Box 413 (93102-0413)
PHONE..................805 898-0442
Gary Hilton, *Principal*
EMP: 60
SALES (est): 47.1K **Privately Held**
SIC: 8631 Labor unions & similar labor organizations

(P-25174)
INTERNATIONAL BRTHRHD OF ELCTR (PA)
Also Called: AFL-CIO #1245
30 Orange Tree Cir, Vacaville (95687-3105)
PHONE..................707 452-2700
Fax: 707 452-2701
Ed Mallory, *President*
James McCulley, *Vice Pres*
Peggy Proschold, *Admin Asst*
Tom Dalzell, *Business Mgr*
Tom Dolza, *Business Mgr*
EMP: 64
SALES: 27.8MM **Privately Held**
WEB: www.ibew1245.com
SIC: 8631 Labor union

(P-25175)
INTERNATIONAL LONGSHOREMENS
Also Called: LONGSHOREMEN'S & WAREHOUSEMENS
22 N Union St, Stockton (95205-4915)
PHONE..................209 464-1827
Marc Cuavas, *President*
Dennis Brueckner, *President*
Lee Flood, *Vice Pres*
Frank Aeonis, *Admin Sec*
EMP: 81 **EST:** 1934
SQ FT: 1,000
SALES: 218.6K **Privately Held**
SIC: 8631 Trade union; labor union

(P-25176)
INTERNTIONAL UN OPER ENGINEERS
Local 12
150 Corson St, Pasadena (91103-3839)
P.O. Box 7109 (91109-7209)
PHONE..................626 792-2519
Fax: 626 792-9039
William C Waggoner, *Manager*
EMP: 50
SQ FT: 32,534
SALES (corp-wide): 48.5MM **Privately Held**
WEB: www.iuoestateunit12.org
SIC: 8631 Labor unions & similar labor organizations
PA: International Union Of Operating Engineers
   1121 L St Ste 401
   Sacramento CA 95814
   916 444-6880

(P-25177)
INTERNTIONAL UN OPER ENGINEERS (PA)
1121 L St Ste 401, Sacramento (95814-3969)
PHONE..................916 444-6880
Fax: 916 444-6877
Tim Neep, *Director*
EMP: 67 **EST:** 1939
SALES (est): 48.5MM **Privately Held**
WEB: www.iuoestateunit12.org
SIC: 8631 Labor union

(P-25178)
LOS ANGLES CNTY EMPLOYEES ASSN
Also Called: Service Employee Intl Un
1545 Wilshire Blvd, Los Angeles (90017-4501)
PHONE..................213 368-8660
Annelle Grajeda, *President*
Kathleen Austria, *Treasurer*
Bob Schoonover, *Vice Pres*
Linda Dent, *Admin Sec*
Annette Jeffrief, *Admin Sec*
EMP: 60
SQ FT: 40,000
SALES (est): 6.9MM **Privately Held**
WEB: www.local660.org
SIC: 8631 Labor union

(P-25179)
MILLMENS LOCAL 1496
6190 N Cecelia Ave, Fresno (93722-3204)
PHONE..................559 275-8676
Norman Avila, *President*
EMP: 50
SALES (est): 800.7K **Privately Held**
SIC: 8631 Labor unions & similar labor organizations

(P-25180)
OPERATING ENGNEERS LOCAL UN 3 (PA)
250 N Canyons Pkwy, Livermore (94551-9470)
PHONE..................925 454-4000
Mike Donahue, *CEO*
Jeff Hampton, *CFO*
Deepak Godhwani, *Assoc VP*
Cyndi Guerzon, *Senior VP*
Joanna Boedecker, *VP Info Sys*
EMP: 58
SALES (est): 19.7MM **Privately Held**
SIC: 8631 Labor unions & similar labor organizations

(P-25181)
PORT OF LONG BCH EMPLOYEES CLB
4801 Airport Plaza Dr, Long Beach (90815-1263)
P.O. Box 570 (90801-0570)
PHONE..................562 590-4102
Paul McArthy, *CEO*
Ofelia Alvarado, *Treasurer*
J Christopher, *Exec Dir*
Richard Steinke, *Director*
EMP: 400
SALES (est): 40.2MM **Privately Held**
SIC: 8631 4499 Employees' association; marine salvaging & surveying services

(P-25182)
SAN BRNRDINO PUB EMPLYEES ASSN
Also Called: SBPEA
433 N Sierra Way, San Bernardino (92410-4831)
P.O. Box 432 (92402-0432)
PHONE..................909 386-1260
Fax: 909 888-7429
Paula Ready, *President*
Robert Blough, *General Mgr*
EMP: 50
SQ FT: 20,000
SALES: 3.6MM **Privately Held**
WEB: www.sbpea.com
SIC: 8631 Employees' association

(P-25183)
SEIU LOCAL 2015
2910 Beverly Blvd, Los Angeles (90057-1012)
PHONE..................213 985-0463
Laphonza Butler, *President*
Dereck Smith, *Director*
EMP: 300
SALES (est): 825K **Privately Held**
SIC: 8631 Labor unions & similar labor organizations

(P-25184)
SEIU UNITED HEALTHCARE WORKERS (PA)
560 Thomas L Berkley Way, Oakland (94612-1602)
PHONE..................510 251-1250
Dave Regan, *President*
Edgard Tajina, *CFO*
Eliseo Medina, *Trustee*
Debbie M Schneider, *Trustee*
Laphonza Butler, *Vice Pres*
EMP: 140
SQ FT: 33,000
SALES: 104.3MM **Privately Held**
WEB: www.seiu-uhw.org
SIC: 8631 Labor union

(P-25185)
SEIU UNITED HEALTHCARE WORKERS
Also Called: Seiu Uhw-West
5480 Ferguson Dr, Commerce (90022-5119)
PHONE..................323 734-8399
Liza Leyva, *Director*
Verna Hampton,
Veronica Chavez, *Asst Director*
Vicki Jackson, *Asst Director*
Jorge Viilanueva, *Representative*
EMP: 50
SALES (corp-wide): 104.3MM **Privately Held**
SIC: 8631 Labor union
PA: Seiu United Healthcare Workers-West Local 2005
   560 Thomas L Berkley Way
   Oakland CA 94612
   510 251-1250

(P-25186)
SERVICE WORKERS LOCAL 715 (PA)
Also Called: Service Employees Intl Union
2302 Zanker Rd, San Jose (95131-1115)
PHONE..................408 678-3300
Fax: 408 954-1538
Rosemary Romo, *President*
Alan Ng, *Admin Asst*
Kristina Sermersheim, *Exec Sec*
EMP: 54
SQ FT: 1,000
SALES: 2.1MM **Privately Held**
WEB: www.seiu715.org
SIC: 8631 8621 Labor unions & similar labor organizations; professional membership organizations

(P-25187)
SOUTHWEST RGNAL CNCIL CRPNTERS (PA)
533 S Fremont Ave Fl 10, Los Angeles (90071-1712)
PHONE..................213 385-1457
Fax: 213 385-3759
Jacky Barnett, *President*
Mike McCarron, *President*

PRODUCTS & SERVICES SECTION

8641 - Civic, Social & Fraternal Associations County (P-25211)

Hal Jensen, *Vice Pres*
Jim Bernsen, *Admin Sec*
EMP: 50
SQ FT: 4,000
SALES (est): 22.7MM **Privately Held**
SIC: 8631 Labor union

(P-25188)
SUGAR WORKERS LOCAL 1
641 Loring Ave, Crockett (94525-1233)
PHONE..................................510 787-1676
Fax: 510 787-1776
Ed Cummings, *President*
Surinder M Bhanot, *President*
EMP: 330
SQ FT: 5,000
SALES: 227.5K **Privately Held**
SIC: 8631 Labor union

(P-25189)
UNITED FARM WORKERS AMERICA (PA)
29700 Wdford Tehachapi Rd, Keene (93531)
P.O. Box 62 (93531-0062)
PHONE..................................661 822-5571
Fax: 661 822-6103
Arturo Rodriguez, *President*
Mary Mecartney, *COO*
Liz Villarino, *CFO*
Tanis Ybarra, *Corp Secy*
Irv Hershenbaum, *Vice Pres*
EMP: 110
SQ FT: 5,000
SALES: 6.5MM **Privately Held**
WEB: www.ufw.org
SIC: 8631 Labor union

(P-25190)
UNITED FOOD AND COMMERCIAL (PA)
Also Called: Ufcw Local 770
630 Shatto Pl Ste 300, Los Angeles (90005-1372)
P.O. Box 770 (90078-0770)
PHONE..................................213 487-7070
Ricardo F Icaza, *President*
Rodney Diamond, *Corp Secy*
Jan Dresner, *Admin Asst*
Johnny Fung, *Controller*
Danny Garcia, *Marketing Mgr*
EMP: 60
SALES: 19MM **Privately Held**
SIC: 8631 Labor unions & similar labor organizations

(P-25191)
UNITED TEACHERS LOS ANGELES
Also Called: U T L A
3303 Wilshire Blvd Fl 10, Los Angeles (90010-1794)
PHONE..................................213 487-5560
Fax: 213 487-1618
Aj Duffy, *President*
David Goldburg, *Treasurer*
David Goldburg, *Treasurer*
Cecily Myart-Cruz, *Vice Pres*
Joshua Pechthalt, *Vice Pres*
EMP: 72 **EST:** 1970
SQ FT: 144,000
SALES: 15.1MM **Privately Held**
WEB: www.utla.net
SIC: 8631 Collective bargaining unit

(P-25192)
WRITERS GUILD AMERICA WEST INC
7000 W 3rd St, Los Angeles (90048-4321)
PHONE..................................323 951-4000
Fax: 323 782-4800
David Young, *CEO*
Don Gor, *CFO*
Elias Davis, *Corp Secy*
Carleton Eastlake, *Bd of Directors*
Sally Burmester, *Officer*
EMP: 160 **EST:** 1954
SQ FT: 67,000
SALES: 29.1MM **Privately Held**
WEB: www.wga.org
SIC: 8631 Labor union

8641 Civic, Social & Fraternal Associations

(P-25193)
ACLU FNDATION SOUTHERN CAL LLC
Also Called: AMERICAN CIVIL LIBERTIES UNION
1313 W 8th St, Los Angeles (90017-4420)
PHONE..................................213 977-9500
Fax: 213 250-3919
James Gilliam, *Deputy Dir*
Ramona Ripston, *Info Tech Mgr*
Glen Eichenblatt, *Information Mgr*
Mark Rosenbaum, *Mng Member*
EMP: 55
SALES: 7.7MM **Privately Held**
SIC: 8641 Civic social & fraternal associations

(P-25194)
ACTION PROPERTY MANAGEMENT INC
530 S Hewitt St, Los Angeles (90013-2286)
PHONE..................................800 400-2284
Mary Moore, *Branch Mgr*
EMP: 119
SALES (corp-wide): 76.5MM **Privately Held**
SIC: 8641 Homeowners' association
PA: Action Property Management, Inc.
2603 Main St Ste 500
Irvine CA 92614
949 450-0202

(P-25195)
ADELANTO YWCA
14938 Binford Ave, Adelanto (92301-4860)
PHONE..................................760 530-1850
Juanita Staley, *Exec Dir*
EMP: 100
SALES: 50K **Privately Held**
SIC: 8641 7991 8351 7032 Youth organizations; physical fitness facilities; child day care services; youth camps; individual & family services

(P-25196)
AMERICAN LEGION AMBULANCE SVC
Also Called: American Legion Hall
11350 American Legion Dr, Sutter Creek (95685)
PHONE..................................209 223-2963
Al Lennox, *General Mgr*
EMP: 70
SQ FT: 800
SALES: 6.8MM **Privately Held**
SIC: 8641 Veterans' organization

(P-25197)
AMERICAN LEGION AUX
Also Called: Fall Christian Unit, The
142 Raylow Ave, Manteca (95336-4821)
PHONE..................................209 823-4406
Sandy Holloway, *President*
Josephine Klingler, *Corp Secy*
EMP: 70
SALES (est): 534.4K **Privately Held**
WEB: www.americanlegionaux.com
SIC: 8641 Veterans' organization

(P-25198)
ANNENBERG FOUNDATION (PA)
2000 Ave Stars Ste 1000s, Los Angeles (90067)
PHONE..................................310 209-4560
Wallis Annenberg, *CEO*
Gregory Weingarten, *Vice Pres*
Leonard J Aube, *Exec Dir*
Shea Irick, *Admin Asst*
Margarita Diaz, *Technician*
EMP: 76
SALES (est): 6MM **Privately Held**
SIC: 8641 Civic social & fraternal associations

(P-25199)
ARTHRTIS FUNDATION PCF REG INC
800 W 6th St Ste 1250, Los Angeles (90017-2721)
PHONE..................................323 954-5760
Manuel Loya, *President*
Mireya Pena, *Director*
EMP: 50
SALES: 12.5MM **Privately Held**
SIC: 8641 Civic social & fraternal associations

(P-25200)
ASSOCIATED STUDENTS CALIFORNI
800 N State College Blvd, Fullerton (92831-3547)
P.O. Box 6828 (92834-6828)
PHONE..................................657 278-2468
Fred Sanchez, *Exec Dir*
Amir Dabirian, *President*
Marsha Farwick, *Finance Dir*
Bobby Weber, *Manager*
EMP: 51 **EST:** 1975
SQ FT: 117,000
SALES: 7.9MM **Privately Held**
SIC: 8641 Civic social & fraternal associations; university club

(P-25201)
ASSOCIATED STUDENTS CALIFORNIA
Also Called: A S I
1212 N Bellflower Blvd # 220, Long Beach (90815-4148)
PHONE..................................562 985-4994
Fax: 562 698-1460
Richard Haller, *Exec Dir*
EMP: 260 **EST:** 1956
SQ FT: 184,000
SALES: 14.1MM **Privately Held**
SIC: 8641 University club

(P-25202)
ASSOCIATED STUDENTS STANFORD (PA)
Also Called: A S S U
201 Tresidder Un, Stanford (94305)
PHONE..................................650 723-4331
Linda Whitcomb, *Director*
Alice Willoughby, *Principal*
EMP: 63
SALES: 1.4MM **Privately Held**
SIC: 8641 University club

(P-25203)
ASSOCIATED STUDENTS UNIV PCF
3601 Pacific Ave, Stockton (95211-0110)
PHONE..................................209 946-2233
Jason Belo, *Director*
Pamela Woodruff, *Treasurer*
EMP: 75
SALES (est): 3.2MM **Privately Held**
SIC: 8641 5411 7832 7389 University club; grocery stores; motion picture theaters, except drive-in; lecture bureau

(P-25204)
BALANCE4KIDS
4500 Soquel Dr, Soquel (95073-2122)
PHONE..................................831 464-8669
Fax: 831 457-0405
Victoria George, *Director*
Shannon Crane, *Treasurer*
Mary Willis, *Director*
EMP: 92
SALES: 3.2MM **Privately Held**
SIC: 8641 Youth organizations

(P-25205)
BAYVIEW HUNTERS POINT Y M C A
Also Called: YMCA
1601 Lane St, San Francisco (94124-2732)
PHONE..................................415 822-7728
Fax: 415 822-7769
Cheryl Smith-Thornton, *Exec Dir*
Tami Minix, *Meeting Planner*
EMP: 64
SALES (est): 2.5MM **Privately Held**
SIC: 8641 7991 8351 7032 Youth organizations; physical fitness facilities; child day care services; youth camps; individual & family services

(P-25206)
BEAR VALLEY SPRINGS ASSN
29541 Rollingoak Dr, Tehachapi (93561-7133)
PHONE..................................661 821-5537
Fax: 661 821-5406
Todd Lander, *President*
Terry Quinn, *President*
Larry Thompson, *Treasurer*
Tim Hawkins, *Vice Pres*
Kerry Brandt, *Controller*
EMP: 200
SQ FT: 2,000
SALES: 6.5MM **Privately Held**
WEB: www.bearinfo.com
SIC: 8641 Dwelling-related associations

(P-25207)
BEL-AIR BAY CLUB LTD
16801 Pacific Coast Hwy, Pacific Palisades (90272-3399)
PHONE..................................310 230-4700
Fax: 310 454-0571
William Howard, *CEO*
Shannon Griffin, *Executive*
Roberto Portillo, *Executive*
Samantha Ladue, *Comms Dir*
Lisa Lavin, *Accountant*
EMP: 200
SQ FT: 7,500
SALES (est): 11MM **Privately Held**
WEB: www.belairbayclub.com
SIC: 8641 Social club, membership

(P-25208)
BODEGA HARBOUR HOMEOWNERS ASSN
Also Called: Bodega Harbour Golf Links
21301 Heron Dr, Bodega Bay (94923-9401)
P.O. Box 368 (94923-0368)
PHONE..................................707 875-3519
Fax: 707 875-6980
Judith A Steeves, *Admin Mgr*
Michelle Gelfang, *Admin Asst*
EMP: 65
SQ FT: 10,000
SALES (est): 3.3MM **Privately Held**
SIC: 8641 5812 5813 7997 Homeowners' association; American restaurant; bars & lounges; yacht club, membership

(P-25209)
BOHEMIAN CLUB (PA)
Also Called: Bohemian Grove
624 Taylor St, San Francisco (94102-1075)
PHONE..................................415 885-2440
Fax: 415 567-2332
Robert L Spence, *CEO*
Lindsey Grant, *Social Dir*
Matt Ogerio, *General Mgr*
Jennifer Robertson, *Human Res Dir*
Chris Cheeseman, *Manager*
EMP: 100 **EST:** 1872
SQ FT: 20,000
SALES: 6.1MM **Privately Held**
WEB: www.bc-owl.org
SIC: 8641 Social club, membership

(P-25210)
BOY SCOUTS OF AMERICA (PA)
2333 Scout Way, Los Angeles (90026-4995)
PHONE..................................213 353-9879
Fax: 213 483-6472
Cash Sutton, *President*
Dennis Cline, *Vice Chairman*
Larry Forbes, *CFO*
Jay Lee, *Webmaster*
Parker Irey, *Manager*
EMP: 82
SALES: 5.9MM **Privately Held**
SIC: 8641 Civic social & fraternal associations

(P-25211)
BOYS & GIRLS CLUB SIMI VLY INC
2850 Lemon Dr, Simi Valley (93063-2193)
PHONE..................................805 527-4437
Fax: 805 527-4516
Linda White, *CEO*
Dee Cavanaugh, *Vice Pres*
Sandee Covone, *Asst Director*
Lauren Guynes, *Director*

Bruce Yi, *Director*
EMP: 50
SALES: 2.5MM **Privately Held**
WEB: www.bgcsimi.com
SIC: 8641 Civic social & fraternal associations

(P-25212)
BOYS & GIRLS CLUBS CENT SONOMA
1400 N Dutton Ave Ste 14, Santa Rosa (95401-7120)
PHONE.....................707 528-7977
Jennifer Weiss, *Exec Dir*
Dawn Holman, *Administration*
Margaret Forbes, *Business Mgr*
Shannon Baron, *Director*
Kirsten Schepp, *Director*
EMP: 187
SALES (est): 6.1MM **Privately Held**
SIC: 8641 Youth organizations

(P-25213)
BOYS AND GIRLS CLUBS OF THE LA (PA)
Also Called: Boys & Girls Club of San Pedro
1200 S Cabrillo Ave, San Pedro (90731-4011)
PHONE.....................310 833-1322
Fax: 310 833-4235
Mike Lansing, *Director*
Robert Nizich, *President*
Dennis Lane, *Treasurer*
Joseph Rich, *Vice Pres*
John Robinson, *Vice Pres*
EMP: 79 EST: 1939
SQ FT: 26,083
SALES: 6MM **Privately Held**
WEB: www.bgclaharbor.org
SIC: 8641 Youth organizations

(P-25214)
BOYS AND GIRLS CLUBS OF THE LA
Also Called: Dana Middle Schl Bys Girls CLB
1501 S Cabrillo Ave, San Pedro (90731-4617)
PHONE.....................310 833-1322
Mike Lansing, *Branch Mgr*
EMP: 99
SALES (corp-wide): 6MM **Privately Held**
SIC: 8641 Civic social & fraternal associations
PA: Boys And Girls Clubs Of The Los Angeles Harbor
1200 S Cabrillo Ave
San Pedro CA 90731
310 833-1322

(P-25215)
BOYS AND GIRLS CLUBS OF THE LA
Also Called: Wilmington Schll Bys & Grls CL
1700 Gulf Ave, Wilmington (90744-1311)
PHONE.....................310 833-1322
Fax: 310 549-5307
Mike Lansing, *Branch Mgr*
EMP: 99
SALES (corp-wide): 6MM **Privately Held**
SIC: 8641 Civic social & fraternal associations
PA: Boys And Girls Clubs Of The Los Angeles Harbor
1200 S Cabrillo Ave
San Pedro CA 90731
310 833-1322

(P-25216)
BOYS GIRLS CLB OF BAKERSFIELD
Also Called: BOY'S & GIRL'S CLUB OF BAKERSF
801 Niles St, Bakersfield (93305-4419)
PHONE.....................661 325-3730
Fax: 661 325-2118
Zane Smith, *Exec Dir*
Ed Kuhn, *President*
Murry Tragish, *President*
Craig Stickler, *Treasurer*
Bill Campbell, *Vice Pres*
EMP: 100
SALES: 5.8MM **Privately Held**
SIC: 8641 8322 Youth organizations; individual & family services

(P-25217)
BOYS GIRLS CLB OF IMPERL BCH
847 Encina Ave, Imperial Beach (91932-2135)
P.O. Box 520 (91933-0520)
PHONE.....................619 424-2266
Fax: 619 424-8266
Ken Blinsman, *Director*
Mark Nagles, *President*
Joy Sprouce, *Director*
EMP: 100
SALES: 2.8MM **Privately Held**
SIC: 8641 5812 Civic social & fraternal associations; eating places

(P-25218)
BOYS GRLS CLB SNTA MONICA INC
1220 Lincoln Blvd, Santa Monica (90401-1704)
PHONE.....................310 361-8500
Fax: 310 458-8857
Aaron Young, *Director*
Jessica Rubecindo, *Volunteer Dir*
Virginia Kato, *General Mgr*
Lauren Savage, *Finance*
Jesse Satterfield, *Athletic Dir*
EMP: 83
SQ FT: 6,000
SALES: 4MM **Privately Held**
WEB: www.smbgc.org
SIC: 8641 7997 Youth organizations; membership sports & recreation clubs

(P-25219)
BOYS GRLS CLUBS GRDN GROVE INC (PA)
10540 Chapman Ave, Garden Grove (92840-3101)
PHONE.....................714 530-0430
Fax: 714 530-0431
Patsy Halbertstadt, *CEO*
Bryce McHale, *Finance*
Joy Aho, *Transptn Dir*
Romy Cisneros, *Director*
Rachelle Gillerman, *Director*
EMP: 86
SQ FT: 12,000
SALES: 10.6MM **Privately Held**
SIC: 8641 Youth organizations

(P-25220)
BOYS GRLS CLUBS GRDN GROVE INC
Also Called: Girls and Boys Club Grdn Grove
13645 Clinton St, Garden Grove (92843-4110)
PHONE.....................714 537-8833
Fax: 714 741-0596
Evelyn Matua, *Branch Mgr*
EMP: 158
SALES (corp-wide): 10.6MM **Privately Held**
SIC: 8641 Youth organizations
PA: Boys & Girls Clubs Of Garden Grove, Inc.
10540 Chapman Ave
Garden Grove CA 92840
714 530-0430

(P-25221)
BOYS TOWN CALIFORNIA INC
2223 E Wellington Ave, Santa Ana (92701-3161)
P.O. Box 148, Boys Town NE (68010-0148)
PHONE.....................714 558-0303
Fax: 714 558-0324
Lawren Ramos, *CEO*
Christina Garkovich, *Director*
Sara Larsen, *Assistant*
EMP: 70
SALES: 5.8MM
SALES (corp-wide): 465.5MM **Privately Held**
SIC: 8641 Youth organizations
PA: Father Flanagan's Boys' Home
14086 Mother Theresa Ln
Boys Town NE 68010
402 498-1111

(P-25222)
BRIDGES CLUB AT RANCHO SA
18550 Seven Bridges Rd, Rancho Santa Fe (92091-0216)
P.O. Box 1322 (92067-1322)
PHONE.....................858 759-7200
Tom Martin, *President*
Jenna Burns, *Executive Asst*
Patty Aguirre, *Controller*
Patty Aguirre, *Controller*
EMP: 140
SALES: 4MM **Privately Held**
SIC: 8641 Social club, membership

(P-25223)
BROADCOM FOUNDATION
5300 California Ave # 14067, Irvine (92617-3038)
P.O. Box 57013 (92619-7013)
PHONE.....................949 926-9500
Scott A McGregor, *President*
Auerello Fernandez, *Vice Pres*
Sean Lee, *Engineer*
Brian Stevens, *Engineer*
Jing Liu, *Buyer*
EMP: 69
SALES: 27.6MM **Privately Held**
SIC: 8641 Civic social & fraternal associations

(P-25224)
BUNKER HILL CLUB INC
Also Called: City Club On Bunker Hill
555 S Flower St Ste 5100, Los Angeles (90071-2400)
PHONE.....................213 620-9662
Fax: 213 620-0895
Isaias Ledesma, *Manager*
Nicole Imlach, *Executive*
Larry Ahlquist, *General Mgr*
EMP: 72
SQ FT: 16,874
SALES (est): 1.6MM
SALES (corp-wide): 1B **Publicly Held**
WEB: www.remington-gc.com
SIC: 8641 Bars & restaurants, members only
HQ: Clubcorp Usa, Inc.
3030 Lyndon B Johnson Fwy
Dallas TX 75234
972 243-6191

(P-25225)
CALIFORNIA CLUB
538 S Flower St, Los Angeles (90071-2548)
PHONE.....................213 622-1391
Fax: 213 624-7093
Robert C Baker, *CEO*
Mark Emerson, *Controller*
Dindo Galanto, *Marketing Staff*
Raj Raghavan, *Director*
Angel Tecun, *Manager*
EMP: 185 EST: 1888
SALES: 14.6MM **Privately Held**
SIC: 8641 7041 Business persons club; bars & restaurants, members only; residence club, organization

(P-25226)
CALIFORNIA CLUB OF CA
1750 Clay St, San Francisco (94109-3613)
PHONE.....................415 474-3516
Eleanor Leith, *President*
Isabelle Brown, *Vice Pres*
EMP: 72
SALES (est): 1MM **Privately Held**
SIC: 8641 7922 Social club, membership; community theater production

(P-25227)
CAMP ROYANEH BOY SCOUT
P.O. Box 39 (95421-0039)
PHONE.....................707 632-5291
Stanley Andrew, *Principal*
Jim Schiechl, *Director*
EMP: 60
SALES (est): 716.3K **Privately Held**
SIC: 8641 Youth organizations

(P-25228)
CANYON LK PROPERTY OWNERS ASSN
31512 Railroad Canyon Rd, Canyon Lake (92587-9400)
PHONE.....................951 244-6841

Fax: 951 244-6845
Carl Armburst, *President*
Marty Gibson, *Treasurer*
Bruce Yarbrough, *Treasurer*
Clint Warrell, *General Mgr*
Harmony Owen, *Admin Asst*
EMP: 93
SQ FT: 18,000
SALES (est): 8.2MM **Privately Held**
SIC: 8641 Homeowners' association

(P-25229)
CARLSBAD INN VACTN CONDO OWNRS
3001 Carlsbad Blvd, Carlsbad (92008-2964)
PHONE.....................760 434-7542
Fax: 760 434-1676
David Brown, *President*
Joe Spirito, *President*
Tim Stripe, *Co-President*
Randall Chapin, *General Mgr*
Eric Segal, *Director*
EMP: 68
SQ FT: 130,000
SALES: 3.5MM **Privately Held**
WEB: www.carlsbadinn.com
SIC: 8641 Homeowners' association

(P-25230)
CENTRAL VLY YNG MNS CHRN ASSOC
Also Called: Central Valley YMCA
4045 N Fresno St Ste 101, Fresno (93726-4099)
PHONE.....................559 225-9191
Jeff Teliha, *President*
Chris Schneider, *Exec Dir*
EMP: 50 EST: 1886
SQ FT: 50,000
SALES: 371.5K **Privately Held**
SIC: 8641 7991 8351 7032 Youth organizations; physical fitness facilities; child day care services; youth camps; individual & family services

(P-25231)
CHANNEL ISLANDS YOUNG MENS CH
Also Called: Lompoc Family YMCA
201 W College Ave, Lompoc (93436-4415)
PHONE.....................805 736-3483
Dan Powell, *Branch Mgr*
Barbara Gooden, *Exec Dir*
Barbara Franks, *CTO*
Kate Schiffelbein, *Program Dir*
EMP: 51
SALES (corp-wide): 16MM **Privately Held**
WEB: www.ciymca.org
SIC: 8641 7991 8351 7032 Youth organizations; physical fitness facilities; child day care services; youth camps; individual & family services
PA: Channel Islands Young Men's Christian Association
105 E Carrillo St
Santa Barbara CA 93101
805 569-1103

(P-25232)
CHANNEL ISLANDS YOUNG MENS CH
Also Called: Camarillo Family YMCA
3111 Village Park Dr, Camarillo (93012)
PHONE.....................805 484-0423
Fax: 805 388-7087
Marge Castellano, *Director*
Ann Wirtz, *Mktg Coord*
Cheri Hays, *Director*
Karen Maass, *Director*
Jane Reed, *Director*
EMP: 85
SALES (corp-wide): 16MM **Privately Held**
WEB: www.ciymca.org
SIC: 8641 7991 8351 7032 Youth organizations; physical fitness facilities; child day care services; youth camps; individual & family services
PA: Channel Islands Young Men's Christian Association
105 E Carrillo St
Santa Barbara CA 93101
805 569-1103

PRODUCTS & SERVICES SECTION
8641 - Civic, Social & Fraternal Associations County (P-25255)

(P-25233)
CHANNEL ISLANDS YOUNG MENS CH
Also Called: Santa Barbara Family YMCA
36 Hitchcock Way, Santa Barbara (93105-3102)
PHONE 805 687-7727
Fax: 805 687-7568
Tim Hardy, *Branch Mgr*
Alicia Cattoni, *Marketing Staff*
Paige Harris, *Director*
Vinny Savelich, *Director*
Traci Costa, *Associate*
EMP: 139
SALES (corp-wide): 16MM Privately Held
WEB: www.ciymca.org
SIC: 8641 7991 8351 7032 Youth organizations; physical fitness facilities; child day care services; youth camps; individual & family services
PA: Channel Islands Young Men's Christian Association
105 E Carrillo St
Santa Barbara CA 93101
805 569-1103

(P-25234)
CHANNEL ISLANDS YOUNG MENS CH
Also Called: Montecito Family YMCA
591 Santa Rosa Ln, Santa Barbara (93108-2145)
PHONE 805 969-3288
Fax: 805 969-4871
Yvonne Rubio, *Director*
Keiko Rankart, *Mktg Coord*
Sheryl Barnard, *Manager*
EMP: 73
SALES (corp-wide): 16MM Privately Held
WEB: www.ciymca.org
SIC: 8641 7991 8351 7032 Youth organizations; physical fitness facilities; child day care services; youth camps; individual & family services
PA: Channel Islands Young Men's Christian Association
105 E Carrillo St
Santa Barbara CA 93101
805 569-1103

(P-25235)
CHANNEL ISLANDS YOUNG MENS CH
Also Called: Ventura Family YMCA
3760 Telegraph Rd, Ventura (93003-3421)
PHONE 805 484-0423
Fax: 805 642-1137
Sarah Abrams, *Director*
Amy Bailey, *Director*
EMP: 144
SALES (corp-wide): 16MM Privately Held
WEB: www.ciymca.org
SIC: 8641 7991 8351 7032 Youth organizations; physical fitness facilities; child day care services; youth camps; individual & family services
PA: Channel Islands Young Men's Christian Association
105 E Carrillo St
Santa Barbara CA 93101
805 569-1103

(P-25236)
CHANNEL ISLANDS YOUNG MENS CH
Also Called: Stuart C. Gildred Family YMCA
900 N Refugio Rd, Santa Ynez (93460-9314)
PHONE 805 686-2037
Fax: 805 686-1424
Paula Parisotto, *Branch Mgr*
EMP: 80
SALES (corp-wide): 16MM Privately Held
WEB: www.ciymca.org
SIC: 8641 7991 8351 7032 Youth organizations; physical fitness facilities; child day care services; youth camps; individual & family services
PA: Channel Islands Young Men's Christian Association
105 E Carrillo St
Santa Barbara CA 93101
805 569-1103

(P-25237)
CHATEAU LAKE SAN MARCOS HOMEOW
1502 Circa Del Lago, San Marcos (92078-7201)
PHONE 760 471-0083
Fax: 760 471-2157
Chris Arvanitis, *President*
EMP: 75
SQ FT: 240,000
SALES: 3MM Privately Held
SIC: 8641 Homeowners' association

(P-25238)
CHINESE CNSLD BENEVOLENT ASSN
843 Stockton St, San Francisco (94108-2120)
PHONE 415 982-6000
Thomas Ng, *Exec Dir*
EMP: 55
SALES: 54.3K Privately Held
SIC: 8641 Community membership club

(P-25239)
COMMUNITY ACTION BRD OF SNT CR
406 Main St Ste 202, Watsonville (95076-4639)
PHONE 831 724-0206
Elena Dela Garza, *Director*
Helen Ewan, *CEO*
EMP: 50
SALES (corp-wide): 3MM Privately Held
SIC: 8641 Civic social & fraternal associations
PA: Community Action Board Of Santa Cruz County Inc
406 Main St Ste 207
Watsonville CA 95076
831 763-2147

(P-25240)
COMMUNITY CATALYSTS CALIFORNIA
229 Pajaro St Ste 201, Salinas (93901-3428)
PHONE 831 769-0934
Fax: 831 769-0893
Greg Murphy, *Branch Mgr*
EMP: 50
SALES (corp-wide): 11.4MM Privately Held
SIC: 8641 Civic social & fraternal associations
PA: Community Catalysts Of California
3760 Convoy St Ste 344
San Diego CA 92111
858 292-2020

(P-25241)
CONEJO VALLEY UNIFIED SCHL DST
620 Velarde Dr, Thousand Oaks (91360-1331)
PHONE 805 492-3531
Fax: 805 492-6071
EMP: 173
SALES (corp-wide): 190.6MM Privately Held
SIC: 8641 Parent-teachers' association
PA: Conejo Valley Unified School District
1400 E Janss Rd
Thousand Oaks CA 91362
805 497-9511

(P-25242)
CONTEMPRARY HSTRICAL VHCL ASSN
430 Oak View Dr, Vacaville (95688-4224)
PHONE 707 448-7266
Eric V Beeby, *Principal*
EMP: 90
SALES (est): 667.6K Privately Held
SIC: 8641 Civic social & fraternal associations

(P-25243)
COUNTY OF SHASTA
Also Called: Shasta Cattle Women
19897 Gas Point Rd, Cottonwood (96022-9115)
P.O. Box 1491 (96022-1491)
PHONE 530 347-6276
Diane Montagner, *President*
EMP: 80 Privately Held
WEB: www.rsdnmp.org
SIC: 8641 Civic social & fraternal associations
PA: County Of Shasta
1450 Court St Ste 308a
Redding CA 96001
530 225-5561

(P-25244)
COWELL HOMEOWNERS ASSOCIATION (PA)
Also Called: Walnut Country
4498 Lawson Ct, Concord (94521-4410)
PHONE 925 825-0250
Fax: 925 677-0182
Michael Demeo, *President*
Katie Herbert, *Manager*
Virginia Balesteri, *Agent*
EMP: 60 EST: 1972
SQ FT: 2,300
SALES (est): 2.1MM Privately Held
WEB: www.walnutcountry.com
SIC: 8641 Homeowners' association; child day care services

(P-25245)
CRENSHAW YMCA
3820 Santa Rosalia Dr, Los Angeles (90008-2516)
PHONE 323 290-9113
Martin Harris, *Director*
EMP: 70
SALES: 2MM Privately Held
SIC: 8641 7991 8351 7032 Youth organizations; physical fitness facilities; child day care services; youth camps; individual & family services

(P-25246)
CRESCENTA-CANADA YMCA (PA)
Also Called: YMCA Crescenta-Canada
1930 Foothill Blvd, La Canada (91011-1933)
PHONE 818 790-0123
Larry Hall, *CEO*
Ken Gorvetzian, *Ch of Bd*
EMP: 150 EST: 1953
SALES: 9MM Privately Held
SIC: 8641 7991 8351 7032 Youth organizations; physical fitness facilities; child day care services; youth camps; individual & family services

(P-25247)
CRESCENTA-CANADA YMCA
Also Called: Learning Tree Pre-School
6840 Foothill Blvd, Tujunga (91042-2711)
PHONE 818 352-3255
Kathi Brink, *Branch Mgr*
EMP: 50
SALES (corp-wide): 9MM Privately Held
SIC: 8641 7991 8351 7032 Youth organizations; physical fitness facilities; child day care services; youth camps; individual & family services
PA: Crescenta-Canada Ymca
1930 Foothill Blvd
La Canada CA 91011
818 790-0123

(P-25248)
CYPRESS COLLEGE FOUNDATION
9200 Valley View Ave, Whittier (90603-1957)
PHONE 714 484-7128
Raul Alvarez, *Principal*
EMP: 77
SALES: 513.9K Privately Held
SIC: 8641 Civic social & fraternal associations

(P-25249)
CYPRESS EDUCATION FOUNDATION
9470 Moody St, Cypress (90630-2919)
PHONE 714 220-6900
William D Eller, *CEO*
EMP: 51
SALES: 456.1K Privately Held
WEB: www.cypressmonterey.com
SIC: 8641 Educator's association

(P-25250)
DELTA KAPPA GAMMA SOCIETY
2350 Elsinore Rd, Riverside (92506-1540)
PHONE 951 686-8630
Paula Wilcoxson, *President*
EMP: 50
SALES (est): 309.1K Privately Held
SIC: 8641 Social associations

(P-25251)
DESERT PRNCESS HOMEOWNERS ASSN
Also Called: Desert Princess Hoa
28211 Desert Princess Dr, Cathedral City (92234-3524)
PHONE 760 322-0567
Mario Gonzales, *CEO*
Tom Adamo, *President*
Marilyn J White, *CEO*
Mark McLaughlin, *Treasurer*
Robin Kauder, *Controller*
EMP: 100
SQ FT: 3,000
SALES (est): 4.4MM Privately Held
WEB: www.desertprincesscc.com
SIC: 8641 Homeowners' association

(P-25252)
EAST PALO ALTO Y M C A
550 Bell St, East Palo Alto (94303-1701)
PHONE 650 328-9622
Robert Huges, *Director*
EMP: 50 EST: 1994
SALES (est): 292.5K Privately Held
SIC: 8641 7991 8351 7032 Youth organizations; physical fitness facilities; child day care services; youth camps; individual & family services

(P-25253)
EMBARCADERO HOMES ASSOCIATION
Lincoln Sq Condos, Stockton (95207)
P.O. Box 7003 (95267-0003)
PHONE 209 951-4420
Kathy Dharnidharka, *President*
Charles Klass, *Treasurer*
Edmund Weiss, *Bd of Directors*
Cheri Margie, *Vice Pres*
Donna Zuckerman, *Admin Sec*
EMP: 73
SALES (est): 810.6K Privately Held
SIC: 8641 Homeowners' association

(P-25254)
EMERSON ELEMENTARY
720 E Cypress Ave, Burbank (91501-1812)
PHONE 818 558-5419
Fax: 818 843-2359
Linda Acuff, *Principal*
EMP: 65
SALES: 31.8K Privately Held
SIC: 8641 Parent-teachers' association

(P-25255)
FORT WASHINGTON PARENT ASSOC
Also Called: FT. WASHINGTON ELEM.
960 E Teague Ave, Fresno (93720-1704)
PHONE 559 327-6600
Fax: 559 327-6690
Sean Osterberg, *Principal*
Anne Kalashian, *Principal*
Brenda R Smith, *Tech/Comp Coord*
Andrew Hendricks, *Network Analyst*
Paula Prince, *Librarian*
EMP: 55
SALES: 58.3K Privately Held
SIC: 8641 Parent-teachers' association

8641 - Civic, Social & Fraternal Associations County (P-25256)

(P-25256)
FOUNDTION FOR HISPANIC EDUCATN (PA)
14271 Story Rd, San Jose (95127-3823)
P.O. Box 730453 (95173-0453)
PHONE.............................408 585-5022
Edward Alvarez, *CEO*
EMP: 86
SQ FT: 60
SALES: 1.5MM **Privately Held**
SIC: 8641 Civic social & fraternal associations

(P-25257)
FRIENDS SANTA CRUZ STATE PARKS
144 School St, Santa Cruz (95060-3726)
PHONE.............................831 429-1840
Bonny Hawley, *Exec Dir*
Peg Danielson, *Executive Asst*
Taylor Dial, *Finance*
EMP: 80
SALES: 3.5MM **Privately Held**
SIC: 8641 Civic social & fraternal associations

(P-25258)
GENERAL GEORGE W SLINEY BASHA
Also Called: China Brma India Veterans Assn
4839 Rio Vista Ave, San Jose (95129-1009)
PHONE.............................408 296-3423
Robert E Burke, *Treasurer*
EMP: 75
SALES (est): 2.8MM **Privately Held**
SIC: 8641 Veterans' organization

(P-25259)
GEOSYNTEC CONSULTANTS INC
2100 Main St Ste 150, Huntington Beach (92648-2460)
PHONE.............................714 969-0800
Fax: 714 969-0820
Bert Palmer, *Manager*
Misty Yanok, *Info Tech Mgr*
Eric Smalstig, *Project Engr*
Paul Hobson, *Engineer*
Julia Ryan, *Engineer*
EMP: 55
SALES (corp-wide): 2.7MM **Privately Held**
SIC: 8641 8711 Environmental protection organization; engineering services
PA: Geosyntec Consultants, Inc.
900 Broken Sound Pkwy Nw
Boca Raton FL 33487
561 995-0900

(P-25260)
GIRL SCOUTS HEART CENTRAL CAL
6601 Elvas Ave, Sacramento (95819-4339)
PHONE.............................916 452-9181
Linda Farley, *CEO*
Kerry Koyasako, *Vice Pres*
Jan Spencer, *Development*
EMP: 127
SALES: 8.5MM **Privately Held**
SIC: 8641 Girl Scout organization

(P-25261)
GIRL SCOUTS NORTHERN CAL (PA)
1650 Harbor Bay Pkwy # 100, Alameda (94502-3013)
PHONE.............................510 562-8470
Fax: 510 633-7925
Marina Park, *CEO*
Robin Macgillivray, *President*
M Whitman, *COO*
Maria Buxbaum, *Officer*
Diana Bell, *Vice Pres*
EMP: 70
SQ FT: 17,000
SALES: 19.2MM **Privately Held**
SIC: 8641 Girl Scout organization

(P-25262)
GIRL SCTS SN DIEGO-IMPRL CNCL (
1231 Upas St, San Diego (92103-5127)
PHONE.............................619 610-0751
Fax: 619 298-2031
Jo Dee C Jacob, *CEO*
Michael Didock, *Controller*
Danielle Russell, *Sales Mgr*
Bob Cornelius, *Manager*
EMP: 112
SQ FT: 7,926
SALES: 11MM **Privately Held**
SIC: 8641 Girl Scout organization

(P-25263)
GIRL SCUTS GREATER LOS ANGELES (PA)
801 S Grand Ave Ste 300, Los Angeles (90017-4621)
PHONE.............................626 677-2200
Lise L Luttgens, *CEO*
Sylvia Rosenberger, *COO*
Sandra Saldana, *Accountant*
James Lim, *Sales Mgr*
Jessica Belanger, *Senior Mgr*
EMP: 72
SQ FT: 7,600
SALES: 20.1MM **Privately Held**
WEB: www.gsmwvc.org
SIC: 8641 Girl Scout organization

(P-25264)
GLENWOOD VILLAGE CMNTY ASSN
Also Called: Seabreeze Management Comp
39 Argonaut Ste 100, Aliso Viejo (92656-4152)
PHONE.............................949 855-1800
Susan Larson, *President*
Annette Chong, *Manager*
EMP: 55
SALES (est): 584.1K **Privately Held**
SIC: 8641 Homeowners' association

(P-25265)
GOLD HILL GRANGE NO 326
1514 5th St, Lincoln (95648-1511)
PHONE.............................916 645-3605
Ron Smith, *Director*
EMP: 75
SALES (est): 2.8MM **Privately Held**
SIC: 8641 Fraternal associations

(P-25266)
GOLDEN RAIN FOUNDATION
800 Rockview Dr, Walnut Creek (94595-3002)
PHONE.............................925 988-7800
Warren Thurlow Salmons, *Branch Mgr*
Mark Marlatte, *Manager*
EMP: 280
SQ FT: 24,100
SALES (corp-wide): 24MM **Privately Held**
WEB: www.rossmoornews.com
SIC: 8641 Civic social & fraternal associations
PA: Golden Rain Foundation Of Walnut Creek
1001 Golden Rain Rd
Walnut Creek CA 94595
925 988-7700

(P-25267)
GORDON BETTY MOORE FOUNDATION
1661 Page Mill Rd, Palo Alto (94304-1209)
PHONE.............................650 213-3000
Fax: 415 561-7707
Steve McCormick, *President*
Paul Gray, *Bd of Directors*
Aileen Lee,
Susan Baade, *Officer*
Marina Campos, *Officer*
EMP: 89
SALES (est): 4.1MM **Privately Held**
SIC: 8641 Civic social & fraternal associations

(P-25268)
GROSSMONT-CUYAMACA COMMUNITY
Also Called: GCCCD AUXILIARY
8800 Grossmont College Dr, El Cajon (92020-1765)
PHONE.............................619 644-7684
Stanley Schroeder, *Exec Dir*
Sue Rearic, *CFO*
Julianna Barnes, *Vice Pres*

Sally Cox, *Info Tech Mgr*
EMP: 86
SQ FT: 1,000
SALES: 8.1MM **Privately Held**
SIC: 8641 Educator's association

(P-25269)
HACIENDA INVOLVED PARENT STAFF
1290 Kimberly Dr, San Jose (95118-1536)
PHONE.............................408 535-6259
Melissa Mohammed, *Principal*
EMP: 55
SALES: 175.6K **Privately Held**
SIC: 8641 Parent-teachers' association

(P-25270)
HIDDEN VALLEY LAKE ASSOCIATION (PA)
Also Called: Hidden Valley Golf Course
18174 Hidden Valley Rd, Hidden Valley Lake (95467-8690)
PHONE.............................707 987-3146
Fax: 707 987-2752
Wiliiam E Waite, *CEO*
Bill Chapman, *General Mgr*
Jim Freeman, *Corp Comm Staff*
James D Johnson, *Agent*
EMP: 79
SQ FT: 1,000
SALES (est): 7.5MM **Privately Held**
WEB: www.hvla.com
SIC: 8641 7997 5813 Homeowners' association; golf club, membership; swimming club, membership; bar (drinking places)

(P-25271)
HORIZONS 4 CONDOMINIUMS INC
Also Called: Horizon For Hmwners Asscation
2113 Meridan Blvd, Mammoth Lakes (93546)
P.O. Box 175 (93546-0175)
PHONE.............................760 934-6779
Fax: 760 934-4224
Tom Marx, *President*
EMP: 92
SALES (est): 2.5MM **Privately Held**
SIC: 8641 Homeowners' association

(P-25272)
JACK I KAISER
2238 Geary Blvd, San Francisco (94115-3416)
PHONE.............................415 833-8152
Deborah Joyce McNeil, *Principal*
Ramey D Littell, *Obstetrician*
Sandra L Torrente, *Obstetrician*
Eric R Dummel, *Emerg Med Spec*
Laurie Miller, *Med Doctor*
EMP: 54
SALES (est): 1.5MM **Privately Held**
SIC: 8641 Civic social & fraternal associations

(P-25273)
JEFFERSON CALIFORNIA CONGRESS
6225 El Camino Real, Carlsbad (92009-1604)
PHONE.............................760 331-5500
Chad Lund, *Principal*
EMP: 65
SALES: 84.4K **Privately Held**
SIC: 8641 Parent-teachers' association

(P-25274)
JEWISH CMNTY FNDN OF (PA)
6505 Wilshire Blvd, Los Angeles (90048-4906)
PHONE.............................323 761-8700
Fax: 323 761-8060
Richard V Sandler, *Ch of Bd*
J Sanderson, *President*
Jack Klein, *COO*
Ivan Wolkind, *CFO*
Leslie E Bider, *Chairman*
EMP: 150
SQ FT: 100,000
SALES: 52MM **Privately Held**
SIC: 8641 8661 Community membership club; religious organizations

(P-25275)
JONATHAN CLUB (PA)
545 S Figueroa St, Los Angeles (90071-1793)
PHONE.............................213 624-0881
Fax: 213 624-7609
Gregory J Dumas, *President*
Randolph P Sinnott, *CEO*
Hollis Cheek, *CFO*
Plato Skouras, *CFO*
James Abbott, *Principal*
◆ **EMP:** 200
SQ FT: 230,276
SALES: 38.5MM **Privately Held**
WEB: www.jc.org
SIC: 8641 Social club, membership

(P-25276)
KIWANIS INTERNATIONAL INC
Also Called: North Modesto Kiwanis Club
3201 Canterbury Ct, Modesto (95350-1419)
PHONE.............................209 578-1448
Robert Dunbar, *Principal*
EMP: 80
SALES (corp-wide): 15.1MM **Privately Held**
WEB: www.kfne.org
SIC: 8641 Civic social & fraternal associations
PA: Kiwanis International, Inc.
3636 Woodview Trce
Indianapolis IN 46268
317 875-8755

(P-25277)
KNIGHTS OF COLUMBUS
2211 Shamrock Dr, Campbell (95008-6210)
PHONE.............................408 371-1531
Steve Duffy, *Principal*
EMP: 220
SQ FT: 3,024
SALES (corp-wide): 2.1B **Privately Held**
WEB: www.kofc.org
SIC: 8641 Fraternal associations
PA: Knights Of Columbus
1 Columbus Plz Ste 1700
New Haven CT 06510
203 752-4000

(P-25278)
KNIGHTS OF COLUMBUS
1344 Magnolia Dr, Santa Paula (93060-1112)
PHONE.............................805 525-7810
Frank Arpuelles, *President*
EMP: 150
SALES (corp-wide): 2.1B **Privately Held**
WEB: www.kofc.org
SIC: 8641 Fraternal associations
PA: Knights Of Columbus
1 Columbus Plz Ste 1700
New Haven CT 06510
203 752-4000

(P-25279)
LA MESA LIONS CLUB
4387 Summit Dr, La Mesa (91941-7842)
P.O. Box 1441 (91944-1441)
PHONE.............................619 469-9988
Howard C Linke, *Admin Sec*
EMP: 60
SALES: 34K **Privately Held**
SIC: 8641 Civic associations

(P-25280)
LA PUERTA
560 4th Ave, San Diego (92101-6905)
PHONE.............................619 696-3466
Darren Morre, *Owner*
Darren Moore, *Owner*
EMP: 50
SALES (est): 1.9MM **Privately Held**
SIC: 8641 Bars & restaurants, members only

(P-25281)
LACOLINA JR HIGH CA CONGRESS O
4025 Foothill Rd, Santa Barbara (93110-1209)
PHONE.............................805 967-4506
Cristine Gallagher, *President*
EMP: 55

PRODUCTS & SERVICES SECTION
8641 - Civic, Social & Fraternal Associations County (P-25304)

SALES (est): 406.4K Privately Held
SIC: 8641 Civic social & fraternal associations

(P-25282)
LAKE FOREST LI MASTER HOMEOWN
Also Called: Sun & Sail Club
24752 Toledo Ln, Lake Forest (92630-2318)
PHONE...................949 586-0860
Fax: 949 588-1716
Sonny Morper, *President*
Jim Richert, *President*
Clark Dwinell, *Vice Pres*
Ted Brackez, *Principal*
Terri Graham, *Principal*
EMP: 80 EST: 1971
SQ FT: 9,000
SALES: 4.1MM Privately Held
WEB: www.lf2.org
SIC: 8641 Homeowners' association

(P-25283)
LAKE MISSION VIEJO ASSOCIATION
22555 Olympiad Rd, Mission Viejo (92692-1118)
PHONE...................949 770-1313
Fred Mellenbruch, *President*
Sid Wittenberg, *Treasurer*
Jane Chadburn, *Vice Pres*
J Miklaus, *Vice Pres*
Sen Jeff Miklaus, *Vice Pres*
EMP: 90
SQ FT: 7,400
SALES: 6.7MM Privately Held
WEB: www.lakemissionviejo.org
SIC: 8641 Homeowners' association

(P-25284)
LAKE OF THE PINES ASSOCIATION
Also Called: Lake of The Pines Homeowners
11665 Lakeshore N, Auburn (95602-8325)
PHONE...................530 268-1141
Edwin Vitrano, *General Mgr*
Rhonda Saigh, *Accounts Mgr*
Robert A Broyer, *Agent*
EMP: 50
SALES (est): 5.8MM Privately Held
WEB: www.lop.org
SIC: 8641 Homeowners' association

(P-25285)
LAKE WILDWOOD ASSOCIATION
Also Called: LAKE WILDWOOD GOLF COURSE.
11255 Cottontail Way, Penn Valley (95946-9409)
PHONE...................530 432-1152
Fax: 530 432-2951
Tom Cross, *CEO*
Edward Simpkins, *COO*
Phyllis Gurewitz, *Officer*
Debbie Casey, *General Mgr*
Meredith Martin, *Admin Asst*
EMP: 120
SQ FT: 10,000
SALES: 6.9MM Privately Held
SIC: 8641 Homeowners' association

(P-25286)
LEISURE VILLAGE ASSOCIATION
200 Leisure Village Dr, Camarillo (93012-6802)
PHONE...................805 484-2861
Robert Scheaffer, *General Mgr*
Maggie Wolfe, *Accounts Mgr*
EMP: 100 EST: 1973
SQ FT: 6,000
SALES (est): 4.2MM Privately Held
SIC: 8641 Homeowners' association

(P-25287)
LELAND STANFORD JUNIOR UNIV
Also Called: Stanford Alumni Association
326 Galvez St, Stanford (94305-6105)
PHONE...................650 723-2021
Fax: 650 723-7890
Howard Wolf, *Branch Mgr*
EMP: 250

SALES (corp-wide): 1.9B Privately Held
SIC: 8641 8221 Alumni association; university
PA: Leland Stanford Junior University
2575 Sand Hill Rd
Menlo Park CA 94025
650 723-2300

(P-25288)
LOMA LINDA VET ASSOCIATION FOR
Also Called: L L V A R E
710 Brookside Ave Ste 2, Redlands (92373-5181)
P.O. Box 1280 (92373-0421)
PHONE...................909 583-6250
Alan Jacobson, *President*
David Buxbaum, *Treasurer*
Colin Rasmussen, *Exec Dir*
Gayle Rundberg, *Exec Dir*
Robert Miller, *Admin Sec*
EMP: 60
SQ FT: 44,000
SALES: 3.9MM Privately Held
WEB: www.llvare.org
SIC: 8641 Veterans' organization

(P-25289)
LOMA RIVIERA COMMUNITY ASSN
9610 Waples St, San Diego (92121-2955)
PHONE...................619 224-1313
Fax: 619 224-4053
Dale Bredon, *President*
Anne Wagner, *President*
Thomas M Wilson, *Agent*
EMP: 100
SQ FT: 300
SALES (est): 3.7MM Privately Held
SIC: 8641 Homeowners' association

(P-25290)
LOS ANGELES AIRPORT PEACE OFFC
Also Called: Laapoa
6080 Center Dr Fl 6, Los Angeles (90045-9205)
PHONE...................310 242-5218
Marshall E McClain, *President*
Rodney Rouzan, *Treasurer*
Julius Levy, *Vice Pres*
Rupert Staine, *Admin Sec*
Jasmyne Cannick, *Consultant*
EMP: 425
SQ FT: 500
SALES: 820K Privately Held
SIC: 8641 Civic social & fraternal associations

(P-25291)
LOS ANGELES UNIFIED SCHOOL DST
Also Called: YMCA Metro La-52nd St School
816 W 51st St, Los Angeles (90037-3603)
PHONE...................323 753-3175
Beverly Crosby, *Principal*
Katie Gaspard, *Principal*
EMP: 200
SALES (corp-wide): 4.4B Privately Held
WEB: www.lausd.k12.ca.us
SIC: 8641 7991 8351 7032 Youth organizations; physical fitness facilities; child day care services; youth camps; individual & family services
PA: Los Angeles Unified School District
333 S Beaudry Ave Ste 209
Los Angeles CA 90017
213 241-1000

(P-25292)
MADE IN USA FOUNDATION INC
11950 San Vicente Blvd # 220, Los Angeles (90049-5013)
PHONE...................310 623-3872
Joel Joseph, *President*
EMP: 50
SALES: 1.1MM Privately Held
SIC: 8641 Civic social & fraternal associations

(P-25293)
MARAVILLA FOUNDATION (PA)
5729 Union Pacific Ave, Commerce (90022-5134)
PHONE...................323 721-4162

Fax: 323 721-0356
Alex M Sotomayor, *CEO*
Tristen Sotomayor, *COO*
George Ross, *CFO*
Paul Lopez, *Chairman*
Robert Lagunas, *Admin Sec*
EMP: 64
SQ FT: 30,000
SALES (est): 8MM Privately Held
SIC: 8641 Civic associations

(P-25294)
MARINES MEMORIAL ASSOCIATION
Also Called: MARINES' MEMORIAL CLUB & HOTEL
609 Sutter St, San Francisco (94102-1081)
PHONE...................415 673-6672
Fax: 415 441-3649
James M Myatt, *President*
Ruby Wu, *CFO*
Jennifer Paige, *Executive*
Michael Alen, *General Mgr*
Michael Allen, *General Mgr*
EMP: 148 EST: 1946
SQ FT: 160,062
SALES: 14.9MM Privately Held
WEB: www.marineclub.org
SIC: 8641 7011 5921 5813 Veterans' organization; hotels; liquor stores; bar (drinking places); eating places

(P-25295)
MEMORIALCARE MED FOUNDATION (PA)
2742 Dow Ave, Tustin (92780-7242)
PHONE...................714 389-5353
Sherry Sherman, *Purchasing*
Karen Hayashibara, *Info Tech Mgr*
EMP: 80
SALES (est): 8.7MM Privately Held
SIC: 8641 Civic social & fraternal associations

(P-25296)
MERCY MEDICAL GROUP INC
Also Called: Dominican Med Fndtn A Service
1595 Soquel Dr Ste 140, Santa Cruz (95065-1717)
PHONE...................831 475-1111
Michael Walsh, *Branch Mgr*
EMP: 199
SALES (corp-wide): 570.1MM Privately Held
SIC: 8641 Civic social & fraternal associations
PA: Dignity Health Medical Foundation
3400 Data Dr
Rancho Cordova CA 95670
916 379-2840

(P-25297)
METROPOLITAN CLUB
640 Sutter St, San Francisco (94102-1097)
PHONE...................415 673-0600
Fax: 415 922-2059
Clint Prescott, *General Mgr*
Kayne Maynard, *President*
Margaret Handelman, *Treasurer*
Gibbs Freeman, *General Mgr*
Charles Hudak, *Controller*
EMP: 65
SQ FT: 101,662
SALES: 5MM Privately Held
WEB: www.metropolitanclubsf.org
SIC: 8641 Social club, membership

(P-25298)
MIDNIGHT MISSION (PA)
601 S San Pedro St, Los Angeles (90014-2415)
PHONE...................213 624-9258
Fax: 213 553-2359
R Stephen Doan, *Chairman*
Larry Adamson, *President*
Cross Charles, *CFO*
Glenn D Woody, *CFO*
Grace Uwadiale, *Vice Pres*
EMP: 69
SQ FT: 11,550
SALES: 6.5MM Privately Held
WEB: www.midnightmission.org
SIC: 8641 8322 Civic social & fraternal associations; individual & family services

(P-25299)
MONTECITO FIRE PROTECTION DST
595 San Ysidro Rd, Santa Barbara (93108-2124)
PHONE...................805 969-7762
Fax: 805 969-3598
Chip Hickman, *Fire Chief*
Geri Ventura, *Admin Sec*
Joyce Reed, *Admin Asst*
Charlene Lim, *Marketing Staff*
Kevin Wallace, *Fire Chief*
EMP: 50
SALES (est): 2.4MM Privately Held
SIC: 8641 9224 Civic social & fraternal associations; fire protection

(P-25300)
MOOSE INTERNATIONAL INC
Also Called: Moose Family Center 545
2470 El Rancho Dr, Santa Cruz (95060-1106)
P.O. Box 66292, Scotts Valley (95067-6292)
PHONE...................831 438-1817
Perry James, *Administration*
Mark Filipowicz, *Info Tech Dir*
EMP: 208
SQ FT: 2,800
SALES (corp-wide): 55.3MM Privately Held
WEB: www.thalist.com
SIC: 8641 Fraternal associations
PA: Moose International, Incorporated
155 S International Dr
Mooseheart IL 60539
630 859-2000

(P-25301)
MORNINGSIDE COMMUNITY ASSN
82 Mayfair Dr, Rancho Mirage (92270-2562)
PHONE...................760 328-3323
Michelle Abdelnour, *General Mgr*
EMP: 73
SQ FT: 3,500
SALES (est): 3.6MM Privately Held
SIC: 8641 Homeowners' association

(P-25302)
NAPA SUNRISE ROTARY CLUB INC
Also Called: ROTARY CLUB OF NAPA SUNRISE OF
P.O. Box 5324 (94581-0324)
PHONE...................707 257-9564
William Jabin, *Treasurer*
Tyler Cokeley, *Treasurer*
EMP: 80
SALES: 163.4K Privately Held
SIC: 8641 Community membership club

(P-25303)
NATURAL RSRCES DEF COUNCIL INC
1314 2nd St, Santa Monica (90401-1103)
PHONE...................310 434-2300
Fax: 310 434-2399
Frances Beinecke, *Exec Dir*
Rene Leni, *Office Admin*
Ella Tabasky, *CTO*
Robert Norris, *Info Tech Dir*
Lisa Whiteman, *Producer*
EMP: 70
SQ FT: 10,558
SALES (corp-wide): 115.9MM Privately Held
WEB: www.savebiogems.org
SIC: 8641 Environmental protection organization
PA: Natural Resources Defense Council Inc.
40 W 20th St
New York NY 10011
212 727-2700

(P-25304)
OLYMPIC CLUB (PA)
524 Post St, San Francisco (94102-1295)
PHONE...................415 345-5100
Fax: 415 239-2165
John M Jack, *CEO*
Derek Ingraham, *Executive*
Christie Clemens, *Comms Mgr*

8641 - Civic, Social & Fraternal Associations County (P-25305) — PRODUDUCTS & SERVICES SECTION

Jay Bedsworth, *Principal*
Chris Funabashi, *Admin Asst*
EMP: 200
SQ FT: 160,000
SALES: 47MM **Privately Held**
WEB: www.ocrugby.com
SIC: 8641 7997 5812 Civic social & fraternal associations; golf club, membership; health food restaurant

(P-25305)
OLYMPIC CLUB
Also Called: Lakeside Clubhouse
599 Skyline Dr, Daly City (94015-4611)
PHONE.................................415 404-4300
EMP: 81
SALES (corp-wide): 47MM **Privately Held**
SIC: 8641 5812 Civic social & fraternal associations; health food restaurant
PA: The Olympic Club
524 Post St
San Francisco CA 94102
415 345-5100

(P-25306)
ORANGE COUNTY CNCL BSA (PA)
1211 E Dyer Rd Ste 100, Santa Ana (92705-5670)
PHONE.................................714 546-4990
Les Baron, *President*
Robert Neal, *Ch of Bd*
Jeffrie A Herrmann, *President*
Larry Behm, *Principal*
Jan Borja, *Admin Sec*
EMP: 65
SALES: 10MM **Privately Held**
WEB: www.ocbsa.org
SIC: 8641 Boy Scout organization

(P-25307)
ORTEGA ELEMENTARY PTO
1283 Terra Nova Blvd, Pacifica (94044-4341)
PHONE.................................650 738-6670
Jannel Jones, *President*
EMP: 75
SALES (est): 189.2K **Privately Held**
SIC: 8641 Parent-teachers' association

(P-25308)
PACIFIC CAST CLB VNDENBURG AFB
758 Nebraska Ave, Lompoc (93437-6213)
PHONE.................................805 734-4375
Chris Powderoy, *Manager*
EMP: 75
SALES (est): 825.8K **Privately Held**
SIC: 8641 Social club, membership

(P-25309)
PACIFIC UNION CLUB
1000 California St, San Francisco (94108-2280)
PHONE.................................415 775-1234
Thomas Gaston, *General Mgr*
EMP: 62
SQ FT: 54,000
SALES: 10.4MM **Privately Held**
WEB: www.pacificunionclub.com
SIC: 8641 Social club, membership

(P-25310)
PALISADES OPTIMIST FOUNDATION
15312 Whitfield Ave, Pacific Palisades (90272-2547)
PHONE.................................310 454-4111
Harold Vicau, *Treasurer*
EMP: 71
SALES (est): 2.1MM **Privately Held**
SIC: 8641 Social associations

(P-25311)
PALM DESERT GREENS ASSOCIATION
73750 Country Club Dr, Palm Desert (92260-8663)
PHONE.................................760 346-8005
Fax: 760 568-4965
Roberta Hollingsworth, *General Mgr*
Ken Dobson, *President*
Claude Klug, *Treasurer*
Mal Sinclair, *Treasurer*

Barbara Houcek, *Human Res Mgr*
EMP: 75 **EST:** 1971
SQ FT: 12,400
SALES: 5.8MM **Privately Held**
SIC: 8641 Homeowners' association

(P-25312)
PALO ALTO FAMILY Y M C A
3412 Ross Rd, Palo Alto (94303-4411)
PHONE.................................650 856-9622
Scott Glissmeyer, *Manager*
John Logan, *CEO*
Patty Doolittle, *CTO*
Arnold Guinto, *Info Tech Dir*
Laura Gardner, *Marketing Staff*
EMP: 50
SALES (est): 791.5K **Privately Held**
SIC: 8641 7991 8351 7032 Youth organizations; physical fitness facilities; child day care services; youth camps; individual & family services

(P-25313)
PESCADERO CONSERVATION ALIANCE
4100 Cabrillo Hwy, Pescadero (94060-9724)
P.O. Box 873 (94060-0873)
PHONE.................................650 879-1441
John Wade, *Director*
Randy Bennett, *President*
Jack Olsen, *Admin Sec*
Bert Fewss, *Director*
EMP: 50
SALES: 13.2K **Privately Held**
WEB: www.gazos.org
SIC: 8641 Environmental protection organization

(P-25314)
PIEDMONT CNCIL BOY SCOUTS AMER
10 Highland Way, Piedmont (94611-4026)
PHONE.................................510 547-4493
Josephine Hazelett, *Exec Dir*
Terri Ashton, *Vice Pres*
EMP: 78
SALES: 589.6K **Privately Held**
WEB: www.piedmontbsa.org
SIC: 8641 Boy Scout organization

(P-25315)
PINE MOUNTAIN LAKE ASSOCIATION
19228 Pine Mountain Dr, Groveland (95321-9581)
PHONE.................................209 962-4080
Brian Sweeney, *President*
Dana Chavarria, *Treasurer*
Mike Gustafson, *Treasurer*
Ron Maguire, *Vice Pres*
Ian Morcott, *Vice Pres*
EMP: 130
SQ FT: 20,000
SALES: 9.2MM **Privately Held**
SIC: 8641 Homeowners' association

(P-25316)
PLAYWORKS
380 Washington St, Oakland (94607-3800)
PHONE.................................510 893-4180
Fax: 510 893-4378
Jill Violet, *Owner*
Elizabeth Cushing, *COO*
Lisa Frydenlund, *Officer*
Marco Santos, *Director*
Cheryl Lewis, *Manager*
EMP: 50
SALES (est): 1.1MM **Privately Held**
SIC: 8641 Youth organizations

(P-25317)
PROGRESS FOUNDATION
52 Dore St, San Francisco (94103-3828)
PHONE.................................415 553-3100
EMP: 55
SALES (corp-wide): 20.8MM **Privately Held**
SIC: 8641 Civic social & fraternal associations
PA: Progress Foundation
368 Fell St
San Francisco CA 94102
415 861-0828

(P-25318)
PTA CA CONGRESS OF PARENTS
Also Called: Serrania Charter Elementary
5014 Serrania Ave, Woodland Hills (91364-3303)
PHONE.................................818 340-6700
Theresa C Wedaa, *Principal*
Luis Alvoredo, *Principal*
EMP: 50
SALES (est): 112.2K **Privately Held**
SIC: 8641 Parent-teachers' association

(P-25319)
PTA CALIFORNIA CONG P A S ELEM
5280 Irene Way, Livermore (94550-3508)
PHONE.................................925 606-4700
Denise Mathanson, *Principal*
EMP: 50
SALES: 58.5K **Privately Held**
SIC: 8641 Parent-teachers' association

(P-25320)
PTA CALIFORNIA CONGRESS OF PAR
21514 Halldale Ave, Torrance (90501-3016)
PHONE.................................310 328-3100
Deborah Evers-Allen, *Principal*
EMP: 80
SALES (est): 364.2K **Privately Held**
SIC: 8641 Parent-teachers' association

(P-25321)
PTA CALIFORNIA CONGRESS OF PAR
13901 Nordyke Dr, San Jose (95127-3138)
PHONE.................................408 928-7900
Gretchen Dietrich-Wynne, *Principal*
EMP: 50
SALES (est): 202.7K **Privately Held**
SIC: 8641 Educator's association

(P-25322)
PTAC CARMEL VALLEY MID SCHOOL
3800 Mykonos Ln, San Diego (92130-3572)
PHONE.................................858 481-8221
Laurie Brady, *Principal*
Adam Camacho, *Asst Principal*
EMP: 85
SALES (est): 57.8K **Privately Held**
SIC: 8641 Parent-teachers' association

(P-25323)
PTAC RAIL RANCH ELEM SCHOOL
25030 Via Santee, Murrieta (92563-5020)
PHONE.................................951 696-1404
Hunter Wethers, *Principal*
EMP: 60
SALES: 20.4K **Privately Held**
SIC: 8641 Parent-teachers' association

(P-25324)
PUBLIC HLTH FNDATION ENTPS INC
277 S Atlantic Blvd, Los Angeles (90022-1734)
PHONE.................................323 263-0262
Fax: 323 263-8338
Laurie Hill, *Principal*
EMP: 129
SALES (corp-wide): 97.5MM **Privately Held**
SIC: 8641 Civic social & fraternal associations
PA: Public Health Foundation Enterprises, Inc.
12801 Crossrds Pkwy S 200
City Of Industry CA 91746
562 692-4643

(P-25325)
PUBLIC HLTH FNDATION ENTPS INC
Also Called: Wic
1640 W Carson St Ste G, Torrance (90501-3877)
PHONE.................................310 320-5215
EMP: 129

SALES (corp-wide): 97.5MM **Privately Held**
SIC: 8641 Civic social & fraternal associations
PA: Public Health Foundation Enterprises, Inc.
12801 Crossrds Pkwy S 200
City Of Industry CA 91746
562 692-4643

(P-25326)
READING AND BEYOND
4670 E Butler Ave, Fresno (93702-4608)
PHONE.................................559 840-1068
Luis Santana, *President*
EMP: 74
SALES: 3.2MM **Privately Held**
SIC: 8641 Youth organizations

(P-25327)
ROSARY ACADEMY PARENT COUNCIL
1340 N Acacia Ave, Fullerton (92831-1202)
PHONE.................................714 879-6302
Fax: 714 879-0853
Patty Weller, *President*
Kathryn Hennigan, *Principal*
Matt Karcher, *Tech/Comp Coord*
Charlene Romano, *Human Res Mgr*
Nicola Huerta, *Teacher*
EMP: 72
SALES (est): 3.4MM **Privately Held**
SIC: 8641 Parent-teachers' association

(P-25328)
ROTARY INTERNATIONAL
Also Called: Rotary Club
9839 Meadowlark Way, Palo Cedro (96073-8750)
PHONE.................................530 547-5272
Bill Evans Jr, *Admin Sec*
EMP: 62
SALES (corp-wide): 92.9MM **Privately Held**
WEB: www.rotary5340.org
SIC: 8641 Civic associations
PA: Rotary International
1 Rotary Ctr
Evanston IL 60201
847 866-3000

(P-25329)
SAA SIERRA PROGRAMS LLC
Also Called: Stanford Sierra Camp & Lodge
130 Fallen Leaf Rd, South Lake Tahoe (96150-6165)
P.O. Box 10618 (96158-3618)
PHONE.................................530 541-1244
Fax: 530 541-2212
David Bunnett, *Project Mgr*
Antja Thompson, *Asst Director*
Nancy Marzocco, *Director*
EMP: 90
SALES (est): 1.3MM
SALES (corp-wide): 1.9B **Privately Held**
SIC: 8641 Civic associations
PA: Leland Stanford Junior University
2575 Sand Hill Rd
Menlo Park CA 94025
650 723-2300

(P-25330)
SACRAMENTO CY UNIFIED SCHL DST (PA)
5735 47th Ave, Sacramento (95824-4528)
P.O. Box 246870 (95824-6870)
PHONE.................................916 643-7400
Fax: 916 643-9454
Jose Banda, *Superintendent*
Tom Barrinson, *CFO*
Nina Delgadillo, *Security Dir*
Mary Prather, *Admin Mgr*
Gerardo Castillo, *Purch Dir*
EMP: 300 **EST:** 1854
SQ FT: 45,000
SALES (est): 175.8MM **Privately Held**
WEB: www.sachigh.org
SIC: 8641 Veterans' organization; environmental protection organization; Boy Scout organization

PRODUCTS & SERVICES SECTION
8641 - Civic, Social & Fraternal Associations County (P-25355)

(P-25331)
SACROMENTO EDUCTN READNG LIONS
10461 Old Plza Vlle 130 Ste 130 Ville, Sacramento (95827)
PHONE 916 228-2219
Fax: 916 228-2677
Alice Furry, *Director*
Charlotte Barcellos, *E-Business*
EMP: 50
SALES (est): 1.9MM **Privately Held**
SIC: 8641 Civic associations

(P-25332)
SAN DIEGO COUNTRY ESTATES ASSN
Also Called: San Vicente Inn & Golf Club
24157 San Vicente Rd, Ramona (92065-4166)
PHONE 760 789-3788
Jim Piva, *President*
Mario Trejo, *General Mgr*
Juli Elliott, *Finance*
Marcia Lewis, *Human Resources*
Maureen Rabehl, *Exec Sec*
EMP: 147
SQ FT: 14,000
SALES (est): 11.6MM **Privately Held**
WEB: www.sdcea.net
SIC: 8641 7997 7992 7011 Homeowners' association; membership sports & recreation clubs; tennis clubs, membership; golf club, membership; boating & swimming clubs; public golf courses; vacation lodges; restaurant, family: independent; bar (drinking places)

(P-25333)
SAN DIEGO URBAN LEAGUE INC
4305 University Ave # 360, San Diego (92105-8602)
PHONE 619 266-6247
Fax: 619 263-3660
Lenord Stephens, *Ch of Bd*
Benjamin Bagnas, *CFO*
Karen Goss, *Admin Sec*
EMP: 80
SALES: 913.3K **Privately Held**
SIC: 8641 Civic associations

(P-25334)
SAN FRANCISCO-BAY CNCL BSA
Also Called: SAN FRANCISCO BAY AREA COUNCIL
1001 Davis St, San Leandro (94577-1514)
PHONE 510 577-9000
Fax: 510 577-9002
Kenneth Mehlhorn, *CEO*
Cesar Garingan, *VP Finance*
Sarah Oppenheim-Beggs,
EMP: 86 EST: 2008
SALES: 6.1MM **Privately Held**
SIC: 8641 Boy Scout organization

(P-25335)
SAN MARCOS KIDS HELPNG KIDS FN
Also Called: KID HELPING KIDS
4750 Hollister Ave, Santa Barbara (93110-1921)
PHONE 800 659-6411
James Devries, *President*
Marley Miller, *COO*
Jacob Iuele, *CFO*
Evyn Van Homer, *Mktg Dir*
Chris Newton, *Director*
EMP: 147
SALES: 229.5K **Privately Held**
SIC: 8641 Civic social & fraternal associations

(P-25336)
SAN PABLO LODGE 43
342 Georgia St, Vallejo (94590-5907)
PHONE 707 642-1391
Al Hieb, *President*
EMP: 80
SALES (est): 957.4K **Privately Held**
SIC: 8641 Civic social & fraternal associations

(P-25337)
SANTA ANA POLICE OFFICERS ASSN
1607 N Sycamore St, Santa Ana (92701-2352)
PHONE 714 836-1211
Fax: 714 836-6108
Mark R Nichols, *President*
Tino Gallo, *Treasurer*
Bo Herter, *Treasurer*
EMP: 600
SQ FT: 10,157
SALES: 143.1K **Privately Held**
SIC: 8641 Civic social & fraternal associations

(P-25338)
SANTA CLARA VNGARD BOOSTER CLB
Also Called: VANGUARD CADETS
1795 Space Park Dr, Santa Clara (95054-3436)
PHONE 408 727-5532
Fax: 408 727-8730
Jeff Fiedler, *CEO*
Marc Hebert, *President*
Richard Lesher, *Treasurer*
Marie Bienkowski, *Vice Pres*
Linda Garbarino, *Admin Sec*
EMP: 50
SQ FT: 21,000
SALES: 4.2MM **Privately Held**
WEB: www.scvanguard.com
SIC: 8641 Youth organizations

(P-25339)
SANTA MARIA VALLEY YMCA
3400 Skyway Dr, Santa Maria (93455-2504)
PHONE 805 937-8521
Fax: 805 937-7007
Shannon Seifert, *Exec Dir*
Krista Delia, *Volunteer Dir*
Dave Wright, *Treasurer*
Stacey Pennington, *Associate Dir*
Kevin James, *Admin Sec*
EMP: 120
SQ FT: 22,000
SALES: 2.6MM **Privately Held**
WEB: www.smvymca.org
SIC: 8641 7991 8351 7032 Youth organizations; physical fitness facilities; child day care services; youth camps; individual & family services

(P-25340)
SANTA MNICA MNTINS TRILS CNCIL
24735 Mulholland Hwy, Woodland Hills (91302-2327)
P.O. Box 345, Agoura Hills (91376-0345)
PHONE 818 222-4531
Ruth Gerson, *President*
Anita Sneddon, *Treasurer*
Linda Palmer, *Vice Pres*
Georgia Farinella, *Admin Sec*
EMP: 100
SALES (est): 1.1MM **Privately Held**
WEB: www.smmtc.org
SIC: 8641 Environmental protection organization

(P-25341)
SANTA MONICA FAMILY YMCA
1332 6th St, Santa Monica (90401-1604)
P.O. Box 1160 (90406-1160)
PHONE 310 451-7387
Fax: 310 451-9906
Tara Pomposini, *Director*
Jurgen Davila, *Athletic Dir*
Tara Pomtomsini, *Director*
Kellie Fremming, *Manager*
EMP: 80
SQ FT: 157,000
SALES: 4.1MM **Privately Held**
WEB: www.ymcasm.org
SIC: 8641 8351 8322 Youth organizations; recreation association; child day care services; individual & family services

(P-25342)
SAVE OUR SUNOL
2934 Kilkare Rd, Sunol (94586-9428)
PHONE 925 862-2263
Patricia Stillman, *President*

Lois Throop, *Treasurer*
Neil Davies, *Vice Pres*
Andrew Turnvull, *Admin Sec*
EMP: 100
SALES (est): 1.1MM **Privately Held**
WEB: www.sunol.net
SIC: 8641 Environmental protection organization

(P-25343)
SCIOTS TRACT ASSOCIATION
937 Chestnut Ln, Davis (95616-2411)
PHONE 530 753-5219
Robert Monty, *Vice Pres*
Beverly Monty, *Admin Sec*
EMP: 80
SALES (est): 990.3K **Privately Held**
SIC: 8641 Social club, membership

(P-25344)
SCORPION ATHC BOOSTER CLB INC
300 E Esplanade Dr # 250, Oxnard (93036-1238)
PHONE 805 482-2005
Bob Graham, *CEO*
Martin Marietta, *Treasurer*
EMP: 50 EST: 2011
SALES (est): 200.2K **Privately Held**
SIC: 8641 Booster club

(P-25345)
SCRIPPS HEALTH
10010 Campus Point Dr, San Diego (92121-1518)
PHONE 858 678-6966
Jaimie Bottorf, *Human Resources*
EMP: 378
SALES (corp-wide): 1.7B **Privately Held**
SIC: 8641 Civic social & fraternal associations
PA: Scripps Health
  4275 Campus Point Ct
  San Diego CA 92121
  858 678-7000

(P-25346)
SELF HELP ENTERPRISES (PA)
Also Called: S H E
8445 W Elowin Ct, Visalia (93291-9262)
P.O. Box 6520 (93290-6520)
PHONE 559 651-1000
Fax: 559 651-3634
Thomas Collishaw, *President*
Kathy Long-Tence, *CFO*
Kathryn Long-Pence, *Finance*
Carol Glass, *Council Mbr*
Betsy Garcia, *Program Dir*
EMP: 75
SQ FT: 15,000
SALES: 14.7MM **Privately Held**
SIC: 8641 Dwelling-related associations

(P-25347)
SIERRA CLUB (PA)
Also Called: Sierra Club Books
2101 Webster St Ste 1300, Oakland (94612-3011)
PHONE 415 977-5500
Fax: 415 977-5793
Robin Mann, *President*
Lynn Henning, *Vice Chairman*
Tom Larson, *Vice Chairman*
Craig Lubow, *Vice Chairman*
Ken Smokoska, *Vice Chairman*
EMP: 175 EST: 1892
SQ FT: 43,500
SALES: 98.1MM **Privately Held**
WEB: www.youngboglelaw.com
SIC: 8641 8399 Environmental protection organization; advocacy group

(P-25348)
SIERRA MASONIC ASSOCIATION
Also Called: Sierra Lodge 788
2166 Hwy 49, Oakhurst (93644)
P.O. Box 805 (93644-0805)
PHONE 559 683-7713
William Bastian, *Admin Sec*
EMP: 78
SALES (est): 2.4MM **Privately Held**
SIC: 8641 Civic associations

(P-25349)
SILICON VLY CMNTY FOUNDATION
Also Called: Svcf
2440 W El Camin, Mountain View (94040)
PHONE 650 450-5400
Fax: 650 450-5401
Emmett Carson, *CEO*
John M Sobrato Sr, *Vice Chairman*
Lianne Araki, *President*
Sheila Conacciu, *CFO*
Paul Velaski, *CFO*
EMP: 120
SALES (est): 11.3MM **Privately Held**
SIC: 8641 Civic social & fraternal associations

(P-25350)
SILVER LAKES ASSOCIATION
Also Called: Homeowners Association
15273 Orchard Hill Ln, Helendale (92342)
P.O. Box 179 (92342-0179)
PHONE 760 245-1606
Michael Bennett, *General Mgr*
Bud Allen, *Officer*
Denise Hammer, *Executive Asst*
Susan Bellani, *Human Resources*
Robert Solgan, *Food Svc Dir*
EMP: 90
SQ FT: 3,000
SALES (est): 5MM **Privately Held**
WEB: www.silverlakesassociation.com
SIC: 8641 Homeowners' association

(P-25351)
SONOMA VALLEY WOMANS CLUB
574 1st St E, Sonoma (95476-6753)
PHONE 707 938-8313
Carmella A Greco, *Principal*
EMP: 70
SQ FT: 3,216
SALES (est): 2.5MM **Privately Held**
SIC: 8641 Civic social & fraternal associations

(P-25352)
SPYGLASS HILL COMMUNITY ASSN
39 Argonaut Ste 100, Aliso Viejo (92656-4152)
P.O. Box 57063, Irvine (92619-7063)
PHONE 949 855-1800
Susan Larson, *President*
EMP: 50
SALES: 497.4K **Privately Held**
SIC: 8641 Homeowners' association

(P-25353)
SULPHUR SPRINGS UNION PTA
16628 Lost Canyon Rd, Canyon Country (91387-3241)
PHONE 661 252-2725
Jocey Hogan, *President*
EMP: 70 EST: 2001
SALES (est): 851.2K **Privately Held**
SIC: 8641 Parent-teachers' association

(P-25354)
SUN CITY PALM DSERT CMNTY ASSN (PA)
Also Called: Palm Desert Community Assn
38180 Del Webb Blvd, Palm Desert (92211-1256)
PHONE 760 200-2100
Helen McEnerney, *President*
EMP: 80
SQ FT: 4,000
SALES (est): 6.5MM **Privately Held**
SIC: 8641 7992 7997 Dwelling-related associations; public golf courses; country club, membership

(P-25355)
SUTTER CLUB INC
1220 9th St, Sacramento (95814-4897)
PHONE 916 442-0456
Fax: 916 442-0580
Tom Narozonick, *General Mgr*
Marvin Shoultes, *General Mgr*
Ann Daigle, *Executive Asst*
Joy Betlach, *Financial Exec*
EMP: 75
SQ FT: 45,000

8641 - Civic, Social & Fraternal Associations County (P-25356)

SALES: 3.5MM **Privately Held**
WEB: www.sutterclub.com
SIC: **8641** Social club, membership

(P-25356)
SUTTER HEALTH
795 El Camino Real, Palo Alto (94301-2302)
PHONE..................650 853-2975
Fax: 650 853-2852
Paul Tang, *Vice Pres*
Roy W Hong, *Plastic Surgeon*
Marian Piper, *Manager*
EMP: 233
SALES (corp-wide): 11B **Privately Held**
SIC: **8641** Civic social & fraternal associations
PA: Sutter Health
    2200 River Plaza Dr
    Sacramento CA 95833
    916 733-8800

(P-25357)
SUTTER HEALTH
1301 Mission St, Santa Cruz (95060-3530)
PHONE..................831 458-6310
Roger A Larsen, *President*
Karen Landon, *Executive Asst*
Megan E Watkins, *Executive Asst*
Alicia Holloway, *Admin Asst*
Phil Fritz, *Planning*
EMP: 93
SALES (corp-wide): 11B **Privately Held**
SIC: **8641** Civic social & fraternal associations
PA: Sutter Health
    2200 River Plaza Dr
    Sacramento CA 95833
    916 733-8800

(P-25358)
SUTTER HEALTH
2950 Research Park Dr, Soquel (95073-2000)
PHONE..................831 458-6272
Scott Imahara, *Plastic Surgeon*
EMP: 466
SALES (corp-wide): 11B **Privately Held**
SIC: **8641** Civic social & fraternal associations
PA: Sutter Health
    2200 River Plaza Dr
    Sacramento CA 95833
    916 733-8800

(P-25359)
SUTTER HEALTH
Also Called: Sutter Elk Grove Surgery Ctr
8200 Laguna Blvd, Elk Grove (95758-7956)
PHONE..................916 544-5423
EMP: 280
SALES (corp-wide): 11B **Privately Held**
SIC: **8641** Civic social & fraternal associations
PA: Sutter Health
    2200 River Plaza Dr
    Sacramento CA 95833
    916 733-8800

(P-25360)
SUTTER HEALTH
502 Washington Ave, Los Banos (93635-4649)
PHONE..................209 827-4866
EMP: 140
SALES (corp-wide): 11B **Privately Held**
SIC: **8641** Civic social & fraternal associations
PA: Sutter Health
    2200 River Plaza Dr
    Sacramento CA 95833
    916 733-8800

(P-25361)
SUTTER HEALTH
Also Called: Gyneclgic Onclogy Plvic Srgery
360 Dardanelli Ln Ste 2d, Los Gatos (95032-1421)
PHONE..................408 523-3900
EMP: 280
SALES (corp-wide): 11B **Privately Held**
SIC: **8641** Civic social & fraternal associations

PA: Sutter Health
    2200 River Plaza Dr
    Sacramento CA 95833
    916 733-8800

(P-25362)
SUTTER HEALTH
2880 Soquel Ave, Santa Cruz (95062-1423)
PHONE..................831 458-5500
EMP: 187
SALES (corp-wide): 11B **Privately Held**
SIC: **8641** Civic social & fraternal associations
PA: Sutter Health
    2200 River Plaza Dr
    Sacramento CA 95833
    916 733-8800

(P-25363)
SUTTER HEALTH
2449 Summerfield Rd, Santa Rosa (95405-7815)
PHONE..................707 523-7253
Gina Solich, *Human Resources*
James Vaughan, *Manager*
EMP: 187
SALES (corp-wide): 11B **Privately Held**
SIC: **8641** Civic social & fraternal associations
PA: Sutter Health
    2200 River Plaza Dr
    Sacramento CA 95833
    916 733-8800

(P-25364)
SUTTER HEALTH
Also Called: Smf Clinical Lab
2715 K St Ste A, Sacramento (95816-5128)
PHONE..................916 551-9550
EMP: 187
SALES (corp-wide): 11B **Privately Held**
SIC: **8641** Civic social & fraternal associations
PA: Sutter Health
    2200 River Plaza Dr
    Sacramento CA 95833
    916 733-8800

(P-25365)
SUTTER REGIONAL MED FOUNDATION
127 Hospital Dr Ste 102, Vallejo (94589-2500)
PHONE..................707 551-3616
Bobbi Underhill, *Principal*
EMP: 140
SALES (corp-wide): 31.7MM **Privately Held**
SIC: **8641** Civic social & fraternal associations
PA: Sutter Regional Medical Foundation Inc
    2702 Low Ct
    Fairfield CA 94534
    707 427-4900

(P-25366)
TABLE COMMUNITY FOUDATION
3201 W Benjamin Holt Dr, Stockton (95219-3741)
PHONE..................209 951-1753
Tyronne Gross Jr, *President*
EMP: 92
SALES (est): 224.6K **Privately Held**
SIC: **8641** Youth organizations

(P-25367)
TAHOE DONNER ASSOCIATION
12790 Northwoods Blvd, Truckee (96161-6334)
PHONE..................530 587-9437
Fax: 530 587-0947
Leighanne Gachowski, *Vice Pres*
David Gravell, *General Mgr*
Bettye Carmichael, *Admin Sec*
Annie Rosenfeldt, *Human Res Mgr*
EMP: 146
SALES (corp-wide): 18.1MM **Privately Held**
SIC: **8641** Homeowners' association
PA: Donner Tahoe Association
    11509 Northwoods Blvd
    Truckee CA 96161
    530 587-9400

(P-25368)
TAMARACK BCH CONDO OWNERS ASSN
3200 Carlsbad Blvd, Carlsbad (92008-3101)
PHONE..................760 729-3500
Connie Bloem, *President*
EMP: 50
SQ FT: 2,000
SALES (est): 952.2K **Privately Held**
SIC: **8641** Homeowners' association

(P-25369)
TECHSOUP GLOBAL
Also Called: Tech Soup Spock
435 Brannan St Ste 100, San Francisco (94107-1780)
PHONE..................415 633-9325
Rebecca Masisak, *CEO*
Geri Doran, *COO*
Doug Keiller, *Treasurer*
Marnie Webb, *Co-CEO*
Dara Westling, *Vice Pres*
EMP: 175
SALES: 29.6MM **Privately Held**
WEB: www.techsoup.org
SIC: **8641** Social associations

(P-25370)
TEMECULA VLY UNIFIED SCHL DST
33125 Regina Dr, Temecula (92592-1473)
PHONE..................951 302-5140
Fax: 951 302-5146
Kelli Sunderland, *Administration*
EMP: 200
SALES (corp-wide): 208.5MM **Privately Held**
SIC: **8641** Parent-teachers' association
PA: Temecula Valley Unified School District
    31350 Rancho Vista Rd
    Temecula CA 92592
    951 676-2661

(P-25371)
TEMPLE CITY YOUTH DEV FUND
6415 N Muscatel Ave, San Gabriel (91775-1845)
PHONE..................626 548-5085
Kathy Perini, *Principal*
Krista Carlson, *Technology*
EMP: 68
SALES (est): 758.1K **Privately Held**
SIC: **8641** Youth organizations

(P-25372)
THE YOUNG MENS CHRIS ASSOC OF
Also Called: Berkly YMCA Head Start
1222 University Ave, Berkeley (94702-1766)
PHONE..................510 841-4152
EMP: 68
SALES (corp-wide): 27.5MM **Privately Held**
SIC: **8641** 7991 8351 7032 Youth organizations; physical fitness facilities; child day care services; youth camps; individual & family services
PA: Young Men's Christian Association Of The Central Bay Area
    2111 M Lthr Kng Jr Way
    Berkeley CA 94704
    510 542-2120

(P-25373)
THE YOUNG MENS CHRIS ASSOC OF
350 Civic Dr, Pleasant Hill (94523-1921)
PHONE..................925 687-8900
M Saenz, *Exec Dir*
EMP: 62
SALES (corp-wide): 27.5MM **Privately Held**
SIC: **8641** Youth organizations
PA: Young Men's Christian Association Of The Central Bay Area
    2111 M Lthr Kng Jr Way
    Berkeley CA 94704
    510 542-2120

(P-25374)
THE YOUNG MENS CHRIS ASSOC OF
Also Called: Emery Marina
4727 San Pablo Ave, Emeryville (94608-3035)
PHONE..................510 601-8674
Henry Der, *Branch Mgr*
EMP: 68
SALES (corp-wide): 27.5MM **Privately Held**
SIC: **8641** 7991 8351 7032 Youth organizations; physical fitness facilities; child day care services; youth camps; individual & family services
PA: Young Men's Christian Association Of The Central Bay Area
    2111 M Lthr Kng Jr Way
    Berkeley CA 94704
    510 542-2120

(P-25375)
THE YOUNG MENS CHRIS ASSOC OF
Also Called: Y M C A Metro Clinic
2111 Mrtn Lthr King Jr Wa, Berkeley (94704-1108)
PHONE..................510 486-8400
Larry Bush, *Manager*
EMP: 63
SALES (corp-wide): 27.5MM **Privately Held**
SIC: **8641** 7991 8351 7032 Youth organizations; physical fitness facilities; child day care services; youth camps; individual & family services
PA: Young Men's Christian Association Of The Central Bay Area
    2111 M Lthr Kng Jr Way
    Berkeley CA 94704
    510 542-2120

(P-25376)
THE YOUNG MENS CHRIS ASSOC OF
Also Called: YMCA Head Start
2009 10th St, Berkeley (94710-2119)
PHONE..................510 848-9092
Pamela Shaw, *Director*
Rita Harris, *Vice Pres*
Maria Carmona, *Exec Dir*
Janet Skaar, *Director*
EMP: 70
SALES (corp-wide): 27.5MM **Privately Held**
SIC: **8641** 7991 8351 7032 Youth organizations; physical fitness facilities; child day care services; youth camps; individual & family services
PA: Young Men's Christian Association Of The Central Bay Area
    2111 M Lthr Kng Jr Way
    Berkeley CA 94704
    510 542-2120

(P-25377)
THE YOUNG MENS CHRIS ASSOC OF
Also Called: Downtown Berkeley YMCA
2001 Allston Way, Berkeley (94704-1417)
PHONE..................510 848-9622
Fax: 510 848-6835
Fran Gallati, *Exec Dir*
Jay Mullins, *Info Tech Mgr*
Paul Milsap, *Director*
EMP: 130
SQ FT: 70,135
SALES (corp-wide): 27.5MM **Privately Held**
SIC: **8641** 7991 8351 7032 Youth organizations; physical fitness facilities; child day care services; youth camps; individual & family services
PA: Young Men's Christian Association Of The Central Bay Area
    2111 M Lthr Kng Jr Way
    Berkeley CA 94704
    510 542-2120

(P-25378)
THE YOUNG MENS CHRIS ASSOC OF
Also Called: Kids' Club YMCA Oxford School
1130 Oxford St, Berkeley (94707-2624)
PHONE..................510 526-2146

8641 - Civic, Social & Fraternal Associations County (P-25401)

Stephanie Hochman, *Branch Mgr*
EMP: 63
SALES (corp-wide): 27.5MM **Privately Held**
SIC: 8641 7991 8351 7032 Youth organizations; physical fitness facilities; child day care services; youth camps; individual & family services
PA: Young Men's Christian Association Of The Central Bay Area
2111 M Lthr Kng Jr Way
Berkeley CA 94704
510 542-2120

(P-25379)
THE YOUNG MENS CHRIS ASSOC OF
2001 Allston Way, Berkeley (94704-1417)
PHONE 510 848-6800
Peter Gerharz, *Branch Mgr*
Peter Chong, *Vice Pres*
EMP: 62
SALES (corp-wide): 27.5MM **Privately Held**
SIC: 8641 7991 8351 7032 Youth organizations; physical fitness facilities; child day care services; youth camps; individual & family services
PA: Young Men's Christian Association Of The Central Bay Area
2111 M Lthr Kng Jr Way
Berkeley CA 94704
510 542-2120

(P-25380)
THE YOUNG MENS CHRIS ASSOC OF
1422 San Pablo Ave, Berkeley (94702-1024)
PHONE 510 559-2090
Fax: 510 559-2091
Larry Bush, *Branch Mgr*
EMP: 68
SALES (corp-wide): 27.5MM **Privately Held**
SIC: 8641 8322 8351 Youth organizations; individual & family services; head start center, except in conjunction with school
PA: Young Men's Christian Association Of The Central Bay Area
2111 M Lthr Kng Jr Way
Berkeley CA 94704
510 542-2120

(P-25381)
THEAT AND ARTS FOUND OF SAN DI
Also Called: La Jolla Playhouse
2910 La Jolla Village Dr, La Jolla (92093-5100)
P.O. Box 12039 (92039-2039)
PHONE 858 623-3366
Fax: 858 550-1075
Jeffrey Ressler, *Chairman*
Steven Libman, *President*
Michael L Eagle, *CEO*
Lynelle Lynch, *Chairman*
Tim Scott, *Chairman*
EMP: 250 **EST:** 1954
SQ FT: 1,440
SALES: 15.6MM **Privately Held**
WEB: www.lajollaplayhouse.com
SIC: 8641 7922 Civic associations; theatrical producers & services

(P-25382)
TIERRA DEL ORO GIRL SCOUT CNSL
6601 Elvas Ave, Sacramento (95819-4339)
PHONE 916 452-9174
Pamela Saltenberger, *Exec Dir*
EMP: 84
SQ FT: 12,200
SALES: 8.1MM **Privately Held**
WEB: www.tdogs.org
SIC: 8641 Girl Scout organization

(P-25383)
TUOLUMNE ME-WUK TRIBAL COUNCIL
1182 24th St Ste 311, Oakland (94607-2430)
PHONE 707 319-3472
EMP: 153 **Privately Held**
SIC: 8641 Civic social & fraternal associations
PA: Tuolumne Me-Wuk Tribal Council
19595 Mi Wu St
Tuolumne CA 95379
209 928-5300

(P-25384)
TWAIN HARTE HORSEMEN
23580 View Ln, Columbia (95310)
P.O. Box 1326, Twain Harte (95383-1326)
PHONE 209 601-5585
Scott Lewis, *President*
EMP: 99
SALES: 12.3K **Privately Held**
SIC: 8641 Civic social & fraternal associations

(P-25385)
UNITED STATES MARINES YOUTH FD
90 La Venta Dr, Santa Barbara (93110-1716)
PHONE 805 967-7990
EMP: 54
SALES (corp-wide): 105.9K **Privately Held**
WEB: www.usmc.mil
SIC: 8641 Veterans' organization
PA: United States Marines Youth Foundation, Inc.
8626 Lee Hwy Ste 201
Fairfax VA 22031
703 207-9588

(P-25386)
UNIVERSITY STUDENT UNION OF CA
18111 Nordhoff St, Northridge (91330-0001)
PHONE 818 677-2251
Debra Hammond, *Exec Dir*
Joseph Illuminate, *Associate Dir*
Merri Pearson, *Exec Dir*
Carol Henschel, *Psychologist*
Samia Boctor, *Med Doctor*
EMP: 450
SQ FT: 350,000
SALES: 13.2M **Privately Held**
SIC: 8641 Civic social & fraternal associations

(P-25387)
VALLEY HUNT CLUB
520 S Orange Grove Blvd, Pasadena (91105-1799)
PHONE 626 793-7134
Fax: 323 449-8878
David Mole, *CEO*
Donald F Crumrine, *COO*
Bill Roemer, *Controller*
David Gieselman, *Purch Dir*
Tim Pedigo, *Maintenance Dir*
EMP: 85
SQ FT: 40,000
SALES: 9.3MM **Privately Held**
WEB: www.valleyhuntclub.com
SIC: 8641 Social club, membership

(P-25388)
VENTURA COUNTY FIRE DEPARTMENT
165 Durley Ave, Camarillo (93010-8586)
PHONE 805 389-9710
Mark Lorensen, *Chief*
Bob Michels, *Department Mgr*
EMP: 50
SALES (est): 1.6MM **Privately Held**
SIC: 8641 Civic social & fraternal associations

(P-25389)
VENTURA COUNTY OFFICE EDUCATN
1379 Oakridge Ct, Thousand Oaks (91362-1923)
PHONE 805 495-7037
EMP: 77 **Privately Held**
SIC: 8641
PA: Ventura County Office Of Education
5189 Verdugo Way
Camarillo CA 93012
805 383-1900

(P-25390)
VETERANS OF FOREIGN WARS OF US
1525 W Oakland Ave, Hemet (92543-2682)
PHONE 951 202-3792
Louis Morales, *Principal*
EMP: 65
SALES (corp-wide): 105.2MM **Privately Held**
SIC: 8641 Veterans' organization
PA: Veterans Of Foreign Wars Of The United States
406 W 34th St Fl 11
Kansas City MO 64111
816 756-3390

(P-25391)
VETERANS OF FOREIGN WARS OF US
12235 California St, Yucaipa (92399-4349)
PHONE 909 797-1898
EMP: 62
SALES (corp-wide): 105.2MM **Privately Held**
SIC: 8641 Veterans' organization
PA: Veterans Of Foreign Wars Of The United States
406 W 34th St Fl 11
Kansas City MO 64111
816 756-3390

(P-25392)
VETERANS OF FOREIGN WARS OF US
9136 Elk Grove Blvd # 100, Elk Grove (95624-2075)
PHONE 916 786-7757
Jesse Van, *Branch Mgr*
EMP: 65
SALES (corp-wide): 105.2MM **Privately Held**
SIC: 8641 Veterans' organization
PA: Veterans Of Foreign Wars Of The United States
406 W 34th St Fl 11
Kansas City MO 64111
816 756-3390

(P-25393)
VETERANS OF FOREIGN WARS OF US
1251 Oregon St, Redding (96001-0414)
PHONE 530 241-9168
Robert D Arrasmith, *Branch Mgr*
EMP: 62
SALES (corp-wide): 105.2MM **Privately Held**
SIC: 8641 Veterans' organization
PA: Veterans Of Foreign Wars Of The United States
406 W 34th St Fl 11
Kansas City MO 64111
816 756-3390

(P-25394)
VFW POST 6476
1789 N 8th St, Colton (92324-1303)
PHONE 909 754-3828
Joe Quioz, *Principal*
EMP: 130
SALES (est): 647.3K **Privately Held**
SIC: 8641 Veterans' organization

(P-25395)
VIETNAM VETERANS OF SAN DIEGO (PA)
Also Called: VETERANS VILLAGE OF SAN DIEGO
4141 Pacific Hwy, San Diego (92110-2030)
PHONE 619 497-0142
Fax: 619 497-0263
Phil Landis, *President*
Andre Simpson, *COO*
Harry Guess, *CFO*
Hernendez Aida, *Accountant*
EMP: 65
SQ FT: 35,719
SALES: 10.6MM **Privately Held**
WEB: www.vvsd.net
SIC: 8641 Veterans' organization

(P-25396)
VIETNMS-MRCAN YUTH ALANCE CORP
Also Called: Vaya
7968 Arjons Dr Ste 109, San Diego (92126-6362)
P.O. Box 711912 (92171-1912)
PHONE 619 320-8292
Frank Vuong, *Principal*
Roy Valdez, *Area Mgr*
Ed Carey, *MIS Mgr*
Dan Schitea, *Project Mgr*
Peter Turnbull, *Project Mgr*
EMP: 50
SALES: 101K **Privately Held**
SIC: 8641 Civic social & fraternal associations

(P-25397)
VILLA BALBOA COMMUNITY ASSOC
22 Mauchly, Irvine (92618-2306)
P.O. Box 4708 (92616-4708)
PHONE 949 450-1515
Janice Walley, *President*
Frank Jenes, *President*
EMP: 65
SALES (est): 797.3K **Privately Held**
SIC: 8641 Homeowners' association

(P-25398)
VILLA MARIN HOMEOWNERS ASSN
Also Called: Villa Mrin Rtrement Residences
100 Thorndale Dr, San Rafael (94903-4599)
PHONE 415 499-8711
Fax: 415 492-2673
Danel Walker, *CEO*
Dan Walker, *CEO*
Priscilla G Hartman, *Manager*
EMP: 170
SQ FT: 500,000
SALES: 11.7MM **Privately Held**
SIC: 8641 8051 8059 Homeowners' association; skilled nursing care facilities; personal care home, with health care

(P-25399)
VINTAGE CLUB MASTER ASSN INC
75001 Vintage Dr W, Indian Wells (92210-7304)
PHONE 760 340-0500
Art Allen, *Exec Dir*
Red Scott, *President*
EMP: 60
SALES: 3MM **Privately Held**
SIC: 8641 Homeowners' association

(P-25400)
VOICE CNTY AMER & LRNG FOR LF
1211 E Dyer Rd, Santa Ana (92705-5670)
PHONE 714 546-8558
Thomas Hartmann, *Director*
EMP: 75
SALES (est): 399.9K **Privately Held**
WEB: www.voice-lessons.com
SIC: 8641 Boy Scout organization

(P-25401)
WEST END YUNG MNS CHRISTN ASSN
Also Called: Upland Ymca-Valencia
1150 E Foothill Blvd, Upland (91786-4012)
PHONE 909 946-6120
Fax: 909 946-0087
Leeann Faucett, *Branch Mgr*
EMP: 59
SALES (corp-wide): 3.5MM **Privately Held**
WEB: www.westendymca.org
SIC: 8641 7991 8351 7032 Youth organizations; physical fitness facilities; child day care services; youth camps; individual & family services
PA: West End Young Men's Christian Association Inc
10970 Arrow Rte Ste 106
Rancho Cucamonga CA 91730
909 481-0722

8641 - Civic, Social & Fraternal Associations County (P-25402)

(P-25402)
WEST END YUNG MNS CHRISTN ASSN
Also Called: Rancho Cucamonga Family YMCA
11200 Baseline Rd, Rancho Cucamonga (91701-5338)
P.O. Box 248 (91729-0248)
PHONE 909 477-2780
Fax: 909 481-6425
Dianna Lee-Mitchell, *Director*
EMP: 80
SALES (corp-wide): 3.5MM Privately Held
WEB: www.westendymca.org
SIC: 8641 7991 8351 7032 Youth organizations; physical fitness facilities; child day care services; youth camps; individual & family services
PA: West End Young Men's Christian Association Inc
10970 Arrow Rte Ste 106
Rancho Cucamonga CA 91730
909 481-0722

(P-25403)
WOODBRIDGE VILLAGE ASSOCIATION
31 Creek Rd, Irvine (92604-4793)
PHONE 949 786-1800
Fax: 949 786-1212
Kevin Chudy, *Exec Dir*
William Mavity, *Treasurer*
Robert Woodings, *Vice Pres*
Bob Figeira, *Exec Dir*
Bertha Rivera, *Admin Sec*
EMP: 65
SQ FT: 15,000
SALES: 9.5MM Privately Held
WEB: www.wva.org
SIC: 8641 Homeowners' association

(P-25404)
WOODCRAFT RANGERS
2111 Park Grove Ave, Los Angeles (90007-2017)
PHONE 213 749-3031
Fax: 213 749-0409
Cathie Mostovoy, *Branch Mgr*
EMP: 400
SALES (corp-wide): 8.8MM Privately Held
SIC: 8641 Youth organizations
PA: Woodcraft Rangers
340 E 2nd St Ste 200
Los Angeles CA 90012
213 388-6788

(P-25405)
WOODLAND SWIM TEAM BOSTERS CLB
155 West St, Woodland (95695-3162)
P.O. Box 763 (95776-0763)
PHONE 530 662-9783
Mark Morkski, *Manager*
EMP: 60
SALES: 125.2K Privately Held
SIC: 8641 Booster club

(P-25406)
Y W C A OF SONOMA COUNTY
Also Called: YWCA
811 3rd St Ste 100, Santa Rosa (95404-4541)
P.O. Box 3506 (95402-3506)
PHONE 707 546-9922
Madeline O'Connell, *Exec Dir*
Lisa Carreno, *Exec Dir*
Suzy Marcalek, *Exec Dir*
Julie Lafranchi, *General Mgr*
Doreen Lorinczi, *Director*
EMP: 50
SALES: 1.8MM Privately Held
SIC: 8641 7991 8351 7032 Youth organizations; physical fitness facilities; child day care services; youth camps; individual & family services

(P-25407)
YMCA OF EAST BAY
Also Called: Urban Services YMCA
3265 Market St, Oakland (94608-4332)
PHONE 510 654-9622
Fax: 510 654-0474
Chris Chatmon, *Exec Dir*
Crystal Brookter, *Case Mgr*
EMP: 72
SALES (corp-wide): 30.1MM Privately Held
SIC: 8641 7991 8351 7032 Youth organizations; physical fitness facilities; child day care services; youth camps; individual & family services
PA: Ymca Of The East Bay
2350 Broadway
Oakland CA 94612
510 451-8039

(P-25408)
YMCA OF EAST BAY
Also Called: Coronado YMCA
263 S 20th St, Richmond (94804-2709)
PHONE 510 412-5647
Don Lau, *Branch Mgr*
EMP: 325
SQ FT: 16,338
SALES (corp-wide): 30.1MM Privately Held
SIC: 8641 Youth organizations; recreation association
PA: Ymca Of The East Bay
2350 Broadway
Oakland CA 94612
510 451-8039

(P-25409)
YMCA OF EAST BAY
Also Called: Hilltop Family YMCA
4300 Lakeside Dr, Richmond (94806-5717)
PHONE 510 222-9622
Linda Cook, *Branch Mgr*
Lisa Nakamura, *Info Tech Mgr*
EMP: 125
SALES (corp-wide): 30.1MM Privately Held
SIC: 8641 Youth organizations; recreation association
PA: Ymca Of The East Bay
2350 Broadway
Oakland CA 94612
510 451-8039

(P-25410)
YMCA OF EAST VALLEY (PA)
500 E Citrus Ave, Redlands (92373-5285)
PHONE 909 798-9622
Fax: 909 335-2007
Darwin Barnett, *CEO*
Ken Stein, *CEO*
Doug Thorne, *CFO*
Perry Mecate, *Vice Pres*
Crystal Rochsord,
EMP: 125
SQ FT: 100,000
SALES: 13MM Privately Held
WEB: www.ymcaofredlands.com
SIC: 8641 Youth organizations

(P-25411)
YMCA OF EAST VALLEY
Also Called: San Bernardino Family YMCA
808 E 21st St, San Bernardino (92404-4874)
PHONE 909 881-9622
Bill Blank, *Director*
EMP: 50
SALES (corp-wide): 13MM Privately Held
WEB: www.ymcaofredlands.com
SIC: 8641 7991 8351 7032 Youth organizations; physical fitness facilities; child day care services; youth camps; individual & family services
PA: Ymca Of The East Valley
500 E Citrus Ave
Redlands CA 92373
909 798-9622

(P-25412)
YMCA OF EAST VALLEY
7793 Central Ave, Highland (92346-4106)
PHONE 909 425-9622
Fax: 909 864-4925
Ursula Walsh, *Branch Mgr*
EMP: 50
SALES (corp-wide): 13MM Privately Held
WEB: www.ymcaofredlands.com
SIC: 8641 7991 8351 7032 Youth organizations; physical fitness facilities; child day care services; youth camps; individual & family services
PA: Ymca Of The East Valley
500 E Citrus Ave
Redlands CA 92373
909 798-9622

(P-25413)
YMCA OF NORTH ORANGE COUNTY
Also Called: North Orange Cnty Fmly Y M C A
2000 Youth Way, Fullerton (92835-3878)
PHONE 714 879-9622
Fax: 714 879-2820
Jim Lapak, *Exec Dir*
Claire Akenna, *Manager*
EMP: 85
SQ FT: 10,000
SALES (est): 1.1MM Privately Held
SIC: 8641 7991 8351 7032 Youth organizations; physical fitness facilities; child day care services; youth camps; individual & family services

(P-25414)
YMCA OF SAN DIEGO COUNTY
Also Called: Y M C A Childcare Resource Ser
1310 Union Plaza Ct # 200, Oceanside (92054-5604)
PHONE 760 754-6042
Fax: 760 754-6043
Job Moraido, *Branch Mgr*
EMP: 76
SALES (corp-wide): 155.5MM Privately Held
WEB: www.ymcacrs.org
SIC: 8641 7991 8351 7032 Youth organizations; physical fitness facilities; child day care services; youth camps; individual & family services
PA: Ymca Of San Diego County
3708 Ruffin Rd
San Diego CA 92123
858 292-9622

(P-25415)
YMCA OF SAN DIEGO COUNTY
Also Called: La Jolla YMCA
8355 Cliffridge Ave, La Jolla (92037-2107)
PHONE 858 453-3483
Fax: 858 452-3761
Sam Wurtzbacher, *Director*
Anita Smith, *Vice Pres*
Wendy Mahaffy, *Executive Asst*
EMP: 200
SALES (corp-wide): 155.5MM Privately Held
WEB: www.ymcacrs.org
SIC: 8641 8351 7997 Civic social & fraternal associations; child day care services; membership sports & recreation clubs
PA: Ymca Of San Diego County
3708 Ruffin Rd
San Diego CA 92123
858 292-9622

(P-25416)
YMCA OF SAN DIEGO COUNTY (PA)
Also Called: Y, The
3708 Ruffin Rd, San Diego (92123-1812)
PHONE 858 292-9622
Baron Herdelin Doherty, *CEO*
Paul Sullivan, *CFO*
Steve Rowe, *Exec VP*
John Merritt, *Senior VP*
Serena Souza, *Senior VP*
EMP: 101
SQ FT: 19,600
SALES: 155.5MM Privately Held
WEB: www.ymcacrs.org
SIC: 8641 Youth organizations

(P-25417)
YMCA OF SAN DIEGO COUNTY
Also Called: Magdalena Ecke Family YMCA
200 Saxony Rd, Encinitas (92024-2720)
PHONE 858 292-4034
Fax: 760 944-9329
Susan J Cocke, *Branch Mgr*
Marcy Jenne, *Department Mgr*
Mike Grohsman, *Info Tech Dir*
Geoff Doyon, *Info Tech Mgr*
Emily Figueiredo, *Relations*
EMP: 76
SALES (corp-wide): 155.5MM Privately Held
WEB: www.ymcacrs.org
SIC: 8641 8351 8322 7997 Youth organizations; child day care services; youth center; membership sports & recreation clubs
PA: Ymca Of San Diego County
3708 Ruffin Rd
San Diego CA 92123
858 292-9622

(P-25418)
YMCA OF SAN DIEGO COUNTY
8881 Dallas St, La Mesa (91942-3297)
PHONE 619 464-1323
Steve Rowe, *Exec Dir*
EMP: 76
SALES (corp-wide): 155.5MM Privately Held
WEB: www.ymcacrs.org
SIC: 8641 7991 8351 7032 Youth organizations; physical fitness facilities; child day care services; youth camps; individual & family services
PA: Ymca Of San Diego County
3708 Ruffin Rd
San Diego CA 92123
858 292-9622

(P-25419)
YMCA OF SAN DIEGO COUNTY
Also Called: Pelomar Family YMCA
1050 N Broadway, Escondido (92026-3044)
PHONE 760 745-7490
Alfredo Velasco, *Manager*
Fran Waller, *Marketing Mgr*
Lisa Daniels, *Director*
Diana Carlin, *Manager*
Arlene Shaffer, *Manager*
EMP: 500
SALES (corp-wide): 155.5MM Privately Held
WEB: www.ymcacrs.org
SIC: 8641 7991 8351 7032 Youth organizations; physical fitness facilities; child day care services; youth camps; individual & family services
PA: Ymca Of San Diego County
3708 Ruffin Rd
San Diego CA 92123
858 292-9622

(P-25420)
YMCA OF SAN DIEGO COUNTY
Also Called: YMCA Youth & Family Services
2927 Meade Ave, San Diego (92116-4251)
PHONE 619 281-8313
Fax: 619 281-8324
Cesar Marcano, *Exec Dir*
EMP: 72
SALES (corp-wide): 155.5MM Privately Held
SIC: 8641 7991 8351 7032 Youth organizations; physical fitness facilities; child day care services; youth camps; individual & family services
PA: Ymca Of San Diego County
3708 Ruffin Rd
San Diego CA 92123
858 292-9622

(P-25421)
YMCA OF SAN DIEGO COUNTY
Also Called: Peninsula Family YMCA Sunshine
2150 Beryl St Ste 18, San Diego (92109-3617)
PHONE 619 226-8888
Fax: 858 272-0260
Andrea Sanchez, *Director*
Vince Goorioso, *Exec Dir*
EMP: 75
SQ FT: 3,500
SALES (corp-wide): 155.5MM Privately Held
WEB: www.ymcacrs.org
SIC: 8641 8322 Youth organizations; individual & family services

PRODUCTS & SERVICES SECTION
8641 - Civic, Social & Fraternal Associations County (P-25441)

PA: Ymca Of San Diego County
3708 Ruffin Rd
San Diego CA 92123
858 292-9622

(P-25422)
YMCA OF SAN DIEGO COUNTY
Also Called: YMCA Child Care Resource Svcs
3333 Camino Del Rio S # 400, San Diego (92108-3808)
PHONE.....619 521-3055
Fax: 619 521-3050
Debbie Macdonald, *Director*
Debbie M Donald, *Exec Dir*
EMP: 180
SALES (corp-wide): 155.5MM **Privately Held**
WEB: www.ymcacrs.org
SIC: 8641 7991 8351 7032 Youth organizations; physical fitness facilities; child day care services; youth camps; individual & family services
PA: Ymca Of San Diego County
3708 Ruffin Rd
San Diego CA 92123
858 292-9622

(P-25423)
YMCA OF SAN DIEGO COUNTY
Also Called: YMCA Overnight Camp
4761 Pine Hills Rd, Julian (92036)
P.O. Box 2440 (92036-2440)
PHONE.....760 765-0642
Thomas Madeyski, *Exec Dir*
EMP: 50
SALES (corp-wide): 155.5MM **Privately Held**
WEB: www.ymcacrs.org
SIC: 8641 7991 8351 7032 Youth organizations; physical fitness facilities; child day care services; youth camps; individual & family services
PA: Ymca Of San Diego County
3708 Ruffin Rd
San Diego CA 92123
858 292-9622

(P-25424)
YMCA OF SAN DIEGO COUNTY
Also Called: Mission Valley YMCA
5505 Friars Rd, San Diego (92110-2682)
PHONE.....619 298-3576
Fax: 619 298-9262
Dick Webster, *Manager*
EMP: 200
SALES (corp-wide): 155.5MM **Privately Held**
WEB: www.ymcacrs.org
SIC: 8641 7997 Youth organizations; membership sports & recreation clubs
PA: Ymca Of San Diego County
3708 Ruffin Rd
San Diego CA 92123
858 292-9622

(P-25425)
YMCA OF SAN DIEGO COUNTY
Also Called: Cameron Family YMCA
10123 Hoffman Ln, Santee (92071-5295)
PHONE.....619 449-9622
Steve Rowe, *Branch Mgr*
Debbie Lenz, *Director*
Stephanie Thompson, *Manager*
EMP: 100
SQ FT: 32,970
SALES (corp-wide): 155.5MM **Privately Held**
WEB: www.ymcacrs.org
SIC: 8641 8322 Youth organizations; individual & family services
PA: Ymca Of San Diego County
3708 Ruffin Rd
San Diego CA 92123
858 292-9622

(P-25426)
YMCA OF SAN DIEGO COUNTY
Also Called: Joe & Mary Mottino YMCA
4701 Mesa Dr, Oceanside (92056-6568)
PHONE.....760 758-0808
Fax: 760 758-8059
Jeff Guzzardo, *Branch Mgr*
Gary Wegener, *Director*
Brent Ayers, *Manager*
EMP: 100

SALES (corp-wide): 155.5MM **Privately Held**
WEB: www.ymcacrs.org
SIC: 8641 8322 Youth organizations; individual & family services
PA: Ymca Of San Diego County
3708 Ruffin Rd
San Diego CA 92123
858 292-9622

(P-25427)
YMCA OF SAN DIEGO COUNTY
Also Called: Santa Margarita YMCA Garrison
333 Garrison St, Oceanside (92054-4700)
PHONE.....760 757-8270
Margie Oliver, *Branch Mgr*
EMP: 76
SALES (corp-wide): 155.5MM **Privately Held**
WEB: www.ymcacrs.org
SIC: 8641 7991 8351 7032 Youth organizations; physical fitness facilities; child day care services; youth camps; individual & family services
PA: Ymca Of San Diego County
3708 Ruffin Rd
San Diego CA 92123
858 292-9622

(P-25428)
YMCA OF SAN DIEGO COUNTY
50 4th Ave, Chula Vista (91910-1767)
PHONE.....619 422-8068
Sheri Greene, *Manager*
EMP: 76
SQ FT: 2,832
SALES (corp-wide): 155.5MM **Privately Held**
WEB: www.ymcacrs.org
SIC: 8641 7991 8351 7032 Youth organizations; physical fitness facilities; child day care services; youth camps; individual & family services
PA: Ymca Of San Diego County
3708 Ruffin Rd
San Diego CA 92123
858 292-9622

(P-25429)
YMCA OF SAN JOAQUIN COUNTY
2105 W March Ln Ste 1, Stockton (95207-6422)
PHONE.....209 472-9622
Russ Hayward, *CEO*
Rich Good, *Exec Dir*
Sam Prak, *Finance*
EMP: 70
SQ FT: 2,000
SALES: 3.1MM **Privately Held**
WEB: www.ymcasjc.org
SIC: 8641 Social club, membership; youth organizations

(P-25430)
YMCA OF SILICON VALLEY (PA)
80 Saratoga Ave, Santa Clara (95051-7303)
PHONE.....408 351-6400
Kathy Riggins, *President*
Ed Barrantes, *CFO*
James Amaral, *Controller*
EMP: 60
SQ FT: 5,000
SALES (est): 57.6MM **Privately Held**
WEB: www.scvymca.org
SIC: 8641 7991 8351 7032 Youth organizations; physical fitness facilities; child day care services; youth camps; individual & family services

(P-25431)
YMCA OF SILICON VALLEY
1922 The Alameda Ste 300, San Jose (95126-1430)
PHONE.....650 493-9622
EMP: 300
SALES (corp-wide): 57.6MM **Privately Held**
SIC: 8641 7991 8351 7032 Youth organizations; physical fitness facilities; child day care services; youth camps; individual & family services

PA: Ymca Of Silicon Valley
80 Saratoga Ave
Santa Clara CA 95051
408 351-6400

(P-25432)
YMCA OF SILICON VALLEY
Also Called: Central Branch YMCA
1717 The Alameda, San Jose (95126-1794)
PHONE.....408 298-1717
Barbara Cardinez, *Manager*
Phillip Sims Sr, *Senior Partner*
Mike Williams Sr,
EMP: 150
SQ FT: 52,715
SALES (corp-wide): 57.6MM **Privately Held**
WEB: www.scvymca.org
SIC: 8641 8351 8322 7997 Youth organizations; child day care services; individual & family services; membership sports & recreation clubs; physical fitness facilities
PA: Ymca Of Silicon Valley
80 Saratoga Ave
Santa Clara CA 95051
408 351-6400

(P-25433)
YMCA OF SILICON VALLEY
Also Called: El Camino YMCA
2400 Grant Rd, Mountain View (94040-4324)
PHONE.....650 969-9622
Fax: 650 969-1053
Elaine Glissmeyer, *Director*
S T Brigham, *Bd of Directors*
Stephen C Gerrish, *Bd of Directors*
Jan Dale, *Vice Pres*
John Remy, *Vice Pres*
EMP: 300
SALES (corp-wide): 57.6MM **Privately Held**
SIC: 8641 7991 8351 7032 Youth organizations; physical fitness facilities; child day care services; youth camps; individual & family services
PA: Ymca Of Silicon Valley
80 Saratoga Ave
Santa Clara CA 95051
408 351-6400

(P-25434)
YMCA OF SILICON VALLEY
Also Called: YMCA of Santa Clara Valley
5632 Santa Teresa Blvd, San Jose (95123-2698)
PHONE.....408 226-3324
Fax: 408 226-9324
Rick Valdez, *Exec Dir*
EMP: 60
SALES (corp-wide): 57.6MM **Privately Held**
WEB: www.scvymca.org
SIC: 8641 7991 8351 7032 Youth organizations; physical fitness facilities; child day care services; youth camps; individual & family services
PA: Ymca Of Silicon Valley
80 Saratoga Ave
Santa Clara CA 95051
408 351-6400

(P-25435)
YMCA OF THE MID-PENINSULA INC
1922 The Alameda Ste 300, San Jose (95126-1430)
PHONE.....650 493-9622
EMP: 300
SQ FT: 6,000
SALES (est): 847.5K **Privately Held**
SIC: 8641 7991 8351 7032

(P-25436)
YMCA YOUTH & FAMILY SERVICES
4080 Centre St Ste 203, San Diego (92103-2657)
PHONE.....619 543-9850
Laura Mustari, *Principal*
EMP: 64

SALES (est): 1.2MM **Privately Held**
SIC: 8641 7991 8351 7032 Youth organizations; physical fitness facilities; child day care services; youth camps; individual & family services

(P-25437)
YOSEMITE FOUNDATION
Also Called: YOSEMITE CONSERVANCY
101 Montgomery St # 1700, San Francisco (94104-4129)
PHONE.....415 434-1782
Fax: 415 434-0745
Micheal Tollesson, *CEO*
Bob Hansen, *President*
Jerry Edelbrock, *CFO*
Kirstie Kari, *Project Dir*
Greg Immel, *Manager*
EMP: 84
SQ FT: 15,000
SALES: 17.4MM **Privately Held**
WEB: www.yosemitefund.org
SIC: 8641 Civic associations

(P-25438)
YOSEMITE LAKES OWNERS ASSN
30250 Yosemite Springs Pk, Coarsegold (93614-9369)
PHONE.....559 658-7466
Fax: 559 658-7866
Steve Payne, *General Mgr*
Kathy Casey, *Admin Asst*
Patti Bisnett, *Administration*
Kristen Day, *HR Admin*
EMP: 70
SQ FT: 10,000
SALES (est): 2.8MM **Privately Held**
WEB: www.yloa.org
SIC: 8641 Homeowners' association

(P-25439)
YOUNG MENS CHRISTIAN (PA)
Also Called: YMCA
321 E Magnolia Blvd, Burbank (91502-1132)
PHONE.....818 845-8551
Fax: 818 845-0785
JC Holt, *CEO*
Harkmore Lee, *COO*
Doris Umemoto, *Executive Asst*
ARA Bonyadian, *Controller*
Marissa Arreguin, *Director*
EMP: 100
SQ FT: 47,000
SALES: 5.3MM **Privately Held**
SIC: 8641 7991 8351 7032 Youth organizations; physical fitness facilities; child day care services; youth camps; individual & family services

(P-25440)
YOUNG MENS CHRISTIAN ASSNSF
Also Called: Presidio Community YMCA
57 Post St, San Francisco (94104-5003)
PHONE.....415 447-9602
EMP: 86
SALES (corp-wide): 74.5MM **Privately Held**
SIC: 8641 7999 Civic social & fraternal associations; swimming instruction
PA: Young Men's Christian Association Of San Francisco
50 California St Ste 650
San Francisco CA 94111
415 777-9622

(P-25441)
YOUNG MENS CHRISTIAN ASSNSF
Also Called: Presido YMCA
63 Funston Ave, San Francisco (94129-1110)
PHONE.....415 447-9622
Robert Sindelar, *Exec Dir*
Sean Dries, *Director*
EMP: 86
SALES (corp-wide): 74.5MM **Privately Held**
SIC: 8641 7999 Youth organizations; tennis services & professionals

8641 - Civic, Social & Fraternal Associations County (P-25442)

PA: Young Men's Christian Association Of San Francisco
50 California St Ste 650
San Francisco CA 94111
415 777-9622

(P-25442)
YOUNG MENS CHRISTIAN ASSNSF
Also Called: Precidio YMCA
Main Post Gym Bldg 63, San Francisco (94129)
PHONE..................415 447-9645
EMP: 86
SALES (corp-wide): 74.5MM Privately Held
SIC: 8641 7991 8351 7032 Youth organizations; physical fitness facilities; child day care services; youth camps; individual & family services
PA: Young Men's Christian Association Of San Francisco
50 California St Ste 650
San Francisco CA 94111
415 777-9622

(P-25443)
YOUNG MENS CHRISTIAN ASSNSF
Also Called: YMCA Youth & Family Service
1115 3rd St, San Rafael (94901-3017)
PHONE..................415 459-9622
Don Carney, *Director*
EMP: 200
SALES (corp-wide): 74.5MM Privately Held
SIC: 8641 7991 8351 7032 Youth organizations; physical fitness facilities; child day care services; youth camps; individual & family services
PA: Young Men's Christian Association Of San Francisco
50 California St Ste 650
San Francisco CA 94111
415 777-9622

(P-25444)
YOUNG MENS CHRISTIAN ASSNSF
Also Called: YMCA Richmond Afterschool Ctr
4545 Anza St, San Francisco (94121-2621)
PHONE..................415 752-0790
Kevin Lee, *Manager*
EMP: 86
SALES (corp-wide): 74.5MM Privately Held
SIC: 8641 7991 8351 7032 Youth organizations; physical fitness facilities; child day care services; youth camps; individual & family services
PA: Young Men's Christian Association Of San Francisco
50 California St Ste 650
San Francisco CA 94111
415 777-9622

(P-25445)
YOUNG MENS CHRISTIAN ASSNSF
Also Called: American Chinese Presb YMCA
914 Clay St, San Francisco (94108-1521)
PHONE..................415 421-5721
Elenore Louie, *Manager*
EMP: 86
SALES (corp-wide): 74.5MM Privately Held
SIC: 8641 7991 8351 7032 Youth organizations; physical fitness facilities; child day care services; youth camps; individual & family services
PA: Young Men's Christian Association Of San Francisco
50 California St Ste 650
San Francisco CA 94111
415 777-9622

(P-25446)
YOUNG MENS CHRISTIAN ASSNSF
Also Called: YMCA San Francisco-Marin Cnty
1500 Los Gamos Dr, San Rafael (94903-1841)
PHONE..................415 492-9622
Fax: 415 492-9703
Luann Jackman, *Exec Dir*

Jamie Bruning, *Senior VP*
Don Hanna, *Vice Pres*
Jane Chandler, *Associate Dir*
Erin Reedy, *Associate Dir*
EMP: 300
SALES (corp-wide): 74.5MM Privately Held
SIC: 8641 8351 7991 Community membership club; child day care services; physical fitness facilities
PA: Young Men's Christian Association Of San Francisco
50 California St Ste 650
San Francisco CA 94111
415 777-9622

(P-25447)
YOUNG MENS CHRISTIAN ASSO
4031 N Moorpark Rd, Thousand Oaks (91360-2660)
PHONE..................805 523-7613
Fax: 805 523-8831
Kelly Dulek, *Director*
Cory Yoshinagaa, *Director*
Janice Wise, *Relations*
Jerrid Meikle, *Associate*
EMP: 100
SALES (corp-wide): 20.9MM Privately Held
SIC: 8641 7997 8351 Civic social & fraternal associations; membership sports & recreation clubs; child day care services
PA: Young Men's Christian Association Of Southeast Ventura County
100 E Thousand Oaks Blvd # 107
Thousand Oaks CA 91360
805 497-3081

(P-25448)
YOUNG MENS CHRISTIAN ASSOC SF
Also Called: Argonne YMCA After School
680 18th Ave, San Francisco (94121-3823)
PHONE..................415 831-4093
Robin Sharp, *Manager*
EMP: 86
SALES (corp-wide): 74.5MM Privately Held
SIC: 8641 7991 8351 7032 Youth organizations; physical fitness facilities; child day care services; youth camps; individual & family services
PA: Young Men's Christian Association Of San Francisco
50 California St Ste 650
San Francisco CA 94111
415 777-9622

(P-25449)
YOUNG MENS CHRISTIAN ASSOC SF
Also Called: Peninsula YMCA
1877 S Grant St, San Mateo (94402-2647)
PHONE..................650 286-9622
Fax: 650 286-0128
Rachel Del Monte, *Manager*
Luann Jackman, *Vice Pres*
Patrizia Guiotto, *Principal*
Elizabeth Jordan, *Exec Dir*
Gary Cockrell, *Facilities Dir*
EMP: 200
SALES (corp-wide): 74.5MM Privately Held
SIC: 8641 7991 8351 Youth organizations; physical fitness facilities; child day care services
PA: Young Men's Christian Association Of San Francisco
50 California St Ste 650
San Francisco CA 94111
415 777-9622

(P-25450)
YOUNG MENS CHRISTIAN ASSOC SF (PA)
Also Called: YMCA of San Francisco
50 California St Ste 650, San Francisco (94111-4607)
PHONE..................415 777-9622
Fax: 415 777-6915
Charles M Collins, *President*
Kathy Cheng, *CFO*
Virginia Richardson, *Bd of Directors*
Linda Griffith, *Vice Pres*
Don Hanna, *Vice Pres*
EMP: 50

SQ FT: 10,000
SALES: 74.5MM Privately Held
SIC: 8641 7991 8351 7032 Youth organizations; physical fitness facilities; child day care services; youth camps; individual & family services

(P-25451)
YOUNG MENS CHRISTIAN ASSOC SF
Also Called: Richmond District YMCA
360 18th Ave, San Francisco (94121-2317)
PHONE..................415 666-9622
Tiffany Patterson, *Branch Mgr*
EMP: 80
SALES (corp-wide): 74.5MM Privately Held
SIC: 8641 7991 8351 7032 Youth organizations; physical fitness facilities; child day care services; youth camps; individual & family services
PA: Young Men's Christian Association Of San Francisco
50 California St Ste 650
San Francisco CA 94111
415 777-9622

(P-25452)
YOUNG MENS CHRISTIAN ASSOC SF
Also Called: YMCA
169 Steuart St, San Francisco (94105-1206)
PHONE..................415 957-9622
Larry Bush, *Branch Mgr*
Sandy Lasalle, *Personnel*
Megan Schroder, *Marketing Staff*
Jon Kaufman, *Director*
EMP: 100
SQ FT: 54,186
SALES (corp-wide): 74.5MM Privately Held
SIC: 8641 7991 8351 7032 Youth organizations; physical fitness facilities; child day care services; youth camps; individual & family services
PA: Young Men's Christian Association Of San Francisco
50 California St Ste 650
San Francisco CA 94111
415 777-9622

(P-25453)
YOUNG MENS CHRISTIAN ASSOC SF
Also Called: Shih Yu-Lang Central YMCA
246 Eddy St, San Francisco (94102-2716)
PHONE..................415 885-0460
Fax: 415 885-5439
Carmela Gold, *Exec Dir*
Mike Ross, *Officer*
Rick White, *MIS Dir*
Lara Hitchcock, *Director*
EMP: 100
SALES (corp-wide): 74.5MM Privately Held
SIC: 8641 7997 8322 7999 Civic social & fraternal associations; membership sports & recreation clubs; senior citizens' center or association; swimming instruction; aerobic dance & exercise classes; hotels
PA: Young Men's Christian Association Of San Francisco
50 California St Ste 650
San Francisco CA 94111
415 777-9622

(P-25454)
YOUNG MENS CHRISTIAN ASSOC SF
3 Hamilton Landing # 140, Novato (94949-8248)
PHONE..................415 883-9622
Jayne Blote, *Branch Mgr*
Maria C Reyes, *Controller*
EMP: 88
SALES (corp-wide): 74.5MM Privately Held
SIC: 8641 7991 8351 7032 Youth organizations; physical fitness facilities; child day care services; youth camps; individual & family services

PRODUDUCTS & SERVICES SECTION

PA: Young Men's Christian Association Of San Francisco
50 California St Ste 650
San Francisco CA 94111
415 777-9622

(P-25455)
YOUNG MENS CHRISTIAN ASSOCIAT
Also Called: Downtown Community Dev YMCA
525 E 7th St, Long Beach (90813-4559)
PHONE..................562 624-2376
Robert Cabeza, *Exec Dir*
Noel Burcelis, *Exec Dir*
Emilio Sosa, *Exec Dir*
Lenore Gabel, *Director*
EMP: 99
SALES: 3.3MM Privately Held
SIC: 8641 7991 8351 7032 Youth organizations; physical fitness facilities; child day care services; youth camps; individual & family services

(P-25456)
YOUNG MENS CHRISTN ASSN ORANGE
146 N Grand St, Orange (92866-1512)
PHONE..................714 771-1287
Fax: 714 633-4337
Dolores Marikian, *CEO*
Danny Escobar, *Site Mgr*
Liz Martinez, *Director*
EMP: 60
SQ FT: 6,500
SALES: 510.2K Privately Held
SIC: 8641 Youth organizations

(P-25457)
YOUNG MENS CHRSTN ASSC GR L B
Also Called: Lakewood Y M C A Gymnastics
4116 South St, Lakewood (90712-1005)
PHONE..................562 272-4884
Rick Carlson, *Branch Mgr*
EMP: 89
SALES (corp-wide): 19.4MM Privately Held
WEB: www.lbymca.org
SIC: 8641 7991 8351 7032 Youth organizations; physical fitness facilities; child day care services; youth camps; individual & family services
PA: Young Men's Christian Association Of Greater Long Beach
3605 Lngbach Blvd Ste 210
Long Beach CA 90807
562 279-1700

(P-25458)
YOUNG MENS CHRSTN ASSC GR L B
Also Called: Los Altos YMCA
1720 N Bellflower Blvd, Long Beach (90815-4011)
PHONE..................562 596-3394
Fax: 562 596-7911
Sierra Lahera, *Director*
Mayra Gonzalez, *Director*
EMP: 500
SQ FT: 9,740
SALES (corp-wide): 19.4MM Privately Held
WEB: www.lbymca.org
SIC: 8641 7991 8351 7032 Youth organizations; physical fitness facilities; child day care services; youth camps; individual & family services
PA: Young Men's Christian Association Of Greater Long Beach
3605 Lngbach Blvd Ste 210
Long Beach CA 90807
562 279-1700

(P-25459)
YOUNG MENS CHRSTN ASSC GR L B
Also Called: Y M C A Los Cerritos
15530 Woodruff Ave, Bellflower (90706-4014)
PHONE..................562 925-1292
Michele Janssen, *Director*
Jessica Lopez, *Director*
EMP: 80
SQ FT: 6,190

PRODUCTS & SERVICES SECTION

8641 - Civic, Social & Fraternal Associations County (P-25477)

SALES (corp-wide): 19.4MM **Privately Held**
WEB: www.lbymca.org
SIC: **8641** 8351 Community membership club; child day care services
PA: Young Men's Christian Association Of Greater Long Beach
3605 Lngbach Blvd Ste 210
Long Beach CA 90807
562 279-1700

(P-25460)
YOUNG MENS CHRSTN ASSC GR L B
Also Called: Weingart-Lakewood Family YMCA
5835 Carson St, Lakewood (90713-3056)
PHONE.................................562 425-7431
Chanelle Collo, *Director*
EMP: 125
SALES (corp-wide): 19.4MM **Privately Held**
WEB: www.lbymca.org
SIC: **8641** 7991 8351 7032 Youth organizations; physical fitness facilities; child day care services; youth camps; individual & family services
PA: Young Men's Christian Association Of Greater Long Beach
3605 Lngbach Blvd Ste 210
Long Beach CA 90807
562 279-1700

(P-25461)
YOUNG MENS CHRSTN ASSC GR L B
Also Called: Fairfield Family YMCA
4949 Atlantic Ave, Long Beach (90805-6505)
PHONE.................................562 423-0491
Ricky Grober, *Director*
Terry Griffin, *Director*
EMP: 60
SALES (corp-wide): 19.4MM **Privately Held**
WEB: www.lbymca.org
SIC: **8641** 8351 8322 Youth organizations; child day care services; youth center
PA: Young Men's Christian Association Of Greater Long Beach
3605 Lngbach Blvd Ste 210
Long Beach CA 90807
562 279-1700

(P-25462)
YOUNG MENS CHRSTN ASSC GR L B
Also Called: YMCA Glb Grant
4949 Atlantic Ave, Long Beach (90805-6505)
PHONE.................................562 423-0491
Fax: 562 984-9611
Katherine Tarlecky, *Director*
EMP: 89
SALES (corp-wide): 19.4MM **Privately Held**
WEB: www.lbymca.org
SIC: **8641** 8351 Civic social & fraternal associations; child day care services
PA: Young Men's Christian Association Of Greater Long Beach
3605 Lngbach Blvd Ste 210
Long Beach CA 90807
562 279-1700

(P-25463)
YOUNG MENS CHRSTN ASSC GR L B
Also Called: Y M C A The
6125 Coke Ave, Long Beach (90805-3925)
PHONE.................................562 633-0106
Lyle Yballe, *Branch Mgr*
EMP: 89
SALES (corp-wide): 19.4MM **Privately Held**
WEB: www.lbymca.org
SIC: **8641** 7999 8351 Civic social & fraternal associations; recreation center; group day care center
PA: Young Men's Christian Association Of Greater Long Beach
3605 Lngbach Blvd Ste 210
Long Beach CA 90807
562 279-1700

(P-25464)
YOUNG MENS CHRSTN ASSN OF LA
Also Called: Mid-Valley Y M C A
6901 Lennox Ave, Van Nuys (91405-4002)
PHONE.................................818 989-3800
Fax: 818 901-9609
Wendy Sunders, *Exec Dir*
EMP: 50
SQ FT: 37,223
SALES (corp-wide): 103.1MM **Privately Held**
SIC: **8641** 7991 8351 7032 Youth organizations; physical fitness facilities; child day care services; youth camps; individual & family services
PA: Young Men's Christian Association Of Metropolitan Los Angeles
625 S New Hampshire Ave
Los Angeles CA 90005
213 351-2256

(P-25465)
YOUNG MENS CHRSTN ASSN OF LA
Also Called: South Pasadena San Marino YMCA
1605 Garfield Ave, South Pasadena (91030-4968)
PHONE.................................626 799-9119
Fax: 626 799-3670
Sue Marasco, *Director*
Michael Henderson, *Exec Dir*
EMP: 65
SQ FT: 23,031
SALES (corp-wide): 103.1MM **Privately Held**
SIC: **8641** 7991 8351 7032 Youth organizations; physical fitness facilities; child day care services; youth camps; individual & family services
PA: Young Men's Christian Association Of Metropolitan Los Angeles
625 S New Hampshire Ave
Los Angeles CA 90005
213 351-2256

(P-25466)
YOUNG MENS CHRSTN ASSN OF LA (PA)
Also Called: YMCA
625 S New Hampshire Ave, Los Angeles (90005-1342)
PHONE.................................213 351-2256
Fax: 213 251-9720
Alan Hostrup, *President*
W J Ellison, *Ch of Bd*
Dan Cooper, *CFO*
Marsha Bowman, *Exec VP*
Robert Shafer, *Executive*
EMP: 70
SQ FT: 16,000
SALES: 103.1MM **Privately Held**
SIC: **8641** Youth organizations

(P-25467)
YOUNG MENS CHRSTN ASSN OF LA
Also Called: YMCA of Westchester
8015 S Sepulveda Blvd, Los Angeles (90045-2940)
PHONE.................................310 216-9036
Fax: 310 338-9752
Patricia De Frelice, *Exec Dir*
Carol Baer, *Business Mgr*
Chad Mender, *Manager*
EMP: 50
SALES (corp-wide): 103.1MM **Privately Held**
SIC: **8641** 8322 Youth organizations; individual & family services
PA: Young Men's Christian Association Of Metropolitan Los Angeles
625 S New Hampshire Ave
Los Angeles CA 90005
213 351-2256

(P-25468)
YOUNG MENS CHRSTN ASSN OF LA
Also Called: YMCA Metro La Summit Park
26147 Mcbean Pkwy, Valencia (91355-2015)
PHONE.................................661 253-3593
Fax: 661 799-6945
Brian Thorn, *Exec Dir*
Mike Irwin, *Software Dev*
EMP: 130
SQ FT: 13,124
SALES (corp-wide): 103.1MM **Privately Held**
SIC: **8641** 7991 8351 7032 Youth organizations; physical fitness facilities; child day care services; youth camps; individual & family services
PA: Young Men's Christian Association Of Metropolitan Los Angeles
625 S New Hampshire Ave
Los Angeles CA 90005
213 351-2256

(P-25469)
YOUNG MENS CHRSTN ASSN OF LA
Also Called: Downey Family Y M C A
11531 Downey Ave, Downey (90241-4936)
PHONE.................................562 862-4201
George Saikali, *Director*
EMP: 100
SALES (corp-wide): 103.1MM **Privately Held**
SIC: **8641** 7991 8351 7032 Youth organizations; physical fitness facilities; child day care services; youth camps; individual & family services
PA: Young Men's Christian Association Of Metropolitan Los Angeles
625 S New Hampshire Ave
Los Angeles CA 90005
213 351-2256

(P-25470)
YOUNG MENS CHRSTN ASSN OF LA
Also Called: Ketchum YMCA
401 S Hope St, Los Angeles (90071-1903)
PHONE.................................213 624-2348
Fax: 213 627-8151
Laurie Goganzer, *Director*
Shawn Berry, *Manager*
EMP: 100
SALES (corp-wide): 103.1MM **Privately Held**
SIC: **8641** 8322 Youth organizations; youth center
PA: Young Men's Christian Association Of Metropolitan Los Angeles
625 S New Hampshire Ave
Los Angeles CA 90005
213 351-2256

(P-25471)
YOUNG MENS CHRSTN ASSN OF LA
Also Called: Young Mens Christian Assn
1605 Garfield Ave, South Pasadena (91030-4968)
PHONE.................................323 682-2147
Fax: 323 799-3670
Sue Marasco, *Manager*
Hailey Morris, *Director*
EMP: 75
SALES (corp-wide): 103.1MM **Privately Held**
SIC: **8641** 7991 8351 7032 Youth organizations; physical fitness facilities; child day care services; youth camps; individual & family services
PA: Young Men's Christian Association Of Metropolitan Los Angeles
625 S New Hampshire Ave
Los Angeles CA 90005
213 351-2256

(P-25472)
YOUNG MENS CHRSTN ASSN ORANGE
2300 University Dr, Newport Beach (92660-3313)
PHONE.................................949 642-9990
Fax: 949 645-3570
Joy Hyde, *General Mgr*
EMP: 65
SQ FT: 17,976
SALES (corp-wide): 30.6MM **Privately Held**
WEB: www.ymcaoc.com
SIC: **8641** 7991 Youth organizations; physical fitness facilities
PA: Young Men's Christian Association Of Orange County
13821 Newport Ave Ste 200
Tustin CA 92780
714 549-9622

(P-25473)
YOUNG MENS CHRSTN ASSN ORANGE
Also Called: YMCA
2000 Youth Way, Fullerton (92835-3812)
PHONE.................................714 879-9622
Clare McKenna, *Director*
EMP: 60
SALES (corp-wide): 30.6MM **Privately Held**
WEB: www.ymcaoc.com
SIC: **8641** 8322 7991 Youth organizations; individual & family services; athletic club & gymnasiums, membership
PA: Young Men's Christian Association Of Orange County
13821 Newport Ave Ste 200
Tustin CA 92780
714 549-9622

(P-25474)
YOUNG MENS CHRSTN ASSN ORANGE
Also Called: Saddle Back Valley YMCA
27341 Trabuco Cir, Mission Viejo (92692-1939)
PHONE.................................949 859-9622
Mary J Goodrick, *Exec Dir*
Kevin Trump, *Property Mgr*
EMP: 100
SALES (corp-wide): 30.6MM **Privately Held**
WEB: www.ymcaoc.com
SIC: **8641** 7991 8351 7032 Youth organizations; physical fitness facilities; child day care services; youth camps; individual & family services
PA: Young Men's Christian Association Of Orange County
13821 Newport Ave Ste 200
Tustin CA 92780
714 549-9622

(P-25475)
YOUNG MENS CHRSTN ASSN STANIS
Also Called: YMCA of Stanislaus County
2700 Mchenry Ave, Modesto (95350-2348)
PHONE.................................209 578-9622
Steve Smith, *CEO*
EMP: 78
SQ FT: 40,000
SALES (est): 4.8MM **Privately Held**
SIC: **8641** 7991 8351 7032 Youth organizations; physical fitness facilities; child day care services; youth camps; individual & family services

(P-25476)
YOUNG MENS CHRSTN ASSOC GNDL
Also Called: GLENDALE YMCA SWIM SCHOOL
140 N Louise St, Glendale (91206-4226)
PHONE.................................818 484-8256
Fax: 818 500-1737
Tom Tyler, *CEO*
Adrineh Salam, *CFO*
Ryan Nekota, *Director*
Mineh Petrosian, *Director*
EMP: 86 EST: 1924
SQ FT: 15,000
SALES: 3.7MM **Privately Held**
WEB: www.glenymca.org
SIC: **8641** Civic social & fraternal associations; youth organizations; social club, membership; community membership club

(P-25477)
YOUNG WOMENS CHRISTIAN ASSOCI
375 S 3rd St, San Jose (95112-3649)
PHONE.................................408 295-4011
Keri Procunier McLain, *President*
Tanis Crosby, *CEO*
Lorraine Michelle, *Officer*
Sue Barnes, *Principal*
Adriana Caldera, *Principal*

8641 - Civic, Social & Fraternal Associations County (P-25478)

PRODUDCTS & SERVICES SECTION

EMP: 83
SALES: 5MM **Privately Held**
WEB: www.ywca-sv.org
SIC: **8641** 8322 Community membership club; individual & family services

(P-25478)
YUEN SOO BENEVOLENT ASSN
119 Chung Wah Ln, Stockton (95202-3221)
PHONE..................................209 464-3048
Maw L Louie, *President*
Kim Fong, *Vice Pres*
EMP: 250
SALES: 28K **Privately Held**
SIC: **8641** Dwelling-related associations

(P-25479)
YWCA OF SAN DIEGO COUNTY (PA)
1012 C St, San Diego (92101-5544)
PHONE..................................619 239-0355
Heather Finlay, *CEO*
Susan Conner, *Bd of Directors*
Diane Pearson, *Senior VP*
Jill Townson, *Exec Dir*
Shalia Ford, *Director*
EMP: 52
SQ FT: 59,100
SALES: 11MM **Privately Held**
SIC: **8641** 8322 Youth organizations; individual & family services; emergency shelters

8651 Political Organizations

(P-25480)
COUNTY OF ORANGE
Also Called: Registrar of Voters
1300 S Grand Ave Ste C, Santa Ana (92705-4434)
P.O. Box 11298 (92711-1298)
PHONE..................................714 567-7500
Fax: 714 567-7627
Neal Kelly, *Director*
Ron Minekime, *Senior VP*
Margaret Furbank, *Vice Pres*
Kenneth Inouye, *Executive*
Jim Lehmann, *Executive*
EMP: 50 **Privately Held**
SIC: **8651** 9199 Political campaign organization; general government administration;
PA: County Of Orange
333 W Santa Ana Blvd 3f
Santa Ana CA 92701
714 834-6200

(P-25481)
LEAGUE OF WMEN VOTERS WHITTIER
10011 Melgar Dr, Whittier (90603-1458)
PHONE..................................562 947-5818
Margo Reeg, *Treasurer*
EMP: 50
SALES (est): 1.3MM **Privately Held**
SIC: **8651** Political organizations

8699 Membership Organizations, NEC

(P-25482)
AAUW ACTION FUND INC
P.O. Box 1239 (94401-0816)
PHONE..................................650 574-9160
Lowla Ghompson, *President*
EMP: 100
SALES (corp-wide): 269K **Privately Held**
SIC: **8699** Personal interest organization
PA: Aauw Action Fund, Inc.
1111 16th St Nw Ste Milrm
Washington DC 20036
202 785-7700

(P-25483)
ABINGDON ROUGH RIDERS TOU
1231 12th Ave, San Francisco (94122-2211)
PHONE..................................415 566-9796

Allan Chalmer, *Admin Sec*
EMP: 100
SALES (est): 1.2MM **Privately Held**
SIC: **8699** Personal interest organization

(P-25484)
AFFINITY DEVELOPMENT GROUP INC
Also Called: A D G
10251 Vista Sorrento Pkwy # 300, San Diego (92121-3774)
PHONE..................................858 643-9324
Fax: 858 643-9354
Jeff Skeen, *President*
Gary Drean, *COO*
Greg Siebenthal, *CFO*
Josie Herschel, *Senior VP*
Mark Stcyr, *Senior VP*
EMP: 120
SQ FT: 46,000
SALES (est): 14.6MM **Privately Held**
WEB: www.affinitydev.com
SIC: **8699** Automobile owners' association

(P-25485)
AGUA CLNTE BAND CHILLA INDIANS (PA)
5401 Dinah Shore Dr, Palm Springs (92264-5970)
PHONE..................................760 699-6800
Jeff L Grubbe, *Chairman*
Vincent Gonzales III, *Corp Secy*
Larry N Olinger, *Principal*
Kari Smith, *Exec Dir*
Rebecca Mejia, *Admin Asst*
EMP: 148
SALES (est): 182MM **Privately Held**
SIC: **8699** 6552 7999 Reading rooms & other cultural organizations; subdividers & developers; tour & guide services

(P-25486)
ALL SOUTH BAY CENTRAL OFFICE
1411 Marcelina Ave, Torrance (90501-3210)
PHONE..................................310 618-1180
Liza Ferguson, *Manager*
EMP: 80
SALES: 54.2K **Privately Held**
WEB: www.southbayaa.org
SIC: **8699** Charitable organization

(P-25487)
ALLIANCE FC
Also Called: INLAND EMPIRE SURF SOCCER CLUB
3496 Little League Dr, San Bernardino (92407)
P.O. Box 90211 (92427-1211)
PHONE..................................909 784-0005
Bryan Young, *President*
Taisha Wick, *Treasurer*
John Green, *Vice Pres*
Brian Jensen, *Vice Pres*
Rodney Nelson, *Vice Pres*
EMP: 50
SALES: 1.2MM **Privately Held**
SIC: **8699** Personal interest organization

(P-25488)
ALLIANCE MEMBER SERVICES INC
333 Front St Ste 200, Santa Cruz (95060-4533)
P.O. Box 8507 (95061-8507)
PHONE..................................831 459-0980
Pamela Davis, *President*
Tim Demetres, *Treasurer*
EMP: 63
SQ FT: 25,000
SALES: 12.3MM **Privately Held**
SIC: **8699** Charitable organization

(P-25489)
AMERICAN AUTOMOBILE ASSCTN
1982 Pleasant Valley Ave A, Oakland (94611-4250)
P.O. Box 23392 (94623-0392)
PHONE..................................510 350-2042
Annette Kwan, *Branch Mgr*
EMP: 191

SALES (corp-wide): 1.1B **Privately Held**
SIC: **8699** 6331 6311 Automobile owners' association; automobile insurance; life insurance carriers
PA: American Automobile Association Of Northern California, Nevada & Utah
1900 Powell St Ste 1200
Emeryville CA 94608
800 922-8228

(P-25490)
AMERICAN AUTOMOBILE ASSCTN
Also Called: Csaa Travel Agency
3116 W March Ln Ste 100, Stockton (95219-2374)
PHONE..................................209 952-4100
Fax: 209 473-1018
Jim Owens, *Manager*
EMP: 50
SALES (corp-wide): 1.1B **Privately Held**
WEB: www.californiastateautomobileassociation.c
SIC: **8699** Automobile owners' association
PA: American Automobile Association Of Northern California, Nevada & Utah
1900 Powell St Ste 1200
Emeryville CA 94608
800 922-8228

(P-25491)
AMERICAN NATIONAL RED CROSS
601 N Golden Circle Dr, Santa Ana (92705-3902)
P.O. Box 11364 (92711-1364)
PHONE..................................714 481-5300
Fax: 714 547-7903
Stanley Perdue, *Branch Mgr*
William Fredericks, *Info Systems*
George Chitty, *Director*
EMP: 50
SQ FT: 30,092
SALES (corp-wide): 2.6B **Privately Held**
WEB: www.redcross.org
SIC: **8699** Charitable organization
PA: American Red Cross
431 18th St Nw
Washington DC 20006
202 737-8300

(P-25492)
ASSOCIATED STUDENTS SAN DIEGO (PA)
Also Called: Mission Bay Aquatic Center
5500 Campanile Dr, San Diego (92182-0001)
PHONE..................................619 594-0234
Fax: 619 594-6423
Christina Brown, *Exec Dir*
Cameron Salce, *Production*
Anne Bialowas, *Teacher*
Kevin Waldick, *Asst Director*
Radbeh Ravaz, *Accounts Exec*
EMP: 900
SALES: 22.8MM **Privately Held**
SIC: **8699** Automobile owners' association

(P-25493)
AUTO KNIGHT MOTOR CLUB INC
1009 N Palm Canyon Dr, Palm Springs (92262-4419)
PHONE..................................760 969-4300
Jeffery Rizzo, *President*
EMP: 85
SQ FT: 3,500
SALES (est): 1.5MM
SALES (corp-wide): 440.1MM **Publicly Held**
SIC: **8699** Automobile owners' association
HQ: Fortegra Financial Corporation
10151 Deerwood Park Blvd # 330
Jacksonville FL 32256
866 961-9529

(P-25494)
AUTOMOBILE CLUB SOUTHERN CAL
Also Called: AAA
15503 Ventura Blvd # 150, Encino (91436-3115)
PHONE..................................818 997-6230
Jim Okun, *Branch Mgr*
EMP: 50

SALES (corp-wide): 4.8B **Privately Held**
SIC: **8699** 4724 6331 Automobile owners' association; travel agencies; fire, marine & casualty insurance
PA: Automobile Club Of Southern California
2601 S Figueroa St
Los Angeles CA 90007
213 741-3686

(P-25495)
AUTOMOBILE CLUB SOUTHERN CAL
Also Called: AAA
23001 Hawthorne Blvd, Torrance (90505-3702)
P.O. Box 4298 (90510-4298)
PHONE..................................310 325-3111
Bud Hudson, *Branch Mgr*
EMP: 60
SQ FT: 34,720
SALES (corp-wide): 4.8B **Privately Held**
SIC: **8699** Automobile owners' association
PA: Automobile Club Of Southern California
2601 S Figueroa St
Los Angeles CA 90007
213 741-3686

(P-25496)
AUTOMOBILE CLUB SOUTHERN CAL
Also Called: AAA
1501 S Victoria Ave, Ventura (93003-6539)
P.O. Box 3618 (93006-3618)
PHONE..................................805 644-7171
Fax: 805 658-0470
Sigmund Grant, *Manager*
Leticia Garcia, *Agent*
EMP: 70
SALES (corp-wide): 4.8B **Privately Held**
SIC: **8699** 4724 6331 Automobile owners' association; travel agencies; fire, marine & casualty insurance
PA: Automobile Club Of Southern California
2601 S Figueroa St
Los Angeles CA 90007
213 741-3686

(P-25497)
AUTOMOBILE CLUB SOUTHERN CAL
Also Called: AAA
1301s S Grand Ave, Glendora (91740-5040)
PHONE..................................626 963-8531
Fax: 626 963-8590
Connie Stelzer, *Manager*
EMP: 50
SQ FT: 8,261
SALES (corp-wide): 4.8B **Privately Held**
SIC: **8699** Automobile owners' association
PA: Automobile Club Of Southern California
2601 S Figueroa St
Los Angeles CA 90007
213 741-3686

(P-25498)
AUTOMOBILE CLUB SOUTHERN CAL
Also Called: AAA
1500 Commercial Way, Bakersfield (93309-0625)
PHONE..................................661 327-4661
Fax: 661 325-3276
Jeff Goldsmith, *Branch Mgr*
Cheryl Watkins, *Office Mgr*
EMP: 50
SALES (corp-wide): 4.8B **Privately Held**
SIC: **8699** Automobile owners' association
PA: Automobile Club Of Southern California
2601 S Figueroa St
Los Angeles CA 90007
213 741-3686

(P-25499)
AUTOMOBILE CLUB SOUTHERN CAL
Also Called: AAA
9440 Reseda Blvd, Northridge (91324-6014)
PHONE..................................818 993-1616
Fax: 818 727-0730
Freedom Homes, *Branch Mgr*
Richard Greene, *Manager*
EMP: 54
SQ FT: 15,624

PRODUCTS & SERVICES SECTION
8699 - Membership Organizations, NEC County (P-25522)

SALES (corp-wide): 4.8B **Privately Held**
SIC: **8699** Automobile owners' association
PA: Automobile Club Of Southern California
2601 S Figueroa St
Los Angeles CA 90007
213 741-3686

(P-25500)
AUTOMOBILE CLUB SOUTHERN CAL
Also Called: AAA
22708 Victory Blvd, Woodland Hills (91367-1697)
PHONE.....................................818 883-2660
Fax: 818 340-2457
Glenn Lumley, *Branch Mgr*
EMP: 50
SQ FT: 15,624
SALES (corp-wide): 4.8B **Privately Held**
SIC: **8699** 4724 6331 Automobile owners' association; travel agencies; fire, marine & casualty insurance
PA: Automobile Club Of Southern California
2601 S Figueroa St
Los Angeles CA 90007
213 741-3686

(P-25501)
AUTOMOBILE CLUB SOUTHERN CAL
3700 Central Ave, Riverside (92506-2421)
P.O. Box 2217 (92516-2217)
PHONE.....................................951 684-4250
Fax: 951 788-4932
Richard Meyer, *Branch Mgr*
Anwar Othman, *Sr Corp Ofcr*
EMP: 80
SALES (corp-wide): 4.8B **Privately Held**
SIC: **8699** Automobile owners' association
PA: Automobile Club Of Southern California
2601 S Figueroa St
Los Angeles CA 90007
213 741-3686

(P-25502)
AUTOMOBILE CLUB SOUTHERN CAL
Also Called: A A A Automobile Club So Cal
25181 Paseo De Alicia, Laguna Hills (92653-4614)
PHONE.....................................949 951-1400
Fax: 949 598-3447
Cindy Raymond, *Manager*
Miriam Moritz, *Prdtn Mgr*
Cindy Coultier, *Manager*
Stacey Fetch, *Manager*
EMP: 50
SQ FT: 13,948
SALES (corp-wide): 4.8B **Privately Held**
SIC: **8699** Automobile owners' association
PA: Automobile Club Of Southern California
2601 S Figueroa St
Los Angeles CA 90007
213 741-3686

(P-25503)
AUTOMOBILE CLUB SOUTHERN CAL
Also Called: AAA
8765 Fletcher Pkwy, La Mesa (91942-3200)
PHONE.....................................619 464-7001
Marria Porter, *Manager*
Ruth Myers, *Human Resources*
Luis Alarcon, *Manager*
EMP: 75
SQ FT: 42,441
SALES (corp-wide): 4.8B **Privately Held**
SIC: **8699** Automobile owners' association
PA: Automobile Club Of Southern California
2601 S Figueroa St
Los Angeles CA 90007
213 741-3686

(P-25504)
AUTOMOTIVE SERVICE COUNCIL
10813 Airport Dr, El Cajon (92020-1202)
PHONE.....................................800 810-4272
Steve Vanlandingham, *President*
EMP: 90
SALES: 42.4K **Privately Held**
SIC: **8699** Automobile owners' association

(P-25505)
BEAD SOCIETY
Also Called: Bead Society , The
1454 Valley High Ave, Thousand Oaks (91362-1906)
P.O. Box 1456, Culver City (90232-1456)
PHONE.....................................805 495-2550
Adel Boehm-Mabe, *President*
Adel B Mabe, *President*
Joan Eppen, *CFO*
EMP: 250
SALES: 36.9K **Privately Held**
SIC: **8699** Personal interest organization

(P-25506)
BERKELEY CLINIC AUXUILLARY
Also Called: TURNABOUT SHOP
10052 San Pablo Ave, El Cerrito (94530-3927)
PHONE.....................................510 525-7844
Barbara Coleman, *President*
VI Galardo, *President*
Peggy Eanaman, *Chairman*
Kay Jevons, *Chairman*
Dorothy Zwoyer, *Treasurer*
EMP: 60
SQ FT: 1,800
SALES: 85.7K **Privately Held**
SIC: **8699** 5932 Charitable organization; used merchandise stores

(P-25507)
BEST FRIENDS ANIMAL SOCIETY
15321 Brand Blvd, Mission Hills (91345-1438)
PHONE.....................................818 643-3989
Marc Peralta, *Manager*
EMP: 362
SALES (corp-wide): 65.5MM **Privately Held**
SIC: **8699** Animal humane society
PA: Best Friends Animal Society
5001 Angel Canyon Rd
Kanab UT 84741
435 644-2001

(P-25508)
BRIARPATCH COOP NEV CNTY INC
Also Called: Briarpatch Coop-Community Mkt
290 Sierra College Dr A, Grass Valley (95945-5762)
PHONE.....................................530 272-5333
Christopher Maher, *CEO*
EMP: 180 **EST**: 1976
SALES (est): 16.2MM **Privately Held**
WEB: www.briarpatchcoop.com
SIC: **8699** Food co-operative

(P-25509)
BUTTE COUNTY OFFICE EDUCATION
1859 Bird St, Oroville (95965-4854)
PHONE.....................................530 532-5786
Don McNelis, *Superintendent*
Hector Gonzalez, *Associate Dir*
Bruce Baldwin, *Exec Dir*
Becca Cerveri, *Admin Sec*
Anne Lake, *Software Dev*
EMP: 400
SALES (corp-wide): 23.4MM **Privately Held**
SIC: **8699** Charitable organization
PA: Butte County Office Of Education
1859 Bird St
Oroville CA 95965
530 532-5650

(P-25510)
CALIF STAT UNIV FRES FOUN (PA)
Also Called: Z The Fresno State Foundation
4910 N Chestnut Ave, Fresno (93726-1852)
PHONE.....................................559 278-0850
Debbie Astome, *Exec Dir*
Chris Morgan, *Technical Staff*
Rachel Viramontes, *Human Res Mgr*
Jesse Arreguin, *Director*
Keith Kompsi, *Director*
EMP: 121
SQ FT: 8,800

SALES: 75.7MM **Privately Held**
WEB: www.auxiliary.com
SIC: **8699** Charitable organization

(P-25511)
CALIF STAT UNIV FRES FOUN
5370 N Chestnut Ave, Fresno (93725)
PHONE.....................................559 278-0850
Linda Alatorre, *Branch Mgr*
Lynn Hemink, *Finance*
David Doleoske, *Director*
EMP: 140
SALES (corp-wide): 75.7MM **Privately Held**
WEB: www.auxiliary.com
SIC: **8699** Amateur sports promotion
PA: California State University, Fresno Foundation
4910 N Chestnut Ave
Fresno CA 93726
559 278-0850

(P-25512)
CALIFRNIA YOUTH SOCCER ASSN INC
1040 Serpentine Ln # 206, Pleasanton (94566-4754)
PHONE.....................................925 426-5437
Fax: 925 426-9473
John Murphy, *Chairman*
Ilona Montoya, *CFO*
Gurdev Mann, *General Mgr*
Debbie Alvarez, *Executive Asst*
Margaret Gordon, *Accounting Mgr*
EMP: 87
SALES (est): 4.8MM **Privately Held**
WEB: www.cysanorth.com
SIC: **8699** Personal interest organization

(P-25513)
CASAS - COMPREHENSIVE
5151 Murphy Canyon Rd # 220, San Diego (92123-4440)
PHONE.....................................858 292-2900
Robert S Muir, *Director*
Anthony Castle, *Software Dev*
Stacey Downey, *Director*
Jim Harrison, *Director*
EMP: 55
SALES: 6.1MM **Privately Held**
SIC: **8699** Charitable organization

(P-25514)
CATHEDRAL CENTER OF ST PAUL
Also Called: Cathedral Bookstore
840 Echo Park Ave, Los Angeles (90026-4209)
P.O. Box 512164 (90051-0164)
PHONE.....................................213 482-2040
Fax: 213 482-5304
Bishop Jon Bruno,
Peter Mann, *Treasurer*
Janet Wild, *Admin Sec*
EMP: 75 **EST**: 1898
SALES: 3.5MM **Privately Held**
WEB: www.cathedralbookstore.com
SIC: **8699** 5942 Charitable organization; books, religious

(P-25515)
CCNA VONS ATHLETES FOR LIFE
Also Called: AFL
10670 6th St Ste 113, Rancho Cucamonga (91730-5912)
PHONE.....................................805 453-2499
Greg Bell, *President*
EMP: 60
SALES (est): 203.3K **Privately Held**
SIC: **8699** 7389 Athletic organizations; fund raising organizations

(P-25516)
CHINESE YOUTH ARTS
3592 Rsemead Blud Ste 220, Rosemead (91770)
PHONE.....................................323 985-4699
Xin Tan, *President*
EMP: 60 **EST**: 2013
SALES: 1MM **Privately Held**
SIC: **8699** Charitable organization

(P-25517)
CITY IMPACT
230 Jones St Fl 1, San Francisco (94102-2619)
PHONE.....................................415 292-1770
Christian Huang, *Exec Dir*
EMP: 50
SALES (est): 203.6K **Privately Held**
SIC: **8699** Charitable organization

(P-25518)
CITY OF LOS ANGELES
Also Called: Department of Cultural Affairs
201 N Figueroa St # 1400, Los Angeles (90012-2623)
PHONE.....................................213 202-5500
Karen Constine, *General Mgr*
Helen Santella, *Controller*
Teresa Abraham, *Manager*
EMP: 64 **Privately Held**
WEB: www.lacity.org
SIC: **8699** 9512 Literary, film or cultural club; recreational program administration, government
PA: City Of Los Angeles
200 N Spring St Ste 303
Los Angeles CA 90012
213 978-0600

(P-25519)
COUNTY OF FRESNO
Also Called: Sheriffs Fndtion For Pub Sfety
2221 Kern St, Fresno (93721-2613)
P.O. Box 1512 (93716-1512)
PHONE.....................................559 600-8135
Harry Gill, *President*
EMP: 137 **Privately Held**
SIC: **8699** Charitable organization
PA: County Of Fresno
2420 Mariposa St
Fresno CA 93721
559 600-1710

(P-25520)
COUNTY OF MONTEREY
Also Called: Monterey County Sheriffs Dept
1414 Natividad Rd, Salinas (93906-3102)
PHONE.....................................831 755-3700
Fax: 831 755-3810
Mike Kanalakis, *Sheriff*
Hye-Weon Kim, *Manager*
EMP: 474 **Privately Held**
WEB: www.montereycountyfarmbureau.org
SIC: **8699** Personal interest organization
PA: County Of Monterey
168 W Alisal St Fl 3
Salinas CA 93901
831 755-5040

(P-25521)
CROCKER ART MUSEUM ASSOCIATION
Also Called: Crocker Art Museum
216 O St, Sacramento (95814-5324)
PHONE.....................................916 808-7000
Fax: 916 264-7372
Lial Jones, *CEO*
Jay Drury, *Admin Dir*
Cheri Johnson, *Administration*
Cindy Gudeman, *Finance*
Donna M Natsoulas, *Buyer*
EMP: 66 **EST**: 1875
SQ FT: 150,000
SALES: 7MM **Privately Held**
WEB: www.crockerartmuseum.org
SIC: **8699** 5942 8412 Art council; book stores; museum

(P-25522)
CSULB 49ER FOUNDATION
6300 E State Univ Dr Ste, Long Beach (90815-4669)
PHONE.....................................562 985-5778
Michael Thomas Losquadro, *Administration*
EMP: 934
SALES: 16.9MM **Privately Held**
SIC: **8699** Charitable organization
HQ: California State University, Long Beach
1250 N Bellflower Blvd
Long Beach CA 90840
562 985-4111

8699 - Membership Organizations, NEC County (P-25523)

(P-25523)
DEATH VALLEY 49ERS INC
1442 Carson Ave, Clovis (93611-6906)
P.O. Box 997, Kernville (93238-0997)
PHONE...............................559 297-5691
Bill Pool, *President*
Edtytat Pool, *Treasurer*
Richard Gering, *Vice Pres*
Marv Jensen, *Vice Pres*
EMP: 80 **EST:** 1949
SALES: 78.9K **Privately Held**
WEB: www.deathvalley49ers.org
SIC: 8699 Charitable organization

(P-25524)
DELTA RESCUE INC
P.O. Box 9, Glendale (91209-0009)
PHONE...............................661 269-4010
Leo Grillo, *President*
EMP: 60
SALES (est): 1MM **Privately Held**
SIC: 8699 Animal humane society

(P-25525)
DFA OF CALIFORNIA
6100 Wilson Landing Rd, Chico (95973-8902)
PHONE...............................530 345-5077
Fax: 530 345-5077
Marie Cowan, *Branch Mgr*
EMP: 166
SALES (corp-wide): 9.5MM **Privately Held**
SIC: 8699 Athletic organizations
PA: Dfa Of California
  710 Striker Ave
  Sacramento CA 95834
  916 561-5900

(P-25526)
EARLY LEARNING ART-TECH GROUP
1697 N Sierra Way, San Bernardino (92405-4628)
PHONE...............................866 491-2432
David Morrow, *CEO*
EMP: 50
SALES: 158.6K **Privately Held**
SIC: 8699 Charitable organization

(P-25527)
EARTH ISLAND INSTITUTE INC
2150 Allston Way Ste 460, Berkeley (94704-1375)
PHONE...............................510 859-9100
Michael Mitrani, *CEO*
John A Knox, *Principal*
David Phillips, *Exec Dir*
Susan Kamprath, *Sls & Mktg Exec*
Trixie Concepcion, *Director*
EMP: 76
SQ FT: 4,400
SALES: 11.1MM **Privately Held**
WEB: www.earthisland.org
SIC: 8699 8748 8641 Charitable organization; business consulting; environmental protection organization

(P-25528)
EMPLOYMENT TRAINING ACADEMY
4045 Coronado Ave, Stockton (95204-2311)
PHONE...............................209 475-1529
EMP: 50
SALES (est): 144.2K **Privately Held**
SIC: 8699 Charitable organization

(P-25529)
FAMILY SERVICES
807 W Oak Ave, Visalia (93291-6033)
PHONE...............................559 741-7310
Kaitey Meader, *Director*
Susan Munten, *Deputy Dir*
EMP: 50
SALES (est): 1.9MM **Privately Held**
SIC: 8699 Charitable organization

(P-25530)
FARMS OF AMADOR
12200b Airport Rd, Jackson (95642-9527)
PHONE...............................209 257-0112
Sean Kriletich, *Principal*
EMP: 99
SALES (est): 2.6MM **Privately Held**
SIC: 8699 Membership organizations

(P-25531)
FREMONT CANDLE LIGHTERS
Also Called: CANDLE LIGHTERS THE
39261 Fremont Hub, Fremont (94538-1329)
P.O. Box 174 (94537-0174)
PHONE...............................510 796-0595
Claire Douglas, *President*
Linda Genter, *Ch of Bd*
EMP: 110
SALES: 58K **Privately Held**
SIC: 8699 Charitable organization

(P-25532)
FRIENDS FOR LIFE
12282 Brewster Dr, Moreno Valley (92555-1818)
PHONE...............................951 601-6722
Rena Fisher, *CEO*
EMP: 80
SALES (est): 2.7MM **Privately Held**
SIC: 8699 Charitable organization

(P-25533)
FRIENDS OF ANGELES CHAPTER
Also Called: Sierra Club Angeles Chapter
3435 Wilshire Blvd # 660, Los Angeles (90010-1907)
PHONE...............................213 387-4287
Linda Hoyer, *Manager*
Jack Bochlka, *Director*
EMP: 50
SALES (est): 1.3MM **Privately Held**
SIC: 8699 Charitable organization

(P-25534)
FRIENDS OF BEAR GULCH
8355 Bear Gulch Pl, Rancho Cucamonga (91730-3469)
PHONE...............................909 989-9396
Susan Kohn, *Principal*
EMP: 50
SALES (est): 1.7MM **Privately Held**
SIC: 8699 Membership organizations

(P-25535)
GLOBAL HEALTH FELLOWS PROGRAM
555 12th St Ste 1050, Oakland (94607-3630)
PHONE...............................510 285-5660
Sharon Rudy, *Director*
EMP: 50
SALES (est): 647.2K **Privately Held**
WEB: www.cfhl.org
SIC: 8699 Charitable organization

(P-25536)
GOODWILL INDS ORANGE CNTY CAL
2910 W Garry Ave, Santa Ana (92704-6510)
PHONE...............................714 754-7808
EMP: 135
SALES (corp-wide): 69.6MM **Privately Held**
SIC: 8699 Charitable organization
PA: Goodwill Industries Of Orange County, California
  410 N Fairview St
  Santa Ana CA 92703
  714 547-6308

(P-25537)
GOODWILL INDS SAN DIEGO CNTY
3841 Plaza Dr Ste 902, Oceanside (92056-4649)
PHONE...............................760 806-7670
Tim Hurley, *Manager*
EMP: 574
SALES (corp-wide): 75.9MM **Privately Held**
SIC: 8699 8331 5932 Charitable organization; vocational rehabilitation agency; used merchandise stores
PA: Goodwill Industries Of San Diego County
  3663 Rosecrans St
  San Diego CA 92110
  619 225-2200

(P-25538)
GOODWILL INDUSTRIES OF SACRAME
8031 Watt Ave, Sacramento (95843-9793)
PHONE...............................916 331-0237
EMP: 50
SALES (corp-wide): 64.8MM **Privately Held**
SIC: 8699 8331 5932 Charitable organization; vocational rehabilitation agency; used merchandise stores
PA: Goodwill Industries Of Sacramento Valley & Northern Nevada, Inc.
  8001 Folsom Blvd
  Sacramento CA 95826
  916 395-9000

(P-25539)
HALO
4916 Chism Way, Antioch (94531-8148)
P.O. Box 2011 (94531-2011)
PHONE...............................925 473-4642
Karen Kops, *President*
Linda Mills, *Admin Sec*
EMP: 50
SALES (est): 624.8K **Privately Held**
SIC: 8699 Animal humane society

(P-25540)
HELEN WOODWARD ANIMAL CENTER (PA)
6461 El Apajo, Rancho Santa Fe (92067)
P.O. Box 64 (92067-0064)
PHONE...............................858 756-4117
Fax: 858 756-0613
Michael A Arms, *President*
Bryce Rhoades, *Ch of Bd*
Marcie Grube, *Admin Asst*
Renee Simmons, *Finance Mgr*
Renee Simons, *Controller*
EMP: 84
SQ FT: 45,000
SALES: 12.2MM **Privately Held**
WEB: www.sddac.com
SIC: 8699 Animal humane society

(P-25541)
HEWLETT WLLIAM FLORA FNDATION
Also Called: HEWLETT FOUNDATION
2121 Sand Hill Rd, Menlo Park (94025-6909)
PHONE...............................650 234-4500
Fax: 650 234-4501
Paul Brest, *President*
Charlene Cooper, *CFO*
William F Nichols, *Treasurer*
Luisa Smith, *Treasurer*
Jean Bordewich, *Officer*
EMP: 60
SALES (est): 624.6MM **Privately Held**
SIC: 8699 Charitable organization

(P-25542)
HOPLAND BAND POMO INDIANS INC (PA)
3000 Shanel Rd, Hopland (95449-9809)
PHONE...............................707 472-2100
Fax: 707 744-1506
Romen Carrillo, *President*
Rachel Whetstone, *CFO*
Rod Clarke, *Administration*
EMP: 90
SQ FT: 3,800
SALES (est): 19.8MM **Privately Held**
WEB: www.hoplandtribe.com
SIC: 8699 Personal interest organization

(P-25543)
HUBBARD DIANETICS FOUNDATION
4833 Fountain Ave, Los Angeles (90029-1600)
PHONE...............................323 953-3206
Fax: 323 953-3206
Jenie Ivert, *President*
EMP: 95
SALES (est): 816.7K **Privately Held**
SIC: 8699 Charitable organization

(P-25544)
INLAND EMPIRE CHAPTER-ASSN OF
4200 Concours Ste 360, Ontario (91764-4982)
PHONE...............................512 478-9000
Todd Christopher Landry Cfe, *CPA*
EMP: 82
SALES: 5.4K **Privately Held**
SIC: 8699 Membership organizations

(P-25545)
INLAND VALLEY BUSINESS AND COM
Also Called: IVBCF
40335 Winchester Rd, Temecula (92591-5500)
PHONE...............................951 378-5316
Steve Matley, *President*
Steve Matly, *President*
Dena Lansford, *Treasurer*
Wendy Johnson, *Bd of Directors*
Hans R Monod De Froideville, *Vice Pres*
EMP: 80
SALES: 17.4K **Privately Held**
SIC: 8699 Charitable organization

(P-25546)
IRVINE COMPANY LLC
Also Called: Oak Creek Golf Club
1 Golf Club Dr, Irvine (92618-5210)
PHONE...............................949 653-5300
Fax: 949 653-5305
John McCook, *Manager*
Janet Muller, *Senior Mgr*
David Jacobo, *Director*
John Mc Cook, *Director*
Michael Tripp, *Manager*
EMP: 70
SALES (corp-wide): 2B **Privately Held**
WEB: www.irvineco.com
SIC: 8699 Professional golf association
PA: The Irvine Company Llc
  550 Newport Center Dr # 160
  Newport Beach CA 92660
  949 720-2000

(P-25547)
KNIGHTS OF COLUMBUS
871 Founders Ln, Milpitas (95035-3345)
PHONE...............................408 262-6609
EMP: 80
SALES (est): 2.6MM **Privately Held**
SIC: 8699 Charitable organization

(P-25548)
LAVA BEDS NATIONAL MONUMENTS
Also Called: U S GOVERNMENT
1 Indian Wells Hqtrs, Tulelake (96134-8216)
P.O. Box 1240 (96134-1240)
PHONE...............................530 667-2282
Fax: 530 667-3299
EMP: 50 **EST:** 1963
SALES: 55.2K **Publicly Held**
SIC: 8699 8412
PA: Government Of The United States
  1600 Pennsylvania Ave Nw
  Washington DC 20500
  202 456-1414

(P-25549)
LEWIS FAMILY PLAYHOUSE
Also Called: City of Rancho Cucamonga, The
12505 Cultural Center Dr, Rancho Cucamonga (91739-8546)
PHONE...............................909 477-2775
Nettie Nielsen, *Superintendent*
Kevin Macardo, *Director*
Susan Sluka, *Supervisor*
EMP: 70
SALES (est): 2.1MM **Privately Held**
SIC: 8699 Literary, film or cultural club

(P-25550)
LINCOLN CHILD CENTER
1266 14th St, Oakland (94607-2205)
PHONE...............................510 531-3111
C Stoner-Mertz, *President*
Christine Stoner-Mertz, *President*
EMP: 200
SQ FT: 300
SALES (est): 11.6MM **Privately Held**
SIC: 8699 Charitable organization

PRODUCTS & SERVICES SECTION
8699 - Membership Organizations, NEC County (P-25578)

(P-25551)
LIVE LOVE LAUGH GLOBAL
8306 Wilshire Blvd # 350, Beverly Hills (90211-2304)
PHONE.................310 362-1783
Maksim Zaslavskiy, *President*
EMP: 55
SQ FT: 500
SALES: 3MM **Privately Held**
SIC: 8699 Charitable organization

(P-25552)
LOS ANGELES 2024
10960 Wilshire Blvd Fl 16, Los Angeles (90024-3802)
PHONE.................310 407-0204
Casey Wasserman, *Chairman*
EMP: 50
SALES (est): 144.2K **Privately Held**
SIC: 8699 Charitable organization

(P-25553)
LOS ANGELES POLICE COMMAND
100 W 1st St, Los Angeles (90012-4112)
P.O. Box 53188 (90053-0188)
PHONE.................877 275-5273
Deborah A Gonzales, *Principal*
EMP: 405
SALES: 258K **Privately Held**
SIC: 8699 Membership organizations

(P-25554)
MARIN HUMANE SOCIETY
171 Bel Marin Keys Blvd, Novato (94949-6183)
PHONE.................415 883-4621
Fax: 415 382-1349
Suzanne Golt, *Exec Dir*
John Reese, *COO*
Marilyn Castellblanch, *CFO*
Lisa Nausin, *Officer*
Dave Stapp, *Officer*
EMP: 91
SQ FT: 42,500
SALES: 10.1MM **Privately Held**
WEB: www.marinhumanesociety.com
SIC: 8699 Animal humane society

(P-25555)
MARTINEZ CERT
129 Midhill Rd, Martinez (94553-4201)
PHONE.................925 228-0911
Gilford Patton, *Chairman*
EMP: 99
SALES (est): 889.3K **Privately Held**
SIC: 8699 Membership organizations

(P-25556)
N F L ALUMNI
1311 Madison Ave, Redwood City (94061-1547)
PHONE.................650 366-3659
Jerry Murkins, *President*
EMP: 200
SALES (est): 2.5MM **Privately Held**
SIC: 8699 Charitable organization

(P-25557)
NATIONAL ASSN LTR CARRIERS
Also Called: National Assn Ltr Crrers BR 52
4251 S Higuera St, San Luis Obispo (93401-7700)
PHONE.................805 543-7329
Edward L Somogyi, *Branch Mgr*
EMP: 300
SALES (corp-wide): 1.4B **Privately Held**
SIC: 8699 Athletic organizations
PA: National Association Of Letter Carriers
100 Indana Ave Nw Ste 709
Washington DC 20001
202 393-4695

(P-25558)
NATIONAL ASSN LTR CARRIERS
2310 Mason St Fl 4, San Francisco (94133-1800)
PHONE.................415 362-0214
John Beaumont, *Manager*
Sheila Gardner, *Trustee*
Karen Eshabarr, *Exec VP*
EMP: 300
SALES (corp-wide): 1.4B **Privately Held**
WEB: www.nalc.org
SIC: 8699 Charitable organization
PA: National Association Of Letter Carriers
100 Indana Ave Nw Ste 709
Washington DC 20001
202 393-4695

(P-25559)
NATIONAL COUNCIL NEGRO WOMEN
Also Called: Golden Gate Section
784 Cole St, San Francisco (94117-3912)
PHONE.................415 564-4153
Catherine J Bradford, *President*
EMP: 99
SALES: 25K **Privately Held**
WEB: www.co.rappahannock.comm-rev.state.va.us
SIC: 8699 Membership organizations

(P-25560)
NATUREBRIDGE
1033 Fort Cronkhite, Sausalito (94965-2609)
PHONE.................415 332-5771
Amanda Zvirblis, *Comms Mgr*
EMP: 54 **Privately Held**
SIC: 8699 Charitable organization
PA: Naturebridge
28 Geary St Ste 650
San Francisco CA 94108

(P-25561)
NORTH ISLAND HISPANIC ASSN
1878 Port Albans, Chula Vista (91913-1225)
PHONE.................619 545-6156
Joseph Garcia, *Principal*
EMP: 99
SALES (est): 589.8K **Privately Held**
SIC: 8699 Membership organizations

(P-25562)
ORANGEWOOD CHLD FOUNDATION
1575 E 17th St, Santa Ana (92705-8506)
PHONE.................714 480-2300
Fax: 714 619-0251
William Lyon Homes, *CEO*
Eugene Howard, *President*
C Chris, *CFO*
Michael Yusko, *CFO*
Gaddi Vasquez, *Vice Pres*
EMP: 85
SQ FT: 22,340
SALES: 12.8MM **Privately Held**
WEB: www.orangewoodfoundation.org
SIC: 8699 Charitable organization

(P-25563)
ORGANZTION AMRCN KDALY EDCTORS
10801 National Blvd # 590, Los Angeles (90064-4139)
PHONE.................310 441-3555
Roger D Chittum Esq, *Principal*
Beth Pontiff, *Editor*
EMP: 50
SALES: 592.7K **Privately Held**
SIC: 8699 Charitable organization

(P-25564)
PASADENA HUMANE SOCIETY
361 S Raymond Ave, Pasadena (91105-2687)
PHONE.................626 792-7151
Steven R Mc Nall, *President*
Ryne Meadors, *Officer*
Elizabeth Baronowski, *Vice Pres*
Elizabeth Campo, *Vice Pres*
Kymberly Pietsch, *Vice Pres*
EMP: 70
SQ FT: 26,000
SALES: 8.3MM **Privately Held**
WEB: www.phsspca.org
SIC: 8699 0752 Animal humane society; animal specialty services

(P-25565)
PENINSULA HUMANE SOC & SPCA
1450 Rollins Rd, Burlingame (94010-2307)
PHONE.................650 340-7022
Katie Dinneen, *Vice Pres*
Linda Janowitz, *Persnl Dir*
Katy Schwarz, *Education*
EMP: 74
SALES (corp-wide): 13.8MM **Privately Held**
SIC: 8699 Animal humane society
PA: Peninsula Humane Society And Spca
12 Airport Blvd
San Mateo CA 94401
650 340-7022

(P-25566)
PETS UNLIMITED
2343 Fillmore St, San Francisco (94115-1812)
PHONE.................415 563-6700
Fax: 415 775-2573
Suzanne Troxel, *President*
Pat Boyd, *Volunteer Dir*
Brandyn Denico, *COO*
Theresa L Smith, *CFO*
Sally Wortman, *Vice Pres*
EMP: 110
SALES (est): 8.6MM **Privately Held**
WEB: www.petsunlimited.org
SIC: 8699 Animal humane society

(P-25567)
POINT REYES BIRD OBSERVATOR
Also Called: Point Blue Cnservation Science
3820 Cypress Dr Ste 11, Petaluma (94954-6964)
P.O. Box 69, Bolinas (94924-0069)
PHONE.................415 868-0371
Allie Cohen, *CEO*
Padmini Srinivasan, *CFO*
Ellie Cohen, *Exec Dir*
EMP: 86 **EST:** 2011
SQ FT: 20,000
SALES (est): 3.4MM **Privately Held**
SIC: 8699 Charitable organization

(P-25568)
RACELEGAL COM
Also Called: Center For Injury Prevention
315 4th Ave, Chula Vista (91910-3801)
P.O. Box 600943, San Diego (92160-0943)
PHONE.................619 265-8159
Fax: 619 265-8117
Charles Chris, *Chairman*
EMP: 50
SALES: 239K **Privately Held**
WEB: www.racelegal.com
SIC: 8699 Charitable organization

(P-25569)
READING PARTNERS (PA)
180 Grand Ave Ste 800, Oakland (94612-3748)
PHONE.................510 444-9800
Michael Lombardo, *CEO*
Matt Aguiar, *COO*
Mike Barr, *CFO*
David Kuizenga, *CFO*
Hagar Berlin, *Vice Pres*
EMP: 68
SALES: 23.5MM **Privately Held**
SIC: 8699 Charitable organization

(P-25570)
RESCUE MISSION ALLIANCE (PA)
Also Called: Mission Bargain Center
315 N A St, Oxnard (93030-4901)
P.O. Box 5545 (93031-5545)
PHONE.................805 487-1234
Fax: 805 385-3139
Gary Gray, *President*
David Chittenden, *CFO*
Jim Ownes, *Chairman*
Andy Stay, *Treasurer*
Larry Cooney, *Director*
EMP: 77
SQ FT: 30,000
SALES: 24.8MM **Privately Held**
WEB: www.erescuemission.com
SIC: 8699 Charitable organization

(P-25571)
SAN DIEGO FAMILY HOUSING LLC
3360 Murray Ridge Rd, San Diego (92123-2264)
PHONE.................858 874-8100
Carol Klepper, *Managing Prtnr*
Drew Schunk, *Vice Pres*
Bonnie New, *Administration*
Tom Vogt, *Mng Member*
EMP: 350
SALES (est): 19.1MM **Privately Held**
SIC: 8699 Charitable organization

(P-25572)
SAN FRANCISCO BAY AR TRAN ASSN
915 San Antonio Ave, Alameda (94501-3959)
PHONE.................510 501-5318
Jahan Byrne, *President*
Monte Boscovich, *Treasurer*
EMP: 150
SALES: 89.7K **Privately Held**
SIC: 8699 7389 Athletic organizations; fund raising organizations

(P-25573)
SAN JOAQUIN VALLEY INTERGRP
Also Called: Sjvi
6048 E Cimarron Ave, Fresno (93727-6810)
P.O. Box 8302 (93747-8302)
PHONE.................559 856-0559
Marjorie J Donovan, *Ch of Bd*
EMP: 50
SALES (est): 248.9K **Privately Held**
SIC: 8699 Charitable organization

(P-25574)
SANKARA EYE FOUNDATION USA
1900 Mccarthy Blvd # 302, Milpitas (95035-7440)
PHONE.................408 456-0555
Krishan Murlidharan, *Chairman*
EMP: 50 **EST:** 1998
SALES: 10.1MM **Privately Held**
WEB: www.giftofvision.org
SIC: 8699 7929 Personal interest organization; entertainers & entertainment groups

(P-25575)
SANTA MONICA BAY WOMENS CLUB
1210 4th St, Santa Monica (90401-1304)
PHONE.................310 395-1308
Darlene Bahr, *President*
Jessica Hankey, *Admin Sec*
EMP: 50
SQ FT: 12,226
SALES (est): 1MM **Privately Held**
SIC: 8699 6732 Charitable organization; trusts: educational, religious, etc.

(P-25576)
SJSU FOUNDATION
210 N 4th St Ste 300, San Jose (95112-5569)
PHONE.................408 924-1410
Mary Sidney, *COO*
Danny Ta, *Info Tech Mgr*
Max Talebi, *Analyst*
Sandy Xiao, *Analyst*
Steve Barranti, *Human Resources*
EMP: 750
SALES (est): 6.9MM **Privately Held**
WEB: www.foundation.sjsu.edu
SIC: 8699 Charitable organization

(P-25577)
SKIRBALL CULTURAL CENTER
2701 N Sepulveda Blvd, Los Angeles (90049-6833)
PHONE.................310 440-4500
Fax: 310 440-4545
Uri D Herscher, *President*
Baron Saldanah, *Controller*
EMP: 150
SQ FT: 65,000
SALES: 30.7MM **Privately Held**
SIC: 8699 Literary, film or cultural club

(P-25578)
SKOLL FOUNDATION
250 University Ave Lbby, Palo Alto (94301-1725)
PHONE.................650 331-1031
Jeffrey S Skoll, *Owner*
James G Demartini III, *Managing Prtnr*
Richard Fahey, *COO*

8699 - Membership Organizations, NEC County (P-25579)

Peter Hero, *Treasurer*
Sally F Kassab, *Officer*
EMP: 50
SALES (est): 43.1MM **Privately Held**
SIC: 8699 Charitable organization

(P-25579)
SOCIETY FOR INFO DISPLAY
Also Called: Bay Area Chapter of Sid
236 N Santa Cruz Ave, Los Gatos (95030-7244)
PHONE 408 399-6000
Joel Pollack, *Director*
John L Miller, *Treasurer*
EMP: 350
SALES (est): 12MM **Privately Held**
SIC: 8699 Membership organizations

(P-25580)
SOCIETY FOR SAN FRANCISCO
201 Alabama St, San Francisco (94103-4217)
PHONE 415 554-3000
Katherine Brown, *Ch of Bd*
Jane McHugh-Smith, *President*
David Tateosian, *Treasurer*
Eric Roberts, *Vice Ch Bd*
Becky Corea, *Controller*
EMP: 200
SQ FT: 57,000
SALES: 28.4MM **Privately Held**
WEB: www.sfspca.org
SIC: 8699 Animal humane society

(P-25581)
SOCIETY OF ST VINCENT (PA)
9235 San Leandro St, Oakland (94603-1237)
PHONE 510 638-7600
Blase Bova, *Exec Dir*
Ron Dean, *Principal*
Inga Lewis, *Executive Asst*
Nelijah Carminer, *Admin Asst*
Gary Flinders, *Human Res Mgr*
EMP: 80
SALES: 7.8MM **Privately Held**
SIC: 8699 Charitable organization

(P-25582)
SOCIETY OF ST VINCENT DE PAUL (PA)
Also Called: St Vincent De Paul of La
210 N Avenue 21, Los Angeles (90031-1713)
PHONE 323 224-6214
James Bibb, *CEO*
Ching Cahill, *Controller*
Justin Mammen, *Social Worker*
Jose J Rossier, *Director*
EMP: 85
SQ FT: 6,500
SALES (est): 19.1MM **Privately Held**
SIC: 8699 Charitable organization

(P-25583)
SOROPTOMIST INTL TAHOE SIERRA
3050 Lake Tahoe Blvd, South Lake Tahoe (96150-7810)
P.O. Box 18727 (96151-8727)
PHONE 530 573-1657
Lydia Rogers, *President*
EMP: 50
SALES: 55.9K **Privately Held**
SIC: 8699 Charitable organization

(P-25584)
SOUTH BAY HISTORICAL RR SOC
1005 Railroad Ave, Santa Clara (95050-4319)
PHONE 408 243-3969
Robert Dolci, *President*
EMP: 50
SALES: 61.2K **Privately Held**
WEB: www.sbhrs.org
SIC: 8699 8412 Personal interest organization; museum

(P-25585)
SOUTHERN CAL BLLDOG RESCUE INC
2219 N Spurgeon St, Santa Ana (92706-2962)
PHONE 714 547-5725

Gilbertt Van Der Marliere, *President*
EMP: 50 **EST:** 2008
SALES: 300K **Privately Held**
SIC: 8699 Animal humane society

(P-25586)
ST VINCENT DE PAUL VLG INC
Also Called: Joan Kroc Center
1501 Imperial Ave, San Diego (92101-7638)
PHONE 619 233-8500
Richard Swain, *Principal*
Ruth Bruland, *Branch Mgr*
Carol M Kleinke, *Nurse Practr*
Bill Ludwig, *Manager*
EMP: 150
SALES (corp-wide): 24MM **Privately Held**
WEB: www.neighbor.org
SIC: 8699 Charitable organization
PA: St. Vincent De Paul Village, Inc.
3350 E St
San Diego CA 92102
619 687-1000

(P-25587)
STUDENT UN SAN JOSE STATE UNIV
Also Called: Student Union Building
211 S. 9th Street, San Jose (95192-0001)
PHONE 408 924-6405
Terry Gregory, *Manager*
EMP: 60
SALES (corp-wide): 9.1MM **Privately Held**
SIC: 8699 Personal interest organization
PA: Student Union Of San Jose State University
1 Washington Sq
San Jose CA
408 924-6315

(P-25588)
THE DAVID LCILE PCKARD FNDTION
300 2nd St, Los Altos (94022-3694)
PHONE 650 917-7167
Carol S Larson, *President*
Katy Lnp, *Principal*
Julie Packard, *Exec Dir*
Gene Lewit, *Program Mgr*
Cathy Winter, *Executive Asst*
EMP: 85
SALES: 283MM **Privately Held**
SIC: 8699 Personal interest organization

(P-25589)
THE FOR SACRAMENTO SOCIETY
Also Called: SSPCA
6201 Florin Perkins Rd, Sacramento (95828-1012)
PHONE 916 383-7387
Fax: 916 383-7062
Maryann Subbotin, *Director*
Jeannie Biskup, *CFO*
Rebecca Wright, *Administration*
Candace Taylor, *Development*
Lety Sanchez,
EMP: 76
SQ FT: 40,000
SALES: 5.8MM **Privately Held**
WEB: www.sspca.org
SIC: 8699 Animal humane society

(P-25590)
TRIO CONSULTING LLC
Also Called: Trio Vntura Cnty W Vly Chapter
15763 Kenneth Pl, Santa Clarita (91387-4430)
PHONE 818 309-7919
EMP: 127 **Privately Held**
SIC: 8699 Charitable organization
PA: Trio Consulting, Llc
3244 Ridge View Ct # 104
Woodbridge VA 22192

(P-25591)
UCP WORK INC
2040 Alameda Padre Serra, Santa Barbara (93103-1760)
PHONE 805 962-6699
Jeffrey Cowen, *Branch Mgr*
EMP: 135

SALES (corp-wide): 8.5MM **Privately Held**
SIC: 8699 Charitable organization
PA: Ucp Work, Inc.
5464 Carpinteria Ave B
Carpinteria CA 93013
805 566-9000

(P-25592)
UNITED CEREBRAL PALSY ASSN SAN (PA)
8525 Gibbs Dr Ste 209, San Diego (92123-1765)
PHONE 858 495-3155
David Carrucci, *Exec Dir*
James O'Leary, *President*
Daniel Alessio, *Treasurer*
Joan Ewing, *Manager*
EMP: 50 **EST:** 1958
SALES: 4MM **Privately Held**
WEB: www.readystamps.com
SIC: 8699 Charitable organization

(P-25593)
UNITED STTES BOWL CONGRESS INC
12895 Arbor Ln, Red Bluff (96080-9387)
PHONE 530 527-9049
Fred Zastrow, *Branch Mgr*
EMP: 51
SALES (corp-wide): 37.2MM **Privately Held**
SIC: 8699 Athletic organizations
PA: United States Bowling Congress, Inc.
621 Six Flags Dr
Arlington TX 76011
817 385-8200

(P-25594)
USC SHOAH FNDN INST FOR VISUAL
650 W 35th St Ste 114, Los Angeles (90089-0033)
PHONE 213 740-6001
Linda Sturm, *Executive Asst*
Linda Sturmm, *Executive Asst*
ARI Zev, *Administration*
Satish Bon, *Project Mgr*
Anna Kanauka, *Manager*
EMP: 100
SALES (est): 2.5MM **Privately Held**
WEB: www.vhf.org
SIC: 8699 Historical club

(P-25595)
VICKIE LOBELLO
Also Called: Saint Baldricks Foundation
1333 S Mayflower Ave 40 Ste 400, Simi Valley (93063)
PHONE 805 750-2327
Kathleen Ruddy, *CEO*
EMP: 65 **EST:** 2010
SALES (est): 2.3MM **Privately Held**
SIC: 8699 Charitable organization

(P-25596)
WALNUT VALLEY UNIFIED SCHOOL
Child Care Program
880 S Lemon Ave, Walnut (91789-2931)
PHONE 909 444-3415
Josephine Jones, *Director*
EMP: 67
SALES (corp-wide): 146.8MM **Privately Held**
SIC: 8699 8351 Charitable organization; child day care services
PA: Walnut Valley Unified School District
880 S Lemon Ave
Walnut CA 91789
909 595-1261

(P-25597)
WENMAT INC
Also Called: Signature Athletic Club The
6001 Fair Oaks Blvd, Carmichael (95608-4816)
PHONE 916 485-0714
Edward Orta, *Branch Mgr*
Ed Yu, *Branch Mgr*
Amber Wilkendorf, *Manager*
EMP: 100
SALES (corp-wide): 5MM **Privately Held**
WEB: www.wenmat.com
SIC: 8699 Athletic organizations

PA: Wenmat, Inc.
6001 Fair Oaks Blvd
Carmichael CA 95608
916 485-0714

(P-25598)
WIKIMEDIA FOUNDATION INC
149 New Montgomery St # 6, San Francisco (94105-3739)
PHONE 415 839-6885
Lila Tretikov, *Exec Dir*
V Ronique Kessler, *COO*
Garfield Byrd, *Treasurer*
Stuart West, *Trustee*
Quim Gil, *Comms Mgr*
EMP: 240
SALES: 52.8MM **Privately Held**
SIC: 8699 6732 Charitable organization; trusts: educational, religious, etc.

(P-25599)
WISDOM UNIVERSITY
35 Miller Ave, Mill Valley (94941-1903)
PHONE 415 259-7122
Rhonda Britten, *Principal*
EMP: 51
SALES: 659.6K **Privately Held**
SIC: 8699 Charitable organization

(P-25600)
WOMANS THURSDAY CLUB FAIR OAK
10625 Fair Oaks Blvd, Fair Oaks (95628-7210)
P.O. Box 396 (95628-0396)
PHONE 916 967-7891
Lucy Strom, *President*
EMP: 80
SALES (est): 1.3MM **Privately Held**
SIC: 8699 Membership organizations

(P-25601)
WORLD VISION INTERNATIONAL (HQ)
Also Called: Vision Fund International
800 W Chestnut Ave, Monrovia (91016-3198)
PHONE 626 303-8811
Dean Hirsch, *President*
Valdir Steuernagel, *Ch of Bd*
Kevin Jenkins, *President*
Oloo Tobias, *Associate Dir*
Denis St Amour, *Admin Sec*
EMP: 196
SQ FT: 94,000
SALES (est): 32.8MM
SALES (corp-wide): 1B **Privately Held**
SIC: 8699 Charitable organization
PA: World Vision, Inc.
34834 Weyerhaeuser Way S
Federal Way WA 98001
253 815-1000

(P-25602)
YMCA OF SILICON VALLEY
Also Called: Southwest YMCA
13500 Quito Rd, Saratoga (95070-4749)
PHONE 408 370-1877
Fax: 408 370-1333
Maria Drake, *Exec Dir*
EMP: 160
SALES (corp-wide): 57.6MM **Privately Held**
WEB: www.scvymca.org
SIC: 8699 8641 Personal interest organization; youth organizations
PA: Ymca Of Silicon Valley
80 Saratoga Ave
Santa Clara CA 95051
408 351-6400

(P-25603)
YOUR MAN TOURS INC
100 N Sepulveda Blvd # 1700, El Segundo (90245-5662)
PHONE 513 772-4411
Jerrey Fuque, *President*
Katja Jahn, *Manager*
EMP: 100
SALES (corp-wide): 22.1B **Privately Held**
WEB: www.ymtvacations.com
SIC: 8699 Travel club
HQ: Your Man Tours, Inc.
100 N Sepulveda Blvd # 1700
El Segundo CA 90245
310 649-3820

8711 Engineering Services

(P-25604)
7 LAYERS INC
15 Musick, Irvine (92618-1638)
PHONE..................................949 716-6512
Fax: 949 716-6521
Hans Jrgen Meckelburg, *CEO*
Fernando Rodriguez, *COO*
Don Newton, *Vice Pres*
Thomas Jaeger, *Business Dir*
Dan Baker, *Administration*
EMP: 81 **EST:** 1999
SQ FT: 20,000
SALES (est): 15.9MM
SALES (corp-wide): 14.3MM **Privately Held**
WEB: www.7layers.com
SIC: 8711 Engineering services
PA: 7layers Gmbh
  Borsigstr. 11
  Ratingen 40880
  210 274-90

(P-25605)
A P H TECHNOLOGICAL CONSULTING
2500 E Colo Blvd Ste 300, Pasadena (91107)
PHONE..................................626 796-0331
Fax: 626 449-6021
Steve Rodgers, *President*
EMP: 50
SQ FT: 5,000
SALES (est): 3.9MM **Privately Held**
SIC: 8711 Engineering services; consulting engineer

(P-25606)
A URSGI-BMDC JOINT VENTURE
4225 Executive Sq # 1600, La Jolla (92037-9122)
PHONE..................................858 812-9292
Martin Koffel, *CEO*
Burns McDonnell Engineering, *Principal*
EMP: 70
SALES (est): 3MM **Privately Held**
SIC: 8711 Engineering services

(P-25607)
A-C ELECTRIC COMPANY
Also Called: Automated Ctrl Technical Svcs
315 30th St, Bakersfield (93301-2511)
P.O. Box 81376 (93380-1376)
PHONE..................................661 633-5368
Fax: 661 324-2761
Dave Morton, *VP Opers*
Baron Alexander, *General Mgr*
Daren Alexander, *General Mgr*
Paul Calvillo, *Project Mgr*
Rusty Stone, *Manager*
EMP: 60
SALES (corp-wide): 62.4MM **Privately Held**
SIC: 8711 Engineering services
PA: A-C Electric Company
  2921 Hanger Way
  Bakersfield CA 93308
  661 410-0000

(P-25608)
ABBOOD ZEYAD
Also Called: Nafithat Alsharq
7914 La Mesa Blvd Apt 6, La Mesa (91942-5056)
PHONE..................................619 212-2820
Zeyad Abbood, *Owner*
EMP: 50
SALES (est): 810.9K **Privately Held**
SIC: 8711 0761 1731 1623 Electrical or electronic engineering; crew leaders, farm labor: contracting services; electric power systems contractors; electric power line construction; excavation & grading, building construction

(P-25609)
ABM FACILITY SERVICES LLC (DH)
Also Called: A B M
152 Technology Dr, Irvine (92618-2401)
PHONE..................................949 330-1555
Henrik C Slipsager, *CEO*
James P McClure, *President*
James S Lusk, *Exec VP*
EMP: 148
SALES (est): 216.7MM
SALES (corp-wide): 4.9B **Publicly Held**
SIC: 8711 Engineering services
HQ: Abm Facility Solutions Group, Llc
  1221 Lamar St Ste 1500
  Houston TX 77010
  832 214-5500

(P-25610)
ABS CONSULTING INC
Also Called: ABS Group
300 Commerce Ste 200, Irvine (92602-1305)
PHONE..................................714 734-4242
Doug Frazier, *CEO*
Peter Yanev, *President*
Jim Johnson, *COO*
George Reitter, *CFO*
William R Fuller, *Vice Pres*
EMP: 100
SQ FT: 16,700
SALES (est): 9.6MM
SALES (corp-wide): 1.1B **Privately Held**
SIC: 8711 8742 Consulting engineer; management consulting services
HQ: Abs Group Of Companies, Inc.
  16855 Northchase Dr
  Houston TX 77060

(P-25611)
ACCEL BIOTECH LLC
103 Cooper Ct, Los Gatos (95032-7604)
PHONE..................................408 354-1700
Bruce James Richardson, *CEO*
Jeff Thomas, *CFO*
Wayne Hopp, *Vice Pres*
Brian Lewis, *Vice Pres*
Rick Rubin, *Vice Pres*
EMP: 68 **EST:** 2008
SALES (est): 5.3MM
SALES (corp-wide): 34MM **Privately Held**
SIC: 8711 Mechanical engineering; consulting engineer; electrical or electronic engineering
PA: Ximedica, Llc
  55 Dupont Dr
  Providence RI 02907
  401 330-3163

(P-25612)
ACETECH CONSTRUCTION INC
3699 Wilshire Blvd # 655, Los Angeles (90010-2742)
PHONE..................................213 637-4702
Chong Lee, *President*
EMP: 50
SALES (est): 10MM **Privately Held**
SIC: 8711 Building construction consultant

(P-25613)
ACL CONSTRUCTION COMPANY INC
207 W State St, Ontario (91762-4360)
P.O. Box 1929, Chino Hills (91709-0065)
PHONE..................................909 391-4477
Fax: 909 391-4472
Jonathan Jordan, *President*
Joyce Oleyinka, *Administration*
Liz Evans, *Controller*
Parker Negus, *Manager*
EMP: 50
SQ FT: 800
SALES: 5MM **Privately Held**
SIC: 8711 Engineering services

(P-25614)
ACRONICS SYSTEMS INC
2102 Commerce Dr, San Jose (95131-1804)
PHONE..................................408 432-0888
Kim Tran, *CEO*
Michael Nguyen, *Project Mgr*
Tram Bui, *Accountant*
Jessica Tran, *Accountant*
Vivian Nguyen, *Purch Mgr*
EMP: 110
SQ FT: 16,000
SALES (est): 17.8MM **Privately Held**
WEB: www.acronics.com
SIC: 8711 7373 Engineering services; systems engineering, computer related

(P-25615)
ADAMS STREETER CIVIL ENGINEERS
15 Corporate Park, Irvine (92606-5109)
PHONE..................................949 474-2330
Fax: 949 474-0251
Jan A Adams, *President*
Randal Streeter, *Vice Pres*
Randal Streetr, *Software Engr*
Jerry Johnstone, *Project Mgr*
Jeff Otley, *Technical Staff*
EMP: 57
SQ FT: 14,000
SALES (est): 7.3MM **Privately Held**
SIC: 8711 Civil engineering

(P-25616)
ADKISON ENGINEERS INC
Also Called: Adkan Engineers
6879 Airport Dr, Riverside (92504-1903)
PHONE..................................951 688-0241
Fax: 951 688-0599
Ed Adkison, *President*
Jerry Snell, *Exec VP*
Chrissa Leach, *Vice Pres*
Lailah E Espritt, *General Mgr*
Tammy Phillips, *Admin Asst*
EMP: 52
SALES (est): 7.8MM **Privately Held**
WEB: www.adkan.com
SIC: 8711 8713 Civil engineering; surveying services

(P-25617)
ADTEK ENGINEERING SERVICE
2090 N Tustin Ave Ste 160, Santa Ana (92705-7868)
PHONE..................................800 451-0782
Joel R Spellacy, *President*
Lisa Fritz, *Office Mgr*
Lisa Smith, *Office Mgr*
EMP: 75 **EST:** 1974
SALES: 8.7MM **Privately Held**
WEB: www.adtekjobs.com
SIC: 8711 7361 Consulting engineer; employment agencies

(P-25618)
ADVANTEDGE TECHNOLOGY INC
271 Market St Ste 15, Port Hueneme (93041-3219)
PHONE..................................805 488-0405
Tim Edward Huggins, *CEO*
Tim Huggins, *Exec Dir*
Bruce Underwood, *Administration*
Julie Graves, *Sr Associate*
Vickie Dewolfe, *Director*
EMP: 60
SQ FT: 2,000
SALES (est): 12.4MM **Privately Held**
WEB: www.advantedgetechnology.com
SIC: 8711 Engineering services

(P-25619)
AECOM (PA)
1999 Avenue Of The Stars # 2600, Los Angeles (90067-6033)
PHONE..................................213 593-8000
Fax: 213 593-8729
Michael S Burke, *Ch of Bd*
Stephen M Kadenacy, *President*
Richard Silos, *President*
Matthew Sutton, *CEO*
W Troy Rudd, *CFO*
EMP: 148
SQ FT: 31,500
SALES: 17.9B **Publicly Held**
SIC: 8711 8712 Engineering services; architectural engineering

(P-25620)
AECOM C&E INC
Also Called: Aecom Environment
1220 Avenida Acaso, Camarillo (93012-8750)
PHONE..................................805 388-3775
Rick Simon, *Manager*
Mike Hale, *Manager*
EMP: 100
SALES (corp-wide): 17.9B **Publicly Held**
SIC: 8711 Engineering services
HQ: Aecom C&E, Inc
  250 Apollo Dr
  Chelmsford MA 01824
  978 905-2100

(P-25621)
AECOM E&C HOLDINGS INC (DH)
1999 Avenue Of Ste 2600, Los Angeles (90067)
PHONE..................................213 593-8000
Robert W Zaist, *CEO*
Gary V Jandegian, *President*
H Thomas Hicks, *CFO*
Judy L Rodgers, *Treasurer*
Hugh Blackwood, *Senior VP*
EMP: 148
SALES (est): 5.6B
SALES (corp-wide): 17.9B **Publicly Held**
SIC: 8711 1611 1629 1623 Engineering services; general contractor, highway & street construction; dams, waterways, docks & other marine construction; industrial plant construction; power plant construction; pipeline construction; industrial buildings, new construction; bridge construction; tunnel construction; highway construction, elevated
HQ: Urs Holdings, Inc.
  600 Montgomery St Fl 25
  San Francisco CA 94111
  415 774-2700

(P-25622)
AECOM ENERGY & CNSTR INC
Also Called: Washington Group
16711 Knott Ave, La Mirada (90638-6013)
PHONE..................................714 228-4300
Nancy Delvon, *Branch Mgr*
EMP: 120
SALES (corp-wide): 17.9B **Publicly Held**
WEB: www.wgint.com
SIC: 8711 Engineering services
HQ: Aecom Energy & Construction, Inc.
  6200 S Quebec St
  Greenwood Village CO 80111
  303 228-3000

(P-25623)
AECOM GLOBAL II LLC
1320 S Simpson Cir, Anaheim (92806-5531)
PHONE..................................415 774-2700
Bill Prior, *Branch Mgr*
EMP: 73
SALES (corp-wide): 17.9B **Publicly Held**
SIC: 8711 Engineering services
HQ: Aecom Global Ii, Llc
  1999 Avenue Of Ste 2600
  Los Angeles CA 90067
  213 593-8100

(P-25624)
AECOM GLOBAL II LLC
130 Robin Hill Rd Ste 100, Goleta (93117-3153)
PHONE..................................805 692-0600
Tim Cohen, *Senior Partner*
Eric McMurtry, *CTO*
EMP: 74
SALES (corp-wide): 17.9B **Publicly Held**
SIC: 8711 Consulting engineer
HQ: Aecom Global Ii, Llc
  1999 Avenue Of Ste 2600
  Los Angeles CA 90067
  213 593-8100

(P-25625)
AECOM GLOBAL II LLC
500 12th St, Oakland (94607-4076)
PHONE..................................510 874-3000
EMP: 73
SALES (corp-wide): 17.9B **Publicly Held**
SIC: 8711 Engineering services
HQ: Aecom Global Ii, Llc
  1999 Avenue Of Ste 2600
  Los Angeles CA 90067
  213 593-8100

(P-25626)
AECOM GLOBAL II LLC (HQ)
1999 Avenue Of Ste 2600, Los Angeles (90067)
PHONE..................................213 593-8100
Michael Burke, *Mng Member*
Tommy Bell, *President*

8711 - Engineering Services County (P-25627)

PRODUDUCTS & SERVICES SECTION

Rick L Randall, *President*
David Scripter, *Data Proc Exec*
Jay Mills, *Info Tech Dir*
EMP: 65 **EST:** 1976
SALES (est): 11.9B
SALES (corp-wide): 17.9B **Publicly Held**
SIC: 8711 8712 8741 Engineering services; consulting engineer; architectural engineering; construction management
PA: Aecom
 1999 Avenue Of The Stars # 2600
 Los Angeles CA 90067
 213 593-8000

(P-25627)
AECOM GLOBAL II LLC
2870 Gateway Oaks Dr # 150, Sacramento (95833-3577)
PHONE...................916 679-2000
Sujan Punyamurthuai, *General Mgr*
EMP: 300
SALES (corp-wide): 17.9B **Publicly Held**
SIC: 8711 Engineering services
HQ: Aecom Global Ii, Llc
 1999 Avenue Of Ste 2600
 Los Angeles CA 90067
 213 593-8100

(P-25628)
AECOM GLOBAL II LLC
2020 E 1st St Ste 400, Santa Ana (92705-4032)
PHONE...................714 835-6886
Davies Kristen, *Branch Mgr*
Richard Hart, *Office Mgr*
EMP: 280
SALES (corp-wide): 17.9B **Publicly Held**
SIC: 8711 Engineering services
HQ: Aecom Global Ii, Llc
 1999 Avenue Of Ste 2600
 Los Angeles CA 90067
 213 593-8100

(P-25629)
AECOM GLOBAL II LLC
600 Montgomery St, San Francisco (94111-2702)
PHONE...................415 774-2700
EMP: 83
SALES (corp-wide): 17.9B **Publicly Held**
SIC: 8711 Engineering services
HQ: Aecom Global Ii, Llc
 1999 Avenue Of Ste 2600
 Los Angeles CA 90067
 213 593-8100

(P-25630)
AECOM GLOBAL II LLC
16525 Worthley Dr, San Lorenzo (94580-1811)
PHONE...................510 258-0152
Ken Knott, *Branch Mgr*
EMP: 73
SALES (corp-wide): 17.9B **Publicly Held**
SIC: 8711 Engineering services
HQ: Aecom Global Ii, Llc
 1999 Avenue Of Ste 2600
 Los Angeles CA 90067
 213 593-8100

(P-25631)
AECOM GLOBAL II LLC
74 C St, Herlong (96113-7400)
P.O. Box 30 (96113-0030)
PHONE...................530 827-2406
Mike Rhodes, *Branch Mgr*
EMP: 73
SALES (corp-wide): 17.9B **Publicly Held**
SIC: 8711 Engineering services
HQ: Aecom Global Ii, Llc
 1999 Avenue Of Ste 2600
 Los Angeles CA 90067
 213 593-8100

(P-25632)
AECOM GLOBAL II LLC
5168 E Dakota Ave, Fresno (93727-7404)
PHONE...................559 347-5669
EMP: 105
SALES (corp-wide): 17.9B **Publicly Held**
SIC: 8711 Aviation &/or aeronautical engineering
HQ: Aecom Global Ii, Llc
 1999 Avenue Of Ste 2600
 Los Angeles CA 90067
 213 593-8100

(P-25633)
AECOM GLOBAL II LLC
Reeves Boulevard, Lemoore (93246-0001)
PHONE...................559 998-1820
EMP: 73
SALES (corp-wide): 17.9B **Publicly Held**
SIC: 8711 Engineering services
HQ: Aecom Global Ii, Llc
 1999 Avenue Of Ste 2600
 Los Angeles CA 90067
 213 593-8100

(P-25634)
AECOM GLOBAL II LLC
3990 Old Town Ave A, San Diego (92110-2930)
PHONE...................619 241-4568
EMP: 73
SALES (corp-wide): 17.9B **Publicly Held**
SIC: 8711 Engineering services
HQ: Aecom Global Ii, Llc
 1999 Avenue Of Ste 2600
 Los Angeles CA 90067
 213 593-8100

(P-25635)
AECOM GLOBAL II LLC
576th Flts, Vandenberg Afb (93437)
PHONE...................805 260-8440
EMP: 73
SALES (corp-wide): 17.9B **Publicly Held**
SIC: 8711 Engineering services
HQ: Aecom Global Ii, Llc
 1999 Avenue Of Ste 2600
 Los Angeles CA 90067
 213 593-8100

(P-25636)
AECOM GLOBAL II LLC
Also Called: URS Energy & Consruction
600 Montgomery St Fl 26, San Francisco (94111-2728)
PHONE...................415 774-2700
EMP: 84
SALES (corp-wide): 17.9B **Publicly Held**
SIC: 8711 Engineering services; consulting engineer
HQ: Aecom Global Ii, Llc
 1999 Avenue Of Ste 2600
 Los Angeles CA 90067
 213 593-8100

(P-25637)
AECOM TECHNICAL SERVICES INC
1333 Broadway Ste 800, Oakland (94612-1924)
PHONE...................510 834-4304
EMP: 180
SALES (corp-wide): 17.9B **Publicly Held**
WEB: www.earthtech.com
SIC: 8711 8742 Engineering services; transportation consultant
HQ: Aecom Technical Services, Inc.
 300 S Grand Ave Ste 1100
 Los Angeles CA 90071
 213 593-8000

(P-25638)
AECOM TECHNICAL SERVICES INC
901 Via Piemonte Ste 400, Ontario (91764-6597)
PHONE...................909 554-5000
Brian Weith, *Manager*
EMP: 65
SQ FT: 15,000
SALES (corp-wide): 17.9B **Publicly Held**
WEB: www.earthtech.com
SIC: 8711 8748 Engineering services; environmental consultant
HQ: Aecom Technical Services, Inc.
 300 S Grand Ave Ste 1100
 Los Angeles CA 90071
 213 593-8000

(P-25639)
AECOM TECHNOLOGY CORPORATION
2020 L St Ste 400, Sacramento (95811-4267)
PHONE...................916 414-5800
Colleen Johnston, *Branch Mgr*
EMP: 66

SALES (corp-wide): 17.9B **Publicly Held**
SIC: 8711 Consulting engineer
PA: Aecom
 1999 Avenue Of The Stars # 2600
 Los Angeles CA 90067
 213 593-8000

(P-25640)
AECOM TECHNOLOGY CORPORATION
501 2nd St, San Francisco (94107-1469)
PHONE...................415 908-6135
EMP: 58
SALES (corp-wide): 17.9B **Publicly Held**
SIC: 8711 Engineering services
PA: Aecom
 1999 Avenue Of The Stars # 2600
 Los Angeles CA 90067
 213 593-8000

(P-25641)
AEROSPACE CORPORATION
1650 Hotel Cir N, San Diego (92108-2816)
PHONE...................619 491-3557
Fax: 619 491-3563
Lynn T Wells, *Manager*
EMP: 64
SALES (corp-wide): 916.6MM **Privately Held**
SIC: 8711 Aviation &/or aeronautical engineering
PA: The Aerospace Corporation
 2310 E El Segundo Blvd
 El Segundo CA 90245
 310 336-5000

(P-25642)
AFFILIATED ENGINEERS INC
123 Mission St Fl 7, San Francisco (94105-5122)
PHONE...................415 764-3700
Fax: 415 764-3701
Nancy Yu, *Principal*
Zach Goldsworthy, *Electrical Engi*
Orlando Zaraspe, *Electrical Engi*
EMP: 50
SALES (est): 782.7K **Privately Held**
SIC: 8711 Engineering services

(P-25643)
AFFILIATED ENGINEERS W INC (HQ)
123 Mission St Fl 7, San Francisco (94105-5122)
PHONE...................925 933-8400
Fax: 925 933-8401
Mike Bove, *Principal*
Bora Akca, *Sales Staff*
Michael Fahey, *Sales Staff*
Elton Kam, *Sales Staff*
Matt Kovatch, *Director*
EMP: 75
SQ FT: 11,000
SALES (est): 5.4MM
SALES (corp-wide): 96.6MM **Privately Held**
WEB: www.aeieng.com
SIC: 8711 Mechanical engineering; electrical or electronic engineering
PA: Affiliated Engineers, Inc.
 5802 Research Park Blvd
 Madison WI 53719
 608 238-2616

(P-25644)
AFFORDABLE ENGRG SVCS INC
120 C Ave Ste 110, Coronado (92118-1992)
PHONE...................973 890-8915
Jason Kamdar, *Branch Mgr*
EMP: 86
SALES (corp-wide): 39.9MM **Privately Held**
SIC: 8711 Engineering services
PA: Affordable Engineering Services, Inc.
 120 C Ave Ste 110
 Coronado CA 92118
 619 522-9800

(P-25645)
ALAMEDA CORRIDOR ENGRG TEAM
1 Civic Plaza Dr Ste 600, Carson (90745-7980)
PHONE...................310 816-0460

Fax: 310 816-0464
Rachel Vandenberg, *Admin Mgr*
Moffatt Nichol Engineers, *Partner*
Daniel Mann Johnson and Menden, *Partner*
East Los Angeles Community UNI, *Partner*
EMP: 65
SALES (est): 4.2MM **Privately Held**
WEB: www.trenchteam.com
SIC: 8711 Engineering services

(P-25646)
ALBERT A WEBB ASSOCIATES (PA)
3788 Mccray St, Riverside (92506-2927)
PHONE...................951 686-1070
Fax: 951 788-1256
A Hubert Webb, *Chairman*
Matt Webb, *President*
Scott Webb, *CFO*
Mohammad A Faghihi, *Senior VP*
MO Faghihi, *Senior VP*
EMP: 127
SQ FT: 20,000
SALES (est): 30.1MM **Privately Held**
WEB: www.webbassociates.com
SIC: 8711 Civil engineering

(P-25647)
ALFA TECH CNSLTING ENGNERS INC (PA)
Also Called: Alfa Tech Consulting Entps
1321 Ridder Park Dr 50, San Jose (95131-2306)
PHONE...................408 487-1200
Jeff Fini, *Ch of Bd*
Susanne Dixon, *Office Mgr*
Jaime Smyth, *Executive Asst*
Reza Zare, *Admin Sec*
Jensen Leong, *Info Tech Dir*
EMP: 67
SQ FT: 22,000
SALES: 22.2MM **Privately Held**
WEB: www.atcginc.net
SIC: 8711 Engineering services

(P-25648)
ALION SCIENCE AND TECH CORP
266 E Scott St, Port Hueneme (93041-2918)
PHONE...................805 488-8761
Christopher Learned, *Manager*
Lynzy Williams, *Engineer*
EMP: 57
SQ FT: 1,000
SALES (corp-wide): 885.2MM **Privately Held**
SIC: 8711 8731 Engineering services; commercial physical research; commercial physical research
PA: Alion Science And Technology Corporation
 1750 Tysons Blvd Ste 1300
 Mc Lean VA 22102
 703 918-4480

(P-25649)
ALTA VISTA SOLUTIONS
3260 Blume Dr Ste 500, Richmond (94806-5715)
PHONE...................510 594-0510
Mazen A Wahbeh, *CEO*
Patrick S Lowry, *President*
Stacy Garcia, *Admin Asst*
Margaret Thomas, *Manager*
EMP: 120
SALES (est): 12.6MM **Privately Held**
SIC: 8711 Engineering services; consulting engineer

(P-25650)
AMEC E & C SERVICES INC
Also Called: AMEC E & C SERVICES, INC.
250 E Rincon St Ste 204, Corona (92879-1363)
PHONE...................951 273-7400
Thomas Cheahan, *Vice Pres*
EMP: 113
SALES (corp-wide): 6.3B **Privately Held**
SIC: 8711 Engineering services
HQ: Amec Foster Wheeler E&C Services, Inc.
 1979 Lkeside Pkwy Ste 400
 Tucker GA 30084
 770 688-2500

PRODUCTS & SERVICES SECTION

8711 - Engineering Services County (P-25672)

(P-25651)
AMEC FSTR WHLR ENVRNMNT INFRST
180 Grand Ave Fl 11, Oakland (94612-3741)
PHONE 510 663-4100
Susan Gallardo, *Branch Mgr*
Lester Feldman, *Vice Pres*
Calvin Hardcastle, *Vice Pres*
Thomas Jones, *Info Tech Dir*
John Egan, *Project Mgr*
EMP: 150
SALES (corp-wide): 8.2B **Privately Held**
SIC: 8711 8999 8744 Engineering services; pollution control engineering; earth science services; facilities support services
HQ: Amec Foster Wheeler Environment & Infrastructure, Inc.
1105 Lakewood Pkwy # 300
Alpharetta GA 30009
770 360-0600

(P-25652)
AMEC FSTR WHLR ENVRNMNT INFRST
6001 Rickenbacker Rd, Commerce (90040-3031)
PHONE 323 889-5300
Bruce Corkel, *Branch Mgr*
Carmen Mendoza, *General Mgr*
Jerry Haffley, *Project Mgr*
Matt Fraychineaud, *Project Engr*
Martin B Hudson, *Engineer*
EMP: 85
SQ FT: 30,000
SALES (corp-wide): 8.2B **Privately Held**
SIC: 8711 8748 Engineering services; environmental consultant
HQ: Amec Foster Wheeler Environment & Infrastructure, Inc.
1105 Lakewood Pkwy # 300
Alpharetta GA 30009
770 360-0600

(P-25653)
AMERICAN GNC CORPORATION
888 E Easy St, Simi Valley (93065-1812)
PHONE 805 582-0582
Fax: 805 582-0098
Dr Ching-Fang Lin, *President*
Emily Melgarejo, *General Mgr*
Traci Ho, *Engineer*
Rebecca Lin, *Manager*
EMP: 50
SQ FT: 30,000
SALES (est): 4.6MM **Privately Held**
WEB: www.americangnc.com
SIC: 8711 Engineering services

(P-25654)
AMERICAN PRIDE GEN ENGRG INC
529 W 4th Ave Ste B, Escondido (92025-4037)
PHONE 760 736-4056
James H Hatter, *CEO*
Barry Blanchard, *Vice Pres*
Bubba Riggins, *Administration*
David Eveland, *Controller*
EMP: 50
SQ FT: 3,000
SALES (est): 7.3MM **Privately Held**
SIC: 8711 Engineering services

(P-25655)
AMERICAN TECHNICAL SVCS INC
9520 Topanga Canyon Blvd, Chatsworth (91311-4045)
PHONE 818 590-7784
Alen Petrossian, *President*
EMP: 70
SQ FT: 2,040
SALES (est): 3.4MM **Privately Held**
WEB: www.americantechnicalservices.net
SIC: 8711 Engineering services

(P-25656)
AMG HUNTINGTON BEACH LLC
Also Called: Notthoff Engineering
5416 Argosy Ave, Huntington Beach (92649-1039)
PHONE 714 894-9802
Fax: 714 894-9803
David L Patterson, *CEO*
J Ross Feeney, *COO*
Robert Taylor, *Exec VP*
Kelley Kaller, *Vice Pres*
John Nicklos, *Vice Pres*
EMP: 50
SALES (est): 11.2MM **Privately Held**
SIC: 8711 Engineering services
HQ: Aerospace Manufacturing Group Inc
5401 Business Dr
Huntington Beach CA 92649
714 373-4300

(P-25657)
ANATEC INTERNATIONAL INC (HQ)
38 Executive Park Ste 350, Irvine (92614-6745)
PHONE 949 498-3350
Fax: 949 498-9405
Blaine Curtis, *President*
Tammy Holden, *Vice Pres*
Allen Gallaher, *Project Mgr*
Dorane Palm, *Controller*
Neal Farenbaugh, *Manager*
EMP: 60
SQ FT: 12,000
SALES (est): 8.2MM
SALES (corp-wide): 2.2B **Publicly Held**
WEB: www.anatectexas.com
SIC: 8711 Consulting engineer
PA: Curtiss-Wright Corporation
13925 Balntyn Corp Pl
Charlotte NC 28277
704 869-4600

(P-25658)
APEX MACHINE WORKS INC
2118 Wilshire Blvd # 258, Santa Monica (90403-5704)
PHONE 310 393-5987
EMP: 100
SALES (est): 3.3MM **Privately Held**
SIC: 8711

(P-25659)
APPLIED COMPANIES INC (PA)
28020 Avenue Stanford, Santa Clarita (91355-1105)
P.O. Box 802078 (91380-2078)
PHONE 661 257-0090
Mary Elizabeth Klinger, *CEO*
Jun Huh, *Design Engr*
James Ronga, *Project Mgr*
Joe Klinger, *Engineer*
Elizabeth Klinger, *Opers Mgr*
EMP: 60
SQ FT: 58,000
SALES (est): 21.4MM **Privately Held**
WEB: www.appliedcompanies.net
SIC: 8711 3585 3443 3621 Mechanical engineering; ice making machinery; cylinders, pressure: metal plate; motors & generators

(P-25660)
APPLIED GEOKINETICS
77 Bunsen, Irvine (92618-4218)
PHONE 949 502-5353
Fax: 949 502-5354
Glenn Tofani, *President*
Felicity Meek, *Treasurer*
Berge Basmadjian, *Vice Pres*
Melita Murphy, *Admin Asst*
Kevin Lea, *Engineer*
EMP: 65
SALES (est): 9.3MM **Privately Held**
WEB: www.appliedgeokinetics.com
SIC: 8711 Engineering services

(P-25661)
ARCHITRENDS INC
Also Called: ATI
3860 Blackhawk Rd Ste 160, Danville (94506-4615)
PHONE 925 648-8800
Robert Desauteis, *President*
Paul Didonato, *Vice Pres*
Grace Kam, *Office Mgr*
EMP: 70
SQ FT: 3,500
SALES (est): 4.2MM **Privately Held**
WEB: www.architrends.com
SIC: 8711 8741 Structural engineering; construction management

(P-25662)
ARES PROJECT MANAGEMENT LLC (HQ)
Also Called: Ares Prism
1440 Chapin Ave Ste 390, Burlingame (94010-4058)
PHONE 650 401-7100
Stanley C Lynch, *Mng Member*
Joyce Grant, *Controller*
Michael Jackson,
Larry E Shipley,
EMP: 54
SALES (est): 31MM **Privately Held**
SIC: 8711 Consulting engineer

(P-25663)
ARGON ST INC A BOEING COMPANY
6696 Mesa Ridge Rd Ste A, San Diego (92121-2950)
PHONE 312 544-2537
Fax: 858 623-9433
Jay Grove, *Manager*
Robert Gamos, *Manager*
EMP: 66
SALES (corp-wide): 96.1B **Publicly Held**
WEB: www.argonst.com
SIC: 8711 Engineering services
HQ: Argon St. Inc.
12701 Fair Lakes Cir # 800
Fairfax VA 22033
703 322-0881

(P-25664)
ARIA GROUP INCORPORATED
17395 Daimler St, Irvine (92614-5510)
PHONE 949 475-2915
Fax: 949 475-2916
Clive Hawkins, *President*
Charles Taylor, *Exec VP*
Pam Gaudreau, *Admin Asst*
Danh Le, *Design Engr*
Robert M Taylor, *Design Engr*
EMP: 70
SQ FT: 45,489
SALES (est): 14.4MM **Privately Held**
WEB: www.getbedbugs.com
SIC: 8711 Engineering services

(P-25665)
ARINC INCORPORATED
4553 Glencoe Ave Ste 100, Marina Del Rey (90292-7917)
PHONE 310 301-9040
Fax: 310 751-3202
John Belcher, *CEO*
Pascal Mermoz, *Manager*
EMP: 100 **Publicly Held**
SIC: 8711 Engineering services
HQ: Arinc Incorporated
2551 Riva Rd
Annapolis MD 21401
410 266-4000

(P-25666)
ARQ LLC
19517 Pauling, Foothill Ranch (92610-2619)
PHONE 888 384-0971
Kunal Hinduja, *Mng Member*
Arjun Dua, *CFO*
Jawan Salman, *Vice Pres*
Robert Danner, *Project Mgr*
Dionese Vela, *Project Mgr*
EMP: 85
SALES (est): 14.6MM **Privately Held**
SIC: 8711 Electrical or electronic engineering

(P-25667)
ARTIMISA & CO
220 Forest Knoll Ln, Quincy (95971-9350)
P.O. Box 3585 (95971-3585)
PHONE 530 283-3700
Chris D Kennedy, *President*
EMP: 54
SALES (est): 3.2MM **Privately Held**
WEB: www.mainecoon.com
SIC: 8711 Engineering services

(P-25668)
ARUP NORTH AMERICA LIMITED
12777 W Jefferson Blvd, Los Angeles (90066-7048)
PHONE 310 578-4182
Tony Panossian, *Branch Mgr*
Oswaldo Mercado, *Vice Pres*
EMP: 101
SALES (corp-wide): 48.3MM **Privately Held**
SIC: 8711 Engineering services
HQ: Arup North America Limited
560 Mission St Fl 7
San Francisco CA 94105
415 957-9445

(P-25669)
ARUP NORTH AMERICA LIMITED (DH)
560 Mission St Fl 7, San Francisco (94105-0915)
PHONE 415 957-9445
Fax: 415 957-9096
Mahadev Ramen, *President*
Stuart Robertson, *Officer*
Andrew Howard, *Vice Pres*
Brian Jackson, *Vice Pres*
James Quiter, *Vice Pres*
EMP: 200
SALES (est): 93.7MM
SALES (corp-wide): 48.3MM **Privately Held**
SIC: 8711 Engineering services
HQ: Arup Americas Inc.
77 Water St
New York NY 10005
212 896-3000

(P-25670)
ASTRO AEROSPACE
6384 Via Real, Carpinteria (93013-2928)
PHONE 805 684-6641
Fax: 805 684-3372
Richard Nelson, *President*
Al Lacroix, *Data Proc Staff*
Danny Chae, *Project Mgr*
Mark Gralewski, *Research*
Kelley Ristau, *Engineer*
EMP: 110
SQ FT: 70,000
SALES (est): 17MM **Publicly Held**
WEB: www.trw.com
SIC: 8711 Structural engineering
HQ: Northrop Grumman Space & Mission Systems Corp.
6377 San Ignacio Ave
San Jose CA 95119
703 280-2900

(P-25671)
ATA ENGINEERING INC (PA)
13290 Evening Creek Dr S # 250, San Diego (92128-4424)
PHONE 858 480-2000
Fax: 858 792-8932
Mary Baker, *President*
Robin Ash, *CFO*
William Cherom, *CFO*
David L Hunt, *Treasurer*
Paul A Blelloch, *Vice Pres*
EMP: 60
SQ FT: 50,215
SALES (est): 22.9MM **Privately Held**
WEB: www.ata-e.com
SIC: 8711 Consulting engineer

(P-25672)
ATIEVA USA INC
125 Constitution Dr, Menlo Park (94025-1118)
PHONE 650 802-8181
Jeffery Jia, *CEO*
Derek Jenkins, *Vice Pres*
Henry LI, *Vice Pres*
Sam Weng, *Vice Pres*
Mike Hambleton, *Creative Dir*
EMP: 320 **EST:** 2007
SQ FT: 65,000
SALES (est): 29.6MM **Privately Held**
SIC: 8711 3711 Engineering services; motor vehicles & car bodies
PA: Atieva Inc
C/O: Maples Corporate Services Limited
George Town GR CAYMAN
345 949-8066

8711 - Engineering Services County (P-25673)

PRODUDUCTS & SERVICES SECTION

(P-25673)
ATKINS NORTH AMERICA INC
9275 Sky Park Ct Ste 200, San Diego (92123-4905)
PHONE.................................858 874-1810
Marc Cavallero, *Branch Mgr*
Elyse Avella, *Office Mgr*
EMP: 100
SALES (corp-wide): 2.7B **Privately Held**
WEB: www.cargillemt.com
SIC: 8711 Consulting engineer
HQ: Atkins North America, Inc.
2001 Nw 107th Ave
Doral FL 33172
813 282-7275

(P-25674)
AUSENCO PSI LLC (HQ)
1320 Willow Pass Rd # 300, Concord (94520-5241)
PHONE.................................925 939-4420
Ed Meka, *President*
Andrew Fletcher, *Treasurer*
Delbert Boyle, *Senior VP*
Craig Allen, *Admin Sec*
Kenneth Bennert, *Finance Mgr*
EMP: 59
SALES (est): 20MM **Privately Held**
SIC: 8711 Engineering services
PA: Ausenco Usa Inc.
1320 Willow Pass Rd
Concord CA 94520
925 939-4420

(P-25675)
AUSGAR TECHNOLOGIES INC
10721 Treena St, San Diego (92131-1016)
PHONE.................................855 428-7427
Jonathan Dien, *President*
Cretia Bowman, *Vice Pres*
Yen Doan, *Manager*
EMP: 115
SQ FT: 16,000
SALES (est): 20MM **Privately Held**
SIC: 8711 7371 7373 7379 Engineering services; custom computer programming services; computer integrated systems design; computer related consulting services; testing laboratories

(P-25676)
AZTEC ENGINEERING GROUP INC
18510 Pasadena St Ste C, Lake Elsinore (92530-2772)
PHONE.................................951 471-6190
Robert L Lemke Jr Pe, *Branch Mgr*
EMP: 61
SALES (corp-wide): 34.8MM **Privately Held**
SIC: 8711 Construction & civil engineering
PA: Aztec Engineering Group, Inc.
4561 E Mcdowell Rd
Phoenix AZ 85008
602 454-0402

(P-25677)
B&C TRANSIT INC (PA)
Also Called: B & C
7955 Edgewater Dr, Oakland (94621-2003)
PHONE.................................510 483-3560
Fax: 510 483-0122
Alberto Fernandez, *President*
Tanya Powell, *CFO*
Steven Falk, *Vice Pres*
Jerome S Furman, *Vice Pres*
Rita Roquez, *Admin Sec*
EMP: 60
SQ FT: 25,000
SALES (est): 33.7MM **Privately Held**
SIC: 8711 Engineering services

(P-25678)
BAE SYSTEMS LAND ARMAMENTS LP
6331 San Ignacio Ave, San Jose (95119-1202)
P.O. Box 5300958 (95153-5398)
PHONE.................................408 289-0111
Mark Pedrazzi, *Manager*
Robert Sankovich, *Vice Pres*
Loren Van Huystee, *Program Mgr*
Raj Jacapl, *General Mgr*
Arthur Roberts, *General Mgr*
EMP: 1000

SALES (corp-wide): 25.3B **Privately Held**
WEB: www.udlp.com
SIC: 8711 Engineering services
HQ: Bae Systems Land & Armaments L.P.
2000 15th Nw Fl 11
Arlington VA 22201
703 312-6100

(P-25679)
BAE SYSTEMS MARITIME ENGINEERI
7330 Engineer Rd Ste A, San Diego (92111-1434)
P.O. Box 13308 (92170-3308)
PHONE.................................619 238-1000
Peter Henning, *General Mgr*
David A Herr, *CEO*
Irene Falo, *Administration*
Diana Edwards, *Info Tech Mgr*
Bill Fitzpatrick, *Finance Dir*
EMP: 370
SALES (est): 18.7MM
SALES (corp-wide): 25.3B **Privately Held**
WEB: www.baesystemsmaritimeengineeringandservices.com
SIC: 8711 Engineering services
HQ: Bae Systems Ship Repair Inc.
750 W Berkley Ave
Norfolk VA 23523
757 494-4000

(P-25680)
BARA INFOWARE INC (PA)
Also Called: BARA CONSTRUCTION
4115 Blackhawk Plaza Cir, Danville (94506-4901)
PHONE.................................925 465-5354
Elina Singh, *President*
Menginder Singh, *Vice Pres*
Tonya Morales, *Office Mgr*
Gary Heinz, *Business Mgr*
EMP: 50
SQ FT: 600
SALES: 6.6MM **Privately Held**
SIC: 8711 1542 Engineering services; custom builders, non-residential

(P-25681)
BAY-TEC ENGINEERING (PA)
5130 Fulton Dr Ste X, Fairfield (94534-4223)
PHONE.................................707 252-6575
John Justus, *President*
Rick Cavalli, *Treasurer*
Adam Beaddy, *Vice Pres*
Alan Kelm, *Admin Sec*
Duane North, *Senior Engr*
EMP: 53
SQ FT: 22,000
SALES (est): 5.7MM **Privately Held**
WEB: www.bay-tec.com
SIC: 8711 1731 3823 3829 Engineering services; electronic controls installation; industrial instrmnts msrmnt display/control process variable; measuring & controlling devices

(P-25682)
BECHTEL CORPORATION (HQ)
50 Beale St, San Francisco (94105-1813)
P.O. Box 193965 (94119-3965)
PHONE.................................415 768-1234
Fax: 415 276-2500
Bill Dudley, *CEO*
Riley Bechtel, *Ch of Bd*
Brendan Bechtel, *President*
Steve Katzman, *President*
Peter Dawson, *CFO*
EMP: 685
SQ FT: 300,000
SALES (est): 7.4B
SALES (corp-wide): 7.7B **Privately Held**
WEB: www.bechteltelecoms.com
SIC: 8711 1629 8742 Civil engineering; industrial plant construction; power plant construction; construction project management consultant
PA: Bechtel Group, Inc.
50 Beale St Bsmt 1
San Francisco CA 94105
415 768-1234

(P-25683)
BECHTEL ENERGY CORPORATION
50 Beale St Bsmt 1, San Francisco (94105-1819)
P.O. Box 193965 (94119-3965)
PHONE.................................415 768-1234
R P Bechtel, *Chairman*
G C Proctor, *Senior VP*
J D Carter, *Director*
A Zaccaria, *Director*
EMP: 1588
SQ FT: 300,000
SALES (est): 36MM
SALES (corp-wide): 7.7B **Privately Held**
SIC: 8711 8741 Construction & civil engineering; construction management
HQ: Bechtel Power Corporation
50 Beale St Bsmt 2
San Francisco CA 94105
415 768-1234

(P-25684)
BECHTEL ENTERPRISES HOLDINGS (HQ)
50 Beale St Ste 2200, San Francisco (94105-1827)
P.O. Box 193965 (94119-3965)
PHONE.................................415 768-1234
Riley P Bechtel, *Ch of Bd*
V P Unruh, *President*
Marcia B Burkey, *CFO*
H J Haynes, *Vice Ch Bd*
C W Hull, *Vice Ch Bd*
EMP: 85
SQ FT: 300,000
SALES (est): 7.3MM
SALES (corp-wide): 7.7B **Privately Held**
SIC: 8711 Engineering services
PA: Bechtel Group, Inc.
50 Beale St Bsmt 1
San Francisco CA 94105
415 768-1234

(P-25685)
BECHTEL GROUP INC (PA)
50 Beale St Bsmt 1, San Francisco (94105-1819)
PHONE.................................415 768-1234
Fax: 415 768-9038
Bill Dudley, *Vice Chairman*
Brendan Bechtel, *President*
Adrian Zaccaria, *President*
Peter Dawson, *CFO*
Georgeann Proctor, *CFO*
EMP: 2100
SQ FT: 300,000
SALES (est): 7.7B **Privately Held**
WEB: www.bechtelgroup.com
SIC: 8711 1629 8742 Engineering services; civil engineering; industrial plant construction; construction project management consultant

(P-25686)
BEDON CONSTRUCTION INC
27989 Holland Rd, Menifee (92584-9703)
PHONE.................................951 246-9005
Don Parker, *President*
Crystal Boussaksou, *Administration*
Marti Manser, *Manager*
Marti Maser, *Manager*
Jerry Mayes, *Superintendent*
EMP: 68
SQ FT: 2,000
SALES (est): 7.9MM **Privately Held**
WEB: www.bedonconstruction.com
SIC: 8711 Construction & civil engineering

(P-25687)
BENTLEY COMPANY
12647 Alcosta Blvd # 500, San Ramon (94583-4439)
PHONE.................................925 543-3500
Lou L Pai, *Ch of Bd*
Lee Jestings, *President*
Malcom Adkins, *Technology*
Tom Krowley, *Technology*
Donald C Bentley, *Director*
EMP: 91
SQ FT: 45,000

SALES (est): 3.7MM
SALES (corp-wide): 2.9B **Privately Held**
SIC: 8711 8712 1541 1629 Engineering services; construction & civil engineering; architectural engineering; industrial buildings & warehouses; power plant construction; energy research; construction management
HQ: Enron Energy Services Inc
1400 Smith St Ste 501
Houston TX 77002
713 853-6161

(P-25688)
BIGGS CARDOSA ASSOCIATES INC (PA)
865 The Alameda, San Jose (95126-3133)
PHONE.................................408 296-5515
Fax: 408 296-8114
Steven A Biggs, *President*
Mark Cardosa, *Vice Pres*
Carrie Bibolet, *Admin Asst*
Yvonne Mac, *Admin Asst*
Roberto Castro, *Technical Staff*
EMP: 70
SQ FT: 7,237
SALES (est): 12.8MM **Privately Held**
SIC: 8711 Structural engineering

(P-25689)
BIT MEDTECH LLC
15870 Bernardo Center Dr, San Diego (92127-2320)
PHONE.................................858 613-1200
Brian S Kelleher, *Mng Member*
EMP: 60
SALES (est): 5.4MM **Privately Held**
SIC: 8711 3841 Engineering services; surgical & medical instruments

(P-25690)
BKF ENGINEERS
1730 N 1st St Ste 600, San Jose (95112-4508)
PHONE.................................408 467-9100
Fax: 408 436-1194
David Lavelle, *President*
EMP: 57
SALES (corp-wide): 46MM **Privately Held**
SIC: 8711 Engineering services
PA: Bkf Engineers
255 Shoreline Dr Ste 200
Redwood City CA 94065
650 482-6300

(P-25691)
BKF ENGINEERS (PA)
255 Shoreline Dr Ste 200, Redwood City (94065-1428)
PHONE.................................650 482-6300
David Lavelle, *President*
Maureen Nevin, *CFO*
Max Keech, *Corp Secy*
Todd Adair, *Vice Pres*
Dave Evans, *Vice Pres*
EMP: 90
SQ FT: 18,155
SALES (est): 46MM **Privately Held**
SIC: 8711 8713 Civil engineering; surveying services

(P-25692)
BLACK & VEATCH CORPORATION
265 E River Park Cir, Fresno (93720-1575)
PHONE.................................913 458-9406
EMP: 81
SALES (corp-wide): 2.9B **Privately Held**
SIC: 8711 Engineering services
HQ: Black & Veatch Corporation
11401 Lamar Ave
Overland Park KS 66211
913 458-2000

(P-25693)
BLACK & VEATCH CORPORATION
15615 Alton Pkwy Ste 300, Irvine (92618-7311)
PHONE.................................913 458-2000
Fax: 949 753-1252
Steve Foellmi, *Vice Pres*
Lynn Allen, *Managing Dir*
Jacob Holden, *Research*

PRODUCTS & SERVICES SECTION

8711 - Engineering Services County (P-25714)

Ronald Chen, *Electrical Engi*
Robert Kaessner, *Engineer*
EMP: 50
SALES (corp-wide): 2.9B **Privately Held**
WEB: www.bv.com
SIC: 8711 Consulting engineer
HQ: Black & Veatch Corporation
11401 Lamar Ave
Overland Park KS 66211
913 458-2000

(P-25694)
BLACK & VEATCH CORPORATION
5 Peters Canyon Rd # 300, Irvine (92606-1791)
PHONE..............................562 345-9332
Adan Madrid, *Manager*
Yvonne Conley, *Manager*
Nardo Del Rosario, *Manager*
EMP: 84
SALES (corp-wide): 2.9B **Privately Held**
SIC: 8711 Consulting engineer
HQ: Black & Veatch Corporation
11401 Lamar Ave
Overland Park KS 66211
913 458-2000

(P-25695)
BLACK & VEATCH-BALFOUR BEATTY
300 Rancheros Dr Ste 250, San Marcos (92069-2969)
PHONE..............................760 510-7715
James Waller, *Managing Prtnr*
Crandall Bates, *General Ptnr*
Connie Nikravan, *Finance Dir*
EMP: 60
SQ FT: 10,000
SALES (est): 4.2MM **Privately Held**
SIC: 8711 Consulting engineer

(P-25696)
BMT SCIENTIFIC MARINE SVCS INC (HQ)
955 Borra Pl Ste 100, Escondido (92029-2011)
PHONE..............................760 737-3505
Thomas L Johnson, *President*
Cynthia Ballard, *CFO*
Campman Craig, *Vice Pres*
Rod Edwards, *Vice Pres*
R Peter Johnson, *Vice Pres*
EMP: 65
SQ FT: 25,000
SALES (est): 26MM
SALES (corp-wide): 266.9MM **Privately Held**
WEB: www.scimar.com
SIC: 8711 Marine engineering
PA: Bmt Group Limited
Goodrich House
Teddington MIDDX TW11
208 943-5544

(P-25697)
BOEING COMPANY
5301 Bolsa Ave, Huntington Beach (92647-2048)
PHONE..............................714 896-1301
Dave Bullock, *CFO*
EMP: 559
SALES (corp-wide): 96.1B **Publicly Held**
SIC: 8711 Engineering services
PA: The Boeing Company
100 N Riverside Plz
Chicago IL 60606
312 544-2000

(P-25698)
BOEING COMPANY
5800 Woolsey Canyon Rd, Canoga Park (91304-1148)
PHONE..............................818 466-8800
Philip Condit, *Branch Mgr*
T Peterson, *Program Mgr*
Chris Maddox, *Engineer*
EMP: 50
SALES (corp-wide): 96.1B **Publicly Held**
SIC: 8711 8748 Engineering services; safety training service
PA: The Boeing Company
100 N Riverside Plz
Chicago IL 60606
312 544-2000

(P-25699)
BOOZ ALLEN HAMILTON INC
2250 E Imperial Hwy # 450, El Segundo (90245-3543)
PHONE..............................310 524-1557
Fax: 310 322-4474
Loren Caddick, *Manager*
Nader Nejadhashemi, *Engineer*
Christine Campbell, *Marketing Mgr*
Christine Jana, *Facilities Mgr*
EMP: 60 **Publicly Held**
SIC: 8711 Engineering services
HQ: Booz Allen Hamilton Inc.
8283 Greensboro Dr # 700
Mc Lean VA 22102
703 902-5000

(P-25700)
BOYLE ENGINEERING CORPORATION (HQ)
999 W Town And Country Rd, Orange (92868-4713)
PHONE..............................949 476-3300
Fax: 949 721-7141
Phil Petrocelli, *President*
Keith T Campbell, *President*
Jon S Holmgren, *CFO*
Salvatore D'Angelo, *Vice Pres*
Janet Hegland, *Executive*
EMP: 100 **EST:** 1945
SQ FT: 50,000
SALES (est): 50MM
SALES (corp-wide): 17.9B **Publicly Held**
WEB: www.boyleengineering.com
SIC: 8711 8712 Engineering services; architectural engineering
PA: Aecom
1999 Avenue Of The Stars # 2600
Los Angeles CA 90067
213 593-8000

(P-25701)
BOYLE ENGINEERING CORPORATION
999 W Town And Country Rd, Orange (92868-4713)
P.O. Box 7350, Newport Beach (92658-7350)
PHONE..............................714 543-5274
EMP: 80
SALES (corp-wide): 8.3B **Publicly Held**
SIC: 8711 8712
HQ: Boyle Engineering Corporation
999 W Town And Country Rd
Orange CA 92868
949 476-3300

(P-25702)
BRADY GCE II
3710 Ruffin Rd, San Diego (92123-1812)
PHONE..............................858 496-0500
Marisol Canales, *Principal*
Richard Brady, *Principal*
Jon Owens, *Principal*
EMP: 99 **EST:** 2013
SQ FT: 20,000
SALES (est): 2.7MM **Privately Held**
SIC: 8711 1542 1623 8744 Civil engineering; commercial & office building, new construction; water & sewer line construction;

(P-25703)
BRINDERSON LP (HQ)
19000 Macarthur Blvd 8, Irvine (92612-1438)
PHONE..............................714 466-7100
Fax: 714 466-7320
Gary L Brinderson, *CEO*
Russel Conda, *President*
Ian Cairns, *Vice Pres*
Kris Schramm, *General Mgr*
Teresa Franco, *Administration*
EMP: 150
SQ FT: 30,000
SALES (est): 322.6MM
SALES (corp-wide): 1.3B **Publicly Held**
SIC: 8711 1629 Engineering services; dams, waterways, docks & other marine construction
PA: Aegion Corporation
17988 Edison Ave
Chesterfield MO 63005
636 530-8000

(P-25704)
BRINDERSON LP
19000 Macarthur Blvd 8, Irvine (92612-1438)
PHONE..............................714 466-7100
Allan Updyke, *President*
Jon Rodriguez, *CFO*
EMP: 60
SALES (est): 2.2MM
SALES (corp-wide): 1.3B **Publicly Held**
SIC: 8711 Engineering services
HQ: Energy & Mining Holding Company Llc
17988 Edison Ave
Chesterfield MO 63005
636 530-8000

(P-25705)
BRINDERSON & ASSOCIATES
Also Called: Environmental Compliance Svcs
19000 Macarthur Blvd 8, Irvine (92612-1438)
PHONE..............................714 466-7100
Gary Brinderson, *President*
EMP: 50
SALES (est): 4.1MM
SALES (corp-wide): 1.3B **Publicly Held**
SIC: 8711 8748 Engineering services; testing services
HQ: Brinderson, L.P.
19000 Macarthur Blvd 8
Irvine CA 92612
714 466-7100

(P-25706)
BROWN AND CALDWELL (PA)
201 N Civic Dr Ste 115, Walnut Creek (94596-3865)
P.O. Box 8045 (94596-1220)
PHONE..............................925 937-9010
Fax: 925 932-9026
Craig Goehring, *CEO*
Richard D' Amanto, *President*
James Miller, *Vice Ch Bd*
Cindy Paulson, *Officer*
Steve Wilson, *Project Mgr*
EMP: 131
SQ FT: 24,000
SALES (est): 514.2MM **Privately Held**
SIC: 8711 Civil engineering; sanitary engineers; consulting engineer

(P-25707)
BROWN AND CALDWELL
1590 Drew Ave Ste 210, Davis (95618-7848)
PHONE..............................530 747-0650
Fax: 916 635-8805
Dave Zuber, *Branch Mgr*
Cathy Boyd, *Admin Mgr*
Tina Bauer, *Project Mgr*
Tom Mingee, *Project Engr*
Robb McComb, *Electrical Engi*
EMP: 80
SQ FT: 4,000
SALES (est): 514.2MM **Privately Held**
SIC: 8711 Consulting engineer
PA: Brown And Caldwell
201 N Civic Dr Ste 115
Walnut Creek CA 94596
925 937-9010

(P-25708)
BROWN AND CALDWELL
9665 Chesapeake Dr # 201, San Diego (92123-1367)
PHONE..............................858 514-8822
Fax: 858 514-8833
George Khoury, *Vice Pres*
Victor Occiano, *Vice Pres*
Boris Pastushenko, *Vice Pres*
Larry Finnerty, *CIO*
Robert Coleman, *Project Mgr*
EMP: 56
SALES (corp-wide): 514.2MM **Privately Held**
SIC: 8711 Civil engineering; sanitary engineers; consulting engineer
PA: Brown And Caldwell
201 N Civic Dr Ste 115
Walnut Creek CA 94596
925 937-9010

(P-25709)
BSK ASSOCIATES
Also Called: B S K Analytical Laboratories
1414 Stanislaus St, Fresno (93706-1623)
PHONE..............................559 497-2888
Fax: 559 485-6935
Jeff Koelewyn, *Director*
Brad Meadows, *Vice Pres*
Kasanna Coulter, *Comp Lab Dir*
Robert Coulter, *Info Tech Mgr*
Jacqueline Murphy, *Project Dir*
EMP: 60
SQ FT: 6,316
SALES (corp-wide): 41.7MM **Privately Held**
WEB: www.bskinc.com
SIC: 8711 8734 Professional engineer; testing laboratories
PA: Bsk Associates
550 W Locust Ave
Fresno CA 93650
559 497-2880

(P-25710)
BURNS & MCDONNELL INC
1 Pointe Dr Ste 540, Brea (92821-7634)
PHONE..............................714 256-1595
Ken Gerling, *Manager*
EMP: 50
SALES (corp-wide): 1.4B **Privately Held**
SIC: 8711 Engineering services
PA: Burns & Mcdonnell, Inc.
9400 Ward Pkwy
Kansas City MO 64114
816 333-9400

(P-25711)
C D LYON CONSTRUCTION INC (PA)
380 W Stanley Ave, Ventura (93001-1350)
P.O. Box 1456 (93002-1456)
PHONE..............................805 653-0173
Christopher D Lyon, *CEO*
Debra C Lyon, *Corp Secy*
Lisa Sess, *Accountant*
Eddie Garcia, *Opers Mgr*
Vincent Torres, *Opers Mgr*
EMP: 80
SALES (est): 25.6MM **Privately Held**
WEB: www.cdlyon.com
SIC: 8711 Petroleum engineering

(P-25712)
C S G CONSULTANTS INC
1257 Quarry Ln Ste 100, Pleasanton (94566-8400)
PHONE..............................925 931-0370
George Barnes, *Branch Mgr*
EMP: 50
SALES (corp-wide): 28.3MM **Privately Held**
SIC: 8711 Consulting engineer
PA: C S G Consultants, Inc.
550 Pilgrim Dr
Foster City CA 94404
650 522-2525

(P-25713)
C S G CONSULTANTS INC (PA)
Also Called: C S C Consultants
550 Pilgrim Dr, Foster City (94404-1253)
PHONE..............................650 522-2525
Fax: 650 522-2599
Cyrus Kianpour, *CEO*
Dave Gottlieb, *CFO*
Hatem Ahmed, *Vice Pres*
Khoa Duong, *Vice Pres*
Bradley Donohue, *Admin Sec*
EMP: 50
SQ FT: 16,000
SALES (est): 15.8MM **Privately Held**
SIC: 8711 Engineering services

(P-25714)
CALIFORNIA MFG TECH CONSULTING
Also Called: Cmtc
690 Knox St Ste 200, Torrance (90502-1323)
PHONE..............................310 263-3060
Fax: 310 263-3062
James Watson, *President*
Jack Buren, *CFO*
John J Vanburen, *CFO*
Tom Lightner, *Vice Pres*

8711 - Engineering Services County (P-25715) — PRODUDUCTS & SERVICES SECTION

Fabio Gomez, *Business Dir*
EMP: 73
SQ FT: 10,000
SALES: 26.5MM **Privately Held**
SIC: 8711 8742 Consulting engineer; management consulting services; marketing consulting services

(P-25715)
CALNEV PIPE LINE LLC
1100 W Town And Cntry Rd, Orange (92868-4600)
PHONE.................................714 560-4400
Richard Kinder,
Gary Prim, *Controller*
EMP: 200
SALES (est): 8.8MM
SALES (corp-wide): 14.4B **Publicly Held**
WEB: www.kindermorgan.com
SIC: 8711 Energy conservation engineering
HQ: Kinder Morgan Energy Partners, L.P.
  1001 La St Ste 1000
  Houston TX 77002
  713 369-9000

(P-25716)
CAMBRIDGE DESIGN PARTNR INC
22 8 Camelton Ave Fl 3, Palo Alto (94301)
PHONE.................................650 387-7812
EMP: 85 **EST:** 2015
SALES (est): 1.2MM **Privately Held**
SIC: 8711 Engineering services

(P-25717)
CAPITAL ENGINEERING CONS (PA)
11020 Sun Center Dr # 100, Rancho Cordova (95670-6287)
PHONE.................................916 851-3500
Fax: 916 631-4424
Lowell E Shields, *President*
Thomas Duval, *Treasurer*
John Lionakis, *Vice Pres*
Tatyana Pivnik, *Info Tech Mgr*
Thomas Montgomery, *Network Mgr*
EMP: 76
SQ FT: 6,800
SALES: 7.6MM **Privately Held**
WEB: www.capital-engineering.com
SIC: 8711 Mechanical engineering

(P-25718)
CARLILEMACY INC
15 3rd St, Santa Rosa (95401-6204)
PHONE.................................707 542-6451
David Hanson, *President*
Mark Hale, *Treasurer*
Curtis Nichols, *Vice Pres*
Bruce Jarvis, *Admin Sec*
Nikki Todeschini, *Admin Asst*
EMP: 50
SQ FT: 10,000
SALES (est): 6.8MM **Privately Held**
WEB: www.carlilemacy.com
SIC: 8711 Civil engineering

(P-25719)
CARLSON BARBEE & GIBSON INC
2633 Camino Ramon Ste 350, San Ramon (94583-9139)
PHONE.................................925 866-0322
Fax: 925 866-8575
David Carlson, *President*
Grant Gibson, *Vice Pres*
Heather Daun, *Admin Mgr*
Michael Barbee, *Admin Sec*
Danny D Santos, *Systs Prg Mgr*
EMP: 100
SQ FT: 6,800
SALES (est): 14.3MM **Privately Held**
WEB: www.cbandg.com
SIC: 8711 Civil engineering

(P-25720)
CAROLLO ENGINEERS PC (PA)
2700 Ygnacio Valley Rd # 300, Walnut Creek (94598-3466)
PHONE.................................925 932-1710
Balakrishnan Narayanan, *President*
Gary Meyerhofer, *Partner*
Rick D Wheadon, *Treasurer*
Larry E Elliott, *Vice Pres*

Robb Grantham, *Vice Pres*
EMP: 100
SQ FT: 20,000
SALES (est): 225.9MM **Privately Held**
SIC: 8711 Consulting engineer

(P-25721)
CARTER & BURGESS INC
180 Promenade Cir Ste 300, Sacramento (95834-2952)
PHONE.................................916 929-3323
William M Romzick, *Branch Mgr*
Frank Joyce, *Contract Mgr*
EMP: 50
SALES (corp-wide): 12.1B **Publicly Held**
WEB: www.jacobs.com
SIC: 8711 8713 8712 8742 Engineering services; surveying services; architectural services; site location consultant
HQ: Carter & Burgess, Inc.
  777 Main St Ste 2500
  Fort Worth TX 76102
  817 735-6000

(P-25722)
CB&I GOVERNMENT SOLUTIONS INC
18100 Von Karman Ave # 450, Irvine (92612-7197)
PHONE.................................949 261-6441
Richard Fowler, *Branch Mgr*
Patricia Olson, *Manager*
EMP: 63 **Privately Held**
SIC: 8711 1521 1542 Pollution control engineering; single-family housing construction; nonresidential construction
HQ: Cb&I Government Solutions, Inc.
  4171 Essen Ln
  Baton Rouge LA 70809
  225 932-2500

(P-25723)
CB&I GOVERNMENT SOLUTIONS INC
4005 Port Chicago Hwy # 200, Concord (94520-1181)
PHONE.................................925 288-9898
David McMurtry, *Branch Mgr*
Frank Hackett, *Branch Mgr*
Julie Hoover, *Purch Agent*
Patricia Olson, *Manager*
EMP: 181 **Privately Held**
SIC: 8711 8734 8748 Engineering services; testing laboratories; business consulting
HQ: Cb&I Government Solutions, Inc.
  4171 Essen Ln
  Baton Rouge LA 70809
  225 932-2500

(P-25724)
CBS BROADCASTING INC
7800 Beverly Blvd, Los Angeles (90036-2112)
PHONE.................................212 975-3240
Michael Klausman, *Senior VP*
Kingsley Wood, *Software Dev*
Titus Canet, *Foreman/Supr*
Michael Skinner, *Director*
Laura Moss, *Manager*
EMP: 90
SALES (corp-wide): 27.1B **Publicly Held**
SIC: 8711 Engineering services
HQ: Cbs Broadcasting Inc.
  51 W 52nd St
  New York NY 10019
  212 975-4321

(P-25725)
CDI MARINE COMPANY LLC
694 Moss St, Chula Vista (91911-1616)
PHONE.................................619 407-4010
M S Karlovic, *CEO*
Stephen Karlovic, *CEO*
Francesco Anderson, *Manager*
EMP: 50
SALES (corp-wide): 985.4MM **Publicly Held**
SIC: 8711 Engineering services
HQ: Cdi Marine Company, Llc
  4600 Village Ave
  Norfolk VA 23502
  757 763-6666

(P-25726)
CDM SMITH INC
111 Academy Ste 150, Irvine (92617-3053)
PHONE.................................949 752-5452
Steve Brewer, *Manager*
Robin Ijams, *Vice Pres*
Jeffrey Pitchford, *Vice Pres*
R B Chalmers, *Principal*
Bob Huguenard, *Sr Project Mgr*
EMP: 72
SALES (corp-wide): 1.2B **Privately Held**
WEB: www.cdm.com
SIC: 8711 Engineering services
PA: Cdm Smith Inc
  75 State St Ste 701
  Boston MA 02109
  617 452-6000

(P-25727)
CDM SMITH INC
703 Palomar Airport Rd, Carlsbad (92011-1040)
PHONE.................................760 438-7755
Fax: 760 438-7411
Kelly Burn-Roy, *Director*
Paul G Camell, *Exec VP*
Keith London, *Principal*
Charlotte Files, *Admin Asst*
Stephen F Shumaker, *Project Leader*
EMP: 60
SALES (corp-wide): 1.2B **Privately Held**
WEB: www.cdm.com
SIC: 8711 Sanitary engineers
PA: Cdm Smith Inc
  75 State St Ste 701
  Boston MA 02109
  617 452-6000

(P-25728)
CDM SMITH INC
100 Pringle Ave Ste 300, Walnut Creek (94596-3580)
PHONE.................................617 452-6000
Fax: 925 933-4174
Randall Smith, *Manager*
Paul Meyerhofer, *Vice Pres*
B Zeiler, *Design Engr*
Robert Allen, *Project Mgr*
John Mooney, *Technology*
EMP: 80
SALES (corp-wide): 1.2B **Privately Held**
WEB: www.cdm.com
SIC: 8711 Engineering services
PA: Cdm Smith Inc
  75 State St Ste 701
  Boston MA 02109
  617 452-6000

(P-25729)
CE2 KLEINFELDER JV
6140 Stoneridge Mall Rd, Pleasanton (94588-3232)
PHONE.................................925 463-7301
Clyde Wong, *Mng Member*
Edward Kilduff, *CFO*
Celia Robertson, *Controller*
EMP: 99
SQ FT: 300
SALES (est): 4.3MM **Privately Held**
SIC: 8711 8748 Engineering services; energy conservation engineering; systems analysis & engineering consulting services

(P-25730)
CECOS
Also Called: Csfe
3502 Goodspeed St Ste 1, Port Hueneme (93043-4335)
PHONE.................................805 982-5400
Peter Sanders,
EMP: 50
SALES (est): 2.7MM **Privately Held**
WEB: www.cecos.com
SIC: 8711 Civil engineering

(P-25731)
CEM BUILDERS INC
Also Called: Dirtmarket , The
37 S 4th St, Campbell (95008-2943)
PHONE.................................408 395-1490
David Rossi, *CEO*
Lesley Matheson, *President*
Leslie Horton, *CFO*
Nathan Stanley, *Vice Pres*
Rachel Haas, *Admin Asst*

EMP: 50
SQ FT: 3,000
SALES: 2MM **Privately Held**
WEB: www.dirtmarket.com
SIC: 8711 5093 Engineering services; scrap & waste materials

(P-25732)
CH2M HILL INC
2525 Airpark Dr, Redding (96001-2443)
PHONE.................................530 243-5832
Fax: 530 243-1654
Ed Christopherson, *Manager*
Kent Galloway, *Comp Spec*
Barbara Schmitz, *Comp Spec*
Bernice Kidd, *Project Dir*
Bill Fox, *Project Mgr*
EMP: 220
SALES (corp-wide): 5.4B **Privately Held**
SIC: 8711 Consulting engineer
HQ: Ch2m Hill, Inc.
  9191 S Jamaica St
  Englewood CO 80112
  303 771-0900

(P-25733)
CH2M HILL INC
2485 Natomas Park Dr # 600, Sacramento (95833-2975)
PHONE.................................916 920-0300
J Hartley, *Branch Mgr*
Lorene Liebert, *Data Proc Mgr*
EMP: 1200
SALES (corp-wide): 5.4B **Privately Held**
SIC: 8711 Engineering services
HQ: Ch2m Hill, Inc.
  9191 S Jamaica St
  Englewood CO 80112
  303 771-0900

(P-25734)
CH2M HILL INC
155 Grand Ave Ste 800, Oakland (94612-3767)
P.O. Box 12681 (94604-2681)
PHONE.................................510 604-4144
Robert Keyes, *Manager*
Ana Demorest, *Project Mgr*
Andrea Gardner, *Project Mgr*
Michael Walkowiak, *Project Mgr*
David Larter, *Human Resources*
EMP: 200
SALES (corp-wide): 5.4B **Privately Held**
SIC: 8711 Consulting engineer; civil engineering
HQ: Ch2m Hill, Inc.
  9191 S Jamaica St
  Englewood CO 80112
  303 771-0900

(P-25735)
CHADUXTT JV
1230 Columbia St Ste 1000, San Diego (92101-8588)
PHONE.................................619 525-7188
Michael J Wanta, *President*
Ed Philemonof, *Principal*
EMP: 83
SALES (est): 3.1MM **Privately Held**
SIC: 8711 Engineering services

(P-25736)
CHEVRON ENERGY TECHNOLOGY CO (HQ)
100 Chevron Way, Richmond (94801-2016)
PHONE.................................510 242-5059
R William Potter, *Principal*
Andrew Sorley, *Engineer*
EMP: 78
SALES (est): 24.4MM
SALES (corp-wide): 138.4B **Publicly Held**
WEB: www.chevrontexaco.com
SIC: 8711 Engineering services
PA: Chevron Corporation
  6001 Bollinger Canyon Rd
  San Ramon CA 94583
  925 842-1000

(P-25737)
CIERRA WIRELESS
2738 Loker Ave W Ste A, Carlsbad (92010-6629)
PHONE.................................760 476-8700
Jason Collinhower, *President*

PRODUCTS & SERVICES SECTION
8711 - Engineering Services County (P-25760)

Tracy Bolognese, *Finance*
EMP: 110
SALES (est): 4.2MM **Privately Held**
WEB: www.sierrawireless.com
SIC: 8711 4813 Engineering services;

(P-25738)
CITY OF DALY CITY
Also Called: Public Works Engineering Div
333 90th St Fl 1, Daly City (94015-1808)
PHONE.................................650 991-8064
Fax: 650 991-8243
John Fuller, *Director*
Corum Chan, *Purch Agent*
Bonnie Lippi, *Clerk*
EMP: 70 **Privately Held**
WEB: www.dalycity.org
SIC: 8711 9111 Engineering services; mayors' offices
PA: City Of Daly City
333 90th St
Daly City CA 94015
650 991-8000

(P-25739)
CITY OF GLENDALE
Also Called: Engineering Public Works
633 E Broadway Ste 205, Glendale (91206-4310)
PHONE.................................818 548-3945
Fax: 818 242-7087
Lou Le Blanc, *Director*
EMP: 60 **Privately Held**
WEB: www.glendaleca.com
SIC: 8711 9511 Engineering services; air, water & solid waste management;
PA: City Of Glendale
141 N Glendale Ave Fl 2
Glendale CA 91206
818 548-2085

(P-25740)
CITY OF LOS ANGELES
Also Called: Public Works Dept
600 S Spring St Unit 200, Los Angeles (90014-1979)
PHONE.................................213 978-0259
Deborah Weignard, *Branch Mgr*
EMP: 1000 **Privately Held**
WEB: www.lacity.org
SIC: 8711 9532 Mechanical engineering; electrical or electronic engineering; urban & community development;
PA: City Of Los Angeles
200 N Spring St Ste 303
Los Angeles CA 90012
213 978-0600

(P-25741)
CITY OF LOS ANGELES
6262 Van Nuys Blvd # 451, Van Nuys (91401-2793)
PHONE.................................818 756-8022
Fax: 818 374-3310
Michael Kantor, *Branch Mgr*
Claudia Rodriguez, *Bd of Directors*
EMP: 508 **Privately Held**
WEB: www.lacity.org
SIC: 8711 9224 Fire protection engineering; fire protection
PA: City Of Los Angeles
200 N Spring St Ste 303
Los Angeles CA 90012
213 978-0600

(P-25742)
CITY OF SAN DIEGO
9485 Aero Dr, San Diego (92123-1801)
PHONE.................................858 627-3210
Hossein Ruhi, *Branch Mgr*
EMP: 250 **Privately Held**
SIC: 8711 Engineering services
PA: City Of San Diego
202 C St
San Diego CA 92101
619 236-6330

(P-25743)
CITY OF VACAVILLE
Also Called: Public Works Office
650 Merchant St, Vacaville (95688-6992)
PHONE............................,707 449-5170
Fax: 707 449-5170
Dale Pfeiffer, *Manager*
Paul Hom, *Director*
EMP: 400 **Privately Held**

WEB: www.lenaugustine.com
SIC: 8711 Engineering services
PA: City Of Vacaville
650 Merchant St
Vacaville CA 95688
707 449-5100

(P-25744)
CITY OF WOODLAND
Also Called: Public Works Department
42929 County Road 24, Woodland (95776-9111)
PHONE.................................530 661-5961
Gary Wagner, *Director*
EMP: 75 **Privately Held**
WEB: www.ci.woodland.ca.us
SIC: 8711 8748 Engineering services; city planning
PA: City Of Woodland
300 1st St
Woodland CA 95695
530 661-5830

(P-25745)
CLARK RICHARDSON AND BISKUP
75 E Santa Clara St # 350, San Jose (95113-1827)
PHONE.................................408 931-6030
Mark Von Stwolinski, *Branch Mgr*
EMP: 51
SALES (corp-wide): 123.1MM **Privately Held**
SIC: 8711 Consulting engineer
PA: Clark, Richardson And Biskup Consulting Engineers, Inc.
1251 Nw Briarcliff Pkwy # 500
Kansas City MO 64116
816 880-9800

(P-25746)
CLDWLL/VRSAR A BROWN JINT VNTR
10540 White Rock Rd, Rancho Cordova (95670-6088)
PHONE.................................916 444-0123
Thomas Rowe, *Partner*
Patty McElroy, *Accounting Mgr*
EMP: 200 **EST:** 2012
SALES (est): 4.9MM **Privately Held**
SIC: 8711 Engineering services

(P-25747)
COMPREHENSIVE ENVIRO
1615 Murray Canyon Rd, San Diego (92108-4314)
PHONE.................................619 294-9400
Steve Briginar, *Director*
EMP: 50
SALES (est): 1.5MM **Privately Held**
SIC: 8711 Engineering services

(P-25748)
CONNEXSYS ENGINEERING INC
3075 Research Dr, Richmond (94806-5206)
PHONE.................................510 243-2050
John Mentil, *CEO*
Leonard George, *President*
Mark Daughtry, *Admin Sec*
Gina Baker, *Admin Asst*
Carol Avila, *Administration*
EMP: 100
SQ FT: 10,000
SALES (est): 14.3MM **Privately Held**
WEB: www.connexsysinc.com
SIC: 8711 Consulting engineer

(P-25749)
CONSTRUCTION TSTG & ENGRG INC (PA)
1441 Montiel Rd Ste 115, Escondido (92026-2239)
PHONE.................................760 746-4955
Fax: 760 746-9806
Thomas Gaeto, *CEO*
Rodney Ballard, *Vice Pres*
Greg Guy, *Sales Executive*
EMP: 60
SQ FT: 4,800
SALES (est): 18.3MM **Privately Held**
SIC: 8711 Construction & civil engineering

(P-25750)
CONTINENTAL GRAPHICS CORP
Also Called: Continental Datagraphics
2401 E Wardlow Rd, Long Beach (90807-5309)
PHONE.................................714 503-4200
Steve Meade, *Manager*
James Mills, *CFO*
Michael Sandifer, *Exec VP*
Jose Madrid, *Vice Pres*
Warren Smith, *Vice Pres*
EMP: 1200
SALES (corp-wide): 96.1B **Publicly Held**
WEB: www.cdgnow.com
SIC: 8711 Engineering services
HQ: Continental Graphics Corporation
4060 N Lakewood Blvd
Long Beach CA 90808
714 503-4200

(P-25751)
CONTROL POINT CORPORATION (PA)
110 Castilian Dr Ste 200, Goleta (93117-3028)
PHONE.................................805 685-6390
Fax: 805 882-1883
Edward Marcarelli, *President*
Jonathan Dorny, *Exec VP*
Rick Wyrembelski, *Vice Pres*
Scott G Grant, *General Mgr*
Stephen Saputo, *Software Engr*
EMP: 50
SALES (est): 12MM **Privately Held**
WEB: www.control-pt.com
SIC: 8711 Consulting engineer

(P-25752)
COOPER VALI & ASSOCIATES INC (PA)
2000 Powell St Ste 500, Emeryville (94608-1842)
PHONE.................................510 446-8301
Fax: 510 215-0760
Gary Bedey, *CEO*
Agnes Weber, *President*
Marian Ross, *CFO*
Gary Baker, *Exec VP*
Connie Fremier, *Exec VP*
EMP: 80
SQ FT: 3,000
SALES (est): 28.7MM **Privately Held**
SIC: 8711 Engineering services

(P-25753)
CORA CONSTRUCTORS INC
Also Called: General Contractor
75140 Saint Charles Pl A, Palm Desert (92211-9044)
PHONE.................................760 674-3201
Fax: 760 674-3202
Dennis Stockton, *CEO*
Lynne Cazeaulp, *Office Mgr*
Penny Ham, *Manager*
Lyle Schultz, *Manager*
EMP: 50
SQ FT: 2,500
SALES (est): 9.9MM **Privately Held**
WEB: www.coraconstructors.com
SIC: 8711 Engineering services

(P-25754)
COUNTY ENGINEERS ASSN CAL
120 Round Ct, Petaluma (94952-4720)
PHONE.................................707 762-3492
Phil Demery, *President*
Mehdi Sadji, *Treasurer*
EMP: 58
SALES: 353.7K **Privately Held**
SIC: 8711 Engineering services

(P-25755)
COUNTY OF LOS ANGELES
Also Called: Engineering Division
44933 Fern Ave, Lancaster (93534-2461)
PHONE.................................661 723-6088
Bert Perry, *Branch Mgr*
Jonathan Dang, *Engineer*
EMP: 130 **Privately Held**
WEB: www.co.la.ca.us
SIC: 8711 9111 Engineering services; executive offices

PA: County Of Los Angeles
500 W Temple St Ste 375
Los Angeles CA 90012
213 974-1101

(P-25756)
COUNTY OF LOS ANGELES
Public Works, Dept of
14747 Ramona Blvd, Baldwin Park (91706-3435)
PHONE.................................626 337-1277
William Wolfer, *Branch Mgr*
Dennis Slavin, *Manager*
EMP: 130 **Privately Held**
WEB: www.co.la.ca.us
SIC: 8711 9199 Engineering services; general government administration;
PA: County Of Los Angeles
500 W Temple St Ste 375
Los Angeles CA 90012
213 974-1101

(P-25757)
COUNTY OF MARIN
Also Called: Department of Public Works
1600 Los Gamos Dr Ste 200, San Rafael (94903-1807)
P.O. Box 4186 (94913-4186)
PHONE.................................415 499-7877
Fax: 415 499-3724
Mehdi Sadjadi, *Director*
Allan Kristal, *Technical Mgr*
Laura Armor, *Human Res Dir*
EMP: 200 **Privately Held**
SIC: 8711 1611 7349 6552 Civil engineering; highway & street construction; building maintenance services; subdividers & developers; automotive & apparel trimmings
PA: County Of Marin
1600 Los Gamos Dr Ste 200
San Rafael CA 94903
415 473-6358

(P-25758)
COUNTY OF SAN LUIS OBISPO
Also Called: County Government
Government Center Rm 207, San Luis Obispo (93408-0001)
PHONE.................................805 781-5258
Fax: 805 781-1229
Tim Nanson, *Branch Mgr*
EMP: 170 **Privately Held**
SIC: 8711 Engineering services
PA: County Of San Luis Obispo
Government Center Rm. 300
San Luis Obispo CA 93408
805 781-5040

(P-25759)
CURTISS-WRIGHT CONTROLS
28965 Avenue Penn, Santa Clarita (91355-4185)
PHONE.................................661 257-4430
Val Zarov, *Branch Mgr*
Marc O'Casal, *Asst Treas*
EMP: 109
SALES (corp-wide): 2.2B **Publicly Held**
SIC: 8711 Engineering services
HQ: Curtiss-Wright Controls Electronic Systems, Inc.
28965 Avenue Penn
Santa Clarita CA 91355
661 702-1494

(P-25760)
CURTISS-WRIGHT CONTROLS (DH)
28965 Avenue Penn, Santa Clarita (91355-4185)
PHONE.................................661 702-1494
Thomas P Quinly, *CEO*
David Dietz, *President*
Jerri Charbonneau, *CTO*
Paul Bubendorf, *Info Tech Mgr*
Paul Dubendorf, *Info Tech Mgr*
EMP: 172
SQ FT: 18,700
SALES (est): 52MM
SALES (corp-wide): 2.2B **Publicly Held**
WEB: www.cwcembedded.com
SIC: 8711 8731 3769 3625 Engineering services; commercial physical research; guided missile & space vehicle parts & auxiliary equipment; relays & industrial controls

8711 - Engineering Services County (P-25761)

HQ: Curtiss-Wright Controls, Inc.
15801 Brixham Hill Ave # 200
Charlotte NC 28277
704 869-4600

(P-25761)
D & K ENGINEERING
Also Called: D&K Engineering
15890 Bernardo Center Dr, San Diego (92127-2320)
PHONE..................858 451-8999
Fax: 858 451-9989
Scott M Dennis, *CEO*
Alex Kunczynski, *President*
Jodi Zebenbergen, *CFO*
Jody Zevenbergen, *CFO*
Bruce Pinkston, *Officer*
▲ EMP: 520
SQ FT: 60,000
SALES (est): 81.2MM **Privately Held**
WEB: www.dkengineering.com
SIC: **8711** 3824 Acoustical engineering; mechanical & electromechanical counters & devices

(P-25762)
D A WOOD CONSTRUCTION INC
601 Albers Rd, Modesto (95357-1015)
P.O. Box 1810, Empire (95319-1810)
PHONE..................209 491-4970
Danny Wood, *President*
Kristine Wood, *Admin Sec*
EMP: 56
SQ FT: 960
SALES (est): 9.6MM **Privately Held**
WEB: www.dawoodinc.com
SIC: **8711** Construction & civil engineering

(P-25763)
DAVID EVANS AND ASSOCIATES INC
4200 Concours Ste 200, Ontario (91764-7976)
PHONE..................909 481-5750
Cliff Simental, *Branch Mgr*
Karen Padova, *Manager*
EMP: 50
SALES (corp-wide): 155.5MM **Privately Held**
WEB: www.deainc.com
SIC: **8711** Engineering services
PA: David Evans And Associates, Inc.
2100 Sw River Pkwy
Portland OR 97201
503 223-6663

(P-25764)
DAVID EVANS ENTERPRISES INC
201 S Figueroa St Ste 240, Los Angeles (90012-2543)
PHONE..................213 337-3680
EMP: 704
SALES (corp-wide): 21MM **Privately Held**
SIC: **8711** 7389 Consulting engineer; design services
PA: David Evans Enterprises, Inc.
2100 Sw River Pkwy
Portland OR 97201
503 223-6663

(P-25765)
DCS CORPORATION
7510 Hazard Center Dr, San Diego (92108-4521)
PHONE..................619 278-3600
Fax: 619 278-3699
EMP: 176
SALES (corp-wide): 327.2MM **Privately Held**
SIC: **8711** Engineering services
PA: Dcs Corporation
6909 Metro Park Dr # 500
Alexandria VA 22310
571 227-6000

(P-25766)
DEGENKOLB ENGINEERS (PA)
235 Montgomery St Ste 500, San Francisco (94104-2908)
PHONE..................415 392-6952
Stacy Bartoletti, *CEO*
Chris Poland, *Ch of Bd*
Robert Beggs, *CFO*
Thomas Diblasi, *Vice Pres*

Jay Love, *Vice Pres*
EMP: 66
SQ FT: 22,800
SALES (est): 38.6MM **Privately Held**
WEB: www.degenkolb.com
SIC: **8711** Structural engineering

(P-25767)
DESIGNWORKS/USA INC (HQ)
2201 Corporate Center Dr, Newbury Park (91320-1421)
PHONE..................805 499-9590
Fax: 805 499-9650
Laurenz Schaffer, *President*
Alexandra McGill, *COO*
Alissa Kloner, *Associate Dir*
Johannes Lampela, *Creative Dir*
Evelyn Gonzales, *Executive Asst*
EMP: 67 EST: 1971
SQ FT: 78,000
SALES (est): 16.8MM
SALES (corp-wide): 99B **Privately Held**
WEB: www.designworksusa.com
SIC: **8711** Designing: ship, boat, machine & product
PA: Bayerische Motoren Werke Ag
Petuelring 130
Munchen 80788
893 820-

(P-25768)
DEVELOPMENT RESOURCE CONS INC (PA)
160 S Old Springs Rd # 210, Anaheim (92808-1226)
PHONE..................714 685-6860
Lawrence Gates, *President*
Lena Starbird, *Info Tech Mgr*
Wayne Pena, *Project Mgr*
Gregory Schlarbaum, *Project Mgr*
Inocencio A Briones, *Project Engr*
EMP: 90
SQ FT: 12,000
SALES (est): 11.7MM **Privately Held**
SIC: **8711** Engineering services

(P-25769)
DEX CORPORATION
Also Called: Data Exchange
3600 Via Pescador, Camarillo (93012-5051)
PHONE..................805 388-1711
◆ EMP: 150
SALES (est): 4.8MM **Privately Held**
SIC: **8711** 5065 Engineering services; electronic parts

(P-25770)
DIVERSIFIED PRJ SVCS INTL INC (PA)
5351 Olive Dr Ste 100, Bakersfield (93308-2921)
PHONE..................661 371-2800
Robert Chambers, *President*
Stefanie Frei, *Admin Asst*
Ryan Gardea, *Admin Asst*
Jenna Paculba, *Admin Asst*
Lindsey Richter, *Admin Asst*
EMP: 63
SALES (est): 17.6MM **Privately Held**
SIC: **8711** Engineering services

(P-25771)
DMS FACILITY SERVICES LLC
5735 Krny Vlla Rd Ste 108, San Diego (92123)
PHONE..................858 560-4191
John Harris, *Branch Mgr*
EMP: 150
SALES (corp-wide): 43.8MM **Privately Held**
WEB: www.dmsfacilityservices.com
SIC: **8711** 7349 0781 Engineering services; janitorial service, contract basis; landscape services
PA: Dms Facility Services, Llc
1040 Arroyo Dr
South Pasadena CA 91030
626 305-8500

(P-25772)
DOKKEN ENGINEERING (PA)
110 Blue Ravine Rd # 200, Folsom (95630-4713)
PHONE..................916 858-0642
Fax: 916 858-0643

Richard Dokken, *CEO*
Richard Liptak, *President*
Bradley Dokken, *CFO*
Cathy Chan, *Executive*
Lynne Castillo, *Executive Asst*
EMP: 70
SQ FT: 12,931
SALES (est): 21.1MM **Privately Held**
WEB: www.dokkenengineering.com
SIC: **8711** 8741 Construction & civil engineering; construction management

(P-25773)
DUDEK (PA)
605 3rd St, Encinitas (92024-3513)
PHONE..................760 942-5147
Frank J Dudek, *Ch of Bd*
Dave Carter, *CFO*
June Collins, *Vice Pres*
Chuck Duffy, *General Mgr*
Nathan Sweetman, *Administration*
EMP: 100 EST: 1980
SQ FT: 50,000
SALES (est): 47.6MM **Privately Held**
SIC: **8711** Civil engineering

(P-25774)
DZYNE TECHNOLOGIES INC
11 Vanderbilt, Irvine (92618-2011)
PHONE..................703 291-6663
Darrell Gillette, *CEO*
David Sammons, *CFO*
Craig Werley, *Research*
EMP: 50 EST: 2013
SALES (est): 5.3MM **Privately Held**
SIC: **8711** Mechanical engineering; aviation &/or aeronautical engineering

(P-25775)
E2 CONSULTING ENGINEERS INC
1900 Powell St Ste 250, Emeryville (94608-1807)
PHONE..................510 652-1164
Fax: 510 652-5604
Matthew Rindiera, *Office Mgr*
Aurora Abbott, *Project Mgr*
Dominic Charles, *Engineer*
Rick Sugarek, *Consultant*
EMP: 300
SALES (corp-wide): 40MM **Privately Held**
SIC: **8711** Consulting engineer
PA: E2 Consulting Engineers, Inc.
450 E 17th Ave Unit 200
Denver CO 80203
303 232-9800

(P-25776)
E2 MANAGETECH INC (PA)
5001 Airport Plaza Dr # 260, Long Beach (90815-1369)
PHONE..................562 740-1060
Julie Reynolds, *CFO*
Daryl Hernandez, *Vice Pres*
Jennifer Conard, *Office Mgr*
Richard Mock, *Planning*
David Low, *Technical Mgr*
EMP: 51
SALES (est): 14.8MM **Privately Held**
SIC: **8711** 8741 Engineering services; management services

(P-25777)
EARTH SYSTEMS SOUTHWEST (HQ)
79811 Country Club Dr B, Bermuda Dunes (92203-1290)
PHONE..................760 345-1588
Fax: 760 348-7315
Mark Spykerman, *President*
Jerol Brown, *Corp Secy*
Scot Stormo, *Senior VP*
Kevin Paul, *Vice Pres*
Ji Shin, *Admin Sec*
EMP: 59 EST: 1998
SQ FT: 6,750
SALES: 3.6MM
SALES (corp-wide): 16.3MM **Privately Held**
WEB: www.earthsystems.com
SIC: **8711** Engineering services
PA: Earth Systems, Inc.
895 Aerovista Pl Ste 102
San Luis Obispo CA 93401
805 781-0112

(P-25778)
EDO LLC
Edo Technical Svcs Operations
3500 Willow Ln, Thousand Oaks (91361-4921)
PHONE..................914 641-2000
Thomas J Gardiner, *General Mgr*
Louis Stein, *Project Mgr*
David Davis, *Controller*
EMP: 140
SALES (corp-wide): 7.4B **Publicly Held**
WEB: www.nycedo.com
SIC: **8711** 3728 Engineering services; aircraft training equipment
HQ: Edo Llc
1500 New Horizons Blvd
Amityville NY 11701
631 630-4000

(P-25779)
EDSI
Also Called: E D S I
504 E Alvarado St Ste 109, Fallbrook (92028-2363)
PHONE..................760 728-1899
Fax: 760 723-4981
Dan Allegro, *Branch Mgr*
Michael Rodriguez, *Info Tech Mgr*
Jan Corley, *Technology*
Frances Raymond, *Purch Agent*
Sandy Koester, *Manager*
EMP: 50
SQ FT: 4,000
SALES (corp-wide): 15.9MM **Privately Held**
SIC: **8711** Engineering services
PA: Edsi
1095 Montecito Dr
Corona CA 92879
951 272-8689

(P-25780)
EFS WEST
28472 Constellation Rd, Valencia (91355-5081)
PHONE..................661 705-8200
Arthur Babcock, *CEO*
Robert Golden, *President*
Dante Jumanan, *Vice Pres*
Tom Soper, *Vice Pres*
Ines Parr, *Safety Mgr*
EMP: 50
SQ FT: 41,000
SALES (est): 10.1MM **Privately Held**
SIC: **8711** Engineering services

(P-25781)
EICHLEAY ENGINEERS INC CAL
3780 Kilroy Airport Way # 440, Long Beach (90806-2498)
PHONE..................562 256-8600
Lori M Lofstrom, *Branch Mgr*
EMP: 150
SALES (corp-wide): 47.7MM **Privately Held**
SIC: **8711** Consulting engineer
PA: Eichleay Inc
1390 Willow Pass Rd # 600
Concord CA 94520
925 689-7000

(P-25782)
EICHLEAY INC (PA)
1390 Willow Pass Rd # 600, Concord (94520-5200)
PHONE..................925 689-7000
Fax: 925 689-7006
George F Eichleay Jr, *President*
Theodore Nelson, *Vice Pres*
Todd Hancock, *Project Dir*
Steven S Chan, *Project Engr*
Chad Dupuis, *Electrical Engi*
EMP: 150
SQ FT: 17,000
SALES (est): 47.7MM **Privately Held**
WEB: www.eichleay.com
SIC: **8711** Consulting engineer

(P-25783)
ELECTROSONIC INC (DH)
3320 N San Fernando Blvd, Burbank (91504-2530)
PHONE..................818 333-3600
Fax: 818 566-4923
James Bowie, *President*
Scott Meyer, *CFO*

PRODUCTS & SERVICES SECTION
8711 - Engineering Services County (P-25807)

David Mitchell, *Admin Sec*
Jim Maddux, *IT/INT Sup*
Dan Lauf, *Project Engr*
EMP: 70
SALES (est): 55.1MM
SALES (corp-wide): 101.6MM **Privately Held**
WEB: www.mediasonic.com
SIC: 8711 7359 7812 Engineering services; audio-visual equipment & supply rental; audio-visual program production
HQ: Electrosonic Group Oy Ab
Kalevankatu 4
Helsinki 00100
956 549-301

(P-25784)
ELITE ENGINEERING SERVICES INC
1641-1645 Reynolds, Irvine (92614)
PHONE..........................949 536-7199
Dustin Tillman, *CEO*
EMP: 50
SALES (est): 3MM **Privately Held**
SIC: 8711 Engineering services

(P-25785)
EMERY SMITH LABORATORIES INC
Also Called: Inspection and Testing
1195 N Tustin Ave, Anaheim (92807-1736)
PHONE..........................714 238-6133
Mark Lastufka, *Manager*
Rob Greeley, *Branch Mgr*
EMP: 99
SALES (est): 5.3MM **Privately Held**
SIC: 8711 8071 Engineering services; testing laboratories

(P-25786)
ENCORE SEMI INC
9444 Waples St Ste 150, San Diego (92121-2941)
PHONE..........................858 225-4993
Olivier Lauvray, *President*
EMP: 67
SALES: 15.3MM **Privately Held**
SIC: 8711 Electrical or electronic engineering

(P-25787)
ENERTIS SOLAR INC
1750 Montgomery St # 127, San Francisco (94111-1000)
PHONE..........................415 400-5271
Jose Galindo, *President*
Inaki Herrero, *General Mgr*
EMP: 50
SALES (est): 3MM **Privately Held**
SIC: 8711 Engineering services

(P-25788)
ENGILITY CORPORATION
Also Called: Tasc
1843 Hotel Cir S, San Diego (92108-3320)
PHONE..........................703 708-1400
Victoria Nguyen, *Administration*
EMP: 60
SALES (est): 1.1MM **Privately Held**
SIC: 8711 Engineering services

(P-25789)
ENGILITY LLC
2001 Solar Dr Ste 250, Oxnard (93036-2648)
PHONE..........................805 383-7551
Victoria Nguyen, *Administration*
EMP: 86
SALES (est): 4.8MM **Privately Held**
SIC: 8711 Engineering services

(P-25790)
ENGILITY LLC
Also Called: Command & Control Systems
7580 Metro Dr Ste 207, San Diego (92108)
PHONE..........................858 552-9500
Mike Lawson, *Branch Mgr*
Mike Harbeck, *Data Proc Exec*
EMP: 202
SALES (corp-wide): 2B **Publicly Held**
SIC: 8711 Engineering services
HQ: Engility Llc
4803 Stonecroft Blvd
Chantilly VA 20151
703 708-1400

(P-25791)
ENGILITY LLC
Also Called: Titan Pulse Sciences Division
2700 Merced St, San Leandro (94577-5602)
PHONE..........................510 357-4610
David Price, *Manager*
EMP: 125
SALES (corp-wide): 2B **Publicly Held**
SIC: 8711 Engineering services
HQ: Engility Llc
4803 Stonecroft Blvd
Chantilly VA 20151
703 708-1400

(P-25792)
ENGILITY LLC
200 W Los Angeles Ave, Simi Valley (93065-1650)
PHONE..........................703 664-6274
Sewanee Johnson, *Branch Mgr*
Anthony Smeraglinolo, *CEO*
Michael J Alber, *CFO*
Edward P Boykin, *Officer*
Darryll J Pines, *Officer*
EMP: 6000
SALES (corp-wide): 2B **Publicly Held**
SIC: 8711 Engineering services
HQ: Engility Llc
4803 Stonecroft Blvd
Chantilly VA 20151
703 708-1400

(P-25793)
ENGINEERING & TSTG SVCS CORP
7757 Bell Rd, Windsor (95492-8519)
PHONE..........................707 838-1113
Fax: 707 838-1114
Gary M Cappa, *CEO*
EMP: 304
SALES (corp-wide): 3.3MM **Privately Held**
SIC: 8711 Consulting engineer
PA: Engineering & Testing Services Corporation
2001 Crow Canyon Rd # 110
San Ramon CA 94583
925 314-7100

(P-25794)
ENGINRING SFTWR SYS SLTONS INC (PA)
Also Called: E S 3
550 W C St Ste 1630, San Diego (92101-3569)
PHONE..........................619 338-0380
Fax: 619 338-0324
Teri Sgammato, *President*
Doug Wiser, *COO*
Chuck Dahms, *CFO*
Jon Robertson, *Creative Dir*
Clint Forrest, *Principal*
EMP: 80
SQ FT: 8,000
SALES (est): 44.8MM **Privately Held**
WEB: www.es3inc.com
SIC: 8711 Engineering services

(P-25795)
ENGLEKIRK INSTITUTIONAL INC (PA)
888 S Figueroa St Ste 180, Los Angeles (90017-5307)
PHONE..........................323 733-2640
Tom Sabol, *President*
Bente Martinez, *Bookkeeper*
EMP: 50
SQ FT: 12,000
SALES (est): 6.9MM **Privately Held**
SIC: 8711 Engineering services

(P-25796)
ENGLEKIRK STRUCTURAL ENGINEERS (PA)
888 S Figueroa St # 1800, Los Angeles (90017-5326)
PHONE..........................323 733-6673
Tom Sabol, *President*
Christopher Rosien, *CFO*
Maria Bravo, *Design Engr*
Carlos Gonzalez, *Design Engr*
Ed Shiosaki, *Opers Mgr*
EMP: 50

SALES (est): 8.1MM **Privately Held**
SIC: 8711 Structural engineering

(P-25797)
ENVIRONMENTAL CHEMICAL CORP (PA)
Also Called: Ecc
1240 Bayshore Hwy, Burlingame (94010-1805)
PHONE..........................650 347-1555
Fax: 650 347-4571
Manjiv Vohra, *President*
Paul Sabharwal, *Shareholder*
Steve Anderson, *CFO*
Tom Delmastro, *Treasurer*
Terry Kohl, *Vice Pres*
EMP: 75
SQ FT: 21,000
SALES (est): 190.2MM **Privately Held**
WEB: www.ecc.net
SIC: 8711 1542 8744 Engineering services; commercial & office building contractors;

(P-25798)
EPRISOLUTIONS INC
Also Called: Epri Csg
3412 Hillview Ave, Palo Alto (94304-1395)
PHONE..........................650 855-8900
Fax: 650 855-1008
Philip Curtis, *President*
Ric Rudman, *CFO*
Roger Ailshie, *Treasurer*
Walter Bak, *Vice Pres*
Mark Graham, *Administration*
EMP: 80
SQ FT: 20,000
SALES (est): 9.1MM **Privately Held**
WEB: www.eprictcenter.com
SIC: 8711 Engineering services

(P-25799)
EPSILON MISSION SOLUTIONS INC
9242 Lightwave Ave # 100, San Diego (92123-6402)
PHONE..........................619 702-1700
Alan Stewart, *CFO*
Robin Nordberg, *Vice Pres*
EMP: 99
SALES (est): 4.7MM **Privately Held**
SIC: 8711 Engineering services

(P-25800)
EPSILON SYSTEMS SOLUTIONS INC
Also Called: Rugged Engineered Pdts Sector
5482 Complex St Ste 109, San Diego (92123-1125)
PHONE..........................619 702-1700
Roy Erickson, *Branch Mgr*
Lauren Eschborn, *Graphic Designe*
EMP: 115
SALES (corp-wide): 110MM **Privately Held**
SIC: 8711 Engineering services
PA: Epsilon Systems Solutions, Inc.
9242 Lightwave Ave # 100
San Diego CA 92123
619 702-1700

(P-25801)
EPSILON SYSTEMS SOLUTIONS INC (PA)
9242 Lightwave Ave # 100, San Diego (92123-6402)
PHONE..........................619 702-1700
Fax: 619 702-1711
Bryan Min, *CEO*
Stuart Teshima, *CFO*
Ralph Staples, *Senior VP*
Richard Benedetto, *Vice Pres*
Jim Blasko, *Vice Pres*
EMP: 100
SQ FT: 16,000
SALES: 110MM **Privately Held**
WEB: www.epsilonsystems.com
SIC: 8711 Engineering services

(P-25802)
ERM-WEST INC (DH)
Also Called: ENVIRONMENTAL RESOURCES MANAGEMENT
1277 Treat Blvd Ste 500, Walnut Creek (94597-7989)
PHONE..........................925 946-0455
Jonathan Beevers, *President*
Paul Douglass, *Managing Prtnr*
Josie Rosidi, *CFO*
Cindy Buitrago, *Treasurer*
Rita Harvey, *Corp Secy*
EMP: 72
SQ FT: 19,455
SALES: 120.9MM
SALES (corp-wide): 521.3K **Privately Held**
SIC: 8711 8742 Consulting engineer; management consulting services
HQ: Erm North America, Inc.
75 Valley Stream Pkwy
Malvern PA 19355
484 913-0300

(P-25803)
ES ENGINEERING INC
1036 W Taft Ave, Orange (92865-4121)
PHONE..........................714 919-6500
Niu Jinghui, *President*
Marla Lunsford, *Administration*
Kevin O'Malley, *Manager*
EMP: 60
SQ FT: 2,300
SALES: 25MM **Privately Held**
SIC: 8711 Acoustical engineering

(P-25804)
EXP US SERVICES INC
5670 Oberlin Dr, San Diego (92121-1721)
PHONE..........................858 597-0555
Paul Gibson, *Branch Mgr*
EMP: 70
SALES (corp-wide): 478MM **Privately Held**
SIC: 8711 Consulting engineer
HQ: Exp U.S. Services Inc.
205 N Mich Aveste 3600
Chicago IL 60601
312 616-0000

(P-25805)
EXPONENT INC (PA)
149 Commonwealth Dr, Menlo Park (94025-1133)
PHONE..........................650 326-9400
Toll Free:..........................888 -
Paul R Johnston, *President*
Michael R Gaulke, *Ch of Bd*
Catherine Corrigan, *President*
Paul Johnston, *CEO*
Richard L Schlenker Jr, *CFO*
EMP: 118
SQ FT: 153,738
SALES: 304.7MM **Publicly Held**
SIC: 8711 8742 8999 Consulting engineer; management consulting services; scientific consulting

(P-25806)
FATA TRAVEL
1040 Iowa Ave Ste 100, Riverside (92507-2106)
PHONE..........................951 328-0200
Anthony Choviano, *President*
EMP: 50
SALES (est): 967.3K **Privately Held**
WEB: www.fatahunter.com
SIC: 8711 Engineering services
HQ: Danieli Fata Hunter, Inc.
1040 Iowa Ave Ste 100
Riverside CA 92507
951 328-0200

(P-25807)
FEHR & PEERS (PA)
100 Pringle Ave Ste 600, Walnut Creek (94596-3582)
PHONE..........................925 977-3200
Fax: 925 933-8007
Matthew Henry, *CEO*
Marion Donnelly, *President*
Steven Brown, *Vice Pres*
Alan Telford, *Vice Pres*
Mary Garcia, *Admin Asst*
EMP: 60
SQ FT: 16,000

8711 - Engineering Services County (P-25808)

SALES (est): 52.6MM **Privately Held**
SIC: 8711 Engineering services

(P-25808)
FICCADENTI & WAGGONER CONSUL (PA)
16969 Von Karman Ave # 240, Irvine (92606-4944)
PHONE.................................949 474-0502
Seb Ficcadenti, *President*
Michael Waggoner, *Vice Pres*
Jeff Kersh, *Project Engr*
Rui Kuroiwa, *Project Engr*
Tom Waggoner, *Project Engr*
EMP: 52
SALES (est): 8.4MM **Privately Held**
WEB: www.fwcse.com
SIC: 8711 Structural engineering

(P-25809)
FIRE SAFE SYSTEMS INC
1312 Kingsdale Ave, Redondo Beach (90278-3926)
PHONE.................................310 542-0585
Michael Moller, *CEO*
Joyce Moller, *President*
Sandra Marquez, *Office Mgr*
Mark Brancato, *Supervisor*
EMP: 60
SQ FT: 3,000
SALES (est): 10.6MM **Privately Held**
WEB: www.firesafesystems.com
SIC: 8711 Fire protection engineering

(P-25810)
FLINTCO PACIFIC INC
401 Derek Pl, Roseville (95678-7153)
PHONE.................................916 757-1000
John R Bates, *CEO*
David P Parkes, *President*
Craig Smart, *Administration*
EMP: 80
SALES (est): 9.9MM
SALES (corp-wide): 1.8B **Privately Held**
SIC: 8711 Building construction consultant
HQ: Flintco, Llc
1624 W 21st St
Tulsa OK 74107
918 587-8451

(P-25811)
FLUOR CORPORATION
Also Called: Trs Staffing Solutions
3 Polaris Way, Aliso Viejo (92656-5338)
PHONE.................................949 349-2000
Tim Kirk, *Principal*
Terry Gohde, *Executive*
David Parker, *Exec Dir*
Marcel Vliegenthart, *Branch Mgr*
Maryann Mayshaw, *Executive Asst*
EMP: 99
SALES (corp-wide): 18.1B **Publicly Held**
SIC: 8711 7363 Engineering services; help supply services
PA: Fluor Corporation
6700 Las Colinas Blvd
Irving TX 75039
469 398-7000

(P-25812)
FLUOR ENTERPRISES INC
5600 Cottle Rd, San Jose (95123-3696)
PHONE.................................408 256-0853
Barry Subotkin, *Branch Mgr*
EMP: 60
SALES (corp-wide): 18.1B **Publicly Held**
SIC: 8711 1799 Building construction consultant; decontamination services
HQ: Fluor Enterprises, Inc.
6700 Las Colinas Blvd
Irving TX 75039
469 398-7000

(P-25813)
FLUOR ENTERPRISES INC
9701 Jeronimo Rd, Irvine (92618-2076)
PHONE.................................949 349-2000
Fax: 949 609-9818
Philip J Carroll Jr, *Principal*
Tim Kernan, *Div Sub Head*
Gary Mack, *Engineer*
Marcia Hamilton, *Training Spec*
Ronald Peterson, *QC Dir*
EMP: 100
SALES (corp-wide): 18.1B **Publicly Held**
SIC: 8711 Consulting engineer

HQ: Fluor Enterprises, Inc.
6700 Las Colinas Blvd
Irving TX 75039
469 398-7000

(P-25814)
FLUOR PLANT SERVICES INTL INC (HQ)
Also Called: Fluor Daniel
1 Enterprise, Aliso Viejo (92656-2606)
PHONE.................................949 349-2000
Fax: 949 349-5271
D Michael Steuert, *CFO*
Glenn Gilkey, *President*
Jim Scotti, *Vice Pres*
Mark S Strukelj, *Vice Pres*
Patricia Whaley, *Executive*
EMP: 100
SALES (est): 25.2MM
SALES (corp-wide): 18.1B **Publicly Held**
SIC: 8711 Engineering services
PA: Fluor Corporation
6700 Las Colinas Blvd
Irving TX 75039
469 398-7000

(P-25815)
FLUORAMEC LLC (HQ)
1 Enterprise, Aliso Viejo (92656-2606)
PHONE.................................949 349-2000
Michelle Bell, *Director*
Lorna Calvin, *Admin Sec*
EMP: 50
SALES (est): 30MM
SALES (corp-wide): 18.1B **Publicly Held**
SIC: 8711 Engineering services
PA: Fluor Corporation
6700 Las Colinas Blvd
Irving TX 75039
469 398-7000

(P-25816)
FORWARD SLOPE INCORPORATED
Also Called: Forward Slope.
2020 Camino Del Rio N # 400, San Diego (92108-1543)
PHONE.................................619 299-4400
Carlos Persichetti, *President*
Kevin Noonan, *Vice Pres*
Adham Shaaban, *CIO*
Jacquelyn Hernandez, *Engineer*
John Morgan, *Engineer*
EMP: 80
SALES (est): 13.6MM **Privately Held**
WEB: www.forwardslope.com
SIC: 8711 7371 7389 Engineering services; software programming applications; financial services

(P-25817)
FORZA SILICON CORPORATION
2947 Bradley St Ste 130, Pasadena (91107-1566)
PHONE.................................626 796-1182
Barmak Mansoorian, *President*
Mel Stinebaugh, *Exec VP*
John Winn, *Vice Pres*
Daniel Van Blerkom, *CTO*
Daniel Vanblerkom, *CTO*
EMP: 61
SALES (est): 8.9MM **Privately Held**
WEB: www.forzasilicon.com
SIC: 8711 Engineering services

(P-25818)
FRANK M BOOTH INC (PA)
Also Called: Valley Sheet Metal Co
222 3rd St, Marysville (95901-5948)
P.O. Box 5 (95901-0001)
PHONE.................................650 871-8292
Fax: 530 742-8109
Lawrence R Booth, *President*
Richard Gabel, *CFO*
Clint Studebaker, *Officer*
Lance Blanchard, *Project Mgr*
Steve Guttman, *Engineer*
EMP: 80
SQ FT: 75,000
SALES (est): 52.3MM **Privately Held**
WEB: www.frankbooth.com
SIC: 8711 Mechanical engineering

(P-25819)
FRICTION MATERIALS LLC
Also Called: Honeywell
2525 W 190th St, Torrance (90504-6002)
PHONE.................................248 362-3600
Andre Bezuszka, *Mng Member*
Chris Sumrell, *Manager*
EMP: 116
SALES (est): 17.9MM
SALES (corp-wide): 38.5B **Publicly Held**
SIC: 8711 Engineering services
PA: Honeywell International Inc.
115 Tabor Rd
Morris Plains NJ 07950
973 455-2000

(P-25820)
FTI CONSULTING INC
633 W 5th St Ste 1600, Los Angeles (90071-2030)
PHONE.................................213 689-1200
Fax: 213 689-1220
Stewart Kahn, *President*
Tamara McGrath, *Managing Dir*
Scott Sizemore, *Info Tech Dir*
Emily Kirsch, *Sales Dir*
Amir Agam, *Director*
EMP: 80
SALES (corp-wide): 1.7B **Publicly Held**
SIC: 8711 8748 8742 Consulting engineer; business consulting; management consulting services
PA: Fti Consulting, Inc.
1101 K St Nw Ste B100
Washington DC 20005
202 312-9100

(P-25821)
FUGRO CONSULTANTS INC
1777 Botelho Dr Ste 262, Walnut Creek (94596-5132)
PHONE.................................925 256-6070
Richard Baird, *Controller*
Osman El Manchawi, *Manager*
EMP: 50
SALES (est): 810.9K **Privately Held**
SIC: 8711 Engineering services

(P-25822)
FUGRO WEST INC (DH)
4820 Mcgrath St Ste 100, Ventura (93003-7778)
PHONE.................................805 650-7000
Fax: 805 658-6679
Timothy N Dunne, *President*
Brian Aikens, *Corp Secy*
David Gardner, *Exec VP*
Thomas Blake, *Engineer*
Cindy Rivera, *Safety Mgr*
EMP: 97
SALES (est): 17.5MM
SALES (corp-wide): 2.5B **Privately Held**
SIC: 8711 Consulting engineer
HQ: Fugro (Usa) Inc.
6100 Hillcroft St Ste 700
Houston TX 77081
713 772-3700

(P-25823)
FUJITSU ELECTRONICS AMER INC (DH)
Also Called: Fujitsu Semiconductor Amer Inc
1250 E Arques Ave, Sunnyvale (94085-5401)
PHONE.................................408 737-5600
Shinichi Machida, *President*
Irene Mason, *Assoc VP*
Kazuhiko Kato, *Exec VP*
Ajison Nair, *Executive*
Jason So, *Surgery Dir*
EMP: 84
SQ FT: 49,000
SALES (est): 23.4MM
SALES (corp-wide): 40.5B **Privately Held**
WEB: www.fma.fujitsu.com
SIC: 8711 5065 Engineering services; electronic parts & equipment
HQ: Fujitsu Semiconductor Limited
2-100-45, Shin-Yokohama, Kohoku-Ku
Yokohama KNG 222-0
457 557-000

(P-25824)
FUSCOE ENGINEERING INC (PA)
16795 Von Karman Ave # 100, Irvine (92606-4974)
PHONE.................................949 474-1960
Fax: 949 474-5315
Patrick Fuscoe, *President*
Jill Littley, *Officer*
J T Yean, *Division Mgr*
Jennifer Palmer, *Office Mgr*
Barbara Fox, *Admin Asst*
EMP: 85
SQ FT: 16,000
SALES (est): 25.4MM **Privately Held**
WEB: www.fuscoe.com
SIC: 8711 Civil engineering

(P-25825)
FUTURE ENERGY CORPORATION
9701 Elk Grove Florin Rd, Elk Grove (95624-2277)
PHONE.................................916 685-4200
Jeffrey Adkins, *Branch Mgr*
EMP: 76
SALES (corp-wide): 33MM **Privately Held**
SIC: 8711 Building construction consultant
PA: Future Energy Corporation
8980 Grant Line Rd
Upland CA 91786
800 985-0733

(P-25826)
G2 SOFTWARE SYSTEMS INC
4025 Hancock St Ste 105, San Diego (92110-5167)
PHONE.................................619 222-8025
Georgia D Griffiths, *CEO*
Bill Long, *CFO*
William Long, *CFO*
Charlie Hopkins, *Program Mgr*
Dennis Ahern, *Sr Software Eng*
EMP: 140
SQ FT: 4,000
SALES: 38MM **Privately Held**
SIC: 8711 Engineering services

(P-25827)
GARRAD HASSAN AMERICA INC (DH)
Also Called: GL
9665 Chesapeake Dr # 435, San Diego (92123-1378)
PHONE.................................858 836-3370
Carole Barbeau, *CEO*
Phil Dutton, *Vice Pres*
Bridget McEwen, *Info Tech Mgr*
Darrell Orban, *Manager*
EMP: 70
SQ FT: 1,380
SALES (est): 13MM
SALES (corp-wide): 2.7B **Privately Held**
SIC: 8711 Consulting engineer

(P-25828)
GAS TRANSMISSION SYSTEMS INC
Also Called: GTS
130 Amber Grove Dr # 134, Chico (95973-5880)
PHONE.................................530 893-6711
Fax: 530 892-9297
Katie Clapp, *President*
Kathleen B Clapp, *President*
Robert Gross, *Vice Pres*
Scott R Clapp, *Admin Sec*
Eric Weesner, *Database Admin*
EMP: 220
SQ FT: 4,500
SALES (est): 33.4MM **Privately Held**
WEB: www.gtsinc.us
SIC: 8711 Professional engineer

(P-25829)
GATAN INC (HQ)
5794 W Las Positas Blvd, Pleasanton (94588-4083)
PHONE.................................925 463-0200
Fax: 925 463-0204
Benjamin Wood, *President*
Ed Morrissey, *Treasurer*
Tom Balutis, *Vice Pres*
Jack Buhsmer, *Vice Pres*

PRODUCTS & SERVICES SECTION

8711 - Engineering Services County (P-25849)

John Hunt, *Vice Pres*
EMP: 55
SQ FT: 30,000
SALES (est): 61.3MM
SALES (corp-wide): 3.5B **Publicly Held**
SIC: 8711 3826 Designing: ship, boat, machine & product; analytical optical instruments
PA: Roper Technologies, Inc.
6901 Prof Pkwy E Ste 200
Sarasota FL 34240
941 556-2601

(P-25830)
GDA TECHNOLOGIES INC (HQ)
25 Metro Dr Ste 300, San Jose (95110-1340)
PHONE 408 753-1191
Isaac Sundarajan, *CEO*
Gopa Periyadan, *Exec VP*
Prakppash Bare, *Vice Pres*
Gopakumar K Periyadan, *Vice Pres*
Ravi Thummarukudy, *Vice Pres*
EMP: 100
SALES (est): 24.6MM
SALES (corp-wide): 8.7B **Privately Held**
WEB: www.gdatech.com
SIC: 8711 Electrical or electronic engineering
PA: Larsen And Toubro Limited
L&T House,
Mumbai MH 40000
226 752-5734

(P-25831)
GENERAL DYNAMICS ADVANCED INFO
General Dynamics Adv Info Sys
100 Ferguson Dr, Mountain View (94043-5239)
P.O. Box 7188 (94039)
PHONE 650 966-2000
John Stewart, *Branch Mgr*
Nancy Sturges, *Vice Pres*
Rich Riveron, *Program Mgr*
Dave Lukens, *Technical Mgr*
Brian Kravitz, *Technical Staff*
EMP: 4000
SALES (corp-wide): 31.4B **Publicly Held**
SIC: 8711 8731 Engineering services; commercial physical research
HQ: General Dynamics Mission Systems, Inc
12450 Fair Lakes Cir # 800
Fairfax VA 22033
703 263-2800

(P-25832)
GENERAL DYNAMICS CORPORATION
General Dynamics Nassco
2798 Harbor Dr, San Diego (92113-3650)
PHONE 619 544-3400
Steven Strobel, *Vice Pres*
Michael Askew, *President*
Christopher Barnes, *President*
Kevin Mooney, *Vice Pres*
Jim Gill, *Comms Dir*
EMP: 98
SALES (corp-wide): 31.4B **Publicly Held**
SIC: 8711 Designing: ship, boat, machine & product
PA: General Dynamics Corporation
2941 Frview Pk Dr Ste 100
Falls Church VA 22042
703 876-3000

(P-25833)
GENERAL DYNAMICS INFO TECH INC
1615 Murray Canyon Rd # 600, San Diego (92108-4322)
PHONE 619 881-8989
Dan Morrissey, *Branch Mgr*
John Long, *Vice Pres*
John Perrin, *Engineer*
Pem Smith, *Senior Mgr*
Jim Harlow, *Manager*
EMP: 50
SALES (corp-wide): 31.4B **Publicly Held**
SIC: 8711 Professional engineer
HQ: General Dynamics Information Technology, Inc.
3211 Jermantown Rd
Fairfax VA 22030
703 995-8700

(P-25834)
GENERAL ELECTRIC COMPANY
2120 Diamond Blvd Ste 100, Concord (94520-5720)
PHONE 925 602-5950
Fax: 925 602-5901
Malcolm Jepson, *Principal*
Tony Montano, *Administration*
EMP: 100
SALES (corp-wide): 117.3B **Publicly Held**
SIC: 8711 7629 Engineering services; electrical repair shops
PA: General Electric Company
41 Farnsworth St
Boston MA 02210
617 443-3000

(P-25835)
GENERAL SERVICES CAL DEPT
Also Called: Telecommunications Division
601 Sequoia Pacific Blvd, Sacramento (95811-0231)
PHONE 916 657-9960
Wendell McCullough, *Branch Mgr*
EMP: 500 **Privately Held**
WEB: www.4c.net
SIC: 8711 9199 Electrical or electronic engineering; general government administration;
HQ: California Department Of General Services
707 3rd St
West Sacramento CA 95605

(P-25836)
GENERAL SERVICES CAL DEPT
Telecommunications Division
601 Sequoia Pacific Blvd, Sacramento (95811-0231)
PHONE 916 657-9903
Fax: 916 657-9233
Wendell McCullough, *Director*
EMP: 450 **Privately Held**
WEB: www.4c.net
SIC: 8711 9199 Electrical or electronic engineering; general government administration;
HQ: California Department Of General Services
707 3rd St
West Sacramento CA 95605

(P-25837)
GEOCON INCORPORATED
6960 Flanders Dr, San Diego (92121-3992)
PHONE 858 558-6900
Michael Chapin, *CEO*
William Lydon, *CFO*
Neal Berliner, *Office Mgr*
EMP: 54
SALES: 8MM **Privately Held**
SIC: 8711 Engineering services

(P-25838)
GEORGE G SHARP INC
1065 Bay Blvd Ste D, Chula Vista (91911-1626)
PHONE 619 425-4211
Joseph Aven, *Manager*
Lisa Mackie, *Counsel*
Andy Hargreaves, *Manager*
Ron Petty, *Manager*
EMP: 75
SALES (corp-wide): 81.6MM **Privately Held**
WEB: www.ggsharp.com
SIC: 8711 Consulting engineer
PA: George G. Sharp, Inc.
160 Broadway Fl 8
New York NY 10038
212 732-2800

(P-25839)
GEOSYNTEC CONSULTANTS INC
Also Called: Geo Mmi Engineering
1111 Broadway Fl 6th, Oakland (94607-4139)
PHONE 510 836-3034
Fax: 510 836-3036
Pat Lucia, *Branch Mgr*
R J Dunn, *Principal*
Patrick Lucia, *Principal*

Hari Sharma, *Project Mgr*
Syed Rehan, *Senior Engr*
EMP: 50
SALES (corp-wide): 2.7MM **Privately Held**
SIC: 8711 8748 Consulting engineer; environmental consultant
PA: Geosyntec Consultants, Inc.
900 Broken Sound Pkwy Nw
Boca Raton FL 33487
561 995-0900

(P-25840)
GHD INC
718 3rd St, Eureka (95501-0504)
P.O. Box 1010 (95502-1010)
PHONE 707 443-8326
Steve Allen, *Principal*
Steve Cox, *Vice Pres*
Wayne McFarland, *Manager*
EMP: 50
SALES (corp-wide): 1.2B **Privately Held**
SIC: 8711 Engineering services
HQ: Ghd Inc.
4747 N 22nd St Ste 200
Phoenix AZ 85016
602 216-7200

(P-25841)
GHD INC
2235 Mercury Way Ste 150, Santa Rosa (95407-5470)
PHONE 707 523-1010
Alex Culick, *Branch Mgr*
Peggy Dezurik, *Info Tech Mgr*
Mary Grace Pawson, *Project Mgr*
Marc Solomon, *Project Mgr*
Jim Winter, *Project Engr*
EMP: 100
SALES (corp-wide): 1.2B **Privately Held**
WEB: www.sjoeng.com
SIC: 8711 Consulting engineer
HQ: Ghd Inc.
4747 N 22nd St Ste 200
Phoenix AZ 85016
602 216-7200

(P-25842)
GILBANE FEDERAL (DH)
1655 Grant St Fl 12, Concord (94520-2445)
PHONE 925 946-3100
Sarabjit Singh, *CEO*
Steve Schneider, *CFO*
Jon Verlinde, *Senior VP*
Subhash Pantakar, *Vice Pres*
Brian Helberg, *Info Tech Mgr*
EMP: 110
SALES (est): 169.7MM
SALES (corp-wide): 3.8B **Privately Held**
WEB: www.itsi.com
SIC: 8711 8748 Building construction consultant; environmental consultant
HQ: Gilbane Building Company
7 Jackson Walkway Ste 2
Providence RI 02903
401 456-5800

(P-25843)
GLENN A RICK ENGRG & DEV CO (PA)
Also Called: Rick Engineering Company
5620 Friars Rd, San Diego (92110-2513)
PHONE 619 291-0708
Fax: 619 291-4165
Roger Ball, *Principal*
William R Rick, *President*
Deborah B Ragione, *CFO*
Dennis C Bowling, *Vice Pres*
Paul J Iezzi, *Vice Pres*
EMP: 212 **EST:** 1955
SQ FT: 50,000
SALES (est): 58.7MM **Privately Held**
SIC: 8711 Civil engineering

(P-25844)
GPA TECHNOLOGIES INC
2368 Eastman Ave Ste 8, Ventura (93003-5770)
PHONE 805 643-7878
Fax: 805 643-7474
Michael Vaswani, *President*
Darrell Boynton, *Program Mgr*
Miranda Wong, *VP Opers*
Chris Hammons, *Sales Executive*
EMP: 55

SQ FT: 6,580
SALES (est): 8.9MM **Privately Held**
WEB: www.gpatech.com
SIC: 8711 Engineering services

(P-25845)
GRADIENT ENGINEERS INC
Also Called: Leighton & Associates
17781 Cowan Ste 140, Irvine (92614-6009)
PHONE 949 477-0555
Terry Brennan, *Chairman*
Kris Lutton, *President*
Tom Mills, *Vice Pres*
EMP: 70
SALES (est): 3.7MM
SALES (corp-wide): 26.8MM **Privately Held**
WEB: www.gradientengineers.com
SIC: 8711 8744 Engineering services;
PA: Leighton Group, Inc.
17781 Cowan
Irvine CA 92614
949 477-4040

(P-25846)
GULFSTREAM AEROSPACE CORP GA
4150 E Donald Douglas Dr, Long Beach (90808-1725)
PHONE 562 420-1818
Fax: 562 420-5090
Barry Russell, *Vice Pres*
Noe Rodriguez, *Info Tech Mgr*
Bela Kalapos, *Engineer*
Robert Nilson, *Engineer*
Joan Caterino, *Human Res Dir*
EMP: 800
SALES (corp-wide): 31.4B **Publicly Held**
WEB: www.gdavservices.net
SIC: 8711 3721 Engineering services; aircraft
HQ: Gulfstream Aerospace Corporation (Georgia)
500 Gulfstream Rd
Savannah GA 31408
912 965-3000

(P-25847)
H M H ENGINEERS
1570 Oakland Rd, San Jose (95131-2430)
PHONE 408 487-2200
William J Wagner, *President*
Valarie Kitaura, *CFO*
Tom Armstrong, *Vice Pres*
EMP: 54 **EST:** 1976
SALES (est): 7.9MM **Privately Held**
SIC: 8711 8713 Consulting engineer; surveying services

(P-25848)
HARRIS & ASSOCIATES INC
22 Executive Park Ste 200, Irvine (92614-2704)
PHONE 949 655-3900
Fax: 949 655-3995
Jeff Cooper, *Branch Mgr*
Dave Seevers, *Vice Pres*
Ray Polidoro, *Branch Mgr*
Chere Eulogil, *Administration*
Randall Berry, *Project Engr*
EMP: 60
SALES (corp-wide): 78.5MM **Privately Held**
WEB: www.harris-assoc.com
SIC: 8711 8712 Construction & civil engineering; civil engineering; sanitary engineers; architectural engineering
PA: Harris & Associates, Inc.
1401 Wllw Pca Rd 500
Concord CA 94520
925 827-4900

(P-25849)
HARRIS & ASSOCIATES INC (PA)
Also Called: Harris & Associates Cnstr MGT
1401 Wllw Pca Rd 500, Concord (94520)
PHONE 925 827-4900
Lisa Larrabee, *CEO*
Carl Harris, *Ch of Bd*
Don Coulter, *Vice Chairman*
Guy Erickson, *President*
Gary Yagade, *President*
EMP: 104
SQ FT: 23,000

8711 - Engineering Services County (P-25850)

SALES (est): 83.7MM **Privately Held**
WEB: www.harris-assoc.com
SIC: 8711 8712 Construction & civil engineering; civil engineering; sanitary engineers; architectural engineering

(P-25850)
HARRIS CORPORATION
1400 S Shamrock Ave, Monrovia (91016-4267)
PHONE.................................626 584-4527
Pat Carr, *Branch Mgr*
Marwah Buck, *Network Enginr*
Chad Bouchey, *Research*
Eduardo Andres, *Technology*
EMP: 299
SALES (corp-wide): 7.4B **Publicly Held**
WEB: www.ittind.com
SIC: 8711 Electrical or electronic engineering
PA: Harris Corporation
1025 W Nasa Blvd
Melbourne FL 32919
321 727-9100

(P-25851)
HATCH MOTT MACDONALD GROUP INC
4301 Hacienda Dr Ste 300, Pleasanton (94588-2724)
PHONE.................................925 469-8010
Tony Purdon, *Branch Mgr*
Craig Velasquez, *Treasurer*
Melanie Graham, *Executive*
EMP: 75
SALES (corp-wide): 507.4MM **Privately Held**
WEB: www.hatchmott.com
SIC: 8711 Engineering services
PA: Hatch Mott Macdonald Group, Inc.
111 Wood Ave S Ste 5
Iselin NJ 08830
973 379-3400

(P-25852)
HDR ARCHITECTURE INC
Also Called: H D R
251 S Lake Ave Ste 1000, Pasadena (91101-3020)
PHONE.................................626 584-1700
Fax: 626 584-1750
Al Korth, *Manager*
EMP: 100
SQ FT: 5,905
SALES (corp-wide): 1.8B **Privately Held**
SIC: 8711 8712 Designing: ship, boat, machine & product; architectural services
HQ: Hdr Architecture, Inc.
8404 Indian Hills Dr
Omaha NE 68114
402 399-1000

(P-25853)
HDR ARCHITECTURE INC
560 Mission St Ste 900, San Francisco (94105-0918)
PHONE.................................415 546-4242
Bill Brinkman, *Director*
EMP: 55
SALES (corp-wide): 1.8B **Privately Held**
SIC: 8711 8712 Designing: ship, boat, machine & product; architectural services
HQ: Hdr Architecture, Inc.
8404 Indian Hills Dr
Omaha NE 68114
402 399-1000

(P-25854)
HDR ENGINEERING INC
3230 El Camino Real # 200, Irvine (92602-1333)
PHONE.................................714 730-2300
Fax: 949 224-3500
William Bennet, *Manager*
Gregorio Estrada, *Project Engr*
EMP: 150
SALES (corp-wide): 1.8B **Privately Held**
SIC: 8711 8742 Engineering services; management consulting services
HQ: Hdr Engineering, Inc.
8404 Indian Hills Dr
Omaha NE 68114
402 399-1000

(P-25855)
HDR ENGINEERING INC
401 B St Ste 1110, San Diego (92101-4271)
PHONE.................................619 231-4865
Melissa Kiscoan, *Branch Mgr*
Abby Jacobsen, *Manager*
EMP: 100
SALES (corp-wide): 1.8B **Privately Held**
SIC: 8711 Consulting engineer
HQ: Hdr Engineering, Inc.
8404 Indian Hills Dr
Omaha NE 68114
402 399-1000

(P-25856)
HDR ENGINEERING INC
100 Pringle Ave Ste 400, Walnut Creek (94596-7326)
PHONE.................................925 974-2500
Fax: 925 974-2533
Zuraile Wilson, *Principal*
Tracy Maher, *General Mgr*
EMP: 70
SALES (corp-wide): 1.8B **Privately Held**
SIC: 8711 8742 Engineering services; construction project management consultant
HQ: Hdr Engineering, Inc.
8404 Indian Hills Dr
Omaha NE 68114
402 399-1000

(P-25857)
HDR ENGINEERING INC
Also Called: Hydro Power Service
2379 Gateway Oaks Dr # 200, Sacramento (95833-4238)
PHONE.................................916 564-4214
Kevin Snyder, *General Mgr*
Melissa Kiscoan, *Admin Sec*
Gary Hicks, *Manager*
EMP: 74
SALES (corp-wide): 1.8B **Privately Held**
SIC: 8711 Engineering services
HQ: Hdr Engineering, Inc.
8404 Indian Hills Dr
Omaha NE 68114
402 399-1000

(P-25858)
HDR ENGINEERING INC
431 W Baseline Rd, Claremont (91711-1608)
PHONE.................................909 626-0967
Graham E Bell, *Branch Mgr*
EMP: 56
SALES (corp-wide): 1.8B **Privately Held**
SIC: 8711 Engineering services
HQ: Hdr Engineering, Inc.
8404 Indian Hills Dr
Omaha NE 68114
402 399-1000

(P-25859)
HDR/CARDNO ENTRIX JOINT VENTR
2365 Iron Point Rd # 300, Folsom (95630-8711)
PHONE.................................916 817-4700
Dave Lecureux, *Senior VP*
EMP: 99
SALES (est): 7MM **Privately Held**
SIC: 8711 Engineering services

(P-25860)
HENKEL CORPORATION
Also Called: Aerospace Material Division
2850 Willow Pass Rd, Bay Point (94565-3237)
P.O. Box 312 (94565-0031)
PHONE.................................925 458-8086
Lyndon Smith, *Vice Pres*
Michael Cichon, *Program Mgr*
Dennis Cardoza, *General Mgr*
Cindy Garcia, *Info Tech Dir*
Manette Gebhardt, *Project Mgr*
EMP: 170
SQ FT: 6,325
SALES (corp-wide): 19.4B **Privately Held**
SIC: 8711 Engineering services
HQ: Henkel Corporation
1 Henkel Way
Rocky Hill CT 06067
860 571-5100

(P-25861)
HENWOOD ENERGY SERVICES INC (DH)
2379 Gateway Oaks Dr # 110, Sacramento (95833-4239)
PHONE.................................916 955-6031
Fax: 916 569-0999
Mark Henwood, *President*
Andy Bane, *Vice Pres*
David Branchcomb, *Vice Pres*
John Fisher, *Vice Pres*
Vikram Janardhan, *Vice Pres*
EMP: 118
SALES (est): 8.5MM
SALES (corp-wide): 35.4B **Privately Held**
WEB: www.globalenergydecisions.com
SIC: 8711 Consulting engineer
HQ: Global Energy Decisions Llc
1495 Canyon Blvd Ste 100
Boulder CO 80302
720 221-5700

(P-25862)
HNTB CORPORATION
601 W 5th St Ste 1000, Los Angeles (90071-2028)
PHONE.................................213 403-1000
Fax: 213 403-1001
Tony Gonzales, *Branch Mgr*
Lanson Nichols, *Vice Pres*
Bill Marek, *Manager*
EMP: 50
SALES (corp-wide): 907.8MM **Privately Held**
WEB: www.hntb.com
SIC: 8711 Consulting engineer
HQ: Hntb Corporation
715 Kirk Dr
Kansas City MO 64105
816 472-1201

(P-25863)
HNTB CORPORATION
200 Sandpointe Ave # 200, Santa Ana (92707-8797)
PHONE.................................714 460-1600
Fax: 714 460-1610
Andres Ocon, *Branch Mgr*
Tushar Mehta, *Engineer*
EMP: 57
SALES (corp-wide): 907.8MM **Privately Held**
WEB: www.hntb.com
SIC: 8711 Consulting engineer
HQ: Hntb Corporation
715 Kirk Dr
Kansas City MO 64105
816 472-1201

(P-25864)
HNTB CORPORATION
36 Executive Park Ste 200, Irvine (92614-4717)
PHONE.................................949 460-1700
Fax: 949 724-0865
Ron Hartje, *Branch Mgr*
EMP: 54
SALES (corp-wide): 907.8MM **Privately Held**
SIC: 8711 8712 Consulting engineer; architectural services
HQ: Hntb Corporation
715 Kirk Dr
Kansas City MO 64105
816 472-1201

(P-25865)
HNTB GERWICK WATER SOLUTIONS
200 Sandpointe Ave, Santa Ana (92707-5751)
PHONE.................................714 460-1600
Larry Davis, *Partner*
Dale Berner, *Partner*
Rob Vining, *Vice Pres*
Michael O'Hagan, *Project Mgr*
EMP: 150
SALES (est): 3.9MM **Privately Held**
SIC: 8711 8712 Engineering services; architectural services

(P-25866)
HOLDREGE KULL CONSULTIMG ENGR
48 Bellarmine Ct Ste 40, Chico (95928-7261)
PHONE.................................530 894-2487
Fax: 530 894-2437
Tom Hodrege, *President*
EMP: 70
SALES (est): 4.2MM **Privately Held**
SIC: 8711 Consulting engineer

(P-25867)
HOLMES & NARVER INC (HQ)
999 W Town And Country Rd, Orange (92868-4713)
P.O. Box 6240 (92863-6240)
PHONE.................................714 567-2400
Fax: 714 567-2649
Danny Seal, *CEO*
Raymond Landy, *President*
Dennis Deslatte, *CFO*
William Autrey, *Vice Pres*
Michel Flynn, *Vice Pres*
EMP: 250 **EST:** 1933
SQ FT: 100,000
SALES (est): 19.4MM
SALES (corp-wide): 17.9B **Publicly Held**
SIC: 8711 8742 8741 1542 Engineering services; training & development consultant; construction management; nonresidential construction
PA: Aecom
1999 Avenue Of The Stars # 2600
Los Angeles CA 90067
213 593-8000

(P-25868)
HONEYWELL INTERNATIONAL INC
22 Centerpointe Dr # 100, La Palma (90623-2504)
PHONE.................................714 562-9003
Garry Grodp, *Branch Mgr*
EMP: 70
SALES (corp-wide): 38.5B **Publicly Held**
WEB: www.honeywell.com
SIC: 8711 Pollution control engineering
PA: Honeywell International Inc.
115 Tabor Rd
Morris Plains NJ 07950
973 455-2000

(P-25869)
HONEYWELL INTERNATIONAL INC
13475 Danielson St # 100, Poway (92064-8855)
PHONE.................................858 679-4140
Jeffrey Goodrich, *Branch Mgr*
EMP: 68
SALES (corp-wide): 38.5B **Publicly Held**
SIC: 8711 Engineering services
PA: Honeywell International Inc.
115 Tabor Rd
Morris Plains NJ 07950
973 455-2000

(P-25870)
HUNSAKER & ASSOC IRVINE INC (PA)
3 Hughes, Irvine (92618-2021)
PHONE.................................949 583-1010
Fax: 949 583-0759
Richard Hunsaker, *CEO*
Douglas Snyder, *President*
Chuck Cater, *Vice Pres*
Kamal Karam, *Vice Pres*
Doug Staley, *Vice Pres*
EMP: 100
SQ FT: 27,000
SALES (est): 55.8MM **Privately Held**
WEB: www.hunsaker.com
SIC: 8711 8713 Civil engineering; surveying services

(P-25871)
IACCESS TECHNOLOGIES INC
1251 E Dyer Rd Ste 160, Santa Ana (92705-5655)
P.O. Box 53545, Irvine (92619-3545)
PHONE.................................714 922-9158
Hasan I Ramlaoui, *CEO*
Marie Fujita, *Business Dir*
Neil Duong, *General Mgr*

PRODUCTS & SERVICES SECTION

8711 - Engineering Services County (P-25893)

Dung Nguyen, *Sr Software Eng*
Michael Steven, *Sr Software Eng*
EMP: 57
SQ FT: 20,000
SALES: 26.6MM **Privately Held**
SIC: 8711 8748 Engineering services; business consulting

(P-25872)
IBI GROUP (US) INC (HQ)
18401 Von Karman Ave # 110, Irvine (92612-8543)
PHONE 949 477-5030
Fax: 949 833-5511
Scott Stewart, *CEO*
Alistair Baillie, *President*
David Thom, *President*
Tony Long, *CFO*
David Chow, *Vice Pres*
EMP: 50 **EST:** 1979
SQ FT: 10,000
SALES (est): 22.9MM
SALES (corp-wide): 261.3MM **Privately Held**
SIC: 8711 0781 Civil engineering; consulting engineer; landscape architects
PA: Ibi Group Inc
  55 St Clair Ave W Suite 700
  Toronto ON M4V 2
  416 596-1930

(P-25873)
ICI SERVICES CORPORATION
1000 Town Center Dr # 225, Oxnard (93036-1155)
PHONE 805 988-3210
Vicki Ervin, *Branch Mgr*
Julie Banks, *Administration*
EMP: 320
SALES (corp-wide): 63.6MM **Privately Held**
SIC: 8711 Engineering services
PA: Ici Services Corporation
  500 Viking Dr Ste 200
  Virginia Beach VA 23452
  757 340-6970

(P-25874)
INDUS TECHNOLOGY INC
2243 San Diego Ave # 200, San Diego (92110-2069)
PHONE 619 299-2555
Fax: 619 299-2444
James B Lasswell, *President*
Rebecca Spane, *CFO*
Will Nevilles, *Senior VP*
Steve Chiodini, *Vice Pres*
Eric Macgregor, *Vice Pres*
EMP: 230
SQ FT: 12,000
SALES (est): 39.8MM **Privately Held**
WEB: www.industechnology.com
SIC: 8711 Engineering services

(P-25875)
INFINITE TECHNOLOGIES INC (PA)
2140 E Bidwell St Ste 100, Folsom (95630-6453)
PHONE 916 987-3261
John A Runnberg, *CEO*
Michael P Whittle, *President*
Paul Friedrich, *Program Mgr*
Clint Lackey, *Manager*
EMP: 63
SQ FT: 3,450
SALES (est): 11.5MM **Privately Held**
WEB: www.infintech.com
SIC: 8711 7371 7379 Engineering services; custom computer programming services; computer related maintenance services

(P-25876)
INFORMATION SYSTEMS LABS INC (PA)
10070 Barnes Canyon Rd, San Diego (92121-2722)
PHONE 858 535-9680
Fax: 858 535-9848
Richard G Miller, *CEO*
William Gang, *COO*
Peter Kuebler, *CFO*
Bill Arcieri, *Vice Pres*
David Honey, *Vice Pres*
EMP: 50

SQ FT: 31,000
SALES (est): 30.2MM **Privately Held**
WEB: www.islinc.com
SIC: 8711 Engineering services

(P-25877)
INFRASTRUCTURE ENGRG CORP
301 Mission Ave Ste 202, Oceanside (92054-2591)
PHONE 760 529-0795
Preston Lewis, *President*
EMP: 50
SALES (est): 2.9MM **Privately Held**
WEB: www.iecorporation.com
SIC: 8711 Engineering services

(P-25878)
INGENIUM TECHNOLOGIES CORP
5665 Oberlin Dr Ste 202, San Diego (92121-1739)
PHONE 858 227-4422
Duane Wingate, *Principal*
EMP: 80
SALES (corp-wide): 23.3MM **Privately Held**
SIC: 8711 Consulting engineer
PA: Ingenium Technologies Corp.
  4216 Maray Dr
  Rockford IL 61107
  815 399-8803

(P-25879)
INNOVATIVE ENGRG SYSTEMS INC
Also Called: Ies Engineering
8800 Crippen St, Bakersfield (93311-9686)
P.O. Box 20610 (93390-0610)
PHONE 661 381-7800
David Wolfer, *President*
Bill Shipp, *Division Mgr*
Ben Gough, *Admin Sec*
Mike Opperman, *Project Mgr*
Dinesh Peeramsetty, *Electrical Engi*
EMP: 100
SQ FT: 20,000
SALES: 20.4MM **Privately Held**
SIC: 8711 1731 Engineering services; electrical work

(P-25880)
INSIGHT ENVIRONMENTAL WSTN LLC
3010 E Miraloma Ave, Anaheim (92806-1810)
PHONE 714 678-6700
Aqeel Mohammad, *President*
EMP: 62
SALES (est): 4.7MM **Privately Held**
SIC: 8711 Construction & civil engineering

(P-25881)
INSIGHT ENVMTL ENGRG CNSTR INC (PA)
2749 Saturn St, Brea (92821-6705)
PHONE 714 678-6700
Aqeel Mohammad, *President*
Tasawwar Ali, *Vice Pres*
Asrar Faheem, *Admin Sec*
Khoa Tran, *Info Tech Dir*
Dave Marks, *Project Mgr*
EMP: 54
SQ FT: 5,000
SALES: 18MM **Privately Held**
SIC: 8711 8741 Engineering services; construction management

(P-25882)
INSPIRIA INC (PA)
Also Called: Audiovisions
25741 Atl Ocn Dr Ste A, Lake Forest (92630-8864)
PHONE 949 206-0606
Fax: 949 206-0602
Mark Hoffenberg, *President*
Ted Taylor, *Vice Pres*
Bob Walpert, *Vice Pres*
Kim Cain, *Executive*
John Salow, *Info Tech Mgr*
EMP: 64
SQ FT: 20,000

SALES (est): 13.1MM **Privately Held**
WEB: www.avisions.com
SIC: 8711 Electrical or electronic engineering

(P-25883)
INTELLIGENT AUTOMATION CORP
Also Called: I A C
13475 Danielson St # 100, Poway (92064-8855)
PHONE 858 679-4140
Fax: 858 679-4144
Jeffery A Goodrich, *President*
Thomas W Brotherton, *Ch of Bd*
Paul J Grabill, *Vice Pres*
Stacy Neilson, *Program Mgr*
William A Lawler, *Admin Sec*
EMP: 50
SQ FT: 7,000
SALES (est): 3.4MM
SALES (corp-wide): 38.5B **Publicly Held**
WEB: www.iac-online.com
SIC: 8711 Engineering services
PA: Honeywell International Inc.
  115 Tabor Rd
  Morris Plains NJ 07950
  973 455-2000

(P-25884)
INTER ACT PMTI INC (PA)
4567 Telephone Rd Ste 203, Ventura (93003-5665)
PHONE 805 658-5600
Fax: 805 658-5605
Tom Kennedy, *President*
S E Asia, *Engineer*
Scott Carey, *Controller*
Vicky Johnson Moore, *Manager*
EMP: 54
SQ FT: 6,000
SALES (est): 7.7MM **Privately Held**
WEB: www.interactpmti.com
SIC: 8711 Consulting engineer

(P-25885)
INTERNATIONAL DESIGN SERVICES
2437 Michicorena St, Los Angeles (90039-2531)
PHONE 323 662-3963
Zigmas Tanaka, *Ch of Bd*
Betty Tanaka, *President*
Steve Murray, *Exec Dir*
EMP: 57
SQ FT: 3,600
SALES (est): 4.4MM **Privately Held**
SIC: 8711 Engineering services

(P-25886)
IQA SOLUTIONS INC
4089 E Conant St, Long Beach (90808-1777)
PHONE 562 420-1000
Mohsem H Hashemi, *CEO*
David Hellier, *Vice Pres*
Andrew Stasio, *Vice Pres*
Paul Rodelo, *Project Engr*
EMP: 62
SQ FT: 8,500
SALES: 6.8MM **Privately Held**
WEB: www.iqasolutions.com
SIC: 8711 Engineering services

(P-25887)
JACOBS CIVIL INC
1500 Hughes Way Ste B400, Long Beach (90810-1882)
PHONE 310 847-2500
Frank Joyce, *Contract Mgr*
EMP: 78
SALES (corp-wide): 12.1B **Publicly Held**
SIC: 8711 Engineering services
HQ: Jacobs Civil Inc.
  501 N Broadway Ste 185
  Saint Louis MO
  314 335-4000

(P-25888)
JACOBS ENGINEERING COMPANY
1111 S Arroyo Pkwy, Pasadena (91105-3254)
P.O. Box 7084 (91109-7084)
PHONE 626 449-2171

Noel G Watson, *CEO*
C L Martin, *President*
EMP: 4000
SALES (est): 98.4MM
SALES (corp-wide): 12.1B **Publicly Held**
WEB: www.jacobs.com
SIC: 8711 1629 Engineering services; chemical plant & refinery construction
PA: Jacobs Engineering Group Inc.
  155 N Lake Ave
  Pasadena CA 91101
  626 578-3500

(P-25889)
JACOBS ENGINEERING GROUP INC
3451 Unicorn Rd, Bakersfield (93308-6829)
PHONE 661 393-3922
EMP: 98
SALES (corp-wide): 12.7B **Publicly Held**
SIC: 8711
PA: Jacobs Engineering Group Inc.
  155 N Lake Ave
  Pasadena CA 91101
  626 578-3500

(P-25890)
JACOBS ENGINEERING GROUP INC
3161 Michelson Dr Ste 500, Irvine (92612-4405)
PHONE 949 224-7585
Fax: 714 503-3999
Dan Grubb, *Branch Mgr*
Constance A Kolajtowicz, *Area Mgr*
Sarah Borton, *Admin Asst*
Jason Blackburn, *Info Tech Dir*
Bobby Curtis, *Systs Prg Mgr*
EMP: 88
SALES (corp-wide): 12.1B **Publicly Held**
WEB: www.jacobs.com
SIC: 8711 Engineering services
PA: Jacobs Engineering Group Inc.
  155 N Lake Ave
  Pasadena CA 91101
  626 578-3500

(P-25891)
JACOBS ENGINEERING GROUP INC
37528 Morning Cir, Palmdale (93550-2578)
PHONE 661 275-5685
EMP: 93
SALES (corp-wide): 12.1B **Publicly Held**
SIC: 8711 Aviation &/or aeronautical engineering
PA: Jacobs Engineering Group Inc.
  155 N Lake Ave
  Pasadena CA 91101
  626 578-3500

(P-25892)
JACOBS ENGINEERING GROUP INC
420 Stevens Ave Ste 150, Solana Beach (92075-2077)
PHONE 858 793-0461
Lawrence Costello, *Branch Mgr*
EMP: 88
SALES (corp-wide): 12.1B **Publicly Held**
SIC: 8711 Engineering services
PA: Jacobs Engineering Group Inc.
  155 N Lake Ave
  Pasadena CA 91101
  626 578-3500

(P-25893)
JACOBS ENGINEERING GROUP INC
2300 Clayton Rd, Concord (94520-2100)
PHONE 925 356-3900
EMP: 92
SALES (corp-wide): 12.7B **Publicly Held**
SIC: 8711
PA: Jacobs Engineering Group Inc.
  155 N Lake Ave
  Pasadena CA 91101
  626 578-3500

8711 - Engineering Services County (P-25894)

PRODUDUCTS & SERVICES SECTION

(P-25894)
JACOBS ENGINEERING GROUP INC
1500 Hughes Way Ste B400, Long Beach (90810-1882)
PHONE.....................310 847-2500
Janet Van Peursem, *Project Engr*
Tom Gipe, *Manager*
EMP: 91
SALES (corp-wide): 12.1B **Publicly Held**
SIC: 8711 Engineering services
PA: Jacobs Engineering Group Inc.
  155 N Lake Ave
  Pasadena CA 91101
  626 578-3500

(P-25895)
JACOBS ENGINEERING GROUP INC (PA)
155 N Lake Ave, Pasadena (91101-1849)
PHONE.....................626 578-3500
Steven J Demetriou, *President*
Terence D Hagen, *President*
Andrew F Kremer, *President*
Joseph G Mandel, *President*
Kevin C Berryman, *CFO*
EMP: 300
SALES: 12.1B **Publicly Held**
WEB: www.jacobs.com
SIC: 8711 1629 1541 8748 Engineering services; construction & civil engineering; building construction consultant; industrial plant construction; chemical plant & refinery construction; oil refinery construction; waste disposal plant construction; industrial buildings & warehouses; pharmaceutical manufacturing plant construction; industrial buildings, new construction; systems analysis & engineering consulting services; systems analysis or design

(P-25896)
JACOBS ENGINEERING GROUP INC
404 Camino Del Rio S, San Diego (92108-3503)
PHONE.....................619 795-8872
Fax: 619 725-5079
David Roberts, *Manager*
Jennifer Farrell, *Office Mgr*
Frank Joyce, *Contract Mgr*
EMP: 88
SALES (corp-wide): 12.1B **Publicly Held**
WEB: www.jacobs.com
SIC: 8711 Engineering services
PA: Jacobs Engineering Group Inc.
  155 N Lake Ave
  Pasadena CA 91101
  626 578-3500

(P-25897)
JACOBS ENGINEERING GROUP INC
3257 E Guasti Rd Ste 130, Ontario (91761-1237)
PHONE.....................909 974-2700
Chao Chen, *Manager*
Frank Joyce, *Contract Mgr*
EMP: 88
SALES (corp-wide): 12.1B **Publicly Held**
SIC: 8711 Engineering services
PA: Jacobs Engineering Group Inc.
  155 N Lake Ave
  Pasadena CA 91101
  626 578-3500

(P-25898)
JACOBS ENGINEERING GROUP INC
1050 20th St Ste 200, Sacramento (95811-3155)
PHONE.....................916 273-5500
Margaret Bell, *Branch Mgr*
Craig Martin, *CEO*
Kenneth Luttrell, *Vice Pres*
Ben Faircloth, *Engineer*
Frank Joyce, *Contract Mgr*
EMP: 50
SALES (corp-wide): 12.1B **Publicly Held**
WEB: www.jacobs.com
SIC: 8711 1629 Engineering services; industrial plant construction
PA: Jacobs Engineering Group Inc.
  155 N Lake Ave
  Pasadena CA 91101
  626 578-3500

(P-25899)
JACOBS ENGINEERING GROUP INC
1050 20th St Ste 200, Sacramento (95811-3155)
PHONE.....................916 929-3323
Andrew Freeman, *Branch Mgr*
Craig Anderson, *President*
Jeff Smith, *Vice Pres*
Frank Joyce, *Contract Mgr*
Patrick Flynn, *Manager*
EMP: 113
SALES (corp-wide): 12.1B **Publicly Held**
WEB: www.jacobs.com
SIC: 8711 Engineering services
PA: Jacobs Engineering Group Inc.
  155 N Lake Ave
  Pasadena CA 91101
  626 578-3500

(P-25900)
JACOBS ENGINEERING GROUP INC
95 S Market St Ste 300, San Jose (95113-2350)
PHONE.....................408 995-3257
Chris R Bartos, *Branch Mgr*
EMP: 88
SALES (corp-wide): 12.1B **Publicly Held**
WEB: www.jacobs.com
SIC: 8711 Engineering services
PA: Jacobs Engineering Group Inc.
  155 N Lake Ave
  Pasadena CA 91101
  626 578-3500

(P-25901)
JACOBS ENGINEERING GROUP INC
600 Wilshire Blvd # 1000, Los Angeles (90017-3212)
PHONE.....................213 362-4336
Fax: 213 239-1357
Bruce Russell, *Branch Mgr*
Reddy Cherukupally, *Vice Pres*
Joe Siebold, *Vice Pres*
Frank Joyce, *Contract Mgr*
E Jensen, *Opers Mgr*
EMP: 250
SALES (corp-wide): 12.1B **Publicly Held**
SIC: 8711 Engineering services
PA: Jacobs Engineering Group Inc.
  155 N Lake Ave
  Pasadena CA 91101
  626 578-3500

(P-25902)
JACOBS ENGINEERING INC (HQ)
155 N Lake Ave, Pasadena (91101-1849)
P.O. Box 7084 (91109-7084)
PHONE.....................626 578-3500
Fax: 626 578-6801
Craig L Martin, *CEO*
Gregory Gassett, *Info Tech Dir*
Mark Wishart, *Info Tech Mgr*
John Pratt, *Network Mgr*
Christopher Foust, *Engineer*
EMP: 84
SALES (est): 166.6MM
SALES (corp-wide): 12.1B **Publicly Held**
SIC: 8711 Engineering services
PA: Jacobs Engineering Group Inc.
  155 N Lake Ave
  Pasadena CA 91101
  626 578-3500

(P-25903)
JACOBS INTERNATIONAL LTD INC
155 N Lake Ave, Pasadena (91101-1849)
P.O. Box 7084 (91109-7084)
PHONE.....................626 578-3500
Craig Martin, *President*
John W Prosser Jr, *Treasurer*
Bruce Mills, *Senior VP*
Jeff Sanders, *Vice Pres*
George A Kunberger Jr, *Director*
EMP: 300
SQ FT: 120,000
SALES: 85MM
SALES (corp-wide): 12.1B **Publicly Held**
SIC: 8711 Engineering services
PA: Jacobs Engineering Group Inc.
  155 N Lake Ave
  Pasadena CA 91101
  626 578-3500

(P-25904)
JACOBS PROJECT MANAGEMENT CO
3161 Michelson Dr Ste 500, Irvine (92612-4405)
PHONE.....................949 224-7695
Les Steinberger, *Manager*
Frank Joyce, *Contract Mgr*
EMP: 99
SALES: 950K
SALES (corp-wide): 12.1B **Publicly Held**
SIC: 8711 Engineering services
PA: Jacobs Engineering Group Inc.
  155 N Lake Ave
  Pasadena CA 91101
  626 578-3500

(P-25905)
JACOBS TECHNOLOGY INC
1550 N Norma St, Ridgecrest (93555-2556)
PHONE.....................760 446-7084
Chuck Schroeder, *Branch Mgr*
Harvey Nelson, *Senior Engr*
Jean Helm, *Marketing Mgr*
EMP: 100
SALES (corp-wide): 12.1B **Publicly Held**
SIC: 8711 Engineering services
HQ: Jacobs Technology, Inc.
  600 William Northern Blvd
  Tullahoma TN 37388
  931 455-6400

(P-25906)
JACOBS TECHNOLOGY INC
Ames Division
M S 213 15, Mountain View (94035)
PHONE.....................650 604-5946
Ron Marmol, *Vice Pres*
Edward J Donahue, *Engineer*
EMP: 50
SALES (corp-wide): 12.1B **Publicly Held**
SIC: 8711 Aviation &/or aeronautical engineering
HQ: Jacobs Technology, Inc.
  600 William Northern Blvd
  Tullahoma TN 37388
  931 455-6400

(P-25907)
JACOBS TECHNOLOGY INC
1550 N Norma St, Ridgecrest (93555-2556)
PHONE.....................760 446-1549
Penny Hersley, *Manager*
EMP: 150
SALES (corp-wide): 12.1B **Publicly Held**
SIC: 8711 Aviation &/or aeronautical engineering
HQ: Jacobs Technology, Inc.
  600 William Northern Blvd
  Tullahoma TN 37388
  931 455-6400

(P-25908)
JAS PACIFIC
201 N Euclid Ave Ste A, Upland (91786-8308)
P.O. Box 2 (91785-0002)
PHONE.....................909 605-7777
Jason Addison Smith, *CEO*
Addison Smith, *CEO*
Lacey Wochuk, *Executive Asst*
Harley J Jenkins, *Manager*
EMP: 110 **EST:** 1992
SALES (est): 7.4MM **Privately Held**
WEB: www.jaspacific.com
SIC: 8711 Engineering services

(P-25909)
JENSEN DESIGN & SURVEY INC
1672 Donlon St, Ventura (93003-5617)
PHONE.....................805 654-6977
Fax: 805 654-6979
Don Jensen, *CEO*
Lynn Gray, *COO*
John Marler, *Executive*
Robert Talmadge, *Planning Mgr*
Lisa Woodburn, *Planning Mgr*
EMP: 50
SALES (est): 5.5MM **Privately Held**
WEB: www.jdscivil.com
SIC: 8711 8713 Engineering services; surveying services

(P-25910)
JOHNSON CONTROLS INC
2226 Northpoint Pkwy, Santa Rosa (95407-7398)
PHONE.....................707 546-3042
Glen Nold, *Branch Mgr*
EMP: 82 **Privately Held**
SIC: 8711 7623 Heating & ventilation engineering; air conditioning repair
HQ: Johnson Controls, Inc.
  5757 N Green Bay Ave
  Milwaukee WI 53209
  414 524-1200

(P-25911)
JSL TECHNOLOGIES INC
1701 Pacific Ave Ste 270, Oxnard (93033-1887)
PHONE.....................805 985-7700
Joseph T Black III, *President*
Ben Fujikawa, *Exec VP*
Jim Savage, *Exec VP*
Jed Williams, *Exec VP*
Brenda Massey, *Admin Asst*
EMP: 79
SQ FT: 6,000
SALES (est): 4.7MM **Privately Held**
SIC: 8711 Engineering services

(P-25912)
JT3 LLC
190 S Wolfe Ave Bldg 1260, Edwards (93524-6501)
PHONE.....................661 277-4900
James Tedeschi, *Manager*
Josephine Newman, *HR Admin*
EMP: 900
SALES (corp-wide): 395.5MM **Privately Held**
WEB: www.jt3.com
SIC: 8711 Engineering services
PA: Jt3, L.L.C.
  821 Grier Dr
  Las Vegas NV 89119
  702 492-2100

(P-25913)
K&B ENGINEERING
290 Corporate Terrace Cir, Corona (92879-6033)
PHONE.....................951 808-9501
Trey Gibbs, *Owner*
Luke Polling, *Technology*
Sandee Gibbs, *Human Resources*
EMP: 200
SALES (est): 27.2MM **Privately Held**
SIC: 8711 Engineering services

(P-25914)
KAISER FOUNDATION HOSPITALS
Also Called: Kaiser Engineering
1850 California Ave, Corona (92881-3378)
PHONE.....................951 270-1220
Jonathan Kim, *Info Tech Mgr*
EMP: 60000
SALES (corp-wide): 27.8B **Privately Held**
SIC: 8711 Engineering services
HQ: Kaiser Foundation Hospitals Inc
  1 Kaiser Plz
  Oakland CA 94612
  510 271-6611

(P-25915)
KAISER GROUP HOLDINGS INC
Also Called: Earthtech
2101 Webster St Ste 1000, Oakland (94612-3060)
PHONE.....................510 419-6000
Fundar Rajan, *Manager*
Jacques F Romaguera, *Manager*
EMP: 90
SALES (corp-wide): 578.9MM **Publicly Held**
SIC: 8711 Engineering services
PA: Kaiser Group Holdings, Inc.
  9300 Lee Hwy
  Fairfax VA 22031
  703 934-3000

PRODUCTS & SERVICES SECTION
8711 - Engineering Services County (P-25936)

(P-25916)
KBRWYLE TECH SOLUTIONS LLC
Honeywell
850 E Main St, Barstow (92311-2347)
PHONE..................760 255-8322
EMP: 200
SALES (corp-wide): 5.1B Publicly Held
WEB: www.honeywell-tsi.com
SIC: 8711 Pollution control engineering
HQ: Kbrwyle Technology Solutions, Llc
7000 Columbia Gateway Dr # 100
Columbia MD 21046
410 964-7000

(P-25917)
KENNEDY/JENKS CONSULTANTS INC (PA)
303 2nd St Ste 300s, San Francisco (94107-3632)
PHONE..................415 243-2150
Fax: 415 896-0999
Keith A London, *CEO*
Patrick J Courtney, *CFO*
Lynn Takaichi, *Chairman*
Don Weiden, *Officer*
Michael Greenspan, *Vice Pres*
EMP: 100
SQ FT: 45,000
SALES (est): 137MM Privately Held
SIC: 8711 Consulting engineer

(P-25918)
KEVCOMP INC
Also Called: Kevcomp Engineering
4300 Long Beach Blvd # 720, Long Beach (90807-2019)
PHONE..................562 423-3028
Fax: 562 423-3286
Kevin Ngo, *President*
Mike T Diep, *CEO*
Tien Le, *Admin Mgr*
Dennis Romano, *Human Res Mgr*
EMP: 80
SQ FT: 1,500
SALES (est): 7.9MM Privately Held
WEB: www.kevcomp.com
SIC: 8711 7379 Engineering services; computer related consulting services

(P-25919)
KIMLEY-HORN AND ASSOCIATES INC
517 4th Ave Ste 301, San Diego (92101-6870)
PHONE..................619 234-9411
James Roberts, *Manager*
Chuck Spinks, *Vice Pres*
EMP: 60
SALES (corp-wide): 583.5MM Privately Held
WEB: www.itscareers.com
SIC: 8711 Consulting engineer
HQ: Kimley-Horn And Associates, Inc.
421 Fayetteville St # 600
Raleigh NC 27601
919 677-2000

(P-25920)
KINEMETRICS INC (DH)
222 Vista Ave, Pasadena (91107-3295)
PHONE..................626 795-2220
Fax: 323 795-2220
Tadashi Jimbo, *CEO*
Michelle Harrington, *Treasurer*
Melvin Lund, *Exec VP*
Ogie Kuraica, *Vice Pres*
Ian Standley, *Vice Pres*
EMP: 59 EST: 1969
SQ FT: 50,000
SALES (est): 21.6MM
SALES (corp-wide): 399.7MM Privately Held
WEB: www.kinemetrics.com
SIC: 8711 3829 Engineering services; seismographs

(P-25921)
KLEINFELDER INC (HQ)
550 W C St Ste 1200, San Diego (92101-3532)
P.O. Box 51958, Los Angeles (90051-6258)
PHONE..................619 831-4600
Fax: 858 320-2001
Kevin Pottmeyer, *Ch of Bd*
Jon Holmgren, *CFO*
Carl Lowman, *CFO*
Michael P Kesler, *Vice Pres*
John Moossazaeeh, *Principal*
EMP: 160
SQ FT: 5,000
SALES: 175.4MM
SALES (corp-wide): 258.9MM Privately Held
WEB: www.kleinfelder.com
SIC: 8711 8712 Consulting engineer; architectural engineering
PA: The Kleinfelder Group Inc
550 W C St Ste 1200
San Diego CA 92101
619 831-4600

(P-25922)
KLEINFELDER INC
5125 N Gates Ave Ste 102, Fresno (93722-6414)
PHONE..................559 486-0750
Fax: 559 442-5081
Walt Placata, *Manager*
Paul Geitner, *Lab Dir*
David Pearson, *Project Engr*
Neva Popenoe, *Engineer*
EMP: 60
SALES (corp-wide): 258.9MM Privately Held
WEB: www.kleinfelder.com
SIC: 8711 8734 8731 Consulting engineer; testing laboratories; commercial physical research
HQ: Kleinfelder, Inc.
550 W C St Ste 1200
San Diego CA 92101
619 831-4617

(P-25923)
KLEINFELDER INC
6700 Koll Center Pkwy # 120, Pleasanton (94566-7032)
PHONE..................925 484-1700
Fax: 925 484-5838
Mike Majchrzak, *Manager*
Chris Dacey, *Lab Dir*
Fred Schafer, *Sales Executive*
EMP: 60
SALES (corp-wide): 258.9MM Privately Held
WEB: www.kleinfelder.com
SIC: 8711 8742 8734 8748 Consulting engineer; management consulting services; testing laboratories; environmental consultant
HQ: Kleinfelder, Inc.
550 W C St Ste 1200
San Diego CA 92101
619 831-4617

(P-25924)
KLEINFELDER INC
2882 Prospect Park Dr # 200, Rancho Cordova (95670-6058)
PHONE..................916 366-1701
Fax: 916 366-7013
John Baker, *Manager*
Jim Hughes, *Administration*
Ru Carey, *CTO*
Qassim Siddiqyar, *CTO*
Julie Ster, *Safety Mgr*
EMP: 90
SALES (corp-wide): 258.9MM Privately Held
WEB: www.kleinfelder.com
SIC: 8711 Consulting engineer
HQ: Kleinfelder, Inc.
550 W C St Ste 1200
San Diego CA 92101
619 831-4617

(P-25925)
KOCH-ARMSTRONG GENERAL ENGRG
15315 Olde Highway 80, El Cajon (92021-2408)
P.O. Box 1190, Lakeside (92040-0906)
PHONE..................619 561-2005
Fax: 619 561-0317
Monte J Koch, *CEO*
Christopher Armstrong, *Vice Pres*
Sara Schmidt, *Administration*
Lynda Brewer, *Accounting Mgr*
EMP: 65
SALES (est): 10.2MM Privately Held
WEB: www.koch-armstrong.com
SIC: 8711 Construction & civil engineering

(P-25926)
KPFF INC
Also Called: K P F F Consulting Engineers
6080 Center Dr Ste 300, Los Angeles (90045-1591)
PHONE..................310 665-1536
Fax: 310 665-9070
John Gavan, *Manager*
Rob Fecarotta, *Engineer*
Kelly Graf, *Engineer*
Mario Leon, *Engineer*
Rodrigo Toro, *Engineer*
EMP: 114
SALES (corp-wide): 172.6MM Privately Held
WEB: www.kpff.com
SIC: 8711 Consulting engineer
PA: Kpff, Inc.
1601 5th Ave Ste 1600
Seattle WA 98101
206 622-5822

(P-25927)
KPFF INC
400 Oceangate Ste 500, Long Beach (90802-4392)
PHONE..................562 437-9100
Fax: 562 437-9200
Todd Graham, *Branch Mgr*
Nick Murphy, *Associate*
EMP: 71
SALES (corp-wide): 172.6MM Privately Held
WEB: www.kpff.com
SIC: 8711 Construction & civil engineering
PA: Kpff, Inc.
1601 5th Ave Ste 1600
Seattle WA 98101
206 622-5822

(P-25928)
KPFF INC
Also Called: Kpff Consulting Engineers
45 Fremont St Fl 28, San Francisco (94105-2209)
PHONE..................415 989-1004
Fax: 415 989-1552
Marc Press, *Manager*
Patrick Macdonald, *Project Engr*
Susie Smith, *Marketing Staff*
EMP: 56
SALES (corp-wide): 172.6MM Privately Held
WEB: www.kpff.com
SIC: 8711 Consulting engineer
PA: Kpff, Inc.
1601 5th Ave Ste 1600
Seattle WA 98101
206 622-5822

(P-25929)
KSI ENGINEERING INC
6205 District Blvd, Bakersfield (93313-2141)
PHONE..................661 617-1700
Fax: 661 631-0368
Kevin Small, *President*
Glenda Sue Small, *Corp Secy*
Matthew Bouchard, *Manager*
EMP: 50
SQ FT: 7,000
SALES: 6.5MM Privately Held
WEB: www.dcck.com
SIC: 8711 Electrical or electronic engineering

(P-25930)
L-3 COMMUNICATIONS MARIPRO INC
1522 Cook Pl, Goleta (93117-3124)
PHONE..................805 683-3881
Dan Chabot, *Vice Pres*
Kerri Churchill, *General Mgr*
Roger Barranco, *Senior Engr*
Peter Yinger, *Business Mgr*
Donna Kramer, *Accountant*
EMP: 90
SQ FT: 100,000
SALES (est): 2.6MM
SALES (corp-wide): 10.4B Publicly Held
WEB: www.nautronix.com
SIC: 8711 Marine engineering
HQ: L-3 Communications Corporation
600 3rd Ave
New York NY 10016
212 697-1111

(P-25931)
LACO ASSOCIATES (PA)
21 W 4th St, Eureka (95501-0216)
P.O. Box 1023 (95502-1023)
PHONE..................707 443-5054
Fax: 707 443-0553
Leonard Osborne, *President*
David Lindberg, *Vice Pres*
Peggy Shea, *Office Mgr*
Frank R Bickner, *Admin Sec*
Veronica L Ruse, *Admin Asst*
EMP: 50
SQ FT: 6,000
SALES (est): 6MM Privately Held
WEB: www.lacoassociates.us
SIC: 8711 8999 0711 Structural engineering; mechanical engineering; building construction consultant; civil engineering; geological consultant; soil testing services

(P-25932)
LANWAVE TECHNOLOGY INC
20111 Stevens Creek Blvd, Cupertino (95014-2399)
PHONE..................408 253-3883
Kenneth Chan, *President*
Alan Chan, *CFO*
EMP: 53
SQ FT: 3,000
SALES (est): 1.9MM Privately Held
WEB: www.lanwave.com
SIC: 8711 Engineering services

(P-25933)
LEE & RO INC (PA)
1199 Fullerton Rd, City of Industry (91748-1232)
PHONE..................626 912-3391
Fax: 626 912-2015
Myong S Ro, *President*
Gregory Holmes, *CFO*
Lee Badertscher, *Vice Pres*
Kelly Mardorf, *Vice Pres*
Dhirus Patel Sr, *Vice Pres*
EMP: 50 EST: 1979
SQ FT: 19,000
SALES: 10.5MM Privately Held
WEB: www.lee-ro.com
SIC: 8711 Civil engineering; mechanical engineering; sanitary engineers

(P-25934)
LEIDOS ENGINEERING LLC
590 W Central Ave Ste I, Brea (92821-3019)
PHONE..................714 257-6400
Sherif Philobos, *Branch Mgr*
EMP: 54
SALES (corp-wide): 5B Publicly Held
SIC: 8711 Engineering services
HQ: Leidos Engineering, Llc
11951 Freedom Dr
Reston VA 20190
571 526-6000

(P-25935)
LEIDOS ENGINEERING LLC
1671 Dell Ave Ste 100, Campbell (95008-6900)
PHONE..................408 364-4700
April Pierson, *Branch Mgr*
EMP: 54
SALES (corp-wide): 5B Publicly Held
SIC: 8711 Engineering services
HQ: Leidos Engineering, Llc
11951 Freedom Dr
Reston VA 20190
571 526-6000

(P-25936)
LEIDOS ENGINEERING LLC
4161 Campus Point Ct E, San Diego (92121-1513)
PHONE..................858 826-6000
David Bernal, *Branch Mgr*
EMP: 54
SALES (corp-wide): 5B Publicly Held
SIC: 8711 Engineering services

8711 - Engineering Services County (P-25937)

HQ: Leidos Engineering, Llc
11951 Freedom Dr
Reston VA 20190
571 526-6000

(P-25937)
LINQUEST CORPORATION (PA)
5140 W Goldleaf Cir # 400, Los Angeles (90056-1299)
PHONE 323 924-1600
Fax: 323 924-1601
Leon Biederman, *Ch of Bd*
Ronald B Gorda, *COO*
Matthew C Lyons, *CFO*
Joe Dodd, *Vice Pres*
Scott Stowe, *Vice Pres*
EMP: 200
SQ FT: 20,000
SALES (est): 96.5MM **Privately Held**
WEB: www.linquest.com
SIC: 8711 Aviation &/or aeronautical engineering

(P-25938)
LIONAKIS
20371 Irvine Ave Ste 120, Newport Beach (92660-0119)
PHONE 949 955-1919
Fax: 949 955-9175
Jeffrey Gill, *Principal*
Greg P Pires, *Manager*
EMP: 156
SALES (corp-wide): 52.4MM **Privately Held**
WEB: www.lbdg.com
SIC: 8711 7389 Engineering services; design, commercial & industrial
PA: Lionakis
1919 19th St
Sacramento CA 95811
916 558-1901

(P-25939)
LIONAKIS (PA)
1919 19th St, Sacramento (95811-6714)
PHONE 916 558-1901
Fax: 916 558-1919
Tim Fry, *President*
Andy Deeble, *CFO*
Jeff Farley, *Treasurer*
Maynard Feist, *Social Dir*
Valerie Hoffman, *Social Dir*
EMP: 150 EST: 1909
SQ FT: 38,000
SALES (est): 52.4MM **Privately Held**
WEB: www.lbdg.com
SIC: 8711 7389 8712 Engineering services; interior design services; architectural services

(P-25940)
LOCKHEED MARTIN CORPORATION
275 Battery St Ste 750, San Francisco (94111-3376)
PHONE 415 402-0406
Marc Mansour, *Manager*
Ronald Coll, *Administration*
David Paton, *Opers Mgr*
EMP: 232
SALES (corp-wide): 46.1B **Publicly Held**
WEB: www.lockheedmartin.com
SIC: 8711 3721 Aviation &/or aeronautical engineering; aircraft
PA: Lockheed Martin Corporation
6801 Rockledge Dr
Bethesda MD 20817
301 897-6000

(P-25941)
LOCKHEED MARTIN CORPORATION
Also Called: Lockheed Martin Naval
1121 W Reeves Ave, Ridgecrest (93555-2313)
PHONE 760 446-1700
Fax: 760 446-8891
John Polak, *Branch Mgr*
William Kenny, *Engineer*
EMP: 232
SALES (corp-wide): 46.1B **Publicly Held**
SIC: 8711 Engineering services
PA: Lockheed Martin Corporation
6801 Rockledge Dr
Bethesda MD 20817
301 897-6000

(P-25942)
LUND CONSTRUCTION CO
5302 Roseville Rd, North Highlands (95660-5000)
PHONE 916 344-5800
Fax: 916 338-2725
Jerry A Lund, *President*
Alta M Lund, *Treasurer*
Jeff Lund, *Vice Pres*
Kevin Lund, *Vice Pres*
Patricia Thomas, *Controller*
EMP: 75
SQ FT: 7,500
SALES (est): 10MM **Privately Held**
SIC: 8711 Construction & civil engineering

(P-25943)
LUNDSTROM & ASSOCIATES INC
4804 Sunrise Hills Dr, El Cajon (92020-8259)
PHONE 619 641-5900
Fax: 619 641-5910
Jeffrey R Lundstrom, *President*
Bill Lundstrom, *Vice Pres*
EMP: 50
SALES (est): 4.1MM **Privately Held**
SIC: 8711 Civil engineering; consulting engineer

(P-25944)
M+W US INC
Also Called: Mw U.S.
1453 Mission St Fl 2, San Francisco (94103-2560)
PHONE 415 621-1199
Mike Hammarstrom, *Branch Mgr*
EMP: 50 **Privately Held**
SIC: 8711 8712 Mechanical engineering; architectural engineering
HQ: M+W U.S., Inc.
201 Fuller Rd Ste 400
Albany NY 12203
518 266-3400

(P-25945)
M-E ENGINEERS INC
10113 Jefferson Blvd, Culver City (90232-3519)
PHONE 310 842-8700
Fax: 310 842-7700
Akira Hiruma, *General Mgr*
Simon Younan, *Treasurer*
EMP: 65
SALES (corp-wide): 43.4MM **Privately Held**
WEB: www.meengineers.com
SIC: 8711 Consulting engineer
PA: M-E Engineers, Inc.
14143 Denver West Pkwy # 300
Lakewood CO 80401
303 421-6655

(P-25946)
MACDONALD MOTT GROUP INC
3699 Crenshaw Blvd, Los Angeles (90016-4849)
PHONE 323 903-4100
EMP: 70
SALES (corp-wide): 507.4MM **Privately Held**
SIC: 8711 Consulting engineer
PA: Macdonald Mott Group Inc
111 Wood Ave S Ste 5
Iselin NJ 08830
973 379-3400

(P-25947)
MACDONALD MOTT LLC
3103 N 1st St Bldg B, San Jose (95134-1934)
PHONE 408 321-5900
EMP: 64
SALES (corp-wide): 507.4MM **Privately Held**
SIC: 8711 Engineering services
HQ: Macdonald Mott Llc
4301 Hacienda Dr Ste 300
Pleasanton CA 94588

(P-25948)
MACDONALD MOTT LLC
Also Called: Railroad Technology
2495 Natomas Park Dr # 530, Sacramento (95833-2935)
PHONE 916 399-0580
Fax: 916 399-0582
Cara Stromm, *Office Mgr*
Don Dali, *Vice Pres*
EMP: 64
SALES (corp-wide): 507.4MM **Privately Held**
SIC: 8711 Consulting engineer
HQ: Macdonald Mott Llc
4301 Hacienda Dr Ste 300
Pleasanton CA 94588

(P-25949)
MACKAY SMPS CVIL ENGINEERS INC (PA)
5142 Franklin Dr Ste C, Pleasanton (94588-3368)
PHONE 925 416-1790
James C Ray, *President*
Bob Chan, *Vice Pres*
John F Kuzia, *Admin Sec*
Gary Seigal, *Manager*
EMP: 62 EST: 1953
SALES (est): 8.8MM **Privately Held**
WEB: www.msce.com
SIC: 8711 Civil engineering

(P-25950)
MANGAN INC (PA)
3901 Via Oro Ave, Long Beach (90810-1800)
PHONE 310 835-8080
Richard Mangan, *President*
Amin Solehjou, *CEO*
Russell Seward, *CFO*
Bruce Craven, *Vice Pres*
Leon Juckett, *Managing Dir*
EMP: 90
SQ FT: 15,000
SALES: 49.4MM **Privately Held**
WEB: www.mangan.com
SIC: 8711 Engineering services

(P-25951)
MARQUES PIPELINE INC
7225 26th St, Rio Linda (95673-1814)
PHONE 916 923-3434
Jeremy R Jaeger, *CEO*
Jeremy Jaeger, *President*
Dennis Loosli, *Vice Pres*
Carlene Riva, *Administration*
Torrie Sorenson, *Accounting Mgr*
EMP: 50
SQ FT: 2,000
SALES (est): 12.2MM **Privately Held**
WEB: www.marquespipeline.com
SIC: 8711 Engineering services

(P-25952)
MARTIN ASSOCIATES GROUP INC (PA)
Also Called: Martin, John A & Associates
950 S Grand Ave Fl 4, Los Angeles (90015-1436)
PHONE 213 483-6490
Fax: 213 483-3084
John A Martin Jr, *CEO*
Barry Schindler, *Vice Pres*
Michael McCoy, *Business Dir*
Diane Duvand, *Project Mgr*
Larry Pitkin, *Engineer*
EMP: 63
SQ FT: 70,000
SALES (est): 53.1MM **Privately Held**
WEB: www.johnmartin.com
SIC: 8711 Structural engineering

(P-25953)
MAZDA RESEARCH & DEV OF N AMER
1421 Reynolds Ave, Irvine (92614-5531)
PHONE 949 852-8898
Fax: 949 475-2609
Kelvin Hiraishi, *Manager*
Charles Simmons, *COO*
Tetsuro Takiguchi, *Info Tech Mgr*
Yvonne Burkhouse, *Engng Exec*
Evon Burkhouse, *Manager*
EMP: 100
SQ FT: 127,000
SALES (est): 6.8MM
SALES (corp-wide): 29.1B **Privately Held**
WEB: www.mazdamotorsports.com
SIC: 8711 Designing; ship, boat, machine & product
HQ: Mazda Motor Of America, Inc.
7755 Irvine Center Dr
Irvine CA 92618
949 727-1990

(P-25954)
MAZZETTI INC (PA)
Also Called: Mazzetti GBA
220 Montgomery St Ste 650, San Francisco (94104-3491)
PHONE 415 362-3266
Fax: 415 362-3267
Walt Vernon, *CEO*
Darryl Wandry, *CFO*
Brigette Thomas, *Chief Mktg Ofcr*
Christine Nagayama, *Office Mgr*
David Hobson, *Admin Asst*
EMP: 50
SQ FT: 17,700
SALES (est): 33.1MM **Privately Held**
WEB: www.mazzetti.com
SIC: 8711 Electrical or electronic engineering; mechanical engineering; consulting engineer

(P-25955)
MC CONSULTANTS INC (PA)
2055 Corte Del Nogal, Carlsbad (92011-1412)
PHONE 760 930-9966
Dan Ducomnun, *President*
Kai Loedel, *CFO*
Kristina Ashcraft, *Vice Pres*
Chantell Cornett, *Plan/Corp Dev D*
Rose Martinet, *Principal*
EMP: 55
SALES (est): 10.8MM **Privately Held**
SIC: 8711 8111 Building construction consultant; legal services

(P-25956)
MDA US SYSTEMS LLC (HQ)
1250 Lincoln Ave Ste 100, Pasadena (91103-2466)
PHONE 626 296-1373
Daniel Friedmann,
Mohammad Manki, *Principal*
Frank Bleisch, *General Mgr*
EMP: 86
SALES (est): 32.4MM
SALES (corp-wide): 1.5B **Privately Held**
SIC: 8711 8731 Engineering services; commercial physical research
PA: Macdonald, Dettwiler And Associates Ltd
13800 Commerce Pky
Richmond BC V6V 2
604 278-3411

(P-25957)
MDA US SYSTEMS LLC
Also Called: Space Dvson-Integrated Systems
1250 Lincoln Ave Ste 100, Pasadena (91103-2466)
PHONE 626 296-1373
Fax: 626 296-0048
Mohammad Manki, *Branch Mgr*
Eric Kucher, *President*
Don Atkinson, *Business Mgr*
Jill Staats, *Recruiter*
Dave Kwan, *Program Dir*
EMP: 65
SALES (corp-wide): 1.5B **Privately Held**
SIC: 8711 8731 Engineering services; commercial physical research
HQ: Mda Us Systems Llc
1250 Lincoln Ave Ste 100
Pasadena CA 91103
626 296-1373

(P-25958)
MDA US SYSTEMS LLC
4398 Corporate Center Dr, Los Alamitos (90720-2537)
PHONE 626 296-1373
Ted Cheng, *General Mgr*
EMP: 150

PRODUCTS & SERVICES SECTION

8711 - Engineering Services County (P-25982)

SALES (corp-wide): 1.5B **Privately Held**
SIC: 8711 Aviation &/or aeronautical engineering
HQ: Mda Us Systems Llc
1250 Lincoln Ave Ste 100
Pasadena CA 91103
626 296-1373

(P-25959)
MDR INC
Also Called: Accu-Bore Directional Drilling
100 Oak Rd, Benicia (94510)
P.O. Box 639 (94510-0639)
PHONE.................................707 750-5376
Michael Robirds, *Principal*
Michael Burton, *Controller*
EMP: 90
SQ FT: 3,000
SALES: 26MM **Privately Held**
SIC: 8711 Construction & civil engineering

(P-25960)
MDS CONSULTING (PA)
17320 Red Hill Ave # 350, Irvine (92614-5644)
PHONE.................................949 251-8821
Fax: 949 251-0516
Stanley C Morse, *Chairman*
Jerry R Schultz, *Co-Owner*
Chris Bergh, *Vice Pres*
Brian Butchko, *Vice Pres*
Ed Lenth, *Vice Pres*
EMP: 71 EST: 1976
SQ FT: 8,837
SALES (est): 9.2MM **Privately Held**
WEB: www.mdsconsulting.net
SIC: 8711 Civil engineering

(P-25961)
MEC INTERNATIONAL
1932 Gauguin Pl, Davis (95618-0541)
PHONE.................................415 866-4497
Franz Campero, *President*
EMP: 200 EST: 2014
SALES (est): 6.2MM **Privately Held**
SIC: 8711 Engineering services

(P-25962)
MERCURY DEFENSE SYSTEMS INC (HQ)
Also Called: Mercury Systems
10855 Bus Ctr Dr Bldg A, Cypress (90630)
PHONE.................................714 898-8200
Mark Aslett, *CEO*
Brian Perry, *President*
Kevin M Bisson, *CFO*
Gerald M Haines II, *Senior VP*
Rich Beeber, *Vice Pres*
EMP: 84
SQ FT: 35,000
SALES (est): 23MM
SALES (corp-wide): 270.1MM **Publicly Held**
WEB: www.korelectronics.com
SIC: 8711 7374 Engineering services; data processing service
PA: Mercury Systems, Inc.
201 Riverneck Rd
Chelmsford MA 01824
978 256-1300

(P-25963)
MGGB INC
Also Called: Alltech Services
10841 Noel St Ste 110, Los Alamitos (90720-6701)
P.O. Box 1065, Sunset Beach (90742-1065)
PHONE.................................714 226-0520
Miles D Sleeth, *CEO*
Phil Gentile, *Director*
Dan Jakary, *Director*
EMP: 114
SQ FT: 3,900
SALES (est): 8.6MM **Privately Held**
SIC: 8711 8748 Pollution control engineering; construction & civil engineering; environmental consultant

(P-25964)
MICHAEL BAKER JR INC
5051 Verdugo Way Ste 300, Camarillo (93012-8683)
PHONE.................................805 383-3373
Kurt Bergman, *CEO*
Louis Levner, *Assistant VP*
EMP: 99
SALES (est): 3.7MM **Privately Held**
SIC: 8711 Engineering services

(P-25965)
MICHAEL BAKER INTL INC
1 Kaiser Plz Ste 1150, Oakland (94612-3601)
PHONE.................................510 879-0950
Mike Conrad, *Branch Mgr*
EMP: 140
SALES (corp-wide): 592.9MM **Privately Held**
SIC: 8711 Engineering services
HQ: Baker Michael International Inc
100 Airside Dr
Coraopolis PA 15219
724 495-7711

(P-25966)
MILLENNIUM ENGRG INTEGRATION
350 N Akron Rd Bldg 19, Moffett Field (94035)
PHONE.................................703 413-7750
Rick Maurer, *Branch Mgr*
Dianne Thomas, *Vice Pres*
EMP: 99
SALES (corp-wide): 117.1MM **Privately Held**
SIC: 8711 Engineering services
PA: Millennium Engineering And Integration Co.
1400 Crystal Dr Ste 800
Arlington VA 22202
703 413-7750

(P-25967)
MISTRAS GROUP INC
Also Called: Mistras Impro
21215 Kratzmeyer Rd A, Bakersfield (93314-9482)
PHONE.................................661 829-1192
Jorky Kidwell, *General Mgr*
Michele Herstad, *QA Dir*
Kelly Brown, *Manager*
EMP: 70 **Publicly Held**
SIC: 8711 Engineering services
PA: Mistras Group, Inc.
195 Clarksville Rd Ste 2
Princeton Junction NJ 08550

(P-25968)
MISTRAS GROUP INC
2230 E Artesia Blvd, Long Beach (90805-1739)
PHONE.................................562 597-3932
EMP: 58 **Publicly Held**
SIC: 8711 Engineering services
PA: Mistras Group, Inc.
195 Clarksville Rd Ste 2
Princeton Junction NJ 08550

(P-25969)
MISTRAS GROUP INC
8427 Atlantic Ave, Cudahy (90201-5809)
PHONE.................................323 583-1653
Victor Altomare, *General Mgr*
EMP: 58 **Publicly Held**
SIC: 8711 Engineering services
PA: Mistras Group, Inc.
195 Clarksville Rd Ste 2
Princeton Junction NJ 08550

(P-25970)
MIYAMOTO INTERNATIONAL INC (PA)
1450 Halyard Dr Ste 1, West Sacramento (95691-5038)
PHONE.................................916 373-1995
Fax: 916 373-1466
Hideki Kit Miyamoto, *President*
Richard Miyamoto, *COO*
Lon Determan, *Bd of Directors*
Diana Erwin, *Comms Dir*
Denise Cisneros, *Admin Asst*
EMP: 59
SQ FT: 6,000
SALES (est): 14MM **Privately Held**
SIC: 8711 Consulting engineer; structural engineering

(P-25971)
MNS ENGINEERS INC (PA)
201 N Calle Cesar, Santa Barbara (93103)
PHONE.................................805 692-6921
Fax: 805 692-6931
James A Salvito, *CEO*
Mark E Reinhardt, *CFO*
Gregory A Chelini, *Vice Pres*
Jeffrey L Edwards, *Vice Pres*
Shawn M Kowalewski, *Admin Sec*
EMP: 94
SQ FT: 7,000
SALES (est): 18.4MM **Privately Held**
WEB: www.mnsengineers.com
SIC: 8711 8713 Civil engineering; surveying services

(P-25972)
MOBILENET SERVICES INC (PA)
18 Morgan Ste 200, Irvine (92618-2074)
PHONE.................................949 951-4444
Fax: 949 951-3667
Richard Grant, *President*
Eugene Powell, *Vice Pres*
Michael Ellison, *Engineer*
Felix Flores, *Engineer*
Earl Melendres, *Engineer*
EMP: 180
SQ FT: 17,500
SALES (est): 54MM **Privately Held**
WEB: www.mobilenetservices.net
SIC: 8711 4813 Engineering services; telephone communication, except radio

(P-25973)
MOFFATT & NICHOL
2185 N Calif Blvd Ste 500, Walnut Creek (94596-3543)
PHONE.................................925 944-5411
Robin Rhodes, *Manager*
Sarah Agoncillo, *Administration*
Bo Jensen, *Manager*
EMP: 50
SQ FT: 150,000
SALES (corp-wide): 204.2MM **Privately Held**
SIC: 8711 Engineering services
PA: Moffatt & Nichol
3780 Kilroy Arprt Way
Long Beach CA 90806
562 590-6500

(P-25974)
MOFFATT & NICHOL
3780 Kilroy Arprt Way # 600, Long Beach (90806-2457)
PHONE.................................562 426-9551
Mike McCarthy, *Manager*
Eric Nichol, *CEO*
Christine Norman, *Manager*
Donald L Powers, *Agent*
EMP: 55
SALES (corp-wide): 204.2MM **Privately Held**
WEB: www.moffattnichol.com
SIC: 8711 Engineering services
PA: Moffatt & Nichol
3780 Kilroy Arprt Way
Long Beach CA 90806
562 590-6500

(P-25975)
MOOG INC
2581 Leghorn St, Mountain View (94043-1613)
PHONE.................................650 210-9000
Christopher Head, *CEO*
Leslie Chrzan, *Senior Engr*
Rainer Growitz, *Business Mgr*
EMP: 57
SALES (corp-wide): 2.5B **Publicly Held**
SIC: 8711 Engineering services
PA: Moog Inc.
400 Jamison Rd Plant26
Elma NY 14059
716 652-2000

(P-25976)
MORTON & PITALO INC (PA)
75 Iron Point Cir Ste 120, Folsom (95630-8813)
PHONE.................................916 984-7621
Fax: 916 984-9617
Eddie Kho, *President*
Vincent Doyle, *CFO*
Gregory J Bardini, *Vice Pres*
Christopher J Gorges, *Vice Pres*
Renee Brandit, *Administration*
EMP: 64
SQ FT: 5,200
SALES (est): 11.4MM **Privately Held**
WEB: www.mpengr.com
SIC: 8711 Civil engineering

(P-25977)
MULTIPOINT WIRELESS LLC
2549 Eastbluff Dr Ste 474, Newport Beach (92660-3500)
PHONE.................................714 262-4172
Rick Luch, *CEO*
Rob Brownjohn, *CFO*
Ilaha Omar, *Vice Pres*
Pete Wu, *Recruiter*
Apurva Sheth, *Manager*
EMP: 50
SALES (est): 6.6MM **Privately Held**
WEB: www.multipointllc.com
SIC: 8711 Engineering services

(P-25978)
MVE INC (PA)
Also Called: M V E
1117 L St, Modesto (95354-0833)
PHONE.................................209 526-4214
Kirk Delamare, *CEO*
Catherine De La Mare, *Vice Pres*
Jason Boyd, *Finance Dir*
Mora Nevels, *Controller*
Cindy Martina, *Accounts Mgr*
EMP: 52
SQ FT: 10,000
SALES (est): 10.2MM **Privately Held**
WEB: www.mve.net
SIC: 8711 8713 Civil engineering; surveying services

(P-25979)
MWH AMERICAS INC
437 2nd St, Solvang (93463-2763)
PHONE.................................805 683-2409
EMP: 77
SALES (corp-wide): 1.5B **Privately Held**
SIC: 8711
HQ: Mwh Americas, Inc.
370 Interlocken Blvd
Broomfield CO 80021
303 410-4000

(P-25980)
MWH AMERICAS INC
2121 N Calif Blvd Ste 600, Walnut Creek (94596-7350)
PHONE.................................925 627-4500
Fax: 925 627-4501
Jennel Cook, *Manager*
Ellen Seymour, *Admin Asst*
Maria Chryssofos, *Manager*
Jack Storace, *Manager*
EMP: 130
SALES (corp-wide): 2.1B **Privately Held**
WEB: www.mw.com
SIC: 8711 Engineering services
HQ: Mwh Americas, Inc.
370 Interlocken Blvd
Broomfield CO 80021
303 410-4000

(P-25981)
MWH AMERICAS INC
19800 Macarthur Blvd # 550, Irvine (92612-2434)
PHONE.................................949 328-2400
Michael Moore, *Manager*
Ellen Seymour, *Admin Asst*
EMP: 74
SALES (corp-wide): 2.1B **Privately Held**
WEB: www.mw.com
SIC: 8711 Mechanical engineering
HQ: Mwh Americas, Inc.
370 Interlocken Blvd
Broomfield CO 80021
303 410-4000

(P-25982)
MWH AMERICAS INC
300 N Lake Ave 4001040, Pasadena (91101-4109)
PHONE.................................626 796-9141
Paul Boulos, *Branch Mgr*
Marc Strasen, *Manager*
EMP: 74

8711 - Engineering Services County (P-25983)

SALES (corp-wide): 2.1B **Privately Held**
WEB: www.mw.com
SIC: **8711** Engineering services
HQ: Mwh Americas, Inc.
370 Interlocken Blvd
Broomfield CO 80021
303 410-4000

(P-25983)
MWH AMERICAS INC
3301 C St Ste 1900, Sacramento (95816-3394)
PHONE..................916 924-8844
Mike Watson, *Manager*
Joe Niland, *Principal*
Ellen Seymour, *Administration*
Kelley Guerrero, *Manager*
Peggy Kearney-Hoffman, *Manager*
EMP: 50
SALES (corp-wide): 2.1B **Privately Held**
WEB: www.mw.com
SIC: **8711** Engineering services
HQ: Mwh Americas, Inc.
370 Interlocken Blvd
Broomfield CO 80021
303 410-4000

(P-25984)
MWH AMERICAS INC
44 Montgomery St Ste 1400, San Francisco (94104-4717)
PHONE..................415 430-1800
Fax: 415 430-1801
Janell Cook, *Branch Mgr*
Kathy Gibbons, *Office Admin*
Rose Rivera, *Administration*
Nita Sullivan, *Administration*
Micki Charlton, *CIO*
EMP: 74
SALES (corp-wide): 2.1B **Privately Held**
WEB: www.mwh-inc.com
SIC: **8711** Engineering services
HQ: Mwh Americas, Inc.
370 Interlocken Blvd
Broomfield CO 80021
303 410-4000

(P-25985)
MWH AMERICAS INC
618 Michilinda Ave # 200, Arcadia (91007-1625)
PHONE..................626 796-9141
Ellen Seymour, *Branch Mgr*
James Borchardt, *Vice Pres*
Geoff Carthew, *Vice Pres*
Jerome Fisher, *Engineer*
Robert Malcomson, *Engineer*
EMP: 74
SALES (corp-wide): 2.1B **Privately Held**
SIC: **8711** Engineering services
HQ: Mwh Americas, Inc.
370 Interlocken Blvd
Broomfield CO 80021
303 410-4000

(P-25986)
NATIONAL SECURITY TECH LLC
Also Called: Bechtel
161 S Vasco Rd Ste A, Livermore (94551-5131)
PHONE..................925 960-2500
Gary Still, *Branch Mgr*
Dan Wagner, *COO*
Amy S Thompson, *Admin Asst*
Brian Ward, *CTO*
Jason Moore, *Mktg Dir*
EMP: 80
SALES (corp-wide): 584.5MM **Privately Held**
SIC: **8711** 1629 Civil engineering; industrial plant construction
PA: National Security Technologies, Llc
2621 Losee Rd
North Las Vegas NV 89030
702 295-1000

(P-25987)
NATIONAL TELECONSULTANTS INC (PA)
550 N Brand Blvd Fl 17, Glendale (91203-1944)
PHONE..................818 265-4400
Fax: 818 265-4455
Eliot P Graham, *Mng Member*
Eliot Gram, *Managing Prtnr*
Charles C Phelan, *Exec VP*

Kevin Scott, *Senior VP*
Andre Abed, *Vice Pres*
EMP: 91
SQ FT: 35,400
SALES (est): 34.5MM **Privately Held**
WEB: www.ntc.com
SIC: **8711** Electrical or electronic engineering

(P-25988)
NAVAL FAC ENG CMMD SW WRKNG CA
1220 Pacific Hwy, San Diego (92132-5190)
PHONE..................619 532-1158
Shahraam Plaseied, *Principal*
Capt Darius Banaji, *COO*
Nancy Wright, *Accountant*
EMP: 99 EST: 2014
SQ FT: 4,000
SALES (est): 5.9MM **Privately Held**
SIC: **8711** 1623 8744 Pollution control engineering; civil engineering; underground utilities contractor; base maintenance (providing personnel on continuing basis)

(P-25989)
NEK SERVICES INC
2280 Historic Decatur Rd, San Diego (92106-6132)
PHONE..................858 277-8760
Bill Toti, *President*
Angela Hartley, *Admin Sec*
Angela Mansell, *Administration*
EMP: 95
SALES (est): 6.8MM **Privately Held**
SIC: **8711** Engineering services

(P-25990)
NEW ENGLAND SHTMTL WORKS INC
2731 S Cherry Ave, Fresno (93706-5423)
P.O. Box 11158 (93771-1158)
PHONE..................559 268-7375
Fax: 559 268-5018
Michael Hensley, *CEO*
Paul R Kapigian, *CFO*
Tia Eastham, *Finance*
EMP: 150
SQ FT: 43,000
SALES (est): 34.2MM **Privately Held**
WEB: www.nesmw.com
SIC: **8711** 8741 1542 Engineering services; construction management; commercial & office building, new construction; commercial & office buildings, renovation & repair; hospital construction; school building construction

(P-25991)
NORTHWEST CIRCUITS CORP
8660 Avenida Costa Blanca, San Diego (92154-6232)
PHONE..................619 661-1701
Fax: 619 661-1735
Toribio Lobato, *President*
Joe Leon, *Production*
EMP: 65
SQ FT: 12,000
SALES (est): 9.7MM **Privately Held**
WEB: www.northwestcircuitscorp.com
SIC: **8711** Electrical or electronic engineering

(P-25992)
NOVARIANT INC (HQ)
Also Called: Autofarm
46610 Landing Pkwy, Fremont (94538-6420)
PHONE..................510 933-4800
Dave Vaughn, *President*
Mike Manning, *CFO*
Mark Bittner, *Vice Pres*
Alex Cortez, *Vice Pres*
Jim Tan, *Vice Pres*
EMP: 60
SQ FT: 20,000
SALES (est): 33.9MM **Privately Held**
WEB: www.novariant.com
SIC: **8711** Engineering services
PA: Agjunction, Inc.
2207 Iowa St
Hiawatha KS 66434
785 742-2976

(P-25993)
NOVO ENGINEERING INC (PA)
1350 Specialty Dr Ste A, Vista (92081-8565)
PHONE..................760 598-6686
Fax: 760 598-6616
Dan Kline, *CEO*
Rajan Ramaswamy, *President*
Dave Peterson, *Vice Pres*
Kerry McKay, *Program Mgr*
Josh Villanueva, *Info Tech Mgr*
EMP: 60
SQ FT: 18,000
SALES (est): 20.7MM **Privately Held**
WEB: www.novoengineering.com
SIC: **8711** Consulting engineer

(P-25994)
NV5 INC (DH)
Also Called: Nolte Associates
2525 Natomas Park Dr # 300, Sacramento (95833-2933)
PHONE..................916 641-9100
Fax: 916 641-9222
Dickerson Wright, *CEO*
Joanne Keiter, *Admin Asst*
Aaron Andren, *Info Tech Dir*
Lesley Richard, *Info Tech Mgr*
Darcy Smith, *Technical Mgr*
EMP: 60
SQ FT: 27,000
SALES (est): 41.4MM
SALES (corp-wide): 154.6MM **Publicly Held**
WEB: www.nolte.com
SIC: **8711** Construction & civil engineering

(P-25995)
NV5 INC
Also Called: Nolte, George S & Associates
15092 Avenue Of Science # 200, San Diego (92128-3404)
PHONE..................858 385-0500
Bill Miller, *Senior VP*
Larry Shaw, *Sales Executive*
EMP: 74
SALES (corp-wide): 154.6MM **Publicly Held**
WEB: www.nolte.com
SIC: **8711** 8713 Civil engineering; surveying services
HQ: Nv5, Inc.
2525 Natomas Park Dr # 300
Sacramento CA 95833
916 641-9100

(P-25996)
NV5 INC
2495 Natomas Park Dr # 300, Sacramento (95833-2923)
PHONE..................916 641-9100
Steve Hiatt, *Vice Pres*
EMP: 72
SALES (corp-wide): 154.6MM **Publicly Held**
WEB: www.nolte.com
SIC: **8711** 8713 Engineering services; surveying services
HQ: Nv5, Inc.
2525 Natomas Park Dr # 300
Sacramento CA 95833
916 641-9100

(P-25997)
OC ENGINEERING
300 N Flower St, Santa Ana (92703-5001)
PHONE..................714 667-3212
Ignacio G Ochoa, *Principal*
EMP: 99
SALES (est): 3.7MM **Privately Held**
SIC: **8711** Engineering services

(P-25998)
OPTERRA ENERGY SERVICES INC (DH)
500 12th St Ste 300, Oakland (94607-4087)
PHONE..................844 678-3772
John Mahoney, *CEO*
Ryan Blair, *President*
John Sullivan, *CFO*
Mark Emerson, *Chief Mktg Ofcr*
Brad Boerger, *Vice Pres*
EMP: 68
SQ FT: 17,250

SALES (est): 354.3K
SALES (corp-wide): 21.3B **Privately Held**
SIC: **8711** Energy conservation engineering
HQ: Gdf Suez Energy North America, Inc.
1990 Post Oak Blvd # 1900
Houston TX 77056
713 636-0000

(P-25999)
OPTIMUM DESIGN ASSOCIATES INC (PA)
1075 Serpentine Ln Ste A, Pleasanton (94566-4809)
PHONE..................925 401-2004
Fax: 925 401-2010
Nick A Barbin, *CEO*
Roger Hileman, *CFO*
Harold Carpenter, *Vice Pres*
Sherrie Hubbard, *Business Dir*
Clinton Gann, *Engineer*
EMP: 63
SQ FT: 22,000
SALES: 19MM **Privately Held**
WEB: www.optimumdesign.com
SIC: **8711** 3679 3577 Engineering services; electronic circuits; computer peripheral equipment

(P-26000)
P & D CONSULTANTS INC (HQ)
999 W Town And Country Rd, Orange (92868-4713)
P.O. Box 5367 (92863-5367)
PHONE..................714 835-4447
Fax: 714 285-0102
John L Kinley, *President*
Roeena Devega, *Controller*
EMP: 50
SQ FT: 23,000
SALES (est): 11.5MM
SALES (corp-wide): 17.9B **Publicly Held**
SIC: **8711** 8742 Civil engineering; planning consultant
PA: Aecom
1999 Avenue Of The Stars # 2600
Los Angeles CA 90067
213 593-8000

(P-26001)
P2S ENGINEERING INC
Also Called: P2s Commissioning
5000 E Spring St Ste 800, Long Beach (90815-5247)
PHONE..................562 497-2999
Kevin L Peterson, *CEO*
Kent Peterson, *COO*
Marie E Nissen, *CFO*
Ivan Thomas Pe Leed AP, *Principal*
Jagjit Singh, *Principal*
EMP: 91
SQ FT: 20,000
SALES (est): 14MM **Privately Held**
WEB: www.p2seng.com
SIC: **8711** Engineering services

(P-26002)
PACIFIC ADVNCED CVIL ENGRG INC (PA)
17520 Newhope St Ste 200, Fountain Valley (92708-8206)
PHONE..................714 481-7300
Mark E Krebs, *President*
Andy Komor, *Vice Pres*
Sonny Sim, *Vice Pres*
Michelle Grau, *Software Engr*
David Imam, *Design Engr*
EMP: 61
SQ FT: 18,254
SALES (est): 17.8MM **Privately Held**
WEB: www.pacificadvanceengineering.com
SIC: **8711** Civil engineering

(P-26003)
PACIFIC AIRWORKS GROUP LLC
255 S Leland Norton Way, San Bernardino (92408-0103)
PHONE..................909 815-7012
Jose L Gonzalez,
Jose Gonzalez,
Dale Stix,
EMP: 84
SQ FT: 15,000

PRODUCTS & SERVICES SECTION

8711 - Engineering Services County (P-26026)

SALES (est): 3.6MM **Privately Held**
SIC: 8711 7699 Aviation &/or aeronautical engineering; aircraft & heavy equipment repair services

(P-26004)
PACIFIC CIVIL & STRL CONS LLC
7415 Greenhaven Dr # 100, Sacramento (95831-5167)
PHONE................................916 421-1000
Fax: 916 421-1002
Fred Huang, *Partner*
EMP: 50
SALES: 5MM **Privately Held**
SIC: 8711 Engineering services

(P-26005)
PACIFIC HYDROTECH CORPORATION
314 E 3rd St, Perris (92570-2225)
PHONE................................951 943-8803
J Kirk Harns, *President*
Mary White, *CFO*
Kris Bertuco, *Vice Pres*
Sean Finnegan, *Vice Pres*
Joselito Guintu, *Vice Pres*
EMP: 135
SQ FT: 1,500
SALES (est): 37.9MM **Privately Held**
WEB: www.pachydro.com
SIC: 8711 Construction & civil engineering

(P-26006)
PACIFIC MARINE DEVELOPMENT
16870 W Bernardo Dr, San Diego (92127-1677)
PHONE................................858 674-6642
George Pappas, *CEO*
Tom Wilkins, *Vice Pres*
EMP: 50
SQ FT: 6,000
SALES (est): 1.7MM **Privately Held**
SIC: 8711 Engineering services

(P-26007)
PACIFICA SERVICES INC
106 S Mentor Ave Ste 200, Pasadena (91106-2931)
PHONE................................626 405-0131
Fax: 626 405-0059
Ernest M Camacho, *President*
Stephen Caropino, *CFO*
Paul Jackowski, *Project Mgr*
EMP: 84 **EST:** 1979
SQ FT: 15,000
SALES (est): 14.1MM **Privately Held**
WEB: www.pacificaservices.com
SIC: 8711 7629 8741 Civil engineering; electronic equipment repair; construction management

(P-26008)
PADRE ASSOCIATES INC
3500 Coffee Rd Ste B, Bakersfield (93308-5001)
PHONE................................661 829-2686
EMP: 57 **Privately Held**
SIC: 8711 Consulting engineer
PA: Padre Associates, Inc.
 1861 Knoll Dr
 Ventura CA 93003

(P-26009)
PARSONS BRINCKERHOFF INC
505 S Main St Ste 900, Orange (92868-4529)
PHONE................................714 973-4880
Fax: 714 973-0358
Charline Talmer, *General Mgr*
Mark Briggs, *Vice Pres*
Bedros Agopovich, *Manager*
Jiun Liao, *Manager*
Jerry Azzato, *Supervisor*
EMP: 100
SALES (corp-wide): 2.5B **Privately Held**
SIC: 8711 Consulting engineer
HQ: Parsons Brinckerhoff, Inc.
 1 Penn Plz Ste 200
 New York NY 10119
 212 465-5000

(P-26010)
PARSONS BRINCKERHOFF INC
444 S Flower St Ste 800, Los Angeles (90071-2962)
PHONE................................212 465-5000
Fax: 213 362-9480
Carl Enson, *General Mgr*
Danny Wu, *Planning Mgr*
Isanower Jesiah, *Director*
EMP: 50
SALES (corp-wide): 2.5B **Privately Held**
SIC: 8711 Consulting engineer
HQ: Parsons Brinckerhoff, Inc.
 1 Penn Plz Ste 200
 New York NY 10119
 212 465-5000

(P-26011)
PARSONS BRINCKERHOFF INC
425 Market St Fl 17, San Francisco (94105-2531)
PHONE................................415 243-4600
Fax: 415 243-9501
Stuart Sunshine, *Branch Mgr*
Robert Stromsted, *Vice Pres*
Teresa Carroll, *Admin Asst*
Scott Osten, *Info Tech Dir*
Tiffany Batac, *Project Mgr*
EMP: 180
SALES (corp-wide): 2.5B **Privately Held**
SIC: 8711 Consulting engineer
HQ: Parsons Brinckerhoff, Inc.
 1 Penn Plz Ste 200
 New York NY 10119
 212 465-5000

(P-26012)
PARSONS BRINCKERHOFF INC
451 E Vanderbilt Way # 200, San Bernardino (92408-3614)
PHONE................................909 888-1106
Fax: 909 889-1884
Danika Bragg, *Branch Mgr*
EMP: 70
SQ FT: 10,000
SALES (corp-wide): 2.5B **Privately Held**
SIC: 8711 Consulting engineer
HQ: Parsons Brinckerhoff, Inc.
 1 Penn Plz Ste 200
 New York NY 10119
 212 465-5000

(P-26013)
PARSONS ENGRG SCIENCE INC (DH)
100 W Walnut St, Pasadena (91124-0001)
P.O. Box 88954, Chicago IL (60695-1954)
PHONE................................626 440-2000
Charles Harrington, *CEO*
Mary Ann Hopkins, *President*
Curtis A Bower, *Exec VP*
Brian Curin, *Senior VP*
Nicholas L Presecan, *Senior VP*
EMP: 500
SALES (est): 143.4MM
SALES (corp-wide): 7.9B **Privately Held**
SIC: 8711 Consulting engineer
HQ: Parsons Government Services Inc.
 100 W Walnut St
 Pasadena CA 91124
 626 440-2000

(P-26014)
PARSONS GOVERNMENT SVCS INC (HQ)
100 W Walnut St, Pasadena (91124-0001)
PHONE................................626 440-2000
Charles L Harrington, *Ch of Bd*
Mary Ann Hopkins, *President*
Anthony F Leketa, *Senior VP*
Gary L Stone, *Vice Pres*
Joseph M Zika, *Vice Pres*
EMP: 500
SQ FT: 900,000
SALES (est): 484.9MM
SALES (corp-wide): 7.9B **Privately Held**
SIC: 8711 Engineering services; designing: ship, boat, machine & product; petroleum engineering; chemical engineering
PA: The Parsons Corporation
 100 W Walnut St
 Pasadena CA 91124
 626 440-2000

(P-26015)
PARSONS GOVERNMENT SVCS INC
2000 Marina Vista Ave, Martinez (94553-1301)
PHONE................................925 313-3217
Dean Lunsford, *Manager*
EMP: 75
SALES (corp-wide): 7.9B **Privately Held**
SIC: 8711 Engineering services
HQ: Parsons Government Services Inc.
 100 W Walnut St
 Pasadena CA 91124
 626 440-2000

(P-26016)
PARSONS TECHNICAL SERVICES INC
100 W Walnut St, Pasadena (91124-0001)
PHONE................................626 440-3998
Mary Ann Hopkins, *President*
Charles Harrington, *Treasurer*
Milton Hunter, *Senior VP*
Gary L Stone, *Senior VP*
Robert W Jones, *Vice Pres*
EMP: 99
SALES (est): 6.3MM
SALES (corp-wide): 7.9B **Privately Held**
SIC: 8711 Engineering services
PA: The Parsons Corporation
 100 W Walnut St
 Pasadena CA 91124
 626 440-2000

(P-26017)
PARSONS WTR INFRASTRUCTURE INC
100 W Walnut St, Pasadena (91124-0001)
PHONE................................626 440-7000
Virginia Grebbien, *CEO*
Anthony F Leketa, *President*
Brian Kehne, *Controller*
EMP: 1522
SQ FT: 1,220,000
SALES (est): 71.6MM
SALES (corp-wide): 7.9B **Privately Held**
SIC: 8711 Engineering services
PA: The Parsons Corporation
 100 W Walnut St
 Pasadena CA 91124
 626 440-2000

(P-26018)
PARTNER ASSESSMENT CORPORATION (PA)
Also Called: Partner Engineering & Science
2154 Torrance Blvd # 200, Torrance (90501-2609)
PHONE................................800 419-4923
Joseph P Derhake, *President*
Dana Derhake, *Shareholder*
Sandy Ross, *Executive*
Mike Giuliano, *Admin Dir*
Nancy Friedmann, *Executive Asst*
EMP: 148
SQ FT: 10,000
SALES (est): 66.5MM **Privately Held**
WEB: www.partneresi.com
SIC: 8711 Engineering services

(P-26019)
PERRY & SHAW INC
9029 Park Plaza Dr # 104, La Mesa (91942-3450)
PHONE................................619 390-6500
Michael Shaw, *President*
Harold Perry, *Vice Pres*
Robin Schaefer, *Manager*
EMP: 85 **EST:** 1995
SALES: 48.5MM **Privately Held**
WEB: www.perry-shaw.com
SIC: 8711 Engineering services

(P-26020)
PGS SUBSIDIARY II COMPANY
100 W Walnut St, Pasadena (91124-0001)
PHONE................................626 440-2000
Mary Ann Hopkins, *President*
Yolanda Smalling, *Admin Sec*
EMP: 241 **EST:** 2014
SQ FT: 39,600
SALES (est): 6.1MM **Privately Held**
SIC: 8711 8713 Engineering services; surveying services

(P-26021)
POWER ENGINEERS INCORPORATED
731 E Ball Rd Ste 100, Anaheim (92805-5951)
PHONE................................714 507-2700
Douglas M Sharpe, *Branch Mgr*
Mark Conroy, *Project Dir*
Trish Webb, *Director*
Kevin Franklin, *Manager*
Jim Hays, *Manager*
EMP: 51
SALES (corp-wide): 395.1MM **Privately Held**
SIC: 8711 Engineering services
PA: Power Engineers, Incorporated
 3940 Glenbrook Dr
 Hailey ID 83333
 208 788-3456

(P-26022)
POWER ENGINEERS INCORPORATED
218 Loreto Ct, Martinez (94553-3551)
P.O. Box 2037 (94553-0203)
PHONE................................925 372-9284
EMP: 52
SALES (corp-wide): 298.6MM **Privately Held**
SIC: 8711
PA: Power Engineers, Incorporated
 3940 Glenbrook Dr
 Hailey ID 83333
 208 788-3456

(P-26023)
PSOMAS
1075 Crkside Rdg Dr # 200, Roseville (95678-3504)
PHONE................................916 788-8122
Paul Enneking, *Manager*
Mike Thalhamer, *Vice Pres*
Sharon Hill, *Office Admin*
Robert A Blasberg, *Project Mgr*
Matthew Heideman, *Project Mgr*
EMP: 140
SALES (corp-wide): 121.4MM **Privately Held**
SIC: 8711 8713 Civil engineering; surveying services
PA: Psomas
 555 S Flower St Ste 4300
 Los Angeles CA 90071
 310 954-3700

(P-26024)
PTS STAFFING SOLUTIONS
9960 Research Dr Ste 200, Irvine (92618-4323)
PHONE................................949 268-4000
Fax: 949 268-4040
June Stein, *President*
David Stein, *Vice Pres*
Ronald Stein, *Vice Pres*
Russell Stein, *Vice Pres*
Fran Barbata, *Tech Recruiter*
EMP: 220
SQ FT: 4,950
SALES: 30.6MM **Privately Held**
WEB: www.ptsstaffing.com
SIC: 8711 Engineering services

(P-26025)
PTSI MANAGED SERVICES INC
100 W Walnut St, Pasadena (91124-0001)
PHONE................................626 440-3118
Mary Ann Hopkins, *President*
EMP: 99 **EST:** 1983
SALES (est): 5.2MM **Privately Held**
SIC: 8711 Engineering services

(P-26026)
QUAD KNOPF INC (PA)
901 E Main St, Visalia (93292-6546)
P.O. Box 3699 (93278-3699)
PHONE................................559 733-0440
Michael Knopf, *President*
Janel Freeman, *CFO*
Ron Wathen, *Vice Pres*
Natali Carrera, *Executive*
Harry Pe, *Executive*
EMP: 50
SQ FT: 11,000

8711 - Engineering Services County (P-26027)

SALES: 15.3MM Privately Held
WEB: www.quadknopf.com
SIC: 8711 8712 Civil engineering; consulting engineer; architectural services

(P-26027)
QUARTUS ENGINEERING INC (PA)
10251 Vista Sorrento Pkwy # 250, San Diego (92121-3774)
PHONE 858 875-6000
Fax: 858 373-1208
Mark Stabb, *Principal*
Doug Botos, *CEO*
Christopher Flanigan, *CFO*
Chris Flanigan, *Vice Pres*
Jeff Frantz, *Vice Pres*
EMP: 70 EST: 1997
SQ FT: 3,100
SALES (est): 20.9MM Privately Held
WEB: www.quartus.com
SIC: 8711 Mechanical engineering

(P-26028)
R AND L LOPEZ ASSOCIATES INC (PA)
Also Called: Lopez & Associates Engineers
3649 Tyler Ave, El Monte (91731-2505)
PHONE 626 336-9655
Lourdes P Lopez, *President*
Remberto Lopez, *Vice Pres*
EMP: 80
SQ FT: 2,700
SALES (est): 6.1MM Privately Held
SIC: 8711 Consulting engineer

(P-26029)
R G VANDERWEIL ENGINEERS LLP
3760 Kilroy Airport Way # 230, Long Beach (90806-2455)
PHONE 562 256-8623
Jeff Duncan, *Principal*
EMP: 110
SALES (corp-wide): 55.3MM Privately Held
SIC: 8711 Engineering services
PA: R. G. Vanderweil Engineers, Llp
   274 Summer St Fl 2
   Boston MA 02210
   617 423-7423

(P-26030)
R M A GROUP INC (PA)
Also Called: RMA Group
12130 Santa Margarita Ct, Rancho Cucamonga (91730-6138)
PHONE 909 980-6096
Edward Duane Lyon, *Chairman*
Ed Lyon, *President*
Melinda Metzler, *CFO*
Sue Lyon, *Corp Secy*
Slawek Dymerski, *Vice Pres*
EMP: 75
SQ FT: 9,600
SALES (est): 25.4MM Privately Held
WEB: www.rmagrp.com
SIC: 8711 Engineering services

(P-26031)
RAILPROS INC (PA)
1 Ada Ste 200, Irvine (92618-5341)
PHONE 714 734-8765
Fax: 949 734-8755
Eric Hankinson, *President*
Johnny Johnson, *Vice Pres*
EMP: 50 EST: 2000
SQ FT: 1,200
SALES (est): 12.3MM Privately Held
WEB: www.railpros.com
SIC: 8711 Civil engineering

(P-26032)
RAMSGATE ENGINEERING INC
2331 Cepheus Ct, Bakersfield (93308-6944)
P.O. Box 20068 (93390-0068)
PHONE 661 392-0050
Fax: 661 392-9606
Donald C Nelson, *President*
Eric Berger, *Engineer*
Mike Houghton, *Manager*
Frank Lawrence, *Manager*
EMP: 95

SALES (est): 12.3MM Privately Held
SIC: 8711 Engineering services

(P-26033)
RANGE GENERATION NEXT LLC
Also Called: Rgnext
105 13th St Bldg 6525, Vandenberg Afb (93437-5209)
PHONE 310 647-9438
Tom Kennedy, *CEO*
Donna Mc Cullough, *Manager*
Donna McCullough, *Manager*
EMP: 99
SQ FT: 100
SALES (est): 3.2MM Privately Held
SIC: 8711 Engineering services

(P-26034)
RAYTHEON COMPANY
9985 Pcf Hts Blvd Ste 200, San Diego (92121)
PHONE 858 455-9741
EMP: 187
SALES (corp-wide): 23.2B Publicly Held
SIC: 8711 8733 5045 Aviation &/or aeronautical engineering; scientific research agency; computer software
PA: Raytheon Company
   870 Winter St
   Waltham MA 02451
   781 522-3000

(P-26035)
RAYTHEON COMPANY
2000 E El Segundo Blvd, El Segundo (90245-4501)
PHONE 310 647-9438
Donna McCullough, *Branch Mgr*
EMP: 220
SALES (corp-wide): 23.2B Publicly Held
SIC: 8711 Electrical or electronic engineering
PA: Raytheon Company
   870 Winter St
   Waltham MA 02451
   781 522-3000

(P-26036)
RBF CONSULTING
40810 County Center Dr # 100, Temecula (92591-6049)
PHONE 951 676-8042
William Green, *Vice Pres*
EMP: 60
SALES (corp-wide): 592.9MM Privately Held
WEB: www.rbf.com
SIC: 8711 8713 Engineering services; surveying services
HQ: Rbf Consulting
   14725 Alton Pkwy
   Irvine CA 92618
   949 472-3505

(P-26037)
REAUME AND ASSOCIATES INC
Also Called: Reaume, E M & Associates
11527 W Washington Blvd, Los Angeles (90066-5913)
PHONE 310 398-5768
Fax: 310 870-5258
John Wilmer, *President*
Allen John Wilmer, *Vice Pres*
EMP: 80
SQ FT: 1,500
SALES (est): 1.1MM Privately Held
SIC: 8711 Consulting engineer

(P-26038)
RELATIONEDGE LLC
1917 Palomar Oaks Way # 310, Carlsbad (92008-5521)
PHONE 858 227-2955
Matthew Stoyka,
Luke Laurin, *Sales Staff*
Ryan Peddycord,
Brent Rivard,
EMP: 52
SALES (est): 3MM Privately Held
SIC: 8711 Industrial engineers

(P-26039)
RIALTO BIOENERGY FACILITY LLC
5780 Fleet St Ste 310, Carlsbad (92008-4714)
PHONE 760 436-8870
Rakesh Dewan, *CEO*
Arun Sharma, *President*
EMP: 250 EST: 2013
SQ FT: 12,937
SALES (est): 5.4MM
SALES (corp-wide): 24.2MM Privately Held
SIC: 8711 Energy conservation engineering
PA: Anaergia Inc
   4210 South Service Rd
   Burlington ON L7L 4
   905 766-3333

(P-26040)
RICHARD BRADY & ASSOCIATES INC
18837 Brookhurst St, Fountain Valley (92708-7301)
PHONE 657 204-9124
EMP: 65
SALES (corp-wide): 67.1MM Privately Held
SIC: 8711 Consulting engineer
PA: Richard Brady & Associates, Inc.
   3710 Ruffin Rd
   San Diego CA 92123
   858 496-0500

(P-26041)
RICHARDSON A CLARK
2701 Loker Ave W Ste 145, Carlsbad (92010-6637)
PHONE 760 496-3714
Mark Ginestro, *Branch Mgr*
EMP: 51
SALES (corp-wide): 123.1MM Privately Held
SIC: 8711 Consulting engineer
PA: Clark, Richardson And Biskup Consulting Engineers, Inc.
   1251 Nw Briarcliff Pkwy # 500
   Kansas City MO 64116
   816 880-9800

(P-26042)
RIVER CY GEOPROFESSIONALS INC
Also Called: Wallace-Kuhl & Associates
3050 Industrial Blvd, West Sacramento (95691-3470)
PHONE 916 372-1434
David R Gius, *President*
Andrew Wallace, *CFO*
Steve French, *Treasurer*
EMP: 56
SALES (est): 5.2MM Privately Held
SIC: 8711 Engineering services

(P-26043)
ROBERT CONSL ENGLEKIRK STRCTRL (PA)
2116 Arlington Ave Lbby, Los Angeles (90018-1365)
PHONE 323 733-6673
Fax: 323 733-8682
Robert E Englekirk, *President*
Solveig Jensen, *Treasurer*
Diana Nishl, *Vice Pres*
Jason Hernandez, *Info Tech Mgr*
Yangbo Chen, *IT/INT Sup*
EMP: 55
SQ FT: 12,000
SALES (est): 4.3MM Privately Held
SIC: 8711 Structural engineering

(P-26044)
ROQUE DEVELOPMENT AND INV INC
Also Called: Rdi Engineering
227 E Pomona Blvd Ste B, Monterey Park (91755-7226)
PHONE 626 427-9077
Hector Mendoza Jr, *CEO*
Jason Roque, *Real Est Agnt*
EMP: 99
SQ FT: 5,000
SALES (est): 7.8MM Privately Held
SIC: 8711 Civil engineering

(P-26045)
ROSS F CARROLL INC
8873 Warnerville Rd, Oakdale (95361-9411)
P.O. Box 1308 (95361-1308)
PHONE 209 848-5959
Fax: 209 848-5955
Sean Carroll, *President*
Sheila M Carroll, *Corp Secy*
Tina Erickson, *Controller*
John Negele, *VP Opers*
EMP: 50
SALES (est): 9.4MM Privately Held
WEB: www.rossfcarrollinc.com
SIC: 8711 Engineering services

(P-26046)
RWC ENTERPRISES INC
Also Called: Professional Construction Svcs
9130 Santa Anita Ave, Rancho Cucamonga (91730-6143)
PHONE 909 373-4100
Robert William Casey, *President*
Diane Casey, *Admin Sec*
EMP: 50
SQ FT: 16,000
SALES (est): 8.1MM Privately Held
SIC: 8711 0781 Civil engineering; landscape counseling services

(P-26047)
S E C C CORPORATION
900 W Los Angeles Ave, Simi Valley (93065-1636)
PHONE 805 578-3596
Fax: 805 578-3598
Dan Brown, *Manager*
EMP: 53
SALES (corp-wide): 22.8MM Privately Held
SIC: 8711 Engineering services
PA: S E C C Corporation
   14945 La Palma Dr
   Chino CA 91710
   909 393-5419

(P-26048)
SAALEX CORP (PA)
Also Called: Saalex Solutions
811 Camarillo Springs Rd A, Camarillo (93012-9465)
PHONE 805 482-1070
Fax: 805 385-3682
Travis Mack, *President*
Jim Brenner, *COO*
Devin Sappington, *Business Dir*
Dennis Meehan, *Program Mgr*
Kelly Nguyen, *Program Mgr*
EMP: 148
SQ FT: 7,000
SALES: 36.5MM Privately Held
SIC: 8711 7379 Engineering services; computer related consulting services

(P-26049)
SAIFUL/BOUQUET CON STRU ENG (PA)
155 N Lake Ave Fl 6, Pasadena (91101-1849)
PHONE 626 304-2616
Fax: 626 304-2676
Saiful Islam, *CEO*
Tom Bouquet, *CFO*
Y K Low, *Admin Sec*
Carlos Buenrostro, *Senior Engr*
Andrea Hammer, *Exec Sec*
EMP: 53 EST: 1997
SQ FT: 25,000
SALES (est): 10.5MM Privately Held
WEB: www.sbise.com
SIC: 8711 Engineering services

(P-26050)
SALAS OBRIEN ENGINEERS INC (PA)
305 S 11th St, San Jose (95112-2218)
PHONE 408 282-1500
Fax: 408 279-2995
Paul Silva, *CEO*
Rick Gunter, *Vice Pres*
Carl Salas, *Principal*
John Salas, *Principal*
Stephen Graham, *Controller*
EMP: 50
SQ FT: 10,000

PRODUCTS & SERVICES SECTION
8711 - Engineering Services County (P-26073)

SALES (est): 19.4MM **Privately Held**
WEB: www.salasobrien.com
SIC: 8711 Consulting engineer

(P-26051)
SAMROD CORPORATION
28425 Calex Dr, Valencia (91354-1500)
PHONE..................................661 945-3602
Fax: 661 949-8536
Michael Rodriguez, *President*
EMP: 60
SALES (est): 6.8MM **Privately Held**
WEB: www.samrodcorp.com
SIC: 8711 Engineering services

(P-26052)
SAN BERNARDINO CALIFORNIA CITY
Also Called: City Hall Pblc Wrks Eng Dpt
300 N D St Fl 3, San Bernardino (92418-0001)
PHONE..................................909 384-5111
James Funt, *Manager*
Robert Sepulveda, *Systs Prg Mgr*
EMP: 70 **Privately Held**
SIC: 8711 Engineering services
PA: California City Of San Bernardino
    300 N D St
    San Bernardino CA 92418
    909 384-5128

(P-26053)
SAN DIEGO TESTING ENGINEERS
Also Called: Testing Engineers San Diego
7895 Convoy Ct Ste 18, San Diego (92111-1215)
PHONE..................................858 715-5800
Fax: 858 715-5810
Mark Baron, *President*
Dickerson Wright, *CEO*
Julie Reyes, *Office Mgr*
EMP: 94
SQ FT: 13,000
SALES (est): 6.6MM **Privately Held**
WEB: www.uslaboratories.com
SIC: 8711 8734 8742 Engineering services; testing laboratories; construction project management consultant

(P-26054)
SAN-JOAQUIN HELICOPTERS INC
15216 County Line Rd, Delano (93215-9427)
PHONE..................................661 725-2682
Andy Laeno, *Principal*
EMP: 221
SALES (corp-wide): 35.6MM **Privately Held**
SIC: 8711 Professional engineer
PA: San-Joaquin Helicopters Inc.
    1408 S Lexington St
    Delano CA 93215
    661 725-1898

(P-26055)
SC WRIGHT CONSTRUCTION INC
3838 Camino Del Rio Nth S Ste 370, San Diego (92108)
P.O. Box 3250, La Mesa (91944-3250)
PHONE..................................619 698-6909
Fax: 619 698-6951
Steven C Wright, *President*
Laurie Beckham, *Admin Asst*
Jim Barker, *Human Res Mgr*
Debbie Chapman, *Manager*
David Gulczynski, *Consultant*
EMP: 400
SALES (est): 28.6MM **Privately Held**
WEB: www.scwright.com
SIC: 8711 Building construction consultant

(P-26056)
SCHILLING ROBOTICS LLC
Also Called: Manufacturing Facility
260 Cousteau Pl Ste 200, Davis (95618-5497)
PHONE..................................530 753-6718
Tyler Schilling, *Manager*
Greg Engemann, *Vice Pres*
Sally Larocca, *Vice Pres*
Scott Callori, *Admin Asst*
Tim Ranstrom, *Technical Mgr*

EMP: 100
SALES (corp-wide): 6.3B **Publicly Held**
SIC: 8711 3593 Engineering services; fluid power cylinders & actuators
HQ: Schilling Robotics, Llc
    260 Cousteau Pl
    Davis CA 95618
    530 753-6718

(P-26057)
SCICON TECHNOLOGIES CORP (PA)
27525 Newhall Ranch Rd # 2, Valencia (91355-4003)
PHONE..................................661 295-8630
Fax: 661 295-6611
Thomas J Bulger, *President*
Marie Bulger, *Admin Sec*
Randy Doyle, *Info Tech Mgr*
Mitch Greenwood, *Info Tech Mgr*
Omar Pacheco, *Info Tech Mgr*
EMP: 50
SQ FT: 25,000
SALES (est): 18.4MM **Privately Held**
WEB: www.scicontech.com
SIC: 8711 3999 Engineering services; models, except toy

(P-26058)
SCICON TECHNOLOGIES CORP
1300 Quail St Ste 208, Newport Beach (92660-2710)
PHONE..................................949 252-1341
Fax: 949 252-1341
Tom Bulger, *Manager*
Mary Myint, *HR Admin*
Hoche Steffen, *Sales Staff*
EMP: 60
SALES (corp-wide): 18.4MM **Privately Held**
WEB: www.scicontech.com
SIC: 8711 Engineering services
PA: Scicon Technologies Corp
    27525 Newhall Ranch Rd # 2
    Valencia CA 91355
    661 295-8630

(P-26059)
SERCO INC
9350 Waxie Way Ste 400, San Diego (92123-1056)
PHONE..................................858 569-8979
Kent Brown, *Branch Mgr*
Mike Baker, *Project Dir*
Karen Russell, *Engineer*
Olen Hanf, *Purchasing*
Edith Zazuta, *Purchasing*
EMP: 132
SALES (corp-wide): 4.7B **Privately Held**
WEB: www.serco.com
SIC: 8711 Engineering services
HQ: Serco Inc.
    1818 Library St Ste 1000
    Reston VA 20190

(P-26060)
SHAW ENVMTL & INFRASTRUCTURE
1326 N Market Blvd, Sacramento (95834-1912)
PHONE..................................916 928-3300
Patricia Olson, *Principal*
EMP: 6000
SALES (est): 86.8MM **Privately Held**
SIC: 8711 Engineering services

(P-26061)
SHN CONSULTING ENGIN (PA)
Also Called: Shn Cnslting Engnrs-Geologists
812 W Wabash Ave, Eureka (95501-2138)
PHONE..................................707 441-8855
Kenneth Jeffrey Nelson, *President*
Mike Foget, *Executive*
Tom Herman, *Regional Mgr*
John Franklin, *Technical Staff*
Brenda Howell, *Engineer*
EMP: 60
SQ FT: 14,000
SALES (est): 16.8MM **Privately Held**
WEB: www.shn-engr.com
SIC: 8711 8999 Consulting engineer; geological consultant

(P-26062)
SIA ENGINEERING (USA) INC
7001 W Imperial Hwy, Los Angeles (90045-6313)
PHONE..................................310 693-7108
Chiuyen Tseng, *CFO*
EMP: 51
SALES: 8.6MM **Privately Held**
SIC: 8711 Engineering services

(P-26063)
SIEMENS AG
685 E Middlefield Rd, Mountain View (94043-4045)
PHONE..................................650 969-9112
Faid Bolorforfh, *CEO*
Franz Wiehler, *CFO*
Marty Munoz, *Telecomm Dir*
Sandhya Patel, *Software Engr*
Jessica Chame, *Project Mgr*
◆ EMP: 250
SALES (est): 2MM **Privately Held**
SIC: 8711 8721 8742 Engineering services; accounting, auditing & bookkeeping; marketing consulting services

(P-26064)
SIEMENS INDUSTRY INC
25821 Industrial Blvd # 300, Hayward (94545-2919)
PHONE..................................510 783-6000
John P Nichols, *Manager*
Joven Manlutac, *Engineer*
Kevin Healy, *Natl Sales Mgr*
Dale McGrath, *Marketing Staff*
Brian Bonham, *Director*
EMP: 300
SALES (corp-wide): 83.5B **Privately Held**
SIC: 8711 Building construction consultant
HQ: Siemens Industry, Inc.
    1000 Deerfield Pkwy
    Buffalo Grove IL 60089
    847 215-1000

(P-26065)
SIERRA LOBO INC
465 N Halstead St Ste 130, Pasadena (91107-3144)
PHONE..................................626 510-6340
EMP: 54 **Privately Held**
SIC: 8711 Engineering services
PA: Sierra Lobo, Inc.
    102 Pinnacle Dr
    Fremont OH 43420

(P-26066)
SIERRA NEVADA CORPORATION
985 University Ave Ste 4, Los Gatos (95032-7639)
PHONE..................................408 395-2004
Michael Weiland, *Branch Mgr*
Eren Ozmen, *President*
Fatih Ozmen, *CEO*
Brian Simpson, *Asst Controller*
Tony Hoskins, *Director*
EMP: 123
SALES (corp-wide): 1.2B **Privately Held**
SIC: 8711 Engineering services
PA: Sierra Nevada Corporation
    444 Salomon Cir
    Sparks NV 89434
    775 331-0222

(P-26067)
SIMPSON GUMPERTZ & HEGER INC
100 Pine St Ste 1600, San Francisco (94111-5202)
PHONE..................................415 495-3700
Fax: 415 495-3550
John Sumnchit, *Systems Mgr*
John Sumnicht, *Managing Prtnr*
Ryan Magner, *Executive*
Dr Rene W Luff, *Principal*
Marianne Reynolds, *Admin Asst*
EMP: 90
SALES (corp-wide): 114.7MM **Privately Held**
WEB: www.sgh.com
SIC: 8711 8741 Engineering services; construction management
PA: Simpson Gumpertz & Heger Inc.
    41 Seyon St Ste 500
    Waltham MA 02453
    781 907-9000

(P-26068)
SIMPSON GUMPERTZ & HEGER INC
500 12th St, Oakland (94607-4076)
PHONE..................................510 835-0705
Glenn R Bell, *CEO*
EMP: 114
SALES (corp-wide): 114.7MM **Privately Held**
SIC: 8711 Consulting engineer
PA: Simpson Gumpertz & Heger Inc.
    41 Seyon St Ste 500
    Waltham MA 02453
    781 907-9000

(P-26069)
SOLOPOINT SOLUTIONS INC
150 Paularino Ave Ste 282, Costa Mesa (92626-3302)
PHONE..................................714 708-3639
Dinh Le, *Branch Mgr*
Breanne Myers, *Tech Recruiter*
Ryan Golod, *Accounts Mgr*
EMP: 50
SALES (corp-wide): 8MM **Privately Held**
SIC: 8711 Consulting engineer
PA: Solopoint Solutions, Inc.
    3350 Scott Blvd Bldg 2
    Santa Clara CA 95054
    408 246-5945

(P-26070)
SONIC INDUSTRIES INC
Also Called: Airframer R
20030 Normandie Ave, Torrance (90502-1210)
PHONE..................................310 532-8382
Steven Scott Stil, *CEO*
Michael Cagliano, *Vice Pres*
James Edwards, *MIS Dir*
Sharon Couturiaux, *Director*
Bill Buckson, *Manager*
▲ EMP: 150
SQ FT: 65,000
SALES (est): 26.8MM
SALES (corp-wide): 597.4MM **Publicly Held**
SIC: 8711 7699 Machine tool design; aviation propeller & blade repair
HQ: Roller Bearing Company Of America,
    102 Willenbrock Rd
    Oxford CT 06478
    203 267-7001

(P-26071)
SPEC SERVICES INC
10540 Talbert Ave 100e, Fountain Valley (92708-6051)
PHONE..................................714 963-8077
Chris Smart, *Manager*
EMP: 100
SALES (corp-wide): 68.1MM **Privately Held**
SIC: 8711 Consulting engineer
PA: Spec Services, Inc.
    10540 Talbert Ave 100e
    Fountain Valley CA 92708
    714 963-8077

(P-26072)
SPEC SERVICES INC (PA)
10540 Talbert Ave 100e, Fountain Valley (92708-6051)
PHONE..................................714 963-8077
Fax: 714 963-0364
Kim R Henry, *President*
Chris Smart, *COO*
Dan Letcher, *CFO*
Chuck Lake, *Vice Pres*
Jim Molders, *CIO*
EMP: 190
SQ FT: 16,000
SALES (est): 68.1MM **Privately Held**
WEB: www.specservices.com
SIC: 8711 Consulting engineer

(P-26073)
SPIRAL TECHNOLOGY INC
229 E Avenue K8 Ste 105, Lancaster (93535-4517)
PHONE..................................661 723-3148
Archie L Moore, *President*
Steve McCarter, *Ch of Bd*
Daniel Hare, *COO*
Barbara Moore, *Officer*

8711 - Engineering Services County (P-26074)

Robyn Barton, *General Mgr*
EMP: 56
SQ FT: 4,984
SALES (est): 12.3MM **Privately Held**
WEB: www.spiraltechinc.com
SIC: 8711 Industrial engineers

(P-26074)
SSC CONSTRUCTION INC
2073 Railroad St, Corona (92880-5431)
PHONE...................................951 278-1177
Fax: 951 278-2538
Gregory E Larkin, *CEO*
Neil Nehmens, *Senior VP*
Dave Larsen, *Project Mgr*
Dara Kargari, *Controller*
David Larkin, *Safety Dir*
EMP: 200
SALES (est): 41.1MM **Privately Held**
WEB: www.sscconstruction.com
SIC: 8711 Engineering services

(P-26075)
STANTEC ARCH & ENGRG PC
100 California St # 1000, San Francisco (94111-4505)
PHONE...................................415 882-9500
Reshma Panjanani, *Information Mgr*
Christina Han, *Marketing Staff*
Lori Van Dermark, *Marketing Staff*
EMP: 100
SALES (corp-wide): 2.1B **Privately Held**
SIC: 8711 8712 Engineering services; architectural services
HQ: Stantec Architecture And Engineering P.C.
311 Summer St
Boston MA 02210

(P-26076)
STANTEC ARCH & ENGRG PC
38 Technology Dr Ste 100, Irvine (92618-5312)
PHONE...................................949 923-6000
Reshma Panjanani, *Information Mgr*
Christina Han, *Marketing Staff*
Lori Van Dermark, *Marketing Staff*
EMP: 117
SALES (corp-wide): 2.1B **Privately Held**
SIC: 8711 8712 Engineering services; architectural services
HQ: Stantec Architecture And Engineering P.C.
311 Summer St
Boston MA 02210

(P-26077)
STANTEC ARCHITECTURE INC
100 California St # 1000, San Francisco (94111-4575)
PHONE...................................415 882-9500
Michael Gambucci, *CEO*
Reshma Panjanani, *Information Mgr*
Christina Han, *Marketing Staff*
Lori Van Dermark, *Marketing Staff*
EMP: 96
SALES (corp-wide): 2.2B **Privately Held**
SIC: 8711 8712 Engineering services; architectural services
HQ: Stantec Architecture Inc.
301 N Main St Ste 2452
Winston Salem NC 27101
336 714-7413

(P-26078)
STANTEC CONSULTING SVCS INC
100 California St # 1000, San Francisco (94111-4505)
PHONE...................................415 882-9500
Nicole Collins, *Manager*
Reshma Panjanani, *Information Mgr*
Christina Han, *Marketing Staff*
Lori Van Dermark, *Marketing Staff*
Rebecca Leonardis-Grefski, *Manager*
EMP: 96
SALES (corp-wide): 2.1B **Privately Held**
WEB: www.keithco.com
SIC: 8711 8712 Engineering services; architectural services
HQ: Stantec Consulting Services Inc.
50 W 23rd St Fl 8
New York NY 10010
212 366-5600

(P-26079)
STRUCTURAL INTEGRITY ASSOC INC (PA)
5215 Hellyer Ave Ste 210, San Jose (95138-1079)
PHONE...................................408 978-8200
Fax: 408 978-8964
Laney H Bisbee, *CEO*
Stager Dave, *CFO*
Ricard A Mattson, *Chairman*
David Stager, *Treasurer*
Nathaniel G Cofie, *Vice Pres*
EMP: 89
SQ FT: 17,000
SALES (est): 90.7MM **Privately Held**
SIC: 8711 Consulting engineer

(P-26080)
STURGEON SON GRADING & PAV INC
Also Called: Sturgeon Services Intl
6516 Cat Canyon Rd, Santa Maria (93454-9605)
PHONE...................................805 938-0618
Fax: 805 938-0894
Keith Kidwell, *Branch Mgr*
EMP: 114
SALES (corp-wide): 63MM **Privately Held**
WEB: www.sturgeonandson.com
SIC: 8711 1794 Engineering services; excavation work
PA: Sturgeon & Son Grading & Paving, Inc.
3511 Gilmore Ave
Bakersfield CA 93308
661 322-4408

(P-26081)
SUTTER HEALTH
2340 Clay St Rm 121, San Francisco (94115-1932)
P.O. Box 7999 (94120-7999)
PHONE...................................415 600-1020
Mark Brady, *Project Mgr*
Konstantin J Ovodov, *Anesthesiology*
James A Davis, *Rheumtlgy Spec*
Stewart Cooper, *Med Doctor*
George Horng, *Med Doctor*
EMP: 140
SALES (corp-wide): 11B **Privately Held**
SIC: 8711 Engineering services
PA: Sutter Health
2200 River Plaza Dr
Sacramento CA 95833
916 733-8800

(P-26082)
SYSKA & HENNESSY ENGINEERS INC
800 Crprate Pinte Ste 200, Culver City (90230)
PHONE...................................310 312-0200
Fax: 310 473-7468
Gary A Brennen, *President*
Ann Banning-Wright, *Vice Pres*
Jennifer Crawford, *Principal*
EMP: 99
SALES (est): 9.3MM **Privately Held**
SIC: 8711 Engineering services

(P-26083)
SYSTEMS APPLICATION & TECH INC
Also Called: Sa-Tech
1000 Town Center Dr # 110, Oxnard (93036-1100)
P.O. Box 25, Port Hueneme (93044-0025)
PHONE...................................805 487-7373
Fax: 805 240-7390
Geoff Dezavala, *Senior VP*
Harry Sherman, *Vice Pres*
Vince Carrasco, *Info Tech Dir*
Tom McVey, *Network Mgr*
EMP: 80
SALES (corp-wide): 45MM **Privately Held**
WEB: www.sa-techinc.com
SIC: 8711 Engineering services
PA: Systems Application & Technologies, Inc.
1101 Merc Ln Ste 200
Largo MD 20774
301 322-8880

(P-26084)
SYZYGY TECHNOLOGIES INC
12526 High Bluff Dr, San Diego (92130-2064)
P.O. Box 1422, Solana Beach (92075-7422)
PHONE...................................619 297-0970
Fax: 619 297-0975
Keith H Sutton, *President*
Eileen M Parkhurst, *CFO*
Al Crespo, *Vice Pres*
Merv Cutler, *Vice Pres*
Joe Discar, *Vice Pres*
EMP: 60
SALES (est): 2.3MM **Privately Held**
SIC: 8711 7371 Engineering services; computer software development

(P-26085)
T Y LIN INTERNATIONAL (HQ)
345 California St Fl 23, San Francisco (94104-2646)
PHONE...................................415 291-3700
Fax: 415 433-0807
Alvaro J Piedrahita, *President*
Robert A Peterson, *CFO*
Man Chung Tang, *Chairman*
Veronica Fennie, *Officer*
Maribel Castillo, *Assoc VP*
EMP: 84
SQ FT: 18,000
SALES (est): 128.3MM
SALES (corp-wide): 139.6MM **Privately Held**
WEB: www.tyli.com
SIC: 8711 Consulting engineer
PA: T.Y. Lin International Group
345 California St Fl 23
San Francisco CA 94104
415 291-3700

(P-26086)
TALENTSCALE LLC
31805 Temecula Pkwy 204, Temecula (92592-8203)
PHONE...................................951 744-0053
Douglas Poldrugo, *President*
Steve Santich, *President*
Richard Nester, *Vice Pres*
Kristen Wolfam, *Human Res Mgr*
EMP: 83
SALES (est): 7.5MM
SALES (corp-wide): 12.2MM **Privately Held**
SIC: 8711 Engineering services
PA: Scst, Inc.
6280 Riverdale St
San Diego CA 92120
619 280-4321

(P-26087)
TECHNIP USA INC
Also Called: TP USA
555 W Arrow Hwy, Claremont (91711-4805)
PHONE...................................909 447-3600
Fax: 909 447-3700
Gary Keyser, *Branch Mgr*
Niken Warihanjari, *Executive*
Ana Franqueville, *Admin Asst*
Sanjiv Ratan, *CTO*
Bill Mead, *Technical Mgr*
EMP: 400
SALES (corp-wide): 203.9MM **Privately Held**
WEB: www.technip.com
SIC: 8711 Petroleum engineering
HQ: Technip Usa, Inc.
11740 Katy Fwy Ste 100
Houston TX 77079
281 870-1111

(P-26088)
TED JACOB ENGRG GROUP INC (PA)
1763 Broadway, Oakland (94612-2105)
PHONE...................................510 763-4880
Fax: 510 763-5099
Ted Jacob, *President*
Octavian Dragos, *Executive*
Marina Taruch, *Engineer*
Shad Shabbas, *Controller*
Shulamit Rabinovich, *Sheriff*
EMP: 60
SQ FT: 12,000
SALES (est): 21MM **Privately Held**
WEB: www.tjeg.com
SIC: 8711 Mechanical engineering; electrical or electronic engineering

(P-26089)
TETER LLP (PA)
7535 N Palm Ave Ste 201, Fresno (93711-5504)
PHONE...................................559 437-0887
Glen Teter, *Partner*
Clay Davis, *Partner*
Byron Dietrich, *Partner*
Paul Halajian, *Partner*
Jamie Hickman, *Partner*
EMP: 50
SALES (est): 11MM **Privately Held**
WEB: www.tetercon.com
SIC: 8711 8712 Engineering services; architectural services

(P-26090)
TETRA TECH INC
17885 Von Karman Ave # 500, Irvine (92614-5227)
PHONE...................................949 263-0846
Jack Chicca, *Branch Mgr*
EMP: 85
SALES (corp-wide): 2.3B **Publicly Held**
SIC: 8711 Engineering services; civil engineering; consulting engineer
PA: Tetra Tech, Inc.
3475 E Foothill Blvd
Pasadena CA 91101
626 351-4664

(P-26091)
TETRA TECH INC
Also Called: Tetra Tech Engrg & Arch Svcs
17885 Von Karman Ave # 500, Irvine (92614-5227)
PHONE...................................949 809-5000
Steve Tedesco, *Branch Mgr*
EMP: 91
SALES (corp-wide): 2.3B **Publicly Held**
WEB: www.tetratech.com
SIC: 8711 Civil engineering
PA: Tetra Tech, Inc.
3475 E Foothill Blvd
Pasadena CA 91107
626 351-4664

(P-26092)
TETRA TECH BAS INC (HQ)
Also Called: B A S
1360 Valley Vista Dr, Diamond Bar (91765-3910)
PHONE...................................909 860-7777
Fax: 909 860-8017
Bryan A Stirrat, *President*
Ira Snyder, *CFO*
Jeanne Stirrat, *Admin Sec*
Ashley Orsaba, *Technical Staff*
Patti Dickason, *Human Res Dir*
EMP: 65
SQ FT: 20,000
SALES (est): 11.3MM
SALES (corp-wide): 2.3B **Publicly Held**
WEB: www.bas.com
SIC: 8711 Civil engineering; pollution control engineering
PA: Tetra Tech, Inc.
3475 E Foothill Blvd
Pasadena CA 91107
626 351-4664

(P-26093)
TETRA TECH TECHNICAL SERVICES
3475 E Foothill Blvd Fl 3, Pasadena (91107-6024)
PHONE...................................626 351-4664
Dan Batrack, *CEO*
EMP: 244
SALES (est): 11.7MM
SALES (corp-wide): 2.3B **Publicly Held**
WEB: www.tetratech.com
SIC: 8711 Consulting engineer
PA: Tetra Tech, Inc.
3475 E Foothill Blvd
Pasadena CA 91107
626 351-4664

PRODUCTS & SERVICES SECTION
8711 - Engineering Services County (P-26114)

(P-26094)
TGCON INC (HQ)
Also Called: Goodfellow Top Grade Cnstr LLC
50 Contractors St, Livermore (94551-4863)
PHONE...................925 449-5764
Fax: 925 449-5875
William L Gates, *President*
Brian L Gates, *COO*
Scott Blaine, *CFO*
Bob Fisher, *Exec VP*
Brian Gates, *Exec VP*
EMP: 108
SQ FT: 25,000
SALES (est): 56.2MM
SALES (corp-wide): 203MM **Privately Held**
WEB: www.topgradeconstruction.com
SIC: 8711 Engineering services; construction & civil engineering
PA: Goodfellow Bros., Inc.
1407 Walla Walla Ave
Wenatchee WA 98801
509 667-9095

(P-26095)
THERMASOURCE LLC (PA)
235 Pine St Ste 1150, San Francisco (94104-2748)
PHONE...................707 523-2960
Fax: 707 523-1029
Richard Chow, *CEO*
Louis Capuano Jr, *President*
Gerald Hamblin, *COO*
Christopher T Schofield, *CFO*
Linda Capuano, *Treasurer*
EMP: 80
SALES (est): 45.4MM **Privately Held**
WEB: www.thermasource.com
SIC: 8711 Consulting engineer

(P-26096)
THERMASOURCE LLC
333 S Grand Ave Ste 4070, Los Angeles (90071-1544)
PHONE...................530 476-3333
Louis Capuano Jr, *Branch Mgr*
EMP: 76
SALES (corp-wide): 45.4MM **Privately Held**
SIC: 8711 Consulting engineer
PA: Thermasource, Llc
235 Pine St Ste 1150
San Francisco CA 94104
707 523-2960

(P-26097)
THOMAS MARK & COMPANY INC (PA)
2290 N 1st St Ste 304, San Jose (95131-2017)
PHONE...................408 453-5373
Fax: 408 453-5390
Mike Lohman, *President*
Robert A Himes, *President*
Richard K Tanaka, *Chairman*
Sasha D Dansky, *Principal*
David E Ross, *Principal*
EMP: 50
SQ FT: 10,600
SALES (est): 32.2MM **Privately Held**
WEB: www.markthomas.com
SIC: 8711 8713 Consulting engineer; surveying services

(P-26098)
THOMPSON HYSELL ENGINEERS
1016 12th St, Modesto (95354-0812)
PHONE...................209 521-8986
Fax: 209 521-9045
Ken Stepan, *President*
William Hysell, *President*
Tom Holstrom, *Vice Pres*
Kent Hysell, *Vice Pres*
Stan Thompson, *Vice Pres*
EMP: 65
SQ FT: 8,000
SALES: 540.3K **Privately Held**
SIC: 8711 8713 Civil engineering; surveying services

(P-26099)
THORNTON TOMASETTI INC
650 California St Fl 14, San Francisco (94108-2792)
PHONE...................415 365-6900
Fax: 415 365-6901
Joseph R Sutton, *Office Mgr*
Cristina Medina, *Office Mgr*
EMP: 60
SALES (corp-wide): 260MM **Privately Held**
SIC: 8711 Structural engineering
PA: Thornton Tomasetti, Inc.
51 Madison Ave Fl 19
New York NY 10010
917 661-7800

(P-26100)
TJ CROSS ENGINEERS INC
200 New Stine Rd Ste 270, Bakersfield (93309-2658)
PHONE...................661 831-8782
Fax: 661 831-5019
Timothy Couch, *Principal*
Kent Halley, *Principal*
Stuart Heisler, *Principal*
Chuck Soderstrom, *Principal*
Lisa Wong, *Principal*
EMP: 130
SQ FT: 22,000
SALES (est): 20.6MM
SALES (corp-wide): 7.9B **Privately Held**
WEB: www.tjcross.com
SIC: 8711 Engineering services; consulting engineer
PA: The Parsons Corporation
100 W Walnut St
Pasadena CA 91124
626 440-2000

(P-26101)
TOYON RESEARCH CORPORATION (PA)
6800 Cortona Dr, Goleta (93117-3139)
PHONE...................805 968-6787
Fax: 805 685-8089
Joel R Garbarino, *Ch of Bd*
Tom Geyer, *Vice Pres*
Michael Grace, *Vice Pres*
Ryan Strader, *Vice Pres*
Larry Romero, *Managing Dir*
EMP: 84 EST: 1980
SQ FT: 16,000
SALES (est): 32.7MM **Privately Held**
WEB: www.toyon.com
SIC: 8711 7371 Engineering services; custom computer programming services

(P-26102)
TRANDES CORP
4250 Pacific Hwy Ste 209, San Diego (92110-3222)
PHONE...................619 398-0464
Fax: 858 268-4603
Rollin Cross, *Program Mgr*
Scott Iwanowski, *Vice Pres*
Paul Anderson, *Engineer*
David Pate, *Engineer*
Tess Spaulding, *QC Mgr*
EMP: 121
SALES (corp-wide): 13.7MM **Privately Held**
WEB: www.trandes.com
SIC: 8711 7378 7371 Consulting engineer; computer maintenance & repair; custom computer programming services
PA: Trandes Corp.
4601 Presidents Dr # 360
Lanham MD 20706
301 459-0200

(P-26103)
TREADWELL & ROLLO INC (DH)
555 Montgomery St # 1300, San Francisco (94111-2561)
PHONE...................415 955-9040
Fax: 415 955-9041
Philip Ttringale, *Director*
Philip G Smith, *Exec VP*
Philip Smith, *Exec VP*
Maria G Flessas, *Vice Pres*
Maria Flessas, *Vice Pres*
EMP: 50
SQ FT: 12,500
SALES (est): 12.4MM
SALES (corp-wide): 189.1MM **Privately Held**
WEB: www.treadwellrollo.com
SIC: 8711 Engineering services
HQ: Langan Engineering And Environmental Services, Inc.
300 Kimball Dr
Parsippany NJ 07054
201 794-6900

(P-26104)
TRIAD HOMES ASSOC
Also Called: Triad-Holmes Associates
873 N Main St Ste 150, Bishop (93514-2479)
PHONE...................760 873-4273
Thomas Platz, *President*
David Laverty, *Project Mgr*
Andy Holmes, *Personnel Exec*
EMP: 60
SQ FT: 800
SALES (est): 4.5MM
SALES (corp-wide): 6.2MM **Privately Held**
SIC: 8711 8713 6552 Civil engineering; surveying services; subdividers & developers
PA: Holmes Triad Associates
549 Old Mmmoth Rd Ste 202
Mammoth Lakes CA
760 934-7588

(P-26105)
TRUST AUTOMATION INC
143 Suburban Rd Ste 100, San Luis Obispo (93401-1102)
PHONE...................805 544-0761
Fax: 805 544-4621
Ty Safreno, *CEO*
Brett Keegan, *COO*
Trudie Safreno, *CFO*
Chuck Kass, *Exec VP*
Dave Rennie, *Vice Pres*
EMP: 65
SQ FT: 50,000
SALES (est): 13MM **Privately Held**
WEB: www.trustautomation.com
SIC: 8711 3812 3731 3621 Machine tool design; antennas, radar or communications; submersible marine robots, manned or unmanned; generators for gas-electric or oil-electric vehicles; automation & robotics consultant

(P-26106)
TTG ENGINEERS
222 S Harbor Blvd Ste 800, Anaheim (92805-3715)
PHONE...................714 490-5555
Albert Chiu, *Branch Mgr*
Saurin Chakrabarti, *Vice Pres*
Sunil Patel, *Vice Pres*
EMP: 55
SALES (corp-wide): 55MM **Privately Held**
WEB: www.tmadengineers.com
SIC: 8711 Consulting engineer
PA: Ttg Engineers
300 N Lake Ave Fl 14
Pasadena CA 91101
626 463-2800

(P-26107)
TTG ENGINEERS (PA)
Also Called: Mbe
300 N Lake Ave Fl 14, Pasadena (91101-4164)
PHONE...................626 463-2800
Fax: 626 351-5319
Zareh Astourian, *President*
Stephen Boase, *CFO*
Ed Gharabans, *Vice Pres*
Sunil Patel, *Vice Pres*
Ron Sheldon, *Vice Pres*
EMP: 160
SQ FT: 16,000
SALES (est): 55MM **Privately Held**
WEB: www.tmadengineers.com
SIC: 8711 Consulting engineer

(P-26108)
TY LIN INTERNATIONAL GROUP (PA)
345 California St Fl 23, San Francisco (94104-2646)
PHONE...................415 291-3700
Robert A Peterson, *President*
Meg Brown, *Human Res Dir*
EMP: 109
SQ FT: 34,000
SALES (est): 139.6MM **Privately Held**
SIC: 8711 Consulting engineer

(P-26109)
U S ARMY CORPS OF ENGINEERS
1645 Riverbank Rd, West Sacramento (95605-1743)
PHONE...................916 557-7491
EMP: 66 **Publicly Held**
SIC: 8711 9199 Engineering services; general government administration
HQ: U S Army Corps Of Engineers
441 G Street Nw
Washington DC 20314
804 435-9362

(P-26110)
U S ARMY CORPS OF ENGINEERS
300 N Los Angeles St, Los Angeles (90012-3308)
PHONE...................213 452-3139
EMP: 65 **Publicly Held**
SIC: 8711 Engineering services
HQ: U S Army Corps Of Engineers
441 G Street Nw
Washington DC 20314
804 435-9362

(P-26111)
U S ARMY CORPS OF ENGINEERS
2194 Ascot Ave, Rio Linda (95673-5337)
PHONE...................916 649-0133
EMP: 65 **Publicly Held**
SIC: 8711 9711 Engineering services; Army;
HQ: U S Army Corps Of Engineers
441 G Street Nw
Washington DC 20314
804 435-9362

(P-26112)
U S ARMY CORPS OF ENGINEERS
3900 Roseville Rd, North Highlands (95660-5707)
PHONE...................916 925-7001
Ed Fager, *Branch Mgr*
EMP: 66 **Publicly Held**
SIC: 8711 Engineering services
HQ: U S Army Corps Of Engineers
441 G Street Nw
Washington DC 20314
804 435-9362

(P-26113)
U S ARMY CORPS OF ENGINEERS
2100 Bridgeway, Sausalito (94965-1753)
PHONE...................415 289-3067
Linda Holm, *Manager*
EMP: 65 **Publicly Held**
SIC: 8711 Engineering services
HQ: U S Army Corps Of Engineers
441 G Street Nw
Washington DC 20314
804 435-9362

(P-26114)
UCI CONSTRUCTION INC
3900 Fruitvale Ave, Bakersfield (93308-5114)
PHONE...................661 587-0192
David Krugh, *Manager*
Jeff Holz, *Opers Mgr*
Charles D Martin, *Agent*
EMP: 98
SALES (est): 17.7MM **Privately Held**
SIC: 8711 1521 Professional engineer; new construction, single-family houses

8711 - Engineering Services County (P-26115)

(P-26115)
UNITED INFRSTRCTURE PRJCTS INC
Also Called: Uiprojects
9891 Irvine Center Dr # 200, Irvine (92618-4317)
PHONE.....................213 402-1232
Mazin Sadiq, *President*
Brian Poyant, *Vice Pres*
EMP: 99
SALES: 950K **Privately Held**
WEB: www.uiprojects.net
SIC: 8711 1542 Engineering services; custom builders, non-residential

(P-26116)
UNITED STATES DEPT OF ARMY
1325 J St, Sacramento (95814-2928)
PHONE.....................916 557-5100
Lina Terprestra, *Administration*
Miki Fujitsubo, *Project Mgr*
Jane Rinck, *Manager*
EMP: 302 **Publicly Held**
SIC: 8711 Engineering services
HQ: United States Department Of The Army
1400 Defense Pentagon
Washington DC 20310
703 695-1717

(P-26117)
UNITED STATES DEPT OF NAVY
Also Called: Navfac-Southwest General Funds
1220 Pacific Hwy, San Diego (92132-5190)
PHONE.....................619 532-2317
Fax: 619 532-3830
Lynn Biederman, *Branch Mgr*
Capt Darius Banaji, *COO*
Lee Saunders, *Officer*
Robert Phillips, *Office Mgr*
Joseph Cook, *Info Tech Dir*
EMP: 200 **Publicly Held**
SIC: 8711 9711 Engineering services; Navy;
HQ: United States Department Of The Navy
1200 Navy Pentagon
Washington DC 20350
703 545-6700

(P-26118)
UNIVERSAL GENERAL BUILDERS
871 Industrial Rd Ste A, San Carlos (94070-3389)
PHONE.....................650 591-3104
EMP: 99
SALES (est): 2.8MM **Privately Held**
SIC: 8711 Building construction consultant

(P-26119)
URS GROUP INC
1333 Broadway Ste 800, Oakland (94612-1924)
PHONE.....................510 893-3600
Louise Armstrong, *Manager*
Said Salah-Mars, *President*
Adam Krpan, *Info Tech Mgr*
Robert Michna, *Project Mgr*
Ivan Wong, *Project Engr*
EMP: 200
SALES (corp-wide): 17.9B **Publicly Held**
SIC: 8711 4953 Engineering services; refuse systems
HQ: Urs Group, Inc.
300 S Grand Ave Ste 1100
Los Angeles CA 90071
213 593-8000

(P-26120)
URS GROUP INC
1 Montgomery St Ste 900, San Francisco (94104-4538)
PHONE.....................415 896-5858
Simon Kim, *Branch Mgr*
EMP: 100
SALES (corp-wide): 17.9B **Publicly Held**
SIC: 8711 8712 8741 Consulting engineer; architectural engineering; construction management
HQ: Urs Group, Inc.
300 S Grand Ave Ste 1100
Los Angeles CA 90071
213 593-8000

(P-26121)
URS GROUP INC
915 Wilshire Blvd Ste 700, Los Angeles (90017-3436)
P.O. Box 116183, Atlanta GA (30368-6183)
PHONE.....................213 996-2200
Paul Ryan, *Manager*
Helen Kerschner, *Branch Mgr*
Dave Wu, *Branch Mgr*
Hal McGee, *CTO*
Tom Lych, *Info Tech Mgr*
EMP: 99
SALES (corp-wide): 17.9B **Publicly Held**
SIC: 8711 8712 8741 Consulting engineer; architectural engineering; construction management
HQ: Urs Group, Inc.
300 S Grand Ave Ste 1100
Los Angeles CA 90071
213 593-8000

(P-26122)
URS GROUP INC
901 Via Piemonte Ste 500, Ontario (91764-8502)
PHONE.....................909 980-4000
Brian Winne, *Branch Mgr*
EMP: 69
SALES (corp-wide): 17.9B **Publicly Held**
SIC: 8711 8712 8741 Consulting engineer; architectural engineering; construction management
HQ: Urs Group, Inc.
300 S Grand Ave Ste 1100
Los Angeles CA 90071
213 593-8000

(P-26123)
URS GROUP INC
915 Wilshire Blvd Ste 700, Los Angeles (90017-3436)
P.O. Box 116183, Atlanta GA (30368-6183)
PHONE.....................213 996-2200
Shahram Bahbagu, *Branch Mgr*
EMP: 100
SALES (corp-wide): 17.9B **Publicly Held**
SIC: 8711 Engineering services
HQ: Urs Group, Inc.
300 S Grand Ave Ste 1100
Los Angeles CA 90071
213 593-8000

(P-26124)
URS GROUP INC
2300 Clayton Rd Ste 1400, Concord (94520-2173)
PHONE.....................925 446-3800
Sam Capps, *Branch Mgr*
EMP: 69
SALES (corp-wide): 17.9B **Publicly Held**
SIC: 8711 8712 8741 Consulting engineer; architectural engineering; construction management
HQ: Urs Group, Inc.
300 S Grand Ave Ste 1100
Los Angeles CA 90071
213 593-8000

(P-26125)
URS GROUP INC
4225 Executive Sq # 1600, La Jolla (92037-9122)
PHONE.....................619 294-9400
Fax: 858 812-9293
Norbert Schulz, *Manager*
Steve Brinigar, *General Mgr*
Leo Handfelt, *General Mgr*
Sunnie House, *Project Mgr*
Lauren Wittmann, *Project Mgr*
EMP: 100
SALES (corp-wide): 17.9B **Publicly Held**
SIC: 8711 Engineering services
HQ: Urs Group, Inc.
300 S Grand Ave Ste 1100
Los Angeles CA 90071
213 593-8000

(P-26126)
URS GROUP INC
130 Robin Hill Rd Ste 100, Santa Barbara (93117-3153)
PHONE.....................805 964-6010
Timothy Cohen, *Manager*
Kim Young, *Office Admin*
Pablo Landriz, *Info Tech Dir*
Richard Rosenbaum, *Safety Mgr*
EMP: 80
SQ FT: 29,621
SALES (corp-wide): 17.9B **Publicly Held**
SIC: 8711 Engineering services
HQ: Urs Group, Inc.
300 S Grand Ave Ste 1100
Los Angeles CA 90071
213 593-8000

(P-26127)
URS GROUP INC
2870 Gateway Oaks Dr # 150, Sacramento (95833-3577)
PHONE.....................916 679-2000
Fax: 916 679-2900
Gary Horton, *Manager*
Rob Trojan, *Admin Asst*
Lukas Allred, *Project Leader*
Lisa Lanterman, *Project Mgr*
Shabad Khalsa, *Senior Engr*
EMP: 64
SALES (corp-wide): 17.9B **Publicly Held**
SIC: 8711 8712 8741 Engineering services; consulting engineer; architectural engineering; construction management
HQ: Urs Group, Inc.
300 S Grand Ave Ste 1100
Los Angeles CA 90071
213 593-8000

(P-26128)
URS GROUP INC
100 W San Fernando St # 200, San Jose (95113-2219)
PHONE.....................408 297-9585
William Hadaya, *Branch Mgr*
Rick Moreland, *Project Mgr*
Lan Ho, *Project Engr*
Ramsey Hissen, *Sr Project Mgr*
Millette Litzinger, *Sr Project Mgr*
EMP: 55
SALES (corp-wide): 17.9B **Publicly Held**
SIC: 8711 Engineering services
HQ: Urs Group, Inc.
300 S Grand Ave Ste 1100
Los Angeles CA 90071
213 593-8000

(P-26129)
URS GROUP INC
999 W Town And Country Rd, Orange (92868-4713)
PHONE.....................714 835-6886
Steve Pearson, *Branch Mgr*
Doug Smith, *Project Mgr*
Julie Hines, *Human Resources*
EMP: 69
SALES (corp-wide): 17.9B **Publicly Held**
SIC: 8711 8712 8741 Consulting engineer; architectural engineering; construction management
HQ: Urs Group, Inc.
300 S Grand Ave Ste 1100
Los Angeles CA 90071
213 593-8000

(P-26130)
URS GROUP INC
2870 Gateway Oaks Dr # 300, Sacramento (95833-3577)
PHONE.....................916 929-2346
Fax: 916 929-7263
Victor Auvinen, *Branch Mgr*
Kevin Wong, *Sales Executive*
EMP: 200
SALES (corp-wide): 17.9B **Publicly Held**
SIC: 8711 Engineering services
HQ: Urs Group, Inc.
300 S Grand Ave Ste 1100
Los Angeles CA 90071
213 593-8000

(P-26131)
URS GROUP INC
1 Montgomery St Ste 900, San Francisco (94104-4538)
PHONE.....................415 896-5858
Rob Robinson, *Branch Mgr*
Dale Shileikis, *Vice Pres*
EMP: 69
SALES (corp-wide): 17.9B **Publicly Held**
SIC: 8711 Engineering services
HQ: Urs Group, Inc.
300 S Grand Ave Ste 1100
Los Angeles CA 90071
213 593-8000

(P-26132)
URS HOLDINGS INC (DH)
600 Montgomery St Fl 25, San Francisco (94111-2727)
PHONE.....................415 774-2700
Thomas W Bishop, *CEO*
Martin M Koffel, *Ch of Bd*
W D Balfour, *Senior VP*
Dhamo S Dhamotharan, *Senior VP*
Robert M Gallen, *Senior VP*
EMP: 470
SALES (est): 5.6B
SALES (corp-wide): 17.9B **Publicly Held**
SIC: 8711 7389 6531 8249 Consulting engineer; financial services; real estate agents & managers; aviation school; aircraft maintenance & repair services
HQ: Aecom Global Ii, Llc
1999 Avenue Of Ste 2600
Los Angeles CA 90067
213 593-8100

(P-26133)
URS-GEI JOINT VENTURE
1333 Broadway Ste 800, Oakland (94612-1924)
PHONE.....................510 874-3051
Said Salah-Mars, *Principal*
EMP: 50
SALES (est): 2.1MM **Privately Held**
SIC: 8711 Engineering services

(P-26134)
URS-WESTON JOINT VENTURE
2020 E 1st St Ste 400, Santa Ana (92705-4032)
PHONE.....................714 433-7710
Terri McDaniel, *Principal*
EMP: 50
SALES (est): 3.6MM **Privately Held**
SIC: 8711 Engineering services

(P-26135)
US ARMY CORPS OF ENGINEERS
1325 J St Frnt, Sacramento (95814-2922)
PHONE.....................916 557-7490
Fax: 916 557-7853
Thomas Chapman, *Director*
EMP: 800 **Publicly Held**
WEB: www.sac.usace.army.mil
SIC: 8711 9711 Engineering services; Army;
HQ: U S Army Corps Of Engineers
441 G Street Nw
Washington DC 20314
804 435-9362

(P-26136)
US ARMY CORPS OF ENGINEERS
915 Wilshire Blvd Ste 930, Los Angeles (90017-3489)
PHONE.....................213 452-3967
Col Richard Thompson, *Manager*
David Turk, *Vice Pres*
Bob Coplin, *Chief*
Mark Durham, *Chief*
EMP: 650 **Publicly Held**
WEB: www.sac.usace.army.mil
SIC: 8711 9711 Engineering services; Army;
HQ: U S Army Corps Of Engineers
441 G Street Nw
Washington DC 20314
804 435-9362

(P-26137)
VANDORPE CHOU ASSOCIATES INC
Also Called: VCA Engineering
1845 W Orangewood Ave # 210, Orange (92868-2051)
PHONE.....................714 978-9780
Fax: 714 978-9788
Daniel T Van Dorpe, *President*
Neil Evans, *Shareholder*
Margaret Van Dorpe, *Corp Secy*
Mark Gaale, *Vice Pres*
Charles Russell, *Vice Pres*
EMP: 50 **EST:** 1979
SQ FT: 3,000

PRODUCTS & SERVICES SECTION
8712 - Architectural Services County (P-26159)

SALES (est): 7.9MM **Privately Held**
WEB: www.vcaengineers.com
SIC: **8711** Civil engineering; structural engineering

(P-26138)
VCA CODE GROUP
2200 W Orangewood Ave # 150, Orange (92868-1948)
PHONE..................................714 363-4700
Dan Van Dope, *President*
Tom Van Dorpe, *Senior Partner*
Dan Vandope, *President*
Bob Chou, *Vice Pres*
Kathryn Ito, *Admin Asst*
EMP: 50
SALES (est): 7.2MM **Privately Held**
WEB: www.vcacodegroup.com
SIC: **8711** Engineering services

(P-26139)
VECTOR RESOURCES INC
Also Called: Vector USA
9808 Waples St, San Diego (92121-2921)
PHONE..................................858 546-1014
Fax: 858 546-1086
Debra Treece, *Branch Mgr*
EMP: 50
SALES (corp-wide): 83MM **Privately Held**
SIC: **8711** Consulting engineer
PA: Vector Resources, Inc.
3530 Voyager St
Torrance CA 90503
310 436-1000

(P-26140)
VELOCITEL RF INC
2415 Campus Dr Ste 200, Irvine (92612-8530)
PHONE..................................949 809-4999
John Powers, *CEO*
Dan Southwick, *President*
Steve Chiotti, *CFO*
Thor Erickson, *Vice Pres*
Bill Zlotnick, *Vice Pres*
EMP: 200
SALES (est): 6.1MM
SALES (corp-wide): 800MM **Privately Held**
WEB: www.velocitel.net
SIC: **8711** Engineering services
PA: Velocitel, Inc.
1033 Skokie Blvd Ste 320
Northbrook IL 60062
224 757-0001

(P-26141)
VERSA ENGINEERING & TECH INC
1320 Willow Pass Rd S500, Concord (94520-5232)
PHONE..................................925 405-4505
Fred Fong, *President*
Flavio Santini, *Chairman*
Cynthia Wiggins-Wyrick, *Business Dir*
Tom Nollie, *Principal*
EMP: 55
SALES (est): 6MM **Privately Held**
SIC: **8711** Engineering services

(P-26142)
VT MILCOM INC
2232 Verus St Ste A, San Diego (92154-4706)
PHONE..................................619 424-9024
Fax: 619 424-9097
Brian Upthegrove, *Branch Mgr*
Paul Becher, *Project Mgr*
Jim Williams, *Manager*
EMP: 178
SALES (corp-wide): 369.7MM **Privately Held**
WEB: www.milcom-systems.com
SIC: **8711** Engineering services
HQ: Vt Milcom Inc.
529 Viking Dr
Virginia Beach VA 23452
757 463-2800

(P-26143)
W M LYLES CO
2810 Unicorn Rd, Bakersfield (93308-6853)
PHONE..................................661 387-1600
Fax: 661 387-1620
Patrick Saleen, *Assistant VP*
EMP: 50
SALES (corp-wide): 31.9MM **Privately Held**
WEB: www.wmlyles.com
SIC: **8711** 1623 Engineering services; pipeline construction
HQ: W. M. Lyles Co.
1210 W Olive Ave
Fresno CA 93728
951 973-7393

(P-26144)
WALLACE-KUHL INVESTMENTS LLC (PA)
3050 Industrial Blvd, West Sacramento (95691-3470)
P.O. Box 1137 (95691-1137)
PHONE..................................916 372-1434
Fax: 916 372-2565
Douglas J Kuhl,
Thomas S Wallace,
Eric Trotter, *Manager*
EMP: 65
SQ FT: 11,300
SALES (est): 14.4MM **Privately Held**
WEB: www.wallace-kuhl.com
SIC: **8711** **8748** Engineering services; business consulting

(P-26145)
WEST YOST & ASSOCIATES INC (PA)
2020 Res Pk Dr Ste 100, Davis (95618)
PHONE..................................530 756-5905
Fax: 530 756-5991
Charles Duncan, *President*
Bruce West, *President*
Steven R Dalrymple, *Corp Secy*
John Bergen, *Vice Pres*
John Goodwin, *Vice Pres*
EMP: 76
SQ FT: 25,000
SALES (est): 28.1MM **Privately Held**
WEB: www.westyost.com
SIC: **8711** Civil engineering

(P-26146)
WESTWIND ENGINEERING INC
553 N Pcf Coastte B179 B, Redondo Beach (90277)
PHONE..................................310 831-3454
Carl Graves, *President*
Mary Ann Graves, *CEO*
Howard Wong, *Treasurer*
Ben Loya, *Exec VP*
Bob Wong, *Vice Pres*
EMP: 70
SALES (est): 2.7MM **Privately Held**
SIC: **8711** Engineering services

(P-26147)
WILLDAN ENGINEERING
2401 E Katella Ave # 300, Anaheim (92806-5909)
PHONE..................................714 978-8200
Lisa Penna, *Manager*
EMP: 86
SALES (corp-wide): 135.1MM **Publicly Held**
WEB: www.willdan.com
SIC: **8711** **8742** Civil engineering; business planning & organizing services
HQ: Willdan Engineering
2401 E Katella Ave # 300
Anaheim CA 92806
714 978-8200

(P-26148)
WILLDAN GROUP INC (PA)
2401 E Katella Ave # 300, Anaheim (92806-5909)
PHONE..................................800 424-9144
Fax: 714 940-4920
Thomas D Brisbin, *President*
Win Westfall, *Ch of Bd*
Marc Tipermas, *President*
John Rinard, *CEO*
Rebekah Smith, *COO*
EMP: 121
SQ FT: 18,000
SALES: 135.1MM **Publicly Held**
WEB: www.willdangroup.com
SIC: **8711** **8748** Civil engineering; consulting engineer; urban planning & consulting services

(P-26149)
WILLIAM E HEINSELMAN
3303 Luyung Dr, Rancho Cordova (95742-6860)
PHONE..................................916 920-0220
William E Heinselman, *Owner*
EMP: 50 EST: 2011
SALES: 10MM **Privately Held**
SIC: **8711** Sanitary engineers

(P-26150)
WIND RIVER SYSTEMS INC
10505 Sorrento Valley Rd, San Diego (92121-1618)
PHONE..................................858 824-3100
Brad Murdoch, *Vice Pres*
Damien Art, *Vice Pres*
Veronica Andres, *Manager*
Shelley Schwartz, *Manager*
EMP: 100
SALES (corp-wide): 55.3MM **Publicly Held**
WEB: www.windriver.com
SIC: **8711** Electrical or electronic engineering
HQ: Wind River Systems, Inc.
500 Wind River Way
Alameda CA 94501
510 748-4100

(P-26151)
WINZLER & KELLY
2235 Mercury Way Ste 150, Santa Rosa (95407-5470)
PHONE..................................707 523-1010
Theodore B Whiton, *Sales & Mktg St*
Julie Cardinale, *Officer*
Chuck Bove, *Regional Mgr*
Daren Dalby, *Regional Mgr*
Fred Smith, *Regional Mgr*
EMP: 95
SQ FT: 7,000
SALES (corp-wide): 8.9MM **Privately Held**
WEB: www.sjoeng.com
SIC: **8711** **8748** **8742** Consulting engineer; environmental consultant; industrial hygiene consultant
PA: Winzler & Kelly
2235 Mercury Way Ste 150
Santa Rosa CA 95407
707 523-1010

(P-26152)
WOOD RODGERS INC (PA)
3301 C St Ste 100b, Sacramento (95816-3350)
PHONE..................................916 341-7760
Mark Rodgers, *President*
Steve Balbierz, *Vice Pres*
Gerardo Calvillo, *Vice Pres*
Mark Rayback, *Vice Pres*
Peter Tobia, *Vice Pres*
EMP: 120 EST: 1996
SQ FT: 5,500
SALES (est): 49.1MM **Privately Held**
WEB: www.woodrodgers.com
SIC: **8711** Civil engineering

(P-26153)
WORLEYPARSONS GROUP INC
125 W Huntington Dr, Arcadia (91007-3050)
PHONE..................................626 294-3300
William Hall, *Manager*
Thinh Pham, *Database Admin*
Greg Grigorian, *Project Mgr*
Mark Lim, *Engineer*
Vicente Panganiban, *Engineer*
EMP: 60
SALES (corp-wide): 5.7B **Privately Held**
SIC: **8711** **8742** Engineering services; construction project management consultant
HQ: Worleyparsons Group Inc.
6330 West Loop S
Bellaire TX 77401
713 407-5000

(P-26154)
WORLEYPARSONS GROUP INC
721 Charles E Young Dr S, Los Angeles (90095-8342)
PHONE..................................610 855-2000
Christopher L Parker, *CEO*
EMP: 329

SALES (corp-wide): 5.7B **Privately Held**
SIC: **8711** Acoustical engineering
HQ: Worleyparsons Group Inc.
6330 West Loop S
Bellaire TX 77401
713 407-5000

(P-26155)
WSP USA CORP
405 Howard St Ste 500, San Francisco (94105-2928)
PHONE..................................415 398-3833
Randy J Meyers, *Branch Mgr*
Edward Michel, *CFO*
Tom Smith, *Bd of Directors*
Robert Gracilieri, *Exec VP*
Michael Mangione, *Exec VP*
EMP: 120
SALES (corp-wide): 2.5B **Privately Held**
WEB: www.flackandkurtz.com
SIC: **8711** **8748** Consulting engineer; telecommunications consultant
HQ: Wsp Usa Corp.
512 Fashion Ave Fl 13
New York NY 10018
914 747-1120

(P-26156)
YUPANA LLC
201 N Civic Dr Ste 180, Walnut Creek (94596-8226)
PHONE..................................925 482-0657
John McWeeny,
Hatice Erdec, *Human Resources*
Buse Ur, *Marketing Staff*
John McWeeney, *Mng Member*
Hakan Evircan, *Manager*
EMP: 50
SALES (est): 4.1MM **Privately Held**
SIC: **8711** Engineering services

(P-26157)
ZEEAERO INC
2700 Broderick Way, Mountain View (94043-1108)
PHONE..................................650 964-4570
Eric Allison, *CEO*
Dave Castelletti, *Technology*
EMP: 85
SQ FT: 30,000
SALES (est): 21.7MM **Privately Held**
SIC: **8711** Aviation &/or aeronautical engineering

8712 Architectural Services

(P-26158)
5 DESIGN INC
Also Called: 5design
1024 N Orange Dr Ste 215, Los Angeles (90038-2348)
PHONE..................................323 308-3558
Stan Hathaway, *President*
Michael Ellis, *Treasurer*
Arthur Benedetti Jr, *Vice Pres*
Melissa Zukerman, *Executive*
Tina Washington, *Executive Asst*
EMP: 76
SALES: 12MM **Privately Held**
WEB: www.5plusdesign.com
SIC: **8712** Architectural services

(P-26159)
A SMWM CALIFORNIA CORPORATION
Also Called: Simon Mrtn-Vgue Wnklstein Mris
185 Berry St Ste 5100, San Francisco (94107-1772)
PHONE..................................415 546-0400
Cathy Simon, *President*
Karen Alschuler, *Chairman*
John Long, *Vice Pres*
Prakash Pinto, *Vice Pres*
Evan Rose, *Vice Pres*
EMP: 60
SQ FT: 16,200
SALES: 10MM **Privately Held**
WEB: www.smwm.com
SIC: **8712** Architectural services

8712 - Architectural Services County (P-26160)

(P-26160)
AECOM SERVICES INC (HQ)
Also Called: Aecom Design
555 S Flower St Ste 3700, Los Angeles (90071-2432)
PHONE.................213 593-8000
John M Dionisio, *CEO*
Daniel R Streett, *Vice Chairman*
Michael S Burke, *President*
Raymond Landy, *President*
Jane Chmielinski, *COO*
EMP: 250 **EST:** 1946
SALES (est): 1B
SALES (corp-wide): 17.9B **Publicly Held**
WEB: www.dmjmhn.com
SIC: 8712 8741 8711 Architectural services; management services; engineering services
PA: Aecom
1999 Avenue Of The Stars # 2600
Los Angeles CA 90067
213 593-8000

(P-26161)
AECOM TECHNOLOGY CORPORATION
41235 11th St W Ste B, Palmdale (93551-1435)
PHONE.................661 266-0802
EMP: 120
SALES (corp-wide): 17.9B **Publicly Held**
SIC: 8712 Architectural engineering
PA: Aecom
1999 Avenue Of The Stars # 2600
Los Angeles CA 90067
213 593-8000

(P-26162)
ALTOON PARTNERS LLP (PA)
Also Called: Altoon Porter
617 W 7th St Ste 400, Los Angeles (90017-3889)
PHONE.................213 225-1900
Fax: 213 225-1901
Ronald A Altoon, *Partner*
James Auld, *Partner*
Gary Dempster, *Partner*
William Sebring, *Partner*
Christine Anderson, *Principal*
EMP: 50
SQ FT: 20,000
SALES (est): 7.8MM **Privately Held**
WEB: www.altoonporter.com
SIC: 8712 Architectural services

(P-26163)
ANOVA ARCHITECTS INC
1990 3rd St Ste 500, Sacramento (95811-6925)
PHONE.................530 626-1810
Charles Downs, *President*
EMP: 50
SALES (est): 4MM **Privately Held**
SIC: 8712 Architectural services

(P-26164)
ARCHITECTS ORANGE
144 N Orange St, Orange (92866-1400)
PHONE.................714 639-9860
Fax: 714 639-5286
Jack Selman, *Senior Partner*
Selman Jack, *Senior Partner*
RC Alley III, *Partner*
Jim Dietze, *Partner*
Darrel Hebenstreit, *Partner*
EMP: 200 **EST:** 1973
SQ FT: 10,000
SALES (est): 41.5MM **Privately Held**
WEB: www.architectsorange.com
SIC: 8712 Architectural engineering

(P-26165)
ATI ENGINEERING SERVICES INC (PA)
Also Called: ATI Architects & Engineers
3860 Blackhawk Rd Ste 160, Danville (94506-4615)
PHONE.................925 648-8800
Fax: 925 648-8811
Robert Desautels, *President*
Paul Didonato, *COO*
Gmichael Goldsworthy, *Vice Pres*
Mike Rojansky, *Vice Pres*
Donna Foster, *Admin Asst*
EMP: 74
SQ FT: 14,000
SALES (est): 11.3MM **Privately Held**
WEB: www.atiengineering.com
SIC: 8712 8711 Architectural services; structural engineering

(P-26166)
AUSTIN VEUM RBBINS PRTNERS INC (PA)
501 W Broadway Ste A, San Diego (92101-3562)
PHONE.................619 231-1960
Douglas H Austin, *CEO*
Chris Vium, *President*
Christopher Venum, *COO*
Doreen Austin, *CFO*
Jeffrey Parshalle, *Vice Pres*
EMP: 83
SQ FT: 12,500
SALES (est): 5.3MM **Privately Held**
SIC: 8712 Architectural services

(P-26167)
BAR ARCHITECTS
901 Battery St Ste 300, San Francisco (94111-1350)
PHONE.................415 293-5700
Robert Hunter, *President*
Victor Chu, *Executive*
Randy Simonson, *Executive*
Earl Wilson, *Principal*
Jackson Ng, *MIS Dir*
EMP: 80
SQ FT: 13,500
SALES (est): 10.2MM **Privately Held**
WEB: www.bararch.com
SIC: 8712 Architectural services

(P-26168)
BASSENIAN/LAGONI ARCHITECTS
2031 Orchard Dr Ste 100, Newport Beach (92660-0753)
PHONE.................949 553-9100
Fax: 949 553-0548
Aram Bassenian, *CEO*
Carl Lagoni, *President*
Lee R Rogaliner, *CFO*
Hans Anderle, *Assoc VP*
Robert Chavez, *Exec VP*
EMP: 65 **EST:** 1979
SQ FT: 22,800
SALES (est): 13.3MM **Privately Held**
WEB: www.bassenianlagoni.com
SIC: 8712 Architectural engineering

(P-26169)
CALLISON LLC
1453 3rd Street Promenade # 400, Santa Monica (90401-3428)
PHONE.................310 394-8460
Fax: 310 394-4970
EMP: 205
SALES (corp-wide): 48.2MM **Privately Held**
SIC: 8712 Architectural services
PA: Callison Llc
1420 5th Ave Ste 2400
Seattle WA 98101
206 623-4646

(P-26170)
CALLISONRTKL INC
818 W 7th St Ste 300, Los Angeles (90017-3426)
PHONE.................213 627-7373
EMP: 140
SALES (corp-wide): 2.5B **Privately Held**
SIC: 8712
HQ: Callisonrtkl Inc
901 S Bond St
Baltimore MD 21231
410 528-8600

(P-26171)
CALLISONRTKL INC
333 S Hope St Ste C200, Los Angeles (90071-3005)
PHONE.................213 633-6000
Fax: 213 633-6060
Barbara Proano, *Branch Mgr*
Patricia Caripa, *Marketing Mgr*
EMP: 143
SALES (corp-wide): 2.7B **Privately Held**
WEB: www.rtkl.com
SIC: 8712 Architectural services
HQ: Callisonrtkl Inc.
901 S Bond St
Baltimore MD 21231
410 528-8600

(P-26172)
CANNON DESIGN INC
Also Called: Cannondworsky
1901 Avenue Of The Stars # 175, Los Angeles (90067-6000)
PHONE.................310 229-2700
Fax: 310 229-2800
Kevin Sticht, *Manager*
Cathryn Bang, *Vice Pres*
Daniel L Dworsky, *Principal*
Timothy Rommell, *Principal*
Dean Geib, *Technical Staff*
EMP: 56
SALES (corp-wide): 97.4MM **Privately Held**
WEB: www.cannondesign.com
SIC: 8712 Architectural engineering
HQ: Cannon Design, Inc.
2170 Whitehaven Rd
Grand Island NY 14072
716 774-3366

(P-26173)
CARRIER JOHNSON (PA)
Also Called: Culture
1301 3rd Ave, San Diego (92101-4012)
PHONE.................619 236-9462
Gordon Carrier, *President*
Michael Johnson, *Vice Pres*
EMP: 68
SQ FT: 13,000
SALES (est): 17MM **Privately Held**
WEB: www.carrierjohnson.com
SIC: 8712 7389 Architectural services; interior design services

(P-26174)
CH2M HILL INC
2485 Natomas Park Dr # 600, Sacramento (95833-2975)
PHONE.................916 920-0300
Fax: 916 920-8463
Craig Eldrich, *Branch Mgr*
Cindy Erickson, *Project Mgr*
Julie Spahn, *Project Mgr*
Mary Blankenship, *Manager*
Jim Hartley, *Manager*
EMP: 50
SALES (corp-wide): 5.4B **Privately Held**
SIC: 8712 Architectural services
HQ: Ch2m Hill, Inc.
9191 S Jamaica St
Englewood CO 80112
303 771-0900

(P-26175)
CH2M HILL INC
1737 N 1st St Ste 300, San Jose (95112-4585)
PHONE.................408 436-4936
Mark Janay, *Finance Other*
Michael Alonzo, *Project Mgr*
James Isles, *Project Mgr*
Steve Long, *Project Mgr*
Jerry Lillston, *VP Finance*
EMP: 50
SALES (corp-wide): 5.4B **Privately Held**
SIC: 8712 8711 1622 1611 Architectural services; engineering services; bridge, tunnel & elevated highway; highway & street construction
HQ: Ch2m Hill, Inc.
9191 S Jamaica St
Englewood CO 80112
303 771-0900

(P-26176)
CHONG PARTNERS ARCHITECHER INC
901 Market St Ste 600, San Francisco (94103-1740)
PHONE.................613 995-8210
Gordon H Chong, *President*
David A Englund, *CFO*
Sam Nunes, *Vice Pres*
Jeff Warner, *Vice Pres*
John Ruffo, *Admin Sec*
EMP: 125
SQ FT: 16,000
SALES: 4.2MM **Privately Held**
SIC: 8712 Architectural services

(P-26177)
CITY OF FREMONT
Also Called: Building & Safety Department
39550 Liberty St, Fremont (94538-2211)
P.O. Box 5006 (94537-5006)
PHONE.................510 494-4460
Neil Hawkins, *General Mgr*
Fred Diaz, *City Mgr*
EMP: 150 **Privately Held**
WEB: www.ci.fremont.ca.us
SIC: 8712 Architectural services
PA: City Of Fremont
3300 Capitol Ave
Fremont CA 94538
510 284-4000

(P-26178)
CITY OF LOS ANGELES
Also Called: Architecture Division
1149 S Broadway Ste 800, Los Angeles (90015-2237)
PHONE.................213 485-4282
Mahmood Karimzadeh, *Manager*
EMP: 65 **Privately Held**
WEB: www.lacity.org
SIC: 8712 Architectural engineering
PA: City Of Los Angeles
200 N Spring St Ste 303
Los Angeles CA 90012
213 978-0600

(P-26179)
CUNINGHAM GROUP ARCH INC
Also Called: Cuningham Group, The
8665 Hayden Pl, Culver City (90232-2901)
PHONE.................310 895-2200
Fax: 310 327-1822
John Cuiter, *President*
EMP: 50
SALES (corp-wide): 26.6MM **Privately Held**
WEB: www.cuningham.com
SIC: 8712 Architectural services
PA: Cuningham Group Architecture, Inc.
201 Se Main St Ste 325
Minneapolis MN 55414
612 379-3400

(P-26180)
DAHLIN GROUP INC (PA)
5865 Owens Dr, Pleasanton (94588-3942)
PHONE.................925 251-7200
Nancy K Keenan, *President*
Doug Dahlin, *Vice Pres*
Karl Danielson, *Vice Pres*
Charles Meyer, *Vice Pres*
Harrison Pierson, *Vice Pres*
EMP: 60
SQ FT: 300,000
SALES (est): 17.5MM **Privately Held**
WEB: www.dahlingroup.com
SIC: 8712 Architectural services

(P-26181)
DARDEN ARCHITECTS INC
6790 N West Ave Ste 104, Fresno (93711-4306)
PHONE.................559 448-8051
Martin Dietz, *President*
Chuck Aby, *Systs Prg Mgr*
EMP: 75 **EST:** 1959
SQ FT: 5,000
SALES (est): 12.6MM **Privately Held**
SIC: 8712 7389 Architectural engineering; interior designer

(P-26182)
DES ARCHITECTS + ENGINEERS INC
399 Bradford St Ste 300, Redwood City (94063-1585)
P.O. Box 3599 (94064-3599)
PHONE.................650 364-6453
Fax: 650 364-2618
Thomas Gilman, *President*
Stephen D Mincey, *CFO*
Craig Ivancovich, *Corp Secy*
Brandi Reyes, *Executive*
Jessica Langford, *Admin Asst*
EMP: 115
SQ FT: 35,000
SALES (est): 19.3MM **Privately Held**
WEB: www.des-ae.com
SIC: 8712 8711 Architectural engineering; engineering services

PRODUCTS & SERVICES SECTION
8712 - Architectural Services County (P-26203)

(P-26183)
DG ARCHITECTS INC (PA)
Also Called: Dga Plnning L Arch L Interiors
550 Ellis St, Mountain View (94043-2236)
PHONE..................650 943-1660
Fax: 650 943-1670
Randall Dowler, *President*
Nancy Escano, *Treasurer*
Mark Davis, *CTO*
Warren Young, *Project Mgr*
Gloria Magliari, *Prdtn Mgr*
EMP: 60
SQ FT: 15,000
SALES (est): 11.3MM **Privately Held**
WEB: www.dga-mv.com
SIC: **8712** Architectural services

(P-26184)
DLR GROUP INC OF CALIFORNIA (HQ)
3130 Wilshire Blvd Fl 6, Santa Monica (90403-2349)
PHONE..................310 828-0040
Adrian O Cohen, *President*
Dale Hallock, *Managing Prtnr*
Dennis Wiederholt, *Treasurer*
Jon P Anderson, *Vice Pres*
Brian Arial, *Vice Pres*
EMP: 73 EST: 1997
SALES (est): 14.8MM
SALES (corp-wide): 109.7MM **Privately Held**
SIC: **8712** **8711** Architectural services; engineering services; mechanical engineering
PA: Dlr Holding Company
6457 Frances St Ste 200
Omaha NE
402 393-4100

(P-26185)
GEHRY PARTNERS LLP
12541 Beatrice St, Los Angeles (90066-7001)
PHONE..................310 482-3000
Frank Gehry, *Partner*
Brian Aamoth, *Partner*
John Bowers, *Partner*
Anand Devarajan, *Partner*
Berta Gehry, *Partner*
EMP: 130
SQ FT: 12,100
SALES (est): 17.5MM **Privately Held**
SIC: **8712** Architectural services

(P-26186)
GENERAL SERVICES CAL DEPT
Also Called: Division of State Architect
1515 Clay St Ste 1201, Oakland (94612-1474)
PHONE..................510 622-3101
Fax: 510 622-3140
Lee Roy Tam, *Manager*
EMP: 60 **Privately Held**
WEB: www.4c.net
SIC: **8712** **9199** Architectural services; general government administration;
HQ: California Department Of General Services
707 3rd St
West Sacramento CA 95605

(P-26187)
GENERAL SERVICES CAL DEPT
Also Called: Division of State Architect
700 N Alameda St Ste 500, Los Angeles (90012-3352)
PHONE..................213 897-3995
Sharqat Ullah, *Manager*
EMP: 55 **Privately Held**
WEB: www.4c.net
SIC: **8712** **9199** Architectural services; general government administration;
HQ: California Department Of General Services
707 3rd St
West Sacramento CA 95605

(P-26188)
GENSLER ARCH DESIGN & PLG PC
2 Harrison St Fl 4, San Francisco (94105-6127)
PHONE..................415 433-3700
Fax: 415 836-4599
Daniel W Winey, *Principal*
Joan Price, *Principal*
EMP: 316
SALES (est): 2MM
SALES (corp-wide): 1B **Privately Held**
SIC: **8712** Architectural services
PA: M. Arthur Gensler Jr. & Associates, Inc.
2 Harrison St Fl 4
San Francisco CA 94105
415 433-3700

(P-26189)
GKK CORPORATION
1775 Hancock St Ste 150, San Diego (92110-2039)
PHONE..................619 398-0215
Unknown T Logan, *Branch Mgr*
EMP: 59
SALES (corp-wide): 117.5MM **Privately Held**
SIC: **8712** Architectural engineering
PA: Gkk Corporation
2355 Main St Ste 220
Irvine CA 92614
949 250-1500

(P-26190)
GKK CORPORATION (PA)
Also Called: Gkkworks
2355 Main St Ste 220, Irvine (92614-4251)
PHONE..................949 250-1500
Fax: 949 955-2708
Praful Kulkarni, *President*
James Staley, *CFO*
David Hunt, *Vice Pres*
Charles G Merrick, *Vice Pres*
Vanessa Oozano, *General Mgr*
EMP: 85
SQ FT: 11,000
SALES: 117.5MM **Privately Held**
SIC: **8712** **8711** Architectural engineering; building construction consultant

(P-26191)
GONZALEZ/GOODALE ARCHITECTS
Also Called: Chcg Architects
135 W Green St Ste 200, Pasadena (91105-4131)
PHONE..................626 568-1428
Fax: 626 568-8026
Armando L Gonzalez, *Owner*
Ali Barar, *Principal*
Harry Drake, *Principal*
John Ferguson, *Principal*
David Goodale, *Principal*
EMP: 52
SQ FT: 8,000
SALES: 9.8MM **Privately Held**
WEB: www.gonzalezgoodale.com
SIC: **8712** **7389** Architectural engineering; interior designer

(P-26192)
GOULD EVANS P C
95 Brady St, San Francisco (94103-1241)
PHONE..................415 503-1411
Fax: 415 503-1471
Robert Baum, *Manager*
Lauren Maass, *Assoc VP*
Anthony Rohr, *Design Engr*
Sherry Michalske, *Opers Mgr*
John Westell, *Associate*
EMP: 75
SALES (corp-wide): 27.3MM **Privately Held**
SIC: **8712** Architectural services
PA: Gould Evans, P C
4041 Mill St Ste A
Kansas City MO 64111
816 931-6655

(P-26193)
GRUEN ASSOCIATES
Also Called: Gruen Assoc Archtects Planners
6330 San Vicente Blvd # 200, Los Angeles (90048-5441)
PHONE..................323 937-4270
Fax: 323 937-6001
Ki Suh Park, *Partner*
Michael A Enomoto, *Partner*
Larry Schlossberg, *Partner*
Michael Enomoto, *Managing Prtnr*
Karl Swope, *Vice Pres*
EMP: 75 EST: 1947
SQ FT: 14,000
SALES (est): 13.7MM **Privately Held**
WEB: www.gruenassociates.com
SIC: **8712** Architectural services

(P-26194)
HAMMEL GREEN & ABRAHAMSON INC
Also Called: Hga Architects and Engineers
1200 R St Ste 100, Sacramento (95811-5807)
PHONE..................916 787-5100
Brent Forslin, *Director*
Stephen Ours, *Assoc VP*
Richard Tannahill, *Assoc VP*
Dale Wenkus, *Associate*
EMP: 65
SALES (corp-wide): 142.8MM **Privately Held**
WEB: www.hga.com
SIC: **8712** **8711** Architectural services; engineering services
PA: Hammel, Green And Abrahamson, Inc.
420 N 5th St Ste 100
Minneapolis MN 55401
612 758-4000

(P-26195)
HAMMEL GREEN & ABRAHAMSON INC
1918 Main St Fl 3, Santa Monica (90405-1006)
PHONE..................310 557-7600
Michael Ross, *Branch Mgr*
Bonnie Walker, *Vice Pres*
Linda Pederson, *Opers Mgr*
EMP: 182
SALES (corp-wide): 142.8MM **Privately Held**
SIC: **8712** Architectural engineering
PA: Hammel, Green And Abrahamson, Inc.
420 N 5th St Ste 100
Minneapolis MN 55401
612 758-4000

(P-26196)
HARLEY ELLIS DEVEREAUX CORP
417 Montgomery St Ste 400, San Francisco (94104-1111)
PHONE..................510 268-3800
Fax: 510 268-3820
Lee Vandekerchove, *President*
EMP: 64
SALES (corp-wide): 43.5MM **Privately Held**
SIC: **8712** Architectural services
PA: Harley Ellis Devereaux Corp
26913 Nrthwstrn Hwy 200
Southfield MI 48033
248 262-1500

(P-26197)
HARLEY ELLIS DEVEREAUX CORP
Also Called: Harley Ellis Devereuax
601 Suth Fgroa St Ste 500, Los Angeles (90017)
PHONE..................213 542-4500
Derrick Washington, *Principal*
EMP: 125
SALES (corp-wide): 43.5MM **Privately Held**
WEB: www.harleyellis.com
SIC: **8712** Architectural engineering
PA: Harley Ellis Devereaux Corp
26913 Nrthwstrn Hwy 200
Southfield MI 48033
248 262-1500

(P-26198)
HDR ENVIRONMENTAL OPE
8690 Balboa Ave Ste 200, San Diego (92123-6507)
PHONE..................858 712-8400
Dean Gipson, *Branch Mgr*
EMP: 70
SALES (corp-wide): 1.8B **Privately Held**
SIC: **8712** **8711** **8748** **8999** Architectural services; engineering services; business consulting; communication services
HQ: Hdr Environmental, Operations And Construction, Inc.
9781 S Meridian Blvd # 400
Englewood CO 80112
303 754-4200

(P-26199)
HELLMUTH OBATA & KASSABAUM INC (DH)
Also Called: H O K
1 Bush St Ste 200, San Francisco (94104-4404)
PHONE..................415 243-0555
Fax: 415 882-7763
Patrick Macleamy, *CEO*
William Hellmuth, *President*
Lisa Green, *Treasurer*
Thomas Robson, *Officer*
Dave Troup, *Senior VP*
EMP: 193
SALES (est): 30.9MM
SALES (corp-wide): 386MM **Privately Held**
SIC: **8712** **8711** **8742** **7389** Architectural services; engineering services; management consulting services; interior design services; landscape architects

(P-26200)
HELLMUTH OBATA & KASSABAUM INC
9530 Jefferson Blvd, Culver City (90232-2918)
PHONE..................310 838-9555
Jeff Mayer, *Manager*
Janice Dannebaum, *Office Mgr*
Bob Elliot, *Design Engr*
Peter Mosanyi,
Douglas Fisher, *Sr Associate*
EMP: 50
SALES (corp-wide): 386MM **Privately Held**
SIC: **8712** **8711** Architectural services; engineering services
HQ: Hellmuth, Obata & Kassabaum, Inc.
1 Bush St Ste 200
San Francisco CA 94104
415 243-0555

(P-26201)
HKS ARCHITECTS INC
500 Howard St Fl 4, San Francisco (94105-3040)
PHONE..................415 356-3800
Kirk Teske, *COO*
Brendan Dunnigan, *Vice Pres*
EMP: 50
SALES (est): 148.6K **Privately Held**
SIC: **8712** Architectural services

(P-26202)
HMC GROUP (PA)
Also Called: HMC Architects
3546 Concours, Ontario (91764-5583)
PHONE..................909 989-9979
Fax: 909 483-1400
Brian Staton, *CEO*
Randal Peterson, *President*
Beverly Prior, *President*
Robert J Kain, *Chairman*
John Nichols, *Data Proc Staff*
EMP: 165
SQ FT: 58,000
SALES (est): 74.1MM **Privately Held**
WEB: www.hmcarchitects.com
SIC: **8712** Architectural services

(P-26203)
HMC GROUP
2930 Inland Empire Blvd # 100, Ontario (91764-4802)
PHONE..................909 980-8058
Fax: 909 944-3088
Lauie L McCoy, *Manager*
EMP: 56
SALES (corp-wide): 74.1MM **Privately Held**
SIC: **8712** Architectural services
PA: Hmc Group
3546 Concours
Ontario CA 91764
909 989-9979

8712 - Architectural Services County (P-26204)

PRODUCUCTS & SERVICES SECTION

(P-26204)
HNTB CORPORATION
49 Stevenson St Ste 600, San Francisco (94105-2953)
PHONE..................415 963-6700
Ladonna Golden, *Branch Mgr*
EMP: 86
SALES (corp-wide): 907.8MM **Privately Held**
SIC: 8712 Architectural services
HQ: Hntb Corporation
715 Kirk Dr
Kansas City MO 64105
816 472-1201

(P-26205)
HNTB-GERWICK JV
1300 Clay St Fl 7, Oakland (94612-1425)
PHONE..................510 839-8972
Dale Berner, *Partner*
EMP: 70
SALES (est): 3.2MM **Privately Held**
SIC: 8712 8711 8742 8741 Architectural services; engineering services; business planning & organizing services; construction management

(P-26206)
HOK GROUP INC
1 Bush St Ste 200, San Francisco (94104-4404)
PHONE..................415 243-0555
Russ Drinker, *Branch Mgr*
EMP: 233
SALES (corp-wide): 386MM **Privately Held**
SIC: 8712 8742 8711 Architectural services; planning consultant; engineering services
PA: Hok Group, Inc
10 S Broadway Ste 200
Saint Louis MO 63102
314 421-2000

(P-26207)
HOK GROUP INC
9530 Jefferson Blvd, Culver City (90232-2918)
PHONE..................310 838-9555
John L Conley, *Branch Mgr*
Alicia Wachtel, *Vice Pres*
Sharon Burton, *Principal*
Jeffrey Greenbaum, *Manager*
EMP: 150
SALES (corp-wide): 386MM **Privately Held**
SIC: 8712 Architectural services
PA: Hok Group, Inc
10 S Broadway Ste 200
Saint Louis MO 63102
314 421-2000

(P-26208)
HORNBERGER WORSTELL ASSOC INC
Also Called: Hornberger, Mark R
170 Maiden Ln Ste 600, San Francisco (94108-5334)
PHONE..................415 391-1080
Fax: 415 986-6387
Mark Hornberger, *President*
Francine Larose, *CFO*
Mike Larose, *CFO*
Jack Worstell, *Exec VP*
John Davis, *Senior VP*
EMP: 50
SALES (est): 8MM **Privately Held**
WEB: www.hornbergerworstell.com
SIC: 8712 Architectural services

(P-26209)
HOSPITLITY FCSED SOLUTIONS INC
3229 E Spring St Ste 200, Long Beach (90806-2472)
PHONE..................562 424-1720
Chien An Lee, *Chairman*
John Marner, *President*
John W Wong, *CEO*
David Chen, *Vice Pres*
Bill Legg, *Vice Pres*
EMP: 100
SALES (est): 17.4MM **Privately Held**
WEB: www.concepts4inc.com
SIC: 8712 Architectural services

(P-26210)
HUNTER MC CLELLAN INC
120 W Bellevue Dr Ste 200, Pasadena (91105-2538)
PHONE..................626 397-2700
Fax: 323 304-2785
Robert Hunter, *Ch of Bd*
Vic Marovish, *Vice Pres*
EMP: 51
SALES (est): 5.1MM **Privately Held**
WEB: www.mcclellanhunter.com
SIC: 8712 1531 1542 Architectural services; operative builders; nonresidential construction

(P-26211)
HUNTSMAN ARCHITECTURAL GROUP (PA)
50 California St Fl 7, San Francisco (94111-4677)
PHONE..................415 394-1212
Sascha Wagner, *President*
Daniel Huntsman, *President*
Susan Williams, *Senior VP*
Linda H Parker, *Vice Pres*
Linda Parker, *Vice Pres*
EMP: 65
SQ FT: 19,000
SALES (est): 14.3MM **Privately Held**
WEB: www.huntsmanag.com
SIC: 8712 Architectural services

(P-26212)
JACK P SELMAN
144 N Orange St, Orange (92866-1413)
PHONE..................714 639-9860
Jack P Selman, *Partner*
R C Alley, *Partner*
Ed Cadavona, *Partner*
Jim Dietze, *Partner*
Darrel Hidenstreit, *Partner*
EMP: 80
SQ FT: 800
SALES (est): 4.3MM **Privately Held**
SIC: 8712 Architectural services

(P-26213)
JANGHO CURTAIN WALL AMERICAS
2181 Meyers Ave Ste C, Escondido (92029-1033)
PHONE..................650 588-9688
Yizeng Ll, *CEO*
Haifeng Ren, *Manager*
EMP: 53
SALES (est): 16.6MM **Privately Held**
SIC: 8712 Architectural services

(P-26214)
JEFFREY ROME & ASSOCIATES
131 Innovation Dr Ste 100, Irvine (92617-3072)
PHONE..................949 760-3929
Fax: 949 760-3931
Jeffery Rome, *President*
EMP: 60
SALES (est): 2.8MM **Privately Held**
SIC: 8712 Architectural engineering

(P-26215)
JOHNSON FAIN INC
1201 N Broadway, Los Angeles (90012-1407)
PHONE..................323 224-6000
Fax: 213 224-6040
William H Fain Jr, *Co-President*
R Scott Johnson, *Co-President*
Dana Smith, *Business Dir*
Natalie Egnatchik, *Executive Asst*
Sherry Miller, *Admin Sec*
EMP: 80
SQ FT: 26,000
SALES (est): 13MM **Privately Held**
WEB: www.johnsonfain.com
SIC: 8712 7389 Architectural engineering; interior design services

(P-26216)
KAA DESIGN GROUP INC
4201 Redwood Ave, Los Angeles (90066-5605)
PHONE..................310 821-1400
Fax: 310 821-1440
Grant Kirkpatrick, *President*
Joyce Lopez, *Executive Asst*
John Margolis, *Project Mgr*
Todd Paolillo, *Project Mgr*
Michael McGowan, *Sr Project Mgr*
EMP: 55
SQ FT: 2,520
SALES (est): 8.3MM **Privately Held**
WEB: www.kaa-architects.com
SIC: 8712 Architectural services

(P-26217)
KMD ARCHITECTS (PA)
222 Vallejo St, San Francisco (94111-1335)
PHONE..................415 398-5191
Fax: 415 394-7158
Herbert P McLaughlin, *Chairman*
Roy Latka, *President*
James R Diaz, *Admin Sec*
Ryan Denny, *Admin Asst*
Carl Gabrielson, *Technology*
EMP: 150
SQ FT: 35,000
SALES (est): 31.6MM **Privately Held**
SIC: 8712 Architectural services

(P-26218)
KTGY GROUP INC
580 2nd St Ste 200, Oakland (94607-3545)
PHONE..................510 463-2097
Tricia Esser, *CEO*
Thomas Foley, *Associate*
EMP: 50
SALES (corp-wide): 29.5MM **Privately Held**
SIC: 8712 Architectural services
PA: Ktgy Group, Inc.
17911 Von Karman Ave # 250
Irvine CA 92614
949 851-2133

(P-26219)
KTGY GROUP INC (PA)
17911 Von Karman Ave # 250, Irvine (92614-4243)
PHONE..................949 851-2133
Fax: 949 851-5156
Tricia Esser, *CEO*
Stan Braden, *President*
Michael Kingsley, *Vice Pres*
Michael Saenz, *Associate Dir*
Nick Lehnert, *Exec Dir*
EMP: 70
SQ FT: 21,000
SALES (est): 29.5MM **Privately Held**
SIC: 8712 Architectural services

(P-26220)
KTGY GROUP INC
12555 W Jefferson Blvd # 100, Los Angeles (90066-7033)
PHONE..................310 394-2625
Stan Braden, *Branch Mgr*
Sonia Lopez, *Project Mgr*
Lara M McKissick, *Purch Mgr*
Gary Leus, *Sr Project Mgr*
EMP: 50
SALES (corp-wide): 29.5MM **Privately Held**
SIC: 8712 Architectural services
PA: Ktgy Group, Inc.
17911 Von Karman Ave # 250
Irvine CA 92614
949 851-2133

(P-26221)
LEE BURKHART LIU INC (PA)
5510 Lincoln Blvd Ste 250, Playa Vista (90094-3008)
PHONE..................310 829-2249
Kenneth Lee, *President*
Erich Burkart, *Principal*
Ken Liu, *Principal*
Teague Clement, *CIO*
EMP: 73
SQ FT: 11,000
SALES (est): 11.6MM **Privately Held**
WEB: www.lblarch.com
SIC: 8712 Architectural services

(P-26222)
LEO A DALY COMPANY
Also Called: Leo Daly Company
550 S Hope St Ste 2700, Los Angeles (90071-2675)
PHONE..................213 627-9300
Brian A Kite, *Branch Mgr*
R Follmuth, *Vice Pres*
Joseph Vaccaro, *Vice Pres*
Michael Walden, *Vice Pres*
Edmund Buch, *Architect*
EMP: 60
SALES (corp-wide): 162.2MM **Privately Held**
SIC: 8712 8742 8711 Architectural engineering; planning consultant; consulting engineer
PA: Leo A. Daly Company
8600 Indian Hills Dr
Omaha NE 68114
808 521-8889

(P-26223)
LEO A DALY COMPANY
550 S Hope St Ste 2700, Los Angeles (90071-2675)
PHONE..................213 533-8855
Leo A Daly, *Branch Mgr*
EMP: 62
SALES (corp-wide): 162.2MM **Privately Held**
SIC: 8712 Architectural engineering
PA: Leo A. Daly Company
8600 Indian Hills Dr
Omaha NE 68114
808 521-8889

(P-26224)
LEO A DALY COMPANY
Also Called: Leo A Daly Company
2150 River Plaza Dr, Sacramento (95833-3883)
PHONE..................916 564-3259
EMP: 63
SALES (corp-wide): 162.2MM **Privately Held**
SIC: 8712 Architectural services
PA: Leo A. Daly Company
8600 Indian Hills Dr
Omaha NE 68114
808 521-8889

(P-26225)
LPA INC (PA)
Also Called: L P A
5161 California Ave # 100, Irvine (92617-8002)
PHONE..................949 261-1001
Robert O Kupper, *President*
Dan Heinfeld, *President*
Charles Pruitt, *CFO*
James Kelly, *Vice Pres*
Chris Torrey, *Admin Mgr*
EMP: 180
SQ FT: 33,700
SALES (est): 56.4MM **Privately Held**
WEB: www.lpainc.com
SIC: 8712 8711 0781 Architectural services; engineering services; landscape counseling & planning

(P-26226)
LPA INC
60 S Market St Ste 150, San Jose (95113-2368)
PHONE..................408 780-7200
Bob Kupper, *President*
EMP: 110
SALES (corp-wide): 56.4MM **Privately Held**
SIC: 8712 Architectural services
PA: Lpa, Inc.
5161 California Ave # 100
Irvine CA 92617
949 261-1001

(P-26227)
LPAS INC
2484 Natomas Park Dr # 100, Sacramento (95833-2928)
PHONE..................916 443-0335
Theressa Page, *Owner*
EMP: 60 **EST:** 1975
SQ FT: 12,000
SALES (est): 8MM **Privately Held**
WEB: www.lpasacramento.com
SIC: 8712 Architectural engineering

(P-26228)
M ARTHUR GENSLER JR ASSOC INC
225 W Santa Clara St, San Jose (95113-1723)
PHONE..................408 885-8100

PRODUCTS & SERVICES SECTION

8712 - Architectural Services County (P-26250)

Kevin Schaeffer, *Branch Mgr*
EMP: 50
SALES (corp-wide): 915.3MM **Privately Held**
SIC: 8712 Architectural services
PA: M. Arthur Gensler Jr. & Associates, Inc.
2 Harrison St Fl 4
San Francisco CA 94105
415 433-3700

(P-26229)
M ARTHUR GENSLER JR ASSOC INC
225 S 1st St, San Jose (95113-2702)
PHONE 408 858-8100
Fax: 408 885-8199
Kevin Heinly, *Managing Dir*
EMP: 199
SALES (corp-wide): 1B **Privately Held**
SIC: 8712 Architectural services
PA: M. Arthur Gensler Jr. & Associates, Inc.
2 Harrison St Fl 4
San Francisco CA 94105
415 433-3700

(P-26230)
M ARTHUR GENSLER JR ASSOC INC (PA)
2 Harrison St Fl 4, San Francisco (94105-6127)
PHONE 415 433-3700
Andy Cohen, *Co-CEO*
Robin Klehr Avia, *Ch of Bd*
Linda Harvard, *CFO*
Diane Hoskins, *Co-CEO*
Robert Clough, *Officer*
EMP: 360 **EST:** 1965
SQ FT: 57,000
SALES: 1B **Privately Held**
SIC: 8712 Architectural services

(P-26231)
M ARTHUR GENSLER JR ASSOC INC
2101 Webster St Ste 2000, Oakland (94612-3032)
PHONE 510 625-7400
EMP: 207
SALES (corp-wide): 915.3MM **Privately Held**
SIC: 8712
PA: M. Arthur Gensler Jr. & Associates, Inc.
2 Harrison St Fl 4
San Francisco CA 94105
415 433-3700

(P-26232)
M ARTHUR GENSLER JR ASSOC INC
Also Called: Gensler and Associates
500 S Figueroa St, Los Angeles (90071-1705)
PHONE 213 927-3600
Fax: 310 449-5850
Rob Jernigan, *Branch Mgr*
Daniel Brents, *Vice Pres*
John Gaulden, *Vice Pres*
Jeff Henry, *Vice Pres*
Steve McCartt, *Vice Pres*
EMP: 249
SALES (corp-wide): 915.3MM **Privately Held**
SIC: 8712 7389 Architectural services; design, commercial & industrial
PA: M. Arthur Gensler Jr. & Associates, Inc.
2 Harrison St Fl 4
San Francisco CA 94105
415 433-3700

(P-26233)
M ARTHUR GENSLER JR ASSOC INC
4675 Macarthur Ct Ste 100, Newport Beach (92660-8811)
PHONE 949 863-9434
Fax: 949 553-1676
Darla Farnell, *Branch Mgr*
Darla Callahan, *Vice Pres*
Laurie Tartagni, *Human Res Dir*
Richard T Fleming, *Architect*
EMP: 69
SALES (corp-wide): 915.3MM **Privately Held**
SIC: 8712 Architectural services

PA: M. Arthur Gensler Jr. & Associates, Inc.
2 Harrison St Fl 4
San Francisco CA 94105
415 433-3700

(P-26234)
MARMOL RADZINER
12210 Nebraska Ave, Los Angeles (90025-3620)
PHONE 310 826-6222
Ron Radziner, *CEO*
Leo Marmol, *President*
Scott Tran, *Info Tech Dir*
Patrick McHugh, *Comp Tech*
Eli Daniel, *Project Mgr*
EMP: 70
SQ FT: 6,500
SALES (est): 12.7MM **Privately Held**
WEB: www.marmol-radziner.com
SIC: 8712 1521 1542 Architectural services; general remodeling, single-family houses; new construction, single-family houses; commercial & office building, new construction; commercial & office buildings, renovation & repair

(P-26235)
MARTIN AC PARTNERS INC
444 S Flower St Ste 1200, Los Angeles (90071-2977)
PHONE 213 683-1900
Fax: 213 614-6002
Robert Newsom, *President*
Christopher C Martin, *CEO*
David C Martin, *Principal*
Virginia Dussy, *Administration*
Patrick Rivera, *Director*
EMP: 116 **EST:** 1906
SALES (est): 19.7MM **Privately Held**
SIC: 8712 Architectural services

(P-26236)
MBH ARCHITECTS INC
960 Atlantic Ave, Alameda (94501-1086)
PHONE 510 865-8663
Dennis Heath, *President*
Clay Fry, *Treasurer*
Joseph Smart, *Vice Pres*
John McNulty, *Principal*
Teresa Doroliat, *Admin Mgr*
EMP: 210
SQ FT: 55,000
SALES (est): 43.3MM **Privately Held**
WEB: www.mbharch.com
SIC: 8712 Architectural services

(P-26237)
MCCLIER CORPORATION
999 W Town And Country Rd, Orange (92868-4713)
PHONE 714 835-8923
Luanne Sheffner, *Manager*
EMP: 400
SALES (corp-wide): 17.9B **Publicly Held**
WEB: www.aecomconsulting.com
SIC: 8712 Architectural services
HQ: The Mcclier Corporation
303 E Wacker Dr Ste 900
Chicago IL 60601
312 938-0300

(P-26238)
MORPHOSIS ARCHITECTS
3440 Wesley St, Culver City (90232-2328)
PHONE 310 453-2247
Thom Mayne, *President*
Blythe Allison Mayne, *Vice Pres*
Jared Brunk, *Office Mgr*
Marty Doscher, *Info Tech Dir*
Scott Smith, *Info Tech Dir*
EMP: 62 **EST:** 1975
SQ FT: 10,000
SALES (est): 14.2MM **Privately Held**
WEB: www.morphosis.net
SIC: 8712 Architectural engineering

(P-26239)
MVE + PARTNERS INC (PA)
1900 Main St Ste 800, Irvine (92614-7318)
PHONE 949 809-3388
Carl F McLarand, *CEO*
Lori Ichisaka, *Partner*
Geoff Miasnik, *Partner*
Ernesto M Vasquez, *President*
Richard Castillo, *Vice Pres*
EMP: 60

SQ FT: 22,000
SALES (est): 15.4MM **Privately Held**
WEB: www.mve-architects.com
SIC: 8712 Architectural services

(P-26240)
NADEL INC (PA)
1990 S Bundy Dr Ste 400, Los Angeles (90025-5243)
PHONE 310 826-2100
Fax: 310 826-0182
Herbert Nadel, *CEO*
Brent Bland, *Assoc VP*
Norman Viray, *Vice Pres*
Patrick Winters, *Vice Pres*
Heather Chavez, *Admin Mgr*
EMP: 55
SQ FT: 29,000
SALES (est): 12.4MM **Privately Held**
SIC: 8712 Architectural services

(P-26241)
NBBJ LP
523 W 6th St Ste 300, Los Angeles (90014-1227)
PHONE 213 243-3333
Brenda Clark, *Manager*
EMP: 50
SALES (corp-wide): 107.4MM **Privately Held**
SIC: 8712 7389 Architectural services; interior design services
PA: Nbbj Lp
223 Yale Ave N
Seattle WA 98109
206 223-5555

(P-26242)
NEWMA GARRIS GILMO + PARTNE I
3100 Bristol St Ste 400, Costa Mesa (92626-7333)
PHONE 949 756-0818
Kevin Newman, *Chairman*
Donald J Meeks, *President*
Bruce Hargens, *Sr Project Mgr*
Louis Marinelli, *Director*
EMP: 70 **EST:** 1974
SQ FT: 7,000
SALES (est): 7.1MM **Privately Held**
WEB: www.nggpartners.com
SIC: 8712 Architectural services

(P-26243)
OEL/HHH INC
1833 Victory Blvd, Glendale (91201-2557)
PHONE 818 246-6050
Fax: 818 240-0430
EMP: 80 **EST:** 1978
SQ FT: 20,000
SALES (est): 4.5MM **Privately Held**
WEB: www.lhaarchitects.com
SIC: 8712

(P-26244)
RATCLIFF ARCHITECTS
5856 Doyle St, Emeryville (94608-2520)
PHONE 510 899-6400
Fax: 415 655-6654
Christopher P Ratcliff, *President*
David Dersch, *CFO*
Crodd Chin, *Vice Pres*
Joseph Nicola, *Business Dir*
Rich Steele, *CIO*
EMP: 71
SQ FT: 20,000
SALES (est): 12.6MM **Privately Held**
WEB: www.ratcliffarch.com
SIC: 8712 Architectural services

(P-26245)
RBB ARCHITECTS INC (PA)
10980 Wilshire Blvd, Los Angeles (90024-3944)
PHONE 310 479-1473
Fax: 310 312-3646
Joseph A Balbona, *CEO*
Deneys Purcell, *President*
Frank Bostrom, *Treasurer*
Kevin Boots, *Senior VP*
Arthur E Border, *Senior VP*
EMP: 54
SQ FT: 15,837
SALES (est): 9.1MM **Privately Held**
WEB: www.rbbinc.com
SIC: 8712 Architectural engineering

(P-26246)
RIM ARCHITECTS CALIFORNIA INC
639 Front St Fl 2, San Francisco (94111-1970)
PHONE 415 247-0400
Fax: 415 296-8323
Larry S Cash, *CEO*
Eric R Nelson, *President*
David L McVeigh, *Senior VP*
Virginia Kelly, *Principal*
Michelle M Jones, *Admin Sec*
EMP: 56
SQ FT: 4,350
SALES (est): 161.6K **Privately Held**
SIC: 8712 Architectural services
PA: Rim Architects, Llc
645 G St Ste 400
Anchorage AK 99501

(P-26247)
RJC ARCHITECTS INC
320 Laurel St, San Diego (92101-1631)
PHONE 619 239-9292
James K Robbins, *President*
Janene K Christopher, *Vice Pres*
Dan Stewart, *Sr Associate*
Don Goldman, *Architect*
John Hinkel, *Director*
EMP: 51
SQ FT: 5,000
SALES (est): 8.5MM **Privately Held**
WEB: www.rjcarch.com
SIC: 8712 Architectural services

(P-26248)
RRM DESIGN GROUP (PA)
3765 S Higuera St Ste 102, San Luis Obispo (93401-1577)
PHONE 805 439-0442
Fax: 805 543-4609
Victor Montgomery, *Ch of Bd*
John Wilbanks, *President*
Keith Gurnee, *Senior VP*
Steven Jobst, *Vice Pres*
Erik P Justesen, *Principal*
EMP: 99
SQ FT: 23,000
SALES (est): 23MM **Privately Held**
WEB: www.rrmdesign.com
SIC: 8712 Architectural engineering

(P-26249)
RUTH PERKOWITZ INC (PA)
Also Called: Perkowitz & Ruth Architects
111 W Ocean Blvd Ste 21, Long Beach (90802-4653)
PHONE 562 628-8000
Fax: 562 628-8001
Simon Perkowitz, *President*
Steven J Ruth, *Vice Pres*
Renee Barot, *Business Dir*
Miguel Avila, *Project Mgr*
Danelle R Plunkett, *Human Res Dir*
EMP: 144
SALES (est): 36.4MM **Privately Held**
SIC: 8712 Architectural services

(P-26250)
SKIDMORE OWINGS & MERRILL LLP
1 Front St Ste 2500, San Francisco (94111-5332)
PHONE 415 981-1555
Fax: 415 398-3214
Gene Schnair, *Partner*
Craig W Hartman, *Partner*
John Kriken, *Partner*
Ryan Crawford, *Info Tech Mgr*
Amy Keller, *Research*
EMP: 240
SALES (corp-wide): 128.1MM **Privately Held**
SIC: 8712 Architectural engineering
PA: Skidmore, Owings & Merrill Llp
224 S Michigan Ave # 1000
Chicago IL 60604
312 554-9090

8712 - Architectural Services County (P-26251)

(P-26251)
SKIDMORE OWINGS & MERRILL LLP
10100 Santa Monica Blvd, Beverly Hills (90210)
PHONE..................310 651-9924
Michael Mann, *Manager*
EMP: 228
SALES (corp-wide): 128.1MM **Privately Held**
SIC: 8712 Architectural services
PA: Skidmore, Owings & Merrill Llp
224 S Michigan Ave # 1000
Chicago IL 60604
312 554-9090

(P-26252)
SKIDMORE OWINGS & MERRILL LLP
555 W 5th St Fl 30, Los Angeles (90013-1048)
PHONE..................213 996-8366
Jeffrey McCarthy, *Partner*
EMP: 228
SALES (corp-wide): 128.1MM **Privately Held**
SIC: 8712 Architectural services
PA: Skidmore, Owings & Merrill Llp
224 S Michigan Ave # 1000
Chicago IL 60604
312 554-9090

(P-26253)
SMITHGROUPJJR INC
Also Called: Smithgroup California
301 Battery St Fl 7, San Francisco (94111-3237)
PHONE..................313 442-8351
Michael Medici, *President*
Thomas Golden, *Administration*
EMP: 146
SALES (corp-wide): 78.8MM **Privately Held**
WEB: www.dc.smithgroup.com
SIC: 8712 Architectural services
HQ: Smithgroupjjr, Inc.
1700 New York Ave Nw # 100
Washington DC 20006
602 265-2200

(P-26254)
STAFFORD-KING-WIESE ARCHITECTS
622 20th St, Sacramento (95811-1712)
PHONE..................916 930-5900
Fax: 916 443-0719
Pat Derickson, *President*
Kelly Reynolds, *Vice Pres*
Karen Carr, *Mktg Dir*
Gary Fabian, *Associate*
Bill Heinicke, *Associate*
EMP: 50
SQ FT: 12,800
SALES: 9MM **Privately Held**
WEB: www.skwaia.com
SIC: 8712 Architectural services

(P-26255)
STANTEC ARCHITECTURE INC
38 Technology Dr Ste 100, Irvine (92618-5312)
PHONE..................949 923-6000
Eric Nielsen, *Vice Pres*
Reshma Panjanani, *Information Mgr*
Christina Han, *Marketing Staff*
Lori Van Dermark, *Marketing Staff*
EMP: 117
SALES (corp-wide): 2.2B **Privately Held**
SIC: 8712 8711 4111 Architectural services; engineering services; local & suburban transit
HQ: Stantec Architecture Inc.
301 N Main St Ste 2452
Winston Salem NC 27101
336 714-7413

(P-26256)
STANTEC ARCHITECTURE INC
1340 Treat Blvd Ste 300, Walnut Creek (94597-7966)
PHONE..................925 941-1400
Lori Van Dermark, *Marketing Staff*
Christina Han, *Marketing Staff*
EMP: 65
SALES (corp-wide): 2.1B **Privately Held**
SIC: 8712 Architectural services
HQ: Stantec Architecture Inc.
301 N Main St Ste 2452
Winston Salem NC 27101
336 714-7413

(P-26257)
STANTEC CONSULTING SVCS INC
3875 Atherton Rd, Rocklin (95765-3716)
PHONE..................916 773-8100
Charles Bunker, *Branch Mgr*
Reshma Panjanani, *Information Mgr*
Jason Foster, *Software Dev*
Joseph Digiorgio, *Senior Engr*
Christina Han, *Marketing Staff*
EMP: 60
SALES (corp-wide): 2.2B **Privately Held**
SIC: 8712 8711 Architectural services; engineering services
HQ: Stantec Consulting Services Inc.
50 W 23rd St Fl 8
New York NY 10010
212 366-5600

(P-26258)
STANTEC CONSULTING SVCS INC
38 Technology Dr Ste 100, Irvine (92618-5312)
PHONE..................949 923-6000
Bob Gomes, *Manager*
Reshma Panjanani, *Information Mgr*
Christina Han, *Marketing Staff*
Lori Van Dermark, *Marketing Staff*
Jeff Crawford, *Manager*
EMP: 117
SALES (corp-wide): 2.2B **Privately Held**
WEB: www.keithco.com
SIC: 8712 8711 Architectural services; engineering services
HQ: Stantec Consulting Services Inc.
50 W 23rd St Fl 8
New York NY 10010
212 366-5600

(P-26259)
STEINBERG ARCHITECTS (PA)
Also Called: Steinberg Group Architects
125 S Market St Ste 110, San Jose (95113-2210)
PHONE..................408 295-5446
David Hart, *President*
Robert Steinberg, *Ch of Bd*
Hong Chen, *COO*
Ernest Yamana, *Treasurer*
Renee Charland, *Executive*
EMP: 74 EST: 1953
SQ FT: 14,000
SALES (est): 19.8MM **Privately Held**
WEB: www.tsgarch.com
SIC: 8712 Architectural services

(P-26260)
STV ARCHITECTS INC
1055 W 7th St Ste 3150, Los Angeles (90017-2556)
PHONE..................213 482-9444
Wagih Andraos, *Manager*
EMP: 60
SALES (corp-wide): 274.2MM **Privately Held**
WEB: www.stvinc.com
SIC: 8712 8742 8711 Architectural services; transportation consultant; consulting engineer
HQ: Stv Architects Inc
205 W Welsh Dr
Douglassville PA 19518
610 385-8200

(P-26261)
TAYLOR & ASSOC ARCHITECTS INC
Also Called: Taylor Design
17850 Fitch, Irvine (92614-6002)
PHONE..................949 574-1325
Fax: 949 574-1338
Linda Taylor, *Ch of Bd*
D Randy Regier, *President*
Gary Davidson, *CFO*
Kristy Jordan, *Executive*
David Taylor, *Executive*
EMP: 73
SQ FT: 12,000
SALES (est): 15.2MM **Privately Held**
WEB: www.taa1.com
SIC: 8712 Architectural services

(P-26262)
THOMAS P COX ARCHITECTS INC
19782 Macarthur Blvd # 300, Irvine (92612-2417)
PHONE..................949 862-0270
Fax: 949 862-0289
Thomas P Cox, *President*
Aram C Chahbazian, *President*
Harry Steinway, *CFO*
Larry Scott, *Senior VP*
Heidi Mather, *Vice Pres*
EMP: 63
SQ FT: 14,368
SALES (est): 11.5MM **Privately Held**
SIC: 8712 Architectural services

(P-26263)
VARSITY CONTRACTORS INC
5880 District Blvd Ste 1, Bakersfield (93313-2137)
PHONE..................661 398-0275
Fax: 661 398-0358
Tony Avila, *Manager*
EMP: 150
SALES (corp-wide): 85MM **Privately Held**
SIC: 8712 7349 Architectural services; building maintenance services
PA: Varsity Contractors, Inc.
315 S 5th Ave
Pocatello ID 83201
208 232-8598

(P-26264)
WALTER J CONN & ASSOCIATES
Also Called: Charleston Company
800 W 6th St Ste 600, Los Angeles (90017-2709)
PHONE..................213 683-0500
Walter J Conn, *Partner*
Sally K Conn, *Partner*
Alan Lui, *Director*
EMP: 60
SALES (est): 6.7MM **Privately Held**
WEB: www.charlestoncompany.com
SIC: 8712 Architectural services

(P-26265)
WARE MALCOMB (PA)
10 Edelman, Irvine (92618-4312)
PHONE..................949 660-9128
Fax: 949 863-1581
Lawrance R Armstrong, *CEO*
James E Williams, *President*
Kevin Kim, *COO*
Melissa Wehrberg, *Sr Corp Ofcr*
Kenneth Wink, *Exec VP*
EMP: 100
SQ FT: 22,000
SALES (est): 37.1MM **Privately Held**
SIC: 8712 7336 8711 7389 Architectural services; commercial art & graphic design; civil engineering; interior design services; design, commercial & industrial

(P-26266)
WILL PERKINS INC
617 W 7th St Fl 12, Los Angeles (90017-3807)
PHONE..................213 270-8400
Fax: 213 270-8401
Gabriella Bullock, *Principal*
Phyllis Dubinsky, *Principal*
EMP: 129
SALES (corp-wide): 232.7MM **Privately Held**
SIC: 8712 Architectural services
HQ: Will Perkins Inc
1250 24th St Nw Ste 800
Washington DC 20037
312 755-0770

(P-26267)
WILL PERKINS INC
2 Bryant St Ste 300, San Francisco (94105-1641)
PHONE..................415 896-0800
Fax: 415 856-3001
Russ Drinker, *Branch Mgr*
Luc Deckinga, *Manager*
Jay Manzo, *Associate*
Reinhardt Muir, *Associate*
EMP: 60
SALES (corp-wide): 232.7MM **Privately Held**
SIC: 8712 Architectural services
HQ: Will Perkins Inc
1250 24th St Nw Ste 800
Washington DC 20037
312 755-0770

(P-26268)
WILLIAM HZMLHLCH ARCHTECTS INC
2850 Redhill Ave Ste 200, Santa Ana (92705-5543)
PHONE..................949 250-0607
William Hezmalhalch, *CEO*
Don Ancheta, *Administration*
Jeremy Leach, *Systs Prg Mgr*
Brian Crooker, *Information Mgr*
Ken Stover, *Project Mgr*
EMP: 75
SALES (est): 14.6MM **Privately Held**
SIC: 8712 Architectural services

(P-26269)
WIMBERLY ALLISON TONG GOO INC
Also Called: Watg
300 Spectrum Center Dr # 500, Irvine (92618-4989)
PHONE..................949 574-8500
Monica Cuervo, *Managing Dir*
Paul Ignacio, *Executive*
Ric Gomez, *Systs Prg Mgr*
Manish Desai, *Engineer*
Diane Rprins, *Human Res Dir*
EMP: 100
SQ FT: 63
SALES (corp-wide): 37.5MM **Privately Held**
SIC: 8712 Architectural services
PA: Wimberly Allison Tong & Goo, Inc.
700 Bishop St Ste 1800
Honolulu HI 96813
808 521-8888

(P-26270)
WRNS STUDIO
501 2nd St Ste 402, San Francisco (94107-4132)
PHONE..................415 489-2268
Fax: 415 358-9100
Jeff Warner, *CEO*
David Englund, *Corp Secy*
Sam Nunes, *Senior VP*
John Ruffo, *Senior VP*
Bryan Shiles, *Senior VP*
EMP: 52
SALES: 19.3MM **Privately Held**
WEB: www.wrnsstudio.com
SIC: 8712 Architectural services

(P-26271)
ZIMMER GUNSUL
Also Called: Zimmer Gnsul Frsca Partnr Amer
515 S Flower St Ste 3700, Los Angeles (90071-2221)
PHONE..................213 617-1901
Fax: 213 617-0047
Rachel Morris, *Manager*
Rachell J Morris, *Executive*
Yuwei MA, *Info Tech Dir*
Debra Barbour, *Manager*
Deb Barbour, *Assistant*
EMP: 63
SALES (corp-wide): 130.5MM **Privately Held**
SIC: 8712 7389 Architectural services; interior designer
PA: Zimmer Gunsul Frasca Architects Llp
1223 Sw Washington St # 200
Portland OR 97205
503 224-3860

8713 Surveying Services

(P-26272)
ANDREGG GEOMATICS
11661 Blocker Dr Ste 200, Auburn (95603-4649)
PHONE..................530 885-7072
Fax: 530 885-5798

PRODUCTS & SERVICES SECTION
8721 - Accounting, Auditing & Bookkeeping Svcs County (P-26294)

Dennis Meyer, *President*
Mark Bardakjian, *COO*
Jean Granato, *CFO*
Adam Kelly, *Officer*
Christine Johnson, *Admin Sec*
EMP: 65
SALES: 4.5MM **Privately Held**
WEB: www.andregg.com
SIC: 8713 Surveying services

(P-26273)
CANNON CORPORATION (PA)
1050 Southwood Dr, San Luis Obispo (93401-5813)
PHONE...........................805 544-7407
Fax: 805 544-3863
Michael F Cannon, *CEO*
Bob Stets, *CFO*
John Evans, *Vice Pres*
Daniel Hutchinson, *Vice Pres*
Liz Jaeger, *Business Dir*
EMP: 60
SQ FT: 4,200
SALES (est): 16.6MM **Privately Held**
WEB: www.cannoncorp.us
SIC: 8713 8711 1611 Surveying services; civil engineering; highway & street construction

(P-26274)
F3 AND ASSOCIATES INC (PA)
701 E H St, Benicia (94510-3567)
P.O. Box 5099, Petaluma (94955-5099)
PHONE...........................707 748-4300
Fax: 707 347-4500
Fred Feickert, *President*
Gene Feickert, *Partner*
Sean Finn, *Partner*
Devin Finn, *Info Tech Mgr*
Shawn Harmon, *Asst Controller*
EMP: 70
SALES (est): 17.5MM **Privately Held**
WEB: www.f3-inc.com
SIC: 8713 Surveying services

(P-26275)
HUITT - ZOLLARS INC
2603 Main St Ste 400, Irvine (92614-4250)
PHONE...........................949 988-5815
Fax: 714 734-5155
Mark Harlinger, *Manager*
Tim Gillen, *Vice Pres*
Carl Taylor, *Vice Pres*
Russell Parr, *Engineer*
Brenda Fullmer, *VP Finance*
EMP: 50
SALES (corp-wide): 62.6MM **Privately Held**
WEB: www.huitt-zollars.com
SIC: 8713 8711 Surveying services; consulting engineer
PA: Huitt - Zollars, Inc.
1717 Mckinney Ave # 1400
Dallas TX 75202
214 871-3311

(P-26276)
KIER & WRIGHT CIVIL ENGRS&SRVY
2850 Collier Canyon Rd, Livermore (94551-9201)
PHONE...........................925 245-8788
Tony McCants, *Manager*
Emad Ddine, *Project Mgr*
EMP: 50
SALES (corp-wide): 8.9MM **Privately Held**
WEB: www.kierwright.com
SIC: 8713 8711 Surveying services; civil engineering
PA: Kier & Wright Civil Engineers & Surveyors Inc
3350 Scott Blvd Bldg 22
Santa Clara CA 95054
408 727-6665

(P-26277)
PSOMAS
Also Called: Psomas & Associates
3 Hutton Cntre Dr Ste 200, Santa Ana (92707)
PHONE...........................714 751-7373
Ryan McLean, *Principal*
Arief Naftali, *Project Mgr*
EMP: 125

SALES (corp-wide): 121.4MM **Privately Held**
SIC: 8713 8711 Surveying services; consulting engineer
PA: Psomas
555 S Flower St Ste 4300
Los Angeles CA 90071
310 954-3700

(P-26278)
PSOMAS
14369 Park Ave Ste 101b, Victorville (92392-2392)
PHONE...........................760 843-5700
John Thornton, *Vice Pres*
Steve Gregerson, *Vice Pres*
Ken Stram, *Vice Pres*
EMP: 50
SALES (corp-wide): 121.4MM **Privately Held**
SIC: 8713 8711 Surveying services; construction & civil engineering
PA: Psomas
555 S Flower St Ste 4300
Los Angeles CA 90071
310 954-3700

(P-26279)
PSOMAS (PA)
555 S Flower St Ste 4300, Los Angeles (90071-2405)
PHONE...........................310 954-3700
Fax: 213 223-1444
Blake Murillo, *CEO*
Jacob Lipa, *President*
Loren Sokolow, *Treasurer*
Brian Bullock, *Vice Pres*
Sean P Vargas, *Vice Pres*
EMP: 125
SQ FT: 30,000
SALES (est): 121.4MM **Privately Held**
SIC: 8713 8711 Surveying services; engineering services

(P-26280)
SANDIS CIVIL ENGINEERS (PA)
1700 Winchester Blvd, Campbell (95008-1163)
P.O. Box 640, Mountain View (94042-0640)
PHONE...........................408 636-0900
Fax: 408 636-0999
Ken Olcott, *President*
Tony Brubaker, *Treasurer*
Jeff Setera, *Vice Pres*
Jack Frusetta, *Admin Asst*
Erik Easterly, *Design Engr*
EMP: 61 EST: 1965
SQ FT: 12,000
SALES (est): 15.7MM **Privately Held**
SIC: 8713 8711 Surveying services; civil engineering

(P-26281)
STANTEC CONSULTING SVCS INC
46 Discovery Ste 250, Irvine (92618-3133)
PHONE...........................949 474-1000
Robert Gomes, *CEO*
Christina Han, *Marketing Staff*
Lori Van Dermark, *Marketing Staff*
EMP: 70
SALES (corp-wide): 2.1B **Privately Held**
SIC: 8713 8711 8742 Surveying services; civil engineering; planning consultant
HQ: Stantec Consulting Services Inc.
50 W 23rd St Fl 8
New York NY 10010
212 366-5600

(P-26282)
STANTEC CONSULTING SVCS INC
111 E Victoria St, Santa Barbara (93101-2018)
PHONE...........................805 963-9532
Christina Han, *Marketing Staff*
Lori Van Dermark, *Marketing Staff*
EMP: 55
SALES (corp-wide): 2.2B **Privately Held**
WEB: www.penfieldsmith.com
SIC: 8713 Surveying services
HQ: Stantec Consulting Services Inc.
50 W 23rd St Fl 8
New York NY 10010
212 366-5600

(P-26283)
STANTEC ENERGY & RESOURCES INC (HQ)
5500 Ming Ave Ste 300, Bakersfield (93309-4627)
PHONE...........................661 396-3770
Robert Gomes, *President*
Richard Allen, *COO*
Daniel Lefaivre, *Treasurer*
Kirk Morrison, *Exec VP*
Paul Alpern, *Senior VP*
EMP: 182 EST: 2015
SALES (est): 6.1MM
SALES (corp-wide): 20.7MM **Privately Held**
SIC: 8713 Surveying services
PA: Stantec Holdings (Delaware) Iii Inc.
5500 Ming Ave Ste 300
Bakersfield CA 93309
661 396-3770

8721 Accounting, Auditing & Bookkeeping Svcs

(P-26284)
A K P LLP
Also Called: Grice Lund Tarkington
312 S Juniper St Ste 100, Escondido (92025-4943)
PHONE...........................760 746-1560
Fax: 760 746-7048
Kevin Camperell, *Partner*
Judy Howell, *CPA*
EMP: 55
SALES (est): 2.1MM **Privately Held**
SIC: 8721 8742 8111 6411 Accounting, auditing & bookkeeping; management consulting services; general practice attorney, lawyer; pension & retirement plan consultants

(P-26285)
AAA ACCOUNTING SERVICES
2 Enterprise Apt 1211, Aliso Viejo (92656-7079)
PHONE...........................949 791-7368
Frazier Shayla, *CEO*
EMP: 99
SALES (est): 2MM **Privately Held**
SIC: 8721 Auditing services

(P-26286)
ABBOTT STRINGHAM LYNCH ACCTG
1550 Leigh Ave, San Jose (95125-5301)
PHONE...........................408 377-8700
Morgan Lynch, *President*
Ray Scheaffer, *President*
Franceen Borrillo, *Principal*
Bill Melton, *Principal*
Todd Robinson, *Principal*
EMP: 60
SALES (est): 5.6MM **Privately Held**
WEB: www.aslcpa.com
SIC: 8721 Accounting services, except auditing

(P-26287)
ACCOUNTANTS 4 CONTRACT
235 Montgomery St Ste 630, San Francisco (94104-2922)
PHONE...........................415 781-8644
Fax: 415 781-6450
Daniel M Maisler, *CEO*
Marla Broude, *General Mgr*
EMP: 80
SQ FT: 2,300
SALES (est): 8.1MM **Privately Held**
SIC: 8721 Accounting, auditing & bookkeeping

(P-26288)
AGRI VALLEY SERVICES
1532 N West Ave, Fresno (93728-1306)
PHONE...........................559 233-5633
Carmalee Kossaras, *Owner*
EMP: 100
SALES (est): 3.8MM **Privately Held**
SIC: 8721 7363 Payroll accounting service; labor resource services

(P-26289)
ARMANINO LLP
11512 El Camino Real, San Diego (92130-2087)
PHONE...........................858 794-9401
EMP: 60
SALES (corp-wide): 95.3MM **Privately Held**
SIC: 8721 Certified public accountant
PA: Armanino Llp
12657 Alcosta Blvd # 500
San Ramon CA 94583
925 790-2600

(P-26290)
ARMANINO LLP
11766 Wilshire Blvd Fl 9, Los Angeles (90025-6548)
PHONE...........................310 478-4148
EMP: 150
SALES (corp-wide): 95.3MM **Privately Held**
SIC: 8721 Certified public accountant
PA: Armanino Llp
12657 Alcosta Blvd # 500
San Ramon CA 94583
925 790-2600

(P-26291)
ARMANINO LLP (PA)
12657 Alcosta Blvd # 500, San Ramon (94583-4600)
PHONE...........................925 790-2600
Fax: 925 790-2601
Andy Armanino, *Managing Prtnr*
Linda Antonelli, *Partner*
Esther Ratteree, *Partner*
Matt Armanino, *COO*
Frank Siskowski, *Vice Pres*
EMP: 160
SQ FT: 5,500
SALES (est): 95.3MM **Privately Held**
WEB: www.amllp.com
SIC: 8721 8742 Certified public accountant; management consulting services

(P-26292)
BARTLETT PRINGLE & WOLF LLP
1123 Chapala St Ste 300, Santa Barbara (93101-3163)
PHONE...........................805 564-2103
Fax: 805 564-2103
Robert Maloy, *General Ptnr*
Camey Barber-Olds, *Admin Asst*
Eileen Sheridan, *CPA*
Jacob Sheffield, *Senior Mgr*
Laura Copple, *Manager*
EMP: 50
SALES (est): 4.8MM **Privately Held**
SIC: 8721 Certified public accountant

(P-26293)
BDO USA LLP
1 Market Spear Tower Ste 1100, San Francisco (94104)
PHONE...........................415 397-7900
Fax: 415 397-2161
Brian Minnihan, *Partner*
Terry Lloyd, *Partner*
Peter Meeks, *Partner*
Suzanna Musick, *Partner*
Jonathan Huynh, *Research*
EMP: 150
SQ FT: 1,500
SALES (corp-wide): 647.9MM **Privately Held**
WEB: www.bdo.com
SIC: 8721 Certified public accountant
PA: Bdo Usa, Llp
130 E Randolph St # 2800
Chicago IL 60601
312 240-1236

(P-26294)
BDO USA LLP
4250 Executive Sq Ste 600, La Jolla (92037-9105)
PHONE...........................858 404-9200
Wayne Berson, *Branch Mgr*
EMP: 78
SALES (corp-wide): 647.9MM **Privately Held**
SIC: 8721 Certified public accountant

8721 - Accounting, Auditing & Bookkeeping Svcs County (P-26295)

PRODUCTS & SERVICES SECTION

PA: Bdo Usa, Llp
130 E Randolph St # 2800
Chicago IL 60601
312 240-1236

(P-26295)
BDO USA LLP
50 W San Fernando St # 200, San Jose (95113-2429)
PHONE...........................408 278-0220
Doug Sirotta, *Partner*
Linda Leclair, *CPA*
Ahmad Ejaz, *Manager*
Steven Hurok, *Manager*
EMP: 60
SALES (corp-wide): 647.9MM **Privately Held**
WEB: www.bdo.com
SIC: 8721 Accounting, auditing & bookkeeping
PA: Bdo Usa, Llp
130 E Randolph St # 2800
Chicago IL 60601
312 240-1236

(P-26296)
BDO USA LLP
600 Anton Blvd Ste 500, Costa Mesa (92626-7167)
PHONE...........................714 957-3200
Christopher Tower, *Partner*
Vanessa Romo, *Admin Asst*
Alan Whiley, *Sr Associate*
Patricia Bottomly, *Director*
Stephanie Sum, *Director*
EMP: 65
SALES (corp-wide): 647.9MM **Privately Held**
WEB: www.bdo.com
SIC: 8721 Certified public accountant
PA: Bdo Usa, Llp
130 E Randolph St # 2800
Chicago IL 60601
312 240-1236

(P-26297)
BMS PARENT INC (PA)
1220 Dewey Way Ste F, Upland (91786-1101)
PHONE...........................909 981-2341
John Wallace, *CEO*
Barbara Gillet, *Vice Pres*
John Connors, *General Mgr*
EMP: 68 **EST:** 1997
SQ FT: 9,000
SALES (est): 11.9MM **Privately Held**
WEB: www.bmsreimbursement.com
SIC: 8721 Billing & bookkeeping service

(P-26298)
BROWN ARMSTRONG ACCNTANCY CORP
Also Called: Brown Armstrong Cpas
4200 Truxtun Ave Ste 300, Bakersfield (93309-0668)
PHONE...........................661 324-4971
Andrew J Paulden, *President*
Benjamin P Reyes, *Corp Secy*
Christina M Thornburgh, *Corp Secy*
Burton H Armstrong, *Vice Pres*
Diana H Branthoover, *Vice Pres*
EMP: 65
SQ FT: 30,000
SALES (est): 7.8MM **Privately Held**
WEB: www.bacpas.com
SIC: 8721 Accounting services, except auditing

(P-26299)
BURR PILGER MAYER INC
110 Stony Point Rd # 210, Santa Rosa (95401-4118)
PHONE...........................707 544-4078
Carolyn Amster, *Principal*
Maggie Castro, *Admin Mgr*
Cynthia Craig, *Manager*
EMP: 63
SALES (corp-wide): 54.1MM **Privately Held**
SIC: 8721 Accounting, auditing & bookkeeping
PA: Burr Pilger Mayer, Inc.
600 California St Ste 600
San Francisco CA 94108
415 421-5757

(P-26300)
BURR PILGER MAYER INC
432a Main St, Saint Helena (94574)
PHONE...........................707 968-5207
EMP: 63
SALES (corp-wide): 54.1MM **Privately Held**
SIC: 8721 Certified public accountant
PA: Burr Pilger Mayer, Inc.
600 California St Ste 600
San Francisco CA 94108
415 421-5757

(P-26301)
BURR PILGER MAYER INC (PA)
600 California St Ste 600, San Francisco (94108-2733)
PHONE...........................415 421-5757
Fax: 415 288-6288
James Wallace, *CEO*
Mark Loveless, *Managing Prtnr*
Stephen Mayer, *Managing Prtnr*
Andrea Cope, *Shareholder*
Robert Houston, *Shareholder*
EMP: 110
SQ FT: 20,824
SALES (est): 54.1MM **Privately Held**
SIC: 8721 Certified public accountant

(P-26302)
BURR PILGER MAYER INC
60 S Market St Ste 800, San Jose (95113-2340)
PHONE...........................408 961-6355
Fax: 408 961-6324
Mark Loveless, *Manager*
EMP: 50
SALES (corp-wide): 54.1MM **Privately Held**
SIC: 8721 Certified public accountant
PA: Burr Pilger Mayer, Inc.
600 California St Ste 600
San Francisco CA 94108
415 421-5757

(P-26303)
BURR PILGER MAYER INC
2000 University Ave, East Palo Alto (94303-2214)
PHONE...........................650 855-6800
Mark Loveless, *Branch Mgr*
Adriana Lewis, *Tax Mgr*
Rich McDonnell, *CPA*
Rebecca Teutschel, *CPA*
David Sherve, *Mktg Dir*
EMP: 50
SALES (corp-wide): 54.1MM **Privately Held**
SIC: 8721 Certified public accountant
PA: Burr Pilger Mayer, Inc.
600 California St Ste 600
San Francisco CA 94108
415 421-5757

(P-26304)
C D PAYROLL INC
2300 W Empire Ave, Burbank (91504-3341)
PHONE...........................818 848-1562
Ed Spietel, *President*
Ed Spiegel, *President*
EMP: 60
SQ FT: 12,000
SALES (est): 3.1MM **Privately Held**
SIC: 8721 Payroll accounting service

(P-26305)
CALSTARS
915 L St Fl 7, Sacramento (95814-3705)
PHONE...........................916 445-0211
Freda Luan-Dun, *Co-Owner*
Gordon Kobayashi, *Webmaster*
EMP: 50
SALES (est): 1.7MM **Privately Held**
SIC: 8721 Accounting, auditing & bookkeeping

(P-26306)
CAPINCROUSE LLP
5990 Stoneridge Dr, Pleasanton (94588-4517)
PHONE...........................925 201-1187
EMP: 88
SALES (corp-wide): 2MM **Privately Held**
SIC: 8721 Accounting, auditing & bookkeeping
PA: Capincrouse Llp
972 Emerson Pkwy Ste A
Greenwood IN 46143
317 885-2620

(P-26307)
CAST & CREW PAYROLL LLC (HQ)
Also Called: Cast and Crew Entrmt Svcs
2300 W Empire Ave Fl 5, Burbank (91504-3341)
PHONE...........................818 848-6022
Fax: 818 848-9556
Eric Belcher, *VP Sales*
Sally Knutson, *CFO*
Ken Goldstein, *Senior VP*
Sharon Babkes, *Vice Pres*
Shirley White, *Vice Pres*
EMP: 195
SQ FT: 12,000
SALES (est): 60.2MM **Privately Held**
SIC: 8721 Payroll accounting service
PA: Zm Capital, L.P.
19 W 44th St Fl 18
New York NY 10036
212 223-1383

(P-26308)
CBIZ SOUTHERN CALIFORNIA LLC
Also Called: Cks Business Services
5060 California Ave # 800, Bakersfield (93309-0731)
PHONE...........................661 325-7500
EMP: 50
SALES (est): 3.1MM **Publicly Held**
SIC: 8721 Accounting, auditing & bookkeeping
PA: Cbiz, Inc.
6050 Oak Tree Blvd # 500
Cleveland OH 44131

(P-26309)
CERIDIAN LLC
1515 W 190th St Ste 100, Gardena (90248-4913)
PHONE...........................310 719-7400
Fax: 310 719-7485
Chris Byers, *Branch Mgr*
Chuck Patterson, *Production*
EMP: 60
SALES (corp-wide): 615.9MM **Privately Held**
WEB: www.ceridian.com
SIC: 8721 Payroll accounting service
HQ: Ceridian Llc
3311 E Old Shakopee Rd
Minneapolis MN 55425
952 853-8100

(P-26310)
CERIDIAN TAX SERVICE INC
17390 Brookhurst St # 100, Fountain Valley (92708-3704)
P.O. Box 20805 (92728-0805)
PHONE...........................714 963-1311
Webster Hill, *General Mgr*
Joshua Duston, *Engineer*
Bryan Odenwald, *Director*
Addie Brunskow, *Manager*
Cheryl Eaton, *Manager*
EMP: 300
SQ FT: 130,000
SALES (est): 25.1MM
SALES (corp-wide): 615.9MM **Privately Held**
WEB: www.ceridian.com
SIC: 8721 Payroll accounting service
HQ: Ceridian Llc
3311 E Old Shakopee Rd
Minneapolis MN 55425
952 853-8100

(P-26311)
CITY OF BERKELEY
Also Called: Police Department
2180 Milvia St, Berkeley (94704-1122)
PHONE...........................510 981-6750
Fax: 510 981-6760
Doug Hambleton, *Chief*
Henry A Borders, *Info Tech Mgr*
David Hodgkins, *Human Res Dir*
EMP: 1500 **Privately Held**
WEB: www.berkeleycamps.com
SIC: 8721 Auditing services

PA: City Of Berkeley
2120 Milvia St
Berkeley CA 94704
510 981-7300

(P-26312)
COHNREZNICK LLP
21700 Oxnard St, Woodland Hills (91367-3642)
PHONE...........................818 205-2600
Cott Sachs, *Office Mgr*
EMP: 59
SALES (corp-wide): 585.1MM **Privately Held**
SIC: 8721 Certified public accountant
PA: Cohnreznick Llp
1301 Ave Of The Americas
New York NY 10019
212 297-0400

(P-26313)
COHNREZNICK LLP
11755 Wilshire Blvd # 1700, Los Angeles (90025-1500)
PHONE...........................310 477-3722
Thomas J Marino, *Branch Mgr*
EMP: 50
SALES (corp-wide): 585.1MM **Privately Held**
SIC: 8721 Certified public accountant
PA: Cohnreznick Llp
1301 Ave Of The Americas
New York NY 10019
212 297-0400

(P-26314)
COLLABRUS INC
Also Called: M Squared Consulting
111 Sutter St Ste 900, San Francisco (94104-4523)
PHONE...........................415 288-1826
Alex Todd, *CEO*
Russel Orelowitz, *CFO*
Larry Blumsack, *Exec VP*
David Graves, *Vice Pres*
Mike Hagerthy, *Vice Pres*
EMP: 240
SQ FT: 8,000
SALES (est): 13MM
SALES (corp-wide): 47.8MM **Privately Held**
WEB: www.collabrusinc.com
SIC: 8721 Billing & bookkeeping service
HQ: M Squared Consulting, Inc.
111 Sutter St Ste 900
San Francisco CA 94104
415 391-1038

(P-26315)
CONSIDINE & CONSIDINE AN ACCO
1501 5th Ave Ste 400, San Diego (92101-3297)
PHONE...........................619 231-1977
Fax: 619 231-8244
Perry S Wright, *CEO*
Timothy Considine, *President*
Jerry Hotz, *Treasurer*
Michael Boardman, *Vice Pres*
Don Bonk, *Vice Pres*
EMP: 80
SQ FT: 20,000
SALES (est): 7MM **Privately Held**
WEB: www.cccpa.com
SIC: 8721 Certified public accountant

(P-26316)
CORWE HORWATH
1 Embarcadero Ctr # 1330, San Francisco (94111-3628)
PHONE...........................415 576-1100
Ken Astle, *Branch Mgr*
EMP: 71
SALES (corp-wide): 8.4MM **Privately Held**
SIC: 8721 8748 Accounting, auditing & bookkeeping; business consulting
PA: Corwe Horwath
400 Capitol Mall Ste 1400
Sacramento CA 95814
916 441-1000

PRODUCTS & SERVICES SECTION
8721 - Accounting, Auditing & Bookkeeping Svcs County (P-26337)

(P-26317)
COUNTY OF SAN BERNARDINO
Also Called: Auditor Controller Department
222 W Hospitality Ln, San Bernardino (92415-0013)
PHONE 909 386-8818
Larry Walker, *Principal*
Patrick Honny, *Info Tech Dir*
A B Brand, *Controller*
Oscar Valdez, *Assistant*
EMP: 200
SQ FT: 12,700 **Privately Held**
SIC: 8721 9311 Auditing services; finance, taxation & monetary policy;
PA: County Of San Bernardino
    385 N Arrowhead Ave
    San Bernardino CA 92415
    909 387-3841

(P-26318)
COUNTY OF VENTURA
Auditor /controller
800 S Victoria Ave 1540, Ventura (93009-0003)
PHONE 805 654-3152
Fax: 805 654-5081
Christine Cohens, *Manager*
EMP: 61 **Privately Held**
WEB: www.vcoe.org
SIC: 8721 9311 Auditing services; controllers' office, government;
PA: County Of Ventura
    800 S Victoria Ave
    Ventura CA 93009
    805 654-2551

(P-26319)
CROWE HORWATH LLP
15233 Ventura Blvd Fl 9, Sherman Oaks (91403-2250)
PHONE 818 501-5200
Ray Calvey, *Manager*
Mark Taylor, *Executive*
Cassandra Johnson, *Technology*
Todd Hein, *CPA*
Sue Tomlinson, *CPA*
EMP: 120
SALES (corp-wide): 745.1MM **Privately Held**
SIC: 8721 Certified public accountant
PA: Crowe Horwath Llp
    225 W Wacker Dr Ste 2600
    Chicago IL 60606
    312 899-7000

(P-26320)
DELOITTE & TOUCHE LLP
555 W 5th St Ste 2700, Los Angeles (90013-1024)
PHONE 213 688-0800
Fax: 213 694-5265
Byron David, *Branch Mgr*
David N Bowen, *Partner*
Jim Moffat, *Managing Dir*
Hiroko Barker, *Admin Asst*
Terry Feit, *Admin Asst*
EMP: 1000
SALES (corp-wide): 9.5B **Privately Held**
WEB: www.deloitte.com
SIC: 8721 Accounting services, except auditing
HQ: Deloitte & Touche Llp
    30 Rockefeller Plz # 4350
    New York NY 10112
    212 492-4000

(P-26321)
DELOITTE & TOUCHE LLP
655 W Broadway Ste 700, San Diego (92101-8480)
PHONE 619 232-6500
Fax: 619 237-1755
Cathy Jennings, *Manager*
Robert Lee, *MIS Mgr*
Madhura Deshpande, *IT/INT Sup*
Prajakta Kemkar, *IT/INT Sup*
Aimee Sando, *IT/INT Sup*
EMP: 200
SALES (corp-wide): 9.5B **Privately Held**
WEB: www.deloitte.com
SIC: 8721 7291 Accounting, auditing & bookkeeping; tax return preparation services

HQ: Deloitte & Touche Llp
    30 Rockefeller Plz # 4350
    New York NY 10112
    212 492-4000

(P-26322)
DELOITTE & TOUCHE LLP
555 Mission St Ste 1400, San Francisco (94105-0942)
PHONE 415 783-4000
Fax: 415 247-4329
Mark Edmonds, *Branch Mgr*
Mike Deverell, *Principal*
David Gully, *Principal*
Mack Schwing, *Principal*
Lyn Nicholson, *Admin Asst*
EMP: 350
SALES (corp-wide): 9.5B **Privately Held**
WEB: www.deloitte.com
SIC: 8721 Accounting services, except auditing
HQ: Deloitte & Touche Llp
    30 Rockefeller Plz # 4350
    New York NY 10112
    212 492-4000

(P-26323)
DELOITTE & TOUCHE LLP
695 Town Center Dr # 1200, Costa Mesa (92626-7188)
PHONE 714 436-7419
Fax: 714 436-7200
Bob Grant, *Director*
Jeffrey D Egertson, *Partner*
Vito Francone, *Partner*
Curtis Hildt, *Partner*
Ken Salgado, *Partner*
EMP: 700
SALES (corp-wide): 9.5B **Privately Held**
WEB: www.deloitte.com
SIC: 8721 7291 Accounting services, except auditing; tax return preparation services
HQ: Deloitte & Touche Llp
    30 Rockefeller Plz # 4350
    New York NY 10112
    212 492-4000

(P-26324)
DELOITTE & TOUCHE LLP
225 W Santa Clara St # 600, San Jose (95113-1728)
PHONE 408 704-4000
Jonathan Tharmapalan, *Manager*
Monty Arslan, *MIS Mgr*
Larry Moore, *MIS Mgr*
Michael Reichert, *Accounting Dir*
Yoko Soma, *Tax Mgr*
EMP: 450
SALES (corp-wide): 9.5B **Privately Held**
WEB: www.deloitte.com
SIC: 8721 8742 6282 Certified public accountant; management consulting services; investment advice
HQ: Deloitte & Touche Llp
    30 Rockefeller Plz # 4350
    New York NY 10112
    212 492-4000

(P-26325)
DELOITTE & TOUCHE LLP
5250 N Palm Ave Ste 300, Fresno (93704-2200)
PHONE 559 449-6300
Fax: 559 226-1533
Nada Barrett, *Branch Mgr*
Mary Richardson, *Admin Asst*
Kenneth Beard, *CIO*
Bernadette Bixler, *Auditing Mgr*
Kevin Emerzian, *Auditing Mgr*
EMP: 70
SALES (corp-wide): 9.5B **Privately Held**
WEB: www.deloitte.com
SIC: 8721 Certified public accountant
HQ: Deloitte & Touche Llp
    30 Rockefeller Plz # 4350
    New York NY 10112
    212 492-4000

(P-26326)
DELOITTE & TOUCHE LLP
6210 Stoneridge Mall Rd, Pleasanton (94588-3268)
PHONE 415 782-4020
EMP: 244

SALES (corp-wide): 9.5B **Privately Held**
SIC: 8721 Certified public accountant
HQ: Deloitte & Touche Llp
    30 Rockefeller Plz # 4350
    New York NY 10112
    212 492-4000

(P-26327)
DELOITTE & TOUCHE LLP
555 W 5th St Ste 2700, Los Angeles (90013-1024)
PHONE 213 688-0800
EMP: 244
SALES (corp-wide): 12.3B **Privately Held**
SIC: 8721
HQ: Deloitte & Touche Llp
    30 Rockefeller Plz # 4350
    New York NY 10112
    212 492-4000

(P-26328)
DELOITTE TAX LLP
555 Mission St Ste 1400, San Francisco (94105-0942)
PHONE 415 783-4000
Mark Edmunds, *Branch Mgr*
Scott Rosenberger, *Senior Partner*
Sharon Zorbach, *Treasurer*
William Long, *Security Dir*
Donna Bernalsilva, *Admin Asst*
EMP: 294
SALES (corp-wide): 9.5B **Privately Held**
SIC: 8721 Auditing services; certified public accountant
HQ: Deloitte Tax Llp
    30 Rockefeller Plz
    New York NY 10112
    212 492-4000

(P-26329)
DELOITTE TAX LLP
225 W Santa Clara St # 600, San Jose (95113-1728)
PHONE 408 704-4000
Fax: 408 704-3083
Teresa Briggs, *Branch Mgr*
Wen H Chow, *Admin Asst*
Theresa Hauckes, *Admin Asst*
Julie Ichinaga, *Admin Asst*
Silvia Kandah, *Admin Asst*
EMP: 294
SALES (corp-wide): 9.5B **Privately Held**
SIC: 8721 Auditing services; certified public accountant
HQ: Deloitte Tax Llp
    30 Rockefeller Plz
    New York NY 10112
    212 492-4000

(P-26330)
DFS GROUP LP
Duty Free
1580 Francisco St, Torrance (90501-1323)
PHONE 310 783-6600
Fax: 310 783-6603
Claudia Gerard, *Branch Mgr*
Bruce Tweitmann, *Business Dir*
Duman Wong, *Director*
Rachel Centeno, *Manager*
EMP: 64
SALES (corp-wide): 255.7MM **Privately Held**
SIC: 8721 5947 Payroll accounting service; gift shop
HQ: Dfs Group L.P.
    525 Market St Fl 33
    San Francisco CA 94105
    415 977-2701

(P-26331)
ECONA CORP
1344 Paizay Pl Unit 732, Chula Vista (91913-3972)
P.O. Box 296, Alpine (91903-0296)
PHONE 619 722-6555
Branden B Moss, *CEO*
EMP: 50 EST: 2013
SALES (est): 1.8MM **Privately Held**
SIC: 8721 7389 Payroll accounting service;

(P-26332)
EDF RENEWABLE ENERGY INC
15445 Innovation Dr, San Diego (92128-3432)
P.O. Box 504080 (92150-4080)
PHONE 760 329-1437
Arlondo Flores, *Branch Mgr*
Larry Barr, *Exec VP*
Deborah Gronvold, *Exec VP*
David Kirkpatrick, *Vice Pres*
EMP: 150
SALES (corp-wide): 769.9MM **Privately Held**
SIC: 8721 Accounting, auditing & bookkeeping
PA: Edf Renewable Energy, Inc.
    15445 Innovation Dr
    San Diego CA 92128
    858 521-3300

(P-26333)
EDWARD E STRAINE CPA
1760 Creekside Oaks Dr, Sacramento (95833-3632)
PHONE 916 646-6464
Edward E Straine, *Principal*
EMP: 60
SALES (est): 1.8MM **Privately Held**
SIC: 8721 Certified public accountant

(P-26334)
EGO INC
Also Called: Emergency Groups Office
444 E Huntington Dr # 300, Arcadia (91006-6203)
PHONE 626 447-0296
Fax: 626 447-6036
Andrea Brault, *President*
Del Brault, *President*
Jane Brault, *Treasurer*
Sharon Richardson, *Officer*
James Blakeman, *Senior VP*
EMP: 150
SQ FT: 8,500
SALES (est): 16.6MM **Privately Held**
SIC: 8721 Billing & bookkeeping service

(P-26335)
EISNERAMPER LLP
1 Market Ste 620, San Francisco (94105-5105)
PHONE 415 974-6000
John Williamson, *Managing Prtnr*
Corina Evans, *Manager*
Yvonne Yang, *Manager*
EMP: 70
SALES (corp-wide): 276.3MM **Privately Held**
SIC: 8721 Certified public accountant
PA: Eisneramper Llp
    750 3rd Ave
    New York NY 10017
    212 949-8700

(P-26336)
ENTERTAINMENT PARTNERS (PA)
2835 N Naomi St, Burbank (91504-2000)
PHONE 818 955-6000
Fax: 818 845-7120
Mark Goldstein, *CEO*
George Vaughan, *CFO*
Rebecca Harshberger, *Vice Pres*
Tom Johnson, *Vice Pres*
Elza Martirosyan, *Executive Asst*
EMP: 295
SQ FT: 38,000
SALES (est): 52.4MM **Privately Held**
WEB: www.epservices.com
SIC: 8721 Payroll accounting service

(P-26337)
ERNST & YOUNG LLP
Also Called: Ey
725 S Figueroa St Ste 200, Los Angeles (90017-5403)
PHONE 213 977-3200
Fax: 213 977-3729
Jeff Kaufman, *Manager*
Allison Somphou, *Auditing Mgr*
Andrew Mokhov, *CPA*
Amy Cerna, *Personnel Assit*
Kara D Croce, *Senior Mgr*
EMP: 1000

8721 - Accounting, Auditing & Bookkeeping Svcs County (P-26338)

SALES (corp-wide): 5.9B Privately Held
WEB: www.ey.com
SIC: 8721 8742 7291 Certified public accountant; auditing services; business consultant; management information systems consultant; tax return preparation services
PA: Ernst & Young Llp
  5 Times Sq Fl Conlv1
  New York NY 10036
  212 773-3000

(P-26338)
ERNST & YOUNG LLP
Also Called: Ey
200 N Sepulveda Blvd Fl 2, El Segundo (90245-4340)
PHONE.....................310 725-1764
Fax: 310 727-8848
Kristen Schmitt, *Branch Mgr*
Valerie Logan, *CFO*
Sylvie Harton, *Sales Executive*
Thomas Brodeur, *Manager*
Mike Terpin, *Manager*
EMP: 228
SALES (corp-wide): 5.9B Privately Held
SIC: 8721 Certified public accountant
PA: Ernst & Young Llp
  5 Times Sq Fl Conlv1
  New York NY 10036
  212 773-3000

(P-26339)
ERNST & YOUNG LLP
Also Called: Ey
560 Mission St Ste 1600, San Francisco (94105-2990)
PHONE.....................415 894-8000
Michael Strachan, *Manager*
Gregory Martin, *Partner*
Monica Fox, *Business Dir*
James Oneil, *Principal*
Barak Ravid, *Exec Dir*
EMP: 100
SALES (corp-wide): 5.9B Privately Held
WEB: www.ey.com
SIC: 8721 8742 Accounting services, except auditing; management consulting services
PA: Ernst & Young Llp
  5 Times Sq Fl Conlv1
  New York NY 10036
  212 773-3000

(P-26340)
ERNST & YOUNG LLP
Also Called: Ey
1451 S California Ave, Palo Alto (94304-1109)
PHONE.....................650 496-1600
Fax: 650 496-1600
Alex Turco, *Branch Mgr*
Adam Barrow, *Auditor*
EMP: 230
SALES (corp-wide): 5.9B Privately Held
SIC: 8721 Certified public accountant
PA: Ernst & Young Llp
  5 Times Sq Fl Conlv1
  New York NY 10036
  212 773-3000

(P-26341)
ERNST & YOUNG LLP
Also Called: Ey
303 Almaden Blvd Ste 1000, San Jose (95110-2723)
PHONE.....................408 947-5500
Fax: 408 947-4975
Teri Shaffer, *Partner*
Dave Price, *Partner*
John Wills, *Partner*
Kevin McAuliffe, *Principal*
Phyrne Bourke, *Admin Mgr*
EMP: 650
SALES (corp-wide): 5.9B Privately Held
WEB: www.ey.com
SIC: 8721 8742 Certified public accountant; auditing services; business consultant; management information systems consultant
PA: Ernst & Young Llp
  5 Times Sq Fl Conlv1
  New York NY 10036
  212 773-3000

(P-26342)
ERNST & YOUNG LLP
Also Called: Ey
18111 Von Karman Ave # 1000, Irvine (92612-7101)
PHONE.....................949 794-2300
Fax: 949 437-0595
Ronda L Spires, *Manager*
Chris Abston, *Partner*
Kathy Dagestino, *Partner*
Mike Denning, *Partner*
John F Fritz, *Partner*
EMP: 300
SALES (corp-wide): 5.9B Privately Held
WEB: www.ey.com
SIC: 8721 8742 Certified public accountant; auditing services; business consultant; management information systems consultant
PA: Ernst & Young Llp
  5 Times Sq Fl Conlv1
  New York NY 10036
  212 773-3000

(P-26343)
ERNST & YOUNG LLP
Also Called: Ey
4370 La Jolla Village Dr # 500, San Diego (92122-1251)
PHONE.....................858 535-7200
Michael J Hartnett, *Manager*
Riju Parakh, *Manager*
Wendy Roy, *Manager*
EMP: 135
SALES (corp-wide): 5.9B Privately Held
WEB: www.ey.com
SIC: 8721 8742 7291 Certified public accountant; auditing services; business consultant; management information systems consultant; tax return preparation services
PA: Ernst & Young Llp
  5 Times Sq Fl Conlv1
  New York NY 10036
  212 773-3000

(P-26344)
ERNST & YOUNG LLP
Also Called: Ey
18006 Sky Park Cir # 106, Irvine (92614-6406)
PHONE.....................949 838-3300
Ted Esau, *Principal*
EMP: 228
SALES (corp-wide): 5.9B Privately Held
WEB: www.ey.com
SIC: 8721 Certified public accountant
PA: Ernst & Young Llp
  5 Times Sq Fl Conlv1
  New York NY 10036
  212 773-3000

(P-26345)
ERNST & YOUNG LLP
Also Called: Ey
2931 Townsgate Rd Ste 100, Westlake Village (91361-5874)
PHONE.....................805 778-7000
Brian Ladin, *Branch Mgr*
Todd Moody, *Advisor*
EMP: 80
SALES (corp-wide): 5.9B Privately Held
WEB: www.ey.com
SIC: 8721 8742 8748 Certified public accountant; auditing services; business consultant; management information systems consultant; business consulting
PA: Ernst & Young Llp
  5 Times Sq Fl Conlv1
  New York NY 10036
  212 773-3000

(P-26346)
ERNST & YOUNG LLP
Also Called: Ey
275 Shoreline Dr Ste 600, Redwood City (94065-1493)
PHONE.....................650 802-4500
Donna Frazer, *Branch Mgr*
David Hickox, *Accounting Dir*
Sunil Bhat, *Consultant*
David Ward, *Consultant*
EMP: 250

(P-26347)
ERNST & YOUNG LLP
Also Called: Ey
2901 Douglas Blvd Ste 300, Roseville (95661-4247)
PHONE.....................916 218-1900
Fax: 916 218-1999
Craig Pickett, *Manager*
James Markham, *Senior Mgr*
EMP: 228
SALES (corp-wide): 5.9B Privately Held
WEB: www.ey.com
SIC: 8721 Certified public accountant; auditing services
PA: Ernst & Young Llp
  5 Times Sq Fl Conlv1
  New York NY 10036
  212 773-3000

(P-26348)
ERNST & YOUNG LLP
4301 Hacienda Dr Ste 450, Pleasanton (94588-2791)
PHONE.....................925 734-6388
Karen Amato, *Manager*
EMP: 228
SALES (corp-wide): 5.9B Privately Held
WEB: www.ey.com
SIC: 8721 Certified public accountant
PA: Ernst & Young Llp
  5 Times Sq Fl Conlv1
  New York NY 10036
  212 773-3000

(P-26349)
ERNST & YOUNG LLP
560 Mission St Ste 1600, San Francisco (94105-0911)
PHONE.....................415 894-8000
EMP: 700
SALES (corp-wide): 3B Privately Held
SIC: 8721
PA: Ernst & Young Llp
  5 Times Sq Fl Conlv1
  New York NY 10036
  212 773-3000

(P-26350)
FILM PAYROLL SERVICES INC (PA)
Also Called: Quantos Payroll
500 S Sepulveda Blvd Fl 4, Los Angeles (90049-3550)
PHONE.....................310 440-9600
Fax: 310 472-9970
Gregory Pickert, *CEO*
Maureen Macneil, *Executive*
Roger Jones, *Business Dir*
Elijah Lee, *Info Tech Mgr*
Mala Mathur, *Technology*
EMP: 100
SQ FT: 5,000
SALES (est): 6.6MM Privately Held
SIC: 8721 Payroll accounting service

(P-26351)
FRANK RIMERMAN & CO LLP
1 Embarcadero Ctr # 2410, San Francisco (94111-3628)
PHONE.....................415 439-1144
Fax: 415 296-8208
Bryan Polster, *Managing Prtnr*
Chris Glick, *Programmer Anys*
Candace Curtis, *CPA*
Robert Hoffman, *CPA*
Elaine Leung, *CPA*
EMP: 62
SALES (corp-wide): 30.8MM Privately Held
SIC: 8721 Certified public accountant
PA: Frank, Rimerman & Co. Llp
  1801 Page Mill Rd Ste 100
  Palo Alto CA
  650 845-8100

(P-26352)
GELFAND RENNERT & FELDMAN LLP (PA)
1880 Century Park E # 1600, Los Angeles (90067-1661)
PHONE.....................310 553-1707
Fax: 310 557-8412
Marshall R Gelfand, *Partner*
Tyson Beem, *Partner*
Todd Gelfand, *Partner*
Judy Chesky, *Admin Sec*
Jeff Gilman, *Admin Asst*
EMP: 200
SALES: 5K Privately Held
WEB: www.grfllp.com
SIC: 8721 Certified public accountant

(P-26353)
GELFAND RENNERT & FELDMAN LLP
1880 Century Park E # 1600, Los Angeles (90067-1661)
PHONE.....................310 553-1707
Todd M Gelfand, *Manager*
EMP: 200
SALES (corp-wide): 5K Privately Held
WEB: www.grfllp.com
SIC: 8721 8741 Certified public accountant; business management
PA: Gelfand, Rennert & Feldman, L.L.P.
  1880 Century Park E # 1600
  Los Angeles CA 90067
  310 553-1707

(P-26354)
GLENN BURDETTE PHILLIPS BRYSON
Also Called: A Professional
1150 Palm St, San Luis Obispo (93401-3176)
PHONE.....................805 544-1441
Fax: 805 544-4351
David Bryson, *Shareholder*
Gary Wintermeyer, *Shareholder*
Kristy Wilson, *Officer*
Dave Phillip0s, *Principal*
Jennie L Hackett, *Admin Asst*
EMP: 55
SQ FT: 3,000
SALES (est): 5MM Privately Held
WEB: www.gbpb.net
SIC: 8721 Certified public accountant

(P-26355)
GRANT THORNTON LLP
101 California St # 2700, San Francisco (94111-5830)
PHONE.....................415 986-3900
Jeff Pera, *Manager*
Lucy Lee, *Vice Pres*
Daniel Allustiarti, *Admin Asst*
Rimma Tabakh, *Senior Mgr*
Orus Dearman, *Director*
EMP: 70
SALES (corp-wide): 74MM Privately Held
WEB: www.gt.com
SIC: 8721 Accounting services, except auditing
HQ: Grant Thornton Llp
  171 N Clark St Ste 200
  Chicago IL 60601
  312 856-0200

(P-26356)
GRANT THORNTON LLP
150 Almaden Blvd Ste 600, San Jose (95113-2016)
PHONE.....................408 275-9000
Fax: 408 275-0582
Harry Smith, *Branch Mgr*
Gary J Gemoll, *Managing Prtnr*
Steve Singer, *Business Dir*
Bill Heppner, *Principal*
Rocky Williams, *Managing Dir*
EMP: 50
SALES (corp-wide): 74MM Privately Held
WEB: www.gt.com
SIC: 8721 Certified public accountant
HQ: Grant Thornton Llp
  171 N Clark St Ste 200
  Chicago IL 60601
  312 856-0200

PRODUCTS & SERVICES SECTION **8721 - Accounting, Auditing & Bookkeeping Svcs County (P-26378)**

(P-26357)
GRANT THORNTON LLP
1000 Wilshire Blvd # 300, Los Angeles (90017-2457)
PHONE..................213 627-1717
Fax: 213 624-6793
Mark Bagaason, *Manager*
Stephen Legg, *CFO*
Jim Hayden, *Principal*
Joe A Monti, *Principal*
Robert Garcia, *Admin Asst*
EMP: 50
SALES (corp-wide): 74MM **Privately Held**
WEB: www.gt.com
SIC: 8721 8742 7291 Accounting services, except auditing; auditing services; management consulting services; tax return preparation services
HQ: Grant Thornton Llp
   171 N Clark St Ste 200
   Chicago IL 60601
   312 856-0200

(P-26358)
GRANT THORNTON LLP
515 S Flower St Ste 700, Los Angeles (90071-2209)
PHONE..................213 627-1717
Don Dahl, *Manager*
Jeff White, *Department Mgr*
Rosemarie Brown, *Director*
EMP: 99
SALES (corp-wide): 74MM **Privately Held**
WEB: www.gt.com
SIC: 8721 Accounting, auditing & bookkeeping; auditing services; accounting services, except auditing
HQ: Grant Thornton Llp
   171 N Clark St Ste 200
   Chicago IL 60601
   312 856-0200

(P-26359)
GRANT THORNTON LLP
12220 El Camino Real, San Diego (92130-2091)
PHONE..................858 704-8000
Don Williams,
EMP: 113
SALES (corp-wide): 74MM **Privately Held**
WEB: www.gt.com
SIC: 8721 Accounting, auditing & bookkeeping; auditing services; accounting services, except auditing
HQ: Grant Thornton Llp
   171 N Clark St Ste 200
   Chicago IL 60601
   312 856-0200

(P-26360)
GREEN HASSON & JANKS LLP
10990 Wilshire Blvd Fl 16, Los Angeles (90024-3925)
PHONE..................310 873-1600
Fax: 310 873-6600
Leon Janks, *Partner*
William Cline, *CFO*
Jill Farley, *CFO*
Sherri Gastelum, *Business Dir*
Derrick Coleman, *Branch Mgr*
EMP: 120
SQ FT: 22,000
SALES (est): 15.5MM **Privately Held**
WEB: www.ghjadvisors.com
SIC: 8721 Certified public accountant

(P-26361)
GROBSTEIN HORWATH & CO
Also Called: Grobstein, Horwath & Company
15233 Ventura Blvd Fl 9, Van Nuys (91403-2250)
PHONE..................818 501-5200
Michael Grobstein, *Partner*
David Agler, *Partner*
Michael Fenstein, *Partner*
David Gottlieb, *Partner*
Jerry Levine, *Partner*
EMP: 70
SQ FT: 11,000
SALES (est): 4.1MM **Privately Held**
WEB: www.horwathcal.com
SIC: 8721 Certified public accountant

(P-26362)
GURSEY SCHNEIDER & CO LLC (PA)
1888 Century Park E # 900, Los Angeles (90067-1735)
PHONE..................310 552-0960
Fax: 310 557-3468
Stephan H Wasserman,
Jeff Bagge, *COO*
Carmen Corral, *Administration*
Michael Kamen, *Info Tech Mgr*
Jhesse Garcia, *Technology*
EMP: 82
SQ FT: 12,000
SALES (est): 19.3MM **Privately Held**
SIC: 8721 Certified public accountant

(P-26363)
HAGEN STREIFF NEWTON & OSHIRO
300 Montgomery St Ste 500, San Francisco (94104-1916)
PHONE..................415 982-4704
Fax: 415 982-4705
Peter Hagen, *CEO*
EMP: 50
SALES (est): 3.4MM **Privately Held**
SIC: 8721 Accounting, auditing & bookkeeping

(P-26364)
HAGEN STREIFF NEWTON OSHIRO
1990 N Calif Blvd Ste 320, Walnut Creek (94596-3781)
PHONE..................925 941-1050
Fax: 925 941-1055
Mark Newton, *Partner*
EMP: 50
SALES (est): 1.4MM **Privately Held**
SIC: 8721 Accounting, auditing & bookkeeping

(P-26365)
HANSEN ICC LLC
2111 Palomar Airport Rd, Carlsbad (92011-1418)
PHONE..................760 268-7299
Guy Tennant, *General Mgr*
Michelle Royce, *Accounting Mgr*
Tammy Culp, *Controller*
EMP: 100 EST: 2013
SQ FT: 8,016
SALES (est): 7.6MM
SALES (corp-wide): 109.3MM **Privately Held**
SIC: 8721 Billing & bookkeeping service
HQ: Hansen North America Inc.
   350 5th Ave Ste 6510
   New York NY 10118
   212 268-6000

(P-26366)
HASKELL & WHITE (PA)
300 Spectrum Center Dr # 300, Irvine (92618-4987)
PHONE..................949 450-6200
Fax: 949 753-1224
Wayne Pinnell, *Partner*
Gary L Curtis, *Partner*
Peter Dolbee, *Partner*
Brad Graves, *Partner*
John Poth, *Partner*
EMP: 62
SALES (est): 13.6MM **Privately Held**
WEB: www.hwcpa.com
SIC: 8721 Certified public accountant

(P-26367)
HEALTHCARE COST SOLUTIONS INC
Also Called: H C S
1200 Newprt Cntr Dr 190, Newport Beach (92660)
PHONE..................949 721-2795
Bridget T Gallagher, *CEO*
Melanie Moore, *Marketing Staff*
Monica Leisch, *Director*
EMP: 60
SALES (est): 3.3MM **Privately Held**
WEB: www.hcsstat.com
SIC: 8721 8742 Auditing services; hospital & health services consultant

(P-26368)
HMWC CPAS & BUSINESS ADVISORS
Also Called: Yosemite Capital Manggement
17501 17th St Ste 100, Tustin (92780-7924)
PHONE..................714 505-9000
Fax: 714 505-9200
Steven Williams, *President*
Phr A Ferran, *COO*
Michaele Garcia, *Executive Asst*
Debra Leon, *Executive Asst*
Curtis Campbell, *Admin Sec*
EMP: 57 EST: 1972
SALES (est): 5.4MM **Privately Held**
SIC: 8721 Certified public accountant

(P-26369)
HOLTHOUSE CARLIN VAN TRIGT LLP
350 W Colo Blvd Fl 5, Pasadena (91105)
PHONE..................626 243-5100
Kevin Cordano, *Principal*
EMP: 70
SALES (corp-wide): 36.1MM **Privately Held**
SIC: 8721 Certified public accountant
PA: Holthouse Carlin Van Trigt Llp
   11444 W Olympic Blvd # 11
   Los Angeles CA 90064
   310 477-5551

(P-26370)
HOLTHOUSE CARLIN VAN TRIGT LLP
400 W Ventura Blvd # 250, Camarillo (93010-9137)
PHONE..................805 374-8555
Jeffrey Strug, *Executive*
Kathleen H Jones, *Principal*
Beth Salverson, *Principal*
Rebecca Gibb, *CPA*
EMP: 70
SALES (corp-wide): 36.1MM **Privately Held**
SIC: 8721 Certified public accountant
PA: Holthouse Carlin Van Trigt Llp
   11444 W Olympic Blvd # 11
   Los Angeles CA 90064
   310 477-5551

(P-26371)
HOLTHOUSE CARLIN VAN TRIGT LLP
15760 Ventura Blvd # 1700, Encino (91436-3028)
PHONE..................818 849-3140
EMP: 70
SALES (corp-wide): 36.1MM **Privately Held**
SIC: 8721 Certified public accountant
PA: Holthouse Carlin Van Trigt Llp
   11444 W Olympic Blvd # 11
   Los Angeles CA 90064
   310 477-5551

(P-26372)
HOLTHOUSE CARLIN VAN TRIGT LLP
555 Anton Blvd Ste 700, Costa Mesa (92626-7659)
PHONE..................714 361-7600
Donna Hansen, *Owner*
Carol Carlile, *Managing Dir*
EMP: 70
SALES (corp-wide): 36.1MM **Privately Held**
SIC: 8721 Certified public accountant
PA: Holthouse Carlin Van Trigt Llp
   11444 W Olympic Blvd # 11
   Los Angeles CA 90064
   310 477-5551

(P-26373)
HOLTHOUSE CARLIN VAN TRIGT LLP (PA)
11444 W Olympic Blvd # 11, Los Angeles (90064-1500)
PHONE..................310 477-5551
Fax: 310 477-2633
Philip Holthouse, *Managing Prtnr*
David Bierhorst, *Partner*
James Carlin, *Partner*
Blake Christian, *Partner*
Greg Hutchins, *Partner*
EMP: 110
SALES (est): 36.1MM **Privately Held**
WEB: www.hcvt.com
SIC: 8721 Certified public accountant

(P-26374)
HOOD & STRONG LLP (PA)
100 1st St Fl 14, San Francisco (94105-4631)
PHONE..................415 781-0793
Fax: 415 421-2976
Robert Raffo, *Managing Prtnr*
Raul Hernandez, *Partner*
Steve Piuma, *Partner*
Ngu Phan, *Tax Mgr*
Barbara Bond, *CPA*
EMP: 75
SQ FT: 13,000
SALES (est): 12.2MM **Privately Held**
WEB: www.hoodstrong.com
SIC: 8721 Certified public accountant

(P-26375)
HUTCHINSON & BLOODGOOD LLP (PA)
550 N Brand Blvd Fl 14, Glendale (91203-1952)
P.O. Box 1917 (91209-1917)
PHONE..................818 637-5000
Fax: 323 240-0949
Richard Preciado, *Managing Prtnr*
Michael Benneian, *Partner*
Gary Carruthers, *Partner*
Jenny Chen, *Partner*
Juan Daukowski, *Partner*
EMP: 59
SALES (est): 26.2MM **Privately Held**
WEB: www.hbllp.com
SIC: 8721 Accounting, auditing & bookkeeping

(P-26376)
I L S WEST INC
17501 17th St Ste 100, Tustin (92780-7924)
PHONE..................714 505-7530
Steve Williams, *President*
Gerry Herter, *President*
Andrea Ferran, *CFO*
Andrea Serran, *Exec Dir*
Robyne Wilkerson, *Technology*
EMP: 50
SALES (est): 1.6MM **Privately Held**
SIC: 8721 Accounting, auditing & bookkeeping

(P-26377)
INNOVTIVE EMPLYEE SLUTIONS INC
9665 Gran Rdge Dr Ste 420, San Diego (92123)
PHONE..................858 715-5100
Karla Hertzog, *CEO*
Gaby Mergenphal, *President*
Peter Limone, *CFO*
Darlene Bruder, *Vice Pres*
Tania Fiero, *Vice Pres*
EMP: 1500
SQ FT: 6,641
SALES (est): 82.9MM **Privately Held**
WEB: www.innovative-solution.com
SIC: 8721 Payroll accounting service

(P-26378)
INTERNATIONAL RECTIFIER CORP
Interntnal Rctfr/Ccunting Dept
222 Kansas St, El Segundo (90245-4315)
PHONE..................310 726-8000
Michael McGee, *Manager*
Mike Seidl, *President*
Michael P McGee, *CFO*
Linda J Pahl, *CFO*
Michael Barrow, *Exec VP*
EMP: 699
SALES (corp-wide): 6.4B **Privately Held**
WEB: www.irf.com
SIC: 8721 3674 Accounting, auditing & bookkeeping; semiconductors & related devices
HQ: Infineon Technologies Americas Corp.
   101 N Sepulveda Blvd
   El Segundo CA 90245
   310 726-8000

8721 - Accounting, Auditing & Bookkeeping Svcs County (P-26379)

(P-26379)
INTUIT INC
21215 Burbank Blvd, Woodland Hills (91367-7090)
PHONE..................................818 436-7800
Fax: 805 419-8679
Michael Ermi, *Branch Mgr*
Phil Warden, *Program Mgr*
Jasvinder Grover, *Admin Asst*
Phu Thi, *Administration*
Raghu Doppalapudi, *Sr Software Eng*
EMP: 51
SALES (corp-wide): 4.6B **Publicly Held**
SIC: 8721 Payroll accounting service
PA: Intuit Inc.
2700 Coast Ave
Mountain View CA 94043
650 944-6000

(P-26380)
JOSHUA J BODENSTADT CPA A PROF
4225 Executive Sq Ste 900, La Jolla (92037-1485)
PHONE..................................858 642-5050
Joshua J Bodenstadt, *Partner*
EMP: 50
SALES (est): 108.7K **Privately Held**
SIC: 8721 Certified public accountant

(P-26381)
JPMORGAN XIGN CORPORATION
7077 Koll Center Pkwy, Pleasanton (94566-3142)
PHONE..................................925 469-9446
Fax: 925 469-9447
Thomas M Glassanos, *President*
Jerry Ulrich, *Treasurer*
Mahmood Masghati, *Senior VP*
Ken Daly, *Vice Pres*
Allen F Nordgren, *Vice Pres*
EMP: 85
SQ FT: 26,000
SALES (est): 33.4K
SALES (corp-wide): 101B **Publicly Held**
WEB: www.xign.com
SIC: 8721 Billing & bookkeeping service
HQ: Jpmorgan Chase Bank, National Association
1111 Polaris Pkwy
Columbus OH 43240
614 436-3055

(P-26382)
KELLOGG ANDLSON ACCNTANCY CORP (PA)
21700 Oxnard St Ste 800, Woodland Hills (91367-7500)
PHONE..................................818 971-5100
Christian Payne, *CEO*
James F Walters, *President*
William Wall, *Vice Pres*
Manuel Acevedo, *CTO*
Tarah Scott, *Recruiter*
EMP: 60
SALES (est): 13.6MM **Privately Held**
WEB: www.k-a.com
SIC: 8721 Accounting, auditing & bookkeeping

(P-26383)
KIECKHAFER SCHIFFER & CO LLP (PA)
6201 Oak Cyn Ste 200, Irvine (92618-5231)
PHONE..................................949 250-3900
Jim Kieckhafer, *Partner*
Scott Schiffer, *Partner*
Susan E Chubbuck, *CPA*
Ana Felkai, *CPA*
Brandy Gilbert, *Opers Mgr*
EMP: 53
SALES (est): 9.1MM **Privately Held**
WEB: www.ksandco.com
SIC: 8721 Accounting, auditing & bookkeeping

(P-26384)
KPMG LLP
9171 Wilshire Blvd # 500, Beverly Hills (90210-5530)
PHONE..................................310 273-2770
Fax: 310 273-6649
Melvin Ozur, *Branch Mgr*
Michael Barton, *CFO*
EMP: 50
SALES (corp-wide): 5.2B **Privately Held**
WEB: www.rkco.com
SIC: 8721 Accounting, auditing & bookkeeping
PA: Kpmg Llp
345 Park Ave Lowr L-4
New York NY 10154
212 758-9700

(P-26385)
KPMG LLP
4747 Executive Dr Ste 600, San Diego (92121-3100)
PHONE..................................858 750-7100
Kelli Beane, *Branch Mgr*
Elton E Winston, *Principal*
Michael Grossi, *Admin Asst*
Stephanie Isaacson, *Auditing Mgr*
Reyna Estremera, *Human Res Mgr*
EMP: 150
SALES (corp-wide): 5.2B **Privately Held**
SIC: 8721 Certified public accountant
PA: Kpmg Llp
345 Park Ave Lowr L-4
New York NY 10154
212 758-9700

(P-26386)
KPMG LLP
55 2nd St Ste 1400, San Francisco (94105-4557)
PHONE..................................415 963-5100
Louis P Miramontes, *Managing Prtnr*
Barbara Carbone, *Partner*
Alan Chinn, *Partner*
Glenn M Farrell, *Partner*
Brad Fisher, *Partner*
EMP: 50
SQ FT: 4,325
SALES (corp-wide): 5.2B **Privately Held**
SIC: 8721 Certified public accountant
PA: Kpmg Llp
345 Park Ave Lowr L-4
New York NY 10154
212 758-9700

(P-26387)
KPMG LLP
550 S Hope St Ste 1500, Los Angeles (90071-2629)
PHONE..................................212 758-9700
Joseph T Boyle, *Manager*
Steven Melloy, *Administration*
Peter Berman, *Engrg Dir*
William Sand, *Engrg Dir*
Curtis Conover, *Finance Other*
EMP: 3000
SALES (corp-wide): 5.2B **Privately Held**
SIC: 8721 Certified public accountant
PA: Kpmg Llp
345 Park Ave Lowr L-4
New York NY 10154
212 758-9700

(P-26388)
KPMG LLP
500 Capitol Mall Ste 2100, Sacramento (95814-4754)
PHONE..................................916 448-4700
Fax: 916 554-1199
Rich Wise, *Partner*
Tiffany Ellis, *Manager*
EMP: 110
SALES (corp-wide): 5.2B **Privately Held**
SIC: 8721 Certified public accountant
PA: Kpmg Llp
345 Park Ave Lowr L-4
New York NY 10154
212 758-9700

(P-26389)
KPMG LLP
2175 N Calif Blvd # 1000, Walnut Creek (94596-3579)
PHONE..................................925 946-1300
Todd Goldman, *Manager*
Robert Jinkins, *CPA*
EMP: 50
SALES (corp-wide): 5.2B **Privately Held**
WEB: www.rkco.com
SIC: 8721 Certified public accountant
PA: Kpmg Llp
345 Park Ave Lowr L-4
New York NY 10154
212 758-9700

(P-26390)
KPMG LLP
21700 Oxnard St Ste 1800, Woodland Hills (91367-3659)
PHONE..................................818 227-6900
Mort Erlich, *Manager*
Claudia Sabedra, *Director*
EMP: 50
SALES (corp-wide): 5.2B **Privately Held**
SIC: 8721 Certified public accountant
PA: Kpmg Llp
345 Park Ave Lowr L-4
New York NY 10154
212 758-9700

(P-26391)
KRANZ & ASSOC HOLDINGS LLC
830 Menlo Ave Ste 100, Menlo Park (94025-4734)
PHONE..................................650 854-4400
Deborah Kranz,
EMP: 90
SQ FT: 750
SALES (est): 1.3MM **Privately Held**
SIC: 8721 Accounting services, except auditing

(P-26392)
L RUHLAND
1877 Centro West St, Belvedere Tiburon (94920-1910)
PHONE..................................415 435-5992
Leslie Ruhland, *Owner*
EMP: 50
SALES (est): 3.5MM **Privately Held**
SIC: 8721 Certified public accountant

(P-26393)
LAVANTE INC
5285 Hellyer Ave Ste 200, San Jose (95138-1087)
P.O. Box 41058 (95160-1058)
PHONE..................................408 754-0505
Frank Harbist, *President*
Sanjeev Srivastav, *COO*
Robert Habig, *CFO*
Angela Bandlow, *Chief Mktg Ofcr*
Joe Flynn, *Officer*
EMP: 50
SALES (est): 5.8MM **Privately Held**
WEB: www.auditsolutions.com
SIC: 8721 8741 Auditing services; management services

(P-26394)
LAVINE LOFGREN MORRIS & ENGE
4180 La Jolla Village Dr # 315, La Jolla (92037-1402)
PHONE..................................858 455-1200
Fax: 858 455-0898
Von Morris, *Mng Member*
Romy Brown, *COO*
Robert Hasse, *COO*
David Saunders, *Senior VP*
Shawn Goll, *Admin Asst*
EMP: 50
SQ FT: 5,000
SALES (est): 6.8MM **Privately Held**
SIC: 8721 Certified public accountant

(P-26395)
LINDQUIST LLP (PA)
5000 Executive Pkwy # 400, San Ramon (94583-4210)
PHONE..................................925 277-9100
Fax: 925 277-9552
Barry Omahen, *Partner*
Alan C Lindquist, *Partner*
Kimberly Ray, *Partner*
Pamela Lorenz, *Info Tech Dir*
Mike Fahy, *Info Tech Mgr*
EMP: 57
SALES (est): 10.5MM **Privately Held**
SIC: 8721 Certified public accountant

(P-26396)
LLP MOSS ADAMS
3100 Zinfandel Dr Ste 500, Rancho Cordova (95670-6074)
PHONE..................................916 503-8100
Fax: 916 503-8101
Robert Ahern, *Branch Mgr*
Amy Allison, *Accountant*
Carolyn Watts, *Human Res Mgr*
Sharyl David, *Senior Mgr*
Patricia Hewitt, *Manager*
EMP: 78
SALES (corp-wide): 318.8MM **Privately Held**
SIC: 8721 Certified public accountant
PA: Moss Adams Llp
999 3rd Ave Ste 3300
Seattle WA 98104
206 302-6500

(P-26397)
LLP MOSS ADAMS
21700 Oxnard St Ste 300, Woodland Hills (91367-7561)
PHONE..................................818 577-1822
Gidget Furness, *COO*
Star Fischer, *Bd of Directors*
Bob Terada, *Office Mgr*
Robyn Wassom, *Office Mgr*
Nicholas Hansen, *Manager*
EMP: 78
SALES (corp-wide): 318.8MM **Privately Held**
SIC: 8721 Certified public accountant
PA: Moss Adams Llp
999 3rd Ave Ste 3300
Seattle WA 98104
206 302-6500

(P-26398)
LLP MOSS ADAMS
3121 W March Ln Ste 100, Stockton (95219-2367)
PHONE..................................209 955-6100
Raymond Wiggins, *Technology*
Donald Butwill, *Senior Mgr*
Heidi Berenbrok, *Manager*
Shonda Furr, *Manager*
EMP: 50
SALES (corp-wide): 318.8MM **Privately Held**
SIC: 8721 Certified public accountant
PA: Moss Adams Llp
999 3rd Ave Ste 3300
Seattle WA 98104
206 302-6500

(P-26399)
LLP MOSS ADAMS
101 2nd St Ste 900, San Francisco (94105-3650)
PHONE..................................415 956-1500
Joy Robinson, *Branch Mgr*
Dan Cheyney, *Partner*
Caryl Thorp, *Partner*
Eric Tostenrud, *Partner*
Paul Tucci, *Partner*
EMP: 140
SALES (corp-wide): 318.8MM **Privately Held**
WEB: www.mossadams.com
SIC: 8721 Certified public accountant
PA: Moss Adams Llp
999 3rd Ave Ste 3300
Seattle WA 98104
206 302-6500

(P-26400)
LLP MOSS ADAMS
635 Campbell Tech Pkwy # 100, Campbell (95008-5075)
PHONE..................................408 369-2400
Fax: 408 879-9485
Joe Costa, *Branch Mgr*
Steven Brunk, *Business Dir*
Clare Piech, *Admin Asst*
Liana Felix, *Auditor*
Kevin Maddock, *Auditor*
EMP: 78
SALES (corp-wide): 318.8MM **Privately Held**
SIC: 8721 Accounting, auditing & bookkeeping

PRODUCTS & SERVICES SECTION

8721 - Accounting, Auditing & Bookkeeping Svcs County (P-26421)

PA: Moss Adams Llp
999 3rd Ave Ste 3300
Seattle WA 98104
206 302-6500

(P-26401)
LLP MOSS ADAMS
10960 Wilshire Blvd # 1100, Los Angeles (90024-3714)
PHONE.................................310 278-5850
Fax: 213 477-8424
Rod Green, *Partner*
Shirley Maimoni, *Officer*
Lynda Blake, *Admin Mgr*
Carmen Swetland, *Executive Asst*
Penni Kotsalis, *Admin Asst*
EMP: 150
SALES (corp-wide): 318.8MM **Privately Held**
WEB: www.mossadams.com
SIC: 8721 Certified public accountant
PA: Moss Adams Llp
999 3rd Ave Ste 3300
Seattle WA 98104
206 302-6500

(P-26402)
LLP MOSS ADAMS
4747 Executive Dr # 1300, San Diego (92121-3114)
PHONE.................................858 627-1400
Laura Roos, *Partner*
Carisa Wisniewski, *Managing Prtnr*
Beth Gayvert, *Executive Asst*
Simone Edwards, *Admin Asst*
Kim Bryant, *Sales Mgr*
EMP: 65
SALES (corp-wide): 318.8MM **Privately Held**
WEB: www.mossadams.com
SIC: 8721 Certified public accountant
PA: Moss Adams Llp
999 3rd Ave Ste 3300
Seattle WA 98104
206 302-6500

(P-26403)
LLP MOSS ADAMS
2040 Main St Ste 900, Irvine (92614-8213)
PHONE.................................949 221-4000
Roger Weninger, *Branch Mgr*
Peggy Grobe, *Office Mgr*
Linda Lamar, *Office Mgr*
Simon Dufour, *Auditing Mgr*
Doug Buurma, *Senior Mgr*
EMP: 50
SALES (corp-wide): 318.8MM **Privately Held**
WEB: www.mossadams.com
SIC: 8721 Certified public accountant
PA: Moss Adams Llp
999 3rd Ave Ste 3300
Seattle WA 98104
206 302-6500

(P-26404)
LODGEN LACHER GOLDITCH SARD
16530 Ventura Blvd # 305, Encino (91436-4554)
PHONE.................................818 783-0570
Fax: 310 783-7902
Ben Frankel, *Partner*
Patricia Bates, *Partner*
Bernard S Golditch, *Partner*
Dan Howard, *Partner*
Stephen P Lacher, *Partner*
EMP: 50
SQ FT: 12,000
SALES (est): 4.2MM **Privately Held**
WEB: www.fllgsh.com
SIC: 8721 Certified public accountant

(P-26405)
MACIAS GINI & OCONNELL LLP (PA)
3000 S St Ste 300, Sacramento (95816-7014)
PHONE.................................916 928-4600
Kenneth A Macias, *Partner*
Ernest Gini, *Partner*
Jim Godsey, *Partner*
Rick Green, *Partner*
Scott Hammon, *Partner*
EMP: 75
SQ FT: 12,000
SALES: 33.4MM **Privately Held**
WEB: www.mgocpa.com
SIC: 8721 Accounting, auditing & bookkeeping

(P-26406)
MARCUM LLP
303 2nd St Ste 950, San Francisco (94107-1366)
PHONE.................................415 543-6900
Jeffrey M Weiner, *Branch Mgr*
EMP: 55
SALES (corp-wide): 273MM **Privately Held**
SIC: 8721 Certified public accountant
PA: Marcum Llp
750 3rd Ave Fl 11
New York NY 10017
212 485-5500

(P-26407)
MARCUM LLP
2049 Century Park E # 300, Los Angeles (90067-3105)
PHONE.................................310 432-7400
Ron Friedman, *Branch Mgr*
Claudia Herrera, *Office Admin*
Ken Gryske, *Director*
Lori Rock, *Manager*
EMP: 75
SALES (corp-wide): 273MM **Privately Held**
SIC: 8721 Accounting services, except auditing
PA: Marcum Llp
750 3rd Ave Fl 11
New York NY 10017
212 485-5500

(P-26408)
MED-DATA INCORPORATED
3741 Douglas Blvd Ste 170, Roseville (95661-4271)
PHONE.................................916 771-1362
Bruce Stewart, *Branch Mgr*
EMP: 100
SALES (corp-wide): 18.1MM **Privately Held**
SIC: 8721 Accounting services, except auditing
PA: Med-Data, Incorporated
1407 116th Ave Ne Ste 104
Bellevue WA 98004
800 835-7474

(P-26409)
MEDAMERICA BILLING SVCS INC (HQ)
Also Called: California Emergency Physician
1601 Cummins Dr Ste D, Modesto (95358-6411)
PHONE.................................209 491-7710
Fax: 209 526-6808
Michael F Harrington, *CEO*
Charles Ayers, *Senior Partner*
Alice Hunter, *Senior Partner*
Robert Kollen, *Senior Partner*
John Naftel, *Senior Partner*
EMP: 73
SQ FT: 75,000
SALES (est): 31.6MM
SALES (corp-wide): 500MM **Privately Held**
WEB: www.cep.com
SIC: 8721 Billing & bookkeeping service
PA: California Emergency Physicians Foundation
2100 Powell St Ste 900
Emeryville CA 94608
510 350-2700

(P-26410)
MEDEX PRATICE SOLUTIONS INC
4725 Enterprise Way Ste 1, Modesto (95356-8967)
P.O. Box 188, Oakdale (95361-0188)
PHONE.................................209 845-1346
Bryan Williamson, *President*
Michael Mc Gann, *Vice Pres*
Phyllis Waters, *Opers Mgr*
EMP: 60
SALES (est): 3MM **Privately Held**
SIC: 8721 Billing & bookkeeping service

(P-26411)
MOHLER NIXON & WILLIAMS ACCOUN (PA)
635 Campbell Tech Pkwy # 100, Campbell (95008-5075)
PHONE.................................408 369-2400
Chris Schmidt, *CEO*
Greg Finley, *President*
Dick Fohn, *President*
Steve Vidlock, *Treasurer*
Bud Fallon, *Vice Pres*
EMP: 90
SQ FT: 25,000
SALES (est): 10.4MM **Privately Held**
SIC: 8721 Certified public accountant

(P-26412)
MSC SERVICE CO
Also Called: Morley Construction
3330 Ocean Park Blvd # 101, Santa Monica (90405-3211)
PHONE.................................310 399-1600
Mark Benjamin, *CEO*
Burt Lewitt, *President*
Todd Paris, *CFO*
Arun Asher, *Vice Pres*
EMP: 85
SQ FT: 20,000
SALES (est): 2.8MM
SALES (corp-wide): 166MM **Privately Held**
WEB: www.mscservice.com
SIC: 8721 1542 1522 1521 Auditing services; nonresidential construction; residential construction; single-family housing construction
PA: Morley Builders, Inc.
3330 Ocean Park Blvd # 101
Santa Monica CA 90405
310 399-1600

(P-26413)
NOVOGRADAC AND CO LLP
246 1st St Ste 500, San Francisco (94105-4699)
PHONE.................................415 356-8000
M J Novogradac, *Partner*
EMP: 50
SALES (est): 991.8K **Privately Held**
SIC: 8721 Certified public accountant

(P-26414)
NSBN LLP (PA)
Also Called: Nanas Stern Biers Neinstein Co
1925 Century Park E Fl 16, Los Angeles (90067-2701)
PHONE.................................310 273-2501
Ken Miles, *Partner*
Joseph B Burton, *Partner*
Peter M Craig, *Partner*
Bill Esenstein, *Partner*
Harold W Jaffe, *Partner*
EMP: 56
SALES (est): 11.3MM **Privately Held**
SIC: 8721 Accounting services, except auditing

(P-26415)
OUM & CO LLP (PA)
465 California St Ste 700, San Francisco (94104-1818)
PHONE.................................415 434-3744
Fax: 415 788-2260
Chris Millias, *Managing Prtnr*
Paul Ainslie, *Partner*
Chris S Millias, *Partner*
John Muranishi, *Partner*
James E Ullakko, *Partner*
EMP: 68 **EST:** 1976
SQ FT: 7,700
SALES (est): 15.2MM **Privately Held**
WEB: www.oumcpa.com
SIC: 8721 Certified public accountant

(P-26416)
PASADENA BILLING ASSOCIATES
225 S Lake Ave Ste 535, Pasadena (91101-3010)
PHONE.................................626 795-6596
Dale W Zeh Jr, *President*
Lauri G Zeh, *Vice Pres*
Kerith Kelly, *Manager*
Theresa Latino, *Manager*
EMP: 70
SQ FT: 5,000
SALES (est): 3.4MM **Privately Held**
WEB: www.dobilling.com
SIC: 8721 Billing & bookkeeping service

(P-26417)
PAYCHEX INC
9 E River Park Pl E # 210, Fresno (93720-1530)
PHONE.................................559 432-1100
Kevin Hardwick, *Manager*
Martin Howell, *Branch Mgr*
Erin Nestor, *Consultant*
EMP: 60
SALES (corp-wide): 2.9B **Publicly Held**
WEB: www.paychex.com
SIC: 8721 Payroll accounting service
PA: Paychex, Inc.
911 Panorama Trl S
Rochester NY 14625
585 385-6666

(P-26418)
PAYCHEX INC
10150 Meanley Dr Ste 200, San Diego (92131-3008)
PHONE.................................858 547-2920
Ed Nunn, *Manager*
Candy Wolles, *Data Proc Staff*
Corinne Hirt, *Manager*
Margaret Laird, *Manager*
Jerry Vitovsky, *Manager*
EMP: 100
SALES (corp-wide): 2.9B **Publicly Held**
WEB: www.paychex.com
SIC: 8721 8742 7374 Payroll accounting service; management consulting services; data processing & preparation
PA: Paychex, Inc.
911 Panorama Trl S
Rochester NY 14625
585 385-6666

(P-26419)
PAYCHEX INC
300 Crprate Pinte Ste 150, Culver City (90230)
PHONE.................................310 338-7900
Fax: 310 338-7960
Debbie Woods, *Manager*
Bob Gilbow, *General Mgr*
Caroline Carmona, *Purch Dir*
Debi Wood, *Mktg Dir*
David Beach, *Sales Mgr*
EMP: 100
SALES (corp-wide): 2.9B **Publicly Held**
WEB: www.paychex.com
SIC: 8721 Payroll accounting service
PA: Paychex, Inc.
911 Panorama Trl S
Rochester NY 14625
585 385-6666

(P-26420)
PAYCHEX INC
1420 Iowa Ave Ste 100, Riverside (92507-0510)
PHONE.................................951 682-6100
Karry Zolz, *Manager*
R Remson, *Manager*
EMP: 50
SALES (corp-wide): 2.9B **Publicly Held**
WEB: www.paychex.com
SIC: 8721 Payroll accounting service
PA: Paychex, Inc.
911 Panorama Trl S
Rochester NY 14625
585 385-6666

(P-26421)
PAYROLLINGCOM CORP
Also Called: Kaizen Staffing
4626 Albuquerque St Uppr, San Diego (92109-3858)
PHONE.................................858 866-2626
Laverne Kato, *CEO*
Samer Khouli, *CEO*
Susan Kelly, *Principal*
Ashley Reinholtz, *Human Resources*
EMP: 50
SQ FT: 10,000
SALES (est): 4.6MM **Privately Held**
WEB: www.payrolling.com
SIC: 8721 Payroll accounting service

(PA)=Parent Co (HQ)=Headquarters (DH)=Div Headquarters
✚ = New Business established in last 2 years

8721 - Accounting, Auditing & Bookkeeping Svcs County (P-26422)

(P-26422)
PHYSICIANS CHOICE LLC
21860 Burbank Blvd # 120, Woodland Hills
(91367-6477)
P.O. Box 4419 (91365-4419)
PHONE....................................818 340-9988
John D Uphold,
Lynn Graziano, *Vice Pres*
Clare Nicholson, *Vice Pres*
Jonathan Sturm, *Vice Pres*
Michelle Reckleff,
EMP: 80
SQ FT: 10,000
SALES (est): 6.2MM **Privately Held**
WEB: www.physchoice.com
SIC: 8721 Billing & bookkeeping service

(P-26423)
PKF CERTIF PUB ACCTS A PROF (PA)
550 N Brand Blvd Ste 950, Glendale
(91203-1973)
PHONE....................................818 630-7630
Rex H Poulsen, *President*
Mark Hennelly, *Treasurer*
John Engelbrecht, *Vice Pres*
Barbara Fitchett, *Office Mgr*
EMP: 65
SALES (est): 3.1MM **Privately Held**
WEB: www.pkfla.com
SIC: 8721 Accounting, auditing & bookkeeping; auditing services; certified public accountant; accounting services, except auditing

(P-26424)
PRICEWATERHOUSECOOPERS LLP
2020 Main St Ste 400, Irvine (92614-8243)
PHONE....................................949 437-5200
Diana Franklin, *Manager*
Gautam Agarwal, *Sr Associate*
Michael Wellington, *Sr Associate*
Joanna Kraynek, *Senior Mgr*
Rony Mansour, *Senior Mgr*
EMP: 260
SALES (corp-wide): 9.4B **Privately Held**
WEB: www.pwcglobal.com
SIC: 8721 Certified public accountant
PA: Pricewaterhousecoopers Llp
  300 Madison Ave Fl 24
  New York NY 10017
  646 471-4000

(P-26425)
PRICEWATERHOUSECOOPERS LLP
488 Almaden Blvd Ste 1800, San Jose
(95110-2768)
PHONE....................................408 817-3700
Fax: 408 537-1390
Don McGovern, *Branch Mgr*
Kenneth Sharkey, *Managing Prtnr*
Robert Gittings, *COO*
Rose Telles, *Executive*
Thomas Ciccolella, *Managing Dir*
EMP: 700
SALES (corp-wide): 9.4B **Privately Held**
WEB: www.pwcglobal.com
SIC: 8721 Certified public accountant
PA: Pricewaterhousecoopers Llp
  300 Madison Ave Fl 24
  New York NY 10017
  646 471-4000

(P-26426)
PRICEWATERHOUSECOOPERS LLP
5375 Mira Sorrento Pl, San Diego
(92121-3809)
PHONE....................................858 677-2400
Christina Nordvall, *Manager*
EMP: 275
SALES (corp-wide): 9.4B **Privately Held**
SIC: 8721 Certified public accountant
PA: Pricewaterhousecoopers Llp
  300 Madison Ave Fl 24
  New York NY 10017
  646 471-4000

(P-26427)
PRICEWATERHOUSECOOPERS LLP
400 Capitol Mall Ste 600, Sacramento
(95814-4423)
PHONE....................................916 930-8100
Robert Kittredge, *Branch Mgr*
Douglas Anderson, *Admin Mgr*
Diana Pfanner, *Office Mgr*
Susan Coleman, *Admin Sec*
Eric Drew, *Client Mgr*
EMP: 84
SQ FT: 1,000
SALES (corp-wide): 9.4B **Privately Held**
WEB: www.pwcglobal.com
SIC: 8721 Certified public accountant
PA: Pricewaterhousecoopers Llp
  300 Madison Ave Fl 24
  New York NY 10017
  646 471-4000

(P-26428)
PRICEWATERHOUSECOOPERS LLP
3 Embarcadero Ctr Fl 20, San Francisco
(94111-4004)
PHONE....................................415 498-5000
Fax: 415 498-7100
Deanne Aguirre, *Senior Partner*
Ajay Bhatia, *Managing Dir*
Doran McClellan, *Managing Dir*
Bebe Lach, *Executive Asst*
Maria C Luevanos, *Executive Asst*
EMP: 275
SALES (corp-wide): 9.4B **Privately Held**
WEB: www.pwcglobal.com
SIC: 8721 Accounting, auditing & bookkeeping
PA: Pricewaterhousecoopers Llp
  300 Madison Ave Fl 24
  New York NY 10017
  646 471-4000

(P-26429)
PROTIVITI INC
2613 Camino Ramon, San Ramon
(94583-4289)
PHONE....................................415 402-3663
Keith Waddell, *Principal*
Kimberly Dickerson, *Associate Dir*
Lisa O'Brien, *Auditor*
Brad Rachmiel, *Director*
Adam Brand, *Manager*
EMP: 58
SALES (corp-wide): 5B **Publicly Held**
SIC: 8721 8742 Accounting, auditing & bookkeeping; management consulting services
HQ: Protiviti Inc.
  2884 Sand Hill Rd Ste 200
  Menlo Park CA 94025
  650 234-6000

(P-26430)
RAND MEDICAL BILLING INC
1633 Erringer Rd Fl 1, Simi Valley
(93065-3557)
PHONE....................................805 578-8300
Marvin Retsky, *President*
Patty Artist, *Office Mgr*
EMP: 100
SQ FT: 10,000
SALES (est): 5.8MM
SALES (corp-wide): 54.2MM **Publicly Held**
SIC: 8721 Billing & bookkeeping service
PA: Orion Healthcorp, Inc.
  368 W Pike St Ste 102
  Lawrenceville GA 30046
  678 832-1800

(P-26431)
ROSERYAN INC
35473 Dumbarton Ct, Newark
(94560-1100)
PHONE....................................510 456-3056
Fax: 510 456-3063
Kathleen M Ryan, *President*
Maureen Ryan, *President*
Pat Voll, *Vice Pres*
Lawrence Lau, *Executive*
Stan Fels, *Business Dir*
EMP: 60

SALES (est): 3.9MM **Privately Held**
WEB: www.roseryan.com
SIC: 8721 Accounting, auditing & bookkeeping

(P-26432)
RSM US LLP
44 Montgomery St Ste 3900, San Francisco
(94104-4812)
PHONE....................................415 848-5300
Fax: 415 848-5353
Victor Howe, *Branch Mgr*
EMP: 99
SALES (corp-wide): 1.8B **Privately Held**
SIC: 8721 Certified public accountant
PA: Rsm Us Llp
  1 S Wacker Dr Ste 800
  Chicago IL 60606
  312 634-3400

(P-26433)
RSM US LLP
18401 Von Karman Ave # 500, Irvine
(92612-1542)
PHONE....................................949 255-6500
Gebauer Jutta, *Branch Mgr*
Ryan Lemond, *Auditing Mgr*
EMP: 71
SALES (corp-wide): 1.8B **Privately Held**
SIC: 8721 Auditing services
PA: Rsm Us Llp
  1 S Wacker Dr Ste 800
  Chicago IL 60606
  312 634-3400

(P-26434)
RSM US LLP
100 W San Fernando St, San Jose
(95113-2219)
PHONE....................................408 572-4440
Dennis Young, *Branch Mgr*
EMP: 84
SALES (corp-wide): 1.7B **Privately Held**
SIC: 8721 Accounting, auditing & bookkeeping
PA: Rsm Us Llp
  1 S Wacker Dr Ste 800
  Chicago IL 60606
  312 634-3400

(P-26435)
S L G G CONSULTING GROUP LLC (PA)
10960 Wilshire Blvd # 1100, Los Angeles
(90024-3714)
PHONE....................................310 477-3924
Harvey Goldstein,
Norman Greebaum,
Donald Leve,
Eric Ouellette,
Simon William,
EMP: 150
SALES (est): 10.8MM **Privately Held**
SIC: 8721 Accounting, auditing & bookkeeping

(P-26436)
SANTA CLARA COUNTY OF
Also Called: Valley Med Ctr Billing Dept
2325 Enborg Ln Fl 4, San Jose
(95128-2649)
PHONE....................................408 885-7200
Mary Wells, *Director*
EMP: 150 **Privately Held**
WEB: www.countyairports.org
SIC: 8721 9311 Billing & bookkeeping service; finance, taxation & monetary policy;
PA: County Of Santa Clara
  3180 Newberry Dr Ste 150
  San Jose CA 95118
  408 299-5105

(P-26437)
SANTA CLARA COUNTY OF
Also Called: Santa Clara Vlly Health/Hosptl
751 S Bascom Ave Fl 4, San Jose
(95128-2604)
PHONE....................................408 885-7354
Fax: 408 295-0703
Art Gamez, *Branch Mgr*
John M Bauman, *Radiology Dir*
Narinder Singh, *Pharmacy Dir*
Jim Murphy, *Sls & Mktg Exec*
Jacqueline Doctolero,
EMP: 160 **Privately Held**

WEB: www.countyairports.org
SIC: 8721 Billing & bookkeeping service; administration of public health programs;
PA: County Of Santa Clara
  3180 Newberry Dr Ste 150
  San Jose CA 95118
  408 299-5105

(P-26438)
SEILER LLP (PA)
3 Lagoon Dr Ste 400, Redwood City
(94065-5157)
P.O. Box 8043 (94063-0943)
PHONE....................................650 365-4646
Fax: 650 368-4055
James G B Demartini III, *Partner*
Mark Berryman, *Partner*
James G B Demartini III, *Partner*
Brian J Dinsmore, *Partner*
Kenneth Everett, *Partner*
EMP: 102
SQ FT: 31,142
SALES (est): 27.9MM **Privately Held**
SIC: 8721 Certified public accountant

(P-26439)
SHEA LABAGH DOBBERSTEIN CPA (PA)
505 Montgomery St Ste 500, San Francisco
(94111-2588)
PHONE....................................415 731-0100
Fax: 415 981-0898
James Dobberstein, *President*
Pei Asay, *COO*
Ron Simonian, *Treasurer*
Gregory T Labagh, *Vice Pres*
Tom Jackson, *Admin Sec*
EMP: 50
SQ FT: 15,000
SALES (est): 9.4MM **Privately Held**
SIC: 8721 Accounting, auditing & bookkeeping

(P-26440)
SIERRA BOOKKEEPING & TAX SVC
5777 Madison Ave Ste 615, Sacramento
(95841-3312)
PHONE....................................916 349-7610
Joannie D Utley, *Principal*
EMP: 60
SALES (est): 1.8MM **Privately Held**
SIC: 8721 Billing & bookkeeping service

(P-26441)
SIERRA HEALTH SERVICES LLC
2423 W March Ln Ste 100, Stockton
(95207-8250)
P.O. Box 7096 (95267-0096)
PHONE....................................209 956-7725
Fax: 209 956-7733
Earl Ohgman, *Mng Member*
Allan Ebbin, *Vice Pres*
Paul Tausendfreund, *Info Tech Mgr*
Anthony L Watson, *Finance*
Marcia Weist, *Mktg Dir*
EMP: 50
SALES (est): 3.4MM **Privately Held**
SIC: 8721 8011 Billing & bookkeeping service; specialized medical practitioners, except internal; physicians' office, including specialists

(P-26442)
SINGERLEWAK LLP (PA)
10960 Wilshire Blvd, Los Angeles
(90024-3702)
PHONE....................................310 477-3924
Fax: 310 478-6070
David W Krajanowski, *Managing Prtnr*
Marc Abrams, *Partner*
David Free, *Partner*
Norman Greenbaum, *Partner*
Janice McKenna, *Partner*
EMP: 120
SQ FT: 24,000
SALES (est): 47.2MM **Privately Held**
WEB: www.singerlewak.com
SIC: 8721 8742 Certified public accountant; business consultant

(P-26443)
SINGERLEWAK LLP
2050 Main St Ste 700, Irvine (92614-8259)
PHONE....................................949 261-8600

PRODUCTS & SERVICES SECTION **8731 - Commercial Physical & Biological Research County (P-26464)**

Fax: 949 261-8610
David Krajanowski, *Branch Mgr*
EMP: 52
SALES (corp-wide): 47.2MM **Privately Held**
SIC: 8721 8742 Certified public accountant; business consultant
PA: Singerlewak Llp
10960 Wilshire Blvd
Los Angeles CA 90024
310 477-3924

(P-26444)
SINGERLEWAK LLP
21550 Oxnard St Ste 1000, Woodland Hills (91367-7148)
PHONE.................818 999-3924
Elizabeth Vanderroest, *Branch Mgr*
EMP: 52
SALES (corp-wide): 47.2MM **Privately Held**
SIC: 8721 8742 Certified public accountant; business consultant
PA: Singerlewak Llp
10960 Wilshire Blvd
Los Angeles CA 90024
310 477-3924

(P-26445)
SOREN MCADAM CHRISTIANSON LLP
2068 Orange Tree Ln # 100, Redlands (92374-4555)
P.O. Box 8010 (92375-1210)
PHONE.................909 798-2222
Fax: 909 798-9772
James L Soren, *Partner*
Gary Christianson, *Partner*
Doug McAdam, *Partner*
Kirk Stitt, *Partner*
David Tuttle, *Partner*
EMP: 59
SQ FT: 14,000
SALES (est): 5.3MM **Privately Held**
WEB: www.smc-cpas.com
SIC: 8721 Certified public accountant

(P-26446)
SQUAR MILNER PETERSON MIRAN (PA)
4100 Nwport Pl Dr Ste 300, Newport Beach (92660)
PHONE.................949 222-2999
Steve Milner, *Managing Prtnr*
Scott Burack, *Partner*
Ray Hermanson, *Partner*
Stan Luker, *Partner*
Steve Speier, *Partner*
EMP: 117
SQ FT: 11,500
SALES (est): 42.5MM **Privately Held**
WEB: www.squarmilner.com
SIC: 8721 Accounting services, except auditing

(P-26447)
SURGICAL CARE AFFILIATE
Also Called: TAC Rbo
2450 Venture Oaks Way # 120, Sacramento (95833-3292)
PHONE.................916 529-4590
EMP: 50 **EST:** 2011
SALES (est): 2.7MM **Privately Held**
SIC: 8721

(P-26448)
TANNER MAINSTAIN BLATT & GLY
10866 Wilshire Blvd Fl 10, Los Angeles (90024-4350)
PHONE.................310 446-2700
William Tanner, *President*
Steve Blatt, *Vice Pres*
Michael Glynn, *Vice Pres*
Brad Johnson, *Vice Pres*
Linda Jhee, *Admin Asst*
EMP: 70
SQ FT: 13,000
SALES: 7MM **Privately Held**
WEB: www.tmbgcpa.com
SIC: 8721 Accounting services, except auditing

(P-26449)
TAXRESOURCES INC (PA)
Also Called: Taxaudit.com
7803 Madison Ave Ste 100, Citrus Heights (95610-7694)
PHONE.................877 369-7827
Fax: 916 966-5417
Mark D Olander, *CEO*
Dave E Du Val, *Vice Pres*
David E Duval, *Vice Pres*
Nancy K Farwell, *Vice Pres*
Jane T Smith, *Vice Pres*
EMP: 120
SQ FT: 3,000
SALES: 40MM **Privately Held**
WEB: www.taxaudit.com
SIC: 8721 Auditing services

(P-26450)
TEAM COMPANIES INC (PA)
Also Called: Team Services
901 W Alameda Ave Ste 100, Burbank (91506-2801)
PHONE.................818 558-3261
Gerald K Schwartz, *President*
An De Vooght, *CFO*
Justin Kramer, *Exec VP*
Judy Santi, *Senior VP*
Lori Tedds, *Vice Pres*
EMP: 90
SQ FT: 20,000
SALES: 1.3B **Privately Held**
WEB: www.teamservices.net
SIC: 8721 Payroll accounting service

(P-26451)
THOMAS WIRIG DOLL & CO CPAS
Also Called: Thomas Doll & Company
165 Lennon Ln Ste 200, Walnut Creek (94598-2447)
P.O. Box 30307 (94598-9307)
PHONE.................925 939-2500
Fax: 925 945-8371
Brent P Thomas, *President*
Sherman Doll, *Admin Sec*
Joseph E Kalinowski, *CPA*
EMP: 66
SQ FT: 9,000
SALES (est): 5.6MM **Privately Held**
SIC: 8721 Certified public accountant

(P-26452)
TRI CITY EMERGENCY MED GROUP
5050 Avenida Encinas # 200, Carlsbad (92008-4383)
PHONE.................760 439-1963
Fax: 760 439-1831
Richard P Buruss, *Partner*
Joe Brockman, *Physician Asst*
Chad M Bernhardt, *Emerg Med Spec*
Sue Kruger, *Manager*
EMP: 50
SALES (est): 5MM **Privately Held**
SIC: 8721 8011 Billing & bookkeeping service; physicians' office, including specialists

(P-26453)
UNIVERSITY CAL SAN FRANCISCO
Also Called: Behalf of San Francisco Campus
1855 Folsom St Ste 425, San Francisco (94103-4249)
PHONE.................415 476-2075
Vanessa Long, *Branch Mgr*
Mary Catherine Gaisbauer, *Officer*
Francine Sneddon, *Info Tech Mgr*
John Ellis, *Controller*
Jason Stout, *Human Res Mgr*
EMP: 150 **Privately Held**
WEB: www.uchastings.edu
SIC: 8721 8221 9411 Accounting services, except auditing; university; administration of educational programs;
HQ: University Of California, San Francisco
505 Parnassus Ave
San Francisco CA 94143
415 476-9000

(P-26454)
US LOAN AUDITORS LLC
7485 Rush Rver Dr Ste 710, Sacramento (95831)
PHONE.................916 248-8625
Shane Barker, *Mng Member*
Alex Polyak, *Auditor*
Trevor Fisher, *Bookkeeper*
EMP: 100 **EST:** 2009
SALES (est): 3.7MM **Privately Held**
SIC: 8721 Accounting, auditing & bookkeeping

(P-26455)
VAVRINEK TRINE DAY AND CO LLP (PA)
10681 Fthill Blvd Ste 300, Rancho Cucamonga (91730)
PHONE.................909 466-4410
Fax: 909 466-4431
Ron White, *Partner*
Joe Aguilar, *Partner*
Roger E Alfaro, *Partner*
Rick Alonzo, *Partner*
Heidi L Aschenbrenner, *Partner*
EMP: 140 **EST:** 1948
SQ FT: 10,000
SALES (est): 35.7MM **Privately Held**
WEB: www.vtdcpa.com
SIC: 8721 Certified public accountant

(P-26456)
VICENTI LLOYD & STUTZMAN
2210 E Route 66 Ste 100, Glendora (91740-4676)
PHONE.................626 857-7300
Fax: 626 857-7302
Carl Pon, *Managing Prtnr*
Peter Gautreau, *Partner*
Renee Graves, *Partner*
Linda Saddlemire, *Partner*
Mary Ann Quay, *Managing Prtnr*
EMP: 55
SALES: 8.1MM **Privately Held**
WEB: www.vlsllp.com
SIC: 8721 Certified public accountant

(P-26457)
WHITE NELSON & CO CPAS LLP
2875 Michelle Ste 300, Irvine (92606-1020)
PHONE.................714 978-1300
David Doran, *Partner*
Gary Belz, *Partner*
Brian Donnelly, *Partner*
Brian Wilterink, *Partner*
Nitin Patel, *Managing Prtnr*
EMP: 90 **EST:** 1950
SQ FT: 12,000
SALES (est): 8.6MM **Privately Held**
WEB: www.whitenelson.com
SIC: 8721 Certified public accountant

(P-26458)
WINDES MCCLGHRY ACCNTANCY CORP (PA)
Also Called: W M
111 W Ocean Blvd Ste 22, Long Beach (90802-4653)
P.O. Box 87 (90801-0087)
PHONE.................562 435-1191
Fax: 562 495-1665
John L Dicarlo, *CEO*
Jim Jimenez, *Partner*
Jack E Hinsche, *President*
Anna McGregor, *Social Dir*
Moses Bass, *Controller*
EMP: 120
SQ FT: 18,483
SALES (est): 23.3MM **Privately Held**
WEB: www.windes.com
SIC: 8721 Certified public accountant

8731 Commercial Physical & Biological Research

(P-26459)
ACHATES POWER INC
4060 Sorrento Valley Blvd A, San Diego (92121-1428)
PHONE.................858 535-9920
David Johnson, *CEO*
John Koszewnik, *Principal*
Carol Mottershead, *Finance Dir*
Minerva Hess, *Controller*
Jerome Paye, *Opers Staff*
EMP: 95
SALES (est): 12.8MM **Privately Held**
WEB: www.achatespower.com
SIC: 8731 Commercial physical research

(P-26460)
ACTIVE MOTIF INC (PA)
Also Called: Timelogic
1914 Palomar Oaks Way # 150, Carlsbad (92008-6509)
PHONE.................760 431-1263
Fax: 760 431-1351
Joseph Fernandez, *CEO*
Joel Harris, *Managing Prtnr*
Theodore Defrank, *President*
Laura Carpenter, *Vice Pres*
Adam Blattler, *Research*
EMP: 53
SQ FT: 16,000
SALES (est): 11.3MM **Privately Held**
WEB: www.activemotif.com
SIC: 8731 Biotechnical research, commercial

(P-26461)
ADESTO TECHNOLOGIES CORP
3600 Peterson Way, Santa Clara (95054-2808)
PHONE.................408 400-0578
Narbeh Derhacobian, *CEO*
Barry L Cox, *Ch of Bd*
Ron Shelton, *CFO*
Shane Hollmer, *Vice Pres*
Ishai Naveh, *Vice Pres*
EMP: 65
SALES: 43.2MM **Privately Held**
SIC: 8731 Commercial research laboratory

(P-26462)
ADVANCED CELL DIAGNOSTICS INC (HQ)
Also Called: A C D
7707 Gateway Blvd, Newark (94560-1160)
PHONE.................510 576-8800
Yuling Luo, *President*
Steve Chen, *COO*
Jessie Qian Wang, *CFO*
Tom Olenic, *Ch Credit Ofcr*
Rob Monroe, *Chief Mktg Ofcr*
EMP: 79
SQ FT: 2,500
SALES (est): 5.3MM
SALES (corp-wide): 499MM **Publicly Held**
WEB: www.genospectra.com
SIC: 8731 2835 Biotechnical research, commercial; microbiology & virology diagnostic products
PA: Bio-Techne Corporation
614 Mckinley Pl Ne
Minneapolis MN 55413
612 379-8854

(P-26463)
AFFYMETRIX INC
10255 Science Center Dr, San Diego (92121-1117)
PHONE.................858 642-2058
EMP: 200
SALES (corp-wide): 16.9B **Publicly Held**
SIC: 8731 Biotechnical research, commercial
HQ: Affymetrix, Inc.
3420 Central Expy
Santa Clara CA 95051
408 731-5000

(P-26464)
ALLIANT TCHSYSTEMS OPRTONS LLC
9401 Corbin Ave, Northridge (91324-2400)
PHONE.................818 887-8195
Ronald Hill, *Principal*
John Uppendahl, *Vice Pres*
Nancy Stoehr-Campbell, *Comms Mgr*
Salvador Villagrana, *Info Tech Mgr*
Amparo Llanes, *Software Engr*
EMP: 400
SALES (est): 48.1MM
SALES (corp-wide): 6.8B **Publicly Held**
WEB: www.mrcwdc.com
SIC: 8731 Commercial physical research

8731 - Commercial Physical & Biological Research County (P-26465)

PRODUDUCTS & SERVICES SECTION

PA: Orbital Atk, Inc.
45101 Warp Dr
Dulles VA 20166
703 406-5000

(P-26465)
ALPHA TEKNOVA INC
2290 Bert Dr, Hollister (95023-2567)
PHONE................................831 637-1100
Fax: 831 637-2355
Thomas Davis, *CEO*
Richard Alan Goozh, *CFO*
Sean McVeigh, *CTO*
Luis Alvarez, *Info Tech Mgr*
Carl Clarke, *Engineer*
EMP: 50
SQ FT: 34,000
SALES (est): 9.1MM **Privately Held**
WEB: www.teknova.com
SIC: 8731 Biotechnical research, commercial

(P-26466)
AMAZON LAB126
1100 Enterprise Way, Sunnyvale (94089-1412)
PHONE................................206 266-1000
Fax: 408 790-6401
Gregg Zehr, *Vice Pres*
Toby Smith, *Vice Pres*
Robert Kim, *Program Mgr*
Shellie Ambrozik, *Executive Asst*
Aldon Almeida, *Sr Software Eng*
EMP: 683
SALES (est): 91.9MM
SALES (corp-wide): 107B **Publicly Held**
SIC: 8731 Electronic research
PA: Amazon.Com, Inc.
410 Terry Ave N
Seattle WA 98109
206 266-1000

(P-26467)
AMSEC LLC
9444 Balboa Ave Ste 400, San Diego (92123-4378)
PHONE................................858 522-6319
Michelle Wurl, *Director*
Karl W Jahn Jr, *CFO*
EMP: 289 **Publicly Held**
SIC: 8731 8711 Commercial physical research; engineering services
HQ: Amsec Llc
5701 Cleveland St Ste 110
Virginia Beach VA 23462
757 463-6666

(P-26468)
ANAPTYSBIO INC
10421 Pcf Ctr Ct Ste 200, San Diego (92121)
PHONE................................858 362-6295
Hamza Suria, *President*
Carol G Gallagher, *Ch of Bd*
Robert E Hoffman, *CFO*
Marco Londei, *Officer*
Matthew Moyle, *Security Dir*
EMP: 50
SALES (est): 5.1MM **Privately Held**
WEB: www.anaptysbio.com
SIC: 8731 8733 Biotechnical research, commercial; biotechnical research, non-commercial

(P-26469)
ANASPEC INC (HQ)
Also Called: Anaspec Egt Group
34801 Campus Dr, Fremont (94555-3606)
PHONE................................800 452-5530
Philippe Cronet, *President*
Masanobu Sugawara, *President*
Xiaohe Tong, *CTO*
Kathy Chen, *Info Tech Mgr*
Lan Luo, *Controller*
EMP: 50
SALES (est): 20.7MM
SALES (corp-wide): 4.7B **Privately Held**
WEB: www.anaspec.com
SIC: 8731 Chemical laboratory, except testing
PA: Kaneka Corporation
2-3-18, Nakanoshima, Kita-Ku
Osaka OSK 530-0
662 265-050

(P-26470)
APPLIED BIOSYSTEMS
1149 Chess Dr, Foster City (94404-1102)
PHONE................................800 327-3002
Lilly Voong, *Senior Partner*
EMP: 99
SALES (est): 4.3MM **Privately Held**
SIC: 8731 Biotechnical research, commercial

(P-26471)
APPLIED MOLECULAR EVOLUTION (HQ)
10300 Campus Point Dr # 200, San Diego (92121-1504)
PHONE................................858 597-4990
Thomas Bumol, *President*
Melissa Baker, *Officer*
Binzy Kiske, *Executive Asst*
Cheryl C Gabele, *Director*
EMP: 50
SQ FT: 43,000
SALES (est): 11.1MM
SALES (corp-wide): 19.9B **Publicly Held**
WEB: www.amevolution.com
SIC: 8731 Commercial physical research
PA: Eli Lilly And Company
Lilly Corporate Center
Indianapolis IN 46285
317 276-2000

(P-26472)
APPLIED P & CH LABORATORY SOUT
Also Called: APC Lab
13760 Magnolia Ave, Chino (91710-7018)
PHONE................................909 590-1828
Fax: 909 590-1498
Jack Zhang, *President*
Mary Luo, *Corp Secy*
EMP: 60
SQ FT: 30,000
SALES (est): 3.6MM **Privately Held**
WEB: www.apclab.com
SIC: 8731 Environmental research

(P-26473)
APPLIED RESEARCH ASSOC INC
735 State St, Santa Barbara (93101-3351)
PHONE................................805 962-4810
Joan Rothenberg, *Branch Mgr*
Rob Sues, *President*
Antoinette Vigil, *Administration*
EMP: 61
SALES (corp-wide): 209MM **Privately Held**
SIC: 8731 8711 Commercial physical research; consulting engineer
PA: Applied Research Associates, Inc.
4300 San Mateo Blvd Ne A220
Albuquerque NM 87110
505 883-3636

(P-26474)
AQUATIC SCIENCE CENTER
4911 Central Ave, Richmond (94804-5803)
PHONE................................510 746-7334
Warner Chabot, *Exec Dir*
Jim Kelly, *Exec Dir*
EMP: 50
SALES (est): 1.7MM **Privately Held**
SIC: 8731 Environmental research

(P-26475)
ARAGEN BIOSCIENCE INC
380 Woodview Ave, Morgan Hill (95037-2823)
PHONE................................408 779-1700
William R Srigley, *CEO*
Oren Beske, *President*
Leonard Miller, *Vice Pres*
Chris Simonsen, *Vice Pres*
Kenneth Meek, *Sales Dir*
EMP: 50
SALES (est): 8.4MM **Privately Held**
WEB: www.aragenbio.com
SIC: 8731 Biotechnical research, commercial
PA: Gvk Biosciences Private Limited
Plot No. 28a,
Hyderabad TS 50007

(P-26476)
ARETE ASSOCIATES
103 Johnson St, Windsor (95492-7435)
PHONE................................818 885-2200
Dave Kier, *CEO*
David Campion, *COO*
Victoria Brundage, *Administration*
EMP: 57
SALES (corp-wide): 78MM **Privately Held**
SIC: 8731 Commercial physical research
PA: Arete Associates
9301 Corbin Ave Unit 2000
Northridge CA 91324
818 885-2200

(P-26477)
ARETE ASSOCIATES (PA)
9301 Corbin Ave Unit 2000, Northridge (91324-2508)
PHONE................................818 885-2200
Lee Buchanan, *CEO*
Chris Choi, *CFO*
Charles Agnew, *Officer*
David Campion, *Vice Pres*
Doug Deprospo, *Vice Pres*
EMP: 125
SQ FT: 170,000
SALES (est): 78MM **Privately Held**
WEB: www.arete-dc.com
SIC: 8731 Commercial physical research

(P-26478)
ARIOSA DIAGNOSTICS INC
5945 Optical Ct, San Jose (95138-1400)
PHONE................................408 229-7500
Kenneth Song MD, *CEO*
Dave Mullarkey, *COO*
Thomas Musci MD, *Chief Mktg Ofcr*
Thomas J Musci, *Vice Pres*
Enzo Altomare, *Executive*
EMP: 140
SALES (est): 37.5MM
SALES (corp-wide): 47.9B **Publicly Held**
SIC: 8731 Commercial physical research, commercial
HQ: Roche Holdings, Inc.
1 Dna Way
South San Francisco CA 94080
625 225-1000

(P-26479)
ATK SPACE SYSTEMS INC
370 N Halstead St, Pasadena (91107-3122)
PHONE................................626 351-0205
Joe Tellegrino, *Manager*
Dean Grayson, *General Counsel*
Joe Pellegrino, *Manager*
EMP: 70
SALES (corp-wide): 6.8B **Publicly Held**
SIC: 8731 3826 8711 Commercial physical research; engineering laboratory, except testing; instruments measuring thermal properties; engineering services
HQ: Atk Space Systems Inc.
11310 Frederick Ave
Beltsville MD 20705
301 595-5500

(P-26480)
AURORA ALGAE INC (PA)
3325 Investment Blvd, Hayward (94545-3808)
PHONE................................510 266-5000
Paul Angelico, *President*
Bill Roeschlein, *CFO*
Dawn McGuire, *Sr Corp Ofcr*
Lee Covert, *Senior VP*
Connie Sandusky, *Senior VP*
EMP: 68
SALES (est): 16.2MM **Privately Held**
WEB: www.aurorabiofuels.com
SIC: 8731 Commercial physical research

(P-26481)
AUTOGENOMICS INC
1600 Faraday Ave, Carlsbad (92008-7313)
PHONE................................760 477-2248
Fareed Kureshy, *CEO*
Thomas V Hennessey, *COO*
Robert B Cole, *CFO*
Peter Wilding, *Bd of Directors*
Jim Canfield, *Vice Pres*
EMP: 80
SQ FT: 120,000

SALES (est): 16.5MM **Privately Held**
WEB: www.autogenomics.com
SIC: 8731 Biotechnical research, commercial

(P-26482)
AVERY CORP
207 N Goode Ave Fl 6, Glendale (91203-1364)
PHONE................................626 304-2000
Dean Scarborough, *President*
Marsha Erickson, *Info Tech Mgr*
Tom Apodaca, *Marketing Staff*
David Maxson, *Director*
EMP: 200
SALES (est): 9.8MM
SALES (corp-wide): 5.9B **Publicly Held**
WEB: www.avery.com
SIC: 8731 Biological research
PA: Avery Dennison Corporation
207 N Goode Ave Fl 6
Glendale CA 91203
626 304-2000

(P-26483)
AVIVA SYSTEMS BIOLOGY CORP
5754 Pcf Ctr Blvd Ste 201, San Diego (92121)
PHONE................................858 552-6979
Lingxun Duan, *President*
Huajie Wen, *Exec VP*
Steve Zmina, *Vice Pres*
Stephen Hill, *Controller*
Sherri Botzbach, *Marketing Mgr*
EMP: 55
SQ FT: 2,600
SALES: 3MM **Privately Held**
WEB: www.avivasysbio.com
SIC: 8731 Commercial physical research; biotechnical research, commercial

(P-26484)
BAY AREA ENVMTL RES INST
Also Called: Baer Institute
625 2nd St Ste 209, Petaluma (94952-5159)
PHONE................................707 938-9387
Robert W Bergstrom, *President*
Mark Sittloh, *Exec Dir*
Mark T Sittloh, *Exec Dir*
Helene Hendriks, *Analyst*
Aparna Kar, *Consultant*
EMP: 87
SQ FT: 750
SALES: 13.8MM **Privately Held**
WEB: www.baeri.org
SIC: 8731 Environmental research

(P-26485)
BAYER HEALTHCARE LLC
455 Mission Bay Blvd S # 493, San Francisco (94158-2160)
PHONE................................415 437-5800
Douglas Schneider, *Manager*
Taneshia Ezeb, *QA Dir*
David M Weinreich, *Med Doctor*
Arnel Agapito, *Manager*
EMP: 252
SALES (corp-wide): 49.7B **Privately Held**
SIC: 8731 Commercial physical research
HQ: Bayer Healthcare Llc
100 Bayer Blvd
Whippany NJ 07981
862 404-3000

(P-26486)
BAYER HEALTHCARE LLC
Biological Products Division
717 Potter St Street-2, Berkeley (94710-2722)
PHONE................................510 705-7539
Jay Keasling, *Branch Mgr*
EMP: 252
SALES (corp-wide): 49.7B **Privately Held**
SIC: 8731 Commercial physical research
HQ: Bayer Healthcare Llc
100 Bayer Blvd
Whippany NJ 07981
862 404-3000

(P-26487)
BIO-RAD LABORATORIES INC
2000 Alfred Nobel Dr, Hercules (94547-1804)
PHONE................................510 232-7000

PRODUCTS & SERVICES SECTION
8731 - Commercial Physical & Biological Research County (P-26508)

Fax: 510 724-5445
Norman Swartz, *CEO*
Susan Milam, *Program Mgr*
Rob Downes, *Info Tech Mgr*
Sonia Mills, *Design Engr*
Saul Saucedo, *Design Engr*
EMP: 1500
SALES (corp-wide): 2B **Publicly Held**
WEB: www.bio-rad.com
SIC: 8731 Commercial physical research
PA: Bio-Rad Laboratories, Inc.
　1000 Alfred Nobel Dr
　Hercules CA 94547
　510 724-7000

(P-26488)
BIOCLINCA (PA)
Also Called: Synarc's
7707 Gateway Blvd Fl 3, Newark (94560-1160)
PHONE 415 817-8900
Fax: 415 817-8999
Claus Christiansen, *CEO*
Harry K Genant, *Chairman*
Ciaran Cooper, *Vice Pres*
Vivek Swarnakar, *Vice Pres*
Aaron Timm, *Vice Pres*
EMP: 153
SQ FT: 40,000
SALES (est): 42MM **Privately Held**
WEB: www.synarc.com
SIC: 8731 Commercial physical research

(P-26489)
BIOMEDICURE LLC
7940 Silverton Ave # 107, San Diego (92126-6340)
PHONE 858 586-1888
Yong Qian,
EMP: 55
SALES: 100K **Privately Held**
SIC: 8731 Commercial physical research

(P-26490)
BME CMGI UC DAVIS
1 Shields Ave, Davis (95616-5270)
PHONE 530 754-5488
Fax: 530 752-6363
Uc Davis, *Principal*
Ross Obrien, *Accounting Mgr*
Paul Hawley, *Analyst*
EMP: 394 **EST:** 2010
SALES (est): 71.6MM **Privately Held**
SIC: 8731 Biotechnical research, commercial

(P-26491)
CALIFORNIA INSTITUTE TECH
360 S Wilson Ave, Pasadena (91106-3268)
PHONE 626 395-8700
Bill Nunez, *Manager*
EMP: 200
SQ FT: 3,536
SALES (corp-wide): 2.3B **Privately Held**
WEB: www.caltech.edu
SIC: 8731 Biological research
PA: California Institute Of Technology
　1200 E California Blvd
　Pasadena CA 91125
　626 395-6811

(P-26492)
CARDIUM BIOLOGICS INC
Also Called: Tissue Repair Co
11750 Sorrento Valley Rd # 250, San Diego (92121-1025)
PHONE 858 436-1000
Christopher J Reinhard, *President*
Barbara Sosnowski, *COO*
Dennis M Mulroy, *CFO*
Randall Morehadith, *Chief Mktg Ofcr*
Matthias Blume, *Officer*
EMP: 50
SALES (est): 89.5K
SALES (corp-wide): 109.2K **Publicly Held**
WEB: www.t-r-co.com
SIC: 8731 Biotechnical research, commercial
PA: Taxus Cardium Pharmaceuticals Group Inc.
　11750 Sorrento Valley Rd
　San Diego CA 92121
　858 436-1000

(P-26493)
CCINTEGRATION INC
2060 Corporate Ct, San Jose (95131-1753)
PHONE 408 228-1314
Fax: 510 661-2742
Hank C Ta, *President*
Diana Jackman, *Admin Asst*
Diana Jackson, *Admin Asst*
Philisia Vuong, *Admin Asst*
Chan Chep, *Technician*
EMP: 50
SQ FT: 235,000
SALES (est): 15.3MM **Privately Held**
WEB: www.ccintegration.com
SIC: 8731 7371 Computer (hardware) development; computer software development

(P-26494)
CELGENE CORPORATION
10300 Campus Point Dr # 100, San Diego (92121-1504)
PHONE 858 558-7500
Alan Louis, *President*
David Anderson, *Vice Pres*
Thu Thai, *Executive*
Heather K Raymon, *Associate Dir*
Paul Ryan, *Associate Dir*
EMP: 100
SALES (corp-wide): 9.2B **Publicly Held**
WEB: www.celgene.com
SIC: 8731 Medical research, commercial
PA: Celgene Corporation
　86 Morris Ave
　Summit NJ 07901
　908 673-9000

(P-26495)
CGI TECHNOLOGIES SOLUTIONS INC
860 Stillwater Rd Ste 210, West Sacramento (95605-1684)
PHONE 916 281-3200
EMP: 50
SALES (corp-wide): 7.8B **Privately Held**
SIC: 8731 Commercial physical research
HQ: Cgi Technologies And Solutions Inc.
　11325 Random Hills Rd
　Fairfax VA 22030
　703 267-8000

(P-26496)
CIR
1745 Celeste Dr, San Mateo (94402-2603)
PHONE 650 574-6900
Dan Collins, *Owner*
EMP: 105
SQ FT: 13,500
SALES (est): 4.2MM **Privately Held**
WEB: www.cirlabs.com
SIC: 8731 5169 5191 2899 Industrial laboratory, except testing; chemicals & allied products; chemicals, industrial & heavy; pesticides; fertilizer & fertilizer materials; chemical preparations; insecticides & pesticides; phosphatic fertilizers

(P-26497)
COGENT SYSTEMS INCORPORATED (DH)
639 N Rosemead Blvd, Pasadena (91107-2147)
PHONE 626 325-9600
Ming Hsieh, *CEO*
Taul Kim, *CFO*
James Xie, *Info Tech Mgr*
Xian Tang, *Research*
Carleen Chen, *Engineer*
EMP: 51
SALES: 12.9MM
SALES (corp-wide): 30.2B **Publicly Held**
SIC: 8731 Biotechnical research, commercial
HQ: 3m Cogent, Inc.
　639 N Rosemead Blvd
　Pasadena CA 91107
　626 325-9600

(P-26498)
COLSA CORPORATION
41240 12th St W, Palmdale (93551-1449)
PHONE 661 273-3859
Tom Berard, *Director*
EMP: 238

SALES (corp-wide): 190.1MM **Privately Held**
SIC: 8731 Computer (hardware) development
PA: Colsa Corporation
　6728 Odyssey Dr Nw
　Huntsville AL 35806
　256 964-5361

(P-26499)
COMPARENETWORKS INC (PA)
Also Called: Biocompare
395 Oyster Point Blvd # 321, South San Francisco (94080-1931)
PHONE 650 873-9031
Fax: 650 873-9038
Brian Cowley, *CEO*
Paul Gatti, *President*
Matthew McLean, *COO*
Bo Purtic, *Officer*
Ben Grady, *Info Tech Mgr*
EMP: 75
SQ FT: 16,152
SALES (est): 10.9MM **Privately Held**
WEB: www.biocompare.com
SIC: 8731 Commercial physical research

(P-26500)
COVANCE INC
10300 Campus Point Dr # 225, San Diego (92121-1515)
PHONE 858 352-2300
MO Chaudry, *Manager*
Vinita Roy, *Sales Staff*
Marivic Turman, *Assistant*
Pamela Phillips, *Associate*
EMP: 85
SALES (corp-wide): 8.6B **Publicly Held**
SIC: 8731 Commercial physical research
HQ: Covance Inc.
　210 Carnegie Ctr Ste 106
　Princeton NJ 08540

(P-26501)
CPU TECHNOLOGY INC
5753 W Las Positas Blvd, Pleasanton (94588-4084)
PHONE 925 398-7659
Chris D Wedewer, *President*
Dan Jurchenko, *President*
Stephen Lanza, *Exec VP*
Dave Bennett, *Vice Pres*
Richard Comfort, *Vice Pres*
EMP: 63
SALES (est): 118.7K
SALES (corp-wide): 96.1B **Publicly Held**
WEB: www.cputech.com
SIC: 8731 8711 3674 3672 Computer (hardware) development; engineering services; semiconductors & related devices; printed circuit boards
PA: The Boeing Company
　100 N Riverside Plz
　Chicago IL 60606
　312 544-2000

(P-26502)
CTK BIOTECH INC
10110 Mesa Rim Rd, San Diego (92121-3936)
PHONE 858 457-8698
Fax: 858 535-1739
Catherine Yaping Chen, *CEO*
Joel Heidecker, *Vice Pres*
Yin Wushan, *Principal*
Angie Cai, *Opers Staff*
Dan Hanlon, *Sales Staff*
EMP: 50
SALES (est): 5.9MM **Privately Held**
WEB: www.ctkbiotech.com
SIC: 8731 Commercial physical research

(P-26503)
DART NEUROSCIENCE LLC
12278 Scripps Summit Dr, San Diego (92131-3697)
PHONE 858 736-3060
Kenneth E Johns Jr, *CEO*
Ted Stmartin, *CFO*
Tim Tully, *Officer*
Ali Tabatabaei, *Associate Dir*
Linda Soimany, *Executive Asst*
EMP: 220

SALES (est): 50.4MM **Privately Held**
SIC: 8731 8733 Biotechnical research, commercial; medical research

(P-26504)
DEPOSITION SCIENCES INC
Also Called: D S I
3300 Coffey Ln, Santa Rosa (95403-1917)
PHONE 707 573-6700
Fax: 707 579-0731
Lee Bartolomei, *President*
Kevin Gibbons, *Program Mgr*
Stephanie Ferguson, *Human Res Mgr*
Linda Svenson, *Human Res Mgr*
Mary Cody, *Buyer*
EMP: 96
SQ FT: 8,400
SALES (est): 14.9MM
SALES (corp-wide): 46.1B **Publicly Held**
WEB: www.depsci.com
SIC: 8731 3827 Industrial laboratory, except testing; lens coating equipment
PA: Lockheed Martin Corporation
　6801 Rockledge Dr
　Bethesda MD 20817
　301 897-6000

(P-26505)
DSM BIOMEDICAL INC
Also Called: Polymer Technology Group, The
2810 7th St, Berkeley (94710-2703)
PHONE 510 841-8800
Fax: 510 841-7800
Christophe Dardel, *CEO*
Richard Alsterberg, *Vice Pres*
Mike Comstock, *Controller*
Margaret Macedo, *Human Resources*
Nelson Cooke, *Manager*
EMP: 120
SQ FT: 55,000
SALES (est): 30.4MM **Privately Held**
WEB: www.polymertech.com
SIC: 8731 2836 Commercial physical research; biological products, except diagnostic
PA: Koninklijke Dsm N.V.
　Het Overloon 1
　Heerlen 6411
　455 788-111

(P-26506)
DT RESEARCH INC (PA)
2000 Concourse Dr, San Jose (95131-1701)
PHONE 408 934-6220
Yuan D Tsai, *President*
Yuan-Daw Tsai, *President*
David Hale, *Vice Pres*
Rick Wysocki, *Vice Pres*
Yong Chen, *Executive*
EMP: 63
SQ FT: 20,000
SALES (est): 26.8MM **Privately Held**
WEB: www.dtresearch.com
SIC: 8731 Computer (hardware) development

(P-26507)
E-SCEPTRE INC
16800 Gale Ave, City of Industry (91745-1804)
PHONE 888 350-8989
Stephen Liu, *President*
Steven Liu, *CEO*
Richard Gallegos, *Exec VP*
EMP: 60
SQ FT: 80,000
SALES (est): 4.7MM **Privately Held**
SIC: 8731 Computer (hardware) development
PA: Sceptre Industries Inc
　16800 Gale Ave
　City Of Industry CA 91745

(P-26508)
ECOLOGY ACTION OF SANTA CRUZ
877 Cedar St Ste 240, Santa Cruz (95060-3938)
PHONE 831 426-5925
Fax: 831 425-1404
Jennifer Smith-Grub, *President*
Ilse Lopes, *Treasurer*
Marc Adato, *Vice Pres*
Michael Brown, *Exec Dir*

8731 - Commercial Physical & Biological Research County (P-26509)
PRODUDUCTS & SERVICES SECTION

Ellen Yeoman, *Admin Sec*
EMP: 110
SQ FT: 14,000
SALES: 22.3MM **Privately Held**
SIC: 8731 Environmental research

(P-26509)
ELAN DRUG DELIVERY INC
Also Called: Elan Drug Technologies
180 Oyster Point Blvd, South San Francisco (94080-1909)
PHONE..................770 531-8100
David Czekai, *President*
James L Botkin, *Senior VP*
John B Moriarty Jr, *Senior VP*
Patrick Pollard, *Vice Pres*
Kevin Barrett, *CIO*
EMP: 52
SALES (est): 3.1MM **Privately Held**
SIC: 8731 4215 Medical research, commercial; courier services, except by air
PA: Alkermes Public Limited Company
Connaught House
Dublin 4

(P-26510)
ELECTRIC POWER RES INST INC (PA)
3420 Hillview Ave, Palo Alto (94304-1382)
P.O. Box 10412 (94303-0813)
PHONE..................650 855-2000
Fax: 650 855-1080
Michael Howard, *CEO*
Gil C Quiniones, *Ch of Bd*
Terry Boston, *President*
Steve Yamamoto, *CFO*
Patricia Vincent-Collawn, *Vice Ch Bd*
EMP: 600
SQ FT: 300,000
SALES: 406MM **Privately Held**
WEB: www.epri.com
SIC: 8731 Energy research

(P-26511)
ENDOVASCULAR TECHNOLOGIES INC
1360 Obrien Dr, Menlo Park (94025-1436)
PHONE..................650 325-1600
W James Fitzsimmons, *President*
G Bradley Cole, *CFO*
Lori Adels, *Vice Pres*
Vic Bernhard, *Vice Pres*
Ron Giannotti, *Vice Pres*
EMP: 74
SQ FT: 20,000
SALES (est): 2.9MM
SALES (corp-wide): 7.4B **Publicly Held**
WEB: www.guidant.com
SIC: 8731 Medical research, commercial
HQ: Guidant Sales Llc
4100 Hamline Ave N
Saint Paul MN 55112
800 949-9459

(P-26512)
ENERGY INNOVATIONS INC
130 W Union St, Pasadena (91103-3628)
PHONE..................626 585-6900
Joseph Budano, *CEO*
Bill Gross, *President*
Marcia Goodstein, *COO*
Greg Chrisney, *CFO*
Doug McPherson, *Executive*
EMP: 200
SALES (est): 14.4MM **Privately Held**
WEB: www.energyinnovations.com
SIC: 8731 Commercial physical research

(P-26513)
ENTELOS INC
110 Marsh Dr Ste 200, Foster City (94404-1131)
PHONE..................650 578-2900
Fax: 650 572-5401
Jim Neal, *President*
Charles Sholtz, *Vice Pres*
Mikhail Gishizky, *Security Dir*
Greg Thompson, *Info Tech Dir*
Mark Zhang, *Database Admin*
EMP: 50
SQ FT: 21,000
SALES (est): 3.9MM **Privately Held**
WEB: www.entelos.com
SIC: 8731 Medical research, commercial

(P-26514)
ENVIRONMENTAL SCIENCE ASSOC (PA)
Also Called: ESA
550 Kearny St Ste 800, San Francisco (94108-2512)
PHONE..................415 896-5900
Gary Oates, *Ch of Bd*
Greg Thornton, *CFO*
Bruce Mackey, *Bd of Directors*
Marty Abell, *Vice Pres*
Jean Chen, *Vice Pres*
EMP: 65
SQ FT: 20,000
SALES (est): 31.2MM **Privately Held**
WEB: www.esassoc.com
SIC: 8731 8748 Environmental research; environmental consultant

(P-26515)
EXECUTIVE OFFICE STATE OF CA
Also Called: Governors Office Plg & RES
1400 10th St Rm 100, Sacramento (95814-5502)
PHONE..................916 322-2318
Sean Walsh, *Director*
Wade Crowfoot, *Deputy Dir*
EMP: 80 **Privately Held**
SIC: 8731 9111 Environmental research; governors' offices;
HQ: Executive Office Of The State Of California
Governors Ofc
Sacramento CA 95814
916 445-2841

(P-26516)
EXELIXIS INC
210 E Grand Ave, South San Francisco (94080-4811)
P.O. Box 511 (94083-0511)
PHONE..................650 837-7000
Michael M Morrissey, *President*
Frank L Karbe, *CFO*
Frances K Heller, *Vice Pres*
Peter Lamb, *Vice Pres*
Lupe M Rivera, *Vice Pres*
EMP: 100
SALES (est): 7MM **Privately Held**
SIC: 8731 Commercial physical research

(P-26517)
FERRING RESEARCH INSTITUTE INC
4245 Sorrento Valley Blvd, San Diego (92121-1408)
PHONE..................858 657-1400
Pierre Riviere, *President*
Joshua Heitzmann, *Vice Pres*
Halina W Niewska, *Vice Pres*
Dawn Painter, *Executive Asst*
Robert Meadows, *Info Tech Dir*
EMP: 65
SQ FT: 30,000
SALES (est): 9.6MM **Privately Held**
SIC: 8731 Commercial physical research
HQ: Ferring Pharmaceuticals Sa
Chemin De La Vergognausaz 50
Saint-Prex VD
583 010-000

(P-26518)
FIT ELECTRONICS INC (HQ)
Also Called: Foxconn Electronics
500 S Kraemer Blvd # 100, Brea (92821-6763)
PHONE..................714 988-9388
Mike Unger, *President*
Ralph Gillespie, *CEO*
Helen Pearsall, *Buyer*
EMP: 140 **EST:** 1997
SALES (est): 43.7MM **Privately Held**
SIC: 8731 5065 Electronic research; electronic parts
PA: Hon Hai Precision Industry Co., Ltd.
66, Zhongshan Rd.,
New Taipei City
222 683-477

(P-26519)
FUJITSU LABORATORIES AMER INC (DH)
1240 E Arques Ave 345, Sunnyvale (94085-5401)
PHONE..................408 530-4500
Hiromu Hayashi, *President*
Nobuaki Kawato, *Exec VP*
Hitoshi Funatogawa, *Senior VP*
Nobuhiko Hara, *Senior VP*
Kazuhiro Matsuo, *Senior VP*
EMP: 80
SALES (est): 640.4MM
SALES (corp-wide): 40.5B **Privately Held**
WEB: www.fujitsulabs.com
SIC: 8731 Commercial physical research
HQ: Fujitsu Laboratories Ltd.
4-1-1, Kamikodanaka, Nakahara-Ku
Kawasaki KNG 211-0
447 542-613

(P-26520)
GEN-PROBE INCORPORATED (HQ)
10210 Genetic Center Dr, San Diego (92121-4394)
PHONE..................858 410-8000
Fax: 858 410-8001
Carl W Hull, *President*
Henry L Nordhoff, *President*
Herm Rosenman, *CFO*
Daniel L Kacian PHD, *Exec VP*
R William Bowen, *Senior VP*
EMP: 202
SQ FT: 262,000
SALES (est): 201.8MM
SALES (corp-wide): 2.7B **Publicly Held**
SIC: 8731 Biological research
PA: Hologic, Inc.
250 Campus Dr
Marlborough MA 01752
508 263-2900

(P-26521)
GENEOHM SCIENCES INC
11085 N Torrey Pines Rd # 210, La Jolla (92037-1015)
PHONE..................201 847-5824
Peter Klemm, *President*
Jamie Condy, *President*
Kurt Klassen, *Finance*
Steve Lundy, *VP Mktg*
EMP: 150
SQ FT: 22,000
SALES (est): 7.9MM
SALES (corp-wide): 10.2B **Publicly Held**
WEB: www.geneohm.com
SIC: 8731 Commercial physical research
PA: Becton, Dickinson And Company
1 Becton Dr
Franklin Lakes NJ 07417
201 847-6800

(P-26522)
GENERAL ATOMIC AERON
9779 Yucca Rd, Adelanto (92301-2265)
PHONE..................760 246-3660
Jim Machin, *Manager*
Amber Streets, *Planning*
Mark Churchman, *Engineer*
Brandon Hackney, *Engineer*
Richard Huff, *Engineer*
EMP: 135
SALES (corp-wide): 3.5B **Privately Held**
WEB: www.ga-asi.com
SIC: 8731 Commercial physical research
HQ: General Atomics Aeronautical Systems, Inc.
14200 Kirkham Way
Poway CA 92064
858 312-2810

(P-26523)
GENERAL ATOMICS (HQ)
3550 General Atomics Ct, San Diego (92121-1194)
P.O. Box 85608 (92186-5608)
PHONE..................858 455-2810
Fax: 858 455-2232
J Neal Blue, *President*
Liam Kelly, *CFO*
Karen Baldwin, *Treasurer*
Mary Cowen, *Treasurer*
Anthony Navarra, *Treasurer*
EMP: 2000 **EST:** 1955
SQ FT: 1,000,000
SALES (est): 2.3B
SALES (corp-wide): 3.5B **Privately Held**
WEB: www.generalatomics.com
SIC: 8731 Commercial physical research; energy research
PA: General Atomic Technologies Corporation
3550 General Atomics Ct
San Diego CA 92121
858 455-3000

(P-26524)
GENERAL ATOMICS
16969 Mesamint St, San Diego (92127-2407)
PHONE..................858 676-7100
Anthony Navarra, *Vice Pres*
Robert Laird, *Research*
Tom Gogg, *Engineer*
Puja Gupta, *Engineer*
Todd Meyer, *Engineer*
EMP: 99
SALES (corp-wide): 3.5B **Privately Held**
WEB: www.generalatomics.com
SIC: 8731 Commercial physical research
HQ: General Atomics
3550 General Atomics Ct
San Diego CA 92121
858 455-2810

(P-26525)
GENERAL ATOMICS
Also Called: General Atomics Energy Pdts
4949 Greencraig Ln, San Diego (92123-1675)
PHONE..................858 455-4000
Fax: 858 522-8301
Joel Ennis, *General Mgr*
Kristin Spivey, *Program Mgr*
Emelie Galace, *Admin Asst*
Tony Rockwell, *Admin Asst*
Julio Dominguez, *Administration*
EMP: 170
SALES (corp-wide): 3.5B **Privately Held**
WEB: www.generalatomics.com
SIC: 8731 7371 3823 Commercial physical research; custom computer programming services; industrial instrmnts msrmnt display/control process variable
HQ: General Atomics
3550 General Atomics Ct
San Diego CA 92121
858 455-2810

(P-26526)
GENTEX CORPORATION
Also Called: Western Operations
9859 7th St, Rancho Cucamonga (91730-5244)
PHONE..................909 481-7667
Fax: 909 481-7759
Robert McCay, *Branch Mgr*
John Ash, *Officer*
Cay Mc, *Executive*
Michael Tran, *Technology*
John Kern, *Engineer*
EMP: 90
SALES (corp-wide): 177.5MM **Privately Held**
WEB: www.gentex.net
SIC: 8731 3845 3841 Commercial research laboratory; biological research; electromedical equipment; surgical & medical instruments
PA: Gentex Corporation
324 Main St
Simpson PA 18407
570 282-3550

(P-26527)
GEOLOGICAL SURVEY US DEPT
345 Middlefield Rd, Menlo Park (94025-3561)
PHONE..................650 329-5229
Maria McNutt, *Director*
EMP: 70 **Publicly Held**
SIC: 8731 9511 Commercial physical research; air, water & solid waste management;
HQ: United States Dept Of Geological Survey
12201 Sunrise Valley Dr
Reston VA 20192

PRODUCTS & SERVICES SECTION
8731 - Commercial Physical & Biological Research County (P-26549)

(P-26528)
GRAIL INC
Also Called: Grail Bio
800 Saginaw Dr, Redwood City (94063-4740)
PHONE.................................858 766-1512
Jeff Huber, *CEO*
Michael Myers, *Finance Dir*
EMP: 50
SALES (est): 1.8MM **Privately Held**
SIC: 8731 Biotechnical research, commercial

(P-26529)
HMCLAUSE INC
Also Called: Harris Moran
9241 Mace Blvd, Davis (95618-9614)
PHONE.................................530 747-3235
Fax: 530 756-1016
Lincoln Moehle, *Manager*
Shaunese Lambel, *Manager*
John Shobein, *Manager*
John Shovein, *Manager*
EMP: 80 **Privately Held**
WEB: www.harrismoran.com
SIC: 8731 Agricultural research
HQ: Hm.Clause, Inc.
555 Codoni Ave
Modesto CA 95357
530 747-3700

(P-26530)
HOWARD HUGHES MEDICAL INST
Also Called: H H M I
279 Campus Dr Rm B202, Stanford (94305-5101)
PHONE.................................650 725-8252
Fax: 650 725-8112
John Kennedy, *Manager*
EMP: 100
SALES (corp-wide): 2.7B **Privately Held**
SIC: 8731 6732 Medical research, commercial; trusts: educational, religious, etc.
PA: Howard Hughes Medical Institute Inc
4000 Jones Bridge Rd
Chevy Chase MD 20815
301 215-8500

(P-26531)
HOWARD HUGHES MEDICAL INST
1550 4th St Rm 190, San Francisco (94143-2324)
PHONE.................................415 476-9668
Fax: 415 514-4250
Martha Drews, *Admin Asst*
EMP: 120
SALES (corp-wide): 2.7B **Privately Held**
SIC: 8731 Biological research
PA: Howard Hughes Medical Institute Inc
4000 Jones Bridge Rd
Chevy Chase MD 20815
301 215-8500

(P-26532)
HP INC
1501 Page Mill Rd, Palo Alto (94304-1126)
PHONE.................................650 857-4946
Fax: 650 857-7868
Richard D Lampman, *Senior VP*
Chandra Venkatraman, *Project Leader*
Yong Yan, *Research*
Johnny Fung, *Engineer*
Jun LI, *Engineer*
EMP: 3000
SALES (corp-wide): 103.3B **Publicly Held**
SIC: 8731 Computer (hardware) development
PA: Hp Inc.
1501 Page Mill Rd
Palo Alto CA 94304
650 857-1501

(P-26533)
IBIS BIOSCIENCES INC
2251 Faraday Ave Ste 150, Carlsbad (92008-7209)
PHONE.................................760 476-3200
Andrea Wainer, *CEO*
Jayme Laforte, *Administration*
Lee Ann Paaton, *Administration*
Maria Tobar, *Research*
Jose Gutierrez, *Engineer*
EMP: 120
SALES (est): 16.4MM
SALES (corp-wide): 20.4B **Publicly Held**
SIC: 8731 Commercial physical research
PA: Abbott Laboratories
100 Abbott Park Rd
Abbott Park IL 60064
224 667-6100

(P-26534)
IMPACT ASSESSMENT INC
2166 Avenida De La Playa F, La Jolla (92037-3214)
PHONE.................................858 459-0142
Fax: 858 459-9461
John S Petterson, *President*
Kristen Nelson, *Financial Exec*
EMP: 60
SQ FT: 1,700
SALES (est): 5.8MM **Privately Held**
WEB: www.impactassessment.net
SIC: 8731 Environmental research; commercial research laboratory

(P-26535)
INCLIN INC
2000 Alameda De Las Pulga, San Mateo (94403-1271)
PHONE.................................650 961-3422
Taylor Kilfoil, *CEO*
Dirk Thye, *CEO*
Tony Pantuso, *COO*
Arnold Wong, *CFO*
Marc R Perry, *Senior VP*
EMP: 75
SQ FT: 9,800
SALES (est): 10.4MM **Privately Held**
SIC: 8731 Biological research

(P-26536)
INTEGRA LIFESCIENCES CORP
2 Goodyear Ste A, Irvine (92618-2052)
PHONE.................................949 595-8710
Eugene Reu, *Branch Mgr*
Tom Tarca, *Vice Pres*
Brandon Alvarado, *Executive*
Nancy Toledo, *Administration*
Janet Reyes, *Purchasing*
EMP: 150
SALES (corp-wide): 882.7MM **Publicly Held**
SIC: 8731 Biological research
HQ: Integra Lifesciences Corporation
311 Enterprise Dr
Plainsboro NJ 08536
609 275-2700

(P-26537)
INTEGRIUM LLC (PA)
Also Called: Integrex Innovations
14351 Myford Rd Ste A, Tustin (92780-7038)
PHONE.................................714 541-5591
David Smith MD,
Adam Steadman, *CFO*
Junya Yamamoto, *Vice Pres*
Emily Machale, *Associate Dir*
Kevin Vernarec, *Exec Dir*
EMP: 67
SQ FT: 40,000
SALES (est): 12.5MM **Privately Held**
WEB: www.integrium.com
SIC: 8731 8742 Medical research, commercial; industry specialist consultants

(P-26538)
INTERNATIONAL BUS MCHS CORP
Also Called: IBM
650 Harry Rd, San Jose (95120-6001)
PHONE.................................408 927-1080
Fax: 408 927-2100
Mark Dean, *Vice Pres*
David Zhang, *Vice Pres*
Tom Randel, *Administration*
Guillermo Alvarez, *Info Tech Mgr*
Kraisit Vittinanon, *Info Tech Mgr*
EMP: 500
SALES (corp-wide): 81.7B **Publicly Held**
WEB: www.ibm.com
SIC: 8731 Commercial research laboratory
PA: International Business Machines Corporation
1 New Orchard Rd Ste 1
Armonk NY 10504
914 499-1900

(P-26539)
ISE CORPORATION
Also Called: I S E
12302 Kerran St, Los Angeles (90064)
PHONE.................................858 413-1720
Richard J Sander, *CEO*
David Mazaika, *Ch of Bd*
Johan Lecoutere, *CEO*
Eric Hohl, *CFO*
Alex Bernasconi, *Senior VP*
EMP: 140
SQ FT: 15,000
SALES (est): 11.9MM **Privately Held**
WEB: www.isecorp.com
SIC: 8731 3621 Commercial physical research; electric motor & generator parts

(P-26540)
ISOTIS ORTHOBIOLOGICS INC
2 Goodyear Ste A, Irvine (92618-2052)
PHONE.................................949 595-8711
Fax: 949 595-8711
Keith Valentine, *CEO*
Peter J Arduini, *President*
Christian S Schade, *Exec VP*
Alan Donze, *Vice Pres*
Nancy Toledo, *Principal*
EMP: 150
SALES (est): 21.3MM
SALES (corp-wide): 2.3MM **Privately Held**
SIC: 8731 5047 Biological research; surgical equipment & supplies
HQ: Isotis International Sarl
C/O Fidulem Sa
Lausanne VD 1005
216 132-501

(P-26541)
JANSSEN ALZHEIMER IMMUNOTHERA
700 Gateway Blvd, South San Francisco (94080-7020)
PHONE.................................650 794-2500
Fax: 650 794-2504
Dr Stefaan Heylen, *President*
Nadine De Leeuw, *Manager*
EMP: 100
SALES (est): 6.9MM
SALES (corp-wide): 70B **Publicly Held**
SIC: 8731 Commercial physical research
HQ: Janssen Research & Development, Llc
920 Us Highway 202
Raritan NJ 08869
908 704-4000

(P-26542)
KAPL INC
1126 N Brookhurst St, Anaheim (92801-1702)
PHONE.................................714 991-9543
EMP: 254
SALES (corp-wide): 315.9MM **Privately Held**
SIC: 8731 Energy research
PA: Kapl, Inc.
2401 River Rd
Schenectady NY 12309
877 527-5522

(P-26543)
KINEMED INC
40 Lincoln Ave, Piedmont (94611-3845)
PHONE.................................510 655-6525
Fax: 510 655-6506
Robert Stein, *CEO*
David Fineman, *President*
Hank Settle, *CFO*
Patrick James Doyle, *Officer*
Bill Evans, *Exec VP*
EMP: 54 EST: 2001
SQ FT: 10,000
SALES (est): 7.6MM **Privately Held**
WEB: www.kinemed.com
SIC: 8731 Biotechnical research, commercial

(P-26544)
KITE PHARMA INC (PA)
2225 Colorado Ave, Santa Monica (90404-3505)
PHONE.................................310 824-9999
Arie Belldegrun, *Ch of Bd*
Cynthia M Butitta, *COO*
Paul L Jenkinson, *CFO*
David Chang, *Chief Mktg Ofcr*
Shawn Tomasello, *Officer*
EMP: 74
SQ FT: 20,000
SALES: 17.2MM **Publicly Held**
SIC: 8731 2836 Commercial physical research; biological products, except diagnostic

(P-26545)
KOSAN BIOSCIENCES INCORPORATED
3832 Bay Center Pl, Hayward (94545-3619)
P.O. Box 4000, Princeton NJ (08543-4000)
PHONE.................................510 732-8400
Fax: 510 732-8401
EMP: 91
SALES (est): 7.2MM
SALES (corp-wide): 16.5B **Publicly Held**
WEB: www.kosan.com
SIC: 8731 2834
PA: Bristol-Myers Squibb Company
345 Park Ave Bsmt Lc3
New York NY 10154
212 546-4000

(P-26546)
L-3 APPLIED TECHNOLOGIES INC
2700 Merced St, San Leandro (94577-5602)
PHONE.................................510 577-7100
Fax: 510 577-7129
Janet Luna, *Director*
EMP: 109
SALES (corp-wide): 10.4B **Publicly Held**
SIC: 8731 Commercial physical research
HQ: L-3 Applied Technologies, Inc.
10180 Barnes Canyon Rd
San Diego CA 92121
858 404-7824

(P-26547)
LA JOLLA PHARMACEUTICAL CO (PA)
10182 Telesis Ct Ste 600, San Diego (92121-4777)
PHONE.................................858 207-4264
Fax: 858 626-2851
George F Tidmarsh, *President*
Kevin C Tang, *Ch of Bd*
Dennis M Mulroy, *CFO*
Lakhmir S Chawla, *Chief Mktg Ofcr*
Jennifer A Carver, *Senior VP*
EMP: 58
SQ FT: 18,599
SALES: 1MM **Publicly Held**
WEB: www.ljpc.com
SIC: 8731 2834 Biological research; pharmaceutical preparations

(P-26548)
LEIDOS INC
1411 Marsh St, San Luis Obispo (93401-2957)
PHONE.................................805 546-0307
Lauren Brown,
EMP: 82
SALES (corp-wide): 5B **Publicly Held**
WEB: www.saic.com
SIC: 8731 Commercial physical research
HQ: Leidos, Inc.
11951 Freedom Dr Ste 500
Reston VA 20190
571 526-6000

(P-26549)
LEIDOS INC
1874 S Pacific Coast Hwy, Redondo Beach (90277-6117)
PHONE.................................310 791-9671
Alexander Preston, *Branch Mgr*
EMP: 82
SALES (corp-wide): 5B **Publicly Held**
WEB: www.saic.com
SIC: 8731 Commercial physical research
HQ: Leidos, Inc.
11951 Freedom Dr Ste 500
Reston VA 20190
571 526-6000

8731 - Commercial Physical & Biological Research County (P-26550)

PRODUDUCTS & SERVICES SECTION

(P-26550)
LEIDOS INC
Saic
590 W Central Ave Ste I, Brea
(92821-3019)
PHONE.................................714 257-6400
Ed Morland, *Manager*
EMP: 93
SALES (corp-wide): 5B **Publicly Held**
WEB: www.saic.com
SIC: 8731 Commercial physical research;
  energy research
HQ: Leidos, Inc.
  11951 Freedom Dr Ste 500
  Reston VA 20190
  571 526-6000

(P-26551)
LEIDOS INC
3700 State St Ste 300, Santa Barbara
(93105-3128)
PHONE.................................805 563-9597
Arthur McNary, *Branch Mgr*
EMP: 93
SALES (corp-wide): 5B **Publicly Held**
WEB: www.saic.com
SIC: 8731 Commercial physical research
HQ: Leidos, Inc.
  11951 Freedom Dr Ste 500
  Reston VA 20190
  571 526-6000

(P-26552)
LEIDOS INC
300 N Sepulveda Blvd # 3000, El Segundo
(90245-4472)
PHONE.................................310 524-3134
Ronald Graves, *Manager*
Craig Yamachika, *Controller*
EMP: 182
SALES (corp-wide): 5B **Publicly Held**
WEB: www.saic.com
SIC: 8731 Commercial physical research
HQ: Leidos, Inc.
  11951 Freedom Dr Ste 500
  Reston VA 20190
  571 526-6000

(P-26553)
LEIDOS INC
10740 Thornmint Rd, San Diego
(92127-2700)
PHONE.................................858 826-6616
Sarita Ambris, *Branch Mgr*
EMP: 93
SALES (corp-wide): 5B **Publicly Held**
WEB: www.saic.com
SIC: 8731 Commercial physical research
HQ: Leidos, Inc.
  11951 Freedom Dr Ste 500
  Reston VA 20190
  571 526-6000

(P-26554)
LEIDOS INC
139 N 5th St, Coalinga (93210-1901)
PHONE.................................559 935-2305
Dr J Robert Beyster, *President*
EMP: 50
SALES (corp-wide): 5B **Publicly Held**
WEB: www.saic.com
SIC: 8731 Commercial physical research;
  energy research; environmental research;
  medical research, commercial
HQ: Leidos, Inc.
  11951 Freedom Dr Ste 500
  Reston VA 20190
  571 526-6000

(P-26555)
LEIDOS INC
2000 Powell St Ste 1090, Emeryville
(94608-1780)
PHONE.................................510 428-2550
Sarita Ambris, *Manager*
EMP: 93
SALES (corp-wide): 5B **Publicly Held**
WEB: www.saic.com
SIC: 8731 Commercial physical research;
  energy research; environmental research;
  medical research, commercial
HQ: Leidos, Inc.
  11951 Freedom Dr Ste 500
  Reston VA 20190
  571 526-6000

(P-26556)
LEIDOS INC
Also Called: National Security
4065 Hancock St, San Diego (92110-5151)
PHONE.................................858 826-6000
Gordon Saakamodo, *Manager*
EMP: 93
SALES (corp-wide): 5B **Publicly Held**
WEB: www.saic.com
SIC: 8731 Commercial physical research;
  energy research; environmental research;
  medical research, commercial
HQ: Leidos, Inc.
  11951 Freedom Dr Ste 500
  Reston VA 20190
  571 526-6000

(P-26557)
LEIDOS INC
Also Called: Saic
475 14th St, Oakland (94612-1928)
PHONE.................................408 364-4700
April Pierson, *Manager*
EMP: 93
SALES (corp-wide): 5B **Publicly Held**
SIC: 8731 Commercial physical research
HQ: Leidos, Inc.
  11951 Freedom Dr Ste 500
  Reston VA 20190
  571 526-6000

(P-26558)
LEIDOS INC
10010 Campus Point Dr, San Diego
(92121-1518)
PHONE.................................858 826-7129
Joel Colbourn, *Branch Mgr*
James Barber, *Vice Pres*
Miriam John, *Director*
EMP: 241
SQ FT: 64,800
SALES (corp-wide): 5B **Publicly Held**
WEB: www.saic.com
SIC: 8731 Energy research; environmental
  research; medical research, commercial
HQ: Leidos, Inc.
  11951 Freedom Dr Ste 500
  Reston VA 20190
  571 526-6000

(P-26559)
LEIDOS INC
N Depo Rd Bldg 4530, Fort Irwin (92310)
PHONE.................................910 574-4597
Cassidy Smith, *Manager*
EMP: 93
SALES (corp-wide): 5B **Publicly Held**
SIC: 8731 Commercial physical research
HQ: Leidos, Inc.
  11951 Freedom Dr Ste 500
  Reston VA 20190
  571 526-6000

(P-26560)
LEIDOS ENGRG & SCIENCES LLC
1330 30th St Ste A, San Diego
(92154-3471)
PHONE.................................619 542-3130
Karen Parizeau, *Manager*
James Sleeth, *Principal*
Maryanne Dykes, *Administration*
Mike Crawford, *Programmer Anys*
Deirdre Newton, *Business Mgr*
EMP: 95
SALES (corp-wide): 5B **Publicly Held**
SIC: 8731 Natural resource research
HQ: Leidos Engineering & Sciences, Llc
  700 N Frederick Ave
  Gaithersburg MD 20879
  301 240-7000

(P-26561)
LIGHTWAVES 2020 INC
1323 Great Mall Dr, Milpitas (95035-8013)
PHONE.................................408 503-8888
Fax: 408 503-8988
J J Pan, *Ch of Bd*
Jewel Chang, *Principal*
Roger Liu, *Data Proc Staff*
Jonathan Zhang, *Sales Staff*
EMP: 50
SALES (est): 7.5MM **Privately Held**
WEB: www.lightwaves2020.com
SIC: 8731 Commercial physical research

(P-26562)
LOCKHEED MARTIN CORPORATION
3251 Hanover St Bldg 245, Palo Alto
(94304-1121)
PHONE.................................650 424-2000
Fax: 408 742-9999
Aram Mica, *Vice Pres*
Marillyn Lewson, *President*
Mark Ferraro, *Administration*
Theo-Alice Pierce, *Administration*
Mike Kretzer, *Systems Staff*
EMP: 625
SQ FT: 350,000
SALES (corp-wide): 46.1B **Publicly Held**
WEB: www.lockheedmartin.com
SIC: 8731 Commercial physical research
PA: Lockheed Martin Corporation
  6801 Rockledge Dr
  Bethesda MD 20817
  301 897-6000

(P-26563)
MA LABORATORIES INC
Also Called: MA Labs
18725 San Jose Ave, City of Industry
(91748-1324)
PHONE.................................626 820-8988
Fax: 626 820-8188
Christine Pan, *Manager*
Albert Herrera, *Marketing Staff*
EMP: 59
SALES (corp-wide): 241.3MM **Privately Held**
SIC: 8731 Commercial physical research
PA: Ma Laboratories, Inc.
  2075 N Capitol Ave
  San Jose CA 95132
  408 941-0808

(P-26564)
MANNKIND CORPORATION (PA)
25134 Rye Canyon Loop # 300, Valencia
(91355-5031)
PHONE.................................661 775-5300
Fax: 661 775-2080
Matthew J Pfeffer, *CEO*
Kent Kresa, *Ch of Bd*
Raymond W Urbanski, *Chief Mktg Ofcr*
Michael E Castagna, *Officer*
Linda Adreveno, *Senior VP*
EMP: 146
SQ FT: 142,000
SALES (est): 69.7MM **Publicly Held**
WEB: www.mannkindcorp.com
SIC: 8731 2834 Biotechnical research,
  commercial; pharmaceutical preparations

(P-26565)
MEDICAL TECHNOLOGIES INTL
75145 Saint Charles Pl B, Palm Desert
(92211-9048)
PHONE.................................760 837-4778
Fax: 760 837-4779
Gary Thompson, *President*
Jessica Goldberg, *Admin Asst*
Pam Montellano, *VP Finance*
EMP: 50
SALES (est): 3.2MM **Privately Held**
SIC: 8731 Commercial physical research

(P-26566)
MEMBRANE TECHNOLOGY & RES INC (PA)
Also Called: M T R
39630 Eureka Dr, Newark (94560-4805)
PHONE.................................650 328-2228
Fax: 650 328-6580
Colin Bailey, *Chairman*
Hans Wijmans, *President*
Nicolas Wynn, *COO*
Meryl Rains, *CFO*
Janet Farrant, *Exec VP*
EMP: 68
SQ FT: 60,000
SALES (est): 31.4MM **Privately Held**
WEB: www.mtrinc.com
SIC: 8731 3823 Commercial research laboratory; on-stream gas/liquid analysis instruments, industrial

(P-26567)
MEMORIAL HEALHTEC LABRATORIES
9920 Talbert Ave, Fountain Valley
(92708-5153)
PHONE.................................714 962-4677
Marcia Manker, *Manager*
Debbie Marino, *MIS Dir*
Lori Debold, *Med Doctor*
Susan Worley, *Manager*
Mynor Trinidad, *Supervisor*
EMP: 875
SALES (corp-wide): 2B **Privately Held**
SIC: 8731 Commercial physical research
HQ: Memorial Healhtec Labratories Inc
  2865 Atlantic Ave Ste 203
  Long Beach CA 90806

(P-26568)
MERCEDES-BENZ RE
4035 Via Oro Ave, Long Beach
(90810-1458)
PHONE.................................310 549-7600
John Espeleta, *Branch Mgr*
EMP: 50
SALES (corp-wide): 160.5B **Privately Held**
SIC: 8731 Commercial physical research
HQ: Mercedes-Benz Research & Development North America, Inc.
  309 N Pastoria Ave
  Sunnyvale CA 94085
  650 845-2500

(P-26569)
MIDWEST ENVIROMENTAL CONTROL
22430 13th St, Santa Clarita (91321-1104)
PHONE.................................661 255-0722
Dale Brouhl, *Owner*
EMP: 50
SALES (est): 2.8MM **Privately Held**
SIC: 8731 Environmental research

(P-26570)
MONTEREY BAY AQUARIUM RES INST
Also Called: Mbari
7700 Sandholdt Rd, Moss Landing
(95039-9644)
PHONE.................................831 775-1700
Fax: 831 775-1620
Christopher A Scholin, *President*
Marcia McNutt, *President*
Keith Raybould, *COO*
Dan Chamberlain, *Officer*
Julie Packard, *Vice Pres*
EMP: 220
SQ FT: 17,000
SALES: 47MM **Privately Held**
WEB: www.mbari.org
SIC: 8731 Commercial physical research

(P-26571)
MOTECH AMERICAS LLC
Also Called: GE Energy
1300 Valley Vista Dr # 207, Diamond Bar
(91765-3940)
PHONE.................................302 451-7500
Peng Heng Chang, *CEO*
Eric Kuo, *President*
Dr Alan Wu, *President*
Tiffany Walker, *Analyst*
EMP: 320
SALES (est): 29.4MM
SALES (corp-wide): 761.7MM **Privately Held**
SIC: 8731 3674 Energy research; solar cells
PA: Motech Industries Inc.
  6f, 248, Pei Shen Rd., Sec. 3,
  New Taipei City 22204
  226 625-093

(P-26572)
NATIONAL MARINE FISHERIES SVC
Also Called: Southwest Fsheries Science Ctr
8604 La Jolla Shores Dr, La Jolla
(92037-1508)
PHONE.................................858 546-7081
Fax: 858 546-7000
William W Fox Jr, *Director*
Anne Allen, *Admin Asst*

PRODUCTS & SERVICES SECTION **8731 - Commercial Physical & Biological Research County (P-26592)**

Matthew Bones, *Info Tech Mgr*
Rich Cosgrove, *Analyst*
Milton Lopez, *Manager*
EMP: 150 **Publicly Held**
SIC: 8731 9512 Biological research; land, mineral & wildlife conservation;
HQ: Western Pacific Regional Fishery Management Council
1315 E West Hwy
Silver Spring MD 20910
-

(P-26573)
NEBULA INC
Also Called: Nebula Systems
215 Castro St Fl 3, Mountain View (94041-2821)
PHONE.................................650 539-9900
Gordon Stitt, *CEO*
Chris C Kemp, *CEO*
Herb Schneider, *Senior VP*
Kim Broadbeck, *Vice Pres*
Jon Mittelhauser, *Vice Pres*
EMP: 67
SALES (est): 10.2MM **Privately Held**
WEB: www.nebula.com
SIC: 8731 7373 Computer (hardware) development; computer integrated systems design

(P-26574)
NEOGENOMICS INC
5 Jenner Ste 100, Irvine (92618-3854)
PHONE.................................239 768-0600
Robert Gasparini, *Principal*
Lori Ross, *Manager*
EMP: 209
SALES (corp-wide): 99.8MM **Publicly Held**
SIC: 8731 Biological research
PA: Neogenomics, Inc.
12701 Commwl Dr Ste 9
Fort Myers FL 33913
239 768-0600

(P-26575)
NEUROPACE INC
455 Bernardo Ave, Mountain View (94043-5237)
PHONE.................................650 237-2700
Fax: 650 237-2701
Frank Fischer, *President*
Rebecca Kuhn, *CFO*
Laura Lysen, *CFO*
Isabella Abati, *Vice Pres*
Debra Smolley, *Vice Pres*
EMP: 90
SQ FT: 37,500
SALES (est): 19MM **Privately Held**
WEB: www.neuropace.com
SIC: 8731 Medical research, commercial

(P-26576)
NORTHROP GRMMN SPCE & MSSN SYS
1 Rancho Carmel Dr, San Diego (92128-3403)
PHONE.................................858 592-3000
Rudy Lozano, *Manager*
David Vandervoet, *Vice Pres*
Jerry Wheeler, *Admin Asst*
Gail Hutson, *Administration*
Christopher Love, *Sr Software Eng*
EMP: 1300
SQ FT: 211,000 **Publicly Held**
WEB: www.trw.com
SIC: 8731 8711 7373 3812 Commercial physical research; engineering services; computer integrated systems design; search & navigation equipment
HQ: Northrop Grumman Space & Mission Systems Corp.
6377 San Ignacio Ave
San Jose CA 95119
703 280-2900

(P-26577)
NORTHROP GRMMN SPCE & MSSN SYS
Space Technology Sector
862 E Hospitality Ln, San Bernardino (92408-3530)
PHONE.................................909 382-6800
Fax: 909 382-6249
Bert Yamada, *Branch Mgr*
Bruce Palser, *Comp Spec*

Ron Pipes, *Manager*
EMP: 200 **Publicly Held**
WEB: www.trw.com
SIC: 8731 7373 Commercial physical research; computer integrated systems design
HQ: Northrop Grumman Space & Mission Systems Corp.
6377 San Ignacio Ave
San Jose CA 95119
703 280-2900

(P-26578)
ORBITAL SCIENCES CORPORATION
Also Called: Advanced Programs Group
2401 E El Segundo Blvd # 200, El Segundo (90245-4631)
PHONE.................................703 406-5000
Antonio Elias, *Exec VP*
Brad Bolstad, *General Mgr*
EMP: 500
SALES (corp-wide): 6.8B **Publicly Held**
SIC: 8731 Commercial physical research
HQ: Orbital Sciences Corporation
45101 Warp Dr
Dulles VA 20166
703 406-5000

(P-26579)
OSTENDO TECHNOLOGIES INC (PA)
6185 Paseo Del Norte # 200, Carlsbad (92011-1152)
PHONE.................................760 710-3003
Hussein S El-Ghoroury, *CEO*
Benjamin Haskell, *President*
Joaquin Silva, *President*
Seongsoo Kim, *Vice Pres*
Wayne Lutje, *Vice Pres*
EMP: 52
SQ FT: 10,000
SALES (est): 23.1MM **Privately Held**
WEB: www.ostendotech.com
SIC: 8731 Electronic research

(P-26580)
PALL FORTEBIO CORP
1360 Willow Rd Ste 201, Menlo Park (94025-1524)
PHONE.................................650 322-1360
Fax: 650 322-1370
Joseph D Keegan, *CEO*
Jack H Fuchs, *CFO*
Robert Wicke, *Vice Pres*
Patricia Friedman, *Executive Asst*
Andrey Klishin, *Electrical Engi*
EMP: 94
SALES (est): 17.9MM
SALES (corp-wide): 20.5B **Publicly Held**
WEB: www.fortebio.com
SIC: 8731 Biological research
HQ: Pall Corporation
25 Harbor Park Dr
Port Washington NY 11050
516 484-5400

(P-26581)
PALO ALTO MEDICAL FOUNDATION
Research Institute
795 El Camino Real, Palo Alto (94301-2302)
PHONE.................................650 326-8120
EMP: 50
SALES (corp-wide): 11B **Privately Held**
SIC: 8731 Medical research, commercial
HQ: Palo Alto Medical Foundation For Health Care, Research And Education (Inc)
795 El Camino Real
Palo Alto CA 94301
650 321-4121

(P-26582)
PALO ALTO RESEARCH CENTER INC
Also Called: Parc
3333 Coyote Hill Rd, Palo Alto (94304-1314)
PHONE.................................650 812-4000
Fax: 650 812-4970
Mark Bernstein, *President*
John Knights, *President*
Stephen Hoover, *CEO*

John Pauksta, *CFO*
Jonathan R Wolter, *CFO*
EMP: 250
SQ FT: 200,000
SALES (est): 49.1MM
SALES (corp-wide): 18B **Publicly Held**
WEB: www.parc.com
SIC: 8731 Commercial physical research
PA: Xerox Corporation
45 Glover Ave Ste 700
Norwalk CT 06850
203 968-3000

(P-26583)
PANASONIC CORP NORTH AMERICA
Panasonic Research & Dev
10900 N Tantau Ave 200, Cupertino (95014-0713)
PHONE.................................408 861-3900
Thomas Eccleston, *Branch Mgr*
EMP: 140
SALES (corp-wide): 64.5B **Privately Held**
SIC: 8731 Electronic research
HQ: Panasonic Corporation Of North America
2 Riverfront Plz Ste 200
Newark NJ 07102
201 348-7000

(P-26584)
PAREXEL INTERNATIONAL CORP
1560 E Chevy Chase Dr # 140, Glendale (91206-4197)
PHONE.................................818 254-7076
Mollie Barrett, *Director*
Sabrina Palmateer, *Admin Asst*
Simon Soden, *Info Tech Mgr*
Muhammad Toori, *Software Dev*
Carla Raassi, *Project Mgr*
EMP: 200
SALES (corp-wide): 2.4B **Publicly Held**
SIC: 8731 Commercial physical research
PA: Parexel International Corporation
195 West St
Waltham MA 02451
781 487-9900

(P-26585)
PARSONS GOVERNMENT SVCS INC (HQ)
25531 Commercentre Dr, Lake Forest (92630-8873)
PHONE.................................949 768-8161
Charles L Harrington, *CEO*
Garth Bloxham, *Vice Pres*
Michael Byers, *Vice Pres*
John Dyer, *Vice Pres*
Joe Hidalgo, *Vice Pres*
EMP: 53
SALES (est): 105.2MM
SALES (corp-wide): 7.9B **Privately Held**
WEB: www.sparta.com
SIC: 8731 Commercial physical research
PA: The Parsons Corporation
100 W Walnut St
Pasadena CA 91124
626 440-2000

(P-26586)
PAXVAX INC
3985 Sorrento Valley Blvd A, San Diego (92121-1421)
PHONE.................................858 450-9595
Ali Pina, *Branch Mgr*
EMP: 50
SALES (corp-wide): 15.1MM **Privately Held**
SIC: 8731 Biotechnical research, commercial
PA: Paxvax, Inc.
900 Veterans Blvd Ste 500
Redwood City CA 94063
650 847-1075

(P-26587)
PERLEGEN SCIENCES INC
35473 Dumbarton Ct, Newark (94560-1100)
PHONE.................................650 625-4500
Bradley Margus, *President*
Stephen Fodor, *Ch of Bd*
William W Sims, *CFO*
David R Cox MD, *Officer*
Mark McCamish MD, *Officer*

EMP: 102
SQ FT: 58,000
SALES (est): 7.4MM **Privately Held**
WEB: www.perlegen.com
SIC: 8731 8071 Biotechnical research, commercial; medical laboratories

(P-26588)
PERSONALIS INC
1330 Obrien Dr, Menlo Park (94025-1436)
PHONE.................................650 752-1300
John West, *CEO*
Richard Chen, *Vice Pres*
Michael Fitzpatrick, *Vice Pres*
Carol Tillis, *Vice Pres*
Christian D Haudenschild, *Lab Dir*
EMP: 70
SQ FT: 12,000
SALES (est): 12.5MM **Privately Held**
SIC: 8731 Commercial research laboratory

(P-26589)
PETER H MATTSON & CO INC
383 Vintage Park Dr, Foster City (94404-1135)
PHONE.................................650 356-2500
Steve Gundrum, *President*
Peter H Mattson, *Chairman*
Patricia Mattson, *Corp Secy*
Barbara Stuckey, *Officer*
Samson Hsia, *Vice Pres*
EMP: 70
SQ FT: 20,000
SALES (est): 12.3MM **Privately Held**
WEB: www.protothink.com
SIC: 8731 Food research

(P-26590)
PHYSICAL OPTICS CORPORATION (PA)
1845 W 205th St, Torrance (90501-1510)
PHONE.................................310 320-3088
Fax: 310 320-4667
Joanna Jannson, *CEO*
Min-Yi Shih, *President*
Robert Waldo, *President*
Gajendra Savant, *COO*
Gordon Drew, *CFO*
EMP: 80
SQ FT: 45,000
SALES (est): 53.2MM **Privately Held**
WEB: www.poc.com
SIC: 8731 7299 Commercial physical research; information services, consumer

(P-26591)
PROFIL INST FOR CLNCAL RES INC
855 3rd Ave Ste 4400, Chula Vista (91911-1350)
PHONE.................................619 427-1300
Fax: 619 427-1307
Marcus Hompesch, *CEO*
Linda Morrow, *COO*
Christian Weyer, *Officer*
Abigail Devine, *Associate Dir*
Yeonjoo Kang, *Associate Dir*
EMP: 200
SQ FT: 20,000
SALES (est): 36.4MM
SALES (corp-wide): 51.8MM **Privately Held**
WEB: www.profilinstitute.com
SIC: 8731 Biotechnical research, commercial
PA: Profil Institut Fur Stoffwechselforschung Gmbh
Hellersbergstr. 9
Neuss 41460
213 140-180

(P-26592)
PROMAB BIOTECHNOLOGIES INC
2600 Hilltop Dr, San Pablo (94806-1971)
PHONE.................................510 860-4615
Lijun Wu, *President*
Martyn Lewis, *Manager*
EMP: 80 **EST:** 2001
SALES: 1.5MM **Privately Held**
SIC: 8731 Biological research

8731 - Commercial Physical & Biological Research County (P-26593)

PRODUDUCTS & SERVICES SECTION

(P-26593)
PULSE-LINK INC
2730 Loker Ave W, Carlsbad (92010-6603)
PHONE..................760 496-2136
Fax: 760 607-0861
John Santhoff, *CEO*
Paul Dillon, *President*
Bruce Watkins, *President*
Jeff Torpey, *Controller*
Ivan Krivokapic, *Director*
EMP: 75
SQ FT: 33,000
SALES (est): 6.3MM **Privately Held**
WEB: www.pulselink.net
SIC: 8731 Electronic research

(P-26594)
RAVEN BIOTECHNOLOGIES INC
1 Corporate Dr, South San Francisco (94080-7043)
PHONE..................650 624-2600
Fax: 650 620-9431
George Schreiner, *CEO*
Michael Kranda, *Ch of Bd*
John B Whelan, *COO*
William R Rohn, *Vice Ch Bd*
Lucille W S Chang, *Vice Pres*
EMP: 66
SQ FT: 68,000
SALES (est): 7MM
SALES (corp-wide): 100.8MM **Publicly Held**
WEB: www.ravenbio.com
SIC: 8731 Biotechnical research, commercial; commercial research laboratory
PA: Macrogenics, Inc.
    9704 Medical Center Dr
    Rockville MD 20850
    301 251-5172

(P-26595)
ROCHE MOLECULAR SYSTEMS INC
1145 Atlantic Ave Ste 100, Alameda (94501-1145)
PHONE..................510 814-2800
Fax: 510 522-1285
Terrance Taford, *Branch Mgr*
Tony Le, *Research*
Kristin Aquino, *Asst Director*
EMP: 135
SALES (corp-wide): 47.9B **Publicly Held**
SIC: 8731 Biotechnical research, commercial
HQ: Roche Molecular Systems, Inc.
    4300 Hacienda Dr
    Pleasanton CA 94588
    925 730-8000

(P-26596)
ROCHE MOLECULAR SYSTEMS INC (DH)
4300 Hacienda Dr, Pleasanton (94588-2722)
P.O. Box 9002 (94566-9002)
PHONE..................925 730-8000
Paul Brown, *President*
Frederick C Kentz III, *Admin Sec*
Fidel Fampo, *Software Dev*
Pmp Talluri, *Engineer*
Peter Saladin, *VP Finance*
EMP: 400
SALES (est): 194.4MM
SALES (corp-wide): 47.9B **Publicly Held**
SIC: 8731 Biotechnical research, commercial
HQ: Roche Holdings, Inc.
    1 Dna Way
    South San Francisco CA 94080
    625 225-1000

(P-26597)
SAMSUNG RESEARCH AMERICA INC (DH)
Also Called: Sisa
665 Clyde Ave, Mountain View (94043-2235)
PHONE..................408 544-5700
Fax: 408 544-5924
Young Joon Gil, *President*
Doochan Daniel Eum, *CEO*
Oh-Hyun Kwon, *CEO*
K E Jang, *CFO*
Ju-Hwa Yoon, *CFO*
EMP: 50
SQ FT: 32,000
SALES (est): 74.4MM
SALES (corp-wide): 118.4B **Privately Held**
WEB: www.cnl-samsung.com
SIC: 8731 7371 Computer (hardware) development; computer software development & applications
HQ: Samsung Electronics America, Inc.
    85 Challenger Rd
    Ridgefield Park NJ 07660
    201 229-4000

(P-26598)
SANDCRAFT INC
3003 Bunker Hill Ln # 101, Santa Clara (95054-1144)
PHONE..................925 253-8311
Fax: 408 490-3111
Paul H F Vroomen, *President*
Sidney S Faulkner, *CFO*
Mayank Gupta, *Principal*
Terence Chin, *Engineer*
Ramesh Kunchtham, *Engineer*
EMP: 69
SQ FT: 10,000
SALES (est): 5.6MM **Privately Held**
WEB: www.sandcraft.com
SIC: 8731 Commercial physical research

(P-26599)
SANSA TECHNOLOGY LLC
6232 Murdock Way, San Ramon (94582-5944)
PHONE..................866 204-3710
Sony Prasad,
EMP: 50
SALES (est): 3.8MM **Privately Held**
SIC: 8731 Commercial physical research

(P-26600)
SANTA CRUZ BIOTECHNOLOGY INC
2145 Delaware Ave, Santa Cruz (95060-5706)
PHONE..................831 457-3800
Matt Mullin, *Branch Mgr*
Chris App, *CTO*
Kevin Tran, *Info Tech Mgr*
Shannon Anderson, *Research*
Jennifer Bachman, *Research*
EMP: 80
SALES (corp-wide): 20.8MM **Privately Held**
SIC: 8731 Medical research, commercial
PA: Santa Cruz Biotechnology, Inc.
    10410 Finnell St
    Dallas TX 75220
    214 902-3900

(P-26601)
SCIENTIFIC APPLICATIONS & RES (PA)
Also Called: SARA
6300 Gateway Dr, Cypress (90630-4844)
PHONE..................714 828-1465
Fax: 714 224-1710
Parviz Parhami, *CEO*
James Wes, *President*
William Hutchinson, *Vice Pres*
Michael Zintl, *Program Mgr*
Janet Raska, *Admin Sec*
EMP: 58
SQ FT: 43,000
SALES (est): 27.9MM **Privately Held**
WEB: www.sarainc.com
SIC: 8731 Commercial physical research

(P-26602)
SCRIPPS HEALTH
Scripps Health Research
11025 N Torrey Pines Rd # 200, La Jolla (92037-1030)
PHONE..................858 652-5504
Fax: 858 652-5404
Robert Sarnoff, *Branch Mgr*
Victoria R Thein, *Meeting Planner*
EMP: 108
SALES (corp-wide): 1.7B **Privately Held**
SIC: 8731 Medical research, commercial
PA: Scripps Health
    4275 Campus Point Ct
    San Diego CA 92121
    858 678-7000

(P-26603)
SEMINIS INC
500 Lucy Brown Rd, San Juan Bautista (95045-9713)
PHONE..................831 623-4554
Nancy Bergamini, *Manager*
EMP: 60
SALES (corp-wide): 13.5B **Publicly Held**
WEB: www.seminis.com
SIC: 8731 Agricultural research
HQ: Seminis, Inc.
    2700 Camino Del Sol
    Oxnard CA 93030

(P-26604)
SEMINIS INC (HQ)
2700 Camino Del Sol, Oxnard (93030-7967)
PHONE..................805 485-7317
Fax: 805 918-2542
Bruno Ferrari, *President*
W Paine, *Vice Chairman*
Eugenio N Solorzano, *President*
Andy Kuchan, *CFO*
Charles E Green, *Senior VP*
EMP: 300
SALES (est): 75.4MM
SALES (corp-wide): 13.5B **Publicly Held**
WEB: www.seminis.com
SIC: 8731 8742 2099 Agricultural research; food research; productivity improvement consultant; marketing consulting services; food preparations
PA: Monsanto Company
    800 N Lindbergh Blvd
    Saint Louis MO 63167
    314 694-1000

(P-26605)
SENOMYX INC
4767 Nexus Center Dr, San Diego (92121-3051)
PHONE..................858 646-8300
John Poyhonen, *President*
Kent Snyder, *Ch of Bd*
Antony E Rogers, *CFO*
Donald S Karanewsky, *Senior VP*
Sharon Wicker, *Senior VP*
EMP: 90
SQ FT: 65,000
SALES (est): 24.8MM **Privately Held**
WEB: www.senomyx.com
SIC: 8731 6794 Food research; franchises, selling or licensing

(P-26606)
SEQUENOM INC (HQ)
3595 John Hopkins Ct, San Diego (92121-1121)
PHONE..................858 202-9000
Dirk Van Den Boom, *President*
Carolyn D Beaver, *CFO*
Daniel S Grosu, *Chief Mktg Ofcr*
Jeffrey D Linton, *Senior VP*
Rob Lozuk, *Senior VP*
EMP: 80
SALES: 128.2MM
SALES (corp-wide): 8.6B **Publicly Held**
WEB: www.sequenom.com
SIC: 8731 Biological research
PA: Laboratory Corporation Of America Holdings
    358 S Main St
    Burlington NC 27215
    336 229-1127

(P-26607)
SIMBOL INC (PA)
Also Called: Simbol Materials
6920 Koll Center Pkwy # 216, Pleasanton (94566-3156)
PHONE..................925 226-7400
Luka Erceg, *President*
Darin Redabaugh, *Finance*
EMP: 92
SALES (est): 20.2MM **Privately Held**
SIC: 8731 Natural resource research

(P-26608)
SORRENTO THERAPEUTICS INC (PA)
9380 Judicial Dr, San Diego (92121-3830)
PHONE..................858 210-3700
Fax: 858 210-3759
Henry Ji, *President*
William S Marth, *Ch of Bd*
Jeffrey Su, *COO*
Kevin M Herde, *CFO*
George Ng, *Officer*
EMP: 62 EST: 2006
SQ FT: 43,000
SALES: 4.5MM **Publicly Held**
SIC: 8731 Commercial physical research; biological research

(P-26609)
SPREADTRUM CMMNCATIONS USA INC
10180 Telesis Ct Ste 500, San Diego (92121-2787)
PHONE..................858 546-0895
Daniel Li, *CFO*
Joe Zou, *CTO*
Tiger Xu, *Director*
Shawn Pallard, *Manager*
Ping Wu, *Manager*
EMP: 70
SALES (est): 10.5MM
SALES (corp-wide): 1.4B **Privately Held**
WEB: www.spreadtrum.com
SIC: 8731 Electronic research
PA: Spreadtrum Communications (Shanghai) Co., Ltd.
    Bldg No.1, Lane 2288, Zu Chongzhi Rd., Zhangjiang, Pudong New Ar
    Shanghai 20120
    212 036-0600

(P-26610)
STELLARTECH RESEARCH CORP (PA)
560 Cottonwood Dr, Milpitas (95035-7403)
PHONE..................408 331-3134
Fax: 408 964-5743
Roger A Stern, *President*
Barrett Craner, *Vice Pres*
Jerome Jackson, *Vice Pres*
Jerry Smith, *Vice Pres*
Vincent Sullivan, *Vice Pres*
EMP: 100
SQ FT: 20,000
SALES (est): 34MM **Privately Held**
SIC: 8731 3842 Medical research, commercial; surgical appliances & supplies

(P-26611)
STRATEGY FOR WATER & LAND RESO
49 Donovan, Irvine (92620-3882)
PHONE..................949 572-3034
Douglas Hamilton,
EMP: 50
SALES (est): 1.1MM **Privately Held**
SIC: 8731 Natural resource research

(P-26612)
SUN INNOVATIONS INC
43241 Osgood Rd, Fremont (94539-5657)
PHONE..................510 573-3913
Ted Sun, *President*
EMP: 50
SQ FT: 2,200
SALES (est): 3.2MM **Privately Held**
WEB: www.superimaging.com
SIC: 8731 Commercial physical research

(P-26613)
SUN PHARMACEUTICALS INC
Also Called: Research
13718 Sorbonne Ct, San Diego (92128-4760)
PHONE..................858 380-8865
Meng Sun, *President*
Zuolin Zhu, *CTO*
EMP: 102
SALES (est): 3MM **Privately Held**
SIC: 8731 Biotechnical research, commercial

(P-26614)
SYNTERACTHCR INC (DH)
5759 Fleet St Ste 100, Carlsbad (92008-4710)
PHONE..................760 268-8200
Wendel Barr, *CEO*
Ellen Morgan, *President*
Keith Kelson, *CFO*
Richard Paul, *Chief Mktg Ofcr*
Francisco Harrison, *Exec VP*
EMP: 330

PRODUCTS & SERVICES SECTION **8731 - Commercial Physical & Biological Research County (P-26634)**

SQ FT: 30,000
SALES (est): 87.3MM **Privately Held**
WEB: www.synteract.com
SIC: 8731 Commercial physical research
HQ: Synteracthcr Corporation
5759 Fleet St Ste 100
Carlsbad CA 92008
760 268-8200

(P-26615)
SYNTERACTHCR
CORPORATION (HQ)
5759 Fleet St Ste 100, Carlsbad (92008-4710)
PHONE..................................760 268-8200
Fax: 760 929-1419
Wendel Barr, *CEO*
Stewart Bieler, *President*
Keith Kelson, *CFO*
Matthew Smith, *Senior VP*
Martine Dehlinger-Kremer, *Vice Pres*
EMP: 330 **EST:** 2008
SALES (est): 87.3MM **Privately Held**
SIC: 8731 Commercial physical research
PA: Synteracthcr Holdings Corporation
5759 Fleet St Ste 100
Carlsbad CA 92008
760 268-8200

(P-26616)
SYNTERACTHCR HOLDINGS
CORP (PA)
5759 Fleet St Ste 100, Carlsbad (92008-4710)
PHONE..................................760 268-8200
Wendel Barr, *CEO*
Keith Kelson, *CFO*
Stewart Bieler, *Officer*
Dieter Seitz-Tutter, *Opers Staff*
Matthew Smith, *Opers Staff*
EMP: 350 **EST:** 2008
SALES (est): 87.3MM **Privately Held**
SIC: 8731 Commercial physical research

(P-26617)
SYNTHETIC GENOMICS INC
(DH)
11149 N Torrey Pines Rd, La Jolla (92037-1009)
PHONE..................................858 754-2900
Fax: 858 754-2988
Oliver Fetzer, *CEO*
J Craig Venter, *Ch of Bd*
Aristides Patrinos, *President*
Joseph Mahler, *CFO*
Fernanda Gandara, *Vice Pres*
EMP: 118
SQ FT: 45,000
SALES (est): 57MM
SALES (corp-wide): 4.5K **Privately Held**
WEB: www.syntheticgenomics.com
SIC: 8731 Biotechnical research, commercial
HQ: Genting Plantations Berhad
10th Floor Wisma Genting
Kuala Lumpur KLP
323 336-408

(P-26618)
TAKARA BIO USA INC
Also Called: Clontech Laboratories, Inc.
1290 Terra Bella Ave, Mountain View (94043-1837)
PHONE..................................650 237-5700
Carol Lou, *President*
Leslee McLennan Bonino, *Vice Pres*
Michael Haugwitz, *Associate Dir*
Elizabeth Quinn, *Associate Dir*
Kazuki Yamamoto, *Principal*
EMP: 112
SQ FT: 100,000
SALES (est): 35.4MM
SALES (corp-wide): 1.9B **Privately Held**
WEB: www.clontech.com
SIC: 8731 2836 Biotechnical research, commercial; biological products, except diagnostic
HQ: Takara Bio Inc.
7-4-38, Nojihigashi
Kusatsu SGA 525-0
775 656-920

(P-26619)
TEGILE SYSTEMS INC
7999 Gateway Blvd Ste 120, Newark (94560-1144)
PHONE..................................510 791-7900
Rohit Kshetrapal, *CEO*
James Yu, *President*
Ian Edmundson, *CFO*
Michael Morgan, *CFO*
Narayan Venkat, *Chief Mktg Ofcr*
EMP: 130
SQ FT: 6,500
SALES (est): 29.8MM **Privately Held**
SIC: 8731 3572 Computer (hardware) development; computer storage devices

(P-26620)
TELEDYNE SCENTIFIC IMAGING
LLC
5212 Verdugo Way, Camarillo (93012-8662)
PHONE..................................805 373-4979
Kadri Vural, *Vice Pres*
Dennis Edwall, *Research*
Craig Cabelli, *Technical Staff*
Scott Cabelli, *Engineer*
Vic Evangelista, *Engineer*
EMP: 150
SQ FT: 54,295
SALES (corp-wide): 2.3B **Publicly Held**
SIC: 8731 Commercial physical research
HQ: Teledyne Scientific & Imaging, Llc
1049 Camino Dos Rios
Thousand Oaks CA 91360
-

(P-26621)
TELEDYNE SCENTIFIC IMAGING
LLC (HQ)
Also Called: Teledyne Imaging Sensors
1049 Camino Dos Rios, Thousand Oaks (91360-2362)
PHONE..................................805 373-4545
Robert Mehrabian,
Jagmohan Bajaj, *President*
Tucker Grant, *Officer*
Lisa Porter, *Senior VP*
Bertrand Bovard, *Vice Pres*
EMP: 225
SQ FT: 161,000
SALES (est): 95.4MM
SALES (corp-wide): 2.3B **Publicly Held**
WEB: www.teledyne-si.com
SIC: 8731 8732 8733 Commercial physical research; commercial nonphysical research; noncommercial research organizations
PA: Teledyne Technologies Inc
1049 Camino Dos Rios
Thousand Oaks CA 91360
805 373-4545

(P-26622)
TERRAVIA HOLDINGS INC (PA)
225 Gateway Blvd, South San Francisco (94080-7019)
PHONE..................................650 780-4777
Fax: 650 989-6700
Jonathan S Wolfson, *CEO*
Jerry Fiddler, *Ch of Bd*
Tyler W Painter, *COO*
Cameron Byers, *Senior VP*
Troy J Campione, *Senior VP*
EMP: 148
SQ FT: 106,000
SALES: 46.1MM **Publicly Held**
WEB: www.solazyme.com
SIC: 8731 2836 2844 2869 Biotechnical research, commercial; biological products, except diagnostic; toilet preparations; fuels

(P-26623)
TRI ALPHA ENERGY INC
27121 Towne Centre Dr # 150, Foothill Ranch (92610-2825)
P.O. Box 7010, Rcho STA Marg (92688-7010)
PHONE..................................949 830-2117
Dale Prouty, *President*
Michl Binderbauer, *Vice Pres*
Chad Davis, *Controller*
EMP: 100
SALES (est): 17.3MM **Privately Held**
SIC: 8731 Energy research

(P-26624)
TRILINK BIOTECHNOLOGIES
INC
9955 Mesa Rim Rd, San Diego (92121-2911)
PHONE..................................858 546-0004
Fax: 858 546-0020
Richard Hogrefe, *President*
Terry Beck, *Senior VP*
Debbie Rigler, *Admin Asst*
Jenn Chall, *Accountant*
Lisa Olivier, *Mktg Dir*
EMP: 72
SQ FT: 40,000
SALES (est): 12.8MM **Privately Held**
WEB: www.trilinkbiotech.com
SIC: 8731 8748 Biotechnical research, commercial; biological research; test development & evaluation service

(P-26625)
TRUESDAIL LABORATORIES
INC
3337 Michelson Dr, Irvine (92612-1699)
PHONE..................................714 730-6239
Fax: 714 730-6462
Ed Wilson, *CEO*
John Hill, *President*
Brian K Service, *Chairman*
Anthony Fontana, *Info Tech Mgr*
Sanjay Ray, *Director*
EMP: 50 **EST:** 1931
SQ FT: 40,000
SALES: 4.8MM **Privately Held**
WEB: www.truesdail.com
SIC: 8731 8734 1711 Commercial physical research; water testing laboratory; plumbing contractors

(P-26626)
UNITED STATES DEPT OF
ENERGY
1 Cyclotron Rd, Berkeley (94720-8099)
PHONE..................................510 486-4936
Fax: 510 486-7192
EMP: 2351 **Publicly Held**
SIC: 8731
HQ: United States Dept Of Energy
1000 Independence Ave Sw
Washington DC 20585
202 586-5000

(P-26627)
UNITED STATES DEPT OF
ENERGY
Also Called: Lawrence Livermore Nat Lab
7000 East Ave, Livermore (94550-9698)
P.O. Box 808 (94551-0808)
PHONE..................................925 422-1100
Fax: 925 423-3597
EMP: 7000 **Publicly Held**
SIC: 8731 9611
HQ: United States Dept Of Energy
1000 Independence Ave Sw
Washington DC 20585
202 586-5000

(P-26628)
UNITED STATES DEPT OF NAVY
Also Called: Naval Research
937 N Harbor Dr, San Diego (92132-5001)
PHONE..................................619 532-1897
Erickson Gary, *Branch Mgr*
EMP: 50 **Publicly Held**
SIC: 8731 9711 Commercial physical research; Navy;
HQ: United States Department Of The Navy
1200 Navy Pentagon
Washington DC 20350
703 545-6700

(P-26629)
UNITED STATES DEPT OF NAVY
Also Called: Naval Research Lab
7 Grace Hopper Ave Stop 2, Monterey (93943-5598)
PHONE..................................831 656-4613
Fax: 831 656-4489
Phillip Merilees, *Branch Mgr*
Don Cunningham, *Administration*
EMP: 64 **Publicly Held**
SIC: 8731 9711 Commercial physical research; Navy;

HQ: United States Department Of The Navy
1200 Navy Pentagon
Washington DC 20350
703 545-6700

(P-26630)
UNIVERSITY SOUTHERN
CALIFORNIA
1000 S Fremont Ave Unit 7, Alhambra (91803-8897)
PHONE..................................626 457-4240
Mary Ann Pentz, *Director*
Mario Galdamez, *Associate Dir*
Laura Navarette, *Manager*
EMP: 100
SALES (corp-wide): 4.7B **Privately Held**
WEB: www.usc.edu
SIC: 8731 8221 Medical research, commercial; university
PA: University Of Southern California
3720 S Flower St Fl 3
Los Angeles CA 90007
213 740-7762

(P-26631)
US DEPT OF THE AIR FORCE
Also Called: Chem Lab Rkfe
10 E Saturn Dr, Edwards (93524-7201)
PHONE..................................661 275-5410
Joan Larue, *Manager*
Buddy R Bocock, *Engineer*
EMP: 85 **Publicly Held**
WEB: www.af.mil
SIC: 8731 9711 Chemical laboratory, except testing; Air Force;
HQ: United States Department Of The Air Force
1000 Air Force Pentagon
Washington DC 20330
703 545-6700

(P-26632)
USDA FOREST SERVICE
4955 Canyon Crest Dr, Riverside (92507-6071)
PHONE..................................951 680-1560
Fax: 909 276-6426
Irene Powell, *Administration*
EMP: 75 **Publicly Held**
WEB: www.defendtheforests.org
SIC: 8731 9512 Environmental research; land conservation agencies;
HQ: Usda Forest Service
201 14th St Sw
Washington DC 20024
-

(P-26633)
VENTURE DESIGN SERVICES
INC (PA)
1051 S East St, Anaheim (92805-5749)
PHONE..................................714 765-3740
Wong Ngit Liong, *Chairman*
Tan Kian Seng, *President*
E H SOO, *CEO*
Bernie Chong, *CFO*
Soin Sign, *Treasurer*
EMP: 66
SQ FT: 60,000
SALES (est): 15.7MM **Privately Held**
SIC: 8731 Commercial physical research

(P-26634)
VERINATA HEALTH INC
Also Called: Illumina-Redwood City
800 Saginaw Dr, Redwood City (94063-4740)
PHONE..................................650 632-1680
Jeff Bird, *CEO*
Vance Vanier, *President*
Suzanne Yokota, *Vice Pres*
Lito Carbonel, *Technology*
Elizabeth Kerr, *VP Mktg*
EMP: 55
SQ FT: 16,800
SALES (est): 7.2MM
SALES (corp-wide): 2.2B **Publicly Held**
WEB: www.livingmicrosystems.com
SIC: 8731 2835 Biotechnical research, commercial; in vitro & in vivo diagnostic substances
PA: Illumina, Inc.
5200 Illumina Way
San Diego CA 92122
858 202-4500

8731 - Commercial Physical & Biological Research County (P-26635)

PRODUDUCTS & SERVICES SECTION

(P-26635)
VERTEX PHRMCTCALS SAN DEGO LLC (HQ)
11010 Torreyana Rd, San Diego (92121-1103)
PHONE 858 404-6600
Fax: 858 404-6726
Joshua S Boger,
Peter Coassin, *Vice Pres*
Pam Fritz, *Vice Pres*
Erik Bradbury, *Controller*
Jeff Barbee, *Opers Mgr*
EMP: 235
SQ FT: 81,000
SALES (est): 19.4MM
SALES (corp-wide): 1B **Publicly Held**
SIC: 8731 Biological research
PA: Vertex Pharmaceuticals Incorporated
50 Northern Ave
Boston MA 02210
617 341-6100

(P-26636)
VIA COMMUNICATIONS INC
940 Mission Ct, Fremont (94539-8202)
PHONE 510 687-4650
Wen-CHI Chen, *CEO*
Jonathan Chang, *CFO*
EMP: 250
SQ FT: 3,300
SALES (est): 9.1MM **Privately Held**
SIC: 8731 Computer (hardware) development

(P-26637)
VIRIDENT SYSTEMS INC
1745 Tech Dr Ste 700, San Jose (95110)
PHONE 408 573-5000
Mike Gustafson, *Senior VP*
Bruce Horn, *CFO*
Mark Delsman, *Vice Pres*
Terrence Flynn, *Vice Pres*
Kumar Ganapathy, *Vice Pres*
EMP: 110
SALES (est): 18.6MM
SALES (corp-wide): 12.9B **Publicly Held**
SIC: 8731 Computer (hardware) development
HQ: Hgst, Inc.
3403 Yerba Buena Rd
San Jose CA 95135
800 801-4618

(P-26638)
WESTON SOLUTIONS INC
5817 Dryden Pl Ste 101, Carlsbad (92008-5576)
PHONE 760 795-6900
Lisa Marie Kay, *Branch Mgr*
Bruce Ferguson, *Officer*
Andrea Crumpacker, *Opers Mgr*
Michelle Patzius, *Manager*
EMP: 65
SALES (corp-wide): 518.2MM **Privately Held**
WEB: www.rfweston.com
SIC: 8731 Environmental research
HQ: Weston Solutions, Inc.
1400 Weston Way
West Chester PA 19380
610 701-3000

(P-26639)
WILLOW GARAGE INC
921 E Charleston Rd, Palo Alto (94303-4903)
PHONE 650 322-2584
Scott Wendell Hassan, *CEO*
Steve Cousins, *President*
Bob Bauer, *Exec Dir*
Suzanne Dunn, *Research*
Ryan Bahadur, *Mfg Dir*
EMP: 59
SQ FT: 10,000
SALES (est): 6.1MM **Privately Held**
SIC: 8731 Electronic research

(P-26640)
ZYMO RESEARCH CORP
17062 Murphy Ave, Irvine (92614-5914)
PHONE 949 679-1190
Fax: 714 288-9643
Xiyu Jia MD, *President*
LI Zhang, *Shareholder*
Michelle Rabot, *General Mgr*
Onyi Chima, *Human Res Mgr*
Diana Jia, *Marketing Staff*
EMP: 57
SQ FT: 10,000
SALES (est): 10.3MM **Privately Held**
WEB: www.zymoresearch.com
SIC: 8731 Biotechnical research, commercial; medical research, commercial

8732 Commercial Economic, Sociological & Educational Research

(P-26641)
ACCESS INTELLIGENCE LLC
SRI Consulting Division
3975 Freedom Cir Ste 300, Santa Clara (95054-1242)
PHONE 650 384-4300
Fax: 650 330-1190
John Pearson, *Senior VP*
Ping Jiang, *CFO*
Russell Heinen, *Vice Pres*
Michael Hogsett, *CTO*
Marcelo Hoffmann, *Info Tech Mgr*
EMP: 60
SALES (corp-wide): 95MM **Privately Held**
WEB: www.accessintel.com
SIC: 8732 8731 Market analysis or research; commercial physical research
PA: Access Intelligence Llc
9211 Corp Blvd Fl 4
Rockville MD 20850
301 354-2000

(P-26642)
ADEPT CONSUMER TESTING INC
16130 Ventura Blvd # 200, Encino (91436-2580)
PHONE 310 279-4600
Fax: 310 285-0925
Mark Tobias, *President*
EMP: 50
SQ FT: 12,000
SALES (est): 6.4MM **Privately Held**
WEB: www.adeptconsumer.com
SIC: 8732 Market analysis or research

(P-26643)
AMER ZOETROPE RESEARCH LLC
1991 Saint Helana Hwy, Rutherford (94573)
P.O. Box 208 (94573-0208)
PHONE 707 963-9230
Jay Shoemaker, *President*
EMP: 150
SALES (est): 4.7MM **Privately Held**
SIC: 8732 Market analysis or research

(P-26644)
BANK AMERICA NATIONAL ASSN
555 California St Ste 4, San Francisco (94104-1532)
PHONE 415 913-3438
John Walter, *Senior VP*
Hatem Amdouni, *Project Mgr*
EMP: 100
SALES (corp-wide): 93B **Publicly Held**
WEB: www.bofa.com
SIC: 8732 Business analysis
HQ: Bank Of America, National Association
101 S Tryon St
Charlotte NC 28280
704 386-5681

(P-26645)
BAY ALARM COMPANY
9836 Kitty Ln, Oakland (94603-1070)
PHONE 510 452-3211
Fax: 510 834-4174
Delores Nielsen, *Manager*
Alex Ledesma, *Marketing Staff*
Jonathan Mealley, *Marketing Staff*
Laurie Santos, *Marketing Staff*
Scott Hoppe, *Manager*
EMP: 81
SALES (corp-wide): 160.6MM **Privately Held**
WEB: www.bayalarm.com
SIC: 8731 7382 5063 Commercial nonphysical research; electrical work; security systems services; electrical apparatus & equipment
PA: Bay Alarm Company
60 Berry Dr
Pacheco CA 94553
925 935-1100

(P-26646)
BERKELEY RESEARCH GROUP LLC
2049 Century Park E # 2525, Los Angeles (90067-3225)
PHONE 310 499-4750
Fax: 310 557-8982
David Teece, *Chairman*
EMP: 74 **Privately Held**
SIC: 8732 Research services, except laboratory
PA: Berkeley Research Group, Llc
2200 Powell St Ste 1200
Emeryville CA 94608

(P-26647)
BUSINESS INDEX GROUP INC
Also Called: National Shopping Service
2510 Warren Dr, Rocklin (95677-2176)
PHONE 916 577-1010
Matt Wozniak, *President*
Nerrissa Coleman, *Vice Pres*
Tony Yorba, *Vice Pres*
Shawn Grant, *Business Mgr*
Britney Eason, *Opers Mgr*
EMP: 50
SALES (est): 3MM **Privately Held**
WEB: www.nationalshoppingservice.com
SIC: 8732 7389 Market analysis or research; brokers, business: buying & selling business enterprises

(P-26648)
CAPITOL CORPORATE SERVICES
455 Capitol Mall Ste 217, Sacramento (95814-4405)
PHONE 916 444-6787
John H Robinson, *Vice Pres*
Cheryl Roberts, *President*
Tess Sartel, *Manager*
EMP: 50
SALES (est): 4.7MM **Privately Held**
WEB: www.capitolcorporateservices.com
SIC: 8732 Research services, except laboratory

(P-26649)
CIC RESEARCH INC
8361 Vickers St Ste 308, San Diego (92111-2112)
PHONE 858 637-4000
Fax: 858 637-4040
Gordon H Kubota PHD, *President*
Janet Muller, *Treasurer*
Joyce G Revlett, *Vice Pres*
Warren L Hull, *Admin Sec*
Randy Landis, *Admin Sec*
EMP: 65 EST: 1965
SQ FT: 15,000
SALES (est): 3.1MM **Privately Held**
WEB: www.cicresearch.com
SIC: 8732 Economic research; market analysis or research

(P-26650)
COHERENT INC
1100 La Avenida St, Mountain View (94043-1452)
PHONE 408 764-4000
Richard Pierce, *CEO*
Keith Morton, *Senior VP*
John H N Fisher, *Principal*
Mike Mielke, *Security Dir*
Steve P Sapers, *VP Opers*
EMP: 82
SQ FT: 42,000
SALES (est): 15.9MM **Privately Held**
WEB: www.raydiance-inc.com
SIC: 8732 3826 3821 Research services, except laboratory; laser scientific & engineering instruments; laser beam alignment devices

(P-26651)
COMPETITIVE EDGE RES COMM INC
2170 4th Ave, San Diego (92101-2110)
PHONE 619 702-2372
Fax: 619 702-2272
John E Nienstedt, *President*
Steve Danon, *Vice Pres*
Shari Ciancio, *Office Mgr*
Ken Luce, *Opers Staff*
Jacques Ballard, *Manager*
EMP: 60
SQ FT: 4,000
SALES: 1.5MM **Privately Held**
WEB: www.cerc.net
SIC: 8732 Opinion research

(P-26652)
CORNERSTONE RESEARCH INC
633 W 5th St Fl 31, Los Angeles (90071-2005)
PHONE 213 553-2500
Fax: 213 553-2699
Jeanene Maclean, *Admin Asst*
Maria Rivas, *Admin Asst*
Jordan Finley, *Administration*
Stacy Johnson, *Technician*
Sonia Lara, *Technician*
EMP: 103
SALES (corp-wide): 99.2MM **Privately Held**
SIC: 8732 Market analysis, business & economic research
PA: Cornerstone Research, Inc.
1000 El Camino Real # 250
Menlo Park CA 94025
650 853-1660

(P-26653)
DAS GLOBAL CAPITAL CORP
42 Peninsula Ctr Ste 317, Rlng HLS Est (90274-3506)
PHONE 702 967-1688
EMP: 59 **Privately Held**
SIC: 8732 Merger, acquisition & reorganization research
PA: Das Global Capital Corp
1785 E Sahara Ave Ste 490
Las Vegas NV 89104

(P-26654)
DAVIS RESEARCH LLC
23801 Calabasas Rd # 1036, Calabasas (91302-3319)
PHONE 818 591-2408
William A Davis III, *Mng Member*
Robert Davis,
EMP: 150
SQ FT: 16,000
SALES (est): 8MM **Privately Held**
WEB: www.davisresearch.com
SIC: 8732 Market analysis or research

(P-26655)
DECIPHER INC (HQ)
7 E River Park Pl E # 110, Fresno (93720-1669)
PHONE 559 436-6940
Fax: 559 436-6944
Jamin Brazil, *President*
Kristin Luck, *President*
Ian Duffield, *COO*
Ian Staller, *COO*
Jeffrey Bergman, *CFO*
EMP: 60
SQ FT: 13,000
SALES (est): 12.5MM
SALES (corp-wide): 37.1MM **Privately Held**
WEB: www.decipherinc.com
SIC: 8732 Economic research
PA: Focusvision Worldwide, Inc.
1266 E Main St Ste 3
Stamford CT 06902
203 961-1715

(P-26656)
DIRECTLINE TECHNOLOGIES INC
1600 N Carpenter Rd, Modesto (95351-1185)
PHONE 209 491-2020
Fax: 209 491-2091

PRODUCTS & SERVICES SECTION
8732 - Commercial Economic, Sociological & Educational Research County (P-26677)

Martha Connor, *CEO*
Gary Connor, *Admin Sec*
Marian De Ramos-Maverro, *Accountant*
EMP: 75
SQ FT: 9,000
SALES (est): 2.8MM **Privately Held**
WEB: www.directline-tech.com
SIC: 8732 Market analysis or research

(P-26657)
DSG ASSOCIATES INC
15500 Erwin St Ste 4007, Van Nuys (91411-1010)
PHONE..........................714 835-3020
Donna Guido, *CEO*
Mike Guido, *President*
Robert Tenney, *Network Mgr*
Jennifer Mason, *Opers Staff*
EMP: 50
SQ FT: 6,700
SALES (est): 2.8MM **Privately Held**
WEB: www.dsgai.com
SIC: 8732 Market analysis, business & economic research

(P-26658)
ECKER CONSUMER RECRUITING INC (PA)
Also Called: Ecker & Associates
1303 Melbourne St, Foster City (94404-3739)
PHONE..........................650 871-6800
Fax: 650 871-6815
Leon Ecker, *President*
Bette Rosenthal, *Vice Pres*
EMP: 50
SQ FT: 5,300
SALES: 2.5MM **Privately Held**
WEB: www.eckersf.com
SIC: 8732 Opinion research

(P-26659)
ELECTRONIC ENTRMT DESIGN & RES
Also Called: Eedar
2075 Corte Del Nogal B, Carlsbad (92011-1413)
PHONE..........................760 579-7100
Gregory Short, *CEO*
Geoffrey Zatkin, *President*
Paul Matthys, *Vice Pres*
EMP: 53
SQ FT: 11,000
SALES (est): 4.9MM **Privately Held**
WEB: www.eedar.com
SIC: 8732 Market analysis or research

(P-26660)
ERNEST GALLO CLINIC & RES CTR
5980 Horton St Ste 370, Emeryville (94608-2058)
PHONE..........................510 985-3856
Fax: 510 648-7116
Raymond L White PHD, *President*
Randy Soares, *CFO*
John De Luca, *Chairman*
William Sawyers, *Vice Pres*
Steve Lum, *Info Tech Mgr*
EMP: 115
SQ FT: 87,200
SALES: 1.4MM **Privately Held**
WEB: www.gallo.ucsf.edu
SIC: 8732 8731 Commercial nonphysical research; commercial physical research

(P-26661)
EXIMEX INC
503 Beacon Pl, Chula Vista (91910-7503)
PHONE..........................619 585-1327
Fax: 619 585-8799
Homero Reyes, *President*
Rose M Reyes, *Vice Pres*
EMP: 70
SALES (est): 4.2MM **Privately Held**
SIC: 8732 Market analysis, business & economic research

(P-26662)
FLEISCHMAN FIELD RESEARCH INC
250 Sutter St Fl 2, San Francisco (94108-4462)
P.O. Box 641620 (94164-1620)
PHONE..........................415 398-4140
Fax: 415 989-4506
Molly Fleischman, *President*
Andrew Fleischman, *CEO*
EMP: 130
SALES (est): 8.9MM **Privately Held**
WEB: www.ffrsf.com
SIC: 8732 Market analysis or research

(P-26663)
FRANCE TELECOM RES & DEV LLC
Also Called: Orange Labs
60 Spear St Ste 1100, San Francisco (94105-1599)
PHONE..........................415 284-9765
Fax: 650 875-1505
Elie Girard,
Xavier Pichon, *CFO*
Gilles Coullon, *Officer*
Sylvie Raby, *Officer*
Christian Luginbuhl, *Senior VP*
EMP: 65
SALES (est): 15.5MM
SALES (corp-wide): 25.3B **Privately Held**
WEB: www.francetelecom.com
SIC: 8732 Commercial nonphysical research
PA: Orange
78 Rue Olivier De Serres
Paris Cedex 15 75505
144 442-222

(P-26664)
FRANK N MAGID ASSOCIATES INC
15260 Ventura Blvd # 1840, Sherman Oaks (91403-5379)
PHONE..........................818 263-3300
Brent Magid, *Owner*
Tyler Goetz, *Research*
Aaron Hoffman, *Analyst*
EMP: 70 EST: 2001
SALES (est): 3.9MM **Privately Held**
SIC: 8732 Market analysis or research

(P-26665)
FRANK N MAGID ASSOCIATES INC
15260 Vntr Blvd Ste 1840, Sherman Oaks (91403)
PHONE..........................818 263-3300
Fax: 818 263-3311
Frank N Magid, *Branch Mgr*
EMP: 105
SALES (corp-wide): 30.5MM **Privately Held**
SIC: 8732 Commercial nonphysical research
PA: Frank N. Magid Associates, Inc.
1 Research Ctr
Marion IA 52302
319 377-7349

(P-26666)
FROST & SULLIVAN
3211 Scott Blvd Ste 203, Santa Clara (95054-3009)
PHONE..........................650 475-4500
Wyman Bravard, *Principal*
EMP: 75
SALES (corp-wide): 255.1MM **Privately Held**
WEB: www.frost.com
SIC: 8732 Commercial nonphysical research
PA: Frost & Sullivan
7550 W Ih 10 Ste 400
San Antonio TX 78229
210 348-1000

(P-26667)
GFK CUSTOM RESEARCH LLC
360 Pine St Fl 6, San Francisco (94104-3226)
PHONE..........................415 398-2812
Xiaoyan Zhao, *Branch Mgr*
Erik Andersen, *Senior VP*
Rob Hernandez, *Senior VP*
Robert Benford, *Vice Pres*
Suzanne Davis, *Vice Pres*
EMP: 54
SALES (corp-wide): 2.1MM **Privately Held**
WEB: www.gfknop.com
SIC: 8732 8713 Market analysis or research; surveying services

HQ: Gfk Custom Research, Llc
200 Liberty St Fl 4
New York NY 10281
212 240-5300

(P-26668)
GFK CUSTOM RESEARCH LLC
879 W 190th St Ste 390, Gardena (90248-4229)
PHONE..........................310 527-2100
Fax: 310 523-2996
Donna Miller, *Senior VP*
Maikel Verhaaren, *Director*
EMP: 112
SALES (corp-wide): 2.1MM **Privately Held**
SIC: 8732 Market analysis or research
HQ: Gfk Custom Research, Llc
200 Liberty St Fl 4
New York NY 10281
212 240-5300

(P-26669)
GFK ETILIZE INC
18662 Macarthur Blvd # 200, Irvine (92612-1285)
PHONE..........................888 608-1212
Azhar Hameed, *President*
Pervaiz Khan, *COO*
Sawera Khan, *Officer*
Sherry Frederick, *Vice Pres*
Adnan Memon, *Technology*
EMP: 54
SQ FT: 4,000
SALES (est): 4.5MM
SALES (corp-wide): 2.1MM **Privately Held**
WEB: www.etilize.com
SIC: 8732 Market analysis or research
HQ: Gfk North America Holding Gmbh
Nordwestring 101
Nurnberg
911 395-0

(P-26670)
GLASS LEWIS & CO LLC (HQ)
1 Sansome St Fl 33, San Francisco (94104-4436)
PHONE..........................415 678-4110
Katherine Rabin, *CEO*
John Wieck, *COO*
Robert McCormick,
Kathy Appuhn, *Officer*
Kevin Ferguson, *Senior VP*
EMP: 60
SALES (est): 21.4MM
SALES (corp-wide): 14.2B **Privately Held**
WEB: www.glasslewis.com
SIC: 8732 Business analysis
PA: Ontario Teachers' Pension Plan Board
5650 Yonge St Suite 300
North York ON M2M 4
416 228-5900

(P-26671)
GLOBAL INDUSTRY ANALYSTS INC
6150 Hellyer Ave Ste 100, San Jose (95138-1072)
PHONE..........................408 528-9966
Fax: 408 528-9977
Kalakoti S Reddy, *CEO*
EMP: 700
SALES (est): 29.5MM **Privately Held**
WEB: www.sisinfotech.com
SIC: 8732 Market analysis or research

(P-26672)
HANLEY WOOD MKT INTELLIGENCE (HQ)
Also Called: Meyers Group
555 Anton Blvd Ste 950, Costa Mesa (92626-7811)
PHONE..........................714 540-8500
Jeff Meyers, *CEO*
Tom Flynn, *President*
Shawn Dacy, *Associate*
EMP: 55
SALES (est): 6.4MM
SALES (corp-wide): 193.5MM **Privately Held**
SIC: 8732 Market analysis, business & economic research

PA: Hw Holdco Llc
1 Thomas Cir Nw Ste 600
Washington DC 20005
202 452-0800

(P-26673)
HONDA R&D AMERICAS INC
7514 Reseda Blvd, Reseda (91335-2820)
PHONE..........................818 345-7922
David Colby, *Branch Mgr*
Kerry Crutchfield, *Finance Mgr*
Chet Bredemeir, *Controller*
Randy Gauvin, *Manager*
EMP: 50
SALES (corp-wide): 124.7B **Privately Held**
WEB: www.hra.com
SIC: 8732 Market analysis or research
HQ: Honda R&D Americas, Inc.
1900 Harpers Way
Torrance CA 90501
310 781-5500

(P-26674)
IBISWORLD INC (DH)
11755 Wilshire Blvd # 1100, Los Angeles (90025-1549)
PHONE..........................800 330-3772
Phil Ruthven, *Chairman*
Justin Ruthven, *President*
Jason Baker, *COO*
Harvey Jones, *COO*
Kerryn Ruthven, *Vice Pres*
EMP: 71
SALES (est): 17.6MM **Privately Held**
SIC: 8732 Market analysis or research
HQ: Ibisworld Pty Ltd
L 3 1 Collins St
Melbourne VIC 3000
396 553-800

(P-26675)
INTERVIEWING SERVICE AMER INC (PA)
Also Called: I S A
15400 Sherman Way Fl 4, Van Nuys (91406-4271)
PHONE..........................818 989-1044
Arnold Fishman, *Chairman*
Michael Halberstam, *President*
Tony Kretzmer, *COO*
Jesse Galvez, *CFO*
Daniel Gascoyne, *Exec VP*
EMP: 680
SQ FT: 20,000
SALES (est): 57.4MM **Privately Held**
SIC: 8732 Market analysis, business & economic research

(P-26676)
INTERVIEWING SERVICE AMER INC
200 S Grfield Ave Ste 302, Alhambra (91801)
PHONE..........................626 979-4140
Kelly Simmoms, *Manager*
EMP: 100
SALES (corp-wide): 57.4MM **Privately Held**
SIC: 8732 Market analysis, business & economic research
PA: Interviewing Service Of America, Inc.
15400 Sherman Way Fl 4
Van Nuys CA 91406
818 989-1044

(P-26677)
IPSOS PUBLIC AFFAIRS INC
3402 N Blackstone Ave, Fresno (93726-5395)
PHONE..........................559 451-2820
Jorge Zelada, *Branch Mgr*
EMP: 111
SALES (corp-wide): 451.8K **Privately Held**
SIC: 8732 Business economic service
HQ: Ipsos Public Affairs, Inc.
222 S Riverside Plz # 350
Chicago IL 60606
312 526-4000

8732 - Commercial Economic, Sociological & Educational Research County (P-26678)   PRODUDUCTS & SERVICES SEC-

(P-26678)
J PAUL GETTY TRUST
Also Called: Getty Conservation Institute
1200 Getty Center Dr # 400, Los Angeles
(90049-1657)
PHONE..................310 440-7325
Tim Wayland, *Branch Mgr*
EMP: 70
SALES (corp-wide): 117.5MM **Privately Held**
SIC: 8732 Commercial nonphysical research
PA: The J Paul Getty Trust
   1200 Getty Center Dr # 500
   Los Angeles CA 90049
   310 440-7300

(P-26679)
JD POWER AND ASSOCIATES (PA)
3200 Park Center Dr Fl 13, Costa Mesa
(92626-7163)
PHONE..................714 621-6200
Finbarr O'Neill, *President*
Deirdre Borrego, *Exec VP*
Gary Tucker, *Senior VP*
Deidre Borrego, *Vice Pres*
Frances Caille, *Vice Pres*
EMP: 250
SQ FT: 45,000
SALES (est): 161.3MM **Privately Held**
WEB: www.jdpower.com
SIC: 8732 Survey service: marketing, location, etc.

(P-26680)
KELLY SLATER WAVE COMPANY LLC
3300 La Cienega Pl, Los Angeles
(90016-3117)
PHONE..................310 202-9283
Kelly Slater,
Noah Grimmett, *General Mgr*
Jeff Bizzack,
Terry Hardy,
EMP: 50
SALES (est): 2.4MM **Privately Held**
SIC: 8732 Commercial nonphysical research

(P-26681)
LELAND STANFORD JUNIOR UNIV
Stanf CNT Rsch & Ds Prntn
1070 Arastradero Rd # 100, Palo Alto
(94304-1336)
PHONE..................650 723-6254
Steven Fortmann, *Director*
EMP: 163
SALES (corp-wide): 1.9B **Privately Held**
SIC: 8732 8221 Educational research; university
PA: Leland Stanford Junior University
   2575 Sand Hill Rd
   Menlo Park CA 94025
   650 723-2300

(P-26682)
LELAND STANFORD JUNIOR UNIV
476 Lomita Mall, Palo Alto (94305-4008)
PHONE..................650 723-7546
EMP: 300
SALES (corp-wide): 1.9B **Privately Held**
SIC: 8732 8221 Educational research; university
PA: Leland Stanford Junior University
   2575 Sand Hill Rd
   Menlo Park CA 94025
   650 723-2300

(P-26683)
LIEBERMAN RES WORLDWIDE INC (PA)
1900 Ave Of The Sts 160 Ste 1600, Los Angeles (90067)
PHONE..................310 553-7721
Fax: 310 553-4607
David Sackman, *President*
Arnold Fishman, *Ch of Bd*
Nancy Alfaro, *Research*
Kristin Caiella, *Research*
Nicholas Christiansen, *Research*
EMP: 140 EST: 1973
SQ FT: 24,560
SALES (est): 45.1MM **Privately Held**
WEB: www.lrwonline.com
SIC: 8732 Market analysis or research

(P-26684)
LOS ANGELES BIO MED RES INST
1124 W Carson St Rm 5l2, Torrance
(90502-2006)
PHONE..................310 222-3604
Fax: 310 533-6972
Eli Ipp, *Principal*
EMP: 50
SALES: 75MM **Privately Held**
SIC: 8732 Research services, except laboratory

(P-26685)
LUTH RESEARCH INC (PA)
Also Called: Surveysavvy.com
1365 4th Ave, San Diego (92101-4208)
PHONE..................619 234-5884
Fax: 619 234-5888
Roseanne Luth, *President*
Charles Rosen, *Exec VP*
Becky Wu, *Vice Pres*
Candice Rab, *VP Bus Dvlpt*
Sean Miller, *Managing Dir*
EMP: 305
SQ FT: 15,000
SALES (est): 57.5MM **Privately Held**
WEB: www.luthresearch.com
SIC: 8732 Market analysis or research

(P-26686)
MARITZCX RESEARCH LLC
3901 Via Oro Ave Ste 200, Long Beach
(90810-1800)
PHONE..................310 525-1300
Christopher Gerth, *Branch Mgr*
Lucero Rodriguez, *Sales Dir*
EMP: 526
SALES (corp-wide): 1.2B **Privately Held**
SIC: 8732 Commercial nonphysical research
HQ: Maritzcx Research Llc
   1355 N Highway Dr
   Fenton MO 63026
   636 827-4000

(P-26687)
MARKETSHARE PARTNERS LLC (HQ)
11150 Santa Monica Blvd # 500, Los Angeles (90025-0480)
PHONE..................310 914-5677
Fax: 310 914-5155
Wes Nichols,
Anupam Singh, *President*
Dirk Beyer, *Exec VP*
Jeanette Carlsson, *Exec VP*
Ivan Markman, *Exec VP*
EMP: 54
SQ FT: 3,000
SALES (est): 12.1MM
SALES (corp-wide): 1B **Publicly Held**
WEB: www.marketsharepartners.com
SIC: 8732 Market analysis, business & economic research
PA: Neustar, Inc.
   21575 Ridgetop Cir
   Sterling VA 20166
   571 434-5400

(P-26688)
MCCANN-ERICKSON USA INC
Also Called: McKann World Group
600 Battery St Fl 1, San Francisco
(94111-1834)
PHONE..................415 262-5600
Mike Parsons, *Branch Mgr*
Joe Burton, *COO*
Whitman Jon, *Creative Dir*
Elizabeth Tranzillo, *Database Admin*
Kaersten Hill, *Accounting Mgr*
EMP: 200
SALES (corp-wide): 7.6B **Publicly Held**
SIC: 8732 7311 Market analysis or research; advertising agencies
HQ: Mccann-Erickson Usa, Inc.
   622 3rd Ave Fl 16
   New York NY 10017
   646 865-2000

(P-26689)
MICHAEL A MECZKA
5757 W Century Blvd # 120, Los Angeles
(90045-6401)
PHONE..................310 670-4824
Michael A Meczka, *President*
Dona Browne, *Vice Pres*
EMP: 50
SALES (est): 2MM **Privately Held**
WEB: www.mmrcinc.com
SIC: 8732 Commercial nonphysical research

(P-26690)
MILLWARD BROWN LLC
2425 Olympic Blvd 240e, Santa Monica
(90404-4076)
PHONE..................310 309-3352
Fax: 310 309-3401
Nile Rowan, *Branch Mgr*
Alex Creed, *Director*
EMP: 50
SALES (corp-wide): 18.4B **Privately Held**
SIC: 8732 Market analysis or research
HQ: Millward Brown, Llc
   11 Madison Ave Ste 1200
   New York NY 10010
   212 548-7200

(P-26691)
MILLWARD BROWN LLC
Also Called: Millward Brown International
6500 Wilshire Blvd # 460, Los Angeles
(90048-4920)
PHONE..................323 966-5770
Fax: 323 653-1150
Mike Moloney, *Vice Pres*
EMP: 78
SQ FT: 1,000
SALES (corp-wide): 18.4B **Privately Held**
WEB: www.us.millwardbrown.com
SIC: 8732 Market analysis or research
HQ: Millward Brown, Llc
   11 Madison Ave Ste 1200
   New York NY 10010
   212 548-7200

(P-26692)
MONTEREY COUNTY OFFICE EDUCATN
Technology Information Svcs
901 Blanco Cir, Salinas (93901-4401)
PHONE..................831 755-0324
Dave Paulson, *CTO*
Barry Brown, *Executive*
Jessica Herfurth, *Executive Asst*
Linda Sweet, *Executive Asst*
Maricela Cruz, *Admin Asst*
EMP: 94
SALES (corp-wide): 51.3MM **Privately Held**
SIC: 8732 7374 Educational research; computer processing services
PA: Monterey County Office Of Education
   901 Blanco Cir
   Salinas CA 93901
   831 755-0301

(P-26693)
NATIONAL RESEARCH GROUP INC
6255 W Sunset Blvd Fl 19, Los Angeles
(90028-7420)
PHONE..................323 817-2000
Eric Dale, *CEO*
Michael Flamberg, *Research*
Scott Crowley, *Engineer*
Michael McLean, *Engineer*
Sarah Miller, *Engineer*
EMP: 400
SALES (est): 23.5MM
SALES (corp-wide): 43.6K **Privately Held**
WEB: www.nrg.com
SIC: 8732 Market analysis or research; business research service
HQ: The Nielsen Company Us Llc
   85 Broad St
   New York NY 10004

(P-26694)
NIELSEN COMPANY (US) LLC
Also Called: Nielsen Media Research
6255 W Sunset Blvd Fl 20, Los Angeles
(90028-7405)
PHONE..................323 817-2000
Tom Borys, *Manager*
EMP: 400
SALES (corp-wide): 43.6K **Privately Held**
WEB: www.nielsenmedia.com
SIC: 8732 Market analysis or research
HQ: The Nielsen Company Us Llc
   85 Broad St
   New York NY 10004

(P-26695)
NIELSEN COMPANY (US) LLC
5375 Mira Sorrento Pl # 400, San Diego
(92121-3809)
PHONE..................858 677-9542
Teri Jacobson, *Branch Mgr*
Keith Peterson, *COO*
Hugo Borda, *Vice Pres*
Doug Diem, *Vice Pres*
Mark Nelson, *Vice Pres*
EMP: 127
SALES (corp-wide): 43.6K **Privately Held**
SIC: 8732 Market analysis or research
HQ: The Nielsen Company Us Llc
   85 Broad St
   New York NY 10004

(P-26696)
NITTO DENKO TECHNICAL CORP
501 Via Del Monte, Oceanside
(92058-1251)
PHONE..................760 435-7011
Kenji Matsumoto, *President*
Mehrdad Tabrizi, *Principal*
Jesse D Froehlich, *Research*
Brett T Harding, *Research*
Amane Mochizuki, *Research*
EMP: 100
SALES (est): 18.4MM
SALES (corp-wide): 6.7B **Privately Held**
WEB: www.nitto.co.jp
SIC: 8732 3089 3462 Commercial nonphysical research; automotive parts, plastic; automotive & internal combustion engine forgings
PA: Nitto Denko Corporation
   4-20, Ofukacho, Kita-Ku
   Osaka OSK 530-0
   676 322-101

(P-26697)
NOVOZYMES INC (DH)
Also Called: Novo Nordisk Biotech
1445 Drew Ave, Davis (95618-4880)
PHONE..................530 757-8100
Peder Holk Nielsen, *CEO*
Ejner B Jensen, *President*
Maarit Pokkinen, *CFO*
Julia Waterson, *Executive Asst*
Kieu Le, *Info Tech Mgr*
EMP: 83
SQ FT: 64,000
SALES (est): 27.4MM
SALES (corp-wide): 2B **Privately Held**
WEB: www.novozymesbiotech.com
SIC: 8732 Commercial nonphysical research
HQ: Novozymes North America, Inc.
   77 Perry Chapel Church Rd
   Franklinton NC 27525
   919 494-2014

(P-26698)
PACIFICA KATIE AVENUE LLC
1775 Hancock St Ste 100, San Diego
(92110-2035)
PHONE..................619 296-9000
Deepak Israni,
Alison Shovlain, *Executive Asst*
EMP: 80
SALES (est): 5.7MM **Privately Held**
SIC: 8732 Merger, acquisition & reorganization research

PRODUCTS & SERVICES SECTION
8733 - Noncommercial Research Organizations County (P-26721)

(P-26699)
PROSEARCH STRATEGIES INC
3250 Wilshire Blvd # 301, Los Angeles (90010-1577)
PHONE..................213 355-1260
Julia Kim Hasenzahl, *Owner*
Ken Graulich, *President*
Michael Gamelin, *Administration*
Bryan D Corlett, *Project Mgr*
Lisa K Douglas, *Project Mgr*
EMP: 50
SALES (est): 11.4MM **Privately Held**
SIC: 8732 Research services, except laboratory

(P-26700)
QUINTILES PACIFIC INCORPORATED (DH)
448 E Middlefield Rd, Mountain View (94043-4006)
PHONE....................650 567-2000
Joe Colintino, *President*
John Sneed, *Director*
EMP: 50
SQ FT: 13,500
SALES (est): 15.2MM
SALES (corp-wide): 5.7B **Publicly Held**
SIC: 8732 Research services, except laboratory
HQ: Quintiles Transnational Corp.
4820 Emperor Blvd
Durham NC 27703
919 998-2000

(P-26701)
QURI INC
475 Brannan St Ste 400, San Francisco (94107-5421)
PHONE....................888 886-8423
Justin Behar, *CEO*
John Mecklenburg, *COO*
Anna Lo, *Software Engr*
Alex Rockwell, *Software Engr*
Karishma Barua, *Accounts Mgr*
EMP: 50
SALES (est): 5MM **Privately Held**
SIC: 8732 Market analysis or research

(P-26702)
RDP ACQUISITION COMPANY
Also Called: Dreyers Grnd Ice Cream Hldings
5929 College Ave, Oakland (94618-1325)
PHONE....................510 652-8187
Gary T Rogers, *Principal*
EMP: 350
SALES (est): 5.8MM
SALES (corp-wide): 88.3B **Privately Held**
SIC: 8732 Merger, acquisition & reorganization research
HQ: Dreyer's Grand Ice Cream Holdings, Inc.
5929 College Ave
Oakland CA 94618
510 652-8187

(P-26703)
REDHILL GROUP INC
Also Called: SCR
18010 Sky Park Cir # 275, Irvine (92614-6487)
PHONE....................949 752-5900
Fax: 949 752-2900
Mark McCourt, *President*
Judith McCourt, *Vice Pres*
Linda Weinberger, *QA Dir*
John Slocovich, *Project Mgr*
Ryan Mak, *Research Analys*
EMP: 61
SQ FT: 4,000
SALES (est): 5.8MM **Privately Held**
WEB: www.redhillgroup.com
SIC: 8732 Market analysis or research

(P-26704)
RETAILNEXT INC
845 Market St Ste 450, San Francisco (94103-1938)
PHONE....................408 298-2585
EMP: 150
SALES (corp-wide): 60.3MM **Privately Held**
SIC: 8732 Market analysis or research
PA: Retailnext, Inc.
60 S Market St Ste 1000
San Jose CA 95113
408 884-2162

(P-26705)
S K & A INFORMATION SVCS INC (DH)
Also Called: SK&a
2601 Main St Ste 650, Irvine (92614-4228)
PHONE....................949 476-2051
David Escalante Jr, *President*
Al M Cosentino, *CFO*
Manus Gallagher, *Vice Pres*
Daphne Nguyen, *Exec Dir*
Dan Ortlip, *MIS Dir*
EMP: 87
SQ FT: 12,000
SALES (est): 11.9MM
SALES (corp-wide): 65.3MM **Privately Held**
WEB: www.skainfo.com
SIC: 8732 Market analysis or research
HQ: Cegedim Inc.
1425 Us Highway 206
Bedminster NJ 07921
908 443-2000

(P-26706)
SMARTREVENUECOM INC
101 Cooper St Ste 205, Santa Cruz (95060-4526)
PHONE....................203 733-9156
John Dranow, *CEO*
EMP: 655
SALES (corp-wide): 44.1MM **Privately Held**
SIC: 8732 Commercial nonphysical research
PA: Smartrevenue.Com, Inc.
60 Twin Ridge Rd
Ridgefield CT 06877
203 733-9156

(P-26707)
SOLEIL COMMUNICATIONS LLC
Also Called: Prodata Research
2655 Camino Dl Rio N 11 Ste 110, San Diego (92108)
PHONE....................619 624-2888
Michael Gehrig, *Mng Member*
John Lewis,
EMP: 70
SALES (est): 6.2MM
SALES (corp-wide): 119.4MM **Privately Held**
SIC: 8732 Market analysis or research
PA: The Welk Group Inc
8860 Lawrence Welk Dr
Escondido CA 92026
760 749-3000

(P-26708)
SUNING CMMERCE R D CTR USA INC
845 Page Mill Rd, Palo Alto (94304-1011)
PHONE....................650 834-9800
Jin Ming, *President*
Jingxi Wang, *General Mgr*
EMP: 60
SQ FT: 9,800
SALES (est): 5.8MM
SALES (corp-wide): 21.3B **Privately Held**
SIC: 8732 Commercial nonphysical research
PA: Suning Commerce Group Co.,Ltd.
No.1, Suning Avenue, Xuanwu District
Nanjing 21004
256 699-6699

(P-26709)
SURVEY SAMPLING INTL LLC
Also Called: Instantly
16501 Ventura Blvd # 300, Encino (91436-2007)
PHONE....................866 872-4006
EMP: 200
SALES (corp-wide): 188.3MM **Privately Held**
SIC: 8732 Market analysis or research; market analysis, business & economic research; survey service: marketing, location, etc.
PA: Survey Sampling International, Llc
6 Research Dr Ste 200
Shelton CT 06484
203 225-6191

(P-26710)
SYSTEM SOLDING (USA) INC
2301 E Del Amo Blvd, Compton (90220-6304)
PHONE....................310 608-5588
Chunming Li, *President*
Tony WEI, *Manager*
EMP: 52
SALES (est): 8.9MM **Privately Held**
SIC: 8732 Market analysis or research

(P-26711)
TECHAISLE LLC
5053 Doyle Rd Ste 105, San Jose (95129-4228)
PHONE....................408 253-4416
Anurag Agrawal,
Arun Mishra, *Managing Dir*
Lavanya Agrawal, *Info Tech Mgr*
Gitika Bajaj, *Research*
EMP: 50
SALES: 172K **Privately Held**
WEB: www.techaisle.com
SIC: 8732 Market analysis or research

(P-26712)
TIGER ANALYTICS LLC
2701 Patrick Henry Dr Bldg 16, Santa Clara (95054)
PHONE....................408 508-4430
Mahesh Kumar,
Pooja Agarwal, *Manager*
EMP: 60 **EST:** 2012
SALES: 2.3MM **Privately Held**
SIC: 8732 Business analysis

(P-26713)
TOSHIBA EDUCATION CENTER
9740 Irvine Blvd, Irvine (92618-1608)
PHONE....................949 583-3000
Ted Flati, *Principal*
Jim Magness, *COO*
Lisa Cortes, *Vice Pres*
Kathy Wilbur, *Vice Pres*
Jon Arvik, *Business Dir*
EMP: 84
SALES (est): 8.5MM
SALES (corp-wide): 48.4B **Privately Held**
WEB: www.tams.com
SIC: 8732 Educational research
HQ: Toshiba America Medical Systems Inc
2441 Michelle Dr
Tustin CA 92780
714 730-5000

(P-26714)
TRENDSOURCE INC
Also Called: Examine Your Practice
4891 Pacific Hwy Ste 200, San Diego (92110-4026)
PHONE....................619 718-7467
Rodney Moll, *Chairman*
Bob Post, *COO*
Neil A Wykes, *CFO*
Michelle Foley, *VP Finance*
Jaime Sandoval, *Mktg Dir*
EMP: 57
SQ FT: 7,500
SALES (est): 9.5MM **Privately Held**
WEB: www.trendsource.com
SIC: 8732 Market analysis, business & economic research

(P-26715)
TROTTA ASSOCIATES
13160 Mindanao Way # 100, Marina Del Rey (90292-7900)
PHONE....................310 306-6866
Fax: 310 827-5198
Diane Trotta, *CEO*
Allyce Chappell, *Project Dir*
Rebecca Hanner, *Project Dir*
Allyce Marshall, *Project Dir*
EMP: 80
SALES (est): 7.7MM **Privately Held**
SIC: 8732 Market analysis or research

(P-26716)
UNIV OF CA
1156 High St, Santa Cruz (95064-1077)
PHONE....................831 459-5041
Donald Smith, *Manager*
Deb Culmer, *Office Mgr*
Jerry Cabak, *Administration*
Christopher Ratliff, *Engineer*
Wally Goldfrank, *Teacher*
EMP: 105
SALES (est): 9.7MM **Privately Held**
SIC: 8732 Commercial nonphysical research

(P-26717)
US MKTG PROMOTIONS AGCY INC
4721 Alla Rd, Marina Del Rey (90292-6311)
PHONE....................310 754-3000
Simon Temperley, *President*
Jennifer Henry, *Controller*
EMP: 50
SALES (est): 4.1MM
SALES (corp-wide): 15.1B **Publicly Held**
WEB: www.uspmagency.com
SIC: 8732 8742 7311 Market analysis or research; marketing consulting services; advertising consultant
HQ: Das Holdings, Inc.
437 Madison Ave
New York NY 10022
212 415-3700

(P-26718)
VERANCE CORPORATION
10089 Willow Creek Rd, San Diego (92131-1697)
PHONE....................858 202-2800
Linesh Shah, *CEO*
Clifford Friedman, *Ch of Bd*
F Mario Petrocco, *CFO*
Dr Joe Winograd, *Exec VP*
Greg Hampton, *Senior VP*
EMP: 65
SALES (est): 8.6MM **Privately Held**
WEB: www.verance.com
SIC: 8732 Research services, except laboratory

(P-26719)
WELK GROUP INC
6150 Micaion Gorge Rd 1 Ste 140, San Diego (92120)
PHONE....................619 516-7800
EMP: 345
SALES (corp-wide): 119.4MM **Privately Held**
SIC: 8732 Market analysis or research
PA: The Welk Group Inc
8860 Lawrence Welk Dr
Escondido CA 92026
760 749-3000

(P-26720)
XDBS CORPORATION
Also Called: Xdbsb2b
3501 Jack Northrop Ave, Hawthorne (90250-4433)
PHONE....................302 566-3006
Kartik Anand, *CEO*
EMP: 100
SQ FT: 4,000
SALES (est): 3.6MM **Privately Held**
SIC: 8732 7389 5963 8742 Survey service: marketing, location, etc.; telemarketing services; direct sales, telemarketing; sales (including sales management) consultant

---

8733 Noncommercial Research Organizations

(P-26721)
ACADIA PHARMACEUTICALS INC (PA)
3611 Valley Centre Dr # 300, San Diego (92130-3331)
PHONE....................858 558-2871
Fax: 858 558-2872
Stephen R Davis, *President*
Stephen R Biggar, *Ch of Bd*
Todd S Young, *CFO*
Terrence O Moore, *Ch Credit Ofcr*
Bill Keller, *Chief Mktg Ofcr*
EMP: 128
SQ FT: 51,000
SALES: 61K **Publicly Held**
WEB: www.acadia-pharm.com
SIC: 8733 2834 Noncommercial research organizations; pharmaceutical preparations

8733 - Noncommercial Research Organizations County (P-26722)   PRODUDUCTS & SERVICES SECTION

(P-26722)
AEROSPACE CORPORATION (PA)
2310 E El Segundo Blvd, El Segundo (90245-4609)
P.O. Box 92957, Los Angeles (90009-2957)
PHONE..................310 336-5000
Fax: 310 336-1433
Dr Wanda M Austin, *President*
Wanda M Austin, *President*
Ellen M Beatty, *CFO*
Barbara M Barrett, *Chairman*
Thomas Oconnor, *Treasurer*
EMP: 2313 EST: 1960
SQ FT: 1,167,251
SALES: 916.6MM **Privately Held**
SIC: 8733 8731 8711 Scientific research agency; commercial physical research; engineering services

(P-26723)
AEROSPACE CORPORATION
2745 E Sherman Ave, Orange (92869-3216)
PHONE..................714 248-1194
EMP: 345
SALES (corp-wide): 916.6MM **Privately Held**
SIC: 8733 Noncommercial research organizations
PA: The Aerospace Corporation
2310 E El Segundo Blvd
El Segundo CA 90245
310 336-5000

(P-26724)
AEROSPACE CORPORATION
P.O. Box 5068 (93437-0068)
PHONE..................805 320-9599
Fax: 805 606-2003
William Sandberg, *Branch Mgr*
Matthew Ogan, *Project Engr*
EMP: 99
SALES (corp-wide): 916.6MM **Privately Held**
SIC: 8733 Noncommercial research organizations
PA: The Aerospace Corporation
2310 E El Segundo Blvd
El Segundo CA 90245
310 336-5000

(P-26725)
AEROSPACE CORPORATION
3171 Grangemount Rd, Glendale (91206)
PHONE..................818 952-6075
Milton F Pope, *Branch Mgr*
EMP: 345
SALES (corp-wide): 916.6MM **Privately Held**
SIC: 8733 Noncommercial research organizations
PA: The Aerospace Corporation
2310 E El Segundo Blvd
El Segundo CA 90245
310 336-5000

(P-26726)
AEROSPACE CORPORATION
624 N Guadalupe Ave, Redondo Beach (90277-2953)
PHONE..................310 374-8866
Robert W Hosken, *Branch Mgr*
EMP: 99
SALES (corp-wide): 916.6MM **Privately Held**
SIC: 8733 Noncommercial research organizations
PA: The Aerospace Corporation
2310 E El Segundo Blvd
El Segundo CA 90245
310 336-5000

(P-26727)
AEROSPACE CORPORATION
2009 Harkness St, Manhattan Beach (90266-4112)
PHONE..................310 336-1025
Joe Barger, *Branch Mgr*
EMP: 345
SALES (corp-wide): 916.6MM **Privately Held**
SIC: 8733 Noncommercial research organizations

PA: The Aerospace Corporation
2310 E El Segundo Blvd
El Segundo CA 90245
310 336-5000

(P-26728)
AFFYMAX RESEARCH INSTITUTE
4001 Miranda Ave, Palo Alto (94304-1218)
PHONE..................650 812-8700
Fax: 650 424-0832
Gordon Ringold PHD, *CEO*
Lauren Stevens, *President*
Mark Thompson, *CFO*
Helen S Kim, *Officer*
Emily Lee Kelly, *Vice Pres*
EMP: 50
SQ FT: 103,000
SALES (est): 3.8MM **Privately Held**
SIC: 8733 8732 8731 Medical research; commercial nonphysical research; commercial physical research

(P-26729)
AIR FORCE US DEPT OF
Also Called: Aerospace Federally Funded RES
2310 E El Segundo Blvd, El Segundo (90245-4609)
PHONE..................310 336-5000
EMP: 391 **Publicly Held**
SIC: 8733 9711 Noncommercial research organizations; Air Force;
HQ: United States Department Of The Air Force
1000 Air Force Pentagon
Washington DC 20330
703 545-6700

(P-26730)
AIR FORCE US DEPT OF
Also Called: Project Air Force
1776 Main St, Santa Monica (90401-3208)
PHONE..................310 393-0411
EMP: 391 **Publicly Held**
SIC: 8733 9711 Noncommercial research organizations; Air Force;
HQ: United States Department Of The Air Force
1000 Air Force Pentagon
Washington DC 20330
703 545-6700

(P-26731)
AKELA PHARMA INC
11011 Torreyana Rd 100, San Diego (92121-1104)
PHONE..................512 391-3525
Rudy Emmelot, *President*
Seth E Lemler, *Ch of Bd*
Fr D Ric Dumais, *Vice Pres*
Jeff Laforce, *Finance Dir*
EMP: 50 EST: 2008
SALES (est): 5.5MM **Privately Held**
SIC: 8733 Noncommercial research organizations

(P-26732)
AMERICAN CANCER SOC CAL DIV (PA)
1001 Marina Village Pkwy, Alameda (94501-1091)
PHONE..................510 893-7900
Fax: 510 465-0535
Carolyn F Katzin, *CEO*
Marilyn Broussard, *CFO*
David Veneziano, *Bd of Directors*
Marilyn Brossard, *Vice Pres*
Cathy Chenard, *Vice Pres*
▲ EMP: 100
SQ FT: 47,000
SALES (est): 36.7MM **Privately Held**
SIC: 8733 Noncommercial research organizations

(P-26733)
AMERICAN INSTITUTE OF AERONAUT
3198 E Fox Run Way, San Diego (92111-7721)
PHONE..................619 545-3736
Keith Glassman, *Principal*
EMP: 99

SALES (est): 3.3MM **Privately Held**
SIC: 8733 Noncommercial research organizations

(P-26734)
AMERICAN INSTITUTE RESEARCH
2151 River Plaza Dr # 320, Sacramento (95833-3881)
PHONE..................916 286-8800
EMP: 329
SALES (corp-wide): 488.3MM **Privately Held**
SIC: 8733 Noncommercial social research organization
PA: American Institutes For Research In The Behavioral Sciences
1000 Thmas Jfferson St Nw
Washington DC 20007
202 403-5000

(P-26735)
AMERICAN INSTITUTE RESEARCH
2800 Campus Dr Ste 200, San Mateo (94403-2555)
PHONE..................650 843-8100
Jennifer O'Day, *Branch Mgr*
EMP: 78
SALES (corp-wide): 488.3MM **Privately Held**
SIC: 8733 8742 Noncommercial research organizations; management consulting services
PA: American Institutes For Research In The Behavioral Sciences
1000 Thmas Jfferson St Nw
Washington DC 20007
202 403-5000

(P-26736)
AMGEN PHARMACEUTICALS INC
1 Amgen Center Dr, Thousand Oaks (91320-1799)
PHONE..................805 447-1000
Gordon Binder, *President*
Kevin Wilcox, *Senior Mgr*
EMP: 4200
SALES (corp-wide): 21.6B **Publicly Held**
SIC: 8733 Biotechnical research, noncommercial
PA: Amgen Inc.
1 Amgen Center Dr
Thousand Oaks CA 91320
805 447-1000

(P-26737)
ATK SPACE SYSTEMS INC
Also Called: Space Components Division
7130 Miramar Rd Ste 100b, San Diego (92121-2340)
PHONE..................858 621-5700
Doan La, *Manager*
EMP: 300
SALES (corp-wide): 6.8B **Publicly Held**
SIC: 8733 Scientific research agency
HQ: Atk Space Systems Inc.
6033 Bandini Blvd
Commerce CA 90040
323 722-0222

(P-26738)
BECKMAN RESEARCH INST HOPE
1500 Duarte Rd, Duarte (91010-3012)
PHONE..................626 359-8111
Michael A Friedman, *CEO*
Robert Stone, *President*
Harlan Levine, *CEO*
William Sargeant, *COO*
Terry Blackwood, *CFO*
EMP: 250
SALES: 298.9MM **Privately Held**
SIC: 8733 Medical research

(P-26739)
BRENTWOOD BMDICAL RES INST INC
11301 Wilshire Blvd, Los Angeles (90073-1003)
P.O. Box 25027 (90025-0027)
PHONE..................310 312-1554
Kenneth Hickman, *CEO*

Thoyd Ellis, *CFO*
Zenaida Feliciano, *Cardiovascular*
EMP: 130
SQ FT: 1,500
SALES: 10.3MM **Privately Held**
SIC: 8733 Noncommercial biological research organization

(P-26740)
BUCK INST FOR RES ON AGING (PA)
8001 Redwood Blvd, Novato (94945-1400)
PHONE..................415 209-2000
Brian K Kennedy, *CEO*
Dale Bredesen MD, *President*
Maryann Sinkkonen, *Treasurer*
Mary McEachron, *Officer*
Raja Kamal, *Senior VP*
EMP: 148
SQ FT: 185,000
SALES (est): 34.6MM **Privately Held**
SIC: 8733 Medical research

(P-26741)
CALIFORNIA INSTITUTE TECH (PA)
Also Called: CALTECH
1200 E California Blvd, Pasadena (91125-0001)
PHONE..................626 395-6811
Fax: 626 795-4571
Chameau A Jean-Lou, *President*
Kent Kresa, *Ch of Bd*
Robert L O'Rourke, *President*
Edward M Stolper, *President*
Daniel I Meron, *CFO*
EMP: 3908
SQ FT: 2,600,000
SALES: 2.3B **Privately Held**
WEB: www.caltech.edu
SIC: 8733 Research institute

(P-26742)
CALIFRNIA INST FOR BMDICAL RES
11119 N Torrey Pines Rd, La Jolla (92037-1046)
PHONE..................858 242-1000
Peter G Schultz, *Director*
EMP: 110
SQ FT: 6,320
SALES: 18.3MM **Privately Held**
SIC: 8733 Biotechnical research, noncommercial

(P-26743)
CANCER PREVENTION INST CAL (PA)
Also Called: CPIC
2201 Walnut Ave Ste 300, Fremont (94538-2334)
PHONE..................510 608-5000
Fax: 510 608-5095
Donna M Randall, *CEO*
Reed Goertler, *COO*
Jay Yu, *Vice Pres*
Debroah Rubie,
Don Neilsen, *Exec Dir*
EMP: 115 EST: 1974
SQ FT: 33,598
SALES: 15MM **Privately Held**
SIC: 8733 Medical research

(P-26744)
CANJI INC
3525 John Hopkins Ct, San Diego (92121-1121)
PHONE..................858 597-0177
Steven Chang, *Vice Pres*
Donald R Conklin, *Ch of Bd*
Raul E Cesan, *President*
Joseph C Conners, *Exec VP*
Thomas H Kelly, *Exec VP*
EMP: 78
SQ FT: 48,000
SALES (est): 1.6MM
SALES (corp-wide): 39.5B **Publicly Held**
WEB: www.canji.com
SIC: 8733 Biotechnical research, noncommercial
PA: Merck & Co., Inc.
2000 Galloping Hill Rd
Kenilworth NJ 07033
908 740-4000

PRODUCTS & SERVICES SECTION
8733 - Noncommercial Research Organizations County (P-26766)

(P-26745)
CAPRION PROTEOMICS USA LLC
1455 Adams Dr Ste 2124, Menlo Park (94025-1438)
P.O. Box 16044, San Francisco (94116-0044)
PHONE..................................650 470-2300
Martin Leblanc, *CEO*
Dr Daniel Chelsky, *Principal*
Suman Gupta, *Director*
Andrew Zwiebel, *Director*
EMP: 50
SALES (est): 5.3MM
SALES (corp-wide): 3MM **Privately Held**
SIC: 8733 Scientific research agency
PA: Caprion Proteomique Inc
   201 Av Du President-Kennedy Bureau 3900
   Montreal QC H2X 3
   514 360-3600

(P-26746)
CARNEGIE INSTITUTION WASH
Also Called: Observatories of The Carnegie
813 Santa Barbara St, Pasadena (91101-1232)
PHONE..................................626 577-1122
Fax: 626 795-8136
Wendy L Freedman, *Director*
Sonia Ochoa, *Purch Mgr*
Elsa Luna, *Manager*
EMP: 100
SQ FT: 24,075
SALES (corp-wide): 126.6MM **Privately Held**
WEB: www.gl.ciw.edu
SIC: 8733 7999 Scientific research agency; observation tower operation
PA: Carnegie Institution Of Washington
   1530 P St Nw
   Washington DC 20005
   202 387-6400

(P-26747)
CARNEGIE INSTITUTION WASH
Also Called: Department of Global Ecology
260 Panama St, Stanford (94305-4150)
PHONE..................................650 319-8904
Chris Field, *Director*
Lee Evana, *Accountant*
EMP: 139
SALES (corp-wide): 126.6MM **Privately Held**
SIC: 8733 Scientific research agency
PA: Carnegie Institution Of Washington
   1530 P St Nw
   Washington DC 20005
   202 387-6400

(P-26748)
CATHOLIC CHARITIES OF LA INC (PA)
1531 James M Wood Blvd, Los Angeles (90015-1112)
P.O. Box 15095 (90015-0095)
PHONE..................................213 251-3400
Fax: 213 251-3400
Monsignor G Cox, *Exec Dir*
James E Bathker, *CFO*
John Gutierrez, *CFO*
Ronald Lopez, *Officer*
Sarah Elder, *Vice Pres*
EMP: 85
SQ FT: 18,000
SALES: 29MM **Privately Held**
SIC: 8733 8322 Noncommercial research organizations; individual & family services

(P-26749)
CELERA CORPORATION (HQ)
33608 Ortega Hwy, San Juan Capistrano (92675-2042)
PHONE..................................510 749-4200
Fax: 510 749-6200
Kathy Ordoez, *CEO*
Mathew J Budoff, *Co-Owner*
Timothy Brandon, *COO*
Kim Lickteig, *CFO*
H R Superko MD, *Officer*
EMP: 119
SQ FT: 48,000
SALES (est): 74.5MM
SALES (corp-wide): 7.4B **Publicly Held**
SIC: 8733 8731 Scientific research agency; commercial physical research

PA: Quest Diagnostics Incorporated
   3 Giralda Farms
   Madison NJ 07940
   973 520-2700

(P-26750)
CENTER FOR CIVIC EDUCATION (PA)
5115 Douglas Fir Rd Ste J, Calabasas (91302-2590)
PHONE..................................818 591-9321
Fax: 818 591-9330
Charles N Quigley, *Exec Dir*
James B Heredia, *CFO*
Michael Fischer, *Executive*
John Hale, *Associate Dir*
N Quigley, *Exec Dir*
EMP: 60
SQ FT: 16,000
SALES: 1.1MM **Privately Held**
WEB: www.civiced.org
SIC: 8733 8748 Educational research agency; educational consultant

(P-26751)
CENTRAL CALIFORNIA TR
22847 Road 140, Tulare (93274-9367)
PHONE..................................559 686-4973
Fax: 559 686-5496
Marylou Polek, *Prgrmr*
Vic Corkins, *Chairman*
Dean Gillette, *Admin Sec*
Jill Barnier, *Manager*
EMP: 55
SQ FT: 12,500
SALES: 1.6MM **Privately Held**
WEB: www.cctea.org
SIC: 8733 Bacteriological research

(P-26752)
CHILDRENS HOSP OKLAND RES INST
5700 Martin Luther, Oakland (94609)
PHONE..................................510 450-7600
Antonie H Paap, *President*
Jenison Soriano, *Receiver*
Suzanne Haendel, *Officer*
Barbara Swiatkiewicz, *Lab Dir*
Betsy Lathrop, *Administration*
EMP: 100
SALES (est): 10.1MM
SALES (corp-wide): 178.6MM **Privately Held**
SIC: 8733 Scientific research agency
PA: Children's Hospital & Research Center At Oakland
   747 52nd St
   Oakland CA 94609
   510 428-3000

(P-26753)
CHILDRENS INST LOS ANGELES (PA)
2121 W Temple St, Los Angeles (90026-4915)
PHONE..................................213 385-5100
Mary Emmons, *Principal*
EMP: 150
SALES: 790.3K **Privately Held**
SIC: 8733 Noncommercial research organizations

(P-26754)
COMPLETE GENOMICS INC
2071 Stierlin Ct, Mountain View (94043-4655)
PHONE..................................650 943-2800
Clifford A Reid PHD, *Ch of Bd*
Ajay Bansal, *CFO*
Keith Raffel, *Ch Credit Ofcr*
Radoje Drmanac, *Officer*
Arthur W Homan, *Senior VP*
EMP: 255
SQ FT: 66,000
SALES (est): 69MM **Privately Held**
SIC: 8733 Biotechnical research, noncommercial
PA: Bgi Research
   Building 11, Beishan Industrial Zone, Yantian District
   Shenzhen
   755 252-7381

(P-26755)
EMOR CONSULTING INC
1570 Heritage Bay Dr, San Jose (95138-2751)
P.O. Box 612551 (95161-2551)
PHONE..................................408 505-0453
Rome Johnson, *President*
Rome Johnso, *President*
EMP: 52
SQ FT: 1,500
SALES: 1.1MM **Privately Held**
SIC: 8733 Scientific research agency

(P-26756)
ENERGY BERKELEY OFFICE US DEPT
Also Called: Lawrence Berkeley National Lab
5885 Hollis St, Emeryville (94608-2404)
PHONE..................................510 495-2490
Tina Clarke, *Human Resources*
EMP: 1039 **Privately Held**
SIC: 8733 9611 Noncommercial research organizations; energy development & conservation agency, government;
PA: United States Department Of Energy Berkeley Office
   1 Cyclotron Rd
   Berkeley CA 94720
   510 486-4000

(P-26757)
ENERGY BERKELEY OFFICE US DEPT
Also Called: Lawrence Berkeley National Lab
555 W Imperial Hwy, Brea (92821-4802)
PHONE..................................510 486-7089
EMP: 346 **Privately Held**
SIC: 8733 9611 Noncommercial research organizations; energy development & conservation agency, government;
PA: United States Department Of Energy Berkeley Office
   1 Cyclotron Rd
   Berkeley CA 94720
   510 486-4000

(P-26758)
ENERGY BERKELEY OFFICE US DEPT
Also Called: Lawrence Berkeley National Lab
1226 Cornell Ave, Albany (94706-2308)
PHONE..................................510 701-1089
EMP: 519 **Privately Held**
SIC: 8733 9611 Noncommercial research organizations; energy development & conservation agency, government;
PA: United States Department Of Energy Berkeley Office
   1 Cyclotron Rd
   Berkeley CA 94720
   510 486-4000

(P-26759)
ENERGY BERKELEY OFFICE US DEPT
Also Called: Lawrence Berkeley National Lab
225 University Hall, Berkeley (94720-3541)
PHONE..................................510 642-1440
EMP: 519 **Privately Held**
SIC: 8733 9611 Noncommercial research organizations; energy development & conservation agency, government;
PA: United States Department Of Energy Berkeley Office
   1 Cyclotron Rd
   Berkeley CA 94720
   510 486-4000

(P-26760)
ENERGY BERKELEY OFFICE US DEPT
Also Called: Lawrence Berkeley National Lab
523 Buena Vista Ave # 315, Alameda (94501-2075)
PHONE..................................510 468-5662
EMP: 346 **Privately Held**
SIC: 8733 9611 Noncommercial research organizations; energy development & conservation agency, government;
PA: United States Department Of Energy Berkeley Office
   1 Cyclotron Rd
   Berkeley CA 94720
   510 486-4000

(P-26761)
ENERGY BERKELEY OFFICE US DEPT
Also Called: Lawrence Berkeley National Lab
419 Latimer Hall, Berkeley (94720-1461)
PHONE..................................510 486-4033
EMP: 692 **Privately Held**
SIC: 8733 9611 Noncommercial research organizations; energy development & conservation agency, government;
PA: United States Department Of Energy Berkeley Office
   1 Cyclotron Rd
   Berkeley CA 94720
   510 486-4000

(P-26762)
ENERGY LIVERMORE OFF US DEPT
Also Called: Lawrence Livermore Nat Lab
539 Peralta Ave, San Francisco (94110-5338)
PHONE..................................415 648-3878
Thomas McVey, *Research*
EMP: 636 **Privately Held**
SIC: 8733 9611 Noncommercial research organizations; energy development & conservation agency, government;
PA: United States Department Of Energy Livermore Office
   7000 East Ave
   Livermore CA 94550
   925 422-1100

(P-26763)
ENERGY LIVERMORE OFF US DEPT
Also Called: Lawrence Livermore Nat Lab
1413 Willowtree Ct, San Jose (95118-1155)
PHONE..................................408 267-1413
David Zalk, *Branch Mgr*
EMP: 477 **Privately Held**
SIC: 8733 9611 Noncommercial research organizations; energy development & conservation agency, government;
PA: United States Department Of Energy Livermore Office
   7000 East Ave
   Livermore CA 94550
   925 422-1100

(P-26764)
EPITOMICS INC (HQ)
863 Mitten Rd Ste 103, Burlingame (94010-1311)
PHONE..................................650 583-6688
Guo-Liang Yu, *Ch of Bd*
Liang Yu, *Bd of Directors*
Zhiqiang An, *Officer*
Brad S Lee, *Exec VP*
Weimin Zhu, *Senior VP*
EMP: 85
SALES (est): 16.6MM
SALES (corp-wide): 222.1MM **Privately Held**
WEB: www.epitomics.com
SIC: 8733 Scientific research agency
PA: Abcam Plc
   330 Cambridge Science Park
   Cambridge CAMBS CB4 0
   122 369-6000

(P-26765)
FAIR TRADE USA
1500 Broadway Ste 400, Oakland (94612-2079)
PHONE..................................510 663-5260
Fax: 510 663-5264
Paul Rice, *President*
Dave Rochlin, *COO*
Joan Catherine Braun, *CFO*
Lynn Lohr, *Vice Pres*
Carmen Iezzi, *Exec Dir*
EMP: 80
SQ FT: 23,600
SALES: 12.1MM **Privately Held**
SIC: 8733 Noncommercial social research organization

(P-26766)
FOCUS PSYCHO EDUCATIONAL
1427 N La Brea Ave, Los Angeles (90028-7505)
PHONE..................................323 851-4577

Susan Brown, *Director*
EMP: 100
SALES: 1.8MM **Privately Held**
SIC: 8733 Noncommercial social research organization

(P-26767)
GARY MARY W WIRELESS HLTH INST
10350 N Torrey Pines Rd, La Jolla (92037-1018)
PHONE....................858 412-8600
Donald M Casey Jr, *CEO*
Shelley Lyford, *COO*
Michael Caponetto, *CFO*
Gary West, *Chairman*
Dr Joseph Smith, *Chief Mktg Ofcr*
EMP: 50
SALES: 184.6K **Privately Held**
SIC: 8733 Medical research

(P-26768)
GNF
10675 John J Hopkins Dr, San Diego (92121-1127)
PHONE....................858 812-1976
Elena Rodriguez, *Principal*
Andrey Santrosyan, *Project Leader*
Jason Matzen, *Research*
Josh Lewis, *Technology*
Daniel Rines, *Marketing Staff*
EMP: 51
SALES (est): 9.2MM **Privately Held**
SIC: 8733 Research institute

(P-26769)
HRL LABORATORIES LLC
3011 Malibu Canyon Rd, Malibu (90265-4797)
PHONE....................310 317-5000
Penrose Albright, *President*
Dr Penrose Parney C Albright, *CEO*
Mary Y Asui-Amabe, *CFO*
Charles Fields, *CFO*
Roger Gronwald, *CFO*
EMP: 500
SQ FT: 250,000
SALES: 6MM **Privately Held**
WEB: www.hrl.com
SIC: 8733 8731 Research institute; commercial physical research

(P-26770)
HUNTINGTON MED RES INSTITUTES
734 Fairmount Ave, Pasadena (91105-3104)
PHONE....................626 397-5804
Fax: 626 397-5808
William Opel, *Manager*
Marguerite Duncan-Abrams, *Director*
EMP: 60
SALES (corp-wide): 11.8MM **Privately Held**
WEB: www.hmri.org
SIC: 8733 Scientific research agency
PA: Huntington Medical Research Institutes
99 N El Molino Ave
Pasadena CA 91101
626 795-4343

(P-26771)
IDUN PHARMACEUTICALS INC
9380 Judicial Dr, San Diego (92121-3830)
PHONE....................858 622-3000
Martin Mackay, *CEO*
David Shapiro, *Exec VP*
David Higgins, *Business Dir*
Robert Ternansky, *Director*
David Hecht, *Manager*
EMP: 50
SQ FT: 43,000
SALES (est): 3.2MM **Publicly Held**
SIC: 8733 Medical research
PA: Conatus Pharmaceuticals Inc.
16745 W Bernardo Dr # 200
San Diego CA 92127
858 376-2600

(P-26772)
INSTITUTE FOR LA JOLLA
Also Called: Didnri
9420 Athena Cir, La Jolla (92037-1387)
PHONE....................858 752-6500
Mitchell Kronenberg, *President*
Harold G Buchanan II, *Managing Prtnr*

Skip Carpowich, *CFO*
Charles A Carpowich Jr, *Exec VP*
Stephen Wilson, *Exec VP*
EMP: 240
SQ FT: 87,000
SALES: 49.3MM **Privately Held**
SIC: 8733 Medical research

(P-26773)
INTERNTIONAL CMPT SCIENCE INST
Also Called: I C S I
1947 Center St Ste 600, Berkeley (94704-1159)
PHONE....................510 643-9153
Fax: 510 643-7684
Rebecca Pieraccini, *President*
Scott McComas, *Admin Asst*
Cindy Ngu, *Admin Asst*
Albert Park, *Admin Asst*
Theresa Hogg, *Info Tech Mgr*
EMP: 50
SQ FT: 26,000
SALES: 12.3MM **Privately Held**
SIC: 8733 Research institute

(P-26774)
IRHYTHM TECHNOLOGIES INC
Also Called: Irhythm Tech Inc Orange Cnty
11085 Knott Ave, Cypress (90630-5152)
PHONE....................714 855-4030
Alan Shell, *Branch Mgr*
EMP: 107
SALES (corp-wide): 36.1MM **Publicly Held**
SIC: 8733 Medical research
PA: Irhythm Technologies, Inc.
650 Townsend St Ste 500
San Francisco CA 94103
415 632-5700

(P-26775)
JAYCOR INC
3394 Carmel Mountain Rd, San Diego (92121-1065)
PHONE....................858 720-4000
Eric M Demarco, *CEO*
Rajiv Bendale, *Director*
EMP: 500
SQ FT: 47,000
SALES (est): 28.7MM **Privately Held**
WEB: www.jaycor.com
SIC: 8733 8711 Scientific research agency; engineering services

(P-26776)
JBS INTERNATIONAL INC
555 Airport Blvd Ste 400, Burlingame (94010-2036)
PHONE....................650 373-4900
Cynthia Currin, *Principal*
EMP: 55
SALES (corp-wide): 69.1MM **Privately Held**
SIC: 8733 Medical research
PA: Jbs International, Inc.
5515 Security Ln Ste 800
North Bethesda MD 20852
301 495-1080

(P-26777)
JOHN WAYNE INSTITUTE FOR CTR
2200 Santa Monica Blvd, Santa Monica (90404-2312)
PHONE....................310 449-5253
Patrick Wayne, *Ch of Bd*
Gary Grubbs, *COO*
Linda Burt, *CFO*
EMP: 160
SQ FT: 57,000
SALES: 13.9MM **Privately Held**
SIC: 8733 Research institute

(P-26778)
JWCH INSTITUTE INC
6912 Ajax Ave, Bell (90201-4057)
PHONE....................323 562-5813
Fax: 323 326-1146
Annabel Munoz, *Manager*
Teresa I Bertao, *Nurse Practr*
EMP: 72
SALES (corp-wide): 27.6MM **Privately Held**
SIC: 8733 Noncommercial research organizations

PA: Jwch Institute, Inc.
5650 Jillson St
Commerce CA 90040
323 477-1171

(P-26779)
JWCH INSTITUTE INC
12360 Firestone Blvd, Norwalk (90650-4324)
PHONE....................562 281-0306
Oyamendan Itohan, *COO*
Jonathan Wada, *Gnrl Med Prac*
EMP: 72
SALES (corp-wide): 27.6MM **Privately Held**
SIC: 8733 Noncommercial research organizations
PA: Jwch Institute, Inc.
5650 Jillson St
Commerce CA 90040
323 477-1171

(P-26780)
KECK GRADUATE INSTITUTE (PA)
Also Called: Kgi
535 Watson Dr, Claremont (91711-4817)
PHONE....................909 621-8000
Fax: 909 607-8086
Sheldon M Schuster, *President*
T Gregory Dewey, *President*
Robert W Caragher, *CFO*
Andy Davenport, *CFO*
Kerry Howell, *Vice Pres*
EMP: 65 **EST:** 1997
SQ FT: 156,992
SALES: 22.5MM **Privately Held**
SIC: 8733 Research institute

(P-26781)
LAS CUMBRES OBSERVATORY GLOBAL
6740 Cortona Dr Ste 102, Goleta (93117-5575)
PHONE....................805 880-1600
Wayne Rosing, *President*
Dorothy Largay, *Treasurer*
Michael Falarsky, *Exec VP*
Ann Brooks, *Manager*
EMP: 50
SQ FT: 9,000
SALES: 9.7MM **Privately Held**
WEB: www.lcogt.net
SIC: 8733 Scientific research agency

(P-26782)
LELAND STANFORD JUNIOR UNIV
Blum, John Erthquake Engrg Ctr
Melcode 4020 Bldg 540, Stanford (94305)
PHONE....................650 723-4150
Greg Dierlein, *Director*
EMP: 70
SALES (corp-wide): 1.9B **Privately Held**
SIC: 8733 8221 Research institute; university
PA: Leland Stanford Junior University
2575 Sand Hill Rd
Menlo Park CA 94025
650 723-2300

(P-26783)
LELAND STANFORD JUNIOR UNIV
Also Called: Ginzton Laboratory
450 Via Palou Mall, Stanford (94305-4014)
PHONE....................650 723-0107
Marilynn Elverson, *Director*
Jack Zeng, *Info Tech Dir*
Babak B Mortezai, *Info Tech Mgr*
EMP: 150
SALES (corp-wide): 1.9B **Privately Held**
SIC: 8733 8221 Physical research, noncommercial; university
PA: Leland Stanford Junior University
2575 Sand Hill Rd
Menlo Park CA 94025
650 723-2300

(P-26784)
LELAND STANFORD JUNIOR UNIV
Also Called: Stanford Univ Earth Secinces
397 Panama Mall Ste 360, Stanford (94305-2237)
PHONE....................650 724-8899
Pamila Matson, *Principal*
EMP: 150
SALES (corp-wide): 1.9B **Privately Held**
SIC: 8733 8731 Scientific research agency; commercial physical research
PA: Leland Stanford Junior University
2575 Sand Hill Rd
Menlo Park CA 94025
650 723-2300

(P-26785)
LELAND STANFORD JUNIOR UNIV
Diagnostic Radiology
1201 Welch Rd, Palo Alto (94305-5102)
PHONE....................650 723-4733
Fax: 650 723-5795
Robert Herfkens, *Principal*
Lanzie Rivera, *Administration*
EMP: 67
SALES (corp-wide): 2.7B **Privately Held**
SIC: 8733 8221 Medical research; university
PA: Leland Stanford Junior University
2575 Sand Hill Rd
Menlo Park CA 94025
650 723-2300

(P-26786)
MEDIDATA SOLUTIONS INC
343 Sansome St Ste 1400, San Francisco (94104-5607)
PHONE....................415 295-4300
John Kingery, *CEO*
SAI Pendyam, *Database Admin*
Kelly Kingdon, *Engineer*
EMP: 169
SALES (corp-wide): 392.5MM **Publicly Held**
SIC: 8733 Noncommercial research organizations
PA: Medidata Solutions, Inc.
350 Hudson St Fl 9
New York NY 10014
212 918-1800

(P-26787)
MILKEN INSTITUTE
1250 4th St Fl 2, Santa Monica (90401-1418)
PHONE....................310 570-4600
Fax: 310 570-4601
Michael L Klowden, *President*
Michael Milken, *Ch of Bd*
Paul H Irving, *COO*
Nancy McHose, *Associate Dir*
Cecilia Arradaza, *Comms Dir*
EMP: 50
SALES: 61.8MM **Privately Held**
WEB: www.milkeninstitute.com
SIC: 8733 Economic research, noncommercial

(P-26788)
MIND RESEARCH INSTITUTE
Also Called: Music Intllgnce Neuro Dev Inst
111 Academy Ste 100, Irvine (92617-3046)
PHONE....................949 345-8700
Matthew Peterson, *CEO*
Andrew R Coulson, *President*
Brett Woudenberg, *COO*
John Bishop, *Vice Pres*
Jim Lund, *Vice Pres*
EMP: 160
SALES: 30.7MM **Privately Held**
WEB: www.mindinst.org
SIC: 8733 Noncommercial research organizations

(P-26789)
MONTEREY INST OF INTL STUDIES
460 Pierce St, Monterey (93940-2658)
PHONE....................831 647-4100
Sunder Ramaswamy, *President*
Molly Laughlin, *Officer*
Maggie Peters, *Associate Dir*
Steven Baker, *Principal*

PRODUCTS & SERVICES SECTION
8733 - Noncommercial Research Organizations County (P-26810)

Amy C McGill, *Exec Dir*
EMP: 101
SALES (est): 11.8MM **Privately Held**
SIC: 8733 Noncommercial research organizations

(P-26790)
NANOSYS INC
233 S Hillview Dr, Milpitas (95035-5417)
PHONE 408 240-6700
Fax: 650 331-2101
Jason Hartlove, *CEO*
John Hanlow, *Senior VP*
Catherine Cotell, *Vice Pres*
Andrew Filler, *Vice Pres*
Charlie Hotz, *Vice Pres*
EMP: 130
SQ FT: 32,000
SALES (est): 37.7MM **Privately Held**
WEB: www.nanosysinc.com
SIC: 8733 Research institute

(P-26791)
NT SUNSET INC
2220 Livingston St # 201, Oakland (94606-5216)
PHONE 510 420-3772
Wilbur Ross, *Ch of Bd*
James Curley, *President*
Peter David, *CFO*
Mark Brutten, *Senior VP*
Dirk Keunen, *Senior VP*
EMP: 50
SALES (est): 7MM **Privately Held**
WEB: www.nano-tex.com
SIC: 8733 Noncommercial research organizations

(P-26792)
OLIVE VIEW/UCLA EDUCATION &
14445 Olive View Dr, Sylmar (91342-1437)
PHONE 818 364-3434
Denise Tritt, *General Mgr*
Lisa Gipti, *Accountant*
EMP: 75
SQ FT: 1,326
SALES: 3.7MM **Privately Held**
SIC: 8733 Medical research

(P-26793)
PALO ALTO VTERANS INST FOR RES
Also Called: Pavir
3801 Miran Ave Bldg 101a, Palo Alto (94304)
PHONE 650 858-3970
Kerstin Lynam, *CEO*
Mary Thornton, *COO*
Barclay Kamb, *Bd of Directors*
Daniel Harris, *Admin Asst*
Jenny Dao, *Accounting Mgr*
EMP: 218
SQ FT: 5,500
SALES: 24.2MM **Privately Held**
WEB: www.paire.org
SIC: 8733 Noncommercial research organizations; noncommercial biological research organization; scientific research agency

(P-26794)
PARKINSONS INSTITUTE
675 Almanor Ave Ste 101, Sunnyvale (94085-2930)
PHONE 800 786-2958
Fax: 408 734-8522
Carrolee Barlow, *CEO*
Irwin Helford, *Ch of Bd*
Michelle Knapik, *CFO*
Peter Nosler, *Executive*
Douglas Palmer, *Executive*
EMP: 85
SQ FT: 40,000
SALES: 11.8MM **Privately Held**
WEB: www.parkinsonsinstitute.org
SIC: 8733 8011 Medical research; clinic, operated by physicians

(P-26795)
POINT REYES BIRD OBSERVATORY
Also Called: PRBO
3820 Cypress Dr Ste 11, Petaluma (94954-6964)
PHONE 707 781-2555
Fax: 707 868-1946
Ellie M Cohen, *President*
Edward Sarti, *Ch of Bd*
Laurie Tahcott, *CFO*
Laurie Talcott, *CFO*
Steven Thal, *Chairman*
EMP: 85
SQ FT: 2,000
SALES: 10.9MM **Privately Held**
SIC: 8733 8748 Noncommercial biological research organization; business consulting

(P-26796)
PREMIER SOURCE LLC
999 Bayhill Dr Fl 3, San Bruno (94066-3070)
PHONE 415 349-2010
Kenneth Wicks,
Sinead Foley,
EMP: 65
SQ FT: 13,000
SALES (est): 4.3MM
SALES (corp-wide): 135.9B **Publicly Held**
SIC: 8733 Scientific research agency
PA: Amerisourcebergen Corporation
1300 Morris Dr Ste 100
Chesterbrook PA 19087
610 727-7000

(P-26797)
PROTHENA BIOSCIENCES INC
650 Gateway Blvd, South San Francisco (94080-7014)
PHONE 650 837-8550
Dale Schenk, *CEO*
A W Homan, *Principal*
Martin Koller MD, *Principal*
EMP: 50
SALES (est): 9.2MM **Privately Held**
SIC: 8733 Medical research

(P-26798)
PUBLIC HEALTH INSTITUTE (PA)
555 12th St Ste 1050, Oakland (94607-3630)
PHONE 510 285-5500
Fax: 510 285-5501
Mary Pittman, *President*
Melange Matthews, *COO*
Bob Wolfson, *COO*
Tamar Dorfman, *CFO*
Matthew Marsom, *Vice Pres*
EMP: 100
SQ FT: 50,000
SALES: 106.7MM **Privately Held**
WEB: www.bmsg.org
SIC: 8733 Scientific research agency; medical research

(P-26799)
RADIABEAM TECHNOLOGIES LLC
1717 Stuart St, Santa Clara (95054)
PHONE 310 822-5845
Salime Boubher,
EMP: 50
SALES: 5MM **Privately Held**
SIC: 8733 3826 Physical research, noncommercial; laser scientific & engineering instruments

(P-26800)
RANCHO RESEARCH INSTITUTE
Also Called: RRI
7601 Imperial Hwy, Downey (90242-3456)
P.O. Box 3500 (90242-3500)
PHONE 562 401-8111
Julia Laplount, *CEO*
Yaga Szlachcic, *President*
Susan Bejer, *Admin Asst*
Conrad Cutchon, *Hum Res Coord*
EMP: 175
SQ FT: 15,000

SALES: 6.7MM **Privately Held**
WEB: www.larei.org
SIC: 8733 Educational research agency; scientific research agency

(P-26801)
RAPTOR PHARMACEUTICAL CORP (PA)
7 Hamilton Landing # 100, Novato (94949-8209)
PHONE 415 408-6200
Julie Anne Smith, *President*
Gregg Lapointe, *Ch of Bd*
Michael P Smith, *CFO*
David A Happel, *Ch Credit Ofcr*
Krishna R Polu, *Chief Mktg Ofcr*
EMP: 94
SQ FT: 52,319
SALES: 94.2MM **Privately Held**
WEB: www.torreypinestherapeutics.com
SIC: 8733 2834 Medical research; pharmaceutical preparations

(P-26802)
RENAL TREATMENT CENTERS INC (HQ)
601 Hawaii St, El Segundo (90245-4814)
PHONE 310 536-2400
Kent Thiry, *Chairman*
David Barry, *COO*
Richard Whitney, *CFO*
Georgina Randolph,
EMP: 100
SALES: 18.3MM
SALES (corp-wide): 13.7B **Publicly Held**
SIC: 8733 Medical research
PA: Davita Inc.
2000 16th St
Denver CO 80202
303 405-2100

(P-26803)
RIVERSIDE RESEARCH INSTITUTE
Also Called: Newport Beach Dialysis Center
3333 W Coast Hwy Ste 101, Newport Beach (92663-4039)
PHONE 949 631-0107
Fax: 949 631-5960
Rosemary Ellis, *Director*
EMP: 50
SALES (corp-wide): 84.5MM **Privately Held**
SIC: 8733 8092 Research institute; kidney dialysis centers
PA: Riverside Research Institute
156 William St Fl 9
New York NY 10038
212 563-4545

(P-26804)
SAFC CARLSBAD INC
6211 El Camino Real, Carlsbad (92009-1604)
PHONE 760 918-0007
David M Backer, *Manager*
Mark A Logomasini, *Finance Dir*
Jefferey L Strobel, *Director*
EMP: 65
SQ FT: 24,000
SALES (est): 2.9MM
SALES (corp-wide): 13.8B **Publicly Held**
WEB: www.molecularmed.com
SIC: 8733 Medical research
HQ: Safc, Inc.
645 Science Dr
Madison WI 53711
608 233-3115

(P-26805)
SANFORD BURNHAM PREBYS MEDICAL (PA)
Also Called: SBP
10901 N Torrey Pines Rd, La Jolla (92037-1005)
PHONE 858 795-5000
Perry Nisen, *CEO*
Kristiina Vuori, *President*
Gary Chessum, *CFO*
Nicole Deberg, *CFO*
Robert Walsh, *CFO*
EMP: 966
SQ FT: 397,000
SALES (est): 2.5MM **Privately Held**
SIC: 8733 Research institute

(P-26806)
SANTEN INCORPORATED
2100 Powell St Fl 16, Emeryville (94608-1826)
PHONE 415 268-9100
Fax: 707 254-1755
Akihiro Aki Tsujimura, *Principal*
Akihiro Tsujimura, *COO*
Cerina Letty, *CFO*
Murata Masashi, *Officer*
Yusuf Aii, *Vice Pres*
EMP: 100
SQ FT: 40,000
SALES (est): 22.6MM
SALES (corp-wide): 1.6B **Privately Held**
WEB: www.santeninc.com
SIC: 8733 8011 8731 Noncommercial biological research organization; offices & clinics of medical doctors; commercial physical research
PA: Santen Pharmaceutical Co., Ltd.
4-20, Ofukacho, Kita-Ku
Osaka OSK 530-0
663 217-000

(P-26807)
SCRIPPS RESEARCH INSTITUTE (PA)
10550 N Torrey Pines Rd, La Jolla (92037-1000)
PHONE 858 784-1000
Fax: 858 784-8480
Peter G Schultz, *CEO*
Lawrence Horowitz, *General Ptnr*
Steve A Kay, *President*
Cary E Thomas, *CFO*
Donna J Weston, *CFO*
EMP: 99
SALES (est): 60.3MM **Privately Held**
SIC: 8733 Research institute

(P-26808)
SETI INSTITUTE
Also Called: Seti Institute, The
189 Bernardo Ave 100, Mountain View (94043-5203)
PHONE 650 961-6633
Edna Devor, *CEO*
Shannon Atkinson, *CFO*
Dr Greg Papadopolous, *Chairman*
A R Taylor, *Exec Sec*
Melissa Loo, *Director*
EMP: 115
SQ FT: 19,737
SALES: 15.9MM **Privately Held**
WEB: www.voyagesthroughtime.org
SIC: 8733 Noncommercial research organizations

(P-26809)
SRI INTERNATIONAL (PA)
333 Ravenswood Ave, Menlo Park (94025-3493)
P.O. Box 2203 (94026-2203)
PHONE 650 859-2000
Fax: 650 326-5512
William Jeffrey, *President*
Mariann Byerwalter, *Ch of Bd*
John Prausa, *CEO*
Luther Lau, *CFO*
Richard B Brewer, *Bd of Directors*
EMP: 1430
SQ FT: 1,300,000
SALES: 507.7MM **Privately Held**
WEB: www.sri.com
SIC: 8733 8748 Scientific research agency; noncommercial social research organization; business consulting

(P-26810)
SRI INTERNATIONAL
4111 Broad St Ste 220, San Luis Obispo (93401-8743)
PHONE 805 542-9330
EMP: 142
SALES (corp-wide): 550MM **Privately Held**
SIC: 8733
PA: Sri International
333 Ravenswood Ave
Menlo Park CA 94025
650 859-2000

8733 - Noncommercial Research Organizations

(P-26811)
STUDY US RESEARCH INST INC
1335 N La Brea Ave 2-205, Los Angeles (90028-3905)
PHONE..................213 840-9575
Tiffany S Bennett, *President*
EMP: 99
SALES: 250K Privately Held
SIC: 8733 Noncommercial research organizations

(P-26812)
TAKEDA CALIFORNIA INC
Also Called: Tcal
10410 Science Center Dr, San Diego (92161-1119)
PHONE..................858 622-8528
Fax: 858 550-0526
Keith Wilson, *President*
Toshiro Hayes, *Senior VP*
Joe Carney, *Vice Pres*
Keith Williams, *Vice Pres*
Richard Czerniak, *Associate Dir*
EMP: 220
SALES (est): 44.6MM
SALES (corp-wide): 15.4B Privately Held
WEB: www.takedasd.com
SIC: 8733 Biotechnical research, noncommercial
PA: Takeda Pharmaceutical Company Limited
4-1-1, Doshomachi, Chuo-Ku
Osaka OSK 541-0
662 042-111

(P-26813)
THE NATIONAL FOOD LAB LLC
365 N Canyons Pkwy # 201, Livermore (94551-7703)
PHONE..................925 828-1440
Fax: 925 243-0117
Austin Sharp, *President*
Bill Pappas, *CFO*
Julie Hill, *Vice Pres*
Debbie Lohmeyer, *Vice Pres*
Jena Roberts, *Vice Pres*
EMP: 150
SQ FT: 21,000
SALES (est): 28MM
SALES (corp-wide): 8.6B Publicly Held
WEB: www.thenfl.com
SIC: 8733 Scientific research agency
HQ: Safe Foods International Holdings, Llc
111 S Wacker Dr
Chicago IL
-

(P-26814)
TORREY PINES INSTITUTE FOR MO
3550 General Atomics Ct, San Diego (92121-1122)
PHONE..................858 455-3803
Fax: 858 455-3804
Richard Houghten, *President*
Eli Sercarz, *Top Exec*
Libby Handel, *Business Dir*
Donna Freher-Lyons, *General Mgr*
Rosita Moya, *Research*
EMP: 160
SQ FT: 35,000
SALES: 17.3MM Privately Held
WEB: www.pain-research.org
SIC: 8733 Medical research

(P-26815)
UNITED STATES DEPT OF ENERGY
Also Called: Lawrence Berkeley National Lab
1 Cyclotron Rd, Berkeley (94720-8099)
PHONE..................510 486-4000
EMP: 5000 Publicly Held
SIC: 8733 9611
HQ: United States Dept Of Energy
1000 Independence Ave Sw
Washington DC 20585
202 586-5000

(P-26816)
UNIVERSITY CAL SAN FRANCISCO
Also Called: Uscf Caps Department Medicine
500 Parnassus Ave, San Francisco (94143-2203)
PHONE..................415 476-9000
Sam Hawgood, *Chancellor*
David Orth,
Joyce Abe, *Officer*
Maria Dacosta, *Lab Dir*
Mara Fellouris, *Exec Dir*
EMP: 97 Privately Held
SIC: 8733 8221 9411 Medical research; university; administration of educational programs;
HQ: University Of California, San Francisco
505 Parnassus Ave
San Francisco CA 94143
415 476-9000

(P-26817)
VETERANS MEDICAL RESEARCH FUND
3350 La Jolla Village Dr, San Diego (92161-0002)
PHONE..................858 642-3080
Kerstin B Lynam, *CEO*
Barabara Dovenbarger, *CFO*
Eileen Costa, *General Mgr*
Paul Clopton, *Network Mgr*
Thomas Mercer, *Comp Spec*
EMP: 250
SALES: 21.4MM Privately Held
WEB: www.vapop.ucsd.edu
SIC: 8733 Medical research

(P-26818)
VIACYTE INC
3550 General Atomics Ct B2-503, San Diego (92121-1122)
PHONE..................858 455-3708
Paul K Laikind, *President*
Kevin D'Amour, *Officer*
Anthony Gringeri, *Officer*
Allan Robins, *Senior VP*
Howard Foyt, *Vice Pres*
EMP: 55
SQ FT: 12,000
SALES (est): 12.5MM Privately Held
WEB: www.novocell.com
SIC: 8733 2836 Noncommercial research organizations; biological products, except diagnostic

(P-26819)
WCCT GLOBAL LLC (PA)
3545 Howard Way, Costa Mesa (92626-1418)
PHONE..................714 668-1500
Kenneth T Kim, *Mng Member*
Ron Fikert, *CFO*
Melton Affrime, *Senior VP*
Lee Barsky, *Vice Pres*
Talia Nikolao, *Exec Dir*
EMP: 73
SALES (est): 23.4MM Privately Held
SIC: 8733 Research institute

(P-26820)
WESTED
300 Lakeside Dr Fl 25th, Oakland (94612-3534)
PHONE..................510 302-4200
Fax: 510 302-4242
Teresa Johnson, *Branch Mgr*
Richard Whitmore, *Administration*
Brian Williams, *Human Res Mgr*
Robert Montgomery, *Sr Project Mgr*
EMP: 62
SALES (corp-wide): 154.4MM Privately Held
WEB: www.edgateway.net
SIC: 8733 8732 Educational research agency; commercial nonphysical research
PA: Wested
730 Harrison St Ste 500
San Francisco CA 94107
415 565-3000

(P-26821)
WESTED
180 Harbor Dr Ste 112, Sausalito (94965-2845)
PHONE..................415 289-2300
Peter Mangione, *Branch Mgr*
Kim Luttgen, *Research*
Consuelo Espinosa, *Manager*
EMP: 51
SALES (corp-wide): 154.4MM Privately Held
WEB: www.edgateway.net
SIC: 8733 8732 Educational research agency; commercial nonphysical research
PA: Wested
730 Harrison St Ste 500
San Francisco CA 94107
415 565-3000

(P-26822)
WESTED (PA)
730 Harrison St Ste 500, San Francisco (94107-1242)
PHONE..................415 565-3000
Fax: 415 512-2024
Glen H Harvey, *CEO*
Jeff Kuwabara, *Treasurer*
Tacy C Ashby, *Bd of Directors*
Jorge O Ayala, *Bd of Directors*
John M Baracy, *Bd of Directors*
EMP: 115
SQ FT: 85,000
SALES (est): 154.4MM Privately Held
WEB: www.edgateway.net
SIC: 8733 Educational research agency

(P-26823)
WESTED
730 Harrison St Ste 500, San Francisco (94107-1242)
PHONE..................415 565-3000
Judy Gilbert, *Manager*
EMP: 172
SALES (corp-wide): 154.4MM Privately Held
WEB: www.edgateway.net
SIC: 8733 8732 Educational research agency; commercial nonphysical research
PA: Wested
730 Harrison St Ste 500
San Francisco CA 94107
415 565-3000

(P-26824)
WESTERN STATES INFO NETWRK INC
1825 Bell St Ste 205, Sacramento (95825-1020)
PHONE..................916 263-1180
Karen Aumond, *Exec Dir*
EMP: 78
SALES: 5.2MM Privately Held
SIC: 8733 Noncommercial research organizations

(P-26825)
WHITTIER INST FOR DIABETES
10140 Campus Point Dr, San Diego (92121-1520)
PHONE..................877 944-8843
Fax: 858 535-0894
Athena Tsimikas, *Exec Dir*
EMP: 80 EST: 1980
SALES (est): 4MM
SALES (corp-wide): 1.7B Privately Held
WEB: www.scripps.org
SIC: 8733 Medical research
PA: Scripps Health
4275 Campus Point Ct
San Diego CA 92121
858 678-7000

(P-26826)
WILLIAM LETTIS & ASSOCIATES
1777 Botelho Dr Ste 262, Walnut Creek (94596-5132)
PHONE..................713 369-5400
William Lettis, *Owner*
EMP: 80
SALES (est): 3.2MM Privately Held
SIC: 8733 Scientific research agency

(P-26827)
ZONARE MEDICAL SYSTEMS INC (HQ)
420 Bernardo Ave, Mountain View (94043-5209)
PHONE..................650 230-2800
Fax: 650 887-2419
Donald Southard, *CEO*
Timothy A Marcotte, *President*
Dan Bradford, *Vice Pres*
Stephen Edwards, *Vice Pres*
Steve Edwards, *Vice Pres*
EMP: 65
SALES (est): 32.5MM Privately Held
WEB: www.zonare.com
SIC: 8733 5047 Research institute; hospital equipment & supplies

8734 Testing Laboratories

(P-26828)
AGRICULTURE AND PRIORITY POLLU (PA)
Also Called: Appl
908 N Temperance Ave, Clovis (93611-8606)
PHONE..................559 275-2175
Diane Anderson, *President*
Bradford Anderson, *Corp Secy*
Sharon Dehmlow, *General Mgr*
Sue Bonds, *Admin Sec*
Robb Pendergrass, *Marketing Staff*
EMP: 50
SQ FT: 8,000
SALES (est): 4.8MM Privately Held
SIC: 8734 Pollution testing

(P-26829)
AIRCRAFT XRAY LABORATORIES INC
5216 Pacific Blvd, Huntington Park (90255-2595)
PHONE..................323 587-0164
Fax: 323 588-6410
Jim Newton, *President*
Thomas Newton, *Executive*
Sandi Spelic, *Admin Mgr*
Donald Kautz, *Credit Mgr*
Brenda Deegan, *Controller*
EMP: 67
SQ FT: 60,000
SALES (est): 11MM Privately Held
WEB: www.aircraftxray.com
SIC: 8734 7384 3471 Testing laboratories; photograph developing & retouching; plating & polishing

(P-26830)
ALS SERVICES USA CORP
1875 Coronado Ave, Long Beach (90755-1245)
PHONE..................562 597-3932
Pete Guebara, *Branch Mgr*
Juan Guevara, *Sales Executive*
EMP: 100
SALES (corp-wide): 967.1MM Privately Held
SIC: 8734 Testing laboratories
HQ: Als Services Usa, Corp.
10450 Stncliff Rd Ste 210
Houston TX 77099
281 530-5656

(P-26831)
AMBRY GENETICS CORPORATION (PA)
15 Argonaut, Aliso Viejo (92656-1423)
P.O. Box 55064, Irvine (92619-5064)
PHONE..................949 900-5500
Fax: 949 900-5501
Charles Lm Dunlop, *President*
Charles Caporale, *CFO*
Michael Squier, *Treasurer*
Aaron Elliott, *Vice Pres*
Humberto Huerta, *Vice Pres*
EMP: 94
SQ FT: 20,000
SALES (est): 55.5MM Privately Held
WEB: www.ambrygen.com
SIC: 8734 Testing laboratories

(P-26832)
BABCOCK LABORATORIES INC
Also Called: E. S. Babcock & Sons
6100 Quail Valley Ct, Riverside (92507-0704)
P.O. Box 432 (92502-0432)
PHONE..................951 653-3351
Fax: 951 653-1662
Allison Mackenzie, *CEO*
Carol Kase, *COO*
Tiffany Gomez, *CFO*
Tami Kearns, *Admin Asst*
Taylor Cariaga, *Project Mgr*
EMP: 70
SQ FT: 20,000

PRODUCTS & SERVICES SECTION

8734 - Testing Laboratories County (P-26854)

SALES (est): 13MM **Privately Held**
WEB: www.babcocklabs.com
SIC: 8734 Water testing laboratory; food testing service

(P-26833)
BC LABORATORIES INC
4100 Atlas Ct, Bakersfield (93308-4510)
PHONE................................661 327-4911
Fax: 661 327-1918
Carolyn I Jackson, *President*
Richard Eglin, *Shareholder*
Stuart Buttram, *Lab Dir*
Robert Cortez, *Department Mgr*
Chrissy Herndon, *Project Mgr*
EMP: 93
SQ FT: 18,000
SALES: 9.5MM **Privately Held**
WEB: www.bclabs.com
SIC: 8734 Testing laboratories

(P-26834)
BIO RAD LABORATORIES
2000 Alfred Nobel Dr, Hercules (94547-1804)
PHONE................................510 741-1000
Fax: 510 741-1053
Lincoln Fong, *Principal*
Brad U Crutchfield, *Vice Pres*
Lanette Ewing, *Branch Mgr*
Prabhat Mastey, *Sr Software Eng*
Jaya Chitithoti, *Info Tech Mgr*
EMP: 89
SALES (est): 17.2MM **Privately Held**
SIC: 8734 Testing laboratories

(P-26835)
BIOSCREEN TESTING SERVICES INC (PA)
3904 Del Amo Blvd Ste 801, Torrance (90503-2183)
PHONE................................602 277-1154
Fax: 310 370-3642
Bradford L Rope, *President*
Ranil M Fernando, *Vice Pres*
Susan Small, *QA Dir*
Valerie Hoback, *Research*
Kelly Ruffino, *Sales Mgr*
EMP: 85
SQ FT: 20,000
SALES (est): 17.3MM **Privately Held**
WEB: www.bioscreen.com
SIC: 8734 8731 Testing laboratories; commercial physical research

(P-26836)
CALIFORNIA LAB SCIENCES LLC
Also Called: West Pacific Medical Lab
10200 Pioneer Blvd # 500, Santa Fe Springs (90670-6000)
PHONE................................562 758-6900
William McDonald,
EMP: 300
SALES (est): 30.4MM **Privately Held**
SIC: 8734 Testing laboratories

(P-26837)
CENTRAL COUNTIES
241 Business Park Way, Atwater (95301-9487)
PHONE................................209 356-0355
Christine Hackler, *Principal*
EMP: 70
SALES (est): 5.6MM **Privately Held**
SIC: 8734 Testing laboratories

(P-26838)
CLANDESTINE LABORATORY INVEST
1704 E Bullard Ave, Fresno (93710-5856)
PHONE................................760 597-7946
Pam Smith, *Owner*
EMP: 99
SALES (est): 2.6MM **Privately Held**
SIC: 8734 Testing laboratories

(P-26839)
CONSTRUCTION TESTING SERVICES (PA)
2118 Rheem Dr, Pleasanton (94588-2775)
PHONE................................925 462-5151
Fax: 925 462-5183
Patrick Greenan, *President*
Rachel Dodds, *Engineer*
David Zetterlund, *Opers Mgr*
Kimberly Goodrich, *Marketing Staff*
Emily Stanton, *Mktg Coord*
EMP: 62 EST: 1994
SQ FT: 5,000
SALES (est): 13.9MM **Privately Held**
WEB: www.cts-1.com
SIC: 8734 8741 Testing laboratories; construction management

(P-26840)
COOPER & JACKSON INC
310 Shaw Rd Ste D, South San Francisco (94080-6615)
PHONE................................408 437-2750
Fax: 650 244-4110
Kevin Waldron, *President*
Jeanine Waldron, *Vice Pres*
Vicky Cooper, *Accounts Mgr*
EMP: 200
SQ FT: 52,000
SALES (est): 11.8MM **Privately Held**
SIC: 8734 1521 Testing laboratories; repairing fire damage, single-family houses; single-family home remodeling, additions & repairs

(P-26841)
DACOR HOLDINGS INC
14425 Clark Ave, City of Industry (91745-1235)
P.O. Box 90070 (91715-0070)
PHONE................................626 626-4461
Michael Joseph, *President*
Ben Flores, *Controller*
EMP: 150
SALES (est): 11.4MM **Privately Held**
SIC: 8734 Testing laboratories

(P-26842)
DE PAR INC
Also Called: Associated Laboratories
806 N Batavia St, Orange (92868-1225)
PHONE................................714 771-6900
Fax: 714 538-1209
Tito L Parola, *President*
Robert Webber, *Treasurer*
Kim Holtman, *Officer*
Brad Schultz, *Vice Pres*
John Yokoyama, *Lab Dir*
EMP: 85
SQ FT: 17,000
SALES (est): 11.8MM **Privately Held**
WEB: www.associatedlabs.com
SIC: 8734 Testing laboratories

(P-26843)
DICKSON TESTING CO INC (DH)
11126 Palmer Ave, South Gate (90280-7492)
PHONE................................562 862-8378
Fax: 562 862-3143
Robert Lyddon, *President*
Jim Scanell, *Vice Pres*
ARA Kesheshian, *Engineer*
J Maclean, *Human Res Mgr*
Imtiyaz Ahmed, *Manager*
EMP: 80
SQ FT: 40,000
SALES (est): 21.4MM
SALES (corp-wide): 210.8B **Publicly Held**
WEB: www.dicksontesting.com
SIC: 8734 Metallurgical testing laboratory
HQ: Precision Castparts Corp.
    4650 Sw Mcdam Ave Ste 300
    Portland OR 97239
    503 946-4800

(P-26844)
DRUG ENFORCEMENT ADM
Also Called: DEA
2815 Scott St, Vista (92081-8547)
PHONE................................760 597-7955
Scott R Oulton, *Lab Dir*
EMP: 50 **Publicly Held**
SIC: 8734 Forensic laboratory
HQ: Drug Enforcement Administration
    8701 Morrissette Dr
    Springfield VA 22152
    202 307-1000

(P-26845)
EAG INC (PA)
2710 Walsh Ave, Santa Clara (95051-0963)
PHONE................................408 454-4600
Siddhartha Kadia, *CEO*
Lance Jones, *President*
Christeen Russel, *CFO*
Patricia M Lindley, *Exec VP*
John D Bucksath, *Senior VP*
EMP: 148
SQ FT: 70,000
SALES (est): 292.9MM **Privately Held**
WEB: www.eaglabs.com
SIC: 8734 Product testing laboratories

(P-26846)
ELEMENT MTRLS TECH HB INC
18100 S Wilmington Ave, Compton (90220-5909)
PHONE................................310 632-8500
Chuck Gee, *General Mgr*
Karla Chairez, *Purchasing*
Frank Kashou, *Manager*
Julie Nguyen, *Manager*
David Podrug, *Manager*
EMP: 86 **Privately Held**
WEB: www.stork.com
SIC: 8734 Metallurgical testing laboratory
HQ: Element Materials Technology Huntington Beach Inc.
    15062 Bolsa Chica St
    Huntington Beach CA 92649
    714 892-1961

(P-26847)
ELEMENT MTRLS TECH HB INC (HQ)
15062 Bolsa Chica St, Huntington Beach (92649-1023)
PHONE................................714 892-1961
Charles Noall, *President*
Eelco Niermeijer, *CFO*
Pete Regan, *Chairman*
Jeff Joyce, *Exec VP*
Jo Wetz, *Exec VP*
EMP: 80
SQ FT: 4,500
SALES (est): 44.8MM **Privately Held**
WEB: www.stork.com
SIC: 8734 Metallurgical testing laboratory
PA: Element B.V.
    Maerten Trompstraat 29
    Delft
    152 190-885

(P-26848)
EMAX LABORATORIES INC
1835 W 205th St, Torrance (90501-1510)
PHONE................................310 618-8889
Caspar J Pang, *CEO*
Kam P Yee, *President*
Sing C Pang, *Admin Sec*
Khoa Vu, *Research*
Ye Myint, *Sr Project Mgr*
EMP: 50
SQ FT: 14,000
SALES (est): 11.4MM **Privately Held**
WEB: www.emaxlabs.com
SIC: 8734 8748 8731 Pollution testing; environmental consultant; environmental research

(P-26849)
EMERY SMITH LABORATORIES INC
781 E Washington Blvd, Los Angeles (90021-3043)
PHONE................................213 745-5333
Fax: 213 746-0744
James E Partridge, *CEO*
John Latiolait, *Vice Pres*
Tamey Irons, *Office Mgr*
Janeth Quintero, *Project Mgr*
Ayesha Syeda, *Safety Mgr*
EMP: 135
SALES (est): 14.7MM **Privately Held**
SIC: 8734 Testing laboratories

(P-26850)
EMLAB P&K LLC (DH)
Also Called: Test America
1150 Bayhill Dr Ste 100, San Bruno (94066-3004)
PHONE................................650 829-5800
Fax: 650 829-5852
Belinda Vaga, *Mng Member*
David Gallup, *Ch of Bd*
Sicilia Bertoldi, *Controller*
Michael Berg, *Director*
Eric Ciotti, *Director*
EMP: 69
SQ FT: 18,000
SALES (est): 6.3MM
SALES (corp-wide): 3.7B **Privately Held**
WEB: www.emlabpk.com
SIC: 8734 Testing laboratories
HQ: Testamerica Holdings, Inc.
    4101 Shuffel St Nw
    North Canton OH 44720
    330 497-9396

(P-26851)
ENVIRONMENTAL HEALTH HAZARD
1515 Clay St Ste 1600, Oakland (94612-1499)
PHONE................................510 622-3200
Joan Denton, *Director*
EMP: 70 **Privately Held**
WEB: www.oehha.ca.gov
SIC: 8734 9511 Hazardous waste testing; air, water & solid waste management;
HQ: California Office Of Environmental Health Hazard Assessment
    1001 I St
    Sacramento CA 95814
    916 324-7572

(P-26852)
EUROFINS AIR TOXICS INC
180 Blue Ravine Rd Ste B, Folsom (95630-4719)
PHONE................................916 985-1000
Fax: 916 985-1020
J Wilson Hershey, *Ch of Bd*
Robert Mitzel, *President*
Thomas E Wolgemuth, *Corp Secy*
Heidi Hayes, *Vice Pres*
Stephany Mason, *Vice Pres*
EMP: 55
SQ FT: 24,000
SALES (est): 9.7MM
SALES (corp-wide): 12.1MM **Privately Held**
WEB: www.airtoxics.com
SIC: 8734 Testing laboratories
PA: Eurofins Environment Testing Us Holdings, Inc.
    2200 Rittenhouse St # 175
    Des Moines IA 50321
    515 698-5039

(P-26853)
EVANS ANALYTICAL GROUP LLC (HQ)
Also Called: Wildlife International
2710 Walsh Ave, Santa Clara (95051-0963)
PHONE................................408 454-4600
Fax: 408 588-0051
Steve Hall, *Manager*
Jeff Mayer, *Info Tech Mgr*
Aram Sarkissian, *VP Sales*
Lance Jones, *Director*
Shaida Kashani, *Accounts Exec*
EMP: 148
SALES (est): 36.4MM
SALES (corp-wide): 292.9MM **Privately Held**
SIC: 8734 Assaying service
PA: Eag Inc.
    2710 Walsh Ave
    Santa Clara CA 95051
    408 454-4600

(P-26854)
GARWOOD LABORATORIES INC
Also Called: Garwood Labs
143 Calle Iglesia, San Clemente (92672-7501)
PHONE................................562 949-2727
Fax: 562 692-8757
Vernon J Armstrong, *CEO*
Jim Armstrong, *President*
Heather Armstrong Bennett, *General Mgr*
Heather Armstrong, *Admin Sec*
Becky Maraz, *Accountant*
EMP: 65
SQ FT: 35,000

8734 - Testing Laboratories County (P-26855)

PRODUDUCTS & SERVICES SECTION

SALES (est): 8.5MM
SALES (corp-wide): 209MM Privately Held
WEB: www.garwoodlabs.com
SIC: 8734 Testing laboratories
HQ: National Technical Systems, Inc.
  24007 Ventura Blvd # 200
  Calabasas CA 91302
  818 591-0776

(P-26855)
GENERAL ATOMIC AERON
73 El Mirage Airport Rd B, Adelanto (92301-9540)
PHONE.............................760 246-3662
Fax: 760 388-4040
Gary Bener, *Branch Mgr*
Bart Roper, *Vice Pres*
Steven Blair, *Info Tech Mgr*
Kathy Reinhart, *Senior Buyer*
Mark Deffley, *Manager*
EMP: 200
SQ FT: 34,425
SALES (corp-wide): 3.5B Privately Held
WEB: www.generalatomics.com
SIC: 8734 Product testing laboratory, safety or performance
HQ: General Atomics Aeronautical Systems, Inc.
  14200 Kirkham Way
  Poway CA 92064
  858 312-2810

(P-26856)
GENERAL TESTING & INSPTN INC
8427 Atlantic Ave, Cudahy (90201-5809)
PHONE.............................323 583-1653
Fax: 323 560-1627
Jay Haber, *President*
Vick Altomare, *COO*
Dave Polidan, *Vice Pres*
Isy Ratz, *Purchasing*
Greg Nygaard, *VP Sales*
EMP: 92
SQ FT: 36,000
SALES (est): 6.9MM Privately Held
WEB: www.generalinspection.com
SIC: 8734 Testing laboratories

(P-26857)
GENZYME CORPORATION
2440 S Sepulveda Blvd # 100, Los Angeles (90064-1744)
PHONE.............................310 482-5000
Richard Adleson, *Branch Mgr*
Ellie Ghonsuli, *Program Mgr*
Lara Flores, *Project Mgr*
Lydia Balatian-Flores, *Pathologist*
Patrick Browne, *Pathologist*
EMP: 200
SALES (corp-wide): 421.5MM Privately Held
WEB: www.genzyme.com
SIC: 8734 8731 Testing laboratories; commercial physical research
HQ: Genzyme Corporation
  500 Kendall St
  Cambridge MA 02142
  617 252-7500

(P-26858)
HORIZON WEST INC
Also Called: Oakwood Village
3388 Bell Rd, Auburn (95603-9242)
PHONE.............................530 889-8122
Fax: 530 888-9761
Roubah Moredhesal, *President*
EMP: 55
SALES (corp-wide): 99MM Privately Held
SIC: 8734 8361 Food testing service; residential care
PA: Horizon West, Inc.
  4020 Sierra College Blvd
  Rocklin CA 95677
  916 624-6230

(P-26859)
IMAGING HLTHCARE SPCALISTS LLC
6386 Alvarado Ct, San Diego (92120-4985)
PHONE.............................619 229-2299
Eric Chou, *Med Doctor*
EMP: 61

SALES (corp-wide): 11.2MM Privately Held
SIC: 8734 Testing laboratories
PA: Imaging Healthcare Specialists, Llc
  150 W Washington St
  San Diego CA 92103
  619 295-9729

(P-26860)
INTERTEK TESTING SVCS NA INC
25800 Commercentre Dr, Lake Forest (92630-8804)
PHONE.............................949 448-4100
EMP: 65
SALES (corp-wide): 3.2B Privately Held
SIC: 8734 Testing laboratories
HQ: Intertek Testing Services Na, Inc.
  3933 Us Route 11
  Cortland NY 13045
  607 753-6711

(P-26861)
INVITAE CORPORATION (PA)
458 Brannan St, San Francisco (94107-1713)
PHONE.............................415 374-7782
Randy Scott, *CEO*
Sean George, *President*
Lee Bendekgey, *CFO*
Cristi Radford, *Regional Mgr*
Rawand Tbeileh, *Administration*
EMP: 61
SQ FT: 7,795
SALES: 8.3MM Publicly Held
SIC: 8734 Testing laboratories

(P-26862)
IRVINE PHARMACEUTICAL SVCS INC (PA)
10 Vanderbilt, Irvine (92618-2010)
PHONE.............................949 951-4425
Assad Kazeminy, *President*
Adam Fox, *Exec VP*
Mujtaba Ali, *Vice Pres*
Jack Wright, *Vice Pres*
Tiffany Murphy, *Business Dir*
▲ **EMP:** 113
SQ FT: 62,000
SALES (est): 41.4MM Privately Held
WEB: www.irvinepharma.com
SIC: 8734 Product testing laboratories

(P-26863)
ISE LABS INC
46800 Bayside Pkwy, Fremont (94538-6592)
PHONE.............................510 687-2500
Cezar Simoniak, *Manager*
EMP: 50
SALES (corp-wide): 8.7B Privately Held
WEB: www.iselabs.com
SIC: 8734 8731 Testing laboratories; commercial physical research
HQ: Ise Labs, Inc.
  46800 Bayside Pkwy
  Fremont CA 94538
  510 687-2500

(P-26864)
ISE LABS INC (DH)
46800 Bayside Pkwy, Fremont (94538-6592)
PHONE.............................510 687-2500
Fax: 925 687-2413
Tien Wu, *CEO*
Jeff Thompson, *Vice Pres*
Nada Yacobe, *Database Admin*
You Tian, *Controller*
EMP: 200
SQ FT: 69,000
SALES (est): 54.3MM
SALES (corp-wide): 8.7B Privately Held
WEB: www.iselabs.com
SIC: 8734 3672 Testing laboratories; printed circuit boards

(P-26865)
MCCAMPBELL ANALYTICAL INC
1534 Willow Pass Rd, Pittsburg (94565-1701)
PHONE.............................925 252-9262
Edward Hamilton, *CEO*
Yen Cao, *Admin Asst*
Blake Brown, *Project Mgr*
Jennifer Lagerbom, *Project Mgr*

Alicia Rinne, *Accountant*
EMP: 63
SQ FT: 12,896
SALES (est): 10.5MM Privately Held
WEB: www.mccampbell.com
SIC: 8734 Testing laboratories

(P-26866)
MICHELSON LABORATORIES INC (PA)
6280 Chalet Dr, Commerce (90040-3761)
PHONE.............................562 928-0553
Fax: 562 927-6625
Grant Michelson, *President*
Jack E Michelson, *CEO*
Peggy McCrum, *Lab Dir*
Eva Vasco, *Administration*
Benjamin Garcia, *Info Tech Mgr*
EMP: 69
SQ FT: 20,000
SALES (est): 11.8MM Privately Held
WEB: www.michelsonlab.com
SIC: 8734 Food testing service

(P-26867)
MILLENNIUM HEALTH LLC (PA)
16981 Via Tazon Ste F, San Diego (92127-1645)
PHONE.............................877 451-3534
Fax: 858 451-3636
Ronald A Rittenmeyer, *CEO*
Howard Appel, *President*
David Cohen, *COO*
Mark A Winham, *COO*
Michael Keane, *CFO*
EMP: 148
SALES (est): 133.6MM Privately Held
SIC: 8734 Testing laboratories

(P-26868)
MIRION TECHNOLOGIES GDS INC (HQ)
Also Called: Global Dosimetry Solutions
2652 Mcgaw Ave, Irvine (92614-5840)
PHONE.............................949 419-1000
Fax: 949 296-1144
Thomas Logan, *CEO*
Sander Perle, *President*
James Hippel, *CFO*
Jack Pacheco, *CFO*
Antony Besso, *Exec VP*
EMP: 125
SALES (est): 40MM
SALES (corp-wide): 173.7MM Privately Held
WEB: www.mirion.com
SIC: 8734 Radiation dosimetry laboratory
PA: Mirion Technologies, Inc.
  3000 Executive Pkwy # 518
  San Ramon CA 94583
  925 543-0800

(P-26869)
MISTRAS GROUP INC
6170 Egret Ct, Benicia (94510-1269)
PHONE.............................707 746-5870
Chuck Penley, *General Mgr*
Patrick Brady, *Analyst*
Jennifer Urban, *Human Resources*
Fergal Oconnell, *Accounts Mgr*
Robert Beaver, *Consultant*
EMP: 50 Publicly Held
SIC: 8734 Testing laboratories
PA: Mistras Group, Inc.
  195 Clarksville Rd Ste 2
  Princeton Junction NJ 08550

(P-26870)
MONTROSE ENVMTL GROUP INC
2825 Verne Roberts Cir, Antioch (94509-7902)
PHONE.............................925 680-4300
WEi Marcus Tan, *Principal*
EMP: 444
SALES (corp-wide): 22.2MM Privately Held
SIC: 8734 Pollution testing
PA: Montrose Environmental Group, Inc.
  1 Park Plz Ste 1000
  Irvine CA 92614
  949 988-3500

(P-26871)
MOORE TWINING ASSOCIATES INC (PA)
2527 Fresno St, Fresno (93721-1804)
Rural Route 2527 Fresno St (93721)
PHONE.............................559 268-7021
Fax: 559 268-7126
Harry D Moore, *President*
Ruth E Moore, *Corp Secy*
Brian Boudreau, *Vice Pres*
Andy Seruntine, *Lab Dir*
Michael Shwiyhat, *Manager*
EMP: 85 **EST:** 1898
SQ FT: 22,500
SALES (est): 18.8MM Privately Held
WEB: www.mooretwining.com
SIC: 8734 8711 Testing laboratories; engineering services

(P-26872)
MWH AMERICAS INC
M W H Laboratories
750 Royal Oaks Dr Ste 100, Monrovia (91016-6359)
PHONE.............................626 386-1100
Mona Alteri, *Managing Dir*
Patrick Mullen, *Treasurer*
Lisa Zhao, *Research*
Andrew Eiche, *Sls & Mktg Exec*
Jim Hein, *Cust Mgr*
EMP: 129
SALES (corp-wide): 2.1B Privately Held
WEB: www.mw.com
SIC: 8734 Water testing laboratory
HQ: Mwh Americas, Inc.
  370 Interlocken Blvd
  Broomfield CO 80021
  303 410-4000

(P-26873)
NANOLAB TECHNOLOGIES INC (PA)
Also Called: Fib Lab
1708 Mccarthy Blvd, Milpitas (95035-7454)
PHONE.............................408 433-3320
John P Traub, *President*
Carol Traub, *Treasurer*
Xiu Han, *Vice Pres*
John Olson, *Vice Pres*
Jein Shyue, *Vice Pres*
EMP: 65
SQ FT: 15,000
SALES (est): 14.1MM Privately Held
WEB: www.nanolab1.com
SIC: 8734 Testing laboratories

(P-26874)
NATIONAL EVERCLEAN SVCS INC
28632 Roadside Dr Ste 275, Agoura Hills (91301-6052)
PHONE.............................877 532-5326
Fax: 310 865-0465
John McShane, *President*
EMP: 100
SQ FT: 2,500
SALES (est): 9.7MM
SALES (corp-wide): 1.8B Privately Held
WEB: www.evercleanservices.com
SIC: 8734 Food testing service
PA: Underwriters Laboratories Inc.
  333 Pfingsten Rd
  Northbrook IL 60062
  847 272-8800

(P-26875)
NATIONAL TECHNICAL SYSTEMS INC
3505 E 3rd St, San Bernardino (92408-0201)
P.O. Box 160, Norco (92860-0160)
PHONE.............................909 382-2360
Fax: 714 382-2359
Doug Anderson, *Branch Mgr*
William McGinnis, *CEO*
Mari Abe, *Manager*
Mac McClanahan, *Consultant*
EMP: 105
SALES (corp-wide): 209MM Privately Held
WEB: www.wylelabs.com
SIC: 8734 Testing laboratories

PRODUCTS & SERVICES SECTION

8734 - Testing Laboratories County (P-26896)

HQ: National Technical Systems, Inc.
24007 Ventura Blvd # 200
Calabasas CA 91302
818 591-0776

(P-26876)
NATIONAL TECHNICAL SYSTEMS INC
Also Called: NTS Technical Systems
1536 E Valencia Dr, Fullerton (92831-4797)
PHONE................................714 998-4351
Fax: 714 879-6117
Hector Paez, *General Mgr*
Rachel Joshi, *Business Dir*
Audrey Harris, *Admin Asst*
Ba Nguyen, *Engineer*
John Smith, *Engineer*
EMP: 100
SALES (corp-wide): 209MM Privately Held
WEB: www.ntscorp.com
SIC: 8734 8711 Radiation laboratories; sanitary engineers
HQ: National Technical Systems, Inc.
24007 Ventura Blvd # 200
Calabasas CA 91302
818 591-0776

(P-26877)
NATIONAL TECHNICAL SYSTEMS INC
Also Called: Saugus Division
20970 Centre Pointe Pkwy, Santa Clarita (91350-2975)
PHONE................................661 259-8184
Fax: 661 254-4814
Rick Reyes, *General Mgr*
Bob Carpenter, *Program Mgr*
Katherine Higgs, *Manager*
Pat Leblanc, *Manager*
EMP: 65
SALES (corp-wide): 209MM Privately Held
WEB: www.ntscorp.com
SIC: 8734 8748 Testing laboratories; product testing laboratories; environmental consultant
HQ: National Technical Systems, Inc.
24007 Ventura Blvd # 200
Calabasas CA 91302
818 591-0776

(P-26878)
NATIONAL TECHNICAL SYSTEMS INC
Also Called: NTS Technical Systems
5320 W 104th St, Los Angeles (90045-6010)
PHONE................................310 671-6488
Fax: 310 322-4093
George Melton, *President*
Leslie Lott, *Officer*
Scot J Butkis, *Vice Pres*
Cindy Cook, *Vice Pres*
John R Jordan, *Vice Pres*
EMP: 170
SALES (corp-wide): 209MM Privately Held
WEB: www.wylelabs.com
SIC: 8734 8731 Testing laboratories; commercial physical research
HQ: National Technical Systems, Inc.
24007 Ventura Blvd # 200
Calabasas CA 91302
818 591-0776

(P-26879)
NORTH AMERCN SCIENCE ASSOC INC
NAMSA
9 Morgan, Irvine (92618-2005)
PHONE................................949 951-3110
Fax: 949 951-3280
Dennis Nivens, *Vice Pres*
Gina Skolmowski, *Opers Mgr*
Judi Gorski, *VP Mktg*
Terry Langerderfer, *Marketing Mgr*
Nuzhat Hussain, *Manager*
EMP: 60
SQ FT: 40,000

SALES (corp-wide): 124.9MM Privately Held
WEB: www.namsa.com
SIC: 8734 8071 8999 Testing laboratories; medical laboratories; chemical consultant
PA: North American Science Associates, Inc.
6750 Wales Rd
Northwood OH 43619
419 666-9455

(P-26880)
NTS TECHNICAL SYSTEMS (PA)
Also Called: N T S
24007 Ventura Blvd # 200, Calabasas (91302-1430)
PHONE................................818 591-0776
William McGinnis, *CEO*
Rachel Joshi, *Controller*
EMP: 100
SALES (est): 21.4MM Privately Held
SIC: 8734 Product testing laboratories

(P-26881)
OILFIELD ENVMTL COMPLIANCE INC
Also Called: O E C
307 Roemer Way Ste 300, Santa Maria (93454-1105)
PHONE................................805 922-4772
Fax: 805 925-3376
Stefanie Haynes, *CEO*
Julius Carstens, *Vice Pres*
Dwain Zsadanyi, *Department Mgr*
Meredith Sprister, *Project Mgr*
Kevin Calcagno, *Sales Dir*
EMP: 55
SQ FT: 1,667
SALES: 6MM Privately Held
WEB: www.oecusa.com
SIC: 8734 Testing laboratories

(P-26882)
PHAMATECH INCORPORATED
15175 Innovation Dr, San Diego (92128-3401)
PHONE................................858 643-5555
Tuan Pham, *CEO*
Tuan H Pham, *CEO*
David Powers, *Manager*
Jodee Callaghan, *Accounts Mgr*
EMP: 200
SQ FT: 50,000
SALES (est): 32.9MM Privately Held
WEB: www.phamatech.com
SIC: 8734 5047 Forensic laboratory; medical laboratory equipment

(P-26883)
PHARMATEK LABORATORIES INC
7330 Carroll Rd Ste 200, San Diego (92121-2364)
PHONE................................858 805-6383
Jeffrey A Bibbs, *CEO*
Timothy Scott, *President*
Mark G Foletta, *Vice Pres*
Nancy Hori, *Info Tech Mgr*
Rina Fong, *Research*
EMP: 120
SQ FT: 5,500
SALES: 18MM Privately Held
WEB: www.pharmatek.com
SIC: 8734 8731 Testing laboratories; commercial research laboratory

(P-26884)
PHYSICIANS AUTOMATED LAB INC
Also Called: Physicians Automated Lab
107 Adkisson Way, Taft (93268-3602)
PHONE................................661 765-4522
EMP: 201
SALES (corp-wide): 25MM Privately Held
SIC: 8734 8071 8011 Testing laboratories; medical laboratories; offices & clinics of medical doctors
PA: Physician's Automated Laboratory, Inc.
820 34th St Ste 102
Bakersfield CA 93301
661 325-0744

(P-26885)
SCST INC (PA)
6280 Riverdale St, San Diego (92120-3308)
PHONE................................619 280-4321
Fax: 619 280-4717
Neal W Clements, *CEO*
John Kirschbaum, *COO*
Royce Parker, *Vice Pres*
EMP: 74
SQ FT: 15,482
SALES: 12.2MM Privately Held
WEB: www.scst.com
SIC: 8734 8711 Testing laboratories; engineering services

(P-26886)
SGS ACCUTEST INC
2105 Lundy Ave, San Jose (95131-1849)
PHONE................................408 588-0200
James A Gordon, *Director*
EMP: 95
SALES (corp-wide): 1.4B Privately Held
SIC: 8734 Testing laboratories
HQ: Sgs Accutest Inc.
201 Route 17
Rutherford NJ 07070
201 508-3000

(P-26887)
SHAW GROUP INC
4005 Port Chicago Hwy, Concord (94520-1180)
PHONE................................925 288-2011
Karen Cracken, *Branch Mgr*
Tom Machen, *Director*
EMP: 502 Privately Held
SIC: 8734 Testing laboratories
HQ: The Shaw Group Inc
4171 Essen Ln
Baton Rouge LA 70809
225 932-2500

(P-26888)
SHAW GROUP INC
Also Called: CB&i
18100 Von Karman Ave # 450, Irvine (92612-0169)
PHONE................................949 261-6441
Seyed Miri, *Project Mgr*
EMP: 502 Privately Held
SIC: 8734 Pollution testing
HQ: The Shaw Group Inc
4171 Essen Ln
Baton Rouge LA 70809
225 932-2500

(P-26889)
SILLIKER LABS GROUP INC
6360 Gateway Dr, Cypress (90630-4844)
PHONE................................714 226-0000
Vidyha Ganger, *Managing Dir*
Helen Andrews, *Opers Mgr*
L Smoot, *Manager*
EMP: 50
SALES (est): 4.2MM Privately Held
SIC: 8734 Product testing laboratories
HQ: Silliker, Inc.
111 E Wacker Dr Ste 2300
Chicago IL 60601
312 938-5151

(P-26890)
SIMCO ELECTRONICS (PA)
3131 Jay St Ste 100, Santa Clara (95054-3336)
PHONE................................408 734-9750
Fax: 408 734-9754
Brian Kenna, *CEO*
Bradford G Phillips, *CFO*
Marianne Bloomberg, *Administration*
Montgomery Tidwell, *Prgrmr*
Brian Searfass, *Technician*
EMP: 75 EST: 1962
SQ FT: 24,222
SALES (est): 51.8MM Privately Held
WEB: www.simco.com
SIC: 8734 5045 Calibration & certification; computer software

(P-26891)
SUPERTEX INC
Supertex Wafer Foundry
71 Vista Montana, San Jose (95134-1510)
PHONE................................408 222-8880
Fax: 408 222-8804

Melissa Chal, *Branch Mgr*
Robin Liu, *Engineer*
Rita Ferreira, *Manager*
EMP: 50
SALES (corp-wide): 2.1B Publicly Held
SIC: 8734 Testing laboratories
HQ: Supertex, Inc.
1235 Bordeaux Dr
Sunnyvale CA 94089
408 222-8888

(P-26892)
TESTAMERICA LABORATORIES INC
17461 Derian Ave Ste 100, Irvine (92614-5845)
PHONE................................949 261-1022
Fred Haley, *Branch Mgr*
EMP: 177
SALES (corp-wide): 3.7B Privately Held
WEB: www.stl-inc.com
SIC: 8734 Water testing laboratory
HQ: Testamerica Laboratories, Inc.
4101 Shuffel St Nw
North Canton OH 44720
800 456-9396

(P-26893)
TESTAMERICA LABORATORIES INC
880 Riverside Pkwy, West Sacramento (95605-1500)
PHONE................................916 373-5600
Roger Freize, *Manager*
Mark Lund, *Analyst*
Pam Schemmer, *QC Mgr*
EMP: 100
SALES (corp-wide): 3.7B Privately Held
WEB: www.stl-inc.com
SIC: 8734 8731 2899 Testing laboratories; commercial physical research; chemical preparations
HQ: Testamerica Laboratories, Inc.
4101 Shuffel St Nw
North Canton OH 44720
800 456-9396

(P-26894)
TUV SUD AMERICA INC
10040 Mesa Rim Rd, San Diego (92121-2912)
PHONE................................858 546-3999
Fax: 858 546-0364
Gerhard Abel, *Branch Mgr*
EMP: 58 Privately Held
WEB: www.tuvamerica.com
SIC: 8734 Product testing laboratories
HQ: Tuv Sud America Inc.
10 Centennial Dr Fl 2a
Peabody MA 01960
978 573-2500

(P-26895)
TWINING LABS SOUTHERN CAL INC (PA)
2883 E Spring St Ste 300, Long Beach (90806-6847)
PHONE................................562 426-3355
Edward Butch M Twining Jr, *CEO*
Brian Kramer, *President*
Talin Astourian, *Vice Pres*
Richard S Hazen, *Vice Pres*
Boris Stein, *Vice Pres*
EMP: 110
SQ FT: 13,600
SALES (est): 41.7MM Privately Held
WEB: www.twininglabs.com
SIC: 8734 Testing laboratories

(P-26896)
UNDERWRITERS LABORATORIES INC
455 E Trimble Rd, San Jose (95131-1230)
PHONE................................248 427-5300
Fax: 408 689-5600
Eric Swerrie, *Branch Mgr*
Paul Nguyen, *Info Tech Mgr*
Thomas M Burke, *Senior Engr*
Richard Olesen, *Manager*
Steve Undorte, *Manager*
EMP: 300
SALES (corp-wide): 1.8B Privately Held
WEB: www.ul.com
SIC: 8734 Testing laboratories

8734 - Testing Laboratories County (P-26897) PRODUDUCTS & SERVICES SECTION

PA: Underwriters Laboratories Inc.
333 Pfingsten Rd
Northbrook IL 60062
847 272-8800

(P-26897)
UNDERWRITERS LABORATORIES INC
47173 Benicia St, Fremont (94538-7366)
PHONE..................510 771-1000
Robert W Miller, *Branch Mgr*
Charlie Griffin, *Info Systems*
EMP: 487
SALES (corp-wide): 1.8B **Privately Held**
WEB: www.ul.com
SIC: 8734 Testing laboratories
PA: Underwriters Laboratories Inc.
333 Pfingsten Rd
Northbrook IL 60062
847 272-8800

(P-26898)
UNDERWRITERS LABORATORIES INC
4510 Riding Club Ct, Hayward (94542-2238)
PHONE..................408 754-6500
Crystal Vanderpan, *Principal*
EMP: 180
SALES (corp-wide): 1.8B **Privately Held**
SIC: 8734 Testing laboratories
PA: Underwriters Laboratories Inc.
333 Pfingsten Rd
Northbrook IL 60062
847 272-8800

(P-26899)
UNDERWRITERS LABORATORIES INC
2191 Zanker Rd, San Jose (95131-2109)
PHONE..................408 493-9910
EMP: 102
SALES (corp-wide): 1.8B **Privately Held**
SIC: 8734 Product testing laboratory, safety or performance
PA: Underwriters Laboratories Inc.
333 Pfingsten Rd
Northbrook IL 60062
847 272-8800

(P-26900)
UNITED MFG ASSEMBLY INC
44169 Fremont Blvd, Fremont (94538-6044)
PHONE..................510 490-1065
Fax: 510 490-4380
Yonwen Chou, *President*
Joe Loh, *General Mgr*
Lisian Pan, *Project Mgr*
May Mah, *Finance*
May Wah, *Controller*
EMP: 95
SALES (est): 13.2MM **Privately Held**
WEB: www.umai.com
SIC: 8734 3672 Testing laboratories; printed circuit boards

(P-26901)
VALLEY INDUSTRIAL X-RA
3700 Pegasus Dr 100, Bakersfield (93308-6825)
PHONE..................661 399-8497
Fax: 661 393-8497
Larry Williams, *President*
Greg Williams, *COO*
Terry Campbell, *Vice Pres*
Don Carlon, *Executive*
EMP: 200
SQ FT: 18,000
SALES (est): 20.5MM
SALES (corp-wide): 69.9MM **Privately Held**
WEB: www.vxray.com
SIC: 8734 X-ray inspection service, industrial
HQ: Rontgen Technische Dienst B.V.
Delftweg 144
Rotterdam 3046
102 088-208

(P-26902)
ZYMAX ENVIROTECHNOLOGY INC
Also Called: Zymax Forensics
600 S Andreasen Dr, Escondido (92029-1917)
PHONE..................760 781-3338
Fax: 805 544-8226
Sandra G Nielsen, *President*
Dr Jesper Nielsen, *VP Finance*
Mike Ng, *Finance Mgr*
John Culpepper, *Controller*
Chad Messer, *Pub Rel Dir*
EMP: 60
SQ FT: 12,000
SALES (est): 3.9MM **Privately Held**
SIC: 8734 Pollution testing; hazardous waste testing; soil analysis; water testing laboratory

8741 Management Services

(P-26903)
800 DEGREES LLC
10889 Lindbrook Dr, Los Angeles (90024-3027)
PHONE..................310 443-1911
Adam Fleischman,
Anthony Carron,
Allen Ravert,
EMP: 50
SQ FT: 2,900
SALES (est): 4.3MM **Privately Held**
SIC: 8741 Restaurant management

(P-26904)
ACCESS INFO MGT SHRED SVCS LLC
13950 Cerritos Corprt Dr C, Cerritos (90703-2468)
PHONE..................805 529-6866
Elaine Pahulu, *Branch Mgr*
Joanne Dorr, *Opers Mgr*
EMP: 71
SALES (corp-wide): 12MM **Privately Held**
SIC: 8741 Management services
PA: Access Information Management Shared Services, Llc
6818 Patterson Pass Rd A
Livermore CA 94550
925 461-5352

(P-26905)
ACE PARKING MANAGEMENT INC
300 Capitol Mall Bsmt, Sacramento (95814-4338)
PHONE..................916 498-9852
Charles Blottin, *Principal*
EMP: 436
SALES (corp-wide): 273.2MM **Privately Held**
SIC: 8741 Management services
PA: Ace Parking Management, Inc.
645 Ash St
San Diego CA 92101
619 233-6624

(P-26906)
ACE PARKING MANAGEMENT INC
3400 E Tahquitz Cyn Way, Palm Springs (92262-6970)
PHONE..................760 320-8974
EMP: 436
SALES (corp-wide): 273.2MM **Privately Held**
SIC: 8741 7521 Business management; parking lots
PA: Ace Parking Management, Inc.
645 Ash St
San Diego CA 92101
619 233-6624

(P-26907)
ACEPEX MANAGEMENT CORPORATION
13401 Yorba Ave, Chino (91710-5055)
PHONE..................909 591-1999
Charles Kidd, *Director*
EMP: 300

SALES (corp-wide): 37.5MM **Privately Held**
SIC: 8741 Management services
PA: Acepex Management Corporation
10643 Mills Ave
Montclair CA 91763
909 625-6900

(P-26908)
ACTIVCARE LIVING INC (PA)
9619 Chesapeake Dr # 103, San Diego (92123-1368)
PHONE..................858 565-4424
Fax: 858 565-1508
William Major Chance, *CEO*
Todd A Shetter, *COO*
B Renee Barnard, *CFO*
Jack Rowe, *CFO*
Dkevin Moriarty, *Vice Pres*
EMP: 180
SQ FT: 9,000
SALES (est): 33.2MM **Privately Held**
WEB: www.healthcaregrp.com
SIC: 8741 Nursing & personal care facility management

(P-26909)
ACTIVE WELLNESS LLC
4000 Bridgeway Ste 101, Sausalito (94965-4800)
PHONE..................415 331-1600
Jill Stevens Kinney, *Chairman*
William Joseph McBride III, *President*
Carey White, *CFO*
EMP: 1400
SQ FT: 5,000
SALES: 40MM **Privately Held**
SIC: 8741 Hospital management; nursing & personal care facility management

(P-26910)
ADVANCED BIOSERVICES LLC (PA)
19255 Vanowen St, Reseda (91335-5021)
PHONE..................818 342-0100
Anna Kane,
EMP: 65
SALES (est): 13.9MM **Privately Held**
SIC: 8741 Administrative management

(P-26911)
ADVANCED MEDICAL MGT INC
5000 Arprt Plz Dr Ste 150, Long Beach (90815)
PHONE..................562 766-2000
Stephen Hegstrom, *CEO*
Kathy Hegstrom, *President*
Paul Pew, *Exec VP*
EMP: 60
SALES (est): 8.2MM **Privately Held**
WEB: www.duongnet.com
SIC: 8741 8721 Hospital management; nursing & personal care facility management; accounting, auditing & bookkeeping

(P-26912)
AEG MANAGEMENT LACC LLC
Also Called: Los Angeles Convention Center
1201 S Figueroa St, Los Angeles (90015-1308)
PHONE..................213 741-1151
Fax: 213 765-4440
Brad Gessner, *Senior VP*
Keith Hilsgen, *Vice Pres*
Carisa Malanum, *Vice Pres*
Greg Rosicky, *Vice Pres*
Ellen Schwartz, *Vice Pres*
EMP: 220
SALES (est): 15MM
SALES (corp-wide): 15.2MM **Privately Held**
SIC: 8741 Business management
PA: Aeg Facilities, Llc
800 W Olympic Blvd # 305
Los Angeles CA 90015
213 763-7700

(P-26913)
AIR FORCE US DEPT OF
Also Called: 30th Cpts-Financial Management
1031 California Blvd # 11777, Lompoc (93437-6248)
PHONE..................805 606-5355
Steve Kam, *Branch Mgr*
EMP: 65 **Publicly Held**
WEB: www.af.mil

SIC: 8741 9711 Management services; Air Force;
HQ: United States Department Of The Air Force
1000 Air Force Pentagon
Washington DC 20330
703 545-6700

(P-26914)
AJIT HEALTHCARE INC
316 S Westlake Ave, Los Angeles (90057-4500)
PHONE..................213 484-0510
Jasvant N Modi, *President*
Reuben Barrera, *Maintenance Dir*
EMP: 80
SALES (est): 6.2MM **Privately Held**
SIC: 8741 Nursing & personal care facility management

(P-26915)
ALFATECH CAMBRIDGE GROUP GP
345 S California Ave # 3, Palo Alto (94306-1866)
PHONE..................650 543-3030
William Hammerson, *Partner*
Jeff Fini, *Partner*
Marlene Groff, *Controller*
EMP: 70
SALES: 150MM **Privately Held**
SIC: 8741 8742 Construction management; management engineering

(P-26916)
ALL IN ONE INC
Also Called: Act 1 Personnel Services
1999 W 190th St, Torrance (90504-6202)
P.O. Box 29048, Glendale (91209-9048)
PHONE..................310 538-3374
Janice B Howroyd, *President*
Michael A Hoyal, *CFO*
Charles Ng, *Vice Pres*
Carvalhl Peter, *Vice Pres*
Tina Bryant, *Admin Sec*
EMP: 120
SALES (est): 12.1MM **Privately Held**
SIC: 8741 Administrative management

(P-26917)
ALLEGIS RESIDENTIAL SVCS INC
Also Called: Aspm-Sandiego
9340 Hazard Way Ste B2, San Diego (92123-1228)
PHONE..................858 430-5700
Karen Martinez, *CEO*
Steve Howe, *COO*
Jorge Martinez, *CFO*
Barbara Wilkinson, *Treasurer*
Bill Carnley, *Vice Pres*
EMP: 65
SQ FT: 4,000
SALES (est): 1.4MM
SALES (corp-wide): 6.4MM **Privately Held**
SIC: 8741 Management services
PA: S.H.E. Manages Properties, Inc.
9340 Hazard Way Ste B2
San Diego CA 92123
619 291-6300

(P-26918)
AMERICAN MZHOU DNGPO GROUP INC
4520 Maine Ave, Baldwin Park (91706-2671)
PHONE..................626 820-9239
Gang Wang, *CEO*
EMP: 100
SALES (est): 478.2K **Privately Held**
SIC: 8741 Restaurant management

(P-26919)
AMERISOURCEBERGEN CORPORATION
1368 Metropolitan Dr, Orange (92868)
P.O. Box 247, Thorofare NJ (08086-0247)
PHONE..................610 727-7000
Daniel Ramirez, *Manager*
Leilane Buendia, *Technology*
Jim Morales, *Technology*
Mark Webb, *Technology*
Wesley Behar, *Sales Staff*
EMP: 180

PRODUCTS & SERVICES SECTION

8741 - Management Services County (P-26942)

SALES (corp-wide): 135.9B Publicly Held
WEB: www.amerisourcebergen.net
SIC: 8741 Administrative management
PA: Amerisourcebergen Corporation
1300 Morris Dr Ste 100
Chesterbrook PA 19087
610 727-7000

(P-26920)
AMERISOURCEBERGEN CORPORATION
505 City Pkwy W, Orange (92868-2924)
PHONE...................714 704-4407
EMP: 180
SALES (corp-wide): 135.9B Publicly Held
SIC: 8741 Administrative management
PA: Amerisourcebergen Corporation
1300 Morris Dr Ste 100
Chesterbrook PA 19087
610 727-7000

(P-26921)
ANAHEIM FIRST FMLY DNTL GROUP
Also Called: Affd
1161 N Euclid St, Anaheim (92801-1938)
PHONE...................714 999-5050
Fax: 714 999-1786
Mary Ann De Santiago, *President*
John Delaney DDS, *Vice Pres*
EMP: 54
SALES (est): 4MM Privately Held
SIC: 8741 Office management

(P-26922)
APEX GROUP
17101 Superior St, Northridge (91325-1961)
PHONE...................818 885-0513
Damon Zumwalt, *President*
Robert Brockway, *Vice Pres*
Brian Beppel, *Regional Mgr*
Michael Davidson, *Regional Mgr*
Dan Denz, *Regional Mgr*
EMP: 200
SALES (est): 9.4MM Privately Held
SIC: 8741 8721 Administrative management; accounting, auditing & bookkeeping

(P-26923)
APPLECARE MEDICAL MGT LLC
18 Centerpointe Dr # 100, La Palma (90623-1066)
PHONE...................714 443-4507
Vinod Jivrajka, *Principal*
Gabriela Castaneda, *COO*
Richard Greene, *CFO*
Vangie Bigalbal, *Vice Pres*
Yvonne Miller, *Vice Pres*
EMP: 108
SALES (est): 14.1MM Privately Held
SIC: 8741 Nursing & personal care facility management

(P-26924)
ARCHIVES MANAGEMENT CORP (PA)
Also Called: Bay Management
2301 S El Camino Real, San Mateo (94403-2213)
PHONE...................650 544-2200
Fax: 415 468-6297
Harlan Shapers, *President*
Thelma Imperio, *Controller*
EMP: 180
SQ FT: 12,000
SALES (est): 18.9MM Privately Held
WEB: www.adultsupersource.com
SIC: 8741 8742 Business management; management consulting services

(P-26925)
ARES MANAGEMENT LLC
1999 Ave Of Stars Fl 37, Los Angeles (90067-4650)
PHONE...................310 201-4100
Tony Ressler, *Branch Mgr*
Pamela Bloom, *Director*
Allison Sternberg, *Director*
EMP: 170
SALES (corp-wide): 814.4MM Publicly Held
SIC: 8741 Management services
HQ: Ares Management Llc
2000 Avenue Of The Stars
Los Angeles CA 90067
310 201-4100

(P-26926)
ARNEL INTERIOR CORP
Also Called: Arnel and Affiliate
949 S Coast Dr Ste 600, Costa Mesa (92626-7734)
PHONE...................714 481-5100
George Argyrox, *Ch of Bd*
Dan Russo, *CEO*
Tony Roxtrom, *Vice Pres*
Jeannie Rennwald, *Office Mgr*
EMP: 300
SQ FT: 4,000
SALES (est): 7.4MM Privately Held
SIC: 8741 Management services

(P-26927)
ARNOLD PALMER GOLF MGT LLC
300 Finley Rd, San Francisco (94129-1196)
P.O. Box 29063 (94129-0063)
PHONE...................415 561-4670
Jamie Miller, *Manager*
Don Chelemedos, *General Mgr*
Becky Jensen, *Marketing Staff*
EMP: 70
SALES (corp-wide): 44.9MM Privately Held
SIC: 8741 7992 Management services; public golf courses
HQ: Arnold Palmer Golf Management, Llc
5080 Spctrum Dr Ste 1000e
Dallas TX 75240
972 419-1400

(P-26928)
ASHFORD TRS NICKEL LLC
Also Called: Sheraton Sn Diego Htl Msn Vly
1433 Camino Del Rio S, San Diego (92108-3521)
PHONE...................619 260-0111
Fax: 619 497-0813
Mike Rice, *Manager*
Chris Feastern, *Chief Engr*
Mark Luttik, *Sales Dir*
EMP: 60
SALES (corp-wide): 6MM Privately Held
SIC: 8741 5813 5812 Hotel or motel management; drinking places; eating places
PA: Ashford Trs Nickel, Llc
1345 Treat Blvd
Walnut Creek CA 94597
925 934-2500

(P-26929)
ASSET ATHENE MANAGEMENT L P (HQ)
2121 Rosecrans Ave # 5300, El Segundo (90245-4750)
PHONE...................310 698-4444
James R Belardi, *CEO*
Jeff Boland, *Exec VP*
Nancy De Liban, *Exec VP*
James Hassett, *Exec VP*
Laura Hodges, *Senior VP*
EMP: 69
SALES (est): 15.6MM Publicly Held
SIC: 8741 Financial management for business

(P-26930)
ATRIA SENIOR LIVING GROUP INC
Also Called: Golden
33 Creek Rd Side, Irvine (92604-4792)
PHONE...................949 786-5665
Fax: 949 786-3745
Sandra McDaniel, *Manager*
EMP: 60
SALES (corp-wide): 3.2B Publicly Held
WEB: www.atriacom.com
SIC: 8741 6531 Hotel or motel management; real estate brokers & agents
HQ: Atria Senior Living Group Inc
300 E Market St Ste 100
Louisville KY 40202

(P-26931)
AUDIO VISUAL MGT SOLUTIONS
Also Called: AV Management
12812 Garden Grove Blvd M, Garden Grove (92843-2009)
PHONE...................714 590-8755
Just Cameron, *Branch Mgr*
EMP: 173 Privately Held
SIC: 8741 Business management
PA: Audio Visual Management Solutions, Inc
814 6th Ave S
Seattle WA 98134

(P-26932)
AVIATION CONSULTANTS INC (PA)
Also Called: Epic Jet Centre
945 Airport Dr, San Luis Obispo (93401-8354)
PHONE...................805 548-1300
William Borgsmiller, *President*
Nathan Ross, *CFO*
Anna Valsing, *Info Tech Mgr*
Julia Lojacono, *Human Res Mgr*
Crystal Heavers, *Mktg Dir*
EMP: 62
SQ FT: 6,100
SALES (est): 10.6MM Privately Held
WEB: www.aviationconsultants.net
SIC: 8741 7363 Management services; pilot service, aviation

(P-26933)
AWI MANAGEMENT CORPORATION
1800 E Lakeshore Dr, Lake Elsinore (92530-4469)
PHONE...................951 674-8200
Angelica Chaidez, *Branch Mgr*
EMP: 241
SALES (corp-wide): 13.7MM Privately Held
SIC: 8741 Business management
PA: Awi Management Corporation
120 Center St
Auburn CA 95603
530 745-6170

(P-26934)
BACCHUS VINEYARD MGT LLC
930 Shiloh Rd Bldg 17, Windsor (95492-6628)
PHONE...................707 837-8304
James G Alexander, *Mng Member*
Olga Mendova, *Manager*
Armando Miranda, *Manager*
Morgan Marengo, *Assistant*
EMP: 60
SALES (est): 7.2MM Privately Held
SIC: 8741 Business management

(P-26935)
BANK AMERICA NATIONAL ASSN
73525 El Paseo, Palm Desert (92260-4341)
PHONE...................760 636-7500
EMP: 138
SALES (corp-wide): 93B Publicly Held
SIC: 8741 6282 6029 6021 Business management; investment advice; commercial banks; national commercial banks
HQ: Bank Of America, National Association
101 S Tryon St
Charlotte NC 28280
704 386-5681

(P-26936)
BANK AMERICA NATIONAL ASSN
555 Capitol Mall, Sacramento (95814-4504)
PHONE...................916 326-3161
Maria Barry, *Branch Mgr*
EMP: 138
SALES (corp-wide): 93B Publicly Held
SIC: 8741 6282 6029 6021 Business management; investment advice; commercial banks; national commercial banks
HQ: Bank Of America, National Association
101 S Tryon St
Charlotte NC 28280
704 386-5681

(P-26937)
BARRETT BUSINESS SERVICES INC
1840 Gateway Dr, San Mateo (94404-4027)
PHONE...................650 653-7588
EMP: 5004
SALES (corp-wide): 740.8MM Publicly Held
SIC: 8741 Business management
PA: Barrett Business Services Inc
8100 Ne Parkway Dr # 200
Vancouver WA 98662
360 828-0700

(P-26938)
BAYSCAPE MANAGEMENT INC
Also Called: Coast Landscape Management
1350 Pacific Ave, Alviso (95002)
P.O. Box 880 (95002-0880)
PHONE...................408 288-2940
Thomas Ellington, *President*
EMP: 70
SALES (est): 9.6MM Privately Held
SIC: 8741 Management services

(P-26939)
BAYVIEW PROPERTIES INC (PA)
Also Called: Best Western, The Beach Resort
2600 Sand Dunes Dr, Monterey (93940-3838)
PHONE...................831 394-3321
Theodore Richter, *President*
EMP: 99
SALES (est): 9MM Privately Held
WEB: www.montereybeachhotel.com
SIC: 8741 Hotels & motels

(P-26940)
BECHTEL CAPITAL MGT CORP
50 Beale St, San Francisco (94105-1813)
PHONE...................415 768-1234
Riley Bechtel, *Chairman*
Brendan Bechtel, *President*
Bill Dudley, *CEO*
Peter Dawson, *CFO*
Anshul Maheshwari, *Treasurer*
EMP: 2000
SQ FT: 600,000
SALES (est): 53.3MM
SALES (corp-wide): 7.7B Privately Held
WEB: www.bechtelgroup.com
SIC: 8741 Financial management for business
PA: Bechtel Group, Inc.
50 Beale St Bsmt 1
San Francisco CA 94105
415 768-1234

(P-26941)
BEECH STREET CORPORATION (DH)
25500 Commercentre Dr # 100, Lake Forest (92630-8862)
PHONE...................949 672-1000
Fax: 949 672-1111
William Fickling Jr, *Chairman*
William Hale, *President*
Jon Bird, *CFO*
Terry Harris, *Exec VP*
Rick Markus, *Exec VP*
EMP: 350
SQ FT: 60,000
SALES (est): 22.6MM
SALES (corp-wide): 3.7B Publicly Held
WEB: www.beechstreet.com
SIC: 8741 Administrative management
HQ: Concentra Operating Corporation
5080 Spectrum Dr Ste 400w
Addison TX 75001
972 364-8000

(P-26942)
BEVERLY HEALTH CARE CORP (PA)
5445 Everglades St, Ventura (93003-6523)
PHONE...................805 642-1736
Carol Tradeway, *Director*
Rose Taylor-Calhoun, *CEO*
Philip Drescher, *Principal*
Harry Maynard, *Principal*
Gary Wolfe, *Principal*
EMP: 50
SQ FT: 85,000

8741 - Management Services County (P-26943)

SALES (est): 16.9MM **Privately Held**
SIC: 8741 Management services

(P-26943)
BML WORKS NA LLC
228 Hamilton Ave Fl 3, Palo Alto (94301-2583)
PHONE.....................650 268-8305
George Ferrier,
EMP: 52
SALES (est): 2.5MM **Privately Held**
SIC: 8741 Management services

(P-26944)
BOARDVANTAGE INC (HQ)
4300 Bohannon Dr Ste 110, Menlo Park (94025-1042)
PHONE.....................650 614-6000
Joe Ruck, *President*
Anirban Datta, *Chief Mktg Ofcr*
Mary De Frnchi, *Exec VP*
Junaid Syed, *CTO*
Randy Hollingsworth, *QA Dir*
EMP: 120
SQ FT: 7,000
SALES (est): 40.1MM
SALES (corp-wide): 3.4B **Publicly Held**
WEB: www.boardvantage.com
SIC: 8741 8742 Management services; personnel management consultant
PA: Nasdaq, Inc.
1 Liberty Plz Ste 4900
New York NY 10006
212 401-8700

(P-26945)
BOEING COMPANY
2401 E Wardlow Rd, Long Beach (90807-5309)
P.O. Box 200 (90801-0200)
PHONE.....................562 593-5511
Linda Van Reeden, *Manager*
Frank Tetnowski, *Info Tech Dir*
Matthew Matsuoka, *Human Resources*
EMP: 1400
SALES (corp-wide): 96.1B **Publicly Held**
SIC: 8741 Administrative management
PA: The Boeing Company
100 N Riverside Plz
Chicago IL 60606
312 544-2000

(P-26946)
BPG STORAGE SOLUTIONS INC
2033 N Main St Ste 340, Walnut Creek (94596-3727)
PHONE.....................562 467-2000
Michael Barker, *President*
Jae Ho, *Manager*
EMP: 60
SALES (est): 3.4MM
SALES (corp-wide): 14.5MM **Privately Held**
WEB: www.barkerpacific.com
SIC: 8741 Management services
PA: Barker Pacific Group, Inc.
2033 N Main St Ste 340
Walnut Creek CA 94596
415 884-9977

(P-26947)
BRET BOYLAN PROPERTY MGT
Also Called: Bret Boylan
35 N Alboni Pl Apt 409, Long Beach (90802-5438)
P.O. Box 14690 (90853-4690)
PHONE.....................562 437-7886
Bret Boylan, *Owner*
EMP: 50
SQ FT: 300
SALES (est): 2MM **Privately Held**
SIC: 8741 Business management

(P-26948)
BUCKINGHAM AFFRDBL APRTMNTS LP
Also Called: Buckingham Apartments
11911 San Vicente Blvd, Los Angeles (90049-5086)
PHONE.....................424 273-6162
Adam Cutler, *Vice Pres*
EMP: 60
SALES (est): 1.7MM **Privately Held**
SIC: 8741 Business management

(P-26949)
BUCKLAND VINEYARD MANAGEMENT (PA)
4560 Slodusty Rd, Garden Valley (95633-9244)
PHONE.....................530 333-1534
Fax: 707 252-1438
Alfred Buckland, *President*
EMP: 60
SALES (est): 3.2MM **Privately Held**
SIC: 8741 Management services

(P-26950)
BUONA TERRA FARMING CO INC
2380 A St, Santa Maria (93455-1009)
PHONE.....................805 614-9229
John Belfy, *President*
EMP: 100
SALES (est): 11.2MM **Privately Held**
SIC: 8741 0762 Management services; farm management services

(P-26951)
C/O UC SAN FRANCISCO (PA)
Also Called: University of CA Office
1111 Franklin St Fl 12, Oakland (94607-5201)
PHONE.....................858 534-7323
John Fox, *Principal*
Arthur A Castillo, *Officer*
Marina Arseniev, *Associate Dir*
Ronald James, *Associate Dir*
Carol Buge, *Exec Dir*
EMP: 148
SALES (est): 49.8MM **Privately Held**
SIC: 8741 Restaurant management

(P-26952)
CAL PINNACLE MLTARY CMMUNITIES
3200 4th Ave Ste 201, San Diego (92103-5716)
P.O. Box 10034, Fort Irwin (92310-0034)
PHONE.....................619 764-5087
Shawn Sommerville, *Director*
EMP: 55
SALES (est): 1.4MM **Privately Held**
SIC: 8741 Management services

(P-26953)
CAL POLY CORPORATION
Also Called: Cal Poly Foundation
Bldg 15, San Luis Obispo (93407)
PHONE.....................805 756-1131
Hank A Mumford, *Exec Dir*
EMP: 210
SALES (corp-wide): 44.1MM **Privately Held**
WEB: www.calpolyarts.org
SIC: 8741 Business management
PA: Cal Poly Corporation
1 Grand Ave Bldg 15
San Luis Obispo CA 93407
805 756-1131

(P-26954)
CALIFORNIA STATE UNIV AUX SVCS
Also Called: UNIVERSITY BOOKSTORE
5151 State University Dr Ge314, Los Angeles (90032-4226)
PHONE.....................323 343-2531
R Dean Calvo, *Exec Dir*
Rowena Tran, *Associate Dir*
Tuyet Castille, *Admin Asst*
EMP: 600
SQ FT: 108,000
SALES (est): 30.8MM **Privately Held**
SIC: 8741 5942 5651 5812 Business management; financial management for business; college book stores; unisex clothing stores; cafeteria

(P-26955)
CALIFORNIA STATE UNIVERSITY
25976 Carlos Bee Blvd, Hayward (94542-1602)
PHONE.....................510 885-2700
Curt Robinson, *Director*
EMP: 78
SQ FT: 32,500
SALES: 20.3MM **Privately Held**
SIC: 8741 5942 Management services; administrative management; financial management for business; book stores

(P-26956)
CALTROP CORPORATION
2415 Campus Dr Ste 265, Irvine (92612-8550)
PHONE.....................949 337-4280
Fax: 714 263-0327
David Saber, *President*
Derich Sukow, *Manager*
EMP: 78
SALES (corp-wide): 64.5MM **Privately Held**
WEB: www.caltrop.com
SIC: 8741 Construction management
PA: Caltrop Corporation
9337 Milliken Ave
Rancho Cucamonga CA 91730
909 931-9331

(P-26957)
CAMARILLO HEALTHCARE CENTER
205 Granada St, Camarillo (93010-7715)
PHONE.....................805 482-9805
Angie Chavz, *Administration*
Brett Watson, *Administration*
EMP: 1201
SALES (est): 2.2MM
SALES (corp-wide): 1.3B **Publicly Held**
SIC: 8741 Nursing & personal care facility management
PA: The Ensign Group Inc
27101 Puerta Real Ste 450
Mission Viejo CA 92691
949 487-9500

(P-26958)
CAREMORE MEDICAL MANAGEMENT A (HQ)
Also Called: Caremore AP
12900 Park Plaza Dr # 150, Cerritos (90703-9329)
PHONE.....................562 741-4300
Ken Westbrook, *Partner*
John KAO, *Exec VP*
Eric V Horn, *General Mgr*
Cindy Grave, *Accountant*
Demetra Crandall,
EMP: 80
SALES (est): 44.7MM
SALES (corp-wide): 79.1B **Publicly Held**
SIC: 8741 5047 Business management; hospital management; medical equipment & supplies
PA: Anthem, Inc.
120 Monument Cir Ste 200
Indianapolis IN 46204
317 488-6000

(P-26959)
CARGILL INCORPORATED
4344 S Eldorado St, Stockton (95206)
P.O. Box 369 (95201-3069)
PHONE.....................209 982-4632
Fax: 209 982-5649
Matt Budine, *Principal*
Jessica King, *Executive*
Terry Quadros, *CPA*
Russell Riecken, *Manager*
EMP: 100
SALES (corp-wide): 107.1B **Privately Held**
WEB: www.cargill.com
SIC: 8741 2048 Administrative management; prepared feeds
PA: Cargill, Incorporated
15407 Mcginty Rd W
Wayzata MN 55391
952 742-7575

(P-26960)
CARRINGTON MORTGAGE SERVICES
1600 S Douglass Rd 110, Anaheim (92806-5948)
PHONE.....................888 267-0584
Phil Grassbaugh, *Principal*
Mark Allanach, *President*
Ron Nicolas, *CFO*
Ryan George, *Officer*
Jennifer Rakaphoume, *Officer*
EMP: 123

SQ FT: 192,000
SALES (est): 21.1MM
SALES (corp-wide): 32.5MM **Privately Held**
SIC: 8741 Management services
PA: Carrington Capital Management Llc
7 Greenwich Office Park
Greenwich CT 06831
203 661-6186

(P-26961)
CASE SHELLA MANAGEMENT SERVICE
26010 Mccall Blvd Ste B, Sun City (92586-1983)
P.O. Box 263 (92586-0263)
PHONE.....................951 723-8460
Michael Foster, *Owner*
Michael Kassens, *Manager*
EMP: 145
SQ FT: 600
SALES (est): 10.4MM **Privately Held**
SIC: 8741 Business management

(P-26962)
CASTLEBLACK OWNER HOLDINGS LLC
601 James Way, Pismo Beach (93449-3502)
PHONE.....................805 773-6020
Gordon Jackson, *Manager*
EMP: 50
SALES (corp-wide): 31.8MM **Privately Held**
SIC: 8741 Hotel or motel management
PA: Castleblack Owner Holdings, Llc
399 Park Ave Fl 18
New York NY 10022
212 547-2609

(P-26963)
CHEVRON INVESTOR INC
100 Chevron Way, Richmond (94801-2016)
PHONE.....................510 242-3000
Mark Logan, *Branch Mgr*
Jirong Xiao, *Vice Pres*
Morgan Clark, *VP Mfg*
Pat Wyffels, *Manager*
EMP: 100
SALES (corp-wide): 138.4B **Publicly Held**
SIC: 8741 8731 Management services; commercial physical research
HQ: Chevron Investor Inc
6001 Bollinger Canyon Rd
San Ramon CA 94583
925 842-1000

(P-26964)
CHILIS 898 CORONA
3579 Grand Oaks, Corona (92881-4634)
PHONE.....................951 734-7275
Deann Demarso, *President*
Deann De Marso, *President*
Perry Schoulten, *Office Mgr*
EMP: 90
SALES (est): 3.2MM **Privately Held**
SIC: 8741 Restaurant management

(P-26965)
CIK POWER DISTRIBUTORS LLC
240 W Grove Ave, Orange (92865-3204)
PHONE.....................714 938-0297
Chris A Christopher, *Mng Member*
Stephen G Carter,
Robert M Tulley,
EMP: 59
SALES (est): 10.8MM **Privately Held**
SIC: 8741 Construction management

(P-26966)
CIRCLE WOOD SERVICES INC
3670 W Temple Ave, Pomona (91768-2588)
PHONE.....................909 784-0733
Don Watson, *President*
EMP: 70 EST: 2007
SQ FT: 1,400
SALES (est): 6.4MM **Privately Held**
SIC: 8741 Management services

PRODUCTS & SERVICES SECTION
8741 - Management Services County (P-26988)

(P-26967)
CITIZENHAWK INC
Also Called: Wolters Kluwer Corp Legal Svcs
135 Columbia, Aliso Viejo (92656-4108)
PHONE..................................949 427-3002
Richard Flynn, *CEO*
Robert Ofee, *Business Dir*
Thomas Nestor, *VP Finance*
EMP: 54
SALES (est): 21MM
SALES (corp-wide): 4.5B **Privately Held**
SIC: 8741 Management services
HQ: C T Corporation System
111 8th Ave Fl 13
New York NY 10011
212 894-8940

(P-26968)
CITRUS VLY HLTH PARTNERS INC (PA)
Also Called: Inter Community Hospital
210 W San Bernardino Rd, Covina (91723-1515)
P.O. Box 6108 (91722-5108)
PHONE..................................626 331-7331
Fax: 626 859-5848
Robert Curry, *CEO*
James Yoshioka, *President*
Alvia Polk, *COO*
Lois Conyers, *CFO*
Paveljit Bindra, *Chief Mktg Ofcr*
EMP: 1200
SQ FT: 237,000
SALES: 58.1MM **Privately Held**
WEB: www.cvhp.com
SIC: 8741 Administrative management

(P-26969)
CITY & COUNTY OF SAN FRANCISCO
Also Called: Administrative Services
1 Carlton B Goodlett Pl # 234, San Francisco (94102-4604)
PHONE..................................415 554-4799
Corrine Mehgan, *Mng Officer*
Alvin C Moses, *Manager*
EMP: 100 **Privately Held**
SIC: 8741 9199 Management services; general government administration; ;
PA: City & County Of San Francisco
1 Dr Carlton B Goodlett P
San Francisco CA 94102
415 554-7500

(P-26970)
CITY ALAMEDA HEALTH CARE CORP
2070 Clinton Ave, Alameda (94501-4399)
PHONE..................................510 814-4000
Deborah E Stebbins, *Branch Mgr*
EMP: 457
SALES (corp-wide): 0 **Privately Held**
SIC: 8741 Hospital management
PA: City Of Alameda Health Care Corporation
2070 Clinton Ave
Alameda CA 94501
510 522-3700

(P-26971)
CLARIZEN INC
2755 Campus Dr Ste 300, San Mateo (94403-2538)
PHONE..................................866 502-9813
Boaz Chalamish, *CEO*
Jason Schwartz, *CFO*
Ted Purcell, *Senior VP*
Amber Tallerico, *Sales Staff*
Jen Howard, *Senior Mgr*
EMP: 64
SALES (est): 15.2MM
SALES (corp-wide): 59.9K **Privately Held**
SIC: 8741 Management services
PA: Clarizen Ltd
4 Hacharash
Hod Hasharon
979 443-00

(P-26972)
CLOROX SERVICES COMPANY
5060 Johnson Dr, Pleasanton (94588-3333)
PHONE..................................925 425-6748
Tinoco Adelita, *Manager*
Bob Miller, *Research*
Dan Faubion, *Chief Engr*
Ryan Elvers, *Marketing Mgr*
EMP: 70
SALES (corp-wide): 5.7B **Publicly Held**
SIC: 8741 Management services
HQ: Clorox Services Company
1221 Broadway Ste 13
Oakland CA 94612

(P-26973)
CLOROX SERVICES COMPANY (HQ)
1221 Broadway Ste 13, Oakland (94612-1829)
PHONE..................................510 271-7000
R A Llenado, *Ch of Bd*
C E Williams, *President*
Lyle Hoover, *Treasurer*
Ausfahl Cutter, *Vice Pres*
Wayne Delker, *Vice Pres*
EMP: 100
SALES (est): 61.5MM
SALES (corp-wide): 5.7B **Publicly Held**
WEB: www.clorox.com
SIC: 8741 Management services
PA: The Clorox Company
1221 Broadway Ste 1300
Oakland CA 94612
510 271-7000

(P-26974)
CMTS LLC
5777 W Century Blvd # 1105, Los Angeles (90045-5637)
PHONE..................................310 215-0237
Fax: 310 390-9847
K Hezekiah Harris II, *CEO*
Bill Blalock, *President*
Winifred Harris, *Vice Pres*
Glenna Spencer, *Admin Asst*
Todd Britten, *Analyst*
EMP: 120
SQ FT: 1,500
SALES (est): 11.9MM **Privately Held**
SIC: 8741 Construction management

(P-26975)
COLLECTIVE MGT GROUP LLC
8383 Wilshire Blvd # 1050, Beverly Hills (90211-2415)
PHONE..................................323 655-8585
Fax: 310 888-1555
Michael Green, *CEO*
Jordan Toplitzky, *CFO*
Jordan Berliant,
Gary Binkow,
Reza Izad,
EMP: 110
SQ FT: 15,000
SALES: 50MM **Privately Held**
SIC: 8741 Management services

(P-26976)
COMMONWEALTH HOTELS LLC
Also Called: Courtyard Vallejo
1000 Fairgrounds Dr, Vallejo (94589-4000)
PHONE..................................707 644-1200
Nader Elkabbany, *General Mgr*
EMP: 133
SALES (corp-wide): 95.2MM **Privately Held**
WEB: www.commonwealth-hotels.com
SIC: 8741 Circuit management for motion picture theaters
PA: Commonwealth Hotels, Llc
100 E Rivercenter Blvd # 1050
Covington KY 41011
859 392-2264

(P-26977)
COMMUNITY DEVELOPMENT COMM
Also Called: Construction Development Div
700 W Main St, Alhambra (91801-3312)
PHONE..................................626 262-4511
Sean Rogan, *Director*
Tom Foreman, *Info Tech Mgr*
Esther E Kosababian, *Manager*
EMP: 50 **Privately Held**
WEB: www.co.la.ca.us
SIC: 8741 Construction management
HQ: Community Development Commission
700 W Main St
Alhambra CA 91801
626 262-4511

(P-26978)
COMMUNITY HOSPITAL FOUNDATION (PA)
23625 Holman Hwy, Monterey (93940-5902)
P.O. Box Hh (93942-6032)
PHONE..................................831 625-4830
Fax: 831 625-4784
Steven Packer MD, *President*
William C Vogelpohl, *Ch OB/GYN*
Terril Lowe, *Vice Pres*
Tim Nylen, *Vice Pres*
Cynthia Peck, *Vice Pres*
EMP: 1650
SQ FT: 350,000
SALES: 200MM **Privately Held**
SIC: 8741 Hospital management

(P-26979)
COMMUNITY HOUSING OPPORT
Also Called: Sterling Asset Management
5030 Bus Center Dr # 260, Fairfield (94534-6884)
PHONE..................................707 759-6043
Fax: 530 757-4454
Nancy Conk, *Exec Dir*
EMP: 50 **Privately Held**
WEB: www.chochousing.org
SIC: 8741 Management services
PA: Community Housing Opportunities Corporation
5030 Business Center Dr # 260
Fairfield CA 94534
530 757-4444

(P-26980)
COMPUTERIZED MGT SVCS INC
Also Called: CMS
4100 Guardian St Ste 205, Simi Valley (93063-6721)
P.O. Box 190 (93062-0190)
PHONE..................................805 522-5940
J Daryl Favale, *President*
Jimitria Smith, *Division Mgr*
Robb Charlton, *Info Tech Mgr*
EMP: 100
SQ FT: 7,500
SALES (est): 9.3MM **Privately Held**
SIC: 8741 Business management

(P-26981)
CONVENIENCE MANAGEMENT GROUP
3781 Telegraph Rd, Ventura (93003-3420)
PHONE..................................805 644-6784
William E Thompson, *President*
Kay Thompson, *Treasurer*
Gary Carson, *Exec VP*
Anna McCowan, *Manager*
EMP: 90
SALES (est): 5MM **Privately Held**
SIC: 8741 5172 Business management; petroleum products

(P-26982)
CORLAND COMPANIES (PA)
Also Called: Carlson
17542 17th St Ste 420, Tustin (92780-7928)
P.O. Box 807 (92781-0807)
PHONE..................................714 573-7780
Chis Hide, *President*
Christopher Hite, *Treasurer*
Patrick Galentine, *Vice Pres*
Wendy Guvban, *Office Mgr*
Brooke Casey, *Executive Asst*
EMP: 50
SALES (est): 9.5MM **Privately Held**
SIC: 8741 Management services

(P-26983)
CORNERSTONE HOTEL MANAGEMENT (DH)
222 Kearny St Ste 200, San Francisco (94108-4537)
PHONE..................................415 397-5572
Tom La Tour, *President*
J Kirke Wrench, *CFO*
Nir Margalit, *Admin Sec*
EMP: 75
SALES (est): 7.1MM
SALES (corp-wide): 1.8B **Privately Held**
SIC: 8741 Management services
HQ: Alexis Hotel Management Inc
222 Kearny St Ste 200
San Francisco CA
415 397-5572

(P-26984)
CORVEL CORPORATION (PA)
2010 Main St Ste 600, Irvine (92614-7272)
PHONE..................................949 851-1473
Fax: 949 851-1469
V Gordon Clemons, *Ch of Bd*
Richard J Schweppe, *CFO*
Shari Muniz, *Treasurer*
Diane J Blaha, *Senior VP*
Laura Schumacher, *District Mgr*
EMP: 133
SQ FT: 13,000
SALES: 503.5MM **Publicly Held**
WEB: www.corvel.com
SIC: 8741 8011 Nursing & personal care facility management; internal medicine practitioners; medical insurance associations

(P-26985)
COUNTRY VILLA SERVICE CORP
3002 Rowena Ave, Los Angeles (90039-2005)
PHONE..................................323 666-1544
Stephen Rissman, *President*
Mauricio Bajar, *MIS Dir*
EMP: 120
SALES (corp-wide): 154.7MM **Privately Held**
WEB: www.countryvillahealth.com
SIC: 8741 8051 Nursing & personal care facility management; skilled nursing care facilities
PA: Country Villa Service Corp.
2400 E Katella Ave # 800
Anaheim CA 92806
310 574-3733

(P-26986)
COUNTRY VILLA SERVICE CORP (PA)
Also Called: Country Villa Health Services
2400 E Katella Ave # 800, Anaheim (92806-5955)
PHONE..................................310 574-3733
Fax: 310 574-1322
Stephen Reissman, *CEO*
Diane Reissman, *Exec VP*
Cheryl Petterson, *Vice Pres*
Andy Levin, *Exec Dir*
Larry Huffman, *Administration*
EMP: 80 **EST:** 1972
SQ FT: 24,000
SALES (est): 154.7MM **Privately Held**
WEB: www.countryvillahealth.com
SIC: 8741 Nursing & personal care facility management; hospital management

(P-26987)
COUNTRY VILLA SERVICE CORP
1730 Grand Ave, Long Beach (90804-2011)
PHONE..................................562 597-8817
Nenita Bartolome, *Financial Exec*
EMP: 110
SALES (corp-wide): 154.7MM **Privately Held**
SIC: 8741 Management services
PA: Country Villa Service Corp.
2400 E Katella Ave # 800
Anaheim CA 92806
310 574-3733

(P-26988)
COUNTRY VILLA SERVICE CORP
615 W Duarte Rd, Monrovia (91016-4436)
PHONE..................................626 358-4547
Sam Chia, *Branch Mgr*
EMP: 110
SALES (corp-wide): 154.7MM **Privately Held**
SIC: 8741 Management services
PA: Country Villa Service Corp.
2400 E Katella Ave # 800
Anaheim CA 92806
310 574-3733

8741 - Management Services County (P-26989)

PRODUDUCTS & SERVICES SECTION

(P-26989)
COUNTRY VILLA SERVICE CORP
Also Called: Country Villa E Convalescent
2415 S Western Ave, Los Angeles (90018-2608)
PHONE...................323 734-1101
Phadra Johnson, *Manager*
Alisha Thimbrel, *Records Dir*
Christina Arias, *Social Dir*
Butch Alindogan, *Office Mgr*
Monica Urena, *Administration*
EMP: 120
SALES (corp-wide): 154.7MM **Privately Held**
WEB: www.countryvillahealth.com
SIC: 8741 8051 8011 8059 Nursing & personal care facility management; skilled nursing care facilities; clinic, operated by physicians; convalescent home
PA: Country Villa Service Corp.
   2400 E Katella Ave # 800
   Anaheim CA 92806
   310 574-3733

(P-26990)
COUNTRY VILLA SERVICE CORP
3533 Motor Ave, Los Angeles (90034-4806)
PHONE...................310 574-3733
EMP: 110
SALES (corp-wide): 154.7MM **Privately Held**
SIC: 8741 Nursing & personal care facility management
PA: Country Villa Service Corp.
   2400 E Katella Ave # 800
   Anaheim CA 92806
   310 574-3733

(P-26991)
COUNTRY VILLA SERVICE CORP
3233 W Pico Blvd, Los Angeles (90019-3640)
PHONE...................323 734-9122
Mike Demchuck, *Manager*
Bella Bonds, *Records Dir*
Carlos Zaragoza, *Envir Svcs Dir*
Norma Rojas, *Office Mgr*
Cynvilin Ramillano, *Nursing Dir*
EMP: 100
SALES (corp-wide): 154.7MM **Privately Held**
WEB: www.countryvillahealth.com
SIC: 8741 8051 Nursing & personal care facility management; skilled nursing care facilities
PA: Country Villa Service Corp.
   2400 E Katella Ave # 800
   Anaheim CA 92806
   310 574-3733

(P-26992)
COUNTRYSIDE INN-CORONA LP
1015 W Colton Ave, Redlands (92374-2933)
PHONE...................909 335-9024
Donald B Ayres Jr, *Branch Mgr*
EMP: 50
SALES (corp-wide): 45.4MM **Privately Held**
SIC: 8741 Management services
PA: Countryside Inn-Corona, L.P.
   1900 Frontage Rd
   Corona CA 92882
   714 540-6060

(P-26993)
COUNTRYSIDE INN-CORONA LP
12850 Seal Beach Blvd, Seal Beach (90740-2714)
PHONE...................562 596-8330
Bill Tolen, *Manager*
EMP: 50
SALES (corp-wide): 45.4MM **Privately Held**
WEB: www.ayreshotelsealbeach.com
SIC: 8741 1531 Management services; operative builders
PA: Countryside Inn-Corona, L.P.
   1900 Frontage Rd
   Corona CA 92882
   714 540-6060

(P-26994)
COUNTY OF SAN MATEO
Also Called: Human Resources Department
400 County Ctr, Redwood City (94063-1662)
PHONE...................650 363-4915
Fax: 650 363-1819
Greg Munks, *Sheriff*
EMP: 145 **Privately Held**
WEB: www.ci.sanmateo.ca.us
SIC: 8741 9441 Personnel management;
PA: County Of San Mateo
   400 County Ctr
   Redwood City CA 94063
   650 363-4123

(P-26995)
COUNTY OF SAN MATEO
Also Called: Human Resources Department
455 County Ctr, Redwood City (94063-1663)
PHONE...................650 363-4343
Fax: 650 363-4822
Donna Vaillancourt, *Director*
EMP: 50 **Privately Held**
WEB: www.ci.sanmateo.ca.us
SIC: 8741 9441 Personnel management;
PA: County Of San Mateo
   400 County Ctr
   Redwood City CA 94063
   650 363-4123

(P-26996)
COUNTY OF SAN MATEO
Also Called: Human Resources Department
455 County Ctr Fl 5, Redwood City (94063-1663)
PHONE...................650 363-4321
Donna Vaillancourt, *Director*
EMP: 58 **Privately Held**
WEB: www.ci.sanmateo.ca.us
SIC: 8741 9441 Personnel management;
PA: County Of San Mateo
   400 County Ctr
   Redwood City CA 94063
   650 363-4123

(P-26997)
CRESTLINE HOTELS & RESORTS LLC
535 S Grand Ave, Los Angeles (90071-2601)
PHONE...................213 624-0000
Eddie Andre, *Manager*
EMP: 88 **Publicly Held**
SIC: 8741 Hotel or motel management
HQ: Crestline Hotels & Resorts, Llc
   3950 University Dr # 301
   Fairfax VA 22030
   571 529-6100

(P-26998)
CRESTLINE HOTELS & RESORTS LLC
1250 Columbus Ave, San Francisco (94133-1327)
PHONE...................415 775-7555
Amy Arbuckle, *Manager*
EMP: 175 **Publicly Held**
SIC: 8741 Hotel or motel management
HQ: Crestline Hotels & Resorts, Llc
   3950 University Dr # 301
   Fairfax VA 22030
   571 529-6100

(P-26999)
CSI FINANCIAL SERVICES LLC
3636 Nobel Dr Ste 250, San Diego (92122-1042)
PHONE...................858 200-9200
Janet Shanks, *CFO*
Vince Koch, *Vice Pres*
Craig Webster, *CIO*
Dusty Harkleroad, *Info Tech Mgr*
Lewis Harkleroad, *Info Tech Mgr*
EMP: 50
SQ FT: 4,050
SALES (est): 7MM **Privately Held**
WEB: www.csifinancial.com
SIC: 8741 8742 Management services; hospital & health services consultant

(P-27000)
CYMETRIX CORPORATION
1515 W 190th St Ste 350, Gardena (90248-4910)
PHONE...................424 201-6300
Jeff Macdonald, *Branch Mgr*
Karen Ladika, *Principal*
EMP: 125
SALES (corp-wide): 919.4MM **Publicly Held**
WEB: www.hmsintl.com
SIC: 8741 Management services
HQ: Cymetrix Corporation
   2875 Michelle Ste 250
   Irvine CA 92606
   714 361-6800

(P-27001)
D BAILEY MANAGEMENT COMP
Also Called: McDonald's
121 S Hope St Apt 307, Los Angeles (90012-5005)
PHONE...................213 626-2665
Fax: 323 731-0394
Donald Bailey Sr, *President*
EMP: 500
SALES (est): 35.8MM **Privately Held**
SIC: 8741 Management services

(P-27002)
DELTA STEWARDSHIP COUNCIL
980 9th St Ste 1500, Sacramento (95814-2735)
PHONE...................916 445-5511
Chris Knopp, *CEO*
Jessica Pearson, *Exec Officer*
EMP: 60
SALES (est): 5.4MM **Privately Held**
SIC: 8741 Administrative management
HQ: California Natural Resources Agency
   1416 9th St Ste 1311
   Sacramento CA 95814
   916 653-5656

(P-27003)
DERJJAN ASSOCIATES INC (PA)
2025 Soquel Ave, Santa Cruz (95062-1323)
PHONE...................831 423-4111
Larry Deghetaldi, *President*
Gary Loveridge, *Ch of Bd*
Wayne Boss, *President*
Lowell M Sprague, *VP Finance*
EMP: 185
SQ FT: 60,000
SALES (est): 11.2MM **Privately Held**
WEB: www.williamrichards.com
SIC: 8741 6512 Administrative management; bank building operation

(P-27004)
DEWOLF REALTY CO INC
4330 California St, San Francisco (94118-1316)
P.O. Box 591540 (94159-1540)
PHONE...................415 221-2032
William A Talmage, *President*
Marie Wayne, *Corp Secy*
Aaron Sinel, *Vice Pres*
William Fuson, *Manager*
EMP: 60
SALES (est): 5.9MM **Privately Held**
WEB: www.dewolfsf.com
SIC: 8741 6531 Management services; appraiser, real estate; real estate brokers & agents

(P-27005)
DIRECTORATE OF MWR FMD USAG
420 Montgomery St, San Francisco (94104-1207)
PHONE...................210 466-1376
Christine Brunner, *Manager*
EMP: 99
SALES (est): 1.7MM **Privately Held**
SIC: 8741 Management services

(P-27006)
DOCTORS OF AFFILIATED
600 City Pkwy W Ste 400, Orange (92868-2900)
PHONE...................714 539-3100
Fax: 714 539-3131
Frank Rubino, *President*
John Ernsberger, *CEO*
Prakesh Bondade, *Chairman*
Veronica Palafox, *Office Mgr*
Son Tran, *Accountant*
EMP: 59
SQ FT: 10,000
SALES (est): 6.4MM **Privately Held**
WEB: www.adoc.us
SIC: 8741 Management services

(P-27007)
DONALD LUCKY LLC
Also Called: Babe's Bbq Grill
4029 Westerly Pl Ste 111, Newport Beach (92660-2329)
PHONE...................949 752-0647
Donald Callender,
EMP: 120
SALES (est): 5.1MM **Privately Held**
SIC: 8741 Restaurant management

(P-27008)
E3 HEALTHCARE MANAGEMENT LLC
375 Forest Ave, Palo Alto (94301-2521)
PHONE...................650 324-0600
Carole Wilson, *Mng Member*
Patrick Murphy, *Info Tech Mgr*
Karen Jansen, *Director*
EMP: 100
SALES (est): 4.4MM **Privately Held**
SIC: 8741 Hospital management

(P-27009)
ECHO PCF COMMUNICATIONS LLC
2066 Aldergrove Ave, Escondido (92029-1901)
PHONE...................760 737-3003
EMP: 95
SALES (est): 65MM **Privately Held**
SIC: 8741 1542 Management services; nonresidential construction

(P-27010)
ECONNECTIONS INC
75 N Fair Oaks Ave, Pasadena (91103-3651)
PHONE...................626 307-6200
Robert Rodin, *President*
Henry W Chin, *Exec VP*
EMP: 150
SALES (est): 5.3MM **Privately Held**
WEB: www.econnections.com
SIC: 8741 5065 8742 Management services; electronic parts & equipment; management consulting services

(P-27011)
EDUCATION FOR CHANGE
Also Called: Ascend
3709 E 12th St, Oakland (94601-4001)
PHONE...................510 879-3140
Morgan Alconcher, *Principal*
Robert Litt, *Comp Lab Dir*
Kathryn Fireman, *Librarian*
EMP: 157
SALES (corp-wide): 23.7MM **Privately Held**
SIC: 8741 Management services
PA: Education For Change
   3265 Logan St
   Oakland CA 94601
   510 568-7936

(P-27012)
EDUCATION MANAGEMENT CORP
11128 Magnolia Blvd, North Hollywood (91601-3812)
PHONE...................818 487-0201
EMP: 272
SALES (corp-wide): 2.2B **Publicly Held**
SIC: 8741 Management services
PA: Education Management Corporation
   210 6th Ave Fl 33
   Pittsburgh PA 15222
   412 562-0900

(P-27013)
EDUCATION MANAGEMENT CORP
7650 Mission Valley Rd, San Diego (92108-4423)
PHONE...................858 810-0215
Lia Miller, *General Mgr*

PRODUCTS & SERVICES SECTION

8741 - Management Services County (P-27036)

EMP: 181
SALES (corp-wide): 2.2B **Publicly Held**
SIC: 8741 Management services
PA: Education Management Corporation
210 6th Ave Fl 33
Pittsburgh PA 15222
412 562-0900

(P-27014)
ELATERAL INC
101 1st St Ste 192, Los Altos (94022-2750)
PHONE....................650 917-9141
Alexandre Perry Kamel, *CEO*
Mark Schlief, *Vice Pres*
Perry Kamel, *Exec Dir*
Julie Best, *Manager*
Adam Kottler, *Manager*
EMP: 75
SALES (est): 5.2MM **Privately Held**
SIC: 8741 Management services

(P-27015)
EMULEX CORPORATE SERVICES CORP
3333 Susan St, Costa Mesa (92626-1632)
PHONE....................714 662-5600
Paul Folino, *President*
Barry Massey, *President*
Michael J Rockenbach, *Vice Pres*
Jeff Hoogenboom, *Info Tech Dir*
Natalie Smith, *Controller*
EMP: 79
SQ FT: 30,000
SALES (est): 8.1MM **Privately Held**
SIC: 8741 Business management

(P-27016)
ENERGY SALVAGE INC
8231 Alpine Ave Ste 3, Sacramento (95826-4746)
P.O. Box 255009 (95865-5009)
PHONE....................916 737-8640
Michael P Lien, *President*
Norman Lien, *CFO*
Timothy S Lien, *Vice Pres*
EMP: 50
SALES (est): 2.1MM **Privately Held**
SIC: 8741 6512 Business management; financial management for business; non-residential building operators

(P-27017)
EPIC MANAGEMENT LP (PA)
1615 Orange Tree Ln, Redlands (92374-4501)
P.O. Box 19020, San Bernardino (92423-9020)
PHONE....................909 799-1818
John D Goodman, *CEO*
David Hutchinson, *CFO*
Jean Meeks, *Treasurer*
Fred Hollaus, *Senior VP*
Brian R Fraser, *Vice Pres*
EMP: 148
SALES (est): 52.3MM **Privately Held**
SIC: 8741 Nursing & personal care facility management

(P-27018)
EUGENE BURGER MANAGEMENT CORP
555 Capitol Mall Ste 725, Sacramento (95814-4515)
PHONE....................916 443-6637
Eugene Burger, *Principal*
Karen Oyanguren, *Admin Asst*
Carol Melendez, *Supervisor*
EMP: 240
SALES (corp-wide): 19.1MM **Privately Held**
SIC: 8741 Management services
PA: Eugene Burger Management Corp
6600 Hunter Dr
Rohnert Park CA 94928
707 584-5123

(P-27019)
EVENTBRITE INC (PA)
155 5th St Fl 7, San Francisco (94103-2919)
PHONE....................888 541-9753
Julia Hartz, *CEO*
Mark Rubash, *CFO*
Kevin Hartz, *Chairman*
Roelof Botha, *Bd of Directors*
Matt Rosenberg, *Senior VP*

EMP: 56
SALES (est): 73.9MM **Privately Held**
SIC: 8741 8734 Business management; water testing laboratory

(P-27020)
EVOLUTION HOSPITALITY LLC (PA)
1211 Puerta Del Sol # 170, San Clemente (92673-6353)
PHONE....................949 498-2056
John Murphy, *President*
Sean Maddock, *Shareholder*
Bhavesh Patel, *Senior VP*
Matt Greene, *Vice Pres*
Lynn Kozlowski, *Vice Pres*
EMP: 111 EST: 2010
SALES (est): 265.6MM **Privately Held**
SIC: 8741 Hotel or motel management

(P-27021)
FACILITY SERVICES PARTNERS
1 University Dr, Aliso Viejo (92656-8081)
PHONE....................949 480-4090
Malcolm Thomas, *President*
Scott Collins, *Corp Secy*
EMP: 62 EST: 2008
SALES (est): 4MM **Privately Held**
SIC: 8741 7349 Industrial management; building maintenance services

(P-27022)
FAIRMONT HOTEL PARTNERS LLC (DH)
950 Mason St, San Francisco (94108-2098)
PHONE....................415 772-5000
Fax: 415 772-5013
April Sheesley, *General Mgr*
Don Voncent, *Chief Engr*
Guadalupe Alamilla, *Controller*
Michele Gaul, *Human Res Dir*
Michelle Gilman, *Sales Staff*
EMP: 1000
SQ FT: 2,100
SALES (est): 229.2MM
SALES (corp-wide): 27.3MM **Privately Held**
SIC: 8741 Hotel or motel management
HQ: Fairmont Hotels & Resorts Inc
155 Wellington St W Suite 3300
Toronto ON M5V 0
416 874-2600

(P-27023)
FALCON AEROSPACE HOLDINGS LLC
Also Called: Wesco Aircraft
27727 Avenue Scott, Valencia (91355-1219)
PHONE....................661 775-7200
Randy J Snyder, *Ch of Bd*
Gregory A Hann, *Exec VP*
Tommy Lee, *Exec VP*
EMP: 1250
SALES (est): 32.8MM **Privately Held**
SIC: 8741 Management services

(P-27024)
FBD VANGUARD CONSTRUCTION INC
651 Enterprise Ct, Livermore (94550-5200)
PHONE....................925 245-1300
Fax: 925 245-1007
Billie Sposeto, *President*
Dominic Spofeto, *COO*
Dominic Sposeto, *COO*
Troy Ravazza, *Manager*
EMP: 120
SALES (est): 19.9MM **Privately Held**
SIC: 8741 Construction management

(P-27025)
FIVE STAR QUALITY CARE INC
Also Called: Palm Springs Health Care Ctr
277 S Sunrise Way, Palm Springs (92262-6738)
PHONE....................760 327-8541
Fax: 760 325-0289
Darrin Tharp, *Administration*
EMP: 100

SALES (corp-wide): 1.3B **Publicly Held**
WEB: www.fivestarqualitycare.com
SIC: 8741 8322 Nursing & personal care facility management; rehabilitation services
PA: Five Star Quality Care, Inc.
400 Centre St
Newton MA 02458
617 796-8387

(P-27026)
FOR HOSPITAL COMMITTEE
Also Called: Valleycare Health System
1111 E Stanley Blvd, Livermore (94550-4115)
PHONE....................925 447-7000
Marcelina L Feit, *CEO*
Virgil De Leon, *Network Analyst*
Jeff Klassen, *Network Analyst*
Linda Hedley, *Human Res Mgr*
EMP: 1000
SALES (est): 269.2MM **Privately Held**
SIC: 8741 Administrative management; hospital management

(P-27027)
FORT JAMES CORPORATION
Also Called: Fort James Communications Pprs
2000 Powell St, Emeryville (94608-1804)
PHONE....................510 594-4900
Miles Marsh, *Branch Mgr*
EMP: 100
SALES (corp-wide): 26.7B **Privately Held**
WEB: www.fortjames.com
SIC: 8741 Administrative management
HQ: Fort James Corporation
133 Peachtree St Ne
Atlanta GA 30303
404 652-4000

(P-27028)
FORTE ENTERPRISES INC (PA)
Also Called: St Francis Pavillion
99 Escuela Dr, Daly City (94015-4003)
PHONE....................650 994-3200
Thomas J Nico, *President*
EMP: 240
SQ FT: 14,000
SALES (est): 8.9MM **Privately Held**
SIC: 8741 8721 Nursing & personal care facility management; accounting, auditing & bookkeeping

(P-27029)
FPI MANAGEMENT INC
1107 Luchessi Dr, San Jose (95118-3739)
PHONE....................408 267-3952
EMP: 250
SALES (corp-wide): 73.9MM **Privately Held**
SIC: 8741 6513 Business management; apartment building operators
PA: Fpi Management, Inc.
800 Iron Point Rd
Folsom CA 95630
916 357-5300

(P-27030)
FRITO-LAY NORTH AMERICA INC
1500 Francisco St, Torrance (90501-1329)
PHONE....................310 224-5600
Dexter Matt, *General Mgr*
EMP: 200
SQ FT: 75,861
SALES (corp-wide): 63B **Publicly Held**
WEB: www.fritolay.com
SIC: 8741 2099 2096 Management services; food preparations; potato chips & similar snacks
HQ: Frito-Lay North America, Inc.
7701 Legacy Dr
Plano TX 75024

(P-27031)
FRONT LINE MGT GROUP INC
1100 Glendon Ave Ste 2000, Los Angeles (90024-3524)
PHONE....................310 209-3100
Irving Azoff, *President*
Susan Markheim, *Manager*
EMP: 90

SALES (est): 5.3MM
SALES (corp-wide): 7.2B **Publicly Held**
SIC: 8741 Management services
HQ: Flmg Holdings Corp.
9348 Civic Center Dr
Beverly Hills CA 90210
310 867-7000

(P-27032)
GAFCON INC (PA)
5960 Cornerstone Ct W # 100, San Diego (92121-3780)
PHONE....................858 875-0010
Fax: 619 231-6995
Yehudi Gaffen, *CEO*
Pam Gaffen, *President*
Robin Duveen, *COO*
James Baum, *CFO*
Jon Rodriguez, *CFO*
EMP: 60
SQ FT: 14,000
SALES (est): 28.6MM **Privately Held**
SIC: 8741 8111 Construction management; legal services

(P-27033)
GARDNER NEUROLOGIC ORTHOPEDIC
Also Called: Internal Associates Med Group
6167 Bristol Pkwy Ste 200, Culver City (90230-6649)
PHONE....................310 649-5824
Elias Munoz, *Principal*
EMP: 70
SALES (est): 4.4MM **Privately Held**
SIC: 8741 Management services

(P-27034)
GEO GROUP INC
10400 Rancho Rd, Adelanto (92301-2237)
P.O. Box 6005 (92301-1190)
PHONE....................760 246-1171
Jerardo Acevedo, *Warden*
EMP: 100
SALES (corp-wide): 1.8B **Privately Held**
WEB: www.thegeogroupinc.com
SIC: 8741 Management services
PA: The Geo Group Inc
621 Nw 53rd St Ste 700
Boca Raton FL 33487
561 893-0101

(P-27035)
GEO GROUP INC
Also Called: Golden State Crrctional Fcilty
611 Frontage Rd, Mc Farland (93250-1075)
P.O. Box 1518 (93250-0118)
PHONE....................661 792-2731
Fax: 661 792-6131
Wanda Wilson, *Warden*
EMP: 120
SALES (corp-wide): 1.8B **Privately Held**
WEB: www.thegeogroupinc.com
SIC: 8741 Management services
PA: The Geo Group Inc
621 Nw 53rd St Ste 700
Boca Raton FL 33487
561 893-0101

(P-27036)
GILARDI & CO LLC
3301 Kerner Blvd Ste 100, San Rafael (94901-4896)
PHONE....................415 461-0410
Bryan Butvick, *CEO*
Daniel Burke, *Exec VP*
Lara McDermott, *Exec VP*
Kim Wagner, *Exec VP*
Jason Cahill, *Network Enginr*
EMP: 80
SQ FT: 16,000
SALES (est): 16MM
SALES (corp-wide): 1.4B **Privately Held**
WEB: www.gilardi.com
SIC: 8741 8111 Management services; legal services
HQ: Kurtzman Carson Consultants, Inc
2335 Alaska Ave
El Segundo CA 90245
310 823-9000

8741 - Management Services County (P-27037)

PRODUDUCTS & SERVICES SECTION

(P-27037)
GILBANE BUILDING COMPANY
Also Called: Gilbane Construction
1798 Tech Dr Ste 120, San Jose (95110)
PHONE..................................408 660-4400
Fax: 408 660-4402
Bob Crowder, Director
EMP: 64
SALES (corp-wide): 3.8B **Privately Held**
WEB: www.gilbaneco.com
SIC: 8741 1542 Construction management; commercial & office building, new construction
HQ: Gilbane Building Company
7 Jackson Walkway Ste 2
Providence RI 02903
401 456-5800

(P-27038)
GKK WORKS (HQ)
Also Called: Transitworks
2355 Main St Ste 220, Irvine (92614-4251)
PHONE..................................949 250-1500
Praful Kulkarni, CEO
Sam Porter, CFO
Juan Caldentey, Vice Pres
David Hunt, Vice Pres
Charlie Merrick, Vice Pres
EMP: 50
SALES (est): 16.5MM
SALES (corp-wide): 117.5MM **Privately Held**
SIC: 8741 8712 7389 Construction management; architectural services; interior design services
PA: Gkk Corporation
2355 Main St Ste 220
Irvine CA 92614
949 250-1500

(P-27039)
GLOBAL 360 INC
1080 Marina Village Pkwy # 300, Alameda (94501-6427)
PHONE..................................510 263-4800
Nina Abbott, Branch Mgr
Paul Winsberg, Director
EMP: 65
SALES (corp-wide): 1.8B **Privately Held**
WEB: www.global360.com
SIC: 8741 Management services
PA: Open Text Corporation
275 Frank Tompa Dr
Waterloo ON N2L 0
519 888-7111

(P-27040)
GLOBAL-DINING INC CALIFORNIA
1212 3rd Street Promenade, Santa Monica (90401-1308)
PHONE..................................310 576-9922
Kozo Hasegawa, CEO
EMP: 140
SALES: 6.2MM **Privately Held**
SIC: 8741 Restaurant management

(P-27041)
GOLDEN GATE CAPITAL MGT II LLC
1 Embarcadero Ctr 39th, San Francisco (94111-3628)
PHONE..................................415 983-2700
David Dominik, Mng Member
Rishi Chandra,
Josh Cohen,
Felix Lo,
Jim Rauh,
EMP: 56
SALES (est): 4.1MM **Privately Held**
SIC: 8741 Management services

(P-27042)
GOLDMAN AVRAM
Also Called: Nrt
1855 Gateway Blvd Ste 750, Concord (94520-3290)
PHONE..................................925 275-3000
Avram Goldman, President
Jamie A Schlicher, Vice Pres
EMP: 75
SALES (est): 3MM **Privately Held**
SIC: 8741 6531 Management services; real estate brokers & agents

(P-27043)
GONZALEZ MANAGEMENT CO INC
10147 San Fernando Rd, Pacoima (91331-2617)
PHONE..................................818 485-0596
Luis Gonzalez, President
James Lodenquai, Director
EMP: 65 EST: 2004
SQ FT: 20,000
SALES (est): 6.8MM **Privately Held**
SIC: 8741 Management services

(P-27044)
GRANVILLE GLENDALE INC
16133 Ventura Blvd # 1085, Encino (91436-2403)
PHONE..................................818 981-1171
Jonathan Weiss, President
EMP: 80 EST: 2008
SALES (est): 3.4MM **Privately Held**
SIC: 8741 Restaurant management

(P-27045)
GREYSTAR MANAGEMENT SVCS LP
17885 Von Karman Ave, Irvine (92614-5223)
PHONE..................................949 705-0010
EMP: 347
SALES (corp-wide): 264.3MM **Privately Held**
SIC: 8741 Business management
PA: Greystar Management Services, L.P.
750 Bering Dr Ste 300
Houston TX 77057
713 966-5000

(P-27046)
GRIFFIN SLR MANAGEMENT INC
9454 Wilshire Blvd # 700, Beverly Hills (90212-2931)
PHONE..................................310 270-4031
Sol L Rabin, President
Coleen Rabin, Principal
EMP: 66
SALES (est): 3.1MM **Privately Held**
SIC: 8741 Management services

(P-27047)
GRM INFORMATION MGT SERVICES
8500 Mercury Ln, Pico Rivera (90660-3796)
PHONE..................................562 373-9000
Jerry Glatt, Exec VP
Dave Symanski, VP Opers
John Buglino, Marketing Staff
EMP: 50
SALES (est): 1.6MM **Privately Held**
SIC: 8741 Management services

(P-27048)
GRM INFORMATION MGT SVCS INC
8500 Mercury Ln, Pico Rivera (90660-3796)
PHONE..................................562 373-9000
Fax: 562 373-9031
Jack Grimdjean, Manager
EMP: 54
SALES (corp-wide): 82.9MM **Privately Held**
SIC: 8741 Management services
PA: Grm Information Management Services, Inc.
215 Coles St
Jersey City NJ 07310
201 798-7100

(P-27049)
GSG ASSOCIATES INC
1010 E Union St Ste 203, Pasadena (91106-1756)
PHONE..................................626 585-1808
Glenda S Garrard, CEO
Jay Garrard, President
Maureen Stratton, President
EMP: 100
SQ FT: 3,800
SALES (est): 10MM **Privately Held**
WEB: www.gsga.net
SIC: 8741 Management services; nursing & personal care facility management

(P-27050)
HALL MANAGEMENT CORP
Also Called: Land & Personnel Management
759 S Madera Ave, Kerman (93630-1744)
PHONE..................................559 846-7382
Stacy Hampton, President
James Randles, Vice Pres
EMP: 2000
SQ FT: 5,000
SALES (est): 98.4MM **Privately Held**
SIC: 8741 Management services; personnel management

(P-27051)
HARBOR-UCLA MED FOUNDATION INC (PA)
Also Called: Harbor Ucla Med Foundation
21840 S Norm Ave Ste 100, Torrance (90502)
PHONE..................................310 222-5015
Fax: 310 328-1415
Chester Choi, CEO
Mary Davila, Ch Nursing Ofcr
Chris Eke, Controller
David Plurad, Surgeon
EMP: 100
SQ FT: 45,000
SALES: 12.3MM **Privately Held**
WEB: www.harborucla.org
SIC: 8741 Hospital management

(P-27052)
HDL COREN & CONE
Also Called: Hdl Companies, The
1340 Valley Vista Dr # 200, Diamond Bar (91765-3913)
PHONE..................................909 861-4335
Fax: 909 861-7726
Paula Cone, President
Nichole Cone, Vice Pres
Robert Scherer, Vice Pres
David Schey, Vice Pres
Jess Schmehr, Office Mgr
EMP: 51
SQ FT: 11,400
SALES (est): 6.5MM **Privately Held**
WEB: www.hdlcompanies.com
SIC: 8741 7371 Administrative management; custom computer programming services

(P-27053)
HEALTHCARE MGT PARTNERS LLC
20 Executive Park Ste 155, Irvine (92614-4733)
PHONE..................................949 263-8620
Claudia Dwyer,
Jay Lichman, Engineer
Richard Taketa, Senior Engr
Gloria Rull, Controller
Linda Longfellow, Human Res Dir
EMP: 260 EST: 1997
SALES (est): 12.3MM **Privately Held**
WEB: www.hmpllc.com
SIC: 8741 8721 Hospital management; nursing & personal care facility management; accounting, auditing & bookkeeping

(P-27054)
HONEYWELL INTERNATIONAL INC
6 Center Pt Ste 300, La Palma (90623)
PHONE..................................714 562-3114
Fax: 714 562-4388
John Gruss, General Mgr
Ed Mathews, Manager
Robert Norcutt, Manager
EMP: 75
SALES (corp-wide): 38.5B **Publicly Held**
WEB: www.honeywell.com
SIC: 8741 Business management
PA: Honeywell International Inc.
115 Tabor Rd
Morris Plains NJ 07950
973 455-2000

(P-27055)
HOSTMARK INVESTORS LTD PARTNR
Also Called: Santa Clara Hilton, The
4949 Great America Pkwy, Santa Clara (95054-1216)
PHONE..................................408 330-0001
Roy Truitt, General Mgr
EMP: 180
SALES (corp-wide): 122.9MM **Privately Held**
SIC: 8741 7991 5813 5812 Hotel or motel management; physical fitness facilities; drinking places; eating places; hotel, franchised
PA: Hostmark Investors Limited Partnership
1300 E Wdfield Rd Ste 400
Schaumburg IL 60173
847 517-9100

(P-27056)
HOTCHKIS WILEY CAPITL MGT LLC (PA)
725 S Figueroa St # 3900, Los Angeles (90017-5439)
PHONE..................................213 430-1000
Fax: 213 430-1001
George Davis,
Anna Lopez, COO
Patrick McMenamin, Managing Dir
Matt Michaelson, Managing Dir
David Green, Office Mgr
EMP: 50
SQ FT: 12,000
SALES (est): 19.4MM **Privately Held**
WEB: www.hwcm.com
SIC: 8741 6211 Financial management for business; security brokers & dealers

(P-27057)
HOTEL MANAGERS GROUP LLC
11590 W Bernardo Ct # 211, San Diego (92127-1624)
PHONE..................................858 673-1534
Joel Biggs, Mng Member
Randy Hulce, President
Cha M Demayo, Exec VP
Michelle Demayo, Exec VP
Alan Bowles, Vice Pres
EMP: 400
SALES (est): 36MM **Privately Held**
WEB: www.hotelmanagersgroup.com
SIC: 8741 7011 7041 Hotel or motel management; hotels & motels; membership-basis organization hotels

(P-27058)
HRONOPOULOS
110 W A St Ste 900, San Diego (92101-3705)
PHONE..................................619 237-6161
Andreas Hronopoulos, CEO
George Hronopoulos, CFO
Kevin Kachman,
EMP: 50 EST: 2010
SQ FT: 10,000
SALES: 4MM **Privately Held**
SIC: 8741 Business management

(P-27059)
HUNT CONVENIENCE STORES LLC
5750 S Watt Ave, Sacramento (95829-9349)
P.O. Box 277670 (95827-7670)
PHONE..................................916 383-4868
Joshua M Hunt, Mng Member
Daniel Maue, CFO
EMP: 50 EST: 2014
SQ FT: 3,200
SALES: 5MM **Privately Held**
SIC: 8741 Administrative management

(P-27060)
IDEAL LIVING MANAGEMENT LLC
14724 Ventura Blvd Fl 200, Sherman Oaks (91403-3514)
P.O. Box 9169, Van Nuys (91409-9169)
PHONE..................................818 217-2000
Katie Williams, President
Peter Spiegel, President
Michael Badar, COO
Richard Sheiner,

PRODUCTS & SERVICES SECTION
8741 - Management Services County (P-27082)

Joshua Levine, *Mng Member*
EMP: 52
SALES (est): 10MM **Privately Held**
SIC: 8741 Management services

(P-27061)
IKEA PURCHASING SVCS US INC
600 N San Fernando Blvd, Burbank (91502-1021)
PHONE 818 841-3500
Chris Maynard, *Manager*
EMP: 300 **Privately Held**
SIC: 8741 8721 5712 Administrative management; accounting, auditing & bookkeeping; furniture stores
HQ: Ikea Purchasing Services (Us) Inc.
7810 Katy Fwy
Houston TX 77024
888 888-4532

(P-27062)
IMA EUROPE MWR SINGLE FUND
420 Montgomery St, San Francisco (94104-1207)
PHONE 210 466-1376
Marion W Maynard, *Administration*
EMP: 99
SALES (est): 2.3MM **Privately Held**
SIC: 8741 Management services

(P-27063)
INDUSTRIAL PHARMACY MGT LLC
3198 Arprt Loop Dr Ste F, Costa Mesa (92626)
PHONE 949 777-3100
Michael R Drobot,
Laura Beran, *Info Tech Mgr*
EMP: 52
SALES (est): 7.5MM **Privately Held**
SIC: 8741 Hospital management

(P-27064)
INLAND CNTIES REGIONAL CTR INC (PA)
Also Called: Inland Regional Center
1365 S Waterman Ave, San Bernardino (92408-2804)
P.O. Box 19037 (92423-9037)
PHONE 909 890-3000
Fax: 909 890-3001
Carol A Fitzgibbons, *CEO*
Carol Fitzgibbons, *Exec Dir*
Lawana Blair, *Program Mgr*
Mia Gurri, *Program Mgr*
Stephen Hughes, *Office Admin*
EMP: 111
SQ FT: 82,000
SALES: 335.1MM **Privately Held**
SIC: 8741 Management services

(P-27065)
INNOVATIVE EDUCATION MGT INC
1166 Broadway Ste Q, Placerville (95667-5745)
PHONE 530 295-3566
Fax: 530 295-3583
Randy Gaschler, *President*
Jennifer Sanchez, *Vice Pres*
Jacey Marsh, *Teacher*
Susan Clark, *Manager*
EMP: 53
SQ FT: 2,000
SALES: 31.6MM **Privately Held**
SIC: 8741 Management services

(P-27066)
INTEGRAL SENIOR LIVING LLC (PA)
2333 State St Ste 300, Carlsbad (92008-1691)
PHONE 760 547-2863
Sue Farrow,
Mike Korin, *Shareholder*
Mike Zeug, *Shareholder*
Terry Ervin, *President*
Tracee Degrande, *CFO*
EMP: 148
SALES (est): 19.4MM **Privately Held**
SIC: 8741 Nursing & personal care facility management

(P-27067)
INTERSTATE HOTELS RESORTS INC
4685 Macarthur Ct Ste 480, Newport Beach (92660-8850)
PHONE 949 783-2500
Mark Burden, *Branch Mgr*
EMP: 61
SALES (corp-wide): 1.7B **Privately Held**
SIC: 8741 Hotel or motel management
HQ: Interstate Hotels & Resorts, Inc.
4501 Fairfax Dr Ste 500
Arlington VA 22203
703 387-3100

(P-27068)
INTERSTATE HOTELS RESORTS INC
Also Called: Hilton Garden Inn Carlsbad Bch
6450 Carlsbad Blvd, Carlsbad (92011-1058)
PHONE 760 476-0800
Bob Moore, *Manager*
EMP: 70
SALES (corp-wide): 1.7B **Privately Held**
WEB: www.sheratonokc.com
SIC: 8741 Hotel or motel management
HQ: Interstate Hotels & Resorts, Inc.
4501 Fairfax Dr Ste 500
Arlington VA 22203
703 387-3100

(P-27069)
INTERSTATE HOTELS RESORTS INC
Also Called: Doral Palm Sprngs Rsrt & Golf
67 967 Vst Chno At Lndau, Palm Springs (92263)
P.O. Box 1644 (92263-1644)
PHONE 760 322-7000
Elie Zod, *Manager*
Jeff Kulek, *Manager*
EMP: 200
SALES (corp-wide): 1.7B **Privately Held**
WEB: www.sheratonokc.com
SIC: 8741 Hotel or motel management
HQ: Interstate Hotels & Resorts, Inc.
4501 Fairfax Dr Ste 500
Arlington VA 22203
703 387-3100

(P-27070)
INTERSTATE HOTELS RESORTS INC
Also Called: Embassy Suites Walnut Creek
1345 Treat Blvd, Walnut Creek (94597-2173)
PHONE 925 934-2500
David Cano, *Manager*
Lisa Drew, *Human Res Dir*
Josephine Segraves, *Manager*
EMP: 130
SALES (corp-wide): 1.7B **Privately Held**
WEB: www.sheratonokc.com
SIC: 8741 Hotel or motel management
HQ: Interstate Hotels & Resorts, Inc.
4501 Fairfax Dr Ste 500
Arlington VA 22203
703 387-3100

(P-27071)
INTERSTATE HOTELS RESORTS INC
Also Called: Santa Barbara Inn
901 E Cabrillo Blvd, Santa Barbara (93103-3642)
P.O. Box 5634 (93150-5634)
PHONE 805 966-2285
Fax: 805 966-6584
Clark Sarchet, *Branch Mgr*
Mary Gregg, *General Mgr*
Marilou Deang, *Manager*
EMP: 75
SALES (corp-wide): 1.7B **Privately Held**
WEB: www.sheratonokc.com
SIC: 8741 Hotel or motel management
HQ: Interstate Hotels & Resorts, Inc.
4501 Fairfax Dr Ste 500
Arlington VA 22203
703 387-3100

(P-27072)
INTERSTATE HOTELS RESORTS INC
Also Called: Hilton Irvne/Orange Cnty Arprt
18800 Macarthur Blvd, Irvine (92612-1410)
PHONE 949 833-9999
Fax: 949 833-3317
Ted Holmquist, *General Mgr*
Cathy Dutton, *Marketing Mgr*
EMP: 185
SALES (corp-wide): 1.7B **Privately Held**
WEB: www.sheratonokc.com
SIC: 8741 Hotel or motel management
HQ: Interstate Hotels & Resorts, Inc.
4501 Fairfax Dr Ste 500
Arlington VA 22203
703 387-3100

(P-27073)
INVESTORS CAPITAL MGT GROUP
Also Called: Cuisine Partners USA
10390 Santa Monica Blvd, Los Angeles (90025-5058)
PHONE 310 553-5175
Edward Lindor, *President*
Manfred Gordon, *CFO*
Richere Altoport, *Vice Pres*
Jason Graham, *Vice Pres*
Ray I Ledford II, *Vice Pres*
EMP: 277
SQ FT: 7,800
SALES (est): 11MM **Privately Held**
SIC: 8741 Restaurant management

(P-27074)
JBWO INC
3955 Kingsbarns Dr, Roseville (95747-6359)
PHONE 916 239-7013
William Osborne, *CEO*
EMP: 50
SALES (est): 2.8MM **Privately Held**
SIC: 8741 Management services

(P-27075)
JC RESORTS LLC
Also Called: Surf Sand Hotel
1555 S Coast Hwy, Laguna Beach (92651-3226)
PHONE 949 376-2779
Fax: 949 494-2897
Blaise Bartell, *Branch Mgr*
Joanna Bear, *Director*
Jan Henningsen, *Manager*
EMP: 300 **Privately Held**
WEB: www.surfandsandresort.com
SIC: 8741 5813 5812 7011 Hotel or motel management; drinking places; eating places; hotels
PA: Jc Resorts Llc
533 Coast Blvd S
La Jolla CA 92037

(P-27076)
JC RESORTS LLC
Also Called: Encinitas Ranch Golf Course
1275 Quail Gardens Dr, Encinitas (92024-2368)
PHONE 760 944-1936
Rod Landville, *Manager*
Jace Schwarm, *Executive*
EMP: 100 **Privately Held**
WEB: www.surfandsandresort.com
SIC: 8741 7992 Hotel or motel management; public golf courses
PA: Jc Resorts Llc
533 Coast Blvd S
La Jolla CA 92037

(P-27077)
JENKINS GALES & MARTINEZ INC
6033 W Century Blvd # 601, Los Angeles (90045-6414)
PHONE 310 645-0561
Earl Gales Jr, *Ch of Bd*
Ray David, *Corp Secy*
Starla Gale, *Vice Pres*
Glenn Haller, *Vice Pres*
Renato Davis, *Financial Exec*
EMP: 70
SQ FT: 5,000

SALES: 3.9MM **Privately Held**
WEB: www.jgminc.com
SIC: 8741 8712 7389 8711 Construction management; architectural engineering; mapmaking or drafting, including aerial; construction & civil engineering

(P-27078)
JESSE LEE GROUP INC
Also Called: Castro Valley Care Centers
300 Crprate Pinte Ste 550, Culver City (90230)
PHONE 510 351-3700
Fax: 510 889-7955
George Davis, *Manager*
Cynthia Letatez, *Exec Dir*
Ebi Davis, *Nursing Dir*
EMP: 91
SALES (corp-wide): 7.6MM **Privately Held**
SIC: 8741 8051 8059 Hospital management; skilled nursing care facilities; convalescent home
PA: Jesse Lee Group, Inc
5212 Village Creek Dr
Plano TX 75093
972 931-3800

(P-27079)
JESSE LEE GROUP INC
Also Called: New Hope Care Center
2586 Buthmann Ave, Tracy (95376-2165)
PHONE 209 832-2273
Fax: 209 832-0743
Ruby Rakow, *President*
EMP: 120
SALES (corp-wide): 7.6MM **Privately Held**
SIC: 8741 8051 Hospital management; convalescent home with continuous nursing care
PA: Jesse Lee Group, Inc
5212 Village Creek Dr
Plano TX 75093
972 931-3800

(P-27080)
JIPC MANAGEMENT INC
Also Called: John's Incredible Pizza Co
22342 Avenida Empresa # 220, Rcho STA Marg (92688-2161)
PHONE 949 916-2000
Fax: 949 916-2600
John M Parlet, *President*
EMP: 1000
SALES (est): 82.3MM **Privately Held**
SIC: 8741 Restaurant management

(P-27081)
JOIE DE VIVRE HOSPITALITY LLC (PA)
530 Bush St Ste 501, San Francisco (94108-3633)
PHONE 415 835-0300
Fax: 415 835-0310
Niki Leondakis, *CEO*
Stephen T Conley Jr, *CEO*
Ingrid Summerfield, *COO*
Rick Colangelo, *Exec VP*
Greg Smith, *Exec VP*
EMP: 50
SALES: 231.8MM **Privately Held**
WEB: www.hotelbijou.com
SIC: 8741 Hotel or motel management

(P-27082)
JOIE DE VIVRE HOSPITALITY LLC
Also Called: Maxwell Hotel, The
386 Geary St, San Francisco (94102-1802)
PHONE 415 986-2000
Fax: 415 986-2193
Steven Conley, *Manager*
EMP: 60
SALES (corp-wide): 231.8MM **Privately Held**
WEB: www.hotelbijou.com
SIC: 8741 7011 Hotel or motel management; motels
PA: Joie De Vivre Hospitality, Llc
530 Bush St Ste 501
San Francisco CA 94108
415 835-0300

8741 - Management Services County (P-27083) — PRODUCTS & SERVICES SECTION

(P-27083)
JOIE DE VIVRE HOSPITALITY LLC
Also Called: Costanoa
2001 Rossi Rd, Pescadero (94060-9732)
PHONE..................................650 879-1100
Daniel Medellin, *Branch Mgr*
EMP: 65
SALES (corp-wide): 231.8MM **Privately Held**
WEB: www.hotelbijou.com
SIC: 8741 Hotel or motel management
PA: Joie De Vivre Hospitality, Llc
530 Bush St Ste 501
San Francisco CA 94108
415 835-0300

(P-27084)
JT2 INTEGRATED RESOURCES (PA)
519 17th St, Oakland (94612-1527)
P.O. Box 8021, Pleasanton (94588-8604)
PHONE..................................925 556-7012
Jeff Sandford, *Ch of Bd*
John Casas, *President*
Tom Blake, *COO*
Tabatha Bettencourt, *Senior VP*
Theresa Fernandez, *Vice Pres*
EMP: 58
SQ FT: 4,200
SALES (est): 11.5MM **Privately Held**
SIC: 8741 Administrative management

(P-27085)
JUVENILE JUSTICE DIVISION CAL
Also Called: Ventura Yuth Crrctional Fcilty
3100 Wright Rd, Camarillo (93010-8307)
PHONE..................................805 485-7951
Vivian Craford, *Superintendent*
Gary Collins, *Principal*
EMP: 350 **Privately Held**
WEB: www.cya.ca.gov
SIC: 8741 9223 Office management; house of correction, government
HQ: Juvenile Justice Division, California
1515 S St Ste 502s
Sacramento CA 95811
916 323-2848

(P-27086)
KA MANAGEMENT INC
5820 Oberlin Dr Ste 201, San Diego (92121-3743)
PHONE..................................858 404-6080
Kayvon Agahnia, *CEO*
Jill Muller, *Manager*
EMP: 90
SALES: 12MM **Privately Held**
SIC: 8741 Management services

(P-27087)
KAISER HLTH PLAN ASSET MGT INC
Also Called: KAISER PERMANENTE
1 Kaiser Plz Ste 1333, Oakland (94612-3604)
PHONE..................................510 271-5910
Thomas R Meier, *President*
EMP: 50
SALES: 31.6MM
SALES (corp-wide): 27.8B **Privately Held**
WEB: www.kaiser.com
SIC: 8741 Hospital management
PA: Kaiser Foundation Health Plan, Inc.
1 Kaiser Plz
Oakland CA 94612
510 271-5800

(P-27088)
KEIRO SERVICES
Also Called: Keiro Senior Health Care
420 E 3rd St Ste 1000, Los Angeles (90013-1648)
PHONE..................................213 873-5700
Shawn Miyake, *CEO*
Susan Lara, *Executive*
Patty Flores, *Personnel Assit*
Lance Maemori, *Chf Purch Ofc*
Brandon Leong, *Manager*
EMP: 500
SQ FT: 26,000
SALES: 4.2MM **Privately Held**
SIC: 8741 Nursing & personal care facility management

(P-27089)
KELLEYAMERIT HOLDINGS INC
Also Called: Kelleyamerit Fleet Services
1331 N Calif Blvd Ste 150, Walnut Creek (94596-4535)
PHONE..................................877 512-6374
Gary Herbold, *CEO*
Robert Brauer, *President*
Amein Punjani, *COO*
Dan Williams, *CFO*
Lorraine Brady, *Vice Pres*
EMP: 1300
SQ FT: 5,000
SALES (est): 98.4MM **Privately Held**
SIC: 8741 Management services

(P-27090)
KENDO BRANDS INC
525 Market St Fl 15, San Francisco (94105-2723)
PHONE..................................415 284-3700
EMP: 200
SALES (est): 2MM **Privately Held**
SIC: 8741 Business management

(P-27091)
KERN AROUND CLOCK FOUNDATION
Also Called: AROUND THE CLOCK LINKAGE
5251 Office Park Dr # 400, Bakersfield (93309-0667)
PHONE..................................661 395-5800
Fax: 661 864-0732
Mary Vasinda, *President*
John Vasinda, *Vice Pres*
Stacie Dollar, *Program Mgr*
EMP: 50
SALES: 264.8K **Privately Held**
WEB: www.bakersfieldcare.com
SIC: 8741 8322 Business management; individual & family services

(P-27092)
KFI
1 Sansome St Fl 32, San Francisco (94104-4436)
PHONE..................................415 956-9812
Gary Burison, *CEO*
EMP: 50
SALES (est): 1.5MM **Privately Held**
SIC: 8741 Management services

(P-27093)
KIMPTON HOTEL & REST GROUP LLC (HQ)
222 Kearny St Ste 200, San Francisco (94108-4537)
PHONE..................................415 397-5572
Fax: 415 296-8031
Mike Depatie, *CEO*
Donald Ogrady, *President*
Mike Defrino, *COO*
Niki Leondakis, *COO*
Ben Rowe, *CFO*
EMP: 100
SALES (est): 1B
SALES (corp-wide): 1.8B **Privately Held**
WEB: www.kuletos.com
SIC: 8741 Hotel or motel management
PA: Intercontinental Hotels Group Plc
Broadwater Park North Orbital Road
Uxbridge MIDDX UB9 5
189 551-2000

(P-27094)
KIMPTON HOTEL & REST GROUP LLC
Also Called: Triton Hotel, The
342 Grant Ave, San Francisco (94108-3607)
PHONE..................................415 394-0500
Fax: 415 394-0555
Brian Danwick, *Manager*
Janet Leong, *CFO*
Melinda Macfarlane, *General Mgr*
Louis Zelidon, *Chief Engr*
EMP: 50
SALES (corp-wide): 1.8B **Privately Held**
WEB: www.kuletos.com
SIC: 8741 7011 Hotel or motel management; restaurant management; hotels & motels

HQ: Kimpton Hotel & Restaurant Group Llc
222 Kearny St Ste 200
San Francisco CA 94108
415 397-5572

(P-27095)
KIMPTON HOTEL & REST GROUP LLC
Also Called: Hotel Moneco
501 Geary St, San Francisco (94102-1640)
PHONE..................................415 292-0100
Jimmy Hord, *Manager*
EMP: 88
SALES (corp-wide): 1.8B **Privately Held**
WEB: www.kuletos.com
SIC: 8741 7011 5812 Hotel or motel management; hotels & motels; eating places
HQ: Kimpton Hotel & Restaurant Group Llc
222 Kearny St Ste 200
San Francisco CA 94108
415 397-5572

(P-27096)
KINTETSU ENTERPRISES
328 E 1st St, Los Angeles (90012-3902)
PHONE..................................213 687-2000
Takenori Kakutani, *President*
Akimasa Yoneda, *Exec VP*
Dinh Le, *Director*
EMP: 90
SALES: 5MM
SALES (corp-wide): 10.4B **Privately Held**
WEB: www.miyakoinn.com
SIC: 8741 6531 Hotel or motel management; real estate managers
PA: Kintetsu Group Holdings Co., Ltd.
6-1-55, Uehonmachi, Tennoji-Ku
Osaka OSK 543-0
667 753-355

(P-27097)
KISCO SENIOR LIVING LLC
Also Called: Bridgepoint At San Francisco
1601 19th Ave Ofc, San Francisco (94122-3478)
PHONE..................................415 664-6264
Fax: 415 664-9806
Susan Edwards, *Branch Mgr*
EMP: 66
SALES (corp-wide): 135.3MM **Privately Held**
WEB: www.kiscosl.com
SIC: 8741 Management services
PA: Senior Kisco Living Llc
5790 Fleet St Ste 300
Carlsbad CA 92008
760 804-5900

(P-27098)
KISCO SENIOR LIVING LLC
1100 E Spruce Ave Ofc, Fresno (93720-3314)
PHONE..................................559 449-8070
EMP: 55
SALES (corp-wide): 135.3MM **Privately Held**
WEB: www.kiscosl.com
SIC: 8741 Management services
PA: Senior Kisco Living Llc
5790 Fleet St Ste 300
Carlsbad CA 92008
760 804-5900

(P-27099)
KISCO SENIOR LIVING LLC
Also Called: KRC Santa Margarita
21952 Buena Suerte, Rcho STA Marg (92688-3903)
PHONE..................................949 888-2250
Rick Lansford, *Branch Mgr*
Bill Ireland, *Envir Svcs Dir*
Dixie King, *Exec Dir*
Colleen Ramsdale, *Marketing Staff*
Paula Tobin, *Marketing Staff*
EMP: 100
SALES (corp-wide): 135.3MM **Privately Held**
WEB: www.kiscosl.com
SIC: 8741 Management services
PA: Senior Kisco Living Llc
5790 Fleet St Ste 300
Carlsbad CA 92008
760 804-5900

(P-27100)
KISCO SENIOR LIVING LLC
Also Called: Oak View Snoma Hlls Apartments
1350 Oak View Cir, Rohnert Park (94928-6411)
PHONE..................................707 585-1800
Fax: 707 585-1900
Kim Healis, *Branch Mgr*
EMP: 66
SALES (corp-wide): 135.3MM **Privately Held**
WEB: www.kiscosl.com
SIC: 8741 Management services
PA: Senior Kisco Living Llc
5790 Fleet St Ste 300
Carlsbad CA 92008
760 804-5900

(P-27101)
KISCO SENIOR LIVING LLC
Also Called: KRC Los Altos
1174 Los Altos Ave Ofc, Los Altos (94022-1059)
PHONE..................................650 948-7337
Felora Lotfi, *Branch Mgr*
MEI Chuang, *Director*
EMP: 50
SALES (corp-wide): 123MM **Privately Held**
WEB: www.kiscosl.com
SIC: 8741 Management services
PA: Senior Kisco Living Llc
5790 Fleet St Ste 300
Carlsbad CA 92008
760 804-5900

(P-27102)
KOR HOTEL GROUPS INC
530 Pico Blvd, Santa Monica (90405-1223)
PHONE..................................310 309-8066
Micheal D'Amodio, *President*
Joji Nakano, *Vice Pres*
Faisal Yousuf, *Controller*
EMP: 99
SALES (est): 3.3MM **Privately Held**
SIC: 8741 Hotel or motel management

(P-27103)
KRM RISK MANAGEMENT SVCS INC
4270 W Richert Ave # 101, Fresno (93722-6334)
PHONE..................................559 277-4800
Fax: 559 277-4950
Steve Wigh, *Vice Pres*
Luis Feliz, *CIO*
Mike Sernasky, *Manager*
EMP: 51
SALES (corp-wide): 19MM **Privately Held**
WEB: www.krmrisk.com
SIC: 8741 Management services
PA: Krm Risk Management Services, Inc.
4270 W Richert Ave 101
Fresno CA 93722
714 560-9200

(P-27104)
KSL II MNGEMENT OPERATIONS LLC
50905 Avenida Bermudas, La Quinta (92253-8910)
PHONE..................................760 564-8000
Scott Dalecio, *President*
Sam Barton, *Controller*
EMP: 60
SALES (est): 5MM **Privately Held**
SIC: 8741 Management services

(P-27105)
LA JOIE JERRY
Also Called: La Joie Construction
418 Sonora Dr, San Mateo (94402-2342)
PHONE..................................650 375-1808
Jerry La Joie, *Owner*
EMP: 50
SALES (est): 2.9MM **Privately Held**
SIC: 8741 1542 1521 Construction management; commercial & office building, new construction; new construction, single-family houses

PRODUCTS & SERVICES SECTION
8741 - Management Services County (P-27131)

(P-27106)
LA RESTAURANT MANAGEMENT INC
Also Called: King Taco
45 N Arroyo Pkwy, Pasadena (91103-3901)
PHONE....................626 792-0405
Luis A Martinez, *President*
EMP: 70
SALES (est): 2.6MM **Privately Held**
SIC: 8741 Management services

(P-27107)
LA VOIE & SONS CONSTRUCTION
1061 Nichols Ct, Rocklin (95765-1325)
PHONE....................916 408-6900
Timothy Lavoie, *President*
Jodia Lavoie, *Vice Pres*
Magia Kvach, *Manager*
EMP: 50
SALES (est): 2.6MM **Privately Held**
SIC: 8741 Construction management

(P-27108)
LAKESIDE SYSTEMS INC
Also Called: Lakeside Medical Systems
8510 Balboa Blvd Ste 150, Northridge (91325-5810)
PHONE....................866 654-3471
Fax: 818 637-2770
Richard Merkin, *CEO*
Karol Cabrera, *Executive*
Kenneth B Epstein, *Med Doctor*
EMP: 700
SQ FT: 20,000
SALES (est): 31.2MM
SALES (corp-wide): 43.9MM **Privately Held**
SIC: 8741 8742 6411 Management services; management consulting services; insurance agents, brokers & service
PA: Heritage Provider Network Inc
    8510 Balboa Blvd Ste 285
    Northridge CA 91325
    818 654-3461

(P-27109)
LEAVITT GROUP ENTERPRISES INC
785 E Washington Blvd # 4, Crescent City (95531-8343)
PHONE....................707 465-6508
Debbie Koehlerschmidt, *Branch Mgr*
EMP: 130
SALES (corp-wide): 211MM **Privately Held**
SIC: 8741 Management services
PA: Leavitt Group Enterprises Inc
    216 S 200 W
    Cedar City UT 84720
    435 586-1555

(P-27110)
LEDCOR MANAGEMENT SERVICES INC
6405 Mira Mesa Blvd Ste 1, San Diego (92121-4147)
PHONE....................858 527-6400
EMP: 55
SALES (est): 5.1MM **Privately Held**
SIC: 8741 Business management

(P-27111)
LEDESMA & MEYER DEV INC
9441 Haven Ave, Rancho Cucamonga (91730-5844)
PHONE....................909 476-0590
Fax: 909 476-0592
Joseph Ledesma, *CEO*
Kris Meyer, *Vice Pres*
EMP: 55
SQ FT: 16,480
SALES (est): 3.3MM **Privately Held**
SIC: 8741 Construction management

(P-27112)
LEGACY PRTNERS RESIDENTIAL INC (HQ)
4000 E 3rd Ave Ste 600, Foster City (94404-4828)
PHONE....................650 571-2250
C Preston Butcher, *Ch of Bd*
Tim McCarthy, *CFO*
Gary J Rossi, *CFO*
Spencer R Stuart Jr, *Managing Dir*
Sharon Cassidy, *Executive Asst*
EMP: 180
SALES (est): 57.1MM
SALES (corp-wide): 199.1MM **Privately Held**
SIC: 8741 Management services
PA: Steelwave, Inc.
    4000 E 3rd Ave Ste 600
    Foster City CA 94404
    650 571-2200

(P-27113)
LENDLEASE US CONSTRUCTION INC
800 W 6th St Ste 1600, Los Angeles (90017-2719)
PHONE....................213 430-4660
Todd Pennington, *Branch Mgr*
EMP: 100
SALES (corp-wide): 57.5MM **Privately Held**
SIC: 8741 8742 1541 1542 Management services; construction project management consultant; industrial buildings, new construction; nonresidential construction
HQ: Lendlease (Us) Construction Inc.
    200 Park Ave Fl 9
    New York NY 10166
    212 592-6700

(P-27114)
LEXXIOM INC
7945 Cartilla Ave A, Rancho Cucamonga (91730-3069)
PHONE....................909 481-2536
Robert Lemelin, *President*
Brian Lemelin, *COO*
Leo Lemelin, *CFO*
Tracie Marcelin, *Controller*
EMP: 360
SALES (est): 24MM **Privately Held**
WEB: www.thedebtmediator.com
SIC: 8741 Administrative management

(P-27115)
LIBSOURCE LLC
10390 Santa Monica Blvd, Los Angeles (90025-5058)
PHONE....................323 852-1083
Deborah Schwarz, *CEO*
Robert Corrao, *COO*
Laura Wang, *Vice Pres*
EMP: 140
SQ FT: 2,500
SALES: 20MM **Privately Held**
SIC: 8741 Financial management for business

(P-27116)
LIFELONG LEARNING ADM CORP
177 Holston Dr, Lancaster (93535-4570)
PHONE....................661 272-1225
Dante R Simi, *CEO*
EMP: 99
SALES (est): 1.3MM **Privately Held**
SIC: 8741 Business management

(P-27117)
LION-VALLEN LTD PARTNERSHIP
22 Area Aven A Bldg 2234, Camp Pendleton (92055)
P.O. Box 555045 (92055-5045)
PHONE....................760 385-4885
EMP: 50 **Privately Held**
SIC: 8741 Management services
PA: Lion-Vallen Limited Partnership
    7200 Poe Ave Ste 400
    Dayton OH 45414

(P-27118)
LIVINGSTON MEM VNA HLTH CORP
Also Called: Livingston Mem Vst Nrs Associa
1996 Eastman Ave Ste 101, Ventura (93003-5768)
PHONE....................805 642-0239
Lanyard K Dial MD, *President*
Charles Hair MD, *Ch of Bd*
Judy Hecox, *President*
Jeffrey Paul, *Treasurer*
John Macias, *Office Mgr*
EMP: 200
SQ FT: 12,600
SALES: 16.6MM **Privately Held**
WEB: www.lmvna.org
SIC: 8741 8082 Hospital management; nursing & personal care facility management; home health care services

(P-27119)
LWI FINANCIAL INC
3055 Olin Ave Ste 2000, San Jose (95128-2069)
PHONE....................408 260-3100
John Bowen, *President*
Michael Clinton, *COO*
Marcus Beisel, *Chief Mktg Ofcr*
Steven Atkinson, *Exec VP*
Bernadette Calvo, *Vice Pres*
EMP: 50
SALES: 1.4MM **Privately Held**
SIC: 8741 Management services

(P-27120)
MARINER HEALTH CARE INC
Also Called: Vale Healthcare Center
13484 San Pablo Ave, San Pablo (94806-3904)
PHONE....................510 232-5945
Remy Dise, *Director*
Julie Evans, *Senior VP*
Braziel Carter, *Director*
EMP: 210
SALES (corp-wide): 4.1B **Privately Held**
WEB: www.marinerhealth.com
SIC: 8741 Nursing & personal care facility management
HQ: Mariner Health Care, Inc.
    1 Ravinia Dr Ste 1500
    Atlanta GA 30346
    678 443-7000

(P-27121)
MAVERICK HOTEL PARTNERS LLC
Also Called: Filament Hospitality
466 Green St Ste 302, San Francisco (94133-4067)
PHONE....................415 655-9526
Ingrid Summerfield, *Mng Member*
EMP: 300
SQ FT: 2,000
SALES: 75K **Privately Held**
SIC: 8741 Hotel or motel management

(P-27122)
MCKINLEY PLAZA LLC
2401 E Division St, National City (91950-1901)
PHONE....................619 405-6307
Roshan Gupta,
EMP: 99
SALES: 950K **Privately Held**
SIC: 8741 Hotel or motel management

(P-27123)
MCMILLAN FARM MANAGEMENT
29379 Rancho California R, Temecula (92591-5208)
PHONE....................951 676-2045
Gary McMillan, *Owner*
EMP: 150
SALES (est): 14MM **Privately Held**
SIC: 8741 0174 Management services; citrus fruits

(P-27124)
MEDEANALYTICS INC (PA)
5858 Horton St Ste 170, Emeryville (94608-2007)
PHONE....................510 647-1300
Andrew Hurd, *CEO*
James Quist, *Ch of Bd*
Anthony McKeever, *CEO*
Salvatore Detrane, *Officer*
Terry Fouts, *Officer*
EMP: 148
SQ FT: 25,000
SALES (est): 51.1MM **Privately Held**
WEB: www.medefinance.com
SIC: 8741 Financial management for business

(P-27125)
MEDICAL NETWORK INC
Also Called: MBC Systems
1809 E Dyer Rd Ste 311, Santa Ana (92705-5740)
PHONE....................949 863-0022
Fax: 949 863-0023
David Conrad, *President*
Mardi C Morillo, *CIO*
Kimmie Le, *Director*
EMP: 80
SQ FT: 3,500
SALES (est): 9.4MM **Privately Held**
WEB: www.mbcsystems.org
SIC: 8741 Hospital management; nursing & personal care facility management

(P-27126)
MENTOR MEDIA (USA) SUP
3768 Milliken Ave Ste A, Eastvale (91752-1037)
PHONE....................909 930-0800
Kok Khoon Lim, *CEO*
▲ EMP: 80
SALES: 15MM
SALES (corp-wide): 4.8B **Privately Held**
SIC: 8741 8742 Business management; business planning & organizing services
HQ: Mentor Media Ltd
    1 Bukit Batok Street 22
    Singapore 65959
    663 133-98

(P-27127)
MERITAGE GROUP LP
The Embarcad Pier 5 St Pier, San Francisco (94111)
PHONE....................415 399-5330
Mark Mindich, *Principal*
EMP: 1500
SALES (est): 94.1MM **Privately Held**
SIC: 8741 Management services

(P-27128)
MG RESTAURANTS INC
475 Sansome St Ste 100s, San Francisco (94111-3181)
PHONE....................415 296-8222
David Silverglide, *CEO*
EMP: 90
SALES: 8.5MM **Privately Held**
SIC: 8741 Restaurant management

(P-27129)
MGT INDUSTRIES INC
19034 S Vermont Ave, Gardena (90248-4412)
PHONE....................310 324-3152
EMP: 64
SALES (corp-wide): 63.5MM **Privately Held**
SIC: 8741 Management services
PA: Mgt Industries, Inc.
    13889 S Figueroa St
    Los Angeles CA 90061
    310 516-5900

(P-27130)
MIDNIGHT SNACK LP
Also Called: Ford's Filling Station
4182 Irving Pl, Culver City (90232-2812)
PHONE....................310 202-1470
Benjamin Ford, *Partner*
Wild Hog, *Partner*
Derek Tilley, *Manager*
EMP: 50
SALES (est): 4.8MM **Privately Held**
SIC: 8741 8742 Restaurant management; restaurant & food services consultants

(P-27131)
MIG MANAGEMENT SERVICES LLC
660 Newport Center Dr # 1300, Newport Beach (92660-6492)
PHONE....................949 474-5800
Paul Merage,
Matt Drevlow, *Controller*
EMP: 80
SALES (est): 4.1MM
SALES (corp-wide): 133.7K **Privately Held**
SIC: 8741 Management services

8741 - Management Services County (P-27132)

PA: Mig Capital, Llc
660 Newport Center Dr # 1300
Newport Beach CA 92660
949 474-5800

(P-27132)
MIKE ROVNER CONSTRUCTION INC
22600 Lambert St, Lake Forest (92630-6201)
PHONE..................949 458-1562
Mike Rovner, *Branch Mgr*
EMP: 163 **Privately Held**
SIC: **8741** 1522 1521 Construction management; residential construction; single-family housing construction
PA: Mike Rovner Construction, Inc.
5400 Tech Cir
Moorpark CA 93021

(P-27133)
MIMG MEDICAL MANAGEMENT LLC
26522 La Alameda Ste 120, Mission Viejo (92691-6330)
PHONE..................949 282-1600
EMP: 60
SQ FT: 1,800
SALES (est): 2.6MM **Privately Held**
SIC: **8741**

(P-27134)
MORRISON MGT SPECIALISTS INC
Also Called: Morrison Health Care
1150 N Indian Canyon Dr, Palm Springs (92262-4872)
PHONE..................760 323-6296
Rick Tinsley, *Director*
EMP: 97
SALES (corp-wide): 27.3B **Privately Held**
SIC: **8741** 5812 8742 5813 Management services; eating places; food & beverage consultant; drinking places
HQ: Morrison Management Specialists, Inc.
5801 Pachtree Dunwoody Rd
Atlanta GA 30342

(P-27135)
MORRISON MGT SPECIALISTS INC
1531 Esplanade, Chico (95926-3310)
PHONE..................530 332-7557
EMP: 97
SALES (corp-wide): 27.3B **Privately Held**
WEB: www.iammorrison.com
SIC: **8741** Management services
HQ: Morrison Management Specialists, Inc.
5801 Pachtree Dunwoody Rd
Atlanta GA 30342
-

(P-27136)
MORRISON MGT SPECIALISTS INC
14445 Olive View Dr, Sylmar (91342-1437)
PHONE..................818 364-4219
Kathy Dagg, *Manager*
EMP: 78
SALES (corp-wide): 27.3B **Privately Held**
WEB: www.iammorrison.com
SIC: **8741** 5812 Restaurant management; eating places
HQ: Morrison Management Specialists, Inc.
5801 Pachtree Dunwoody Rd
Atlanta GA 30342
-

(P-27137)
MOSAIC
Also Called: Mosaic Quest
10991 Via Banco, San Diego (92126-7423)
PHONE..................858 397-2261
EMP: 79
SALES (corp-wide): 240.8MM **Privately Held**
SIC: **8741** Management services
PA: Mosaic
4980 S 118th St
Omaha NE 68137
402 896-3884

(P-27138)
NB ENTERPRISES & DIST INC
603 Wilshire Blvd, Los Angeles (90017-3207)
PHONE..................866 216-1515
Neal B Platt, *President*
William Saller, *Vice Pres*
EMP: 85
SQ FT: 1,500
SALES: 15.3MM **Privately Held**
SIC: **8741** Management services

(P-27139)
NETWORK MANAGEMENT GROUP INC (PA)
1100 S Flower St Ste 3110, Los Angeles (90015-2287)
PHONE..................323 263-2632
John Park, *President*
Kelly Hutson, *Human Res Dir*
Frederick Miller, *Director*
Evan Gracia, *Manager*
EMP: 160
SQ FT: 2,039
SALES (est): 12MM **Privately Held**
WEB: www.networkm.com
SIC: **8741** 8742 Business management; management consulting services

(P-27140)
NETWORK MEDICAL MANAGEMENT INC
14120 Victory Blvd, Van Nuys (91401-1927)
PHONE..................818 370-9125
Thomas Lam, *CEO*
EMP: 130
SQ FT: 14,000
SALES (est): 7.2MM **Privately Held**
WEB: www.nmm.cc
SIC: **8741** Hospital management; nursing & personal care facility management

(P-27141)
NEW SOLAR INCORPORATED
1525 Mccarthy Blvd, Milpitas (95035-7451)
PHONE..................888 886-0103
Charles Ng, *President*
Porter Wong, *Corp Secy*
Ralph Chern, *Sales Executive*
EMP: 50
SALES (est): 2MM **Privately Held**
WEB: www.newsolarinc.com
SIC: **8741** 5063 1731 4931 Financial management for business; electrical apparatus & equipment; electrical work; electric & other services combined; solar energy contractor

(P-27142)
NEWPORT GROUP INC (PA)
1350 Treat Blvd Ste 300, Walnut Creek (94597-7959)
PHONE..................925 328-4540
Greg W Tschider, *CEO*
John McCormack, *President*
Nancy Worth, *COO*
Purvi Chekuri, *CFO*
Martha Sadler, *Exec VP*
EMP: 112
SALES (est): 46.7MM **Privately Held**
SIC: **8741** Administrative management

(P-27143)
NO SHNACKS INC
7480 Harvard Ct, Fontana (92336-3432)
PHONE..................909 293-8747
Gary Clark, *Owner*
EMP: 50
SALES (est): 2MM **Privately Held**
SIC: **8741** Business management

(P-27144)
NORTH AMERICAN HEALTH CARE
Also Called: Cottonwood Post-Acute Rehab
625 Cottonwood St, Woodland (95695-3614)
PHONE..................530 662-9193
Jason Bliss, *Manager*
Donald Laws, *Principal*
James Ellissherinian, *Info Tech Mgr*
Deborah Larson, *Personnel*
Earl Keck, *Plant Mgr*
EMP: 80

SALES (corp-wide): 60.3MM **Privately Held**
WEB: www.nahci.com
SIC: **8741** 8051 Nursing & personal care facility management; skilled nursing care facilities
PA: North American Health Care, Inc.
32836 Pacific Coast Hwy
Dana Point CA 92629
949 240-2423

(P-27145)
NORTH AMERICAN HEALTH CARE INC (PA)
32836 Pacific Coast Hwy, Dana Point (92629-3472)
PHONE..................949 240-2423
Fax: 949 240-6557
John L Sorensen, *Ch of Bd*
Timothy J Paulsen, *CEO*
Tim Paulson, *CFO*
Donald G Laws, *Chairman*
Darian Dahl, *Vice Pres*
▲ EMP: 175
SALES (est): 60.3MM **Privately Held**
WEB: www.nahci.com
SIC: **8741** Nursing & personal care facility management

(P-27146)
NORTH AMERICAN MED MGT CAL INC (DH)
3281 E Guasti Rd Fl 7, Ontario (91761-7622)
PHONE..................909 605-8012
Richard A Shinto MD, *CEO*
Glen Marconcini, *Exec VP*
Diane Moon, *Accountant*
Crystal Leonard, *Mktg Dir*
EMP: 75
SALES (est): 7.9MM
SALES (corp-wide): 714.8MM **Privately Held**
SIC: **8741** Nursing & personal care facility management
HQ: Namm Holdings, Inc.
3281 E Guasti Rd Ste 700
Ontario CA 91761
909 605-8000

(P-27147)
NORTHROP GRUMMAN ENTERPRISE MG
806 S Loop Rd, Fort Irwin (92310)
P.O. Box 11159 (92310-1159)
PHONE..................760 380-4268
David Booze, *Branch Mgr*
EMP: 500 **Publicly Held**
SIC: **8741** 7699 Business management; miscellaneous automotive repair services
HQ: Northrop Grumman Enterprise Management Services Corporation
2340 Dulles Corner Blvd
Herndon VA 20171
703 713-4000

(P-27148)
NORTHSTAR SENIOR LIVING INC
Also Called: Mountain Lakes Senior Living
2334 Washington Ave Ste A, Redding (96001-2159)
PHONE..................530 242-8300
Rick Jensen, *CEO*
Lucian Luca, *President*
Brian Uhlir, *CFO*
EMP: 586
SALES (est): 43.8MM **Privately Held**
SIC: **8741** Nursing & personal care facility management

(P-27149)
NTREPID CORPORATION
10201 Wtridge Cir Ste 300, San Diego (92121)
PHONE..................800 921-2414
Mike Simpson, *Program Mgr*
Chris Bertolero, *Director*
EMP: 77 **Privately Held**
SIC: **8741** 7371 Management services; software programming applications
PA: Ntrepid Corporation
12801 Worldgate Dr # 800
Herndon VA 20170
-

(P-27150)
ONRAD INC
Also Called: Onrad Medical Group
1770 Iowa Ave Ste 280, Riverside (92507-7401)
PHONE..................800 848-5876
Samuel Salen, *CEO*
Scott Castle, *CFO*
Daniel Brazell, *Vice Pres*
Alice Reuter, *Vice Pres*
Jesse Salen, *Vice Pres*
EMP: 79
SQ FT: 1,500
SALES: 9MM **Privately Held**
SIC: **8741** Business management

(P-27151)
ORANGE COUNTY DEPT EDUCATION
Tustin Unified School District
300 S C St, Tustin (92780-3633)
PHONE..................714 730-7301
Peter Gorman, *Superintendent*
EMP: 1600
SALES (corp-wide): 123MM **Privately Held**
WEB: www.ocprob.com
SIC: **8741** Administrative management
PA: Orange County Superintendent Of Schools
200 Kalmus Dr
Costa Mesa CA 92626
714 966-4000

(P-27152)
OREQ CORPORATION
Also Called: Pool Pals Division
42306 Remington Ave, Temecula (92590-2512)
PHONE..................951 296-5076
Jess L Hetzner, *CEO*
Ron Hetzner, *Exec VP*
Luis Baroso, *Controller*
Maurine Sparks, *Sales Staff*
EMP: 50
SALES (est): 11.9MM **Privately Held**
WEB: www.oreqcorp.com
SIC: **8741** 5091 5087 Business management; spa equipment & supplies; beauty parlor equipment & supplies

(P-27153)
OVATIONS FANFARE
Also Called: Fanfare Enterprises
88 Fair Dr, Costa Mesa (92626-6521)
PHONE..................714 708-1880
Fax: 714 708-1882
Juan Quintero, *Manager*
Biancba Kulback, *Executive*
EMP: 75
SALES (corp-wide): 5.6MM **Privately Held**
SIC: **8741** 5812 Management services; caterers
PA: Ovations Fanfare
61 Haas Pavilion
Berkeley CA 94720
510 704-8361

(P-27154)
PACIFIC PROGRAM/DESIGN MANAGEM
100 W Walnut St, Pasadena (91124-0001)
PHONE..................626 440-2000
Mary Ann Hopkins, *Manager*
Lily Hidalgo, *Admin Sec*
Ann Hick, *Administration*
Ozzie Gallo, *Controller*
Matt Miller, *Controller*
EMP: 99
SALES (est): 37.5K **Privately Held**
SIC: **8741** 8711 Business management; engineering services

(P-27155)
PACIFIC VENTURES LTD
Also Called: Jacmar Companies, The
2200 W Valley Blvd, Alhambra (91803-1928)
PHONE..................626 576-0737
William H Tilley, *CEO*
Jim Dalpozzo, *President*
Randy Hill, *Exec VP*
EMP: 250 **EST:** 1976
SQ FT: 20,000

PRODUCTS & SERVICES SECTION 8741 - Management Services County (P-27179)

SALES (est): 11.5MM **Privately Held**
SIC: 8741 6722 Restaurant management; management investment, open-end

(P-27156)
PACKARD HOSPITALITY GROUP LLC
9555 Chesapeake Dr # 202, San Diego (92123-6394)
PHONE...................................858 277-4305
Michael Goldstein,
Steve Carr,
EMP: 120
SQ FT: 4,000
SALES: 75MM **Privately Held**
SIC: 8741 Hotel or motel management

(P-27157)
PAMA MANAGEMENT CO
123 N Inez St Ste 16, Hemet (92543-4169)
PHONE...................................951 929-0340
EMP: 50
SALES (est): 2.4MM **Privately Held**
SIC: 8741

(P-27158)
PARAMUNT MADOWS NURSING CTR LP
Also Called: Paramount Meadows Nursing Ctr
7039 Alondra Blvd, Paramount (90723-3925)
PHONE...................................562 531-0990
Carlos Aragon, *Administration*
EMP: 99 EST: 2015
SQ FT: 10,000
SALES (est): 1.9MM **Privately Held**
SIC: 8741 Nursing & personal care facility management

(P-27159)
PARSONS CONSTRUCTORS INC
Also Called: Operations/Risk Group
100 W Walnut St, Pasadena (91124-0001)
PHONE...................................626 440-2000
Fax: 626 440-2516
Chuck Harrington, *CEO*
Robert Camp, *Admin Sec*
Thomas L Johanson, *Assistant*
EMP: 10000
SALES (est): 98.4MM
SALES (corp-wide): 7.9B **Privately Held**
SIC: 8741 8711 Management services; engineering services
PA: The Parsons Corporation
100 W Walnut St
Pasadena CA 91124
626 440-2000

(P-27160)
PARTHENON DCS HOLDINGS LLC
4 Embarcadero Ctr, San Francisco (94111-4106)
PHONE...................................925 960-4800
Mari Machado, *Controller*
Collin R Lesser, *Associate*
EMP: 1400
SALES (est): 25.5MM **Privately Held**
SIC: 8741 Management services

(P-27161)
PATHWAY CAPITAL MANAGEMENT LP (PA)
2211 Michelson Dr Ste 900, Irvine (92612-1395)
PHONE...................................949 622-1000
Milt M Best,
Gerard Branka, *President*
Curtis Gerlach, *CFO*
Paul De Groot, *Senior VP*
Matthew Lugar, *Senior VP*
EMP: 67
SQ FT: 13,302
SALES (est): 19.9MM **Privately Held**
WEB: www.pathwaycapital.com
SIC: 8741 6282 Financial management for business; investment advice

(P-27162)
PEN-CAL ADMINISTRATORS INC
Also Called: P C A
7633 Suthfront Rd Ste 120, Livermore (94551)
PHONE...................................925 251-3400
Bob Penland, *Ch of Bd*
Kirk Penland, *CEO*
Terry Oprey, *COO*
Freevan Ching, *Executive*
Stephen Nell, *Managing Dir*
EMP: 75
SQ FT: 15,000
SALES (est): 9.5MM **Privately Held**
WEB: www.pencal.com
SIC: 8741 Financial management for business

(P-27163)
PHYSICIAN MANAGEMENT GROUP INC
Also Called: Childrens Specialist San Diego
3860 Calle Fortunada # 210, San Diego (92123-4800)
PHONE...................................858 309-6300
Fax: 858 309-6298
Larry Nichols, *President*
Wade Blundell, *Partner*
Judy Pruitt, *Marketing Mgr*
EMP: 105
SALES (est): 7.2MM **Privately Held**
WEB: www.pmgservices.org
SIC: 8741 Business management

(P-27164)
PHYSICIAN WEBLINK OF CAL (HQ)
7 Technology Dr, Irvine (92618-2302)
PHONE...................................949 923-3201
Jay Cohen, *President*
Bartley Asner, *CEO*
Jacob Furgacth, *COO*
Richard Greene, *CFO*
Jackie Kinton, *Human Resources*
EMP: 145
SQ FT: 25,000
SALES (est): 6.2MM
SALES (corp-wide): 25MM **Privately Held**
SIC: 8741 Business management
PA: Syntiro Healthcare Services Inc
7 Technology Dr
Irvine CA 92618
949 923-3438

(P-27165)
PIERCEY MANAGEMENT SVCS INC (PA)
Also Called: Piercey Automotive Group
16901 Millikan Ave, Irvine (92606-5011)
PHONE...................................949 379-3701
William R Piercey, *President*
Tom A Chadwell, *CFO*
Ve Pham, *Engineer*
EMP: 56 EST: 1994
SALES (est): 61.9MM **Privately Held**
WEB: www.pierceyautomotivegroup.com
SIC: 8741 Management services

(P-27166)
PIONEER HEALTH CARE SERVICES
1640 School St Ste 100, Moraga (94556-1119)
PHONE...................................925 631-9100
Charles Patterson, *President*
EMP: 200
SQ FT: 2,300
SALES (est): 7.3MM **Privately Held**
WEB: www.pioneerhealthcareservices.com
SIC: 8741 Hospital management; nursing & personal care facility management

(P-27167)
PK MANAGEMENT LLC
15301 Ventura Blvd # 570, Sherman Oaks (91403-3102)
PHONE...................................818 808-0600
Robert Krensky, *Mng Member*
Leann Harris, *Executive Asst*
Gregory Perlman,
EMP: 500
SALES (est): 19.7MM **Privately Held**
SIC: 8741 Management services

(P-27168)
POLYCOM INC (PA)
6001 America Center Dr, San Jose (95002-2562)
P.O. Box 641390 (95164-1390)
PHONE...................................408 586-6000
Fax: 925 924-6100
Peter A Leav, *President*
Gary J Daichendt, *Ch of Bd*
Jeff Garratt, *COO*
Laura J Durr, *CFO*
Scott Hillis, *Treasurer*
▲ EMP: 148
SALES: 1.2B **Privately Held**
WEB: www.polycom.com
SIC: 8741 Management services

(P-27169)
PRE CON INDUSTRIES INC
Also Called: Premier Drywall
514 Work St, Salinas (93901-4350)
P.O. Box 5728, Santa Maria (93456-5728)
PHONE...................................805 345-3147
John Amburgey, *CEO*
Jose Rosas,
EMP: 50
SALES (est): 1.8MM **Privately Held**
SIC: 8741 Management services

(P-27170)
PREMIER HLTHCARE SOLUTIONS INC
Also Called: Premier IMS Insurance Services
12225 El Camino Real, San Diego (92130-2084)
PHONE...................................858 569-8629
Susan Devore, *Branch Mgr*
David Osman, *Vice Pres*
Rina Wolf, *Vice Pres*
Robert Hall, *Executive*
Carmen Wade, *Executive Asst*
EMP: 305
SALES (corp-wide): 1.1B **Publicly Held**
SIC: 8741 Management services
HQ: Premier Healthcare Solutions, Inc.
13034 Balntyn Corp Pl
Charlotte NC 28277
704 357-0022

(P-27171)
PRIMARY CARE ASSOD MED GROUP (PA)
1635 Lake San Marcos Dr # 105, San-Marcos (92078-4661)
PHONE...................................760 471-7505
Robert Mongeon, *President*
Chris Schlade, *Admin Sec*
EMP: 70
SALES (est): 6.6MM **Privately Held**
SIC: 8741 Administrative management

(P-27172)
PRIMARY PROVIDER MGT CO INC (PA)
Also Called: Ppmc
2115 Compton Ave Ste 301, Corona (92881-7272)
PHONE...................................951 280-7700
Robert Dukes, *CEO*
Maureen B Tyson, *President*
Carl Mathenge, *CTO*
Sandy Fuerfich, *Manager*
EMP: 90
SQ FT: 23,500
SALES (est): 16.1MM **Privately Held**
WEB: www.missionmedicalgroup.net
SIC: 8741 Management services

(P-27173)
PRIMED MGT CONSULTING SVCS INC
2409 Camino Ramon, San Ramon (94583-4285)
P.O. Box 5080 (94583-0980)
PHONE...................................925 327-6710
Cardoza Darryl, *CEO*
Steve McDermott, *President*
Rick Messman, *CFO*
Robert Ramsey, *Vice Pres*
Wendy Chow, *Admin Sec*
EMP: 500
SQ FT: 30,000
SALES (est): 49MM **Privately Held**
SIC: 8741 8742 Management services; management consulting services

(P-27174)
PRO UNLIMITED INC
1350 Bayshore Hwy Ste 350, Burlingame (94010-1831)
PHONE...................................650 344-1099
Fax: 650 548-0314
Allie Shlomo, *COO*
Terrie L Weinand, *CFO*
Henry Huang, *Vice Pres*
Anita Raman, *Vice Pres*
Dana Inverso, *Program Mgr*
EMP: 50 **Privately Held**
SIC: 8741 Financial management for business
HQ: Pro Unlimited, Inc.
7777 Glades Rd Ste 208
Boca Raton FL 33434
800 291-1099

(P-27175)
PRO-MED HLTH CARE ADMNISTRATOR
4150 Concours Ste 100, Ontario (91764-5914)
PHONE...................................909 932-1045
Kit Thapar, *CEO*
Jeereddi A Prasad, *President*
Karen Harvey, *Executive Asst*
EMP: 75
SQ FT: 20,000
SALES (est): 1.8MM
SALES (corp-wide): 90MM **Privately Held**
WEB: www.promedhealth.com
SIC: 8741 Administrative management
PA: Pamona Valley Medical Group Inc
9302 Pttsbrgh Ave Ste 220
Rancho Cucamonga CA 91730
909 932-1045

(P-27176)
PROACTIVE BUS SOLUTIONS INC
428 13th St Fl 5, Oakland (94612-2617)
PHONE...................................510 302-0120
Deidrie Towery, *CEO*
Jay A Copeland, *CFO*
Franklin Dearaujo, *Project Leader*
Darren Graham, *Project Leader*
Scott Jenkins, *Technician*
EMP: 250 EST: 1998
SQ FT: 3,000
SALES: 5.7MM **Privately Held**
WEB: www.proactiveok.com
SIC: 8741 8742 Management services; business consultant

(P-27177)
PROFESSIONAL GOLF MGT LLC
49155 Vista Estrella, La Quinta (92253-6343)
P.O. Box 5566 (92248-5565)
PHONE...................................760 564-0804
Raymond Holohan, *Mng Member*
Carol Holohan,
EMP: 70
SALES (est): 5.8MM **Privately Held**
WEB: www.professionalgolfmanagement.com
SIC: 8741 Management services

(P-27178)
PROJECT MANAGEMENT INSTITUTE
8895 Towne Centre Dr, San Diego (92122-5542)
Drawer 8895 (92122)
PHONE...................................760 458-6198
Tieman Chang, *Vice Pres*
EMP: 99
SALES: 258.4K **Privately Held**
SIC: 8741 Office management

(P-27179)
PROSPECT MEDICAL GROUP INC (HQ)
1920 E 17th St Ste 200, Santa Ana (92705-8626)
PHONE...................................714 796-5900
Jacob Y Terner MD, *President*
Mitchell Lew, *CEO*
Lily Kam, *COO*
Mike Heather, *CFO*
Elaine Lucas, *Executive Asst*
EMP: 350

8741 - Management Services County (P-27180)

PRODUDUCTS & SERVICES SECTION

SQ FT: 2,420
SALES (est): 41.5MM
SALES (corp-wide): 637.4MM Privately Held
WEB: www.prospectcorona.com
SIC: 8741 Hospital management; nursing & personal care facility management
PA: Prospect Medical Holdings, Inc.
3415 S Sepulveda Blvd # 9
Los Angeles CA 90034
310 943-4500

(P-27180)
PROSPECT MEDICAL SYSTEMS INC (HQ)
Also Called: Genesis Health Care
600 City Pkwy W Ste 800, Orange (92868-2948)
PHONE.................................714 667-8156
Mitchell Lew MD, *CEO*
Terri Holmes, *Vice Pres*
Brice Keyser, *Surgery Dir*
Amy Hugaert, *Admin Asst*
Ashley Fishback, *Network Mgr*
EMP: 165
SALES (est): 24.9MM
SALES (corp-wide): 637.4MM Privately Held
SIC: 8741 Hospital management; nursing & personal care facility management
PA: Prospect Medical Holdings, Inc.
3415 S Sepulveda Blvd # 9
Los Angeles CA 90034
310 943-4500

(P-27181)
PROVIDENCE LITTLE CO OF MARY (DH)
Also Called: Little Company Mary Svc Area
4101 Torrance Blvd, Torrance (90503-4607)
PHONE.................................310 540-7676
Fax: 310 316-6120
Blair Contratto, *CEO*
Louise Pilati, *Chief Mktg Ofcr*
Joseph M Zanetta, *Exec Dir*
Patti Hamaguchi, *QA Dir*
Chris Nowell, *Engineer*
EMP: 200
SQ FT: 300,000
SALES (est): 152.6MM
SALES (corp-wide): 10.1B Privately Held
WEB: www.littlecompanyofmary.org
SIC: 8741 Hospital management
HQ: Providence Health System-Southern California
1801 Lind Ave Sw
Renton WA 98057
425 525-3355

(P-27182)
PROVIDENCE LITTLE CO OF MARY
Little Company Mary Pathology
4101 Torrance Blvd, Torrance (90503-4607)
PHONE.................................310 303-6970
Fax: 310 543-9671
Angie Bugg, *Branch Mgr*
EMP: 102
SALES (corp-wide): 10.1B Privately Held
SIC: 8741 8071 Hospital management; pathological laboratory
HQ: Providence Little Company Of Mary Medical Center-Torrance
4101 Torrance Blvd
Torrance CA 90503
310 540-7676

(P-27183)
PROVIDENT FINANCIAL MANAGEMENT
2850 Ocean Park Blvd # 300, Santa Monica (90405-6216)
P.O. Box 4084 (90411-4084)
PHONE.................................310 282-0477
Ivan Axelrod, *Managing Prtnr*
Barry Siegel, *Partner*
Vicki M Lubben, *Admin Sec*
Liz Clements, *Human Res Dir*
Deannon Moore, *Purchasing*
EMP: 95
SQ FT: 34,000
SALES (est): 2MM Privately Held
WEB: www.providentfm.com
SIC: 8741 Business management

(P-27184)
PTR GROUP INC
Also Called: Glad I'M Not Driving.com
652 S Joyce Ave, Rialto (92376-7178)
PHONE.................................951 965-1822
Paul Rodriguez, *President*
EMP: 50 EST: 2013
SALES (est): 1.4MM Privately Held
SIC: 8741 7389 Business management;

(P-27185)
PUBLIC HLTH FNDATION ENTPS INC (PA)
Also Called: Phfe
12801 Crossrds Pkwy S 200, City of Industry (91746)
PHONE.................................562 692-4643
Mark J Bertler, *President*
Gerald D Jensen, *President*
Michael R Gomez, *CEO*
Michael Ascher, *Chairman*
Azhar K Qureshi, *Chairman*
EMP: 148
SQ FT: 19,426
SALES (est): 97.5MM Privately Held
SIC: 8741 Management services

(P-27186)
QC (US) INTERNATIONAL INC
205 E Rver Pk Cir Ste 310, Fresno (93720)
PHONE.................................559 447-1390
Warren Williams, *Principal*
EMP: 76
SALES (est): 17.4MM
SALES (corp-wide): 19.8B Privately Held
SIC: 8741 Management services
HQ: Olam Holdings Partnership
25 Union Pl Fl 2
Summit NJ 07901

(P-27187)
QUICK QUACK CAR WASH (PA)
6505 Fair Oaks Blvd, Carmichael (95608-4023)
P.O. Box 2703 (95609-2703)
PHONE.................................888 772-2792
Jason Johnson, *Owner*
EMP: 65
SALES (est): 19.8MM Privately Held
SIC: 8741 Management services

(P-27188)
QUICKHEALTH INC
9 41st Ave, San Mateo (94403-5105)
PHONE.................................650 286-1986
David Mandelkern, *President*
Crystal Carrasco, *Controller*
EMP: 90
SALES (est): 3.2MM Privately Held
WEB: www.quickhealth.com
SIC: 8741 Business management

(P-27189)
R & V MANAGEMENT CORPORATION
768 Hollister St, San Diego (92154-1333)
PHONE.................................619 429-3305
EMP: 103
SALES (corp-wide): 25.7MM Privately Held
SIC: 8741 Management services
PA: R & V Management Corporation
3444 Camno Dl Rio N 202
San Diego CA 92108
619 285-5500

(P-27190)
RADNET MANAGEMENT INC
Also Called: Modesto Imaging Center
157 E Coolidge Ave, Modesto (95350-4504)
PHONE.................................209 524-6800
Kim Davis, *Branch Mgr*
EMP: 60
SALES (corp-wide): 809.6MM Publicly Held
WEB: www.radnetmgt.com
SIC: 8741 Management services
HQ: Radnet Management, Inc.
1510 Cotner Ave
Los Angeles CA 90025
310 445-2800

(P-27191)
RADNET MANAGEMENT INC
8750 Wilshire Blvd # 100, Beverly Hills (90211-2708)
PHONE.................................323 549-3000
Taryn D Dartz, *Branch Mgr*
Phillip Hahn, *Med Doctor*
Maggie Malaro, *Med Doctor*
EMP: 100
SALES (corp-wide): 809.6MM Publicly Held
WEB: www.radnetmgt.com
SIC: 8741 Management services
HQ: Radnet Management, Inc.
1510 Cotner Ave
Los Angeles CA 90025
310 445-2800

(P-27192)
RADY CHLD HOSPITAL-SAN DIEGO
Also Called: Bernardy Ctr For Medcly Frgled
8022 Birmingham Dr # 22, San Diego (92123-2707)
PHONE.................................858 966-5833
Kathleen Sellick, *Manager*
Kim Looney, *Software Dev*
Jeffrey Max, *Psychiatry*
Xenia Hom, *Med Doctor*
Pamela Dixon, *Director*
EMP: 60
SALES (corp-wide): 838.7MM Privately Held
SIC: 8741 8051 Nursing & personal care facility management; skilled nursing care facilities
PA: Rady Children's Hospital-San Diego
3020 Childrens Way
San Diego CA 92123
858 576-1700

(P-27193)
RAINMAKER SYSTEMS INC
Also Called: Rmkr
1821 S Bascom Ave 385, Campbell (95008-2309)
PHONE.................................408 659-1800
Terry Lydon, *CEO*
Bryant Tolles, *CFO*
Andy Sheehan, *Bd of Directors*
David Guerci, *Senior VP*
Thomas Venable, *Senior VP*
EMP: 150
SALES (est): 17.6MM Privately Held
WEB: www.rmkr.com
SIC: 8741 8742 Management services; marketing consulting services; sales (including sales management) consultant

(P-27194)
RANDOM HOLDINGS INC
Also Called: Sutra Lounge
1599 Superior Ave Ste A1, Costa Mesa (92627-3625)
PHONE.................................949 722-7103
Brittney Ellison, *Manager*
EMP: 85
SALES (corp-wide): 18MM Privately Held
SIC: 8741 Restaurant management
PA: Random Holdings, Inc.
620 Nwport Ctr Dr Ste 525
Newport Beach CA

(P-27195)
RAYMOND GROUP (PA)
Also Called: Orange Cnty George M Raymond N
520 W Walnut Ave, Orange (92868-5008)
P.O. Box 1727 (92856-0727)
PHONE.................................714 771-7670
Fax: 714 633-1558
Travis Winsor, *CEO*
James Watson, *President*
Tom O'Brien, *CFO*
Mary Raymond, *Corp Secy*
Buster Peterson, *Exec VP*
EMP: 95
SQ FT: 20,000
SALES (est): 47.3MM Privately Held
SIC: 8741 Construction management

(P-27196)
REIGN ACCESSORIES INC
4000 Redondo Beach Ave, Redondo Beach (90278-1109)
PHONE.................................310 297-6400
Jon Hirschberg, *President*
EMP: 50
SALES (est): 2MM Privately Held
WEB: www.rainforestventures.com
SIC: 8741 Business management

(P-27197)
RELIABLE INTERIORS INC
104 S Maple St, Corona (92880-1704)
P.O. Box 2618 (92878-2618)
PHONE.................................951 371-3390
Gerald C Crowther, *President*
William J Klotz, *President*
Glenn L Crowther, *Vice Pres*
Ralph G Prentiss, *Vice Pres*
Lee Scott, *Vice Pres*
EMP: 200
SALES (est): 7.3MM Privately Held
SIC: 8741 1742 Construction management; drywall

(P-27198)
RESIDNTIAL ALZHEIMERS CARE INC
9619 Chesapeake Dr # 103, San Diego (92123-1368)
PHONE.................................858 565-4424
William M Chance, *President*
EMP: 180
SQ FT: 9,000
SALES (est): 4.5MM Privately Held
SIC: 8741 Nursing & personal care facility management

(P-27199)
RESPONSELOGIX INC
2001 Gateway Pl Ste 750w, San Jose (95110-1080)
PHONE.................................408 220-6505
Lionel Thomas Mohr, *CEO*
EMP: 150
SALES (corp-wide): 17.9MM Privately Held
SIC: 8741 Management services
PA: Responselogix, Inc.
6991 E Camelback Rd B300
Scottsdale AZ 85251
408 220-6545

(P-27200)
REYES HOLDINGS LLC
1625 S Lewis St, Anaheim (92805-6437)
PHONE.................................714 445-3392
Thomas Reyes, *Principal*
Dan Schmidt, *Vice Pres*
Andy Chin, *Info Tech Mgr*
Paul Rizzo, *VP Opers*
Keith Triscele, *Director*
EMP: 64 Privately Held
SIC: 8741 Management services
PA: Reyes Holdings, L.L.C.
6250 N River Rd Ste 9000
Rosemont IL 60018

(P-27201)
RHS CORP
Also Called: Redlands Community Hospital
350 Terracina Blvd, Redlands (92373-4850)
PHONE.................................909 335-5500
James R Holmes, *President*
Cindy Ruiz,
Todd Sexton, *COO*
Curt Forbes, *Vice Pres*
Maria Lopez, *Admin Sec*
EMP: 1450
SQ FT: 265,000
SALES: 210.7K Privately Held
SIC: 8741 Hospital management

(P-27202)
RROMEO CORPORATION
535 Anton Blvd Ste 200, Costa Mesa (92626-7680)
PHONE.................................714 640-3800
Richard Putnam, *Branch Mgr*
John Casasante, *Vice Pres*

PRODUCTS & SERVICES SECTION
8741 - Management Services County (P-27225)

EMP: 80
SALES (corp-wide): 8.8B **Privately Held**
WEB: www.rref.com
SIC: 8741 6531 Management services; real estate managers
HQ: The Rromeo Corporation
101 California St Fl 24
San Francisco CA 94111
415 781-3300

(P-27203)
S W K PROPERTIES LLC (PA)
Also Called: Sheraton Ontario Airport Hotel
3807 Wilshire Blvd # 1226, Los Angeles (90010-3101)
PHONE 213 383-9204
Eric Cha,
EMP: 70
SQ FT: 3,000
SALES (est): 10MM **Privately Held**
SIC: 8741 7011 Hotel or motel management; hotels

(P-27204)
SAN JOSE ARENA MANAGEMENT LLC
44388 Old Warm Sprng Blvd, Fremont (94538-6148)
PHONE 510 623-7200
Greg Jamison, *Branch Mgr*
EMP: 127
SALES (corp-wide): 16.1MM **Privately Held**
SIC: 8741 Management services
PA: San Jose Arena Management, Llc
525 W Santa Clara St
San Jose CA 95113
408 287-7070

(P-27205)
SANTA CLARITA HEALTH CARE ASSN (PA)
23845 Mcbean Pkwy, Santa Clarita (91355-2001)
PHONE 661 253-8000
Roger Seaver, *President*
Paul Salomon, *COO*
C R Hudson, *CFO*
James D Hicken, *Treasurer*
John Barstis, *Admin Sec*
EMP: 65
SQ FT: 130,000
SALES (est): 22.6MM **Privately Held**
SIC: 8741 Hospital management; nursing & personal care facility management

(P-27206)
SCCH INC
Also Called: COURTYARD CARE CENTER
1880 Dawson Ave, Signal Hill (90755-5913)
PHONE 562 494-5188
Fax: 562 494-8758
Julie Javier, *Administration*
Spencer Olsen, *Treasurer*
EMP: 99
SALES: 6.9MM **Privately Held**
WEB: www.nahci.com
SIC: 8741 8052 8051 Management services; intermediate care facilities; skilled nursing care facilities

(P-27207)
SCRIPPS CLINIC FOUNDATION
12395 El Camino Real, San Diego (92130-3082)
PHONE 858 554-9000
Fax: 858 554-6941
Dr Hugh Greenway, *CEO*
Giacomo Delaria, *Surgeon*
George Dailey, *Endocrinology*
Christopher W Marx, *Endocrinology*
Thomas Deuel, *Oncology*
EMP: 1600
SALES (est): 96.5MM
SALES (corp-wide): 1.7B **Privately Held**
WEB: www.scripps.org
SIC: 8741 Management services
PA: Scripps Health
4275 Campus Point Ct
San Diego CA 92121
858 678-7000

(P-27208)
SEABREEZE MANAGEMENT COMPANY (PA)
39 Argonaut Ste 100, Aliso Viejo (92656-4152)
PHONE 949 855-1800
Fax: 949 855-6678
Lisa Dale, *CEO*
Susan Larson, *President*
Nancy Burke, *General Mgr*
Brian Fleming, *General Mgr*
Laurene Cail, *Admin Asst*
EMP: 69
SQ FT: 22,000
SALES (est): 13.6MM **Privately Held**
WEB: www.seabreezemgmt.com
SIC: 8741 Management services

(P-27209)
SETHI MANAGEMENT INC
6100 Innovation Way, Carlsbad (92009-1728)
P.O. Box 235927, Encinitas (92023-5927)
PHONE 760 692-5288
Jeetander Sethi, *CEO*
EMP: 154 **EST**: 2009
SALES: 40MM **Privately Held**
SIC: 8741 Management services

(P-27210)
SHELL VACATIONS LLC
Also Called: Donatello
501 Post St, San Francisco (94102-1228)
PHONE 415 441-7100
Fax: 415 885-8842
Sheldon Ginsburg, *Owner*
EMP: 60
SALES (corp-wide): 5.5B **Publicly Held**
SIC: 8741 7011 7389 Hotel or motel management; hotels & motels; office facilities & secretarial service rental
HQ: Shell Vacations L.L.C.
40 Skokie Blvd Ste 350
Northbrook IL 60062
847 564-4600

(P-27211)
SILVER CREEK HOME OWNERS
Also Called: Silver Crk Vlly Ctry CLB HM Ow
1935 Dry Creek Rd Ste 203, Campbell (95008-3631)
PHONE 408 559-1977
Tim Johnson, *CEO*
Marianne Hudkins, *Principal*
EMP: 50
SALES (est): 3.7MM **Privately Held**
SIC: 8741 Management services

(P-27212)
SIMPSON & SIMPSON
633 W 5th St Ste 3320, Los Angeles (90071-3542)
PHONE 213 736-6664
Fax: 213 736-6692
Brainard Simpson, *Principal*
Carl P Simpson, *Principal*
Joey Williams, *Info Tech Mgr*
Susanna Leung, *Manager*
Grace Yuen, *Manager*
EMP: 61
SQ FT: 5,500
SALES (est): 7.4MM **Privately Held**
WEB: www.simpsonandsimpsoncpas.com
SIC: 8741 8721 Financial management for business; accounting, auditing & bookkeeping; certified public accountant

(P-27213)
SIX PER CENT MANAGEMENT
2800 Neilson Way Apt 601, Santa Monica (90405-4034)
PHONE 310 399-2611
Robert Fidler, *Owner*
Michael Fidler, *Manager*
EMP: 75 **EST**: 1971
SALES (est): 2.6MM **Privately Held**
SIC: 8741 Restaurant management

(P-27214)
SJ HOTEL MANAGER LLC
Also Called: AC Hotel San Jose Downtown
350 W Santa Clara St, San Jose (95113-1501)
PHONE 401 946-4600
Elizabeth Procaccianti,
Michelle Joyal, *Administration*

EMP: 75
SALES (est): 951.8K **Privately Held**
SIC: 8741 Hotel or motel management

(P-27215)
SMART MANAGEMENT & COMPANIES
Also Called: G Moroni Comp
1501 Corp Way Ste 200, Sacramento (95831)
PHONE 916 392-3000
Fax: 916 428-2795
Tony Lutsi, *Owner*
Greg Moroni, *Co-Owner*
EMP: 400
SQ FT: 2,000
SALES (est): 15.1MM **Privately Held**
WEB: www.smartmanagement.us
SIC: 8741 8742 Management services; management consulting services

(P-27216)
SMILE BRANDS GROUP INC (PA)
Also Called: Bright Now Dental
100 Spectrum Center Dr # 1500, Irvine (92618-4962)
PHONE 714 668-1300
Steven C Bilt, *CEO*
Stan Andrakowicz, *President*
Bradley Schmidt, *CFO*
Victoria Harvey,
Cheryl Dore, *Senior VP*
EMP: 90
SQ FT: 15,000
SALES (est): 538.4MM **Privately Held**
WEB: www.brightnow.com
SIC: 8741 8021 Management services; dental clinics & offices

(P-27217)
SMITH BROADCASTING GROUP INC (PA)
2315 Red Rose Way, Santa Barbara (93109-1259)
PHONE 805 965-0400
Debrah Egar, *Exec Sec*
David A Fitz, *Vice Pres*
Margaret Williams, *VP Finance*
EMP: 165 **EST**: 1985
SALES (est): 15.4MM **Privately Held**
SIC: 8741 8742 Business management; management consulting services

(P-27218)
SMITH BROTHERS RESTAURANT INC
100 Corson St Lbby, Pasadena (91103-3854)
PHONE 626 577-2400
Robert Smith, *President*
Jason Tirona, *CFO*
Greg Smith, *Admin Sec*
Ines Zapatero, *Controller*
Will Van Leuven, *Consultant*
EMP: 55
SALES (est): 5.5MM **Privately Held**
SIC: 8741 8742 8721 Restaurant management; management consulting services; accounting, auditing & bookkeeping

(P-27219)
SNF MANAGEMENT
9200 W Sunset Blvd # 700, West Hollywood (90069-3502)
PHONE 310 385-1090
Lee Samson, *President*
Ken Cess, *Shareholder*
Lawrence Feigen, *COO*
Christine Houser, *CFO*
John Minor, *Vice Pres*
EMP: 67
SALES (est): 14.5MM **Privately Held**
SIC: 8741 Management services

(P-27220)
SOC/GENERAL SERVICES/BPM
455 Golden Gate Ave # 2600, San Francisco (94102-3670)
PHONE 415 703-5341
Sam Flores, *General Mgr*
Erika Monterroza, *Comms Dir*
Lee Ratcliff, *Regional Mgr*
EMP: 60
SALES (est): 3.8MM **Privately Held**
SIC: 8741 Construction management

(P-27221)
SODEXO MANAGEMENT INC
Also Called: Cific Energy Center
851 Howard St, San Francisco (94103-3009)
PHONE 925 325-9657
Jim Wasley, *Branch Mgr*
EMP: 82
SALES (corp-wide): 96.3MM **Privately Held**
SIC: 8741 Management services
HQ: Sodexo Management Inc.
9801 Washingtonian Blvd
Gaithersburg MD 20878
301 987-4000

(P-27222)
SODEXO MANAGEMENT INC
1 University Cir, Turlock (95382-3200)
PHONE 209 667-3634
Tom Welton, *Manager*
Anne Dean, *General Mgr*
Lam Silva, *Admin Asst*
Sean Lovely, *Opers Mgr*
EMP: 75
SALES (corp-wide): 96.3MM **Privately Held**
WEB: www.compass-mgmt.com
SIC: 8741 Management services
HQ: Sodexo Management Inc.
9801 Washingtonian Blvd
Gaithersburg MD 20878
301 987-4000

(P-27223)
SODEXO OPERATIONS LLC
100 Campus Ctr Bldg 16, Seaside (93955-8000)
PHONE 831 582-3838
Charles Wesley, *General Mgr*
EMP: 100
SALES (corp-wide): 96.3MM **Privately Held**
SIC: 8741 5812 Restaurant management; eating places
HQ: Sodexo Operations, Llc
9801 Washingtonian Blvd
Gaithersburg MD 20878
301 987-4000

(P-27224)
SOLPAC CONSTRUCTION INC
Also Called: Soltek Pacific Construction Co
2424 Congress St, San Diego (92110-2819)
PHONE 619 296-6247
Steven Thompson, *CEO*
Dave Carlin, *President*
John Myers, *Senior VP*
Kevin Cammall, *Vice Pres*
William Naylor, *Vice Pres*
EMP: 235
SQ FT: 12,291
SALES: 121.2MM **Privately Held**
SIC: 8741 1542 1611 Construction management; commercial & office building contractors; design & erection, combined: non-residential; general contractor, highway & street construction

(P-27225)
SOUTHERN CALIFORNIA GAS CO
1801 S Atlantic Blvd, Monterey Park (91754-5207)
PHONE 213 244-1200
W J Torres, *Branch Mgr*
Warren Mitchell, *President*
Jim Nguyen, *Info Tech Dir*
Hong Ly, *Network Engnr*
Lester Larson, *Systems Staff*
EMP: 293
SALES (corp-wide): 10.2B **Publicly Held**
WEB: www.gasselect.com
SIC: 8741 Administrative management
HQ: Southern California Gas Company
555 W 5th St Fl 31
Los Angeles CA 90013
213 244-1200

8741 - Management Services County (P-27226)

(P-27226)
SOUTHERN CALIFORNIA PHYSICIA
6760 Top Gun St Ste 100, San Diego (92121-4152)
PHONE...................858 824-7000
Joyce Cook, *CEO*
Arlys Bartholomew, *President*
Marcia Aeschaleman, *CFO*
Marcia Aeschleman, *CFO*
Noemi Marton, *Administration*
EMP: 65 **EST:** 1996
SQ FT: 17,000
SALES: 5MM **Privately Held**
WEB: www.scpmcs.org
SIC: 8741 Administrative management

(P-27227)
SRG MANAGEMENT LLC
500 Stevens Ave Ste 100, Solana Beach (92075-2055)
PHONE...................858 792-9300
Michael S Grust, *CEO*
Tony Daloisio, *Bd of Directors*
EMP: 189
SALES (est): 41.2K
SALES (corp-wide): 70.7MM **Privately Held**
SIC: 8741 Management services
HQ: Srg Holdings, Llc
500 Stevens Ave Ste 100
Solana Beach CA 92075
858 792-9300

(P-27228)
SRHT PROPERTY MGMT CO
1317 E 7th St, Los Angeles (90021-1101)
PHONE...................213 683-0522
Michael Alvidrez, *Director*
Joanne Cohen, *Admin Asst*
EMP: 100 **EST:** 1994
SALES: 4.3MM **Privately Held**
SIC: 8741 Management services

(P-27229)
STAN TASHMAN & ASSOCIATES INC
8675 Wash Blvd Ste 203, Culver City (90232-7486)
PHONE...................310 460-7600
Richard Tashman, *CEO*
Ellen Chargualaf, *CFO*
Stan Tashman, *CFO*
Ty Olson, *Vice Pres*
EMP: 650
SQ FT: 14,000
SALES (est): 38.1MM **Privately Held**
WEB: www.tashman.com
SIC: 8741 Management services

(P-27230)
STANFORD MANAGEMENT COMPANY
635 Knight Way, Stanford (94305-7297)
PHONE...................650 721-2200
John F Powers, *CEO*
EMP: 60
SALES (est): 233.8K **Privately Held**
SIC: 8741 Management services

(P-27231)
STEWARDSHIP COMPANY LLC
1 Rancho San Carlos Rd, Carmel (93923-7999)
PHONE...................831 620-6700
Thomas A Gray,
Anthony Lombardi, *Controller*
Don W Wilcoxon,
EMP: 200
SQ FT: 2,000
SALES (est): 13MM **Privately Held**
SIC: 8741 Management services

(P-27232)
STONE PUBLISHING INC (PA)
Also Called: Almaden Press
2549 Scott Blvd, Santa Clara (95050-2508)
PHONE...................408 450-7910
Fax: 408 450-7917
Eric T Stern, *President*
H Gene Timmons, *CFO*
Ed Schultz, *General Mgr*
Zach Abad, *Web Proj Mgr*
Charlotta Gallo, *Project Mgr*
EMP: 70
SQ FT: 15,000
SALES (est): 28MM **Privately Held**
WEB: www.almadenpress.com
SIC: 8741 Management services

(P-27233)
STRAIGHT LANDER INC
8335 W Sunset Blvd # 320, Los Angeles (90069-1500)
PHONE...................323 337-9075
David Yashar, *President*
EMP: 58 **EST:** 1998
SALES (est): 1.8MM **Privately Held**
SIC: 8741 Business management

(P-27234)
SUMITOMO ELC USA HOLDINGS INC
21250 Hawthorne Blvd # 730, Torrance (90503-5513)
PHONE...................310 792-6016
Shelly Yang, *Branch Mgr*
EMP: 51
SALES (corp-wide): 25B **Privately Held**
SIC: 8741 Financial management for business
HQ: Sumitomo Electric U.S.A. Holdings, Inc.
600 5th Ave Fl 18
New York NY 10020
212 490-6610

(P-27235)
SUN MAR MANAGEMENT SERVICES
Also Called: Anaheim Health Care Center
501 S Beach Blvd, Anaheim (92804-1810)
PHONE...................714 827-9263
Rob Koontz, *Administration*
EMP: 200
SALES (corp-wide): 59MM **Privately Held**
WEB: www.extendedcarehospital.com
SIC: 8741 8051 Management services; skilled nursing care facilities
PA: Sun Mar Management Services
3050 Saturn St Ste 201
Brea CA 92821
714 577-3880

(P-27236)
SUN MAR MANAGEMENT SERVICES
Also Called: Laurel Convelescent Center
7509 Laurel Ave, Fontana (92336-2315)
PHONE...................909 822-8066
Blaine Hendrickson, *President*
Yousuf Sadiq, *Director*
EMP: 86
SALES (corp-wide): 59MM **Privately Held**
WEB: www.extendedcarehospital.com
SIC: 8741 8051 Management services; skilled nursing care facilities
PA: Sun Mar Management Services
3050 Saturn St Ste 201
Brea CA 92821
714 577-3880

(P-27237)
SUN MAR MANAGEMENT SERVICES
Also Called: Sun Mar Health Care
3136 Del Mar Ave, Rosemead (91770-2326)
PHONE...................626 288-8353
Steve Montelli, *Administration*
Carlos Zavala, *Envir Svcs Dir*
Angelo Jesus, *Director*
Tina Tsai, *Director*
Sunny Wong, *Director*
EMP: 60
SALES (corp-wide): 59MM **Privately Held**
WEB: www.extendedcarehospital.com
SIC: 8741 8051 Management services; skilled nursing care facilities
PA: Sun Mar Management Services
3050 Saturn St Ste 201
Brea CA 92821
714 577-3880

(P-27238)
SUN MAR MANAGEMENT SERVICES
Also Called: North Valley Nursing Center
7660 Wyngate St, Tujunga (91042-1736)
PHONE...................818 352-1454
Fax: 818 352-3995
Katherine Rodriguez, *Manager*
Matilde Sandoval, *Office Mgr*
EMP: 100
SALES (corp-wide): 59MM **Privately Held**
WEB: www.extendedcarehospital.com
SIC: 8741 8059 Management services; convalescent home
PA: Sun Mar Management Services
3050 Saturn St Ste 201
Brea CA 92821
714 577-3880

(P-27239)
SUNAMERICA INVESTMENTS INC (DH)
1 Sun America Ctr Fl 37, Los Angeles (90067-6103)
PHONE...................310 772-6000
Eli Broad, *President*
Michael Thomas, *Director*
EMP: 80
SQ FT: 76,000
SALES: 2B
SALES (corp-wide): 58.3B **Publicly Held**
WEB: www.opfa.com
SIC: 8741 6211 6282 7311 Administrative management; financial management for business; security brokers & dealers; investment advisory service; advertising agencies
HQ: Sunamerica Inc.
1 Sun America Ctr Fl 38
Los Angeles CA 90067
310 772-6000

(P-27240)
SUPERIOR SUPPORT SERVICES INC
Also Called: Superior Services
702 Civic Center Dr, Oceanside (92054-2504)
PHONE...................559 458-0507
Fax: 559 458-0539
Sheila Guarderas, *President*
Richard Meissner, *Controller*
Marsy Nikkel, *Controller*
Cassandra Sumner, *Personnel Assit*
EMP: 500
SQ FT: 6,000
SALES: 17MM **Privately Held**
WEB: www.superiorservices.com
SIC: 8741 7349 Restaurant management; janitorial service, contract basis

(P-27241)
SUTHERLAND HALTHCARE SOLUTIONS
9841 Arprt Blvd Ste 1414, Los Angeles (90045)
PHONE...................310 464-5000
Noel Coppinger, *Vice Pres*
EMP: 131
SALES (corp-wide): 61.7MM **Privately Held**
SIC: 8741 Management services
PA: Sutherland Healthcare Solutions Inc.
2 Brighton Rd Ste 300
Clifton NJ 07012
973 405-5002

(P-27242)
SUTTER HEALTH
2015 Steiner St Fl 1, San Francisco (94115-2627)
PHONE...................415 600-4280
Angela Morris-Bates, *Internal Med*
EMP: 140
SALES (corp-wide): 11B **Privately Held**
SIC: 8741 Administrative management
PA: Sutter Health
2200 River Plaza Dr
Sacramento CA 95833
916 733-8800

(P-27243)
SYLMARK INC (PA)
Also Called: Sylmark Group
7821 Orion Ave Ste 200, Van Nuys (91406-2032)
PHONE...................818 217-2000
Peter Spiegel, *President*
Mark Funk, *CFO*
Michael Badar, *Senior VP*
Jorge Noa, *Vice Pres*
Steven Ober, *Vice Pres*
EMP: 90
SALES (est): 22MM **Privately Held**
SIC: 8741 Management services

(P-27244)
SYMTECH INDUSTRIES INC (PA)
800 E Colorado Blvd, Pasadena (91101-2103)
PHONE...................626 683-7555
Cole Harris, *President*
EMP: 100
SQ FT: 30,000
SALES (est): 7.1MM **Privately Held**
SIC: 8741 Management services

(P-27245)
SYMTECH INDUSTRIES INC
100 N Lake Ave, Pasadena (91101-1883)
PHONE...................626 683-7555
Fax: 626 628-3855
Cole Harris, *Branch Mgr*
EMP: 150
SALES (corp-wide): 7.1MM **Privately Held**
SIC: 8741 Management services
PA: Symtech Industries Inc
800 E Colorado Blvd
Pasadena CA 91101
626 683-7555

(P-27246)
SYNERMED
711 W College St Fl 4, Los Angeles (90012-3177)
P.O. Box 2002, Monterey Park (91754-0952)
PHONE...................213 626-4556
John Edwards, *President*
EMP: 65
SALES (est): 5.8MM **Privately Held**
SIC: 8741 Hospital management

(P-27247)
TCM GROUP LLC
3130 Inland Empire Blvd, Ontario (91764-6569)
PHONE...................909 527-8580
Rima Tahan, *President*
S Michael Tahan, *Vice Pres*
Carol Larsen, *Administration*
Bryce Nielsen, *Controller*
Ivan Benavidez, *Sr Project Mgr*
EMP: 50
SALES (est): 2.7MM
SALES (corp-wide): 720.6MM **Publicly Held**
SIC: 8741 8742 Construction management; construction project management consultant
PA: Hill International, Inc.
2005 Market St Fl 17
Philadelphia PA 19103
215 309-7700

(P-27248)
TCV MANAGEMENT 2004 LLC
528 Ramona St, Palo Alto (94301-1709)
PHONE...................650 614-8200
Jay C Hoag, *Manager*
Suzann Curley, *Office Mgr*
EMP: 50
SALES: 2.5MM **Privately Held**
SIC: 8741 Management services

(P-27249)
TCW SPECIALIZED CASH MGT LTD
865 S Figueroa St # 1800, Los Angeles (90017-2543)
PHONE...................213 244-0000
Tcw Capital, *Principal*
EMP: 65
SALES (est): 6.2MM **Privately Held**
SIC: 8741 Management services

PRODUCTS & SERVICES SECTION
8741 - Management Services County (P-27274)

(P-27250)
TEXTAINER GROUP HOLDINGS LTD (HQ)
650 California St Fl 16, San Francisco (94108-2720)
PHONE.................................415 434-0551
John A Maccarone, *CEO*
Ernest J Furtado, *CFO*
Lionel Vargas, *Admin Asst*
Kenneth Chow, *Network Enginr*
Lynda Kwong, *Controller*
EMP: 55 EST: 1994
SALES (est): 12.5MM Privately Held
SIC: 8741 Management services
PA: Textainer Equipment Management Limited
  C/O Continental Management Limited
  Hamilton
  441 292-2487

(P-27251)
TICKETMOB LLC
11833 Mississippi Ave, Los Angeles (90025-6134)
PHONE.................................800 927-0939
Scot Richardson, *CEO*
Nasi Peretz, *CTO*
EMP: 1145
SALES (est): 29.6MM
SALES (corp-wide): 187.7MM Publicly Held
SIC: 8741 Management services
PA: Cvent, Inc.
  1765 Grnsboro Stn Pl Fl 7
  Tysons Corner VA 22102
  703 226-3500

(P-27252)
TISHMAN CONSTRUCTION CORP CAL
444 S Flower St Ste 2500, Los Angeles (90071-2926)
PHONE.................................213 542-6400
Fax: 213 362-1002
John L Tishman, *Ch of Bd*
Larry Schwarzwalder, *Treasurer*
Thomas McCaslin, *Exec VP*
James L Riccio, *Senior VP*
James M Ostrom, *Vice Pres*
EMP: 70
SQ FT: 14,000
SALES (est): 5.8MM
SALES (corp-wide): 17.9B Publicly Held
SIC: 8741 Construction management
HQ: Tishman Realty & Construction Co, Inc.
  100 Park Ave Fl 5
  New York NY 10017
  212 708-6800

(P-27253)
TOFASCO OF AMERICA INC (PA)
1661 Fairplex Dr, La Verne (91750-5871)
PHONE.................................909 392-8282
Fax: 909 392-8283
Edward Zheng, *President*
Stephen Chan, *CFO*
Joe Greenfeld, *Vice Pres*
Xiu Jun Liang, *Vice Pres*
Albert Sheih, *Vice Pres*
EMP: 60
SQ FT: 160,554
SALES: 9MM Privately Held
SIC: 8741 Financial management for business

(P-27254)
TOP OF MARKET
Also Called: San Diego Fish Market
750 N Harbor Dr, San Diego (92101-5806)
PHONE.................................619 234-4867
Jim Wentler, *Owner*
Alfonso Deanda, *Owner*
Bob Wilson, *Owner*
Fred Ducket, *Partner*
Dan Houte, *Manager*
EMP: 280
SALES (est): 9.7MM Privately Held
SIC: 8741 5813 Restaurant management; cocktail lounge

(P-27255)
TRAFFIC MANAGEMENT INC
1244 S Claudina St, Anaheim (92805-6232)
PHONE.................................562 264-2353
Christopher Spano, *Principal*
EMP: 69 Privately Held
SIC: 8741 Business management
PA: Traffic Management, Inc.
  2435 Lemon Ave
  Signal Hill CA 90755

(P-27256)
TRAFFIC MANAGEMENT INC
5806 Perrin Ave, McClellan (95652-2410)
PHONE.................................916 394-2200
Chris Spano, *Branch Mgr*
EMP: 57 Privately Held
SIC: 8741 Business management
PA: Traffic Management, Inc.
  2435 Lemon Ave
  Signal Hill CA 90755

(P-27257)
TRILAR MANAGEMENT GROUP
1025 S Gilbert St, Hemet (92543-7090)
PHONE.................................951 925-2021
Susan A York, *Branch Mgr*
EMP: 123
SALES (corp-wide): 9MM Privately Held
SIC: 8741 Management services
PA: Trilar Management Group
  2101 Camino Vida Roble A
  Carlsbad CA 92011
  760 603-3205

(P-27258)
TRIMARINE FISHING MGT LLC
Also Called: Trimarine Fish Group
220 Cannery St, San Pedro (90731-7308)
PHONE.................................310 547-1144
Vince Torre, *Manager*
Phil Roberts, *Principal*
Kevin Stark, *Technology*
Renato Curto,
Renato C Member,
EMP: 50
SQ FT: 8,000
SALES (est): 2.8MM Privately Held
SIC: 8741 Management services

(P-27259)
TRITON MANAGEMENT SERVICES LLC
1000 Aviara Dr Ste 300, Carlsbad (92011-4218)
PHONE.................................760 431-9911
Bob Lloyd, *Principal*
EMP: 59
SALES (est): 11.5MM Privately Held
SIC: 8741 Management services

(P-27260)
TROON GOLF LLC
Also Called: Indian Wells Golf Resort
44500 Indian Wells Ln, Indian Wells (92210-8746)
PHONE.................................760 346-4653
Fax: 760 340-1035
Rich Carter, *General Mgr*
Judy A Hill, *General Mgr*
Amy Spittle, *Mktg Dir*
George Edwards, *Facilities Mgr*
Brian Hampson, *Director*
EMP: 130 Privately Held
WEB: www.americangolf.com
SIC: 8741 7997 Management services; country club, membership
PA: Troon Golf, L.L.C.
  15044 N Scottsdale Rd # 300
  Scottsdale AZ 85254

(P-27261)
TWENTY4SEVEN HOTELS CORP
567 San Nicolas Dr # 100, Newport Beach (92660-6513)
PHONE.................................949 734-6400
David Wani, *CEO*
Drew Hardy, *President*
EMP: 200
SQ FT: 15,000
SALES (est): 15.7MM Privately Held
SIC: 8741 Hotel or motel management

(P-27262)
UCD MC HOME CARE SERVICES
Also Called: Uc David Home Care Services
3630 Business Dr, Sacramento (95820-2163)
PHONE.................................916 734-2458
Glenda Wegner, *Manager*
Kim Jacobs, *Executive*
John McMillan, *Director*
EMP: 200
SALES (est): 8MM Privately Held
SIC: 8741 Nursing & personal care facility management

(P-27263)
UNITED BEHAVIORAL HEALTH
3111 Cmino Del Rio N 50 Ste 500, San Diego (92108)
P.O. Box 601370 (92160-1370)
PHONE.................................619 641-6800
Fax: 619 641-6801
Chris Janick, *Manager*
EMP: 100
SALES (corp-wide): 157.1B Publicly Held
WEB: www.unitedbehavioralhealth.com
SIC: 8741 8322 Nursing & personal care facility management; individual & family services
HQ: United Behavioral Health
  425 Market St Fl 18
  San Francisco CA 94105
  415 547-1403

(P-27264)
UNITED BEHAVIORAL HEALTH (HQ)
425 Market St Fl 18, San Francisco (94105-2493)
PHONE.................................415 547-1403
Fax: 415 547-5800
Saul Feldman, *Ch of Bd*
Keith Dickson, *President*
Ann Mc Clanathan, *COO*
Karen Schievelbein, *CFO*
Karen Shievelbien, *CFO*
EMP: 250
SQ FT: 20,000
SALES: 24.5MM
SALES (corp-wide): 157.1B Publicly Held
WEB: www.unitedbehavioralhealth.com
SIC: 8741 8742 Management services; management consulting services
PA: Unitedhealth Group Incorporated
  9900 Bren Rd E Ste 300w
  Minnetonka MN 55343
  952 936-1300

(P-27265)
UNITED PARADYNE CORPORATION
P.O. Box 5368 (93150-5368)
PHONE.................................805 734-2359
Randy Cobb, *Manager*
EMP: 52
SALES (corp-wide): 19.1MM Privately Held
SIC: 8741 Management services
PA: United Paradyne Corporation
  2415 Professional Pkwy
  Santa Maria CA
  805 348-3150

(P-27266)
UNIVERSAL PAIN MGT MED CORP (PA)
819 Auto Center Dr Ste A, Palmdale (93551-4599)
PHONE.................................661 267-6876
Fax: 661 538-9483
Francis X Riegler, *President*
Lance Jackson, *COO*
Omid Mahgerefteh, *Chiropractor*
EMP: 50
SALES (est): 9.9MM Privately Held
WEB: www.universalmedica.com
SIC: 8741 Management services

(P-27267)
UNYCOM INC
Also Called: Unycom Intellectual
2600 10th St Ste 622, Berkeley (94710-3107)
PHONE.................................415 513-0316
Don Manvel, *CEO*
Hans Jrgen Wels, *CFO*
EMP: 80
SALES (est): 4MM Privately Held
SIC: 8741 Management services

(P-27268)
USAG ANSBACH FINANCIAL MGT DIV
420 Montgomery St, San Francisco (94104-1207)
PHONE.................................210 466-1376
Karen McGrail, *Manager*
EMP: 99
SALES (est): 5.1MM Privately Held
SIC: 8741 Management services

(P-27269)
USAG RHEINLAND PFALZ FINCL MGT
420 Montgomery St, San Francisco (94104-1207)
PHONE.................................210 466-1376
Tanja Lee, *Manager*
EMP: 99
SALES (est): 5.4MM Privately Held
WEB: www.usajobs.org
SIC: 8741 Management services

(P-27270)
USAG VICENZA ITALY DMWR F M D
420 Montgomery St, San Francisco (94104-1207)
PHONE.................................210 466-1376
David Floyd, *Manager*
EMP: 99
SALES (est): 1.6MM Privately Held
SIC: 8741 Financial management for business

(P-27271)
USAG WIESBADEN FINCL MGT DIV
420 Montgomery St, San Francisco (94104-1207)
PHONE.................................210 466-1376
Sabine Norton, *Manager*
EMP: 99
SALES (est): 5.5MM Privately Held
SIC: 8741 Management services

(P-27272)
VALLEY MANAGEMENT SERVICES
Also Called: Valley Power System
425 S Hacienda Blvd, City of Industry (91745-1123)
PHONE.................................626 333-1243
H Clark Lee, *Chairman*
EMP: 425
SALES (est): 22.2MM Privately Held
SIC: 8741 Business management; administrative management

(P-27273)
VANIR CONSTRUCTION MGT INC (PA)
4540 Duckhorn Dr Ste 300, Sacramento (95834-2597)
PHONE.................................916 444-3700
Fax: 916 575-8887
Dorene C Dominguez, *Ch of Bd*
John Kuprenas, *CEO*
Alex Leon, *CFO*
Andrew Morgan, *Vice Pres*
Miles Phippen, *Vice Pres*
EMP: 70
SQ FT: 16,000
SALES (est): 79.5MM Privately Held
WEB: www.vanir.com
SIC: 8741 Construction management

(P-27274)
VB GOLF LLC
Also Called: Mariner's Point Golf Course
2401 E 3rd Ave, Foster City (94404-1067)
PHONE.................................650 573-7888
Fax: 650 577-1074
Chris Aliaga, *Manager*
Sergio Garcia, *Partner*
William Verbrugge, *Partner*
Mick Soli, *Exec Dir*
Stewart Reichlyn, *General Mgr*

8741 - Management Services County (P-27275)

EMP: 55
SALES (est): 4.5MM Privately Held
SIC: 8741 Management services

(P-27275)
VENDOR DIRECT SOLUTIONS LLC
515 S Figueroa St # 1900, Los Angeles (90071-3336)
PHONE 213 362-5622
Jules Buenabenta, *Principal*
Jim Young, *Exec VP*
James Higdon, *Senior VP*
Michelle Cartwright, *Vice Pres*
Ken Tan, *Administration*
EMP: 250
SQ FT: 1,200
SALES (est): 37.6MM Privately Held
SIC: 8741 Business management

(P-27276)
VPM MANAGEMENT INC
2400 Main St Ste 201, Irvine (92614-6271)
PHONE 949 863-1500
Philip H McNamee, *CEO*
Mark Ellis,
Steve Tomlin,
Scott J Barker, *Mng Member*
EMP: 150
SALES (est): 19.4MM Privately Held
SIC: 8741 Management services

(P-27277)
WARNER BROS DISTRIBUTING INC
Warner Bros. Pictures Domestic
4000 Warner Blvd Bldg 154, Burbank (91522-0002)
PHONE 818 954-6000
Dan Fellman, *Branch Mgr*
Annaliese S Kambour, *Treasurer*
Roseann Cacciola, *Senior VP*
Michael A Russo, *Senior VP*
Ronald B Sunderland, *Senior VP*
EMP: 122
SALES (corp-wide): 28.1B Publicly Held
SIC: 8741 7822 Management services; distribution, exclusive of production: motion picture
HQ: Warner Bros. Distributing Inc.
    4000 Warner Blvd
    Burbank CA 91522
    818 954-6000

(P-27278)
WEALTH EDUCATORS INC
5209 Wilshire Blvd, Los Angeles (90036-4311)
PHONE 310 623-9145
Veronica Sesma, *CEO*
EMP: 112
SQ FT: 1,800
SALES (est): 4.8MM Privately Held
SIC: 8741 Financial management for business

(P-27279)
WESTERN MEDICAL MANAGEMENT LLC
3333 Michelson Dr Ste 735, Irvine (92612-7679)
PHONE 949 260-6575
Fax: 949 833-3736
Baruch Fogel, *Partner*
Rachel Fogel, *Partner*
Karen Brandenburg, *Vice Pres*
Deborah Lusk, *Office Mgr*
Yoav Shtainman, *Info Tech Dir*
EMP: 50
SALES (est): 4.4MM Privately Held
WEB: www.1wmm.com
SIC: 8741 Hospital management; nursing & personal care facility management

(P-27280)
WESTERN NATIONAL CONTRACTORS
8 Executive Cir, Irvine (92614-6746)
PHONE 949 862-6200
Michael Hayde, *CEO*
Randy Avery, *Vice Pres*
John Townsend, *Vice Pres*
Sally Packer, *Executive Asst*
Jeffrey R Scott, *Admin Sec*
EMP: 88

SALES (est): 16.2MM Privately Held
SIC: 8741 Construction management

(P-27281)
WESTLAKE DEVELOPMENT GROUP LLC
520 El Camino Real Fl 9, Belmont (94002-2121)
PHONE 650 579-1010
T M Chang, *Branch Mgr*
EMP: 100
SQ FT: 600
SALES (corp-wide): 8.4MM Privately Held
WEB: www.westlake-global.com
SIC: 8741 Administrative management
PA: Westlake Development Group, Llc
    520 S El Camino Real # 900
    San Mateo CA 94402
    650 579-1010

(P-27282)
WHISKEY GIRL
702 5th Ave, San Diego (92101-6918)
PHONE 619 236-1616
Jerry Lopez, *General Mgr*
David Schissman, *Co-Owner*
EMP: 83
SALES (est): 5.5MM
SALES (corp-wide): 5.6MM Privately Held
SIC: 8741 5813 Restaurant management; night clubs
PA: Buffalo Joe's Lp
    1620 5th Ave Ste 770
    San Diego CA 92101
    619 235-6796

(P-27283)
WHITE CARNIVAL LLC
11812 San Vicente Blvd # 4, Los Angeles (90049-5022)
PHONE 310 914-1600
Matt Lichtenberg,
EMP: 50
SALES (est): 1.1MM Privately Held
SIC: 8741 Management services

(P-27284)
WORD & BROWN INSURANCE
Also Called: Conexis
721 S Parker St Ste 200, Orange (92868-4772)
PHONE 714 567-4398
John Word, *President*
Eva Boucher, *Vice Pres*
Ivonne Roca, *Executive*
John Ball, *Managing Dir*
Andrew Russell, *Broker*
EMP: 215
SALES (corp-wide): 357.5MM Privately Held
SIC: 8741 Administrative management
PA: Word & Brown, Insurance Administrators, Inc.
    721 S Parker St Ste 300
    Orange CA 92868
    714 835-5006

(P-27285)
WYNDHAM IRVN-ORANGE CNTY ARPRT
17941 Von Karman Ave, Irvine (92614-6253)
PHONE 949 863-1999
Fax: 949 863-1999
Paul Gibbs, *Principal*
Bill Acuna, *Director*
EMP: 90
SQ FT: 1,000
SALES: 15MM Privately Held
SIC: 8741 7011 7389 Management services; hotels & motels; hotel & motel reservation service

(P-27286)
XTRA DEPARTMENT INC
12631 Imperial Hwy F106, Santa Fe Springs (90670-4710)
PHONE 562 462-3800
Richard Anzalone, *President*
EMP: 60
SALES (est): 3.7MM Privately Held
WEB: www.xtradepartment.com
SIC: 8741 Business management

(P-27287)
ZAHARONI HOLDINGS
5400 W Rosecrans Ave Lowr, Hawthorne (90250-6686)
PHONE 310 297-9722
Isaac Zaharoni, *Principal*
Dan Zaharoni, *Treasurer*
Patty Steiman, *Vice Pres*
Gil Zaharoni, *Admin Sec*
EMP: 50
SQ FT: 75,000
SALES: 80MM Privately Held
WEB: www.zaharoni.com
SIC: 8741 Financial management for business

(P-27288)
ZERO WASTE SOLUTIONS INC
1850 Gateway Blvd # 1030, Concord (94520-3279)
P.O. Box 5097 (94524-0097)
PHONE 925 270-3339
Fax: 510 581-8741
Shavila Singh, *CEO*
Crystel Castillo, *Personnel Assit*
Jai Sharma, *Manager*
Teresa One, *Assistant*
EMP: 200
SQ FT: 3,000
SALES (est): 29.2MM Privately Held
WEB: www.zerowastesolutions.com
SIC: 8741 Business management

8742 Management Consulting Services

(P-27289)
A T KEARNEY INC
555 Mission St Ste 1800, San Francisco (94105-0924)
PHONE 415 490-4000
Charity Reyes, *Office Mgr*
Steffen Oder, *Associate*
EMP: 98
SALES (corp-wide): 1.1B Privately Held
SIC: 8742 Management consulting services
HQ: A. T. Kearney, Inc.
    227 W Monroe St Fl 40
    Chicago IL 60606
    312 648-0111

(P-27290)
A WORLD FIT FOR KIDS
678 S La Fayette Park Pl, Los Angeles (90057-3206)
PHONE 213 387-7712
Fax: 213 387-7717
Normandie Nigh, *Exec Dir*
Samantha Sorbo, *Vice Pres*
Kevin Campbell, *Program Mgr*
Martha Cordero, *Program Mgr*
Hovik Kasamanyan, *Opers Staff*
EMP: 110
SQ FT: 4,800
SALES: 1.9MM Privately Held
WEB: www.worldfitforkids.org
SIC: 8742 8641 8322 Management consulting services; civic social & fraternal associations; youth center

(P-27291)
ABS CAPITAL PARTNERS III LP
101 California St Fl 24, San Francisco (94111-5898)
PHONE 415 617-2800
Fax: 415 477-3229
John Mallon, *Branch Mgr*
EMP: 100 Privately Held
SIC: 8742 Banking & finance consultant
PA: Abs Capital Partners Iii, L.P.
    400 E Pratt St Ste 910
    Baltimore MD 21202

(P-27292)
ABSOLUTELYNEW INC
Also Called: Absolutelynew.com
650 Townsend St Ste 475, San Francisco (94103-6225)
PHONE 415 865-6200
Richard Donat, *CEO*
Henry Lo, *CFO*
Phillip Levers, *Technology*

Amit Pendyal, *Finance*
Greg Waples, *Sales Executive*
EMP: 70
SQ FT: 20,000
SALES (est): 5.2MM
SALES (corp-wide): 9.7MM Privately Held
WEB: www.absolutelynew.com
SIC: 8742 5722 Marketing consulting services; electric household appliances
PA: Absolutelynew Holdings, Inc.
    650 Townsend St Ste 475
    San Francisco CA

(P-27293)
ACCENTURE FEDERAL SERVICES LLC
Also Called: Accenture National SEC Svcs
1615 Murray Canyon Rd # 400, San Diego (92108-4314)
PHONE 619 574-2400
Jim Wangler, *Branch Mgr*
Danni Kanatsky, *Executive Asst*
EMP: 145
SIC: 8742 7361 8711 7373 Management consulting services; employment agencies; engineering services; computer integrated systems design; computer software development
HQ: Accenture Federal Services Llc
    800 N Glebe Rd Ste 300
    Arlington VA 22203
    703 947-2000

(P-27294)
ACCENTURE LLP
2141 Rosecrans Ave # 3100, El Segundo (90245-7518)
PHONE 310 726-2700
Fax: 310 726-2950
Joyce Nitz, *Branch Mgr*
Bob Macniven, *CFO*
Fielding Walker, *Vice Pres*
Kenneth McQuarrie, *Executive*
Cenk Ozdemir, *Executive*
EMP: 350 Privately Held
WEB: www.wavesecurities.com
SIC: 8742 Business consultant
HQ: Accenture Llp
    161 N Clark St Ste 1100
    Chicago IL 60601
    312 693-0161

(P-27295)
ACCENTURE LLP
1255 Treat Blvd Ste 400, Walnut Creek (94597-7985)
PHONE 925 974-5220
EMP: 100 Privately Held
WEB: www.wavesecurities.com
SIC: 8742 Business consultant
HQ: Accenture Llp
    161 N Clark St Ste 1100
    Chicago IL 60601
    312 693-0161

(P-27296)
ACCENTURE LLP
2 Santa Ana Ct, Belvedere Tiburon (94920-1620)
PHONE 415 537-5860
Bill Moon, *Vice Pres*
Ming Wong, *Software Dev*
EMP: 208 Privately Held
WEB: www.wavesecurities.com
SIC: 8742 Management consulting services
HQ: Accenture Llp
    161 N Clark St Ste 1100
    Chicago IL 60601
    312 693-0161

(P-27297)
ACCENTURE LLP
560 Mission St Fl 12, San Francisco (94105-2927)
PHONE 415 537-5000
Fax: 415 537-5042
Christopher S Digiorgio, *Principal*
Howard Glazier, *Executive*
Kirk Kirkpatrick, *Principal*
Courtney Rosen, *Principal*
Maria Xavier, *Marketing Mgr*
EMP: 310 Privately Held
WEB: www.wavesecurities.com

PRODUCTS & SERVICES SECTION

8742 - Management Consulting Services County (P-27319)

SIC: 8742 Management consulting services
HQ: Accenture Llp
161 N Clark St Ste 1100
Chicago IL 60601
312 693-0161

(P-27298)
ACCENTURE LLP
50 W San Fernando St # 1208, San Jose (95113-2429)
PHONE..................408 817-2100
Jackson Wilson, *Manager*
Nobuyuki Idei, *Exec Dir*
Robert Lipp, *Exec Dir*
Maria Xavier, *General Mgr*
Dushyant Sethi, *Sr Software Eng*
EMP: 218 **Privately Held**
WEB: www.wavesecurities.com
SIC: 8742 Management consulting services
HQ: Accenture Llp
161 N Clark St Ste 1100
Chicago IL 60601
312 693-0161

(P-27299)
ACCENTURE LLP
50 W San Fernando St # 1200, San Jose (95113-2429)
PHONE..................650 213-2000
Fax: 650 213-2222
Christopher S Digiorgio, *Manager*
Paul Hasenwinkel, *Principal*
Vincent Hui, *Principal*
Clifford Jury, *Principal*
Carlisle Kirkpatrick, *Principal*
EMP: 175 **Privately Held**
SIC: 8742 8748 Management consulting services; business consulting
HQ: Accenture Llp
161 N Clark St Ste 1100
Chicago IL 60601
312 693-0161

(P-27300)
ACCENTURE LLP
1415 L St Ste 700, Sacramento (95814-3964)
PHONE..................916 557-2200
Christopher S Digiorgio, *Branch Mgr*
Paul Dalglish, *Senior VP*
EMP: 175 **Privately Held**
WEB: www.wavesecurities.com
SIC: 8742 Business consultant; management information systems consultant
HQ: Accenture Llp
161 N Clark St Ste 1100
Chicago IL 60601
312 693-0161

(P-27301)
ACCOUNTNOW INC
2603 Camino Ramon Ste 485, San Ramon (94583-9131)
P.O. Box 1966 (94583-6966)
PHONE..................925 498-1800
James G Jones, *CEO*
David J Petrini, *CFO*
Paul Rosenfeld, *Chief Mktg Ofcr*
Simon Williams, *Vice Pres*
Daniel Davis, *CTO*
EMP: 76
SALES (est): 15MM **Privately Held**
SIC: 8742 Financial consultant

(P-27302)
ADDED VALUE LLC
Also Called: (OWNED BY WPP IN U.K.)
3400 Cahuenga Blvd W B, Los Angeles (90068-1376)
PHONE..................323 254-4326
Fax: 323 254-8756
Meggy Taylor, *President*
Ruth Moss, *Exec VP*
Zoe Dowling, *Vice Pres*
Lisa Noble, *Vice Pres*
Scott Porter, *Vice Pres*
EMP: 190
SQ FT: 9,800
SALES (est): 23.1MM
SALES (corp-wide): 18.4B **Privately Held**
WEB: www.us.millwardbrown.com
SIC: 8742 Marketing consulting services

HQ: Millward Brown, Llc
11 Madison Ave Ste 1200
New York NY 10010
212 548-7200

(P-27303)
ADIVO ASSOCIATES LLC
1 Post St Ste 2750, San Francisco (94104-5246)
PHONE..................415 992-1449
Maik Klasen, *Managing Dir*
Darren Ewaniuk, *Managing Dir*
EMP: 90
SQ FT: 2,000
SALES (est): 3.7MM **Privately Held**
SIC: 8742 Management consulting services

(P-27304)
ADMINISTRATIVE SVCS COOP INC
2129 W Rosecrans Ave, Gardena (90249-2933)
PHONE..................310 715-1968
Fax: 310 327-7975
Martiros Manukyan, *CEO*
Raymond McGreevy, *President*
William J Rouse, *General Mgr*
Ruth Knap, *Marketing Staff*
Mike Heffeman, *Manager*
EMP: 200
SALES (est): 18MM **Privately Held**
SIC: 8742 Administrative services consultant

(P-27305)
AECOM C&E INC
Also Called: Aecom Consulting
1999 Avenue Of The Stars, Los Angeles (90067-6022)
PHONE..................213 593-8100
Bill Mehol, *Branch Mgr*
Paul Gennaro Jr, *Senior VP*
Barry Hawkins, *Senior VP*
Ernest Kartinen, *Vice Pres*
James Lynch, *Vice Pres*
EMP: 200
SALES (corp-wide): 17.9B **Publicly Held**
SIC: 8742 9441 Human resource consulting services; administration of social & human resources
HQ: Aecom C&E, Inc
250 Apollo Dr
Chelmsford MA 01824
978 905-2100

(P-27306)
AEG GLOBAL PARTNERSHIPS LLC
1100 S Flower St Ste 3200, Los Angeles (90015-2125)
PHONE..................213 763-7700
Todd Goldstein, *President*
Dan Beckerman, *Creative Dir*
Jonathan Lowe, *Marketing Mgr*
Jonah Chodosh, *Sales Associate*
EMP: 50
SALES (est): 1.6MM
SALES (corp-wide): 110.6MM **Privately Held**
SIC: 8742 Management consulting services
HQ: Anschutz Entertainment Group, Inc.
1100 S Flower St
Los Angeles CA 90015
213 763-7700

(P-27307)
AEROMEDEVAC INC
681 Kenney St, El Cajon (92020-1278)
PHONE..................619 284-7910
Fax: 619 284-7918
Adam Williams, *President*
John Olson, *CEO*
Raul Mendoza, *Vice Pres*
Michael Weiland, *Business Dir*
Sheila Navarro, *Info Tech Mgr*
EMP: 54
SALES (est): 6.4MM **Privately Held**
WEB: www.aeromedevac.com
SIC: 8742 Management consulting services

(P-27308)
AGAMA SOLUTIONS INC
39159 Paseo Padre Pkwy # 216, Fremont (94538-1689)
PHONE..................510 796-9300
Shivani G Sanan, *CEO*
Tanu Kalra, *President*
Pankaj Kalra, *Vice Pres*
Ashish Sanan, *Vice Pres*
Shail Gupta, *Business Mgr*
EMP: 175
SQ FT: 9,000
SALES (est): 22.3MM **Privately Held**
SIC: 8742 7371 Management consulting services; computer software development

(P-27309)
AGR GROUP INC
13902 Harbor Blvd Ste 2c, Garden Grove (92843-4013)
PHONE..................714 245-7151
Matt Judkin, *President*
Adolfo Quintero, *COO*
Herb Zerden, *CFO*
Kim Larsen, *Vice Pres*
Desiree Arnold, *Office Mgr*
EMP: 750
SQ FT: 15,500
SALES: 16MM **Privately Held**
WEB: www.agrgroupinc.com
SIC: 8742 Management consulting services

(P-27310)
AGREEYA SOLUTIONS INC (PA)
605 Coolidge Dr Ste 200, Folsom (95630-4210)
PHONE..................916 294-0075
Neerja Khosla, *President*
Sangeeta Khazanchi, *CFO*
David Price, *Exec VP*
Sanjay Khosla, *Vice Pres*
Ajay Kaul, *Admin Sec*
EMP: 55
SQ FT: 14,000
SALES (est): 39.4MM **Privately Held**
WEB: www.agreeya.com
SIC: 8742 7371 Management consulting services; computer software systems analysis & design, custom

(P-27311)
AIMIA PROPRIETARY LOYALTY
180 Montgomery St, San Francisco (94104-4205)
PHONE..................415 398-3534
Joyce Clark, *Branch Mgr*
EMP: 100
SALES (corp-wide): 2.1B **Privately Held**
WEB: www.carlsonmarketing.com
SIC: 8742 Marketing consulting services
HQ: Aimia Proprietary Loyalty U.S. Inc.
100 N 6th St Ste 700b
Minneapolis MN 55403
763 445-3000

(P-27312)
AIMIA PROPRIETARY LOYALTY
735 Battery St Fl 1, San Francisco (94111-1535)
PHONE..................415 844-2200
Fax: 415 844-2248
Keith Rose, *Manager*
EMP: 70
SALES (corp-wide): 2.1B **Privately Held**
WEB: www.carlsonmarketing.com
SIC: 8742 Marketing consulting services
HQ: Aimia Proprietary Loyalty U.S. Inc.
100 N 6th St Ste 700b
Minneapolis MN 55403
763 445-3000

(P-27313)
AKQA INC (HQ)
360 3rd St Ste 500, San Francisco (94107-2165)
PHONE..................415 645-9400
Tom Bedecarre, *CEO*
Lester Feintuck, *CFO*
Veronica Kavanagh, *CFO*
Rei Inamoto, *Ch Credit Ofcr*
Andy Almquist, *Executive*
EMP: 400
SQ FT: 28,000

SALES (est): 119.5MM
SALES (corp-wide): 18.4B **Privately Held**
WEB: www.akqa.com
SIC: 8742 Management consulting services; marketing consulting services
PA: Wpp Plc
27 Farm Street
London W1J 5
207 408-2204

(P-27314)
ALAN B WHITSON COMPANY INC
1507 W Alton Ave, Santa Ana (92704-7219)
P.O. Box 9229, Newport Beach (92658-9229)
PHONE..................949 955-1200
Alan B Whitson, *President*
EMP: 750
SQ FT: 18,000
SALES: 41.4MM **Privately Held**
SIC: 8742 1389 5411 Corporation organizing; servicing oil & gas wells; convenience stores, chain

(P-27315)
ALTEGRA HEALTH
3415 S Sepulveda Blvd # 900, Los Angeles (90034-6981)
PHONE..................310 776-4001
EMP: 99
SALES (est): 6.6MM **Privately Held**
SIC: 8742

(P-27316)
ALVAREZ & MARSAL HOLDINGS LLC
100 Pine St Fl 9, San Francisco (94111-5111)
PHONE..................415 490-2300
Fax: 415 837-1684
Bill Kosturos, *Manager*
Mark Alvarez, *Managing Dir*
Paul Aversano, *Managing Dir*
James Barratt, *Managing Dir*
Joseph Bondi, *Managing Dir*
EMP: 180
SALES (corp-wide): 217.6MM **Privately Held**
SIC: 8742 3523 3448 Financial consultant; farm machinery & equipment; prefabricated metal buildings
HQ: Alvarez & Marsal, Inc.
600 Madison Ave Fl 8
New York NY 10022
212 759-4433

(P-27317)
AMCO FOODS INC
601 E Glenoaks Blvd # 108, Glendale (91207-1760)
PHONE..................818 247-4716
Bobken Amirian, *President*
Brian Polthow, *CFO*
Nick Amirian, *Corp Secy*
Nareg Amirian, *Principal*
EMP: 475 EST: 1999
SALES: 5.8MM **Privately Held**
SIC: 8742 Business consultant

(P-27318)
AMERICAN ALL RISK LOSS ADM
4270 W Richert Ave # 101, Fresno (93722-6334)
P.O. Box 9783 (93794-9783)
PHONE..................559 277-4960
Fax: 559 277-4961
Steve Wigh, *President*
Brandi Kwiatkowski, *Vice Pres*
Luis Feliz, *Admin Sec*
Patrick Humphrey, *Director*
EMP: 125
SALES (est): 12.6MM **Privately Held**
SIC: 8742 Administrative services consultant

(P-27319)
AMERICAN FINANCIAL NETWORK INC
14241 Firestone Blvd, La Mirada (90638-5530)
PHONE..................562 926-2401
Dan Piumpunyalerd, *Branch Mgr*
EMP: 222

8742 - Management Consulting Services County (P-27320)

PRODUCTS & SERVICES SECTION

SALES (corp-wide): 82MM **Privately Held**
SIC: **8742** 7389 6162 Financial consultant; financial services; mortgage bankers & correspondents
PA: American Financial Network, Inc.
3110 Chino Ave Ste 290
Chino CA 91710
909 606-3905

(P-27320)
AMGREEN SOLUTIONS INC
1367 Venice Blvd Fl 2, Los Angeles (90006-5519)
PHONE..................213 388-5647
Changhwan Ko, *President*
Michael Kim, *Sales Dir*
David Ko, *Manager*
Daniel Choi, *Consultant*
EMP: 50
SALES: 8MM **Privately Held**
SIC: **8742** 7389 Management engineering; water softener service

(P-27321)
AMMUNITION LLC
1500 Sansome St Ste 110, San Francisco (94111-1015)
PHONE..................415 632-1170
Peter Rack, *CFO*
Nick Barrett, *Vice Pres*
Victoria Slaker, *Vice Pres*
David Summers, *Vice Pres*
Vivian Wu, *Program Mgr*
EMP: 51
SQ FT: 5,200
SALES: 16.3MM **Privately Held**
SIC: **8742** Industrial consultant

(P-27322)
AMTROW GROUP INC
8306 Wilshire Blvd 1042, Beverly Hills (90211-2304)
PHONE..................310 557-0857
Samuel Neiderberg, *President*
Mikhail Aptor, *Vice Pres*
EMP: 86
SQ FT: 1,400
SALES (est): 3.6MM **Privately Held**
SIC: **8742** 8741 1542 1522 Industry specialist consultants; construction management; nonresidential construction; residential construction

(P-27323)
ANDERSON KAYNE INV MGT INC (PA)
1800 Avenue Of The Stars # 200, Los Angeles (90067-4204)
PHONE..................310 556-2721
Richard Kayne, *Ch of Bd*
John Anderson, *CEO*
John Daley, *CFO*
Paul Stapleton, *Treasurer*
David J Shladovsky, *Admin Sec*
EMP: 55
SQ FT: 20,000
SALES (est): 21.9MM **Privately Held**
SIC: **8742** 6211 6726 6282 Financial consultant; investment firm, general brokerage; investment offices; investment advice

(P-27324)
ANDERSONPENNA PARTNERS INC
3737 Birch St Ste 250, Newport Beach (92660-2682)
PHONE..................949 428-1500
Mallory McCamant, *Ch of Bd*
Lisa Penna, *President*
Angelique M Lucero, *CFO*
David R Anderson, *Exec VP*
Dino D'Emilia, *Vice Pres*
EMP: 62
SALES (est): 8.7MM **Privately Held**
SIC: **8742** 8711 Transportation consultant; engineering services

(P-27325)
ANJANEYAP INC
830 Hillview Ct Ste 140, Milpitas (95035-4552)
PHONE..................408 922-9690
Sundeep Bhandal, *President*
Swapnil Anand, *Vice Pres*

Taresh Anand, *Vice Pres*
Puja Kumar, *Tech Recruiter*
Nishant Gupta, *Marketing Mgr*
EMP: 53
SQ FT: 4,300
SALES: 37.7MM **Privately Held**
SIC: **8742** Business consultant

(P-27326)
AON CONSULTING INC
2570 N 1st St Ste 500, San Jose (95131-1018)
PHONE..................408 321-2500
Steve Radford, *Manager*
John Burg, *Vice Pres*
Julia Reeder, *Analyst*
James Garlit, *Safety Mgr*
Karyn Gans, *Sales Executive*
EMP: 65
SALES (corp-wide): 11.6B **Privately Held**
WEB: www.radford.com
SIC: **8742** Compensation & benefits planning consultant
HQ: Aon Consulting, Inc.
315 W 3rd St
Little Rock AR 72201
501 374-9300

(P-27327)
AON HEWITT LLC
100 Bayview Cir Ste 100, Newport Beach (92660-2963)
P.O. Box 6300 (92658-6300)
PHONE..................949 725-4500
Fax: 949 725-0668
Eric Watkins, *Manager*
Chris Rogers, *President*
Mark Murray, *Info Systems*
Steven Camferdam, *Investment Ofcr*
Amy M Liu, *Investment Ofcr*
EMP: 200
SALES (corp-wide): 11.6B **Privately Held**
WEB: www.hewitt.com
SIC: **8742** 8748 Human resource consulting services; business consulting
HQ: Aon Hewitt Llc
200 E Randolph St Ll3
Chicago IL 60601
312 381-1000

(P-27328)
AP-REDLANDS LLC
12447 Lewis St Ste 203, Garden Grove (92840-6601)
PHONE..................562 435-2100
Fred Leland, *Controller*
Paul Fabela, *Property Mgr*
EMP: 50
SALES (est): 1MM **Privately Held**
SIC: **8742** 6512 Real estate consultant; shopping center, property operation only

(P-27329)
APA INCORPORATED
405 S Beverly Dr Ste 500, Beverly Hills (90212-4425)
P.O. Box 45 (90213-0045)
PHONE..................310 888-4200
Kat Cafeler, *President*
Ben Mehlman, *Assistant*
EMP: 150
SALES (est): 11.4MM **Privately Held**
SIC: **8742** Business consultant

(P-27330)
APERIAN GLOBAL INC (PA)
1 Kaiser Plz Ste 785, Oakland (94612-3611)
PHONE..................415 749-2920
Ernest Gundling, *President*
Dave Eaton, *President*
Theodore Dale, *COO*
David Reilly, *CFO*
Michael Billard, *Vice Pres*
EMP: 75
SQ FT: 4,000
SALES (est): 10MM **Privately Held**
WEB: www.meridianglobal.com
SIC: **8742** Management consulting services

(P-27331)
ARCH HEALTH PARTNERS INC (HQ)
15611 Pomerado Rd Ste 575, Poway (92064-2438)
PHONE..................858 675-3100
Deanna Kyrimis, *Principal*
Robert Trifunovic, *CEO*
Nancy Burnham, *Office Mgr*
Mary Payne, *Info Tech Dir*
Mark Casas, *Data Proc Staff*
EMP: 130 EST: 2010
SALES: 57MM
SALES (corp-wide): 614.2MM **Privately Held**
SIC: **8742** Hospital & health services consultant
PA: Palomar Health
456 E Grand Ave
Escondido CA 92025
442 281-5000

(P-27332)
ARCO ENVMTL REMEDIATION LLC
5472 Orangethorpe Ave, La Palma (90623-1005)
PHONE..................714 523-5674
Bruce Niemeyer, *President*
EMP: 68 EST: 1996
SALES (est): 1.7MM
SALES (corp-wide): 222.8B **Privately Held**
WEB: www.bpamoco.com
SIC: **8742** 8748 Management consulting services; environmental consultant
HQ: Bp Corporation North America Inc.
501 Westlake Park Blvd
Houston TX 77079
281 366-2000

(P-27333)
ASHLEY MANAGEMENT GROUP
300 Spectrum Center Dr # 400, Irvine (92618-4925)
PHONE..................949 754-3120
Lance Ashley, *President*
EMP: 50
SALES: 5MM **Privately Held**
SIC: **8742** Business consultant

(P-27334)
ASSET MARKETING SYSTEMS INSU
Also Called: AMS
15050 Ave Of Science # 100, San Diego (92128-3418)
PHONE..................888 303-8755
Mike Botkin, *CEO*
Dee Costa, *President*
David Creaven, *COO*
Louise Erdman, *COO*
Chris Gladheim, *COO*
EMP: 70
SQ FT: 19,000
SALES (est): 9.6MM **Privately Held**
WEB: www.assetmarketingsystems.net
SIC: **8742** Marketing consulting services

(P-27335)
AUTISM PARTNERSHIP INC
200 Marina Dr C, Seal Beach (90740-6023)
PHONE..................562 431-9293
Ronald Leaf, *President*
John McEachin, *Admin Sec*
EMP: 95
SALES (est): 6.1MM **Privately Held**
WEB: www.autismpartnership.com
SIC: **8742** Hospital & health services consultant

(P-27336)
B A TECHNOLINKS CORPORATION
4677 Old Ironsides Dr # 440, Santa Clara (95054-1826)
PHONE..................408 940-5921
Kiran Maruvada, *CEO*
Krishna Vemuri, *President*
EMP: 70 EST: 2010
SALES (est): 5.8MM **Privately Held**
SIC: **8742** Business consultant

(P-27337)
BAIN & COMPANY INC
1901 Ave Of The Sts 200 Ste 2000, Los Angeles (90067)
PHONE..................310 229-3000
Fax: 310 229-3050
Kevin Badkoubehi, *Branch Mgr*
Peter Ratajczak, *Mktg Coord*
Erik Hauge, *Sr Associate*
Hubert Shen, *Sr Associate*
Edouard Didier, *Senior Mgr*
EMP: 80
SALES (corp-wide): 660.6MM **Privately Held**
WEB: www.bain.com
SIC: **8742** Management consulting services
PA: Bain & Company, Inc.
131 Dartmouth St Ste 901
Boston MA 02116
617 572-2000

(P-27338)
BAIN & COMPANY INC
1 Embarcadero Ctr # 3500, San Francisco (94111-3628)
PHONE..................415 627-1000
Fax: 415 627-1033
Vernon Altman, *Manager*
Yesenia Pulido, *Executive Asst*
Anja Wittrup, *Info Tech Mgr*
Randy Hughes, *Analyst*
Amber Markley, *Human Resources*
EMP: 109
SALES (corp-wide): 660.6MM **Privately Held**
WEB: www.bain.com
SIC: **8742** Management consulting services
PA: Bain & Company, Inc.
131 Dartmouth St Ste 901
Boston MA 02116
617 572-2000

(P-27339)
BASELINE CONSULTING GROUP INC
15300 Ventura Blvd # 200, Sherman Oaks (91403-3138)
PHONE..................818 906-7638
Evan Levy, *President*
Jill Dyche, *Vice Pres*
Richard Weimar, *Vice Pres*
Gordon Lewy, *Controller*
Tamara Dull, *VP Mktg*
EMP: 50
SQ FT: 5,000
SALES (est): 4.1MM
SALES (corp-wide): 2.9B **Privately Held**
WEB: www.baseline-consulting.com
SIC: **8742** Management consulting services
HQ: Dataflux Corporation Llc
100 Sas Campus Dr
Cary NC 27513
919 447-3000

(P-27340)
BASKETBALL MARKETING CO INC
Also Called: and 1
101 Enterprise Ste 100, Aliso Viejo (92656-2604)
PHONE..................866 866-1232
Kevin Wulff, *President*
Jerome A Turner, *Treasurer*
Bob Schott, *Vice Pres*
Marcina Turner, *Managing Dir*
David Hoffman, *Info Tech Mgr*
▲ EMP: 67
SALES (est): 3.8MM
SALES (corp-wide): 2.5B **Publicly Held**
WEB: www.avia.com
SIC: **8742** Management consulting services
HQ: American Sporting Goods Corp
101 Enterprise Ste 200
Aliso Viejo CA 92656
949 267-2800

PRODUCTS & SERVICES SECTION
8742 - Management Consulting Services County (P-27364)

(P-27341)
BEACON ACCUNTING RESOURCES LLC
1818 Glenwood Ln, Newport Beach (92660-4317)
PHONE....................949 981-5946
EMP: 50
SALES (est): 1.8MM **Privately Held**
SIC: 8742 Business planning & organizing services

(P-27342)
BEACON RESOURCES LLC
4 Corporate Plaza Dr # 101, Newport Beach (92660-7906)
PHONE....................949 955-1773
Colleen Freeman,
Mike Kelly,
EMP: 50
SALES (est): 3.4MM **Privately Held**
SIC: 8742 Business planning & organizing services
HQ: David M. Lewis Company, Llc
21800 Oxnard St Ste 980
Woodland Hills CA 91367
818 936-2612

(P-27343)
BEATING WALL STREET INC (PA)
14934 Dickens St Apt 16, Sherman Oaks (91403-3419)
PHONE....................818 332-9696
Hamed Khorsand, *President*
Vahid Khorsand, *Research*
EMP: 230
SQ FT: 8,000
SALES (est): 7.6MM **Privately Held**
WEB: www.beatingwallstreet.com
SIC: 8742 Financial consultant

(P-27344)
BENETECH INC (PA)
3947 Lennane Dr Ste 250, Sacramento (95834-1972)
PHONE....................916 484-6811
Robert L Brandon, *President*
James Casalegno, *Senior VP*
Chris Blazek, *Vice Pres*
Charles Bridges, *Vice Pres*
Roberta Brosnahan, *Vice Pres*
EMP: 60 EST: 1974
SQ FT: 20,000
SALES (est): 16.6MM **Privately Held**
SIC: 8742 Administrative services consultant

(P-27345)
BENTLEY HEALTH CARE INC
9777 Wilshire Blvd Fl 4, Beverly Hills (90212-1904)
PHONE....................310 967-3300
Bernard Salick MD, *President*
Barbara Bromley-Williams, *Vice Pres*
EMP: 70
SQ FT: 32,000
SALES (est): 3.8MM **Privately Held**
SIC: 8742 Hospital & health services consultant

(P-27346)
BITE COMMUNICATIONS LLC (HQ)
100 Montgomery St # 1103, San Francisco (94104-4388)
PHONE....................415 365-0222
Fax: 415 365-0223
Tim Dyson, *Mng Member*
Andrea Cunningham, *President*
Alisa Macdonnell, *Senior VP*
Will Willis, *Senior VP*
Steven Brewster, *Vice Pres*
EMP: 75
SQ FT: 10,000
SALES (est): 13.7MM
SALES (corp-wide): 248.8MM **Privately Held**
WEB: www.bitepr.com
SIC: 8742 8743 Marketing consulting services; public relations services

(P-27347)
BIZ VISION INC
4800 Kokomo Dr Apt 3014, Sacramento (95835-1832)
PHONE....................916 792-2124
Raymond M Williams Jr, *President*
EMP: 72
SALES (est): 4.7MM **Privately Held**
SIC: 8742 Planning consultant

(P-27348)
BLACKSTONE CONSULTING INC (PA)
11726 San Vicente Blvd # 550, Los Angeles (90049-5089)
PHONE....................310 826-4389
Fax: 310 826-7269
Ronald Joseph Blackstone, *President*
Sean Dundon, *Senior Partner*
James Brown, *COO*
Anna Chavez, *Vice Pres*
Joe Blackstone, *General Mgr*
EMP: 148
SQ FT: 1,500
SALES (est): 135MM **Privately Held**
WEB: www.blackstone-consulting.com
SIC: 8742 Management consulting services

(P-27349)
BLANCHARD TRAINING AND DEV INC (PA)
Also Called: Ken Blanchard Companies, The
125 State Pl, Escondido (92029-1323)
PHONE....................760 489-5005
Fax: 760 489-8407
Thomas J McKee, *CEO*
Howard Farfel, *President*
John Slater, *COO*
Allison A Pico, *CFO*
Deborah K Blanchard, *Exec VP*
EMP: 200
SALES (est): 65.9MM **Privately Held**
SIC: 8742 Training & development consultant

(P-27350)
BLB RESOURCES INC (PA)
16845 Von Karman Ave # 100, Irvine (92606-4961)
PHONE....................949 261-9155
Rod Gaston, *CEO*
Susan Gaston, *President*
Denise Johnson, *CFO*
Khiem Nguyen, *Info Tech Dir*
Katherine Gartin, *Business Anlyst*
EMP: 105
SQ FT: 20,000
SALES (est): 15.6MM **Privately Held**
SIC: 8742 Management consulting services

(P-27351)
BON APPETIT MANAGEMENT CO
1259 E Colton Ave, Redlands (92374-3755)
PHONE....................909 748-8970
Fax: 909 335-5243
Bret Martin, *General Mgr*
EMP: 120
SALES (corp-wide): 27.3B **Privately Held**
WEB: www.cafebonappetit.com
SIC: 8742 Administrative services consultant
HQ: Bon Appetit Management Co.
100 Hamilton Ave Ste 400
Palo Alto CA 94301
650 798-8000

(P-27352)
BOOZ ALLEN HAMILTON INC
5220 Pacific Concourse Dr, Los Angeles (90045-6277)
PHONE....................310 297-2100
Fax: 310 297-2179
Ralph Shrader, *CEO*
Lam Nguyen, *Admin Asst*
Matthew Trinca, *Associate*
EMP: 52 **Publicly Held**
SIC: 8742 Management consulting services
HQ: Booz Allen Hamilton Inc.
8283 Greensboro Dr # 700
Mc Lean VA 22102
703 902-5000

(P-27353)
BOOZ ALLEN HAMILTON INC
1615 Murray Canyon Rd # 220, San Diego (92108-4329)
PHONE....................619 725-6500
Fax: 619 725-6699
Foster Rich, *Vice Pres*
David J Karp, *Vice Pres*
Tim Newman, *Social Dir*
Philip Summerly, *Social Dir*
Erik Olson, *Administration*
EMP: 52 **Publicly Held**
WEB: www.bah.com
SIC: 8742 Management consulting services
HQ: Booz Allen Hamilton Inc.
8283 Greensboro Dr # 700
Mc Lean VA 22102
703 902-5000

(P-27354)
BOOZ ALLEN HAMILTON INC
555 S Flower St Fl 36, Los Angeles (90071-2300)
PHONE....................213 620-1900
Fax: 213 622-2464
Wayne Gilles, *Branch Mgr*
Michael Quant, *MIS Mgr*
Albert Scala, *Manager*
EMP: 52 **Publicly Held**
WEB: www.bah.com
SIC: 8742 Management consulting services
HQ: Booz Allen Hamilton Inc.
8283 Greensboro Dr # 700
Mc Lean VA 22102
703 902-5000

(P-27355)
BRANDREP INC
16812 Armstrong Ave, Irvine (92606-4916)
PHONE....................800 405-7119
Banir Ganatra, *Owner*
EMP: 50 EST: 2013
SALES (est): 6.9MM **Privately Held**
SIC: 8742 Management consulting services

(P-27356)
BRICKWALK SYSTEMS INTEGRATION
425 Market St Fl 22, San Francisco (94105-2532)
PHONE....................800 495-5779
Matthew Williams, *President*
William Masurat, *Exec VP*
EMP: 100
SALES: 16.7MM **Privately Held**
SIC: 8742 Business consultant

(P-27357)
BRIGHTCURRENT INC
55 Harrison St Ste 300, Oakland (94607-3760)
PHONE....................877 896-3306
Jack Bertuzzi, *CFO*
EMP: 75
SQ FT: 20,000
SALES (est): 3.8MM **Privately Held**
SIC: 8742 Sales (including sales management) consultant

(P-27358)
BRINCKERHOFF PARSONS GROUP LLC
2329 Oakes Dr Ste 200, Sacramento (95833)
PHONE....................916 567-2500
Fax: 916 925-3517
Michelle Poe, *Manager*
EMP: 70
SALES (corp-wide): 2.5B **Privately Held**
SIC: 8742 Management consulting services
HQ: Parsons Brinckerhoff Group Llc
1 Penn Plz 2nd
New York NY 10119
212 465-5000

(P-27359)
BROKER SOLUTIONS INC
800 N Haven Ave Ste 330, Ontario (91764-4976)
PHONE....................909 458-0718
Brett Reichel, *Branch Mgr*
EMP: 102
SALES (corp-wide): 107.4MM **Privately Held**
SIC: 8742 6162 Financial consultant; bond & mortgage companies
PA: Broker Solutions, Inc.
14511 Myford Rd
Tustin CA 92780
800 450-2010

(P-27360)
BROKER SOLUTIONS INC (PA)
Also Called: New American Funding
14511 Myford Rd, Tustin (92780-7068)
PHONE....................800 450-2010
Rick Arvielo, *CEO*
Enrico Arvielo, *President*
Patricia Arvielo, *President*
Christy Bunce, *COO*
Sam Ellsworth, *Senior VP*
EMP: 650
SALES (est): 107.4MM **Privately Held**
SIC: 8742 6162 Financial consultant; bond & mortgage companies

(P-27361)
BROWN AND STREZA LLP
40 Pacifica Ste 1500, Irvine (92618-7496)
PHONE....................949 453-2900
Richard Streza, *President*
David Brown, *Vice Pres*
Michael Offenheiser, *Planning*
Joe McCarthy, *Info Tech Dir*
Kj Nguyen, *Info Tech Mgr*
EMP: 60
SQ FT: 1,000
SALES (est): 8.6MM **Privately Held**
WEB: www.brownandstreza.com
SIC: 8742 8111 Business planning & organizing services; general practice attorney, lawyer

(P-27362)
BUSINESS INTELLIGENCE
2131 Palomar Airport Rd, Carlsbad (92011-1433)
P.O. Box 99973, San Diego (92169-1973)
PHONE....................858 452-8200
Sean Lesher, *Mng Member*
John Vasek,
Chris Stoffel, *Consultant*
EMP: 50
SQ FT: 700
SALES: 12MM **Privately Held**
SIC: 8742 Management information systems consultant

(P-27363)
BUSINESSCOM INC
2120 Colorado Ave Fl 3, Santa Monica (90404-5510)
PHONE....................310 586-4000
Ryan Peddycord, *CEO*
Brian Barnum, *President*
Katie Hand, *Vice Pres*
Grant Reinero, *Creative Dir*
Jim Gilliam, *CTO*
EMP: 52
SQ FT: 22,000
SALES (est): 5.6MM
SALES (corp-wide): 69.4MM **Privately Held**
WEB: www.business.com
SIC: 8742 7375 Management consulting services; information retrieval services
HQ: Business.Com Media, Inc.
1900 Wright Pl Ste 250
Carlsbad CA 92008
888 441-4466

(P-27364)
CAFEPRESSCOM INC
24301 Suthland Dr Ste 300, Hayward (94545)
PHONE....................650 655-3000
Sumant Sridharan, *Branch Mgr*
Jason Domina, *Software Engr*
Vidya Gopalan, *Software Engr*
George Chappell, *Production*
Amy Maniatis, *VP Mktg*

8742 - Management Consulting Services County (P-27365)

PRODUDUCTS & SERVICES SECTION

EMP: 53
SALES (corp-wide): 104.5MM **Publicly Held**
SIC: 8742 Business consultant
HQ: Cafepress.Com Inc.
6901a Riverport Dr
Louisville KY 40258
502 995-2220

(P-27365)
CAL CARE INC
Also Called: Atherton Healthcare
1275 Crane St, Menlo Park (94025-4212)
PHONE.................................650 325-8600
Nana Cocachvili, *Administration*
David Dediachvili, *Office Mgr*
Oliver Berber, *Business Mgr*
Phillip Ng, *Director*
EMP: 115
SALES: 11.2MM **Privately Held**
SIC: 8742 Hospital & health services consultant

(P-27366)
CALIF INSTITUTE HUMAN SER
1801 E Cotati Ave, Rohnert Park (94928-3613)
PHONE.................................707 664-2416
Tony Apolloni, *Director*
Kimberly Krawchuk, *Technician*
EMP: 70 EST: 1980
SALES (est): 2.6MM **Privately Held**
SIC: 8742 Human resource consulting services

(P-27367)
CALIFRNIA IND SYS OPRATOR CORP
110 Blue Ravine Rd, Folsom (95630-4711)
PHONE.................................916 608-7000
Terry Winter, *President*
William J Regan, *CFO*
EMP: 150 **Privately Held**
WEB: www.caiso.com
SIC: 8742 Human resource consulting services
PA: California Independent System Operator Corporation
250 Outcropping Way
Folsom CA 95630

(P-27368)
CANON SOLUTIONS AMERICA INC
3237 E Guasti Rd Ste 200, Ontario (91761-1243)
PHONE.................................909 390-7400
Larry Candejas, *Branch Mgr*
Damian Hawthorne, *Analyst*
Adrienne Hill, *Manager*
EMP: 65
SALES (corp-wide): 30.8B **Privately Held**
SIC: 8742 Sales (including sales management) consultant
HQ: Canon Solutions America, Inc.
1 Canon Park
Melville NY 11747
631 330-5000

(P-27369)
CAPTAIN MARKETING INC
3577 N Figueroa St, Los Angeles (90065-2445)
PHONE.................................310 402-9709
EMP: 72
SALES (corp-wide): 11.9MM **Privately Held**
SIC: 8742 Marketing consulting services
PA: Captain Marketing, Inc.
4505 Las Virgenes Rd
Calabasas CA 91302
888 297-9977

(P-27370)
CARANYTHINGCOM INC
Also Called: Customerlink Systems
1376 Lead Hill Blvd # 150, Roseville (95661-2946)
PHONE.................................916 781-4344
Mark Hockridge, *CEO*
Jim Bonfield, *Senior VP*
Kennan Bridge, *VP Mktg*
Shanna Chaney, *Manager*
EMP: 59
SQ FT: 11,366
SALES (est): 7MM **Privately Held**
WEB: www.customerlink.com
SIC: 8742 Marketing consulting services

(P-27371)
CARLETON BOOKER MARKETING INC
5042 Wilshire Blvd # 31584, Los Angeles (90036-4305)
PHONE.................................925 752-1973
Carleton C Booker, *CEO*
EMP: 52
SALES (est): 3.5MM **Privately Held**
SIC: 8742 Marketing consulting services

(P-27372)
CAROLLO ENGINEERS INC
2700 Ygnacio Valley Rd # 300, Walnut Creek (94598-3466)
PHONE.................................925 932-1710
Gary Deis, *CEO*
Daniel Ramey, *Manager*
EMP: 110
SALES (corp-wide): 225.9MM **Privately Held**
SIC: 8742 8711 Management engineering; engineering services
PA: Carollo Engineers Pc
2700 Ygnacio Valley Rd # 300
Walnut Creek CA 94598
925 932-1710

(P-27373)
CASA ALLEGRA COMMUNITY SVCS
35 Mitchell Blvd Ste 8, San Rafael (94903-2012)
PHONE.................................415 499-1116
Jeannie Santaneelo, *Director*
Jeanne Santangelo, *Director*
EMP: 70
SALES: 3.2MM **Privately Held**
SIC: 8742 Human resource consulting services

(P-27374)
CATAPULT MARKETING
10940 Wilshire Blvd Fl 6, Los Angeles (90024-3940)
PHONE.................................203 682-4000
William R Fenoglio, *Principal*
Patricia Kinkead, *Vice Pres*
Anne Gallagher, *Creative Dir*
Ines Henrich, *Managing Dir*
Alysia Margiloff, *Managing Dir*
EMP: 50
SALES (corp-wide): 27.2MM **Privately Held**
SIC: 8742 Management consulting services
PA: Catapult Marketing
55 Post Rd W Ste 1
Westport CT 06880
203 682-4000

(P-27375)
CBRE GLOBAL INVESTORS LLC (DH)
Also Called: Global Innovation Partner
515 S Flower St Ste 3100, Los Angeles (90071-2233)
PHONE.................................213 683-4200
Ritson Ferguson, *CEO*
Peter Di Corpo, *COO*
Stuart Savidge, *COO*
Maurice Voskuilen, *CFO*
Kathy Matson, *Vice Pres*
EMP: 150 EST: 1972
SQ FT: 60,000
SALES (est): 148.2MM
SALES (corp-wide): 10.8B **Publicly Held**
WEB: www.cbreglobalindestors.com
SIC: 8742 Real estate consultant
HQ: Cbre, Inc.
400 S Hope St Ste 25
Los Angeles CA 90071
310 477-5876

(P-27376)
CBRE GLOBAL INVESTORS LLC
3501 Jamboree Rd Ste 100, Newport Beach (92660-2940)
PHONE.................................949 725-8500
Steven Swerdlow, *Principal*
Dan Hensgen, *Technology*
EMP: 350
SALES (corp-wide): 10.8B **Publicly Held**
SIC: 8742 6531 Management consulting services; real estate agent, commercial
HQ: Cbre Global Investors, Llc
515 S Flower St Ste 3100
Los Angeles CA 90071
213 683-4200

(P-27377)
CERTIFIEDSAFETY INC
3070 Bay Vista Courtste B, Benicia (94510)
PHONE.................................707 747-9400
EMP: 78
SALES (corp-wide): 19.9MM **Privately Held**
SIC: 8742 Business consultant
PA: Certifiedsafety, Inc.
1177 Butler Rd
League City TX 77573
281 680-1200

(P-27378)
CHASE GROUP LLC
Also Called: Center At Parkwest, The
6740 Wilbur Ave, Reseda (91335-5179)
PHONE.................................818 708-3533
Phil Chase, *Branch Mgr*
Elizabeth J Casey, *CFO*
Diana Lopez, *Social Dir*
Jorge Samayoa, *Facilities Dir*
Kamran Rabbani, *Director*
EMP: 100 **Privately Held**
SIC: 8742 8049 Management consulting services; nurses & other medical assistants
PA: The Chase Group Llc
3075 E Thousand Oaks Blvd
Thousand Oaks CA 91362

(P-27379)
CHASE GROUP LLC
Also Called: Simi Vly Care & Rehabilitation
5270 E Los Angeles Ave, Simi Valley (93063-4137)
PHONE.................................805 522-9155
Fax: 805 581-3879
Phil Chase, *Manager*
Maria Curiel, *Office Mgr*
Floyd Rhoades, *Administration*
EMP: 100 **Privately Held**
SIC: 8742 8732 Management consulting services; research services, except laboratory
PA: The Chase Group Llc
3075 E Thousand Oaks Blvd
Thousand Oaks CA 91362

(P-27380)
CHECK DISC LABS
4121 W Vanowen Pl, Burbank (91505-1131)
PHONE.................................818 847-2255
Jonathan Burk, *General Mgr*
EMP: 70
SQ FT: 8,000
SALES (est): 4MM **Privately Held**
SIC: 8742 Quality assurance consultant

(P-27381)
CIPHERMAX INC (PA)
1975 Concourse Dr, San Jose (95131-1708)
PHONE.................................408 382-6500
Fax: 408 382-6599
Nelson Bye, *President*
Ray KAO, *Ch of Bd*
George Vaiser, *Vice Pres*
Tsunyi Tuan, *Director*
EMP: 55
SQ FT: 23,000
SALES (est): 5.3MM **Privately Held**
WEB: www.maxxan.com
SIC: 8742 Management consulting services

(P-27382)
CITY OF FULLERTON
Maintenance Dept
1580 W Commonwealth Ave, Fullerton (92833-2728)
PHONE.................................714 738-6897
Robert Savage, *Director*
Charles Kovac, *Project Mgr*
Kevin Coe, *Supervisor*
Bill Roseberry, *Supervisor*
EMP: 150 **Privately Held**
SIC: 8742 Maintenance management consultant
PA: City Of Fullerton
303 W Commonwealth Ave
Fullerton CA 92832
714 738-6300

(P-27383)
CITY OF IRVINE
Also Called: Dept of Public Works
6427 Oak Cyn, Irvine (92618-5202)
P.O. Box 19575 (92623-9575)
PHONE.................................949 724-7600
Fax: 949 724-7607
Allison Hart, *Manager*
Thomas Roberts, *Analyst*
Dave Flanagan, *Sr Project Mgr*
EMP: 70 **Privately Held**
SIC: 8742 9111 8748 7349 Public utilities consultant; mayors' offices; business consulting; building maintenance services; lawn & garden services
PA: City Of Irvine
1 Civic Center Plz
Irvine CA 92606
949 724-6000

(P-27384)
CLOUDTRIGGER INC
760 Garden View Ct # 120, Encinitas (92024-2473)
PHONE.................................858 367-5272
Doug McLean, *Vice Pres*
Carter Wigell, *COO*
Janis Hom, *VP Mktg*
EMP: 70
SALES (est): 5.9MM **Privately Held**
SIC: 8742 Management consulting services

(P-27385)
COHEN BROWN MGT GROUP INC (PA)
11835 W Olympic Blvd 920e, Los Angeles (90064-5836)
PHONE.................................310 966-1001
Martin L Cohen, *CEO*
Edward G Brown, *President*
Alex Monteiro, *President*
Ruben Rubinstein, *COO*
Christopher Phillips, *Vice Pres*
EMP: 64
SQ FT: 5,500
SALES (est): 10.1MM **Privately Held**
WEB: www.cbmg.com
SIC: 8742 Training & development consultant

(P-27386)
COLLEGE TRACK
111 Broadway Ste 101, Oakland (94607-3730)
PHONE.................................510 834-3295
Elissa Salas, *CEO*
Richard Rodrigo, *Program Mgr*
Julia Chih, *VP Finance*
Cynthia Creswell, *Bookkeeper*
Margaret Winnen, *Human Res Dir*
EMP: 191
SALES (est): 13.3MM **Privately Held**
SIC: 8742 School, college, university consultant

(P-27387)
COMPSPEC INC
425 E Colorado St Ste 410, Glendale (91205-1675)
PHONE.................................818 551-4200
Nabil Haddad, *President*
Shelly Murph, *Marketing Staff*
Shelle Mitchell, *Director*
EMP: 100
SALES (est): 10.9MM **Privately Held**
WEB: www.compspecinc.com
SIC: 8742 7299 Hospital & health services consultant; debt counseling or adjustment service, individuals

PRODUCTS & SERVICES SECTION
8742 - Management Consulting Services County (P-27409)

(P-27388)
CONSUMER RESOURCE NETWORK LLC
Also Called: Launchpad Communications
4420 E Miraloma Ave Ste J, Anaheim (92807-1839)
PHONE.................................800 291-4794
Mark Osborne,
Alex Kim, *CFO*
Brian Pick, *Vice Pres*
Greg Hall,
Benjamin Kim,
EMP: 340
SQ FT: 27,519
SALES (est): 19.5MM **Privately Held**
WEB: www.consumerresourcenetwork.net
SIC: 8742 Marketing consulting services

(P-27389)
COOPERATIVE PERSONNEL SERVICES (PA)
Also Called: CPS Hr Consulting
241 Lathrop Way, Sacramento (95815-4242)
PHONE.................................916 263-3600
Fax: 916 263-3613
Jerry Greenwell, *CEO*
Tim Howald, *CFO*
Pamela Derby, *Info Tech Dir*
Lynne Harris, *Info Tech Mgr*
Rosanne McHenry, *Project Mgr*
EMP: 139
SQ FT: 34,000
SALES (est): 31.7MM **Privately Held**
SIC: 8742 Personnel management consultant

(P-27390)
CORPORATE VISIONS INC
Also Called: CORPORATE VISIONS INC.
2705 Avenida De Anita # 29, Carlsbad (92010-8355)
PHONE.................................760 458-0914
Mark Valle, *Principal*
EMP: 127
SALES (corp-wide): 5.4MM **Privately Held**
SIC: 8742 Management consulting services
PA: Corporate Visions Inc
  3875 Hopyard Rd Ste 275
  Pleasanton CA 94588
  415 464-4400

(P-27391)
COUNTY OF ALAMEDA
Also Called: Civil Service Commission
1405 Lakeside Dr, Oakland (94612-4306)
PHONE.................................510 272-6442
Fax: 510 272-6424
Denise Etonmay, *Director*
Stephen Amano, *Deputy Dir*
Elsie Lum, *Director*
EMP: 60 **Privately Held**
WEB: www.co.alameda.ca.us
SIC: 8742 9441 Human resource consulting services; administration of social & manpower programs
PA: County of Alameda
  1221 Oak St Ste 555
  Oakland CA 94612
  510 272-6691

(P-27392)
COVARIO INC (PA)
9255 Towne Centre Dr # 600, San Diego (92121-3039)
PHONE.................................858 397-1500
Fax: 858 397-1598
Russ Mann, *CEO*
Claire Long, *COO*
Curt Nelson, *Chairman*
James Latham, *Chief Mktg Ofcr*
Craig Macdonald, *Chief Mktg Ofcr*
EMP: 84
SALES (est): 22.4MM **Privately Held**
WEB: www.covario.com
SIC: 8742 Marketing consulting services

(P-27393)
CPE HR INC
9000 W Sunset Blvd # 900, West Hollywood (90069-5801)
PHONE.................................310 270-9800
Fax: 310 385-1068
Harold Walt, *CEO*
Faith Branvold, *President*
Grace Drulias, *CFO*
Shameem Hussain, *Vice Pres*
Shameem Sain, *CIO*
EMP: 90
SALES (est): 14.8MM **Privately Held**
SIC: 8742 Human resource consulting services

(P-27394)
CPG SOLUTIONS LLC
111 Woodmere Rd Ste 200, Folsom (95630-4750)
PHONE.................................561 988-8611
James Daleen, *Mng Member*
James Cramer,
Ali Safadi,
Barbara Herman, *Manager*
EMP: 50 **EST:** 2001
SQ FT: 12,000
SALES (est): 4.8MM
SALES (corp-wide): 200MM **Privately Held**
SIC: 8742 Business consultant
HQ: Kpit Infosystems Incorporated
  379 Thornall St Ste 6
  Edison NJ 08837
  732 321-0921

(P-27395)
CREATIVE CHANNEL SERVICES LLC (HQ)
Also Called: C C S
12777 W Jefferson Blvd # 120, Los Angeles (90066-7038)
PHONE.................................310 482-6500
Fax: 310 482-6596
Andy Restivo, *CEO*
Michael Butler, *CFO*
Hanoz Gandhi, *Exec VP*
George Thorn, *Exec VP*
Gregg Nole, *Senior VP*
EMP: 96
SALES (est): 51.6MM
SALES (corp-wide): 15.1B **Publicly Held**
WEB: www.creativechannel.com
SIC: 8742 Distribution channels consultant
PA: Omnicom Group Inc.
  437 Madison Ave
  New York NY 10022
  212 415-3600

(P-27396)
CREATIVE EVENTS ENTERPRISES
4872 Topanga Canyon Blvd # 406, Woodland Hills (91364-4229)
PHONE.................................818 610-7000
Frank Biedka, *President*
Irving Shanske, *Vice Pres*
Arthur Webb, *Vice Pres*
EMP: 170
SALES (est): 7.2MM **Privately Held**
SIC: 8742 7389 7999 Business consultant; convention & show services; picnic ground operation

(P-27397)
CROWN GOLF PROPERTIES LP
Also Called: Tustin Ranch Golf Club
12442 Tustin Ranch Rd, Tustin (92782-1000)
PHONE.................................714 730-1611
Fax: 714 730-1991
Steve Plummer, *Manager*
Tracy Saracino, *Admin Mgr*
Jessica Tjan, *Manager*
Christian Estrada, *Supervisor*
Kyle Herbold, *Supervisor*
EMP: 200
SALES (corp-wide): 77.7MM **Privately Held**
WEB: www.rvrgolf.com
SIC: 8742 7997 7992 Business consultant; membership sports & recreation clubs; public golf courses
PA: Crown Golf Properties, Lp
  222 N La Salle St # 2000
  Chicago IL 60601
  312 395-7701

(P-27398)
CROWN GOLF PROPERTIES LP
Also Called: Empire Lake Golf Course
791 Camarillo Springs Rd, Camarillo (93012-8111)
PHONE.................................909 481-6663
Fax: 909 481-6763
Eugene Park, *Manager*
Dolores Joiner, *Manager*
Eugene Parks, *Manager*
EMP: 60
SALES (corp-wide): 77.7MM **Privately Held**
WEB: www.rvrgolf.com
SIC: 8742 Business consultant
PA: Crown Golf Properties, Lp
  222 N La Salle St # 2000
  Chicago IL 60601
  312 395-7701

(P-27399)
CT LIEN SOLUTION
330 N Brand Blvd Ste 700, Glendale (91203-2336)
PHONE.................................818 662-4100
CT Cor System, *Branch Mgr*
EMP: 124
SALES (corp-wide): 4.5B **Privately Held**
SIC: 8742 Management consulting services
HQ: Ct Lien Solution
  2929 Allen Pkwy Ste 3300
  Houston TX 77019
  713 533-4600

(P-27400)
CUMMING CORPORATION
25220 Hancock Ave Ste 440, Murrieta (92562-0903)
PHONE.................................951 200-7860
Finlay Cumming, *CEO*
Peter Heald, *President*
Michael Jensen, *COO*
Brian Ruttencutter, *CFO*
Marty Breen, *Vice Pres*
EMP: 50
SALES (est): 9.8MM **Privately Held**
SIC: 8742 Industry specialist consultants

(P-27401)
CUNNINGHAM GROUP INC
5616 Circle View Dr, Bonsall (92003-5301)
PHONE.................................303 295-1982
Paul Cunningham, *CEO*
Troy Cunningham, *President*
EMP: 57
SALES (est): 3MM **Privately Held**
SIC: 8742 Financial consultant

(P-27402)
CUSA PCSTC LLC
Also Called: Coach USA
2001 S Manchester Ave, Anaheim (92802-3803)
PHONE.................................714 978-8855
Tony Hancuff,
Daniel Ferry, *Info Tech Mgr*
Vanessa Dejong, *Controller*
EMP: 225
SQ FT: 10,000
SALES (est): 21.3MM
SALES (corp-wide): 5.4B **Privately Held**
SIC: 8742 Transportation consultant
HQ: Coach Usa, Inc.
  160 S Route 17 N
  Paramus NJ 07652

(P-27403)
CUSTOMER LOYALTY BUILDERS INC
Also Called: Service Quality
1063 Todos Santos, Concord (94522)
PHONE.................................888 478-7787
Jeff Kasper, *President*
Michael Mendona, *Principal*
EMP: 100
SALES (est): 3.9MM **Privately Held**
SIC: 8742 8211 Management consulting services; seminary

(P-27404)
CUSTOMIZED DIST SVCS INC
3355 E Cedar St, Ontario (91761-7632)
PHONE.................................909 947-0084
Fax: 909 947-8740
Mark Tuttle, *Branch Mgr*
Melinda Ramirez, *Executive*
Randall Wright, *Opers Mgr*
EMP: 100
SALES (corp-wide): 104MM **Privately Held**
WEB: www.cds3pl.com
SIC: 8742 7319 8741 Transportation consultant; distribution of advertising material or sample services; management services
PA: Customized Distribution Services, Inc.
  20 Harry Shupe Blvd
  Wharton NJ 07885
  973 366-5090

(P-27405)
DEEP FOCUS INC
6922 Hollywood Blvd Fl 10, Hollywood (90028-6130)
PHONE.................................323 790-5340
EMP: 600
SALES (corp-wide): 132.7MM **Privately Held**
SIC: 8742 8743 Marketing consulting services; promotion service
HQ: Deep Focus, Inc.
  229 W 43rd St Fl 8
  New York NY 10036
  212 792-6800

(P-27406)
DELOITTE CONSULTING LLP
Also Called: Bersin By Deloitte
180 Grand Ave Ste 320, Oakland (94612-3778)
PHONE.................................510 251-4400
Joshua Bersin, *Principal*
EMP: 63
SALES (corp-wide): 9.5B **Privately Held**
SIC: 8742 Financial consultant
HQ: Deloitte Consulting Llp
  30 Rockefeller Plz
  New York NY 10112
  212 492-4000

(P-27407)
DELOITTE CONSULTING LLP
695 Town Center Dr # 1200, Costa Mesa (92626-1924)
PHONE.................................714 436-7100
Robert Lupcenpi, *Branch Mgr*
Jay Monson, *Auditing Mgr*
EMP: 63
SALES (corp-wide): 9.5B **Privately Held**
WEB: www.dctoolset.com
SIC: 8742 Management consulting services
HQ: Deloitte Consulting Llp
  30 Rockefeller Plz
  New York NY 10112
  212 492-4000

(P-27408)
DENTISTAT INC
Also Called: Insurance Dentists Amer Idoa
1688 Dell Ave Ste 210, Campbell (95008-6926)
PHONE.................................408 376-0336
Richard H Guenther, *Ch of Bd*
Richard H Guenther DMD, *Ch of Bd*
Bret W Guenther, *President*
Richard L Garwood DDS, *CEO*
Harry J Kaplan, *Corp Secy*
EMP: 65
SQ FT: 7,661
SALES (est): 7.1MM **Privately Held**
WEB: www.dentistat.com
SIC: 8742 8748 Hospital & health services consultant; business consulting

(P-27409)
DEVELPMENT DIMENSIONS INTL INC
4160 Dublin Blvd Ste 450, Dublin (94568-7723)
PHONE.................................925 361-4246
Daniel Prachar, *Director*
EMP: 288
SALES (corp-wide): 234.9MM **Privately Held**
SIC: 8742 Training & development consultant

8742 - Management Consulting Services County (P-27410)

PA: Development Dimensions International, Inc.
1225 Washington Pike
Bridgeville PA 15017
412 257-0600

(P-27410)
DIAMOND CONCESSIONS LLC
6140 Stoneridge Mall Rd # 550, Pleasanton (94588-3232)
PHONE...........................925 226-2889
Amit Patel,
Greg Coleman, *Vice Pres*
Dave Kaval,
Kevin Outcalt,
EMP: 60
SQ FT: 1,500
SALES (est): 3.8MM **Privately Held**
SIC: 8742 Food & beverage consultant

(P-27411)
DIGITAL NIRVANA INC
3984 Washington Blvd # 355, Fremont (94538-4954)
PHONE...........................510 226-9000
Hirendra Hindocha, *President*
Vishnu Beri, *COO*
John M Stephens, *Vice Pres*
Ned Chini, *VP Sls/Mktg*
Michael Collins, *Cust Mgr*
EMP: 500
SQ FT: 4,000
SALES (est): 25.1MM **Privately Held**
WEB: www.digital-nirvana.com
SIC: 8742 Management consulting services

(P-27412)
DIGITALMOJO INC
3111 Camino Del Rio N # 400, San Diego (92108-5724)
PHONE...........................800 346-7147
Megan Gates, *Branch Mgr*
EMP: 71
SALES (corp-wide): 14.2MM **Privately Held**
SIC: 8742 4813 Marketing consulting services;
PA: Digitalmojo, Inc.
3111 Camino Del Rio N # 400
San Diego CA 92108
800 413-5916

(P-27413)
DIGITALTHINK INC (DH)
601 Brannan St, San Francisco (94107-1511)
PHONE...........................415 625-4000
Michael W Pope, *President*
Jon Madonna, *Ch of Bd*
Robert J Krolik, *CFO*
Adam D Levy, *Vice Pres*
Terri Brncic, *Controller*
EMP: 250
SQ FT: 51,000
SALES (est): 16.5MM
SALES (corp-wide): 2.9B **Publicly Held**
WEB: www.digitalthink.com
SIC: 8742 Marketing consulting services
HQ: Convergys Customer Management Group Inc.
201 E 4th St Bsmt
Cincinnati OH 45202
513 723-6104

(P-27414)
DPK CONSULTING
Also Called: Tetra Tech Dpk
605 Market St Ste 800, San Francisco (94105-3210)
PHONE...........................415 495-7772
Fax: 415 495-6017
Robert W Page, *President*
Tammy Lovlie, *General Mgr*
Allen Shannon, *Manager*
EMP: 100
SALES (est): 7.7MM
SALES (corp-wide): 2.3B **Publicly Held**
WEB: www.dpkconsulting.com
SIC: 8742 Management consulting services
HQ: Ard, Inc.
159 Bank St Ste 300
Burlington VT 05401
802 658-3890

(P-27415)
DRAWBRIDGE INC
2121 S El Camino Real 7th, San Mateo (94403-1855)
PHONE...........................650 513-2323
Kamakshi Sivaramakrishnan, *CEO*
Charles Tseng, *Analyst*
Brian Ferrario, *VP Mktg*
Diana Epstein, *Accounts Exec*
EMP: 85
SALES (est): 706.4K **Privately Held**
SIC: 8742 Marketing consulting services

(P-27416)
DUFF & PHELPS LLC
1950 University Ave # 400, East Palo Alto (94303-2281)
PHONE...........................650 798-5500
Fax: 650 798-5510
Jim Behrens, *Manager*
EMP: 65
SALES (corp-wide): 377.4MM **Privately Held**
SIC: 8742 Financial consultant
HQ: Duff & Phelps, Llc
55 E 52nd St Fl 31
New York NY 10055
212 871-2000

(P-27417)
DUFF & PHELPS LLC
350 S Grand Ave Ste 3100, Los Angeles (90071-3420)
PHONE...........................213 270-2300
EMP: 67
SALES (corp-wide): 97.4MM **Privately Held**
SIC: 8742
HQ: Duff & Phelps, Llc
55 E 52nd St Fl 31
New York NY 10055
212 871-6777

(P-27418)
EASTERN GOLDFIELDS INC
1660 Hotel Cir N Ste 207, San Diego (92108-2803)
PHONE...........................619 497-2555
Michael McChesney, *CEO*
Mike Tonkins, *Manager*
EMP: 218
SALES (est): 4.6MM **Privately Held**
SIC: 8742 Management consulting services

(P-27419)
EBISU MARKETING CORP
1930 Wilshire Blvd # 400, Los Angeles (90057-3605)
PHONE...........................213 674-2330
Takehisa Naito, *CEO*
EMP: 64 **EST:** 2010
SALES: 3.5MM **Privately Held**
SIC: 8742 Marketing consulting services

(P-27420)
ECORP CONSULTING INC (PA)
2525 Warren Dr, Rocklin (95677-2167)
PHONE...........................916 782-9100
James Stewart, *President*
James D Stewart, *CEO*
Bjorn Gregersen, *CFO*
Peter Balfour, *Vice Pres*
Harold Freeman, *Vice Pres*
EMP: 55
SQ FT: 6,950
SALES (est): 20.2MM **Privately Held**
WEB: www.ecorpconsulting.com
SIC: 8742 8748 Industry specialist consultants; business consulting

(P-27421)
EILEEN SHI
2635 N 1st St Ste 149, San Jose (95134-2043)
PHONE...........................866 777-6104
Ying Shi, *President*
Wutai Shi, *Senior VP*
EMP: 100
SALES (est): 3.1MM **Privately Held**
SIC: 8742 Management information systems consultant

(P-27422)
EK HEALTH SERVICES INC
992 S De Anza Blvd Ste 10, San Jose (95129-2777)
PHONE...........................408 973-0888
Fax: 408 973-2508
Eunhee Kim, *President*
Sang Kim, *CFO*
Douglas Benner, *Chief Mktg Ofcr*
Sherry Busbee, *Assoc VP*
Anita Breedlove, *Exec VP*
EMP: 155
SQ FT: 6,500
SALES (est): 18.2MM **Privately Held**
WEB: www.ekhealth.com
SIC: 8742 Hospital & health services consultant; human resource consulting services; personnel management consultant

(P-27423)
EMMIS COMMUNICATIONS CORP
Emmis Marketting Group
2600 W Olive Ave Fl 8, Burbank (91505-4553)
PHONE...........................818 238-6705
Fax: 818 238-9158
Val Maki, *Branch Mgr*
EMP: 175
SALES (corp-wide): 231.4MM **Publicly Held**
WEB: www.emmis.com
SIC: 8742 Marketing consulting services
PA: Emmis Communications Corp
40 Monument Cir Ste 700
Indianapolis IN 46204
317 266-0100

(P-27424)
ENSIGHTEN INC (HQ)
1741 Tech Dr Ste 500, San Jose (95110)
PHONE...........................650 249-4712
Josh Manion, *CEO*
Dan Dal Degan, *President*
Fuad Ahmad, *CFO*
Pelin Thorogood, *Officer*
Wolfgang Allisat, *Senior VP*
EMP: 81 **EST:** 2012
SALES (est): 36.3MM **Privately Held**
SIC: 8742 8741 Management consulting services; management services
PA: Tagman Limited
Henry Wood House 7th Floor
London SE1 3
203 465-9250

(P-27425)
ENTERPRISE EVENTS GROUP INC
950 Northgate Dr Ste 100, San Rafael (94903-3430)
PHONE...........................415 499-4444
Fax: 415 499-7979
Matt Gillam, *CEO*
Rich A Calcaterra, *Vice Pres*
Erin Clark, *Executive*
Priscilla Mack, *Executive*
Christopher Shavor, *Executive*
EMP: 150
SQ FT: 18,000
SALES (est): 29.3MM **Privately Held**
WEB: www.eegweb.com
SIC: 8742 8743 Incentive or award program consultant; promotion service

(P-27426)
EXCEL MANAGED CARE DISA
3840 Watt Ave Bldg C, Sacramento (95821-2640)
PHONE...........................916 944-7185
Fax: 916 944-0211
Judy Lawson-Bailey, *President*
Bill Spaller, *CEO*
Steve Smetana, *Vice Pres*
Brenda Smith, *Vice Pres*
William V Spaller, *Principal*
EMP: 92
SQ FT: 3,600
SALES (est): 10.3MM **Privately Held**
WEB: www.excelmanagedcare.com
SIC: 8742 Management consulting services; hospital & health services consultant

(P-27427)
EXECUTIVE MARKETING FIRM
4924 Balboa Blvd 375, Encino (91316-3402)
PHONE...........................818 713-1998
Ladona Colletto, *Owner*
EMP: 50
SALES (est): 1.5MM **Privately Held**
SIC: 8742 Management consulting services

(P-27428)
EXPERIAN INFO SOLUTIONS INC
Also Called: Experian Marketing
841 Apollo St Ste 200, El Segundo (90245-4722)
PHONE...........................310 343-6700
Dana Shupe, *Branch Mgr*
Stephen Benelisha, *Sr Software Eng*
EMP: 110
SALES (corp-wide): 4.5B **Privately Held**
SIC: 8742 Marketing consulting services
HQ: Experian Information Solutions, Inc.
475 Anton Blvd
Costa Mesa CA 92626
714 830-7000

(P-27429)
EXPRESSWORKS INTERNATIONAL LLC (PA)
2010 Crow Canyon Pl # 260, San Ramon (94583-4634)
PHONE...........................925 244-0900
John Quereto, *President*
Jeff Mahach, *Vice Pres*
Maria Walker, *Office Mgr*
Deborah Bernardi, *Info Tech Mgr*
Laura Stone, *Accountant*
EMP: 100
SQ FT: 1,450
SALES (est): 10.1MM **Privately Held**
WEB: www.expressworks.com
SIC: 8742 Management consulting services

(P-27430)
EXULT INC
121 Innovation Dr Ste 200, Irvine (92617-3094)
P.O. Box 6300, Newport Beach (92658-6300)
PHONE...........................949 856-8800
Fax: 949 856-8813
James C Madden, *Ch of Bd*
Jim Aselta, *Partner*
Kevin Campbell, *President*
John Adams, *CFO*
Robert E Ball, *CFO*
EMP: 2424
SQ FT: 22,000
SALES (est): 83.8MM
SALES (corp-wide): 11.6B **Privately Held**
SIC: 8742 Human resource consulting services
HQ: Aon Hewitt Llc
200 E Randolph St Ll3
Chicago IL 60601
312 381-1000

(P-27431)
FAMILY FIRST FINANCIAL SERVICE
13658 Hawthorne Blvd # 307, Hawthorne (90250-5824)
PHONE...........................310 355-1788
Alex Islas, *Owner*
EMP: 54
SALES (est): 3.9MM **Privately Held**
SIC: 8742 Financial consultant

(P-27432)
FDSI LOGISTICS LLC
5703 Corsa Ave, Westlake Village (91362-4001)
PHONE...........................818 971-3300
David Kolchins, *Vice Pres*
Ivan Martinez, *Accountant*
Elizabeth Derderian, *Auditor*
Jennifer Osborn, *Human Resources*
Gina Ortiz-Wunder, *Opers Staff*
EMP: 75
SQ FT: 8,000

PRODUCTS & SERVICES SECTION
8742 - Management Consulting Services County (P-27456)

SALES: 13MM
SALES (corp-wide): 121.5B **Publicly Held**
WEB: www.fdsi.com
SIC: 8742 4731 Transportation consultant; freight transportation arrangement
PA: Cardinal Health, Inc.
  7000 Cardinal Pl
  Dublin OH 43017
  614 757-5000

(P-27433)
FINANCIAL CONSULTING &
Also Called: Fcti
11766 Wilshire Blvd # 1100, Los Angeles (90025-6561)
PHONE 310 201-2535
Fax: 310 201-2538
Gabriel Frem, *President*
Jesus Carrillo, *Vice Pres*
Sal Carrillo, *Vice Pres*
Marc Lewis, *Vice Pres*
Anthony Roque, *Vice Pres*
EMP: 139
SALES (est): 21MM **Privately Held**
WEB: www.fcti.net
SIC: 8742 6099 Financial consultant; automated teller machine (ATM) network

(P-27434)
FINANCIAL ENGINES INC (PA)
1050 Enterprise Way Fl 3, Sunnyvale (94089-1411)
PHONE 408 498-6000
Fax: 650 565-4905
Lawrence M Raffone, *President*
Blake R Grossman, *Ch of Bd*
Raymond J Sims, *CFO*
Christopher L Jones, *Ch Invest Ofcr*
John B Bunch, *Exec VP*
EMP: 170 **EST:** 1996
SQ FT: 80,995
SALES: 310.7MM **Publicly Held**
WEB: www.financialadvice.com
SIC: 8742 6282 6411 Management consulting services; investment advice; pension & retirement plan consultants

(P-27435)
FINANCIAL HEALTHCARE SERVICES
690 E Green St Ste 300, Pasadena (91101-2121)
PHONE 626 356-7950
Fax: 626 356-7977
Esther Yatman, *President*
Lon Yatman, *Treasurer*
Weng Tang, *Controller*
EMP: 50
SQ FT: 10,000
SALES (est): 3.4MM **Privately Held**
WEB: www.uai-unifi.com
SIC: 8742 Administrative services consultant

(P-27436)
FIRST AMERICAN FINANCIAL CORP
Also Called: 1st American Financial
39465 Paseo Padre Pkwy, Fremont (94538-5350)
PHONE 510 252-1563
EMP: 293 **Publicly Held**
SIC: 8742 7389 Financial consultant; financial services
PA: First American Financial Corporation
  1 First American Way
  Santa Ana CA 92707

(P-27437)
FOOD MANAGEMENT ASSOCIATES INC
22349 La Palma Ave # 115, Yorba Linda (92887-3810)
PHONE 714 694-2828
Fax: 714 694-2829
Richard Warmolts, *President*
Laura Warmolts, *Vice Pres*
Amy Leadbetter, *Admin Asst*
Darlene Riego, *Sales Executive*
Rich Warmolts, *Marketing Mgr*
EMP: 50
SQ FT: 1,800
SALES (est): 7.2MM **Privately Held**
SIC: 8742 Business consultant

(P-27438)
FOSTERING EXECUTIVE LEADERSHIP
4790 Irvine Blvd 105-432, Irvine (92620-1973)
PHONE 949 651-6250
Tammy Wong, *President*
Chris Martell, *Opers Staff*
EMP: 99
SALES (est): 4.1MM **Privately Held**
SIC: 8742 Management consulting services

(P-27439)
FRANK GATES SERVICE COMPANY
1107 Investment Blvd, El Dorado Hills (95762-5736)
PHONE 916 934-0812
Fax: 916 939-8230
Chanteo Kvigne, *Manager*
Brenda Remington, *Director*
EMP: 70
SALES (corp-wide): 4.3B **Privately Held**
WEB: www.fgsc.com
SIC: 8742 Management consulting services
HQ: The Frank Gates Service Company
  5000 Bradenton Ave # 100
  Dublin OH 43017
  614 793-8000

(P-27440)
FREDERICK LABS LLC
535 Mission St, San Francisco (94105-2997)
PHONE 646 738-8303
Josh McCarter, *CEO*
EMP: 172
SALES (est): 471.7K
SALES (corp-wide): 41.4MM **Privately Held**
SIC: 8742 Marketing consulting services
PA: Booker Software, Inc.
  22 Cortlandt St Fl 18
  New York NY 10007
  646 738-8303

(P-27441)
FREIGHT MANAGEMENT INC
Also Called: F M I
2900 E La Palma Ave, Anaheim (92806-2616)
PHONE 714 632-1440
Robert J Walters, *President*
Dennis Rihn, *COO*
Heidi Calamusa, *Vice Pres*
Tim Ponder, *Vice Pres*
Angela Shackford, *Vice Pres*
EMP: 53
SQ FT: 9,000
SALES: 60.6MM **Privately Held**
SIC: 8742 Management consulting services; transportation consultant

(P-27442)
FRONTRANGE SOLUTIONS INC (HQ)
490 N Mccarthy Blvd, Milpitas (95035-5118)
PHONE 408 601-2800
Fax: 925 398-1305
Udo Waibel, *CTO*
Bill Heise, *Partner*
John Hillyard, *CFO*
Kevin Thompson, *CFO*
David Puglia, *Chief Mktg Ofcr*
EMP: 85
SQ FT: 88,000
SALES (est): 45.1MM
SALES (corp-wide): 1B **Privately Held**
SIC: 8742 Management consulting services
PA: Francisco Partners Management, L.P.
  1 Letterman Dr Ste 410
  San Francisco CA 94129
  415 418-2500

(P-27443)
FUNDBOX INC
300 Montgomery St Ste 900, San Francisco (94104-1921)
PHONE 415 509-1343
EMP: 75
SALES (est): 2.8MM **Privately Held**
SIC: 8742 Management consulting services
PA: Fundbox Ltd
  23 Yehuda Halevy, Floor 19
  Tel Aviv-Jaffa
  362 468-06

(P-27444)
FUTUREDONTICS INC (PA)
Also Called: 1-800 Dentist
6060 Center Dr Fl 7, Los Angeles (90045-1596)
PHONE 310 215-6400
Fax: 310 215-6629
Michael Turner, *CEO*
Ronald Joyal, *COO*
Gary Kim, *CFO*
Gary St Denis, *Chairman*
Alfred Joyal, *Bd of Directors*
EMP: 126
SQ FT: 35,000
SALES (est): 45.5MM **Privately Held**
WEB: www.futuredontics.com
SIC: 8742 Marketing consulting services

(P-27445)
GALLUP INC
Also Called: Gallup Organization, The
18300 Von Karman Ave # 1000, Irvine (92612-0182)
PHONE 949 474-2700
Fax: 949 474-2782
Kelly Aylward, *Manager*
Lawrence M Edond, *Chief Mktg Ofcr*
Craig Kamins, *Associate*
EMP: 50
SALES (corp-wide): 249.1MM **Privately Held**
SIC: 8742 Management consulting services
PA: Gallup, Inc.
  901 F St Nw Ste 400
  Washington DC 20004
  202 715-3030

(P-27446)
GARTNER INC
11845 W Olympic Blvd 505w, Los Angeles (90064-1149)
PHONE 310 479-2108
Bill Kumagai, *Manager*
Amy Cooper, *Sales Staff*
Dina Demko, *Sales Staff*
Mark Gilbert, *Director*
Ed Fraga, *Manager*
EMP: 55
SALES (corp-wide): 2.1B **Publicly Held**
WEB: www.gartner.com
SIC: 8742 Business consultant
PA: Gartner, Inc.
  56 Top Gallant Rd
  Stamford CT 06902
  203 316-1111

(P-27447)
GAVIN DE BECKER & ASSOCIATES
11684 Ventura Blvd # 440, Studio City (91604-2699)
PHONE 818 760-4213
Gavin De Becker, *President*
Michael La Fever, *Exec VP*
Jeff Marquart, *Exec VP*
Robert C Martin, *Vice Pres*
Stuart Sullivan, *Executive*
EMP: 180
SQ FT: 1,600
SALES (est): 26.4MM **Privately Held**
SIC: 8742 Management consulting services

(P-27448)
GLOBAL MANAGEMENT COMPANY LLC
3150 E Pico Blvd, Los Angeles (90023-3632)
PHONE 323 261-8114
Sandra Berg,
EMP: 100
SALES: 2.5MM **Privately Held**
SIC: 8742 Management consulting services

(P-27449)
GLOBAL WORK GROUP LLC
Also Called: Global Realty Group
17224 San Fernando, Granada Hills (91344)
PHONE 424 220-9994
Geoff Mills, *Mng Member*
Jill Henson, *Treasurer*
EMP: 75
SALES: 30MM **Privately Held**
SIC: 8742 7389 Materials mgmt. (purchasing, handling, inventory) consultant;

(P-27450)
GOETZMAN GROUP INC (PA)
21700 Oxnard St Ste 1540, Woodland Hills (91367-3644)
PHONE 818 595-1112
Fax: 818 595-1525
Greg Goetzman, *President*
EMP: 75
SQ FT: 4,500
SALES (est): 9.9MM **Privately Held**
WEB: www.goetzmangroup.com
SIC: 8742 8721 Management consulting services; accounting, auditing & bookkeeping

(P-27451)
GOLD TREE INC
Also Called: New Wave Transport
2170 W Esther St, Long Beach (90813-1026)
PHONE 562 801-0218
Jose S Funes, *President*
Tiego Enciso, *Office Mgr*
EMP: 60
SALES (est): 3MM **Privately Held**
SIC: 8742 Transportation consultant

(P-27452)
GORILLA TECH AMERICAS INC
2678 Bishop Dr Ste 290, San Ramon (94583-4455)
PHONE 925 365-1161
Carlo Tortora, *President*
EMP: 99
SALES (est): 5.4MM **Privately Held**
SIC: 8742 Marketing consulting services

(P-27453)
GRAND VIEW RESEARCH INC
28 2nd St Ste 3036, San Francisco (94105-3460)
PHONE 415 349-0058
Brian Haven, *CEO*
Rachel Brown, *Sales Mgr*
Sherry James, *Sales Staff*
EMP: 50
SQ FT: 1,000
SALES (est): 2.6MM **Privately Held**
SIC: 8742 Marketing consulting services

(P-27454)
GRAPHIC ORB INC
8687 Melrose Ave Ste 8, West Hollywood (90069-5746)
PHONE 310 967-2350
John Thompson, *President*
Denis Adair, *Vice Pres*
Jacquie Reynolds, *Human Res Mgr*
Lisa Boryslewski, *Opers Staff*
EMP: 64 **EST:** 1970
SQ FT: 35,000
SALES (est): 4.7MM **Privately Held**
WEB: www.graphicorb.com
SIC: 8742 Marketing consulting services

(P-27455)
GREAT DESTINATIONS INC
25510 Commercentre Dr, Lake Forest (92630-8855)
PHONE 949 667-9401
Andrew Gennuso, *President*
Nishant Machado, *Vice Pres*
EMP: 95
SQ FT: 3,000
SALES: 9MM **Privately Held**
SIC: 8742 Marketing consulting services

(P-27456)
GSTC LLC
555 Bryant St Ste 400, Palo Alto (94301-1704)
PHONE 650 773-7700
Ann Marie Williams, *Principal*

8742 - Management Consulting Services County (P-27457)

EMP: 99
SALES (est): 2.9MM **Privately Held**
SIC: 8742 Management consulting services

(P-27457) HAMILTON PARTNERS
1301 Shoreway Rd Ste 250, Burlingame (94010)
PHONE..................650 347-8800
Fax: 650 373-1617
John Hamilton, *President*
EMP: 55 EST: 2000
SALES (est): 4.3MM **Privately Held**
SIC: 8742 Training & development consultant

(P-27458) HARRIS MYCFO INC
2200 Geng Rd Ste 100, Palo Alto (94303-3358)
PHONE..................480 348-7725
Michael Montgomery, *President*
John Benevides, *President*
Craig Rawlins, *President*
Rudolph Galera, *Officer*
Harvey Armstrong, *Exec Dir*
EMP: 90
SALES (est): 18MM **Privately Held**
SIC: 8742 Financial consultant

(P-27459) HDR ENGINEERING INC
8690 Balboa Ave Ste 200, San Diego (92123-6507)
PHONE..................858 712-8400
Fax: 858 712-8333
Bill Bennett, *Branch Mgr*
Eric Scherch, *Engineer*
EMP: 50
SALES (corp-wide): 1.8B **Privately Held**
SIC: 8742 8711 Management consulting services; engineering services
HQ: Hdr Engineering, Inc.
    8404 Indian Hills Dr
    Omaha NE 68114
    402 399-1000

(P-27460) HDR ENGINEERING INC
251 S Lake Ave Ste 1000, Pasadena (91101-3020)
PHONE..................626 584-1700
Al Korth, *Manager*
Bill Naprsteki, *Manager*
EMP: 130
SALES (corp-wide): 1.8B **Privately Held**
SIC: 8742 8711 Management consulting services; engineering services
HQ: Hdr Engineering, Inc.
    8404 Indian Hills Dr
    Omaha NE 68114
    402 399-1000

(P-27461) HDR ENGINEERING INC
560 Mission St, San Francisco (94105-2907)
PHONE..................415 546-4200
Mike Greenberg, *Manager*
EMP: 99
SALES (corp-wide): 1.8B **Privately Held**
SIC: 8742 8711 Management consulting services; engineering services
HQ: Hdr Engineering, Inc.
    8404 Indian Hills Dr
    Omaha NE 68114
    402 399-1000

(P-27462) HDR ENGINEERING INC
2365 Iron Point Rd # 300, Folsom (95630-8711)
PHONE..................916 817-4700
Fax: 916 817-4747
Brent Felker, *Branch Mgr*
Tim Fleming, *District Mgr*
Peter Bukowski, *MIS Mgr*
EMP: 86
SALES (corp-wide): 1.8B **Privately Held**
SIC: 8742 Construction project management consultant
HQ: Hdr Engineering, Inc.
    8404 Indian Hills Dr
    Omaha NE 68114
    402 399-1000

(P-27463) HEALTH EDUC ECONOMIC DEVLPMNT
304 Coral Reef Rd, Alameda (94501-5929)
PHONE..................510 604-6143
Leeda Rashid, *President*
EMP: 99
SALES (est): 2MM **Privately Held**
SIC: 8742 Hospital & health services consultant

(P-27464) HIGH ROAD SPORTS
423 Oconnor Way, San Luis Obispo (93405-7839)
PHONE..................805 545-7940
Bob Stapleton, *Owner*
Kristy Scrymgeour, *Marketing Staff*
Rolf Aldag, *Manager*
Bryanna Baker, *Manager*
Allan Peiper, *Manager*
EMP: 90
SALES (est): 4.3MM **Privately Held**
SIC: 8742 Marketing consulting services

(P-27465) HIS MANNA INC
Also Called: Workforce
150 Felker St Ste B, Santa Cruz (95060-2849)
P.O. Box 1527 (95061-1527)
PHONE..................831 423-5515
Fax: 831 457-3743
Gordon Agrella, *President*
Carolyn Agrella, *Vice Pres*
Sue Belanger, *Executive Asst*
Baisy Alvarez, *Admin Asst*
Jessica Perry, *Financial Exec*
EMP: 200 EST: 1972
SQ FT: 4,200
SALES (est): 13.4MM **Privately Held**
WEB: www.hismanna.com
SIC: 8742 7549 7349 Management consulting services; automotive maintenance services; building maintenance, except repairs

(P-27466) HORIZON ACTUARIAL SERVICES LLC
5200 Lankershim Blvd, North Hollywood (91601-3155)
PHONE..................818 691-2000
Larry H Weitzner,
Mark Lewis, *Owner*
Cary Franklin, *Investment Ofcr*
EMP: 92
SALES (corp-wide): 9.6MM **Privately Held**
SIC: 8742 Compensation & benefits planning consultant
PA: Horizon Actuarial Services Llc
    8601 Georgia Ave Ste 700
    Silver Spring MD 20910
    240 247-4600

(P-27467) HORNBLOWER YACHTS INC
2825 5th Ave, San Diego (92103-6326)
PHONE..................619 234-8687
Fax: 619 686-8733
Jim Unger, *Branch Mgr*
EMP: 160
SALES (corp-wide): 104.6MM **Privately Held**
WEB: www.hornbloweryachts.com
SIC: 8742 7999 7389 7299 Restaurant & food services consultants; pleasure boat rental; convention & show services; wedding chapel, privately operated
PA: Hornblower Yachts, Llc
    On The Embarcadero Pier 3 St Pier
    San Francisco CA 94111
    415 788-8866

(P-27468) HUMBLE HUSTLE INCORPORATED
1101 California Ave # 100, Corona (92881-6470)
PHONE..................951 444-0263
Jonathan Stewart, *CEO*
EMP: 50 EST: 1990

SALES (est): 1MM **Privately Held**
SIC: 8742 Management consulting services

(P-27469) HUMETRIX INC
1155 Camino Del Mar Ste 5, Del Mar (92014-2605)
PHONE..................858 259-8987
Bettina Experton, *President*
Randy Ullrich, *Senior VP*
Claudia M Ellison, *Vice Pres*
Jack Guastaferro, *Exec Dir*
EMP: 50
SALES (est): 4.3MM **Privately Held**
WEB: www.humetrix.com
SIC: 8742 5047 3841 Hospital & health services consultant; medical & hospital equipment; surgical & medical instruments

(P-27470) ICF CONSULTING GROUP INC
101 Lucas Valley Rd # 249, San Rafael (94903-1700)
PHONE..................703 934-3000
Berlin Brett, *Branch Mgr*
EMP: 509
SALES (corp-wide): 1.1B **Publicly Held**
SIC: 8742 Management consulting services
HQ: Icf Consulting Group, Inc.
    9300 Lee Hwy
    Fairfax VA 22031
    703 934-3000

(P-27471) ICF JONES & STOKES INC
1 Ada Ste 100, Irvine (92618-5339)
PHONE..................949 333-6600
David Freytag, *Manager*
EMP: 99
SALES (corp-wide): 1.1B **Publicly Held**
SIC: 8742 8748 Management consulting services; business consulting
HQ: Icf Jones & Stokes, Inc
    630 K St Ste 400
    Sacramento CA 95814
    916 737-3000

(P-27472) INDIGO HOSPITALITY MANAGEMENT
Also Called: Indigo Hotels
1817 N Sepulveda Blvd, Manhattan Beach (90266-2901)
PHONE..................310 787-7795
B C Patel, *President*
Barrett Patel, *Director*
EMP: 50
SALES (est): 2.3MM **Privately Held**
WEB: www.indigohotels.com
SIC: 8742 Real estate consultant

(P-27473) INDVLS
401 Rockefeller B1407, Irvine (92612-7179)
PHONE..................949 339-0575
EMP: 50
SQ FT: 3,000
SALES: 5MM **Privately Held**
SIC: 8742 7311 Marketing consulting services; advertising agencies

(P-27474) INFORMA RESEARCH SERVICES INC (DH)
26565 Agoura Rd Ste 300, Calabasas (91302-1942)
PHONE..................818 880-8877
Michael E Adler, *President*
Charles A Miwa, *COO*
Charles Miwa, *COO*
Lori Jomsky, *Senior VP*
Brian Richards, *Senior VP*
EMP: 193
SQ FT: 16,000
SALES (est): 42.6MM **Privately Held**
WEB: www.informars.com
SIC: 8742 Banking & finance consultant
HQ: Informa Financial Information, Inc.
    1 Research Dr Ste 400a
    Westborough MA 01581
    508 616-5550

(P-27475) INFOTECH GLOBAL SERVICES
Also Called: Infotech Consulting
301 Battery St Fl 2, San Francisco (94111-3237)
PHONE..................415 986-5400
Brad Miller, *Owner*
EMP: 200
SALES: 8MM **Privately Held**
SIC: 8742 Management information systems consultant

(P-27476) INKLING SYSTEMS INC
343 Sansome St 8, San Francisco (94104-1303)
PHONE..................415 975-4420
Matt Macinnis, *CEO*
Rob Cromwell, *President*
Charles Macinnis, *President*
Harper Casimiro, *Admin Asst*
Lilith Wu, *Software Dev*
EMP: 66
SALES (est): 11.4MM **Privately Held**
SIC: 8742 Management consulting services

(P-27477) INNOTAS
111 Sutter St Ste 300, San Francisco (94104-4508)
PHONE..................415 263-9800
Kevin Kern, *President*
Scott McPhail, *President*
John Tingleff, *CFO*
Tim Madewell, *Senior VP*
Cliff McBride, *Senior VP*
EMP: 55
SALES (est): 12.3MM
SALES (corp-wide): 145MM **Privately Held**
SIC: 8742 7371 Management consulting services; computer software development & applications
PA: Planview, Inc.
    12301 Research Blvd 5-100
    Austin TX 78759
    512 346-8600

(P-27478) INNOVATIVE MERCH SOLUTIONS LLC
Also Called: IMS
21215 Burbank Blvd, Woodland Hills (91367-7090)
PHONE..................818 936-7800
Fax: 818 936-7903
Joe Kaplan,
May Judal, *Analyst*
Tim Jochner,
Mark Lowry, *Manager*
EMP: 250 EST: 1999
SQ FT: 50,000
SALES (est): 16.3MM
SALES (corp-wide): 4.6B **Publicly Held**
WEB: www.innovativeclub.com
SIC: 8742 Management consulting services
PA: Intuit Inc.
    2700 Coast Ave
    Mountain View CA 94043
    650 944-6000

(P-27479) INSPERITY INC
1440 Bridgegate Dr # 200, Diamond Bar (91765-3935)
PHONE..................909 569-1000
Fax: 909 569-1305
Richard Cleek, *General Mgr*
Connie Yeh, *Executive*
Janice Morgan, *HR Admin*
EMP: 100
SALES (corp-wide): 2.6B **Publicly Held**
WEB: www.administaff.com
SIC: 8742 Business planning & organizing services
PA: Insperity, Inc.
    19001 Crescent Springs Dr
    Kingwood TX 77339
    281 358-8986

PRODUCTS & SERVICES SECTION
8742 - Management Consulting Services County (P-27502)

(P-27480)
INTER CON SECURITY INC
2801 Camino Del Rio S 300h, San Diego (92108-3800)
PHONE..................619 523-0291
Rick Hernadez, *President*
Jeff Jamison, *Opers Staff*
Jack Schneider, *Supervisor*
EMP: 50
SALES (est): 2.7MM **Privately Held**
WEB: www.interconsecurity.com
SIC: 8742 7381 Industry specialist consultants; security guard service

(P-27481)
INTERNATIONAL BUS MCHS CORP
Also Called: IBM
4000 Executive Pkwy # 300, San Ramon (94583-4257)
PHONE..................925 277-5000
Fax: 925 277-5001
Lynn Dail, *Branch Mgr*
Richard Hernandez, *Branch Mgr*
Richard Sweda, *Analyst*
Jamie Mendez, *Marketing Mgr*
Karin Ball, *Marketing Staff*
EMP: 186
SALES (corp-wide): 81.7B **Publicly Held**
WEB: www.ibm.com
SIC: 8742 Sales (including sales management) consultant
PA: International Business Machines Corporation
    1 New Orchard Rd Ste 1
    Armonk NY 10504
    914 499-1900

(P-27482)
INTERNET MARKETING ASSN INC
10 Mar Del Rey, San Clemente (92673-2761)
PHONE..................949 443-9300
Sinan Kanatsiz, *Principal*
EMP: 72
SALES (est): 4.7MM **Privately Held**
SIC: 8742 Management consulting services

(P-27483)
INTERSTATE ELECTRONICS CORP
Also Called: Human Resources
708 E Vermont Ave, Anaheim (92805-5611)
PHONE..................714 758-0500
EMP: 600
SALES (corp-wide): 10.4B **Publicly Held**
SIC: 8742 Human resource consulting services
HQ: Interstate Electronics Corporation
    602 E Vermont Ave
    Anaheim CA 92805
    714 758-0500

(P-27484)
INTRAVAS INC
Also Called: Review Boost
5840 El Camino Real, Carlsbad (92008-8851)
PHONE..................760 650-4040
Guillermo Rivas, *CEO*
EMP: 65
SALES (est): 3.7MM **Privately Held**
SIC: 8742 Management consulting services

(P-27485)
IRVINE TECHNOLOGY CORPORATION
17900 Von Karman Ave # 100, Irvine (92614-6249)
PHONE..................714 445-2624
Fax: 714 434-8869
John Thornby, *President*
Mike Rose, *Treasurer*
Kevin Orlando, *Vice Pres*
Colin Crane, *Tech Recruiter*
Amanda Pierce, *Human Res Mgr*
EMP: 400 EST: 2000
SQ FT: 8,000
SALES (est): 45.2MM **Privately Held**
WEB: www.irvinetechcorp.com
SIC: 8742 Management consulting services

(P-27486)
ISYS SOLUTIONS INC
2601 Saturn St Ste 302, Brea (92821-6702)
PHONE..................714 521-7656
Fax: 714 521-7820
Chris Loumakis, *CEO*
Joseph Archibald, *Supervisor*
EMP: 69
SALES (est): 11.3MM **Privately Held**
WEB: www.isyscal.com
SIC: 8742 Hospital & health services consultant

(P-27487)
ITA GROUP INC
350 Sansome St, San Francisco (94104-1304)
PHONE..................415 277-3200
Deborah Ebsen, *General Mgr*
EMP: 119
SALES (corp-wide): 155MM **Privately Held**
SIC: 8742 Incentive or award program consultant
PA: Ita Group, Inc
    4600 Westown Pkwy Ste 100
    West Des Moines IA 50266
    515 326-3400

(P-27488)
J P CONSULTING
4690 E 2nd St Ste 3, Benicia (94510-1008)
PHONE..................707 747-4800
Jody Hoberson, *Co-Owner*
Robert Perkey, *Co-Owner*
EMP: 50
SALES (est): 3.6MM **Privately Held**
SIC: 8742 Management consulting services

(P-27489)
JACK NADEL INC (PA)
Also Called: Jack Nadel International
8701 Bellanca Ave, Los Angeles (90045-4411)
P.O. Box 8342, Pasadena (91109-8342)
PHONE..................310 815-2600
Fax: 310 839-9486
Craig Nadel, *CEO*
Jann Jaskol, *COO*
Robert Kritzler, *CFO*
Jack Nadel, *Chairman*
Debbie Abergel, *Senior VP*
EMP: 70
SQ FT: 30,000
SALES (est): 91.4MM **Privately Held**
WEB: www.nadel.com
SIC: 8742 5199 Incentive or award program consultant; gifts & novelties

(P-27490)
JACOBS CENTER FOR NGHBRHOOD (PA)
404 Euclid Ave Ste 101, San Diego (92114-2200)
PHONE..................619 527-6161
Fax: 619 527-6162
Reginald Jones, *President*
Susan Halliday, *CFO*
Leilani A Rasmussen, *CFO*
Norm Hapke, *Chairman*
Elenore Garton, *Vice Pres*
EMP: 60
SQ FT: 30,000
SALES: 10.8MM **Privately Held**
WEB: www.jacobscenter.org
SIC: 8742 Management consulting services

(P-27491)
JACOBS PROJECT MANAGEMENT CO
300 Frank H Ogawa Plz, Oakland (94612-2037)
PHONE..................510 457-2436
Steve Paquette, *Manager*
Frank Joyce, *Contract Mgr*
EMP: 95
SALES (est): 3.5MM
SALES (corp-wide): 12.1B **Publicly Held**
SIC: 8742 Management consulting services

PA: Jacobs Engineering Group Inc.
    155 N Lake Ave
    Pasadena CA 91101
    626 578-3500

(P-27492)
JACOBUS CONSULTING INC
15375 Barranca Pkwy B202, Irvine (92618-2213)
PHONE..................949 713-2101
Sandra Jacobs, *President*
Gayle Consiglio, *Vice Pres*
Alan Hall, *Vice Pres*
Matt Kopp, *Vice Pres*
Arizdelsy Vega, *Executive Asst*
EMP: 50
SQ FT: 1,800
SALES (est): 7.9MM **Privately Held**
SIC: 8742 Management consulting services

(P-27493)
JB UPLAND LTD LIABILITY CO
9087 Arrow Rte Ste 140, Rancho Cucamonga (91730-4431)
PHONE..................909 944-5456
Mary R McDonagh,
EMP: 50
SALES (est): 2.4MM **Privately Held**
SIC: 8742 Marketing consulting services

(P-27494)
JNR INC
19900 Macarthur Blvd # 700, Irvine (92612-8416)
PHONE..................949 476-2788
Fax: 949 955-3825
James Jalet III, *CEO*
Luann Jalet, *COO*
Greg Moody, *CFO*
Matt Kisser, *Plan/Corp Dev D*
Jenna Paseka, *Planning Mgr*
EMP: 60
SQ FT: 15,000
SALES (est): 10.3MM **Privately Held**
WEB: www.jnrinc.com
SIC: 8742 7389 4724 Incentive or award program consultant; convention & show services; tourist agency arranging transport, lodging & car rental

(P-27495)
JOBVITE INC
1300 S El Camino Real # 400, San Mateo (94402-2970)
PHONE..................650 376-7200
Dan Finnigan, *CEO*
Charles Stryker, *President*
Peter Maloney, *CFO*
Andy Priest, *Ch Credit Ofcr*
Kimberley Kasper, *Chief Mktg Ofcr*
EMP: 100
SALES (est): 15.9MM **Privately Held**
SIC: 8742 Human resource consulting services

(P-27496)
K & S TOWING & TRANSPORT
Also Called: K & S Auto, Truck & Tractor
2780 Willow Pass Rd, Bay Point (94565-6603)
PHONE..................925 709-0759
Khurram Shah, *Owner*
Bashir Shah, *Office Mgr*
EMP: 55
SQ FT: 10,000
SALES: 5.6MM **Privately Held**
WEB: www.kandstowing.com
SIC: 8742 7299 Transportation consultant; personal item care & storage services

(P-27497)
KABLER CONSTRUCTION SVCS INC
467 Miller Ave, Mill Valley (94941-2941)
PHONE..................415 888-8812
Sophia Kabler Cowley, *President*
John Kabler, *Vice Pres*
EMP: 50
SALES: 536K **Privately Held**
SIC: 8742 1771 8741 Construction project management consultant; concrete work; construction management

(P-27498)
KASPICK & CO LLC (HQ)
203 Redwood Shores Pkwy # 300, Redwood City (94065-6121)
PHONE..................650 585-4100
Fax: 650 595-1400
Thomas Grenville, *Officer*
Warwick Stirling, *Vice Pres*
Lindy Sherwood, *Managing Dir*
Casey Yeh, *Program Mgr*
Dwnell Testa, *Admin Mgr*
EMP: 54
SALES (est): 7.8MM
SALES (corp-wide): 10.4B **Privately Held**
WEB: www.kaspick.com
SIC: 8742 Financial consultant
PA: Teachers Insurance And Annuity Association-College Retirement Equities Fund
    730 3rd Ave Ste 2a
    New York NY 10017
    212 490-9000

(P-27499)
KENSHOO INC
22 4th St Fl 7, San Francisco (94103-3141)
PHONE..................877 536-7462
Yoav Izhar-Prato, *CEO*
Shirley Grill-Rachman, *COO*
Sarit Firon, *CFO*
Igal Shany, *CFO*
Ted Krantz, *Senior VP*
EMP: 110
SALES (est): 22.5MM **Privately Held**
SIC: 8742 Management consulting services
PA: Kenshoo Ltd
    6 Habarzel
    Tel Aviv-Jaffa
    503 335-115

(P-27500)
KETCHUM SHEPPARD INC
340 Main St 100, Venice (90291-2524)
PHONE..................310 584-8300
Sean Fitzgerald, *CEO*
Terry McKenzie, *President*
Barbara Standke, *Exec VP*
Susan Wendell, *Senior VP*
Millie Delgado, *MIS Dir*
EMP: 50
SQ FT: 18,500
SALES (est): 3.1MM
SALES (corp-wide): 15.1B **Publicly Held**
WEB: www.ketchum.com
SIC: 8742 Compensation & benefits planning consultant; business consultant; marketing consulting services
HQ: Ketchum Inc.
    1285 Avenue Of The Americ
    New York NY 10019
    646 935-3900

(P-27501)
KORN/FERRY INTERNATIONAL (PA)
Also Called: KORN FERRY
1900 Avenue Stars, Los Angeles (90067)
PHONE..................310 552-1834
Fax: 310 553-6452
Gary D Burnison, *President*
George T Shaheen, *Ch of Bd*
Melanie Kusin, *Vice Chairman*
Stephen Kaye, *CEO*
Byrne Mulrooney, *CEO*
EMP: 109 EST: 1969
SALES: 1.3B **Publicly Held**
WEB: www.kornferry.com
SIC: 8742 7361 Management consulting services; executive placement

(P-27502)
KYRIBA CORP (HQ)
9620 Towne Cntre Dr 200, San Diego (92121)
PHONE..................858 210-3560
Fax: 858 210-3561
Jean-Luc Robert, *CEO*
Didier Martineau, *COO*
Fabrice Lvy, *CFO*
Gene Lynes, *CFO*
Julie Roy, *Chief Mktg Ofcr*
EMP: 50

8742 - Management Consulting Services County (P-27503)

SALES (est): 39.6MM
SALES (corp-wide): 18.8MM Privately Held
WEB: www.kyriba.com
SIC: 8742 Financial consultant

(P-27503)
LABMED PARTNERS
5000 Birch St, Newport Beach (92660-2127)
PHONE.....................949 242-9925
Mohamad Elmannan, President
Andrew Doyle, Vice Pres
EMP: 50
SALES (est): 1.1MM Privately Held
SIC: 8742 Hospital & health services consultant

(P-27504)
LANCASHIRE GROUP INCORPORATED
Also Called: Tlg
37053 Cherry St Ste 210, Newark (94560-3782)
P.O. Box 1138 (94560-6138)
PHONE.....................510 792-9384
Ian McDonnell, President
John Cerelli, CFO
John Lambert, Senior VP
Rosie Abigana, Office Mgr
EMP: 279
SQ FT: 2,400
SALES (est): 25.4MM Privately Held
WEB: www.tlg-inc.com
SIC: 8742 Industry specialist consultants

(P-27505)
LEEKILPATRICK MANAGEMENT INC
Also Called: Management Success
412 W Broadway Fl 3, Glendale (91204-1297)
PHONE.....................818 500-9631
Fax: 818 552-1006
Bill Kilpatrick, President
EMP: 60
SQ FT: 18,200
SALES (est): 6.8MM Privately Held
SIC: 8742 7538 Management consulting services; general automotive repair shops

(P-27506)
LEGACY MARKETING GROUP (PA)
2090 Marina Ave, Petaluma (94954-6714)
PHONE.....................707 778-8638
Lynda R Pitts, CEO
Preston Pitts, President
Chris Eaken, Vice Pres
Dayna Wells, Vice Pres
Lynda Regan, Executive
EMP: 215
SALES (est): 13.9MM Privately Held
WEB: www.legacynet.com
SIC: 8742 Marketing consulting services

(P-27507)
LEK CONSULTING LLC
1100 Glendon Ave Ste 2100, Los Angeles (90024-3592)
PHONE.....................310 209-9800
Fax: 310 209-9125
Sherice Lenons, Manager
Manny Picciola, Vice Pres
Chelsey Kobuch, Admin Asst
Laura Kotzeff, Director
Dan Horsley, Manager
EMP: 60
SALES (corp-wide): 69.3MM Privately Held
WEB: www.lek.com
SIC: 8742 8748 Business consultant; business consulting
PA: L.E.K. Consulting, Llc
75 State St Ste 1901
Boston MA 02109
617 737-1725

(P-27508)
LEVEL STUDIOS INC (DH)
4800 Morabito Pl, San Luis Obispo (93401-8748)
PHONE.....................805 781-0546
Tom Adamski, CEO
Dan Connolly, President

Paul Rappoport, COO
Alexander Mahernia, Ch Credit Ofcr
Michael Phillips, Senior VP
EMP: 110
SQ FT: 12,000
SALES (est): 22.3MM
SALES (corp-wide): 65.7MM Privately Held
WEB: www.webassociates.com
SIC: 8742 Marketing consulting services
HQ: Rosetta Llc
100 American Metro Blvd # 201
Hamilton NJ 08619
609 689-6100

(P-27509)
LEVITY ENTERTAINMENT GROUP LLC
Also Called: L E G
6701 Center Dr W Fl 11, Los Angeles (90045-1535)
PHONE.....................310 417-4861
Robert Hartmann, Mng Member
Stuart Schreiberg, Mng Member
Roddy Swearngin, Director
EMP: 50 EST: 2009
SALES (est): 5.5MM Privately Held
SIC: 8742 Personnel management consultant

(P-27510)
LOS ANGELES FREE CLINIC (PA)
Also Called: SABAN COMMUNITY CLINIC
8405 Beverly Blvd, Los Angeles (90048-3401)
PHONE.....................323 653-8622
Fax: 323 651-5026
Jeffrey Bujer, CEO
Shannon Cisch, COO
Muriel Nouwezem, CFO
Eric Jung, Treasurer
Johni Robinson, Officer
EMP: 79
SQ FT: 26,615
SALES (est): 17.4MM Privately Held
SIC: 8742 Management consulting services

(P-27511)
LOS ANGELES GUILD LLC
Also Called: Guild, The
3437 W El Segundo Blvd, Hawthorne (90250-4816)
PHONE.....................323 733-5033
Peter Brown,
Sam Ewan,
Jeffrey Hatfield,
EMP: 201 EST: 2007
SALES (est): 24.6MM Privately Held
SIC: 8742 7319 Marketing consulting services; display advertising service

(P-27512)
LOS ANGELES CLIPPERS FOUNDATION
Also Called: Lac Club
1111 S Figueroa St # 1100, Los Angeles (90015-1300)
PHONE.....................213 742-7555
Fax: 213 742-7570
Donald Sterling, President
Zachary Gano, Accounts Exec
EMP: 55
SALES (est): 1.3MM Privately Held
SIC: 8742 Sales (including sales management) consultant

(P-27513)
LOTUS INTERWORKS INC
10801 National Blvd # 500, Los Angeles (90064-4152)
PHONE.....................310 442-3330
Bhaskarpilai Gopinath, Ch of Bd
April Hall, General Mgr
Valerie Trejill, Accountant
EMP: 200
SQ FT: 10,000
SALES (est): 13.3MM Privately Held
WEB: www.lotusinterworks.com
SIC: 8742 Management consulting services

(P-27514)
LUCKY PACIFIC LLC
2000 Broadway St 102, Redwood City (94063-1802)
PHONE.....................650 330-0263
Doug Karlson,
Reid Behrendt, Managing Dir
EMP: 50
SALES (est): 3.4MM Privately Held
SIC: 8742 Marketing consulting services

(P-27515)
LWI FINANCIAL INC
Also Called: Loring Ward
10 Almaden Blvd, San Jose (95113-2226)
PHONE.....................408 217-8886
Steven Atkinson, Vice Pres
Steve Ncginnis, Exec VP
Vincent J Crivello, Vice Pres
Jennifer Yee, Executive Asst
EMP: 108
SQ FT: 40,000
SALES (est): 5.9MM Privately Held
SIC: 8742 Financial consultant

(P-27516)
LYNUP CORPORATION
16875 W Bernardo Dr # 110, San Diego (92127-1670)
PHONE.....................858 207-4610
Parvin Garbo-Inkumsah, President
Aaron J Gaeir, Vice Pres
Mike Matamala, Director
EMP: 60 EST: 2010
SALES (est): 5.7MM Privately Held
SIC: 8742 Marketing consulting services

(P-27517)
M E NOLLKAMPER INC (PA)
940 Manor Way, Corona (92882-7979)
PHONE.....................951 737-9300
Milton Nollkamper, President
EMP: 50
SALES (est): 3MM Privately Held
SIC: 8742 8711 Public utilities consultant; consulting engineer

(P-27518)
M F SALTA CO INC (PA)
Also Called: Atlas Advertising
20 Executive Park Ste 150, Irvine (92614-4732)
PHONE.....................562 421-2512
Mike Salta, President
James Smith, Treasurer
EMP: 70
SALES (est): 3.6MM Privately Held
SIC: 8742 Management consulting services

(P-27519)
MACDONALD-BEDFORD LLC
2100 Embarcadero, Oakland (94606-5302)
PHONE.....................510 436-4020
Daniel Herrera, Principal
EMP: 54
SALES (corp-wide): 8.9MM Privately Held
SIC: 8742 Management consulting services
PA: Macdonald-Bedford Llc
2900 Main St Ste 200
Alameda CA 94501
510 521-4020

(P-27520)
MALCO SERVICES INC
3703 E Melville Way, Anaheim (92806-2122)
PHONE.....................714 630-0194
Duane Malone, President
EMP: 100
SQ FT: 15,831
SALES (est): 4MM Privately Held
SIC: 8742 Maintenance management consultant

(P-27521)
MANAGEMENT TRUST ASSN INC
12607 Hiddencreek Way R, Cerritos (90703-2146)
PHONE.....................562 926-3372
Christie Alviso, Administration
EMP: 100

SALES (corp-wide): 135MM Privately Held
SIC: 8742 8741 Management consulting services; business management
PA: The Management Trust Association Inc
15661 Red Hill Ave # 201
Tustin CA 92780
714 285-2626

(P-27522)
MANSION HOSPITALITY SERVICES
3410 Westover St, McClellan (95652-1005)
PHONE.....................916 643-6222
Russell A Dazzio, Chairman
Roland Moritz, Corp Secy
EMP: 60
SALES (est): 2.3MM Privately Held
SIC: 8742 Management consulting services

(P-27523)
MARKET MOTIVE
10 Victor Sq Ste 250, Scotts Valley (95066-3562)
PHONE.....................831 706-2369
Michael Stebbins, CEO
Patrick James, Opers Mgr
Chip Street, Marketing Mgr
Barbara Young, Marketing Mgr
Kim Nadeau, Director
EMP: 246
SALES (est): 381.3K
SALES (corp-wide): 6.1MM Privately Held
SIC: 8742 Training & development consultant
PA: Simplilearn Americas Llc
10685 Hazelhurst Dr Ste B
Houston TX 77043
281 881-8180

(P-27524)
MARKETING PROFESSIONALS INC
5100 E La Palma Ave # 116, Anaheim (92807-2081)
PHONE.....................714 578-0500
Joseph L Smith, President
Cynthia A Simms, CFO
George M Schnitzer, Chairman
EMP: 350
SQ FT: 900
SALES (est): 18.5MM Privately Held
WEB: www.marketingprofessionals.org
SIC: 8742 7319 Marketing consulting services; retail trade consultant; display advertising services

(P-27525)
MARS & CO CONSULTING LLC
600 Montgomery St # 4200, San Francisco (94111-2801)
PHONE.....................415 288-6970
Dominique Mars, Manager
EMP: 188
SALES (corp-wide): 21.9MM Privately Held
SIC: 8742 Management consulting services
PA: Mars & Co. Consulting Llc
124 Mason St Ste 1
Greenwich CT 06830
203 862-5200

(P-27526)
MATERIALS MARKETING
250 Baker St E Ste 100, Costa Mesa (92626-4574)
PHONE.....................949 729-9881
John Cina, Manager
EMP: 100
SALES (est): 4.9MM Privately Held
SIC: 8742 Marketing consulting services

(P-27527)
MATT CONSTRUCTION CORPORATION (PA)
9814 Norwalk Blvd Ste 100, Santa Fe Springs (90670-2997)
PHONE.....................562 903-2277
Paul J Matt, CEO
Steve F Matt, President
Alan B Matt, Corp Secy
Kenneth Blakeley, Senior VP

PRODUCTS & SERVICES SECTION
8742 - Management Consulting Services County (P-27548)

Michael Fedorchek, *Vice Pres*
EMP: 131
SQ FT: 21,000
SALES (est): 39.9MM **Privately Held**
WEB: www.mattconstruction.com
SIC: 8742 Construction project management consultant

(P-27528)
MAXIMUS INC
Also Called: Maximus CA Healthy Family
625 Coolidge Dr Ste 100, Folsom (95630-3197)
PHONE.................916 673-2175
John Antifino, *Principal*
Jon Lemelin, *Vice Pres*
Susan Norris, *Vice Pres*
Jerry Musheno, *Project Dir*
Awilda Martinez, *Project Mgr*
EMP: 70
SALES (corp-wide): 2.1B **Publicly Held**
WEB: www.maxinc.com
SIC: 8742 Management consulting services
PA: Maximus, Inc.
1891 Metro Center Dr
Reston VA 20190
703 251-8500

(P-27529)
MAXIMUS INC
625 Coolidge Dr Ste 100, Folsom (95630-3197)
PHONE.................916 673-4162
Michael Lemburg, *Manager*
EMP: 50
SALES (corp-wide): 2.1B **Publicly Held**
WEB: www.maxinc.com
SIC: 8742 Management consulting services
PA: Maximus, Inc.
1891 Metro Center Dr
Reston VA 20190
703 251-8500

(P-27530)
MAXWELL PETERSEN ASSOCIATES
Also Called: Dynamic Chiropractic
13950 Milton Ave Ste 200, Westminster (92683-2939)
PHONE.................714 230-3150
Fax: 714 899-4273
Donald M Petersen, *President*
Gabrielle Lindsley, *Business Mgr*
Evelyn Petersen, *Payroll Mgr*
Michael Robins, *Sales Mgr*
Betsey Montague, *Marketing Staff*
EMP: 50
SQ FT: 2,000
SALES (est): 5.4MM **Privately Held**
WEB: www.mpamedia.com
SIC: 8742 Business consultant

(P-27531)
MCB-CJS LLC
5312 Bolsa Ave, Huntington Beach (92649-1051)
PHONE.................714 230-3600
Joan Heid, *Partner*
Chet Seto, *Partner*
David Dowell, *Finance*
EMP: 99 EST: 2013
SQ FT: 70,000
SALES (est): 2.9MM **Privately Held**
SIC: 8742 Management consulting services

(P-27532)
MCCLELLAN BUSINESS PARK LLC
Also Called: Mp Holdings
3140 Peacekeeper Way, McClellan (95652-2508)
PHONE.................916 965-7100
Larry Kelley, *President*
Jay Hecklively, *Exec VP*
Debra Compton, *Senior VP*
Ken Giannotti, *Senior VP*
Alan Hersh, *Senior VP*
EMP: 99 EST: 1999
SQ FT: 22,000
SALES (est): 19.8MM **Privately Held**
WEB: www.mcclellanpark.com
SIC: 8742 Real estate consultant

(P-27533)
MCKINSEY & COMPANY INC
2000 Avenue Of The Stars # 800, Los Angeles (90067-4714)
PHONE.................424 249-1000
John Durat, *General Mgr*
Cynthia Liu, *Business Anlyst*
Joseph Percoco, *Business Anlyst*
Paul Brownkenyon, *Clerk*
Ashwin Rajendra, *Associate*
EMP: 50
SALES (corp-wide): 3.4B **Privately Held**
WEB: www.mckinsey.com
SIC: 8742 Management consulting services
PA: Mckinsey & Company, Inc.
55 E 52nd St Fl 21
New York NY 10055
212 446-7000

(P-27534)
MCKINSEY & COMPANY INC
555 California St # 4800, San Francisco (94104-1779)
PHONE.................415 981-0250
Fax: 415 954-5200
Gary Pinkus, *Manager*
Ann Lightbody, *Admin Asst*
Debbie Maley, *Human Res Mgr*
Robert Kaplan, *Director*
Roberta Casey, *Manager*
EMP: 300
SALES (corp-wide): 3.4B **Privately Held**
WEB: www.mckinsey.com
SIC: 8742 Management consulting services
PA: Mckinsey & Company, Inc.
55 E 52nd St Fl 21
New York NY 10055
212 446-7000

(P-27535)
MCKINSEY & COMPANY INC
3075 Hansen Way Bldg A, Palo Alto (94304-1025)
PHONE.................650 494-6262
Fax: 650 842-5800
Jon Duane, *Manager*
Kristina Colangelo, *Executive Asst*
Gail Gohsman, *Executive Asst*
Melody Radmacher, *Admin Asst*
Kelly Kramer, *Info Tech Mgr*
EMP: 75
SALES (corp-wide): 3.4B **Privately Held**
WEB: www.mckinsey.com
SIC: 8742 Management consulting services
PA: Mckinsey & Company, Inc.
55 E 52nd St Fl 21
New York NY 10055
212 446-7000

(P-27536)
MEDICAL MANAGEMENT CONS INC
Also Called: MMC
6046 Cornerstone Ct W, San Diego (92121-4758)
PHONE.................858 587-0609
Rahmani, *Manager*
EMP: 4950
SALES (corp-wide): 71.4MM **Privately Held**
WEB: www.mmchr.com
SIC: 8742 Hospital & health services consultant
PA: Medical Management Consultants, Inc.
8150 Beverly Blvd
Los Angeles CA 90048
310 659-3835

(P-27537)
MEDICAL RECEIVABLES SOLUTIONS
Also Called: M R S
101 W American Canyon Rd, American Canyon (94503-1162)
PHONE.................707 980-6733
Aleshia L Hunter, *President*
EMP: 50
SALES (est): 7.2MM **Privately Held**
SIC: 8742 Business consultant

(P-27538)
MEDICAL SPECIALTIES MANAGERS
Also Called: Medical Specialty Billing
1 City Blvd W Ste 1100, Orange (92868-3647)
PHONE.................714 571-5000
Barry Haberman, *President*
Uri Klugman, *CFO*
Mark Kelly, *Bd of Directors*
Randy Brooks, *Vice Pres*
David Hertzgaard, *Vice Pres*
EMP: 115
SQ FT: 29,000
SALES (est): 19.1MM **Privately Held**
WEB: www.msmnet.com
SIC: 8742 8721 Hospital & health services consultant; billing & bookkeeping service

(P-27539)
MEDPHARM COMMUNICATIONS
1734 Caminito Ardiente, La Jolla (92037-7134)
PHONE.................858 412-6848
Dr Marc Henis, *President*
EMP: 60
SALES (est): 2.3MM **Privately Held**
SIC: 8742 Hospital & health services consultant

(P-27540)
MEDSPHERE SYSTEMS CORPORATION (PA)
1903 Wright Pl Ste 120, Carlsbad (92008-6584)
PHONE.................760 692-3700
Irv Lichtenwald, *CEO*
Kenneth W Kizer, *Ch of Bd*
Irv H Lichtenwald, *CEO*
Edmund Billings, *Vice Pres*
Bobbie Peterson, *Vice Pres*
EMP: 96
SALES (est): 20.5MM **Privately Held**
WEB: www.medsphere.com
SIC: 8742 Hospital & health services consultant

(P-27541)
MELTWATER NEWS US INC (DH)
225 Bush St Ste 1000, San Francisco (94104-4218)
PHONE.................415 829-5900
Fax: 415 829-5936
Jorn Lyseggen, *CEO*
Martin Hernandez, *CFO*
Niklas De Besche, *Exec Dir*
Paal Larsen, *Exec Dir*
Kevin Lorenz, *Exec Dir*
EMP: 54
SALES (est): 43.2MM
SALES (corp-wide): 87.9MM **Privately Held**
SIC: 8742 Marketing consulting services
HQ: Meltwater Us Holdings Inc.
225 Bush St Ste 1000
San Francisco CA 94104
415 236-3144

(P-27542)
MERCER (US) INC
777 S Figueroa St # 2000190, Los Angeles (90017-5800)
PHONE.................213 346-2200
Fax: 213 346-2680
Nancy McLean, *Manager*
Steve Pastore, *Office Mgr*
Elizabeth Dill, *Investment Ofcr*
Roy Kudla, *Finance*
Amy Kawabori, *Sr Associate*
EMP: 200
SALES (corp-wide): 12.8B **Publicly Held**
SIC: 8742 Human resource consulting services
HQ: Mercer (Us) Inc.
1166 Ave Of The Americ
New York NY 10036
212 345-7000

(P-27543)
MERCER (US) INC
4 Embarcadero Ctr Fl 4, San Francisco (94111-4156)
PHONE.................415 743-8700
Jerry Murphy, *Manager*
Neal Murphy, *Senior VP*
Christopher Pease, *Senior VP*
Andrea Gargan, *Vice Pres*
Susan Snow, *Mng Officer*
EMP: 250
SALES (corp-wide): 12.8B **Publicly Held**
SIC: 8742 Compensation & benefits planning consultant
HQ: Mercer (Us) Inc.
1166 Ave Of The Americ
New York NY 10036
212 345-7000

(P-27544)
MERCER (US) INC
Also Called: Mercer Consulting
17901 Von Karman Ave # 1100, Irvine (92614-6297)
PHONE.................949 222-1300
Kathy Spear, *Manager*
Longiaotti Chuck, *Exec VP*
Bubphawadee Oy, *Managing Dir*
Krzysztof Nowak, *Info Tech Dir*
Corrina Rygalski, *Engineer*
EMP: 100
SALES (corp-wide): 12.8B **Publicly Held**
SIC: 8742 Compensation & benefits planning consultant; personnel management consultant
HQ: Mercer (Us) Inc.
1166 Ave Of The Americ
New York NY 10036
212 345-7000

(P-27545)
MERCER HEALTH & BENEFITS LLC
3 Embarcadero Ctr, San Francisco (94111-4003)
PHONE.................415 743-8751
Susan Snow, *Principal*
Jerry Murphy, *Manager*
EMP: 99
SALES (corp-wide): 12.8B **Publicly Held**
SIC: 8742 Human resource consulting services
HQ: Mercer Health & Benefits Llc
1166 Ave Of The Americas
New York NY 10036
212 345-7000

(P-27546)
MERIT TECHNOLOGIES LLC
Also Called: MTI
10509 Vista Sorrento Pkwy # 100, San Diego (92121-2743)
PHONE.................858 623-9800
Donald Wang PHD, *Mng Member*
Mabel Uyeda, *Project Mgr*
Steeve Higgins, *Controller*
EMP: 60
SQ FT: 2,000
SALES (est): 4MM **Privately Held**
SIC: 8742 Construction project management consultant

(P-27547)
METRON INCORPORATED
12250 El Camino Real # 260, San Diego (92130-2226)
PHONE.................858 792-8904
Sam Brown, *Branch Mgr*
EMP: 50
SALES (corp-wide): 39.9MM **Privately Held**
SIC: 8742 8731 8733 8711 Management consulting services; commercial physical research; scientific research agency; engineering services
PA: Metron, Incorporated
1818 Library St Ste 600
Reston VA 20190
703 467-5641

(P-27548)
MF SERVICES COMPANY LLC (HQ)
4350 Von Karman Ave # 400, Newport Beach (92660-2007)
PHONE.................949 474-5800
Paul Merage, *Mng Member*
Jared Klumker, *Controller*
Jenni Weinard, *Cust Svc Mgr*
Richard Merage,
EMP: 60

8742 - Management Consulting Services County (P-27549)

PRODUDUCTS & SERVICES SECTION

SALES (est): 3MM
SALES (corp-wide): 133.7K **Privately Held**
SIC: 8742 Financial consultant
PA: Mig Capital, Llc
660 Newport Center Dr # 1300
Newport Beach CA 92660
949 474-5800

(P-27549)
MICHAELSON CONNOR & BOUL (PA)
5312 Bolsa Ave Ste 200, Huntington Beach (92649-1062)
PHONE.................714 846-6099
Joan Heid, *President*
Firmin Boul, *Corp Secy*
Pam Santos, *Senior VP*
Michael Ryan, *Vice Pres*
Dan Boul, *CTO*
EMP: 100
SQ FT: 12,500
SALES (est): 20.4MM **Privately Held**
WEB: www.mcbreo.com
SIC: 8742 Real estate consultant

(P-27550)
MILLENNIA HOLDINGS INC
Also Called: Mellennia Holdings
3731 Wilshire Blvd # 618, Los Angeles (90010-2876)
PHONE.................213 252-1230
Fax: 213 252-1235
Hiroki Tarui, *CEO*
Eric Chen, *CFO*
Chugo Rionie, *CFO*
Yumiko Pardi, *Human Resources*
EMP: 60
SALES (est): 8.4MM **Privately Held**
WEB: www.mhiholdings.com
SIC: 8742 Management consulting services

(P-27551)
MLSLISTINGS INC
Also Called: RE Infolink
350 Oakmead Pkwy Ste 200, Sunnyvale (94085-5423)
PHONE.................408 874-0200
Gerald J Harrison, *President*
Jan Bruce, *Executive Asst*
Carol Martin, *Admin Asst*
Robert Bustamante, *Info Tech Mgr*
Archana Bajracharya, *Software Engr*
EMP: 58 EST: 2007
SALES: 14MM **Privately Held**
SIC: 8742 Real estate consultant

(P-27552)
MONITOR COMPANY GROUP GP LLC
555 Mission St Ste 1400, San Francisco (94105-0942)
PHONE.................415 932-5300
Fax: 415 278-5800
Pepe Govender, *Branch Mgr*
Rebecca Brian, *Consultant*
Gabriel Kasper, *Consultant*
EMP: 140
SALES (corp-wide): 9.5B **Privately Held**
SIC: 8742 Management information systems consultant
HQ: Monitor Company Group Gp Llc
140 Bradford Dr Ste A
West Berlin NJ 08091

(P-27553)
MUNISERVICES LLC (HQ)
7625 N Palm Ave Ste 108, Fresno (93711-5785)
PHONE.................800 800-8181
Marc Herman, *President*
Brenda Narayan, *Chief Mktg Ofcr*
Randy Dryden, *Vice Pres*
Hannes Leifsson, *Info Tech Mgr*
Kevin Stocks, *Info Tech Mgr*
EMP: 113
SQ FT: 16,000
SALES (est): 11.7MM
SALES (corp-wide): 942MM **Publicly Held**
WEB: www.muniservices.com
SIC: 8742 Industry specialist consultants

PA: Pra Group, Inc.
120 Corporate Blvd # 100
Norfolk VA 23502
888 772-7326

(P-27554)
MV MEDICAL MANAGEMENT
1860 Colo Blvd Ste 200, Los Angeles (90041)
PHONE.................323 257-7637
Fax: 323 257-7329
Eva Vargas, *President*
Daniel E Vargas Jr, *COO*
Alma Moreno, *Treasurer*
Evy Vargas, *Admin Sec*
Margaret Shao, *Administration*
EMP: 60
SQ FT: 7,400
SALES (est): 8.9MM **Privately Held**
WEB: www.mvmedical.com
SIC: 8742 Management consulting services

(P-27555)
MW2 CONSULTING LLC
981 Manor Way, Los Altos (94024-5622)
PHONE.................408 573-6310
Fax: 408 773-8455
Michael Morris,
Yuliya Vlasova, *Opers Mgr*
Alice Harmon,
Uwe Wienkauf,
EMP: 85
SQ FT: 5,700
SALES (est): 5.1MM **Privately Held**
WEB: www.mw2consulting.com
SIC: 8742 Management consulting services

(P-27556)
N COMPASS INTERNATIONAL INC
Also Called: Ncompass International
8223 Santa Monica Blvd, West Hollywood (90046-5912)
PHONE.................323 785-1700
Fax: 323 785-1701
Donna Direnzo Graves, *CEO*
Kae Erickson, *COO*
Matt Mayer, *Vice Pres*
Michaela McCoy, *Vice Pres*
Aaron Miller, *Vice Pres*
EMP: 138
SQ FT: 20,000
SALES: 37.7MM **Privately Held**
WEB: www.ncompassinternational.com
SIC: 8742 Marketing consulting services

(P-27557)
NAN MCKAY AND ASSOCIATES INC
1810 Gillespie Way # 202, El Cajon (92020-0920)
PHONE.................619 258-1855
Fax: 619 258-5791
Nan McKay, *President*
John McKay, *CEO*
Raymond Adair, *Vice Pres*
Dorian Jenkins, *Vice Pres*
James McKay, *Vice Pres*
EMP: 58
SQ FT: 14,000
SALES: 29.7MM **Privately Held**
WEB: www.nanmckay.com
SIC: 8742 7371 2731 Training & development consultant; computer software development; textbooks: publishing & printing

(P-27558)
NATIONAL EMPLOYEE BENEFITS LLC
3200 E Guasti Rd Ste 100, Ontario (91761-8661)
PHONE.................877 778-8330
Cheryl Gollnick, *Mng Member*
EMP: 208
SALES (est): 10.7MM **Privately Held**
WEB: www.manageyouremployees.com
SIC: 8742 Compensation & benefits planning consultant

(P-27559)
NATIONAL FNCL SRVCS CNSRTM LLC
3161 Los Prados St, San Mateo (94403-2013)
PHONE.................650 572-2872
Tony Quintero,
EMP: 99
SALES (est): 2.6MM **Privately Held**
SIC: 8742 Management consulting services

(P-27560)
NAVIGANT CONSULTING INC
300 S Grand Ave Ste 3850, Los Angeles (90071-3174)
PHONE.................213 452-4516
Fax: 818 670-3250
Mike Wallace, *Vice Pres*
Angela Sabbe, *Associate Dir*
Amy H Workman, *CPA*
Benjamin WEI, *Director*
EMP: 100
SALES (corp-wide): 919.4MM **Publicly Held**
WEB: www.navigantconsulting.com
SIC: 8742 Management consulting services
PA: Navigant Consulting, Inc.
30 S Wacker Dr Ste 3550
Chicago IL 60606
312 573-5600

(P-27561)
NEARDATA INC
Also Called: Neardata Systems
4502 Dyer St Ste 103, La Crescenta (91214-2854)
PHONE.................818 249-2469
Samuel S Chilingurian, *President*
EMP: 76
SQ FT: 5,600
SALES (est): 6.5MM **Privately Held**
SIC: 8742 7371 Management consulting services; computer software development

(P-27562)
NET4SITE LLC
3350 Scott Blvd Bldg 34b, Santa Clara (95054-3105)
PHONE.................408 427-3004
C K Singla,
EMP: 78
SQ FT: 3,000
SALES: 10MM **Privately Held**
SIC: 8742 Management information systems consultant

(P-27563)
NETBASE SOLUTIONS INC (PA)
3960 Freedom Cir 201, Santa Clara (95054-1204)
PHONE.................650 810-2100
Fax: 650 968-4872
Peter M Caswell, *CEO*
Andy Johnson, *President*
Bob Pape, *CFO*
Pernille Bruun-Jensen, *Chief Mktg Ofcr*
Patrick Williams, *Officer*
EMP: 56
SALES (est): 15.4MM **Privately Held**
WEB: www.accelovation.com
SIC: 8742 Business planning & organizing services

(P-27564)
NEWMARK & COMPANY RE INC
Also Called: Newmark Grubb Knight Frank
1551 N Tustin Ave Ste 300, Santa Ana (92705-8638)
PHONE.................714 667-8252
Audra Cunningham, *Managing Dir*
EMP: 60
SALES (corp-wide): 2.5B **Publicly Held**
SIC: 8742 6531 Real estate consultant; real estate agent, commercial; housing authority operator
HQ: Newmark & Company Real Estate, Inc.
125 Park Ave
New York NY 10017
212 372-2000

(P-27565)
NEX CORONADO NAB
Also Called: Navy Exchange
3632 Guadalcanal Rd, San Diego (92155-5504)
PHONE.................619 522-7403
Fax: 619 522-7433
Edward Pearson, *Principal*
Selita Perry, *Facilities Mgr*
EMP: 50
SALES (est): 5.3MM **Privately Held**
SIC: 8742 Retail trade consultant

(P-27566)
NEXT IMAGE MEDICAL INC (PA)
3390 Carmel Mountain Rd # 150, San Diego (92121-1055)
PHONE.................858 847-9185
Fax: 858 847-9135
Elizabeth Griggs, *CEO*
Robert Bilow, *Technology*
EMP: 63
SALES (est): 7.6MM **Privately Held**
SIC: 8742 Business consultant

(P-27567)
NEXT MANAGEMENT LLC
Also Called: Next Management Co
8447 Wilshire Blvd # 301, Beverly Hills (90211-3226)
PHONE.................323 782-0038
Faith Kates, *President*
EMP: 50
SALES (corp-wide): 11.1MM **Privately Held**
SIC: 8742 8021 Management consulting services; offices & clinics of dentists
PA: Next Management, Llc
15 Watts St Fl 6
New York NY 10013
212 925-5100

(P-27568)
NFP PROPERTY & CASUALTY SVCS
Also Called: Nfp Advisors
2450 Tapo St, Simi Valley (93063-2454)
PHONE.................805 579-1900
Mary Lue, *CEO*
EMP: 50
SALES (est): 86.4K **Privately Held**
SIC: 8742 Financial consultant

(P-27569)
NINES RESTAURANT
Also Called: Bunkers Grille
100 Summerset Dr, Brentwood (94513-6426)
PHONE.................925 516-3413
James A Shoemaker, *President*
Sally Shoemaker, *Vice Pres*
EMP: 60
SQ FT: 14,000
SALES (est): 4.2MM **Privately Held**
WEB: www.bunkersgrille.com
SIC: 8742 Management consulting services

(P-27570)
NORTHBOUND LLC
2870 Zanker Rd Ste 210, San Jose (95134-2133)
P.O. Box 730, Campbell (95009-0730)
PHONE.................408 245-6500
Hetel Mehta,
Yasir Aladdin, *Vice Pres*
Srikant Sharma, *General Mgr*
Leena Menon,
Britney Barnes, *Manager*
EMP: 128
SQ FT: 20,000
SALES (est): 21.5MM **Privately Held**
WEB: www.northboundllc.com
SIC: 8742 Management information systems consultant

(P-27571)
NPS MARKETING
3381 Sage Rose Ln, Placerville (95667-5452)
P.O. Box 2392 (95667-2392)
PHONE.................916 941-5510
Scott Becker, *Owner*
EMP: 300

PRODUCTS & SERVICES SECTION
8742 - Management Consulting Services County (P-27596)

SALES: 2.5MM **Privately Held**
SIC: **8742** 7389 Marketing consulting services;

(P-27572)
OMEGA 2 ALPHA SERVICES LLC
Also Called: O2a
935 Riverside Ave Ste 23, Paso Robles (93446-2605)
PHONE.....................805 610-2249
Daniel McGee,
Robert Cidemiller, *Mng Member*
EMP: 53 EST: 2014
SALES (est): 1.1MM **Privately Held**
SIC: **8742** Construction project management consultant

(P-27573)
OMEGA WASTE MANAGEMENT INC
Also Called: Omega Management Services
957 Colusa St, Corning (96021-2224)
P.O. Box 495 (96021-0495)
PHONE.....................530 824-1890
Fax: 530 824-1895
Robert O Conner, *President*
Karen O'Conner, *Vice Pres*
Dan O'Connor, *Vice Pres*
Laurie Spindler, *Human Res Mgr*
Lois Ballard, *Accounts Mgr*
EMP: 68
SQ FT: 6,000
SALES (est): 13.2MM **Privately Held**
WEB: www.omegawastemanagement.com
SIC: **8742** Management consulting services

(P-27574)
OMNI CONSULTING GROUP LLP
Also Called: Omni Research Group
3531 Mono Pl Ste 100, Davis (95618-6049)
P.O. Box 4128 (95617-4128)
PHONE.....................530 750-5199
Frank J Bernard, *Partner*
Michael G Ashworth, *Partner*
Lawrence C Barrington, *Partner*
Frank J Bernhard, *Partner*
John P Evans, *Partner*
EMP: 78 EST: 1989
SQ FT: 8,500
SALES (est): 4.1MM **Privately Held**
WEB: www.omniconsultinggroup.com
SIC: **8742** Management consulting services

(P-27575)
ONE CALL MEDICAL INC
8501 Fllbrook Ave Ste 100, Canoga Park (91304)
PHONE.....................818 346-8700
Julie Moss, *Manager*
James F Simmons, *Vice Pres*
EMP: 90
SALES (corp-wide): 900MM **Privately Held**
SIC: **8742** Compensation & benefits planning consultant
PA: One Call Medical Inc.
841 Prudential Dr Ste 900
Jacksonville FL 32207
904 646-0199

(P-27576)
OPEN HARBOR INC
1123 Industrial Rd, San Francisco (94111)
PHONE.....................650 413-4200
Bill Walsh, *President*
Jacques Clay, *Vice Pres*
EMP: 83
SALES (est): 3.1MM **Privately Held**
SIC: **8742** Management consulting services

(P-27577)
OTX CORPORATION (HQ)
10567 Jefferson Blvd, Culver City (90232-3513)
PHONE.....................310 736-3400
Fax: 310 736-3301
Shelley Zalis, *CEO*
Jeff Dean, *CFO*
David Klein, *Senior VP*
Derek Jackson, *Technical Mgr*
EMP: 210

SALES (est): 17.6MM
SALES (corp-wide): 451.8K **Privately Held**
SIC: **8742** Management consulting services
PA: Ipsos
35 Rue Du Val De Marne
Paris 75013
141 989-000

(P-27578)
P H S MANAGEMENT GROUP (PA)
721 N Eckhoff St, Orange (92868-1005)
PHONE.....................714 547-7551
Kevin O Lewand, *President*
EMP: 50
SALES (est): 5.3MM **Privately Held**
SIC: **8742** Hospital & health services consultant

(P-27579)
PACIFIC SECURED EQUITIES INC (PA)
Also Called: Intercare Holdings Insur Svcs
6020 W Oaks Blvd Ste 100, Rocklin (95765-5472)
P.O. Box 579, Roseville (95661-0579)
PHONE.....................916 677-2500
Fax: 916 677-2608
EMP: 100
SQ FT: 21,000
SALES (est): 48.5MM **Privately Held**
WEB: www.intercareins.com
SIC: **8742**

(P-27580)
PACIFIC THEATRES ENTRMT CORP (HQ)
120 N Robertson Blvd Fl 3, Los Angeles (90048-3113)
PHONE.....................310 657-8420
Christopher Forman, *Ch of Bd*
Joe Robinson, *Administration*
Jill Saperstein, *Technology*
EMP: 100
SQ FT: 3,000
SALES (est): 13MM
SALES (corp-wide): 200.2MM **Privately Held**
WEB: www.pacifictheatres.com
SIC: **8742** Business consultant
PA: The Decurion Corporation
120 N Robertson Blvd Fl 3
Los Angeles CA 90048
310 659-9432

(P-27581)
PALOMAR HEALTH
150 W Crest St, Escondido (92025-1706)
PHONE.....................760 739-2243
Robert G Walsh, *Assistant VP*
EMP: 75
SALES (corp-wide): 614.2MM **Privately Held**
WEB: www.sunbridge.com
SIC: **8742** Management consulting services
PA: Palomar Health
456 E Grand Ave
Escondido CA 92025
442 281-5000

(P-27582)
PALORAS CORPORATION
228 Hamilton Ave Fl 3, Palo Alto (94301-2583)
PHONE.....................650 440-7663
Ramki Pitchuiyer, *CEO*
Bruce Young, *Recruiter*
EMP: 55
SALES: 8MM **Privately Held**
SIC: **8742** Management consulting services

(P-27583)
PARSONS BRINCKERHOFF INC
1818 Gilbreth Rd, Burlingame (94010-1225)
PHONE.....................650 697-1869
EMP: 61
SALES (corp-wide): 2.5B **Privately Held**
SIC: **8742** Management consulting services

HQ: Parsons Brinckerhoff, Inc.
1 Penn Plz Ste 200
New York NY 10119
212 465-5000

(P-27584)
PARTNERS IN LEADERSHIP INTERME (PA)
27555 Ynez Rd, Temecula (92591-4687)
PHONE.....................951 506-6878
EMP: 86
SALES (est): 31MM **Privately Held**
SIC: **8742** Management consulting services

(P-27585)
PAUL KITTLE
Also Called: Knowledge Folk
4495 Mt Vernon Ave, Riverside (92507-4855)
PHONE.....................951 684-0918
Paul Kittle, *Owner*
EMP: 50
SALES (est): 2.6MM **Privately Held**
WEB: www.knowledgefolk.com
SIC: **8742** Management information systems consultant

(P-27586)
PERKSTREET FINANCIAL INC
1100 La Avenida St Ste A, Mountain View (94043-1453)
PHONE.....................978 801-1177
Laurence Stock, *CFO*
EMP: 50 EST: 2008
SALES (est): 4.4MM **Privately Held**
SIC: **8742** Banking & finance consultant

(P-27587)
PERMANENTE FEDERATION LLC
1800 Harrison St Fl 22, Oakland (94612-3466)
PHONE.....................510 625-6920
Cal James, *CEO*
Claire Tamo, *CFO*
EMP: 80 EST: 1997
SQ FT: 18,663
SALES (est): 9.4MM **Privately Held**
SIC: **8742** Management consulting services

(P-27588)
PG&E CAPITAL LLC
1 Market, San Francisco (94105-1596)
PHONE.....................415 321-4600
Anthony Earley Hr, *Chairman*
EMP: 210
SALES (est): 84.4K **Publicly Held**
SIC: **8742** Marketing consulting services
PA: Pg&E Corporation
77 Beale St
San Francisco CA 94105

(P-27589)
PHENOMENON MKTG & ENTRMT INC (PA)
5900 Wilshire Blvd Fl 28, Los Angeles (90036-5013)
PHONE.....................323 648-4035
Krishnan Menon, *CEO*
Greg Hampar, *Executive*
Ali Filsoof, *Creative Dir*
Ray Dollete, *Info Tech Mgr*
Marco Icardo, *Accountant*
EMP: 60
SQ FT: 15,289
SALES: 20MM **Privately Held**
SIC: **8742** Marketing consulting services

(P-27590)
PNC REALTY INVESTORS INC
26901 Agoura Rd Ste 200, Calabasas (91301-5109)
PHONE.....................818 880-3300
Tim White, *Branch Mgr*
Joe G Basurto, *Senior VP*
Gary Baratta, *Vice Pres*
EMP: 80
SALES (corp-wide): 16.2B **Publicly Held**
SIC: **8742** Financial consultant

HQ: Pnc Bank, National Association
249 5th Ave Ste 1200
Pittsburgh PA 15222
412 762-2000

(P-27591)
PRECISE ENTERPRISES LLC
Also Called: Precise Auto Protection
751 W 9th St, Azusa (91702-2340)
P.O. Box 305 (91702-0305)
PHONE.....................818 599-6450
Harry Pambuckchyan, *Mng Member*
Gina Pambuckchyan,
Sitta Saghoejian,
EMP: 50
SQ FT: 6,500
SALES (est): 3.4MM **Privately Held**
SIC: **8742** Marketing consulting services

(P-27592)
PRESCRIPTION SOLUTIONS
2858 Loker Ave E Ste 100, Carlsbad (92010-6673)
PHONE.....................760 804-2370
Bobby Robert Bliatout, *President*
Phil Haworth, *Info Tech Mgr*
Sumiyo Avans, *Accountant*
Shaun Davis, *Senior Mgr*
Zachary Crnecki, *Manager*
EMP: 1000
SALES (est): 81.5MM **Privately Held**
SIC: **8742** Hospital & health services consultant

(P-27593)
PREVENTION INSTITUTE
221 Oak St Ste A, Oakland (94607-4595)
PHONE.....................510 444-4133
Fax: 510 663-1280
Larry Cohen, *Exec Dir*
Anthony Iton, *Vice Pres*
Jessica Berthold, *Comms Mgr*
Lauren Sharp, *Managing Dir*
Virginia Lee, *Program Mgr*
EMP: 56 EST: 2001
SQ FT: 2,612
SALES (est): 7.5MM **Privately Held**
SIC: **8742** Training & development consultant

(P-27594)
PRIMUS GROUP INC (PA)
Also Called: Primus Labs
2810 Industrial Pkwy, Santa Maria (93455-1812)
PHONE.....................805 922-0055
Robert F Stovicek, *President*
Brian Mansfield, *Business Dir*
Yuri Hernandez, *Admin Asst*
Jayson Garin, *Administration*
Janice Jones, *Administration*
EMP: 50
SQ FT: 12,000
SALES (est): 20.4MM **Privately Held**
WEB: www.primuslabs.com
SIC: **8742** 8734 8731 Food & beverage consultant; food testing service; commercial physical research

(P-27595)
PRIZE PROZ
1500 S Hellman Ave, Ontario (91761-7634)
PHONE.....................909 509-8600
Dennis Foland, *Owner*
EMP: 50 EST: 2011
SALES (est): 3.4MM **Privately Held**
SIC: **8742** Incentive or award program consultant

(P-27596)
PROMO SHOP INC (PA)
5420 Mcconnell Ave, Los Angeles (90066-7037)
PHONE.....................208 333-0881
Guillermo Kahan, *President*
Jim Buescher, *COO*
Matthew Mason, *Vice Pres*
Frank Nordyke, *Vice Pres*
Christina Navarro, *Principal*
EMP: 55
SALES (est): 30.3MM **Privately Held**
WEB: www.promoshopinc.com
SIC: **8742** Marketing consulting services

8742 - Management Consulting Services County (P-27597)

PRODUDUCTS & SERVICES SECTION

(P-27597)
PROPHET BRAND STRATEGY (PA)
1 Bush St Fl 7, San Francisco (94104-4413)
PHONE...............415 677-0909
Fax: 415 677-9020
Michael Dunn, *President*
David A Ker, *Vice Chairman*
Rune Gustafson, *President*
Simon Marlow, *COO*
Jeani Vance, *CIO*
EMP: 50
SQ FT: 1,744
SALES: 100MM **Privately Held**
SIC: 8742 Marketing consulting services

(P-27598)
PROTIVITI INC (HQ)
2884 Sand Hill Rd Ste 200, Menlo Park (94025-7072)
PHONE...............650 234-6000
Carol M Beaumier, *Exec VP*
Brian Christensen, *Exec VP*
James Pajakowski, *Exec VP*
Scott Redfearn, *Exec VP*
Rick Beyer, *Associate Dir*
EMP: 100
SALES (est): 349.1MM
SALES (corp-wide): 5B **Publicly Held**
SIC: 8742 8721 Industry specialist consultants; auditing services
PA: Robert Half International Inc.
    2884 Sand Hill Rd Ste 200
    Menlo Park CA 94025
    650 234-6000

(P-27599)
PROTIVITI INC
400 S Hope St Ste 900, Los Angeles (90071-2808)
PHONE...............213 327-1400
Paul Sacks, *Branch Mgr*
Jonathon Bronson, *Exec Dir*
Annette Christensen, *CPA*
Matthew Timbol, *Sr Consultant*
Golreez Jalali, *Manager*
EMP: 100
SALES (corp-wide): 5B **Publicly Held**
SIC: 8742 Food & beverage consultant
HQ: Protiviti Inc.
    2884 Sand Hill Rd Ste 200
    Menlo Park CA 94025
    650 234-6000

(P-27600)
PROVIDENCE SEMINARS INC
6349 Palomar Oaks Ct, Carlsbad (92011-1428)
PHONE...............760 827-2100
Russell Carroll, *President*
EMP: 75
SQ FT: 15,000
SALES (est): 2.7MM **Privately Held**
SIC: 8742 Real estate consultant

(P-27601)
PUBLIC CONSULTING GROUP INC
Also Called: Pcg Technology Consulting
2150 River Plaza Dr # 380, Sacramento (95833-3883)
PHONE...............916 565-8090
Lori Duff, *Manager*
Barbara Moesta, *Administration*
Maren Stark, *Administration*
Paul Olalde, *Business Anlyst*
Jeff Field, *Consultant*
EMP: 60
SALES (corp-wide): 341.4MM **Privately Held**
SIC: 8742 Business consultant
PA: Public Consulting Group, Inc.
    148 State St Fl 10
    Boston MA 02109
    617 426-2026

(P-27602)
PWC STRATEGY& (US) LLC
2141 Rosecrans Ave # 5100, El Segundo (90245-4747)
PHONE...............281 685-8325
Glenna Heller, *Branch Mgr*
EMP: 99
SALES (corp-wide): 9.4B **Privately Held**
SIC: 8742 Management consulting services
HQ: Pwc Strategy& (Us) Llc
    300 Campus Dr Ste 100
    Florham Park NJ 07932

(P-27603)
PWC STRATEGY& (US) LLC
101 California St # 3300, San Francisco (94111-5802)
PHONE...............415 391-1900
Ralph W Shrader, *Branch Mgr*
Brian Fischer, *Vice Pres*
William T Reed, *Principal*
EMP: 200
SALES (corp-wide): 9.4B **Privately Held**
SIC: 8742 Management consulting services
HQ: Pwc Strategy& (Us) Llc
    300 Campus Dr Ste 100
    Florham Park NJ 07932

(P-27604)
Q ANALYSTS LLC (PA)
5201 Great America Pkwy # 238, Santa Clara (95054-1126)
PHONE...............408 907-8500
Ross Fernandes,
Joe Lawlor, *President*
Ilisa Kim, *Senior VP*
Thuy To, *Executive*
Raul Deleon, *QA Dir*
EMP: 70
SALES (est): 13.7MM **Privately Held**
WEB: www.qanalysts.com
SIC: 8742 7379 Quality assurance consultant; computer related consulting services

(P-27605)
QLM CONSULTING INC
2400 Bridgeway Ste 290, Sausalito (94965-2851)
P.O. Box 982 (94966-0982)
PHONE...............415 331-9292
Fax: 415 381-1080
Michael McCartney, *CEO*
Alex Unongo, *Office Mgr*
EMP: 50
SALES (est): 3.8MM **Privately Held**
WEB: www.qlmconsulting.com
SIC: 8742 Management consulting services

(P-27606)
QUALITY PLANNING CORPORATION
388 Market St Ste 750, San Francisco (94111-5352)
PHONE...............415 369-0707
Fax: 415 369-0709
Raj Bhat, *President*
Carissa Clarkson, *Admin Sec*
Michael Garcia, *Administration*
Patrick Clancy, *Info Tech Mgr*
Edward Dao, *Software Engr*
EMP: 54
SALES (est): 5.3MM
SALES (corp-wide): 2B **Publicly Held**
WEB: www.qualityplanning.com
SIC: 8742 Management consulting services
HQ: Insurance Services Office, Inc.
    545 Washington Blvd Fl 12
    Jersey City NJ 07310
    201 469-2000

(P-27607)
QUANTUMSCAPE CORPORATION
1730 Technology Dr, San Jose (95110-1303)
PHONE...............408 452-2051
Jagdeep Singh, *CEO*
EMP: 52
SALES (est): 13.2MM **Privately Held**
SIC: 8742 Marketing consulting services

(P-27608)
R3 STRATEGIC SUPPORT GROUP INC
1050 B Ave Ste A, Coronado (92118-3430)
PHONE...............800 418-2040
Randall Packard, *President*
Clark Nichols, *Principal*
Mark Sanders, *Principal*
David Sadler, *General Mgr*
Patrick Gokey, *Technician*
EMP: 67
SALES (est): 700K **Privately Held**
SIC: 8742 Management consulting services

(P-27609)
RAY W CHOI
Also Called: Ictp
731 E Ball Rd Ste 100, Anaheim (92805-5951)
PHONE...............714 783-1000
Ray W Choi, *Owner*
Alexandria Chang, *Technical Staff*
Carol Brock, *Finance Mgr*
EMP: 92
SQ FT: 10,000
SALES (est): 4.2MM **Privately Held**
SIC: 8742 7379 Training & development consultant; computer related consulting services

(P-27610)
RED PEAK GROUP LLC
23975 Park Sorrento # 365, Calabasas (91302-4020)
PHONE...............818 222-7762
Michael Birkin, *CEO*
EMP: 90
SALES (est): 4.6MM **Privately Held**
SIC: 8742 Marketing consulting services

(P-27611)
REDHORSE CORPORATION (PA)
Also Called: Redhorse Technical Services
1370 India St Ste 200, San Diego (92101-3432)
PHONE...............619 241-4609
David L Inmon, *CEO*
David Loran Inmon, *CEO*
Mark Walsh, *COO*
Jo Blais, *Program Mgr*
Kaisha Brown, *Admin Asst*
EMP: 53
SALES (est): 27.1MM **Privately Held**
SIC: 8742 Management consulting services

(P-27612)
REDSTONE PRINT & MAIL INC
910 Riverside Pkwy Ste 40, West Sacramento (95605-1510)
PHONE...............916 318-6450
Ledi Cody, *President*
EMP: 60 EST: 2015
SALES: 20MM **Privately Held**
SIC: 8742 Marketing consulting services

(P-27613)
REPUTATION IMPRESSION LLC
9245 Activity Rd Ste 106, San Diego (92126-4442)
PHONE...............858 633-4500
Scott Spencer, *CEO*
Jason Wong, *Info Tech Dir*
Mark Spencer, *Opers Staff*
Joe Ibanez, *Sales Dir*
EMP: 85
SALES (est): 8.3MM **Privately Held**
SIC: 8742 Industry specialist consultants

(P-27614)
REPUTATION MANAGEMENT CONS INC
1720 E Garry Ave Ste 103, Santa Ana (92705-5831)
P.O. Box 92, Irvine (92650-0092)
PHONE...............949 682-7906
Gary P Hagins, *President*
Steve Boccone, *Controller*
Alex Sandoval, *Marketing Staff*
EMP: 65
SQ FT: 4,000
SALES: 9MM **Privately Held**
SIC: 8742 Business consultant

(P-27615)
RESEARCH TRIANGLE INSTITUTE
2150 Shattuck Ave Ste 800, Berkeley (94704-1352)
PHONE...............510 849-4942
E Wayne Holden, *Branch Mgr*
EMP: 72
SALES (corp-wide): 831.5MM **Privately Held**
SIC: 8742 8732 Management consulting services; educational research
PA: Research Triangle Institute Inc
    3040 Cornwallis Rd
    Durham NC 27709
    919 541-6000

(P-27616)
RESORT PROCOMM INC
9550 Waples St Ste 105, San Diego (92121-2984)
PHONE...............858 866-6280
Will Dougherty, *President*
EMP: 61
SALES (est): 2.6MM **Privately Held**
SIC: 8742 Marketing consulting services

(P-27617)
RESOURCES CONNECTION INC (PA)
17101 Armstrong Ave, Irvine (92614-5730)
PHONE...............714 430-6400
Anthony Cherbak, *President*
Susan Hicks, *Managing Prtnr*
Donald B Murray, *Ch of Bd*
Tracy B Stephens, *COO*
Nathan W Franke, *CFO*
EMP: 772
SQ FT: 56,200
SALES: 598.5MM **Publicly Held**
SIC: 8742 7389 8721 Management consulting services; business planning & organizing services; financial services; legal & tax services; accounting, auditing & bookkeeping; auditing services

(P-27618)
RHODES RETAIL SERVICES INC
8603 Excelsior Rd, Elk Grove (95624-9661)
PHONE...............916 714-9233
Fax: 916 714-9225
Chris Rhodes, *President*
Valerie Rhodes, *CFO*
Richard Lang, *Project Mgr*
Deanne McCullough, *Human Res Mgr*
EMP: 90
SQ FT: 1,200
SALES (est): 9.3MM **Privately Held**
WEB: www.rhodesretail.com
SIC: 8742 Merchandising consultant

(P-27619)
RICHARD HEATH & ASSOCIATES INC
7847 Convoy Ct Ste 102, San Diego (92111-1220)
PHONE...............858 514-4025
Fax: 858 514-4047
Cassandra Schaeg, *Branch Mgr*
John Jensen, *Program Mgr*
Norma Kaufman, *Manager*
EMP: 80
SALES (corp-wide): 180.5MM **Privately Held**
WEB: www.rhainc.com
SIC: 8742 Management consulting services
PA: Richard Heath & Associates, Inc.
    590 W Locust Ave Ste 103
    Fresno CA 93650
    559 447-7000

(P-27620)
RIVIERA PARTNERS LLC (PA)
141 10th St, San Francisco (94103-2604)
PHONE...............877 748-4372
Michael Morell, *Managing Prtnr*
Kevin Buckby, *Partner*
Andy Grosso, *Partner*
Zack Isaacson, *Tech Recruiter*
Majed Itani, *VP Engrg*
EMP: 53
SALES (est): 10.6MM **Privately Held**
SIC: 8742 Business consultant

PRODUCTS & SERVICES SECTION

8742 - Management Consulting Services County (P-27644)

(P-27621)
ROBANY INC
21550 Oxnard St Fl 3, Woodland Hills
(91367-7105)
PHONE.................................818 721-2150
Tracy Hampton, *President*
Linda Mintor, *Human Resources*
EMP: 84
SALES (est): 3.5MM **Privately Held**
SIC: 8742 6799 Real estate consultant; real estate investors, except property operators

(P-27622)
ROBERT HALF MGT RESOURCES
1999 Harrison St Ste 1100, Oakland
(94612-4708)
PHONE.................................510 271-0910
Robert Gardener, *Manager*
Alice Fisher, *Accounts Exec*
EMP: 50
SALES (est): 2.4MM **Privately Held**
SIC: 8742 Management consulting services

(P-27623)
ROBERTSON PIPER MANAGEMENT LLC
963 Fremont Ave, Los Altos (94024-6098)
PHONE.................................650 625-8333
Robertson Piper, *Principal*
EMP: 185
SALES (est): 4.8MM **Privately Held**
SIC: 8742 Management consulting services

(P-27624)
ROCKPORT ADM SVCS LLC (PA)
Also Called: Rockport Healthcare Services
5900 Wilshire Blvd # 1600, Los Angeles
(90036-5016)
PHONE.................................323 330-6500
Vincent S Hambright, *CEO*
Brad Gibson, *CFO*
Yehuda Kaplan, *Benefits Mgr*
Steven Stroll, *Mng Member*
EMP: 75
SQ FT: 4,800
SALES (est): 36MM **Privately Held**
SIC: 8742 Hospital & health services consultant

(P-27625)
ROSENTHAL & COMPANY LLC
75 Rowland Way Ste 250, Novato
(94945-5018)
PHONE.................................415 884-1100
Dan Rosenthal, *Mng Member*
James Smith, *Info Tech Dir*
Jim Rothmuller, *Marketing Mgr*
Carma Sten, *Manager*
EMP: 60
SQ FT: 7,000
SALES (est): 3.1MM
SALES (corp-wide): 1.4B **Privately Held**
WEB: www.rosenthalco.com
SIC: 8742 Administrative services consultant
HQ: Kurtzman Carson Consultants, Inc
2335 Alaska Ave
El Segundo CA 90245
310 823-9000

(P-27626)
ROSETTA LLC
60 S Market St Ste 750, San Jose
(95113-2362)
PHONE.................................408 275-7117
EMP: 154
SALES (corp-wide): 65.7MM **Privately Held**
SIC: 8742 Management consulting services
HQ: Rosetta Llc
100 American Metro Blvd # 201
Hamilton NJ 08619
609 689-6100

(P-27627)
ROSETTA LLC
4800 Morabito Pl, San Luis Obispo
(93401-8748)
PHONE.................................347 332-7659
Chris Kuenne, *Chairman*

Josh Demolar, *Info Tech Dir*
Giana Ronzani, *Project Mgr*
David Nau, *Technology*
Chris Cunningham, *Manager*
EMP: 154
SALES (corp-wide): 65.7MM **Privately Held**
SIC: 8742 Marketing consulting services
HQ: Rosetta Llc
100 American Metro Blvd # 201
Hamilton NJ 08619
609 689-6100

(P-27628)
RUBY CREEK RESOURCES
1835 W Olympic Blvd, Los Angeles
(90006-3701)
PHONE.................................212 671-0404
Robert Slavik, *CEO*
EMP: 50
SALES: 10MM **Privately Held**
SIC: 8742 Business planning & organizing services

(P-27629)
RUSSON FINANCIAL SERVICES INC
Also Called: New England Financial
19935 Ventura Blvd # 100, Woodland Hills
(91364-9605)
PHONE.................................818 999-2800
Fax: 818 999-6100
Tony Russon, *CEO*
R Russon, *Agent*
EMP: 60
SQ FT: 10,000
SALES (est): 3.8MM **Privately Held**
SIC: 8742 Financial consultant

(P-27630)
S E O P INC
1720 E Garry Ave Ste 103, Santa Ana
(92705-5831)
PHONE.................................949 682-7906
Gary Hagins, *CEO*
Rhonda Spears, *President*
Caroline Lane, *Controller*
EMP: 150
SALES (est): 13.9MM **Privately Held**
WEB: www.seop.com
SIC: 8742 Marketing consulting services

(P-27631)
SABAL FINANCIAL GROUP LP
465 N Halstead St Ste 105, Pasadena
(91107-6075)
PHONE.................................626 351-6859
Whitney Macdonnell, *Manager*
EMP: 51
SALES (corp-wide): 90.5MM **Privately Held**
SIC: 8742 6282 Financial consultant; futures advisory service
PA: Sabal Financial Group, L.P.
4675 Macarthur Ct Fl 15
Newport Beach CA 92660
949 255-2660

(P-27632)
SABAN BRANDS LLC (HQ)
10100 Santa Monica Blvd # 500, Los Angeles (90067-4003)
PHONE.................................310 557-5230
Elie Dekel, *President*
Jack Sorensen, *President*
Janet Scardino, *COO*
William Kehoe, *CFO*
Michael Bayer, *Senior VP*
EMP: 88
SQ FT: 605,000
SALES (est): 28.9MM
SALES (corp-wide): 44.4MM **Privately Held**
SIC: 8742 General management consultant
PA: Saban Music Group, Inc
10100 Santa Monica Blvd # 1050
Los Angeles CA 90067
310 557-5100

(P-27633)
SACKETT NATIONAL HOLDINGS INC
2605 Camino Del Rio S # 400, San Diego
(92108-3706)
PHONE.................................866 834-6242

EMP: 63
SALES (corp-wide): 38.2MM **Privately Held**
SIC: 8742 7389 Management consulting services; financial services
PA: Sackett National Holdings, Inc.
7373 Peak Dr
Las Vegas NV 89128
702 900-1791

(P-27634)
SAMSUNG ELECTRONICS AMER INC
665 Clyde Ave, Mountain View
(94043-2235)
PHONE.................................650 210-1000
Evan Maxei, *Director*
Insun Lee, *Vice Pres*
Ted Kim, *Business Dir*
Anshul Khandelwal, *Sr Software Eng*
Sam Kim, *Engineer*
EMP: 1000
SQ FT: 395
SALES (corp-wide): 118.4B **Privately Held**
WEB: www.samsung.com
SIC: 8742 Marketing consulting services
HQ: Samsung Electronics America, Inc.
85 Challenger Rd
Ridgefield Park NJ 07660
201 229-4000

(P-27635)
SANDISK CORPORATION
951 Sandisk Dr, Milpitas (95035-7933)
PHONE.................................408 801-1000
Dennis Segers, *Branch Mgr*
EMP: 104
SALES (corp-wide): 12.9B **Publicly Held**
WEB: www.sdcard.com
SIC: 8742 Management consulting services
HQ: Sandisk Corporation
951 Sandisk Dr
Milpitas CA 95035
408 801-1000

(P-27636)
SCORPION DESIGN LLC
28480 Ave Stnford Ste 140, Valencia
(91355)
PHONE.................................661 702-0100
Rustin Kretz, *President*
Steven Mauser, *President*
Andrew Krowne, *CFO*
Matthew Shepherd, *CFO*
Jamie Adams, *Senior VP*
EMP: 130
SALES (est): 23MM **Privately Held**
WEB: www.scorpiondesign.com
SIC: 8742 Marketing consulting services

(P-27637)
SEARCH OPTICS LLC (PA)
5770 Oberlin Dr, San Diego (92121-1723)
PHONE.................................858 678-0707
David Ponn, *CEO*
Eduardo Cortez, *President*
Troy Smith, *President*
Jason Stesney, *Treasurer*
Christian Fuller, *Vice Pres*
EMP: 60
SQ FT: 16,500
SALES (est): 26.3MM **Privately Held**
WEB: www.searchoptics.com
SIC: 8742 Marketing consulting services

(P-27638)
SECOVA INC
5000 Birch St Ste 1400, Newport Beach
(92660-2150)
PHONE.................................714 384-0530
Venkat Tadanki, *President*
V Chandrasekaran, *COO*
Joel Carter, *Senior VP*
Robert G Parke, *Senior VP*
EMP: 186
SQ FT: 13,734
SALES (est): 9.6MM **Privately Held**
WEB: www.secova.com
SIC: 8742 Human resource consulting services
HQ: Secova Eservices, Inc.
5000 Birch St
Newport Beach CA 92660
714 384-0655

(P-27639)
SECOVA ESERVICES INC (HQ)
5000 Birch St, Newport Beach
(92660-2127)
PHONE.................................714 384-0655
Venkat R Tadanki, *CEO*
Brian Perrine, *Vice Pres*
Vinod Kumar, *Executive*
Robert G Parke, *Admin Sec*
V Chandrasekaran, *CTO*
EMP: 84
SQ FT: 6,713
SALES (est): 33MM **Privately Held**
WEB: www.ultralink.com
SIC: 8742 Human resource consulting services

(P-27640)
SEQUOIA BNEFITS INSUR SVCS LLC
1850 Gateway Dr Ste 600, San Mateo
(94404-4064)
PHONE.................................650 369-0200
Greg Golub,
Ned Sizer, *CFO*
Michele Floriani, *Chief Mktg Ofcr*
Manish Kumar, *Vice Pres*
Lucy Camplin, *Accountant*
EMP: 70 **EST:** 2001
SQ FT: 2,000
SALES (est): 11.8MM **Privately Held**
WEB: www.sequoiabenefits.com
SIC: 8742 Compensation & benefits planning consultant

(P-27641)
SERVICESOURCE INTL INC (PA)
760 Market St Fl 4, San Francisco
(94102-2306)
PHONE.................................415 901-6030
Fax: 415 962-3230
Christopher M Carrington, *CEO*
Brian J Delaney, *CEO*
Robert N Pinkerton, *CFO*
EMP: 148
SQ FT: 24,394
SALES: 252.2MM **Publicly Held**
WEB: www.servicesource.com
SIC: 8742 Business consultant

(P-27642)
SET FREE SERVICES INC
3300 Veda St, Redding (96001-3511)
P.O. Box 993544 (96099-3544)
PHONE.................................530 243-3373
Robert Lincoln Hancock, *President*
Jim Dahl,
Lisa Freres,
Tammy Lucarelli,
Dan Mullens,
EMP: 53
SQ FT: 10,000
SALES (est): 3.7MM **Privately Held**
SIC: 8742 8748 Management consulting services; business consulting

(P-27643)
SEVILLE CONSTRUCTION SVCS INC
199 S Hudson Ave, Pasadena
(91101-2917)
PHONE.................................626 204-0800
Jeffrey S Flores, *President*
Vince Quinones, *Vice Pres*
Jim Rogers, *Manager*
Bernadette Vargas, *Business Mgr*
Michelle Acero, *Manager*
EMP: 75
SQ FT: 3,300
SALES (est): 8.7MM **Privately Held**
WEB: www.sevillecs.com
SIC: 8742 Construction project management consultant

(P-27644)
SHANNON RANCHES INC
12601 E Highway 20, Clearlake Oaks
(95423-8312)
P.O. Box 2037 (95423-2037)
PHONE.................................707 998-9656
Fax: 707 998-0139
Clay Shannon, *President*
Margarita Shannon, *Corp Secy*
Craig Shannon, *Vice Pres*
Keith Brandt, *Manager*

8742 - Management Consulting Services County (P-27645)

EMP: 250 **EST:** 1993
SQ FT: 2,100
SALES (est): 33.6MM **Privately Held**
WEB: www.shannonridge.com
SIC: 8742 Administrative services consultant

(P-27645)
SHERATON HTL SAN DIEGO MSN VLY
Also Called: Sheraton San Diego Mission Vly
1433 Camino Del Rio S, San Diego (92108-3521)
PHONE..................................619 321-4602
Cynthia Adams Carlin, *Administration*
Sabra Baran, *General Mgr*
Kheam Taing, *General Mgr*
Brooke Vandenbrink, *Controller*
Anna Maria, *Director*
EMP: 100
SALES (est): 9.9MM **Privately Held**
SIC: 8742 Hospital & health services consultant

(P-27646)
SIGMAWAYS INC
39737 Paseo Padre Pkwy, Fremont (94538-2996)
PHONE..................................510 573-4208
Prakash Sadasivam, *CEO*
Sudha Kadirvelu, *Human Res Mgr*
EMP: 60
SQ FT: 5,000
SALES (est): 7.4MM **Privately Held**
SIC: 8742 7379 7373 Management consulting services; computer related consulting services; systems software development services

(P-27647)
SIMI RADIOLOGY & IMAGING
Also Called: Computerized Management Svcs
4100 Guardian St Ste 205, Simi Valley (93063-6721)
P.O. Box 190 (93062-0190)
PHONE..................................805 522-5978
Fax: 805 522-6401
Daryl Favale, *Owner*
Christine H Kim, *Radiology*
EMP: 100
SALES (est): 5.7MM **Privately Held**
SIC: 8742 Hospital & health services consultant

(P-27648)
SITESTUFF YARDI SYSTEMS I
430 S Fairview Ave, Goleta (93117-3637)
PHONE..................................805 966-3666
Steven Sewell, *Principal*
Gordon Morrel, *COO*
John Bennett, *Vice Pres*
Fritz Schindelbeck, *Vice Pres*
Richard Runswick, *Admin Asst*
EMP: 103
SALES (est): 19.9MM **Privately Held**
SIC: 8742 Real estate consultant

(P-27649)
SITRICK BRINCKO GROUP LLC
1840 Century Park E # 800, Los Angeles (90067-2109)
PHONE..................................310 788-2850
Michael Sitrick, *Mng Member*
John Brincko,
EMP: 60
SALES (est): 3.7MM
SALES (corp-wide): 598.5MM **Publicly Held**
SIC: 8742 8743 Management consulting services; public relations services
PA: Resources Connection, Inc.
17101 Armstrong Ave
Irvine CA 92614
714 430-6400

(P-27650)
SKYLIGHT HALTHCARE SYSTEMS INC
10935 Vista Sorrento Pkwy # 350, San Diego (92130-2651)
PHONE..................................858 523-3700
David J Schofield, *CEO*
Fitz Patrick, *CFO*
Lisa Romano, *Ch Credit Ofcr*
Robin Wygal, *Administration*

Mike Barksdale, *Sr Software Eng*
EMP: 56
SQ FT: 11,000
SALES (est): 13.2MM
SALES (corp-wide): 84.9MM **Privately Held**
WEB: www.skylight.com
SIC: 8742 Hospital & health services consultant
PA: Getwellnetwork, Inc.
7700 Old Georgetown Rd 4t
Bethesda MD 20814
240 482-3200

(P-27651)
SKYLINE CONSULTING GROUP
13186 Skyline Blvd, Woodside (94062-4542)
PHONE..................................650 529-3455
Gustavo Rabin, *Owner*
Stacy McCarthy, *Principal*
EMP: 119
SALES (est): 7.8MM **Privately Held**
WEB: www.skylineconsulting.com
SIC: 8742 Training & development consultant

(P-27652)
SMG HOLDINGS INC
Also Called: Palm Springs Convention Center
277 N Avenida Caballeros, Palm Springs (92262-6440)
PHONE..................................760 325-6611
Fax: 760 778-4102
Jim Dunn, *Branch Mgr*
Kristie Dore, *Social Dir*
Gabe Rios, *Opers Mgr*
Dave Allen, *Opers Staff*
Amy Guzzetta, *Sales Mgr*
EMP: 60
SALES (corp-wide): 410.9MM **Privately Held**
WEB: www.smgworld.com
SIC: 8742 7389 Business consultant; convention & show services
PA: Smg Holdings, Inc
300 Cnshohckn State Rd # 450
Conshohocken PA 19428
610 729-7900

(P-27653)
SMITH-EMERY COMPANY (PA)
781 E Washington Blvd, Los Angeles (90021-3091)
PHONE..................................213 745-5312
Fax: 213 746-7228
James Partridge, *Ch of Bd*
James E Partridge, *Ch of Bd*
Helen Choe, *CFO*
Daniel Slater, *Vice Pres*
Rob Benjamin, *Info Tech Mgr*
EMP: 70
SQ FT: 35,000
SALES (est): 28.1MM **Privately Held**
WEB: www.smithemery.com
SIC: 8742 Construction project management consultant

(P-27654)
SNAP TECHNOLOGIES INC
130 W Union St, Pasadena (91103-3628)
PHONE..................................626 585-6900
Tom McGovern, *President*
EMP: 50 **EST:** 2004
SALES: 10MM **Privately Held**
SIC: 8742 4813 Financial consultant;

(P-27655)
SOAPROJECTS INC (PA)
495 N Whisman Rd Ste 100, Mountain View (94043-5725)
PHONE..................................650 960-9900
Manpreet Grover, *President*
Namitha Sajeev, *CFO*
Dineshni Anumala, *Admin Asst*
Wennie Wang, *Admin Asst*
James Stoddard, *Accounting Mgr*
EMP: 51
SALES (est): 17MM **Privately Held**
SIC: 8742 7379 8721 Financial consultant; computer related consulting services; accounting, auditing & bookkeeping

(P-27656)
SODEXO INC
1812 Verdugo Blvd Fl 1, Glendale (91208-1407)
PHONE..................................818 952-2201
Ron Reed, *Manager*
Dominic Bull, *Manager*
Maurice Parson, *Manager*
EMP: 90
SALES (corp-wide): 96.3MM **Privately Held**
SIC: 8742 Hospital & health services consultant
HQ: Sodexo, Inc.
9801 Washingtonian Blvd # 1
Gaithersburg MD 20878
301 987-4000

(P-27657)
SOLO W-2 INC
Also Called: Solo Workforce
3478 Buskirk Ave Ste 1000, Pleasant Hill (94523-4378)
PHONE..................................925 680-0200
James R Ziegler, *President*
Sara M Wilkison, *CFO*
Gina Acosta, *Admin Asst*
Chris Race, *Administration*
Sandi Buchanan, *Human Res Dir*
EMP: 110 **EST:** 1997
SQ FT: 800
SALES: 10MM **Privately Held**
WEB: www.pacepros.com
SIC: 8742 8721 Compensation & benefits planning consultant; billing & bookkeeping service

(P-27658)
SOUTH PACIFIC FINANCIAL CORP
2299 W Adams Ave Ste 113, El Centro (92243-9445)
PHONE..................................760 353-1080
EMP: 74
SALES (corp-wide): 29.4MM **Privately Held**
SIC: 8742 6141 Financial consultant; personal credit institutions
PA: South Pacific Financial Corp
2 Ada Ste 150
Irvine CA 92618
909 476-4182

(P-27659)
SPECTRUM STTLMENT RECOVERY LLC
100 Shrline Hwy Ste B-125, San Francisco (94111)
PHONE..................................415 392-5900
Howard Yellen,
John D'Agate, *Sales Staff*
Josh Camire,
David Morgenstein,
Donna Hart, *Manager*
EMP: 50
SQ FT: 10,000
SALES (est): 4.8MM **Privately Held**
SIC: 8742 Management consulting services

(P-27660)
SQA SERVICES INC
550 Silver Spur Rd # 300, Rllng HLS Est (90275-3605)
PHONE..................................310 544-6888
James C McKay, *CEO*
J Michael McKay, *President*
Gerard Pearce, *Vice Pres*
Fred Williams, *Vice Pres*
Stephanie Dizon, *Office Admin*
EMP: 267
SQ FT: 8,000
SALES (est): 36MM **Privately Held**
WEB: www.sqaservices.com
SIC: 8742 Quality assurance consultant

(P-27661)
ST JUDE HOSPITAL YORBA LINDA (PA)
251 Imperial Hwy Ste 481, Fullerton (92835-1058)
PHONE..................................714 449-4800
Lee Penrose, *Partner*
Iris Chow, *Executive*
Man Chow, *Manager*

EMP: 64
SALES (est): 9.9MM **Privately Held**
SIC: 8742 Management consulting services

(P-27662)
STARBUCKS CORPORATION
2950 N Hollywood Way # 175, Burbank (91505-1074)
PHONE..................................818 565-3510
Sarosh Mistry, *Branch Mgr*
Jessica Picard, *District Mgr*
EMP: 75
SALES (corp-wide): 19.1B **Publicly Held**
SIC: 8742 Restaurant & food services consultants
PA: Starbucks Corporation
2401 Utah Ave S
Seattle WA 98134
206 447-1575

(P-27663)
STARBUCKS CORPORATION
17700 Newhope St Ste 200, Fountain Valley (92708-5433)
PHONE..................................714 378-1107
Fax: 714 424-1919
Maureen Schuller, *Manager*
Jim Spillane, *Vice Pres*
Kevin B Joy, *Opers Staff*
Judy Han, *Instructor*
Bridgette Flores, *Legal Staff*
EMP: 75
SALES (corp-wide): 19.1B **Publicly Held**
SIC: 8742 Restaurant & food services consultants
PA: Starbucks Corporation
2401 Utah Ave S
Seattle WA 98134
206 447-1575

(P-27664)
STARBUCKS CORPORATION
1451 Francis Ave, Upland (91786-2343)
PHONE..................................626 203-1862
Carrie Valore, *Principal*
EMP: 75
SALES (corp-wide): 19.1B **Publicly Held**
SIC: 8742 Restaurant & food services consultants
PA: Starbucks Corporation
2401 Utah Ave S
Seattle WA 98134
206 447-1575

(P-27665)
STARBUCKS CORPORATION
60 Spear St Ste 700, San Francisco (94105-1513)
PHONE..................................415 537-7170
Fax: 415 865-0651
Moana Stolz, *Branch Mgr*
David Razon, *Human Resources*
EMP: 75
SALES (corp-wide): 19.1B **Publicly Held**
SIC: 8742 Restaurant & food services consultants
PA: Starbucks Corporation
2401 Utah Ave S
Seattle WA 98134
206 447-1575

(P-27666)
STATE GROUP LLC
Also Called: Seven Hospitality
36 Umbria, Irvine (92618-8877)
PHONE..................................949 612-2879
Matt Pannek,
Michelle Pannek,
EMP: 280
SQ FT: 8,800
SALES (est): 17.6MM **Privately Held**
SIC: 8742 Restaurant & food services consultants

(P-27667)
STEELE INTERNATIONAL INC
1350 Treat Blvd Ste 250, Walnut Creek (94597-8802)
PHONE..................................415 781-4300
Todd Lane, *CFO*
EMP: 549 **Privately Held**
SIC: 8742 7381 Management consulting services; detective & armored car services

PA: Steele International, Inc.
1 Sansome St Ste 3500
San Francisco CA 94104
-

(P-27668)
STERLING CONSULTING GROUP LLC
Also Called: Sterling Brand
55 Union St Fl 3, San Francisco (94111-1244)
PHONE.................................415 248-7900
Austin McGhie, *Manager*
EMP: 84
SALES (corp-wide): 12.1MM **Privately Held**
SIC: 8742 Marketing consulting services
PA: Sterling Consulting Group Llc
75 Varick St Fl 8
New York NY 10013
212 329-4600

(P-27669)
STERLING MKTG & FINCL CORP
Also Called: T3 Direct
4660 Spyres Way Ste 1, Modesto (95356-9801)
PHONE.................................209 593-1140
Albert W Dadesho, *President*
Susie Dadesho, *Vice Pres*
Jonathan Dadesho, *Mktg Dir*
Jonathan Mason, *Marketing Staff*
EMP: 50
SQ FT: 8,000
SALES (est): 6.2MM **Privately Held**
SIC: 8742 Marketing consulting services

(P-27670)
STRATEGIC BUS INSIGHTS INC (PA)
333 Ravenswood Ave, Menlo Park (94025-3453)
PHONE.................................650 859-4600
William Guns, *CEO*
William Ralston, *CFO*
Eilif Trondsen, *Senior VP*
Chulho Park, *Principal*
Elen Boykin, *Administration*
EMP: 63 EST: 2000
SQ FT: 10,000
SALES (est): 10.4MM **Privately Held**
WEB: www.sricbi.com
SIC: 8742 Management consulting services

(P-27671)
STRATEGIC ENLACE INC
281 N Puente St, Brea (92821-3825)
PHONE.................................714 256-8648
Fax: 714 256-8638
Alberto Fernandez, *President*
Marina Arreola, *Office Mgr*
Joe Cannarozzi, *VP Sales*
EMP: 55
SQ FT: 6,000
SALES (est): 4.8MM **Privately Held**
WEB: www.strategicenlace.com
SIC: 8742 Marketing consulting services; sales (including sales management) consultant

(P-27672)
SULLIVANCURTISMONROE INSURANCE (PA)
1920 Main St Ste 600, Irvine (92614-7226)
P.O. Box 19763 (92623-9763)
PHONE.................................800 427-3253
Fax: 949 852-9762
John Monroe, *CEO*
David Kummer, *President*
Mark Eckenweiler, *CFO*
Frances Leiva, *CFO*
Veronica Kimble, *Officer*
EMP: 103
SQ FT: 22,000
SALES (est): 46.5MM **Privately Held**
WEB: www.sullicurt.com
SIC: 8742 6411 Management consulting services; insurance brokers

(P-27673)
SUMMIT HR WORLDWIDE INC
Also Called: Echo Staffing
220 Main St Ste 208a, San Jose (95112)
PHONE.................................408 884-7100
Priyaranjan Sinha, *Ch of Bd*
Vidhya Singaradel, *Info Tech Mgr*
Maxwell Samueal, *Controller*
Rex Fernando, *Manager*
EMP: 100
SALES (est): 4.1MM **Privately Held**
SIC: 8742 Human resource consulting services

(P-27674)
SUTTER CONNECT LLC (HQ)
Also Called: Sutter Physician Services
10470 Old Placrvl Rd # 100, Sacramento (95827-2539)
P.O. Box 254707 (95865-4707)
PHONE.................................916 854-6600
Fax: 916 854-6610
Charles V Wirth, *CEO*
Gabrielle Gaspar, *Vice Pres*
Robert Raymond, *Info Tech Dir*
Balbir Singh, *Database Admin*
Kevin Yamamoto, *Financial Analy*
EMP: 800
SQ FT: 87,000
SALES (est): 35.9MM
SALES (corp-wide): 11B **Privately Held**
WEB: www.sutterconnect.com
SIC: 8742 8741 8721 Hospital & health services consultant; management information systems consultant; management services; accounting, auditing & bookkeeping
PA: Sutter Health
2200 River Plaza Dr
Sacramento CA 95833
916 733-8800

(P-27675)
SUTTER HEALTH
633 Folsom St Fl 5, San Francisco (94107-3623)
PHONE.................................415 600-3311
Phillip Kay, *Sr Project Mgr*
EMP: 93
SALES (corp-wide): 11B **Privately Held**
SIC: 8742 Business planning & organizing services
PA: Sutter Health
2200 River Plaza Dr
Sacramento CA 95833
916 733-8800

(P-27676)
SWANDER PACE CAPITAL LLC
101 Mission St Ste 1900, San Francisco (94105-1726)
PHONE.................................415 477-8500
Fax: 415 477-8510
Andrew Richards, *Managing Dir*
Ann Kim, *Vice Pres*
Nathan Ngai, *Vice Pres*
Heather Smith Thorne, *Vice Pres*
Valerie Scott, *Principal*
EMP: 567
SQ FT: 5,000
SALES (est): 39.1MM **Privately Held**
WEB: www.spcap.com
SIC: 8742 Management consulting services; restaurant & food services consultants

(P-27677)
SYNERGY HEALTH AST LLC (DH)
Also Called: Americas Regional Division
9020 Activity Rd Ste D, San Diego (92126-4454)
PHONE.................................858 586-1166
Fax: 858 586-6641
▲ EMP: 60
SALES (est): 11.2MM
SALES (corp-wide): 2.2B **Privately Held**
WEB: www.beam-one.com
SIC: 8742 Hospital & health services consultant
HQ: Steris Corporation
5960 Heisley Rd
Mentor OH 44060
440 354-2600

(P-27678)
TAJ MARKETING LLC
3550 Wilshire Blvd, Los Angeles (90010-2401)
PHONE.................................213 232-0150
Jin Young Kim, *CEO*
Young Min Yoo, *CFO*
Ilho Lee, *Chief Mktg Ofcr*
Yang Sum Shin, *Vice Pres*
Sang Young Yi, *Admin Sec*
EMP: 50
SQ FT: 2,250
SALES (est): 135.1K **Privately Held**
SIC: 8742 Marketing consulting services

(P-27679)
TECHNOLOGY ASSOCIATES EC INC
3115 Melrose Dr Ste 110, Carlsbad (92010-6531)
PHONE.................................760 765-5275
Walter Oleski, *CEO*
Susan Kimbrough, *Business Dir*
Wilma Gozaga, *Administration*
James Watkins, *Engineer*
Wilma Gamboa, *Controller*
EMP: 74
SALES (est): 12.4MM **Privately Held**
SIC: 8742 General management consultant

(P-27680)
TECOLOTE RESEARCH INC
2120 E Grand Ave Ste 200, El Segundo (90245-5024)
PHONE.................................310 640-4700
Fax: 310 536-9922
James Takayesu, *President*
Derek Lettman, *Technology*
Donna Delonti, *Human Res Dir*
Jim Schmitz, *Director*
EMP: 114
SALES (corp-wide): 96.2MM **Privately Held**
WEB: www.tecolote.com
SIC: 8742 8731 Management consulting services; commercial physical research
PA: Tecolote Research, Inc.
420 S Fairview Ave # 201
Goleta CA 93117
805 571-6366

(P-27681)
TEJON MARKETING COMPANY
4436 Lebec Rd, Lebec (93243-9705)
PHONE.................................661 248-3000
Robert A Stine, *President*
Dennis Atkinson, *Agent*
EMP: 75
SALES: 458.4K
SALES (corp-wide): 51.1MM **Publicly Held**
WEB: www.tejonfilm.com
SIC: 8742 Marketing consulting services
PA: Tejon Ranch Co.
4436 Lebec Rd
Lebec CA 93243
661 248-3000

(P-27682)
TELEGRAPH HILL PARTNERS INVEST
360 Post St Ste 601, San Francisco (94108-4909)
PHONE.................................415 765-6980
Fax: 415 765-6983
J Matthew Mackowski, *Chairman*
Rob C Hart Cfa, *Vice Pres*
Alexandra J Frankel, *Administration*
Toto N Granucci, *Administration*
M Celeste Salvatto, *Administration*
EMP: 50
SALES: 1.2MM **Privately Held**
SIC: 8742 6799 Management consulting services; investors

(P-27683)
TELESTAR CONSULTING INC
519 N Alta Dr, Beverly Hills (90210-3501)
PHONE.................................310 748-0008
Karl Angel, *President*
EMP: 50
SALES (est): 2.5MM **Privately Held**
SIC: 8742 Hospital & health services consultant

(P-27684)
TERRACARE ASSOCIATES LLC
921 Arnold Dr, Martinez (94553-4102)
PHONE.................................925 374-0060
Todd Williams, *Principal*
Jason Holley, *Business Mgr*
Kris Dasso, *Manager*
Mike Farrell, *Accounts Exec*
EMP: 77
SALES (corp-wide): 62.3MM **Privately Held**
SIC: 8742 Management consulting services
PA: Terracare Associates, Llc
8201 Southpark Ln Ste 110
Littleton CO 80120
720 587-2520

(P-27685)
TETRA TECH INC
1230 Columbia St Ste 1000, San Diego (92101-8588)
PHONE.................................619 525-7188
Fax: 619 525-7186
Roger Argus, *Branch Mgr*
Lawrence D Romine Jr, *Engineer*
EMP: 68
SALES (corp-wide): 2.3B **Publicly Held**
SIC: 8742 8744 8711 Management consulting services; facilities support services; engineering services
PA: Tetra Tech, Inc.
3475 E Foothill Blvd
Pasadena CA 91107
626 351-4664

(P-27686)
THE BOSTON CNSULTING GROUP INC
355 S Grand Ave Ste 3300, Los Angeles (90071-1592)
PHONE.................................213 621-2772
Fax: 213 621-1639
Angela Johnson, *Director*
William Burnside, *Vice Pres*
Chris Bennington, *Info Tech Mgr*
Reggie Gilyard, *Info Tech Mgr*
Linda Adams, *VP Mktg*
EMP: 70
SALES (corp-wide): 875.7MM **Privately Held**
WEB: www.bcg.com
SIC: 8742 Management consulting services
PA: The Boston Consulting Group Inc
1 Beacon St Fl 10
Boston MA 02108
617 850-3700

(P-27687)
THRESHOLD DIGITAL RESEARCH LAB
1649 11th St, Santa Monica (90404-3707)
PHONE.................................310 452-8885
Larry Kasanoff, *President*
EMP: 50 EST: 1996
SALES (est): 2.9MM **Privately Held**
WEB: www.threshold-digital.com
SIC: 8742 Management consulting services

(P-27688)
TMG FINANCIAL
3478 Buskirk Ave Ste 1031, Pleasant Hill (94523-4344)
PHONE.................................925 989-0632
Troy Holland, *Owner*
EMP: 82
SALES (est): 4.8MM **Privately Held**
SIC: 8742 Marketing consulting services

(P-27689)
TOP TIER CONSULTING
21550 Oxnard St Fl 3, Woodland Hills (91367-7105)
PHONE.................................818 338-2121
Brad Armstrong, *Principal*
Gregory Anderson, *Principal*
Christopher Downey, *Principal*
Susan Linard, *Controller*
EMP: 70
SQ FT: 2,000
SALES: 19MM **Privately Held**
SIC: 8742 7379 Management consulting services; computer related consulting services

(P-27690)
TOPDOWN CONSULTING INC
530 Divisadero St Ste 310, San Francisco (94117-2213)
PHONE.................................888 644-8445

8742 - Management Consulting Services County (P-27691)

PRODUCDUCTS & SERVICES SECTION

Juan Porter, *President*
Mike Davies, *COO*
Lee Spencer, *Vice Pres*
David Beverly, *Info Tech Mgr*
Katie Fenech, *Finance*
EMP: 80
SALES (est): 10.7MM **Privately Held**
WEB: www.topdownconsulting.com
SIC: 8742 Financial consultant

(P-27691)
TOWERS WATSON & CO
Also Called: Watson Wyatt Worldwide 421
345 California St Fl 15, San Francisco (94104-2629)
PHONE..................................415 733-4100
Jacque Leger, *Principal*
Mia Saetern, *Finance Asst*
Jennifer Miller, *Corp Comm Staff*
EMP: 125 **Privately Held**
WEB: www.watsonwyatt.com
SIC: 8742 8999 7371 6411 Compensation & benefits planning consultant; human resource consulting services; actuarial consultant; computer software systems analysis & design, custom; computer software development; pension & retirement plan consultants
HQ: Towers Watson Delaware Holdings Inc.
335 Madison Ave Fl 20
New York NY 10017
212 309-3400

(P-27692)
TOWERS WATSON PENNSYLVANIA INC
Also Called: Towers Perrin
300 S Grand Ave Ste 2000, Los Angeles (90071-3109)
PHONE..................................310 551-5600
Fax: 310 551-5757
Michael Fox, *Manager*
Raymond L Bille, *Principal*
Emily Lawrence, *Consultant*
Jennifer Lee, *Consultant*
Ryan Patschke, *Consultant*
EMP: 110 **Privately Held**
WEB: www.towers.com
SIC: 8742 Management consulting services
HQ: Towers Watson Pennsylvania Inc.
263 Tresser Blvd Ste 700
Stamford CT 06901
203 326-5400

(P-27693)
TRACE3 INC
2120 E Grand Ave Ste 145, El Segundo (90245-5024)
PHONE..................................310 220-0164
Teresa Chavez, *Office Mgr*
EMP: 85
SALES (corp-wide): 130.1MM **Privately Held**
SIC: 8742 Sales (including sales management) consultant
PA: Trace3, Inc.
7565 Irvine Center Dr # 200
Irvine CA 92618
949 333-1801

(P-27694)
TRACE3 INC (PA)
7565 Irvine Center Dr # 200, Irvine (92618-4919)
PHONE..................................949 333-1801
Fax: 949 333-2400
Hayes Drumwright, *CEO*
Tyler Beecher, *CEO*
Paul Wiederkehr, *Chief Mktg Ofcr*
Paul Markel, *Senior VP*
Terri Cooper, *Vice Pres*
EMP: 100
SQ FT: 10,000
SALES (est): 130.1MM **Privately Held**
WEB: www.trace3.com
SIC: 8742 Sales (including sales management) consultant

(P-27695)
TRADING AMERICA CORP
535 N Brand Blvd Ste 275, Glendale (91203-3395)
PHONE..................................786 842-7888
Timothy Richard, *President*
EMP: 50

SALES: 8MM **Privately Held**
SIC: 8742 Foreign trade consultant

(P-27696)
TRANSIRIS CORPORATION
900 Industrial Rd Ste B, San Carlos (94070-4140)
PHONE..................................650 303-3495
Silvian Centiu, *CEO*
Simona Nan, *Director*
Simina Simion, *Director*
EMP: 75
SALES (est): 5.1MM **Privately Held**
SIC: 8742 Marketing consulting services

(P-27697)
TREELINE AND ASSOCIATES
9330 Baseline Rd Ste 106, Rancho Cucamonga (91701-5827)
PHONE..................................909 476-2757
John Metters, *Owner*
EMP: 99
SALES (est): 2.8MM **Privately Held**
SIC: 8742 Marketing consulting services

(P-27698)
TRIAGE CONSULTING GROUP (PA)
221 Main St Ste 1100, San Francisco (94105-1949)
PHONE..................................415 512-9400
Fax: 415 512-9404
Brian Neece, *President*
Damon Lewis, *Treasurer*
Melissa Beard, *Program Mgr*
Kim Mc Lemore, *Office Mgr*
Kim McLemore, *Office Admin*
EMP: 280
SQ FT: 21,665
SALES: 98MM **Privately Held**
WEB: www.triageconsulting.com
SIC: 8742 8748 Hospital & health services consultant; business consulting

(P-27699)
TRINET HR CORPORATION
1100 San Leandro Blvd # 300, San Leandro (94577-1599)
PHONE..................................972 789-3900
Burton Goldfield, *Principal*
Garth Hobden, *Vice Pres*
Afton Lewis, *Executive Asst*
Richard Pagador, *Engineer*
Chris Fitzjarrald, *Marketing Staff*
EMP: 723
SALES (est): 25.9MM
SALES (corp-wide): 2.6B **Publicly Held**
SIC: 8742 Human resource consulting services
PA: Trinet Group, Inc.
1100 San Leandro Blvd # 300
San Leandro CA 94577
510 352-5000

(P-27700)
TRIPLE RING TECHNOLOGIES INC
39655 Eureka Dr, Newark (94560-4806)
PHONE..................................510 592-3000
Joseph A Heanue, *CEO*
Marc Whyte, *Ch of Bd*
Peter Clark, *CFO*
Gurinder Parhar, *Officer*
Barclay Dorman, *Vice Pres*
EMP: 50
SALES (est): 13MM **Privately Held**
WEB: www.tripleringtech.com
SIC: 8742 Business consultant

(P-27701)
TRIPLECURVE LLC
5716 Corsa Ave Ste 110, Westlake Village (91362-7354)
PHONE..................................855 874-2878
Joseph Demike,
Brianna Demike, *Partner*
EMP: 100 **EST:** 2012
SALES (est): 3.7MM **Privately Held**
SIC: 8742 2741 7371 Management consulting services; ; custom computer programming services

(P-27702)
TSMC NORTH AMERICA (HQ)
2851 Junction Ave, San Jose (95134-1910)
PHONE..................................408 382-8000

Richard B Cassidy II, *CEO*
Rick Cassidy, *President*
John Yue, *Vice Pres*
Joyce Huang, *Executive*
Katy Liu, *Executive*
EMP: 148
SALES (est): 45.4MM
SALES (corp-wide): 25.9B **Privately Held**
SIC: 8742 8711 5065 3674 Marketing consulting services; consulting engineer; electronic parts & equipment; semiconductor circuit networks
PA: Taiwan Semiconductor Manufacturing Company Limited
8, Li Hsing 6th Rd.,
Hsinchu City 30077
350 559-32

(P-27703)
UNGER & ASSOCIATES INC
29805 Weatherwood Ste 200, Laguna Niguel (92677-1945)
PHONE..................................949 249-2800
Walter Unger, *Branch Mgr*
EMP: 50
SALES (corp-wide): 3.9MM **Privately Held**
SIC: 8742 Hospital & health services consultant
PA: Unger & Associates, Inc.
1845 Summit Ave Ste 406
Plano TX 75074
972 424-6773

(P-27704)
UNITED TALENT AGENCY INC
1880 Century Park E, Los Angeles (90067-1600)
PHONE..................................310 385-2800
Fax: 310 385-1220
Grant Ledger, *Owner*
Ron Bleiweiss, *Vice Pres*
Mark Bennett, *Agent*
Anna Bewers, *Agent*
Sean Goulding, *Agent*
EMP: 120
SALES (corp-wide): 22.1MM **Privately Held**
SIC: 8742 Management consulting services
PA: United Talent Agency, Llc
9336 Civic Center Dr
Beverly Hills CA 90210
310 273-6700

(P-27705)
US TOURNAMENT GOLF LTD LBLTY
10808 Stamfield Dr, Rancho Cucamonga (91730-6607)
P.O. Box 3373 (91729-3373)
PHONE..................................909 987-6695
Robert E Harrington, *Mng Member*
EMP: 50
SQ FT: 1,000
SALES: 5MM **Privately Held**
SIC: 8742 Business planning & organizing services

(P-27706)
USA FACT INC (PA)
6200 Box Springs Blvd, Riverside (92507-0790)
PHONE..................................951 656-7800
Matt Davidson, *CEO*
Mike Curran, *President*
Laurie Beem, *Vice Pres*
Daniel Doherty, *Vice Pres*
Cheryl Franklin, *Vice Pres*
EMP: 54
SALES (est): 10.9MM **Privately Held**
WEB: www.usafact.com
SIC: 8742 Human resource consulting services

(P-27707)
VAN ETTEN SUZUMOTO BECKET LLP
1620 26th St Ste 6000n, Santa Monica (90404-4074)
PHONE..................................310 315-8284
Fax: 310 315-8210
David Van Etten,
EMP: 65

SALES (est): 3.3MM **Privately Held**
SIC: 8742 Management consulting services

(P-27708)
VARIS LLC
3915 Security Park Dr B, Rancho Cordova (95742-6903)
PHONE..................................916 294-0860
Dean B Wilkie, *Manager*
Padra Randall, *Senior Mgr*
EMP: 70
SALES (corp-wide): 8.1MM **Privately Held**
SIC: 8742 Management consulting services
PA: Varis Llc
9245 Sierra College Blvd
Roseville CA 95661
916 294-0860

(P-27709)
VAYAN MARKETING GROUP LLC
10877 Wilshire Blvd Fl 12, Los Angeles (90024-4332)
PHONE..................................310 943-4990
Jesse Lo RE,
Curt Shaffer, *CFO*
Laura Kall,
Michael Medema,
Brad Morrison,
EMP: 50
SQ FT: 7,000
SALES (est): 3.3MM **Privately Held**
WEB: www.vayan.com
SIC: 8742 Marketing consulting services

(P-27710)
VERIFI INC
8391 Beverly Blvd Ste 310, Los Angeles (90048-2633)
PHONE..................................323 655-5789
Fax: 323 655-5537
Matthew G Katz, *CEO*
Rick Lynch, *President*
Jennifer Schulz, *CEO*
Sara Craven, *COO*
Ronald B Cushey, *CFO*
EMP: 65
SALES (est): 10.8MM **Privately Held**
SIC: 8742 Quality assurance consultant

(P-27711)
VERTICALRESPONSE INC
50 Beale St Fl 10, San Francisco (94105-1813)
PHONE..................................415 905-6880
Fax: 415 808-2480
Janine Popick, *President*
David Shiba, *COO*
Anthony Ginn, *Vice Pres*
John McNulty, *Vice Pres*
Arturo Zacarias, *Admin Asst*
EMP: 110
SALES (est): 23.5MM
SALES (corp-wide): 1.7B **Publicly Held**
WEB: www.verticalresponse.com
SIC: 8742 Marketing consulting services
PA: Deluxe Corporation
3680 Victoria St N
Shoreview MN 55126
651 483-7111

(P-27712)
VISIO INTEG PROFE LLC (HQ)
Also Called: Visionary Intgrtion Prfssonals
80 Iron Point Cir Ste 100, Folsom (95630-8592)
PHONE..................................916 608-8320
Jonna A Ward, *Mng Member*
Jason Marceau, *COO*
Terry Miller, *COO*
Karen Davis, *CFO*
David Perroni, *Exec VP*
EMP: 95
SQ FT: 9,000
SALES: 100MM
SALES (corp-wide): 82.8MM **Privately Held**
SIC: 8742 7379 Management consulting services; computer related maintenance services

PRODUCTS & SERVICES SECTION
8743 - Public Relations Svcs County (P-27734)

PA: Visionary Integration Professionals, Inc.
2001 Edmund Halley Dr
Reston VA 20191
703 322-9565

(P-27713)
VISIONSTAR INC
3435 Wilsh Blvd Ste 2120, Los Angeles (90010)
PHONE.................213 387-3700
Mark Anav, CEO
EMP: 90
SALES (est): 8.5MM **Privately Held**
SIC: 8742 Marketing consulting services

(P-27714)
VISTAGE INTERNATIONAL INC (PA)
Also Called: Executive Committee, The
11452 El Camino Real # 400, San Diego (92130-2043)
PHONE.................858 523-6800
Rafael Pastor, Ch of Bd
Peter J Campbell, Managing Prtnr
Richard Carr, President
Gaye Van Den Hombergh, President
Ken Jacobson, CEO
EMP: 115
SALES (est): 46.3MM **Privately Held**
WEB: www.teconline.com
SIC: 8742 Business planning & organizing services

(P-27715)
VISTANCIA MARKETING LLC
Also Called: Shea Homes Ltd Prtnershp
655 Brea Canyon Rd, Walnut (91789-3078)
PHONE.................909 594-9500
EMP: 107
SALES (est): 3.9MM
SALES (corp-wide): 2B **Privately Held**
SIC: 8742 Marketing consulting services
HQ: Shea Homes Limited Partnership, A California Limited Partnership
655 Brea Canyon Rd
Walnut CA 91789

(P-27716)
WAGEWORKS INC (PA)
1100 Park Pl Fl 4, San Mateo (94403-1599)
PHONE.................650 577-5200
Joseph L Jackson, CEO
John W Larson, Ch of Bd
Edgar O Montes, COO
Colm M Callan, CFO
Kimberly L Wilford, Senior VP
EMP: 113
SQ FT: 37,937
SALES: 334.3MM **Publicly Held**
SIC: 8742 Compensation & benefits planning consultant

(P-27717)
WASSERMAN MEDIA GROUP LLC (PA)
10960 Wilshire Blvd, Los Angeles (90024-3702)
PHONE.................310 407-0200
Casey Wasserman, Mng Member
Tim Chadwick, COO
Michael Watts, COO
Dean Christopher, CFO
Hugh Boss, Vice Pres
EMP: 115
SQ FT: 40,000
SALES (est): 52.4MM **Privately Held**
SIC: 8742 Marketing consulting services

(P-27718)
WEISSCOMM GROUP LTD
50 Francisco St Ste 400, San Francisco (94133-2114)
PHONE.................415 362-5018
EMP: 56
SALES (corp-wide): 131.7MM **Privately Held**
SIC: 8742 8748 Marketing consulting services; communications consulting
PA: The Weisscomm Group Ltd
50 Francisco St Ste 400
San Francisco CA 94133
415 362-5018

(P-27719)
WEST COAST AVIATION SVCS LLC (PA)
Also Called: West Coast Charters
19711 Campus Dr Ste 200, Santa Ana (92707-5203)
PHONE.................949 852-8340
Gary Standell, President
Barbara Hunt, Sales Dir
Gina Roe, Program Dir
Annie Akmakjian, Manager
EMP: 50
SQ FT: 2,000
SALES (est): 9.1MM **Privately Held**
WEB: www.westcoastcharters.com
SIC: 8742 5088 Industry specialist consultants; aircraft & parts

(P-27720)
WILSHIRE ASSOCIATES INC (PA)
1299 Ocean Ave Ste 700, Santa Monica (90401-1085)
PHONE.................310 451-3051
Fax: 310 458-0520
Dennis A Tito, CEO
John Hindman, President
Andrew Junkin, President
Jamie Ohl, CFO
Gareth Alli, Vice Pres
EMP: 210
SQ FT: 57,530 **Privately Held**
WEB: www.wilshire.com
SIC: 8742 Financial consultant

(P-27721)
WINSTON RETAIL SOLUTIONS LLC (PA)
456 Montgomery St Lowr 5, San Francisco (94104-1233)
PHONE.................415 558-9000
Fax: 415 558-9191
Jan Croatt, Partner
Steve Riegler, CFO
Diane Blake, Exec VP
Jon Bilock, Senior VP
Terry Healy, Recruiter
EMP: 50
SALES (est): 6.7MM **Privately Held**
WEB: www.winston-usa.com
SIC: 8742 Retail trade consultant

(P-27722)
WIPFLI LLP
Also Called: Wipli HFS Consultants
505 14th St Fl 5, Oakland (94612-1406)
PHONE.................510 768-0066
EMP: 100
SALES (corp-wide): 296.2MM **Privately Held**
SIC: 8742 Hospital & health services consultant
PA: Wipfli Llp
10000 W Innovation Dr 250-260
Milwaukee WI 53226
414 431-9300

(P-27723)
WORKFORCE LOGIC LLC
19080 Lomita Ave Bldg 3, Sonoma (95476-5453)
PHONE.................866 296-3343
Gary D Nelson, Mng Member
Stephanie Ellis, Executive
Britney Anderson, Admin Asst
Ed Pearson, Technology
Hed Buckleyon,
EMP: 613
SALES (est): 48.7MM
SALES (corp-wide): 214.2MM **Privately Held**
SIC: 8742 Management information systems consultant
PA: Zerochaos, Llc
420 S Orange Ave Ste 600
Orlando FL 32801
407 770-6161

(P-27724)
WTW DELAWARE HOLDINGS LLC
Also Called: Willis Towers Watson
10955 Vista Sorrento Pkwy # 300, San Diego (92130-8699)
PHONE.................858 523-5500

Ken Platt, CIO
EMP: 80 **Privately Held**
WEB: www.watsonwyatt.com
SIC: 8742 Management consulting services
HQ: Wtw Delaware Holdings Llc
901 N Glebe Rd
Arlington VA 22203
703 258-8000

(P-27725)
XAD INC
189 Bernardo Ave 100, Mountain View (94043-5203)
PHONE.................650 386-6867
EMP: 150
SALES (corp-wide): 52.8MM **Privately Held**
SIC: 8742 Marketing consulting services
PA: Xad, Inc.
1 World Trade Ctr Fl 60
New York NY 10007
347 271-2258

(P-27726)
YODLEE INC (HQ)
3600 Bridge Pkwy Ste 200, Redwood City (94065-6139)
PHONE.................650 980-3600
Fax: 650 980-3602
Anil Arora, President
Mike Armsby, CFO
Brad Beals, Treasurer
Bill Parsons, Ch Credit Ofcr
Bruce Felt, Bd of Directors
EMP: 146
SQ FT: 35,000
SALES: 89MM
SALES (corp-wide): 348.7MM **Publicly Held**
SIC: 8742 Banking & finance consultant
PA: Envestnet, Inc.
35 E Wacker Dr Ste 2400
Chicago IL 60601
312 827-2800

(P-27727)
ZS ASSOCIATES INC
2535 W Hillcrest Dr # 100, Thousand Oaks (91320-2457)
PHONE.................805 413-5900
EMP: 62
SALES (corp-wide): 469.9MM **Privately Held**
SIC: 8742 Marketing consulting services
PA: Zs Associates, Inc.
1800 Sherman Ave Ste 37
Evanston IL 60201
858 677-2200

(P-27728)
ZS ASSOCIATES INC
4365 Executive Dr # 1530, San Diego (92121-2129)
PHONE.................858 677-2200
EMP: 62
SALES (corp-wide): 469.9MM **Privately Held**
SIC: 8742 7378 Marketing consulting services; computer maintenance & repair
PA: Zs Associates, Inc.
1800 Sherman Ave Ste 37
Evanston IL 60201
858 677-2200

8743 Public Relations Svcs

(P-27729)
ACCESS PUBLIC RELATIONS LLC
Also Called: Access Communications
650 California St Fl 30, San Francisco (94108-2611)
PHONE.................415 904-7070
Fax: 415 904-7055
Susan Butenhoff,
Leana Wood, Exec VP
Danielle Caff, Senior VP
Matthew Afflixio, Vice Pres
Cori Barrett, Vice Pres
EMP: 64 EST: 1982
SQ FT: 17,000

SALES (est): 11MM
SALES (corp-wide): 15.1B **Publicly Held**
WEB: www.accesspr.com
SIC: 8743 Public relations & publicity
HQ: Ketchum Inc.
1285 Avenue Of The Americ
New York NY 10019
646 935-3900

(P-27730)
ARYAKA NETWORKS INC
691 S Milpitas Blvd # 206, Milpitas (95035-5476)
PHONE.................408 273-8420
Shawn Farshchi, President
Kelly Hicks, CFO
Jim Hilbert, Senior VP
Nikesh Kalra, Senior VP
Mark Fogel, Vice Pres
EMP: 200
SALES (est): 25.6MM **Privately Held**
SIC: 8743 Sales promotion

(P-27731)
AT&T CORP
50 Fremont St, San Francisco (94105-2276)
PHONE.................415 442-5900
Fax: 415 442-3644
Dennis Williams, Branch Mgr
EMP: 150
SALES (corp-wide): 146.8B **Publicly Held**
WEB: www.att.com
SIC: 8743 Sales promotion
HQ: At&T Corp.
1 At&T Way
Bedminster NJ 07921
800 403-3302

(P-27732)
B T B EVENTS INC
Also Called: California Special Events
10950 Virginia Cir, Fountain Valley (92708-7010)
PHONE.................714 415-3313
Christopher P Chapin, CEO
Robert G Traxel, President
Roger Janke, Vice Pres
John P Regas, VP Opers
David Fitzpatrick,
EMP: 75
SALES (est): 12.9MM **Privately Held**
SIC: 8743 8742 7359 6512 Sales promotion; public relations & publicity; sales (including sales management) consultant; equipment rental & leasing; nonresidential building operators

(P-27733)
BAKER WINOKUR
Also Called: Bwrpr
9100 Wilshire Blvd 64w, Beverly Hills (90212-3415)
PHONE.................310 248-6169
M Sorel, President
EMP: 70
SALES: 10MM **Privately Held**
WEB: www.bwrpr.com
SIC: 8743 Public relations services

(P-27734)
BEHR PROCESS SALES COMPANY
3000 S Main St Apt 84e, Santa Ana (92707-4225)
P.O. Box 1287 (92702-1287)
PHONE.................714 545-7101
Fax: 714 241-1002
Kevin Jaffe, Partner
John V Croul, Partner
Parker Pace, COO
Michael Stecher, COO
Jim Dybevik, Human Res Dir
EMP: 150
SQ FT: 54,000
SALES (est): 9.8MM **Privately Held**
SIC: 8743 2851 5198 Sales promotion; varnishes; paints & paint additives; stains: varnish, oil or wax; lacquer: bases, dopes, thinner; paints, varnishes & supplies

8743 - Public Relations Svcs County (P-27735)

(P-27735)
BNI ENTERPRISES INC
Also Called: B N I
545 College Commerce Way, Upland (91786-4377)
PHONE.................................909 305-1818
Fax: 909 608-7676
Ivan Misner, *Chairman*
Michael Budd, *Vice Pres*
David Castro, *Vice Pres*
Rey Descalso, *Vice Pres*
Greg Ezell, *Vice Pres*
EMP: 600
SQ FT: 33,000
SALES (est): 81.7MM Privately Held
WEB: www.bni.com
SIC: 8743 Promotion service

(P-27736)
BWR PUBLIC RELATIONS
Also Called: Baker Winokur Ryder
9100 Wilshire Blvd 500w, Beverly Hills (90212-3415)
PHONE.................................310 248-6100
Fax: 310 550-1701
Larry Winokur, *President*
Paul Gillis, *Info Tech Mgr*
EMP: 67
SALES (est): 1.7MM Privately Held
SIC: 8743 Public relations services

(P-27737)
CALIBRE INTERNATIONAL LLC (PA)
Also Called: High Caliber Line
6250 N Irwindale Ave, Irwindale (91702-3208)
PHONE.................................626 969-4660
Fax: 626 969-4661
Daniel Oas,
Catherine Oas,
Patty Gomez, *Accounts Exec*
EMP: 120
SQ FT: 100,000
SALES (est): 39.8MM Privately Held
WEB: www.calibr.com
SIC: 8743 2759 Promotion service; promotional printing

(P-27738)
CAROLINE PROMOTIONS INC
809 S Adams St Apt 7, Glendale (91205-4424)
PHONE.................................818 507-7666
Caroline Jovenich, *President*
Delia Armenda, *Manager*
EMP: 55
SQ FT: 600
SALES (est): 3.4MM Privately Held
WEB: www.carolinepromotions.com
SIC: 8743 Sales promotion

(P-27739)
CATALINA MARKETING CORPORATION
18191 Von Karman Ave # 200, Irvine (92612-7105)
PHONE.................................949 930-6500
Tracey Jones, *Branch Mgr*
Gurleen Suri, *Comptroller*
EMP: 50
SALES (corp-wide): 229.2MM Privately Held
WEB: www.catalinamktg.com
SIC: 8743 Promotion service
HQ: Catalina Marketing Corporation
200 Carillon Pkwy
Saint Petersburg FL 33716
727 579-5000

(P-27740)
CHANDLER CHICCO AGENCY LLC (DH)
Also Called: CCA Advertising
474 Alvarado St, San Francisco (94114-3305)
PHONE.................................415 643-1101
Gianfranco Chicco,
Robert Chandler, *Principal*
Peggy Stanton, *Manager*
Charlotte Noble, *Agent*
EMP: 66
SQ FT: 30,000
SALES (est): 4MM Privately Held
SIC: 8743 8732 Public relations services; market analysis, business & economic research
HQ: Inventiv Health, Inc.
1 Van De Graaff Dr
Burlington MA 01803
800 416-0555

(P-27741)
CITY OF CORONA
400 S Vicentia Ave, Corona (92882-2187)
PHONE.................................951 279-3647
Kit Field, *Branch Mgr*
EMP: 250 Privately Held
SIC: 8743 Public relations services
PA: City Of Corona
400 S Vicentia Ave
Corona CA 92882
951 736-2372

(P-27742)
CMP FILM & DESIGN BURBANK LLC
Also Called: Mocean
2717 W Olive Ave, Burbank (91505-4532)
PHONE.................................818 729-0800
Craig Murray, *Mng Member*
Raluca Hirnna, *Controller*
Matthew Hurst, *Production*
EMP: 65
SQ FT: 12,000
SALES (est): 4.6MM Privately Held
SIC: 8743 7812 Promotion service; video tape production

(P-27743)
COMPETITOR GROUP EVENTS INC
5452 Oberlin Dr, San Diego (92121-1715)
PHONE.................................858 450-6510
Fax: 858 450-6905
Tim Murphy, *President*
Maura Callan, *Manager*
EMP: 50
SQ FT: 12,500
SALES (est): 4.1MM
SALES (corp-wide): 151.6MM Privately Held
WEB: www.eliteracing.com
SIC: 8743 Promotion service
HQ: Competitor Group, Inc.
9477 Waples St Ste 150
San Diego CA 92121
858 450-6510

(P-27744)
D L RYAN COMPANIES LLC
Also Called: Ryan Partnership
12121 Wilshire Blvd # 100, Los Angeles (90025-1123)
PHONE.................................310 442-0400
Fax: 310 442-0459
David L Ryan, *Principal*
EMP: 106
SALES (corp-wide): 6.4B Publicly Held
SIC: 8743 8742 Sales promotion; marketing consulting services
HQ: D. L. Ryan Companies, Llc
50 Danbury Rd Ste 101
Wilton CT 06897
203 210-3000

(P-27745)
DANIEL J EDELMAN INC
Also Called: Edelman Public Relations
525 Market St, San Francisco (94105-2708)
PHONE.................................415 222-9944
Fax: 415 222-9924
Jay Porter, *General Mgr*
Tom Parker, *Creative Dir*
EMP: 99
SALES (corp-wide): 868.7MM Privately Held
SIC: 8743 Public relations services
HQ: Daniel J. Edelman, Inc.
200 E Randolph St Fl 63
Chicago IL 60601
312 240-3000

(P-27746)
DANIEL J EDELMAN INC
Also Called: Edelman Public Relations
5670 Wilshire Blvd # 2500, Los Angeles (90036-5679)
PHONE.................................323 857-9100
Fax: 323 857-9117
Gail Becker, *Principal*
Lorie Fiber, *Senior VP*
Thomas J Goff, *Senior VP*
Regan Phillips, *Vice Pres*
Drew Cary, *Accounting Mgr*
EMP: 65
SALES (corp-wide): 868.7MM Privately Held
SIC: 8743 7313 Public relations & publicity; electronic media advertising representatives; printed media advertising representatives
HQ: Daniel J. Edelman, Inc.
200 E Randolph St Fl 63
Chicago IL 60601
312 240-3000

(P-27747)
FENTON COMMUNICATIONS INC
182 2nd St Ste 400, San Francisco (94105-3801)
PHONE.................................415 255-1946
Fax: 415 901-0110
Parker Blackman, *Manager*
Justin J Cole, *Vice Pres*
Bill Hamilton, *Comms Dir*
Llewellyn Powers, *CTO*
Molly McGovern, *Senior Mgr*
EMP: 50
SALES (corp-wide): 13.2MM Privately Held
WEB: www.dhs.gov
SIC: 8743 Public relations & publicity
PA: Fenton Communications, Inc.
1010 Vermont Ave Nw # 1100
Washington DC 20005
202 822-5200

(P-27748)
FLEISHMAN-HILLARD INC
720 California St Fl 6, San Francisco (94108-2478)
PHONE.................................415 318-4000
Fax: 415 318-4010
Tim Keeff, *General Mgr*
Pam Miracle, *Vice Pres*
Michael Schuppenhauer, *Vice Pres*
Tiffany Pence, *VP Mktg*
EMP: 50
SALES (corp-wide): 15.1B Publicly Held
WEB: www.fleishmanhillard.com
SIC: 8743 Public relations services
HQ: Fleishman-Hillard Inc.
200 N Broadway
Saint Louis MO 63102
314 982-1700

(P-27749)
GOLIN/HARRIS INTERNATIONAL INC
601 W 5th St Ste 400, Los Angeles (90071-2004)
PHONE.................................213 623-4200
Fax: 213 895-4745
Judy Johnson, *Director*
Stephen Jones, *Exec VP*
Jered Thorp, *Vice Pres*
Cary Kwok, *Accounting Mgr*
Clleen Farrell, *Accounts Exec*
EMP: 65
SALES (corp-wide): 7.6B Publicly Held
WEB: www.golinharris.com
SIC: 8743 Public relations services
HQ: Golin/Harris International, Inc.
875 N Michigan Ave
Chicago IL 60611
312 729-4000

(P-27750)
HAVAS FORMULA LLC
Also Called: Formula PR Inc.
1215 Cushman Ave, San Diego (92110-3904)
PHONE.................................619 234-0345
Fax: 619 234-0360
Michael A Olguin, *President*
Tara Reid, *Assoc VP*
Alexis McCance, *Senior VP*
Ditas Mauricio, *Vice Pres*
Sera Christonson, *Executive Asst*
EMP: 100
SQ FT: 2,700
SALES (est): 20.1MM
SALES (corp-wide): 104.6MM Privately Held
WEB: www.formulapr.com
SIC: 8743 Public relations services
PA: Havas
29 Quai De Dion Bouton
Puteaux Cedex 92817
158 478-000

(P-27751)
HILL & KNOWLTON STRATEGIES LLC
Blanc & Otus
60 Green St, San Francisco (94111-1435)
PHONE.................................415 281-7120
Fax: 415 281-7121
Quinn Daly, *General Mgr*
Kim Barsi, *Senior VP*
Barbara Edler, *Senior VP*
Anna Leonard, *General Mgr*
Syreeta Mussante, *Account Dir*
EMP: 55
SALES (corp-wide): 18.4B Privately Held
SIC: 8743 Public relations services
HQ: Hill And Knowlton Strategies, Llc
466 Lexington Ave Frnt 4
New York NY 10017
212 885-0300

(P-27752)
KETCHUM INCORPORATED
1050 Battery St, San Francisco (94111-1286)
PHONE.................................415 984-6100
Fax: 415 984-6102
Dave Chapman, *Director*
Marcus Peterzell, *Exec VP*
Rajat Chandihok, *Senior VP*
Monica Marshall, *Senior VP*
Steve Moylan, *Senior VP*
EMP: 75
SALES (corp-wide): 15.1B Publicly Held
WEB: www.imsfastpak.com
SIC: 8743 Public relations services
HQ: Ketchum Inc.
1285 Avenue Of The Americ
New York NY 10019
646 935-3900

(P-27753)
KETCHUM INC
12555 W Jefferson Blvd # 250, Los Angeles (90066-7032)
PHONE.................................310 295-3300
Amy Wallendeck, *Office Mgr*
Maxine Enciso, *Vice Pres*
EMP: 60
SALES (corp-wide): 15.1B Publicly Held
SIC: 8743 7311 Public relations services; advertising agencies
HQ: Ketchum Inc.
1285 Avenue Of The Americ
New York NY 10019
646 935-3900

(P-27754)
LEAGUE OF CALIFORNIA CITIES (PA)
Also Called: Western City Magazine
1400 K St Fl 4, Sacramento (95814-3916)
PHONE.................................916 341-0140
Judy Mitchell, *President*
Bill Bogaard, *President*
Chris McKenzie, *CFO*
Darren Hernandez, *Vice Pres*
Adrienne Sprenger, *Comms Mgr*
EMP: 65
SQ FT: 32,000
SALES: 295.6K Privately Held
WEB: www.cacities.org
SIC: 8743 2721 Lobbyist; magazines: publishing only, not printed on site

(P-27755)
LEWIS PR INC (PA)
575 Market St Ste 1200, San Francisco (94105-2851)
PHONE.................................415 432-2400
Chris Lewis, *CEO*
Paul Charles, *COO*
James Oehlcke, *CFO*

PRODUCTS & SERVICES SECTION

8744 - Facilities Support Mgmt Svcs County (P-27778)

Fernando Batista, *Top Exec*
Alba Roig, *Top Exec*
EMP: 89
SALES (est): 10.5MM **Privately Held**
SIC: 8743 Public relations services

(P-27756)
MAGIC WORKFORCE SOLUTIONS LLC
9100 Wilsh Blvd Ste 700e, Beverly Hills (90212)
PHONE.................................310 246-6153
Earvin Johnson, *CEO*
Eric Holoman, *President*
Kawanna Brown, *COO*
EMP: 4532 **EST:** 2007
SALES: 2.1MM
SALES (corp-wide): 505.2MM **Privately Held**
SIC: 8743 Promotion service
PA: Magic Johnson Enterprises, Inc.
9100 Wilshire Blvd 700e
Beverly Hills CA 90212
310 247-2033

(P-27757)
MURPHY OBRIEN INC
11444 W Olympic Blvd # 600, Los Angeles (90064-1549)
PHONE.................................310 453-2539
Fax: 310 264-0083
Karen Murphy O'Brien, *CEO*
Brett O'Brien, *Managing Prtnr*
Shelli Jarrett, *Exec VP*
Kimi Ozawa, *Vice Pres*
Wendi Shapiro, *Vice Pres*
EMP: 55
SQ FT: 7,159
SALES (est): 4.6MM **Privately Held**
WEB: www.murphyobrien.com
SIC: 8743 Public relations & publicity

(P-27758)
NATIONAL PRODUCT SERVICES LLC
1005 Marvista Ave, Seal Beach (90740-5841)
PHONE.................................562 594-8206
Nancy Sawyer,
EMP: 50 **EST:** 2001
SQ FT: 600
SALES (est): 2.6MM **Privately Held**
SIC: 8743 Sales promotion

(P-27759)
OGILVY PUB RLTONS WRLDWIDE INC
1530 J St, Sacramento (95814-2052)
PHONE.................................916 231-7700
EMP: 74
SALES (corp-wide): 18.4B **Privately Held**
SIC: 8743 Public relations & publicity
HQ: Ogilvy Public Relations Worldwide Inc.
636 11th Ave
New York NY 10036
212 880-5200

(P-27760)
OUTCAST AGENCY LLC
100 Montgomery St # 1200, San Francisco (94104-4331)
PHONE.................................415 392-8282
Tim Dyson,
Darlyn Phillips, *CFO*
Zak Brazen, *Creative Dir*
Alex Plant, *Mktg Dir*
Michelle Barczak, *Art Dir*
EMP: 120
SALES (est): 16.1MM **Privately Held**
SIC: 8743 Public relations service

(P-27761)
PMK-BNC INC (PA)
8687 Melrose Ave Fl 8th, Los Angeles (90069-5746)
PHONE.................................310 854-0455
Fax: 310 854-4848
Michael Nyman, *CEO*
Chris Robichaud, *President*
John Lundy, *CFO*
Brad Cafarelli, *Bd of Directors*
Doug Piwinski, *Exec VP*
EMP: 80
SQ FT: 4,000

SALES (est): 34.7MM **Privately Held**
SIC: 8743 Public relations & publicity

(P-27762)
PMK-BNC INC
8687 Melrose Ave Fl 8th, Los Angeles (90069-5746)
PHONE.................................310 854-4800
Eunice Ko, *Branch Mgr*
Erica Gray, *Vice Pres*
EMP: 50
SALES (corp-wide): 34.7MM **Privately Held**
SIC: 8743 Public relations & publicity
PA: Pmk-Bnc, Inc.
8687 Melrose Ave Fl 8th
Los Angeles CA 90069
310 854-0455

(P-27763)
POSITEA INV & PUB RELATIONS
Also Called: Mathews & Clark Communications
710 Lakeway Dr, Sunnyvale (94085-4006)
PHONE.................................408 736-1120
Stuart Chalmers, *President*
Stephen Howse, *Manager*
EMP: 50
SALES (est): 1.6MM **Privately Held**
SIC: 8743 Public relations services

(P-27764)
QUEST TRANSPORTATION INC
241b Prado Rd, San Luis Obispo (93401-7309)
PHONE.................................805 545-8400
Fax: 805 545-8404
Jim Galusha, *President*
Sharon Galusha, *CFO*
EMP: 60
SQ FT: 7,500
SALES (est): 2.9MM **Privately Held**
WEB: www.silveradotours.com
SIC: 8743 Promotion service

(P-27765)
RADIUMONE INC (PA)
55 2nd St Ste 1800, San Francisco (94105-3498)
PHONE.................................415 418-2840
Bill Lonergan, *CEO*
Alex Gove, *President*
Anna Baird, *CFO*
Bob Hall, *Senior VP*
Mike Werner, *Senior VP*
EMP: 82
SALES (est): 43.7MM **Privately Held**
SIC: 8743 Promotion service

(P-27766)
ROGERS & COWAN (HQ)
8687 Melrose Ave Ste G700, West Hollywood (90069-5721)
PHONE.................................310 854-8100
Fax: 310 854-8101
Mark Owens, *CEO*
Jeff Raymond, *Assoc VP*
Fran Curtis, *Exec VP*
Maggie Gallant, *Exec VP*
Melissa Schumer, *Exec VP*
EMP: 72
SALES (est): 13.3MM
SALES (corp-wide): 7.6B **Publicly Held**
SIC: 8743 Public relations services
PA: The Interpublic Group Of Companies Inc
909 3rd Ave Fl 7
New York NY 10022
212 704-1200

(P-27767)
SCHWARTZ MSL LLC
100 California St Fl 9, San Francisco (94111-4514)
PHONE.................................415 817-2500
Fax: 415 882-5787
Gary Thompson, *Manager*
Merrill Freund, *Senior VP*
Nigel Smith, *Senior VP*
Lauren Arnold, *Vice Pres*
Steve Cragle, *Vice Pres*
EMP: 70
SALES (corp-wide): 65.7MM **Privately Held**
WEB: www.schwartz-pr.com
SIC: 8743 Public relations services

HQ: Schwartz Msl, Llc
300 5th Ave Ste 1
Waltham MA 02451
781 684-0770

(P-27768)
WEBER SHANDWICK
600 Battery St Fl 1, San Francisco (94111-1820)
PHONE.................................415 262-5600
Luca Penati, *Vice Pres*
EMP: 60
SALES (est): 405.2K **Privately Held**
SIC: 8743 Public relations services

(P-27769)
YOUNG & RUBICAM INC
Also Called: Burson Marsteller
303 2nd St Ste N350, San Francisco (94107-1368)
PHONE.................................415 591-4000
Kevin Elliott, *Managing Dir*
Morgan Mauritz, *Manager*
Ruben Simpliciano, *Associate*
EMP: 78
SALES (corp-wide): 18.4B **Privately Held**
WEB: www.sfo.bm.com
SIC: 8743 Public relations services
HQ: Young & Rubicam Inc.
3 Columbus Cir Fl 8
New York NY 10019
212 210-3000

8744 Facilities Support Mgmt Svcs

(P-27770)
ACEPEX MANAGEMENT CORPORATION (PA)
10643 Mills Ave, Montclair (91763-4612)
PHONE.................................909 625-6900
Henry C Rhee, *CEO*
Nancy Escobar, *Executive Asst*
Drew Feldmann, *Engineer*
EMP: 148 **EST:** 1989
SQ FT: 7,000
SALES: 37.5MM **Privately Held**
WEB: www.acepex.com
SIC: 8744 7349 1799 1521 Base maintenance (providing personnel on continuing basis); janitorial service, contract basis; coating, caulking & weather, water & fireproofing; single-family housing construction; nonresidential construction

(P-27771)
ADVANCED CLEANUP TECH INC (PA)
20928 S Lamberton Ave, Carson (90810-1024)
PHONE.................................310 763-1423
Fax: 310 763-9076
Ruben Garcia, *CEO*
Douglas Orban, *Branch Mgr*
Senaka Ekanayake, *Controller*
Miles Cronin, *Safety Dir*
James Karsten, *Safety Mgr*
EMP: 120
SALES (est): 38.2MM **Privately Held**
WEB: www.actird.com
SIC: 8744

(P-27772)
AGUATIERRA ASSOCIATES INC (PA)
Also Called: Weiss Associates
2200 Powell St Ste 925, Emeryville (94608-1879)
PHONE.................................510 450-6000
Fax: 510 547-5043
Michael D Dresen, *President*
Richard B Weiss, *CFO*
Scott Bourne, *Vice Pres*
Robert Devany, *Vice Pres*
Udit Minocha, *MIS Dir*
EMP: 55
SQ FT: 13,000
SALES (est): 11.3MM **Privately Held**
SIC: 8744 4959 8748 Facilities support services; environmental cleanup services; environmental consultant

(P-27773)
AMERICAN INTEGRATED SVCS INC (PA)
1502 E Opp St, Wilmington (90744-3927)
P.O. Box 92316, Long Beach (90809-2316)
PHONE.................................310 522-1168
Fax: 310 522-0474
Paul David Herrera, *President*
Gary Runnells, *Vice Pres*
Sandi Schafer, *Vice Pres*
Ryan Harding, *General Mgr*
Lisa Huizenga, *Executive Asst*
EMP: 50
SQ FT: 77,000
SALES (est): 31.7MM **Privately Held**
WEB: www.americanintegrated.com
SIC: 8744

(P-27774)
AMERITAC INC (PA)
640 Logan Ln, Danville (94526-1512)
P.O. Box 279 (94526-0279)
PHONE.................................925 743-8398
Isiah Harris, *President*
Lawrence Stevens, *Vice Pres*
EMP: 80
SQ FT: 2,024
SALES (est): 4.7MM **Privately Held**
WEB: www.ameritac.net
SIC: 8744 Base maintenance (providing personnel on continuing basis)

(P-27775)
ARGUS MANAGEMENT COMPANY LLC
Also Called: Argus Medical Management
1045 S Atl Ave Ste 705, Long Beach (90813)
PHONE.................................562 491-9673
Robert C Boullon,
Shing Huang, *CFO*
Misun Kim, *Analyst*
Barry Allswang MD,
Peter Ferrera MD,
EMP: 300
SQ FT: 2,500
SALES (est): 18.4MM **Privately Held**
WEB: www.argusmso.com
SIC: 8744 Facilities support services

(P-27776)
CAPE ENVIRONMENTAL MGT INC
24 Executive Park Ste 200, Irvine (92614-2753)
PHONE.................................949 236-3000
Amir Matin, *Manager*
EMP: 265
SALES (corp-wide): 261.3MM **Privately Held**
SIC: 8744
PA: Cape Environmental Management Inc.
500 Pinnacle Ct Ste 100
Norcross GA 30071
770 908-7200

(P-27777)
CASA DSCANSO CONVALESCENT HOSP
Also Called: Huntington Child Care Center
4515 Huntington Dr S, Los Angeles (90032-1940)
PHONE.................................323 225-5991
Fax: 323 225-6685
Jack Gindi, *President*
EMP: 107
SALES (est): 5.6MM **Privately Held**
SIC: 8744 Facilities support services

(P-27778)
CITY OF BREA
Also Called: Maintenance Dept
1 Civic Center Cir Fl 3, Brea (92821-5758)
PHONE.................................714 990-7650
Fax: 714 671-1493
Bill Higgins, *Director*
EMP: 57 **Privately Held**
WEB: www.cityofbrea.net
SIC: 8744 Base maintenance (providing personnel on continuing basis)
PA: City Of Brea
1 Civic Center Cir Fl 3
Brea CA 92821
714 990-7600

8744 - Facilities Support Mgmt Svcs County (P-27779) PRODUCTS & SERVICES SECTION

(P-27779)
CITY OF WOODLAND
Also Called: Public Works Department
655 N Pioneer Ave, Woodland (95776-6112)
PHONE..................530 661-5962
Greg Mayer, *Director*
EMP: 200 Privately Held
WEB: www.ci.woodland.ca.us
SIC: 8744 Base maintenance (providing personnel on continuing basis)
PA: City Of Woodland
   300 1st St
   Woodland CA 95695
   530 661-5830

(P-27780)
CORRECTIONAL SERVICES CORP
7805 Arjons Dr, San Diego (92126-4368)
PHONE..................858 566-9816
Fax: 858 566-9837
EMP: 51
SALES (corp-wide): 1.8B Privately Held
SIC: 8744 Correctional facility
HQ: Correctional Services Corporation, Llc
   621 Nw 53rd St Ste 700
   Boca Raton FL 33487
   561 893-0101

(P-27781)
CORRECTIONS CORP AMERICA
Also Called: San Diego Correctional Fcilty
446 Alta Rd, San Diego (92158-0001)
P.O. Box 439049, San Ysidro (92143-9049)
PHONE..................619 661-9119
Martha Honorato, *Personnel Assit*
Alfred A Joshua, *Emerg Med Spec*
Anita L Ballance, *Manager*
Karl Stansel, *Assistant*
EMP: 243
SALES (corp-wide): 1.7B Publicly Held
WEB: www.correctionscorp.com
SIC: 8744 Correctional facility
PA: Corrections Corporation Of America
   10 Burton Hills Blvd
   Nashville TN 37215
   615 263-3000

(P-27782)
CORRECTIONS CORP AMERICA
Also Called: California Cy Correctional Ctr
22844 Virginia Blvd, California City (93505)
P.O. Box 2590 (93504-0590)
PHONE..................760 373-1764
Fax: 760 373-1764
Charles Gilkey, *Warden*
EMP: 150
SALES (corp-wide): 1.7B Publicly Held
WEB: www.correctionscorp.com
SIC: 8744 Correctional facility
PA: Corrections Corporation Of America
   10 Burton Hills Blvd
   Nashville TN 37215
   615 263-3000

(P-27783)
COUNTY OF MONTEREY
Also Called: County Jail
1410 Natividad Rd, Salinas (93906-3102)
PHONE..................831 755-3782
John Davidson, *Principal*
EMP: 179 Privately Held
WEB: www.montereycountyfarmbureau.org
SIC: 8744 Jails, privately operated
PA: County Of Monterey
   168 W Alisal St Fl 3
   Salinas CA 93901
   831 755-5040

(P-27784)
COUNTY OF SACRAMENTO
Also Called: Sheriff's Dept
12500 Bruceville Rd, Elk Grove (95757-9784)
PHONE..................916 874-1927
James Babcock, *Branch Mgr*
EMP: 250 Privately Held
WEB: www.sna.com
SIC: 8744 9223 Correctional facility; correctional institutions;
PA: County Of Sacramento
   700 H St Ste 7650
   Sacramento CA 95814
   916 874-5544

(P-27785)
CVE NB CONTRACTING GROUP INC
Also Called: Central Valley Environmental
135 Utility Ct A, Rohnert Park (94928-1616)
PHONE..................707 584-1900
Tim Williamson, *CEO*
Glenn Accornero, *COO*
EMP: 50 EST: 2015
SQ FT: 4,700
SALES: 12.5MM Privately Held
SIC: 8744

(P-27786)
GEI CONSULTANTS INC
2868 Prospect Park Dr # 400, Rancho Cordova (95670-6065)
PHONE..................916 631-4500
Frank Leathers, *President*
EMP: 76
SALES (corp-wide): 202.1MM Privately Held
WEB: www.geiconsultants.com
SIC: 8744 Facilities support services
PA: Gei Consultants, Inc.
   400 Unicorn Park Dr Ste 8
   Woburn MA 01801
   781 721-4000

(P-27787)
GEO GROUP INC
Also Called: Taft Correctional Institution
1500 Cadet Rd, Taft (93268-4800)
P.O. Box 7000 (93268-7000)
PHONE..................661 763-2510
Michael Denop, *Warden*
EMP: 387
SALES (corp-wide): 1.8B Privately Held
WEB: www.thegeogroupinc.com
SIC: 8744 Correctional facility
PA: The Geo Group Inc
   621 Nw 53rd St Ste 700
   Boca Raton FL 33487
   561 893-0101

(P-27788)
GEO GROUP INC
Also Called: Leo Chesney Fccf
2800 Apricot St, Live Oak (95953-2272)
PHONE..................530 695-1846
Amanda Valencia, *Manager*
EMP: 50
SALES (corp-wide): 1.8B Privately Held
SIC: 8744 Correctional facility
PA: The Geo Group Inc
   621 Nw 53rd St Ste 700
   Boca Raton FL 33487
   561 893-0101

(P-27789)
GEO REENTRY INC
111 Taylor St, San Francisco (94102-2802)
PHONE..................415 346-9769
EMP: 92
SALES (corp-wide): 1.8B Privately Held
SIC: 8744 Correctional facility
HQ: Geo Reentry, Inc.
   621 Nw 53rd St Ste 700
   Boca Raton FL 33487
   561 893-0101

(P-27790)
GERWEND ENTERPRISES INC
Also Called: Integrity Management Entps
2952 Mkt St Pizarro Bldg, San Diego (92102)
PHONE..................619 254-5018
Fax: 619 234-2629
Carlos Buzon, *President*
Tony Pizarro, *Vice Pres*
Emma Misch, *Accountant*
EMP: 150
SQ FT: 4,000
SALES (est): 6.9MM Privately Held
SIC: 8744 Facilities support services

(P-27791)
GILBANE AECOM JV
1655 Grant St Fl 12, Concord (94520-2445)
PHONE..................925 946-3100
Dave Farraiolo, *Principal*
Kara Baharyan, *Principal*
EMP: 99

SALES (est): 1MM Privately Held
SIC: 8744 Facilities support services

(P-27792)
HUMAN POTENTIAL CONS LLC
373 Van Ness Ave Ste 160, Torrance (90501-6244)
PHONE..................310 756-1560
Fax: 310 756-1562
Garnett Newcombe, *CEO*
Tiffani Clegg, *General Mgr*
Camille Chapman, *Administration*
Richard Brown, *Training Spec*
Deidre Norville, *Director*
EMP: 63 EST: 1997
SQ FT: 3,500
SALES: 3.5MM Privately Held
SIC: 8744 7349 8741 Facilities support services; janitorial service, contract basis; personnel management

(P-27793)
IAP WORLD SERVICES INC
567 Dugan South Akron Rd, Mountain View (94035)
PHONE..................650 604-0451
Travis Durano, *Project Mgr*
EMP: 68
SALES (corp-wide): 546.7MM Privately Held
WEB: www.jcwsi.com
SIC: 8744 Facilities support services
HQ: Iap World Services, Inc.
   7315 N Atlantic Ave
   Cape Canaveral FL 32920
   321 784-7100

(P-27794)
IAP WORLD SERVICES INC
510 S Loop 1st St Bldg T, Fort Irwin (92310)
PHONE..................760 380-6772
Jeffrey D Williamson, *Manager*
EMP: 290
SALES (corp-wide): 546.7MM Privately Held
WEB: www.jcwsi.com
SIC: 8744 Facilities support services
HQ: Iap World Services, Inc.
   7315 N Atlantic Ave
   Cape Canaveral FL 32920
   321 784-7100

(P-27795)
INDYNE INC
105 13thstbld6525rma 7 Bldg 6525, Vandenberg Afb (93437)
P.O. Box 5009, Lompoc (93437-0009)
PHONE..................805 606-7225
Kenneth A Cinal, *Branch Mgr*
David Miller, *Principal*
Dave Salm, *Director*
Dan Nunnelee, *Manager*
EMP: 700
SALES (corp-wide): 283.1MM Privately Held
WEB: www.indyneinc.com
SIC: 8744 Base maintenance (providing personnel on continuing basis)
PA: Indyne, Inc.
   11800 Sunrise Valley Dr # 250
   Reston VA 20191
   703 903-6900

(P-27796)
INNOVATIVE CNSTR SOLUTIONS
4011 W Chandler Ave, Santa Ana (92704-5201)
PHONE..................714 893-6366
Hirad Emadi, *President*
John R White, *Vice Pres*
Adam Herrera, *Project Mgr*
Mary Krist, *Project Mgr*
Bill Lewis, *Project Mgr*
EMP: 105 EST: 1999
SQ FT: 2,000
SALES (est): 19.6MM Privately Held
SIC: 8744 1795 ; demolition, buildings & other structures

(P-27797)
JLS ENVIRONMENTAL SERVICES INC
3460 Swetzer Rd, Loomis (95650-7624)
PHONE..................916 660-1525
Fax: 916 660-0465

Larry Walker, *President*
John G Sheehan, *CEO*
David Locke, *CFO*
Lucille Mandeville, *Executive*
Cigi Ramesbottom, *Office Mgr*
EMP: 70
SALES (est): 7.7MM Privately Held
WEB: www.jls-inc.com
SIC: 8744 8999 ; earth science services

(P-27798)
ONE WORKPLACE L FERRARI LLC
Also Called: One Work Place
475 Brannan St Ste 210, San Francisco (94107-5498)
PHONE..................415 357-2200
Mark Smith, *VP Sales*
EMP: 73
SALES (corp-wide): 186.4MM Privately Held
WEB: www.oneworkplace.com
SIC: 8744 Facilities support services
PA: One Workplace L. Ferrari, Llc
   2500 De La Cruz Blvd
   Santa Clara CA 95050
   669 800-2500

(P-27799)
SUPPORT ASSOCIATES INC
22901 Mill Creek Dr, Laguna Hills (92653-1215)
PHONE..................949 595-4379
Fax: 949 595-2110
John Shadwick, *President*
Larry Cory, *Shareholder*
Peggy Norman, *Shareholder*
Norman Bouchard, *Program Dir*
EMP: 170
SALES (est): 10MM Privately Held
WEB: www.supportassociates.com
SIC: 8744 Facilities support services

(P-27800)
SWISS PORT CORP
Also Called: Swissport
11001 Aviation Blvd, Los Angeles (90045-6123)
PHONE..................310 417-0258
Fax: 310 215-3263
Armin Unternaehrer, *Vice Pres*
Steve Gomez, *Vice Pres*
Dion Fatafehi, *Manager*
EMP: 500
SALES (est): 37.3MM Privately Held
SIC: 8744 4581 Facilities support services; airports, flying fields & services

(P-27801)
VANGUARD RESOURCES CORP
13816 Fontanelle Pl, San Diego (92128-4755)
P.O. Box 420355 (92142-0355)
PHONE..................858 336-7147
Nicole Murray, *President*
EMP: 60
SALES: 2MM Privately Held
WEB: www.vanguardresourcescorp.com
SIC: 8744 Facilities support services

(P-27802)
WEST COAST STORM INC (PA)
9701 Wilshire Blvd # 1000, Beverly Hills (90212-2010)
PHONE..................909 890-5700
Michelle Padilla, *President*
Renata Salo, *CFO*
Rafael Padilla, *Vice Pres*
Sarah Moore, *Manager*
EMP: 50
SQ FT: 48,000
SALES (est): 6.3MM Privately Held
WEB: www.wcstorm.net
SIC: 8744

(P-27803)
WORKCARE INC
300 S Harbor Blvd Ste 600, Anaheim (92805-3718)
PHONE..................714 978-7488
Dr Peter P Greaney, *CEO*
Suzann Vincent, *President*
Bill Nixon, *CFO*
William E Nixon, *CFO*
Johanna F Amaya, *Ch Credit Ofcr*
EMP: 181

PRODUCTS & SERVICES SECTION
8748 - Business Consulting Svcs, NEC County (P-27827)

SQ FT: 11,000
SALES (est): 22.1MM Privately Held
WEB: www.workcare.com
SIC: 8744 8011 Facilities support services; offices & clinics of medical doctors

8748 Business Consulting Svcs, NEC

(P-27804)
8020 CONSULTING LLC
6303 Owensmouth Ave Fl 10, Woodland Hills (91367-2262)
PHONE.................................818 523-3201
David Lewis, *Mng Member*
EMP: 50
SALES: 15MM Privately Held
SIC: 8748 Business consulting

(P-27805)
ABSG CONSULTING INC
505 14th St Ste 900, Oakland (94612-1468)
PHONE.................................510 508-6289
Fax: 510 663-1046
William Keogh, *Branch Mgr*
Omar Khemici, *Vice Pres*
Ryan Holland, *Info Tech Dir*
Branimir Betov, *Software Engr*
EMP: 50
SALES (corp-wide): 1.1B Privately Held
WEB: www.absconsulting.com
SIC: 8748 Safety training service; systems analysis & engineering consulting services; testing services
HQ: Absg Consulting Inc.
16855 Northchase Dr
Houston TX 77060
281 673-2800

(P-27806)
ABSG CONSULTING INC
300 Commerce Ste 200, Irvine (92602-1305)
PHONE.................................714 734-4242
Melinda Arjonilla, *Branch Mgr*
EMP: 68
SALES (corp-wide): 1.1B Privately Held
WEB: www.absconsulting.com
SIC: 8748 Safety training service; testing services; systems analysis & engineering consulting services
HQ: Absg Consulting Inc.
16855 Northchase Dr
Houston TX 77060
281 673-2800

(P-27807)
AC SQUARE INC
4590 Qantas Ln, Stockton (95206-3903)
PHONE.................................650 293-2730
EMP: 239
SALES (corp-wide): 43.7MM Privately Held
SIC: 8748
PA: Ac Square, Inc.
371 Foster City Blvd
Foster City CA 94404
650 293-2730

(P-27808)
ACC-GWG LLC
Also Called: American Commodity Co.
6133 Abel Rd, Williams (95987-5816)
P.O. Box 236 (95987-0236)
PHONE.................................530 473-2827
Chris Crutchfield, *President*
Bob Watts, *President*
Nicole Montna Van Vleck, *Admin Sec*
Paul Crutchfield,
Al Montna,
EMP: 60
SALES (est): 5.6MM Privately Held
SIC: 8748 Agricultural consultant

(P-27809)
ACIONTALK INTERNATIONAL INC
1398 Poinsettia Ave # 101, Vista (92081-8504)
PHONE.................................619 393-1710
Steven Truong, *President*
Khris Thetsy, *CFO*
EMP: 300

SQ FT: 15,000
SALES: 10MM Privately Held
SIC: 8748 Telecommunications consultant

(P-27810)
AE & ASSOCIATES LLC
506 Queensland Cir, Corona (92879-1381)
PHONE.................................951 278-3477
Fax: 951 278-3670
Arnold Ardevela,
Ester Ardevela, *Info Tech Mgr*
EMP: 60
SQ FT: 3,755
SALES (est): 750K Privately Held
SIC: 8748 Business consulting

(P-27811)
AECOM C&E INC
Also Called: Aecom Environment
2101 Webster St Ste 1900, Oakland (94612-3042)
PHONE.................................510 622-6600
Mark Lutrell, *Manager*
Scott Kelsey, *Engineer*
EMP: 99
SALES (corp-wide): 17.9B Publicly Held
SIC: 8748 Environmental consultant
HQ: Aecom C&E, Inc
250 Apollo Dr
Chelmsford MA 01824
978 905-2100

(P-27812)
AECOM GLOBAL II LLC
2870 Gateway Oaks Dr # 300, Sacramento (95833-3577)
PHONE.................................916 679-8700
Victor Auvinen, *Branch Mgr*
Debora Monahan, *Executive*
David Anderson, *Engineer*
Walter Lafranchi, *Engineer*
Jennifer Hames, *Manager*
EMP: 185
SQ FT: 12,000
SALES (corp-wide): 17.9B Publicly Held
SIC: 8748 Environmental consultant
HQ: Aecom Global Ii, Llc
1999 Avenue Of Ste 2600
Los Angeles CA 90067
213 593-8100

(P-27813)
AECOM GLOBAL II LLC
915 Wilshire Blvd Ste 800, Los Angeles (90017-3488)
PHONE.................................213 996-2200
Dave Wu, *Branch Mgr*
Bernard Pyska, *Manager*
EMP: 200
SALES (corp-wide): 17.9B Publicly Held
SIC: 8748 Systems analysis & engineering consulting services
HQ: Aecom Global Ii, Llc
1999 Avenue Of Ste 2600
Los Angeles CA 90067
213 593-8100

(P-27814)
AECOM GLOBAL II LLC
310 Golden Shore Ste 100, Long Beach (90802-4240)
PHONE.................................310 343-6977
Edward Andrechak, *Branch Mgr*
EMP: 65
SALES (corp-wide): 17.9B Publicly Held
SIC: 8748 Environmental consultant
HQ: Aecom Global Ii, Llc
1999 Avenue Of Ste 2600
Los Angeles CA 90067
213 593-8100

(P-27815)
AECOM TECHNICAL SERVICES INC
1333 Broadway Ste 800, Oakland (94612-1924)
PHONE.................................510 285-2010
EMP: 55
SALES (corp-wide): 17.9B Publicly Held
SIC: 8748 Systems engineering consultant, ex. computer or professional
HQ: Aecom Technical Services, Inc.
300 S Grand Ave Ste 1100
Los Angeles CA 90071
213 593-8000

(P-27816)
AECOM USA INC
515 S Figueroa St Ste 400, Los Angeles (90071-3323)
PHONE.................................213 330-7200
EMP: 104
SALES (corp-wide): 17.9B Publicly Held
SIC: 8748 Business consulting
HQ: Aecom Usa, Inc.
605 3rd Ave
New York NY 10158
212 973-2900

(P-27817)
AECOM USA INC
100 W San Fernando St, San Jose (95113-2219)
PHONE.................................408 392-0670
EMP: 104
SALES (corp-wide): 17.9B Publicly Held
SIC: 8748 Business consulting
HQ: Aecom Usa, Inc.
605 3rd Ave
New York NY 10158
212 973-2900

(P-27818)
AECOM USA INC
300 S Grand Ave Ste 1100, Los Angeles (90071-3173)
PHONE.................................213 593-8000
Tom Joldersma, *CFO*
Dennis Deslatte, *Treasurer*
Robyn Miller, *Admin Sec*
Donald Dwore, *Director*
Julio Grabiel, *Director*
EMP: 500
SALES (corp-wide): 17.9B Publicly Held
SIC: 8748 Business consulting
HQ: Aecom Usa, Inc.
605 3rd Ave
New York NY 10158
212 973-2900

(P-27819)
AECOM USA INC
999 W Town And Country Rd, Orange (92868-4713)
PHONE.................................714 567-2501
Bruce Toro, *Manager*
Norm Andres, *Info Tech Mgr*
Linda Rudawiat, *MIS Staff*
Sean Faircloth, *IT/INT Sup*
EMP: 60
SALES (corp-wide): 17.9B Publicly Held
SIC: 8748 Business consulting
HQ: Aecom Usa, Inc.
605 3rd Ave
New York NY 10158
212 973-2900

(P-27820)
AHTNA-CDM SMITH JV
3200 El Camino Real, Irvine (92602-1378)
PHONE.................................714 824-3471
Craig O'Rourke, *Partner*
John Czapor, *Partner*
David Fehrenbach, *CFO*
EMP: 99
SALES (est): 2.7MM Privately Held
SIC: 8748 1794 8711 1611 Environmental consultant; excavation & grading; building construction; building construction consultant; highway & street construction

(P-27821)
AIMS EDUCATION FOUNDATION
1595 S Chestnut Ave, Fresno (93702-4706)
P.O. Box 8120 (93747-8120)
PHONE.................................559 255-4094
Fax: 559 255-6396
Richard Thiessen PHD, *President*
Robert Lippert, *Administration*
Johann Weber, *Administration*
Terry Walthers, *Info Tech Mgr*
Lynn Gies, *Purch Mgr*
EMP: 220
SQ FT: 18,000
SALES: 2.8MM Privately Held
SIC: 8748 8733 5999 Educational consultant; noncommercial research organizations; training materials, electronic

(P-27822)
AIR POLLUTION CONTROL DISTRICT
Also Called: STA Barbara Cnty Air Pltn Cntr
260 N San Antonio Rd A, Santa Barbara (93110-1315)
PHONE.................................805 961-8800
Terry Dressler, *Director*
Barbara Spriggs, *Info Tech Dir*
Linda Alexander, *Financial Exec*
Elizabeth Zavala, *Manager*
EMP: 55
SALES (est): 4.1MM Privately Held
SIC: 8748 Environmental consultant

(P-27823)
ALIANTEL INC
1940 W Corporate Way, Anaheim (92801-5373)
PHONE.................................800 274-7074
Suresh Sachdeva, *CEO*
John Kelly, *Principal*
EMP: 90
SALES (est): 14.3MM Privately Held
SIC: 8748 7389 Telecommunications consultant; telephone services

(P-27824)
ALL ENVIRONMENTAL INC
Also Called: Aei Consultants
1200 Main St Ste D, Irvine (92614-6749)
PHONE.................................949 752-9300
Craig Hertz, *Owner*
Ken Bachrach, *Marketing Staff*
EMP: 76
SALES (corp-wide): 111.8MM Privately Held
SIC: 8748 Business consulting
PA: All Environmental, Inc.
2500 Camino Diablo
Walnut Creek CA 94597
925 746-6000

(P-27825)
ALL ENVIRONMENTAL INC
Also Called: Aei Consultants
2447 Pcf Cast Hwy Ste 101, Hermosa Beach (90254)
PHONE.................................310 798-4255
Fax: 310 798-2841
Adam Bennett, *Manager*
Jennifer Keahey, *Project Mgr*
Mohammad I Kleit, *Senior Engr*
Danny Huerta, *Manager*
EMP: 150
SALES (corp-wide): 111.8MM Privately Held
WEB: www.allenvironmental.com
SIC: 8748 Environmental consultant
PA: All Environmental, Inc.
2500 Camino Diablo
Walnut Creek CA 94597
925 746-6000

(P-27826)
ALL-CITY MANAGEMENT SVCS INC
10440 Pioneer Blvd Ste 5, Santa Fe Springs (90670-8238)
PHONE.................................310 202-8284
Fax: 310 202-8325
Baron Farwell, *CEO*
Ron Farwell, *Admin Sec*
EMP: 1800
SQ FT: 3,500
SALES (est): 96.9MM Privately Held
SIC: 8748 Traffic consultant

(P-27827)
ALLIED INDUSTRIES INC (PA)
Also Called: Allied Environmental Services
21650 Oxnard St Ste 500, Woodland Hills (91367-4911)
PHONE.................................818 781-2490
Ernesto Gutierrez, *President*
Fernando Gutierrez, *COO*
Jeffrey Hall, *Project Mgr*
Noah Vaughan, *Cust Mgr*
Fernando Guitterez, *Manager*
EMP: 150
SQ FT: 11,000
SALES (est): 30.3MM Privately Held
SIC: 8748 Environmental consultant

8748 - Business Consulting Svcs, NEC County (P-27828)

(P-27828)
AMEC FSTR WHLR ENVRNMNT INFRST
121 Innovation Dr Ste 200, Irvine (92617-3094)
PHONE..................949 642-0245
Jay River, *Principal*
Greg Hamer, *Project Mgr*
Calvin Hardcastle, *Project Mgr*
Tim Keuscher, *Project Mgr*
Anne McQueen, *Project Mgr*
EMP: 95
SALES (corp-wide): 8.2B **Privately Held**
SIC: 8748 Environmental consultant
HQ: Amec Foster Wheeler Environment & Infrastructure, Inc.
1105 Lakewood Pkwy # 300
Alpharetta GA 30009
770 360-0600

(P-27829)
AMERICAN INFRASTRUCTURE MLP FU
950 Tower Ln Ste 800, Foster City (94404-2191)
PHONE..................650 854-6000
George McCown, *Partner*
Judy Bornstein, *CFO*
Jon Contos, *Vice Pres*
Matthew Carbone, *Managing Dir*
Ed Diffendal, *Managing Dir*
EMP: 51
SALES (est): 7.5MM **Privately Held**
SIC: 8748 Business consulting

(P-27830)
AMERICAN NURSING HOME MGT INC
Also Called: Briercrest Inglewoodhealthcare
301 Centinela Ave, Inglewood (90302-3231)
PHONE..................310 672-1012
Bill Belamger, *Administration*
Edwin David, *Executive*
EMP: 100
SALES (corp-wide): 7.5MM **Privately Held**
SIC: 8748 8051 Business consulting; skilled nursing care facilities
PA: American Nursing Home Management, Inc.
17000 Ventura Blvd # 211
Encino CA
-

(P-27831)
AMERICAN TECHNOLOGIES INC
8444 Miralani Dr Ste 200, San Diego (92126-4389)
PHONE..................858 530-2400
Fax: 858 530-2401
Eric Gotsom, *Branch Mgr*
Robin Moorhead, *Admin Asst*
Eric Gotham, *Project Mgr*
Mike Carroll, *Superintendent*
EMP: 55
SALES (corp-wide): 138.4MM **Privately Held**
WEB: www.amer-tech.com
SIC: 8748 Business consulting
PA: American Technologies Inc.
210 W Baywood Ave
Orange CA 92865
714 283-9990

(P-27832)
AMTEL INC
950 S Bascom Ave Ste 2002, San Jose (95128-3538)
PHONE..................408 615-0522
Fax: 408 615-1524
Pankaj Gupta, *CEO*
Chet Jackson, *President*
Raghu Nath, *President*
Humberto Bengochea, *Info Tech Mgr*
EMP: 50
SALES (est): 10.6MM
SALES (corp-wide): 24.6MM **Privately Held**
WEB: www.amtelnet.com
SIC: 8748 7371 Telecommunications consultant; computer software development

HQ: Netplus Buyer, Inc.
704 Quince Orch
Gaithersburg MD 20878
800 989-5566

(P-27833)
ANELLO SEC & CONSULTING LLC
17348 Tiara St, Encino (91316-1355)
PHONE..................818 632-3277
Michael Anello,
EMP: 65 **EST:** 2008
SALES (est): 2.5MM **Privately Held**
SIC: 8748 Business consulting

(P-27834)
APX INC (PA)
2001 Gateway Pl Ste 315w, San Jose (95110-1045)
PHONE..................408 899-3300
Brian Storms, *CEO*
Matt Ledna, *Vice Pres*
Robert Sarkes, *Director*
EMP: 52
SALES (est): 18.5MM **Privately Held**
WEB: www.apx.com
SIC: 8748 Energy conservation consultant

(P-27835)
ASCEND LEARNING LLC
2185 N California Blvd, Walnut Creek (94596-3500)
PHONE..................925 300-3203
Rick Willet, *Branch Mgr*
Vikki Watson, *Comms Dir*
EMP: 536
SALES (corp-wide): 330MM **Privately Held**
SIC: 8748 Educational consultant
PA: Ascend Learning, Llc
11161 Overbrook Rd
Leawood KS 66211
800 667-7531

(P-27836)
ASSOCIATED RESEARCH SVCS INC
Also Called: ARS
9333 Genesee Ave Ste 260, San Diego (92121-2139)
PHONE..................858 551-0008
Jeff Swartz, *President*
Raymond Keneipp, *COO*
Thomas Greason, *Senior VP*
Mary Beth Jones, *Vice Pres*
EMP: 60
SALES (est): 3MM
SALES (corp-wide): 100.4MM **Privately Held**
SIC: 8748 Business consulting
HQ: Current Analysis, Inc.
179 South St Fl 2
Boston MA 02111
703 404-9200

(P-27837)
ASSURE CONSULTING INC
257 Castro St Ste 205, Mountain View (94041-1287)
PHONE..................650 966-1967
Murugesh Ramiah, *Chairman*
Vina Vivek, *President*
Renjana Gopinath, *Top Exec*
EMP: 90
SALES (est): 3.4MM **Privately Held**
WEB: www.assure-usa.com
SIC: 8748 Business consulting

(P-27838)
AT&T CORP
330 R, San Ramon (94583)
PHONE..................925 823-6949
Leon P Davis, *Area Mgr*
EMP: 416
SALES (corp-wide): 146.8B **Publicly Held**
WEB: www.swbell.com
SIC: 8748 Telecommunications consultant
HQ: At&T Corp.
1 At&T Way
Bedminster NJ 07921
800 403-3302

(P-27839)
AT&T CORP
16201 Raymer St, Van Nuys (91406-1210)
PHONE..................818 997-5998
Laurie Tossie, *Manager*
Blanca Barrera, *General Mgr*
EMP: 100
SALES (corp-wide): 146.8B **Publicly Held**
WEB: www.swbell.com
SIC: 8748 Telecommunications consultant
HQ: At&T Corp.
1 At&T Way
Bedminster NJ 07921
800 403-3302

(P-27840)
AT&T SERVICES INC
Also Called: SBC
5650 Aldrin Ct, Bakersfield (93313-2110)
PHONE..................661 324-2046
Tim Frazure, *Manager*
Patty Sullivan, *Purchasing*
EMP: 120
SALES (corp-wide): 146.8B **Publicly Held**
WEB: www.dsdllc.com
SIC: 8748 Telecommunications consultant
HQ: At&T Services, Inc.
208 S Akard St Ste 110
Dallas TX 75202
210 821-4105

(P-27841)
ATKINS NORTH AMERICA INC
332 Pine St Fl 5, San Francisco (94104-3206)
PHONE..................916 325-4800
Rod Jeung, *Manager*
Heather Madonna, *Admin Asst*
EMP: 50
SALES (corp-wide): 2.7B **Privately Held**
WEB: www.cargillemt.com
SIC: 8748 8742 8711 Environmental consultant; planning consultant; consulting engineer
HQ: Atkins North America, Inc.
2001 Nw 107th Ave
Doral FL 33172
813 282-7275

(P-27842)
AUCTIVA CORPORATION
360 E 6th St, Chico (95928-5631)
PHONE..................530 894-7400
Jeff Schlicht, *President*
Mark A Schwartz, *CEO*
Shawn Horswill, *Info Tech Mgr*
Kathleen Spanos, *Software Dev*
Michael Davies, *Cust Mgr*
EMP: 80
SALES (est): 6.4MM **Privately Held**
WEB: www.theonlineseller.com
SIC: 8748 Business consulting

(P-27843)
AVA THE RABBIT HAVEN INC
Also Called: RABBIT HAVEN THE
1261 S Mary St, Scotts Valley (95067)
P.O. Box 66594 (95067-6594)
PHONE..................831 600-7479
Heather Bechtel, *Director*
Richard Jacobel, *President*
EMP: 80
SALES: 111.1K **Privately Held**
SIC: 8748 Testing service, educational or personnel

(P-27844)
AXIOM GLOBAL TECHNOLOGIES INC
220 N Wiget Ln, Walnut Creek (94598-2404)
PHONE..................925 393-5800
Fax: 925 932-1950
Mohit Sishu Arora, *CEO*
Priya Arora, *General Mgr*
Raman Sharma, *Software Dev*
Arun Sharma, *Tech Recruiter*
Alok Singh, *Tech Recruiter*
EMP: 125
SALES (est): 1.3MM **Privately Held**
WEB: www.acg-usa.com
SIC: 8748 Business consulting

(P-27845)
B & L CONSULTING LLC
152 N 2nd Ave, Upland (91786-6001)
PHONE..................682 238-6994
Bayandre Lewis, *Mng Member*
EMP: 63
SQ FT: 5,000
SALES: 5.2MM **Privately Held**
SIC: 8748 Business consulting

(P-27846)
BALBOA WATER GROUP LLC
28545 Livingston Ave, Valencia (91355-4166)
PHONE..................661 678-5109
Fax: 714 384-0385
Eric Kownacki, *CEO*
EMP: 76
SALES (corp-wide): 67.9MM **Privately Held**
SIC: 8748 Business consulting
PA: Balboa Water Group, Llc
1382 Bell Ave
Tustin CA 92780
714 384-0384

(P-27847)
BARSTOW REDEVELOPMENT AGENCY
220 E Mountain View St B, Barstow (92311-7304)
PHONE..................760 256-3531
Paul Warrner, *General Mgr*
EMP: 126
SQ FT: 1,039
SALES (est): 60K **Privately Held**
SIC: 8748 Economic consultant

(P-27848)
BERKELEY RESEARCH GROUP LLC (PA)
2200 Powell St Ste 1200, Emeryville (94608-1833)
PHONE..................510 285-3300
Fax: 510 654-7857
David Teece, *Chairman*
Marvin Tenenbaum, *President*
Sebastien Belanger, *COO*
Kimberly Starr, *CFO*
David Salat, *Exec VP*
EMP: 148
SALES (est): 137.2MM **Privately Held**
SIC: 8748 Business consulting

(P-27849)
BLACKSTONE CONSULTING INC
2710 N Harbor Dr, San Diego (92101-1028)
PHONE..................619 293-0043
EMP: 125
SALES (corp-wide): 135MM **Privately Held**
SIC: 8748 Business consulting
PA: Blackstone Consulting, Inc.
11726 San Vicente Blvd # 550
Los Angeles CA 90049
310 826-4389

(P-27850)
BLACKSTONE CONSULTING INC
8300 Santa Cruz St, Sacramento (95828-0909)
PHONE..................916 383-8060
Fax: 916 383-8064
Hellynn Gaines, *Manager*
EMP: 125
SALES (corp-wide): 135MM **Privately Held**
SIC: 8748 Business consulting
PA: Blackstone Consulting, Inc.
11726 San Vicente Blvd # 550
Los Angeles CA 90049
310 826-4389

(P-27851)
BLACKSTONE TECHNOLOGY GROUP (PA)
150 California St Fl 9, San Francisco (94111-4560)
PHONE..................415 837-1400
David Mysona, *CEO*
Casey Courneen, *President*

PRODUCTS & SERVICES SECTION
8748 - Business Consulting Svcs, NEC County (P-27875)

Mark Coggeshall, *COO*
Patrick James, *COO*
Rakesh Agrawal, *Exec VP*
EMP: 100
SQ FT: 10,000
SALES (est): 37.2MM **Privately Held**
WEB: www.bstonetech.com
SIC: 8748 Business consulting

(P-27852)
BOCA MESA INCORPORATED
3130 Skyway Dr Ste 701, Santa Maria (93455-1800)
PHONE..................805 934-9470
EMP: 69
SALES (est): 4.7MM **Privately Held**
SIC: 8748 7349

(P-27853)
BON SUISSE INC
392 W Walnut Ave, Fullerton (92832-2351)
PHONE..................714 578-0001
EMP: 66
SALES (corp-wide): 87.9MM **Privately Held**
SIC: 8748 5149 2052 Agricultural consultant; bakery products; cones, ice cream
PA: Bon Suisse Inc.
    11860 Cmnty Rd Ste 100
    Poway CA 92064
    858 486-0005

(P-27854)
BRANDNET INC
724 Battery St 3, San Francisco (94111-1559)
PHONE..................415 216-4152
Fax: 650 638-1781
John Farrar, *President*
Andy Atherton, *COO*
Jay Beckley, *Vice Pres*
Dylan Parks, *Vice Pres*
Matt Gallatin, *VP Finance*
EMP: 60
SALES (est): 8.1MM
SALES (corp-wide): 5.3B **Privately Held**
SIC: 8748 Business consulting
HQ: Valassis Communications, Inc.
    19975 Victor Pkwy
    Livonia MI 48152
    734 591-3000

(P-27855)
BROCADE CMMNCTIONS SYSTEMS INC
110 Holger Way, San Jose (95134-1376)
PHONE..................408 333-4300
Jeff Achtzehn, *Program Mgr*
Catherine Ferandin, *Admin Asst*
Kent Nichols, *Admin Asst*
Jason Gary, *Administration*
Rajib Dutta, *Software Engr*
EMP: 98 **Publicly Held**
SIC: 8748 Communications consulting
PA: Brocade Communications Systems, Inc.
    130 Holger Way
    San Jose CA 95134

(P-27856)
BURBANK PLG & ZONING DIV OF
150 N 3rd St Fl 2, Burbank (91502-1264)
PHONE..................818 238-5250
Joy Forbes, *Director*
EMP: 50
SALES (est): 82.9K **Privately Held**
SIC: 8748 Urban planning & consulting services

(P-27857)
BUREAU VERITAS NORTH AMER INC
Also Called: Clayton Group Services
1665 Scenic Ave Ste 200, Costa Mesa (92626-1441)
PHONE..................714 431-4100
Sandi Schafer, *Vice Pres*
Lisa Townsend, *Social Dir*
Trevor Donaghu, *Project Mgr*
John Olson, *Project Mgr*
Bob Kay, *Business Mgr*
EMP: 70

SALES (corp-wide): 10.5MM **Privately Held**
SIC: 8748 Business consulting
HQ: Bureau Veritas North America, Inc.
    1601 Sawgrs Corp Pkwy
    Sunrise FL 33323
    954 236-8100

(P-27858)
BUXTON CONSULTING
6140 Stoneridge Mall Rd # 100, Pleasanton (94588-3155)
PHONE..................925 467-0700
Fax: 510 467-0717
James T Buxton, *President*
Chandra Reddy, *Vice Pres*
Arno Fritz, *Regional Mgr*
Sudha Parameswaran, *Tech Recruiter*
Leah Beltran, *Accountant*
EMP: 90
SQ FT: 6,500
SALES (est): 11.8MM **Privately Held**
WEB: www.us-buxton.com
SIC: 8748 Systems analysis & engineering consulting services

(P-27859)
BY REFERRAL ONLY INC
2035 Corte Del Nogal # 200, Carlsbad (92011-1445)
PHONE..................760 707-1300
Joseph F Stumpf, *President*
Robert Sherrell, *Info Tech Dir*
EMP: 100
SALES (est): 10.1MM **Privately Held**
SIC: 8748 Educational consultant

(P-27860)
CA SAFETY COMPLIANCE CORP
Also Called: Cscc
1122 W Wash Blvd Fl 3, Los Angeles (90015-3352)
PHONE..................213 747-0805
Fax: 213 747-4028
Carol Pender, *President*
EMP: 70
SALES (est): 3.4MM
SALES (corp-wide): 1.8B **Privately Held**
SIC: 8748 Safety training service
HQ: UI Verification Services Inc.
    85 John Rd
    Canton MA 02021
    781 821-2200

(P-27861)
CAL SOUTHERN ASSN GOVERNMENTS (PA)
Also Called: S C A G
818 W 7th St Fl 12, Los Angeles (90071-3435)
PHONE..................213 236-1800
Fax: 213 236-1825
Hasan Ikhrata, *Exec Dir*
Lambertus Becker, *CFO*
Basil Panas, *CFO*
Jim Gosnell, *Deputy Dir*
Karen Tachiki, *Legal Staff*
EMP: 116
SQ FT: 50,000
SALES: 40MM **Privately Held**
SIC: 8748 Urban planning & consulting services

(P-27862)
CALIFORNIA COML INV GROUP INC
Also Called: Ccig
4530 E Thousand Oaks Blvd # 100, Westlake Village (91362-3897)
PHONE..................805 495-8400
Gary Collett, *President*
Louis Mellman, *Vice Pres*
EMP: 50
SALES (est): 4.8MM **Privately Held**
SIC: 8748 Urban planning & consulting services

(P-27863)
CALIFORNIA ENVMTL HLTH ASSN
Also Called: C E H A
2000 A De Las Pulgas 10 Ste 100, San Mateo (94403)
PHONE..................650 363-4726
Liberty Cerezo, *Treasurer*

Todd A Frantz, *President*
EMP: 70
SQ FT: 500
SALES (est): 6.1MM **Privately Held**
SIC: 8748 Environmental consultant

(P-27864)
CALIFORNIA TRAFFIC SAFETY INST
Also Called: CTSI
209 E Avenue K8 Ste 210, Lancaster (93535-4535)
PHONE..................661 940-1907
Fax: 661 546-0046
Wanda Paulson, *President*
Michael Atmore, *CFO*
Tiffany Coronado, *Exec Dir*
Diana Clark, *Executive Asst*
EMP: 160
SQ FT: 42,000
SALES: 4.5MM **Privately Held**
WEB: www.ctsi-courtnetwork.org
SIC: 8748 Educational consultant

(P-27865)
CAPITAL OVERSIGHT INC
2118 Wilshire Blvd, Santa Monica (90403-5704)
PHONE..................310 453-8000
Patricia Sewell, *Admin Sec*
Douglas Rand, *CEO*
Matthew Denti, *Vice Pres*
Dane Williams, *Vice Pres*
Tamara Stewart, *Human Resources*
EMP: 307 **EST:** 2002
SALES: 6.7MM **Privately Held**
SIC: 8748 7323 7389 7299 Business consulting; credit clearinghouse; ; personal financial services

(P-27866)
CARBER HOLDINGS INC
15350 Texaco Ave, Paramount (90723-3920)
PHONE..................562 531-2400
EMP: 133
SALES (corp-wide): 45.1MM **Privately Held**
SIC: 8748 Business consulting
PA: Carber Holdings, Inc.
    12600 N Featherwood Dr # 450
    Houston TX 77034
    800 592-8378

(P-27867)
CATALINA ENTERPRISE INC
206 Catalina Rd, Fullerton (92835-2506)
PHONE..................949 637-3091
Easter Johnson, *Vice Pres*
Stanley Johnson, *Asst Sec*
EMP: 52 **EST:** 2015
SALES (est): 698.5K **Privately Held**
SIC: 8748 Systems engineering consultant, ex. computer or professional

(P-27868)
CB&I ENVMTL INFRASTRUCTURE INC
18100 Von Karman Ave # 450, Irvine (92612-0169)
PHONE..................949 261-6441
Richard Fowler, *Branch Mgr*
Patricia Olson, *Manager*
EMP: 63 **Privately Held**
SIC: 8748 Business consulting
HQ: Cb&I Environmental & Infrastructure, Inc.
    4171 Essen Ln
    Baton Rouge LA 70809
    225 932-2500

(P-27869)
CB&I ENVMTL INFRASTRUCTURE INC
180 Promenade Cir Ste 320, Sacramento (95834-2922)
PHONE..................916 928-3300
Charles Metcinger, *Branch Mgr*
Patricia Olson, *Manager*
EMP: 50 **Privately Held**
SIC: 8748 Environmental consultant

HQ: Cb&I Environmental & Infrastructure, Inc.
    4171 Essen Ln
    Baton Rouge LA 70809
    225 932-2500

(P-27870)
CB&I ENVMTL INFRASTRUCTURE INC
1230 Columbia St Ste 1200, San Diego (92101-8517)
PHONE..................619 239-1690
Debra Morris, *Branch Mgr*
James Pawlisch, *Sales Executive*
Patricia Olson, *Manager*
EMP: 260 **Privately Held**
SIC: 8748 Environmental consultant
HQ: Cb&I Environmental & Infrastructure, Inc.
    4171 Essen Ln
    Baton Rouge LA 70809
    225 932-2500

(P-27871)
CB&I ENVMTL INFRASTRUCTURE INC
4005 Port Chicago Hwy, Concord (94520-1180)
PHONE..................925 288-9898
Ron Fiore, *Manager*
Tom Machen, *Director*
Patricia Olson, *Manager*
EMP: 220 **Privately Held**
SIC: 8748 Business consulting
HQ: Cb&I Environmental & Infrastructure, Inc.
    4171 Essen Ln
    Baton Rouge LA 70809
    225 932-2500

(P-27872)
CDSNET LLC
Also Called: Frmsinfoserv
6053 W Century Blvd, Los Angeles (90045-6430)
PHONE..................310 981-9500
Michael Griffus, *President*
Francis G Homan, *CFO*
Susan Soh, *Accounts Mgr*
EMP: 65
SALES (est): 3.5MM **Privately Held**
WEB: www.tectransinc.com
SIC: 8748 Business consulting
HQ: Keolis Transit America, Inc.
    6053 W Century Blvd # 900
    Los Angeles CA 90045
    310 981-9500

(P-27873)
CENTER FOR AUTISM RELATED SVCS
5949 Lankershim Blvd, North Hollywood (91601-1006)
PHONE..................323 850-7177
Susan Kumaer, *Administration*
EMP: 50
SALES (est): 107.4K **Privately Held**
WEB: www.center4autism.com
SIC: 8748 7361 Educational consultant; employment agencies

(P-27874)
CENTER FOR SUSTAINABLE ENERGY
9325 Sky Park Ct Ste 100, San Diego (92123-4380)
PHONE..................858 244-1177
Michael Akavan, *Chairman*
Fred Baranowski, *Treasurer*
Len Hering, *Exec Dir*
Benjamin Airth, *Program Mgr*
Tamara Gishri, *Program Mgr*
EMP: 87
SALES: 90MM **Privately Held**
WEB: www.sdenergy.org
SIC: 8748 Business consulting

(P-27875)
CETECOM INC (DH)
411 Dixon Landing Rd, Milpitas (95035-2579)
PHONE..................408 586-6200
Fax: 408 586-6299
Maan Ghanma, *CEO*
Willfried Klassmann, *President*

8748 - Business Consulting Svcs, NEC County (P-27876)

Heiko Strehlow, *COO*
Clorinda Sammis, *Corp Secy*
Timothy Vago, *Vice Pres*
EMP: 85
SQ FT: 48,000
SALES (est): 22.2MM
SALES (corp-wide): 300.2MM **Privately Held**
WEB: www.cetecomusa.com
SIC: 8748   8734   Communications consulting; testing laboratories
HQ: Cetecom Gmbh
    Im Teelbruch 116
    Essen 45219
    205 495-190

(P-27876)
CHALLENGER INDUSTRIES INC
Also Called: Challenger Ent
2971 E White Star Ave, Anaheim (92806-2630)
PHONE..........................714 630-4344
Fax: 714 632-7324
Gregory Joseph Martin, *President*
Ron Flicker, *Exec VP*
Melody Fahee, *Manager*
EMP: 60
SQ FT: 4,000
SALES (est): 8.1MM **Privately Held**
WEB: www.challengerenterprises.com
SIC: 8748 Systems analysis & engineering consulting services

(P-27877)
CHAMBERS GROUP INC
17671 Cowan Ste 100, Irvine (92614-6074)
P.O. Box N Centre D, Santa Ana (92707)
PHONE..........................949 261-5414
Fax: 949 261-8950
Sherman Smith, *President*
Noel Davis, *Finance Mgr*
Bob Wilson, *Facilities Mgr*
EMP: 50
SALES (corp-wide): 15.2MM **Privately Held**
WEB: www.chambersgroupinc.com
SIC: 8748 Environmental consultant
PA: Chambers Group, Inc.
    5 Hutton Cntre Dr Ste 750
    Santa Ana CA 92707
    949 261-5414

(P-27878)
CHC CONSULTING LLC
1845 W Orangewood Ave # 300, Orange (92868-2053)
PHONE..........................949 250-0004
Chris Cook, *CEO*
Susan Cook, *President*
Paul Cook, *Vice Pres*
Christine Havey, *Vice Pres*
Lorrie Pope, *Vice Pres*
EMP: 300
SALES (est): 19.7MM **Privately Held**
SIC: 8748 Telecommunications consultant

(P-27879)
CHIKPEA INC
1 Market St Spear Spear Tower, San Francisco (94127)
PHONE..........................888 342-3828
Adam Kleinberg, *CEO*
Kitty Russack, *Business Mgr*
Scott Gray, *Director*
EMP: 50
SALES (est): 3.7MM **Privately Held**
SIC: 8748 Telecommunications consultant

(P-27880)
CITY OF MORGAN HILL
Also Called: Public Works Department
100 Edes St, Morgan Hill (95037-5301)
PHONE..........................408 776-7333
Fax: 408 779-6282
Jim Ashcraft, *Director*
Mario Iglesias, *Systs Prg Mgr*
EMP: 52 **Privately Held**
WEB: www.mhcommunitycenter.com
SIC: 8748 9111 City planning; mayors' offices
PA: City Of Morgan Hill
    17575 Peak Ave
    Morgan Hill CA 95037
    408 778-6480

(P-27881)
CITY OF SAN DIEGO
Also Called: Enginring Capitl Projects Dept
1010 2nd Ave Ste 800, San Diego (92101-4907)
PHONE..........................619 533-3012
Patti Boekamp, *Deputy Dir*
Sandy Rugglero, *Analyst*
Brian P Fennessy, *Fire Chief*
EMP: 50 **Privately Held**
WEB: www.eayo.com
SIC: 8748 9621 Traffic consultant; regulation, administration of transportation;
PA: City Of San Diego
    202 C St
    San Diego CA 92101
    619 236-6330

(P-27882)
CLEARESULT CONSULTING INC
Also Called: Peci
1 Sansome St Fl 35, San Francisco (94104-4436)
PHONE..........................415 848-1250
Karen Healey, *Branch Mgr*
EMP: 77
SALES (corp-wide): 232.5MM **Privately Held**
SIC: 8748 Energy conservation consultant
HQ: Clearesult Consulting Inc.
    4301 Westbank Dr Ste A250
    Austin TX 78746
    512 327-9200

(P-27883)
COASSURE INC
4100 Moorpark Ave Ste 122, San Jose (95117-1707)
P.O. Box 234, Los Altos (94023-0234)
PHONE..........................408 244-0400
Zaydoon Jawadi, *President*
EMP: 100
SALES (est): 2.9MM **Privately Held**
WEB: www.coassure.com
SIC: 8748 Testing services

(P-27884)
COHEN VENTURES INC (PA)
Also Called: Energy Solutions
449 15th St Ste 402, Oakland (94612-2828)
PHONE..........................510 482-4420
Samuel D Cohen, *President*
Walter Harrower, *CFO*
Chris Burmester, *Vice Pres*
Simone Young-Tem, *Executive Asst*
Raina Carter, *Software Engr*
EMP: 74
SQ FT: 11,000
SALES (est): 16.5MM **Privately Held**
WEB: www.energy-solution.com
SIC: 8748 Energy conservation consultant

(P-27885)
COMBINE RESIDENTIAL CNSTR
Also Called: Conterra Residential Cnstr
8413 63rd St, Riverside (92509-6006)
PHONE..........................951 360-1260
Rachel Stanhoff, *President*
EMP: 60
SQ FT: 5,000
SALES (est): 4.2MM **Privately Held**
SIC: 8748 Business consulting

(P-27886)
COMMODITY DISTRIBUTION SERVICE
10035 Painter Ave, Santa Fe Springs (90670-3015)
PHONE..........................562 777-9969
Dan Nagel, *President*
Mitchell Patton, *CFO*
EMP: 50
SQ FT: 40,000
SALES (est): 2.3MM **Privately Held**
WEB: www.cdsold.com
SIC: 8748 Business consulting

(P-27887)
CONSORTM ON REACHNG EXCELLNCE
Also Called: Core
3112 Cedar Ravine Rd, Placerville (95667-6506)
PHONE..........................510 540-4200
Fax: 510 540-4242
Linda Diamond, *CEO*
Bill Honig, *President*
Mark Simmons, *COO*
Jennifer Ogden, *Treasurer*
Jack Gerson, *Vice Pres*
EMP: 50
SALES (est): 4.1MM **Privately Held**
WEB: www.corelearn.com
SIC: 8748 Educational consultant

(P-27888)
CORNERSTONE CNSULTING TECH INC
44 Montgomery St Ste 3360, San Francisco (94104-4806)
PHONE..........................415 705-7800
Fax: 415 705-7801
Wayne Perry, *CEO*
Charles Jones, *Officer*
Martin Banas, *Manager*
EMP: 50
SQ FT: 1,400
SALES (est): 4MM **Privately Held**
WEB: www.cornerstoneconcilium.com
SIC: 8748 Business consulting

(P-27889)
CORNERSTONE RESEARCH INC (PA)
1000 El Camino Real # 250, Menlo Park (94025-4315)
PHONE..........................650 853-1660
Fax: 650 324-9204
Cynthia Zollinger, *Chairman*
Michael E Burton, *President*
Lee Reamy, *CFO*
Catherine Galley, *Senior VP*
Michael Keeley, *Senior VP*
EMP: 100
SQ FT: 40,000
SALES (est): 99.2MM **Privately Held**
WEB: www.cornerstone.com
SIC: 8748 7389 Economic consultant; financial services

(P-27890)
CORNERSTONE RESEARCH INC
2 Embarcadero Ctr Fl 20, San Francisco (94111-3922)
PHONE..........................415 229-8100
Cynthia Zollinger, *CEO*
EMP: 52
SALES (corp-wide): 110.2MM **Privately Held**
SIC: 8748 Economic consultant
PA: Cornerstone Research, Inc.
    1000 El Camino Real # 250
    Menlo Park CA 94025
    650 853-1660

(P-27891)
COUNTY OF SAN DIEGO
Human Resources Dept
1600 Pacific Hwy Ste 207, San Diego (92101-2422)
PHONE..........................619 236-2191
Janice Horning, *Branch Mgr*
EMP: 150 **Privately Held**
WEB: www.sdlcc.org
SIC: 8748 9441 Employee programs administration; administration of social & human resources
PA: County Of San Diego
    1600 Pacific Hwy Ste 209
    San Diego CA 92101
    619 531-5880

(P-27892)
CSC CONSULTING INC
3113 E Laurel Ave, Visalia (93292-3337)
PHONE..........................559 739-8180
Brian Greaves, *Principal*
EMP: 250
SALES (corp-wide): 12.1B **Publicly Held**
SIC: 8748 Business consulting
HQ: Csc Consulting, Inc.
    404 Wyman St Ste 355
    Waltham MA 02451
    781 890-7446

(P-27893)
DATA RECOGNITION CORPORATION
Also Called: C T B
20 Ryan Ranch Rd, Monterey (93940-5703)
PHONE..........................831 393-0700
Mike Limbach, *Vice Pres*
Premratan Kalani, *Sr Software Eng*
Jim Ekstrand, *MIS Dir*
Randy Bradley, *Info Tech Mgr*
David Bogart, *Software Engr*
EMP: 50
SALES (corp-wide): 201MM **Privately Held**
SIC: 8748 Business consulting
PA: Data Recognition Corporation
    13490 Bass Lake Rd
    Maple Grove MN 55311
    763 268-2000

(P-27894)
DATASTAX INC (PA)
Also Called: (FORMARLY RIPTANO, INC)
3975 Freedom Cir Ste 400, Santa Clara (95054-1258)
PHONE..........................650 389-6000
Billy Bosworth, *CEO*
Glenn Johnson, *President*
Dennis Wolf, *CFO*
Karl Van Den Bergh, *Chief Mktg Ofcr*
Tony Kavanagh, *Chief Mktg Ofcr*
EMP: 97 **EST:** 2011
SALES (est): 49.9MM **Privately Held**
SIC: 8748 Telecommunications consultant

(P-27895)
DECISION TOOLBOX INC
5319 University Dr 521, Irvine (92612-2965)
PHONE..........................562 377-5600
Fax: 562 377-5640
Kim Shepherd, *President*
Loren Miner, *COO*
Jay Barnett, *Founder*
Staci Detwiler, *Officer*
Melissa Edelman, *Project Mgr*
EMP: 85
SQ FT: 300
SALES (est): 8.8MM **Privately Held**
SIC: 8748 Business consulting

(P-27896)
DELOITTE CONSULTING LLP
350 S Grand Ave Ste 200, Los Angeles (90071-3469)
PHONE..........................212 489-1600
Laura Conlin, *Branch Mgr*
Previn Waas, *Auditing Mgr*
Kurt Conger, *Senior Mgr*
EMP: 117
SALES (corp-wide): 9.5B **Privately Held**
SIC: 8748 Business consulting
HQ: Deloitte Consulting Llp
    30 Rockefeller Plz
    New York NY 10112
    212 492-4000

(P-27897)
DESTINATION SCIENCE LLC
953 N Elm St, Orange (92867-5454)
PHONE..........................714 289-9100
Fax: 714 289-9102
Heena Desai,
Sharon Fogg, *Bd of Directors*
Kathy Heraghty, *Bd of Directors*
Jan Holland, *Administration*
Colleen Segale, *Teacher*
EMP: 150
SQ FT: 5,000
SALES: 1MM **Privately Held**
WEB: www.destinationscience.org
SIC: 8748 Educational consultant

(P-27898)
DEUTSCHE TELEKOM INC
295 Bernardo Ave Ste 200, Mountain View (94043-5205)
PHONE..........................650 335-4100
Ramesh Menon, *Branch Mgr*
Frank Schwarz, *CFO*
Roman Baumgaertner, *Senior Mgr*
Jatinder Singh, *Manager*
EMP: 100
SALES (corp-wide): 74.3B **Publicly Held**
SIC: 8748 Telecommunications consultant

PRODUCTS & SERVICES SECTION
8748 - Business Consulting Svcs, NEC County (P-27924)

HQ: Deutsche Telekom, Inc.
1 Rockefeller Plz Fl 16
New York NY 10020
212 301-6111

(P-27899)
DIVERSIFIED RE PACKAGING CORP
1118 S La Cienega Blvd, Los Angeles (90035-2519)
PHONE.................310 855-1946
Jeffrie Green, *President*
EMP: 700
SALES (est): 15MM **Privately Held**
SIC: 8748 Business consulting

(P-27900)
E & J GALLO WINERY
Also Called: Ranch Winery The
105a Zinfandel Ln, Saint Helena (94574-1631)
PHONE.................707 967-9284
EMP: 50
SALES (corp-wide): 4.1B **Privately Held**
SIC: 8748 5182 Business consulting; wine
PA: E. & J. Gallo Winery
600 Yosemite Blvd
Modesto CA 95354
209 341-3111

(P-27901)
E2C INC
3016 Scott Blvd, Santa Clara (95054-3323)
PHONE.................408 327-5700
Fax: 408 327-5707
Sako Noravian, *Ch of Bd*
Benjamin Berman, *Project Mgr*
EMP: 50
SQ FT: 13,000
SALES (est): 3.1MM **Privately Held**
SIC: 8748 Environmental consultant

(P-27902)
EAG HOLDINGS LLC
2710 Walsh Ave, Santa Clara (95051-0963)
PHONE.................408 530-3500
Siddhartha Kadia, *CEO*
Cindy Gentile, *Director*
EMP: 700
SQ FT: 70,000
SALES (est): 18.6MM **Privately Held**
SIC: 8748 Business consulting

(P-27903)
EALLIANT LLC
1202 Morena Blvd Ste 100, San Diego (92110-3842)
PHONE.................619 255-9344
Allen F Maxwell, *Mng Member*
Clarence Carter,
EMP: 50 **EST:** 2012
SALES (est): 1.7MM **Privately Held**
SIC: 8748 Business consulting

(P-27904)
ECHELON SECURITY INC
1604 Kerley Dr, San Jose (95112-4815)
PHONE.................408 436-8844
Steve Brown, *President*
EMP: 67
SQ FT: 2,000
SALES (est): 5.1MM **Privately Held**
SIC: 8748 7381 Business consulting; guard services; security guard service

(P-27905)
ECO BAY SERVICES INC
1501 Minnesota St, San Francisco (94107-3521)
PHONE.................415 643-7777
Trent Michels, *President*
Hector Borrayo, *Controller*
EMP: 150
SQ FT: 80,000
SALES (est): 16MM **Privately Held**
SIC: 8748 Business consulting

(P-27906)
ECOLOGY AND ENVIRONMENT INC
505 Sansome St Ste 300, San Francisco (94111-3155)
PHONE.................510 893-6700
Craig Tiballi, *Manager*

EMP: 64
SALES (corp-wide): 126.7MM **Publicly Held**
SIC: 8748 5099 Environmental consultant; firearms & ammunition, except sporting
PA: Ecology And Environment, Inc.
368 Pleasant View Dr
Lancaster NY 14086
716 684-8060

(P-27907)
ECONOMIC DEV CORP OF LA COUNTY
Also Called: Los Angeles Cnty Economic Dev
444 S Flower St Ste 3700, Los Angeles (90071-2972)
PHONE.................213 622-4300
William C Allen, *President*
Jill Yoshimi, *President*
David A Flaks, *COO*
Susan D Stel, *CFO*
Christine Cooper, *Vice Pres*
EMP: 50 **EST:** 1981
SQ FT: 18,000
SALES (est): 6.1MM **Privately Held**
WEB: www.laedc.org
SIC: 8748 Business consulting

(P-27908)
EDGE MORTGAGE ADVISORY CO LLC
2125 E Katella Ave # 350, Anaheim (92806-6072)
PHONE.................714 564-5800
Robin Auerbach, *President*
Doug Speaker, *Senior VP*
EMP: 88
SALES (est): 9.5MM **Privately Held**
SIC: 8748 Business consulting

(P-27909)
ELLITE MANAGEMENT INC
7340 Firestone Blvd # 218, Downey (90241-4100)
PHONE.................562 806-2062
Franscisco Porras, *CEO*
Angie Ramirez, *President*
Mariano Ramirez, *Treasurer*
Yesenai Porras, *Admin Sec*
Linda Shlultz, *Sales Mgr*
EMP: 83
SALES (est): 5.8MM **Privately Held**
SIC: 8748 Business consulting

(P-27910)
ELS
Also Called: Els Architecture
2040 Addison St, Berkeley (94704-1104)
PHONE.................510 549-2929
Fax: 510 843-3304
Barry Elbasani, *President*
Janette Gross, *Treasurer*
Carol Shen, *Admin Sec*
George Omura, *Applctn Conslt*
William Gordon, *Project Mgr*
EMP: 65 **EST:** 1967
SQ FT: 12,000
SALES (est): 7.4MM **Privately Held**
WEB: www.elsarch.com
SIC: 8748 8712 Urban planning & consulting services; architectural services

(P-27911)
EMERGENT VENTURES INTL INC
1156 Clement St, San Francisco (94118-2115)
PHONE.................415 655-6617
Ashutosh Pandey, *President*
Thomas Rosenberg, *Vice Pres*
EMP: 99
SALES (est): 3.2MM **Privately Held**
SIC: 8748 Business consulting

(P-27912)
ENERGY EXPERTS INTERNATIONAL
7111 N Fresno St, Fresno (93720-2965)
PHONE.................559 449-1724
EMP: 118
SALES (corp-wide): 847K **Privately Held**
SIC: 8748 8742 Energy conservation consultant; management consulting services

PA: Energy Experts International
555 Twin Dolphin Dr # 185
Redwood City CA 94065
650 593-4261

(P-27913)
ENERGY EXPERTS INTERNATIONAL
37310 Cedar Blvd, Newark (94560-4156)
PHONE.................510 574-1822
EMP: 118
SALES (corp-wide): 847K **Privately Held**
SIC: 8748 8742 Energy conservation consultant; management consulting services
PA: Energy Experts International
555 Twin Dolphin Dr # 185
Redwood City CA 94065
650 593-4261

(P-27914)
ENGINEERING/REMDTN RSRCS GRP (PA)
Also Called: Errg
4585 Pacheco Blvd Ste 200, Martinez (94553-2228)
PHONE.................925 839-2200
Cynthia A Liu, *CEO*
James Hudson, *CFO*
Hudson M James, *CFO*
Guy Remo, *Manager*
Kenneth Wall, *Manager*
EMP: 70
SQ FT: 31,000
SALES: 50.4MM **Privately Held**
WEB: www.errg.com
SIC: 8748 Systems analysis & engineering consulting services

(P-27915)
ENTERPRISE SOLUTIONS INC
2855 Kifer Rd, Santa Clara (95051-0814)
PHONE.................408 727-3627
Lucy Phang, *CFO*
Sachin Kumar, *Tech Recruiter*
Ravi Sharma, *Business Mgr*
EMP: 185
SALES (corp-wide): 31.8MM **Privately Held**
SIC: 8748 Systems engineering consultant, ex. computer or professional
PA: Enterprise Solutions, Inc.
500 E Diehl Rd Ste 130
Naperville IL 60563
630 955-5984

(P-27916)
ENVENT CORPORATION (PA)
3220 E 29th St, Long Beach (90806-2321)
PHONE.................562 997-9465
Fax: 562 997-9485
Steve Sellinger, *President*
Thomas L Kerscher, *Vice Pres*
Nancy Savady, *Office Admin*
Michelle Figueroa, *Admin Asst*
Jessica Jones, *Admin Asst*
EMP: 135
SQ FT: 6,400
SALES: 33.3MM **Privately Held**
WEB: www.enventcorporation.com
SIC: 8748 Environmental consultant

(P-27917)
EPCM PROF SVC PARTNERS LLC
2017 Palo Verde Ave, Long Beach (90815-3300)
PHONE.................562 936-1000
F P Kallina, *Mng Member*
David Perez, *COO*
Frederick Paul Kallina, *Mng Member*
EMP: 52 **EST:** 2008
SQ FT: 5,000
SALES (est): 785K **Privately Held**
SIC: 8748 Business consulting; systems analysis & engineering consulting services

(P-27918)
EUROGENTEC NORTH AMERICA INC
34801 Campus Dr, Fremont (94555-3606)
PHONE.................510 791-9560
Jean-Pierre Delwart, *President*
Gopal Inamati, *Project Mgr*
Luke Marion, *Opers Mgr*

Pascal Bolon, *Sales Staff*
Lamarr Kelley, *Manager*
EMP: 115
SQ FT: 11,000
SALES: 2.5MM
SALES (corp-wide): 4.7B **Privately Held**
WEB: www.eurogentec.com
SIC: 8748 Business consulting
HQ: Eurogentec Sa
Rue Du Bois Saint-Jean 5
Seraing 4102
437 274-00

(P-27919)
FAITH COM INC (PA)
Also Called: Fci Management
3850 E Gilman St, Long Beach (90815-1752)
PHONE.................562 719-9300
Patricia Watts, *President*
Donald Gregg, *COO*
Joyce Clarke, *Admin Asst*
Deloris Banks, *Manager*
EMP: 58
SQ FT: 7,000
SALES (est): 14.1MM **Privately Held**
WEB: www.fcimgt.com
SIC: 8748 Energy conservation consultant

(P-27920)
FAME ASSISTANCE CORPORATION
1968 W Adams Blvd, Los Angeles (90018-3515)
PHONE.................323 373-7720
Denise Hunter, *President*
Cyndia Soloway, *Director*
EMP: 75
SQ FT: 33,748
SALES (est): 1.8MM **Privately Held**
SIC: 8748 Business consulting

(P-27921)
FAMILY AND CHILDREN SERVICES
950 W Julian St, San Jose (95126-2719)
PHONE.................408 292-9353
Diana Nemen, *CEO*
John Harland, *Treasurer*
James Ochsner, *Admin Sec*
Cristina Trujillo, *Admin Asst*
Charles Barley, *Director*
EMP: 70
SQ FT: 9,500
SALES (est): 4.7MM **Privately Held**
SIC: 8748 Business consulting

(P-27922)
FIELD DATA SERVICES
Also Called: Southland Car Counters
380 S Tustin St, Orange (92866-2502)
PHONE.................714 997-4498
Abraham Tashman, *President*
Michael Blitz, *CFO*
Douglas Bowen, *Corp Secy*
Roger Fiske, *Vice Pres*
Steve Souter, *Vice Pres*
EMP: 55
SQ FT: 1,200
SALES (est): 2.4MM **Privately Held**
WEB: www.fielddataservices.com
SIC: 8748 8742 Traffic consultant; transportation consultant

(P-27923)
FORMA SYSTEMS VISUART
3050 Pullman St, Costa Mesa (92626-5901)
PHONE.................949 660-1900
Van Stephens, *President*
Christopher Lee, *Vice Pres*
Carol Macfarlane, *Vice Pres*
H Gene Shieh, *Vice Pres*
Haley Beamon, *Principal*
EMP: 60
SQ FT: 15,500
SALES (est): 4.8MM **Privately Held**
WEB: www.formacompanies.com
SIC: 8748 0781 7336 City planning; landscape architects; graphic arts & related design

(P-27924)
FORTUNA TECHNOLOGIES INC
44721 Aguila Ter, Fremont (94539-6293)
PHONE.................510 687-9797

8748 - Business Consulting Svcs, NEC County (P-27925)

PRODUCTS & SERVICES SECTION

Ashok Thummalachetty, *President*
Surajit Duttachoudhury, *COO*
Swami Nathan, *COO*
Dayakar Anne, *Vice Pres*
William Lynch, *Vice Pres*
EMP: 115
SQ FT: 3,000
SALES (est) 5.6MM **Privately Held**
WEB: www.fortuna.com
SIC: 8748 7379 1731 Business consulting; computer related consulting services; electrical work

(P-27925)
FOX TRANSPORTATION INC (PA)
8610 Helms Ave, Rancho Cucamonga (91730-4520)
P.O. Box 3119 (91729-3119)
PHONE 909 291-4646
Michael K Fox, *CEO*
Mary Anne Fox, *Shareholder*
Chad Shearer, *President*
David Langrehr, *Senior VP*
David Burns, *Vice Pres*
EMP: 60
SALES (est): 22MM **Privately Held**
SIC: 8748 4213 Business consulting; trucking, except local

(P-27926)
FRYS ELECTRONICS INC
4100 Northgate Blvd, Sacramento (95834-1240)
PHONE 916 286-5800
Fax: 916 286-5818
Mark Ashby, *Branch Mgr*
EMP: 300
SALES (corp-wide): 17.4MM **Privately Held**
WEB: www.frys.com
SIC: 8748 5731 Business consulting; radio, television & electronic stores
PA: Fry's Electronics, Inc.
     600 E Brokaw Rd
     San Jose CA 95112
     408 350-1484

(P-27927)
FTI CONSULTING INC
1 Front St Ste 1600, San Francisco (94111-5353)
PHONE 415 283-4200
Jerry Keeler, *Manager*
Jody Ball, *Managing Dir*
Torsten Hartmann, *Managing Dir*
Dido Laurimore, *Managing Dir*
Michael WEI, *Managing Dir*
EMP: 80
SALES (corp-wide): 1.7B **Publicly Held**
SIC: 8748 Business consulting
PA: Fti Consulting, Inc.
     1101 K St Nw Ste B100
     Washington DC 20005
     202 312-9100

(P-27928)
FUSE PROJECT LLC
1401 16th St, San Francisco (94103-5109)
PHONE 415 908-1492
Yves Behar, *President*
Helen Fu Thomas, *Ch of Bd*
Mitch Pergola, *COO*
Graham Humphreys, *Vice Pres*
Cody Carroll, *Business Dir*
EMP: 60
SQ FT: 22,000
SALES (est): 3.1MM **Privately Held**
WEB: www.fuseproject.com
SIC: 8748 Business consulting

(P-27929)
G T TECHNOLOGY INC
12306 Brooksglen Dr, Saratoga (95070-3411)
PHONE 408 257-5245
Gregory Tenengolts, *President*
Derek Smid, *Mfg Staff*
Svetlana Reznikov, *Manager*
EMP: 50
SALES (est): 4.5MM **Privately Held**
SIC: 8748 Business consulting

(P-27930)
GARCO ENTERPRISES INC
Also Called: McDonald's
5930 W Pico Blvd, Los Angeles (90035-2658)
PHONE 323 933-1089
Fax: 323 933-0367
Ginger Cox, *President*
Jose Cortez, *Manager*
EMP: 50
SALES (est): 2.5MM **Privately Held**
SIC: 8748 Business consulting

(P-27931)
GEOCON CONSULTANTS INC (PA)
6960 Flanders Dr, San Diego (92121-3992)
PHONE 858 558-6900
Fax: 858 558-6159
Michael Chapin, *CEO*
Joe Vettel, *President*
Joseph Vettel, *COO*
William J Lydon, *CFO*
John Hoobs, *Vice Pres*
EMP: 85
SQ FT: 10,000
SALES (est): 22.2MM **Privately Held**
WEB: www.geoconinc.com
SIC: 8748 8711 Environmental consultant; engineering services

(P-27932)
GLASSFAB TEMPERING SERVICES (PA)
1448 Mariani Ct, Tracy (95376-2825)
PHONE 209 229-1060
Jagmohan Singh, *CEO*
Surinderpal Bains, *President*
Usha Mhay, *CFO*
EMP: 60
SQ FT: 60,000
SALES (est): 15.7MM **Privately Held**
SIC: 8748 Business consulting

(P-27933)
GLOBAL INFOTECH CORPORATION
2890 Zanker Rd Ste 202, San Jose (95134-2118)
PHONE 408 567-0600
Fax: 408 567-0810
Atul Sharma, *President*
Nitin Prasad, *Vice Pres*
Srikant Gupta, *Manager*
EMP: 550 **EST:** 1995
SQ FT: 3,000
SALES: 46.1MM **Privately Held**
WEB: www.global-infotech.com
SIC: 8748 Systems analysis & engineering consulting services

(P-27934)
GOLDEN GATE CAPITOL
1 Embarcadero Ctr # 3900, San Francisco (94111-3628)
PHONE 415 983-2700
Jacob Mizrahi, *Principal*
Alan Dillsaver, *Senior VP*
EMP: 500
SALES (est): 11.6MM **Privately Held**
SIC: 8748 Business consulting

(P-27935)
GOLDEN WEST PARTNERS INC (PA)
Also Called: Golden West Casino
18101 Von Karman Ave # 1280, Irvine (92612-0168)
PHONE 949 477-3090
Franklin R Elfend, *President*
Bob Patty, *Vice Pres*
EMP: 53
SALES (est): 6.6MM **Privately Held**
SIC: 8748 Business consulting

(P-27936)
GORDON E BTTY I MORE FUNDATION
1661 Page Mill Rd, Palo Alto (94304-1209)
PHONE 650 213-3000
Lewis W Coleman, *President*
Kathleen Justice-Moore, *Bd of Directors*
Kenneth F Siebel, *Bd of Directors*
George W Bo-Linn,

Alice A Ruth, *Ch Invest Ofcr*
EMP: 75
SALES: 423.7MM **Privately Held**
WEB: www.moorefoundation.org
SIC: 8748 Economic consultant

(P-27937)
GTE CORPORATION
Also Called: Verizon
180 N Mirage Ave, Lindsay (93247-2538)
PHONE 559 562-0000
Seiden Berg, *Manager*
EMP: 53
SALES (corp-wide): 131.6B **Publicly Held**
WEB: www.gte.com
SIC: 8748 Telecommunications consultant
HQ: Gte Corporation
     140 West St
     New York NY 10007
     212 395-1000

(P-27938)
H & F GRAIN FARMS LLC
1181 S Wolff Rd, Oxnard (93033-2105)
PHONE 805 754-4449
Robert Boelts,
EMP: 70
SALES: 4.5MM **Privately Held**
SIC: 8748 0191 Agricultural consultant; general farms, primarily crop

(P-27939)
HANLEY WOOD MKT INTELLIGENCE (PA)
555 Anton Blvd Ste 950, Costa Mesa (92626-7811)
PHONE 714 540-8500
Fax: 949 540-8555
Thomas Flynn, *President*
Shawn Edwards, *Vice Pres*
Munoz Doug, *Manager*
EMP: 65
SQ FT: 15,000
SALES: 20MM **Privately Held**
SIC: 8748 8742 Publishing consultant; real estate consultant

(P-27940)
HARRIS & SLOAN CONSULTING
2295 Gateway Oaks Dr # 165, Sacramento (95833-4211)
PHONE 916 921-2800
Fax: 916 753-5380
Timothy Sloan, *President*
Christopher Antonucci, *Human Resources*
EMP: 50
SALES (est): 1.4MM **Privately Held**
WEB: www.hscgi.com
SIC: 8748 Business consulting

(P-27941)
HERE FILMS
10990 Wilshire Blvd, Los Angeles (90024-3913)
PHONE 310 806-4288
EMP: 50
SALES (est): 1.2MM **Privately Held**
SIC: 8748

(P-27942)
HESPERIA SENIOR LIVING LLC
17581 Sultana St, Hesperia (92345-6552)
PHONE 760 244-5579
Wesley Brown,
Tony Alvarez, *Accountant*
Greg Anderson,
Cipriano Bautista,
EMP: 75
SALES (est): 2.7MM **Privately Held**
SIC: 8748 Business consulting

(P-27943)
HETROSYS LLC
3858 Carrera Ct, San Jose (95148-3716)
PHONE 408 270-0240
Harpreet Soni, *Mng Member*
EMP: 56
SQ FT: 2,800
SALES: 3.1MM **Privately Held**
SIC: 8748 7389 Telecommunications consultant;

(P-27944)
HFS NORTH AMERICA LLC (PA)
Also Called: Link Canada Distribution
231 G St Ste 4, Davis (95616-4568)
PHONE 530 758-8253
Jeff Nicholson, *Mng Member*
EMP: 200
SALES (est): 11MM **Privately Held**
SIC: 8748 Business consulting

(P-27945)
HINTTECH INC
505 Montgomery St Fl 11, San Francisco (94111-2585)
PHONE 415 874-3200
Egbert Hendricks, *President*
EMP: 120
SALES: 17MM **Privately Held**
SIC: 8748 Business consulting

(P-27946)
HUMBOLDT STATE UNIVERSITY SPON
Also Called: HSU FOUNDATION
1 Harpst St, Arcata (95521-8299)
P.O. Box 1185 (95518-1185)
PHONE 707 826-4189
Fax: 707 826-4783
Jacob Varkey, *President*
Martha Traphagen, *Principal*
Donna Sorensen, *Admin Sec*
Jeff Borgeld, *Professor*
Dixie L Johnson, *Director*
EMP: 50
SALES: 20.6MM **Privately Held**
WEB: www.hsujacks.com
SIC: 8748 Educational consultant

(P-27947)
HUNTER-LA PURISIMA CORP
5060 California Ave # 640, Bakersfield (93309-0728)
PHONE 661 616-0600
Kenneth J Hunter III, *President*
EMP: 52 **EST:** 1984
SALES (est): 1.9MM **Privately Held**
SIC: 8748 Urban planning & consulting services

(P-27948)
IBASET INC
27442 Portola Pkwy # 300, Foothill Ranch (92610-2822)
PHONE 949 598-5200
Ladeira Poonian, *CEO*
Vikram Sial, *President*
EMP: 99
SQ FT: 28,000
SALES (est): 1.7MM **Privately Held**
SIC: 8748 7371 7372 Business consulting; custom computer programming services; application computer software

(P-27949)
ICF JONES & STOKES INC (DH)
630 K St Ste 400, Sacramento (95814-3331)
PHONE 916 737-3000
Fax: 916 737-3030
Sergio Ostria, *President*
Sandra Murray, *CFO*
Terrance Mc Govern, *Treasurer*
Mike Arnold, *Controller*
Stacy Gorajewski, *Asst Director*
EMP: 140 **EST:** 1970
SQ FT: 49,532
SALES (est): 53.9MM
SALES (corp-wide): 1.1B **Publicly Held**
WEB: www.icfi.com
SIC: 8748 Environmental consultant
HQ: Icf Consulting Group, Inc.
     9300 Lee Hwy
     Fairfax VA 22031
     703 934-3000

(P-27950)
INSIDE TRACK INC
1620 Montgomery St # 230, San Francisco (94111-1016)
PHONE 415 243-4440
Alan Tripp, *CEO*
Kai Drekmeier, *President*
ARI Blum, *CFO*
Marijean Hamilton, *Senior VP*
Ruth White, *Vice Pres*
EMP: 300

PRODUCTS & SERVICES SECTION 8748 - Business Consulting Svcs, NEC County (P-27974)

SALES (est): 31.2MM **Privately Held**
WEB: www.insidetrack.net
SIC: **8748** Educational consultant

(P-27951)
INSTITUTE FOR MLTCLTRL CNSLNG
3580 Wilshire Blvd # 2000, Los Angeles (90010-2501)
PHONE...................213 381-1239
Fax: 213 383-4803
Tara Pir, *CEO*
EMP: 80
SALES: 4.7MM **Privately Held**
SIC: **8748** Educational consultant

(P-27952)
INTERFACE MASTERS TECH INC
150 E Brokaw Rd, San Jose (95112-4203)
PHONE...................408 441-9341
Benjamin Askarinam, *CEO*
Sima Askarinam, *President*
WEI Liu, *Design Engr*
Shijie Cheng, *Engineer*
Jennifer Tam, *Engineer*
EMP: 50
SQ FT: 3,000
SALES (est): 20MM **Privately Held**
SIC: **8748** 8711 Communications consulting; engineering services

(P-27953)
INTERNATIONAL ADVISORS LLC
31248 Oak Crest Dr, Westlake Village (91361-4692)
PHONE...................497 961-7988
Steven Bronson, *President*
EMP: 100
SALES: 8MM **Privately Held**
SIC: **8748** Business consulting

(P-27954)
INTERNATIONAL MGT SYSTEMS
Also Called: IMS
4640 Admiralty Way # 500, Marina Del Rey (90292-6621)
PHONE...................310 822-2022
Fax: 310 305-8683
Harry M Thorpe Jr, *President*
Pam Barrie, *Administration*
Becky Valdez, *Administration*
Shirley Holt, *Human Res Dir*
Kristi Newman, *Human Res Mgr*
EMP: 90
SQ FT: 6,000
SALES (est): 5MM **Privately Held**
WEB: www.imssvs.com
SIC: **8748** 7374 Systems engineering consultant, ex. computer or professional; data processing & preparation

(P-27955)
INTRINSIK ENVMTL SCIENCES INC
1608 Pacific Ave Ste 201, Venice (90291-5112)
PHONE...................310 392-6462
EMP: 67
SALES (corp-wide): 3.5MM **Privately Held**
SIC: **8748**
PA: Intrinsik Environmental Sciences Inc
6605 Hurontario St Suite 605
Mississauga ON L5T 0
905 364-7800

(P-27956)
ITC SERVICE GROUP INC (PA)
Also Called: I T C
7777 Greenback Ln Ste 201, Citrus Heights (95610-5800)
PHONE...................877 370-4482
Timothy S Sauer, *President*
Teresa Aranda, *Admin Asst*
Jamie Gladden, *Admin Asst*
Dena Maynor, *Admin Asst*
Debi Richir, *Admin Asst*
EMP: 150
SQ FT: 11,843
SALES (est): 37.6MM **Privately Held**
WEB: www.callitc.com
SIC: **8748** Communications consulting; telecommunications consultant

(P-27957)
JACOBS CONSULTANCY INC
555 Airport Blvd Ste 300, Burlingame (94010-2036)
PHONE...................650 579-7722
Nick Davidson, *Branch Mgr*
Warren Adams, *Associate Dir*
Ken Bukauskas, *Associate Dir*
Gary Davies, *Associate Dir*
Bill Flock, *Associate Dir*
EMP: 85
SALES (corp-wide): 12.1B **Publicly Held**
WEB: www.jacobsconsultancy.com
SIC: **8748** 8742 Business consulting; management consulting services
HQ: Jacobs Consultancy Inc.
5995 Rogerdale Rd
Houston TX 77072
832 351-7800

(P-27958)
JAG PROFESSIONAL SERVICES INC
2008 Walnut Ave, Manhattan Beach (90266-2841)
P.O. Box 3007, El Segundo (90245-8107)
PHONE...................310 945-5648
Judith Hinkley, *CEO*
EMP: 126
SQ FT: 1,000
SALES (est): 10MM **Privately Held**
WEB: www.jagprof.com
SIC: **8748** Business consulting

(P-27959)
JILL TAYLOR MACARI
17 Hemway Ter, San Francisco (94117-1221)
PHONE...................781 315-2597
Jill Taylor Macari, *Owner*
EMP: 54
SALES (est): 719.5K **Privately Held**
SIC: **8748** Business consulting

(P-27960)
JK CONSULTANTS
1257 Sanguinetti Rd, Sonora (95370-6215)
PHONE...................209 532-7772
Fred Khachi, *President*
Elaine Khachi, *Exec VP*
Wilhelmina M Rodriguez, *Administration*
EMP: 50
SQ FT: 3,000
SALES: 25MM **Privately Held**
WEB: www.jksuccess.com
SIC: **8748** 8742 Business consulting; management consulting services

(P-27961)
JULIO GONZALEZ
1417 S Fairfax Ave Apt 4, Los Angeles (90019-3736)
PHONE...................310 310-4055
Julio Gonzalez, *Owner*
EMP: 99
SALES: 950K **Privately Held**
SIC: **8748** Business consulting

(P-27962)
JUSTICE CALIFORNIA DEPARTMENT
Also Called: Testing and Selection
1300 I St Ste 720, Sacramento (95814-2958)
PHONE...................916 324-5039
Richard Busman, *Branch Mgr*
Jeanne Wolfe,
EMP: 1000 **Privately Held**
WEB: www.doj.state.wi.us
SIC: **8748** 9222 Testing services; systems engineering consultant, ex. computer or professional; legal counsel & prosecution;
HQ: California Department Of Justice
1300 I St Ste 1142
Sacramento CA 95814
916 324-5437

(P-27963)
KATZ MEDIA GROUP INC
5700 Wilshire Blvd # 100, Los Angeles (90036-3889)
PHONE...................323 966-5000
K Thornton, *Manager*
EMP: 85

SALES (corp-wide): 6.2B **Publicly Held**
WEB: www.ctvsales.com
SIC: **8748** Business consulting
HQ: Katz Media Group Inc
125 W 55th St Fl 11
New York NY 10019
212 315-0956

(P-27964)
KEMA INC
Also Called: K E M A
155 Grand Ave Ste 500, Oakland (94612-3747)
PHONE...................510 891-0446
Rich Barnes, *Director*
Dirk Fenske, *COO*
David Cesio, *Business Dir*
William Vail, *Administration*
Michael Rufo, *Director*
EMP: 50
SALES (corp-wide): 2.7B **Privately Held**
SIC: **8748** Energy conservation consultant
HQ: Kema, Inc.
67 S Bedford St Ste 201e
Burlington MA 01803
781 273-5700

(P-27965)
KLEINFELDER INC
3880 Lemon St Ste 300, Riverside (92501-3301)
PHONE...................951 801-3681
Fax: 909 396-1324
John Lohman, *Manager*
Aaron Kidd, *Lab Dir*
Pam Massa, *Branch Mgr*
Kim Harlow, *Purch Agent*
Lisa Campbell, *Marketing Mgr*
EMP: 55
SALES (corp-wide): 258.9MM **Privately Held**
WEB: www.kleinfelder.com
SIC: **8748** 7389 Environmental consultant; systems engineering consultant, ex. computer or professional; air pollution measuring service
HQ: Kleinfelder, Inc.
550 W C St Ste 1200
San Diego CA 92101
619 831-4617

(P-27966)
KLEINFELDER ASSOCIATES
550 W C St Ste 1200, San Diego (92101-3532)
PHONE...................619 831-4600
William Siegel, *CEO*
Bart Patton, *COO*
John Pilkington, *CFO*
Larry Peterson, *Senior VP*
Russ Carey, *Vice Pres*
EMP: 1500
SALES (est): 51MM
SALES (corp-wide): 258.9MM **Privately Held**
SIC: **8748** Environmental consultant
PA: The Kleinfelder Group Inc
550 W C St Ste 1200
San Diego CA 92101
619 831-4600

(P-27967)
KLH CONSULTING INC
2235 Mercury Way Ste 210, Santa Rosa (95407-5472)
PHONE...................707 575-9986
Fax: 707 575-8758
Soni Lampert, *CEO*
Hub Lampert, *CFO*
EMP: 55 EST: 1978
SALES (est): 8.7MM **Privately Held**
WEB: www.klhconsulting.com
SIC: **8748** 7371 7372 Systems engineering consultant, ex. computer or professional; custom computer programming services; business oriented computer software

(P-27968)
KRAZAN & ASSOCIATES (PA)
215 W Dakota Ave, Clovis (93612-5608)
PHONE...................559 348-2200
Fax: 559 348-2201
Dean L Alexander, *President*
Jodi Ragsdale, *CFO*
Emilo Vargas, *CFO*

Thomas P Krazan, *Chairman*
Mike Thomas, *Lab Dir*
EMP: 68
SQ FT: 21,000
SALES: 19MM **Privately Held**
WEB: www.krazan.com
SIC: **8748** 8734 8742 Environmental consultant; product testing laboratory, safety or performance; management engineering

(P-27969)
KROS-WISE
4250 Pacific Hwy Ste 205, San Diego (92110-3222)
PHONE...................619 223-1980
Lily Aragon, *President*
EMP: 85
SALES (est): 4.3MM **Privately Held**
WEB: www.kroswise.com
SIC: **8748** Business consulting

(P-27970)
L S A ASSOCIATES INC (PA)
20 Executive Park Ste 200, Irvine (92614-4739)
PHONE...................949 553-0666
Les Card, *CEO*
Rob McCann, *President*
James Baum, *CFO*
Christina Belsito, *Chief Mktg Ofcr*
Jeff Bray, *Admin Mgr*
EMP: 110
SQ FT: 22,000
SALES (est): 35.9MM **Privately Held**
WEB: www.lsa-assoc.com
SIC: **8748** Environmental consultant

(P-27971)
LAND DESIGN CONSULTANTS INC
2700 E Foothill Blvd # 200, Pasadena (91107-3443)
PHONE...................626 578-7000
Fax: 626 578-7373
Robert Sims, *President*
Larry Mar, *CFO*
Steve Hunter, *Vice Pres*
EMP: 70
SALES: 9.6MM **Privately Held**
WEB: www.ldcla.com
SIC: **8748** 8711 8713 Urban planning & consulting services; environmental consultant; civil engineering; surveying services

(P-27972)
LEED INTERNATIONAL LLC
1583 Shanghai Cir, San Jose (95131-2411)
PHONE...................650 861-7883
Hong Zhang, *Chairman*
EMP: 50
SALES (est): 405.8K **Privately Held**
SIC: **8748** 5961 Business consulting; catalog & mail-order houses

(P-27973)
LEIGHTON AND ASSOCIATES INC (PA)
17781 Cowan, Irvine (92614-6009)
PHONE...................949 250-1421
Fax: 949 250-1114
Terry Brennan, *President*
Robert Riha, *COO*
Brendan Oconnell, *CFO*
Gareth Mills, *Vice Pres*
Iraj Poormand, *Vice Pres*
EMP: 70
SQ FT: 30,000
SALES (est): 16.3MM **Privately Held**
SIC: **8748** 8711 Environmental consultant; engineering services

(P-27974)
LESLEY FOUNDATION
701 Arnold Way Bldg A, Half Moon Bay (94019-2199)
PHONE...................650 726-4888
Fax: 650 726-5888
Sarah Lambert, *Exec Dir*
Galyn Evans, *Director*
Lesley Plaza, *Manager*
EMP: 65
SALES: 5.4MM **Privately Held**
SIC: **8748** Urban planning & consulting services

8748 - Business Consulting Svcs, NEC County (P-27975)

PRODUDUCTS & SERVICES SECTION

(P-27975)
LEVEL FOUR BUSINESS MGT LLC
11812 San Vicente Blvd # 400, Los Angeles (90049-6625)
PHONE.................................310 914-1600
Mark Friedman, *Mng Member*
Bill Olson, *Business Mgr*
Karen Malloy, *Manager*
John Rigney, *Manager*
Shiela Thompson, *Manager*
EMP: 50
SALES (est): 1.1MM **Privately Held**
SIC: 8748 Business consulting

(P-27976)
LIVEVOX INC (PA)
655 Montgomery St # 1190, San Francisco (94111-2647)
PHONE.................................415 671-6000
Louis Summe, *CEO*
Larry Siegel, *COO*
Michael Leraris, *CFO*
Randy Nelson, *Vice Pres*
Chris Pigott, *Vice Pres*
EMP: 107
SALES (est): 33.8MM **Privately Held**
WEB: www.tfhinc.net
SIC: 8748 Telecommunications consultant

(P-27977)
LUMETRA HEALTHCARE SOLUTIONS
550 Kearny St Ste 300, San Francisco (94108-2597)
PHONE.................................415 677-2000
Patricia Daniel, *CEO*
Lewy Roth, *Office Mgr*
Consuela Bejan, *Executive Asst*
Mike Snell, *Systems Staff*
Merry Tantaros, *Project Mgr*
EMP: 50
SQ FT: 5,000
SALES: 4MM **Privately Held**
WEB: www.lumetra.com
SIC: 8748 Business consulting

(P-27978)
LUSIVE DECOR
3400 Medford St, Los Angeles (90063-2530)
PHONE.................................323 227-9207
Jason Kai Cooper, *CEO*
Terra M Clark, *General Mgr*
Michelle Seminaris, *Sales Dir*
Audre McKenzie, *Sales Associate*
EMP: 57 EST: 2006
SALES (est): 7.4MM **Privately Held**
SIC: 8748 3646 Lighting consultant; ceiling systems, luminous

(P-27979)
LYLE COMPANY
3140 Gold Camp Dr Ste 30, Rancho Cordova (95670-6192)
P.O. Box 2255 (95741-2255)
PHONE.................................916 266-7000
Fax: 916 266-7001
Lanny G Lyle, *Ch of Bd*
Melanie Wertenberger, *Admin Sec*
Andrew Williams, *Admin Sec*
Tim Daniels, *Telecom Exec*
Tom Assad, *Info Tech Mgr*
EMP: 60 EST: 1989
SALES (est): 6.8MM **Privately Held**
WEB: www.lyleco.com
SIC: 8748 Business consulting

(P-27980)
MANAGEMENT TECH CONSULTING LLC
7738 Skyhill Dr, Los Angeles (90068-1232)
PHONE.................................323 851-5008
Darryl Henderson, *CEO*
EMP: 65
SQ FT: 2,800
SALES (est): 3.7MM **Privately Held**
SIC: 8748 Business consulting

(P-27981)
MANTECH SYSTEMS ENGRG CORP
8328 Clairemont Mesa Blvd # 100, San Diego (92111-1328)
PHONE.................................858 292-9000
Brad Geiger, *Systems Mgr*
Ron Renfor, *Exec Dir*
EMP: 70
SALES (corp-wide): 1.5B **Publicly Held**
SIC: 8748 Business consulting
HQ: Mantech Systems Engineering Corporation
12015 Lee Jackson Hwy
Fairfax VA 22033
703 218-6000

(P-27982)
MASSDROP INC
100 Bush St Ste 1000, San Francisco (94104-3912)
PHONE.................................415 340-2999
Steve El-Hage, *CEO*
Anne Morrissey, *Vice Pres*
Pari Patel, *Controller*
EMP: 70
SQ FT: 11,839
SALES (est): 13MM **Privately Held**
SIC: 8748 Business consulting

(P-27983)
MAXIM PLANNING GROUP
1214 E Colorado Blvd, Pasadena (91106-1899)
PHONE.................................818 425-4343
Steve Vivanco, *Owner*
EMP: 60
SALES (est): 3MM **Privately Held**
SIC: 8748 Business consulting

(P-27984)
MCWONG ENVMTL & ENRGY GROUP
1921 Arena Blvd, Sacramento (95834-3770)
PHONE.................................916 371-8080
Margaret Wong, *President*
Julie Yu, *Manager*
EMP: 50 EST: 2001
SQ FT: 7,800
SALES: 16MM **Privately Held**
WEB: www.mcwonginc.com
SIC: 8748 Energy conservation consultant; environmental consultant

(P-27985)
MEDIA LINK LLC
1901 Avenue Of The Stars # 1775, Los Angeles (90067-6057)
PHONE.................................646 722-3632
Michael Kassan,
EMP: 102
SALES: 40MM **Privately Held**
SIC: 8748 Business consulting

(P-27986)
MICHAEL BAKER INTL INC
2729 Prospect Park Dr # 220, Rancho Cordova (95670-6291)
PHONE.................................916 361-8384
Phil Carter, *Manager*
Kurt Bergman, *CEO*
Louis Levner, *Vice Pres*
EMP: 99
SALES (corp-wide): 592.9MM **Privately Held**
SIC: 8748 Business consulting
HQ: Baker Michael International Inc
500 Grant St Ste 5400
Pittsburgh PA 15219
412 269-6300

(P-27987)
MICHAEL BAKER INTL INC
6020 Cornerstone Ct W, San Diego (92121-3730)
PHONE.................................858 453-3602
Fax: 858 614-5001
Phil Carter, *Manager*
Louis Levner, *Vice Pres*
Larry Tortuya, *Engineer*
Pat Bossio, *Accounts Mgr*
EMP: 75
SALES (corp-wide): 592.9MM **Privately Held**
WEB: www.rbf.com
SIC: 8748 Business consulting
HQ: Baker Michael International Inc
500 Grant St Ste 5400
Pittsburgh PA 15219
412 269-6300

(P-27988)
MICHAEL BAKER INTL INC
3300 E Guasti Rd Ste 100, Ontario (91761-8656)
PHONE.................................909 974-4900
Ron Craig, *Manager*
EMP: 50
SALES (corp-wide): 592.9MM **Privately Held**
SIC: 8748 Business consulting
HQ: Baker Michael International Inc
14725 Alton Pkwy
Irvine CA 92618
949 472-3505

(P-27989)
MICROCONSTANTS INC
9050 Camino Santa Fe, San Diego (92121-3203)
PHONE.................................858 652-4600
Fax: 858 362-5698
Gilbert Lam, *President*
John Jintong, *Chairman*
Jose Buenviaje, *Vice Pres*
David Beyerlein, *Lab Dir*
Michelle Mason, *General Mgr*
EMP: 50 EST: 1998
SQ FT: 34,000
SALES (est): 7MM **Privately Held**
SIC: 8748 Business consulting

(P-27990)
MIND DRAGON INC
36002 Pansy St, Winchester (92596-8735)
PHONE.................................877 367-6060
Jefferson Nunn, *President*
Fern Rudin, *CFO*
Jim Alexander, *Vice Pres*
Alan Gerson, *Vice Pres*
EMP: 50
SQ FT: 1,700
SALES: 600K **Privately Held**
WEB: www.mindragon.com
SIC: 8748 Business consulting

(P-27991)
MIRAMED GLOBAL SERVICES INC
Also Called: On Call Consulting
199 E Thsand Oaks Blvd, Thousand Oaks (91360)
PHONE.................................805 277-1017
Ron Manzani, *Branch Mgr*
EMP: 1737
SALES (corp-wide): 98.4MM **Privately Held**
SIC: 8748 Business consulting
PA: Miramed Global Services, Inc.
255 W Michigan Ave
Jackson MI 49201
866 544-6647

(P-27992)
MONTE VSTA MEM SCHLRSHP ASSOC
2 School Way, Watsonville (95076-9716)
PHONE.................................831 722-8178
Stephen Sharp, *Administration*
EMP: 50
SALES (est): 3MM **Privately Held**
SIC: 8748 Business consulting

(P-27993)
MOORE IACOFANO GOLTSMAN INC (PA)
Also Called: M I G
800 Hearst Ave, Berkeley (94710-2018)
PHONE.................................510 845-7549
Fax: 510 845-8750
Susan M Goltsman, *President*
Daniel Iacofano, *CEO*
Carolyn Verheyen, *COO*
Dave Banks, *Sr Software Eng*
Andy Pendoley, *Project Mgr*
EMP: 63
SQ FT: 6,000
SALES (est): 21.1MM **Privately Held**
WEB: www.migcom.com
SIC: 8748 Environmental consultant; communications consulting

(P-27994)
MSLA MANAGEMENT LLC
1294 E Colorado Blvd, Pasadena (91106-1901)
PHONE.................................626 824-6020
Michael Lambert, *CEO*
Sahniah Siciarz-Lambert, *President*
Robert Worth Oberrender, *Treasurer*
Thomas Shaun McGlinch, *Asst Treas*
Paul Timothy Runice, *Asst Treas*
EMP: 134
SALES (est): 1.5MM
SALES (corp-wide): 157.1B **Publicly Held**
SIC: 8748 Business consulting
HQ: Logistics Health, Inc.
328 Front St S
La Crosse WI 54601
866 284-8788

(P-27995)
MYOSCIENCE INC
46400 Fremont Blvd, Fremont (94538-6469)
PHONE.................................510 933-1500
Fax: 650 474-2900
Larry Hicks, *President*
Robert E Grant, *Ch of Bd*
Matt Franklin, *CFO*
Peter Osborne, *CFO*
Bill Brodie, *Vice Pres*
EMP: 50
SALES (est): 12MM **Privately Held**
SIC: 8748 Business consulting

(P-27996)
NATIONAL ECONOMIC RES ASSOC
777 S Figueroa St # 1950, Los Angeles (90017-5800)
PHONE.................................213 346-3000
Fax: 213 346-3030
Gary Dorman, *Manager*
Pamala Leonard, *Senior VP*
Amparo Nieto, *Senior VP*
Hethie Parmesano, *Vice Pres*
Andrew Hund, *Human Res Mgr*
EMP: 62
SALES (corp-wide): 12.8B **Publicly Held**
SIC: 8748 Economic consultant
HQ: National Economic Research Associates, Inc
1166 Ave Of The Americas
New York NY 10036
212 345-3000

(P-27997)
NATIONAL SAFETY SERVICES
3400 Avenue Of The Arts, Costa Mesa (92626-1927)
PHONE.................................714 679-9118
EMP: 50
SALES (est): 2.7MM **Privately Held**
SIC: 8748 8999

(P-27998)
NEWTON SOFTED INC
Also Called: Pm2net
30 Corporate Park Ste 101, Irvine (92606-5132)
PHONE.................................949 396-6192
Carson Synh, *CEO*
EMP: 50
SALES (est): 1.5MM **Privately Held**
SIC: 8748 7379 Systems analysis & engineering consulting services; computer related consulting services

(P-27999)
NEXANT INC (PA)
101 2nd St Ste 1000, San Francisco (94105-3651)
PHONE.................................415 369-1000
Fax: 415 369-9700
Basam Y Sarandah, *CEO*
Basam Sarandah, *President*
Michael Alvarez, *CFO*
Arjun Gupta, *Chairman*
Richard Balzhiser, *Bd of Directors*
EMP: 80
SQ FT: 17,462
SALES (est): 146.9MM **Privately Held**
WEB: www.nexant.com
SIC: 8748 Energy conservation consultant

PRODUCTS & SERVICES SECTION
8748 - Business Consulting Svcs, NEC County (P-28023)

(P-28000)
NINYO & MOORE GEOTECHNICAL (PA)
5710 Ruffin Rd, San Diego (92123-1013)
PHONE.................................858 576-1000
Avram Ninyo, *CEO*
Stephen Waide, *COO*
Faith Logsdon, *Vice Pres*
Ellen Roe, *Admin Mgr*
Pat Zaby, *Admin Mgr*
EMP: 80
SQ FT: 24,000
SALES: 50.9MM **Privately Held**
SIC: 8748 Business consulting; environmental consultant

(P-28001)
NINYO & MOORE GEOTECHNICAL
Also Called: Ninyo & AMP Moore Geotechnical
475 Goddard Ste 200, Irvine (92618-4622)
PHONE.................................949 753-7070
Fax: 949 753-7071
Carol Price, *Manager*
Avram Ninyo, *President*
Ruth Dolecki, *Administration*
Andy Murphy, *Info Tech Mgr*
EMP: 65
SALES (corp-wide): 50.9MM **Privately Held**
SIC: 8748 8711 8734 Environmental consultant; pollution control engineering; soil analysis
PA: Ninyo & Moore Geotechnical & Environmental Sciences Consultants
5710 Ruffin Rd
San Diego CA 92123
858 576-1000

(P-28002)
NMS DATA INC
Also Called: Neilson Marketing Services
23172 Plaza Pointe Dr # 205, Laguna Hills (92653-1477)
PHONE.................................949 472-2700
Lawrence Neilson, *CEO*
Jeffrey Neilson, *President*
Paul Neilson, *VP Sales*
EMP: 50
SQ FT: 9,500
SALES: 5MM **Privately Held**
SIC: 8748 Business consulting

(P-28003)
NORTH LA COUNTY REGIONAL CTR (PA)
15400 Sherman Way Ste 170, Van Nuys (91406-4272)
PHONE.................................818 778-1900
Fax: 818 756-6140
George Stevens, *Director*
K Jennifr, *Bd of Directors*
Thompson Kelly, *Exec Dir*
Kimberly Benjamin, *Program Mgr*
Michel Marra, *Human Res Dir*
EMP: 280
SQ FT: 57,000
SALES: 345.9MM **Privately Held**
SIC: 8748 Test development & evaluation service

(P-28004)
NORTH LA COUNTY REGIONAL CTR
Also Called: Regional Center For Devlpmtnly
43210 Gingham Ave Ste 6, Lancaster (93535-4512)
PHONE.................................661 945-6761
Fax: 661 942-4050
Joan Daniels, *Manager*
Marra Michelle, *Personnel Exec*
Michelle Marra, *Human Res Dir*
Latonia Rogers, *Manager*
EMP: 70
SALES (corp-wide): 345.9MM **Privately Held**
SIC: 8748 Test development & evaluation service
PA: North La County Regional Center Inc
15400 Sherman Way Ste 170
Van Nuys CA 91406
818 778-1900

(P-28005)
NORTHROP GRMMN SPCE & MSSN SYS
1 Space Park Blvd, Redondo Beach (90278-1071)
PHONE.................................855 737-8364
Jack Distaso, *Technical Staff*
Felipe Rico, *Electrical Engi*
Todd Sebastian, *Engineer*
EMP: 140
SQ FT: 500,000 **Publicly Held**
WEB: www.trw.com
SIC: 8748 Systems analysis & engineering consulting services
HQ: Northrop Grumman Space & Mission Systems Corp.
6377 San Ignacio Ave
San Jose CA 95119
703 280-2900

(P-28006)
O C JONES & SONS INC
155 Filbert St Ste 209, Oakland (94607-2524)
PHONE.................................510 663-6911
Carla Radosta, *Branch Mgr*
EMP: 100
SALES (corp-wide): 114.3MM **Privately Held**
SIC: 8748 Business consulting
PA: O. C. Jones & Sons, Inc.
1520 4th St
Berkeley CA 94710
510 526-3424

(P-28007)
OCEAN PARK COMMUNITY CENTER
Turning Point
1447 16th St, Santa Monica (90404-2715)
PHONE.................................310 828-6717
Patricia Bauman, *Director*
Lindsey Hirsch, *Exec Dir*
Luther Richert, *Director*
EMP: 60
SALES (corp-wide): 12.1MM **Privately Held**
SIC: 8748 Urban planning & consulting services
PA: Ocean Park Community Center
1453 16th St
Santa Monica CA 90404
310 264-6646

(P-28008)
OFFICE OF THE LEGISLATIVE COUN
Also Called: Legislative Counsel Tstg Off
925 L St Ste 900, Sacramento (95814-3702)
PHONE.................................916 445-3796
Alison Raymer, *Manager*
Steve Abrams, *Manager*
EMP: 1000 **Privately Held**
WEB: www.lc.ca.gov
SIC: 8748 9121 Testing services; legislative bodies;
HQ: Office Of The Legislative Counsel
State Cpitol Bldg Rm 3021
Sacramento CA 95814
916 341-8000

(P-28009)
ONSITE CONSULTING LLC
5042 Wilshire Blvd # 135, Los Angeles (90036-4305)
PHONE.................................323 401-3190
James D Sinclair, *Mng Member*
EMP: 65
SALES: 9.5MM **Privately Held**
SIC: 8748 Business consulting

(P-28010)
OPALLIOS INC
3211 Scott Blvd Ste 205, Santa Clara (95054-3009)
PHONE.................................408 769-4594
Omcar Paradkar, *CEO*
EMP: 50 EST: 2015
SALES (est): 2.2MM **Privately Held**
SIC: 8748 Business consulting

(P-28011)
OPERATION SAMAHAN INC
2835 Highland Ave Ste C, National City (91950-7406)
PHONE.................................619 477-4451
Joel San Juan, *Director*
Gilda Martinez, *Treasurer*
Shaila St Serpas, *Obstetrician*
EMP: 66
SQ FT: 6,687
SALES (corp-wide): 10.7MM **Privately Held**
SIC: 8748 Urban planning & consulting services
PA: Operation Samahan, Inc.
1428 Highland Ave
National City CA 91950
619 474-2284

(P-28012)
ORANGE SILICON VALLEY
60 Spear St Ste 1100, San Francisco (94105-1599)
PHONE.................................415 243-1500
EMP: 60 EST: 2012
SALES (est): 3.6MM **Privately Held**
SIC: 8748

(P-28013)
OUTSOURCE TESTING INC
Also Called: Ostcs
1278 Center Court Dr, Covina (91724-3601)
PHONE.................................909 592-8898
Brian Steven Pinkus, *President*
Christie Moses, *Vice Pres*
Matthew Pifer, *Vice Pres*
Denny Tao, *Vice Pres*
Melanie Pinkus, *Director*
EMP: 75
SQ FT: 8,000
SALES (est): 5.6MM **Privately Held**
WEB: www.outsourcetesting.com
SIC: 8748 Testing services

(P-28014)
P8GE CONSULTING INC
Also Called: Fame Hardwood Floors
8406 Beverly Blvd, Los Angeles (90048-3402)
PHONE.................................310 666-2301
Pedram Youav Nazarian, *CEO*
EMP: 50
SQ FT: 1,500
SALES: 10MM **Privately Held**
SIC: 8748 Business consulting

(P-28015)
PACIFIC COMMUNICATIONS ASSOC
761 2nd St, Brentwood (94513-1352)
P.O. Box 1147 (94513-3147)
PHONE.................................925 634-1203
Fax: 925 634-9403
Peter Petrovich, *President*
Fred Valverde, *CFO*
Rhonda Petrovich, *Vice Pres*
Mark Isidoro, *VP Opers*
EMP: 50
SQ FT: 600
SALES (est): 2.7MM **Privately Held**
WEB: www.pacific-communications.com
SIC: 8748 Communications consulting

(P-28016)
PARAGON PARTNERS LTD (PA)
5762 Bolsa Ave Ste 201, Huntington Beach (92649-1172)
PHONE.................................714 379-3376
Fax: 714 373-1234
Neilia A La Valle, *President*
Tammie Bedlington, *Vice Pres*
Joel Sewell, *Vice Pres*
Robert Segawa, *CIO*
William McCawley, *VP Finance*
EMP: 65
SQ FT: 10,000
SALES (est): 20.6MM **Privately Held**
WEB: www.paragon-partners.com
SIC: 8748 Business consulting

(P-28017)
PCS LINK INC
Also Called: Greenwood & Hall
12424 Wilshire Blvd # 1030, Los Angeles (90025-1031)
PHONE.................................949 655-5000
John R Hall, *CEO*
Jonathan Newcomb, *Ch of Bd*
Zantine Greenwood, *CFO*
Brad Johnson, *Exec VP*
Harvey Ross, *Exec VP*
EMP: 310
SQ FT: 25,000
SALES (est): 37.4MM **Privately Held**
WEB: www.pcslink.com
SIC: 8748 Communications consulting

(P-28018)
PINNACLE ELECTRICAL SVCS INC
Also Called: Pinnacle Networking Services
730 Fairmont Ave Ste 100, Glendale (91203-1079)
PHONE.................................818 241-6009
Avo Amirian, *CEO*
Joe Lucurst, *President*
Ramela Asaguryan, *Accounts Mgr*
EMP: 56
SQ FT: 2,500
SALES (est): 3.1MM **Privately Held**
SIC: 8748 Telecommunications consultant

(P-28019)
POLARIS RESEARCH & DEVELOPMENT
390 4th St Fl 1, San Francisco (94107-1289)
PHONE.................................415 777-3229
Mike Jang, *Vice Pres*
Ernie Fazio, *President*
Rosa Osman, *CFO*
Carol McGruder, *Project Dir*
EMP: 70
SQ FT: 10,000
SALES (est): 4.9MM **Privately Held**
SIC: 8748 Business consulting

(P-28020)
PRAGITI INC
2560 N 1st St Ste 210, San Jose (95131-1041)
PHONE.................................408 891-7423
Praveen Pahwa, *CEO*
Lei Zhang, *Engineer*
EMP: 55
SALES (est): 3MM **Privately Held**
SIC: 8748 Business consulting

(P-28021)
PREMIER EXEC SOLUTIONS INC
269 S Beverly Dr Ste 981, Beverly Hills (90212-3851)
PHONE.................................310 989-9925
Manny Salazar, *President*
EMP: 50
SALES (est): 1.7MM **Privately Held**
SIC: 8748 Business consulting

(P-28022)
PRESCOTT COMMUNICATIONS INC
Also Called: Cable Engineering Services
10640 Sepulveda Blvd # 1, Mission Hills (91345-1919)
PHONE.................................818 898-2352
Fax: 818 898-9186
Lynn Prescott, *CEO*
Martin Prescott, *President*
Ken Goddard, *Info Tech Dir*
Paul Smolarski, *Project Mgr*
Elizabeth Villalobos, *Project Mgr*
EMP: 135
SQ FT: 12,000
SALES: 15.5MM **Privately Held**
WEB: www.cableeng.com
SIC: 8748 Telecommunications consultant

(P-28023)
PROFIT RECOVERY PARTNERS LLC
Also Called: P R P
2995 Red Hill Ave Ste 200, Costa Mesa (92626-5984)
PHONE.................................949 851-2777
Donald Steiner, *President*

Marty Bozarth, COO
Edward Lyon, CFO
Jeremy Linehan, Exec VP
Brett Rodewald, Exec VP
EMP: 75
SQ FT: 260,000
SALES (est): 12.1MM **Privately Held**
WEB: www.prpllc.com
SIC: 8748 Business consulting

(P-28024)
PROJECT CONSULTING SPECIALISTS
425 N Whisman Rd Ste 600, Mountain View (94043-5733)
PHONE 650 265-2400
Brendan McIntyre, President
Kevin Cahalan, Accounts Exec
EMP: 50
SQ FT: 2,200
SALES (est): 5.7MM **Privately Held**
SIC: 8748 Business consulting

(P-28025)
PROJECT DESIGN CONSULTANTS
701 B St Ste 800, San Diego (92101-8162)
PHONE 619 235-6471
Fax: 619 234-0349
Gregory M Shields, CEO
William R Dick, President
Debby Reese, President
Gary Hus, Vice Pres
Debby Reece, Vice Pres
EMP: 100
SQ FT: 22,000
SALES (est): 11.3MM **Privately Held**
WEB: www.projectdesign.com
SIC: 8748 8711 8713 Urban planning & consulting services; civil engineering; surveying services

(P-28026)
PS ARTS
Also Called: Crossroads Cmnty Foundation
6701 Center Dr W Ste 550, Los Angeles (90045-1556)
PHONE 310 586-1017
Kristin Paglia, Exec Dir
Amy Shario, Exec Dir
Stephanie Kistner, Program Mgr
Matthew Martin, Finance Mgr
Christopher Lor, Financial Analy
EMP: 50
SALES: 2.6MM **Privately Held**
WEB: www.psarts.org
SIC: 8748 Educational consultant

(P-28027)
QUADRIX INFORMATION TECH INC
Also Called: Quadrixit
10736 Jefferson Blvd # 132, Culver City (90230-4933)
PHONE 424 603-2140
Joseph Gutwirth, CEO
Naida Gutwirth, COO
Dennis Rojas, Exec VP
David Hopkins, Director
EMP: 50 **EST:** 2010
SALES (est): 2.1MM **Privately Held**
SIC: 8748 7379 Systems engineering consultant, ex. computer or professional; computer related consulting services

(P-28028)
QUOVA INC
401 Castro St Fl 3, Mountain View (94041-2089)
PHONE 650 965-2898
Fax: 650 625-9809
Marie Alexander, President
Gary P Jackson, COO
Jean-Louis Casabonne, CFO
Kevin Brannon, Vice Pres
Kevin Wandryk, Vice Pres
EMP: 60
SQ FT: 10,000
SALES (est): 4.6MM
SALES (corp-wide): 1B **Publicly Held**
WEB: www.quova.com
SIC: 8748 Business consulting
PA: Neustar, Inc.
   21575 Ridgetop Cir
   Sterling VA 20166
   571 434-5100

(P-28029)
QUOVERA INC (PA)
788 Stone Ln, Palo Alto (94303-4413)
PHONE 650 691-0114
Austin R Erlich, CEO
Metin Gokcen, Vice Pres
Guy Wilnai, Vice Pres
Mary Mosham, Sr Consultant
EMP: 90
SQ FT: 8,000
SALES (est): 8MM **Privately Held**
WEB: www.quovera.com
SIC: 8748 Business consulting; systems analysis & engineering consulting services; systems engineering consultant, ex. computer or professional

(P-28030)
QUOVERA INC
19800 Macarthur Blvd, Irvine (92612-2421)
PHONE 949 224-3825
Hector Rodriguez, Branch Mgr
EMP: 50
SALES (corp-wide): 8MM **Privately Held**
WEB: www.quovera.com
SIC: 8748 Business consulting
PA: Quovera, Inc
   788 Stone Ln
   Palo Alto CA 94303
   650 691-0114

(P-28031)
RAMBOLL ENVIRON US CORPORATION
18100 Von Karman Ave # 600, Irvine (92612-0169)
PHONE 949 798-3604
Anne Pena, Manager
Greg Sullivan, Controller
EMP: 50
SALES (corp-wide): 210.3MM **Privately Held**
SIC: 8748 8999 Business consulting; environmental consultant; earth science services
HQ: Ramboll Environ Us Corporation
   4350 Fairfax Dr Ste 300
   Arlington VA 22203
   703 516-2300

(P-28032)
RAMBOLL ENVIRON US CORPORATION
2200 Powell St Ste 700, Emeryville (94608-1877)
PHONE 510 655-7400
Fax: 510 655-9517
Robert Powell, IT/INT Sup
Cathy Smith, Executive
Richard Dear, IT/INT Sup
Renee Van De Griend, Project Engr
Anne W Gates, Project Engr
EMP: 70
SALES (corp-wide): 210.3MM **Privately Held**
WEB: www.environcorp.com
SIC: 8748 Environmental consultant
HQ: Ramboll Environ Us Corporation
   4350 Fairfax Dr Ste 300
   Arlington VA 22203
   703 516-2300

(P-28033)
RAMBOLL ENVIRON US CORPORATION
18100 Von Karman Ave # 600, Irvine (92612-0169)
PHONE 949 261-5151
Fax: 949 261-6202
George Linkletter, Manager
Jeff Raumin, Project Mgr
Devon Rowe, Project Mgr
Rebekah Wale, Project Mgr
Houshang Dezfulian, Senior Engr
EMP: 65
SALES (corp-wide): 210.3MM **Privately Held**
WEB: www.environcorp.com
SIC: 8748 8711 Environmental consultant; pollution control engineering
HQ: Ramboll Environ Us Corporation
   4350 Fairfax Dr Ste 300
   Arlington VA 22203
   703 516-2300

(P-28034)
RANGE GENERATION NEXT LLC
Also Called: Rgnext
Pillar Point Air Sta, El Granada (94018)
PHONE 310 647-9438
Tom Kennedy, CEO
Donna Mc Cullough, Manager
EMP: 50
SQ FT: 100
SALES (est): 2.5MM **Privately Held**
SIC: 8748 Systems analysis or design

(P-28035)
RAPID PRODUCT DEV GROUP INC
300 W Grand Ave, Escondido (92025-2659)
PHONE 760 703-5770
Tony Moran, CEO
Steve Forney, Business Mgr
Stephanie Gelinas, Business Mgr
Robert Wazny, Manager
EMP: 110
SALES (est): 5.7MM **Privately Held**
WEB: www.rpdg.com
SIC: 8748 Business consulting

(P-28036)
RCG INTERNATIONAL
Also Called: Rahmati Consulting Group
4570 Campus Dr Ste 100, Newport Beach (92660-1835)
PHONE 714 956-7027
Mike Rahmati, Principal
EMP: 499
SALES: 80MM **Privately Held**
SIC: 8748 Systems analysis & engineering consulting services

(P-28037)
RECON ENVIRONMENTAL INC (PA)
1927 5th Ave Ste 200, San Diego (92101-2357)
PHONE 520 325-9977
Fax: 619 308-9334
Charles Bull, Ch of Bd
Bill Berto, Senior Partner
Robert Macaller, President
Diane Pearson Bull, CFO
Linda Evans, Vice Pres
EMP: 100
SQ FT: 18,500
SALES (est): 29.6MM **Privately Held**
WEB: www.recon-us.com
SIC: 8748 Environmental consultant

(P-28038)
REDEVELOPMENT AGENCY OF THE CI
Also Called: SUISUN REDEVELOPMENT AGENCY
701 Civic Center Blvd, Suisun City (94585-2617)
PHONE 707 421-7309
Fax: 707 429-3758
Suzanne Bragdon, Manager
Mark Joseph, Finance Mgr
Pete Sanchez, Mayor
Jason Garben, Director
Randy Starbuck, Manager
EMP: 68
SALES: 12.6MM **Privately Held**
SIC: 8748 Urban planning & consulting services

(P-28039)
REGENESIS BIOREMEDIATION PDTS (PA)
1011 Calle Sombra, San Clemente (92673-4204)
PHONE 949 366-8000
Fax: 949 366-8090
Scott B Wilson, President
Christopher Graham, CFO
Gavin Herbert Jr, Chairman
Rick Gillespie, Vice Pres
Craig Sandefur, Vice Pres
▲ **EMP:** 50
SQ FT: 15,000
SALES: 24.3MM **Privately Held**
SIC: 8748 Environmental consultant

(P-28040)
RESEARCH MANAGEMENT CONS INC (PA)
816 Camarillo Springs Rd J, Camarillo (93012-9441)
PHONE 805 987-5538
Fax: 805 987-2868
Raydean Acevedo, President
Cynthia Burns, CFO
Holly Kwon, Database Admin
Elizabeth De La Pena, Technology
EMP: 95
SQ FT: 2,700
SALES (est): 13.7MM **Privately Held**
SIC: 8748 8711 Environmental consultant; systems engineering consultant, ex. computer or professional; engineering services

(P-28041)
RESOURCE MANAGEMENT GROUP INC (PA)
Also Called: Express Waste Rolloff
4686 Mercury St, San Diego (92111-2428)
PHONE 858 677-0884
Armen Derderian, President
Robert Garcia, COO
Josie Pantangco, CFO
Saba Salloum, Managing Dir
Mitch Lee, Info Tech Dir
EMP: 50
SQ FT: 3,000
SALES (est): 16.7MM **Privately Held**
WEB: www.rmgrecycling.com
SIC: 8748 Environmental consultant

(P-28042)
RETINAL CONSULTANTS INC
Also Called: Vitreo Retinal Medical Group
19 Ilahee Ln, Chico (95973-7205)
PHONE 530 899-2251
David Telander, Branch Mgr
EMP: 55
SALES (corp-wide): 11.9MM **Privately Held**
WEB: www.retinalmd.com
SIC: 8748 Business consulting
PA: Retinal Consultants Inc
   3939 J St Ste 106
   Sacramento CA 95819
   916 454-4861

(P-28043)
RISK MANAGEMENT STRATEGIES INC
Also Called: Trust Employee ADM & MGT
8530 La Mesa Blvd Ste 200, La Mesa (91942-0966)
PHONE 619 281-1100
Terence J Keating, President
Arthur D Candland, CFO
Cheryl Doss, Vice Pres
Sharon Novak, Human Resources
EMP: 2500
SALES (est): 98.4MM **Privately Held**
SIC: 8748 Employee programs administration

(P-28044)
ROI COMMUNICATIONS INC (PA)
5274 Scotts Valley Dr # 107, Scotts Valley (95066-3538)
PHONE 831 430-0170
Fax: 831 430-0176
Barbara Fagan Smith, President
Joann Webster, CFO
Sheri Austin, Vice Pres
Michelle Glover, Vice Pres
Karen Faber, Executive
EMP: 65
SALES (est): 13.2MM **Privately Held**
WEB: www.roico.com
SIC: 8748 Business consulting

(P-28045)
ROSE INTERNATIONAL INC
4000 Executive Pkwy # 150, San Ramon (94583-4314)
PHONE 636 812-4000
Fax: 925 867-9722
Mary Coats, Branch Mgr
Jonnie Gray, Associate Dir
Ed Francisco, Technician

PRODUCTS & SERVICES SECTION
8748 - Business Consulting Svcs, NEC County (P-28068)

Samar Singh, *Tech Recruiter*
EMP: 200
SALES (corp-wide): 293.5MM **Privately Held**
SIC: 8748 7371 7363 7361 Systems engineering consultant, ex. computer or professional; computer software development; help supply services; employment agencies
PA: Rose International, Inc.
16401 Swingley Ridge Rd
Chesterfield MO 63017
636 812-4000

(P-28046)
ROSE INTERNATIONAL INC
18952 Macarthur Blvd # 440, Irvine (92612-1402)
PHONE..................636 812-4000
Fax: 949 250-6081
Jonnie Gray, *Branch Mgr*
EMP: 50
SALES (corp-wide): 293.5MM **Privately Held**
SIC: 8748 7371 7363 7361 Systems engineering consultant, ex. computer or professional; computer software development; help supply services; employment agencies
PA: Rose International, Inc.
16401 Swingley Ridge Rd
Chesterfield MO 63017
636 812-4000

(P-28047)
ROUX ASSOCIATES INC
5150 E Pacific Coast Hwy # 450, Long Beach (90804-3328)
PHONE..................562 446-8600
EMP: 51
SALES (corp-wide): 71.4MM **Privately Held**
SIC: 8748 Business consulting
PA: Roux Associates, Inc.
209 Shafter St
Islandia NY 11749
631 232-2600

(P-28048)
S R I C B I
333 Ravenswood Ave, Menlo Park (94025-3453)
PHONE..................650 859-4865
William Guns, *President*
William Rolston, *CFO*
EMP: 70
SALES: 9MM **Privately Held**
SIC: 8748 Business consulting

(P-28049)
SA PHOTONICS INC
120 Knowles Dr, Los Gatos (95032-1828)
PHONE..................408 560-3500
James Coward, *President*
Andrea Singewald, *Officer*
David Upham, *Vice Pres*
Michael Brown, *General Mgr*
Michael Browne, *General Mgr*
EMP: 51
SQ FT: 30,000
SALES (est): 5.6MM **Privately Held**
WEB: www.saphotonics.com
SIC: 8748 Business consulting

(P-28050)
SAN DIEGO COMMUNITY HSING CORP
230 Catania St, San Diego (92113-1864)
PHONE..................619 527-4633
Garl Vaughn, *CEO*
John Piper, *CFO*
EMP: 250
SQ FT: 2,200
SALES: 1.2MM **Privately Held**
SIC: 8748 Urban planning & consulting services

(P-28051)
SAN JOAQUIN VALLEY A P C D
Also Called: Air Polution Control District
1990 E Gettysburg Ave, Fresno (93726-0244)
PHONE..................559 230-6000
David L Crow, *Director*
Alex Krivobok, *Administration*
Brad Schwegel, *Administration*

Brian Clerico, *Manager*
EMP: 100
SALES (est): 6.1MM **Privately Held**
SIC: 8748 Environmental consultant

(P-28052)
SAN JOSE REDEVELOPMENT AGENCY
200 E Santa Clara St 14th, San Jose (95113-1903)
PHONE..................408 535-8500
Fax: 408 292-6755
Harry Mavrogenes, *Exec Dir*
Julie Amato, *Officer*
Geraldine S Smith, *Administration*
John Wise, *Deputy Dir*
Dave Keys, *Assistant*
EMP: 140
SQ FT: 10,045
SALES (est): 8.1MM **Privately Held**
WEB: www.sjredevelopment.org
SIC: 8748 Urban planning & consulting services
PA: City Of San Jose
200 E Santa Clara St
San Jose CA 95113
408 535-3500

(P-28053)
SEALASKA ENVMTL SVCS LLC
3838 Camino Del Rio N # 240, San Diego (92108-1741)
PHONE..................619 564-8329
Derik Frederiksen,
Alfonso Arana, *MIS Dir*
Thomas Wilson, *Manager*
EMP: 65
SALES (est): 2.8MM **Privately Held**
SIC: 8748 4959 Environmental consultant; environmental cleanup services

(P-28054)
SENSITY SYSTEMS INC (PA)
1237 E Arques Ave, Sunnyvale (94085-4701)
PHONE..................408 774-9492
Hugh Martin, *CEO*
Phil Rehkemper, *CFO*
Scott Shipman,
David Tucker, *Vice Pres*
Barb Campisi, *Executive Asst*
EMP: 58
SALES (est): 27.6MM **Privately Held**
SIC: 8748 Lighting consultant

(P-28055)
SHELTER INC
1333 Willow Pass Rd # 206, Concord (94520-7931)
PHONE..................925 335-0698
Timothy O'Keefe, *Exec Dir*
Timothy Okeefe, *Exec Dir*
Michelle Schimberg, *Controller*
Cynthia Dial, *Director*
Jose Villa, *Manager*
EMP: 70
SALES (est): 8MM **Privately Held**
WEB: www.shelter.com
SIC: 8748 Urban planning & consulting services

(P-28056)
SIGNATURE CONSULTANTS LLC
8560 W Sunset Blvd, Los Angeles (90069-2311)
PHONE..................310 229-5731
EMP: 94 **Privately Held**
SIC: 8748 Business consulting
PA: Signature Consultants Llc
200 W Cypress Creek Rd # 400
Fort Lauderdale FL 33309

(P-28057)
SILV COMMUNICATION INC
3460 Wilshire Blvd # 1100, Los Angeles (90010-2224)
PHONE..................213 381-7999
John Shaikh, *President*
Sk Golam Ahia, *Vice Pres*
Marai Zepeda, *Manager*
EMP: 56
SQ FT: 7,500
SALES: 8MM **Privately Held**
SIC: 8748 Telecommunications consultant

(P-28058)
SOLUGENIX CORPORATION (PA)
601 Valencia Ave, Brea (92823-6358)
PHONE..................866 749-7658
Shashi Jasthi, *CEO*
Suneetha Menon, *COO*
Damola Akinola, *Vice Pres*
Sanjay RAO, *Vice Pres*
Crystal A Kolosick, *Executive Asst*
EMP: 72
SQ FT: 1,600
SALES (est): 50.7MM **Privately Held**
WEB: www.solugenix.com
SIC: 8748 Telecommunications consultant

(P-28059)
SONOMA TECHNOLOGY INC
1450 N Mcdowell Blvd, Petaluma (94954-6515)
PHONE..................707 665-9900
Fax: 707 665-9800
Lyle R Chinkin, *President*
Fred Lurmann, *Shareholder*
Donald L Blumenthal, *Chairman*
Barbara A Austin, *Exec VP*
Paul T Roberts, *Exec VP*
EMP: 65
SQ FT: 18,272
SALES: 9.7MM **Privately Held**
WEB: www.sonomatech.com
SIC: 8748 Environmental consultant

(P-28060)
SOURCE 44 LLC
Also Called: Source Intelligence
1921 Palomar Oaks Way # 205, Carlsbad (92008-6524)
PHONE..................877 916-6337
Jess F Kraus, *CEO*
Matt Thorn, *COO*
Dan Dague, *Officer*
Jennifer Kraus, *Officer*
Lina Ramos, *Senior VP*
EMP: 111
SALES (est): 10.2MM **Privately Held**
SIC: 8748 7371 Business consulting; computer software development

(P-28061)
SOUTH CAPITOL COTTAGE
15054 Daisy Rd, Adelanto (92301-4824)
PHONE..................951 662-3026
Carol James, *Exec Dir*
Felica Taylor, *President*
Dorothy Shorter, *CFO*
Emma Nash, *Exec VP*
Theodore Nash, *Vice Pres*
EMP: 80
SALES: 450K **Privately Held**
SIC: 8748 Urban planning & consulting services

(P-28062)
SPECTRUM SERVICES GROUP INC
4600 Northgate Blvd # 120, Sacramento (95834-1159)
PHONE..................916 760-7913
Tasawwar Ali, *CEO*
Shane Ali, *President*
Hasain Ali, *Principal*
Darrel Calipo, *Program Mgr*
Shannon Dawson, *Info Tech Mgr*
EMP: 85
SQ FT: 800
SALES (est): 12.4MM **Privately Held**
SIC: 8748 8744 8741 Business consulting; facilities support services; construction management

(P-28063)
SUCCESSOR TO SAN FRANCISCO
Also Called: Office Cmnty Inv Infrstructure
1 S Van Ness Ave Fl 5, San Francisco (94103-5416)
PHONE..................415 749-2400
Fax: 415 749-2590
Marcia Rosen, *Principal*
Tiffany Bohee, *Exec Dir*
Don Rice, *Accounts Mgr*
EMP: 99
SALES (est): 6.7MM **Privately Held**
SIC: 8748 Urban planning & consulting services

(P-28064)
SWCA INCORPORATED
Also Called: Swca Environmental Consultants
150 S Arroyo Pkwy Fl 2, Pasadena (91105-4150)
PHONE..................626 240-0587
Cara Corsetti, *Branch Mgr*
EMP: 89
SALES (corp-wide): 146.6MM **Privately Held**
WEB: www.swca.com
SIC: 8748 8733 Environmental consultant; archeological expeditions
PA: Swca, Incorporated
3033 N Central Ave # 145
Phoenix AZ 85012
505 254-1115

(P-28065)
SYNAGRO WEST LLC
1499 Bayshore Hwy Ste 111, Burlingame (94010-1723)
PHONE..................650 652-6531
Sue Gregory,
EMP: 99
SALES: 950K
SALES (corp-wide): 208MM **Privately Held**
WEB: www.synagro.com
SIC: 8748 Business consulting
HQ: Synagro Technologies, Inc.
435 Williams Ct Ste 100
Baltimore MD 21220
800 370-0035

(P-28066)
SYPARTNERS LLC (HQ)
475 Brannan St Ste 100, San Francisco (94107-5419)
PHONE..................415 536-6600
Susan Schuman, *CEO*
Michael Gizzo, *CFO*
Mickey Stretton, *Creative Dir*
Jessica Tillyer, *Creative Dir*
Matthew Grabis, *Business Dir*
EMP: 90
SALES (est): 21.7MM
SALES (corp-wide): 10.3B **Privately Held**
WEB: www.sypartners.com
SIC: 8748 Business consulting
PA: Hakuhodo Dy Holdings Incorporated
5-3-1, Akasaka
Minato-Ku TKY 107-0
364 419-033

(P-28067)
T-FORCE INC (PA)
4695 Macarthur Ct, Newport Beach (92660-1882)
PHONE..................949 208-1527
Fax: 949 216-3010
Raid Al-Khawaldeh, *President*
Ally Adnan, *COO*
Tareq Amin, *Senior VP*
Peter Nguyen, *Vice Pres*
Thao Le, *Administration*
EMP: 98
SALES (est): 9.8MM **Privately Held**
WEB: www.t-force.com
SIC: 8748 7379 Telecommunications consultant;

(P-28068)
TARGETSOLUTIONS INC (HQ)
10805 Rancho Bernardo Rd # 200, San Diego (92127-5701)
PHONE..................858 592-6880
Fax: 858 487-8762
Jon Handy, *President*
James Henfel, *CFO*
Dale Johnson, *Bd of Directors*
Jody Hillier, *Human Resources*
Mike Butler, *Mktg Dir*
EMP: 53 **EST:** 1999
SQ FT: 10,000
SALES (est): 8.3MM
SALES (corp-wide): 30.6MM **Privately Held**
WEB: www.targetsafety.com
SIC: 8748 8299 Safety training service; educational service, nondegree granting: continuing educ.
PA: Redvector.Com, Llc
4890 W Kennedy Blvd
Tampa FL 33609
866 546-1212

(P-28069)
TC3 HEALTH INC (DH)
1901 E Alton Ave Ste 100, Santa Ana
(92705-5849)
PHONE..............................949 943-8700
Robert Gerger, *COO*
Sindi Corwin, *Vice Pres*
Roberta Patrow, *Vice Pres*
Jeong Lee, *Sr Software Eng*
Barb Deyoung, *CIO*
EMP: 75
SALES (est): 11.8MM
SALES (corp-wide): 1.4B Privately Held
WEB: www.tc3health.com
SIC: 8748 Business consulting
HQ: Medifax-Edi, Llc
    26 Century Blvd
    Nashville TN 37214
    615 932-3226

(P-28070)
TELECOM TECHNOLOGY SVCS INC
Also Called: Tts
7901 Stoneridge Dr # 500, Pleasanton
(94588-3969)
PHONE..............................925 224-7812
Lin Weng, *CEO*
Paul Arevalo, *Engineer*
Tom Chan, *Controller*
Joan Shimizu, *Human Res Mgr*
Mike Yglesias, *VP Sales*
EMP: 130
SQ FT: 7,102
SALES (est): 16.9MM Privately Held
WEB: www.ttswireless.com
SIC: 8748 Telecommunications consultant

(P-28071)
TEMPEST TELECOM SOLUTIONS LLC (PA)
136 W Canon Perdido St A, Santa Barbara
(93101-3242)
PHONE..............................805 879-4800
Fax: 805 690-3345
Jessica Firestone, *CEO*
Dan Firestone, *COO*
Julie Lubin, *CFO*
Dave Smargon, *Vice Pres*
Richard Smith, *Vice Pres*
EMP: 60
SQ FT: 9,000
SALES (est): 52.4MM Privately Held
WEB: www.tempesttelecom.com
SIC: 8748 Systems analysis & engineering consulting services; telecommunications consultant

(P-28072)
TETRA TECH INC
3201 Airpark Dr Ste 108, Santa Maria
(93455-1834)
PHONE..............................805 739-2600
Fax: 805 739-2605
Jeff Matthew, *Branch Mgr*
Andrew Smith, *Manager*
EMP: 63
SALES (corp-wide): 2.3B Publicly Held
WEB: www.tetratech.com
SIC: 8748 Environmental consultant
PA: Tetra Tech, Inc.
    3475 E Foothill Blvd
    Pasadena CA 91107
    626 351-4664

(P-28073)
TETRA TECH EC INC
1230 Columbia St Ste 750, San Diego
(92101-8536)
PHONE..............................619 234-8690
Niel Hart, *Branch Mgr*
David Rodriguez, *Webmaster*
Randy Monohan, *Manager*
EMP: 67
SALES (corp-wide): 2.3B Publicly Held
SIC: 8748 Testing services
HQ: Tetra Tech Ec, Inc.
    1000 The American Rd # 1
    Morris Plains NJ 07950
    973 630-8000

(P-28074)
TETRA TECH EC INC
2969 Prospect Park Dr # 100, Rancho Cordova (95670-6187)
PHONE..............................916 852-8300
Anh Nghiem, *Manager*
EMP: 1000
SALES (corp-wide): 2.3B Publicly Held
SIC: 8748 Environmental consultant
HQ: Tetra Tech Ec, Inc.
    1000 The American Rd # 1
    Morris Plains NJ 07950
    973 630-8000

(P-28075)
TETRA TECH NUS INC
3475 E Foothill Blvd, Pasadena
(91107-6024)
PHONE..............................412 921-7090
Dan L Batrack, *CEO*
Steven M Burdick, *Exec VP*
John Trepanowski, *Vice Pres*
Ronald Chu, *Principal*
Janet Mandel, *Director*
▲ EMP: 100
SALES (est): 6.6MM
SALES (corp-wide): 2.3B Publicly Held
WEB: www.ttnus.com
SIC: 8748 Environmental consultant
PA: Tetra Tech, Inc.
    3475 E Foothill Blvd
    Pasadena CA 91107
    626 351-4664

(P-28076)
THOMSON FINANCIAL SERVICES
633 W 5th St, Los Angeles (90071-2005)
PHONE..............................213 955-5902
Maria Cavazos, *Manager*
EMP: 50
SALES (est): 1.9MM
SALES (corp-wide): 3.8B Publicly Held
SIC: 8748 Systems engineering consultant, ex. computer or professional
HQ: Thomson Reuters Corporation
    3 Times Sq Lbby Mailroom
    New York NY 10036
    646 223-4000

(P-28077)
THOMSON REUTERS (LEGAL) INC
2440 W El Camino Real, Mountain View
(94040-1497)
PHONE..............................650 210-1900
Steve Robinson, *Manager*
EMP: 100
SALES (corp-wide): 3.8B Publicly Held
SIC: 8748 Business consulting
HQ: Thomson Reuters (Legal) Inc.
    610 Opperman Dr
    Eagan MN 55123
    651 687-7000

(P-28078)
THOMSON REUTERS (LEGAL) INC
50 California St Ste 200, San Francisco
(94111-4605)
PHONE..............................415 344-6000
Heather Cameron, *Manager*
Chris Rodrigues, *Database Admin*
Brian Houston, *Analyst*
Allison Spalding, *Marketing Mgr*
EMP: 100
SALES (corp-wide): 3.8B Publicly Held
SIC: 8748 Business consulting
HQ: Thomson Reuters (Legal) Inc.
    610 Opperman Dr
    Eagan MN 55123
    651 687-7000

(P-28079)
TM FINANCIAL FORENSICS LLC (PA)
2 Embarcadero Ctr # 2510, San Francisco
(94111-3924)
PHONE..............................415 692-6350
Paul Meyer, *Mng Member*
Jeff Colditz, *Vice Pres*
Brian Hammer, *Vice Pres*
John Hansen, *Vice Pres*
Angela Izuel, *Vice Pres*
EMP: 50

SALES (est): 11.5MM Privately Held
SIC: 8748 Communications consulting

(P-28080)
TO CELERITY EDUCATIONAL GROUP
4501 Wadsworth Ave, Los Angeles
(90011-3637)
PHONE..............................323 231-7005
Grace Canada, *CEO*
EMP: 75
SALES (est): 4.5MM Privately Held
SIC: 8748 Business consulting

(P-28081)
TOTAL EDUCATION SOLUTIONS INC (PA)
625 Fair Oaks Ave Ste 300, South
Pasadena (91030-5805)
PHONE..............................323 341-5580
Nancy Lavelle, *President*
Piero Stillitano, *CFO*
Meaghan Donahue, *Vice Pres*
Edward Ayme, *Managing Dir*
Tawnia Novak, *Regional Mgr*
EMP: 50
SALES (est): 43.6MM Privately Held
SIC: 8748 Educational consultant

(P-28082)
TRC SOLUTIONS INC (HQ)
Also Called: Alton Geoscience
9685 Research Dr Ste 100, Irvine
(92618-4657)
PHONE..............................949 753-0101
Fax: 949 753-0111
Christopher P Vincze, *Ch of Bd*
Thomas W Bennet Jr, *CFO*
Bernard Bethke, *Vice Pres*
Rich Roda, *Human Res Mgr*
EMP: 125
SQ FT: 47,000
SALES (est): 30.4MM
SALES (corp-wide): 465.1MM Publicly Held
WEB: www.trcsolutions.com
SIC: 8748 8711 Environmental consultant; engineering services
PA: Trc Companies, Inc.
    650 Suffolk St
    Lowell MA 01854
    978 970-5600

(P-28083)
TRIAD SYSTEMS INTERNATIONAL (PA)
23801 Calabasas Rd # 2022, Calabasas
(91302-1568)
PHONE..............................818 222-6811
Fax: 818 222-0116
Cyril Cianflone, *President*
EMP: 260
SQ FT: 4,800
SALES (est): 24.5MM Privately Held
WEB: www.worktek.com
SIC: 8748 8711 Systems engineering consultant, ex. computer or professional; electrical or electronic engineering

(P-28084)
TRIMARK ASSOCIATES INC
2365 Iron Point Rd # 100, Folsom
(95630-8714)
PHONE..............................916 357-5970
Fax: 916 357-5971
Mark J Morosky, *President*
Dean Schoeder, *COO*
Bob Wood, *CTO*
Robert Hinchman, *Director*
Jae Kim, *Director*
EMP: 53 EST: 2000
SQ FT: 108,000
SALES (est): 11.3MM Privately Held
WEB: www.trimarkmdma.com
SIC: 8748 Business consulting

(P-28085)
ULLMEN ASSOCIATES LLC
22129 Martinez St, Woodland Hills
(91364-1614)
PHONE..............................310 444-3915
John Ullmen, *Managing Dir*
EMP: 100 EST: 2002
SALES (est): 8.9MM Privately Held
SIC: 8748 Business consulting

(P-28086)
UNIVERSAL NETWORK DEV CORP (PA)
Also Called: Undc
2555 3rd St Ste 112, Sacramento
(95818-1100)
PHONE..............................916 475-1200
Fax: 916 475-1202
Cinthia Larkin Kazee, *President*
Sharan Goldrupe, *Bookkeeper*
EMP: 108
SQ FT: 1,600
SALES (est): 11.3MM Privately Held
WEB: www.undc.com
SIC: 8748 8711 Communications consulting; telecommunications consultant; professional engineer

(P-28087)
VALLE SANIT AND FLOOD CONTR DI
450 Ryder St, Vallejo (94590-7217)
PHONE..............................707 644-8949
Fax: 707 644-8949
Ron Matheson, *CEO*
Melissa Morton, *District Mgr*
Jason Kaduk, *Info Tech Mgr*
Michele Dold, *Finance*
Eileen White, *Accountant*
EMP: 86 EST: 1952
SQ FT: 10,000
SALES (est): 27.4MM Privately Held
WEB: www.vsfcd.com
SIC: 8748 Environmental consultant; traffic consultant; economic consultant

(P-28088)
VENCORE INC
1315 Dell Ave, Campbell (95008-6609)
PHONE..............................571 313-6000
John Curtis, *CEO*
Zachary McCready, *Manager*
EMP: 50
SQ FT: 10,000
SALES (est): 1MM Privately Held
SIC: 8748 7373 Systems analysis & engineering consulting services; systems engineering, computer related

(P-28089)
VENUE MANAGEMENT SERVICES INC
500 N 1st Ave Ste 4, Arcadia (91006-2898)
PHONE..............................626 445-6000
Fax: 626 445-6110
Charles E McIntyre, *President*
EMP: 280
SALES (est): 6.8MM Privately Held
WEB: www.venueservices.com
SIC: 8748 Business consulting

(P-28090)
VETERANS AFFAIRS CAL DEPT
Also Called: Veterans Affairs Testing Off
1227 O St Ste 105, Sacramento
(95814-5891)
PHONE..............................916 653-2535
Karen Escobar, *Director*
EMP: 347 Privately Held
WEB: www.californiachronicle.com
SIC: 8748 9451 Testing services; administration of veterans' affairs;
HQ: California Department Of Veterans Affairs
    1227 O St Ste 105
    Sacramento CA 95814
    800 952-5626

(P-28091)
VIMO INC
Also Called: Getinsured.com
1305 Terra Bella Ave, Mountain View
(94043-1851)
PHONE..............................650 618-4600
Srinivasan Krishnan, *CEO*
Shankar Srinivasan, *COO*
Krzysztof Kujawa, *Vice Pres*
Scott Osler, *Vice Pres*
Saurin Pandya, *VP Bus Dvlpt*
EMP: 100
SQ FT: 20,000

PRODUCTS & SERVICES SECTION

8999 - Services Not Elsewhere Classified County (P-28115)

SALES (est): 18.5MM Privately Held
WEB: www.vimo.com
SIC: 8748 6411 7371 7373 Business consulting; insurance brokers; computer software development & applications; systems software development services

(P-28092)
VINCULUMS SERVICES INC
10 Pasteur Ste 100, Irvine (92618-3823)
PHONE.................................949 783-3552
Bart V Aardenne, *CEO*
Paul Foster, *President*
Bart Von Aardenne, *CEO*
Brian Woodward, *COO*
Norm Alexander, *CFO*
EMP: 220 EST: 2005
SQ FT: 8,000
SALES (est): 44MM Privately Held
SIC: 8748 Telecommunications consultant

(P-28093)
VOLT TELECOM GROUP INC
Also Called: Volt Telecom Group
218 Helicopter Cir, Corona (92880-2531)
PHONE.................................727 571-2268
Fax: 951 582-5963
Frank Dalessio, *CEO*
Shelby Best, *Executive*
Lori Morin, *General Mgr*
Freddie Hernandez, *Director*
EMP: 50
SALES (corp-wide): 1.5B Publicly Held
SIC: 8748 Telecommunications consultant
HQ: Volt Telecommunications Group, Inc.
    560 Lexington Ave Fl 14
    New York NY 10022
    212 704-2400

(P-28094)
VOLT TELECOM GROUP INC
Also Called: Volt Telecom Group
218 Helicopter Cir, Corona (92880-2531)
PHONE.................................951 493-8900
Frank D'Alessio, *CEO*
Kingsley H Nelson, *Principal*
Lon Johnson, *Manager*
Achim Wehren, *Manager*
EMP: 250
SALES (corp-wide): 1.5B Publicly Held
SIC: 8748 Telecommunications consultant
HQ: Volt Telecommunications Group, Inc.
    560 Lexington Ave Fl 14
    New York NY 10022
    212 704-2400

(P-28095)
VOX NETWORK SOLUTIONS INC
8000 Marina Blvd Ste 130, Brisbane (94005-1882)
PHONE.................................650 989-1000
Scott Landis, *Ch of Bd*
Edwin L Kingen, *Vice Pres*
Pat McCarthy, *Executive*
Jerome Hoban, *Engineer*
Kevin Mott, *Engineer*
EMP: 90
SQ FT: 3,904
SALES: 35.8MM Privately Held
WEB: www.voxnetworksolutions.com
SIC: 8748 Telecommunications consultant

(P-28096)
W CORPORATION
Also Called: Vantage Company
1643 W Orange Grove Ave, Orange (92868-1116)
PHONE.................................949 861-2927
Kenneth Watkins, *President*
Marvin Anderson, *CFO*
Jim Watkins, *Office Mgr*
Amanda Munoz, *Office Admin*
Sonya Burton, *Manager*
EMP: 80 EST: 2001
SALES: 7.5MM Privately Held
SIC: 8748 1542 1522 Telecommunications consultant; commercial & office building, new construction; residential construction

(P-28097)
WARNER BROS CONSUMER PDTS INC (DH)
4001 W Olive Ave, Burbank (91505-4272)
PHONE.................................818 954-7980
Brad Globe, *President*
Dan Romanelli, *President*
Randy Blotky, *Senior VP*
Ana De Castro, *Senior VP*
John Schulman, *Admin Sec*
▲ EMP: 112
SALES (est): 21.2MM
SALES (corp-wide): 28.1B Publicly Held
SIC: 8748 5961 Business consulting; novelty merchandise, mail order
HQ: Warner Bros. Entertainment Inc.
    4000 Warner Blvd
    Burbank CA 91522
    818 954-6000

(P-28098)
WEISSCOMM GROUP LTD (PA)
Also Called: Wcg World
50 Francisco St Ste 400, San Francisco (94133-2114)
PHONE.................................415 362-5018
Fax: 415 362-5019
James Weiss, *CEO*
Chris Deri, *President*
Diane Weiser, *President*
Tony Esposito, *CFO*
Tim Malone, *Vice Pres*
EMP: 75
SQ FT: 16,000
SALES (est): 131.7MM Privately Held
WEB: www.wcgworld.com
SIC: 8748 Communications consulting

(P-28099)
WILLIAM S HART PONY & SOFTBALL
Also Called: Wm S Hart Pony & Softball
23437 Valencia Blvd, Valencia (91355-1702)
PHONE.................................661 254-9780
Dave Scripture, *President*
Mike Clare, *Treasurer*
Ken Underwood, *Exec VP*
Paul Silveri, *Admin Sec*
EMP: 55
SALES (est): 2.3MM Privately Held
SIC: 8748 Environmental consultant

(P-28100)
WNC & ASSOCIATES INC
17782 Sky Park Cir, Irvine (92614-6404)
PHONE.................................714 662-5565
Will Cooper Sr, *CEO*
Anil Advani, *Vice Pres*
Lisa Castillo, *Vice Pres*
Christine Cormier, *Vice Pres*
Amy Dosen, *Vice Pres*
EMP: 65
SALES (est): 11.1MM Privately Held
WEB: www.wncinc.com
SIC: 8748 Urban planning & consulting services

(P-28101)
WRIGHT BROADBAND GROUP INC
4413 La Jolla Village Dr, San Diego (92122-1264)
PHONE.................................858 362-0380
Leroy Wright, *President*
EMP: 75
SQ FT: 3,000
SALES: 7MM Privately Held
SIC: 8748 Telecommunications consultant

(P-28102)
X3 MANAGEMENT SERVICES INC
2128 Auto Park Way, Escondido (92029-1344)
PHONE.................................760 597-9336
David G Cranford, *CEO*
Arlette Zuniga, *CFO*
Linda Cue-Roden, *Manager*
Anthony Kachinsky, *Manager*
Janell Arce, *Assistant*
EMP: 72
SALES: 7.8MM Privately Held
SIC: 8748 1731 1531 1541 Telecommunications consultant; electrical work; fiber optic cable installation; operative builders; industrial buildings & warehouses; solar energy contractor

(P-28103)
YCG LLC
Also Called: You Consulting Group
566 Shanas Ln, Encinitas (92024-2435)
P.O. Box 231423 (92023-1423)
PHONE.................................760 230-8016
David Hackett, *Mng Member*
Dr Zannah Hackett,
EMP: 52
SALES (est): 250K Privately Held
SIC: 8748 Business consulting

(P-28104)
YUCAIPA COMPANIES LLC (PA)
9130 W Sunset Blvd, Los Angeles (90069-3110)
PHONE.................................310 789-7200
Fax: 310 228-2873
Ronald W Burkle, *Mng Member*
Scott Stedman,
EMP: 150
SALES (est): 4.1B Privately Held
SIC: 8748 6719 6726 Business consulting; investment holding companies, except banks; investment offices

(P-28105)
ZELOS CONSULTING LLC
2400 Wyandotte St B103, Mountain View (94043-2373)
PHONE.................................650 968-2881
Fax: 650 968-4001
Stephen Chiu,
Clyde Booth, *Engineer*
Poline Chiu,
Tony Quintong,
EMP: 50
SQ FT: 5,000
SALES (est): 3.5MM Privately Held
WEB: www.zelos.com
SIC: 8748 Systems analysis & engineering consulting services

8999 Services Not Elsewhere Classified

(P-28106)
ACTIVE LAWYERS REFERRAL SVC
9301 Wilshire Blvd # 508, Beverly Hills (90210-5424)
PHONE.................................310 247-0425
Paul Mehdizadeh, *President*
Vincent Mehdizadeh, *Manager*
EMP: 60
SALES (est): 2.6MM Privately Held
SIC: 8999 7299 Information bureau; information services, consumer

(P-28107)
ADVENTIST HEALTH SYSTEM/WEST
111 Raley Blvd, Chico (95928-8351)
PHONE.................................530 342-4576
EMP: 60
SALES (corp-wide): 251.4MM Privately Held
SIC: 8999 Artists & artists' studios
PA: Adventist Health System/West
    2100 Douglas Blvd
    Roseville CA 95661
    916 781-2000

(P-28108)
AEROSPACE & MARINE INTL
6910 Santa Teresa Blvd, San Jose (95119-1339)
PHONE.................................408 360-0440
Fax: 408 360-0450
George Carlsgaard, *President*
Jason Snyder, *Software Engr*
Mark Bailon, *Associate*
EMP: 50
SALES (est): 1.9MM Privately Held
WEB: www.amiwx.com
SIC: 8999 Weather related services

(P-28109)
AGEIS LIVING
Also Called: Aegis of San Francisco
2280 Gellert Blvd, South San Francisco (94080-5411)
PHONE.................................650 952-6100
Wayne Clark, *President*
Sylvia M Chu, *Exec Dir*
EMP: 50 EST: 2010
SALES (est): 898.4K Privately Held
SIC: 8999 Services

(P-28110)
AHTNA ENVIRONMENTAL INC
2255 Contra Costa Blvd, Pleasant Hill (94523-3772)
PHONE.................................907 433-0729
Karen Pearson, *Manager*
EMP: 72
SALES (est): 626.9K Privately Held
SIC: 8999 Earth science services

(P-28111)
ALLIANCE ENVMTL GROUP INC
680 Flinn Ave Unit 32, Moorpark (93021-2076)
PHONE.................................805 378-6590
Fax: 805 378-6594
Joe McLean, *Manager*
EMP: 85 Privately Held
WEB: www.alliance-enviro.com
SIC: 8999 Earth science services
PA: Alliance Environmental Group, Inc.
    978 W 10th St
    Azusa CA 91702

(P-28112)
ALLIANCE HEALTH INC
5300 Lennox Ave Ste 103, Bakersfield (93309-1662)
PHONE.................................661 325-6937
Abraham Nesheiwat, *Branch Mgr*
EMP: 317 Privately Held
SIC: 8999 Artists & artists' studios
PA: Alliance Health, Inc.
    134 Rumford Ave Ste 306
    Auburndale MA 02466

(P-28113)
ANKA BEHAVIORAL HEALTH INC
2507 Evelyn Ave, Rosemead (91770-3070)
PHONE.................................626 573-5902
EMP: 69
SALES (corp-wide): 41.6MM Privately Held
SIC: 8999 Actuarial consultant
PA: Anka Behavioral Health, Incorporated
    1850 Gateway Blvd Ste 900
    Concord CA 94520
    925 825-4700

(P-28114)
APPLIED WEATHER TECHNOLOGY INC
Also Called: Awt Worlwide
140 Kifer Ct, Sunnyvale (94086-5120)
PHONE.................................408 731-8600
Robert Haydn Jones, *CEO*
Haydn Jones, *President*
William Lapworth, *CFO*
Cynthia Lin, *CFO*
Richard Brown, *Vice Pres*
EMP: 166
SQ FT: 19,000
SALES (est): 10.3MM
SALES (corp-wide): 52.6MM Privately Held
SIC: 8999 Weather forecasting
HQ: Stormgeo As
    Nordre Nostekaien 1
    Bergen 5011
    557 061-70

(P-28115)
ASSISTED HOME RECOVERY INC
1900 W Garvey Ave S # 210, West Covina (91790-2656)
PHONE.................................626 915-5595
Fax: 626 851-4041
EMP: 66
SALES (corp-wide): 10.9MM Privately Held
SIC: 8999 Artists & artists' studios
PA: Assisted Home Recovery Inc
    8550 Balboa Blvd Lbby
    Northridge CA 91325
    818 894-8117

8999 - Services Not Elsewhere Classified County (P-28116) — PRODUDUCTS & SERVICES SECTION

(P-28116)
ASSOCIATED STUDENTS INC
Also Called: Associated Students, Inc.
1 Grand Ave, San Luis Obispo (93407-9000)
PHONE 805 756-1281
Richard Johnson, *Exec Dir*
Carol Brizendine, *Human Res Mgr*
EMP: 68
SALES (corp-wide): 12.7MM **Privately Held**
SIC: 8999 Artists & artists' studios
PA: Associated Students Inc Of California
Polytechnic State University At San Luis Obispo
University Un Bldg 65
San Luis Obispo CA 93407
805 756-1281

(P-28117)
AT&T CORP
1188 W Evelyn Ave, Sunnyvale (94086-5742)
PHONE 650 960-2313
EMP: 68
SALES (corp-wide): 146.8B **Publicly Held**
SIC: 8999 Communication services
HQ: At&T Corp.
1 At&T Way
Bedminster NJ 07921
800 403-3302

(P-28118)
AT&T CORP
1705 Story Rd, San Jose (95122-1935)
PHONE 408 729-8400
EMP: 68
SALES (corp-wide): 146.8B **Publicly Held**
SIC: 8999 Artists & artists' studios
HQ: At&T Corp.
1 At&T Way
Bedminster NJ 07921
800 403-3302

(P-28119)
BUCK CONSULTANTS LLC
1801 Century Park E # 500, Los Angeles (90067-2307)
PHONE 310 282-8232
Fax: 310 282-0881
Harold Love, *Branch Mgr*
EMP: 55
SALES (corp-wide): 18B **Publicly Held**
SIC: 8999 8742 6282 2741 Actuarial consultant; compensation & benefits planning consultant; investment advice; technical papers: publishing only, not printed on site
HQ: Buck Consultants, Llc
485 Lexington Ave Fl 10
New York NY 10017
212 330-1000

(P-28120)
BUCK CONSULTANTS LLC
7676 Hazard Center Dr # 400, San Diego (92108-4554)
PHONE 619 725-1769
Mike Schinning, *Manager*
EMP: 59
SALES (corp-wide): 18B **Publicly Held**
SIC: 8999 Actuarial consultant
HQ: Buck Consultants, Llc
485 Lexington Ave Fl 10
New York NY 10017
212 330-1000

(P-28121)
CALIFORNIA TAHOE CONSERVANCY
1061 3rd St, South Lake Tahoe (96150-3475)
PHONE 530 542-5580
Fax: 530 542-5591
Patrick Wright, *Exec Dir*
Russell Maloney, *Principal*
Bryan Lossberg, *Exec Dir*
Debra Harric, *Executive Asst*
David Gregorich, *Administration*
EMP: 50
SALES (est): 1.9MM **Privately Held**
SIC: 8999 Natural resource preservation service
HQ: California Natural Resources Agency
1416 9th St Ste 1311
Sacramento CA 95814
916 653-5656

(P-28122)
CARDINAL CARTRIDGE INC
20450 Plummer St, Chatsworth (91311-5372)
PHONE 818 727-9740
Dan Ghammachi, *Principal*
EMP: 69
SALES (corp-wide): 50.1MM **Privately Held**
SIC: 8999 Artists & artists' studios
HQ: Cardinal Cartridge, Inc.
20450 Plummer St
Chatsworth CA 91311
775 624-8135

(P-28123)
CITY OF HOPE
2701 Santa Rosa Ave, Altadena (91001-1940)
PHONE 626 256-4673
Kimlin Tam Ashing-Giwa, *Owner*
Alexander Kaye, *Research*
Abrahm Levi, *Research*
Traci Biondi, *Anesthesiology*
Diana Chia, *Nurse*
EMP: 359
SALES (corp-wide): 1.4B **Privately Held**
SIC: 8999 Scientific consulting
PA: City Of Hope
1500 E Duarte Blvd
Duarte CA 91010
626 256-4673

(P-28124)
CONSERVATION LIQUIDATION
100 Pine St Ste 2600, San Francisco (94111-5212)
PHONE 415 676-5000
David Wilson, *CEO*
EMP: 75
SALES (est): 3MM **Privately Held**
SIC: 8999 Natural resource preservation service

(P-28125)
COUNTY OF SAN MATEO
Also Called: Information Services Dept
455 County Ctr Fl 3, Redwood City (94063-1663)
PHONE 650 363-4548
Jon Walton, *CIO*
Eric Fan, *Manager*
EMP: 150 **Privately Held**
WEB: www.ci.sanmateo.ca.us
SIC: 8999 9199 Information bureau;
PA: County Of San Mateo
400 County Ctr
Redwood City CA 94063
650 363-4123

(P-28126)
CWS UTILITY SERVICES CORP
1720 N 1st St, San Jose (95112-4508)
PHONE 408 367-8200
Robert W Foye, *Principal*
EMP: 382
SALES (est): 4.4MM
SALES (corp-wide): 588.3MM **Publicly Held**
SIC: 8999 Services
WEB: www.calwater.com
PA: California Water Service Group
1720 N 1st St
San Jose CA 95112
408 367-8200

(P-28127)
DATA TRACE INFO SVCS LLC (HQ)
4 First American Way, Santa Ana (92707-5913)
PHONE 714 250-6700
Fax: 714 250-6933
Mike Henney Sr,
Calvin Powell, *President*
Felix Uy, *Technical Mgr*
Andrea Henney, *Project Mgr*
Rio Sells, *Technology*
EMP: 100

(P-28128)
DURHAM SCHOOL SERVICES
Also Called: Perterman
3001 Ross Ave Ste 11, San Jose (95124-2358)
PHONE 408 448-0740
Ron Mahler, *Branch Mgr*
EMP: 80
SALES (corp-wide): 2.8B **Privately Held**
SIC: 8999 Artists & artists' studios
HQ: Durham School Services
506 Se 15th St
Oak Grove MO

(P-28129)
ENVIROBUSINESS INC
Also Called: Ebi Consulting
3703 Long Beach Blvd Fl 2, Long Beach (90807-3329)
PHONE 562 481-3365
EMP: 83
SALES (corp-wide): 109.4MM **Privately Held**
SIC: 8999 Scientific consulting
PA: Envirobusiness, Inc.
21 B St
Burlington MA 01803
781 273-2500

(P-28130)
FORT MASON CENTER
2 Marina Blvd Bldg A, San Francisco (94123-1284)
PHONE 415 345-7500
Fax: 415 441-3405
Caroline Werth, *President*
Jovanne Reilly, *Executive*
Rich Hillis, *Exec Dir*
Lisa Phillips, *Office Mgr*
Matt Sauerman, *Info Tech Mgr*
EMP: 56
SQ FT: 300,000
SALES: 11.4MM **Privately Held**
WEB: www.fortmason.org
SIC: 8999 Art related services

(P-28131)
GLOBAL BUILDING SERVICES INC
17618 Murphy Pkwy, Lathrop (95330-8629)
PHONE 209 858-9501
EMP: 298
SALES (corp-wide): 37.3MM **Privately Held**
SIC: 8999 Actuarial consultant
PA: Global Building Services, Inc.
25129 The Old Rd Ste 102
Stevenson Ranch CA 91381
661 288-5733

(P-28132)
GOLDEN GATE NAT PRKS CNSRVANCY (PA)
Fort Mason Bldg 201, San Francisco (94123)
PHONE 415 561-3000
Fax: 415 561-3003
Greg Moore, *CEO*
David H Courtney, *Trustee*
Alexander H Scilling, *Trustee*
Nicolas Elsishans, *Exec VP*
Cathie Barner, *Vice Pres*
▲ **EMP:** 70
SQ FT: 5,000
SALES: 52.3MM **Privately Held**
WEB: www.parksconservancy.org
SIC: 8999 Natural resource preservation service

(P-28133)
HEALTHCARE SERVICES GROUP INC
5199 E Pacific Coast Hwy # 402, Long Beach (90804-3309)
PHONE 562 494-7939
Fax: 562 494-8039
Mike Hammond, *Principal*
Tom Freeland, *Regional Mgr*
Michael Fiorella, *Director*
EMP: 1893
SALES (corp-wide): 1.4B **Publicly Held**
SIC: 8999 Artists & artists' studios
PA: Healthcare Services Group Inc
3220 Tillman Dr Ste 300
Bensalem PA 19020
215 639-4274

(P-28134)
HEALY & CO
268 Bush St 2704, San Francisco (94104-3503)
PHONE 925 543-5700
Fax: 925 543-5720
Eileen Healy, *President*
Richard Collins, *CFO*
EMP: 60
SQ FT: 5,500
SALES (est): 3.3MM **Privately Held**
WEB: www.healy-co.com
SIC: 8999 Communication services

(P-28135)
INDYME SOLUTIONS LLC
8295 Aero Pl Ste 260, San Diego (92123-2029)
PHONE 858 268-0717
Joe Joseph Eudano, *CEO*
Jack Hetzel, *CFO*
Larry Cleary, *Vice Pres*
Bill Kepner, *Vice Pres*
Jay Standiford, *Vice Pres*
EMP: 50
SQ FT: 18,000
SALES (est): 3.9MM **Privately Held**
SIC: 8999 Communication services

(P-28136)
INTERIM INC
Also Called: Interim Services
339 Pajaro St Ste B, Salinas (93901-3400)
PHONE 831 754-3838
Fred Harris, *Branch Mgr*
EMP: 116
SALES (corp-wide): 10.4MM **Privately Held**
SIC: 8999 Personal services
PA: Interim, Inc.
604 Pearl St Frnt
Monterey CA 93940
831 649-4399

(P-28137)
ISO SERVICES INC
388 Market St Ste 800, San Francisco (94111-5383)
PHONE 415 434-4599
Scott G Stephenson, *Branch Mgr*
EMP: 2864
SALES (corp-wide): 140.8MM **Privately Held**
SIC: 8999 Artists & artists' studios
PA: Iso Services, Inc.
545 Washington Blvd Fl 12
Jersey City NJ 07310
201 469-2000

(P-28138)
J RIVERA ASSOCIATES INC
Also Called: 4 Su Salud Medical Contact Ctr
139 S Guild Ave, Lodi (95240-0867)
PHONE 415 617-5660
Jose R Rivera MPH, *CEO*
Aros Resmini, *CIO*
EMP: 92
SQ FT: 5,000
SALES: 2MM **Privately Held**
SIC: 8999 Communication services

(P-28139)
KCI ENVIRONMENTAL INC
207 Suburban Rd Ste 6, San Luis Obispo (93401-7559)
P.O. Box 3307 (93403-3307)
PHONE 805 543-3311
Curt Boutwell, *President*
Janice Pepper, *General Mgr*
Ernie Peterson, *Project Mgr*
Yolanda Inguito, *Accountant*
EMP: 50
SALES (est): 3.4MM **Privately Held**
WEB: www.kcienv.com
SIC: 8999 Earth science services

▲ = Import ▼ = Export
◆ = Import/Export

PRODUCTS & SERVICES SECTION
8999 - Services Not Elsewhere Classified County (P-28165)

(P-28140)
KINGS RIVER CONSERVATION DST
4886 E Jensen Ave, Fresno (93725-1899)
PHONE..................................559 237-5567
Fax: 559 237-5560
Mark McKean, *President*
Brent Graham, *Vice Pres*
Cristel Tufenkjian, *Executive*
David Orth, *General Mgr*
Eric Osterling, *General Mgr*
EMP: 77
SQ FT: 8,500
SALES (est): 7.6MM **Privately Held**
WEB: www.krcd.org
SIC: **8999** Natural resource preservation service

(P-28141)
LIFTECH ELEVATOR SERVICES INC
1901 E 29th St, Signal Hill (90755-1907)
PHONE..................................562 997-3639
Fax: 562 997-3680
Daniel M Simon, *CEO*
Linda Gutierrez, *Manager*
EMP: 51
SALES (est): 5.6MM **Privately Held**
SIC: **8999** Artists & artists' studios

(P-28142)
LUCILE SALTER PACKARD CHIL
725 Welch Rd, Palo Alto (94304-1601)
PHONE..................................650 736-4030
Simone Esson, *Branch Mgr*
EMP: 388
SALES (corp-wide): 1.1B **Privately Held**
SIC: **8999** Artists & artists' studios
PA: Lucile Salter Packard Children's Hospital At Stanford
725 Welch Rd
Palo Alto CA 94304
650 736-7398

(P-28143)
M4 WIND SERVICES INC
4020 Long Beach Blvd Fl 2, Long Beach (90807-2683)
PHONE..................................562 981-7797
Myles Baker, *President*
Scott Young, *Manager*
EMP: 99
SALES (est): 1.4MM **Privately Held**
SIC: **8999** Artists & artists' studios

(P-28144)
MALKA COMMUNICATIONS GROUP INC
15260 Ventura Blvd # 1430, Sherman Oaks (91403-5307)
PHONE..................................818 990-0278
Nataly Malka, *CEO*
Robert Malka, *COO*
EMP: 50
SQ FT: 1,900
SALES (est): 1.5MM **Privately Held**
SIC: **8999** Communication services

(P-28145)
MAXIM HEALTHCARE SERVICES INC
500 E Esplanade Dr, Oxnard (93036-2110)
PHONE..................................805 278-4593
EMP: 856
SALES (corp-wide): 1.2B **Privately Held**
SIC: **8999** Artists & artists' studios
PA: Maxim Healthcare Services, Inc.
7227 Lee Deforest Dr
Columbia MD 21046
410 910-1500

(P-28146)
MAXUS USA
6300 Wilshire Blvd # 720, Los Angeles (90048-5204)
PHONE..................................323 202-4650
EMP: 444
SALES (est): 62.8K
SALES (corp-wide): 18.4B **Privately Held**
SIC: **8999** Communication services
HQ: Maxus Communications Llc
498 Fashion Ave
New York NY 10018
212 297-8300

(P-28147)
MCCLATCHY COMPANY
2100 Q St, Sacramento (95816-6816)
PHONE..................................916 321-1941
EMP: 10000
SALES (est): 72.8K **Privately Held**
SIC: **8999**

(P-28148)
MIDPENINSUL RGNL OPN SP
330 Distel Cir, Los Altos (94022-1404)
PHONE..................................650 691-1200
Fax: 650 691-0485
Craig Britton, *President*
Matt Freeman, *Bd of Directors*
Ira Ruskin, *Bd of Directors*
Jennifer Kavanagh, *Admin Asst*
Benny Hsieh, *Info Tech Mgr*
EMP: 65
SQ FT: 12,000
SALES: 37.9MM **Privately Held**
SIC: **8999** Natural resource preservation service

(P-28149)
MILLIMAN INC
650 California St Fl 17, San Francisco (94108-2721)
PHONE..................................415 403-1333
Terry Haney, *Facilities Mgr*
Bob Helliesen, *Principal*
Jim Walbridge, *Principal*
Rich Wright, *General Mgr*
Gale I Yarymowicz, *Office Mgr*
EMP: 55
SALES (corp-wide): 828.2MM **Privately Held**
WEB: www.millimanglobal.com
SIC: **8999** **6411** Actuarial consultant; ratemaking organizations, insurance
PA: Milliman, Inc.
1301 5th Ave Ste 3800
Seattle WA 98101
206 624-7940

(P-28150)
OPTIMA NETWORK SERVICES INC (DH)
15345 Fairfield Ranch Rd # 225, Chino Hills (91709-8859)
PHONE..................................305 599-1800
Fax: 909 597-7008
Robert E Apple, *CEO*
Michael Mosel, *President*
Jeff L Mock, *Executive*
Chris Dunn, *General Mgr*
Michael Manfre, *Project Mgr*
EMP: 75
SQ FT: 6,475
SALES (est): 9.6MM
SALES (corp-wide): 4.2B **Publicly Held**
WEB: www.optimanet.net
SIC: **8999** Communication services
HQ: Mastec North America, Inc.
800 S Douglas Rd Ste 1200
Coral Gables FL 33134
305 599-1800

(P-28151)
ORACLE CORP
17901 Von Karman Ave # 800, Irvine (92614-5241)
PHONE..................................650 506-7000
EMP: 567
SALES (est): 27.1MM **Privately Held**
SIC: **8999**

(P-28152)
OVERSEAS SERVICE CORPORATION
Also Called: Ocean Service
8221 Arjons Dr Ste B2, San Diego (92126-6319)
PHONE..................................858 408-0751
Tomoko Phillips, *Buyer*
Glen Maxwell, *Mktg Dir*
EMP: 229
SALES (corp-wide): 36.6MM **Privately Held**
SIC: **8999** Actuarial consultant
PA: Overseas Service Corporation
1100 Northpoint Pkwy # 200
West Palm Beach FL 33407
561 683-4090

(P-28153)
PANGEA CORPORATION
34145 Pacific Coast Hwy, Dana Point (92629-2808)
PHONE..................................949 443-0666
Fax: 949 443-0066
John Schulte, *CEO*
John Besmehn, *CEO*
Cheryl Ann Wong, *Director*
EMP: 50
SALES (est): 1.2MM **Privately Held**
WEB: www.pangeacorp.com
SIC: **8999** **8742 7336 8743** Advertising copy writing; writing for publication; new products & services consultants; creative services to advertisers, except writers; graphic arts & related design; public relations services; video tape production; audio-visual program production

(P-28154)
PARADIGM INFORMATION SERVICES
10755 F Scrps Pwy Pkwy424, San Diego (92131)
PHONE..................................858 693-6115
Elizabeth Bentz, *CEO*
Richard Scheiner, *President*
Gwen Scheiner, *Corp Secy*
Layne Scheiner, *Project Mgr*
Kristi Jennings, *Assistant*
EMP: 75
SALES (est): 2.1MM **Privately Held**
WEB: www.paradigmplacements.com
SIC: **8999** **8711 7336 7371** Technical writing; consulting engineer; electrical or electronic engineering; graphic arts & related design; computer software development & applications; educational services

(P-28155)
PLACER COUNTY ADM SVCS
2962 Richardson Dr, Auburn (95603-2640)
PHONE..................................530 886-5401
Fax: 530 889-4280
Jerry Gamaz, *Director*
Cathy Buchanan, *Info Tech Mgr*
EMP: 126
SALES (est): 5.7MM **Privately Held**
SIC: **8999** **9199** Information bureau; general government administration

(P-28156)
PRIDE INDUSTRIES
1281 National Dr, Sacramento (95834-1902)
PHONE..................................916 649-9499
Fax: 916 649-3854
Allan Ruzick, *Branch Mgr*
Bob Gonzales, *Info Tech Dir*
Valerie Seldon, *Software Dev*
Jonathan Brownell, *Business Anlyst*
Debbie Olmstead, *Business Anlyst*
EMP: 220
SALES (corp-wide): 279.8MM **Privately Held**
SIC: **8999** Personal services
PA: Pride Industries
10030 Foothills Blvd
Roseville CA 95747
916 788-2100

(P-28157)
PROVIDENCE HEALTH & SERVICES
27875 Smyth Dr, Santa Clarita (91355-6063)
PHONE..................................661 257-9999
Hu Howard, *Branch Mgr*
EMP: 69
SALES (corp-wide): 10.1B **Privately Held**
SIC: **8999** Artists & artists' studios
PA: Providence Health & Services
1801 Lind Ave Sw
Renton WA 98057
425 525-3355

(P-28158)
QUALITY CONSERVATION SVCS INC
264 Michelle Ct, South San Francisco (94080-6201)
PHONE..................................650 266-9490
Jame P Maitilasso, *Branch Mgr*
EMP: 168
SALES (corp-wide): 40.7MM **Privately Held**
SIC: **8999** Artists & artists' studios
PA: Quality Conservation Services, Inc.
5678 Berkshire Valley Rd C
Oak Ridge NJ 07438
973 697-9552

(P-28159)
RADAR MEDICAL SYSTEMS INC
1510 Cotner Ave, Los Angeles (90025-3303)
PHONE..................................440 337-9521
Florence Present, *Principal*
EMP: 101 EST: 2015
SALES (est): 44.6K
SALES (corp-wide): 809.6MM **Publicly Held**
SIC: **8999** Communication services
HQ: Radnet Managed Imaging Services, Inc.
1510 Cotner Ave
Los Angeles CA 90025
310 445-2800

(P-28160)
SIGNATURE CONSULTANTS LLC
44 Montgomery St Ste 1450, San Francisco (94104-4701)
PHONE..................................415 544-7510
EMP: 235 **Privately Held**
SIC: **8999** Scientific consulting
PA: Signature Consultants Llc
200 W Cypress Creek Rd # 400
Fort Lauderdale FL 33309

(P-28161)
SINTEX SECURITY SERVICES INC
650 W 20th St, Merced (95340-3702)
PHONE..................................510 208-0474
Jerry Sterner, *Branch Mgr*
EMP: 51
SALES (corp-wide): 4MM **Privately Held**
SIC: **8999** Artists & artists' studios
PA: Sintex Security Services, Inc.
501 Bangs Ave Ste D
Modesto CA 95356
209 543-9044

(P-28162)
SSG HOP SP
5811 S San Pedro St, Los Angeles (90011-5323)
PHONE..................................323 432-4399
Herbert Hatanaka, *Principal*
Michelle Huerta, *Admin Asst*
EMP: 450
SALES (est): 1.6MM **Privately Held**
SIC: **8999** Actuarial consultant

(P-28163)
THRIVE SUPPORT SERVICES INC
324 G St, Antioch (94509-1255)
PHONE..................................510 292-5058
Eric Partridge, *President*
Stanley Lamontagne, *Program Mgr*
EMP: 50 EST: 2009
SALES (est): 2.4MM **Privately Held**
SIC: **8999** Services

(P-28164)
UCDE - CENTER FOR HUMAN SVCS
1632 Da Vinci Ct, Davis (95618-4860)
PHONE..................................530 757-8538
Ken Ly, *Principal*
EMP: 50 EST: 2008
SALES (est): 504.1K **Privately Held**
SIC: **8999** Services

(P-28165)
UNIVERSAL CYLINDER EXCH INC
692 N Cypress St Ste B, Orange (92867-6665)
P.O. Box 6147 (92863-6147)
PHONE..................................714 744-1036
Pamela A Ogier, *President*
Darlene Thompson, *Accounts Mgr*
EMP: 85

8999 - Services Not Elsewhere Classified County (P-28166)

SALES (est): 2MM **Privately Held**
SIC: **8999** Natural resource preservation service

(P-28166)
UNIVERSAL SERVICES AMERICA LP
77725 Enfield Ln, Palm Desert (92211-0468)
PHONE..................760 200-2865
EMP: 5001
SALES (corp-wide): 2B **Privately Held**
SIC: **8999** Artists & artists' studios
PA: Universal Services Of America, Lp
  1551 N Tustin Ave
  Santa Ana CA 92705
  714 619-9700

(P-28167)
VERITY HEALTH SYSTEM CAL INC
203 Redwood Shr Pkwy # 800, Redwood City (94065-1198)
PHONE..................650 551-6700
Wahid Choudhury, *Branch Mgr*
EMP: 996
SALES (corp-wide): 225.4MM **Privately Held**
SIC: **8999** Artists & artists' studios
PA: Verity Health System Of California, Inc.
  203 Redwood Shores Pkwy
  Redwood City CA 94065
  650 551-6650

(P-28168)
VICTOR CMNTY SUPPORT SVCS INC
900 E Main St Ste 201, Grass Valley (95945-5853)
PHONE..................530 273-2244
Rachel Pena, *Exec Dir*
EMP: 205
SALES (corp-wide): 37.7MM **Privately Held**
SIC: **8999** Artists & artists' studios
PA: Victor Community Support Services, Inc.
  1360 E Lassen Ave
  Chico CA 95973
  530 893-0758

(P-28169)
WESTOWER COMMUNICATIONS INC
2017 Opportunity Dr Ste 4, Roseville (95678-3006)
PHONE..................916 783-6400
Mike Jarvis, *Branch Mgr*
Richard Chavez, *Manager*
EMP: 69
SALES (corp-wide): 4.2B **Publicly Held**
SIC: **8999** Communication services
HQ: Westower Communications Inc.
  4401 Northside Pkwy Nw # 600
  Atlanta GA 30327
  360 306-3300

(P-28170)
WOODMONT REAL ESTATE SVCS LP
3883 Airway Dr, Santa Rosa (95403-1670)
PHONE..................707 569-0582
Ron Granville, *Branch Mgr*
Donette Moix, *Property Mgr*
EMP: 279
SALES (corp-wide): 20.8MM **Privately Held**
SIC: **8999** Artists & artists' studios
PA: Woodmont Real Estate Services, L.P.
  1050 Ralston Ave
  Belmont CA 94002
  650 592-3960

(P-28171)
WU YEE CHILDRENS SERVICES
Also Called: Wu Yee Child Care Center
831 Broadway, San Francisco (94133-4218)
PHONE..................415 677-0100
Fax: 415 391-4716
Alyson Suzueki, *Program Dir*
EMP: 68
SALES (corp-wide): 20.4MM **Privately Held**
SIC: **8999** Artists & artists' studios
PA: Wu Yee Children's Services
  827 Broadway
  San Francisco CA 94133
  415 230-7504

(P-28172)
ZOE HOLDING COMPANY INC
44 Montgomery St, San Francisco (94104-4602)
PHONE..................415 421-4900
John Unick, *Branch Mgr*
Michael Murphy, *Manager*
EMP: 112
SALES (corp-wide): 55.7MM **Privately Held**
SIC: **8999** Artists & artists' studios
PA: Zoe Holding Company, Inc.
  3131 E Camelback Rd # 200
  Phoenix AZ 85016
  602 508-1883

ALPHABETIC SECTION

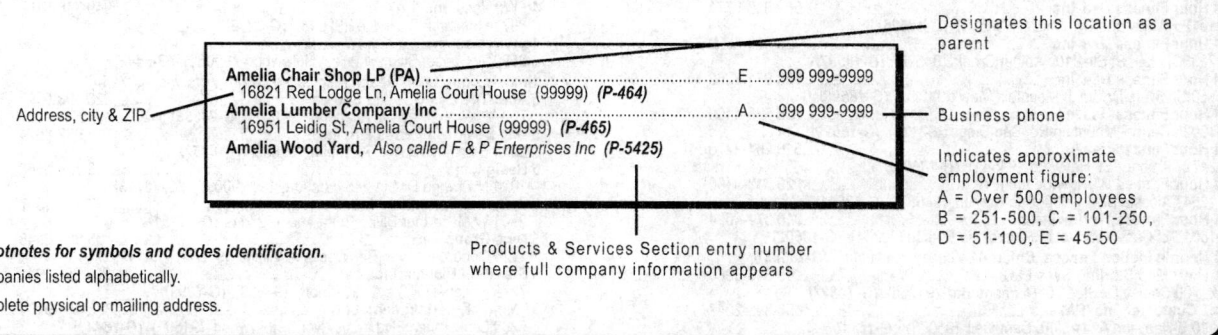

See footnotes for symbols and codes identification.
* Companies listed alphabetically.
* Complete physical or mailing address.

(a) Tool Shed Inc (PA)...831 477-7133
  3700 Soquel Ave Santa Cruz (95062) **(G-14503)**
0epi, Carmichael Also called Eskaton Properties Inc **(G-24653)**
1-800 Dentist, Los Angeles Also called Futuredontics Inc **(G-27444)**
1-800 Radiator & A/C (PA)..707 747-7400
  4401 Park Rd Benicia (94510) **(G-6702)**
1-800-4-insure Insurance Svcs......................................818 701-3733
  9310 Reseda Blvd Northridge (91324) **(G-10574)**
1-800-Radiator, Benicia Also called 1-800 Radiator & A/C **(G-6702)**
1000 Aguajito Op Co LLC..831 373-6141
  1000 Aguajito Rd Monterey (93940) **(G-12356)**
1000 Executive Parkway LLC..530 533-7335
  1000 Executive Pkwy Oroville (95966) **(G-20362)**
101communications Holdings LLC (HQ).........................818 734-1520
  9201 Oakdale Ave Ste 101 Chatsworth (91311) **(G-13957)**
102.9 Kblx-FM Radio, San Francisco Also called Inner City Broadcasting Corp **(G-5789)**
106 Sacramento Mhrc, Sacramento Also called Crestwood Behavioral Hlth Inc **(G-22060)**
107 San Jose Mhrc, San Jose Also called Crestwood Behavioral Hlth Inc **(G-24621)**
10up LLC...888 571-7130
  2765 Carradale Dr Roseville (95661) **(G-15888)**
11 Main Inc...530 892-9191
  527 Flume St Chico (95928) **(G-5437)**
1105 Government Group, Chatsworth Also called 101communications Holdings LLC **(G-13957)**
1105 Media Inc..949 265-1520
  4 Venture Ste 150 Irvine (92618) **(G-6059)**
111 Vallejo IMD, Vallejo Also called Crestwood Behavioral Hlth Inc **(G-22064)**
112 Modesto Snf, Modesto Also called Crestwood Behavioral Hlth Inc **(G-22059)**
1125 Sir Francis Drake Bouleva....................................415 456-9680
  1125 Sir Francis Drake Bl Kentfield (94904) **(G-22112)**
1130 W La Palma Ave Inc..562 930-0777
  4115 E Broadway Long Beach (90803) **(G-20363)**
1135 N Leisure Ct Inc..714 772-1353
  1135 N Leisure Ct Anaheim (92801) **(G-20364)**
115 Bakersfield Mhrc, Bakersfield Also called Crestwood Behavioral Hlth Inc **(G-22061)**
120 Fremont Snf, Redding Also called Crestwood Behavioral Hlth Inc **(G-24620)**
120 Fremont Snf, Fremont Also called Crestwood Behavioral Hlth Inc **(G-24624)**
120 South Los Angeles Street H...................................213 629-1200
  120 S Los Angeles St Los Angeles (90012) **(G-12357)**
1260 Bb Property LLC...805 969-2261
  1260 Channel Dr Santa Barbara (93108) **(G-12358)**
1334 Partners LP..310 546-5656
  1330 Park View Ave Manhattan Beach (90266) **(G-18839)**
134 Alameda Snf, Fremont Also called Crestwood Behavioral Hlth Inc **(G-24623)**
137 Bakersfield Bridge, Bakersfield Also called Crestwood Behavioral Hlth Inc **(G-22135)**
1370 Realty Corp..818 817-0092
  14545 Friar St Ste 101 Van Nuys (91411) **(G-11265)**
144 Pleasant Hill The Pathway, Pleasant Hill Also called Crestwood Behavioral Hlth Inc **(G-22066)**
145 Fresno Bridge, Fresno Also called Crestwood Behavioral Hlth Inc **(G-22062)**
14545 Friar LLC...818 817-0082
  14545 Friar St Ste 105 Van Nuys (91411) **(G-10950)**
152 Vallejo Rcfe, Vallejo Also called Crestwood Behavioral Hlth Inc **(G-24622)**
153 American River PHF, Carmichael Also called Crestwood Behavioral Hlth Inc **(G-22065)**
15th & L Investors LLC..916 267-6805
  1121 15th St Sacramento (95814) **(G-12359)**
15th Island LLC..619 321-1111
  405 15th St San Diego (92101) **(G-11266)**
16 3 Inc..619 588-2000
  529 Front St El Cajon (92020) **(G-3134)**
1658 Camden LLC...818 769-1944
  12147 Riverside Dr North Hollywood (91607) **(G-11076)**
16700 Roscoe Associates LLC....................................818 989-2300
  16700 Roscoe Blvd Van Nuys (91406) **(G-18840)**
1755 Efm 1 LLC...323 231-4174
  1755 E M L King Jr Blvd Los Angeles (90058) **(G-11267)**
1800-R-Ado, Los Angeles Also called Wilshire Consumer Credit **(G-9767)**
180la LLC...310 382-1400
  1733 Ocean Ave Ste 400 Santa Monica (90401) **(G-13807)**
1835 Columbia Street LP..619 564-3993
  1835 Columbia St San Diego (92101) **(G-12360)**
19 Entertainment Worldwide LLC..................................310 777-1940
  8560 W Sunset Blvd Fl 8 West Hollywood (90069) **(G-18447)**

19 Management, West Hollywood Also called 19 Entertainment Worldwide LLC **(G-18447)**
1906 Lodge, Coronado Also called Four Sisters Inns **(G-12650)**
1k Studios, Burbank Also called One K Studios LLC **(G-14157)**
1life Healthcare Inc...415 644-5265
  130 Sutter St Fl 2 San Francisco (94104) **(G-22869)**
1st American Financial, Fremont Also called First American Financial Corp **(G-27436)**
1st Century Bancshares Inc..310 270-9500
  1875 Century Park E # 1400 Los Angeles (90067) **(G-9467)**
1st Class Laundry Services, Union City Also called Specialized Laundry Svcs Inc **(G-13657)**
1st Interstate Bank Building, Oakland Also called San Francisco Bay Area Rapid **(G-3700)**
1st Light Energy Inc (PA)..209 824-5500
  1869 Moffat Blvd Manteca (95336) **(G-3483)**
1st Team Real Estate, Tustin Also called First Team RE - Orange Cnty **(G-11537)**
1st United Services Credit Un (PA)..............................800 649-0193
  5901 Gibraltar Dr Pleasanton (94588) **(G-9649)**
2 G Fitness LLC...925 838-9200
  730 Camino Ramon Ste 200 Danville (94526) **(G-18577)**
20/20 Plumbing & Heating Inc.....................................951 396-2020
  7343 Orangewood Dr Ste B Riverside (92504) **(G-2098)**
20/20 Recycle Centers, Redlands Also called Contain-A-Way Inc **(G-6467)**
2100 Trust LLC (PA)..877 469-7344
  625 N Grand Ave Santa Ana (92701) **(G-12167)**
211 La County, San Gabriel Also called Information & Referral Fed Los **(G-13768)**
21st Century Health Club (PA).....................................707 795-0400
  680a E Cotati Ave Cotati (94931) **(G-22647)**
21st Century Insurance Company (HQ)........................877 310-5687
  6301 Owensmouth Ave Woodland Hills (91367) **(G-10575)**
21st Century Insurance Company.................................858 637-9070
  9325 Sky Park Ct Ste 100 San Diego (92123) **(G-10576)**
21st Century Lf & Hlth Co Inc (PA)..............................818 887-4436
  21600 Oxnard St Ste 1500 Woodland Hills (91367) **(G-10230)**
21st Century Super Stars., Rcho STA Marg Also called C-21 Super Stars **(G-11336)**
2300 West El Secundo LP...310 769-6669
  11916 Eucalyptus Ave Hawthorne (90250) **(G-11268)**
24 Hour Fitness Usa Inc...916 984-1924
  1006 Riley St Folsom (95630) **(G-18578)**
24 Hour Fitness Usa Inc...707 536-0048
  6345 Commerce Blvd Rohnert Park (94928) **(G-22870)**
24 Hour Fitness Usa Inc...510 795-6666
  39300 Paseo Padre Pkwy Fremont (94538) **(G-18579)**
24 Hour Fitness Usa Inc...818 531-0257
  1903 W Empire Ave Burbank (91504) **(G-22871)**
24 Hour Fitness Usa Inc...949 610-0651
  1870 Harbor Blvd Ste 124 Costa Mesa (92627) **(G-22872)**
24 Hour Fitness Usa Inc...760 602-5001
  1265 Laurel Tree Ln # 100 Carlsbad (92011) **(G-18580)**
24 Hour Fitness Usa Inc...714 525-9924
  1430 N Lemon St Anaheim (92801) **(G-18581)**
24 Hour Fitness Usa Inc...619 425-6600
  1660 Broadway Ste 19 Chula Vista (91911) **(G-18582)**
24 Hour Fitness Usa Inc (HQ).....................................925 543-3100
  12647 Alcosta Blvd # 500 San Ramon (94583) **(G-18583)**
24 Hour Fitness Usa Inc...310 553-7600
  9911 W Pico Blvd Ste A Los Angeles (90035) **(G-18584)**
24 Hour Fitness Usa Inc...626 795-7121
  525 E Colorado Blvd Bsmt Pasadena (91101) **(G-18585)**
24 Hour Fitness Usa Inc...909 944-1000
  11787 Foothill Blvd Rancho Cucamonga (91730) **(G-18586)**
24 Hour Fitness Usa Inc...310 652-7440
  8612 Santa Monica Blvd West Hollywood (90069) **(G-18587)**
24 Hour Fitness Usa Inc...949 650-3600
  555 W 19th St Costa Mesa (92627) **(G-18588)**
24 Hour Fitness Usa Inc...916 722-7588
  12647 Alcosta Blvd # 500 San Ramon (94583) **(G-18589)**
24 Hour Fitness Usa Inc...818 247-4334
  450 N Brand Blvd Ste 100 Glendale (91203) **(G-18590)**
24 Hour Fitness Usa Inc...310 450-4464
  2929 31st St Santa Monica (90405) **(G-18591)**
24 Hour Fitness Usa Inc...949 830-4213
  26781 Rancho Pkwy Lake Forest (92630) **(G-18592)**
24 Hour Fitness Usa Inc...650 343-7922
  500 El Camino Real Burlingame (94010) **(G-18593)**
24 Hour Fitness Usa Inc...619 294-2424
  1640 Camino Del Rio N # 315 San Diego (92108) **(G-18594)**

24 Hour Fitness Usa Inc 818 887-2582
6653 Fallbrook Ave Canoga Park (91307) ***(G-18595)***
24 Hour Fitness Usa Inc 562 943-3771
10125 Whittwood Dr Whittier (90603) ***(G-18596)***
24 Hour Fitness Usa Inc 925 930-7900
2033 N Main St Ste 110 Walnut Creek (94596) ***(G-18597)***
24 Hour Fitness Usa Inc 650 941-2268
550 Showers Dr Ste 1 Mountain View (94040) ***(G-18598)***
24 Hour Fitness Usa Inc 858 538-4400
10025 Carmel Mountain Rd San Diego (92129) ***(G-18599)***
24 Hour Fitness Usa Inc 510 264-3275
24727 Amador St Hayward (94544) ***(G-18600)***
24 Hour Fitness Worldwide Inc (PA) 925 543-3100
12647 Alcosta Blvd # 500 San Ramon (94583) ***(G-18601)***
24 Hour Fitness Worldwide Inc 310 374-4524
1601 Pcf Cast Hwy Ste 100 Hermosa Beach (90254) ***(G-18602)***
24 Hour In Motion Fitness, Chico *Also called B A M I Inc* ***(G-18605)***
24-Hour Med Staffing Svcs LLC 909 895-8960
21700 Copley Dr Ste 270 Diamond Bar (91765) ***(G-14827)***
24/7 Customer Inc (PA) 650 385-2247
910 E Hamilton Ave # 240 Campbell (95008) ***(G-16310)***
24hr Homecare LLC 310 906-3683
300 N Sepulveda Blvd # 1065 El Segundo (90245) ***(G-24537)***
29 Palms Enterprises Corp 760 775-5566
46200 Harrison Pl Coachella (92236) ***(G-19129)***
2h Construction Inc 562 490-2897
2653 Walnut Ave Signal Hill (90755) ***(G-1394)***
2nd Floor Main Street Concepts 714 969-9000
126 Main St Ste 201 Huntington Beach (92648) ***(G-11077)***
2wire Inc (HQ) 678 473-2907
1764 Automation Pkwy San Jose (95131) ***(G-5438)***
3-Way Air Charter, Santa Clara *Also called Three Way Inc* ***(G-4380)***
3-Way Farms (PA) 831 722-0748
428 Browns Valley Rd Watsonville (95076) ***(G-263)***
3067 Orange Avenue LLC 714 827-2440
3067 W Orange Ave Anaheim (92804) ***(G-20365)***
30th Cpts-Financial Management, Lompoc *Also called Air Force US Dept of* ***(G-26913)***
314e Corporation 510 371-6736
47102 Mission Falls Ct # 219 Fremont (94539) ***(G-14988)***
32nd District-Orange Cnty Fair, Costa Mesa *Also called Food & Agriculture Cal Dept* ***(G-19215)***
3900 West Lane Bowl Inc 209 466-6100
3900 West Ln Stockton (95204) ***(G-18506)***
3ality Digital LLC (PA) 818 759-5551
55 E Orange Grove Ave Burbank (91502) ***(G-18035)***
3ality Technica, Burbank *Also called 3ality Digital LLC* ***(G-18035)***
3dna Corp 213 394-4623
520 S Grand Ave Fl 2 Los Angeles (90071) ***(G-14989)***
3k Technologies LLC 408 716-5900
1114 Cadillac Ct Milpitas (95035) ***(G-15889)***
3M Cogent Inc (HQ) 626 325-9600
639 N Rosemead Blvd Pasadena (91107) ***(G-15890)***
3M Company 909 974-3004
5151 E Philadelphia St Ontario (91761) ***(G-4512)***
3m/Pharmaceuticals 818 341-1300
19901 Nordhoff St Northridge (91324) ***(G-2801)***
3share Acquisition Inc 888 505-1625
1902 Wright Pl Carlsbad (92008) ***(G-14990)***
3vr Security Inc 415 513-4577
814 Mission St Fl 4 San Francisco (94103) ***(G-16858)***
4 C'S, Santa Rosa *Also called Community Chld Cre Cncl Sonoma* ***(G-24445)***
4 CS Council 408 487-0747
2515 N 1st St San Jose (95131) ***(G-24408)***
4 Seasons Roofing 530 865-4998
11 Commerce Ct Ste 1 Chico (95928) ***(G-3135)***
4 Su Salud Medical Contact Ctr, Lodi *Also called J Rivera Associates Inc* ***(G-28138)***
4 Wheel Parts Performance Ctrs, Compton *Also called Tap Worldwide LLC* ***(G-6776)***
40 Hours Staffing, San Jose *Also called 40 Hrs Inc* ***(G-14593)***
40 Hrs Inc 408 414-0158
1669 Flanigan Dr San Jose (95121) ***(G-14593)***
425 North Point Street LLC 800 648-4626
101 California St Ste 950 San Francisco (94111) ***(G-12361)***
4290 El Camino Properties LP 650 857-0787
4290 El Camino Real Palo Alto (94306) ***(G-12362)***
42nd Street Moon 415 255-8207
601 Van Ness Ave San Francisco (94102) ***(G-18448)***
48123 CA Investors LLC 831 667-2331
48123 Highway 1 Big Sur (93920) ***(G-12363)***
495 Geary LLC 415 775-4700
495 Geary St San Francisco (94102) ***(G-12364)***
4d Inc 408 557-4600
95 S Market St Ste 240 San Jose (95113) ***(G-14991)***
4g Wireless Inc 562 928-2972
7220 Eastern Ave Bell (90201) ***(G-5439)***
4g Wireless Inc 925 307-8990
4620 Tassajara Rd Dublin (94568) ***(G-5440)***
4g Wireless Inc 310 429-9048
8342 Lincoln Blvd Los Angeles (90045) ***(G-5441)***
4g Wireless Inc 323 679-9991
4925 Eagle Rock Blvd Los Angeles (90041) ***(G-5442)***
4g Wireless Inc 760 705-7133
501 W Felicita Ave # 104 Escondido (92025) ***(G-5443)***
4g Wireless Inc 760 828-2543
2635 Gateway Rd Ste 103 Carlsbad (92009) ***(G-5444)***
4g Wireless Inc 951 210-7980
2560 N Perris Blvd Ste G8 Perris (92571) ***(G-5445)***
4g Wireless Inc 310 376-2299
407 N Pacific Coast Hwy # 101 Redondo Beach (90277) ***(G-5446)***
4g Wireless Inc 562 432-7744
285 E 5th St Long Beach (90802) ***(G-5447)***
4g Wireless Inc (PA) 949 748-6100
8871 Research Dr Irvine (92618) ***(G-5252)***
4g Wireless Inc 310 310-7998
8590 W Sunset Blvd 9.1 West Hollywood (90069) ***(G-5448)***
4inkjets.com, Long Beach *Also called Ld Products Inc* ***(G-7154)***
5 Acrs-The Bys Grls Aid Soc La 626 798-6793
760 Mountain View St Altadena (91001) ***(G-24538)***
5 Day Business Forms Mfg Inc 714 632-8674
2921 E La Cresta Ave Anaheim (92806) ***(G-8157)***
5 Design Inc 323 308-3558
1024 N Orange Dr Ste 215 Los Angeles (90038) ***(G-26158)***
5 Diamond Protection Inc 949 466-1367
2901 W Macarthur Blvd Santa Ana (92704) ***(G-10951)***
5 Nine Group Inc 805 880-2948
1125 Lindero Canyon Rd Westlake Village (91362) ***(G-14992)***
5 Star Pool Plaster Inc 209 599-3111
7275 National Dr Ste A Livermore (94550) ***(G-1395)***
51 Minds Entertainment LLC 323 466-9200
5200 Lankershim Blvd # 200 North Hollywood (91601) ***(G-18449)***
51st St & 8th Ave Corp 619 424-4000
4000 Coronado Bay Rd Coronado (92118) ***(G-12365)***
525 Studios Inc 310 525-1234
1632 5th St Santa Monica (90401) ***(G-18210)***
550 Flower St Operations LLC 213 892-8080
550 S Flower St Los Angeles (90071) ***(G-12366)***
5design, Los Angeles *Also called 5 Design Inc* ***(G-26158)***
5th & Sunset Productions, Los Angeles *Also called Fifth & Sunset Enterprises LLC* ***(G-14541)***
5th Avenue Partners LLC 619 515-3000
1047 5th Ave San Diego (92101) ***(G-12367)***
600b Ag-Lo Owner L P 619 234-7036
600 B St Ste 2480 San Diego (92101) ***(G-11269)***
61st Communication Squadron, El Segundo *Also called US Dept of the Air Force* ***(G-16072)***
6th & Island Investments 619 236-0624
454 6th Ave San Diego (92101) ***(G-10110)***
7 Diamonds Clothing, Tustin *Also called M & S Trading Inc* ***(G-8352)***
7 Layers Inc 949 716-6512
15 Musick Irvine (92618) ***(G-25604)***
711 Hope LP 213 488-3500
711 S Hope St Los Angeles (90017) ***(G-12368)***
72andsunny LLC 310 215-9009
12101 Bluff Creek Dr Playa Vista (90094) ***(G-13808)***
7410 Woodman Avenue LLC 805 496-4336
22837 Ventura Blvd # 201 Woodland Hills (91364) ***(G-11078)***
76, San Diego *Also called Cosco Fire Protection Inc* ***(G-17097)***
7days Inc 424 255-5872
3503 Jack Northrop Ave Hawthorne (90250) ***(G-7514)***
7th Avenue Center LLC 831 476-1700
1171 7th Ave Santa Cruz (95062) ***(G-22036)***
7th Standard Ranch Company 661 399-0416
33374 Lerdo Hwy Bakersfield (93308) ***(G-139)***
800 Degrees LLC 310 443-1911
10889 Lindbrook Dr Los Angeles (90024) ***(G-26903)***
8020 Consulting LLC 818 523-3201
6303 Owensmouth Ave Fl 10 Woodland Hills (91367) ***(G-27804)***
8110 Aero Holding LLC 858 277-8888
8110 Aero Dr San Diego (92123) ***(G-12369)***
834 W Arrow Highway LP 213 355-1024
4032 Wilshire Blvd # 600 Los Angeles (90010) ***(G-21065)***
8520 Western Ave Inc 714 828-8222
10811 Kiowa Rd Apt 2a Apple Valley (92308) ***(G-21120)***
8x8 Inc (PA) 408 727-1885
2125 Onel Dr San Jose (95131) ***(G-5449)***
901 West Olympic Blvd LP 347 992-5707
901 W Olympic Blvd Los Angeles (90015) ***(G-12370)***
95cs/Scxc Comp, Edwards *Also called US Dept of the Air Force* ***(G-6097)***
989 Studios, San Diego *Also called Sony Intrctive Entrtmt Amer LLC* ***(G-8054)***
9th Medical Group, Marysville *Also called US Dept of the Air Force* ***(G-22006)***
A & A Home Care Services 760 416-6769
7756 Cntry Clb Dr Bldg A Palm Springs (92263) ***(G-22314)***
A & A Mechanical Contractors 408 225-1321
2943 Daylight Way San Jose (95111) ***(G-2099)***
A & A Plastering Co Inc 559 439-2500
3787 W Bullard Ave Fresno (93711) ***(G-2843)***
A & C Convatescent Hospital, Millbrae *Also called A & C Health Care Services Inc* ***(G-19314)***
A & C Health Care Services Inc 650 689-5784
33 Mateo Ave Millbrae (94030) ***(G-19314)***
A & D Fire Protection Inc 619 258-7697
11465 Woodside Ave Fl 1 Santee (92071) ***(G-2100)***
A & D General Contracting, Santee *Also called A & D Fire Protection Inc* ***(G-2100)***
A & D Hauling Services Inc 310 514-8969
13337 South St Cerritos (90703) ***(G-3964)***
A & G Grove Service 760 728-5447
32731 Mesa Lilac Rd Escondido (92026) ***(G-488)***
A & H Communications Inc 949 250-4555
1791 Reynolds Ave Irvine (92614) ***(G-1900)***
A & I Color Laboratory, Burbank *Also called Jake Hey Incorporated* ***(G-16953)***
A & M Gyms LLC 916 788-4241
5110 Foothills Blvd Roseville (95747) ***(G-18603)***
A & P Towing-Metropro Rd Svcs, Santa Ana *Also called Metropro Road Services Inc* ***(G-17887)***
A & R Electric, Fullerton *Also called Swinford Electric Inc* ***(G-2762)***
A & R Wholesale Distrs Inc 714 777-7742
1765 W Penhall Way Anaheim (92801) ***(G-8608)***
A & S Technologies, Northridge *Also called Ikano Communications Inc* ***(G-16145)***

ALPHABETIC SECTION A.M. Ortega Construction, Corona

A & W Maintenance ... 310 619-8694
7573 Cibola Trl Yucca Valley (92284) *(G-1118)*
A A A Automobile Club So Cal, Los Angeles *Also called Automobile Club Southern Cal (G-10635)*
A A A Automobile Club So Cal, Laguna Hills *Also called Automobile Club Southern Cal (G-25502)*
A A A Five Star Adventures ... 760 320-1500
611 S Palm Canyon Dr Palm Springs (92264) *(G-18841)*
A A A Furnace AC Co ... 408 293-4717
1712 Stone Ave Ste 1 San Jose (95125) *(G-2101)*
A A A Furnace Company, San Jose *Also called Rando AAA Hvac Inc (G-2339)*
A A A Packing and Shipping Inc ... 626 310-7787
806 W 47th St Los Angeles (90037) *(G-3965)*
A A Gonzalez Inc ... 818 367-2242
13264 Ralston Ave Sylmar (91342) *(G-2844)*
A A U C, Los Angeles *Also called African American Unity Center (G-23645)*
A B C D Associates ... 916 363-4843
10410 Coloma Rd Rancho Cordova (95670) *(G-20366)*
A B M, Irvine *Also called ABM Facility Services LLC (G-25609)*
A B S Auto Auctions, Colton *Also called Auto Buyline Systems Inc (G-17011)*
A Better Life Together, Spring Valley *Also called Kim Wilson (G-22493)*
A Better Solution In Home Care ... 619 447-1528
1409 N 2nd St El Cajon (92021) *(G-22315)*
A C D, Newark *Also called Advanced Cell Diagnostics Inc (G-26462)*
A C F, Covina *Also called Acf Components & Fasteners Inc (G-7665)*
A C Freight Systems Inc (PA) ... 408 392-8900
850 Service St San Jose (95112) *(G-4096)*
A C I Communications, Calabasas *Also called Able Cable Inc (G-17928)*
A C M, Santa Ana *Also called Advanced Clnroom McRclean Corp (G-14215)*
A C N, City of Industry *Also called America Chung Nam LLC (G-8060)*
A C Rentals LLC ... 858 271-8571
8540 Production Ave Ste A San Diego (92121) *(G-2102)*
A C S Security, Los Angeles *Also called ACS Security Industries Inc (G-16859)*
A C T Box Office, San Francisco *Also called American Conservatory (G-18369)*
A C T S, Bloomington *Also called Acts For Children (G-24540)*
A Caos Medical Corporation ... 800 362-2731
2655 Camino Del R Ste 330 San Diego (92108) *(G-22316)*
A Caregiver LLC ... 951 676-4190
31520 Rr Cyn Rd Ste A Canyon Lake (92587) *(G-22317)*
A Coach USA Company, Sacramento *Also called All West Coachlines Inc (G-3897)*
A Colmenero Plastering Inc ... 559 435-3606
1710 W San Madele Ave Fresno (93711) *(G-2845)*
A Comcast, Modesto *Also called Comcast Corporation (G-5955)*
A Community For Peace ... 916 728-5613
6060 Sunrise Vista Dr Citrus Heights (95610) *(G-24860)*
A Community of Friends ... 213 480-0809
3701 Wilshire Blvd # 700 Los Angeles (90010) *(G-11079)*
A Complete Drywall Co, San Rafael *Also called Michael B Mayock Inc (G-2932)*
A Csg-Nova Joint Venture ... 916 371-7303
3960 Industrial Blvd # 500 West Sacramento (95691) *(G-1722)*
A D Bilich Inc ... 925 820-5557
11 Crow Canyon Ct Ste 100 San Ramon (94583) *(G-9809)*
A D G, San Diego *Also called Affinity Development Group Inc (G-25484)*
A D S, Los Angeles *Also called Advanced Digital Services Inc (G-18038)*
A Development Stage Company, San Francisco *Also called Brience Inc (G-15064)*
A Dti Company, Dublin *Also called Micro Dental Laboratories (G-22311)*
A E W/Careage Ops, Bakersfield *Also called Glenwood Gardens (G-20601)*
A F Evans Company Inc ... 925 937-1700
1700 Tice Valley Blvd Ofc Walnut Creek (94595) *(G-16960)*
A F Gilmore Company ... 323 939-1191
6301 W 3rd St Los Angeles (90036) *(G-11270)*
A F V W Health Center ... 951 697-2025
17050 Arnold Dr Ofc Riverside (92518) *(G-20367)*
A Filml Inc ... 213 977-8600
6255 W Sunset Blvd Fl 12 Los Angeles (90028) *(G-18211)*
A G A, Fremont *Also called Homelegance Inc (G-6818)*
A G Hacienda Incorporated ... 661 792-2418
32794 Sherwood Ave Mc Farland (93250) *(G-3966)*
A G Paceman Inc ... 650 592-7282
1100 Industrial Rd Ste 11 San Carlos (94070) *(G-11247)*
A G Spanos Management Inc ... 209 478-7954
10100 Trinity Pkwy Fl 5 Stockton (95219) *(G-11271)*
A Growing Concern Landscapes ... 714 843-5137
17382 Gothard St Huntington Beach (92647) *(G-736)*
A I H, Glendale *Also called Access Integrated Healthcare (G-21124)*
A I S-Auto Insur Specialists, Long Beach *Also called Auto Insur Spcialists-Long Bch (G-10634)*
A I T Development Corp ... 818 407-5533
21021 Devonshire St # 102 Chatsworth (91311) *(G-1119)*
A Is For Apple Inc ... 877 991-0009
1485 Saratoga Ave Ste 200 San Jose (95129) *(G-20303)*
A J Esprit ... 619 223-8171
5102 N Harbor Dr San Diego (92106) *(G-12371)*
A J Parent Company Inc (PA) ... 714 521-1100
6910 Aragon Cir Ste 6 Buena Park (90620) *(G-16961)*
A J R Trucking Inc ... 562 989-9555
915 Monterey Rd Glendale (91206) *(G-3967)*
A K P LLP ... 760 746-1560
312 S Juniper St Ste 100 Escondido (92025) *(G-26284)*
A L Gilbert Company ... 209 537-0766
4431 Jessup Rd Keyes (95328) *(G-8959)*
A L S Industries Inc (PA) ... 310 532-9262
1942 Artesia Blvd Torrance (90504) *(G-8035)*
A Lighting By Design, Anaheim *Also called Albd Electric and Cable (G-2513)*
A M I Encn-Trzana Rgnal Med Ce, Tarzana *Also called AMI-Hti Tarzana Encino Joint V (G-21449)*
A M Ortega Construction Inc ... 951 360-1352
58 Kellogg St Ventura (93001) *(G-1120)*
A M Ortega Construction Inc (PA) ... 619 390-1988
10125 Channel Rd Lakeside (92040) *(G-2505)*
A M Ortega Construction Inc ... 951 360-1352
224 N Sherman Ave Corona (92882) *(G-2506)*
A M R, Irwindale *Also called American Med (G-3743)*
A M S Partnership (PA) ... 310 312-6698
1517 S Sepulveda Blvd Los Angeles (90025) *(G-11944)*
A Meissners Hhld & Indus Svc ... 916 920-2121
2417 Cormorant Way Sacramento (95815) *(G-7816)*
A O Reed & Co ... 858 565-4131
4777 Ruffner St San Diego (92111) *(G-2103)*
A P Express Worldwide, Pico Rivera *Also called AP Express LLC (G-5027)*
A P H Technological Consulting ... 626 796-0331
2500 E Colo Blvd Ste 300 Pasadena (91107) *(G-25605)*
A P R Inc ... 805 379-3400
100 E Thsnd Oaks Blvd Ste 240 Thousand Oaks (91360) *(G-14828)*
A Professional, San Luis Obispo *Also called Glenn Burdette Phillips Bryson (G-26354)*
A R C Fastener Supply, Corona *Also called ARC Fastener Supply & Mfg (G-7914)*
A R Wilson Quarry & Asp Plant, Aromas *Also called Granite Rock Co (G-6987)*
A Ruiz Cnstr Co & Assoc Inc ... 415 647-4010
1601 Cortland Ave San Francisco (94110) *(G-1480)*
A S A P Professional Services ... 800 303-2727
2440 Camino Ramon Ste 313 San Ramon (94583) *(G-14594)*
A S E C International Inc ... 803 939-4809
11400 W Olympic Blvd Los Angeles (90064) *(G-16087)*
A S I, Long Beach *Also called Associated Students California (G-25201)*
A S I, Fremont *Also called Asi Computer Technologies Inc (G-7094)*
A S I Corporation ... 714 526-5533
1308 N Patt St Anaheim (92801) *(G-13809)*
A S S U, Stanford *Also called Associated Students Stanford (G-25202)*
A Smwm California Corporation ... 415 546-0400
185 Berry St Ste 5100 San Francisco (94107) *(G-26159)*
A Sutton Carlos ... 310 286-0010
9903 Santa Monica Blvd Beverly Hills (90212) *(G-16534)*
A T Associates Inc ... 510 649-6670
2223 Ashby Ave Berkeley (94705) *(G-21121)*
A T Associates Inc ... 510 261-8564
2919 Fruitvale Ave Oakland (94602) *(G-21122)*
A T Associates Inc (PA) ... 925 808-6540
535 School St Pittsburg (94565) *(G-21123)*
A T Kearney Inc ... 415 490-4000
555 Mission St Ste 1800 San Francisco (94105) *(G-27289)*
A T S, Los Angeles *Also called Authorized Taxi Cab (G-16869)*
A Taxi Cab, Santa Ana *Also called A White and Yellow Cab Inc (G-3861)*
A Teichert & Son Inc (HQ) ... 916 484-3011
3500 American River Dr Sacramento (95864) *(G-6971)*
A Tool Shed Equipment Rentals, Santa Cruz *Also called (a) Tool Shed Inc (G-14503)*
A Touch of Kindness ... 323 997-6500
353 1/2 N La Brea Ave Los Angeles (90036) *(G-23639)*
A Ursgi-Bmdc Joint Venture ... 858 812-9292
4225 Executive Sq # 1600 La Jolla (92037) *(G-25606)*
A V Nursing Care Center, Lancaster *Also called Antelope Vly Retirement HM Inc (G-21141)*
A W Properties West LLC ... 858 832-1462
16236 San Dieguito Rd # 310 Rancho Santa Fe (92091) *(G-1121)*
A White and Yellow Cab Inc ... 714 258-1000
2406 S Main St Santa Ana (92707) *(G-3861)*
A World Fit For Kids ... 213 387-7712
678 S La Fayette Park Pl Los Angeles (90057) *(G-27290)*
A Yafa Pen Company ... 818 704-8888
21306 Gault St Canoga Park (91303) *(G-8158)*
A&E Television Networks LLC ... 310 201-6015
2049 Century Park E # 800 Los Angeles (90067) *(G-5932)*
A&S Floors, Benicia *Also called Anthony Trevino (G-3105)*
A-1 Delivery Co ... 909 444-1220
19805 Business Pkwy Walnut (91789) *(G-3968)*
A-1 Electric Service Co Inc ... 310 204-1077
4204 Sepulveda Blvd Culver City (90230) *(G-2507)*
A-1 Elite Painting Inc ... 760 365-6702
56409 Yuma Trl Yucca Valley (92284) *(G-2425)*
A-1 Event & Party Rentals ... 626 967-0500
251 E Front St Covina (91723) *(G-13729)*
A-1 Party Rentals, Covina *Also called Cwf Inc (G-14534)*
A-1 Pomona Linen, Paramount *Also called Braun Linen Service Inc (G-13539)*
A-Able Inc (PA) ... 323 658-5779
17801 Ventura Blvd Encino (91316) *(G-14170)*
A-C Electric Company ... 661 633-5368
315 30th St Bakersfield (93301) *(G-25607)*
A-Check America Inc (PA) ... 951 750-1501
1501 Research Park Dr Riverside (92507) *(G-14053)*
A-Check America Inc ... 800 872-2677
1501 Research Park Dr Riverside (92507) *(G-14054)*
A-Check America, Member Act 1, Riverside *Also called A-Check America Inc (G-14053)*
A-One Greeting Card Service, Costa Mesa *Also called Frank Gustafson (G-9265)*
A-Para Transit Corp ... 510 732-9400
1400 Doolittle Dr San Leandro (94577) *(G-3738)*
A-Star Staffing Inc ... 619 574-7600
2835 Camino Del Rio S # 220 San Diego (92108) *(G-14595)*
A-Throne Co Inc ... 562 981-1197
1850 E 33rd St Long Beach (90807) *(G-14504)*
A-Z Bus Sales Inc (PA) ... 951 781-7188
1900 S Riverside Ave Colton (92324) *(G-6657)*
A.M. Ortega Construction, Corona *Also called A M Ortega Construction Inc (G-2506)*

ALPHABETIC

A1 Building Management Inc   ALPHABETIC SECTION

A1 Building Management Inc 714 447-3800
  2461 E Orangethorpe Ave # 200 Fullerton (92831) *(G-14198)*
A1 Event & Party Rentals, Covina *Also called A-1 Event & Party Rentals* *(G-13729)*
A1 Protective Services Inc 916 421-3000
  7000 Franklin Blvd # 665 Sacramento (95823) *(G-16535)*
A10 Networks Inc (PA) 408 325-8668
  3 W Plumeria Dr San Jose (95134) *(G-15891)*
AA Autmtive Personnel Svcs Inc 310 914-3012
  2251 Federal Ave Los Angeles (90064) *(G-17868)*
Aa/Acme Locksmiths Inc 510 483-6584
  1660 Factor Ave San Leandro (94577) *(G-2508)*
AAA, Oakland *Also called American Automobile Assctn* *(G-25489)*
AAA, Encino *Also called Automobile Club Southern Cal* *(G-25494)*
AAA, Torrance *Also called Automobile Club Southern Cal* *(G-25495)*
AAA, Ventura *Also called Automobile Club Southern Cal* *(G-25496)*
AAA, Glendora *Also called Automobile Club Southern Cal* *(G-25497)*
AAA, Bakersfield *Also called Automobile Club Southern Cal* *(G-25498)*
AAA, Northridge *Also called Automobile Club Southern Cal* *(G-25499)*
AAA, Woodland Hills *Also called Automobile Club Southern Cal* *(G-25500)*
AAA, Capitola *Also called CA Ste Atom Assoc Intr-Ins Bur* *(G-17877)*
AAA, San Mateo *Also called CA Ste Atom Assoc Intr-Ins Bur* *(G-10404)*
AAA, Mountain View *Also called CA Ste Atom Assoc Intr-Ins Bur* *(G-10653)*
AAA, Costa Mesa *Also called Automobile Club Southern Cal* *(G-17784)*
AAA, La Mesa *Also called Automobile Club Southern Cal* *(G-25503)*
AAA Accounting Services 949 791-7368
  2 Enterprise Apt 1211 Aliso Viejo (92656) *(G-26285)*
AAA Drain Patrol 916 348-3098
  3437 Myrtle Ave Ste 440 North Highlands (95660) *(G-2104)*
AAA Elctrcal Cmmunications Inc (PA) 800 892-4784
  25007 Anza Dr Valencia (91355) *(G-2509)*
AAA Fire Protection Service, Union City *Also called AAA Restaurant Fire Ctrl Inc* *(G-16962)*
AAA Northern Cal Nev & Utah 510 596-3669
  1900 Powell St Ste 1200 Emeryville (94608) *(G-10393)*
AAA Property Services, Valencia *Also called AAA Elctrcal Cmmunications Inc* *(G-2509)*
AAA Restaurant Fire Ctrl Inc 510 786-9555
  30113 Union City Blvd Union City (94587) *(G-16962)*
AAA Restoration Inc 951 471-5828
  29850 2nd St Lake Elsinore (92532) *(G-3484)*
AAA Signs Inc 916 568-3456
  2020 Railroad Dr Sacramento (95815) *(G-17779)*
AAA Travel 650 572-5600
  1650 S Delaware St San Mateo (94402) *(G-10394)*
AAA Yellow Cab, San Mateo *Also called Yellow A Cab* *(G-3872)*
AAAA Investors, Orinda *Also called Mason-Mcduffie Real Estate Inc* *(G-11662)*
Aaaaa Rent-A-Space, Castro Valley *Also called Ras Management Inc* *(G-4628)*
Aaaza Inc 213 380-8333
  3250 Wilshire Blvd # 1901 Los Angeles (90010) *(G-13810)*
Aab Water Company Inc 559 497-2700
  226 S Avenue 54 Los Angeles (90042) *(G-6309)*
Aadlen Brothers Auto Wrecking (PA) 323 875-1400
  11590 Tuxford St Sun Valley (91352) *(G-8057)*
Aah Hudson LP 626 794-9179
  1255 N Hudson Ave Pasadena (91104) *(G-11080)*
Aall Care In Home Services, San Diego *Also called Faith Jones & Associates Inc* *(G-22436)*
AAM, Anaheim *Also called Anaheim Arena Management LLC* *(G-18534)*
Aamcom LLC 310 318-8100
  800 N Pacific Coast Hwy Redondo Beach (90277) *(G-5450)*
AAR Defense Systems Logistics, San Diego *Also called AAR Parts Trading Inc* *(G-4513)*
AAR Manufacturing Inc 916 830-7011
  5307 Luce Ave Bldg 243e McClellan (95652) *(G-17926)*
AAR Manufacturing Inc 800 422-2213
  5239 Luce Ave Bldg 243d McClellan (95652) *(G-17927)*
AAR Parts Trading Inc 858 627-6029
  4400 Ruffin Rd San Diego (92123) *(G-4513)*
Aardex Inc 805 928-7600
  1550 E Main St Santa Maria (93454) *(G-1481)*
Aardvark Staffing Inc 916 774-7115
  3017 Douglas Blvd Fl 3 Roseville (95661) *(G-14829)*
Aaron Dowling Incorporated 559 432-4500
  8080 N Palm Ave Ste 300 Fresno (93711) *(G-23079)*
Aaron Thomas Company Inc (PA) 714 894-4468
  7421 Chapman Ave Garden Grove (92841) *(G-16963)*
Aat Kings Tours USA Inc 714 456-0505
  801 E Katella Ave Fl 3 Anaheim (92805) *(G-4983)*
Aat Sorrento Pointe LLC 858 350-2600
  11455 El Camino Real San Diego (92130) *(G-12232)*
Aat Torrey Reserve 6 LLC 858 350-2600
  11455 El Cmino Real Ste 2 San Diego (92130) *(G-10952)*
Aatcaa Headstart, Sonora *Also called Amador Tlmne Cmnty Action Agcy* *(G-24865)*
Aauw Action Fund Inc 650 574-9160
  P.O. Box 1239 San Mateo (94401) *(G-25482)*
AB Cellular Holding LLC 562 468-6846
  1452 Edinger Ave Tustin (92780) *(G-5451)*
AB Closing Corporation 707 766-1777
  1304 Southpoint Blvd Petaluma (94954) *(G-14596)*
AB Health Inc 949 464-4300
  9340 Santa Anita Ave # 100 Rancho Cucamonga (91730) *(G-10577)*
Ab/SW 70 S Lake Owner LLC 650 571-2200
  70 S Lake Ave Pasadena (91101) *(G-11248)*
Aba Holdings LLC 858 565-4131
  4777 Ruffner St San Diego (92111) *(G-12046)*
Abacus Business Solutions Inc 408 200-0977
  3333 Bowers Ave Ste 130 Santa Clara (95054) *(G-16311)*
Abacus Service Corporation 916 288-8948
  1725 23rd St Sacramento (95816) *(G-14993)*
Abad Foam Inc 714 994-2223
  6560 Caballero Blvd Buena Park (90620) *(G-9241)*

ABB Enterprise Software Inc 415 527-2850
  60 Spear St San Francisco (94105) *(G-15563)*
Abb/Con-Cise Optical Group LLC 800 852-8089
  1750 N Loop Rd Ste 150 Alameda (94502) *(G-7328)*
Abb/Con-Cise Optical Group LLC 800 852-8089
  1750 N Loop Rd Ste 150 Alameda (94502) *(G-7329)*
Abbey Management Company LLC 562 243-2100
  330 Golden Shore Ste 300 Long Beach (90802) *(G-12047)*
Abbey Partner VI 951 785-8800
  7207 Arlington Ave Ste D Riverside (92503) *(G-11272)*
Abbey-Properties LLC (PA) 562 435-2100
  12447 Lewis St Ste 203 Garden Grove (92840) *(G-10953)*
Abbood Zeyad 619 212-2820
  7914 La Mesa Blvd Apt 6 La Mesa (91942) *(G-25608)*
Abbott Stringham Lynch Acctg 408 377-8700
  1550 Leigh Ave San Jose (95125) *(G-26286)*
Abbyson Living Corp 805 465-5500
  26500 Agoura Rd 102-875 Calabasas (91302) *(G-6798)*
Abbyy USA Software House Inc (PA) 408 457-9777
  880 N Mccarthy Blvd # 220 Milpitas (95035) *(G-14994)*
Abc Inc 818 863-7801
  500 Circle Seven Dr Glendale (91201) *(G-5831)*
ABC 30, Fresno *Also called Kfsn Television LLC* *(G-5880)*
ABC Bus Inc 714 444-5888
  1485 Dale Way Costa Mesa (92626) *(G-6658)*
ABC Bus Inc 650 368-3364
  3508 Haven Ave Redwood City (94063) *(G-6659)*
ABC Cable Networks Group 415 954-7911
  900 Front St San Francisco (94111) *(G-5832)*
ABC Cable Networks Group 818 560-4365
  698 S Buena Vista St Burbank (91521) *(G-18268)*
ABC Cable Networks Group (HQ) 818 460-7477
  500 S Buena Vista St Burbank (91521) *(G-5745)*
ABC Cable Networks Group 323 860-5900
  6834 Hollywood Blvd Los Angeles (90028) *(G-5746)*
ABC Family Worldwide Inc (HQ) 818 560-1000
  500 S Buena Vista St Burbank (91521) *(G-18036)*
ABC School Equipment Inc 951 817-2200
  1451 E 6th St Corona (92879) *(G-7338)*
ABC Security Service Inc 916 442-7001
  3065 Freeport Blvd Sacramento (95818) *(G-16536)*
Abc7 Broadcast Center, San Francisco *Also called Kgo Television Inc* *(G-5882)*
Abco Insulation, Azusa *Also called Oj Insulation LP* *(G-2943)*
Abd Insurance & Fincl Svcs Inc (PA) 650 488-8565
  3 Waters Park Dr Ste 100 San Mateo (94403) *(G-10578)*
Abd Insurance and Fincl Svcs, San Carlos *Also called Wells Fargo Insur Svcs USA Inc* *(G-10932)*
Abe Entercom Holdings LLC 619 291-9797
  1615 Murray Canyon Rd # 710 San Diego (92108) *(G-5747)*
Abe-El Produce 559 528-3030
  42143 Road 120 Orosi (93647) *(G-35)*
Aberdeen Group, The, San Diego *Also called Harte-Hanks Mkt Intelligence* *(G-16139)*
ABF Freight System Inc 408 435-8550
  2135 Otoole Ave San Jose (95131) *(G-4097)*
ABF Freight System Inc 323 773-2580
  8001 Telegraph Rd Pico Rivera (90660) *(G-4098)*
ABF Freight System Inc 510 533-8575
  4575 Tidewater Ave Oakland (94601) *(G-4099)*
ABF Freight System Inc 714 974-2485
  1601 N Batavia St Orange (92867) *(G-4100)*
ABF Freight System Inc 916 428-3531
  3250 47th Ave Sacramento (95824) *(G-4101)*
ABF Freight System Inc 909 355-9805
  10744 Almond Ave Fontana (92337) *(G-4102)*
Abhe & Svoboda Inc 619 659-1320
  880 Tavern Rd Alpine (91901) *(G-1482)*
ABI Attorneys Service Inc (PA) 909 793-0613
  2015 W Park Ave Redlands (92373) *(G-14098)*
ABI Document Support Service, Sacramento *Also called Edco Health Info Solution* *(G-17142)*
ABI Document Support Services, Redlands *Also called Edco Health Info Solution* *(G-17143)*
ABI VIP Attorney Service, Redlands *Also called ABI Attorneys Service Inc* *(G-14098)*
Ability Counts Inc (PA) 951 734-6595
  775 Trademark Cir Ste 101 Corona (92879) *(G-24302)*
Abilityfirst 213 748-7309
  3812 S Grand Ave Los Angeles (90037) *(G-23640)*
Abilty First 562 426-6161
  3770 E Willow St Long Beach (90815) *(G-24539)*
Abingdon Rough Riders Tou 415 566-9796
  1231 12th Ave San Francisco (94122) *(G-25483)*
Abington Homes Inc 619 208-9486
  4364 Bonita Rd Ste 442 Bonita (91902) *(G-11273)*
ABLE, Azusa *Also called California Pediatric Fmly Svcs* *(G-23699)*
Able Building Maintenance, Santa Ana *Also called Crown Building Maintenance Co* *(G-14274)*
Able Building Maintenance, Los Angeles *Also called Crown Building Maintenance Co* *(G-14277)*
Able Cable Inc (PA) 818 223-3600
  5115 Douglas Fir Rd Ste A Calabasas (91302) *(G-17928)*
Able Engineering Services, Los Angeles *Also called Crown Energy Services Inc* *(G-14278)*
Able Exterminators Inc 408 251-6500
  68 N Sunset Ave San Jose (95116) *(G-14171)*
Able Hands Inc 626 965-2233
  18780 Amar Rd Ste 207 Walnut (91789) *(G-22318)*
Able Industries, Visalia *Also called Tulare Cty Trng Ctr Hndcpd* *(G-24397)*
Able Patrol & Guard, San Diego *Also called Locator Services Inc* *(G-16724)*
Ablitt's Fine Cleaners, Santa Barbara *Also called Santa Barbara Fabricare Inc* *(G-13585)*

ALPHABETIC SECTION　　Acco Engineered Systems Inc

ABM Distributors Inc 310 401-0434
811 W 7th St Ste 1040 Los Angeles (90017) *(G-18037)*
ABM Electrical & Ltg Solutions (HQ)....877 546-2937
152 Technology Dr Irvine (92618) *(G-14199)*
ABM Engineering, Oakland *Also called ABM Facility Services Inc (G-14200)*
ABM Facility Services Inc (HQ)....510 251-0381
1266 14th St Ste 103 Oakland (94607) *(G-14200)*
ABM Facility Services LLC (HQ)....949 330-1555
152 Technology Dr Irvine (92618) *(G-25609)*
ABM Industries Incorporated....323 720-4020
5300 S Eastrn Ave Ste 110 Los Angeles (90040) *(G-14201)*
ABM Janitorial Services Inc....213 384-0600
3580 Wilshire Blvd # 1130 Los Angeles (90010) *(G-9956)*
ABM Janitorial Services Inc....559 276-9096
4747 N Bendel Ave Ste 104 Fresno (93722) *(G-14202)*
ABM Janitorial Services Inc....925 924-0270
6671 Owens Dr Pleasanton (94588) *(G-14203)*
ABM Janitorial Services Inc....916 374-1739
830 Riverside Pkwy Ste 40 West Sacramento (95605) *(G-14204)*
ABM Janitorial Services Inc....909 987-3700
11955 Jack Benny Dr # 104 Rancho Cucamonga (91739) *(G-14205)*
ABM Janitorial Services Inc....209 983-3923
2385 Arch Airport Rd # 100 Stockton (95206) *(G-14206)*
ABM Jntrial Svcs - Sthwest Inc....661 322-3280
1400 Easton Dr Ste 149 Bakersfield (93309) *(G-14207)*
ABM Jntrial Svcs - Sthwest Inc....559 276-9096
4747 N Bendel Ave Fresno (93722) *(G-14208)*
ABM Office Solutions Inc....909 527-8145
9550 Hermosa Ave Rancho Cucamonga (91730) *(G-6799)*
ABM Parking Services (PA)....619 235-4500
3585 Corporate Ct San Diego (92123) *(G-17708)*
ABM Securities, Los Angeles *Also called ABM Janitorial Services Inc (G-9956)*
Abode Communities....213 629-2702
1149 S Hill St Fl 7 Los Angeles (90015) *(G-11274)*
Abode Services (PA)....510 657-7409
40849 Fremont Blvd Fremont (94538) *(G-23641)*
Above Hlth HM Care Sltions LLC....714 585-2185
960 S Peregrine Pl Anaheim (92806) *(G-22319)*
Abp Liquidating Corp....650 871-7689
299 Lawrence Ave South San Francisco (94080) *(G-8692)*
Abraham Jsha Hschl Dy Schl Wst....818 707-2365
27400 Canwood St Agoura (91301) *(G-24409)*
Abrams Kazan McClain....510 465-7728
171 12th St Ste 300 Oakland (94607) *(G-23080)*
ABRAZAR ELDERLY ASSISTANCE, Westminster *Also called Abrazar Inc (G-23642)*
Abrazar Inc....714 893-3581
7101 Wyoming St Westminster (92683) *(G-23642)*
ABS Capital Partners III LP....415 617-2800
101 California St Fl 24 San Francisco (94111) *(G-27291)*
ABS Computer Technologies, Whittier *Also called Magnell Associate Inc (G-4595)*
ABS Computer Technologies, City of Industry *Also called Magnell Associate Inc (G-7157)*
ABS Computer Technologies, City of Industry *Also called Magnell Associate Inc (G-7158)*
ABS Consulting Inc....714 734-4242
300 Commerce Ste 200 Irvine (92602) *(G-25610)*
ABS Group, Irvine *Also called ABS Consulting Inc (G-25610)*
ABS HARWARE PURCHASING, Fontana *Also called American Bolt & Screw Mfg Corp (G-7669)*
Abs-American Building Supply, Sacramento *Also called American Building Supply Inc (G-6906)*
ABS-Cbn International (HQ)....800 527-2820
150 Shoreline Dr Redwood City (94065) *(G-5933)*
Absg Consulting Inc....510 508-6289
505 14th St Ste 900 Oakland (94612) *(G-27805)*
Absg Consulting Inc....714 734-4242
300 Commerce Ste 200 Irvine (92602) *(G-27806)*
Abshear Landscape Development....916 660-1617
3171b Rippey Rd Loomis (95650) *(G-737)*
Abso....800 943-2589
101 Creekside Ridge Ct # 2 Roseville (95678) *(G-14597)*
Absolutdata Technologies Inc....510 748-9922
1851 Harbor Bay Pkwy # 125 Alameda (94502) *(G-16964)*
Absolute Exhibits Inc (PA)....714 685-2800
1382 Valencia Ave Ste H Tustin (92780) *(G-16965)*
Absolute Return Portfolio....800 800-7646
700 Newport Center Dr Newport Beach (92660) *(G-12099)*
Absolute Towing-Hollenbeck Div....323 225-9294
4760 Valley Blvd Los Angeles (90032) *(G-17869)*
Absolutelynew Inc....415 865-6200
650 Townsend St Ste 475 San Francisco (94103) *(G-27292)*
Absolutelynew.com, San Francisco *Also called Absolutelynew Inc (G-27292)*
Abtech Support, Carlsbad *Also called Abtech Technologies Inc (G-16312)*
Abtech Technologies Inc....760 827-5100
2042 Corte Del Nogal D Carlsbad (92011) *(G-16312)*
Abx Engineering Inc....650 552-2300
875 Stanton Rd Burlingame (94010) *(G-15892)*
Abzooba Inc....650 453-8760
1551 Mccarthy Blvd # 204 Milpitas (95035) *(G-14995)*
AC Hotel San Jose Downtown, San Jose *Also called Sj Hotel Manager LLC (G-27214)*
AC Square Inc....650 293-2730
4590 Qantas Ln Stockton (95206) *(G-27807)*
AC Transit, Oakland *Also called Alameda-Contra Costa Trnst Dst (G-3634)*
Aca Financial Guaranty Corp....323 255-3583
7189 N Figueroa St Los Angeles (90042) *(G-9909)*
Academy Foundation (HQ)....310 247-3000
8949 Wilshire Blvd Beverly Hills (90211) *(G-18212)*
Academy Mpic Arts & Sciences (PA)....310 247-3000
8949 Wilshire Blvd Beverly Hills (90211) *(G-25112)*
Academy TV Arts & Sciences....818 754-2800
5220 Lankershim Blvd North Hollywood (91601) *(G-25113)*
Acadia Pharmaceuticals Inc (PA)....858 558-2871
3611 Valley Centre Dr # 300 San Diego (92130) *(G-26721)*
ACC....310 558-6100
9599 Jefferson Blvd Culver City (90232) *(G-610)*
ACC-Gwg LLC....530 473-2827
6133 Abel Rd Williams (95987) *(G-27808)*
Accel Biotech LLC....408 354-1700
103 Cooper Ct Los Gatos (95032) *(G-25611)*
Accel North America Inc....408 514-5199
4633 Old Ironsides Dr # 400 Santa Clara (95054) *(G-7080)*
Accel-KKR Company LLC (PA)....650 233-9723
2500 Sand Hill Rd Ste 300 Menlo Park (94025) *(G-14996)*
Accela Inc (PA)....925 659-3200
2633 Camino Ramon Ste 500 San Ramon (94583) *(G-15564)*
Accelerated Envmtl Svcs Inc....661 765-4003
23601 Taft Hwy Bakersfield (93311) *(G-14209)*
Accelon Inc....925 216-5735
2603 Camino Ramon Ste 200 San Ramon (94583) *(G-14598)*
Accent Service Company Inc....714 557-2837
2770 S Harbor Blvd Ste J Santa Ana (92704) *(G-14210)*
Accentcare Inc....707 792-2211
1301 Redwood Way Petaluma (94954) *(G-22320)*
Accentcare Inc....858 576-7410
5050 Mrphy Knyan Rd St200 Ste 200 San Diego (92123) *(G-22321)*
Accentcare HM Hlth Scrmnto Inc....916 852-5888
2880 Sunrise Blvd Ste 218 Rancho Cordova (95742) *(G-22322)*
Accentcare Home Health....760 352-4022
2344 S 2nd St Ste A El Centro (92243) *(G-22323)*
Accentcare Home Health Cal Inc....925 356-6066
2300 Contra Costa Blvd # 125 Pleasant Hill (94523) *(G-22324)*
Accentcare Home Health Cal Inc....818 528-8855
16461 Sherman Way Ste 178 Van Nuys (91406) *(G-22325)*
Accentcare Home Health Cal Inc....909 605-7000
1455 Auto Center Dr # 200 Ontario (91761) *(G-22326)*
Accentcare Home Health Cal Inc....626 568-9478
2549 Huntington Dr San Marino (91108) *(G-22327)*
Accentcare Home Health Cal Inc....858 576-7410
5050 Murphy Canyon Rd # 200 San Diego (92123) *(G-22328)*
Accentcare Home Health Cal Inc....626 869-0250
750 Terrado Plz Ste 221 Covina (91723) *(G-22329)*
Accentcare Home Health Cal Inc....949 250-0133
3636 Birch St Ste 195 Newport Beach (92660) *(G-22330)*
Accenture Federal Services LLC....619 574-2400
1615 Murray Canyon Rd # 400 San Diego (92108) *(G-27293)*
Accenture LLP....310 726-2700
2141 Rosecrans Ave # 3100 El Segundo (90245) *(G-27294)*
Accenture LLP....925 974-5220
1255 Treat Blvd Ste 400 Walnut Creek (94597) *(G-27295)*
Accenture LLP....415 537-5860
2 Santa Ana Ct Belvedere Tiburon (94920) *(G-27296)*
Accenture LLP....415 537-5000
560 Mission St Fl 12 San Francisco (94105) *(G-27297)*
Accenture LLP....408 817-2100
50 W San Fernando St # 1208 San Jose (95113) *(G-27298)*
Accenture LLP....650 213-2000
50 W San Fernando St # 1200 San Jose (95113) *(G-27299)*
Accenture LLP....916 557-2200
1415 L St Ste 700 Sacramento (95814) *(G-27300)*
Accenture National SEC Svcs, San Diego *Also called Accenture Federal Services LLC (G-27293)*
Access Biologicals LLC....760 597-9749
995 Park Center Dr Vista (92081) *(G-8225)*
Access Communications, San Francisco *Also called Access Public Relations LLC (G-27729)*
Access Control Centres Inc....858 455-1500
6450 Sequence Dr San Diego (92121) *(G-5934)*
Access Dental Centers, Sacramento *Also called Access Dental Plan (G-20242)*
Access Dental Plan (PA)....916 922-5000
8890 Cal Center Dr Sacramento (95826) *(G-20242)*
Access Hollywood, Burbank *Also called Nbcuniversal Media LLC (G-18118)*
Access Hollywood....818 840-4444
3000 W Alameda Ave Burbank (91523) *(G-5833)*
Access Info MGT Shred Svcs LLC....805 529-6866
13950 Cerritos Corprt Dr C Cerritos (90703) *(G-26904)*
Access Info MGT Shred Svcs LLC (PA)....925 461-5352
6818 Patterson Pass Rd A Livermore (94550) *(G-16214)*
Access Integrated Healthcare....866 460-7465
550 N Brand Blvd Fl 20 Glendale (91203) *(G-21124)*
Access Intelligence LLC....650 384-4300
3975 Freedom Cir Ste 300 Santa Clara (95054) *(G-26641)*
Access Nurses Inc....858 458-4400
5935 Cornerstone Ct W San Diego (92121) *(G-14599)*
Access Pacific Inc....626 792-0616
755 E Washington Blvd Pasadena (91104) *(G-1483)*
Access Paratransit, El Monte *Also called Access Services (G-3630)*
Access Public Relations LLC....415 904-7070
650 California St Fl 30 San Francisco (94108) *(G-27729)*
Access Services....213 270-6000
3449 Santa Anita Ave El Monte (91731) *(G-3630)*
Access Systems Americas Inc....408 400-3000
1188 E Arques Ave Sunnyvale (94085) *(G-14997)*
Access To Loans For Learning....310 979-4700
6701 Center Dr W Ste 500 Los Angeles (90045) *(G-9910)*
Accessory Power, Westlake Village *Also called AP Global Inc (G-7520)*
Accidental Fire & Casualty, Lancaster *Also called Wilshire Insurance Company (G-10939)*
Acco Engineered Systems Inc....323 727-7765
3421 S Malt Ave Commerce (90040) *(G-17916)*

ALPHABETIC

Acco Engineered Systems Inc...510 346-4300
1133 Aladdin Ave San Leandro (94577) ***(G-2105)***
Acco Engineered Systems Inc...323 201-0931
6446 E Washington Blvd Commerce (90040) ***(G-16966)***
Accor Bus & Leisure N Amer Inc...650 598-9000
223 Twin Dolphin Dr Redwood City (94065) ***(G-12372)***
Accor Corp...310 278-5444
8555 Beverly Blvd Los Angeles (90048) ***(G-12373)***
Account Control Technology Inc...661 395-5702
5531 Bus Park S Ste 100 Bakersfield (93309) ***(G-14015)***
Accountable Health Staff Inc...916 286-7667
7777 Greenback Ln Ste 205 Citrus Heights (95610) ***(G-14830)***
Accountants 4 Contract...415 781-8644
235 Montgomery St Ste 630 San Francisco (94104) ***(G-26287)***
Accountemps, Cerritos *Also called Robert Half International Inc* ***(G-14761)***
Accountemps, San Francisco *Also called Robert Half International Inc* ***(G-14765)***
Accountemps, Menlo Park *Also called Robert Half International Inc* ***(G-14766)***
Accountnow Inc...925 498-1800
2603 Camino Ramon Ste 485 San Ramon (94583) ***(G-27301)***
Accounts Payable Department, Ontario *Also called Technicolor HM Entrmt Svcs Inc* ***(G-18261)***
Accredited Nursing Care, Pasadena *Also called Accredited Nursing Services* ***(G-20368)***
Accredited Nursing Care, Woodland Hills *Also called Dunn & Berger Inc* ***(G-22427)***
Accredited Nursing Care, Costa Mesa *Also called Accredited Nursing Services* ***(G-20369)***
Accredited Nursing Services...626 573-1234
80 S Lake Ave Ste 630 Pasadena (91101) ***(G-20368)***
Accredited Nursing Services...714 973-1234
950 S Coast Dr Ste 215 Costa Mesa (92626) ***(G-20369)***
Accriva Dgnostics Holdings Inc (PA)...858 263-2300
6260 Sequence Dr San Diego (92121) ***(G-12048)***
Accs, San Clemente *Also called American Corrective Counseling* ***(G-23657)***
Acct Holdings LLC...916 971-1981
5949 Fair Oaks Blvd Carmichael (95608) ***(G-16967)***
ACCU, Glendora *Also called Americas Christian Credit Un* ***(G-9652)***
Accu-Bore Directional Drilling, Benicia *Also called Mdr Inc* ***(G-25959)***
Accu-Count Inventory Svcs Inc...805 231-6310
1024 N Citrus Ave Covina (91722) ***(G-16968)***
Accumen Inc (PA)...858 777-8160
9246 Lightwave Ave # 320 San Diego (92123) ***(G-22331)***
Accunex Inc...818 882-5858
20700 Lassen St Chatsworth (91311) ***(G-2510)***
Accurate Background LLC...800 784-3911
7515 Irvine Center Dr Irvine (92618) ***(G-16215)***
Accurate Courier Services Inc...310 481-3937
11022 Santa Monica Blvd # 360 Los Angeles (90025) ***(G-3969)***
Accurate Delivery Systems Inc...951 823-8870
173 Resource Dr Bloomington (92316) ***(G-3970)***
Accurate Electronics, Chatsworth *Also called Accunex Inc* ***(G-2510)***
Accurate Express, Los Angeles *Also called Accurate Services Inc* ***(G-9705)***
Accurate Services Inc...323 906-1000
3429 Glendale Blvd Los Angeles (90039) ***(G-9705)***
Ace Beverage Co...323 266-6238
550 S Mission Rd Los Angeles (90033) ***(G-9036)***
Ace Cash Express Inc...951 509-3506
6302 Van Buren Blvd Riverside (92503) ***(G-9706)***
Ace Duraflo Pipe Restoration, Santa Ana *Also called Pipe Restoration Inc* ***(G-2322)***
Ace Financial Services Inc...510 790-4600
39300 Civic Center Dr # 290 Fremont (94538) ***(G-10579)***
Ace Hardware, Fresno *Also called Fresno Plumbing & Heating Inc* ***(G-2230)***
Ace High Entertainnment LLC...916 243-5515
125 Sconce Way Sacramento (95838) ***(G-18532)***
Ace Parking Management Inc...916 498-9852
300 Capitol Mall Bsmt Sacramento (95814) ***(G-26905)***
Ace Parking Management Inc...949 727-1470
71 Fortune Dr Ste 916 Irvine (92618) ***(G-17709)***
Ace Parking Management Inc...760 320-8974
3400 E Tahquitz Cyn Way Palm Springs (92262) ***(G-26906)***
Ace Parking Management Inc (PA)...619 233-6624
645 Ash St San Diego (92101) ***(G-17710)***
Ace Property & Casualty, Fremont *Also called Ace Financial Services Inc* ***(G-10579)***
Ace Reforestation, Porterville *Also called Raul Acevedo* ***(G-997)***
Ace Relocation Systems Inc (PA)...858 677-5500
5608 Eastgate Dr San Diego (92121) ***(G-4103)***
Ace Relocation Systems Inc...310 632-2800
189 W Victoria St Long Beach (90805) ***(G-3971)***
Ace Tomato Company Inc...209 982-0734
777 N Pershing Ave Ste 1a Stockton (95203) ***(G-36)***
Ace USA...510 790-4695
39300 Civic Center Dr # 290 Fremont (94538) ***(G-10580)***
Ace Usa Inc...415 547-4400
455 Market St Ste 500 San Francisco (94105) ***(G-10581)***
Ace Usa Inc...818 428-3600
9200 Oakdale Ave Chatsworth (91311) ***(G-10582)***
Ace Usa Inc...619 563-2400
3131 Camino Del Rio N San Diego (92108) ***(G-10583)***
Acemi Nursery Inc...559 842-7766
3626 N Howard Ave Kerman (93630) ***(G-212)***
Acepex Management Corporation...909 591-1999
13401 Yorba Ave Chino (91710) ***(G-26907)***
Acepex Management Corporation (PA)...909 625-6900
10643 Mills Ave Montclair (91763) ***(G-27770)***
Acer America Corporation (HQ)...408 533-7700
333 W San Carlos St San Jose (95110) ***(G-16313)***
Acera, Oakland *Also called Alameda County Employees Retir* ***(G-10539)***
Acetech Construction Inc...213 637-4702
3699 Wilshire Blvd # 655 Los Angeles (90010) ***(G-25612)***
Aceteck Roofing Co Inc...323 231-6060
5830 Woodlawn Ave Los Angeles (90003) ***(G-3136)***

ALPHABETIC

Aceva Technologies Inc...650 227-5500
1810 Gateway Dr Ste 360 San Mateo (94404) ***(G-14055)***
Acf Components & Fasteners Inc...949 833-0506
742 Arrow Grand Cir Covina (91722) ***(G-7665)***
Achates Power Inc...858 535-9920
4060 Sorrento Valley Blvd A San Diego (92121) ***(G-26459)***
Achates Security Agency, Salinas *Also called J Waters Inc* ***(G-16714)***
Achem Industry America Inc (PA)...562 802-0998
13226 Alondra Blvd Cerritos (90703) ***(G-7910)***
Achiever Christian Pre-Schl &...408 264-2345
540 Sands Dr San Jose (95125) ***(G-24410)***
Achievo Corporation (PA)...925 498-8864
1400 Terra Bella Ave E Mountain View (94043) ***(G-14998)***
Aci International (PA)...310 889-3400
844 Moraga Dr Los Angeles (90049) ***(G-8419)***
Aciontalk International Inc...619 393-1710
1398 Poinsettia Ave # 101 Vista (92081) ***(G-27809)***
ACI Construction Company Inc...909 391-4477
207 W State St Ontario (91762) ***(G-25613)***
Aclu Fndation Southern Cal LLC...213 977-9500
1313 W 8th St Los Angeles (90017) ***(G-25193)***
Acm Technologies Inc (PA)...951 738-9898
2535 Research Dr Corona (92882) ***(G-7039)***
Acma Computers Inc...214 587-1829
1565 Reliance Way Fremont (94539) ***(G-15893)***
Acme Building Maintenance Co (HQ)...408 263-5911
941 Catherine St Alviso (95002) ***(G-14211)***
Acme Building Maintenance Co...408 526-5939
3750 Zanker Rd San Jose (95134) ***(G-14212)***
Acme Construction Company Inc...209 523-2674
1565 Cummins Dr Modesto (95358) ***(G-1396)***
Acme Furniture Industry Inc (PA)...626 964-3456
18895 Arenth Ave City of Industry (91748) ***(G-6800)***
Acme Laundry Products Inc...818 341-0700
21600 Lassen St Chatsworth (91311) ***(G-6840)***
Acme Metals & Steel Supply Inc...310 329-2263
14930 S San Pedro St Gardena (90248) ***(G-7353)***
Acme Staffing, El Centro *Also called I N C Builders Inc* ***(G-14886)***
Acme Trading, City of Industry *Also called Acme Furniture Industry Inc* ***(G-6800)***
Acme-Cisco Systems, San Jose *Also called Acme Building Maintenance Co* ***(G-14212)***
Acom Solutions Inc (PA)...562 424-7899
2850 E 29th St Long Beach (90806) ***(G-15894)***
Acosta Inc...925 600-3500
5735 W Las Positas Blvd # 300 Pleasanton (94588) ***(G-8447)***
Acoustical Contractor, Thousand Oaks *Also called S A Cali-U Acoustics Inc* ***(G-2974)***
Acrobat Staffing, San Diego *Also called SE Scher Corporation* ***(G-14781)***
Acrobat Staffing, Rocklin *Also called SE Scher Corporation* ***(G-14782)***
Acronics Systems Inc...408 432-0888
2102 Commerce Dr San Jose (95131) ***(G-25614)***
Across Systems Inc...877 922-7677
100 N Brand Blvd Ste 100 Glendale (91203) ***(G-7081)***
ACS, Huntington Beach *Also called Applied Computer Solutions* ***(G-15023)***
ACS Security Industries Inc...310 475-9016
100 Bel Air Rd Los Angeles (90077) ***(G-16859)***
Acss, Beaumont *Also called Anderson Chrnesky Strl Stl Inc* ***(G-3362)***
Act 1 Group Inc...310 532-1529
1999 W 190th St Torrance (90504) ***(G-14600)***
Act 1 Group Inc (PA)...310 532-1529
1999 W 190th St Torrance (90504) ***(G-14601)***
Act 1 Personnel Services, Torrance *Also called All In One Inc* ***(G-26916)***
Act Associates, Folsom *Also called Matthew Burns* ***(G-1610)***
Act Fulfillment Inc...909 930-9083
3155 Universe Dr Mira Loma (91752) ***(G-4514)***
Act Home Health Inc...714 560-0800
12431 Lewis St Ste 101 Garden Grove (92840) ***(G-22332)***
Actelis Networks Inc (PA)...510 545-1045
47800 Westinghouse Dr Fremont (94539) ***(G-5452)***
Actelis USA, Fremont *Also called Actelis Networks Inc* ***(G-5452)***
Actian Corporation (PA)...650 587-5500
2300 Geng Rd Ste 150 Palo Alto (94303) ***(G-15895)***
Action Day Nrseries Prmry Plus...408 370-0350
18720 Bucknall Rd Saratoga (95070) ***(G-24411)***
Action Day Nrseries Prmry Plus...408 266-8952
2148 Lincoln Ave San Jose (95125) ***(G-24412)***
Action Force Security...310 715-6053
1212 W Gardena Blvd Ste C Gardena (90247) ***(G-16537)***
Action Home Nursing Services...530 756-2600
1190 Suncast Ln Ste 6 El Dorado Hills (95762) ***(G-22333)***
Action Messenger Service, Los Angeles *Also called Peach Inc* ***(G-4420)***
Action Property Management Inc...800 400-2284
530 S Hewitt St Los Angeles (90013) ***(G-25194)***
Action Property Management Inc (PA)...949 450-0202
2603 Main St Ste 500 Irvine (92614) ***(G-11232)***
Action Roofing, Santa Barbara *Also called JM Roofing Company Inc* ***(G-3181)***
Action Sales, Monterey Park *Also called JC Foodservice Inc* ***(G-7220)***
Action Sports Retailer...949 226-5744
31910 Del Obispo St # 200 San Juan Capistrano (92675) ***(G-16969)***
Action Technologies Inc...510 638-8300
21 Orinda Way Ste 124c Orinda (94563) ***(G-15565)***
Activ Identity Corporation...510 574-0100
6623 Dumbarton Cir Fremont (94555) ***(G-16088)***
Activcare Living Inc (PA)...858 565-4424
9619 Chesapeake Dr # 103 San Diego (92123) ***(G-26908)***
Active Lawyers Referral Svc...310 247-0425
9301 Wilshire Blvd # 508 Beverly Hills (90210) ***(G-28106)***
Active Motif Inc (PA)...760 431-1263
1914 Palomar Oaks Way # 150 Carlsbad (92008) ***(G-26460)***

Active Storage Inc 818 709-1133
2295 Jefferson St Torrance (90501) *(G-16970)*
Active Wellness LLC 415 331-1600
4000 Bridgeway Ste 101 Sausalito (94965) *(G-26909)*
Activision Blizzard Inc 415 881-9100
4 Hamilton Landing Novato (94949) *(G-15566)*
Activision Blizzard Inc 310 581-4700
3420 Ocean Park Blvd # 2000 Santa Monica (90405) *(G-14999)*
Activision Blizzard Inc (PA) 310 255-2000
3100 Ocean Park Blvd Santa Monica (90405) *(G-15567)*
Activision Blizzard Inc 949 955-1380
16205 Alton Pkwy Irvine (92618) *(G-15568)*
Activision Blizzard Inc 310 431-4000
4247 S Minnewawa Ave Fresno (93725) *(G-4515)*
Acts For Children (PA) 909 877-5499
18136 Jurupa Ave Bloomington (92316) *(G-24540)*
Actual Reality Pictures Inc 818 325-8800
16030 Ventura Blvd # 380 Encino (91436) *(G-11275)*
Acumen LLC 650 558-8882
500 Airport Blvd Ste 365 Burlingame (94010) *(G-15896)*
Acutus Medical Inc 858 673-1621
2210 Faraday Ave Ste 100 Carlsbad (92008) *(G-22873)*
Acwd, Fremont *Also called Alameda County Water District (G-6310)*
Acxiom Corporation 650 356-3400
100 Redwood Shores Pkwy Redwood City (94065) *(G-16216)*
Ad Force Private Security, Stockton *Also called California Guard Inc (G-16589)*
Ad Land Venture LP 916 853-9015
3217 Fitzgerald Rd Rancho Cordova (95742) *(G-804)*
Ad Media, Burbank *Also called Adcom Interactive Media Inc (G-16314)*
Adair Enterprises 714 998-5551
2390 N American Way Orange (92865) *(G-18365)*
Adams & Barnes Inc 626 358-1858
433 W Foothill Blvd Monrovia (91016) *(G-11276)*
Adams Pool Specialties, Sacramento *Also called Dave Gross Enterprises Inc (G-3511)*
Adams Steel, Anaheim *Also called Self Serve Auto Dismantlers (G-8083)*
Adams Streeter Civil Engineers 949 474-2330
15 Corporate Park Irvine (92606) *(G-25615)*
Adaptive Consolidation, Palo Alto *Also called Adaptive Insights Inc (G-15569)*
Adaptive Insights Inc (PA) 800 303-6346
3350 W Byshore Rd Ste 200 Palo Alto (94303) *(G-15569)*
Adaptive Spectrum and Signal A 650 264-2667
333 Twin Dolphin Dr # 300 Redwood City (94065) *(G-5453)*
Adaptv Inc (HQ) 650 286-4420
2 Waters Park Dr Ste 200 San Mateo (94403) *(G-7082)*
Adassured, Oceanside *Also called Pepperjam LLC (G-15373)*
Adco Container Company 818 998-2565
9959 Canoga Ave Chatsworth (91311) *(G-7911)*
Adcolony, Los Angeles *Also called Jirbo Inc (G-15263)*
Adcom Interactive Media Inc 800 296-7104
901 W Alameda Ave 102 Burbank (91506) *(G-16314)*
Adconion Media Inc (PA) 310 382-5521
3301 Exposition Blvd Fl 1 Santa Monica (90404) *(G-13811)*
Adconion Media Group, Santa Monica *Also called Adconion Media Inc (G-13811)*
Add Media, Los Angeles *Also called Admarketing Inc (G-13813)*
Added Value LLC 323 254-4326
3400 Cahuenga Blvd W B Los Angeles (90068) *(G-27302)*
Addepar Inc (PA) 855 692-3337
1215 Terra Bella Ave Mountain View (94043) *(G-15000)*
Addiction RES & Trtmnt Inc 415 928-7800
433 Turk St San Francisco (94102) *(G-22648)*
Addus Healthcare Inc 209 526-8451
817 Coffee Rd Ste B1 Modesto (95355) *(G-14602)*
Addus Healthcare Inc 530 566-0405
936 Mangrove Ave Chico (95926) *(G-22334)*
Addus Healthcare Inc 650 638-7943
1730 S Amphlett Blvd San Mateo (94402) *(G-22335)*
Addus Healthcare Inc 530 247-0858
926 E Cypress Ave Ste 800 Redding (96002) *(G-20304)*
Adee Plumbing and Heating Inc (PA) 323 296-8787
5457 Crenshaw Blvd Los Angeles (90043) *(G-2106)*
Adelanto YWCA 760 530-1850
14938 Binford Ave Adelanto (92301) *(G-25195)*
Adelphia, Fullerton *Also called Time Warner Cable Inc (G-6043)*
Adelson Testan Brundo Novel (PA) 805 367-5663
31330 Oak Crest Dr Westlake Village (91361) *(G-23081)*
Adept Consumer Testing Inc 310 279-4600
16130 Ventura Blvd # 200 Encino (91436) *(G-26642)*
Adept Fasteners Inc (PA) 661 257-6600
28709 Industry Dr Valencia (91355) *(G-7666)*
Aderans Hair Goods Inc 818 428-1626
9135 Independence Ave Chatsworth (91311) *(G-8308)*
Aderholt Specialty Company Inc 209 526-2000
1557 Cummins Dr Modesto (95358) *(G-2846)*
Adesa Auction, Sacramento *Also called Adesa Corporation LLC (G-6660)*
Adesa Corporation LLC 916 388-8899
8649 Kiefer Blvd Sacramento (95826) *(G-6660)*
Adesa Corporation LLC 951 361-9400
11625 Nino Way Mira Loma (91752) *(G-6661)*
Adesa Corporation LLC 619 661-5565
2175 Cactus Rd San Diego (92154) *(G-6662)*
Adesso Inc 909 839-2929
160 Commerce Way Walnut (91789) *(G-7083)*
Adeste Program Company 213 251-3551
1531 James M Wood Blvd Los Angeles (90015) *(G-24413)*
Adesto Technologies Corp 408 400-0578
3600 Peterson Way Santa Clara (95054) *(G-26461)*
Adexa Inc (PA) 310 642-2100
5777 W Century Blvd # 1100 Los Angeles (90045) *(G-15570)*
Adexis, San Francisco *Also called Fusionstorm (G-16376)*
Adg Corporation 415 864-4090
1871 Market St San Francisco (94103) *(G-12280)*
Adhei Enterprises Inc 818 788-7680
4627 Lemona Ave Sherman Oaks (91403) *(G-14213)*
ADI, San Bernardino *Also called Aviation & Defense Inc (G-4903)*
Adia LLC 310 370-0555
3625 Del Amo Blvd Ste 225 Torrance (90503) *(G-22336)*
Adicio Inc 760 602-9502
5993 Avenida Encinas Carlsbad (92008) *(G-5454)*
Adir International LLC 213 639-7716
4444 Ayers Ave Vernon (90058) *(G-1397)*
Adir International LLC 213 386-4412
4444-46 Ayers Ave Los Angeles (90023) *(G-4516)*
Adir Money Transfer Corp 213 639-2195
1605 W Olympic Blvd Los Angeles (90015) *(G-13730)*
Adivo Associates LLC 415 992-1449
1 Post St Ste 2750 San Francisco (94104) *(G-27303)*
Adkan Engineers, Riverside *Also called Adkison Engineers Inc (G-25616)*
Adkison Engineers Inc 951 688-0241
6879 Airport Dr Riverside (92504) *(G-25616)*
Adlink Cable Advertising LLC 310 477-3994
11150 Santa Monica Blvd # 100 Los Angeles (90025) *(G-13812)*
Adlware, San Clemente *Also called Kinnser Software Inc (G-15269)*
ADM Furniture Inc 310 762-2800
11680 Wright Rd Lynwood (90262) *(G-6801)*
Admarketing Inc 310 203-8400
1801 Century Park E # 2100 Los Angeles (90067) *(G-13813)*
Admhs, Santa Barbara *Also called County of Santa Barbara Alcoho (G-22711)*
Admin, Bakersfield *Also called County of Kern (G-19465)*
Administration, Fullerton *Also called St Jude Hospital (G-21926)*
Administration, Los Angeles *Also called County of Los Angeles (G-25017)*
Administration of Public Works, Martinez *Also called County of Contra Costa (G-1754)*
Administrative Office, Redding *Also called Mercy HM Svcs A Cal Ltd Partnr (G-19747)*
Administrative Services, San Francisco *Also called City & County of San Francisco (G-26969)*
Administrative Services SD 619 398-2314
3473 Kurtz St San Diego (92110) *(G-3862)*
Administrative Svcs Coop Inc 310 715-1968
2129 W Rosecrans Ave Gardena (90249) *(G-27304)*
Administrative Systems Inc 916 563-1121
1651 Response Rd Ste 350 Sacramento (95815) *(G-16971)*
Adminstrtive Office of US Crts 408 535-5200
280 S 1st St San Jose (95113) *(G-23643)*
Adminstrtive Office of US Crts 619 557-6650
101 W Broadway Ste 700 San Diego (92101) *(G-23644)*
Admiral Home Health Inc 562 421-0777
4010 Watson Plaza Dr # 140 Lakewood (90712) *(G-22337)*
Admiral Security Services Inc 888 471-1128
2151 Salvio St Ste 260 Concord (94520) *(G-16860)*
Admiralty Partners Inc 310 471-3772
1170 Somera Rd Los Angeles (90077) *(G-12281)*
Adobe Animal Hospital Inc 650 948-9661
4470 El Camino Real Los Altos (94022) *(G-611)*
Adobe Packing Company (PA) 831 753-6195
367 W Market St Salinas (93901) *(G-504)*
Adobe Systems Incorporated 415 832-2000
601 And 625 Townsend St San Francisco (94103) *(G-15571)*
Adobe Systems Incorporated (PA) 408 536-6000
345 Park Ave San Jose (95110) *(G-15572)*
Adolph Gasser Inc (PA) 415 495-3852
181 2nd St San Francisco (94105) *(G-7028)*
Adopt-A-Beach, Costa Mesa *Also called Adopt-A-Highway Maintenance (G-1723)*
Adopt-A-Highway Maintenance 800 200-0003
3158 Red Hill Ave Ste 200 Costa Mesa (92626) *(G-1723)*
Adorno Construction Inc 408 369-8675
520 Westchester Dr Ste A Campbell (95008) *(G-3225)*
ADP, Buena Park *Also called Automatic Data Processing Inc (G-16090)*
ADP, Rancho Cucamonga *Also called Automatic Data Processing Inc (G-16091)*
ADP, Camarillo *Also called Automatic Data Processing Inc (G-16092)*
ADP, South San Francisco *Also called Automatic Data Processing Inc (G-16093)*
ADP, San Dimas *Also called Automatic Data Processing Inc (G-16094)*
ADP, Redwood City *Also called Automatic Data Processing Inc (G-16095)*
ADP, Novato *Also called Automatic Data Processing Inc (G-16096)*
ADP, Milpitas *Also called Automatic Data Processing Inc (G-16097)*
ADP, La Palma *Also called Automatic Data Processing Inc (G-16098)*
ADP, San Dimas *Also called Automatic Data Processing Inc (G-16100)*
ADP, Woodland Hills *Also called Automatic Data Processing Inc (G-16101)*
ADP, Culver City *Also called Automatic Data Processing Inc (G-16102)*
ADP, San Diego *Also called Automatic Data Processing Inc (G-16103)*
Adroit Energy Inc 858 483-3568
1135 Garnet Ave Ste 32 San Diego (92109) *(G-2107)*
Adroll Inc (PA) 877 723-7655
972 Mission St Fl 3 San Francisco (94103) *(G-13814)*
ADS, Bloomington *Also called Accurate Delivery Systems Inc (G-3970)*
ADS Techonlogy, Walnut *Also called Adesso Inc (G-7083)*
Adstream North America Inc 212 459-0290
2400 W Empire Ave Burbank (91504) *(G-15897)*
Adtek Engineering Service 800 451-0782
2090 N Tustin Ave Ste 160 Santa Ana (92705) *(G-25617)*
Adult & Childrens Dental Group, South Gate *Also called Scott Jacks DDS Inc (G-20277)*
Adult Health Center At Sierra 559 459-1550
3837 N Clark St Fresno (93726) *(G-19315)*
Adult Mddlhlth Otptient Clinic, Fairfield *Also called County of Solano (G-21076)*

ALPHABETIC

Adult Probation Department, San Francisco *Also called City & County of San Francisco (G-23747)*
Adult Probation Department, San Jose *Also called Santa Clara County of (G-24192)*
Advance Beverage Co Inc....661 833-3783
5200 District Blvd Bakersfield (93313) *(G-9037)*
Advance Building Maintenance....310 247-0077
9601 Wilshire Blvd Gl25 Beverly Hills (90210) *(G-14214)*
Advance Critical Care of La, Culver City *Also called ACC (G-610)*
Advance Disposal Company, Hesperia *Also called Best Way Disposal Co Inc (G-6438)*
Advance Health Solutions LLC....858 876-0136
7825 Fay Ave Ste 200 La Jolla (92037) *(G-22338)*
Advance Semiconductor Engrg, Sunnyvale *Also called Ase (us) Inc (G-7525)*
Advance Services Inc....408 767-2797
8021 Kern Ave Gilroy (95020) *(G-17949)*
Advance Staffing Inc....408 205-6154
189 Easy St Unit C Mountain View (94043) *(G-14831)*
Advanced Acoustics....925 299-0515
3430 Golden Gate Way Lafayette (94549) *(G-2847)*
Advanced Bioservices LLC (PA)....818 342-0100
19255 Vanowen St Reseda (91335) *(G-26910)*
Advanced Cell Diagnostics Inc (HQ)....510 576-8800
7707 Gateway Blvd Newark (94560) *(G-26462)*
Advanced Cleanup Tech Inc....661 392-7765
4548 Wesley Ln Bakersfield (93308) *(G-3972)*
Advanced Cleanup Tech Inc (PA)....310 763-1423
20928 S Lamberton Ave Carson (90810) *(G-27771)*
Advanced Clnroom McRclean Corp....714 751-1152
3250 S Susan St Ste A Santa Ana (92704) *(G-14215)*
Advanced Commercial Corporatio....760 431-8500
5900 Pasteur Ct Ste 200 Carlsbad (92008) *(G-12100)*
Advanced Communication Service....909 210-9328
2650 Flora Spiegel Way Corona (92881) *(G-16972)*
Advanced Critical Care Emerge....818 887-2262
20051 Ventura Blvd Ste I Woodland Hills (91364) *(G-612)*
Advanced Data Center, Montebello *Also called Advanced Data Transcribing Ctr (G-16089)*
Advanced Data Transcribing Ctr....626 571-1570
1401 Cuesta Way Montebello (90640) *(G-16089)*
Advanced Dental Imaging LLC....805 687-5571
4028 Via Laguna Santa Barbara (93110) *(G-22300)*
Advanced Digital Services Inc (PA)....323 962-8585
948 N Cahuenga Blvd Los Angeles (90038) *(G-18038)*
Advanced Discovery Inc....866 342-3282
350 Sansome St Ste 510 San Francisco (94104) *(G-23082)*
Advanced Discovery Inc....408 294-0091
115 E Gish Rd Ste 500 San Jose (95112) *(G-16315)*
Advanced Electronic Solutions, El Cajon *Also called Patric Communications Inc (G-2681)*
Advanced Environmental Inc....909 356-9025
13579 Whittram Ave Fontana (92335) *(G-3973)*
Advanced Fabrication Tech, Hayward *Also called R2g Enterprises Inc (G-3206)*
Advanced HM Hlth & Hospice Inc....916 978-0744
4370 Auburn Blvd Sacramento (95841) *(G-20243)*
Advanced Home Health Inc....916 978-0744
4370 Auburn Blvd Sacramento (95841) *(G-22339)*
Advanced Home House, Sacramento *Also called Advanced HM Hlth & Hospice Inc (G-20243)*
Advanced Image Direct, Fullerton *Also called Real Estate Image (G-14088)*
Advanced Industrial Cmpt Inc (PA)....909 895-8989
21808 Garcia Ln City of Industry (91789) *(G-7084)*
Advanced Industrial Services, Bakersfield *Also called CL Knox Inc (G-1071)*
Advanced Industrial Svcs Cal, Paramount *Also called Advanced Industrial Svcs Inc (G-2426)*
Advanced Industrial Svcs Inc....562 940-8305
7831 Alondra Blvd Paramount (90723) *(G-2426)*
Advanced Logistics MGT Inc....310 638-0715
19067 S Reyes Ave Compton (90221) *(G-4104)*
Advanced Medical Imaging, Fresno *Also called Community Medical Centers (G-21506)*
Advanced Medical MGT Inc....562 766-2000
5000 Arprt Plz Dr Ste 150 Long Beach (90815) *(G-26911)*
Advanced Medical Placement....818 996-9812
18401 Burbank Blvd # 201 Tarzana (91356) *(G-24861)*
Advanced Medical Reviews Inc....310 575-0900
2950 31st St Ste 100 Santa Monica (90405) *(G-14832)*
Advanced Mp Technology Inc (PA)....949 492-6589
1010 Calle Sombra San Clemente (92673) *(G-7515)*
Advanced Network Tech Inc....909 428-9030
7950 Cherry Ave Ste 107 Fontana (92336) *(G-1901)*
Advanced Office, Santa Ana *Also called Integrus LLC (G-7054)*
Advanced Programs Group, El Segundo *Also called Orbital Sciences Corporation (G-26578)*
Advanced Protection Inds Inc....949 215-8000
25341 Commercentre Dr # 100 Lake Forest (92630) *(G-16861)*
Advanced Quality Logistics LLC....310 221-6651
350 Westmont Dr San Pedro (90731) *(G-5014)*
Advanced Rehabilitation Tech....858 621-5959
7950 Dunbrook Rd San Diego (92126) *(G-7231)*
Advanced Resources, Fontana *Also called Advanced Environmental Inc (G-3973)*
Advanced Rsrvation Systems Inc....858 300-8600
2445 Truxtun Rd Ste 205 San Diego (92106) *(G-16316)*
Advanced Software Design Inc....925 975-0691
1371 Oakland Blvd Ste 100 Walnut Creek (94596) *(G-15001)*
Advanced Software Dynamics Inc, Walnut Creek *Also called Advanced Software Design Inc (G-15001)*
Advanced Sterlization....909 350-6987
13135 Napa St Fontana (92335) *(G-4517)*
Advanced Surgery Institute LLC....707 528-6331
1739 4th St Santa Rosa (95404) *(G-19316)*
Advanced Test Equipment Corp....858 558-6500
10401 Roselle St San Diego (92121) *(G-14505)*
ADVANCED TEST EQUIPMENT RENTAL, San Diego *Also called Advanced Test Equipment Corp (G-14505)*
Advanced Trans Grp, Compton *Also called Advanced Logistics MGT Inc (G-4104)*
Advanced Veterinary Care Ctr....310 542-8018
15926 Hawthorne Blvd Lawndale (90260) *(G-613)*
Advantacare Health Inc (PA)....831 373-1111
5 Mandeville Ct Monterey (93940) *(G-14468)*
Advantacare Medical, Monterey *Also called Advantacare Health Inc (G-14468)*
Advantage Ground Trnsp, Costa Mesa *Also called Advantage Ground Trnsp Corp (G-3631)*
Advantage Ground Trnsp Corp....714 557-2465
2960 Airway Ave Ste B102 Costa Mesa (92626) *(G-3631)*
Advantage Logistics Inc....408 943-6300
2071 Ringwood Ave Ste D San Jose (95131) *(G-5015)*
Advantage Mailing Inc (PA)....714 538-3881
1600 N Kraemer Blvd Anaheim (92806) *(G-14064)*
Advantage Mailing Service, Anaheim *Also called Advantage Mailing Inc (G-14064)*
Advantage Media Services Inc....661 705-7588
28220 Industry Dr Valencia (91355) *(G-4518)*
Advantage Media Services Inc (PA)....661 775-0611
29010 Commerce Center Dr Valencia (91355) *(G-5196)*
Advantage Medical Group Inc....510 614-3700
15035 E 14th St San Leandro (94578) *(G-19317)*
Advantage Plumbing Group Inc....714 898-6020
3331 Orangewood Ave Los Alamitos (90720) *(G-2108)*
Advantage Produce Inc....213 627-2777
1511 Bay St Los Angeles (90021) *(G-8693)*
Advantage Sales & Marketing....925 463-5600
5064 Franklin Dr Pleasanton (94588) *(G-8448)*
Advantage Sales & Mktg Inc....310 321-6869
200 N Sepulveda Blvd # 1000 El Segundo (90245) *(G-8449)*
Advantage Sales & Mktg Inc (PA)....949 797-2900
18100 Von Karman Ave # 900 Irvine (92612) *(G-8450)*
Advantage Sales & Mktg LLC....925 463-5600
6700 Koll Center Pkwy # 300 Pleasanton (94566) *(G-8451)*
Advantage Sales & Mktg LLC (HQ)....949 797-2900
18100 Von Karman Ave # 900 Irvine (92612) *(G-8452)*
Advantage Solutions, Irvine *Also called Advantage Sales & Mktg Inc (G-8450)*
Advantage Solutions, Irvine *Also called Advantage Sales & Mktg LLC (G-8452)*
Advantage Waypoint LLC....717 424-4973
235 Baker St E Costa Mesa (92626) *(G-8453)*
Advantage-Crown Sls & Mktg LLC (HQ)....714 780-3000
1400 S Douglass Rd # 200 Anaheim (92806) *(G-8454)*
Advantech Corporation (HQ)....408 519-3800
380 Fairview Way Milpitas (95035) *(G-7085)*
Advantedge Technology Inc....805 488-0405
271 Market St Ste 15 Port Hueneme (93041) *(G-25618)*
Advantel Incorporated (PA)....408 954-5100
2222 Trade Zone Blvd San Jose (95131) *(G-17929)*
Advantel Networks, San Jose *Also called Advantel Incorporated (G-17929)*
Advantis Global Inc (PA)....415 395-4444
301 Howard St Ste 1400 San Francisco (94105) *(G-16317)*
Advent Group Ministries Inc....408 281-0708
90 Great Oaks Blvd # 108 San Jose (95119) *(G-24541)*
Advent Resources Inc....310 241-1500
235 W 7th St San Pedro (90731) *(G-15002)*
Advent Securities Investments (PA)....562 920-5467
9631 Alondra Blvd Ste 202 Bellflower (90706) *(G-9957)*
Advent Software Inc (HQ)....415 543-7696
600 Townsend St Fl 5 San Francisco (94103) *(G-15003)*
Adventis Chldren Hlth Care Ctr, Reedley *Also called Adventist Health System/West (G-19323)*
ADVENTIST HEALTH, Hanford *Also called Hanford Community Hospital (G-21589)*
ADVENTIST HEALTH, Glendale *Also called Glendale Adventist Medical Ctr (G-21576)*
ADVENTIST HEALTH, Simi Valley *Also called Simi Vly Hosp & Hlth Care Svcs (G-20353)*
ADVENTIST HEALTH, Hanford *Also called Central Valley General Hosp (G-21475)*
Adventist Health Clearlake (HQ)....707 994-6486
15630 18th Ave Clearlake (95422) *(G-21430)*
ADVENTIST HEALTH SYSTEM, Los Angeles *Also called White Memorial Medical Center (G-22031)*
Adventist Health System/West....530 342-4576
111 Raley Blvd Chico (95928) *(G-28107)*
Adventist Health System/West....559 891-2611
2141 High St Ste E Selma (93662) *(G-19318)*
Adventist Health System/West....707 987-8344
18990 Coyote Valley Rd # 11 Hidden Valley Lake (95467) *(G-19319)*
Adventist Health System/West....559 537-0305
1524 W Lacey Blvd Ste 102 Hanford (93230) *(G-19320)*
Adventist Health System/West....323 454-4481
3191 Casitas Ave Ste 216 Los Angeles (90039) *(G-22874)*
Adventist Health System/West....661 763-5131
501 6th St Taft (93268) *(G-22875)*
Adventist Health System/West....559 537-2299
125 Mall Dr Hanford (93230) *(G-22876)*
Adventist Health System/West....888 443-2273
1025 N Douty St Hanford (93230) *(G-22877)*
Adventist Health System/West....707 995-4888
14880 Olympic Dr Clearlake (95422) *(G-19321)*
Adventist Health System/West....559 638-8155
372 W Cypress Ave Reedley (93654) *(G-22878)*
Adventist Health System/West....818 246-5900
1560 E Chevy Chase Dr # 245 Glendale (91206) *(G-19322)*
Adventist Health System/West (PA)....916 781-2000
2100 Douglas Blvd Roseville (95661) *(G-21431)*
Adventist Health System/West....559 537-2860
460 Kings County Dr # 105 Hanford (93230) *(G-22340)*
Adventist Health System/West....559 537-2510
470 Greenfield Ave Hanford (93230) *(G-22649)*
Adventist Health System/West....818 409-8540
381 Merrill Ave Glendale (91206) *(G-21432)*

ALPHABETIC

Adventist Health System/West 559 637-2384
1433 N Acacia Ave Reedley (93654) ***(G-19323)***
Adventist Health System/West 707 459-1818
100 San Hedrin Cir Willits (95490) ***(G-22341)***
Adventist Health System/West 707 995-4500
15230 Lakeshore Dr Clearlake (95422) ***(G-21433)***
Adventist Health System/West 707 994-6486
18th Ave Hwy 53 Clearlake (95422) ***(G-19324)***
Adventist Health System/West 209 536-5700
20100 Cedar Rd N Sonora (95370) ***(G-22879)***
Adventist Hlth Cmnty Care-Taft, Taft *Also called Adventist Health System/West* ***(G-22875)***
Adventist Hlth Med Foundation, Glendale *Also called Adventist Health System/West* ***(G-21432)***
Adventist Med Center-Reedley 559 638-8155
372 W Cypress Ave Reedley (93654) ***(G-21434)***
Adventist Media Center Inc 805 955-7777
11291 Pierce St Riverside (92505) ***(G-18366)***
Adventres Rlling Cross-Country 415 332-5075
242 Redwd Hwy Frntge 1 Mill Valley (94941) ***(G-13457)***
Adventure City Inc 714 821-3311
1238 S Beach Blvd Anaheim (92804) ***(G-19130)***
Adventure Connection Inc 530 626-7385
986 Lotus Rd Lotus (95651) ***(G-19131)***
Adventureplex 310 546-7708
1701 Marine Ave Manhattan Beach (90266) ***(G-18604)***
Adventures Cross-Country, Mill Valley *Also called Adventres Rlling Cross-Country* ***(G-13457)***
Adventures In Hospitality Inc 760 356-2806
633 W Canal St Calexico (92231) ***(G-18842)***
Advertising, Santa Ana *Also called Dgwb Ventures LLC* ***(G-13839)***
Advertising Consultants Inc (PA) 310 233-2750
330 Golden Shore Ste 410 Long Beach (90802) ***(G-13986)***
Advertising Department, Long Beach *Also called Comcast Corporation* ***(G-5967)***
Advintist Hlth Clearlake Hosp 707 994-6486
18th Ave & Hwy 53 Clearlake (95422) ***(G-21435)***
Advisorsquare, Culver City *Also called Liveoffice LLC* ***(G-15734)***
Advisory Board Company 415 671-7750
23 Geary St San Francisco (94108) ***(G-22342)***
Ae & Associates LLC 951 278-3477
506 Queensland Cir Corona (92879) ***(G-27810)***
Aecom (PA) 213 593-8000
1999 Avenue Of The Stars # 2600 Los Angeles (90067) ***(G-25619)***
Aecom C&E Inc 510 622-6600
2101 Webster St Ste 1900 Oakland (94612) ***(G-27811)***
Aecom C&E Inc 805 388-3775
1220 Avenida Acaso Camarillo (93012) ***(G-25620)***
Aecom C&E Inc 213 593-8100
1999 Avenue Of The Stars Los Angeles (90067) ***(G-27305)***
Aecom Consulting, Los Angeles *Also called Aecom C&E Inc* ***(G-27305)***
Aecom Design, Los Angeles *Also called Aecom Services Inc* ***(G-26160)***
Aecom E&C Holdings Inc (HQ) 213 593-8000
1999 Avenue Of Ste 2600 Los Angeles (90067) ***(G-25621)***
Aecom Energy & Cnstr Inc 858 481-9502
2850 Carmel Valley Rd Del Mar (92014) ***(G-1724)***
Aecom Energy & Cnstr Inc 714 228-4300
16711 Knott Ave La Mirada (90638) ***(G-25622)***
Aecom Environment, Oakland *Also called Aecom C&E Inc* ***(G-27811)***
Aecom Environment, Camarillo *Also called Aecom C&E Inc* ***(G-25620)***
Aecom Global II LLC 415 774-2700
1320 S Simpson Cir Anaheim (92806) ***(G-25623)***
Aecom Global II LLC 805 692-0600
130 Robin Hill Rd Ste 100 Goleta (93117) ***(G-25624)***
Aecom Global II LLC 510 874-3000
500 12th St Oakland (94607) ***(G-25625)***
Aecom Global II LLC (HQ) 213 593-8100
1999 Avenue Of Ste 2600 Los Angeles (90067) ***(G-25626)***
Aecom Global II LLC 916 679-2000
2870 Gateway Oaks Dr # 150 Sacramento (95833) ***(G-25627)***
Aecom Global II LLC 916 679-8700
2870 Gateway Oaks Dr # 300 Sacramento (95833) ***(G-27812)***
Aecom Global II LLC 714 835-6886
2020 E 1st St Ste 400 Santa Ana (92705) ***(G-25628)***
Aecom Global II LLC 415 774-2700
600 Montgomery St San Francisco (94111) ***(G-25629)***
Aecom Global II LLC 510 258-0152
16525 Worthley Dr San Lorenzo (94580) ***(G-25630)***
Aecom Global II LLC 530 827-2406
74 C St Herlong (96113) ***(G-25631)***
Aecom Global II LLC 559 347-5669
5168 E Dakota Ave Fresno (93727) ***(G-25632)***
Aecom Global II LLC 559 998-1820
Reeves Boulevard Lemoore (93246) ***(G-25633)***
Aecom Global II LLC 619 241-4568
3990 Old Town Ave A San Diego (92110) ***(G-25634)***
Aecom Global II LLC 805 260-8440
576th Flts Vandenberg Afb (93437) ***(G-25635)***
Aecom Global II LLC 213 996-2200
915 Wilshire Blvd Ste 800 Los Angeles (90017) ***(G-27813)***
Aecom Global II LLC 310 343-6977
310 Golden Shore Ste 100 Long Beach (90802) ***(G-27814)***
Aecom Global II LLC 415 774-2700
600 Montgomery St Fl 26 San Francisco (94111) ***(G-25636)***
Aecom Services Inc (HQ) 213 593-8000
555 S Flower St Ste 3700 Los Angeles (90071) ***(G-26160)***
Aecom Technical Services Inc (HQ) 213 593-8000
300 S Grand Ave Ste 1100 Los Angeles (90071) ***(G-6421)***
Aecom Technical Services Inc 510 285-2010
1333 Broadway Ste 800 Oakland (94612) ***(G-27815)***
Aecom Technical Services Inc 510 834-4304
1333 Broadway Ste 800 Oakland (94612) ***(G-25637)***
Aecom Technical Services Inc 909 554-5000
901 Via Piemonte Ste 400 Ontario (91764) ***(G-25638)***
Aecom Technology Corporation 916 414-5800
2020 L St Ste 400 Sacramento (95811) ***(G-25639)***
Aecom Technology Corporation 661 266-0802
41235 11th St W Ste B Palmdale (93551) ***(G-26161)***
Aecom Technology Corporation 415 908-6135
501 2nd St San Francisco (94107) ***(G-25640)***
Aecom Usa Inc 213 330-7200
515 S Figueroa St Ste 400 Los Angeles (90071) ***(G-27816)***
Aecom Usa Inc 408 392-0670
100 W San Fernando St San Jose (95113) ***(G-27817)***
Aecom Usa Inc 213 593-8000
300 S Grand Ave Ste 1100 Los Angeles (90071) ***(G-27818)***
Aecom Usa Inc 714 567-2501
999 W Town And Country Rd Orange (92868) ***(G-27819)***
AEG Global Partnerships LLC 213 763-7700
1100 S Flower St Ste 3200 Los Angeles (90015) ***(G-27306)***
AEG Live LLC (HQ) 323 930-5700
425 W 11th St Ste 300 Los Angeles (90015) ***(G-18367)***
AEG Management Lacc LLC 213 741-1151
1201 S Figueroa St Los Angeles (90015) ***(G-26912)***
AEG Ontario Arena LLC 909 244-5500
4000 E Ontario Ctr Pkwy Ontario (91764) ***(G-18533)***
AEG Worldwide, Los Angeles *Also called Anschutz Entrmt Group Inc* ***(G-18450)***
Aegis Assisted Living, Aptos *Also called Aegis Senior Communities LLC* ***(G-22346)***
Aegis Asssted Living Prpts LLC 510 739-1515
3850 Walnut Ave 228 Fremont (94538) ***(G-21125)***
Aegis Asssted Living Prpts LLC 760 806-3600
1440 S Melrose Dr Oceanside (92056) ***(G-24542)***
Aegis At Shadowridge, Oceanside *Also called Aegis Asssted Living Prpts LLC* ***(G-24542)***
Aegis Enterprises Inc 925 417-5550
500 Boulder Ct Ste A Pleasanton (94566) ***(G-2109)***
Aegis Film Group Inc 323 848-7977
7510 W Sunset Blvd # 275 Los Angeles (90046) ***(G-18269)***
Aegis Fire Systems, Pleasanton *Also called Aegis Enterprises Inc* ***(G-2109)***
Aegis Gardens, Fremont *Also called Aegis Senior Communities LLC* ***(G-22344)***
Aegis Living, Pleasant Hill *Also called Aegis Senior Communities LLC* ***(G-22345)***
AEgis of Carmichael 916 972-1313
4050 Walnut Ave Carmichael (95608) ***(G-24543)***
Aegis of Corte Madera, Corte Madera *Also called Aegis Senior Communities LLC* ***(G-22343)***
Aegis of Fremont, Fremont *Also called Aegis Asssted Living Prpts LLC* ***(G-21125)***
Aegis of Granada Hills, Granada Hills *Also called Aegis Senior Communities LLC* ***(G-22348)***
Aegis of Laguna Niguel, Laguna Niguel *Also called Aegis Senior Communities LLC* ***(G-22347)***
Aegis of San Francisco, South San Francisco *Also called Ageis Living* ***(G-28109)***
Aegis Senior Communities LLC 415 483-1399
5555 Paradise Dr Corte Madera (94925) ***(G-22343)***
Aegis Senior Communities LLC 510 739-0909
36281 Fremont Blvd Fremont (94536) ***(G-22344)***
Aegis Senior Communities LLC 925 588-7030
1660 Oak Park Blvd Pleasant Hill (94523) ***(G-22345)***
Aegis Senior Communities LLC 831 684-2700
125 Heather Ter Aptos (95003) ***(G-22346)***
Aegis Senior Communities LLC 949 496-8080
32170 Niguel Rd Laguna Niguel (92677) ***(G-22347)***
Aegis Senior Communities LLC 818 363-3373
10801 Lindley Ave Granada Hills (91344) ***(G-22348)***
Aegis Software Inc 858 551-1652
5580 La Jolla Blvd # 436 La Jolla (92037) ***(G-13987)***
Aegis Treatment Centers LLC (PA) 818 206-0360
7246 Remmet Ave Canoga Park (91303) ***(G-22650)***
Aei Consultants, Irvine *Also called All Environmental Inc* ***(G-27824)***
Aei Consultants, Hermosa Beach *Also called All Environmental Inc* ***(G-27825)***
AEP Span Inc 916 372-0933
2110 Enterprise Blvd West Sacramento (95691) ***(G-3137)***
Aer Electronics Inc (PA) 510 300-0500
42744 Boscell Rd Fremont (94538) ***(G-6422)***
Aer Technologies Inc 714 871-7357
650 Columbia St Brea (92821) ***(G-17956)***
Aera Energy LLC (HQ) 661 665-5000
10000 Ming Ave Bakersfield (93311) ***(G-1053)***
Aera Energy LLC 661 768-3100
25401 Highway 33 Fellows (93224) ***(G-1054)***
Aera Energy LLC 661 665-3200
29235 Highway 33 Maricopa (93252) ***(G-1055)***
Aera Energy South Midway, Maricopa *Also called Aera Energy LLC* ***(G-1055)***
Aerelectronics, Fremont *Also called Aer Electronics Inc* ***(G-6422)***
Aerial Applicators, Biggs *Also called Chuck Jones Flying Service* ***(G-478)***
Aeris Communications Inc 408 557-1900
2350 Mission College Blvd # 600 Santa Clara (95054) ***(G-5455)***
Aero Port Services Inc (PA) 310 623-8230
216 W Florence Ave Inglewood (90301) ***(G-16862)***
Aero Precision Industries LLC 925 579-5327
201 Lindbergh Ave Livermore (94551) ***(G-7991)***
Aero-Engines Inc 323 663-3961
2641 Roseview Ave Los Angeles (90065) ***(G-17957)***
Aeroflot Rssina Internatl Arln, Beverly Hills *Also called Aeroflot Russian Airlines* ***(G-4777)***
Aeroflot Russian Airlines 323 272-4861
8383 Wilshire Blvd # 648 Beverly Hills (90211) ***(G-4777)***
Aeroground Inc (HQ) 650 266-6965
270 Lawrence Ave South San Francisco (94080) ***(G-4891)***
Aerohive Networks Inc 408 988-9918
2899 Toyon Dr Santa Clara (95051) ***(G-15898)***
Aerohive Networks Inc (PA) 408 510-6100
1011 Mccarthy Blvd Milpitas (95035) ***(G-15899)***
Aeromedevac Inc 619 284-7910
681 Kenney St El Cajon (92020) ***(G-27307)***

ALPHABETIC

Aeronautical Radio Inc ALPHABETIC SECTION

Aeronautical Radio Inc ... 925 294-8400
6011 Industrial Way Livermore (94551) *(G-5253)*

Aerospace & Marine Intl ... 408 360-0440
6910 Santa Teresa Blvd San Jose (95119) *(G-28108)*

Aerospace Corporation (PA) ... 310 336-5000
2310 E El Segundo Blvd El Segundo (90245) *(G-26722)*

Aerospace Corporation ... 714 248-1194
2745 E Sherman Ave Orange (92869) *(G-26723)*

Aerospace Corporation ... 805 320-9599
P.O. Box 5068 Lompoc (93437) *(G-26724)*

Aerospace Corporation ... 818 952-6075
3171 Grangemount Rd Glendale (91206) *(G-26725)*

Aerospace Corporation ... 310 374-8866
624 N Guadalupe Ave Redondo Beach (90277) *(G-26726)*

Aerospace Corporation ... 310 336-1025
2009 Harkness St Manhattan Beach (90266) *(G-26727)*

Aerospace Corporation ... 619 491-3557
1650 Hotel Cir N San Diego (92108) *(G-25641)*

Aerospace Fclities Support LLC ... 661 723-3148
244 E Avenue K4 Lancaster (93535) *(G-16274)*

Aerospace Federally Funded RES, El Segundo *Also called Air Force US Dept of (G-26729)*

Aerospace Material Division, Bay Point *Also called Henkel Corporation (G-25860)*

Aerotransporte De Carge Union ... 310 649-0069
5625 W Imperial Hwy Los Angeles (90045) *(G-4778)*

Aerounion, Los Angeles *Also called Aerotransporte De Carge Union (G-4778)*

Aerovironment Inc ... 805 581-2187
900 Innovators Way Simi Valley (93065) *(G-25074)*

AES, Oceanside *Also called Automation Engrg Systems Inc (G-15907)*

AES Corporation ... 310 318-7510
1100 N Harbor Dr Redondo Beach (90277) *(G-11277)*

AES Huntington Beach LLC ... 714 374-1476
21730 Newland St Huntington Beach (92646) *(G-6103)*

AES Networks, San Jose *Also called Vormetric Inc (G-16524)*

AES Southland LLC ... 562 430-8685
690 N Studebaker Rd Long Beach (90803) *(G-6104)*

Aesthetic Maintenance Corp ... 213 353-1525
1625 Palo Alto St Ste 301 Los Angeles (90026) *(G-14216)*

Aestiva Software Inc ... 310 697-0338
3551 Voyager St Ste 201 Torrance (90503) *(G-15004)*

Aetna Health California Inc ... 415 645-8200
1 Embarcadero Ctr Ste 300 San Francisco (94111) *(G-10251)*

Aetna Health California Inc ... 619 656-3104
727 Pueblo Pl Chula Vista (91914) *(G-10252)*

Aetna Health California Inc (HQ) ... 925 543-9000
2409 Camino Ramon San Ramon (94583) *(G-10253)*

AFA Constrctn Grp/Cal Inc JV ... 707 446-7996
2040 Peabody Rd Ste 400 Vacaville (95687) *(G-1484)*

Afex, Woodland Hills *Also called Associated Foreign Exch Inc (G-9708)*

Affd, Anaheim *Also called Anaheim First Fmly Dntl Group (G-26921)*

Affiliated Communications Inc ... 805 650-4949
3601 Calle Tecate Ste 200 Camarillo (93012) *(G-16973)*

Affiliated Engineers Inc ... 415 764-3700
123 Mission St Fl 7 San Francisco (94105) *(G-25642)*

Affiliated Engineers W Inc (HQ) ... 925 933-8400
123 Mission St Fl 7 San Francisco (94105) *(G-25643)*

Affiliated Funding Corporation ... 714 619-3100
5 Hutton Centre Dr # 1100 Santa Ana (92707) *(G-9911)*

Affiliated Temporary Help ... 323 771-1383
4359 Florence Ave Bell (90201) *(G-14833)*

Affinity Auto Programs Inc ... 858 643-9324
10251 Vista Cerento Pkwy Ste 300 San Diego (92121) *(G-16974)*

Affinity Development Group Inc ... 858 643-9324
10251 Vista Sorrento Pkwy # 300 San Diego (92121) *(G-25484)*

Affinity Group, Ventura *Also called Agi Holding Corp (G-18843)*

Affirm Inc ... 415 984-0490
225 Bush St Ste 1600 San Francisco (94104) *(G-9768)*

Affirm Identity, San Francisco *Also called Affirm Inc (G-9768)*

Affordable Engrg Svcs Inc ... 973 890-8915
120 C Ave Ste 110 Coronado (92118) *(G-25644)*

Affordable Installations, Nevada City *Also called Patrick Dean Bryan (G-3566)*

Affymax Research Institute ... 650 812-8700
4001 Miranda Ave Palo Alto (94304) *(G-26728)*

Affymetrix Inc ... 858 642-2058
10255 Science Center Dr San Diego (92121) *(G-26463)*

AFL, Rancho Cucamonga *Also called Ccna Vons Athletes For Life (G-25515)*

AFL-CIO #1245, Vacaville *Also called International Brthrhd of Elctr (G-25174)*

African American Unity Center ... 323 789-7300
944 W 53rd St Los Angeles (90037) *(G-23645)*

Afshan Baig MD ... 760 344-6471
900 Main St Brawley (92227) *(G-19325)*

After Market Group Inc (HQ) ... 916 361-1687
10173 Croydon Way Ste 1 Sacramento (95827) *(G-7232)*

After-Party2 Inc (HQ) ... 310 202-0011
901 W Hillcrest Blvd Inglewood (90301) *(G-14506)*

After-Party2 Inc ... 310 535-3660
2310 E Imperial Hwy El Segundo (90245) *(G-14507)*

Afternoon Delight, Los Angeles *Also called Drinks Holdings LLC (G-9097)*

AG Air Conditioning & Htg Inc ... 818 988-5388
14620 Keswick St Van Nuys (91405) *(G-2110)*

AG Facilities Operations LLC ... 323 651-1808
6380 Wilshire Blvd # 800 Los Angeles (90048) *(G-21126)*

AG Heating and AC, Van Nuys *Also called AG Air Conditioning & Htg Inc (G-2110)*

AG Redlands LLC ... 909 793-2678
700 E Highland Ave Redlands (92374) *(G-21127)*

Ag-Wise Enterprises Inc (PA) ... 661 325-1567
5100 California Ave # 209 Bakersfield (93309) *(G-689)*

Ag/LPC Griffin Towers LP ... 714 662-5902
5 Hutton Cntre Dr Ste 120 Santa Ana (92707) *(G-12282)*

Agama Solutions Inc ... 510 796-9300
39159 Paseo Padre Pkwy # 216 Fremont (94538) *(G-27308)*

Agamerica Fcb (PA) ... 651 282-8800
3636 American River Dr # 100 Sacramento (95864) *(G-9726)*

Agape In Home Care Inc ... 661 835-0364
4800 District Blvd Ste A Bakersfield (93313) *(G-22349)*

Age Advantage HM Care Svcs ... 619 449-5900
5480 Baltimore Dr Ste 214 La Mesa (91942) *(G-21128)*

Age Concerns Inc ... 619 544-1622
2650 Camino Del Rio N # 203 San Diego (92108) *(G-23646)*

Ageis Living ... 650 952-6100
2280 Gellert Blvd South San Francisco (94080) *(G-28109)*

Agemark Corporation (PA) ... 925 257-4671
25 Avenida De Orinda Orinda (94563) *(G-20370)*

Agency For Performing Arts Inc (PA) ... 310 557-9049
405 S Beverly Dr Ste 500 Beverly Hills (90212) *(G-16975)*

Agencycom LLC (HQ) ... 415 817-3800
5353 Grosvenor Blvd Los Angeles (90066) *(G-15573)*

Agendia Inc ... 949 540-6300
22 Morgan Irvine (92618) *(G-22651)*

Agent Franchise LLC ... 949 930-5025
9518 9th St Ste C2 Rancho Cucamonga (91730) *(G-10231)*

Aggregate West Coast, Thermal *Also called West Coast Aggregate Supply (G-1109)*

Aggressive Action Security ... 858 829-2516
17489 Plaza Del Curtidor San Diego (92128) *(G-16538)*

Agi Holding Corp (PA) ... 805 667-4100
2575 Vista Del Mar Dr Ventura (93001) *(G-18843)*

Agile 1, Torrance *Also called Act 1 Group Inc (G-14601)*

Agile Sourcing Partners Inc ... 951 279-4154
2385 Railroad St Corona (92880) *(G-6299)*

Agilepoint Inc ... 650 968-6789
1916 Old Middlefield Way Mountain View (94043) *(G-15574)*

Agiliance Inc ... 408 200-0400
845 Stewart Dr Ste D Sunnyvale (94085) *(G-16318)*

Agility Holdings Inc (HQ) ... 714 617-6300
240 Commerce Irvine (92602) *(G-5016)*

Agility Logistics, Irvine *Also called Agility Holdings Inc (G-5016)*

Agility Logistics Corp ... 310 507-6700
21906 Arnold Center Rd Carson (90810) *(G-5017)*

Agility Logistics Corp ... 650 645-5800
111 Anza Blvd Ste 122 Burlingame (94010) *(G-5018)*

Agilysys Inc ... 702 759-4879
1900 Powell St Ste 230 Emeryville (94608) *(G-7086)*

Agilysys Inc ... 805 692-6339
5383 Hollister Ave # 120 Santa Barbara (93111) *(G-15900)*

Aging & Adult Services, Bakersfield *Also called County of Kern (G-23815)*

Aging & Adult Services, Taft *Also called County of Kern (G-23817)*

Aging & Adult Services, Bakersfield *Also called County of Kern (G-23819)*

Aging & Adult Services, Victorville *Also called County of San Bernardino (G-23894)*

Agire Mortgage Corporation ... 714 564-5821
2125 E Katella Ave # 350 Anaheim (92806) *(G-9810)*

Agostini and Associates Inc ... 925 691-7300
1470 Civic Ct Ste 1760 Concord (94520) *(G-14834)*

Agostini Health Care Staffing, Concord *Also called Agostini and Associates Inc (G-14834)*

Agoura Hills Renaissance Hotel, Agoura Hills *Also called Davidson Hotel Partners Lp (G-12564)*

AGR Group Inc ... 714 245-7151
13902 Harbor Blvd Ste 2c Garden Grove (92843) *(G-27309)*

Agreeya Solutions Inc (PA) ... 916 294-0075
605 Coolidge Dr Ste 200 Folsom (95630) *(G-27310)*

Agreserves Inc ... 530 343-5365
6100 Wilson Landing Rd Chico (95973) *(G-194)*

Agri Valley Services ... 559 233-5633
1532 N West Ave Fresno (93728) *(G-26288)*

Agri-Cal Venture Associates ... 760 398-9520
52300 Enterprise Way Coachella (92236) *(G-690)*

Agri-Feed Industries, Imperial *Also called Western Meat Processors Inc (G-414)*

Agri-Mix Transport Inc ... 661 833-6280
1400 S Union Ave Ste 110 Bakersfield (93307) *(G-3974)*

Agri-World Cooperative ... 559 673-1306
31545 Donald Ave Madera (93636) *(G-691)*

Agrichem, Fowler *Also called Kandarian Agri Enterprises (G-161)*

Agriculture and Priority Pollu (PA) ... 559 275-2175
908 N Temperance Ave Clovis (93611) *(G-26828)*

Agriland Holding Inc ... 559 665-2100
23400 Road 24 Chowchilla (93610) *(G-252)*

Agro-Jal Farms Inc ... 805 928-2682
257 Kathleen Ct Santa Maria (93458) *(G-505)*

Agsource Services LLC ... 559 735-9700
222 N Garden St Ste 400 Visalia (93291) *(G-647)*

Agua Caliente Casino & Resort, Rancho Mirage *Also called Agua Clnte Band Chilla Indians (G-12374)*

Agua Caliente Development Auth ... 760 699-6800
5401 Dinah Shore Dr Palm Springs (92264) *(G-11278)*

Agua Clnte Band Chilla Indians ... 760 321-2000
32250 Bob Hope Dr Rancho Mirage (92270) *(G-12374)*

Agua Clnte Band Chilla Indians (PA) ... 760 699-6800
5401 Dinah Shore Dr Palm Springs (92264) *(G-25485)*

Agua Clnte Band Chilla Indians ... 800 854-1279
401 E Amado Rd Palm Springs (92262) *(G-12375)*

Aguatierra Associates Inc (PA) ... 510 450-6000
2200 Powell St Ste 925 Emeryville (94608) *(G-27772)*

Ahern Agribusiness Inc ... 619 661-9450
9465 Customhouse Plz G San Diego (92154) *(G-9124)*

Ahern International, San Diego *Also called Ahern Agribusiness Inc (G-9124)*

Ahm Gemch Inc ... 626 579-7777
1701 Santa Anita Ave El Monte (91733) *(G-21436)*

Ahmc, Anaheim *Also called Anaheim Regional Medical Ctr (G-19346)*

ALPHABETIC

Ahmc Garfield Medical Ctr LP....626 573-2222
525 N Garfield Ave Monterey Park (91754) *(G-20371)*
Ahmc Healthcare....626 570-0612
55 S Raymond Ave Ste 105 Alhambra (91801) *(G-21437)*
Ahmc Healthcare Inc....626 248-3452
500 E Main St Alhambra (91801) *(G-22880)*
Ahmc Healthcare Inc (PA)....626 943-7526
1000 S Fremont Ave Unit 6 Alhambra (91803) *(G-21438)*
Ahmc Healthcare Inc....626 579-7777
1701 Santa Anita Ave South El Monte (91733) *(G-21439)*
Ahmc Whittier Hosp Med Ctr LP....562 945-3561
9080 Colima Rd Whittier (90605) *(G-21440)*
Ahr Professionals, Lake Forest *Also called Validus Group Inc (G-14814)*
Ahrens Landscape & Maintenance, Sacramento *Also called Jma Investments Ltd (G-880)*
Ahtna Environmental Inc....907 433-0729
2255 Contra Costa Blvd Pleasant Hill (94523) *(G-28110)*
Ahtna Government Services Corp....916 372-2000
3100 Beacon Blvd West Sacramento (95691) *(G-1485)*
Ahtna-CDM Smith JV....714 824-3471
3200 El Camino Real Irvine (92602) *(G-27820)*
Ai Inc/CSC Grou....661 775-8400
28001 Smyth Dr Ste 107 Valencia (91355) *(G-16539)*
AIA Holdings Inc (PA)....818 222-4999
26560 Agoura Rd Ste 100 Calabasas (91302) *(G-10488)*
Aic Inc USA, City of Industry *Also called Advanced Industrial Cmpt Inc (G-7084)*
Aicent Inc....408 324-1316
900 E Hamilton Ave # 600 Campbell (95008) *(G-16319)*
Aichinger International Inc....310 375-1533
5423 Littlebow Rd Pls Vrds Pnsl (90275) *(G-6663)*
Aico, Pico Rivera *Also called Amini Innovation Corp (G-6803)*
Aids Healthcare Foundation....661 723-3244
1669 W Avenue J Ste 301 Lancaster (93534) *(G-19326)*
Aids Healthcare Foundation....323 662-0492
1300 N Vermont Ave Los Angeles (90027) *(G-19327)*
Aids Healthcare Foundation....562 693-2654
9200 Colima Rd Whittier (90605) *(G-19328)*
Aids Project La, Los Angeles *Also called Aids Project Los Angeles (G-23647)*
Aids Project Los Angeles (PA)....213 201-1600
611 S Kingsley Dr Los Angeles (90005) *(G-23647)*
Aids Svcs Fndation Orange Cnty....949 809-5700
17982 Sky Park Cir Ste J Irvine (92614) *(G-23648)*
AIDS WALK ORANGE COUNTY, Irvine *Also called Aids Svcs Fndation Orange Cnty (G-23648)*
AIG, San Francisco *Also called American Gen Lf Insur Co Del (G-10594)*
AIG Direct Insurance Svcs Inc....858 309-3000
9640 Gran Rdge Dr Ste 200 San Diego (92123) *(G-10584)*
AIG Private Client Group, San Diego *Also called American Intl Group Inc (G-10597)*
AIG Sun America, Los Angeles *Also called Sun America Housing Fund (G-11058)*
Aimia Proprietary Loyalty....415 398-3534
180 Montgomery St San Francisco (94104) *(G-27311)*
Aimia Proprietary Loyalty....415 844-2200
735 Battery St Fl 1 San Francisco (94111) *(G-27312)*
Aimloan.com, A Direct Lender, San Diego *Also called American Internet Mortgage Inc (G-9814)*
Aims Education Foundation....559 255-4094
1595 S Chestnut Ave Fresno (93702) *(G-27821)*
Air Cargo Handling Service, South San Francisco *Also called Aeroground Inc (G-4891)*
Air Control Systems Inc....714 572-6880
1940 S Grove Ave Ontario (91761) *(G-2111)*
Air Force US Dept of....805 606-5355
1031 California Blvd # 11777 Lompoc (93437) *(G-26913)*
Air Force US Dept of....310 336-5000
2310 E El Segundo Blvd El Segundo (90245) *(G-26729)*
Air Force US Dept of....310 393-0411
1776 Main St Santa Monica (90401) *(G-26730)*
Air Force Village West Inc....951 697-2000
17050 Arnold Dr Ofc Riverside (92518) *(G-20372)*
Air France (air Nationale)....415 877-0179
San Francisco Intl A San Francisco (94125) *(G-4779)*
Air Lease Corporation (PA)....310 553-0555
2000 Avenue Of The Stars 1000n Los Angeles (90067) *(G-14508)*
Air Mechanical Inc....714 995-3947
608 S Vicki Ln Anaheim (92804) *(G-2112)*
Air New Zealand Limited....310 648-7000
222 N Sepulveda Blvd # 900 El Segundo (90245) *(G-4780)*
Air Pollution Control District....805 961-8800
260 N San Antonio Rd A Santa Barbara (93110) *(G-27822)*
Air Polution Control District, Fresno *Also called San Joaquin Valley A P C D (G-28051)*
Air Serv Corporation....650 872-5400
601 Gateway Blvd Ste 1145 South San Francisco (94080) *(G-4892)*
Air Systems Inc....408 280-1666
940 Remillard Ct Frnt San Jose (95122) *(G-2113)*
Air Systems Sacramento Inc....916 368-0336
10381 Old Placerville Rd # 100 Sacramento (95827) *(G-2114)*
Air Tiger Express (usa) Inc....626 965-8647
17000 Gale Ave City of Industry (91745) *(G-5019)*
Air Treatment Corporation (PA)....909 869-7975
640 N Puente St Brea (92821) *(G-7733)*
Air-Sea Forwarders Inc (PA)....310 216-1616
9009 S La Cienega Blvd Inglewood (90301) *(G-5020)*
Air-TEC, Carson *Also called Clay Dunn Enterprises Inc (G-2182)*
Airbnb Inc (PA)....415 800-5959
888 Brannan St Ste 400 San Francisco (94103) *(G-13486)*
Airco Mechanical Inc....916 381-4523
8210 Demetre Ave Sacramento (95828) *(G-2115)*
Aircraft Service International....909 937-3210
Ontario Intl Airport Ontario (91761) *(G-4893)*
Aircraft Service Intl Inc....310 646-2990
5720 Avion Dr Los Angeles (90045) *(G-14217)*
Aircraft Service Intl Inc....909 937-3998
1049 S Vineyard Ave Ontario (91761) *(G-4894)*
Aircraft Service Intl Inc....909 937-3210
2161 E Avion Ave Ontario (91761) *(G-4895)*
Aircraft Xray Laboratories Inc....323 587-0164
5216 Pacific Blvd Huntington Park (90255) *(G-26829)*
Airdrome Orchards Inc (PA)....408 297-6461
610 E Gish Rd San Jose (95112) *(G-213)*
Aire-Rite AC & Rfrgn Inc....714 895-2338
15122 Bolsa Chica St Huntington Beach (92649) *(G-2116)*
Airemasters Air Conditioning, Santa Fe Springs *Also called Scorpio Enterprises (G-2361)*
Airespring Inc....818 786-8990
6060 Sepulveda Blvd # 220 Van Nuys (91411) *(G-5456)*
Airfield Maintenance, Sacramento *Also called County of Sacramento (G-14270)*
Airflite Inc....562 490-6200
3250 Airflite Way Long Beach (90807) *(G-4896)*
Airframer R, Torrance *Also called Sonic Industries Inc (G-26070)*
Airgas Inc....530 241-1544
653 N Market St Redding (96003) *(G-8970)*
Airgas Inc....858 279-8200
9010 Clairemont Mesa Blvd San Diego (92123) *(G-8971)*
Airgas Safety Inc....562 699-5239
2355 Workman Mill Rd City of Industry (90601) *(G-8972)*
Airgas Usa LLC- West Division....562 497-1991
3737 Worsham Ave Long Beach (90808) *(G-8973)*
Airgas USA LLC....858 279-8200
9010 Clairemont Mesa Blvd San Diego (92123) *(G-8974)*
Airgas USA LLC....323 568-2244
11711 S Alameda St Los Angeles (90059) *(G-8975)*
Airgas USA LLC....562 497-1991
3737 Worsham Ave Long Beach (90808) *(G-8976)*
Airgas USA LLC....408 998-6380
441 Hobson St San Jose (95110) *(G-7817)*
Airline Coach Service Inc (PA)....650 697-7733
863 Malcolm Rd Burlingame (94010) *(G-3632)*
Airmagnet Inc....408 400-0200
830 E Arques Ave Sunnyvale (94085) *(G-7087)*
Airmotive Carburetor Co, Burbank *Also called William F Kellogg Corporation (G-8010)*
Airpark Partners, Riverside *Also called Abbey Partner VI (G-11272)*
Airport Century Inn....310 649-4000
5547 W Century Blvd Los Angeles (90045) *(G-12376)*
Airport Cinemas 12, Santa Rosa *Also called North American Cinemas Inc (G-18339)*
Airport Club....707 528-2582
432 Aviation Blvd Santa Rosa (95403) *(G-18844)*
Airport Commisions....650 821-5000
San Francisco Intl Arprt San Francisco (94128) *(G-4897)*
Airport Connection Inc....805 389-8196
240 S Glenn Dr Camarillo (93010) *(G-3633)*
Airport Health Club, Santa Rosa *Also called Airport Club (G-18844)*
Airport Parking Services, San Bruno *Also called Skypark Inc (G-13794)*
Airpush Inc....877 944-2490
11400 W Olympic Blvd Los Angeles (90064) *(G-13815)*
Airtek Indoor Air Solutions, Azusa *Also called Applebee & Sheehan Inc (G-14231)*
Ais Construction Company....805 928-9467
1811 W Betteravia Rd Santa Maria (93455) *(G-1486)*
Ait Worldwide Logistics Inc....310 538-4383
19901 Hamilton Ave Ste D Torrance (90502) *(G-5021)*
AJ Kirkwood & Associates Inc....714 505-1977
2752 Walnut Ave Tustin (92780) *(G-2511)*
Ajax Portable Services....831 384-5000
11240 Commercial Pkwy Castroville (95012) *(G-14509)*
Ajc Sandblasting Inc....562 436-3606
932 Schley Ave Wilmington (90744) *(G-3485)*
Ajit Healthcare Inc....213 484-0510
316 S Westlake Ave Los Angeles (90057) *(G-26914)*
AJM Packaging Corporation....619 448-4007
1160 Vernon Way El Cajon (92020) *(G-9242)*
Ajr Trucking Inc....562 989-9555
2700 Rose Ave Ste A Signal Hill (90755) *(G-3975)*
AK Constructors Inc....951 280-0269
1828 Railroad St Corona (92880) *(G-1487)*
Akamai Holding Inc....951 922-2419
515 W Ramsey St Ste A Banning (92220) *(G-13718)*
Akela Pharma Inc....512 391-3525
11011 Torreyana Rd 100 San Diego (92121) *(G-26731)*
Akin Gump Strauss....310 229-1000
2029 Century Park E # 2400 Los Angeles (90067) *(G-23083)*
Akin Gump Strauss....415 765-9500
580 California St # 1500 San Francisco (94104) *(G-23084)*
Akland Healthcare Wellness Ctr, Oakland *Also called Oakland Healthcare & Wellness (G-20817)*
Akqa Inc (HQ)....415 645-9400
360 3rd St Ste 500 San Francisco (94107) *(G-27313)*
Al - Amir Group Llc....408 505-9458
380 Northlake Dr Apt 28 San Jose (95117) *(G-6105)*
Al Anwa USA Incorporated....310 301-2000
4200 Admiralty Way Marina Del Rey (90292) *(G-12377)*
Al Barcellos Et....209 826-2636
17599 Ward Rd Los Banos (93635) *(G-9)*
ALABBASI, Perris *Also called Mamco Inc (G-1819)*
Aladdin Bail Bonds, Fairfield *Also called Two Jinn Inc (G-17547)*
Aladdin Bail Bonds, Carlsbad *Also called Two Jinn Inc (G-17548)*
Aladdin Sonora Motor Inn....209 533-4971
14260 Mono Way Sonora (95370) *(G-12378)*
Alaidandrew Corporation....661 334-2200
1205 8th St Bakersfield (93304) *(G-21129)*

ALPHABETIC

Alain Pinel Realtors 831 622-1040
Junipero Between 5 & 6 # 56 Carmel (93921) ***(G-11279)***
Alain Pinel Realtors Inc 415 814-6690
2001 Union St Ste 200 San Francisco (94123) ***(G-11280)***
Alain Pinel Realtors Inc 415 755-1111
101 Nellen Ave Corte Madera (94925) ***(G-11281)***
Alain Pinel Realtors Inc 650 548-1111
520 S El Camino Real # 100 San Mateo (94402) ***(G-11282)***
Alain Pinel Realtors Inc 408 358-1111
750 University Ave # 150 Los Gatos (95032) ***(G-11283)***
Alain Pinel Realtors Inc 707 636-3800
2911 Cleveland Ave Santa Rosa (95403) ***(G-11284)***
Alain Pinel Realtors Inc 925 251-1111
900 Main St Ste 101 Pleasanton (94566) ***(G-11285)***
Alain Pinel Realtors Inc 650 375-1111
1440 Chapin Ave Ste 200 Burlingame (94010) ***(G-11286)***
Alain Pinel Realtors Inc 650 323-1111
578 University Ave Palo Alto (94301) ***(G-11287)***
Alain Pinel Realtors Inc 650 941-1111
167 S San Antonio Rd # 1 Los Altos (94022) ***(G-11288)***
Alain Pinel Realtors Inc 650 462-1111
1550 El Camino Real # 100 Menlo Park (94025) ***(G-11289)***
Alakor Healthcare LLC 626 408-9800
323 S Heliotrope Ave Monrovia (91016) ***(G-21441)***
Alameda Alliance For Health 510 747-4555
1240 S Loop Rd Alameda (94502) ***(G-10254)***
Alameda Bureau Elec Imprv Corp (PA) 510 748-3901
2000 Grand St Alameda (94501) ***(G-6106)***
Alameda Care Center, Burbank *Also called Artesia Healthcare Inc* ***(G-20383)***
Alameda Care Center, Alameda *Also called Shoreline S Intermediate Care* ***(G-21107)***
Alameda Chapel of The Chimes, Hayward *Also called Chapel of Chimes* ***(G-12028)***
Alameda Cnty Cmnty Fd Bnk Inc 510 635-3663
7900 Edgewater Dr Oakland (94621) ***(G-23649)***
Alameda Corridor Engrg Team 310 816-0460
1 Civic Plaza Dr Ste 600 Carson (90745) ***(G-25645)***
Alameda County 510 383-1556
2000 Embarcadero Ste 101 Oakland (94606) ***(G-23650)***
Alameda County AG Fair Assn 925 426-7600
4501 Pleasanton Ave Pleasanton (94566) ***(G-19132)***
Alameda County Employees Retir 510 628-3000
475 14th St Ste 1000 Oakland (94612) ***(G-10539)***
Alameda County Fair, Pleasanton *Also called Alameda County AG Fair Assn* ***(G-19132)***
Alameda County Industries Inc 510 357-7282
610 Aladdin Ave San Leandro (94577) ***(G-6423)***
Alameda County Water District (PA) 510 668-4200
43885 S Grimmer Blvd Fremont (94538) ***(G-6310)***
Alameda Family Services 510 629-6300
2325 Clement Ave Alameda (94501) ***(G-24414)***
Alameda Halthcare Wellness Ctr, Alameda *Also called Alameda Hlthcare & Wellnss Ctr* ***(G-20373)***
Alameda Hlthcare & Wellnss Ctr 510 523-8857
430 Willow St Alameda (94501) ***(G-20373)***
Alameda Hospital, Alameda *Also called City Alameda Health Care Corp* ***(G-21494)***
Alameda Municpal Power, Alameda *Also called Alameda Bureau Elec Imprv Corp* ***(G-6106)***
Alameda Produce Market LLC 213 221-3400
761 Terminal St Ste 2 Los Angeles (90021) ***(G-11290)***
Alameda, County Medical Center, San Leandro *Also called County of Alameda* ***(G-19464)***
Alameda-Contra Costa Trnst Dst (PA) 510 891-4777
1600 Franklin St Oakland (94612) ***(G-3634)***
Alameda-Contra Costa Trnst Dst 510 577-8816
10626 International Blvd Oakland (94603) ***(G-3954)***
Alamitos Blmont Rhbltion Hosp, Long Beach *Also called Alamitos-Belmont Rehab Inc* ***(G-22113)***
Alamitos Convalescent Hospital, Los Alamitos *Also called Goodman Group Inc* ***(G-11558)***
Alamitos Enterprises LLC (PA) 562 596-1827
3311 Katella Ave Los Alamitos (90720) ***(G-17870)***
Alamitos W Convalescent Hosp, Los Alamitos *Also called Katella Properties* ***(G-20694)***
Alamitos-Belmont Rehab Inc 562 434-8421
3901 E 4th St Long Beach (90814) ***(G-22113)***
Alamo Medical Group, Alamo *Also called John Muir Physician Network* ***(G-19577)***
Alamo Rent A Car, Inglewood *Also called Alamo Rental (us) Inc* ***(G-17659)***
Alamo Rent A Car, Newport Beach *Also called Alamo Rental (us) Inc* ***(G-17660)***
Alamo Rental (us) Inc 310 649-2242
9020 Aviation Blvd Inglewood (90301) ***(G-17659)***
Alamo Rental (us) Inc 949 852-0403
4361 Birch St Newport Beach (92660) ***(G-17660)***
Alan B Whitson Company Inc 949 955-1200
1507 W Alton Ave Santa Ana (92704) ***(G-27314)***
Alan Smith Pool Plastering Inc 714 628-9494
227 W Carleton Ave Orange (92867) ***(G-2848)***
Alaska Airlines Inc 800 426-0333
Ontario Intl Arprt Ontario (91761) ***(G-4781)***
Alaska Airlines Inc 310 342-4401
300 World Way Los Angeles (90045) ***(G-4782)***
Alaska Airlines Inc 619 238-2042
3665 N Harbor Dr Ste 228 San Diego (92101) ***(G-4783)***
Alaska Airlines Inc 510 577-5813
1 Airport Dr Ste 24 Oakland (94621) ***(G-4784)***
Alaska Diesel Electric 626 934-6211
425 S Hacienda Blvd City of Industry (91745) ***(G-17819)***
Alaska Experiment Inc 323 904-4680
3800 Barham Blvd Ste 410 Los Angeles (90068) ***(G-2512)***
Albany Inventory Services 818 505-8138
11490 Burbank Blvd Ste 1 North Hollywood (91601) ***(G-16976)***
Albd Electric and Cable 949 440-1216
2912 E Blue Star St Anaheim (92806) ***(G-2513)***
Albert A Webb Associates (PA) 951 686-1070
3788 Mccray St Riverside (92506) ***(G-25646)***

ALPHABETIC

Albert D Seeno Cnstr Co Inc 925 671-7711
4021 Port Chicago Hwy Concord (94520) ***(G-1355)***
Albertsons LLC 714 578-4670
777 S Harbor Blvd La Habra (90631) ***(G-4519)***
Albertsons LLC 714 990-8200
200 N Puente St Brea (92821) ***(G-4520)***
Albertsons Brea Dist Ctr, Brea *Also called Albertsons LLC* ***(G-4520)***
Albertsons Dist Ctr 8760, La Habra *Also called Albertsons LLC* ***(G-4519)***
Albertsons Dist Ctr 8795, Vacaville *Also called Albertsons LLC* ***(G-4521)***
Albertsons LLC 707 446-5922
700 Crocker Dr Vacaville (95688) ***(G-4521)***
Albion River Inn Incorporated 707 937-1919
3790 N Highway 1 Albion (95410) ***(G-12379)***
Alcatraz Cruises LLC 415 981-7625
Hornb Alcat Landi Pier 33 St Pier San Francisco (94111) ***(G-4984)***
Alco Iron & Metal Co (PA) 510 562-1107
2140 Davis St San Leandro (94577) ***(G-8058)***
Alcoa Global Fasteners, Inc., Simi Valley *Also called Arconic Global Fas & Rings Inc* ***(G-7918)***
Alcohol DRG Program Yolo Cnty 530 666-8650
137 N Cottonwood St Ste 1 Woodland (95695) ***(G-22652)***
Alcone Marketing Group Inc (HQ) 949 595-5322
4 Studebaker Irvine (92618) ***(G-13816)***
Alcorn Fence Company (PA) 818 983-0650
9901 Glenoaks Blvd Sun Valley (91352) ***(G-3486)***
Alcott Rehabilitation Hospital, Los Angeles *Also called Inland Medical Enterprises* ***(G-20686)***
Aldersly Retirement Center 415 453-9271
326 Mission Ave San Rafael (94901) ***(G-11081)***
ALDERSLY RETIREMENT COMMUNITY, San Rafael *Also called Aldersly Retirement Center* ***(G-11081)***
ALDERSON CONVALESCENT HOSPITAL, Woodland *Also called United Health Systems Inc* ***(G-20999)***
Alderwood Inc 626 289-4439
115 Bridge St San Gabriel (91775) ***(G-21130)***
Alderwoods (delaware) Inc 209 883-0411
900 Santa Fe Ave Hughson (95326) ***(G-12027)***
Aldoc Inc 714 836-8477
304 N Townsend St Ste D Santa Ana (92703) ***(G-2117)***
Aldon Ter Convalsent Hosptial, Los Angeles *Also called Longwood Management Corp* ***(G-21299)***
Aldridge Pite LLP 858 750-7700
4375 Jutland Dr Ste 200 San Diego (92117) ***(G-23085)***
Alecto Healthcare Services LLC (PA) 323 938-3161
16310 Bake Pkwy Ste 200 Irvine (92618) ***(G-21442)***
Alegrecare Inc 415 974-3530
1375 Sutter St Ste 110 San Francisco (94109) ***(G-16977)***
Aleks Corporation 714 245-7191
15640 Laguna Canyon Rd Irvine (92618) ***(G-15575)***
Aleks Educational Systems, Irvine *Also called Aleks Corporation* ***(G-15575)***
Alemeda County Industries LLC 510 357-7282
610 Aladdin Ave San Leandro (94577) ***(G-6424)***
Alert Communications, Camarillo *Also called Affiliated Communications Inc* ***(G-16973)***
Alert Insulation Company Inc 626 961-9113
15913 Old Valley Blvd A La Puente (91744) ***(G-2849)***
Alert One, San Jose *Also called Responselink LLC* ***(G-19912)***
Alex Moving & Storage, Anaheim *Also called Uribe Trucking Inc* ***(G-4385)***
Alexander Delu 209 334-6660
15175 N Devries Rd Lodi (95242) ***(G-140)***
Alexander Properties Company 925 866-0100
1 Annabel Ln San Ramon (94583) ***(G-10954)***
Alexander's Grand Salon & Spa, Anaheim *Also called Alexanders Grand Salon* ***(G-13666)***
Alexanders Grand Salon 714 282-6438
5579 E Santa Ana Cyn Rd Anaheim (92807) ***(G-13666)***
Alexanders Mobility Services 714 731-1658
2942 Dow Ave Tustin (92780) ***(G-5211)***
Alexandre Ecodairy Farms, Crescent City *Also called Blake Alexandre* ***(G-418)***
Alexandria Care Center LLC 323 660-1800
1515 N Alexandria Ave Los Angeles (90027) ***(G-21131)***
Alfa Marine Services, Imperial Beach *Also called Offshore Service Vessels LLC* ***(G-4751)***
Alfa Tech Cnslting Engners Inc (PA) 408 487-1200
1321 Ridder Park Dr 50 San Jose (95131) ***(G-25647)***
Alfa Tech Consulting Entps, San Jose *Also called Alfa Tech Cnslting Engners Inc* ***(G-25647)***
Alfatech Cambridge Group GP 650 543-3030
345 S California Ave # 3 Palo Alto (94306) ***(G-26915)***
Alfreds Pictures Frames Inc 714 434-4838
1580 Sunflower Ave Costa Mesa (92626) ***(G-16978)***
Alfresco Software Inc (PA) 888 317-3395
1825 S Grant St Ste 900 San Mateo (94402) ***(G-15576)***
Alg Worldwide Logistics LLC 800 932-3383
220 W Victoria St Rancho Dominguez (90220) ***(G-5022)***
Algonquin Power and Utilities 530 543-5288
933 Eloise Ave South Lake Tahoe (96150) ***(G-2514)***
Algos Inc A Medical Corp (PA) 626 696-1400
224 N Fair Oaks Ave Pasadena (91103) ***(G-22653)***
Alhambra, San Francisco *Also called Ds Services of America Inc* ***(G-8828)***
Alhambra Convalescent Hosp LLC 925 228-2020
331 Ilene St Martinez (94553) ***(G-20374)***
Alhambra Healthcare & Wellness 626 282-3151
415 S Garfield Ave Alhambra (91801) ***(G-20375)***
Alhambra Hospital Med Ctr LP 626 570-1606
100 S Raymond Ave Alhambra (91801) ***(G-21443)***
Alhambra Hospital Medical Ctr, Alhambra *Also called Alhambra Hospital Med Ctr LP* ***(G-21443)***
Alhambra/Sierra Springs 408 727-0677
485 Vista Way Milpitas (95035) ***(G-8793)***
Aliantel Inc 800 274-7074
1940 W Corporate Way Anaheim (92801) ***(G-27823)***

Alicia Arroyo Inc......831 675-2850
800 Johnson Cyn Rd 4 Gonzales (93926) ***(G-648)***
Alienvault LLC (PA)......650 713-3333
1875 S Grant St Ste 200 San Mateo (94402) ***(G-15577)***
Align Aerospace LLC (HQ)......818 727-7800
21123 Nordhoff St Chatsworth (91311) ***(G-7992)***
Alignment Health Plan......323 728-7232
1100 W Town & Country Orange (92868) ***(G-10255)***
Alion Science and Tech Corp......805 488-8761
266 E Scott St Port Hueneme (93041) ***(G-25648)***
Aliphcom (PA)......415 230-7600
99 Rhode Island St Fl 3 San Francisco (94103) ***(G-7516)***
Alisal Guest Ranch, Solvang *Also called Alisal Properties* ***(G-13458)***
Alisal Health Center, Salinas *Also called County of Monterey* ***(G-19476)***
Alisal Properties (PA)......805 688-6411
1054 Alisal Rd Solvang (93463) ***(G-13458)***
Alisam Oxnard Operating......310 877-7179
212 26th St Ste 246 Santa Monica (90402) ***(G-10955)***
Aliso Air Conditioning & Htg, Rancho Santa Margari *Also called Jct Company LLC* ***(G-2261)***
Aliso Creek Inn and Golf Crse, Laguna Beach *Also called Laguna Bch Golf Bnglow Vlg LLC* ***(G-18752)***
Aliso Mechanical Incorporated......949 544-1601
29736 A De Las Bandera Rancho Santa Margari (92688) ***(G-2118)***
Aliso Viejo Country Club, Aliso Viejo *Also called Aliso Viejo Golf Club Inc* ***(G-18845)***
Aliso Viejo Golf Club Inc......949 598-9200
33 Santa Barbara Dr Aliso Viejo (92656) ***(G-18845)***
Aliso Viejo Medical Offices, Aliso Viejo *Also called Kaiser Foundation Hospitals* ***(G-19580)***
Alix Technologies Inc......714 630-6000
2929 E White Star Ave Anaheim (92806) ***(G-8226)***
All Action Security Inc......800 482-7371
20501 Ventura Blvd # 275 Woodland Hills (91364) ***(G-16540)***
All American Agrigate, Corona *Also called All American Asphalt* ***(G-1725)***
All American Asphalt (PA)......951 736-7600
400 E 6th St Corona (92879) ***(G-1725)***
All American Asphalt......951 736-7617
1776 All American Way Corona (92879) ***(G-1726)***
All American Asphalt......951 736-7617
1776 All American Way Corona (92879) ***(G-1727)***
All American Maintenance, Chatsworth *Also called Marotto Corporation* ***(G-14350)***
All American Service & Sups......951 736-3880
1776 All American Way Corona (92879) ***(G-17958)***
All Area Plumbing Inc......323 939-9990
5742 Venice Blvd Los Angeles (90019) ***(G-2119)***
All Axis Enterprise Inc......510 451-1200
4408 Market St Ste E Oakland (94608) ***(G-1122)***
All Care Industries Inc......562 623-4009
16747 1/2 Parkside Ave Cerritos (90703) ***(G-14218)***
All Care Medical Group Inc......408 278-3550
31 Crescent St Huntington Park (90255) ***(G-19329)***
All Care Services Inc......714 669-1148
17671 Irvine Blvd Ste 110 Tustin (92780) ***(G-23651)***
All Commercial Landscape Svc......559 453-1670
5213 E Pine Ave Fresno (93727) ***(G-805)***
All Control Cleaning Inc......805 987-4210
124 N Aviador St Ste 1 Camarillo (93010) ***(G-14219)***
All Counties Courier Inc......949 224-0900
14811 Myford Rd Tustin (92780) ***(G-4394)***
All Day Electric Company Inc......707 748-1036
4620 W America Dr B Fairfield (94534) ***(G-2515)***
All Direct Mail Services Inc......818 833-7773
5091 4th St Baldwin Park (91706) ***(G-14065)***
All Environmental Inc......949 752-9300
1200 Main St Ste D Irvine (92614) ***(G-27824)***
All Environmental Inc......310 798-4255
2447 Pcf Cast Hwy Ste 101 Hermosa Beach (90254) ***(G-27825)***
All Fab Prcsion Sheetmetal Inc......408 279-1099
1015 Timothy Dr San Jose (95133) ***(G-3138)***
All For You Home Care, Sacramento *Also called Careability Health Svcs Corp* ***(G-22395)***
All Hallows Garden Apartments, San Francisco *Also called All Hallows Preservation LP* ***(G-11082)***
All Hallows Preservation LP......415 285-3909
54 Navy Rd San Francisco (94124) ***(G-11082)***
All Health Services Corp (PA)......559 583-9101
206 W 8th St Hanford (93230) ***(G-14603)***
All Hnds Crwash Dtail Ctr Lube......949 716-3600
22952 Pacific Park Dr Aliso Viejo (92656) ***(G-17828)***
All In One Inc......310 538-3374
1999 W 190th St Torrance (90504) ***(G-26916)***
All In One Complete Bldg Svcs, Vacaville *Also called Mark Garcia* ***(G-14349)***
All Motorists Insurance Agency......818 880-9070
5230 Las Virgenes Rd # 100 Calabasas (91302) ***(G-10585)***
All Phase Business Supplies......310 631-1900
1920 E Gladwick St Compton (90220) ***(G-8159)***
All Pro Drywall......530 722-5182
22148 Buckeye Pl Cottonwood (96022) ***(G-2850)***
All Pro Tools Inc......888 425-5776
1040 S Mount Vernon Ave G292 Colton (92324) ***(G-7667)***
ALL SAINTS SUBACUTE REHABILITA, Hayward *Also called Ty Five Star Corporation* ***(G-21975)***
All Seasons Framing Corp......714 634-2324
644 N Eckhoff St Orange (92868) ***(G-3028)***
All South Bay Central Office......310 618-1180
1411 Marcelina Ave Torrance (90501) ***(G-25486)***
All Star Automotive Products......626 960-5164
4150 Puente Ave Baldwin Park (91706) ***(G-6703)***
All Star Glass Inc (PA)......619 275-3343
1845 Morena Blvd San Diego (92110) ***(G-17781)***
All Star Maintenance Inc......858 259-0900
12250 El Camino Real # 300 San Diego (92130) ***(G-3487)***
All Star Seed (PA)......760 482-9400
2015 Silsbee Rd El Centro (92243) ***(G-506)***
All Stars......858 259-0900
12250 El Camino Real # 300 San Diego (92130) ***(G-3488)***
All State Association Inc......877 425-2558
11487 San Fernando Rd San Fernando (91340) ***(G-3976)***
All Taxi Electronics, San Francisco *Also called Yellow Cab Cooperative Inc* ***(G-3875)***
All Tmperatures Controlled Inc......818 882-1478
9720 Topanga Canyon Pl Chatsworth (91311) ***(G-2120)***
All Types of Baseboard, San Diego *Also called Juan Lopez* ***(G-1199)***
All Valley Home Care, San Diego *Also called All Valley Home Hlth Care Inc* ***(G-22881)***
All Valley Home Hlth Care Inc......619 276-8001
3665 Ruffin Rd Ste 103 San Diego (92123) ***(G-22881)***
All Valley Washer Service Inc......818 787-1100
15008 Delano St Van Nuys (91411) ***(G-13572)***
All West Coachlines, Sacramento *Also called Cusa AWC LLC* ***(G-3640)***
All West Coachlines Inc......916 423-4000
7701 Wilbur Way Sacramento (95828) ***(G-3897)***
All-Battery.com, Fremont *Also called Tenergy Corporation* ***(G-7478)***
All-City Management Svcs Inc......310 202-8284
10440 Pioneer Blvd Ste 5 Santa Fe Springs (90670) ***(G-27826)***
All-Guard Alarm Systems Inc (PA)......510 887-7055
1306 Stealth St Livermore (94551) ***(G-2516)***
All-Phase Electric Supply, Burbank *Also called Consolidated Elec Distrs Inc* ***(G-7431)***
All-Points Petroleum LLC......707 745-1116
640 Noyes Ct Benicia (94510) ***(G-9011)***
All-Pro Bail Bonds Inc (PA)......858 481-1200
512 Via De La Valle # 301 Solana Beach (92075) ***(G-16979)***
All-Pro Bail Bonds Inc......760 941-4100
530 Hacienda Dr Ste 104d Vista (92081) ***(G-16980)***
All-Pro Remodeling......714 288-1314
706 N Tustin St Orange (92867) ***(G-1289)***
All-Rite Leasing Company Inc......714 530-7074
3420 Bristol St Ste 210 Costa Mesa (92626) ***(G-14220)***
Allan Automatic Sprinkler Corp......714 993-9500
3233 Enterprise St Brea (92821) ***(G-2121)***
Allan Company, Baldwin Park *Also called Cedarwood-Young Company* ***(G-8067)***
Allan Company, Baldwin Park *Also called Cedarwood-Young Company* ***(G-8068)***
Allaquaria LLC......310 645-1107
5420 W 104th St Los Angeles (90045) ***(G-9243)***
Alldata LLC (HQ)......916 684-5200
9650 W Taron Dr Ste 100 Elk Grove (95757) ***(G-15578)***
Alldayeveryday Productions LLC......323 556-6200
662 N Crescent Hts Blvd Los Angeles (90048) ***(G-18039)***
Alldrin Brothers Inc......855 667-4231
584 Hi Tech Pkwy Oakdale (95361) ***(G-507)***
Alldrin Brothers Almonds, Oakdale *Also called Alldrin Brothers Inc* ***(G-507)***
Allegis Group Inc......650 425-6950
1 Waters Park Dr San Mateo (94403) ***(G-14835)***
Allegis Residential Svcs Inc......858 430-5700
9340 Hazard Way Ste B2 San Diego (92123) ***(G-26917)***
Allen Spees Family Homes......559 432-3664
524 W Roberts Ave Fresno (93704) ***(G-24544)***
Allen Construction Inc......818 879-5334
31356 Via Colinas Ste 107 Westlake Village (91362) ***(G-3029)***
Allen Development Partners LLC (PA)......559 732-5425
125 Sbridge 100 Visalia (93291) ***(G-11945)***
Allen Drywall & Associates......650 579-0664
380 Lang Rd Burlingame (94010) ***(G-2851)***
Allen L Bender Inc......916 372-2190
2798 Industrial Blvd West Sacramento (95691) ***(G-1488)***
Allen Lee Rose Inc......858 587-3100
9370 Sky Park Ct Ste 250 San Diego (92123) ***(G-14604)***
Allen Lund Company Inc (PA)......818 790-8412
4529 Angeles Crest Hwy La Canada Flintridge (91011) ***(G-5023)***
Allen Lund Company LLC (HQ)......818 790-1110
4529 Angeles Crest Hwy # 300 La Canada Flintridge (91011) ***(G-5024)***
Allen Lund Company LLC......650 358-9454
1825 S Grant St Ste 320 San Mateo (94402) ***(G-5025)***
Allen Matkins, San Francisco *Also called Eileen Nottoli* ***(G-23232)***
Allen Matkins Leck Gmble......415 837-1515
3 Embarcadero Ctr Fl 12 San Francisco (94111) ***(G-23086)***
Allen Matkins Leck Gmble......949 553-1313
1900 Main St Fl 5 Irvine (92614) ***(G-23087)***
Allen Matkins Leck Gmble (PA)......213 622-5555
515 S Figueroa St Fl 9 Los Angeles (90071) ***(G-23088)***
Allen Medical Group Inc......818 698-8444
14416 Victory Blvd # 211 Van Nuys (91401) ***(G-19330)***
Allen Transportation Co, Sacramento *Also called Amador Stage Lines Inc* ***(G-3890)***
Allergan Sales LLC (HQ)......714 246-4500
2525 Dupont Dr 14th Irvine (92612) ***(G-8227)***
Alliance Bay Funding Inc......510 742-6600
37600 Central Ct Ste 264 Newark (94560) ***(G-11291)***
Alliance Capital Markets, Orange *Also called Alliance Funding Group* ***(G-9791)***
Alliance Construction, Costa Mesa *Also called Empire Leasing Inc* ***(G-3046)***
Alliance Credit Union (PA)......408 445-3386
3315 Almaden Expy Ste 55 San Jose (95118) ***(G-9650)***
Alliance Envmtl Group Inc......805 378-6590
680 Flinn Ave Unit 32 Moorpark (93021) ***(G-28111)***
Alliance Fc......909 784-0005
3496 Little League Dr San Bernardino (92407) ***(G-25487)***
Alliance Funding Group......714 940-0653
3745 W Chapman Ave # 200 Orange (92868) ***(G-9791)***
Alliance Ground Intl LLC......310 646-2446
6181 W Imperial Hwy Los Angeles (90045) ***(G-4898)***

A L P H A B E T I C

Alliance Ground Intl LLC...650 821-0855
648 Rest Field Rd San Francisco (94128) **(G-4899)**
Alliance Health Inc...661 325-6937
5300 Lennox Ave Ste 103 Bakersfield (93309) **(G-28112)**
Alliance Healthcare Svcs Inc (PA)...949 242-5300
100 Bayview Cir Ste 400 Newport Beach (92660) **(G-22188)**
Alliance Hospital Services...650 697-6900
100 S San Mateo Dr San Mateo (94401) **(G-22350)**
Alliance Medical Center Inc...707 431-8234
1381 University St Healdsburg (95448) **(G-19331)**
Alliance Member Services Inc...831 459-0980
333 Front St Ste 200 Santa Cruz (95060) **(G-25488)**
Alliance Nrsing Rhbltation Ctr, El Monte *Also called Georgia Atkison Snf LLC* **(G-20596)**
Alliance Rdwods Cnfrnce Grunds...707 874-3507
6250 Bohemian Hwy Occidental (95465) **(G-13459)**
Alliance Roofing Company Inc (PA)...800 579-2595
630 Martin Ave Santa Clara (95050) **(G-3139)**
Alliance Rvrside Hsptality LLC...949 229-3168
21520 Yorba Linda Blvd Yorba Linda (92887) **(G-12380)**
Alliance Title, Glendale *Also called Wfg National Title Insur Co* **(G-10538)**
Alliance Wall Systems Inc...530 740-7800
4638 Skyway Dr Marysville (95901) **(G-2852)**
Alliance Work Net, Modesto *Also called County of Stanislaus* **(G-24333)**
Alliancebernstein LP...310 286-6000
1999 Ave Of The Sts 215 Ste 2150 Los Angeles (90067) **(G-10111)**
Alliant Asset MGT Co LLC (PA)...818 668-2805
21600 Oxnard St Ste 1200 Woodland Hills (91367) **(G-11292)**
Alliant Educational Foundation...559 456-2777
5130 E Clinton Way Fresno (93727) **(G-22654)**
Alliant Insurance Services Inc (PA)...949 756-0271
1301 Dove St Ste 200 Newport Beach (92660) **(G-10586)**
Alliant Insurance Services Inc...619 238-1828
701 B St Ste 600 San Diego (92101) **(G-10587)**
Alliant Tchsystems Oprtons LLC...818 887-8195
9401 Corbin Ave Northridge (91324) **(G-26464)**
Allianz Globl Corp & Specialty, Burbank *Also called Allianz Underwriters Insur Co* **(G-10396)**
Allianz Globl Investors US LLC...415 954-5400
555 Mission St Ste 1700 San Francisco (94105) **(G-10112)**
Allianz Globl Invstors Amer LP...949 219-2200
680 New Port Dr Ste 250 Newport Beach (92660) **(G-10113)**
Allianz Globl Invstors Amer LP (HQ)...949 219-2200
680 Nwport Ctr Dr Ste 250 Newport Beach (92660) **(G-10114)**
Allianz Globl Risks US Insur (HQ)...818 260-7500
2350 W Empire Ave Burbank (91504) **(G-10395)**
Allianz Life, San Francisco *Also called Allianz Globl Investors US LLC* **(G-10112)**
Allianz Underwriters Insur Co...818 260-7500
2350 W Empire Ave Burbank (91504) **(G-10396)**
Allied Anesthesia Med Group...951 830-9816
400 N Tustin Ave Santa Ana (92705) **(G-19332)**
Allied Artists International, City of Industry *Also called Allied Entertainment Group Inc* **(G-18040)**
Allied Auto Store, Fremont *Also called Serrato-Mcdermott Inc* **(G-6762)**
Allied Barton Security Svcs, Palm Desert *Also called Alliedbarton Security Svcs LLC* **(G-16551)**
Allied Beverage LLC...818 493-6400
13235 Golden State Rd Sylmar (91342) **(G-7752)**
Allied Beverages Incorporated (PA)...818 493-6400
13235 Golden State Rd Sylmar (91342) **(G-9038)**
Allied Building Products Corp...714 647-9792
111 S Minnie St Santa Ana (92701) **(G-7005)**
Allied Building Products Corp...909 796-6926
456 Industrial Rd San Bernardino (92408) **(G-7023)**
Allied Building Products Corp...707 584-7599
4159 Santa Rosa Ave Santa Rosa (95407) **(G-7006)**
Allied Building Products Corp...323 721-9011
1620 S Maple Ave Montebello (90640) **(G-6905)**
Allied Digital Services LLC (HQ)...310 431-2375
680 Knox St Ste 200 Torrance (90502) **(G-16275)**
Allied Electric Motor Svc Inc (PA)...559 486-4222
4690 E Jensen Ave Fresno (93725) **(G-7411)**
Allied Entertainment Group Inc (PA)...626 330-0600
273 W Allen Ave City of Industry (91746) **(G-18040)**
Allied Environmental Services, Woodland Hills *Also called Allied Industries Inc* **(G-27827)**
Allied Farming Company, Exeter *Also called Sun Pacific Farming Coop Inc* **(G-724)**
Allied Fire Protection...510 533-5516
555 High St Oakland (94601) **(G-2122)**
Allied Food Distributors Inc...925 432-1625
1225 California Ave Pittsburg (94565) **(G-8794)**
Allied Framers Inc...707 452-7050
4990 Allison Pkwy Vacaville (95688) **(G-3030)**
Allied Gardens Towing Inc (HQ)...619 563-4060
9150 Chesapeake Dr # 240 San Diego (92123) **(G-17871)**
Allied High Tech Products Inc...310 635-2466
2376 E Pacifica Pl Rancho Dominguez (90220) **(G-7912)**
Allied Industries Inc (PA)...818 781-2490
21650 Oxnard St Ste 500 Woodland Hills (91367) **(G-27827)**
Allied Information & Services...510 769-9648
7750 Pardee Ln Ste 200 Oakland (94621) **(G-10588)**
Allied International, Sylmar *Also called AWI Acquisition Company* **(G-7674)**
Allied Interstate Inc (HQ)...818 575-5400
30699 Russell Ranch Rd # 250 Westlake Village (91362) **(G-14016)**
Allied Intl San Franisco, Hayward *Also called Nor-Cal Moving Services* **(G-4366)**
Allied Lube Texas LP (PA)...949 486-4008
4440 Von Karman Ave # 100 Newport Beach (92660) **(G-17872)**
Allied Medical Service of Cal...415 931-1400
2570 Bush St San Francisco (94115) **(G-3739)**
Allied Merchandising Industry, Corona *Also called Core-Mark Interrelated* **(G-9256)**
Allied Physicians...626 282-2116
1680 S Garfield Ave Alhambra (91801) **(G-22351)**
Allied Physicians, IPA, Alhambra *Also called Allied Physicians* **(G-22351)**
Allied Prof Nursing Care...909 949-1066
2345 W Fthlls Blvd Ste 14 Upland (91786) **(G-22352)**
Allied Protection Services Inc...310 330-8314
5757 W Century Blvd Los Angeles (90045) **(G-16541)**
Allied Refrigeration Inc...310 202-2220
3650 Holdrege Ave Los Angeles (90016) **(G-7734)**
Allied Risk Management Inc...661 305-0455
2010 W Avenue K 395 Lancaster (93536) **(G-16542)**
Allied Steel Co Inc...951 241-7000
1027 Palmyrita Ave Riverside (92507) **(G-3361)**
Allied Swift, Oceanside *Also called Allied Swiss Limited* **(G-10956)**
Allied Swiss Limited...760 941-1702
2636 Vista Pacific Dr Oceanside (92056) **(G-10956)**
Alliedbarton Security Svcs LLC...626 213-3100
765 The City Dr S Ste 150 Orange (92868) **(G-16543)**
Alliedbarton Security Svcs LLC...951 801-7300
3120 Chicago Ave Ste 190 Riverside (92507) **(G-16544)**
Alliedbarton Security Svcs LLC...310 324-1219
637 E Albertoni St # 202 Carson (90746) **(G-16545)**
Alliedbarton Security Svcs LLC...916 489-8280
8950 Cal Center Dr # 150 Sacramento (95826) **(G-16546)**
Alliedbarton Security Svcs LLC...805 480-3563
3529 Old Conejo Rd # 119 Newbury Park (91320) **(G-16547)**
Alliedbarton Security Svcs LLC...562 906-4800
10330 Pioneer Blvd # 235 Santa Fe Springs (90670) **(G-16863)**
Alliedbarton Security Svcs LLC...510 839-4041
1600 Riviera Ave Ste 375 Walnut Creek (94596) **(G-16864)**
Alliedbarton Security Svcs LLC...408 954-8274
2540 N 1st St Ste 101 San Jose (95131) **(G-16548)**
Alliedbarton Security Svcs LLC...858 874-8200
7670 Opportunity Rd # 210 San Diego (92111) **(G-16549)**
Alliedbarton Security Svcs LLC...800 418-6423
3701 Wilshire Blvd # 600 Los Angeles (90010) **(G-16550)**
Alliedbarton Security Svcs LLC...760 568-5550
41 945 Boardwalk Ste T Palm Desert (92211) **(G-16551)**
Alliedbarton Security Svcs LLC...714 260-0805
765 The City Dr S Ste 105 Orange (92868) **(G-16865)**
Allison Dowdy...707 303-3472
1045 College Ave Santa Rosa (95404) **(G-11293)**
Allison, Amanda Dvm, Elk Grove *Also called Bradshaw Veterinary Clinic* **(G-616)**
Allmark Inc (PA)...909 989-7556
10070 Arrow Rte Rancho Cucamonga (91730) **(G-11294)**
Allpro Industry Solutions LLC...661 854-3613
7850 White Ln Bakersfield (93309) **(G-5026)**
Allpro Tools.com, Colton *Also called All Pro Tools Inc* **(G-7667)**
Allred Child Developement Ctr, San Bernardino *Also called San Bernardino City Unf School* **(G-24509)**
Allstar Commercial Cleaning...858 715-0500
4805 Mercury St Ste H San Diego (92111) **(G-14221)**
Allstate, Corona *Also called Acm Technologies Inc* **(G-7039)**
Allstate, Torrance *Also called Janet Hilton* **(G-10753)**
Allstate Building Maintenance...714 739-8080
4890 Saint Andrews Ave Buena Park (90621) **(G-14222)**
Allstate Communications ASC, Chatsworth *Also called US Interstate Distrg Inc* **(G-5713)**
Allstate Construction Co...310 652-6942
1364 Londonderry Pl Los Angeles (90069) **(G-1123)**
Allstate Imaging Inc (PA)...818 678-4550
21621 Nordhoff St Chatsworth (91311) **(G-7040)**
Allstate Insurance Company...909 612-5504
21950 Copley Dr Ste 130 Diamond Bar (91765) **(G-10397)**
Allstate Research and Plg Ctr...650 833-6200
4200 Bohannon Dr Ste 200 Menlo Park (94025) **(G-10589)**
Alltech Services, Los Alamitos *Also called Mggb Inc* **(G-25963)**
Alltek Company U S A Inc...714 375-9785
18281 Gothard St Ste 102 Huntington Beach (92648) **(G-7818)**
Alltrade Tools LLC...310 522-9008
1431 W Via Plata St Long Beach (90810) **(G-7668)**
Ally Financial Inc...925 370-7200
2530 Arnold Dr Ste 300 Martinez (94553) **(G-9792)**
Alma Construction Co Inc...909 825-1328
1377 N La Cadena Dr Colton (92324) **(G-2853)**
ALMA VIA OF CAMARILLO, Alameda *Also called Elder Care Alliance Camarillo* **(G-24642)**
Almaden Golf & Country Club...408 323-4812
6663 Hampton Dr San Jose (95120) **(G-18846)**
Almaden Health & Rehab Ctr, San Jose *Also called Mariner Health Care Inc* **(G-20770)**
Almaden Press, Santa Clara *Also called Stone Publishing Inc* **(G-27232)**
Almaden Valley Athletic Club...408 445-4900
5400 Camden Ave San Jose (95124) **(G-18847)**
Almavia of San Francisco...415 337-1339
1 Thomas More Way San Francisco (94132) **(G-20376)**
Aloft El Sgnd-Los Angles Arprt, El Segundo *Also called Rubicon B Hacienda LLC* **(G-13179)**
Aloft Ontario-Rancho Cucamonga...909 484-2018
10480 4th St Rancho Cucamonga (91730) **(G-12381)**
Aloft Sfo, Millbrae *Also called Millbrae Wcp Hotel II LLC* **(G-12997)**
Alom Technologies Corporation (PA)...510 360-3600
48105 Warm Springs Blvd Fremont (94539) **(G-18213)**
Alondra Golf Course Inc...310 217-9915
16400 Prairie Ave Lawndale (90260) **(G-18710)**
Alonso Construction, Spring Valley *Also called Hugo Alonso Inc* **(G-1438)**
Alonzo Farms Inc...707 678-5282
7481 Batavia Rd Dixon (95620) **(G-344)**
Alorica Inc (PA)...949 527-4600
5 Park Plz Ste 1100 Irvine (92614) **(G-16981)**
Alpert & Alpert Iron & Met Inc...562 624-8833
2350 W 16th St Long Beach (90813) **(G-7354)**

ALPHABETIC SECTION

ALPERT JEWISH COMMUNITY CENTRE, Long Beach *Also called Jewish Community Ctr Long Bch* *(G-24043)*
Alpha Connection Group Home..................760 247-6370
  22675 Anoka Rd Apple Valley (92308) *(G-25164)*
ALPHA CONNECTION YOUTH FAMILY, Apple Valley *Also called Alpha Connection Group Home* *(G-25164)*
Alpha Entrprneur Hlth Fndation..................323 735-0873
  3655 Ruthelen St Los Angeles (90018) *(G-21444)*
Alpha Mechanical Inc..................858 278-3500
  4990 Greencraig Ln Ste A San Diego (92123) *(G-2123)*
Alpha Mechanical Inc (PA)..................858 278-3500
  4885 Greencraig Ln San Diego (92123) *(G-2124)*
Alpha Professional Resources, Thousand Oaks *Also called A P R Inc* *(G-14828)*
Alpha Shirt Company..................562 802-9919
  14061 Borate St Santa Fe Springs (90670) *(G-8331)*
Alpha Swimming Pool & Spa..................714 879-4667
  2600 Athena Pl Fullerton (92833) *(G-16982)*
Alpha Systems Fire Protection..................323 227-0700
  7356 Fulton Ave North Hollywood (91605) *(G-8104)*
Alpha Teknova Inc..................831 637-1100
  2290 Bert Dr Hollister (95023) *(G-26465)*
Alpha-Winfield Contractors Inc..................510 652-4712
  1096 Yerba Buena Ave Emeryville (94608) *(G-1124)*
Alphavista Services Inc..................408 331-2181
  1290 Kifer Rd Ste 301 Sunnyvale (94086) *(G-20305)*
Alpine Camp Conference Ctr Inc..................909 337-6287
  415 Clubhouse Dr Blue Jay (92317) *(G-19133)*
Alpine Convalescent Center..................619 659-3120
  2120 Alpine Blvd Alpine (91901) *(G-22655)*
Alpine Electronics America Inc..................310 783-7391
  2012 Abalone Ave Ste D Torrance (90501) *(G-7488)*
Alpine Electronics America Inc (HQ)..................310 326-8000
  19145 Gramercy Pl Torrance (90501) *(G-7489)*
Alpine Inn Restaurant, Torrance *Also called Alpine Village* *(G-10957)*
Alpine Meadows Ski Area..................530 583-4232
  2600 Alpine Meadows Rd Alpine Meadows (96146) *(G-12382)*
Alpine Meadows Ski Resort, Alpine Meadows *Also called Alpine Meadows Ski Area* *(G-12382)*
Alpine Special Treatment Ctr, Alpine *Also called Alpine Convalescent Center* *(G-22655)*
Alpine Village..................310 327-4384
  833 Torrance Blvd Ste 1a Torrance (90502) *(G-10957)*
Als Services Usa Corp..................562 597-3932
  1875 Coronado Ave Long Beach (90755) *(G-26830)*
Alsco - Geyer Irrigation Inc..................530 476-2253
  700 5th St Arbuckle (95912) *(G-7798)*
Alsco Inc..................510 237-9634
  1009 Factory St Richmond (94801) *(G-13510)*
Alsco Inc..................323 465-5111
  900 N Highland Ave Los Angeles (90038) *(G-13511)*
Alsco Inc..................805 650-6578
  2215 Palma Dr Ventura (93003) *(G-13512)*
Alsco Inc..................619 234-7291
  705 W Grape St San Diego (92101) *(G-13513)*
Alsco Inc..................415 648-9266
  1575 Indiana St San Francisco (94107) *(G-13514)*
Alsco Inc..................714 774-4165
  1750 S Zeyn St Anaheim (92802) *(G-13515)*
Alsco Inc..................707 523-3311
  3311 Industrial Dr Santa Rosa (95403) *(G-13516)*
Alsco Inc..................408 279-2345
  2275 Junction Ave San Jose (95131) *(G-13517)*
Alsco Inc..................707 751-0652
  5159 Commercial Cir Concord (94520) *(G-13518)*
Alsco Inc..................916 454-5545
  3391 Lanatt St Sacramento (95819) *(G-13519)*
Alston & Bird LLP..................213 626-8830
  333 S Hope St Ste 1600 Los Angeles (90071) *(G-23089)*
Alston & Bird LLP..................202 239-3673
  2815 Townsgate Rd Ste 200 Westlake Village (91361) *(G-23090)*
Alston Construction Co Inc (PA)..................916 340-2400
  8775 Folsom Blvd Ste 201 Sacramento (95826) *(G-1398)*
Alta Bates Summit Medical Ctr, Berkeley *Also called Surgery Center of Alta Bates* *(G-21937)*
Alta Bates Summit Medical Ctr, Berkeley *Also called Sutter East Bay Hospitals* *(G-21944)*
Alta Btes Cmprhnsive Cncer Ctr, Berkeley *Also called Surgery Center of Alta Bates* *(G-22842)*
Alta Cal Regional Ctr Inc..................530 674-3070
  950 Tharp Rd Ste 202 Yuba City (95993) *(G-23652)*
Alta Care Center LLC..................714 530-6322
  13075 Blackbird St Garden Grove (92843) *(G-21132)*
Alta Drywall, Escondido *Also called Innovative Drywall Systems Inc* *(G-2910)*
Alta Equipment Leasing Company..................415 875-1000
  50 California St Fl 24 San Francisco (94111) *(G-14510)*
Alta Healthcare System LLC..................818 787-1511
  14433 Emelita St Van Nuys (91401) *(G-24862)*
Alta Healthcare System LLC (HQ)..................323 267-0477
  4081 E Olympic Blvd Los Angeles (90023) *(G-24863)*
Alta Hollywood Community Hsptl..................818 787-1511
  14433 Emelita St Van Nuys (91401) *(G-22037)*
Alta Home Care Inc..................760 778-3443
  1059 N Palm Canyon Dr Palm Springs (92262) *(G-22353)*
Alta Home Care Inc..................714 744-8191
  1740 W Katella Ave Ste B Orange (92867) *(G-14605)*
Alta Hospitals System LLC..................323 267-0477
  4081 E Olympic Blvd Los Angeles (90023) *(G-21445)*
Alta Hospitals System LLC (HQ)..................310 943-4500
  10780 Santa Monica Blvd # 400 Los Angeles (90025) *(G-21446)*
Alta Interiors Inc..................951 784-1400
  847 Palmyrita Ave Riverside (92507) *(G-2854)*

Alta Loma Assisted Living LLC..................909 481-2600
  9428 19th St Murrieta (92562) *(G-23653)*
Alta Los Angeles Hospitals Inc..................323 267-0477
  4081 E Olympic Blvd Los Angeles (90023) *(G-21447)*
ALTA ONE FCU, Ridgecrest *Also called Altaone Federal Credit Union* *(G-9587)*
Alta Resources Corp..................714 672-9700
  975 W Imperial Hwy # 200 Brea (92821) *(G-16983)*
Alta Sierra Country Club Inc..................530 273-2041
  11897 Tammy Way Grass Valley (95949) *(G-18848)*
Alta Vista Country Club LLC..................714 524-1591
  777 Alta Vista St Placentia (92870) *(G-18849)*
Alta Vista Healthcare and Well..................951 688-8200
  9020 Garfield St Riverside (92503) *(G-19333)*
Alta Vista Healthcare Center, Riverside *Also called Kindred Healthcare Operating* *(G-21284)*
Alta Vista Solutions..................510 594-0510
  3260 Blume Dr Ste 500 Richmond (94806) *(G-25649)*
Alta-Dena Certified Dairy LLC..................858 292-6930
  4656 Cardin St San Diego (92111) *(G-8576)*
Altadena Town and Country Club..................626 345-9088
  2290 Country Club Dr Altadena (91001) *(G-18850)*
Altaf Zahid Engineering Svcs..................760 481-9072
  42051 Orange Blossom Dr Temecula (92591) *(G-16984)*
Altamed Health Services Corp..................323 980-4466
  5427 Whittier Blvd Los Angeles (90022) *(G-19334)*
Altamed Health Services Corp (PA)..................323 725-8751
  2040 Camfield Ave Commerce (90040) *(G-19335)*
Altamed Health Services Corp..................323 869-5448
  5427 Whittier Blvd Los Angeles (90022) *(G-19336)*
Altamed Health Services Corp..................562 949-8717
  9436 Slauson Ave Pico Rivera (90660) *(G-22882)*
Altametrics LLC..................800 676-1281
  3191 Red Hill Ave Ste 100 Costa Mesa (92626) *(G-7088)*
Altamont Infrastructure Co..................925 245-5500
  6185 Industrial Way Livermore (94551) *(G-6107)*
Altaone Federal Credit Union (PA)..................760 371-7000
  701 S China Lake Blvd Ridgecrest (93555) *(G-9587)*
Altcare Cedar Creek LLC..................510 527-7282
  868 Ensenada Ave Berkeley (94707) *(G-24545)*
Altec Products Inc (PA)..................949 727-1248
  23422 Mill Creek Dr # 225 Laguna Hills (92653) *(G-16985)*
Altegra Health..................310 776-4001
  3415 S Sepulveda Blvd # 900 Los Angeles (90034) *(G-27315)*
Alten Calsoftlabs, Santa Clara *Also called Calsoft Labs Inc* *(G-15913)*
Alten Construction Inc..................510 234-4200
  720 12th St Richmond (94801) *(G-1489)*
Altenheim Inc..................510 530-4013
  1720 Macarthur Blvd Oakland (94602) *(G-11083)*
Altera Real Estate..................949 547-7351
  33522 Niguel Rd Ste 200 Dana Point (92629) *(G-11295)*
Altium Inc (HQ)..................858 864-1661
  4275 Executive Sq Ste 825 La Jolla (92037) *(G-15005)*
Altium LLC..................858 864-1500
  4225 Executive Sq Ste 700 La Jolla (92037) *(G-15579)*
Altman Plants, Vista *Also called Altman Specialty Plants Inc* *(G-9176)*
Altman Specialty Plants Inc (PA)..................760 744-8191
  3742 Blue Bird Canyon Rd Vista (92084) *(G-9176)*
Alto Lucero Transitional Care, Santa Barbara *Also called Compass Health Inc* *(G-20469)*
Alton Geoscience, Irvine *Also called TRC Solutions Inc* *(G-28082)*
Alton Irvine Inc..................949 428-4141
  2052 Alton Pkwy Irvine (92606) *(G-6802)*
Altoon Partners LLP (PA)..................213 225-1900
  617 W 7th St Ste 400 Los Angeles (90017) *(G-26162)*
Altoon Porter, Los Angeles *Also called Altoon Partners LLP* *(G-26162)*
Altour International Inc..................310 571-6000
  12100 W Olympic Blvd # 300 Los Angeles (90064) *(G-4953)*
Altour International Inc (PA)..................310 571-6000
  12100 W Olympic Blvd # 300 Los Angeles (90064) *(G-4954)*
Altour Travel Master, Los Angeles *Also called Altour International Inc* *(G-4953)*
Altria Group Distribution Co..................804 274-2000
  300 N Lake Ave Ste 1100 Pasadena (91101) *(G-8963)*
Altria Group Distribution Co..................626 792-2900
  300 N Lake Ave Ste 1100 Pasadena (91101) *(G-9231)*
Altschool Inc..................415 255-9766
  1245 Folsom St San Francisco (94103) *(G-15006)*
Altura Centers For Health..................559 686-9097
  1201 N Cherry St Tulare (93274) *(G-19337)*
Altura Comm Solutions LLC (HQ)..................714 948-8400
  1335 S Acacia Ave Fullerton (92831) *(G-7517)*
Altura Credit Union (PA)..................888 883-7228
  2847 Campus Pkwy Riverside (92507) *(G-9651)*
Alumatec Inc..................818 609-7460
  18411 Sherman Way Reseda (91335) *(G-1056)*
Alvarado Parkway Institute, La Mesa *Also called Helix Healthcare Inc* *(G-22073)*
Alvarez & Marsal Holdings LLC..................415 490-2300
  100 Pine St Fl 9 San Francisco (94111) *(G-27316)*
Alvarion Inc (HQ)..................650 314-2500
  555 N Mathilda Ave # 210 Sunnyvale (94085) *(G-7518)*
Alves, Robert L, Selma *Also called Robert Alves Farms Inc* *(G-180)*
Alvizia Landscape Co LLC..................619 661-6557
  2520 Cactus Rd San Diego (92154) *(G-806)*
Always Best, City of Industry *Also called Rongcheng Trading LLC* *(G-8683)*
Always Home Nursing Svc Inc..................916 989-6420
  7777 Greenback Ln Ste 208 Citrus Heights (95610) *(G-22354)*
Always There Live In Care LLC..................888 606-8880
  7121 Magnolia Ave Riverside (92504) *(G-22355)*
Alzheimer's Center, Fullerton *Also called Fullerton Guest Home Inc* *(G-21229)*
Alzheimer's Living Center, Fresno *Also called Community Medical Centers* *(G-21504)*

Alzheimers Care Since 1983....714 641-0959
3730 S Greenville St Santa Ana (92704) *(G-22356)*
Alzheimers Family Services Ctr....714 593-9630
9451 Indianapolis Ave Huntington Beach (92646) *(G-23654)*
Alzheimers Greater Los Angeles....323 938-3379
4221 Wilshire Blvd # 400 Los Angeles (90010) *(G-23655)*
AM Cor Capital, Coachella *Also called Agri-Cal Venture Associates (G-690)*
AM Products Inc....714 662-4454
1661 Palm St Santa Ana (92701) *(G-7355)*
Am-PM Sewer & Drain Cleaning, San Diego *Also called Bill Howe Plumbing Inc (G-2167)*
Amada America Inc (HQ)....714 739-2111
7025 Firestone Blvd Buena Park (90621) *(G-7819)*
Amada Capital Corporation....714 739-2111
7025 Firestone Blvd Buena Park (90621) *(G-14511)*
Amada Enterprises Inc....323 757-1881
12619 Avalon Blvd Los Angeles (90061) *(G-20377)*
Amador Development, Azusa *Also called David L Amador Inc (G-3253)*
Amador Stage Lines Inc....916 444-7880
1331 C St Sacramento (95814) *(G-3890)*
Amador Tlmne Cmnty Action Agcy (PA)....209 296-2785
935 S State Highway 49 Jackson (95642) *(G-24864)*
Amador Tlmne Cmnty Action Agcy....209 533-1397
427 Highway 49 Sonora (95370) *(G-24865)*
Amador Water Agency....209 223-3018
12800 Ridge Rd Sutter Creek (95685) *(G-6311)*
Amador-Tolumne Cmnty Resources....209 223-1485
935 S State Highway 49 Jackson (95642) *(G-24866)*
Amanecer Cmnty Counseling Svc....213 481-7464
1200 Wilshire Blvd # 510 Los Angeles (90017) *(G-22656)*
Amar Transportation Inc (PA)....831 728-8209
144 W Lake Ave Ste C Watsonville (95076) *(G-4105)*
AMARAL RANCHES, Chualar *Also called C & G Farms Inc (G-44)*
Amato Industries Incorporated....650 697-2087
1550 Gilbreth Rd Burlingame (94010) *(G-3740)*
Amaturo Sonoma Media Group LLC....707 543-0126
1410 Neotomas Ave Ste 200 Santa Rosa (95405) *(G-5748)*
Amax Computer, Fremont *Also called Amax Engineering Corporation (G-7089)*
Amax Engineering Corporation (PA)....510 651-8886
1565 Reliance Way Fremont (94539) *(G-7089)*
Amazon Lab126....206 266-1000
1100 Enterprise Way Sunnyvale (94089) *(G-26466)*
Ambassador Gaming Inc....714 969-8730
660 Newport Center Dr # 1050 Newport Beach (92660) *(G-19134)*
Amber Holding Inc....415 765-6500
150 California St San Francisco (94111) *(G-15007)*
Amberfin Limited....818 768-8948
7590 N Glenoaks Blvd # 101 Burbank (91504) *(G-7090)*
Ambiente Enterprises Inc....760 674-1905
73726 Alessandro Dr # 203 Palm Desert (92260) *(G-22357)*
Amblin/Reliance Holding Co LLC....818 733-6272
100 Universal City Plz Universal City (91608) *(G-18041)*
Ambrose Recreation & Park Dst....925 458-1601
3105 Willow Pass Rd Bay Point (94565) *(G-19135)*
Ambry Genetics Corporation (PA)....949 900-5500
15 Argonaut Aliso Viejo (92656) *(G-26831)*
Ambulnz Health LLC....310 968-3999
12527 Vanowen St North Hollywood (91605) *(G-16217)*
AMC, Burbank *Also called American Multi-Cinema Inc (G-18294)*
AMC, San Diego *Also called American Multi-Cinema Inc (G-18295)*
AMC, Monterey Park *Also called American Multi-Cinema Inc (G-18296)*
AMC, Covina *Also called American Multi-Cinema Inc (G-18297)*
AMC, San Francisco *Also called American Multi-Cinema Inc (G-18298)*
AMC, Torrance *Also called American Multi-Cinema Inc (G-18299)*
AMC, Orange *Also called American Multi-Cinema Inc (G-18300)*
AMC, Fullerton *Also called American Multi-Cinema Inc (G-18301)*
AMC, Pasadena *Also called American Multi-Cinema Inc (G-18302)*
AMC, Norwalk *Also called American Multi-Cinema Inc (G-18303)*
AMC, Los Angeles *Also called Aesthetic Maintenance Corp (G-14216)*
AMC, Los Angeles *Also called American Multi-Cinema Inc (G-18304)*
AMC, San Diego *Also called American Multi-Cinema Inc (G-18305)*
AMC, City of Industry *Also called American Multi-Cinema Inc (G-18306)*
AMC, Montebello *Also called American Multi-Cinema Inc (G-18307)*
AMC Entertainment Inc....909 476-1288
4549 Mills Cir Ontario (91764) *(G-18293)*
AMC&, Los Angeles *Also called Anderson McPharlin Conners LLP (G-23092)*
Amcal Communities Inc....818 706-0694
30141 Agoura Rd Ste 100 Agoura Hills (91301) *(G-11946)*
Amcap Fund Inc....213 486-9200
333 S Hope St Ste Levb Los Angeles (90071) *(G-12101)*
Amco Foods Inc....818 247-4716
601 E Glenoaks Blvd # 108 Glendale (91207) *(G-27317)*
Amcom Food Service, City of Industry *Also called Klm Management Company (G-8586)*
AMD Trading Company Inc....415 391-0601
1021 Stockton St San Francisco (94108) *(G-9244)*
Amdal In-Home Care Inc (PA)....559 686-6611
147 N K St Tulare (93274) *(G-21133)*
Amdal In-Home Care Inc....559 227-1701
4848 N 1st St Ste 104 Fresno (93726) *(G-21134)*
Amdocs Inc....916 934-7000
1104 Investment Blvd El Dorado Hills (95762) *(G-15008)*
Amdocs Bcs Inc....916 934-7000
1104 Investment Blvd El Dorado Hills (95762) *(G-15009)*
Amdx Laboratory Sciences, San Diego *Also called Progenity Inc (G-22260)*
Amec E & C Services Inc....951 273-7400
250 E Rincon St Ste 204 Corona (92879) *(G-25650)*
AMEC E & C SERVICES, INC., Corona *Also called Amec E & C Services Inc (G-25650)*
Amec Fstr Whlr Envrnmnt Infrst....949 642-0245
121 Innovation Dr Ste 200 Irvine (92617) *(G-27828)*
Amec Fstr Whlr Envrnmnt Infrst....510 663-4100
180 Grand Ave Fl 11 Oakland (94612) *(G-25651)*
Amec Fstr Whlr Envrnmnt Infrst....323 889-5300
6001 Rickenbacker Rd Commerce (90040) *(G-25652)*
Amen Clinics Inc A Med Corp (PA)....888 564-2700
3150 Bristol St Ste 400 Costa Mesa (92626) *(G-22189)*
Amen Clinics Inc A Med Corp....650 416-7830
1000 Marina Blvd Ste 100 Brisbane (94005) *(G-19338)*
Amer Zoetrope Research LLC....707 963-9230
1991 Saint Helana Hwy Rutherford (94573) *(G-26643)*
Ameri-Kleen....831 722-8888
313 W Beach St Watsonville (95076) *(G-14223)*
Ameri-Kleen....805 546-0706
1023 E Grand Ave Arroyo Grande (93420) *(G-14224)*
Ameri-Kleen Building Services, Watsonville *Also called Ameri-Kleen (G-14223)*
Ameri-Kleen Building Services, Arroyo Grande *Also called Ameri-Kleen (G-14224)*
America Chung Nam (group) (PA)....909 839-8383
1163 Fairway Dr City of Industry (91789) *(G-8059)*
America Chung Nam LLC (HQ)....909 839-8383
1163 Fairway Dr Fl 3 City of Industry (91789) *(G-8060)*
America West Airlines Inc....619 231-7340
3835 N Harbor Dr Ste 128 San Diego (92101) *(G-4785)*
America West Airlines Inc....949 852-5471
18601 Airport Way Ste 238 Santa Ana (92707) *(G-4786)*
American AC Distrs LLC....407 850-0147
16900 Chestnut St City of Industry (91748) *(G-2125)*
American Academy of Opthalmlgy (PA)....415 561-8500
655 Beach St Fl 1 San Francisco (94109) *(G-25114)*
American Ace International Co....626 937-6116
313 Newquist Pl Ste A City of Industry (91745) *(G-8455)*
American Ace Intl Trdg Co, City of Industry *Also called American Ace International Co (G-8455)*
American Advisors Group (PA)....866 948-0003
3800 W Chapman Ave Fl 3 Orange (92868) *(G-10115)*
American Agcredit Flca (PA)....707 545-1200
400 Aviation Blvd Ste 100 Santa Rosa (95403) *(G-9793)*
American Air, Visalia *Also called American Incorporated (G-2127)*
American Airlines Inc....408 291-3800
2077 Airport Blvd Ste 103 San Jose (95110) *(G-4787)*
American Airlines Inc....650 877-6000
International Airport San Francisco (94128) *(G-4788)*
American Airlines Inc....310 215-7054
5950 Avion Dr Los Angeles (90045) *(G-4789)*
American Airlines Inc....760 778-2878
3400 E Tahqtz Cyn Way # 12 Palm Springs (92262) *(G-4790)*
American Airlines Inc....213 935-6045
7000 World Way W Los Angeles (90045) *(G-5005)*
American Airlines Inc....949 852-5470
18601 Airport Way Ste 213 Santa Ana (92707) *(G-4791)*
American Airlines Inc....310 646-0093
100 World Way Ste D Los Angeles (90045) *(G-4900)*
American Airlines Inc....310 646-3013
7183 World Way W Los Angeles (90045) *(G-4792)*
American Airlines Inc....805 988-0407
3100 Wright Rd Camarillo (93010) *(G-4901)*
American Airlines Group Inc....310 251-9184
3543 Carlisle St Perris (92571) *(G-4793)*
American All Risk Loss Adm....559 277-4960
4270 W Richert Ave # 101 Fresno (93722) *(G-27318)*
American Alliance Always Avail....209 948-9220
503 Bangs Ave Ste H Modesto (95356) *(G-17959)*
American Ambulance, Fresno *Also called K W P H Enterprises (G-3808)*
American Asp Repr Rsrfcing Inc (PA)....510 723-0280
24200 Clawiter Rd Hayward (94545) *(G-1728)*
American Asphalt South Inc....909 427-8276
14436 Santa Ana Ave Fontana (92337) *(G-1729)*
American Assets Trust Inc (PA)....858 350-2600
11455 El Camino Real # 200 San Diego (92130) *(G-12233)*
American Automobile....707 566-4000
1500 Farmers Ln Santa Rosa (95405) *(G-10398)*
American Automobile....925 279-2300
3055 Oak Rd Walnut Creek (94597) *(G-10590)*
American Automobile Assctn....510 350-2042
1982 Pleasant Valley Ave A Oakland (94611) *(G-25489)*
American Automobile Assctn....209 952-4100
3116 W March Ln Ste 100 Stockton (95219) *(G-25490)*
American Baptist Homes of West, Redlands *Also called American Baptist Homes of West (G-11084)*
American Baptist Homes of West....909 335-3077
460 E Fern Ave Redlands (92373) *(G-11084)*
American Baptist Homes of West....559 439-4770
5555 N Fresno St Fresno (93710) *(G-24546)*
American Baptist Homes of West....510 654-7172
110 41st St Ofc Oakland (94611) *(G-24547)*
American Baptist Homes of West....661 834-0620
1401 New Stine Rd Bakersfield (93309) *(G-21135)*
American Baptist Homes of West....909 793-1233
900 Salem Dr Redlands (92373) *(G-21136)*
American Baptist Homes of West (PA)....925 924-7100
6120 Stoneridge Mall Rd # 300 Pleasanton (94588) *(G-21137)*
American Baptist Homes of West....650 948-8291
373 Pine Ln Los Altos (94022) *(G-21138)*
American Baptist Homes of West....805 687-1571
900 Calle De Los Amigos Santa Barbara (93105) *(G-11085)*
American Baptist Homes of West....408 357-1100
800 Blossom Hill Rd Ofc Los Gatos (95032) *(G-21139)*

ALPHABETIC

American Beef Packers Inc 909 628-4888
13677 Yorba Ave Chino (91710) ***(G-635)***
American Bldg Maint Co of Ill 510 573-1618
44870 Osgood Rd Fremont (94539) ***(G-14225)***
American Bldg Maint Co-West (HQ) 415 733-4000
75 Broadway Ste 111 San Francisco (94111) ***(G-14226)***
American Bolt & Screw Mfg Corp (PA) 909 390-0522
14650 Miller Ave Ste 200 Fontana (92336) ***(G-7669)***
American Brdge/Fluor Entps Inc 510 808-4623
1390 Willow Pass Rd Concord (94520) ***(G-1886)***
American Building Maint Co NY 415 733-4000
101 California St San Francisco (94111) ***(G-14227)***
American Building Maintenance, Los Angeles *Also called Century Plaza Garage* ***(G-17715)***
American Building Service 510 483-5120
4578 Crow Canyon Pl Castro Valley (94552) ***(G-14228)***
American Building Supply Inc (PA) 916 503-4100
8360 Elder Creek Rd Sacramento (95828) ***(G-6906)***
American Building Supply Inc 209 941-8852
1488 Tillie Lewis Dr Stockton (95206) ***(G-6907)***
American Cancer Soc Cal Div (PA) 510 893-7900
1001 Marina Village Pkwy Alameda (94501) ***(G-26732)***
American Cancer Soc Cal Div 408 265-5535
1103 Branham Ln San Jose (95118) ***(G-24867)***
American Care Givers Westwood 310 208-8005
947 Tiverton Ave Ste 533 Los Angeles (90024) ***(G-23656)***
American Carequest Inc 415 752-9100
3921 Geary Blvd San Francisco (94118) ***(G-22358)***
American Century Inv MGT Inc 650 965-8300
1665 Charleston Rd Mountain View (94043) ***(G-10116)***
American Century Investments, Mountain View *Also called American Century Inv MGT Inc* ***(G-10116)***
American Chem & Sani Sup Inc 714 632-3010
3800 E Miraloma Ave Anaheim (92806) ***(G-6618)***
American Chinese Presb YMCA, San Francisco *Also called Young Mens Christian Assnsf* ***(G-25445)***
American Civil Const 707 746-8028
2990 Bay Vista Ct Ste D Benicia (94510) ***(G-1887)***
American Civil Constrs LLC 707 746-8028
3701 Mallard Dr Benicia (94510) ***(G-2020)***
American Civil Constrs W Coast, Benicia *Also called American Civil Const* ***(G-1887)***
AMERICAN CIVIL LIBERTIES UNION, Los Angeles *Also called Aclu Fndation Southern Cal LLC* ***(G-25193)***
American College Phlebology 510 346-6800
101 Callan Ave Ste 210 San Leandro (94577) ***(G-25115)***
American Commercial SEC Svcs 415 856-1020
420 Taylor St Fl 2 San Francisco (94102) ***(G-16552)***
American Commodity Co., Williams *Also called ACC-Gwg LLC* ***(G-27808)***
American Companies, Pico Rivera *Also called Three Sons Inc* ***(G-8687)***
American Concrete 760 471-9907
1125 Linda Vista Dr Ste 1 San Marcos (92078) ***(G-3226)***
American Concrete Cutting Inc 714 547-7181
620 N Poinsettia St Santa Ana (92701) ***(G-3447)***
American Conservatory 415 749-2228
415 Geary St San Francisco (94102) ***(G-18368)***
American Conservatory 415 749-2228
405 Geary St San Francisco (94102) ***(G-18369)***
American Conservatory Theater 415 439-2379
1117 Market St San Francisco (94103) ***(G-13731)***
American Contractors Inc 714 282-5700
404 W Blueridge Ave Orange (92865) ***(G-2126)***
American Contrs Indemnity Co (HQ) 213 330-1309
601 S Figueroa St # 1600 Los Angeles (90017) ***(G-10565)***
American Corporate SEC Inc (PA) 562 216-7440
1 World Trade Ctr # 1240 Long Beach (90831) ***(G-16553)***
American Corporation 310 274-1800
315 N Doheny Dr Beverly Hills (90211) ***(G-6794)***
American Corrective Counseling 949 369-6210
180 Avenida La Pata # 200 San Clemente (92673) ***(G-23657)***
American Cotton Coop Assn, Bakersfield *Also called Calcot Ltd* ***(G-8964)***
American Crclation Innovations, Long Beach *Also called Advertising Consultants Inc* ***(G-13986)***
American Cstm Private SEC Inc 209 369-1200
446 E Vine St Ste A Stockton (95202) ***(G-16554)***
American Datamed (PA) 949 250-4000
325 Maple Ave Torrance (90503) ***(G-13732)***
American De Rosa Lamparts LLC (PA) 323 728-6300
1945 S Tubeway Ave Commerce (90040) ***(G-7412)***
American Deck Systems, San Diego *Also called Magnesite Specialties Inc* ***(G-3125)***
American Dept of Inspections 510 683-9360
1550 Washington Blvd Fremont (94539) ***(G-16986)***
American Dj Group of Companies, Commerce *Also called D J American Supply Inc* ***(G-8109)***
American Dmlton/Concrete Cutng, Santa Ana *Also called American Concrete Cutting Inc* ***(G-3447)***
American Dntl Partners of Cal 951 689-5031
7251 Magnolia Ave Riverside (92504) ***(G-20244)***
American Dream 916 613-4917
300 Portinao Cir Sacramento (95831) ***(G-1125)***
American Eagle Services Inc 574 859-2055
1320 Arrow Hwy La Verne (91750) ***(G-14836)***
American Eagle Wheel Corp (PA) 909 590-8828
5780 Soestern Ct Chino (91710) ***(G-6704)***
American Electric Supply Inc (PA) 951 734-7910
361 S Maple St Corona (92880) ***(G-7413)***
American Electrical Svcs Inc 831 638-1737
501 San Benito St Fl 3 Hollister (95023) ***(G-2517)***
American Engrg Contrs Inc 209 229-1591
1204 Holly Dr Tracy (95376) ***(G-2518)***
American Etc Inc 650 873-5353
1140 San Mateo Ave South San Francisco (94080) ***(G-13499)***
American Express Travel 714 547-7116
1851 E 1st St Ste 600 Santa Ana (92705) ***(G-9769)***
American Express Travel 949 453-7123
15353 Barranca Pkwy Irvine (92618) ***(G-4955)***
American Farms LLC 831 424-1815
1107 Harkins Rd Salinas (93901) ***(G-37)***
American Faucet Coatings Corp 760 598-5895
3280 Corporate Vw Vista (92081) ***(G-6841)***
American Fidelity Assurance Co 909 941-1175
3200 Inland Empire Blvd # 260 Ontario (91764) ***(G-10591)***
American Fidelity Assurance Co 559 230-2107
3649 W Beechwood Ave # 103 Fresno (93711) ***(G-10592)***
American Financial Network Inc 909 606-3905
10 Pointe Dr Ste 330 Brea (92821) ***(G-9736)***
American Financial Network Inc 562 861-1414
8505 Florence Ave Downey (90240) ***(G-10117)***
American Financial Network Inc 562 926-2401
14241 Firestone Blvd La Mirada (90638) ***(G-27319)***
American Financial Network Inc 760 291-1059
333 S Juniper St 102 Escondido (92025) ***(G-9811)***
American Financial Network Inc (PA) 909 606-3905
3110 Chino Ave Ste 290 Chino (91710) ***(G-9812)***
American First Credit Union (PA) 562 691-1112
700 N Harbor Blvd La Habra (90631) ***(G-9588)***
American Fish and Seafood, Los Angeles *Also called Prospect Enterprises Inc* ***(G-8649)***
American Force Private SEC Inc 909 384-9820
1585 S D St Ste 208 San Bernardino (92408) ***(G-16555)***
American Freightways LP 866 326-5902
10845 Rancho Bernardo Rd # 100 San Diego (92127) ***(G-4106)***
American Funding 408 269-4238
5369 Camden Ave Ste 240 San Jose (95124) ***(G-9912)***
American Funds Distrs Inc (HQ) 213 486-9200
333 S Hope St Ste Levb Los Angeles (90071) ***(G-12102)***
American Funds Service Company 949 975-5000
6455 Irvine Center Dr Irvine (92618) ***(G-10195)***
American Future Tech Corp 888 462-3899
529 Baldwin Park Blvd City of Industry (91746) ***(G-7091)***
American Gen Lf Accident Insur 619 299-5213
2650 Camino Dl Rio N 20 Ste 205 San Diego (92108) ***(G-10593)***
American Gen Lf Insur Co Del 415 836-2700
121 Spear St Fl 5 San Francisco (94105) ***(G-10594)***
American General Life Insur 650 994-6679
455 Hickey Blvd Ste 500 Daly City (94015) ***(G-10595)***
American GNC Corporation 805 582-0582
888 E Easy St Simi Valley (93065) ***(G-25653)***
American Golf Construction, Canoga Park *Also called American Landscape Inc* ***(G-738)***
American Golf Corporation 858 755-6768
Lomas Snta Fe Highland Dr Solana Beach (92075) ***(G-18851)***
American Golf Corporation 805 495-5407
4155 Erbes Rd Thousand Oaks (91360) ***(G-18852)***
American Golf Corporation 949 786-1224
1 Ethel Coplen Way Irvine (92612) ***(G-18853)***
American Golf Corporation (PA) 310 664-4000
6080 Center Dr Ste 500 Los Angeles (90045) ***(G-18854)***
American Golf Corporation 562 421-0550
3101 Carson St Lakewood (90712) ***(G-18711)***
American Golf Corporation 805 343-1214
1490 Golf Course Ln Nipomo (93444) ***(G-18855)***
American Golf Corporation 714 536-8866
6501 Palm Ave Huntington Beach (92648) ***(G-18856)***
American Golf Corporation 714 779-2461
19400 Mountain View Ave Yorba Linda (92886) ***(G-18857)***
American Golf Corporation 562 494-4424
5001 Deukmejian Dr Long Beach (90804) ***(G-18858)***
American Golf Corporation 760 737-9762
17166 Stonerdg Cntry Clb Poway (92064) ***(G-18859)***
American Golf Corporation 702 431-2191
68311 Paseo Real Cathedral City (92234) ***(G-18860)***
American Golf Corporation 209 477-4653
6301 W Eight Mile Rd Stockton (95219) ***(G-18861)***
American Golf Corporation 310 476-2411
12445 Mountain Gate Dr Los Angeles (90049) ***(G-18862)***
American Golf Corporation 909 861-5757
22751 Golden Springs Dr Diamond Bar (91765) ***(G-18863)***
American Golf Corporation 925 672-9737
1001 Peacock Creek Dr Clayton (94517) ***(G-18864)***
American Golf Corporation 408 262-8813
1500 Country Club Dr Milpitas (95035) ***(G-18865)***
American Golf Corporation 760 757-2100
3202 Vista Way Oceanside (92056) ***(G-18866)***
American Golf Corporation 310 377-7370
7000 Los Verdes Dr Ste 1 Rancho Palos Verdes (90275) ***(G-18867)***
American Golf Corporation 714 846-1364
16782 Graham St Huntington Beach (92649) ***(G-18868)***
American Golf Corporation 831 688-3213
610 Clubhouse Dr Rear Aptos (95003) ***(G-18869)***
American Golf Corporation 760 568-9311
41500 Monterey Ave Palm Desert (92260) ***(G-18870)***
American Golf Corporation 562 943-7123
15501 Alicante Rd La Mirada (90638) ***(G-18871)***
American Golf Corporation 805 522-0803
5031 Alamo St Simi Valley (93063) ***(G-18872)***
American Golf Corporation 805 527-9663
301 Wood Ranch Pkwy Simi Valley (93065) ***(G-18712)***
American Golf Corporation 714 672-6800
1440 E Bastanchury Rd Fullerton (92835) ***(G-18713)***
American Guard Services Inc (PA) 310 645-6200
1299 E Artesia Blvd # 200 Carson (90746) ***(G-16556)***

American Health Care, Rocklin *Also called American Hlthcare ADM Svcs Inc* ***(G-22883)***

American Health Connection...424 226-0420
8484 Wilshire Blvd # 501 Beverly Hills (90211) ***(G-16987)***

American Health Services LLC...661 254-6630
26460 Summit Cir Santa Clarita (91350) ***(G-19339)***

American Heart Association Inc...213 291-7000
816 S Figueroa St Los Angeles (90017) ***(G-24868)***

American Hlthcare ADM Svcs Inc...916 773-7227
3850 Atherton Rd Rocklin (95765) ***(G-22883)***

American Home Assurance Co...213 689-3500
777 S Figueroa St Ste 300 Los Angeles (90017) ***(G-10399)***

American Homeowners & Renters...310 913-9263
334 W 120th St Apt 7 Los Angeles (90061) ***(G-11296)***

American Homes 4 Rent (PA)...805 413-5300
30601 Agoura Rd Ste 200 Agoura Hills (91301) ***(G-12234)***

American Homes Trust...619 694-7821
450 Camino Hermoso San Marcos (92078) ***(G-12235)***

American Honda, Mira Loma *Also called Meiko America Inc* ***(G-4598)***

American Honda Finance Corp (HQ)...310 972-2239
20800 Madrona Ave Torrance (90503) ***(G-9737)***

American Honda Finance Corp...714 816-8110
10801 Walker St Ste 140 Cypress (90630) ***(G-9738)***

American Honda Motor Co Inc (HQ)...310 783-2000
1919 Torrance Blvd Torrance (90501) ***(G-6664)***

American Hospital Mgt Corp (PA)...707 822-3621
3800 Janes Rd Arcata (95521) ***(G-21448)***

American Hritg Protection Svcs, Winnetka *Also called Memon Aamir* ***(G-16734)***

American Incorporated...559 651-1776
1345 N American St Visalia (93291) ***(G-2127)***

American Indian Health & Svcs...805 681-7356
4141 State St Ste B11 Santa Barbara (93110) ***(G-22884)***

American Industrial Supply...818 841-7788
9817 Variel Ave Chatsworth (91311) ***(G-7913)***

American Infrastructure Mlp Fu...650 854-6000
950 Tower Ln Ste 800 Foster City (94404) ***(G-27829)***

American Institute of Aeronaut...619 545-3736
3198 E Fox Run Way San Diego (92111) ***(G-26733)***

American Institute Research...916 286-8800
2151 River Plaza Dr # 320 Sacramento (95833) ***(G-26734)***

American Institute Research...650 843-8100
2800 Campus Dr Ste 200 San Mateo (94403) ***(G-26735)***

American Insurance Company Inc...415 899-2000
1465 N Mcdowell Blvd Petaluma (94954) ***(G-10400)***

American Integrated Svcs Inc (PA)...310 522-1168
1502 E Opp St Wilmington (90744) ***(G-27773)***

American Interbanc Mrtg LLC...714 957-9430
4 Park Plz Ste 650 Irvine (92614) ***(G-9813)***

American International Group, San Diego *Also called American Gen Lf Accident Insur* ***(G-10593)***

American International Inds, Camarillo *Also called Bml Industries Inc* ***(G-7419)***

American International Inds (PA)...323 728-2999
2220 Gaspar Ave Commerce (90040) ***(G-8228)***

American Internet Mortgage Inc...619 610-9900
4121 Camino Del Rio S San Diego (92108) ***(G-9814)***

American Intl Group Inc...213 689-3500
777 S Figueroa St # 1800 Los Angeles (90017) ***(G-10596)***

American Intl Group Inc...619 682-4058
9350 Waxie Way Ste 300 San Diego (92123) ***(G-10597)***

American Intl Telephonics LLC...800 600-6151
9601 Wilshire Blvd Beverly Hills (90210) ***(G-5457)***

American Janitor Services, Thousand Oaks *Also called American Services and Products* ***(G-14229)***

American Kal Enterprises Inc (PA)...626 338-7308
4265 Puente Ave Baldwin Park (91706) ***(G-7670)***

American Labor Pool Inc...408 496-9950
1725 De La Cruz Blvd # 2 Santa Clara (95050) ***(G-14606)***

American Landscape Inc...818 999-2041
7013 Owensmouth Ave Canoga Park (91303) ***(G-738)***

American Landscape Management...805 647-5077
1607 Los Angeles Ave I Ventura (93004) ***(G-807)***

American Landscape Management (PA)...818 999-2041
7013 Owensmouth Ave Canoga Park (91303) ***(G-739)***

American Leak Detection Inc...714 836-8477
304 N Townsend St Ste D Santa Ana (92703) ***(G-2128)***

American Legal Copy-Or LLC...415 777-4449
98 Battery St Ste 220 San Francisco (94111) ***(G-14099)***

American Legion Ambulance Svc...209 223-2963
11350 American Legion Dr Sutter Creek (95685) ***(G-25196)***

American Legion Aux...209 823-4406
142 Raylow Ave Manteca (95336) ***(G-25197)***

American Legion Hall, Sutter Creek *Also called American Legion Ambulance Svc* ***(G-25196)***

American Liberty Capital Corp...949 623-0288
19000 Macarthur Blvd # 400 Irvine (92612) ***(G-9913)***

American Liberty Funding, Irvine *Also called American Liberty Capital Corp* ***(G-9913)***

American Linehaul Corporation...323 418-8900
12333 S Van Ness Ave Hawthorne (90250) ***(G-4107)***

American Loss Prevention Svcs, San Francisco *Also called American Commercial SEC Svcs* ***(G-16552)***

American Marketing Systems Inc...800 747-7784
2800 Van Ness Ave San Francisco (94109) ***(G-11297)***

American Mdsg Specialists Inc...925 516-3220
958 Dainty Ave Brentwood (94513) ***(G-13988)***

American Med...925 602-1300
5151 Port Chicago Hwy Concord (94520) ***(G-3741)***

American Med...909 793-7676
600 Iowa St Redlands (92373) ***(G-3742)***

American Med...626 633-4600
5257 Vincent Ave Irwindale (91706) ***(G-3743)***

American Med...650 235-1333
1510 Rollins Rd Burlingame (94010) ***(G-3744)***

American Med...760 883-5000
1111 Montalvo Way Palm Springs (92262) ***(G-3745)***

American Med...909 948-1714
7925 Center Ave Rancho Cucamonga (91730) ***(G-3746)***

American Med...510 895-7600
7575 Southfront Rd Livermore (94551) ***(G-3747)***

American Med Resp Amblnc Svc...707 536-0400
930 S A St Santa Rosa (95404) ***(G-3748)***

American Med Rspnse Sthern Cal...661 945-9310
1055 W Avenue J Lancaster (93534) ***(G-3749)***

American Medical Response, Palm Springs *Also called Springs Ambulance Service Inc* ***(G-3847)***

American Medical Response...925 454-6000
2400 Bisso Ln Concord (94520) ***(G-3750)***

American Medical Response...916 563-0600
1041 Fee Dr Sacramento (95815) ***(G-3751)***

American Medical Response...415 922-9400
1300 Illinois St San Francisco (94107) ***(G-3752)***

American Medical Response...831 423-7030
116 Hubbard St Santa Cruz (95060) ***(G-3753)***

American Medical Response (HQ)...951 782-5200
879 Marlborough Ave Riverside (92507) ***(G-3754)***

American Medical Response...650 235-1333
1510 Rollins Rd Burlingame (94010) ***(G-3755)***

American Medical Response Inc...951 658-2826
208 E Devonshire Ave A Hemet (92543) ***(G-3756)***

American Medical Response Inc...858 492-3500
8808 Balboa Ave Ste 150 San Diego (92123) ***(G-3757)***

American Medical Response Inc...805 688-6550
240 E Highway 246 Ste 300 Buellton (93427) ***(G-3758)***

American Medical Response Inc...760 322-4134
1111 Montalvo Way Palm Springs (92262) ***(G-3759)***

American Medical Response Inc...831 718-9555
4548 A St Marina (93933) ***(G-3760)***

American Medical Response Inc...951 765-3900
208 E Devonshire Ave A Hemet (92543) ***(G-3761)***

American Medical Response Inc...831 636-9391
1870 Hillcrest Rd Hollister (95023) ***(G-3762)***

American Medical Response Inc...530 887-9440
13146 Lincoln Way Auburn (95603) ***(G-3763)***

American Medical Response Inc...209 567-4030
1420 Lander Ave Turlock (95380) ***(G-3764)***

American Medical Rspnse Amblnc...303 495-1217
879 Marlborough Ave Riverside (92507) ***(G-3765)***

American Medical Tech Inc...949 553-0359
17595 Cartwright Rd Irvine (92614) ***(G-7233)***

American Medical Technologies, Irvine *Also called Gordian Medical Inc* ***(G-7266)***

American Merchant Center Inc...818 947-1700
6819 Sepulveda Blvd # 311 Van Nuys (91405) ***(G-9770)***

American Messaging Svcs LLC...510 889-2300
2181 W Winton Ave Hayward (94545) ***(G-5458)***

American Metal & Iron Inc...408 452-0777
2377 Tulip Rd San Jose (95128) ***(G-8061)***

American Metals Corporation (HQ)...916 371-7700
1499 Parkway Blvd West Sacramento (95691) ***(G-7356)***

American Mobile Healthcare, San Diego *Also called Amn Healthcare Services Inc* ***(G-20306)***

American Multi-Cinema Inc...818 953-4020
125 E Palm Ave Burbank (91502) ***(G-18294)***

American Multi-Cinema Inc...619 296-0370
7037 Friars Rd San Diego (92108) ***(G-18295)***

American Multi-Cinema Inc...626 407-0240
450 N Atlantic Blvd Monterey Park (91754) ***(G-18296)***

American Multi-Cinema Inc...626 974-8624
1414 N Azusa Ave Covina (91722) ***(G-18297)***

American Multi-Cinema Inc...415 674-4630
1000 Van Neca Ave Ste A San Francisco (94109) ***(G-18298)***

American Multi-Cinema Inc...310 326-5011
2591 Airport Dr Torrance (90505) ***(G-18299)***

American Multi-Cinema Inc...714 769-4288
20 City Blvd W Ste E1 Orange (92868) ***(G-18300)***

American Multi-Cinema Inc...714 992-6961
1001 S Lemon St Ste A Fullerton (92832) ***(G-18301)***

American Multi-Cinema Inc...626 585-8900
42 Miller Aly Pasadena (91103) ***(G-18302)***

American Multi-Cinema Inc...562 864-6206
12300 Civic Center Dr Norwalk (90650) ***(G-18303)***

American Multi-Cinema Inc...310 228-5500
10250 Snta Mnca Bld Ste 196 Los Angeles (90067) ***(G-18304)***

American Multi-Cinema Inc...619 296-2737
1640 Cmino Del Rio N 20 San Diego (92108) ***(G-18305)***

American Multi-Cinema Inc...626 810-7949
1560 S Azusa Ave City of Industry (91748) ***(G-18306)***

American Multi-Cinema Inc...323 722-4583
1475 N Montebello Blvd Montebello (90640) ***(G-18307)***

American Mutual Fund Inc...213 486-9200
333 S Hope St Fl 51 Los Angeles (90071) ***(G-12103)***

American Mzhou Dngpo Group Inc...626 820-9239
4520 Maine Ave Baldwin Park (91706) ***(G-26918)***

American National Red Cross...510 594-5100
6230 Claremont Ave Oakland (94618) ***(G-22885)***

American National Red Cross...415 427-8134
1663 Market St San Francisco (94103) ***(G-23658)***

American National Red Cross...714 481-5300
601 N Golden Circle Dr Santa Ana (92705) ***(G-25491)***

American National Red Cross...925 603-7400
1300 Alberta Way Concord (94521) ***(G-23659)***

American National Red Cross...909 859-7006
100 Red Cross Cir Pomona (91768) ***(G-22886)***

American National Red Cross....858 309-1200
3950 Calle Fortunada San Diego (92123) *(G-23660)*
American Nursing Home MGT Inc....310 672-1012
301 Centinela Ave Inglewood (90302) *(G-27830)*
American Nwland Communities LP (PA)....858 455-7503
9820 Towne Centre Dr # 100 San Diego (92121) *(G-11947)*
American Pacific Mortgage Corp (PA)....916 960-1325
3000 Lava Ridge Ct # 200 Roseville (95661) *(G-9815)*
American Paper & Plastics Inc....626 444-0000
550 S 7th Ave City of Industry (91746) *(G-8184)*
American Paper & Provisions, City of Industry *Also called American Paper & Plastics Inc (G-8184)*
American Patriot Security....916 706-2449
10293 Rockingham Dr # 104 Sacramento (95827) *(G-16557)*
American Paving Co....559 268-9886
315 N Thorne Ave Fresno (93706) *(G-1730)*
American Postal Workers Union....661 775-8174
28201 Franklin Pkwy Santa Clarita (91383) *(G-25165)*
American Pride Gen Engrg Inc....760 736-4056
529 W 4th Ave Ste B Escondido (92025) *(G-25654)*
American Private Duty Inc....818 386-6358
13111 Ventura Blvd # 100 Studio City (91604) *(G-22359)*
American Prof Ambulance Corp....818 996-2200
16945 Sherman Way Van Nuys (91406) *(G-3766)*
American Professional Security....213 487-2100
2500 Wilshire Blvd # 1030 Los Angeles (90057) *(G-16558)*
American Property Management....925 463-8000
7050 Johnson Dr Pleasanton (94588) *(G-12383)*
American Prprty-Mnagement Corp....619 232-3121
326 Broadway San Diego (92101) *(G-12384)*
American Realty, San Jose *Also called American Funding (G-9912)*
American Realty Advisors....818 545-1152
801 N Brand Blvd Ste 800 Glendale (91203) *(G-12236)*
American Realty Centre Inc....323 666-6111
120 S Glendale Ave Glendale (91205) *(G-11298)*
American Recovery Center, Pomona *Also called Behavioral Health Services Inc (G-23681)*
American Recovery Service, El Dorado Hills *Also called Patrick K Willis and Co Inc (G-17405)*
American Red Cross, Concord *Also called American National Red Cross (G-23659)*
American Red Cross....310 445-9900
11355 Ohio Ave Los Angeles (90025) *(G-23661)*
American Red Cross La Chapter (PA)....310 445-9900
11355 Ohio Ave Los Angeles (90025) *(G-24869)*
American Red Cross San Diego (PA)....858 309-1200
3950 Calle Fortunada San Diego (92123) *(G-24870)*
American Reprographics Co LLC....213 745-3145
934 Venice Blvd Los Angeles (90015) *(G-14100)*
American Reprographics Co LLC....916 443-1322
1322 V St Sacramento (95818) *(G-14101)*
American Reprographics Co LLC....626 289-5021
616 Monterey Pass Rd Monterey Park (91754) *(G-14102)*
American Reprographics Co LLC....408 295-5770
821 Martin Ave Santa Clara (95050) *(G-14103)*
American Reprographics Co LLC....714 751-2680
345 Clinton St Costa Mesa (92626) *(G-14104)*
American Reprographics Co LLC....951 686-0530
4295 Main St Riverside (92501) *(G-14105)*
AMERICAN RESIDENTIAL SERVICES L.L.C., San Diego *Also called American Residential Svcs LLC (G-2129)*
AMERICAN RESIDENTIAL SERVICES L.L.C., Gardena *Also called American Residential Svcs LLC (G-2130)*
American Residential Svcs LLC....858 457-5547
9895 Olson Dr Ste A San Diego (92121) *(G-2129)*
American Residential Svcs LLC....310 637-1454
15707 S Main St Gardena (90248) *(G-2130)*
American Residential Svcs LLC....858 677-5445
6162 Nncy Rdge Dr Ste 100 San Diego (92121) *(G-2131)*
American Residential Svcs LLC....858 292-4452
P.O. Box 1592 El Cajon (92022) *(G-2132)*
American Residential Svcs LLC....650 856-1612
1965 Kyle Park Ct San Jose (95125) *(G-2133)*
American Residential Svcs LLC....951 341-9371
1520 W Linden St Riverside (92507) *(G-2134)*
American Residential Svcs LLC....650 652-1050
825 Mahler Rd Burlingame (94010) *(G-2135)*
American Residential Svcs LLC....510 657-7601
29196 Simms Ct Hayward (94544) *(G-2136)*
American Residential Svcs LLC....408 435-3810
2305 Paragon Dr San Jose (95131) *(G-17960)*
American Residential Svcs LLC....714 634-1826
740 N Hariton St Orange (92868) *(G-2137)*
American Residential Svcs LLC....818 833-6677
12507 San Fernando Rd Sylmar (91342) *(G-2138)*
American Residential Svcs LLC....858 277-2606
8949 Kenamar Dr Ste 110 San Diego (92121) *(G-2139)*
American Restoration Services, Hayward *Also called American Technologies Inc (G-3490)*
American Restoration Services, Simi Valley *Also called American Technologies Inc (G-1128)*
American Retirement Corp....310 399-3227
2107 Ocean Ave Santa Monica (90405) *(G-24548)*
American River Care, Carmichael *Also called Sunbridge Brittany Rehab Centr (G-20939)*
American Rlction Logistics Inc....562 229-3600
13565 Larwin Cir Santa Fe Springs (90670) *(G-4327)*
American Security Force Inc....323 722-8585
5400 E Olympic Blvd # 225 Commerce (90022) *(G-16559)*
American Service Industries....323 779-4000
2930 W Imperial Hwy # 332 Inglewood (90303) *(G-16866)*
American Services and Products....805 375-2858
949 Camino Dos Rios Thousand Oaks (91360) *(G-14229)*
American Sign, Van Nuys *Also called Dee Sign Co (G-17118)*
American Solar Direct Inc....626 435-9211
217 N Sunset Ave City of Industry (91744) *(G-2140)*
American Solar Solution Inc....877 946-8855
6400 Laurel Canyon Blvd # 400 North Hollywood (91606) *(G-1126)*
American Spclty Hlth Group Inc (HQ)....858 754-2000
10221 Wateridge Cir # 201 San Diego (92121) *(G-22360)*
American Specialty Health Inc (PA)....858 754-2000
10221 Wateridge Cir # 201 San Diego (92121) *(G-10598)*
American State Water Company, San Dimas *Also called Golden State Water Company (G-6352)*
American Sunrise Inc....858 610-4766
7404 Santa Fe Canyon Pl San Diego (92129) *(G-15010)*
American Synergy Asbestos Remo....510 444-2333
28436 Satellite St Hayward (94545) *(G-3489)*
American Team Managers Inc....714 414-1200
1030 N Armando St Anaheim (92806) *(G-10599)*
American Technical Svcs Inc....818 590-7784
9520 Topanga Canyon Blvd Chatsworth (91311) *(G-25655)*
American Technologies Inc....510 429-5000
25000 Industrial Blvd Hayward (94545) *(G-3490)*
American Technologies Inc (PA)....714 283-9990
210 W Baywood Ave Orange (92865) *(G-1127)*
American Technologies Inc....818 700-5060
2688 Westhills Ct Simi Valley (93065) *(G-1128)*
American Technologies Inc....858 530-2400
8444 Miralani Dr Ste 200 San Diego (92126) *(G-27831)*
American Textile Maint Co....213 749-4433
1705 Hooper Ave Los Angeles (90021) *(G-13520)*
American Textile Maint Co....562 438-7656
3001 E Anaheim St Long Beach (90804) *(G-13521)*
American Textile Maint Co....562 438-1126
3001 E Anaheim St Long Beach (90804) *(G-6842)*
American Textile Maint Co....323 735-1661
1664 W Washington Blvd Los Angeles (90007) *(G-13522)*
American Textile Maint Co....562 424-1607
2201 E Carson St Long Beach (90807) *(G-13523)*
American Tile Brick Veneer Inc....562 595-9293
1389 E 28th St Signal Hill (90755) *(G-3004)*
American Transport Inc....714 567-8000
3080 S Harbor Blvd Santa Ana (92704) *(G-9816)*
American Travel Solutions LLC....800 243-2724
26707 Agoura Rd Ste 204 Calabasas (91302) *(G-4956)*
American Two-Way, North Hollywood *Also called Emergency Technologies Inc (G-7439)*
American Union Fincl Svcs Inc....714 619-2520
210 S Orange Grove Blvd # 1 Pasadena (91105) *(G-9739)*
American Unique Staff Provider....818 908-9051
14545 Victory Blvd # 404 Van Nuys (91411) *(G-14607)*
American Untd HM Care Crp-Priv, Studio City *Also called American Private Duty Inc (G-22359)*
American Vision Windows Inc....805 582-1833
2125 N Madera Rd Ste A Simi Valley (93065) *(G-17961)*
American Water Works Co Inc....916 568-4236
4701 Beloit Dr Sacramento (95838) *(G-6312)*
American Way Cultural Center, Orange *Also called Adair Enterprises (G-18365)*
American West....805 926-2800
511 Zaca Ln Ste 120 San Luis Obispo (93401) *(G-4108)*
American West Worldwide Ex Inc (PA)....800 788-4534
51 Zaca Ln Ste 120 San Luis Obispo (93401) *(G-4328)*
American Wht Mssn In Sthrn....714 522-4599
7212 Orangethorpe Ave 7a Buena Park (90621) *(G-23662)*
American Wrecking Inc....626 350-8303
2459 Lee Ave South El Monte (91733) *(G-3448)*
American Zettler Inc (HQ)....949 360-5830
75 Columbia Aliso Viejo (92656) *(G-7519)*
American-1 Airtight SEC Co....714 997-0605
2510 N Grand Ave Ste 207 Santa Ana (92705) *(G-16560)*
Americantours Intl LLC (HQ)....310 641-9953
6053 W Century Blvd Los Angeles (90045) *(G-4985)*
Americare Ambulance Service, Carson *Also called Americare Medservices Inc (G-3767)*
Americare Hlth Retirement Inc....760 744-4484
1550 Security Pl Ofc San Marcos (92078) *(G-10958)*
Americare Medservices Inc (PA)....310 632-1141
1059 E Bedmar St Carson (90746) *(G-3767)*
Americas Christian Credit Un (PA)....626 208-5400
2100 E Route 66 Ste 100 Glendora (91740) *(G-9652)*
Americas Finest Carpet Co, Chula Vista *Also called Home Carpet Investment Inc (G-3117)*
Americas Flood Services Inc....916 636-9460
3350 Country Club Dr # 201 Cameron Park (95682) *(G-10600)*
Americas Home Loans Inc....707 577-7464
131 Stony Cir Ste 500a Santa Rosa (95401) *(G-9914)*
Americas Lemonade Stand Inc....707 745-1274
5100 Park Rd Benicia (94510) *(G-16988)*
Americas Printer.com, Buena Park *Also called A J Parent Company Inc (G-16961)*
Americas Regional Division, San Diego *Also called Synergy Health Ast LLC (G-27677)*
Americash....714 994-7554
3080 Bristol St Ste 300 Costa Mesa (92626) *(G-9817)*
Americold Logistics LLC....831 424-1537
950 S Sanborn Rd Salinas (93901) *(G-4485)*
Americold Logistics LLC....714 993-3533
2750 Orbiter St Brea (92821) *(G-4486)*
Americold Logistics LLC....909 390-4950
700 Malaga St Ontario (91761) *(G-4487)*
Americold Logistics LLC....323 581-0025
3420 E Vernon Ave Vernon (90058) *(G-4488)*
Americold Realty, Ontario *Also called Americold Logistics LLC (G-4487)*
Amerifleet Transportation Inc....916 331-2355
3044 Elkhorn Blvd Ste J North Highlands (95660) *(G-5212)*

A L P H A B E T I C

Amerifleet Transportation Inc 562 420-5604
5000 E Spring St Ste 350 Long Beach (90815) *(G-5213)*
Ameriflight LLC 510 569-6000
21889 Skywest Dr Hayward (94541) *(G-4794)*
Amerifreight Inc 909 839-2600
218 Machlin Ct Walnut (91789) *(G-4522)*
AmeriGas Propane LP 916 852-7400
11030 White Rock Rd # 100 Rancho Cordova (95670) *(G-9012)*
Amerine Systems Incorporated 209 847-5968
10866 Cleveland Ave Oakdale (95361) *(G-740)*
Ameripath Mortgage Corporation 949 753-9211
6410 Oak Cyn Ste 200 Irvine (92618) *(G-9818)*
Ameripride Services Inc 805 239-9449
109 Calle Propano Ste C Paso Robles (93446) *(G-13524)*
Ameripride Services Inc 530 242-0564
3750 Eastside Rd Redding (96001) *(G-13525)*
Ameripride Services Inc 661 324-7941
335 Washington St Bakersfield (93307) *(G-13526)*
Ameripride Services Inc 559 266-0627
1050 W Whites Bridge Ave Fresno (93706) *(G-13601)*
Ameripride Services Inc 209 982-0020
4206 S B St Stockton (95206) *(G-13527)*
Ameripride Services Inc 714 385-8991
2230 W Chapman Ave Orange (92868) *(G-13528)*
Ameripride Services Inc 800 748-6178
3701 Collins Ave Ste 5b Richmond (94806) *(G-13529)*
Ameripride Services Inc 800 882-5326
1356 Dayton St Ste R Salinas (93901) *(G-13530)*
Ameripride Unifom Svcs, Bakersfield *Also called Ameripride Services Inc (G-13526)*
Ameripride Uniform Services, Fresno *Also called Ameripride Services Inc (G-13601)*
Ameriquest Capital Corporation (PA) 714 564-0600
1100 W Twn Cntry Rd R Orange (92868) *(G-9915)*
Amerisourcebergen Corporation 661 257-6400
24903 Avenue Kearny Valencia (91355) *(G-8229)*
Amerisourcebergen Corporation 714 385-4000
500 N State College Blvd # 900 Orange (92868) *(G-8230)*
Amerisourcebergen Corporation 610 727-7000
1368 Metropolitan Dr Orange (92868) *(G-26919)*
Amerisourcebergen Corporation 951 493-2339
215 Deininger Cir Corona (92880) *(G-8231)*
Amerisourcebergen Corporation 916 830-4500
1325 Striker Ave Sacramento (95834) *(G-8232)*
Amerisourcebergen Corporation 714 704-4407
505 City Pkwy W Orange (92868) *(G-26920)*
Amerisourcebergen Corporation 951 371-2000
1851 California Ave Corona (92881) *(G-8233)*
Amerisuites, Ontario *Also called Todays Vi LLC (G-13348)*
Amerit Fleet Solutions Inc (PA) 877 512-6374
1331 N Calif Blvd Ste 150 Walnut Creek (94596) *(G-17873)*
Ameritac Inc (PA) 925 743-8398
640 Logan Ln Danville (94526) *(G-27774)*
Ameritech Mortgage, Walnut Creek *Also called Izt Mortgage Inc (G-9930)*
Ameriwest Industries Inc 909 930-1898
2910 S Archibald Ave A Ontario (91761) *(G-7671)*
Ames Construction Inc 951 697-9094
14427 Meridian Pkwy March ARB (92518) *(G-1290)*
Ames Taping Tool Systems, Ceres *Also called Ames Taping Tools (G-14512)*
Ames Taping Tools 209 538-0113
1842 Herndon Rd Ste A Ceres (95307) *(G-14512)*
AMF Bowling Centers Inc 323 728-9161
1201 W Beverly Blvd Montebello (90640) *(G-18507)*
AMF Bowling Centers Inc 661 324-4966
1819 30th St Bakersfield (93301) *(G-18508)*
AMF Bowling Centers Inc 949 770-0055
22771 Centre Dr Lake Forest (92630) *(G-18509)*
AMG Huntington Beach LLC 714 894-9802
5416 Argosy Ave Huntington Beach (92649) *(G-25656)*
Amgen Distribution Inc 760 438-2538
1910 Palomar Oaks Way Carlsbad (92008) *(G-4109)*
Amgen Distribution Inc 760 989-4424
1244 Valley View Rd # 119 Glendale (91202) *(G-4110)*
Amgen Pharmaceuticals Inc 805 447-1000
1 Amgen Center Dr Thousand Oaks (91320) *(G-26736)*
Amgreen Solar and Electrics 213 388-5647
1367 Venice Blvd Los Angeles (90006) *(G-2141)*
Amgreen Solutions Inc 213 388-5647
1367 Venice Blvd Fl 2 Los Angeles (90006) *(G-27320)*
Amh Portfolio One LLC 480 921-4600
30601 Agoura Rd Ste 200 Agoura Hills (91301) *(G-12237)*
AMI Electrical & Telecom Inc 714 531-0872
11572 Carnation Cir Fountain Valley (92708) *(G-2519)*
AMI Manufacturing, Sacramento *Also called Airco Mechanical Inc (G-2115)*
AMI-Hti Tarzana Encino Joint V 818 881-0800
18321 Clark St Tarzana (91356) *(G-21449)*
Amica Mutual Insurance Company 877 972-6422
3200 Park Center Dr # 650 Costa Mesa (92626) *(G-10401)*
Amini Innovation Corp 562 222-2500
8725 Rex Rd Pico Rivera (90660) *(G-6803)*
Amir Ahmad MD 805 545-8100
628 California Blvd Ste D San Luis Obispo (93401) *(G-19340)*
Amisub (irvine Regional Hospi) 949 916-7556
1400 S Douglass Rd # 250 Anaheim (92806) *(G-21450)*
Amisub of California Inc (HQ) 818 881-0800
18321 Clark St Tarzana (91356) *(G-21451)*
Amk Foodservices Inc 805 544-7600
830 Capitolio Way San Luis Obispo (93401) *(G-8456)*
Amkotron Inc 562 921-3330
12620 Hiddencreek Way Cerritos (90703) *(G-16285)*
Ammunition LLC 415 632-1170
1500 Sansome St Ste 110 San Francisco (94111) *(G-27321)*
Amn Healthcare Inc (HQ) 858 792-0711
12400 High Bluff Dr San Diego (92130) *(G-19341)*
Amn Healthcare Services Inc 858 792-0711
12400 High Bluff Dr # 100 San Diego (92130) *(G-20306)*
Amn Healthcare Services Inc (PA) 866 871-8519
12400 High Bluff Dr San Diego (92130) *(G-14837)*
Amobee Inc (HQ) 650 802-8871
950 Tower Ln Ste 2000 Foster City (94404) *(G-15011)*
Amoeba Music Inc 415 831-1200
1855 Haight St San Francisco (94117) *(G-16989)*
Amos of America Inc 899 415-2000
1465 N Mcdowell Blvd Petaluma (94954) *(G-16320)*
AMP Technologies LLC (PA) 877 442-2824
2420 Camino Ramon Ste 210 San Ramon (94583) *(G-15012)*
Ampac, Los Angeles *Also called Viva Vina Inc (G-17596)*
Ampam Parks Mechanical Inc 310 835-1532
1060 N Wilmington Blvd Wilmington (90744) *(G-2142)*
Ampco Contracting Inc 949 955-2255
1540 S Lewis St Anaheim (92805) *(G-6619)*
Ampla Health (PA) 530 674-4261
935 Market St Yuba City (95991) *(G-20245)*
Ampla Health 530 342-4395
680 Cohasset Rd Chico (95926) *(G-19342)*
Ampla Health 530 743-4614
4941 Olivehurst Ave Olivehurst (95961) *(G-19343)*
Amplify Education Inc 562 209-7875
1032 Irving St Ste 445 San Francisco (94122) *(G-15013)*
Ampronix Inc 949 273-8000
15 Whatney Irvine (92618) *(G-7234)*
AMR, Los Angeles *Also called American Airlines Inc (G-4789)*
AMR, Riverside *Also called American Medical Rspnse Amblnc (G-3765)*
AMR Appraisals Inc 925 400-6066
5000 Executive Pkwy # 270 San Ramon (94583) *(G-11299)*
AMR Eagle, San Diego *Also called Envoy Air Inc (G-4799)*
AMR Eagle, San Diego *Also called Envoy Air Inc (G-4916)*
AMS, Anaheim *Also called Walnut Investment Corp (G-6969)*
AMS, San Diego *Also called Asset Marketing Systems Insu (G-27334)*
AMS, San Bernardino *Also called Allied Building Products Corp (G-7023)*
AMS, Montebello *Also called Allied Building Products Corp (G-6905)*
AMS - Exotic LLC 213 612-5888
720 S Alameda St Los Angeles (90021) *(G-8694)*
AMS American Mech Svcs MD Inc 714 888-6820
2116 E Walnut Ave Fullerton (92831) *(G-2143)*
AMS Bekins Van Lines, Burlingame *Also called AMS Relocation Incorporated (G-4329)*
AMS Electric Inc 925 961-1600
6905 Sierra Ct Dublin (94568) *(G-2520)*
AMS Fulfillement, Valencia *Also called Advantage Media Services Inc (G-5196)*
AMS Fulfillment, Valencia *Also called Advantage Media Services Inc (G-4518)*
AMS Paving Inc (PA) 909 357-0711
11060 Rose Ave Fontana (92337) *(G-1731)*
AMS Relocation Incorporated 650 697-3530
1873 Rollins Rd Burlingame (94010) *(G-4329)*
Amsec LLC 858 522-6319
9444 Balboa Ave Ste 400 San Diego (92123) *(G-26467)*
Amsi Real Estate Services, San Francisco *Also called American Marketing Systems Inc (G-11297)*
Amsnet Inc (PA) 925 245-6100
502 Commerce Way Livermore (94551) *(G-15901)*
Amstar/Davidson Robles LLC 626 577-1000
168 S Los Robles Ave Pasadena (91101) *(G-12385)*
Amsurg, Torrance *Also called Torrance Surgery Center LP (G-20138)*
Amsurg, San Diego *Also called Mission Valley Hts Surgery Ctr (G-19756)*
Amtel Inc 408 615-0522
950 S Bascom Ave Ste 2002 San Jose (95128) *(G-27832)*
Amtel LLC 510 529-3220
1074 University Ave Berkeley (94710) *(G-5254)*
Amtrak, San Diego *Also called National Railroad Pass Corp (G-3614)*
Amtrav, Calabasas *Also called American Travel Solutions LLC (G-4956)*
Amtrow Group Inc 310 557-0857
8306 Wilshire Blvd 1042 Beverly Hills (90211) *(G-27322)*
Amwins Insurance Brkg Cal LLC (HQ) 818 772-1774
21550 Oxnard St Ste 1100 Woodland Hills (91367) *(G-10601)*
An Companion Hospice 877 303-0692
150 E Colorado Blvd # 100 Pasadena (91105) *(G-22361)*
An Open Check, Costa Mesa *Also called North American Acceptance Corp (G-9760)*
Ana Nacapa Surgical Associates, Ventura *Also called Ventura County Medical Center (G-20193)*
Anabella Hotel The, Anaheim *Also called Fjs Inc (G-12638)*
Anaheim Arena, Anaheim *Also called City of Anaheim (G-10971)*
Anaheim Arena Management LLC 714 704-2400
2695 E Katella Ave Anaheim (92806) *(G-18534)*
Anaheim Arts Council 714 868-6094
P.O. Box 1364 Anaheim (92815) *(G-25001)*
Anaheim Ca LLC 714 634-4500
100 The City Dr S Orange (92868) *(G-12386)*
Anaheim Crest Nursing Center, Anaheim *Also called 3067 Orange Avenue LLC (G-20365)*
Anaheim Ducks Hockey Club LLC 714 940-2900
2695 E Katella Ave Anaheim (92806) *(G-18873)*
Anaheim First Fmly Dntl Group 714 999-5050
1161 N Euclid St Anaheim (92801) *(G-26921)*
Anaheim Gateway Sport Club, Anaheim *Also called 24 Hour Fitness Usa Inc (G-18581)*
Anaheim Global Medical Center 714 533-6220
1025 S Anaheim Blvd Anaheim (92805) *(G-21452)*
Anaheim Harbor Medical Group (PA) 714 533-4511
710 N Euclid St Anaheim (92801) *(G-19344)*
Anaheim Health Care Center, Anaheim *Also called Sun Mar Management Services (G-27235)*

ALPHABETIC SECTION Anixter International Inc

Anaheim Hills Auto Body Inc 714 632-8266
3500 E La Palma Ave Anaheim (92806) ***(G-17747)***
Anaheim Hills Medical Offices, Anaheim *Also called Kaiser Foundation Hospitals* ***(G-19599)***
Anaheim Hilton & Towers, Anaheim *Also called Makar Anaheim LLC* ***(G-12937)***
Anaheim Hotel LLC 714 750-1811
1855 S Harbor Blvd Anaheim (92802) ***(G-12387)***
Anaheim Ice 714 518-3200
300 W Lincoln Ave Anaheim (92805) ***(G-19136)***
Anaheim Kraemer Medical Offs, Anaheim *Also called Kaiser Foundation Hospitals* ***(G-19601)***
Anaheim Majestic Garden Hotel, Anaheim *Also called Ken Real Estate Lease Ltd* ***(G-12878)***
Anaheim Medical Center 714 774-1450
1111 W La Palma Ave Anaheim (92801) ***(G-19345)***
Anaheim Park Hotel 714 992-1700
222 W Houston Ave Fullerton (92832) ***(G-12388)***
Anaheim Park Inn and Camelot 714 635-7275
1520 S Harbor Blvd Anaheim (92802) ***(G-12389)***
Anaheim Plaza Hotel & Suites, Anaheim *Also called Anaheim Plaza Hotel Inc* ***(G-12390)***
Anaheim Plaza Hotel Inc 714 772-5900
1700 S Harbor Blvd Anaheim (92802) ***(G-12390)***
Anaheim Regional Medical Ctr 714 999-3847
1211 W La Palma Ave # 104 Anaheim (92801) ***(G-19346)***
Anaheim V A Clinic, Anaheim *Also called Veterans Health Administration* ***(G-20218)***
Anaheim/Orange Cnty Visitor Bu (PA) 714 765-8888
800 W Katella Ave Anaheim (92802) ***(G-16990)***
Anaheim/Orange Hilton Suites, Orange *Also called Hilton Suites Inc* ***(G-12712)***
Analytic US Market Neutral Off 213 688-3015
555 W 5th St Fl 50 Los Angeles (90013) ***(G-9958)***
Anaplan Inc (PA) 415 742-8199
625 2nd St Ste 101 San Francisco (94107) ***(G-16321)***
Anaptysbio Inc 858 362-6295
10421 Pcf Ctr Ct Ste 200 San Diego (92121) ***(G-26468)***
Anaspec Inc (HQ) 800 452-5530
34801 Campus Dr Fremont (94555) ***(G-26469)***
Anaspec Egt Group, Fremont *Also called Anaspec Inc* ***(G-26469)***
Anatec International Inc (HQ) 949 498-3350
38 Executive Park Ste 350 Irvine (92614) ***(G-25657)***
Anberry Rehabilitation Hosp, Atwater *Also called Tjd LLC* ***(G-21391)***
Ancca Corporation 949 553-0084
17401 Armstrong Ave Irvine (92614) ***(G-2855)***
Anchor General Insurance Agcy 858 527-3600
10256 Meanley Dr San Diego (92131) ***(G-10602)***
Anchor J Dairy, Stevinson *Also called James J Stevinson A Corp* ***(G-430)***
Ancillary Medical Solutions, San Diego *Also called Drx LLC* ***(G-22949)***
and 1, Aliso Viejo *Also called Basketball Marketing Co Inc* ***(G-27340)***
and Syndicated Productions Inc 818 308-5200
3500 W Olive Ave Ste 1000 Burbank (91505) ***(G-18042)***
Andatha International Inc (PA) 415 398-8600
611 Mission St Fl 4 San Francisco (94105) ***(G-23091)***
Andaz Sandiego, San Diego *Also called Hyatt Corporation* ***(G-12822)***
Andco Farms, Davis *Also called Anderson Farms Inc* ***(G-3)***
Andersen & Sons Shelling Inc 530 839-2236
4530 Rowles Rd Vina (96092) ***(G-508)***
Andersen Hotels Inc 949 494-1151
425 S Coast Hwy Laguna Beach (92651) ***(G-12391)***
Andersen Tax LLC 213 593-2300
400 Suth Hope St Ste 2000 Los Angeles (90071) ***(G-13719)***
Andersncttonwood Disposal Svcs 530 824-4700
3281 State Highway 99w S Corning (96021) ***(G-3977)***
Anderson Rowe & Buckley Inc 415 282-1625
2833 3rd St San Francisco (94107) ***(G-2144)***
Anderson & Howard Electric Inc 949 250-4555
1791 Reynolds Ave Irvine (92614) ***(G-2521)***
Anderson & Martella Inc 925 934-3831
1200 Mt Diablo Blvd # 400 Walnut Creek (94596) ***(G-3473)***
Anderson Air Conditioning LP 714 998-6850
2100 E Walnut Ave Fullerton (92831) ***(G-2145)***
Anderson Associates Staffing (PA) 323 930-3170
8200 Wilshire Blvd # 200 Beverly Hills (90211) ***(G-14838)***
Anderson Burton Construction 626 441-2464
1510 Oxley St Ste G South Pasadena (91030) ***(G-1490)***
Anderson Chrnesky Strl Stl Inc 951 769-5700
353 Risco Cir Beaumont (92223) ***(G-3362)***
Anderson Direct Marketing, Poway *Also called T G T Enterprises Inc* ***(G-14092)***
Anderson Farms Inc 530 753-5695
4600 2nd St Davis (95618) ***(G-3)***
Anderson Homes, Lodi *Also called Lodi Development Inc* ***(G-11979)***
Anderson House, Concord *Also called Youth Homes Incorporated* ***(G-24859)***
Anderson Howard, Irvine *Also called Anderson & Howard Electric Inc* ***(G-2521)***
Anderson Kayne Inv MGT Inc (PA) 310 556-2721
1800 Avenue Of The Stars # 200 Los Angeles (90067) ***(G-27323)***
Anderson Lumber, North Highlands *Also called Pacific Coast Supply LLC* ***(G-6943)***
Anderson McPharlin Conners LLP (PA) 213 688-0080
707 Wilshire Blvd # 4000 Los Angeles (90017) ***(G-23092)***
Anderson News LLC 714 892-7766
15172 Goldenwest Cir Westminster (92683) ***(G-9160)***
Anderson Nut Company 209 854-6820
3050 S Hunt Rd Gustine (95322) ***(G-509)***
Anderson PCF Engrg Cnstr Inc 408 970-9900
1390 Norman Ave Santa Clara (95054) ***(G-2021)***
Anderson Plbg Htg A Condition, El Cajon *Also called Walter Anderson Plumbing Inc* ***(G-2413)***
Andersonpenna Partners Inc 949 428-1500
3737 Birch St Ste 250 Newport Beach (92660) ***(G-27324)***
Andover Maintenance Inc 626 254-1651
45 La Porte St Arcadia (91006) ***(G-14230)***
Andregg Geomatics 530 885-7072
11661 Blocker Dr Ste 200 Auburn (95603) ***(G-26272)***
Andreini & Company (PA) 650 573-1111
220 W 20th Ave San Mateo (94403) ***(G-10603)***
Andres Bermudez 530 795-1000
121 E Grant Ave Ste 4 Winters (95694) ***(G-649)***
Andrew and Williamson Sales Co (PA) 619 661-6000
9940 Marconi Dr San Diego (92154) ***(G-8695)***
Andrew L Youngquist Cnstr Inc 949 862-5611
3187 Red Hill Ave Ste 200 Costa Mesa (92626) ***(G-1491)***
Andrew Lauren Company Inc 949 861-4222
15225 Alton Pkwy Unit 300 Irvine (92618) ***(G-16991)***
Andrew M Golden MD 619 528-5342
4647 Zion Ave San Diego (92120) ***(G-19347)***
Andrew M Martin Company Inc 310 323-2000
16539 S Main St Gardena (90248) ***(G-16992)***
Andrew Williamson Fresh Prod, San Diego *Also called Andrew and Williamson Sales Co* ***(G-8695)***
Andrews International Inc 818 260-9586
455 N Moss St Burbank (91502) ***(G-16561)***
Andrews International Inc 805 409-4160
455 N Moss St Burbank (91502) ***(G-16562)***
Andrews International Inc (PA) 661 775-8400
28001 Smyth Dr Ste 107 Valencia (91355) ***(G-16563)***
Andrews International Inc 626 407-2290
455 N Moss St Burbank (91502) ***(G-16564)***
Andrighetto Produce Inc 650 588-0930
155 Terminal Ct Stalls 15 Stalls South San Francisco (94083) ***(G-3491)***
Andwin Corporation (PA) 818 999-2828
6636 Variel Ave Woodland Hills (91303) ***(G-8185)***
Andwin Scientific, Woodland Hills *Also called Andwin Corporation* ***(G-8185)***
Andy Boy, Salinas *Also called DArrigo Broscoof California* ***(G-56)***
Andy Gump Inc 818 255-0650
11551 Hart St North Hollywood (91605) ***(G-14513)***
Ane Productions Inc 818 972-0777
3500 W Olive Ave Ste 1000 Burbank (91505) ***(G-18043)***
Anello SEC & Consulting LLC 818 632-3277
17348 Tiara St Encino (91316) ***(G-27833)***
Anesthesia Business Cons Inc 925 951-1366
1600 Riviera Ave Ste 420 Walnut Creek (94596) ***(G-19348)***
Anesthesia Consultants of Cont, Walnut Creek *Also called Anesthesia Business Cons Inc* ***(G-19348)***
Anesthesia Svc Med Group Inc 858 277-4767
3626 Ruffin Rd San Diego (92123) ***(G-19349)***
Anfinson Lumber Sales Inc (PA) 951 681-4707
13041 Union Ave Fontana (92337) ***(G-6908)***
Angel Care Home Health Inc 818 248-8811
850 Colorado Blvd Ste 103 Los Angeles (90041) ***(G-22362)***
Angel View Inc 760 322-2440
454 N Indian Canyon Dr Palm Springs (92262) ***(G-24549)***
Angel View Resale Store, Palm Springs *Also called Angel View Inc* ***(G-24549)***
Angeles Contractor Inc (PA) 714 523-1021
8461 Commonwealth Ave Buena Park (90621) ***(G-1399)***
Angeles Home Health Care Inc 213 487-5131
3701 Wilshire Blvd # 900 Los Angeles (90010) ***(G-22363)***
Angeles Los Equestrian Center 818 840-9063
480 W Riverside Dr Burbank (91506) ***(G-19137)***
Angelica Corporation 925 473-2520
701 Willow Pass Rd Ste 10 Pittsburg (94565) ***(G-13531)***
Angelica Textile, Pittsburg *Also called Angelica Corporation* ***(G-13531)***
Angelica Textile Services Inc 714 998-6109
1575 N Case St Orange (92867) ***(G-13532)***
Angelica Textile Services Inc 909 623-5135
300 E Commercial St Pomona (91767) ***(G-13533)***
Angelika Film Center and Cafe, San Diego *Also called Reading International Inc* ***(G-18345)***
Angels Baseball LP (PA) 714 940-2000
2000 E Gene Autry Way Anaheim (92806) ***(G-18535)***
Angels Everyday Inc 909 793-7788
330 Sixth St Ste 201 Redlands (92374) ***(G-22364)***
Angels In Motion LLC 909 590-9102
4091 Riverside Dr Ste 111 Chino (91710) ***(G-22365)***
Angels Nursing Center, Los Angeles *Also called Gva Enterprises Inc* ***(G-21258)***
Angels Nursing Center, Los Angeles *Also called Gva Enterprises Inc* ***(G-21259)***
Angels of Vly Hospice Care LLC 818 542-3070
2600 Foothill Blvd # 202 La Crescenta (91214) ***(G-22366)***
Angelus Western Ppr Fibers Inc 213 623-9221
2474 Porter St Los Angeles (90021) ***(G-8062)***
Angioscore Inc 510 933-7900
5055 Brandin Ct Fremont (94538) ***(G-7235)***
Anheuser-Busch LLC 707 429-7595
3101 Busch Dr Fairfield (94534) ***(G-7820)***
Anheuser-Busch LLC 951 782-3935
1400 Marlborough Ave Riverside (92507) ***(G-9039)***
Anheuser-Busch LLC 310 761-4600
20499 S Reeves Ave Carson (90810) ***(G-9040)***
Anheuser-Busch LLC 949 263-9270
18952 Macarthur Blvd Irvine (92612) ***(G-9041)***
Animal Care Center 707 584-4343
6470 Redwood Dr Rohnert Park (94928) ***(G-614)***
Animoto LLC 415 987-3139
333 Kearny St Fl 6 San Francisco (94108) ***(G-15014)***
Anitsa Inc 213 237-0533
6032 Shull St Bell Gardens (90201) ***(G-13500)***
Anixter Inc 858 505-1950
4775 Viewridge Ave San Diego (92123) ***(G-7960)***
Anixter Inc 510 477-2400
30061 Ahern Ave Union City (94587) ***(G-7414)***
Anixter Inc 925 469-8500
4464 Willow Rd Ste 101 Pleasanton (94588) ***(G-7415)***
Anixter International Inc 858 571-6571
7140 Opportunity Rd San Diego (92111) ***(G-7961)***

ALPHABETIC

Anixter International Inc......858 974-6714
4775 Viewridge Ave San Diego (92123) *(G-7962)*
Anjana Software Solutions Inc......805 583-0121
1445 E Los Angeles Ave # 305 Simi Valley (93065) *(G-15015)*
Anjaneyap Inc......408 922-9690
830 Hillview Ct Ste 140 Milpitas (95035) *(G-27325)*
Anka Behavioral Health Inc......626 573-5902
2507 Evelyn Ave Rosemead (91770) *(G-28113)*
Anka Behavioral Health Inc......209 982-4697
458 Almond Dr Lodi (95240) *(G-22887)*
Anka Behavioral Health Inc......916 722-3700
7515 Willow Way Citrus Heights (95610) *(G-22888)*
Anka Behavioral Health Inc......951 929-2744
2100 S State Hemet (92543) *(G-10604)*
Anka Behavioral Health Inc......510 494-1567
5149 Winston Ct Fremont (94536) *(G-22889)*
Anka Behavioral Health Inc (PA)......925 825-4700
1850 Gateway Blvd Ste 900 Concord (94520) *(G-22657)*
Anka Behavioral Health Inc......909 622-8217
942 Barbara Ln Pomona (91767) *(G-19350)*
Anna Corporation......951 736-6037
2078 2nd St Norco (92860) *(G-2427)*
Annabel Investment Company......925 866-0100
2600 Camino Ramon Ste 201 San Ramon (94583) *(G-11948)*
Annandale Golf Club......626 796-6125
1 N San Rafael Ave Pasadena (91105) *(G-18874)*
Anne Sppi Clnic Riverside Rnch, Bakersfield *Also called Sippi Anne Riverside Ranch LLP (G-24812)*
Annenberg Foundation (PA)......310 209-4560
2000 Ave Stars Ste 1000s Los Angeles (90067) *(G-25198)*
Annenberg Foundation Trust (PA)......760 202-2222
71231 Tamarisk Ln Rancho Mirage (92270) *(G-12168)*
Annie App Inc (PA)......844 277-2664
23 Geary St Ste 400800 San Francisco (94108) *(G-15016)*
Annies Homegrown Inc......510 558-7500
1610 5th St Berkeley (94710) *(G-8795)*
Anning-Johnson Company......510 670-0100
22955 Kidder St Hayward (94545) *(G-2856)*
Anning-Johnson Company......626 369-7131
13250 Temple Ave City of Industry (91746) *(G-2857)*
Annuzzi Concrete Service Inc......415 468-2795
85 Elmira St San Francisco (94124) *(G-1732)*
Anomali Incorporated......408 800-4050
2317 Broadway St Fl 3 Redwood City (94063) *(G-15017)*
Anonymous Content LLC (PA)......310 558-6000
3532 Hayden Ave Culver City (90232) *(G-18044)*
Anova Architects Inc......530 626-1810
1990 3rd St Ste 500 Sacramento (95811) *(G-26163)*
Ans World Service Inc......714 441-2400
2751 E Chapman Ave # 204 Fullerton (92831) *(G-5214)*
Ansafone Contact Centers, Santa Ana *Also called Ephonamationcom Inc (G-17152)*
Ansar Gallery......949 220-0000
2505 El Camino Rd Tustin (92782) *(G-8457)*
Anschutz Entrmt Group Inc (HQ)......213 763-7700
1100 S Flower St Los Angeles (90015) *(G-18450)*
Anschutz Film Group......310 887-1000
1888 Century Park E # 1400 Los Angeles (90067) *(G-2858)*
Anschutz So Calif Sports Compl......310 630-2000
18400 Avalon Blvd Ste 100 Carson (90746) *(G-18536)*
Ansett Aircraft Spares & Svcs, Sylmar *Also called Ansett Arcft Spares & Svcs Inc (G-7993)*
Ansett Arcft Spares & Svcs Inc (PA)......818 362-1100
12675 Encinitas Ave Sylmar (91342) *(G-7993)*
Ansira Partners Inc......818 461-6100
5000 Van Nuys Blvd Sherman Oaks (91403) *(G-16993)*
Answer Financial Inc (HQ)......818 644-4000
15910 Ventura Blvd Fl 6 Encino (91436) *(G-16994)*
Ant Farm LLC......323 850-0700
110 S Fairfax Ave Ste 200 Los Angeles (90036) *(G-18214)*
Antech Diagnostics Inc (HQ)......800 745-4725
17672 Cowan Bldg B Irvine (92614) *(G-615)*
Antelope Valley Distributing, Pomona *Also called FBC Industries (G-11967)*
Antelope Valley Foundation......661 945-7290
646 W Lancaster Blvd # 109 Lancaster (93534) *(G-23663)*
Antelope Valley Health Center, Lancaster *Also called County of Los Angeles (G-22703)*
ANTELOPE VALLEY HLTH CARE DST, Lancaster *Also called Antelope Valley Hospital Aux (G-21453)*
Antelope Valley Hospital, Lancaster *Also called Kaiser Foundation Hospitals (G-21644)*
Antelope Valley Hospital Aux......661 949-1550
1601 W Avenue J Lancaster (93534) *(G-19351)*
Antelope Valley Hospital Aux......661 726-6180
1600 W Avenue J Lancaster (93534) *(G-19352)*
Antelope Valley Hospital Aux (PA)......661 949-5000
1600 W Avenue J Lancaster (93534) *(G-21453)*
Antelope Valley Mall......661 266-9150
1233 W Rancho Vista Blvd # 405 Palmdale (93551) *(G-10959)*
Antelope Valley Medical Group......661 945-2783
44469 10th St W Lancaster (93534) *(G-19353)*
Antelope Vly Convalecent Hosp, Lancaster *Also called Antelope Vly Retirement HM Inc (G-21140)*
Antelope Vly Retirement HM Inc......661 948-7501
44445 15th St W Lancaster (93534) *(G-21140)*
Antelope Vly Retirement HM Inc......661 949-5524
44567 15th St W Lancaster (93534) *(G-21141)*
Antelope Vly Schl Trnsp Agcy......661 945-3621
670 W Avenue L8 Lancaster (93534) *(G-3911)*
Anthem Inc......805 557-6655
2100 Corporate Center Dr Newbury Park (91320) *(G-10232)*
Anthem Insurance Companies Inc......858 571-8136
9655 Granite Ridge Dr San Diego (92123) *(G-10256)*
Anthem Insurance Companies Inc......805 557-6655
1 Wellpoint Way Westlake Village (91362) *(G-10257)*
Anthem Insurance Companies Inc......805 557-6655
5653 Camino Ruiz Ste A Camarillo (93012) *(G-10258)*
Anthony Botelho......831 623-4228
382 Olympia Ave San Juan Bautista (95045) *(G-227)*
Anthony Harvesting Inc......831 385-6460
401 S Vanderhurst Ave King City (93930) *(G-489)*
Anthony Lambe......559 268-0709
1521 W Nielsen Ave Ste 69 Fresno (93706) *(G-6705)*
Anthony P Garofalo A Dental......619 440-0071
742 Broadway El Cajon (92021) *(G-20246)*
Anthony Robbins & Associates......858 535-9900
9888 Carroll Cntre Rd 1 Ste 100 San Diego (92126) *(G-12210)*
Anthony Soto Emplyment Trining, Santa Rosa *Also called California Human Dev Corp (G-24318)*
Anthony Trevino......707 747-4776
938 Adams St Ste A Benicia (94510) *(G-3105)*
Anthony Vineyards Inc......760 391-5400
52301 Enterprise Way Coachella (92236) *(G-692)*
Anthony Vineyards Inc (PA)......661 858-6211
5512 Valpredo Ave Bakersfield (93307) *(G-141)*
Anthonys Fish Grotto......619 713-1853
5575 Lake Park Way # 211 La Mesa (91942) *(G-8626)*
Antimite Associates Inc......619 231-2900
5458 Complex St 401 San Diego (92123) *(G-14172)*
Antioch Cab, Pacheco *Also called Yellow Cab Company (G-3873)*
Antioch Convalescent Hospital, Antioch *Also called Norcal Care Centers Inc (G-21328)*
Antioch Public Golf Corp......925 706-4220
4800 Golf Course Rd Antioch (94531) *(G-18714)*
Antioch Rotary Club......925 757-1800
324 G St Antioch (94509) *(G-18875)*
Antonelli & Sons Fish & Plty......650 952-7413
119 S Linden Ave South San Francisco (94080) *(G-8627)*
Anvil Builders Inc......415 397-4925
1475 Donner Ave San Francisco (94124) *(G-1733)*
Anvil Iron, Gardena *Also called Anvil Steel Corporation (G-3363)*
Anvil Steel Corporation......310 329-5811
134 W 168th St Gardena (90248) *(G-3363)*
AOC Technologies Inc......925 875-0808
5960 Inglewood Dr Pleasanton (94588) *(G-7357)*
AON, Los Angeles *Also called Schirmer Fire Protection Eng (G-10862)*
AON Benfield Fac Inc......415 486-6900
199 Fremont St Fl 15 San Francisco (94105) *(G-10233)*
AON Consulting Inc......559 449-7200
5260 N Palm Ave Ste 400 Fresno (93704) *(G-10605)*
AON Consulting Inc......408 321-2500
2570 N 1st St Ste 500 San Jose (95131) *(G-27326)*
AON Consulting Inc......818 506-4300
707 Wilshire Blvd # 2500 Los Angeles (90017) *(G-10606)*
AON Consulting Inc......800 558-0655
3461 Fair Oaks Blvd Sacramento (95864) *(G-10607)*
AON Consulting Inc......213 630-2900
707 Wilshire Blvd # 2500 Los Angeles (90017) *(G-10608)*
AON Consulting Inc......562 345-4600
16969 Von Karman Ave Irvine (92606) *(G-10609)*
AON Consulting Inc......562 345-4900
1600 Iowa Ave Ste 100 Riverside (92507) *(G-10610)*
AON Consulting Inc......562 345-4700
21900 Burbank Blvd # 101 Woodland Hills (91367) *(G-10611)*
AON Consulting Inc......800 283-1667
851 Van Ness Ave Fl 2 San Francisco (94109) *(G-10612)*
AON Consulting Inc......800 815-1823
160 Via Verde Ste 200 San Dimas (91773) *(G-10613)*
AON Consulting Inc......415 486-6226
199 Fremont St Fl 11 San Francisco (94105) *(G-10614)*
AON Consulting Inc......408 288-8000
307 Main St Ste 340 Salinas (93901) *(G-10615)*
AON Consulting Inc......562 496-2888
5000 E Spring St Ste 100 Long Beach (90815) *(G-10616)*
AON Consulting Inc......626 683-5200
255 S Lake Ave Ste 900 Pasadena (91101) *(G-10617)*
AON Consulting & Insur Svcs......415 486-7500
199 Fremont St Fl 14 San Francisco (94105) *(G-10618)*
AON Hewitt LLC......949 725-4500
100 Bayview Cir Ste 100 Newport Beach (92660) *(G-27327)*
Aopen America Incorporated......408 586-1200
2150 N 1st St Ste 300 San Jose (95131) *(G-7092)*
AP Express LLC......562 236-2250
8500 Rex Rd Pico Rivera (90660) *(G-5027)*
AP Express International LLC......562 236-2250
8500 Rex Rd Pico Rivera (90660) *(G-5215)*
AP Global Inc......818 707-3167
31352 Via Colinas Ste 101 Westlake Village (91362) *(G-7520)*
Ap-Redlands LLC......562 435-2100
12447 Lewis St Ste 203 Garden Grove (92840) *(G-27328)*
APA Incorporated......310 888-4200
405 S Beverly Dr Ste 500 Beverly Hills (90212) *(G-27329)*
APAC Customer Services Inc......619 298-7103
8885 Rio San Diego Dr San Diego (92108) *(G-16995)*
APC Lab, Chino *Also called Applied P & Ch Laboratory Sout (G-26472)*
Aperian Global Inc (PA)......415 749-2920
1 Kaiser Plz Ste 785 Oakland (94612) *(G-27330)*
Aperio Group LLC......415 339-4300
3 Harbor Dr Ste 315 Sausalito (94965) *(G-16996)*
Apex Bulk Commodities Inc......909 854-9991
14080 Slover Ave Fontana (92337) *(G-10104)*
Apex Communications, Fremont *Also called Netversant - Silicon Vly Inc (G-2665)*

ALPHABETIC

Apex Computer Systems Inc 562 926-6820
13875 Cerritos Corprt Dr A Cerritos (90703) *(G-16286)*
Apex Development Inc 818 887-0400
23679 Calabasas Rd # 764 Calabasas (91302) *(G-1291)*
Apex Group 818 885-0513
17101 Superior St Northridge (91325) *(G-26922)*
Apex Logistics Intl Inc 310 665-0288
17511 S Susana Rd Compton (90221) *(G-5028)*
Apex Machine Works Inc 310 393-5987
2118 Wilshire Blvd # 258 Santa Monica (90403) *(G-25658)*
Apex Mechanical Systems Inc 858 536-8700
7440 Trade St Ste A San Diego (92121) *(G-2146)*
Apex Mortgage Solutions, Hercules *Also called Unipark LLC (G-17745)*
Apex Parks Group LLC (PA) 949 349-8461
27061 Aliso Creek Rd Aliso Viejo (92656) *(G-18811)*
Apex Parks Group LLC 909 981-5251
1500 W 7th St Upland (91786) *(G-19138)*
Apex Parks Group LLC 210 341-6663
27061 Aliso Creek Rd # 100 Aliso Viejo (92656) *(G-19139)*
Apex Staffing Service 909 941-0267
10134 6th St Ste A Rancho Cucamonga (91730) *(G-14839)*
Apfeld & Neal Insurance Svcs 714 821-7041
11022 Winners Cir Ste 100 Los Alamitos (90720) *(G-10619)*
Apical Industries Inc 760 724-5300
3030 Enterprise Ct Ste A Vista (92081) *(G-7994)*
Apigee Corporation 408 343-7300
10 Almaden Blvd Ste 1600 San Jose (95113) *(G-15902)*
APL Logistics Ltd 310 548-8700
614 Terminal Way San Pedro (90731) *(G-4713)*
Apla Health & Wellness 213 201-1546
611 S Kingsley Dr Los Angeles (90005) *(G-19354)*
APM Terminals Pacific LLC 310 221-4000
2500 Navy Way Pier 400 San Pedro (90731) *(G-5029)*
APM Terminals Pacific LLC (HQ) 704 571-2768
2500 Navy Way San Pedro (90731) *(G-4742)*
APM Terminals Pacific Ltd 510 992-6430
5801 Christie Ave Emeryville (94608) *(G-5030)*
Apn Software Services Inc (PA) 510 623-5050
39899 Balentine Dr # 385 Newark (94560) *(G-16322)*
Apollo Cpr, Pico Rivera *Also called Ionics Altrpure Wtr Crparation (G-8856)*
Apollo Div Ionics Ultrapure, San Jose *Also called GE Ionics Inc (G-7721)*
Apollo Electric 714 256-8414
330 N Basse Ln Brea (92821) *(G-2522)*
App Wholesale LLC 323 980-8315
3686 E Olympic Blvd Los Angeles (90023) *(G-8796)*
Apparel Concepts Intl Inc 626 233-9198
4804 Laurel Canyon Blvd # 59 Valley Village (91607) *(G-8332)*
Appcelerator Inc (HQ) 650 200-4255
1732 N 1st St Ste 150 San Jose (95112) *(G-15018)*
Appdirect Inc (PA) 415 852-3924
650 California St Fl 25 San Francisco (94108) *(G-15580)*
Appdynamics Inc (PA) 415 442-8400
303 2nd St Ste N450 San Francisco (94107) *(G-15019)*
Appellation Tours Inc 707 938-9390
21707 8th St E Sonoma (95476) *(G-4986)*
Apperience Corporation 415 813-2995
665 3rd St Ste 150 San Francisco (94107) *(G-15020)*
Appery LLC 925 602-5504
1340 Treat Blvd Ste 375 Walnut Creek (94597) *(G-15581)*
Appfabrix Software Inc 408 834-4435
691 S Milpitas Blvd # 210 Milpitas (95035) *(G-15021)*
Appfolio Inc (PA) 805 364-6093
50 Castilian Dr Ste 101 Goleta (93117) *(G-15582)*
Appirio Inc (PA) 415 663-4433
760 Market St Ste 1150 San Francisco (94102) *(G-15022)*
Appl, Clovis *Also called Agriculture and Priority Pollu (G-26828)*
Apple Eght Hospitality MGT Inc 714 827-1010
5865 Katella Ave Cypress (90630) *(G-12392)*
Apple Hospitality Reit Inc 916 568-5400
2540 Venture Oaks Way Sacramento (95833) *(G-12393)*
Apple Inns Inc 510 895-1311
68 Monarch Bay Dr San Leandro (94577) *(G-12394)*
Apple One Employment, Glendale *Also called Howroyd-Wright Emplymnt Agcy (G-14675)*
Apple One Service Arizona Inc 714 848-2610
16371 Beach Blvd Ste 22 Huntington Beach (92647) *(G-14608)*
Apple Store Glendale Galleria, Glendale *Also called Glendale Associates Ltd (G-10989)*
Apple Valley Care & Rehab, Sebastopol *Also called Apple Vly Cnvalescent Hosp Inc (G-20378)*
Apple Valley Care Center, Apple Valley *Also called Front Porch Communities & Svcs (G-20585)*
Apple Valley Farms Inc 559 498-7115
1828 E Hedges Ave Fresno (93703) *(G-3492)*
Apple Valley Golf Club 760 242-3653
15200 Rancherias Rd Apple Valley (92307) *(G-18876)*
Apple Valley Golf Course, Apple Valley *Also called Apple Valley Golf Club (G-18876)*
Apple Vlley/ Vctrvlle Cnsrtium 760 240-7000
14955 Dale Evans Pkwy Apple Valley (92307) *(G-13733)*
Apple Vly Cnvalescent Hosp Inc 707 823-7675
1035 Gravenstein Hwy N Sebastopol (95472) *(G-20378)*
Applebee & Sheehan Inc (PA) 800 200-8872
978 W 10th St Azusa (91702) *(G-14231)*
Applebee Leasing Inc 818 612-6218
4 Maidstone Dr Newport Beach (92660) *(G-16997)*
Applecare Medical MGT LLC 714 443-4507
18 Centerpointe Dr # 100 La Palma (90623) *(G-26923)*
Appleone Employment Services, Glendale *Also called Howroyd-Wright Emplymnt Agcy (G-14676)*
Applewood Care Center 916 446-2506
1090 Rio Ln Sacramento (95822) *(G-20379)*
Applewood Operating, Redding *Also called Copper Ridge Care Center (G-20471)*
Appliance Distribution Inc 916 497-0274
915 N B St Sacramento (95811) *(G-7490)*
Appliance Recycl Ctrs of Amer 310 223-2800
1920 S Acacia Ave Compton (90220) *(G-6425)*
Applied Biosystems 800 327-3002
1149 Chess Dr Foster City (94404) *(G-26470)*
Applied Companies Inc (PA) 661 257-0090
28020 Avenue Stanford Santa Clarita (91355) *(G-25659)*
Applied Computer Solutions (PA) 714 861-2200
15461 Springdale St Huntington Beach (92649) *(G-15023)*
Applied Engineering MGT Corp 805 484-1909
760 Paseo Camarillo # 101 Camarillo (93010) *(G-15024)*
Applied Geokinetics 949 502-5353
77 Bunsen Irvine (92618) *(G-25660)*
Applied Language Solutions LLC 800 579-5010
1250 W Sunflower La Habra (90631) *(G-16998)*
Applied Materials, Roseville *Also called Cokeva Inc (G-16289)*
Applied Materials Inc 408 727-5555
3340 Scott Blvd Santa Clara (95054) *(G-1292)*
Applied Materials Inc 408 727-5555
2821 Scott Blvd Bldg 17 Santa Clara (95050) *(G-4523)*
Applied Molecular Evolution (HQ) 858 597-4990
10300 Campus Point Dr # 200 San Diego (92121) *(G-26471)*
Applied P & Ch Laboratory Sout 909 590-1828
13760 Magnolia Ave Chino (91710) *(G-26472)*
Applied Research Assoc Inc 805 962-4810
735 State St Santa Barbara (93101) *(G-26473)*
Applied Underwriters Inc 415 656-5000
950 Tower Ln Ste 1400 Foster City (94404) *(G-10620)*
Applied Weather Technology Inc 408 731-8600
140 Kifer Ct Sunnyvale (94086) *(G-28114)*
Applimotion Inc 916 652-3118
5915 Jetton Ln Loomis (95650) *(G-7416)*
Appraisal Trend, Encino *Also called Valuation Concepts LLC (G-11896)*
Appraiser Loft LLC 858 832-8334
3027 Townsgate Rd Ste 140 Westlake Village (91361) *(G-11300)*
Apprentice & Journeymen Traini 818 464-4579
7850 Haskell Ave Van Nuys (91406) *(G-2147)*
Apprentice & Journeymen Trn Tr 323 636-9871
7850 Haskell Ave Van Nuys (91406) *(G-24303)*
Approvalfinder.com, Irvine *Also called Loangeniecom Inc (G-9934)*
Appsflyer Ltd 415 636-9430
111 New Montgomery St San Francisco (94105) *(G-13958)*
Appster Inc 415 926-2741
180 Sansome St Fl 4 San Francisco (94104) *(G-15025)*
Apptivo Inc 650 906-1034
34364 Eucalyptus Ter Fremont (94555) *(G-15026)*
Apria Healthcare LLC 530 669-6441
1680 Tide Ct Ste B Woodland (95776) *(G-22890)*
Apria Healthcare LLC 209 223-7727
220 Scttslle Blvd Bldg A Jackson (95642) *(G-22891)*
Apria Healthcare LLC 650 588-9744
480 Carlton Ct South San Francisco (94080) *(G-7236)*
Apria Healthcare LLC 805 278-6700
2150 Trabajo Dr Ste B Oxnard (93030) *(G-14469)*
Apria Healthcare LLC 858 653-6800
10090 Willow Creek Rd San Diego (92131) *(G-14470)*
Apria Healthcare LLC 714 508-3000
15091 Bake Pkwy Irvine (92618) *(G-14471)*
Apria Healthcare LLC (HQ) 949 616-2606
26220 Enterprise Ct Lake Forest (92630) *(G-7237)*
Apria Healthcare LLC 530 677-2713
1450 Expo Pkwy Sacramento (95815) *(G-7238)*
Apria Healthcare LLC 925 827-8800
2510 Dean Lesher Dr Ste D Concord (94520) *(G-7239)*
Apria Healthcare LLC 408 383-4400
2040 Corporate Ct San Jose (95131) *(G-14472)*
Apria Healthcare LLC 707 543-0979
3636 N Laughlin Rd # 190 Santa Rosa (95403) *(G-14473)*
Apria Healthcare LLC 951 320-1100
1565 Eastwood Ct Riverside (92507) *(G-22367)*
Apria Healthcare LLC 510 346-4000
2476 Verna Ct San Leandro (94577) *(G-22368)*
Apriso Corporation 562 951-8000
301 E Ocean Blvd Ste 1200 Long Beach (90802) *(G-15903)*
Apteligent 415 371-1402
760 Market St Ste 1101 San Francisco (94102) *(G-15027)*
Aptiv Digital Inc 818 295-6789
2210 W Olive Ave Fl 2 Burbank (91506) *(G-15583)*
Aptos Berry Farms Inc 831 726-3256
730 S A St Oxnard (93030) *(G-103)*
Apttus Corporation 650 445-7700
1400 Fashi Islan Blvd Ste San Mateo (94404) *(G-15028)*
Apttus Corporation 650 722-1619
560 S Winchester Blvd San Jose (95128) *(G-16323)*
Apu Inc (PA) 661 948-2880
14939 Oxnard St Van Nuys (91411) *(G-6706)*
Apumac LLC 888 248-7775
6404 Wilshire Blvd # 106 Los Angeles (90048) *(G-7521)*
Apumac.com, Los Angeles *Also called Apumac LLC (G-7521)*
Apw Construction Inc 626 855-1720
15135 Salt Lake Ave City of Industry (91746) *(G-3493)*
Apw International Inc 310 884-5003
1073 E Artesia Blvd Carson (90746) *(G-6707)*
Apw Knox-Seeman Warehouse Inc (HQ) 310 604-4373
1073 E Artesia Blvd Carson (90746) *(G-6708)*

A
L
P
H
A
B
E
T
I
C

Apx Inc (PA)...408 899-3300
2001 Gateway Pl Ste 315w San Jose (95110) ***(G-27834)***
Aqua Gunite Inc...408 271-2782
5830 S Naylor Rd Livermore (94551) ***(G-3494)***
Aqua-Serv Engineers Inc (HQ)...951 681-9696
13560 Colombard Ct Fontana (92337) ***(G-8977)***
Aqualine Piping Inc...408 745-7100
2108 Bering Dr Ste C San Jose (95131) ***(G-2148)***
Aquamatic Fire Protection Inc (PA)...925 753-0420
540 Garcia Ave Ste A Pittsburg (94565) ***(G-16999)***
Aquantia Corp (PA)...408 228-8300
105 E Tasman Dr San Jose (95134) ***(G-17000)***
Aquarium of Pacific...562 590-3100
310 Golden Shore Ste 300 Long Beach (90802) ***(G-25056)***
Aquarium of Pacific (PA)...562 590-3100
100 Aquarium Way Long Beach (90802) ***(G-25057)***
Aquarium of The Bay, The, San Francisco *Also called Bayorg* ***(G-25058)***
Aquatic Desigining Inc...707 822-4629
4801 West End Rd Arcata (95521) ***(G-1400)***
Aquatic Science Center...510 746-7334
4911 Central Ave Richmond (94804) ***(G-26474)***
Aquinas Corporation...408 248-7100
3580 Payne Ave San Jose (95117) ***(G-20380)***
Aquirecorps Norwalk Auto Auctn...562 864-7464
12405 Rosecrans Ave Norwalk (90650) ***(G-6665)***
AR Preservation LP...415 776-2151
201 Eddy St San Francisco (94102) ***(G-11086)***
AR Wilson Quarry, Aromas *Also called Granite Rock Co* ***(G-1104)***
Aragen Bioscience Inc...408 779-1700
380 Woodview Ave Morgan Hill (95037) ***(G-26475)***
Aragon Commercial Ldscpg Inc...408 998-0600
530 Stockton Ave San Jose (95126) ***(G-808)***
Aragon Construction Inc...909 621-2200
5440 Arrow Hwy Montclair (91763) ***(G-1492)***
Arakelian Enterprises Inc...818 768-0689
11121 Pendleton St Sun Valley (91352) ***(G-6426)***
Arakelian Enterprises Inc...626 336-3636
15045 Salt Lake Ave City of Industry (91746) ***(G-6427)***
Arakelian Enterprises Inc...951 342-3300
687 Iowa Ave Riverside (92507) ***(G-6428)***
Arakelian Enterprises Inc (PA)...626 336-3636
14048 Valley Blvd City of Industry (91746) ***(G-6429)***
Arakelyan Aram...818 247-0191
2115 Balmain Way Glendale (91206) ***(G-11301)***
Aramark Facility Services LLC...213 740-8968
941 W 35th St Los Angeles (90007) ***(G-14232)***
Aramark Facility Services LLC...714 372-0683
5301 Bolsa Ave Bldg 10 Huntington Beach (92647) ***(G-14233)***
Aramark MGT Svcs Ltd Partnr...562 593-2724
2401 E Wardlow Rd Ste C Long Beach (90807) ***(G-14234)***
Aramark Services Inc...831 372-8016
800 Asilomar Blvd Pacific Grove (93950) ***(G-18451)***
Aramark Services Inc...323 587-7661
1405 E 58th Pl Los Angeles (90001) ***(G-13650)***
Aramark Services Inc...925 798-3321
2000 Kirker Pass Rd Concord (94521) ***(G-19140)***
Aramark Spt & Entrmt Group LLC...213 740-1224
3400 S Figueroa St Los Angeles (90007) ***(G-18452)***
Aramark Spt & Entrmt Group LLC...530 740-4758
2677 Forty Mile Rd Marysville (95901) ***(G-18453)***
Aramark Spt & Entrmt Group LLC...831 648-9809
886 Cannery Row Monterey (93940) ***(G-18454)***
Aramark Spt & Entrmt Group LLC...408 748-7030
5001 Great America Pkwy Santa Clara (95054) ***(G-18455)***
Aramark Unf & Career AP LLC...209 368-9785
1617 Jim Way Modesto (95358) ***(G-13602)***
Aramark Unf & Career AP LLC...818 973-3700
115 N First St Burbank (91502) ***(G-13603)***
Aramark Unf & Career AP LLC...323 774-4216
15525 Garfield Ave Paramount (90723) ***(G-13534)***
Aramark Unf & Career AP LLC...510 835-9285
330 Chestnut St Oakland (94607) ***(G-13604)***
Aramark Unf & Career AP LLC...323 266-0555
4422 Dunham St Los Angeles (90023) ***(G-13605)***
Aramark Unf & Career AP LLC...408 243-9824
855 Mckendrie St San Jose (95126) ***(G-13535)***
Aramark Unf & Career AP LLC...530 241-6433
755 Butte St Redding (96001) ***(G-13606)***
Aramark Unf & Career AP LLC (HQ)...818 973-3700
115 N First St Ste 203 Burbank (91502) ***(G-13607)***
Aramark Unf & Career AP LLC...916 286-4100
1419 National Dr Sacramento (95834) ***(G-13608)***
Aramark Unf & Career AP LLC...559 291-6631
3333 N Sabre Dr Fresno (93727) ***(G-13536)***
Aramark Unf & Career AP LLC...510 487-1855
31148 San Antonio St Hayward (94544) ***(G-13609)***
Aramark Unf & Career AP LLC...858 550-1131
5665 Eastgate Dr San Diego (92121) ***(G-13537)***
Aramark Unf & Career AP LLC...714 545-4877
3101 W Adams St Santa Ana (92704) ***(G-13610)***
Aramark Unf & Career AP LLC...925 827-3782
5000 Forni Dr Concord (94520) ***(G-13611)***
Aramark Unf & Career AP LLC...909 888-4272
1135 Hall Ave Riverside (92509) ***(G-13612)***
Aramark Unf & Career AP LLC...818 364-8272
15372 Cobalt St Sylmar (91342) ***(G-13613)***
Aramark Unf & Career AP LLC...650 244-9332
440 N Canal St South San Francisco (94080) ***(G-13614)***
Aramark Unf & Career AP LLC...415 244-8332
440 Carolina St San Francisco (94107) ***(G-13538)***
Aramark Unf Svcs Midwest LLC...800 388-3300
115 N First St Burbank (91502) ***(G-13615)***
Aramark Uniform Services...916 286-4100
1419 National Dr Sacramento (95834) ***(G-13616)***
Ararat Home of Los Angeles...818 837-1800
15099 Mission Hills Rd Mission Hills (91345) ***(G-21142)***
Ararat Nursing Facility, Mission Hills *Also called Ararat Home of Los Angeles* ***(G-21142)***
Arb Inc (HQ)...949 598-9242
26000 Commercentre Dr Lake Forest (92630) ***(G-2022)***
Arb Inc...925 432-3649
1875 Loveridge Rd Pittsburg (94565) ***(G-4524)***
Arb Inc...805 643-4188
2235 N Ventura Ave Ventura (93001) ***(G-1902)***
Arb Inc...415 206-1015
50 Quint St San Francisco (94124) ***(G-1903)***
Arbitech LLC...949 376-6650
15330 Barranca Pkwy Irvine (92618) ***(G-7093)***
Arbor Employment & Training, Canoga Park *Also called Canoga Park Worksource Center* ***(G-14620)***
Arbor Vly Nrsing Rhblttion Ctr, Modesto *Also called Kissito Health Case Inc* ***(G-20710)***
Arbormed Inc (PA)...714 689-1500
725 W Town And Country Rd Orange (92868) ***(G-22892)***
Arbors, The, San Diego *Also called G & L Penasquitos Inc* ***(G-23992)***
Arborwell Inc (PA)...510 881-4260
2337 American Ave Hayward (94545) ***(G-983)***
ARC, Torrance *Also called Good Sports Plus Ltd* ***(G-15209)***
ARC...310 857-5759
1740 Stanford St Santa Monica (90404) ***(G-14106)***
ARC - Imperial Valley (PA)...760 352-0180
298 E Ross Ave El Centro (92243) ***(G-23664)***
ARC - Imperial Valley...760 768-1944
340 E 1st St Calexico (92231) ***(G-22658)***
ARC - SD E Cnty Training Ctrs, El Cajon *Also called ARC of San Diego* ***(G-24872)***
ARC Community Enrichment, Ojai *Also called ARC of Ventura County Inc* ***(G-22659)***
ARC Document Solutions Inc...818 242-6555
655 N Central Ave Glendale (91203) ***(G-14107)***
ARC Document Solutions Inc...626 333-7005
1207 John Reed Ct Ste A City of Industry (91745) ***(G-14108)***
ARC Document Solutions Inc...415 495-8700
2430 Mariner Square Loop Alameda (94501) ***(G-14109)***
ARC Document Solutions Inc...415 495-8700
945 Bryant St Ste 1000 San Francisco (94103) ***(G-14110)***
ARC Document Solutions Inc...818 908-0222
15019 Califa St Van Nuys (91411) ***(G-14111)***
ARC Enterprises, San Diego *Also called ARC of San Diego* ***(G-24871)***
ARC Fastener Supply & Mfg...909 481-8171
2104 Wembley Ln Corona (92881) ***(G-7914)***
ARC Fresno/Madera Counties (PA)...559 226-6268
4490 E Ashlan Ave Fresno (93726) ***(G-24304)***
ARC Hosp Portfolio II NTC Trs...760 431-9399
5835 Owens Ave Carlsbad (92008) ***(G-12395)***
ARC Hospitality Portfolio...310 333-0888
2135 E El Segundo Blvd El Segundo (90245) ***(G-12396)***
ARC Imaging Resources, Monterey Park *Also called American Reprographics Co LLC* ***(G-14102)***
ARC Industries...805 520-0399
5143 Cochran St Ste 93063 Simi Valley (93063) ***(G-24550)***
ARC Mid-Cities Inc...310 329-9272
14208 Towne Ave Los Angeles (90061) ***(G-24305)***
ARC of Alameda County...510 582-8151
1101 Walpert St Hayward (94541) ***(G-24306)***
ARC of Butte County (PA)...530 891-5865
2030 Park Ave Chico (95928) ***(G-23665)***
ARC of San Diego, Chula Vista *Also called ARC Starlight Center* ***(G-23667)***
ARC of San Diego (PA)...619 685-1175
3030 Market St San Diego (92102) ***(G-24871)***
ARC of San Diego...619 448-2415
1855 John Towers Ave El Cajon (92020) ***(G-24872)***
ARC of Southern California, El Cajon *Also called 16 3 Inc* ***(G-3134)***
ARC of Ventura County Inc...805 650-8611
210 Canada St Ojai (93023) ***(G-22659)***
ARC of Ventura County Inc...805 644-0880
4277 Transport St Ste D Ventura (93003) ***(G-22660)***
ARC Partners Inc...703 757-0402
3 Vanderbilt Irvine (92618) ***(G-16324)***
ARC San Francisco...650 756-1304
6644 Mission St Daly City (94014) ***(G-23666)***
ARC Starlight Center...619 427-7524
1280 Nolan Ave Chula Vista (91911) ***(G-23667)***
Arca Los Angeles, Compton *Also called Appliance Recycl Ctrs of Amer* ***(G-6425)***
Arcadia Convalescent Hosp Inc (PA)...323 681-1504
1601 S Baldwin Ave Arcadia (91007) ***(G-21143)***
Arcadia Gardens MGT Corp...626 574-8571
720 W Camino Real Ave Arcadia (91007) ***(G-21066)***
Arcadia Health Care Center, Arcadia *Also called Arcadia Convalescent Hosp Inc* ***(G-21143)***
Arcadia Health Care Inc...415 472-2273
4340 Redwood Hwy Ste 123 San Rafael (94903) ***(G-22369)***
Arcadia Health Services Inc...209 572-7650
1400 Florida Ave Ste 206 Modesto (95350) ***(G-22370)***
Arcadia Healthcare, Redding *Also called Northern California Hlth Care* ***(G-22515)***
Arcadia Management Service Co...408 286-4440
150 Almaden Blvd Ste 1100 San Jose (95113) ***(G-11302)***
Arcadia Services Inc...248 352-7530
4340 Redwood Hwy Ste 123 San Rafael (94903) ***(G-14840)***
Arcadia Transit Inc...818 252-0630
7955 San Fernando Rd Sun Valley (91352) ***(G-3635)***
Arcana Corporation...805 882-1305
118 Nopalitos Way Santa Barbara (93103) ***(G-17001)***

Arch Bay Holdings LLC 949 679-2400
327 W Maple Ave Monrovia (91016) *(G-12049)*
Arch Health Partners Inc (HQ) 858 675-3100
15611 Pomerado Rd Ste 575 Poway (92064) *(G-27331)*
Arch Mortgage Insurance Co 800 909-4264
Pmi Plaza 3003 Oak Rd Walnut Creek (94597) *(G-10489)*
Archer Norris A Prof Law Corp (PA) 925 930-6600
2033 N Main St Ste 800 Walnut Creek (94596) *(G-23093)*
Archer Western Contractors LLC 858 715-7200
9915 Mira Mesa Blvd # 230 San Diego (92131) *(G-1734)*
Architects Orange 714 639-9860
144 N Orange St Orange (92866) *(G-26164)*
Architectural Coatings Inc 714 701-1360
1565 E Edinger Ave Santa Ana (92705) *(G-2428)*
Architectural GL & Alum Co Inc (PA) 925 583-2460
6400 Brisa St Livermore (94550) *(G-7358)*
Architecture Division, Los Angeles *Also called City of Los Angeles (G-26178)*
Architrends Inc 925 648-8800
3860 Blackhawk Rd Ste 160 Danville (94506) *(G-25661)*
Archives Management Corp (PA) 650 544-2200
2301 S El Camino Real San Mateo (94403) *(G-26924)*
Arclight Cinema Company 818 501-0753
15301 Ventura Blvd Bldg A Sherman Oaks (91403) *(G-18308)*
Arclight Cinema Company 323 464-1465
120 N Robertson Blvd Fl 3 Los Angeles (90048) *(G-18309)*
Arco Envmtl Remediation LLC 714 523-5674
5472 Orangethorpe Ave La Palma (90623) *(G-27332)*
Arco Olympic Training Center, Chula Vista *Also called United Sttes Olympic Committee (G-18565)*
Arconic Fastening Systems, Torrance *Also called Arconic Global Fas & Rings Inc (G-7917)*
Arconic Fastening Systems, Torrance *Also called Arconic Global Fas & Rings Inc (G-7921)*
Arconic Fstening Systems Rings, City of Industry *Also called Arconic Global Fas & Rings Inc (G-7915)*
Arconic Fstening Systems Rings, Torrance *Also called Arconic Global Fas & Rings Inc (G-7916)*
Arconic Fstening Systems Rings, Fullerton *Also called Arconic Global Fas & Rings Inc (G-7919)*
Arconic Fstening Systems Rings, Torrance *Also called Arconic Global Fas & Rings Inc (G-7920)*
Arconic Fstening Systems Rings, Tracy *Also called Arconic Global Fas & Rings Inc (G-7672)*
Arconic Global Fas & Rings Inc 626 968-3831
135 N Unruh Ave City of Industry (91744) *(G-7915)*
Arconic Global Fas & Rings Inc 310 784-0700
3000 Lomita Blvd Torrance (90505) *(G-7916)*
Arconic Global Fas & Rings Inc 310 530-2220
3014 Lomita Blvd Torrance (90505) *(G-7917)*
Arconic Global Fas & Rings Inc (HQ) 310 530-2220
3990a Heritage Oak Ct Simi Valley (93063) *(G-7918)*
Arconic Global Fas & Rings Inc 714 871-1550
800 S State College Blvd Fullerton (92831) *(G-7919)*
Arconic Global Fas & Rings Inc 310 530-2220
3000 Lomita Blvd Torrance (90505) *(G-7920)*
Arconic Global Fas & Rings Inc 209 839-3005
1925 N Macarthur Dr # 200 Tracy (95376) *(G-7672)*
Arconic Global Fas & Rings Inc 310 530-2220
3018 Lomita Blvd Torrance (90505) *(G-7921)*
Arconix USA, Camarillo *Also called Arconix/Usa Inc (G-7522)*
Arconix/Usa Inc 805 388-2525
880 Avenida Acaso Ste 100 Camarillo (93012) *(G-7522)*
Arcs Commercial Mortgage Co LP (HQ) 818 676-3274
26901 Agoura Rd Ste 200 Calabasas (91301) *(G-9819)*
Arcsight LLC 408 864-2600
5 Results Way Cupertino (95014) *(G-15029)*
Arcsoft Inc (PA) 510 440-9901
46601 Fremont Blvd Fremont (94538) *(G-15030)*
Arctouch LLC 415 944-2000
340 Brannan St Ste 302 San Francisco (94107) *(G-15031)*
Ardcore Senior Living 714 974-2226
525 S Anaheim Hills Rd Anaheim (92807) *(G-24551)*
Arden Health & Rehab Ctr, Sacramento *Also called Mariner Health Care Inc (G-20775)*
Arden Hills Country Club Inc 916 482-6111
1220 Arden Hills Ln Sacramento (95864) *(G-18877)*
Arden Realty Inc (HQ) 310 966-2600
11601 Wilshire Blvd Fl 4 Los Angeles (90025) *(G-10960)*
Arden-Mayfair Inc 310 638-2842
6191 Peachtree St Commerce (90040) *(G-4525)*
Ardenwood Farm, Fremont *Also called City of Fremont (G-25010)*
Ardmore Home Design Inc 626 939-1177
4700 Littlejohn St Baldwin Park (91706) *(G-6843)*
Ardwin Freight, Burbank *Also called Ardwin Inc (G-4111)*
Ardwin Inc 818 767-7777
2940 N Hollywood Way Burbank (91505) *(G-4111)*
Are- Maryland No 31 LLC 626 578-0777
385 E Colo Blvd Ste 299 Pasadena (91101) *(G-10961)*
Area Distributing Company, San Jose *Also called J T R Company Inc (G-4579)*
Area Housing Authority (PA) 805 480-9991
1400 W Hillcrest Dr Newbury Park (91320) *(G-11303)*
Arena Painting Contractors Inc 310 316-2446
525 E Alondra Blvd Gardena (90248) *(G-2429)*
Arena Solutions Inc (PA) 650 513-3500
989 E Hillsdale Blvd # 250 Foster City (94404) *(G-15032)*
Arent Fox LLP 213 629-7400
555 W 5th St Ste 4800 Los Angeles (90013) *(G-23094)*
Ares Management LP (PA) 310 201-4100
2000 Avenue Of The Stars Los Angeles (90067) *(G-10118)*
Ares Management LLC (HQ) 310 201-4100
2000 Avenue Of The Stars Los Angeles (90067) *(G-12283)*
Ares Management LLC 310 201-4100
1999 Ave Of Stars Fl 37 Los Angeles (90067) *(G-26925)*
Ares Prism, Burlingame *Also called Ares Project Management LLC (G-25662)*
Ares Project Management LLC (HQ) 650 401-7100
1440 Chapin Ave Ste 390 Burlingame (94010) *(G-25662)*
Arete Associates 818 885-2200
103 Johnson St Windsor (95492) *(G-26476)*
Arete Associates (PA) 818 885-2200
9301 Corbin Ave Unit 2000 Northridge (91324) *(G-26477)*
AREY JONES EDUCATIONAL SOLUTIO, San Diego *Also called Broadway Typewriter Co Inc (G-7103)*
Argent Hotel, The, San Francisco *Also called L-O Soma Hotel Inc (G-12895)*
Argent Management Co LLC 949 777-4070
2392 Morse Ave Irvine (92614) *(G-11304)*
Argon Enterprises Inc 310 349-8777
13658 Hawthorne Blvd # 306 Hawthorne (90250) *(G-11305)*
Argon St Inc A Boeing Company 312 544-2537
6696 Mesa Ridge Rd Ste A San Diego (92121) *(G-25663)*
Argonaut Constructors 707 542-4862
1236 Cent Ave Santa Rosa (95401) *(G-1735)*
Argonaut Hotel, San Francisco *Also called Maritime Hotel Associates LP (G-12943)*
Argonaut Kensington Associates 925 943-1121
1580 Geary Rd Ofc Walnut Creek (94597) *(G-23668)*
Argonne YMCA After School, San Francisco *Also called Young Mens Christian Assoc SF (G-25448)*
Argus Management Company LLC 562 491-9673
1045 S Atl Ave Ste 705 Long Beach (90813) *(G-27775)*
Argus Medical Management, Long Beach *Also called Argus Management Company LLC (G-27775)*
Aria Group Incorporated 949 475-2915
17395 Daimler St Irvine (92614) *(G-25664)*
Ariba Inc (HQ) 650 849-4000
3420 Hillview Ave Bldg 3 Palo Alto (94304) *(G-15584)*
Aricent Inc (HQ) 650 632-4310
303 Twin Dolphin Dr # 600 Redwood City (94065) *(G-15033)*
Aries Filterworks 323 262-1600
8722 Burton Way 40 West Hollywood (90048) *(G-7922)*
ARINC Incorporated 310 301-9040
4553 Glencoe Ave Ste 100 Marina Del Rey (90292) *(G-25665)*
Arinwine Arcft Maint Svcs LLC 310 338-0063
1720 E Holly Ave El Segundo (90245) *(G-4902)*
Ariosa Diagnostics Inc 408 229-7500
5945 Optical Ct San Jose (95138) *(G-26478)*
Aris Vision Ins of CA A Medcl 310 914-0150
11400 W Olympic Blvd # 200 Los Angeles (90064) *(G-19355)*
Arise LLC 559 485-0881
1033 Van Ness Ave Fresno (93721) *(G-19141)*
Arise Construction Inc 559 449-8989
5390 E Pine Ave Fresno (93727) *(G-2149)*
Arise Solar, Fresno *Also called Arise Construction Inc (G-2149)*
Arizona and 21st Corp 310 829-5377
2021 Arizona Ave Santa Monica (90404) *(G-21144)*
Arizona Pipe Line Company (PA) 760 244-8212
17372 Lilac St Hesperia (92345) *(G-1904)*
Arizona Pipe Line Company 951 270-3100
1745 Sampson Ave Corona (92879) *(G-1905)*
Arizona Tile LLC 714 978-6403
1620 S Lewis St Anaheim (92805) *(G-6972)*
Arkebauer Properties, Irvine *Also called Western National Properties (G-1351)*
Arlene Keller MD 415 923-3598
2100 Webster St Ste 423 San Francisco (94115) *(G-19356)*
Arlington Gardens Care Center, Riverside *Also called Honeyflower Holdings LLC (G-20673)*
Armand Hammer Museum 310 443-7000
10899 Wilshire Blvd Los Angeles (90024) *(G-25002)*
Armando Gonzalez Contracting 661 792-3785
32380 Elmo Hwy Mc Farland (93250) *(G-650)*
Armanino LLP 858 794-9401
11512 El Camino Real San Diego (92130) *(G-26289)*
Armanino LLP 310 478-4148
11766 Wilshire Blvd Fl 9 Los Angeles (90025) *(G-26290)*
Armanino LLP (PA) 925 790-2600
12657 Alcosta Blvd # 500 San Ramon (94583) *(G-26291)*
ARMC, Colton *Also called Arrowhead Regional Medical Ctr (G-21454)*
Armed Courier Service, Santa Clara *Also called Dan Connolly Inc (G-16621)*
Armed Forces Officials Assn 858 672-1438
14532 Penasquitos Dr San Diego (92129) *(G-25116)*
Armenian Amercn Thea Musical S, Los Angeles *Also called Armenian Amrcn Thea Msical Soc (G-18370)*
Armenian Amrcn Cuncil On Aging 818 241-8690
407 E Colorado St Glendale (91205) *(G-23669)*
Armenian Amrcn Thea Msical Soc 323 668-1030
3111 Los Feliz Blvd # 103 Los Angeles (90039) *(G-18370)*
ARMENIAN-AMERICAN COUNCIL ON A, Glendale *Also called Armenian Amrcn Cuncil On Aging (G-23669)*
Armstrong Construction Co, Emeryville *Also called Armstrong Installation Service (G-2430)*
Armstrong Garden Centers In C 760 414-1490
1492 Wilshire Rd Fallbrook (92028) *(G-9177)*
Armstrong Installation Service 408 777-1234
4575 San Pablo Ave Emeryville (94608) *(G-2430)*
Armstrong Logistics LLC 323 721-1500
5655 Union Pacific Ave Commerce (90022) *(G-5031)*
Arnaudo Bros Transport Inc (PA) 209 835-0406
16505 S Tracy Blvd Tracy (95304) *(G-345)*
Arnaudo Bros Trucking, Tracy *Also called Arnaudo Bros Transport Inc (G-345)*
Arnel and Affliate, Costa Mesa *Also called Arnel Interior Corp (G-26926)*
Arnel Development Company 760 599-6111
3146 Tiger Run Ct Ste 108 Carlsbad (92010) *(G-1293)*

A L P H A B E T I C

Arnel Interior Corp....714 481-5100
949 S Coast Dr Ste 600 Costa Mesa (92626) ***(G-26926)***
Arnies Supplies Service Ltd....323 263-1696
1501 N Ditman Ave Los Angeles (90063) ***(G-17962)***
Arnold & Porter PC....415 434-1600
3 Embarcadero Ctr Fl 7 San Francisco (94111) ***(G-23095)***
Arnold Palmer Golf MGT LLC....415 561-4670
300 Finley Rd San Francisco (94129) ***(G-26927)***
Arntz Builders Inc....415 382-1188
19 Pamaron Way Novato (94949) ***(G-1401)***
Aroma Spa & Sports LLC....213 387-2111
3680 Wilshire Blvd # 301 Los Angeles (90010) ***(G-19142)***
Aroma Wilshire Center, Los Angeles *Also called Hanil Development Inc* ***(G-12032)***
Aroma Wilshire Center, Los Angeles *Also called Aroma Spa & Sports LLC* ***(G-19142)***
Around The Clock Home Care, Bakersfield *Also called Vasindas Around The Clock Care* ***(G-24844)***
AROUND THE CLOCK LINKAGE, Bakersfield *Also called Kern Around Clock Foundation* ***(G-27091)***
Arpi Reit LLC....805 413-5300
30601 Agoura Rd Ste 200 Agoura Hills (91301) ***(G-12238)***
Arpom Inc....626 798-6777
1920 N Fair Oaks Ave Pasadena (91103) ***(G-20381)***
Arq LLC....888 384-0971
19517 Pauling Foothill Ranch (92610) ***(G-25666)***
Arrand Properties LLC....925 289-1032
5032 Westside Dr San Ramon (94583) ***(G-1129)***
Array Networks Inc (PA)....408 240-8700
1371 Mccarthy Blvd Milpitas (95035) ***(G-5459)***
Arraycon LLC (PA)....916 925-0201
1143 Blumenfeld Dr # 200 Sacramento (95815) ***(G-2150)***
Arreolas Complete Ldscp Svc, Sacramento *Also called Arreolas Complete Ldscp Svc* ***(G-809)***
Arreolas Complete Ldscp Svc....916 387-6777
8671 Morrison Creek Dr # 100 Sacramento (95828) ***(G-809)***
Arriaga Usa Inc....818 982-9559
11831 Vose St North Hollywood (91605) ***(G-3005)***
Arrival Communications Inc (HQ)....661 322-7375
1800 19th St Bakersfield (93301) ***(G-17002)***
Arrow Alliance Group, Santa Clara *Also called Arrow Electronics Inc* ***(G-7523)***
Arrow Bell, Woodland Hills *Also called Arrow Electronics Inc* ***(G-7524)***
Arrow Disposal Services Inc....626 336-2255
14332 Valley Blvd La Puente (91746) ***(G-6430)***
Arrow Electronics Inc....631 847-2918
3000 Bowers Ave Santa Clara (95051) ***(G-7523)***
Arrow Electronics Inc....818 932-1022
20935 Warner Center Ln A Woodland Hills (91367) ***(G-7524)***
Arrow Tools Fas & Saw Inc....818 780-1464
7635 Burnet Ave Van Nuys (91405) ***(G-7673)***
Arrow USA....951 845-6144
1105 Highland Ct Beaumont (92223) ***(G-7963)***
Arrowhead Central Credit Union (PA)....866 212-4333
550 E Hospitality Ln # 200 San Bernardino (92408) ***(G-9589)***
Arrowhead Convalescent Home....909 886-4731
4343 N Sierra Way San Bernardino (92407) ***(G-20382)***
Arrowhead Gen Insur Agcy Inc (HQ)....619 881-8600
701 B St Ste 2100 San Diego (92101) ***(G-10402)***
Arrowhead Home, San Bernardino *Also called Arrowhead Convalescent Home* ***(G-20382)***
Arrowhead Management Company (HQ)....800 669-1889
701 B St Ste 2100 San Diego (92101) ***(G-10621)***
Arrowhead Mountain Spring Wtr, El Monte *Also called Nestle Waters North Amer Inc* ***(G-8886)***
Arrowhead Mountain Spring Wtr, Los Angeles *Also called Nestle Waters North Amer Inc* ***(G-8887)***
Arrowhead Mountain Spring Wtr, Brea *Also called Nestle Waters North Amer Inc* ***(G-8889)***
Arrowhead Regional Medical Ctr....909 580-1000
400 N Pepper Ave Colton (92324) ***(G-21454)***
Arrowhead Water, Orange *Also called Nestle Waters North Amer Inc* ***(G-8885)***
Arroyo & Coates Inc....415 445-7800
425 California St # 2000 San Francisco (94104) ***(G-11306)***
Arroyo Developmental Services....626 307-2240
1839 Potrero Grande Dr Monterey Park (91755) ***(G-23670)***
Arroyo Grande Care Center, Arroyo Grande *Also called Compass Health Inc* ***(G-21191)***
Arroyo Grande Community Hosp, Arroyo Grande *Also called Dignity Health* ***(G-21535)***
Arroyo Insurance Services Inc (PA)....626 799-9532
440 E Huntington Dr # 100 Arcadia (91006) ***(G-10622)***
Arroyo Labor Contracting Svc, Gonzales *Also called Alicia Arroyo Inc* ***(G-648)***
Arroyo Seco Medical Group (PA)....626 795-7556
301 S Fair Oaks Ave # 300 Pasadena (91105) ***(G-19357)***
ARS, Whittier *Also called Assocted Reproduction Svcs Inc* ***(G-14112)***
ARS, San Diego *Also called Associated Research Svcs Inc* ***(G-27836)***
ARS, Los Angeles *Also called Asian Rehabilitation Svc Inc* ***(G-24308)***
ARS American Residential (HQ)....760 941-7000
2373 La Mirada Dr Vista (92081) ***(G-2151)***
ARS National Services Inc (PA)....800 456-5053
201 W Grand Ave Escondido (92025) ***(G-14017)***
ARS of San Diego Hvac, San Diego *Also called American Residential Svcs LLC* ***(G-2139)***
ARS of San Diego-8112, San Diego *Also called American Residential Svcs LLC* ***(G-2131)***
ARS West LLC....760 480-6631
780 W El Norte Pkwy Escondido (92026) ***(G-17874)***
Art & Logic Inc....818 500-1933
2 N Lake Ave Ste 1050 Pasadena (91101) ***(G-15904)***
Art Piccadilly Shaw LLC....559 375-7760
5115 E Mckinley Ave Fresno (93727) ***(G-12397)***
Art Piccadilly Shaw LLC....559 224-4200
4961 N Cedar Ave Fresno (93726) ***(G-12398)***
Arta Western Medical Group....949 260-6575
1665 Scenic Ave Ste 100 Costa Mesa (92626) ***(G-10234)***
Artesia Christian Home Inc....562 865-5218
11614 183rd St Artesia (90701) ***(G-21145)***
Artesia Healthcare Inc....818 843-1771
925 W Alameda Ave Burbank (91506) ***(G-20383)***
Arthrtis Fundation PCF Reg Inc....323 954-5760
800 W 6th St Ste 1250 Los Angeles (90017) ***(G-25199)***
Arthur J Gallagher & Co....949 349-9800
18201 Von Karman Ave # 200 Irvine (92612) ***(G-10623)***
Arthur J Gallagher & Co....818 539-2300
505 N Brand Blvd Ste 600 Glendale (91203) ***(G-10624)***
Arthur J Gallagher & Co....415 546-9300
1 Market Spear Tower San Francisco (94105) ***(G-10625)***
Arthur J Gallagher & Co....559 436-0833
7910 N Ingram Ave Ste 201 Fresno (93711) ***(G-10626)***
Arthur J Gallagher & Co....925 299-1112
3697 Mt Diablo Blvd # 300 Lafayette (94549) ***(G-10627)***
Arthur Kunde & Sons Inc....707 833-5501
9825 Sonoma Hwy Kenwood (95452) ***(G-693)***
Arthur Loussararian MD, Mission Viejo *Also called Mission Internal Med Group Inc* ***(G-19752)***
Artic Mechanical Inc (PA)....909 980-2539
10440 Trademark St Rancho Cucamonga (91730) ***(G-2152)***
Artichoke Joe's Casino, San Bruno *Also called Artichoke Joes Inc* ***(G-19143)***
Artichoke Joes Inc....650 589-8812
659 Huntington Ave San Bruno (94066) ***(G-19143)***
Artificial Solutions Inc....650 943-2325
800 W El Camino Real Mountain View (94040) ***(G-15034)***
Artimisa & Co....530 283-3700
220 Forest Knoll Ln Quincy (95971) ***(G-25667)***
Artisan Bakers....707 939-1765
21684 8th St E Ste 400 Sonoma (95476) ***(G-8797)***
Artisan Pictures Inc....310 449-9200
2700 Colorado Ave Fl 2 Santa Monica (90404) ***(G-8105)***
Artisan Sotheby's Intl. Realty, Santa Rosa *Also called Realogy Holdings Corp* ***(G-11798)***
Artistic Entrmt Svcs LLC....626 334-9388
120 N Aspan Ave Azusa (91702) ***(G-18456)***
Artistic Maintenance Inc....949 733-8690
16092 Construction Cir E Irvine (92606) ***(G-810)***
Artists of River Town....530 534-7690
56 Highlands Blvd Oroville (95966) ***(G-25117)***
Artists Studio Gallery....424 206-9902
5504 Crestridge Rd Rancho Palos Verdes (90275) ***(G-19144)***
Artizen Incorporated....650 261-9400
101 Golf Course Dr # 300 Rohnert Park (94928) ***(G-15035)***
Artlogic, Pasadena *Also called Art & Logic Inc* ***(G-15904)***
Artwear Inc....310 217-1393
13621 S Main St Los Angeles (90061) ***(G-8333)***
Arup North America Limited....310 578-4182
12777 W Jefferson Blvd Los Angeles (90066) ***(G-25668)***
Arup North America Limited (HQ)....415 957-9445
560 Mission St Fl 7 San Francisco (94105) ***(G-25669)***
Arvin-Edison Water Storage Dst (PA)....661 854-5573
20401 E Bear Mtn Blvd Arvin (93203) ***(G-6642)***
Arya Design Group, Los Angeles *Also called Arya Group Inc* ***(G-1130)***
Arya Group Inc....310 446-7000
10490 Santa Monica Blvd Los Angeles (90025) ***(G-1130)***
Arya Ice Cream Distrg Co Inc....323 234-2994
914 E 31st St Los Angeles (90011) ***(G-8577)***
Aryaka Networks Inc....408 273-8420
691 S Milpitas Blvd # 206 Milpitas (95035) ***(G-27730)***
Aryzta LLC....909 472-3500
1220 S Baker Ave Ontario (91761) ***(G-8798)***
Aryzta LLC....214 630-8292
14490 Catalina St San Leandro (94577) ***(G-8799)***
Aryzta LLC....704 357-0369
14490 Catalina St San Leandro (94577) ***(G-8800)***
Aryzta LLC....209 462-3601
920 Shaw Rd Stockton (95215) ***(G-8801)***
Asai, Glendale *Also called Automated Systems America Inc* ***(G-17963)***
Asana Integrated Medical Group....888 212-7545
26135 Mureau Rd Ste 101 Calabasas (91302) ***(G-23671)***
ASAP Professional Services, San Ramon *Also called A S A P Professional Services* ***(G-14594)***
ASAP Staffing Inc....562 499-2120
11 Golden Shore Ste 360 Long Beach (90802) ***(G-14609)***
Asbestos Instant Response Inc....323 733-0508
3517 W Washington Blvd Los Angeles (90018) ***(G-3495)***
Asbury Environmental Services (PA)....310 886-3400
1300 S Santa Fe Ave Compton (90221) ***(G-3978)***
Asbury Pk Nrsing Rhblttion Ctr....916 649-2000
2257 Fair Oaks Blvd Sacramento (95825) ***(G-21146)***
Asbury Transportation Co....661 327-2271
2144 Parker Ln Bakersfield (93308) ***(G-4112)***
Ascend, Oakland *Also called Education For Change* ***(G-27011)***
Ascend Distribution, City of Industry *Also called Eforcity Corp - Nfm* ***(G-7559)***
Ascend Learning LLC....925 300-3203
2185 N California Blvd Walnut Creek (94596) ***(G-27835)***
Ascendantfx Capital USA Inc....201 633-4667
3478 Buskirk Ave Ste 1000 Pleasant Hill (94523) ***(G-9707)***
Ascendify Corporation....415 528-5503
530 Bush St Ste 104 San Francisco (94108) ***(G-15036)***
Ascension Bnfits Insur Sltions, Walnut Creek *Also called Portal Insurance Agency Inc* ***(G-10830)***
Ascension Insurance Inc....661 321-3290
7673 N Ingram Ave Ste 103 Fresno (93711) ***(G-10628)***

Ascension Insurance Inc...800 537-1777
  12121 Wilshire Blvd # 1001 Los Angeles (90025) *(G-10629)*
Ascent Services Group Inc...925 627-4900
  3000 Oak Rd Ste 200 Walnut Creek (94597) *(G-16325)*
Asco, Fontana Also called Automotive Sup Co Southern Cal *(G-6711)*
Ascon Recycle Company..661 533-0154
  6500 E Avenue T Littlerock (93543) *(G-6431)*
Ascon Recycling Co...760 948-1538
  17671 Bear Valley Rd Hesperia (92345) *(G-6432)*
Ase (us) Inc (HQ)..408 636-9500
  1255 E Arques Ave Sunnyvale (94085) *(G-7525)*
Asec Group, Los Angeles Also called A S E C International Inc *(G-16087)*
Ash Holdings LLC..909 793-2609
  1620 W Fern Ave Redlands (92373) *(G-20384)*
Ashbury Market Inc...650 952-8889
  179 Starlite St South San Francisco (94080) *(G-8802)*
Ashford Trs Nickel LLC..619 260-0111
  1433 Camino Del Rio S San Diego (92108) *(G-26928)*
Ashland Distribution, Commerce Also called Ashland Inc *(G-8979)*
Ashland Inc..310 223-3505
  20915 S Wilmington Ave Carson (90810) *(G-8978)*
Ashland Inc..323 767-1300
  6608 E 26th St Commerce (90040) *(G-8979)*
Ashland Performance Materials, Carson Also called Ashland Inc *(G-8978)*
Ashley Lane Cherry Orchards LP..................................209 546-0426
  500 N Jack Tone Rd Stockton (95215) *(G-228)*
Ashley Ltc Inc..707 528-2100
  446 Arrowood Dr Santa Rosa (95407) *(G-20385)*
Ashley Management Group...949 754-3120
  300 Spectrum Center Dr # 400 Irvine (92618) *(G-27333)*
Ashunya Inc..714 385-1900
  642 N Eckhoff St Orange (92868) *(G-15037)*
Ashwood Construction Inc...559 253-7240
  5755 E Kings Canyon Rd # 110 Fresno (93727) *(G-1294)*
Asi Computer Technologies Inc (PA)............................510 226-8000
  48289 Fremont Blvd Fremont (94538) *(G-7094)*
ASI Hastings Inc..619 590-9300
  4870 Vewridge Ave Ste 200 San Diego (92123) *(G-2153)*
Asi Heating, Air and Solar, San Diego Also called ASI Hastings Inc *(G-2153)*
Asia Foundation (PA)...415 982-4640
  465 California St Fl 9 San Francisco (94104) *(G-12152)*
Asia Pacific Capital..213 628-8800
  345 Suth Fgroa St Ste 100 Los Angeles (90071) *(G-12133)*
Asia Pacific Management, Palo Alto Also called H & Q Asia Pacific Ltd *(G-10150)*
Asiainfo-Linkage Inc..408 970-9788
  5201 Great America Pkwy # 356 Santa Clara (95054) *(G-5460)*
Asian Amercn Recovery Svcs Inc.................................408 271-3900
  1340 Tully Rd Ste 304 San Jose (95122) *(G-22114)*
Asian Art Meusuem of SF, San Francisco Also called Asian Art Museum Found San Fra *(G-25003)*
Asian Art Museum, San Francisco Also called City & County of San Francisco *(G-25009)*
Asian Art Museum Found San Fra................................415 581-3701
  200 Larkin St San Francisco (94102) *(G-25003)*
Asian Cmnty Mental Hlth Svcs, Oakland Also called Asian Community Mental Hlth Bd *(G-22661)*
Asian Community Center of Sac...................................916 393-9020
  7801 Rush River Dr Sacramento (95831) *(G-24552)*
Asian Community Mental Hlth Bd.................................510 625-1650
  310 8th St Ste 201 Oakland (94607) *(G-22661)*
Asian Health Services..510 986-0601
  270 13th St Oakland (94612) *(G-19358)*
Asian Health Services (PA)..510 986-6800
  818 Webster St Oakland (94607) *(G-19359)*
Asian Legal Workforce...650 703-2190
  1046 Rudder Ln Foster City (94404) *(G-651)*
Asian PCF Hlth Care Ventr Inc (PA).............................323 644-3880
  4216 Fountain Ave Los Angeles (90029) *(G-24873)*
Asian Rehabilitation Svc Inc (PA)................................213 743-9242
  4322 Wilshire Blvd # 310 Los Angeles (90010) *(G-24307)*
Asian Rehabilitation Svc Inc..213 680-3790
  312 N Spring St Ste B30 Los Angeles (90012) *(G-24308)*
Asiana Airlines Inc...213 365-2000
  3530 Wilshire Blvd # 1700 Los Angeles (90010) *(G-4795)*
Asics America Corporation (HQ)..................................949 453-8888
  80 Technology Dr Irvine (92618) *(G-8420)*
Asics Tiger, Irvine Also called Asics America Corporation *(G-8420)*
Asig, Ontario Also called Aircraft Service Intl Inc *(G-4894)*
Asilomar Conference Center, Pacific Grove Also called Pacific Grove Aslmar Oper Corp *(G-13056)*
Asistencia Villa, Redlands Also called Redlands Cmnty Hosp Foundation *(G-21357)*
Asistencia Villa Rehab & Care, Redlands Also called Silverscreen Healthcare Inc *(G-21378)*
Ask.com, Oakland Also called IAC Search & Media Inc *(G-16244)*
Askew Industrial Corporation (PA)...............................323 727-7772
  13071 Arctic Cir Santa Fe Springs (90670) *(G-7923)*
Asmg, San Diego Also called Anesthesia Svc Med Group Inc *(G-19349)*
Asociacon De Bomberos Del Esta.................................949 355-4249
  1100 Calle Del Cerro 52d San Clemente (92672) *(G-25075)*
Aspect Software Inc..408 595-5002
  101 Academy Ste 130 Irvine (92617) *(G-15585)*
Aspects Furniture Mfg Inc..909 606-5806
  15830 El Prado Rd Ste A Chino (91708) *(G-6804)*
Aspen Apts I..415 673-5879
  165 Eddy St San Francisco (94102) *(G-11087)*
Aspen Grove Apartments LLC......................................408 848-6400
  450 E 8th St Gilroy (95020) *(G-11088)*
Aspen Ranch LLC...435 836-2080
  20400 Stevens Creek Blvd Cupertino (95014) *(G-24553)*

Aspiranet...415 759-3690
  3925 Noriega St San Francisco (94122) *(G-24554)*
Aspiranet...209 669-2582
  151 E Canal Dr Turlock (95380) *(G-24555)*
Aspiranet...209 667-0327
  2513 Youngstown Rd Turlock (95380) *(G-23672)*
Aspiriant LLC...415 371-7800
  50 California St Ste 2600 San Francisco (94111) *(G-17003)*
Asplundh Construction Co., Cypress Also called Asplundh Tree Expert Co *(G-987)*
Asplundh Tree Expert Co...805 964-9216
  6100 Francis Botello Rd C Goleta (93117) *(G-984)*
Asplundh Tree Expert Co...951 352-3144
  10730 Campbell Ave Riverside (92505) *(G-985)*
Asplundh Tree Expert Co...805 641-0528
  2055 N Ventura Ave Ventura (93001) *(G-986)*
Asplundh Tree Expert Co...714 893-2405
  6101 Gateway Dr Cypress (90630) *(G-987)*
Aspm-Sandiego, San Diego Also called Allegis Residential Svcs Inc *(G-26917)*
Asr, San Juan Capistrano Also called Action Sports Retailer *(G-16969)*
Asr Constructors Inc...951 779-6580
  33891 Mission Trl Wildomar (92595) *(G-1493)*
Assembly Member Ammiano, San Francisco Also called San Francisco City & County *(G-21846)*
Assertive Security Services &.....................................818 888-2405
  20501 Ventura Blvd # 150 Woodland Hills (91364) *(G-16867)*
Assessor-Recorder's Office, Fresno Also called County of Fresno *(G-25132)*
Asset Athene Management L P (HQ)............................310 698-4444
  2121 Rosecrans Ave # 5300 El Segundo (90245) *(G-26929)*
Asset Marketing Investment Svc, Pleasant Hill Also called Assetmark Capital Corp *(G-9959)*
Asset Marketing Systems Insu....................................888 303-8755
  15050 Ave Of Science # 100 San Diego (92128) *(G-27334)*
Assetmark Inc (HQ)...925 521-1040
  1655 Grant St Concord (94520) *(G-10119)*
Assetmark Capital Corp...925 521-1040
  2300 Contra Costa Blvd # 600 Pleasant Hill (94523) *(G-9959)*
Assi Security (PA)...949 955-0244
  1370 Reynolds Ave Ste 201 Irvine (92614) *(G-2523)*
ASSICIATED STUDENTS, San Luis Obispo Also called Associated Students Inc *(G-23673)*
Assign Corporation..818 247-7100
  801 N Brand Blvd Ste 905 Glendale (91203) *(G-16326)*
Assist 65 Plus...323 557-4426
  111 W 7th St Ste 211 Los Angeles (90014) *(G-17004)*
Assistance In Home Care, Garden Grove Also called Our Watch *(G-22526)*
Assistance Leag San Bernardino.................................909 885-2045
  580 W 6th St San Bernardino (92410) *(G-12153)*
Assistance League Covina Vly....................................626 966-7550
  636 E San Bernardino Rd Covina (91723) *(G-24874)*
Assistance League Foothill Com.................................909 987-2813
  8555 Archibald Ave 8593 Rancho Cucamonga (91730) *(G-24875)*
Assistance League of Redlands..................................909 792-2675
  506 W Colton Ave Redlands (92374) *(G-24876)*
ASSISTANCE LEAGUE THRIFT SHOP, Redlands Also called Assistance League of Redlands *(G-24876)*
Assisted Home Care, Northridge Also called Assisted Home Recovery Inc *(G-14610)*
Assisted Home Recovery Inc.......................................626 915-5595
  1900 W Garvey Ave S # 210 West Covina (91790) *(G-28115)*
Assisted Home Recovery Inc (PA)...............................818 894-8117
  8550 Balboa Blvd Lbby Northridge (91325) *(G-14610)*
Assoc For Retarded Citizens.......................................909 884-6484
  796 E 6th St San Bernardino (92410) *(G-24309)*
Associate Mechanical Contrs......................................760 294-3517
  622 S Vinewood St Escondido (92029) *(G-2154)*
Associated Bond, Calabasas Also called AIA Holdings Inc *(G-10488)*
Associated Entrmt Releasing (PA)..............................323 934-7044
  4401 Wilshire Blvd Los Angeles (90010) *(G-18045)*
Associated Feed & Supply Co (PA)............................209 667-2708
  5213 W Main St Turlock (95380) *(G-9125)*
Associated Foreign Exch Inc (HQ)..............................888 307-2339
  21045 Califa St Woodland Hills (91367) *(G-9708)*
Associated Group, Commerce Also called Associated Landscape *(G-17005)*
Associated Indemnity Corp..415 899-2000
  1465 N Mcdowell Blvd # 100 Petaluma (94954) *(G-10200)*
Associated Internal Medicine (PA).............................510 465-6700
  350 30th St Ste 320 Oakland (94609) *(G-19360)*
Associated Intl Insur Co, Woodland Hills Also called Markel Corp *(G-10769)*
Associated Koi Clubs America....................................949 650-5225
  P.O. Box 10879 Costa Mesa (92627) *(G-18878)*
Associated Laboratories, Orange Also called De Par Inc *(G-26842)*
Associated Landscape..714 558-6100
  2420 S Eastern Ave Commerce (90040) *(G-17005)*
Associated Pathology Med Group...............................831 462-7625
  1555 Soquel Dr Santa Cruz (95065) *(G-19361)*
Associated Pension Cons Inc (PA).............................530 343-4233
  2035 Forest Ave Chico (95928) *(G-10630)*
Associated Press..213 626-1200
  221 S Figueroa St Ste 300 Los Angeles (90012) *(G-16944)*
Associated Realtors..949 813-1888
  27411 Viana Mission Viejo (92692) *(G-11307)*
Associated Research Svcs Inc....................................858 551-0008
  9333 Genesee Ave Ste 260 San Diego (92121) *(G-27836)*
Associated Roofing Contractors, Carson Also called Defcon Inc *(G-3163)*
Associated Students Californi.....................................657 278-2468
  800 N State College Blvd Fullerton (92831) *(G-25200)*
Associated Students California..................................562 985-4994
  1212 N Bellflower Blvd # 220 Long Beach (90815) *(G-25201)*
Associated Students Cdc..408 924-6988
  460 S 8th St San Jose (95112) *(G-24415)*

Associated Students Inc — ALPHABETIC SECTION

Associated Students Inc 760 750-4990
  333 S Twin Oaks Valley Rd San Marcos (92096) *(G-13487)*
Associated Students Inc (PA) 805 756-1281
  University Un Bldg 65 San Luis Obispo (93407) *(G-23673)*
Associated Students Inc 805 756-1281
  1 Grand Ave San Luis Obispo (93407) *(G-28116)*
Associated Students San Diego (PA) 619 594-0234
  5500 Campanile Dr San Diego (92182) *(G-25492)*
Associated Students Stanford (PA) 650 723-4331
  201 Tresidder Un Stanford (94305) *(G-25202)*
Associated Students Uc Irvine, Irvine Also called Student Government Associat *(G-4975)*
Associated Students UCLA (PA) 310 825-4321
  308 Westwood Plz Los Angeles (90024) *(G-24877)*
Associated Students UCLA 310 794-0242
  924 Westwood Blvd Los Angeles (90024) *(G-24878)*
Associated Students UCLA 310 825-9451
  650 Chrls Yng S Rm 23 120 Los Angeles (90095) *(G-19362)*
Associated Students Univ PCF 209 946-2233
  3601 Pacific Ave Stockton (95211) *(G-25203)*
Associated Students, Inc., San Luis Obispo Also called Associated Students Inc *(G-28116)*
Associated Television Intl, Los Angeles Also called Associated Entrmt Releasing *(G-18045)*
Association For Retarded (PA) 562 597-7716
  4519 E Stearns St Long Beach (90815) *(G-24310)*
Association For Retarded Citzn (PA) 562 803-1556
  12049 Woodruff Ave Downey (90241) *(G-24311)*
Associations of United Nurses (PA) 909 599-8622
  955 Overland Ct Ste 150 San Dimas (91773) *(G-25166)*
Assocted Fgn Exch Holdings Inc (PA) 818 386-2702
  21045 Califa St Woodland Hills (91367) *(G-9709)*
Assocted Reproduction Svcs Inc 562 696-1181
  13925 Whittier Blvd Whittier (90605) *(G-14112)*
Assocted Third Pty Admnstrtors 619 358-8140
  2831 Camino Del Rio S San Diego (92108) *(G-10540)*
Assocted Third Pty Admnstrtors 415 777-3707
  642 Harrison St San Francisco (94107) *(G-10541)*
Assurant Inc 714 571-3900
  2677 N Main St Ste 600 Santa Ana (92705) *(G-10631)*
Assure Consulting Inc 650 966-1967
  257 Castro St Ste 205 Mountain View (94041) *(G-27837)*
Assure Detective Agency, Corona Also called Chief Protective Services Inc *(G-16596)*
Assured Regulatory Compliance, Irvine Also called Mavent Inc *(G-15993)*
Assyrian Cultural Center, Ceres Also called Bet-Nahrain Inc *(G-17030)*
Astoria Convalescent Hospital 818 367-5881
  14040 Astoria St Sylmar (91342) *(G-20386)*
Astoria Nursing & Rehab Center, Sylmar Also called Astoria Convalescent Hospital *(G-20386)*
Astoria Nursing and Rehab Ctr, Sylmar Also called G and E Healthcare Svcs LLC *(G-20588)*
Astoria Software 415 956-3917
  160 Spear St Ste 1100 San Francisco (94105) *(G-15038)*
Astro Aerospace 805 684-6641
  6384 Via Real Carpinteria (93013) *(G-25670)*
Astro Realty Inc 562 924-3381
  11305 183rd St Cerritos (90703) *(G-11308)*
Asus Computer International 510 739-3777
  800 Corp Way Fremont (94539) *(G-7095)*
At & T Wireless Service, Tustin Also called AB Cellular Holding LLC *(G-5451)*
At Home Caregivers, Novato Also called Bear Flag Marketing Corp *(G-22377)*
At Home Nursing 707 546-8773
  2227 Capricorn Way # 105 Santa Rosa (95407) *(G-22371)*
At Road Inc (HQ) 510 668-1638
  888 Tasman Dr Milpitas (95035) *(G-15905)*
At Your Home Familycare 858 625-0406
  6540 Lusk Blvd Ste C266 San Diego (92121) *(G-13734)*
At Your Svc Htg & Coolg LLC 602 550-6946
  333 H St Ste 5000 Chula Vista (91910) *(G-1494)*
AT&T, Artesia Also called New Cingular Wireless Svcs Inc *(G-5667)*
AT&T Corp 714 965-4685
  10035 Adams Ave Huntington Beach (92646) *(G-5461)*
AT&T Corp 925 603-9476
  2390 Monument Blvd Pleasant Hill (94523) *(G-5462)*
AT&T Corp 415 970-8520
  2410 Mission St San Francisco (94110) *(G-5463)*
AT&T Corp 619 448-1798
  50 Town Center Pkwy Santee (92071) *(G-5464)*
AT&T Corp 415 442-2600
  795 Folsom St San Francisco (94107) *(G-5465)*
AT&T Corp 714 258-8290
  2219 Park Ave Ste 8a Tustin (92782) *(G-5466)*
AT&T Corp 909 646-9644
  12379 S Mainstreet Rancho Cucamonga (91739) *(G-5467)*
AT&T Corp 925 673-2120
  5434 Ygnacio Valley Rd Concord (94521) *(G-5468)*
AT&T Corp 909 930-6508
  2508 S Grove Ave Ontario (91761) *(G-5255)*
AT&T Corp 951 253-3304
  29273 Central Ave Lake Elsinore (92532) *(G-5469)*
AT&T Corp 626 382-0241
  810 E Valley Blvd Alhambra (91801) *(G-5470)*
AT&T Corp 310 225-3028
  20810 Avalon Blvd Carson (90746) *(G-5471)*
AT&T Corp 323 589-7045
  6833 Pacific Blvd Huntington Park (90255) *(G-5256)*
AT&T Corp 949 559-1457
  6328 Irvine Blvd Irvine (92620) *(G-5257)*
AT&T Corp 310 473-3649
  2333 S Sepulveda Blvd Los Angeles (90064) *(G-5258)*
AT&T Corp 626 396-0100
  83 E Colorado Blvd Pasadena (91105) *(G-5472)*
AT&T Corp 805 562-0121
  7060 Market Place Dr Goleta (93117) *(G-5259)*
AT&T Corp 925 823-6949
  330 R San Ramon (94583) *(G-27838)*
AT&T Corp 310 547-0400
  980 N Western Ave Ste H San Pedro (90732) *(G-5473)*
AT&T Corp 661 297-1720
  26453 Bouquet Canyon Rd Santa Clarita (91350) *(G-5474)*
AT&T Corp 714 284-3818
  217 N Lemon St Rm 205 Anaheim (92805) *(G-5260)*
AT&T Corp 661 799-0800
  24935 Pico Canyon Rd Stevenson Ranch (91381) *(G-5475)*
AT&T Corp 951 275-8801
  3977 Chicago Ave Riverside (92507) *(G-5476)*
AT&T Corp 323 568-2006
  4332 Tweedy Blvd South Gate (90280) *(G-5477)*
AT&T Corp 949 364-4052
  27762 Antonio Pkwy Ste L3 Ladera Ranch (92694) *(G-5478)*
AT&T Corp 310 303-3888
  1100 Pacific Coast Hwy # 5 Hermosa Beach (90254) *(G-5261)*
AT&T Corp 626 576-3616
  501 S Marengo Ave Alhambra (91803) *(G-5479)*
AT&T Corp 925 356-6204
  2745 Cloverdale Ave Concord (94518) *(G-5480)*
AT&T Corp 530 891-2025
  3750 Morrow Ln Chico (95928) *(G-5262)*
AT&T Corp 530 274-8255
  151 W Mcknight Way Ste F Grass Valley (95949) *(G-5481)*
AT&T Corp 559 353-3999
  8817 N Cedar Ave Fresno (93720) *(G-5263)*
AT&T Corp 805 445-6562
  1955 E Daily Dr Camarillo (93010) *(G-5482)*
AT&T Corp 530 822-2700
  1054 Harter Pkwy Ste 9 Yuba City (95993) *(G-5483)*
AT&T Corp 951 654-2081
  1821 S San Jacinto Ave G San Jacinto (92583) *(G-5484)*
AT&T Corp 209 954-1033
  7860 West Ln Stockton (95210) *(G-5485)*
AT&T Corp 760 752-3273
  133 S Las Posas Rd # 141 San Marcos (92078) *(G-5486)*
AT&T Corp 213 787-0055
  624 S Grand Ave Ste 2940 Los Angeles (90017) *(G-5487)*
AT&T Corp 619 660-0637
  2883 Jamacha Rd Ste A-D El Cajon (92019) *(G-5264)*
AT&T Corp 415 721-1470
  835 4th St San Rafael (94901) *(G-5265)*
AT&T Corp 707 591-9500
  1620 Mendocino Ave Santa Rosa (95401) *(G-5266)*
AT&T Corp 831 465-6771
  1855 41st Ave Capitola (95010) *(G-5267)*
AT&T Corp 805 583-9483
  1263 Simi Town Center Way Simi Valley (93065) *(G-5268)*
AT&T Corp 209 956-8324
  1610 W Yosemite Ave Ste 2 Manteca (95337) *(G-5488)*
AT&T Corp 949 581-1600
  24321 Avend D La Carlt Carlota Laguna Hills (92653) *(G-5269)*
AT&T Corp 858 693-0815
  8225 Mira Mesa Blvd San Diego (92126) *(G-5489)*
AT&T Corp 530 661-7724
  1810 E Main St Woodland (95776) *(G-5270)*
AT&T Corp 818 374-6458
  6920 Van Nuys Blvd Rm 100 Van Nuys (91405) *(G-5490)*
AT&T Corp 831 457-8255
  550 River St Ste D Santa Cruz (95060) *(G-5271)*
AT&T Corp 650 960-2313
  1188 W Evelyn Ave Sunnyvale (94086) *(G-28117)*
AT&T Corp 650 780-1005
  1121 Jefferson Ave Rm 222 Redwood City (94063) *(G-5491)*
AT&T Corp 818 373-6896
  14709 Vanoan St Van Nuys (91405) *(G-5492)*
AT&T Corp 714 284-2878
  Rm 620 Anaheim (92805) *(G-17006)*
AT&T Corp 323 874-7000
  7100 Santa Monica Blvd # 125 West Hollywood (90046) *(G-5272)*
AT&T Corp 925 327-7100
  134 Sunset Dr San Ramon (94583) *(G-5273)*
AT&T Corp 408 729-8400
  1705 Story Rd San Jose (95122) *(G-28118)*
AT&T Corp 408 871-3870
  1546 Saratoga Ave San Jose (95129) *(G-5493)*
AT&T Corp 949 622-8240
  17675 Harvard Ave Ste B Irvine (92614) *(G-5494)*
AT&T Corp 818 506-9118
  6000 Lankershim Blvd North Hollywood (91606) *(G-5495)*
AT&T Corp 415 394-3000
  2600 Camino Ramon San Ramon (94583) *(G-5496)*
AT&T Corp 760 240-3592
  18805 Bear Valley Rd Apple Valley (92308) *(G-5497)*
AT&T Corp 805 461-6400
  6917 El Camino Real Atascadero (93422) *(G-5498)*
AT&T Corp 714 940-9976
  2400 E Katella Ave Anaheim (92806) *(G-5499)*
AT&T Corp 925 275-8048
  2600 Camino Ramon San Ramon (94583) *(G-5500)*
AT&T Corp 925 560-5011
  5130 Hacienda Dr Fl 1 Dublin (94568) *(G-17007)*
AT&T Corp 310 659-7600
  998 S Robertson Blvd # 103 Los Angeles (90035) *(G-5274)*
AT&T Corp 925 823-5388
  2600 Camino Ramon 2w856 San Ramon (94583) *(G-5501)*

AT&T Corp 818 997-5998
16201 Raymer St Van Nuys (91406) *(G-27839)*
AT&T Corp 415 442-5900
50 Fremont St San Francisco (94105) *(G-27731)*
AT&T Corp 916 830-5000
4130 S Market Ct Sacramento (95834) *(G-5502)*
AT&T Corp 559 294-5431
3375 Peach Ave Clovis (93612) *(G-5503)*
AT&T Corp 909 381-7378
I 15 & Razor Yermo (92398) *(G-5504)*
AT&T Corp 909 381-7729
455 W 2nd St San Bernardino (92401) *(G-5505)*
AT&T Corp 408 980-2004
3025 Raymond St Santa Clara (95054) *(G-5506)*
AT&T Corp 530 251-0666
2980 Main St Susanville (96130) *(G-5275)*
AT&T Corp 510 965-9714
2105 Macdonald Ave Richmond (94801) *(G-5507)*
AT&T Corp 831 642-0100
400 Del Monte Ctr Monterey (93940) *(G-5276)*
AT&T Corp 562 923-3032
8420 Firestone Blvd Downey (90241) *(G-5508)*
AT&T Corp 800 222-0300
3175 Spring St Redwood City (94063) *(G-5509)*
AT&T Corp 415 276-0039
625 Ellis St Ste 205 Mountain View (94043) *(G-5510)*
AT&T Corp 213 787-0055
700 S Flower St Ste 810 Los Angeles (90017) *(G-5511)*
AT&T Corp 925 776-1200
2701 Verne Roberts Cir Antioch (94509) *(G-5512)*
AT&T Corp 818 920-1216
14500 Roscoe Blvd Panorama City (91402) *(G-5513)*
AT&T Corp 925 823-9700
2600 Camino Ramon 4cn100 San Ramon (94583) *(G-5514)*
AT&T Interactive, Glendale *Also called Ypcom LLC (G-17637)*
AT&T Services 925 901-9318
2 Circle E Ranch Pl San Ramon (94583) *(G-5515)*
AT&T Services 661 327-6030
50101 Office Park Dr Bakersfield (93304) *(G-5516)*
AT&T Services 916 972-2248
3464 El Camino Ave Sacramento (95821) *(G-5517)*
AT&T Services 707 428-2512
1122 Western St Fairfield (94533) *(G-5518)*
AT&T Services 925 831-4443
39 Beta Ct Rm 235 San Ramon (94583) *(G-5519)*
AT&T Services 415 774-1957
2345 Pine St San Francisco (94115) *(G-5520)*
AT&T Services 760 722-7261
2727 Oceanside Blvd Oceanside (92054) *(G-5521)*
AT&T Services 916 972-2423
3707 Kings Way Sacramento (95821) *(G-5522)*
AT&T Services 925 943-4383
1755 Locust St Fl 2 Walnut Creek (94596) *(G-5523)*
AT&T Services 415 823-0993
2600 Camino Ramon Rm 1-E San Ramon (94583) *(G-5524)*
AT&T Services Inc 619 515-5100
101 Broadway San Diego (92101) *(G-5525)*
AT&T Services Inc 661 398-2000
4300 Ming Ave Bakersfield (93309) *(G-5526)*
AT&T Services Inc 831 394-2690
161 Calle Del Oaks Monterey (93940) *(G-5527)*
AT&T Services Inc 415 545-9051
610 Brannan St San Francisco (94107) *(G-5528)*
AT&T Services Inc 209 578-7161
1548 N Carpenter Rd Modesto (95351) *(G-5529)*
AT&T Services Inc 209 223-0012
303 Church St Jackson (95642) *(G-5530)*
AT&T Services Inc 559 454-3579
5555 E Olive Ave Ste A315 Fresno (93727) *(G-5531)*
AT&T Services Inc 714 259-4441
1834 W Victoria Ave Anaheim (92804) *(G-5532)*
AT&T Services Inc 805 237-9503
908 28th St Paso Robles (93446) *(G-5533)*
AT&T Services Inc 831 649-2029
787 Munras Ave Monterey (93940) *(G-5534)*
AT&T Services Inc 858 886-2762
7337 Trade St Rm 3600 San Diego (92121) *(G-5535)*
AT&T Services Inc 210 886-4922
200 W Center Street Prome Anaheim (92805) *(G-5536)*
AT&T Services Inc 650 960-2255
360 Pioneer Way Mountain View (94041) *(G-5537)*
AT&T Services Inc 661 324-2046
5650 Aldrin Ct Bakersfield (93313) *(G-27840)*
AT&T Services Inc 818 242-4102
720 Western Ave Glendale (91201) *(G-1906)*
AT&T Services Inc 213 975-4089
1010 Wilshire Blvd Los Angeles (90017) *(G-5538)*
AT&T Services Inc 925 823-1443
2600 Camino Ramon 2e750ll San Ramon (94583) *(G-5539)*
AT&T Services Inc 916 638-6096
2615 Mercantile Dr Rancho Cordova (95742) *(G-5540)*
AT&T Services Inc 800 662-6252
4734 E Carmen Ave Fresno (93703) *(G-5541)*
AT&T Services Inc 714 575-8320
3939 E Coronado St Anaheim (92807) *(G-5542)*
AT&T Services Inc 661 398-4650
5101 Office Park Dr # 303 Bakersfield (93309) *(G-5543)*
AT&T Services Inc 707 545-5000
2125 Occidental Rd Santa Rosa (95401) *(G-5544)*
AT&T Services Inc 650 579-5266
1480 Burlingame Ave Burlingame (94010) *(G-5545)*
AT&T Services Inc 213 741-3111
1900 S Grand Ave Rm 100 Los Angeles (90007) *(G-5546)*
AT&T Services Inc 415 394-3000
140 New Montgomery St San Francisco (94105) *(G-5547)*
AT&T Services Inc 510 791-6605
44900 Industrial Dr Fremont (94538) *(G-5548)*
AT&T Services Inc 760 489-3519
146 S Broadway Escondido (92025) *(G-5549)*
AT&T Services Inc 714 992-3359
8925 Orangethorpe Ave Buena Park (90621) *(G-5550)*
AT&T Services Inc 925 671-1902
1714 Colfax St Ste 300 Concord (94520) *(G-5551)*
AT&T Services Inc 510 732-0830
7701 Artesia Blvd Buena Park (90621) *(G-5552)*
AT&T Services Inc 916 453-6267
1821 24th St Rm 122 Sacramento (95816) *(G-5553)*
AT&T Services Inc 925 671-1059
1033 Shary Cir Ste A Concord (94518) *(G-5554)*
AT&T Services Inc 858 495-3907
7650 Convoy Ct Ste 106 San Diego (92111) *(G-5555)*
AT&T Services Inc 760 489-3187
950 W Washington Ave Escondido (92025) *(G-5556)*
AT&T Services Inc 858 268-6751
8335 Century Park Ct # 150 San Diego (92123) *(G-5557)*
AT&T Services Inc 323 468-6813
1429 N Gower St Los Angeles (90028) *(G-5558)*
AT&T Services Inc 626 308-8582
501 S Marengo Ave Alhambra (91803) *(G-5559)*
AT&T Services Inc 408 973-7504
5285 Doyle Rd Rm 3 San Jose (95129) *(G-5560)*
AT&T Services Inc 916 376-2006
3900 Channel Dr West Sacramento (95691) *(G-5561)*
AT&T Wireless, Santa Fe Springs *Also called New Cingular Wireless Svcs Inc (G-5402)*
Ata Engineering Inc (PA) 858 480-2000
13290 Evening Creek Dr S # 250 San Diego (92128) *(G-25671)*
Ata Retail Services LLC (PA) 925 621-4700
7133 Koll Center Pkwy # 100 Pleasanton (94566) *(G-9245)*
Atac (PA) 408 736-2822
2770 De La Cruz Blvd Santa Clara (95050) *(G-15906)*
Atascadero Hotel Partners LLC 805 462-3500
900 El Camino Real Atascadero (93422) *(G-12399)*
Atascadero State Hospital, Atascadero *Also called Califrnia Dept State Hospitals (G-22050)*
Atcaa, Jackson *Also called Amador Tlmne Cmnty Action Agcy (G-24864)*
Atchesons Express Inc 714 808-9199
201 E La Palma Ave Anaheim (92801) *(G-3979)*
Atcr, Jackson *Also called Amador-Tolumne Cmnty Resources (G-24866)*
Atech Logistics Inc 707 526-1910
7 College Ave Santa Rosa (95401) *(G-5032)*
Atech Warehousing & Dist Inc (PA) 707 526-1910
7 College Ave Santa Rosa (95401) *(G-4113)*
Atel Capital Group (PA) 415 989-8800
600 Montgomery St Fl 9 San Francisco (94111) *(G-9794)*
Aten Technology Inc 949 428-1111
15365 Barranca Pkwy Irvine (92618) *(G-7096)*
Athenahealth Inc 415 416-3500
50 Hawthorne St San Francisco (94105) *(G-15586)*
Athens Administrators, Concord *Also called Athens Insurance Service Inc (G-10632)*
Athens Disposal Company Inc (PA) 626 336-3636
14048 Valley Blvd La Puente (91746) *(G-6433)*
Athens Insurance, Concord *Also called James C Jenkins Insur Svc Inc (G-10751)*
Athens Insurance Service Inc 925 826-1000
2552 Stanwell Dr Ste 100 Concord (94520) *(G-10632)*
Athens Services, City of Industry *Also called Arakelian Enterprises Inc (G-6427)*
Athens Services, City of Industry *Also called Arakelian Enterprises Inc (G-6429)*
Atherton Baptist Homes 626 289-4178
214 S Atlantic Blvd Alhambra (91801) *(G-20387)*
Atherton Healthcare, Menlo Park *Also called Cal Care Inc (G-27365)*
Athletic Department, Stockton *Also called University of Pacific (G-19301)*
Athletics Investment Group LLC (PA) 510 638-4900
7000 Coliseum Way Oakland (94621) *(G-18537)*
Athoc Inc 650 685-3000
2988 Campus Dr Ste 200 San Mateo (94403) *(G-15039)*
ATI, Danville *Also called Architrends Inc (G-25661)*
ATI, Orange *Also called American Technologies Inc (G-1127)*
Ati Inc 408 942-1780
2123 Ringwood Ave San Jose (95131) *(G-16327)*
ATI Architects & Engineers, Danville *Also called ATI Engineering Services Inc (G-26165)*
ATI Engineering Services Inc (PA) 925 648-8800
3860 Blackhawk Rd Ste 160 Danville (94506) *(G-26165)*
ATI Machinery Inc 559 884-2471
21436 S Lassen Ave Five Points (93624) *(G-7799)*
Atieva Usa Inc 650 802-8181
125 Constitution Dr Menlo Park (94025) *(G-25672)*
Atk Audiotek 661 705-3700
28238 Avenue Crocker Valencia (91355) *(G-2524)*
Atk Services, Valencia *Also called Atk Audiotek (G-2524)*
Atk Space Systems Inc 626 351-0205
370 N Halstead St Pasadena (91107) *(G-26479)*
Atk Space Systems Inc 858 621-5700
7130 Miramar Rd Ste 100b San Diego (92121) *(G-26737)*
Atkins North America Inc 858 874-1810
9275 Sky Park Ct Ste 200 San Diego (92123) *(G-25673)*
Atkins North America Inc 916 325-4800
332 Pine St Fl 5 San Francisco (94104) *(G-27841)*
Atkinson And Ly Rd & Rm Lw (PA) 562 653-3200
12800 Center Court Dr S # 300 Cerritos (90703) *(G-23096)*
Atkinson & Mullen Travel Inc 408 452-0202
2025 Gateway Pl San Jose (95110) *(G-4957)*

Atkinson Andelson Loya, Cerritos *Also called Atkinson And Ly Rd & Rm Lw* ***(G-23096)***
Atkinson Construction Inc 303 410-2540
18201 Von Karman Ave # 800 Irvine (92612) ***(G-1736)***
Atkinson Youth Services Inc 916 927-1863
4253 Balsam St Sacramento (95838) ***(G-23674)***
Atkinson-Baker Inc (PA) 818 551-7300
500 N Brand Blvd Fl 3 Glendale (91203) ***(G-14166)***
ATL Services 714 712-4220
2390 E Orangewood Ave Anaheim (92806) ***(G-14235)***
Atlanta Seafoods LLC 626 626-4900
1301 S Sunkist St Anaheim (92806) ***(G-8628)***
Atlantic Aviation, Santa Ana *Also called Newport Beach Fbo LLC* ***(G-14917)***
Atlantic Express of California, Long Beach *Also called Atlantic Express Trnsp* ***(G-3768)***
Atlantic Express Trnsp 562 997-6868
2450 Long Beach Blvd Long Beach (90806) ***(G-3768)***
Atlantic Mem Healthcare Assoc (PA) 562 424-8101
2750 Atlantic Ave Long Beach (90806) ***(G-20388)***
Atlantic Mem Healthcare Ctr, Long Beach *Also called Atlantic Mem Healthcare Assoc* ***(G-20388)***
Atlantic Optical Co Inc 818 407-1890
20801 Nordhoff St Chatsworth (91311) ***(G-7330)***
Atlantic Recording Corporation 818 238-6800
3400 W Olive Ave Burbank (91505) ***(G-17008)***
Atlas Advertising, Irvine *Also called M F Salta Co Inc* ***(G-27518)***
Atlas Construction Supply Inc (PA) 858 277-2100
4640 Brinnell St San Diego (92111) ***(G-6973)***
Atlas Database Software Corp (PA) 818 340-7080
26679 Agoura Rd Ste 200 Calabasas (91302) ***(G-15040)***
Atlas Development, Calabasas *Also called Atlas Database Software Corp* ***(G-15040)***
Atlas Digital LLC (PA) 323 762-2626
170 S Flower St Burbank (91502) ***(G-18046)***
Atlas Disposal Industries LLC 916 455-2800
3000 Power Inn Rd Sacramento (95826) ***(G-6434)***
Atlas Entertainment Inc 310 786-4900
9200 W Sunset Blvd Ste 10 West Hollywood (90069) ***(G-18047)***
Atlas General Insur Svcs LLC 858 529-6700
4365 Executive Dr Ste 400 San Diego (92121) ***(G-10633)***
Atlas Heating, San Jose *Also called American Residential Svcs LLC* ***(G-2133)***
ATLAS MOVER SERVICES, Rancho Dominguez *Also called Mover Services Inc* ***(G-4363)***
Atlas Security & Patrol Inc 510 791-7380
39465 Paseo Padre Pkwy # 2800 Fremont (94538) ***(G-16565)***
Atlas Security Inc 323 876-1401
11862 Balboa Blvd Ste 395 Granada Hills (91344) ***(G-16868)***
Atlas Textile Co Inc 818 881-8862
6047 Tampa Ave Ste 103 Tarzana (91356) ***(G-6844)***
Atlas/Eastern Van Lines, Pomona *Also called W Why W Enterprises Inc* ***(G-4390)***
Atlassian Inc (HQ) 415 701-1110
1098 Harrison St San Francisco (94103) ***(G-15587)***
Atlaz Inc 415 671-6142
914 S St Sacramento (95811) ***(G-15041)***
Atm Insurance, Anaheim *Also called American Team Managers Inc* ***(G-10599)***
Atpa, Alameda *Also called Joint Labor MGT Retirement Tr* ***(G-10242)***
Atrenta Inc (HQ) 408 453-3333
690 E Middlefield Rd Mountain View (94043) ***(G-15042)***
Atria Grand Oaks, Thousand Oaks *Also called Atria Senior Living Inc* ***(G-24556)***
Atria Senior Living Inc 805 370-5400
2177 E Thousand Oaks Blvd Thousand Oaks (91362) ***(G-24556)***
Atria Senior Living Group Inc 805 482-9771
24 Las Posas Rd Camarillo (93010) ***(G-24557)***
Atria Senior Living Group Inc 949 661-1220
32353 San Juan Creek Rd San Juan Capistrano (92675) ***(G-24558)***
Atria Senior Living Group Inc 925 938-6611
1400 Montego Walnut Creek (94598) ***(G-11089)***
Atria Senior Living Group Inc 408 266-1660
1660 Gaton Dr Ofc San Jose (95125) ***(G-11090)***
Atria Senior Living Group Inc 415 892-0944
853 Tamalpais Ave Ofc Novato (94947) ***(G-24559)***
Atria Senior Living Group Inc 949 786-5665
33 Creek Rd Side Irvine (92604) ***(G-26930)***
Atria Senior Living Group Inc 916 488-5722
2426 Garfield Ave Ofc Carmichael (95608) ***(G-11091)***
Atria Senior Living Group Inc 760 341-0890
44600 Monterey Ave Ofc Palm Desert (92260) ***(G-24560)***
Atrium Capital Corp 650 233-7878
3000 Sand Hill Rd 2-130 Menlo Park (94025) ***(G-9960)***
Atrium Hotel, Irvine *Also called Golden Hotels Ltd Partnership* ***(G-12668)***
Atrium Hotels LP 510 658-9300
1800 Powell St Oakland (94608) ***(G-12400)***
Atrium Hotels LP 916 446-0100
300 J St Sacramento (95814) ***(G-12401)***
Atrium Hotels LP 916 446-0100
300 J St Sacramento (95814) ***(G-12402)***
Atrium Hotels LP 831 393-1115
1441 Canyon Del Rey Blvd Seaside (93955) ***(G-12403)***
Atrium of San Jose, San Jose *Also called Brookdale Lving Cmmunities Inc* ***(G-24570)***
Atrium Plaza LLC 650 653-6000
1770 S Amphlett Blvd San Mateo (94402) ***(G-12404)***
Atsugi Kokusai Kanko USA Inc 951 924-4444
28095 John F Kennedy Dr Moreno Valley (92555) ***(G-18879)***
Attendant Care Referrals Inc 310 399-2904
2801 Ocean Park Blvd # 192 Santa Monica (90405) ***(G-22372)***
Attom Data Solutions, Irvine *Also called Renwood Realtytrac LLC* ***(G-11810)***
Attorney Recovery Systems Inc (PA) 818 774-1420
18757 Burbank Blvd # 300 Tarzana (91356) ***(G-14018)***
Attorneys At Law, Fresno *Also called Lang Richert & Patch* ***(G-23364)***
Auberge Du Soleil, Rutherford *Also called Terre Du Soleil Ltd* ***(G-13341)***
Auburn Constructors Inc 916 924-0344
730 W Stadium Ln Sacramento (95834) ***(G-2023)***
Auburn Gardens Care Center, Auburn *Also called Madera Convalescent Hospital* ***(G-21304)***
Auburn Oaks Care Center 650 949-7777
3400 Bell Rd Auburn (95603) ***(G-20389)***
Auburn Old Town Gallery 530 887-9150
218 Washington St Ste A Auburn (95603) ***(G-19145)***
Auburn Placer Disposal Service 530 885-3735
12305 Shale Ridge Ln Auburn (95602) ***(G-6435)***
Auburn Pride, Auburn *Also called Pride Industries* ***(G-24380)***
Auburn Ravine Terrace, Auburn *Also called Retirement Housing Foundation* ***(G-24786)***
Auburn Ravine Terrace, Auburn *Also called Congrgtnal Ch Retirement Cmnty* ***(G-24901)***
Auburn-Placer Recycling Center, Auburn *Also called Auburn Placer Disposal Service* ***(G-6435)***
Auchante Inc 562 231-1880
6730 Florence Ave Bell Gardens (90201) ***(G-11309)***
Auction.com, Irvine *Also called Ten-X LLC* ***(G-11868)***
Auctioncom Inc 800 499-6199
1 Mauchly Ste 27 Irvine (92618) ***(G-11310)***
Auctiva Corporation 530 894-7400
360 E 6th St Chico (95928) ***(G-27842)***
Audaexplore, San Diego *Also called Audatex North America Inc* ***(G-15588)***
Audatex North America Inc (HQ) 858 946-1900
15030 Ave Of Ste 100 San Diego (92128) ***(G-15588)***
Audio Visual Headquarters (HQ) 310 603-0652
16320 Arthur St Cerritos (90703) ***(G-14514)***
Audio Visual MGT Solutions 714 590-8755
12812 Garden Grove Blvd M Garden Grove (92843) ***(G-26931)***
Audiobahn Inc 714 988-0400
114 S Berry St Brea (92821) ***(G-7526)***
Audioquest, Irvine *Also called Quest Group* ***(G-8134)***
Audiovisions, Lake Forest *Also called Inspiria Inc* ***(G-25882)***
Auditor Controller Department, San Bernardino *Also called County of San Bernardino* ***(G-26317)***
Audrey Adams MD 408 354-2114
718 University Ave # 211 Los Gatos (95032) ***(G-19363)***
Augmedix Inc 954 903-4993
1161 Mission St Ste 210 San Francisco (94103) ***(G-17009)***
Augustine Ideas, Roseville *Also called D Augustine & Associates* ***(G-13829)***
Aurora Algae Inc (PA) 510 266-5000
3325 Investment Blvd Hayward (94545) ***(G-26480)***
Aurora Behavioral Health 707 800-7700
1287 Fulton Rd Santa Rosa (95401) ***(G-22038)***
Aurora Behavioral Health Care 858 487-3200
11878 Avenue Of Industry San Diego (92128) ***(G-22039)***
Aurora Behavioral Hlth Care, San Diego *Also called Aurora Healthcare Inc* ***(G-21455)***
Aurora Healthcare Inc 858 487-3200
11878 Avenue Of Industry San Diego (92128) ***(G-21455)***
Aurora Las Encinas LLC 626 356-2500
2900 E Del Mar Blvd Pasadena (91107) ***(G-22040)***
Aurora Las Encinas Hospital, Pasadena *Also called Aurora Las Encinas LLC* ***(G-22040)***
Aurora San Diego, San Diego *Also called Aurora Behavioral Health Care* ***(G-22039)***
Aurora World Inc 562 205-1222
8820 Mercury Ln Pico Rivera (90660) ***(G-8036)***
Aus Decking Inc 916 373-5320
2999 Promenade St Ste 100 West Sacramento (95691) ***(G-3227)***
Ausenco PSI LLC (HQ) 925 939-4420
1320 Willow Pass Rd # 300 Concord (94520) ***(G-25674)***
Ausgar Technologies Inc 855 428-7427
10721 Treena St San Diego (92131) ***(G-25675)***
Austin Builders 714 879-1100
151 1/2 N Yale Ave Fullerton (92831) ***(G-1131)***
Austin Construction 805 610-0622
330 L P Ranch Rd Templeton (93465) ***(G-1132)***
Austin Security Patrol Inc 916 631-9877
11300 Sanders Dr Ste 24 Rancho Cordova (95742) ***(G-16566)***
Austin Veum Rbbins Prtners Inc (PA) 619 231-1960
501 W Broadway Ste A San Diego (92101) ***(G-26166)***
Authority Tax Services LLC 213 486-5135
777 S Figueroa St # 1900 Los Angeles (90017) ***(G-17010)***
Authorized Taxi Cab 323 776-5324
6150 W 96th St Los Angeles (90045) ***(G-16869)***
Autism Partnership Inc 562 431-9293
200 Marina Dr C Seal Beach (90740) ***(G-27335)***
Auto Body Management Inc 818 888-7654
7654 Tampa Ave Reseda (91335) ***(G-17748)***
Auto Buyline Systems Inc (PA) 909 881-7828
1620 Fairway Dr Colton (92324) ***(G-17011)***
Auto Club Enterprises (PA) 714 850-5111
3333 Fairview Rd Msa451 Costa Mesa (92626) ***(G-10235)***
Auto Club Enterprises 310 914-8500
1950 Century Park E Los Angeles (90067) ***(G-10236)***
Auto Club Speedway, Fontana *Also called California Speedway Corp* ***(G-18567)***
Auto Collection, Escondido *Also called Lincoln Witt Mercury* ***(G-17804)***
Auto Edge Solutions, Pacoima *Also called Moc Products Company Inc* ***(G-8994)***
Auto Expressions LLC 310 639-0666
505 E Euclid Ave Compton (90222) ***(G-6709)***
Auto Insur Spcialists-Long Bch 562 496-2888
5000 E Spring St Ste 100 Long Beach (90815) ***(G-10634)***
Auto Knight Motor Club Inc 760 969-4300
1009 N Palm Canyon Dr Palm Springs (92262) ***(G-25493)***
Auto Parts Group, Rancho Cordova *Also called Pick Pull Auto Dismantling Inc* ***(G-8079)***
Auto Parts Warehouse Inc (PA) 800 913-6119
16941 Keegan Ave Carson (90746) ***(G-6710)***
Auto Pride, Anaheim *Also called Cal-State Auto Parts Inc* ***(G-6720)***
Auto Town Inc 209 473-2513
2150 E Hammer Ln Stockton (95210) ***(G-17783)***
Auto Value, San Bernardino *Also called Metropolitan Automotive Whse* ***(G-6748)***

ALPHABETIC

ALPHABETIC SECTION
Aviar Golf Club, Carlsbad

Auto World Car Wash LLC ... 408 345-6532
15951 Los Gatos Blvd Los Gatos (95032) *(G-17829)*
Auto-Chlor System LLC ... 650 967-3085
450 Ferguson Dr Mountain View (94043) *(G-14515)*
Autobody Depot, San Diego *Also called Tcp Global Corporation* *(G-9240)*
Autobytel Inc (PA) ... 949 225-4500
18872 Macarthur Blvd # 200 Irvine (92612) *(G-16218)*
Autocrib Inc ... 714 274-0400
2882 Dow Ave Tustin (92780) *(G-17012)*
Autodesk Inc ... 415 356-0700
1 Market St San Francisco (94105) *(G-15589)*
Autodesk Inc (PA) ... 415 507-5000
111 Mcinnis Pkwy San Rafael (94903) *(G-15590)*
Autodesk Inc ... 415 507-5000
3950 Civic Center Dr San Rafael (94903) *(G-15591)*
Autofarm, Fremont *Also called Novariant Inc* *(G-25992)*
Autogenomics Inc ... 760 477-2248
1600 Faraday Ave Carlsbad (92008) *(G-26481)*
Automate Parking Inc ... 310 674-3396
8405 Pershing Dr Ste 100 Playa Del Rey (90293) *(G-17711)*
Automated Ctrl Technical Svcs, Bakersfield *Also called A-C Electric Company* *(G-25607)*
Automated Systems America Inc ... 877 500-0002
101 N Brand Blvd Ste 1230 Glendale (91203) *(G-17963)*
Automatic Data Processing Inc ... 714 690-7000
7000 Village Dr Ste 200 Buena Park (90621) *(G-16090)*
Automatic Data Processing Inc ... 909 477-4266
9445 Fairway View Pl # 200 Rancho Cucamonga (91730) *(G-16091)*
Automatic Data Processing Inc ... 805 383-8630
5153 Camino Ruiz Ste 100 Camarillo (93012) *(G-16092)*
Automatic Data Processing Inc ... 650 829-6900
601 Gateway Blvd Ste 900 South San Francisco (94080) *(G-16093)*
Automatic Data Processing Inc ... 909 592-6411
620 W Covina Blvd San Dimas (91773) *(G-16094)*
Automatic Data Processing Inc ... 800 225-5237
720 Bay Rd Redwood City (94063) *(G-16095)*
Automatic Data Processing Inc ... 415 899-7300
505 San Marin Dr Ste A110 Novato (94945) *(G-16096)*
Automatic Data Processing Inc ... 408 876-6600
820 N Mccarthy Blvd # 120 Milpitas (95035) *(G-16097)*
Automatic Data Processing Inc ... 714 994-2000
5355 Orangethorpe Ave La Palma (90623) *(G-16098)*
Automatic Data Processing Inc ... 925 251-5300
4125 Hopyard Rd Pleasanton (94588) *(G-16099)*
Automatic Data Processing Inc ... 800 225-5237
400 W Covina Blvd San Dimas (91773) *(G-16100)*
Automatic Data Processing Inc ... 661 631-1456
6300 Canoga Ave Ste 400 Woodland Hills (91367) *(G-16101)*
Automatic Data Processing Inc ... 800 226-5237
600 Crprate Pinte Ste 450 Culver City (90230) *(G-16102)*
Automatic Data Processing Inc ... 619 293-4800
1450 Frazee Rd Ste 601 San Diego (92108) *(G-16103)*
Automation Engrg Systems Inc ... 858 967-8650
3520 Seagate Way Ste 115 Oceanside (92056) *(G-15907)*
Automattic Inc ... 650 388-0901
132 Hawthorne St San Francisco (94107) *(G-5562)*
Automobile Club Southern Cal (PA) ... 213 741-3686
2601 S Figueroa St Los Angeles (90007) *(G-10635)*
Automobile Club Southern Cal ... 818 997-6230
15503 Ventura Blvd # 150 Encino (91436) *(G-25494)*
Automobile Club Southern Cal ... 310 325-3111
23001 Hawthorne Blvd Torrance (90505) *(G-25495)*
Automobile Club Southern Cal ... 805 644-7171
1501 S Victoria Ave Ventura (93003) *(G-25496)*
Automobile Club Southern Cal ... 626 963-8531
1301s S Grand Ave Glendora (91740) *(G-25497)*
Automobile Club Southern Cal ... 661 327-4661
1500 Commercial Way Bakersfield (93309) *(G-25498)*
Automobile Club Southern Cal ... 818 993-1616
9440 Reseda Blvd Northridge (91324) *(G-25499)*
Automobile Club Southern Cal ... 818 883-2660
22708 Victory Blvd Woodland Hills (91367) *(G-25500)*
Automobile Club Southern Cal ... 951 684-4250
3700 Central Ave Riverside (92506) *(G-25501)*
Automobile Club Southern Cal ... 949 951-1400
25181 Paseo De Alicia Laguna Hills (92653) *(G-25502)*
Automobile Club Southern Cal ... 714 885-1343
3333 Fairview Rd Costa Mesa (92626) *(G-10636)*
Automobile Club Southern Cal ... 909 392-1444
2488 Foothill Blvd Ste A La Verne (91750) *(G-10637)*
Automobile Club Southern Cal ... 760 247-4110
19201 Bear Valley Rd C Apple Valley (92308) *(G-10638)*
Automobile Club Southern Cal ... 909 980-0233
10540 Fthill Blvd Ste 100 Rancho Cucamonga (91730) *(G-10639)*
Automobile Club Southern Cal ... 858 481-7181
2666 Del Mar Heights Rd Del Mar (92014) *(G-10640)*
Automobile Club Southern Cal ... 714 850-5111
3333 Fairview Rd Costa Mesa (92626) *(G-17784)*
Automobile Club Southern Cal ... 619 464-7001
8765 Fletcher Pkwy La Mesa (91942) *(G-25503)*
Automotive Service Council ... 800 810-4272
10813 Airport Dr El Cajon (92020) *(G-25504)*
Automotive Services Division, Ontario *Also called Securitas SEC Svcs USA Inc* *(G-16793)*
Automotive Services Division, Northridge *Also called Securitas SEC Svcs USA Inc* *(G-16812)*
Automotive Sup Co Southern Cal (PA) ... 909 428-9072
10580 Mulberry Ave Fontana (92337) *(G-6711)*
Automotive Tstg & Dev Svcs Inc (PA) ... 909 390-1100
400 Etiwanda Ave Ontario (91761) *(G-17875)*
Autonomy Interwoven, Sunnyvale *Also called Interwoven Inc* *(G-15709)*
Autoreturn, San Francisco *Also called Tegsco LLC* *(G-17896)*
Autowebcom Inc ... 949 862-1371
18872 Macarthur Blvd Irvine (92612) *(G-16219)*
Autry Museum of American West ... 323 667-2000
4700 Western Heritage Way Los Angeles (90027) *(G-25004)*
Autry National Centre, Los Angeles *Also called Autry Museum of American West* *(G-25004)*
Autumn LP ... 415 277-1245
1 Kaiser Plz Ste 505 Oakland (94612) *(G-17013)*
Autumn Hills Convalescent Home, Glendale *Also called Mariner Health Care Inc* *(G-20764)*
Auxiliary of Mission ... 949 364-1400
27700 Medical Center Rd Mission Viejo (92691) *(G-21456)*
Auxilio Inc (PA) ... 949 614-0700
27271 Las Ramblas Ste 200 Mission Viejo (92691) *(G-14113)*
Auxilio Solutions Inc ... 949 614-0700
27271 Las Ramblas Ste 200 Mission Viejo (92691) *(G-14114)*
AV Courtyard SD Spectrum ... 858 573-0700
8651 Spectrum Center Blvd San Diego (92123) *(G-12405)*
AV Management, Garden Grove *Also called Audio Visual MGT Solutions* *(G-26931)*
AV Occupational Medicine, Lancaster *Also called Daniel O Mongiano MD A PR* *(G-19485)*
Ava Enterprises Inc ... 805 988-0192
3451 Lunar Ct Oxnard (93030) *(G-7491)*
Ava The Rabbit Haven Inc ... 831 600-7479
1261 S Mary St Scotts Valley (95067) *(G-27843)*
Avac, San Jose *Also called Almaden Valley Athletic Club* *(G-18847)*
Avad LLC (PA) ... 818 742-4800
5805 Sepulvda Blvd # 750 Sherman Oaks (91411) *(G-7527)*
Avadyne Health, San Diego *Also called H & R Accounts Inc* *(G-15218)*
Avalon A Cerritos ... 562 865-9500
11000 New Falcon Way Ofc # 177 Cerritos (90703) *(G-23675)*
Avalon At Newport, Newport Beach *Also called Ventage Senior Housing* *(G-24845)*
Avalon At Newport LLC ... 949 631-3555
393 Hospital Rd Newport Beach (92663) *(G-24561)*
Avalon At Newport Beach, Newport Beach *Also called Avalon At Newport LLC* *(G-24561)*
Avalon Building Maintenance (PA) ... 714 693-2407
3148 E La Palma Ave Ste A Anaheim (92806) *(G-14236)*
Avalon Care Center - Merced Fr ... 209 722-6231
3169 M St Merced (95348) *(G-20390)*
Avalon Care Cntr Merced Hy ... 209 384-8839
3170 Main St Merced (95340) *(G-20391)*
Avalon Care Ctr - Madera LLC ... 559 673-9278
1700 Howard Rd Madera (93637) *(G-20392)*
Avalon Care Ctr - Modesto LLC ... 209 529-0516
515 E Orangeburg Ave Modesto (95350) *(G-20393)*
Avalon Care Ctr - Newman LLC ... 209 862-2862
709 N St Newman (95360) *(G-20394)*
Avalon Golden Gate LLC ... 415 664-6264
1601 19th Ave Apt 122 San Francisco (94122) *(G-24562)*
Avalon Health Care Inc ... 209 526-1775
1900 Coffee Rd Modesto (95355) *(G-20395)*
Avalon Health Care Inc ... 707 433-4877
725 Grove St Healdsburg (95448) *(G-20396)*
Avalon Health Care Inc ... 209 754-3823
900 Mountain Ranch Rd San Andreas (95249) *(G-20397)*
Avalon Health Care Inc ... 559 665-4826
1010 Ventura Ave Chowchilla (93610) *(G-20398)*
Avalon Health Care Inc ... 209 533-2500
19929 Greenley Rd Sonora (95370) *(G-20399)*
Avalon Health Care - Madera, Madera *Also called Avalon Care Ctr - Madera LLC* *(G-20392)*
Avalon Hotel, Beverly Hills *Also called Honeymoon Real Estate LP* *(G-12757)*
Avalon Staffing, Westlake Village *Also called Jackie Hoofring* *(G-14688)*
Avalon Transportation Co, Culver City *Also called Virgin Fish Inc* *(G-3855)*
Avamar Technologies Inc ... 949 743-5100
135 Technology Dr Irvine (92618) *(G-15043)*
Avanquest North America Inc (HQ) ... 818 223-8967
23801 Calabasas Rd # 2005 Calabasas (91302) *(G-15044)*
Avanti Agency Corporation ... 714 935-0900
282 S Anita Dr Orange (92868) *(G-17014)*
Avanti Hospitals LLC ... 323 268-5514
4060 Whittier Blvd Los Angeles (90023) *(G-17015)*
Avanti Hospitals LLC ... 323 583-1931
2623 E Slauson Ave Huntington Park (90255) *(G-17016)*
Avanti Hospitals LLC ... 310 532-4200
1145 W Redondo Beach Blvd Gardena (90247) *(G-21457)*
Avanti Hospitals LLC ... 562 868-3751
13100 Studebaker Rd Norwalk (90650) *(G-21458)*
Avantica Technologies, Mountain View *Also called Group Avantica Inc* *(G-15215)*
Avantra Financial, Arcadia *Also called Avantra Real Estate Services* *(G-11311)*
Avantra Real Estate Services ... 626 357-7028
148 E Fthill Blvd Ste 100 Arcadia (91006) *(G-11311)*
Avar Construction Inc ... 510 354-2000
47375 Fremont Blvd Fremont (94538) *(G-1737)*
Avaya Inc ... 805 581-6119
2989 Flanagan Dr Simi Valley (93063) *(G-5563)*
Ave Maria Convalescent Hosp ... 831 373-1216
1249 Josselyn Canyon Rd Monterey (93940) *(G-20400)*
Ave Maria Senior Living, Monterey *Also called Ave Maria Convalescent Hosp* *(G-20400)*
Avenue H LLC ... 909 795-2476
35253 Avenue H Yucaipa (92399) *(G-20401)*
Avenue of Arts Wyndham Hotel, Costa Mesa *Also called Rosanna Inc* *(G-13167)*
Avenuesocial Inc ... 510 275-4485
440 N Wolfe Rd Sunnyvale (94085) *(G-15045)*
Aver Information Inc ... 408 263-3828
668 Mission Ct Fremont (94539) *(G-7097)*
Avery Corp ... 626 304-2000
207 N Goode Ave Fl 6 Glendale (91203) *(G-26482)*
Avia Tech LLC ... 858 777-5000
7220 Trade St Ste 300 San Diego (92121) *(G-13817)*
Aviar Golf Club, Carlsbad *Also called Four Seasons Resort Aviara* *(G-18741)*

ALPHABETIC

Aviara Fsrc Associates Limited.....760 603-6800
7100 Aviara Resort Dr Carlsbad (92011) ***(G-12406)***
Aviara Resort Associates (PA).....760 448-1234
7100 Aviara Resort Dr Carlsbad (92011) ***(G-12407)***
Aviation & Defense Inc.....909 382-3487
255 S Leland Norton Way San Bernardino (92408) ***(G-4903)***
Aviation Consultants Inc (PA).....805 548-1300
945 Airport Dr San Luis Obispo (93401) ***(G-26932)***
Aviation Port Services LLC, San Leandro *Also called Aviation Port Services LLc* ***(G-4743)***
Aviation Port Services LLc.....510 636-8790
2081 Adams Ave San Leandro (94577) ***(G-4743)***
Aviation Safeguards, Los Angeles *Also called Command Security Corporation* ***(G-16604)***
Aviation Safeguards, San Jose *Also called Command Security Corporation* ***(G-16605)***
Avid Bioservices Inc.....714 508-6100
14282 Franklin Ave Tustin (92780) ***(G-8234)***
Avida Caregivers Inc.....323 498-1500
11500 W Olympic Blvd # 400 Los Angeles (90064) ***(G-22373)***
Avis Budget Car Rentals, San Leandro *Also called Avis Rent A Car System Inc* ***(G-17663)***
Avis Budget Group Inc.....650 616-0150
513 Eccles Ave Ste A South San Francisco (94080) ***(G-17661)***
Avis Rent A Car System Inc.....909 974-2192
3450 E Airport Dr Ste 500 Ontario (91761) ***(G-17662)***
Avis Rent A Car System Inc.....510 562-8828
390 Doolittle Dr San Leandro (94577) ***(G-17663)***
Avis Rent A Car System Inc.....916 922-5601
6520 Mcnair Cir Sacramento (95837) ***(G-17664)***
Avis Rent A Car System Inc.....818 566-3001
4209 W Vanowen Pl Burbank (91505) ***(G-17665)***
Avis Rent A Car Systems, Sacramento *Also called Avis Rent A Car System Inc* ***(G-17664)***
Aviva Center, Los Angeles *Also called Hamburger Home* ***(G-24676)***
Aviva Systems Biology Corp.....858 552-6979
5754 Pcf Ctr Blvd Ste 201 San Diego (92121) ***(G-26483)***
Avnet Inc.....949 789-4100
220 Commerce Ste 100 Irvine (92602) ***(G-7528)***
Avnet Inc.....818 594-8310
20951 Burbank Blvd Ste A Woodland Hills (91367) ***(G-7529)***
Avnet Inc.....408 501-3925
2110 Zanker Rd San Jose (95131) ***(G-7530)***
Avnet Inc.....858 385-7500
15231 Avenue Of Science # 150 San Diego (92128) ***(G-7531)***
Avnet Emg, Woodland Hills *Also called Avnet Inc* ***(G-7529)***
Avnet USI, Irvine *Also called Avnet Inc* ***(G-7528)***
Avoca Productions Inc.....310 244-4000
10202 Washington Blvd Culver City (90232) ***(G-18048)***
Avolent Inc.....415 553-6400
444 De Haro St Ste 100 San Francisco (94107) ***(G-15592)***
Avongard Products USa Ltd.....310 319-2300
1700 W El Segundo Blvd Gardena (90249) ***(G-18215)***
Aware Point, San Diego *Also called Awarepoint Corporation* ***(G-15046)***
Awarepoint Corporation (PA).....858 345-5000
600 W Broadway Ste 250 San Diego (92101) ***(G-15046)***
Awe, San Diego *Also called Herring Networks Inc* ***(G-5870)***
AWH Burbank Hotel LLC.....813 843-6000
2500 N Hollywood Way Burbank (91505) ***(G-12408)***
AWI Acquisition Company (PA).....818 364-2333
13207 Bradley Ave Sylmar (91342) ***(G-7674)***
AWI Management Corporation.....951 674-8200
1800 E Lakeshore Dr Lake Elsinore (92530) ***(G-26933)***
Awm LLC.....916 381-4200
8180 Industrial Pkwy Sacramento (95824) ***(G-6909)***
Awt Worlwide, Sunnyvale *Also called Applied Weather Technology Inc* ***(G-28114)***
Axa Advisors LLC.....213 251-1600
3435 Wilshire Blvd # 2500 Los Angeles (90010) ***(G-10120)***
Axa Advisors LLC.....619 239-0018
701 B St Ste 1500 San Diego (92101) ***(G-10201)***
Axa Advisors LLC.....415 276-2100
88 Kearny St Fl 20 San Francisco (94108) ***(G-12134)***
Axa Equitable Life Insur Co.....858 552-1234
3777 La Jolla Village Dr San Diego (92122) ***(G-10641)***
Axcient Inc (PA).....650 314-7300
1161 San Antonio Rd Mountain View (94043) ***(G-15047)***
Axiom Global Technologies Inc.....925 393-5800
220 N Wiget Ln Walnut Creek (94598) ***(G-27844)***
Axis, Culver City *Also called Rick Solomon Enterprises Inc* ***(G-8359)***
Axis Community Health Inc.....925 462-1755
4361 Railroad Ave Pleasanton (94566) ***(G-22662)***
Axis Construction, Hayward *Also called Axis Services Inc* ***(G-1295)***
Axis Services Inc.....510 732-6111
2566 Barrington Ct Hayward (94545) ***(G-1295)***
Axminster Medical Group Inc (PA).....310 670-3255
11539 Hawthorne Blvd Fl 6 Hawthorne (90250) ***(G-19364)***
Axolotl Corp.....408 920-0800
160 W Santa Clara St San Jose (95113) ***(G-15593)***
Aya Healthcare Inc.....858 458-4410
5930 Cornerstone Ct W # 300 San Diego (92121) ***(G-14841)***
Ayala Corporation.....559 867-5700
21510 S Chteau Fresno Ave Riverdale (93656) ***(G-14611)***
Ayala Drywall.....805 487-3392
2600 Alexander St Oxnard (93033) ***(G-2859)***
Ayala Farms, Riverdale *Also called Ayala Corporation* ***(G-14611)***
Ayco Company LP.....949 955-1544
17885 Von Karman Ave # 300 Irvine (92614) ***(G-10121)***
Ayoob & Peery Plumbing Co Inc.....415 550-0975
975 Indiana St San Francisco (94107) ***(G-2155)***
Ayres Group (PA).....714 540-6060
355 Bristol St Costa Mesa (92626) ***(G-12409)***
Ayres Hotel Laguna Woods, Aliso Viejo *Also called Countryside Inn-Corona LP* ***(G-12542)***

Ayzenberg Group Inc.....626 584-4070
49 E Walnut St Pasadena (91103) ***(G-13818)***
AZ West, Compton *Also called Az/CFS West Inc* ***(G-4676)***
Az/CFS West Inc.....310 898-2090
250 W Manville St Compton (90220) ***(G-4676)***
Azalea & Rose Co.....909 949-2442
1420 N Campus Ave Upland (91786) ***(G-264)***
Azcona Harvesting LLC.....831 674-2526
44 El Camino Real Unit A Greenfield (93927) ***(G-652)***
Aztec Engineering Group Inc.....951 471-6190
18510 Pasadena St Ste C Lake Elsinore (92530) ***(G-25676)***
Aztec Harvesting.....760 922-7348
1075 N Broadway Blythe (92225) ***(G-653)***
Aztec Landscaping Inc (PA).....619 464-3303
7980 Lemon Grove Way Lemon Grove (91945) ***(G-811)***
Aztec Sheet Metal Inc.....619 937-0005
11222 Woodside Ave N Santee (92071) ***(G-3140)***
Azteca America, Glendale *Also called Stations Group LLC* ***(G-5913)***
Azteca Landscape.....951 369-9210
4073 Mennes Ave Riverside (92509) ***(G-741)***
Aztlan Graphics, Chico *Also called Gonzales Enterprises Inc* ***(G-8343)***
Azubu North America Inc.....310 759-9529
15303 Ventura Blvd # 220 Sherman Oaks (91403) ***(G-8037)***
Azure Acres, Sebastopol *Also called Camp Recovery Centers LP* ***(G-22119)***
B & B Concrete, Santa Clara *Also called Robert A Bothman Inc* ***(G-3322)***
B & B Nurseries Inc.....951 352-8383
9505 Cleveland Ave Riverside (92503) ***(G-9178)***
B & B Plastics Recyclers Inc (PA).....909 829-3606
3040 N Locust Ave Rialto (92377) ***(G-8063)***
B & B Specialties Inc.....714 985-3075
4321 E La Palma Ave Anaheim (92807) ***(G-7675)***
B & B Specialty Metals, Bakersfield *Also called B & B Surplus Inc* ***(G-7359)***
B & B Surplus Inc (PA).....661 589-0381
7020 Rosedale Hwy Bakersfield (93308) ***(G-7359)***
B & C, Oakland *Also called B&C Transit Inc* ***(G-25677)***
B & E Convalescent Center Inc (PA).....562 923-9449
11627 Telg Rd Ste 200 Santa Fe Springs (90670) ***(G-21147)***
B & E Farms Inc.....714 893-8166
9112 Mcfadden Ave Westminster (92683) ***(G-104)***
B & G Delivery System Inc.....916 921-4401
2549 Harris Ave Sacramento (95838) ***(G-3980)***
B & L Consulting LLC.....682 238-6994
152 N 2nd Ave Upland (91786) ***(G-27845)***
B & M Contractors Inc.....805 581-5480
4473 Cochran St Simi Valley (93063) ***(G-3228)***
B & M Racing, Santa Rosa *Also called B&M Racing & Prfmce Pdts Inc* ***(G-6712)***
B & R Farm Labor Contractor.....805 524-1346
422 Mockingbird Ln Fillmore (93015) ***(G-14612)***
B & R Tevelde.....559 583-1277
2911 Hanford Armona Rd Hanford (93230) ***(G-417)***
B A M I Inc.....530 343-5678
1293 E 1st Ave Chico (95926) ***(G-18605)***
B A S, Diamond Bar *Also called Tetra Tech Bas Inc* ***(G-26092)***
B A Technolinks Corporation.....408 940-5921
4677 Old Ironsides Dr # 440 Santa Clara (95054) ***(G-27336)***
B B & K Fund Services Inc.....650 571-5800
950 Tower Ln Ste 1900 Foster City (94404) ***(G-9961)***
B B & T Management Corp.....916 428-8060
1453 Blair Ave Sacramento (95822) ***(G-6910)***
B B G Management Group (PA).....909 797-9581
12164 California St Yucaipa (92399) ***(G-8609)***
B C C S Inc (PA).....408 379-5500
1711 Dell Ave Campbell (95008) ***(G-1495)***
B C Life & Health Insurance Co.....818 703-2345
21555 Oxnard St Woodland Hills (91367) ***(G-10237)***
B C Rentals Inc.....714 974-1190
638 W Southern Ave Orange (92865) ***(G-7821)***
B C S, Canoga Park *Also called Buyers Consultation Svc Inc* ***(G-7539)***
B F C Inc.....415 495-3085
45 Broadway San Francisco (94111) ***(G-2525)***
B F Management.....323 931-7776
117 N Fuller Ave Los Angeles (90036) ***(G-11312)***
B H C Alhambra Hospital, Rosemead *Also called Psychiatric Solutions Inc* ***(G-22813)***
B H R Operations LLC.....408 321-9500
777 Bellew Dr Milpitas (95035) ***(G-12410)***
B I A, Emeryville *Also called Behavioral Intervention Assn* ***(G-14846)***
B Jacqueline and Assoc Inc.....626 844-1400
1192 N Lake Ave Pasadena (91104) ***(G-15048)***
B L S Limousine Service, Los Angeles *Also called Bls Lmsine Svc Los Angeles Inc* ***(G-3775)***
B M D, Galt *Also called Building Material Distrs Inc* ***(G-6911)***
B M S, Irvine *Also called Bankruptcy MGT Solutions Inc* ***(G-23104)***
B M W of North America, Oxnard *Also called BMW of North America LLC* ***(G-6717)***
B N B, Redwood City *Also called Bnbuilders* ***(G-1742)***
B N E U S A, City of Industry *Also called Eastern Broadcasting Amer Corp* ***(G-5997)***
B N I, Upland *Also called Bni Enterprises Inc* ***(G-27735)***
B R Funsten & Co.....209 825-5375
105 Lndustrial Park Manteca (95337) ***(G-6845)***
B R Funsten & Co.....707 863-8300
5200 Watt Ct Ste B Fairfield (94534) ***(G-6846)***
B Riley Financial Inc (PA).....818 884-3737
21860 Burbank Blvd Woodland Hills (91367) ***(G-17017)***
B S A Partners.....714 523-2800
14419 Firestone Blvd La Mirada (90638) ***(G-12411)***
B S I Holdings Inc.....831 622-1840
100 Clock Tower Pl # 200 Carmel (93923) ***(G-2860)***
B S K Analytical Laboratories, Fresno *Also called BSK Associates* ***(G-25709)***
B S R, San Francisco *Also called Business For Social Responsibi* ***(G-25077)***

ALPHABETIC SECTION
Bali Construction Inc

B T & T Travel Inc 559 237-9410
2609 E Mckinley Ave Ste N Fresno (93703) ***(G-4958)***
B T B Events Inc 714 415-3313
10950 Virginia Cir Fountain Valley (92708) ***(G-27732)***
B T Mancini Co Inc (PA) 408 942-7900
876 S Milpitas Blvd Milpitas (95035) ***(G-3106)***
B T W, West Sacramento *Also called Bytheways Manufacturing Inc* ***(G-6851)***
B Z Plumbing Company Inc 916 645-1600
1901 Aviation Blvd Lincoln (95648) ***(G-2156)***
B&B Industrial Services Inc (PA) 909 428-3167
14549 Manzanita Dr Fontana (92335) ***(G-2802)***
B&C Transit Inc (PA) 510 483-3560
7955 Edgewater Dr Oakland (94621) ***(G-25677)***
B&M Racing & Prfmce Pdts Inc (PA) 707 544-4761
100 Stony Point Rd # 125 Santa Rosa (95401) ***(G-6712)***
B-Per Electronic Inc 626 912-0600
1600 N Broadway Ste 810 Santa Ana (92706) ***(G-5277)***
B-Spring Valley LLC 619 797-3991
9009 Campo Rd Spring Valley (91977) ***(G-20402)***
B.T. Mancini Company, Milpitas *Also called B T Mancini Co Inc* ***(G-3106)***
B2b Payroll Services, Cypress *Also called B2b Staffing Services Inc* ***(G-14842)***
B2b Staffing Services Inc 714 243-4104
4141 Ball Rd Ste 150 Cypress (90630) ***(G-14842)***
Ba Leasing & Capital Corp (HQ) 415 765-1804
555 California St Fl 4 San Francisco (94104) ***(G-14516)***
Baart Behavioral Hlth Svcs Inc 415 928-7800
433 Turk St San Francisco (94102) ***(G-22663)***
Baart Behavioral Hlth Svcs Inc (PA) 415 552-7914
1145 Market St Fl 10 San Francisco (94103) ***(G-22664)***
Baart Community Healthcare 415 928-7800
433 Turk St San Francisco (94102) ***(G-22665)***
Babcock & Brown Holdings Inc (HQ) 415 512-1515
1 Pier Ste 3 San Francisco (94111) ***(G-9962)***
Babcock & Brown Latin America 415 512-1515
2 Harrison St Fl 6 San Francisco (94105) ***(G-9795)***
Babcock Laboratories Inc 951 653-3351
6100 Quail Valley Ct Riverside (92507) ***(G-26832)***
Babe Farms 805 928-3728
1293 W Stowell Rd Santa Maria (93458) ***(G-346)***
Babe's Bbq Grill, Newport Beach *Also called Donald Lucky LLC* ***(G-27007)***
Baby Dica Inc 818 988-0671
14501 Calvert St Van Nuys (91411) ***(G-18049)***
Babycenter LLC (HQ) 415 537-0900
163 Freelon St San Francisco (94107) ***(G-13735)***
Bacara Resorts and Spa, Santa Barbara *Also called Bcra Resort Services Inc* ***(G-12428)***
Bacchus Vineyard MGT LLC 707 837-8304
930 Shiloh Rd Bldg 17 Windsor (95492) ***(G-26934)***
Bacci Glinn Physcl Therapy Inc 559 733-2478
5533 W Hillsdale Ave A Visalia (93291) ***(G-20307)***
Bachelor Productions Inc 310 567-9249
2121 Avenue Of The Stars Los Angeles (90067) ***(G-18050)***
Bachem Americas Inc 760 597-8820
1271 Avenida Chelsea Vista (92081) ***(G-8980)***
Back Street Fitness Inc 707 254-7200
3175 California Blvd NAPA (94558) ***(G-18606)***
Backproject Corporation 408 730-1111
170 N Wolfe Rd Sunnyvale (94086) ***(G-7240)***
Backroads (PA) 510 527-1555
801 Cedar St Berkeley (94710) ***(G-4987)***
Backweb Technologies Inc 408 933-1700
2727 Walsh Ave Ste 102 Santa Clara (95051) ***(G-7098)***
Baco Realty Corporation 916 974-9898
6310 Stockton Blvd Sacramento (95824) ***(G-16567)***
Bacome Insurance Agency, Fresno *Also called James G Parker Insurance Assoc* ***(G-10752)***
Bacon's Multivision, Oakland *Also called Multivision Inc* ***(G-17343)***
Bacr, San Francisco *Also called Ruth Barajas* ***(G-24162)***
Bad Boys Bail Bonds Inc (PA) 408 298-3333
595 Park Ave Ste 200 San Jose (95110) ***(G-17018)***
Badalian Enterprises Inc 714 635-4082
1540 S Harbor Blvd Anaheim (92802) ***(G-12412)***
Badger Farming Company Inc 559 592-5520
150 W Pine St Exeter (93221) ***(G-214)***
Badgeville Inc 650 323-6668
805 Veterans Blvd Ste 307 Redwood City (94063) ***(G-15594)***
Bae Sys Sierra Detroit Allison (HQ) 510 635-8991
1755 Adams Ave San Leandro (94577) ***(G-17785)***
Bae Systems Inc 619 788-5000
10920 Technology Pl San Diego (92127) ***(G-17019)***
Bae Systems Land Armaments LP 408 289-0111
6331 San Ignacio Ave San Jose (95119) ***(G-25678)***
Bae Systems Maritime Engineeri 619 238-1000
7330 Engineer Rd Ste A San Diego (92111) ***(G-25679)***
Baechler Investigative Svcs 619 464-5600
4910 70th St San Diego (92115) ***(G-16568)***
Baer Institute, Petaluma *Also called Bay Area Envmtl Res Inst* ***(G-26484)***
Baghouse and Indus Shtmtl Svcs, Corona *Also called MS Industrial Shtmtl Inc* ***(G-3193)***
Baghouse Parts & Services Inc 800 584-4720
600 W Freedom Ave Orange (92865) ***(G-1402)***
Bagley, William T, San Francisco *Also called Nossaman LLP* ***(G-23474)***
Bahia Resort Hotels, San Diego *Also called Bh Partn A Calif Limit Partne* ***(G-12448)***
Bahia Sternwheelers Inc 858 539-7720
998 W Mission Bay Dr San Diego (92109) ***(G-4730)***
Baid Vivek 888 550-8553
2335 Irvine Ave Newport Beach (92660) ***(G-5564)***
Bail Hotline Bail Bonds, Riverside *Also called Dmcg Inc* ***(G-17128)***
Bailey, Rollin C MD, Lompoc *Also called Valley Medical Group of Lompoc* ***(G-20183)***
Bain & Company Inc 310 229-3000
1901 Ave Of The Sts 200 Ste 2000 Los Angeles (90067) ***(G-27337)***
Bain & Company Inc 415 627-1000
1 Embarcadero Ctr # 3500 San Francisco (94111) ***(G-27338)***
Baird-Neece Packing Corp 559 784-3393
60 S E St Porterville (93257) ***(G-510)***
Baja Construction Co Inc (PA) 925 229-0732
223 Foster St Martinez (94553) ***(G-3364)***
Baja Fresh, Chino Hills *Also called Gateway Fresh LLC* ***(G-12065)***
Baja Life Online Partners 949 376-4619
P.O. Box 4917 Laguna Beach (92652) ***(G-15049)***
Baja Metal Shredder LLC 847 622-9898
402 W Broadway Ste 1120 San Diego (92101) ***(G-8064)***
Bakbone Software Inc (HQ) 858 450-9009
9540 Towne Centre Dr # 100 San Diego (92121) ***(G-15050)***
Baked In Sun 760 591-9045
2560 Progress St Vista (92081) ***(G-8803)***
Baker Keener & Nahra 213 241-0900
633 W 5th St Fl 49 Los Angeles (90071) ***(G-23097)***
Baker & Hostetler LLP 310 820-8800
11601 Wilshire Blvd Fl 14 Los Angeles (90025) ***(G-23098)***
Baker & McKenzie LLP 415 576-3000
2 Embarcadero Ctr Fl 11 San Francisco (94111) ***(G-23099)***
Baker & McKenzie LLP 650 856-2400
660 Hansen Way Ste 1 Palo Alto (94304) ***(G-23100)***
Baker & Taylor LLC 858 457-2500
10350 Barnes Canyon Rd # 100 San Diego (92121) ***(G-9161)***
Baker Distributing Company LLC 760 708-4201
241 Market Pl Escondido (92029) ***(G-7753)***
Baker Hughes Incorporated 661 831-7686
3901 Fanucchi Way E Shafter (93263) ***(G-1068)***
Baker Keener & Nahra, Los Angeles *Also called Baker Keener & Nahra* ***(G-23097)***
Baker Mnock Jensen A Prof Corp 559 432-5400
5260 N Palm Ave Ste 421 Fresno (93704) ***(G-23101)***
Baker Mnock Jnsen Attys At Law, Fresno *Also called Baker Mnock Jensen A Prof Corp* ***(G-23101)***
Baker Petrolite Corporation 661 325-4138
5125 Boylan St Bakersfield (93308) ***(G-1069)***
Baker Places Inc 415 503-3137
101 Gough St San Francisco (94102) ***(G-22666)***
Baker Winokur 310 248-6169
9100 Wilshire Blvd 64w Beverly Hills (90212) ***(G-27733)***
Baker Winokur Ryder, Beverly Hills *Also called Bwr Public Relations* ***(G-27736)***
Bakercorp (HQ) 562 430-6262
3020 Old Ranch Pkwy # 220 Seal Beach (90740) ***(G-14517)***
Bakersfield Assc Rrtd Ctzns 661 834-2272
2240 S Union Ave Bakersfield (93307) ***(G-24312)***
Bakersfield Community Based, Bakersfield *Also called Veterans Health Administration* ***(G-20219)***
Bakersfield Country Club 661 871-4000
4200 Country Club Dr Bakersfield (93306) ***(G-18880)***
Bakersfield Dialysis Center 661 325-4741
5143 Office Park Dr Bakersfield (93309) ***(G-22617)***
Bakersfield District Office, Bakersfield *Also called State Compensation Insur Fund* ***(G-10462)***
Bakersfield Family Med Group 661 861-1835
4570 California Ave Bakersfield (93309) ***(G-17020)***
Bakersfield Family Medical Ctr, Bakersfield *Also called Heritage Medical Group* ***(G-19556)***
Bakersfield Healthcare 661 872-2121
2211 Mount Vernon Ave Bakersfield (93306) ***(G-20403)***
Bakersfield Heart Hospital, Bakersfield *Also called Medcath Incorporated* ***(G-22158)***
Bakersfield Kitchen & Bath 661 836-2284
3529 Pegasus Dr Bakersfield (93308) ***(G-2157)***
Bakersfield Memorial Hospital 661 327-1792
420 34th St Bakersfield (93301) ***(G-21459)***
Bakersfield Pipe and Sup Inc (PA) 661 589-9141
3301 Zachary Ave Shafter (93263) ***(G-7360)***
Bakersfield Rodeway Inn Inc 661 324-6666
818 Real Rd Bakersfield (93309) ***(G-12413)***
Bakersfield Symphony Orch 661 323-7928
1328 34th St Ste A Bakersfield (93301) ***(G-18457)***
Bakersfield Vet Center, Bakersfield *Also called Veterans Health Administration* ***(G-20221)***
Bakery Ex Southern Cal LLC 714 446-9470
1910 W Malvern Ave Fullerton (92833) ***(G-8804)***
Balance Staffing, San Jose *Also called Staffing Solutions Inc* ***(G-14795)***
Balance4kids 831 464-8669
4500 Soquel Dr Soquel (95073) ***(G-25204)***
Balboa Bay Club Inc (HQ) 949 645-5000
1221 W Coast Hwy Ste 145 Newport Beach (92663) ***(G-18881)***
Balboa Bay Club and Resort, Newport Beach *Also called International Bay Clubs LLC* ***(G-18962)***
Balboa Capital Corporation (PA) 949 756-0800
575 Anton Blvd Fl 12 Costa Mesa (92626) ***(G-9740)***
Balboa Enterprises Inc 650 961-6161
2530 Solace Pl Mountain View (94040) ***(G-20404)***
Balboa Plaza Admin Offices, Granada Hills *Also called Kaiser Foundation Hospitals* ***(G-19619)***
Balboa Water Group LLC 661 678-5109
28545 Livingston Ave Valencia (91355) ***(G-27846)***
Balboa Yacht Club 949 673-3515
1801 Bayside Dr Corona Del Mar (92625) ***(G-18882)***
Bald Eagle Security Svcs Inc 619 230-0022
3626 Main St San Diego (92113) ***(G-16569)***
Baldwin Hospitality LLC 626 962-6000
14635 Baldwin Ave Baldwin Park (91706) ***(G-12414)***
Balfour Beatty Cnstr LLC 510 903-2060
2335 Broadway Ste 300 Oakland (94612) ***(G-1496)***
Balfour Beatty Construction, San Diego *Also called Barnhart-Balfour Beatty Inc* ***(G-1498)***
Bali Construction Inc 626 442-8003
9852 Joe Vargas Way South El Monte (91733) ***(G-1907)***

ALPHABETIC

Ball Horticultural Company..........805 343-2723
400 Obispo St Guadalupe (93434) ***(G-265)***
Ball Tagawa Growers..........805 481-7526
819 Zenon Way Arroyo Grande (93420) ***(G-266)***
Ballard Clothing Design, Los Angeles *Also called W Scott Bllard Dsign Arch Inc* ***(G-17604)***
Ballard Rehabilitation Hosp, San Bernardino *Also called Vibra Hosp San Bernardino LLC* ***(G-22023)***
Ballard Rehabilitation Hosp, San Bernardino *Also called Robert Ballard Rehab Hospital* ***(G-20351)***
Ballard Spahr LLP..........424 204-4400
2029 Century Park E # 800 Los Angeles (90067) ***(G-23102)***
Ballard Spahr LLP..........619 696-9200
655 W Broadway Ste 1600 San Diego (92101) ***(G-23103)***
Balliet Bros Construction Corp..........650 871-9000
390 Swift Ave Ste 14 South San Francisco (94080) ***(G-1497)***
Bally Total Fitness Corp (HQ)..........562 484-2000
12440 Imperial Hwy # 300 Norwalk (90650) ***(G-18607)***
Bally Total Fitness Corp..........310 204-2030
3827 Overland Ave Wstsdew Culver City (90232) ***(G-18608)***
Bally Total Fitness Corp..........310 732-2100
28901 S Wstrn 315321 Rancho Palos Verdes (90275) ***(G-18609)***
Bally Total Fitness Corp..........858 831-0773
9850 Hibert St San Diego (92131) ***(G-18610)***
Bally Total Fitness Corp..........714 952-3101
310 S Magnolia Ave Anaheim (92804) ***(G-18611)***
Bally Total Fitness Corp..........909 625-2411
9385 Monte Vista Ave Montclair (91763) ***(G-18612)***
Bally Total Fitness Corp..........323 722-0994
2222 W Beverly Blvd Montebello (90640) ***(G-18613)***
Bally Total Fitness Corp..........619 474-6392
1910 Sweetwater Rd National City (91950) ***(G-18614)***
Baloian Farm, Fresno *Also called Baloian Packing Co Inc* ***(G-38)***
Baloian Farms, Fresno *Also called Baloian Packing Co Inc* ***(G-39)***
Baloian Packing Co Inc (PA)..........559 485-9200
446 N Blythe Ave Fresno (93706) ***(G-38)***
Baloian Packing Co Inc..........559 441-7043
3138 W Whites Bridge Ave Fresno (93706) ***(G-39)***
Baltazar Construction Inc..........626 339-8620
236 E Arrow Hwy Covina (91722) ***(G-3229)***
Bamko Inc..........310 470-5859
11620 Wilshire Blvd # 610 Los Angeles (90025) ***(G-13950)***
Bamko LLC..........310 470-5859
11620 Wilshire Blvd # 610 Los Angeles (90025) ***(G-17021)***
Banamex USA (HQ)..........310 203-3400
2029 Century Park E Fl 42 Los Angeles (90067) ***(G-9468)***
Banamex USA..........800 222-1234
2029 Century Park E # 4200 Los Angeles (90067) ***(G-9469)***
Banamex USA Bancorp (HQ)..........310 203-3440
2029 Century Park E Fl 42 Los Angeles (90067) ***(G-12039)***
Banc America Lsg & Capitl LLC (HQ)..........415 765-7349
555 California St Fl 4 San Francisco (94104) ***(G-9796)***
Banc California National Assn..........310 286-0710
10100 Santa Monica Blvd Los Angeles (90067) ***(G-9470)***
Banc California National Assn (HQ)..........877 770-2262
18500 Von Karman Ave Irvine (92612) ***(G-9567)***
BANC HOME LOANS, Irvine *Also called Banc California National Assn* ***(G-9567)***
Banc of California Inc..........714 569-0451
1403 N Tustin Ave Santa Ana (92705) ***(G-9317)***
Banc of California Inc..........310 835-9826
125 E Anaheim St Unit A Wilmington (90744) ***(G-9318)***
Banc of California Inc (PA)..........855 361-2262
18500 Von Karman Ave # 1100 Irvine (92612) ***(G-9319)***
Bandai Namco Entrmt Amer Inc..........408 235-2000
2051 Mission College Blvd Santa Clara (95054) ***(G-8038)***
Baney Corporation..........530 899-9090
2035 Business Ln Chico (95928) ***(G-12415)***
Bangkit (usa) Inc..........626 672-0888
10511 Valley Blvd El Monte (91731) ***(G-8160)***
Bangs Avenue Medical Offices, Modesto *Also called Kaiser Foundation Hospitals* ***(G-19630)***
Banister Electrical Inc..........925 778-7801
2532 Verne Roberts Cir Antioch (94509) ***(G-2526)***
Bank America National Assn..........559 445-7731
5292 N Palm Ave Fresno (93704) ***(G-9320)***
Bank America National Assn..........800 432-1000
1525 Market St San Francisco (94103) ***(G-9321)***
Bank America National Assn..........805 520-5100
450 American St Simi Valley (93065) ***(G-9771)***
Bank America National Assn..........415 913-5891
345 Montgomery St San Francisco (94104) ***(G-9322)***
Bank America National Assn..........530 891-7019
400 Broadway St Chico (95928) ***(G-9323)***
Bank America National Assn..........800 432-1000
345 N Brand Blvd Glendale (91203) ***(G-9324)***
Bank America National Assn..........562 624-4330
6351 E Spring St Long Beach (90808) ***(G-9325)***
Bank America National Assn..........818 898-3033
120 S Brand Blvd San Fernando (91340) ***(G-9326)***
Bank America National Assn..........800 432-1000
212 E Main St Visalia (93291) ***(G-9327)***
Bank America National Assn..........760 636-7500
73525 El Paseo Palm Desert (92260) ***(G-26935)***
Bank America National Assn..........310 384-4562
550 S Hill St Ste 101 Los Angeles (90013) ***(G-9328)***
Bank America National Assn..........916 326-3161
555 Capitol Mall Sacramento (95814) ***(G-26936)***
Bank America National Assn..........714 973-8495
13220 Harbor Blvd Garden Grove (92843) ***(G-9329)***
Bank America National Assn..........951 929-8614
1687 E Florida Ave Hemet (92544) ***(G-9330)***
Bank America National Assn..........800 432-1000
1450 W Redondo Beach Blvd Gardena (90247) ***(G-9331)***
Bank America National Assn..........909 393-3002
4100 Chino Hills Pkwy Chino Hills (91709) ***(G-9332)***
Bank America National Assn..........818 577-2000
5901 Canoga Ave Woodland Hills (91367) ***(G-9333)***
Bank America National Assn..........951 676-4114
27489 Ynez Rd Temecula (92591) ***(G-9334)***
Bank America National Assn..........415 913-3438
555 California St Ste 4 San Francisco (94104) ***(G-26644)***
Bank Leumi Le, Los Angeles *Also called Bank Leumi USA* ***(G-9335)***
Bank Leumi USA..........323 966-4700
555 W 5th St Fl 33 Los Angeles (90013) ***(G-9335)***
Bank of America, San Francisco *Also called Bankamerica Financial Inc* ***(G-9772)***
Bank of Commerce Mortgage, San Ramon *Also called Simonich Corporation* ***(G-9951)***
Bank of Hope (HQ)..........213 639-1700
3731 Wilshire Blvd # 400 Los Angeles (90010) ***(G-9336)***
Bank of Marin..........415 472-2265
4460 Redwood Hwy Ste 1 San Rafael (94903) ***(G-9471)***
Bank of Marin Bancorp (PA)..........415 763-4520
504 Redwood Blvd Fl 1 Novato (94947) ***(G-9472)***
Bank of Orient (HQ)..........415 338-0668
100 Pine St Ste 600 San Francisco (94111) ***(G-9473)***
Bank of Sierra, San Luis Obispo *Also called Bank of Sierra* ***(G-9337)***
Bank of Sierra..........805 541-0400
500 Marsh St San Luis Obispo (93401) ***(G-9337)***
Bank of Sierra (HQ)..........559 782-4300
90 N Main St Porterville (93257) ***(G-9474)***
Bank of Stockton (HQ)..........209 929-1600
301 E Miner Ave Stockton (95202) ***(G-9475)***
BANK OF THE WEST (HQ)..........415 765-4800
180 Montgomery St # 1400 San Francisco (94104) ***(G-9476)***
Bank of Tky-Mitsubishi Ufj Ltd..........213 488-3700
777 S Figueroa St Ste 600 Los Angeles (90017) ***(G-9544)***
Bankamerica Financial Inc..........415 622-3521
315 Montgomery St San Francisco (94104) ***(G-9772)***
Bankcard Services, Torrance *Also called Credit Card Services Inc* ***(G-17105)***
Bankcard Services (PA)..........213 365-1122
21281 S Western Ave Torrance (90501) ***(G-17022)***
Bankcard USA Merchant Srvc..........818 597-7000
5701 Lindero Canyon Rd Westlake Village (91362) ***(G-7041)***
Bankers Diversified Mortgage, Santa Ana *Also called American Transport Inc* ***(G-9816)***
Bankruptcy Management Cons, El Segundo *Also called BMC Group Inc* ***(G-23124)***
Bankruptcy MGT Solutions Inc..........949 222-1212
5 Peters Canyon Rd # 200 Irvine (92606) ***(G-23104)***
Bankserv, San Francisco *Also called Bserv Inc* ***(G-9712)***
Banner Bank..........916 648-2100
1750 Howe Ave Ste 100 Sacramento (95825) ***(G-9568)***
Banner Bank..........916 685-6546
9340 E Stockton Blvd Elk Grove (95624) ***(G-9338)***
Banner Bank..........619 243-7900
1350 Rosecrans St San Diego (92106) ***(G-9339)***
Banner Health..........530 251-3147
1800 Spring Ridge Dr Susanville (96130) ***(G-21460)***
Banner Lassen Medical Center..........530 252-2000
1800 Spring Ridge Dr Susanville (96130) ***(G-21461)***
Banquet Facilities..........951 360-2081
6000 Camino Real Riverside (92509) ***(G-13736)***
Banyan Solutions Inc..........650 766-9338
1067 Bryant Way Sunnyvale (94087) ***(G-14843)***
Banyon Transcription, Sunnyvale *Also called Banyan Solutions Inc* ***(G-14843)***
Bapko Metal Inc..........714 639-9380
838 N Cypress St Orange (92867) ***(G-3365)***
Bar Architects..........415 293-5700
901 Battery St Ste 300 San Francisco (94111) ***(G-26167)***
Bar Asscation of San Francisco (PA)..........415 982-1600
301 Battery St Fl 3 San Francisco (94111) ***(G-25118)***
BARA CONSTRUCTION, Danville *Also called Bara Infoware Inc* ***(G-25680)***
Bara Construction Services..........925 790-0130
2678 Bishop Dr Ste 116 San Ramon (94583) ***(G-1356)***
Bara Infoware Inc (PA)..........925 465-5354
4115 Blackhawk Plaza Cir Danville (94506) ***(G-25680)***
Barazani Outdoors Inc..........818 701-6977
14101 Valleyheart Dr # 104 Sherman Oaks (91423) ***(G-742)***
Barazani Pave Stone Inc..........818 701-6977
14546 Hamlin St Ste 201 Van Nuys (91411) ***(G-2803)***
Barbaccia Properties..........408 225-1010
165 Blossom Hill Rd San Jose (95123) ***(G-11244)***
Barbara Worth Resort, Calexico *Also called Adventures In Hospitality Inc* ***(G-18842)***
Barbour & Floyd Medical Assoc, Lynwood *Also called South Cntl Health & Rehab Prog* ***(G-22836)***
Barcelo Enterprises Inc..........760 728-3444
4400 Macarthur Blvd # 980 Newport Beach (92660) ***(G-267)***
Barcelon Associates MGT Corp..........925 627-7000
590 Lennon Ln Ste 110 Walnut Creek (94598) ***(G-11313)***
Barclays Capital Inc..........650 289-6000
155 Linfield Dr Menlo Park (94025) ***(G-9963)***
Barclays Capital Inc..........310 481-4100
10250 Santa Monica Blvd # 24 Los Angeles (90067) ***(G-9964)***
Barclays Globl Investors Funds..........415 597-2000
45 Fremont St Bsmt San Francisco (94105) ***(G-12104)***
Barco Fashions, Sun Valley *Also called Gilbert Barco* ***(G-17186)***
Barcott Frank A SEC Invstgtons..........714 891-8556
6446 San Andres Ave Cypress (90630) ***(G-16570)***
Barcott SEC & Investigations, Cypress *Also called Barcott Frank A SEC Invstgtons* ***(G-16570)***
Bare Elegance, Valley Village *Also called Imperial Project Inc* ***(G-18474)***

ALPHABETIC

ALPHABETIC SECTION
Bay City Flower Co (PA)

Barger & Wolen LLP ...415 434-2800
275 Battery St Ste 480 San Francisco (94111) ***(G-23105)***
Barkers Food Machinery, Irwindale *Also called Service Solutions Group LLC* ***(G-17943)***
Barlow Group (PA) ...213 250-4200
2000 Stadium Way Los Angeles (90026) ***(G-22115)***
Barlow Respiratory Hospital (PA) ...213 250-4200
2000 Stadium Way Los Angeles (90026) ***(G-22116)***
Barlow Respitory Hospital, Los Angeles *Also called Barlow Group* ***(G-22115)***
Barnes & Thornburg LLP ...310 284-3880
2029 Century Park E # 300 Los Angeles (90067) ***(G-23106)***
Barnes and Berger ...760 922-6136
1091 S Intake Blvd Blythe (92225) ***(G-490)***
Barney & Barney Inc (HQ) ...800 321-4696
9171 Twne Cntre Dr 500 San Diego (92122) ***(G-10642)***
Barnhart-Balfour Beatty Inc (HQ) ...858 635-7400
10620 Treena St Ste 300 San Diego (92131) ***(G-1498)***
Barnum & Celillo Electric Inc (PA) ...916 564-9976
135 Main Ave Ste A Sacramento (95838) ***(G-2527)***
Baron Pool Plst Sthern Cal Inc ...909 792-8891
495 Industrial Rd San Bernardino (92408) ***(G-3496)***
Barona Creek Golf Club ...619 387-7018
1932 Wildcat Canyon Rd Lakeside (92040) ***(G-18715)***
Barona Resort & Casino ...619 443-2300
1932 Wildcat Canyon Rd Lakeside (92040) ***(G-12416)***
Baronhr LLC ...909 517-3800
13085 Central Ave Ste 4 Chino (91710) ***(G-14613)***
Barr Engineering Inc ...562 944-1722
12612 Clark St Santa Fe Springs (90670) ***(G-2158)***
Barra LLC (HQ) ...510 548-5442
2100 Milvia St Berkeley (94704) ***(G-15595)***
Barra, Inc., Berkeley *Also called Barra LLC* ***(G-15595)***
Barracuda Networks Inc (PA) ...408 342-5400
3175 Winchester Blvd Campbell (95008) ***(G-15596)***
Barranca Medical Offices, Irvine *Also called Kaiser Foundation Hospitals* ***(G-21629)***
Barraza Farm Labor Contractor, Calipatria *Also called Frank Barraza* ***(G-662)***
Barrel Ten Quarter Circle Inc ...707 265-4000
33 Harlow Ct NAPA (94558) ***(G-9090)***
Barrett Business Services Inc ...650 653-7588
1840 Gateway Dr San Mateo (94404) ***(G-26937)***
Barrick Gold Corporation ...707 995-6070
26775 Morgan Valley Rd Lower Lake (95457) ***(G-1021)***
Barry McPherson Inc ...425 343-5000
1932 E Deere Ave Ste 240 Santa Ana (92705) ***(G-10643)***
Barrys Security Services Inc (PA) ...951 789-7575
16739 Van Buren Blvd Riverside (92504) ***(G-16571)***
Barrys Security Services Inc ...562 493-7007
5480 Katella Ave Ste 203 Los Alamitos (90720) ***(G-16572)***
Barstow Community Hospital, Barstow *Also called Hospital of Barstow Inc* ***(G-21607)***
Barstow Redevelopment Agency ...760 256-3531
220 E Mountain View St B Barstow (92311) ***(G-27847)***
Bart, Oakland *Also called San Francisco Bay Area Rapid* ***(G-3705)***
Bartco Lighting Inc ...714 230-3200
5761 Research Dr Huntington Beach (92649) ***(G-7417)***
Bartell Hotels ...619 224-3411
2303 Shelter Island Dr San Diego (92106) ***(G-12417)***
Bartell Hotels ...619 222-6440
1710 W Mission Bay Dr San Diego (92109) ***(G-12418)***
Bartell Hotels ...858 581-3500
610 Diamond St San Diego (92109) ***(G-12419)***
Bartell Hotels ...619 222-0561
2051 Shelter Island Dr San Diego (92106) ***(G-12420)***
Bartell Hotels ...858 453-5500
3299 Holiday Ct La Jolla (92037) ***(G-12421)***
Bartholomew Barry & Associates ...818 543-4000
701 N Brand Blvd Ste 800 Glendale (91203) ***(G-23107)***
Bartko Zankel Tarrant & Mil ...415 956-1900
1 Embarcadero Ctr Ste 800 San Francisco (94111) ***(G-23108)***
Bartlett Pringle & Wolf LLP ...805 564-2103
1123 Chapala St Ste 300 Santa Barbara (93101) ***(G-26292)***
Bartley Optical, Irwindale *Also called Essilor Laboratories Amer Inc* ***(G-7331)***
Barton Home Health and Hospice, South Lake Tahoe *Also called Barton Memorial Hospital* ***(G-24563)***
Barton Hospital ...530 543-5685
2170 South Ave South Lake Tahoe (96150) ***(G-21462)***
Barton Memorial Hospital ...530 543-5581
2092 Lake Tahoe Blvd # 500 South Lake Tahoe (96150) ***(G-24563)***
Barton Memorial Hospital ...530 659-7434
1111 Sierra At Tahoe Rd Twin Bridges (95735) ***(G-19365)***
Barton Ski Clinic At Sierra, Twin Bridges *Also called Healthcare Barton System* ***(G-17210)***
Barton Ski Clinic At Sierra, Twin Bridges *Also called Barton Memorial Hospital* ***(G-19365)***
Baseline Consulting Group Inc ...818 906-7638
15300 Ventura Blvd # 200 Sherman Oaks (91403) ***(G-27339)***
Basic Occpational Training Ctr, Perris *Also called Basic Occpational Training Ctr* ***(G-24879)***
Basic Occpational Training Ctr ...951 657-8028
1323 Jet Way Perris (92571) ***(G-24879)***
Basic Resources Inc (PA) ...209 521-9771
928 12th St Ste 700 Modesto (95354) ***(G-1738)***
Basile Construction Inc ...858 278-2739
7952 Armour St San Diego (92111) ***(G-1908)***
Bask Jewelry Inc ...831 479-8849
2607 S Main St Soquel (95073) ***(G-8094)***
Basket Basics, Carson *Also called Kole Imports* ***(G-9274)***
Basketball Marketing Co Inc ...866 866-1232
101 Enterprise Ste 100 Aliso Viejo (92656) ***(G-27340)***
Basquez Tiburcio Health Center ...510 471-5907
33255 9th St Union City (94587) ***(G-22667)***
Bass Tickets, Concord *Also called Bay Area Seating Service Inc* ***(G-19146)***
Bassard Convalescent & Med Hm (PA) ...510 537-6700
3269 D St Hayward (94541) ***(G-21148)***
Bassard Convalscent Home, Hayward *Also called Bassard Convalescent & Med Hm* ***(G-21148)***
Bassenian/Lagoni Architects ...949 553-9100
2031 Orchard Dr Ste 100 Newport Beach (92660) ***(G-26168)***
Basslake LLC ...559 642-3121
39255 Marina Dr Bass Lake (93604) ***(G-12422)***
Bassmnt, Newport Beach *Also called Downtown SD Ventures LLC* ***(G-19199)***
Bastanchury Waters Company Inc (PA) ...909 824-2430
2 Sterling Irvine (92618) ***(G-8805)***
Batchmaster Software, Laguna Hills *Also called Eworkplace Solutions Inc* ***(G-7130)***
Bateman Eichler Hill Richards, Woodland Hills *Also called Wells Fargo Advisors LLC* ***(G-10101)***
Bates Display & Packaging, Chino Hills *Also called Bates Sample Case Company Inc* ***(G-17023)***
Bates Sample Case Company Inc ...951 371-4922
5995 W Park Dr Chino Hills (91709) ***(G-17023)***
Battery Assist, Los Angeles *Also called Club Assist US LLC* ***(G-6721)***
Battery Ventures LP ...650 372-3939
2884 Sand Hill Rd Ste 101 Menlo Park (94025) ***(G-17024)***
Battery-Biz Inc ...805 437-7777
1380 Flynn Rd Camarillo (93012) ***(G-7099)***
Batth Farms, Caruthers *Also called Charanjit Singh Batth* ***(G-196)***
Bauer Hockey Inc ...818 782-6445
7855 Haskell Ave Ste 200 Van Nuys (91406) ***(G-8012)***
Bauers Intelligent Trnsp Inc (PA) ...415 522-1212
50 Pier San Francisco (94158) ***(G-3769)***
Bautista, Jennifer L, San Jose *Also called Robinson and Wood Inc* ***(G-23535)***
Bavarian Lion Company Cal (PA) ...707 545-8530
2777 4th St Santa Rosa (95405) ***(G-12423)***
Bavc, San Francisco *Also called Bay Area Video Coalition Inc* ***(G-18216)***
Baxter Healthcare Corporation ...805 372-3000
1 Baxter Way Ste 100 Westlake Village (91362) ***(G-8235)***
Baxter Healthcare Corporation ...303 222-6837
4551 E Philadelphia St Ontario (91761) ***(G-7241)***
Baxter Healthcare Corporation ...503 285-0212
700 Vaughn Rd Dixon (95620) ***(G-7242)***
Bay Advanced Tech 0045, Newark *Also called Bay Advanced Technologies LLC* ***(G-7822)***
Bay Advanced Technologies LLC ...510 857-0900
8100 Central Ave Newark (94560) ***(G-7822)***
Bay Alarm Company (PA) ...925 935-1100
60 Berry Dr Pacheco (94553) ***(G-2528)***
Bay Alarm Company ...510 452-3211
9836 Kitty Ln Oakland (94603) ***(G-26645)***
Bay Area Beverage, Richmond *Also called T F Louderback Inc* ***(G-9087)***
Bay Area Beverage Co ...510 965-6120
700 National Ct Richmond (94804) ***(G-9091)***
Bay Area Chapter of Sid, Los Gatos *Also called Society For Info Display* ***(G-25579)***
Bay Area Cnstr Framers Inc ...925 454-8514
1150 W Center St Ste 105 Manteca (95337) ***(G-3031)***
Bay Area Community Med Group, Los Angeles *Also called Santa Monica Bay Physicians He* ***(G-19961)***
Bay Area Community Svcs Inc (PA) ...510 613-0330
629 Oakland Ave Oakland (94611) ***(G-23676)***
Bay Area Credit Service LLC (PA) ...408 392-4425
1901 W 10th St Antioch (94509) ***(G-14019)***
Bay Area Credit Service LLC ...858 653-3824
10562 Caminito Flores San Diego (92126) ***(G-9653)***
Bay Area Distributing Coinc ...510 232-8554
1061 Factory St Richmond (94801) ***(G-9042)***
Bay Area Envmtl Res Inst ...707 938-9387
625 2nd St Ste 209 Petaluma (94952) ***(G-26484)***
Bay Area Garment, Hayward *Also called Early Transportation Services* ***(G-4144)***
Bay Area Installations Inc (PA) ...510 895-8196
2481 Verna Ct San Leandro (94577) ***(G-3497)***
Bay Area Intl Translation Svcs ...510 673-8912
46921 Warm Springs Blvd # 111 Fremont (94539) ***(G-17025)***
Bay Area Kenworth, San Leandro *Also called Ssmb Pacific Holding Co Inc* ***(G-6695)***
Bay Area News Group E Bay LLC (HQ) ...925 302-1683
6270 Houston Pl Ste A Dublin (94568) ***(G-13989)***
Bay Area Rescue Mission, Richmond *Also called Richmond Rescue Mission* ***(G-24158)***
Bay Area Seating Service Inc ...925 671-4000
1855 Gateway Blvd Ste 630 Concord (94520) ***(G-19146)***
Bay Area Senior Services Inc ...650 579-5500
1 Baldwin Ave Ofc San Mateo (94401) ***(G-23677)***
Bay Area Surgical MGT LLC ...408 297-3432
2110 Forest Ave Fl 2 San Jose (95128) ***(G-19366)***
Bay Area Techworkers ...925 359-2200
2000 Crow Canyon Pl # 150 San Ramon (94583) ***(G-14614)***
Bay Area Video Coalition Inc ...415 861-3282
2727 Mariposa St Fl 2 San Francisco (94110) ***(G-18216)***
Bay Area/Diablo Petroleum Co (HQ) ...925 228-2222
1340 Arnold Dr Ste 231 Martinez (94553) ***(G-9013)***
Bay Area/Diablo Petroleum Co ...925 228-2222
1800 Sutter St Concord (94520) ***(G-9014)***
Bay Bread LLC ...415 440-0356
2325 Pine St San Francisco (94115) ***(G-8806)***
Bay Brokerage Inc ...650 413-1721
17 Woodleaf Ave Redwood City (94061) ***(G-8458)***
Bay Cities Pav & Grading Inc ...925 687-6666
1450 Civic Ct Bldg B Concord (94520) ***(G-3419)***
Bay City Equipment Inds Inc ...619 938-8200
13625 Danielson St Poway (92064) ***(G-7418)***
Bay City Flower Co (PA) ...650 726-5535
2265 Cabrillo Hwy S Half Moon Bay (94019) ***(G-268)***

ALPHABETIC

Bay City Flower Co.......650 712-8147
1450 Cabrillo Hwy S Half Moon Bay (94019) *(G-269)*
Bay City Mechanical Inc.......510 233-7000
4124 Lakeside Dr Richmond (94806) *(G-2159)*
Bay City Television Inc (PA).......858 279-6666
8253 Ronson Rd San Diego (92111) *(G-5834)*
Bay Club Golden Gateway Inc.......415 616-8800
370 Drumm St San Francisco (94111) *(G-18883)*
Bay Club Hotel and Marina A C.......619 222-0314
2131 Shelter Island Dr San Diego (92106) *(G-12424)*
Bay Club Marin, Corte Madera *Also called Western Athletic Clubs Inc (G-18703)*
Bay Clubs Inc (HQ).......415 781-1874
1 Lombard St San Francisco (94111) *(G-18615)*
Bay Clubs Inc.......818 884-5034
22235 Sherman Way Canoga Park (91303) *(G-18884)*
Bay Counties Waste Svcs Inc.......408 565-9900
3355 Thomas Rd Santa Clara (95054) *(G-6436)*
Bay Equity Home Loans, Sausalito *Also called Bay Equity LLC (G-9820)*
Bay Equity LLC (PA).......415 632-5150
28 Liberty Ship Way # 2800 Sausalito (94965) *(G-9820)*
Bay Federal Credit Union (PA).......831 479-6000
3333 Clares St Capitola (95010) *(G-9590)*
Bay Grove Capital Group LLC (PA).......415 229-7953
423 Washington St Fl 7 San Francisco (94111) *(G-12105)*
Bay Imaging Cons Med Group Inc (PA).......925 296-7150
175 Lennon Ln Ste 100 Walnut Creek (94598) *(G-19367)*
Bay Management, San Mateo *Also called Archives Management Corp (G-26924)*
Bay Meadows Racing Association.......650 573-4500
2600 S Delaware St San Mateo (94403) *(G-18566)*
Bay Medic Transportation Inc.......800 689-9511
959 Detroit Ave Concord (94518) *(G-3770)*
Bay Medical Management LLC.......925 296-7150
2125 Oak Grove Rd Ste 200 Walnut Creek (94598) *(G-19368)*
Bay Photo Inc.......831 475-6090
2959 Park Ave Ste A Soquel (95073) *(G-13659)*
Bay Point Healthcare Center, Hayward *Also called Kissito Health Care Inc (G-22495)*
Bay Porter Ex Arprt Shuttle.......415 467-1800
27 Industrial Way Brisbane (94005) *(G-3636)*
Bay Rosie Hotel LLP.......619 276-4010
1775 E Mission Bay Dr San Diego (92109) *(G-12425)*
Bay Span Inc.......707 863-4949
260 Link Rd Ste D Fairfield (94534) *(G-14844)*
Bay Standard Inc.......925 634-1181
24485 Marsh Creek Rd Brentwood (94513) *(G-7924)*
Bay Standard Manufacturing Inc (PA).......925 634-1181
24485 Marsh Creek Rd Brentwood (94513) *(G-7676)*
Bay Valley Medical Group Inc (PA).......510 785-5000
27212 Calaroga Ave Hayward (94545) *(G-19369)*
Bay View Rhbilitation Hosp LLC.......510 521-5600
516 Willow St Alameda (94501) *(G-20405)*
Bay West Shwplace Invstors LLC (PA).......415 490-5800
2 Henry Adams St Ste 450 San Francisco (94103) *(G-10962)*
Bay-TEC Engineering (PA).......707 252-6575
5130 Fulton Dr Ste X Fairfield (94534) *(G-25681)*
Baybridge Employment Services, Eureka *Also called Humboldt Commnty Accss Resrc (G-24016)*
Bayco Financial Corporation (PA).......310 378-8181
24050 Madison St Ste 101 Torrance (90505) *(G-11314)*
Bayer Healthcare LLC.......415 437-5800
455 Mission Bay Blvd S # 493 San Francisco (94158) *(G-26485)*
Bayer Healthcare LLC.......510 705-7539
717 Potter St Street-2 Berkeley (94710) *(G-26486)*
Bayer Protective Services Inc.......916 486-5800
3436 Amrcn Rver Dr Ste 10 Sacramento (95864) *(G-16870)*
Baymarr Constructors Inc (PA).......661 395-1676
6950 Mcdivitt Dr Bakersfield (93313) *(G-3230)*
Baynote Inc.......866 921-0919
333 W San Carlos St # 700 San Jose (95110) *(G-16220)*
Bayonet/Blackhorse Golf Course, Seaside *Also called Bsl Golf Corp (G-18718)*
Bayorg.......415 623-5300
Embarcadero At Beach St San Francisco (94133) *(G-25058)*
Baypoint Trading, San Francisco *Also called Btig LLC (G-9967)*
Baysand Inc.......408 960-8263
6910 Santa Teresa Blvd San Jose (95119) *(G-7532)*
Bayscape Management Inc.......408 288-2940
1350 Pacific Ave Alviso (95002) *(G-26938)*
Bayshore Ambulance Inc (PA).......650 525-9700
370 Hatch Dr Foster City (94404) *(G-3771)*
Bayshore Healthcare Inc.......805 544-5100
3033 Augusta St San Luis Obispo (93401) *(G-20406)*
Bayside Care Center, Morro Bay *Also called Compass Health Inc (G-21190)*
Bayside Interiors Inc (PA).......510 580-3950
3220 Darby Cmn Fremont (94539) *(G-2861)*
Bayside Medical Group, San Ramon *Also called Lucile Salter Packard Chil (G-19723)*
Bayside Rhabilitation Care Ctr, San Diego *Also called Preferred Care West Inc (G-20858)*
Bayside Solutions Inc.......760 448-2970
1917 Palomar Oaks Way # 130 Carlsbad (92008) *(G-14845)*
Bayspring Medical Group A Pro.......415 674-2600
1199 Bush St Ste 500 San Francisco (94109) *(G-19370)*
Bayview Engrg & Cnstr Co Inc.......916 939-8986
5040 Rbert J Mathews Pkwy El Dorado Hills (95762) *(G-2160)*
Bayview Hospital and Mental.......619 426-6311
330 Moss St Chula Vista (91911) *(G-22041)*
Bayview Hunters Point Y M C A.......415 822-7728
1601 Lane St San Francisco (94124) *(G-25205)*
Bayview Preservation LP.......415 285-7344
5 Commer Ct San Francisco (94124) *(G-11092)*
Bayview Properties Inc.......831 655-7650
2600 Sand Dunes Dr Monterey (93940) *(G-12426)*
Bayview Properties Inc.......831 624-1841
3665 Rio Rd Carmel (93923) *(G-12427)*
Bayview Properties Inc (PA).......831 394-3321
2600 Sand Dunes Dr Monterey (93940) *(G-26939)*
Baywood Court (PA).......510 733-2102
21966 Dolores St Apt 279 Castro Valley (94546) *(G-22374)*
Baywood Court Retirement Ctr, Castro Valley *Also called Baywood Court (G-22374)*
Bazan Mario AG Services & Vine.......707 945-0718
1984 Yountville Cross Rd Yountville (94599) *(G-142)*
Bazan Mrio Vinyrd Mgmt AG Svcs, Yountville *Also called Bazan Mario AG Services & Vine (G-142)*
Bazic Product, El Monte *Also called Bangkit (usa) Inc (G-8160)*
BB&k, Riverside *Also called Best Best & Krieger LLP (G-23113)*
Bbam Arcft Holdings 137 Labuan.......415 267-1600
50 California St Fl 14 San Francisco (94111) *(G-14518)*
Bbam Arcft Holdings 139 Labuan, San Francisco *Also called Bbam US LP (G-9965)*
Bbam US LP.......415 267-1600
50 California St Fl 14 San Francisco (94111) *(G-9965)*
Bbcn Bank.......213 389-5550
550 S Western Ave Los Angeles (90020) *(G-9477)*
BBDO Worldwide Inc.......415 808-6200
600 California St Fl 8 San Francisco (94108) *(G-13819)*
Bbhs, San Francisco *Also called Baart Behavioral Hlth Svcs Inc (G-22664)*
Bbk Performance Inc.......951 296-1771
27440 Bostik Ct Temecula (92590) *(G-6713)*
Bbt Health LLC.......559 222-0007
5105 E Dakota Ave Fresno (93727) *(G-22375)*
Bc Contractors, Gonzales *Also called Bulmaro Castro Contractors (G-14617)*
Bc Laboratories Inc.......661 327-4911
4100 Atlas Ct Bakersfield (93308) *(G-26833)*
Bc Traffic Specialists, Orange *Also called B C Rentals Inc (G-7821)*
Bc2 Environmental, Orange *Also called Beks Acquisition Inc (G-3353)*
Bcbg Max Azria Group LLC.......213 624-2224
2865 Fruitland Ave Ste F Vernon (90058) *(G-8367)*
Bcbg Max Azria Group LLC.......323 589-2224
2761 Fruitland Ave Vernon (90058) *(G-8368)*
Bcbg Max Azria Group LLC (PA).......323 589-2224
2761 Fruitland Ave Vernon (90058) *(G-8369)*
Bcci Builders, San Francisco *Also called Bcci Construction Company (G-1499)*
Bcci Construction Company (PA).......415 817-5100
1160 Battery St Ste 250 San Francisco (94111) *(G-1499)*
BCI Coca-Cola Btlg Los Angeles.......818 362-4307
12925 Bradley Ave Sylmar (91342) *(G-8807)*
BCII, North Hills *Also called Brentwood Cmmncations Intl Inc (G-18053)*
BCM Construction Company Inc.......530 342-1722
2990 State Highway 32 # 100 Chico (95973) *(G-1403)*
Bcp Systems Inc.......714 202-3900
1560 S Sinclair St Anaheim (92806) *(G-16287)*
Bcra Resort Services Inc.......805 571-3176
8301 Hollister Ave Santa Barbara (93117) *(G-12428)*
Bdc Distribution Center, Redlands *Also called Becton Dickinson and Company (G-7243)*
Bdl, Torrance *Also called Bio-Diagnostics Laboratories (G-22190)*
Bdl Prosthetics, Irvine *Also called James R Glidewell Dental (G-22308)*
Bdna Corporation (PA).......650 625-9530
339 Bernardo Ave Ste 206 Mountain View (94043) *(G-15597)*
Bdo Usa LLP.......415 397-7900
1 Market Spear Tower Ste 1100 San Francisco (94104) *(G-26293)*
Bdo Usa LLP.......858 404-9200
4250 Executive Sq Ste 600 La Jolla (92037) *(G-26294)*
Bdo Usa LLP.......408 278-0220
50 W San Fernando St # 200 San Jose (95113) *(G-26295)*
Bdo Usa LLP.......714 957-3200
600 Anton Blvd Ste 500 Costa Mesa (92626) *(G-26296)*
Bdp Bowl Inc.......650 878-0300
900 King Plz Daly City (94015) *(G-18510)*
BDR Industries Inc (PA).......661 940-8554
820 E Avenue L12 Lancaster (93535) *(G-5935)*
BDS Marketing Inc (PA).......949 472-6700
10 Holland Irvine (92618) *(G-13820)*
BDS Plumbing Inc.......925 939-1004
2125 Youngs Ct Walnut Creek (94596) *(G-2161)*
Be Wise Ranch, San Diego *Also called William Brammer (G-8791)*
Bea Systems Inc (HQ).......650 506-7000
2315 N 1st St San Jose (95131) *(G-15051)*
Beach & Tennis Club, Pebble Beach *Also called Lone Cypress Company LLC (G-18981)*
Beach and La Mirada Car Wash.......714 994-1099
5231 Beach Blvd Buena Park (90621) *(G-17830)*
Beach Cities 16 Cinemas, El Segundo *Also called Pacific Theaters Inc (G-18341)*
Beach Cities Eldercare Inc (PA).......562 596-4884
5500 E Atherton St # 204 Long Beach (90815) *(G-22376)*
Beach Cities Health District.......310 318-7939
514 N Prospect Ave Fl 3 Redondo Beach (90277) *(G-24880)*
Beach Cities Invest & Protctn.......310 322-4724
2500 Via Cabrillo Marina San Pedro (90731) *(G-16573)*
Beach Cities Memory Care Cmnty, Redondo Beach *Also called Silverado Senior Living Inc (G-20916)*
Beach Club.......310 395-3254
201 Palisades Beach Rd Santa Monica (90402) *(G-18885)*
Beach Motel Partners Ltd.......800 755-0222
28 W Cabrillo Blvd Santa Barbara (93101) *(G-12429)*
Beachbody LLC (PA).......310 883-9000
3301 Exposition Blvd Fl 3 Santa Monica (90404) *(G-13959)*
BEACHSIDE NURSING CENTER, Huntington Beach *Also called Sea Breeze Health Care Inc (G-20900)*
Beachside Realtors (PA).......714 969-6100
19671 Beach Blvd Ste 101 Huntington Beach (92648) *(G-11315)*

ALPHABETIC

Beachside Realtors....909 606-1299
4197 Chino Hills Pkwy Chino Hills (91709) ***(G-3498)***
Beachside Realtors....562 947-7834
15820 Whittier Blvd Ste B Whittier (90603) ***(G-11316)***
Beachsports Inc....310 372-2202
600 N Catalina Ave Redondo Beach (90277) ***(G-13460)***
Beacon Accunting Resources LLC....949 981-5946
1818 Glenwood Ln Newport Beach (92660) ***(G-27341)***
Beacon Health Options Inc....714 763-2405
10805 Holder St Ste 300 Cypress (90630) ***(G-23678)***
Beacon Healthcare Services....949 650-9750
1501 E 16th St Newport Beach (92663) ***(G-22042)***
Beacon Resources LLC....949 955-1773
4 Corporate Plaza Dr # 101 Newport Beach (92660) ***(G-27342)***
Beacon Roofing Supply Inc....408 293-5947
200 San Jose Ave San Jose (95125) ***(G-7007)***
Beacon Sales Acquisition Inc....714 288-1974
1201 E Mcfadden Ave Santa Ana (92705) ***(G-7008)***
Bead Society....805 495-2550
1454 Valley High Ave Thousand Oaks (91362) ***(G-25505)***
Bead Society , The, Thousand Oaks *Also called Bead Society* ***(G-25505)***
Beador Construction Co Inc....951 674-7352
26320 Lester Cir Corona (92883) ***(G-1739)***
Beam "easy Living" Center, Grass Valley *Also called Beam Vacuums California Inc* ***(G-2529)***
Beam Vacuums California Inc....916 564-3279
422 Henderson St Grass Valley (95945) ***(G-2529)***
Bear Creek Golf & Country Club, Murrieta *Also called Bear Creek Golf Club Inc* ***(G-18886)***
Bear Creek Golf Club Inc....951 677-8621
22640 Bear Creek Dr N Murrieta (92562) ***(G-18886)***
Bear Creek Manor....209 723-4674
2929 M St Merced (95348) ***(G-11093)***
Bear Creek Partners LLC....951 677-8621
22640 Bear Creek Dr N Murrieta (92562) ***(G-18887)***
Bear Data Solutions Inc....415 788-1501
300 Broadway Ste 24 San Francisco (94133) ***(G-7100)***
Bear Data Solutions Inc....858 824-2920
11189 Sorrento Valley Rd # 103 San Diego (92121) ***(G-15908)***
Bear Data Solutions Inc....949 833-3282
2485 Mccabe Way Ste 100 Irvine (92614) ***(G-15909)***
Bear Flag Marketing Corp....415 899-8466
7599 Redwood Blvd Ste 200 Novato (94945) ***(G-22377)***
Bear River Casino....707 733-9644
11 Bear Paws Way Loleta (95551) ***(G-12430)***
Bear River Casino Hotel, Loleta *Also called Bear River Casino* ***(G-12430)***
Bear River Veterinary Clinic....530 633-2957
6998 Eric Ln Wheatland (95692) ***(G-636)***
Bear Stearns, Del Mar *Also called JP Morgan Securities LLC* ***(G-10021)***
Bear Stearns Companies LLC....949 856-8300
1833 Alton Pkwy Irvine (92606) ***(G-9821)***
Bear Stern Residential Mrtg, Irvine *Also called Bear Stearns Companies LLC* ***(G-9821)***
Bear Trucking Inc....909 799-1616
19768 Kendall Dr San Bernardino (92407) ***(G-4330)***
Bear Valley Mountain Resort, Bear Valley *Also called Bear Valley Ski Co* ***(G-19147)***
Bear Valley Ski Co....209 753-2301
2280 State Rte 207 Bear Valley (95223) ***(G-19147)***
Bear Valley Springs Assn....661 821-5537
29541 Rollingoak Dr Tehachapi (93561) ***(G-25206)***
Bear Vly Cmnty Healthcare Dst (PA)....909 866-6501
41870 Garstin Dr Big Bear Lake (92315) ***(G-21463)***
Bear Vly Fbrcators Stl Sup Inc....760 247-5381
22060 Bear Valley Rd Apple Valley (92308) ***(G-1404)***
Bearing Engineers Inc (PA)....949 586-7442
27 Argonaut Aliso Viejo (92656) ***(G-7925)***
Beating Wall Street Inc (PA)....818 332-9696
14934 Dickens St Apt 16 Sherman Oaks (91403) ***(G-27343)***
Beats Music LLC....415 590-5104
235 2nd St San Francisco (94105) ***(G-15598)***
Beau Wine Tours, Sonoma *Also called Appellation Tours Inc* ***(G-4986)***
Beauchamp Distributing Company....310 639-5320
1911 S Santa Fe Ave Compton (90221) ***(G-9043)***
Beaulieu Group LLC....714 522-2080
15130 Northam St La Mirada (90638) ***(G-6847)***
Beaumont Care Center, Cherry Valley *Also called David-Kleis Inc* ***(G-20512)***
Beaumont Unified School Dst....951 845-3010
1001 Cougar Way Beaumont (92223) ***(G-3912)***
Beautitudes Beauty Supply LLC....800 830-6076
7850 White Ln Ste E Bakersfield (93309) ***(G-7964)***
Beauty 21 Cosmetics Inc....909 945-2220
2021 S Archibald Ave Ontario (91761) ***(G-8236)***
Beauty Bazar Inc....650 326-8522
36 Stanford Shopping Ctr Palo Alto (94304) ***(G-13667)***
Beauty Recognized LP....310 278-7646
224 Via Rodeo Dr Beverly Hills (90210) ***(G-13668)***
Beauty Service Inc....760 434-4141
2946 State St Ste F Carlsbad (92008) ***(G-13669)***
Beaver Medical Clinic, Highland *Also called Beaver Medical Group LP* ***(G-19372)***
Beaver Medical Clinic Inc (PA)....909 793-3311
1615 Orange Tree Ln Redlands (92374) ***(G-19371)***
Beaver Medical Group LP (HQ)....909 425-3321
7000 Boulder Ave Highland (92346) ***(G-19372)***
Beazer Pre-Owned Rental Homes, Agoura Hills *Also called Amh Portfolio One LLC* ***(G-12237)***
Becho Inc....818 362-8391
15901 Olden St Sylmar (91342) ***(G-1740)***
Bechtel, Livermore *Also called National Security Tech LLC* ***(G-25986)***
Bechtel Capital MGT Corp....415 768-1234
50 Beale St San Francisco (94105) ***(G-26940)***
Bechtel Corporation (HQ)....415 768-1234
50 Beale St San Francisco (94105) ***(G-25682)***
Bechtel Energy Corporation....415 768-1234
50 Beale St Bsmt 1 San Francisco (94105) ***(G-25683)***
Bechtel Enterprises Holdings (HQ)....415 768-1234
50 Beale St Ste 2200 San Francisco (94105) ***(G-25684)***
Bechtel Entps Holdings Inc....415 768-6745
50 Beale St Bsmt 1 San Francisco (94105) ***(G-1500)***
Bechtel Group Inc (PA)....415 768-1234
50 Beale St Bsmt 1 San Francisco (94105) ***(G-25685)***
Beck Group, The, Beverly Hills *Also called Beck International Inc* ***(G-1405)***
Beck International Inc....310 281-2980
9641 Sunset Blvd Beverly Hills (90210) ***(G-1405)***
Beckman Research Inst Hope....626 359-8111
1500 Duarte Rd Duarte (91010) ***(G-26738)***
Becton Dickinson and Company....909 748-7300
2200 W San Bernardino Ave Redlands (92374) ***(G-7243)***
Bedon Construction Inc....951 246-9005
27989 Holland Rd Menifee (92584) ***(G-25686)***
Bedrock Company....951 273-1931
2970 Myers St Riverside (92503) ***(G-3231)***
Bedrosian Farms Inc....559 834-5981
8333 S Sunnyside Ave Fowler (93625) ***(G-143)***
Beech Street Corporation (HQ)....949 672-1000
25500 Commercentre Dr # 100 Lake Forest (92630) ***(G-26941)***
Been Enterprises....559 298-8864
755 N Peach Ave Ste F11 Clovis (93611) ***(G-1133)***
Beethoven Holdings Inc....559 733-4100
400 E Main St Ste 110 Visalia (93291) ***(G-11317)***
Begroup (PA)....818 638-4563
516 Burchett St Glendale (91203) ***(G-21149)***
Begroup....714 282-1409
1525 E Taft Ave Orange (92865) ***(G-20407)***
Begroup....626 359-9371
1763 Royal Oaks Dr Ofc Duarte (91010) ***(G-20408)***
Behalf of San Francisco Campus, San Francisco *Also called University Cal San Francisco* ***(G-26453)***
Behappy.me, Chatsworth *Also called Idea Bits LLC* ***(G-16951)***
Behavioral H Bakersfield....661 398-1800
5201 White Ln Bakersfield (93309) ***(G-22043)***
Behavioral Health, Lancaster *Also called Kaiser Foundation Hospitals* ***(G-19624)***
Behavioral Health and Recovery, Ceres *Also called Stanislaus Recovery Center* ***(G-22841)***
Behavioral Health Care Svcs, Oakland *Also called Alameda County* ***(G-23650)***
Behavioral Health Resources....951 275-8400
5900 Brockton Ave Riverside (92506) ***(G-22044)***
Behavioral Health Services, Mount Shasta *Also called County of Siskiyou* ***(G-22712)***
Behavioral Health Services Inc (PA)....310 679-9031
15519 Crenshaw Blvd Gardena (90249) ***(G-23679)***
Behavioral Health Services Inc....562 599-4194
1775 Chestnut Ave Long Beach (90813) ***(G-23680)***
Behavioral Health Services Inc....909 865-2336
2180 Valley Blvd Pomona (91768) ***(G-23681)***
Behavioral Health Svcs Dept, Long Beach *Also called Childnet Youth & Fmly Svcs Inc* ***(G-24593)***
Behavioral Hlth Recovery Svcs, Modesto *Also called County of Stanislaus* ***(G-24911)***
Behavioral Intervention Assn....510 652-7445
2354 Powell St A Emeryville (94608) ***(G-14846)***
Behavioral Medicine Center, Redlands *Also called Loma Linda University Med Ctr* ***(G-21714)***
Behavioral Support Partnership, Villa Park *Also called Melissa Sweitzer PHD Inc* ***(G-22083)***
Behr Process Sales Company....714 545-7101
3000 S Main St Apt 84e Santa Ana (92707) ***(G-27734)***
Behringer Harvard Wilshire....310 475-8711
10740 Wilshire Blvd Los Angeles (90024) ***(G-12431)***
Behringer Harvard Wilshire Blv....310 475-8711
10740 Wilshire Blvd Los Angeles (90024) ***(G-12432)***
Being Fit Inc....858 483-9294
4971 Clairemont Dr Ste A San Diego (92117) ***(G-18616)***
Beitler & Associates Inc (PA)....310 820-2955
825 S Barrington Ave Los Angeles (90049) ***(G-11318)***
Beitler Commercial Realty Svcs, Los Angeles *Also called Beitler & Associates Inc* ***(G-11318)***
Bejac Corporation (PA)....714 528-6224
569 S Van Buren St Placentia (92870) ***(G-7823)***
Bekins Moving & Storage, Santa Fe Springs *Also called Bekins Moving Solutions Inc* ***(G-4331)***
Bekins Moving Solutions Inc (PA)....714 736-6100
12610 Shoemaker Ave Santa Fe Springs (90670) ***(G-4331)***
Beks Acquisition Inc....714 744-2990
1150 W Trenton Ave Orange (92867) ***(G-3353)***
Bel Air Security Solutions, Beverly Hills *Also called A Sutton Carlos* ***(G-16534)***
Bel Esprit Builders Inc....949 709-3500
20902 Bake Pkwy Ste 100 Lake Forest (92630) ***(G-1501)***
Bel Vista Convalescent Hosp, Long Beach *Also called Villa De La Mar Inc* ***(G-21412)***
Bel Vista Convalescent Hosp, Pasadena *Also called Robert C Hamilton* ***(G-24790)***
Bel-Air Bay Club Ltd....310 230-4700
16801 Pacific Coast Hwy Pacific Palisades (90272) ***(G-25207)***
Bel-Air Country Club....310 472-9563
10768 Bellagio Rd Los Angeles (90077) ***(G-18888)***
Belcampo Butchery....530 842-5200
329 N Phillipe Ln Yreka (96097) ***(G-13737)***
Belcampo Group Inc....510 250-7810
65 Webster St Oakland (94607) ***(G-461)***
Belcampo Meat, Yreka *Also called Belcampo Butchery* ***(G-13737)***
Belectric Inc (HQ)....510 896-3940
951 Mariners Island Blvd San Mateo (94404) ***(G-2024)***
Belinda, Los Angeles *Also called Xenos Fashion Inc* ***(G-8417)***
Belkin Components, Playa Vista *Also called Belkin International Inc* ***(G-7533)***

Belkin International Inc (PA) — 310 751-5100
  12045 Waterfront Dr Playa Vista (90094) *(G-7533)*
Bell Gardens Bicycle Club Inc — 562 806-4646
  888 Bicycle Casino Dr Bell Gardens (90201) *(G-19148)*
Bell Pipe & Supply Co — 714 772-3200
  215 E Ball Rd Anaheim (92805) *(G-7926)*
Bell Private Security Inc — 714 964-9381
  18030 Brookhurst St Fountain Valley (92708) *(G-16574)*
Bell Products Inc — 707 255-1811
  722 Soscol Ave NAPA (94559) *(G-2162)*
Bella Limousines — 619 302-4062
  4502 Melisa Way San Diego (92117) *(G-3772)*
Bella Terra Carwash, Huntington Beach Also called Russell Fisher Partnership *(G-17861)*
Bella Terra Technologies Inc — 650 316-6660
  1600 Amphitheatre Pkwy Mountain View (94043) *(G-6060)*
Bella Vista Healthcare Center — 909 985-2731
  933 E Deodar St Ontario (91764) *(G-20409)*
Bellavsta Trnstional Care Ctr, San Luis Obispo Also called Bayshore Healthcare Inc *(G-20406)*
Bellavista Landscape Svcs Inc — 831 461-1761
  340 Twin Pines Dr Scotts Valley (95066) *(G-743)*
Bellflower Dental Group, Bellflower Also called Peter Wylan DDS *(G-20270)*
Bellis Steel Company Inc (PA) — 818 886-5601
  8740 Vanalden Ave Northridge (91324) *(G-3366)*
Belmont Athletic Club — 562 438-3816
  4918 E 2nd St Long Beach (90803) *(G-18889)*
Belmont Bruns Construction Inc — 408 977-1708
  1125 Mabury Rd San Jose (95133) *(G-1502)*
Belmont Convalescent Hospital, Long Beach Also called Country Villa Blmnt Hght Hlth *(G-21193)*
Belmont Corporation — 530 542-1101
  901 Park Ave South Lake Tahoe (96150) *(G-12433)*
Belmont Oaks Academy — 650 593-6175
  2200 Carlmont Dr Belmont (94002) *(G-24416)*
Belmont Shores Kindercare, Long Beach Also called Kindercare Learning Ctrs LLC *(G-24474)*
Belmont Village LP — 408 720-8498
  1039 E El Camino Real Sunnyvale (94087) *(G-11094)*
Belmont Village LP — 858 486-5020
  13075 Evening Creek Dr S San Diego (92128) *(G-21150)*
Belmont Village LP — 818 972-2405
  455 E Angeleno Ave Burbank (91501) *(G-11095)*
Belmont Village LP — 310 377-9977
  5701 Crestridge Rd Rancho Palos Verdes (90275) *(G-11096)*
Belmont Village LP — 323 874-7711
  2051 N Highland Ave Los Angeles (90068) *(G-11097)*
Belmont Village At Sabre Sprng, San Diego Also called Belmont Village LP *(G-21150)*
Belmont Village of Hollywood, Los Angeles Also called Belmont Village LP *(G-11097)*
Belmont Village of Sunnyvale, Sunnyvale Also called Belmont Village LP *(G-11094)*
Belvedere Hotel Partnership — 310 551-2888
  9882 Santa Monica Blvd Beverly Hills (90212) *(G-12434)*
Belvedere Partnership — 310 551-2888
  9882 Santa Monica Blvd Beverly Hills (90212) *(G-12435)*
Belville Enterprises Inc — 858 652-6960
  6225 Nancy Ridge Dr San Diego (92121) *(G-19373)*
Bemus Landscape Inc — 714 557-7910
  1225 Puerta Del Sol # 500 San Clemente (92673) *(G-2025)*
Ben Bennett Inc (PA) — 949 209-9712
  3419 Via Lido 646 Newport Beach (92663) *(G-21151)*
Ben Bollinger Productions Inc — 909 626-3296
  455 W Foothill Blvd Claremont (91711) *(G-18371)*
Ben F Smith Inc — 858 271-4320
  8655 Miramar Pl Ste B San Diego (92121) *(G-3232)*
Ben Myerson Candy Co Inc (PA) — 323 724-1700
  6550 E Washington Blvd Commerce (90040) *(G-9092)*
Ben Myerson Candy Co Inc — 510 236-2233
  3463 Collins Ave Richmond (94806) *(G-9093)*
Benchmark Internet Group LLC — 562 286-6820
  10621 Calle Lee Ste 141 Los Alamitos (90720) *(G-16328)*
Benchmark Landscape Inc — 858 513-7190
  12575 Stowe Dr Poway (92064) *(G-812)*
Benchmark-Tech Corporation — 831 475-5600
  1 Chaminade Ln Santa Cruz (95065) *(G-17026)*
Benchmaster Furniture LLC — 714 414-0240
  1481 N Hundley St Anaheim (92806) *(G-6805)*
Benco Dental Supply Co — 714 424-0977
  3590 Harbor Gtwy N Costa Mesa (92626) *(G-7244)*
Beneficent Technology Inc — 650 644-3400
  480 S California Ave # 201 Palo Alto (94306) *(G-17027)*
Beneficial Administration Co — 949 756-1000
  17701 Mitchell N Irvine (92614) *(G-10644)*
Benefit & Risk Management Svcs — 916 467-1200
  80 Iron Point Cir Ste 200 Folsom (95630) *(G-10645)*
Benefit Planning, Marina Del Rey Also called Veba Administrators Inc *(G-10922)*
Benefit Programs ADM, City of Industry Also called Management Applied Programming *(G-16156)*
Benefitvision Inc — 818 348-3100
  5550 Topanga Canyon Blvd # 180 Woodland Hills (91367) *(G-24313)*
Benetech, Palo Alto Also called Beneficent Technology Inc *(G-17027)*
Benetech Inc (PA) — 916 484-6811
  3947 Lennane Dr Ste 250 Sacramento (95834) *(G-27244)*
Benetech Inc — 916 484-6811
  4420 Auburn Blvd Fl 2 Sacramento (95841) *(G-10646)*
Benetrac, San Diego Also called Paychex Benefit Tech Inc *(G-5680)*
Benettis Italia Inc — 310 537-8036
  18554 S Susana Rd Compton (90221) *(G-6806)*
Benicia Plumbing Inc — 707 745-2930
  265 W Channel Rd Benicia (94510) *(G-2163)*

Bennathon Corp (PA) — 916 405-2100
  10291 Iron Rock Way Elk Grove (95624) *(G-1503)*
Bennett Enterprises A CA — 310 534-3543
  25889 Belle Porte Ave Harbor City (90710) *(G-813)*
Bennett Landscape, Harbor City Also called Bennett Enterprises A CA *(G-813)*
Benq America Corp (HQ) — 714 559-4900
  3200 Park Center Dr # 150 Costa Mesa (92626) *(G-7101)*
Bens Asphalt & Maint Co Inc — 951 248-1103
  2537 Rubidoux Blvd Riverside (92509) *(G-1741)*
Bent Tree Nursing Center Inc — 760 945-3033
  247 E Bobier Dr Vista (92084) *(G-20410)*
Bentley Company — 925 543-3500
  12647 Alcosta Blvd # 500 San Ramon (94583) *(G-25687)*
Bentley Health Care Inc — 310 967-3300
  9777 Wilshire Blvd Fl 4 Beverly Hills (90212) *(G-27345)*
Bentley Systems Incorporated — 925 933-2525
  1600 Riviera Ave Ste 300 Walnut Creek (94596) *(G-15052)*
Bentley-Simonson Inc — 805 650-2794
  1746 S Victoria Ave Ste F Ventura (93003) *(G-1028)*
Bento Box Entertainment LLC — 818 333-7900
  5161 Lankershim Blvd # 1 North Hollywood (91601) *(G-18458)*
Benz - One Complete Operation, Tehachapi Also called Benz Sanitation Inc *(G-6437)*
Benz Sanitation Inc (PA) — 661 822-5273
  1401 Goodrick Dr Tehachapi (93561) *(G-6437)*
Berding & Weil LLP (PA) — 925 838-2090
  2175 N Calif Blvd Ste 500 Walnut Creek (94596) *(G-23109)*
Beres Consulting — 310 476-9941
  470 S Bentley Ave Los Angeles (90049) *(G-25076)*
Beresford Arms, The, San Francisco Also called Beresford Corporation *(G-12436)*
Beresford Corp — 415 981-7386
  582 Market St Ste 912 San Francisco (94104) *(G-215)*
Beresford Corporation — 415 673-9900
  635 Sutter St San Francisco (94102) *(G-12436)*
Berg Lacquer Co (PA) — 323 261-8114
  3150 E Pico Blvd Los Angeles (90023) *(G-9237)*
Bergelectric Corp (PA) — 310 337-1377
  5650 W Centinela Ave Los Angeles (90045) *(G-2530)*
Bergelectric Corp — 760 746-1003
  650 Opper St Escondido (92029) *(G-2531)*
Bergelectric Corp — 916 636-1880
  11333 Sunrise Park Dr Rancho Cordova (95742) *(G-2532)*
Bergelectric Corp — 949 250-7005
  1935 Deere Ave Irvine (92606) *(G-2533)*
Bergen Brunswig Drug Company — 714 385-4000
  4000 W Metropolitan Dr # 200 Orange (92868) *(G-8237)*
Bergensons Property Svcs Inc — 760 631-5111
  3605 Ocean Ranch Blvd # 200 Oceanside (92056) *(G-14237)*
Berger Kahn (PA) — 310 578-6800
  4551 Glencoe Ave Ste 245 Marina Del Rey (90292) *(G-23110)*
Berger Kahn — 310 821-9000
  2 Park Plz Ste 650 Irvine (92614) *(G-23111)*
Berglund & Johnson Law Office, Woodland Hills Also called Law Offices Berglund & Johnson *(G-23377)*
Bergman Kprs LLC (PA) — 714 924-7000
  2850 Saturn St Ste 100 Brea (92821) *(G-1504)*
Berkeley 75 Hsing Partners LP — 510 705-1488
  1936 University Ave # 130 Berkeley (94704) *(G-11319)*
Berkeley Cement Inc — 510 525-8175
  1200 6th St Berkeley (94710) *(G-3233)*
Berkeley Clinic Auxuillary — 510 525-7844
  10052 San Pablo Ave El Cerrito (94530) *(G-25506)*
Berkeley E Convalescent Hosp, Santa Monica Also called Berkeley E Convalescent Hosp *(G-21152)*
Berkeley E Convalescent Hosp — 310 829-5377
  2021 Arizona Ave Santa Monica (90404) *(G-21152)*
Berkeley Electronic Press, Berkeley Also called Internet-Journals Inc *(G-16410)*
Berkeley Farms LLC (HQ) — 510 265-8600
  25500 Clawiter Rd Hayward (94545) *(G-8578)*
Berkeley Pines Care Center, Berkeley Also called A T Associates Inc *(G-21121)*
Berkeley Repertory Theatre Co — 510 204-8901
  2025 Addison St Berkeley (94704) *(G-18372)*
Berkeley Research Group LLC — 310 499-4750
  2049 Century Park E # 2525 Los Angeles (90067) *(G-26646)*
Berkeley Research Group LLC (PA) — 510 285-3300
  2200 Powell St Ste 1200 Emeryville (94608) *(G-27848)*
Berkeley Student Coop Inc — 510 848-1936
  2424 Ridge Rd Berkeley (94709) *(G-13488)*
Berkeley Symphony Orchestra — 510 841-2800
  1942 University Ave # 207 Berkeley (94704) *(G-18459)*
Berkeley Unified School Dst — 510 644-6182
  1314 7th St Berkeley (94710) *(G-3913)*
Berkley East Convalescent Hosp, Santa Monica Also called Arizona and 21st Corp *(G-21144)*
Berkley International LLC — 310 900-1771
  2725 E El Presidio St Carson (90810) *(G-9246)*
Berkley Vly Cnvlscent Hosp Inc — 818 786-0020
  6600 Sepulveda Blvd Van Nuys (91411) *(G-20411)*
Berkly YMCA Head Start, Berkeley Also called The Young Mens Chris Assoc of *(G-25372)*
Berkshire Hathaway, Lancaster Also called V Troth Inc *(G-11895)*
Berkshire Hathaway Homestates — 619 686-8424
  2020 Camino Del Rio N San Diego (92108) *(G-10647)*
Berkshire Hattaway Home Servcs — 626 913-2808
  16404 Colima Rd Hacienda Heights (91745) *(G-11320)*
Berkshire Mortgage Fin Corp — 949 754-6300
  7575 Irvine Center Dr # 200 Irvine (92618) *(G-9822)*
Berlin Tire Centers, Fontana Also called Tire Centers LLC *(G-6791)*
Berlitz Language Center, Beverly Hills Also called Berlitz Languages Inc *(G-17028)*

ALPHABETIC SECTION
Beverly Healthcare, Newman

Berlitz Languages Inc...310 858-8931
9454 Wilshire Blvd # 100 Beverly Hills (90212) ***(G-17028)***

Bermuda Dunes Country Club...760 360-2481
42765 Adams St Bermuda Dunes (92203) ***(G-18890)***

Bermuda Dunes Learning Ctr Inc...760 772-7127
42115 Yucca Ln Bermuda Dunes (92203) ***(G-24417)***

Bermudez Brothers, Winters *Also called Andres Bermudez* ***(G-649)***

Bernard Osher Marin Jewish Com...415 444-8000
200 N San Pedro Rd San Rafael (94903) ***(G-23682)***

Bernard Perrin Supowitz Inc...323 981-2800
5496 Lindbergh Ln Bell (90201) ***(G-8459)***

Bernardo Hts Healthcare Inc...858 673-0101
11895 Avenue Of Industry San Diego (92128) ***(G-21153)***

Bernards Bros Inc...909 941-5225
3633 Inland Empire Blvd # 860 Ontario (91764) ***(G-1505)***

Bernardy Ctr For Medcly Frgled, San Diego *Also called Rady Chld Hospital-San Diego* ***(G-27192)***

Bernel Inc...714 778-6070
501 W Southern Ave Orange (92865) ***(G-2164)***

Berry & Berry Law Firm...510 250-0200
475 14th St Ste 550 Oakland (94612) ***(G-23112)***

Berry Seed & Feed, Keyes *Also called A L Gilbert Company* ***(G-8959)***

Berry-Hinckley, Auburn *Also called Western Energetix LLC* ***(G-9010)***

Berryman Health Inc...707 462-8864
1349 S Dora St Ukiah (95482) ***(G-21154)***

Bershtel Enterprises LLC (PA)...626 301-9214
2745 Huntington Dr Duarte (91010) ***(G-17029)***

Bersin By Deloitte, Oakland *Also called Deloitte Consulting LLP* ***(G-27406)***

Bert E Jessup Transportation...408 848-3390
641 Old Gilroy St Gilroy (95020) ***(G-4114)***

Bertram Capital Management LLC...650 358-5000
800 Concar Dr Ste 100 San Mateo (94402) ***(G-12284)***

Bess Testlab Inc...408 988-0101
2461 Tripaldi Way Hayward (94545) ***(G-1909)***

Best Best & Krieger LLP (PA)...951 686-1450
3390 University Ave # 500 Riverside (92501) ***(G-23113)***

Best Cheer Stone Inc (PA)...714 399-1588
3190 E Miraloma Ave Anaheim (92806) ***(G-6974)***

Best Contracting Services Inc...510 886-7240
4301 Bettencourt Way Union City (94587) ***(G-3141)***

Best Contracting Services Inc (PA)...310 328-6969
19027 S Hamilton Ave Gardena (90248) ***(G-3142)***

Best Financial, The, Signal Hill *Also called First American Team Realty Inc* ***(G-11523)***

Best Friends Animal Society...818 643-3989
15321 Brand Blvd Mission Hills (91345) ***(G-25507)***

Best Interiors Inc (PA)...714 490-7999
2100 E Via Burton Anaheim (92806) ***(G-2862)***

Best Label Company Inc (PA)...562 926-1452
13260 Moore St Cerritos (90703) ***(G-7824)***

Best Life and Health Insur Co...949 253-4080
17701 Mitchell N Irvine (92614) ***(G-10202)***

Best Overnight Express, Irwindale *Also called Best Overnite Express Inc* ***(G-3981)***

Best Overnite Express Inc (PA)...626 256-6340
406 Live Oak Ave Irwindale (91706) ***(G-3981)***

Best Plans, Irvine *Also called Beneficial Administration Co* ***(G-10644)***

Best Tours & Travel, Fresno *Also called B T & T Travel Inc* ***(G-4958)***

Best Valet Parking Corporation...800 708-2538
12792 Valley View St # 201 Garden Grove (92845) ***(G-13738)***

Best Way Disposal Co Inc...760 244-9773
17105 Mesa St Hesperia (92345) ***(G-6438)***

Best Western, San Simeon *Also called Cavalier Inn Incorporated* ***(G-12501)***

Best Western, Monterey *Also called Bayview Properties Inc* ***(G-12426)***

Best Western, South Lake Tahoe *Also called Belmont Corporation* ***(G-12433)***

Best Western, Aptos *Also called Seacliff Inn Inc* ***(G-13227)***

Best Western, San Diego *Also called Tic World-Wide Corp* ***(G-13345)***

Best Western, Bakersfield *Also called Salimar Inc* ***(G-13191)***

Best Western, Victorville *Also called L & S Investment Co Inc* ***(G-12893)***

Best Western, South San Francisco *Also called Grosvenor Properties Ltd* ***(G-12679)***

Best Western, Santa Barbara *Also called Encina Pepper Tree Joint Ventr* ***(G-12620)***

Best Western Amador Inn, Jackson *Also called Sita Ram LLC* ***(G-13260)***

Best Western Bayside Inn, San Diego *Also called T I C Hotels Inc* ***(G-13334)***

Best Western Canterbury Hotel, San Francisco *Also called Canterbury Hotel Corp* ***(G-12486)***

Best Western Golden Sails Ht, Long Beach *Also called Long Beach Golden Sails Inc* ***(G-12929)***

Best Western Half Moon Bay, Half Moon Bay *Also called Pacifica Hotel Company* ***(G-13068)***

Best Western Hilltop Inn...530 221-6100
2300 Hilltop Dr Redding (96002) ***(G-12437)***

Best Western Hotel Tomo...415 921-4000
1800 Sutter St San Francisco (94115) ***(G-12438)***

Best Western International Inc...559 592-8118
805 S Kaweah Ave Exeter (93221) ***(G-12439)***

Best Western Island Palms, San Diego *Also called Bartell Hotels* ***(G-12420)***

Best Western Oxnard Inn...805 483-9581
1156 S Oxnard Blvd Oxnard (93030) ***(G-12440)***

Best Western Park Place, Anaheim *Also called Best Western Stovalls Inn* ***(G-12442)***

Best Western Pasada At Harbor, San Diego *Also called Tesi Investment Company LLC* ***(G-13342)***

BEST WESTERN PEPPER TREE INN, Santa Barbara *Also called Encina Pepper Tree Joint Ventr* ***(G-12619)***

Best Western Royal Host Inn...209 810-2619
5414 Brook Hollow Ct Stockton (95219) ***(G-12441)***

Best Western Stockton Inn, Stockton *Also called Westland Hotel Corporation* ***(G-13406)***

Best Western Stovalls Inn...714 776-4800
1544 S Harbor Blvd Anaheim (92802) ***(G-12442)***

Best Western Stovalls Inn (PA)...714 956-4430
1110 W Katella Ave Anaheim (92802) ***(G-12443)***

Best Western, The Beach Resort, Monterey *Also called Bayview Properties Inc* ***(G-26939)***

Best Wstn Carmel Mission Inn, Carmel *Also called Trevi Partners A Calif LP* ***(G-13357)***

Best Wstn El Rancho Inn Suites, Millbrae *Also called El Rancho Motel Inc* ***(G-12614)***

Best Wstn Golden Pheasant Inn, Willows *Also called Paul P Ortner DDS* ***(G-13081)***

Best Wstn Half Moon Bay Lodge, Half Moon Bay *Also called Iwf Half Moon Bay LP* ***(G-12860)***

Best-Way Distributing Co, Sylmar *Also called Allied Beverages Incorporated* ***(G-9038)***

Bestitcom Inc (PA)...602 667-5613
1464 Madera Rd Simi Valley (93065) ***(G-16329)***

Beston Development...619 232-6315
1055 1st Ave San Diego (92101) ***(G-12444)***

Bestway Delivery, Van Nuys *Also called Mercury Messenger Service Inc* ***(G-17329)***

Bestway Recycling Company Inc (PA)...323 588-8157
2268 Firestone Blvd Los Angeles (90002) ***(G-8065)***

Bet Tzedek...323 939-0506
3250 Wilshire Blvd Fl 13 Los Angeles (90010) ***(G-23114)***

Bet-Nahrain Inc...209 538-4111
3119 Central Ave Ceres (95307) ***(G-17030)***

Beta Offshore, Long Beach *Also called Beta Operating Company LLC* ***(G-1029)***

Beta Operating Company LLC...562 628-1526
111 W Ocean Blvd Ste 1240 Long Beach (90802) ***(G-1029)***

Bethel Lutheran Home Inc...559 896-4900
2280 Dockery Ave Selma (93662) ***(G-21155)***

Bethel Retirement Community...209 577-1901
2345 Scenic Dr Modesto (95355) ***(G-21156)***

BETHESDA CHRISTIAN UNIVERSITY, Anaheim *Also called Bethesda University California* ***(G-12154)***

Bethesda Lthran Cmmunities Inc...559 636-6300
5440 W Wren Ave Visalia (93291) ***(G-24564)***

Bethesda University California...714 517-1945
730 N Euclid St Ste 314 Anaheim (92801) ***(G-12154)***

Bettendorf Enterprises Inc...530 365-1937
20943 Bettendorf Way Anderson (96007) ***(G-4115)***

Bettendorf Trucking, Anderson *Also called Bettendorf Enterprises Inc* ***(G-4115)***

Better Homes and Gardens Mason...925 776-2740
5887 Lone Tree Way Ste A Antioch (94531) ***(G-11321)***

Better Life Organic Produce, Los Angeles *Also called Better Life Produce Inc* ***(G-8696)***

Better Life Produce Inc...213 623-0640
2020 E 7th Pl Los Angeles (90021) ***(G-8696)***

Better Living Brands LLC...888 723-3929
11555 Dublin Canyon Rd Pleasanton (94588) ***(G-17031)***

Better Mens Clothes, Los Angeles *Also called Hirsh Inc* ***(G-1082)***

Better Way Services...661 326-6444
5329 Office Center Ct # 100 Bakersfield (93309) ***(G-23683)***

Betty Ford Center (HQ)...760 773-4100
39000 Bob Hope Dr Rancho Mirage (92270) ***(G-22117)***

Betty Jimenez, Brawley *Also called Clinicas De Slud Del Peblo Inc* ***(G-19448)***

Beutler Heating & AC, Suisun City *Also called Villara Corporation* ***(G-3222)***

Beutler Heating & AC, Manteca *Also called Villara Corporation* ***(G-2410)***

Beutler Heating & Air, McClellan *Also called Villara Corporation* ***(G-2411)***

Beven-Herron Inc...714 523-5870
14511 Industry Cir La Mirada (90638) ***(G-3143)***

Beverly, Fresno *Also called Golden Living LLC* ***(G-20603)***

Beverly, Fowler *Also called Golden Living LLC* ***(G-20604)***

Beverly, Beverly Hills *Also called Bhrac LLC* ***(G-17666)***

Beverly, Ridgecrest *Also called Golden Living LLC* ***(G-22445)***

Beverly Blvd Leaseco LLC...310 278-5444
8555 Beverly Blvd Los Angeles (90048) ***(G-12445)***

Beverly Center, Los Angeles *Also called La Cienega Associates* ***(G-11624)***

Beverly Community Hosp Assn...323 889-2452
101 E Beverly Blvd # 104 Montebello (90640) ***(G-21464)***

Beverly Community Hosp Assn (PA)...323 726-1222
309 W Beverly Blvd Montebello (90640) ***(G-21465)***

Beverly Community Hosp Assn...323 725-1519
1920 W Whittier Blvd Montebello (90640) ***(G-21466)***

Beverly Health Care Corp (PA)...805 642-1736
5445 Everglades St Ventura (93003) ***(G-26942)***

Beverly Healthcare, Panorama City *Also called Golden Living LLC* ***(G-21238)***

Beverly Healthcare, Costa Mesa *Also called Golden Living LLC* ***(G-20605)***

Beverly Healthcare, Montrose *Also called Golden Living LLC* ***(G-21239)***

Beverly Healthcare, San Francisco *Also called Golden Living LLC* ***(G-20608)***

Beverly Healthcare, Modesto *Also called Golden Living LLC* ***(G-21241)***

Beverly Healthcare, Sonora *Also called Golden Living LLC* ***(G-21242)***

Beverly Healthcare, Los Gatos *Also called Golden Living LLC* ***(G-21243)***

Beverly Healthcare, Seal Beach *Also called Golden Living LLC* ***(G-21244)***

Beverly Healthcare, Oxnard *Also called Golden Living LLC* ***(G-20611)***

Beverly Healthcare, Lodi *Also called Golden Living LLC* ***(G-20612)***

Beverly Healthcare, Big Sur *Also called Golden Living LLC* ***(G-22444)***

Beverly Healthcare, West Covina *Also called Golden Living LLC* ***(G-20614)***

Beverly Healthcare, Ventura *Also called Golden Living LLC* ***(G-20615)***

Beverly Healthcare, Capistrano Beach *Also called Golden Living LLC* ***(G-20616)***

Beverly Healthcare, Murrieta *Also called Golden Living LLC* ***(G-23996)***

Beverly Healthcare, Madera *Also called Golden Living LLC* ***(G-21247)***

Beverly Healthcare, Fresno *Also called Golden Living LLC* ***(G-20621)***

Beverly Healthcare, San Jose *Also called Golden Living LLC* ***(G-24669)***

Beverly Healthcare, Modesto *Also called Golden Living LLC* ***(G-20622)***

Beverly Healthcare, Los Gatos *Also called Golden Living LLC* ***(G-20623)***

Beverly Healthcare, Chico *Also called Golden Living LLC* ***(G-20626)***

Beverly Healthcare, Merced *Also called Golden Living LLC* ***(G-21249)***

Beverly Healthcare, Newman *Also called Golden Living LLC* ***(G-20627)***

ALPHABETIC

Beverly Hills Active Club, Los Angeles *Also called 24 Hour Fitness Usa Inc* ***(G-18584)***
Beverly Hills Country Club 310 836-4400
3084 Motor Ave Los Angeles (90064) ***(G-11949)***
Beverly Hills Hotel, Beverly Hills *Also called Sajahtera Inc* ***(G-13190)***
Beverly Hills Luxury Hotel LLC 310 274-9999
1801 Century Park E # 1200 Los Angeles (90067) ***(G-12446)***
Beverly Hills Luxury Interiors, Los Angeles *Also called Kenneth Brdwick Intr Dsgns Inc* ***(G-17270)***
Beverly Hills Plaza Hotel, Los Angeles *Also called Donald T Sterling Corporation* ***(G-12587)***
BEVERLY HOSPITAL, Montebello *Also called Beverly Community Hosp Assn* ***(G-21465)***
Beverly Lving Ctr Cnty Vw Alzh 559 275-4785
925 N Cornelia Ave Fresno (93706) ***(G-21157)***
Beverly Pl Memory Care Cmnty, Los Angeles *Also called Silverado Senior Living Inc* ***(G-21377)***
Beverly Sunstone Hills LLC 310 228-4100
1177 S Beverly Dr Los Angeles (90035) ***(G-12447)***
Beverly West Health Care Inc 323 938-2451
1020 S Fairfax Ave Los Angeles (90019) ***(G-20412)***
Beverlywood Realty Inc 310 836-8322
2800 S Robertson Blvd Los Angeles (90034) ***(G-11322)***
Beyer Park Villas LLC 209 236-1900
3529 Forest Glenn Dr Modesto (95355) ***(G-24565)***
Beyond International Corp, San Francisco *Also called Bynd LLC* ***(G-15070)***
BFI Waste Services LLC 559 275-1551
5501 N Golden State Blvd Fresno (93722) ***(G-6439)***
BFI Waste Systems N Amer Inc 805 965-5248
800 Cacique St Santa Barbara (93103) ***(G-6440)***
BFI Waste Systems N Amer Inc 831 775-3850
271 Rianda St Salinas (93901) ***(G-6441)***
BFI Waste Systems N Amer Inc 510 657-1350
42600 Boyce Rd Fremont (94538) ***(G-6442)***
Bfp Fire Protection Inc 831 461-1100
17 Janis Way Scotts Valley (95066) ***(G-2165)***
Bgm, San Jose *Also called Brilliant General Maintinc* ***(G-14240)***
Bh Partn A Calif Limit Partne (PA) 858 539-7635
998 W Mission Bay Dr San Diego (92109) ***(G-12448)***
Bh Partn A Calif Limit Partne 858 453-4420
11480 N Torrey Pines Rd A La Jolla (92037) ***(G-12449)***
Bh-SD Opco LLC 619 465-4411
7050 Parkway Dr La Mesa (91942) ***(G-22045)***
Bhai Group Co, Los Angeles *Also called Yogibotanicals* ***(G-8958)***
Bhandal Bros Inc 831 728-2691
2490 San Juan Rd Hollister (95023) ***(G-4116)***
Bhandal Bros Trucking Inc 831 728-2691
2490 San Juan Rd Hollister (95023) ***(G-4117)***
Bho LLC 951 845-2220
5801 Sun Lakes Blvd Banning (92220) ***(G-24566)***
Bhrac LLC 310 862-1933
9777 Wilshire Blvd # 517 Beverly Hills (90212) ***(G-17666)***
Bi-County Ambulance Service 530 674-2780
1700 Poole Blvd Yuba City (95993) ***(G-3773)***
BI-RITE FOODSERVICE DISTRIBUTO, Brisbane *Also called Bi-Rite Restaurant Sup Co Inc* ***(G-8460)***
Bi-Rite Restaurant Sup Co Inc 415 656-0187
123 S Hill Dr Brisbane (94005) ***(G-8460)***
Biagi Bros Inc 707 642-4412
1200 Green Island Rd American Canyon (94503) ***(G-4526)***
Biagi Bros Inc 909 390-6910
3655 E Airport Dr Ontario (91761) ***(G-4527)***
Biagi Bros Inc 707 745-8115
650 Stone Rd Benicia (94510) ***(G-4332)***
Biagi Brothers Bezzerides Co, Benicia *Also called Biagi Bros Inc* ***(G-4332)***
Bianchi Ag Services Inc 530 923-7675
3056 Colusa Hwy Yuba City (95993) ***(G-694)***
Bianchi Plumbing Co Inc 916 772-7364
2130 March Rd Ste D Roseville (95747) ***(G-2166)***
Bic Real Estate Dev Corp 661 847-9691
8800 Stockdale Hwy # 100 Bakersfield (93311) ***(G-9773)***
Bicara Ltd (PA) 310 316-6222
1611 S Catalina Ave Redondo Beach (90277) ***(G-8664)***
Bickmore and Associates Inc (HQ) 916 244-1100
1750 Creekside Oaks Dr # 200 Sacramento (95833) ***(G-10648)***
Bickmore Risk Svcs Consulting, Sacramento *Also called Bickmore and Associates Inc* ***(G-10648)***
Bicycle Casino LP 562 806-4646
888 Bicycle Casino Dr Bell Gardens (90201) ***(G-12450)***
Bicycle Club, Bell Gardens *Also called Bicycle Casino LP* ***(G-12450)***
Bicycle Club Casino, Bell Gardens *Also called Bell Gardens Bicycle Club Inc* ***(G-19148)***
Bidmail, Tustin *Also called Internet Blueprint Inc* ***(G-15252)***
Bienvenidos Community Hlth Ctr, Los Angeles *Also called Via Care Cmnty Hlth Ctr Inc* ***(G-20223)***
Big 5 Sporting Goods Corp 323 755-2663
11310 Crenshaw Blvd Inglewood (90303) ***(G-19149)***
Big Bulb Ideas Inc 408 888-2346
5655 Silver Creek Vlley R San Jose (95138) ***(G-15053)***
Big Canyon Country Club 949 706-5260
1 Big Canyon Dr Newport Beach (92660) ***(G-18891)***
Big City Access Inc (PA) 916 428-4090
3131 52nd Ave West Sacramento (95691) ***(G-7762)***
Big Creek Division Office, Big Creek *Also called Southern California Edison Co* ***(G-6223)***
Big F Company Inc 805 928-2333
3130 Skyway Dr Ste 405 Santa Maria (93455) ***(G-9126)***
Big Four Restaurant, San Francisco *Also called Nob Hill Properties Inc* ***(G-13023)***
Big Joe California North Inc (PA) 510 785-6900
25932 Eden Landing Rd Hayward (94545) ***(G-7825)***
Big Joe Handling Systems, Hayward *Also called Big Joe California North Inc* ***(G-7825)***
Big League Dreams Jurupa LLC 951 685-6900
10550 Cntu Gllano Rnch Rd Mira Loma (91752) ***(G-18538)***
Big Lgue Drams Chino Hills LLC 909 287-6900
16333 Fairfield Ranch Rd Chino Hills (91709) ***(G-18539)***
Big Lgue Dreams Consulting LLC 619 846-8855
2155 Trumble Rd Perris (92571) ***(G-18540)***
Big Lgue Dreams Consulting LLC 760 324-5600
33700 Date Palm Dr Cathedral City (92234) ***(G-13461)***
Big Lgue Dreams Consulting LLC 530 223-1177
20155 Viking Way Redding (96003) ***(G-18892)***
Big Lgue Dreams Consulting LLC 626 839-1100
2100 S Azusa Ave West Covina (91792) ***(G-1506)***
Big O Tires LLC (HQ) 707 829-9864
742 S Main St Sebastopol (95472) ***(G-6714)***
Big Oak Hardwood Floor Co Inc 650 591-8651
1731 Leslie St San Mateo (94402) ***(G-3107)***
Big River Lodge, Mendocino *Also called Big River Ltd-Design* ***(G-12451)***
Big River Ltd-Design 707 937-5615
44850 Comptche Ukiah Rd Mendocino (95460) ***(G-12451)***
Big Sandy Rancheria, Auberry *Also called Mono Wind Casino* ***(G-13003)***
Big Sky Country Club LLC 805 522-4653
3301 Lost Canyons Dr Simi Valley (93063) ***(G-18716)***
Big Star, South Gate *Also called Koos Manufacturing Inc* ***(G-17276)***
Big Valley Mortgage, Roseville *Also called American Pacific Mortgage Corp* ***(G-9815)***
Bigbyte Corporation 510 249-1100
47430 Seabridge Dr Fremont (94538) ***(G-16288)***
Biggest Lser Ftnes Rdge Malibu, Malibu *Also called Fitness Ridge Malibu LLC* ***(G-12637)***
Biggie Crane and Ritting, San Leandro *Also called Galena Equipment Rental LLC* ***(G-14482)***
Biggs Cardosa Associates Inc (PA) 408 296-5515
865 The Alameda San Jose (95126) ***(G-25688)***
Bigham Taylor Roofing Corp 510 886-0197
22721 Alice St Hayward (94541) ***(G-3144)***
Bighorn Golf Club 760 773-2468
255 Palowet Dr Palm Desert (92260) ***(G-18893)***
Bigrentz Inc 855 999-5438
1063 Mcgaw Ave Ste 200 Irvine (92614) ***(G-14478)***
Bigrentz.com, Irvine *Also called Bigrentz Inc* ***(G-14478)***
Bikrams Yoga College of India 415 346-2480
910 Columbus Ave San Francisco (94133) ***(G-19150)***
Bill & Wag's, Ontario *Also called United Road Towing Inc* ***(G-17901)***
Bill & Wag's, Redlands *Also called United Road Towing Inc* ***(G-17902)***
Bill Brown Construction Co 408 297-3738
242 Phelan Ave San Jose (95112) ***(G-1296)***
Bill Brown Construction Co 408 297-3738
242 Phelan Ave San Jose (95112) ***(G-1134)***
Bill Howe Plumbing Inc 800 245-5469
9085 Aero Dr Ste B San Diego (92123) ***(G-2167)***
Bill Nelson GEC, Fresno *Also called Bill Nlson Gen Engrg Cnstr Inc* ***(G-1910)***
Bill Nlson Gen Engrg Cnstr Inc 559 439-1756
2741 E Malaga Ave Fresno (93725) ***(G-1910)***
Bill Papich Construction Inc 805 489-9420
800 Farroll Rd Grover Beach (93433) ***(G-2026)***
Bill Wilson Center (PA) 408 243-0222
3490 The Alameda Santa Clara (95050) ***(G-23684)***
Billcom Inc 650 353-3301
1810 Embarcadero Rd Palo Alto (94303) ***(G-15599)***
Bilt-Well Roofing & Mtl Co, Los Angeles *Also called Sbb Roofing Inc* ***(G-3212)***
Biltmore Hotel 408 988-8411
2151 Laurelwood Rd Santa Clara (95054) ***(G-12452)***
Biltwell Roofing, Los Angeles *Also called R F R Corporation* ***(G-12004)***
Bimbo Bakeries Usa Inc 714 634-8068
1220 Howell St Anaheim (92805) ***(G-8808)***
Binding Site Inc 858 453-9177
6730 Mesa Ridge Rd San Diego (92121) ***(G-7245)***
Binex Line Corp (PA) 310 416-8600
19515 S Vermont Ave Torrance (90502) ***(G-5033)***
Bio Industries Inc 530 529-3290
2060 Montgomery Rd Red Bluff (96080) ***(G-474)***
Bio Mdcal Applications Fla Inc 559 221-6311
3636 N 1st St Ste 144 Fresno (93726) ***(G-22618)***
Bio RAD Laboratories 510 741-1000
2000 Alfred Nobel Dr Hercules (94547) ***(G-26834)***
Bio-Diagnostics Laboratories (PA) 818 780-3300
19951 Mariner Ave Ste 150 Torrance (90503) ***(G-22190)***
Bio-Mdcal Applications Cal Inc 562 920-2070
10116 Rosecrans Ave Bellflower (90706) ***(G-22619)***
Bio-Mdcal Applications Cal Inc 626 457-9002
1801 W Valley Blvd # 102 Alhambra (91803) ***(G-22620)***
Bio-Mdcal Applications Cal Inc 951 343-7700
3470 La Sierra Ave Ste E Riverside (92503) ***(G-22621)***
Bio-Med Services Inc 909 235-4400
3300 E Guasti Rd Ontario (91761) ***(G-22893)***
Bio-RAD Laboratories Inc 510 741-1000
2000 Alfred Nobel Dr Hercules (94547) ***(G-7339)***
Bio-RAD Laboratories Inc 510 232-7000
2000 Alfred Nobel Dr Hercules (94547) ***(G-26487)***
Bio-Reference Laboratories Inc 408 341-8600
2605 Winchester Blvd Campbell (95008) ***(G-22191)***
Biocept Inc 858 320-8200
5810 Nancy Ridge Dr # 150 San Diego (92121) ***(G-22192)***
Bioclinca (PA) 415 817-8900
7707 Gateway Blvd Fl 3 Newark (94560) ***(G-26488)***
Biocompare, South San Francisco *Also called Comparenetworks Inc* ***(G-26499)***
Biofusion LLC 310 803-8100
19110 Van Ness Ave Torrance (90501) ***(G-19374)***
Bioimagene Inc 408 207-4200
919 Hermosa Ct Sunnyvale (94085) ***(G-22193)***

Biomat Usa Inc ... 310 772-7777
2410 Lillyvale Ave Los Angeles (90032) *(G-22894)*
Biomat Usa Inc (HQ) ... 323 225-2221
2410 Lillyvale Ave Los Angeles (90032) *(G-22895)*
Biomat Usa Inc ... 661 863-0621
246 Bernard St Bakersfield (93305) *(G-22896)*
Biomedical Engineering Center, Sacramento *Also called Sutter Health (G-22843)*
Biomedicure LLC ... 858 586-1888
7940 Silverton Ave # 107 San Diego (92126) *(G-26489)*
Bionano Genomics Inc (PA) ... 858 888-7600
9640 Twne Cntre Dr 100 San Diego (92121) *(G-22194)*
Bioscreen Testing Services Inc (PA) ... 602 277-1154
3904 Del Amo Blvd Ste 801 Torrance (90503) *(G-26835)*
Biosite Inc ... 510 683-9063
9975 Summers Ridge Rd San Diego (92121) *(G-7246)*
Biotheranostics Inc (HQ) ... 858 678-0940
9640 Towne Centre Dr # 200 San Diego (92121) *(G-22195)*
Birch Aquarium At Scripps ... 858 534-4109
2300 Expedition Way La Jolla (92037) *(G-25059)*
Birch Ptrick Convalescent Cntr, Chula Vista *Also called Sharp Healthcare (G-20909)*
Bird Mrlla Bxer Wlpert A Prof ... 310 201-2100
1875 Century Park E Fl 23 Los Angeles (90067) *(G-23115)*
Bird Street Media Project ... 530 534-1200
2360 Oro Quincy Hwy Oroville (95966) *(G-5749)*
Birkenstock Usa Lp (HQ) ... 415 884-3200
8171 Redwood Blvd Novato (94945) *(G-8421)*
Birnam Wood Golf Club ... 805 969-2223
1941 E Valley Rd Santa Barbara (93108) *(G-18894)*
Birst Inc (PA) ... 415 766-4800
45 Fremont St Ste 1800 San Francisco (94105) *(G-15054)*
Birtcher Andrson Investors LLC ... 949 545-0526
31910 Del Obispo St # 100 San Juan Capistrano (92675) *(G-12285)*
Birtcher Andrson Property Svcs (PA) ... 949 831-0707
27611 La Paz Rd Ste D Laguna Niguel (92677) *(G-11323)*
Birtcher N Goodman Amer LLC ... 949 407-0100
18201 Von Karman Ave Irvine (92612) *(G-11324)*
Birtcher/Aetna Laguna Hills ... 949 458-2311
24903 Moulton Pkwy Ofc Laguna Hills (92653) *(G-11098)*
Birth Choice of San Marco ... 760 744-1313
277 S Rancho Santa Fe Rd San Marcos (92078) *(G-23685)*
Birth Family Services Inc ... 310 323-8181
1968 W Adams Blvd Apt 1 Los Angeles (90018) *(G-23686)*
Bishop Barry Howe Haney & Ryde ... 510 596-0888
6001 Shellmound St # 875 Emeryville (94608) *(G-23116)*
Bishop Paiute Gaming Corp ... 760 872-6005
2742 N Sierra Hwy Bishop (93514) *(G-19151)*
Bishop Waste Disposal Inc ... 760 872-6561
100 Snland Reservation Rd Bishop (93514) *(G-6443)*
Bissell Bros Bldg Maint Servic, Rancho Cordova *Also called Bissell Brothers Janitorial (G-14238)*
Bissell Brothers Janitorial ... 916 635-1852
3207 Luyung Dr Rancho Cordova (95742) *(G-14238)*
Bit Medtech LLC ... 858 613-1200
15870 Bernardo Center Dr San Diego (92127) *(G-25689)*
Bitas ... 310 324-2273
990 W 190th St Ste 120 Torrance (90502) *(G-20413)*
Bite Communications LLC (HQ) ... 415 365-0222
100 Montgomery St # 1103 San Francisco (94104) *(G-27346)*
Bitech-Ace A Joint Venture ... 714 521-1477
7371 Walnut Ave Buena Park (90620) *(G-3234)*
Bitfone Corporation (PA) ... 949 234-7000
32451 Golden Lantern # 301 Laguna Niguel (92677) *(G-15055)*
Bitgravity, Burlingame *Also called Tata Communications Amer Inc (G-17517)*
Bixby Ranch Co A California LP ... 562 596-4425
3901 Lampson Ave Seal Beach (90740) *(G-11950)*
Bixby Ranch Company, Seal Beach *Also called Bixby Ranch Co A California LP (G-11950)*
Biz Vision Inc ... 916 792-2124
4800 Kokomo Dr Apt 3014 Sacramento (95835) *(G-27347)*
Bizcom Electronics Inc (HQ) ... 408 262-7877
1171 Montague Expy Milpitas (95035) *(G-7102)*
Bizmatics Inc (PA) ... 408 873-3030
4010 Moorpark Ave Ste 222 San Jose (95117) *(G-15600)*
Bizringer.com, Newport Beach *Also called Baid Vivek (G-5564)*
Bjj Company LLC (PA) ... 209 941-8361
1040 W Kettleman Ln Lodi (95240) *(G-4118)*
BJs Restaurants Inc ... 209 526-8850
3401 Dale Rd Ste 840 Modesto (95356) *(G-8095)*
Bkf Engineers ... 408 467-9100
1730 N 1st St Ste 600 San Jose (95112) *(G-25690)*
Bkf Engineers (PA) ... 650 482-6300
255 Shoreline Dr Ste 200 Redwood City (94065) *(G-25691)*
BKK Corporation (PA) ... 626 965-0911
2210 S Azusa Ave West Covina (91792) *(G-6444)*
BKM Officeworks, San Diego *Also called Wmk Office San Diego LLC (G-6839)*
Blach Construction Company (PA) ... 408 244-7100
2244 Blach Pl Ste 100 San Jose (95131) *(G-1406)*
Black & Veatch Corporation ... 913 458-9406
265 E River Park Cir Fresno (93720) *(G-25692)*
Black & Veatch Corporation ... 913 458-2000
15615 Alton Pkwy Ste 300 Irvine (92618) *(G-25693)*
Black & Veatch Corporation ... 562 345-9332
5 Peters Canyon Rd # 300 Irvine (92606) *(G-25694)*
Black & Veatch-Balfour Beatty ... 760 510-7715
300 Rancheros Dr Ste 250 San Marcos (92069) *(G-25695)*
Black & White TV Inc ... 310 855-1040
8756 Dorrington Ave West Hollywood (90048) *(G-17906)*
Black Bear Security Services ... 415 559-5159
2016 Oakdale Ave Ste B San Francisco (94124) *(G-16575)*
Black Box Inc ... 760 804-3300
371 2nd St Ste 1 Encinitas (92024) *(G-8334)*
Black Box Network Services, Los Angeles *Also called Scottel Voice & Data Inc (G-17942)*
Black Diamond Electric Inc ... 925 777-3440
2595 W 10th St Antioch (94509) *(G-2534)*
Black Dog Farms of California ... 760 356-2951
530 W 6th St Holtville (92250) *(G-40)*
Black Dot Wireless LLC ... 949 502-3800
27271 Las Ramblas Ste 300 Mission Viejo (92691) *(G-5278)*
Black Gold Golf Club ... 714 961-0060
1 Black Gold Dr Yorba Linda (92886) *(G-18717)*
Black Lake Golf Course, Nipomo *Also called American Golf Corporation (G-18855)*
Black Meadow Landing ... 760 663-4901
156100 Black Meadow Rd Parker Dam (92267) *(G-12453)*
Black Oak Casino ... 209 928-9300
19400 Tuolumne Rd N Tuolumne (95379) *(G-19152)*
Black Tie Transportation LLC ... 925 847-0747
7080 Comm Dr Pleasanton (94588) *(G-3774)*
Blackarrow Inc (HQ) ... 408 642-6400
65 N San Pedro St San Jose (95110) *(G-15056)*
Blackbaud Internet Solutions, San Diego *Also called Kintera Inc (G-15723)*
Blackbeard's Family Fun Center, Fresno *Also called GLad Entertainment Inc (G-19217)*
Blackbird, San Francisco *Also called Palomino Db Inc (G-16453)*
Blackhawk Country Club ... 925 736-6500
599 Blackhawk Club Dr Danville (94506) *(G-18895)*
Blackhawk Information Services ... 925 244-6701
22 Beta Ct San Ramon (94583) *(G-15057)*
Blackhawk Network Inc (HQ) ... 925 226-9990
6220 Stoneridge Mall Rd Pleasanton (94588) *(G-9710)*
Blackhawk Network Holdings Inc (PA) ... 925 226-9990
6220 Stoneridge Mall Rd Pleasanton (94588) *(G-9711)*
Blackline Inc ... 818 223-9008
21300 Victory Blvd Fl 12 Woodland Hills (91367) *(G-15058)*
Blackline Systems Inc (PA) ... 818 746-4700
21300 Victory Blvd Fl 12 Woodland Hills (91367) *(G-15601)*
Blackrock Global Investors ... 415 670-2000
400 Howard St San Francisco (94105) *(G-10122)*
Blackrock Holdco 2 Inc ... 415 678-2000
50 California St Ste 200 San Francisco (94111) *(G-11325)*
Blackrock Instnl Tr Nat Assn (HQ) ... 415 597-2000
400 Howard St San Francisco (94105) *(G-12106)*
Blackrock Logistics Inc ... 925 523-3878
5870 Stoneridge Mall Rd # 208 Pleasanton (94588) *(G-5034)*
Blackstone Consulting Inc ... 619 293-0043
2710 N Harbor Dr San Diego (92101) *(G-27849)*
Blackstone Consulting Inc ... 916 383-8060
8300 Santa Cruz St Sacramento (95828) *(G-27850)*
Blackstone Consulting Inc (PA) ... 310 826-4389
11726 San Vicente Blvd # 550 Los Angeles (90049) *(G-27348)*
Blackstone Technology Group (PA) ... 415 837-1400
150 California St Fl 9 San Francisco (94111) *(G-27851)*
Blacktalon Enterprises Inc ... 707 256-1810
481 Technology Way NAPA (94558) *(G-16576)*
Blacktalon Security Solutions, NAPA *Also called Blacktalon Enterprises Inc (G-16576)*
Bladium Inc (PA) ... 510 814-4999
800 W Tower Ave Bldg 40 Alameda (94501) *(G-18896)*
Bladium Sports Clubs, Alameda *Also called Bladium Inc (G-18896)*
Blaine Convention Services Inc ... 714 522-8270
114 S Berry St Brea (92821) *(G-17032)*
Blair Television Inc ... 714 537-5923
11111 Santa Monica Blvd # 1900 Los Angeles (90025) *(G-18051)*
Blair TV Communication, Los Angeles *Also called Blair Television Inc (G-18051)*
Blake Alexandre ... 707 487-1000
8371 Lower Lake Rd Crescent City (95531) *(G-418)*
Blake H Brown Inc (HQ) ... 310 764-0110
1300 W Artesia Blvd Compton (90220) *(G-7826)*
Blakely Skloff Tylor Zfman LLP (PA) ... 310 207-3800
12400 Wilshire Blvd # 700 Los Angeles (90025) *(G-23117)*
Blakely Skloff Tylor Zfman LLP ... 408 720-8300
1279 Oakmead Pkwy Sunnyvale (94085) *(G-23118)*
Blanchard Training and Dev Inc (PA) ... 760 489-5005
125 State Pl Escondido (92029) *(G-27349)*
Blanchardcoachingcom Inc ... 760 489-5005
125 State Pl Escondido (92029) *(G-24314)*
Blank Rome LLP ... 424 239-3400
2029 Century Park E Fl 6 Los Angeles (90067) *(G-23119)*
Blank Rome LLP ... 650 690-9500
2049 Century Park E # 700 Los Angeles (90067) *(G-23120)*
Blank Rome LLP ... 310 772-8300
2049 Century Park E # 700 Los Angeles (90067) *(G-23121)*
Blare's Air & Ground Services, Lemoore *Also called R & D Leasing Inc (G-14574)*
Blayne Pacelli ... 310 383-6281
12345 Ventura Blvd Ste A Studio City (91604) *(G-11326)*
Blazer Wilkinson LP ... 831 455-3700
19040 Portola Dr Salinas (93908) *(G-105)*
Blazing Industrial Steel Inc ... 951 360-8340
9040 Jurupa Rd Riverside (92509) *(G-3367)*
Blazona Concrete Cnstr Inc ... 916 375-8337
525 Harbor Blvd Ste 10 West Sacramento (95691) *(G-1507)*
Blb Resources Inc (PA) ... 949 261-9155
16845 Von Karman Ave # 100 Irvine (92606) *(G-27350)*
Bleacher Report Inc ... 415 777-5505
609 Mission St San Francisco (94105) *(G-16104)*
Bleacher Report Inc ... 415 777-5505
153 Kearny St Fl 2 San Francisco (94108) *(G-18270)*
Bledsoe Masonry Inc ... 951 360-6140
4680 Felspar St Ste A Riverside (92509) *(G-2804)*
Bleu Chateau Assisted Living, Burbank *Also called Le Bleu Chateau Inc (G-24708)*

Blh Construction Company...818 905-3837
21031 Ventura Blvd # 200 Woodland Hills (91364) *(G-1297)*
Blize Healthcare Cal Inc...800 343-2549
828 San Pablo Ave Ste 105 Albany (94706) *(G-22378)*
Blizzard Entertainment Inc (HQ)...949 955-1380
16215 Alton Pkwy Irvine (92618) *(G-15602)*
Blocka Construction Inc...510 657-3686
4455 Enterprise St Fremont (94538) *(G-2168)*
Blois Construction Inc...805 485-0011
3201 Sturgis Rd Oxnard (93030) *(G-1911)*
Blomberg Window, Sacramento *Also called B B & T Management Corp (G-6910)*
Blood Bank of San Bernardino A (PA)...909 885-6503
384 W Orange Show Rd San Bernardino (92408) *(G-22897)*
Blood Centers of Pacific (PA)...415 567-6400
270 Masonic Ave San Francisco (94118) *(G-22898)*
Blood Centers of Pacific...707 428-6001
1325 Gateway Blvd Ste C1 Fairfield (94533) *(G-22899)*
Blood Systems Inc...805 543-1077
4119 Broad St Ste 100 San Luis Obispo (93401) *(G-22900)*
Blood Systems Inc...831 751-1993
4119 Broad St Ste 100 San Luis Obispo (93401) *(G-22901)*
Bloodsource Inc (PA)...916 456-1500
10536 Peter A Mccuen Blvd Mather (95655) *(G-22902)*
Bloodsource Inc...209 724-0428
382 E Yosemite Ave Merced (95340) *(G-22903)*
Bloodsource Inc...916 488-1701
3099 Fair Oaks Blvd Sacramento (95864) *(G-22904)*
Bloom David Law Offices of...323 938-5248
3699 Wilshire Blvd Fl 10 Los Angeles (90010) *(G-23122)*
Bloom Hergott Diemer Cook LLC...310 859-6800
150 S Rodeo Dr Fl 3 Beverly Hills (90212) *(G-23123)*
Bloom, Jacob A, Beverly Hills *Also called Bloom Hergott Diemer Cook LLC (G-23123)*
Bloomberg LP...415 912-2960
345 California St Fl 35 San Francisco (94104) *(G-16945)*
Bloss Memorial Health Care Dst (PA)...209 381-2000
3605 Hospital Rd Ste A Atwater (95301) *(G-19375)*
Blossom Valley Cnstr Inc...408 993-0766
1125 Mabury Rd San Jose (95133) *(G-814)*
Blower-Dempsay Corporation (PA)...714 481-3800
4042 W Garry Ave Santa Ana (92704) *(G-8151)*
Bls Lmsine Svc Los Angeles Inc (PA)...323 644-7166
2860 Fletcher Dr Los Angeles (90039) *(G-3775)*
BLT & Associates Inc...323 860-4000
6430 W Sunset Blvd # 800 Los Angeles (90028) *(G-14134)*
Blu Homes Inc...415 625-0809
1245 Nimitz Ave Vallejo (94592) *(G-1135)*
Blu Homes Inc...707 674-5368
1245 Nimitz Ave Bldg 680 Vallejo (94592) *(G-1136)*
Blue and Gold Fleet...415 705-8200
Marine Terminal Pier 41 St Pier San Francisco (94133) *(G-4731)*
Blue Banner Company Inc (PA)...951 682-6183
2601 3rd St Riverside (92507) *(G-511)*
Blue Box Opco LLC (PA)...800 840-4916
4920 Carroll Canyon Rd # 200 San Diego (92121) *(G-8039)*
Blue Bus Tours LLC...415 353-5310
50 Quint St San Francisco (94124) *(G-19153)*
Blue Chip Inventory Service...818 461-1765
14852 Ventura Blvd # 112 Sherman Oaks (91403) *(G-17033)*
Blue Chip Mayflower, Hawthorne *Also called Blue Chip Moving and Stor Inc (G-4119)*
Blue Chip Moving and Stor Inc...323 463-6888
13525 Crenshaw Blvd Hawthorne (90250) *(G-4119)*
Blue Coat Systems LLC (HQ)...408 220-2200
384 Santa Trinita Ave Sunnyvale (94085) *(G-15603)*
Blue Cross & Blue Shield Mich...323 782-3046
6300 Wilshire Blvd # 970 Los Angeles (90048) *(G-10259)*
Blue Cross of California (HQ)...805 557-6050
4553 La Tienda Rd Westlake Village (91362) *(G-10260)*
Blue Devils Lessee LLC...310 399-9344
530 Pico Blvd Santa Monica (90405) *(G-12454)*
Blue Diamond Growers...209 545-6221
4800 Sisk Rd Modesto (95356) *(G-512)*
Blue Diamond Materials, Brea *Also called Sully-Miller Contracting Co (G-1869)*
Blue Eagle Contracting Inc...530 272-0287
2059 Nev Cy Hwy Ste 204 Grass Valley (95945) *(G-3982)*
Blue Freight, Tarzana *Also called Blue Sky Services Inc (G-5035)*
Blue Harbor, Aliso Viejo *Also called Blueyield Inc (G-15059)*
Blue Lake Casino...707 668-5101
777 Casino Way Blue Lk Blue Lake Blue Lake (95525) *(G-12455)*
Blue Mountain Air, Vacaville *Also called Blue Mountain Cnstr Svcs Inc (G-2169)*
Blue Mountain Cnstr Svcs Inc...707 820-2323
707 Aldridge Rd Ste B Vacaville (95688) *(G-2169)*
Blue Planet International Inc...213 742-9999
1526 E Washington Blvd Los Angeles (90021) *(G-8370)*
Blue River Seafood Inc...510 300-6800
25447 Industrial Blvd Hayward (94545) *(G-8629)*
Blue Rose Concrete Contrs Inc...909 823-6190
14636 Ceres Ave Fontana (92335) *(G-3235)*
Blue Sheild of California, Walnut Creek *Also called California Physicians Service (G-10262)*
Blue Shield of California, San Francisco *Also called California Physicians Service (G-10263)*
Blue Shield of California, El Dorado Hills *Also called California Physicians Service (G-10265)*
Blue Shield of California, El Segundo *Also called California Physicians Service (G-10266)*
Blue Shield of California, Woodland Hills *Also called California Physicians Service (G-10267)*
Blue Skies Landscape Maint, San Diego *Also called Cielo Azul Inc (G-824)*
Blue Sky Lodge Motel...831 659-2935
10 Flight Rd Carmel Valley (93924) *(G-12456)*
Blue Sky Services Inc...818 609-8779
5530 Corbin Ave Ste 220 Tarzana (91356) *(G-5035)*
Bluegill Solar, Moreno Valley *Also called Bluegill Technologies LLC (G-16871)*
Bluegill Technologies LLC...877 765-2770
11884 Welby Pl Ste 101 Moreno Valley (92557) *(G-16871)*
Blueline Construction, Rancho Cordova *Also called Ron Nurss Inc (G-3323)*
Bluevine...888 452-7805
401 Warren St Ste 300 Redwood City (94063) *(G-9774)*
Bluewater Envmtl Svcs Inc...510 346-8800
2075 Williams St San Leandro (94577) *(G-3499)*
Blueyield Inc...949 385-6219
15 Enterprise Ste 520 Aliso Viejo (92656) *(G-15059)*
Blufocus Inc...818 294-7695
10911 Riverside Dr 200 North Hollywood (91602) *(G-15060)*
Blumenthal Distributing Inc (PA)...909 930-2000
1901 S Archibald Ave Ontario (91761) *(G-6807)*
Bluprint Clothing Corp...323 780-4347
5600 Bandini Blvd Bell (90201) *(G-8371)*
Blx Group Inc...760 776-6622
71534 Sahara Rd Rancho Mirage (92270) *(G-270)*
Blx Group LLC...213 612-2400
777 S Figueroa St # 3200 Los Angeles (90017) *(G-10123)*
Blythe Nursing Care Center...760 922-8176
285 W Chanslor Way Blythe (92225) *(G-20414)*
BMA Long Beach, Long Beach *Also called Fresenius Med Care Long Beach (G-22627)*
BMA San Gabriel, Alhambra *Also called Bio-Mdcal Applications Cal Inc (G-22620)*
BMC Group Inc...310 321-5555
300 N Cntntl Blvd Ste 570 El Segundo (90245) *(G-23124)*
BMC Software Inc...713 918-8800
10620 Treena St Ste 130 San Diego (92131) *(G-15604)*
BMC Stock Holdings Inc...707 301-4475
3333 Vaca Valley Pkwy Vacaville (95688) *(G-3032)*
Bme Cmgi Uc Davis...530 754-5488
1 Shields Ave Davis (95616) *(G-26490)*
Bmi Imaging Systems Inc...916 924-6666
749 W Stadium Ln Sacramento (95834) *(G-7042)*
Bml Industries Inc...805 388-6800
1040 Avenida Acaso Camarillo (93012) *(G-7419)*
Bml Works Na LLC...650 268-8305
228 Hamilton Ave Fl 3 Palo Alto (94301) *(G-26943)*
Bmp, Van Nuys *Also called Bunim-Murray Productions (G-18056)*
Bmr 21 Erie St LLC...858 485-9840
17190 Bernardo Center Dr San Diego (92128) *(G-11327)*
Bmr Apps Inc...954 651-1412
548 Market St San Francisco (94104) *(G-16330)*
Bms Parent Inc (PA)...909 981-2341
1220 Dewey Way Ste F Upland (91786) *(G-26297)*
Bmt International SEC Svcs, Oakland *Also called Rory V Parker (G-16775)*
Bmt Scientific Marine Svcs Inc (HQ)...760 737-3505
955 Borra Pl Ste 100 Escondido (92029) *(G-25696)*
BMW of North America LLC...909 975-7355
2201 Corporate Center Dr Newbury Park (91320) *(G-6715)*
BMW of North America LLC...805 271-2400
5900 Arcturus Ave Oxnard (93033) *(G-6716)*
BMW of North America LLC...805 271-2400
5650 Arcturus Ave Oxnard (93033) *(G-6717)*
Bnb Norcal, Redwood City *Also called Truebeck Construction (G-1697)*
Bnbuilders...650 227-1957
201 Redwood Shores Pkwy Redwood City (94065) *(G-1742)*
Bni Enterprises Inc...909 305-1818
545 College Commerce Way Upland (91786) *(G-27735)*
BNP Paribas Asset MGT Inc...415 772-1300
1 Front St Fl 23 San Francisco (94111) *(G-9701)*
Bnsf Railway Company...909 386-4002
740 Carnegie Dr San Bernardino (92408) *(G-3607)*
Bnsf Railway Company...760 255-7803
200 N Avenue H Barstow (92311) *(G-3608)*
Bnsf Railway Company...323 869-3002
6300 Sheila St Commerce (90040) *(G-3609)*
Bnsf Railway Company...323 267-4133
3770 E Washington Blvd Vernon (90058) *(G-3610)*
Boardvantage Inc (HQ)...650 614-6000
4300 Bohannon Dr Ste 110 Menlo Park (94025) *(G-26944)*
Boardwalk and Parkway Bowl, El Cajon *Also called Newport Diversified Inc (G-17358)*
Boatworks, San Leandro *Also called Stepping Stn Grwth Ctr Fr Chld (G-24393)*
Bob Dillon Construction Inc...805 495-2607
856 Calle Margarita Thousand Oaks (91360) *(G-3033)*
BOB HOPE HEALTH CENTER, Woodland Hills *Also called Motion Picture and TV Fund (G-21753)*
Bob Hubbard Horse Trnsp Inc (PA)...951 369-3770
3730 S Riverside Ave Colton (92324) *(G-3983)*
Bobcat West, Fremont *Also called Pape Material Handling Inc (G-7874)*
Bobco Metals LLC...213 748-5171
2000 S Alameda St Vernon (90058) *(G-7361)*
Boboli International LLC (PA)...209 473-3507
1718 Boeing Way Ste 100 Stockton (95206) *(G-8809)*
Boca Mesa Incorporated...805 934-9470
3130 Skyway Dr Ste 701 Santa Maria (93455) *(G-27852)*
Bockmon & Woody Elc Co Inc...209 464-2615
1528 El Pinal Dr Stockton (95205) *(G-2535)*
Bodega Bay Associates...650 330-8888
1100 Alma St Ste 106 Menlo Park (94025) *(G-12457)*
Bodega Bay Lodge, Bodega Bay *Also called NAPA Valley Lodge LP (G-13013)*
Bodega Bay Lodge, Menlo Park *Also called Bodega Bay Associates (G-12457)*
Bodega Harbour Golf Links, Bodega Bay *Also called Bodega Harbour Homeowners Assn (G-25208)*
Bodega Harbour Homeowners Assn...707 875-3519
21301 Heron Dr Bodega Bay (94923) *(G-25208)*
Body Balance, Sherman Oaks *Also called Body Conqueror Inc (G-22668)*
Body Conqueror Inc...310 651-0387
4570 Van Nuys Blvd B Sherman Oaks (91403) *(G-22668)*

ALPHABETIC

Body Transformations, Lodi *Also called R DS For Healthcare (G-20346)*
Boeing Company......559 998-8260
Lemoore Nval Base Hnger 1 Lemoore (93245) ***(G-17930)***
Boeing Company......805 606-6340
Slc 2 Bldg 1628 San Luis Obispo (93401) ***(G-4904)***
Boeing Company......714 896-1301
5301 Bolsa Ave Huntington Beach (92647) ***(G-25697)***
Boeing Company......562 593-5511
2401 E Wardlow Rd Long Beach (90807) ***(G-26945)***
Boeing Company......818 466-8800
5800 Woolsey Canyon Rd Canoga Park (91304) ***(G-25698)***
Boeing Satellite Systems......310 662-9000
2000 E El Segundo Blvd El Segundo (90245) ***(G-7995)***
Boething Treeland Farms Inc......650 851-4770
2923 Alpine Rd Portola Valley (94028) ***(G-1004)***
Boething Treeland Farms Inc (PA)......818 883-1222
23475 Long Valley Rd Woodland Hills (91367) ***(G-1005)***
Boething Treeland Farms Inc......209 727-3741
20601 E Kettleman Ln Lodi (95240) ***(G-1006)***
Boething Treeland Nursery, Lodi *Also called Boething Treeland Farms Inc (G-1006)*
Bofi Federal Bank (HQ)......858 350-6200
4350 La Jolla Village Dr # 140 San Diego (92122) ***(G-9741)***
Bogart Construction Inc......949 453-1400
9980 Irvine Center Dr # 200 Irvine (92618) ***(G-1508)***
Boghosian Raisin Pkg Co Inc......559 834-5348
726 S 8th St Fowler (93625) ***(G-513)***
Bohemian Club (PA)......415 885-2440
624 Taylor St San Francisco (94102) ***(G-25209)***
Bohemian Grove, San Francisco *Also called Bohemian Club (G-25209)*
Boiling Point Rest Sca Inc......626 551-5181
13668 Valley Blvd Unit C2 City of Industry (91746) ***(G-14615)***
Boku Inc (PA)......415 375-3160
735 Battery St Fl 2 San Francisco (94111) ***(G-15061)***
Bolin Builders Inc......209 772-9721
3848 Berkesey Ln Valley Springs (95252) ***(G-1137)***
Bollingers Candelight Pavilion, Claremont *Also called Ben Bollinger Productions Inc (G-18371)*
Bolthouse Farms......661 366-7205
3200 E Brundage Ln Bakersfield (93304) ***(G-41)***
Bomel Construction Co Inc (PA)......714 921-1660
8195 E Kaiser Blvd Anaheim (92808) ***(G-1407)***
Bon Appetit Management Co......909 748-8970
1259 E Colton Ave Redlands (92374) ***(G-27351)***
Bon Suisse Inc......714 578-0001
392 W Walnut Ave Fullerton (92832) ***(G-27853)***
Bonanza Productions Inc......818 954-4212
4000 Warner Blvd Burbank (91522) ***(G-18460)***
Bond Manufacturing Co Inc......925 252-1135
1700 W 4th St Antioch (94509) ***(G-7800)***
Bonded Carpet, San Diego *Also called Bonded Inc (G-13590)*
Bonded Inc (PA)......858 576-8400
7831 Ostrow St San Diego (92111) ***(G-13590)***
Bondi-Nderson Assoc Insur Brks, Santa Rosa *Also called Northwest Insurance Agency (G-10813)*
Bonhams Bttrflds Actneers Corp (HQ)......415 861-7500
220 San Bruno Ave San Francisco (94103) ***(G-17034)***
Bonhams Corporation......415 861-7500
220 San Bruno Ave San Francisco (94103) ***(G-17035)***
Bonita Golf Club, Bonita *Also called Crockett & Coinc (G-18729)*
Bonita House Inc......510 923-0180
6333 Telg Ave Ste 102 Oakland (94609) ***(G-23687)***
Bonita Medical Offices, Bonita *Also called Kaiser Foundation Hospitals (G-21669)*
Bonne Bridge Muell Okeef & (PA)......213 480-1900
3699 Wilsh Boule Fl 10 Los Angeles (90010) ***(G-23125)***
Bonneville International Corp......323 634-1800
5900 Wilshire Blvd # 1900 Los Angeles (90036) ***(G-5750)***
Bonneville International Corp......415 777-0965
201 3rd St Fl 12 San Francisco (94103) ***(G-5751)***
Bonneville Steel Inc......866 956-8323
13654 Live Oak Ln Irwindale (91706) ***(G-3368)***
Bonnie Brae Cnvlscent Hosp Inc (PA)......213 483-8144
420 S Bonnie Brae St Los Angeles (90057) ***(G-21158)***
Bontadelli Inc......831 423-8572
2611 Mission St Santa Cruz (95060) ***(G-8697)***
Boom-Boom Jeans, Los Angeles *Also called Blue Planet International Inc (G-8370)*
Boomers, Newport Beach *Also called Festival Fun Parks LLC (G-19208)*
Boomers, Vista *Also called Festival Fun Parks LLC (G-19210)*
Boornazian Jensen & Garthe A......510 834-4350
555 12th St Oakland (94607) ***(G-23126)***
Boost Mobile LLC (PA)......949 451-1563
6316 Irvine Blvd Irvine (92620) ***(G-17036)***
Booth Ranches LLC......559 626-4472
440 Anchor Ave Orange Cove (93646) ***(G-464)***
Booz Allen Hamilton Inc......310 297-2100
5220 Pacific Concourse Dr Los Angeles (90045) ***(G-27352)***
Booz Allen Hamilton Inc......619 725-6500
1615 Murray Canyon Rd # 220 San Diego (92108) ***(G-27353)***
Booz Allen Hamilton Inc......310 524-1557
2250 E Imperial Hwy # 450 El Segundo (90245) ***(G-25699)***
Booz Allen Hamilton Inc......213 620-1900
555 S Flower St Fl 36 Los Angeles (90071) ***(G-27354)***
Bops Inc......650 254-2800
1200 Charleston Rd Mountain View (94043) ***(G-15605)***
Boq......619 556-0266
N9 56 Bldg 804 Rm 108 Lemoore (93246) ***(G-11233)***
Borbon Incorporated......714 994-0170
7312 Walnut Ave Buena Park (90620) ***(G-2431)***
Border Valley Trading Ltd......760 344-6700
604 Mead Rd Brawley (92227) ***(G-9127)***
Boreal Ridge Corporation......530 426-1012
19749 Boreal Ridge Rd Soda Springs (95728) ***(G-12458)***
Boreal Ski Area, Soda Springs *Also called Boreal Ridge Corporation (G-12458)*
Boretech Resrce Recovry Engine......209 373-2588
1820 Industrial Dr Stockton (95206) ***(G-7827)***
Boretech Rsurce Recovery Engrg, Stockton *Also called Boretech Resrce Recovry Engine (G-7827)*
Borg Produce Inc......213 305-6621
1601 E Olympic Blvd # 103 Los Angeles (90021) ***(G-514)***
Borgens & Borgens Inc......209 547-2980
141 E Acacia St Ste D Stockton (95202) ***(G-16577)***
Borjon Iscander......209 245-6289
18586 Highway 49 Plymouth (95669) ***(G-654)***
Borland Software Corporation......650 286-1900
951 Mariners Isl Blvd # 460 San Mateo (94404) ***(G-15606)***
Borrego Cmnty Hlth Foundation......760 765-1223
2721 Washington Julian (92036) ***(G-19376)***
Borrego Springs Bank......619 668-5159
7777 Alvarado Rd Ste 515 La Mesa (91942) ***(G-9545)***
Borrego Springs Country Club......760 767-3289
1112 Tilting Tee Dr Borrego Springs (92004) ***(G-18897)***
Borrmann Metal Center (PA)......818 846-7171
110 W Olive Ave Burbank (91502) ***(G-7362)***
Borunda Private SEC Patrol Inc......559 299-2662
1070 Brookhaven Dr Clovis (93612) ***(G-16578)***
Boshart Automotive Tstg Svcs......909 466-1602
1840 S Carlos Ave 15 Ontario (91761) ***(G-17037)***
Boskovich Farms Inc (PA)......805 487-2299
711 Diaz Ave Oxnard (93030) ***(G-515)***
Boskovich Farms Inc......805 987-1443
4224 Pleasant Valley Rd Camarillo (93012) ***(G-42)***
Bosman Dairy......559 752-1012
6802 Avenue 120 A Tipton (93272) ***(G-419)***
Boss Audio Systems, Oxnard *Also called Ava Enterprises Inc (G-7491)*
Boss Poultry......559 897-7507
4068 Avenue 404 Dinuba (93618) ***(G-450)***
Bossard North America Inc......562 906-2003
2000 Chabot Ct Tracy (95304) ***(G-7927)***
Boston Brick & Stone Inc......626 269-2622
2005 Lincoln Ave Pasadena (91103) ***(G-2805)***
Boston Properties Ltd Partnr......415 772-0500
4 Embarcadero Ctr Lbby 1 San Francisco (94111) ***(G-11951)***
Bostonia Medical Offices, El Cajon *Also called Kaiser Foundation Hospitals (G-21651)*
Botanica Landscapes, Yuba City *Also called United Landscape Resource Inc (G-972)*
Bottomley Distributing Co Inc......408 945-0660
755 Yosemite Dr Milpitas (95035) ***(G-9044)***
Boulder Active Club, Carlsbad *Also called 24 Hour Fitness Usa Inc (G-18580)*
Boulder Creek Post Acute, Poway *Also called Pomerado Operations LLC (G-20857)*
Boulevard Entertainment Inc......818 840-6969
903 S Lake St Ste 202 Burbank (91502) ***(G-17038)***
Bowers Ambulance Service, Long Beach *Also called Bowers Companies Inc (G-3776)*
Bowers Ambulance Service, Long Beach *Also called Bowers Companies Inc (G-3777)*
Bowers Companies Inc (HQ)......562 988-6460
3355 E Spring St Ste 301 Long Beach (90806) ***(G-3776)***
Bowers Companies Inc......562 988-6460
3355 E Spring St Ste 301 Long Beach (90806) ***(G-3777)***
Bowie Enterprises......559 732-2988
1920 S Mooney Blvd Visalia (93277) ***(G-17831)***
Bowie Enterprises (PA)......559 227-6221
4411 N Blackstone Ave Fresno (93726) ***(G-17832)***
Bowie Enterprises......559 292-6565
801 W Shaw Ave Clovis (93612) ***(G-17833)***
Bowie Enterprises......559 227-3400
4411 N Blackstone Ave Fresno (93726) ***(G-17876)***
Bowles & Verna......925 935-3300
2121 N Calif Blvd Ste 875 Walnut Creek (94596) ***(G-23127)***
Bowles Farming Co Inc......209 827-3000
11609 Hereford Rd Los Banos (93635) ***(G-347)***
Bowlmor AMF Corp......626 339-1286
1060 W San Bernardino Rd Covina (91722) ***(G-18511)***
Bowlmor AMF Corp......626 960-3636
675 S Glendora Ave West Covina (91790) ***(G-18512)***
Bowlmor AMF Corp......909 945-9392
7930 Haven Ave Ste 101 Rancho Cucamonga (91730) ***(G-18513)***
Bowlmor AMF Corp......951 698-2202
40440 California Oaks Rd Murrieta (92562) ***(G-18514)***
Bowman & Brooke-Attys, Torrance *Also called Bowman and Brooke LLP (G-23128)*
Bowman and Brooke LLP......310 768-3068
970 W 190th St Ste 700 Torrance (90502) ***(G-23128)***
Bowsmith Inc (PA)......559 592-9485
131 2nd St Exeter (93221) ***(G-13617)***
Box Inc (PA)......877 729-4269
900 Jefferson Ave Redwood City (94063) ***(G-15607)***
Box Bros Corp......310 394-8660
825 Wilshire Blvd Santa Monica (90401) ***(G-17039)***
Boy Scouts of America (PA)......213 353-9879
2333 Scout Way Los Angeles (90026) ***(G-25210)***
BOY'S & GIRL'S CLUB OF BAKERSF, Bakersfield *Also called Boys Girls CLB of Bakersfield (G-25216)*
Boyd & Associates......805 988-8298
445 E Esplanade Dr # 210 Oxnard (93036) ***(G-16579)***
Boyd & Associates (PA)......818 752-1888
2191 E Thompson Blvd Ventura (93001) ***(G-16580)***
Boyd & Associates......714 835-5423
3151 Airway Ave Ste K105 Costa Mesa (92626) ***(G-16581)***
Boyd Flotation Inc......909 357-6400
7551 Cherry Ave Fontana (92336) ***(G-6808)***

ALPHABETIC

Boyett Construction Inc (PA).....510 264-9100
2404 Tripaldi Way Hayward (94545) ***(G-2863)***
Boykin Mgt Co Ltd Lblty Co.....619 299-6633
3888 Greenwood St San Diego (92110) ***(G-12459)***
Boykin Mgt Co Ltd Lblty Co.....510 548-7920
200 Marina Blvd Berkeley (94710) ***(G-12460)***
Boykin Mgt Co Ltd Lblty Co.....619 298-8281
875 Hotel Cir S San Diego (92108) ***(G-12461)***
Boyle Engineering Corporation (HQ).....949 476-3300
999 W Town And Country Rd Orange (92868) ***(G-25700)***
Boyle Engineering Corporation.....714 543-5274
999 W Town And Country Rd Orange (92868) ***(G-25701)***
Boys & Girls CLB of Peninsula.....650 322-6255
401 Pierce Rd Menlo Park (94025) ***(G-18898)***
Boys & Girls Club of San Pedro, San Pedro *Also called Boys and Girls Clubs of The La* ***(G-25213)***
Boys & Girls Club Silicon Vly.....408 957-9685
518 Valley Way Milpitas (95035) ***(G-23688)***
Boys & Girls Club Simi Vly Inc.....805 527-4437
2850 Lemon Dr Simi Valley (93063) ***(G-25211)***
Boys & Girls Clubs Cent Sonoma.....707 528-7977
1400 N Dutton Ave Ste 14 Santa Rosa (95401) ***(G-25212)***
Boys & Girls Clubs of Marin A.....707 769-5322
203 Maria Dr Petaluma (94954) ***(G-24881)***
Boys and Girls Clubs of The La (PA).....310 833-1322
1200 S Cabrillo Ave San Pedro (90731) ***(G-25213)***
Boys and Girls Clubs of The La.....310 833-1322
1501 S Cabrillo Ave San Pedro (90731) ***(G-25214)***
Boys and Girls Clubs of The La.....310 833-1322
1700 Gulf Ave Wilmington (90744) ***(G-25215)***
Boys Girls CLB Huntington Vly (PA).....714 531-2582
16582 Brookhurst St Fountain Valley (92708) ***(G-23689)***
Boys Girls CLB of Bakersfield.....661 325-3730
801 Niles St Bakersfield (93305) ***(G-25216)***
Boys Girls CLB of Imperl Bch.....619 424-2266
847 Encina Ave Imperial Beach (91932) ***(G-25217)***
Boys Grls CLB Dsert Hot Sprng.....760 329-1312
42600 Cook St Ste 120 Palm Desert (92211) ***(G-23690)***
Boys Grls CLB Snta Monica Inc.....310 361-8500
1220 Lincoln Blvd Santa Monica (90401) ***(G-25218)***
Boys Grls Clubs Grdn Grove Inc (PA).....714 530-0430
10540 Chapman Ave Garden Grove (92840) ***(G-25219)***
Boys Grls Clubs Grdn Grove Inc.....714 537-8833
13645 Clinton St Garden Grove (92843) ***(G-25220)***
Boys Grls Clubs of Squoias Inc.....559 592-4074
1003 San Juan Ave Exeter (93221) ***(G-23691)***
Boys Republic (PA).....909 902-6690
1907 Boys Republic Dr Chino Hills (91709) ***(G-24567)***
Boys Town California Inc.....714 558-0303
2223 E Wellington Ave Santa Ana (92701) ***(G-25221)***
BP Arco, La Palma *Also called BP West Coast Products LLC* ***(G-1032)***
BP Industries Incorporated.....909 481-0227
5300 Concours Ontario (91764) ***(G-6848)***
BP Products W Coast Refinery, Carson *Also called BP West Coast Products LLC* ***(G-9004)***
BP West Coast Products LLC.....310 816-8787
22600 Wilmington Ave Carson (90745) ***(G-1030)***
BP West Coast Products LLC.....510 231-4724
1306 Canal Blvd Richmond (94804) ***(G-1031)***
BP West Coast Products LLC.....310 549-6204
1801 E Sepulveda Blvd Carson (90745) ***(G-9004)***
BP West Coast Products LLC.....714 670-5400
4 Centerpointe Dr La Palma (90623) ***(G-1032)***
Bpg Storage Solutions Inc.....562 467-2000
2033 N Main St Ste 340 Walnut Creek (94596) ***(G-26946)***
Bpo Management Services Inc (PA).....714 972-2670
8175 E Kaiser Blvd 100 Anaheim (92808) ***(G-15062)***
BQE Software Inc.....310 602-4020
3825 Del Amo Blvd Trrance Torrance Torrance (90503) ***(G-15608)***
BR Funsten, Manteca *Also called B R Funsten & Co* ***(G-6845)***
Bracket Global LLC.....415 293-1340
303 2nd St Ste 700 San Francisco (94107) ***(G-15063)***
Brad Rambo & Associates Inc (PA).....949 366-9911
1341 Calle Avanzado San Clemente (92673) ***(G-8335)***
Brad Watkins Masonry Inc.....818 360-3796
10315 Woodley Ave Ste 130 Granada Hills (91344) ***(G-2806)***
Braddock & Logan Group II LP.....925 736-4000
4155 Blackhawk Plaza Cir # 201 Danville (94506) ***(G-11952)***
Braddock & Logan Inc.....925 229-1747
3600 Pine St Apt 3600 Martinez (94553) ***(G-11099)***
Braddock & Logan Services Inc.....925 736-4000
4155 Blackhawk Plaza Cir # 201 Danville (94506) ***(G-1509)***
Braden Partners LP A Calif.....661 632-1979
7500 District Blvd Bakersfield (93313) ***(G-7247)***
Braden Partners LP A Calif (HQ).....415 893-1518
773 San Marin Dr Ste 2230 Novato (94945) ***(G-22379)***
Bradford & Barthel LLP (PA).....916 569-0790
2518 River Plaza Dr Sacramento (95833) ***(G-23129)***
Bradford Building Services.....323 720-4020
5200 S Eastern Ave Los Angeles (90040) ***(G-14239)***
Bradford Messenger Service.....559 252-0775
4955 E Andersen Ave # 118 Fresno (93727) ***(G-17040)***
Bradley Court, Chula Vista *Also called Healthcare MGT Systems Inc* ***(G-20659)***
Bradley Grdns Convalescent Ctr, San Jacinto *Also called Healthcare MGT Systems Inc* ***(G-20660)***
Bradley Melissa Real Estate.....415 459-1010
851 Irwin St Ste 104 San Rafael (94901) ***(G-11328)***
Bradshaw International Inc (PA).....909 476-3884
9409 Buffalo Ave Rancho Cucamonga (91730) ***(G-6849)***

Bradshaw Veterinary Clinic.....916 685-2494
9609 Bradshaw Rd Elk Grove (95624) ***(G-616)***
Brady Vorwerck Rydr & Cspno (PA).....480 456-9888
19200 Von Karman Ave Irvine (92612) ***(G-23130)***
Brady Company/Central Cal.....831 633-3315
13540 Blackie Rd Castroville (95012) ***(G-2864)***
Brady Company/Los Angeles Inc.....714 533-9850
1010 N Olive St Anaheim (92801) ***(G-2865)***
Brady Company/San Diego Inc.....619 462-2600
8100 Center St La Mesa (91942) ***(G-2866)***
Brady Gce II.....858 496-0500
3710 Ruffin Rd San Diego (92123) ***(G-25702)***
Brady Socal Incorporated.....619 462-2600
8100 Center St La Mesa (91942) ***(G-2867)***
Brady-Fortitude.....858 496-0500
3710 Ruffin Rd San Diego (92123) ***(G-1510)***
Braemar Country Club Inc.....323 873-6880
4001 Reseda Blvd Tarzana (91356) ***(G-18899)***
Braemar Partnership.....858 539-8600
3999 Mission Blvd San Diego (92109) ***(G-12462)***
Braga Fresh Family Farms Inc.....831 675-2154
33750 Moranda Rd Soledad (93960) ***(G-43)***
Bragg Crane & Rigging, Long Beach *Also called Bragg Investment Company Inc* ***(G-17041)***
Bragg Investment Company Inc (PA).....562 984-2400
6251 N Paramount Blvd Long Beach (90805) ***(G-17041)***
Braille Institute America Inc (PA).....323 663-1111
741 N Vermont Ave Los Angeles (90029) ***(G-23692)***
Brake Parts Inc LLC.....559 665-5781
711 S 3rd St Chowchilla (93610) ***(G-6718)***
Brand Energy Solutions LLC.....559 444-1970
4755 E Commerce Ave Fresno (93725) ***(G-3500)***
Brand Flower Farms Inc (PA).....805 684-5531
5300 Foothill Rd Carpinteria (93013) ***(G-9179)***
Brand Precision, Benicia *Also called Veolia Es Industrial Svcs Inc* ***(G-18032)***
Brand Precision Services, Benicia *Also called Veolia Es Industrial Svcs Inc* ***(G-14463)***
Brand Scaffold Service, Richmond *Also called Brand Services LLC* ***(G-3501)***
Brand Services Inc.....707 603-3400
535 Watt Dr Fairfield (94534) ***(G-7763)***
Brand Services LLC.....510 231-9640
940 Hensley St Richmond (94801) ***(G-3501)***
Brand Services of California, Fairfield *Also called Brand Services Inc* ***(G-7763)***
Brandel Manor, Turlock *Also called Emanuel Medical Center Inc* ***(G-21555)***
Branderscom Inc (PA).....650 292-2752
2551 Casey Ave Mountain View (94043) ***(G-9247)***
Brandes Inv Partners Inc (PA).....858 755-0239
11988 El Cmino Real Ste 6 San Diego (92130) ***(G-10124)***
Brandnet Inc.....415 216-4152
724 Battery St 3 San Francisco (94111) ***(G-27854)***
Brandrep Inc.....800 405-7119
16812 Armstrong Ave Irvine (92606) ***(G-27355)***
Brandt Cattle, Calipatria *Also called Brandt Co Inc* ***(G-407)***
Brandt Co Inc.....760 348-2295
7015 Brandt Rd Calipatria (92233) ***(G-407)***
Brandvia Alliance Inc.....408 955-0500
2159 Bering Dr San Jose (95131) ***(G-9248)***
Branlyn Prominence Inc.....760 843-5655
13334 Amargosa Rd Victorville (92392) ***(G-23693)***
Branlyn Prominence Inc (PA).....909 476-9030
9213 Archibald Ave Rancho Cucamonga (91730) ***(G-22380)***
Brannon Inc.....805 621-5000
1340 W Betteravia Rd Santa Maria (93455) ***(G-1408)***
Braswell Col Care Redlands CA.....909 792-6050
1618 Laurel Ave Redlands (92373) ***(G-21159)***
Braswells Villa Monte Vista.....858 487-6242
12696 Monte Vista Rd Poway (92064) ***(G-21160)***
Braswells Yucaipa Valley C.....909 795-2476
35253 Avenue H Yucaipa (92399) ***(G-20415)***
Braun Electric Company Inc (HQ).....661 633-1451
3000 E Belle Ter Bakersfield (93307) ***(G-2536)***
Braun Electric Company Inc.....661 763-1531
111 Main St Taft (93268) ***(G-2537)***
Braun Linen Service Inc (PA).....909 623-2678
16514 Garfield Ave Paramount (90723) ***(G-13539)***
Braun Linen Service Inc.....909 623-2678
396 La Mesa St Pomona (91766) ***(G-13501)***
Bravante Produce, Reedley *Also called Cal Packing & Storage LP* ***(G-4489)***
Bravo Tech Inc.....714 230-8333
6185 Phyllis Dr Unit D Cypress (90630) ***(G-5279)***
Brayton Purcell APC (PA).....415 898-1555
222 Rush Landing Rd Novato (94945) ***(G-23131)***
BRC Imagination Arts Inc.....818 841-8084
2711 Winona Ave Burbank (91504) ***(G-18052)***
Bre Diamond Hotel LLC.....650 712-7000
1 Miramontes Point Rd Half Moon Bay (94019) ***(G-12463)***
Bre/Japantown Owner LLC.....415 922-3200
1625 Post St San Francisco (94115) ***(G-12464)***
Break Floor Productions LLC.....212 247-7277
5446 Satsuma Ave North Hollywood (91601) ***(G-18373)***
Break Media, Beverly Hills *Also called Nextpoint Inc* ***(G-5670)***
Breakout Prison Outreach.....408 702-2405
1560 Berger Dr San Jose (95112) ***(G-23694)***
Breast Diagnostic Center.....310 517-4709
3275 Skypark Dr Ste A Torrance (90505) ***(G-19377)***
Breast Imaging Center, Sacramento *Also called Sutter Health* ***(G-20106)***
Brehm Communities (PA).....760 448-2420
1935 Camino Vida Roble # 200 Carlsbad (92008) ***(G-1138)***
Breitburn Energy Co, Santa Fe Springs *Also called Strand Energy Company* ***(G-1051)***
Breitburn Energy Partners I LP.....213 225-5900
707 Wilshire Blvd # 4600 Los Angeles (90017) ***(G-1033)***

ALPHABETIC

Breitburn GP LLC....213 225-5900
707 Wilshire Blvd # 4600 Los Angeles (90017) ***(G-1034)***
Bremer & Whyte LLP (PA)....949 221-1000
20320 Sw Birch St Ste 200 Newport Beach (92660) ***(G-23132)***
Bremer Whyte Brown Omeara, Newport Beach *Also called Bremer & Whyte LLP* ***(G-23132)***
Brendan Tours (PA)....818 428-6000
801 E Katella Ave Anaheim (92805) ***(G-4988)***
Brendan Worldwide Vacations, Anaheim *Also called Brendan Tours* ***(G-4988)***
Brenden Theatre Corporation....707 469-0180
531 Davis St Vacaville (95688) ***(G-18310)***
Brenden Theatre Corporation....209 491-7770
1021 10th St Frnt Modesto (95354) ***(G-18311)***
Brenden Theatre Corporation (PA)....925 677-0462
1985 Willow Pass Rd Ste C Concord (94520) ***(G-18312)***
Brennan Electric Inc....909 772-2263
460 S Stoddard Ave Ste 3 San Bernardino (92401) ***(G-2538)***
Brenner Info Tech Staffing Inc....818 705-7500
21300 Victory Blvd # 240 Woodland Hills (91367) ***(G-14616)***
Brenntag Pacific Inc (HQ)....562 903-9626
10747 Patterson Pl Santa Fe Springs (90670) ***(G-8981)***
Brentwood Bmdical RES Inst Inc....310 312-1554
11301 Wilshire Blvd Los Angeles (90073) ***(G-26739)***
Brentwood Cmmncations Intl Inc....818 333-3680
16135 Roscoe Blvd North Hills (91343) ***(G-18053)***
Brentwood Country Club....310 451-8011
590 S Burlingame Ave Los Angeles (90049) ***(G-18900)***
BRENTWOOD HEALTH CARE CENTER, Santa Monica *Also called Coastal Health Care Inc* ***(G-20463)***
Brentwood Skill Nursng & Rehab....530 527-2046
1795 Walnut St Red Bluff (96080) ***(G-21161)***
Brentwood Sklled Nursng Rhbltn, Red Bluff *Also called Brentwood Skill Nursng & Rehab* ***(G-21161)***
Brer Affiliates Inc (HQ)....949 794-7900
18500 Von Karman Ave # 400 Irvine (92612) ***(G-12211)***
Bret Boylan, Long Beach *Also called Bret Boylan Property Mgt* ***(G-26947)***
Bret Boylan Property Mgt....562 437-7886
35 N Alboni Pl Apt 409 Long Beach (90802) ***(G-26947)***
Brethren Inc....714 836-4800
1170 E Fruit St Santa Ana (92701) ***(G-8106)***
Brethren Hillcrest Homes....909 593-4917
2705 Mountain View Dr Ofc La Verne (91750) ***(G-24568)***
Breville Usa Inc....310 755-3000
19400 S Western Ave Torrance (90501) ***(G-6850)***
Brewster Marble Co Inc....818 834-2195
13576 Desmond St Pacoima (91331) ***(G-3006)***
Brewsters Automotive Inc....714 528-4683
17357 Los Angeles St Yorba Linda (92886) ***(G-17786)***
Briar Golf LP....760 328-6571
68311 Paseo Real Cathedral City (92234) ***(G-19154)***
Briarcrest Nursing Center Inc....562 927-2641
5648 Gotham St Bell (90201) ***(G-20416)***
Briarpatch Coop Nev Cnty Inc....530 272-5333
290 Sierra College Dr A Grass Valley (95945) ***(G-25508)***
Briarpatch Coop-Community Mkt, Grass Valley *Also called Briarpatch Coop Nev Cnty Inc* ***(G-25508)***
Briarwood Health Care Inc....916 383-2741
5901 Lemon Hill Ave Sacramento (95824) ***(G-21162)***
Brickley Construction Co Inc....909 888-2010
957 Reece St San Bernardino (92411) ***(G-3502)***
Brickley Environmental, San Bernardino *Also called Brickley Construction Co Inc* ***(G-3502)***
Brickwalk Systems Integration....800 495-5779
425 Market St Fl 22 San Francisco (94105) ***(G-27356)***
Bricsnet FM America Inc....202 756-1840
1820 Harvest Rd Pleasanton (94566) ***(G-16331)***
Bridge Bank, San Jose *Also called Western Alliance Bank* ***(G-9539)***
Bridge Housing Acquisition....415 989-1111
1 Hawthorne St Ste 400 San Francisco (94105) ***(G-10963)***
Bridge Housing Corporation (PA)....415 989-1111
600 California St Ste 900 San Francisco (94108) ***(G-11953)***
Bridge Medical Inc....858 350-0100
120 S Sierra Ave Solana Beach (92075) ***(G-8238)***
Bridgepoint At San Francisco, San Francisco *Also called Kisco Senior Living LLC* ***(G-27097)***
Bridger Commercial Funding LLC....707 953-7475
249 Boas Dr Santa Rosa (95409) ***(G-9916)***
Bridges At Gale Ranch LLC....925 735-4253
9000 S Gale Ridge Rd San Ramon (94582) ***(G-18901)***
Bridges At Sn Pdro Pnnsla Hspt....310 514-5359
1300 W 7th St Fl 4 San Pedro (90732) ***(G-22669)***
Bridges Club At Rancho SA....858 759-7200
18550 Seven Bridges Rd Rancho Santa Fe (92091) ***(G-25222)***
Bridges From School To Work, Oakland *Also called Marriott Foundation For People* ***(G-24362)***
Bridges Golf Club, The, San Ramon *Also called Bridges At Gale Ranch LLC* ***(G-18901)***
Bridgford Foods, Anaheim *Also called A S I Corporation* ***(G-13809)***
Bridgford Marketing Company (HQ)....714 526-5533
1308 N Patt St Anaheim (92801) ***(G-8665)***
Brieck Restoration Inc....858 679-9928
13750 Danielson St Poway (92064) ***(G-1139)***
Brience Inc (HQ)....415 974-5300
128 Spear St Fl 3 San Francisco (94105) ***(G-15064)***
Brier Oak On Sunset LLC....323 663-3951
5154 W Sunset Blvd Los Angeles (90027) ***(G-21163)***
Brier Oak On Sunset Rehab, Los Angeles *Also called Skilled Healthcare LLC* ***(G-20918)***
Brier Oak On Sunset Rehab Ctr, Los Angeles *Also called Brier Oak On Sunset LLC* ***(G-21163)***
Briercrest Inglewoodhealthcare, Inglewood *Also called American Nursing Home MGT Inc* ***(G-27830)***
Briggs Electric Inc (PA)....714 544-2500
14381 Franklin Ave Tustin (92780) ***(G-2539)***
Bright Bristol Street LLC....714 557-3000
3131 Bristol St Costa Mesa (92626) ***(G-12465)***
Bright Caregivers, Huntington Beach *Also called Medical Diagnostic* ***(G-21312)***
Bright Expectations....951 360-2070
8175 Limonite Ave Ste C Riverside (92509) ***(G-22381)***
Bright Health Physicians (PA)....562 947-8478
15725 Whittier Blvd # 500 Whittier (90603) ***(G-19378)***
Bright Horizons Chld Ctrs LLC....408 853-2196
800 Barber Ln Milpitas (95035) ***(G-24418)***
Bright Horizons Chld Ctrs LLC....805 447-6793
1 Amgen Center Dr Thousand Oaks (91320) ***(G-24419)***
Bright House Networks LLC....661 634-2200
4450 California Ave Ste A Bakersfield (93309) ***(G-5936)***
Bright Now Dental, Irvine *Also called Smile Brands Group Inc* ***(G-27216)***
Bright Pharmaceutical Services....818 981-9100
4570 Van Nuys Blvd Sherman Oaks (91403) ***(G-8239)***
Brightcloud Inc....858 652-4803
4370 La Jolla Village Dr # 820 San Diego (92122) ***(G-16872)***
Brightcurrent Inc....877 896-3306
55 Harrison St Ste 300 Oakland (94607) ***(G-27357)***
Brightedge Technologies Inc (PA)....800 578-8023
999 Baker Way Ste 500 San Mateo (94404) ***(G-15065)***
Brighter Beginnings (PA)....510 903-7503
3478 Buskirk Ave Ste 105 Pleasant Hill (94523) ***(G-23695)***
Brighterion Inc....415 986-5600
150 Spear St Fl 10 San Francisco (94105) ***(G-15066)***
Brighton Convalescent Center....626 798-9124
1836 N Fair Oaks Ave Pasadena (91103) ***(G-21164)***
Brighton Gardens Inc....858 259-2222
13101 Hartfield Ave San Diego (92130) ***(G-20417)***
Brighton Gardens of Camarillo, Camarillo *Also called Sunrise Senior Living LLC* ***(G-20982)***
Brighton Gardens of Sunrise, Palm Desert *Also called Sunrise Senior Living Inc* ***(G-20948)***
Brighton Health Alliance (PA)....619 461-0376
8322 Clairemont Mesa Blvd San Diego (92111) ***(G-20418)***
Brighton Place East Inc....619 461-3222
8625 Lamar St Spring Valley (91977) ***(G-20419)***
Brighton Place of San Diego, San Diego *Also called Brighton Health Alliance* ***(G-20418)***
Brighton Place San Diego....619 263-2166
1350 Euclid Ave San Diego (92105) ***(G-20420)***
BRIGHTON PLACE SPRING VALLEY, Spring Valley *Also called B-Spring Valley LLC* ***(G-20402)***
Brightroll Inc (HQ)....415 677-9222
343 Sansome St Ste 600 San Francisco (94104) ***(G-13821)***
Brightscope Inc....858 452-7500
9191 Towne Centre Dr # 400 San Diego (92122) ***(G-15609)***
Brightsource Energy Inc (PA)....510 550-8161
1999 Harrison St Ste 2150 Oakland (94612) ***(G-2027)***
Brightstar Health, Torrance *Also called Smart Choice Investments Inc* ***(G-14788)***
Brightview Companies LLC....209 993-9277
2447 Stagecoach Rd Stockton (95215) ***(G-744)***
Brightview Companies LLC....626 574-3940
201 Longden Ave Irwindale (91706) ***(G-745)***
Brightview Companies LLC (HQ)....818 223-8500
24151 Ventura Blvd Calabasas (91302) ***(G-2028)***
Brightview Companies LLC....714 437-1586
11555 Coley River Cir Fountain Valley (92708) ***(G-815)***
Brightview Golf Maint Inc....805 968-6400
405 Glen Annie Rd Santa Barbara (93117) ***(G-2029)***
Brightview Golf Maint Inc (HQ)....818 223-8500
24151 Ventura Blvd Calabasas (91302) ***(G-2030)***
Brightview Landscape Dev Inc (HQ)....818 223-8500
24151 Ventura Blvd Calabasas (91302) ***(G-746)***
Brightview Landscape Dev Inc....858 458-9900
8450 Miramar Pl San Diego (92121) ***(G-2031)***
Brightview Landscape Dev Inc....818 838-4700
13571 Vaughn St San Fernando (91340) ***(G-816)***
Brightview Landscape Dev Inc....714 546-7975
11555 Cley Rver Cir Ste A Fountain Valley (92708) ***(G-2032)***
Brightview Landscape Dev Inc....714 414-0914
2890 E Miraloma Ave Anaheim (92806) ***(G-747)***
Brightview Landscape Svcs Inc....510 723-0690
20551 Corsair Blvd Hayward (94545) ***(G-748)***
Brightview Landscape Svcs Inc....858 458-1900
8500 Miramar Pl San Diego (92121) ***(G-749)***
Brightview Landscape Svcs Inc....925 957-8831
4677 Pacheco Blvd Martinez (94553) ***(G-750)***
Brightview Landscape Svcs Inc....714 546-7843
1960 S Yale St Santa Ana (92704) ***(G-751)***
Brightview Landscape Svcs Inc....916 381-1121
5745 Alder Ave Sacramento (95828) ***(G-752)***
Brightview Landscape Svcs Inc....925 373-9500
7039 Commerce Cir Ste B Pleasanton (94588) ***(G-753)***
Brightview Landscape Svcs Inc....310 327-8700
17813 S Main St Ste 105 Gardena (90248) ***(G-754)***
Brightview Landscapes LLC....951 657-4603
144 Malbert St Ste A Perris (92570) ***(G-755)***
Brightview Landscapes LLC....760 929-8509
2420 Cougar Dr Carlsbad (92010) ***(G-756)***
Brightview Landscapes LLC....619 644-8584
9090 Birch St Spring Valley (91977) ***(G-757)***
Brightview Tree Company....661 305-3312
9500 Foothill Blvd Sunland (91040) ***(G-1007)***
Brightview Tree Company....805 524-3939
3200 W Telegraph Rd Fillmore (93015) ***(G-1008)***

A L P H A B E T I C

Brightview Tree Company 925 862-2485
8501 Calaveras Rd Sunol (94586) ***(G-1009)***
Brightview Tree Company 209 886-5511
28915 E Funck Rd Farmington (95230) ***(G-1010)***
Brilliance Investment LLC 510 568-1880
8350 Edes Ave Oakland (94621) ***(G-12466)***
Brilliant General Maintinc 408 287-6708
954 Chestnut St San Jose (95110) ***(G-14240)***
Brilliant Sftwr Solutions Inc 510 742-5120
39350 Civic Center Dr # 310 Fremont (94538) ***(G-15910)***
Brillstein Entrmt Partners LLC (PA) 310 205-5100
9150 Wilshire Blvd # 350 Beverly Hills (90212) ***(G-18054)***
Brillstein Grey Entertainment, Beverly Hills *Also called Brillstein Entrmt Partners LLC* ***(G-18054)***
Brinckerhoff Parsons Group LLC 916 567-2500
2329 Oakes Dr Ste 200 Sacramento (95833) ***(G-27358)***
Brinderson LP (HQ) 714 466-7100
19000 Macarthur Blvd 8 Irvine (92612) ***(G-25703)***
Brinderson LP 714 466-7100
19000 Macarthur Blvd 8 Irvine (92612) ***(G-25704)***
Brinderson & Associates 714 466-7100
19000 Macarthur Blvd 8 Irvine (92612) ***(G-25705)***
Brinks Incorporated 818 503-8630
1120 Venice Blvd Los Angeles (90015) ***(G-16582)***
Brinks Incorporated 619 263-6615
4520 Federal Blvd Ste A San Diego (92102) ***(G-16583)***
Brinks Incorporated 916 452-5279
8178 Alpine Ave Unit A Sacramento (95826) ***(G-16584)***
Brinks Incorporated 408 436-7717
1630 Old Bayshore Hwy San Jose (95112) ***(G-16585)***
Brinks Incorporated 323 262-2646
1821 S Soto St Los Angeles (90023) ***(G-16586)***
Brisam Lax (de) LLC 310 649-5151
9901 S La Cienega Blvd Los Angeles (90045) ***(G-12467)***
Brisbane Mechanical, Brisbane *Also called FW Spencer & Son Inc* ***(G-2232)***
Bristlecone Incorporated 650 386-4000
10 Almaden Blvd Ste 600 San Jose (95113) ***(G-15067)***
Bristol Hotel 619 232-6141
1055 1st Ave San Diego (92101) ***(G-12468)***
Bristol Park Medical Group, Fountain Valley *Also called St Jude Hospital Yorba Linda* ***(G-20059)***
Bristol, The, San Diego *Also called Beston Development* ***(G-12444)***
Brita Products Company 510 271-7000
1221 Broadway Ste 290 Oakland (94612) ***(G-7705)***
Brite Media Group LLC 877 479-7777
50 1st St Ste 600 San Francisco (94105) ***(G-13960)***
Brite Media LLC 818 849-3560
16027 Ventura Blvd # 210 Encino (91436) ***(G-13961)***
Brite Promotions, Encino *Also called Brite Media LLC* ***(G-13961)***
Briteworks Inc 626 337-0099
620 N Commercial Ave Covina (91723) ***(G-14241)***
Brithinee Electric 909 825-7971
620 S Rancho Ave Colton (92324) ***(G-7420)***
Brittany House LLC 562 421-4717
5401 E Centralia St Long Beach (90808) ***(G-24569)***
Brittney House 562 421-4717
5401 E Centralia St Long Beach (90808) ***(G-22382)***
Britz Fertilizers Inc 559 659-2033
35836 W Bullard Ave Firebaugh (93622) ***(G-9128)***
Britz Fertilizers Inc 559 884-2421
21817 S Frsno Coalinga Rd Five Points (93624) ***(G-9129)***
Brix Group Inc (PA) 559 457-4700
838 N Laverne Ave Fresno (93727) ***(G-7534)***
Brix Group Inc 559 499-1890
80 Van Ness Ave Fresno (93721) ***(G-7535)***
Broad Beach Films Inc 323 468-5120
1438 N Gower St Ste 48 Los Angeles (90028) ***(G-14135)***
Broadcast Co of Americas LLC (PA) 858 453-0658
6160 Cornerstone Ct E San Diego (92121) ***(G-5752)***
Broadcom Foundation 949 926-9500
5300 California Ave # 14067 Irvine (92617) ***(G-25223)***
Broadmoor Hotel (PA) 415 776-7034
1499 Sutter St San Francisco (94109) ***(G-11100)***
Broadmoor Hotel 415 673-8445
1465 65th St Apt 274 Emeryville (94608) ***(G-12469)***
Broadmoor Hotel 415 673-2511
1000 Sutter St San Francisco (94109) ***(G-12470)***
Broadrach Cpitl Prtners Fund I 650 331-2500
248 Homer Ave Palo Alto (94301) ***(G-12107)***
Broadreach Capitl Partners LLC 310 691-5760
6430 W Sunset Blvd # 504 Los Angeles (90028) ***(G-12286)***
Broadreach Capitl Partners LLC (PA) 650 331-2500
248 Homer Ave Palo Alto (94301) ***(G-9966)***
Broadreach Capitl Partners LLC 415 354-4640
235 Montgomery St # 1018 San Francisco (94104) ***(G-12287)***
Broadsoft Contact Center Inc 408 338-0900
930 Hamlin Ct Sunnyvale (94089) ***(G-15068)***
Broadspire Inc 213 785-8043
19425 Soled Canyo Rd Ste Santa Clarita (91351) ***(G-5565)***
Broadstone Raquet Club, Folsom *Also called Spare-Time Inc* ***(G-19086)***
Broadview Inc 323 221-9174
4570 Griffin Ave Los Angeles (90031) ***(G-20421)***
Broadvision Inc (PA) 650 331-1000
1700 Seaport Blvd Ste 210 Redwood City (94063) ***(G-15610)***
Broadway By Bay 650 579-5565
1155 Broadway St Ste 206 Redwood City (94063) ***(G-18374)***
Broadway Manor Care Center, Glendale *Also called Longwood Management Corp* ***(G-21296)***
Broadway Mech - Contrs Inc 510 746-4000
873 81st Ave Oakland (94621) ***(G-2170)***
Broadway Typewriter Co Inc 619 645-0253
1055 6th Ave Ste 101 San Diego (92101) ***(G-7103)***
Brocade Cmmnctions Systems Inc 408 333-4300
110 Holger Way San Jose (95134) ***(G-27855)***
Brocchini Farms Inc 209 599-4229
27011 S Austin Rd Ripon (95366) ***(G-144)***
Brock G and L Cnstr Co Inc 209 931-3626
4145 Calloway Ct Stockton (95215) ***(G-1912)***
Broder Bros Co 559 233-9900
3443 E Central Ave Fresno (93725) ***(G-8336)***
Broker Solutions Inc 800 450-2010
233 Milford Dr Corona Del Mar (92625) ***(G-9775)***
Broker Solutions Inc 951 637-2300
11820 Pierce St Riverside (92505) ***(G-17042)***
Broker Solutions Inc 760 633-0102
662 Encinitas Blvd Encinitas (92024) ***(G-9776)***
Broker Solutions Inc 909 458-0718
800 N Haven Ave Ste 330 Ontario (91764) ***(G-27359)***
Broker Solutions Inc (PA) 800 450-2010
14511 Myford Rd Tustin (92780) ***(G-27360)***
Brokerage Lgstics Slutions Inc 619 671-0276
1659 Gailes Blvd San Diego (92154) ***(G-5036)***
Bronco Concrete Inc 559 323-5005
3197 E North Ave 101 Fresno (93725) ***(G-3236)***
Brook Furniture Clearance Ctr, Hayward *Also called Brook Furniture Rental Inc* ***(G-14519)***
Brook Furniture Rental Inc 510 487-4440
30985 Santana St Hayward (94544) ***(G-14519)***
Brook Side Development, Stockton *Also called Groupe Development Associates* ***(G-11972)***
Brookdale Elk Grove, Elk Grove *Also called Brookdale Senior Living Inc* ***(G-21067)***
Brookdale Folsom, Folsom *Also called Brookdale Senior Living Inc* ***(G-20423)***
Brookdale Fresno, Fresno *Also called Brookdale Lving Cmmunities Inc* ***(G-11101)***
Brookdale Lving Cmmunities Inc 559 321-8624
1715 E Alluvial Ave Fresno (93720) ***(G-11101)***
Brookdale Lving Cmmunities Inc 408 445-7770
1009 Blossom River Way San Jose (95123) ***(G-24570)***
Brookdale Lving Cmmunities Inc 650 366-3900
485 Woodside Rd Ofc Redwood City (94061) ***(G-20422)***
Brookdale Senior Living Inc 714 671-7898
285 W Central Ave Brea (92821) ***(G-23696)***
Brookdale Senior Living Inc 209 839-6623
355 W Grant Line Rd Ofc Tracy (95376) ***(G-22383)***
Brookdale Senior Living Inc 916 725-7418
7418 Stock Ranch Rd Citrus Heights (95621) ***(G-18801)***
Brookdale Senior Living Inc 818 718-1547
20801 Devonshire St Chatsworth (91311) ***(G-10649)***
Brookdale Senior Living Inc 760 340-5999
72201 Country Club Dr Rancho Mirage (92270) ***(G-11102)***
Brookdale Senior Living Inc 626 301-0204
201 E Foothill Blvd Monrovia (91016) ***(G-11103)***
Brookdale Senior Living Inc 916 683-1881
6727 Laguna Park Dr Elk Grove (95758) ***(G-21067)***
Brookdale Senior Living Inc 951 929-5988
1177 S Palm Ave Hemet (92543) ***(G-24571)***
Brookdale Senior Living Inc 714 489-8966
2050 Gondar Ave Long Beach (90815) ***(G-21165)***
Brookdale Senior Living Inc 760 346-7772
72750 Country Club Dr Rancho Mirage (92270) ***(G-24572)***
Brookdale Senior Living Inc 209 823-0164
430 N Union Rd Manteca (95337) ***(G-17787)***
Brookdale Senior Living Inc 916 983-9300
780 Harrington Way Folsom (95630) ***(G-20423)***
Brookdale Senior Living Inc 951 744-9861
1001 N Lyon Ave Hemet (92545) ***(G-21166)***
Brookdale Senior Living Inc 951 808-9387
2005 Kellogg Ave Corona (92879) ***(G-24573)***
Brookdale Snior Lving Cmmnties 909 796-5421
25585 Van Leuven St Loma Linda (92354) ***(G-21167)***
Brookdale Sunwest, Hemet *Also called Brookdale Senior Living Inc* ***(G-21166)***
Brooker Associates 949 559-4877
16372 Cnstr Cir E 5 Irvine (92618) ***(G-988)***
Brookfeld Bay Area Hldings LLC 925 743-8000
500 La Gonda Way Ste 100 Danville (94526) ***(G-11954)***
Brookfeld Sthland Holdings LLC 714 427-6868
3200 Park Center Dr # 1000 Costa Mesa (92626) ***(G-1140)***
Brookfield 1996 California, Del Mar *Also called Brookfield Homes of California* ***(G-1141)***
Brookfield Dtla Fund Office 626 792-2727
191 N Los Robles Ave Pasadena (91101) ***(G-12471)***
Brookfield Dtla Fund Office 213 626-3300
355 S Grand Ave Ste 3300 Los Angeles (90071) ***(G-12239)***
Brookfield Homes, Danville *Also called Brookfeld Bay Area Hldings LLC* ***(G-11954)***
Brookfield Homes of California 858 481-8500
12865 Pointe Del Mar Way # 200 Del Mar (92014) ***(G-1141)***
Brookfield Homes Pacific Inc (HQ) 858 481-8500
12865 Pointe Del 200 Del Mar (92014) ***(G-1142)***
Brookfield Properties, Los Angeles *Also called Trz Holdings II Inc* ***(G-11886)***
Brookfield Relocation Inc (HQ) 949 794-7900
3333 Michelson Dr # 1000 Irvine (92612) ***(G-12212)***
Brookfield Residential, Costa Mesa *Also called Brookfeld Sthland Holdings LLC* ***(G-1140)***
Brookside Community Health Ctr 510 215-5001
1030 Nevin Ave Richmond (94801) ***(G-19379)***
Brookside Country Club 209 956-6200
3603 Saint Andrews Dr Stockton (95219) ***(G-18902)***
Brookside Golf Course, Pasadena *Also called City of Pasadena* ***(G-18725)***
Brooktrails Lodge LLC 707 459-1596
24675 Birch St Willits (95490) ***(G-12472)***
Brosamer & Wall LLC 925 932-7900
1777 Oakland Blvd Ste 300 Walnut Creek (94596) ***(G-11329)***

ALPHABETIC

Brotman Medical Partners, Culver City *Also called Southern Cal Hosp At Culver Cy* ***(G-21900)***
Broward Builders Inc..........530 406-1815
1200 E Kentucky Ave Woodland (95776) ***(G-1511)***
Brower Mechanical Inc..........530 749-0808
4060 Alvis Ct Rocklin (95677) ***(G-17917)***
Brown & Brown Inc..........805 965-0071
1025 Chapala St Santa Barbara (93101) ***(G-10650)***
Brown & Toland Medical Group (PA)..........415 972-4162
1221 Broadway Ste 700 Oakland (94612) ***(G-19380)***
Brown & Toland Medical Group..........415 923-3015
2100 Webster St Ste 109 San Francisco (94115) ***(G-19381)***
Brown and Caldwell (PA)..........925 937-9010
201 N Civic Dr Ste 115 Walnut Creek (94596) ***(G-25706)***
Brown and Caldwell..........530 747-0650
1590 Drew Ave Ste 210 Davis (95618) ***(G-25707)***
Brown and Caldwell..........858 514-8822
9665 Chesapeake Dr # 201 San Diego (92123) ***(G-25708)***
Brown and Streza LLP..........949 453-2900
40 Pacifica Ste 1500 Irvine (92618) ***(G-27361)***
Brown Armstrong Accntancy Corp..........661 324-4971
4200 Truxtun Ave Ste 300 Bakersfield (93309) ***(G-26298)***
Brown Armstrong Cpas, Bakersfield *Also called Brown Armstrong Accntancy Corp* ***(G-26298)***
Brown Construction Inc..........916 374-8616
1465 Entp Blvd Ste 100 West Sacramento (95691) ***(G-1298)***
Brownco Construction Co Inc..........714 935-9600
1000 E Katella Ave Anaheim (92805) ***(G-1512)***
Browne Child Development Ctr, Oceanside *Also called Business and Support Services* ***(G-24420)***
Brownie's Digital Imaging, Sacramento *Also called American Reprographics Co LLC* ***(G-14101)***
Browning Apartments..........213 252-8847
1104 Browning Blvd Los Angeles (90037) ***(G-11104)***
Browning Mnor Cnvalescent Hosp, Delano *Also called Moyles Health Care Inc* ***(G-21321)***
Browning-Ferris Inds Cal Inc..........650 637-1411
333 Shoreway Rd San Carlos (94070) ***(G-6445)***
Browning-Ferris Industries Inc..........408 262-1401
1601 Dixon Landing Rd Milpitas (95035) ***(G-6446)***
Browning-Ferris Industries Inc..........818 790-5410
9200 Glenoaks Blvd Sun Valley (91352) ***(G-6447)***
Brownstone Companies Inc..........310 297-3600
2629 Manhattan Beach Blvd # 100 Redondo Beach (90278) ***(G-7536)***
Brownstone Security, Redondo Beach *Also called Brownstone Companies Inc* ***(G-7536)***
Browsercam..........415 378-6936
915 Cole St Ste 220 San Francisco (94117) ***(G-16221)***
Brsc Inc..........310 549-9180
12801 Leffingwell Ave Santa Fe Springs (90670) ***(G-7677)***
Bruce Olson Construction Inc..........530 581-1087
7320 River Rd Tahoe City (96145) ***(G-1299)***
Bruce Olson Construction Inc..........530 581-1087
7320 River Rd Olympic Valley (96146) ***(G-1143)***
Bruck Lighting, Tustin *Also called Ledra Brands Inc* ***(G-6871)***
Brunswick Cal Oaks Bowl, Murrieta *Also called Bowlmor AMF Corp* ***(G-18514)***
Brunswick Corner Partnership..........916 649-7500
550 Howe Ave Ste 200 Sacramento (95825) ***(G-11330)***
Brunswick Covino Lanes, Covina *Also called Bowlmor AMF Corp* ***(G-18511)***
Brunswick Deer Creks Lnes 213, Rancho Cucamonga *Also called Bowlmor AMF Corp* ***(G-18513)***
Brunton Enterprises Inc..........562 945-0013
8815 Sorensen Ave Santa Fe Springs (90670) ***(G-3369)***
Brutoco Engrg & Cnstr Inc..........909 350-3535
1272 Center Court Dr # 101 Covina (91724) ***(G-1743)***
Bryan Cave LLP..........415 675-3400
333 Market St Fl 25 San Francisco (94105) ***(G-23133)***
Bryan Cave LLP..........949 223-7000
3161 Michelson Dr # 1500 Irvine (92612) ***(G-23134)***
Bryan Cave LLP..........310 576-2100
120 Broadway Ste 300 Santa Monica (90401) ***(G-23135)***
Bryant Ranch Prepack..........818 764-7225
1919 N Victory Pl Burbank (91504) ***(G-8240)***
Bserv Inc (PA)..........415 277-9900
333 Bush St Fl 26 San Francisco (94104) ***(G-9712)***
Bsgs Five Points, Five Points *Also called Britz Fertilizers Inc* ***(G-9129)***
Bsia Natural Resources Co..........805 650-2794
4475 Dupont Ct Ste 4 Ventura (93003) ***(G-1070)***
BSK Associates..........559 497-2888
1414 Stanislaus St Fresno (93706) ***(G-25709)***
Bsl Golf Corp..........831 899-7271
1 Mcclure Way Seaside (93955) ***(G-18718)***
Bsmi, Brentwood *Also called Bay Standard Manufacturing Inc* ***(G-7676)***
Bssp, Sausalito *Also called Butler Shine Stern Prtners LLC* ***(G-13822)***
Bst Enterprises Inc..........310 638-1222
17801 S Susana Rd Compton (90221) ***(G-6719)***
Bstz, Los Angeles *Also called Blakely Skloff Tylor Zfman LLP* ***(G-23117)***
BT Americas Inc..........310 335-2600
2160 E Grand Ave El Segundo (90245) ***(G-7537)***
BT Americas Inc..........646 487-7400
2160 E Grand Ave El Segundo (90245) ***(G-7538)***
BT Holdings Inc..........707 279-4317
4150 Soda Bay Rd Kelseyville (95451) ***(G-229)***
BT Infonet, El Segundo *Also called Infonet Services Corporation* ***(G-5636)***
Bti Wireless, Cypress *Also called Bravo Tech Inc* ***(G-5279)***
Btig LLC (PA)..........415 248-2200
600 Montgomery St Fl 6 San Francisco (94111) ***(G-9967)***
Bubbia Inc..........818 884-2000
7931 Deering Ave Canoga Park (91304) ***(G-9249)***
Buchalter Nemer A Prof Corp (PA)..........213 891-0700
1000 Wilshire Blvd # 1500 Los Angeles (90017) ***(G-23136)***
Buchalter Nemer A Prof Corp..........714 549-5150
18400 Von Karman Ave # 800 Irvine (92612) ***(G-23137)***
Buchanan Dental Center, San Francisco *Also called U C S F School of Dentistry* ***(G-20281)***
Buchanan Fund I LLC..........949 721-1414
620 Nwport Ctr Dr Ste 850 Newport Beach (92660) ***(G-12288)***
Buchanan Street Partners LP..........949 721-1414
3501 Jamboree Rd Ste 4200 Newport Beach (92660) ***(G-11331)***
Buck Consultants LLC..........310 282-8232
1801 Century Park E # 500 Los Angeles (90067) ***(G-28119)***
Buck Consultants LLC..........619 725-1769
7676 Hazard Center Dr # 400 San Diego (92108) ***(G-28120)***
Buck Inst For RES On Aging (PA)..........415 209-2000
8001 Redwood Blvd Novato (94945) ***(G-26740)***
Buckelew Programs (PA)..........415 457-6964
555 Northgate Dr Ste 200 San Rafael (94903) ***(G-23697)***
Buckingham Affrdbl Aprtmnts LP..........424 273-6162
11911 San Vicente Blvd Los Angeles (90049) ***(G-26948)***
Buckingham Apartments, Los Angeles *Also called Buckingham Affrdbl Aprtmnts LP* ***(G-26948)***
Buckingham Property Management..........559 322-1105
12609 Moffatt Ln Fresno (93730) ***(G-13739)***
Buckland Vineyard Management (PA)..........530 333-1534
4560 Slodusty Rd Garden Valley (95633) ***(G-26949)***
Buckles-Smith Electric Company (PA)..........408 280-7777
801 Savaker Ave San Jose (95126) ***(G-7828)***
Budget Electric, Tracy *Also called American Engrg Contrs Inc* ***(G-2518)***
Budget Electrical Contrs Inc..........909 381-2646
25051 5th St San Bernardino (92410) ***(G-2540)***
Budget Rent-A-Car, Beverly Hills *Also called Star Lax LLC* ***(G-17693)***
Budget Rent-A-Car, San Diego *Also called Bw-Budget-Sda LLC* ***(G-17667)***
Buds & Son Trucking Inc..........619 443-4200
12570 Highway 67 Lakeside (92040) ***(G-3984)***
Budway Enterprises Inc (PA)..........909 463-0500
13600 Napa St Fontana (92335) ***(G-4120)***
Budway Trucking & Warehousing, Fontana *Also called Budway Enterprises Inc* ***(G-4120)***
Buena Park Medical Group Inc (PA)..........714 994-5290
6301 Beach Blvd Ste 101 Buena Park (90621) ***(G-19382)***
Buena Park Nursing Center, Apple Valley *Also called 8520 Western Ave Inc* ***(G-21120)***
Buena Park Police Association..........714 562-3901
6650 Beach Blvd Buena Park (90621) ***(G-25167)***
Buena Ventura Care Center Inc (PA)..........323 268-0106
1016 S Record Ave Los Angeles (90023) ***(G-20424)***
Buena Ventura Care Center Inc..........818 247-4476
1505 Colby Dr Glendale (91205) ***(G-21168)***
Buena Vista Care Center, Santa Barbara *Also called Covenant Care California LLC* ***(G-20495)***
Buena Vista Care Center Inc..........714 535-7264
1440 S Euclid St Anaheim (92802) ***(G-20425)***
Buena Vista Food Products Inc..........626 815-8859
823 W 8th St Azusa (91702) ***(G-8810)***
Buena Vista International Inc (HQ)..........818 560-1000
500 S Buena Vista St Burbank (91521) ***(G-18271)***
Buena Vista International Inc (HQ)..........818 295-5200
350 S Buena Vista St Burbank (91521) ***(G-18055)***
Buena Vista Manor, Duarte *Also called Cal Southern Presbt Homes* ***(G-20430)***
Buena Vista Pictures Dist, Burbank *Also called ABC Cable Networks Group* ***(G-18268)***
Buena Vista Television (HQ)..........818 560-1878
500 S Buena Vista St Burbank (91521) ***(G-16946)***
Buena Vista TV Advg Sls, Burbank *Also called Buena Vista Television* ***(G-16946)***
Buenaventura Medical Group (PA)..........805 477-6000
888 S Hill Rd Ventura (93003) ***(G-19383)***
Buenaventura Medical Group..........805 477-6220
2601 E Main St Ste 104 Ventura (93003) ***(G-19384)***
Buffalo Distribution..........510 475-9810
1624 Pacific St Union City (94587) ***(G-8422)***
Buffini & Company (PA)..........760 827-2100
6349 Palomar Oaks Ct Carlsbad (92011) ***(G-24315)***
Build Group Inc..........415 777-4070
457 Minna St Ste 100 San Francisco (94103) ***(G-1513)***
Buildcom Inc..........800 375-3403
402 Otterson Dr Ste 100 Chico (95928) ***(G-7706)***
Builders & Tradesmens..........916 772-9200
6610 Sierra College Blvd Rocklin (95677) ***(G-10651)***
Builders & Tradesmens Insur..........916 772-9200
6610 Sierra College Blvd Rocklin (95677) ***(G-10203)***
Building & Safety Department, Fremont *Also called City of Fremont* ***(G-26177)***
Building and Property MGT BR, Los Angeles *Also called General Services Cal Dept* ***(G-14310)***
Building Cleaning Systems, Santa Ana *Also called Carrasco Heleo* ***(G-14245)***
Building Elctronic Contrls Inc (PA)..........909 305-1600
2246 Lindsay Way Glendora (91740) ***(G-2541)***
Building Inspection, Long Beach *Also called City of Long Beach* ***(G-17075)***
Building Material Distrs Inc (PA)..........209 745-3001
225 Elm Ave Galt (95632) ***(G-6911)***
Building Material Distrs Inc..........951 341-0708
100 Sinclair St Perris (92571) ***(G-6912)***
Building Services, San Bernardino *Also called San Bernardino City Unf School* ***(G-14416)***
Building Services Maint Inc..........510 636-1224
7677 Oakport St Oakland (94621) ***(G-4121)***
BUILDING SERVICES MAINTENANCE,INC., Oakland *Also called Building Services Maint Inc* ***(G-4121)***
Building Services/System Inc..........925 688-1234
2575 Stanwell Dr Concord (94520) ***(G-10964)***
Bulk Transportation (PA)..........909 594-2855
415 S Lemon Ave Walnut (91789) ***(G-4122)***

ALPHABETIC

Bulmaro Castro Contractors 831 675-2927
349 Belden St Gonzales (93926) *(G-14617)*
Bunchball Inc 408 215-2924
1820 Gateway Dr Ste 300 San Mateo (94404) *(G-15069)*
Bungalow 16 Entertainment LLC 310 226-7870
8113 Melrose Ave Los Angeles (90046) *(G-8096)*
Bunim-Murray Productions 818 756-5100
6007 Sepulveda Blvd Van Nuys (91411) *(G-18056)*
Bunker Hill Club Inc 213 620-9662
555 S Flower St Ste 5100 Los Angeles (90071) *(G-25224)*
Bunkers Grille, Brentwood *Also called Nines Restaurant (G-27569)*
Bunzl Usa Inc 314 997-5959
15959 Piuma Ave Cerritos (90703) *(G-8186)*
Buona Terra Farming Co Inc 805 614-9229
2380 A St Santa Maria (93455) *(G-26950)*
Burbank Airport Mariott Hotel, Burbank *Also called PHF II Burbank LLC (G-13091)*
Burbank Bob Hope Airport, Burbank *Also called Jetblue Airways Corporation (G-4806)*
Burbank Dental Laboratory Inc 818 841-2256
2101 Floyd St Burbank (91504) *(G-7248)*
Burbank Housing Dev Corp 707 526-9782
790 Sonoma Ave Santa Rosa (95404) *(G-11955)*
Burbank Plg & Zoning Div of 818 238-5250
150 N 3rd St Fl 2 Burbank (91502) *(G-27856)*
Burbank Television Entps LLC 818 954-6000
4000 Warner Blvd Burbank (91522) *(G-5835)*
Burbank Water & Power, Burbank *Also called City of Burbank (G-6284)*
Burbank Water & Power 818 238-3706
164 W Magnolia Blvd Burbank (91502) *(G-17043)*
Burch Construction Company Inc 760 788-9370
405 Maple St Ste C-101 Ramona (92065) *(G-1514)*
Burdette De Cock Inc 310 542-0563
3625 Del Amo Blvd Ste 105 Torrance (90503) *(G-22384)*
Burdick Painting 408 567-1330
705 Nuttman St Santa Clara (95054) *(G-3503)*
Bureau Veritas North Amer Inc 714 431-4100
1665 Scenic Ave Ste 200 Costa Mesa (92626) *(G-27857)*
Burger Physcl Thrapy Svcs Inc (HQ) 916 983-5900
1301 E Bidwell St Ste 201 Folsom (95630) *(G-20308)*
Burger Physcl Thrapy Rhbltion, Folsom *Also called Burger Physcl Therapy Svcs Inc (G-20308)*
Burger Physical Therapy 916 983-5900
1301 E Bidwell St Ste 101 Folsom (95630) *(G-20309)*
Burger Rhblitation Systems Inc 916 617-2400
2101 Stone Blvd Ste 175 West Sacramento (95691) *(G-20310)*
Burger Rhblitation Systems Inc 916 863-5785
6614 Mercy Ct Ste C Fair Oaks (95628) *(G-20311)*
Burger Rhblitation Systems Inc (PA) 800 900-8491
1301 E Bidwell St Ste 201 Folsom (95630) *(G-20312)*
Burgett Incorporated 916 567-9999
4111a N Freeway Blvd Sacramento (95834) *(G-8107)*
Burke Williams & Sorensen LLP (PA) 213 236-0600
444 S Flower St Ste 2400 Los Angeles (90071) *(G-23138)*
Burkshire Has A Way Home Servc 818 501-4800
16810 Ventura Blvd Fl 1 Encino (91436) *(G-11332)*
Burlingame Country Club 650 696-8100
80 New Place Rd Hillsborough (94010) *(G-18903)*
Burlingame Healtcare Center, Burlingame *Also called Burlingame Senior Care LLC (G-21169)*
Burlingame Industries Inc (PA) 909 355-7000
3546 N Riverside Ave Rialto (92377) *(G-13475)*
Burlingame Industries Inc 909 887-7038
277 Lytle Creek Rd Lytle Creek (92358) *(G-13476)*
Burlingame Industries Inc 209 464-9001
4555 Mckinley Ave Stockton (95206) *(G-7009)*
Burlingame Long Term Care, Burlingame *Also called San Mateo Healthcare & Wellnes (G-20892)*
Burlingame Senior Care LLC 650 692-3758
1100 Trousdale Dr Burlingame (94010) *(G-21169)*
Burlington Convalescent Hosp (PA) 213 381-5585
845 S Burlington Ave Los Angeles (90057) *(G-20426)*
Burlington Convalescent Hosp 323 295-7737
3737 Don Felipe Dr Los Angeles (90008) *(G-21170)*
Burlington Northern, San Bernardino *Also called Bnsf Railway Company (G-3607)*
Burlington Northern, Barstow *Also called Bnsf Railway Company (G-3608)*
Burlington Northern, Commerce *Also called Bnsf Railway Company (G-3609)*
Burlington Northern, Vernon *Also called Bnsf Railway Company (G-3610)*
Burnham & Brown, Oakland *Also called Burnham Brown A Prof Corp (G-23139)*
Burnham Brown A Prof Corp 510 444-6800
1901 Harrison St Ste 1100 Oakland (94612) *(G-23139)*
Burnham Real Estate, San Diego *Also called Christian and Wakefield (G-11389)*
Burns & McDonnell Inc 714 256-1595
1 Pointe Dr Ste 540 Brea (92821) *(G-25710)*
Burns and Sons Trucking Inc 619 460-5394
9210 Olive Dr Spring Valley (91977) *(G-3985)*
Burr Pilger Mayer Inc 707 544-4078
110 Stony Point Rd # 210 Santa Rosa (95401) *(G-26299)*
Burr Pilger Mayer Inc 707 968-5207
432a Main St Saint Helena (94574) *(G-26300)*
Burr Pilger Mayer Inc (PA) 415 421-5757
600 California St Ste 600 San Francisco (94108) *(G-26301)*
Burr Pilger Mayer Inc 408 961-6355
60 S Market St Ste 800 San Jose (95113) *(G-26302)*
Burr Pilger Mayer Inc 650 855-6800
2000 University Ave East Palo Alto (94303) *(G-26303)*
Burrtec Waste Group Inc 760 256-2730
2340 W Main St Barstow (92311) *(G-3986)*
Burrtec Waste Industries Inc (HQ) 909 429-4200
9890 Cherry Ave Fontana (92335) *(G-6448)*
Burson Marsteller, San Francisco *Also called Young & Rubicam Inc (G-27769)*
Burtch Construction, Bakersfield *Also called Burtch Trucking Inc (G-1744)*
Burtch Trucking Inc 661 399-1736
18815 Highway 65 Bakersfield (93308) *(G-1744)*
Burtech Pipeline Incorporated 760 634-2822
102 2nd St Encinitas (92024) *(G-1913)*
Burton P Scott, Los Angeles *Also called Morgan Lewis & Bockius LLP (G-23446)*
Burton-Way House Ltd A CA 805 214-8075
2 Dole Dr Westlake Village (91362) *(G-12473)*
Burton-Way House Ltd A CA 310 273-2222
300 S Doheny Dr Los Angeles (90048) *(G-12474)*
Burton-Way House Ltd A CA (PA) 310 552-6623
2029 Century Park E # 2200 Los Angeles (90067) *(G-12475)*
Bus Company, Santa Clarita *Also called Santa Clarita City of (G-3886)*
Bushnell Gardens 916 791-4199
5255 Douglas Blvd Granite Bay (95746) *(G-9180)*
Bushnell's Landscape Creations, Granite Bay *Also called Bushnell Gardens (G-9180)*
Business and Support Services 760 830-6873
P.O. Box 6001 Twentynine Palms (92278) *(G-18904)*
Business and Support Services 760 725-5187
Camp Pendleton Mc Base Oceanside (92055) *(G-20247)*
Business and Support Services 760 725-2817
Santa Jancinto Rd 20286 Bldg 202860 Oceanside (92054) *(G-24420)*
Business and Support Services 858 577-4786
Mccs Bldg 2273 Elrod Ave San Diego (92145) *(G-19155)*
Business Connections 530 527-6229
332 Pine St Red Bluff (96080) *(G-14618)*
Business Department, Murrieta *Also called Southwest Healthcare Sys Aux (G-21909)*
Business For Social Responsibi (PA) 415 984-3200
88 Kearny St Fl 12 San Francisco (94108) *(G-25077)*
Business Index Group Inc 916 577-1010
2510 Warren Dr Rocklin (95677) *(G-26647)*
Business Intelligence 858 452-8200
2131 Palomar Airport Rd Carlsbad (92011) *(G-27362)*
Business Objects Inc (HQ) 650 849-4000
3410 Hillview Ave Palo Alto (94304) *(G-7104)*
Business of Finance, San Francisco *Also called Airport Commisions (G-4897)*
Business Services Network 415 282-8161
1275 Fairfax Ave Ste 103 San Francisco (94124) *(G-14066)*
Businesscom Inc 310 586-4000
2120 Colorado Ave Fl 3 Santa Monica (90404) *(G-27363)*
Buswest LLC (HQ) 310 984-3900
21107 Chico St Carson (90745) *(G-3891)*
Butcher's Brand, San Leandro *Also called Webers Quality Meats Inc (G-8690)*
Butler International Inc (PA) 805 882-2200
3820 State St Ste A Santa Barbara (93105) *(G-14847)*
Butler Service Group Inc (HQ) 201 891-5312
3820 State St Ste A Santa Barbara (93105) *(G-14848)*
Butler Shine Stern Prtners LLC 415 331-6049
20 Liberty Ship Way Sausalito (94965) *(G-13822)*
Butte County Employment Center, Oroville *Also called County of Butte (G-23799)*
Butte County Mental Hlth Svcs, Chico *Also called County of Butte (G-22693)*
Butte County Office Education 530 532-5786
1859 Bird St Oroville (95965) *(G-25509)*
Butte County Probation, Oroville *Also called County of Butte (G-23794)*
Butte Home Health & Hospice, Chico *Also called Butte Home Health Inc (G-22385)*
Butte Home Health Inc 530 895-0462
10 Constitution Dr Chico (95973) *(G-22385)*
Butte Primary Care Med Group 530 877-0762
6585 Clark Rd Ste 200 Paradise (95969) *(G-19385)*
Butte-Yb-Stter Wtr Qlty Cltion 530 673-5131
625 Cooper Ave Yuba City (95991) *(G-4481)*
Butter Paddle 408 395-1678
33 N Santa Cruz Ave Los Gatos (95030) *(G-17044)*
Butter Paddle, The, Los Gatos *Also called Butter Paddle (G-17044)*
Butterfield Electric Inc 530 666-2116
2101 Freeway Dr Ste A Woodland (95776) *(G-2542)*
Butterfield Electric Inc (PA) 530 666-2116
2101 Freeway Dr Ste A Woodland (95776) *(G-2543)*
Butterwick Dr Kimberly Jane MD 858 657-1002
9339 Genesee Ave Ste 300 San Diego (92121) *(G-19386)*
Button & Turkovich 530 795-2090
24604 Buckeye Rd Winters (95694) *(G-348)*
Button Transportation Inc 707 678-1983
8629 Robben Rd Dixon (95620) *(G-4123)*
Buttonwillow Warehouse Co Inc (HQ) 661 764-5234
125 Front St Buttonwillow (93206) *(G-9130)*
Buxton Consulting 925 467-0700
6140 Stoneridge Mall Rd # 100 Pleasanton (94588) *(G-27858)*
Buyers Consultation Svc Inc (PA) 818 341-4820
8735 Remmet Ave Canoga Park (91304) *(G-7539)*
Buzz Oates Management Services 916 381-3843
555 Capitol Mall Ste 900 Sacramento (95814) *(G-11333)*
Buzztime Inc 760 476-1976
2231 Rutherford Rd # 210 Carlsbad (92008) *(G-5836)*
BV General Inc 323 651-0043
619 N Fairfax Ave Los Angeles (90036) *(G-21171)*
Bvls, Plymouth *Also called Borjon Iscander (G-654)*
Bvs Entertainment Inc (HQ) 818 460-6917
500 S Buena Vista St Burbank (91521) *(G-18057)*
Bw-Budget-Sda LLC 619 542-8686
3125 Pacific Hwy San Diego (92101) *(G-17667)*
Bwr Public Relations 310 248-6100
9100 Wilshire Blvd 500w Beverly Hills (90212) *(G-27736)*
Bwrpr, Beverly Hills *Also called Baker Winokur (G-27733)*
Bx Construction LLC 951 509-9412
11671 Sterling Ave Ste K Riverside (92503) *(G-1144)*

By Referral Only Inc...760 707-1300
2035 Corte Del Nogal # 200 Carlsbad (92011) ***(G-27859)***
By The Blue Sea LLC...310 458-0030
1 Pico Blvd Santa Monica (90405) ***(G-12476)***
By-The-Bay Investments Inc...510 793-2581
37000 Fremont Blvd Fremont (94536) ***(G-12289)***
Bycor General Contractors Inc...858 587-1901
6490 Marindustry Dr Ste A San Diego (92121) ***(G-1515)***
Byers Enterprises Inc...530 272-7777
11773 Slow Poke Ln Grass Valley (95945) ***(G-3145)***
Byers Leafguard Gutter Systems, Grass Valley *Also called Byers Enterprises Inc* ***(G-3145)***
Bynd LLC...415 944-2293
100 Montgomery St # 1102 San Francisco (94104) ***(G-15070)***
Byrd Harvest Inc...805 343-1608
192 Guadalupe St Guadalupe (93434) ***(G-491)***
Byrd Produce, Guadalupe *Also called Byrd Harvest Inc* ***(G-491)***
Byrom-Davey Inc...858 513-7199
13220 Evnng Crk Dr S # 103 San Diego (92128) ***(G-2033)***
Byron Park, Walnut Creek *Also called A F Evans Company Inc* ***(G-16960)***
Byte Mobile, Santa Clara *Also called Bytemobile Inc* ***(G-6061)***
Bytemobile Inc (HQ)...408 327-7700
2860 De La Cruz Blvd # 200 Santa Clara (95050) ***(G-6061)***
Bytheways Manufacturing Inc...916 453-1212
2080 Enterprise Blvd West Sacramento (95691) ***(G-6851)***
C & B Delivery Services...909 623-4708
230 Diamond St Laguna Beach (92651) ***(G-4528)***
C & C Boats Inc...805 445-9456
1861 Baja Vista Way Camarillo (93010) ***(G-4774)***
C & C Construction Inc...916 434-5280
7941 E Hidden Lakes Dr Granite Bay (95746) ***(G-1516)***
C & C Security Patrol Inc...925 227-1400
4600 Willow Rd Pleasanton (94588) ***(G-16587)***
C & G Farms Inc...831 679-2978
25453 Iverson Rd Chualar (93925) ***(G-44)***
C & I, Spring Valley *Also called Commercial Indus Roofg Co Inc* ***(G-3153)***
C & L Refrigeration Corp...800 901-4822
479 Nibus Brea (92821) ***(G-2171)***
C & M Transfer San Diego Inc...619 562-6111
8787 Olive Ln Santee (92071) ***(G-3987)***
C & O Painting Inc...408 279-8011
1500 N 4th St San Jose (95112) ***(G-2432)***
C & R Systems Inc (PA)...951 270-0255
1835 Capital St Corona (92880) ***(G-2544)***
C & S Draperies Inc...209 466-5371
4210 Kiernan Ave Modesto (95356) ***(G-13591)***
C & S Wholesale Grocers Inc...916 383-5275
8301 Fruitridge Rd Sacramento (95826) ***(G-4529)***
C A A, Los Angeles *Also called Creative Artists Agency LLC* ***(G-18386)***
C A C, Goleta *Also called Community Action Commsn Santa* ***(G-24895)***
C A C H Inc...530 877-9316
1633 Cypress Ln Paradise (95969) ***(G-20427)***
C A H H S...916 552-7507
1215 K St Ste 800 Sacramento (95814) ***(G-25078)***
C A Hofmann Construction Inc...909 484-5888
8923 Laramie Dr Rancho Cucamonga (91737) ***(G-2868)***
C A L M, Santa Barbara *Also called Child Abuse Lstening Mediation* ***(G-23730)***
C A Rasmussen Inc (PA)...661 367-9040
28548 Livingston Ave Valencia (91355) ***(G-2034)***
C and E Inc...714 236-5790
3103 W Vallejo Dr Anaheim (92804) ***(G-17668)***
C B B Z S Inc...818 908-1900
7015 Valjean Ave Van Nuys (91406) ***(G-2433)***
C B Coast Newport Properties...949 644-1600
840 Nwport Ctr Dr Ste 100 Newport Beach (92660) ***(G-11334)***
C B Richard Ellis Investors, Los Angeles *Also called T C W Realty Fund VI* ***(G-12275)***
C B S Marketwatch, San Francisco *Also called Marketwatch Inc* ***(G-16948)***
C C Connection Inc...925 937-0100
2950 Buskirk Ave Ste 140 Walnut Creek (94597) ***(G-11335)***
C C S, Los Angeles *Also called Creative Channel Services LLC* ***(G-27395)***
C D C, Costa Mesa *Also called Creative Design Cons Inc* ***(G-17103)***
C D I, Sacramento *Also called Creative Design Interiors Inc* ***(G-3109)***
C D Lyon Construction Inc (PA)...805 653-0173
380 W Stanley Ave Ventura (93001) ***(G-25711)***
C D Payroll Inc...818 848-1562
2300 W Empire Ave Burbank (91504) ***(G-26304)***
C D R, Oxnard *Also called Child Development Resources of* ***(G-23736)***
C D R Enterprises Inc...661 940-0344
42302 8th St E Lancaster (93535) ***(G-2869)***
C E B M Inc...909 975-4440
3100 E Cedar St Ste 17 Ontario (91761) ***(G-14242)***
C E D, Orange *Also called County Whl Elc Co Los Angeles* ***(G-7433)***
C E H A, San Mateo *Also called California Envmtl Hlth Assn* ***(G-27863)***
C E I, Oakland *Also called Center For Elders Independence* ***(G-10269)***
C E P...909 580-1456
400 N Pepper Ave Ste 107 Colton (92324) ***(G-19387)***
C E T, Gardena *Also called Charles E Thomas Company Inc* ***(G-7833)***
C E T, San Jose *Also called Center For Employment Training* ***(G-24321)***
C E Toland & Son...707 747-1000
5300 Industrial Way Benicia (94510) ***(G-3504)***
C F I, Los Angeles *Also called Commodity Forwarders Inc* ***(G-5050)***
C F X, Carson *Also called City Fashion Express Inc* ***(G-5048)***
C H I, Modesto *Also called Community Hospice Inc* ***(G-21072)***
C H Reynolds Electric Inc...408 436-9280
1281 Wayne Ave San Jose (95131) ***(G-2545)***
C H Robinson Intl Inc...310 763-6080
680 Knox St Ste 210 Torrance (90502) ***(G-5037)***
C H Stone, Baldwin Park *Also called CH Stone Plumbing Co Inc* ***(G-2179)***
C H W, Bakersfield *Also called Bakersfield Memorial Hospital* ***(G-21459)***
C H W, San Francisco *Also called St Marys Med Ctr Foundation* ***(G-21929)***
C H W, Santa Cruz *Also called Dominican Hospital Foundation* ***(G-21546)***
C H W Mercy Healthcare...916 453-4545
4001 J St Sacramento (95819) ***(G-21467)***
C H W Mercy Healthcare...916 423-3000
7500 Hospital Dr Sacramento (95823) ***(G-21468)***
C I Container Line, Los Angeles *Also called Carmichael International Svc* ***(G-5040)***
C I Design, Lake Forest *Also called Commercial Indus Design Co Inc* ***(G-7109)***
C I G A, Glendale *Also called Califrnia Insur Guarantee Assn* ***(G-10566)***
C I W, Pittsburg *Also called Concord Iron Works Inc* ***(G-3380)***
C J Foods, Los Angeles *Also called CJ America Inc* ***(G-8983)***
C J Health Services Inc...510 793-3000
38650 Mission Blvd Fremont (94536) ***(G-20428)***
C J Vandergeest Ldscp Care Inc...805 650-0726
2476 Palma Dr Ste G Ventura (93003) ***(G-817)***
C L A, Van Nuys *Also called Clay Lacy Aviation Inc* ***(G-4911)***
C L Bryant Inc...209 566-5000
7401 Del Cielo Way Modesto (95356) ***(G-9005)***
C M A, Sacramento *Also called California Medical Association* ***(G-19396)***
C M A Alliance...818 981-0800
16542 Ventura Blvd # 210 Encino (91436) ***(G-10652)***
C M C Steel Fabricators Inc...909 899-9993
12451 Arrow Rte Etiwanda (91739) ***(G-3370)***
C M C Steel Fabricators Inc...909 873-3060
2755 S Willow Ave Bloomington (92316) ***(G-3371)***
C M I Management Inc...323 465-8044
5640 Santa Monica Blvd # 116 Los Angeles (90038) ***(G-11105)***
C M S Hospitality, Los Angeles *Also called Concession Management Svcs Inc* ***(G-19186)***
C N B Commercial Banking Ctr, Riverside *Also called City National Bank* ***(G-9386)***
C N L Hotel Del Partners LP...619 522-8299
1500 Orange Ave San Diego (92118) ***(G-12477)***
C Overaa & Co...510 234-0926
200 Parr Blvd Richmond (94801) ***(G-1409)***
C Overaa & Co/Bayview...510 234-0926
200 Parr Blvd Richmond (94801) ***(G-1410)***
C P Construction Co Inc...909 981-1091
105 N Loma Pl Upland (91786) ***(G-1914)***
C P Document Technologies LLC (PA)...213 617-4040
800 W 6th St Ste 1400 Los Angeles (90017) ***(G-7540)***
C P Holiday Manor Inc...818 341-9800
20554 Roscoe Blvd Canoga Park (91306) ***(G-21172)***
C P S Express (HQ)...951 685-1041
3401 Etiwanda Ave 711a Mira Loma (91752) ***(G-3988)***
C P T C, Anaheim *Also called California Private Trnsp Co LP* ***(G-5207)***
C P Technologies, Irvine *Also called Corner Products Company* ***(G-7550)***
C R S Drywall Inc...408 998-4360
135 San Jose Ave San Jose (95125) ***(G-2870)***
C S C, Northridge *Also called Contemporary Services Corp* ***(G-14628)***
C S C Consultants, Foster City *Also called C S G Consultants Inc* ***(G-25713)***
C S D P, Irvine *Also called Customer Srvc Dlvry Pltfrm Crp* ***(G-16349)***
C S G Consultants Inc...925 931-0370
1257 Quarry Ln Ste 100 Pleasanton (94566) ***(G-25712)***
C S G Consultants Inc (PA)...650 522-2525
550 Pilgrim Dr Foster City (94404) ***(G-25713)***
C S I, Simi Valley *Also called Cardservice International Inc* ***(G-17054)***
C S I, Santa Fe Springs *Also called Csi Electrical Contractors Inc* ***(G-2566)***
C S I Patrol Services...562 981-8988
3605 Long Beach Blvd # 205 Long Beach (90807) ***(G-16588)***
C S P, Santa Ana *Also called Community Service Programs Inc* ***(G-23777)***
C S S, Bakersfield *Also called Construction Specialty Svc Inc* ***(G-1922)***
C T and F Inc...562 927-2339
7228 Scout Ave Bell Gardens (90201) ***(G-2546)***
C T B, Monterey *Also called Data Recognition Corporation* ***(G-27893)***
C T Corporation System...925 287-9801
1350 Treat Blvd Ste 350 Walnut Creek (94597) ***(G-23140)***
C T I, Rancho Cucamonga *Also called Collection Technology Inc* ***(G-14027)***
C V Productions Inc...714 352-4446
812 N Broadway Santa Ana (92701) ***(G-5937)***
C V S Optical Lab Div, Rancho Cordova *Also called Vision Service Plan* ***(G-10390)***
C V Water District, Coachella *Also called Coachella Valley Water Dst* ***(G-6330)***
C W 5, San Diego *Also called Kswb Inc* ***(G-5888)***
C W Construction Inc...909 989-9099
8380 Maple Pl Ste 100 Rancho Cucamonga (91730) ***(G-3034)***
C W Driver Incorporated (PA)...626 351-8800
468 N Rosemead Blvd Pasadena (91107) ***(G-1517)***
C W Driver Incorporated...650 308-4001
2248 N 1st St San Jose (95131) ***(G-1145)***
C W S, San Diego *Also called Communction Wirg Spcalists Inc* ***(G-2559)***
C Y S, Fresno *Also called Comprehensive Youth Ser* ***(G-23784)***
C&M Relocation Systems, Santee *Also called C & M Transfer San Diego Inc* ***(G-3987)***
C&S Wholesale Grocers Inc...559 442-4700
2797 S Orange Ave Fresno (93725) ***(G-8461)***
C-21 Super Stars...949 389-1600
22342 Avenida Empresa Rcho STA Marg (92688) ***(G-11336)***
C-Air International Inc...310 695-3400
9841 Arprt Blvd Ste 1400 Los Angeles (90045) ***(G-5038)***
C.E.G. Construction, Pico Rivera *Also called Chalmers Corporation* ***(G-1413)***
C.H.M.B., Escondido *Also called California Healthcare* ***(G-10658)***
C.O.M.P.A.S.S., Redding *Also called Care Options Management Plans* ***(G-22390)***
C/O Longwood Management, Los Angeles *Also called Magnolia Ventures Ltd* ***(G-17310)***
C/O Uc San Francisco...310 794-1841
1245 16th St Ste 225 Santa Monica (90404) ***(G-19388)***
C/O Uc San Francisco (PA)...858 534-7323
1111 Franklin St Fl 12 Oakland (94607) ***(G-26951)***

ALPHABETIC

C2 Imaging (PA) ALPHABETIC SECTION

C2 Imaging (PA)..........714 668-5955
3180 Pullman St Costa Mesa (92626) ***(G-14115)***
C3 Inc..........650 503-2200
1300 Seaport Blvd Ste 500 Redwood City (94063) ***(G-15611)***
C3 Iot, Redwood City *Also called C3 Inc* ***(G-15611)***
C9 Edge Inc..........650 561-7855
177 Bovet Rd Ste 520 San Mateo (94402) ***(G-7105)***
Ca Inc..........800 225-5224
3965 Freedom Cir Fl 6 Santa Clara (95054) ***(G-15612)***
Ca Inc..........631 342-6000
10180 Telesis Ct Ste 500 San Diego (92121) ***(G-15613)***
CA Landscape and Design, Upland *Also called California Ldscp & Design Inc* ***(G-820)***
CA Safety Compliance Corp..........213 747-0805
1122 W Wash Blvd Fl 3 Los Angeles (90015) ***(G-27860)***
CA Ste Atom Assoc Intr-Ins Bur..........415 565-2012
150 Van Ness Ave San Francisco (94102) ***(G-10403)***
CA Ste Atom Assoc Intr-Ins Bur..........831 824-9128
4400 Capitola Rd Ste 100 Capitola (95010) ***(G-17877)***
CA Ste Atom Assoc Intr-Ins Bur..........650 572-5600
1650 S Delaware St San Mateo (94402) ***(G-10404)***
CA Ste Atom Assoc Intr-Ins Bur..........650 623-3200
900 Miramonte Ave Mountain View (94040) ***(G-10653)***
Cabana Hotel, Palo Alto *Also called 4290 El Camino Properties LP* ***(G-12362)***
Cabazon Band Mission Indians..........760 342-5000
84245 Indio Springs Dr Indio (92203) ***(G-12478)***
Cabinda Gulf Oil Co Inc..........925 842-1000
6001 Bollinger Canyon Rd San Ramon (94583) ***(G-1035)***
Cabinet Supply, Indio *Also called GE Holdings Inc* ***(G-3050)***
Cable Car Eyewear, Hollister *Also called Icu Eyewear Inc* ***(G-8121)***
Cable Doctors Inc..........619 595-4650
8677 Villa La Jolla Dr La Jolla (92037) ***(G-5938)***
Cable Engineering Services, Mission Hills *Also called Prescott Communications Inc* ***(G-28022)***
Cableconn Industries Inc..........858 571-7111
7198 Convoy Ct San Diego (92111) ***(G-7421)***
Cabrillo College Children Ctr..........831 479-6352
6500 Soquel Dr Aptos (95003) ***(G-24421)***
Cabrillo Gen Insur Agcy Inc..........858 244-0550
7071 Convoy Ct Ste 201 San Diego (92111) ***(G-10654)***
Cac Studios, Santa Monica *Also called Creating Arts Company* ***(G-18385)***
Cache Creek Casino Resort..........530 796-3118
14455 State Highway 16 Brooks (95606) ***(G-12479)***
Cacho Landscape Maintenance Co..........818 365-0773
711 Truman St San Fernando (91340) ***(G-818)***
Caci Inc - Federal..........619 881-6000
1455 Frazee Rd Ste 700 San Diego (92108) ***(G-15911)***
Caci Nss Inc..........703 841-7800
3201 Airpark Dr Ste 109 Santa Maria (93455) ***(G-7106)***
Cacique Distributors US..........626 961-3399
14923 Proctor Ave La Puente (91746) ***(G-8579)***
Caden TV..........408 275-1908
6979 Rockton Pl San Jose (95119) ***(G-17907)***
Cadence Design Systems Inc (PA)..........408 943-1234
2655 Seely Ave Bldg 5 San Jose (95134) ***(G-15614)***
Cadent Inc..........408 470-1000
2560 Orchard Pkwy San Jose (95131) ***(G-15912)***
Cadforce Inc..........310 876-1800
10811 Wash Blvd Ste 302 Culver City (90232) ***(G-17045)***
Cadnchev Inc..........562 944-6422
13603 Foster Rd Santa Fe Springs (90670) ***(G-6795)***
Cae Online, Palo Alto *Also called Capital Asset Exch & Trdg LLC* ***(G-7831)***
Caesar and Seider Insur Svcs (PA)..........805 682-2571
40 E Alamar Ave Ste 4 Santa Barbara (93105) ***(G-10655)***
Cafepresscom Inc..........650 655-3000
24301 Suthland Dr Ste 300 Hayward (94545) ***(G-27364)***
Caffeine Productions..........323 860-8111
1040 N Las Palmas Ave Los Angeles (90038) ***(G-18058)***
Cafta..........562 860-9808
16625 Gridley Rd Unit 5 Cerritos (90703) ***(G-7249)***
Cahill Contractors Inc (PA)..........415 986-0600
425 California St # 2200 San Francisco (94104) ***(G-1518)***
Cahuilla Creek Casino, Anza *Also called Cahuilla Creek Rest & Casino* ***(G-19156)***
Cahuilla Creek Rest & Casino..........951 763-1200
52702 Us Highway 371 Anza (92539) ***(G-19156)***
Cai, Corona *Also called Combustion Associates Inc* ***(G-6118)***
Cai Company, Brea *Also called California Automobile Insur Co* ***(G-10405)***
Cai International Inc (PA)..........415 788-0100
1 Market Plz Ste 900 San Francisco (94105) ***(G-14520)***
Caine & Weiner Company Inc (PA)..........818 226-6000
21210 Erwin St Woodland Hills (91367) ***(G-14020)***
Cake Corporation..........650 215-7777
101 Redwood Ave Redwood City (94061) ***(G-15071)***
Cal Americas Wholesale Florist, Vista *Also called United Floral Exchange Inc* ***(G-9222)***
Cal Bowl Enterprises LLC..........562 421-8448
2500 Carson St Lakewood (90712) ***(G-18515)***
Cal Care Inc..........650 325-8600
1275 Crane St Menlo Park (94025) ***(G-27365)***
Cal Chamber, Sacramento *Also called California Chamber Commerce* ***(G-25081)***
Cal Citrus Packing Co..........559 562-2536
111 N Mount Vernon Ave Lindsay (93247) ***(G-516)***
Cal Coast Telecom, San Jose *Also called Radonich Corp* ***(G-2694)***
Cal Coffee Shop, Lakewood *Also called Nationwide Theatres Corp* ***(G-18527)***
Cal Color Growers LLC..........408 778-0835
330 Peebles Ave Morgan Hill (95037) ***(G-9181)***
Cal Consolidated Communications..........916 786-6141
211 Lincoln St Roseville (95678) ***(G-5566)***
Cal Custom Tile, Sanger *Also called Rick Berry Inc* ***(G-3023)***
Cal Facilities Management Co, San Jose *Also called Yang C Park* ***(G-14823)***
Cal Fed Investments Inc..........916 614-2440
3900 Lennane Dr Sacramento (95834) ***(G-12135)***
Cal Fresco LLC..........714 690-7700
6850 Artesia Blvd Buena Park (90620) ***(G-8698)***
Cal Gran Theatres LLC..........805 934-1582
3170 Santa Maria Way Santa Maria (93455) ***(G-18313)***
Cal Micro, Ontario *Also called Ruuhwa Dann and Associates Inc* ***(G-7181)***
Cal North Cellular Inc..........530 467-6128
30 Telco Way Etna (96027) ***(G-5280)***
Cal Packing & Storage LP..........559 638-2929
1356 S Buttonwillow Ave Reedley (93654) ***(G-4489)***
Cal Pinnacle Mltary Cmmunities..........619 764-5087
3200 4th Ave Ste 201 San Diego (92103) ***(G-26952)***
Cal Poly Corporation..........805 756-1587
Cal Poly Bldg 31 San Luis Obispo (93407) ***(G-13449)***
Cal Poly Corporation..........805 756-1131
Bldg 15 San Luis Obispo (93407) ***(G-26953)***
Cal Poly Foundation, San Luis Obispo *Also called Cal Poly Corporation* ***(G-26953)***
CAL SHAKES, Berkeley *Also called California Shakespeare Theater* ***(G-18376)***
Cal Sierra Construction Inc..........916 416-7901
5904 Van Alstine Ave 1 Carmichael (95608) ***(G-1915)***
Cal Southern Assn Governments (PA)..........213 236-1800
818 W 7th St Fl 12 Los Angeles (90017) ***(G-27861)***
Cal Southern Illumination..........949 622-3000
1881 Mcgaw Ave Irvine (92614) ***(G-7422)***
Cal Southern Presbt Homes..........949 854-9500
19191 Harvard Ave Ofc Irvine (92612) ***(G-11106)***
Cal Southern Presbt Homes..........858 454-4201
7450 Olivetas Ave Ofc La Jolla (92037) ***(G-24574)***
Cal Southern Presbt Homes (PA)..........818 247-0420
516 Burchett St Glendale (91203) ***(G-20429)***
Cal Southern Presbt Homes..........818 244-7219
1230 E Windsor Rd Ofc Glendale (91205) ***(G-11107)***
Cal Southern Presbt Homes..........626 359-8141
802 Buena Vista St Duarte (91010) ***(G-20430)***
Cal Southern Presbt Homes..........818 247-0420
516 Burchett St Glendale (91203) ***(G-11108)***
Cal Southern Presbt Homes..........626 357-1632
1763 Royal Oaks Dr Ofc Duarte (91010) ***(G-11109)***
Cal Southern Presbt Homes..........760 747-4306
710 W 13th Ave Escondido (92025) ***(G-24575)***
Cal Southern Presbt Homes..........760 737-5110
500 E Valley Pkwy Ofc Escondido (92025) ***(G-24576)***
Cal Southern Seafood Inc..........805 698-8262
125 Salinas Rd Ste 5b Royal Oaks (95076) ***(G-8630)***
Cal Southern Services..........626 281-5942
419 Mcgroarty St San Gabriel (91776) ***(G-13540)***
Cal Southern Sound Image Inc (PA)..........760 737-3900
2415 Auto Park Way Escondido (92029) ***(G-2547)***
Cal Southern United Food..........714 220-2297
6425 Katella Ave Cypress (90630) ***(G-10542)***
Cal Strs, West Sacramento *Also called Califor State Teach Retire Sys* ***(G-10543)***
Cal West Enterprises, San Diego *Also called Wamc Company Inc* ***(G-11227)***
Cal West General Engrg Inc..........619 469-5811
5480 Baltimore Dr Ste 215 La Mesa (91942) ***(G-14521)***
Cal West Underground Inc..........951 371-6775
951 6th St Norco (92860) ***(G-2035)***
Cal Western Foreclosure Svcs, El Cajon *Also called EC Closing Corp* ***(G-9838)***
Cal-A-Vie, Vista *Also called Spa Havens LP* ***(G-18686)***
Cal-Coast Healthcare Inc..........415 479-5149
81 Professional Ctr Pkwy San Rafael (94903) ***(G-20431)***
Cal-Lift Inc..........562 566-1400
13027 Crossroads Pkwy S La Puente (91746) ***(G-7829)***
Cal-Med Ambulance, Whittier *Also called California Med Response Inc* ***(G-3779)***
Cal-North Wireless..........707 442-8334
1209 Broadway Eureka (95501) ***(G-5281)***
Cal-Organic Farms, Lamont *Also called Grimmway Enterprises Inc* ***(G-8738)***
Cal-Pacific Construction Inc..........650 557-1238
1009 Terra Nova Blvd Pacifica (94044) ***(G-1519)***
Cal-State Auto Parts Inc (PA)..........714 630-5954
1361 N Red Gum St Anaheim (92806) ***(G-6720)***
Cal-State Steel Corporation..........310 632-2772
1801 W Compton Blvd Compton (90220) ***(G-3372)***
Cal-Steam Supply..........415 861-3071
777 Mariposa St San Francisco (94107) ***(G-7707)***
Cal-West Nurseries Inc..........951 270-0667
138 North Dr Norco (92860) ***(G-819)***
Cal/Pac Paintings & Coatings..........714 628-1514
608 N Eckhoff St Orange (92868) ***(G-2434)***
Calabasas Country Club, Calabasas *Also called Knight-Calabasas LLC* ***(G-18966)***
Calabasas Country Club..........818 222-8111
4515 Park Entrada Calabasas (91302) ***(G-18905)***
Calance, Buena Park *Also called Partners Information Tech Inc* ***(G-16454)***
Calatlantic Group Inc (PA)..........949 789-1600
15360 Barranca Pkwy Irvine (92618) ***(G-1357)***
Calatlantic Group Inc..........760 476-0104
5750 Fleet St Ste 200 Carlsbad (92008) ***(G-1146)***
Calatlantic Group Inc..........951 898-5500
355 E Rincon St Ste 300 Corona (92879) ***(G-1147)***
Calatlantic Group Inc..........925 847-8700
3825 Hopyard Rd Ste 195 Pleasanton (94588) ***(G-1358)***
Calatlantic Group Inc..........949 789-1600
15360 Barranca Pkwy Irvine (92618) ***(G-1300)***
Calatlantic Group Inc..........310 821-9843
13200 Fiji Way Marina Del Rey (90292) ***(G-1148)***
Calatlantic Group Inc..........760 931-4414
5740 Fleet St Ste 200 Carlsbad (92008) ***(G-1359)***
CALATLANTIC HOMES, Irvine *Also called Calatlantic Group Inc* ***(G-1357)***

ALPHABETIC

Calaveras County Water Dst...209 754-3543
120 Toma Ct San Andreas (95249) ***(G-6313)***
Calavo Foods, Santa Paula *Also called Calavo Growers Inc* ***(G-5197)***
Calavo Growers Inc (PA)...805 525-1245
1141 Cummings Rd Ste A Santa Paula (93060) ***(G-8699)***
Calavo Growers Inc...805 525-5511
15765 W Telegraph Rd Santa Paula (93060) ***(G-5197)***
Calavo Growers Inc...951 676-7331
28410 Vincent Moraga Dr Temecula (92590) ***(G-8700)***
Calbee North America LLC...707 427-2500
2600 Maxwell Way Fairfield (94534) ***(G-8552)***
Calbond, Rancho Dominguez *Also called Calpipe Industries Inc* ***(G-7363)***
Calcedar Export Inc...209 944-5800
400 S Fresno St Stockton (95203) ***(G-8161)***
Calcom Solar, Visalia *Also called California Coml Solar Inc* ***(G-2173)***
Calcot Ltd (PA)...661 327-5961
1900 E Brundage Ln Bakersfield (93307) ***(G-8964)***
Calderon Building Maintenance...619 269-5940
3822 Sherman St San Diego (92110) ***(G-14243)***
Caldwell Banker Inc...760 941-6888
40 Main St Ste E100 Vista (92083) ***(G-11337)***
Caldwell Realty...562 907-5655
14831 Whittier Blvd # 102 Whittier (90605) ***(G-11338)***
Caldwell Ventures LLC...530 899-0814
1351 E Lassen Ave Ofc Chico (95973) ***(G-20432)***
Calenergy LLC...402 231-1527
7030 Gentry Rd Calipatria (92233) ***(G-2548)***
Calex, Northridge *Also called Valley Hospital Medical Center* ***(G-22009)***
Calex Engineering Inc...661 254-1866
23651 Pine St Newhall (91321) ***(G-3420)***
Calfornia Fruit Exchange LLC (PA)...209 365-2340
6011 E Pine St Lodi (95240) ***(G-8701)***
Calgene LLC...530 753-6313
37437 State Highway 16 Woodland (95695) ***(G-45)***
Calhot Illinios LLC...310 536-9800
5250 W El Segundo Blvd Hawthorne (90250) ***(G-12480)***
Calhoun Construction Inc...916 434-8356
150 Flocchini Cir Lincoln (95648) ***(G-1149)***
Caliber Bodyworks Inc...310 392-7662
1100 Colorado Ave Santa Monica (90401) ***(G-17749)***
Caliber Bodyworks Inc...714 436-5010
1399 Logan Ave Costa Mesa (92626) ***(G-17750)***
Caliber Bodyworks Inc...909 598-1113
20601 Valley Blvd Walnut (91789) ***(G-17751)***
Caliber Capital Group LLC...714 507-1998
5900 Katella Ave Ste A101 Cypress (90630) ***(G-10125)***
Caliber Home Loans Inc...707 432-1000
3700 Hilborn Rd Ste 700 Fairfield (94534) ***(G-9823)***
Calibre International LLC (PA)...626 969-4660
6250 N Irwindale Ave Irwindale (91702) ***(G-27737)***
Calico Brands...909 930-5000
2055 S Haven Ave Ontario (91761) ***(G-9250)***
Calico Building Services Inc...949 380-8707
15550 Rockfield Blvd C Irvine (92618) ***(G-1520)***
Calidad Industries Inc...510 534-6666
1301 30th Ave Oakland (94601) ***(G-24316)***
Calif Institute Human Ser...707 664-2416
1801 E Cotati Ave Rohnert Park (94928) ***(G-27366)***
Calif Land Management, South Lake Tahoe *Also called California Land Mgt Svcs Corp* ***(G-13477)***
Calif Stat Univ Fres Foun (PA)...559 278-0850
4910 N Chestnut Ave Fresno (93726) ***(G-25510)***
Calif Stat Univ Fres Foun...559 278-0850
5370 N Chestnut Ave Fresno (93725) ***(G-25511)***
Califor State Teach Retire Sys (HQ)...800 228-5453
100 Waterfront Pl West Sacramento (95605) ***(G-10543)***
California Academy Sciences (PA)...415 379-8000
55 Music Concourse Dr San Francisco (94118) ***(G-25060)***
California Access Scaffold LLC...310 324-3388
16525 Avalon Blvd Carson (90746) ***(G-3505)***
California American Water Co (HQ)...619 409-7703
655 W Broadway Ste 1410 San Diego (92101) ***(G-6314)***
California American Water Co...831 373-3051
511 Forest Lodge Rd 100 Pacific Grove (93950) ***(G-6315)***
California American Water Co...619 656-2400
880 Kuhn Dr Chula Vista (91914) ***(G-6316)***
California American Water Co...707 542-1717
4787 Old Redwood Hwy Santa Rosa (95403) ***(G-6317)***
California American Water Co...916 568-4216
4701 Beloit Dr Sacramento (95838) ***(G-6318)***
California Anesthesia Asso Med...800 888-2186
400 N Tustin Ave Ste 400 Santa Ana (92705) ***(G-19389)***
California Armenian Home, Fresno *Also called California HM For The Aged Inc* ***(G-21174)***
California Artichoke & Vegetab...831 633-2144
10855 Ocean Mist Pkwy Castroville (95012) ***(G-517)***
California Assn Realtors Inc (PA)...213 739-8200
525 S Virgil Ave Los Angeles (90020) ***(G-25079)***
California Association O (PA)...916 443-7401
1215 K St Ste 800 Sacramento (95814) ***(G-25119)***
California Automobile Insur Co...714 232-8669
555 W Imperial Hwy Brea (92821) ***(G-10405)***
California Baking Company...619 591-8289
681 Anita St Chula Vista (91911) ***(G-8811)***
California Bank & Trust, Culver City *Also called Zb National Association* ***(G-9466)***
California Basic, Santa Fe Springs *Also called Mias Fashion Mfg Co Inc* ***(G-8401)***
California Bistro At Fo...760 603-3700
7100 Aviara Resort Dr Carlsbad (92011) ***(G-12481)***
California Bread Co., Chula Vista *Also called California Baking Company* ***(G-8811)***
California Broadcast Ctr LLC...310 233-2425
3800 Via Oro Ave Long Beach (90810) ***(G-5939)***
California Building Maint...858 451-9111
11315 Rancho Bernardo Rd San Diego (92127) ***(G-14244)***
California Business Bureau Inc (PA)...626 303-1515
1711 S Mountain Ave Monrovia (91016) ***(G-14021)***
California Cancer Assctes...559 447-4949
7130 N Millbrook Ave Fresno (93720) ***(G-19390)***
California Cancer Center, Fresno *Also called Community Medical Centers* ***(G-21505)***
California Cancer Specialists (PA)...626 775-3200
1333 S Mayflower Ave # 200 Monrovia (91016) ***(G-25120)***
California Capital Insur Co (PA)...831 233-5500
2300 Garden Rd Monterey (93940) ***(G-10406)***
California Cartage Company LLC...562 590-8591
2401 E Pacific Coast Hwy Wilmington (90744) ***(G-4677)***
California Casuality, San Mateo *Also called California Casualty Mgt Co* ***(G-10407)***
California Casualty Mgt Co (PA)...650 574-4000
1900 Almeda De Las Pulgas San Mateo (94403) ***(G-10407)***
California Cereal Products Inc (PA)...510 452-4500
1267 14th St Oakland (94607) ***(G-8960)***
California Certified Organic...831 423-2263
2155 Delaware Ave Ste 150 Santa Cruz (95060) ***(G-25080)***
California Chamber Commerce (PA)...916 444-6670
1215 K St Ste 1400 Sacramento (95814) ***(G-25081)***
California Chamber Commerce...916 928-2124
920 Riverside Pkwy Ste 30 West Sacramento (95605) ***(G-25082)***
California Charter Inc...562 634-7969
3333 E 69th St Long Beach (90805) ***(G-3892)***
California Child Care Resourc...510 658-0381
5232 Claremont Ave Oakland (94618) ***(G-23698)***
California Choice, Orange *Also called Choic Admini Insur Servi* ***(G-10669)***
California Citrus Cooperative...951 683-4045
859 Center St Riverside (92507) ***(G-216)***
California Classics, Vernon *Also called Randall Foods Inc* ***(G-8604)***
California Clinical Trials...310 945-1780
3828 Delmas Ter 2 Culver City (90232) ***(G-10656)***
California Closet Co, San Diego *Also called Dehart Inc* ***(G-3512)***
California Closet Co O...714 899-4905
5921 Skylab Rd Huntington Beach (92647) ***(G-3506)***
California Club...213 622-1391
538 S Flower St Los Angeles (90071) ***(G-25225)***
California Club Lucky Lady...619 287-6690
5526 El Cajon Blvd San Diego (92115) ***(G-19157)***
California Club of CA...415 474-3516
1750 Clay St San Francisco (94109) ***(G-25226)***
California Cmnty Foundation (PA)...213 413-4130
221 S Figueroa St Ste 400 Los Angeles (90012) ***(G-12155)***
California Coast Credit Union (PA)...858 495-1600
9201 Spectrum Center Blvd # 300 San Diego (92123) ***(G-9654)***
California Coast Credit Union...858 495-1600
5890 Pcf Ctr Blvd Frnt San Diego (92121) ***(G-9655)***
California Coast Credit Union...858 495-1600
8131 Allison Ave La Mesa (91942) ***(G-9656)***
California Comfort Systems USA...858 564-1100
7740 Kenamar Ct San Diego (92121) ***(G-2172)***
California Coml Inv Group Inc...805 495-8400
4530 E Thousand Oaks Blvd # 100 Westlake Village (91362) ***(G-27862)***
California Coml Solar Inc...559 667-9200
635 S Atwood St Visalia (93277) ***(G-2173)***
California Commerce Club Inc...323 721-2100
6131 Telegraph Rd Commerce (90040) ***(G-12482)***
California Community Colleges...916 445-8752
1102 Q St Fl 4 Sacramento (95811) ***(G-24317)***
California Contrs Sups Inc...818 785-8823
7729 Burnet Ave Van Nuys (91405) ***(G-7764)***
California Convalescent Center, Los Angeles *Also called Bonnie Brae Cnvlscent Hosp Inc* ***(G-21158)***
California Convalescent Hosp...805 682-1355
2225 De La Vina St Santa Barbara (93105) ***(G-21173)***
California Convalescent Hosptl...626 793-5114
120 Bellefontaine St Pasadena (91105) ***(G-20433)***
California Correctnl Peace Ofc (PA)...916 372-6060
755 Riverpoint Dr West Sacramento (95605) ***(G-25168)***
California Country Club...626 333-4571
1509 Workman Mill Rd City of Industry (90601) ***(G-18906)***
California Creations Inc...323 722-9832
1100 S Vail Ave Montebello (90640) ***(G-6809)***
California Credit Union (PA)...818 291-6700
701 N Brand Blvd Ste 100 Glendale (91203) ***(G-9657)***
California Credits Group LLC...626 584-9800
251 S Lake Ave Ste 400 Pasadena (91101) ***(G-17046)***
California Cryobank Inc (PA)...310 443-5244
11915 La Grange Ave Los Angeles (90025) ***(G-22905)***
California Cy Correctional Ctr, California City *Also called Corrections Corp America* ***(G-27782)***
California Dental Arts LLC...408 255-1020
20421 Pacifica Dr Cupertino (95014) ***(G-22301)***
California Dental Association (PA)...916 443-0505
1201 K St Fl 14 Sacramento (95814) ***(G-25121)***
California Drywall Co (PA)...408 292-7500
2290 S 10th St San Jose (95112) ***(G-2871)***
California Eastern Labs Inc (PA)...408 919-2500
4590 Patrick Henry Dr Santa Clara (95054) ***(G-7541)***
California Emergency Physician, Modesto *Also called Medamerica Billing Svcs Inc* ***(G-26409)***
California Empire Bancorp Inc...909 484-7988
10681 Fthill Blvd Ste 200 Rancho Cucamonga (91730) ***(G-9824)***
California Endive Farm, Rio Vista *Also called California Vegetable Spc Inc* ***(G-46)***

ALPHABETIC

California Endowment (PA)........800 449-4149
1000 N Alameda St Los Angeles (90012) ***(G-24882)***
California Envmtl Hlth Assn........650 363-4726
2000 A De Las Pulgas 10 Ste 100 San Mateo (94403) ***(G-27863)***
California Exteriors, San Bernardino *Also called Michael Grove* ***(G-13777)***
California Eye Institute........559 449-5000
Low Vision Dept St Agnes Fresno (93720) ***(G-19391)***
California Fair Plan Assn........213 487-0111
3435 Wilshire Blvd # 1200 Los Angeles (90010) ***(G-10657)***
California Family Fitness, Elk Grove *Also called California Family Health LLC* ***(G-18617)***
California Family Health LLC........916 685-3355
8569 Bond Rd Ste 130 Elk Grove (95624) ***(G-18617)***
California Field Ironwrkrs, San Bernardino *Also called Iron Workers Local 433* ***(G-12178)***
California First National Bank........949 255-0500
28 Executive Park Ste 200 Irvine (92614) ***(G-9546)***
California Floral and Home, City of Industry *Also called California Floral Imports Inc* ***(G-6852)***
California Floral Imports Inc........562 696-1039
14711 Clark Ave City of Industry (91745) ***(G-6852)***
California Forensic Med Group........858 694-4690
2801 Meadow Lark Dr San Diego (92123) ***(G-22906)***
California Forensic Med Group........831 755-3886
1410 Natividad Rd Salinas (93906) ***(G-19392)***
California Forensic Med Group........805 654-3343
800 S Victoria Ave Ventura (93009) ***(G-22907)***
California Forensic Med Group........209 525-5670
200 E Hackett Rd Modesto (95358) ***(G-19393)***
California Friends Homes........714 530-9100
12151 Dale Ave Stanton (90680) ***(G-24577)***
California Fuji International........818 889-6680
901 Encinal Canyon Rd Malibu (90265) ***(G-18719)***
California Golden Realty........408 822-6000
26752 Calaroga Ave Hayward (94545) ***(G-11339)***
California Golf Association........831 625-4653
3200 Lopez Rd Pebble Beach (93953) ***(G-18907)***
California Govrnmnt Opr Agncy........800 228-5453
7667 Folsom Blvd Fl 3 Sacramento (95826) ***(G-10544)***
California Guard Inc........209 465-8420
3108 N Cherryland Ave Stockton (95215) ***(G-16589)***
California Healthcare, Van Nuys *Also called Golden Living LLC* ***(G-22443)***
California Healthcare........760 520-1333
700 La Terraza Blvd # 200 Escondido (92025) ***(G-10658)***
CALIFORNIA HEALTHCARE AND REHA, Van Nuys *Also called Normand/Wlshire Rtrment Ht Inc* ***(G-11174)***
California Hispanic Com........562 942-9625
9033 Washington Blvd Pico Rivera (90660) ***(G-22118)***
California Hlth Collaborative (PA)........559 221-6315
1680 W Shaw Ave Fresno (93711) ***(G-17047)***
California HM For The Aged Inc........559 251-8414
6720 E Kings Canyon Rd Fresno (93727) ***(G-21174)***
California Home Care Inc........619 521-5858
3078 El Cajon Blvd San Diego (92104) ***(G-22386)***
California Hospital Assn Cha, Sacramento *Also called California Association O* ***(G-25119)***
California Hospital Med Ctr, Los Angeles *Also called Dignity Health* ***(G-21539)***
California Human Dev Corp (PA)........707 523-1155
3315 Airway Dr Santa Rosa (95403) ***(G-24318)***
California Hydronics Corp (PA)........510 293-1993
2293 Tripaldi Way Hayward (94545) ***(G-7735)***
California Imaging Inst LLC........559 447-4000
6297 N Fresno St Fresno (93710) ***(G-19394)***
California Imaging Nework, Los Angeles *Also called Oaks Diagnostics Inc* ***(G-19787)***
California Institute Tech (PA)........626 395-6811
1200 E California Blvd Pasadena (91125) ***(G-26741)***
California Institute Tech........626 395-8700
360 S Wilson Ave Pasadena (91106) ***(G-26491)***
CALIFORNIA ISO, Folsom *Also called Califrnia Ind Sys Oprator Corp* ***(G-6108)***
California Kidney Med Group........805 497-7775
375 Rolling Oaks Dr # 100 Thousand Oaks (91361) ***(G-19395)***
California Lab Sciences LLC........562 758-6900
10200 Pioneer Blvd # 500 Santa Fe Springs (90670) ***(G-26836)***
California Land Mgt Svcs Corp........530 544-5994
2165 Fallen Leaf Rd South Lake Tahoe (96150) ***(G-13477)***
California Ldscp & Design Inc........909 949-1601
273 N Benson Ave Upland (91786) ***(G-820)***
California Limousines........949 581-7531
23016 Lake Forest Dr A Laguna Hills (92653) ***(G-3778)***
California Linen, Pasadena *Also called Dydee Service of Pasedena* ***(G-13653)***
California Linen Service, Pasadena *Also called Dy-Dee Service Pasadena Inc* ***(G-13652)***
California Linen Services Inc........626 564-4576
40 E California Blvd Pasadena (91105) ***(G-13541)***
California Lmcc/Ibew-Neca, Dublin *Also called Joint Labor Mgmt Coop Committe* ***(G-2628)***
California Marine Cleaning Inc (PA)........619 231-8788
2049 Main St San Diego (92113) ***(G-6449)***
California Marketing, San Diego *Also called Mabie Marketing Group Inc* ***(G-17305)***
California Mart LLC........213 630-3600
110 E 9th St Ste A727 Los Angeles (90079) ***(G-10965)***
California Mart Parking, Los Angeles *Also called California Mart LLC* ***(G-10965)***
California Materials Inc........209 472-7422
3736 S Highway 99 Stockton (95215) ***(G-3989)***
California Mayoreo-Y-Menudeo, Calexico *Also called California Super Market* ***(G-4530)***
California Med Response Inc........562 968-1818
12409 Slauson Ave Ste B Whittier (90606) ***(G-3779)***
California Medical Association (PA)........916 444-5532
1201 J St Ste 200 Sacramento (95814) ***(G-19396)***
California Mfg Tech Consulting........310 263-3060
690 Knox St Ste 200 Torrance (90502) ***(G-25714)***
California Mission Inn, Rosemead *Also called Ensign Group Inc* ***(G-20542)***

California Motorcycle Club........510 534-6222
742 45th Ave Oakland (94601) ***(G-18908)***
California Nurses Association (PA)........510 273-2200
155 Grand Ave Oakland (94612) ***(G-25122)***
California Nursing and Rehab........760 325-2937
2299 N Indian Ave Palm Springs (92262) ***(G-20434)***
California Oak Valley Golf........951 769-9771
1888 Golf Club Dr Beaumont (92223) ***(G-18909)***
California Odd Fellows (PA)........707 257-7885
1800 Atrium Pkwy NAPA (94559) ***(G-11110)***
California Odd Fellows........707 257-7885
1800 Atrium Pkwy NAPA (94559) ***(G-11111)***
California Omicron Chapter........310 979-3857
1990 S Bundy Dr Ste 500 Los Angeles (90025) ***(G-13489)***
California Oregon Broadcasting (HQ)........530 243-7777
755 Auditorium Dr Redding (96001) ***(G-5837)***
California Overnight, Anaheim *Also called Express Messenger Systems Inc* ***(G-4404)***
California Overnight, Sacramento *Also called Express Messenger Systems Inc* ***(G-4407)***
California Overnight, San Francisco *Also called Express Messenger Systems Inc* ***(G-4408)***
California Pacific CA........415 345-0940
2100 Webster St Ste 516 San Francisco (94115) ***(G-19397)***
California Pacific Medical Ctr, San Francisco *Also called Sutter Bay Hospitals* ***(G-21940)***
California Pacific Medical Ctr........415 600-1378
2100 Webster St Ste 115 San Francisco (94115) ***(G-21469)***
California Pajarosa........831 722-6374
133 Hughes Rd Watsonville (95076) ***(G-271)***
California Pajarosa Floral........831 722-6374
133 Hughes Rd Watsonville (95076) ***(G-9182)***
California Pavement Maint Inc........916 381-8033
9390 Elder Creek Rd Sacramento (95829) ***(G-1745)***
California Pediatric Fmly Svcs........626 812-0055
326 E Foothill Blvd Azusa (91702) ***(G-23699)***
California Peo Home........626 300-0400
700 N Stoneman Ave Alhambra (91801) ***(G-24578)***
California Pharmacy MGT LLC........714 777-3100
3198 Arprt Loop Dr Ste F Costa Mesa (92626) ***(G-14022)***
California Physicians Service........661 631-2277
2020 17th St Bakersfield (93301) ***(G-10261)***
California Physicians Service........925 927-7419
2066 Camel Ln Apt 24 Walnut Creek (94596) ***(G-10262)***
California Physicians Service (PA)........415 229-5000
50 Beale St Bsmt 2 San Francisco (94105) ***(G-10263)***
California Physicians Service........530 351-6115
4700 Bechelli Ln Redding (96002) ***(G-10264)***
California Physicians Service........916 350-7800
4203 Town Center Blvd El Dorado Hills (95762) ***(G-10265)***
California Physicians Service........310 744-2668
100 N Sepulveda Blvd # 2000 El Segundo (90245) ***(G-10266)***
California Physicians Service........818 598-8000
6300 Canoga Ave Ste A Woodland Hills (91367) ***(G-10267)***
California Preferred Bldrs Inc........818 402-3345
20335 Ventura Blvd # 422 Woodland Hills (91364) ***(G-1150)***
California Private Trnsp Co LP........714 637-9191
180 N Rverview Dr Ste 200 Anaheim (92808) ***(G-5207)***
California Produce, San Juan Bautista *Also called Christopher Ranch LLC* ***(G-51)***
California Produce Wholsalers........562 776-5770
6818 Watcher St Commerce (90040) ***(G-8702)***
California Public Emplyees Ret........916 795-3000
400 P St Ste 1204 Sacramento (95814) ***(G-10545)***
California Public Emplyees Ret (HQ)........916 795-3000
400 Q St Sacramento (95811) ***(G-10546)***
California Rain Company Inc........213 624-1771
1213 E 14th St A Los Angeles (90021) ***(G-8372)***
California Repertory Company........562 985-7891
1250 N Bellflower Blvd # 124 Long Beach (90840) ***(G-18375)***
California Resources Corp........661 763-6107
1320 4th St Los Osos (93402) ***(G-1036)***
California Resources Corp........661 395-8000
5000 Stockdale Hwy Bakersfield (93309) ***(G-1037)***
California Resources Corp........562 624-3400
111 W Ocean Blvd Ste 800 Long Beach (90802) ***(G-1038)***
California Resources Corp........310 208-8800
270 Quail Ct Ste 100 Santa Paula (93060) ***(G-1039)***
California Resources Prod Corp........805 483-8017
3450 E 5th St Oxnard (93033) ***(G-1040)***
California Resources Prod Corp (HQ)........661 869-8000
11109 River Run Blvd Bakersfield (93311) ***(G-1041)***
California Rural Indian Health........916 437-0104
4400 Auburn Blvd Fl 2 Sacramento (95841) ***(G-24883)***
California Safety Agency........866 996-6990
8932 Katella Ave Ste 108 Anaheim (92804) ***(G-16590)***
California Schl Employees Assn (PA)........408 473-1000
2045 Lundy Ave San Jose (95131) ***(G-25169)***
California Schl Employees Assn........626 258-3300
4600 Santa Anita Ave El Monte (91731) ***(G-14849)***
California School Boards Assn........916 371-4691
3251 Beacon Blvd West Sacramento (95691) ***(G-25123)***
California Search Services, Red Bluff *Also called Business Connections* ***(G-14618)***
California Security Cons........209 465-8420
3108 N Cherryland Ave Stockton (95215) ***(G-16591)***
California Shakespeare Theater........510 548-3422
701 Heinz Ave Berkeley (94710) ***(G-18376)***
California Shellfish Co Inc........707 542-9490
1280 Columbus Ave 300r San Francisco (94133) ***(G-8631)***
California Shtmtl Works Inc........619 562-7010
1020 N Marshall Ave El Cajon (92020) ***(G-1411)***
California Sierra Express Inc........916 375-7070
2975 Oates St Ste 30 West Sacramento (95691) ***(G-5039)***
California Silver-Agriculture........559 562-3795
831 Ash Ave Lindsay (93247) ***(G-1014)***

ALPHABETIC

California Skateparks 909 949-1601
285 N Benson Ave Upland (91786) *(G-17048)*
California Special Events, Fountain Valley *Also called B T B Events Inc (G-27732)*
California Speedway Corp 909 429-5000
9300 Cherry Ave Fontana (92335) *(G-18567)*
California State Automobile (HQ) 925 287-7600
1276 S California Blvd Walnut Creek (94596) *(G-10408)*
California State Automobile 916 472-2701
908 Pleasant Grove Blvd Roseville (95678) *(G-10409)*
California State Univ Aux Svcs 323 343-2531
5151 State University Dr Ge314 Los Angeles (90032) *(G-26954)*
California State University 510 885-2700
25976 Carlos Bee Blvd Hayward (94542) *(G-26955)*
California Strl Concepts Inc 661 257-6903
14431 Ventura Blvd # 587 Sherman Oaks (91423) *(G-1521)*
California Sun Centers Inc 916 789-9767
8265 Sierra College Blvd Roseville (95661) *(G-13740)*
California Suncare Inc 310 578-4400
12777 W Jefferson Blvd Los Angeles (90066) *(G-8241)*
California Super Market 760 357-3065
363 W 2nd St Calexico (92231) *(G-4530)*
California Supply Inc (PA) 310 532-2500
491 E Compton Blvd Gardena (90248) *(G-8187)*
California Survey Res Svcs 818 780-2777
15350 Sherman Way Ste 480 Van Nuys (91406) *(G-16105)*
California Tahoe Conservancy 530 542-5580
1061 3rd St South Lake Tahoe (96150) *(G-28121)*
California Tan, Los Angeles *Also called California Suncare Inc (G-8241)*
California Teachers Assn 530 622-8013
222 Judy Dr Kelsey (95667) *(G-25124)*
California Teachers Assn (PA) 650 697-1400
1705 Murchison Dr Burlingame (94010) *(G-25125)*
California Ticketscom Inc 925 671-4000
1855 Gateway Blvd Ste 630 Concord (94520) *(G-18377)*
California Ticketscom Inc (HQ) 714 327-5400
555 Anton Blvd Fl 11 Costa Mesa (92626) *(G-18378)*
California Tile Installers, San Jose *Also called U S Perma Inc (G-3027)*
California Title Co Nthrn Cal 909 825-8800
1955 Hunts Ln Ste 102 San Bernardino (92408) *(G-10498)*
California Title Company 619 516-5227
2365 Northside Dr Ste 250 San Diego (92108) *(G-10499)*
California Traffic Control 562 595-7575
3333 Cherry Ave Long Beach (90807) *(G-17049)*
California Traffic Ctrl Svcs, Long Beach *Also called California Traffic Control (G-17049)*
California Traffic Safety Inst 661 940-1907
209 E Avenue K8 Ste 210 Lancaster (93535) *(G-27864)*
California Transit Inc 323 234-8750
3201 Hooper Ave Los Angeles (90011) *(G-3637)*
California United Bank (HQ) 213 430-7000
818 W 7th St Ste 220 Los Angeles (90017) *(G-9478)*
California United Mech Inc (PA) 408 232-9000
2185 Oakland Rd San Jose (95131) *(G-2174)*
California University Long Bch, Long Beach *Also called California Repertory Company (G-18375)*
California Untd Terminals Inc 310 521-5000
2525 Navy Way San Pedro (90731) *(G-4744)*
California Valley Land Co Inc (PA) 559 945-9292
18036 Gale Huron (93234) *(G-477)*
California Vegetable Spc Inc 707 374-2111
15 Poppy House Rd Rio Vista (94571) *(G-46)*
California Villa, Van Nuys *Also called Longwood Management Corp (G-11159)*
California Vocations Inc 530 877-0937
1620 Cypress Ln Paradise (95969) *(G-21175)*
California Waste Services LLC 310 538-5998
621 W 152nd St Gardena (90247) *(G-6450)*
California Waste Solutions Inc 408 292-0830
1820 10th St Oakland (94607) *(G-6451)*
California Waste Solutions Inc (PA) 510 832-8111
1005 Timothy Dr San Jose (95133) *(G-6452)*
California Water Service Co (HQ) 408 367-8200
1720 N 1st St San Jose (95112) *(G-6319)*
California Water Service Co 661 396-2400
3725 S H St Bakersfield (93304) *(G-6320)*
California Water Service Co 209 547-7900
1505 E Sonora St Stockton (95205) *(G-6321)*
California Watercress Inc (PA) 805 524-4808
550 E Telegraph Rd Fillmore (93015) *(G-47)*
California Wireless Solutions 408 771-1249
4095 Evergrn Vlg S 200 Milpitas (95035) *(G-5282)*
California Yacht Club, Marina Del Rey *Also called Laaco Ltd (G-18973)*
California Youth Outreach, San Jose *Also called Breakout Prison Outreach (G-23694)*
Californian-Pasadena, Pasadena *Also called California Convalescent Hosptl (G-20433)*
Califrn/Nvada Developments LLC 714 677-5721
3010 Old Ranch Pkwy # 330 Seal Beach (90740) *(G-11249)*
Califrnia Auto Dalers Exch LLC 714 996-2400
1320 N Tustin Ave Anaheim (92807) *(G-6666)*
Califrnia Cnema Invstments Inc 760 827-6700
6941 El Camino Real Carlsbad (92009) *(G-18314)*
Califrnia CPA Edcatn Fundation 800 922-5272
1800 Gateway Dr Ste 200 San Mateo (94404) *(G-25126)*
Califrnia Cslty Indemnity Exch (PA) 650 574-4000
1900 Almeda De Las Pulgas San Mateo (94403) *(G-10410)*
Califrnia Dept State Hospitals 559 935-4300
24511 W Jayne Ave Coalinga (93210) *(G-22046)*
Califrnia Dept State Hospitals 714 957-5000
2501 Harbor Blvd Costa Mesa (92626) *(G-22047)*
Califrnia Dept State Hospitals 707 253-5000
2100 Napa Vallejo Hwy NAPA (94558) *(G-22048)*
Califrnia Dept State Hospitals 909 425-7000
3102 E Highland Ave Patton (92369) *(G-22049)*
Califrnia Dept State Hospitals 805 468-2000
10333 El Camino Real Atascadero (93422) *(G-22050)*
Califrnia Dsster Med Svcs Assn 408 970-9202
101 Dale Ave San Carlos (94070) *(G-22908)*
Califrnia Erctors Bay Area Inc 707 746-1990
4500 California Ct Benicia (94510) *(G-3373)*
Califrnia Fmly Hlth Cuncil Inc (PA) 213 386-5614
3600 Wilshire Blvd # 600 Los Angeles (90010) *(G-24884)*
Califrnia Golf CLB San Frncsco 650 588-9021
844 W Orange Ave South San Francisco (94080) *(G-18910)*
Califrnia High Speed Rail Auth 916 324-1541
770 L St Ste 800 Sacramento (95814) *(G-3611)*
Califrnia Hlth Care Foundation (PA) 510 891-3963
1438 Webster St Ste 400 Oakland (94612) *(G-24885)*
Califrnia Hlth Humn Srvcs Agcy 916 739-7640
3301 S St Sacramento (95816) *(G-16106)*
Califrnia Hosp Med Ctr Fndtion 213 748-2411
1401 S Grand Ave Los Angeles (90015) *(G-21470)*
Califrnia Ind Sys Oprator Corp 916 608-7000
110 Blue Ravine Rd Folsom (95630) *(G-27367)*
Califrnia Ind Sys Oprator Corp (PA) 916 351-4400
250 Outcropping Way Folsom (95630) *(G-6108)*
Califrnia Inst For Bmdical RES 858 242-1000
11119 N Torrey Pines Rd La Jolla (92037) *(G-26742)*
Califrnia Insur Guarantee Assn 818 844-4300
101 N Brand Blvd Ste 600 Glendale (91203) *(G-10566)*
Califrnia Intermodal Assoc Inc (PA) 323 562-7788
6666 E Washington Blvd Commerce (90040) *(G-4124)*
Califrnia Nrsing Rhbltion Ctr, Palm Springs *Also called Cnrc LLC (G-20461)*
Califrnia Nrsing Rhbltion Ctr, Palm Springs *Also called California Nursing and Rehab (G-20434)*
Califrnia Physcn Reimbursement 530 241-0473
1321 Butte St Redding (96001) *(G-10659)*
Califrnia Psychtric Trnsitions 209 667-9304
9234n Hinton Ave Delhi (95315) *(G-19398)*
Califrnia Rgional Intranet Inc 858 974-5080
8929 Complex Dr Ste A San Diego (92123) *(G-5567)*
Califrnia Scnce Ctr Foundation 213 744-2545
700 Exposition Park Dr Los Angeles (90037) *(G-25005)*
Califrnia Shock Truma A Rescue (PA) 916 921-4000
4933 Bailey Loop McClellan (95652) *(G-4879)*
Califrnia State Employees Assn (PA) 916 444-8134
1108 O St Ste 405 Sacramento (95814) *(G-25170)*
Califrnia Tchers Rtirement Sys, Sacramento *Also called California Govrnmnt Opr Agncy (G-10544)*
Califrnia Yuth Soccer Assn Inc 925 426-5437
1040 Serpentine Ln # 206 Pleasanton (94566) *(G-25512)*
Califrnia-Nevada Methdst Homes 510 835-5511
1850 Alice St Ofc Oakland (94612) *(G-21176)*
Califrnias Gnite Pool Plst Inc 925 960-9500
510 Greenville Rd Livermore (94550) *(G-3237)*
Califronia Department of State 805 468-2501
10333 El Camino Real Atascadero (93422) *(G-22051)*
Calistoga Spa Hot Springs, Calistoga *Also called Calistoga Spa Inc (G-18618)*
Calistoga Spa Inc 707 942-6269
1006 Washington St Calistoga (94515) *(G-18618)*
Calko Transport Company Inc 310 816-0602
720 E Watson Center Rd Carson (90745) *(G-4333)*
Call & Jensen APC 949 717-3000
610 Nwport Ctr Dr Ste 700 Newport Beach (92660) *(G-23141)*
Call To Action LLC 310 996-7200
11601 Wilshire Blvd Fl 23 Los Angeles (90025) *(G-12290)*
Callan Associates Inc (PA) 415 974-5060
600 Montgomery St Ste 800 San Francisco (94111) *(G-10126)*
Callan Management Corporation 818 846-2215
2919 W Burbank Blvd Ste C Burbank (91505) *(G-16873)*
Callaway Golf Ball Oprtons Inc 760 931-1771
2180 Rutherford Rd Carlsbad (92008) *(G-8013)*
Callcatchers Inc 800 477-1477
169 Saxony Rd Ste 212 Encinitas (92024) *(G-5568)*
Calleguas Municipal Water Dict 805 526-9323
2100 E Olsen Rd Thousand Oaks (91360) *(G-6322)*
Callfire Inc 213 221-2289
1410 2nd St Ste 200 Santa Monica (90401) *(G-15072)*
Callidus Software Inc (PA) 925 251-2200
4140 Dublin Blvd Ste 400 Dublin (94568) *(G-15073)*
Calliduscloud, Dublin *Also called Callidus Software Inc (G-15073)*
Callison LLC 310 394-8460
1453 3rd Street Promenade # 400 Santa Monica (90401) *(G-26169)*
Callisonrtkl Inc 213 627-7373
818 W 7th St Ste 300 Los Angeles (90017) *(G-26170)*
Callisonrtkl Inc 213 633-6000
333 S Hope St Ste C200 Los Angeles (90071) *(G-26171)*
Calmet Inc (PA) 323 721-8120
7202 Petterson Ln Paramount (90723) *(G-6453)*
Calmet Inc 562 869-0901
7202 Petterson Ln Paramount (90723) *(G-3990)*
Calmet Services Inc 562 259-1239
7202 Petterson Ln Paramount (90723) *(G-6454)*
Calmex Engineering Inc 909 546-1311
2764 S Vista Ave Bloomington (92316) *(G-3238)*
Calnev Pipe Line LLC 714 560-4400
1100 W Town And Cntry Rd Orange (92868) *(G-25715)*
Calpella Distribution Center, Calpella *Also called Mendocino Forest Pdts Co LLC (G-6937)*
Calpers, Sacramento *Also called Public Employees Retirement (G-10560)*
Calpers Investment Office, Sacramento *Also called California Public Emplyees Ret (G-10545)*

ALPHABETIC

Calpine Containers Inc..........559 591-6555
42779 Road 80 Dinuba (93618) ***(G-8188)***
Calpipe Industries Inc..........562 803-4388
19440 S Dminguez Hills Dr Rancho Dominguez (90220) ***(G-7363)***
Calply, San Diego *Also called L & W Supply Corporation* ***(G-6989)***
Calply, Hayward *Also called L & W Supply Corporation* ***(G-6990)***
Calpoint..........310 274-6680
9860 Wilshire Blvd Beverly Hills (90210) ***(G-5569)***
Calsoft Labs Inc (HQ)..........408 755-3001
2903 Bunker Hill Ln Santa Clara (95054) ***(G-15913)***
Calstar, McClellan *Also called Califrnia Shock Truma A Rescue* ***(G-4879)***
Calstars..........916 445-0211
915 L St Fl 7 Sacramento (95814) ***(G-26305)***
CALTECH, Pasadena *Also called California Institute Tech* ***(G-26741)***
CALTECH EFCU, La Canada Flintridge *Also called Caltech Emplyees Federal Cr Un* ***(G-9658)***
Caltech Emplyees Federal Cr Un..........818 952-4444
528 Foothill Blvd La Canada Flintridge (91011) ***(G-9658)***
Calteck USA Inc..........949 786-4854
33 Goldenrod Irvine (92614) ***(G-17820)***
Caltrain, San Carlos *Also called Peninsula Crrdor Jint Pwers Bd* ***(G-3690)***
Caltrans, Fairfield *Also called Transportation California Dept* ***(G-1878)***
Caltrans Eastern Reg Rd Maint, Whittier *Also called Transportation California Dept* ***(G-1877)***
Caltronics Business Systems, Sacramento *Also called JJR Enterprises Inc* ***(G-17936)***
Caltrop Corporation..........949 337-4280
2415 Campus Dr Ste 265 Irvine (92612) ***(G-26956)***
Calvary Baptist Ch Los Gatos..........408 356-5126
16330 Los Gatos Blvd Los Gatos (95032) ***(G-24422)***
Calvary Cemetery, Santa Barbara *Also called Roman Cath Arch of Los Angels* ***(G-13713)***
Calvary Church Santa Ana Inc..........714 973-4800
1010 N Tustin Ave Santa Ana (92705) ***(G-24423)***
Calvary Infant Care Center, Los Gatos *Also called Calvary Baptist Ch Los Gatos* ***(G-24422)***
Calvin Klein Inc..........951 849-9538
48650 Seminole Dr Ste 182 Cabazon (92230) ***(G-17964)***
Calvin Klein Inc..........408 842-9132
8300 Arroyo Cir Ste 260 Gilroy (95020) ***(G-17965)***
Calworks Partnr Conference..........858 292-2900
5151 Murphy Canyon Rd # 220 San Diego (92123) ***(G-12156)***
CAM Services, Culver City *Also called Common Area Maint Svcs Inc* ***(G-14259)***
Camanche Lake, Ione *Also called Parks and Recreation Cal Dept* ***(G-19258)***
Camanche Northshore Store, Ione *Also called Concessionaires Urban Park* ***(G-19189)***
CAMANCHE RECREATION COMPANY, Red Bluff *Also called Concessionaires Urban Park* ***(G-19187)***
Camanche Recreation-North, Ione *Also called Concessionaires Urban Park* ***(G-19188)***
Camarillo Family YMCA, Camarillo *Also called Channel Islands Young Mens Ch* ***(G-25232)***
Camarillo Healthcare Center..........805 482-9805
205 Granada St Camarillo (93010) ***(G-26957)***
Camarillo Ranch Foundation..........805 389-8182
201 Camarillo Ranch Rd Camarillo (93012) ***(G-17050)***
Cambium Business Group Inc (PA)..........714 670-1171
6950 Noritsu Ave Buena Park (90620) ***(G-6810)***
Cambium Networks Inc..........847 640-3809
2010 N 1st St San Jose (95131) ***(G-6062)***
Camble Center..........818 242-2434
6512 San Fernando Rd Glendale (91201) ***(G-24319)***
Cambria El Segundo Lax, El Segundo *Also called Fc El Segundo LLC* ***(G-12632)***
Cambria Global Tactical Fund 2..........310 683-5500
2321 Rosecrans Ave # 3225 El Segundo (90245) ***(G-12108)***
Cambria Pines Lodge, Cambria *Also called Pacific Cambria Inc* ***(G-13055)***
Cambrian Homecare Inc..........951 301-4300
27994 Bradley Rd Ste A Sun City (92586) ***(G-22387)***
Cambridge Design Partnr Inc..........650 387-7812
22 8 Camelton Ave Fl 3 Palo Alto (94301) ***(G-25716)***
Cambridge Home Loans Inc FN..........858 481-2929
201 Lomas Santa Fe Dr # 340 Solana Beach (92075) ***(G-9825)***
Camellia Gardens Care Center, Pasadena *Also called Arpom Inc* ***(G-20381)***
Camelot Apartments, Reseda *Also called Statewide Enterprises Inc* ***(G-11207)***
Camelot Park Santa Maria, Santa Maria *Also called Festival Fun Parks LLC* ***(G-19209)***
Cameron Family YMCA, Santee *Also called YMCA of San Diego County* ***(G-25425)***
Cameron Health Inc..........949 940-4000
905 Calle Amanecer # 300 San Clemente (92673) ***(G-7250)***
Cameron Pace Group LLC..........818 565-0005
4534 Atoll Ave Sherman Oaks (91423) ***(G-18379)***
Cameron Park Country Club Inc..........530 672-9840
3201 Royal Dr Cameron Park (95682) ***(G-18911)***
Cameron Surface Systems, Bakersfield *Also called Cameron West Coast Inc* ***(G-7765)***
Cameron West Coast Inc..........661 837-4980
4316 Yeager Way Bakersfield (93313) ***(G-7765)***
Camflor Inc..........831 726-1330
2364 Riverside Rd Watsonville (95076) ***(G-272)***
Camico Mutual Insurance Co (PA)..........650 378-6874
1800 Gateway Dr Ste 300 San Mateo (94404) ***(G-10660)***
Caminar..........530 343-4472
376 Rio Lindo Ave Chico (95926) ***(G-22670)***
Camino Dialysis Svcs Oak 110, Mountain View *Also called El Camino Hospital* ***(G-22626)***
Camino Real Group LLC..........650 964-1700
840 E El Camino Real Mountain View (94040) ***(G-12483)***
Camp Amgen, Thousand Oaks *Also called Bright Horizons Chld Ctrs LLC* ***(G-24419)***
Camp Fire USA Long Beach Cncl..........562 421-2725
7070 E Carson St Long Beach (90808) ***(G-23700)***
Camp Harmon Easter Seal Soc, Boulder Creek *Also called Easter Seals Inc* ***(G-13463)***
Camp Pendleton Billeting Fund, Camp Pendleton *Also called Marine Corps United States* ***(G-12942)***
Camp Pendleton Hospital, Oceanside *Also called Marine Corps United States* ***(G-22157)***
Camp Recovery Centers LP..........707 823-3385
2264 Green Hill Rd Sebastopol (95472) ***(G-22119)***
Camp Recovery Centers LLP..........831 438-1868
3192 Glen Canyon Rd Santa Cruz (95066) ***(G-22671)***
Camp Royaneh Boy Scout..........707 632-5291
P.O. Box 39 Cazadero (95421) ***(G-25227)***
Campanile II LP..........323 939-6813
17001 Ventura Blvd Encino (91316) ***(G-8812)***
Campanile Restaurant, Encino *Also called Campanile II LP* ***(G-8812)***
Campbell Certified Inc..........760 842-5226
1629 Ord Way Oceanside (92056) ***(G-3374)***
Campbell Hhg Hotel Dev LP..........408 626-9590
655 Creekside Way Campbell (95008) ***(G-12484)***
Campion, Catherine A MD, Newport Beach *Also called Newport Fmly Mdcne/A Med Group* ***(G-19774)***
Campo Band Missions Indians..........619 938-6000
1800 Golden Acorn Way Campo (91906) ***(G-18802)***
Campos Dmetrio Frm Labor Contr, Woodland *Also called Campos Dmetrio Frm Labor Contr* ***(G-14619)***
Campos Dmetrio Frm Labor Contr..........530 662-4143
117 W Main St Ste 19 Woodland (95695) ***(G-14619)***
Camps Fred Miller, Malibu *Also called County of Los Angeles* ***(G-24612)***
Campton Place Hotel, San Francisco *Also called Southbourne Inc* ***(G-13275)***
Campton Place, A Taj Hotel, San Francisco *Also called Ihms (sf) LLC* ***(G-12835)***
Campus Explorer Inc..........310 574-2243
2850 Ocean Park Blvd # 310 Santa Monica (90405) ***(G-5570)***
Campus Laundry, Watsonville *Also called Monterey Bay Acadamy Laundry* ***(G-13504)***
Campus Laundry, Watsonville *Also called Oceanside Laundry LLC* ***(G-13576)***
Camstar International Inc..........909 931-2540
939 W 9th St Upland (91786) ***(G-7678)***
Can-AM Plumbing Inc..........925 846-1833
151 Wyoming St Pleasanton (94566) ***(G-2175)***
Can-Do..........646 228-7049
578 Washington Blvd 39o Marina Del Rey (90292) ***(G-23701)***
Canadian Imperial Bank..........949 759-4718
620 Newport Center Dr Newport Beach (92660) ***(G-9340)***
Canary Hotel, Santa Barbara *Also called Due West LLC* ***(G-12603)***
Cancer Center of Santa Barbara, Santa Barbara *Also called Cancer Foundation Trtmnt Ctr* ***(G-19399)***
Cancer Foundation Trtmnt Ctr..........805 682-7300
300 W Pueblo St Santa Barbara (93105) ***(G-19399)***
Cancer Prevention Inst Cal (PA)..........510 608-5000
2201 Walnut Ave Ste 300 Fremont (94538) ***(G-26743)***
CANDLE LIGHTERS THE, Fremont *Also called Fremont Candle Lighters* ***(G-25531)***
Candlewood Suites, Santa Clara *Also called Hpt Trs Ihg-2 Inc* ***(G-12797)***
Candor-Ags Inc (PA)..........559 439-2365
9491 N Fort Washington Rd # 102 Fresno (93730) ***(G-195)***
Candy Cane Inn, Anaheim *Also called Cinderella Motel* ***(G-12522)***
Canedy Court Reporting, San Diego *Also called Rett Inc* ***(G-14167)***
Canessa Investments N V..........310 273-8543
9434 Cherokee Ln Beverly Hills (90210) ***(G-12291)***
Canew Inc..........818 703-5100
22135 Roscoe Blvd Canoga Park (91304) ***(G-22302)***
Canfab, Corona *Also called Cannon Fabrication Inc* ***(G-3146)***
Canine Cmpnons For Indpendence (PA)..........707 577-1700
2965 Dutton Ave Santa Rosa (95407) ***(G-637)***
Canji Inc..........858 597-0177
3525 John Hopkins Ct San Diego (92121) ***(G-26744)***
Cannon Corporation (PA)..........805 544-7407
1050 Southwood Dr San Luis Obispo (93401) ***(G-26273)***
Cannon Design Inc..........310 229-2700
1901 Avenue Of The Stars # 175 Los Angeles (90067) ***(G-26172)***
Cannon Fabrication Inc..........951 278-1830
182 Granite St Ste 101 Corona (92879) ***(G-3146)***
Cannondworsky, Los Angeles *Also called Cannon Design Inc* ***(G-26172)***
Canoga Hotel Corporation..........818 595-1000
6360 Canoga Ave Woodland Hills (91367) ***(G-12485)***
Canoga Park Worksource Center..........818 596-4448
21010 Vanowen St Canoga Park (91303) ***(G-14620)***
Canoga Park/West Hills Club, Canoga Park *Also called 24 Hour Fitness Usa Inc* ***(G-18595)***
Canon Bus Solutions-West Inc..........310 217-3000
110 W Walnut St Gardena (90248) ***(G-7043)***
Canon Recruiting Group LLC..........661 252-7400
26531 Summit Cir Santa Clarita (91350) ***(G-14850)***
Canon Solutions America Inc..........213 629-6733
1055 W 7th St Ste 1600 Los Angeles (90017) ***(G-7044)***
Canon Solutions America Inc..........818 871-6700
26901 Agoura Rd Ste 110 Agoura Hills (91301) ***(G-7045)***
Canon Solutions America Inc..........800 323-4827
203 S Waterman Ave El Centro (92243) ***(G-17051)***
Canon Solutions America Inc..........800 333-6395
15975 Alton Pkwy Irvine (92618) ***(G-7830)***
Canon Solutions America Inc..........760 438-6990
2382 Faraday Ave Ste 250 Carlsbad (92008) ***(G-17052)***
Canon Solutions America Inc..........909 390-7400
3237 E Guasti Rd Ste 200 Ontario (91761) ***(G-27368)***
Canon Solutions America Inc..........415 743-7300
201 California St Ste 100 San Francisco (94111) ***(G-7046)***
Canon Solutions America Inc..........949 753-4200
123 Paularino Ave Costa Mesa (92626) ***(G-7047)***
Canon USA Inc..........949 753-4000
15955 Alton Pkwy Irvine (92618) ***(G-7029)***
Canon USA Inc..........323 461-1862
6060 W Sunset Blvd Los Angeles (90028) ***(G-7048)***
Canon USA Inc..........213 629-6700
1055 W 7th St Ste 1600 Los Angeles (90017) ***(G-7049)***
Canopy Energy, Van Nuys *Also called Energy Enterprises USA Inc* ***(G-2218)***
Cantamar Property MGT Inc..........562 862-4470
9550 Firestone Blvd # 105 Downey (90241) ***(G-11340)***

A L P H A B E T I C

Canteen Vending, Garden Grove *Also called Compass Group Usa Inc* ***(G-14524)***
Cantel Medical Corp......925 609-6328
140 Mason Cir Concord (94520) ***(G-2036)***
Canterbury Hotel Corp......415 474-1452
750 Sutter St San Francisco (94109) ***(G-12486)***
Canterbury Woods, Pacific Grove *Also called Episcopal Senior Communities* ***(G-24647)***
Canterbury, The, Pls Vrds Pnsl *Also called Episcopal Communities & Servic* ***(G-20547)***
Canton Food Co Inc......213 688-7707
750 S Alameda St Los Angeles (90021) ***(G-8462)***
Cantor Art Ctr Stanford Univ, Palo Alto *Also called Leland Stanford Junior Univ* ***(G-21699)***
Canyon Country Medical Offices, Santa Clarita *Also called Kaiser Foundation Hospitals* ***(G-19647)***
Canyon Crest Country Club Inc......951 274-7900
975 Country Club Dr Riverside (92506) ***(G-18912)***
Canyon Crest Mental Hlth Offs, Riverside *Also called Kaiser Foundation Hospitals* ***(G-19639)***
Canyon Hills Club, Anaheim *Also called Ardcore Senior Living* ***(G-24551)***
Canyon Insulation Inc......951 278-9200
645 E Harrison St Ste 100 Corona (92879) ***(G-2872)***
Canyon Lk Property Owners Assn......951 244-6841
31512 Railroad Canyon Rd Canyon Lake (92587) ***(G-25228)***
Canyon Manor Residential Treat, Novato *Also called Marin County Sart Program* ***(G-22082)***
Canyon Partners Incorporated (PA)......310 272-1000
2000 Ave Of The Sts Fl 11 Los Angeles (90067) ***(G-9968)***
Canyon Properties III LLC......818 890-0430
11723 Fenton Ave Sylmar (91342) ***(G-21177)***
Canyon Ridge Hospital Inc......909 590-3700
5353 G St Chino (91710) ***(G-22052)***
Canyon View Capital Inc......831 480-6335
331 Soquel Ave Ste 100 Santa Cruz (95062) ***(G-12240)***
Canyon Way Nursery, Studio City *Also called Wurzel Landscape Maintenance* ***(G-981)***
Cap-Mpt, Los Angeles *Also called Coopertive Amrcn Physcians Inc* ***(G-25131)***
Cap-Mpt (PA)......213 473-8600
333 S Hope St Fl 8 Los Angeles (90071) ***(G-10490)***
Capacity LLC......732 745-7770
19852 Business Pkwy Walnut (91789) ***(G-4678)***
Capario Inc......949 553-1974
1901 E Alton Ave Ste 100 Santa Ana (92705) ***(G-10661)***
Capax Management and Services......209 526-3110
1150 9th St Ste 1400 Modesto (95354) ***(G-10662)***
Capax, Giddings, Corby & Hynes, Modesto *Also called G C H Insurance Group* ***(G-10723)***
Capay Fruits and Vegetables, West Sacramento *Also called Capay Incorporated* ***(G-48)***
Capay Incorporated (PA)......916 303-7145
3880 Seaport Blvd West Sacramento (95691) ***(G-48)***
Capc Inc......562 693-8826
7200 Greenleaf Ave # 170 Whittier (90602) ***(G-24886)***
Capcom Entertainment Inc......650 350-6500
185 Berry St Ste 1200 San Francisco (94107) ***(G-8040)***
Capcom U S A Inc (HQ)......650 350-6500
185 Berry St Ste 1200 San Francisco (94107) ***(G-8041)***
Capcom U.S.a, San Francisco *Also called Capcom Entertainment Inc* ***(G-8040)***
Cape Clear Software Inc......408 879-7365
900 E Hamilton Ave # 100 Campbell (95008) ***(G-15074)***
Cape Environmental MGT Inc......949 236-3000
24 Executive Park Ste 200 Irvine (92614) ***(G-27776)***
Capeconnect, Campbell *Also called Cape Clear Software Inc* ***(G-15074)***
Capincrouse LLP......925 201-1187
5990 Stoneridge Dr Pleasanton (94588) ***(G-26306)***
Capiot Software Inc......650 766-2469
2820 Ramona St Palo Alto (94306) ***(G-16332)***
Capistrano Beach Extended......949 496-5786
35410 Del Rey Capistrano Beach (92624) ***(G-20435)***
Capital Asset Exch & Trdg LLC......650 326-3313
870 E Charleston Rd # 210 Palo Alto (94303) ***(G-7831)***
Capital Athletic Club Inc......916 442-3927
1515 8th St Sacramento (95814) ***(G-13741)***
Capital Beverage Company (PA)......916 371-8164
2500 Del Monte St West Sacramento (95691) ***(G-9045)***
Capital Brands LLC......310 996-7200
11601 Wilshire Blvd Fl 23 Los Angeles (90025) ***(G-8813)***
Capital Builders, Brentwood *Also called V Development Inc* ***(G-1349)***
Capital City Drywall Inc......916 331-9200
6525 32nd St Ste B1 North Highlands (95660) ***(G-2873)***
Capital Commercial Flrg Inc......916 569-1960
3709 Bradview Dr Ste 100 Sacramento (95827) ***(G-3108)***
Capital Commercial Property, Culver City *Also called Property Management Assoc Inc* ***(G-11772)***
Capital Engineering Cons (PA)......916 851-3500
11020 Sun Center Dr # 100 Rancho Cordova (95670) ***(G-25717)***
Capital Eye Medical Group......916 241-9378
6620 Coyle Ave Ste 408 Carmichael (95608) ***(G-19400)***
Capital Group Companies Inc......310 996-6238
11100 Santa Monica Blvd # 1500 Los Angeles (90025) ***(G-10127)***
Capital Group Companies Inc (PA)......213 486-9200
333 S Hope St Fl 55 Los Angeles (90071) ***(G-10128)***
Capital Group Companies Inc......213 486-1698
1 Market Plz Ste 1800 San Francisco (94105) ***(G-10129)***
Capital Group Companies Inc......949 975-5000
6455 Irvine Center Dr Irvine (92618) ***(G-10130)***
Capital Group, The, Los Angeles *Also called Capital Group Companies Inc* ***(G-10128)***
Capital Group, The, Irvine *Also called Capital Group Companies Inc* ***(G-10130)***
Capital Guardian Trust Company (HQ)......213 486-9200
333 S Hope St Fl 52 Los Angeles (90071) ***(G-12169)***
Capital Insurance Group, Monterey *Also called California Capital Insur Co* ***(G-10406)***
Capital Invstmnts Vntures Corp (PA)......949 858-0647
30151 Tomas Rcho STA Marg (92688) ***(G-25127)***
Capital Mortgage Services, Ventura *Also called E&S Financial Group Inc* ***(G-9919)***
Capital Network Funding Svcs, Los Angeles *Also called Capnet Financial Services Inc* ***(G-9797)***
Capital Oversight Inc......310 453-8000
2118 Wilshire Blvd Santa Monica (90403) ***(G-27865)***
Capital Pacific Holdings Inc......951 279-2447
4100 Macarthur Blvd # 150 Newport Beach (92660) ***(G-1360)***
Capital Plus Financial Corp......619 744-1900
909 W Laurel St Ste 250 San Diego (92101) ***(G-9826)***
Capital Public Radio Inc......916 278-8900
7055 Folsom Blvd Sacramento (95826) ***(G-5753)***
Capital Research and MGT Co (HQ)......213 486-9200
333 S Hope St Fl 55 Los Angeles (90071) ***(G-10131)***
Capital Research and MGT Co......949 975-5000
6455 Irvine Center Dr Irvine (92618) ***(G-10132)***
Capital Transitional Care, Sacramento *Also called Covenant Care California LLC* ***(G-20494)***
Capitol Casino......916 446-0700
411 N 16th St Sacramento (95811) ***(G-19158)***
Capitol Corporate Services......916 444-6787
455 Capitol Mall Ste 217 Sacramento (95814) ***(G-26648)***
Capitol Fitness Network LLC......916 928-4999
15333 State Highway 88 Jackson (95642) ***(G-18619)***
Capitol Regency LLC......916 443-1234
1209 L St Sacramento (95814) ***(G-12487)***
Capitola Care Center Inc......831 477-0329
1098 38th Ave Santa Cruz (95062) ***(G-21178)***
Capitola Manor, Santa Cruz *Also called Capitola Care Center Inc* ***(G-21178)***
Capnet Financial Services Inc (PA)......818 859-8377
11901 Santa Monica Blvd Los Angeles (90025) ***(G-9797)***
Caprion Proteomics USA LLC......650 470-2300
1455 Adams Dr Ste 2124 Menlo Park (94025) ***(G-26745)***
Capstar San Francisco Co LLC......415 937-6084
2500 Mason St San Francisco (94133) ***(G-12488)***
Captain Marketing Inc......310 402-9709
3577 N Figueroa St Los Angeles (90065) ***(G-27369)***
Captiva Software Corporation (HQ)......858 320-1000
10145 Pacific Hts Blvd San Diego (92121) ***(G-15914)***
Captiva Verde Farming Corp......760 771-3333
78080 Calle Amigo Ste 201 La Quinta (92253) ***(G-349)***
Captured Sea Inc......714 856-3358
5901 Warner Ave Huntington Beach (92649) ***(G-1522)***
Capurro Farms, Moss Landing *Also called Capurro Marketing LLC* ***(G-8703)***
Capurro Marketing LLC......831 728-1767
2250 Highway 1 Moss Landing (95039) ***(G-8703)***
Car Spa Inc......951 279-1422
996 Mountain Ave Norco (92860) ***(G-17878)***
Car Wash of America......714 528-0833
120 S Placentia Ave Placentia (92870) ***(G-17834)***
Cara Communications Corp......310 442-5600
12233 W Olympic Blvd # 255 Los Angeles (90064) ***(G-18059)***
Caranythingcom Inc......916 781-4344
1376 Lead Hill Blvd # 150 Roseville (95661) ***(G-27370)***
Carat Usa Inc......310 255-1000
2700 Penn Ave Fl 2 Santa Monica (90404) ***(G-13990)***
Caraustar Industries Inc......209 476-7710
2575 Grand Canal Blvd # 202 Stockton (95207) ***(G-6455)***
Carber Holdings Inc......562 531-2400
15350 Texaco Ave Paramount (90723) ***(G-27866)***
Carbon Five, San Francisco *Also called Carbonfive Incorporated* ***(G-15075)***
Carbonfive Incorporated......415 546-0500
585 Howard St Fl 2 San Francisco (94105) ***(G-15075)***
Cardenas Bros Farming Company......805 928-1559
1141 Tama Ln Santa Maria (93455) ***(G-106)***
Cardflex Inc......714 361-1900
2900 Bristol St Bldg F Costa Mesa (92626) ***(G-17053)***
Cardiac Noninvasive Laboratory, Los Angeles *Also called Cedars-Sinai Medical Center* ***(G-19413)***
Cardic Arithmias......650 617-8100
770 Welch Rd Ste 100 Palo Alto (94304) ***(G-19401)***
Cardiff Transportation, Palm Desert *Also called Gary Cardiff Enterprises Inc* ***(G-3797)***
Cardinal Cartridge Inc......818 727-9740
20450 Plummer St Chatsworth (91311) ***(G-28122)***
Cardinal Health Inc......909 824-1820
793 Via Lata Colton (92324) ***(G-7251)***
Cardinal Health Inc......951 360-2199
1100 Bird Center Dr Palm Springs (92262) ***(G-7252)***
Cardinal Health Inc......916 372-9880
3238 Dwight Rd Elk Grove (95758) ***(G-8242)***
Cardinal Health Inc......530 406-3600
700 Vaughn Rd Dixon (95620) ***(G-7253)***
Cardinal Health Inc......510 232-2030
1007 Canal Blvd Richmond (94804) ***(G-8243)***
Cardinal Health Inc......559 448-0788
7330 N Palm Ave Ste 104 Fresno (93711) ***(G-8244)***
Cardinal Health Inc......530 225-8735
1935 Pine St Redding (96001) ***(G-8245)***
Cardinal Health Inc......916 372-9880
3238 Dwight Rd West Sacramento (95605) ***(G-8246)***
Cardinal Health Inc......909 605-0900
4551 E Philadelphia St Ontario (91761) ***(G-7254)***
Cardinal Health Inc......661 295-6100
27680 Avenue Mentry Valencia (91355) ***(G-8247)***
Cardinal Health 200 LLC......951 686-8900
3750 Torrey View Ct San Diego (92130) ***(G-7255)***
Cardinal Point Captains Inc......760 438-7361
3508 Seagate Way Ste 140 Oceanside (92056) ***(G-14851)***
Cardinal Trnsp Group Inc......310 769-2400
14800 S Avalon Blvd Gardena (90248) ***(G-3914)***
Cardio Pulmonary Services, La Jolla *Also called Professional Health Tech* ***(G-19879)***

ALPHABETIC

Cardiodx Inc......650 475-2788
600 Saginaw Dr Redwood City (94063) *(G-22196)*
Cardiology Department, Los Angeles *Also called Usc Care Medical Group Inc (G-22007)*
Cardiovascular Consultants Hea......559 432-4303
1207 E Herndon Ave Fresno (93720) *(G-19402)*
Cardiovascular Medical Group, Beverly Hills *Also called Tabak Steven William M MD (G-20127)*
Cardium Biologics Inc......858 436-1000
11750 Sorrento Valley Rd # 250 San Diego (92121) *(G-26492)*
Cardivsclr Mdcl Grp of Sthrn......310 278-3400
414 N Camden Dr Ste 1100 Beverly Hills (90210) *(G-19403)*
Cardservice International Inc......800 217-4622
4565 Industrial St Ste 7k Simi Valley (93063) *(G-17054)*
Cardservice International Inc......714 773-1778
1538 W Commonwealth Ave Fullerton (92833) *(G-17055)*
Cardservice International Inc (HQ)......805 648-1425
5898 Condor Dr 220 Moorpark (93021) *(G-17056)*
Care Inc......818 232-7940
15315 Magnolia Blvd # 306 Sherman Oaks (91403) *(G-21068)*
Care 1st Health Plan (PA)......323 889-6638
601 Potrero Grande Dr # 2 Monterey Park (91755) *(G-22909)*
Care 1st Health Plan......626 299-4299
1000 S Fremont Ave Unit 4 Alhambra (91803) *(G-22910)*
Care 4 U LLC......818 593-7911
22726 Eccles St West Hills (91304) *(G-23702)*
Care A Van Transport, Carlsbad *Also called CAV Inc (G-3780)*
Care Ambulance, San Diego *Also called Care Medical Trnsp Inc (G-14852)*
Care Associates Inc......626 330-4048
15125 Gale Ave Hacienda Heights (91745) *(G-24579)*
Care Health Services of Fla......619 692-1020
2223 Avenida Delaplya 103 La Jolla (92037) *(G-22388)*
Care Medical Trnsp Inc......858 653-4520
9770 Candida St San Diego (92126) *(G-14852)*
Care Options Management Plans......925 551-3227
7000 Village Pkwy Ste A Dublin (94568) *(G-22389)*
Care Options Management Plans (PA)......530 242-8580
475 Knollcrest Dr Redding (96002) *(G-22390)*
Care Plus Home Care Inc......949 716-2273
22931 Triton Way Ste 133 Laguna Hills (92653) *(G-22391)*
Care Plus Home Health, Laguna Hills *Also called Care Plus Nursing Services Inc (G-22392)*
Care Plus North of San Diego......619 421-0807
2337 Eastridge Loop Chula Vista (91915) *(G-14621)*
Care Plus Nursing Services Inc......949 600-7194
22931 Triton Way Ste 236 Laguna Hills (92653) *(G-22392)*
Care Solution Associates LLC......925 443-1000
179 Contractors Ave Livermore (94551) *(G-22393)*
Care Tech Inc......909 882-2965
4280 Cypress Dr San Bernardino (92407) *(G-20436)*
Care Unlimited Health Systems......626 332-3767
1025 W Arrow Hwy Ste 105 Glendora (91740) *(G-22394)*
Care With Dignity Healthcare......619 447-1020
1340 E Madison Ave El Cajon (92021) *(G-20437)*
Care Wst-Wrner Mtn Nursing Ctr, Alturas *Also called County of Modoc (G-20480)*
Careability Health Svcs Corp......916 479-8554
1321 Howe Ave Ste 111 Sacramento (95825) *(G-22395)*
Careage Inc......408 238-9751
2501 Alvin Ave San Jose (95121) *(G-20438)*
Carecredit LLC......800 300-3046
2995 Red Hill Ave Ste 100 Costa Mesa (92626) *(G-17057)*
Caredx Inc (PA)......415 287-2300
3260 Bayshore Blvd Brisbane (94005) *(G-22197)*
Career Group Inc (PA)......310 277-8188
10100 Santa Monica Blvd # 900 Los Angeles (90067) *(G-14622)*
Career Transition Center......562 570-9675
3447 Atlantic Ave Ste 100 Long Beach (90807) *(G-24320)*
Carefusion Corporation......800 231-2466
22745 Savi Ranch Pkwy Yorba Linda (92887) *(G-22911)*
Carefusion Solutions LLC (HQ)......858 617-2100
3750 Torrey View Ct San Diego (92130) *(G-7256)*
Caremark Rx Inc......909 822-1164
1851 N Riverside Ave Rialto (92376) *(G-19404)*
Caremark Rx LLC......760 948-6606
15576 Main St Hesperia (92345) *(G-19405)*
Caremark Rx LLC......209 957-7050
800 Douglas Rd Stockton (95207) *(G-19406)*
Caremore AP, Cerritos *Also called Caremore Medical Management A (G-26958)*
Caremore Health Plan (HQ)......562 622-2950
12900 Park Plaza Dr # 150 Cerritos (90703) *(G-19407)*
Caremore Insurance Services, Cerritos *Also called Caremore Health Plan (G-19407)*
Caremore Medical Group, Downey *Also called Conrad A Cox (G-19460)*
Caremore Medical Group......562 622-2900
12900 Park Plz Ste 150 Lakewood (90805) *(G-10238)*
Caremore Medical Group......714 256-1345
420 W Central Ave Ste A Brea (92821) *(G-19408)*
Caremore Medical Management A (HQ)......562 741-4300
12900 Park Plaza Dr # 150 Cerritos (90703) *(G-26958)*
Careonsite Inc......562 437-0381
1805 Arnold Dr Martinez (94553) *(G-19409)*
Careonsite Inc (PA)......562 437-0831
1250 Pacific Ave Long Beach (90813) *(G-19410)*
Cares, San Diego *Also called Center For Autsm Rsrch Evltn (G-22676)*
CARES COMMUNITY HEALTH, Sacramento *Also called Center For Aids Research (G-19415)*
Carescope LLC......916 780-1384
1455 Response Rd Ste 115 Sacramento (95815) *(G-23703)*
Caresouth Home Health Svcs LLC......408 378-6131
815 Pollard Rd Los Gatos (95032) *(G-22396)*
Carfax Studios......562 377-0223
3937 Carfax Ave Long Beach (90808) *(G-13742)*

ALPHABETIC

Carfinance Capital LLC......800 900-5150
7525 Irvine Center Dr # 250 Irvine (92618) *(G-12292)*
Cargill Incorporated......209 982-4632
4344 S Eldorado St Stockton (95206) *(G-26959)*
Cargo Service Center, Los Angeles *Also called Swissport Cargo Services LP (G-4940)*
Caribbean South Amercn Council......925 709-3433
12 Ambrose Ave Bay Point (94565) *(G-4959)*
Carinet, San Diego *Also called Califrnia Rgional Intranet Inc (G-5567)*
Caring Cmpanions Referral Agcy, Hemet *Also called Caring Companions Home (G-22397)*
Caring Companions Home......951 765-1441
116 Las Lunas St Hemet (92543) *(G-22397)*
Caritas Management Corporation......415 647-7191
1358 Valencia St San Francisco (94110) *(G-11341)*
Carl J Woods Construction Inc......530 673-7877
1321 Gray Ave Yuba City (95991) *(G-2037)*
Carleton Booker Marketing Inc......925 752-1973
5042 Wilshire Blvd # 31584 Los Angeles (90036) *(G-27371)*
Carlilemacy Inc......707 542-6451
15 3rd St Santa Rosa (95401) *(G-25718)*
Carlisle Construction Mtls Inc......909 591-7425
5635 Schaefer Ave Chino (91710) *(G-7010)*
Carlisle Construction Mtls Inc......707 678-6900
1155 Business Park Dr Dixon (95620) *(G-7011)*
Carlisle Research Corporation......818 785-8677
7100 Hayvenhurst Ave Ph F Van Nuys (91406) *(G-15915)*
Carlsbad By The Sea, Carlsbad *Also called Front Porch Communities (G-21220)*
Carlsbad Inn Vactn Condo Ownrs......760 434-7542
3001 Carlsbad Blvd Carlsbad (92008) *(G-25229)*
Carlsbad Medical Offices, Carlsbad *Also called Kaiser Foundation Hospitals (G-19680)*
Carlsbad Municipal Water Dst......760 438-2722
5950 El Camino Real Carlsbad (92008) *(G-6323)*
Carlsbad Surgery Center LLC......760 448-2488
6121 Paseo Del Norte # 100 Carlsbad (92011) *(G-22672)*
Carlson, Tustin *Also called Corland Companies (G-26982)*
Carlson Barbee & Gibson Inc......925 866-0322
2633 Camino Ramon Ste 350 San Ramon (94583) *(G-25719)*
Carlton Hotel Properties LP......415 673-0242
1075 Sutter St San Francisco (94109) *(G-12489)*
Carlton Plaza of Fremont, Fremont *Also called Retirement Lf Care Communities (G-24787)*
Carlton Plaza of San Leandro, San Leandro *Also called Carlton Senior Living (G-11342)*
Carlton Senior Living......925 935-1001
175 Cleaveland Rd Pleasant Hill (94523) *(G-22398)*
Carlton Senior Living......510 636-0660
1000 E 14th St San Leandro (94577) *(G-11342)*
Carlton Senior Living Inc......408 972-1400
380 Branham Ln Ofc Ofc San Jose (95136) *(G-10663)*
Carlton Senior Living Inc......916 714-2404
6915 Elk Grove Blvd Elk Grove (95758) *(G-11343)*
Carlton Senior Living Inc......925 935-1660
2770 Pleasant Hill Rd Ofc Concord (94523) *(G-11956)*
Carlton Senior Living Inc......916 971-4800
1075 Fulton Ave Sacramento (95825) *(G-24580)*
Carmel Architectural Sales......714 630-7221
2300 E Katella Ave # 370 Anaheim (92806) *(G-3147)*
Carmel Hills Care Center, Monterey *Also called Pater Digintas Inc (G-20845)*
Carmel Marina, Castroville *Also called USA Waste of California Inc (G-4081)*
Carmel Mission Inn, Carmel *Also called Bayview Properties Inc (G-12427)*
Carmel Mission Inn......831 624-1841
3665 Rio Rd Carmel (93923) *(G-12490)*
Carmel Mtn Rhab Healthcare Ctr, San Diego *Also called Bernardo Hts Healthcare Inc (G-21153)*
Carmel Valley Manor, Carmel *Also called Northern CA Cngrgtnl Rtmt (G-21329)*
Carmel Valley Medical Offices, San Diego *Also called Kaiser Foundation Hospitals (G-19641)*
Carmel Valley Packing Inc......831 771-8860
26965 Encinal Rd Salinas (93908) *(G-518)*
Carmel Valley Ranch......831 625-9500
1 Old Ranch Rd Carmel (93923) *(G-12491)*
Carmel Valley Ranch Hotel, Carmel *Also called Carmel Valley Ranch (G-12491)*
Carmel Valley Resort, Carmel *Also called Carmel Vly Mrtg Borrower LLC (G-12492)*
Carmel Vlg Rtirement Residence......714 962-6667
17077 San Mateo St # 3113 Fountain Valley (92708) *(G-11112)*
Carmel Vly Mrtg Borrower LLC......831 625-9500
1 Old Ranch Rd Carmel (93923) *(G-12492)*
Carmen Casa Inc......626 852-9477
315 W Dawson Ave Glendora (91740) *(G-21179)*
Carmichael Care Inc......916 483-8103
6041 Fair Oaks Blvd Carmichael (95608) *(G-20439)*
Carmichael International Svc (HQ)......213 353-0800
533 Glendale Blvd Ste 102 Los Angeles (90026) *(G-5040)*
Carmichael Recreation & Pk Dst......916 485-5322
5750 Grant Ave Carmichael (95608) *(G-23704)*
Carnahan Occupational Therapy......805 737-1604
116 E College Ave Ste G Lompoc (93436) *(G-22673)*
Carnegie Agency Inc......805 445-1470
2101 Corp Cntr Dr Ste 150 Newbury Park (91320) *(G-10664)*
Carnegie Institution Wash......626 577-1122
813 Santa Barbara St Pasadena (91101) *(G-26746)*
Carnegie Institution Wash......650 319-8904
260 Panama St Stanford (94305) *(G-26747)*
Carneros Inn LLC......707 299-4880
4048 Sonoma Hwy NAPA (94559) *(G-12493)*
Carnival Corporation......562 901-3232
231 Windsor Way Long Beach (90802) *(G-4960)*
Carol Electric Company Inc......562 431-1870
3822 Cerritos Ave Los Alamitos (90720) *(G-2549)*
Caroline Promotions Inc......818 507-7666
809 S Adams St Apt 7 Glendale (91205) *(G-27738)*

Carollo Engineers Inc.....925 932-1710
2700 Ygnacio Valley Rd # 300 Walnut Creek (94598) *(G-27372)*
Carollo Engineers PC (PA).....925 932-1710
2700 Ygnacio Valley Rd # 300 Walnut Creek (94598) *(G-25720)*
Carolyn E Wylie Center.....951 683-5193
4164 Brockton Ave Ste A Riverside (92501) *(G-24424)*
Carone & Company Inc.....925 602-8800
5009 Forni Dr Ste A Concord (94520) *(G-3421)*
Carparts Technologies.....949 488-8860
32122 Camn Capistrano # 100 San Juan Capistrano (92675) *(G-15615)*
Carpe Diem Enterprises Inc.....866 251-0852
665 Calumet Ave Beaumont (92223) *(G-7423)*
Carpenter Fund Manager Gp LLC.....949 261-8888
5 Park Plz Ste 950 Irvine (92614) *(G-9341)*
Carpenter Funds.....510 633-0333
265 Hegenberger Rd # 100 Oakland (94621) *(G-12170)*
Carpenters Southwest ADM Corp (PA).....213 386-8590
533 S Fremont Ave Los Angeles (90071) *(G-12494)*
Carpet Care By Tri-Star, Northridge *Also called Tri - Star Win Coverings Inc (G-6896)*
Carpet Solutions.....310 886-3800
17100 Margay Ave Carson (90746) *(G-13592)*
Carquinez Dialysis, Vallejo *Also called Total Renal Care Inc (G-22645)*
Carr & Ferrell.....650 812-3400
120 Constitution Dr Menlo Park (94025) *(G-23142)*
Carr & Ferrell LLP (PA).....650 812-3400
120 Constitution Dr Menlo Park (94025) *(G-23143)*
Carr Mc Clellan Ingersoll Thom (PA).....650 342-9600
216 Park Rd Burlingame (94010) *(G-23144)*
Carr, McClellan, Burlingame *Also called Carr Mc Clellan Ingersoll Thom (G-23144)*
Carrara Marble Company America (PA).....626 961-6010
15939 Phoenix Dr City of Industry (91745) *(G-3007)*
Carrasco Heleo.....714 639-1759
2510 N Grand Ave Ste 102 Santa Ana (92705) *(G-14245)*
Carriage Inn, Daly City *Also called Reneson Hotels Inc (G-13144)*
Carrier Commercial Service, Sacramento *Also called Carrier Corporation (G-17918)*
Carrier Corporation.....916 928-9500
1168 National Dr Ste 60 Sacramento (95834) *(G-17918)*
Carrier Iq Inc (HQ).....650 625-5400
1100 La Avenida St Mountain View (94043) *(G-15076)*
Carrier Johnson (PA).....619 236-9462
1301 3rd Ave San Diego (92101) *(G-26173)*
Carrington Mortgage Services.....888 267-0584
1600 S Douglass Rd 110 Anaheim (92806) *(G-26960)*
Carroll Burdick Mc Donough LLP (PA).....415 989-5900
275 Battery St Ste 2600 San Francisco (94111) *(G-23145)*
Carroll Shelby Licensing Inc.....310 914-1843
19021 S Figueroa St Gardena (90248) *(G-4531)*
Carrollco Inc.....559 396-3939
4054 W Ashcroft Ave Fresno (93722) *(G-1151)*
Carson Community Center, Carson *Also called City of Carson (G-23752)*
Carson Frank Ldscp & Maint Inc.....916 856-5400
9530 Elder Creek Rd Sacramento (95829) *(G-821)*
Carson Gang Diversion Team, Carson *Also called County of Los Angeles (G-25171)*
Carson Kurtzman Consultants (HQ).....310 823-9000
2335 Alaska Ave El Segundo (90245) *(G-23146)*
CARSON LANDSCAPE INDUSTRIES, Sacramento *Also called Carson Frank Ldscp & Maint Inc (G-821)*
Carson Medical Offices, Gardena *Also called Kaiser Foundation Hospitals (G-19618)*
Carson Operating Company LLC.....310 830-9200
2 Civic Plaza Dr Carson (90745) *(G-12495)*
Carson Senior Assisted Living, Carson *Also called Secrom Inc (G-21368)*
Carson Senior Assisted Living.....310 830-4010
345 E Carson St Carson (90745) *(G-24581)*
Cartel Marketing Inc.....818 483-1130
5230 Las Virgenes Rd # 250 Calabasas (91302) *(G-10665)*
Carter & Burgess Inc.....916 929-3323
180 Promenade Cir Ste 300 Sacramento (95834) *(G-25721)*
Carters Details Plus, Burbank *Also called Jim & Doug Carters Automotive (G-17724)*
Cartridge Family Inc.....510 658-0400
1940 Union St Ste 29 Oakland (94607) *(G-8162)*
Cartridge Family Ink, Oakland *Also called Cartridge Family Inc (G-8162)*
Cartwright Termite & Pest Ctrl.....760 771-6091
51360 Calle Guatemala La Quinta (92253) *(G-14173)*
Caruso MGT Ltd A Cal Ltd Prtnr.....323 900-8100
101 The Grove Dr Los Angeles (90036) *(G-11344)*
Caruthers Raisin Pkg Co Inc (PA).....559 864-9448
12797 S Elm Ave Caruthers (93609) *(G-519)*
Casa Allegra Community Svcs.....415 499-1116
35 Mitchell Blvd Ste 8 San Rafael (94903) *(G-27373)*
Casa Carmen Guest Home, Glendora *Also called Carmen Casa Inc (G-21179)*
Casa Clina Ctrs For Rhbltation, Pomona *Also called Casa Colina Hospital and Cente (G-21471)*
Casa Colin Comprehensive.....909 596-7733
255 E Bonita Ave Pomona (91767) *(G-22674)*
Casa Colina Inc (PA).....909 596-7733
255 E Bonita Ave Pomona (91767) *(G-23705)*
Casa Colina Hospital and Cente (HQ).....909 596-7733
255 E Bonita Ave Pomona (91767) *(G-21471)*
Casa Coloma Health Care Center, Rancho Cordova *Also called A B C D Associates (G-20366)*
Casa De Amparo (PA).....760 754-5500
325 Buena Creek Rd San Marcos (92069) *(G-24582)*
Casa De Las Campanas Inc.....760 789-4746
24317 Del Amo Rd Ramona (92065) *(G-24583)*
Casa De Las Campanas Inc (PA).....858 451-9152
18655 W Bernardo Dr # 489 San Diego (92127) *(G-24584)*
Casa De Santa Fe of Rocklin.....916 435-8800
3201 Santa Fe Way Apt 1 Rocklin (95765) *(G-21180)*
Casa Dorinda, Santa Barbara *Also called Montecito Retirement Assn (G-20795)*
Casa Dscanso Convalescent Hosp.....323 225-5991
4515 Huntington Dr S Los Angeles (90032) *(G-27777)*
Casa Fremont, Fremont *Also called Anka Behavioral Health Inc (G-22889)*
Casa Madrona Hotel and Spa LLC.....415 332-0502
801 Bridgeway Sausalito (94965) *(G-12496)*
Casa Munras Garden Hotel, Monterey *Also called Portfolio Hotels & Resorts LLC (G-13105)*
Casa Munras Hotel LLC.....831 375-2411
700 Munras Ave Monterey (93940) *(G-12497)*
Casa Pacifica Adult Day H, San Diego *Also called J Gelt Corporation (G-24038)*
Casa Pacifica Centers (PA).....805 482-3260
1722 S Lewis Rd Camarillo (93012) *(G-23706)*
Casa Palmera Care Center, Del Mar *Also called Lee Johnson (G-21288)*
Casa Real Estate Ltd Partnr.....760 320-4117
415 S Belardo Rd Palm Springs (92262) *(G-12498)*
Casa Sandoval LLC.....510 727-1700
1200 Russell Way Hayward (94541) *(G-11113)*
Casa-Pacifica Inc.....951 658-3369
2200 W Acacia Ave Ofc Hemet (92545) *(G-24585)*
Casa-Pacifica Inc.....949 586-4466
23442 El Toro Rd Lake Forest (92630) *(G-24586)*
Casa-Pacifica Inc.....951 766-5116
2400 W Acacia Ave Hemet (92545) *(G-24587)*
Casablanca Alzheimer's Care, Oak View *Also called Casablanca Alzheimers Resid (G-24588)*
Casablanca Alzheimers Resid.....805 649-5143
158 Rockaway Rd Oak View (93022) *(G-24588)*
Casanova Pndrill Pblicidad Inc (PA).....949 474-5001
275 Mccormick Ave Ste 1a Costa Mesa (92626) *(G-13823)*
Casas - Comprehensive.....858 292-2900
5151 Murphy Canyon Rd # 220 San Diego (92123) *(G-25513)*
Casas International Brkg Inc (PA).....619 661-6162
9355 Airway Rd Ste 4 San Diego (92154) *(G-4532)*
Casavina Foundation Corp.....408 238-9751
2501 Alvin Ave San Jose (95121) *(G-20440)*
Casbn Investment Inc.....650 991-2800
345 Gellert Blvd Ste A Daly City (94015) *(G-11345)*
Cascade Drilling LP.....909 946-1605
1333 W 9th St Upland (91786) *(G-3354)*
Cascade Logistics, Tracy *Also called Es3 LLC (G-4549)*
Cascade Logistics LLC.....209 832-4205
857 Stonebridge Dr Tracy (95376) *(G-4533)*
Casden Builders LLC.....310 274-5553
9090 Wilshire Blvd Fl 3 Beverly Hills (90211) *(G-10966)*
Casden Company LLC.....310 274-5553
9606 Santa Monica Blvd # 3 Beverly Hills (90210) *(G-11957)*
Case Dealer Holding Co LLC.....916 649-0096
1751 Bell Ave Sacramento (95838) *(G-7766)*
Case Medical Group, Sacramento *Also called Central Anesthesia Service (G-19417)*
Case Shella Management Service.....951 723-8460
26010 Mccall Blvd Ste B Sun City (92586) *(G-26961)*
Case Vlott Cattle.....559 665-7399
20330 Road 4 Chowchilla (93610) *(G-420)*
Casecentral Inc (HQ).....415 989-2300
1055 E Colo Blvd Ste 400 Pasadena (91106) *(G-17058)*
Casecentral.com, Pasadena *Also called Casecentral Inc (G-17058)*
Casestack Inc (PA).....310 473-8885
3000 Ocean Park Blvd Santa Monica (90405) *(G-5041)*
Casewise Systems Inc (HQ).....424 284-4101
9465 Wilshire Blvd # 300 Beverly Hills (90212) *(G-7107)*
Casey Securities Inc (PA).....415 544-5030
301 Pine St San Francisco (94104) *(G-9969)*
Casey-Fogli Con Contrs Inc.....510 887-0837
1970 National Ave Hayward (94545) *(G-3239)*
Cash It Here, Santa Ana *Also called Continental Currency Svcs Inc (G-9714)*
Cashcall Inc.....949 752-4600
1 City Blvd W Ste 102 Orange (92868) *(G-9742)*
Cashedge Inc.....408 541-3900
525 Almanor Ave Ste 150 Sunnyvale (94085) *(G-17059)*
Casino, Hopland *Also called Hopland Band Pomo Indians Inc (G-19223)*
Casino Morongo.....951 849-3080
49500 Seminole Dr Cabazon (92230) *(G-18812)*
Casino Morongo Resort Spa.....951 846-5100
49500 Seminole Dr Cabazon (92230) *(G-18620)*
Casino San Pablo, San Pablo *Also called Lytton Rancheria (G-19243)*
Caspar Community.....707 964-4997
15051 Caspar Rd Caspar (95420) *(G-23707)*
Casper Company.....619 589-6001
3825 Bancroft Dr Spring Valley (91977) *(G-3449)*
Caspian Commercial Plbg Inc.....818 649-2500
711 Ivy St Glendale (91204) *(G-2176)*
Cass Inc (PA).....510 893-6476
2730 Peralta St Oakland (94607) *(G-8066)*
Cass Construction Inc (PA).....619 590-0929
1100 Wagner Dr El Cajon (92020) *(G-1916)*
Cassidy Medical Group Inc (PA).....760 630-5487
145 Thunder Dr Vista (92083) *(G-19411)*
Cassidy Trly Prop MGT Sn Frncs.....415 781-8100
201 California St Ste 800 San Francisco (94111) *(G-11346)*
Cast & Crew Payroll LLC (HQ).....818 848-6022
2300 W Empire Ave Fl 5 Burbank (91504) *(G-26307)*
Cast and Crew Entrmt Svcs, Burbank *Also called Cast & Crew Payroll LLC (G-26307)*
Caster Family Enterprises Inc.....619 287-8893
4607 Mission Gorge Pl San Diego (92120) *(G-12293)*
Castlblack Pismo Bch Owner LLC.....805 773-6020
601 James Way Pismo Beach (93449) *(G-12499)*
Castle & Cooke Inc.....661 664-6500
10000 Stockdale Hwy # 300 Bakersfield (93311) *(G-6456)*
Castle & Cooke Commercial CA.....661 665-1540
10000 Stockdale Hwy # 300 Bakersfield (93311) *(G-11958)*

ALPHABETIC

Castle Access Inc (PA)....858 836-0200
9606 Aero Dr Ste 1900 San Diego (92123) ***(G-5571)***
Castle Dental....323 567-1227
4433 Tweedy Blvd South Gate (90280) ***(G-20248)***
Castle Family Health Ctrs Inc (PA)....209 381-2000
3605 Hospital Rd Ste H Atwater (95301) ***(G-22675)***
Castle Manor Convalescent Ctr, National City *Also called Castle Manor Inc* ***(G-21181)***
Castle Manor Inc....619 791-7900
541 S V Ave National City (91950) ***(G-21181)***
Castle Rock Enrichment Program, Diamond Bar *Also called Walnut Valley Unified Schl Dst* ***(G-24529)***
Castleblack Owner Holdings LLC....805 773-6020
601 James Way Pismo Beach (93449) ***(G-26962)***
Castlehill Properties Inc (PA)....209 472-9800
3240 W March Ln Stockton (95219) ***(G-12500)***
Castlewood Country Club....925 846-2871
707 Country Club Cir Pleasanton (94566) ***(G-18913)***
Castlight Health Inc....415 829-1400
150 Spear St Ste 400 San Francisco (94105) ***(G-16107)***
Caston Inc....909 381-1619
354 S Allen St San Bernardino (92408) ***(G-2874)***
Castro Valley Care Centers, Culver City *Also called Jesse Lee Group Inc* ***(G-27078)***
Castro Valley Health Inc....510 690-1930
2410 Camino Ramon Ste 331 San Ramon (94583) ***(G-22399)***
Caswell Bay Inc....925 933-8181
1777 N Calif Blvd Ste 210 Walnut Creek (94596) ***(G-22400)***
CAT Logistics Inc....909 390-1920
5491 E Francis St Ontario (91761) ***(G-4534)***
Catalina Business Entps Inc....310 510-1600
635 Crescent Ave Avalon (90704) ***(G-19159)***
Catalina Channel Express Inc (HQ)....310 519-7971
400 Oceangate Ste 300 Long Beach (90802) ***(G-4732)***
Catalina Channel Express Inc....562 435-8686
320 Golden Shore Lbby Long Beach (90802) ***(G-4745)***
Catalina Channel Express Inc....562 495-3565
1046 Queens Hwy Long Beach (90802) ***(G-4733)***
Catalina Enterprise Inc....949 637-3091
206 Catalina Rd Fullerton (92835) ***(G-27867)***
Catalina Express, Long Beach *Also called Catalina Channel Express Inc* ***(G-4745)***
Catalina Express, Long Beach *Also called Catalina Channel Express Inc* ***(G-4733)***
Catalina Express Cruises, Long Beach *Also called Catalina Channel Express Inc* ***(G-4732)***
Catalina Glassbottom Boat Inc....310 510-2888
1 Cabrillo Mole Avalon (90704) ***(G-4734)***
Catalina Marketing Corporation....949 930-6500
18191 Von Karman Ave # 200 Irvine (92612) ***(G-27739)***
Catalina Slar Lssee Holdco LLC....888 903-6926
15445 Innovation Dr San Diego (92128) ***(G-6109)***
Catalina Solar 2 LLC....888 903-6926
15445 Innovation Dr San Diego (92128) ***(G-6110)***
Catalina Solar Lessee LLC....888 903-6926
11585 Willow Springs Rd Rosamond (93560) ***(G-6111)***
Catalyst Development Corp....760 228-9653
56925 Yucca Trl Yucca Valley (92284) ***(G-15616)***
Catamaran Resort Hotel, San Diego *Also called Braemar Partnership* ***(G-12462)***
Catamount Broadcasting of Chic (PA)....530 893-2424
3460 Silverbell Rd Chico (95973) ***(G-5838)***
Catania Hijar Corporation....800 400-3401
11487 Woodside Ave Santee (92071) ***(G-1917)***
Cataphora Inc (PA)....650 622-9840
3425 Edison Way Menlo Park (94025) ***(G-15077)***
Catapult Marketing....203 682-4000
10940 Wilshire Blvd Fl 6 Los Angeles (90024) ***(G-27374)***
Catati Rohnert Park Inc....707 792-4531
1400 Magnolia Ave Rohnert Park (94928) ***(G-17060)***
Catered Manor, Long Beach *Also called Covenant Care California LLC* ***(G-20486)***
Caterpillar, Ontario *Also called CAT Logistics Inc* ***(G-4534)***
Caterpillar, San Diego *Also called Hawthorne Machinery Co* ***(G-17801)***
Caterpillar Authorized Dealer, Riverside *Also called Johnson Machinery Co* ***(G-7777)***
Caterpillar Authorized Dealer, West Sacramento *Also called Holt of California* ***(G-7773)***
Caterpillar Authorized Dealer, San Diego *Also called Hawthorne Machinery Co* ***(G-14484)***
Caterpillar Authorized Dealer, City of Industry *Also called Quinn Shepherd Machinery* ***(G-7785)***
Caterpillar Authorized Dealer, Salinas *Also called Quinn Lift Inc* ***(G-7879)***
Caterpillar Authorized Dealer, San Diego *Also called Hawthorne Machinery Co* ***(G-14485)***
Caterpillar Authorized Dealer, City of Industry *Also called Quinn Company* ***(G-7878)***
Caterpillar Authorized Dealer, Oxnard *Also called Quinn Group Inc* ***(G-7806)***
Caterpillar Authorized Dealer, Imperial *Also called Empire Southwest LLC* ***(G-7768)***
Caterpillar Authorized Dealer, Bakersfield *Also called Quinn Company* ***(G-7781)***
Caterpillar Authorized Dealer, Oxnard *Also called Quinn Company* ***(G-7782)***
Caterpillar Authorized Dealer, Santa Maria *Also called Quinn Company* ***(G-7783)***
Caterpillar Authorized Dealer, Salinas *Also called Quinn Group Inc* ***(G-7784)***
Caterpillar Authorized Dealer, San Diego *Also called Hawthorne Machinery Co* ***(G-7770)***
Cathay Bank (HQ)....626 279-3698
9650 Flair Dr El Monte (91731) ***(G-9479)***
Cathay Bank....213 896-0098
800 W 6th St Ste 200 Los Angeles (90017) ***(G-9480)***
Cathay Bank....626 452-1582
4128 Temple City Blvd Rosemead (91770) ***(G-9702)***
Cathay General Bancorp....626 574-9530
1139 W Huntington Dr Arcadia (91007) ***(G-9481)***
Cathay Pacific Airways Limited....310 615-1113
1960 E Grand Ave Ste 540 El Segundo (90245) ***(G-5006)***
Cathedral Bookstore, Los Angeles *Also called Cathedral Center of St Paul* ***(G-25514)***
Cathedral Center of St Paul....213 482-2040
840 Echo Park Ave Los Angeles (90026) ***(G-25514)***
Cathedral Cyn Golf Tennis CLB, Cathedral City *Also called Briar Golf LP* ***(G-19154)***
Cathedral Oaks Athletic Club, Goleta *Also called Cathedral Oaks Tennis Swim Ath* ***(G-18914)***
Cathedral Oaks Tennis Swim Ath....805 964-7762
5800 Cathedral Oaks Rd Goleta (93117) ***(G-18914)***
Cathedral Pioneer Church Homes (PA)....916 442-4906
415 P St Ofc Sacramento (95814) ***(G-20441)***
Catholic Charities....408 468-0100
2625 Zanker Rd Ste 200 San Jose (95134) ***(G-19412)***
Catholic Charities Diocese San....619 286-1100
6360 El Cajon Blvd San Diego (92115) ***(G-23708)***
Catholic Charities Diocese San....619 287-9454
4575 Mission Gorge Pl A San Diego (92120) ***(G-23709)***
Catholic Charities of East Bay, Oakland *Also called Catholic Charities of The Dioc* ***(G-23714)***
Catholic Charities of La Inc (PA)....213 251-3400
1531 James M Wood Blvd Los Angeles (90015) ***(G-26748)***
Catholic Charities of La Inc....818 883-6015
21600 Hart St Canoga Park (91303) ***(G-23710)***
Catholic Charities of La Inc....213 251-3400
1400 James M Wood Blvd Los Angeles (90015) ***(G-23711)***
Catholic Charities of Santa CL (PA)....408 468-0100
2625 Zanker Rd Ste 200 San Jose (95134) ***(G-23712)***
Catholic Charities of Santa CL....805 643-4694
303 N Ventura Ave Ste A Ventura (93001) ***(G-23713)***
Catholic Charities of The Dioc (PA)....510 768-3100
433 Jefferson St Oakland (94607) ***(G-23714)***
Catholic Chrts Cyo Archdiocs....415 743-0017
810 Avenue D San Francisco (94130) ***(G-23715)***
Catholic Chrts Cyo Archdiocs....415 405-2000
141 Leland Ave San Francisco (94134) ***(G-23716)***
Catholic Chrts Cyo Archdiocs....650 757-2110
699 Serramonte Blvd 210 Daly City (94015) ***(G-3915)***
Catholic Chrts Cyo Archdiocs....415 334-5550
1111 Junipero Serra Blvd San Francisco (94132) ***(G-23717)***
Catholic Chrts Cyo Archdiocs (PA)....415 972-1200
990 Eddy St San Francisco (94109) ***(G-23718)***
Catholic Chrts Cyo Archdiocs....415 553-8700
20 Franklin St San Francisco (94102) ***(G-23719)***
Catholic Chrts Cyo Archdiocs....415 507-2000
1 Saint Vincents Dr San Rafael (94903) ***(G-23720)***
Catholic Hlthcare W Sthern Cal (HQ)....562 491-9000
1050 Linden Ave Long Beach (90813) ***(G-21472)***
CATHOLIC YOUTH ORGANIZATION, Daly City *Also called Catholic Chrts Cyo Archdiocs* ***(G-3915)***
Caton Moving & Storage, Alameda *Also called Chipman Corporation* ***(G-4334)***
Cats U S A Pest Control, North Hollywood *Also called Cats USA Inc* ***(G-14174)***
Cats USA Inc....818 506-1000
5683 Whitnall Hwy North Hollywood (91601) ***(G-14174)***
Catta Verdera Country Club....916 645-7200
1111 Catta Verdera Lincoln (95648) ***(G-18915)***
Cattail Farms Inc....916 207-6580
3970 Cr95b Knights Landing (95645) ***(G-4)***
Cattlemens....925 447-1224
2882 Kitty Hawk Rd Livermore (94551) ***(G-13743)***
Cattlemens Restaurant, Livermore *Also called Cattlemens* ***(G-13743)***
Cattrac Construction Inc....909 355-1146
15030 Slover Ave Fontana (92337) ***(G-2038)***
CAV Inc....760 729-5199
5411 Avenida Encinas # 210 Carlsbad (92008) ***(G-3780)***
Cavalier Inn Incorporated....805 927-6444
250 San Simeon Ave Ste 4c San Simeon (93452) ***(G-12501)***
Cavallo Point LLC (PA)....415 339-4700
601 Murray Cir Sausalito (94965) ***(G-12502)***
Cavaya Inc....831 338-1008
100 Marine Pkwy Ste 400 Redwood City (94065) ***(G-15916)***
Cavendish Kinetics Inc....408 240-7370
2960 N 1st St San Jose (95134) ***(G-7542)***
CB Associates Inc....818 284-3699
11659 Haynes St North Hollywood (91606) ***(G-14023)***
CB C&C Properties/Comm Di Inc....530 221-7551
2120 Churn Creek Rd Redding (96002) ***(G-11347)***
CB North LLC....831 786-1642
480 W Beach St Watsonville (95076) ***(G-350)***
CB Richard Ellis RE Svcs LLC....213 613-3333
355 S Grand Ave Ste 2700 Los Angeles (90071) ***(G-11348)***
CB Richard Ellis Services Inc, Los Angeles *Also called Cbre Services Inc* ***(G-11360)***
CB Richard Ellis Strategic Par....213 614-6862
515 S Flower St Ste 3100 Los Angeles (90071) ***(G-12294)***
CB Richard Ellis Strtgc Prtnrs....213 683-4200
515 S Flower St Los Angeles (90071) ***(G-10967)***
CB&i, Irvine *Also called Shaw Group Inc* ***(G-26888)***
CB&i Envmtl Infrastructure Inc....949 261-6441
18100 Von Karman Ave # 450 Irvine (92612) ***(G-27868)***
CB&i Envmtl Infrastructure Inc....916 928-3300
180 Promenade Cir Ste 320 Sacramento (95834) ***(G-27869)***
CB&i Envmtl Infrastructure Inc....619 239-1690
1230 Columbia St Ste 1200 San Diego (92101) ***(G-27870)***
CB&i Envmtl Infrastructure Inc....925 288-9898
4005 Port Chicago Hwy Concord (94520) ***(G-27871)***
CB&i Government Solutions Inc....949 261-6441
18100 Von Karman Ave # 450 Irvine (92612) ***(G-25722)***
CB&i Government Solutions Inc....925 288-9898
4005 Port Chicago Hwy # 200 Concord (94520) ***(G-25723)***
CB&i Inc....909 962-6400
250 W 1st St Ste 346 Claremont (91711) ***(G-3375)***
Cb-1 Hotel....415 633-3838
757 Market St San Francisco (94103) ***(G-12503)***
Cbabr Inc (PA)....951 640-7056
31620 Rr Cyn Rd Ste A Canyon Lake (92587) ***(G-11349)***
Cbest Inc....310 445-2378
11620 Wilshire Blvd # 450 Los Angeles (90025) ***(G-22120)***

ALPHABETIC

Cbiz Southern California LLC 661 325-7500
5060 California Ave # 800 Bakersfield (93309) **(G-26308)**
Cbol Corporation 818 704-8200
19850 Plummer St Chatsworth (91311) **(G-7543)**
Cbr Systems Inc (HQ) 650 635-1420
1200 Bayhill Dr Fl 3 San Bruno (94066) **(G-22912)**
Cbre Inc 916 446-6800
500 Capitol Mall Fl 24 Sacramento (95814) **(G-11350)**
Cbre Inc (HQ) 310 477-5876
400 S Hope St Ste 25 Los Angeles (90071) **(G-12136)**
Cbre Inc 714 939-2100
2125 E Katella Ave # 100 Anaheim (92806) **(G-11351)**
Cbre Inc 626 814-7900
4900 Rivergrade Rd A110 Baldwin Park (91706) **(G-11352)**
Cbre Inc 818 907-4600
15303 Ventura Blvd # 200 Van Nuys (91403) **(G-11353)**
Cbre Inc 408 453-7400
225 W Santa Clara St # 1050 San Jose (95113) **(G-9827)**
Cbre Inc 818 502-6700
234 S Brand Blvd Ste 800 Glendale (91204) **(G-11354)**
Cbre Inc 310 363-4900
2221 Rosecrans Ave # 100 El Segundo (90245) **(G-11355)**
Cbre Inc 310 550-2500
1840 Century Park E # 900 Los Angeles (90067) **(G-11356)**
Cbre Inc 858 546-4600
4365 Executive Dr # 1600 San Diego (92121) **(G-11357)**
Cbre Inc 909 418-2000
4141 Inland Empire Blvd # 100 Ontario (91764) **(G-11358)**
Cbre Global Investors LLC (HQ) 213 683-4200
515 S Flower St Ste 3100 Los Angeles (90071) **(G-27375)**
Cbre Global Investors LLC 949 725-8500
3501 Jamboree Rd Ste 100 Newport Beach (92660) **(G-27376)**
Cbre Group Inc 415 772-0123
101 California St Fl 44 San Francisco (94111) **(G-10968)**
Cbre Group Inc (PA) 213 613-3333
400 S Hope St Ste 25 Los Angeles (90071) **(G-11359)**
Cbre Services Inc 213 613-3333
400 S Hope St Ste 25 Los Angeles (90071) **(G-11360)**
Cbre Valuation and Advisory, Los Angeles *Also called CB Richard Ellis RE Svcs LLC* **(G-11348)**
CBS Broadcasting Inc 415 765-0928
855 Battery St San Francisco (94111) **(G-5839)**
CBS Broadcasting Inc 415 765-4097
A65 Bettery St San Francisco (94111) **(G-5754)**
CBS Broadcasting Inc 310 577-3457
12641 Beatrice St Los Angeles (90066) **(G-5840)**
CBS Broadcasting Inc 310 284-6835
1888 Century Park E # 1900 Los Angeles (90067) **(G-9777)**
CBS Broadcasting Inc 818 655-2000
4200 Radford Ave Studio City (91604) **(G-5841)**
CBS Broadcasting Inc 212 975-3240
7800 Beverly Blvd Los Angeles (90036) **(G-25724)**
CBS Corporation 323 575-2345
7800 Beverly Blvd Los Angeles (90036) **(G-5842)**
CBS Corporation 415 765-4000
865 Battery St Fl 2/3 San Francisco (94111) **(G-5755)**
CBS Corporation 760 343-5700
31276 Dunham Way Thousand Palms (92276) **(G-5843)**
CBS Interactive Inc 818 556-1538
2900 W Alameda Ave Burbank (91505) **(G-13991)**
CBS Interactive Inc (HQ) 415 344-2000
235 2nd St San Francisco (94105) **(G-13992)**
CBS Maxpreps Inc 530 676-6440
4080 Plaza Goldorado Cir Cameron Park (95682) **(G-5572)**
CBS Network News, Los Angeles *Also called Merlot Film Productions Inc* **(G-18109)**
CBS Paramount Television, Los Angeles *Also called CBS Studios Inc* **(G-18060)**
CBS Radio 916 923-6800
280 Commerce Cir Sacramento (95815) **(G-5756)**
CBS Radio Inc 559 490-0106
1071 W Shaw Ave Fresno (93711) **(G-5757)**
CBS Radio Inc 858 560-1037
8033 Linda Vista Rd San Diego (92111) **(G-5758)**
CBS Radio Inc 415 765-4097
865 Battery St Fl 3 San Francisco (94111) **(G-5759)**
CBS Radio Inc 323 525-0980
5670 Wilshire Blvd # 200 Los Angeles (90036) **(G-5760)**
CBS Radio Inc 909 825-9525
900 E Washington St # 315 Colton (92324) **(G-5761)**
CBS Radio Inc 323 930-1067
5901 Venice Blvd Los Angeles (90034) **(G-5762)**
CBS Radio Inc 323 930-7580
5901 Venice Blvd Los Angeles (90034) **(G-5763)**
CBS Studio Center, Studio City *Also called Radford Studio Center Inc* **(G-18428)**
CBS Studios Inc (HQ) 323 634-3519
6100 Wilshire Blvd # 1000 Los Angeles (90048) **(G-18060)**
CBS Television City 323 651-0255
7800 Beverly Blvd Los Angeles (90036) **(G-5844)**
Cbsi, San Francisco *Also called CBS Interactive Inc* **(G-13992)**
Cbsj Financial Corporation 408 792-4600
1735 N 1st St Ste 250 San Jose (95112) **(G-14024)**
Cbsrr Inc 909 336-2131
27206 Hwy 189 Blue Jay (92317) **(G-11361)**
CC Wellness LLC (HQ) 661 295-1700
29000 Hancock Pkwy Valencia (91355) **(G-8248)**
Cc-Palo Alto Inc 650 853-5000
620 Sand Hill Rd Palo Alto (94304) **(G-21069)**
CCA Advertising, San Francisco *Also called Chandler Chicco Agency LLC* **(G-27740)**
Ccare West, Fresno *Also called California Cancer Assctes* **(G-19390)**
Ccbc Reference Lab, Fresno *Also called Central California Blood Ctr* **(G-22915)**
CCC Property Holdings LLC 310 609-1957
500 S Alameda St Compton (90221) **(G-12050)**
Cccc Growth Fund LLC 626 441-8770
899 El Centro St South Pasadena (91030) **(G-12295)**
Cch Computax, Torrance *Also called CCH Incorporated* **(G-16108)**
CCH Incorporated 310 800-9800
20101 Hamilton Ave # 200 Torrance (90502) **(G-16108)**
Ccig, Westlake Village *Also called California Coml Inv Group Inc* **(G-27862)**
Ccintegration Inc 408 228-1314
2060 Corporate Ct San Jose (95131) **(G-26493)**
Ccna Vons Athletes For Life 805 453-2499
10670 6th St Ste 113 Rancho Cucamonga (91730) **(G-25515)**
CCOF CERTIFICATION SERVICES, Santa Cruz *Also called California Certified Organic* **(G-25080)**
CCPOA, West Sacramento *Also called California Correctnl Peace Ofc* **(G-25168)**
CCS, Hayward *Also called Controlled Contamination Svcs* **(G-14263)**
Ccts, Santa Ana *Also called Satellite Management Co* **(G-11834)**
Cdc San Francisco LLC 415 616-6512
888 Howard St San Francisco (94103) **(G-12504)**
Cdcf III Pacific Catalina 562 453-1353
320 Golden Shore Ste 320 Long Beach (90802) **(G-12109)**
Cdcr - California Men's Colony, San Luis Obispo *Also called Correctons Rhbltation Cal Dept* **(G-22692)**
Cdcr Cal Instn For Men Hosp, Chino *Also called Correctons Rhbltation Cal Dept* **(G-21512)**
CDI, Woodland Hills *Also called Child Development Institute* **(G-23735)**
CDI Marine Company LLC 619 407-4010
694 Moss St Chula Vista (91911) **(G-25725)**
CDM Constructors Inc 909 579-3500
9220 Cleveland Ave # 100 Rancho Cucamonga (91730) **(G-1918)**
CDM Field Services Inc 936 537-7786
25 Crescent Dr 253a Pleasant Hill (94523) **(G-14131)**
CDM SMITH INC 949 752-5452
111 Academy Ste 150 Irvine (92617) **(G-25726)**
CDM SMITH INC 760 438-7755
703 Palomar Airport Rd Carlsbad (92011) **(G-25727)**
CDM SMITH INC 617 452-6000
100 Pringle Ave Ste 300 Walnut Creek (94596) **(G-25728)**
Cdnetworks Inc (HQ) 408 228-3379
1919 S Bascom Ave Ste 600 Campbell (95008) **(G-5573)**
Cds Moving Equipment Inc (PA) 310 631-1100
375 W Manville St Rancho Dominguez (90220) **(G-7832)**
Cdsnet LLC 310 981-9500
6053 W Century Blvd Los Angeles (90045) **(G-27872)**
Cdw, Anaheim *Also called Consolidated Design West Inc* **(G-14139)**
CE Allencompany Inc 562 989-6100
2109 Gundry Ave Long Beach (90755) **(G-2039)**
Ce2 Kleinfelder JV 925 463-7301
6140 Stoneridge Mall Rd Pleasanton (94588) **(G-25729)**
Cea-Pack Logistics, Cerritos *Also called Cea-Pack Services Inc* **(G-4395)**
Cea-Pack Services Inc 562 407-0660
12607 Hiddencreek Way Cerritos (90703) **(G-4395)**
Cec, La Canada *Also called Child Educational Center* **(G-24433)**
Cecchini & Cecchini, Brentwood *Also called Robert Cecchini Inc* **(G-90)**
Cecelia Packing Corporation 559 626-5000
24780 E South Ave Orange Cove (93646) **(G-520)**
Cecico Inc 323 269-7000
1016 Towne Ave Unit 110 Los Angeles (90021) **(G-8373)**
Cecico Town, Los Angeles *Also called Cecico Inc* **(G-8373)**
Cecil Hotel Company LLC 213 213-7829
640 S Main St Los Angeles (90014) **(G-12505)**
Cecos 805 982-5400
3502 Goodspeed St Ste 1 Port Hueneme (93043) **(G-25730)**
Cedar Creek Alzhimers Dementia, Berkeley *Also called Altcare Cedar Creek LLC* **(G-24545)**
Cedar Crest Nrsing & Rehab, Sunnyvale *Also called Ghc of Sunnyvale LLC* **(G-21233)**
Cedar Fair LP 408 988-1776
4701 Great America Pkwy Santa Clara (95054) **(G-18813)**
Cedar Holdings LLC 909 862-0611
7534 Palm Ave Highland (92346) **(G-20442)**
Cedar House Rehabilitation Ctr, Bloomington *Also called Social Science Service Center* **(G-22176)**
Cedar Management LLC 310 396-3100
3233 Dnald Douglas Loop S Santa Monica (90405) **(G-11362)**
Cedar Signature, Santa Monica *Also called Cedar Management LLC* **(G-11362)**
Cedar Sinai Medical Group, Beverly Hills *Also called Medical Group Bverly Hills Inc* **(G-19738)**
Cedars Sinai Medical Group, Beverly Hills *Also called Medical Group Bverly Hills Inc* **(G-19737)**
Cedars-Sinai Medical Center 310 423-3849
127 S San Vicente Blvd # 3417 Los Angeles (90048) **(G-19413)**
Cedars-Sinai Medical Center 323 866-8483
8631 W 3rd St Ste 730 Los Angeles (90048) **(G-19414)**
Cedars-Sinai Medical Center 310 385-3400
250 N Robertson Blvd # 101 Beverly Hills (90211) **(G-21473)**
Cedarwood-Young Company (PA) 626 962-4047
14620 Joanbridge St Baldwin Park (91706) **(G-8067)**
Cedarwood-Young Company 626 962-4047
14618 Arrow Hwy Baldwin Park (91706) **(G-8068)**
Cei, San Jose *Also called Cupertino Electric Inc* **(G-2568)**
Celebrity Casinos Inc 310 631-3838
123 E Artesia Blvd Compton (90220) **(G-12506)**
Celebrity Valet, Los Angeles *Also called Premiere Valet Service Inc* **(G-17739)**
Celera Corporation (HQ) 510 749-4200
33608 Ortega Hwy San Juan Capistrano (92675) **(G-26749)**
Celerity Consulting Group Inc (PA) 415 986-8850
2 Gough St Ste 300 San Francisco (94103) **(G-16109)**

ALPHABETIC

Celestica LLC ...909 418-6986
821 S Rockefeller Ave Ontario (91761) ***(G-7544)***
Celex Solutions, Brea *Also called Contract Services Group Inc* ***(G-14261)***
Celgene Corporation...858 558-7500
10300 Campus Point Dr # 100 San Diego (92121) ***(G-26494)***
Celgene Corporation...858 677-0034
10300 Campus Point Dr # 100 San Diego (92121) ***(G-8249)***
Celgene Signal Research, San Diego *Also called Celgene Corporation* ***(G-8249)***
Cell Site Management Group LLC ...800 906-9778
25109 Jefferson Ave Murrieta (92562) ***(G-5283)***
Cell-Crete Corporation...510 471-7257
995 Zephyr Ave Hayward (94544) ***(G-3240)***
Cellco Partnership ...951 769-0985
1484 E 2nd St Beaumont (92223) ***(G-5284)***
Cellco Partnership ...951 296-3499
26480 Ynez Rd Temecula (92591) ***(G-5285)***
Cellco Partnership ...310 891-6991
24329 Crenshaw Blvd Ste D Torrance (90505) ***(G-5286)***
Cellco Partnership ...925 245-0494
2428 Las Positas Rd Livermore (94551) ***(G-5287)***
Cellco Partnership ...831 644-0858
1680 Del Monte Ctr Monterey (93940) ***(G-5288)***
Cellco Partnership ...714 921-5130
1500 E Village Way # 2205 Orange (92865) ***(G-5289)***
Cellco Partnership ...925 626-3480
6471 Lone Tree Way Brentwood (94513) ***(G-5290)***
Cellco Partnership ...951 697-3035
2851 Canyon Springs Pkwy Riverside (92507) ***(G-5291)***
Cellco Partnership ...805 376-8917
2535 W Hillcrest Dr Thousand Oaks (91320) ***(G-5292)***
Cellco Partnership ...212 395-1000
255 Parkshore Dr Folsom (95630) ***(G-5293)***
Cellco Partnership ...805 596-2300
1101 Los Olivos Ave Los Osos (93402) ***(G-5294)***
Cellco Partnership ...559 454-0803
550 S Clovis Ave Ste 105 Fresno (93727) ***(G-5295)***
Cellco Partnership ...714 427-0733
901 S Coast Dr Ste K120 Costa Mesa (92626) ***(G-5296)***
Cellco Partnership ...951 361-1850
12459 Limonite Ave Mira Loma (91752) ***(G-5297)***
Cellco Partnership ...916 786-6151
1900 Douglas Blvd Ste D Roseville (95661) ***(G-5298)***
Cellco Partnership ...949 286-7000
15505 Sand Canyon Ave Irvine (92618) ***(G-5299)***
Cellco Partnership ...831 786-0267
1051 S Green Valley Rd Watsonville (95076) ***(G-5300)***
Cellco Partnership ...562 694-8630
1401 W Imperial Hwy Ste C La Habra (90631) ***(G-5301)***
Cellco Partnership ...714 564-0050
691 S Main St Ste 80 Orange (92868) ***(G-5302)***
Cellco Partnership ...760 738-0088
711 Center Dr Ste 6a San Marcos (92069) ***(G-5303)***
Cellco Partnership ...831 475-3100
1440 41st Ave Ste B Capitola (95010) ***(G-5304)***
Cellco Partnership ...661 827-8728
2701 Ming Ave Spc 100a Bakersfield (93304) ***(G-5305)***
Cellco Partnership ...760 720-8400
1846 Marron Rd Carlsbad (92008) ***(G-5306)***
Cellco Partnership ...415 924-9084
125 Corte Madera Town Ctr Corte Madera (94925) ***(G-5307)***
Cellco Partnership ...619 596-7201
1571 N Magnolia Ave # 212 El Cajon (92020) ***(G-5308)***
Cellco Partnership ...559 451-0556
7723 N Blackstone Ave # 102 Fresno (93720) ***(G-5309)***
Cellco Partnership ...562 809-5650
12607 Artesia Blvd Cerritos (90703) ***(G-5310)***
Cellco Partnership ...530 892-6900
1950 E 20th St Ste 803 Chico (95928) ***(G-5311)***
Cellco Partnership ...951 549-6400
2210 Griffin Way Ste 101 Corona (92879) ***(G-5312)***
Cellco Partnership ...510 490-3800
39050 Argonaut Way Fremont (94538) ***(G-5313)***
Cellco Partnership ...714 256-6015
2500 E Imperial Hwy # 178 Brea (92821) ***(G-5314)***
Cellco Partnership ...619 409-4600
67 N Broadway Ste A Chula Vista (91910) ***(G-5315)***
Cellco Partnership ...951 679-6083
30098 Haun Rd Menifee (92584) ***(G-5574)***
Cellco Partnership ...818 500-7779
1023 E Colorado St Glendale (91205) ***(G-5316)***
Cellco Partnership ...619 209-5818
980 Camino De La Reina D San Diego (92108) ***(G-5317)***
Cellco Partnership ...858 625-7751
10525 Vista Sorrento Pkwy # 150 San Diego (92121) ***(G-5318)***
Cellco Partnership ...818 920-4848
8300 Van Nuys Blvd Panorama City (91402) ***(G-5319)***
Cellco Partnership ...805 650-0410
488 S Mills Rd Ventura (93003) ***(G-5320)***
Cellco Partnership ...805 237-8200
205 Oak Hill Rd Paso Robles (93446) ***(G-5321)***
Cellco Partnership ...530 233-2100
204 W 12th St Ste 1 Alturas (96101) ***(G-5322)***
Cellco Partnership ...760 642-0430
258 N El Cmino Real Ste A Encinitas (92024) ***(G-5323)***
Cellco Partnership ...951 898-0980
2540 Tuscany St Corona (92881) ***(G-5324)***
Cellco Partnership ...661 296-7585
26445 Bouquet Canyon Rd Santa Clarita (91350) ***(G-5325)***
Cellco Partnership ...916 408-7958
125 Cyber Ct Rocklin (95765) ***(G-5326)***

Cellco Partnership ...818 842-2722
1729 N Victory Pl Burbank (91502) ***(G-5327)***
Cellco Partnership ...626 472-6196
14510 Baldwn Prk Town Ctr Baldwin Park (91706) ***(G-5328)***
Cellco Partnership ...408 846-5170
6965 Camino Arroyo Ste 60 Gilroy (95020) ***(G-5329)***
Cellco Partnership ...626 395-0956
368 S Lake Ave Pasadena (91101) ***(G-5330)***
Cellco Partnership ...916 331-6833
5051 Auburn Blvd Sacramento (95841) ***(G-5331)***
Cellco Partnership ...760 568-5542
71800 Highway 111 A110 Rancho Mirage (92270) ***(G-5332)***
Cellco Partnership ...408 263-1960
172 Ranch Dr Milpitas (95035) ***(G-5333)***
Cellco Partnership ...949 472-0700
23718 El Toro Rd Ste A Lake Forest (92630) ***(G-5334)***
Cellco Partnership ...818 316-0865
6600 Topanga Canyon Blvd # 9001 Canoga Park (91303) ***(G-5335)***
Cellco Partnership ...415 402-0640
768 Market St San Francisco (94102) ***(G-5336)***
Cellco Partnership ...209 668-9579
3202 W Monte Vista Ave Turlock (95380) ***(G-5337)***
Cellco Partnership ...925 743-9327
18012 Bollinger Canyon Rd San Ramon (94583) ***(G-5338)***
Cellco Partnership ...661 663-9451
5508 Young St Bakersfield (93311) ***(G-6063)***
Cellco Partnership ...714 258-8870
2687 Park Ave Tustin (92782) ***(G-5339)***
Cellco Partnership ...818 990-4610
17237 Ventura Blvd Encino (91316) ***(G-5340)***
Cellco Partnership ...415 258-8404
333 Biscayne Dr San Rafael (94901) ***(G-5341)***
Cellco Partnership ...213 380-2299
3458 Wilshire Blvd Los Angeles (90010) ***(G-5342)***
Cellco Partnership ...916 419-6200
3635 N Freeway Blvd Sacramento (95834) ***(G-5343)***
Cellco Partnership ...818 980-4200
11265 Ventura Blvd Studio City (91604) ***(G-5344)***
Cellco Partnership ...925 472-0487
1199 Dunsyre Dr Lafayette (94549) ***(G-5345)***
Cellco Partnership ...562 401-1045
12006 Lakewood Blvd Downey (90242) ***(G-5346)***
Cellco Partnership ...760 662-5914
12821 Main St Hesperia (92345) ***(G-5347)***
Cellco Partnership ...619 216-5840
2015 Birch Rd Ste 1805 Chula Vista (91915) ***(G-5348)***
Cellco Partnership ...510 267-0731
3264 Lakeshore Ave Oakland (94610) ***(G-5349)***
Cellco Partnership ...559 325-1420
1398 Shaw Ave Clovis (93612) ***(G-5350)***
Cellco Partnership...661 274-2112
39575 Trade Center Dr Palmdale (93551) ***(G-5351)***
Cellco Partnership ...714 847-8799
16120 Beach Blvd Huntington Beach (92647) ***(G-5352)***
Cellco Partnership ...310 659-0775
100 N La Cienega Blvd # 233 Los Angeles (90048) ***(G-5353)***
Cellco Partnership...916 357-1000
255 Parkshore Dr Bldg B Folsom (95630) ***(G-5354)***
Cellco Partnership ...209 543-6500
3801 Pelandale Ave Ste B3 Modesto (95356) ***(G-5355)***
Cellco Partnership ...213 738-9771
3785 Wilshire Blvd Los Angeles (90010) ***(G-5356)***
Cellco Partnership ...310 329-9325
20820 Avalon Blvd Carson (90746) ***(G-5357)***
Cellco Partnership ...323 465-0640
1503 Vine St Hollywood (90028) ***(G-5358)***
Cellco Partnership ...323 603-0369
7100 Santa Monica Blvd West Hollywood (90046) ***(G-5359)***
Cellco Partnership ...415 695-8400
2654 Mission St San Francisco (94110) ***(G-5360)***
Cellco Partnership ...510 324-5740
30935 Courthouse Dr Spc 1 Union City (94587) ***(G-5361)***
Cellco Partnership ...530 223-0420
900 Dana Dr Ste 6 Redding (96003) ***(G-5362)***
Cellco Partnership ...661 286-2399
24201 Valencia Blvd Valencia (91355) ***(G-5363)***
Cellco Partnership ...714 899-4690
6856 Katella Ave Cypress (90630) ***(G-5364)***
Cellco Partnership ...760 337-5508
880 N Imperial Ave El Centro (92243) ***(G-5365)***
Cellco Partnership ...805 955-9035
1555 Simi Town Center Way Simi Valley (93065) ***(G-5366)***
Cellco Partnership ...818 715-9143
6600 Topanga Canyon Blvd Canoga Park (91303) ***(G-5367)***
Cellco Partnership ...831 421-0753
110 Cooper St Ste A Santa Cruz (95060) ***(G-5368)***
Cellco Partnership ...909 381-0576
500 Inland Ctr 459 San Bernardino (92408) ***(G-5369)***
Cellco Partnership ...916 536-0440
6065 Sunrise Blvd Citrus Heights (95610) ***(G-5370)***
Cellco Partnership ...415 351-1700
1 Daniel Burnham Ct Bsmt San Francisco (94109) ***(G-5371)***
Cellco Partnership...562 789-0911
12376 Washington Blvd A Whittier (90606) ***(G-5372)***
Cellco Partnership ...858 614-0011
7061 Clairemont Mesa Blvd San Diego (92111) ***(G-5373)***
Cellco Partnership ...909 591-9740
3825 Grand Ave Chino (91710) ***(G-5374)***
Cellco Partnership ...530 674-8007
1145 Colusa Ave Ste A Yuba City (95991) ***(G-5375)***

Cellco Partnership 949 831-3955
27040 Alicia Pkwy Ste E Laguna Niguel (92677) ***(G-5376)***
Cellco Partnership 909 899-8910
12475 N Mainstreet Rancho Cucamonga (91739) ***(G-5377)***
Cellco Partnership 805 569-2525
2980 State St Santa Barbara (93105) ***(G-5378)***
Cellco Partnership 707 525-5010
844 4th St Santa Rosa (95404) ***(G-5379)***
Cellco Partnership 714 449-0715
503 N State College Blvd Fullerton (92831) ***(G-5380)***
Cellco Partnership 650 323-6127
219 University Ave Palo Alto (94301) ***(G-5381)***
Cellco Partnership 925 847-0320
5221 Martinelli Way Dublin (94568) ***(G-5382)***
Cellco Partnership 805 549-6260
994 Mill St Ste 100 San Luis Obispo (93401) ***(G-5383)***
Cellco Partnership 714 775-0600
3770 W Mcfadden Ave Ste H Santa Ana (92704) ***(G-5384)***
Cellco Partnership 323 826-9880
6400 Pacific Blvd Huntington Park (90255) ***(G-6064)***
Cellco Partnership 858 618-2100
11134 Rancho Carmel Dr # 101 San Diego (92128) ***(G-5742)***
Cellco Partnership 714 669-3500
2792 Walnut Ave Tustin (92780) ***(G-5385)***
Cellco Partnership 661 726-4762
43458 10th St W Ste C Lancaster (93534) ***(G-5386)***
Cellco Partnership 949 488-9990
638 Camino De Ls Mrs H140 Ste H San Clemente (92673) ***(G-5387)***
Cellco Partnership 323 725-9750
5438 Whittier Blvd Commerce (90022) ***(G-5388)***
Cellco Partnership 562 942-8527
8724 Washington Blvd Pico Rivera (90660) ***(G-5389)***
Cellmark Inc (HQ) 415 927-1700
22 Pelican Way San Rafael (94901) ***(G-8108)***
Cellmatics 760 692-2424
2309 Masters Rd Carlsbad (92008) ***(G-15917)***
Cello & Maudru Cnstr Co Inc 707 257-0454
2505 Oak St NAPA (94559) ***(G-1523)***
Cellular Palace Inc 310 278-2007
10435 Santa Monica Blvd F Los Angeles (90025) ***(G-7545)***
Celluphone LLC 323 727-9131
6119 E Washington Blvd Commerce (90040) ***(G-7546)***
Celmol Inc 714 259-1000
1611 E Saint Andrew Pl Santa Ana (92705) ***(G-9251)***
Cels Enterprises Inc (PA) 310 838-0280
3485 S La Cienega Blvd A Los Angeles (90016) ***(G-8423)***
Cem - Victorville River Plant, Victorville *Also called Cemex Cnstr Mtls PCF LLC* ***(G-6976)***
Cem Builders Inc 408 395-1490
37 S 4th St Campbell (95008) ***(G-25731)***
Cemak Trucking Inc 949 253-2800
3252 E 70th St Long Beach (90805) ***(G-3991)***
Cement Cutting Inc 619 296-9592
3610 Hancock St Frnt Frnt San Diego (92110) ***(G-3241)***
Cement Mason Health & Welfare 707 864-3300
220 Campus Ln Suisun City (94534) ***(G-24887)***
Cemex Cement Inc 626 969-1747
1201 W Gladstone St Azusa (91702) ***(G-6975)***
Cemex Cnstr Mtls PCF LLC 760 381-7600
16888 E St Victorville (92394) ***(G-6976)***
Cen Cal Plastering Inc 209 858-1045
1256 W Lathrop Rd Manteca (95336) ***(G-2875)***
Cencal Health, Santa Barbara *Also called Santa Barbara San Luis Obispo* ***(G-10248)***
Centene Corporation 530 626-5773
550 Main St Placerville (95667) ***(G-10268)***
Center At Parkwest, The, Reseda *Also called Chase Group Llc* ***(G-27378)***
Center Cnslng Edctn & Crisis 925 462-1755
4361 Railroad Ave Pleasanton (94566) ***(G-23721)***
Center Coast Home Help Care, Monterey *Also called Visiting Nurse Association* ***(G-22593)***
Center For Achievement Center, Bakersfield *Also called New Advances For People Disabi* ***(G-24946)***
Center For Aids Research 916 443-3299
1500 21st St Sacramento (95811) ***(G-19415)***
Center For Autism & (PA) 818 345-2345
21600 Oxnard St Ste 1800 Woodland Hills (91367) ***(G-20313)***
Center For Autism Related Svcs 323 850-7177
5949 Lankershim Blvd North Hollywood (91601) ***(G-27873)***
Center For Autsm Rsrch Evltn 858 444-8823
10065 Old Grove Rd # 200 San Diego (92131) ***(G-22676)***
Center For Better Health and 714 751-8110
1520 Nutmeg Pl Ste 220 Costa Mesa (92626) ***(G-22913)***
Center For Children Protection, San Diego *Also called Rady Chld Hospital-San Diego* ***(G-22166)***
Center For Civic Education (PA) 818 591-9321
5115 Douglas Fir Rd Ste J Calabasas (91302) ***(G-26750)***
Center For Discovery, Lakewood *Also called Discovery Practice Management* ***(G-19505)***
Center For Dscovery Adoloscent 562 425-6404
4136 Ann Arbor Rd Lakewood (90712) ***(G-22121)***
Center For Elders Independence 510 433-1150
510 17th St Ste 400 Oakland (94612) ***(G-10269)***
Center For Employment Training (PA) 408 287-7924
701 Vine St San Jose (95110) ***(G-24321)***
Center For Human Services (PA) 209 526-1476
2000 W Briggsmore Ave I Modesto (95350) ***(G-23722)***
Center For Indvdual and Fam Th 714 558-9266
840 W Town And Country Rd Orange (92868) ***(G-23723)***
Center For Injury Prevention, Chula Vista *Also called Racelegal Com* ***(G-25568)***
Center For Sustainable Energy 858 244-1177
9325 Sky Park Ct Ste 100 San Diego (92123) ***(G-27874)***
Center For Ventr Philanthropy, San Mateo *Also called Peninsula Community Foundation* ***(G-12162)***
Center Glass Co No 3 ....619 469-6181
7853 El Cajon Blvd La Mesa (91942) ***(G-3408)***
Center Medical Company 626 575-7500
12100 Valley Blvd 109a El Monte (91732) ***(G-19416)***
Center Point Inc (PA) 415 492-4444
135 Paul Dr San Rafael (94903) ***(G-23724)***
Center Thtre Group Los Angeles (PA) 213 972-7344
601 W Temple St Los Angeles (90012) ***(G-18380)***
Center To Promote Healthcare A (PA) 510 834-1300
1333 Broadway Ste 604 Oakland (94612) ***(G-22914)***
CENTER, THE, San Diego *Also called San Diego Lesbian Gay Bisexu* ***(G-24175)***
Centerplate, San Francisco *Also called Volume Services Inc* ***(G-19305)***
Centerplate, Lake Elsinore *Also called Volume Services Inc* ***(G-19307)***
Centex Homes Inc 949 453-0113
27101 Puerta Real Ste 300 Mission Viejo (92691) ***(G-1152)***
Centex Homes Inc 949 453-0113
250 Commerce Ste 100 Irvine (92602) ***(G-1153)***
Centimark Corporation 909 652-9280
1420 S Archibald Ave Ontario (91761) ***(G-1412)***
Centimark Corporation 510 614-1140
2380 W Winton Ave Hayward (94545) ***(G-3148)***
Centimark Roofing Systems, Hayward *Also called Centimark Corporation* ***(G-3148)***
Centinela Frman Rgonal Med Ctr, Marina Del Rey *Also called Cfhs Holdings Inc* ***(G-21476)***
Centinela Frman Rgonal Med Ctr, Marina Del Rey *Also called Cfhs Holdings Inc* ***(G-21477)***
Centinela Frman Rgonal Med Ctr, Inglewood *Also called Cfhs Holdings Inc* ***(G-21478)***
Centinela Hospital Medical Ctr, Inglewood *Also called Prime Healthcare Centinela LLC* ***(G-21810)***
Centinela Skilled Nursing and 310 674-3216
950 S Flower St Inglewood (90301) ***(G-21474)***
Centinela Skld Nrng Wlns Cntr, Inglewood *Also called West Cntinela Vly Care Ctr Inc* ***(G-21030)***
Centinela Skld Nrsng & Wllnss 310 674-3216
1001 S Osage Ave Inglewood (90301) ***(G-20443)***
Centinela Valley Care Center 310 674-3216
950 S Flower St Inglewood (90301) ***(G-24589)***
Centra Freight Services Inc (PA) 650 873-8147
279 Lawrence Ave South San Francisco (94080) ***(G-5198)***
Central Anesthesia Service 916 481-6800
3315 Watt Ave Sacramento (95821) ***(G-19417)***
Central Branch YMCA, San Jose *Also called YMCA of Silicon Valley* ***(G-25432)***
Central Cal Healthcare Sys, Fresno *Also called Veterans Health Administration* ***(G-20199)***
Central Cal Nikkei Foundation 559 237-4006
540 S Peach Ave Fresno (93727) ***(G-23725)***
Central California Blood Ctr 559 389-5433
4343 W Herndon Ave Fresno (93722) ***(G-22915)***
Central California Blood Ctr 559 324-1211
8094 N Cedar Ave Fresno (93720) ***(G-22916)***
Central California Blood Ctr (PA) 559 389-5433
4343 W Herndon Ave Fresno (93722) ***(G-22917)***
Central California Ear Nose 559 432-3724
1351 E Spruce Ave Fresno (93720) ***(G-19418)***
Central California Faculty Med 209 620-6937
1085 W Minnesota Ave Turlock (95382) ***(G-22918)***
Central California Faculty Med (PA) 559 453-5200
2625 E Divisadero St Fresno (93721) ***(G-19419)***
Central California Tr 559 686-4973
22847 Road 140 Tulare (93274) ***(G-26751)***
Central Cardiology Med Clinic 661 395-0000
2901 Sillect Ave Ste 100 Bakersfield (93308) ***(G-19420)***
Central Cast Vsting Nurse Assn, Monterey *Also called Central Coast Cmnty Hlth Care* ***(G-22919)***
Central Cleaning Co, Pleasanton *Also called Dan Lofgren* ***(G-14280)***
Central Coast Cmnty Hlth Care 831 372-6668
5 Lower Ragsdale Dr # 102 Monterey (93940) ***(G-21182)***
Central Coast Cmnty Hlth Care 831 648-4200
40 Ragsdale Dr Ste 150 Monterey (93940) ***(G-22919)***
Central Coast Cooling LLC 831 422-7265
1107 Merrill St Salinas (93901) ***(G-4490)***
Central Coast Distributing LLC 805 922-2108
815 S Blosser Rd Santa Maria (93458) ***(G-9046)***
Central Coast Packing, Soledad *Also called Vasquez Brothers Inc* ***(G-601)***
Central Coast Pathology Lab, Bakersfield *Also called Physicians Automated Lab Inc* ***(G-22256)***
Central Coast Pub Safety Inc 805 556-4450
222 Carmen Ln Ste 202 Santa Maria (93458) ***(G-16592)***
Central Coast Vna & Hospice (PA) 831 372-6668
5 Lower Ragsdle Dr 102 Monterey (93940) ***(G-22401)***
Central Coast Vna & Hospice 831 758-8243
6 Quail Run Cir Ste 101 Salinas (93907) ***(G-22402)***
Central Cold Storage, Castroville *Also called Vps Companies Inc* ***(G-8573)***
Central Contra Costa Sanit 925 228-9500
5019 Imhoff Pl Martinez (94553) ***(G-6410)***
Central Counties 209 356-0355
241 Business Park Way Atwater (95301) ***(G-26837)***
Central Courier LLC 805 654-1145
1957 Eastman Ave Ste C Ventura (93003) ***(G-3992)***
Central Freight Lines Inc 800 782-5036
1621 Main Ave Sacramento (95838) ***(G-4709)***
Central Freight Lines Inc 559 233-5559
4575 S Chestnut Ave Fresno (93725) ***(G-3993)***
Central Garden & Pet Company 858 695-0743
9235 Activity Rd San Diego (92126) ***(G-9252)***
Central Garden & Pet Company 562 926-5252
13227 Orden Dr Santa Fe Springs (90670) ***(G-9253)***

ALPHABETIC

Central Gardens Inc ... 415 567-2967
1355 Ellis St San Francisco (94115) *(G-20444)*
Central Grdns Cnvalescent Hosp, San Francisco *Also called Central Gardens Inc (G-20444)*
Central Health Plan Cal Inc ... 626 938-7120
1055 Park View Dr Ste 355 Covina (91724) *(G-22403)*
Central Medical Offices, Bakersfield *Also called Kaiser Foundation Hospitals (G-19600)*
Central Orange County Svc Ctr, Santa Ana *Also called Southern California Edison Co (G-6224)*
Central Parking Corporation ... 510 832-7227
1624 Franklin St Ste 722 Oakland (94612) *(G-17712)*
Central Parking System Inc ... 714 751-2855
3420 Bristol St Ste 225 Costa Mesa (92626) *(G-17713)*
Central Parking System Inc ... 916 441-1074
716 10th St Ste 101 Sacramento (95814) *(G-17714)*
Central Payment Co LLC ... 415 462-8335
2350 Kerner Blvd Ste 300 San Rafael (94901) *(G-17061)*
Central Purchasing LLC (PA) ... 805 388-1000
3491 Mission Oaks Blvd Camarillo (93012) *(G-7928)*
Central Reference Lab Inc (PA) ... 909 861-6966
1470 Valley Vista Dr # 100 Pomona (91765) *(G-22198)*
Central Refill Pharmaceuticals ... 562 401-4214
9521 Dalen St Downey (90242) *(G-8250)*
Central Reinforcing Corp ... 909 773-0840
14166 Slover Ave Fontana (92337) *(G-3376)*
Central Retail Pharmaceuticals, Downey *Also called Central Refill Pharmaceuticals (G-8250)*
Central Roofing Company, Gardena *Also called Claud Townsley Inc (G-3151)*
Central State Pre-School ... 760 432-2499
2310 Aldergrove Ave Escondido (92029) *(G-24425)*
Central Technologies, Irvine *Also called Inductors Inc (G-7585)*
Central Valley AG Grinding ... 209 544-9246
5509 Langworth Rd Oakdale (95361) *(G-2040)*
Central Valley AG Transload, Oakdale *Also called Central Valley AG Grinding (G-2040)*
Central Valley Autism Project ... 209 521-4791
3425 Coffee Rd Ste C2 Modesto (95355) *(G-23726)*
Central Valley Cheese Inc ... 209 664-1080
115 S Kilroy Rd Turlock (95380) *(G-8580)*
Central Valley Clinic Inc ... 408 885-5400
2425 Enborg Ln San Jose (95128) *(G-22677)*
Central Valley Cmnty Bancorp (PA) ... 559 298-1775
7100 N Fincl Dr Ste 101 Fresno (93720) *(G-9482)*
Central Valley Community Bank ... 559 625-8733
120 N Floral St Visalia (93291) *(G-9483)*
Central Valley Community Bank (HQ) ... 559 323-3384
600 Pollasky Ave Clovis (93612) *(G-12040)*
Central Valley Community Bank ... 559 298-1775
7100 N Fincl Dr Ste 101 Fresno (93720) *(G-12041)*
Central Valley Concrete Inc ... 209 383-7292
3371 N Highway 59 Merced (95348) *(G-6977)*
Central Valley Concrete Inc (PA) ... 209 723-8846
3823 N State Highway 59 Merced (95348) *(G-3994)*
Central Valley Environmental, Rohnert Park *Also called Cve Nb Contracting Group Inc (G-27785)*
Central Valley Family Heal, Selma *Also called Adventist Health System/West (G-19318)*
Central Valley General Hosp (HQ) ... 559 583-2100
1025 N Douty St Hanford (93230) *(G-21475)*
Central Valley Indian Hlth Inc (PA) ... 559 299-2578
2740 Herndon Ave Clovis (93611) *(G-19421)*
Central Valley Oprtnty Ctr Inc (PA) ... 209 357-0062
6838 W Bridgett Ct Winton (95388) *(G-24322)*
Central Valley Presort Inc ... 559 498-6151
1931 G St Fresno (93706) *(G-14067)*
Central Valley Trucking, Merced *Also called Central Valley Concrete Inc (G-6977)*
Central Valley Trucking, Merced *Also called Central Valley Concrete Inc (G-3994)*
Central Valley YMCA, Fresno *Also called Central Vly Yng MNS Chrn Assoc (G-25230)*
Central Vly Chld Svcs Netwrk ... 559 456-1100
1911 N Helm Ave Fresno (93727) *(G-23727)*
Central Vly Regional Ctr Inc ... 559 738-2200
5441 W Cypress Ave Visalia (93277) *(G-22678)*
Central Vly Specialty Hosp Inc ... 209 248-7700
730 17th St Modesto (95354) *(G-20445)*
Central Vly Yng MNS Chrn Assoc ... 559 225-9191
4045 N Fresno St Ste 101 Fresno (93726) *(G-25230)*
Central Whl Elec Distrs Inc ... 925 245-9310
6611 Preston Ave Ste E Livermore (94551) *(G-7424)*
Centre Care Management Co LLC ... 858 613-6255
15611 Pomerado Rd Ste 400 Poway (92064) *(G-19422)*
Centre For Health Care, Poway *Also called Centre Care Management Co LLC (G-19422)*
Centre For Neuro Skills (PA) ... 661 872-3408
5215 Ashe Rd Bakersfield (93313) *(G-22679)*
Centrelink Ins & Fincl Svcs, Woodland Hills *Also called Centrelink Insur & Fincl Svcs (G-17062)*
Centrelink Insur & Fincl Svcs ... 818 587-2001
20750 Ventura Blvd # 300 Woodland Hills (91364) *(G-17062)*
Centrescapes Inc ... 909 392-3303
165 Gentry St Pomona (91767) *(G-822)*
Centrify Corporation ... 669 444-5200
3300 Tannery Way Santa Clara (95054) *(G-15078)*
Centrl Territrl Salvation Army ... 714 832-7100
10200 Pioneer Rd Tustin (92782) *(G-23728)*
Centro Inc ... 415 788-6190
115 Sansome St San Francisco (94104) *(G-15918)*
Centro De Salud De La (PA) ... 619 428-4463
4004 Beyer Blvd San Ysidro (92173) *(G-22680)*
Centro De Salud De La ... 619 477-0165
1420 E Plaza Blvd Ste E4 National City (91950) *(G-23729)*
Centurion Group, The, Los Angeles *Also called Mulholland SEC & Patrol Inc (G-16741)*
Centurion Group, The, Los Angeles *Also called Centurion Security Inc (G-16593)*
Centurion Security Inc ... 818 755-0202
11454 San Vicente Blvd Los Angeles (90049) *(G-16593)*
Centurion Security Services ... 949 474-0444
20102 Sw Cypress St Newport Beach (92660) *(G-16594)*
Century 14, Roseville *Also called Century Theatres Inc (G-18356)*
Century 21, Downey *Also called First Family Homes (G-11525)*
Century 21, Inglewood *Also called Smith Coleman Inc (G-11848)*
Century 21, Huntington Beach *Also called Beachside Realtors (G-11315)*
Century 21, Downey *Also called Steve Roberson (G-11858)*
Century 21, Redlands *Also called Lois Lauer Realty (G-11635)*
Century 21, Monrovia *Also called Adams & Barnes Inc (G-11276)*
Century 21, Laguna Woods *Also called Rainbow Realty Corporation (G-11784)*
Century 21, Porter Ranch *Also called Coast To Coast Realty (G-11400)*
Century 21, Walnut Creek *Also called Kropa Realty (G-11623)*
Century 21, Lakewood *Also called Rainbow Properties Inc (G-11783)*
Century 21, Fresno *Also called Century Adanalian & Vasquez (G-11382)*
Century 21, Rancho Cucamonga *Also called Excellnce of Inland Empire Inc (G-11500)*
Century 21, Fullerton *Also called John G Shipley (G-11598)*
Century 21, San Dimas *Also called National Credit Industries Inc (G-9941)*
Century 21, Bellflower *Also called Leroy Durbin (G-11633)*
Century 21, Cerritos *Also called Astro Realty Inc (G-11308)*
Century 21, Whittier *Also called Beachside Realtors (G-11316)*
Century 21 ... 707 429-2121
301 Dickson Hill Rd Ste A Fairfield (94533) *(G-11363)*
Century 21 A Better Svc Rlty ... 562 287-0230
8077 2nd St Fl Fl Downey (90241) *(G-11364)*
Century 21 A Better Svc Rlty ... 562 806-1000
5831 Firestone Blvd Ste J South Gate (90280) *(G-10666)*
Century 21 Able Inc ... 858 450-2100
3202 Governor Dr Ste 100 San Diego (92122) *(G-11365)*
Century 21 Alpha LLC ... 408 369-2000
1630 W Campbell Ave Campbell (95008) *(G-11366)*
Century 21 Amber Realty Inc ... 310 625-4363
21024 Wood Ave Apt A Torrance (90503) *(G-11367)*
Century 21 Beachside ... 562 430-2121
6265 E 2nd St Ste 103 Long Beach (90803) *(G-11368)*
Century 21 Beverlywood Realty ... 310 836-8321
2800 S Robertson Blvd Los Angeles (90034) *(G-11369)*
Century 21 Champion ... 408 725-4000
10420 S De Anza Blvd Cupertino (95014) *(G-11370)*
Century 21 Crest ... 818 248-9100
4005 Foothill Blvd La Crescenta (91214) *(G-11371)*
Century 21 Dstnctive Prpts Inc ... 707 678-9211
1450 Ary Ln Ste A Dixon (95620) *(G-11372)*
Century 21 E, Diamond Bar *Also called E-N Realty II (G-11484)*
Century 21 Excellence ... 562 948-4553
5207 Rosemead Blvd Ste 1 Pico Rivera (90660) *(G-11373)*
Century 21 Exclusive Realtors ... 310 373-5252
22831 Hawthorne Blvd Torrance (90505) *(G-11374)*
Century 21 Experience, Alta Loma *Also called Expreal Inc (G-11501)*
Century 21 Golden Hills, San Jose *Also called Qal Affiliate Inc (G-11781)*
Century 21 Golden Realty ... 626 204-2400
1332 N Lake Ave Pasadena (91104) *(G-11375)*
Century 21 Green Gable RE, Dixon *Also called Century 21 Dstnctive Prpts Inc (G-11372)*
Century 21 Haley & Associates ... 916 782-1500
699 Wshington Blvd Ste B5 Roseville (95678) *(G-11376)*
Century 21 Hill Top Realtors, Simi Valley *Also called First & La Realty Corp (G-11520)*
Century 21 Home Realtors ... 909 980-8000
8338 Day Creek Blvd # 101 Rancho Cucamonga (91739) *(G-11377)*
Century 21 King Realtors, Rancho Cucamonga *Also called Century 21 Home Realtors (G-11377)*
Century 21 Landmark Properties ... 562 422-0911
1650 Ximeno Ave Ste 120 Long Beach (90804) *(G-11378)*
Century 21 Les Ryan Realty ... 707 577-7777
1057 College Ave Ofc Ste Santa Rosa (95404) *(G-11379)*
Century 21 Ludecke Inc (PA) ... 626 445-0123
20 E Foothill Blvd # 105 Arcadia (91006) *(G-11380)*
Century 21 Powerhouse Realty, Huntington Park *Also called Powerhouse Realty Inc (G-11757)*
Century 21 Showcase Inc ... 909 936-9334
7835 Church St Highland (92346) *(G-11381)*
Century 8, North Hollywood *Also called Century Theatres Inc (G-18358)*
Century Adanalian & Vasquez ... 559 244-6000
1415 W Shaw Ave Fresno (93711) *(G-11382)*
Century Bankcard Services ... 818 700-3100
25129 The Old Rd Ste 222 Stevenson Ranch (91381) *(G-17063)*
Century City Primary Care ... 310 553-3189
2080 Century Park E # 1605 Los Angeles (90067) *(G-19423)*
Century Contract Services Inc ... 858 672-4118
15815 Camino Codorniz San Diego (92127) *(G-14246)*
Century Finance Incorporated ... 310 281-3081
2461 Santa Monica Blvd Santa Monica (90404) *(G-9828)*
Century Lighting and Electric ... 530 823-1004
12820 Earhart Ave Auburn (95602) *(G-7425)*
Century National, Encino *Also called Kramer-Wilson Company Inc (G-10431)*
Century National Properties (PA) ... 818 760-0880
12200 Sylvan St Ste 250 North Hollywood (91606) *(G-10969)*
Century Pk Capitl Partners LLC (PA) ... 310 867-2210
2101 Rosecrans Ave # 4275 El Segundo (90245) *(G-12137)*
Century Plaza Garage ... 310 226-7495
2049 Century Park E Ste D Los Angeles (90067) *(G-17715)*
Century Properties Owners Assn ... 310 272-8580
1 W Century Dr Los Angeles (90067) *(G-11383)*
Century Skilled Nursing Care, Inglewood *Also called Oplv Inc (G-20827)*

ALPHABETIC SECTION
Change Healthcare Inc

Century Theatres Inc 916 797-3466
1555 Eureka Rd Roseville (95661) ***(G-18356)***

Century Theatres Inc 510 758-9626
3200 Klose Way Richmond (94806) ***(G-18357)***

Century Theatres Inc 818 508-1943
12827 Victory Blvd North Hollywood (91606) ***(G-18358)***

Century Vision Developers Inc 925 682-4830
3000 Oak Rd Ste 360 Walnut Creek (94597) ***(G-1524)***

Century West Plumbing, Westlake Village *Also called Sdg Enterprises* ***(G-2362)***

Century Wilshire Hotel, Culver City *Also called Century Wilshire Inc* ***(G-12507)***

Century Wilshire Inc 310 558-9400
9400 Culver Blvd Culver City (90232) ***(G-12507)***

Century, The, Los Angeles *Also called Century Properties Owners Assn* ***(G-11383)***

Century-Coast Building Pdts, Salinas *Also called Coast Building Products* ***(G-2879)***

Century-National Insurance Co (HQ) 818 760-0880
16650 Sherman Way Van Nuys (91406) ***(G-10204)***

Cenzic Inc 408 200-0700
655 Campbell Tech Pkwy # 100 Campbell (95008) ***(G-7547)***

Cep America LLC 510 350-2691
2100 Powell St Ste 900 Emeryville (94608) ***(G-19424)***

Ceramic Decorating Company Inc 323 268-5135
4900 Zambrano St Commerce (90040) ***(G-17064)***

Ceramic Tile Art Inc 818 767-9088
11601 Pendleton St Sun Valley (91352) ***(G-3008)***

Cerenzia Foods Inc 909 989-4000
8585 White Oak Ave Rancho Cucamonga (91730) ***(G-8463)***

Ceridian LLC 310 719-7400
1515 W 190th St Ste 100 Gardena (90248) ***(G-26309)***

Ceridian Tax Service Inc 714 963-1311
17390 Brookhurst St # 100 Fountain Valley (92708) ***(G-26310)***

Cerium Systems Inc 408 623-0787
4701 Patrick Henry Dr Santa Clara (95054) ***(G-16333)***

Cerritos Cinemas 10, Artesia *Also called Edwards Theatres Circuit Inc* ***(G-18330)***

Cerritos Medical Office Bldg, Cerritos *Also called Kaiser Foundation Hospitals* ***(G-19605)***

Certain Inc (PA) 415 353-5330
75 Hawthorne St Ste 550 San Francisco (94105) ***(G-15079)***

Certainteed Gypsum Inc 949 282-5300
27442 Portola Pkwy # 100 El Toro (92610) ***(G-6913)***

Certapro Painters, San Francisco *Also called Norcal Painters Inc* ***(G-2470)***

Certified Air Conditioning Inc 858 292-5740
7912 Armour St San Diego (92111) ***(G-2177)***

Certified Coatings Company 707 639-4414
2320 Cordelia Rd Fairfield (94534) ***(G-2435)***

Certified Frt Logistics Inc (PA) 805 925-9900
1344 White Ct Santa Maria (93458) ***(G-4125)***

Certified Nursing Registry Inc 626 912-1877
2707 E Valley Blvd # 309 West Covina (91792) ***(G-14623)***

Certified Trnsp Svcs Inc 714 835-8676
1038 N Custer St Santa Ana (92701) ***(G-3916)***

Certifiedsafety Inc 707 747-9400
3070 Bay Vista Courtste B Benicia (94510) ***(G-27377)***

Cerutti Bros Inc 209 862-2249
26118 Mcclintock Rd Newman (95360) ***(G-49)***

Cesar Chavez Student Center 415 338-7362
1650 Holloway Ave Rm C134 San Francisco (94132) ***(G-10970)***

Cesars Productions 415 821-1156
91 Miguel St San Francisco (94131) ***(G-17065)***

Cessna Aircraft Company 916 929-5656
5850 Citation Way Sacramento (95837) ***(G-4905)***

Cessna Scrmnto Ctation Svc Ctr, Sacramento *Also called Cessna Aircraft Company* ***(G-4905)***

Cetecom Inc (HQ) 408 586-6200
411 Dixon Landing Rd Milpitas (95035) ***(G-27875)***

Cetera Financial Group Inc (HQ) 800 879-8100
200 N Sepulveda Blvd # 1200 El Segundo (90245) ***(G-17066)***

Ceva Freight LLC 310 972-5500
19600 S Western Ave Torrance (90501) ***(G-4841)***

Ceva Freight LLC 916 379-6000
8670 Younger Creek Dr Sacramento (95828) ***(G-5042)***

Ceva Logistics LLC 310 223-6500
18120 Bishop Ave Carson (90746) ***(G-5043)***

Ceva Logistics US Inc 951 332-3202
11290 Cntu Gllano Rnch Rd Mira Loma (91752) ***(G-4679)***

Ceva Ocean Line, Torrance *Also called Ceva Freight LLC* ***(G-4841)***

Ceva Ocean Line, Sacramento *Also called Ceva Freight LLC* ***(G-5042)***

CF Merced La Sierra LLC 209 723-4224
2424 M St Merced (95340) ***(G-20446)***

CF Quincy LLC 530 283-2110
50 E Central Ave Quincy (95971) ***(G-20447)***

CF San Rafael LLC 415 479-5161
81 Professional Ctr Pkwy San Rafael (94903) ***(G-20448)***

CF Watsonville LLC 831 724-7505
525 Auto Center Dr Watsonville (95076) ***(G-20449)***

CF Watsonville East LLC 310 574-3733
535 Auto Center Dr Watsonville (95076) ***(G-20450)***

CF Watsonville West LLC 831 724-7505
525 Auto Center Dr Watsonville (95076) ***(G-20451)***

CFHC, Los Angeles *Also called Califrnia Fmly Hlth Cuncil Inc* ***(G-24884)***

Cfhs Holdings Inc 310 823-8911
4650 Lincoln Blvd Marina Del Rey (90292) ***(G-21476)***

Cfhs Holdings Inc 310 448-7800
4640 Admiralty Way # 650 Marina Del Rey (90292) ***(G-21477)***

Cfhs Holdings Inc 310 673-4660
555 E Hardy St Inglewood (90301) ***(G-21478)***

Cfp Fire Protection Inc 949 338-4280
17461 Derian Ave Ste 114 Irvine (92614) ***(G-2178)***

Cfr Line Rinkens International, Paramount *Also called Cfr Rinken LLC* ***(G-5044)***

Cfr Rinken LLC 310 223-0474
15501 Texaco Ave Paramount (90723) ***(G-5044)***

CFS Income Tax, Simi Valley *Also called CFS Tax Software* ***(G-15617)***

CFS Tax Software 805 522-1157
1445 E Los Angeles Ave # 214 Simi Valley (93065) ***(G-15617)***

CGB, Gardena *Also called Pulp Studio Incorporated* ***(G-14160)***

Cgi Technologies Solutions Inc 916 281-3200
860 Stillwater Rd Ste 210 West Sacramento (95605) ***(G-26495)***

Cgi Technologies Solutions Inc 510 238-5300
505 14th St Fl 9 Oakland (94612) ***(G-16334)***

Cgtech (PA) 949 753-1050
9000 Research Dr Irvine (92618) ***(G-15919)***

Ch Cupertino Owner LLC 408 253-8900
10050 S De Anza Blvd Cupertino (95014) ***(G-12508)***

Ch Market Center Inc 909 628-9100
4200 Chino Health Ste 325 Chino Hills (91709) ***(G-11384)***

Ch Reynolds, San Jose *Also called C H Reynolds Electric Inc* ***(G-2545)***

CH Robinson Freight Svcs Ltd 310 515-7755
680 Knox St Ste 210 Torrance (90502) ***(G-5045)***

CH Stone Plumbing Co Inc 626 962-5001
13170 Spring St Baldwin Park (91706) ***(G-2179)***

Ch2m Hill Inc 916 920-0300
2485 Natomas Park Dr # 600 Sacramento (95833) ***(G-26174)***

Ch2m Hill Inc 530 243-5832
2525 Airpark Dr Redding (96001) ***(G-25732)***

Ch2m Hill Inc 916 920-0300
2485 Natomas Park Dr # 600 Sacramento (95833) ***(G-25733)***

Ch2m Hill Inc 510 604-4144
155 Grand Ave Ste 800 Oakland (94612) ***(G-25734)***

Ch2m Hill Inc 408 436-4936
1737 N 1st St Ste 300 San Jose (95112) ***(G-26175)***

Ch2m Hill Constructors Inc 916 920-0212
2485 Natomas Park Dr # 600 Sacramento (95833) ***(G-1919)***

Cha Hollywood Medical Ctr LP (PA) 213 413-3000
1300 N Vermont Ave Los Angeles (90027) ***(G-21479)***

Cha-Dor Realty 916 624-0627
4243 Dominguez Rd Rocklin (95677) ***(G-6914)***

Chad Garrett Investigations, North Hollywood *Also called Protection Specialists* ***(G-16768)***

Chadlor Enterprises Inc 209 577-1001
2633 W Rumble Rd Modesto (95350) ***(G-20452)***

Chaduxtt JV 619 525-7188
1230 Columbia St Ste 1000 San Diego (92101) ***(G-25735)***

Chadwick Center For Children & 858 966-5814
3020 Childrens Way San Diego (92123) ***(G-19425)***

Challenge Dairy Products Inc 323 724-3130
5741 Smithway St Commerce (90040) ***(G-8581)***

Challenge Dairy Products Inc (HQ) 925 828-6160
6701 Donlon Way Dublin (94568) ***(G-8582)***

Challenger Ent, Anaheim *Also called Challenger Industries Inc* ***(G-27876)***

Challenger Industries Inc 714 630-4344
2971 E White Star Ave Anaheim (92806) ***(G-27876)***

Challenger Schools 408 266-7073
4949 Harwood Rd San Jose (95124) ***(G-24426)***

Challenger Sheet Metal Inc 619 596-8040
9353 Abraham Way Ste A Santee (92071) ***(G-3149)***

Chalmers Corporation 562 948-4850
7901 Crossway Dr Pico Rivera (90660) ***(G-1413)***

Chamber Maid Lessee Inc 310 657-7400
1000 Westmount Dr West Hollywood (90069) ***(G-12509)***

Chamberlain West Hollywood, West Hollywood *Also called Chamber Maid Lessee Inc* ***(G-12509)***

Chamberlains Children Ctr Inc 831 636-2121
1850 Cienega Rd Hollister (95023) ***(G-24590)***

Chamberpac, San Jose *Also called San Jose Silicon Valley Cham* ***(G-25102)***

Chambers Belt Company 760 602-9688
5840 El Camino Real Ste 1 Carlsbad (92008) ***(G-8424)***

Chambers Group Inc 949 261-5414
17671 Cowan Ste 100 Irvine (92614) ***(G-27877)***

Chameleon Associates, Woodland Hills *Also called Chameleon Group Inc* ***(G-16595)***

Chameleon Group Inc 818 734-8448
22020 Clarendon St # 112 Woodland Hills (91367) ***(G-16595)***

Chaminade At Santa Cruz, Santa Cruz *Also called Chaminade Ltd* ***(G-17067)***

Chaminade Ltd 831 475-5600
1 Chaminade Ln Santa Cruz (95065) ***(G-17067)***

Chaminade of Santa Cruz, Santa Cruz *Also called Lho Santa Cruz One Lesse Inc* ***(G-12918)***

Chaminade of Santa Cruz, Santa Cruz *Also called Benchmark-Tech Corporation* ***(G-17026)***

Champagne Landscape Nurs Inc 559 277-8188
3233 N Cornelia Ave Fresno (93722) ***(G-823)***

Champion Electric Inc 951 276-9619
3950 Garner Rd Riverside (92501) ***(G-2550)***

Champion Lumber Co 951 684-5670
1313 Chicago Ave Ste 100 Riverside (92507) ***(G-6915)***

Champion Signs Incorporated 858 751-2900
7835 Wilkerson Ct San Diego (92111) ***(G-14136)***

Champion Transportation Svcs, Pico Rivera *Also called AP Express International LLC* ***(G-5215)***

Championship Golf Services Inc 951 272-4340
2340 Silver Oak Cir Corona (92882) ***(G-18720)***

Chamson Management Inc 714 751-2400
7 Hutton Centre Dr Santa Ana (92707) ***(G-12510)***

Chancellor Hlth Care Cal I Inc (PA) 909 796-0235
25383 Cole St Loma Linda (92354) ***(G-21183)***

Chandler Chicco Agency LLC (HQ) 415 643-1101
474 Alvarado St San Francisco (94114) ***(G-27740)***

Chandler Convalescent Hospital 818 240-1610
525 S Central Ave Glendale (91204) ***(G-20453)***

Change Healthcare Inc 805 777-7773
241 Lombard St Thousand Oaks (91360) ***(G-16110)***

ALPHABETIC

Changeorg Inc

ALPHABETIC SECTION

Changeorg Inc 415 817-1840
  383 Rhode Island St Fl 3 San Francisco (94103) *(G-16222)*
Channel 4-NBC 4 Television, Burbank *Also called Access Hollywood (G-5833)*
Channel 40 Inc 916 454-4422
  4655 Fruitridge Rd Sacramento (95820) *(G-5845)*
Channel 47, Fresno *Also called Iheartcommunications Inc (G-5872)*
Channel Intelligence Inc (HQ) 321 939-5600
  1600 Amphitheatre Pkwy Mountain View (94043) *(G-5575)*
Channel Islands Young Mens Ch 805 736-3483
  201 W College Ave Lompoc (93436) *(G-25231)*
Channel Islands Young Mens Ch 805 484-0423
  3111 Village Park Dr Camarillo (93012) *(G-25232)*
Channel Islands Young Mens Ch 805 687-7727
  36 Hitchcock Way Santa Barbara (93105) *(G-25233)*
Channel Islands Young Mens Ch 805 969-3288
  591 Santa Rosa Ln Santa Barbara (93108) *(G-25234)*
Channel Islands Young Mens Ch 805 484-0423
  3760 Telegraph Rd Ventura (93003) *(G-25235)*
Channel Islands Young Mens Ch 805 686-2037
  900 N Refugio Rd Santa Ynez (93460) *(G-25236)*
Channel Islnds Vgtble Frms Inc (PA) 805 984-1910
  595 Victoria Ave Oxnard (93030) *(G-327)*
Channel Medical Center, Stockton *Also called Community Medical Centers Inc (G-21507)*
Channing House 650 327-0950
  850 Webster St Ofc Palo Alto (94301) *(G-21184)*
Chap, Pasadena *Also called Community Hlth Alance Pasadena (G-21497)*
Chapa-De Indian Health (PA) 530 887-2800
  11670 Atwood Rd Auburn (95603) *(G-19426)*
Chaparral Foundation 510 848-8774
  1309 Allston Way Berkeley (94702) *(G-20454)*
Chaparral House, Berkeley *Also called Chaparral Foundation (G-20454)*
Chapel Funding Corporation 949 580-1800
  26521 Rancho Pkwy S Lake Forest (92630) *(G-9829)*
Chapel of Chimes (HQ) 510 471-3363
  32992 Mission Blvd Hayward (94544) *(G-12028)*
Chapel of Chimes 510 654-1288
  4499 Piedmont Ave Oakland (94611) *(G-13702)*
Chapel of Memories Crematorium, Oakland *Also called Chapel of Chimes (G-13702)*
Chapman Global Medical Center 714 633-0011
  2601 E Chapman Ave Orange (92869) *(G-21480)*
Chapman Golf Development LLC 760 564-8723
  78505 Avenue 52 La Quinta (92253) *(G-18721)*
Chapman Hbr Sklled Nrsing Care 714 971-5517
  12232 Chapman Ave Garden Grove (92840) *(G-20455)*
Chapman Medical Center Inc., Orange *Also called Chapman Global Medical Center (G-21480)*
Chapman University 714 997-6821
  625 N Glassell St Orange (92867) *(G-17068)*
Chapman/Leonard Studio Eqp Inc (PA) 323 877-5309
  12950 Raymer St North Hollywood (91605) *(G-18217)*
Chapmn-Hrbor Sklled Nrsing Ctr, Garden Grove *Also called Chapman Hbr Sklled Nrsing Care (G-20455)*
Chappellet Vineyard 707 286-4219
  1581 Sage Canyon Rd Saint Helena (94574) *(G-145)*
Charanjit Singh Batth 559 864-9421
  5434 W Kamm Ave Caruthers (93609) *(G-196)*
Chardonnay Golf Club, NAPA *Also called Chardonnay/ Club Shakespeare (G-18916)*
Chardonnay/ Club Shakespeare 707 257-1900
  2555 Jamieson Canyon Rd NAPA (94558) *(G-18916)*
Chargers Football Company LLC (PA) 619 280-2121
  4020 Murphy Canyon Rd San Diego (92123) *(G-18541)*
Chariot, Carmichael *Also called Laurels Medical Services (G-3864)*
Chariot Travelware, Ontario *Also called Damao Luggage Intl Inc (G-8110)*
Charlee Family Care 951 845-3588
  136 E 6th St Beaumont (92223) *(G-24591)*
Charles & Cynthia Eberly Inc 323 937-6468
  8383 Wilshire Blvd # 906 Beverly Hills (90211) *(G-11114)*
Charles Brooks Cmnty Swim Ctr, Woodland *Also called City of Woodland (G-19184)*
Charles Culberson Inc 650 335-4730
  1084 Allen Way Campbell (95008) *(G-2876)*
Charles Drew Univ Mdcine Scnce 310 605-0164
  135 W Victoria St Long Beach (90805) *(G-24427)*
Charles Dunn Co Inc 213 481-1800
  800 W 6th St Ste 800 Los Angeles (90017) *(G-11385)*
Charles Dunn Raltor State Svcs, Los Angeles *Also called Charles Dunn Co Inc (G-11385)*
Charles Dunn RE Svcs Inc (PA) 213 270-6200
  800 W 6th St Ste 600 Los Angeles (90017) *(G-11386)*
Charles E Thomas Company Inc (PA) 310 323-6730
  13701 Alma Ave Gardena (90249) *(G-7833)*
Charles Fenley Enterprises 209 523-2832
  1109 Oakdale Rd Modesto (95355) *(G-17835)*
Charles M Kamiya and Sons Inc 310 781-2066
  373 Van Ness Ave Ste 200 Torrance (90501) *(G-10667)*
Charles McMurray Co (PA) 559 292-5751
  2520 N Argyle Ave Fresno (93727) *(G-7679)*
Charles Pankow Bldrs Ltd A Cal (PA) 626 304-1190
  199 S Los Robles Ave # 300 Pasadena (91101) *(G-1525)*
Charles Pankow Bldrs Ltd A Cal 510 893-5170
  1111 Broadway Ste 200 Oakland (94607) *(G-1526)*
Charles Schwab Corporation (PA) 415 667-7000
  211 Main St Fl 17 San Francisco (94105) *(G-9970)*
Charles Schwab Corporation 951 587-2840
  27580 Ynez Rd Ste A Temecula (92591) *(G-17069)*
Charles Schwab Corporation 858 523-2454
  12481 High Bluff Dr # 100 San Diego (92130) *(G-9971)*
Charles W Bowers Museum Corp 714 567-3600
  2002 N Main St Santa Ana (92706) *(G-25006)*
Charleston Company, Los Angeles *Also called Walter J Conn & Associates (G-26264)*

Charlie Mitchell Chld Clinic, Madera *Also called Valley Childrens Hospital (G-20181)*
Charlie W Shaeffer Jr MD 760 346-0642
  39000 Bob Hope Dr Rancho Mirage (92270) *(G-19427)*
Charlies Enterprises 559 445-8600
  1888 S East Ave Fresno (93721) *(G-8704)*
Charming Trim & Packaging 415 302-7021
  28 Brookside Ct Novato (94947) *(G-8309)*
Charolais Care V Inc 415 921-5038
  1426 Fillmore St Ste 207 San Francisco (94115) *(G-22404)*
Charter Behavioral Health Syst 626 966-1632
  1161 E Covina Blvd Covina (91724) *(G-22053)*
Charter Cmmnctons Oprating LLC 760 452-8609
  12180 Ridgecrest Rd # 102 Victorville (92395) *(G-5940)*
Charter Cmmnctons Oprating LLC 310 971-4001
  4031 Via Oro Ave Long Beach (90810) *(G-5941)*
Charter Cmmnctons Oprating LLC 530 241-7352
  5797 Eastside Rd Redding (96001) *(G-5942)*
Charter Hospice Inc 909 825-2969
  1012 E Cooley Dr Ste G Colton (92324) *(G-21070)*
Charter Oak Hospital, Covina *Also called Charter Behavioral Health Syst (G-22053)*
Charter Oak Investments Inc 925 447-1753
  5571 Stacy Ct Livermore (94550) *(G-10668)*
Chase Bros Dairy, Ventura *Also called Hailwood Inc (G-10995)*
Chase Care Center Inc 323 935-8490
  1101 Crenshaw Blvd Los Angeles (90019) *(G-21185)*
Chase Credit Systems Inc 818 762-6262
  300 E Magnolia Blvd # 502 Burbank (91502) *(G-15080)*
Chase Group Llc 818 708-3533
  6740 Wilbur Ave Reseda (91335) *(G-27378)*
Chase Group Llc 805 522-9155
  5270 E Los Angeles Ave Simi Valley (93063) *(G-27379)*
Chase Home Finance 925 277-3700
  2633 Camino Ramon Ste 300 San Ramon (94583) *(G-9830)*
Chase Manhattan, San Ramon *Also called Chase Home Finance (G-9830)*
Chase Receivables, Sonoma *Also called Credit Bureau NAPA County Inc (G-14029)*
Chase Suite and Woodfin Hotels, San Diego *Also called Woodfin Suite Hotels LLC (G-13427)*
Chaser, Gardena *Also called Houston Salem Inc (G-8346)*
Chateau At River's Edge, Sacramento *Also called Hank Fisher Properties Inc (G-21260)*
Chateau La Jolla Inn 858 459-4451
  233 Prospect St La Jolla (92037) *(G-11115)*
Chateau Lake San Marcos Homeow 760 471-0083
  1502 Circa Del Lago San Marcos (92078) *(G-25237)*
Chateau On Capitol Avenue, The, Sacramento *Also called Hank Fisher Properties Inc (G-24677)*
Chateau Pleasant Hill 2, Concord *Also called Carlton Senior Living Inc (G-11956)*
Chateau San Juan, San Juan Capistrano *Also called Atria Senior Living Group Inc (G-24558)*
Chateaux Framing Inc. 209 537-6799
  3701 Georgeann Pl Ceres (95307) *(G-3035)*
Chater Oak Real Estate Co, Livermore *Also called Charter Oak Investments Inc (G-10668)*
Chatsworth Health & Rehab, Chatsworth *Also called Golden State Health Ctrs Inc (G-21253)*
Chatsworth Park Hlth Care Ctr, Chatsworth *Also called Cpcc Inc (G-21200)*
Chc, Los Angeles *Also called Covenant House California (G-24616)*
Chc Consulting LLC 949 250-0004
  1845 W Orangewood Ave # 300 Orange (92868) *(G-27878)*
Chcg Architects, Pasadena *Also called Gonzalez/Goodale Architects (G-26191)*
Check Disc Labs 818 847-2255
  4121 W Vanowen Pl Burbank (91505) *(G-27380)*
Check Point Software Tech Inc (HQ) 800 429-4391
  959 Skyway Rd Ste 300 San Carlos (94070) *(G-15618)*
Checkfree Corporation 310 954-5600
  1640 S Sepulveda Blvd # 400 Los Angeles (90025) *(G-15920)*
Cheema Freightlines LLC 209 599-0777
  223 W 5th St Ripon (95366) *(G-4126)*
Cheese Plant, Hanford *Also called Marquez Brothers Intl Inc (G-8496)*
Chefs Warehouse Westcoast LLC (HQ) 626 465-4200
  16633 Gale Ave City of Industry (91745) *(G-8464)*
Chelbay Schuler & Chelbay (PA) 408 288-4400
  6800 Santa Teresa Blvd # 100 San Jose (95119) *(G-10547)*
Chelsio Communications Inc 408 962-3600
  209 N Fair Oaks Ave Sunnyvale (94085) *(G-15081)*
Chem Lab Rkfe, Edwards *Also called US Dept of the Air Force (G-26631)*
Chem Quip Inc. 916 923-5091
  2551 Land Ave Sacramento (95815) *(G-8014)*
Chemical Dependency Recovery 916 482-1132
  2829 Watt Ave Ste 150 Sacramento (95821) *(G-8982)*
Chemical Waste Management Inc 559 386-9711
  35251 Old Skyline Rd Kettleman City (93239) *(G-6457)*
Chemtrans, Gardena *Also called Radford Alexander Corporation (G-4053)*
Cher Ae Heights Casino, Trinidad *Also called Cher-Ae Heights Indian Cmnty (G-19160)*
Cher-Ae Heights Indian Cmnty 707 677-3611
  27 Scenic Dr Trinidad (95570) *(G-19160)*
Cherne Contracting Corporation 952 944-4300
  150 Solano Way Pacheco (94553) *(G-3507)*
Cherokee Freight Lines, Stockton *Also called Scan-Vino LLC (G-4260)*
Cherokee Inc (PA) 818 908-9868
  5990 Sepulvda Blvd # 600 Sherman Oaks (91411) *(G-12213)*
Cherry Avenue Auction Inc 559 266-9856
  4640 S Cherry Ave Fresno (93706) *(G-17070)*
Cherry City Electric, City of Industry *Also called Morrow-Meadows Corporation (G-2657)*
Chesapeake Lodging Trust 415 296-2900
  333 Battery St Lbby San Francisco (94111) *(G-12511)*
Chester Avenue Medical Offices, Bakersfield *Also called Kaiser Foundation Hospitals (G-19602)*
Chester Avenue Medical Offs II, Bakersfield *Also called Kaiser Foundation Hospitals (G-19603)*

Chester C Lehmann Co Inc (PA).....408 293-5818
1135 Auzerais Ave San Jose (95126) *(G-7426)*
Chester Public Utility Dst.....530 258-2171
251 Chester Airport Rd Chester (96020) *(G-6300)*
Chevron, Modesto *Also called Charles Fenley Enterprises (G-17835)*
Chevron Energy Technology Co (HQ).....510 242-5059
100 Chevron Way Richmond (94801) *(G-25736)*
Chevron Investor Inc (HQ).....925 842-1000
6001 Bollinger Canyon Rd San Ramon (94583) *(G-12296)*
Chevron Investor Inc.....510 242-3000
100 Chevron Way Richmond (94801) *(G-26963)*
Chevron Mining Inc.....760 856-7625
67750 Bailey Rd Mountain Pass (92366) *(G-1024)*
Chevron USA Inc.....925 842-0855
6001 Bollinger Canyon Rd San Ramon (94583) *(G-1042)*
Chhp Holdings II LLC (PA).....323 583-1931
2623 E Slauson Ave Huntington Park (90255) *(G-21481)*
Chhp Management LLC.....323 583-1931
2623 E Slauson Ave Huntington Park (90255) *(G-21482)*
Chiala, George Packing, Morgan Hill *Also called George Chiala Farms Inc (G-67)*
CHIBI CHAN PRESCHOOL, San Francisco *Also called Japanese Cmnty Youth Council (G-24930)*
Chicago Title & Escrow.....760 746-3882
316 W Mission Ave Ste 110 Escondido (92025) *(G-11387)*
Chicago Title and Trust Co.....818 548-0222
535 N Brnd Blvrd Fl 3 Glendale (91203) *(G-10500)*
Chicago Title Company.....619 230-6340
701 B St Ste 1120 San Diego (92101) *(G-10501)*
Chicago Title Company.....213 488-4375
725 S Figueroa St Ste 200 Los Angeles (90017) *(G-10502)*
Chicago Title Company.....559 451-3700
7330 N Palm Ave Ste 101 Fresno (93711) *(G-10503)*
Chicago Title Company.....559 733-3814
120 N Floral St Visalia (93291) *(G-10504)*
Chicago Title Insurance Co.....209 952-5500
3127 Transworld Dr # 103 Stockton (95206) *(G-11937)*
Chicago Title Insurance Co.....916 985-0300
105 Lake Forest Way Folsom (95630) *(G-10505)*
Chicago Title Insurance Co.....805 656-1300
500 E Esplanade Dr # 102 Oxnard (93036) *(G-10506)*
Chicago Title Insurance Co.....760 546-1000
316 W Mission Ave Ste 110 Escondido (92025) *(G-10507)*
Chicago Title Insurance Co.....916 783-7195
516 Gibson Dr Ste 200 Roseville (95678) *(G-10508)*
Chicago Title Insurance Co (HQ).....805 565-6900
4050 Calle Real Santa Barbara (93110) *(G-10509)*
Chick-Fil-A, Long Beach *Also called Howard John (G-12794)*
Chicken of Sea International, San Diego *Also called Tri-Union Seafoods LLC (G-8660)*
Chicken Ranch Bingo & Casino.....209 984-3000
16929 Chicken Ranch Rd Jamestown (95327) *(G-19161)*
Chico Area Recreation & Pk Dst (PA).....530 895-4711
545 Vallombrosa Ave Chico (95926) *(G-19162)*
Chico Creek Care Rhabilitation, Chico *Also called Helios Healthcare LLC (G-21263)*
Chico Csu Research Foundation.....530 898-6811
Csuc Bldg 25 Ste 203 Chico (95929) *(G-17071)*
Chico Electric.....530 891-1933
36 W Eaton Rd Chico (95973) *(G-2551)*
Chico Family Health Center, Chico *Also called Ampla Health (G-19342)*
Chico Immdate Care Med Ctr Inc (PA).....530 891-1676
376 Vallombrosa Ave Chico (95926) *(G-19428)*
Chico Paramedic Rescue, Chico *Also called First Rsponder Emrgncy Med Svc (G-3793)*
Chico Produce Inc (PA).....530 893-0596
70 Pepsi Way Durham (95938) *(G-8705)*
Chico Sports Club, Chico *Also called Jeff Stover Inc (G-18648)*
Chico V A Outpatient Clinic, Chico *Also called Veterans Health Administration (G-20207)*
Chidren's Hospital Center, Los Angeles *Also called Childrens Hospital Los Angeles (G-22126)*
Chief Engineering Co, Lake Elsinore *Also called Chief Trnsp & Engrg Contrs Inc (G-1746)*
Chief Executive Office, Los Angeles *Also called County of Los Angeles (G-16226)*
Chief Protective Services Inc.....951 738-0881
1344 W 6th St Ste 300 Corona (92882) *(G-16596)*
Chief San Diego Hotel LLC.....619 239-2400
601 Pacific Hwy San Diego (92101) *(G-12512)*
Chief Trnsp & Engrg Contrs Inc.....951 258-6607
32220 Terra Cotta St Lake Elsinore (92530) *(G-1746)*
Chikpea Inc.....888 342-3828
1 Market St Spear Spear Tower San Francisco (94127) *(G-27879)*
Child & Family Services, Orland *Also called Glenn County Office Education (G-24465)*
Child & Youth Services.....831 583-1050
841 Sherman Ct Marina (93933) *(G-24428)*
Child Abuse Lstening Mediation.....805 965-2376
1236 Chapala St Santa Barbara (93101) *(G-23730)*
Child and Family Guidance Ctr.....661 265-8627
310 E Plmdle Blvd G Palmdale (93550) *(G-22681)*
Child and Family Guidance Ctr (PA).....818 739-5140
9650 Zelzah Ave Northridge (91325) *(G-22682)*
Child and Family Guidance Ctr.....818 830-0200
8550 Balboa Blvd Ste 150 Northridge (91325) *(G-22683)*
Child Care, Fresno *Also called Kid Iq 24 Hr Childcare (G-24471)*
Child Care Coordinating Counsi.....650 517-1400
330 Twin Dolphin Dr # 119 Redwood City (94065) *(G-23731)*
Child Care Resource Center Inc (PA).....818 717-1000
20001 Prairie St Chatsworth (91311) *(G-23732)*
Child Care Resource Center Inc.....661 255-2474
20001 Prairie St Chatsworth (91311) *(G-23733)*
Child Care Resource Center Inc.....661 723-3246
250 Grand Cypress Ave # 601 Palmdale (93551) *(G-23734)*
Child Development Assoc Inc (PA).....619 427-4411
180 Otay Lakes Rd Ste 310 Bonita (91902) *(G-24429)*
Child Development Center.....858 794-7160
309 N Rios Ave Solana Beach (92075) *(G-24430)*
Child Development Centers, San Jose *Also called Child Development Incorporated (G-24431)*
Child Development Incorporated (PA).....408 556-7300
20 Great Oaks Blvd # 200 San Jose (95119) *(G-24431)*
Child Development Incorporated.....714 842-4064
17341 Jacquelyn Ln Huntington Beach (92647) *(G-11388)*
Child Development Incorporated.....949 854-5060
5151 Amalfi Dr Irvine (92603) *(G-24432)*
Child Development Institute.....818 888-4559
6340 Variel Ave Ste A Woodland Hills (91367) *(G-23735)*
Child Development Office, The, Santa Monica *Also called Santa Monica City of (G-24512)*
Child Development Resources of (PA).....805 485-7878
221 E Ventura Blvd Oxnard (93036) *(G-23736)*
Child Educational Center.....818 354-3418
140 Foothill Blvd La Canada (91011) *(G-24433)*
Child Family & Cmnty Svcs Inc.....510 796-9512
32980 Alvarado Niles Rd # 846 Union City (94587) *(G-24434)*
Child Help Head Start Center, Beaumont *Also called Childhelp Inc (G-24592)*
Child Nutrition Center, San Bernardino *Also called San Bernardino City Unf School (G-23045)*
Child Support Services, Commerce *Also called County of Los Angeles (G-23826)*
Child Support Services, San Francisco *Also called San Francisco City & County (G-24183)*
Child Support Svcs Cal Dept (HQ).....916 464-5000
11120 International Dr Rancho Cordova (95670) *(G-23737)*
Childcare Careers LLC.....650 372-0211
1700 S El Camino Real # 201 San Mateo (94402) *(G-14853)*
Childerns Spec of San Deigo, San Diego *Also called Stanley M Kirkpatrick MD (G-20065)*
Childhelp Inc.....951 845-6737
14700 Manzanita Rd Beaumont (92223) *(G-24592)*
Childnet Youth & Fmly Svcs Inc (PA).....562 498-5500
4155 Outer Traffic Cir Long Beach (90804) *(G-24888)*
Childnet Youth & Fmly Svcs Inc.....562 492-9983
5150 E Pacific Cst Hwy # 100 Long Beach (90804) *(G-24593)*
Children & Family Serivces, Orange *Also called County of Orange (G-23874)*
Children & Family Svcs Dept, Santa Fe Springs *Also called County of Los Angeles (G-23828)*
Children & Family Svcs Dept, Los Angeles *Also called County of Los Angeles (G-23837)*
Children of Rainbow Inc (PA).....619 615-0652
4890 Logan Ave San Diego (92113) *(G-24435)*
Children of The Rainbow Head.....619 266-7311
4890 Logan Ave San Diego (92113) *(G-24436)*
Children Services, San Bernardino *Also called County of San Bernardino (G-24615)*
Children's Discovery Museum, Rancho Mirage *Also called Childrens Museum of Desert (G-25008)*
Children's Health Center, Chico *Also called Enloe Medical Center (G-19516)*
Children's Protective Services, Redding *Also called County of Shasta (G-23918)*
Childrens Angelcare Aid Intl.....619 795-6234
6457 Elmhurst Dr San Diego (92120) *(G-23738)*
Childrens Assoc Medical Group.....858 576-1700
3020 Chld Way Mc5004 5004 Mc San Diego (92123) *(G-19429)*
Childrens Associated Med Group, San Diego *Also called Childrens Specialist of San D (G-19435)*
Childrens Botique, The, Rancho Cucamonga *Also called Childrens Btq At Stevens Hope (G-8374)*
Childrens Btq At Stevens Hope.....909 256-0100
10730 Fthill Blvd Ste 170 Rancho Cucamonga (91730) *(G-8374)*
Childrens Bureau Southern Cal (PA).....213 342-0100
1910 Magnolia Ave Los Angeles (90007) *(G-24594)*
Childrens Clinic serving Chl.....562 264-4638
701 E 28th St Ste 200 Long Beach (90806) *(G-19430)*
Childrens Creativity Museum.....415 820-3320
221 4th St San Francisco (94103) *(G-25007)*
Childrens Crisis Cntr Stanisls.....209 577-4413
1244 Fiori Ave Modesto (95350) *(G-23739)*
Childrens Day School.....415 861-5432
333 Dolores St San Francisco (94110) *(G-24437)*
Childrens Dental Health Center, San Bernardino *Also called Assistance Leag San Bernardino (G-12153)*
Childrens Healthcare Cal.....714 997-3000
455 S Main St Orange (92868) *(G-19431)*
Childrens Healthcare Cal (PA).....714 997-3000
455 S Main St Orange (92868) *(G-22122)*
Childrens Home of Stockton.....209 466-0853
430 N Pilgrim St Stockton (95205) *(G-24595)*
Childrens Hosp La Med Group, Los Angeles *Also called Childrens Hospital Los (G-19432)*
Childrens Hosp Okland Res Inst.....510 450-7600
5700 Martin Luther Oakland (94609) *(G-26752)*
Childrens Hospital Los (PA).....323 361-2336
6430 W Sunset Blvd # 600 Los Angeles (90028) *(G-19432)*
Childrens Hospital Los Angeles.....818 728-4930
5353 Balboa Blvd Ste 100 Encino (91316) *(G-22199)*
Childrens Hospital Los Angeles.....323 361-2153
5000 W Sunset Blvd # 400 Los Angeles (90027) *(G-22123)*
Childrens Hospital Los Angeles (PA).....323 660-2450
4650 W Sunset Blvd Los Angeles (90027) *(G-22124)*
Childrens Hospital Los Angeles.....626 795-7177
468 E Santa Clara St Arcadia (91006) *(G-21483)*
Childrens Hospital Los Angeles.....323 361-2119
4650 W Sunset Blvd Los Angeles (90027) *(G-19433)*
Childrens Hospital Los Angeles.....310 820-8608
1301 20th St Ste 460 Santa Monica (90404) *(G-19434)*

ALPHABETIC

Childrens Hospital Los Angeles 310 303-3890
3440 Torrance Blvd # 100 Torrance (90503) ***(G-22684)***
Childrens Hospital Los Angeles 323 361-2215
800 N Brand Blvd Glendale (91203) ***(G-22125)***
Childrens Hospital Los Angeles 714 841-4990
7891 Talbert Ave Ste 103 Huntington Beach (92648) ***(G-20249)***
Childrens Hospital Los Angeles 323 660-2450
4650 W Sunset Blvd Los Angeles (90027) ***(G-21484)***
Childrens Hospital Los Angeles 323 361-5702
4661 W Sunset Blvd Los Angeles (90027) ***(G-22126)***
Childrens Hospital Orange Cnty (PA) 714 997-3000
1201 W La Veta Ave Orange (92868) ***(G-22127)***
Childrens Hospital Orange Cnty 949 631-2062
500 Superior Ave Newport Beach (92663) ***(G-24438)***
Childrens Hospital Orange Cnty 949 365-2416
455 S Main St Orange (92868) ***(G-22128)***
Childrens Hospotal & Research (PA) 510 428-3000
747 52nd St Oakland (94609) ***(G-21485)***
Childrens Hunger Fund (PA) 818 979-7100
13931 Balboa Blvd Sylmar (91342) ***(G-23740)***
Childrens Inst Intrntnal-Burto, Torrance *Also called Childrens Institute Inc* ***(G-23743)***
Childrens Inst Los Angeles 213 383-2765
679 S New Hampshire Ave Los Angeles (90005) ***(G-23741)***
Childrens Inst Los Angeles (PA) 213 385-5100
2121 W Temple St Los Angeles (90026) ***(G-26753)***
Childrens Institute Inc (PA) 213 385-5100
2121 W Temple St Los Angeles (90026) ***(G-23742)***
Childrens Institute Inc 310 783-4677
21810 Normandie Ave Torrance (90502) ***(G-23743)***
Childrens Laboratory, Encino *Also called Childrens Hospital Los Angeles* ***(G-22199)***
Childrens Law Center Cal 916 520-2000
8950 Cal Center Dr # 101 Sacramento (95826) ***(G-23147)***
Childrens Law Center Cal (PA) 323 980-8700
201 Centre Plaza Dr Ste 8 Monterey Park (91754) ***(G-23148)***
Childrens Law Ctr - Sacramento, Sacramento *Also called Childrens Law Center Cal* ***(G-23147)***
Childrens Museum of Desert 760 321-0602
71701 Gerald Ford Dr Rancho Mirage (92270) ***(G-25008)***
Childrens Protective Services 530 749-6311
5730 Packard Ave Marysville (95901) ***(G-23744)***
Childrens Rcvery Ctr Nthrn Cal, Campbell *Also called Subacute Childrens Hosp of Cal* ***(G-22179)***
Childrens Recvg Hm Sacramento 916 482-2370
3555 Auburn Blvd Sacramento (95821) ***(G-24596)***
Childrens Services 530 458-0300
345 5th St Ste A Colusa (95932) ***(G-23745)***
Childrens Specialist of San D (PA) 858 576-1700
3030 Chld Way Ste 401 San Diego (92123) ***(G-19435)***
Childrens Specialist San Diego, San Diego *Also called Physician Management Group Inc* ***(G-27163)***
Childrens Theraputic Community 951 789-4410
17675 Van Buren Blvd A Riverside (92504) ***(G-24597)***
Childrens Vlg of Sonoma Cnty 707 566-7044
1321 Lia Ln Santa Rosa (95404) ***(G-24598)***
Chilis 898 Corona 951 734-7275
3579 Grand Oaks Corona (92881) ***(G-26964)***
China Airlines Ltd (HQ) 310 646-4233
11201 Aviation Blvd Los Angeles (90045) ***(G-4796)***
China Brma India Veterans Assn, San Jose *Also called General George W Sliney Basha* ***(G-25258)***
China Japan Global Inc (PA) 510 441-2993
1684 Decoto Rd Union City (94587) ***(G-9972)***
China Peak Mountain Resort LLC 559 233-2500
59265 Hwy 168 Lakeshore (93634) ***(G-12513)***
China Pearl, Pacoima *Also called CPI Luxury Group* ***(G-8097)***
China Shipg N Amer Holdg Ltd 562 590-3845
111 W Ocean Blvd Ste 1700 Long Beach (90802) ***(G-5046)***
China Shipg N Amer Holdg Ltd 562 590-0900
444 W Ocean Blvd Long Beach (90802) ***(G-5047)***
China Yngxin Phrmceuticals Inc 626 581-9098
927 Canada Ct City of Industry (91748) ***(G-7257)***
Chinaamerica Film Distributors, San Marino *Also called Tricor Entertainment Inc* ***(G-18171)***
Chinatown Service Center 213 808-1700
320 S Grfield Ave Ste 118 Alhambra (91801) ***(G-24323)***
Chinese Cnsld Benevolent Assn 415 982-6000
843 Stockton St San Francisco (94108) ***(G-25238)***
Chinese Hospital Association (PA) 415 982-2400
845 Jackson St San Francisco (94133) ***(G-21486)***
Chinese Laundry Inc 310 945-3299
3485 S La Cienega Blvd Los Angeles (90016) ***(G-8425)***
Chinese Laundry Shoes, Los Angeles *Also called Cels Enterprises Inc* ***(G-8423)***
Chinese Laundry Shoes, Los Angeles *Also called Chinese Laundry Inc* ***(G-8425)***
Chinese Youth Arts 323 985-4699
3592 Rsemead Blud Ste 220 Rosemead (91770) ***(G-25516)***
Chino Grading Inc 909 364-8667
3613 Philadelphia St Chino (91710) ***(G-3422)***
Chino Medical Group Inc 909 591-6446
5475 Walnut Ave Chino (91710) ***(G-19436)***
Chino Rdological Registry Corp 909 591-6688
6719 Eagle Dr Chino (91710) ***(G-21487)***
Chino Valley Healthcare Center 909 628-1245
2351 S Towne Ave Pomona (91766) ***(G-20456)***
Chino Valley Medical Center, Chino *Also called Veritas Health Services Inc* ***(G-22012)***
Chino Valley Rock, Ontario *Also called Chino Valley Sawdust Inc* ***(G-6458)***
Chino Valley Sawdust Inc 909 947-5983
13434 S Ontario Ave Ontario (91761) ***(G-6458)***
Chino-Pacific Warehouse Corp (PA) 909 545-8100
3601 Jurupa St Ontario (91761) ***(G-4535)***

Chipman Corporation (PA) 510 748-8700
1040 Marina Village Pkwy # 100 Alameda (94501) ***(G-4334)***
Chipman Corporation 510 748-8787
1555 Zephyr Ave Hayward (94544) ***(G-4127)***
Chipton-Ross Inc (wisconsin) 310 414-7800
343 Main St El Segundo (90245) ***(G-14624)***
Chiquita Brands Intl Inc 213 488-0925
746 Market Ct Los Angeles (90021) ***(G-8706)***
Chiquita Fresh North Amer LLC 954 924-5642
1440 E 3rd St Oxnard (93030) ***(G-253)***
Chirag Hospitality Inc 415 922-0244
2440 Lombard St San Francisco (94123) ***(G-12514)***
Chiro Inc (PA) 909 879-1160
2260 S Vista Ave Bloomington (92316) ***(G-7965)***
Chlb LLC 562 997-2000
2776 Pacific Ave Long Beach (90806) ***(G-22054)***
Choa Hope LLC 712 277-4101
515 W Washington Ave Escondido (92025) ***(G-12515)***
CHOC, Orange *Also called Childrens Hospital Orange Cnty* ***(G-22127)***
Choc Health Alliance 714 565-5100
1120 W La Veta Ave # 450 Orange (92868) ***(G-10270)***
Choc Mission, Orange *Also called Childrens Hospital Orange Cnty* ***(G-22128)***
Chodorow De Castro West 310 478-2541
10960 Wilshire Blvd # 1400 Los Angeles (90024) ***(G-23149)***
Choic Admini Insur Servi 714 542-4200
721 S Parker St Ste 200 Orange (92868) ***(G-10669)***
Choice Hotels Intl Inc 661 764-5207
20688 Tracy Ave Buttonwillow (93206) ***(G-12516)***
Choice Internet, Irvine *Also called Cie Digital Labs LLC* ***(G-13993)***
Choice Medical Group Inc 916 483-2885
2322 Butano Dr Ste 205 Sacramento (95825) ***(G-22685)***
Choice Pak Products, Maywood *Also called Jack H Caldwell & Sons Inc* ***(G-8742)***
CHOICESS, Arcadia *Also called Community Housing Options* ***(G-23774)***
Chong Partners Architecher Inc 613 995-8210
901 Market St Ste 600 San Francisco (94103) ***(G-26176)***
Chooljian & Sons Inc (PA) 559 888-2031
5287 S Del Rey Ave Del Rey (93616) ***(G-521)***
Chooljian Bros Packing Co Inc 559 875-5501
3192 S Indianola Ave Sanger (93657) ***(G-8814)***
Chopra Center For Wellbeing, Carlsbad *Also called Chopra Cntre For Wll-Being LLC* ***(G-19163)***
Chopra Cntre For Wll-Being LLC 760 494-1600
2013 Costa Del Mar Rd Carlsbad (92009) ***(G-19163)***
Choura Events 310 320-6200
540 Hawaii Ave Torrance (90503) ***(G-14522)***
Choura Venue Services 562 426-0555
4101 E Willow St Long Beach (90815) ***(G-13744)***
Choura Vnue Svcs At Carson Ctr, Long Beach *Also called Choura Venue Services* ***(G-13744)***
Chowchilla Conv. Center, Chowchilla *Also called Avalon Health Care Inc* ***(G-20398)***
Chowchilla Convalescent, Chowchilla *Also called Golden Living LLC* ***(G-24670)***
Chowchilla Medical Center, Chowchilla *Also called Madera Community Hospital* ***(G-21721)***
Chowchilla Mem Hlth Care Dst (PA) 559 665-3781
1104 Ventura Ave Chowchilla (93610) ***(G-20457)***
Chownow Inc 888 707-2469
12181 Bluff Creek Dr # 200 Playa Vista (90094) ***(G-15619)***
Chrisp Company (PA) 510 656-2840
43650 Osgood Rd Fremont (94539) ***(G-1747)***
Christensen & Giannini LLC 831 449-2494
1588 Moffett St Ste B Salinas (93905) ***(G-50)***
Christian and Wakefield (PA) 619 236-1555
110 W A St Ste 900 San Diego (92101) ***(G-11389)***
Christian Church Homes 510 893-2998
251 28th St Oakland (94611) ***(G-11390)***
Christian Community Credit Un (PA) 626 915-7551
255 N Lone Hill Ave San Dimas (91773) ***(G-9659)***
Christian Conference Grounds, Mount Hermon *Also called Mount Hermon Association Inc* ***(G-13469)***
Christian Counseling Centers 408 559-1115
3880 S Bascom Ave Ste 202 San Jose (95124) ***(G-19437)***
Christian Salvesen, Brea *Also called Americold Logistics LLC* ***(G-4486)***
Christiansen Amusements Corp 760 735-8542
1725 S Escondido Blvd E Escondido (92025) ***(G-19164)***
Christie Dgtal Systems USA Inc (HQ) 714 527-7056
10550 Camden Dr Cypress (90630) ***(G-7030)***
Christmas Bonus Fund of The Pl 213 385-6161
501 Shatto Pl Ste 5 Los Angeles (90020) ***(G-12171)***
Christopher Ranch LLC (PA) 408 847-1100
305 Bloomfield Ave Gilroy (95020) ***(G-21)***
Christopher Ranch LLC 831 636-8722
1690 Freitas Rd San Juan Bautista (95045) ***(G-51)***
Chroma Systems 714 557-8480
3201 S Susan St Santa Ana (92704) ***(G-13593)***
Chromalloy San Diego Corp 858 877-2800
7007 Consolidated Way San Diego (92121) ***(G-17966)***
Chrome River Technologies Inc 323 857-5800
5757 Wilshire Blvd # 270 Los Angeles (90036) ***(G-15082)***
Chronicle Broadcasting Co 415 561-8000
900 Front St San Francisco (94111) ***(G-5846)***
Chrysler Plymouth Dodge Jeep, Watsonville *Also called Marty Franich Leasing Co* ***(G-17702)***
Chsp Trs Fisherman Wharf LLC 415 563-1234
555 N Point St San Francisco (94133) ***(G-12517)***
Chsp Trs Los Angeles LLC 213 624-0000
535 S Grand Ave Los Angeles (90071) ***(G-12518)***
Chubb, Los Angeles *Also called Pacific Indemnity Company* ***(G-10821)***
Chubb, San Francisco *Also called Federal Insurance Company* ***(G-10716)***

A L P H A B E T I C

ALPHABETIC SECTION CIT Bank National Association

Chuck Jones Flying Service (PA).....530 868-5798
216 W Hamilton Rd Biggs (95917) *(G-478)*
Chukchansi Gold Resort Casino.....866 794-6946
711 Lucky Ln Coarsegold (93614) *(G-12519)*
Chula Vista Active Club, Chula Vista *Also called 24 Hour Fitness Usa Inc (G-18582)*
Chula Vista Veterans Center, Chula Vista *Also called Veterans Health Administration (G-20209)*
Chumash Casino Resort.....805 688-7997
100 Via Juana Rd Santa Ynez (93460) *(G-19165)*
Chumash Casino Resort (PA).....805 686-0855
3400 E Highway 246 Santa Ynez (93460) *(G-19166)*
Church & Larsen Inc.....626 303-8741
16103 Avenida Padilla Irwindale (91702) *(G-2877)*
Church Brothers LLC (PA).....831 796-1000
19065 Portola Dr Ste C Salinas (93908) *(G-52)*
Church of Scientology.....650 969-5262
3226 Scott Blvd Santa Clara (95054) *(G-23746)*
Church of Vly Rtrment Hmes Inc.....408 241-7750
390 N Winchester Blvd Ofc Santa Clara (95050) *(G-24599)*
Churchill Downs Incorporated.....502 638-3879
800 W El Camino Real Mountain View (94040) *(G-18568)*
Churchill MGT Group Corp.....877 937-7110
5900 Wilshire Blvd # 400 Los Angeles (90036) *(G-10133)*
Churchill PCF Asset MGT LLC.....213 489-3810
601 S Figueroa St # 2400 Los Angeles (90017) *(G-12110)*
Ciba Insurance Svcs Cal Inc (PA).....818 638-8525
655 N Central Ave # 2100 Glendale (91203) *(G-10670)*
CIC Research Inc.....858 637-4000
8361 Vickers St Ste 308 San Diego (92111) *(G-26649)*
Cicileo Landscapes.....805 967-3939
4565 Hollister Ave Santa Barbara (93110) *(G-758)*
Cie Digital Labs LLC (PA).....949 381-6200
19900 Macarthur Blvd # 1000 Irvine (92612) *(G-13993)*
Cie Games LLC.....415 800-6100
500 Howard St Ste 300 San Francisco (94105) *(G-15083)*
Cielo Azul Inc.....858 565-8344
7986 Dagget St San Diego (92111) *(G-824)*
Cierra Wireless.....760 476-8700
2738 Loker Ave W Ste A Carlsbad (92010) *(G-25737)*
Cific Energy Center, San Francisco *Also called Sodexo Management Inc (G-27221)*
Cigna Healthcare Cal Inc.....415 374-2500
1 Front St Ste 700 San Francisco (94111) *(G-10271)*
Cigna Healthcare Cal Inc (HQ).....818 500-6262
400 N Brand Blvd Ste 400 Glendale (91203) *(G-10272)*
Cigna Healthcare Cal Inc.....805 230-8300
2801 Townsgate Rd Ste 121 Thousand Oaks (91361) *(G-10273)*
Cigna Healthcare Cal Inc.....559 738-2000
5300 W Tulare Ave Ste 100 Visalia (93277) *(G-10274)*
Cignex Datamatics Inc (PA).....408 327-9900
2350 Mission College Blvd Santa Clara (95054) *(G-15084)*
Cik Power Distributors LLC.....714 938-0297
240 W Grove Ave Orange (92865) *(G-26965)*
Cim Group Inc (PA).....323 860-4900
4700 Wilshire Blvd Ste 1 Los Angeles (90010) *(G-11391)*
Cim/J Street Ht Sacramento Inc.....916 447-1700
1230 J St Sacramento (95814) *(G-12520)*
Cim/Oakland City Center LLC.....510 451-4000
1001 Broadway Oakland (94607) *(G-12521)*
Cimatron Gibbs LLC.....805 523-0004
323 Science Dr Moorpark (93021) *(G-15085)*
Cinderella Motel.....559 432-0118
1747 S Harbor Blvd Anaheim (92802) *(G-12522)*
Cinelease Inc (HQ).....855 441-5500
5375 W San Fernando Rd Los Angeles (90039) *(G-18218)*
Cinema City Theaters.....714 970-0865
5635 E La Palma Ave Anaheim (92807) *(G-18315)*
Cinemark 16 Bayfair.....510 276-9684
15555 E 14th St Ste 600 San Leandro (94578) *(G-18316)*
Cinemastar Luxury Theaters.....760 945-2500
1949 Avenida Del Oro # 100 Oceanside (92056) *(G-18317)*
Cinicas De Salud Del Pueblo, Brawley *Also called Afshan Baig MD (G-19325)*
Cinnabar.....818 842-8190
4571 Electronics Pl Los Angeles (90039) *(G-14137)*
Cinnabar California Inc.....818 842-8190
4571 Electronics Pl Los Angeles (90039) *(G-14138)*
Cinnabar Hills Golf Club, San Jose *Also called Traditions Golf LLC (G-18795)*
Cinovation Inc.....818 246-3160
6527 San Fernando Rd Glendale (91201) *(G-18061)*
Cintas Corporation.....925 743-1745
3201 Dnville Blvd Ste 285 Alamo (94507) *(G-13542)*
Cintas Corporation No 2.....310 635-8713
18050 Central Ave Carson (90746) *(G-13745)*
Cintas Corporation No 2.....408 292-6700
2188 Del Franco St Ste 70 San Jose (95131) *(G-13618)*
Cintas Corporation No 2.....714 288-8400
4320 E Miraloma Ave Anaheim (92807) *(G-9254)*
Cintas Corporation No 3.....661 282-4300
5500 Young St Bakersfield (93311) *(G-13619)*
Cintas Corporation No 3.....619 239-1001
675 32nd St San Diego (92102) *(G-13620)*
Cintas Corporation No 3.....562 692-8741
2829 Workman Mill Rd Whittier (90601) *(G-13543)*
Cintas Corporation No 3.....510 352-6330
777 139th Ave San Leandro (94578) *(G-13746)*
Cintas Corporation No 3.....909 930-9096
2150 Proforma Ave Ontario (91761) *(G-13544)*
Cintas Corporation No 3.....661 310-7400
28334 Industry Dr Valencia (91355) *(G-13545)*
Cintas Corporation No 3.....408 337-2910
904 Holloway Rd Gilroy (95020) *(G-13621)*
Cintas Corporation No 3.....510 352-6330
20929 Cabot Blvd Hayward (94545) *(G-13622)*
Cintas Corporation No 3.....310 725-2850
20100 S Susana Rd Compton (90221) *(G-13623)*
Cintas Corporation No 3.....916 419-8519
1231 National Dr Sacramento (95834) *(G-13624)*
Cintas Corporation No 3.....909 390-4912
1851 S Wineville Ave Ontario (91761) *(G-13625)*
Cintas Corporation No 3.....650 278-4004
370 Shaw Rd South San Francisco (94080) *(G-13626)*
Cintas Corporation No 3.....650 589-4300
220 Demeter St East Palo Alto (94303) *(G-13627)*
Cintas Corporation No 3.....510 573-5300
45133 Industrial Dr Fremont (94538) *(G-13628)*
Cintiva Financial Corporation.....858 526-0955
10145 Pacific Hts 800 San Diego (92121) *(G-9917)*
Ciphermax Inc (PA).....408 382-6500
1975 Concourse Dr San Jose (95131) *(G-27381)*
Cir.....650 574-6900
1745 Celeste Dr San Mateo (94402) *(G-26496)*
Circle K Ranch.....559 834-1571
8640 E Manning Ave Selma (93662) *(G-146)*
Circle Marina Car Wash Inc.....562 494-4698
4800 E Pacific Coast Hwy Long Beach (90804) *(G-17836)*
Circle Marina Hand Car Wash, Long Beach *Also called Circle Marina Car Wash Inc (G-17836)*
Circle W Enterprises Inc.....661 257-2400
27737 Avenue Hopkins Valencia (91355) *(G-7427)*
Circle Wood Services Inc.....909 784-0733
3670 W Temple Ave Pomona (91768) *(G-26966)*
Circulating Air Inc (PA).....818 764-0530
7337 Varna Ave North Hollywood (91605) *(G-2180)*
Cirks Construction Inc.....916 362-5460
3300 Industrial Blvd West Sacramento (95691) *(G-1527)*
Cirrus Enterprises LLC.....310 204-6159
18027 Bishop Ave Carson (90746) *(G-8967)*
Cirrus Health II LP.....949 855-0562
24331 El Toro Rd Ste 150 Laguna Hills (92637) *(G-19438)*
CIS Security, Fresno *Also called Geil Enterprises Inc (G-16664)*
Cisco Ironport Systems LLC (HQ).....650 989-6500
170 W Tasman Dr San Jose (95134) *(G-15620)*
Cisco Systems, Rancho Cordova *Also called Cisco Webex LLC (G-5576)*
Cisco Webex LLC.....916 861-3135
2868 Prospect Park Dr # 500 Rancho Cordova (95670) *(G-5576)*
Cisco Webex LLC (HQ).....408 435-7000
3979 Freedom Cir Ste 100 Santa Clara (95054) *(G-17072)*
CIT Bank NA.....310 477-0546
11310 National Blvd Los Angeles (90064) *(G-9342)*
CIT Bank NA.....949 598-9621
23072 Alicia Pkwy Mission Viejo (92692) *(G-9343)*
CIT Bank NA (HQ).....626 535-4300
888 E Walnut St Pasadena (91101) *(G-9344)*
CIT Bank NA.....805 379-5520
199 E Thousand Oaks Blvd Thousand Oaks (91360) *(G-9345)*
CIT Bank National Association.....818 885-9065
20505 Devonshire St Chatsworth (91311) *(G-9346)*
CIT Bank National Association.....323 767-1180
900 Huntington Dr San Marino (91108) *(G-9347)*
CIT Bank National Association.....760 771-3498
78010 Main St La Quinta (92253) *(G-9348)*
CIT Bank National Association.....310 727-5660
1570 Rosecrans Ave Manhattan Beach (90266) *(G-9349)*
CIT Bank National Association.....626 435-2260
220 N Hacienda Blvd City of Industry (91744) *(G-9350)*
CIT Bank National Association.....909 631-2560
3410 Grand Ave Ste A Chino Hills (91709) *(G-9351)*
CIT Bank National Association.....310 475-4594
2920 N Beverly Glen Cir Los Angeles (90077) *(G-9352)*
CIT Bank National Association.....310 372-8473
1100 Pacific Coast Hwy Hermosa Beach (90254) *(G-9353)*
CIT Bank National Association.....818 502-8400
1111 N Brand Blvd Ste A Glendale (91202) *(G-9354)*
CIT Bank National Association.....310 394-1640
401 Wilshire Blvd Santa Monica (90401) *(G-9355)*
CIT Bank National Association.....310 826-2741
11611 San Vicente Blvd Los Angeles (90049) *(G-9356)*
CIT Bank National Association.....310 452-3802
1750 Ocean Park Blvd Santa Monica (90405) *(G-9357)*
CIT Bank National Association.....310 390-7745
5573 Sepulveda Blvd Culver City (90230) *(G-9358)*
CIT Bank National Association.....310 399-9262
2827 Main St Santa Monica (90405) *(G-9359)*
CIT Bank National Association.....805 465-1053
1727 E Daily Dr Camarillo (93010) *(G-9360)*
CIT Bank National Association.....818 525-3760
1001 N San Fernando Blvd Burbank (91504) *(G-9361)*
CIT Bank National Association.....949 454-4100
25624 Alicia Pkwy Laguna Hills (92653) *(G-9362)*
CIT Bank National Association.....949 347-7014
28311 Marguerite Pkwy B Mission Viejo (92692) *(G-9363)*
CIT Bank National Association.....818 817-5320
17050 Ventura Blvd # 100 Encino (91316) *(G-9364)*
CIT Bank National Association.....310 559-7222
10784 Jefferson Blvd Culver City (90230) *(G-9365)*
CIT Bank National Association.....562 433-0972
3500 E 7th St Long Beach (90804) *(G-9366)*
CIT Bank National Association.....805 496-4034
3835 E Thusand Oaks Blvd Westlake Village (91362) *(G-9367)*
CIT Bank National Association.....310 577-6142
13405 Washington Blvd Marina Del Rey (90292) *(G-9368)*

ALPHABETIC

CIT Bank National Association 310 820-9650
12401 Wilshire Blvd Los Angeles (90025) ***(G-9369)***
CIT Bank National Association 310 829-4477
1630 Montana Ave Santa Monica (90403) ***(G-9370)***
CIT Bank National Association 949 675-2890
3700 E Coast Hwy Corona Del Mar (92625) ***(G-9371)***
CIT Bank National Association 323 838-6881
5701 S Eastrn Ave Ste 108 Commerce (90040) ***(G-9372)***
CIT Bank National Association 310 265-1656
30019 Hawthorne Blvd Rancho Palos Verdes (90275) ***(G-9373)***
Citadel Broadcasting Corp 310 840-4900
3321 S La Cienega Blvd Los Angeles (90016) ***(G-5764)***
Citadel Broadcasting Corp 209 766-5103
3136 Boeing Way 125 Stockton (95206) ***(G-5765)***
Citadel Group Solutions LLC 310 649-7500
6601 Center Dr W Fl 5 Los Angeles (90045) ***(G-15921)***
Citadel Roofing & Solar 707 446-5500
4980 Allison Pkwy Vacaville (95688) ***(G-3150)***
Citadel Security Inc 562 248-2300
5199 E Pacific Cst Hwy # 200 Long Beach (90804) ***(G-16597)***
Citco Fund Svcs San Francisco 415 228-0390
560 Mission St Fl 26 San Francisco (94105) ***(G-10134)***
Citibank National Association 415 431-6940
150 Pennsylvania Ave San Francisco (94107) ***(G-9374)***
Citibank National Association 619 870-0609
2240 Otay Lakes Rd 304-3 Chula Vista (91915) ***(G-9375)***
Citibank N A 805 497-7361
3967 E Thousand Oaks Blvd Westlake Village (91362) ***(G-9376)***
Citibank N A 800 627-3999
3580 Tyler St Riverside (92503) ***(G-9377)***
Citibank N A 415 627-6000
1 Sansome St Fl 28 San Francisco (94104) ***(G-9569)***
Citigroup Global Markets Inc 213 486-8811
444 S Flower St Fl 35 Los Angeles (90071) ***(G-9973)***
Citigroup Global Markets Inc 310 285-6500
9665 Wilshire Blvd # 600 Beverly Hills (90212) ***(G-9974)***
Citigroup Global Markets Inc 310 727-9533
2381 Rosecrans Ave # 115 El Segundo (90245) ***(G-9975)***
Citigroup Global Markets Inc 916 567-2056
155 Cadillac Dr Fl 1 Sacramento (95825) ***(G-9976)***
Citigroup Global Markets Inc 858 597-7777
4350 La Jolla Village Dr San Diego (92122) ***(G-9977)***
Citigroup Global Markets Inc 310 540-9511
21250 Hawthorne Blvd # 650 Torrance (90503) ***(G-9978)***
Citigroup Global Markets Inc 949 955-7500
1901 Main St Ste 800 Irvine (92614) ***(G-9979)***
Citigroup Global Markets Inc 858 456-4900
1225 Prospect St La Jolla (92037) ***(G-9980)***
Citigroup Global Markets Inc 559 438-2542
5250 N Palm Ave Ste 321 Fresno (93704) ***(G-9981)***
Citigroup Global Markets Inc 310 544-3600
609 Deep Valley Dr # 400 Rllng HLS Est (90274) ***(G-9982)***
Citigroup Global Markets Inc 909 625-0781
456 W Foothill Blvd Claremont (91711) ***(G-9983)***
Citigroup Global Markets Inc 650 926-7600
2775 Sand Hill Rd Ste 120 Menlo Park (94025) ***(G-9984)***
Citigroup Inc 805 557-0930
325 E Hillcrest Dr Thousand Oaks (91360) ***(G-9378)***
Citigroup Inc 909 335-0547
300 E State St Redlands (92373) ***(G-9379)***
Citigroup Inc 818 638-5714
787 W 5th St Los Angeles (90071) ***(G-9380)***
Citigroup Inc 949 726-5124
3996 Barranca Pkwy # 130 Irvine (92606) ***(G-9381)***
Citigroup Inc 619 498-3158
352 H St Chula Vista (91910) ***(G-9382)***
Citigroup Inc 415 617-8524
1 Sansome St Fl 27 San Francisco (94104) ***(G-9985)***
Citigroup Inc 714 938-0748
840 N Eckhoff St Ste 140 Orange (92868) ***(G-9831)***
Citimortgage Inc 925 730-3800
6160 Stoneridge Mall Rd # 150 Pleasanton (94588) ***(G-9986)***
Citiscape Prprty MGT Group LLC 415 674-1440
3450 3rd St Ste 1a San Francisco (94124) ***(G-11392)***
Citisite Co, Jackson *Also called Citisite Inc* ***(G-7548)***
Citisite Inc 209 418-7620
11400 State Highway 49 Jackson (95642) ***(G-7548)***
Citivest Inc 949 474-0440
4340 Von Karman Ave # 110 Newport Beach (92660) ***(G-11393)***
Citizen Potawatomi Nation 559 635-1039
31150 Road 180 Visalia (93292) ***(G-9383)***
Citizenhawk Inc 949 427-3002
135 Columbia Aliso Viejo (92656) ***(G-26967)***
Citizens Business Bank (HQ) 909 980-4030
701 N Haven Ave Ste 350 Ontario (91764) ***(G-9484)***
Citizens Business Bank 949 440-5200
1401 Dove St Ste 100 Newport Beach (92660) ***(G-9485)***
Citizens Business Bank 818 843-0707
4100 W Alameda Ave # 101 Burbank (91505) ***(G-9384)***
Citizens Business Bank 661 281-0300
1230 17th St Bakersfield (93301) ***(G-9486)***
Citizens Business Bank Arena, Ontario *Also called AEG Ontario Arena LLC* ***(G-18533)***
Citizens Choice Health Plan, Orange *Also called Alignment Health Plan* ***(G-10255)***
Citizens Development Corp (PA) 760 744-0120
1105 La Bonita Dr San Marcos (92078) ***(G-18917)***
Citrix Systems Inc 805 690-6400
7414 Hollister Ave Goleta (93117) ***(G-15086)***
Citrix Systems Inc 408 790-8000
4988 Great America Pkwy Santa Clara (95054) ***(G-15087)***
Citrus Heights Sport Club, San Ramon *Also called 24 Hour Fitness Usa Inc* ***(G-18589)***
Citrus Valley Home Health, West Covina *Also called Citrus Valley Hospice* ***(G-20458)***
Citrus Valley Hospice 626 859-2263
820 N Phillips Ave West Covina (91791) ***(G-20458)***
Citrus Valley Medical Ctr Inc (PA) 626 962-4011
1115 S Sunset Ave West Covina (91790) ***(G-21488)***
Citrus Valley Medical Ctr Inc 626 858-8515
140 W College St Covina (91723) ***(G-21489)***
Citrus Valley Medical Ctr Inc 626 963-8411
1115 S Sunset Ave West Covina (91790) ***(G-21490)***
Citrus Valley Medical Ctr Inc 626 331-7331
210 W San Bernardino Rd Covina (91723) ***(G-21491)***
Citrus Vly Hlth Partners Inc 626 962-4011
1115 S Sunset Ave West Covina (91790) ***(G-19439)***
Citrus Vly Hlth Partners Inc (PA) 626 331-7331
210 W San Bernardino Rd Covina (91723) ***(G-26968)***
Citrus Vly Hlth Partners Inc 626 732-3100
1325 N Grand Ave Ste 300 Covina (91724) ***(G-22920)***
City & County of San Francisco 415 553-1706
850 Bryant St Ste 200 San Francisco (94103) ***(G-23747)***
City & County of San Francisco 415 621-6600
401 Van Ness Ave Ste 110 San Francisco (94102) ***(G-18381)***
City & County of San Francisco 415 621-6600
401 Van Ness Ave Ste 110 San Francisco (94102) ***(G-18382)***
City & County of San Francisco 415 581-3500
200 Larkin St San Francisco (94102) ***(G-25009)***
City & County of San Francisco 415 206-8000
1001 Potrero Ave San Francisco (94110) ***(G-21492)***
City & County of San Francisco 415 557-4713
30 Van Ness Ave Ste 4100 San Francisco (94102) ***(G-25128)***
City & County of San Francisco 415 759-2300
375 Laguna Honda Blvd San Francisco (94116) ***(G-21493)***
City & County of San Francisco 415 554-4700
1 Carlton B Goodlett Pl # 234 San Francisco (94102) ***(G-23150)***
City & County of San Francisco 415 553-1752
850 Bryant St Ste 600 San Francisco (94103) ***(G-23151)***
City & County of San Francisco 415 753-7561
375 Woodside Ave 1 San Francisco (94127) ***(G-23748)***
City & County of San Francisco 415 554-4799
1 Carlton B Goodlett Pl # 234 San Francisco (94102) ***(G-26969)***
City Alameda Health Care Corp (PA) 510 522-3700
2070 Clinton Ave Alameda (94501) ***(G-21494)***
City Alameda Health Care Corp 510 814-4000
2070 Clinton Ave Alameda (94501) ***(G-26970)***
CITY ARTS ACADEMY, San Diego *Also called Harmonium Inc* ***(G-24466)***
City Attorney, Los Angeles *Also called City of Los Angeles* ***(G-23155)***
City Attorney, San Francisco *Also called City & County of San Francisco* ***(G-23150)***
City Attorneys Office, Long Beach *Also called City of Long Beach* ***(G-23153)***
City Charter School 310 273-2489
11625 W Pico Blvd Los Angeles (90064) ***(G-3898)***
City Club On Bunker Hill, Los Angeles *Also called Bunker Hill Club Inc* ***(G-25224)***
City Corporation Yard, Delano *Also called City of Delano* ***(G-18723)***
City Fashion Express Inc 310 223-1010
2888 E El Presidio St Carson (90810) ***(G-5048)***
City Fibers Inc (PA) 323 583-1013
2500 S Santa Fe Ave Vernon (90058) ***(G-8069)***
City Fibers Inc 323 583-1013
2525 E 25th St Vernon (90058) ***(G-4536)***
City Hall, Ventura *Also called Ventura Streets Dept* ***(G-1280)***
City Hall Pblc Wrks Eng Dpt, San Bernardino *Also called San Bernardino California City* ***(G-26052)***
City Hanford Public Imprv Corp 559 585-2550
900 S 10th Ave Hanford (93230) ***(G-1920)***
City Hope Development Center, Duarte *Also called City of Hope* ***(G-24889)***
City Hope National Medical Ctr 626 256-4673
1500 Duarte Rd Duarte (91010) ***(G-21495)***
City II Enterprises Inc 408 275-1200
845 Earle Ave San Jose (95126) ***(G-825)***
City Impact 415 292-1770
230 Jones St Fl 1 San Francisco (94102) ***(G-25517)***
City Impact Inc 805 983-3636
829 N A St Oxnard (93030) ***(G-23749)***
City Leasing & Rentals 619 276-6171
2111 Morena Blvd San Diego (92110) ***(G-17698)***
City Long Bch Prkg Enforcement, Long Beach *Also called City of Long Beach* ***(G-6622)***
City Los Angeles General Svcs, Los Angeles *Also called City of Los Angeles* ***(G-23154)***
City Mnterey Pk Recreation Ctr, Monterey Park *Also called City of Monterey Park* ***(G-19176)***
City National Bank (HQ) 310 888-6000
555 S Flower St Ste 2500 Los Angeles (90071) ***(G-9385)***
City National Bank 951 276-8800
3484 Central Ave Riverside (92506) ***(G-9386)***
City National Bank 619 645-6100
225 Broadway Ste 500 San Diego (92101) ***(G-9387)***
City National Bank 310 297-6606
2100 Park Pl Ste 150 El Segundo (90245) ***(G-9388)***
City National Investments, San Diego *Also called City National Bank* ***(G-9387)***
City National SEC Svcs Inc 310 641-6666
6151 W Century Blvd # 916 Los Angeles (90045) ***(G-16598)***
City of Anaheim 714 704-2400
2695 E Katella Ave Anaheim (92806) ***(G-10971)***
City of Antioch 925 779-6950
1201 W 4th St Antioch (94509) ***(G-6620)***
City of Arcadia 626 574-5435
240 W Huntington Dr Arcadia (91007) ***(G-3638)***
City of Bakersfield 661 852-7300
1001 Truxtun Ave Bakersfield (93301) ***(G-23750)***
City of Bell 323 773-1596
6330 Pine Ave Bell (90201) ***(G-23751)***

ALPHABETIC

ALPHABETIC SECTION City of Pasadena

City of Berkeley..............510 981-6750
2180 Milvia St Berkeley (94704) ***(G-26311)***
City of Beverly Hills..............310 285-2552
342 Foothill Rd Beverly Hills (90210) ***(G-17716)***
City of Brea..............714 990-7650
1 Civic Center Cir Fl 3 Brea (92821) ***(G-27778)***
City of Burbank..............818 238-3550
164 W Magnolia Blvd Burbank (91502) ***(G-6284)***
City of Calexico (PA)..............760 768-2130
608 Heber Ave Calexico (92231) ***(G-3781)***
City of Carson..............310 835-0212
3 Civic Plaza Dr Carson (90745) ***(G-23752)***
City of Chino..............909 591-9843
5050 Schaefer Ave Chino (91710) ***(G-6621)***
City of Chula Vista..............619 691-5137
276 4th Ave Chula Vista (91910) ***(G-17073)***
City of Commerce..............323 722-4805
2535 Commerce Way Commerce (90040) ***(G-19167)***
City of Compton..............310 635-3484
1108 N Oleander Ave Compton (90222) ***(G-19168)***
City of Concord..............925 692-2400
2000 Kirker Pass Rd Concord (94521) ***(G-18383)***
City of Concord..............925 686-6262
4050 Port Chicago Hwy Concord (94520) ***(G-18722)***
City of Corona..............951 279-3647
400 S Vicentia Ave Corona (92882) ***(G-27741)***
City of Corona..............951 736-2266
400 S Vicentia Ave # 210 Corona (92882) ***(G-6301)***
City of Coronado..............619 522-7342
1845 Strand Way Coronado (92118) ***(G-19169)***
City of Coronado..............619 522-7380
101 B Ave Coronado (92118) ***(G-6285)***
City of Daly City..............650 991-8064
333 90th St Fl 1 Daly City (94015) ***(G-25738)***
City of Delano..............661 721-3350
725 S Lexington St Delano (93215) ***(G-18723)***
City of Downey..............562 861-8211
8435 Firestone Blvd Downey (90241) ***(G-18384)***
City of El Centro..............760 337-4505
307 W Brighton Ave El Centro (92243) ***(G-1748)***
City of Encinitas..............760 633-2850
160 Calle Magdalena Encinitas (92024) ***(G-1749)***
City of Fairfield..............707 428-7435
1000 Webster St Fairfield (94533) ***(G-10972)***
City of Folsom..............916 355-7285
50 Natoma St Folsom (95630) ***(G-19170)***
City of Foster City..............650 286-3380
650 Shell Blvd Foster City (94404) ***(G-19171)***
City of Fremont..............510 791-4196
34600 Ardenwood Blvd Fremont (94555) ***(G-25010)***
City of Fremont..............510 494-4460
39550 Liberty St Fremont (94538) ***(G-26177)***
City of Fresno..............559 621-4500
5175 E Clinton Way Fresno (93727) ***(G-4906)***
City of Fresno..............559 621-5300
1910 E University Ave Fresno (93703) ***(G-6324)***
City of Fresno..............559 445-8200
700 M St Fresno (93721) ***(G-17074)***
City of Fresno..............559 621-7080
2828 Fresno St Ste 201 Fresno (93721) ***(G-12138)***
City of Fullerton..............714 738-6897
1580 W Commonwealth Ave Fullerton (92833) ***(G-27382)***
City of Galt..............209 366-7180
660 Chabolla Ave Galt (95632) ***(G-19172)***
City of Gardena..............310 324-1475
13999 S Western Ave Gardena (90249) ***(G-3639)***
City of Glendale..............818 548-3945
633 E Broadway Ste 205 Glendale (91206) ***(G-25739)***
City of Glendale..............818 548-3950
541 W Chevy Chase Dr Glendale (91204) ***(G-18542)***
City of Glendale..............818 548-3300
141 N Glendale Ave Fl 2 Glendale (91206) ***(G-6112)***
City of Glendale..............818 548-3980
634 Bekins Way Glendale (91201) ***(G-6113)***
City of Glendale..............818 548-2011
800 Air Way Glendale (91201) ***(G-6325)***
City of Hope..............626 396-2900
209 Fair Oaks Ave South Pasadena (91030) ***(G-19440)***
City of Hope..............213 202-5735
1500 Duarte Rd Duarte (91010) ***(G-24889)***
City of Hope..............626 256-4673
2701 Santa Rosa Ave Altadena (91001) ***(G-28123)***
City of Hope Medical Group, South Pasadena *Also called City of Hope* ***(G-19440)***
City of Industry Disposal Co..............626 336-5439
17445 Railroad St City of Industry (91748) ***(G-6459)***
City of Inglewood..............310 412-5370
700 Warren Ln Inglewood (90302) ***(G-19173)***
City of Irvine..............949 724-7600
6427 Oak Cyn Irvine (92618) ***(G-27383)***
City of Irvine..............949 724-7740
6443 Oak Cyn Irvine (92618) ***(G-19174)***
City of Irvine..............949 724-7101
1 Civic Center Plz Irvine (92606) ***(G-25129)***
City of La Habra..............562 905-9708
101 W La Habra Blvd La Habra (90631) ***(G-23753)***
City of La Mesa..............619 667-1450
8152 Commercial St La Mesa (91942) ***(G-1750)***
City of Livermore..............925 960-8100
101 W Jack London Blvd Livermore (94551) ***(G-2041)***
City of Lomita..............310 325-7114
24300 Narbonne Ave Lomita (90717) ***(G-6326)***
City of Lomita..............310 325-9830
24373 Walnut St Lomita (90717) ***(G-6327)***
City of Long Beach..............562 570-7298
333 W Ocean Blvd Fl 4 Long Beach (90802) ***(G-17075)***
City of Long Beach..............562 570-2828
2600 Temple Ave Long Beach (90806) ***(G-17788)***
City of Long Beach..............562 570-5423
2600 Temple Ave Long Beach (90806) ***(G-23152)***
City of Long Beach..............562 570-2890
2929 E Willow St Long Beach (90806) ***(G-6622)***
City of Long Beach..............562 570-2000
2400 E Spring St Long Beach (90806) ***(G-6296)***
City of Long Beach..............562 570-2600
4100 E Don Douglas Dr Fl Flr 2 Long Beach (90808) ***(G-4907)***
City of Long Beach..............562 436-3636
300 E Ocean Blvd Long Beach (90802) ***(G-17076)***
City of Long Beach..............562 570-6919
333 W Ocean Blvd Lbby Long Beach (90802) ***(G-23153)***
City of Long Beach..............562 570-2390
1800 E Wardlow Rd Long Beach (90807) ***(G-6328)***
City of Los Angeles..............213 978-0259
600 S Spring St Unit 200 Los Angeles (90014) ***(G-25740)***
City of Los Angeles..............310 522-1750
161 Island Ave Wilmington (90744) ***(G-6114)***
City of Los Angeles..............213 978-4049
111 E 1st St Ste 401 Los Angeles (90012) ***(G-23154)***
City of Los Angeles..............310 732-3550
500 Pier A Pl Wilmington (90744) ***(G-3955)***
City of Los Angeles..............213 473-0800
2800 E Observatory Ave Los Angeles (90027) ***(G-25011)***
City of Los Angeles..............213 485-4282
1149 S Broadway Ste 800 Los Angeles (90015) ***(G-26178)***
City of Los Angeles..............818 756-8022
6262 Van Nuys Blvd # 451 Van Nuys (91401) ***(G-25741)***
City of Los Angeles..............213 202-5500
201 N Figueroa St # 1400 Los Angeles (90012) ***(G-25518)***
City of Los Angeles..............213 847-2799
3330 W 36th St Los Angeles (90018) ***(G-14247)***
City of Los Angeles..............213 978-8100
200 N Main St Ste 800 Los Angeles (90012) ***(G-23155)***
City of Los Angeles..............310 732-7681
425 S Palos Verdes St San Pedro (90731) ***(G-4746)***
City of Los Angeles..............818 902-3000
6550 Van Nuys Blvd Van Nuys (91401) ***(G-6115)***
City of Los Angeles..............323 467-7193
3200 Canyon Dr Los Angeles (90068) ***(G-13462)***
City of Los Angeles..............213 485-4981
2513 E 24th St Vernon (90058) ***(G-3956)***
City of Los Angeles..............818 908-5950
16461 Sherman Way Ste 210 Van Nuys (91406) ***(G-4908)***
City of Los Angeles..............310 204-6707
1762 S La Cienega Blvd Los Angeles (90035) ***(G-23754)***
City of Los Angeles..............213 978-4551
360 E 2nd St Ste 400 Los Angeles (90012) ***(G-10548)***
City of Mill Valley..............415 383-1370
180 Camino Alto Mill Valley (94941) ***(G-19175)***
City of Mill Valley..............415 388-4033
26 Corte Madera Ave Mill Valley (94941) ***(G-1751)***
City of Monterey Park..............626 307-1388
320 W Newmark Ave Fl 1 Monterey Park (91754) ***(G-19176)***
City of Moorpark..............805 517-6261
799 Moorpark Ave Moorpark (93021) ***(G-23755)***
City of Morgan Hill..............408 776-7333
100 Edes St Morgan Hill (95037) ***(G-27880)***
City of Morro Bay, Morro Bay *Also called Morro Bay Public Works* ***(G-1829)***
City of NAPA..............707 255-7631
1151 Pearl St NAPA (94559) ***(G-3876)***
City of Norwalk, Norwalk *Also called Norwalk Transit System* ***(G-3684)***
City of Oakland..............510 238-6796
150 Frank H Ogawa Plz # 3332 Oakland (94612) ***(G-23756)***
City of Oakland..............510 238-3494
250 Frank H Ogawa Plz # 6301 Oakland (94612) ***(G-19177)***
City of Oakland..............510 268-9000
519 18th St Oakland (94612) ***(G-19178)***
City of Orange..............714 744-7264
230 E Chapman Ave Orange (92866) ***(G-23757)***
City of Orange..............714 744-7272
230 E Chapman Ave Orange (92866) ***(G-19179)***
City of Oxnard..............805 385-8019
350 N C St Oxnard (93030) ***(G-23758)***
City of Oxnard..............805 385-8136
251 S Hayes Ave Oxnard (93030) ***(G-6329)***
City of Oxnard..............805 385-7950
1060 Pacific Ave Oxnard (93030) ***(G-18814)***
City of Oxnard..............805 983-4653
2401 W Vineyard Ave Oxnard (93036) ***(G-18724)***
City of Pacifica-Vallemar..............650 738-7466
170 Santa Maria Ave Pacifica (94044) ***(G-24439)***
City of Palm Springs..............760 318-3800
3400 E Thqitz Cyn Way Ofc Palm Springs (92262) ***(G-4909)***
City of Palmdale..............661 267-5338
39101 3rd St E Palmdale (93550) ***(G-14248)***
City of Palo Alto..............650 329-2598
2501 Embarcadero Way Palo Alto (94303) ***(G-17077)***
City of Pasadena..............626 744-4311
117 E Colorado Blvd Pasadena (91105) ***(G-14249)***
City of Pasadena..............626 405-4409
45 E Glenarm St Pasadena (91105) ***(G-6302)***
City of Pasadena..............626 543-4708
1133 Rosemont Ave Pasadena (91103) ***(G-18725)***

ALPHABETIC

City of Pomona......909 397-5506
2040 W Holt Ave Fl 2 Pomona (91768) **(G-24890)**
City of Pomona......909 620-2361
636 W Monterey Ave Pomona (91768) **(G-6460)**
City of Rancho Cucamonga, The, Rancho Cucamonga *Also called Lewis Family Playhouse* **(G-25549)**
City of Redlands......909 798-7525
35 Cajon St Redlands (92373) **(G-6461)**
City of Richmond......510 620-6788
3230 Macdonald Ave Fl 2 Richmond (94804) **(G-19180)**
City of Riverside......951 346-4700
3485 Mission Inn Ave Riverside (92501) **(G-17078)**
City of Salinas......831 758-7233
426 Work St Salinas (93901) **(G-14250)**
City of San Diego......619 533-3012
1010 2nd Ave Ste 800 San Diego (92101) **(G-27881)**
City of San Diego......619 533-6518
202 C St Ms37c San Diego (92101) **(G-22129)**
City of San Diego......858 627-3210
9485 Aero Dr San Diego (92123) **(G-25742)**
City of San Jose......408 277-5277
408 Almaden Blvd San Jose (95110) **(G-17079)**
City of San Jose......408 794-6400
1300 Senter Rd San Jose (95112) **(G-25061)**
City of San Jose......408 392-3600
1701 Arprt Blvd Ste B1130 San Jose (95110) **(G-4910)**
City of San Jose......408 226-6765
200 Edenvale Ave San Jose (95136) **(G-12523)**
City of San Mateo......650 522-7300
1949 Pacific Blvd San Mateo (94403) **(G-14251)**
City of Santa Clara......408 615-3770
2600 Benton St Santa Clara (95051) **(G-3508)**
City of Santa Clara......408 615-2300
1500 Warburton Ave Santa Clara (95050) **(G-6116)**
City of Santa Clara......408 615-2046
1705 Martin Ave Santa Clara (95050) **(G-6117)**
City of Santa Clra Parks Svc, Santa Clara *Also called City of Santa Clara* **(G-3508)**
City of Santa Monica......310 451-5444
1660 7th St Santa Monica (90401) **(G-3877)**
City of South Lake Tahoe......530 542-6056
1180 Rufus Allen Blvd South Lake Tahoe (96150) **(G-19181)**
City of Sunnyvale......408 730-7451
456 W Olive Ave Sunnyvale (94086) **(G-13490)**
City of Sunnyvale......408 730-7510
221 Commercial St Sunnyvale (94085) **(G-17080)**
City of Sunnyvale Nova......408 730-7232
505 W Olive Ave Ste 550 Sunnyvale (94086) **(G-14625)**
City of Torrance......310 781-6901
20500 Madrona Ave Torrance (90503) **(G-19182)**
City of Tulare......559 684-4200
3981 S K St Tulare (93274) **(G-6462)**
City of Vacaville......707 449-6122
1100 Alamo Dr Vacaville (95687) **(G-23759)**
City of Vacaville......707 449-5170
650 Merchant St Vacaville (95688) **(G-25743)**
City of Vallejo......707 644-4000
1001 Fairgrounds Dr Vallejo (94589) **(G-18815)**
City of Visalia......559 713-4000
303 E Acequia Ave Visalia (93291) **(G-17081)**
City of Vista......760 940-9283
101 Wave Dr Vista (92083) **(G-19183)**
City of Whittier......562 567-9446
7630 Washington Ave Whittier (90602) **(G-23760)**
City of Woodland......530 661-5878
2001 East St Woodland (95776) **(G-19184)**
City of Woodland......530 661-5962
655 N Pioneer Ave Woodland (95776) **(G-27779)**
City of Woodland......530 661-5961
42929 County Road 24 Woodland (95776) **(G-25744)**
City Oxnard Prfrmg Arts Ctr, Oxnard *Also called Oxnard Perfrmn Arts & Convtn* **(G-17387)**
City Park, San Francisco *Also called Imperial Parking (us) LLC* **(G-17718)**
City Rescue Mission, San Diego *Also called San Diego Rescue Mission Inc* **(G-24974)**
City Security Co Inc......626 458-2325
430 S Grfield Ave Ste 401 Alhambra (91801) **(G-16599)**
City Towel & Dust Service Inc......707 542-0391
3016 Dutton Ave Santa Rosa (95407) **(G-13546)**
City Ventures LLC (PA)......949 258-7555
3121 Michelson Dr Ste 150 Irvine (92612) **(G-11394)**
Citywide Limo Services Inc......424 335-9818
3202 E Foothill Blvd Pasadena (91107) **(G-3863)**
Citywide Plumbing Heating......619 231-2022
9825 Carroll Centre Rd San Diego (92126) **(G-2181)**
Civco, Rcho STA Marg *Also called Capital Invstmnts Vntures Corp* **(G-25127)**
Civic Auditorium, Santa Monica *Also called Santa Monica City of* **(G-11040)**
CIVIC THEATRE, San Diego *Also called San Diego Theatres Inc* **(G-11039)**
Civicorps......510 992-7800
6315 San Leandro St Oakland (94621) **(G-6463)**
Civil Service Commission, Oakland *Also called County of Alameda* **(G-27391)**
CJ America Inc (HQ)......213 738-1400
3530 Wilshire Blvd # 1220 Los Angeles (90010) **(G-8983)**
CJ Construction & Dev Inc......760 247-6868
78206 Varner Rd Ste D Palm Desert (92211) **(G-1301)**
CJ Model Home Maintenance Inc......925 485-3280
240 Spring St Pleasanton (94566) **(G-14252)**
CJJ Farming Inc......805 739-1723
125 W Mill St Santa Maria (93458) **(G-107)**
CK Enterprises Inc......760 967-8863
110 Copperwood Way Ste K Oceanside (92058) **(G-17082)**
Ckl Construction Inc......408 244-7042
967 W Hedding St San Jose (95126) **(G-1302)**
Cks Business Services, Bakersfield *Also called Cbiz Southern California LLC* **(G-26308)**
CL Knox Inc......661 837-0477
34933 Imperial St Bakersfield (93308) **(G-1071)**
Claim Jumper Restaurant......949 461-7170
27845 Snta Margarita Pkwy Mission Viejo (92691) **(G-1528)**
Claims Management Inc......916 631-1250
1101 Crksde Rdge Dr 100 Roseville (95678) **(G-10671)**
Clairemont Healthcare......858 278-4750
8060 Frost St San Diego (92123) **(G-20459)**
Clairemont Medical Offices, San Diego *Also called Kaiser Foundation Hospitals* **(G-19660)**
Clairmont Camera Inc (PA)......818 761-4440
4343 Lankershim Blvd North Hollywood (91602) **(G-14523)**
Clandestine Laboratory Invest......760 597-7946
1704 E Bullard Ave Fresno (93710) **(G-26838)**
Clara......415 342-9740
169 11th St San Francisco (94103) **(G-7108)**
Clara Baldwin Stocker Home......626 962-7151
527 S Valinda Ave West Covina (91790) **(G-21186)**
Clarabridge Inc......415 721-1300
900 Larkspur Landing Cir Larkspur (94939) **(G-16335)**
Clarbec Inc......707 996-4012
19368 Orange Ave Sonoma (95476) **(G-147)**
Clare Foundation Inc (PA)......310 314-6200
909 Pico Blvd Santa Monica (90405) **(G-23761)**
Clare Foundation Inc......310 314-6200
1871 9th St Santa Monica (90404) **(G-23762)**
Claremont Club, The, Claremont *Also called Claremont Tennis Club* **(G-18919)**
Claremont Country Club......510 653-6789
5295 Broadway Ter Oakland (94618) **(G-18918)**
Claremont Hotel Club & Spa, Berkeley *Also called Claremont Ht Prpts Ltd Partnr* **(G-12524)**
Claremont House Incorporated......510 658-9266
4500 Gilbert St Oakland (94611) **(G-24600)**
Claremont Ht Prpts Ltd Partnr......510 843-3000
41 Tunnel Rd Berkeley (94705) **(G-12524)**
Claremont Manor, Claremont *Also called Front Porch Communities* **(G-21221)**
Claremont Outpatient Clinic, Claremont *Also called Pomona Valley Hospital Med Ctr* **(G-21803)**
Claremont Resort, Berkeley *Also called Interstate Hotels Resorts Inc* **(G-12851)**
Claremont Retirement MGT, Oakland *Also called Claremont House Incorporated* **(G-24600)**
Claremont Star LP......909 482-0124
555 W Foothill Blvd Claremont (91711) **(G-12525)**
Claremont Tennis Club......909 625-9515
1777 Monte Vista Ave Claremont (91711) **(G-18919)**
Clarence Unruh Farms Inc......559 896-9499
14242 S Mccall Ave Selma (93662) **(G-230)**
Clarient Diagnostic Svcs Inc......888 443-3310
31 Columbia Aliso Viejo (92656) **(G-22200)**
Clarion Construction Inc......909 598-4060
21067 Commerce Point Dr Walnut (91789) **(G-1414)**
Clarion Corporation America (HQ)......310 327-9100
6200 Gateway Dr Cypress (90630) **(G-7492)**
Clarion Hotel, Anaheim *Also called Comfort California Inc* **(G-12536)**
Clarion Hotel, Sacramento *Also called Pacifica Host Inc* **(G-13064)**
Clarion Hotel, Diamond Bar *Also called Joseph Fan* **(G-12868)**
Clarion Hotel San Jose Airport......408 453-5340
1355 N 4th St San Jose (95112) **(G-12526)**
Clarity Medical Systems Inc......925 463-7984
5775 W Las Positas Blvd # 200 Pleasanton (94588) **(G-7258)**
Clarizen Inc......866 502-9813
2755 Campus Dr Ste 300 San Mateo (94403) **(G-26971)**
Clark Richardson and Biskup......408 931-6030
75 E Santa Clara St # 350 San Jose (95113) **(G-25745)**
Clark & Sullivan Builders Inc......916 338-7707
2024 Opportunity Dr # 150 Roseville (95678) **(G-1529)**
Clark Bros Farming Inc......209 392-6144
19772 State Highway 33 Dos Palos (93620) **(G-10)**
Clark Cnstr Group-California......714 754-0764
18201 Von Karman Ave # 800 Irvine (92612) **(G-1415)**
Clark Cnstr Grup-California LP......714 429-9779
18201 Von Karman Ave Irvine (92612) **(G-1530)**
Clark Enterprises Inc......858 320-3900
3655 Nobel Dr Ste 500 San Diego (92122) **(G-11395)**
Clark Pest Ctrl Stockton Inc (PA)......209 368-7152
555 N Guild Ave Lodi (95240) **(G-14175)**
Clark Pest Ctrl Stockton Inc......209 524-6384
480 E Service Rd Modesto (95358) **(G-14176)**
Clark Pest Ctrl Stockton Inc......707 446-9748
811 U Banks Vacaville (95688) **(G-14177)**
Clark Pest Ctrl Stockton Inc......916 723-3390
4750 Beloit Dr Sacramento (95838) **(G-14178)**
Clark Pest Ctrl Stockton Inc......209 474-3204
4816 Clowes St Stockton (95210) **(G-14179)**
Clark Pest Ctrl Stockton Inc......925 449-6203
2313 Research Dr Livermore (94550) **(G-14180)**
Clark Pest Ctrl Stockton Inc......408 945-3600
199 Topaz St Milpitas (95035) **(G-14181)**
Clark Pest Ctrl Stockton Inc......916 635-7770
11285 White Rock Rd Rancho Cordova (95742) **(G-14182)**
Clark Plumbing Co, Van Nuys *Also called Valley Clark Plbg & Htg Co Inc* **(G-2404)**
Clark/Mccarthy A Joint Venture......714 429-9779
18201 Von Karman Ave # 800 Irvine (92612) **(G-1154)**
Clarklift Los Angeles Inc......562 949-1006
8314 Slauson Ave Pico Rivera (90660) **(G-7834)**
Clarklift-West Inc......916 381-5674
4750 Illinois Ave Fair Oaks (95628) **(G-7835)**

ALPHABETIC

Class Act Hair & Nail Salon...530 223-3442
2795 Bechelli Ln Redding (96002) **(G-13670)**
Classic, Torrance *Also called I C Class Components Corp* **(G-7583)**
Classic Bowling Center, Daly City *Also called Bdp Bowl Inc* **(G-18510)**
Classic Car Washes, San Jose *Also called Lark Avenue Car Wash* **(G-17848)**
Classic Custom Vacations, San Jose *Also called Classic Vacations LLC* **(G-4990)**
Classic Custom Vacations Inc...800 221-3949
5893 Rue Ferrari San Jose (95138) **(G-4989)**
Classic Distrg & Bev Group Inc...626 330-8231
120 Puente Ave City of Industry (91746) **(G-9047)**
Classic Hardwood Floors, San Diego *Also called Davenport Development Corp* **(G-3110)**
Classic Installs Inc...951 678-9906
22475 Baxter Rd Wildomar (92595) **(G-3474)**
Classic Park Lane Partnership...831 373-0101
200 Glenwood Cir Ofc Monterey (93940) **(G-11116)**
Classic Parking Inc...408 278-1444
34 S Autumn St San Jose (95110) **(G-17717)**
Classic Party Rentals, NAPA *Also called CP Opco LLC* **(G-14526)**
Classic Party Rentals, San Diego *Also called CP Opco LLC* **(G-14527)**
Classic Party Rentals, Modesto *Also called CP Opco LLC* **(G-14528)**
Classic Party Rentals, Santa Barbara *Also called CP Opco LLC* **(G-14529)**
Classic Party Rentals, Inglewood *Also called CP Opco LLC* **(G-13752)**
Classic Party Rentals, Carpinteria *Also called CP Opco LLC* **(G-14530)**
Classic Party Rentals, Burlingame *Also called CP Opco LLC* **(G-14531)**
Classic Party Rentals, Inglewood *Also called After-Party2 Inc* **(G-14506)**
Classic Party Rentals, Los Angeles *Also called CP Opco LLC* **(G-14532)**
Classic Party Rentals, Santa Ana *Also called CP Opco LLC* **(G-14533)**
Classic Protection Inc...213 742-1238
3208 Royal St Los Angeles (90007) **(G-16600)**
Classic Residential Inc...619 818-5793
1597 Murray Ave El Cajon (92020) **(G-1155)**
Classic Riverdale Inc...831 373-0101
200 Glenwood Cir Monterey (93940) **(G-12527)**
Classic Rsdence Mgt Ltd Partnr...831 373-0101
200 Glenwood Cir Ofc Monterey (93940) **(G-12528)**
Classic Soft Trim Inc...510 782-4911
3201 Diablo Ave Hayward (94545) **(G-9255)**
Classic Tile & Mosaic Inc (PA)...310 538-9605
14463 S Broadway Gardena (90248) **(G-6978)**
Classic Vacations LLC...800 221-3949
5893 Rue Ferrari San Jose (95138) **(G-4990)**
Classmates Media Corporation...818 287-3600
21301 Burbank Blvd Woodland Hills (91367) **(G-13747)**
Claud Townsley Inc...310 527-6770
555 W 182nd St Gardena (90248) **(G-3151)**
Claudia Richard Inc...323 264-3915
4871 S Santa Fe Ave Vernon (90058) **(G-8375)**
Clauss Construction...619 390-4940
8956 Winter Gardens Blvd Lakeside (92040) **(G-3450)**
Clay Dunn Enterprises Inc...310 549-1698
1606 E Carson St Carson (90745) **(G-2182)**
Clay Lacy Aviation Inc (PA)...818 989-2900
7435 Valjean Ave Van Nuys (91406) **(G-4911)**
Clay Miranda Trucking Inc...559 275-6250
3220 W Belmont Ave Fresno (93722) **(G-3995)**
Clayton Group Services, Costa Mesa *Also called Bureau Veritas North Amer Inc* **(G-27857)**
Clayton Place Associates Inc...818 702-0115
20412 Elkwood St Winnetka (91306) **(G-11396)**
CLC Incorporated (PA)...916 789-7600
3001 Lava Ridge Ct # 250 Roseville (95661) **(G-14626)**
Cldwll/Vrsar A Brown Jint Vntr...916 444-0123
10540 White Rock Rd Rancho Cordova (95670) **(G-25746)**
Clean Energy...949 437-1000
4675 Macarthur Ct Ste 800 Newport Beach (92660) **(G-6268)**
Clean Energy Fuels Corp (PA)...949 437-1000
4675 Macarthur Ct Ste 800 Newport Beach (92660) **(G-6269)**
Clean Enviroment...619 521-0543
4570 Alvarado Canyon Rd C San Diego (92120) **(G-14253)**
Clean Harbors Envmtl Svcs Inc...707 747-6699
4101 Industrial Way Benicia (94510) **(G-6464)**
Clean King Laundry Systems Inc...818 363-5500
15431 Chatsworth St Mission Hills (91345) **(G-13573)**
Clean Up, San Bernardino *Also called Universal* **(G-14454)**
Clean-A-Rama Maintenance Co...415 495-5298
526 Columbus Ave San Francisco (94133) **(G-14254)**
CLEANERIFIC, San Francisco *Also called Jewish Family and Chld Svcs* **(G-24044)**
Cleaning Services...408 778-9251
7828 Monterey St Gilroy (95020) **(G-13594)**
Cleanstreet...310 329-3078
1937 W 169th St Gardena (90247) **(G-6623)**
Clear Channel Riverside, Riverside *Also called Iheartcommunications Inc* **(G-5780)**
Clear Credit Capital, Agoura Hills *Also called Quality Home Loans* **(G-9891)**
Clear View Treatment Center...909 794-6688
1131 N Dearborn St Redlands (92374) **(G-22686)**
Clear World Communications...714 445-3900
3100 S Harbor Blvd # 300 Santa Ana (92704) **(G-5577)**
Clearbalance Holdings LLC...858 535-0870
3636 Nobel Dr Ste 250 San Diego (92122) **(G-12051)**
Clearcapitalcom Inc...530 550-2500
10875 Pioneer Trl Truckee (96161) **(G-11397)**
Clearcapitalcom Inc...530 582-5011
1410 Rocky Ridge Dr # 180 Roseville (95661) **(G-11398)**
Clearcaptions LLC...866 868-8695
595 Menlo Dr Rocklin (95765) **(G-5578)**
Clearesult Consulting Inc...415 848-1250
1 Sansome St Fl 35 San Francisco (94104) **(G-27882)**
Clearlake Capital Group LP (PA)...310 400-8800
233 Wilshire Blvd Ste 800 Santa Monica (90401) **(G-12297)**
Clearlake Family Health Center, Clearlake *Also called Adventist Health System/West* **(G-21433)**
Clearpath Workforce MGT Inc...209 239-8700
1215 W Center St Ste 102 Manteca (95337) **(G-14854)**
Clearslide Inc (PA)...877 360-3366
45 Fremont St Ste 3200 San Francisco (94105) **(G-15621)**
Clearvision Funding, Santa Ana *Also called Pacific Union Financial LLC* **(G-10169)**
Clearwater Nursery Inc...805 929-3241
887 Mesa Rd Nipomo (93444) **(G-9183)**
Clearwell Systems Inc...877 253-2793
350 Ellis St Mountain View (94043) **(G-15622)**
Cleary Bros Landscape Inc...925 335-9335
4931 Pacheco Blvd Martinez (94553) **(G-826)**
Clem-Trans Inc...909 877-4450
213 W Valley Blvd Rialto (92376) **(G-3996)**
Clement Support Services Inc...408 227-1171
1001 Yosemite Dr Milpitas (95035) **(G-7364)**
Clendenen Vineyard MGT LLC...707 473-0881
9235 W Dry Creek Rd Healdsburg (95448) **(G-148)**
Cleveland Marble LP...714 998-3280
219 E Bristol Ln Orange (92865) **(G-2807)**
Cleveland Wrecking Company...510 568-2626
999 W Town And Country Rd Orange (92868) **(G-3451)**
Cleveland Wrecking Company (HQ)...626 967-4287
999 W Town And Country Rd Orange (92868) **(G-3452)**
Clh Group, The, Valley Village *Also called Apparel Concepts Intl Inc* **(G-8332)**
Cli, Indio *Also called Commercial Lighting Inds Inc* **(G-7429)**
Click Labs Inc...415 658-5227
315 Montgomery St Fl 8 San Francisco (94104) **(G-15088)**
Clickability Inc...415 200-0410
250 Montgomery St Ste 300 San Francisco (94104) **(G-15089)**
Cliff House Restaurant, Fort Bragg *Also called Tradewinds Lodge* **(G-13353)**
Cliff View Terrace Inc...805 682-7443
623 W Junipero St Santa Barbara (93105) **(G-24601)**
Clifford & Brown A Prof Corp...661 322-6023
1430 Truxtun Ave Ste 900 Bakersfield (93301) **(G-23156)**
Clift Hotel Four Season, San Francisco *Also called Morgans Hotel Group MGT LLC* **(G-13009)**
Clift Hotels, San Francisco *Also called 495 Geary LLC* **(G-12364)**
Clifton Tatum Center...805 652-5727
4333 E Vineyard Ave Oxnard (93036) **(G-24602)**
Clima-Tech Inc...909 613-5513
3610 Placentia Ct Chino (91710) **(G-17919)**
Climate Corporation (HQ)...415 363-0500
201 3rd St Ste 1100 San Francisco (94103) **(G-695)**
Climatec LLC...858 391-7000
13715 Stowe Dr Poway (92064) **(G-2552)**
Clinapps Inc...858 866-0228
9530 Towne Centre Dr # 120 San Diego (92121) **(G-15090)**
Clinic Business, San Diego *Also called Scripps Health* **(G-19982)**
Clinic Inc (PA)...323 730-1920
3834 S Western Ave Los Angeles (90062) **(G-22687)**
Clinica Medica Familiar...714 541-0870
517 N Main St Ste 100 Santa Ana (92701) **(G-19441)**
Clinica Msr Oscar A Romero (PA)...213 989-7700
123 S Alvarado St Los Angeles (90057) **(G-19442)**
Clinica Popular Medical Group...213 381-7175
101 S Rossmore Ave Los Angeles (90004) **(G-19443)**
Clinica Sagrado Corazon...714 491-7777
831 S Harbor Blvd Anaheim (92805) **(G-19444)**
Clinica Salud Del Valle Salns...831 679-0138
24285 Lincoln Chualar (93925) **(G-19445)**
Clinica Sierra Vista...559 457-6900
3727 N 1st St Ste 106 Fresno (93726) **(G-23763)**
Clinica Sierra Vista...661 725-3882
441 Diaz Ave Delano (93215) **(G-20250)**
Clinica Sierra Vista...661 326-6490
1430 Truxtun Ave Ste 300 Bakersfield (93301) **(G-22921)**
Clinica Sierra Vista (PA)...661 635-3050
1430 Truxtun Ave Ste 400 Bakersfield (93301) **(G-19446)**
Clinicas De Slud Del Peblo Inc (PA)...760 344-9951
1166 K St Brawley (92227) **(G-19447)**
Clinicas De Slud Del Peblo Inc...760 344-6471
900 Main St Brawley (92227) **(G-19448)**
Clinicas Del Camino Real Inc...805 487-5351
650 Meta St Oxnard (93030) **(G-22688)**
Clinicomp International Inc (PA)...858 546-8202
9655 Towne Centre Dr San Diego (92121) **(G-15922)**
Clinton Vlg Convalescent Hosp, Oakland *Also called Protean Health Services Inc* **(G-21352)**
Clocktower Inn...805 652-0141
181 E Santa Clara St Ventura (93001) **(G-12529)**
Cloisters Mssion Hills Hosp HM, San Diego *Also called Shea Family Care Mission Hlth* **(G-22831)**
Cloisters of La Jolla Inc...858 459-4361
7160 Fay Ave La Jolla (92037) **(G-20460)**
Clontech Laboratories, Inc., Mountain View *Also called Takara Bio Usa Inc* **(G-26618)**
Clorox Services Company...925 425-6748
5060 Johnson Dr Pleasanton (94588) **(G-26972)**
Clorox Services Company (HQ)...510 271-7000
1221 Broadway Ste 13 Oakland (94612) **(G-26973)**
Closet World Inc...626 855-0846
14438 Don Julian Rd City of Industry (91746) **(G-3036)**
Closingcorp Inc...858 551-1500
6165 Greenwich Dr Ste 300 San Diego (92122) **(G-16336)**
Cloud4wi Inc...415 852-3900
22 Cleveland St San Francisco (94103) **(G-15091)**

A
L
P
H
A
B
E
T
I
C

Employee Codes: A=Over 500 employees, B=251-500
C=101-250, D=51-100, E=45-50

Cloudera Inc (PA)........650 644-3900
1001 Page Mill Rd Bldg 3 Palo Alto (94304) *(G-15092)*
Cloudflare Inc (PA)........650 319-8930
101 Townsend St San Francisco (94107) *(G-16874)*
Cloudike Inc........609 910-0911
3003 N 1st St San Jose (95134) *(G-16337)*
Cloudmark Inc (PA)........415 946-3800
128 King St Fl 2 San Francisco (94107) *(G-15093)*
Cloudpassage Inc........800 215-7404
180 Townsend St Fl 3 San Francisco (94107) *(G-15094)*
Cloudtrigger Inc........858 367-5272
760 Garden View Ct # 120 Encinitas (92024) *(G-27384)*
Clover Network Inc........650 210-7888
415 N Mathilda Ave Sunnyvale (94085) *(G-5579)*
Cloverdale Healthcare Center, Cloverdale *Also called Ensign Cloverdale LLC (G-20536)*
Cloverleaf Bowl, Fremont *Also called Fremont Sports Inc (G-18520)*
Cloverleaf Construction Co........408 776-3122
16470 Vineyard Blvd Morgan Hill (95037) *(G-3037)*
Clovis Community Living, Fresno *Also called Community Medical Centers (G-21503)*
Clovis Custom Drywall Inc........559 297-7073
141 Sunnyside Ave Ste 108 Clovis (93611) *(G-2878)*
Clovis Unified School District........559 327-3900
885 Gettysburg Ave Clovis (93612) *(G-18362)*
Clp Resources Inc........415 508-0910
1485 Bay Shore Blvd # 138 San Francisco (94124) *(G-14855)*
Clp Resources Inc........707 569-0200
1260 N Dutton Ave Santa Rosa (95401) *(G-14856)*
Clp Resources Inc........916 788-0300
1000 Sunrise Ave Ste 8a Roseville (95661) *(G-14857)*
Clp Resources Inc........650 261-2100
570 El Cmino Real Ste 170 Redwood City (94063) *(G-14858)*
Clp Resources Inc........415 446-7000
4460 Redwood Hwy Ste 14 San Rafael (94903) *(G-14859)*
Clp Resources Inc........714 300-0510
741 E Ball Rd Ste 100 Anaheim (92805) *(G-14860)*
Clp Resources Inc........818 260-9190
111 N First St Ste 100 Burbank (91502) *(G-14861)*
Clpf - Sycamore........212 883-2500
6721 Sycamore Canyon Blvd Riverside (92507) *(G-11399)*
Cls Landscape Management Inc........909 628-3005
4711 Schaefer Ave Unit A Chino (91710) *(G-989)*
Cls Trnsprttion Los Angles LLC (HQ)........310 414-8189
600 S Allied Way El Segundo (90245) *(G-3782)*
Club Assist North America Inc (PA)........213 388-4333
3550 Wilshire Blvd # 650 Los Angeles (90010) *(G-12052)*
Club Assist US LLC........213 388-4333
888 W 6th St Ste 300 Los Angeles (90017) *(G-6721)*
Club At Shnndoah Sprng Vlg Inc........760 343-3497
32700 Desert Moon Dr Thousand Palms (92276) *(G-18920)*
Club of Sunrise Country........760 328-6549
71601 Country Club Dr Rancho Mirage (92270) *(G-18921)*
Club One At Petaluma........707 766-8080
1201 Redwood Way Petaluma (94954) *(G-18922)*
Club One Casino Inc........559 497-3000
1033 Van Ness Ave Fresno (93721) *(G-19185)*
Club Quarters San Francisco........415 268-3606
424 Clay St San Francisco (94111) *(G-13491)*
Club Sport of Fremont........510 226-8500
46650 Landing Pkwy Fremont (94538) *(G-17083)*
Club Sport Valley Vista, Pleasanton *Also called Leisure Sports Inc (G-19236)*
Clubcorp Usa Inc........858 756-2471
5690 Cancha De Golf Rancho Santa Fe (92091) *(G-18923)*
Clubcorp Usa Inc........916 434-9100
1525 Highway 193 Lincoln (95648) *(G-18726)*
Clubsport of Fremont, Fremont *Also called Leisure Sports Inc (G-18654)*
Clubsport San Ramon LLC........925 283-4000
4000 Mt Diablo Blvd Lafayette (94549) *(G-18621)*
Clubsport San Ramon LLC (PA)........925 735-1182
350 Bollinger Canyon Ln San Ramon (94582) *(G-18622)*
Clune Construction Company LP........415 395-7245
201 Mission St Ste 1300 San Francisco (94105) *(G-1531)*
Clyde & Co US LLP........415 365-9800
101 2nd St Fl 24 San Francisco (94105) *(G-23157)*
Clyde Miles Cnstr Co Inc........925 427-4473
1110 Burnett Ave Ste C Concord (94520) *(G-1156)*
CM Concrete Inc........805 520-8100
650 E Easy St Simi Valley (93065) *(G-3242)*
CM Laundry LLC........310 436-6170
14919 S Figueroa St Gardena (90248) *(G-13651)*
CMA Baking Co........661 775-0854
28230 Constellation Rd Santa Clarita (91355) *(G-8815)*
CMA Fire Protection (PA)........661 322-9344
4300 Stine Rd Ste 800 Bakersfield (93313) *(G-2183)*
Cmac Cnstr Refinery & Pipeline, Long Beach *Also called Cmac Construction Company (G-1921)*
Cmac Construction Company........562 435-5611
1450 Santa Fe Ave Long Beach (90813) *(G-1921)*
Cmat, Stockton *Also called California Materials Inc (G-3989)*
Cmb Laboratory, Cypress *Also called Consoldted Med Bo-Analysis Inc (G-22202)*
CMC Fontana Steel........909 899-9993
12451 Arrow Rte Rancho Cucamonga (91739) *(G-3377)*
CMC Rebar........909 899-9993
12451 Arrow Rte Rancho Cucamonga (91739) *(G-3378)*
CMC Rebar Fabricators, Bloomington *Also called C M C Steel Fabricators Inc (G-3371)*
Cmf Inc........714 637-2409
1317 W Grove Ave Orange (92865) *(G-3152)*
Cmg Financial Services........925 983-3073
3160 Crow Canyon Rd # 400 San Ramon (94583) *(G-17084)*
Cmg Mortgage Inc (PA)........619 554-1327
3160 Crow Canyon Rd # 400 San Ramon (94583) *(G-9918)*
Cmp Film & Design Burbank LLC........818 729-0800
2717 W Olive Ave Burbank (91505) *(G-27742)*
Cmre Financial Services Inc........714 528-3200
3075 E Imperial Hwy # 200 Brea (92821) *(G-14025)*
CMS, Simi Valley *Also called Computerized Mgt Svcs Inc (G-26980)*
CMS Llnl........925 422-5584
7000 East Ave Msl090 Livermore (94550) *(G-18219)*
Cmsc, San Francisco *Also called Costless Maintenance Svcs Co (G-14266)*
Cmtc, Torrance *Also called California Mfg Tech Consulting (G-25714)*
Cmts LLC........310 215-0237
5777 W Century Blvd # 1105 Los Angeles (90045) *(G-26974)*
CNA Financial Corporation........714 255-2200
1800 E Imperial Hwy # 200 Brea (92821) *(G-10672)*
CNA Insurance, Brea *Also called CNA Financial Corporation (G-10672)*
CNA Surety Corporation........619 682-3550
1455 Frazee Rd Ste 801 San Diego (92108) *(G-10673)*
Cnc Worldwide Inc........310 670-1222
5343 W Imperial Hwy # 300 Los Angeles (90045) *(G-4797)*
Cncml A California Ltd Partnr........530 583-1578
1920 Squaw Valley Rd Olympic Valley (96146) *(G-12530)*
Cnet Networks Inc........415 344-2000
101 California St San Francisco (94111) *(G-15923)*
Cnet Technology Corporation (HQ)........408 392-9966
26291 Prod Ave Ste 205 Hayward (94545) *(G-7549)*
Cnetinc, San Francisco *Also called Cnet Networks Inc (G-15923)*
Cnh Industrial America LLC........510 351-2015
1919 Williams St San Leandro (94577) *(G-7767)*
Cnn America Inc........323 993-5000
6430 W Sunset Blvd # 300 Los Angeles (90028) *(G-5943)*
Cnrc LLC........760 325-2937
2299 N Indian Ave Palm Springs (92262) *(G-20461)*
Cns Industries Inc........661 775-8877
25041 Anza Dr Valencia (91355) *(G-8984)*
Cns Logistics Inc........562 229-1133
108 W Walnut St Ste 270 Gardena (90248) *(G-5049)*
Cntry Vlla Merced Hlthcre Cntr, Merced *Also called Country Villa Service Corp (G-23791)*
CNX Media Inc........415 229-8300
1 Beach St Ste 300 San Francisco (94133) *(G-18062)*
Co Team Staffing........209 578-4286
1608 Sunrise Ave Ste D Modesto (95350) *(G-14862)*
Co-Op Network, Rancho Cucamonga *Also called CU Cooperative Systems Inc (G-9715)*
Co-Optimum, Sherman Oaks *Also called Ansira Partners Inc (G-16993)*
Co-Sales Company........925 327-7322
7133 Koll Center Pkwy Pleasanton (94566) *(G-8465)*
Coa Inc (PA)........562 944-7899
12928 Sandoval St Santa Fe Springs (90670) *(G-6811)*
Coach Bus Lines, San Francisco *Also called Cusa Fl LLC (G-3899)*
Coach USA, Anaheim *Also called Cusa Pcstc LLC (G-27402)*
Coach Usa Inc........714 978-8855
2001 S Manchester Ave Anaheim (92802) *(G-4991)*
Coachella Valley Mosquito Abat........760 342-8287
43420 Trader Pl Indio (92201) *(G-17085)*
Coachella Valley Water Dst (PA)........760 398-2651
85995 Avenue 52 Coachella (92236) *(G-6330)*
Coachella Valley Water Dst........760 398-2651
75515 Hovley Ln E Palm Desert (92211) *(G-6331)*
Coachella Valley Water Dst........760 398-2651
75 525 Hovley Ln Palm Desert (92260) *(G-6332)*
Coachella Vly Rescue Mission........760 347-3512
82873 Via Venecia Indio (92201) *(G-23764)*
Coalinga Dstngished Cmnty Care........559 935-5939
834 Maple Rd Coalinga (93210) *(G-20462)*
Coalinga Regional Medical Ctr........559 935-6400
1191 Phelps Ave Coalinga (93210) *(G-21496)*
Coalinga State Hospital, Coalinga *Also called Califrnia Dept State Hospitals (G-22046)*
Coalition For Family Harmony........805 983-6014
1030 N Ventura Rd Oxnard (93030) *(G-23765)*
Coan Construction Co Inc........909 868-6812
1481 E Grand Ave Pomona (91766) *(G-3243)*
Coassure Inc........408 244-0400
4100 Moorpark Ave Ste 122 San Jose (95117) *(G-27883)*
Coast Alum & Architectural Inc (PA)........562 946-6061
10628 Fulton Wells Ave Santa Fe Springs (90670) *(G-7365)*
Coast Building Products, San Jose *Also called Coast Insulation Contrs Inc (G-2880)*
Coast Building Products........831 757-1089
11 W Lake St Salinas (93901) *(G-2879)*
Coast Carwash LP........562 961-5555
5677 E 7th St Long Beach (90804) *(G-17837)*
Coast Central Credit Union (PA)........707 445-8801
2650 Harrison Ave Eureka (95501) *(G-9591)*
Coast Citrus Distributors (PA)........619 661-7950
7597 Bristow Ct San Diego (92154) *(G-8707)*
Coast Citrus Distributors........213 955-3444
1601 E Olympic Blvd Los Angeles (90021) *(G-8708)*
Coast Citrus Distributors........650 588-0707
131 Terminal Ct 13 South San Francisco (94080) *(G-8709)*
Coast Counties Peterbilt, San Leandro *Also called Coast Counties Truck & Eqp Co (G-6667)*
Coast Counties Truck & Eqp Co........510 568-6933
260 Doolittle Dr San Leandro (94577) *(G-6667)*
Coast Distribution System Inc (HQ)........408 782-6686
350 Woodview Ave Ste 100 Morgan Hill (95037) *(G-6722)*
Coast Environmental Inc........760 929-9570
2221 Las Palmas Dr Ste J Carlsbad (92011) *(G-17086)*
Coast Farms Inc........805 383-0455
645 Laguna Rd Camarillo (93012) *(G-53)*
Coast Hand Car Wash, Long Beach *Also called Coast Carwash LP (G-17837)*

ALPHABETIC

Coast Insulation Contrs Inc (HQ).....386 304-2222
1341 Old Oakland Rd San Jose (95112) *(G-2880)*
Coast Iron & Steel Co.....562 946-4421
12300 Lakeland Rd Santa Fe Springs (90670) *(G-3379)*
Coast Landscape Management, Alviso *Also called Bayscape Management Inc (G-26938)*
Coast Personnel Services Inc (PA).....408 653-2100
2295 De La Cruz Blvd Santa Clara (95050) *(G-14863)*
Coast Produce Company (PA).....213 955-4900
1791 Bay St Los Angeles (90021) *(G-8710)*
Coast To Coast Bus Eqp Inc (PA).....949 457-7300
8 Vanderbilt Ste 200 Irvine (92618) *(G-7050)*
Coast To Coast Realty.....818 360-2609
18879 Brasilia Dr Porter Ranch (91326) *(G-11400)*
Coast To Coast Restoration, Sun Valley *Also called Coast To Coast Water Damage (G-14255)*
Coast To Coast Water Damage.....818 255-3323
10881 La Tuna Canyon Rd Sun Valley (91352) *(G-14255)*
Coast Tropical, South San Francisco *Also called Coast Citrus Distributors (G-8709)*
Coast Waste Management.....760 753-9412
5960 El Camino Real Carlsbad (92008) *(G-6465)*
Coast West Plumbing Inc.....714 446-8686
182 E Liberty Ave Ste A Anaheim (92801) *(G-2184)*
Coastal Alliance Holdings Inc.....562 370-1000
1650 Ximeno Ave Ste 120 Long Beach (90804) *(G-11401)*
Coastal Building Services Inc.....714 775-2855
718 N Hariton St Orange (92868) *(G-14256)*
Coastal Closeouts Inc.....323 589-7900
100 Oceangate Ste 1200 Long Beach (90802) *(G-17087)*
Coastal Cmnty Senior Care LLC.....562 596-4884
5500 E Atherton St # 216 Long Beach (90815) *(G-23766)*
Coastal Community College, Westminster *Also called Orange County One Stop Center (G-14716)*
Coastal Community Hospital, Santa Ana *Also called Health Resources Corp (G-21596)*
Coastal Grading and Excavating.....805 445-6433
756 Calle Plano Camarillo (93012) *(G-3423)*
Coastal Harvesting Inc.....805 525-6250
503 S Palm Ave Santa Paula (93060) *(G-655)*
Coastal Health Care Inc.....310 828-5596
1321 Franklin St Santa Monica (90404) *(G-20463)*
Coastal Hotel Group Inc.....831 646-8900
652 Cannery Row Monterey (93940) *(G-12531)*
Coastal Hotel Group Inc.....831 373-5700
300 Pacific St Monterey (93940) *(G-12532)*
Coastal Hotel Group Inc.....831 373-8000
487 Foam St Monterey (93940) *(G-12533)*
Coastal Industrial Svcs Inc.....661 392-0001
2209 Zeus Ct Bakersfield (93308) *(G-17967)*
Coastal International Inc (PA).....415 339-1700
3 Harbor Dr Ste 211 Sausalito (94965) *(G-17088)*
Coastal Intl Cnstr Svcs, Sausalito *Also called Coastal International Inc (G-17088)*
Coastal Mirage Landscapes.....949 496-7070
26362 Via De Anza San Juan Capistrano (92675) *(G-759)*
Coastal Pacific Fd Distrs Inc (PA).....909 947-2066
1015 Performance Dr Stockton (95206) *(G-8466)*
Coastal Pacific Fd Distrs Inc.....909 947-2066
1520 E Mission Blvd Ste B Ontario (91761) *(G-8467)*
Coastal Pacific Foods, Ontario *Also called Coastal Pacific Fd Distrs Inc (G-8467)*
Coastal Paving Incorporated.....408 988-5559
1295 Norman Ave Santa Clara (95054) *(G-3244)*
Coastal Rubbish, Sun Valley *Also called Crown Disposal Company Inc (G-6471)*
Coastal Select Insurance Co.....707 863-3700
4820 Busineca Ctr Dr 20 Ste 200 Fairfield (94534) *(G-10674)*
Coastal The, North Hollywood *Also called Coastal Tile Inc (G-3009)*
Coastal Tile Inc.....818 988-6134
7403 Greenbush Ave North Hollywood (91605) *(G-3009)*
Coastal Traffic Systems Inc.....714 641-3744
9391 Power Dr Huntington Beach (92646) *(G-7428)*
Coastal Transport Co Inc.....619 584-1055
9950 San Diego Mission Rd F San Diego (92108) *(G-3997)*
Coastal View Hlthcare Ctr LLC.....805 642-4101
4904 Telegraph Rd Ventura (93003) *(G-21187)*
Coaster Company of America, Santa Fe Springs *Also called Coa Inc (G-6811)*
Coasthills Credit Union (PA).....805 733-7600
3880 Constellation Rd Lompoc (93436) *(G-9660)*
Coastline Cnstr & Awng Co Inc.....714 891-9798
5742 Research Dr Huntington Beach (92649) *(G-1157)*
Coastside Senior Housing Limit.....415 355-7100
925 Main St Half Moon Bay (94019) *(G-11402)*
Cobalt Construction Company.....805 577-6222
2259 Ward Ave Ste 200 Simi Valley (93065) *(G-1303)*
Cobb Property Services, Orange *Also called Cobb Waterblasting Inc (G-14257)*
Cobb Waterblasting Inc.....714 769-2622
1145 W Shelley Ct Orange (92868) *(G-14257)*
Coblentz Patch Duffy Bass LLP.....510 655-4598
1 Ferry Building Ste 200 San Francisco (94111) *(G-23158)*
Cockrell Electric Inc.....760 864-6233
79553 Country Club Dr B Bermuda Dunes (92203) *(G-2553)*
Codding Construction Co.....707 795-3550
1400 Valley House Dr # 100 Rohnert Park (94928) *(G-1532)*
Coelho West Custom Farming.....559 884-2566
26979 S Butte Ave Five Points (93624) *(G-351)*
Cofa Media Group LLC.....877 293-2007
5650 El Camino Real Carlsbad (92008) *(G-5580)*
Coffman Specialties Inc (PA).....858 536-3100
9685 Via Excelencia # 200 San Diego (92126) *(G-3245)*
Cogent Financial Group.....562 985-1388
5199 E Pacific Coast Hwy Long Beach (90804) *(G-9778)*
Cogent Systems Incorporated (HQ).....626 325-9600
639 N Rosemead Blvd Pasadena (91107) *(G-26497)*
Cohen Brown MGT Group Inc (PA).....310 966-1001
11835 W Olympic Blvd 920e Los Angeles (90064) *(G-27385)*
Cohen Richard Ldscp & Cnstr.....949 768-0599
20795 Canada Rd El Toro (92630) *(G-827)*
Cohen Ventures Inc (PA).....510 482-4420
449 15th St Ste 402 Oakland (94612) *(G-27884)*
Coherent Inc.....408 764-4000
1100 La Avenida St Mountain View (94043) *(G-26650)*
Cohnreznick LLP.....818 205-2600
21700 Oxnard St Woodland Hills (91367) *(G-26312)*
Cohnreznick LLP.....310 477-3722
11755 Wilshire Blvd # 1700 Los Angeles (90025) *(G-26313)*
Coinmach Corporation (PA).....818 637-4300
3628 San Fernando Rd Glendale (91204) *(G-13574)*
Coinmach Corporation.....510 429-0900
32910 Alvarado Niles Rd # 150 Union City (94587) *(G-13575)*
Coit Clg & Restoration Svcs.....619 726-4734
1080 N Marshall Ave El Cajon (92020) *(G-13595)*
Coit Restoration Services, Modesto *Also called C & S Draperies Inc (G-13591)*
Coit Services Inc.....949 760-0760
1297 Logan Ave Costa Mesa (92626) *(G-13579)*
Cokeva Inc.....916 462-6001
9000 Foothills Blvd Roseville (95747) *(G-16289)*
Colateral Lender Inc.....310 659-4353
9640 Santa Monica Blvd Beverly Hills (90210) *(G-9798)*
Coldwater Care Center LLC.....818 766-6105
12750 Riverside Dr North Hollywood (91607) *(G-20464)*
Coldwell Banker, West Hollywood *Also called Coldwer Banker Previews (G-11440)*
Coldwell Banker, Davis *Also called Doug Arnold Real Estate Inc (G-11476)*
Coldwell Banker, Modesto *Also called Vinson Chase Inc (G-11899)*
Coldwell Banker, Pasadena *Also called Nrt Commercial Utah LLC (G-11716)*
Coldwell Banker, Canyon Lake *Also called Cbabr Inc (G-11349)*
Coldwell Banker, Bakersfield *Also called Preferred Brokers Inc (G-11759)*
Coldwell Banker, Valencia *Also called Vista Valencia Group Inc (G-11901)*
Coldwell Banker, Vista *Also called Caldwell Banker Inc (G-11337)*
Coldwell Banker.....916 447-5900
730 Alhambra Blvd Ste 150 Sacramento (95816) *(G-11403)*
Coldwell Banker.....650 596-5400
580 El Camino Real San Carlos (94070) *(G-10675)*
Coldwell Banker.....619 460-6600
9332 Fuerte Dr La Mesa (91941) *(G-11404)*
Coldwell Banker.....760 753-5616
740 Garden View Ct # 100 Encinitas (92024) *(G-11405)*
Coldwell Banker.....650 726-1100
248 Main St Ste 200 Half Moon Bay (94019) *(G-11406)*
Coldwell Banker.....707 257-7673
1775 Lincoln Ave NAPA (94558) *(G-11407)*
Coldwell Banker Affiliates.....650 941-7040
161 S San Antonio Rd # 1 Los Altos (94022) *(G-11408)*
Coldwell Banker Amaral & Assoc.....925 439-7400
3775 Main St Ste E Oakley (94561) *(G-11409)*
Coldwell Banker Coastl Aliance, Long Beach *Also called Coastal Alliance Holdings Inc (G-11401)*
Coldwell Banker Premier Prpts.....805 565-2200
1498 E Valley Rd Santa Barbara (93108) *(G-11410)*
Coldwell Banker Prof Group.....408 383-1044
2860 Zanker Rd Ste 204 San Jose (95134) *(G-11411)*
Coldwell Banker Property Shop, Ojai *Also called Wilde & Guernsey Inc (G-11921)*
Coldwell Banker RE Corp.....818 995-2424
15490 Ventura Blvd # 100 Sherman Oaks (91403) *(G-11412)*
Coldwell Banker RE Corp.....408 981-7200
1000 Sunset Dr Ste 190 Roseville (95678) *(G-11413)*
Coldwell Banker RE Corp.....909 792-4147
501 W Redlands Blvd Ste A Redlands (92373) *(G-11414)*
Coldwell Banker Real Estate.....408 491-1600
1045 Willow St San Jose (95125) *(G-11415)*
Coldwell Banker Residential BR, San Carlos *Also called Judy Spiegel (G-11604)*
Coldwell Banker Residential RE, San Jose *Also called Tim Brown (G-11876)*
Coldwell Banker Residential RE, San Jose *Also called Terry Meyer (G-11871)*
Coldwell Banker Residential RE (HQ).....949 367-1800
27271 Las Ramblas Mission Viejo (92691) *(G-11416)*
Coldwell Banker Residential RE.....626 445-5500
15 E Foothill Blvd Arcadia (91006) *(G-11417)*
Coldwell Banker Sky Ridge Rlty, Blue Jay *Also called Cbsrr Inc (G-11361)*
Coldwell Banker Solano Pacific, Benicia *Also called Solano Pacific Corporation (G-11850)*
Coldwell Banker Town & Country.....626 966-3688
345 E Rowland St Covina (91723) *(G-11418)*
Coldwell Bankers Residential.....510 583-5400
21060 Redwood Rd Ste 100 Castro Valley (94546) *(G-11419)*
Coldwell Bankers Residential (PA).....818 575-2660
604 Lindero Canyon Rd Agoura Hills (91377) *(G-11420)*
Coldwell Bnkr First Class Rlty.....323 721-7430
7825 Florence Ave A Downey (90240) *(G-11421)*
Coldwell Bnkr Frst Prmier Rlty.....909 395-5400
537 N Euclid Ave Ontario (91762) *(G-11422)*
Coldwell Bnkr Residential Brkg.....650 558-6800
181 2nd Ave Ste 100 San Mateo (94401) *(G-11423)*
Coldwell Bnkr Residential Brkg.....530 823-7653
500 Auburn Folsom Rd # 300 Auburn (95603) *(G-11424)*
Coldwell Bnkr Residential Brkg (HQ).....925 275-3000
1855 Gateway Blvd Ste 750 Concord (94520) *(G-11425)*
Coldwell Bnkr Residential Brkg.....831 462-9000
2140 41st Ave Ste 100 Capitola (95010) *(G-11426)*
Coldwell Bnkr Residential Brkg.....650 558-4200
1427 Chapin Ave Burlingame (94010) *(G-11427)*

ALPHABETIC

Coldwell Bnkr Residential Brkg 415 447-8800
1801 Lombard St San Francisco (94123) *(G-11428)*

Coldwell Bnkr Residential Brkg 760 325-4500
1081 N Palm Canyon Dr Palm Springs (92262) *(G-11429)*

Coldwell Bnkr Residential Brkg 916 966-8200
5034 Sunrise Blvd Fair Oaks (95628) *(G-11430)*

Coldwell Bnkr Residential Brkg 714 832-0020
21580 Yorba Linda Blvd Yorba Linda (92887) *(G-11431)*

Coldwell Bnkr Residential Brkg 818 222-0023
23586 Calabasas Rd # 105 Calabasas (91302) *(G-11432)*

Coldwell Bnkr Residential Brkg 310 273-3113
166 N Canon Dr Ste 200 Beverly Hills (90210) *(G-11433)*

Coldwell Bnkr Residential Brkg 760 776-9898
72605 Highway 111 Ste B2 Palm Desert (92260) *(G-11434)*

Coldwell Bnkr Residential Brkg 760 771-5454
45000 Club Dr Indian Wells (92210) *(G-11435)*

Coldwell Bnkr Residential Brkg 831 420-2628
410 Sims Rd Santa Cruz (95060) *(G-11436)*

Coldwell Bnkr Residential Brkg 510 608-7600
3340 Walnut Ave Ste 110 Fremont (94538) *(G-11437)*

Coldwell Bnkr Rsdential RE LLC 408 355-1500
410 N Santa Cruz Ave Los Gatos (95030) *(G-11438)*

Coldwell Bnkr Rsdntial, Newport Beach *Also called C B Coast Newport Properties (G-11334)*

Coldwell Bnkr Rsdntial RE Svcs 916 933-1155
4370 Town Center Blvd # 270 El Dorado Hills (95762) *(G-11439)*

Coldwer Banker Previews 310 278-9470
9069 W Sunset Blvd # 100 West Hollywood (90069) *(G-11440)*

Cole-Schaefer Ambulance Svc, Pomona *Also called Schaefer Ambulance Service Inc (G-3843)*

Colfin Esh Funding LLC 310 282-8820
2450 Broadway Fl 6 Santa Monica (90404) *(G-12111)*

Colich & Sons, Gardena *Also called Coretco Inc (G-1923)*

Collabnet Inc (PA) 650 228-2500
4000 Shoreline Ct South San Francisco (94080) *(G-15623)*

Collabria Care 707 258-9080
414 S Jefferson St NAPA (94559) *(G-22405)*

Collabrus Inc 415 288-1826
111 Sutter St Ste 900 San Francisco (94104) *(G-26314)*

Collectech Systems Inc (HQ) 818 597-7500
2290 Agate Ct 1a Simi Valley (93065) *(G-14026)*

Collection Technology Inc 800 743-4284
10801 6th St Ste 200 Rancho Cucamonga (91730) *(G-14027)*

Collective Digital Studio, LLC, Beverly Hills *Also called Studio 71 LP (G-13979)*

Collective MGT Group LLC 323 655-8585
8383 Wilshire Blvd # 1050 Beverly Hills (90211) *(G-26975)*

Collectors Universe Inc (PA) 949 567-1234
1921 E Alton Ave Ste 100 Santa Ana (92705) *(G-17968)*

College Hospital Inc (PA) 562 924-9581
10802 College Pl Cerritos (90703) *(G-22055)*

College Hospital Cerritos, Cerritos *Also called College Hospital Inc (G-22055)*

College Housing Northwest 530 345-1393
1400 W 3rd St Chico (95928) *(G-13450)*

College Medical Center, Long Beach *Also called Chlb LLC (G-22054)*

College Movers, San Diego *Also called Student Movers Inc (G-4379)*

College Operations LLC 559 353-0576
1730 S College Ave Dinuba (93618) *(G-24440)*

College Park Realty Inc (PA) 562 594-6753
10791 Los Alamitos Blvd Los Alamitos (90720) *(G-11441)*

College Park Realty Inc 562 982-0300
2610 Los Coyotes Diagonal Long Beach (90815) *(G-11442)*

College Track 510 834-3295
111 Broadway Ste 101 Oakland (94607) *(G-27386)*

College Vsta Convalescent Hosp, Los Angeles *Also called Notellage Corporation (G-21332)*

Collier Warehouse Inc 415 920-9720
90 Dorman Ave San Francisco (94124) *(G-6916)*

Colliers International 415 788-3100
101 2nd St Ste 1100 San Francisco (94105) *(G-11443)*

Colliers International Greater (HQ) 213 627-1214
865 S Figueroa St # 3500 Los Angeles (90017) *(G-11444)*

Colliers Intl Prperty Cons Inc 858 455-1515
4660 La Jolla Village Dr # 100 San Diego (92122) *(G-11445)*

Colliers Intl Prperty Cons Inc 916 929-5999
301 University Ave # 100 Sacramento (95825) *(G-11446)*

Colliers Investment Services, San Jose *Also called Colliers Parrish Intl Inc (G-11447)*

Colliers Parrish Intl Inc 408 282-3800
450 W Santa Clara St San Jose (95113) *(G-11447)*

Colliers Parrish Intl Inc 925 279-1050
1850 Mt Diablo Blvd # 200 Walnut Creek (94596) *(G-11448)*

Collins Avenue LLC 323 930-6633
5410 Wilshire Blvd # 800 Los Angeles (90036) *(G-5847)*

Collins Cllins Muir Stwart LLP 626 243-1100
1100 El Centro St Frnt South Pasadena (91030) *(G-23159)*

Collins Electrical Company Inc (PA) 209 466-3691
3412 Metro Dr Stockton (95215) *(G-2554)*

Collins Electrical Company Inc 209 466-3691
1902 Channel Dr West Sacramento (95691) *(G-2555)*

Collins Pine Company 530 258-2111
1 Chateau Way Chester (96020) *(G-6917)*

Collwood Ter Stellar Care Inc 619 287-2920
4518 54th St San Diego (92115) *(G-21188)*

Colonial Care Center, Long Beach *Also called Longwood Management Corp (G-21301)*

Colonial Gardens Nursing Home, Pico Rivera *Also called Rivera Sanitarium Inc (G-20874)*

Colonial Home Care Svcs Inc 714 289-7220
1224 E Katella Ave # 101 Orange (92867) *(G-14627)*

COLONIAL MANOR CONVALESCENT HOSPITAL, West Covina *Also called Wicoro Inc (G-21421)*

Colony Advisors, Los Angeles *Also called Colony Management Inc (G-11449)*

Colony Capital LLC (PA) 310 282-8820
2450 Broadway Ste 600 Santa Monica (90404) *(G-12298)*

Colony Management, Santa Monica *Also called Colony Capital LLC (G-12298)*

Colony Management Inc 310 282-8820
1999 Ave Of The Ste 1200 Los Angeles (90067) *(G-11449)*

Colony Strwood Homes Partnr LP 510 250-2200
1999 Harrison St Fl 24 Oakland (94612) *(G-1158)*

Color Ad Inc 310 632-5500
18601 S Santa Fe Ave Compton (90221) *(G-13824)*

Color By Deluxe, Burbank *Also called Deluxe Laboratories Inc (G-18222)*

Color Concepts, Canoga Park *Also called Rte Enterprises Inc (G-2487)*

Color Spot Lodi, Lodi *Also called Color Spot Nurseries Inc (G-274)*

Color Spot Nurseries Inc 831 444-0523
420 Espinosa Rd Salinas (93907) *(G-273)*

Color Spot Nurseries Inc 209 369-3018
5400 E Harney Ln Lodi (95240) *(G-274)*

Color Spot Nurseries Inc 310 549-7470
321 W Sepulveda Blvd Carson (90745) *(G-9184)*

Colorado River Adventures Inc (PA) 760 663-3737
2715 Parker Dam Rd Earp (92242) *(G-13478)*

Colorado River Medical Center 760 326-4531
1401 Bailey Ave Needles (92363) *(G-19449)*

Colorama Wholesale Nursery, Azusa *Also called Richard Wilson Wellington (G-313)*

Colorexa, Van Nuys *Also called Exandal Corporation (G-8477)*

Colosseum Athletics Corp 310 667-8341
2400 S Wilmington Ave Compton (90220) *(G-8337)*

Colrich Communities Inc 858 350-7672
444 W Beech St Ste 300 San Diego (92101) *(G-11959)*

Cols Inc 714 720-6100
1611 S Melrose Dr 253&278 Vista (92081) *(G-3783)*

Colsa Corporation 661 273-3859
41240 12th St W Palmdale (93551) *(G-26498)*

Colsa Corporation 619 260-1100
2727 Camino Del Rio S San Diego (92108) *(G-15095)*

Colt Security Services, Palm Desert *Also called Dlo Enterprises Inc (G-16627)*

Colt Services Inc 858 271-9988
9655 Via Excelencia San Diego (92126) *(G-13596)*

Colton Joint Unified Schl Dst 909 876-4240
471 Agua Mansa Rd Colton (92324) *(G-24441)*

Colton Real Estate Group (PA) 949 475-4200
515 Cabrillo Park Dr # 305 Santa Ana (92701) *(G-11250)*

COLUMBIA HCA, Riverside *Also called Riverside Cmnty Hlth Systems (G-21834)*

Columbia Hydronics Co., Hayward *Also called California Hydronics Corp (G-7735)*

Columbia Pictures Inds Inc (HQ) 310 244-4000
10202 Washington Blvd Culver City (90232) *(G-18063)*

Columbia San Clemente Hospital, San Clemente *Also called HCA Inc (G-21595)*

Columbia Woodlake LLC 206 728-9063
500 Leisure Ln Sacramento (95815) *(G-12534)*

Colusa Casino, Colusa *Also called Colusa Indian Cmnty Council (G-24891)*

Colusa City Office Education, Colusa *Also called Childrens Services (G-23745)*

Colusa Cnty Sbstnce Abuse Svcs 530 458-0520
162 E Carson St Ste A Colusa (95932) *(G-23767)*

Colusa County Behavioral Hlth, Colusa *Also called Colusa Cnty Sbstnce Abuse Svcs (G-23767)*

Colusa Indian Cmnty Council 530 458-6572
3740 Highway 45 Colusa (95932) *(G-24891)*

Colusa Produce Corporation 530 696-0121
1954 Progress Rd Meridian (95957) *(G-8816)*

Colusa, Glenn, Trinity Commant, Willows *Also called Glenn Cnty Humn Resource Agcy (G-24342)*

Comak Trading Inc A Cal Corp 323 261-3404
2550 S Soto St Vernon (90058) *(G-8376)*

Combine Residential Cnstr 951 360-1260
8413 63rd St Riverside (92509) *(G-27885)*

Combined Management Svcs Inc 626 856-2263
1500 W West Covina Pkwy # 100 West Covina (91790) *(G-10676)*

Combustion Associates Inc 951 272-6999
555 Monica Cir Corona (92880) *(G-6118)*

Comca Sport Net Bay Area 415 896-2557
360 3rd St Fl 2 San Francisco (94107) *(G-5944)*

Comcast Cable, Fresno *Also called Comcast Corporation (G-5960)*

Comcast Cable, Madera *Also called Comcast Corporation (G-5961)*

Comcast Cable, Fresno *Also called Comcast Corporation (G-5962)*

Comcast Cable, NAPA *Also called Comcast Corporation (G-5963)*

Comcast Cable, Santa Cruz *Also called Comcast Corporation (G-5964)*

Comcast Cable, Sacramento *Also called Comcast Corporation (G-5965)*

Comcast Cable, San Jose *Also called Comcast Corporation (G-5966)*

Comcast California Ix Inc 215 286-3345
1111 Andersen Dr San Rafael (94901) *(G-5945)*

Comcast Cble Cmmunications LLC 310 216-3500
6320 Arizona Cir Los Angeles (90045) *(G-5946)*

Comcast Cble Cmmunications LLC 415 715-0524
1485 Bay Shore Blvd # 125 San Francisco (94124) *(G-5947)*

Comcast Cble Cmmunications LLC 559 253-4050
1031 N Plaza Dr Visalia (93291) *(G-5948)*

Comcast Cble Cmmunications LLC 310 216-3686
6357 Arizona Cir Los Angeles (90045) *(G-5949)*

Comcast Corporation 916 459-2964
2860 Gateway Oaks Dr Sacramento (95833) *(G-5950)*

Comcast Corporation 925 249-2060
2166 Rheem Dr Pleasanton (94588) *(G-5951)*

Comcast Corporation 650 689-5392
860 Stanton Rd Burlingame (94010) *(G-5952)*

Comcast Corporation 415 665-5507
1 La Avanzada St Rm 111 San Francisco (94131) *(G-5953)*

Comcast Corporation 707 266-7584
166 Watson Ln American Canyon (94503) *(G-5954)*

ALPHABETIC

Comcast Corporation 209 222-3656
3801 Pelandale Ave A11 Modesto (95356) *(G-5955)*
Comcast Corporation 415 367-4153
221 2nd St Sausalito (94965) *(G-5956)*
Comcast Corporation 510 266-3200
23525 Clawiter Rd Hayward (94545) *(G-5957)*
Comcast Corporation 415 255-5644
1000 Van Ness Ave San Francisco (94109) *(G-5958)*
Comcast Corporation 951 268-9378
425 Corona Mall Corona (92879) *(G-5959)*
Comcast Corporation 559 389-7251
4991 E Mckinley Ave Fresno (93727) *(G-5960)*
Comcast Corporation 559 474-4194
1300 W Yosemite Ave Madera (93637) *(G-5961)*
Comcast Corporation 559 718-9917
2414 E Acacia Ave Fresno (93726) *(G-5962)*
Comcast Corporation 707 266-7012
810 Randolph St NAPA (94559) *(G-5963)*
Comcast Corporation 831 316-9258
415 River St Santa Cruz (95060) *(G-5964)*
Comcast Corporation 916 520-6813
6500 47th St Sacramento (95823) *(G-5965)*
Comcast Corporation 408 216-2878
203 N 27th St San Jose (95116) *(G-5966)*
Comcast Corporation 800 240-3640
5462 E Del Amo Blvd 239 Long Beach (90808) *(G-5967)*
Comcast Corporation 916 830-6790
1750 Creekside Oaks Dr # 100 Sacramento (95833) *(G-2556)*
Comcast Corporation 925 432-0500
550 Garcia Ave Pittsburg (94565) *(G-5968)*
Comcast Corporation 415 835-5700
50 Francisco St Fl 3 San Francisco (94133) *(G-13962)*
Comcast Corporation 909 390-4777
1500 Auto Center Dr Ontario (91761) *(G-5969)*
Comcast Corporation 209 955-6521
6505 Tam O Shanter Dr Stockton (95210) *(G-5970)*
Comcast Corporation 323 993-8000
900 N Cahuenga Blvd Los Angeles (90038) *(G-5971)*
Comcast Corporation 925 271-9794
2093 Salvio St Concord (94520) *(G-2557)*
Comcast Corporation 831 657-6095
2455 Henderson Way Monterey (93940) *(G-5972)*
Comcast E San Fernando Vly LP 415 233-8328
1111 Andersen Dr San Rafael (94901) *(G-6065)*
Comcast Spotlight Inc 415 675-2300
50 Francisco St Fl 3 San Francisco (94133) *(G-13825)*
Comcast West Bay Area, San Francisco *Also called Comcast Cble Cmmunications LLC (G-5947)*
Come Land Maint Svc Co Inc 818 567-2455
1419 N San Fernando Blvd # 250 Burbank (91504) *(G-14258)*
Comerica Bank 925 941-1900
1442 N Main St Walnut Creek (94596) *(G-9389)*
Comerit Inc 888 556-5990
2201 Francisco Dr # 140283 El Dorado Hills (95762) *(G-16338)*
Comet Building Maintenance Inc 415 383-1035
21 Commercial Blvd Ste 12 Novato (94949) *(G-760)*
Comet Electric Inc 818 340-0965
21625 Prairie St Chatsworth (91311) *(G-2558)*
Comfort Air Inc 209 466-4601
1607 French Camp Tpke Stockton (95206) *(G-2185)*
Comfort California Inc 415 928-5000
2775 Van Ness Ave San Francisco (94109) *(G-12535)*
Comfort California Inc 714 750-3131
616 W Convention Way Anaheim (92802) *(G-12536)*
Comfort Inn, San Francisco *Also called Comfort California Inc (G-12535)*
Comfort Inn, South San Francisco *Also called Comfort Suites (G-12537)*
Comfort Inn, San Diego *Also called A J Esprit (G-12371)*
Comfort Keepers, El Cajon *Also called Way Cool Homecare Inc (G-22614)*
Comfort Suites 650 589-7100
121 E Grand Ave South San Francisco (94080) *(G-12537)*
Comfort Systems Usa Inc 909 390-6677
4189 Santa Ana St Ste D Ontario (91761) *(G-2186)*
Comfort Systems Usa Inc 925 827-0578
5056 Coml Cir Ste E Concord (94520) *(G-2187)*
Comfort Zone, Sacramento *Also called Villara Corporation (G-2409)*
Comglobal Systems Inc (HQ) 619 321-6000
1315 Dell Ave Campbell (95008) *(G-15924)*
Command & Control Systems, San Diego *Also called Engility LLC (G-25790)*
Command Guard Services, Torrance *Also called Resource Collection Inc (G-14406)*
Command International SEC Svcs 818 997-1666
6819 Sepulveda Blvd Van Nuys (91405) *(G-16601)*
Command Security Corporation 714 557-9355
1630 S Sunkist St Ste O Anaheim (92806) *(G-16602)*
Command Security Corporation 510 623-2355
890 Hillview Ct Ste 100 Milpitas (95035) *(G-16603)*
Command Security Corporation 310 981-4530
8929 S Sepulveda Blvd # 300 Los Angeles (90045) *(G-16604)*
Command Security Corporation 650 574-0911
1701 Airport Blvd Ste 205 San Jose (95110) *(G-16605)*
Commerce Casino, Commerce *Also called California Commerce Club Inc (G-12482)*
Commerce Center Theatres 323 722-5577
950 Goodrich Blvd Commerce (90022) *(G-18318)*
Commerce Velocity LLC 949 756-8950
1 Technology Dr Ste J725 Irvine (92618) *(G-15624)*
Commerce West Insurance Co 925 730-6400
6130 Stoneridge Mall Rd # 400 Pleasanton (94588) *(G-9743)*
Commercial Carriers Insur Agcy 562 404-4900
12641 166th St Cerritos (90703) *(G-10411)*
Commercial Casting Co, Fontana *Also called Hartman Industries (G-7374)*
Commercial Coating Company Inc 323 256-1331
2809 W Avenue 37 Los Angeles (90065) *(G-1752)*
Commercial Finance & L 858 866-8525
8445 Camino Sta Ste 202 San Diego (92121) *(G-9547)*
Commercial Indus Design Co Inc 949 273-6199
20372 N Sea Cir Lake Forest (92630) *(G-7109)*
Commercial Indus Roofg Co Inc 619 465-3737
9239 Olive Dr Spring Valley (91977) *(G-3153)*
Commercial Inv MGT Group, Los Angeles *Also called Cim Group Inc (G-11391)*
Commercial Lbr & Pallet Co Inc 626 968-0631
135 Long Ln City of Industry (91746) *(G-6918)*
Commercial Lighting Inds Inc 800 755-0155
81161 Indio Blvd Indio (92201) *(G-7429)*
Commercial Paving, Los Angeles *Also called Commercial Coating Company Inc (G-1752)*
Commercial Prgrm Systems Inc (PA) 818 308-8560
4400 Coldwater Canyon Ave # 200 Studio City (91604) *(G-16339)*
Commercial Property Management (PA) 213 739-2000
3251 W 6th St Ste 109 Los Angeles (90020) *(G-11117)*
Commercial Protective Svcs Inc 310 515-5290
436 W Walnut St Gardena (90248) *(G-16606)*
Commercial Rfrgn Spcialist Inc 510 784-8990
3480 Arden Rd Hayward (94545) *(G-7754)*
Commercial Roofing Systems Inc 626 359-5354
11735 Goldring Rd Arcadia (91006) *(G-3154)*
Commercial Site Imprvs Inc 209 785-1920
192 Poker Flat Rd Copperopolis (95228) *(G-3424)*
Commercial Spport Svcs Antioch, Antioch *Also called Contra Costa ARC (G-24327)*
Commercial Support Services, Richmond *Also called Contra Costa ARC (G-24605)*
Commercial Wood Products Co 760 246-4530
10019 Yucca Rd Adelanto (92301) *(G-3038)*
Commission Junction Inc (HQ) 805 730-8000
530 E Montecito St Santa Barbara (93103) *(G-15096)*
Commodity Distribution Service 562 777-9969
10035 Painter Ave Santa Fe Springs (90670) *(G-27886)*
Commodity Forwarders Inc (PA) 310 348-8855
11101 S La Cienega Blvd Los Angeles (90045) *(G-5050)*
Common Area Maint Svcs Inc (PA) 310 390-3552
5664 Selmaraine Dr Culver City (90230) *(G-14259)*
Common Ground Ldscp MGT Inc 408 278-9847
725 Lenzen Ave San Jose (95126) *(G-828)*
Commons At Calabasas, The, Los Angeles *Also called Caruso MGT Ltd A Cal Ltd Prtnr (G-11344)*
Commonwealth Central Credit Un (PA) 408 531-3100
5890 Silver Creek Vly Rd San Jose (95138) *(G-9661)*
Commonwealth Hotels LLC 707 644-1200
1000 Fairgrounds Dr Vallejo (94589) *(G-26976)*
Commonwealth International 626 279-9201
968 Durfee Ave South El Monte (91733) *(G-16607)*
Commonwealth Land Title Co 949 460-4500
6 Executive Cir Ste 100 Irvine (92614) *(G-10510)*
Communction Wirg Spcalists Inc 858 278-4545
8909 Complex Dr Ste F San Diego (92123) *(G-2559)*
Commune Hotels and Resorts LLC (PA) 415 248-5930
530 Bush St Ste 501 San Francisco (94108) *(G-12538)*
Communicare Health Centers 530 758-2060
2051 John Jones Rd Davis (95616) *(G-19450)*
Communication & Info Tech, Sacramento *Also called County of Sacramento (G-16277)*
Communication Svc For Deaf Inc 209 475-5000
81 W March Ln Stockton (95207) *(G-24892)*
Communications Supply Corp 714 670-7711
6251 Knott Ave Buena Park (90620) *(G-6066)*
Communigate Systems, Larkspur *Also called Stalker Software Inc (G-15847)*
Community & Senior Svcs, Lancaster *Also called County of Los Angeles (G-23831)*
Community Access Network 951 279-1333
2275 S Main St Ste 201 Corona (92882) *(G-23768)*
Community Action Brd of Snt Cr 831 724-0206
406 Main St Ste 202 Watsonville (95076) *(G-25239)*
Community Action Commsn Santa 805 343-0615
4545 10th St Guadalupe (93434) *(G-24893)*
Community Action Commsn Santa 805 614-0786
1890 Sandalwood Dr Santa Maria (93455) *(G-24894)*
Community Action Commsn Santa (PA) 805 964-8857
5638 Hollister Ave # 230 Goleta (93117) *(G-24895)*
Community Action Commsn Santa 805 922-2243
201 W Chapel St Santa Maria (93458) *(G-24896)*
Community Action Marin 415 459-6330
1108 Tamalpais Ave San Rafael (94901) *(G-22689)*
Community Action Marine, San Rafael *Also called Community Action Marin (G-22689)*
Community Action Partnershi 714 897-6670
11870 Monarch St Garden Grove (92841) *(G-23769)*
Community Action Partnership 805 489-4026
1152 E Grand Ave Arroyo Grande (93420) *(G-23160)*
Community Action Partnership (PA) 805 544-4355
1030 Southwood Dr San Luis Obispo (93401) *(G-23770)*
Community Action Partnership O 707 544-0120
141 Stony Cir Ste 210 Santa Rosa (95401) *(G-24897)*
Community Action Partnr Kern 661 758-0129
1600 Poplar Ave Wasco (93280) *(G-24442)*
Community Action Partnr Kern 661 336-0317
2400 Truxtun Ave Bakersfield (93301) *(G-24898)*
Community Action Partnr Kern 760 371-1469
814 N Norma St Ridgecrest (93555) *(G-24899)*
Community Action Partnr Kern 661 366-5953
4404 Pioneer Dr Bakersfield (93306) *(G-24443)*
Community Action Partnr Kern (PA) 661 336-5236
5005 Business Park N Bakersfield (93309) *(G-23771)*
Community Action Prtnrshp (PA) 559 673-9173
1225 Gill Ave Madera (93637) *(G-24444)*

ALPHABETIC

Community Actv Rhbltn & Emplym, Crescent City *Also called Full Spectrum Services Inc (G-23989)*
COMMUNITY ADVOCATE FOR PEOPLE', Whittier *Also called Capc Inc (G-24886)*
Community Bank (PA) 626 577-1700
460 Serra Madre Villa Ave Pasadena (91107) ***(G-9487)***
Community Bank....951 808-8940
255 E Rincon St Ste 312 Corona (92879) ***(G-9488)***
Community Blood Bank Inc 760 773-4190
70025 Highway 111 Ste 101 Rancho Mirage (92270) ***(G-22922)***
COMMUNITY CARE & REHABILITATIO, Riverside *Also called Community Care Rehab Ctr LLC (G-20465)*
Community Care Adhc Inc 626 614-8999
9917 Las Tunas Dr Temple City (91780) ***(G-23772)***
Community Care Center, Duarte *Also called Kf Community Care LLC (G-21279)*
Community Care Health Centers....323 980-4000
5425 Pomona Blvd Los Angeles (90022) ***(G-19451)***
Community Care Rehab Ctr LLC 951 680-6500
4070 Jurupa Ave Riverside (92506) ***(G-20465)***
Community Care Rhblitation Ctr, Newport Beach *Also called Ben Bennett Inc (G-21151)*
Community Catalysts California....831 769-0934
229 Pajaro St Ste 201 Salinas (93901) ***(G-25240)***
Community Chld Cre Cncl Sonoma (PA) 707 522-1413
131 Stony Cir Ste 300 Santa Rosa (95401) ***(G-24445)***
Community Clinics Hlth Netwrk....619 542-4300
7535 Metropolitan Dr San Diego (92108) ***(G-25130)***
Community Convalescent Center....909 621-4751
9620 Fremont Ave Montclair (91763) ***(G-20466)***
Community Convalescent Hospita....626 963-6091
638 E Colorado Ave Glendora (91740) ***(G-20467)***
Community Dev Inst Head Start 858 668-2985
12988 Bowron Rd Poway (92064) ***(G-24446)***
Community Development Comm....626 262-4511
700 W Main St Alhambra (91801) ***(G-26977)***
Community Development Comm....626 262-4511
700 W Main St Alhambra (91801) ***(G-11450)***
Community Facilities Dst No 6, Los Angeles *Also called County of Los Angeles (G-6337)*
Community Family, Riverside *Also called Richard Finn (G-19917)*
Community Gatepath....650 259-8500
350 Twin Dolphin Dr # 123 Redwood City (94065) ***(G-23773)***
Community Health Agency, Riverside *Also called County of Riverside (G-24909)*
Community Health Agency, Riverside *Also called County of Riverside (G-19479)*
Community Health Agency, Moreno Valley *Also called County of Riverside (G-19480)*
COMMUNITY HEALTH CENTER, Bakersfield *Also called Omni Family Health (G-19793)*
Community Health Centers (PA)....805 929-3211
150 Tejas Pl Nipomo (93444) ***(G-19452)***
Community Health Group....619 422-0422
2420 Fenton St 200 Chula Vista (91914) ***(G-19453)***
Community Health Network LLC 951 265-8281
27922 Tamrack Way Murrieta (92563) ***(G-22406)***
Community Health Netwrk of San, San Francisco *Also called Ocean Park Health Center (G-19788)*
Community Health Plan, Alhambra *Also called County of Los Angeles (G-10275)*
Community Health System, Fresno *Also called Community Medical Center (G-21500)*
Community Health Systems Inc 951 571-2300
22675 Alessandro Blvd # 1 Moreno Valley (92553) ***(G-19454)***
Community Hlth Alance Pasadena (PA)....626 398-6300
1855 N Fair Oaks Ave # 200 Pasadena (91103) ***(G-21497)***
Community HM Care & HM Support, Brea *Also called Community Home Care (G-22407)*
Community Home Care 714 671-6877
259 S Randolph Ave # 180 Brea (92821) ***(G-22407)***
Community Home Health Agency, Santa Barbara *Also called Sansum Clinic (G-22556)*
Community Home Partners LLC....408 985-5252
2384 Pacific Dr Santa Clara (95051) ***(G-21071)***
Community Hosp Huntington Pk, Huntington Park *Also called Chhp Management LLC (G-21482)*
Community Hosp Recovery Ctr, Monterey *Also called Monterey Peninsula Hospital (G-21752)*
Community Hosp San Bernardino (HQ)....909 887-6333
1805 Medical Center Dr San Bernardino (92411) ***(G-21498)***
Community Hospice Inc (PA)....209 578-6300
4368 Spyres Way Modesto (95356) ***(G-21072)***
Community Hospice Inc....209 578-6380
2201 Euclid Ave Hughson (95326) ***(G-21073)***
Community Hospital Foundation (PA) 831 625-4830
23625 Holman Hwy Monterey (93940) ***(G-26978)***
Community Hospital Long Beach....562 494-0600
1720 Termino Ave Long Beach (90804) ***(G-21499)***
Community Hospitals Centl Cal....559 459-6000
2823 Fresno St Fresno (93721) ***(G-22130)***
Community Housing Inc....650 328-3300
437 Webster St Palo Alto (94301) ***(G-24603)***
Community Housing Opport....707 759-6043
5030 Bus Center Dr # 260 Fairfield (94534) ***(G-26979)***
Community Housing Options 626 359-3300
348 E Foothill Blvd Arcadia (91006) ***(G-23774)***
Community Infant Tddler Prgram, San Mateo *Also called Peninsula Family Service (G-24129)*
Community Integrated Work Prog....559 276-8564
4623 W Jacquelyn Ave Fresno (93722) ***(G-24324)***
Community Integrated Work Prog....510 487-9768
1875 Whipple Rd Hayward (94544) ***(G-24325)***
Community Integration Program, Sacramento *Also called Develop Disabilities Svc Org (G-23942)*
Community Interface Services....760 729-3866
2621 Roosevelt St Ste 100 Carlsbad (92008) ***(G-23775)***

Community Intgrted Work Prgram, Hayward *Also called Community Integrated Work Prog (G-24325)*
Community MBL Diagnostics LLC 925 516-6851
10948 Bigge St San Leandro (94577) ***(G-22201)***
Community Med Group of Rvrside....951 274-3414
4444 Magnolia Ave Riverside (92501) ***(G-19455)***
Community Medical Center (PA)....559 459-6000
2823 Fresno St Fresno (93721) ***(G-21500)***
Community Medical Centers....559 459-2916
1140 T St Fresno (93721) ***(G-21501)***
Community Medical Centers....559 324-4000
2755 Herndon Ave Clovis (93611) ***(G-21502)***
Community Medical Centers....559 222-7416
3003 N Mariposa St Fresno (93703) ***(G-21503)***
Community Medical Centers....559 320-2200
668 E Bullard Ave Fresno (93710) ***(G-21504)***
Community Medical Centers....559 447-4050
7257 N Fresno St Fresno (93720) ***(G-21505)***
Community Medical Centers....559 447-4000
6297 N Fresno St Fresno (93710) ***(G-21506)***
Community Medical Centers Inc....209 944-4700
701 E Channel St Stockton (95202) ***(G-21507)***
Community Medical Centers Inc (PA) 209 373-2800
7210 Murray Dr Stockton (95210) ***(G-22690)***
Community Medical Ctr Clovis, Clovis *Also called Community Medical Centers (G-21502)*
Community Mem HSP/Sn Benua 805 652-5072
147 N Brent St Ventura (93003) ***(G-21508)***
Community Memorial Health Sys 805 658-5800
120 N Ashwood Ave Ventura (93003) ***(G-21509)***
Community Memorial Health Sys 805 981-3770
2361 E Vineyard Ave Oxnard (93036) ***(G-19456)***
Community Memorial Health Sys 805 482-1282
422 Arneill Rd Ste B Camarillo (93010) ***(G-19457)***
Community Mental Health Clinic, Greenbrae *Also called County of Marin (G-22704)*
Community Mental Health Svcs, San Luis Obispo *Also called County of San Luis Obispo (G-22709)*
Community Orthopedic Medical....949 348-4000
26401 Crown Valley Pkwy # 101 Mission Viejo (92691) ***(G-19458)***
Community Partners....323 780-7605
530 S Boyle Ave Los Angeles (90033) ***(G-23776)***
Community Partners (PA)....213 346-3200
1000 N Alameda St Ste 240 Los Angeles (90012) ***(G-24900)***
Community Recovery 323 525-0961
6708 Melrose Ave Los Angeles (90038) ***(G-22923)***
COMMUNITY REGIONAL MEDICAL CEN, Fresno *Also called Community Hospitals Centl Cal (G-22130)*
Community Retreat Center, Beverly Hills *Also called Labelle Fmly Rtreat Orgnzation (G-24705)*
Community Service Programs Inc (PA) 714 492-1010
1221 E Dyer Rd Ste 120 Santa Ana (92705) ***(G-23777)***
Community Services, Modesto *Also called County of Stanislaus (G-23923)*
Community Services Department, La Habra *Also called City of La Habra (G-23753)*
Community Services For Deaf, Stockton *Also called Communication Svc For Deaf Inc (G-24892)*
Community Support Options Inc....661 758-5331
1401 Poso Dr Wasco (93280) ***(G-23778)***
Community Transit Services, El Monte *Also called First Student Inc (G-3646)*
Community TV Southern Cal, Burbank *Also called Kcetlink (G-5879)*
Community Youth Ministries....559 638-6585
1592 11th St Ste E Reedley (93654) ***(G-23779)***
Communty Convlscnt Hosp Mntclr, Montclair *Also called US Skillserve Inc (G-21000)*
Communty Slns For Chldrn Fmls (PA)....408 779-2113
9015 Murray Ave Ste 100 Gilroy (95020) ***(G-23780)***
Companion Home Hlth & Hospice....714 560-8177
2041 W Orangewood Ave Orange (92868) ***(G-22408)***
Companion Hospice, Orange *Also called Companion Home Hlth & Hospice (G-22408)*
Companion Hospice and....310 338-1257
6133 Bristol Parkday 11 # 110 Culver City (90230) ***(G-22409)***
Companion Hospice Care LLC....562 944-2711
8130 Florence Ave Ste 200 Downey (90240) ***(G-22410)***
Companion Hospice LLC....562 944-2711
8130 Florence Ave Ste 200 Downey (90240) ***(G-22411)***
Company 3 Inc....310 255-6600
1661 Lincoln Blvd Ste 400 Santa Monica (90404) ***(G-18220)***
Comparenetworks Inc (PA) 650 873-9031
395 Oyster Point Blvd # 321 South San Francisco (94080) ***(G-26499)***
Compas Health, Templeton *Also called Compass Health Inc (G-20468)*
Compass Actn Netwk Dirct Outcm, Marina Del Rey *Also called Can-Do (G-23701)*
Compass Bancshares Inc....951 279-7071
195 W Ontario Ave Corona (92882) ***(G-9390)***
Compass Bancshares Inc 951 672-4829
27851 Bradley Rd Ste 125 Sun City (92586) ***(G-9391)***
Compass Bancshares Inc 209 239-1381
201 N Main St Manteca (95336) ***(G-9392)***
Compass Bancshares Inc....209 473-6925
2427 W Hammer Ln Stockton (95209) ***(G-9393)***
Compass Bancshares Inc 209 939-3288
2562 Pacific Ave Stockton (95204) ***(G-9394)***
Compass Bank, Corona *Also called Compass Bancshares Inc (G-9390)*
Compass Bank, Sun City *Also called Compass Bancshares Inc (G-9391)*
Compass Bank, Manteca *Also called Compass Bancshares Inc (G-9392)*
Compass Bank, Stockton *Also called Compass Bancshares Inc (G-9393)*
Compass Bank, Stockton *Also called Compass Bancshares Inc (G-9394)*
Compass Children's Center, San Francisco *Also called Compass Family Services (G-24448)*
Compass Clara House, San Francisco *Also called Compass Family Services (G-23783)*
Compass Connecting Point, San Francisco *Also called Compass Family Services (G-23781)*

ALPHABETIC

Compass Family Services.....415 644-0504
49 Powell St Fl 3 San Francisco (94102) *(G-24447)*
Compass Family Services.....415 644-0504
144 Leavenworth St San Francisco (94102) *(G-24448)*
Compass Family Services.....415 644-0504
995 Market St Fl 6 San Francisco (94103) *(G-23781)*
Compass Family Services.....415 644-0504
626 Polk St San Francisco (94102) *(G-23782)*
Compass Family Services.....415 644-0504
111 Page St San Francisco (94102) *(G-23783)*
Compass Group Usa Inc.....714 899-2520
12640 Knott St Garden Grove (92841) *(G-14524)*
Compass Health Inc.....805 434-3035
290 Heather Ct Templeton (93465) *(G-20468)*
Compass Health Inc.....805 687-6651
3880 Via Lucero Santa Barbara (93110) *(G-20469)*
Compass Health Inc.....805 543-0210
1425 Woodside Dr San Luis Obispo (93401) *(G-21189)*
Compass Health Inc.....805 772-7372
1405 Teresa Dr Morro Bay (93442) *(G-21190)*
Compass Health Inc.....805 489-8137
1212 Farroll Ave Arroyo Grande (93420) *(G-21191)*
Compass Health Inc.....805 466-9254
10805 El Camino Real Atascadero (93422) *(G-21192)*
Compass Home Inc.....909 605-9899
1900 Burgundy Pl Ontario (91761) *(G-6853)*
Compass Transportation Charter, South San Francisco *Also called Sfo Airporter Inc (G-3715)*
Competent Care HM Hlth Nursing, Costa Mesa *Also called Competent Care Inc (G-22412)*
Competent Care Inc.....714 545-4818
2900 Bristol St Ste D107 Costa Mesa (92626) *(G-22412)*
Competitive Edge RES Comm Inc.....619 702-2372
2170 4th Ave San Diego (92101) *(G-26651)*
Competitor Group Events Inc.....858 450-6510
5452 Oberlin Dr San Diego (92121) *(G-27743)*
Compex Legal Services Inc (PA).....310 782-1801
325 Maple Ave Torrance (90503) *(G-23161)*
Complete Coach Works.....951 682-2557
1863 Service Ct Riverside (92507) *(G-17879)*
Complete Equipment Repair.....530 589-1187
143 Willow Pass Rd Oroville (95966) *(G-17969)*
Complete Food Service Inc.....951 685-8490
3815 Wabash Dr Mira Loma (91752) *(G-8817)*
Complete Genomics Inc.....650 943-2800
2071 Stierlin Ct Mountain View (94043) *(G-26754)*
Complete Landscape Care Inc.....562 946-4441
13316 Leffingwell Rd Whittier (90605) *(G-829)*
Complete Linen Services, South San Francisco *Also called Medical Linen Services Inc (G-13551)*
Complete Logistics Company.....909 427-9800
13831 Slover Ave Fontana (92337) *(G-3998)*
Complete Millwork Services Inc.....408 567-9664
405 Aldo Ave Santa Clara (95054) *(G-6919)*
Complete Office California Inc.....714 880-1222
12724 Moore St Cerritos (90703) *(G-6812)*
Complete Relocation Svcs Inc.....714 901-7411
7361 Doig Dr Garden Grove (92841) *(G-4335)*
Completely Fresh Foods Inc.....323 722-9136
4401 S Downey Rd Vernon (90058) *(G-8818)*
Complex The, Los Angeles *Also called W P Media Complex (G-17603)*
Complianceonline, Palo Alto *Also called Metricstream Inc (G-15750)*
Composite Software LLC (HQ).....800 553-6387
755 Sycamore Dr Milpitas (95035) *(G-15625)*
Comppartners Inc.....949 253-3111
333 City Blvd W Ste 1500 Orange (92868) *(G-22413)*
Comprehensive Autism Ctr Inc.....951 813-4035
7839 University Ave # 105 La Mesa (91942) *(G-20314)*
Comprehensive Cmnty Hlth Ctrs.....818 265-2210
801 S Chevy Chase Dr Glendale (91205) *(G-22414)*
Comprehensive Enviro.....619 294-9400
1615 Murray Canyon Rd San Diego (92108) *(G-25747)*
Comprehensive SEC Svcs Inc (PA).....916 683-3605
10535 E Stockton Blvd Elk Grove (95624) *(G-16608)*
Comprehensive SEC Svcs Inc.....530 743-6762
1734 Linda Ave Ste B Marysville (95901) *(G-16609)*
Comprehensive Youth Ser.....559 229-3561
4545 N West Ave Ste 101 Fresno (93705) *(G-23784)*
Compremex LLC.....714 739-1348
14849 Firestone Blvd La Mirada (90638) *(G-4396)*
Comps Inc.....858 658-0576
4535 Towne Centre Ct San Diego (92121) *(G-16223)*
Compspec Inc.....818 551-4200
425 E Colorado St Ste 410 Glendale (91205) *(G-27387)*
Compton Adult Day Care, Compton *Also called Lynwood Developmental Care (G-21302)*
Compton Family Mhc Fsp, Compton *Also called County of Los Angeles (G-22928)*
Compton Hauling, Compton *Also called USA Waste of California Inc (G-6585)*
Compton Service Center, Compton *Also called Southern California Edison Co (G-6229)*
Compton Training Center, Van Nuys *Also called Apprentice & Journeymen Trn Tr (G-24303)*
Compucom Systems Inc.....949 222-0949
16842 Von Karman Ave # 375 Irvine (92606) *(G-7110)*
Compulaw LLC.....310 553-3355
200 Crprate Pinte Ste 400 Culver City (90230) *(G-15097)*
Compulink Business Systems Inc.....805 446-2050
1100 Business Center Cir Newbury Park (91320) *(G-15626)*
Compulink Management Ctr Inc.....562 988-1688
3545 Long Beach Blvd Long Beach (90807) *(G-15627)*
Compumail Information Svcs Inc.....925 689-7100
4057 Port Chicago Hwy # 300 Concord (94520) *(G-17089)*

Computer History Museum.....650 810-1010
1401 N Shoreline Blvd Mountain View (94043) *(G-25012)*
Computer Proc Unlimited Inc.....858 530-0875
9235 Activity Rd Ste 104 San Diego (92126) *(G-15098)*
Computer Programming Dept, Novato *Also called County of Marin (G-16114)*
Computer Resources Group Inc.....415 398-3535
275 Battery St Ste 800 San Francisco (94111) *(G-15099)*
Computer Sciences Corporation.....510 645-3000
1111 Broadway Fl 13 Oakland (94607) *(G-16340)*
Computer Sciences Corporation.....702 558-8092
1520 Railroad Ave Walnut Creek (94595) *(G-16276)*
Computer Task Group Inc.....408 573-6070
2033 Gateway Pl Fl 5 San Jose (95110) *(G-15100)*
Computer Task Group Inc.....800 992-5350
101 Metro Dr Ste 530 San Jose (95110) *(G-15101)*
Computerized Management.....805 522-5999
40 W Cochran St Simi Valley (93065) *(G-14864)*
Computerized Management Svcs, Simi Valley *Also called Simi Radiology & Imaging (G-27647)*
Computerized Mgt Svcs Inc.....805 522-5940
4100 Guardian St Ste 205 Simi Valley (93063) *(G-26980)*
Computrition Inc (HQ).....818 961-3999
8521 Fllbrook Ave Ste 100 Canoga Park (91304) *(G-15102)*
Compuware Corporation.....818 380-3019
15303 Ventura Blvd Fl 9 Sherman Oaks (91403) *(G-15103)*
Compuware Corporation.....858 824-5200
5375 Mira Sorrento Pl # 500 San Diego (92121) *(G-15104)*
Compvue Inc.....408 892-9909
440 N Wolfe Rd Sunnyvale (94085) *(G-15105)*
Compwest Insurance Company.....714 641-9500
3 Hutton Cntre Dr Ste 550 Santa Ana (92707) *(G-10412)*
Comstock Crosser Assoc Dev Inc.....310 546-5781
321 12th St Ste 200 Manhattan Beach (90266) *(G-11960)*
Comstock Homes, Manhattan Beach *Also called Comstock Crosser Assoc Dev Inc (G-11960)*
Comstock Mortgage, San Diego *Also called Guild Mortgage Company (G-9852)*
Comtel Systems Technology.....408 543-5600
1292 Hammerwood Ave Sunnyvale (94089) *(G-2560)*
Comwork.....405 703-8889
6489 Oak Cyn Irvine (92618) *(G-17090)*
Con-Way, Blythe *Also called Xpo Enterprise Services Inc (G-4317)*
Con-Way, Santa Rosa *Also called Xpo Enterprise Services Inc (G-4318)*
Con-Way, Lakeport *Also called Xpo Enterprise Services Inc (G-4319)*
Conam Management Corporation (PA).....858 614-7200
3990 Ruffin Rd Ste 100 San Diego (92123) *(G-11451)*
Concentrix Corporation.....510 668-3717
44201 Nobel Dr Fremont (94538) *(G-16341)*
Concept Enterprises Inc.....626 968-8827
338 Turnbull Canyon Rd City of Industry (91745) *(G-7493)*
Concept Green Enrgy Sltons Inc.....855 459-6535
13824 Yorba Ave Chino (91710) *(G-17091)*
Concerro Inc (HQ).....858 882-8500
9276 Scranton Rd Ste 400 San Diego (92121) *(G-15106)*
Concerto Healthcare Inc.....949 537-3400
2030 Main St Ste 600 Irvine (92614) *(G-23785)*
Concerts West, Los Angeles *Also called AEG Live LLC (G-18367)*
Concession Management Svcs Inc.....310 846-5830
6033 W Century Blvd # 890 Los Angeles (90045) *(G-19186)*
Concessionaires Urban Park (PA).....530 529-1512
2150 Main St Ste 5 Red Bluff (96080) *(G-19187)*
Concessionaires Urban Park.....209 763-5121
2000 Camanche Rd Ofc Ofc Ione (95640) *(G-19188)*
Concessionaires Urban Park.....209 763-5166
2000 Camanche Rd Ofc Ofc Ione (95640) *(G-19189)*
Concessionaires Urban Park.....530 529-1596
34600 Ardenwood Blvd Fremont (94555) *(G-19190)*
Concessionaires Urban Park.....530 529-1513
18013 Bollinger Canyon Rd San Ramon (94583) *(G-19191)*
Conco Cement Company, Concord *Also called Gonsalves & Santucci Inc (G-3268)*
Conco Cement Company, Concord *Also called Gonsalves & Santucci Inc (G-3382)*
Conco Pumping.....909 350-0503
13052 Dahlia St Fontana (92337) *(G-3246)*
Concord Document Services Inc (PA).....213 745-3175
1321 W 12th St Los Angeles (90015) *(G-14116)*
Concord Foods Inc (PA).....909 975-2000
4601 E Guasti Rd Ontario (91761) *(G-8468)*
Concord Hotel LLC.....925 521-3751
45 John Glenn Dr Concord (94520) *(G-12539)*
Concord Iron Works Inc.....925 432-0136
1501 Loveridge Rd Ste 15 Pittsburg (94565) *(G-3380)*
Concord Pavillion, Concord *Also called City of Concord (G-18383)*
Concorde Battery Corporation.....626 962-4006
1125 N Azusa Canyon Rd West Covina (91790) *(G-4537)*
Concorde Career Colleges Inc.....714 620-1000
12951 Euclid St Ste 101 Garden Grove (92840) *(G-21510)*
Concourse Hotel At, Los Angeles *Also called Humnit Hotel At Lax LLC (G-12803)*
Concrete Concepts Inc.....760 737-5470
2317 Auto Park Way Escondido (92029) *(G-3247)*
Concrete Construction, San Diego *Also called Ben F Smith Inc (G-3232)*
Concrete Demolition, Anaheim *Also called Penhall International Corp (G-3464)*
Concrete Holding Co Cal Inc.....818 788-4228
15821 Ventura Blvd # 475 Encino (91436) *(G-12053)*
Concrete Images International.....858 676-1253
17237 Saint Andrews Dr Poway (92064) *(G-3248)*
Concrete North Inc.....209 745-7400
10695 Twin Cities Rd Galt (95632) *(G-3249)*
Concrete Tie Industries Inc (PA).....310 886-1000
130 E Oris St Compton (90222) *(G-6979)*

ALPHABETIC

Condon-Johnson & Assoc Inc (PA).....510 636-2100
480 Roland Way Ste 200 Oakland (94621) ***(G-3250)***
Conduit Lngage Specialists Inc.....859 299-3178
22720 Ventura Blvd # 100 Woodland Hills (91364) ***(G-13748)***
Condusiv Technologies Corp (PA).....818 771-1600
7590 N Glenoaks Blvd Burbank (91504) ***(G-15628)***
Cone Collision Center, Downey *Also called Mullahey Chevrolet Inc* ***(G-17763)***
Conejo Pacific Technologies.....805 498-5315
1560 Newbury Rd Ste 1 Newbury Park (91320) ***(G-1416)***
Conejo Valley Unified Schl Dst.....805 492-3531
620 Velarde Dr Thousand Oaks (91360) ***(G-25241)***
Conestoga Hotel.....714 535-0300
1240 S Walnut St Anaheim (92802) ***(G-12540)***
Conexis, Orange *Also called Word & Brown Insurance* ***(G-27284)***
Conexis Bneft Admnistrators LP (HQ).....714 835-5006
721 S Parker St Ste 300 Orange (92868) ***(G-10677)***
Confie Seguros Inc (HQ).....714 252-2500
7711 Center Ave Ste 200 Huntington Beach (92647) ***(G-10678)***
Conforti Plumbing Inc.....530 622-0202
6080 Pleasant Valley Rd C El Dorado (95623) ***(G-2188)***
Conglobal Industries LLC.....310 518-2850
1711 Alameda St Wilmington (90744) ***(G-4680)***
Congregation of Poor Sisters.....559 237-3444
2121 N 1st St Fresno (93703) ***(G-24604)***
Congress Med Surgery Ctr LLC.....626 396-8100
800 S Raymond Ave Pasadena (91105) ***(G-19459)***
Congrgtnal Ch Retirement Cmnty.....530 823-6131
750 Auburn Ravine Rd Auburn (95603) ***(G-24901)***
Conill Advertising Inc.....424 290-4400
2101 Rosecrans Ave Fl 2 El Segundo (90245) ***(G-13826)***
Conill Advertising Inc.....424 290-4400
2101 Rosecrans Ave Fl 2 El Segundo (90245) ***(G-13827)***
Connect Computers, Santa Ana *Also called General Procurement Inc* ***(G-7138)***
Connect Your Home LLC.....949 777-0100
1 Park Plz Ste 600 Irvine (92614) ***(G-1533)***
Connectx Inc.....310 702-8686
909 N Avi Blvd Unit 6 Manhattan Beach (90266) ***(G-16342)***
Connexity Inc (HQ).....310 571-1235
12200 W Olympic Blvd # 300 Los Angeles (90064) ***(G-5581)***
Connexsys Engineering Inc.....510 243-2050
3075 Research Dr Richmond (94806) ***(G-25748)***
Connotate Technologies Inc.....949 270-1916
2601 Main St Ste 830 Irvine (92614) ***(G-15107)***
Conrad A Cox.....562 927-0033
9040 Telegraph Rd Downey (90240) ***(G-19460)***
Conrad Acceptance Corporation.....760 735-5000
476 W Vermont Ave Escondido (92025) ***(G-9779)***
Conrad Credit, Escondido *Also called Conrad Acceptance Corporation* ***(G-9779)***
Conrad Credit Corporation.....760 735-5000
476 W Vermont Ave Escondido (92025) ***(G-14028)***
Conrad Imports Inc.....415 626-3303
540 Barneveld Ave Ste H San Francisco (94124) ***(G-6854)***
Conrad Lab, The, Lodi *Also called Lodi Memorial Hosp Assn Inc* ***(G-21709)***
Conroy Farms Inc.....805 981-0537
520 Maulhardt Ave Oxnard (93030) ***(G-108)***
Consensus Health, Emeryville *Also called Onebody Inc* ***(G-22521)***
Consensus Orthopedics Inc.....916 355-7110
1115 Windfield Way # 100 El Dorado Hills (95762) ***(G-7259)***
Conservation Corps Long Beach.....562 986-1249
340 Nieto Ave Long Beach (90814) ***(G-24326)***
Conservation Liquidation.....415 676-5000
100 Pine St Ste 2600 San Francisco (94111) ***(G-28124)***
Considine & Considine An Acco.....619 231-1977
1501 5th Ave Ste 400 San Diego (92101) ***(G-26315)***
Consoldted Fire Protection LLC (HQ).....949 727-3277
153 Technology Dr Ste 200 Irvine (92618) ***(G-17092)***
Consoldted Med Bo-Analysis Inc (PA).....714 657-7369
10700 Walker St Cypress (90630) ***(G-22202)***
Consoldted Med Bo-Analysis Inc.....714 657-7389
7631 Wyoming St Ste 105a Westminster (92683) ***(G-22203)***
Consoldted Med Bo-Analysis Inc.....714 467-0240
12665 Garden Grove Blvd Garden Grove (92843) ***(G-22204)***
Consoldted Med Bo-Analysis Inc.....951 243-2600
12980 Frederick St Ste E Moreno Valley (92553) ***(G-22205)***
Consolidated Cleaning Services.....510 663-2585
2515 Willow St Oakland (94607) ***(G-14260)***
Consolidated Design West Inc.....714 999-1476
1345 S Lewis St Anaheim (92805) ***(G-14139)***
Consolidated Disposal Svc LLC.....562 531-2670
2495 E 68th St Long Beach (90805) ***(G-6466)***
Consolidated Elec Distrs Inc.....858 268-1020
5457 Ruffin Rd San Diego (92123) ***(G-7430)***
Consolidated Elec Distrs Inc.....626 345-0000
3020 W Empire Ave Burbank (91504) ***(G-7431)***
Consolidated Plastics Corp (PA).....909 393-8222
14954 La Palma Dr Chino (91710) ***(G-8968)***
Consolidated Reprographics, Costa Mesa *Also called American Reprographics Co LLC* ***(G-14104)***
Consolidated Tribal Health Prj.....707 485-5115
6991 N State St Redwood Valley (95470) ***(G-22691)***
Consortium For Community Svcs, Sacramento *Also called Quality Group Homes Inc* ***(G-1240)***
Consortm On Reachng Excellnce.....510 540-4200
3112 Cedar Ravine Rd Placerville (95667) ***(G-27887)***
Consorzio, Berkeley *Also called Homegrown Natural Foods Inc* ***(G-8485)***
Constance Dehaan Dvm, Rohnert Park *Also called Animal Care Center* ***(G-614)***
Constellation Newenergy Inc.....213 576-6001
350 S Grand Ave Ste 3800 Los Angeles (90071) ***(G-6119)***
Construction, Fresno *Also called Quiring General LLC* ***(G-1643)***
Construction Customer Service.....714 701-1858
1320 N Hancock St Ste A Anaheim (92807) ***(G-1159)***
Construction Development Div, Alhambra *Also called Community Development Comm* ***(G-26977)***
Construction Specialty Svc Inc.....661 864-7573
4550 Buck Owens Blvd Bakersfield (93308) ***(G-1922)***
Construction Temps, Signal Hill *Also called Wannajob Inc* ***(G-14980)***
Construction Testing Services (PA).....925 462-5151
2118 Rheem Dr Pleasanton (94588) ***(G-26839)***
Construction Tstg & Engrg Inc (PA).....760 746-4955
1441 Montiel Rd Ste 115 Escondido (92026) ***(G-25749)***
Consultants For Adhc, Temple City *Also called Community Care Adhc Inc* ***(G-23772)***
Consumer Credit Counseling Svc (PA).....415 788-0288
595 Market St Ste 1500 San Francisco (94105) ***(G-13749)***
Consumer Portfolio Svcs Inc.....949 788-5695
19500 Jamboree Rd Irvine (92612) ***(G-9744)***
Consumer Resource Network LLC.....800 291-4794
4420 E Miraloma Ave Ste J Anaheim (92807) ***(G-27388)***
Contact Security Inc.....714 572-6760
3000 E Birch St Ste 111 Brea (92821) ***(G-16610)***
Contain-A-Way Inc.....909 796-2860
25837 Bus Ctr Dr Ste F Redlands (92374) ***(G-6467)***
Contec Microelectronics USA.....949 250-4025
17811 Gillette Ave Fl 1 Irvine (92614) ***(G-7111)***
Contec USA, Irvine *Also called Contec Microelectronics USA* ***(G-7111)***
Contemporary Services Corp (PA).....818 885-5150
17101 Superior St Northridge (91325) ***(G-14628)***
Contemporary Services Corp.....559 225-9325
2650 E Shaw Ave Fresno (93710) ***(G-16611)***
Contemprary Hstrical Vhcl Assn.....707 448-7266
430 Oak View Dr Vacaville (95688) ***(G-25242)***
Conterra Residential Cnstr, Riverside *Also called Combine Residential Cnstr* ***(G-27885)***
Conti Life Comm Plea LLC.....925 227-6800
3300 Stoneridge Creek Way Pleasanton (94588) ***(G-17093)***
Contiki Holidays, Anaheim *Also called Contiki US Holdings Inc* ***(G-4992)***
Contiki US Holdings Inc.....714 935-0808
801 E Katella Ave Frnt Anaheim (92805) ***(G-4992)***
Continental 155 5th Corp.....310 640-1520
2041 Rosecrans Ave # 200 El Segundo (90245) ***(G-11452)***
Continental Agency Inc (PA).....909 595-8884
1768 W 2nd St Pomona (91766) ***(G-5051)***
Continental Airlines, San Jose *Also called United Airlines Inc* ***(G-4828)***
Continental Airlines, Los Angeles *Also called United Airlines Inc* ***(G-4834)***
Continental Currency Svcs Inc (HQ).....714 569-0300
1108 E 17th St Santa Ana (92701) ***(G-9713)***
Continental Currency Svcs Inc (PA).....714 569-0300
1108 E 17th St Santa Ana (92701) ***(G-9714)***
Continental Datagraphics, Long Beach *Also called Continental Graphics Corp* ***(G-25750)***
Continental Dntl Ceramics Inc.....310 618-8821
1873 Western Way Torrance (90501) ***(G-22303)***
Continental Ex Money Order Co, Santa Ana *Also called Continental Currency Svcs Inc* ***(G-9713)***
Continental Exch Solutions Inc (HQ).....714 522-7044
6565 Knott Ave Buena Park (90620) ***(G-17094)***
Continental Graphics Corp.....714 503-4200
2401 E Wardlow Rd Long Beach (90807) ***(G-25750)***
Continental Sales Co America, Watsonville *Also called Optics East Inc* ***(G-7336)***
Continental Security Guards, Orange *Also called Garda CL West Inc* ***(G-16658)***
Continuing Lf Communities LLC (PA).....760 704-1000
1940 Levante St Carlsbad (92009) ***(G-10679)***
Contra Costa ARC.....925 755-4925
2505 W 10th St Antioch (94509) ***(G-24327)***
Contra Costa ARC.....510 233-7303
1420 Regatta Blvd Richmond (94804) ***(G-24605)***
Contra Costa Country Club.....925 798-7135
801 Golf Club Rd Pleasant Hill (94523) ***(G-18924)***
Contra Costa Electric Inc (HQ).....925 229-4250
825 Howe Rd Martinez (94553) ***(G-2561)***
Contra Costa Electric Inc.....661 322-4036
3208 Landco Dr Bakersfield (93308) ***(G-2562)***
Contra Costa Metal Fabricators, Oakland *Also called Monterey Mechanical Co* ***(G-2069)***
Contra Costa Newspapers Inc.....925 757-2525
1650 Cavallo Rd Antioch (94509) ***(G-9162)***
Contra Costa Powersports, Concord *Also called High Adrenaline Enterprises* ***(G-6680)***
Contra Costa Vet Med Emrgcy CL.....925 798-5830
1145 Turtle Rock Ln Concord (94521) ***(G-617)***
Contra Costa Water District (PA).....925 688-8000
1331 Concord Ave Concord (94520) ***(G-6333)***
Contra Costa Water District.....925 625-6534
3760 Neroly Rd Oakley (94561) ***(G-6334)***
Contra Csta Child Care Council (PA).....925 676-5442
1035 Detroit Ave Ste 200 Concord (94518) ***(G-24902)***
Contra Csta Child Care Council.....925 676-5437
2280 Diamond Blvd Ste 500 Concord (94520) ***(G-24903)***
Contract, San Juan Capistrano *Also called Emerald Expositions LLC* ***(G-17150)***
Contract Services Group Inc.....714 582-1800
480 Capricorn St Brea (92821) ***(G-14261)***
Contractor Warehouse.....562 633-1428
5950 N Paramount Blvd Lakewood (90805) ***(G-1534)***
Contractors Cargo Company, Compton *Also called CCC Property Holdings LLC* ***(G-12050)***
Contractors Cargo Company (PA).....310 609-1957
500 S Alameda St Compton (90221) ***(G-4128)***
Contractors Complete Surety, Wildomar *Also called Asr Constructors Inc* ***(G-1493)***
Contractors Flrg Svc Cal Inc.....714 556-6100
300 E Dyer Rd Santa Ana (92707) ***(G-6855)***
Contractors Labor Pool of La, Burbank *Also called Clp Resources Inc* ***(G-14861)***

ALPHABETIC

Contractors Rigging & Erectors, Compton *Also called Contractors Cargo Company* ***(G-4128)***
Contrlled Cntmination Svcs LLC..........858 457-3157
6150 Lusk Blvd Ste 205 San Diego (92121) ***(G-14262)***
Control Air Conditioning Corp..........760 744-2727
1390 Armorlite Dr San Marcos (92069) ***(G-17920)***
Control Air Conditioning Corp (PA)..........714 777-8600
5200 E La Palma Ave Anaheim (92807) ***(G-2189)***
Control Air Conditioning Svc..........714 777-8600
5200 E La Palma Ave Anaheim (92807) ***(G-2190)***
Control Point Corporation (PA)..........805 685-6390
110 Castilian Dr Ste 200 Goleta (93117) ***(G-25751)***
Controlled Contamination Svcs, San Diego *Also called Contrlled Cntmination Svcs LLC* ***(G-14262)***
Controlled Contamination Svcs..........510 728-1106
23595 Cabot Blvd Ste 115 Hayward (94545) ***(G-14263)***
Convalescent Management Svcs..........408 745-1168
1220 Vienna Dr Spc 573 Sunnyvale (94089) ***(G-20470)***
Convenience Management Group..........805 644-6784
3781 Telegraph Rd Ventura (93003) ***(G-26981)***
Convention Center Booking Off, Richmond *Also called City of Richmond* ***(G-19180)***
Convention Center Los Angeles, Los Angeles *Also called Los Angeles Convention and Exh* ***(G-11012)***
Conventions Arts & Entrmt, San Jose *Also called City of San Jose* ***(G-17079)***
Convergint Technologies LLC..........510 300-2800
5860 W Las Positas Blvd # 7 Pleasanton (94588) ***(G-16875)***
Conversant LLC (HQ)..........818 575-4500
30699 Russell Ranch Rd # 250 Westlake Village (91362) ***(G-16224)***
Converse Consultants Inc (HQ)..........626 930-1200
222 E Huntington Dr # 211 Monrovia (91016) ***(G-17095)***
Converse Inc..........415 433-1174
838 Market St San Francisco (94102) ***(G-8426)***
Converse Inc..........909 625-6655
2150 E Montclair Plaza Ln Montclair (91763) ***(G-8427)***
Converse Inc..........310 451-0314
1437-39 3rd St Promenade Santa Monica (90401) ***(G-8428)***
Converse Inc..........909 974-5695
4450 E Lowell St Ontario (91761) ***(G-8429)***
Convertro Inc..........800 797-0176
13031 W Jeff Blvd 900 Playa Vista (90094) ***(G-15108)***
Convoy Inc..........415 403-2770
463 Pacific Ave San Francisco (94133) ***(G-16290)***
Cook Cabinets Inc..........530 621-0851
6428 Capitol Ave Diamond Springs (95619) ***(G-3039)***
Cook Realty Inc..........916 451-6702
4305 Freeport Blvd Sacramento (95822) ***(G-11453)***
Cook Realty Sales, Sacramento *Also called Cook Realty Inc* ***(G-11453)***
Cookie Jar Entrmt USA Inc..........818 955-5400
4100 W Alameda Ave # 101 Burbank (91505) ***(G-18064)***
Cooks Warehouse Inc..........818 556-2740
2504 N Ontario St Burbank (91504) ***(G-6856)***
Cooksey Toolen Gage Duffy (PA)..........714 431-1100
535 Anton Blvd Fl 10 Costa Mesa (92626) ***(G-23162)***
Cool Roofing Systems Inc (PA)..........209 825-0818
1286 Dupont Ct Manteca (95336) ***(G-3155)***
Cool Transport, Colton *Also called Van Dyk Tank Lines Inc* ***(G-4087)***
Cooley Godward Kronish, San Francisco *Also called Cooley LLP* ***(G-23164)***
Cooley Godward Kronish LLP..........650 842-7201
3000 El Camino Real 5-400 Palo Alto (94306) ***(G-23163)***
Cooley LLP..........415 693-2000
101 California St Fl 5 San Francisco (94111) ***(G-23164)***
Cooley LLP (PA)..........650 843-5000
3175 Hanover St Palo Alto (94304) ***(G-23165)***
Cooley LLP..........650 843-5124
4 Palo Alto Sq Palo Alto (94306) ***(G-23166)***
Cooley LLP..........858 550-6000
4401 Eastgate Mall San Diego (92121) ***(G-23167)***
Cooper & Jackson Inc..........408 437-2750
310 Shaw Rd Ste D South San Francisco (94080) ***(G-26840)***
Cooper Vali & Associates Inc (PA)..........510 446-8301
2000 Powell St Ste 500 Emeryville (94608) ***(G-25752)***
Cooper White & Cooper LLP (PA)..........415 433-1900
201 California St Fl 17 San Francisco (94111) ***(G-23168)***
Cooperative Personnel Services (PA)..........916 263-3600
241 Lathrop Way Sacramento (95815) ***(G-27389)***
Coopertive Amrcn Physcians Inc (PA)..........213 473-8600
333 S Hope St Fl 8 Los Angeles (90071) ***(G-25131)***
Coordnted Dlvry Instlltion Inc..........714 501-4040
905 E Katella Ave Anaheim (92805) ***(G-3999)***
Copia The American C..........707 259-1600
500 1st St NAPA (94559) ***(G-25013)***
Copley Press Inc..........619 718-5200
2375 Northside Dr Ste 300 San Diego (92108) ***(G-15629)***
Coppel Corporation..........760 357-3707
503 Scaroni Ave Calexico (92231) ***(G-6813)***
Copper Eagle Patrol & Security, Santa Clarita *Also called S C Security Inc* ***(G-16777)***
Copper Ridge Care Center..........530 222-2273
201 Hartnell Ave Redding (96002) ***(G-20471)***
Copper River Country Club LP (PA)..........559 434-5200
2140 E Clubhouse Dr Fresno (93730) ***(G-18925)***
Coppersmith Global Logistics, El Segundo *Also called L E Coppersmith Inc* ***(G-5114)***
Coptic Clinics..........562 900-2692
3803 W Mission Blvd Pomona (91766) ***(G-19461)***
Copypage, Los Angeles *Also called C P Document Technologies LLC* ***(G-7540)***
Cora Constructors Inc..........760 674-3201
75140 Saint Charles Pl A Palm Desert (92211) ***(G-25753)***
Coram Alternate Site Svcs Inc..........858 576-6969
12310 World Trade Dr # 100 San Diego (92128) ***(G-22415)***
Coram Specialty Infusion, San Diego *Also called Coram Alternate Site Svcs Inc* ***(G-22415)***
Corcoran District Hospital..........559 992-3300
1310 Hanna Ave Corcoran (93212) ***(G-21511)***
Cordelia Lighting Inc..........310 886-3490
20101 S Santa Fe Ave Compton (90221) ***(G-7432)***
Cordevalle Golf Club LLC..........408 695-4500
1 Cordevalle Club Dr San Martin (95046) ***(G-18926)***
Cordilleras Mental Health Ctr, Redwood City *Also called Telecare Corporation* ***(G-22105)***
Cordoba Corporation..........213 895-0224
1401 N Broadway Los Angeles (90012) ***(G-15925)***
Core, Placerville *Also called Consortm On Reachng Excellnce* ***(G-27887)***
Core Communications Group LLC..........714 729-8404
2749 Saturn St Brea (92821) ***(G-11454)***
Core Group, The, Milpitas *Also called Tcg Builders Inc* ***(G-1688)***
Core Medstaff, Los Angeles *Also called Total Professional Network* ***(G-14805)***
Core Nutrition LLC..........310 424-5077
630 Clinton Pl Beverly Hills (90210) ***(G-8819)***
Core Nutrition LLC..........310 640-0500
1222 E Grand Ave Ste 102 El Segundo (90245) ***(G-8820)***
Core Realty Holdings LLC (PA)..........949 863-1031
1600 Dove St Ste 450 Newport Beach (92660) ***(G-12241)***
Core Realty Holdings MGT Inc..........949 863-1031
1600 Dove St Ste 450 Newport Beach (92660) ***(G-11455)***
Core-Mark International, South San Francisco *Also called Core-Mark Midcontinent Inc* ***(G-9233)***
Core-Mark International Inc..........661 366-2673
200 Coremark Ct Bakersfield (93307) ***(G-8821)***
Core-Mark International Inc..........661 366-2673
8333 Edison Hwy Bakersfield (93307) ***(G-9232)***
Core-Mark International Inc..........323 583-6531
2311 E 48th St Vernon (90058) ***(G-8822)***
Core-Mark International Inc..........916 927-0795
3030 Mulvany Pl West Sacramento (95691) ***(G-8823)***
Core-Mark International Inc (HQ)..........650 589-9445
395 Oyster Point Blvd # 415 South San Francisco (94080) ***(G-8469)***
Core-Mark International Inc..........510 487-3000
31300 Medallion Dr Hayward (94544) ***(G-8824)***
Core-Mark Interrelated (HQ)..........951 272-4790
311 Reed Cir Corona (92879) ***(G-9256)***
Core-Mark Midcontinent Inc (HQ)..........650 589-9445
395 Oyster Point Blvd # 415 South San Francisco (94080) ***(G-9233)***
Corecare I I I..........714 256-8000
800 Morningside Dr Fullerton (92835) ***(G-24606)***
Corecare V A Cal Ltd Partnr..........714 256-1000
2525 Brea Blvd Fullerton (92835) ***(G-20472)***
Corelogic Inc..........714 250-6400
201 Spear St Fl 4 San Francisco (94105) ***(G-11456)***
Corelogic Inc..........714 250-6400
40 Pacifica Ste 900 Irvine (92618) ***(G-11457)***
Corelogic Dorado, Oakland *Also called Dorado Network Systems Corp* ***(G-15644)***
Corelynx Inc..........877 267-3599
11501 Dublin Blvd Ste 200 Dublin (94568) ***(G-15109)***
Coretco Inc..........323 770-2920
547 W 140th St Gardena (90248) ***(G-1923)***
Coretechs Staffing Inc..........650 363-7960
50 Woodside Plz Ste 604 Redwood City (94061) ***(G-15110)***
Corey Delta Constructors Inc..........925 370-9808
261 Arthur Rd Fairfield (94533) ***(G-2191)***
Corey Nursery Co Inc (PA)..........909 621-6886
1650 Monte Vista Ave Claremont (91711) ***(G-9185)***
Corinthian Intl Prkg Svcs Inc..........408 867-7275
19925 Stevens Creek Blvd Cupertino (95014) ***(G-13750)***
Corinthian Parking Services, Cupertino *Also called Corinthian Intl Prkg Svcs Inc* ***(G-13750)***
Corinthian Realty LLC..........510 487-8653
3902 Smith St Union City (94587) ***(G-11458)***
Corinthian Title Company Inc..........619 299-4800
5030 Camino De La Siesta San Diego (92108) ***(G-10511)***
Corizon Health Inc..........707 253-4384
1125 Third St NAPA (94559) ***(G-19462)***
Corizon Health Inc..........925 551-6500
5325 Broder Blvd Dublin (94568) ***(G-19463)***
Corkys Pest Control Inc..........760 432-8801
909 Rancheros Dr San Marcos (92069) ***(G-14183)***
Corland Companies (PA)..........714 573-7780
17542 17th St Ste 420 Tustin (92780) ***(G-26982)***
Cornell Corrections Cal Inc (HQ)..........805 644-8700
1811 Knoll Dr Ventura (93003) ***(G-23786)***
Corner Bakery Store..........714 459-1420
1040 W Imperial Hwy Ste A La Habra (90631) ***(G-8825)***
Corner Products Company..........949 255-3982
1370 Reynolds Ave Ste 100 Irvine (92614) ***(G-7550)***
Cornerstone Affiliates Inc..........925 924-7100
6120 Stoneridge Pleasanton (94588) ***(G-23787)***
Cornerstone Cnsulting Tech Inc..........415 705-7800
44 Montgomery St Ste 3360 San Francisco (94104) ***(G-27888)***
Cornerstone Healthcare Inc..........805 777-1133
143 Triunfo Canyon Rd # 103 Westlake Village (91361) ***(G-21074)***
Cornerstone Hospice Cal LLC..........909 872-8100
1461 E Cooley Dr Ste 220 Colton (92324) ***(G-22416)***
Cornerstone Hotel Management (HQ)..........415 397-5572
222 Kearny St Ste 200 San Francisco (94108) ***(G-26983)***
Cornerstone Marketing Alliance, Encino *Also called C M A Alliance* ***(G-10652)***
Cornerstone Medical Group..........909 890-4353
1881 Commercenter E # 112 San Bernardino (92408) ***(G-20294)***
Cornerstone Ondemand Inc (PA)..........310 752-0200
1601 Cloverfield Blvd 620s Santa Monica (90404) ***(G-15630)***
Cornerstone Research Inc..........213 553-2500
633 W 5th St Fl 31 Los Angeles (90071) ***(G-26652)***
Cornerstone Research Inc (PA)..........650 853-1660
1000 El Camino Real # 250 Menlo Park (94025) ***(G-27889)***

ALPHABETIC

Cornerstone Research Inc...415 229-8100
2 Embarcadero Ctr Fl 20 San Francisco (94111) *(G-27890)*
Coroc, Bakersfield *Also called Weatherford International LLC (G-7796)*
Corodata Corporation (PA)...858 748-1100
12375 Kerran St Poway (92064) *(G-4681)*
Corona - College Heights Ora...951 359-6451
8000 Lincoln Ave Riverside (92504) *(G-522)*
Corona Clipper Inc...951 737-6515
22440 Temescal Canyon Rd # 102 Corona (92883) *(G-7680)*
Corona Division, Corona *Also called Amerisourcebergen Corporation (G-8233)*
Corona Medical Offices, Corona *Also called Kaiser Foundation Hospitals (G-12188)*
Corona Mill Works & Cab Work, Chino *Also called Jose Corona (G-1198)*
Corona Regional Med Ctr Hosp, Corona *Also called Uhs-Corona Inc (G-21978)*
Corona Regional Medical Center, Corona *Also called Uhs-Corona Inc (G-22855)*
Coronado Financial Corp...619 946-1900
940 Eastlake Pkwy Chula Vista (91914) *(G-11459)*
Coronado Royale, Coronado *Also called G & K Management Co Inc (G-11548)*
Coronado YMCA, Richmond *Also called YMCA of East Bay (G-25408)*
Coronel Construction Inc...661 725-4400
2328 Venice Dr Delano (93215) *(G-1160)*
Coronet Carpets, La Mirada *Also called Beaulieu Group LLC (G-6847)*
Corovan Corporation (PA)...858 762-8100
12302 Kerran St Poway (92064) *(G-4336)*
Corovan Moving & Storage Co (HQ)...858 748-1100
12302 Kerran St Poway (92064) *(G-4337)*
Corp of Church of Christ Ld St...323 268-7281
2720 E 11th St Los Angeles (90023) *(G-17951)*
Corp., R.g Barry, Fontana *Also called Uti Integrated Logistics LLC (G-4706)*
Corpinfo Services, Santa Monica *Also called K-Micro Inc (G-7151)*
Corporate Building Svcs Inc...213 252-0999
3325 Wilshire Blvd # 1240 Los Angeles (90010) *(G-14264)*
Corporate Driver Services Inc...626 791-9020
1820 Pasadena Glen Rd Pasadena (91107) *(G-14865)*
Corporate Image Maintenance, Santa Ana *Also called Gamboa Service Inc (G-14306)*
Corporate Production Designs...310 937-9663
1427 Goodman Ave Redondo Beach (90278) *(G-18065)*
Corporate Resource Services...909 230-4510
2414 S Grove Ave Ontario (91761) *(G-14629)*
Corporate Risk Hldings III Inc...949 428-5839
3349 Michelson Dr Ste 150 Irvine (92612) *(G-17096)*
Corporate Security Service Inc...415 626-9271
5 3rd St Ste 314 San Francisco (94103) *(G-16612)*
Corporate Soul LLC...707 431-7781
433 Hudson St Healdsburg (95448) *(G-13751)*
Corporate Visions Inc...760 458-0914
2705 Avenida De Anita # 29 Carlsbad (92010) *(G-27390)*
CORPORATE VISIONS INC., Carlsbad *Also called Corporate Visions Inc (G-27390)*
Corporate Yard, San Mateo *Also called City of San Mateo (G-14251)*
Corporate Yard, Hayward *Also called Hayward Area Recreation Pkdist (G-4568)*
Corporation of The President...916 482-1480
3000 Auburn Blvd Ste B Sacramento (95821) *(G-24328)*
Corporation Service Company...302 636-5400
2710 Gateway Oaks Dr Sacramento (95833) *(G-14265)*
Corportion of Fine Arts Mseums...415 750-3600
50 Hagiwara Tea Garden Dr San Francisco (94118) *(G-25014)*
Corportion of Fine Arts Mseums...415 750-3600
50 Golden Gate Pk Hgiwara San Francisco (94118) *(G-25015)*
Corportion of Fine Arts Mseums (PA)...415 750-3600
50 Hagiwara Tea Garden Dr San Francisco (94118) *(G-25016)*
CORPRATE OFFICE, Blythe *Also called Blythe Nursing Care Center (G-20414)*
Corptax...818 316-2400
21550 Oxnard St Ste 700 Woodland Hills (91367) *(G-15111)*
Corral De Tierra Country Club...831 484-1325
81 Corral De Tierra Rd Salinas (93908) *(G-18927)*
Corral Del Tierra...831 372-6244
81 Corral De Tierra Rd Salinas (93908) *(G-18928)*
Correctional Medical Grp, Monterey *Also called Southwest Correctional Medical (G-22839)*
Correctional Services Corp...858 566-9816
7805 Arjons Dr San Diego (92126) *(G-27780)*
Correctionl Med Grp Co, Inc., Monterey *Also called Northwest Correctnl Med Grp (G-22782)*
Corrections Corp America...619 661-9119
446 Alta Rd San Diego (92158) *(G-27781)*
Corrections Corp America...760 373-1764
22844 Virginia Blvd California City (93505) *(G-27782)*
Correctons Rhbltation Cal Dept...707 445-6520
930 3rd St Ste 100 Eureka (95501) *(G-23788)*
Correctons Rhbltation Cal Dept...909 806-3516
303 W 5th St San Bernardino (92401) *(G-23789)*
Correctons Rhbltation Cal Dept...909 597-1821
14901 Central Ave Chino (91710) *(G-21512)*
Correctons Rhbltation Cal Dept...805 547-7900
Hwy 1 N San Luis Obispo (93409) *(G-22692)*
Correctons Rhbltation Cal Dept...916 358-2319
1920 Alabama Ave Sacramento (95825) *(G-16111)*
Corridor Recycling Inc...310 835-3849
22500 S Alameda St Long Beach (90810) *(G-6468)*
Corru Kraft Buena Pk Div 5058, Buena Park *Also called Orora North America (G-8210)*
Corru Kraft Fullerton Div 5068, Fullerton *Also called Orora North America (G-8209)*
Cort Business Services Corp...562 582-1515
14350 Grfield Ave Ste 500 Paramount (90723) *(G-14525)*
Cortel Inc...650 703-7217
14621 Arroyo Hondo San Diego (92127) *(G-5390)*
Corvel Corporation...909 257-3700
10750 4th St Ste 100 Rancho Cucamonga (91730) *(G-10680)*
Corvel Corporation (PA)...949 851-1473
2010 Main St Ste 600 Irvine (92614) *(G-26984)*
Corvel Enterprise Comp Inc...949 851-1473
2010 Main St Ste 600 Irvine (92614) *(G-10681)*
Corventis Inc (PA)...408 790-9300
2033 Gateway Pl Ste 100 San Jose (95110) *(G-16225)*
Corwe Horwath...415 576-1100
1 Embarcadero Ctr # 1330 San Francisco (94111) *(G-26316)*
Cosco Agencies (los Angeles) (HQ)...213 689-6700
588 Harbor Scenic Way Long Beach (90802) *(G-5052)*
Cosco Fire Protection Inc...925 455-2751
7455 Longard Rd Livermore (94551) *(G-2563)*
Cosco Fire Protection Inc...858 444-2000
4990 Greencraig Ln San Diego (92123) *(G-17097)*
Cosco Fire Protection Inc...714 989-1800
1075 W Lambert Rd Ste D Brea (92821) *(G-2192)*
Cosmogia, San Francisco *Also called Planet Labs Inc (G-16169)*
Cosmopro West Inc...714 258-8301
15773 Gateway Cir Tustin (92780) *(G-22417)*
Coso Operating Company LLC...760 764-1300
2 Gill Station Coso Rd Little Lake (93542) *(G-6120)*
Costa Mesa Country Club, Costa Mesa *Also called Mesa Verde Partners (G-18759)*
Costa Mesa Marriott Suites, Costa Mesa *Also called Host Hotels & Resorts LP (G-12770)*
Costa Mesa Sport Club, Costa Mesa *Also called 24 Hour Fitness Usa Inc (G-18588)*
Costa Sons...831 678-0799
36817 Foothill Rd Soledad (93960) *(G-54)*
Costa View Farms...559 675-3131
16800 Road 15 Madera (93637) *(G-421)*
Costa View Farms Shop, Madera *Also called Costa View Farms (G-421)*
Costanoa, Pescadero *Also called Joie De Vivre Hospitality LLC (G-27083)*
Costanoa, Pescadero *Also called King-Reynolds Ventures LLC (G-17273)*
Costar Group Inc...858 458-4900
8910 University Center Ln # 300 San Diego (92122) *(G-11460)*
Costco Auto Program, San Diego *Also called Affinity Auto Programs Inc (G-16974)*
Costco Wholesale Corporation...909 823-8270
16505 Sierra Lakes Pkwy Fontana (92336) *(G-9257)*
Costless Maintenance Svcs Co...415 550-8819
3254 19th St San Francisco (94110) *(G-14266)*
Coto De Caza Golf Club Inc...949 766-7886
25291 Vista Del Verde Trabuco Canyon (92679) *(G-18543)*
Coto De Caza Golf Racquet CLB, Trabuco Canyon *Also called Coto De Caza Golf Racquet CLB (G-18929)*
Coto De Caza Golf Racquet CLB...949 858-4100
25291 Vista Del Verde Trabuco Canyon (92679) *(G-18929)*
Cottage Care Center...805 682-7111
2415 De La Vina St Santa Barbara (93105) *(G-21513)*
Cottage Health System, Santa Barbara *Also called Goleta Valley Cottage Hospital (G-21581)*
COTTAGE HOSPITAL CHILDREN'S CE, Santa Barbara *Also called Santa Barbara Cottage Hospital (G-21857)*
Cottonwood Cyn Healthcare Ctr, El Cajon *Also called Plum Healthcare Group LLC (G-20854)*
Cottonwood Golf Club, El Cajon *Also called Premier Golf Properties LP (G-18770)*
Cottonwood Post-Acute Rehab, Woodland *Also called North American Health Care (G-27144)*
Couch Distributing Company Inc...831 724-0649
104 Lee Rd Watsonville (95076) *(G-9048)*
Counseling and Research Assoc (PA)...310 715-2020
108 W Victoria St Gardena (90248) *(G-24607)*
Counseling and Research Assoc...661 726-5500
314 E Avenue K4 Lancaster (93535) *(G-24608)*
Country Builders Inc...925 373-1020
5915 Graham Ct Livermore (94550) *(G-1304)*
Country Builders Construction, Livermore *Also called Country Builders Inc (G-1304)*
Country Club Lanes, Sacramento *Also called Pinsetters Inc (G-18528)*
Country Crest Health Center, Oroville *Also called Lake Oroville Country Retireme (G-24706)*
Country Floral Supply Inc (PA)...805 520-8026
3802 Weatherly Cir Westlake Village (91361) *(G-9186)*
Country Furnishings, Westlake Village *Also called Country Floral Supply Inc (G-9186)*
Country Hills Health Care Inc...619 441-8745
1580 Broadway El Cajon (92021) *(G-20473)*
Country Inn &SUite By Carlson...909 937-6000
231 N Vineyard Ave Ontario (91764) *(G-12541)*
Country Manor Health Care, Sylmar *Also called Canyon Properties III LLC (G-21177)*
Country Oaks Care Center, Pomona *Also called Country Oaks Partners LLC (G-20475)*
Country Oaks Care Center Inc...805 922-6657
830 E Chapel St Santa Maria (93454) *(G-20474)*
Country Oaks Partners LLC...909 622-1067
215 W Pearl St Pomona (91768) *(G-20475)*
Country Suites By Carlson, Fremont *Also called Merrill Gardens (G-11237)*
Country Villa Blmnt Hght Hlth...562 597-8817
1730 Grand Ave Long Beach (90804) *(G-21193)*
Country Villa E Convalescent, Los Angeles *Also called Country Villa Service Corp (G-26989)*
Country Villa East LP...323 939-3184
5916 W Pico Blvd Los Angeles (90035) *(G-21194)*
Country Villa Glendale, Glendale *Also called Glendale Healthcare Center (G-20600)*
Country Villa Health Services, Anaheim *Also called Country Villa Service Corp (G-26986)*
Country Villa Imperial LLC...323 666-1544
3002 Rowena Ave Los Angeles (90039) *(G-20476)*
Country Villa La Sierra, Merced *Also called CF Merced La Sierra LLC (G-20446)*
Country Villa Los Feliz, Los Angeles *Also called Country Villa Imperial LLC (G-20476)*
COUNTRY VILLA QUINCY HEALTHCAR, Quincy *Also called CF Quincy LLC (G-20447)*
Country Villa Service Corp...323 666-1544
3002 Rowena Ave Los Angeles (90039) *(G-26985)*
Country Villa Service Corp...562 598-2477
3000 N Gate Rd Seal Beach (90740) *(G-23790)*
Country Villa Service Corp...209 723-2911
510 W 26th St Merced (95340) *(G-23791)*

Country Villa Service Corp (PA)...310 574-3733
2400 E Katella Ave # 800 Anaheim (92806) ***(G-26986)***
Country Villa Service Corp...562 597-8817
1730 Grand Ave Long Beach (90804) ***(G-26987)***
Country Villa Service Corp...818 246-5516
1208 S Central Ave Glendale (91204) ***(G-20477)***
Country Villa Service Corp...626 358-4547
615 W Duarte Rd Monrovia (91016) ***(G-26988)***
Country Villa Service Corp...626 445-2421
400 W Huntington Dr Arcadia (91007) ***(G-20478)***
Country Villa Service Corp...323 734-1101
2415 S Western Ave Los Angeles (90018) ***(G-26989)***
Country Villa Service Corp...310 574-3733
3533 Motor Ave Los Angeles (90034) ***(G-26990)***
Country Villa Service Corp...323 734-9122
3233 W Pico Blvd Los Angeles (90019) ***(G-26991)***
Country Villa Service Corp...310 537-2500
3611 E Imperial Hwy Lynwood (90262) ***(G-20479)***
Country Villa Terrace (PA)...323 653-3980
6050 W Pico Blvd Los Angeles (90035) ***(G-21195)***
Country Villa Terrace...323 939-3184
5916 W Pico Blvd Los Angeles (90035) ***(G-21196)***
Country Villa Westwood Nursing, Los Angeles *Also called Westwood Healthcare Center LP* ***(G-21038)***
Country Vlla Convalescent Hosp, Los Angeles *Also called Country Villa Terrace* ***(G-21195)***
Country Vlla Nrsing Rhbltation, Los Angeles *Also called Country Villa East LP* ***(G-21194)***
Countryside Inn-Corona LP...909 335-9024
1015 W Colton Ave Redlands (92374) ***(G-26992)***
Countryside Inn-Corona LP...949 588-0131
24341 El Toro Rd Aliso Viejo (92653) ***(G-12542)***
Countryside Inn-Corona LP...562 596-8330
12850 Seal Beach Blvd Seal Beach (90740) ***(G-26993)***
Countryside Inn-Corona LP...714 549-0300
325 Bristol St Costa Mesa (92626) ***(G-12543)***
Countryside Mushrooms Inc...408 683-2748
11300 Center Ave Gilroy (95020) ***(G-328)***
Countryside Suites By Ayres, Costa Mesa *Also called Countryside Inn-Corona LP* ***(G-12543)***
Countrywide Capital Mkts LLC (HQ)...818 225-3000
4500 Park Granada Calabasas (91302) ***(G-9832)***
Countrywide Financial Corp (HQ)...818 225-3000
4500 Park Granada Calabasas (91302) ***(G-9833)***
Countrywide Home Loans Inc (HQ)...818 225-3000
225 W Hillcrest Dr Thousand Oaks (91360) ***(G-9834)***
Countrywide Home Loans Inc...818 550-8700
801 N Brand Blvd Ste 750 Glendale (91203) ***(G-9835)***
Countrywide Securities Corp...818 225-3000
4500 Park Granada Calabasas (91302) ***(G-9987)***
County Club of Rancho Bernardo, San Diego *Also called Rancho Bernardo Golf Club* ***(G-19034)***
County Engineers Assn Cal...707 762-3492
120 Round Ct Petaluma (94952) ***(G-25754)***
County General Hospital, San Luis Obispo *Also called County of San Luis Obispo* ***(G-21523)***
County Government, San Luis Obispo *Also called County of San Luis Obispo* ***(G-25758)***
County Jail, Salinas *Also called County of Monterey* ***(G-27783)***
County Lake Health Services...707 263-1090
922 Bevins Ct Lakeport (95453) ***(G-22924)***
County Los Angles Prbtion Dept, Pomona *Also called County of Los Angeles* ***(G-23846)***
County Monterey Social Svcs...831 899-8001
1281 Broadway Ave Seaside (93955) ***(G-23792)***
County of Alameda...510 272-6442
1405 Lakeside Dr Oakland (94612) ***(G-27391)***
County of Alameda...510 670-5455
399 Elmhurst St Hayward (94544) ***(G-1753)***
County of Alameda...510 670-5700
24100 Amador St Ste 130 Hayward (94544) ***(G-24329)***
County of Alameda...510 618-3452
1000 San Leandro Blvd # 200 San Leandro (94577) ***(G-23793)***
County of Alameda...510 481-4141
2060 Fairmont Dr San Leandro (94578) ***(G-19464)***
County of Butte...530 538-7661
25 County Center Dr # 218 Oroville (95965) ***(G-23794)***
County of Butte...530 538-7721
25 County Center Dr # 110 Oroville (95965) ***(G-23795)***
County of Butte...530 872-6328
5910 Clark Rd Ste W Paradise (95969) ***(G-23796)***
County of Butte...530 538-7572
202 Mira Loma Dr Oroville (95965) ***(G-23797)***
County of Butte...530 538-6802
205 Mira Loma Dr Oroville (95965) ***(G-23798)***
County of Butte...530 538-7711
78 Table Mountain Blvd Oroville (95965) ***(G-23799)***
County of Butte...530 891-2850
107 Parmac Rd Ste 4 Chico (95926) ***(G-22693)***
County of Calaveras...209 754-6402
891 Mountain Ranch Rd San Andreas (95249) ***(G-23800)***
County of Contra Costa...925 313-4000
50 Douglas Dr Ste 200 Martinez (94553) ***(G-23801)***
County of Contra Costa...925 313-2000
255 Glacier Dr Martinez (94553) ***(G-1754)***
County of Contra Costa...925 646-5877
2099 Arnold Industrial Wa Concord (94520) ***(G-14267)***
County of Contra Costa...925 313-7052
2467 Waterbird Way Martinez (94553) ***(G-14268)***
County of Contra Costa...925 313-1500
40 Douglas Dr Martinez (94553) ***(G-23802)***
County of Contra Costa...925 370-5000
2500 Alhambra Ave Martinez (94553) ***(G-21514)***
County of Contra Costa...925 646-5480
1420 Willow Pass Rd # 140 Concord (94520) ***(G-22694)***
County of Del Norte...707 464-3191
880 Northcrest Dr Crescent City (95531) ***(G-24904)***
County of El Dorado...530 626-4141
3940 Hwy 49 Diamond Springs (95619) ***(G-6469)***
County of El Dorado...530 621-6210
935b Spring St Placerville (95667) ***(G-22056)***
County of El Dorado...530 621-5845
3000 Fairlane Ct Ste 2 Placerville (95667) ***(G-14269)***
County of El Dorado...530 621-5625
3974 Durock Rd Ste 205 Shingle Springs (95682) ***(G-23803)***
County of El Dorado...530 642-7130
3057 Briw Rd Ste A Placerville (95667) ***(G-23804)***
County of Fresno...559 600-3420
1130 O St Fresno (93724) ***(G-23169)***
County of Fresno...559 600-3800
2212 N Winery Ave Ste 122 Fresno (93703) ***(G-23805)***
County of Fresno...559 600-5127
890 S 10th St Fresno (93702) ***(G-23806)***
County of Fresno...559 600-3546
2220 Tulare St Ste 300 Fresno (93721) ***(G-23170)***
County of Fresno...559 453-4099
4441 E Kings Canyon Rd Fresno (93702) ***(G-23807)***
County of Fresno...559 600-4600
4417 E Inyo St Bldg 333 Fresno (93702) ***(G-22695)***
County of Fresno...559 600-3534
2281 Tulare St Ste 201 Fresno (93721) ***(G-25132)***
County of Fresno...559 600-3996
3333 E American Ave Ste B Fresno (93725) ***(G-23808)***
County of Fresno...559 600-8135
2221 Kern St Fresno (93721) ***(G-25519)***
County of Fresno...559 488-3275
P.O. Box 352 Fresno (93708) ***(G-23809)***
County of Glenn...530 934-6582
247 N Villa Ave Willows (95988) ***(G-22925)***
County of Glenn...530 934-6530
777 N Colusa St Willows (95988) ***(G-1755)***
County of Glenn...530 934-6453
525 W Sycamore St Ste A1 Willows (95988) ***(G-23810)***
County of Glenn...530 934-6514
420 E Laurel St Willows (95988) ***(G-23811)***
County of Glenn...530 934-6582
242 N Villa Ave Willows (95988) ***(G-22696)***
County of Humboldt...707 445-6180
929 Koster St Eureka (95501) ***(G-23812)***
County of Humboldt...707 476-4054
720 Wood St Eureka (95501) ***(G-22697)***
County of Imperial...760 355-1748
304 E 4th St Imperial (92251) ***(G-1756)***
County of Imperial...760 482-4441
935 Broadway Ave El Centro (92243) ***(G-22926)***
County of Imperial...760 336-3581
324 Applestille Rd El Centro (92243) ***(G-23813)***
County of Imperial...760 482-4120
202 N 8th St El Centro (92243) ***(G-22698)***
County of Inyo...760 878-0292
224 N Edwards St Independence (93526) ***(G-17640)***
County of Kern...661 868-4100
2005 Ridge Rd Bakersfield (93305) ***(G-23814)***
County of Kern...661 392-2010
2014 Calloway Dr Bakersfield (93312) ***(G-23815)***
County of Kern...661 336-6800
2001 28th St Ste C Bakersfield (93301) ***(G-23816)***
County of Kern...661 868-8360
1721 Westwind Dr Bakersfield (93301) ***(G-19465)***
County of Kern...661 763-1535
401 Harrison St Taft (93268) ***(G-23817)***
County of Kern...661 326-2054
1700 Mount Vernon Ave Bakersfield (93306) ***(G-21515)***
County of Kern...661 868-2000
1215 Truxtun Ave Bakersfield (93301) ***(G-16112)***
County of Kern...661 763-4246
500 Cascade Pl Taft (93268) ***(G-19192)***
County of Kern...661 721-5134
1816 Cecil Ave Delano (93215) ***(G-23818)***
County of Kern...661 631-6346
100 E California Ave Bakersfield (93307) ***(G-24905)***
County of Kern...661 363-8910
6601 Niles Senior St Bakersfield (93306) ***(G-23819)***
County of Kern...661 868-2000
1215 Truxtun Ave Fl 4 Bakersfield (93301) ***(G-23171)***
County of Kings...559 852-4316
1424 Forum Dr Hanford (93230) ***(G-23820)***
County of Los Angeles...818 364-1555
14445 Olive View Dr 2b Sylmar (91342) ***(G-21516)***
County of Los Angeles...818 837-6969
1212 Pico St San Fernando (91340) ***(G-19466)***
County of Los Angeles...626 356-5281
300 E Walnut St Dept 200 Pasadena (91101) ***(G-23821)***
County of Los Angeles...661 223-8700
30500 Arrastre Canyon Rd Acton (93510) ***(G-22131)***
County of Los Angeles...323 869-7063
5555 Ferguson Dr Commerce (90022) ***(G-24906)***
County of Los Angeles...626 299-5300
1000 S Fremont Ave Unit 4 Alhambra (91803) ***(G-10275)***
County of Los Angeles...909 620-3189
350 W Mcaion Blvd Ste 109 Pomona (91766) ***(G-23822)***
County of Los Angeles...626 575-4059
11234 Valley Blvd Ste 103 El Monte (91731) ***(G-23823)***
County of Los Angeles...213 739-2360
600 S Commwl Ave Fl 2 Los Angeles (90005) ***(G-22927)***

ALPHABETIC

County of Los Angeles ALPHABETIC SECTION

County of Los Angeles......818 896-0571
12653 N Little Tjng Cyn Sylmar (91342) ***(G-24609)***
County of Los Angeles......213 974-1102
500 W Temple St Ste 493 Los Angeles (90012) ***(G-16226)***
County of Los Angeles......310 885-2100
546 W Compton Blvd Compton (90220) ***(G-22928)***
County of Los Angeles......661 940-4181
5300 W Avenue I Lancaster (93536) ***(G-23824)***
County of Los Angeles......562 401-9413
7601 Imperial Hwy Downey (90242) ***(G-23825)***
County of Los Angeles......323 889-3405
5770 S Eastern Ave Fl 4th Commerce (90040) ***(G-23826)***
County of Los Angeles......310 222-2401
1000 W Carson St Fl 8 Palos Verdes Peninsu (90274) ***(G-21517)***
County of Los Angeles......661 723-4051
349 E Avenue K6 Ste B Lancaster (93535) ***(G-23827)***
County of Los Angeles......562 401-7088
7601 Imperial Hwy Downey (90242) ***(G-22699)***
County of Los Angeles......213 974-7284
515 E 6th St Los Angeles (90021) ***(G-22132)***
County of Los Angeles......310 668-4545
12025 Wilmington Ave Los Angeles (90059) ***(G-21518)***
County of Los Angeles......562 903-5000
10355 Slusher Dr Santa Fe Springs (90670) ***(G-23828)***
County of Los Angeles......310 222-4220
1000 W Carson St Torrance (90502) ***(G-19467)***
County of Los Angeles......562 497-3500
4060 Watson Plaza Dr Lakewood (90712) ***(G-23829)***
County of Los Angeles......323 780-2373
245 S Fetterly Ave Los Angeles (90022) ***(G-22418)***
County of Los Angeles......323 226-8611
1605 Eastlake Ave Los Angeles (90033) ***(G-24610)***
County of Los Angeles......323 226-6221
1200 N State St Los Angeles (90033) ***(G-19468)***
County of Los Angeles......323 265-1804
1000 Corp Ctr Dr Ste 200b Monterey Park (91754) ***(G-23830)***
County of Los Angeles......323 846-4122
5850 S Main St Los Angeles (90003) ***(G-22700)***
County of Los Angeles......661 948-2320
777 W Jackman St Lancaster (93534) ***(G-23831)***
County of Los Angeles......213 744-3677
2829 S Grand Ave Los Angeles (90007) ***(G-19469)***
County of Los Angeles......818 374-2161
210 W Temple St Fl 18 Los Angeles (90012) ***(G-23832)***
County of Los Angeles......323 226-8998
1601 Eastlake Ave Ste 4 Los Angeles (90033) ***(G-23172)***
County of Los Angeles......818 364-2011
16350 Filbert St Sylmar (91342) ***(G-24611)***
County of Los Angeles......310 668-6845
921 E Compton Blvd Compton (90221) ***(G-22929)***
County of Los Angeles......626 229-3825
532 E Colorado Blvd Fl 8 Pasadena (91101) ***(G-22930)***
County of Los Angeles......213 922-6210
1 Gateway Plz Los Angeles (90012) ***(G-14140)***
County of Los Angeles......213 744-5730
2707 S Grand Dwntwn S Ave Los Angeles (90007) ***(G-23833)***
County of Los Angeles......213 744-3922
2829 S Grand Ave Rm 116 Los Angeles (90007) ***(G-22931)***
County of Los Angeles......909 620-3330
300 S Park Ave Ste 770 Pomona (91766) ***(G-23173)***
County of Los Angeles......323 586-7263
1740 E Gage Ave Los Angeles (90001) ***(G-23834)***
County of Los Angeles......323 769-7800
5205 Melrose Ave Los Angeles (90038) ***(G-22701)***
County of Los Angeles......213 351-8739
600 S Commwl Ave Ste 700 Los Angeles (90005) ***(G-23835)***
County of Los Angeles......323 226-8511
1601 Eastlake Ave Los Angeles (90033) ***(G-23836)***
County of Los Angeles......323 226-3468
1240 N Mission Rd Los Angeles (90033) ***(G-22133)***
County of Los Angeles......562 462-2094
12400 Imperial Hwy Norwalk (90650) ***(G-16113)***
County of Los Angeles......213 351-5600
425 Shatto Pl Los Angeles (90020) ***(G-23837)***
County of Los Angeles......909 629-1166
1875 Fairplex Dr Pomona (91768) ***(G-18727)***
County of Los Angeles......562 908-3119
8240 Broadway Ave Whittier (90606) ***(G-23838)***
County of Los Angeles......213 974-9331
320 W Temple St Ste 1101 Los Angeles (90012) ***(G-23839)***
County of Los Angeles......213 240-8412
313 N Figueroa St Fl 9 Los Angeles (90012) ***(G-25133)***
County of Los Angeles......818 889-0260
433 Encinal Canyon Rd Malibu (90265) ***(G-24612)***
County of Los Angeles......323 226-6021
1100 N Mission Rd Rm 236 Los Angeles (90033) ***(G-21519)***
County of Los Angeles......661 298-3406
27233 Camp Plenty Rd Canyon Country (91351) ***(G-10549)***
County of Los Angeles......213 351-7800
3530 Wilshire Blvd Fl 9 Los Angeles (90010) ***(G-22932)***
County of Los Angeles......661 948-8581
335 E Avenue I Lancaster (93535) ***(G-19470)***
County of Los Angeles......626 458-3126
900 S Fremont Ave Alhambra (91803) ***(G-6335)***
County of Los Angeles......805 237-3110
530 12th St Fl 1 Paso Robles (93446) ***(G-23840)***
County of Los Angeles......661 723-6088
44933 Fern Ave Lancaster (93534) ***(G-25755)***
County of Los Angeles......213 744-5601
2707 S Grand Ave Los Angeles (90007) ***(G-23841)***
County of Los Angeles......323 727-1639
5445 Whittier Blvd Fl 400 Los Angeles (90022) ***(G-23842)***
County of Los Angeles......323 560-5001
8130 Atlantic Ave Cudahy (90201) ***(G-24907)***
County of Los Angeles......562 945-2581
9402 Greenleaf Ave Whittier (90605) ***(G-3917)***
County of Los Angeles......310 222-2357
1000 W Crson St Bsmnt 404 Basement Torrance (90502) ***(G-8251)***
County of Los Angeles......562 861-0316
5525 Imperial Hwy South Gate (90280) ***(G-22933)***
County of Los Angeles......323 857-6000
5905 Wilshire Blvd Los Angeles (90036) ***(G-25017)***
County of Los Angeles......818 362-6437
14555 Osborne St Ofc Van Nuys (91402) ***(G-23843)***
County of Los Angeles......213 367-3176
6801 E 2nd St Long Beach (90803) ***(G-6336)***
County of Los Angeles......626 854-4987
17171 Gale Ave City of Industry (91745) ***(G-23844)***
County of Los Angeles......213 240-7780
313 N Figueroa St Los Angeles (90012) ***(G-22934)***
County of Los Angeles......626 350-4566
12310 Lower Azusa Rd Arcadia (91006) ***(G-23845)***
County of Los Angeles......626 337-1277
14747 Ramona Blvd Baldwin Park (91706) ***(G-25756)***
County of Los Angeles......909 469-4500
1660 W Mission Blvd Pomona (91766) ***(G-23846)***
County of Los Angeles......818 374-2000
14414 Delano St Van Nuys (91401) ***(G-23847)***
County of Los Angeles......626 821-5858
330 E Live Oak Ave Arcadia (91006) ***(G-23848)***
County of Los Angeles......562 402-0688
17707 Studebaker Rd Artesia (90703) ***(G-22702)***
County of Los Angeles......323 730-3502
3834 S Western Ave Los Angeles (90062) ***(G-19471)***
County of Los Angeles......310 518-8800
1325 Broad Ave Wilmington (90744) ***(G-19472)***
County of Los Angeles......818 896-1903
13300 Van Nuys Blvd Pacoima (91331) ***(G-19473)***
County of Los Angeles......661 947-7173
38126 Sierra Hwy Palmdale (93550) ***(G-1757)***
County of Los Angeles......310 266-3711
1725 Main St Rm 125 Santa Monica (90401) ***(G-23849)***
County of Los Angeles......310 603-7483
200 W Compton Blvd # 700 Compton (90220) ***(G-23174)***
County of Los Angeles......626 455-4700
4024 Durfee Ave Rm 225 El Monte (91732) ***(G-24613)***
County of Los Angeles......213 974-2811
210 W Temple St Fl 19 Los Angeles (90012) ***(G-23175)***
County of Los Angeles......310 603-7271
200 W Compton Blvd Fl 8 Compton (90220) ***(G-23176)***
County of Los Angeles......323 780-2185
4849 Civic Center Way Los Angeles (90022) ***(G-23850)***
County of Los Angeles......562 807-7860
12727 Norwalk Blvd Norwalk (90650) ***(G-23851)***
County of Los Angeles......310 222-3552
20221 Hamilton Ave Torrance (90502) ***(G-23177)***
County of Los Angeles......213 351-7257
501 Shatto Pl Ste 301 Los Angeles (90020) ***(G-23852)***
County of Los Angeles......323 586-6469
8526 Grape St Los Angeles (90001) ***(G-23853)***
County of Los Angeles......310 603-7311
200 W Compton Blvd # 300 Compton (90220) ***(G-23854)***
County of Los Angeles......626 458-1700
1525 Alcazar St Bldg 1 Los Angeles (90033) ***(G-1758)***
County of Los Angeles......626 356-5281
199 N Euclid Ave Pasadena (91101) ***(G-23855)***
County of Los Angeles......818 374-2406
6230 Sylmar Ave Ste 201 Van Nuys (91401) ***(G-23178)***
County of Los Angeles......661 524-2005
335 E Avenue K6 Ste B Lancaster (93535) ***(G-22703)***
County of Los Angeles......562 940-2476
9150 Imperial Hwy Downey (90242) ***(G-23856)***
County of Los Angeles......323 267-2771
1100 N Eastern Ave Los Angeles (90063) ***(G-17098)***
County of Los Angeles......562 599-9200
1975 Long Beach Blvd Long Beach (90806) ***(G-19474)***
County of Los Angeles......562 803-6682
9150 Imperial Hwy Downey (90242) ***(G-23857)***
County of Los Angeles......818 557-4164
3307 N Glenoaks Blvd Burbank (91504) ***(G-23858)***
County of Los Angeles......213 473-6100
450 Bauchet St Los Angeles (90012) ***(G-21520)***
County of Los Angeles......626 308-5542
200 W Woodward Ave Alhambra (91801) ***(G-23859)***
County of Los Angeles......818 889-1353
427 Encinal Canyon Rd Malibu (90265) ***(G-23860)***
County of Los Angeles......213 974-4561
441 Bauchet St Los Angeles (90012) ***(G-5216)***
County of Los Angeles......323 226-6056
1900 Zonal Ave Doc1 Los Angeles (90033) ***(G-19475)***
County of Los Angeles......559 675-7739
209 W Yosemite Ave Madera (93637) ***(G-23861)***
County of Los Angeles......213 974-8301
500 W Temple St Ste 525 Los Angeles (90012) ***(G-6337)***
County of Los Angeles......310 847-4018
21356 Avalon Blvd Carson (90745) ***(G-25171)***
County of Madera......559 675-7811
200 W 4th St Madera (93637) ***(G-17880)***
County of Marin......415 332-6158
164 Donahue St Sausalito (94965) ***(G-23862)***

ALPHABETIC

ALPHABETIC SECTION County of San Diego

County of Marin.....415 499-6970
120 N Redwood Dr San Rafael (94903) *(G-23863)*
County of Marin.....415 499-7060
371 Bel Marin Keys Blvd # 100 Novato (94949) *(G-16114)*
County of Marin.....415 448-1500
250 Bon Air Rd Greenbrae (94904) *(G-22704)*
County of Marin.....415 499-7877
1600 Los Gamos Dr Ste 200 San Rafael (94903) *(G-25757)*
County of Medocina Dept of Mnt, Ukiah *Also called County of Mendocino (G-22705)*
County of Mendocino.....707 463-4363
340 Lake Mendocino Dr Ukiah (95482) *(G-4912)*
County of Mendocino.....707 463-2437
737 S State St Ukiah (95482) *(G-23864)*
County of Mendocino.....707 463-4363
340 Lake Mendocino Dr Ukiah (95482) *(G-6624)*
County of Mendocino.....707 463-4396
860a N Bush St Ukiah (95482) *(G-22705)*
County of Merced.....209 826-2253
715 Martin Luther King Jr Merced (95341) *(G-1759)*
County of Merced.....209 724-2000
1880 Wardrobe Ave Merced (95341) *(G-24330)*
County of Modoc.....530 233-6223
204 S Court St Ste 6 Alturas (96101) *(G-17099)*
County of Modoc.....530 233-6501
120 N Main St Alturas (96101) *(G-23865)*
County of Modoc.....530 233-3416
228 W Mcdowell Ave Alturas (96101) *(G-20480)*
County of Modoc.....530 233-6400
204 S Court St Ste 6 Alturas (96101) *(G-23866)*
County of Monterey.....831 755-4944
855 E Laurel Dr Ste D Salinas (93905) *(G-17100)*
County of Monterey.....831 755-5027
240 Church St Ste 116 Salinas (93901) *(G-17101)*
County of Monterey.....831 755-4500
1270 Natividad Rd Salinas (93906) *(G-24908)*
County of Monterey.....831 755-4201
1441 Constitution Blvd # 100 Salinas (93906) *(G-21521)*
County of Monterey.....831 769-8800
559 E Alisal St Ste 201 Salinas (93905) *(G-19476)*
County of Monterey.....831 755-3700
1414 Natividad Rd Salinas (93906) *(G-25520)*
County of Monterey.....831 755-8500
1000 S Main St Ste 216 Salinas (93901) *(G-23867)*
County of Monterey.....831 755-3782
1410 Natividad Rd Salinas (93906) *(G-27783)*
County of Monterey.....831 755-4800
168 W Alisal St Fl 3 Salinas (93901) *(G-1760)*
County of Monterey.....831 647-7611
1441 Constitution Blvd # 100 Salinas (93906) *(G-21522)*
County of Monterey Social Svcs, Seaside *Also called County Monterey Social Svcs (G-23792)*
County of NAPA.....707 253-4625
650 Imperial Way Ste 101 NAPA (94559) *(G-23868)*
County of NAPA.....707 253-4361
212 Walnut St NAPA (94559) *(G-23869)*
County of NAPA.....707 253-4461
2261 Elm St NAPA (94559) *(G-22706)*
County of Orange.....714 896-7188
8141 13th St Westminster (92683) *(G-23870)*
County of Orange.....714 937-4500
1535 E Orangewood Ave Anaheim (92805) *(G-23871)*
County of Orange.....714 896-7500
14180 Beach Blvd Ste 120 Westminster (92683) *(G-23872)*
County of Orange.....714 834-8385
1729 W 17th St Santa Ana (92706) *(G-22206)*
County of Orange.....714 935-7411
301 City Dr S Orange (92868) *(G-23873)*
County of Orange.....949 252-5006
3160 Airway Ave Costa Mesa (92626) *(G-4913)*
County of Orange.....714 626-3700
1440 N Harbor Blvd # 400 Fullerton (92835) *(G-23179)*
County of Orange.....714 834-4000
300 N Sunflower Ste 400 Santa Ana (92703) *(G-6470)*
County of Orange.....714 704-8000
800 N Eckhoff St Bldg 121 Orange (92868) *(G-23874)*
County of Orange.....714 567-7500
1300 S Grand Ave Ste C Santa Ana (92705) *(G-25480)*
County of Orange.....714 834-8899
2020 W Walnut St Santa Ana (92703) *(G-23875)*
County of Orange.....714 834-6021
405 W 5th St Ofc Santa Ana (92701) *(G-21075)*
County of Orange.....714 935-6435
341 The City Dr S Orange (92868) *(G-23876)*
County of Placer.....530 886-1870
379 Nevada St Auburn (95603) *(G-23877)*
County of Placer.....530 889-7900
2929 Richardson Dr Ste B Auburn (95603) *(G-23878)*
County of Placer.....530 889-7215
11583 C Ave Auburn (95603) *(G-22707)*
County of Placer.....530 823-4300
11512 B Ave Auburn (95603) *(G-23879)*
County of Placer.....530 889-7900
2929 Richardson Dr Ste B Auburn (95603) *(G-23880)*
County of Riverside.....951 955-6000
4200 Orange St Riverside (92501) *(G-23180)*
County of Riverside.....951 272-5400
3178 Hamner Ave Norco (92860) *(G-23881)*
County of Riverside.....951 955-0840
5256 Mission Blvd Riverside (92509) *(G-19477)*
County of Riverside.....951 443-2262
2560 N Perris Blvd Ste N1 Perris (92571) *(G-23882)*
County of Riverside.....951 358-5306
4065 County Circle Dr Riverside (92503) *(G-24909)*
County of Riverside.....951 486-4000
26520 Cactus Ave Moreno Valley (92555) *(G-19478)*
County of Riverside.....951 358-6000
7140 Indiana Ave Riverside (92504) *(G-19479)*
County of Riverside.....951 486-4000
26520 Cactus Ave Moreno Valley (92555) *(G-19480)*
County of Riverside.....951 245-3060
1400 W Minthorn St Lake Elsinore (92530) *(G-23883)*
County of Riverside.....760 863-8283
47923 Oasis St Ste A Indio (92201) *(G-19481)*
County of Riverside.....951 245-3100
1400 W Minthorn St Lake Elsinore (92530) *(G-23884)*
County of Riverside.....951 791-3500
1025 N State St Hemet (92543) *(G-23885)*
County of Riverside.....951 600-6500
43264 Business Park Dr # 102 Temecula (92590) *(G-23886)*
County of Riverside.....760 863-7600
47 665 Oasis St Indio (92201) *(G-24614)*
County of Riverside.....951 275-8783
4168 12th St Riverside (92501) *(G-23887)*
County of Riverside.....760 863-8247
82503 Us Highway 111 Indio (92201) *(G-19193)*
County of Riverside.....951 697-4699
6296 River Crest Dr Ste K Riverside (92507) *(G-23888)*
County of Riverside.....951 486-7700
4080 Lemon St Fl 3 Riverside (92501) *(G-16343)*
County of Riverside.....951 955-0905
3960 Orange St Ste 500 Riverside (92501) *(G-23889)*
County of Riverside.....951 358-4415
10000 County Farm Rd Riverside (92503) *(G-23890)*
County of Riverside.....951 955-4800
3133 Mission Inn Ave Riverside (92507) *(G-1161)*
County of Riverside.....951 955-3100
3403 10th St Ste 500 Riverside (92501) *(G-24331)*
County of Riverside Department.....760 320-1048
554 S Paseo Dorotea Palm Springs (92264) *(G-22935)*
County of Sacramento.....916 874-7752
799 G St Sacramento (95814) *(G-16277)*
County of Sacramento.....916 875-0900
9616 Micron Ave Ste 750 Sacramento (95827) *(G-20481)*
County of Sacramento.....916 875-2711
9700 Goethe Rd Ste D Sacramento (95827) *(G-1888)*
County of Sacramento.....916 874-0746
7207 Earhart Dr Sacramento (95837) *(G-14270)*
County of Sacramento.....916 874-5411
700 H St Ste 270 Sacramento (95814) *(G-23181)*
County of Sacramento.....916 363-8383
4040 Bradshaw Rd Sacramento (95827) *(G-18816)*
County of Sacramento.....916 874-1927
12500 Bruceville Rd Elk Grove (95757) *(G-27784)*
County of Sacramento.....916 875-4467
9750 Bus Park Dr Ste 104 Sacramento (95827) *(G-23891)*
County of San Bernardino.....909 891-3300
412 W Hospitality Ln Fl 2 San Bernardino (92415) *(G-23892)*
County of San Bernardino.....909 580-1000
400 N Pepper Ave Colton (92324) *(G-22207)*
County of San Bernardino.....909 387-5455
385 N Arrowhead Ave San Bernardino (92415) *(G-24449)*
County of San Bernardino.....909 387-2363
250 S Lena Rd San Bernardino (92415) *(G-24450)*
County of San Bernardino.....909 307-2669
2024 Orange Tree Ln Redlands (92374) *(G-25018)*
County of San Bernardino.....909 387-0535
860 E Gilbert St San Bernardino (92415) *(G-24615)*
County of San Bernardino.....909 945-4000
8303 Haven Ave Rancho Cucamonga (91730) *(G-23893)*
County of San Bernardino.....909 386-8818
222 W Hospitality Ln San Bernardino (92415) *(G-26317)*
County of San Bernardino.....760 843-5100
17270 Bear Valley Rd # 108 Victorville (92395) *(G-23894)*
County of San Bernardino.....760 228-5234
56357 Pima Trl Yucca Valley (92284) *(G-23895)*
County of San Bernardino.....909 425-0785
26887 5th St Highland (92346) *(G-24451)*
County of San Diego.....858 694-5141
6950 Levant St San Diego (92111) *(G-23896)*
County of San Diego.....866 262-9881
130 E Alvarado St Fallbrook (92028) *(G-23897)*
County of San Diego.....858 495-5537
5560 Overland Ave Ste 310 San Diego (92123) *(G-23898)*
County of San Diego.....619 515-8202
330 W Broadway Ste 1100 San Diego (92101) *(G-23899)*
County of San Diego.....619 531-4040
330 W Broadway Ste 1020 San Diego (92101) *(G-23182)*
County of San Diego.....619 692-8202
3851 Rosecrans St San Diego (92110) *(G-23900)*
County of San Diego.....619 479-1832
8735 Jamacha Blvd Spring Valley (91977) *(G-23901)*
County of San Diego.....619 236-2191
1600 Pacific Hwy Ste 207 San Diego (92101) *(G-27891)*
County of San Diego.....619 692-8200
3853 Rosecrans St San Diego (92110) *(G-22057)*
County of San Diego.....619 563-2765
3255 Camino Del Rio S San Diego (92108) *(G-23902)*
County of San Diego.....619 531-4521
5570 Overland Ave Ste 101 San Diego (92123) *(G-22936)*

ALPHABETIC

County of San Diego ALPHABETIC SECTION

County of San Diego 619 236-8725
4588 Market St San Diego (92102) ***(G-23903)***
County of San Diego Dept Chil 619 578-6660
225 Broadway Ste 1200 San Diego (92101) ***(G-23904)***
County of San Joaquin 209 468-2601
826 N California St Stockton (95202) ***(G-23905)***
County of San Joaquin 209 468-3021
1810 E Hazelton Ave Stockton (95205) ***(G-24910)***
County of San Joaquin 209 468-8750
1212 N California St Stockton (95202) ***(G-22708)***
County of San Joaquin 209 468-4100
24 S Hunter St Ste 201 Stockton (95202) ***(G-23906)***
County of San Joaquin 209 468-3500
56 S Lincoln St Stockton (95203) ***(G-24332)***
County of San Joaquin 209 468-6966
500 W Hospital Rd French Camp (95231) ***(G-23907)***
County of San Luis Obispo 805 781-4800
2180 Johnson Ave San Luis Obispo (93401) ***(G-21523)***
County of San Luis Obispo 805 781-5437
3433 S Higuera St San Luis Obispo (93401) ***(G-23908)***
County of San Luis Obispo 805 781-4700
2178 Johnson Ave San Luis Obispo (93401) ***(G-22709)***
County of San Luis Obispo 805 781-1864
3433 S Higuera St San Luis Obispo (93401) ***(G-23909)***
County of San Luis Obispo 805 781-5258
Government Center Rm 207 San Luis Obispo (93408) ***(G-25758)***
County of San Mateo 650 599-7336
680 Warren St Redwood City (94063) ***(G-23910)***
County of San Mateo 650 312-5327
222 Paul Scannell Dr San Mateo (94402) ***(G-23911)***
County of San Mateo 650 312-8887
222 Paul Scannell Dr Fl 2 San Mateo (94402) ***(G-23912)***
County of San Mateo 650 363-4915
400 County Ctr Redwood City (94063) ***(G-26994)***
County of San Mateo 650 363-4343
455 County Ctr Redwood City (94063) ***(G-26995)***
County of San Mateo 650 853-3139
2277 University Ave East Palo Alto (94303) ***(G-23913)***
County of San Mateo 650 363-4321
455 County Ctr Fl 5 Redwood City (94063) ***(G-26996)***
County of San Mateo 650 363-4548
455 County Ctr Fl 3 Redwood City (94063) ***(G-28125)***
County of San Mateo 650 363-1910
555 County Ctr Fl 2 Redwood City (94063) ***(G-23914)***
County of San Mateo 650 802-6470
400 Harbor Blvd Bldg B Belmont (94002) ***(G-23915)***
County of San Mateo 650 372-8540
150 W 20th Ave San Mateo (94403) ***(G-22710)***
County of San Mateo 650 312-8803
222 Paul Scannell Dr San Mateo (94402) ***(G-23916)***
County of San Mateo 650 363-4020
455 County Ctr Fl 4 Redwood City (94063) ***(G-13479)***
County of San Mateo 650 312-8803
400 County Ctr Fl 5 Redwood City (94063) ***(G-23917)***
County of Santa Barbara Alcoho 805 681-4093
300 N San Antonio Rd Santa Barbara (93110) ***(G-22711)***
County of Shasta 530 225-5000
1400 California St Redding (96001) ***(G-10550)***
County of Shasta 530 225-5554
1313 Yuba St Redding (96001) ***(G-23918)***
County of Shasta 530 347-6276
19897 Gas Point Rd Cottonwood (96022) ***(G-25243)***
County of Shasta 530 245-6300
1355 West St Redding (96001) ***(G-23183)***
County of Shasta 530 225-2999
43 Hilltop Dr Redding (96003) ***(G-24452)***
County of Siskiyou 530 918-7200
1107 Ream Ave Mount Shasta (96067) ***(G-22712)***
County of Siskiyou 530 841-2700
818 S Main St Yreka (96097) ***(G-23919)***
County of Solano 707 784-8400
275 Beck Ave Fairfield (94533) ***(G-23920)***
County of Solano 707 451-6090
810 Vaca Valley Pkwy # 203 Vacaville (95688) ***(G-6338)***
County of Solano 707 784-7600
475 Union Ave Fairfield (94533) ***(G-23921)***
County of Solano 707 784-2080
2101 Courage Dr Fairfield (94533) ***(G-21076)***
County of Sonoma 707 823-8511
501 Petaluma Ave Sebastopol (95472) ***(G-21524)***
County of Sonoma 707 565-4850
3322 Chanate Rd Santa Rosa (95404) ***(G-22058)***
County of Sonoma 707 527-2911
2615 Paulin Dr Santa Rosa (95403) ***(G-16115)***
County of Sonoma 707 565-2209
600 Administration Dr 212j Santa Rosa (95403) ***(G-23184)***
County of Sonoma 707 527-2641
2300 County Center Dr B100 Santa Rosa (95403) ***(G-23922)***
County of Sonoma 707 527-2911
2300 Prof Dr Rear Door B Santa Rosa (95403) ***(G-16116)***
County of Stanislaus 209 525-4130
1716 Morgan Rd Modesto (95358) ***(G-6625)***
County of Stanislaus 209 525-7000
830 Scenic Dr Modesto (95350) ***(G-21525)***
County of Stanislaus 209 558-8828
830 Scenic Dr Modesto (95350) ***(G-23923)***
County of Stanislaus 209 567-4120
801 11th St Ste 4000 Modesto (95354) ***(G-23924)***
County of Stanislaus 209 558-7377
108 Campus Way Modesto (95350) ***(G-23925)***
County of Stanislaus 209 558-9675
251 E Hackett Rd Modesto (95358) ***(G-23926)***
County of Stanislaus 209 525-6225
800 Scenic Dr Modesto (95350) ***(G-24911)***
County of Stanislaus 209 525-7423
800 Scenic Dr Bldg B Modesto (95350) ***(G-22713)***
County of Stanislaus 209 558-2500
108 Campus Way Modesto (95350) ***(G-23927)***
County of Stanislaus 209 558-2100
251 E Hackett Rd Ste 2 Modesto (95358) ***(G-24333)***
County of Sutter 530 822-7250
1965 Live Oak Blvd Yuba City (95991) ***(G-22714)***
County of Tehama 530 527-5631
1860 Walnut St Red Bluff (96080) ***(G-23928)***
County of Tehama 530 527-4052
1840 Walnut St Red Bluff (96080) ***(G-23929)***
County of Tuolumne 209 533-5561
2 S Green St Sonora (95370) ***(G-16117)***
County of Tuolumne 209 533-5711
20075 Cedar Rd N Sonora (95370) ***(G-23930)***
County of Ventura 805 654-2561
800 S Victoria Ave Ventura (93009) ***(G-23931)***
County of Ventura 805 654-3456
4651 Telephone Rd Ste 300 Ventura (93003) ***(G-23932)***
County of Ventura 805 385-8654
1400 Vanguard Dr Fl 2nd Oxnard (93033) ***(G-23933)***
County of Ventura 805 240-2701
300 W 9th St Oxnard (93030) ***(G-24453)***
County of Ventura 805 654-3152
800 S Victoria Ave 1540 Ventura (93009) ***(G-26318)***
County of Ventura 805 652-6000
3291 Loma Vista Rd Ventura (93003) ***(G-23934)***
County of Ventura 805 654-5529
5171 Verdugo Way Camarillo (93012) ***(G-23935)***
County of Yolo 530 666-8630
292 W Beamer St Woodland (95695) ***(G-22715)***
County of Yuba 530 749-7550
215 5th St Ste 154 Marysville (95901) ***(G-23936)***
County Probation, El Monte *Also called County of Los Angeles* ***(G-23823)***
County Ventura Human Resources, Ventura *Also called County of Ventura* ***(G-23931)***
County Whl Elc Co Los Angeles 714 633-3801
560 N Main St Orange (92868) ***(G-7433)***
Countywide Childrens Case MGT, Los Angeles *Also called County of Los Angeles* ***(G-22927)***
Countywide Mech Systems Inc 619 449-9900
1400 N Johnson Ave # 114 El Cajon (92020) ***(G-2193)***
Coupa Software Incorporated (PA) 650 931-3200
1855 S Grant St Fl 4 San Mateo (94402) ***(G-15631)***
Courier Leasing Inc 619 275-7000
1260 Morena Blvd Ste 200 San Diego (92110) ***(G-16876)***
Court House, Torrance *Also called County of Los Angeles* ***(G-23177)***
Courtland Farming, Courtland *Also called Delta Breeze Farming Inc* ***(G-354)***
Courtney Inc (PA) 949 222-2050
16781 Millikan Ave Irvine (92606) ***(G-3509)***
Courtside Club, Los Gatos *Also called Courtside Tennis Club* ***(G-18930)***
Courtside Tennis Club 408 395-7111
14675 Winchester Blvd Los Gatos (95032) ***(G-18930)***
Courtyard & Residence Inn La, Los Angeles *Also called 901 West Olympic Blvd LP* ***(G-12370)***
Courtyard By Marr San Diego Ai, San Diego *Also called Liberty Station Hhg Hotel LP* ***(G-12920)***
Courtyard By Marriott, San Francisco *Also called Marriot Courtyard* ***(G-12945)***
Courtyard By Marriott, Pleasant Hill *Also called Courtyard Management Corp* ***(G-12549)***
Courtyard By Marriott, Monrovia *Also called Sage Hospitality Resources LLC* ***(G-13188)***
Courtyard By Marriott, San Diego *Also called Kearny Villa Hotel Venture LLC* ***(G-12877)***
Courtyard By Marriott, Pasadena *Also called Rt Pasad Hotel Partners LP* ***(G-13178)***
Courtyard By Marriott, Baldwin Park *Also called Baldwin Hospitality LLC* ***(G-12414)***
Courtyard By Marriott, Rancho Cordova *Also called Courtyard Management Corp* ***(G-12550)***
Courtyard By Marriott, San Diego *Also called San Diego Hotel Lease LLC* ***(G-13198)***
Courtyard By Marriott, El Segundo *Also called Marriott International Inc* ***(G-12968)***
Courtyard By Marriott, Cupertino *Also called Marriott International Inc* ***(G-12970)***
Courtyard By Marriott, Richmond *Also called Pacific Hotel Management LLC* ***(G-13059)***
Courtyard By Marriott, Culver City *Also called Force-Oakleaf LP* ***(G-12641)***
Courtyard By Marriott 619 291-5720
595 Hotel Cir S San Diego (92108) ***(G-12544)***
Courtyard By Marriott 805 786-4200
1605 Calle Joaquin San Luis Obispo (93405) ***(G-12545)***
Courtyard By Marriott 415 925-1800
2500 Larkspur Landing Cir Larkspur (94939) ***(G-12546)***
Courtyard By Marriott 626 965-1700
1905 S Azusa Ave Hacienda Heights (91745) ***(G-12547)***
Courtyard By Marriott S, Sacramento *Also called Gccfc 2005-Gg5 Y St Ltd Partnr* ***(G-12660)***
Courtyard By Marriott San Jose, Campbell *Also called Campbell Hhg Hotel Dev LP* ***(G-12484)***
Courtyard By Marroitt Oxnard, Oxnard *Also called Recp Cy Oxnard LLC* ***(G-13131)***
Courtyard By Mrriott Riverside, Yorba Linda *Also called Alliance Rvrside Hsptality LLC* ***(G-12380)***
COURTYARD CARE CENTER, Signal Hill *Also called SCCH Inc* ***(G-27206)***
Courtyard Care Center, San Jose *Also called SSC San Jose Operating Co LP* ***(G-20927)***
Courtyard Cypress, Cypress *Also called Apple Eght Hospitality MGT Inc* ***(G-12392)***
Courtyard Healthcare, Davis *Also called Covenant Care Courtyard LLC* ***(G-20502)***
Courtyard Management Corp 818 999-2200
21101 Ventura Blvd Woodland Hills (91364) ***(G-12548)***
Courtyard Management Corp 925 691-1444
2250 Contra Costa Blvd Pleasant Hill (94523) ***(G-12549)***

ALPHABETIC

ALPHABETIC SECTION CPS Security Solutions Inc (PA)

Courtyard Management Corp....916 638-3800
10683 White Rock Rd Rancho Cordova (95670) ***(G-12550)***
Courtyard Marriott Mission Vly, San Diego *Also called Mbp Land LLC* ***(G-12986)***
Courtyard Oxnard Ventura, Oxnard *Also called Js Hospitality Group LLC* ***(G-12872)***
Courtyard Plaza....818 780-5005
6951 Lennox Ave Van Nuys (91405) ***(G-20482)***
Courtyard Sacramento-Midtown, Sacramento *Also called Cy Sac Operator LLC* ***(G-12561)***
Courtyard San Diego Carlsbad, Carlsbad *Also called ARC Hosp Portfolio II NTC Trs* ***(G-12395)***
Courtyard Vallejo, Vallejo *Also called Commonwealth Hotels LLC* ***(G-26976)***
Courtyards At Pine Creek Inc....925 798-3900
1081 Mohr Ln Concord (94518) ***(G-22419)***
Couts Heating & Cooling Inc....951 278-5560
1693 Rimpau Ave Corona (92881) ***(G-2194)***
Covad Communications, San Jose *Also called Megapath Group Inc* ***(G-5657)***
Covance Inc....858 352-2300
10300 Campus Point Dr # 225 San Diego (92121) ***(G-26500)***
Covansys Corporation....510 304-3430
34740 Tuxedo Cmn Fremont (94555) ***(G-15112)***
Covanta Delano Inc....661 792-3067
31500 Pond Rd Delano (93215) ***(G-6121)***
Covario Inc (PA)....858 397-1500
9255 Towne Centre Dr # 600 San Diego (92121) ***(G-27392)***
Cove Builders Inc....714 436-2973
3329 W Castor St Santa Ana (92704) ***(G-1305)***
Cove Electric Inc....760 568-9924
77824 Wildcat Dr Palm Desert (92211) ***(G-2564)***
Covenant Aviation Security LLC....650 219-3473
274 Michelle Ct South San Francisco (94080) ***(G-16613)***
Covenant Care LLC....831 476-0770
1935 Wharf Rd Capitola (95010) ***(G-20483)***
Covenant Care LLC....408 779-7347
370 Noble Ct Morgan Hill (95037) ***(G-20484)***
Covenant Care California LLC....562 923-9301
13007 Paramount Blvd Downey (90242) ***(G-20485)***
Covenant Care California LLC....209 477-5252
9289 Branstetter Pl Stockton (95209) ***(G-21197)***
Covenant Care California LLC....562 426-0394
4010 N Virginia Rd Long Beach (90807) ***(G-20486)***
Covenant Care California LLC....415 327-0511
911 Bryant St Palo Alto (94301) ***(G-20487)***
Covenant Care California LLC....408 248-3736
410 N Winchester Blvd Santa Clara (95050) ***(G-20488)***
Covenant Care California LLC....510 261-2628
2124 57th Ave Oakland (94621) ***(G-20489)***
Covenant Care California LLC....562 427-7493
2725 Pacific Ave Long Beach (90806) ***(G-20490)***
Covenant Care California LLC....805 488-3696
5225 S J St Oxnard (93033) ***(G-20491)***
Covenant Care California LLC....323 589-5941
6425 Miles Ave Huntington Park (90255) ***(G-20492)***
Covenant Care California LLC....559 251-8463
577 S Peach Ave Fresno (93727) ***(G-20493)***
Covenant Care California LLC....916 391-6011
6821 24th St Sacramento (95822) ***(G-20494)***
Covenant Care California LLC....805 964-4871
160 S Patterson Ave Santa Barbara (93111) ***(G-20495)***
Covenant Care California LLC....209 632-3821
1111 E Tuolumne Rd Turlock (95382) ***(G-20496)***
Covenant Care California LLC....408 842-9311
8170 Murray Ave Gilroy (95020) ***(G-20497)***
Covenant Care California LLC (HQ)....949 349-1200
27071 Aliso Creek Rd # 100 Aliso Viejo (92656) ***(G-20498)***
Covenant Care California LLC....760 745-1288
1025 W 2nd Ave Escondido (92025) ***(G-20499)***
Covenant Care California LLC....209 521-2094
3620 Dale Rd Ste B Modesto (95356) ***(G-21198)***
Covenant Care California LLC....714 554-9700
1929 N Fairview St Santa Ana (92706) ***(G-20500)***
Covenant Care California LLC....650 964-0543
1949 Grant Rd Mountain View (94040) ***(G-21526)***
Covenant Care California LLC....650 941-5255
809 Fremont Ave Los Altos (94024) ***(G-20501)***
Covenant Care Courtyard LLC....530 756-1800
1850 E 8th St Davis (95616) ***(G-20502)***
Covenant Care La Jolla LLC....858 453-5810
2552 Torrey Pines Rd La Jolla (92037) ***(G-20503)***
Covenant House California....323 461-3131
1325 N Western Ave Los Angeles (90027) ***(G-24616)***
Covenant Industries Inc....951 808-3708
110 Pine Ave Ste 910 Long Beach (90802) ***(G-14630)***
Covenant Rtirement Communities....619 479-4790
325 Kempton St Spring Valley (91977) ***(G-21199)***
Covenant Rtirement Communities....209 632-9976
2125 N Olive Ave Ofc Turlock (95382) ***(G-24617)***
Covenant Village of Turlock, Turlock *Also called Covenant Rtirement Communities* ***(G-24617)***
Coventry Cove Apartments, Fresno *Also called Buckingham Property Management* ***(G-13739)***
Coverity LLC (HQ)....415 321-5200
185 Berry St Ste 6500 San Francisco (94107) ***(G-15113)***
Covey Auto Express Inc (PA)....253 826-0461
1444 El Pinal Dr Stockton (95205) ***(G-17881)***
Covey, The, Carmel *Also called Quail Lodge Inc* ***(G-13117)***
Covina Bowl Inc....626 339-1286
1060 W San Bernardino Rd Covina (91722) ***(G-18516)***
Covina Rehabilitation Center....626 967-3874
261 W Badillo St Covina (91723) ***(G-20504)***
Covina Service Center, San Dimas *Also called Southern California Edison Co* ***(G-6238)***
Covington & Burling LLP....650 632-4700
333 Twin Dolphin Dr # 700 Redwood City (94065) ***(G-23185)***
Covington & Burling LLP....415 591-6000
1 Front St Fl 35 San Francisco (94111) ***(G-23186)***
Covington & Burling LLP....424 332-4800
2029 Century Park E # 3100 Los Angeles (90067) ***(G-23187)***
Cowboy Poetry, Santa Clarita *Also called Santa Clarita City of* ***(G-19278)***
Cowell Homeowners Association (PA)....925 825-0250
4498 Lawson Ct Concord (94521) ***(G-25244)***
Cowell Student Health Center, Davis *Also called University California Davis* ***(G-20168)***
Cowell Student Health Service, Stanford *Also called Leland Stanford Junior Univ* ***(G-19705)***
Cowles California Media Co....831 422-3500
1550 Moffett St Salinas (93905) ***(G-5848)***
Cox Castle & Nicholson LLP (PA)....310 284-2200
2029 Cntury Nicholson Llp Los Angeles (90067) ***(G-23188)***
Cox Automotive Inc....626 573-8001
8001 Garvey Ave Rosemead (91770) ***(G-6668)***
Cox Automotive Inc....404 843-5000
10700 Beech Ave Fontana (92337) ***(G-6669)***
Cox Automotive Inc....510 786-4500
29900 Auction Ct Hayward (94544) ***(G-6670)***
Cox Automotive Inc....951 689-6000
6446 Fremont St Riverside (92504) ***(G-6671)***
Cox Automotive Inc....760 754-3600
691 Calle Joven Oceanside (92057) ***(G-6672)***
Cox California Telcom LLC....310 377-1800
43 Peninsula Ctr Rllng HLS Est (90274) ***(G-5582)***
Cox California Telcom LLC....760 966-0447
1922 Avenida Del Oro Oceanside (92056) ***(G-5583)***
Cox Castle, Los Angeles *Also called Cox Castle & Nicholson LLP* ***(G-23188)***
Cox Communications Inc....949 716-2020
140 Columbia Aliso Viejo (92656) ***(G-5973)***
Cox Communications Inc....858 715-4500
1535 Euclid Ave San Diego (92105) ***(G-5974)***
Cox Communications Inc....619 218-2967
9180 Manor Dr La Mesa (91942) ***(G-6067)***
Cox Communications Inc....949 240-1212
26181 Avenida Aeropuerto San Juan Capistrano (92675) ***(G-5975)***
Cox Communications Inc....949 546-1000
6771 Quail Hill Pkwy Irvine (92603) ***(G-5976)***
Cox Communications Inc....949 546-2000
27121 Towne Centre Dr # 200 Foothill Ranch (92610) ***(G-5977)***
Cox Communications Inc....805 681-6600
3303 State St Santa Barbara (93105) ***(G-5978)***
Cox Communications Cal LLC....619 562-9820
1175 N Cuyamaca St El Cajon (92020) ***(G-5979)***
Cox Communications Cal LLC....619 263-9251
581 Telegraph Canyon Rd Chula Vista (91910) ***(G-5980)***
Cox Communications Cal LLC....619 262-1122
5159 Federal Blvd San Diego (92105) ***(G-5981)***
Cox Petroleum Transport, Bakersfield *Also called H F Cox Inc* ***(G-4194)***
Coyote Creek Consulting Inc....408 383-9200
1551 Mccarthy Blvd # 115 Milpitas (95035) ***(G-16344)***
Coyote Creek Golf Club....408 463-1400
1 Coyote Creek Golf Dr Morgan Hill (95037) ***(G-18728)***
Coyote Hills Golf Course, Fullerton *Also called American Golf Corporation* ***(G-18713)***
CP Opco LLC....707 253-2332
745 Skyway Ct NAPA (94558) ***(G-14526)***
CP Opco LLC....858 496-9700
7069 Cnsld Way Ste 300 San Diego (92121) ***(G-14527)***
CP Opco LLC....209 524-1966
4623 Mchenry Ave Modesto (95356) ***(G-14528)***
CP Opco LLC....805 563-3800
1828 State St Santa Barbara (93101) ***(G-14529)***
CP Opco LLC (HQ)....310 966-4900
901 W Hillcrest Blvd Inglewood (90301) ***(G-13752)***
CP Opco LLC....805 566-3566
1120 Mark Ave Carpinteria (93013) ***(G-14530)***
CP Opco LLC....650 652-0300
1635 Rollins Rd Ste A Burlingame (94010) ***(G-14531)***
CP Opco LLC....310 966-4900
11766 Wilshire Blvd # 380 Los Angeles (90025) ***(G-14532)***
CP Opco LLC....714 540-6111
3101 S Harbor Blvd Santa Ana (92704) ***(G-14533)***
Cpcc Inc....818 882-3200
10610 Owensmouth Ave Chatsworth (91311) ***(G-21200)***
Cpe Hr Inc....310 270-9800
9000 W Sunset Blvd # 900 West Hollywood (90069) ***(G-27393)***
Cpe Peo Inc....310 385-1000
9200 W Sunset Blvd # 700 West Hollywood (90069) ***(G-14866)***
Cpg Solutions LLC....561 988-8611
111 Woodmere Rd Ste 200 Folsom (95630) ***(G-27394)***
Cph Monarch Hotel LLC....949 234-3200
1 Monarch Beach Resort Dana Point (92629) ***(G-12551)***
CPI Econco Division (HQ)....530 662-7553
1318 Commerce Ave Woodland (95776) ***(G-17931)***
CPI International (PA)....707 525-5788
5580 Skylane Blvd Santa Rosa (95403) ***(G-7340)***
CPI Luxury Group....818 249-9888
10220 Norris Ave Pacoima (91331) ***(G-8097)***
CPIC, Fremont *Also called Cancer Prevention Inst Cal* ***(G-26743)***
Cpn Wild Horse Geothermal LLC....707 431-6229
10350 Socrates Mine Rd Middletown (95461) ***(G-6122)***
Cpo Commerce LLC....626 585-3600
120 W Bellevue Dr Ste 300 Pasadena (91105) ***(G-7681)***
CPS, Studio City *Also called Commercial Prgrm Systems Inc* ***(G-16339)***
CPS Hr Consulting, Sacramento *Also called Cooperative Personnel Services* ***(G-27389)***
CPS Security Solutions Inc (PA)....310 818-1030
436 W Walnut St Gardena (90248) ***(G-16614)***

ALPHABETIC

Cpu Medical Management Systems, San Diego *Also called Computer Proc Unlimited Inc* ***(G-15098)***
Cpu Technology Inc 925 398-7659
5753 W Las Positas Blvd Pleasanton (94588) ***(G-26501)***
Cr Drywall, San Jose *Also called C R S Drywall Inc* ***(G-2870)***
CR England Inc 909 946-1555
4131 Etiwanda Ave Mira Loma (91752) ***(G-4000)***
Cr Labs, San Francisco *Also called Jim Couch* ***(G-5642)***
Craft Resources Inc 310 937-3744
220 S Pcifc Cst Hwy 112 Redondo Beach (90277) ***(G-14867)***
Craftworks Rest Breweries Inc 415 292-5800
600 Polk St San Francisco (94102) ***(G-17102)***
Craig and Hamilton Meat Co 916 419-5500
1420 National Dr Sacramento (95834) ***(G-8666)***
Craig Hall College Residences, Chico *Also called College Housing Northwest* ***(G-13450)***
Cramer Painting Inc 909 397-5770
4080 Mission Blvd Montclair (91763) ***(G-2436)***
Crane Acquisition Inc 415 922-1666
2700 Geary Blvd San Francisco (94118) ***(G-14184)***
Crane Co 562 426-2531
3201 Walnut Ave Long Beach (90755) ***(G-7929)***
Crane Pest Control, San Francisco *Also called Crane Acquisition Inc* ***(G-14184)***
Craniofacial Department, Loma Linda *Also called Loma Linda University Med Ctr* ***(G-21711)***
Crash Inc Short Term I 619 282-7274
4161 Marlborough Ave San Diego (92105) ***(G-22716)***
CRAYCROFT YOUTH CENTER, Fresno *Also called Rescue Children Inc* ***(G-24154)***
Crazy Gideons, Los Angeles *Also called F O C Electronics Corporation* ***(G-7497)***
CRC Health Corporate 714 542-3581
2101 E 1st St Santa Ana (92705) ***(G-22717)***
CRC Health Corporate (HQ) 408 367-0044
20400 Stevens Cupertino (95014) ***(G-22718)***
CRC Health Corporation (HQ) 877 272-8668
20400 Stevens Creek Blvd Cupertino (95014) ***(G-22134)***
Crdn of Southern La County, Long Beach *Also called Foasberg Laundry & Clrs Inc* ***(G-13548)***
Creating Arts Company 310 804-0223
3110 Pennsylvania Ave Santa Monica (90404) ***(G-18385)***
Creative Alternatives 209 668-9361
2855 Geer Rd Ste A Turlock (95382) ***(G-24618)***
Creative Artists Agency LLC (PA) 424 288-2000
2000 Avenue Of The Stars # 100 Los Angeles (90067) ***(G-18386)***
Creative Channel Services LLC (HQ) 310 482-6500
12777 W Jefferson Blvd # 120 Los Angeles (90066) ***(G-27395)***
Creative Circle, Los Angeles *Also called Professional Cir Staffing Inc* ***(G-14735)***
Creative Circle LLC (HQ) 323 634-0156
5900 Wilshire Blvd # 1100 Los Angeles (90036) ***(G-14631)***
Creative Design Cons Inc (PA) 714 641-4868
2915 Red Hill Ave G201 Costa Mesa (92626) ***(G-17103)***
Creative Design Interiors Inc (PA) 916 641-1121
737 Del Paso Rd Sacramento (95834) ***(G-3109)***
Creative Energy Foods Inc 510 638-8668
9957 Medford Ave Ste 4 Oakland (94603) ***(G-8826)***
Creative Events Enterprises 818 610-7000
4872 Topanga Canyon Blvd # 406 Woodland Hills (91364) ***(G-27396)***
Creative Group, The, Menlo Park *Also called Robert Half International Inc* ***(G-14767)***
Creative Labs Inc (HQ) 408 428-6600
1901 Mccarthy Blvd Milpitas (95035) ***(G-7112)***
Creative Living Options Inc 916 372-2102
2945 Ramco St Ste 120 West Sacramento (95691) ***(G-24619)***
Creative Maintenance Systems 949 852-2871
1340 Reynolds Ave Ste 111 Irvine (92614) ***(G-14271)***
Creative Nail Design Inc 760 599-2900
9560 Towne Centre Dr # 200 San Diego (92121) ***(G-13671)***
Creative Recreation, Los Angeles *Also called Kommonwealth Inc* ***(G-8438)***
Creative Security Company Inc 408 295-2600
150 S Autumn St Ste B San Jose (95110) ***(G-16615)***
Creative Technology Group Inc (HQ) 818 779-2400
14000 Arminta St Panorama City (91402) ***(G-17104)***
Credit Bureau NAPA County Inc 707 940-3000
1247 Broadway Sonoma (95476) ***(G-14029)***
Credit Card Services Inc (PA) 213 365-1122
21281 S Western Ave Torrance (90501) ***(G-17105)***
Credit Counselor of California, San Francisco *Also called Consumer Credit Counseling Svc* ***(G-13749)***
Credit Interlink America 831 655-7890
6 Harris Ct Monterey (93940) ***(G-14056)***
Credit Management Association (PA) 818 972-5300
40 E Verdugo Ave Burbank (91502) ***(G-14030)***
Credit Solutions Corp 858 650-0812
13520 Evening Creek Dr N # 500 San Diego (92128) ***(G-9745)***
Credit Ssse Securities USA LLC 213 253-2600
10880 Wilshire Blvd Los Angeles (90024) ***(G-9988)***
Credit Suisse (usa) Inc 415 249-2100
650 California St Fl 31 San Francisco (94108) ***(G-9989)***
Credit Suisse (usa) Inc 415 678-3940
650 California St Fl 28 San Francisco (94108) ***(G-9990)***
Credit Union Southern Cal (PA) 562 698-8326
8028 Greenleaf Ave Whittier (90602) ***(G-9592)***
Credit Union Southern Cal 714 671-2700
8101 E Kaiser Blvd # 300 Anaheim (92808) ***(G-9593)***
Credo Mobile Inc 415 369-2000
101 Market St Ste 700 San Francisco (94105) ***(G-5584)***
Creedence Lessee LLC 415 561-1100
425 N Point St San Francisco (94133) ***(G-12552)***
Creekside Cnvalescent Hosp Inc 707 544-7750
850 Sonoma Ave Santa Rosa (95404) ***(G-20505)***
Creekside Rehab and Behavioral 707 524-7030
850 Sonoma Ave Santa Rosa (95404) ***(G-20506)***

ALPHABETIC

Cremation Spclists Los Angeles 323 469-9933
6000 Santa Monica Blvd Los Angeles (90038) ***(G-13703)***
Crenshaw Bowling 310 326-5120
24600 Crenshaw Blvd Torrance (90505) ***(G-18517)***
Crenshaw Nursing, Los Angeles *Also called Longwood Management Corp* ***(G-20745)***
Crenshaw YMCA 323 290-9113
3820 Santa Rosalia Dr Los Angeles (90008) ***(G-25245)***
Crescent Court Nursing Home 209 367-7400
1334 S Ham Ln Lodi (95242) ***(G-21201)***
Crescent Cy Convalescent Hosp, Crescent City *Also called North Shore Investment Inc* ***(G-20809)***
Crescent Healthcare Inc (HQ) 714 520-6300
11980 Telg Rd Ste 100 Santa Fe Springs (90670) ***(G-22420)***
Crescent Solutions, Irvine *Also called Crescent Staffing Inc* ***(G-15114)***
Crescent Staffing Inc (PA) 949 724-0304
17871 Mitchell N Ste 100 Irvine (92614) ***(G-15114)***
Crescenta-Canada YMCA (PA) 818 790-0123
1930 Foothill Blvd La Canada (91011) ***(G-25246)***
Crescenta-Canada YMCA 818 352-3255
6840 Foothill Blvd Tujunga (91042) ***(G-25247)***
Cresse Mark School of Baseball 714 892-6145
58 Fulmar Ln Aliso Viejo (92656) ***(G-19194)***
Crest Beverage, San Diego *Also called Reyes Holdings LLC* ***(G-10074)***
Crest Beverage Company Inc 858 452-2300
3840 Via De La Valle Del Mar (92014) ***(G-9049)***
Crest Digital, Laguna Beach *Also called National Film Laboratories* ***(G-18238)***
Crest Financial Corporation (HQ) 562 733-6500
12641 166th St Cerritos (90703) ***(G-10682)***
Crest R E O & Relocation, La Crescenta *Also called EAM Enterprises Inc* ***(G-11486)***
Cresta Loma, Alameda *Also called Telecare Corporation* ***(G-22106)***
Crestline Funding Corporation 949 863-8600
18851 Pardeen Ave San Diego (92108) ***(G-9836)***
Crestline Hotels & Resorts Inc (HQ) 213 629-1200
120 S Los Angeles St 11 Los Angeles (90012) ***(G-12553)***
Crestline Hotels & Resorts LLC 213 624-0000
535 S Grand Ave Los Angeles (90071) ***(G-26997)***
Crestline Hotels & Resorts LLC 415 775-7555
1250 Columbus Ave San Francisco (94133) ***(G-26998)***
Crestline Hotels & Resorts LLC 760 322-6000
888 E Tahquitz Canyon Way Palm Springs (92262) ***(G-12554)***
Creston Village, Paso Robles *Also called Emeritus Corporation* ***(G-11126)***
Crestview Cnvalescent Hosp Inc 909 877-1361
1471 S Riverside Ave Rialto (92376) ***(G-20507)***
Crestwood Behavioral Hlth Inc 209 526-8050
1400 Celeste Dr Modesto (95355) ***(G-22059)***
Crestwood Behavioral Hlth Inc 530 221-0976
3062 Churn Creek Rd Redding (96002) ***(G-24620)***
Crestwood Behavioral Hlth Inc 408 275-1067
1425 Fruitdale Ave San Jose (95128) ***(G-24621)***
Crestwood Behavioral Hlth Inc 707 552-0215
115 Oddstad Dr Vallejo (94589) ***(G-24622)***
Crestwood Behavioral Hlth Inc 916 452-1431
2600 Stockton Blvd Sacramento (95817) ***(G-22060)***
Crestwood Behavioral Hlth Inc 510 651-1244
4303 Stevenson Blvd Fremont (94538) ***(G-24623)***
Crestwood Behavioral Hlth Inc 510 793-8383
2171 Mowry Ave Fremont (94538) ***(G-24624)***
Crestwood Behavioral Hlth Inc 661 363-8127
6700 Eucalyptus Dr Ste A Bakersfield (93306) ***(G-22061)***
Crestwood Behavioral Hlth Inc 559 445-9094
153 N U St Fresno (93701) ***(G-22062)***
Crestwood Behavioral Hlth Inc 707 558-1777
2201 Tuolumne St Vallejo (94589) ***(G-22063)***
Crestwood Behavioral Hlth Inc 707 552-0215
115 Oddstad Dr Vallejo (94589) ***(G-22064)***
Crestwood Behavioral Hlth Inc 661 363-6711
6744 Eucalyptus Dr Bakersfield (93306) ***(G-22135)***
Crestwood Behavioral Hlth Inc 916 977-0949
4741 Engle Rd Carmichael (95608) ***(G-22065)***
Crestwood Behavioral Hlth Inc 925 938-8050
550 Patterson Blvd Pleasant Hill (94523) ***(G-22066)***
Crew Creative Advertising LLC 310 451-3225
7966 Beverly Blvd Los Angeles (90048) ***(G-13828)***
Crew Inc 310 608-6860
19618 S Susana Rd Compton (90221) ***(G-3425)***
Crh Management, Newport Beach *Also called Core Realty Holdings MGT Inc* ***(G-11455)***
Cri Help Drug Rehabilitation, North Hollywood *Also called Cri-Help Inc* ***(G-24625)***
Cri-Help Inc (PA) 818 985-8323
11027 Burbank Blvd North Hollywood (91601) ***(G-24625)***
Cricket Communications LLC (HQ) 858 882-6000
7337 Trade St San Diego (92121) ***(G-5391)***
Cricket Indiana Property Co 858 587-2648
10307 Pacific Center Ct San Diego (92121) ***(G-5392)***
Cricket Stx, San Diego *Also called Stx Wireless Operations LLC* ***(G-5411)***
Cricket Wireless, San Diego *Also called Cricket Communications LLC* ***(G-5391)***
Crime Impact Security & Patrol, Los Angeles *Also called Crime Impact Security Patrol* ***(G-16616)***
Crime Impact Security Patrol 323 296-6406
3860 Crenshaw Blvd # 223 Los Angeles (90008) ***(G-16616)***
Crimetek Security 209 668-6208
3448 N Golden Ste Bl St G Turlock (95382) ***(G-16617)***
Cripts Health Care 858 554-8646
10666 N Torrey Pines Rd La Jolla (92037) ***(G-19482)***
Crisp California Walnuts, Stratford *Also called Crisp Warehouse Inc* ***(G-523)***
Crisp Warehouse Inc 559 947-9221
20500 Main St Stratford (93266) ***(G-523)***
Crispy Sewing Inc 323 262-9639
3437 E Pico Blvd Los Angeles (90023) ***(G-17106)***

Cristophe Salon, Beverly Hills *Also called Hair Fashion Inc (G-13678)*
Critchfeld Mech Inc Sthern Cal....949 390-2900
1821 Mcgaw Ave Irvine (92614) *(G-2195)*
Critchfield Mechanical Inc....650 321-7801
4085 Campbell Ave Menlo Park (94025) *(G-2196)*
CRITTENTON SERVICES FOR CHILDR, Fullerton *Also called Florence Crittenton Services (G-24659)*
Crmc, Coalinga *Also called Coalinga Regional Medical Ctr (G-21496)*
Crocker Art Museum, Sacramento *Also called Crocker Art Museum Association (G-25521)*
Crocker Art Museum Association....916 808-7000
216 O St Sacramento (95814) *(G-25521)*
Crocker Group LLC....714 221-5621
1101 E Orangewood Ave Anaheim (92805) *(G-11461)*
Crockett & Coinc....619 267-1103
5540 Sweetwater Rd Bonita (91902) *(G-18729)*
Crockett Garbage Service, Richmond *Also called Richmond Sanitary Service Inc (G-6636)*
Crocodile Bay Lodge....707 559-7990
731 Southpoint Blvd Petaluma (94954) *(G-13451)*
Crocus Holdings LLC....916 782-1238
1161 Cirby Way Roseville (95661) *(G-20508)*
Crooks, Jerry C MD, Stockton *Also called Stockton Orthpd Med Group Inc (G-20072)*
Crop Production Services Inc....760 355-1133
305 Larsen Rd Imperial (92251) *(G-9131)*
Crop Production Services Inc....805 922-5848
1335 W Main St Santa Maria (93458) *(G-9132)*
Crop Production Services Inc....559 884-6010
21929 S Lassen Five Points (93624) *(G-9133)*
Crop Production Services Inc....831 757-5391
1143 Terven Ave Salinas (93901) *(G-9134)*
Crosby National Golf Club LLC....858 756-6310
17102 Bing Crosby Blvd Rancho Santa Fe (92067) *(G-18931)*
Cross Country Healthcare Inc....951 786-7683
1700 Iowa Ave Ste 210 Riverside (92507) *(G-14632)*
Cross Link Inc....415 495-3191
Bldg C Pier 50 San Francisco (94158) *(G-4766)*
Cross Rock, Paso Robles *Also called Pearce Services LLC (G-1980)*
Crossmark Inc....714 464-6318
2401 E Katella Ave # 625 Anaheim (92806) *(G-8470)*
Crossmark Incorporated....925 463-3555
3875 Hopyard Rd Ste 250 Pleasanton (94588) *(G-8471)*
Crossmark Sales & Marketing, Pleasanton *Also called Crossmark Incorporated (G-8471)*
Crossroad Services Inc....510 895-5055
2360 Alvarado St San Leandro (94577) *(G-17107)*
Crossroads Cmnty Foundation, Los Angeles *Also called PS Arts (G-28026)*
Crossroads Facility Svcs Inc....916 568-5230
9300 Tech Center Dr # 100 Sacramento (95826) *(G-14272)*
Crossroads Medical Offices, City of Industry *Also called Kaiser Foundation Hospitals (G-19608)*
Crow Canyon Country Club, Danville *Also called Crow Canyon Management Corp (G-18932)*
Crow Canyon Management Corp....925 735-5700
711 Silver Lake Dr Danville (94526) *(G-18932)*
Crowd Management, Fresno *Also called Contemporary Services Corp (G-16611)*
Crowdflower Inc....415 471-1920
2111 Mission St Ste 302 San Francisco (94110) *(G-16118)*
Crowdstrike Holdings Inc....949 954-6785
15440 Laguna Canyon Rd # 250 Irvine (92618) *(G-16345)*
Crowe Horwath LLP....818 501-5200
15233 Ventura Blvd Fl 9 Sherman Oaks (91403) *(G-26319)*
Crowell & Moring LLP....415 986-2800
275 Battery St Ste 2200 San Francisco (94111) *(G-23189)*
Crowell & Moring LLP....949 263-8400
3 Park Plz Ste 2000 Irvine (92614) *(G-23190)*
Crowell, Weedon & Co., Los Angeles *Also called DA Davidson & Co (G-9991)*
Crown Building Maintenance Co....916 920-9556
1832 Tribute Rd Ste J Sacramento (95815) *(G-14273)*
Crown Building Maintenance Co....714 434-9494
3300 W Macarthur Blvd Santa Ana (92704) *(G-14274)*
Crown Building Maintenance Co....303 680-3713
235 Pine St Ste 600 San Francisco (94104) *(G-14275)*
Crown Building Maintenance Co....858 560-5785
5482 Complex St Ste 108 San Diego (92123) *(G-14276)*
Crown Building Maintenance Co....213 765-7800
2601 S Figueroa St # 299 Los Angeles (90007) *(G-14277)*
Crown Cove Senior Care Cmnty....949 760-2800
3901 E Coast Hwy Ofc Corona Del Mar (92625) *(G-24626)*
Crown Disposal Company Inc....818 767-0675
9189 De Garmo Ave Sun Valley (91352) *(G-6471)*
Crown Energy Services Inc....213 765-7800
2601 S Figueroa St Fl 1 Los Angeles (90007) *(G-14278)*
Crown Fence Co....562 864-5177
12118 Bloomfield Ave Santa Fe Springs (90670) *(G-3510)*
Crown Golf Properties LP....714 730-1611
12442 Tustin Ranch Rd Tustin (92782) *(G-27397)*
Crown Golf Properties LP....909 481-6663
791 Camarillo Springs Rd Camarillo (93012) *(G-27398)*
Crown Hardware Inc....760 334-0300
745 S Coast Highway 101 # 104 Encinitas (92024) *(G-7682)*
Crown Limousine L.A., Los Angeles *Also called Crown Transportation Inc (G-3784)*
Crown Media Holdings Inc (HQ)....888 390-7474
12700 Ventura Blvd # 100 Studio City (91604) *(G-5982)*
Crown Media Holdings Inc....818 755-2400
3745 Calle Joaquin Calabasas (91302) *(G-5849)*
Crown Media United States LLC (HQ)....818 755-2400
12700 Ventura Blvd # 100 Studio City (91604) *(G-5983)*
Crown Plaza, Pleasanton *Also called Six Continents Hotels Inc (G-13266)*
Crown Plaza, Milpitas *Also called B H R Operations LLC (G-12410)*
Crown Plaza Los Angeles, Los Angeles *Also called Ihg Management (maryland) LLC (G-12834)*
Crown Plaza SD....619 297-1101
2270 Hotel Cir N San Diego (92108) *(G-12555)*
Crown Pointe Retirement, Corona *Also called Provident Group Crown Pnte LLC (G-11190)*
Crown Transportation Inc....310 737-0888
12300 W Washington Blvd Los Angeles (90066) *(G-3784)*
Crowne Plaza, Irvine *Also called Intercontinental Hotels Group (G-12842)*
Crowne Plaza, Los Angeles *Also called Hpt Trs Ihg-2 Inc (G-12799)*
Crowne Plaza, Redondo Beach *Also called Hpt Trs Ihg-2 inc (G-12800)*
Crowne Plaza, Fullerton *Also called Huoyen International Inc (G-12805)*
Crowne Plaza Concord, Concord *Also called Concord Hotel LLC (G-12539)*
Crowne Plaza Costa Mesa, Costa Mesa *Also called Bright Bristol Street LLC (G-12465)*
Crowne Plaza Hotel, Foster City *Also called Founders Management II Corp (G-12644)*
Crowne Plaza Irvine-Orange Cou, Irvine *Also called Intercntnntal Ht Group Rsurces (G-12841)*
Crowne Plaza Lax LLC....310 258-1321
5985 W Century Blvd Los Angeles (90045) *(G-12556)*
Crowne Plaza Ventura Beach, Ventura *Also called Ventura Hsptality Partners LLC (G-13377)*
Crowne Plz Los Angeles Hbr Ht, San Pedro *Also called Proficient LLC (G-13111)*
Crowne Plz Los Angeles Hbr Ht, San Pedro *Also called Nhca Inc (G-13022)*
Crowner Sheet Metal Pdts Inc....626 960-4971
14346 Arrow Hwy Baldwin Park (91706) *(G-3156)*
Crp Centinela LP....901 821-4117
6161 W Centinela Ave Culver City (90230) *(G-12557)*
CRS, Hayward *Also called Commercial Rfrgn Spcialist Inc (G-7754)*
CRST International Inc....909 829-1313
10641 Calabash Ave Fontana (92337) *(G-4129)*
Crstb Partners LLC....916 645-7200
3075 Twelve Bridges Dr Lincoln (95648) *(G-18730)*
Crucible....510 444-0919
1260 7th St Oakland (94607) *(G-23937)*
Cruise Ship Terminal, San Diego *Also called San Diego Unified Port Dst (G-8004)*
Cruisers Carwash & Diner, Northridge *Also called M K H Inc (G-17855)*
Crum Forster, Los Angeles *Also called United States Fire Insur Co (G-10916)*
Crunch LLC....323 654-4550
8000 W Sunset Blvd # 220 West Hollywood (90046) *(G-18623)*
Crunch LLC....415 495-1939
345 Spear St Ste 104 San Francisco (94105) *(G-18624)*
Crunch Fitness, West Hollywood *Also called Crunch LLC (G-18623)*
Crunch Fitness....805 522-5454
2655 Erringer Rd Simi Valley (93065) *(G-18625)*
Crunchyroll, San Francisco *Also called Ellation Inc (G-15159)*
Cruz Hoffstetter LLC....626 915-5621
519 W Badillo St Covina (91722) *(G-17108)*
Cruz Modular Inc (PA)....714 283-2890
249 W Baywood Ave Ste B Orange (92865) *(G-4338)*
Cruz Veterinary Hospital....831 475-5400
2585 Soquel Dr Santa Cruz (95065) *(G-618)*
Crystal Aire Country Club Golf....661 944-2112
15701 Boca Raton Ave Llano (93544) *(G-18933)*
Crystal Casino & Hotel, Compton *Also called Celebrity Casinos Inc (G-12506)*
Crystal Chrysler Plymuth Dodge....760 324-9375
36444 Auto Park Dr Cathedral City (92234) *(G-17789)*
Crystal Creamery, Modesto *Also called Foster Dairy Farms (G-424)*
Crystal Cruises LLC (HQ)....310 785-9300
11755 Wilshire Blvd # 900 Los Angeles (90025) *(G-4724)*
Crystal Dynamics Inc....650 421-7600
1600 Seaport Blvd Ste 500 Redwood City (94063) *(G-15632)*
Crystal Organic Farms LLC....661 845-5200
6900 Mountain View Rd Bakersfield (93307) *(G-352)*
Crystal Springs Golf Course, Burlingame *Also called Crystal Springs Golf Partners (G-18934)*
Crystal Springs Golf Partners....650 342-4188
6650 Golf Course Dr Burlingame (94010) *(G-18934)*
Crystal Stairs Inc (PA)....323 299-8998
5110 W Goldleaf Cir # 150 Los Angeles (90056) *(G-23938)*
Crystal Valet Parking Inc....323 663-7275
4477 Hollywood Blvd 209 Los Angeles (90027) *(G-13753)*
Crystalaire Country Club, Llano *Also called Crystal Aire Country Club Golf (G-18933)*
Cs Concrete Solutions Inc....949 285-3122
27758 Snta Margarita Pkwy Mission Viejo (92691) *(G-3251)*
Csaa Insur Group Walnut Creek, Irvine *Also called Western United Insurance Co (G-10937)*
Csaa Insurance AAA, Santa Rosa *Also called American Automobile (G-10398)*
Csaa Insurance Exchange (PA)....800 922-8228
3055 Oak Rd Walnut Creek (94597) *(G-10683)*
Csaa Travel Agency, Stockton *Also called American Automobile Assctn (G-25490)*
Csaa Travel Agency, Walnut Creek *Also called American Automobile (G-10590)*
Csac Excess Insurance Auth....916 850-7300
75 Iron Point Cir Ste 200 Folsom (95630) *(G-10684)*
Csba, West Sacramento *Also called California School Boards Assn (G-25123)*
CSC Consulting Inc....310 563-2062
2100 E Grand Ave B360 El Segundo (90245) *(G-16346)*
CSC Consulting Inc....559 739-8180
3113 E Laurel Ave Visalia (93292) *(G-27892)*
Cscc, Los Angeles *Also called CA Safety Compliance Corp (G-27860)*
CSCU, Lompoc *Also called Coasthills Credit Union (G-9660)*
Cse Holdings Inc (HQ)....408 436-1907
650 Brennan St San Jose (95131) *(G-7966)*
Csea, Sacramento *Also called Califrnia State Employees Assn (G-25170)*
Csea, San Jose *Also called California Schl Employees Assn (G-25169)*
Csfe, Port Hueneme *Also called Cecos (G-25730)*
Csi, Fullerton *Also called Cardservice International Inc (G-17055)*
Csi Cold Storage 4150, Anaheim *Also called US Foods Inc (G-8950)*

ALPHABETIC

Csi Electrical Contractors Inc — 661 723-0869
41769 11th St W Ste B Palmdale (93551) *(G-2565)*
Csi Electrical Contractors Inc (PA) — 562 946-0700
10623 Fulton Wells Ave Santa Fe Springs (90670) *(G-2566)*
Csi Financial Services LLC — 858 200-9200
3636 Nobel Dr Ste 250 San Diego (92122) *(G-26999)*
Csi Solutions, Fair Oaks Also called Wightman Enterprises Inc *(G-14983)*
CSRA LLC — 619 225-2600
4045 Hancock St San Diego (92110) *(G-16278)*
CSRA LLC — 951 898-3015
2727 Hamner Ave Norco (92860) *(G-15115)*
CSRA LLC — 310 615-0311
2100 E Grand Ave El Segundo (90245) *(G-16347)*
CSRA LLC — 703 876-1026
1520 Rr Ave Marie Is Vallejo (94592) *(G-16279)*
CSRA System and Solutions LLC — 951 735-3300
2727 Hamner Ave Norco (92860) *(G-16348)*
CSS Holdings Inc — 866 343-7185
7486 La Jolla Blvd La Jolla (92037) *(G-15116)*
Csu Holding Company — 707 746-0353
531 Stone Rd Benicia (94510) *(G-12054)*
Csub Nursing Class of 2006 — 408 219-5914
9001 Stockdale Hwy Bakersfield (93311) *(G-17109)*
Csulb 49er Foundation — 562 985-5778
6300 E State Univ Dr Ste Long Beach (90815) *(G-25522)*
Csus Children's Center, Sacramento Also called Students of Associated *(G-24522)*
CSX Corporation — 626 336-1377
14863 Clark Ave Hacienda Heights (91745) *(G-3612)*
CT Lien Solution — 818 662-4100
330 N Brand Blvd Ste 700 Glendale (91203) *(G-27399)*
Ctc Group Inc (PA) — 310 540-0500
21333 Hawthorne Blvd # 308 Torrance (90503) *(G-12055)*
Ctdn - Redding, Redding Also called Donor Network West *(G-22948)*
Ctg, San Jose Also called Computer Task Group Inc *(G-15101)*
Ctk Biotech Inc — 858 457-8698
10110 Mesa Rim Rd San Diego (92121) *(G-26502)*
Ctm, Gardena Also called Classic Tile & Mosaic Inc *(G-6978)*
CTS Advantage Logistics, San Jose Also called Advantage Logistics Inc *(G-5015)*
CTS Cement Manufacturing Corp — 714 808-1945
1631 W Lincoln Ave Anaheim (92801) *(G-6980)*
CTSI, Lancaster Also called California Traffic Safety Inst *(G-27864)*
CU Cooperative Systems Inc (PA) — 909 948-2500
9692 Haven Ave Rancho Cucamonga (91730) *(G-9715)*
CU Direct Corporation (PA) — 909 481-2300
2855 E Guasti Rd Ste 500 Ontario (91761) *(G-15117)*
Cubic Corporation — 858 277-6780
9233 Balboa Ave San Diego (92123) *(G-15926)*
Cubic Defense Systems, San Diego Also called Cubic Corporation *(G-15926)*
Cubic Global Defense Inc (HQ) — 858 277-6780
9333 Balboa Ave San Diego (92123) *(G-17932)*
Cucamonga Valley Water Dst — 909 987-2591
10440 Ashford St Rancho Cucamonga (91730) *(G-6339)*
Cudahy Medical Offices, Cudahy Also called Kaiser Foundation Hospitals *(G-21652)*
Cudc, Ontario Also called CU Direct Corporation *(G-15117)*
Cuisine Partners USA, Los Angeles Also called Investors Capital MGT Group *(G-27073)*
Culberson Drywall, Campbell Also called Charles Culberson Inc *(G-2876)*
Culinary Hispanic Foods Inc — 619 955-6101
805 Bow St Chula Vista (91914) *(G-8827)*
Culinary Services America Inc — 323 965-7582
6363 Wilshire Blvd # 305 Los Angeles (90048) *(G-14868)*
Culinary Staffing Service, Los Angeles Also called Culinary Services America Inc *(G-14868)*
Culture, San Diego Also called Carrier Johnson *(G-26173)*
Culver City Hsing Partners LP — 562 257-5100
911 N Studebaker Rd Long Beach (90815) *(G-11118)*
Culver City Roofing Company — 323 930-1311
5741 W Adams Blvd Los Angeles (90016) *(G-3157)*
Culver West Health Center LLC — 310 390-9506
4035 Grand View Blvd Los Angeles (90066) *(G-21202)*
Culver-Melin Enterprises — 209 726-9182
2150 Wardrobe Ave Merced (95341) *(G-2808)*
Cumming Corporation — 951 200-7860
25220 Hancock Ave Ste 440 Murrieta (92562) *(G-27400)*
Cummings Transportation, Shafter Also called Cummings Vacuum Service Inc *(G-1072)*
Cummings Vacuum Service Inc — 661 746-1786
19605 Broken Ct Shafter (93263) *(G-1072)*
Cummings-Violich Inc — 530 894-5494
1750 Dayton Rd Chico (95928) *(G-696)*
Cummings-Vlich Inc-Orchard MGT, Chico Also called Cummings-Violich Inc *(G-696)*
Cummins Pacific LLC — 510 351-6101
14775 Wicks Blvd San Leandro (94577) *(G-7836)*
Cumulus Media Inc — 415 835-8120
750 Battery St San Francisco (94111) *(G-6068)*
Cumulus Networks Inc (PA) — 650 383-6700
185 E Dana St Mountain View (94041) *(G-15633)*
Cuneo Black Ward Missler A Law — 916 363-8822
700 University Ave # 110 Sacramento (95825) *(G-23191)*
Cuneo, Black, Ward & Missler, Sacramento Also called Cuneo Black Ward Missler A Law *(G-23191)*
Cunha Draying Inc — 209 858-1400
1500 Madruga Rd Lathrop (95330) *(G-4130)*
Cuningham Group Arch Inc — 310 895-2200
8665 Hayden Pl Culver City (90232) *(G-26179)*
Cuningham Group, The, Culver City Also called Cuningham Group Arch Inc *(G-26179)*
Cunningham Group Inc — 303 295-1982
5616 Circle View Dr Bonsall (92003) *(G-27401)*
Cupertino Dental Group — 408 446-4353
10383 Torre Ave Ste I Cupertino (95014) *(G-20251)*

Cupertino Electric Inc — 408 808-8260
350 Lenore Way Felton (95018) *(G-2567)*
Cupertino Electric Inc (PA) — 408 808-8000
1132 N 7th St San Jose (95112) *(G-2568)*
Cupertino Electric Inc — 415 970-3400
1740 Cesar Chavez Fl 2 San Francisco (94124) *(G-2569)*
Cupertino Healthcare — 408 253-9034
22590 Voss Ave Cupertino (95014) *(G-20509)*
Cupertino Hlthcare Wllness Ctr, Cupertino Also called Cupertino Healthcare *(G-20509)*
Cupertino Inn, Cupertino Also called Forge-Vidovich Motel Limited *(G-12642)*
Curacao Financial, Los Angeles Also called Adir Money Transfer Corp *(G-13730)*
Curatel LLC — 213 427-7411
1605 W Olympic Blvd # 600 Los Angeles (90015) *(G-5585)*
Curran's Disposal, San Bernardino Also called Empire Disposal LLC *(G-6482)*
Current Tv LLC — 415 995-8328
118 King St San Francisco (94107) *(G-17110)*
Curti Family Inc — 559 688-8323
3235 Avenue 199 Tulare (93274) *(G-422)*
Curti's Dairy, Tulare Also called Curtimade Dairy Inc *(G-423)*
Curtimade Dairy Inc — 559 688-8323
Road 24 Tulare (93274) *(G-423)*
Curtis Legal Group A Professi — 209 521-1800
1300 K St Fl 2 Modesto (95354) *(G-23192)*
Curtiss-Wright Controls — 661 257-4430
28965 Avenue Penn Santa Clarita (91355) *(G-25759)*
Curtiss-Wright Controls (HQ) — 661 702-1494
28965 Avenue Penn Santa Clarita (91355) *(G-25760)*
Curvature LLC (HQ) — 805 964-9975
6500 Hollister Ave # 210 Goleta (93117) *(G-5586)*
Cusa AWC LLC — 916 423-4000
7701 Wilbur Way Sacramento (95828) *(G-3640)*
Cusa FI LLC — 415 642-9400
41 Pier San Francisco (94133) *(G-3899)*
Cusa Gcbs LLC — 619 266-7365
3888 Beech St San Diego (92105) *(G-4993)*
Cusa Pcstc LLC — 714 978-8855
2001 S Manchester Ave Anaheim (92802) *(G-27402)*
Cushman & Wakefield Inc — 650 347-3700
1350 Bayshore Hwy Ste 900 Burlingame (94010) *(G-11462)*
Cushman & Wakefield Cal Inc (HQ) — 408 275-6730
1 Maritime Plz Ste 900 San Francisco (94111) *(G-11463)*
Cushman & Wakefield Cal Inc — 949 474-4004
2020 Main St Ste 1000 Irvine (92614) *(G-11464)*
Cuso Financial Services LP — 800 686-4724
10150 Meanley Dr Fl 1 San Diego (92131) *(G-10135)*
Custom Bilt Holdings LLC — 909 664-1587
15133 Sierra Bonita Ln Chino (91710) *(G-7837)*
Custom Building Products Inc — 562 598-8808
7711 Center Ave Ste 500 Huntington Beach (92647) *(G-1162)*
Custom Business Solutions Inc (PA) — 949 380-7674
12 Morgan Irvine (92618) *(G-7051)*
Custom Commercial Dry Clrs Inc (PA) — 510 723-1000
3201 Investment Blvd Hayward (94545) *(G-13580)*
Custom Companies Inc — 310 672-8800
13012 Molette St Santa Fe Springs (90670) *(G-5053)*
Custom Craft Company, Santa Fe Springs Also called Interntonal Win Treatments Inc *(G-6868)*
Custom Crome, Visalia Also called Dae-IL Usa Inc *(G-6724)*
Custom Design Co Inc — 818 507-5959
20969 Ventura Blvd # 217 Woodland Hills (91364) *(G-1163)*
Custom Drywall Inc — 408 263-1616
1570 Gladding Ct Milpitas (95035) *(G-2881)*
Custom Drywall Service, Clovis Also called Clovis Custom Drywall Inc *(G-2878)*
Custom Goods LLC — 310 241-6700
1035 E Watson Center Rd Carson (90745) *(G-4538)*
Custom Hotel LLC — 310 645-0400
8639 Lincoln Blvd Los Angeles (90045) *(G-12558)*
Custom House Hotel LP — 831 649-4511
2 Portola Plz Monterey (93940) *(G-12559)*
Custom Lawn Services, Ventura Also called American Landscape Management *(G-807)*
Custom Lawn Services, Canoga Park Also called American Landscape Management *(G-739)*
Custom Medical Products Inc — 619 461-2068
9680 Alto Dr La Mesa (91941) *(G-7260)*
Custom Metal Fabricators, Orange Also called Cmf Inc *(G-3152)*
Custom Pak West, Sacramento Also called Western Repacking Lllp *(G-17624)*
Custom Product Dev Corp — 925 960-0577
4603 Las Positas Rd Ste A Livermore (94551) *(G-3158)*
Custom Security Services, Temecula Also called Four Star Private Patrol Inc *(G-16645)*
Custom Service Systems, Riverside Also called Ghossain & Truelock Entps Inc *(G-14311)*
Custom Tours Inc — 310 274-8819
24003 Ventura Blvd 100a Calabasas (91302) *(G-5007)*
Custom Vinyls, Fontana Also called Patrick Industries Inc *(G-6992)*
Customcare Home Hlth Svcs Inc — 916 714-1155
9826 Bond Rd Ste A Elk Grove (95624) *(G-22421)*
Customer Loyalty Builders Inc — 888 478-7787
1063 Todos Santos Concord (94522) *(G-27403)*
Customer Srvc Dlvry Pltfrm Crp — 717 896-8489
15615 Alton Pkwy Ste 310 Irvine (92618) *(G-16349)*
Customerlink Systems, Roseville Also called Caranythingcom Inc *(G-27370)*
Customfab Inc — 714 891-9119
7345 Orangewood Ave Garden Grove (92841) *(G-17111)*
Customized Dist Svcs Inc — 909 947-0084
3355 E Cedar St Ontario (91761) *(G-27404)*
Customline Professional — 714 996-1333
567 S Melrose St Placentia (92870) *(G-14141)*
Customzed Svcs Admnstrtors Inc — 858 810-2000
4181 Ruffin Rd Ste 150 San Diego (92123) *(G-10685)*
Cut N Clean Greens, Oxnard Also called San Miguel Produce Inc *(G-92)*

Cutler Group LP 415 645-6745
101 Montgomery St Ste 700 San Francisco (94104) *(G-17112)*
Cutting Edge Drywall Inc 858 408-0870
7046 Convoy Ct San Diego (92111) *(G-2882)*
Cutting Edge Protection I 949 307-1596
381 Crosby St Altadena (91001) *(G-13698)*
Cutting Edge Staffing Inc 951 587-0550
27715 Jefferson Ave Temecula (92590) *(G-14633)*
Cve Nb Contracting Group Inc 707 584-1900
135 Utility Ct A Rohnert Park (94928) *(G-27785)*
Cvh Home Health Services, San Ramon *Also called Castro Valley Health Inc (G-22399)*
Cvoc, Winton *Also called Central Valley Oprtnty Ctr Inc (G-24322)*
Cvpartners Inc (HQ) 415 543-8600
505 Sansome St Ste 1100 San Francisco (94111) *(G-14634)*
CVRM, Indio *Also called Coachella Vly Rescue Mission (G-23764)*
CVS, Camarillo *Also called Kaiser Foundation Hospitals (G-10342)*
Cw Healthcare Inc 510 636-9000
7700 Edgewater Dr Ste 728 Oakland (94621) *(G-14869)*
Cw Network LLC (PA) 818 977-2500
3300 W Olive Ave Fl 3 Burbank (91505) *(G-5850)*
CW Welding Service Inc 661 399-5422
761 Majors Ct Bakersfield (93308) *(G-8098)*
CWC Acquisition, Orange *Also called Cleveland Wrecking Company (G-3452)*
Cwf Inc 626 967-0500
251 E Front St Covina (91723) *(G-14534)*
Cwgp Limited Partnership 310 395-9700
1740 Ocean Ave Santa Monica (90401) *(G-12560)*
Cwi, San Francisco *Also called Collier Warehouse Inc (G-6916)*
Cwip, Fresno *Also called Community Integrated Work Prog (G-24324)*
Cwn Management, Mission Viejo *Also called Claim Jumper Restaurant (G-1528)*
Cwp, Adelanto *Also called Commercial Wood Products Co (G-3038)*
Cwp Cabinets Inc 760 246-4530
10007 Yucca Rd Adelanto (92301) *(G-3040)*
Cwpfl Inc 714 564-7900
1682 Langley Ave Irvine (92614) *(G-17113)*
Cws Utility Services Corp 408 367-8200
1720 N 1st St San Jose (95112) *(G-28126)*
Cwtv, Burbank *Also called Cw Network LLC (G-5850)*
Cy Sac Operator LLC 916 455-6800
4422 Y St Sacramento (95817) *(G-12561)*
Cybercoders Inc 949 885-5151
6591 Irvine Center Dr # 200 Irvine (92618) *(G-14635)*
Cybercsi Inc 408 727-2900
3511 Thomas Rd Ste 5 Santa Clara (95054) *(G-7113)*
Cybernet Entertainment LLC 415 865-0230
1800 Mission St San Francisco (94103) *(G-18066)*
Cyberpower Inc 626 813-7730
730 Baldwin Park Blvd City of Industry (91746) *(G-7114)*
Cyberpower PC, City of Industry *Also called Cyberpower Inc (G-7114)*
Cyberscientific, Irvine *Also called Cybercoders Inc (G-14635)*
Cybersource Corporation (HQ) 650 432-7350
900 Metro Center Blvd Foster City (94404) *(G-16119)*
Cymetrix Corporation 424 201-6300
1515 W 190th St Ste 350 Gardena (90248) *(G-27000)*
Cyphort Inc 408 841-4665
5451 Great America Pkwy Santa Clara (95054) *(G-7115)*
Cypress Acres Cnvalescent Hosp, Paradise *Also called C A C H Inc (G-20427)*
CYPRESS CENTER, Paradise *Also called California Vocations Inc (G-21175)*
Cypress College Foundation 714 484-7128
9200 Valley View Ave Whittier (90603) *(G-25248)*
Cypress Creek Holdings LLC 310 581-6299
3250 Ocean Park Blvd Santa Monica (90405) *(G-2197)*
Cypress Ctr For Fmly Medicine 562 799-4801
10601 Walker St Ste 250 Cypress (90630) *(G-19483)*
Cypress Education Foundation 714 220-6900
9470 Moody St Cypress (90630) *(G-25249)*
Cypress Funeral Services Inc 650 550-8808
1370 El Camino Real Colma (94014) *(G-13704)*
Cypress Garden At Citrus Hts 916 729-2722
7375 Stock Ranch Rd Citrus Heights (95621) *(G-21077)*
Cypress Garden Villas 562 860-9260
21600 Bloomfield Ave Hawaiian Gardens (90716) *(G-11119)*
Cypress Gardens Convalescent H 951 688-3643
9025 Colorado Ave Riverside (92503) *(G-21203)*
Cypress Halthcare Partners LLC (PA) 831 649-1000
100 Wilson Rd Ste 100 Monterey (93940) *(G-19484)*
Cypress Hotel, Cupertino *Also called Ch Cupertino Owner LLC (G-12508)*
Cypress Lawn Funeral Home, Colma *Also called Cypress Funeral Services Inc (G-13704)*
Cypress Private Security, San Jose *Also called Cypress Security LLC (G-16619)*
Cypress Ridge Golf Course 805 474-7979
780 Cypress Ridge Pkwy Arroyo Grande (93420) *(G-18731)*
Cypress Security LLC (PA) 415 240-4494
478 Tehama St San Francisco (94103) *(G-16618)*
Cypress Security LLC 408 217-6063
1762 Tech Dr Ste 122 San Jose (95110) *(G-16619)*
Cypress Security LLC 562 222-4197
9926 Pioneer Blvd Ste 106 Santa Fe Springs (90670) *(G-16620)*
Cytn, Hidden Hills *Also called Cyton Industries Inc (G-6723)*
Cyton Industries Inc 818 999-3398
5558 Bill Cody Rd Hidden Hills (91302) *(G-6723)*
Cytosport Holdings Inc 707 751-3942
1340 Treat Blvd Ste 350 Walnut Creek (94597) *(G-12056)*
Czech Commerce Ltd 831 649-4633
3063 Larkin Rd Pebble Beach (93953) *(G-8985)*
D & C Care Center Inc 626 798-1175
1640 N Fair Oaks Ave Pasadena (91103) *(G-21204)*
D & D Wholesale Distrs Inc 626 333-2111
777 Baldwin Park Blvd City of Industry (91746) *(G-8711)*
D & H Landscaping Inc 510 223-6597
4221 Appian Way El Sobrante (94803) *(G-830)*
D & J Plumbing Inc 916 922-4888
4341 Winters St Sacramento (95838) *(G-2198)*
D & J Tile Company Inc 650 632-4000
1045 Terminal Way San Carlos (94070) *(G-3010)*
D & K Engineering 858 451-8999
15890 Bernardo Center Dr San Diego (92127) *(G-25761)*
D & L Produce, Selma *Also called Serimian M S D L Ranch (G-392)*
D & M Communications, Gardena *Also called Ecamsecure (G-7558)*
D & W LLC 310 345-0075
3501 Rindge Ln Redondo Beach (90278) *(G-12562)*
D - Link, Fountain Valley *Also called D-Link Systems Incorporated (G-7116)*
D A McCosker Construction Co 925 686-1958
3911 Laura Alice Way Concord (94520) *(G-1761)*
D A Wood Construction Inc 209 491-4970
601 Albers Rd Modesto (95357) *(G-25762)*
D A Z, El Segundo *Also called Daz Systems Inc (G-15124)*
D and D Concrete Cnstr Inc 619 518-9737
13795 Blaisdell Pl # 201 Poway (92064) *(G-3252)*
D and S Landscaping Inc 925 455-4630
26901 Hansen Rd Tracy (95377) *(G-831)*
D Augustine & Associates 916 774-9600
532 Gibson Dr Ste 250 Roseville (95678) *(G-13829)*
D B Roberts Inc 805 988-4882
880 Avenida Acaso Ste 100 Camarillo (93012) *(G-7551)*
D B Specialty Farms, Santa Maria *Also called Darensberries LLC (G-109)*
D Bailey Management Comp 213 626-2665
121 S Hope St Apt 307 Los Angeles (90012) *(G-27001)*
D C Golf A CA Partnership 626 797-3821
1456 E Mendocino St Altadena (91001) *(G-18732)*
D C M Data Systems, Fremont *Also called Dcm Technologies Inc (G-15125)*
D C N Wireless, Woodland Hills *Also called Digital Communications Network (G-5393)*
D C S, Brea *Also called Diversfied Cmmnctions Svcs Inc (G-5592)*
D C S, Livermore *Also called Performant Recovery Inc (G-14042)*
D C Taylor Co 925 603-1100
5060 Forni Dr Ste B Concord (94520) *(G-3159)*
D C Vient Inc (PA) 209 578-1224
1556 Cummins Dr Modesto (95358) *(G-2437)*
D E F Express Corporation 559 264-0500
2626 S Railroad Ave Fresno (93725) *(G-4131)*
D E L T A Rescue, Acton *Also called Dedication & Everlasting Love (G-638)*
D E X, Camarillo *Also called Data Exchange Corporation (G-7117)*
D F Rios Construction Inc 510 226-7467
45847 Warm Springs Blvd Fremont (94539) *(G-3041)*
D G A, Los Angeles *Also called Directors Guild America Inc (G-18223)*
D G X, E Rncho Dmngz *Also called Dependable Global Express Inc (G-5057)*
D J American Supply Inc 323 582-2650
6122 S Eastern Ave Commerce (90040) *(G-8109)*
D K Fortune & Associates Inc 310 391-7266
5240 Sepulveda Blvd Culver City (90230) *(G-21205)*
D L Ryan Companies LLC 310 442-0400
12121 Wilshire Blvd # 100 Los Angeles (90025) *(G-27744)*
D M Electric Inc 909 888-8639
336 S Waterman Ave Ste K San Bernardino (92408) *(G-2570)*
D M S, Fremont *Also called DMS Facility Services Inc (G-14283)*
D P I, Azusa *Also called Direct Pack Inc (G-17125)*
D P S Inc 714 564-7900
1682 Langley Ave Irvine (92614) *(G-2438)*
D P Technology Corp (PA) 805 388-6000
1150 Avenida Acaso Camarillo (93012) *(G-15118)*
D R C, Sacramento *Also called Disability Rights California (G-23216)*
D R I Residential Corporation 949 266-1950
2081 Bus Ctr Dr Ste 195 Irvine (92612) *(G-3160)*
D R X, Los Angeles *Also called Destinationrx Inc (G-15132)*
D S I, Santa Rosa *Also called Deposition Sciences Inc (G-26504)*
D S P Janitorial Service, Hayward *Also called D S P Service Inc (G-14279)*
D S P Service Inc 510 782-2200
23762 Foley St Ste 3 Hayward (94545) *(G-14279)*
D S R Inc 805 275-0039
3503 Arundell Cir Ste A Ventura (93003) *(G-17970)*
D S S Company 209 948-0302
655 W Clay St Stockton (95206) *(G-1924)*
D W Nicholson Corporation (PA) 510 887-0900
24747 Clawiter Rd Hayward (94545) *(G-2199)*
D W Powell Construction Inc 909 356-8880
8555 Banana Ave Fontana (92335) *(G-1762)*
D Y U Inc 714 239-2433
223 N Crescent Way Anaheim (92801) *(G-12057)*
D&A Enterprises Inc 510 445-1600
34943 Newark Blvd Newark (94560) *(G-8472)*
D&B, San Francisco *Also called Dun & Bradstreet Inc (G-14057)*
D&D Equipment Rental LLC 562 595-4555
9016 Norwalk Blvd Santa Fe Springs (90670) *(G-14479)*
D&K Engineering, San Diego *Also called D & K Engineering (G-25761)*
D'Andrea Graphics, Los Angeles *Also called DAndrea Graphic Corportion (G-14142)*
D'Angelo, Michael L, Irvine *Also called Sean P OConnor (G-23548)*
D'Best Produce, Fresno *Also called De Benedetto Farms Inc (G-197)*
D+h USA Corporation 714 427-1000
3 Hutton Cntre Dr Ste 700 Santa Ana (92707) *(G-15634)*
D+h USA Corporation 925 463-8356
5000 Franklin Dr Pleasanton (94588) *(G-15635)*
D-Link Systems Incorporated 714 885-6000
17595 Mount Herrmann St Fountain Valley (92708) *(G-7116)*
D/K Mechanical Contractors Inc 714 970-0180
3870 E Eagle Dr Anaheim (92807) *(G-2200)*

ALPHABETIC

D2j Inc 323 589-1374
6351 Regent St Ste 100 Huntington Park (90255) *(G-17114)*
D3publisher of America Inc 310 268-0820
11500 W Olympic Blvd Los Angeles (90064) *(G-15636)*
D7 Roofing Services Inc 916 447-2175
205 23rd St Sacramento (95816) *(G-3161)*
DA Davidson & Co 213 620-1850
624 S Grand Ave Los Angeles (90017) *(G-9991)*
Daart Engineering Company Inc 909 888-8696
1598 N H St San Bernardino (92405) *(G-2201)*
DAC, Palm Springs *Also called Desert Arts Center (G-25019)*
Dacor Holdings Inc 626 626-4461
14425 Clark Ave City of Industry (91745) *(G-26841)*
Dae-IL Usa Inc 559 651-5170
7227 W Sunnyview Ave Visalia (93291) *(G-6724)*
Dahl-Beck Electric Co 510 237-2325
2775 Goodrick Ave Richmond (94801) *(G-7434)*
Dahlin Group Inc (PA) 925 251-7200
5865 Owens Dr Pleasanton (94588) *(G-26180)*
Dailey & Associates 310 360-3100
8687 Melrose Ave Ste G300 Los Angeles (90069) *(G-13830)*
Daily Journal Corporation 213 229-5500
915 E 1st St Los Angeles (90012) *(G-13963)*
Daily Saw Service 323 564-1791
4481 Firestone Blvd South Gate (90280) *(G-7930)*
Daiohs USA Inc (HQ) 562 293-2888
13030 Alondra Blvd # 202 Cerritos (90703) *(G-17115)*
Daiwa Corporation 562 375-6800
11137 Warland Dr Cypress (90630) *(G-8015)*
Daiwa Golf Company Division, Cypress *Also called Daiwa Corporation (G-8015)*
Dako North America Inc (HQ) 805 566-6655
6392 Via Real Carpinteria (93013) *(G-8252)*
Dal Cais Inc 916 381-8080
5101 Florin Perkins Rd Sacramento (95826) *(G-1535)*
Dalaklis McKeown Entertainment 310 545-0120
2517 Crest Dr Manhattan Beach (90266) *(G-18067)*
Daleo Inc 408 846-9621
7190 Forest St Gilroy (95020) *(G-1925)*
Daley, Lakeside *Also called Nicholas Grant Corporation (G-1834)*
Daley & Heft Attorneys 858 755-5666
462 Stevens Ave Ste 201 Solana Beach (92075) *(G-23193)*
Daleys Drywall and Taping Inc 408 378-9500
960 Camden Ave Campbell (95008) *(G-2883)*
Dallas Union Hotel Inc 626 356-1000
150 Corson St Pasadena (91103) *(G-12242)*
Dalton Trucking Inc (PA) 909 823-0663
13560 Whittram Ave Fontana (92335) *(G-4001)*
Damao Luggage Intl Inc 909 923-6531
1909 S Vineyard Ave Ontario (91761) *(G-8110)*
Damco Distribution Svcs Inc 310 661-4600
19801 S Santa Fe Ave Compton (90221) *(G-4539)*
Dameron Hospital Association (PA) 209 944-5550
525 W Acacia St Stockton (95203) *(G-21527)*
Damon Electrical 818 426-3450
7800 Bobbyboyar Ave West Hills (91304) *(G-2571)*
Damrell Nelson Schrimp Pall 209 848-3500
703 W F St Oakdale (95361) *(G-23194)*
Dan Avila and Sons 209 495-3899
2718 Roberts Rd Ceres (95307) *(G-55)*
Dan Connolly Inc 408 241-0910
855 Civic Center Dr Ste 5 Santa Clara (95050) *(G-16621)*
Dan Freitas Electric 559 686-9572
983 E Levin Ave Tulare (93274) *(G-2572)*
Dan Lofgren 925 846-6632
7707 Forsythia Ct Pleasanton (94588) *(G-14280)*
Dan R Costa Inc 209 234-2004
17239 Louise Ave Escalon (95320) *(G-353)*
Dana Middle Schl Bys Girls CLB, San Pedro *Also called Boys and Girls Clubs of The La (G-25214)*
Danco Builders Inc 707 822-9000
5251 Ericson Way Ste A Arcata (95521) *(G-1306)*
Danco Builders Northwest 707 822-9000
5251 Ericson Way Ste A Arcata (95521) *(G-1536)*
Danco Communities 707 822-9000
5251 Ericson Way Ste A Arcata (95521) *(G-11961)*
DAndrea Graphic Corportion 310 642-0260
6341 Arizona Cir Los Angeles (90045) *(G-14142)*
Danell Custom Harvesting LLC 559 582-1251
8265 Hanford Armona Rd Hanford (93230) *(G-492)*
Danerica Enterprises Inc 818 201-3300
6345 Balboa Blvd Ste 285 Encino (91316) *(G-13754)*
Danger Inc 650 323-9700
3101 Park Blvd Palo Alto (94306) *(G-5587)*
Daniel J Edelman Inc 415 222-9944
525 Market St San Francisco (94105) *(G-27745)*
Daniel J Edelman Inc 323 857-9100
5670 Wilshire Blvd # 2500 Los Angeles (90036) *(G-27746)*
Daniel J Edelman Inc 949 330-6760
75 Enterprise Aliso Viejo (92656) *(G-13964)*
Daniel J Edelman Inc 650 762-2800
201 Baldwin Ave San Mateo (94401) *(G-13965)*
Daniel J Edelman Inc 323 857-9100
5900 Wilshire Blvd # 2400 Los Angeles (90036) *(G-13966)*
Daniel Loria Novartis 510 655-8729
4560 Horton St Emeryville (94608) *(G-22136)*
Daniel O Mongiano MD A PR 661 951-9195
42220 10th St W Ste 109 Lancaster (93534) *(G-19485)*
Daniel Robert Knowlton 760 265-5293
68368 Madrid Rd Cathedral City (92234) *(G-23195)*
Daniels Kent Personnel Agency, West Covina *Also called Kent Daniels & Associates Inc (G-14692)*
Daniels Western Mt Packers Inc 562 948-2254
5217 Industry Ave Pico Rivera (90660) *(G-8667)*
Danish Care Center, Atascadero *Also called Compass Health Inc (G-21192)*
Danish Environment Inc 818 992-6722
31125 Via Colinas Chatsworth (91311) *(G-14281)*
Danlil Enterprise Inc 714 776-7705
1440 S State College Blvd Anaheim (92806) *(G-14282)*
Danning Gill Damnd Kollitz LLP 310 277-0077
1900 Avenue Of The Stars # 1100 Los Angeles (90067) *(G-23196)*
Dannis Wlver Klley A Prof Corp (PA) 415 543-4111
71 Stevenson St Fl 19 San Francisco (94105) *(G-23197)*
Danny Mahagna Shapprie 760 341-5070
73280 Highway 111 Palm Desert (92260) *(G-18461)*
Danny Ryan Precision Contg Inc 949 642-6664
1818 N Orangethorpe Park Anaheim (92801) *(G-3453)*
Dans Landscape Service Inc 714 241-9591
718 Aleppo St Newport Beach (92660) *(G-832)*
Dansk Enterprises Inc 714 751-0347
3419 Via Lido 345 Newport Beach (92663) *(G-16622)*
Danville Long-Term Care Inc 925 837-4566
336 Diablo Rd Danville (94526) *(G-20510)*
Danville Post Acute Rehab, Danville *Also called Danville Long-Term Care Inc (G-20510)*
DANVILLE REHSBILITATION, Danville *Also called Danville Village Skilled Nursn (G-22937)*
Danville Village Skilled Nursn 925 837-4566
336 Diablo Rd Danville (94526) *(G-22937)*
Dapcon Inc 408 573-7200
877 Commercial St San Jose (95112) *(G-2439)*
Daps Naval Hosp, Lemoore *Also called United States Dept of Navy (G-21985)*
Daqri LLC (PA) 213 375-8830
1201 W 5th St Ste T800 Los Angeles (90017) *(G-15119)*
Darco Construction, Stanton *Also called Denver D Darling Inc (G-1417)*
Darden Architects Inc 559 448-8051
6790 N West Ave Ste 104 Fresno (93711) *(G-26181)*
Darensberries LLC 805 937-8000
714 S Blosser Rd Santa Maria (93458) *(G-109)*
Darensburg Roghair & Renier 760 256-6891
1520 E Main St Barstow (92311) *(G-12563)*
Darr & Pitcairn AG Inc 661 758-5156
16674 Wasco Ave Wasco (93280) *(G-493)*
Darrell L Green Inc 559 688-0686
12652 Avenue 240 Tulare (93274) *(G-4339)*
DArrigo Broscoof California (PA) 831 455-4500
21777 Harris Rd Salinas (93908) *(G-56)*
Dart Aerospace, Vista *Also called Apical Industries Inc (G-7994)*
Dart Entities, Commerce *Also called Dart International A Corp (G-4340)*
Dart International A Corp (HQ) 323 264-8746
1430 S Eastman Ave Commerce (90023) *(G-4340)*
Dart Neuroscience LLC 858 736-3060
12278 Scripps Summit Dr San Diego (92131) *(G-26503)*
Das Global Capital Corp 702 967-1688
42 Peninsula Ctr Ste 317 Rllng HLS Est (90274) *(G-26653)*
Dassault Systemes Americas 818 999-2500
6320 Canoga Ave Fl 3 Woodland Hills (91367) *(G-15120)*
Dassels Petroleum Inc 831 636-5100
340 El Camino Real S Salinas (93901) *(G-9015)*
Data 911, Alameda *Also called Hubb Systems LLC (G-15962)*
Data Center, Sacramento *Also called Correctons Rhbltation Cal Dept (G-16111)*
Data Control Corporation 916 774-4000
P.O. Box 2069 Granite Bay (95746) *(G-15927)*
Data Domain LLC (HQ) 408 980-4800
2421 Mission College Blvd Santa Clara (95054) *(G-15928)*
Data Exchange, Camarillo *Also called Dex Corporation (G-25769)*
Data Exchange Corporation (PA) 805 388-1711
3600 Via Pescador Camarillo (93012) *(G-7117)*
Data Recognition Corporation 831 393-0700
20 Ryan Ranch Rd Monterey (93940) *(G-27893)*
Data Trace Info Svcs LLC (HQ) 714 250-6700
4 First American Way Santa Ana (92707) *(G-28127)*
Data-Image Systems, Rancho Cordova *Also called Ricoh Usa Inc (G-15422)*
Database Marketing Group Inc 714 727-0800
5 Peters Canyon Rd # 150 Irvine (92606) *(G-14068)*
Databricks Inc 415 494-7672
160 Spear St Fl 13 San Francisco (94105) *(G-15121)*
Datallegro Inc 949 680-3000
85 Enterprise Ste 200 Aliso Viejo (92656) *(G-7118)*
Datameer Inc (PA) 650 286-9100
1550 Bryant St Ste 490 San Francisco (94103) *(G-15122)*
Datapark Inc 510 483-7275
1631 Neptune Dr San Leandro (94577) *(G-15929)*
Dataprose Inc 805 278-7430
1451 N Rice Ave Ste A Oxnard (93030) *(G-16120)*
Datasafe Inc (PA) 650 875-3800
574 Eccles Ave South San Francisco (94080) *(G-4682)*
Datasafe Inc 650 875-3800
3160 W Bayshore Rd Palo Alto (94303) *(G-4683)*
Datastax Inc (PA) 650 389-6000
3975 Freedom Cir Ste 400 Santa Clara (95054) *(G-27894)*
Daughter of Charity, San Jose *Also called Verity Health System Cal Inc (G-22014)*
Davalan Fresh, Los Angeles *Also called Davalan Sales Inc (G-8712)*
Davalan Sales Inc 213 623-2500
1601 E Olympic Blvd # 325 Los Angeles (90021) *(G-8712)*
Dave Gross Enterprises Inc 916 388-2000
7 Wayne Ct Sacramento (95829) *(G-3511)*
Dave Spurr Excavating Inc 805 238-0834
935 Riverside Ave Ste 18 Paso Robles (93446) *(G-3426)*

Dave Wilson Nursery Inc (PA)......209 874-1821
19701 Lake Rd Hickman (95323) ***(G-275)***
Davenport Development Corp......858 300-3333
5160 Mercury Pt Ste D San Diego (92111) ***(G-3110)***
Davey Tree Surgery Company......530 378-2674
6915 Eastside Rd Ste 94 Anderson (96007) ***(G-990)***
Davey Tree Surgery Company (HQ)......925 443-1723
2617 S Vasco Rd Livermore (94550) ***(G-991)***
Davey Tree Surgery Company......760 975-0225
1914 Mission Rd Ste N Escondido (92029) ***(G-992)***
David & Goliath LLC......310 445-5200
909 N Sepulveda Blvd # 700 El Segundo (90245) ***(G-13831)***
David and Margaret Home Inc......909 596-5921
1350 3rd St La Verne (91750) ***(G-24627)***
David Chapman Investments LLC......760 564-3355
78-505 Old Avenue 52 La Quinta (92253) ***(G-18733)***
David Civalier MD Inc......530 244-4034
2510 Airpark Dr Ste 104 Redding (96001) ***(G-19486)***
David D Bohannon Organization (PA)......650 345-8222
60 31st Ave San Mateo (94403) ***(G-10973)***
David E Bland......310 552-0130
2049 Century Park E # 3400 Los Angeles (90067) ***(G-23198)***
David Evans and Associates Inc......909 481-5750
4200 Concours Ste 200 Ontario (91764) ***(G-25763)***
David Evans Enterprises Inc......213 337-3680
201 S Figueroa St Ste 240 Los Angeles (90012) ***(G-25764)***
David King Convalescent Hosp......310 451-9706
1340 15th St Santa Monica (90404) ***(G-21206)***
David L Amador Inc......626 334-2011
762 N Loren Ave Azusa (91702) ***(G-3253)***
David Levy Co Inc......562 404-9998
12753 Moore St Cerritos (90703) ***(G-7552)***
David Margaret Youth Fmly Svcs, La Verne *Also called David and Margaret Home Inc* ***(G-24627)***
David Morse & Assoc., Glendale *Also called Dma Claims Inc* ***(G-10692)***
David Ollis Landscape Dev Inc......909 307-1911
450 Kansas St Ste 104 Redlands (92373) ***(G-833)***
David Ross Inc......323 684-7673
1899 N Raymond Ave Pasadena (91103) ***(G-20511)***
David Santos Farming......209 826-1065
720 Jefferson Ave Los Banos (93635) ***(G-17116)***
David Shaposhnick Inc......760 758-6090
1787 Savannah Way San Marcos (92069) ***(G-2202)***
David-Kleis Inc......951 845-1166
9246 Avenida Miravilla Cherry Valley (92223) ***(G-20512)***
Davidon Five Star Corp......925 945-8000
1600 S Main St Ste 150 Walnut Creek (94596) ***(G-12299)***
Davidon Homes, Walnut Creek *Also called Davidon Five Star Corp* ***(G-12299)***
Davidson Hotel Partners Lp......818 707-1220
30100 Agoura Rd Agoura Hills (91301) ***(G-12564)***
Davie Brown Entertainment Inc......310 979-1980
12777 W Jefferson Blvd # 120 Los Angeles (90066) ***(G-18387)***
Davis Brothers Framing Inc......909 944-4899
8780 Prestige Ct Rancho Cucamonga (91730) ***(G-3042)***
Davis Cmnty Clnic Dntl Program, Davis *Also called Davis Community Clinic* ***(G-19487)***
Davis Community Clinic (PA)......530 758-2060
2040 Sutter Pl Davis (95616) ***(G-19487)***
Davis Framing Inc......619 463-2394
8103 Commercial St La Mesa (91942) ***(G-3043)***
Davis Hallmark Partnership......530 753-3320
110 F St Davis (95616) ***(G-12565)***
Davis Medical Offices, Davis *Also called Kaiser Foundation Hospitals* ***(G-19665)***
Davis Research LLC......818 591-2408
23801 Calabasas Rd # 1036 Calabasas (91302) ***(G-26654)***
Davis Street Community Center (PA)......510 347-4620
3081 Teagarden St San Leandro (94577) ***(G-23939)***
Davis Street Fmly Resource Ctr, San Leandro *Also called Davis Street Community Center* ***(G-23939)***
Davis Wright Tremaine LLP......415 276-6500
505 Montgomery St Ste 800 San Francisco (94111) ***(G-23199)***
Davis Wright Tremaine LLP......213 633-6800
865 S Figueroa St # 2400 Los Angeles (90017) ***(G-23200)***
Davis Ziff Publishing Inc......415 551-4800
235 2nd St San Francisco (94105) ***(G-5588)***
Daviselen Advertising Inc (PA)......213 688-7000
865 S Figueroa St # 1200 Los Angeles (90017) ***(G-13832)***
Daviselen Advertising Inc......858 847-0789
420 Stevens Ave Ste 240 Solana Beach (92075) ***(G-13833)***
Davita Dialysis, Irvine *Also called Renal Treatment Ctrs - Cal Inc* ***(G-22637)***
Davita Hesperia Dialysis Ctr, Hesperia *Also called Total Renal Care Inc* ***(G-22646)***
Davita Inc......949 930-4400
15271 Laguna Canyon Rd Irvine (92618) ***(G-22622)***
Davlor Company......949 244-9748
12 Oakbrook Trabuco Canyon (92679) ***(G-1537)***
Davlor Constructio Corp, Trabuco Canyon *Also called Davlor Company* ***(G-1537)***
Daw Industries Inc......858 622-4955
6610 Nncy Rdge Dr Ste 100 San Diego (92121) ***(G-8111)***
Dawn Ranch Lodge & Rd Hse Rest......707 869-0656
16467 Hwy 116 Guerneville (95446) ***(G-12566)***
Dawson Electric......925 723-3535
3775 Pacheco Blvd Martinez (94553) ***(G-2573)***
Day Star Fixtures......714 838-4613
1802 Riverford Rd Tustin (92780) ***(G-3044)***
Daybreak Care Center (PA)......818 504-6154
9040 Sunland Blvd Sun Valley (91352) ***(G-24628)***
Daybreak Game Company LLC......858 239-0500
15051 Avenue Of Science San Diego (92128) ***(G-15123)***
Daylight Foods Inc......408 284-7300
660 Vista Way Milpitas (95035) ***(G-8713)***
Daylight Transport LLC (PA)......310 507-8200
1501 Hughes Way Ste 200 Long Beach (90810) ***(G-4132)***
Daymark Properties Realty, San Diego *Also called Daymark Realty Advisors Inc* ***(G-11465)***
Daymark Realty Advisors Inc......714 975-2999
750 B St Ste 2620 San Diego (92101) ***(G-11465)***
Daymen US Inc......707 827-4053
1435 N Mcdowell Blvd # 200 Petaluma (94954) ***(G-7031)***
Days Inn, Glendale *Also called JP Allen Extended Stay* ***(G-12871)***
Days Inn, Oakland *Also called Brilliance Investment LLC* ***(G-12466)***
Daystar Foundation, Lancaster *Also called Antelope Valley Foundation* ***(G-23663)***
Daytona Surfise, North Hollywood *Also called Century National Properties* ***(G-10969)***
Daz Systems Inc (PA)......310 640-1300
880 Apollo St Ste 201 El Segundo (90245) ***(G-15124)***
Dazian LLC......818 287-3800
10671 Lorne St Sun Valley (91352) ***(G-8310)***
Dazian's, Sun Valley *Also called Dazian LLC* ***(G-8310)***
Db Custom Farming, Bakersfield *Also called Donald Valpredo Farming Inc* ***(G-59)***
Dbi Beverage Inc......209 524-2477
4140 Brew Master Dr Ceres (95307) ***(G-9050)***
Dbi Beverage Sacramento (HQ)......916 373-5700
3500 Carlin Dr West Sacramento (95691) ***(G-9094)***
Dbi Beverage San Francisco......415 643-9900
245 S Spruce Ave Ste 100 South San Francisco (94080) ***(G-9051)***
Dbi Beverage San Joaquin......209 948-9400
4547 Frontier Way Stockton (95215) ***(G-9052)***
Dbi Services Inc......805 523-7114
5560 Tech Cir Moorpark (93021) ***(G-1926)***
DC Solar Solutions Inc......925 203-1088
4901 Park Rd Benicia (94510) ***(G-2203)***
DC Transport Inc......916 438-0888
5411 Raley Blvd Sacramento (95838) ***(G-4133)***
Dcm Data Systems, Fremont *Also called Dcm Limited* ***(G-16350)***
Dcm Limited......510 494-2321
39159 Paseo Padre Pkwy # 303 Fremont (94538) ***(G-16350)***
Dcm Technologies Inc......510 791-2182
39159 Paseo Padre Pkwy # 303 Fremont (94538) ***(G-15125)***
Dcor LLC (PA)......805 535-2000
290 Maple Ct Ste 290 Ventura (93003) ***(G-1062)***
Dcor LLC......805 576-1200
290 Maple Ct Ste 290 Ventura (93003) ***(G-1063)***
Dcp Rights LLC......310 255-4600
2900 Olympic Blvd Santa Monica (90404) ***(G-18068)***
DCS, Lathrop *Also called Performant Recovery Inc* ***(G-14041)***
DCS Corporation......619 278-3600
7510 Hazard Center Dr San Diego (92108) ***(G-25765)***
Dcss, Modesto *Also called County of Stanislaus* ***(G-23926)***
Dct, Fontana *Also called Desert Coastal Transport Inc* ***(G-4138)***
DDB Worldwide......310 907-1500
10960 Wilshire Blvd Fl 16 Los Angeles (90024) ***(G-13834)***
DDB Worldwide......415 732-3600
600 California St Fl 7 San Francisco (94108) ***(G-13835)***
De Anza Land & Leisure Corp......619 423-2727
2170 Coronado Ave San Diego (92154) ***(G-18359)***
De Anza Square Shopping Center......408 738-4444
1306 S Mary Ave 1370 Sunnyvale (94087) ***(G-1361)***
De Benedetto AG, Chowchilla *Also called Richard De Benedetto* ***(G-718)***
De Benedetto Farms Inc......559 276-2400
1547 N Marks Ave Fresno (93722) ***(G-197)***
De Benedetto Orchards, Chowchilla *Also called Richard De Benedetto* ***(G-719)***
De Hart Plumbing Htg & A Inc......209 523-4578
311 Bitritto Way Modesto (95356) ***(G-2204)***
De La Torre Landscape & Maint......951 549-3525
656 Paseo Grande Corona (92882) ***(G-834)***
De Lasalle Institute, NAPA *Also called Retreat & Conference Center* ***(G-13791)***
De Mattei Construction Inc......408 295-7516
1794 The Alameda San Jose (95126) ***(G-1164)***
De Mello Roofing Inc......415 456-0741
45 Jordan St San Rafael (94901) ***(G-3162)***
De Oliviera Concrete Inc......661 252-7522
14111 Soledad Canyon Rd Santa Clarita (91387) ***(G-3254)***
De Par Inc......714 771-6900
806 N Batavia St Orange (92868) ***(G-26842)***
DEA, Vista *Also called Drug Enforcement ADM* ***(G-26844)***
Dealersocket Inc (PA)......949 900-0300
100 Avenida La Pata San Clemente (92673) ***(G-15126)***
Dealertrack Collte Manag Servi......916 368-5300
9750 Goethe Rd Sacramento (95827) ***(G-16351)***
Dealey Renton and Associates......510 465-3090
530 Water St Fl 7th Oakland (94607) ***(G-10686)***
Dealix Corporation......650 599-5500
720 Bay Rd Ste 200 Redwood City (94063) ***(G-6673)***
Dealstruck Inc......858 218-6703
2223 Avenida De Ln Playa La Jolla (92037) ***(G-9780)***
Dean Goodman Inc......714 229-8999
10833 Valley View St # 500 Cypress (90630) ***(G-11466)***
Dean Socal LLC......951 734-3950
17637 E Valley Blvd City of Industry (91744) ***(G-8583)***
Deanco Healthcare LLC......818 787-2222
14850 Roscoe Blvd Panorama City (91402) ***(G-22067)***
Deardens......909 942-4599
9325 Santa Anita Ave Rancho Cucamonga (91730) ***(G-4540)***
Deardorff Family Farm, Oxnard *Also called Deardorff-Jackson Co* ***(G-8714)***
Deardorff-Jackson Co......805 487-7801
400 Lombard St Oxnard (93030) ***(G-8714)***
Death Valley 49ers Inc......559 297-5691
1442 Carson Ave Clovis (93611) ***(G-25523)***
Debisys Inc (PA)......949 699-1401
27442 Portola Pkwy # 150 Foothill Ranch (92610) ***(G-9716)***

A
L
P
H
A
B
E
T
I
C

Debtmerica LLC......714 389-4200
3100 S Harbor Blvd # 250 Santa Ana (92704) ***(G-13755)***
Debtmerica Relief, Santa Ana *Also called Debtmerica LLC* ***(G-13755)***
Decarta Inc......408 294-8400
1455 Market St Fl 4 San Francisco (94103) ***(G-15127)***
Decathalon Club, San Francisco *Also called Executives Outlet Inc* ***(G-18631)***
Decathlon Club, Santa Clara *Also called Western Athletic Clubs Inc* ***(G-18704)***
Decathlon Club Inc......408 738-2582
3250 Central Expy Santa Clara (95051) ***(G-18626)***
Dechert LLP......949 442-6000
2010 Main St Ste 500 Irvine (92614) ***(G-23201)***
Dechert LLP......213 489-1357
633 W 5th St Ste 3700 Los Angeles (90071) ***(G-23202)***
Dechert LLP......415 262-4500
1 Bush St Ste 1600 San Francisco (94104) ***(G-23203)***
Decipher Inc (HQ)......559 436-6940
7 E River Park Pl E # 110 Fresno (93720) ***(G-26655)***
Decision Sciences Intl Corp......858 602-1600
12345 First American Way # 100 Poway (92064) ***(G-7553)***
Decision Sciences Intl Corp......858 571-1900
12345 First American Way # 100 Poway (92064) ***(G-15128)***
Decision Toolbox Inc......562 377-5600
5319 University Dr 521 Irvine (92612) ***(G-27895)***
Decker Elc Co Inc Elec Contrs......650 635-1390
147 Beacon St South San Francisco (94080) ***(G-2574)***
Decker Landscaping Inc......916 652-1780
13265 Bill Francis Dr Auburn (95603) ***(G-835)***
Deckers Outdoor Corporation......310 395-1120
1451 3rd Street Promenade Santa Monica (90401) ***(G-8430)***
Declara Inc......650 800-7695
977 Commercial St Palo Alto (94303) ***(G-16352)***
Decron Properties Corp......310 363-4887
8601 Lincoln Blvd Los Angeles (90045) ***(G-11467)***
Decurion Corporation (PA)......310 659-9432
120 N Robertson Blvd Fl 3 Los Angeles (90048) ***(G-18319)***
Dedicated Fleet Systems Inc (PA)......909 590-8209
1350 Philadelphia St Pomona (91766) ***(G-4002)***
Dedicated Management Group LLC......209 385-0694
3876 E Childs Ave Merced (95341) ***(G-17117)***
Dedicated Media Inc (PA)......310 524-9400
909 N Sepulveda Blvd # 320 El Segundo (90245) ***(G-13836)***
Dedication & Everlasting Love......661 269-4010
6021 Shannon Valley Rd Acton (93510) ***(G-638)***
Dee Sign Co......818 904-3400
7950 Woodley Ave Van Nuys (91406) ***(G-17118)***
Deep Focus Inc......323 790-5340
6922 Hollywood Blvd Fl 10 Hollywood (90028) ***(G-27405)***
Deepak Chopra LLC......760 494-1600
2013 Costa Del Mar Rd Carlsbad (92009) ***(G-18627)***
DEER PARK PHARMACY, Saint Helena *Also called St Helena Hospital* ***(G-21915)***
Defcon Inc......310 516-5200
20795 Main St Carson (90745) ***(G-3163)***
Defenders Trnsp Svcs Inc......909 854-7000
14562 Slover Ave Fontana (92337) ***(G-5054)***
Defenseweb Technologies Inc......858 272-8505
10188 Telesis Ct Ste 300 San Diego (92121) ***(G-16353)***
Defined Contribution Trust Fun......213 385-6161
501 Shatto Pl Ste 500 Los Angeles (90020) ***(G-12172)***
Degenkolb Engineers (PA)......415 392-6952
235 Montgomery St Ste 500 San Francisco (94104) ***(G-25766)***
Dehart Inc......858 695-0882
7550 Miramar Rd Ste 300 San Diego (92126) ***(G-3512)***
Dejuno Corporation......909 230-6744
1800 S Milliken Ave Ontario (91761) ***(G-9258)***
Dekra-Lite Industries Inc......714 436-0705
3102 W Alton Ave Santa Ana (92704) ***(G-17119)***
Del AMO Construction......310 378-6203
23840 Madison St Torrance (90505) ***(G-1538)***
Del AMO Diagnostic Center......310 316-2424
3531 Fashion Way Torrance (90503) ***(G-22719)***
Del AMO Grdns Cnvalescent Hosp, Torrance *Also called Del AMO Grdns Cnvlscnt Hosp &* ***(G-20513)***
Del AMO Grdns Cnvlscnt Hosp &......310 378-4233
22419 Kent Ave Torrance (90505) ***(G-20513)***
Del AMO Hospital Inc......310 530-1151
23700 Camino Del Sol Torrance (90505) ***(G-22068)***
Del AMO Insurance Services......310 534-3444
910 Lomita Blvd Ste E Harbor City (90710) ***(G-10687)***
Del Contes Landscaping Inc......510 353-6030
41900 Boscell Rd Fremont (94538) ***(G-836)***
Del Mar Convalescent Hospital......626 288-8353
3136 Del Mar Ave Rosemead (91770) ***(G-21528)***
Del Mar Country Club Inc......858 759-5500
6001 Clubhouse Dr Rancho Santa Fe (92067) ***(G-18935)***
Del Mar French Laundry......831 375-9597
508 Del Monte Ave Monterey (93940) ***(G-13502)***
Del Mar Plastering Inc......951 343-5955
7085 Jurupa Rd Ut2 Riverside (92509) ***(G-2884)***
Del Mar Seafoods Inc......805 850-0421
1449 Spinnaker Dr Ventura (93001) ***(G-8632)***
Del Mar Thoroughbred Club......858 755-1141
2260 Jimmy Durante Blvd Del Mar (92014) ***(G-18569)***
Del Monaco Specialty Foods Inc......408 500-4100
18675 Madrone Pkwy # 150 Morgan Hill (95037) ***(G-8473)***
Del Norte Distribution, Oxnard *Also called Seaboard Produce Distrs Inc* ***(G-7810)***
Del Paso Country Club......916 489-3681
3333 Marconi Ave Sacramento (95821) ***(G-18936)***
Del Puerto Health Care Dst......209 892-9100
875 E St Patterson (95363) ***(G-19488)***
Del Puerto Health Center, Patterson *Also called Del Puerto Health Care Dst* ***(G-19488)***
Del Rey Lathing Inc......951 343-1177
10960 Hole Ave Riverside (92505) ***(G-3381)***
DEL REY PACKING CO, Del Rey *Also called Chooljian & Sons Inc* ***(G-521)***
Del Rio Convalescent, Bell Gardens *Also called Del Rio Sanitarium Inc* ***(G-20515)***
Del Rio Convalescent Center, Whittier *Also called Del Rio Health Care Inc* ***(G-20514)***
Del Rio Golf & Country Club......209 341-2414
801 Stewart Rd Modesto (95356) ***(G-18937)***
Del Rio Health Care Inc......562 947-5221
16016 Rio Florida Dr Whittier (90603) ***(G-20514)***
Del Rio Sanitarium Inc......562 927-6586
7002 Gage Ave Bell Gardens (90201) ***(G-20515)***
Del Rosa Villa Inc......909 885-3261
2018 Del Rosa Ave San Bernardino (92404) ***(G-20516)***
Delancey Street Coach Service, San Francisco *Also called Delancey Street Foundation* ***(G-24629)***
Delancey Street Foundation......415 512-5110
600 The Embarcadero San Francisco (94107) ***(G-4003)***
Delancey Street Foundation (PA)......415 957-9800
600 The Embarcadero San Francisco (94107) ***(G-24629)***
Delancey Street Foundation......323 890-9339
1133 S Greenwood Ave Montebello (90640) ***(G-4541)***
Delano Dst Sklled Nrsing Fclty......661 720-2100
1509 Tokay St Delano (93215) ***(G-20517)***
Delano Energy, Delano *Also called Covanta Delano Inc* ***(G-6121)***
Delano Farms Company......661 721-1485
10025 Reed Rd Delano (93215) ***(G-8715)***
Delegata Corporation......916 609-5400
2450 Venture Oaks Way # 400 Sacramento (95833) ***(G-15930)***
Delicate Productions Inc (PA)......415 484-1174
874 Verdulera St Camarillo (93010) ***(G-18388)***
Delimex Holdings Inc......619 210-2700
7878 Airway Rd San Diego (92154) ***(G-12058)***
Delivery Agent Inc (PA)......415 696-5800
300 California St Fl 3 San Francisco (94104) ***(G-13994)***
Delivery Solutions Inc......925 819-1289
650 85th Ave Oakland (94621) ***(G-4004)***
Dell Software Inc......858 450-7153
9540 Towne Centre Dr # 100 San Diego (92121) ***(G-15129)***
Dell Software Inc (HQ)......949 754-8000
4 Polaris Way Aliso Viejo (92656) ***(G-15931)***
Dell Sonicwall, Santa Clara *Also called Sonicwall LLC* ***(G-16057)***
Della Maggiore Tile Inc......408 286-3991
87 N 30th St San Jose (95116) ***(G-3011)***
Delmart Cold Storage Co Inc......661 849-8608
1401 19th St Bakersfield (93301) ***(G-4491)***
Delmart Farms Inc......661 746-2148
30988 Riverside Cntrl Vly Shafter (93263) ***(G-149)***
Deloitte & Touche LLP......213 688-0800
555 W 5th St Ste 2700 Los Angeles (90013) ***(G-26320)***
Deloitte & Touche LLP......619 232-6500
655 W Broadway Ste 700 San Diego (92101) ***(G-26321)***
Deloitte & Touche LLP......415 783-4000
555 Mission St Ste 1400 San Francisco (94105) ***(G-26322)***
Deloitte & Touche LLP......714 436-7419
695 Town Center Dr # 1200 Costa Mesa (92626) ***(G-26323)***
Deloitte & Touche LLP......408 704-4000
225 W Santa Clara St # 600 San Jose (95113) ***(G-26324)***
Deloitte & Touche LLP......559 449-6300
5250 N Palm Ave Ste 300 Fresno (93704) ***(G-26325)***
Deloitte & Touche LLP......415 782-4020
6210 Stoneridge Mall Rd Pleasanton (94588) ***(G-26326)***
Deloitte & Touche LLP......213 688-0800
555 W 5th St Ste 2700 Los Angeles (90013) ***(G-26327)***
Deloitte Consulting LLP......212 489-1600
350 S Grand Ave Ste 200 Los Angeles (90071) ***(G-27896)***
Deloitte Consulting LLP......510 251-4400
180 Grand Ave Ste 320 Oakland (94612) ***(G-27406)***
Deloitte Consulting LLP......714 436-7100
695 Town Center Dr # 1200 Costa Mesa (92626) ***(G-27407)***
Deloitte Tax LLP......415 783-4000
555 Mission St Ste 1400 San Francisco (94105) ***(G-26328)***
Deloitte Tax LLP......408 704-4000
225 W Santa Clara St # 600 San Jose (95113) ***(G-26329)***
Delphi Productions Inc (PA)......510 748-7494
950 W Tower Ave Alameda (94501) ***(G-17120)***
Delphix Corp (PA)......650 494-1645
1400 Saport Blvd Ste 200a Redwood City (94063) ***(G-15637)***
Delta Air Lines Inc......310 646-9614
5625 W Imperial Hwy Los Angeles (90045) ***(G-5055)***
Delta Air Lines Inc......323 417-7374
500 World Way Los Angeles (90045) ***(G-4798)***
Delta Airlines, Los Angeles *Also called Delta Air Lines Inc* ***(G-5055)***
Delta Airlines, Los Angeles *Also called Delta Air Lines Inc* ***(G-4798)***
Delta America Ltd (HQ)......510 668-5100
46101 Fremont Blvd Fremont (94538) ***(G-7554)***
Delta Bank, Manteca *Also called Delta National Bancorp* ***(G-12042)***
Delta Blood Bank......209 943-3830
1900 W Orangeburg Ave Modesto (95350) ***(G-22938)***
Delta Blood Bank (HQ)......800 244-6794
65 N Commerce St Stockton (95202) ***(G-22939)***
Delta Brands Inc......209 522-9044
3700 Finch Rd Modesto (95357) ***(G-9053)***
Delta Breeze Farming Inc......916 775-2055
11566 State Highway 160 Courtland (95615) ***(G-354)***
Delta Computer Consulting......310 541-9440
25550 Hawthorne Blvd # 106 Torrance (90505) ***(G-16354)***
Delta Creative Inc......800 423-4135
2690 Pellissier Pl City of Industry (90601) ***(G-8042)***

ALPHABETIC

Delta Dental of California 619 683-2549
1450 Frazee Rd Ste 200 San Diego (92108) *(G-10276)*
Delta Dental of California (PA) 415 972-8300
100 1st St Fl 4 San Francisco (94105) *(G-10277)*
Delta Dental of California 916 853-7373
11155 International Dr Sacramento (95826) *(G-10278)*
Delta Dental Plan, Sacramento *Also called Delta Dental of California (G-10278)*
Delta Disposal Service Co, Tracy *Also called Tracy Dlta Solid Waste Mgt Inc (G-6570)*
Delta Floral Distributors Inc 323 751-8116
6810 West Blvd Los Angeles (90043) *(G-9187)*
Delta Galil USA Inc 949 296-0380
16912 Von Karman Ave Irvine (92606) *(G-8377)*
Delta Growers, Stockton *Also called Heritage Land Company Inc (G-288)*
Delta Hawkeye Security Inc 209 957-3333
7400 Shoreline Dr Ste 2 Stockton (95219) *(G-16623)*
Delta Health Systems, Stockton *Also called Wm Michael Stemler Inc (G-10942)*
Delta Kappa Gamma Society 951 686-8630
2350 Elsinore Rd Riverside (92506) *(G-25250)*
Delta Max 949 759-8529
23 Curl Dr Corona Del Mar (92625) *(G-16355)*
Delta National Bancorp (PA) 209 824-4000
611 N Main St Manteca (95336) *(G-12042)*
Delta Nrsing Rhabilitation Ctr, Visalia *Also called Delta Nrsing Rhbilitation Hosp (G-20518)*
Delta Nrsing Rhbilitation Hosp 559 625-4003
420 E Murray Ave Visalia (93291) *(G-20518)*
Delta One Security Inc 707 425-9346
342 Acacia St Fairfield (94533) *(G-16624)*
Delta Personnel Services Inc 925 356-3034
1820 Galindo St Ste 3 Concord (94520) *(G-14870)*
DELTA PHI CHAPTER, Goleta *Also called Gamma PHI Beta Sorority Inc (G-13492)*
Delta Products, Fremont *Also called Delta America Ltd (G-7554)*
Delta Products Corporation (HQ) 510 668-5100
46101 Fremont Blvd Fremont (94538) *(G-7555)*
Delta Protective Services, Stockton *Also called Borgens & Borgens Inc (G-16577)*
Delta Rescue Inc 661 269-4010
P.O. Box 9 Glendale (91209) *(G-25524)*
Delta Scientific Corporation (PA) 661 575-1100
40355 Delta Ln Palmdale (93551) *(G-16877)*
Delta Stewardship Council 916 445-5511
980 9th St Ste 1500 Sacramento (95814) *(G-27002)*
Delta Truck Center, French Camp *Also called Fresno Truck Center (G-6677)*
Delta-T Group Inc 619 543-0556
4420 Hotel Circle Ct # 205 San Diego (92108) *(G-22422)*
Deluxe Ad Services Inc, Burbank *Also called Adstream North America Inc (G-15897)*
Deluxe Auto Carriers Inc 909 823-1617
15810 Gale Ave Ste 120 La Puente (91745) *(G-4005)*
Deluxe Digital Dist Inc 818 260-6202
2400 W Empire Ave Ste 200 Los Angeles (90027) *(G-18221)*
Deluxe Entrmt Svcs Group Inc (PA) 818 565-3600
2400 W Empire Ave Ste 200 Burbank (91504) *(G-18462)*
Deluxe Entrmt Svcs Group Inc 661 702-5000
29125 Avenue Paine Valencia (91355) *(G-18069)*
Deluxe Laboratories Inc (HQ) 323 462-6171
2400 W Empire Ave Ste 200 Burbank (91504) *(G-18222)*
Deluxe Media Management, Valencia *Also called Deluxe Entrmt Svcs Group Inc (G-18069)*
Deluxe Media Services 818 526-3700
2130 N Hollywood Way Burbank (91505) *(G-16121)*
Deluxe Media Services LLC 323 462-6171
1377 N Serrano Ave Los Angeles (90027) *(G-18070)*
Demand Chain Inc 800 466-3786
301 Howard St Fl 20 San Francisco (94105) *(G-7119)*
Demand Media Inc (PA) 310 656-6253
1655 26th St Santa Monica (90404) *(G-13967)*
Demandbase Inc (PA) 415 683-2660
680 Folsom St Ste 400 San Francisco (94107) *(G-15638)*
Demandforce Inc 415 904-8080
22 4th St Fl 12 San Francisco (94103) *(G-15130)*
Demaria Landtech Inc 858 481-5500
2789 High Mead Cir Vista (92084) *(G-837)*
Demenno Kerdoon 310 537-7100
2000 N Alameda St Compton (90222) *(G-1064)*
Demenno-Kerdoon 310 898-3848
1300 S Santa Fe Ave Compton (90221) *(G-4006)*
Demko Drywall & Demolition Co 619 590-0025
419 S Marshall Ave El Cajon (92020) *(G-2885)*
Demler Armstrong & Rowland LLP 562 498-8979
4500 E Pacific Cst Hwy # 400 Long Beach (90804) *(G-23204)*
Demler Egg Ranch 661 758-4577
28198 Gromer Ave Wasco (93280) *(G-444)*
Demo Deluxe, Yorba Linda *Also called IMG (G-17234)*
Demptos Glass, Concord *Also called Saxco International LLC (G-9301)*
Dena Corp 415 375-3170
185 Berry St Ste 3000 San Francisco (94107) *(G-15131)*
Denc Services Inc 916 351-1720
1024 Iron Point Rd Folsom (95630) *(G-24334)*
Denevi Digital, San Jose *Also called Far Western Graphics Inc (G-14117)*
Denios Roseville Farmers 916 782-2704
2013 Opportunity Dr Roseville (95678) *(G-9135)*
Deniz Packing Incorporated 559 673-0066
21801 Avenue 16 Madera (93637) *(G-231)*
Dennett Tile & Stone Inc 707 541-3700
3310 Industrial Dr Santa Rosa (95403) *(G-3012)*
Dennis & Leen, Los Angeles *Also called EC Group Inc (G-6814)*
Dennis Allen Associates (PA) 805 884-8777
201 N Milpas St Santa Barbara (93103) *(G-1165)*
Dennis Blazona Construction 916 375-8337
525 Harbor Blvd Ste 10 West Sacramento (95691) *(G-3255)*
Dennis Foland Inc 909 930-9900
1500 S Hellman Ave Ontario (91761) *(G-8112)*
Dennis Hyde Construction Inc 661 393-1077
6212 Patton Way Bakersfield (93308) *(G-1166)*
Dennis M McCoy & Sons Inc (PA) 818 874-3872
32107 Lindero Canyon Rd # 212 Westlake Village (91361) *(G-1763)*
Denova Home Sales Inc 925 852-0545
1500 Willow Pass Ct Concord (94520) *(G-11468)*
Denova Homes, Concord *Also called Denova Home Sales Inc (G-11468)*
Denso Pdts & Svcs Americas Inc (HQ) 310 834-6352
3900 Via Oro Ave Long Beach (90810) *(G-6725)*
Dental, San Diego *Also called Veterans Health Administration (G-20283)*
Dental Office, Oxnard *Also called Clinicas Del Camino Real Inc (G-22688)*
Dental Plus Dental Group, Pasadena *Also called Roisman Leon D DMD Inc (G-20273)*
Dentistat Inc 408 376-0336
1688 Dell Ave Ste 210 Campbell (95008) *(G-27408)*
Dentists Insurance Company (HQ) 916 443-4567
1201 K St Ste 1600 Sacramento (95814) *(G-10688)*
Dentons US LLP 650 798-0300
1530 Page Mill Rd Ste 200 Palo Alto (94304) *(G-23205)*
Dentons US LLP 949 732-3700
2030 Main St Ste 1000 Irvine (92614) *(G-23206)*
Dentons US LLP 619 595-5400
750 B St Ste 3300 San Diego (92101) *(G-23207)*
Dentons US LLP 619 236-1414
4655 Executive Dr Ste 700 San Diego (92121) *(G-23208)*
Dentons US LLP 415 882-5000
1 Market Plz Fl 24 San Francisco (94105) *(G-23209)*
Dentons US LLP 213 623-9300
601 S Figueroa St # 2500 Los Angeles (90017) *(G-23210)*
Dentons US LLP 213 688-1000
300 S Grand Ave Fl 14 Los Angeles (90071) *(G-23211)*
Denver D Darling Inc 714 761-8299
8402 Katella Ave Stanton (90680) *(G-1417)*
Department Behavioral Health, Fresno *Also called County of Fresno (G-22695)*
Department Child Support Svcs, Camarillo *Also called County of Ventura (G-23935)*
Department Children Fmly Svcs, Los Angeles *Also called County of Los Angeles (G-23852)*
Department Health Care Svcs 510 412-3700
850 Marina Bay Pkwy Richmond (94804) *(G-22208)*
Department of Ane, Sacramento *Also called University California Davis (G-22001)*
Department of Cultural Affairs, Los Angeles *Also called City of Los Angeles (G-25518)*
Department of Global Ecology, Stanford *Also called Carnegie Institution Wash (G-26747)*
Department of Health, Los Angeles *Also called County of Los Angeles (G-22932)*
Department of Health Services, Los Angeles *Also called County of Los Angeles (G-22133)*
Department of Health Services, Martinez *Also called County of Contra Costa (G-21514)*
Department of Health Services, Concord *Also called County of Contra Costa (G-22694)*
Department of Mental Health, Willows *Also called County of Glenn (G-22696)*
Department of Public Safety, Stanford *Also called Leland Stanford Junior Univ (G-2637)*
Department of Public Works, Mill Valley *Also called City of Mill Valley (G-1751)*
Department of Public Works, San Rafael *Also called County of Marin (G-25757)*
Department of Radiology, San Francisco *Also called University Cal San Francisco (G-20165)*
Department of Regional Parks, Sacramento *Also called County of Sacramento (G-18816)*
Department of Social Services, Alturas *Also called County of Modoc (G-23865)*
Department of Social Services, San Luis Obispo *Also called County of San Luis Obispo (G-23908)*
Department of Social Services, Placerville *Also called County of El Dorado (G-23804)*
Department of Transportation, Ukiah *Also called County of Mendocino (G-4912)*
Department Public Social Svcs, Cudahy *Also called County of Los Angeles (G-24907)*
Dependable Aircargo Ex Inc 310 537-2000
19201 S Susana Rd Compton (90221) *(G-5056)*
Dependable Auto Shippers Inc 310 719-9915
18004 S Broadway Gardena (90248) *(G-4134)*
Dependable Disposal and Recycl, Spring Valley *Also called Burns and Sons Trucking Inc (G-3985)*
Dependable Global Express Inc 310 537-2000
19201 S Susana Rd E Rncho Dmngz (90221) *(G-5057)*
Dependable Highway Express Inc 909 923-0065
1351 S Campus Ave Ontario (91761) *(G-4135)*
Dependable Highway Express Inc 510 357-2223
3012 Alvarado St San Leandro (94577) *(G-4542)*
Dependable Highway Express Inc (PA) 323 526-2200
2555 E Olympic Blvd Los Angeles (90023) *(G-4136)*
Dependable Highway Express Inc 510 357-2223
3199 Alvarado St San Leandro (94577) *(G-4137)*
Dependable Highway Express Inc 916 374-0782
820 E St West Sacramento (95605) *(G-4007)*
Deploy Hr Inc 925 426-1010
5870 Stoneridge Mall Rd # 208 Pleasanton (94588) *(G-14636)*
Deployment Solutions LLC 317 281-9682
332 Bandini Pl Vista (92083) *(G-2575)*
Depo.com, Glendale *Also called Atkinson-Baker Inc (G-14166)*
Deposition Sciences Inc 707 573-6700
3300 Coffey Ln Santa Rosa (95403) *(G-26504)*
Depot, Porterville *Also called Tharp Truck Rental Inc (G-18024)*
Dept Children and Family Svcs, Lakewood *Also called County of Los Angeles (G-23829)*
Dept of Building Inspection, Salinas *Also called County of Monterey (G-17101)*
Dept of Child Support, Stockton *Also called County of San Joaquin (G-23905)*
Dept of Community Services, Bell *Also called City of Bell (G-23751)*
Dept of Maintenance, Antioch *Also called City of Antioch (G-6620)*
Dept of Mental Health, Woodland *Also called County of Yolo (G-22715)*
Dept of Public Works, Irvine *Also called City of Irvine (G-27383)*
Dept of Social Services, Eureka *Also called County of Humboldt (G-23812)*

ALPHABETIC

Dept of Social Services Dss, San Luis Obispo *Also called County of San Luis Obispo* ***(G-23909)***
Der Mnuel Insur Fincl Svcs Inc...559 447-4600
548 W Cromwell Ave # 101 Fresno (93711) ***(G-10689)***
Derek Silva Community, San Francisco *Also called Catholic Chrts Cyo Archdiocs* ***(G-23719)***
Derjjan Associates Inc (PA)...831 423-4111
2025 Soquel Ave Santa Cruz (95062) ***(G-27003)***
Des Architects + Engineers Inc...650 364-6453
399 Bradford St Ste 300 Redwood City (94063) ***(G-26182)***
Descanso Beach Club, Avalon *Also called Santa Catalina Island Company* ***(G-19063)***
Deser Sands Unifi Schoo Distr...760 777-4200
47950 Dune Palms Rd La Quinta (92253) ***(G-24454)***
Deseret Farms of California, Chico *Also called Agreserves Inc* ***(G-194)***
Deseret Industries, Sacramento *Also called Corporation of The President* ***(G-24328)***
Desert Aids Project (PA)...760 323-2118
1695 N Sunrise Way Bldg 1 Palm Springs (92262) ***(G-23940)***
Desert Air Conditioning Inc...760 323-3383
590 S Williams Rd Palm Springs (92264) ***(G-3164)***
Desert Area Resources Training...760 375-8494
201 E Ridgecrest Blvd Ridgecrest (93555) ***(G-24912)***
Desert Arts Center...760 323-7973
550 N Palm Canyon Dr Palm Springs (92262) ***(G-25019)***
Desert Cardiology Cons Med G, Rancho Mirage *Also called Desert Cardiology Consultants* ***(G-19489)***
Desert Cardiology Consultants...760 346-0642
39000 Bob Hope Dr Ste W30 Rancho Mirage (92270) ***(G-19489)***
Desert Cities Dialysis, Victorville *Also called Jamboor Medical Corporation* ***(G-22631)***
Desert Cncpts Ldscpg Maint Inc...760 200-9007
79469 Country Club Dr I Bermuda Dunes (92203) ***(G-761)***
Desert Coastal Transport Inc (PA)...909 357-3395
10686 Banana Ave Fontana (92337) ***(G-4138)***
Desert Falls Country Club Inc...760 340-5646
1111 Desert Falls Pkwy Palm Desert (92211) ***(G-18938)***
Desert Haven Enterprises (PA)...661 948-8402
43437 Copeland Cir Lancaster (93535) ***(G-838)***
Desert Haven Enterprises...661 948-8402
43437 Copeland Cir Lancaster (93535) ***(G-839)***
DESERT HORIZONS COUNTRY CLUB, Indian Wells *Also called Dhccnp* ***(G-18940)***
Desert Hot Springs Spa Hotel, Desert Hot Springs *Also called Whatever It Takes Inc* ***(G-13409)***
Desert Knlls Convalescent Hosp, Victorville *Also called Knolls Convalescent Hospital* ***(G-20711)***
Desert Knolls Convalescent, Victorville *Also called Knolls Convalescent Hospital* ***(G-20712)***
Desert Manor Care Center LP...760 365-0717
8515 Cholla Ave Yucca Valley (92284) ***(G-24630)***
Desert Mechanical Inc...702 873-7333
15870 Olden St Sylmar (91342) ***(G-2205)***
Desert Medical Group Inc (PA)...760 323-8657
275 N El Cielo Rd Ste C Palm Springs (92262) ***(G-19490)***
Desert Medical Group Inc...760 323-8657
275 N El Cielo Rd Ste C Palm Springs (92262) ***(G-19491)***
Desert Oaks Apartments, Visalia *Also called Kern 2008 Cmnty Partners LP* ***(G-1322)***
Desert Oasis Healthcare, Palm Springs *Also called Desert Medical Group Inc* ***(G-19490)***
Desert Orthopdc Center A Mdcl (PA)...760 568-2684
39000 Bob Hope Dr W301 Rancho Mirage (92270) ***(G-19492)***
Desert Princess Hoa, Cathedral City *Also called Desert Prncess Homeowners Assn* ***(G-25251)***
Desert Princess Home...760 322-1655
28555 Landau Blvd Cathedral City (92234) ***(G-18939)***
Desert Prncess Homeowners Assn...760 322-0567
28211 Desert Princess Dr Cathedral City (92234) ***(G-25251)***
Desert Recreation District (PA)...760 347-3484
45305 Oasis St Indio (92201) ***(G-19195)***
Desert Recycling Inc...760 948-3122
17105 Mesa St Hesperia (92345) ***(G-6472)***
Desert Regional Med Ctr Inc (HQ)...760 323-6374
1150 N Indian Canyon Dr Palm Springs (92262) ***(G-21529)***
Desert Regional Med Ctr Inc...760 323-6640
1695 N Sunrise Way Palm Springs (92262) ***(G-22137)***
Desert Resort Management...760 831-0172
42635 Melanie Pl Ste 103 Palm Desert (92211) ***(G-11469)***
Desert Rose Golf Course, Cathedral City *Also called American Golf Corporation* ***(G-18860)***
Desert Services Inc...760 837-2000
41921 Beacon Hl Palm Desert (92211) ***(G-16625)***
Desert Springs Healthcare, Indio *Also called Indio Hlthcare Wllness Ctr LLC* ***(G-20683)***
Desert Springs Hotel...760 251-3399
10805 Palm Dr Desert Hot Springs (92240) ***(G-10974)***
Desert Star Co...661 259-5848
23119 Drayton St Saugus (91350) ***(G-8986)***
Desert Sun Science Center, The, Idyllwild *Also called Guided Discoveries Inc* ***(G-13464)***
Desert Television LLC...760 343-5700
73185 Highway 111 Ste D Palm Desert (92260) ***(G-5851)***
Desert Valley Date Inc...760 398-0999
86740 Industrial Way Coachella (92236) ***(G-524)***
Desert Valley Hospital Inc (HQ)...760 241-8000
16850 Bear Valley Rd Victorville (92395) ***(G-21530)***
DESERT VALLEY INDUSTRIES, Palm Desert *Also called Desertarc* ***(G-23941)***
Desert Valley Med Group Inc...760 245-2474
12401 Hesperia Rd Ste 9 Victorville (92395) ***(G-19493)***
Desert Valley Med Group Inc (PA)...760 241-8000
16850 Bear Valley Rd Victorville (92395) ***(G-19494)***
Desert View Funeral Home...760 244-0007
11478 Amargosa Rd Victorville (92392) ***(G-13705)***
Desert View Power Inc...916 596-2500
2600 Capitol Ave Sacramento (95816) ***(G-6123)***
Desert Water Agency Fing Corp...760 323-4971
1200 S Gene Autry Trl Palm Springs (92264) ***(G-6340)***
Desert Willow Golf Course, Palm Desert *Also called Desert Willow Golf Resort Inc* ***(G-19196)***
Desert Willow Golf Resort Inc...760 346-0015
38995 Desert Willow Dr Palm Desert (92260) ***(G-19196)***
Desertarc (PA)...760 346-1611
73255 Country Club Dr Palm Desert (92260) ***(G-23941)***
Design Collection Inc...323 277-9200
2209 S Santa Fe Ave Los Angeles (90058) ***(G-8311)***
Design Machine and Mfg...559 897-7374
2491 Simpson St Kingsburg (93631) ***(G-17971)***
Design Masonry Inc...661 252-2784
20703 Santa Clara St Canyon Country (91351) ***(G-2809)***
Designed MBL Systems Inds Inc...209 892-6298
800 S 2nd St Patterson (95363) ***(G-1539)***
Designworks/Usa Inc (HQ)...805 499-9590
2201 Corporate Center Dr Newbury Park (91320) ***(G-25767)***
Desilva Gates Construction LP...916 386-9708
7700 College Town Dr # 230 Sacramento (95826) ***(G-1764)***
Desilva Gates Construction LP (PA)...925 361-1380
11555 Dublin Blvd Dublin (94568) ***(G-1765)***
Desmond Mail Delivery Service...323 262-1085
4600 Worth St Los Angeles (90063) ***(G-4008)***
Destination Residences LLC...858 550-1000
9700 N Torrey Pines Rd La Jolla (92037) ***(G-13756)***
Destination Resort MGT Inc...760 346-4647
45750 San Luis Rey Ave Palm Desert (92260) ***(G-12567)***
Destination Science LLC...714 289-9100
953 N Elm St Orange (92867) ***(G-27897)***
Destination Shuttle Svcs LLC...310 338-9466
6150 W 96th St Los Angeles (90045) ***(G-3641)***
Destination Webcam, La Jolla *Also called Aegis Software Inc* ***(G-13987)***
Destinationrx Inc (HQ)...800 379-9060
600 Wilshire Blvd # 1100 Los Angeles (90017) ***(G-15132)***
Destine One Wholesale Inc...951 202-3545
1660 Kendall Dr Apt 24 San Bernardino (92407) ***(G-8163)***
Destiny Arts Center...510 597-1619
970 Grace Ave Oakland (94608) ***(G-19197)***
Deutsch La Inc...310 862-3000
5454 Beethoven St Los Angeles (90066) ***(G-13837)***
Deutsche Bank National Tr Co (HQ)...213 620-8200
2000 Avenue Of The Stars Los Angeles (90067) ***(G-9727)***
Deutsche Bank National Tr Co...714 247-6000
1761 E Saint Andrew Pl Santa Ana (92705) ***(G-9728)***
Deutsche Bank Tr Co Americas...415 617-4200
101 California St # 4500 San Francisco (94111) ***(G-9992)***
Deutsche Bank Tr Co Americas...213 620-8200
2000 Av Stars N Powers Los Angeles (90067) ***(G-9395)***
Deutsche Inv MGT Americas Inc...415 648-9408
101 California St # 2400 San Francisco (94111) ***(G-10136)***
Deutsche Telekom Inc...650 335-4100
295 Bernardo Ave Ste 200 Mountain View (94043) ***(G-27898)***
Devcon Construction Inc (PA)...408 942-8200
690 Gibraltar Dr Milpitas (95035) ***(G-1418)***
Develop Disabilities Svc Org...916 973-1953
2331 Saint Marks Way G1 Sacramento (95864) ***(G-23942)***
Develop Point Education...805 624-6171
9909 Topanga Canyon Blvd # 346 Chatsworth (91311) ***(G-13757)***
Developers Surety Indemnity Co, Irvine *Also called Insco Insurance Services Inc* ***(G-10743)***
Developers Surety Indemnity Co (HQ)...949 263-3300
17771 Cowan Ste 100 Irvine (92614) ***(G-10491)***
Development Exchange, Mountain View *Also called Devxcom Inc* ***(G-5589)***
Development Resource Cons Inc (PA)...714 685-6860
160 S Old Springs Rd # 210 Anaheim (92808) ***(G-25768)***
Developmental Svcs Cal Dept...559 782-2222
26501 Avenue 140 Porterville (93257) ***(G-20519)***
Developmental Svcs Cal Dept...714 957-5151
2501 Harbor Blvd Costa Mesa (92626) ***(G-24335)***
Developmental Svcs Continuum...619 460-7333
7944 Golden Ave Lemon Grove (91945) ***(G-24631)***
Developmentally Research Ctr, San Marcos *Also called San Diego-Imperial* ***(G-24177)***
Develpment Dimensions Intl Inc...925 361-4246
4160 Dublin Blvd Ste 450 Dublin (94568) ***(G-27409)***
Devereux California Center, Goleta *Also called Devereux Foundation* ***(G-24913)***
Devereux Center In California, Goleta *Also called Devereux Foundation* ***(G-12173)***
Devereux Foundation...805 968-2525
7055 Seaway Dr Goleta (93117) ***(G-24913)***
Devereux Foundation...805 968-2525
El Colegio Rd Goleta (93117) ***(G-12173)***
Device Anywhere...650 655-6400
777 Mariners Isl Blvd # 250 San Mateo (94404) ***(G-15133)***
Devincenzi Concrete Cnstr...707 568-4370
3276 Dutton Ave Santa Rosa (95407) ***(G-3256)***
Devine & Son Trucking Co Inc (PA)...559 486-7440
3870 Channel Dr West Sacramento (95691) ***(G-4721)***
Devine Intermodal, West Sacramento *Also called Devine & Son Trucking Co Inc* ***(G-4721)***
Devonshire Care Center LLC...951 925-2571
1350 E Devonshire Ave Hemet (92544) ***(G-21207)***
Devxcom Inc...650 390-6553
310 Villa St Mountain View (94041) ***(G-5589)***
Dewhurst & Associates...858 456-5345
7533 Girard Ave La Jolla (92037) ***(G-1167)***
Dewmobile USA Inc...408 550-2818
2901 Tasman Dr Ste 107 Santa Clara (95054) ***(G-15134)***
Dewolf Realty Co Inc...415 221-2032
4330 California St San Francisco (94118) ***(G-27004)***
Dex Corporation...805 388-1711
3600 Via Pescador Camarillo (93012) ***(G-25769)***
Deyoung Museum, San Francisco *Also called Corportion of Fine Arts Mseums* ***(G-25016)***
Dfa of California...530 345-5077
6100 Wilson Landing Rd Chico (95973) ***(G-25525)***

ALPHABETIC

Dfa of California 209 465-2289
1050 Diamond St Stockton (95205) *(G-17121)*
Dfs Flooring Inc (PA) 818 374-5200
15651 Saticoy St Van Nuys (91406) *(G-3111)*
Dfs Group LP 310 783-6600
1580 Francisco St Torrance (90501) *(G-26330)*
Dfusion Software Inc 323 617-5577
5900 Wilshire Blvd # 2550 Los Angeles (90036) *(G-15135)*
Dg Architects Inc (PA) 650 943-1660
550 Ellis St Mountain View (94043) *(G-26183)*
Dga Plnning L Arch L Interiors, Mountain View *Also called Dg Architects Inc (G-26183)*
Dga Services Inc (PA) 408 232-4800
540 E Trimble Rd San Jose (95131) *(G-4341)*
Dgwb Inc 714 881-2300
217 N Main St Ste 200 Santa Ana (92701) *(G-13838)*
Dgwb Advg & Communications, Santa Ana *Also called Dgwb Inc (G-13838)*
Dgwb Ventures LLC 714 881-2308
217 N Main St Ste 200 Santa Ana (92701) *(G-13839)*
DH Smith Company Inc 408 532-7617
6000 Hellyer Ave Ste 150 San Jose (95138) *(G-2886)*
Dhap Digital Inc 415 962-4900
465 California St Ste 600 San Francisco (94104) *(G-15136)*
Dharne & Company 949 293-5675
19200 Von Karman Ave # 400 Irvine (92612) *(G-16356)*
Dhccnp 760 340-4646
44900 Desert Horizons Dr Indian Wells (92210) *(G-18940)*
Dhe, Ontario *Also called Dependable Highway Express Inc (G-4135)*
Dhe, San Leandro *Also called Dependable Highway Express Inc (G-4137)*
Dhl Express (usa) Inc 415 826-7338
401 23rd St San Francisco (94107) *(G-4842)*
Dhs Member Services 562 595-5151
3833 Atlantic Ave Long Beach (90807) *(G-20252)*
Dhv Industries Inc 661 392-8948
3451 Pegasus Dr Bakersfield (93308) *(G-7931)*
Dhx-Dependable Hawaiian Ex Inc (PA) 310 537-2000
19201 S Susana Rd Rancho Dominguez (90220) *(G-5058)*
Diabetes Care Center, Tarzana *Also called Providence Health & Services (G-23024)*
Diablo Country Club 925 837-4221
1700 Club House Rd Diablo (94528) *(G-18941)*
Diablo Country Club 925 837-9233
1700 Clubhouse Rd Diablo (94528) *(G-18734)*
Diablo Grande Ltd Partnership 209 892-7421
9521 Morton Davis Dr Patterson (95363) *(G-11962)*
Diablo Landscape Inc 408 487-9620
1655 Berryessa Rd San Jose (95133) *(G-840)*
Diablo Realty Inc 925 933-9300
975 Ygnacio Valley Rd Walnut Creek (94596) *(G-11470)*
Diablo Valley Masonry Inc 916 438-0607
6600 Asher Ln Sacramento (95828) *(G-2810)*
Diablo Valley Rock, Concord *Also called Carone & Company Inc (G-3421)*
Diablo Vly College Foundation (PA) 925 685-1230
321 Golf Club Rd Pleasant Hill (94523) *(G-17122)*
Diageo North America Inc 707 939-6200
21468 8th St E Sonoma (95476) *(G-9095)*
Diageo North America Inc 949 421-3974
30 Journey Aliso Viejo (92656) *(G-9096)*
Diagnostic and Interventio 310 574-0400
13160 Mindanao Way # 150 Marina Del Rey (90292) *(G-19495)*
Diagnostic Labs & Rdlgy, Burbank *Also called Kan-Di-Ki LLC (G-22229)*
Dial Communications, Camarillo *Also called Dial Security (G-16878)*
Dial Global Digital, Culver City *Also called Triton Media Group LLC (G-5825)*
Dial Security (PA) 805 389-6700
760 W Ventura Blvd Camarillo (93010) *(G-16878)*
Dialysis Centers Ventura Cnty 805 658-9211
4567 Telephone Rd Ste 101 Ventura (93003) *(G-22623)*
Dialysis Clinic Inc 916 453-0803
1771 Stockton Blvd # 200 Sacramento (95816) *(G-22624)*
Diamond Bar Golf Course, Diamond Bar *Also called American Golf Corporation (G-18863)*
Diamond Bar Medical Offices, Diamond Bar *Also called Kaiser Foundation Hospitals (G-19611)*
Diamond Concessions LLC 925 226-2889
6140 Stoneridge Mall Rd # 550 Pleasanton (94588) *(G-27410)*
Diamond Environmental Svcs LP 760 744-7191
807 E Mission Rd San Marcos (92069) *(G-14535)*
Diamond Intl Investment LLC 559 226-2200
3737 N Blackstone Ave Fresno (93726) *(G-12568)*
Diamond Learning Center Inc 559 241-0580
1620 W Fairmont Ave Fresno (93705) *(G-23943)*
Diamond Mountain Casino 530 252-1100
900 Skyline Dr Susanville (96130) *(G-12569)*
Diamond Power System Corp 866 882-8088
13980 Mountain Ave Chino (91710) *(G-7435)*
Diamond Reference Laboratory, Pomona *Also called Central Reference Lab Inc (G-22198)*
Diamond Ridge Healthcare Ctr, Pittsburg *Also called SSC Pittsburg Operating Co LP (G-21381)*
Diamond W Floorcovering, City of Industry *Also called W Diamond Supply Co (G-6904)*
Diamondrock San Dego Tnant LLC 619 239-4500
400 W Broadway San Diego (92101) *(G-12570)*
Diana's Beauty Salon, Los Angeles *Also called Dianas Mexican Food Pdts Inc (G-13672)*
Dianas Mexican Food Pdts Inc 323 758-4845
5841 S Figueroa St Los Angeles (90003) *(G-13672)*
Dianetics, Santa Clara *Also called Church of Scientology (G-23746)*
Diani Building Corp (PA) 805 925-9533
351 N Blosser Rd Santa Maria (93458) *(G-1540)*
Dianne Adair Day Care Centers (PA) 925 429-3232
1862 Bailey Rd Concord (94521) *(G-24455)*
Diaz Construction Company Inc 951 352-9960
9782 Indiana Ave Riverside (92503) *(G-3257)*

Diba Fashions Inc 323 232-3775
472 N Bowling Green Way Los Angeles (90049) *(G-17123)*
Dibuduo Dfendis Insur Brks LLC (PA) 559 432-0222
6873 N West Ave Fresno (93711) *(G-10690)*
Dicalite Minerals Corp 530 335-5451
36994 Summit Lake Rd Burney (96013) *(G-17972)*
Dicaperl Corporation (HQ) 610 667-6640
23705 Crenshaw Blvd Torrance (90505) *(G-1114)*
Dick Anderson & Sons Farming 559 945-2511
15900 W Dorris Ave Huron (93234) *(G-355)*
Dickenson Peatman & Fogarty A (PA) 707 252-7122
1455 1st St Ste 301 NAPA (94559) *(G-23212)*
Dickinson, Diane MD, Arcata *Also called Northcountry Clinic (G-19779)*
Dickson Testing Co Inc (HQ) 562 862-8378
11126 Palmer Ave South Gate (90280) *(G-26843)*
Didi Hirsch Community Mental, Culver City *Also called Didi Hirsch Psychiatric Svc (G-23944)*
Didi Hirsch Psychiatric Svc (PA) 310 390-6612
4760 Sepulveda Blvd Culver City (90230) *(G-23944)*
Didnri, La Jolla *Also called Institute For La Jolla (G-26772)*
Diede Construction Inc 209 369-8255
12393 N Hwy 99 Lodi (95240) *(G-1541)*
Diepenbrock Elkin LLP 916 492-5000
500 Capitol Mall Ste 650 Sacramento (95814) *(G-23213)*
Diestel Turkey Ranch 209 984-0826
14111 High Tech Dr C Jamestown (95327) *(G-451)*
Diestel Turkey Ranch (PA) 209 532-4950
22200 Lyons Bald Mtn Rd Sonora (95370) *(G-452)*
Dietrich Post Co Inc 510 596-0080
945 Bryant St San Francisco (94103) *(G-8164)*
Dietz Glmor Chazen A Prof Corp (PA) 858 565-0269
7071 Convoy Ct Ste 300 San Diego (92111) *(G-23214)*
Diez & Leis RE Group Inc 916 487-4287
5120 Manzanita Ave # 120 Carmichael (95608) *(G-11471)*
Digex Inc 408 468-5000
2950 Zanker Rd San Jose (95134) *(G-5590)*
Digicash Incorporated 650 321-0300
2656 E Bayshore Rd Palo Alto (94303) *(G-15137)*
Digicentury Corporation 408 213-0146
2303 Camino Ramon Ste 202 San Ramon (94583) *(G-15138)*
Digimarc Corporation 888 300-9114
1825 S Grant St Ste 600 San Mateo (94402) *(G-15932)*
Digiquest Corp 951 776-4344
989 Talcey Ter Riverside (92506) *(G-7120)*
Digital Communications Network (PA) 818 227-3333
6300 Canoga Ave Ste 1625 Woodland Hills (91367) *(G-5393)*
Digital Domain, Venice *Also called Power Studios Inc (G-18134)*
Digital Domain 30 Inc (PA) 310 314-2800
12641 Beatrice St Los Angeles (90066) *(G-18071)*
Digital Foundry Inc 415 789-1600
1707 Tiburon Blvd Belvedere Tiburon (94920) *(G-15139)*
Digital Insight Corporation 818 879-1010
5601 Lindero Canyon Rd # 100 Westlake Village (91362) *(G-16227)*
Digital Insight Corporation (HQ) 818 879-1010
1300 Seaport Blvd Ste 300 Redwood City (94063) *(G-16228)*
Digital International Corp 818 847-1157
2424 N Ontario St Burbank (91504) *(G-17124)*
Digital Keystone Inc 650 938-7301
21631 Stevns Crk Blvd A Cupertino (95014) *(G-15933)*
Digital Kitchen LLC 310 499-9255
3585 Hayden Ave Culver City (90232) *(G-18072)*
Digital Networks Group Inc 949 428-6333
20382 Hermana Cir Lake Forest (92630) *(G-6069)*
Digital Nirvana Inc 510 226-9000
3984 Washington Blvd # 355 Fremont (94538) *(G-27411)*
Digital Path Inc 800 676-7284
1065 Marauder St Chico (95973) *(G-5591)*
Digital Periph Solutions Inc 714 998-3440
8015 E Crystal Dr Anaheim (92807) *(G-16879)*
Digital Realty Trust Inc (PA) 415 738-6500
4 Embarcadero Ctr # 3200 San Francisco (94111) *(G-12243)*
Digitalmojo Inc 800 346-7147
3111 Camino Del Rio N # 400 San Diego (92108) *(G-27412)*
Digitalpersona Inc (HQ) 650 474-4000
6607 Kaiser Dr Fremont (94555) *(G-7556)*
Digitalthink Inc (HQ) 415 625-4000
601 Brannan St San Francisco (94107) *(G-27413)*
Digitaria, San Diego *Also called Mirum Inc (G-14154)*
Digite Inc 408 418-3834
21060 Homestead Rd # 220 Cupertino (95014) *(G-15140)*
Dignity Health 916 861-1100
3215 Prospect Park Dr Rancho Cordova (95670) *(G-21531)*
Dignity Health 213 484-7111
2131 W 3rd St Los Angeles (90057) *(G-21532)*
Dignity Health 916 983-7400
1650 Creekside Dr Folsom (95630) *(G-19496)*
Dignity Health 805 739-3000
1400 E Church St Santa Maria (93454) *(G-21533)*
Dignity Health 805 384-8071
5051 Verdugo Way Ste 100 Camarillo (93012) *(G-21534)*
Dignity Health 805 489-4261
1054 E Grand Ave Ste A Arroyo Grande (93420) *(G-22423)*
Dignity Health 916 851-2153
3400 Data Dr Rancho Cordova (95670) *(G-19497)*
Dignity Health 805 473-7626
345 S Halcyon Rd Arroyo Grande (93420) *(G-21535)*
Dignity Health 562 491-9000
1050 Linden Ave Long Beach (90813) *(G-21536)*
Dignity Health (PA) 415 438-5500
185 Berry St Ste 300 San Francisco (94107) *(G-21537)*

Dignity Health...916 667-0000
8120 Timberlake Way # 201 Sacramento (95823) *(G-19498)*
Dignity Health...415 438-5500
1700 Montgomery St # 300 San Francisco (94111) *(G-21538)*
Dignity Health...213 748-2411
1401 S Grand Ave Los Angeles (90015) *(G-21539)*
Dignity Health...209 467-6430
2102 N California St Stockton (95204) *(G-22209)*
Dignity Health...661 832-8300
2301 Ashe Rd Bakersfield (93309) *(G-24456)*
Dignity Health...530 225-6345
2175 Rosaline Ave Ste A Redding (96001) *(G-19499)*
Dignity Health...530 666-8828
20 N Cottonwood St Woodland (95695) *(G-19500)*
Dignity Health...831 462-7700
1555 Soquel Dr Santa Cruz (95065) *(G-19501)*
Dignity Health...209 754-3521
768 Mountain Ranch Rd San Andreas (95249) *(G-19502)*
Dignity Health...916 423-5940
7500 Hospital Dr Sacramento (95823) *(G-19503)*
Dignity Health...805 739-3830
124 S College Dr Santa Maria (93454) *(G-22424)*
Dignity Health...805 739-3650
1530 Cypress Way Santa Maria (93454) *(G-20520)*
Dignity Health...661 663-6767
551 Shanley Ct Bakersfield (93311) *(G-22425)*
Dignity Health...805 389-5800
2309 Antonio Ave Camarillo (93010) *(G-21540)*
Dignity Health...805 739-3100
505 Plaza Dr Santa Maria (93454) *(G-22720)*
Dignity Health...805 988-2500
1600 N Rose Ave Oxnard (93030) *(G-21541)*
Dignity Health...562 494-0576
1720 Termino Ave Long Beach (90804) *(G-23945)*
Dignity Health...209 943-4663
2333 W March Ln Ste B Stockton (95207) *(G-22426)*
Dignity Health...661 632-5279
400 Old River Rd Bakersfield (93311) *(G-21542)*
Dignity Health...916 536-2420
8350 Auburn Blvd Ste 200 Citrus Heights (95610) *(G-19504)*
Dignity Health...661 632-5000
2215 Truxtun Ave Bakersfield (93301) *(G-21543)*
Dignity Health Med Foundation...831 535-1560
9515 Soquel Dr Ste 100 Aptos (95003) *(G-22940)*
Dignity Health Med Foundation...831 475-8834
1667 Dominican Way # 134 Santa Cruz (95065) *(G-22941)*
Dignity Health Med Foundation...916 379-2840
3400 Data Dr Rancho Cordova (95670) *(G-22942)*
Dignity Health Med Foundation...916 787-0404
2110 Prfcional Dr Ste 120 Roseville (95661) *(G-22943)*
Dignity Health Med Foundation (PA)...916 379-2840
3400 Data Dr Rancho Cordova (95670) *(G-22944)*
Dignity Health Medical Grp, Santa Cruz *Also called Dignity Health Med Foundation (G-22941)*
Dignity Hlth Med Grp-Dominican, Aptos *Also called Dignity Health Med Foundation (G-22940)*
Dignity Hlth Med Grp-Dominican, Rancho Cordova *Also called Dignity Health Med Foundation (G-22942)*
Dignity Hlth Med Grp-Dominican, Rancho Cordova *Also called Dignity Health Med Foundation (G-22944)*
Dilbeck Inc (PA)...818 790-6774
1030 Foothill Blvd La Canada (91011) *(G-11472)*
Dilbeck Inc...818 248-2248
2943 Foothill Blvd La Crescenta (91214) *(G-11473)*
Dilbeck Inc...626 584-0101
225 E Colorado Blvd Pasadena (91101) *(G-11474)*
Dilbeck Realtors, La Canada *Also called Dilbeck Inc (G-11472)*
Dilbeck Realtors, Pasadena *Also called Dilbeck Inc (G-11474)*
Dimare Company, Newman *Also called Dimare Enterprises Inc (G-57)*
Dimare Enterprises Inc (PA)...209 827-2900
1406 N St Newman (95360) *(G-57)*
Dimare Fresh...916 921-6302
4050 Pell Cir Sacramento (95838) *(G-8716)*
Dimension Data (HQ)...661 257-1500
27202 Turnberry Ln # 100 Valencia (91355) *(G-6070)*
Dimension Data Cloud Solutions (HQ)...408 567-2000
5201 Great America Pkwy # 122 Santa Clara (95054) *(G-15141)*
Dimension Data North Amer Inc...925 226-8378
5000 Hopyard Rd Pleasanton (94588) *(G-15934)*
Dimension Development Two LLC...619 233-8408
1531 Pacific Hwy San Diego (92101) *(G-12571)*
Dimension Development Two LLC...858 485-9250
11611 Bernardo Plaza Ct San Diego (92128) *(G-12572)*
Dincloud Inc...424 286-2300
27520 Hawthorne Blvd Rllng HLS Est (90274) *(G-15639)*
Dinco Inc (HQ)...424 331-1200
27520 Hawthorne Blvd # 1808 Rllng HLS Est (90274) *(G-7121)*
Dino Bones Productions Inc...818 827-5100
4705 Laurel Canyon Blvd Studio City (91607) *(G-18073)*
Dinyari Construction Inc...408 289-5400
500 Phelan Ave San Jose (95112) *(G-1307)*
Diode Led, Emeryville *Also called Elemental Led Inc (G-7438)*
Diplomat Packaging, Sylmar *Also called Winning Performance Pdts Inc (G-17630)*
Diplomatic Security Services, Rancho Cucamonga *Also called Harrison Iyke (G-16886)*
Diplomatic Security Svcs LLC...909 463-8409
7581 Etiwanda Ave Rancho Cucamonga (91739) *(G-16626)*
Direct Delivery Center, Ontario *Also called Sears Roebuck and Co (G-18012)*
Direct Flow Medical Inc (PA)...707 576-0420
451 Aviation Blvd 107a Santa Rosa (95403) *(G-22945)*
Direct Pack Inc...626 380-2360
1025 W 8th St Azusa (91702) *(G-17125)*
Direct Partners Inc (HQ)...310 482-4200
12777 W Jefferson Blvd # 120 Los Angeles (90066) *(G-13840)*
Direct Technology, Roseville *Also called Directapps Inc (G-16357)*
Direct Way Personnel...562 531-8808
7300 Alondra Blvd Ste 103 Paramount (90723) *(G-14637)*
Directapps Inc (PA)...916 787-2200
3009 Douglas Blvd Ste 300 Roseville (95661) *(G-16357)*
Directline Technologies Inc...209 491-2020
1600 N Carpenter Rd Modesto (95351) *(G-26656)*
Directorate of Mwr Fmd Usag...210 466-1376
420 Montgomery St San Francisco (94104) *(G-27005)*
Directors Guild America Inc (PA)...310 289-2000
7920 W Sunset Blvd # 600 Los Angeles (90046) *(G-18223)*
Directv LLC...909 509-4790
1055 E Francis St Ontario (91761) *(G-5984)*
Directv Customer Services Inc (HQ)...310 964-5000
2230 E Imperial Hwy El Segundo (90245) *(G-5985)*
Directv Enterprises LLC...310 535-5000
2230 E Imperial Hwy El Segundo (90245) *(G-5986)*
Directv Group Inc...707 452-7409
340 Commerce Ave Fairfield (94533) *(G-5987)*
Directv Group Inc...510 481-1324
1129 B St San Lorenzo (94580) *(G-5988)*
Directv Group Holdings LLC (HQ)...310 964-5000
2260 E Imperial Hwy El Segundo (90245) *(G-5989)*
Directv Group Inc (HQ)...310 964-5000
2260 E Imperial Hwy El Segundo (90245) *(G-5990)*
Directv International Inc (HQ)...310 964-6460
2230 E Imperial Hwy Fl 10 El Segundo (90245) *(G-5991)*
Dirt Cheap Demolition Inc...619 426-9598
171 Mace St Ste A4 Chula Vista (91911) *(G-3454)*
Dirt Farmer & Co Inc...707 833-2054
9725 Los Guilicos Ave Kenwood (95452) *(G-150)*
Dirtmarket , The, Campbell *Also called Cem Builders Inc (G-25731)*
Disability Group Inc...310 829-5100
604 Arizona Ave Santa Monica (90401) *(G-23215)*
Disability Insurance, Stockton *Also called E D D 2100 (G-10239)*
Disability Rights California (PA)...916 488-9950
1831 K St Sacramento (95811) *(G-23216)*
Disc Marketing In Flight Div...626 795-9510
35 W Dayton St Pasadena (91105) *(G-17126)*
Discharge Resource Group...650 877-8111
400 Oyster Point Blvd # 440 South San Francisco (94080) *(G-14871)*
Discount Builders Supply...415 285-2800
1695 Mission St San Francisco (94103) *(G-6920)*
Discount Hrdwood Flors Mldings, Los Angeles *Also called Superior Home Design Inc (G-6889)*
Discount Tire Center, Northridge *Also called Scl Company Inc (G-17826)*
Discoverready LLC...661 284-6401
27200 Tourney Rd Ste 450 Valencia (91355) *(G-23217)*
Discovery, Castroville *Also called Dorr Distribution Systems (G-3900)*
Discovery Bay Ctry Club, Byron *Also called New Discovery Inc (G-19013)*
Discovery Bay Golf & Cntry CLB, Byron *Also called New Discovery Inc (G-18765)*
Discovery Communications Inc...310 975-5906
10100 Santa Monica Blvd Los Angeles (90067) *(G-6071)*
Discovery Plz Med & Admin Offs, Bakersfield *Also called Kaiser Foundation Hospitals (G-19604)*
Discovery Practice Management...562 425-6404
4136 Ann Arbor Rd Lakewood (90712) *(G-19505)*
Discovery Scnce Ctr Ornge Cnty...714 913-5010
2500 N Main St Santa Ana (92705) *(G-18817)*
Discovery Shop, San Jose *Also called American Cancer Soc Cal Div (G-24867)*
Discovia, San Francisco *Also called Liffey Thames Group LLC (G-16423)*
Dish Network, Santa Ana *Also called C V Productions Inc (G-5937)*
Dish Network Corporation...909 381-4767
396 Orange Show Ln San Bernardino (92408) *(G-5992)*
Dish Network Corporation...818 334-8740
1297 N Verdugo Rd Glendale (91206) *(G-5993)*
Dish Network Corporation...714 424-0503
2602 Halladay St Santa Ana (92705) *(G-5994)*
Dish Network Corporation...916 381-5084
5671 Warehouse Way Sacramento (95826) *(G-5995)*
Dish Systems, Irvine *Also called Connect Your Home LLC (G-1533)*
Disney Construction Inc...650 689-5149
859 Cowan Rd 3 Burlingame (94010) *(G-1766)*
Disney Enterprises Inc (HQ)...818 560-1000
500 S Buena Vista St Burbank (91521) *(G-18074)*
Disney Enterprises Inc...714 817-7317
1150 W Magic Way Anaheim (92802) *(G-12573)*
Disney Enterprises Inc...818 569-7500
3800 W Alameda Ave # 565 Burbank (91505) *(G-5852)*
Disney Enterprises Inc...818 560-3692
3235 S Buena Vista St Burbank (91521) *(G-18075)*
Disney Enterprises Inc...714 956-6425
1717 S Disneyland Dr Anaheim (92802) *(G-12574)*
Disney Incorporated (HQ)...818 560-1000
500 S Buena Vista St Burbank (91521) *(G-18076)*
Disney Interactive Studios Inc...818 560-1000
601 Circle Seven Dr Glendale (91201) *(G-15142)*
Disney Interactive Studios Inc...801 595-1020
622 Circle Seven Dr Glendale (91201) *(G-15143)*
Disney Interactive Studios Inc...818 553-5000
681 W Buena Vista St Burbank (91521) *(G-15144)*

Disney Interfinance Corp....818 560-1000
500 S Buena Vista St Burbank (91521) *(G-18272)*
Disney Regional Entrmt Inc (HQ)....818 560-1000
500 S Buena Vista St Burbank (91521) *(G-19198)*
Disney Worldwide Services Inc (HQ)....818 560-1000
500 S Buena Vista St Burbank (91521) *(G-18077)*
Disneyland, Anaheim *Also called Walt Disney Company (G-13390)*
Disneyland International....714 781-4000
105 S Harbor Blvd Anaheim (92805) *(G-18818)*
Disneyland International....714 956-6746
1580 S Disneyland Dr Anaheim (92802) *(G-12575)*
Disneyland International (HQ)....714 490-3004
770 The Cy Dr S Ste 6000 Orange (92868) *(G-12576)*
Disneyland International Inc (HQ)....818 560-1000
500 S Buena Vista St Burbank (91521) *(G-18819)*
Disneyland International Inc....714 999-4000
1313 S Harbor Blvd Anaheim (92802) *(G-4492)*
Disneys Grand Californian Ht....714 635-2300
1600 S Disneyland Dr Anaheim (92802) *(G-12577)*
Dispatch Office, Oakland *Also called First Transit Inc (G-3652)*
Dispatch Trucking Inc (PA)....909 355-5531
14032 Santa Ana Ave Fontana (92337) *(G-5059)*
Display Works LLC....408 746-9654
854 Stewart Dr Ste B Sunnyvale (94085) *(G-17127)*
Dist Attorney's Office, Redding *Also called County of Shasta (G-23183)*
Distillery Inc....415 505-5446
90 Heron Ct San Quentin (94964) *(G-15640)*
Distinctive Concrete Inc....858 277-9707
9320 Chesapeake Dr # 214 San Diego (92123) *(G-3258)*
Distribution Alternatives Inc....909 673-1000
17820 Slover Ave Bloomington (92316) *(G-4543)*
Distribution Warehouse, Woodland *Also called Apria Healthcare LLC (G-22890)*
District Attorney, Westminster *Also called County of Orange (G-23870)*
District Attorney, Santa Maria *Also called Santa Barbara County of (G-23544)*
District Attorney, Compton *Also called County of Los Angeles (G-23174)*
District Attorney, Santa Rosa *Also called County of Sonoma (G-23184)*
District Attorney, Van Nuys *Also called County of Los Angeles (G-23178)*
District Attorney's Office, San Francisco *Also called City & County of San Francisco (G-23151)*
District Attroney's Office, San Jose *Also called Santa Clara County of (G-23545)*
District Council DC (PA)....510 638-7600
9235 San Leandro St Oakland (94603) *(G-23946)*
District Office East, Bakersfield *Also called Panama-Buena Vista Un Schl Dst (G-14378)*
District Warehouse, Placentia *Also called Linda Placentia-Yorba (G-4587)*
Distritution Center, Ontario *Also called Converse Inc (G-8429)*
Diva Systems Corporation....650 779-3000
800 Saginaw Dr Redwood City (94063) *(G-5996)*
Divecon Services LP....805 488-6428
1180 Eugenia Pl Ste 100 Carpinteria (93013) *(G-2042)*
Diverscape Inc....951 245-1686
21730 Bundy Canyon Rd Wildomar (92595) *(G-841)*
Diverse Journeys Inc (PA)....310 643-7403
525 S Douglas St Ste 210 El Segundo (90245) *(G-23947)*
Diverse Staffing Inc....714 525-8477
211 Imperial Hwy Ste 200 Fullerton (92835) *(G-14638)*
Diversfied Cmmnctions Svcs Inc....562 696-9660
1260 Pioneer St Brea (92821) *(G-5592)*
Diversified Clinical Services....714 579-8400
4225 E La Palma Ave Anaheim (92807) *(G-22946)*
Diversified Health Svcs Del....626 798-6753
2585 E Washington Blvd Pasadena (91107) *(G-24632)*
DIVERSIFIED INDUSTRIES, Montclair *Also called Oparc (G-24373)*
Diversified Landscape Co, Wildomar *Also called Diverscape Inc (G-841)*
Diversified Metal Works, Orange *Also called Rika Corporation (G-3399)*
Diversified Prj Svcs Intl Inc (PA)....661 371-2800
5351 Olive Dr Ste 100 Bakersfield (93308) *(G-25770)*
Diversified RE Packaging Corp....310 855-1946
1118 S La Cienega Blvd Los Angeles (90035) *(G-27899)*
Diversified Transport Systems....559 268-2760
3150 S Willow Ave Fresno (93725) *(G-4544)*
Diversified Transportation LLC....310 981-9500
6053 W Century Blvd # 900 Los Angeles (90045) *(G-3642)*
Diversified Trnsp Svcs, Torrance *Also called DTM Services Inc (G-5061)*
Diversified Utility Svcs Inc....661 325-3212
3105 Unicorn Rd Bakersfield (93308) *(G-1927)*
Divine Home Care, San Leandro *Also called Wild Karma Inc (G-21040)*
Division 7, Venice *Also called Los Angeles County MTA (G-3669)*
Division 8 Inc....619 741-7552
1920 Cordell Ct Ste 105 El Cajon (92020) *(G-3409)*
Division Infectious Diseases, La Jolla *Also called Scripps Clinic Carmel Valley (G-19965)*
Division of Rheumatology, Los Angeles *Also called Childrens Hospital Los Angeles (G-19433)*
Division of State Architect, Oakland *Also called General Services Cal Dept (G-26186)*
Division of State Architect, Los Angeles *Also called General Services Cal Dept (G-26187)*
Division Three Cnstr Svcs....951 609-3043
30620 Plumas St Lake Elsinore (92530) *(G-1542)*
Divx Corporation (HQ)....858 882-0700
4790 Estgate Mall Ste 200 San Diego (92121) *(G-7557)*
Dix Metals Inc....714 677-0777
14801 Able Ln Ste 101 Huntington Beach (92647) *(G-7366)*
DJ Scheffler Inc (PA)....909 595-2924
2500 Pomona Blvd Pomona (91768) *(G-2811)*
Djont/Cmb Ssf....650 589-3400
250 Gateway Blvd South San Francisco (94080) *(G-12578)*
Dkn Hotel LLC (PA)....714 427-4320
42 Corporate Park Ste 200 Irvine (92606) *(G-12579)*
Dkn Hotel LLC....714 535-0300
1240 S Walnut St Anaheim (92802) *(G-12580)*
Dl Imaging, Santa Ana *Also called Dekra-Lite Industries Inc (G-17119)*
DL Long Landscaping Inc....909 628-5531
5475 G St Chino (91710) *(G-762)*
Dla Piper LLP (us)....213 330-7700
550 S Hope St Ste 2300 Los Angeles (90071) *(G-23218)*
Dla Piper LLP (us)....650 833-2000
2000 University Ave # 100 East Palo Alto (94303) *(G-23219)*
Dla Piper LLP (us)....310 595-3000
2000 Avenue Of The Stars 400n Los Angeles (90067) *(G-23220)*
Dla Piper LLP (us)....650 833-2000
2000 University Ave # 100 East Palo Alto (94303) *(G-23221)*
Dla Piper LLP (us)....619 699-2700
401 B St Ste 1700 San Diego (92101) *(G-23222)*
Dla Piper LLP (us)....858 677-1400
4365 Executive Dr # 1100 San Diego (92121) *(G-23223)*
Dlc, Cerritos *Also called David Levy Co Inc (G-7552)*
Dlh Davinci LLC....818 703-5100
22135 Roscoe Blvd West Hills (91304) *(G-22304)*
Dlo Enterprises Inc....760 346-8033
41865 Boardwalk Ste 216 Palm Desert (92211) *(G-16627)*
Dlr Group Inc of California (HQ)....310 828-0040
3130 Wilshire Blvd Fl 6 Santa Monica (90403) *(G-26184)*
Dlt Growers Inc....909 947-8198
13131 S Bon View Ave Ontario (91761) *(G-276)*
Dm Construction Services, Santa Ana *Also called Perennial Engrg & Cnstr Inc (G-1234)*
Dma Claims Inc (PA)....323 342-6800
330 N Brand Blvd Ste 230 Glendale (91203) *(G-10691)*
Dma Claims Inc....323 342-6800
330 N Brand Blvd Ste 230 Glendale (91203) *(G-10692)*
Dma Claims Services, Glendale *Also called Dma Claims Inc (G-10691)*
Dma Greencare Contracting Inc....714 630-9470
3000 E Coronado St Anaheim (92806) *(G-842)*
DMC Construction Incorporated....831 656-1600
2110 Del Monte Ave Monterey (93940) *(G-1543)*
Dmcg Inc (PA)....951 683-9685
3605 10th St Riverside (92501) *(G-17128)*
Dmi, Sylmar *Also called Desert Mechanical Inc (G-2205)*
DMS Facility Services Inc....510 656-9400
3137 Skyway Ct Fremont (94539) *(G-14283)*
DMS Facility Services LLC....858 560-4191
5735 Krny Vlla Rd Ste 108 San Diego (92123) *(G-25771)*
Dna Specialty Inc....310 767-4070
200 W Artesia Blvd Compton (90220) *(G-6726)*
DNC Prks Rsrts At Yosemite Inc....209 372-1001
9001 Village Dr Yosemite Ntpk (95389) *(G-12581)*
Dnow LP....310 900-3900
1111 W Artesia Blvd Compton (90220) *(G-4684)*
Dns Electronics, Sunnyvale *Also called Screen Spe Usa LLC (G-7631)*
Do Rights Plant Growers....805 525-2155
540 Glade Dr Santa Paula (93060) *(G-277)*
Dobler & Sons LLC....831 724-6727
174 Struve Rd Moss Landing (95039) *(G-58)*
Dockside Machine & Ship Repair, Wilmington *Also called Marine Technical Services Inc (G-17311)*
Docler Media LLC (HQ)....424 777-3999
720 N Cahuenga Blvd Los Angeles (90038) *(G-16122)*
Docmagic Inc....800 649-1362
1800 W 213th St Torrance (90501) *(G-17129)*
Doctor On Demand Inc....415 935-4447
275 Battery St Ste 650 San Francisco (94111) *(G-15641)*
Doctors Ambulance Services, Laguna Hills *Also called Herren Enterprises Inc (G-3804)*
Doctors Company....707 226-0289
185 Greenwood Rd NAPA (94558) *(G-19506)*
Doctors Company Insurance Svcs....707 226-0100
185 Greenwood Rd NAPA (94558) *(G-10492)*
Doctors Hospital Manteca Inc....209 823-3111
1205 E North St Manteca (95336) *(G-22138)*
Doctors Hospital W Covina Inc....626 338-8481
725 S Orange Ave West Covina (91790) *(G-21544)*
Doctors Management Company (HQ)....707 226-0100
185 Greenwood Rd NAPA (94558) *(G-10693)*
Doctors Medical Center LLC (HQ)....510 970-5000
2000 Vale Rd San Pablo (94806) *(G-21545)*
Doctors of Affiliated....714 539-3100
600 City Pkwy W Ste 400 Orange (92868) *(G-27006)*
Document Sciences Corporation (HQ)....760 602-0809
5958 Priestly Dr Carlsbad (92008) *(G-15642)*
Document Systems, Torrance *Also called Docmagic Inc (G-17129)*
Document Technologies LLC....415 495-4100
275 Battery St Ste 250 San Francisco (94111) *(G-17130)*
Document Technologies LLC....213 892-9000
350 S Figueroa St Ste 750 Los Angeles (90071) *(G-17131)*
Document Technologies LLC....650 485-2705
3600 W Bayshore Rd Palo Alto (94303) *(G-17132)*
Documentum Inc....925 600-6800
6801 Koll Center Pkwy Pleasanton (94566) *(G-15643)*
Docusign Inc (PA)....415 489-4940
221 Main St Ste 1000 San Francisco (94105) *(G-15935)*
DOD Constructors A JV....707 265-1100
185 Devlin Rd NAPA (94558) *(G-2043)*
DOD Fueling Constructors A JV....707 265-1100
185 Devlin Rd NAPA (94558) *(G-2044)*
DOD Marine Constructors A JV....707 265-1100
185 Devlin Rd NAPA (94558) *(G-2045)*
Dodge & Cox....415 981-1710
555 California St Fl 40 San Francisco (94104) *(G-12112)*

ALPHABETIC

Dodge Ridge Corporation 209 536-5300
1 Dodge Ridge Rd Pinecrest (95364) ***(G-12582)***
Dodge Ridge Winter Sports Area, Pinecrest *Also called Dodge Ridge Corporation* ***(G-12582)***
Dodger Stadium, Los Angeles *Also called Fox BSB Holdco Inc* ***(G-18546)***
Dokken Engineering (PA) 916 858-0642
110 Blue Ravine Rd # 200 Folsom (95630) ***(G-25772)***
Dolan Concrete Construction 408 869-3250
3045 Alfred St Santa Clara (95054) ***(G-3259)***
Dolby Labs Licensing Corp 415 558-0200
100 Potrero Ave San Francisco (94103) ***(G-12214)***
Dolce Hayes Mansion, San Jose *Also called City of San Jose* ***(G-12523)***
Dolce International / NAPA LLC 707 257-0200
1600 Atlas Peak Rd NAPA (94558) ***(G-12583)***
Dole Food Company Inc (HQ) 818 874-4000
1 Dole Dr Westlake Village (91362) ***(G-254)***
Dole Fresh Fruit Company (HQ) 818 874-4000
1 Dole Dr Westlake Village (91362) ***(G-8717)***
Dole Fresh Vegetables Inc 559 945-2591
16199 9th St Huron (93234) ***(G-525)***
Dole Fresh Vegetables Inc 831 678-5030
32655 Camphora Rd Soledad (93960) ***(G-526)***
Dole Holding Company LLC 818 879-6600
1 Dole Dr Westlake Village (91362) ***(G-255)***
Doll Fresh Vegestable, Huron *Also called Royal Packing Dcf* ***(G-91)***
Doll House Footwear, City of Industry *Also called J P Original Corp* ***(G-8437)***
Dollar Smart, Oxnard *Also called G P M M Money Centers Inc* ***(G-9718)***
Dollar Thrifty Auto Group Inc 619 298-7635
4420 Pacific Hwy San Diego (92110) ***(G-17669)***
Dolphin Bay Hotel & Residences, Shell Beach *Also called Dolphin Bay Ht & Residence Inc* ***(G-12584)***
Dolphin Bay Ht & Residence Inc 805 773-4300
2727 Shell Beach Rd Shell Beach (93449) ***(G-12584)***
Dolphin Hkg Ltd (PA) 310 215-3356
1125 W Hillcrest Blvd Inglewood (90301) ***(G-9259)***
Dolphin Imaging MGT Solutions, Chatsworth *Also called Patterson Dental Supply Inc* ***(G-15371)***
Dolphin Imaging Systems LLC 818 435-1368
9200 Eton Ave Chatsworth (91311) ***(G-15145)***
Dolphin International, Inglewood *Also called Dolphin Hkg Ltd* ***(G-9259)***
Dolphins Cove Resort Ltd 714 980-0830
465 W Orangewood Ave Anaheim (92802) ***(G-12585)***
Doma Laszlo 323 478-1313
4041 Eagle Rock Blvd Los Angeles (90065) ***(G-4397)***
Domaine Carneros Ltd 707 257-0101
1240 Duhig Rd NAPA (94559) ***(G-151)***
Domestic Horizons, Beverly Hills *Also called Global Horizons Inc* ***(G-14662)***
Domestic Linen Supply Co Inc (HQ) 213 749-6300
1600 Compton Ave Los Angeles (90021) ***(G-13547)***
Dominator Radiology Systems, San Diego *Also called DR Systems Inc* ***(G-22210)***
Dominguez Landscape Svcs Inc 916 381-8855
8376 Rovana Cir Sacramento (95828) ***(G-843)***
Dominican Hospital Foundation 831 457-7057
610 Frederick St Santa Cruz (95062) ***(G-24633)***
Dominican Hospital Foundation (HQ) 831 462-7700
1555 Soquel Dr Santa Cruz (95065) ***(G-21546)***
Dominican Med Fndtn A Service, Santa Cruz *Also called Mercy Medical Group Inc* ***(G-25296)***
Dominican Oaks Corporation 831 462-6257
3400 Paul Sweet Rd Ofc Santa Cruz (95065) ***(G-11120)***
Dominican Rehab Services, Santa Cruz *Also called Dominican Hospital Foundation* ***(G-24633)***
Dominion International Inc 916 683-9545
2305 Longport Ct Elk Grove (95758) ***(G-12586)***
Dominos Pizza LLC 909 390-1990
301 S Rockefeller Ave Ontario (91761) ***(G-4685)***
Dominos Pizza LLC 510 489-0333
30852 San Antonio St Hayward (94544) ***(G-4545)***
Domus Construction & Design 916 381-7500
8864 Fruitridge Rd Sacramento (95826) ***(G-1168)***
Don Brandel Plumbing Inc 562 408-0400
15100 Texaco Ave Paramount (90723) ***(G-2206)***
Don Gragnani Farms 559 693-4352
12910 S Napa Ave Tranquillity (93668) ***(G-356)***
Don Kinzel Construction Inc 661 322-9105
4300 Easton Dr Ste 2 Bakersfield (93309) ***(G-1544)***
Don Turner and Associates, Fresno *Also called Turner Security Systems Inc* ***(G-16836)***
Don's Auto Body, San Francisco *Also called Shinazy Enterprises Inc* ***(G-17772)***
Donaghy Sales Inc 559 486-0901
2363 S Cedar Ave Fresno (93725) ***(G-9054)***
Donahue Gallager Woods LLP (PA) 415 381-4161
1999 Harrison St Ste 2500 Oakland (94612) ***(G-23224)***
Donahue Schrber Rlty Group Inc (PA) 714 545-1400
200 Baker St E Ste 100 Costa Mesa (92626) ***(G-11475)***
Donahue Schriber Rlty Group LP (PA) 714 545-1400
200 Baker St E Ste 100 Costa Mesa (92626) ***(G-10975)***
Donahue Schriber Rlty Group LP 714 545-1400
5082 N Palm Ave Fresno (93704) ***(G-10976)***
Donahue Schriber Rlty Group LP 714 283-3535
8020 E Santa Ana Cyn Rd Anaheim (92808) ***(G-10977)***
Donahue Schriber Rlty Group LP 858 793-5757
12925 El Camino Real J22 San Diego (92130) ***(G-10978)***
Donald J Schefflers Cnstr, City of Industry *Also called Heidi Corporation* ***(G-1313)***
Donald Lawrence Company, Visalia *Also called Donald Lawrence Fulbright Co* ***(G-1362)***
Donald Lawrence Fulbright Co 559 625-0762
32557 Road 138 Visalia (93292) ***(G-1362)***
Donald Lucky LLC 949 752-0647
4029 Westerly Pl Ste 111 Newport Beach (92660) ***(G-27007)***
Donald P Dick AC Inc (PA) 559 255-1644
1444 N Whitney Ave Fresno (93703) ***(G-2207)***
Donald T Sterling Corporation 310 275-5575
10300 Wilshire Blvd Los Angeles (90024) ***(G-12587)***
Donald Valpredo Farming Inc 661 858-2245
2101 Mttler Frontage Rd E Bakersfield (93307) ***(G-59)***
Donatello, San Francisco *Also called Shell Vacations LLC* ***(G-27210)***
Dongalen Enterprises Inc (PA) 916 422-3110
330 Commerce Cir Sacramento (95815) ***(G-8969)***
Dongyu USI, Irvine *Also called United Samples Inc* ***(G-8301)***
Donor Network West (PA) 925 480-3100
12667 Alcosta Blvd # 500 San Ramon (94583) ***(G-22947)***
Donor Network West 510 418-0336
5800 Airport Rd Ste B Redding (96002) ***(G-22948)***
Donovan Bros Golf LLC 805 531-9300
15187 Tierra Rejada Rd Moorpark (93021) ***(G-18735)***
Donovan Golf Courses MGT 714 528-6400
1800 Carbon Canyon Rd Chino (91708) ***(G-18736)***
Doose Landscape Incorporated 760 591-4500
785 E Mission Rd San Marcos (92069) ***(G-844)***
Dorado Network Systems Corp 650 227-7300
555 12th St Ste 1100 Oakland (94607) ***(G-15644)***
Dorado Software Inc 916 673-1100
4805 Golden Foothill Pkwy El Dorado Hills (95762) ***(G-15146)***
Doral Palm Sprngs Rsrt & Golf, Palm Springs *Also called Interstate Hotels Resorts Inc* ***(G-27069)***
Doremus & Company 415 398-5699
550 3rd St San Francisco (94107) ***(G-13841)***
Dorfman Pacific, Stockton *Also called Dorfman-Pacific Co* ***(G-8338)***
Dorfman-Pacific Co (PA) 209 982-1400
2615 Boeing Way Stockton (95206) ***(G-8338)***
Dorothy Johnson Center, Chico *Also called Chico Area Recreation & Pk Dst* ***(G-19162)***
Dorr Distribution Systems 831 633-7111
11020 Commercial Pkwy Castroville (95012) ***(G-3900)***
Dos Palos Mem Rur Hlth Clinic, Dos Palos *Also called Dos Palos Memorial Hosp Inc* ***(G-19507)***
Dos Palos Memorial Hosp Inc 209 392-6121
2118 Marguerite St Dos Palos (93620) ***(G-19507)***
Dos Pueblos Ranch, Goleta *Also called Schulte Ranches* ***(G-391)***
DOT Foods Inc 209 581-9090
2200 Nickerson Dr Modesto (95358) ***(G-8474)***
DOT Leasing Company 949 474-1100
2424 Mcgaw Ave Irvine (92614) ***(G-8152)***
DOT-Line Transportation Inc 877 900-7768
4366 E 26th St Vernon (90058) ***(G-4139)***
Double D Transportation Co 510 783-2335
22991 Clawiter Rd Hayward (94545) ***(G-4009)***
Double Day Office Services Inc 650 872-6600
340 Shaw Rd South San Francisco (94080) ***(G-4342)***
Double Dutch Inc 800 748-9024
2601 Mission St Ste 800 San Francisco (94110) ***(G-15645)***
Double Eagle Trnsp Corp 760 956-3770
12135 Scarbrough Ct Oak Hills (92344) ***(G-4140)***
Double G Productions Ltd 310 479-0978
11301 W Olympic Blvd # 115 Los Angeles (90064) ***(G-18463)***
Double Three Htlirvinespectrum, Irvine *Also called Spectrum Hotel Group LLC* ***(G-13278)***
Double Tree Club Ht San Diego, San Diego *Also called Pbp Hotel LLC* ***(G-12000)***
Double Tree Past Acute, Sacramento *Also called Sacramento Operating Co LP* ***(G-20886)***
Doubleline Capital LP 213 633-8200
333 S Grand Ave Fl 18 Los Angeles (90071) ***(G-17133)***
Doubletree, Los Angeles *Also called Lenexa Hotel LP* ***(G-12915)***
DoubleTree by Hilton, San Diego *Also called Swvp Del Mar Hotel LLC* ***(G-13331)***
Doubletree By Hilton, San Diego *Also called HLT Operate Dtwc LLC* ***(G-12745)***
Doubletree By Hilton, San Diego *Also called Doubletree LLC* ***(G-12597)***
Doubletree By Hilton Brky Mrna, Berkeley *Also called Westpost Berkeley LLC* ***(G-13407)***
Doubletree By Hilton Carson, Carson *Also called Carson Operating Company LLC* ***(G-12495)***
Doubletree By Hilton Fresno, Fresno *Also called Uniwell Fresno Hotel LLC* ***(G-13368)***
Doubletree By Hilton Hotel 310 322-0999
1985 E Grand Ave El Segundo (90245) ***(G-12588)***
Doubletree By Hilton La - Com, Commerce *Also called Tpg La Commerce LLC* ***(G-13351)***
Doubletree Hotel, Commerce *Also called W2005 Wyn Hotels LP* ***(G-13389)***
Doubletree Hotel, San Diego *Also called Doubletree LLC* ***(G-12590)***
Doubletree Hotel, Santa Ana *Also called Chamson Management Inc* ***(G-12510)***
Doubletree Hotel, Ontario *Also called Doubletree LLC* ***(G-12591)***
Doubletree Hotel, Anaheim *Also called Doubltree Suites By Hilton LLC* ***(G-12601)***
Doubletree Hotel, San Jose *Also called Doubletree LLC* ***(G-12592)***
Doubletree Hotel, Irvine *Also called Spectrum Hotel Group LLC* ***(G-13279)***
Doubletree Hotel, Sacramento *Also called Doubletree LLC* ***(G-12594)***
Doubletree Hotel, Santa Ana *Also called Doubletree LLC* ***(G-12595)***
Doubletree Hotel, Santa Barbara *Also called Fess Prker-Red Lion Gen Partnr* ***(G-12635)***
Doubletree Hotel, El Segundo *Also called European Hotl Invstrs of CA* ***(G-12626)***
Doubletree Hotel, Modesto *Also called Doubletree LLC* ***(G-12596)***
Doubletree Hotel, Claremont *Also called Claremont Star LP* ***(G-12525)***
Doubletree Hotel, Burlingame *Also called Doubletree LLC* ***(G-12598)***
Doubletree Hotel, Santa Monica *Also called Santa Monica Hsr Ltd Partnr* ***(G-13217)***
Doubletree Hotel, Rohnert Park *Also called Doubletree LLC* ***(G-12599)***
Doubletree Hotel, Dana Point *Also called Doubletree LLC* ***(G-12600)***
Doubletree Hotel 323 722-8800
888 Montebello Blvd Rosemead (91770) ***(G-12589)***
Doubletree Hotel Modesto, Modesto *Also called Modesto Hospitality Lessee LLC* ***(G-13002)***
Doubletree Hotel-Lax, El Segundo *Also called Tri-Star Ccw Management L P* ***(G-13359)***

ALPHABETIC

Doubletree Ht San Diego Dwntwn, San Diego *Also called Harbor View Hotel Ventures LLC* ***(G-12690)***
Doubletree LLC 858 485-4145
14455 Penasquitos Dr San Diego (92129) ***(G-12590)***
Doubletree LLC 909 605-4222
222 N Vineyard Ave Ontario (91764) ***(G-12591)***
Doubletree LLC 408 453-4000
2050 Gateway Pl San Jose (95110) ***(G-12592)***
Doubletree LLC 661 323-7111
3100 Camino Del Rio Ct Bakersfield (93308) ***(G-12593)***
Doubletree LLC 916 929-8855
2001 Point West Way Sacramento (95815) ***(G-12594)***
Doubletree LLC 714 825-3333
201 E Macarthur Blvd Santa Ana (92707) ***(G-12595)***
Doubletree LLC 209 526-6000
1150 9th St Frnt Modesto (95354) ***(G-12596)***
Doubletree LLC 619 297-5466
7450 Hazard Center Dr San Diego (92108) ***(G-12597)***
Doubletree LLC 650 344-5500
835 Airport Blvd Burlingame (94010) ***(G-12598)***
Doubletree LLC 707 584-5466
1 Doubletree Dr Rohnert Park (94928) ***(G-12599)***
Doubletree LLC 949 661-1100
34402 Pacific Coast Hwy Dana Point (92624) ***(G-12600)***
Doubletree Suites By Hilton, Santa Monica *Also called I PCA L P* ***(G-12833)***
Doubletwist Inc 510 628-0100
1849 Sawtelle Blvd # 543 Los Angeles (90025) ***(G-15147)***
Doubltree By Hlton Ht Bkrsfeld, Bakersfield *Also called Doubletree LLC* ***(G-12593)***
Doubltree By Hlton Scrmento Ht, Sacramento *Also called Wmk Sacramento LLC* ***(G-13426)***
Doubltree Ht Anhim-Orange Cnty, Orange *Also called Anaheim Ca LLC* ***(G-12386)***
Doubltree Los Angeles Westside, Culver City *Also called Crp Centinela LP* ***(G-12557)***
Doubltree Suites By Hilton LLC 714 750-3000
2085 S Harbor Blvd Anaheim (92802) ***(G-12601)***
Doudell Trucking Company (PA) 408 263-7300
1505 N 4th St San Jose (95112) ***(G-4141)***
Doug Arnold Real Estate Inc (PA) 530 758-3080
505 2nd St Davis (95616) ***(G-11476)***
Douglas & Jayne Starn 209 883-4886
6621 Blue Gum Rd Hughson (95326) ***(G-198)***
Douglas Elliman Real Estate 310 595-3888
9440 Santa Monica Blvd # 710 Beverly Hills (90210) ***(G-11477)***
Douglas Emmett Realty Fund 199 ....310 255-7700
808 Wilshire Blvd Ste 200 Santa Monica (90401) ***(G-11478)***
Douglas Fir Holdings LLC 714 842-5551
8382 Newman Ave Huntington Beach (92647) ***(G-20521)***
Douglas L Myovich Trucking Inc 559 264-1181
1895 W Jefferson Ave Fresno (93706) ***(G-4010)***
Douglas Ross Construction Inc 408 429-7700
1875 S Bascom Ave # 2400 Campbell (95008) ***(G-1308)***
Douglas Steel Supply Inc (PA) 323 587-7676
5764 Alcoa Ave Vernon (90058) ***(G-7367)***
Douglas Steel Supply Co., Vernon *Also called Douglas Steel Supply Inc* ***(G-7367)***
Douglas W Jackson MD 562 424-6666
2760 Atlantic Ave Long Beach (90806) ***(G-19508)***
Doumit Communication Inc 916 362-3519
25 Cadillac Dr Ste 134 Sacramento (95825) ***(G-1767)***
Downey Brand LLP (PA) 916 444-1000
621 Capitol Mall Fl 18 Sacramento (95814) ***(G-23225)***
Downey Care Center, Downey *Also called Covenant Care California LLC* ***(G-20485)***
Downey Civic Theatre, Downey *Also called City of Downey* ***(G-18384)***
Downey Community Health Center 562 862-6506
8425 Iowa St Downey (90241) ***(G-20522)***
Downey Family Y M C A, Downey *Also called Young Mens Chrstn Assn of La* ***(G-25469)***
Downey Orthopedic Med Group, Lawndale *Also called Southwestern Orthpd Med Corp* ***(G-20047)***
Downey Regional Medical 562 698-0811
11500 Brookshire Ave Downey (90241) ***(G-21547)***
Downey Regional Medical Center, Downey *Also called Presbyterian Intrcmmnty Hosptl* ***(G-21806)***
Downey Retirement Ctr 562 869-2416
11500 Dolan Ave Downey (90241) ***(G-11121)***
Downey YMCA, Downey *Also called Young Mens Chrstn Assn of La* ***(G-24295)***
Downs Equipment Rentals Inc (PA) 661 615-6119
4800 Saco Rd Bakersfield (93308) ***(G-14480)***
Downs Fuel Transport Inc 951 256-8286
1296 Magnolia Ave Corona (92879) ***(G-9016)***
Downtown Berkeley YMCA, Berkeley *Also called The Young Mens Chris Assoc of* ***(G-25377)***
Downtown Business Fincl Ctr, Bakersfield *Also called Citizens Business Bank* ***(G-9486)***
Downtown Community Dev YMCA, Long Beach *Also called Young Mens Christian Associat* ***(G-25455)***
Downtown Los Angeles Branch, Los Angeles *Also called Israel Discount Bank New York* ***(G-9504)***
Downtown Metro 760 398-3310
1030 6th St Ste 16 Coachella (92236) ***(G-5394)***
Downtown San Diego Partnr Inc 619 234-8900
1111 6th Ave Ste 101 San Diego (92101) ***(G-25083)***
Downtown SD Ventures LLC 619 231-9200
20162 Sw Birch St Ste 350 Newport Beach (92660) ***(G-19199)***
Dpi Specialty Foods West Inc (HQ) 909 975-1019
601 S Rockefeller Ave Ontario (91761) ***(G-8475)***
Dpk Consulting 415 495-7772
605 Market St Ste 800 San Francisco (94105) ***(G-27414)***
Dppm Inc 415 695-7707
4040 24th St San Francisco (94114) ***(G-11479)***
Dpr Construction 858 646-0757
5010 Shoreham Pl Ste 100 San Diego (92122) ***(G-1419)***
Dpr Construction Inc 408 370-2322
1510 S Winchester Blvd San Jose (95128) ***(G-1420)***
Dpr Construction Inc (PA) 650 474-1450
1450 Veterans Blvd Redwood City (94063) ***(G-1421)***
Dpr Construction Inc 916 568-3434
2480 Natomas Park Dr # 100 Sacramento (95833) ***(G-1545)***
Dpr Construction Inc 949 955-3771
4665 Macarthur Ct Ste 100 Newport Beach (92660) ***(G-1546)***
Dpr Construction A Gen Partnr 650 474-1450
1450 Veterans Blvd Redwood City (94063) ***(G-1422)***
Dpr Holdings LLC 323 761-9829
4804 Laurel Canyon Blvd Studio City (91607) ***(G-12059)***
Dpss, Burbank *Also called County of Los Angeles* ***(G-23858)***
Dr Fresh LLC (PA) 714 690-1573
6645 Caballero Blvd Buena Park (90620) ***(G-7261)***
Dr Fresh Inc 714 690-1573
6645 Caballero Blvd Buena Park (90620) ***(G-7262)***
DR Horton Inc 951 272-9000
2280 Wardlow Cir Ste 100 Corona (92880) ***(G-1363)***
DR Systems Inc 858 625-3344
10140 Mesa Rim Rd San Diego (92121) ***(G-22210)***
Draftfcb, San Francisco *Also called Fcb Worldwide Inc* ***(G-13849)***
Drain Doctor 408 970-3800
480 Aldo Ave Santa Clara (95054) ***(G-2208)***
Drain Patrol, Modesto *Also called American Alliance Always Avail* ***(G-17959)***
Drain Patrol 858 560-1137
7764 Arjons Dr San Diego (92126) ***(G-2209)***
Drake Larson Ranchs 760 399-5494
89780 Ave 60 Thermal (92274) ***(G-152)***
Drake Terrace, San Rafael *Also called Kisco Senior Living LLC* ***(G-11149)***
Drawbridge Inc 650 513-2323
2121 S El Camino Real 7th San Mateo (94403) ***(G-27415)***
Drchronocom Inc 650 600-2079
1001 N Rengstorff Ave # 200 Mountain View (94043) ***(G-15148)***
Dream Home & Investments Rlty, Lomita *Also called Long Beach Investment Group* ***(G-9871)***
Dream Home Care Inc 562 595-9021
4150 Locust Ave Long Beach (90807) ***(G-24634)***
Dream Home Estates Inc 949 415-4646
2901 W Coast Hwy Ste 200 Newport Beach (92663) ***(G-11480)***
Dream River, Commerce *Also called Shason Inc* ***(G-8326)***
Dreamctchers Empwerment Netwrk 925 935-6630
1911 Oak Park Blvd Pleasant Hill (94523) ***(G-24635)***
Dreamctchers Empwerment Netwrk 209 477-4817
6940 Pacific Ave Stockton (95207) ***(G-24636)***
Dreamgear LLC 310 222-5522
20001 S Western Ave Torrance (90501) ***(G-8043)***
Dreamhost.com, Brea *Also called New Dream Network LLC* ***(G-5668)***
Dreamhost.com, Los Angeles *Also called New Dream Network LLC* ***(G-5669)***
Dreamscape Ldscp & Maint Inc 619 583-4439
7192 Mission Gorge Rd San Diego (92120) ***(G-763)***
Dreamworks Animation LLC 818 695-5000
1000 Flower St Glendale (91201) ***(G-18464)***
DREIER'S NURSING CARE CENTER, Glendale *Also called Ksm Healthcare Inc* ***(G-20714)***
Dresick Farms Inc (PA) 559 945-2513
19536 Jayne Ave Huron (93234) ***(G-60)***
Dresser Rand, S, Chula Vista *Also called Siemens Government Tech Inc* ***(G-18015)***
Drew Chain Security Corp 626 457-8626
55 S Raymond Ave Ste 303 Alhambra (91801) ***(G-16880)***
Drew Child Dev Corp Inc (PA) 323 249-2950
1770 E 118th St Los Angeles (90059) ***(G-23948)***
Drew Health Foundation 650 328-1619
1191 Runnymede St East Palo Alto (94303) ***(G-24914)***
Dreyer Bbich Bccola Cllham LLP 916 379-3500
20 Bicentennial Cir Sacramento (95826) ***(G-23226)***
Dreyer's Grand Ice Cream, Walnut *Also called Nestle Dreyers Ice Cream Co* ***(G-8589)***
Dreyers Grand Ice Cream Hold (HQ) 510 652-8187
5929 College Ave Oakland (94618) ***(G-8584)***
Dreyers Grnd Ice Cream Hldings, Oakland *Also called Rdp Acquisition Company* ***(G-26702)***
DRG Health Care Staffing, South San Francisco *Also called Discharge Resource Group* ***(G-14871)***
Dri Companies (PA) 949 266-1900
2081 Bus Ctr Dr Ste 195 Irvine (92612) ***(G-3165)***
Driftwood Convalescent Hosp, Davis *Also called Mariner Health Care Inc* ***(G-20763)***
Driftwood Health Care Ctr, Torrance *Also called Mariner Health Care Inc* ***(G-20757)***
Driftwood Healthcare Center, Hayward *Also called Mariner Health Care Inc* ***(G-20767)***
Drinker Biddle & Reath LLP 310 229-1282
1800 Century Park E # 1400 Los Angeles (90067) ***(G-23227)***
Drinker Biddle & Reath LLP 415 591-7500
50 Fremont St Fl 20 San Francisco (94105) ***(G-23228)***
Drinks Holdings LLC (PA) 310 441-8400
11175 Santa Monica Blvd # 400 Los Angeles (90025) ***(G-9097)***
Driscoll Strawberry Assoc Inc (PA) 831 424-0506
345 Westridge Dr Watsonville (95076) ***(G-8718)***
Driscoll Strawberry Assoc Inc 831 763-5100
1750 San Juan Rd Aromas (95004) ***(G-8719)***
Drive Thru Technology Inc 323 576-1400
1755 N Main St Los Angeles (90031) ***(G-16881)***
Driver Spg 626 351-8800
1501 S Harris Ct Anaheim (92806) ***(G-17134)***
Drivesavers Inc 415 382-2000
400 Bel Marin Keys Blvd Novato (94949) ***(G-16229)***
Drivesavers Data Recovery, Novato *Also called Drivesavers Inc* ***(G-16229)***
Drobo Inc 408 454-4200
2540 Mission College Blvd Santa Clara (95054) ***(G-7122)***
Droisys Inc 408 329-1761
4657 Hedgewick Ave Fremont (94538) ***(G-17135)***
Drop Lot Services, San Juan Capistrano *Also called Merit Integrated Logistics LLC* ***(G-5122)***

A L P H A B E T I C

Drug & Alcohol Services of......805 781-4275
2180 Johnson Ave Ste A San Luis Obispo (93401) *(G-22721)*
Drug Abuse Alternatives Center......707 571-2233
2403 Prof Dr Ste 103 Santa Rosa (95403) *(G-22722)*
Drug Enforcement ADM......760 597-7955
2815 Scott St Vista (92081) *(G-26844)*
Drum Security Service Inc......818 708-7914
45530 Pelican Hill Ct Indio (92201) *(G-16628)*
Drummond Medical Group Inc......760 446-4571
900 N Heritage Dr Ste A Ridgecrest (93555) *(G-19509)*
Drx LLC......888 315-1519
330 A St Ste 80 San Diego (92101) *(G-22949)*
Dry Creek Lath & Plaster Inc......209 367-8607
27940 Kennefick Rd Galt (95632) *(G-2887)*
Dryco Construction Inc (PA)......510 438-6500
42745 Boscell Rd Fremont (94538) *(G-1768)*
Drywall Works Inc......916 383-6667
5900 Warehouse Way Sacramento (95826) *(G-2888)*
Ds Services of America Inc......415 282-1060
2217 Revere Ave San Francisco (94124) *(G-8828)*
Ds Services of America Inc......818 787-9397
7817 Haskell Ave Van Nuys (91406) *(G-8829)*
Ds Services of America Inc......626 472-7201
4548 Azusa Canyon Rd Irwindale (91706) *(G-8830)*
DSC Logistics Inc......909 363-4354
1895 Marigold Ave Redlands (92374) *(G-4142)*
DSC Logistics Inc......540 377-2302
5690 Industrial Pkwy San Bernardino (92407) *(G-5060)*
DSC Logistics Inc......209 833-0200
1565 N Macarthur Dr Tracy (95376) *(G-4546)*
DSC Logistics Inc......909 605-7233
12350 Philadelphia Ave Mira Loma (91752) *(G-4011)*
Dsca, Long Beach *Also called Denso Pdts & Svcs Americas Inc (G-6725)*
Dsd Trucking Inc (PA)......310 338-1210
8840 Bellanca Ave Los Angeles (90045) *(G-4914)*
Dsg Associates Inc......714 835-3020
15500 Erwin St Ste 4007 Van Nuys (91411) *(G-26657)*
Dsh Graphics, Yorba Linda *Also called Dsh West Inc (G-14143)*
Dsh West Inc......714 692-8777
5455 Camino De Bryant Yorba Linda (92887) *(G-14143)*
DSM Biomedical Inc......510 841-8800
2810 7th St Berkeley (94710) *(G-26505)*
Dst Output California Inc......916 939-4617
5220 Rbert J Mathews Pkwy El Dorado Hills (95762) *(G-16291)*
Dt Club Hotel Santa Ana, Santa Ana *Also called Jhc Investment Inc (G-12865)*
Dt Floormasters Inc......510 476-1000
31164 Huntwood Ave Hayward (94544) *(G-3112)*
Dt Research Inc (PA)......408 934-6220
2000 Concourse Dr San Jose (95131) *(G-26506)*
Dtecnet Inc......208 685-1810
2600 W Olive Ave Ste 910 Burbank (91505) *(G-15149)*
Dtex Systems Inc......408 418-3786
300 Santana Row Ste 400 San Jose (95128) *(G-15150)*
Dti Inc......310 635-9002
1628 S Sportsman Dr Compton (90221) *(G-4012)*
Dti Services Inc (PA)......213 670-1100
601 S Figueroa St # 4300 Los Angeles (90017) *(G-16358)*
DTM Services Inc (PA)......310 521-1200
19829 Hamilton Ave Torrance (90502) *(G-5061)*
Dtrs Santa Monica LLC......310 458-6700
1700 Ocean Ave Santa Monica (90401) *(G-12602)*
Dts, Sacramento *Also called Technology Services Cal Dept (G-16504)*
Dts Inc (PA)......818 436-1000
5220 Las Virgenes Rd Calabasas (91302) *(G-18224)*
Dtt, Los Angeles *Also called Drive Thru Technology Inc (G-16881)*
Dtt Surveillance Holdings Inc......323 576-1400
1755 N Main St Los Angeles (90031) *(G-16882)*
Dual Diagnosis Trtmnt Ctr Inc......424 289-9031
12832 Short Ave Los Angeles (90066) *(G-22211)*
Dual Diagnosis Trtmnt Ctr Inc (PA)......949 276-5553
1211 Puerta Del Sol # 270 San Clemente (92673) *(G-22723)*
Dual Diagnosis Trtmnt Ctr Inc......424 207-2220
6167 Bristol Pkwy Culver City (90230) *(G-22724)*
Duane Morris LLP......415 957-3000
1 Market Plz Ste 2000 San Francisco (94105) *(G-23229)*
Duarte Manor, Los Angeles *Also called Emp III Inc (G-12303)*
Duarte Nursery Inc......209 887-3409
23456 E Flood Rd Linden (95236) *(G-278)*
Duarte Nursery Inc (PA)......209 531-0351
1555 Baldwin Rd Hughson (95326) *(G-279)*
Duarte Properties, Hughson *Also called Duarte Nursery Inc (G-279)*
Dublin San Ramon Services Dist......925 846-4565
7399 Johnson Dr Pleasanton (94588) *(G-6341)*
DUBLIN SAN RAMON SERVICES DIST., Pleasanton *Also called Dublin San Ramon Services Dist (G-6341)*
Duckor Spradling Metzger......619 209-3000
3043 4th Ave San Diego (92103) *(G-23230)*
Duckpunk Productions Inc......310 836-3818
9016 W Olympic Blvd Beverly Hills (90211) *(G-18078)*
Ducks Unlimited Inc......916 852-2000
3074 Gold Canal Dr Rancho Cordova (95670) *(G-1020)*
Ducky's Car Wash, San Carlos *Also called Duckys of San Carlos Inc (G-17839)*
Duckys Car Wash Inc......650 375-8100
716 N San Mateo Dr San Mateo (94401) *(G-17838)*
Duckys of San Carlos Inc......650 637-1301
1301 Old County Rd San Carlos (94070) *(G-17839)*
Dudek (PA)......760 942-5147
605 3rd St Encinitas (92024) *(G-25773)*
Due West LLC......805 884-0300
31 W Carrillo St Santa Barbara (93101) *(G-12603)*
Duff & Phelps LLC......650 798-5500
1950 University Ave # 400 East Palo Alto (94303) *(G-27416)*
Duff & Phelps LLC......213 270-2300
350 S Grand Ave Ste 3100 Los Angeles (90071) *(G-27417)*
Duff & Phelps LLC......415 693-5300
345 California St # 2100 San Francisco (94104) *(G-17136)*
Duggan & Associates Inc......323 965-1502
1442 W 135th St Gardena (90249) *(G-2440)*
Dui Program, Santa Monica *Also called Clare Foundation Inc (G-23762)*
Duke Energy Corporation......949 727-7434
8001 Irvine Center Dr Irvine (92618) *(G-6124)*
Duke Pacific Inc......909 591-0191
13950 Monte Vista Ave Chino (91710) *(G-3166)*
Duleys Landscape Inc......559 855-5090
28876 Topaz Rd Tollhouse (93667) *(G-845)*
Dun & Bradstreet Inc......415 343-6540
1 Embarcadero Ctr # 2060 San Francisco (94111) *(G-14057)*
Dun & Bradstreet Emerging (HQ)......310 456-8271
22761 Pacific Coast Hwy # 226 Malibu (90265) *(G-17137)*
Dun & Brdstreet Crdbility Corp, Malibu *Also called Dun & Bradstreet Emerging (G-17137)*
Dun-Rite Maintenance Inc......707 765-2434
438 Petaluma Blvd N Petaluma (94952) *(G-13597)*
Dunbar Armored Inc......510 569-7400
629 Whitney St San Leandro (94577) *(G-16629)*
Dunlap Property Group Inc......714 879-0111
801 E Chapman Ave Ste 233 Fullerton (92831) *(G-11481)*
Dunn & Berger Inc......818 986-1234
5955 De Soto Ave Ste 160 Woodland Hills (91367) *(G-22427)*
Duplo USA Corporation (PA)......949 752-8222
3050 Daimler St Santa Ana (92705) *(G-7052)*
Dura Freight Inc......909 444-1025
525 S Lemon Ave Walnut (91789) *(G-4547)*
Dura Freight Lines, Walnut *Also called Dura Freight Inc (G-4547)*
Dura Metrics Inc (PA)......707 546-5138
816 Piner Rd Santa Rosa (95403) *(G-22305)*
Duran Human Capital Partners......408 540-0070
300 Orchard Cy Dr Ste 142 Campbell (95008) *(G-14639)*
Durham School Services......408 448-0740
3001 Ross Ave Ste 11 San Jose (95124) *(G-28128)*
Durham School Services L P......310 767-5820
16627 Avalon Blvd Ste B Carson (90746) *(G-3918)*
Durham School Services L P......805 495-8338
365 E Avnda De Los Alvare Thousand Oaks (91360) *(G-3919)*
Durham School Services L P......714 542-8989
2818 W 5th St Santa Ana (92703) *(G-3957)*
Durham School Services L P......408 377-6655
1506 White Oaks Rd Campbell (95008) *(G-3920)*
Durham School Services L P......510 887-6005
27577 Industrial Blvd A Hayward (94545) *(G-3921)*
Durham School Services L P......530 273-7282
10701 E Bennett Rd Grass Valley (95945) *(G-3922)*
Durham School Services L P......925 686-3391
5029 Forni Dr Concord (94520) *(G-3923)*
Durham School Services L P......626 573-3769
2713 River Ave Rosemead (91770) *(G-3924)*
Durkee Drayage Company......510 970-7550
3655 Collins Ave San Pablo (94806) *(G-4343)*
Dust Networks Inc......510 400-2900
32990 Alvrdo Niles Rd # 910 Union City (94587) *(G-5395)*
Dutch LLC......323 277-3900
5300 S Santa Fe Ave Vernon (90058) *(G-8378)*
Dutch LLC (HQ)......323 277-3900
5301 S Santa Fe Ave Vernon (90058) *(G-8379)*
Duthie Electric Service Corp......562 790-1772
2335 E Cherry Indus Cir Long Beach (90805) *(G-17933)*
Duthie Power Services, Long Beach *Also called Duthie Electric Service Corp (G-17933)*
Dutra Dredging, San Rafael *Also called Dutra Group (G-2047)*
Dutra Dredging Company (HQ)......415 721-2131
2350 Kerner Blvd Ste 200 San Rafael (94901) *(G-2046)*
Dutra Group (PA)......415 258-6876
2350 Kerner Blvd Ste 200 San Rafael (94901) *(G-2047)*
Dutra Manson JV......415 258-6876
1000 Point San Pedro Rd San Rafael (94901) *(G-2048)*
Dutra Materials, San Rafael *Also called San Rafael Rock Quarry Inc (G-1102)*
Dutra Realty, Pleasanton *Also called Mason-Mcduffie Real Estate Inc (G-11666)*
Duxford Financial Inc......949 471-2010
4490 Von Karman Ave Newport Beach (92660) *(G-9837)*
Dva Renal Healthcare Inc......949 588-9211
23141 Plaza Pointe Dr Laguna Hills (92653) *(G-22625)*
Dventist Health Community, Reedley *Also called Adventist Health System/West (G-22878)*
Dvm Insurance Agency, Brea *Also called Veterinary Pet Insur Svcs Inc (G-10924)*
Dvs Shoe Co Inc (PA)......310 715-8300
1008 Brioso Dr Costa Mesa (92627) *(G-8431)*
Dw Berry Farms LLC......805 795-8403
3960 N Rose Ave Oxnard (93036) *(G-357)*
DW Morgan LLC......925 460-2700
4185 Blackhawk Ste 260 Danville (94506) *(G-5062)*
DWA, Palm Springs *Also called Desert Water Agency Fing Corp (G-6340)*
Dwa Holdings LLC (HQ)......818 695-5000
1000 Flower St Glendale (91201) *(G-18079)*
Dwa Nova LLC......818 695-5000
1000 Flower St Glendale (91201) *(G-15646)*
Dwayne Nash Industries Inc......916 253-1900
8825 Washington Blvd # 100 Roseville (95678) *(G-3167)*
Dwaynes Engineering & Cnstr......661 762-7261
3655 Addie Ave Mc Kittrick (93251) *(G-1073)*

ALPHABETIC

Dwiw Inc......949 574-7147
700 W 16th St Costa Mesa (92627) *(G-846)*
Dwn, Hickman *Also called Dave Wilson Nursery Inc (G-275)*
Dy-Dee Service Pasadena Inc......626 792-6183
40 E California Blvd Pasadena (91105) *(G-13652)*
Dya Assoc......323 364-4270
8335 W Sunset Blvd # 320 Los Angeles (90069) *(G-11963)*
Dydee Service of Pasedena......626 240-0115
40 E California Blvd Pasadena (91105) *(G-13653)*
Dykema Gossett PLLC......213 457-1800
333 S Grand Ave Ste 2100 Los Angeles (90071) *(G-23231)*
Dynalectric Company......805 517-1253
668 Flinn Ave Moorpark (93021) *(G-2576)*
Dynalectric Company......858 712-4700
9505 Chesapeake Dr San Diego (92123) *(G-2577)*
Dynalectric Company......714 236-2242
4462 Corporate Center Dr Los Alamitos (90720) *(G-2578)*
Dynalectric Company......415 487-4700
825 Howe Rd Martinez (94553) *(G-2579)*
Dynamex Inc......209 464-7008
4790 Frontier Way Ste A Stockton (95215) *(G-4398)*
Dynamex Operations West Inc......714 994-1615
16900 Valley View Ave La Mirada (90638) *(G-4399)*
Dynamic Auto Images Inc......714 981-4367
1407 N Batavia St Ste 102 Orange (92867) *(G-17840)*
Dynamic Chiropractic, Westminster *Also called Maxwell Petersen Associates (G-27530)*
Dynamic Detail, Orange *Also called Dynamic Auto Images Inc (G-17840)*
Dynamic Home Care Service Inc (PA)......818 981-4446
14260 Ventura Blvd # 301 Sherman Oaks (91423) *(G-22428)*
Dynamic Maintenance Svcs Inc......925 228-7434
837 Arnold Dr Ste 220 Martinez (94553) *(G-14284)*
Dynamic Medical Systems LLC (HQ)......310 928-0251
2811 E Ana St Compton (90221) *(G-14474)*
Dynamic Plumbing Commercial......951 343-1200
7343 Orangewood Dr Ste B Riverside (92504) *(G-2210)*
Dynamic Plumbing Systems Inc......951 343-1200
5920 Winterhaven Ave Riverside (92504) *(G-2211)*
Dynamic Realty Corp......626 931-3200
800 S Barranca Ave # 260 Covina (91723) *(G-11482)*
Dynamic Worldwide West Inc......310 357-2460
14141 Alondra Blvd Santa Fe Springs (90670) *(G-5063)*
Dynamo Aviation Inc......818 785-9561
16760 Schoenborn St North Hills (91343) *(G-4915)*
Dynasty Farms Inc (PA)......831 755-1398
11900 Big Tujunga Cyn Rd Tujunga (91042) *(G-8720)*
Dyncorp......619 522-2222
Nas Nrth Is Bldg 1479 San Diego (92135) *(G-15936)*
Dynegy Marketing & Trade LLC......831 633-6700
Hwy 1 & Dolan Rd Moss Landing (95039) *(G-6125)*
Dynegy Moss Landing LLC......831 633-6618
7301 Highway 1 Moss Landing (95039) *(G-6126)*
Dyntek Inc (PA)......949 271-6700
4440 Von Karman Ave # 200 Newport Beach (92660) *(G-16359)*
Dzyne Technologies Inc......703 291-6663
11 Vanderbilt Irvine (92618) *(G-25774)*
E & B Ntral Resources Mgt Corp (PA)......661 679-1714
1600 Norris Rd Bakersfield (93308) *(G-1043)*
E & C Fashion Inc......323 262-0099
3600 E Olympic Blvd Los Angeles (90023) *(G-17138)*
E & E Co Ltd......530 669-5991
2222 E Beamer St Woodland (95776) *(G-1169)*
E & E Co Ltd (PA)......510 490-9788
45875 Northport Loop E Fremont (94538) *(G-6857)*
E & J Gallo Winery......707 431-5400
11447 Old Redwood Hwy Healdsburg (95448) *(G-153)*
E & J Gallo Winery......707 967-9284
105a Zinfandel Ln Saint Helena (94574) *(G-27900)*
E & J Gallo Winery......323 720-6400
2650 Commerce Way Commerce (90040) *(G-9098)*
E & J Gallo Winery......209 394-6271
5953 Weir Ave Livingston (95334) *(G-697)*
E & M AG Svc Inc A Cal Corp......559 627-2724
2446 W Border Links Dr Visalia (93291) *(G-698)*
E & M Concrete Construction......805 658-2888
2842 Sherwin Ave Ste A Ventura (93003) *(G-3260)*
E & M Electric and McHy Inc (PA)......707 433-5578
126 Mill St Healdsburg (95448) *(G-7838)*
E & S International Entps Inc (PA)......818 702-2207
7801 Hayvenhurst Ave Van Nuys (91406) *(G-7494)*
E & S Rsidential Care Svcs LLC......559 275-3555
6083 N Marks Ave Fresno (93711) *(G-24637)*
E & T Foods Inc......760 843-7730
14827 Seventh St Victorville (92395) *(G-465)*
E A Com Inc......650 628-1500
209 Redwood Shores Pkwy Redwood City (94065) *(G-15151)*
E B C F, Oakland *Also called East Bay Community Foundation (G-24915)*
E B Stone & Son Inc......707 249-4699
6111 Lambie Rd Suisun City (94585) *(G-9136)*
E C R M C, El Centro *Also called El Centro Regional Medical Ctr (G-21553)*
E Center......530 634-1200
1506 Starr Dr Yuba City (95993) *(G-24457)*
E D C, Torrance *Also called Electronic Data Care Inc (G-15938)*
E D D 2100......209 941-6501
3127 Transworld Dr # 150 Stockton (95206) *(G-10239)*
E D G, Novato *Also called EDG Interior Arch & Design Inc (G-17144)*
E D S I, Fallbrook *Also called Edsi (G-25779)*
E E G and E P, Chico *Also called Enloe Medical Center (G-20316)*
E Film Digital Labratories, Los Angeles *Also called Efilm LLC (G-18082)*
E G Ayers Distributing Inc......707 445-2077
5819 S Broadway St Eureka (95503) *(G-8476)*
E H Summit Inc (PA)......310 476-6571
11461 W Sunset Blvd Los Angeles (90049) *(G-12604)*
E H Summit Inc......310 273-0300
360 N Rodeo Dr Beverly Hills (90210) *(G-12605)*
E I I, Bakersfield *Also called Electrcal Instrumentation Intl (G-2583)*
E J Harrison & Sons Inc......805 647-1414
1589 Lirio Ave Ventura (93004) *(G-6473)*
E J Williams Property MGT......209 473-4022
5637 N Pershing Ave Ste D Stockton (95207) *(G-11122)*
E K T Farms......831 724-0832
105 Logan St Watsonville (95076) *(G-358)*
E L Payne Heating Company......310 275-5331
226 S Lucerne Blvd Los Angeles (90004) *(G-2212)*
E L S, Los Angeles *Also called J C Entertainment Ltg Svcs Inc (G-18400)*
E M Electric Co......415 315-3300
14 Cypress St San Francisco (94110) *(G-6727)*
E M S Trading Inc......909 581-7800
5161 Richton St Montclair (91763) *(G-8432)*
E M Tharp Inc (PA)......559 782-5800
15243 Road 192 Porterville (93257) *(G-6674)*
E O S International, Carlsbad *Also called Electronic Online Systems Intl (G-15939)*
E P A, Sacramento *Also called Environmental Protection Agcy (G-6627)*
E P N Inc......951 279-8877
1580 Magnolia Ave Corona (92879) *(G-18080)*
E P U, Fresno *Also called Exceptnal Prents Unlimited Inc (G-23964)*
E R A First Star Realty......714 974-3111
505 S Villa Real Ste 101a Anaheim (92807) *(G-11483)*
E R G Home Health Provider......562 403-1070
11700 South St Ste 200 Artesia (90701) *(G-22429)*
E R I T Inc (PA)......760 433-6024
251 Airport Rd Oceanside (92058) *(G-24638)*
E R I T Inc......760 721-1706
251 Airport Rd Oceanside (92058) *(G-24639)*
E S 3, San Diego *Also called Enginring Sftwr Sys Sltons Inc (G-25794)*
E T Horn Company (PA)......714 523-8050
16050 Canary Ave La Mirada (90638) *(G-8987)*
E Tradeshowgirlscom......949 661-4177
1 Ocean Rdg Laguna Niguel (92677) *(G-17139)*
E W C H Inc......510 783-4811
1805 West St Hayward (94545) *(G-20523)*
E Z Data Inc (HQ)......626 585-3505
251 S Lake Ave Ste 200 Pasadena (91101) *(G-15152)*
E Z Staffing Inc (PA)......818 845-2500
333 E Glenoaks Blvd # 200 Glendale (91207) *(G-14640)*
E&M, Healdsburg *Also called E & M Electric and McHy Inc (G-7838)*
E&S Building Maintenance Inc......714 961-8078
3315 E Miraloma Ave # 116 Anaheim (92806) *(G-14285)*
E&S Financial Group Inc......805 644-1621
4253 Transport St Ventura (93003) *(G-9919)*
E-Infochips Inc......408 496-1882
1230 Midas Way Ste 200 Sunnyvale (94085) *(G-15153)*
E-Loan Inc (HQ)......925 847-6200
6230 Stoneridge Mall Rd Pleasanton (94588) *(G-9920)*
E-Move Express, Foster City *Also called Rainbow Networking (G-16176)*
E-N Realty II......909 597-1736
1081 Grand Ave Diamond Bar (91765) *(G-11484)*
E-Sceptre Inc......888 350-8989
16800 Gale Ave City of Industry (91745) *(G-26507)*
E-Times Corporation Ltd......213 452-6720
601 S Figueroa St # 5000 Los Angeles (90017) *(G-16230)*
E. S. Babcock & Sons, Riverside *Also called Babcock Laboratories Inc (G-26832)*
E.V. Roberts, Carson *Also called Cirrus Enterprises LLC (G-8967)*
E2 Consulting Engineers Inc......510 652-1164
1900 Powell St Ste 250 Emeryville (94608) *(G-25775)*
E2 Corp......818 904-5660
8121 Van Nuys Blvd # 308 Panorama City (91402) *(G-15937)*
E2 Managetech Inc (PA)......562 740-1060
5001 Airport Plaza Dr # 260 Long Beach (90815) *(G-25776)*
E2 Solutions, Panorama City *Also called E2 Corp (G-15937)*
E21 Corp......510 818-9600
39111 Paseo Padre Pkwy # 208 Fremont (94538) *(G-14144)*
E2c Inc......408 327-5700
3016 Scott Blvd Santa Clara (95054) *(G-27901)*
E3 Healthcare Management LLC......650 324-0600
375 Forest Ave Palo Alto (94301) *(G-27008)*
Ea Consulting Inc......916 357-6767
1024 Iron Point Rd Folsom (95630) *(G-16360)*
Ea Environmental Construction......818 785-0956
15239 Stagg St Van Nuys (91405) *(G-2889)*
Ea Mobile Inc......310 754-7125
5510 Lincoln Blvd Los Angeles (90094) *(G-5396)*
Eag Holdings LLC......408 530-3500
2710 Walsh Ave Santa Clara (95051) *(G-27902)*
Eag Inc (PA)......408 454-4600
2710 Walsh Ave Santa Clara (95051) *(G-26845)*
Eagle Estates Inc......858 484-3829
10175 Rancho Carmel Dr # 124 San Diego (92128) *(G-11485)*
Eagle Glen Country Club LLC......951 272-4653
1800 Eagle Glen Pkwy Corona (92883) *(G-18737)*
Eagle Glen Golf Club, Corona *Also called Eagle Glen Country Club LLC (G-18737)*
Eagle High Reach, La Mirada *Also called Ideal Equipment Rental Inc (G-14548)*
Eagle High Reach Equipment LLC......619 265-2637
14241 Alondra Blvd La Mirada (90638) *(G-14536)*
Eagle Intermodel Services, San Bernardino *Also called Eagle Systems Inc (G-4143)*
Eagle Lath & Plaster Inc......916 925-1435
4350 Warehouse Ct North Highlands (95660) *(G-1547)*

A L P H A B E T I C

Eagle Rafting, Ridgecrest *Also called Kern River Adventures (G-4738)*
Eagle Resources Inc.....805 922-0000
516 W Boone St Santa Maria (93458) *(G-14641)*
Eagle Ridge Golf Club, Gilroy *Also called Eagle Ridge Golf Cntry CLB LLC (G-18942)*
Eagle Ridge Golf Cntry CLB LLC.....408 846-4531
2951 Club Dr Gilroy (95020) *(G-18942)*
Eagle Roofing Products, Rialto *Also called Burlingame Industries Inc (G-13475)*
Eagle Roofing Products, Stockton *Also called Burlingame Industries Inc (G-7009)*
Eagle Security Service Inc.....310 532-1626
12903 S Normandie Ave Gardena (90249) *(G-16630)*
Eagle Systems Inc.....909 386-4343
395 N Mount Vernon Ave San Bernardino (92411) *(G-4143)*
Eagle Systems Intl Inc.....510 259-1700
28436 Satellite St Hayward (94545) *(G-2213)*
Eagle Vnes Vnyrds Golf CLB LLC.....707 257-4470
580 S Kelly Rd American Canyon (94503) *(G-18943)*
EAGLES HALL, Roseville *Also called Fraternal Order Eagles 1582 (G-10984)*
Eah Inc (PA).....415 258-1800
2169 Francisco Blvd E B San Rafael (94901) *(G-11234)*
EAH SAN PABLO, San Rafael *Also called Eah Inc (G-11234)*
Ealliant LLC.....619 255-9344
1202 Morena Blvd Ste 100 San Diego (92110) *(G-27903)*
EAM Enterprises Inc (PA).....818 248-9100
4005 Foothill Blvd La Crescenta (91214) *(G-11486)*
Eappraiseit LLC (PA).....800 281-6200
12395 First American Way Poway (92064) *(G-11487)*
Earl's Organic Produce, San Francisco *Also called Earls Organic (G-8831)*
Earle M Jorgensen Company.....510 487-2700
31100 Wiegman Rd Hayward (94544) *(G-7368)*
Earle M Jorgensen Company.....323 567-1122
350 S Grand Ave Ste 5100 Los Angeles (90071) *(G-7369)*
Earlibest Orange Assn Inc.....559 592-2124
622 Spruce Rd Exeter (93221) *(G-494)*
Earls Organic.....415 824-7419
2101 Jerrold Ave Ste 100 San Francisco (94124) *(G-8831)*
Earlwood LLC.....310 371-1228
20820 Earl St Torrance (90503) *(G-20524)*
Earlwood Convalescent Hospital, Torrance *Also called Earlwood LLC (G-20524)*
Early Childhood Education, La Quinta *Also called Deser Sands Unifi Schoo Distr (G-24454)*
Early Childhood Services, Ridgecrest *Also called Desert Area Resources Training (G-24912)*
Early Learning Art-Tech Group.....866 491-2432
1697 N Sierra Way San Bernardino (92405) *(G-25526)*
Early Transportation Services.....510 324-1119
30796 San Clemente St Hayward (94544) *(G-4144)*
Earth Island Institute Inc.....510 859-9100
2150 Allston Way Ste 460 Berkeley (94704) *(G-25527)*
Earth Systems Southwest (HQ).....760 345-1588
79811 Country Club Dr B Bermuda Dunes (92203) *(G-25777)*
Earth Technology Corp USA.....213 593-8000
1999 Avenue Of Ste 2600 Los Angeles (90067) *(G-6474)*
Earthbound Farm LLC (HQ).....831 623-7880
1721 San Juan Hwy San Juan Bautista (95045) *(G-527)*
Earthbound Productions LLC.....504 734-3337
849 N Occidental Blvd Los Angeles (90026) *(G-18081)*
Earthco, Santa Ana *Also called Morrison Landscaping Inc (G-7410)*
Earthly Delights.....650 726-7227
378 San Pedro Rd Half Moon Bay (94019) *(G-19200)*
Earthtech, Oakland *Also called Kaiser Group Holdings Inc (G-25915)*
Easia Golf Investment LLC.....760 775-2000
84000 Terra Lago Pkwy Indio (92203) *(G-12300)*
East Bay Airport Shuttle, San Jose *Also called South Bay Airport Shuttle (G-3720)*
East Bay Airport Shuttle, Concord *Also called East Bay Connection Inc (G-3643)*
East Bay Asian Local Dev Corp.....510 267-1917
1825 San Pablo Ave # 201 Oakland (94612) *(G-11123)*
East Bay Asian Youth Center.....510 533-1092
2025 E 12th St Oakland (94606) *(G-23949)*
East Bay Btncal Zoological Soc.....510 632-9525
9777 Golf Links Rd Oakland (94605) *(G-19201)*
East Bay Clarklift Inc.....559 268-6621
4646 E Jensen Ave Fresno (93725) *(G-7839)*
East Bay Community Foundation.....510 836-3223
200 Frank H Ogawa Plz Oakland (94612) *(G-24915)*
East Bay Connection Inc.....925 609-1920
1970 Arnold Industrial Pl Concord (94520) *(G-3643)*
East Bay Foundation Grad Med.....510 437-4197
1411 E 31st St Oakland (94602) *(G-22950)*
East Bay Innovations.....510 618-1580
2450 Washington Ave # 240 San Leandro (94577) *(G-17140)*
East Bay Municipl Utilty Distr.....866 403-2683
3999 Lakeside Dr Richmond (94806) *(G-6342)*
East Bay Municipl Utilty Distr (PA).....866 403-2683
375 11th St Oakland (94607) *(G-6343)*
East Bay Municipl Utilty Distr.....866 403-2683
2020 Wake Ave Oakland (94607) *(G-6475)*
East Bay Municipl Utilty Distr.....510 287-0760
375 11th St Oakland (94607) *(G-10551)*
East Bay Regional Park Dst.....510 881-1833
17930 Lake Chabot Rd Castro Valley (94546) *(G-19202)*
East Bay Regional Park Public, Castro Valley *Also called East Bay Regional Park Dst (G-19202)*
East Bay Transitional Homes, Oakland *Also called Bay Area Community Svcs Inc (G-23676)*
East Crson II Hsing Prtners LP.....310 522-9606
401 W Carson St Carson (90745) *(G-11488)*
East Hall Investors Inc.....530 328-1900
11601 Blocker Dr Ste 200 Auburn (95603) *(G-12301)*
East Katella Partnership.....714 978-8088
525 Cabrillo Park Dr # 220 Santa Ana (92701) *(G-12606)*
East Lion Corporation.....626 912-1818
318 Brea Canyon Rd Walnut (91789) *(G-8433)*
East Los Angeles Community Un (PA).....323 721-1655
5400 E Olympic Blvd Commerce (90022) *(G-9781)*
East Los Angeles Doctors.....323 268-5514
4060 Whittier Blvd Los Angeles (90023) *(G-21548)*
East Los Angeles Doctors Hosp, Los Angeles *Also called Eladh LP (G-21554)*
East Los Angeles Employment.....323 838-5710
5301 Whittier Blvd Ste G Los Angeles (90022) *(G-14642)*
East Los Angeles Mental Hlth.....323 725-1337
1436 Goodrich Blvd Commerce (90022) *(G-22725)*
East Palo Alto Hotel Dev Inc.....650 566-1200
2050 University Ave East Palo Alto (94303) *(G-12607)*
East Palo Alto Y M C A.....650 328-9622
550 Bell St East Palo Alto (94303) *(G-25252)*
East San Gbriel Vly Consortium.....626 960-3964
5200 Irwindale Ave # 210 Irwindale (91706) *(G-3785)*
East Valley Cmnty Hlth Ctr Inc (PA).....626 919-3402
420 S Glendora Ave West Covina (91790) *(G-22726)*
East Valley Family YMCA Dcc, North Hollywood *Also called Young Mens Chrstn Assn of La (G-24536)*
East Valley Glendora Hosp LP.....626 335-0231
150 W Route 66 Glendora (91740) *(G-21549)*
East Valley Hospital Med Ctr, Glendora *Also called East Valley Glendora Hosp LP (G-21549)*
East Valley Tourist Dev Auth.....760 342-5000
84245 Indio Springs Dr Indio (92203) *(G-19203)*
East Valley Water District.....909 889-9501
31111 Greenspot Rd Highland (92346) *(G-6344)*
East West, Cerritos *Also called Global Med Services Inc (G-22441)*
East West Bank (HQ).....626 768-6000
135 N Ls Rbls Ave 100 Pasadena (91101) *(G-9489)*
East West Bank.....415 391-8912
555 Montgomery St Bsmt San Francisco (94111) *(G-9490)*
East West Bank.....626 280-1688
228 W Garvey Ave Monterey Park (91754) *(G-9584)*
Eastbiz Corporation (PA).....310 212-7134
3501 Jack Northrop Ave Hawthorne (90250) *(G-19204)*
Eastbrook Construction Inc.....909 394-4994
403 E Arrow Hwy Ste 302 San Dimas (91773) *(G-2890)*
Easter Seal Soc Superior Cal (PA).....916 485-6711
3205 Hurley Way Sacramento (95864) *(G-22951)*
Easter Seal Soc Superior Cal.....530 673-4585
1670 Sierra Ave Ste 601 Yuba City (95993) *(G-23950)*
Easter Seal Society, Lancaster *Also called Easter Seals Southern Cal Inc (G-24917)*
Easter Seals Inc.....831 338-3383
16403 Highway 9 Boulder Creek (95006) *(G-13463)*
Easter Seals Central Cal.....831 684-2166
9010 Soquel Dr Aptos (95003) *(G-23951)*
EASTER SEALS MAIN OFFICE, Sacramento *Also called Easter Seal Soc Superior Cal (G-22951)*
Easter Seals Southern Cal Inc.....818 551-0128
710 W Broadway Glendale (91204) *(G-24916)*
Easter Seals Southern Cal Inc.....661 723-3414
340 E Avenue I Ste 101 Lancaster (93535) *(G-24917)*
Eastern Broadcasting Amer Corp.....626 581-8899
18430 San Jose Ave Ste A City of Industry (91748) *(G-5997)*
Eastern Goldfields Inc.....619 497-2555
1660 Hotel Cir N Ste 207 San Diego (92108) *(G-27418)*
Eastern Los Angeles RE (PA).....626 299-4700
1000 S Fremont Ave # 23 Alhambra (91803) *(G-23952)*
Eastern Municipal Water Dst (PA).....951 928-3777
2270 Trumble Rd Perris (92572) *(G-6345)*
Eastern Plumas Health Care.....530 993-1225
700 3rd St Loyalton (96118) *(G-20525)*
Eastern Plumas Health Care (PA).....530 832-4277
500 1st Ave Portola (96122) *(G-22952)*
Eastern Plumas Hospital, Portola *Also called Eastern Plumas Health Care (G-22952)*
Eastern Sierra Transit Auth.....760 872-1901
703 Airport Rd Bishop (93514) *(G-3878)*
Eastern Sports, Van Nuys *Also called Easton Hockey Inc (G-8016)*
Eastern Star Homes California (PA).....714 986-2380
16850 Bastanchury Rd Yorba Linda (92886) *(G-23953)*
EASTERN STAR PROFESSIONAL BUIL, Yorba Linda *Also called Eastern Star Homes California (G-23953)*
Eastland Executive Office, West Covina *Also called Eastland Tower Partnership (G-11251)*
Eastland Tower Partnership.....626 858-2000
100 N Barranca St Ste 900 West Covina (91791) *(G-11251)*
Easton Hockey, Van Nuys *Also called Bauer Hockey Inc (G-8012)*
Easton Hockey Inc (HQ).....818 782-6445
7855 Haskell Ave Ste 200 Van Nuys (91406) *(G-8016)*
Eastrdge Prsonnel of Las Vegas.....415 248-2567
530 Davis St San Francisco (94111) *(G-14643)*
Eastrdge Prsonnel of Las Vegas (PA).....619 260-2000
2355 Northside Dr Ste 120 San Diego (92108) *(G-14644)*
Eastridge ADM Staffing, San Diego *Also called Eplica Inc (G-14874)*
Eastridge Infotech, San Diego *Also called Eastrdge Prsonnel of Las Vegas (G-14644)*
Eastside Group Corporation.....213 368-9777
1830 W Olympic Blvd # 202 Los Angeles (90006) *(G-16631)*
Eastside Management Co Inc.....209 578-9852
1131 12th St Ste C Modesto (95354) *(G-699)*
Eastwestproto Inc.....888 535-5728
1120 S Maple Ave Ste 200 Montebello (90640) *(G-3786)*
Eastwood Insurance Services (PA).....800 468-5377
155 N Riverview Dr Anaheim (92808) *(G-10694)*
Easun Inc.....916 929-8855
2001 Point West Way Sacramento (95815) *(G-12608)*
Easy Fuel, San Jose *Also called Efuel LLC (G-9017)*

A L P H A B E T I C

Easy Ride Transportation......424 999-8830
1820 W Carson St Ste 202 Torrance (90501) ***(G-5217)***
Eaton Canyon Golf Course, Altadena *Also called D C Golf A CA Partnership* ***(G-18732)***
Eb, Santa Rosa *Also called Exchange Bank* ***(G-9585)***
Ebatts.com, Camarillo *Also called Battery-Biz Inc* ***(G-7099)***
Ebc Inc (PA)......310 753-6407
219 Manhattan Beach Blvd Manhattan Beach (90266) ***(G-1170)***
Ebi Consulting, Long Beach *Also called Envirobusiness Inc* ***(G-28129)***
Ebisu Marketing Corp......213 674-2330
1930 Wilshire Blvd # 400 Los Angeles (90057) ***(G-27419)***
Ebm Inc......213 365-4905
3200 Wilshire Blvd # 1000 Los Angeles (90010) ***(G-14286)***
EBM Janitorial Services Inc......805 523-3700
5260 Bonsai St Ste E Moorpark (93021) ***(G-14287)***
Ebmud, Richmond *Also called East Bay Municipl Utilty Distr* ***(G-6342)***
Ebmud, Oakland *Also called East Bay Municipl Utilty Distr* ***(G-6343)***
Ebmud, Oakland *Also called East Bay Municipl Utilty Distr* ***(G-6475)***
Ebmud, Oakland *Also called East Bay Municipl Utilty Distr* ***(G-10551)***
Ebs Concrete Inc......951 279-6869
1320 E 6th St Ste 100 Corona (92879) ***(G-3261)***
Ebs General Engineering Inc......951 279-6869
1320 E 6th St Ste 100 Corona (92879) ***(G-1769)***
EBSC LP......510 547-2244
3875 Telegraph Ave Oakland (94609) ***(G-19510)***
Ebsco Industries Inc......310 322-5000
898 N Sepulveda Blvd # 800 El Segundo (90245) ***(G-9163)***
Ebuys Inc......858 547-7545
8960 Carroll Way Ste 100 San Diego (92121) ***(G-8434)***
EC Closing Corp......800 546-1531
525 E Main St El Cajon (92020) ***(G-9838)***
EC Davis Health Services, Sacramento *Also called Internal Mdcine Rsdncy Affairs* ***(G-25139)***
EC Group Inc (PA)......310 815-2700
5960 Bowcroft St Los Angeles (90016) ***(G-6814)***
Ecamsecure......800 257-5512
436 W Walnut St Gardena (90248) ***(G-7558)***
Ecc, Burlingame *Also called Environmental Chemical Corp* ***(G-25797)***
ECCU, Brea *Also called Evangelical Christian Cr Un* ***(G-9668)***
Echelon Security Inc......408 436-8844
1604 Kerley Dr San Jose (95112) ***(G-27904)***
Echo Landscape, San Lorenzo *Also called Scyence Inc* ***(G-950)***
Echo PCF Communications LLC......760 737-3003
2066 Aldergrove Ave Escondido (92029) ***(G-27009)***
Echo Staffing, San Jose *Also called Summit Hr Worldwide Inc* ***(G-27673)***
Echo, A Heatlhstream Company, San Diego *Also called Healthstream Inc* ***(G-15689)***
Ecker & Associates, Foster City *Also called Ecker Consumer Recruiting Inc* ***(G-26658)***
Ecker Consumer Recruiting Inc (PA)......650 871-6800
1303 Melbourne St Foster City (94404) ***(G-26658)***
Eclipse Solutions Inc......916 565-8090
2150 River Plaza Dr # 380 Sacramento (95833) ***(G-16361)***
Eco Bay Services Inc......415 643-7777
1501 Minnesota St San Francisco (94107) ***(G-27905)***
Eco Farm Field Inc......951 676-4047
28790 Las Haciendas St Temecula (92590) ***(G-700)***
Eco Farms Avocados Inc (PA)......951 694-3013
28790 Las Haciendas St Temecula (92590) ***(G-528)***
Eco Farms Sales Inc (PA)......951 694-3013
28790 Las Haciendas St Temecula (92590) ***(G-8721)***
Eco Flow Transportation LLC......310 816-0260
18735 S Ferris Pl Rancho Dominguez (90220) ***(G-5064)***
Eco2 Plastics Inc......209 863-6200
5300 Claus Rd Riverbank (95367) ***(G-6476)***
Ecola Services Inc......818 920-7301
15314 Devonshire St Ste C Mission Hills (91345) ***(G-14185)***
Ecologic Brands Inc......209 239-3600
550 Carnegie St Manteca (95337) ***(G-9260)***
Ecology Action of Santa Cruz......831 426-5925
877 Cedar St Ste 240 Santa Cruz (95060) ***(G-26508)***
Ecology and Environment Inc......510 893-6700
505 Sansome St Ste 300 San Francisco (94111) ***(G-27906)***
Ecology Control Industries......510 235-1393
255 Parr Blvd Richmond (94801) ***(G-6626)***
Ecompanies LLC......310 586-4000
2120 Colorado Ave Fl 3 Santa Monica (90404) ***(G-5593)***
Econa Corp......619 722-6555
1344 Paizay Pl Unit 732 Chula Vista (91913) ***(G-26331)***
Econco Broadcast Service, Woodland *Also called CPI Econco Division* ***(G-17931)***
Econnections Inc......626 307-6200
75 N Fair Oaks Ave Pasadena (91103) ***(G-27010)***
Econo Air, Brea *Also called Mddr Inc* ***(G-2291)***
Econo Air Conditioning Inc......714 630-3090
3366 E La Palma Ave Anaheim (92806) ***(G-2214)***
Econo Lodge Inn & Suites, Buttonwillow *Also called Choice Hotels Intl Inc* ***(G-12516)***
Economic Dev Corp of La County......213 622-4300
444 S Flower St Ste 3700 Los Angeles (90071) ***(G-27907)***
Economic Development, Riverside *Also called County of Riverside* ***(G-24331)***
Economic Development Dept, Hemet *Also called County of Riverside* ***(G-23885)***
Economy Inn......760 256-5601
1243 E Main St Barstow (92311) ***(G-12609)***
Econosoft Inc......408 324-1203
2375 Zanker Rd Ste 250 San Jose (95131) ***(G-15154)***
Econtactlive Inc......209 863-8547
6436 Oakdale Rd Riverbank (95367) ***(G-17141)***
Ecorp Consulting Inc (PA)......916 782-9100
2525 Warren Dr Rocklin (95677) ***(G-27420)***
Ecorptech LLC......408 216-8116
4732 Travertino St Dublin (94568) ***(G-14872)***
Ecrio Inc......408 973-7290
19925 Stevens Creek Blvd Cupertino (95014) ***(G-15647)***
Ecs Refining LLC......209 774-5000
2222 S Sinclair Ave Stockton (95215) ***(G-6477)***
Ecs South Bay Head Start, Chula Vista *Also called Episcopal Community* ***(G-24460)***
Ed Rocha Livestock Trnsp Inc......209 538-1302
2400 Nickerson Dr Modesto (95358) ***(G-4145)***
ED Safety Services Inc......209 333-0807
1040 W Kettleman Ln # 388 Lodi (95240) ***(G-1770)***
Ed Silva (PA)......831 675-2327
21 River Rd Gonzales (93926) ***(G-61)***
Ed Thoming & Sons Inc......209 835-2792
33600 S Koster Rd Tracy (95304) ***(G-199)***
Edaw Inc......619 233-1454
401 W A St Ste 1200 San Diego (92101) ***(G-764)***
Edaw Inc......916 414-5800
2020 L St Ste 400 Sacramento (95811) ***(G-765)***
Edaw Inc (HQ)......415 955-2800
300 California St Fl 5 San Francisco (94104) ***(G-11964)***
Edc Probation, Shingle Springs *Also called County of El Dorado* ***(G-23803)***
Edc Service Corporation (del)......909 390-4747
415 N Vineyard Ave # 205 Ontario (91764) ***(G-9717)***
Edco Disposal Corporation Inc (PA)......619 287-7555
2755 California Ave Signal Hill (90755) ***(G-6478)***
Edco Disposal Corporation Inc......714 522-3577
6762 Stanton Ave Buena Park (90621) ***(G-6479)***
Edco Drywall Company, Westminster *Also called Edco Drywall Inc* ***(G-2891)***
Edco Drywall Inc......714 799-9886
7200 Hazard Ave Westminster (92683) ***(G-2891)***
Edco Health Info Solution......909 793-0613
1804 Tribute Rd Ste F Sacramento (95815) ***(G-17142)***
Edco Health Info Solution......909 793-0613
2015 W Park Ave Ste 13 Redlands (92373) ***(G-17143)***
Edco Waste & Recycl Svcs Inc (HQ)......760 744-2700
224 S Las Posas Rd San Marcos (92078) ***(G-6480)***
Edcta, Diamond Springs *Also called El Dorado County Transit Auth* ***(G-3644)***
Edd Payroll Services, Sacramento *Also called Employment Dev Cal Dept* ***(G-14649)***
Edelman Productions, San Francisco *Also called New Paradigm Productions Inc* ***(G-18120)***
Edelman Public Relations, San Francisco *Also called Daniel J Edelman Inc* ***(G-27745)***
Edelman Public Relations, Los Angeles *Also called Daniel J Edelman Inc* ***(G-27746)***
Edelman Public Relations, San Mateo *Also called Daniel J Edelman Inc* ***(G-13965)***
Edelman Public Relations, Los Angeles *Also called Daniel J Edelman Inc* ***(G-13966)***
Eden Area Regnl Occupational P......510 293-2900
26316 Hesperian Blvd Hayward (94545) ***(G-24336)***
Eden Area Rop School, Hayward *Also called Eden Area Regnl Occupational P* ***(G-24336)***
Eden Housing Inc......510 582-1460
22645 Grand St Hayward (94541) ***(G-1309)***
Eden Housing Management Inc (PA)......510 582-1460
22645 Grand St Hayward (94541) ***(G-11489)***
Eden Labs Med Group Inc......510 537-1234
20103 Lake Chabot Rd Castro Valley (94546) ***(G-19511)***
Eden Township Hospital Dst......510 537-1234
20103 Lake Chabot Rd Castro Valley (94546) ***(G-21550)***
Eden Villa, Castro Valley *Also called Ku Kyoung* ***(G-20715)***
Eden West Rehabilitation......510 783-4811
1805 West St Hayward (94545) ***(G-20526)***
Edf Msschstts Spnsor Mmber LLC......888 903-6926
15445 Innovation Dr San Diego (92128) ***(G-6127)***
Edf Renewable Energy, San Diego *Also called Milo Wind Project LLC* ***(G-6148)***
Edf Renewable Energy Inc (PA)......858 521-3300
15445 Innovation Dr San Diego (92128) ***(G-6128)***
Edf Renewable Energy Inc......760 329-1437
15445 Innovation Dr San Diego (92128) ***(G-26332)***
Edf Renewable Services Inc (HQ)......858 521-3575
15445 Innovation Dr San Diego (92128) ***(G-17821)***
Edf Rnwable Asset Holdings Inc......888 903-6926
15445 Innovation Dr San Diego (92128) ***(G-6129)***
EDG Interior Arch & Design Inc......415 454-2277
7 Hamilton Landing # 200 Novato (94949) ***(G-17144)***
Edge Mortgage Advisory Co LLC......714 564-5800
2125 E Katella Ave # 350 Anaheim (92806) ***(G-27908)***
Edge Systems LLC......562 597-0102
2277 Redondo Ave Signal Hill (90755) ***(G-7263)***
Edgemine Inc......323 267-8222
1801 E 50th St Los Angeles (90058) ***(G-8380)***
Edgemoor Hospital......619 956-2880
655 Park Center Dr Santee (92071) ***(G-22139)***
Edgewater Convalescent Hosp......562 434-0974
2625 E 4th St Long Beach (90814) ***(G-20527)***
Edgewater Networks Inc......408 351-7200
5225 Hellyer Ave Ste 100 San Jose (95138) ***(G-5594)***
Edgewater Plumbing of Benicia......707 747-9204
5143 Port Chicago Hwy Concord (94520) ***(G-2215)***
Edgewater Skilled Nursing Ctr, Long Beach *Also called Edgewater Convalescent Hosp* ***(G-20527)***
Edgewave Inc......858 676-2277
15333 Ave Of Sci Ste 100 San Diego (92128) ***(G-15648)***
Edgewood Center, Azusa *Also called RES-Care California Inc* ***(G-21100)***
Edgewood Ctr For Childrens......415 865-3000
101 15th St San Francisco (94103) ***(G-23954)***
Edgewood Ctr For Childrens (PA)......415 681-3211
1801 Vicente St San Francisco (94116) ***(G-24640)***
Edgewood Family Center, San Francisco *Also called Edgewood Ctr For Childrens* ***(G-23954)***
Edgewood Partners Insur Ctr......559 451-3189
8050 N Palm Ave Ste 110 Fresno (93711) ***(G-10695)***
Edgewood Partners Insur Ctr......415 356-3900
135 Main St Fl 21 San Francisco (94105) ***(G-10696)***

ALPHABETIC

Edgewood Partners Insur Ctr (PA)..............................415 356-3900
135 Main St 21f San Francisco (94105) *(G-10697)*
Edison Capital (HQ)..............................909 594-3789
18101 Von Karman Ave Irvine (92612) *(G-12302)*
Edison International (PA)..............................626 302-2222
2244 Walnut Grove Ave Rosemead (91770) *(G-6130)*
Edison Mission Energy (HQ)..............................714 513-8000
3 Macarthur Pl Ste 100 Santa Ana (92707) *(G-6286)*
Edison Mssion Midwest Holdings..............................626 302-2222
2244 Walnut Grove Ave Rosemead (91770) *(G-6131)*
Edith Witt Senior Community, San Francisco *Also called Mercy Hsing California Xxxiv (G-11167)*
Edmin Open Systems Inc (PA)..............................858 712-9341
5471 Krny Vlla Rd Ste 310 San Diego (92123) *(G-16362)*
Edmonds Record Group..............................323 860-1520
1635 N Cahuenga Blvd Fl 6 Los Angeles (90028) *(G-18465)*
Edmunds Holding Company (PA)..............................310 309-6300
1620 26th St Ste 400s Santa Monica (90404) *(G-16231)*
Edmunds.com, Santa Monica *Also called Edmunds Holding Company (G-16231)*
Edo LLC..............................914 641-2000
3500 Willow Ln Thousand Oaks (91361) *(G-25778)*
EDS West LLC..............................323 887-7367
6666 E Washington Blvd Commerce (90040) *(G-4013)*
Edsi..............................760 728-1899
504 E Alvarado St Ste 109 Fallbrook (92028) *(G-25779)*
Education For Change..............................510 879-3140
3709 E 12th St Oakland (94601) *(G-27011)*
Education Management Corp..............................818 487-0201
11128 Magnolia Blvd North Hollywood (91601) *(G-27012)*
Education Management Corp..............................858 810-0215
7650 Mission Valley Rd San Diego (92108) *(G-27013)*
Education Program Associates..............................408 374-3720
1 W Campbell Ave 45e Campbell (95008) *(G-24918)*
Educational Employees Cr Un (PA)..............................559 437-7700
2222 W Shaw Ave Fresno (93711) *(G-9662)*
Educational Employees Cr Un..............................559 587-4460
1460 W 7th St Hanford (93230) *(G-9663)*
Educational Employees Cr Un..............................559 896-0222
3488 W Shaw Ave Fresno (93711) *(G-9664)*
Educational Employees Cr Un..............................209 726-7421
127 W El Portal Dr Ste A Merced (95348) *(G-9665)*
Educational Funding Co LLC..............................858 350-1313
11452 El Camino Real # 110 San Diego (92130) *(G-9729)*
Educational Media Foundation (PA)..............................916 251-1600
5700 W Oaks Blvd Rocklin (95765) *(G-5766)*
Educational Services Division, Ontario *Also called American Fidelity Assurance Co (G-10591)*
Edward B Ward & Company Inc (HQ)..............................415 330-6600
99 S Hill Dr Ste B Brisbane (94005) *(G-7736)*
Edward E Straine CPA..............................916 646-6464
1760 Creekside Oaks Dr Sacramento (95833) *(G-26333)*
Edward Straling..............................760 887-3673
2940 Grace Ln Ste C Costa Mesa (92626) *(G-2580)*
Edward Thomas Companies..............................714 782-7500
640 W Katella Ave Anaheim (92802) *(G-12610)*
Edward Thomas Hospitality Corp..............................310 458-0030
1 Pico Blvd Santa Monica (90405) *(G-12611)*
Edward Vincent Park, Inglewood *Also called City of Inglewood (G-19173)*
Edwardo Z Garcia..............................661 854-5414
380 Tucker St Arvin (93203) *(G-656)*
Edwards Brea 10 West..............................714 672-4136
255 W Birch St Brea (92821) *(G-18320)*
Edwards Cinemas University, Irvine *Also called Edwards Theatres Circuit Inc (G-18333)*
Edwards Frank Co (HQ)..............................801 736-8000
1565 Adrian Rd Burlingame (94010) *(G-7840)*
Edwards Lifesciences LLC (HQ)..............................949 250-2500
1 Edwards Way Irvine (92614) *(G-19512)*
Edwards Technologies Inc..............................310 536-7070
139 Maryland St El Segundo (90245) *(G-2581)*
Edwards Theaters, Camarillo *Also called Edwards Theatres Circuit Inc (G-18332)*
Edwards Theatres Circuit Inc..............................951 361-1917
8032 Limonite Ave Riverside (92509) *(G-18321)*
Edwards Theatres Circuit Inc..............................714 428-0962
901 S Coast Dr Costa Mesa (92626) *(G-18322)*
Edwards Theatres Circuit Inc..............................619 660-3460
2951 Jamacha Rd El Cajon (92019) *(G-18323)*
Edwards Theatres Circuit Inc..............................949 582-4078
27741 Crown Valley Pkwy # 323 Mission Viejo (92691) *(G-18324)*
Edwards Theatres Circuit Inc..............................858 635-7716
10733 Westview Pkwy San Diego (92126) *(G-18325)*
Edwards Theatres Circuit Inc..............................714 557-5701
1561 W Sunflower Ave Santa Ana (92704) *(G-18326)*
Edwards Theatres Circuit Inc (HQ)..............................949 640-4600
300 Newport Center Dr Newport Beach (92660) *(G-18327)*
Edwards Theatres Circuit Inc..............................562 429-3321
7501 Carson Blvd Long Beach (90808) *(G-18328)*
Edwards Theatres Circuit Inc..............................760 471-3734
1180 W San Marcos Blvd San Marcos (92078) *(G-18329)*
Edwards Theatres Circuit Inc..............................562 403-1133
12761 Towne Center Dr Artesia (90703) *(G-18330)*
Edwards Theatres Circuit Inc..............................951 296-0144
40750 Winchester Rd Temecula (92591) *(G-18331)*
Edwards Theatres Circuit Inc..............................805 383-8866
680 Ventura Blvd Camarillo (93010) *(G-18332)*
Edwards Theatres Circuit Inc..............................949 854-8811
4245 Campus Dr Irvine (92612) *(G-18333)*
Edwards Theatres Circuit Inc..............................626 580-7660
10661 Valley Blvd El Monte (91731) *(G-18334)*
Edwards Theatres Circuit Inc..............................805 526-4329
1457 E Los Angeles Ave Simi Valley (93065) *(G-18335)*
Edwards Theatres Circuit Inc..............................805 347-1164
1521 S Bradley Rd Santa Maria (93454) *(G-18336)*
Eedar, Carlsbad *Also called Electronic Entrmt Design & RES (G-26659)*
Ees Residential Group Homes..............................408 265-8780
5369 Camden Ave Ste 280 San Jose (95124) *(G-24641)*
Effort, The, Sacramento *Also called Wellspace Health (G-22864)*
Efilm LLC..............................323 463-7041
1144 N Las Palmas Ave Los Angeles (90038) *(G-18082)*
Efinance Corporation..............................866 433-6878
795 Folsom St Fl 1 San Francisco (94107) *(G-17145)*
Eforcity Corp - Nfm..............................626 442-3168
18525 Railroad St City of Industry (91748) *(G-7559)*
Efs West..............................661 705-8200
28472 Constellation Rd Valencia (91355) *(G-25780)*
Efuel LLC..............................408 280-5235
1346 E Taylor St San Jose (95133) *(G-9017)*
Egain Corporation (PA)..............................408 636-4500
1252 Borregas Ave Sunnyvale (94089) *(G-15649)*
Eggleston Youth Centers Inc (PA)..............................626 480-8107
13001 Ramona Blvd Ste E Irwindale (91706) *(G-23955)*
Egl Holdco Inc..............................800 678-7423
18200 Von Karman Ave # 1000 Irvine (92612) *(G-15650)*
Egnyte Inc (PA)..............................650 968-4018
1350 W Middlefield Rd Mountain View (94043) *(G-15155)*
Ego Inc..............................626 447-0296
444 E Huntington Dr # 300 Arcadia (91006) *(G-26334)*
Eharmony Inc (PA)..............................424 258-1199
10900 Wilshire Blvd Los Angeles (90024) *(G-18628)*
Eharmony.com, Los Angeles *Also called Eharmony Inc (G-18628)*
EHC LIFEBUILDERS, Milpitas *Also called Homefrst Svcs Santa Clara Cnty (G-24011)*
Ehealth Inc (PA)..............................650 584-2700
440 E Middlefield Rd Mountain View (94043) *(G-10698)*
Ehealth Insurance.com, Gold River *Also called Ehealthinsurance Services Inc (G-15156)*
Ehealthinsurance Services Inc (HQ)..............................650 584-2700
440 E Middlefield Rd Mountain View (94043) *(G-10699)*
Ehealthinsurance Services Inc..............................916 608-6101
11919 Foundation Pl # 100 Gold River (95670) *(G-15156)*
Ehealthwirecom Inc..............................916 924-8092
2450 Venture Oaks Way # 100 Sacramento (95833) *(G-22953)*
Ehmcke Sheet Metal Corp..............................619 477-6484
840 W 19th St National City (91950) *(G-3168)*
Ehs Medical Group, Monterey Park *Also called Synermed (G-20126)*
Ehsmd, El Monte *Also called Employee Health System Medical (G-25134)*
Eichleay Engineers Inc Cal..............................562 256-8600
3780 Kilroy Airport Way # 440 Long Beach (90806) *(G-25781)*
Eichleay Inc (PA)..............................925 689-7000
1390 Willow Pass Rd # 600 Concord (94520) *(G-25782)*
Eie Electric, Costa Mesa *Also called Pmd Industries Inc (G-2686)*
Eight Star Commodities, El Centro *Also called All Star Seed (G-506)*
Eight Star Equipment, El Centro *Also called Noblesse Oblige Inc (G-498)*
Eighty One Enterprise Inc..............................626 371-1980
9401 Whitmore St El Monte (91731) *(G-8381)*
Eileen Nottoli..............................415 837-1515
3 Embarcadero Ctr # 1200 San Francisco (94111) *(G-23232)*
Eileen Shi..............................866 777-6104
2635 N 1st St Ste 149 San Jose (95134) *(G-27421)*
Eineridge Care Center, Sylmar *Also called Quality Long Term Care Nev Inc (G-20860)*
Einstein Dental, San Diego *Also called Einstein Industries Inc (G-15157)*
Einstein Industries Inc..............................858 459-1182
6675 Mesa Ridge Rd San Diego (92121) *(G-15157)*
Eis Group Inc..............................415 402-2622
345 California St Fl 10 San Francisco (94104) *(G-15651)*
Eisenberg International Corp (PA)..............................818 365-8161
9128 Jordan Ave Chatsworth (91311) *(G-8339)*
Eisenberg Village, Reseda *Also called Los Angles Jewish HM For Aging (G-20748)*
Eisenhower Desert Crdiolgy Ctr, Rancho Mirage *Also called Charlie W Shaeffer Jr MD (G-19427)*
Eisenhower Medical Center (PA)..............................760 340-3911
39000 Bob Hope Dr Rancho Mirage (92270) *(G-21551)*
Eisner Pediatric Fmly Med Ctr, Los Angeles *Also called Pediatric & Family Medical Ctr (G-22796)*
Eisneramper LLP..............................415 974-6000
1 Market Ste 620 San Francisco (94105) *(G-26335)*
Eiu of California, Bakersfield *Also called Electrical & Instrumentation (G-2586)*
Ek Health Services Inc..............................408 973-0888
992 S De Anza Blvd Ste 10 San Jose (95129) *(G-27422)*
Ekedal Masonry & Concrete Inc..............................949 720-8011
19600 Fairchild Ste 123 Irvine (92612) *(G-2812)*
El & El Wood Products Corp (PA)..............................909 591-0339
6011 Schaefer Ave Chino (91710) *(G-6921)*
El Al Israel Airlines Ltd..............................323 852-1252
6404 Wilshire Blvd # 1250 Los Angeles (90048) *(G-5008)*
El Aviso Magazine..............................323 586-9199
4850 Gage Ave Bell (90201) *(G-9164)*
El Caballero Country Club..............................818 654-3000
18300 Tarzana Dr Tarzana (91356) *(G-18944)*
El Cajon Ford, El Cajon *Also called El Cajon Motors (G-17699)*
El Cajon Medical Offices, El Cajon *Also called Kaiser Foundation Hospitals (G-21653)*
El Cajon Motors (PA)..............................619 579-8888
1595 E Main St El Cajon (92021) *(G-17699)*
El Cajon Plumbing & Htg Sup Co..............................619 449-7300
1655 N Magnolia Ave El Cajon (92020) *(G-7737)*
El Cajon Vly Convalescent Ctr..............................619 440-1211
510 E Washington Ave El Cajon (92020) *(G-20528)*
El Camino Care Center, Carmichael *Also called Helios Healthcare LLC (G-20662)*

ALPHABETIC

El Camino Children & Fmly Svcs......562 364-1258
9900 Lakewood Blvd # 104 Downey (90240) ***(G-23956)***
El Camino Country Club, Oceanside *Also called American Golf Corporation* ***(G-18866)***
El Camino Gardens, Carmichael *Also called Atria Senior Living Group Inc* ***(G-11091)***
El Camino Hospital......650 988-7444
1503 Grant Rd Ste 120 Mountain View (94040) ***(G-23957)***
El Camino Hospital......650 940-7000
2240 Tully Rd San Jose (95122) ***(G-22212)***
El Camino Hospital......650 940-7310
2505 Hospital Dr Ste 1 Mountain View (94040) ***(G-22626)***
El Camino Hospital......650 988-4825
625 Ellis St Ste 100 Mountain View (94043) ***(G-22140)***
El Camino Hospital Auxiliary......650 940-7214
2500 Grant Rd Mountain View (94040) ***(G-22430)***
El Camino Mem Pk & Mortuary, San Diego *Also called Stewart Enterprises Inc* ***(G-13716)***
El Camino Rental......760 722-7368
1833 Oceanside Blvd Ste D Oceanside (92054) ***(G-14537)***
El Camino Rental......760 438-7368
5701 El Camino Real Carlsbad (92008) ***(G-17641)***
El Camino Surgery Center LLC......650 961-1200
2480 Grant Rd Fl 1 Mountain View (94040) ***(G-21552)***
El Camino YMCA, Mountain View *Also called YMCA of Silicon Valley* ***(G-25433)***
El Capitan Canyon, Santa Barbara *Also called El Capitan Ranch LLC* ***(G-13480)***
El Capitan Ranch LLC......805 685-3887
11560 Calle Real Santa Barbara (93117) ***(G-13480)***
El Centro Regional Medical Ctr (PA)......760 339-7100
1415 Ross Ave El Centro (92243) ***(G-21553)***
El Clasificado (PA)......323 837-4095
11205 Imperial Hwy Norwalk (90650) ***(G-13968)***
El Concilio San Mateo Cnty Inc......650 373-1080
1419 Burlingame Ave Ste N Burlingame (94010) ***(G-23958)***
El Cordova Hotel......619 435-4131
1351 Orange Ave Coronado (92118) ***(G-12612)***
El Dorado Country Club......760 346-8081
46000 Fairway Dr Indian Wells (92210) ***(G-18945)***
El Dorado County Transit Auth......530 642-5383
6565 Commerce Way Ste A Diamond Springs (95619) ***(G-3644)***
El Dorado Enterprises Inc......310 719-9800
1000 W Redondo Beach Blvd Gardena (90247) ***(G-12613)***
El Dorado Irrigation District......530 622-4513
2890 Mosquito Rd Placerville (95667) ***(G-6346)***
El Dorado Savings Bank (PA)......530 622-1492
4040 El Dorado Rd Placerville (95667) ***(G-9570)***
El Dorado Wtr & Shower Svc Inc......530 622-8995
5821 Mother Lode Dr Placerville (95667) ***(G-6347)***
El Encanto Healthcare & Rehab......626 336-1274
555 El Encanto Rd City of Industry (91745) ***(G-20529)***
El Encanto Home Health Care, City of Industry *Also called El Encanto Healthcare & Rehab* ***(G-20529)***
El Guapo Spices and Herbs Pkg, Commerce *Also called El Guapo Spices Inc* ***(G-8832)***
El Guapo Spices Inc (PA)......213 312-1300
6200 E Slauson Ave Commerce (90040) ***(G-8832)***
El Macero Country Club Inc......530 753-3363
44571 Clubhouse Dr El Macero (95618) ***(G-18946)***
El Mexicano, Montebello *Also called Marquez Brothers Intl Inc* ***(G-8495)***
El Monte Cinema 8, El Monte *Also called Edwards Theatres Circuit Inc* ***(G-18334)***
El Monte Community Credit Un......626 444-0501
11718 Ramona Blvd El Monte (91732) ***(G-9666)***
El Monte Convalescent Hospital......626 442-1500
4096 Easy St El Monte (91731) ***(G-21208)***
El Monte Rents Inc (PA)......972 562-1900
12818 Firestone Blvd Santa Fe Springs (90670) ***(G-17706)***
El Monte Rv, Santa Fe Springs *Also called El Monte Rents Inc* ***(G-17706)***
El Nido Family Centers (PA)......818 830-3646
10200 Sepulveda Blvd # 350 Mission Hills (91345) ***(G-23959)***
El Pas-Los Angles Lmsne Ex Inc......213 623-2323
260 E 6th St Los Angeles (90014) ***(G-3901)***
El Paseo Limousine, Santa Clara *Also called Worldwide Ground Transportatio* ***(G-3860)***
El Prado Golf Course LP......909 597-1751
6555 Pine Ave Chino (91708) ***(G-18738)***
El Rancho Motel Inc......650 588-8500
1100 El Camino Real Millbrae (94030) ***(G-12614)***
El Rancho Vista Hlth Care Ctr, Pico Rivera *Also called Mariner Health Care Inc* ***(G-20768)***
El Segundo Eductl Foundation......310 615-2650
641 Sheldon St El Segundo (90245) ***(G-24919)***
El Sol, Modesto *Also called McClatchy Newspapers Inc* ***(G-17319)***
El-Com Cabletek, Garden Grove *Also called Elrob Inc* ***(G-7560)***
Eladh LP......323 268-5514
4060 Whittier Blvd Los Angeles (90023) ***(G-21554)***
Elan Drug Delivery Inc......770 531-8100
180 Oyster Point Blvd South San Francisco (94080) ***(G-26509)***
Elan Drug Technologies, South San Francisco *Also called Elan Drug Delivery Inc* ***(G-26509)***
Elance-Odesk, Mountain View *Also called Upwork Inc* ***(G-13933)***
Elance-Odesk, Mountain View *Also called Odesk Corporation* ***(G-14714)***
Elastica Inc......925 699-6714
3055 Olin Ave Ste 2000 San Jose (95128) ***(G-15158)***
Elateral Inc......650 917-9141
101 1st St Ste 192 Los Altos (94022) ***(G-27014)***
Elavon Inc......954 776-7990
1281 9th Ave Unit 706 San Diego (92101) ***(G-16232)***
Elavon Inc......925 734-8939
4234 Hacienda Dr Ste 250 Pleasanton (94588) ***(G-16233)***
Elcor Electric Inc......408 986-1320
3310 Bassett St Santa Clara (95054) ***(G-2582)***
ELDER CARE ALLIANCE, Alameda *Also called Salem Lutheran Home Associatio* ***(G-24796)***
Elder Care Alliance Camarillo......510 769-2700
1301 Marina Village Pkwy # 210 Alameda (94501) ***(G-24642)***
Elder Care Alliance San Rafael......510 769-2700
1301 Marina Village Pkwy # 210 Alameda (94501) ***(G-20530)***
Eldorado Care Center LP......619 440-1211
510 E Washington Ave El Cajon (92020) ***(G-20531)***
Eldorado Community Service Ctr......424 227-7971
335 E Manchester Blvd Inglewood (90301) ***(G-19513)***
Elecnor Inc......909 993-5470
4331 Schaefer Ave Chino (91710) ***(G-2216)***
Electra Owners Assoc......619 236-3310
700 W E St San Diego (92101) ***(G-25084)***
Electrcal Instrumentation Intl......661 836-9466
6950 District Blvd Bakersfield (93313) ***(G-2583)***
Electric Department, Santa Clara *Also called City of Santa Clara* ***(G-6117)***
Electric Motor & Supply Co., Fresno *Also called Electric Motor Shop* ***(G-7436)***
Electric Motor Shop......559 233-1153
250 Broadway St Fresno (93721) ***(G-7436)***
Electric Power RES Inst Inc (PA)......650 855-2000
3420 Hillview Ave Palo Alto (94304) ***(G-26510)***
Electric Sales Unlimited......562 463-8300
9023 Norwalk Blvd Santa Fe Springs (90670) ***(G-7437)***
Electric Svc & Sup Co Pasadena......626 795-8641
2668 E Foothill Blvd Pasadena (91107) ***(G-2584)***
Electric Tech Construction Inc......925 849-5324
1910 Mark Ct Ste 130 Concord (94520) ***(G-1928)***
Electric USA......800 921-1151
480 Aldo Ave Santa Clara (95054) ***(G-2585)***
Electrical & Instrumentation......661 836-9466
6950 District Blvd Bakersfield (93313) ***(G-2586)***
Electrical Distributors Co, San Jose *Also called Chester C Lehmann Co Inc* ***(G-7426)***
ELECTRICAL TRAINING TRUST, Commerce *Also called Los Angeles County Apprentices* ***(G-12160)***
Electro Rent Corporation (PA)......818 786-2525
6060 Sepulveda Blvd # 300 Van Nuys (91411) ***(G-14538)***
Electrolux Home Products Inc......909 605-9448
701 Malaga St Ontario (91761) ***(G-7495)***
Electronic Arts Inc (PA)......650 628-1500
209 Redwood Shores Pkwy Redwood City (94065) ***(G-15652)***
Electronic Clearing House Inc (HQ)......805 419-8700
730 Paseo Camarillo Camarillo (93010) ***(G-15653)***
Electronic Control Systems LLC......858 513-1911
12575 Kirkham Ct Ste 1 Poway (92064) ***(G-2587)***
Electronic Data Care Inc......310 791-2600
23670 Hawthorne Blvd # 208 Torrance (90505) ***(G-15938)***
Electronic Entrmt Design & RES......760 579-7100
2075 Corte Del Nogal B Carlsbad (92011) ***(G-26659)***
Electronic Online Systems Intl......760 431-8400
2292 Faraday Ave Frnt Carlsbad (92008) ***(G-15939)***
Electronic Recyclers America, Fresno *Also called Electronic Recyclers Intl Inc* ***(G-6481)***
Electronic Recyclers Intl Inc (PA)......800 884-8466
7815 N Palm Ave Ste 140 Fresno (93711) ***(G-6481)***
Electrosonic Inc (HQ)......818 333-3600
3320 N San Fernando Blvd Burbank (91504) ***(G-25783)***
Elegance Exotic Wood Flooring, Fontana *Also called Elegance Wood Products Inc* ***(G-6858)***
Elegance Wood Products Inc......909 484-7676
7351 Mcguire Ave Fontana (92336) ***(G-6858)***
Elegant Surfaces......209 823-9388
3640 Amrcn Rver Dr 150 Sacramento (95864) ***(G-6981)***
Element Mtrls Tech HB Inc......310 632-8500
18100 S Wilmington Ave Compton (90220) ***(G-26846)***
Element Mtrls Tech HB Inc (HQ)......714 892-1961
15062 Bolsa Chica St Huntington Beach (92649) ***(G-26847)***
Elemental Led Inc......877 564-5051
1195 Park Ave Ste 211 Emeryville (94608) ***(G-7438)***
Elements Behavioral Health Inc (HQ)......562 741-6470
5000 E Spring St Ste 650 Long Beach (90815) ***(G-22727)***
Elena Villa Healthcare Center......562 868-0591
13226 Studebaker Rd Norwalk (90650) ***(G-21209)***
Elevate Expo Inc......415 625-2821
1361 Lowrie Ave South San Francisco (94080) ***(G-17146)***
Elevate Property Services LP......562 219-2101
19700 Fairchild Ste 150 Irvine (92612) ***(G-11252)***
Eleven Inc......415 707-1111
500 Sansome St San Francisco (94111) ***(G-13842)***
Eleven Agency LLC......949 679-1182
4 Studebaker Irvine (92618) ***(G-13843)***
Eleven Communications, San Francisco *Also called Eleven Inc* ***(G-13842)***
Eleven Western Builders Inc......760 796-6346
2862 Executive Pl Escondido (92029) ***(G-1548)***
Elias Elliott Lampasi Fehn (PA)......951 689-5031
7251 Magnolia Ave Riverside (92504) ***(G-20253)***
Elica Health Centers......916 454-2345
3701 J St Ste 201 Sacramento (95816) ***(G-19514)***
Elim Alzheimers & Rehab......559 320-2200
668 E Bullard Ave Fresno (93710) ***(G-20532)***
Elioco Produce Inc......831 424-5450
26490 Encinal Rd Salinas (93908) ***(G-657)***
Eliseo Esparza Delgadillo......209 745-3937
88 Wildflower Dr Galt (95632) ***(G-658)***
Elite, Culver City *Also called West Publishing Corporation* ***(G-16081)***
Elite & Associates......805 582-0353
18605 Parthenia St Northridge (91324) ***(G-3169)***
Elite Anywhere Corp......917 860-9247
82585 Showcase Pkwy Indio (92203) ***(G-5065)***
Elite Aviation LLC......818 988-5387
7501 Hayvenhurst Pl Van Nuys (91406) ***(G-4880)***
Elite Craftsman (PA)......562 989-3511
2763 Saint Louis Ave Long Beach (90755) ***(G-14288)***
Elite Enfrcment SEC Sltons Inc......866 354-8308
29970 Technology Dr Murrieta (92563) ***(G-16632)***

ALPHABETIC

Elite Engineering Services Inc...949 536-7199
1641-1645 Reynolds Irvine (92614) *(G-25784)*
Elite Information Group Inc (HQ)...323 642-5200
5100 W Goldleaf Cir # 100 Los Angeles (90056) *(G-15940)*
Elite Landscaping Inc...559 292-7760
2972 Larkin Ave Clovis (93612) *(G-847)*
Elite Maintenance Services Inc...619 516-7000
7770 Regents Rd Ste 113 San Diego (92122) *(G-14289)*
Elite Nursing Services Inc...949 475-0700
1700 E Garry Ave Ste 103 Santa Ana (92705) *(G-14645)*
Elite Power Inc...916 739-1580
6530 Asher Ln Sacramento (95828) *(G-2588)*
Elite Roofing Company, Northridge *Also called Elite & Associates (G-3169)*
Elite Security Services Inc...949 222-2203
18006 Sky Park Cir # 205 Irvine (92614) *(G-16633)*
Elite Show Services Inc...619 574-1589
2878 Camino Del Rio S # 260 San Diego (92108) *(G-16634)*
Elite Tek Services Inc...714 881-5301
131 Mercer Way Costa Mesa (92627) *(G-16363)*
Elite Tile, Livermore *Also called Mthuron Inc (G-3020)*
Elitecare Medical Staffing LLC...559 438-7700
761 E Locust Ave Ste 103 Fresno (93720) *(G-14646)*
Elitegroup Cmpt Systems Inc...510 794-2952
6851 Mowry Ave Newark (94560) *(G-7123)*
Elizabeth Glaser Pedia...310 231-0400
16130 Ventura Blvd # 250 Encino (91436) *(G-22954)*
Elizabeth Larson...415 409-7300
3736 Jackson St San Francisco (94118) *(G-11490)*
Elizabethan Inn Associates LP...916 448-1300
1935 Wright St Apt 231 Sacramento (95825) *(G-12615)*
Elk Grove Adult Cmnty Training...916 431-3162
8810 Elk Grove Blvd Elk Grove (95624) *(G-25085)*
Elk Grove Unified School Dst...916 686-7733
8421 Gerber Rd Sacramento (95828) *(G-3925)*
Elk Valley Casino Inc...707 464-1020
2500 Howland Hill Rd Crescent City (95531) *(G-19205)*
Elkay Plastics Co Inc (PA)...323 722-7073
6000 Sheila St Commerce (90040) *(G-8189)*
Elkhorn Berry Farms LLC...831 722-2472
262 E Lake Ave Watsonville (95076) *(G-359)*
Elkor Properties, Santa Monica *Also called Roscoe Real Estate Ltd Partnr (G-13168)*
Ellation Inc...415 796-3560
835 Market St Ste 700 San Francisco (94103) *(G-15159)*
Ellen Degeneres Show, The, Burbank *Also called Wad Productions Inc (G-18188)*
Ellie Fashion Group Inc...818 355-3812
1735 Stewart St Fl 2 Santa Monica (90404) *(G-17147)*
Ellie Mae Inc (PA)...925 227-7000
4420 Rosewood Dr Ste 500 Pleasanton (94588) *(G-15160)*
Ellie Mae Inc...818 223-2000
24025 Park Sorrento # 210 Calabasas (91302) *(G-15161)*
Elliott and Elliott Co...510 444-7270
745 Kevin Ct Oakland (94621) *(G-3170)*
Elliott Auto Supply Co Inc...800 278-6394
448 W Katella Ave Orange (92867) *(G-6728)*
Elliott Auto Supply Co Inc...310 527-2500
1600 E Orangethorpe Ave Fullerton (92831) *(G-6729)*
Elliott Laboratories Inc...510 440-9500
41039 Boyce Rd Fremont (94538) *(G-22213)*
Ellis Building Contractors, Manhattan Beach *Also called Ebc Inc (G-1170)*
Ellis Paint, Los Angeles *Also called Berg Lacquer Co (G-9237)*
Ellison Biner...760 598-6500
2685 S Melrose Dr Vista (92081) *(G-17148)*
Ellison Construction-Framing, Brentwood *Also called Ellison Framing Inc (G-3045)*
Ellison Framing Inc...925 516-9269
160 Guthrie Ln Ste 13 Brentwood (94513) *(G-3045)*
Ellison Machinery Co (HQ)...562 949-8311
9912 Pioneer Blvd Santa Fe Springs (90670) *(G-7841)*
Ellison Technologies, Santa Fe Springs *Also called Ellison Machinery Co (G-7841)*
Ellite Management Inc...562 806-2062
7340 Firestone Blvd # 218 Downey (90241) *(G-27909)*
Elljay Acoustics Inc...714 961-1173
511 Cameron St Placentia (92870) *(G-2892)*
Elmco/Duddy Inc (HQ)...626 333-9942
15070 Proctor Ave City of Industry (91746) *(G-7708)*
Elmer F Karpe Inc...661 847-4800
8501 Camino Media Ste 400 Bakersfield (93311) *(G-11491)*
Elms Convalescent Hospital, Glendale *Also called Elms Sanitarium Inc (G-20533)*
Elms Sanitarium Inc...818 240-6720
212 W Chevy Chase Dr Glendale (91204) *(G-20533)*
Elmwood LNG TRM& Tran Care...510 665-2800
2829 Shattuck Ave Berkeley (94705) *(G-20534)*
Elrob Inc...714 230-6100
12691 Monarch St Garden Grove (92841) *(G-7560)*
Els...510 549-2929
2040 Addison St Berkeley (94704) *(G-27910)*
Els Architecture, Berkeley *Also called Els (G-27910)*
Els Investments...916 388-0308
8380 Rovana Cir Sacramento (95828) *(G-766)*
Elsinore Vly Municpl Wtr Dst (PA)...951 674-3146
31315 Chaney St Lake Elsinore (92530) *(G-6348)*
Elston Masonry Inc...760 728-3593
1422 Santa Margarita Dr Fallbrook (92028) *(G-2813)*
Elvira Sandoval...530 473-5718
2154 Hill Rd Williams (95987) *(G-14647)*
Elvis Schoenberg Production...323 344-1745
549 Marie Ave Los Angeles (90042) *(G-18389)*
Elysium Jennings LLC...661 679-1700
1600 Norris Rd Bakersfield (93308) *(G-1057)*

Elyxir Distributing LLC...831 761-6400
270 W Riverside Dr Watsonville (95076) *(G-9055)*
Emagia Corporation...408 654-6575
4500 Great America Pkwy # 120 Santa Clara (95054) *(G-17149)*
Emagined Security Inc...415 944-2977
2816 San Simeon Way San Carlos (94070) *(G-16883)*
Emanuel Medical Center Inc...209 667-5600
1801 N Olive Ave Turlock (95382) *(G-21555)*
Emanuel Medical Center Inc (HQ)...209 667-4200
825 Delbon Ave Turlock (95382) *(G-21556)*
Emanuel Medical Center Inc...209 664-2520
2121 Colorado Ave Ste A Turlock (95382) *(G-21557)*
Emax Laboratories Inc...310 618-8889
1835 W 205th St Torrance (90501) *(G-26848)*
Embarcadero Homes Association...209 951-4420
Lincoln Sq Condos Stockton (95207) *(G-25253)*
Embarcadero Inn Associates...415 495-2100
155 Steuart St San Francisco (94105) *(G-12616)*
Embarcadero Systems Corp...510 749-7400
1601 Harbor Bay Pkwy # 120 Alameda (94502) *(G-15162)*
Embarcadero, The, San Francisco *Also called Crunch LLC (G-18624)*
Embassador Private Securities...415 822-8811
1341 Evans Ave San Francisco (94124) *(G-9993)*
Embassy Sites-So San Francisco, South San Francisco *Also called Djont/Cmb Ssf (G-12578)*
Embassy Stes Monterey Bay Htl, Seaside *Also called Atrium Hotels LP (G-12403)*
Embassy Stes San Dego-La Jolla, San Diego *Also called Sunstone Top Gun LLC (G-13328)*
Embassy Suites, Milpitas *Also called Hilton Worldwide Inc (G-12716)*
Embassy Suites, Palmdale *Also called Sunstone Hotel Investors LLC (G-13319)*
Embassy Suites, El Segundo *Also called NBC Suite Hotel (G-13017)*
Embassy Suites, NAPA *Also called Hilton Worldwide Inc (G-12721)*
Embassy Suites, Downey *Also called Sanwa Jutaku Co Ltd (G-13219)*
Embassy Suites, Covina *Also called Hilton Worldwide Inc (G-12725)*
Embassy Suites, Burlingame *Also called Hilton Worldwide Inc (G-12728)*
Embassy Suites, Arcadia *Also called Hilton Worldwide Inc (G-12729)*
Embassy Suites, Downey *Also called Hilton Worldwide Inc (G-12730)*
Embassy Suites, Buena Park *Also called Hilton Worldwide Inc (G-12731)*
Embassy Suites, Irvine *Also called Hilton Worldwide Inc (G-12734)*
Embassy Suites, San Diego *Also called Hilton Worldwide Inc (G-12736)*
Embassy Suites, Los Angeles *Also called Sunstone Hotel Investors Inc (G-13315)*
Embassy Suites, San Rafael *Also called Hilton Worldwide Inc (G-12737)*
Embassy Suites, Brea *Also called Windsor Capital Group Inc (G-13419)*
Embassy Suites, Temecula *Also called Windsor Capital Group Inc (G-13420)*
Embassy Suites, Anaheim *Also called Hilton Worldwide Inc (G-12740)*
Embassy Suites, Santa Ana *Also called Windsor Capital Group Inc (G-13423)*
Embassy Suites, South San Francisco *Also called Hilton Worldwide Inc (G-12741)*
Embassy Suites, South Lake Tahoe *Also called Hilton Worldwide Inc (G-12742)*
Embassy Suites Anaheim Orange, Orange *Also called Ergs Aim Hotel Realty LLC (G-12622)*
Embassy Suites Arcadia, Santa Monica *Also called Windsor Capital Group Inc (G-13416)*
Embassy Suites El Paso, Santa Monica *Also called Windsor Capital Group Inc (G-13422)*
Embassy Suites Lompoc, Santa Monica *Also called Windsor Capital Group Inc (G-13417)*
Embassy Suites Management LLC...858 453-0400
4550 La Jolla Village Dr San Diego (92122) *(G-12617)*
Embassy Suites Walnut Creek, Walnut Creek *Also called Interstate Hotels Resorts Inc (G-27070)*
Embassy Suites- Santa Clara, Santa Clara *Also called Msr Hotels & Resorts Inc (G-13012)*
Embassy Suites- Santa Clara, Santa Clara *Also called Santa Clara Tenant Corp (G-13212)*
Embrane Inc...408 550-2700
2350 Mission College Blvd # 703 Santa Clara (95054) *(G-15163)*
EMC Corporation...925 948-9000
6701 Koll Center Pkwy # 150 Pleasanton (94566) *(G-7124)*
EMC Corporation...866 438-3622
17011 Beach Blvd Huntington Beach (92647) *(G-15654)*
EMC Corporation...408 566-2000
2841 Mission College Blvd Santa Clara (95054) *(G-15655)*
EMC Corporation...310 341-1600
2101 Rosecrans Ave # 3200 El Segundo (90245) *(G-16234)*
EMC Corporation...650 871-1970
250 Montgomery St Ste 400 San Francisco (94104) *(G-7125)*
Emc2, San Francisco *Also called EMC Corporation (G-7125)*
Emcor Fclities Svcs N Amer Inc...858 712-4700
9505 Chesapeake Dr San Diego (92123) *(G-2217)*
Emcor Services, Irvine *Also called Mesa Energy Systems Inc (G-2293)*
Emerald Brook LLC...760 345-4770
76000 Frank Sinatra Dr Palm Desert (92211) *(G-13481)*
Emerald Connect LLC (HQ)...800 233-2834
15050 Avenue Of Sci 200 San Diego (92128) *(G-16123)*
Emerald Desert Rv Resort, Palm Desert *Also called Emerald Brook LLC (G-13481)*
Emerald Expositions LLC (HQ)...949 226-5700
31910 Del Obispo St # 200 San Juan Capistrano (92675) *(G-17150)*
Emerald Landscape Services...714 844-2200
1041 N Kemp St Anaheim (92801) *(G-848)*
Emerald Ter Convalescent Hosp, Los Angeles *Also called Equicare Medical Supply Inc (G-20548)*
Emerald Textiles LLC...619 690-7353
1725 Dornoch Ct Ste 101 San Diego (92154) *(G-13503)*
Emercon Construction Inc (PA)...714 630-9615
2906 E Coronado St Anaheim (92806) *(G-1171)*
Emergency Ambulance Service...714 990-1331
3200 E Birch St Ste A Brea (92821) *(G-3787)*
Emergency Groups Office, Arcadia *Also called Ego Inc (G-26334)*
Emergency Medicine Specialist...714 543-8911
1010 W La Veta Ave # 755 Orange (92868) *(G-21558)*

ALPHABETIC SECTION
Encore Trucking Inc

Emergency Physicians Med Group, Citrus Heights *Also called Dignity Health* ***(G-19504)***
Emergency Reporting Systems, El Monte *Also called ERs SEC Alarm Systems Inc* ***(G-7440)***
Emergency Technologies Inc....818 765-4421
7345 Varna Ave North Hollywood (91605) ***(G-7439)***
Emergent Ventures Intl Inc....415 655-6617
1156 Clement St San Francisco (94118) ***(G-27911)***
Emerging Markets Growth Fund, Irvine *Also called American Funds Service Company* ***(G-10195)***
Emerik Hotel Corp....213 748-1291
1020 S Figueroa St Los Angeles (90015) ***(G-12618)***
Emeritus At Casa Glendale, Glendale *Also called Emeritus Corporation* ***(G-11125)***
Emeritus At Villa Colima, Walnut *Also called Emeritus Corporation* ***(G-21081)***
Emeritus Corporation....858 292-8044
5219 Clairemont Mesa Blvd San Diego (92117) ***(G-21078)***
Emeritus Corporation....707 996-7101
800 Oregon St Sonoma (95476) ***(G-21079)***
Emeritus Corporation....707 552-3336
2261 Tuolumne St Vallejo (94589) ***(G-21080)***
Emeritus Corporation....760 741-3055
1351 E Washington Ave Escondido (92027) ***(G-11124)***
Emeritus Corporation....818 246-7457
426 Piedmont Ave Glendale (91206) ***(G-11125)***
Emeritus Corporation....909 544-4871
19850 Colima Rd Walnut (91789) ***(G-21081)***
Emeritus Corporation....805 239-1313
1919 Creston Rd Ofc Paso Robles (93446) ***(G-11126)***
Emerson Elementary....818 558-5419
720 E Cypress Ave Burbank (91501) ***(G-25254)***
Emery Financial Inc (PA)....949 219-0640
620 Nwport Ctr Dr Ste 800 Newport Beach (92660) ***(G-9921)***
Emery Marina, Emeryville *Also called The Young Mens Chris Assoc of* ***(G-25374)***
Emery Smith Laboratories Inc....213 745-5333
781 E Washington Blvd Los Angeles (90021) ***(G-26849)***
Emery Smith Laboratories Inc....714 238-6133
1195 N Tustin Ave Anaheim (92807) ***(G-25785)***
Emeter Corporation....650 227-7770
4000 E 3rd Ave Fl 4 Foster City (94404) ***(G-15164)***
EMI Publishing, Santa Monica *Also called Screen Gems-EMI Music Inc* ***(G-17480)***
Emida Technologies, Foothill Ranch *Also called Debisys Inc* ***(G-9716)***
Eminence Home Health Care Inc....818 830-7113
16921 Parthenia St # 301 Northridge (91343) ***(G-22431)***
EMJ Hayward, Hayward *Also called Earle M Jorgensen Company* ***(G-7368)***
Emlab P&K LLC (HQ)....650 829-5800
1150 Bayhill Dr Ste 100 San Bruno (94066) ***(G-26850)***
Emmanuel Cnvlscent Hosp Almeda....510 521-5765
508 Westline Dr Alameda (94501) ***(G-21210)***
Emmett A Larkin Company Inc (PA)....415 986-2332
22 Battery St Ste 806 San Francisco (94111) ***(G-9994)***
Emmi Inc....213 622-7234
631 S Olive St Ste 302 Los Angeles (90014) ***(G-8099)***
Emmi Universal Fine Jeweller, Los Angeles *Also called Emmi Inc* ***(G-8099)***
Emmis Communications Corp....818 238-6705
2600 W Olive Ave Fl 8 Burbank (91505) ***(G-27423)***
Emmis Communications Corp....626 484-4440
790 E Colorado Blvd Fl 9 Pasadena (91101) ***(G-5767)***
Emmis Radio LLC....818 525-5000
2600 W Olive Ave Fl 8 Burbank (91505) ***(G-5768)***
Emn8, San Diego *Also called Tillster Inc* ***(G-16508)***
Emor Consulting Inc....408 505-0453
1570 Heritage Bay Dr San Jose (95138) ***(G-26755)***
Emotiv Systems Inc....415 503-3601
1770 Post St Ste 350 San Francisco (94115) ***(G-18803)***
Emove Express Company....650 377-0913
688 Matsonia Dr Foster City (94404) ***(G-16124)***
Emovexpress.com, Foster City *Also called Emove Express Company* ***(G-16124)***
Emp III Inc....323 231-4174
1755 Mrtn Lthr Kng Jr Blv Los Angeles (90058) ***(G-12303)***
Empcc Inc....714 564-7900
1682 Langley Ave Fl 2 Irvine (92614) ***(G-2441)***
Emperor's Clge & Clnc Tradtn, Santa Monica *Also called Emperors Clg Trdtnl Orntl Mdc* ***(G-20315)***
Emperors Clg Trdtnl Orntl Mdc....310 453-8383
1807 Wilshire Blvd Ste B Santa Monica (90403) ***(G-20315)***
Empire Building & Envmtl Svcs, Covina *Also called Garcia Asset Management Inc* ***(G-14307)***
Empire Building Services Inc....714 836-7700
1570 E Edinger Ave Ste D Santa Ana (92705) ***(G-14290)***
Empire Chauffeur Service Ltd....310 414-8189
600 S Allied Way El Segundo (90245) ***(G-4014)***
Empire Cls Worldwide, El Segundo *Also called Cls Trnsprttion Los Angles LLC* ***(G-3782)***
Empire Community Painting, Irvine *Also called Empcc Inc* ***(G-2441)***
Empire Community Painting, Irvine *Also called D P S Inc* ***(G-2438)***
Empire Company LLC....951 742-5273
31 Heron Ln Riverside (92507) ***(G-6922)***
Empire Demolition Inc....909 393-8300
1623 Leeson Ln Corona (92879) ***(G-3262)***
Empire Disposal LLC....909 797-9125
5455 Industrial Pkwy San Bernardino (92407) ***(G-6482)***
Empire Enterprises Inc....562 529-2676
8800 Park St Bellflower (90706) ***(G-3788)***
Empire Estates Inc....909 980-3100
10750 Civic Center Dr # 100 Rancho Cucamonga (91730) ***(G-11492)***
Empire Golf Inc (PA)....916 314-3150
14670 Cantova Way Ste 228 Rancho Murieta (95683) ***(G-18739)***
Empire Internation, El Segundo *Also called Empire Chauffeur Service Ltd* ***(G-4014)***
Empire Lake Golf Course, Camarillo *Also called Crown Golf Properties LP* ***(G-27398)***
Empire Leasing Inc....949 646-7400
2045 Placentia Ave Ste A Costa Mesa (92627) ***(G-3046)***
Empire Oil Co....909 877-0226
2756 S Riverside Ave Bloomington (92316) ***(G-9018)***
Empire Parking, Bellflower *Also called Empire Enterprises Inc* ***(G-3788)***
Empire Realty Associates Inc....925 217-5000
380 Diablo Rd Ste 201 Danville (94526) ***(G-11493)***
Empire Southwest LLC....760 545-6200
3393 Us Highway 86 Imperial (92251) ***(G-7768)***
Empire Transportation....562 529-2676
8800 Park St Bellflower (90706) ***(G-3893)***
Employbridge LLC (HQ)....805 882-2200
3820 State St Santa Barbara (93105) ***(G-14873)***
Employee Benefits Security ADM....626 229-1000
1055 E Colo Blvd Ste 200 Pasadena (91106) ***(G-10552)***
Employee Health System Medical....866 430-4288
3131 Santa Anita Ave # 104 El Monte (91733) ***(G-25134)***
Employee Solutions, Van Nuys *Also called ME and ME Inc* ***(G-14906)***
Employment & Community Options....858 565-9870
9370 Sky Park Ct Ste 210 San Diego (92123) ***(G-24337)***
Employment & Human Services, Martinez *Also called County of Contra Costa* ***(G-23802)***
Employment Dev Cal Dept....805 614-1550
1410 S Broadway Ste E Santa Maria (93454) ***(G-14648)***
Employment Dev Cal Dept....916 654-7867
751 N St Fl 6 Sacramento (95814) ***(G-14649)***
Employment Dev Cal Dept....760 339-2709
1550 W Main St El Centro (92243) ***(G-14650)***
Employment Intake Training Ctr, Los Angeles *Also called Swissport Usa Inc* ***(G-4941)***
Employment Training Academy....209 475-1529
4045 Coronado Ave Stockton (95204) ***(G-25528)***
Empolyment Development Dept....916 653-2065
750 N St Sacramento (95814) ***(G-14651)***
Empres Financial Services LLC....707 643-2793
1527 Springs Rd Vallejo (94591) ***(G-20535)***
Empres Post Acute Rhbilitation, Petaluma *Also called Evergreen At Petaluma LLC* ***(G-20558)***
Empress Care Center....408 287-0616
1299 S Bascom Ave San Jose (95128) ***(G-21211)***
Emq Familiesfirst, Campbell *Also called Uplift Family Services* ***(G-24840)***
Emq Familiesfirst, Los Gatos *Also called Uplift Family Services* ***(G-22860)***
Ems Construction Inc....858 679-8292
12185 Dearborn Pl Poway (92064) ***(G-1549)***
Emser International LLC (PA)....323 650-2000
8431 Santa Monica Blvd Los Angeles (90069) ***(G-6982)***
Emser Tile, Los Angeles *Also called Emser International LLC* ***(G-6982)***
Emsoc, Orange *Also called Emergency Medicine Specialist* ***(G-21558)***
Emulex Communications Corp....408 434-6064
2560 N 1st St Ste 300 San Jose (95131) ***(G-15656)***
Emulex Corporate Services Corp....714 662-5600
3333 Susan St Costa Mesa (92626) ***(G-27015)***
En Pointe Technologies Sls LLC....310 337-5200
1940 E Mariposa Ave El Segundo (90245) ***(G-7126)***
Encina Pepper Tree Joint Ventr (PA)....805 687-5511
3850 State St Santa Barbara (93105) ***(G-12619)***
Encina Pepper Tree Joint Ventr....805 682-7277
2220 Bath St Santa Barbara (93105) ***(G-12620)***
Encina Wastewater Authority....760 438-3941
6200 Avenida Encinas Carlsbad (92011) ***(G-6411)***
Encina Water Pollution Control, Carlsbad *Also called Encina Wastewater Authority* ***(G-6411)***
Encinitas Memory Care Cmnty, Encinitas *Also called Silverado Senior Living Inc* ***(G-21376)***
Encinitas Ranch Golf Course, Encinitas *Also called JC Resorts LLC* ***(G-27076)***
Encino Branch, Encino *Also called Umpqua Bank* ***(G-9426)***
Encino Center Car Wash Inc....818 788-6300
16300 Ventura Blvd Encino (91436) ***(G-17841)***
Encino Hospital Medical Center....818 995-5000
16237 Ventura Blvd Encino (91436) ***(G-21559)***
Encino Trzana Regional Med Ctr....818 995-5000
16237 Ventura Blvd Encino (91436) ***(G-21560)***
Enclarity Inc....949 614-8110
16815 Von Karman Ave # 125 Irvine (92606) ***(G-16125)***
Encompass Community Services....831 724-3885
225 Westridge Dr Watsonville (95076) ***(G-23960)***
Encompass Dgtal Mdia Group Inc....323 344-4500
2901 W Alameda Ave Burbank (91505) ***(G-5853)***
Encore Aerospace LLC....562 344-1700
1729 Apollo Ct Seal Beach (90740) ***(G-3513)***
Encore Capital Group Inc (PA)....877 445-4581
3111 Camino Del Rio N # 103 San Diego (92108) ***(G-9782)***
Encore Fund LP....415 676-4000
555 California St # 2975 San Francisco (94104) ***(G-12113)***
Encore Gymnstics Dnce Climbing, Concord *Also called Encore Inc* ***(G-19206)***
Encore Inc....925 932-1033
999 Bancroft Rd Concord (94518) ***(G-19206)***
Encore Media Services Inc....661 705-1323
24853 Avenue Rockefeller Valencia (91355) ***(G-18225)***
Encore Repair Services Inc....805 584-6599
2175 Agate Ct Simi Valley (93065) ***(G-17934)***
Encore Semi Inc....858 225-4993
9444 Waples St Ste 150 San Diego (92121) ***(G-25786)***
Encore Senior Living III LLC....951 360-1616
6280 Clay St Riverside (92509) ***(G-24643)***
Encore Senior Vlg At Riverside, Riverside *Also called Encore Senior Living III LLC* ***(G-24643)***
Encore Software Services Inc....408 573-7337
2025 Gateway Pl Ste 290 San Jose (95110) ***(G-16364)***
Encore Trucking Inc....408 330-7600
650 Aldo Ave Santa Clara (95054) ***(G-4015)***

ALPHABETIC

End-Time Message & Support
ALPHABETIC SECTION

End-Time Message & Support 323 756-6252
855 W 125th St Los Angeles (90044) ***(G-12304)***
Endemol 310 860-9914
9255 W Sunset Blvd # 1100 West Hollywood (90069) ***(G-18390)***
Endocrine Sciences Inc 818 880-8040
4301 Lost Hills Rd Calabasas (91301) ***(G-22214)***
Endovascular Technologies Inc 650 325-1600
1360 Obrien Dr Menlo Park (94025) ***(G-26511)***
Endurance Lending Network, San Francisco *Also called Funding Circle Usa Inc* ***(G-9749)***
Endurance Specialty Insurance 213 270-7700
725 S Figueroa St # 2100 Los Angeles (90017) ***(G-10700)***
Energetic Lath & Plaster, North Highlands *Also called Energetic Pntg & Drywall Inc* ***(G-2893)***
Energetic Pntg & Drywall Inc (PA) 916 488-8455
2929 Orange Grove Ave North Highlands (95660) ***(G-2893)***
Energized Distribution LLC 562 319-0232
8435 Eastern Ave Bell Gardens (90201) ***(G-8833)***
Energy Berkeley Office US Dept 510 495-2490
5885 Hollis St Emeryville (94608) ***(G-26756)***
Energy Berkeley Office US Dept 510 486-7089
555 W Imperial Hwy Brea (92821) ***(G-26757)***
Energy Berkeley Office US Dept 510 701-1089
1226 Cornell Ave Albany (94706) ***(G-26758)***
Energy Berkeley Office US Dept 510 642-1440
225 University Hall Berkeley (94720) ***(G-26759)***
Energy Berkeley Office US Dept 510 468-5662
523 Buena Vista Ave # 315 Alameda (94501) ***(G-26760)***
Energy Berkeley Office US Dept 510 486-4033
419 Latimer Hall Berkeley (94720) ***(G-26761)***
Energy Club Inc 818 834-8222
12950 Pierce St Pacoima (91331) ***(G-8610)***
Energy Enterprises USA Inc 424 339-0005
6736 Vesper Ave Van Nuys (91405) ***(G-2218)***
Energy Experts International 559 449-1124
7111 N Fresno St Fresno (93720) ***(G-27912)***
Energy Experts International 510 574-1822
37310 Cedar Blvd Newark (94560) ***(G-27913)***
Energy Innovations Inc 626 585-6900
130 W Union St Pasadena (91103) ***(G-26512)***
Energy Livermore Off US Dept 415 648-3878
539 Peralta Ave San Francisco (94110) ***(G-26762)***
Energy Livermore Off US Dept 408 267-1413
1413 Willowtree Ct San Jose (95118) ***(G-26763)***
Energy Resource Center, Downey *Also called Southern California Gas Co* ***(G-6279)***
Energy Salvage Inc 916 737-8640
8231 Alpine Ave Ste 3 Sacramento (95826) ***(G-27016)***
Energy Solutions, Oakland *Also called Cohen Ventures Inc* ***(G-27884)***
Energy Store of California Inc 916 825-8751
14958 Venado Dr Rancho Murieta (95683) ***(G-2219)***
Enerpath Services Inc 909 335-1699
1758 Orange Tree Ln Redlands (92374) ***(G-2589)***
Enertis Solar Inc 415 400-5271
1750 Montgomery St # 127 San Francisco (94111) ***(G-25787)***
Engage Bdr Inc 310 954-0751
9000 W Sunset Blvd West Hollywood (90069) ***(G-13844)***
Enganering and Technical Svcs, Santa Maria *Also called Caci Nss Inc* ***(G-7106)***
Engility Corporation 703 708-1400
1843 Hotel Cir S San Diego (92108) ***(G-25788)***
Engility LLC 805 383-7551
2001 Solar Dr Ste 250 Oxnard (93036) ***(G-25789)***
Engility LLC 858 552-9500
7580 Metro Dr Ste 207 San Diego (92108) ***(G-25790)***
Engility LLC 510 357-4610
2700 Merced St San Leandro (94577) ***(G-25791)***
Engility LLC 703 664-6274
200 W Los Angeles Ave Simi Valley (93065) ***(G-25792)***
Engine Yard Inc 866 518-9273
580 Market St Ste 150 San Francisco (94104) ***(G-15165)***
Engineered Forest Products LLC 925 376-0881
1340 Bollinger Cyn Moraga (94556) ***(G-12305)***
Engineered Soil Repairs Inc 408 297-2150
1267 Springbrook Rd Walnut Creek (94597) ***(G-2814)***
Engineered Well Svc Intl Inc 866 913-6283
3120 Standard St Bakersfield (93308) ***(G-1074)***
Engineering & Tstg Svcs Corp 707 838-1113
7757 Bell Rd Windsor (95492) ***(G-25793)***
Engineering Division, Lancaster *Also called County of Los Angeles* ***(G-25755)***
Engineering Public Works, Glendale *Also called City of Glendale* ***(G-25739)***
Engineering/Remdtn Rsrcs Grp (PA) 925 839-2200
4585 Pacheco Blvd Ste 200 Martinez (94553) ***(G-27914)***
Enginring Capitl Projects Dept, San Diego *Also called City of San Diego* ***(G-27881)***
Enginring Sftwr Sys Sltons Inc (PA) 619 338-0380
550 W C St Ste 1630 San Diego (92101) ***(G-25794)***
Englekirk Institutional Inc (PA) 323 733-2640
888 S Figueroa St Ste 180 Los Angeles (90017) ***(G-25795)***
Englekirk Structural Engineers (PA) 323 733-6673
888 S Figueroa St # 1800 Los Angeles (90017) ***(G-25796)***
English Oaks Convalescent & RE, Modesto *Also called Chadlor Enterprises Inc* ***(G-20452)***
Engstrom Lipscomb and Lack A (PA) 310 552-3800
10100 Santa Monica Blvd # 1200 Los Angeles (90067) ***(G-23233)***
Enhanced Landscape MGT Inc 805 557-2737
1938 E Thousand Oaks Blvd Thousand Oaks (91362) ***(G-849)***
Enki Health and RES Systems 626 227-0341
3208 Rosemead Blvd El Monte (91731) ***(G-23961)***
Enky Health 323 725-1337
1436 Goodrich Blvd Commerce (90022) ***(G-22728)***
Enloe Homecare Services, Chico *Also called Enloe Medical Center* ***(G-22432)***
Enloe Hospt-Phys Thrpy 530 891-7300
1444 Magnolia Ave Chico (95926) ***(G-21561)***
Enloe Medical Center 530 332-6745
1448 Esplanade Chico (95926) ***(G-21562)***
Enloe Medical Center 530 332-4111
560 Cohasset Rd Chico (95926) ***(G-20316)***
Enloe Medical Center 530 332-7522
175 W 5th Ave Chico (95926) ***(G-19515)***
Enloe Medical Center 530 332-6050
1390 E Lassen Ave Chico (95973) ***(G-22432)***
Enloe Medical Center 530 332-6138
340 W East Ave Chico (95926) ***(G-20317)***
Enloe Medical Center 530 332-6400
888 Lakeside Vlg Cmns Chico (95928) ***(G-21563)***
Enloe Medical Center 530 332-6000
277 Cohasset Rd Chico (95926) ***(G-19516)***
Enloe Outpatient Center, Chico *Also called Enloe Medical Center* ***(G-21563)***
Enloe Rehabilitation Center, Chico *Also called Enloe Medical Center* ***(G-20317)***
Enmetric Systems Inc 650 489-4441
617 Mountain View Ave # 5 Belmont (94002) ***(G-15166)***
Ennis Inc 951 928-1125
28401 Matthews Rd Sun City (92585) ***(G-8165)***
Enns Farms, Kingsburg *Also called Enns Packing Company Inc* ***(G-232)***
Enns Packing Company Inc 559 897-7700
1911 Bergren Ct Kingsburg (93631) ***(G-232)***
Enpower Management Corp 925 244-1100
2420 Camino Ramon Ste 101 San Ramon (94583) ***(G-6132)***
Enquero Inc 408 406-3203
1851 Mccarthy Blvd # 115 Milpitas (95035) ***(G-15941)***
Enrichment Eductl Experiences 818 989-7509
4400 Coldwater Canyon Ave # 300 Studio City (91604) ***(G-24458)***
Enrichment Program, Rocklin *Also called Star Inc* ***(G-24233)***
Ensighten Inc (HQ) 650 249-4712
1741 Tech Dr Ste 500 San Jose (95110) ***(G-27424)***
Ensign Cloverdale LLC 707 894-5201
300 Cherry Creek Rd Cloverdale (95425) ***(G-20536)***
Ensign Group Inc 949 642-0387
340 Victoria St Costa Mesa (92627) ***(G-20537)***
Ensign Group Inc 805 925-8713
1405 E Main St Santa Maria (93454) ***(G-24644)***
Ensign Group Inc 818 893-6385
9541 Van Nuys Blvd Panorama City (91402) ***(G-20538)***
Ensign Group Inc 562 947-7817
10426 Bogardus Ave Whittier (90603) ***(G-20539)***
Ensign Group Inc 707 525-1250
3751 Montgomery Dr Santa Rosa (95405) ***(G-20540)***
Ensign Group Inc 760 746-0303
201 N Fig St Escondido (92025) ***(G-20541)***
Ensign Group Inc 626 287-0438
8417 Mission Dr Rosemead (91770) ***(G-20542)***
Ensign Group Inc 626 607-2400
4800 Delta Ave Rosemead (91770) ***(G-20543)***
Ensign Palm I LLC 760 323-2638
2990 E Ramon Rd Palm Springs (92264) ***(G-20544)***
Ensign Services Inc 949 487-9500
27101 Puerta Real Ste 450 Mission Viejo (92691) ***(G-20545)***
Ensign Southland LLC 949 487-9500
27101 Puerta Real Ste 450 Mission Viejo (92691) ***(G-20546)***
Ensign Willits LLC 707 459-5592
64 Northbrook Way Willits (95490) ***(G-21212)***
Ent Facial Surgery Center, Fresno *Also called Central California Ear Nose* ***(G-19418)***
Entelos Inc 650 578-2900
110 Marsh Dr Ste 200 Foster City (94404) ***(G-26513)***
Entercom Communications Corp 916 766-5000
5345 Madison Ave Sacramento (95841) ***(G-5769)***
Entercom Communications Corp 610 660-5610
201 3rd St Fl 12 San Francisco (94103) ***(G-5770)***
Entercom Communications Corp 916 334-7777
5345 Madison Ave Ste 100 Sacramento (95841) ***(G-5771)***
Enterprise Events Group Inc 415 499-4444
950 Northgate Dr Ste 100 San Rafael (94903) ***(G-27425)***
Enterprise Holdings Inc 559 261-9221
780 W Pinedale Ave Fresno (93711) ***(G-17670)***
Enterprise Partners MGT LLC 858 731-0300
2223 Avenida De Playa 210 La Jolla (92037) ***(G-12306)***
Enterprise Rent-A-Car 760 772-0281
78385 Varner Rd Ste D Palm Desert (92211) ***(G-17671)***
Enterprise Rent-A-Car 619 297-0311
2942 Kettner Blvd San Diego (92101) ***(G-17672)***
Enterprise Rent-A-Car (HQ) 657 221-4400
333 City Blvd W Ste 1000 Orange (92868) ***(G-17700)***
Enterprise Rent-A-Car 949 373-9350
28112 Camino Capistrano Laguna Niguel (92677) ***(G-17673)***
Enterprise Rent-A-Car Compan 916 576-3164
6320 Mcnair Cir Sacramento (95837) ***(G-17674)***
Enterprise Rent-A-Car Compan (HQ) 916 787-4500
150 N Sunrise Ave Roseville (95661) ***(G-17701)***
Enterprise Roofing Service Inc 925 689-8100
2400 Bates Ave Concord (94520) ***(G-3171)***
Enterprise Solutions Inc 408 727-3627
2855 Kifer Rd Santa Clara (95051) ***(G-27915)***
Enterprise Tech Group Inc 972 373-8800
13428 Maxella Ave 788 Marina Del Rey (90292) ***(G-15167)***
Enterprise Vineyards 707 996-6513
16600 Norrbom Rd Sonoma (95476) ***(G-701)***
Entertainment & Sports Today 213 388-9050
2966 Wilshire Blvd Ste C Los Angeles (90010) ***(G-5854)***
Entertainment Partners (PA) 818 955-6000
2835 N Naomi St Burbank (91504) ***(G-26336)***
Entravision Radio, Sacramento *Also called Entravsion Communications Corp* ***(G-5857)***
Entravsion Communications Corp 831 333-9736
67 Garden Ct Monterey (93940) ***(G-5855)***

ALPHABETIC

Entravsion Communications Corp 323 900-6100
5700 Wilshire Blvd # 250 Los Angeles (90036) *(G-5856)*
Entravsion Communications Corp 916 646-4000
1436 Auburn Blvd Sacramento (95815) *(G-5772)*
Entravsion Communications Corp 916 648-6029
1436 Auburn Blvd Sacramento (95815) *(G-5857)*
Entravsion Communications Corp (PA) 310 447-3870
2425 Olympic Blvd Ste 600 Santa Monica (90404) *(G-5858)*
Entrepreneurial Capital Corp 949 809-3900
4100 Nwport Pl Dr Ste 400 Newport Beach (92660) *(G-10979)*
Entrepreneurial Hospitality 951 346-4700
3485 Mission Inn Ave Riverside (92501) *(G-17151)*
Envent Corporation (PA) 562 997-9465
3220 E 29th St Long Beach (90806) *(G-27916)*
Enviance Inc (HQ) 760 496-0200
5780 Fleet St Ste 200 Carlsbad (92008) *(G-15168)*
Enviro Tech Chemical Svcs Inc (PA) 209 581-9576
500 Winmoore Way Modesto (95358) *(G-8988)*
Envirobusiness Inc 562 481-3365
3703 Long Beach Blvd Fl 2 Long Beach (90807) *(G-28129)*
Environ Hardwood Floors 415 487-0200
2827 Mariposa St San Francisco (94110) *(G-3113)*
Environment Control, Visalia *Also called Tim Hofer Inc (G-14444)*
Environment Control 559 456-9791
1849 N Helm Ave Ste 105 Fresno (93727) *(G-14291)*
Environmental Chemical Corp (PA) 650 347-1555
1240 Bayshore Hwy Burlingame (94010) *(G-25797)*
Environmental Compliance Svcs, Irvine *Also called Brinderson & Associates (G-25705)*
Environmental Construction Inc 818 449-8920
21550 Oxnard St Ste 1050 Woodland Hills (91367) *(G-1550)*
Environmental Health Hazard 510 622-3200
1515 Clay St Ste 1600 Oakland (94612) *(G-26851)*
Environmental Industries, Fillmore *Also called Brightview Tree Company (G-1008)*
Environmental Ldscp Solutions, Sacramento *Also called Els Investments (G-766)*
Environmental Protection Agcy 916 324-7572
1001 I St Ste 19b Sacramento (95814) *(G-6627)*
Environmental Recovery Svcs, Gardena *Also called Waste Management Cal Inc (G-4091)*
ENVIRONMENTAL RESOURCES MANAGEMENT, Walnut Creek *Also called Erm-West Inc (G-25802)*
Environmental Science Assoc (PA) 415 896-5900
550 Kearny St Ste 800 San Francisco (94108) *(G-26514)*
Environmental Systems Inc (PA) 408 980-1711
3353 De La Cruz Blvd Santa Clara (95054) *(G-2220)*
Environmental Systems Research 916 448-2412
1600 K St Ste 4c Sacramento (95814) *(G-7127)*
Environments For Learning Inc (PA) 949 855-5630
24291 Muirlands Blvd Lake Forest (92630) *(G-24459)*
Envivio Inc (HQ) 650 243-2700
535 Mission St Fl 27 San Francisco (94105) *(G-5595)*
Envoy Air Inc 619 231-5452
3707 N Harbor Dr Ste 103 San Diego (92101) *(G-4799)*
Envoy Air Inc 619 260-9069
3707 N Harbor Dr Ste 124 San Diego (92101) *(G-4916)*
Enxco, San Diego *Also called Edf Renewable Services Inc (G-17821)*
Enzennauer Vineyard Managment 707 433-0532
18501 Ida Clayton Rd Calistoga (94515) *(G-702)*
Eoc Resource Development, Fresno *Also called Fresno Cnty Economic Opportunt (G-17176)*
Epairs Inc 408 973-8466
20370 Town Center Ln # 255 Cupertino (95014) *(G-16365)*
Epak9, El Cajon *Also called Executive Protection Agency K- (G-16639)*
Epcm Prof Svc Partners LLC 562 936-1000
2017 Palo Verde Ave Long Beach (90815) *(G-27917)*
Ephesoft Inc 949 335-5335
23041avnda D L Crlota 1 Carlota Laguna Hills (92653) *(G-7128)*
Ephonamationcom Inc 714 560-1000
145 E Columbine Ave Santa Ana (92707) *(G-17152)*
Epic, San Francisco *Also called Edgewood Partners Insur Ctr (G-10697)*
Epic Jet Centre, San Luis Obispo *Also called Aviation Consultants Inc (G-26932)*
Epic Management LP (PA) 909 799-1818
1615 Orange Tree Ln Redlands (92374) *(G-27017)*
Epic Production Tech US Inc 805 278-2400
1401 Maulhardt Ave Ste A Oxnard (93030) *(G-14539)*
Epic Ventures Inc (PA) 831 219-9100
200 Concourse Blvd Santa Rosa (95403) *(G-9099)*
Epic Wines, Santa Rosa *Also called Epic Ventures Inc (G-9099)*
Epicenter Live Inc 424 235-4835
4040 Mahaila Ave Unit A San Diego (92122) *(G-18391)*
Epicentro Advertising Mktg Svc 408 453-0353
2370 Qume Dr Ste B San Jose (95131) *(G-13845)*
Epicor Software Corporation 925 361-9900
4120 Dublin Blvd Ste 300 Dublin (94568) *(G-15657)*
Epicor Software Corporation 858 352-1600
3394 Carmel Mountain Rd # 100 San Diego (92121) *(G-15658)*
Epidendio Construction Inc 707 994-5100
11325 Highway 29 Lower Lake (95457) *(G-3263)*
Episcopal Communities & Servic 310 544-2204
5801 Crestridge Rd Pls Vrds Pnsl (90275) *(G-20547)*
Episcopal Community 619 422-1642
1261 3rd Ave Ste B Chula Vista (91911) *(G-24460)*
Episcopal Senior Communities 510 835-4700
100 Bay Pl Ofc Oakland (94610) *(G-24645)*
Episcopal Senior Communities 408 354-0211
110 Wood Rd Ofc Los Gatos (95030) *(G-24646)*
Episcopal Senior Communities 831 373-3111
651 Sinex Ave Pacific Grove (93950) *(G-24647)*
Episcopal Senior Communities 707 538-8400
5555 Montgomery Dr Santa Rosa (95409) *(G-24648)*
Episcopal Senior Communities 415 776-0500
1661 Pine St Apt 911 San Francisco (94109) *(G-24649)*
Epitome Enterprises LLC 909 625-4728
821 Mary Pl Claremont (91711) *(G-15169)*
Epitomics Inc (HQ) 650 583-6688
863 Mitten Rd Ste 103 Burlingame (94010) *(G-26764)*
Eplica Inc (PA) 619 260-2000
2355 Northside Dr Ste 120 San Diego (92108) *(G-14874)*
Eplus Technology Inc 949 417-7000
2355 Main St Ste 140 Irvine (92614) *(G-15942)*
Epochcom LLC 310 664-5700
2644 30th St Fl 2 Santa Monica (90405) *(G-16126)*
Epocrates Inc (HQ) 650 227-1700
50 Hawthorne St San Francisco (94105) *(G-22955)*
Eppink of California Inc 562 633-1275
11900 Center St South Gate (90280) *(G-3047)*
Epri Csg, Palo Alto *Also called Eprisolutions Inc (G-25798)*
Eprisolutions Inc 650 855-8900
3412 Hillview Ave Palo Alto (94304) *(G-25798)*
Eps Corporate Holdings Inc 714 635-3131
1235 S Lewis St Anaheim (92805) *(G-7709)*
Epsilon Electronics Inc 323 722-3333
1550 S Maple Ave Montebello (90640) *(G-7496)*
Epsilon Mission Solutions Inc 619 702-1700
9242 Lightwave Ave # 100 San Diego (92123) *(G-25799)*
Epsilon Systems Solutions Inc 619 702-1700
5482 Complex St Ste 109 San Diego (92123) *(G-25800)*
Epsilon Systems Solutions Inc (PA) 619 702-1700
9242 Lightwave Ave # 100 San Diego (92123) *(G-25801)*
Epson America Inc 562 290-5855
1650 Glenn Curtiss St Carson (90746) *(G-4548)*
Epson Portland Inc 408 678-0100
150 River Oaks Pkwy San Jose (95134) *(G-15943)*
Epson Research Center, San Jose *Also called Epson Portland Inc (G-15943)*
Epson West, Carson *Also called Epson America Inc (G-4548)*
Epstein Becker & Green PC 310 556-8861
1875 Century Park E # 500 Los Angeles (90067) *(G-23234)*
Eqal Inc 818 276-6300
5250 Lankershim Blvd # 720 North Hollywood (91601) *(G-13846)*
Equal Access International 415 561-4884
1212 Market St Ste 200 San Francisco (94102) *(G-2590)*
Equator LLC (HQ) 310 469-9500
6060 Center Dr Ste 500 Los Angeles (90045) *(G-15170)*
Equator Business Solutions, Los Angeles *Also called Equator LLC (G-15170)*
Equestrian Center, Burbank *Also called Laec Incorporated (G-642)*
Equicare Medical Supply Inc 213 385-1715
1154 S Alvarado St Los Angeles (90006) *(G-20548)*
Equilar Inc 650 241-6600
1100 Marshall St Redwood City (94063) *(G-17153)*
Equinix Inc (PA) 650 598-6000
1 Lagoon Dr Ste 400 Redwood City (94065) *(G-5596)*
Equinix (us) Enterprises Inc 650 598-6363
1 Lagoon Dr Fl 4 Redwood City (94065) *(G-6072)*
Equinox-76th Street Inc 415 398-0747
301 Pine St San Francisco (94104) *(G-18629)*
Equinox-76th Street Inc 949 975-8400
1980 Main St Fl 4 Irvine (92614) *(G-20318)*
Equistar Irvine Company LLC 949 833-3331
18800 Macarthur Blvd Irvine (92612) *(G-12621)*
Equitable Life Assurance, San Diego *Also called Axa Equitable Life Insur Co (G-10641)*
Equitable Variable Lf Insur Co 619 239-0018
701 B St Ste 1500 San Diego (92101) *(G-10205)*
Equity Firm Golden Gate Capitl 415 983-2703
1 Embarcadero Ctr Fl 39th San Francisco (94111) *(G-16366)*
Equity One Incorporated 415 421-5100
3 Serramonte Ctr Daly City (94015) *(G-11494)*
Equity Title Company (HQ) 818 291-4400
425 W Broadway Ste 300 Glendale (91204) *(G-10512)*
ERA, San Diego *Also called Eagle Estates Inc (G-11485)*
ERA, Anaheim *Also called E R A First Star Realty (G-11483)*
ERA Realty Center 530 295-2900
49 Placerville Dr Placerville (95667) *(G-11495)*
Erepublic Inc (PA) 916 932-1300
100 Blue Ravine Rd Folsom (95630) *(G-17154)*
Erewhon Natural Foods Market, Calabasas *Also called Nowher Partners LLC (G-8894)*
Ergs Aim Hotel Realty LLC 714 938-1111
400 N State College Blvd Orange (92868) *(G-12622)*
Eric D Feldman MD Inc 562 424-6666
2760 Atlantic Ave Long Beach (90806) *(G-19517)*
Eric Jones Customs Brokerage 310 348-3777
9841 Arprt Blvd Ste 1400 Los Angeles (90045) *(G-5066)*
Eric Stark Interiors Inc 408 441-6136
2284 Paragon Dr San Jose (95131) *(G-2894)*
Erickson Construction LP 916 774-1100
8350 Industrial Ave Roseville (95678) *(G-3048)*
Erickson Framing AZ LLC 916 774-1100
8350 Industrial Ave Roseville (95678) *(G-3049)*
Erickson-Hall Construction Co (PA) 760 796-7700
500 Corporate Dr Escondido (92029) *(G-1551)*
Ericsson Inc 408 750-5000
300 Holger Way San Jose (95134) *(G-15944)*
Ericsson Inc 408 597-3600
100 Headquarters Dr San Jose (95134) *(G-15945)*
Erlanger Distribution Ctr Inc 951 784-5147
797 Palmyrita Ave Riverside (92507) *(G-9261)*
Erlanger Sales, Riverside *Also called Erlanger Distribution Ctr Inc (G-9261)*
Erm-West Inc (HQ) 925 946-0455
1277 Treat Blvd Ste 500 Walnut Creek (94597) *(G-25802)*

A L P H A B E T I C

Ernest E Pestana Inc....408 432-8110
84 W Santa Clara St # 580 San Jose (95113) ***(G-1929)***
Ernest Gallo Clinic & RES Ctr....510 985-3856
5980 Horton St Ste 370 Emeryville (94608) ***(G-26660)***
Ernest Packaging Solutions Inc (PA)....800 233-7788
5777 Smithway St Commerce (90040) ***(G-8190)***
Ernest Paper, Commerce *Also called Ernest Packaging Solutions Inc* ***(G-8190)***
Ernst & Young LLP....213 977-3200
725 S Figueroa St Ste 200 Los Angeles (90017) ***(G-26337)***
Ernst & Young LLP....310 725-1764
200 N Sepulveda Blvd Fl 2 El Segundo (90245) ***(G-26338)***
Ernst & Young LLP....415 894-8000
560 Mission St Ste 1600 San Francisco (94105) ***(G-26339)***
Ernst & Young LLP....650 496-1600
1451 S California Ave Palo Alto (94304) ***(G-26340)***
Ernst & Young LLP....408 947-5500
303 Almaden Blvd Ste 1000 San Jose (95110) ***(G-26341)***
Ernst & Young LLP....949 794-2300
18111 Von Karman Ave # 1000 Irvine (92612) ***(G-26342)***
Ernst & Young LLP....858 535-7200
4370 La Jolla Village Dr # 500 San Diego (92122) ***(G-26343)***
Ernst & Young LLP....949 838-3300
18006 Sky Park Cir # 106 Irvine (92614) ***(G-26344)***
Ernst & Young LLP....805 778-7000
2931 Townsgate Rd Ste 100 Westlake Village (91361) ***(G-26345)***
Ernst & Young LLP....650 802-4500
275 Shoreline Dr Ste 600 Redwood City (94065) ***(G-26346)***
Ernst & Young LLP....916 218-1900
2901 Douglas Blvd Ste 300 Roseville (95661) ***(G-26347)***
Ernst & Young LLP....925 734-6388
4301 Hacienda Dr Ste 450 Pleasanton (94588) ***(G-26348)***
Ernst & Young LLP....415 894-8000
560 Mission St Ste 1600 San Francisco (94105) ***(G-26349)***
Ero-Tech Corp....415 468-5600
2301 S El Camino Real San Mateo (94403) ***(G-18273)***
Errama Trucking Company Inc....818 381-3341
11336 Montgomery Ave Granada Hills (91344) ***(G-4146)***
Errecas Inc....619 390-6400
12570 Slaughter House Lakeside (92040) ***(G-3427)***
Errg, Martinez *Also called Engineering/Remdtn Rsrcs Grp* ***(G-27914)***
ERs SEC Alarm Systems Inc....626 579-2525
4538 Santa Anita Ave El Monte (91731) ***(G-7440)***
Erwin Street Medical Offices, Woodland Hills *Also called Kaiser Foundation Hospitals* ***(G-21657)***
Es Engineering Inc....714 919-6500
1036 W Taft Ave Orange (92865) ***(G-25803)***
Es3 LLC....209 832-4205
857 Stonebridge Dr Tracy (95376) ***(G-4549)***
ESA, San Francisco *Also called Environmental Science Assoc* ***(G-26514)***
ESA P Prtfolio Oper Lessee LLC....949 851-2711
4881 Birch St Newport Beach (92660) ***(G-12623)***
ESA P Prtfolio Oper Lessee LLC....714 639-8608
1635 W Katella Ave Orange (92867) ***(G-12624)***
ESA Risk Management, San Jose *Also called SCC ESA Dept of Risk Mgmt* ***(G-10861)***
Esaloncom LLC....310 846-9100
10361 Jefferson Blvd Culver City (90232) ***(G-13673)***
Esc Entertainment Inc....818 954-1018
4000 Warner Blvd Burbank (91522) ***(G-18226)***
Escalate Inc (HQ)....858 457-3888
10680 Treena St Ste 170 San Diego (92131) ***(G-15171)***
Escalate Retail, San Diego *Also called Escalate Inc* ***(G-15171)***
Escondido Country Club, Poway *Also called American Golf Corporation* ***(G-18859)***
Escondido Medical Offices, Escondido *Also called Kaiser Foundation Hospitals* ***(G-19661)***
Escondido Memory Care Cmnty, Escondido *Also called Silverado Senior Living Inc* ***(G-21375)***
Escondido Post Acute Rehab, Escondido *Also called Mek Escondido LLC* ***(G-20785)***
Escondido Veterans Center, Escondido *Also called Veterans Health Administration* ***(G-20210)***
Eset LLC (HQ)....619 876-5400
610 W Ash St Ste 1700 San Diego (92101) ***(G-7129)***
Eset North America, San Diego *Also called Eset LLC* ***(G-7129)***
Esi Publishing Inc....310 768-1800
16920 S Main St Gardena (90248) ***(G-15172)***
Esis Inc....949 242-6950
7700 Irvine Center Dr # 900 Irvine (92618) ***(G-10701)***
Esis Health Safety and Envmtl, Irvine *Also called Esis Inc* ***(G-10701)***
Eskaton....916 852-7900
11390 Coloma Rd Ofc Gold River (95670) ***(G-21082)***
Eskaton (PA)....916 334-0296
5105 Manzanita Ave Ste D Carmichael (95608) ***(G-10980)***
Eskaton....916 536-3750
9722 Fair Oaks Blvd Ste A Fair Oaks (95628) ***(G-22433)***
Eskaton Center of Greenhaven, Sacramento *Also called Eskaton Properties Inc* ***(G-20552)***
Eskaton Lodge....916 789-0326
8550 Barton Rd Granite Bay (95746) ***(G-24650)***
Eskaton Properties Inc....916 334-1072
5105 Manzanita Ave Carmichael (95608) ***(G-23962)***
Eskaton Properties Inc....916 974-2060
3847 Walnut Ave Carmichael (95608) ***(G-20549)***
Eskaton Properties Inc....916 331-8513
5318 Manzanita Ave Carmichael (95608) ***(G-20550)***
Eskaton Properties Inc....530 265-2699
625 Eskaton Cir Apt 213 Grass Valley (95945) ***(G-24651)***
Eskaton Properties Inc....916 334-0810
1650 Eskaton Loop Roseville (95747) ***(G-24652)***
Eskaton Properties Inc....916 965-4663
11300 Fair Oaks Blvd Fair Oaks (95628) ***(G-20551)***
Eskaton Properties Inc....916 393-2550
455 Florin Rd Sacramento (95831) ***(G-20552)***
Eskaton Properties Inc (PA)....916 334-0810
5105 Manzanita Ave Ste A Carmichael (95608) ***(G-24653)***
Eskaton Properties Inc....916 974-2000
3939 Walnut Ave Unit 399 Carmichael (95608) ***(G-21213)***
Eskaton Village Care Center, Carmichael *Also called Eskaton Properties Inc* ***(G-20549)***
Eskaton Village Charmichael, Carmichael *Also called Eskaton Properties Inc* ***(G-21213)***
Eskaton Village Roseville, Roseville *Also called Eskaton Properties Inc* ***(G-24652)***
Eskaton Village-Grass Valley, Grass Valley *Also called Eskaton Properties Inc* ***(G-24651)***
Esl, Burbank *Also called Turtle Entertainment America* ***(G-13800)***
Esl Technologies Inc....916 677-4500
8875 Washington Blvd B Roseville (95678) ***(G-16292)***
Esna Corporation....661 206-6010
44300 Lowtree Ave Ste 100 Lancaster (93534) ***(G-9922)***
Esolar Inc (HQ)....818 303-9500
3355 W Empire Ave Ste 200 Burbank (91504) ***(G-2049)***
Esoterix Ctr For Clncal Trails, Calabasas *Also called Endocrine Sciences Inc* ***(G-22214)***
ESP Computer Services Inc (PA)....818 487-4500
12444 Victory Blvd Fl 4 North Hollywood (91606) ***(G-16127)***
ESP Group Ltd....626 301-0280
2397 Bateman Ave Duarte (91010) ***(G-8382)***
Esparza Enterprises Inc....760 344-2031
251 W Main St Ste G&F Brawley (92227) ***(G-703)***
Esparza Enterprises Inc (PA)....661 831-0002
3851 Fruitvale Ave Ste A Bakersfield (93308) ***(G-14652)***
Esparza Enterprises Inc....661 831-0002
3851 Fruitvale Ave A Bakersfield (93308) ***(G-14653)***
Esparza Enterprises Inc....760 398-0349
51335 Harrison St Ste 112 Coachella (92236) ***(G-14654)***
Esparza Enterprises Inc....661 631-0347
500 Workman St Bakersfield (93307) ***(G-4147)***
Espn Inc....212 456-7439
800 W Olympic Blvd Los Angeles (90015) ***(G-5998)***
Esprit, Camarillo *Also called D P Technology Corp* ***(G-15118)***
Esquire, San Diego *Also called Rose Ox Inc* ***(G-14168)***
Esquire Landscape Inc....858 530-2949
8380 Miralani Dr Ste B San Diego (92126) ***(G-850)***
ESS LLC....888 303-6424
23151 Alcalde Dr Ste C1 Laguna Hills (92653) ***(G-2221)***
Essco, Pasadena *Also called Electric Svc & Sup Co Pasadena* ***(G-2584)***
Essendant Co....626 961-0011
918 S Stimson Ave City of Industry (91745) ***(G-8166)***
Essendant Co....916 344-6707
5440 Stationers Way Sacramento (95842) ***(G-8167)***
Essex Management Corporation....650 494-3700
925 E Meadow Dr Palo Alto (94303) ***(G-12244)***
Essex Property, San Mateo *Also called Essex Queen Anne LLC* ***(G-11253)***
Essex Property Trust Inc....916 381-0345
8795 Folsom Blvd Ste 101 Sacramento (95826) ***(G-12245)***
Essex Property Trust Inc (PA)....650 655-7800
1100 Park Pl Ste 200 San Mateo (94403) ***(G-12246)***
Essex Queen Anne LLC....650 849-1600
1100 Park Pl Ste 200 San Mateo (94403) ***(G-11253)***
Essex Realty Management Inc....949 798-8100
18012 Sky Park Cir # 200 Irvine (92614) ***(G-11496)***
Essilor Laboratories Amer Inc....626 969-6181
1300 W Optical Dr Ste 400 Irwindale (91702) ***(G-7331)***
Estancia Estates....707 431-1975
980 Bryant Cyn Soledad (93960) ***(G-11965)***
Estate Investment Group, Dublin *Also called New Home Professionals* ***(G-11705)***
Estes Express Lines Inc....714 994-3770
14727 Alondra Blvd La Mirada (90638) ***(G-4016)***
Estes Express Lines Inc....909 427-9850
10736 Cherry Ave Fontana (92337) ***(G-4148)***
Estes Express Lines Inc....626 333-9090
13327 Temple Ave City of Industry (91746) ***(G-4149)***
Estes Express Lines Inc....408 286-3894
1634 S 7th St San Jose (95112) ***(G-4150)***
Estes Express Lines Inc....510 635-0165
1750 Adams Ave San Leandro (94577) ***(G-4151)***
Estes Express Lines Inc....818 504-4155
9120 San Fernando Rd Sun Valley (91352) ***(G-4152)***
Estes Express Lines Inc....209 982-1841
7611 S Airport Way Stockton (95206) ***(G-4153)***
Estes Express Lines Inc....310 549-7306
1531 Blinn Ave Wilmington (90744) ***(G-4154)***
Estes Express Lines Inc....714 523-1122
14727 Alondra Blvd La Mirada (90638) ***(G-4155)***
Estralla Inn & Spa, Palm Springs *Also called Casa Real Estate Ltd Partnr* ***(G-12498)***
Estrella Inc....562 925-6418
17836 Woodruff Ave Bellflower (90706) ***(G-20553)***
Estrella Communications Inc....818 260-5700
3000 W Alameda Ave Burbank (91523) ***(G-5859)***
Estuate Inc....408 400-0680
1183 Bordeaux Dr Ste 22 Sunnyvale (94089) ***(G-15173)***
Esurance Inc (HQ)....415 875-4500
650 Davis St San Francisco (94111) ***(G-10702)***
Esys Energy Control Company....661 833-1902
4520 Stine Rd Ste 7 Bakersfield (93313) ***(G-7842)***
Et Security, Van Nuys *Also called ET Security Inc* ***(G-16635)***
ET Security Inc....818 988-9617
7100 Hayvenhurst Ave # 318 Van Nuys (91406) ***(G-16635)***
Et Whitehall Seascape LLC....310 581-5533
1910 Ocean Way Santa Monica (90405) ***(G-12625)***
Etairos Consulting....844 219-7027
6711 Studio Pl Riverside (92509) ***(G-16367)***
Etap, Irvine *Also called Operation Technology Inc* ***(G-15353)***

ALPHABETIC

Etchandy Farms LLC 805 983-4700
4324 E Vineyard Ave Oxnard (93036) ***(G-110)***
Etchegaray Farms LLC 661 393-0920
32324 Famoso Rd Mc Farland (93250) ***(G-416)***
Ethan Conrad Properties Inc 916 779-1000
1300 National Dr Ste 100 Sacramento (95834) ***(G-10981)***
Etherwan Systems Inc 714 779-3800
2301 E Winston Rd Anaheim (92806) ***(G-16368)***
Ethiopian World Federation 323 844-1826
422 E 41st St Los Angeles (90011) ***(G-24920)***
Ethosenergy Field Services LLC (HQ) 310 639-3523
10455 Slusher Dr Bldg 12 Santa Fe Springs (90670) ***(G-1075)***
Etiwanda Historical Society 909 899-8432
7150 Etiwanda Ave Rancho Cucamonga (91739) ***(G-25020)***
Etiwanda Power Plant, Rancho Cucamonga *Also called NRG California South LP* ***(G-6154)***
Etna Police Activities League 530 467-3400
448 Main St Etna (96027) ***(G-23963)***
Etrade Financial Corporation 650 331-6435
4748 Touchstone Ter Fremont (94555) ***(G-10137)***
Etrigue Corp 408 490-2900
6399 San Ignacio Ave # 200 San Jose (95119) ***(G-15174)***
Eucalyptus Systems Inc 805 845-8000
6755 Hollister Ave # 200 Goleta (93117) ***(G-15659)***
Euclid Parking, Porterville *Also called Exeter Packers Inc* ***(G-530)***
Eugene Burger Management Corp 916 443-6637
555 Capitol Mall Ste 725 Sacramento (95814) ***(G-27018)***
Eugene N Townsend 619 442-8807
609 S Marshall Ave El Cajon (92020) ***(G-17752)***
Eureka District Office, Eureka *Also called State Compensation Insur Fund* ***(G-10473)***
Eureka Rehab & Wellness Center 707 445-3261
2353 23rd St Eureka (95501) ***(G-20554)***
Eureka Rhbltation Wellness Ctr, Eureka *Also called Eureka Rehab & Wellness Center* ***(G-20554)***
Eureka Veterans Clinic, Eureka *Also called Veterans Health Administration* ***(G-20208)***
Euro Rscg San Francisco LLC 415 345-7700
1355 Sansome St Fl 4 San Francisco (94111) ***(G-14069)***
Euroamerican Propagators LLC 760 731-6029
32149 Aquaduct Rd Bonsall (92003) ***(G-280)***
Eurodent Inc 818 832-1325
9310 Topanga Canyon Blvd Chatsworth (91311) ***(G-22306)***
Eurodrip USA Inc 559 674-2670
1850 W Almond Ave Madera (93637) ***(G-7801)***
Eurofins Air Toxics Inc 916 985-1000
180 Blue Ravine Rd Ste B Folsom (95630) ***(G-26852)***
Eurogentec North America Inc 510 791-9560
34801 Campus Dr Fremont (94555) ***(G-27918)***
European Hotl Invstrs of CA 310 322-0999
1985 E Grandave El Segundo (90245) ***(G-12626)***
European Hotl Invstrs of CA (PA) 949 474-7368
2532 Dupont Dr Irvine (92612) ***(G-11127)***
European Paving Designs Inc 408 283-5230
1474 Berger Dr San Jose (95112) ***(G-2442)***
Ev Ray Inc 818 346-5381
6400 Variel Ave Woodland Hills (91367) ***(G-6859)***
Evangelical Christian Cr Un 714 671-5700
955 W Imperial Hwy Brea (92821) ***(G-9667)***
Evangelical Christian Cr Un (PA) 714 671-5700
955 W Imperial Hwy # 100 Brea (92821) ***(G-9668)***
Evangelical Covenant Church 619 931-1114
325 Kempton St Spring Valley (91977) ***(G-24654)***
Evangelical Covenant Church 805 687-0701
2550 Treasure Dr Santa Barbara (93105) ***(G-24655)***
Evans Hardy & Young Inc 805 963-5841
829 De La Vina St Ste 100 Santa Barbara (93101) ***(G-13847)***
Evans Analytical Group LLC (HQ) 408 454-4600
2710 Walsh Ave Santa Clara (95051) ***(G-26853)***
Evans/Sipes Inc (PA) 805 644-1242
5720 Ralston St Ste 100 Ventura (93003) ***(G-11497)***
Event Center, Paso Robles *Also called Fairgrounds* ***(G-18392)***
Event Guard Services Inc 626 531-6772
1823 Business Center Dr Duarte (91010) ***(G-16636)***
Eventbrite Inc (PA) 888 541-9753
155 5th St Fl 7 San Francisco (94103) ***(G-27019)***
Events Bio Services Inc 626 350-4490
9661 Telstar Ave El Monte (91731) ***(G-8113)***
Ever Win International Corp 626 810-8218
17579 Railroad St City of Industry (91748) ***(G-7561)***
Everbridge Inc 818 230-9700
155 N Lake Ave Ste 900 Pasadena (91101) ***(G-6073)***
Evercom Systems Inc 530 272-8223
10258 Carey Dr Grass Valley (95945) ***(G-5597)***
Everest Consulting Group Inc 510 494-8440
39650 Mission Blvd Fremont (94539) ***(G-15175)***
Everest Wtrprfing Rstrtion Inc 415 282-9800
1270 Missouri St San Francisco (94107) ***(G-13758)***
Everett Basham 408 261-3000
3567 Benton St Ste 300 Santa Clara (95051) ***(G-5598)***
Everett Mall 01 LLC 818 505-6777
12411 Ventura Blvd Studio City (91604) ***(G-11254)***
Evergreen At Lakeport LLC (PA) 707 263-6382
1291 Craig Ave Lakeport (95453) ***(G-20555)***
Evergreen At Lakeport LLC 661 871-3133
6212 Tudor Way Bakersfield (93306) ***(G-20556)***
Evergreen At Oroville LLC 530 533-7335
1000 Executive Pkwy Oroville (95966) ***(G-20557)***
Evergreen At Petaluma LLC 707 763-6887
300 Douglas St Petaluma (94952) ***(G-20558)***
Evergreen Cleaning Systems Inc 213 386-3260
3325 Wilshire Blvd # 622 Los Angeles (90010) ***(G-14292)***
Evergreen Company Inc 916 257-5994
847 E Turner Rd Lodi (95240) ***(G-17155)***
Evergreen Distributors Inc (PA) 858 481-0622
13650 Carmel Valley Rd San Diego (92130) ***(G-281)***
Evergreen Dstntion Hldings LLC 209 379-2606
33160 Evergreen Rd Groveland (95321) ***(G-12627)***
Evergreen Gridley Health Ctr 530 846-6266
246 Spruce St Gridley (95948) ***(G-20559)***
Evergreen Health Care LLC 661 854-4475
323 Campus Dr Arvin (93203) ***(G-20560)***
Evergreen Healthcare Center, Bakersfield *Also called Evergreen At Lakeport LLC* ***(G-20556)***
Evergreen Healthcare Inc 530 342-4885
1200 Springfield Dr Chico (95928) ***(G-20561)***
Evergreen Landcare, Los Angeles *Also called Tog Landscaping Inc* ***(G-801)***
Evergreen Lkport Halthcare Ctr, Lakeport *Also called Evergreen At Lakeport LLC* ***(G-20555)***
Evergreen Lodge, Groveland *Also called Evergreen Dstntion Hldings LLC* ***(G-12627)***
Evergreen Nursery, San Diego *Also called Evergreen Distributors Inc* ***(G-281)***
Evergreen Solar Services, Laguna Hills *Also called ESS LLC* ***(G-2221)***
Evernote Corporation (PA) 650 216-7700
305 Walnut St Redwood City (94063) ***(G-5599)***
Eversoft Inc (PA) 562 495-7766
707 W 16th St Long Beach (90813) ***(G-7710)***
Eversoft Products, Long Beach *Also called Eversoft Inc* ***(G-7710)***
Evidera Archimedes Inc 415 490-0400
450 Sansome St Ste 650 San Francisco (94111) ***(G-10703)***
Evikecom Inc 626 286-0360
2801 W Mission Rd Alhambra (91803) ***(G-8017)***
Evisions Inc (PA) 949 833-1384
440 Exchange Ste 200 Irvine (92602) ***(G-15176)***
Evolent Health Inc 571 389-6000
1 Kearny St Ste 300 San Francisco (94108) ***(G-22956)***
Evolution Fresh Inc (HQ) 909 478-0895
11655 Jersey Blvd Rancho Cucamonga (91730) ***(G-8722)***
Evolution Holdings LLC (PA) 541 826-2113
10250 Constellation Blvd Los Angeles (90067) ***(G-12060)***
Evolution Hospitality LLC (PA) 949 498-2056
1211 Puerta Del Sol # 170 San Clemente (92673) ***(G-27020)***
Evolution Juice, Rancho Cucamonga *Also called Evolution Fresh Inc* ***(G-8722)***
Evolve Discovery, San Francisco *Also called Andatha International Inc* ***(G-23091)***
Evolve Discovery La LLC 213 802-1260
811 Wilshire Blvd # 1400 Los Angeles (90017) ***(G-23235)***
Evolve Growth Initiatives LLC 424 281-5000
9301 Wilshire Blvd # 516 Beverly Hills (90210) ***(G-24656)***
Evolve Media LLC (PA) 310 449-1890
5140 W Goldleaf Cir Fl 3 Los Angeles (90056) ***(G-5600)***
Evolve Treatment Centers, Beverly Hills *Also called Evolve Growth Initiatives LLC* ***(G-24656)***
Evoq Properties Inc 213 988-8890
1318 E 7th St 200 Los Angeles (90021) ***(G-11498)***
Evox Productions LLC (PA) 310 605-1400
2363 E Pacifica Pl 305 Compton (90220) ***(G-15177)***
Evr Lending Inc 949 492-4868
1397 Calle Avanzado San Clemente (92673) ***(G-11499)***
Evriholder Products LLC (PA) 714 490-7878
1500 S Lewis St Anaheim (92805) ***(G-6860)***
EW Scripps Company 619 237-1010
4600 Air Way San Diego (92102) ***(G-5860)***
Ewing-Foley Inc (PA) 408 342-1201
10061 Bubb Rd Ste 100 Cupertino (95014) ***(G-7562)***
Eworkplace Solutions Inc 949 583-1646
23191 La Cadena Dr # 101 Laguna Hills (92653) ***(G-7130)***
Exablox Corporation 408 773-8477
1156 Sonora Ct Sunnyvale (94086) ***(G-16235)***
Exactax Inc (PA) 714 284-4802
1100 E Orangethorpe Ave # 100 Anaheim (92801) ***(G-13720)***
Exadel Inc (PA) 925 363-9510
1340 Treat Blvd Ste 375 Walnut Creek (94597) ***(G-15660)***
Examine Your Practice, San Diego *Also called Trendsource Inc* ***(G-26714)***
Exandal Corporation 818 705-9497
17620 Sherman Way Ste 207 Van Nuys (91406) ***(G-8477)***
Excalibur Well Services Corp (PA) 661 589-5338
22034 Rosedale Hwy Bakersfield (93314) ***(G-1058)***
Exceed, Hemet *Also called Valley Rsrce Ctr For Retarded* ***(G-24994)***
Excel Auto Transporting Towing, La Puente *Also called Deluxe Auto Carriers Inc* ***(G-4005)***
Excel Building Services LLC 650 755-0900
1061 Serpentine Ln Ste H Pleasanton (94566) ***(G-14293)***
Excel Construction Svcs Inc (PA) 714 680-9200
1950 Raymer Ave Fullerton (92833) ***(G-1423)***
Excel Contractors Inc 661 942-6944
348 E Avenue K8 Ste B Lancaster (93535) ***(G-1172)***
Excel Home Health Inc 619 460-6622
5575 Lake Park Way # 220 La Mesa (91942) ***(G-22434)***
Excel Landscape Inc 951 735-9650
710 Rimpau Ave Ste 108 Corona (92879) ***(G-851)***
Excel Managed Care Disa 916 944-7185
3840 Watt Ave Bldg C Sacramento (95821) ***(G-27426)***
Excel Mdular Scaffold Lsg Corp 760 598-0050
2555 Birch St Vista (92081) ***(G-3514)***
Excel Moving Services 800 392-3596
30047 Ahern Ave Union City (94587) ***(G-4344)***
Excel Paving Co, Long Beach *Also called Palp Inc* ***(G-1841)***
Excela Technology Inc 310 607-9400
1960 E Grand Ave Ste 1260 El Segundo (90245) ***(G-15946)***
Excelfore Corporation 510 868-2500
3155 Kearney St Ste 200 Fremont (94538) ***(G-15947)***
Excell Care Ctr, Oakland *Also called Mariner Health Care Inc* ***(G-20771)***
Excell Center, The, Turlock *Also called Aspiranet* ***(G-23672)***
Excell Health Care Center, Oakland *Also called SSC Oakland Excell Oper Co LP* ***(G-20926)***
Excell Sheet Metal, Palm Desert *Also called Jones John* ***(G-3182)***

ALPHABETIC

Excell Staffing & SEC Svcs, El Cajon *Also called Xl Staffing Inc* ***(G-14822)***
Excellence Ventures Inc 323 262-6800
149 S Mednik Ave Los Angeles (90022) ***(G-17156)***
Excellent Building Maintenance, Moorpark *Also called EBM Janitorial Services Inc* ***(G-14287)***
Excellnce of Inland Empire Inc 909 758-4311
9568 Archibald Ave 110 Rancho Cucamonga (91730) ***(G-11500)***
Excelta Corporation (PA) 805 686-4686
60 Easy St Ste F Buellton (93427) ***(G-7683)***
Exceptional Chld Foundation (PA) 310 204-3300
5350 Machado Ln Culver City (90230) ***(G-24338)***
Exceptional Chld Foundation 323 870-2000
5350 Machado Ln Culver City (90230) ***(G-24339)***
Exceptional Chld Foundation 310 204-3300
5350 Machado Ln Culver City (90230) ***(G-24340)***
Exceptnal Prents Unlimited Inc 559 229-2000
4440 N 1st St Fresno (93726) ***(G-23964)***
Exchange Bank (HQ) 707 524-3000
440 Aviation Blvd Santa Rosa (95403) ***(G-9585)***
Exchange Bank 707 524-3399
440 Aviation Blvd Santa Rosa (95403) ***(G-9396)***
Exchange Bank 707 762-5555
2 E Washington St Petaluma (94952) ***(G-9491)***
Exchange Bank/Loan Service Ctr, Santa Rosa *Also called Exchange Bank* ***(G-9396)***
Exchange La, Sherman Oaks *Also called WERM Investments LLC* ***(G-18505)***
Execusheld Prtection Group LLC 707 439-6351
301 Georgia St Ste 307 Vallejo (94590) ***(G-16637)***
Execushield Inc 415 508-0825
4104 24th St Ste 501 San Francisco (94114) ***(G-16638)***
Executive Committee, The, San Diego *Also called Vistage International Inc* ***(G-27714)***
Executive Ex Mssngr-Air Curier, Newport Beach *Also called Executive Express Inc* ***(G-4400)***
Executive Express Inc (PA) 949 852-0450
2007 Quail St Newport Beach (92660) ***(G-4400)***
Executive Financial HM Ln Corp 818 285-5626
12501 Chandler Blvd Valley Village (91607) ***(G-9839)***
Executive Fitness Management 818 259-6753
226 E Palm Ave Burbank (91502) ***(G-18630)***
Executive Home Loan, Valley Village *Also called Executive Financial HM Ln Corp* ***(G-9839)***
Executive Inn Inc 408 245-5330
1217 Wildwood Ave Sunnyvale (94089) ***(G-12628)***
Executive Landscape Inc 760 731-9036
2131 Huffstatler St Fallbrook (92028) ***(G-852)***
Executive Living Apartments, Stockton *Also called Grupe Properties Co* ***(G-4565)***
Executive Marketing Firm 818 713-1998
4924 Balboa Blvd 375 Encino (91316) ***(G-27427)***
Executive Network Entps Inc 310 457-8822
1224 21st St Apt E Santa Monica (90404) ***(G-3789)***
Executive Network Entps Inc (PA) 310 447-2759
13440 Beach Ave Marina Del Rey (90292) ***(G-3790)***
Executive Office State of CA 916 322-2318
1400 10th St Rm 100 Sacramento (95814) ***(G-26515)***
Executive Protection Agency K- 619 442-5771
1175 N 2nd St Ste 102 El Cajon (92021) ***(G-16639)***
Executives Outlet Inc 415 433-6044
1 Lombard St Lbby San Francisco (94111) ***(G-18631)***
Exel Inc 415 531-0596
485 Valley Dr Brisbane (94005) ***(G-5067)***
Exel Inc 510 784-7360
2391 W Winton Ave Hayward (94545) ***(G-4550)***
Exel Inc 623 907-2338
5576 Ontario Mills Pkwy B Ontario (91764) ***(G-4551)***
Exel N Amercn Logistics Inc 209 942-0102
3735 Imperial Way Stockton (95215) ***(G-4493)***
Exel N Amercn Logistics Inc 209 932-2400
4512 Frontier Way Stockton (95215) ***(G-4494)***
Exelixis Inc 650 837-7000
210 E Grand Ave South San Francisco (94080) ***(G-26516)***
Exeter Packers Inc (PA) 559 592-5168
1250 E Myer Ave Exeter (93221) ***(G-529)***
Exeter Packers Inc 661 399-0416
33374 Lerdo Hwy Bakersfield (93308) ***(G-4495)***
Exeter Packers Inc 559 784-8820
23744 Avenue 181 Porterville (93257) ***(G-530)***
Exeter-Ivanhoe Citrus Assn 559 592-3141
901 Rocky Hill Dr Exeter (93221) ***(G-531)***
Exigen (usa) Inc (PA) 415 402-2600
345 California St Fl 22 San Francisco (94104) ***(G-15178)***
Exigen Group, San Francisco *Also called Exigen (usa) Inc* ***(G-15178)***
Eximex Inc 619 585-1327
503 Beacon Pl Chula Vista (91910) ***(G-26661)***
Exis Inc 408 944-4600
1570 The Alameda Ste 150 San Jose (95126) ***(G-7563)***
Exit Twin Advantage Realty, Murrieta *Also called Twin Advantage Inc* ***(G-11889)***
Exmart International Trdg Corp 714 993-1139
2923 Saturn St Ste H Brea (92821) ***(G-9995)***
Exodus Recovery, Fairfield *Also called Solano County Mental Health* ***(G-24216)***
Exodus Recovery Inc (PA) 310 945-3350
9808 Venice Blvd Ste 700 Culver City (90232) ***(G-22729)***
Exodus Recovery Ctr At Brotman (PA) 310 253-9494
3828 Delmas Ter Culver City (90232) ***(G-22141)***
Exodus Wireless Corp 714 665-6500
14352 Chambers Rd Tustin (92780) ***(G-5601)***
Exotic Imports Intl Inc 949 306-8816
32011 Isle Vis Laguna Niguel (92677) ***(G-9262)***
Exp US Services Inc 858 597-0555
5670 Oberlin Dr San Diego (92121) ***(G-25804)***
Expeditors Intl Wash Inc 415 657-3600
425 Valley Dr Brisbane (94005) ***(G-5068)***
Expeditors Intl Wash Inc 919 489-7431
578 Eccles Ave South San Francisco (94080) ***(G-5069)***
Expeditors Intl Wash Inc 310 343-6200
5757 W Century Blvd Los Angeles (90045) ***(G-5070)***
Expeditors Intl Wash Inc 310 343-6200
5757 W Century Blvd Los Angeles (90045) ***(G-5071)***
Expeditors Intl Wash Inc 619 710-1900
1470 Expo Way Ste 110 San Diego (92154) ***(G-5072)***
Experian Corporation 714 830-7000
475 Anton Blvd Santa Ana (92704) ***(G-14058)***
Experian Info Solutions Inc (HQ) 714 830-7000
475 Anton Blvd Costa Mesa (92626) ***(G-14059)***
Experian Info Solutions Inc 310 343-6700
841 Apollo St Ste 200 El Segundo (90245) ***(G-27428)***
Experian Info Solutions Inc 949 567-3731
18500 Von Karman Ave # 400 Irvine (92612) ***(G-14060)***
Experian Marketing, El Segundo *Also called Experian Info Solutions Inc* ***(G-27428)***
Experience Unlimited, Capitola *Also called Profile of Santa Cruz* ***(G-14737)***
Experienced Home Care Registry 760 724-0880
110 Civic Center Dr # 206 Vista (92084) ***(G-22435)***
Expert Building Maint LLC 805 520-1580
4596 Ish Dr Ste 200 Simi Valley (93063) ***(G-14294)***
Experts Exch Exprts-Xchangecom, San Luis Obispo *Also called Experts Exchange LLC* ***(G-16369)***
Experts Exchange LLC 805 787-0603
2701 Mcmillan Ave Ste 160 San Luis Obispo (93401) ***(G-16369)***
Exploratorium (PA) 415 528-4462
17 Pier Ste 100 San Francisco (94111) ***(G-25021)***
Exponent Inc (PA) 650 326-9400
149 Commonwealth Dr Menlo Park (94025) ***(G-25805)***
Exponential Interactive Inc (HQ) 510 250-5500
5858 Horton St Ste 300 Emeryville (94608) ***(G-13848)***
Expreal Inc 909 373-4400
7168 Archibald Ave # 100 Alta Loma (91701) ***(G-11501)***
Exprescom LLC 619 271-0531
10145 Via De La Amistad San Diego (92154) ***(G-7564)***
Exprescom S.A. De C.V., San Diego *Also called Exprescom LLC* ***(G-7564)***
Express Building Maint Co, Los Angeles *Also called Ebm Inc* ***(G-14286)***
Express Cable Communication 951 272-2029
350 S Maple St Ste L Corona (92880) ***(G-5999)***
Express Contractors Inc 951 360-6500
11625 Industry Ave Fontana (92337) ***(G-13598)***
Express Imaging Services Inc 888 846-8804
1805 W 208th St Ste 202 Torrance (90501) ***(G-4686)***
Express Messenger Systems Inc 323 725-2100
5829 Smithway St Commerce (90040) ***(G-4401)***
Express Messenger Systems Inc 818 504-9043
11085 Olinda St Sun Valley (91352) ***(G-4402)***
Express Messenger Systems Inc 209 234-8255
1627 Industrial Dr Stockton (95206) ***(G-4403)***
Express Messenger Systems Inc 949 235-1400
1240 S Allec St Anaheim (92805) ***(G-4404)***
Express Messenger Systems Inc 800 488-2829
914 W Boone St Santa Maria (93458) ***(G-4405)***
Express Messenger Systems Inc 818 504-9043
11085 Olinda St Sun Valley (91352) ***(G-4406)***
Express Messenger Systems Inc 916 921-6016
1635 Main Ave Ste 3 Sacramento (95838) ***(G-4407)***
Express Messenger Systems Inc 559 277-4910
4603 N Brawley Ave # 103 Fresno (93722) ***(G-4843)***
Express Messenger Systems Inc 415 495-7300
101 Spear St Ste A1 San Francisco (94105) ***(G-4408)***
Express Network, Los Angeles *Also called Legal Support Network LLC* ***(G-17291)***
Express Personnel Services, Montebello *Also called Express Services Inc* ***(G-14876)***
Express Personnel Services 530 671-9202
870 W Onstott Frontage Rd E Yuba City (95991) ***(G-14875)***
Express Services Inc 323 832-9405
1433 N Montebello Blvd Montebello (90640) ***(G-14876)***
Express System Intermodal Inc 801 302-6625
2633 Camino Ramon Ste 400 San Ramon (94583) ***(G-5073)***
Express Transport Solutions 626 961-4800
13285 Temple Ave City of Industry (91746) ***(G-4345)***
Express Waste Rolloff, San Diego *Also called Resource Management Group Inc* ***(G-28041)***
Expressworks International LLC (PA) 925 244-0900
2010 Crow Canyon Pl # 260 San Ramon (94583) ***(G-27429)***
Exquisite Dental Technology 626 237-0107
4816 Temple City Blvd Temple City (91780) ***(G-22215)***
Extend A Hand Inc 949 586-5142
24551 Raymond Way Ste 230 Lake Forest (92630) ***(G-23965)***
Extended Care Hosp Westminster 714 891-2769
206 Hospital Cir Westminster (92683) ***(G-20562)***
Extended Stay America, Inc., Newport Beach *Also called ESA P Prtfolio Oper Lessee LLC* ***(G-12623)***
Extended Stay America, Inc., Orange *Also called ESA P Prtfolio Oper Lessee LLC* ***(G-12624)***
Exterior Solutions Inc 310 400-3510
25752 Simpson Pl Calabasas (91302) ***(G-7012)***
Exterran Inc 626 455-0739
3449 Santa Anita Ave El Monte (91731) ***(G-14481)***
Extra Express (cerritos) Inc 714 985-6000
3050 Enterprise St Brea (92821) ***(G-5074)***
Extreme Telecom Inc 818 902-4821
9221 Corbin Ave Ste 260 Northridge (91324) ***(G-5602)***
Exult Inc 949 856-8800
121 Innovation Dr Ste 200 Irvine (92617) ***(G-27430)***
Ey, Los Angeles *Also called Ernst & Young LLP* ***(G-26337)***
Ey, El Segundo *Also called Ernst & Young LLP* ***(G-26338)***
Ey, San Francisco *Also called Ernst & Young LLP* ***(G-26339)***
Ey, Palo Alto *Also called Ernst & Young LLP* ***(G-26340)***

ALPHABETIC

Ey, San Jose *Also called Ernst & Young LLP* ***(G-26341)***
Ey, Irvine *Also called Ernst & Young LLP* ***(G-26342)***
Ey, San Diego *Also called Ernst & Young LLP* ***(G-26343)***
Ey, Irvine *Also called Ernst & Young LLP* ***(G-26344)***
Ey, Westlake Village *Also called Ernst & Young LLP* ***(G-26345)***
Ey, Redwood City *Also called Ernst & Young LLP* ***(G-26346)***
Ey, Roseville *Also called Ernst & Young LLP* ***(G-26347)***
Eye Medical Center of Fresno, Fresno *Also called Eye Medical Clinic Fresno Inc* ***(G-19518)***
Eye Medical Clinic Fresno Inc....559 486-5000
1360 E Herndon Ave # 301 Fresno (93720) ***(G-19518)***
Eye Q Vision Care (PA)....559 486-2000
7075 N Sharon Ave Fresno (93720) ***(G-19519)***
Eyecenter Optometric Inc....916 624-2020
6809 Five Star Blvd # 100 Rocklin (95677) ***(G-20299)***
Eyefinity Inc....877 481-4455
10875 Intl Dr Fl 2 200 Rancho Cordova (95670) ***(G-15179)***
EZ Acceptance Inc....858 278-8351
7651 Ronson Rd San Diego (92111) ***(G-14540)***
EZ Electric, Roseville *Also called Vexillum Inc* ***(G-6250)***
EZ Labor & Harvesting Inc....760 344-6693
1624 Main St Brawley (92227) ***(G-659)***
EZ Lube LLC (PA)....714 556-1312
3540 Howard Way Ste 200 Costa Mesa (92626) ***(G-17882)***
Ez-Flo International Inc (PA)....909 947-5256
2750 E Mission Blvd Ontario (91761) ***(G-7711)***
Eze Trucking LLC (HQ)....909 770-8800
2584 N Locust Ave Rialto (92377) ***(G-4156)***
F & A Federal Credit Union....323 268-1226
2625 Corporate Pl Monterey Park (91754) ***(G-9594)***
F & B Inc....909 203-8436
596 Indian Hill Blvd # 221 Pomona (91767) ***(G-17953)***
F & F Contracting Inc....559 276-2418
4145 W Alamos Ave Fresno (93722) ***(G-660)***
F & G Biagi Transportation, Ontario *Also called Biagi Bros Inc* ***(G-4527)***
F & H Construction (PA)....209 931-3738
1115 E Lockeford St Lodi (95240) ***(G-1552)***
F and A Farms, Stevinson *Also called Frank J Gomes Dairy A Califo* ***(G-425)***
F C I, Anaheim *Also called Fci Lender Services Inc* ***(G-14031)***
F D I C, Roseville *Also called Federal Deposit Insurance Corp* ***(G-10570)***
F E E, Rcho STA Marg *Also called Fakouri Electrical Engrg Inc* ***(G-16293)***
F F L, San Francisco *Also called Ffl Partners LLC* ***(G-12139)***
F F M L R, Moss Beach *Also called Friends Fitzgerald Mar Reserve* ***(G-24921)***
F H One Inc....510 832-3240
1212 Broadway Ste 716 Oakland (94612) ***(G-11966)***
F I N, Van Nuys *Also called Financial Information Network* ***(G-15184)***
F J Hoover Plumbing Inc....951 360-8262
2259 Hamner Ave Norco (92860) ***(G-2222)***
F Korbel & Bros....707 525-1875
4384 Becker Blvd Santa Rosa (95403) ***(G-4917)***
F M I, Anaheim *Also called Freight Management Inc* ***(G-27441)***
F M T, Carlsbad *Also called Fmt Consultants LLC* ***(G-16371)***
F M Tarbell Co....951 471-5333
18295 Collier Ave Lake Elsinore (92530) ***(G-11502)***
F M Tarbell Co....951 677-3565
39028 Winchester Rd # 101 Murrieta (92563) ***(G-11503)***
F M Tarbell Co....714 772-8990
321 S State College Blvd Anaheim (92806) ***(G-11504)***
F M Tarbell Co....714 637-7240
6396 E Santa Ana Cyn Rd Anaheim (92807) ***(G-11505)***
F M Tarbell Co (HQ)....714 972-0988
1403 N Tustin Ave Ste 380 Santa Ana (92705) ***(G-11506)***
F M Tarbell Co....951 280-6040
315 Magnolia Ave Corona (92879) ***(G-11507)***
F M Tarbell Co....949 830-6030
25201 La Paz Rd Laguna Hills (92653) ***(G-11508)***
F M Tarbell Co....951 301-5932
27701 Scott Rd Ste 103 Menifee (92584) ***(G-11509)***
F M Tarbell Co....951 303-0307
31990 Temecula Pkwy # 101 Temecula (92592) ***(G-11510)***
F M Tarbell Co....909 861-3100
22632 Golden Springs Dr # 290 Diamond Bar (91765) ***(G-11511)***
F M Tarbell Co....949 366-8810
1001 Avenida Pico Ste N San Clemente (92673) ***(G-11512)***
F M Tarbell Co....951 471-5333
18295 Collier Ave Lake Elsinore (92530) ***(G-11513)***
F M Tarbell Co....714 639-0677
1403 N Tustin Ave Ste 340 Santa Ana (92705) ***(G-11514)***
F M Tarbell Co....949 559-8451
4000 Barranca Pkwy # 160 Irvine (92604) ***(G-11515)***
F M Tarbell Co....951 270-1022
2409 S Vineyard Ave Ste A Ontario (91761) ***(G-11516)***
F M Tarbell Co....909 982-8881
1365 E 19th St Ste A Upland (91784) ***(G-11517)***
F O C Electronics Corporation....213 625-5775
830 Traction Ave Los Angeles (90013) ***(G-7497)***
F P I, Shafter *Also called Farm Pump & Irrigation Co Inc* ***(G-7843)***
F R A LP....714 633-1442
1702 Fairhaven Ave Santa Ana (92705) ***(G-13706)***
F R Ghianni Drywall Cnstr Co, El Cajon *Also called F R Ghianni Enterprises Inc* ***(G-1173)***
F R Ghianni Enterprises Inc....619 279-1073
1937 Friendship Dr Ste A El Cajon (92020) ***(G-1173)***
F R H I, San Jose *Also called Fertility & Reproductive* ***(G-19526)***
F R T International Inc....909 390-4892
2825 Jurupa St Ontario (91761) ***(G-5075)***
F&E Aircraft Maintenance, El Segundo *Also called Arinwine Arcft Maint Svcs LLC* ***(G-4902)***
F&E Aircraft Maintenance (PA)....310 338-0063
531 Main St El Segundo (90245) ***(G-4918)***
F&M Bank, Long Beach *Also called Farmers Merchants Bnk Long Bch* ***(G-9492)***
F-Secure Inc....408 938-6700
1735 Tech Dr Ste 850 San Jose (95110) ***(G-7131)***
F3 and Associates Inc (PA)....707 748-4300
701 E H St Benicia (94510) ***(G-26274)***
Faberware Div, Fairfield *Also called Meyer Corporation US* ***(G-6874)***
Fabric Barn....562 494-3450
3123 E Anaheim St Long Beach (90804) ***(G-8312)***
Facebook Inc (PA)....650 543-4800
1 Hacker Way Bldg 10 Menlo Park (94025) ***(G-16236)***
Facey Medical Foundation....805 206-2000
2655 1st St Simi Valley (93065) ***(G-20289)***
Facey Medical Foundation....818 861-7831
191 S Buena Vista St Burbank (91505) ***(G-20290)***
Facey Medical Foundation (PA)....818 365-9531
15451 San Fernando Msn Mission Hills (91345) ***(G-22957)***
Facey Medical Foundation....818 837-5677
11211 Sepulveda Blvd Mission Hills (91345) ***(G-22958)***
Facey Medical Foundation....661 250-5225
17909 Soledad Canyon Rd Santa Clarita (91387) ***(G-22959)***
Facey Medical Foundation....661 513-2100
27924 Seco Canyon Rd Santa Clarita (91350) ***(G-22960)***
Facey Medical Foundation....626 576-0800
1237 E Main St San Gabriel (91776) ***(G-22961)***
Facey Medical Foundation....818 734-3600
18460 Roscoe Blvd Northridge (91325) ***(G-22962)***
Facey Medical Group, Santa Clarita *Also called Facey Medical Foundation* ***(G-22959)***
Facey Medical Group, Northridge *Also called Facey Medical Foundation* ***(G-22962)***
Facial Reconstructive Surg &, East Palo Alto *Also called Riley & Powell MD* ***(G-19920)***
Facilities & Operations, San Jacinto *Also called San Jacinto Unified School* ***(G-11264)***
Facilities and Fleet, San Jose *Also called Santa Clara County of* ***(G-14418)***
Facilities Management, Oakland *Also called Oakland Unified School Dst* ***(G-14373)***
Facilities Operation and Trnsp....209 826-1936
2657 E Pacheco Blvd Los Banos (93635) ***(G-3926)***
Facility Masters Inc (PA)....408 436-9090
1604 Kerley Dr San Jose (95112) ***(G-14295)***
Facility Services Partners....949 480-4090
1 University Dr Aliso Viejo (92656) ***(G-27021)***
Facility Solutions Group Inc....714 993-3966
801 Richfield Rd Placentia (92870) ***(G-7441)***
Fact Foundation....818 729-8105
303 N Glenoaks Blvd Burbank (91502) ***(G-17157)***
Facter Direct Ltd....323 634-1999
4751 Wilshire Blvd # 140 Los Angeles (90010) ***(G-17158)***
Factory 2-U Import Export Inc....323 587-9900
13034 Delano St Van Nuys (91401) ***(G-8383)***
Factory Motor Parts, Orange *Also called Elliott Auto Supply Co Inc* ***(G-6728)***
Factory Mutual Insurance Co....925 934-2200
1333 N Calif Blvd Ste 200 Walnut Creek (94596) ***(G-10413)***
Factory Mutual Insurance Co....818 227-2200
6320 Canoga Ave Ste 1100 Woodland Hills (91367) ***(G-10414)***
Factory R D....949 900-3460
23192 Verdugo Dr Laguna Hills (92653) ***(G-7341)***
Factory Remodeling, San Diego *Also called Window Factory Inc* ***(G-3103)***
Faculty Physcans Srgeons Llusm....909 558-4000
11370 Anderson St Loma Linda (92354) ***(G-19520)***
Fair Isaac Corporation (PA)....408 535-1500
181 Metro Dr Ste 700 San Jose (95110) ***(G-15661)***
Fair Isaac International Corp (HQ)....415 446-6000
200 Smith Ranch Rd San Rafael (94903) ***(G-15662)***
Fair Trade USA....510 663-5260
1500 Broadway Ste 400 Oakland (94612) ***(G-26765)***
Fairbanks Ranch Cntry CLB Inc....858 259-8811
15150 San Dieguito Rd Rancho Santa Fe (92067) ***(G-18947)***
FAIRCHILD MEDICAL CENTER, Yreka *Also called Siskiyou Hospital Inc* ***(G-21894)***
Fairfield Community Center, Fairfield *Also called City of Fairfield* ***(G-10972)***
Fairfield Development Inc (PA)....858 457-2123
5510 Morehouse Dr Ste 200 San Diego (92121) ***(G-1310)***
Fairfield Family YMCA, Long Beach *Also called Young Mens Chrstn Assc Gr L B* ***(G-25461)***
Fairfield Healthcare Center, Fairfield *Also called Fairfield Nursing & Rehab Ctr* ***(G-20563)***
Fairfield Inn, San Diego *Also called RPC Old Town Avenue Owner LLC* ***(G-13175)***
Fairfield Inn, Rancho Cordova *Also called Presidio Hotel Group LLC* ***(G-13110)***
Fairfield Inn Suites By M....707 864-6672
315 Pittman Rd Fairfield (94534) ***(G-12629)***
Fairfield Medical Offices, Fairfield *Also called Kaiser Foundation Hospitals* ***(G-19614)***
Fairfield Nursing & Rehab Ctr....707 425-0623
1255 Travis Blvd Fairfield (94533) ***(G-20563)***
Fairfield-Suisun Sewer Dst....707 429-8930
1010 Chadbourne Rd Fairfield (94534) ***(G-6483)***
Fairfight, Pasadena *Also called Myinternetservicescom LLC* ***(G-5662)***
Fairgrounds....805 239-0655
2198 Riverside Ave Paso Robles (93446) ***(G-18392)***
Fairgrounds Golf Center, Rancho Murieta *Also called Empire Golf Inc* ***(G-18739)***
Fairhaven Mem Pk & Mortuary, Santa Ana *Also called R A F LP* ***(G-13711)***
Fairmont Designs, Buena Park *Also called Cambium Business Group Inc* ***(G-6810)***
Fairmont Hotel Partners LLC....310 319-3122
101 Wilshire Blvd Santa Monica (90401) ***(G-12630)***
Fairmont Hotel Partners LLC (HQ)....415 772-5000
950 Mason St San Francisco (94108) ***(G-27022)***
Fairmont Miramar Hotel, Santa Monica *Also called Ocean Avenue LLC* ***(G-13032)***
Fairmont Newport Beach, Newport Beach *Also called Sunstone Hotel Investors Inc* ***(G-13316)***
Fairmont San Francisco, San Francisco *Also called Mason Street Opco LLC* ***(G-12983)***
Fairplex Child Development Ctr....909 623-3899
1101 W Mckinley Ave Pomona (91768) ***(G-24461)***

Fairplex Enterprises Inc.....909 623-3111
1101 W Mckinley Ave Pomona (91768) ***(G-19207)***
Fairplex Rv Park, Pomona *Also called Los Angeles County Fair Assn* ***(G-19240)***
Fairview Developmental Center, Costa Mesa *Also called Califrnia Dept State Hospitals* ***(G-22047)***
Fairview Developmental Center, Costa Mesa *Also called Developmental Svcs Cal Dept* ***(G-24335)***
Fairway Independent Mrtg Corp.....707 361-5342
555 1st St Ste 102 Benicia (94510) ***(G-9996)***
Fairway Independent Mrtg Corp.....951 676-0527
43385 Business Park Dr Temecula (92590) ***(G-9997)***
Fairwinds Woodward Park, Fresno *Also called Leisure Care LLC* ***(G-24710)***
Fairwinds-West Hills, Canoga Park *Also called Leisure Care LLC* ***(G-21089)***
Fairwood Apartments, Carmichael *Also called Fairwood Associates Apts* ***(G-11128)***
Fairwood Associates Apts.....916 944-0152
8893 Fair Oaks Blvd Ofc Carmichael (95608) ***(G-11128)***
Faith Bumper Service, Gilroy *Also called Faith T & B Plating Inc* ***(G-17159)***
Faith Com Inc (PA).....562 719-9300
3850 E Gilman St Long Beach (90815) ***(G-27919)***
Faith Enterprises Inc.....209 835-6034
545 W Beverly Pl Tracy (95376) ***(G-20564)***
Faith Jones & Associates Inc (PA).....619 297-9601
7801 Mission Center Ct # 106 San Diego (92108) ***(G-22436)***
Faith Quality Auto Body Inc.....951 698-8215
41130 Nick Ln Murrieta (92562) ***(G-17753)***
Faith T & B Plating Inc.....408 986-1226
8475 Forest St Gilroy (95020) ***(G-17159)***
Fakouri Electrical Engrg Inc.....949 888-2400
30001 Comercio Rcho STA Marg (92688) ***(G-16293)***
Falcon Aerospace Holdings LLC.....661 775-7200
27727 Avenue Scott Valencia (91355) ***(G-27023)***
Falcon Trading Company (PA).....831 786-7000
423 Salinas Rd Royal Oaks (95076) ***(G-8834)***
Falconwood Inc.....619 297-9080
1011 Camino Del Rio S San Diego (92108) ***(G-16294)***
Falken Tire Corporation, Rancho Cucamonga *Also called Sumitomo Rubber North Amer Inc* ***(G-6790)***
Falken Tire Holdings Inc.....800 723-2553
8656 Haven Ave Rancho Cucamonga (91730) ***(G-6784)***
Falken Tires, Rancho Cucamonga *Also called Falken Tire Holdings Inc* ***(G-6784)***
Fall Christian Unit, The, Manteca *Also called American Legion Aux* ***(G-25197)***
Fallbrook Fire Protection Dst.....760 723-2010
315 E Ivy St Fallbrook (92028) ***(G-17160)***
Fallbrook Hospital, Fallbrook *Also called Fallbrook Sklled Nrsing Fcilty* ***(G-20565)***
Fallbrook Public Utility Dst.....760 728-1125
990 E Mission Rd Fallbrook (92028) ***(G-23236)***
Fallbrook Sklled Nrsing Fcilty.....760 728-2330
325 Potter St Fallbrook (92028) ***(G-20565)***
Fallon Land Company Inc.....213 880-1279
4 Corporate Plaza Dr # 210 Newport Beach (92660) ***(G-7370)***
Fam LLC.....323 888-7755
5553 Ste B Bandini Blvd Bell (90201) ***(G-8340)***
Fam Brands, Bell *Also called Fam LLC* ***(G-8340)***
Famand Inc.....707 255-9295
1604 Airport Blvd Santa Rosa (95403) ***(G-2223)***
Fame Assistance Corporation.....323 373-7720
1968 W Adams Blvd Los Angeles (90018) ***(G-27920)***
Fame Hardwood Floors, Los Angeles *Also called P8ge Consulting Inc* ***(G-28014)***
Fame Systems Inc.....805 485-0808
301 Hearst Dr Oxnard (93030) ***(G-14296)***
Family and Children Services.....408 292-9353
950 W Julian St San Jose (95126) ***(G-27921)***
Family Assessment Cnslng Edctn.....714 547-7345
1651 E 4th St Ste 128 Santa Ana (92701) ***(G-23966)***
Family Bridges Inc.....510 839-2270
168 11th St Oakland (94607) ***(G-23967)***
Family Care Network Inc (PA).....805 503-6240
1255 Kendall Rd San Luis Obispo (93401) ***(G-24462)***
Family Circle Inc.....805 385-4180
2100 Outlet Center Dr # 380 Oxnard (93036) ***(G-23968)***
Family First Financial Service.....310 355-1788
13658 Hawthorne Blvd # 307 Hawthorne (90250) ***(G-27431)***
Family Fun Centers, San Diego *Also called Festival Funparks LLC* ***(G-19212)***
Family Health Center, Pomona *Also called Keith T Kusunis MD* ***(G-22758)***
Family Health Center San Diego, Spring Valley *Also called Family Hlth Ctrs San Diego Inc* ***(G-19524)***
Family Health Program, Long Beach *Also called Healthcare Partners LLC* ***(G-22971)***
Family Health Services Clinic, Madera *Also called Madera Community Hospital* ***(G-19724)***
Family Healthcare Network.....559 798-1877
33025 159th Rd Ivanhoe (93235) ***(G-19521)***
Family Hlth Ctrs San Diego Inc.....619 515-2526
1845 Logan Ave San Diego (92113) ***(G-19522)***
Family Hlth Ctrs San Diego Inc.....619 515-2435
2391 Island Ave San Diego (92102) ***(G-19523)***
Family Hlth Ctrs San Diego Inc.....619 515-2300
1809 National Ave San Diego (92113) ***(G-20254)***
Family Hlth Ctrs San Diego Inc (PA).....619 515-2303
823 Gateway Center Way San Diego (92102) ***(G-22730)***
Family Hlth Ctrs San Diego Inc.....619 515-2550
7592 Broadway Lemon Grove (91945) ***(G-22963)***
Family Hlth Ctrs San Diego Inc.....619 515-2555
8788 Jamacha Rd Spring Valley (91977) ***(G-19524)***
Family Intrnal Mdcn-Plcerville, Placerville *Also called Marshall Medical Center* ***(G-19732)***
Family Mdcine Rsidency Program.....559 499-6450
155 N Fresno St Ste 326 Fresno (93701) ***(G-21564)***
Family Mrale Wlfare Recreation.....760 380-3493
1317 Normandy Dr Fort Irwin (92310) ***(G-18948)***
Family Plg Assoc Med Group.....562 595-5653
2777 Long Beach Blvd # 150 Long Beach (90806) ***(G-17161)***
Family Plg Assoc Med Group (PA).....213 738-7283
3050 E Airport Way Long Beach (90806) ***(G-19525)***
Family Radio, Alameda *Also called Family Stations Inc* ***(G-5773)***
Family Resource & Referral Ctr.....209 948-1553
509 W Weber Ave Ste 101 Stockton (95203) ***(G-23969)***
Family Resource Center.....530 872-4015
6249 Skyway Paradise (95969) ***(G-23970)***
Family Savings Bank, Los Angeles *Also called Oneunited Bank* ***(G-9510)***
Family Service Agency, San Rafael *Also called Family Svcs Agcy Marin Cnty* ***(G-23974)***
Family Service Agency.....805 735-4376
110 S C St Ste A Lompoc (93436) ***(G-23971)***
Family Services.....559 741-7310
807 W Oak Ave Visalia (93291) ***(G-25529)***
Family Services Tulare County.....559 732-1970
815 W Oak Ave Visalia (93291) ***(G-23972)***
Family Stations Inc (PA).....510 568-6200
1350 S Loop Rd Alameda (94502) ***(G-5773)***
Family Stress Center, Northridge *Also called Child and Family Guidance Ctr* ***(G-22683)***
Family Support Bureau, San Francisco *Also called San Francisco City & County* ***(G-24184)***
Family Support Division, Modesto *Also called County of Stanislaus* ***(G-23927)***
Family Svc Agcy San Francisco (PA).....415 474-7310
1500 Franklin St San Francisco (94109) ***(G-14877)***
Family Svc Agcy Santa Barbara.....805 965-1001
123 W Gutierrez St Santa Barbara (93101) ***(G-23973)***
Family Svcs Agcy Marin Cnty (PA).....415 491-5700
555 Northgate Dr San Rafael (94903) ***(G-23974)***
Family Tree Produce Inc.....714 693-5688
5510 E La Palma Ave Anaheim (92807) ***(G-8723)***
Family Urgent Care Center, Anaheim *Also called Anaheim Harbor Medical Group* ***(G-19344)***
Family YMCA of Desert.....760 423-5860
42575 Valley Dr Palm Desert (92210) ***(G-23975)***
Famous Ramona Water Inc.....760 789-0174
250 Aqua Ln Ramona (92065) ***(G-8835)***
Famous Software LLC (PA).....559 438-3600
8080 N Palm Ave Ste 210 Fresno (93711) ***(G-15180)***
Fanfare Enterprises, Costa Mesa *Also called Ovations Fanfare* ***(G-27153)***
Fantasea Yacht Charters, Marina Del Rey *Also called USG Enterprises Inc* ***(G-4741)***
Fantasy Springs Resort Casino, Indio *Also called East Valley Tourist Dev Auth* ***(G-19203)***
Far East Broadcasting Co Inc.....562 947-4651
15700 Imperial Hwy La Mirada (90638) ***(G-5774)***
Far East Home Care Inc.....949 673-3100
3407 W 6th St Ste 710 Los Angeles (90020) ***(G-22437)***
Far East National Bank (HQ).....213 687-1300
977 N Broadway Ste 306 Los Angeles (90012) ***(G-9397)***
Far Northern Coordinating Coun.....530 895-8633
1377 E Lassen Ave Chico (95973) ***(G-23976)***
Far Northern Coordinating Coun (PA).....530 222-4791
1900 Churn Creek Rd # 31 Redding (96002) ***(G-23977)***
Far Northern Regional Center, Redding *Also called Far Northern Coordinating Coun* ***(G-23977)***
Far West Electric Inc.....909 684-8661
6094 Keswick Ave Riverside (92506) ***(G-2591)***
Far West Inc.....559 627-1241
4444 W Meadow Ave Visalia (93277) ***(G-20566)***
Far West Inc.....323 564-7761
8455 State St South Gate (90280) ***(G-20567)***
Far West Inc.....909 884-4781
467 E Gilbert St San Bernardino (92404) ***(G-20568)***
Far West Inc.....559 733-0901
4525 W Tulare Ave Visalia (93277) ***(G-21214)***
Far Western Graphics Inc.....408 481-9777
2642 Heritage Park Cir San Jose (95132) ***(G-14117)***
Farallon Capital MGT LLC (PA).....415 421-2132
1 Maritime Plz Ste 2100 San Francisco (94111) ***(G-12114)***
Fargo Colonial LLC.....858 454-2181
910 Prospect St La Jolla (92037) ***(G-12631)***
Faria Drywall Inc.....408 847-2058
8518 Church St Ste 5 Gilroy (95020) ***(G-2895)***
Farm Pump & Irrigation Co Inc (PA).....661 589-6901
535 N Shafter Ave Shafter (93263) ***(G-7843)***
Farmer Boy Foods Inc (PA).....951 275-9900
3452 University Ave Riverside (92501) ***(G-12215)***
Farmer Boys Restaurants, Riverside *Also called Farmer Boy Foods Inc* ***(G-12215)***
Farmers Group Inc (HQ).....323 932-3200
6301 Owensmouth Ave Woodland Hills (91367) ***(G-10415)***
Farmers Group Inc.....213 615-2500
700 S Flower St Ste 2800 Los Angeles (90017) ***(G-10206)***
Farmers Group Inc.....909 839-2020
13950 Ramona Ave Chino (91710) ***(G-10704)***
Farmers Group Inc.....408 557-1100
429 Llewellyn Ave Campbell (95008) ***(G-10705)***
Farmers Group Inc.....925 847-3100
11555 Dublin Canyon Rd Pleasanton (94588) ***(G-10207)***
Farmers Group Inc.....818 249-3000
550 S Hill St Ste 1309 Los Angeles (90013) ***(G-10706)***
Farmers Group Inc.....916 727-4600
6518 Antelope Rd Citrus Heights (95621) ***(G-10707)***
Farmers Group Inc.....888 327-6335
6303 Owensmouth Ave Woodland Hills (91367) ***(G-10708)***
Farmers Group Inc.....805 583-7400
6303 Owensmouth Ave Fl 1 Woodland Hills (91367) ***(G-10709)***
Farmers Insurance, Woodland Hills *Also called Farmers Group Inc* ***(G-10415)***
Farmers Insurance, Los Angeles *Also called Farmers Group Inc* ***(G-10206)***
Farmers Insurance, Chino *Also called Farmers Group Inc* ***(G-10704)***
Farmers Insurance, Campbell *Also called Farmers Group Inc* ***(G-10705)***
Farmers Insurance, Pleasanton *Also called Farmers Group Inc* ***(G-10207)***

Farmers Insurance, Los Angeles *Also called Farmers Group Inc (G-10706)*
Farmers Insurance, Citrus Heights *Also called Farmers Group Inc (G-10707)*
Farmers Insurance, Woodland Hills *Also called Farmers Group Inc (G-10708)*
Farmers Insurance, Woodland Hills *Also called Farmers Group Inc (G-10709)*
Farmers Insurance.....909 801-3300
1801 Orange Tree Ln # 200 Redlands (92374) **(G-10710)**
Farmers Insurance Exchange (PA).....323 932-3200
6301 Owensmouth Ave # 300 Woodland Hills (91367) **(G-10208)**
Farmers Insurance Exchange.....909 758-7060
7365 Carnelian St Ste 206 Rancho Cucamonga (91730) **(G-10711)**
Farmers Insurance Exchange.....858 677-1100
5280 Carroll Canyon Rd # 230 San Diego (92121) **(G-10712)**
Farmers Insurance Exchange.....559 594-4149
411 E Pine St Ste A Exeter (93221) **(G-10713)**
Farmers Insurance Fed Cred UNI (PA).....323 209-6000
4601 Wilshire Blvd # 110 Los Angeles (90010) **(G-9595)**
Farmers Insurance Group (HQ).....888 327-6335
6301 Owensmouth Ave Los Angeles (90010) **(G-10714)**
Farmers International Inc.....530 566-1405
1260 Muir Ave Chico (95973) **(G-200)**
Farmers Merchants Bnk Long Bch (HQ).....562 437-0011
302 Pine Ave Long Beach (90802) **(G-9492)**
Farmers Merchants Bnk Long Bch.....562 430-4724
1695 Adolfo Lopez Dr Seal Beach (90740) **(G-9493)**
Farmers Mrchants Bnk Centl Cal.....916 394-3200
8799 Elk Grove Blvd Elk Grove (95624) **(G-9494)**
Farmers Services LLC.....323 932-3200
4680 Wilshire Blvd Los Angeles (90010) **(G-10715)**
Farmers W Flowers & Bouquets, Carpinteria *Also called Brand Flower Farms Inc (G-9179)*
Farmex Land Management Inc.....559 875-7181
11156 E Annadale Ave Sanger (93657) **(G-17162)**
Farmhill LLC.....831 726-1986
1800 San Juan Rd Aromas (95004) **(G-111)**
Farmington Fresh Sales LLC (PA).....209 983-9700
7735 S Highway 99 Stockton (95215) **(G-233)**
Farms Golf Club Inc.....858 756-5585
8500 San Andrews Rd Rancho Santa Fe (92067) **(G-18949)**
Farms of Amador.....209 257-0112
12200b Airport Rd Jackson (95642) **(G-25530)**
Faro Logistics, Norwalk *Also called Faro Services Inc (G-4552)*
Faro Services Inc.....562 483-7799
15625 Shoemaker Ave Norwalk (90650) **(G-4552)**
Farwest Corrosion Control Co (PA).....310 532-9524
12029 Regentview Ave Downey (90241) **(G-3515)**
Farwest Insulation Contracting.....310 634-2800
2741 Yates Ave Commerce (90040) **(G-2896)**
Farwest Trading, Turlock *Also called Associated Feed & Supply Co (G-9125)*
Fas Holdings Inc.....619 702-9600
655 W Broadway Fl 11 San Diego (92101) **(G-9998)**
Faschings Car Wash, Arcadia *Also called George Fasching (G-17842)*
Fashion Resources, Los Angeles *Also called Tarrant Apparel Group (G-8413)*
Fashion Wheel, Fresno *Also called Anthony Lambe (G-6705)*
Fast Lane Container Services, Wilmington *Also called Fast Lane Transportation Inc (G-4157)*
Fast Lane Transportation Inc (PA).....562 435-3000
2400 E Pacific Coast Hwy Wilmington (90744) **(G-4157)**
Fast Pro Inc.....408 566-0200
2555 Lafayette St Ste 103 Santa Clara (95050) **(G-6730)**
Fast Undercar, Santa Clara *Also called Fast Pro Inc (G-6730)*
Fast Undercar Stockton, Antioch *Also called Jamm Management LLC (G-6742)*
Fastclick Inc.....805 689-9839
530 E Montecito St Santa Barbara (93103) **(G-13995)**
Fastclick.com, Santa Barbara *Also called Fastclick Inc (G-13995)*
Fastech, Buena Park *Also called Fueling and Service Tech Inc (G-7845)*
Fastly Inc.....415 488-6329
475 Brannan St Ste 320 San Francisco (94107) **(G-15181)**
Fata Travel.....951 328-0200
1040 Iowa Ave Ste 100 Riverside (92507) **(G-25806)**
Fathers of St Charles.....818 768-6500
10631 Vinedale St Sun Valley (91352) **(G-11129)**
Fathom, Oakland *Also called Kemeera Incorporated (G-7152)*
Faucetdirect.com, Chico *Also called Buildcom Inc (G-7706)*
Faulkner Trucking Inc.....559 684-9298
3645 S K St Tulare (93274) **(G-4158)**
Fault Line Plumbing.....925 443-6450
7640 National Dr Livermore (94550) **(G-2224)**
Faurot Ranch.....831 722-1346
703 Hall Rd Royal Oaks (95076) **(G-62)**
FBC Industries (PA).....909 627-6131
2800 S Reservoir St Pomona (91766) **(G-11967)**
Fbd Vanguard Construction Inc.....925 245-1300
651 Enterprise Ct Livermore (94550) **(G-27024)**
Fc El Segundo LLC.....702 439-7945
199 Continental Blvd El Segundo (90245) **(G-12632)**
Fc Landscape Inc.....760 347-6600
43216 Madison St Indio (92201) **(G-767)**
Fc Metropolitan Lofts Inc.....213 488-0010
949 S Hope St Ste 100 Los Angeles (90015) **(G-11968)**
Fcb Worldwide Inc.....415 820-8545
1160 Battery St Ste 250 San Francisco (94111) **(G-13849)**
Fcb Worldwide Inc.....415 820-8000
1160 Battery St Ste 250 San Francisco (94111) **(G-13850)**
Fci Lender Services Inc.....714 974-1945
8180 E Kaiser Blvd Anaheim (92808) **(G-14031)**
Fci Management, Long Beach *Also called Faith Com Inc (G-27919)*
Fcs Medical Corporation.....323 317-9200
1701 E Cesar E Chavez Ave # 230 Los Angeles (90033) **(G-20291)**
Fcs Software Solutions Limited.....408 324-1203
2375 Zanker Rd Ste 250 San Jose (95131) **(G-15182)**
Fcti, Los Angeles *Also called Financial Consulting & (G-27433)*
Fdi Collateral Management, Sacramento *Also called Dealertrack Collte Manag Servi (G-16351)*
FDIC, Los Angeles *Also called Federal Deposit Insurance Corp (G-10569)*
FDIC-San Frncisco Regional Off, San Francisco *Also called Federal Deposit Insurance Corp (G-10568)*
Fdsi Logistics LLC.....818 971-3300
5703 Corsa Ave Westlake Village (91362) **(G-27432)**
Fdx Advisors Inc.....916 920-5293
2399 Gateway Oaks Dr # 200 Sacramento (95833) **(G-10138)**
Feather Falls Casino, Oroville *Also called Mooretown Rancheria (G-18806)*
Feather Falls Casino, Oroville *Also called Mooretown Rancheria (G-19247)*
Feather River Home Health, Paradise *Also called Feather River Hospital (G-21566)*
Feather River Hospital (PA).....530 877-9361
5974 Pentz Rd Paradise (95969) **(G-21565)**
Feather River Hospital.....530 872-3378
6626 Clark Rd Ste P Paradise (95969) **(G-21566)**
Feather River Hospital.....530 876-7216
1295 Bille Rd Paradise (95969) **(G-7264)**
Feather River Hospital HM Oxgn, Paradise *Also called Feather River Hospital (G-7264)*
Fed Air Security Corporation.....626 535-2200
210 S De Lacey Ave Pasadena (91105) **(G-16884)**
Fedelity National Title Co Org.....818 758-6849
5000 Van Nuys Blvd 500 Sherman Oaks (91403) **(G-10513)**
Federal Deposit Insurance Corp.....626 359-7152
1333 S Mayflower Ave # 450 Monrovia (91016) **(G-10567)**
Federal Deposit Insurance Corp.....415 546-0160
25 Jessie St Ste 2300 San Francisco (94105) **(G-10568)**
Federal Deposit Insurance Corp.....323 545-9260
5150 W Goldleaf Cir # 405 Los Angeles (90056) **(G-10569)**
Federal Deposit Insurance Corp.....916 789-8580
1532 Eureka Rd Ste 102 Roseville (95661) **(G-10570)**
Federal Express Corporation.....800 463-3339
3541 Regional Pkwy Petaluma (94954) **(G-4844)**
Federal Express Corporation.....800 463-3339
1650 47th St San Diego (92102) **(G-4845)**
Federal Express Corporation.....800 463-3339
1330 Fortress St Chico (95973) **(G-4846)**
Federal Express Corporation.....800 463-3339
1286 Lawrence Station Rd Sunnyvale (94089) **(G-4847)**
Federal Express Corporation.....800 463-3339
12600 Prairie Ave Hawthorne (90250) **(G-4848)**
Federal Express Corporation.....800 463-3339
11340 Sherman Way Sun Valley (91352) **(G-4800)**
Federal Express Corporation.....800 463-3339
1500 Nichols Dr Rocklin (95765) **(G-4801)**
Federal Express Corporation.....800 463-3339
2660 Research Park Dr Soquel (95073) **(G-4409)**
Federal Express Corporation.....800 463-3339
2495 Faraday Ave Carlsbad (92010) **(G-17163)**
Federal Express Corporation.....800 463-3339
1081 Fullerton Rd City of Industry (91748) **(G-4410)**
Federal Express Corporation.....310 563-4176
200 N Sepulveda Blvd # 800 El Segundo (90245) **(G-17164)**
Federal Express Corporation.....800 463-3339
7275 Johnson Dr Pleasanton (94588) **(G-17165)**
Federal Express Corporation.....800 463-3339
3333 S Grand Ave Los Angeles (90007) **(G-4159)**
Federal Express Corporation.....800 463-3339
1650 Sunflower Ave Costa Mesa (92626) **(G-4849)**
Federal Express Corporation.....510 347-2430
1601 Aurora Dr San Leandro (94577) **(G-4850)**
Federal Express Corporation.....800 463-3339
1111 Bird Center Dr Palm Springs (92262) **(G-4802)**
Federal Express Corporation.....800 463-3339
1 Lower Ragsdale Dr # 4 Monterey (93940) **(G-4851)**
Federal Express Corporation.....800 463-3339
710 Dado St San Jose (95131) **(G-4411)**
Federal Express Corporation.....800 463-3339
8455 Pardee Dr Oakland (94621) **(G-4852)**
Federal Express Corporation.....800 463-3339
7000 Barranca Pkwy Irvine (92618) **(G-17166)**
Federal Express Corporation.....510 465-5209
500 12th St Ste 139 Oakland (94607) **(G-4853)**
Federal Express Corporation.....800 463-3339
6775 Woodrum Cir Redding (96002) **(G-4854)**
Federal Express Corporation.....800 463-3339
935 Performance Dr Stockton (95206) **(G-4855)**
Federal Express Corporation.....800 463-3339
9339 Ann St Santa Fe Springs (90670) **(G-4856)**
Federal Express Corporation.....800 463-3339
9510 W Airport Dr Visalia (93277) **(G-4857)**
Federal Express Corporation.....510 382-2344
9190 Edes Ave Oakland (94603) **(G-4412)**
Federal Express Corporation.....800 463-3339
3371 E Francis St Ontario (91761) **(G-17167)**
Federal Express Corporation.....909 390-3237
2060 S Wineville Ave B Ontario (91761) **(G-4858)**
Federal Express Corporation.....800 463-3339
1600 63rd St Emeryville (94608) **(G-4017)**
Federal Express Corporation.....800 463-3339
2500 Kimberly Ave Fullerton (92831) **(G-4859)**
Federal Express Corporation.....800 463-3339
3150 Paseo Mercado Oxnard (93036) **(G-4860)**
Federal Express Corporation.....916 361-5500
8950 Cal Center Dr # 370 Sacramento (95826) **(G-4861)**

Federal Express Corporation **ALPHABETIC SECTION**

Federal Express Corporation ... 619 688-9203
2221 W Washington St San Diego (92110) ***(G-5076)***
Federal Express Corporation ... 800 463-3339
1875 Marin St San Francisco (94124) ***(G-4862)***
Federal Express Corporation ... 800 463-3339
2451 N Palm Dr Long Beach (90755) ***(G-4863)***
Federal Express Corporation ... 949 862-4500
2601 Main St Ste 1000 Irvine (92614) ***(G-4803)***
Federal Express Corporation ... 562 522-4014
1 World Trade Ctr Ste 191 Long Beach (90831) ***(G-4864)***
Federal Hm Ln Bnk San Frncisco (PA) ... 415 616-1000
600 California St San Francisco (94108) ***(G-9730)***
Federal HM Ln Bnk San Frncisco ... 916 851-6900
11050 White Rock Rd Rancho Cordova (95670) ***(G-9746)***
Federal Insurance Company ... 415 273-6300
275 Battery St Fl 12 San Francisco (94111) ***(G-10716)***
Federal Rsrve Bnk San Frncisco (HQ) ... 415 974-2000
101 Market St San Francisco (94105) ***(G-9315)***
Federal Rsrve Bnk San Frncisco ... 213 683-2300
950 S Grand Ave Los Angeles (90015) ***(G-9316)***
Federico Beauty Institute ... 916 929-4242
1515 Sports Dr Ste 100 Sacramento (95834) ***(G-13674)***
Federted Indans Grton Rncheria ... 707 588-7100
630 Park Ct Rohnert Park (94928) ***(G-12633)***
Fedex, Petaluma *Also called Federal Express Corporation* ***(G-4844)***
Fedex, San Diego *Also called Federal Express Corporation* ***(G-4845)***
Fedex, Chico *Also called Federal Express Corporation* ***(G-4846)***
Fedex, Sunnyvale *Also called Federal Express Corporation* ***(G-4847)***
Fedex, Hawthorne *Also called Federal Express Corporation* ***(G-4848)***
Fedex, Sun Valley *Also called Federal Express Corporation* ***(G-4800)***
Fedex, Rocklin *Also called Federal Express Corporation* ***(G-4801)***
Fedex, Soquel *Also called Federal Express Corporation* ***(G-4409)***
Fedex, Carlsbad *Also called Federal Express Corporation* ***(G-17163)***
Fedex, City of Industry *Also called Federal Express Corporation* ***(G-4410)***
Fedex, El Segundo *Also called Federal Express Corporation* ***(G-17164)***
Fedex, Pleasanton *Also called Federal Express Corporation* ***(G-17165)***
Fedex, Los Angeles *Also called Federal Express Corporation* ***(G-4159)***
Fedex, Costa Mesa *Also called Federal Express Corporation* ***(G-4849)***
Fedex, San Leandro *Also called Federal Express Corporation* ***(G-4850)***
Fedex, Palm Springs *Also called Federal Express Corporation* ***(G-4802)***
Fedex, Monterey *Also called Federal Express Corporation* ***(G-4851)***
Fedex, San Jose *Also called Federal Express Corporation* ***(G-4411)***
Fedex, Oakland *Also called Federal Express Corporation* ***(G-4852)***
Fedex, Irvine *Also called Federal Express Corporation* ***(G-17166)***
Fedex, Oakland *Also called Federal Express Corporation* ***(G-4853)***
Fedex, Redding *Also called Federal Express Corporation* ***(G-4854)***
Fedex, Stockton *Also called Federal Express Corporation* ***(G-4855)***
Fedex, Santa Fe Springs *Also called Federal Express Corporation* ***(G-4856)***
Fedex, Visalia *Also called Federal Express Corporation* ***(G-4857)***
Fedex, Oakland *Also called Federal Express Corporation* ***(G-4412)***
Fedex, Ontario *Also called Federal Express Corporation* ***(G-17167)***
Fedex, Ontario *Also called Federal Express Corporation* ***(G-4858)***
Fedex, Emeryville *Also called Federal Express Corporation* ***(G-4017)***
Fedex, Fullerton *Also called Federal Express Corporation* ***(G-4859)***
Fedex, Oxnard *Also called Federal Express Corporation* ***(G-4860)***
Fedex, Sacramento *Also called Federal Express Corporation* ***(G-4861)***
Fedex, San Diego *Also called Federal Express Corporation* ***(G-5076)***
Fedex, San Francisco *Also called Federal Express Corporation* ***(G-4862)***
Fedex, Long Beach *Also called Federal Express Corporation* ***(G-4863)***
Fedex, Irvine *Also called Federal Express Corporation* ***(G-4803)***
Fedex, Long Beach *Also called Federal Express Corporation* ***(G-4864)***
Fedex Corporation ... 415 657-0403
50 Cypress Ln Brisbane (94005) ***(G-17168)***
Fedex Freight Corporation ... 714 637-9346
310 W Grove Ave Orange (92865) ***(G-4710)***
Fedex Freight Corporation ... 323 269-9800
4500 Bandini Blvd Vernon (90058) ***(G-4160)***
Fedex Freight Corporation ... 714 996-8720
1379 N Miller St Anaheim (92806) ***(G-4161)***
Fedex Freight Corporation ... 909 887-3970
7250 Cajon Blvd San Bernardino (92407) ***(G-4162)***
Fedex Freight Corporation ... 760 873-8655
193 Willow St Bishop (93514) ***(G-4163)***
Fedex Freight Corporation ... 619 710-0268
2250 Airway Ln San Diego (92154) ***(G-4164)***
Fedex Freight Corporation ... 310 323-5230
15200 S Main St Gardena (90248) ***(G-4165)***
Fedex Freight Corporation ... 800 288-0743
3200 Workman Mill Rd Whittier (90601) ***(G-4711)***
Fedex Freight Corporation ... 408 988-2111
3255 Victor St Santa Clara (95054) ***(G-4018)***
Fedex Freight Corporation ... 510 895-0440
29001 Hopkins St Hayward (94545) ***(G-4166)***
Fedex Freight Corporation ... 818 899-1141
11911 Branford St Sun Valley (91352) ***(G-4167)***
Fedex Freight Corporation ... 209 466-7726
4520 S Highway 99 Stockton (95215) ***(G-4168)***
Fedex Freight Corporation ... 800 706-1687
56 Fairbanks Irvine (92618) ***(G-4169)***
Fedex Freight West Inc ... 650 244-9522
3050 Teagarden St San Leandro (94577) ***(G-4170)***
Fedex Freight West Inc ... 559 266-0732
4570 S Maple Ave Fresno (93725) ***(G-4171)***
Fedex Freight West Inc ... 909 357-3555
11153 Mulberry Ave Fontana (92337) ***(G-4172)***
Fedex Freight West Inc ... 707 778-3191
1230 N Mcdowell Blvd Petaluma (94954) ***(G-4173)***
Fedex Ground Package Sys Inc ... 530 247-0935
1497 George Dr Ste G Redding (96003) ***(G-4174)***
Fedex Ground Package Sys Inc ... 714 879-0788
590 E Orangethorpe Ave Anaheim (92801) ***(G-4175)***
Fedex Ground Package Sys Inc ... 619 661-1051
10132 Airway Rd San Diego (92154) ***(G-4413)***
Fedex Ground Package Sys Inc ... 800 463-3339
9999 Olson Dr Ste 100 San Diego (92121) ***(G-4865)***
Fedex Ground Package Sys Inc ... 707 485-8638
1 Carousel Ln Unit B Ukiah (95482) ***(G-4176)***
Fedex Ground Package Sys Inc ... 530 534-5924
101 Book Farm Rd Durham (95938) ***(G-4177)***
Fedex Ground Package Sys Inc ... 760 873-3133
375 Airport Rd Bishop (93514) ***(G-4178)***
Fedex Ground Package Sys Inc ... 707 836-9890
500 Caletti Ave Windsor (95492) ***(G-4179)***
Fedex Ground Package Sys Inc ... 408 943-9960
696 E Trimble Rd Ste 10 San Jose (95131) ***(G-4180)***
Fedex Ground Package Sys Inc ... 909 879-7180
330 Resource Dr Bloomington (92316) ***(G-4181)***
Fedex Ground Package Sys Inc ... 831 786-0751
165 Technology Dr Watsonville (95076) ***(G-4182)***
Fedex Ground Package Sys Inc ... 818 767-7650
9175 San Fernando Rd Sun Valley (91352) ***(G-4183)***
Fedex Office & Print Svcs Inc ... 805 379-1552
2799 E Thousand Oaks Blvd Thousand Oaks (91362) ***(G-14118)***
Fedex Office & Print Svcs Inc ... 562 942-1953
8642 Whittier Blvd Pico Rivera (90660) ***(G-4414)***
Fedex Office & Print Svcs Inc ... 310 827-2297
13488 Maxella Ave Marina Del Rey (90292) ***(G-14119)***
Fedex Office & Print Svcs Inc ... 805 339-2000
4360 E Main St Ste A Ventura (93003) ***(G-14120)***
Fedex Office & Print Svcs Inc ... 213 892-1700
800 Wilshire Blvd Los Angeles (90017) ***(G-14121)***
Fedex Smartpost Inc ... 323 888-8879
5560 Ferguson Dr Commerce (90022) ***(G-4415)***
Fehr & Peers (PA) ... 925 977-3200
100 Pringle Ave Ste 600 Walnut Creek (94596) ***(G-25807)***
Fei Enterprises Inc ... 323 937-0856
5749 Venice Blvd Los Angeles (90019) ***(G-2592)***
Feiwell, Lawrence MD, Los Alamitos *Also called Marinow Harry MD Facs Inc* ***(G-19729)***
Felina Lingerie, Chatsworth *Also called Piege Co* ***(G-8409)***
Felson Companies Inc ... 510 538-1150
1290 B St Ste 210 Hayward (94541) ***(G-11518)***
Felton Institute, San Francisco *Also called Family Svc Agcy San Francisco* ***(G-14877)***
Fencecorp Inc ... 951 686-3170
111 Main St Ste A Riverside (92501) ***(G-3516)***
Fenceworks Inc ... 714 238-0091
2861 E La Cresta Ave Anaheim (92806) ***(G-3517)***
Fenceworks Inc (PA) ... 951 788-5620
870 Main St Riverside (92501) ***(G-3518)***
Fenceworks Inc ... 661 265-0082
891 Corporation St Santa Paula (93060) ***(G-3519)***
Fender Digital LLC ... 480 845-5452
1575 N Gower St Los Angeles (90028) ***(G-15183)***
Fenderscape Inc ... 562 988-2228
1446 E Hill St Signal Hill (90755) ***(G-853)***
Fenton Communications Inc ... 415 255-1946
182 2nd St Ste 400 San Francisco (94105) ***(G-27747)***
Fenton Scripps Landing LLC ... 858 586-0206
9970 Erma Rd San Diego (92131) ***(G-11130)***
Fenwick & West LLP (PA) ... 650 988-8500
801 California St Mountain View (94041) ***(G-23237)***
Fenwick & West LLP ... 415 875-2300
555 California St Fl 12 San Francisco (94104) ***(G-23238)***
Feralloy PDM Steel Service, Stockton *Also called PDM Steel Service Centers* ***(G-7391)***
Fergadis Enterprises, Bell *Also called Bernard Perrin Supowitz Inc* ***(G-8459)***
Ferguson 601, Van Nuys *Also called Ferguson Enterprises Inc* ***(G-7716)***
Ferguson 667, San Diego *Also called Ferguson Enterprises Inc* ***(G-7715)***
Ferguson 677, Garden Grove *Also called Ferguson Enterprises Inc* ***(G-7718)***
Ferguson 679, Salinas *Also called Ferguson Enterprises Inc* ***(G-7717)***
Ferguson Enterprises Inc ... 626 965-0724
18825 San Jose Ave City of Industry (91748) ***(G-7712)***
Ferguson Enterprises Inc ... 559 253-2900
704 N Laverne Ave Fresno (93727) ***(G-7713)***
Ferguson Enterprises Inc ... 909 364-8700
9750 S Town Ave Pomona (91766) ***(G-7714)***
Ferguson Enterprises Inc ... 619 515-0300
3280 Market St San Diego (92102) ***(G-7715)***
Ferguson Enterprises Inc ... 818 786-9720
7651 Woodman Ave Van Nuys (91402) ***(G-7716)***
Ferguson Enterprises Inc ... 831 373-5578
807 Eden St Salinas (93901) ***(G-7717)***
Ferguson Enterprises Inc ... 714 893-1936
11552 Monarch St Garden Grove (92841) ***(G-7718)***
Ferguson Fire Fabrication Inc (HQ) ... 909 517-3085
2750 S Towne Ave Pomona (91766) ***(G-7719)***
Ferguson Salon Management Inc ... 760 434-5008
1104 Knowles Ave Carlsbad (92008) ***(G-13675)***
Fernandes & Sons Gen Contrs ... 408 626-9090
2110 S Bascom Ave Ste 201 Campbell (95008) ***(G-14878)***
Fernview Convalescent Hospital ... 626 285-3131
126 N San Gabriel Blvd San Gabriel (91775) ***(G-20569)***
Ferrado Garden Court LLC ... 650 543-2224
520 Cowper St Ste 100 Palo Alto (94301) ***(G-12634)***

ALPHABETIC

Ferrees Group Home Inc 951 849-1927
878 Highland Home Rd Banning (92220) *(G-24657)*
Ferreira Service Inc (PA)....925 831-9330
2600 Old Crow Canyon Rd # 100 San Ramon (94583) *(G-2225)*
Ferring Research Institute Inc 858 657-1400
4245 Sorrento Valley Blvd San Diego (92121) *(G-26517)*
Fertility & Reproductive....408 358-2500
2581 Samaritan Dr Ste 302 San Jose (95124) *(G-19526)*
Fess Prker-Red Lion Gen Partnr....805 564-4333
633 E Cabrillo Blvd Santa Barbara (93103) *(G-12635)*
Festival Fun Parks LLC 951 785-3000
3500 Polk St Riverside (92505) *(G-18820)*
Festival Fun Parks LLC....954 921-1411
4590 Macarthur Blvd # 400 Newport Beach (92660) *(G-19208)*
Festival Fun Parks LLC 805 922-1574
2250 Preisker Ln Santa Maria (93458) *(G-19209)*
Festival Fun Parks LLC....760 945-9474
1525 W Vista Way Vista (92083) *(G-19210)*
Festival Fun Parks LLC....909 802-2200
111 Raging Waters Dr San Dimas (91773) *(G-8018)*
Festival Fun Parks LLC....949 261-0404
4590 Macarthur Blvd # 400 Newport Beach (92660) *(G-18821)*
Festival Fun Parks LLC 949 559-8336
3405 Michelson Dr Irvine (92612) *(G-19211)*
Festival Funparks LLC....858 560-4213
6999 Clairemont Mesa Blvd San Diego (92111) *(G-19212)*
Festival of Arts Laguna Beach....949 494-1145
650 Laguna Canyon Rd Laguna Beach (92651) *(G-19213)*
Ffd II, San Diego *Also called Fairfield Development Inc* *(G-1310)*
Fff Enterprises Inc (PA) 951 296-2500
41093 County Center Dr Temecula (92591) *(G-8253)*
Ffl Partners LLC (PA)....415 402-2100
1 Maritime Plz Fl 22 San Francisco (94111) *(G-12139)*
Ffna, Foothill Ranch *Also called Frontech N Fujitsu Amer Inc* *(G-15950)*
Fhar Fmly Hsing Adult Rsources 650 573-3341
205 W 20th Ave San Mateo (94403) *(G-23978)*
Fhpa, Gold River *Also called Health Net Inc* *(G-10284)*
Fib Lab, Milpitas *Also called Nanolab Technologies Inc* *(G-26873)*
Fibertron Corporation....714 670-7711
6400 Artesia Blvd Buena Park (90620) *(G-7565)*
Fibrwrap Construction LP (HQ) 909 390-4363
3940 Ruffin Rd Ste C San Diego (92123) *(G-3475)*
Fibrwrap Construction Services, San Diego *Also called Fibrwrap Construction LP* *(G-3475)*
Ficcadenti & Waggoner Consul (PA)....949 474-0502
16969 Von Karman Ave # 240 Irvine (92606) *(G-25808)*
Fidelity Capital Mortgage Brks 323 315-1700
6380 Wilshire Blvd # 1200 Los Angeles (90048) *(G-9923)*
Fidelity Home Energy Inc (PA)....858 220-7784
2235 Polvorosa Ave # 230 San Leandro (94577) *(G-2226)*
Fidelity Nat HM Warranty Co....925 356-0194
1850 Gateway Blvd Ste 400 Concord (94520) *(G-10493)*
Fidelity Nat Title Insur Co (HQ) 949 622-4600
3220 El Camino Real Irvine (92602) *(G-10514)*
Fidelity National Fincl Inc....949 622-5000
1300 Dove St Ste 310 Newport Beach (92660) *(G-10717)*
Fidelity National Title Co 818 881-7800
42544 10th St W Ste E Lancaster (93534) *(G-10515)*
Fidelity National Title Co Cal....916 646-9993
8801 Folsom Blvd Ste 210 Sacramento (95826) *(G-10718)*
Fidelity Roof Company....510 547-6330
1075 40th St Oakland (94608) *(G-3172)*
Fidelity Security Services Inc 661 295-5007
25133 Avenue Tibbitts H Valencia (91355) *(G-16640)*
Field Data Services 714 997-4498
380 S Tustin St Orange (92866) *(G-27922)*
Field Foundation....562 921-3567
15306 Carmenita Rd Santa Fe Springs (90670) *(G-1076)*
Field Fresh Farms LLC....831 722-1422
320 Industrial Rd Watsonville (95076) *(G-8724)*
Fields Construction Services....925 294-8183
5715 Southfront Rd Ste B1 Livermore (94551) *(G-14297)*
Fields Win Clg Win Protection, Livermore *Also called Fields Construction Services* *(G-14297)*
Fieldserver Technologies....408 262-2299
1991 Tarob Ct Milpitas (95035) *(G-6297)*
Fieldstone Co, The, San Diego *Also called Fieldstone Communities Inc* *(G-1174)*
Fieldstone Communities Inc 858 546-8081
5465 Morehouse Dr Ste 250 San Diego (92121) *(G-1174)*
Fieldstone Communities Inc 949 790-5400
16 Technology Dr Ste 125 Irvine (92618) *(G-1175)*
Fieldstone Communities Inc (PA)....949 790-5400
16 Technology Dr Ste 125 Irvine (92618) *(G-1364)*
Fieno Inc....760 352-2996
11583 Big Canyon Ln San Diego (92131) *(G-532)*
Fiesta De Reyes, San Diego *Also called Old Town Fmly Hospitality Corp* *(G-13039)*
Fifth & Sunset Enterprises LLC....310 979-0212
12322 Exposition Blvd Los Angeles (90064) *(G-14541)*
Fifty Peninsula Partners....650 344-8200
850 N El Camino Real Ofc San Mateo (94401) *(G-11131)*
Fig Garden Golf Course Inc 559 439-2928
7700 N Van Ness Blvd Fresno (93711) *(G-18950)*
Fig Holdings LLC 209 524-4817
1310 W Granger Ave Modesto (95350) *(G-20570)*
Figi Acquisition Company LLC....800 678-3444
3636 Gateway Center Ave San Diego (92102) *(G-9263)*
Fiji Water Company LLC (HQ)....310 966-5700
11444 W Olympic Blvd # 250 Los Angeles (90064) *(G-8836)*
Filament Hospitality, San Francisco *Also called Maverick Hotel Partners LLC* *(G-27121)*
Filemaker Inc (HQ) 408 987-7000
5201 Patrick Henry Dr Santa Clara (95054) *(G-15663)*
Filice Insurance Agency, San Jose *Also called Ron Filice Enterprises Inc* *(G-10857)*
Fillmore Convalescent Ctr LLC....805 524-0083
118 B St Fillmore (93015) *(G-21215)*
Fillmore Farm Management, Fillmore *Also called Wonderful Citrus Packing LLC* *(G-224)*
Fillmore Marketplace I, San Francisco *Also called Fillmore Marketplace LP* *(G-11519)*
Fillmore Marketplace LP....415 921-6514
1223 Webster St San Francisco (94115) *(G-11519)*
Fillmore Theatrical Services 310 867-7000
9348 Civic Center Dr Beverly Hills (90210) *(G-18466)*
Film Payroll Services Inc (PA)....310 440-9600
500 S Sepulveda Blvd Fl 4 Los Angeles (90049) *(G-26350)*
Film Roman Llc 818 748-4000
21600 Oxnard St Ste 1700 Woodland Hills (91367) *(G-18083)*
Film Roman LLC....818 748-4000
21600 Oxnard St Ste 1700 Woodland Hills (91367) *(G-18084)*
Filml.a, Los Angeles *Also called A Filml Inc* *(G-18211)*
Filmquest Pictures Corporation 818 905-1006
15331 Stonewood Ter Sherman Oaks (91403) *(G-18085)*
Filoli Center 650 364-8300
86 Canada Rd Woodside (94062) *(G-25062)*
Filoli Garden Shop, Woodside *Also called Filoli Center* *(G-25062)*
Filter Recycling Services Inc (PA)....909 873-4141
180 W Monte Ave Rialto (92376) *(G-6484)*
Filyn Corporation....714 632-0225
2950 E La Jolla St Anaheim (92806) *(G-3791)*
Final Film 323 467-0700
3620 W Valhalla Dr Burbank (91505) *(G-14145)*
Finance America LLC (HQ)....949 440-1000
1901 Main St Ste 150 Irvine (92614) *(G-9840)*
Financial Consulting & 310 201-2535
11766 Wilshire Blvd # 1100 Los Angeles (90025) *(G-27433)*
Financial Credit Network Inc (PA)....559 733-7550
1300 W Main St Visalia (93291) *(G-14032)*
Financial Division, Imperial Beach *Also called Jpmorgan Chase Bank Nat Assn* *(G-9576)*
Financial Engines Inc (PA)....408 498-6000
1050 Enterprise Way Fl 3 Sunnyvale (94089) *(G-27434)*
Financial Group of America 310 860-5160
468 N Camden Dr Ste 2 Beverly Hills (90210) *(G-9924)*
Financial Healthcare Services 626 356-7950
690 E Green St Ste 300 Pasadena (91101) *(G-27435)*
Financial Information Network....818 782-0331
6656 Valjean Ave Van Nuys (91406) *(G-15184)*
Financial Pacific Insur Agcy 916 630-5000
3850 Atherton Rd Rocklin (95765) *(G-10719)*
Financial Pacific Insurance Co....916 630-5000
3850 Atherton Rd Rocklin (95765) *(G-10720)*
Financial Partners Credit Un (PA)....562 904-3000
7800 Imperial Hwy Downey (90242) *(G-9596)*
Financial Statement Svcs Inc (PA) 714 436-3326
3300 S Fairview St Santa Ana (92704) *(G-14070)*
Financial Transaction, Roseville *Also called Safe Credit Union* *(G-9949)*
Financialforcecom Inc (HQ)....866 743-2220
595 Market St Ste 2700 San Francisco (94105) *(G-15185)*
Fine Arts Museum, Santa Barbara *Also called Santa Barbara Museum of Art* *(G-25048)*
Fine Line Group Inc....415 777-4070
457 Minna St San Francisco (94103) *(G-1553)*
Fine Northern Oak, NAPA *Also called Seguin Mreau NAPA Coperage Inc* *(G-7952)*
Finest Produce, Bellflower *Also called Produce Company* *(G-8765)*
Finezi Inc....510 790-4768
31080 Blvd Ste 212 Union City (94587) *(G-14655)*
Finjan Inc 408 452-9700
828 W Taft Ave Orange (92865) *(G-15186)*
Finjan Software, Orange *Also called Finjan Inc* *(G-15186)*
Finley Swim Center....707 543-3760
2060 W College Ave Santa Rosa (95401) *(G-19214)*
Finn Holding Corporation (PA)....310 712-1850
360 N Crescent Dr Beverly Hills (90210) *(G-4722)*
Fiorano Software Inc....650 326-1136
230 S California Ave # 103 Palo Alto (94306) *(G-15664)*
Fircrest Convalescent, Sebastopol *Also called Hermitage Health Care* *(G-22144)*
Fire and Police....562 961-0066
4645 E Anaheim St Long Beach (90804) *(G-25086)*
Fire and Police Pension Dept, Los Angeles *Also called City of Los Angeles* *(G-10548)*
Fire Insurance Exchange (PA)....323 932-3200
4680 Wilshire Blvd Los Angeles (90010) *(G-10721)*
Fire Safe Systems Inc....310 542-0585
1312 Kingsdale Ave Redondo Beach (90278) *(G-25809)*
Fire Safety First, Santa Ana *Also called Brethren Inc* *(G-8106)*
Fire Sprinkler Systems Inc (PA)....951 688-0336
705 E Harrison St Ste 200 Corona (92879) *(G-2227)*
Firearms Academy, Santa Ana *Also called OC Special Events SEC Inc* *(G-16750)*
Fireeye Inc (PA) 408 321-6300
1440 Mccarthy Blvd Milpitas (95035) *(G-15665)*
Firefighter Cancer Support Ntw....866 994-3276
3460 Fletcher Ave El Monte (91731) *(G-23979)*
Firemans Fund Insurance Co (HQ)....415 899-2000
777 San Marin Dr Ste 2160 Novato (94945) *(G-10416)*
Firemans Fund Insurance Co....559 435-5050
7555 N Palm Ave Ste 108 Fresno (93711) *(G-10417)*
Firemans Fund Insurance Co....916 852-4500
3100 Zinfandel Dr Ste 240 Rancho Cordova (95670) *(G-10418)*
Firemans Fund Insurance Co....858 492-3019
9275 Sky Park Ct Ste 450 San Diego (92123) *(G-10419)*
Firemans Fund Insurance Co....949 255-1981
3100 Zinfandel Dr Ste 240 Rancho Cordova (95670) *(G-10420)*

ALPHABETIC

Firemans Fund Insurance Co 818 953-6533
  2350 W Empire Ave Ste 200 Burbank (91504) *(G-10421)*
Firm A Chugh Professional Corp 562 229-1220
  15925 Carmenita Rd Cerritos (90703) *(G-23239)*
Firm A Chugh Professional Corp 408 970-0100
  4800 Great America Pkwy # 310 Santa Clara (95054) *(G-23240)*
First & La Realty Corp (PA) 805 581-0021
  1301 E Los Angeles Ave Simi Valley (93065) *(G-11520)*
First Alarm (PA) 831 476-1111
  1111 Estates Dr Aptos (95003) *(G-16885)*
First Alarm SEC & Patrol Inc (HQ) 831 685-1110
  1731 Tech Dr Ste 800 San Jose (95110) *(G-16641)*
First Allied Facilities Corp 619 702-9600
  655 W Broadway Ste 1100 San Diego (92101) *(G-9999)*
First Allied Securities Inc (PA) 619 702-9600
  655 W Broadway Fl 11 San Diego (92101) *(G-10000)*
First Amercn Lenders Advantage, Concord Also called First American Title Insur Co *(G-10526)*
First Amercn Prof RE Svcs Inc (PA) 714 250-1400
  200 Commerce Irvine (92602) *(G-11521)*
First American Appraisal Svcs (HQ) 619 938-7078
  12395 First American Way Poway (92064) *(G-11522)*
First American Card Service 951 677-8720
  25060 Hancock Ave Ste 103 Murrieta (92562) *(G-17169)*
First American Casualty Insur, Santa Ana Also called First American Title Insur Co *(G-10524)*
First American Financial Corp 805 969-6883
  1150 Coast Village Rd Santa Barbara (93108) *(G-10139)*
First American Financial Corp 510 252-1563
  39465 Paseo Padre Pkwy Fremont (94538) *(G-27436)*
First American Financial Corp 909 376-4247
  231 E Alessandro Blvd Riverside (92508) *(G-10516)*
First American Financial Corp (PA) 714 250-3000
  1 First American Way Santa Ana (92707) *(G-10517)*
First American Mortgage Svcs 714 250-4210
  3 First American Way Santa Ana (92707) *(G-10518)*
First American Team Realty Inc (PA) 562 427-7765
  2501 Cherry Ave Ste 100 Signal Hill (90755) *(G-11523)*
First American Title Company (HQ) 505 881-3300
  1 First American Way Santa Ana (92707) *(G-10519)*
First American Title Insur Co 925 356-7000
  1001 Galaxy Way Ste 101 Concord (94520) *(G-11524)*
First American Title Insur Co (HQ) 800 854-3643
  1 First American Way Santa Ana (92707) *(G-10520)*
First American Title Insur Co 619 238-1776
  411 Ivy St San Diego (92101) *(G-10521)*
First American Title Insur Co 909 889-0311
  1855 W Rdlands Blvd 100 Redlands (92373) *(G-10522)*
First American Title Insur Co 805 543-8900
  899 Pacific St San Luis Obispo (93401) *(G-10523)*
First American Title Insur Co 714 800-3000
  9 First American Way Santa Ana (92707) *(G-10524)*
First American Title Insur Co 831 426-6500
  330 Soquel Ave Santa Cruz (95062) *(G-10525)*
First American Title Insur Co 925 798-2800
  1855 Gateway Blvd Ste 700 Concord (94520) *(G-10526)*
First American Title Insur Co 714 250-4000
  3 First American Way Santa Ana (92707) *(G-10527)*
First American Title Insurance, Los Angeles Also called First Amrcn Cash Advnce SC LLC *(G-10528)*
First American Trust Company (HQ) 714 560-7856
  5 First American Way Santa Ana (92707) *(G-10140)*
First Amrcn Cash Advnce SC LLC 213 271-1700
  777 S Figueroa St Ste 400 Los Angeles (90017) *(G-10528)*
First Amrcn Mrtg Solutions LLC (HQ) 800 333-4510
  30005 Ladyface Ct Agoura Hills (91301) *(G-9925)*
First Avenue Inc 626 856-2076
  5105 Heintz St Baldwin Park (91706) *(G-3173)*
First Bank of San Luis Obispo, San Luis Obispo Also called Mufg Union Bank Na *(G-9411)*
First Baptist Head Start 925 473-2000
  3890 Railroad Ave Pittsburg (94565) *(G-24463)*
First California Mrtg Co II 415 209-0910
  1435 N Mcdowell Blvd # 300 Petaluma (94954) *(G-9841)*
First Call Nursing Svcs Inc 408 262-1533
  1313 N Milpitas Blvd # 210 Milpitas (95035) *(G-14656)*
First Choice Bank (PA) 562 345-9092
  17785 Center Court Dr N # 750 Cerritos (90703) *(G-9495)*
First Choice Coffee Services, Cerritos Also called Daiohs USA Inc *(G-17115)*
First City Credit Union (PA) 213 482-3477
  717 W Temple St Ste 400 Los Angeles (90012) *(G-9597)*
First Databank Inc 650 588-5454
  701 Gateway Blvd Ste 600 San Francisco (94188) *(G-16128)*
First Entertainment Credit Un (PA) 323 851-3673
  6735 Forest Lawn Dr # 100 Los Angeles (90068) *(G-9598)*
First Evang Lutheran Ch & Schl 310 320-9920
  2900 W Carson St Torrance (90503) *(G-24464)*
First Family Homes 562 862-7373
  12027 Paramount Blvd Downey (90242) *(G-11525)*
First Financial Credit Union (PA) 626 814-4611
  1600 W Cameron Ave West Covina (91790) *(G-9599)*
First Fire Systems Inc (PA) 310 559-0900
  5947 Burchard Ave Los Angeles (90034) *(G-2593)*
First Group of America, Santa Maria Also called First Transit *(G-3648)*
First Hotels International Inc 909 884-9364
  295 N E St San Bernardino (92401) *(G-12636)*
First Interstate Security Inc 818 995-6664
  16200 Ventura Blvd # 209 Encino (91436) *(G-16642)*
First Legal Support Svcs LLC (PA) 213 250-1111
  1517 Beverly Blvd Los Angeles (90026) *(G-23241)*

First Marin Realty Inc 415 383-9393
  145 Lomita Dr Mill Valley (94941) *(G-11526)*
First National Bank 760 602-5518
  401 W A St Ste 200 San Diego (92101) *(G-9398)*
First National Bank (PA) 619 233-5588
  401 W A St Ste 200 San Diego (92101) *(G-12174)*
First Nationwide Mortgage Corp 818 209-3134
  18440 Bermuda St Northridge (91326) *(G-9926)*
First Northern Bank of Dixon (HQ) 707 678-4422
  195 N 1st St Dixon (95620) *(G-9496)*
First Northern Community, Dixon Also called First Northern Bank of Dixon *(G-9496)*
First Place For Youth (PA) 510 272-0979
  426 17th St Ste 100 Oakland (94612) *(G-23980)*
First Plus Bank, Irvine Also called Firstplus Bank *(G-9747)*
First Regional Bancorp 310 552-1776
  1801 Century Park E # 800 Los Angeles (90067) *(G-9497)*
First Republic Bank 415 392-1400
  101 Pine St San Francisco (94111) *(G-9548)*
First Republic Bank 415 392-1400
  44 Montgomery St Ste 110 San Francisco (94104) *(G-9549)*
First Republic Bank 650 233-8880
  2550 Sand Hill Rd Ste 100 Menlo Park (94025) *(G-9550)*
First Republic Bank 213 239-8883
  901 W 7th St Los Angeles (90017) *(G-9551)*
First Republic Bank 925 254-8993
  224 Brookwood Rd Orinda (94563) *(G-9552)*
First Republic Bank 310 712-1888
  1888 Century Park E # 200 Los Angeles (90067) *(G-9553)*
First Republic Bank (PA) 415 392-1400
  111 Pine St Ste Bsmt San Francisco (94111) *(G-9498)*
First Responder, Chico Also called Paradise Ambulance Service *(G-3825)*
First Responder Ems Inc 916 381-3780
  10161 Croydon Way Ste 1 Sacramento (95827) *(G-3792)*
First Rsponder Emrgncy Med Svc 530 891-4357
  333 Huss Dr Ste 300 Chico (95928) *(G-3793)*
First State, Huntington Beach Also called First Team RE - Orange Cnty *(G-11533)*
First Step Ind Living Program, Rancho Cucamonga Also called National Mentor Inc *(G-24368)*
First Student Inc 510 237-6677
  436 Parr Blvd Richmond (94801) *(G-3879)*
First Student Inc 707 678-8679
  550 E C St Dixon (95620) *(G-3645)*
First Student Inc 925 676-1976
  2477 Arnold Indus Way Concord (94520) *(G-3902)*
First Student Inc 951 736-3234
  300 S Buena Vista Ave Corona (92882) *(G-3958)*
First Student Inc 650 685-8245
  991 E Poplar Ave San Mateo (94401) *(G-3927)*
First Student Inc 909 383-1640
  234 S I St San Bernardino (92410) *(G-3928)*
First Student Inc 760 320-4659
  5006 E Calle San Raphael Palm Springs (92264) *(G-3929)*
First Student Inc 209 466-7737
  2005 Navy Dr Stockton (95206) *(G-3930)*
First Student Inc 909 383-7104
  844 E 9th St San Bernardino (92410) *(G-3931)*
First Student Inc 310 715-6122
  14800 S Avalon Blvd Gardena (90248) *(G-3932)*
First Student Inc 415 647-9012
  2270 Jerrold Ave San Francisco (94124) *(G-3933)*
First Student Inc 626 448-9446
  4337 Rowland Ave El Monte (91731) *(G-3646)*
First Student Inc 510 237-6365
  436 Parr Blvd Richmond (94801) *(G-3934)*
First Student Inc 818 707-2082
  5320 Derry Ave Ste O Agoura Hills (91301) *(G-3935)*
First Student Inc 714 850-7578
  3401 W Castor St Santa Ana (92704) *(G-3880)*
First Student Inc 925 754-4878
  801 Wilbur Ave Antioch (94509) *(G-3647)*
First Student Inc 818 896-0333
  11233 San Fernando Rd San Fernando (91340) *(G-3936)*
First Student Inc 559 661-7433
  123 N E St Ste 102 Madera (93638) *(G-3794)*
First Team RE - Orange Cnty 760 340-9911
  74855 Country Club Dr Palm Desert (92260) *(G-11527)*
First Team RE - Orange Cnty 909 861-1380
  1950 S Brea Canyon Rd # 1 Diamond Bar (91765) *(G-11528)*
First Team RE - Orange Cnty 714 223-2143
  18180 Yorba Linda Blvd # 501 Yorba Linda (92886) *(G-11529)*
First Team RE - Orange Cnty 562 596-9911
  12501 Seal Beach Blvd # 100 Seal Beach (90740) *(G-11530)*
First Team RE - Orange Cnty 949 759-5747
  4 Corprate Plz Dr Ste 100 Corona Del Mar (92625) *(G-11531)*
First Team RE - Orange Cnty (PA) 888 236-1943
  108 Pacifica Ste 300 Irvine (92618) *(G-11532)*
First Team RE - Orange Cnty 714 965-2244
  20100 Brookhurst St Huntington Beach (92646) *(G-11533)*
First Team RE - Orange Cnty 949 857-0414
  4040 Barranca Pkwy # 100 Irvine (92604) *(G-11534)*
First Team RE - Orange Cnty 562 346-5088
  42 64th Pl Long Beach (90803) *(G-11535)*
First Team RE - Orange Cnty 949 240-7979
  32451 Golden Lantern # 210 Laguna Niguel (92677) *(G-11536)*
First Team RE - Orange Cnty 714 544-5456
  17240 17th St Tustin (92780) *(G-11537)*
First Team RE - Orange Cnty 714 974-9191
  8028 E Santa Ana Cyn Rd Anaheim (92808) *(G-11538)*
First Team S S Estate, Diamond Bar Also called First Team RE - Orange Cnty *(G-11528)*

First Team Walk-In Realty, Irvine *Also called First Team RE - Orange Cnty* ***(G-11532)***
First Technology Federal Cr Un (PA)....855 855-8805
1335 Terra Bella Ave Mountain View (94043) ***(G-9600)***
First Technology Federal Cr Un....855 855-8805
1011 Sunset Blvd Ste 210 Rocklin (95765) ***(G-9601)***
First Transit....805 925-5254
1303 Fairway Dr Santa Maria (93455) ***(G-3648)***
First Transit Inc....310 515-8270
2400 E Dominguez St Long Beach (90810) ***(G-3649)***
First Transit Inc....760 379-1711
6616 Lake Isabella Blvd Lake Isabella (93240) ***(G-3650)***
First Transit Inc....510 535-9192
411 High St Oakland (94601) ***(G-3937)***
First Transit Inc....661 391-3614
5438 Victor St Ste B Bakersfield (93308) ***(G-3651)***
First Transit Inc....510 437-8990
407 High St Oakland (94601) ***(G-3652)***
Firstat Nursing Services Inc....619 220-7600
411 Camino Del Rio S # 100 San Diego (92108) ***(G-22438)***
Firstfed Financial Corp....562 618-0573
6320 Canoga Ave Woodland Hills (91367) ***(G-9399)***
Firstline Trnsp SEC Inc....916 456-5166
1250 Sutterville Rd Sacramento (95822) ***(G-16643)***
Firstmed Ambulance Svcs Inc....800 608-0311
8630 Tamarack Ave Sun Valley (91352) ***(G-3795)***
Firstplus Bank (PA)....949 851-7101
1732 Reynolds Ave Irvine (92614) ***(G-9747)***
Firstsrvice Rsidential Cal Inc (HQ)....909 981-4131
195 N Euclid Ave Upland (91786) ***(G-11539)***
Fischer Inc....909 881-2910
1372 W 26th St San Bernardino (92405) ***(G-2228)***
Fischer Tile and Marble Inc....916 452-1426
1800 23rd St Sacramento (95816) ***(G-3013)***
Fiserv Inc....909 595-9074
19935 E Walnut Dr N City of Industry (91789) ***(G-16129)***
Fiserv Inc....909 598-8700
19935 E Walnut Dr N Walnut (91789) ***(G-16130)***
Fiserv Inc....408 242-3011
525 Almanor Ave Sunnyvale (94085) ***(G-16131)***
Fiserv Inc....805 532-9100
405 Science Dr Moorpark (93021) ***(G-16132)***
Fiserv Inc....909 595-9074
19935 E Walnut Dr N Walnut (91789) ***(G-16133)***
Fish & Richardson PC....650 839-5070
500 Arguello St Ste 500 Redwood City (94063) ***(G-23242)***
Fish & Richardson PC....858 678-5070
12390 El Camino Real San Diego (92130) ***(G-23243)***
Fishel Company....714 668-9268
647 Young St Santa Ana (92705) ***(G-1930)***
Fisher & Paykel Healthcare Inc....949 453-4000
15365 Barranca Pkwy Irvine (92618) ***(G-7265)***
Fisher & Phillips LLP....949 851-2424
2050 Main St Ste 1000 Irvine (92614) ***(G-23244)***
Fisher Communications Inc....661 327-7955
1901 Westwind Dr Bakersfield (93301) ***(G-5861)***
Fisher Ranch LLC....760 922-4151
10610 Ice Plant Rd Blythe (92225) ***(G-533)***
Fisher Scientific Company LLC....909 393-2100
6722 Bickmore Ave Chino (91708) ***(G-7342)***
Fishers Nursery....209 599-3412
24081 S Austin Rd Ripon (95366) ***(G-9188)***
Fisk Electric Company....818 884-1166
15870 Olden St Sylmar (91342) ***(G-2594)***
Fit Electronics Inc (HQ)....714 988-9388
500 S Kraemer Blvd # 100 Brea (92821) ***(G-26518)***
Fitness 2000 Inc....510 791-2481
35145 Newark Blvd Newark (94560) ***(G-18632)***
Fitness International LLC....949 421-6082
24491 Alicia Pkwy Mission Viejo (92691) ***(G-18633)***
Fitness International LLC....858 550-5912
10535 Heater Ct San Diego (92121) ***(G-18634)***
Fitness Ridge Malibu LLC....818 874-1300
277 Latigo Canyon Rd Malibu (90265) ***(G-12637)***
Fitstar Inc....415 409-8348
80 Langton St San Francisco (94103) ***(G-15666)***
Fitz Fresh Inc....831 763-4440
211 Lee Rd Watsonville (95076) ***(G-329)***
Fitzgerald Cantor L P....310 282-6500
1925 Century Park E # 700 Los Angeles (90067) ***(G-10001)***
Fitzgrald Abbott Beardsley LLP....510 451-3300
1221 Broadway Fl 21 Oakland (94612) ***(G-23245)***
Five Acres, Altadena *Also called 5 Acrs-The Bys Grls Aid Soc La* ***(G-24538)***
Five Long Island Properties LL....310 772-6306
1 Sun America Ctr Fl 38 Los Angeles (90067) ***(G-10982)***
Five Star Auto Repair and Wash, Rocklin *Also called Jkf Auto Service Inc* ***(G-17846)***
Five Star Auto Repr & Car Wash, Rocklin *Also called Jemtown Inc* ***(G-17845)***
Five Star Labor, Torrance *Also called Golden Arrow Construction Inc* ***(G-1184)***
Five Star Packing LLC....760 356-4103
437 W 5th St Holtville (92250) ***(G-661)***
Five Star Quality Care Inc....760 479-1818
1350 S El Camino Real Encinitas (92024) ***(G-24658)***
Five Star Quality Care Inc....760 327-8541
277 S Sunrise Way Palm Springs (92262) ***(G-27025)***
Five Star Quality Care Inc....209 951-6500
3530 Deer Park Dr Stockton (95219) ***(G-22439)***
Five Star Quality Care Inc....949 642-8044
466 Flagship Rd Newport Beach (92663) ***(G-20571)***
Five Star Quality Care Inc....209 466-2066
537 E Fulton St Stockton (95204) ***(G-20572)***
Five Star Quality Care Inc....818 997-1841
6835 Hazeltine Ave Van Nuys (91405) ***(G-20573)***
Five Star Quality Care Inc....661 940-0452
1642 W Avenue J Lancaster (93534) ***(G-20574)***
Five Star Quality Care Inc....805 492-2444
93 W Avnida De Los Arbles Thousand Oaks (91360) ***(G-20575)***
Five Star Quality Care Inc....858 673-6300
16925 Hierba Dr San Diego (92128) ***(G-20576)***
Five Star Quality Care Inc....559 446-6226
6075 N Marks Ave Fresno (93711) ***(G-20577)***
Five Star Transportation Inc....310 348-0820
8703 La Tijera Blvd # 102 Los Angeles (90045) ***(G-5009)***
Five9 Inc (PA)....925 201-2000
4000 Executive Pkwy # 400 San Ramon (94583) ***(G-15667)***
Fix Shore, Downey *Also called Westar Manufacturing Inc* ***(G-3603)***
FJ Willert Contracting Co....619 421-1980
1869 Nirvana Ave Chula Vista (91911) ***(G-3428)***
Fjs Inc....714 905-1050
1030 W Katella Ave Anaheim (92802) ***(G-12638)***
Fkc Partners A Cal Ltd Partnr....714 528-9864
180 N Rverview Dr Ste 100 Anaheim (92808) ***(G-11540)***
Fkc Properties, Anaheim *Also called Fkc Partners A Cal Ltd Partnr* ***(G-11540)***
Flagship Credit Acceptance LLC....949 748-7172
7525 Irvine Center Dr Irvine (92618) ***(G-17170)***
Flagship Health Care Center, Newport Beach *Also called Five Star Quality Care Inc* ***(G-20571)***
Flagship Healthcare Center, Newport Beach *Also called SSC Newport Beach Oper Co LP* ***(G-20925)***
Flair Building Maintenance, Santa Clara *Also called Flair Building Services* ***(G-14298)***
Flair Building Services....408 987-4040
3470 Edward Ave Santa Clara (95054) ***(G-14298)***
Flair Cleaners Inc....661 753-9900
27011 Mcbean Pkwy Valencia (91355) ***(G-17973)***
Flamingo Resort Hotel, Santa Rosa *Also called Bavarian Lion Company Cal* ***(G-12423)***
Flanders Pointe Apts, Tustin *Also called Steadfast Management Co Inc* ***(G-11208)***
Flash Point Graphix, Burbank *Also called Final Film* ***(G-14145)***
Flash Transport Inc....909 829-1369
14796 Washington Dr Fontana (92335) ***(G-4184)***
Flatiron Electric Group Inc....714 228-9631
7911 Pine Ave Ste A Chino (91708) ***(G-2595)***
Flatiron West Inc....707 742-6000
2100 Goodyear Rd Benicia (94510) ***(G-1889)***
Flatiron West Inc....909 597-8413
16341 Chino Corona Rd Chino (91708) ***(G-1890)***
Fleet Maintenance Dept, Santa Cruz *Also called Santa Cruz Metro Trnst Dst* ***(G-3888)***
Fleetcor Technologies Inc....800 877-9019
1140 Galaxy Way Concord (94520) ***(G-17171)***
Fleischman Field Research Inc....415 398-4140
250 Sutter St Fl 2 San Francisco (94108) ***(G-26662)***
Fleishman-Hillard Inc....415 318-4000
720 California St Fl 6 San Francisco (94108) ***(G-27748)***
Flexcare LLC....866 564-3589
990 Reserve Dr Ste 200 Roseville (95678) ***(G-14879)***
Flexcare Medical Staffing, Roseville *Also called Flexcare LLC* ***(G-14879)***
Flexera Software LLC....847 466-4000
25 Orinda Way Ste 101 Orinda (94563) ***(G-15187)***
Flexera Software LLC....408 642-3700
101 Metro Dr Ste 375 San Jose (95110) ***(G-15188)***
Flextronics Logistics USA Inc....408 576-7000
6201 America Center Dr San Jose (95002) ***(G-5199)***
Fliesler Dubb Myer Lovejoy LLP....415 362-3800
4 Embarcadero Ctr Ste 400 San Francisco (94111) ***(G-23246)***
Flight Line Products LLC....661 775-8366
28732 Witherspoon Pkwy Valencia (91355) ***(G-3520)***
Flintco Pacific Inc....916 757-1000
401 Derek Pl Roseville (95678) ***(G-25810)***
Flir Commercial Systems Inc (HQ)....805 690-6685
6769 Hollister Ave # 100 Goleta (93117) ***(G-7566)***
Flite Inc....415 992-5870
23 Geary St San Francisco (94108) ***(G-16370)***
Floorgate Inc....323 478-2000
3350 N San Fernando Rd Los Angeles (90065) ***(G-3114)***
Floormasters, The, Hayward *Also called Dt Floormasters Inc* ***(G-3112)***
Flora Ter Convalescent Hosp, Los Angeles *Also called Country Villa Terrace* ***(G-21196)***
Flora Terra Landscape MGT, San Jose *Also called City II Enterprises Inc* ***(G-825)***
Florence Crittenton Services....714 680-9000
801 E Chapman Ave Ste 203 Fullerton (92831) ***(G-24659)***
Florence Filter Corporation....310 637-1137
530 W Manville St Compton (90220) ***(G-7738)***
Florence Office, Los Angeles *Also called County of Los Angeles* ***(G-23834)***
Florence Villa Hotel....415 397-7700
225 Powell St San Francisco (94102) ***(G-12639)***
Florence Villa Hotel LLC....415 397-7700
225 Powell St San Francisco (94102) ***(G-12640)***
Florida Beauty Flora Inc....805 642-1633
6205 Ventura Blvd Ventura (93003) ***(G-13676)***
Florida Conditioning, City of Industry *Also called American AC Distrs LLC* ***(G-2125)***
Flowserve Corporation....323 584-1890
2300 E Vernon Ave Stop 76 Vernon (90058) ***(G-7844)***
Floyd Johnston Cnstr Co Inc....559 299-7373
2301 Herndon Ave Clovis (93611) ***(G-1931)***
Floyd Skeren & Kelly LLP (PA)....818 206-9222
101 Moody Ct Ste 200 Thousand Oaks (91360) ***(G-23247)***
Flt Inc....916 355-1500
12747 Folsom Blvd Folsom (95630) ***(G-17790)***
Fluid Inc (PA)....415 263-7700
222 Sutter St Fl 8 San Francisco (94108) ***(G-15189)***

ALPHABETIC

Fluor Corporation...949 349-2000
3 Polaris Way Aliso Viejo (92656) *(G-25811)*
Fluor Daniel, Aliso Viejo *Also called Fluor Plant Services Intl Inc (G-25814)*
Fluor Daniel Construction Co (HQ)...949 349-2000
3 Polaris Way Aliso Viejo (92656) *(G-1891)*
Fluor Enterprises Inc...408 256-0853
5600 Cottle Rd San Jose (95123) *(G-25812)*
Fluor Enterprises Inc...949 349-2000
9701 Jeronimo Rd Irvine (92618) *(G-25813)*
Fluor Enterprises Inc...949 349-2000
3 Polaris Way Aliso Viejo (92656) *(G-7769)*
Fluor Enterprises Inc...469 398-7000
1 Fluor Daniel Dr Aliso Viejo (92698) *(G-3521)*
Fluor Facility & Plant Svcs...408 256-1333
124 Blossom Hill Rd 1524h San Jose (95123) *(G-14299)*
Fluor Industrial Services Inc...949 439-2000
1 Enterprise Aliso Viejo (92656) *(G-14300)*
Fluor Plant Services Intl Inc (HQ)...949 349-2000
1 Enterprise Aliso Viejo (92656) *(G-25814)*
Fluoramec LLC (HQ)...949 349-2000
1 Enterprise Aliso Viejo (92656) *(G-25815)*
Flurish Inc...855 253-6387
225 Bush St Ste 1100 San Francisco (94104) *(G-9748)*
Fluxx Labs Inc...855 358-9946
77 Maiden Ln Fl 4 San Francisco (94108) *(G-13759)*
Flyers Energy LLC...661 321-9961
4200 Buck Owens Blvd Bakersfield (93308) *(G-9019)*
Flyers Energy LLC...909 877-2441
571 W Slover Ave Bloomington (92316) *(G-9020)*
Flyers Energy LLC...707 546-0766
444 Yolanda Ave Ste A Santa Rosa (95404) *(G-9021)*
Flyers Energy LLC...760 949-3356
11211 G Ave Hesperia (92345) *(G-9006)*
Flynn Properties Inc...415 835-0225
225 Bush St Ste 1470 San Francisco (94104) *(G-11541)*
FM Global, Walnut Creek *Also called Factory Mutual Insurance Co (G-10413)*
FM Global, Woodland Hills *Also called Factory Mutual Insurance Co (G-10414)*
FM Seoul Bang Song Inc...323 525-1650
4525 Wilshire Blvd Fl 3 Los Angeles (90010) *(G-5775)*
FMC Dialysis Svcs Bellflower, Bellflower *Also called Bio-Mdcal Applications Cal Inc (G-22619)*
FMC Dialysis Svcs Riverside, Riverside *Also called Bio-Mdcal Applications Cal Inc (G-22621)*
Fmr LLC...800 225-6447
1995 University Ave Berkeley (94704) *(G-10141)*
Fmr LLC...916 784-3649
1220 Rsville Pkwy Ste 100 Roseville (95678) *(G-10142)*
Fmsinfoserv, Los Angeles *Also called Cdsnet LLC (G-27872)*
Fmt Consultants LLC...760 930-6400
2310 Camino Vida Roble # 101 Carlsbad (92011) *(G-16371)*
Fmwr, Fort Irwin *Also called Family Mrale Wlfare Recreation (G-18948)*
Fnc Inc...714 866-1099
40 Pacifica Ste 900 Irvine (92618) *(G-15190)*
Fni International Inc...916 643-1400
1300 Ethan Way Sacramento (95825) *(G-12307)*
Fns Inc (PA)...661 615-2300
1545 Francisco St Torrance (90501) *(G-5077)*
FNS Customs Brokers Inc...310 667-4880
18301 S Broadwick St Compton (90220) *(G-5078)*
Foam Co, The, Van Nuys *Also called Grht Inc (G-9269)*
Foam Distributors Incorporated...510 441-8377
31009 San Antonio St Hayward (94544) *(G-9264)*
Foam Fabrication For Packaging, Hayward *Also called Foam Distributors Incorporated (G-9264)*
Foasberg Laundry & Clrs Inc (PA)...562 426-7345
640 E Wardlow Rd Long Beach (90807) *(G-13548)*
Focus 360 Inc...949 234-0008
27721 La Paz Rd Ste B Laguna Niguel (92677) *(G-15191)*
Focus Diagnostics Inc...714 220-1900
11331 Valley View St # 150 Cypress (90630) *(G-22216)*
Focus Features LLC...424 214-6360
1540 2nd St Ste 200 Santa Monica (90401) *(G-18086)*
Focus Psycho Educational...323 851-4577
1427 N La Brea Ave Los Angeles (90028) *(G-26766)*
Focus Technologies Holding Co...800 838-4548
10703 Progress Way Cypress (90630) *(G-22217)*
Focus Up LLC...209 545-9055
4120 Dale Rd Ste G Modesto (95356) *(G-18635)*
Focuspoint International...415 446-9418
4660 La Jolla Village Dr San Diego (92122) *(G-16644)*
Foley & Lardner LLP...650 856-3700
975 Page Mill Rd Palo Alto (94304) *(G-23248)*
Foley & Lardner LLP...415 434-4484
555 California St # 1700 San Francisco (94104) *(G-23249)*
Foley & Lardner LLP...213 972-4500
555 S Flower St Ste 3500 Los Angeles (90071) *(G-23250)*
Foley & Lardner LLP...858 847-6700
3579 Vly Cntre Dr Ste 300 San Diego (92130) *(G-23251)*
Folio Wine Company LLC...707 256-2757
1285 Dealy Ln NAPA (94559) *(G-9100)*
Foliodynamix, Sacramento *Also called Fdx Advisors Inc (G-10138)*
Folsom Ambulatory Surgery Ctr, Folsom *Also called Kaiser Foundation Hospitals (G-19617)*
Folsom Lake Toyota, Folsom *Also called Flt Inc (G-17790)*
Folsom Manlove Venture, Sacramento *Also called Oates Buzz Enterprises (G-11026)*
Folsom Recreation Corp...916 983-4411
511 E Bidwell St Folsom (95630) *(G-18518)*
Folsom Sport Club, Folsom *Also called 24 Hour Fitness Usa Inc (G-18578)*
Fontana Mental Health Offices, Fontana *Also called Kaiser Foundation Hospitals (G-19616)*
Fontana Resources At Work...909 428-3833
8608 Live Oak Ave Fontana (92335) *(G-24341)*
Fontana Steel, Etiwanda *Also called C M C Steel Fabricators Inc (G-3370)*
Fontana Water Company, El Monte *Also called San Gabriel Valley Water Co (G-6395)*
Food & Agriculture Cal Dept...714 751-3247
88 Fair Dr Costa Mesa (92626) *(G-19215)*
Food 4 Less, Downey *Also called Ralphs Grocery Company (G-4622)*
Food Express Inc...323 589-1417
5127 Maywood Ave Maywood (90270) *(G-4019)*
Food Management Associates Inc...714 694-2828
22349 La Palma Ave # 115 Yorba Linda (92887) *(G-27437)*
Food Sales West Inc (PA)...714 966-2900
235 Baker St E Costa Mesa (92626) *(G-8478)*
Foodbuzz Inc...415 321-1200
72 Townsend St San Francisco (94107) *(G-16372)*
Foods and Produce, Buena Park *Also called Walong Marketing Inc (G-8955)*
Footh The / Easte Trans Corri...949 754-3400
125 Pacifica Ste 100 Irvine (92618) *(G-1771)*
Footh-De Anza Commun Colleg Di...650 949-7260
12345 S El Monte Rd # 6202 Los Altos Hills (94022) *(G-5776)*
Foothill Community Health Ctr, San Jose *Also called San Jose Foothill Family Comm (G-19946)*
Foothill Distributing Co Inc...530 243-3932
1530 Beltline Rd Redding (96003) *(G-9056)*
Foothill Duplicate Bridge Club...530 677-3771
4050 Durock Rd Ste 8 Shingle Springs (95682) *(G-18951)*
Foothill Estates Inc...831 422-7819
400 Griffin St Salinas (93901) *(G-11969)*
Foothill Hospital-Morris L Jo (PA)...626 857-3145
250 S Grand Ave Glendora (91741) *(G-21567)*
Foothill Oaks Care Center Inc...530 888-6257
3400 Bell Rd Auburn (95603) *(G-20578)*
Foothill Packing Inc...805 925-7900
2255 S Broadway Santa Maria (93454) *(G-8479)*
Foothill Presbyterian Hospital, Glendora *Also called Foothill Hospital-Morris L Jo (G-21567)*
Foothill Ranch Medical Offices, Foothill Ranch *Also called Kaiser Foundation Hospitals (G-19615)*
Foothill Ranch Sport Club, Lake Forest *Also called 24 Hour Fitness Usa Inc (G-18592)*
Foothill Transit Service Corp (PA)...626 967-3147
100 S Vincent Ave Ste 200 West Covina (91790) *(G-3653)*
Foothill Waste Reclamation Inc...818 897-5099
12221 Lopez Canyon Rd Sylmar (91342) *(G-6485)*
For Hospital Committee...925 447-7000
1111 E Stanley Blvd Livermore (94550) *(G-27026)*
Force Electronics, Visalia *Also called Heilind Electronics Inc (G-7576)*
Force Measurement Systems, Anaheim *Also called Wasser Filtration Inc (G-7904)*
Force-Oakleaf LP...310 484-7000
6333 Bristol Pkwy Culver City (90230) *(G-12641)*
Forco Disposal Service, Chico *Also called Mountain Mining Incorporated (G-6507)*
Ford Construction Company Inc...209 333-1116
300 W Pine St Lodi (95240) *(G-2050)*
Ford Graphics, Los Angeles *Also called American Reprographics Co LLC (G-14100)*
Ford Motor Company...949 642-1291
2060 Harbor Blvd Costa Mesa (92627) *(G-17675)*
Ford Motor Company...209 824-6600
1269 Phoenix Dr Manteca (95336) *(G-6731)*
Ford Motor Company...949 341-5800
3 Glen Bell Way Ste 200 Irvine (92618) *(G-23252)*
Ford Plastering Inc...714 921-0624
732 W Grove Ave Orange (92865) *(G-3264)*
Ford Street Project Inc...707 462-1934
139 Ford St Ukiah (95482) *(G-24660)*
Ford's Filling Station, Culver City *Also called Midnight Snack LP (G-27130)*
Forecast 3d, Carlsbad *Also called Product Slingshot Inc (G-17430)*
Foreign Prnt Is Alanz AG Mnchn, Newport Beach *Also called Allianz Globl Invstors Amer LP (G-10114)*
Foreign Trade Corporation (PA)...805 823-8400
685 Cochran St Ste 200 Simi Valley (93065) *(G-7567)*
Foremost Healthcare Centers...760 244-5579
17581 Sultana St Hesperia (92345) *(G-11132)*
Foremost Operations LLC...760 244-5579
17581 Sultana St Hesperia (92345) *(G-24661)*
Foremost Terrace Room, Hesperia *Also called Foremost Operations LLC (G-24661)*
Forensic Toxicology Associates, Chatsworth *Also called Pacific Toxicology Labs (G-22251)*
Forescout Technologies Inc (PA)...408 213-3191
190 W Tasman Dr San Jose (95134) *(G-15192)*
Forest City Rental Prpts Corp...661 266-9150
1233 W Avenue P Ste 900 Palmdale (93551) *(G-10983)*
Forest Lawn Memorial & Mortuar, Cypress *Also called Forest Lawn Memorial-Park Assn (G-12029)*
Forest Lawn Memorial-Park Assn...714 828-3131
4471 Lincoln Ave Cypress (90630) *(G-12029)*
Forest Lawn Memorial-Park Assn...323 254-7251
6300 Forest Lawn Dr Los Angeles (90068) *(G-12030)*
Forest Lawn Memorial-Park Assn...562 424-1631
1500 E San Antonio Dr Long Beach (90807) *(G-12031)*
Forest Park Cabana Club...408 244-1884
2911 Pruneridge Ave Santa Clara (95051) *(G-18952)*
Forest Products Distrs Inc...707 443-7024
1090 W Waterfront Dr Eureka (95501) *(G-6923)*
Forestry and Fire Protection...530 225-2418
875 Cypress Ave Redding (96001) *(G-1015)*
Forever 21 Retail Inc...323 343-9368
3880 N Mission Rd Los Angeles (90031) *(G-8384)*
Forex Capital Markets LLC...415 343-4874
201 Mission St Ste 290 San Francisco (94105) *(G-10002)*

ALPHABETIC

ALPHABETIC SECTION
Four Sisters Inns

Forge-Vidovich Motel Limited....408 996-7700
10889 N De Anza Blvd Cupertino (95014) *(G-12642)*
Forgerock Inc (PA)....415 599-1100
201 Mission St Ste 2900 San Francisco (94105) *(G-15668)*
Foria International Inc (PA)....626 912-8836
18689 Arenth Ave City of Industry (91748) *(G-8341)*
Forma Systems Visuart....949 660-1900
3050 Pullman St Costa Mesa (92626) *(G-27923)*
Formation Brands LLC....650 238-1009
400 Oyster Point Blvd # 200 South San Francisco (94080) *(G-6861)*
Formula PR Inc., San Diego *Also called Havas Formula LLC (G-27750)*
Forrest City Development, Los Angeles *Also called Fc Metropolitan Lofts Inc (G-11968)*
Forsys Inc....844 409-0510
5994 W Las Positas Blvd # 221 Pleasanton (94588) *(G-16373)*
Forsythe Solutions Group Inc....424 217-6500
222 N Sepulveda Blvd # 1426 El Segundo (90245) *(G-16374)*
Fort Hill Construction (PA)....323 656-7425
12711 Ventura Blvd # 390 Studio City (91604) *(G-1176)*
Fort James Communications Pprs, Emeryville *Also called Fort James Corporation (G-27027)*
Fort James Corporation....510 594-4900
2000 Powell St Emeryville (94608) *(G-27027)*
Fort Mason Center....415 345-7500
2 Marina Blvd Bldg A San Francisco (94123) *(G-28130)*
Fort Wash Golf & Cntry CLB....559 434-1702
10272 N Millbrook Ave Fresno (93730) *(G-18953)*
Fort Washington Parent Assoc....559 327-6600
960 E Teague Ave Fresno (93720) *(G-25255)*
FORT, THE, Fresno *Also called Fort Wash Golf & Cntry CLB (G-18953)*
Forta (PA)....626 446-7027
671 W Naomi Ave Arcadia (91007) *(G-20319)*
Fortanasce & Associates, Arcadia *Also called Forta (G-20319)*
Forte Enterprises Inc (PA)....650 994-3200
99 Escuela Dr Daly City (94015) *(G-27028)*
Fortinet Inc (PA)....408 235-7700
899 Kifer Rd Sunnyvale (94086) *(G-15669)*
Fortress Holding Group LLC....714 202-8710
5500 E Sta Ana Cnyn S220 Anaheim (92807) *(G-12061)*
Fortress Investment Group LLC....310 228-3030
10250 Constellation Blvd Los Angeles (90067) *(G-12115)*
Fortress Investment Group LLC....415 284-7400
42 Florida St Flr San Francisco (94103) *(G-12116)*
Fortress Resources LLC (PA)....562 633-9951
14001 Garfield Ave Paramount (90723) *(G-17791)*
Fortuna Enterprises LP....310 410-4000
5711 W Century Blvd Los Angeles (90045) *(G-12643)*
Fortuna Technologies Inc....510 687-9797
44721 Aguila Ter Fremont (94539) *(G-27924)*
Fortune Avenue Foods Inc....909 930-5989
2117 Pointe Ave Ontario (91761) *(G-8480)*
Fortune Dynamic Inc....909 979-8318
21923 Ferrero City of Industry (91789) *(G-8435)*
Forty Four Group LLC....949 407-6360
16351 Gothard St Ste B Huntington Beach (92647) *(G-13851)*
Forty Niners Football Co LLC....408 562-4949
4949 Mrie P Debartolo Way Santa Clara (95054) *(G-18544)*
Forum At Rancho San Antonio, Cupertino *Also called Rancho San Antonio Retirement (G-24779)*
Forum Enterprises Inc....310 330-7300
333 W Florence Ave Inglewood (90301) *(G-18467)*
Forum Healthcare Center....650 944-0200
23600 Via Esplendor Cupertino (95014) *(G-20579)*
Forum, The, Inglewood *Also called Msg Networks Inc (G-18559)*
Forward Air Inc....415 570-6040
427 Valley Dr Brisbane (94005) *(G-5079)*
Forward Management LLC....415 869-6300
101 California St Fl 16 San Francisco (94111) *(G-10143)*
Forward Slope Incorporated....619 299-4400
2020 Camino Del Rio N # 400 San Diego (92108) *(G-25816)*
Forward Slope., San Diego *Also called Forward Slope Incorporated (G-25816)*
Forza Silicon Corporation....626 796-1182
2947 Bradley St Ste 130 Pasadena (91107) *(G-25817)*
Foshay Electric Coinc....858 277-7676
1555 Laurel Bay Ln San Diego (92154) *(G-2596)*
Foss Maritime Company....510 307-4271
1316 Canal Blvd Richmond (94804) *(G-4714)*
Foss Maritime Company....562 435-0171
St Pier D Long Beach (90801) *(G-4715)*
Foster Care Licensing & Svc, Ventura *Also called County of Ventura (G-23932)*
Foster Dairy Farms (PA)....209 576-3400
529 Kansas Ave Modesto (95351) *(G-424)*
Foster Dairy Farms....510 783-1270
3440 Enterprise Ave Hayward (94545) *(G-8585)*
Foster Dairy Farms....209 874-9605
1472 Hall Rd Hickman (95323) *(G-17974)*
Foster Enterprises....909 947-6207
13610 S Archibald Ave Ontario (91761) *(G-8596)*
Foster Farms, Livingston *Also called Foster Poultry Farms (G-454)*
Foster Farms, Waterford *Also called Foster Poultry Farms (G-455)*
Foster Farms, Livingston *Also called Foster Poultry Farms (G-8597)*
Foster Farms LLC....559 793-5501
770 N Plano St Porterville (93257) *(G-445)*
Foster Moore Inc....650 819-3042
650 Page Mill Rd Palo Alto (94304) *(G-14657)*
Foster Poultry Farms (PA)....209 394-6914
1000 Davis St Livingston (95334) *(G-454)*
Foster Poultry Farms....209 394-7901
1307 Ellenwood Rd Waterford (95386) *(G-455)*
Foster Poultry Farms....559 457-6509
4107 Ave 360 Traver (93673) *(G-9137)*
Foster Poultry Farms....209 394-7901
1333 Swan St Livingston (95334) *(G-8597)*
Foster Poultry Farms....209 394-7901
843 Davis St Livingston (95334) *(G-456)*
Foster Poultry Farms....209 668-5922
1033 S Center St Turlock (95380) *(G-457)*
Foster Poultry Farms....559 265-2000
900 W Belgravia Ave Fresno (93706) *(G-458)*
Foster Turkey Live Haul, Turlock *Also called Foster Poultry Farms (G-457)*
Foster Wheeler Energy Svcs Inc....800 500-1993
9645 Scranton Rd Ste 230 San Diego (92121) *(G-3476)*
Fostering Executive Leadership....949 651-6250
4790 Irvine Blvd 105-432 Irvine (92620) *(G-27438)*
Foto Kem Film & Video, Burbank *Also called Foto-Kem Industries Inc (G-18227)*
Foto-Kem Industries Inc (PA)....818 846-3102
2801 W Alameda Ave Burbank (91505) *(G-18227)*
Foto-Kem Industries Inc....818 846-3102
2801 W Olive Ave Burbank (91505) *(G-18228)*
Fotokem, Burbank *Also called Foto-Kem Industries Inc (G-18228)*
Foundation 9 Entertainment Inc (PA)....949 698-1500
30211 A De Las Bandera200 Ste 200 Rancho Santa Margari (92688) *(G-15670)*
Foundation Building Mtls LLC (PA)....714 380-3127
2552 Walnut Ave Ste 160 Tustin (92780) *(G-2897)*
Foundation Building Mtls LLC....951 300-2650
1975 3rd St Riverside (92507) *(G-7371)*
Foundation Constructors Inc (PA)....925 754-6633
81 Big Break Rd Oakley (94561) *(G-2051)*
Foundation For Dance Education....909 482-1590
5050 Arrow Hwy Ste B Montclair (91763) *(G-18393)*
Foundation For Early Childhood (PA)....626 572-5107
3360 Flair Dr Ste 100 El Monte (91731) *(G-23981)*
Foundation Laboratory, Pomona *Also called Latara Enterprise Inc (G-22234)*
Foundation Pile Inc....909 350-1584
8375 Almeria Ave Fontana (92335) *(G-2052)*
Foundation Super Skateboard, San Diego *Also called Tum Yeto Inc (G-8033)*
Founders Healthcare LLC....626 683-5401
170 N Daisy Ave Pasadena (91107) *(G-22440)*
Founders Management II Corp....650 570-5700
1221 Chess Dr Foster City (94404) *(G-12644)*
Foundstone Inc....949 297-5600
27201 Puerta Real Ste 400 Mission Viejo (92691) *(G-15671)*
Foundtion For Hispanic Educatn (PA)....408 585-5022
14271 Story Rd San Jose (95127) *(G-25256)*
Fountain Court Essex....818 227-2100
22102 Clarendon St # 200 Woodland Hills (91367) *(G-11542)*
Fountain Grove Golf & Athc CLB....707 521-3207
1525 Fountaingrove Pkwy Santa Rosa (95403) *(G-18740)*
Fountain Valley Body Works M2....714 751-8812
17481 Newhope St Fountain Valley (92708) *(G-17754)*
Fountain Valley Regl Hospl....714 966-7200
17100 Euclid St Fountain Valley (92708) *(G-21568)*
Fountain Valley School Dst....714 668-5882
17330 Mount Herrmann St Fountain Valley (92708) *(G-14301)*
Fountaingrove Inn LLC....707 578-6101
101 Fountaingrove Pkwy Santa Rosa (95403) *(G-12645)*
Fountains At Sea Bluffs, Dana Point *Also called Sunrise Senior Living Inc (G-20958)*
Fountains At The Carlotta, Palm Desert *Also called Sunrise Senior Living LLC (G-20985)*
Fountains At The Carlotta, The, Palm Desert *Also called Watermark Rtrment Cmmnties Inc (G-21026)*
FOUNTAINS, THE, Yuba City *Also called United Com Serve (G-20998)*
Fountainwood Residential Care....916 988-2200
8773 Oak Ave Orangevale (95662) *(G-24662)*
Fountngrove Inn Conference Ctr, Santa Rosa *Also called Fountaingrove Inn LLC (G-12645)*
Four CS Service Inc....559 237-3990
1560 H St Fresno (93721) *(G-3174)*
Four Medica Inc....310 348-4100
13160 Mindanao Way # 280 Marina Del Rey (90292) *(G-6074)*
Four Points By Sheraton, San Diego *Also called Pinnacle 1617 LLC (G-13097)*
Four Points By Sheraton....310 645-4600
9750 Airport Blvd Los Angeles (90045) *(G-12646)*
Four Points by Sheraton LAX, Los Angeles *Also called Irp Lax Hotel LLC (G-12854)*
Four Points Sheraton Lax, Los Angeles *Also called Lax Hotel Ventures LLC (G-12909)*
Four Points Sheraton Ventura, Ventura *Also called Harbor Island Hotel Group LP (G-12689)*
Four Seasons Healthcare....818 985-1814
5335 Laurel Canyon Blvd North Hollywood (91607) *(G-20580)*
Four Seasons Hotel, Westlake Village *Also called Burton-Way House Ltd A CA (G-12473)*
Four Seasons Hotel, Los Angeles *Also called Burton-Way House Ltd A CA (G-12474)*
Four Seasons Hotel, Los Angeles *Also called Burton-Way House Ltd A CA (G-12475)*
Four Seasons Hotel, San Francisco *Also called Cb-1 Hotel (G-12503)*
Four Seasons Hotel Inc....415 633-3441
735 Market St Fl 6 San Francisco (94103) *(G-12647)*
Four Seasons Hotel Inc....650 566-1200
2050 University Ave East Palo Alto (94303) *(G-12648)*
Four Seasons Hotel Silicon Vly, East Palo Alto *Also called East Palo Alto Hotel Dev Inc (G-12607)*
Four Seasons Landscaping, Van Nuys *Also called S G D Enterprises (G-947)*
Four Seasons Landscaping, Van Nuys *Also called S D Property Management Inc (G-11828)*
Four Seasons Resort Aviara, Carlsbad *Also called California Bistro At Fo (G-12481)*
Four Seasons Resort Aviara....760 603-6900
7447 Batiquitos Dr Carlsbad (92011) *(G-18741)*
Four Seasons Westlake....818 575-3000
2 Dole Dr Westlake Village (91362) *(G-12649)*
Four Sisters Inns....619 437-1900
1060 Adella Ave Coronado (92118) *(G-12650)*

ALPHABETIC

Four Ssons Hotel-San Francisco, San Francisco *Also called Four Seasons Hotel Inc* ***(G-12647)***

Four Ssons Rsort Santa Barbara, Santa Barbara *Also called 1260 Bb Property LLC* ***(G-12358)***

Four Star Private Patrol Inc....951 695-4245
28441 Rancho Ca Rd 105 Temecula (92590) ***(G-16645)***

Fourth Phase Los Angeles, San Fernando *Also called Prg (california) Inc* ***(G-18135)***

Fourth Street Bowl....408 453-5555
1441 N 4th St San Jose (95112) ***(G-18519)***

Fourthfloor Fashion Talent, Los Angeles *Also called Career Group Inc* ***(G-14622)***

Fowler Convalescent Hospital....559 834-2542
1306 E Sumner Ave Fowler (93625) ***(G-21216)***

Fowler Labor Service Inc....559 834-3723
633 W Fresno St Fowler (93625) ***(G-14658)***

Fowler Packing Company Inc....559 834-5911
8570 S Cedar Ave Fresno (93725) ***(G-534)***

Fox Inc (HQ)....310 369-1000
2121 Ave Of The Ste 1100 Los Angeles (90067) ***(G-5862)***

Fox Animation Studios Inc....323 857-8800
5700 Wilshire Blvd # 325 Los Angeles (90036) ***(G-18087)***

Fox Baseball Holdings Inc....323 224-1500
1000 Vin Scully Ave Los Angeles (90090) ***(G-18545)***

Fox Broadcasting Company (HQ)....310 369-1000
10201 W Pico Blvd Los Angeles (90064) ***(G-5863)***

Fox BSB Holdco Inc....323 224-1500
1000 Vin Scully Ave Los Angeles (90090) ***(G-18546)***

Fox Factory Holding Corp....619 768-1800
750 Vernon Way Ste 101 El Cajon (92020) ***(G-6732)***

Fox Family Channel, Burbank *Also called International Fmly Entrmt Inc* ***(G-6008)***

Fox Films Entertainment, Los Angeles *Also called Twentieth Cntury Fox Film Corp* ***(G-18174)***

Fox Head Inc (PA)....408 776-8633
16752 Armstrong Ave Irvine (92606) ***(G-8342)***

Fox Latin American Channel LLC....305 774-4167
10201 W Pico Blvd Los Angeles (90064) ***(G-6000)***

Fox Luggage Inc....323 588-1688
5353 E Slauson Ave Commerce (90040) ***(G-8114)***

Fox Network Center, Los Angeles *Also called Fox Networks Group Inc* ***(G-6001)***

Fox Networks Group Inc....310 369-9369
10201 W Pico Blvd 101 Los Angeles (90064) ***(G-6001)***

Fox Racing, Irvine *Also called Fox Head Inc* ***(G-8342)***

Fox Rent A Car Inc (PA)....310 342-5155
5500 W Century Blvd Los Angeles (90045) ***(G-17676)***

Fox Rothschild LLP....213 624-6560
1800 Century Park E # 300 Los Angeles (90067) ***(G-23253)***

Fox Television Stations LLC (HQ)....310 584-2000
1999 S Bundy Dr Los Angeles (90025) ***(G-5864)***

Fox Transportation Inc (PA)....909 291-4646
8610 Helms Ave Rancho Cucamonga (91730) ***(G-27925)***

Fox US Productions 27 Inc....310 656-6100
1600 Rosecrans Ave 200 Manhattan Beach (90266) ***(G-18274)***

Foxconn, San Jose *Also called Nsg Technology Inc* ***(G-17938)***

Foxconn....510 226-0822
46750 Winema Cmn Fremont (94539) ***(G-17172)***

Foxconn Electronics, Brea *Also called Fit Electronics Inc* ***(G-26518)***

Foxy, Salinas *Also called Nunes Company Inc* ***(G-8756)***

FP, San Francisco *Also called Francisco Partners LP* ***(G-15948)***

Fphs2, Corona *Also called Advanced Communication Service* ***(G-16972)***

FPI Management Inc....408 267-3952
1107 Luchessi Dr San Jose (95118) ***(G-27029)***

FPI Management Inc (PA)....916 357-5300
800 Iron Point Rd Folsom (95630) ***(G-11543)***

Fpk Investigaions, Valencia *Also called Fpk Security Inc* ***(G-16646)***

Fpk Security Inc....661 702-9091
28348 Constellation Rd # 880 Valencia (91355) ***(G-16646)***

Fpl LLC....805 643-6144
550 San Jon Rd Ventura (93001) ***(G-12651)***

Fragomen Del Rey Bernse....858 793-1600
11238 El Camino Real # 100 San Diego (92130) ***(G-23254)***

Fragomen Del Rey Bernse....310 820-3322
11150 W Olympic Blvd # 1000 Los Angeles (90064) ***(G-23255)***

Fragomen Del Rey Bernse....949 660-3504
18401 Von Karman Ave # 255 Irvine (92612) ***(G-23256)***

Fragomen Del Rey Bernse....408 919-0600
2121 Tasman Dr Santa Clara (95054) ***(G-23257)***

Framing Associates Inc....619 336-9991
1320 Coolidge Ave National City (91950) ***(G-17173)***

Fran-Jom Inc....626 443-3028
5101 Tyler Ave Temple City (91780) ***(G-21217)***

France Telecom RES & Dev LLC....415 284-9765
60 Spear St Ste 1100 San Francisco (94105) ***(G-26663)***

Franchisee, Anaheim *Also called Sheraton Pk Ht At Anheim Rsort* ***(G-13246)***

Franciscan Conv. Hospital, Merced *Also called Avalon Care Center - Merced Fr* ***(G-20390)***

Franciscan Lines Inc....415 642-9400
41 Pier San Francisco (94133) ***(G-3796)***

Francisco Emilio Assoc Law Off....949 474-2222
17532 Von Karman Ave Irvine (92614) ***(G-23258)***

Francisco Partners LP (HQ)....415 418-2900
1 Letterman Dr Bldg C San Francisco (94129) ***(G-15948)***

Francisco Partners MGT LP (PA)....415 418-2900
1 Letterman Dr Ste 410 San Francisco (94129) ***(G-12308)***

Francois Annanie....619 846-3438
29131 Escalante Rd Quail Valley (92587) ***(G-14302)***

Franconnect LLC....760 720-5354
300 Carlsbad Village Dr Carlsbad (92008) ***(G-15949)***

Frandeli Group LLC (PA)....714 450-7660
20377 Sw Acacia St # 200 Newport Beach (92660) ***(G-12216)***

Frandzel Share Robins Bloom Lc....323 852-1000
1000 Wilshire Blvd # 1900 Los Angeles (90017) ***(G-23259)***

Frangadakis, Kenneth DDS, Cupertino *Also called Cupertino Dental Group* ***(G-20251)***

Frank Rimerman & Co LLP....415 439-1144
1 Embarcadero Ctr # 2410 San Francisco (94111) ***(G-26351)***

Frank Barraza....760 348-7363
147 E Alamo Calipatria (92233) ***(G-662)***

Frank C Alegre Trucking Inc (PA)....209 334-2112
5100 W Highway 12 Lodi (95242) ***(G-4185)***

FRANK D LANTERMAN REGIONAL CEN, Los Angeles *Also called Los Angeles Cnty Dev Svc Fndtn* ***(G-22995)***

Frank D Yelian MD PC....949 788-1133
3500 Barranca Pkwy # 300 Irvine (92606) ***(G-19527)***

Frank Gates Service Company....916 934-0812
1107 Investment Blvd El Dorado Hills (95762) ***(G-27439)***

Frank Gates Service Company....800 994-4611
2400 E Katella Ave # 650 Anaheim (92806) ***(G-10422)***

Frank Ghiglione Inc (PA)....510 483-7000
14327 Washington Ave San Leandro (94578) ***(G-4020)***

Frank Ghiglione Inc....510 483-2063
2972 Alvarado St Ste H San Leandro (94577) ***(G-4021)***

Frank Gustafson....714 438-1590
1240 Logan Ave Ste N Costa Mesa (92626) ***(G-9265)***

Frank Howard Allen Fincl Corp....415 456-3000
1016 Irwin St San Rafael (94901) ***(G-11544)***

Frank Howard Allen Fincl Corp....707 523-3000
460 Mission Blvd Santa Rosa (95409) ***(G-11545)***

Frank Howard Allen Real Estate, San Rafael *Also called Frank Howard Allen Fincl Corp* ***(G-11544)***

Frank J Gomes Dairy A Califo....209 669-7978
5301 Deangelis Rd Stevinson (95374) ***(G-425)***

Frank M Booth Inc (PA)....650 871-8292
222 3rd St Marysville (95901) ***(G-25818)***

Frank N Magid Associates Inc....818 263-3300
15260 Ventura Blvd # 1840 Sherman Oaks (91403) ***(G-26664)***

Frank N Magid Associates Inc....818 263-3300
15260 Vntr Blvd Ste 1840 Sherman Oaks (91403) ***(G-26665)***

Frank S Smith Masonry Inc....909 468-0525
2830 Pomona Blvd Pomona (91768) ***(G-2815)***

Frank Schipper Construction Co....805 963-4359
610 E Cota St Santa Barbara (93103) ***(G-1554)***

Frank Sciarrino Marble G....858 695-8030
7505 Trade St San Diego (92121) ***(G-6983)***

Frank-Lin Distillers Pdts Ltd (PA)....408 259-8900
2455 Huntington Dr Fairfield (94533) ***(G-9101)***

Franke Con J Electric Inc....209 462-0717
317 N Grant St Stockton (95202) ***(G-2597)***

Franklin Advisers Inc....650 312-2000
1 Franklin Pkwy San Mateo (94403) ***(G-10144)***

Franklin Data, Westlake Village *Also called 5 Nine Group Inc* ***(G-14992)***

Franklin Resources Inc (PA)....650 312-2000
1 Franklin Pkwy San Mateo (94403) ***(G-12117)***

Franklin Templeton Instnl LLC (HQ)....650 312-2000
1 Franklin Pkwy San Mateo (94403) ***(G-9703)***

Franklin Templeton Investment, Rancho Cordova *Also called Franklin Tmpleton Inv Svcs LLC* ***(G-10003)***

Franklin Templeton Svcs LLC....650 312-3000
1 Franklin Pkwy San Mateo (94403) ***(G-10145)***

Franklin Tmpleton Inv Svcs LLC....650 312-2000
3366 Quality Dr Rancho Cordova (95670) ***(G-10146)***

Franklin Tmpleton Inv Svcs LLC....925 875-2619
5130 Hacienda Dr Fl 4 Dublin (94568) ***(G-10147)***

Franklin Tmpleton Inv Svcs LLC (HQ)....916 463-1500
3344 Quality Dr Rancho Cordova (95670) ***(G-10003)***

Frankly Co....415 861-9797
333 Bryant St Ste 240 San Francisco (94107) ***(G-15193)***

Frantz Wholesale Nursery LLC....209 874-1459
12161 Delaware Rd Hickman (95323) ***(G-282)***

Frasco Inc (PA)....818 848-3888
215 W Alameda Ave Burbank (91502) ***(G-16647)***

Frasco Investigative Services, Burbank *Also called Frasco Inc* ***(G-16647)***

Fraternal Order Eagles 1582....916 782-2694
124 Vernon St Roseville (95678) ***(G-10984)***

Frazier Nut Farms Inc....209 522-1406
10830 Yosemite Blvd Waterford (95386) ***(G-201)***

Fred Finch Youth Center....619 797-1090
3434 Grove St Lemon Grove (91945) ***(G-19528)***

Fred Finch Youth Center....510 439-3130
2523 El Portal Dr Ste 103 San Pablo (94806) ***(G-24663)***

Fred H Lundblade Jr....707 442-8049
939 Koster St Ste B Eureka (95501) ***(G-10985)***

Fred Leeds Properties....310 826-2466
1640 S Sepulv Blvd # 320 Los Angeles (90025) ***(G-11133)***

Frederick Labs LLC....646 738-8303
535 Mission St San Francisco (94105) ***(G-27440)***

Frederick Meiswinkel Inc....415 550-0400
850 S Van Ness Ave San Francisco (94110) ***(G-2898)***

Fredericka Manor....619 422-9271
183 3rd Ave Chula Vista (91910) ***(G-24664)***

FREDERICKA MANOR CARE CENTER, Burbank *Also called Fact Foundation* ***(G-17157)***

Fredericka Manor Care Center, Glendale *Also called Front Porch Communities* ***(G-21219)***

Fredericka Manor Care Center, Chula Vista *Also called Front Porch Communities* ***(G-21222)***

Free Conferencing Corporation....562 437-1411
4300 E Pacific Coast Hwy Long Beach (90804) ***(G-5603)***

Free Stream Media Corp....415 889-6404
301 Brannan St Fl 6 San Francisco (94107) ***(G-9266)***

Freeconferencecall.com, Long Beach *Also called Free Conferencing Corporation* ***(G-5603)***

Freedom Cmmnctons Holdings Inc (HQ)....714 796-7000
625 N Grand Ave Santa Ana (92701) ***(G-12062)***

Freedom Colorado Info Inc....719 632-5511
729 N Grand Ave Santa Ana (92701) ***(G-5604)***

Freedom Debt Relief, San Mateo *Also called Freedom Financial Network LLC* ***(G-13760)***
Freedom Financial Network LLC (PA)....650 393-6619
1875 S Grant St Ste 400 San Mateo (94402) ***(G-13760)***
Freedom Mortgage Corporation....760 692-3977
5900 La Place Ct Ste 107 Carlsbad (92008) ***(G-9842)***
Freedom Painting Inc....562 696-0785
8822 Calmada Ave Whittier (90605) ***(G-2443)***
Freedom Properties, Hemet *Also called Casa-Pacifica Inc* ***(G-24585)***
Freedom Properties Village, Hemet *Also called Casa-Pacifica Inc* ***(G-24587)***
Freedom Staff Leasing Inc....310 834-6621
3142 Pacific Coast Hwy Torrance (90505) ***(G-14880)***
Freedom Village, Lake Forest *Also called Casa-Pacifica Inc* ***(G-24586)***
Freedom Village Healthcare Ctr....949 472-4733
23442 El Toro Rd Bldg 2 Lake Forest (92630) ***(G-20581)***
Freedom Voice Systems, Encinitas *Also called Callcatchers Inc* ***(G-5568)***
Freeman Freeman & Smiley LLP (PA)....310 398-6227
1888 Century Park E Fl 19 Los Angeles (90067) ***(G-23260)***
Freeman Audio Visual Inc....714 254-3400
901 E South St Anaheim (92805) ***(G-14542)***
Freeman Expositions Inc....714 254-3400
901 E South St Anaheim (92805) ***(G-17174)***
Freeman Expositions Inc....650 871-1597
245 S Spruce Ave South San Francisco (94080) ***(G-17175)***
Freeman Investments Inc....805 687-4327
2595 Montrose Pl Santa Barbara (93105) ***(G-17778)***
Freemont Health Care Center, Fremont *Also called Mariner Health Care Inc* ***(G-20758)***
Freemont Rideout Health Group....530 751-4000
989 Plumas St Yuba City (95991) ***(G-19529)***
Freemont Rideout Health Group....530 749-4386
939 Live Oak Blvd Ste A4 Yuba City (95991) ***(G-21569)***
Freemont Rideout Hospice, Yuba City *Also called Freemont Rideout Health Group* ***(G-21569)***
Freeport-Mcmoran Oil & Gas LLC....661 322-7600
1200 Discovery Dr Ste 500 Bakersfield (93309) ***(G-1044)***
Freescale Semiconductor Inc....408 518-5500
2680 Zanker Rd Ste 200 San Jose (95134) ***(G-7568)***
Freeway Insurance, Huntington Beach *Also called Confie Seguros Inc* ***(G-10678)***
Freeway Insurance (PA)....714 252-2500
10801 Walker St Ste 250 Cypress (90630) ***(G-10722)***
Freight Management Inc....714 632-1440
2900 E La Palma Ave Anaheim (92806) ***(G-27441)***
Freight Solution Providers, Rancho Cordova *Also called Kls Air Express Inc* ***(G-5108)***
Freitas Brothers....805 343-3134
Hwy 1 Guadalupe (93434) ***(G-63)***
Freixenet Usa Inc....707 996-7256
23555 Arnold Dr Sonoma (95476) ***(G-9102)***
Fremantle Media, Burbank *Also called Prdctions N Fremantle Amer Inc* ***(G-18425)***
Fremont Ambltory Srgery Ctr LP....510 456-4600
39350 Civic Center Dr Fremont (94538) ***(G-19530)***
Fremont Bank (HQ)....510 505-5226
39150 Fremont Blvd Fremont (94538) ***(G-9499)***
Fremont Candle Lighters....510 796-0595
39261 Fremont Hub Fremont (94538) ***(G-25531)***
Fremont Dental Group, Fremont *Also called John J Maguire DDS* ***(G-20258)***
Fremont Group LLC (PA)....415 284-8880
199 Fremont St Ste 2500 San Francisco (94105) ***(G-10148)***
FREMONT HOSPITAL, Mariposa *Also called John C Fremont Healthcare Dst* ***(G-21614)***
Fremont Hospital....530 751-4000
620 J St Marysville (95901) ***(G-21570)***
Fremont Marriott....510 413-3700
46100 Landing Pkwy Fremont (94538) ***(G-12652)***
Fremont Medical Center, Marysville *Also called Fremont Hospital* ***(G-21570)***
Fremont Mutual Funds Inc....800 548-4539
333 Market St Ste 2600 San Francisco (94105) ***(G-10004)***
Fremont Properties Inc....415 284-8500
199 Fremont St Ste 1900 San Francisco (94105) ***(G-10986)***
Fremont Realty Capital LP....415 284-8665
199 Fremont St Fl 19 San Francisco (94105) ***(G-11255)***
Fremont Sports Inc....510 656-1955
40645 Fremont Blvd Ste 3 Fremont (94538) ***(G-18520)***
Fremont Surgery Center, Fremont *Also called Fremont Ambltory Srgery Ctr LP* ***(G-19530)***
Fremont Unified School Dst....510 657-0761
43772 S Grimmer Blvd Fremont (94538) ***(G-14303)***
French Hosp Med Ctr Foundation (HQ)....805 543-5353
1911 Johnson Ave San Luis Obispo (93401) ***(G-21571)***
French Park Care Center....714 973-1656
600 E Washington Ave Santa Ana (92701) ***(G-20582)***
French Redwood Inc....650 598-9000
223 Twin Dolphin Dr Redwood City (94065) ***(G-12653)***
Freschi Air Systems Inc....925 827-9761
715 Fulton Shipyard Rd Antioch (94509) ***(G-2229)***
Freschi Service Experts, Antioch *Also called Freschi Air Systems Inc* ***(G-2229)***
Fresenius Med Care Long Beach....562 432-4444
440 W Ocean Blvd Long Beach (90802) ***(G-22627)***
Fresh Air Environmental Svcs....323 913-1965
10675 Rush St South El Monte (91733) ***(G-3522)***
Fresh Grill LLC....714 444-2126
111 E Garry Ave Santa Ana (92707) ***(G-8837)***
Fresh Leaf Farms LLC (HQ)....831 422-7405
1250 Hansen St Salinas (93901) ***(G-64)***
Fresh Merge, Buena Park *Also called Dr Fresh LLC* ***(G-7261)***
Fresh Origins LLC....760 801-1087
570 Quarry Rd San Marcos (92069) ***(G-22)***
Fresh Start Bakeries, Ontario *Also called Aryzta LLC* ***(G-8798)***
Fresh Start Bakeries, Stockton *Also called Aryzta LLC* ***(G-8801)***
FRESH START CAFE, Reedley *Also called Community Youth Ministries* ***(G-23779)***
Fresh Venture Farms LLC....805 754-4449
1181 S Wolff Rd Oxnard (93033) ***(G-65)***

Freshko Produce Services Inc....559 497-7000
2155 E Muscat Ave Fresno (93725) ***(G-8725)***
Freshlunches Inc....310 478-5705
19431 Business Center Dr # 24 Northridge (91324) ***(G-23982)***
Freshology Inc....818 847-1888
10950 Sherman Way Ste 140 Burbank (91505) ***(G-8838)***
Freshpoint Inc....510 476-5900
30336 Whipple Rd Union City (94587) ***(G-8726)***
Freshpoint Inc....626 855-1400
155 N Orange Ave City of Industry (91744) ***(G-8727)***
Freshpoint Central California....209 216-0200
5900 N Golden State Blvd Turlock (95382) ***(G-8728)***
Freshpoint Las Vegas, City of Industry *Also called Freshpoint Inc* ***(G-8727)***
Freshpoint Southern Cal Inc....626 855-1400
155 N Orange Ave City of Industry (91744) ***(G-8729)***
Freshpoint Southern California, City of Industry *Also called Freshpoint Southern Cal Inc* ***(G-8729)***
Freshway Farms LLC....805 349-7170
2165 W Main St Santa Maria (93458) ***(G-112)***
Fresno AG Hardware Inc....559 224-6441
4590 N 1st St Fresno (93726) ***(G-13761)***
Fresno Airport Hotels LLC....559 252-3611
5090 E Clinton Way Fresno (93727) ***(G-12654)***
Fresno Auto Dealers Auction....559 268-8051
278 N Marks Ave Fresno (93706) ***(G-6675)***
Fresno Beverage Company Inc....559 650-1500
4010 E Hardy Ave Fresno (93725) ***(G-9057)***
Fresno Cmnty Hosp & Med Ctr (HQ)....559 459-6000
2823 Fresno St Fresno (93721) ***(G-21572)***
Fresno Cnty Economic Opportunt....559 263-1000
1900 Mariposa Mall # 300 Fresno (93721) ***(G-23983)***
Fresno Cnty Economic Opportunt (PA)....559 263-1010
1920 Mariposa Mall # 300 Fresno (93721) ***(G-23984)***
Fresno Cnty Economic Opportunt....559 263-1013
1920 Mariposa Mall Fresno (93721) ***(G-17176)***
Fresno Cnty Economic Opportunt....559 485-3733
3120 W Nielsen Ave # 102 Fresno (93706) ***(G-2899)***
Fresno Cnty Supt Schools Cent....559 644-1000
16644 S Elm Ave Caruthers (93609) ***(G-3938)***
Fresno Convention Center, Fresno *Also called City of Fresno* ***(G-17074)***
Fresno County Federal Cr Un (PA)....559 252-5000
2580 W Shaw Ln Frnt Fresno (93711) ***(G-9602)***
Fresno County Private Security....559 233-9800
2150 Tulare St Fresno (93721) ***(G-16648)***
Fresno District Office, Fresno *Also called State Compensation Insur Fund* ***(G-10467)***
Fresno Eoc, Fresno *Also called Fresno Cnty Economic Opportunt* ***(G-23983)***
Fresno Eoc, Fresno *Also called Fresno Cnty Economic Opportunt* ***(G-23984)***
Fresno Hauling, Fresno *Also called USA Waste of California Inc* ***(G-6583)***
Fresno Hauling, Visalia *Also called USA Waste of California Inc* ***(G-6588)***
Fresno Heart Hospital LLC....559 433-8000
15 E Audubon Dr Fresno (93720) ***(G-22142)***
Fresno Heritage Partners....559 446-6226
6075 N Marks Ave Fresno (93711) ***(G-24665)***
Fresno Hotel Partners LP....559 224-4040
324 E Shaw Ave Fresno (93710) ***(G-12655)***
Fresno Irrigation District....559 233-7161
2907 S Maple Ave Fresno (93725) ***(G-6643)***
Fresno Metro Flood Ctrl Dst....559 456-3292
5469 E Olive Ave Fresno (93727) ***(G-17177)***
Fresno Plumbing & Heating Inc (PA)....559 294-0200
2585 N Larkin Ave Fresno (93727) ***(G-2230)***
Fresno Rescue Mission Inc (PA)....559 268-0839
310 G St Fresno (93706) ***(G-23985)***
Fresno Roofing Co Inc....559 255-8377
5950 E Olive Ave Fresno (93727) ***(G-3175)***
Fresno Skilled Nursing....559 268-5361
1665 M St Fresno (93721) ***(G-20583)***
Fresno Surgery Center LP (PA)....559 431-8000
6125 N Fresno St Fresno (93710) ***(G-21573)***
Fresno Surgical Hospital, Fresno *Also called Fresno Surgery Center LP* ***(G-21573)***
Fresno Truck Center....559 486-4310
2727 E Central Ave Fresno (93725) ***(G-6676)***
Fresno Truck Center....209 983-2400
10182 S Harlan Rd French Camp (95231) ***(G-6677)***
Fresno Unified School District....559 457-3074
4600 N Brawley Ave Fresno (93722) ***(G-14304)***
Fresno-Madera Federal Land....559 674-2437
305 N I St Madera (93637) ***(G-9731)***
Fresnos Chaffee Zoo Corp....559 498-5910
894 W Belmont Ave Fresno (93728) ***(G-25063)***
Freund Baking Co, Hayward *Also called Oakhurst Industries Inc* ***(G-8507)***
Frey Farming & Tpsry Vineyards....805 937-1542
2203 Fallen Leaf Dr Santa Maria (93455) ***(G-704)***
Friant Water Users Association....559 562-6305
854 N Harvard Ave Lindsay (93247) ***(G-6349)***
Friant Water Users Authority, Lindsay *Also called Friant Water Users Association* ***(G-6349)***
Frick Paper Company....323 726-8200
2164 N Batavia St Orange (92865) ***(G-8191)***
Friction Materials LLC....248 362-3600
2525 W 190th St Torrance (90504) ***(G-25819)***
Friedas Inc....714 733-7655
4465 Corporate Center Dr Los Alamitos (90720) ***(G-8730)***
Friedman Professional Mgt Co....714 842-1426
17752 Beach Blvd Side Huntington Beach (92647) ***(G-19531)***
Friendly Hills Country Club....562 698-0331
8500 Villaverde Dr Whittier (90605) ***(G-18954)***
Friendly Valley Recrtl Assn....661 252-3223
19345 Avenue Of The Oaks Santa Clarita (91321) ***(G-23986)***

ALPHABETIC

FRIENDLY VILLAGE COMMUNITY ASS, Santa Clarita *Also called Friendly Valley Recrtl Assn (G-23986)*
Friends Abroad 925 939-9420
2173 La Salle Dr Walnut Creek (94598) ***(G-25087)***
Friends Fitzgerald Mar Reserve 650 728-3584
200 Nevada Ave Moss Beach (94038) ***(G-24921)***
Friends For Life 951 601-6722
12282 Brewster Dr Moreno Valley (92555) ***(G-25532)***
Friends Group Express Inc 909 346-6814
14520 Village Dr Apt 1013 Fontana (92337) ***(G-4186)***
Friends of Angeles Chapter 213 387-4287
3435 Wilshire Blvd # 660 Los Angeles (90010) ***(G-25533)***
Friends of Bear Gulch 909 989-9396
8355 Bear Gulch Pl Rancho Cucamonga (91730) ***(G-25534)***
Friends of Family 818 988-4430
16861 Parthenia St Northridge (91343) ***(G-23987)***
Friends of Max Rose LLC 424 901-1260
1639 11th St Ste 260 Santa Monica (90404) ***(G-18088)***
Friends of The Los Angeles 323 653-0440
8405 Beverly Blvd Los Angeles (90048) ***(G-24922)***
Friends Outside 209 955-0701
7272 Murray Dr Stockton (95210) ***(G-23988)***
Friends Santa Cruz State Parks 831 429-1840
144 School St Santa Cruz (95060) ***(G-25257)***
Fritch Eye Care Medical Center 661 665-2020
9000 Ming Ave Ste L2 Bakersfield (93311) ***(G-19532)***
Frito-Lay North America Inc 626 855-1300
14600 Proctor Ave City of Industry (91746) ***(G-8611)***
Frito-Lay North America Inc 310 224-5600
1500 Francisco St Torrance (90501) ***(G-27030)***
Frito-Lay North America Inc 559 226-8153
3630 N Hazel Ave Fresno (93722) ***(G-8612)***
Frito-Lay North America Inc 415 467-1860
151 W Hill Pl Brisbane (94005) ***(G-8613)***
Frito-Lay North America Inc 916 372-5400
3810 Seaport Blvd West Sacramento (95691) ***(G-8614)***
Frito-Lay North America Inc 661 835-0347
6320 District Blvd Bakersfield (93313) ***(G-8615)***
Frito-Lay North America Inc 661 951-1399
751 W Avenue L8 Lancaster (93534) ***(G-8616)***
Frito-Lay North America Inc 510 769-5000
1450 S Loop Rd Alameda (94502) ***(G-8617)***
Frito-Lay North America Inc 760 727-6022
1390 Vantage Ct Vista (92081) ***(G-8618)***
Frito-Lay North America Inc 949 586-4644
26962 Vista Ter El Toro (92630) ***(G-8619)***
Frito-Lay North America Inc 559 651-1334
8316 W Elowin Ct Visalia (93291) ***(G-8620)***
Frito-Lay North America Inc 310 322-5001
1924 E Maple Ave El Segundo (90245) ***(G-4553)***
Fritz Companies Inc (HQ) 650 635-2693
550-1 Eccles Ave San Francisco (94101) ***(G-5080)***
Frize Corporation 626 369-6088
16605 Gale Ave City of Industry (91745) ***(G-1424)***
Frog Design Inc (HQ) 415 442-4804
660 3rd St Fl 4 San Francisco (94107) ***(G-14146)***
Fromer Inc 818 341-3896
22225 Acorn St Chatsworth (91311) ***(G-1177)***
Front Line MGT Group Inc 310 209-3100
1100 Glendon Ave Ste 2000 Los Angeles (90024) ***(G-27031)***
Front Porch Inc (PA) 209 288-5500
14520 Mono Way Ste 200 Sonora (95370) ***(G-15194)***
Front Porch Communities 323 661-1128
1055 N Kingsley Dr Los Angeles (90029) ***(G-20584)***
Front Porch Communities 714 776-7150
1401 W Ball Rd Anaheim (92802) ***(G-21218)***
Front Porch Communities 858 454-2151
849 Coast Blvd La Jolla (92037) ***(G-11134)***
Front Porch Communities (PA) 818 729-8100
800 N Brand Blvd Fl 19 Glendale (91203) ***(G-21219)***
Front Porch Communities 760 729-4983
2855 Carlsbad Blvd Carlsbad (92008) ***(G-21220)***
Front Porch Communities 909 626-1227
650 Harrison Ave Claremont (91711) ***(G-21221)***
Front Porch Communities 619 427-2777
111 3rd Ave Chula Vista (91910) ***(G-21222)***
Front Porch Communities & Svcs 626 796-8162
842 E Villa St Pasadena (91101) ***(G-24666)***
Front Porch Communities & Svcs 858 274-4110
2567 2nd Ave Unit 312 San Diego (92103) ***(G-21223)***
Front Porch Communities & Svcs 818 729-8100
303 N Glenoaks Blvd # 1000 Burbank (91502) ***(G-21224)***
Front Porch Communities & Svcs 626 289-6211
2400 S Fremont Ave Alhambra (91803) ***(G-21225)***
Front Porch Communities & Svcs 562 868-9761
11701 Studebaker Rd Norwalk (90650) ***(G-21226)***
Front Porch Communities & Svcs 760 240-5051
11959 Apple Valley Rd Apple Valley (92308) ***(G-20585)***
Front Prch Cmmunities/Services 805 687-0793
3775 Modoc Rd Santa Barbara (93105) ***(G-21227)***
Front St Inc 831 420-0120
2115 7th Ave Santa Cruz (95062) ***(G-21228)***
Front St Residential Care, Santa Cruz *Also called Front St Inc (G-21228)*
Frontech N Fujitsu Amer Inc 408 982-3697
2933 Bunker Hill Ln # 101 Santa Clara (95054) ***(G-15195)***
Frontech N Fujitsu Amer Inc (HQ) 949 855-5500
27121 Towne Centre Dr # 100 Foothill Ranch (92610) ***(G-15950)***
Frontier California Inc 760 342-0500
83793 Dr Carreon Blvd Indio (92201) ***(G-5605)***
Frontier California Inc 805 925-0000
200 W Church St Santa Maria (93458) ***(G-5606)***
Frontier California Inc 760 256-3511
135 Cozy Ln Barstow (92311) ***(G-5607)***
Frontier California Inc 818 365-0542
510 Park Ave San Fernando (91340) ***(G-5608)***
Frontier California Inc 209 239-4128
525 E Yosemite Ave Manteca (95336) ***(G-5609)***
Frontier California Inc 805 372-6000
112 S Lakeview Canyon Rd Westlake Village (91362) ***(G-7569)***
Frontier California Inc 951 461-7713
800 N Haven Ave Ontario (91764) ***(G-5610)***
Frontier California Inc 805 372-6000
1 Wellpoint Way Westlake Village (91362) ***(G-5611)***
Frontier California Inc 559 592-2100
200 W Firebaugh Ave Exeter (93221) ***(G-5612)***
Frontier California Inc 559 224-9222
5195 N Blackstone Ave Fresno (93710) ***(G-5397)***
Frontier Communities, Rancho Cucamonga *Also called Shii LLC (G-11844)*
Frontier Land Companies 209 957-8112
10100 Trinity Pkwy # 420 Stockton (95219) ***(G-1178)***
Frontier Logistics Services, Ontario *Also called F R T International Inc (G-5075)*
Frontier Mechanical Inc 661 589-6203
6309 Seven Seas Ave Bakersfield (93308) ***(G-2231)***
Frontier Plumbing, Bakersfield *Also called Frontier Mechanical Inc (G-2231)*
Frontiir Corporation 510 996-2071
1586 Parkview Ave Apt 3 San Jose (95130) ***(G-5613)***
Frontrange Holding Inc 408 601-2800
490 N Mccarthy Blvd Milpitas (95035) ***(G-15672)***
Frontrange Solutions Inc (HQ) 408 601-2800
490 N Mccarthy Blvd Milpitas (95035) ***(G-27442)***
Frontrs-Frnters Land Companies, Stockton *Also called Frontier Land Companies (G-1178)*
Frost & Sullivan 650 475-4500
3211 Scott Blvd Ste 203 Santa Clara (95054) ***(G-26666)***
Frsteam By Custom Commercial, Hayward *Also called Custom Commercial Dry Clrs Inc (G-13580)*
Fruit Guys 714 826-2993
4465 Corporate Center Dr Los Alamitos (90720) ***(G-8731)***
Fruitvale Long Term Care LLC 510 261-5613
3020 E 15th St Oakland (94601) ***(G-20586)***
Fry, Opal W & Son Farming, Bakersfield *Also called Opal Fry and Son (G-86)*
Frye Construction Inc 661 588-8870
18807 Highway 65 Bakersfield (93308) ***(G-2900)***
Frys Electronics Inc 916 286-5800
4100 Northgate Blvd Sacramento (95834) ***(G-27926)***
Frys Electronics Inc 925 852-0300
1695 Willow Pass Rd Concord (94520) ***(G-7570)***
Frys Electronics Inc 310 364-3797
3600 N Sepulveda Blvd Manhattan Beach (90266) ***(G-7132)***
FS Commercial Landscape Inc (PA) 951 360-7070
5151 Pedley Rd Riverside (92509) ***(G-854)***
FS&k, Thousand Oaks *Also called Floyd Skeren & Kelly LLP (G-23247)*
FSA, Lompoc *Also called Family Service Agency (G-23971)*
Fscc, Santa Barbara *Also called Frank Schipper Construction Co (G-1554)*
Fsq Rio Las Palmas Business Tr 209 957-4711
877 E March Ln Apt 378 Stockton (95207) ***(G-11135)***
Fssi, Santa Ana *Also called Financial Statement Svcs Inc (G-14070)*
Fst Sand & Gravel Inc 951 277-8440
21780 Temescal Canyon Rd Corona (92883) ***(G-6984)***
FT. WASHINGTON ELEM., Fresno *Also called Fort Washington Parent Assoc (G-25255)*
Fti Consulting Inc 213 689-1200
633 W 5th St Ste 1600 Los Angeles (90071) ***(G-25820)***
Fti Consulting Inc 415 283-4200
1 Front St Ste 1600 San Francisco (94111) ***(G-27927)***
Fuel Delivery Services Inc 209 751-2185
4895 S Airport Way Stockton (95206) ***(G-4187)***
Fuel TV 310 444-8564
1440 S Sepulveda Blvd Los Angeles (90025) ***(G-5865)***
Fueling and Service Tech Inc 714 523-0194
7050 Village Dr Ste D Buena Park (90621) ***(G-7845)***
Fuentes Farms Ag Inc 209 722-7201
2346 Glen Ave Merced (95340) ***(G-14659)***
Fugro Consultants Inc 925 256-6070
1777 Botelho Dr Ste 262 Walnut Creek (94596) ***(G-25821)***
Fugro West Inc (HQ) 805 650-7000
4820 Mcgrath St Ste 100 Ventura (93003) ***(G-25822)***
Fuji Food Products Inc 619 268-3118
8660 Miramar Rd Ste N San Diego (92126) ***(G-8839)***
Fuji Natural Foods Inc (HQ) 909 947-1008
13500 S Hamner Ave Ontario (91761) ***(G-330)***
Fuji Photo Film, Cypress *Also called Fujifilm North America Corp (G-7032)*
Fujifilm North America Corp 714 372-4200
6200 Phyllis Dr Cypress (90630) ***(G-7032)***
Fujitsu America Inc (HQ) 408 746-6000
1250 E Arques Ave Sunnyvale (94085) ***(G-15951)***
Fujitsu America Inc 408 746-8419
3113 Knights Bridge Rd San Jose (95132) ***(G-15952)***
Fujitsu America Inc 408 992-3561
317 Eureka St San Francisco (94114) ***(G-15953)***
Fujitsu America Inc 310 563-7000
2250 E Imperial Hwy # 200 El Segundo (90245) ***(G-15954)***
Fujitsu Computer Pdts Amer Inc (HQ) 408 746-6000
1250 E Arques Ave Sunnyvale (94085) ***(G-7133)***
Fujitsu Electronics Amer Inc (HQ) 408 737-5600
1250 E Arques Ave Sunnyvale (94085) ***(G-25823)***
Fujitsu Glovia Inc (HQ) 310 563-7000
2250 E Imperial Hwy # 200 El Segundo (90245) ***(G-15196)***

Fujitsu Laboratories Amer Inc (HQ) 408 530-4500
1240 E Arques Ave 345 Sunnyvale (94085) *(G-26519)*
Fujitsu Semiconductor Amer Inc, Sunnyvale Also called *Fujitsu Electronics Amer Inc* *(G-25823)*
Fujitsu Ten Corp of America 310 327-2151
19600 S Vermont Ave Torrance (90502) *(G-7498)*
Fulbright & Jaworski LLP 213 244-9941
555 S Flower St Ste 4100 Los Angeles (90071) *(G-23261)*
Full Circle Wireless Inc 949 783-7979
8900 Research Dr Irvine (92618) *(G-7571)*
Full Spectrum Lending Inc (HQ) 626 584-2220
35 N Lake Ave Fl 3 Pasadena (91101) *(G-9843)*
Full Spectrum Services Inc 707 465-1460
1570 S Railroad Ave Crescent City (95531) *(G-23989)*
Fullclip USA, Garden Grove Also called *Customfab Inc* *(G-17111)*
Fullerton College 714 732-5453
321 E Chapman Ave Fullerton (92832) *(G-17792)*
Fullerton Guest Home Inc 714 441-0313
1510 E Commonwealth Ave Fullerton (92831) *(G-21229)*
Fullerton Healthcare 714 992-5701
2222 N Harbor Blvd Fullerton (92835) *(G-20587)*
Fullmer Cattle Nthrn Cal LLC 909 597-3274
16600 Hellman Ave Corona (92880) *(G-410)*
Fullmer Construction 909 947-9467
1725 S Grove Ave Ontario (91761) *(G-1425)*
Fullscreen Inc (HQ) 310 202-3333
12180 Millennium Ste 100 Playa Vista (90094) *(G-13852)*
Fulwider and Patton LLP 310 824-5555
6100 Center Dr Ste 1200 Los Angeles (90045) *(G-23262)*
Fumai Industrial Inc 626 272-1788
735 W Duarte Rd Arcadia (91007) *(G-7572)*
Fume-A-Pest & Termite Control, Encino Also called *A-Able Inc* *(G-14170)*
Fund Services Advisors Inc 213 612-2196
777 S Figueroa St # 3200 Los Angeles (90017) *(G-10149)*
Fundbox Inc 415 509-1343
300 Montgomery St Ste 900 San Francisco (94104) *(G-27443)*
Funding Circle Usa Inc 855 385-5356
747 Front St Fl 4 San Francisco (94111) *(G-9749)*
Funny or Die Inc 650 461-3929
159 2nd Ave San Mateo (94401) *(G-16375)*
Furnace Creek Ranch & Inn, Death Valley Also called *Xanterra Parks & Resorts Inc* *(G-13443)*
Furniture America Cal Inc 909 718-7276
19635 E Walnut Dr N City of Industry (91789) *(G-6815)*
Furniture America California, City of Industry Also called *Furniture America Cal Inc* *(G-6815)*
Furniture Trnsp Systems 909 869-1200
3100 Pomona Blvd Pomona (91768) *(G-5081)*
Fuscoe Engineering Inc (PA) 949 474-1960
16795 Von Karman Ave # 100 Irvine (92606) *(G-25824)*
Fuse Project LLC 415 908-1492
1401 16th St San Francisco (94103) *(G-27928)*
Fusefx Inc 661 644-0783
14823 Califa St Van Nuys (91411) *(G-18229)*
Fusion Contact Centers LLC 805 922-2999
1288 W Mccoy Ln Ste C Santa Maria (93455) *(G-17178)*
Fusion Real Estate Network Inc 916 448-3174
1300 National Dr Ste 170 Sacramento (95834) *(G-11546)*
Fusionone Inc 408 282-1200
55 Almaden Blvd Ste 500 San Jose (95113) *(G-15197)*
Fusionops Inc 408 524-2222
707 California St Mountain View (94041) *(G-15198)*
Fusionstorm (PA) 415 623-2626
2 Bryant St Ste 150 San Francisco (94105) *(G-16376)*
Fusionzone Automotive Inc 888 576-1136
1011 Swarthmore Ave Pacific Palisades (90272) *(G-16377)*
Future Energy Corporation 760 477-9700
4120 Avenida De La Plata Oceanside (92056) *(G-2901)*
Future Energy Corporation 916 685-4200
9701 Elk Grove Florin Rd Elk Grove (95624) *(G-25825)*
Future Homes International, Moraga Also called *Engineered Forest Products LLC* *(G-12305)*
Future Paging & Cellular Inc 408 238-8833
2445 Alvin Ave San Jose (95121) *(G-5398)*
Future State 925 956-4200
2101 Webster St Oakland (94612) *(G-16378)*
Futuredontics Inc (PA) 310 215-6400
6060 Center Dr Fl 7 Los Angeles (90045) *(G-27444)*
Futurenet Technologies Corp 909 396-4000
1320 Valley Vista Dr # 202 Diamond Bar (91765) *(G-15199)*
Futures Explored Inc 925 284-3240
3547 Wilkinson Ln Lafayette (94549) *(G-23990)*
Futurewei Technologies Inc 469 277-5700
2330 Central Expy Santa Clara (95050) *(G-5614)*
Futuris Global Holdings LLC (HQ) 510 771-2333
233 Wilshire Blvd Ste 800 Santa Monica (90401) *(G-12063)*
Futuro Infantil Hispano Ffa 626 339-1824
2227 E Garvey Ave N West Covina (91791) *(G-23991)*
Fvbw, Fountain Valley Also called *Fountain Valley Body Works M2* *(G-17754)*
FW Spencer & Son Inc 415 468-5000
99 S Hill Dr Brisbane (94005) *(G-2232)*
Fx Networks LLC 310 369-1000
10201 W Pico Blvd Los Angeles (90064) *(G-6002)*
G & G Construction Co, Atwater Also called *Gino/Giuseppe Inc* *(G-3265)*
G & H Dental Arts Inc (PA) 310 214-8007
4212 Artesia Blvd Torrance (90504) *(G-22307)*
G & K Management Co Inc (PA) 310 204-2050
5150 Overland Ave Culver City (90230) *(G-11547)*
G & K Management Co Inc 619 437-1777
299 Prospect Pl Coronado (92118) *(G-11548)*
G & K Management Co Inc 818 705-8834
6540 Wilbur Ave Reseda (91335) *(G-11549)*
G & L Penasquitos Inc 858 538-0802
10584 Rancho Carmel Dr San Diego (92128) *(G-23992)*
G and E Healthcare Svcs LLC 818 367-5881
14040 Astoria St Sylmar (91342) *(G-20588)*
G and S Foods, Vernon Also called *Goldberg and Solovy Foods Inc* *(G-8481)*
G B Group Inc (PA) 408 848-8118
8921 Murray Ave Gilroy (95020) *(G-1311)*
G Brothers Construction Inc 714 590-3070
7070 Patterson Dr Garden Grove (92841) *(G-2902)*
G C H Insurance Group 209 526-3110
1150 9th St Ste 1400 Modesto (95354) *(G-10723)*
G D B, San Rafael Also called *Guide Dogs For Blind Inc* *(G-639)*
G I L C Inc 831 724-1011
585 W Beach St Watsonville (95076) *(G-1179)*
G Instruments 858 231-5156
14425 N Church Sq San Diego (92128) *(G-17179)*
G J Sullivan Co Inc 213 626-1000
800 W 6th St Ste 1800 Los Angeles (90017) *(G-10724)*
G K Tool Corp 626 338-7300
4265 Puente Ave Baldwin Park (91706) *(G-7684)*
G Katen Partners Ltd Lblty Co 424 354-3241
9903 Santa Monica Blvd Beverly Hills (90212) *(G-5082)*
G M A C-One Source Realty 619 405-6231
898 Jackman St El Cajon (92020) *(G-11550)*
G M Floral Company 213 489-7055
740 Maple Ave Los Angeles (90014) *(G-9189)*
G M Floral Supply, Los Angeles Also called *G M Floral Company* *(G-9189)*
G M I, San Diego Also called *Guard Management Inc* *(G-16668)*
G Moroni Comp, Sacramento Also called *Smart Management & Companies* *(G-27215)*
G P M M Money Centers Inc 619 288-7607
1460 Doris Ave Oxnard (93030) *(G-9718)*
G P Resources, Compton Also called *General Petroleum Corporation* *(G-9022)*
G P S, Taft Also called *General Production Svc Cal Inc* *(G-1933)*
G R Helm Inc 916 933-9697
5050 Rbert J Mathews Pkwy El Dorado Hills (95762) *(G-14881)*
G S C Ball, Commerce Also called *Grocers Specialty Company* *(G-8484)*
G S I, San Diego Also called *Go-Staff Inc* *(G-14883)*
G S N, Santa Monica Also called *Game Show Network LLC* *(G-6003)*
G S Parsons Co., San Diego Also called *Parsons Airgas Inc* *(G-7875)*
G T Global Staffing, Los Angeles Also called *Global Staffing Inc* *(G-14663)*
G T Technology Inc 408 257-5245
12306 Brooklyn Dr Saratoga (95070) *(G-27929)*
G W Maintenance Inc (PA) 714 541-2211
1101 E 6th St Santa Ana (92701) *(G-7932)*
G&H Dental Arts Cushman Dental, Torrance Also called *G & H Dental Arts Inc* *(G-22307)*
G&K Services Inc 916 381-5500
5900 Alder Ave Sacramento (95828) *(G-13629)*
G/M Business Interiors, San Diego Also called *Goforth & Marti* *(G-6816)*
G2 Direct and Digital 415 421-1000
612 Howard St Ste 400 San Francisco (94105) *(G-15200)*
G2 Software Systems Inc 619 222-8025
4025 Hancock St Ste 105 San Diego (92110) *(G-25826)*
G3 Enterprises, Modesto Also called *United Sttes Intrmdal Svcs LLC* *(G-5183)*
G3 Enterprises Inc (PA) 209 341-7515
502 E Whitmore Ave Modesto (95358) *(G-5083)*
G3 Enterprises Inc 209 341-3441
1300 Camino Diablo Rd Byron (94514) *(G-5084)*
G3 Enterprises Inc 209 341-4045
500 S Santa Rosa Ave Modesto (95354) *(G-5085)*
G4s Secure Solutions (usa) 661 834-3454
4400 Ashe Rd Ste 206 Bakersfield (93313) *(G-16649)*
G4s Secure Solutions (usa) 619 295-2394
5030 Camino De La Siesta San Diego (92108) *(G-16650)*
G4s Secure Solutions (usa) 323 938-9100
4929 Wilshire Blvd # 601 Los Angeles (90010) *(G-16651)*
G4s Secure Solutions (usa) 951 341-3000
1450 Iowa Ave Riverside (92507) *(G-16652)*
G4s Secure Solutions (usa) 415 591-0780
200 Pine St Fl 7 San Francisco (94104) *(G-16653)*
G4s Secure Solutions (usa) 714 939-4900
2300 E Katella Ave # 150 Anaheim (92806) *(G-16654)*
G4s Secure Solutions (usa) 925 543-0008
1 Annabel Ln Ste 208 San Ramon (94583) *(G-16655)*
G4s Secure Solutions (usa) 818 889-1113
5655 Lindero Canyon Rd # 504 Westlake Village (91362) *(G-16656)*
G5 Global Partners Ix LLC 619 291-6500
2151 Hotel Cir S San Diego (92108) *(G-12656)*
G7 Productivity Systems 858 675-1095
16885 W Bernardo Dr # 290 San Diego (92127) *(G-15673)*
GA Services LLC 949 752-6515
1681 Kettering Irvine (92614) *(G-16379)*
Gable House Inc 310 378-2265
22501 Hawthorne Blvd Torrance (90505) *(G-18521)*
Gable House Bowl, Torrance Also called *Gable House Inc* *(G-18521)*
Gables of Ojai LLC 805 646-1446
701 N Montgomery St Ojai (93023) *(G-11136)*
Gabriella Foundation 213 365-2491
639 S Commwl Ave Ste B Los Angeles (90005) *(G-18363)*
Gachina Landscape MGT Inc 650 853-0400
1130 Obrien Dr Menlo Park (94025) *(G-855)*
GAF Holdings Inc 559 734-3333
1300 E Mineral King Ave Visalia (93292) *(G-12064)*
GAF Materials, Stockton Also called *Standard Industries Inc* *(G-7020)*
GAF Materials, Shafter Also called *Standard Industries Inc* *(G-7021)*
Gafcon Inc (PA) 858 875-0010
5960 Cornerstone Ct W # 100 San Diego (92121) *(G-27032)*

Gahvejian Enterprises Inc...559 834-5956
2004 S Temperance Ave Fowler (93625) ***(G-8192)***
Gaia Interactive Inc...408 573-8800
2550 N 1st St Ste 250 San Jose (95131) ***(G-5615)***
Gaia Online, San Jose *Also called Gaia Interactive Inc* ***(G-5615)***
Gaikai Inc...949 330-6850
65 Enterprise Aliso Viejo (92656) ***(G-15674)***
Gaithers Family Home...559 781-0301
1408 S Newcomb St Porterville (93257) ***(G-21230)***
Galaxy Building Systems Inc...818 340-6557
23978 Craftsman Rd Calabasas (91302) ***(G-14305)***
Gale Lina Inc...909 595-8898
230 S 9th Ave City of Industry (91746) ***(G-8254)***
Gale/Triangle, San Pedro *Also called Performance Team Frt Sys Inc* ***(G-4614)***
Galena Equipment Rental LLC...510 638-8100
10700 Bigge St San Leandro (94577) ***(G-14482)***
Galice Inc...323 731-8200
30140 Tuttle Ct Tehachapi (93561) ***(G-17180)***
Galkos Construction Inc (PA)...714 373-8545
15262 Pipeline Ln Huntington Beach (92649) ***(G-13762)***
Gallagher Bassett, Irvine *Also called Arthur J Gallagher & Co* ***(G-10623)***
Gallagher Construction Svcs, San Francisco *Also called Arthur J Gallagher & Co* ***(G-10625)***
Gallagher Pediatric Therapy, Fullerton *Also called Therapy For Kids Inc* ***(G-20358)***
Gallaher Construction Inc...707 535-3200
220 Concourse Blvd Santa Rosa (95403) ***(G-1180)***
Galleano Enterprises Inc...951 685-5376
4231 Wineville Ave Mira Loma (91752) ***(G-154)***
Galleher Corporation (PA)...562 944-8885
9303 Greenleaf Ave Santa Fe Springs (90670) ***(G-6862)***
Galleria Park Associates LLC...415 781-3060
191 Sutter St San Francisco (94104) ***(G-12657)***
Galleria Park Hotel, San Francisco *Also called Galleria Park Associates LLC* ***(G-12657)***
Galli Produce Company...408 436-6100
1650 Old Bayshore Hwy San Jose (95112) ***(G-8732)***
Gallo Cattle Co A Ltd Partnr...209 394-7984
10561 State Highway 140 Atwater (95301) ***(G-426)***
Gallo Sales Company Inc (HQ)...510 476-5000
30825 Wiegman Rd Hayward (94544) ***(G-9103)***
Galloway Lucchese Everson...925 930-9090
2300 Contra Costa Blvd Ste 350 Walnut Creek (94596) ***(G-23263)***
Gallup Inc...949 474-2700
18300 Von Karman Ave # 1000 Irvine (92612) ***(G-27445)***
Gallup & Stribling Orchids LLC...805 684-1998
3450 Via Real Carpinteria (93013) ***(G-283)***
Gallup and Stribling Holdings, Carpinteria *Also called Gallup & Stribling Orchids LLC* ***(G-283)***
Gallup Organization, The, Irvine *Also called Gallup Inc* ***(G-27445)***
Galt Park Recreation, Galt *Also called City of Galt* ***(G-19172)***
Gama Berry Farms LLC...805 483-1000
730 S A St Oxnard (93030) ***(G-113)***
Gamboa Service Inc...714 966-5325
2116 S Wright St Santa Ana (92705) ***(G-14306)***
Game Show Network LLC (HQ)...310 255-6800
2150 Colorado Ave Ste 100 Santa Monica (90404) ***(G-6003)***
Gamefly Inc (PA)...310 568-8224
6080 Center Dr Fl 8 Los Angeles (90045) ***(G-16380)***
Gameworks, Ontario *Also called Sega Entertainment USA Inc* ***(G-18810)***
Gamma PHI Beta Sorority Inc...805 968-4221
890 Camino Pescadero Goleta (93117) ***(G-13492)***
Gammatech Computer Corporation...510 824-6700
48303 Fremont Blvd Fremont (94538) ***(G-7134)***
Gamut Construction Company Inc...909 948-0500
9340 Santa Anita Ave # 105 Rancho Cucamonga (91730) ***(G-1181)***
Ganduglia Trucking...559 251-7101
4737 E Florence Ave Fresno (93725) ***(G-4346)***
Gano Excel (usa) Inc...626 338-8081
4828 4th St Irwindale (91706) ***(G-8840)***
Gar Enterprises (PA)...626 574-1175
418 E Live Oak Ave Arcadia (91006) ***(G-7135)***
Garage Door Specialists, West Sacramento *Also called Singley Enterprises* ***(G-6962)***
Garcia Asset Management Inc...626 289-8755
740 S Corrida Dr Covina (91724) ***(G-14307)***
Garcia Roofing Inc...661 325-5736
201 Mount Vernon Ave Bakersfield (93307) ***(G-3176)***
Garco Enterprises Inc...323 933-1089
5930 W Pico Blvd Los Angeles (90035) ***(G-27930)***
Garda CL Technical Svcs Inc...818 362-7011
15640 Roxford St Sylmar (91342) ***(G-16657)***
Garda CL West Inc...714 771-6010
1602 W Orange Grove Ave Orange (92868) ***(G-16658)***
Garda CL West Inc...909 574-2676
372 S Arrowhead Ave San Bernardino (92408) ***(G-16659)***
Garda CL West Inc (HQ)...213 383-3611
1612 W Pico Blvd Los Angeles (90015) ***(G-16660)***
Garda CL West Inc...800 883-8305
301 N Lake Ave Ste 600 Pasadena (91101) ***(G-16661)***
Garden City Inc...408 244-3333
1887 Matrix Blvd San Jose (95110) ***(G-19216)***
Garden City Casino & Rest, San Jose *Also called Garden City Inc* ***(G-19216)***
Garden City Healthcare Center, Modesto *Also called Fig Holdings LLC* ***(G-20570)***
Garden Court Hotel...650 322-9000
520 Cowper St Ste 100 Palo Alto (94301) ***(G-12658)***
Garden Crest Convalesce...323 663-8281
909 Lucile Ave Los Angeles (90026) ***(G-20589)***
Garden Crest Rtrment Residence, Los Angeles *Also called Garden Crest Convalesce* ***(G-20589)***
Garden Grove Advanced Imaging...310 445-2800
1510 Cotner Ave Los Angeles (90025) ***(G-22218)***
Garden Grove Convales...714 638-9470
12882 Shackelford Ln Garden Grove (92841) ***(G-21231)***
Garden Grove Hospital, Garden Grove *Also called Kenneth Corp* ***(G-21682)***
Garden Grove Hospital Med Ctr, Garden Grove *Also called Prime Health Care Svcs Grdn Gr* ***(G-21808)***
Garden Grove Medical Investors (HQ)...714 534-1041
12332 Garden Grove Blvd Garden Grove (92843) ***(G-20590)***
Garden Grove Rehabilitation, Garden Grove *Also called Garden Grove Medical Investors* ***(G-20590)***
Garden Medical Offices, Downey *Also called Kaiser Foundation Hospitals* ***(G-19613)***
Garden Terrace Health Care Ctr, Vista *Also called Bent Tree Nursing Center Inc* ***(G-20410)***
Garden View Inc...626 303-4043
417 E Huntington Dr Monrovia (91016) ***(G-768)***
Garden View Care Center Inc...626 962-7095
14475 Garden View Ln Baldwin Park (91706) ***(G-20591)***
Garden, The, Santa Ana *Also called Alzheimers Care Since 1983* ***(G-22356)***
Gardena Convalescent Center, Santa Fe Springs *Also called B & E Convalescent Center Inc* ***(G-21147)***
Gardena Flores Inc...310 323-4570
14165 Purche Ave Gardena (90249) ***(G-20592)***
Gardena Hospital LP...310 532-4200
1145 W Redondo Beach Blvd Gardena (90247) ***(G-21574)***
Gardena Medical Offices, Gardena *Also called Kaiser Foundation Hospitals* ***(G-21656)***
Gardena Municipal Bus Lines, Gardena *Also called City of Gardena* ***(G-3639)***
Gardeners Guild Inc...415 457-0400
2780 Goodrick Ave Richmond (94801) ***(G-856)***
Gardens Regional Hosp Med Ctr, Hawaiian Gardens *Also called Gardens Rgnal Hosp Med Ctr Inc* ***(G-21575)***
Gardens Rgnal Hosp Med Ctr Inc...877 877-1104
21530 Pioneer Blvd Hawaiian Gardens (90716) ***(G-21575)***
Gardner Family Care Corp...408 935-3906
160 E Virginia St Ste 280 San Jose (95112) ***(G-22731)***
Gardner Family Hlth Netwrk Inc (PA)...408 918-2682
160 E Virginia St Ste 100 San Jose (95112) ***(G-22732)***
Gardner Neurologic Orthopedic...310 649-5824
6167 Bristol Pkwy Ste 200 Culver City (90230) ***(G-27033)***
Gardner Pool Company Inc (PA)...619 593-8880
801 Gable Way El Cajon (92020) ***(G-3523)***
Gardner Pool Plastering, El Cajon *Also called Gardner Pool Company Inc* ***(G-3523)***
Garfield Nuerobehavioral Ctr, Oakland *Also called Telecare Corporation* ***(G-22100)***
Garfield Nursing Home Inc...510 582-7676
1100 Marina Village Pkwy # 100 Alameda (94501) ***(G-20593)***
Garich Inc (PA)...858 453-1331
6336 Greenwich Dr Ste A San Diego (92122) ***(G-14660)***
Garich Inc...951 302-4750
504 E Alvarado St Ste 201 Fallbrook (92028) ***(G-14661)***
Garlic Company...661 393-4212
18602 Zerker Rd Bakersfield (93314) ***(G-23)***
Garment Industry Laundry...323 752-8335
710 W 58th St Los Angeles (90037) ***(G-13630)***
Garovibridge, Novato *Also called Johann B Garovi* ***(G-1894)***
Garrad Hassan America Inc (HQ)...858 836-3370
9665 Chesapeake Dr # 435 San Diego (92123) ***(G-25827)***
Garrick Motors Inc...760 489-2656
559 S Pine St Escondido (92025) ***(G-17793)***
Garris Plastering, Orange *Also called Padilla Construction Company* ***(G-2952)***
Gartner Inc...310 479-2108
11845 W Olympic Blvd 505w Los Angeles (90064) ***(G-27446)***
Garwood Laboratories Inc...562 949-2727
143 Calle Iglesia San Clemente (92672) ***(G-26854)***
Garwood Labs, San Clemente *Also called Garwood Laboratories Inc* ***(G-26854)***
Gary Cardiff Enterprises Inc...760 568-1403
75255 Sheryl Ave Palm Desert (92211) ***(G-3797)***
Gary Lask...310 825-0631
200 Ucla Medical Plz 4 Los Angeles (90095) ***(G-19533)***
Gary Mary W Wireless Hlth Inst...858 412-8600
10350 N Torrey Pines Rd La Jolla (92037) ***(G-26767)***
Gary R Edwards Inc...619 299-8700
3930 Utah St Ste C San Diego (92104) ***(G-17181)***
Gary Steel Division, Santa Fe Springs *Also called Kloeckner Metals Corporation* ***(G-7380)***
Garys Carpeting Inc...951 272-8210
182 Granite St Ste 102 Corona (92879) ***(G-1426)***
Garys Construction Inc...760 639-4456
2517 Dos Lomas Fallbrook (92028) ***(G-6628)***
GAS COMPANY, THE, Los Angeles *Also called Southern California Gas Co* ***(G-6274)***
Gas Transmission Systems Inc...530 893-6711
130 Amber Grove Dr # 134 Chico (95973) ***(G-25828)***
Gaslamp Hotel Management Inc...619 234-0977
202 Island Ave San Diego (92101) ***(G-12659)***
Gastroenterology Division...415 206-8823
1001 Potrero Ave Ste 1e21 San Francisco (94110) ***(G-19534)***
Gat Airline Ground Support...818 847-9127
2627 N Hollywood Way Burbank (91505) ***(G-5010)***
Gat Airline Ground Support...916 923-2349
6701 Lindbergh Dr Sacramento (95837) ***(G-4919)***
Gatan Inc (HQ)...925 463-0200
5794 W Las Positas Blvd Pleasanton (94588) ***(G-25829)***
Gate City Beverage Bear Trckg, San Bernardino *Also called Bear Trucking Inc* ***(G-4330)***
Gate City Beverage Distrs (PA)...909 799-0281
2505 Steele Rd San Bernardino (92408) ***(G-9058)***
Gate City Beverage Distrs...760 775-5483
82309 Market St Indio (92201) ***(G-9059)***
Gate Five Group LLC...415 339-9500
200 Gate 5 Rd Ste 116 Sausalito (94965) ***(G-6863)***
Gate Three Healthcare LLC...949 770-3348
24962 Calle Aragon Laguna Hills (92637) ***(G-24667)***

ALPHABETIC

Gates of Spain Wibel.....626 441-3078
2545 Mission St Pasadena (91108) ***(G-13677)***
Gateway, Los Angeles *Also called County of Los Angeles* ***(G-14140)***
Gateway Auto Auction Group, Fresno *Also called Gateway Auto Sales & Lsg Inc* ***(G-6678)***
Gateway Auto Sales & Lsg Inc.....800 921-4336
3260 E Annadale Ave Fresno (93725) ***(G-6678)***
Gateway Ctr of Monterey Cnty (PA).....831 372-8002
850 Congress Ave Pacific Grove (93950) ***(G-24668)***
Gateway Fresh LLC.....951 378-5439
3660 Grand Ave Ste A Chino Hills (91709) ***(G-12065)***
Gateway Home Realty, Chino *Also called American Financial Network Inc* ***(G-9812)***
Gateway Landscape Cnstr Inc.....925 875-0000
6735 Sierra Ct Ste A Dublin (94568) ***(G-857)***
Gateway Limousine, Burlingame *Also called Amato Industries Incorporated* ***(G-3740)***
Gateway Security Inc.....310 410-0790
5757 W Century Blvd Los Angeles (90045) ***(G-16662)***
Gateway Security Inc.....310 642-0529
100 World Way Los Angeles (90045) ***(G-16663)***
Gateways Hosp Mental Hlth Ctr.....323 644-2026
340 N Madison Ave Los Angeles (90004) ***(G-22069)***
Gateways Hosp Mental Hlth Ctr (PA).....323 644-2000
1891 Effie St Los Angeles (90026) ***(G-22070)***
Gavin De Becker & Associates.....818 760-4213
11684 Ventura Blvd # 440 Studio City (91604) ***(G-27447)***
Gaw Van Male Smith Myers.....707 425-1250
1411 Oliver Rd Ste 300 Fairfield (94534) ***(G-23264)***
Gazette, The, Santa Ana *Also called Freedom Colorado Info Inc* ***(G-5604)***
Gazillion Inc (PA).....650 393-6500
475 Concar Dr San Mateo (94402) ***(G-15675)***
Gbc Concrete Masnry Cnstr Inc.....951 245-2355
561 Birch St Lake Elsinore (92530) ***(G-2816)***
GBI Tile & Stone Inc (PA).....949 567-1880
5900 Skylab Rd Ste 150 Huntington Beach (92647) ***(G-6985)***
GBS Financial Corp.....310 937-0073
904 Manhattan Ave Ste 3 Manhattan Beach (90266) ***(G-17182)***
GBS Linens Inc (PA).....714 778-6448
305 N Muller St Anaheim (92801) ***(G-13549)***
GBS Party Linens, Anaheim *Also called GBS Linens Inc* ***(G-13549)***
GBT Inc.....626 854-9333
17358 Railroad St City of Industry (91748) ***(G-7136)***
Gc Services Ltd Partnership.....626 851-8227
4900 Rivergrade Rd # 210 Irwindale (91706) ***(G-14033)***
Gcc, Santa Rosa *Also called Ghilotti Construction Co Inc* ***(G-2053)***
GCCCD AUXILIARY, El Cajon *Also called Grossmont-Cuyamaca Community* ***(G-25268)***
Gccfc 2005-Gg5 Y St Ltd Partnr.....916 455-6800
4422 Y St Sacramento (95817) ***(G-12660)***
GCI Construction Inc.....714 957-0233
1031 Calle Recodo Ste D San Clemente (92673) ***(G-1772)***
Gcl Solar Energy Inc.....415 362-2601
1 Market St Steuart To San Francisco (94105) ***(G-2233)***
Gcl W, Los Angeles *Also called Garda CL West Inc* ***(G-16660)***
Gco Inc (PA).....510 786-3333
27750 Industrial Blvd Hayward (94545) ***(G-7720)***
Gcti, Los Angeles *Also called Gentlecare Transport Inc* ***(G-3798)***
Gcu Trucking Inc.....209 845-2117
7819 Crane Rd Oakdale (95361) ***(G-4188)***
GD Heil Inc.....714 687-9100
1031 Segovia Cir Placentia (92870) ***(G-3455)***
GD Nielson Construction Inc.....707 253-8774
147 Camino Oruga NAPA (94558) ***(G-1932)***
Gda Technologies Inc (HQ).....408 753-1191
25 Metro Dr Ste 300 San Jose (95110) ***(G-25830)***
Gdf Parent LLC.....646 262-9635
7119 W Sunset Blvd Los Angeles (90046) ***(G-17183)***
Gdm Concepts.....562 633-0195
15330 Texaco Ave Paramount (90723) ***(G-7215)***
Gdr Group Inc.....949 453-8818
6430 Oak Cyn Ste 200 Irvine (92618) ***(G-16381)***
Gdsa-Lincoln Inc (PA).....916 645-8961
1501 Aviation Blvd Lincoln (95648) ***(G-17935)***
GE, Mission Viejo *Also called Swiss RE America Holding Corp* ***(G-10223)***
GE Aviation Systems LLC.....661 277-7308
295 N Wolfe Ave Bldg 3810 Edwards Afb (93524) ***(G-4920)***
GE Energy, Diamond Bar *Also called Motech Americas LLC* ***(G-26571)***
GE Holdings Inc.....760 343-1299
82545 Showcase Pkwy # 104 Indio (92203) ***(G-3050)***
GE Ionics Inc.....408 360-5900
5900 Silvercreek Vly Rd San Jose (95138) ***(G-7721)***
Geary Darling Lessee Inc.....415 292-0100
501 Geary St San Francisco (94102) ***(G-12661)***
Gebbs Software Intl Inc.....201 227-0088
4640 Admiralty Way Fl 9 Marina Del Rey (90292) ***(G-16382)***
Geek Squad Inc.....800 433-5778
1490 Fitzgerald Dr Pinole (94564) ***(G-16383)***
Geek Squad Inc.....805 278-9555
2300 N Rose Ave Oxnard (93036) ***(G-16384)***
Geek Squad Inc.....800 433-5778
120 Imperial Hwy Fullerton (92835) ***(G-16385)***
Geek Squad Inc.....714 434-0132
901 S Coast Dr Ste F Costa Mesa (92626) ***(G-16386)***
Geek Squad Inc.....408 297-2520
181 Curtner Ave San Jose (95125) ***(G-16387)***
Geek Squad Inc.....714 938-0380
3741 W Chapman Ave Orange (92868) ***(G-16388)***
Gehr Development Corporation (HQ).....323 728-5558
7400 E Slauson Ave Commerce (90040) ***(G-10987)***
Gehry Partners LLP.....310 482-3000
12541 Beatrice St Los Angeles (90066) ***(G-26185)***
Gehry Technologies Inc (HQ).....310 862-1200
12181 Bluff Creek Dr # 200 Playa Vista (90094) ***(G-15201)***
Gei Consultants Inc.....916 631-4500
2868 Prospect Park Dr # 400 Rancho Cordova (95670) ***(G-27786)***
Geico Corporation.....408 286-4342
2195 Monterey Hwy Ste 20 San Jose (95125) ***(G-10725)***
Geico Corporation.....415 330-9999
2340 Monument Blvd Ste A Pleasant Hill (94523) ***(G-10726)***
Geico Corporation.....707 448-7172
2033 Arden Way Ste C Sacramento (95825) ***(G-10727)***
Geico General Insurance Co.....858 848-8200
14111 Danielson St Poway (92064) ***(G-10728)***
Geil Enterprises Inc (PA).....559 495-3000
1945 N Helm Ave Ste 102 Fresno (93727) ***(G-16664)***
Gel Pak LLC.....510 576-2220
31398 Huntwood Ave Hayward (94544) ***(G-14147)***
Gelfand Rennert & Feldman LLP (PA).....310 553-1707
1880 Century Park E # 1600 Los Angeles (90067) ***(G-26352)***
Gelfand Rennert & Feldman LLP.....310 553-1707
1880 Century Park E # 1600 Los Angeles (90067) ***(G-26353)***
Gels Logistics Inc.....909 610-2277
20275 Business Pkwy City of Industry (91789) ***(G-5086)***
Gelshmal Enterprises LLC.....310 672-9090
945 W Hyde Park Blvd Inglewood (90302) ***(G-7033)***
Gem Mobile Treatment Svcs Inc (HQ).....562 436-2999
1196 E Willow St Signal Hill (90755) ***(G-6629)***
Gem Trans Care, Pasadena *Also called Gem Transitional Care Center* ***(G-20594)***
Gem Transitional Care Center.....626 737-0560
716 S Fair Oaks Ave Pasadena (91105) ***(G-20594)***
Gemini Moving Specialists, Toluca Lake *Also called James B Branch Inc* ***(G-4353)***
Gemmm Corp.....805 267-2700
587 W Los Angeles Ave Moorpark (93021) ***(G-11551)***
Gemmm Corp.....818 522-0740
2211 Memory Ln Westlake Village (91361) ***(G-11552)***
Gemmm Corp (PA).....805 496-0555
2860 E Thousand Oaks Blvd Thousand Oaks (91362) ***(G-11553)***
Gemperle Enterprises.....209 667-2651
10218 Lander Ave Turlock (95380) ***(G-446)***
Gemperle Farms, Turlock *Also called Gemperle Enterprises* ***(G-446)***
Gen-Probe Incorporated (HQ).....858 410-8000
10210 Genetic Center Dr San Diego (92121) ***(G-26520)***
Genco Distribution System Inc.....909 605-9210
1670 Champagne Ave Ontario (91761) ***(G-4554)***
Gene A Garcia Construction.....559 352-6173
1663 E Poppy Hills Dr Fresno (93730) ***(G-1182)***
Gene M Accito.....530 674-3179
331 Pelican Pl Yuba City (95993) ***(G-24)***
Gene Townsend's Auto Body, El Cajon *Also called Eugene N Townsend* ***(G-17752)***
Gene Watson Construction A CA.....661 763-5254
801 Kern St Taft (93268) ***(G-1077)***
Gene Wheeler Farms Inc.....661 951-2100
220 W Avenue H6 Lancaster (93534) ***(G-360)***
Gene's Cooperage, El Monte *Also called Pacific Coast Drum Company* ***(G-7944)***
Genea Energy Partners Inc.....714 694-0536
2600 Michelson Dr Ste 720 Irvine (92612) ***(G-2234)***
Geneohm Sciences Inc.....201 847-5824
11085 N Torrey Pines Rd # 210 La Jolla (92037) ***(G-26521)***
General Atomic Aeron.....760 246-3660
9779 Yucca Rd Adelanto (92301) ***(G-26522)***
General Atomic Aeron.....760 246-3662
73 El Mirage Airport Rd B Adelanto (92301) ***(G-26855)***
General Atomics (HQ).....858 455-2810
3550 General Atomics Ct San Diego (92121) ***(G-26523)***
General Atomics.....858 676-7100
16969 Mesamint St San Diego (92127) ***(G-26524)***
General Atomics.....858 455-4000
4949 Greencraig Ln San Diego (92123) ***(G-26525)***
General Atomics Energy Pdts, San Diego *Also called General Atomics* ***(G-26525)***
General Brands Packing, Sun Valley *Also called Sugar Foods Corporation* ***(G-17509)***
General Coatings Corporation.....909 204-4150
9349 Feron Blvd Rancho Cucamonga (91730) ***(G-2444)***
General Coatings Corporation.....858 587-1277
600 W Freedom Ave Orange (92865) ***(G-2445)***
General Coatings Corporation (PA).....858 587-1277
6711 Nancy Ridge Dr San Diego (92121) ***(G-2446)***
General Coatings Corporation.....559 495-4004
1220 E North Ave Fresno (93725) ***(G-2447)***
General Contractor, Palm Desert *Also called Cora Constructors Inc* ***(G-25753)***
General Dynamics Advanced Info.....650 966-2000
100 Ferguson Dr Mountain View (94043) ***(G-25831)***
General Dynamics Corporation.....619 544-3400
2798 Harbor Dr San Diego (92113) ***(G-25832)***
General Dynamics Info Tech Inc.....619 881-8989
1615 Murray Canyon Rd # 600 San Diego (92108) ***(G-25833)***
General Dynmics Mssion Systems.....954 846-3400
250 S Milpitas Blvd Milpitas (95035) ***(G-7137)***
General Electric Capital Corp.....916 286-8020
3100 Zinfandel Dr Ste 255 Rancho Cordova (95670) ***(G-9783)***
General Electric Capital Corp.....714 434-4111
2995 Red Hill Ave Ste 100 Costa Mesa (92626) ***(G-9799)***
General Electric Capital Corp.....949 838-3043
17911 Von Karman Ave Irvine (92614) ***(G-9800)***
General Electric Company.....650 725-0516
288 Campus Dr Bldg 14105 Stanford (94305) ***(G-6133)***
General Electric Company.....707 469-8346
428 Ballindine Dr Vacaville (95688) ***(G-2598)***
General Electric Company.....925 242-6200
2623 Camino Ramon San Ramon (94583) ***(G-15676)***

ALPHABETIC

General Electric Company 626 359-7988
1303 Bloomdale St Duarte (91010) ***(G-16295)***

General Electric Company 925 602-5950
2120 Diamond Blvd Ste 100 Concord (94520) ***(G-25834)***

General Engineering Wstn Inc (PA) 714 630-3200
1140 N Red Gum St Anaheim (92806) ***(G-2235)***

General George W Sliney Basha 408 296-3423
4839 Rio Vista Ave San Jose (95129) ***(G-25258)***

General Motors, Martinez *Also called Ally Financial Inc* ***(G-9792)***

General Motors LLC 800 521-7300
9150 Hermosa Ave Rancho Cucamonga (91730) ***(G-4555)***

General Motors LLC 951 361-6302
11900 Cabernet Dr Dr1 Fontana (92337) ***(G-4556)***

General Networks Corporation 818 249-1962
3524 Ocean View Blvd Glendale (91208) ***(G-16389)***

General Petroleum Corporation (HQ) 562 983-7300
19501 S Santa Fe Ave Compton (90221) ***(G-9022)***

General Petroleum Corporation 209 537-1056
237 E Whitmore Ave Modesto (95358) ***(G-9007)***

General Pool & Spa Supply Inc (PA) 916 853-2401
11285 Sunco Dr Rancho Cordova (95742) ***(G-8019)***

General Procurement Inc (PA) 949 679-7960
800 E Dyer Rd Santa Ana (92705) ***(G-7138)***

General Prod A Cal Ltd Partnr (PA) 916 441-6431
1330 N B St Sacramento (95811) ***(G-8733)***

General Produce, Vernon *Also called V & L Produce Inc* ***(G-8783)***

General Production Svc Cal Inc 661 765-5330
1333 Kern St Taft (93268) ***(G-1933)***

General Restaurant Equipment, Los Angeles *Also called South China Sheet Metal Inc* ***(G-2380)***

General Services, Los Angeles *Also called City of Los Angeles* ***(G-14247)***

General Services, Concord *Also called County of Contra Costa* ***(G-14267)***

General Services, Martinez *Also called County of Contra Costa* ***(G-14268)***

General Services, Vernon *Also called City of Los Angeles* ***(G-3956)***

General Services Cal Dept 916 845-4942
9645 Butterfield Way # 1503 Sacramento (95827) ***(G-14308)***

General Services Cal Dept 510 622-3101
1515 Clay St Ste 1201 Oakland (94612) ***(G-26186)***

General Services Cal Dept 213 897-3995
700 N Alameda St Ste 500 Los Angeles (90012) ***(G-26187)***

General Services Cal Dept 916 657-9960
601 Sequoia Pacific Blvd Sacramento (95811) ***(G-25835)***

General Services Cal Dept 562 342-7212
4665 Lampson Ave Los Alamitos (90720) ***(G-16134)***

General Services Cal Dept 916 657-9903
601 Sequoia Pacific Blvd Sacramento (95811) ***(G-25836)***

General Services Cal Dept 916 445-4566
1304 O St Ste 301 Sacramento (95814) ***(G-14309)***

General Services Cal Dept 213 897-2241
300 S Spring St Ste 1726 Los Angeles (90013) ***(G-14310)***

General Testing & Insptn Inc 323 583-1653
8427 Atlantic Ave Cudahy (90201) ***(G-26856)***

General Tool Inc 949 261-2322
2025 Alton Pkwy Irvine (92606) ***(G-7933)***

General Underground 714 632-8646
701 W Grove Ave Orange (92865) ***(G-2236)***

Generation Construction Inc 909 923-2077
15650 El Prado Rd Chino (91710) ***(G-1555)***

Generation Contracting & Emerg 858 679-9928
13685 Stowe Dr Ste B Poway (92064) ***(G-1183)***

Genesis Health Care, Orange *Also called Prospect Medical Systems Inc* ***(G-27180)***

Genesis Healthcare Corporation 310 391-8266
3951 East Blvd Los Angeles (90066) ***(G-20595)***

Genesis Healthcare Partners PC 619 230-0400
2466 1st Ave Ste B San Diego (92101) ***(G-22733)***

Genesis Home Health Inc 805 520-7100
1687 Erringer Rd Ste 202 Simi Valley (93065) ***(G-14882)***

Genesis Logistics Inc 510 476-0790
4013 Whipple Rd Union City (94587) ***(G-4557)***

Genesis Tech Partners LLC 800 950-2647
21540 Plummer St Ste A Chatsworth (91311) ***(G-17975)***

Genesis Vocational Specialist 213 892-6307
5200 W Century Blvd 305 Los Angeles (90045) ***(G-11554)***

Genesys Telecom Labs, Daly City *Also called Genesys Telecom Labs* ***(G-15677)***

Genesys Telecom Labs (HQ) 650 466-1100
2001 Junipero Serra Blvd Daly City (94014) ***(G-15677)***

Genetic Dsase Screning Program, Richmond *Also called Public Health California Dept* ***(G-19900)***

Genex (HQ) 424 672-9500
800 Corporate Pointe # 100 Culver City (90230) ***(G-15202)***

Genius Products Inc 310 453-1222
3301 Expo Blvd Ste 100 Santa Monica (90404) ***(G-8115)***

Geniuscom Incorporated 650 931-1382
6200 Stoneridge Mall Rd # 500 Pleasanton (94588) ***(G-16390)***

Genomedx Biosciences Corp 888 975-4540
10355 Science Center Dr # 240 San Diego (92121) ***(G-22219)***

Genomic Health Inc (PA) 650 556-9300
301 Penobscot Dr Redwood City (94063) ***(G-22220)***

Genomic Health Inc 650 556-9300
101 Galveston Dr Redwood City (94063) ***(G-22221)***

Genoptix Inc (HQ) 760 268-6200
1811 Aston Ave Ste 100 Carlsbad (92008) ***(G-22222)***

Genoptix Medical Laboratory, Carlsbad *Also called Genoptix Inc* ***(G-22222)***

Genpact Mortgage Services Inc 949 417-5131
15420 Laguna Canyon Rd Irvine (92618) ***(G-9844)***

Gensler and Associates, Los Angeles *Also called M Arthur Gensler Jr Assoc Inc* ***(G-26232)***

Gensler Arch Design & Plg PC 415 433-3700
2 Harrison St Fl 4 San Francisco (94105) ***(G-26188)***

Genstar Capital LP 415 834-2350
4 Embarcadero Ctr # 1500 San Francisco (94111) ***(G-10005)***

Gentek Media Inc 909 476-3818
13900 Sycamore Way Chino (91710) ***(G-7139)***

Gentex Corporation 909 481-7667
9859 7th St Rancho Cucamonga (91730) ***(G-26526)***

Gentiva Hospice 661 324-1232
5001 E Commercecenter Dr # 140 Bakersfield (93309) ***(G-21083)***

Gentle Dental Service Corp (HQ) 310 765-2400
9800 S La Cienega Blvd # 800 Inglewood (90301) ***(G-20255)***

Gentle Giant Studios Inc 818 504-3555
7511 N San Fernando Rd Burbank (91505) ***(G-17184)***

Gentlecare Transport Inc 323 662-8777
3539 Casitas Ave Los Angeles (90039) ***(G-3798)***

Gentry Associates LLC 619 296-0057
525 Spruce St San Diego (92103) ***(G-12662)***

Genuent Usa LLC 916 772-3700
2240 Douglas Blvd Ste 100 Roseville (95661) ***(G-15203)***

Genuine Parts Distributors 562 692-9034
3737 Capitol Ave City of Industry (90601) ***(G-6733)***

Genzyme Corporation 800 255-1616
655 E Huntington Dr Monrovia (91016) ***(G-22223)***

Genzyme Corporation 310 482-5000
2440 S Sepulveda Blvd # 100 Los Angeles (90064) ***(G-26857)***

Genzyme Genetics, Monrovia *Also called Genzyme Corporation* ***(G-22223)***

Geo Group Inc 760 246-1171
10400 Rancho Rd Adelanto (92301) ***(G-27034)***

Geo Group Inc 661 763-2510
1500 Cadet Rd Taft (93268) ***(G-27787)***

Geo Group Inc 661 792-2731
611 Frontage Rd Mc Farland (93250) ***(G-27035)***

Geo Group Inc 530 695-1846
2800 Apricot St Live Oak (95953) ***(G-27788)***

Geo Guidance Drilling Svcs Inc 661 833-9999
200 Old Yard Dr Bakersfield (93307) ***(G-3355)***

Geo H Wilson Inc 831 423-9522
250 Harvey West Blvd Santa Cruz (95060) ***(G-2237)***

Geo Mmi Engineering, Oakland *Also called Geosyntec Consultants Inc* ***(G-25839)***

Geo Reentry Inc 415 346-9769
111 Taylor St San Francisco (94102) ***(G-27789)***

Geo Telecom 949 362-0921
252 Woodcrest Ln Aliso Viejo (92656) ***(G-1934)***

Geocities, Santa Clara *Also called Yahoo Inc* ***(G-5737)***

Geocon Consultants Inc (PA) 858 558-6900
6960 Flanders Dr San Diego (92121) ***(G-27931)***

Geocon Incorporated 858 558-6900
6960 Flanders Dr San Diego (92121) ***(G-25837)***

Geodis Logistics LLC 310 604-8185
301 W Walnut St Compton (90220) ***(G-4558)***

Geodis Logistics LLC 909 801-3145
2301 W San Bernardino Ave Redlands (92374) ***(G-4559)***

Geodis Logistics LLC 909 240-6298
1710 W Base Line Rd Rialto (92376) ***(G-4560)***

Geodis Logistics LLC 951 571-2481
3285 De Forest Cir Mira Loma (91752) ***(G-4561)***

Geodis Wilson Usa Inc 650 692-9850
229 Littlefield Ave Ste 1 South San Francisco (94080) ***(G-5087)***

Geological Survey US Dept 650 329-5229
345 Middlefield Rd Menlo Park (94025) ***(G-26527)***

Georg Fischer Piping, Irvine *Also called George Fischer LLC* ***(G-7372)***

George Amaral Ranches Inc 831 679-2977
25453 Iverson Rd Gonzales (93926) ***(G-66)***

George Brazil Plbg Htg & AC, Culver City *Also called L A Services Inc* ***(G-2271)***

George Brazil Plbg Htg & AC, Santa Ana *Also called Orange County Services Inc* ***(G-2312)***

George Chiala Farms Inc 408 778-0562
15500 Hill Rd Morgan Hill (95037) ***(G-67)***

George E Masker Inc 510 568-1206
7699 Edgewater Dr Oakland (94621) ***(G-2448)***

George Elkins Mrtg Bnkg Co LP (HQ) 310 979-5749
12100 Wilshire Blvd Los Angeles (90025) ***(G-9845)***

George Fasching 626 446-0654
425 N Santa Anita Ave Arcadia (91006) ***(G-17842)***

George Fischer LLC (HQ) 714 731-8800
9271 Jeronimo Rd Irvine (92618) ***(G-7372)***

George G Sharp Inc 619 575-0511
1330 30th St San Diego (92154) ***(G-4562)***

George G Sharp Inc 619 425-4211
1065 Bay Blvd Ste D Chula Vista (91911) ***(G-25838)***

GEORGE L MEE MEMORIAL HOSPITAL, King City *Also called Southern Mnterey Cnty Mem Hosp* ***(G-21906)***

George M Rajacich MD PC 818 787-2020
14914 Sherman Way Van Nuys (91405) ***(G-19535)***

George M Robinson & Co (PA) 510 632-7017
1461 Atteberry Ln San Jose (95131) ***(G-2238)***

George P Johnson Company 650 226-0600
999 Skyway Rd Ste 300 San Carlos (94070) ***(G-9267)***

George Richard 619 805-6751
P.O. Box 712002 Santee (92072) ***(G-1427)***

Georges Yellow Taxi Cab Co, Santa Rosa *Also called Neese Inc* ***(G-3866)***

Georgia Atkison Snf LLC 626 444-2535
3825 Durfee Ave El Monte (91732) ***(G-20596)***

Georgia-Pacific LLC 562 861-6226
9206 Santa Fe Springs Rd Santa Fe Springs (90670) ***(G-8193)***

Georgia-Pacific LLC 562 926-8888
15500 Valley View Ave La Mirada (90638) ***(G-8070)***

Georgian Hotel 310 395-9945
1415 Ocean Ave Santa Monica (90401) ***(G-12663)***

Georgiou, Walnut Creek *Also called Kolonaki* ***(G-8393)***

Geosyntec Consultants Inc....714 969-0800
2100 Main St Ste 150 Huntington Beach (92648) *(G-25259)*
Geosyntec Consultants Inc....510 836-3034
1111 Broadway Fl 6th Oakland (94607) *(G-25839)*
Geovera Specialty Insurance Co....707 863-3700
1455 Oliver Rd Fairfield (94534) *(G-10729)*
Gerawan Farming Partners Inc....559 787-8780
15749 E Ventura Ave Sanger (93657) *(G-479)*
Gerber Ambulance Company Inc....310 542-6464
19801 Mariner Ave Torrance (90503) *(G-3799)*
Gerber Ambulance Service, Torrance *Also called Gerber Ambulance Company Inc (G-3799)*
Gerdau Reinforcing Steel (HQ)....858 737-7700
3880 Murphy Canyon Rd # 100 San Diego (92123) *(G-1428)*
Gerdau Reinforcing Steel....909 713-1130
5425 Industrial Pkwy San Bernardino (92407) *(G-1429)*
Geri Care Inc....310 320-0961
21521 S Vermont Ave Torrance (90502) *(G-20597)*
Geri-Care II Inc....310 328-0812
22035 S Vermont Ave Torrance (90502) *(G-21232)*
German Motors Corporation....415 551-2639
1140 Harrison St San Francisco (94103) *(G-17794)*
Gersh Agency Inc (PA)....310 274-6611
9465 Wilshire Blvd Fl 6 Beverly Hills (90212) *(G-18394)*
Gerson Bakar & Associates, Palo Alto *Also called Oak Creek Apartments (G-11177)*
Gerson Baker & Associates....650 756-0959
333 Park Plaza Dr Ofc Daly City (94015) *(G-11137)*
Gerwend Enterprises Inc....619 254-5018
2952 Mkt St Pizarro Bldg San Diego (92102) *(G-27790)*
Ges, Chula Vista *Also called Global Exprnce Specialists Inc (G-17192)*
Get-A-Lift Handicap Bus Trnsp, Bakersfield *Also called Golden Empire Transit District (G-3654)*
Getinsured.com, Mountain View *Also called Vimo Inc (G-28091)*
Getmedlegal, San Dimas *Also called Legal Solutions Holdings Inc (G-23381)*
Gettler-Ryan Inc (PA)....925 551-7555
6805 Sierra Ct Ste G Dublin (94568) *(G-3524)*
Getty Conservation Institute, Los Angeles *Also called J Paul Getty Trust (G-26678)*
Getty Images Inc....323 202-4200
6300 Wilshire Blvd # 1600 Los Angeles (90048) *(G-17185)*
Gettyone Image Bank, Los Angeles *Also called Getty Images Inc (G-17185)*
Gfk Custom Research LLC....415 398-2812
360 Pine St Fl 6 San Francisco (94104) *(G-26667)*
Gfk Custom Research LLC....310 527-2100
879 W 190th St Ste 390 Gardena (90248) *(G-26668)*
Gfk Etilize Inc....888 608-1212
18662 Macarthur Blvd # 200 Irvine (92612) *(G-26669)*
Gfp Oceanside Block 21 LLC....760 722-1003
110 N Myers St Oceanside (92054) *(G-12664)*
Ggec America Inc....714 750-2280
100 Pacifica Ste 200 Irvine (92618) *(G-7573)*
Ggis Insurance Services Inc....818 553-2110
600 N Brand Blvd Ste 300 Glendale (91203) *(G-10730)*
Ggwh LLC....310 786-1700
9440 Santa Monica Blvd # 610 Beverly Hills (90210) *(G-12665)*
Ghc of Lakeview Terrace LLC....714 241-5600
20371 Irvine Ave Ste A210 Newport Beach (92660) *(G-20598)*
Ghc of Lompoc LLC....805 735-4010
1428 W North Ave Lompoc (93436) *(G-22734)*
Ghc of Sunnyvale LLC....408 738-4880
797 E Fremont Ave Sunnyvale (94087) *(G-21233)*
Ghd Inc....707 443-8326
718 3rd St Eureka (95501) *(G-25840)*
Ghd Inc....707 523-1010
2235 Mercury Way Ste 150 Santa Rosa (95407) *(G-25841)*
Ghg Properties LLC....562 945-8511
7320 Greenleaf Ave Whittier (90602) *(G-12666)*
Ghilotti Bros Inc....415 454-7011
525 Jacoby St San Rafael (94901) *(G-1773)*
Ghilotti Construction Co Inc....707 556-9145
600 S Napa Junction Rd American Canyon (94503) *(G-1774)*
Ghilotti Construction Co Inc (PA)....707 585-1221
246 Ghillotti Ave Santa Rosa (95407) *(G-2053)*
Ghio Seafood Products, La Mesa *Also called Anthonys Fish Grotto (G-8626)*
Ghiringhlli Spcialty Foods Inc....707 561-7670
101 Benicia Rd Vallejo (94590) *(G-1430)*
Ghossain & Truelock Entps Inc....951 781-9345
783 Palmyrita Ave Ste A Riverside (92507) *(G-14311)*
Ghost Management Group LLC....949 870-1400
41 Discovery Irvine (92618) *(G-13969)*
GI Industries....805 522-2150
195 W Los Angeles Ave Simi Valley (93065) *(G-6486)*
GI Partners, San Francisco *Also called Global Innovation Partners LLC (G-17193)*
Giampolini & Co....415 673-1236
1482 67th St Emeryville (94608) *(G-2449)*
Giampolini/Courtney, Emeryville *Also called Giampolini & Co (G-2449)*
Giannas Baking Company....831 633-3700
11165 Commercial Pkwy Castroville (95012) *(G-8841)*
Giant Bicycle Inc (HQ)....805 267-4600
3587 Old Conejo Rd Newbury Park (91320) *(G-8020)*
Giant Creative Strategy Llc....415 655-5200
1700 Montgomery St # 485 San Francisco (94111) *(G-13853)*
Giant Sportz Paintball Park, Bellflower *Also called Hollywood Sports Park LLC (G-17225)*
Giarretto Institute....408 453-7616
232 E Gish Rd San Jose (95112) *(G-23993)*
Gibbs Giden Locher....310 552-3400
1880 Century Park E # 1200 Los Angeles (90067) *(G-23265)*
Gibbs & Associates, Moorpark *Also called Cimatron Gibbs LLC (G-15085)*
Gibbs International Inc (PA)....805 485-0551
2201 E Ventura Blvd Oxnard (93036) *(G-17795)*
Gibbs International Truck Ctrs, Oxnard *Also called Gibbs International Inc (G-17795)*
Gibralter Convalescent Hosp....626 443-9425
2720 Nevada Ave El Monte (91733) *(G-21234)*
Gibson Dunn & Crutcher LLP....650 849-5300
1881 Page Mill Rd Palo Alto (94304) *(G-23266)*
Gibson Dunn & Crutcher LLP....949 451-3800
3161 Michelson Dr # 1200 Irvine (92612) *(G-23267)*
Gibson Dunn & Crutcher LLP (PA)....213 229-8063
333 S Grand Ave Ste 4400 Los Angeles (90071) *(G-23268)*
Gibson Dunn & Crutcher LLP....310 552-8500
2029 Century Park E # 4000 Los Angeles (90067) *(G-23269)*
Gibson Dunn & Crutcher LLP....415 393-8200
555 Mission St Ste 3000 San Francisco (94105) *(G-23270)*
Gibson Dun Law Firm, Palo Alto *Also called Gibson Dunn & Crutcher LLP (G-23266)*
Gibson Dunn, Los Angeles *Also called Gibson Dunn & Crutcher LLP (G-23268)*
Gibson Overseas Inc....323 832-8900
2410 Yates Ave Commerce (90040) *(G-6864)*
Gic Real Estate Inc (HQ)....650 593-3122
255 Shoreline Dr Ste 600 Redwood City (94065) *(G-12309)*
Gico Management....209 599-7131
23073 S Frederick Rd Ripon (95366) *(G-8621)*
Gierahn Dry Wall Inc....661 257-7900
28490 Westinghouse Pl # 150 Santa Clarita (91355) *(G-2903)*
Giga Bite Technology, City of Industry *Also called GBT Inc (G-7136)*
Giga Omni Media Inc....415 974-6355
1613a Lyon St San Francisco (94115) *(G-16947)*
Gigamon Inc (PA)....408 831-4000
3300 Olcott St Santa Clara (95054) *(G-15678)*
Gigya Inc....650 353-7230
2513 E Char Rd Ste 200 Mountain View (94043) *(G-15679)*
Gilardi & Co LLC....415 461-0410
3301 Kerner Blvd Ste 100 San Rafael (94901) *(G-27036)*
Gilbane Aecom JV....925 946-3100
1655 Grant St Fl 12 Concord (94520) *(G-27791)*
Gilbane Building Company....408 660-4400
1798 Tech Dr Ste 120 San Jose (95110) *(G-27037)*
Gilbane Construction, San Jose *Also called Gilbane Building Company (G-27037)*
Gilbane Federal (HQ)....925 946-3100
1655 Grant St Fl 12 Concord (94520) *(G-25842)*
Gilbert Barco....323 232-7672
9034 Terhune Ave Sun Valley (91352) *(G-17186)*
Gilbert Klly Crwley Jnnett LLP (PA)....213 615-7000
550 S Hope St Ste 2200 Los Angeles (90071) *(G-23271)*
Gilbert Service Corp....909 393-7575
6725 Kimball Ave Chino (91708) *(G-4347)*
Gilbert West, Chino *Also called Gilbert Service Corp (G-4347)*
Gilkey Farms Inc....559 992-2136
2411 Whitley Ave Corcoran (93212) *(G-11)*
Gill Transport LLC....805 240-1979
1051 Pacific Ave Oxnard (93030) *(G-4189)*
Gillette Citrus Company....559 626-4236
10175 S Anchor Ave Dinuba (93618) *(G-535)*
Gilliam & Sons Inc....661 589-0913
9831 Rosedale Hwy Bakersfield (93312) *(G-3429)*
Gills Onions LLC....805 240-1983
1051 Pacific Ave Oxnard (93030) *(G-68)*
Gilroy Fitness Inc (PA)....408 848-1234
8540 Church St Gilroy (95020) *(G-18636)*
Gilroy Fitness Inc....408 848-1234
8540 Church St Gilroy (95020) *(G-18637)*
Gilroy Gardens Family Theme Pk....408 840-7100
3050 Hecker Pass Rd Gilroy (95020) *(G-18822)*
Gilroy Health & Rehab Ctr, Gilroy *Also called Mariner Health Care Inc (G-20759)*
Gilroy Health and Fitness, Gilroy *Also called Gilroy Fitness Inc (G-18636)*
Gilroy Health Care, Gilroy *Also called Covenant Care California LLC (G-20497)*
Gilton Resource Recovery....209 527-3781
755 S Yosemite Ave Oakdale (95361) *(G-6487)*
Gilton Solid Waste MGT Inc....209 527-3781
755 S Yosemite Ave # 106 Oakdale (95361) *(G-6488)*
Gina B Ltd Inc....310 366-7926
1601 W 134th St Gardena (90249) *(G-6865)*
Gina B Showroom, Gardena *Also called Gina B Ltd Inc (G-6865)*
Gino Rinaldi Inc....831 761-0195
51 Fremont St Royal Oaks (95076) *(G-3014)*
Gino/Giuseppe Inc....209 358-0556
700 Enterprise Ct Ste A Atwater (95301) *(G-3265)*
Ginzton Laboratory, Stanford *Also called Leland Stanford Junior Univ (G-26783)*
Giovannetti Equipment Sales, Woodland *Also called Half Moon Fruit & Produce Co (G-72)*
Gipson Hoffman & Pancione A....310 556-4660
1901 Avenue Of The Stars # 1100 Los Angeles (90067) *(G-23272)*
Girardi & Keese (PA)....213 977-0211
1126 Wilshire Blvd Los Angeles (90017) *(G-23273)*
Girardi and Keefe....213 489-5330
1126 Wilshire Blvd Los Angeles (90017) *(G-10988)*
Girl Scouts Heart Central Cal....916 452-9181
6601 Elvas Ave Sacramento (95819) *(G-25260)*
Girl Scouts Northern Cal (PA)....510 562-8470
1650 Harbor Bay Pkwy # 100 Alameda (94502) *(G-25261)*
Girl Scts Sn Diego-Imprl Cncl (PA)....619 610-0751
1231 Upas St San Diego (92103) *(G-25262)*
Girl Scuts Greater Los Angeles (PA)....626 677-2200
801 S Grand Ave Ste 300 Los Angeles (90017) *(G-25263)*
Girls and Boys Club Grdn Grove, Garden Grove *Also called Boys Grls Clubs Grdn Grove Inc (G-25220)*
Girls Republic, Chino Hills *Also called Boys Republic (G-24567)*
Giroux Glass Inc (PA)....213 747-7406
850 W Washington Blvd Los Angeles (90015) *(G-3410)*

ALPHABETIC

Employee Codes: A=Over 500 employees, B=251-500
C=101-250, D=51-100, E=45-50
2017 Directory of California
Wholesalers and Services Companies
© Mergent Inc. 1-800-342-5647
1393

Giti Tire (usa) Ltd (HQ)
ALPHABETIC SECTION
ALPHABETIC

Giti Tire (usa) Ltd (HQ).......................................909 527-8800
10404 6th St Rancho Cucamonga (91730) ***(G-6785)***
Giumarra Bros Fruit Co Inc (PA).......................................213 627-2900
1601 E Olympic Blvd # 408 Los Angeles (90021) ***(G-8734)***
Giumarra Companies, Escondido *Also called Rio Vista Ventures LLC* ***(G-8514)***
Giumarra Company, The, Reedley *Also called Rio Vista Ventures LLC* ***(G-8515)***
Giumarra Farms Inc.......................................661 395-7000
11220 Edison Hwy Edison (93220) ***(G-19)***
Giumarra International Berry, Los Angeles *Also called Giumarra Bros Fruit Co Inc* ***(G-8734)***
Giumarra Vineyards Corporation.......................................661 395-7071
1122 O Edison Hwy Bakersfield (93304) ***(G-155)***
Giumarra Vineyards Corporation (PA).......................................661 395-7000
11220 Edison Hwy Edison (93220) ***(G-156)***
Giumarra Winery, Bakersfield *Also called Giumarra Vineyards Corporation* ***(G-155)***
Giusti Farms LLC.......................................650 726-9221
1800 Higgins Canyon Rd Half Moon Bay (94019) ***(G-69)***
Giva Inc.......................................408 260-9000
1030 E El Camino Real Sunnyvale (94087) ***(G-15204)***
Give Something Back Inc (PA).......................................510 635-5500
7730 Pardee Ln Ste A Oakland (94621) ***(G-8168)***
Give Something Back Off Sups, Oakland *Also called Give Something Back Inc* ***(G-8168)***
Givens Farms, Goleta *Also called Givens John* ***(G-70)***
Givens John.......................................805 964-4477
1133 N Fairview Ave Goleta (93117) ***(G-70)***
Gkk Corporation.......................................619 398-0215
1775 Hancock St Ste 150 San Diego (92110) ***(G-26189)***
Gkk Corporation (PA).......................................949 250-1500
2355 Main St Ste 220 Irvine (92614) ***(G-26190)***
Gkk Works (HQ).......................................949 250-1500
2355 Main St Ste 220 Irvine (92614) ***(G-27038)***
Gkkworks, Irvine *Also called Gkk Corporation* ***(G-26190)***
GL, San Diego *Also called Garrad Hassan America Inc* ***(G-25827)***
GL Nemirow Inc.......................................818 562-9433
2550 N Hollywood Way Burbank (91505) ***(G-13854)***
GL Newmirow Inc.......................................818 562-9433
2550 N Hollywood Way Burbank (91505) ***(G-13855)***
GLad Entertainment Inc (PA).......................................559 292-9000
4055 N Chestnut Ave Fresno (93726) ***(G-19217)***
Glad I'M Not Driving.com, Rialto *Also called Ptr Group Inc* ***(G-27184)***
Glad-A-Way Gardens Inc (PA).......................................805 938-0569
2669 E Clark Ave Santa Maria (93455) ***(G-284)***
Gladiator Security Services, Ontario *Also called Mazar Corp* ***(G-16733)***
Gladiolus Holdings LLC.......................................530 622-3400
1040 Marshall Way Placerville (95667) ***(G-20599)***
Glamour Industries Co.......................................323 728-2999
2220 Gaspar Ave Commerce (90040) ***(G-8255)***
Glaser Weil Fink Jacobs (PA).......................................310 553-3000
10250 Constellation Blvd # 1900 Los Angeles (90067) ***(G-23274)***
Glaspy & Glaspy A Prof Corp.......................................408 279-8844
100 Pringle Ave Ste 750 Walnut Creek (94596) ***(G-23275)***
Glass Lewis & Co LLC (HQ).......................................415 678-4110
1 Sansome St Fl 33 San Francisco (94104) ***(G-26670)***
Glass Pak Inc.......................................707 207-0400
5825 Old School Rd Pleasanton (94588) ***(G-5200)***
Glassfab Tempering Services (PA).......................................209 229-1060
1448 Mariani Ct Tracy (95376) ***(G-27932)***
Glaxosmithkline Consumer.......................................559 650-1550
2020 E Vine Ave Fresno (93706) ***(G-8256)***
Glaxosmithkline LLC.......................................858 260-5900
3366 N Torrey Pines Ct La Jolla (92037) ***(G-8257)***
Glaza, Los Angeles *Also called Greater Los Angeles Zoo Assn* ***(G-24924)***
Glazier Steel Inc.......................................510 471-5300
650 Sandoval Way Hayward (94544) ***(G-3430)***
Glen Alpine Building Svcs Inc.......................................510 582-7400
24685 Oneil Ave Hayward (94544) ***(G-14312)***
Glen Ivy Hot Springs.......................................714 990-2090
1001 Brea Mall Brea (92821) ***(G-13763)***
Glenborough LLC (PA).......................................650 343-9300
400 S El Camino Real # 1100 San Mateo (94402) ***(G-11555)***
Glendale Adventist Medical Ctr (HQ).......................................818 409-8000
1509 Wilson Ter Glendale (91206) ***(G-21576)***
Glendale Associates Ltd.......................................818 246-6737
100 W Broadway Ste 700 Glendale (91210) ***(G-10989)***
Glendale Eye Medical Group.......................................818 956-1010
607 N Central Ave Ste 105 Glendale (91203) ***(G-19536)***
Glendale Healthcare Center.......................................818 246-5516
1208 S Central Ave Glendale (91204) ***(G-20600)***
Glendale Medical Offices, Glendale *Also called Kaiser Foundation Hospitals* ***(G-19658)***
Glendale Memorial Breast Ctr, Glendale *Also called Glendale Memorial Health Corp* ***(G-21577)***
Glendale Memorial Health Corp.......................................818 502-2323
222 W Eulalia St Glendale (91204) ***(G-21577)***
Glendale Orange St Med Offs, Glendale *Also called Kaiser Foundation Hospitals* ***(G-19620)***
Glendale Super-Sport Club, Glendale *Also called 24 Hour Fitness Usa Inc* ***(G-18590)***
Glendale Water & Power, Glendale *Also called City of Glendale* ***(G-6112)***
GLENDALE YMCA SWIM SCHOOL, Glendale *Also called Young Mens Chrstn Assoc Gndl* ***(G-25476)***
Glendora Country Club.......................................626 335-4051
2400 Country Club Dr Glendora (91741) ***(G-18955)***
Glenn A Rick Engrg & Dev Co (PA).......................................619 291-0708
5620 Friars Rd San Diego (92110) ***(G-25843)***
Glenn Building Services Inc.......................................626 398-8000
1148 N Lake Ave Apt 1 Pasadena (91104) ***(G-14313)***
Glenn Burdette Phillips Bryson.......................................805 544-1441
1150 Palm St San Luis Obispo (93401) ***(G-26354)***
Glenn Cnty Humn Resource Agcy.......................................530 934-6510
420 E Laurel St Willows (95988) ***(G-24342)***
Glenn County Health Svcs Agcy, Willows *Also called County of Glenn* ***(G-22925)***
Glenn County Humn Resorce Agcy, Willows *Also called County of Glenn* ***(G-23811)***
Glenn County Office Education.......................................530 865-1145
676 E Walker St Fl 2 Orland (95963) ***(G-24465)***
Glenn E Porter.......................................661 615-1500
3955 Coffee Rd Bakersfield (93308) ***(G-10423)***
Glenn E Thomas Company Inc.......................................562 426-5111
2100 E Spring St Long Beach (90755) ***(G-17796)***
Glenn E Thomas Dodge, Long Beach *Also called Glenn E Thomas Company Inc* ***(G-17796)***
Glenn Medical Center Inc.......................................530 934-4681
1133 W Sycamore St Willows (95988) ***(G-21578)***
Glenoaks Convalescent Hosp LP.......................................818 240-4300
409 W Glenoaks Blvd Glendale (91202) ***(G-21579)***
Glenrock Group.......................................408 323-9900
1000 Old Quarry Rd San Jose (95123) ***(G-18742)***
Glentrans, Glendale *Also called Hemodialysis Inc* ***(G-22628)***
Glenview Assisted Living LLP.......................................760 704-6800
1950 Calle Barcelona Carlsbad (92009) ***(G-22964)***
GLENWOOD CARE CENTER, Oxnard *Also called Glenwood Corporation* ***(G-21235)***
Glenwood Corporation.......................................805 983-0305
1300 N C St Oxnard (93030) ***(G-21235)***
Glenwood Gardens.......................................661 587-0221
350 Calloway Dr Unit A1 Bakersfield (93312) ***(G-20601)***
Glenwood Village Cmnty Assn.......................................949 855-1800
39 Argonaut Ste 100 Aliso Viejo (92656) ***(G-25264)***
Gless Ranch Inc (PA).......................................951 780-8458
18541 Van Buren Blvd Riverside (92508) ***(G-705)***
Glidewell Laboratories, Newport Beach *Also called James R Glidewell Dental* ***(G-22309)***
Global 360 Inc.......................................510 263-4800
1080 Marina Village Pkwy # 300 Alameda (94501) ***(G-27039)***
Global Accents Inc.......................................310 639-2600
19808 Normandie Ave Torrance (90502) ***(G-6866)***
Global Ascent Inc.......................................714 930-6860
36 Waterworks Way Irvine (92618) ***(G-17187)***
Global Bakeries Inc.......................................818 896-0525
13336 Paxton St Pacoima (91331) ***(G-8842)***
Global Building Services Inc.......................................209 858-9501
17618 Murphy Pkwy Lathrop (95330) ***(G-28131)***
Global Building Services Inc (PA).......................................661 288-5733
25129 The Old Rd Ste 102 Stevenson Ranch (91381) ***(G-14314)***
Global Business Solutions Inc.......................................714 257-1488
600 Anton Blvd Ste 1050 Costa Mesa (92626) ***(G-16391)***
Global Care Travel, San Diego *Also called Customzed Svcs Admnstrtors Inc* ***(G-10685)***
Global Cellular Inc.......................................925 469-9039
1 Stoneridge Mall Rd Pleasanton (94588) ***(G-7574)***
Global Check Service.......................................619 449-5150
1524 Graves Ave Ste C El Cajon (92021) ***(G-17188)***
Global Data Publications Inc.......................................415 800-0336
425 California St # 1300 San Francisco (94104) ***(G-16392)***
Global Dev Strategies Inc.......................................858 408-1173
9985 Businesspark Ave A San Diego (92131) ***(G-17976)***
Global Domains International.......................................760 602-3000
701 Palomar Airport Rd # 300 Carlsbad (92011) ***(G-5616)***
Global Dosimetry Solutions, Irvine *Also called Mirion Technologies Gds Inc* ***(G-26868)***
Global Eagle Entertainment Inc.......................................949 608-8700
2941 Alton Pkwy Irvine (92606) ***(G-18089)***
Global Entertainment Inds Inc.......................................818 567-0000
2948 N Ontario St Burbank (91504) ***(G-3525)***
Global Eqp Svcs & Mfg Inc.......................................408 441-0682
5215 Hellyer Ave Ste 130 San Jose (95138) ***(G-7216)***
Global Exchange Marketing Inc.......................................949 367-0388
26691 Plaza Ste 100 Mission Viejo (92691) ***(G-17189)***
Global Exprnce Specialists Inc.......................................562 370-1500
5560 Katella Ave Cypress (90630) ***(G-17190)***
Global Exprnce Specialists Inc.......................................818 638-5959
500 N Brand Blvd Ste 1860 Glendale (91203) ***(G-17191)***
Global Exprnce Specialists Inc.......................................619 498-6300
491 C St Chula Vista (91910) ***(G-17192)***
Global Fibernet, Van Nuys *Also called Airespring Inc* ***(G-5456)***
Global Futures Exch & Trdg Co.......................................818 996-0401
19300 Ventura Blvd Tarzana (91356) ***(G-10105)***
Global Garments, Los Angeles *Also called Design Collection Inc* ***(G-8311)***
Global Ground Automation Inc.......................................201 293-4900
1051 E Hillsdale Blvd Foster City (94404) ***(G-7846)***
Global Health Fellows Program.......................................510 285-5660
555 12th St Ste 1050 Oakland (94607) ***(G-25535)***
Global Hobby Distributors, Fountain Valley *Also called Hobby Shack* ***(G-8044)***
Global Holdings Inc.......................................818 905-6000
550 N Brand Blvd Ste 600 Glendale (91203) ***(G-12066)***
Global Horizons Inc.......................................310 234-8475
468 N Camden Dr Ste 200 Beverly Hills (90210) ***(G-14662)***
Global Industry Analysts Inc.......................................408 528-9966
6150 Hellyer Ave Ste 100 San Jose (95138) ***(G-26671)***
Global Infotech Corporation.......................................408 567-0600
2890 Zanker Rd Ste 202 San Jose (95134) ***(G-27933)***
Global Innovation Partner, Los Angeles *Also called Cbre Global Investors LLC* ***(G-27375)***
Global Innovation Partners LLC.......................................650 233-3600
188 The Embarcadero # 700 San Francisco (94105) ***(G-17193)***
Global Language Solutions LLC.......................................949 798-1400
19800 Macarthur Blvd # 750 Irvine (92612) ***(G-17194)***
Global Mail Inc.......................................310 735-0800
921 W Artesia Blvd Compton (90220) ***(G-14071)***
Global Management Company LLC.......................................323 261-8114
3150 E Pico Blvd Los Angeles (90023) ***(G-27448)***
Global Med Services Inc.......................................562 207-6970
11818 South St Ste 201a Cerritos (90703) ***(G-22441)***
Global Meddata Inc.......................................650 369-9734
1725 E Byshore Rd Ste 103 Redwood City (94063) ***(G-22965)***
Global Network Travel, Glendale *Also called Goway Travel Inc* ***(G-4961)***

Global Paratransit Inc...310 715-7550
400 W Compton Blvd Gardena (90248) *(G-3800)*
Global PET Inc...951 657-5466
145 Malbert St Perris (92570) *(G-8071)*
Global Realty Group, Granada Hills *Also called Global Work Group LLC (G-27449)*
Global Risk MGT Solutions LLC...949 759-8500
660 Nwport Ctr Dr Ste 600 Newport Beach (92660) *(G-16237)*
Global Shield Security Inc...818 988-9010
4924 Balboa Blvd Ste 639 Encino (91316) *(G-16665)*
Global Staffing Inc...303 451-5602
5301 Beethoven St Ste 101 Los Angeles (90066) *(G-14663)*
Global Stainless Supply...310 525-1865
17006 S Figueroa St Gardena (90248) *(G-8116)*
Global Tech MGT Resources Inc...760 377-5522
7100 Moanache Mtn Ave Inyokern (93527) *(G-25135)*
Global Understanding Inc...760 812-9650
1190 Encinitas Blvd 237i Encinitas (92024) *(G-24343)*
Global USA Green Card...415 915-4151
201 Spear St Ste 1100 San Francisco (94105) *(G-23276)*
Global Work Group LLC...424 220-9994
17224 San Fernando Granada Hills (91344) *(G-27449)*
Global World Group...760 744-4800
635 N Twin Oaks Valley Rd # 15 San Marcos (92069) *(G-4775)*
Global-Dining Inc California...310 576-9922
1212 3rd Street Promenade Santa Monica (90401) *(G-27040)*
Globalex Corporation (PA)...310 593-4833
2100 Abbot Kinney Blvd A Venice (90291) *(G-15680)*
Globalfoundries Americas Inc (HQ)...408 462-3900
2600 Great America Way Santa Clara (95054) *(G-7575)*
Globallogic Inc (PA)...408 273-8900
1741 Tech Dr Ste 400 San Jose (95110) *(G-15205)*
Globalways Inc (PA)...510 580-1974
42808 Christy St Ste 202 Fremont (94538) *(G-16393)*
Globant LLC...877 798-8104
875 Howard St Fl 3 San Francisco (94103) *(G-15206)*
Globe Shoes, El Segundo *Also called Osata Enterprises Inc (G-8441)*
Globecast America Incorporated (HQ)...212 373-5140
10525 Washington Blvd Culver City (90232) *(G-6004)*
Gloria Ferrer, Sonoma *Also called Freixenet Usa Inc (G-9102)*
Glovia Inc...310 563-7000
2250 E Imperial Hwy # 200 El Segundo (90245) *(G-15207)*
Glovis America Inc (HQ)...714 435-2960
17305 Von Karman Ave # 200 Irvine (92614) *(G-5088)*
Glu Mobile Inc (PA)...415 800-6100
500 Howard St Ste 300 San Francisco (94105) *(G-15208)*
GMAC Insurance, Ontario *Also called National General Insurance Co (G-10451)*
Gmg Janitorial Inc...415 642-2100
2237 Palou Ave San Francisco (94124) *(G-14315)*
Gmg Stone Inc...619 258-6899
7988 Stromesa Ct San Diego (92126) *(G-3015)*
Gmh Inc...805 485-1410
561 Kinetic Dr Ste A Oxnard (93030) *(G-17921)*
GMI Building Services Inc...858 279-6262
8001 Vickers St San Diego (92111) *(G-14316)*
Gms Janitorial Services Inc...858 569-6009
8316 Clairemont Mesa Blvd # 201 San Diego (92111) *(G-14317)*
Gnf...858 812-1976
10675 John J Hopkins Dr San Diego (92121) *(G-26768)*
Go-Staff Inc (PA)...858 292-8562
8798 Complex Dr San Diego (92123) *(G-14883)*
Go-Staff Inc...760 730-8520
9878 Complex Dr Oceanside (92054) *(G-14664)*
Go2 Systems Inc...949 553-0800
18400 Von Karman Ave Fl 9 Irvine (92612) *(G-16238)*
Go2systems, Irvine *Also called Go2 Systems Inc (G-16238)*
Goal Financial LLC...858 731-9000
401 W A St Ste 1300 San Diego (92101) *(G-9846)*
God Help Films Inc...323 556-0699
8200 Wilshire Blvd # 200 Beverly Hills (90211) *(G-6075)*
Goebel Mechanical Inc...707 778-2340
501 Lakeville Cir E Petaluma (94954) *(G-1431)*
Goetzman Group Inc (PA)...818 595-1112
21700 Oxnard St Ste 1540 Woodland Hills (91367) *(G-27450)*
Goforth & Marti (PA)...951 684-0870
110 W A St Ste 140 San Diego (92101) *(G-6816)*
Gogii, Marina Del Rey *Also called Textplus Inc (G-5418)*
Goglanian Bakeries Inc (HQ)...714 549-1524
3401 W Segerstrom Ave Santa Ana (92704) *(G-8843)*
Goguardian, Hermosa Beach *Also called Liminex Inc (G-15275)*
Gold Bond Building Products, Richmond *Also called New Ngc Inc (G-8077)*
Gold Coast Broadcasting, Ventura *Also called Kkzz 1590 (G-5795)*
Gold Coast Design Inc...619 574-0111
7667 Vickers St San Diego (92111) *(G-2450)*
Gold Coast Farms LLC...559 564-6316
32701 Road 204 Woodlake (93286) *(G-285)*
Gold Coast Ingredients Inc...323 724-8935
2429 Yates Ave Commerce (90040) *(G-8844)*
Gold Coast Tours, Fullerton *Also called Hot Dogger Tours Inc (G-3903)*
Gold Country Casino, Oroville *Also called Tyme Maidu Tribe-Berry Creek (G-13363)*
Gold Country Health Center Inc (PA)...530 621-1100
4301 Golden Center Dr Placerville (95667) *(G-24923)*
Gold Country Management Inc...916 929-3003
1825 Bell St Ste 100 Sacramento (95825) *(G-11556)*
Gold Cross Ambulance, Los Angeles *Also called Schaefer Ambulance Service Inc (G-3841)*
Gold Hill Grange No 326...916 645-3605
1514 5th St Lincoln (95648) *(G-25265)*
Gold River Racquet Club, Gold River *Also called Spare-Time Inc (G-19089)*
Gold Rush Coffee...707 629-3460
3864 Lighthouse Rd Petrolia (95558) *(G-8845)*
Gold Star Foods Inc...909 843-9600
3781 E Airport Dr Ontario (91761) *(G-8553)*
Gold Star Insulation Inc...916 928-1100
210 N 10th St Sacramento (95811) *(G-2904)*
Gold Tree Inc...562 801-0218
2170 W Esther St Long Beach (90813) *(G-27451)*
Gold Valley Properties...831 424-1414
333 Salinas St Salinas (93901) *(G-23277)*
Gold's Gym, Redondo Beach *Also called Muscle Improvement Inc (G-18664)*
Gold's Gym, Modesto *Also called Focus Up LLC (G-18635)*
Gold's Gym, Vacaville *Also called Maximum Fitness LLC (G-18659)*
Gold's Gym, Roseville *Also called A & M Gyms LLC (G-18603)*
Gold's Gym, Jackson *Also called Capitol Fitness Network LLC (G-18619)*
Golda & I Chocolatiers Inc...949 660-9581
23052 Alicia Pkwy Ste H Mission Viejo (92692) *(G-8846)*
Goldberg and Solovy Foods Inc...323 581-6161
5925 Alcoa Ave Vernon (90058) *(G-8481)*
Golden, Irvine *Also called Atria Senior Living Group Inc (G-26930)*
Golden 1 Credit Union...877 465-3361
1282 Stabler Ln Ste 640 Yuba City (95993) *(G-9603)*
Golden 1 Credit Union (PA)...916 732-2900
8945 Cal Center Dr Sacramento (95826) *(G-9669)*
Golden Acorn Casino & Trvl Ctr, Campo *Also called Campo Band Missions Indians (G-18802)*
Golden Acres Farms...760 399-1923
87770 62nd Ave Thermal (92274) *(G-71)*
Golden Arrow Construction Inc...310 523-9056
21213 Hawthorne Blvd B Torrance (90503) *(G-1184)*
Golden Bear Rest Assn LLC...415 227-8660
760 2nd St San Francisco (94107) *(G-25088)*
Golden Care Inc...818 763-6275
6120 Vineland Ave North Hollywood (91606) *(G-21236)*
Golden Cross Care II Inc...559 268-3023
1233 A St Fresno (93706) *(G-20602)*
Golden Cross Care Inc...626 791-1948
1450 N Fair Oaks Ave Pasadena (91103) *(G-21237)*
Golden Cross Health Care, Pasadena *Also called Golden Cross Care Inc (G-21237)*
Golden Cross Hlth Care Fresno, Fresno *Also called Golden Cross Care II Inc (G-20602)*
Golden Crust Bakeries Inc...661 294-9750
25170 Anza Dr Santa Clarita (91355) *(G-8847)*
Golden Door Properties LLC...760 744-5777
777 Deer Springs Rd San Marcos (92069) *(G-12667)*
Golden Eagle Insurance Corp (HQ)...619 744-6000
525 B St Ste 1300 San Diego (92101) *(G-10424)*
Golden Eagle Moving Svcs Inc...909 946-7655
1450 N Benson Ave Upland (91786) *(G-4190)*
Golden Empire Concrete Pdts...661 833-4490
8261 Mccutchen Rd Bakersfield (93311) *(G-3266)*
Golden Empire Convalescent Hos...530 273-1316
121 Dorsey Dr Grass Valley (95945) *(G-21580)*
Golden Empire Mortgage...626 967-3236
664 Shoppers Ln Ste A Covina (91723) *(G-9847)*
Golden Empire Mortgage (PA)...661 328-1600
1200 Discovery Dr Ste 300 Bakersfield (93309) *(G-9848)*
Golden Empire Mortgage Inc (PA)...661 328-1600
2130 Chester Ave Bakersfield (93301) *(G-9849)*
Golden Empire Transit District (PA)...661 869-2438
1830 Golden State Ave Bakersfield (93301) *(G-3654)*
Golden Gate...415 455-2000
101 E Sir Francis Drake Larkspur (94939) *(G-5208)*
Golden Gate Brdg Hwy & Transpo (PA)...415 921-5858
Toll Plz San Francisco (94129) *(G-5209)*
Golden Gate Bridge High...415 457-3110
1011 Andersen Dr San Rafael (94901) *(G-5210)*
Golden Gate Capital MGT II LLC...415 983-2700
1 Embarcadero Ctr 39th San Francisco (94111) *(G-27041)*
Golden Gate Capitol...415 983-2700
1 Embarcadero Ctr # 3900 San Francisco (94111) *(G-27934)*
Golden Gate Ferry, Larkspur *Also called Golden Gate (G-5208)*
Golden Gate Fields, Albany *Also called Pacific Racing Association (G-18572)*
Golden Gate Nat Prks Cnsrvancy (PA)...415 561-3000
Fort Mason Bldg 201 San Francisco (94123) *(G-28132)*
Golden Gate Regional Ctr Inc (PA)...415 546-9222
1355 Market St Ste 220 San Francisco (94103) *(G-23994)*
Golden Gate Regional Ctr Inc...650 574-9232
3130 La Selva St Ste 202 San Mateo (94403) *(G-23995)*
Golden Gate Scnic Stmship Corp...415 901-5249
Shed C Pier 45 St Pier San Francisco (94133) *(G-4735)*
Golden Gate Section, San Francisco *Also called National Council Negro Women (G-25559)*
Golden Gate Transit, San Rafael *Also called Golden Gate Bridge High (G-5210)*
Golden Gtwy Tennis & Swim CLB, San Francisco *Also called Bay Club Golden Gateway Inc (G-18883)*
Golden Hotels Ltd Partnership...949 833-2770
18700 Macarthur Blvd Irvine (92612) *(G-12668)*
Golden Hour Data Systems Inc...858 768-2500
10052 Mesa Ridge Ct # 200 San Diego (92121) *(G-5089)*
Golden International...213 628-1388
424 S Los Angeles St # 2 Los Angeles (90013) *(G-12310)*
Golden Living LLC...559 237-8377
1715 S Cedar Ave Fresno (93702) *(G-20603)*
Golden Living LLC...818 893-6385
9541 Van Nuys Blvd Panorama City (91402) *(G-21238)*
Golden Living LLC...559 834-2542
1306 E Sumner Ave Fowler (93625) *(G-20604)*
Golden Living LLC...949 642-0387
340 Victoria St Costa Mesa (92627) *(G-20605)*

ALPHABETIC

Golden Living LLC ... 707 546-0471
1221 Rosemarie Ln Stockton (95207) ***(G-20606)***
Golden Living LLC ... 818 249-3925
2123 Verdugo Blvd Montrose (91020) ***(G-21239)***
Golden Living LLC ... 559 275-4785
925 N Cornelia Ave Fresno (93706) ***(G-20607)***
Golden Living LLC ... 209 745-1537
144 F St Galt (95632) ***(G-22442)***
Golden Living LLC ... 415 563-0565
1477 Grove St San Francisco (94117) ***(G-20608)***
Golden Living LLC ... 707 255-6060
705 Trancas St NAPA (94558) ***(G-21240)***
Golden Living LLC ... 209 529-0516
515 E Orangeburg Ave Modesto (95350) ***(G-21241)***
Golden Living LLC ... 209 533-2500
19929 Greenley Rd Sonora (95370) ***(G-21242)***
Golden Living LLC ... 408 356-8136
14966 Terreno De Flores Los Gatos (95032) ***(G-21243)***
Golden Living LLC ... 562 598-2477
3000 N Gate Rd Seal Beach (90740) ***(G-21244)***
Golden Living LLC ... 661 323-2894
3601 San Dimas St Bakersfield (93301) ***(G-20609)***
Golden Living LLC ... 805 494-4949
6700 Sepulveda Blvd Van Nuys (91411) ***(G-22443)***
Golden Living LLC ... 707 763-4109
217 Lakeville St Apt 3 Petaluma (94952) ***(G-20610)***
Golden Living LLC ... 805 983-0305
1300 N C St Oxnard (93030) ***(G-20611)***
Golden Living LLC ... 209 368-0693
950 S Fairmont Ave Lodi (95240) ***(G-20612)***
Golden Living LLC ... 831 624-1875
23795 Holman Hwy Big Sur (93920) ***(G-22444)***
Golden Living LLC ... 707 546-0471
4650 Hoen Ave Santa Rosa (95405) ***(G-20613)***
Golden Living LLC ... 626 962-3368
850 S Sunkist Ave West Covina (91790) ***(G-20614)***
Golden Living LLC ... 805 642-1736
5445 Everglades St Ventura (93003) ***(G-20615)***
Golden Living LLC ... 949 496-5786
35410 Del Rey Capistrano Beach (92624) ***(G-20616)***
Golden Living LLC ... 530 241-6756
1836 Gold St Redding (96001) ***(G-21245)***
Golden Living LLC ... 559 486-4433
2715 Fresno St Fresno (93721) ***(G-21246)***
Golden Living LLC ... 559 299-2591
111 Barstow Ave Clovis (93612) ***(G-20617)***
Golden Living LLC ... 951 600-4640
24100 Monroe Ave Murrieta (92562) ***(G-23996)***
Golden Living LLC ... 408 923-7232
401 Ridge Vista Ave San Jose (95127) ***(G-20618)***
Golden Living LLC ... 559 222-4807
3510 E Shields Ave Fresno (93726) ***(G-20619)***
Golden Living LLC ... 559 673-9278
1700 Howard Rd Madera (93637) ***(G-21247)***
Golden Living LLC ... 559 638-3577
1090 E Dinuba Ave Reedley (93654) ***(G-20620)***
Golden Living LLC ... 559 227-5383
3672 N 1st St Fresno (93726) ***(G-20621)***
Golden Living LLC ... 408 255-5555
5555 Prospect Rd Ofc San Jose (95129) ***(G-24669)***
Golden Living LLC ... 209 548-0318
1900 Coffee Rd Modesto (95355) ***(G-20622)***
Golden Living LLC ... 408 356-9151
350 De Soto Dr Los Gatos (95032) ***(G-20623)***
Golden Living LLC ... 559 227-4063
3408 E Shields Ave Fresno (93726) ***(G-21248)***
Golden Living LLC ... 209 466-3522
2740 N California St Stockton (95204) ***(G-20624)***
Golden Living LLC ... 707 938-1096
678 2nd St W Sonoma (95476) ***(G-20625)***
Golden Living LLC ... 530 343-6084
188 Cohasset Ln Chico (95926) ***(G-20626)***
Golden Living LLC ... 209 722-6231
3169 M St Merced (95348) ***(G-21249)***
Golden Living LLC ... 760 446-3591
1131 N China Lake Blvd Ridgecrest (93555) ***(G-22445)***
Golden Living LLC ... 559 875-6501
2550 9th St Sanger (93657) ***(G-21250)***
Golden Living LLC ... 209 862-2862
709 N St Newman (95360) ***(G-20627)***
Golden Living LLC ... 559 665-3745
1010 Ventura Ave Chowchilla (93610) ***(G-24670)***
Golden Livingcenter, Sonoma *Also called Golden Living LLC* ***(G-20625)***
Golden Livingcenter - Chateau, Stockton *Also called Golden Living LLC* ***(G-20606)***
Golden Livingcenter - Clovis, Clovis *Also called Golden Living LLC* ***(G-20617)***
Golden Livingcenter - Fresno, Fresno *Also called Golden Living LLC* ***(G-21246)***
Golden Livingcenter - Galt, Galt *Also called Golden Living LLC* ***(G-22442)***
Golden Livingcenter - Hylond, Fresno *Also called Golden Living LLC* ***(G-21248)***
Golden Livingcenter - NAPA, NAPA *Also called Golden Living LLC* ***(G-21240)***
Golden Livingcenter - Petaluma, Petaluma *Also called Golden Living LLC* ***(G-20610)***
Golden Livingcenter - Portside, Stockton *Also called Golden Living LLC* ***(G-20624)***
Golden Livingcenter - Redding, Redding *Also called Golden Living LLC* ***(G-21245)***
Golden Livingcenter - Reedley, Reedley *Also called Golden Living LLC* ***(G-20620)***
Golden Livingcenter - San Jose, San Jose *Also called Golden Living LLC* ***(G-20618)***
Golden Livingcenter - Sanger, Sanger *Also called Golden Living LLC* ***(G-21250)***
Golden Livingctr-Country View, Fresno *Also called Golden Living LLC* ***(G-20607)***
Golden Lvngcenter - Santa Rosa, Santa Rosa *Also called Golden Living LLC* ***(G-20613)***
Golden Lvngcnter - Bakersfield, Bakersfield *Also called Golden Living LLC* ***(G-20609)***

Golden N-Life Diamite Intl Inc (PA) ... 510 651-0405
3500 Gateway Blvd Fremont (94538) ***(G-8258)***
Golden Peterbilt, Porterville *Also called E M Tharp Inc* ***(G-6674)***
Golden Pond LP ... 916 369-8967
3415 Mayhew Rd Ofc Sacramento (95827) ***(G-24671)***
Golden Pond Retirement Cmnty, Sacramento *Also called Golden Pond LP* ***(G-24671)***
Golden Queen Mining Co Inc, Mojave *Also called Golden Queen Mining Co LLC* ***(G-1022)***
Golden Queen Mining Co LLC ... 661 824-4300
15772 K St Mojave (93501) ***(G-1022)***
Golden Rain Foundation (PA) ... 925 988-7700
1001 Golden Rain Rd Walnut Creek (94595) ***(G-11557)***
Golden Rain Foundation ... 562 493-9581
1661 Golden Rain Rd Seal Beach (90740) ***(G-19537)***
Golden Rain Foundation ... 925 988-7800
800 Rockview Dr Walnut Creek (94595) ***(G-25266)***
Golden State Bridge Inc ... 530 865-8400
1227 E South St Orland (95963) ***(G-1775)***
Golden State Care Center, Baldwin Park *Also called Golden State Habilitation Conv* ***(G-20628)***
Golden State Collision Centers ... 916 772-1666
841 Galleria Blvd Roseville (95678) ***(G-17755)***
Golden State Colonial Convales, North Hollywood *Also called Silverscreen Healthcare Inc* ***(G-20917)***
Golden State Crrctional Fcilty, Mc Farland *Also called Geo Group Inc* ***(G-27035)***
Golden State Drilling Inc ... 661 589-0730
3500 Fruitvale Ave Bakersfield (93308) ***(G-1059)***
Golden State Fence, Anaheim *Also called Fenceworks Inc* ***(G-3517)***
Golden State Fence, Santa Paula *Also called Fenceworks Inc* ***(G-3519)***
Golden State Fence Co., Riverside *Also called Fenceworks Inc* ***(G-3518)***
Golden State Flooring, San Diego *Also called H - Investment Company* ***(G-6926)***
Golden State Fruit, Lodi *Also called California Fruit Exchange LLC* ***(G-8701)***
Golden State Habilitation Conv (PA) ... 626 962-3274
1758 Big Dalton Ave Baldwin Park (91706) ***(G-20628)***
Golden State Health Ctrs Inc (PA) ... 818 385-3200
13347 Ventura Blvd Sherman Oaks (91423) ***(G-20629)***
Golden State Health Ctrs Inc ... 626 579-0310
5522 Gracewood Ave Temple City (91780) ***(G-21251)***
Golden State Health Ctrs Inc ... 818 783-4969
13347 Ventura Blvd # 201 Sherman Oaks (91423) ***(G-21252)***
Golden State Health Ctrs Inc ... 818 882-8233
21820 Craggy View St Chatsworth (91311) ***(G-21253)***
Golden State Health Ctrs Inc ... 818 834-5082
12220 Foothill Blvd Sylmar (91342) ***(G-22071)***
Golden State Landscaping, Livermore *Also called J Redfern Inc* ***(G-873)***
Golden State Lumber Inc ... 209 234-7700
3033 S Airport Way Stockton (95206) ***(G-6924)***
Golden State Mutl Lf Insur Co (PA) ... 713 526-4361
1999 W Adams Blvd Los Angeles (90018) ***(G-10209)***
Golden State Plastering ... 559 439-3920
7082 N Harrison Ave Fresno (93650) ***(G-6986)***
Golden State Warriors LLC ... 510 986-2200
1011 Broadway Oakland (94607) ***(G-18547)***
Golden State Water Company ... 714 535-7711
1920 W Corporate Way Anaheim (92801) ***(G-6350)***
Golden State Water Company (HQ) ... 909 394-3600
630 E Foothill Blvd San Dimas (91773) ***(G-6351)***
Golden State Water Company ... 909 394-3600
630 E Foothill Blvd San Dimas (91773) ***(G-6352)***
Golden State Water Company ... 805 583-6400
600 W Los Angeles Ave Simi Valley (93065) ***(G-6353)***
Golden State Water Company ... 909 866-4678
42020 Garstin Rd Big Bear Lake (92315) ***(G-6134)***
Golden State West Valley ... 818 348-8422
7057 Shoup Ave Canoga Park (91307) ***(G-20630)***
Golden Valley Citrus Inc ... 559 568-1768
19875 Meredith Dr Strathmore (93267) ***(G-536)***
Golden Valley Health Centers ... 209 556-5040
1717 Las Vegas St Modesto (95358) ***(G-19538)***
Golden Valley Health Centers (PA) ... 209 383-1848
737 W Childs Ave Merced (95341) ***(G-22735)***
Golden Valley Health Centers ... 209 383-5871
797 W Childs Ave Merced (95341) ***(G-22736)***
Golden Valley Health Centers ... 209 383-7441
727 W Childs Ave Merced (95341) ***(G-19539)***
Golden Vly Occpational Therapy, Oroville *Also called Oroville Hospital* ***(G-20336)***
Golden West Casino, Irvine *Also called Golden West Partners Inc* ***(G-27935)***
Golden West Custom WD Shutters ... 949 951-0600
20561 Pascal Way Lake Forest (92630) ***(G-8117)***
Golden West Partners Inc (PA) ... 949 477-3090
18101 Von Karman Ave # 1280 Irvine (92612) ***(G-27935)***
Golden West Trading Inc ... 323 581-3663
4401 S Downey Rd Vernon (90058) ***(G-8668)***
Goldenpark LLC ... 562 863-5555
16209 Paramount Blvd # 214 Paramount (90723) ***(G-12669)***
Goldenwest Ldry & Valet Svcs ... 714 843-0723
17862 Jamestown Ln Huntington Beach (92647) ***(G-13581)***
Goldfield Stage & Co, El Cajon *Also called Mc Clintock Enterprises* ***(G-3894)***
Goldman Sachs & Co ... 415 393-7500
555 California St # 4500 San Francisco (94104) ***(G-10006)***
Goldman Sachs & Co ... 310 407-5700
2121 Avenue Stars 2600 Los Angeles (90067) ***(G-10007)***
Goldman Avram ... 925 275-3000
1855 Gateway Blvd Ste 750 Concord (94520) ***(G-27042)***
Goldman Sachs, San Francisco *Also called Goldman Sachs & Co* ***(G-10006)***
Goldman Sachs, Los Angeles *Also called Goldman Sachs & Co* ***(G-10007)***
Goldrich & Kest Industries LLC (PA) ... 310 204-2050
5150 Overland Ave Culver City (90230) ***(G-11970)***

ALPHABETIC SECTION

Goldrich and Kest Construction (PA) 310 204-2050
   5150 Overland Ave Culver City (90230) *(G-11971)*
Goldrush Getaways, Citrus Heights Also called Travelmasters Inc *(G-4981)*
Golds Gym, Thousand Oaks Also called Musclebound Inc *(G-18665)*
Golds Gym International Inc 626 304-1133
   39 S Altadena Dr Pasadena (91107) *(G-18638)*
Goldsmith Construction Co Inc 562 595-5975
   2683 Lime Ave Signal Hill (90755) *(G-3267)*
Goldstar Hlthcr Cntr of Chtswr 818 882-8233
   21820 Craggy View St Chatsworth (91311) *(G-21254)*
Goleta Valley Athletic Club, Goleta Also called Millenium Athletic Club LLc *(G-18661)*
Goleta Valley Cottage Hospital 805 681-6468
   351 S Patterson Ave Santa Barbara (93111) *(G-21581)*
Golf & Tennis Pro Shop Inc 650 600-5200
   1751 E Bayshore Rd East Palo Alto (94303) *(G-19218)*
Golf Club At Boulder Ridge, San Jose Also called Glenrock Group *(G-18742)*
Golf Club At Roddy Ranch, Antioch Also called Roddy Ranch Pbc LLC *(G-19046)*
Golf Club At Terra Lago, The, Indio Also called Lb Hills Golf Club LLC *(G-18754)*
Golf Pro Shop, Riverside Also called Canyon Crest Country Club Inc *(G-18912)*
Golf Pro. Shop, Diablo Also called Diablo Country Club *(G-18734)*
Golin/Harris International Inc 213 623-4200
   601 W 5th St Ste 400 Los Angeles (90071) *(G-27749)*
Gomez Farm Labor Contg Inc 760 399-1994
   62610 Monroe St Thermal (92274) *(G-663)*
Gong's Ventures, Sanger Also called Gongs Market of Sanger Inc *(G-10990)*
Gongs Market of Sanger Inc (PA) 559 875-5576
   1825 Academy Ave Sanger (93657) *(G-10990)*
Gonsalves & Santucci Inc (PA) 925 685-6799
   5141 Commercial Cir Concord (94520) *(G-3268)*
Gonsalves & Santucci Inc 707 745-5019
   5141 Commercial Cir Concord (94520) *(G-3382)*
Gonzales Enterprises Inc 530 343-8725
   495 Ryan Ave Chico (95973) *(G-8343)*
Gonzales Painting Corp 951 214-6400
   14437 Meridian Pkwy Riverside (92518) *(G-2451)*
Gonzales Salvador Labor Contrs 209 745-2223
   217 4th St Galt (95632) *(G-664)*
Gonzalez Barba Enterprises 323 233-7995
   1575 E 46th St Los Angeles (90011) *(G-5090)*
Gonzalez Management Co Inc 818 485-0596
   10147 San Fernando Rd Pacoima (91331) *(G-27043)*
Gonzalez/Goodale Architects 626 568-1428
   135 W Green St Ste 200 Pasadena (91105) *(G-26191)*
Good Deal Insurance Services 626 275-6795
   2140 S Hacienda Blvd A Hacienda Heights (91745) *(G-10731)*
Good Neighbor Pharmacy, Fresno Also called Northwest Medical Group Inc *(G-19784)*
Good Samaritan Hosp Southwest, Bakersfield Also called Good Samaritan Hospital *(G-22072)*
Good Samaritan Hospital (PA) 661 399-4461
   901 Olive Dr Bakersfield (93308) *(G-21582)*
Good Samaritan Hospital (PA) 213 977-2121
   1225 Wilshire Blvd Los Angeles (90017) *(G-21583)*
Good Samaritan Hospital 661 398-1800
   5201 White Ln Bakersfield (93309) *(G-22072)*
Good Samaritan Hospital LP (HQ) 408 559-2011
   2425 Samaritan Dr San Jose (95124) *(G-21584)*
Good Samaritan Hospital LP 408 356-4111
   15891 Los Gtos Almaden Rd Los Gatos (95032) *(G-21585)*
Good Samaritan Hospital Aux 213 977-2121
   1225 Wilshire Blvd Los Angeles (90017) *(G-19540)*
GOOD SAMARITAN REHAB AND CARE, Stockton Also called Stockton Edson Healthcare Corp *(G-21385)*
Good Samaritan Shelter 805 346-8185
   245 Inger Dr Ste 103 Santa Maria (93454) *(G-23997)*
Good Shepherd Communities, Porterville Also called Good Shepherd Lutheran Hm of W *(G-24672)*
Good Shepherd Health Care Ce 310 451-4809
   1131 Arizona Ave Santa Monica (90401) *(G-20631)*
Good Shepherd Lutheran Hm of W (PA) 559 791-2000
   119 N Main St Porterville (93257) *(G-24672)*
Good Sports Plus Ltd 310 671-4400
   370 Amapola Ave Ste 208 Torrance (90501) *(G-15209)*
Good Technology Corporation (HQ) 408 212-7500
   430 N Mary Ave Ste 200 Sunnyvale (94085) *(G-15210)*
Good Technology Software Inc 408 212-7500
   430 N Mary Ave Ste 200 Sunnyvale (94085) *(G-15681)*
Good Works LLC 626 584-8130
   1250 E Walnut St Ste 220 Pasadena (91106) *(G-22446)*
Goodall's Charter Bus Company, San Diego Also called Cusa Gcbs LLC *(G-4993)*
Goodby Silverstein & Partners, San Francisco Also called Goodby Slverstein Partners Inc *(G-13856)*
Goodby Slverstein Partners Inc (HQ) 415 392-0669
   720 California St San Francisco (94108) *(G-13856)*
Goodfellow Top Grade Cnstr LLC, Livermore Also called Tgcon Inc *(G-26094)*
Goodhire Llc 650 618-9910
   555 Twin Dolphin Dr Redwood City (94065) *(G-16135)*
Goodland, Goleta Also called Khp III Goleta LLC *(G-12883)*
Goodman Group Inc 562 596-5561
   3902 Katella Ave Los Alamitos (90720) *(G-11558)*
Goodman Usa Inc 408 329-5400
   605 W California Ave Sunnyvale (94086) *(G-19541)*
Goodrich Corporation 562 944-4441
   9920 Freeman Ave Santa Fe Springs (90670) *(G-17977)*
Goodrich Lax A Cal Ltd Partnr 626 254-9988
   310 W Longden Ave Arcadia (91007) *(G-12670)*
Goodridge Usa Inc (HQ) 310 533-1924
   529 Van Ness Ave Torrance (90501) *(G-6734)*

Goodwill Inds Orange Cnty Cal 714 754-7808
   2910 W Garry Ave Santa Ana (92704) *(G-25536)*
Goodwill Inds S Centl Cal 559 366-1030
   1832 E Tulare Ave Tulare (93274) *(G-22737)*
Goodwill Inds S Centl Cal 661 377-0191
   1115 Olive Dr Bakersfield (93308) *(G-24344)*
Goodwill Inds San Diego Cnty 760 806-7670
   3841 Plaza Dr Ste 902 Oceanside (92056) *(G-25537)*
Goodwill Inds San Diego Cnty 619 955-5626
   6386 Del Cerro Blvd San Diego (92120) *(G-24345)*
Goodwill Inds San Frncisco Inc 650 556-9709
   1270 Oddstad Dr Redwood City (94063) *(G-24346)*
Goodwill Industries of Sacrame 916 331-0237
   8031 Watt Ave Sacramento (95843) *(G-25538)*
Goodwill Industrs of San Franc 415 354-8570
   1669 Fillmore St San Francisco (94115) *(G-24347)*
Goodwill of Silicon Valley (PA) 408 998-5774
   1080 N 7th St San Jose (95112) *(G-14884)*
Goodwin Ammonia Company 714 894-0531
   12361 Monarch St Garden Grove (92841) *(G-4563)*
Goodwin Procter LLP 213 426-2500
   601 S Figueroa St # 4100 Los Angeles (90017) *(G-23278)*
Google Checkout, Mountain View Also called Google Payment Corp *(G-17195)*
Google Fiber Inc 650 253-0000
   1600 Amphitheatre Pkwy Mountain View (94043) *(G-5617)*
Google Inc (HQ) 650 253-0000
   1600 Amphitheatre Pkwy Mountain View (94043) *(G-5618)*
Google Inc 650 253-7323
   1945 Charleston Rd Mountain View (94043) *(G-16239)*
Google International LLC (HQ) 650 253-0000
   1600 Amphitheatre Pkwy Mountain View (94043) *(G-5619)*
Google Payment Corp 650 253-0000
   1600 Amphitheatre Pkwy Mountain View (94043) *(G-17195)*
Goplus Corp 909 483-1220
   3900 E Philadelphia St Ontario (91761) *(G-16240)*
Gordian Medical Inc 714 556-0200
   17595 Cartwright Rd Irvine (92614) *(G-7266)*
Gordon & Schwenkmeyer Inc 916 569-1740
   1418 Howe Ave E Sacramento (95825) *(G-17196)*
Gordon Betty Moore Foundation 650 213-3000
   1661 Page Mill Rd Palo Alto (94304) *(G-25267)*
Gordon E Btty I More Fundation 650 213-3000
   1661 Page Mill Rd Palo Alto (94304) *(G-27936)*
Gordon Edelstein Krepack 213 739-7000
   3580 Wilshire Blvd # 1800 Los Angeles (90010) *(G-23279)*
Gordon Hall Conference Center, Chico Also called Graig Hall Service Company *(G-11138)*
Gordon Lane Convalescent Hosp 714 879-7301
   1821 E Chapman Ave Fullerton (92831) *(G-21586)*
Gordon R Levinson A Prof Corp 760 692-2260
   2768 Loker Ave W Ste 101 Carlsbad (92010) *(G-23280)*
Gordon Rees Sclly Mnskhani LLP 916 830-6900
   655 University Ave # 200 Sacramento (95825) *(G-23281)*
Gordon Rees Sclly Mnskhani LLP 949 255-6950
   2211 Michelson Dr Ste 400 Irvine (92612) *(G-23282)*
Gordon Rees Sclly Mnskhani LLP (PA) 415 986-5900
   275 Battery St Ste 2000 San Francisco (94111) *(G-23283)*
Gordon Rees Sclly Mnskhani LLP 213 576-5000
   633 W 5th St Fl 52 Los Angeles (90071) *(G-23284)*
Gordon Rees Sclly Mnskhani LLP 619 696-6700
   101 W Broadway Ste 1600 San Diego (92101) *(G-23285)*
Gordon Rees Sclly Mnskhani LLP 415 986-5900
   101 W Broadway Ste 2000 San Diego (92101) *(G-23286)*
GORDON'S ON THE GREEN, San Marcos Also called San Marcos Country Club *(G-13793)*
Gores Capital Partners LP 310 209-3010
   10877 Wilshire Blvd Fl 18 Los Angeles (90024) *(G-17197)*
Gores Group LLC (PA) 310 209-3010
   9800 Wilshire Blvd Beverly Hills (90212) *(G-10008)*
Gores Norment Holdings Inc (HQ) 310 209-3010
   10877 Wilshire Blvd # 1805 Los Angeles (90024) *(G-12067)*
Gorilla Offroad Lights LLC (HQ) 310 449-1890
   5140 W Goldleaf Cir Fl 3 Los Angeles (90056) *(G-5620)*
Gorilla Tech Americas Inc 925 365-1161
   2678 Bishop Dr Ste 290 San Ramon (94583) *(G-27452)*
Got Appraisals, San Ramon Also called AMR Appraisals Inc *(G-11299)*
Gothic Ground Management, Valencia Also called Gothic Landscaping Inc *(G-858)*
Gothic Grounds Mgmt, Valencia Also called Gothic Landscaping Inc *(G-769)*
Gothic Landscaping Inc 661 257-5085
   27413 Tourney Rd Ste 200 Valencia (91355) *(G-769)*
Gothic Landscaping Inc (PA) 661 257-1266
   27502 Avenue Scott Valencia (91355) *(G-858)*
Gould Electric Inc 858 486-1727
   12975 Brookprinter Pl # 280 Poway (92064) *(G-2599)*
Gould Evans P C 415 503-1411
   95 Brady St San Francisco (94103) *(G-26192)*
Gourmet Foods, Hayward Also called HUG Company *(G-8487)*
Gourmet Foods Inc (PA) 310 632-3300
   2910 E Harcourt St Compton (90221) *(G-8482)*
Gourmet India Food Company LLC 562 698-9763
   12220 Rivera Rd Ste A Whittier (90606) *(G-8848)*
Gourmets Fresh Pasta 626 798-0841
   950 N Fair Oaks Ave Pasadena (91103) *(G-8849)*
Government Technology, Folsom Also called Erepublic Inc *(G-17154)*
Governmentjobscom Inc 310 426-6304
   222 N Sepulveda Blvd El Segundo (90245) *(G-15682)*
Governors Office Plg & RES, Sacramento Also called Executive Office State of CA *(G-26515)*
Goway Travel Inc 800 810-3687
   400 N Brand Blvd Ste 920 Glendale (91203) *(G-4961)*
GPA Technologies Inc 805 643-7878
   2368 Eastman Ave Ste 8 Ventura (93003) *(G-25844)*

Gps Painting Wallcovering Inc 714 730-8904
1307 E Saint Gertrude Pl C Santa Ana (92705) ***(G-2452)***
Gr Hardester LLC 707 987-2325
21088 Calistoga Rd Middletown (95461) ***(G-12247)***
Gracenote Inc (HQ) 510 428-7200
2000 Powell St Ste 1500 Emeryville (94608) ***(G-15211)***
Gradient Engineers Inc 949 477-0555
17781 Cowan Ste 140 Irvine (92614) ***(G-25845)***
Graham Concrete Cnstr Inc 559 292-6571
1323 Dayton Ave Ste 103 Clovis (93612) ***(G-3269)***
Graham Contractors Inc 408 293-9516
860 Lonus St San Jose (95126) ***(G-1776)***
Graham Packaging Company LP 209 572-5187
4500 Finch Rd Modesto (95357) ***(G-9268)***
Graham-Prewett Inc 559 291-3741
2773 N Bus Park Ave # 101 Fresno (93727) ***(G-1556)***
Graig Hall Service Company 530 345-1393
1400 W 3rd St Chico (95928) ***(G-11138)***
Grail Inc 858 766-1512
800 Saginaw Dr Redwood City (94063) ***(G-26528)***
Grail Bio, Redwood City *Also called Grail Inc* ***(G-26528)***
Grainger 732, San Jose *Also called WW Grainger Inc* ***(G-7484)***
Granada Healthcre & Rehab Cntr 707 443-1627
2885 Harris St Eureka (95503) ***(G-21255)***
Granada Hotel, San Francisco *Also called Broadmoor Hotel* ***(G-12470)***
Grancare LLC 510 232-5945
13484 San Pablo Ave San Pablo (94806) ***(G-20632)***
Grancell Village, Reseda *Also called Los Angles Jewish HM For Aging* ***(G-20747)***
Grand Auto Care 626 331-8390
744 N Grand Ave Covina (91724) ***(G-17797)***
Grand Auto Repair, Covina *Also called Grand Auto Care* ***(G-17797)***
Grand Central Communications 415 344-3200
50 Fremont St Fl 16 San Francisco (94105) ***(G-5621)***
Grand Central Station, Livermore *Also called All-Guard Alarm Systems Inc* ***(G-2516)***
Grand Del Mar Resort LP 858 314-2000
5300 Grand Del Mar Ct San Diego (92130) ***(G-12671)***
Grand Events Inc 209 569-0399
4623 Mchenry Ave Modesto (95356) ***(G-14543)***
Grand Hotel The, Sunnyvale *Also called Selvi-Vidovich LP* ***(G-13233)***
Grand Hyatt San Francisco, San Francisco *Also called Hyatt Corporation* ***(G-12811)***
Grand Intelligence LLC 408 954-7368
2880 Zanker Rd Ste 203 San Jose (95134) ***(G-15212)***
Grand Pacific Carlsbad Ht LP 760 827-2400
5480 Grand Pacific Dr Carlsbad (92008) ***(G-12672)***
Grand Pacific Resorts Inc 760 431-8500
5900 Pasteur Ct Ste 200 Carlsbad (92008) ***(G-17198)***
Grand Pacific Resorts Inc (PA) 760 431-8500
5900 Pasteur Ct Ste 200 Carlsbad (92008) ***(G-11559)***
Grand Pacific Resorts Svcs LP 760 431-8500
5900 Pasteur Ct Ste 200 Carlsbad (92008) ***(G-12673)***
Grand Park Convalescent Hosp 213 382-7315
2312 W 8th St Los Angeles (90057) ***(G-20633)***
Grand Performances 213 687-2190
350 S Grand Ave Ste A4 Los Angeles (90071) ***(G-17199)***
Grand Supercenter Inc 562 318-3451
8550 Chetle Ave Ste B Whittier (90606) ***(G-8483)***
Grand Terrace Care Center 909 825-5221
12000 Mount Vernon Ave Grand Terrace (92313) ***(G-20634)***
Grand Valley Health Care Ctr 818 786-3470
13524 Sherman Way Van Nuys (91405) ***(G-20635)***
Grand View Geranium Grdns Inc 310 217-0490
18307 Central Ave Carson (90746) ***(G-286)***
Grand View Research Inc 415 349-0058
28 2nd St Ste 3036 San Francisco (94105) ***(G-27453)***
Grand Vista Hotel, Simi Valley *Also called Simi West Inc* ***(G-13257)***
Grandcare Health Services LLC (PA) 866 554-2447
2555 E Colorado Blvd Fl 4 Pasadena (91107) ***(G-22447)***
Grandcare Home Health Services, Pasadena *Also called Msj Healthcare LLC* ***(G-22510)***
Grande Colonial, La Jolla *Also called Fargo Colonial LLC* ***(G-12631)***
Grani Installation Inc (PA) 714 898-0441
5411 Commercial Dr Huntington Beach (92649) ***(G-1557)***
Granit-Bayashi 2 A Joint Ventr 831 724-1011
585 W Beach St Watsonville (95076) ***(G-1935)***
Granite Bay Golf Club 916 791-5379
9600 Golf Club Dr Granite Bay (95746) ***(G-18956)***
Granite Construction Company (HQ) 831 724-1011
585 W Beach St Watsonville (95076) ***(G-1777)***
Granite Construction Company 661 399-3361
3005 James Rd Bakersfield (93308) ***(G-1778)***
Granite Construction Company 760 775-7500
38000 Monroe St Indio (92203) ***(G-1779)***
Granite Construction Company 916 855-4400
4001 Bradshaw Rd Sacramento (95827) ***(G-2054)***
Granite Construction Company 805 964-9951
5335 Debbie Rd Santa Barbara (93111) ***(G-1892)***
Granite Construction Company 661 854-3051
21541 E Bear Mtn Blvd Arvin (93203) ***(G-1780)***
Granite Construction Company 661 726-4447
213 E Avenue M Lancaster (93535) ***(G-1781)***
Granite Construction Company 408 327-7000
715 Comstock St Santa Clara (95054) ***(G-1782)***
Granite Construction Company 559 441-5700
2716 S Granite Ct Fresno (93706) ***(G-1783)***
Granite Construction Inc 760 337-3030
2095 Us Highway 111 El Centro (92243) ***(G-1784)***
Granite Construction Inc (PA) 831 724-1011
585 W Beach St Watsonville (95076) ***(G-1785)***
Granite Construction Inc 831 657-1700
5 Justin Ct Monterey (93940) ***(G-1786)***
Granite Construction Inc 916 855-4495
4291 Bradshaw Rd Sacramento (95827) ***(G-1787)***
Granite Construction Inc 530 787-2012
15560 County Rd 87 Esparto (95627) ***(G-1788)***
Granite Construction Inc 707 467-4100
1324 S State St Ukiah (95482) ***(G-1789)***
Granite Construction Inc 831 763-5595
25485 Iverson Rd Gonzales (93926) ***(G-1790)***
Granite Construction Inc 831 335-3445
1800 Felton Quarry Rd Felton (95018) ***(G-1791)***
Granite Escrow Services 310 288-0110
439 N Canon Dr Ste 220 Beverly Hills (90210) ***(G-9719)***
Granite Hills Healthcare 619 447-1020
1340 E Madison Ave El Cajon (92021) ***(G-20636)***
Granite Hlls Convalescent Hosp, El Cajon *Also called Care With Dignity Healthcare* ***(G-20437)***
Granite Rock Co (PA) 831 768-2000
350 Technology Dr Watsonville (95076) ***(G-1103)***
Granite Rock Co 831 768-2330
1900 Quarry Rd Aromas (95004) ***(G-1792)***
Granite Rock Co 831 392-3780
End Of Quarry Rd Aromas (95004) ***(G-6987)***
Granite Rock Co 831 768-2300
Quarry Rd Aromas (95004) ***(G-1104)***
Granite Rock Co 650 869-3370
355 Blomquist St Redwood City (94063) ***(G-1793)***
Granite Solutions Groupe Inc 415 963-3999
235 Montgomery St Ste 430 San Francisco (94104) ***(G-14665)***
Granlibakken Ski Racquet Resort, Tahoe City *Also called Granlibakken Management Co Ltd* ***(G-12674)***
Granlibakken Management Co Ltd 800 543-3221
725 Granlibakken Rd Tahoe City (96145) ***(G-12674)***
Granlund Candies, Yucaipa *Also called B B G Management Group* ***(G-8609)***
Grant & Weber (PA) 818 878-7700
26610 Agoura Rd Ste 209 Calabasas (91302) ***(G-14034)***
Grant & Weber Travel, Calabasas *Also called Grant & Weber* ***(G-14034)***
Grant Construction Inc 661 588-4586
7702 Meany Ave Ste 103 Bakersfield (93308) ***(G-3051)***
Grant Thornton LLP 415 986-3900
101 California St # 2700 San Francisco (94111) ***(G-26355)***
Grant Thornton LLP 408 275-9000
150 Almaden Blvd Ste 600 San Jose (95113) ***(G-26356)***
Grant Thornton LLP 213 627-1717
1000 Wilshire Blvd # 300 Los Angeles (90017) ***(G-26357)***
Grant Thornton LLP 213 627-1717
515 S Flower St Ste 700 Los Angeles (90071) ***(G-26358)***
Grant Thornton LLP 858 704-8000
12220 El Camino Real San Diego (92130) ***(G-26359)***
Grant-Cuesta Nursing Center, Mountain View *Also called Covenant Care California LLC* ***(G-21526)***
Grants Custom Cabinets 805 466-9680
7310 Kingsbury Rd Templeton (93465) ***(G-1185)***
Grants Landscape Services Inc 714 444-1903
3046 Orange Ave Santa Ana (92707) ***(G-859)***
Granville Glendale Inc 818 981-1171
16133 Ventura Blvd # 1085 Encino (91436) ***(G-27044)***
Granville Homes Inc 559 268-2000
1396 W Herndon Ave # 101 Fresno (93711) ***(G-1186)***
Granville Hotel Corp 562 863-5555
13111 Sycamore Dr Norwalk (90650) ***(G-12675)***
Grapheex, Simi Valley *Also called Pars Publishing Corp* ***(G-14158)***
Graphic Orb Inc 310 967-2350
8687 Melrose Ave Ste 8 West Hollywood (90069) ***(G-27454)***
Grass Valley LLC 530 272-1055
150 Sutton Way Ofc Grass Valley (95945) ***(G-24673)***
Grasshopper House LLC 310 589-2880
6428 Meadows Ct Malibu (90265) ***(G-22738)***
Gray Systems Inc 619 285-5848
5173 Waring Rd San Diego (92120) ***(G-16296)***
Graybar Electric Company Inc 909 451-4300
1370 Valley Vista Dr # 100 Diamond Bar (91765) ***(G-7442)***
Graybar Electric Company Inc 858 549-9017
8606 Miralani Dr San Diego (92126) ***(G-7443)***
Graybar Electric Company Inc 925 557-3000
3089 Whipple Rd Union City (94587) ***(G-7444)***
Graybill Medical Group Inc (PA) 866 228-2236
225 E 2nd Ave Escondido (92025) ***(G-19542)***
Graycon Inc 626 961-9640
232 S 8th Ave City of Industry (91746) ***(G-2239)***
Grayline of San Francisco, San Francisco *Also called Blue Bus Tours LLC* ***(G-19153)***
Graypay LLC 818 387-6735
6345 Balboa Blvd Ste 115 Encino (91316) ***(G-15683)***
Grayson Service Inc 661 589-5444
4004 Enos Ln Bakersfield (93314) ***(G-1078)***
Great Amercn Seafood Import Co, Carson *Also called Southwind Foods LLC* ***(G-8655)***
Great American Insurance Co 323 937-8600
5750 Wilshire Blvd 360 Los Angeles (90036) ***(G-10425)***
Great American Insurance Co 213 430-4300
725 S Figueroa St # 3400 Los Angeles (90017) ***(G-10426)***
Great Destinations Inc 949 667-9401
25510 Commercentre Dr Lake Forest (92630) ***(G-27455)***
Great Scott Tree Service Inc (PA) 714 826-1750
10761 Court Ave Stanton (90680) ***(G-993)***
Great Western Building Mtl, Tustin *Also called Foundation Building Mtls LLC* ***(G-2897)***
Great Western Building Mtls, Riverside *Also called Foundation Building Mtls LLC* ***(G-7371)***
Great Western Hotels Corp 760 446-6543
1050 N Norma St Ridgecrest (93555) ***(G-12676)***

ALPHABETIC

Great Western Wind Energy LLC....888 903-6926
15445 Innovation Dr San Diego (92128) ***(G-6135)***
Great Wstn Cnvlescent Hosp Inc....818 248-6856
2635 Honolulu Ave Montrose (91020) ***(G-21256)***
Greater Alarm Company Inc (HQ)....949 474-0555
3750 Schaufele Ave # 200 Long Beach (90808) ***(G-2600)***
Greater El Monte Cmnty Hosp, El Monte *Also called Ahm Gemch Inc* ***(G-21436)***
Greater Los Angeles Agency....323 478-8000
2239 Norwalk Ave Los Angeles (90041) ***(G-23998)***
Greater Los Angeles Zoo Assn....323 644-4200
5333 Zoo Dr Los Angeles (90027) ***(G-24924)***
Greater Sacramento Sur....916 929-7229
2288 Auburn Blvd Ste 201 Sacramento (95821) ***(G-22739)***
Greater Sacramento Surgery Ctr, Sacramento *Also called Greater Sacramento Sur* ***(G-22739)***
Greater San Diego AC Co Inc....619 469-7818
3883 Ruffin Rd Ste C San Diego (92123) ***(G-2240)***
Greater South Bay Area HM Hlth....310 329-4835
18726 S Wstn Ave Ste 409 Gardena (90248) ***(G-22448)***
Greater South Bay Home Health, Gardena *Also called Greater South Bay Area HM Hlth* ***(G-22448)***
Greater Vallejo Recreation Dst....707 648-4600
395 Amador St Vallejo (94590) ***(G-19219)***
Greater Valley Medical Group (PA)....818 838-4500
11600 Indian Hills Rd # 300 Mission Hills (91345) ***(G-22740)***
Greatwide Dedicated Transport, Vernon *Also called Greatwide Logistics Svcs LLC* ***(G-4191)***
Greatwide Logistics Svcs LLC....323 268-7100
4310 Bandini Blvd Vernon (90058) ***(G-4191)***
Greatwide Logistics Svcs LLC....877 379-6394
3350 E Cedar St Ontario (91761) ***(G-5091)***
Gree International Inc....415 409-5159
185 Berry St Ste 590 San Francisco (94107) ***(G-15213)***
Green Acres Lodge, Rosemead *Also called Longwood Management Corp* ***(G-20743)***
Green Acres Nursery & Sup LLC....916 782-2273
604 Sutter St Folsom (95630) ***(G-7802)***
Green Again Ldscpg & Con Inc....650 368-9304
851 Charter St Redwood City (94063) ***(G-860)***
Green Diamond Resource Company....707 668-4446
900 Riverside Rd Korbel (95550) ***(G-1011)***
Green Dot Corporation (PA)....626 765-2000
3465 E Foothill Blvd # 100 Pasadena (91107) ***(G-9750)***
Green Energy Innovations, Santa Fe Springs *Also called Sfadia Inc* ***(G-2732)***
Green Equity Investors III L P....310 954-0444
11111 Santa Monica Blvd # 2000 Los Angeles (90025) ***(G-10009)***
Green Farms Inc....858 831-7701
7666 Formula Pl Ste B San Diego (92121) ***(G-8735)***
Green Farms Inc (PA)....213 747-4411
1661 Mcgarry St Los Angeles (90021) ***(G-8736)***
Green Glusk Field Clama & Mach....310 553-3610
1900 Avenue Of The Stars 21f Los Angeles (90067) ***(G-23287)***
Green Hasson & Janks LLP....310 873-1600
10990 Wilshire Blvd Fl 16 Los Angeles (90024) ***(G-26360)***
Green Hills Retirement Center, Millbrae *Also called Hillsdale Group LP* ***(G-21269)***
Green Hills Software Inc (PA)....805 965-6044
30 W Sola St Santa Barbara (93101) ***(G-6735)***
Green House, The, Oceanside *Also called Rocket Farms Inc* ***(G-33)***
Green Ridge Services LLC....925 245-5500
6185 Industrial Way Livermore (94551) ***(G-6136)***
Green River Golf Corporation....714 970-8411
5215 Green River Rd Corona (92880) ***(G-18743)***
Green River Golf Course, Corona *Also called Green River Golf Corporation* ***(G-18743)***
Green Scene Landscape Inc....818 280-0420
21220 Devonshire St # 102 Chatsworth (91311) ***(G-861)***
Green Thumb International Inc....818 340-6400
21812 Sherman Way Canoga Park (91303) ***(G-9190)***
Green Thumb Nursery, Canoga Park *Also called Super Garden Centers Inc* ***(G-9218)***
Green Thumb Produce....951 849-4711
2648 W Ramsey St Banning (92220) ***(G-8737)***
Green Tree Capital LP....760 245-3461
14173 Green Tree Blvd Victorville (92395) ***(G-12677)***
Green Tree Inn, Victorville *Also called Lee-Victorville Hotel Corp* ***(G-12913)***
Green Tree Inn, Victorville *Also called Green Tree Capital LP* ***(G-12677)***
Green Trucking, Tulare *Also called Darrell L Green Inc* ***(G-4339)***
Green Valley Corporation (PA)....408 287-0246
777 N 1st St Fl 5 San Jose (95112) ***(G-1558)***
Green Valley Country Club....707 864-1101
35 Country Club Dr Fairfield (94534) ***(G-18957)***
Green Valley Security Inc....916 797-4058
6049 Douglas Blvd Ste 28 Granite Bay (95746) ***(G-16666)***
Green Valley Trnsp Corp....209 836-5192
30131 Highway 33 Tracy (95304) ***(G-4192)***
Greenall, Suisun City *Also called E B Stone & Son Inc* ***(G-9136)***
Greenball Corp (PA)....714 782-3060
222 S Harbor Blvd Ste 700 Anaheim (92805) ***(G-6786)***
Greenberg Traurig LLP....415 655-1300
4 Embarcadero Ctr # 3000 San Francisco (94111) ***(G-23288)***
Greenberg Traurig LLP....310 586-7708
1840 Century Park E # 1900 Los Angeles (90067) ***(G-23289)***
Greenberg Traurig LLP....650 328-8500
1900 University Ave Fl 5 East Palo Alto (94303) ***(G-23290)***
Greenberg Traurig LLP....949 732-6500
3161 Michelson Dr # 1000 Irvine (92612) ***(G-23291)***
Greenbrea Care Center, Greenbrae *Also called Ocadian Care Centers LLC* ***(G-20821)***
Greenbriar Homes Communities....510 497-8200
4340 Stevens Creek Blvd San Jose (95129) ***(G-1365)***
Greenbriar Homes Community, Fremont *Also called Greenbriar Management Company* ***(G-11560)***
Greenbriar Management Company....510 497-8200
43160 Osgood Rd Fremont (94539) ***(G-11560)***
Greenbrier Lawn Tree Exprt Co....619 469-8720
3616 Bancroft Dr Spring Valley (91977) ***(G-862)***
Greene Rdvsky Maloney Share LP....415 981-1400
4 Embarcadero Ctr # 4000 San Francisco (94111) ***(G-23292)***
Greenes Plumbing, Fresno *Also called Plumbing Limited Inc* ***(G-2324)***
Greenheart Farms Inc (PA)....805 481-2234
902 Zenon Way Arroyo Grande (93420) ***(G-331)***
Greenhill & Co Inc....310 432-4400
10250 Constellation Blvd # 1620 Los Angeles (90067) ***(G-10010)***
Greenland US Consulting Inc....213 362-9300
515 S Figueroa St # 1703 Los Angeles (90071) ***(G-1366)***
Greenlaw Grupe Jr Operating Co, Angels Camp *Also called Motherlode Investors LLC* ***(G-18764)***
Greenleaf, Brisbane *Also called Oakville Produce Partners LLC* ***(G-8757)***
Greenleaf Hotel Inc....562 945-8511
7320 Greenleaf Ave Whittier (90602) ***(G-12678)***
Greenleaf Paper Products....949 348-0048
26431 Crown Valley Pkwy # 150 Mission Viejo (92691) ***(G-8194)***
Greenpath Recovery Recycl Svcs, Colton *Also called Greenpath Recovery West Inc* ***(G-8072)***
Greenpath Recovery West Inc....909 954-0686
330 W Citrus St Ste 250 Colton (92324) ***(G-8072)***
Greenplum Inc....650 286-8023
1900 S Norfolk St Ste 224 San Mateo (94403) ***(G-16136)***
Greenridge Senior Care....510 758-9600
2150 Pyramid Dr El Sobrante (94803) ***(G-24674)***
Greensoft Technology Inc....323 254-5961
155 S El Molino Ave # 100 Pasadena (91101) ***(G-16137)***
Greenteam of San Jose, San Jose *Also called Waste Connections Cal Inc* ***(G-6596)***
Greentree Property MGT Inc....415 347-8600
600 California St Fl 19 San Francisco (94108) ***(G-10991)***
Greenwalds Autobody Frameworks (PA)....619 477-2600
1814 Roosevelt Ave National City (91950) ***(G-17756)***
Greenwaste Recovery Inc....408 283-4804
565 Charles St San Jose (95112) ***(G-6489)***
Greenwaste Recovery Inc (PA)....408 283-4800
625 Charles St San Jose (95112) ***(G-6490)***
Greenway Arts Alliance Inc....323 655-7679
544 N Fairfax Ave Los Angeles (90036) ***(G-18395)***
Greenwood & Hall, Los Angeles *Also called Pcs Link Inc* ***(G-28017)***
Grefco Dicaperl, Torrance *Also called Dicaperl Corporation* ***(G-1114)***
Greg H Carpenter Concrete Inc....209 367-4224
955 N Guild Ave Lodi (95240) ***(G-3270)***
Grega Brooke Sra....707 938-3362
18501 Riverside Dr Sonoma (95476) ***(G-11561)***
Gregg Dilling and Testing, Martinez *Also called Gregg Drilling & Testing Inc* ***(G-3356)***
Gregg Drilling & Testing Inc....925 313-5800
950 Howe Rd Martinez (94553) ***(G-3356)***
Gregg Drilling & Testing Inc (PA)....562 427-6899
2726 Walnut Ave Signal Hill (90755) ***(G-3526)***
Gregg Electric Inc....909 983-1794
608 W Emporia St Ontario (91762) ***(G-2601)***
Greka Inc....805 347-8700
1791 Sinton Rd Santa Maria (93458) ***(G-1025)***
Gresham Savage Nolan & Tilden (PA)....619 794-0050
550 E Hospitality Ln # 300 San Bernardino (92408) ***(G-23293)***
Grey Direct-E Marketing, San Francisco *Also called G2 Direct and Digital* ***(G-15200)***
Greybor Medical Transportation....213 250-4444
119 Belmont Ave Ste 107 Los Angeles (90026) ***(G-3801)***
Greyhound Lines Inc....559 268-1829
1033 Broadway St Fresno (93721) ***(G-3959)***
Greyhound Lines Inc....213 629-8400
1716 E 7th St Los Angeles (90021) ***(G-3960)***
Greyhound Lines Inc....209 466-3568
121 S Center St Stockton (95202) ***(G-4866)***
Greystar Management Svcs LP....818 596-2180
6320 Canoga Ave Ste 1512 Woodland Hills (91367) ***(G-11562)***
Greystar Management Svcs LP....949 705-0010
17885 Von Karman Ave Irvine (92614) ***(G-27045)***
Greystone Homes Inc....925 242-0811
6121 Bollinger Canyon Rd # 500 San Ramon (94583) ***(G-1187)***
Greystone Plastering Inc....408 298-5934
1716 Stone Ave Ste B San Jose (95125) ***(G-2905)***
Grht Inc....323 873-6393
14818 Raymer St Van Nuys (91405) ***(G-9269)***
Grice Lund Tarkington, Escondido *Also called A K P LLP* ***(G-26284)***
Grid Dynamics Intl Inc (PA)....650 523-5000
4600 Bohannon Dr Ste 220 Menlo Park (94025) ***(G-16394)***
Gridiron Systems Inc....201 502-0512
4555 Great America Pkwy # 150 Santa Clara (95054) ***(G-15214)***
Gridley Hlthcare & Wellnss Cen....530 846-6266
246 Spruce St Gridley (95948) ***(G-20637)***
Gridley Packing Inc....530 846-3753
1366 Larkin Rd Gridley (95948) ***(G-537)***
Griffin Motorwerke Inc....510 524-7447
1146 6th St Berkeley (94710) ***(G-17798)***
Griffin Slr Management Inc....310 270-4031
9454 Wilshire Blvd # 700 Beverly Hills (90212) ***(G-27046)***
Griffith Company (PA)....714 984-5500
3050 E Birch St Brea (92821) ***(G-1794)***
Griffith Company....661 831-7331
1128 Carrier Parkway Ave Bakersfield (93308) ***(G-1795)***
Griffith Company....562 929-1128
12200 Bloomfield Ave Santa Fe Springs (90670) ***(G-1796)***
Griffith Company....661 392-6640
1128 Carrier Parkway Ave Bakersfield (93308) ***(G-1797)***

A L P H A B E T I C

Griffith Farms 559 592-1009
504 N Kaweah Ave Exeter (93221) *(G-217)*
Griffith Park Healthcare Ctr, Glendale *Also called Griffith Pk Rhbltation Ctr LLC (G-20638)*
Griffith Pk Rhbltation Ctr LLC 818 845-8507
201 Allen Ave Glendale (91201) *(G-20638)*
Grifols Biologicals Inc 323 255-2221
2410 Lillyvale Ave Los Angeles (90032) *(G-4564)*
Grifols Diagnstc Solutions Inc (HQ) 323 225-2221
4560 Horton St Emeryville (94608) *(G-22224)*
Grifols Shared Svcs N Amer Inc (HQ) 323 225-2221
2410 Lillyvale Ave Los Angeles (90032) *(G-8259)*
Grill On The Alley The Inc 323 856-5530
6801 Hollywood Blvd Los Angeles (90028) *(G-17200)*
Grill Recording Studio 510 531-4351
4770 San Pablo Ave Ste C Emeryville (94608) *(G-17201)*
Grimmway Enterprises Inc 661 854-6240
12020 Malaga Rd Arvin (93203) *(G-1432)*
Grimmway Enterprises Inc 760 344-0204
2171 W Bannister Rd Brawley (92227) *(G-17799)*
Grimmway Enterprises Inc 661 393-3320
6101 S Zerker Rd Shafter (93263) *(G-538)*
Grimmway Enterprises Inc 661 854-6250
830 Sycamore Rd Arvin (93203) *(G-539)*
Grimmway Enterprises Inc 661 854-6200
11412 Malaga Rd Arvin (93203) *(G-540)*
Grimmway Enterprises Inc 661 845-5200
6900 Mountain View Rd Bakersfield (93307) *(G-541)*
Grimmway Enterprises Inc 661 399-0844
6301 S Zerker Rd Shafter (93263) *(G-361)*
Grimmway Enterprises Inc 661 845-3758
12000 Main St Lamont (93241) *(G-8738)*
Grimmway Farms, Arvin *Also called Grimmway Enterprises Inc (G-540)*
Grimmway Farms, Bakersfield *Also called Grimmway Enterprises Inc (G-541)*
Grimmway Farms 760 356-2513
2105 Anderholt Rd Holtville (92250) *(G-362)*
Grimmway Frozen Foods, Arvin *Also called Grimmway Enterprises Inc (G-539)*
Gripp, Temecula *Also called Bbk Performance Inc (G-6713)*
Griswald Industries, Perris *Also called Griswold Industries (G-7934)*
Griswold Industries 951 657-1718
24100 Water Ave Perris (92570) *(G-7934)*
Grizzard Cmmncations Group Inc 818 543-1315
110 N Maryland Ave Glendale (91206) *(G-14072)*
Grm Information MGT Services 562 373-9000
8500 Mercury Ln Pico Rivera (90660) *(G-27047)*
Grm Information MGT Svcs Inc 562 373-9000
8500 Mercury Ln Pico Rivera (90660) *(G-27048)*
Grobstein Horwath & Co 818 501-5200
15233 Ventura Blvd Fl 9 Van Nuys (91403) *(G-26361)*
Grobstein, Horwath & Company, Van Nuys *Also called Grobstein Horwath & Co (G-26361)*
Grocers Specialty Company (HQ) 323 264-5200
5200 Sheila St Commerce (90040) *(G-8484)*
Grolink Plant Company Inc (PA) 805 984-7958
4107 W Gonzales Rd Oxnard (93036) *(G-9191)*
Gross Convalescent Hospital 209 334-3760
321 W Turner Rd Lodi (95240) *(G-20639)*
Grosslight Insurance Inc 310 473-9611
1333 Westwood Blvd # 200 Los Angeles (90024) *(G-10732)*
Grossmont Center Management, La Mesa *Also called Grossmont Shopping Center Co (G-10992)*
Grossmont Family Medical Group 619 644-6500
5525 Grossmont Center Dr # 200 La Mesa (91942) *(G-19543)*
Grossmont Grdns Rtrement Cmnty, La Mesa *Also called Healthcare Group (G-24686)*
Grossmont Home Hlth & Hospice, La Mesa *Also called Grossmont Hospital Corporation (G-21588)*
Grossmont Hospital Corporation (HQ) 619 740-6000
5555 Grossmont Center Dr La Mesa (91942) *(G-21587)*
Grossmont Hospital Corporation 619 667-1900
8881 Fletcher Pkwy # 105 La Mesa (91942) *(G-21588)*
Grossmont Shopping Center Co 619 465-2900
5500 Grsmnt Ctr Dr # 213 La Mesa (91942) *(G-10992)*
Grossmont-Cuyamaca Community 619 644-7684
8800 Grossmont College Dr El Cajon (92020) *(G-25268)*
Grosvenor Properties Ltd 650 873-3200
380 S Airport Blvd South San Francisco (94080) *(G-12679)*
Grosvenor Visalia Associates 559 651-5000
9000 W Airport Dr Visalia (93277) *(G-12680)*
Ground Maintenance Services, Thousand Oaks *Also called Kevin Persons Inc (G-775)*
Groundwork Open Source Inc 415 992-4500
333 Bryant St Ste 100 San Francisco (94107) *(G-16241)*
Groundworks Inc 925 513-0300
2145 Elkins Way Ste C Brentwood (94513) *(G-3271)*
Group 3 Technologies 858 874-3081
4888 Ronson Ct Ste O San Diego (92111) *(G-17908)*
Group Avantica Inc 650 248-9678
2680 Bayshore Pkwy # 416 Mountain View (94043) *(G-15215)*
Group Delphi, Alameda *Also called Delphi Productions Inc (G-17120)*
Groupe Development Associates 209 473-6000
3255 W March Ln Fl 4 Stockton (95219) *(G-11972)*
Groupware Technology Inc (PA) 408 540-0090
541 Division St Campbell (95008) *(G-15955)*
Grove Lumber & Bldg Sups Inc (PA) 909 947-0277
1300 S Campus Ave Ontario (91761) *(G-6925)*
Grover Landscape Services Inc 209 545-4401
6224 Stoddard Rd Modesto (95356) *(G-287)*
Grower Direct Nut Company Inc 209 883-4890
2288 Geer Rd Hughson (95326) *(G-542)*
Growers Company Inc 831 424-3850
21570 Potter Rd Salinas (93908) *(G-14666)*
Growers Express LLC (PA) 831 757-9951
150 Mn St Ste 210 Salinas (93901) *(G-8739)*
Growers Street Cooling LLC 831 424-2929
1080 Growers St Salinas (93901) *(G-543)*
Growers Transplanting Inc (HQ) 831 449-3440
360 Espinosa Rd Salinas (93907) *(G-332)*
Growing Company Inc 916 379-9088
4 Wayne Ct Ste 3 Sacramento (95829) *(G-863)*
Growith Inc 805 650-6650
1069 Camero Way Fremont (94539) *(G-2241)*
Grubb Co Inc 510 339-0400
1960 Mountain Blvd Oakland (94611) *(G-11563)*
Grubb Ellis Rlty Investors LLC 714 667-8252
19700 Fairchild Ste 300 Irvine (92612) *(G-12311)*
Gruen Assoc Archtects Planners, Los Angeles *Also called Gruen Associates (G-26193)*
Gruen Associates 323 937-4270
6330 San Vicente Blvd # 200 Los Angeles (90048) *(G-26193)*
Grupe Co, Stockton *Also called Marchbrook Building Co (G-1212)*
Grupe Company (PA) 209 473-6000
3255 W March Ln Ste 400 Stockton (95219) *(G-11564)*
Grupe Dev Companynorthern Cal 209 473-6000
3255 W March Ln Ste 400 Stockton (95219) *(G-1367)*
Grupe Properties Co 209 956-7885
2944 W Swain Rd Stockton (95219) *(G-4565)*
Grupoex, La Mirada *Also called Mejico Express Inc (G-4868)*
Gs Brothers Inc (PA) 310 833-1369
2215 N Gaffey St San Pedro (90731) *(G-864)*
GS Levine Insurance Svcs Inc 858 481-8692
10505 Sorrento Valley Rd # 200 San Diego (92121) *(G-10733)*
Gs1 Group Inc 626 844-4377
70 S Lake Ave Ste 945 Pasadena (91101) *(G-16667)*
Gsa Design Inc 818 241-2558
4551 San Fernando Rd # 102 Glendale (91204) *(G-17202)*
Gsa Media, San Francisco *Also called Brite Media Group LLC (G-13960)*
GSC Logistics Inc (PA) 510 844-3700
530 Water St Fl 5 Oakland (94607) *(G-4348)*
GSe Construction Company Inc (PA) 925 447-0292
6950 Preston Ave Livermore (94551) *(G-1936)*
Gsf Builders, Placentia *Also called Gsf Enterprises Inc (G-1559)*
Gsf Enterprises Inc 714 524-9500
610 S Jefferson St Ste L Placentia (92870) *(G-1559)*
Gsg Associates Inc 626 585-1808
1010 E Union St Ste 203 Pasadena (91106) *(G-27049)*
Gstc LLC 650 773-7700
555 Bryant St Ste 400 Palo Alto (94301) *(G-27456)*
Gt Diamond, Irvine *Also called General Tool Inc (G-7933)*
Gt Nexus Inc (HQ) 510 808-2222
1111 Broadway 5f Oakland (94607) *(G-5622)*
GTE Corporation 559 562-0000
180 N Mirage Ave Lindsay (93247) *(G-27937)*
GTE Corporation 805 988-5760
1800 Solar Dr Oxnard (93030) *(G-14667)*
GTE Corporation 310 315-7597
2001 Broadway Fl 1 Santa Monica (90404) *(G-17203)*
GTE Corporation 805 441-4001
994 Mill St San Luis Obispo (93401) *(G-5623)*
GTE Corporation 661 328-2226
1220 Oak St Ste M Bakersfield (93304) *(G-5624)*
GTE Corporation 310 319-6148
2943 Exposition Blvd Santa Monica (90404) *(G-5625)*
Gtech, Santa Fe Springs *Also called Igt Global Solutions Corp (G-19228)*
Gtmr, Inyokern *Also called Global Tech MGT Resources Inc (G-25135)*
GTS, Chico *Also called Gas Transmission Systems Inc (G-25828)*
Gtt Communications (mp) Inc 714 327-2000
555 Anton Blvd Ste 200 Costa Mesa (92626) *(G-5626)*
Gtt Communications (mp) Inc (HQ) 925 201-2500
6800 Koll Center Pkwy # 200 Pleasanton (94566) *(G-5627)*
Gtxcel Inc 800 609-8994
2855 Telg Ave Ste 600 Berkeley (94705) *(G-15216)*
Guarachi Wine Partners Inc 818 225-5100
22837 Ventura Blvd # 300 Woodland Hills (91364) *(G-9104)*
Guarantee Mortgage Corporation 415 925-8080
300 Tamal Plz Ste 250 Corte Madera (94925) *(G-9927)*
Guarantee Real Estate 559 650-6030
756 W Shaw Ave Ste 105 Fresno (93704) *(G-11565)*
Guarantee Real Estate Corp 559 431-8600
6710 N West Ave Ste 108 Fresno (93711) *(G-11566)*
Guaranteed Rate Inc 760 310-6008
4180 La Jolla Village Dr # 315 La Jolla (92037) *(G-9850)*
Guaranteed Rate Inc 949 430-0809
31285 Temecula Pkwy Temecula (92592) *(G-9851)*
Guard Management Inc 858 279-8282
8001 Vickers St San Diego (92111) *(G-16668)*
Guard Systems District 1, Monterey Park *Also called Guard-Systems Inc (G-16671)*
Guard-Systems Inc 909 947-5400
1910 S Archibald Ave M2 Ontario (91761) *(G-16669)*
Guard-Systems Inc 323 881-6711
1190 Monterey Pass Rd Monterey Park (91754) *(G-16670)*
Guard-Systems Inc 323 881-6715
1190 Monterey Pass Rd Monterey Park (91754) *(G-16671)*
Guardco Security Services 209 723-4273
1360 W 18th St Merced (95340) *(G-16672)*
Guardian Computer Support 925 251-8800
7075 Commerce Cir Ste D Pleasanton (94588) *(G-16297)*
Guardian Eagle Security Inc 888 990-0002
11400 W Olympic Blvd Fl 2 Los Angeles (90064) *(G-16673)*
Guardian Environmental Inc (PA) 916 641-5695
4330 Pinell St Sacramento (95838) *(G-3527)*
Guardian General Insur Svcs, Glendale *Also called Ggis Insurance Services Inc (G-10730)*

ALPHABETIC

Guardian National Inc.....800 700-1467
20361 Prairie St Ste 1 Chatsworth (91311) *(G-16674)*
Guardian National Security, Chatsworth *Also called Guardian National Inc (G-16674)*
Guardian Rehabilitation Hosp.....323 930-4815
533 S Fairfax Ave Los Angeles (90036) *(G-21257)*
Guardian Security Agency, Concord *Also called Delta Personnel Services Inc (G-14870)*
Guardians of The Los Angeles.....310 479-2468
10780 Santa Monica Blvd # 225 Los Angeles (90025) *(G-20640)*
Guardnow Inc (PA).....877 482-7366
18663 Ventura Blvd # 217 Tarzana (91356) *(G-16675)*
Guardsmark LLC.....310 522-9603
1225 W 190th St Ste 280 Gardena (90248) *(G-16676)*
Guardsmark LLC.....310 216-9081
3000 S Robertson Blvd # 150 Los Angeles (90034) *(G-16677)*
Guardsmark LLC.....925 484-4412
4713 1st St Ste 215 Pleasanton (94566) *(G-16678)*
Guardsmark LLC (HQ).....714 619-9700
1551 N Tustin Ave Ste 650 Santa Ana (92705) *(G-16679)*
Guardsmark LLC.....415 956-6070
350 Sansome St San Francisco (94104) *(G-16680)*
Guardsmark LLC.....949 757-4693
1600 Dove St Ste 201 Newport Beach (92660) *(G-16681)*
Guardsmark LLC.....408 241-1493
4970 Ocamino Ste 110 Los Altos (94022) *(G-16682)*
Guardsmark LLC.....209 575-4972
1816 Tribute Rd Ste 150 Sacramento (95815) *(G-16683)*
Guardsmark LLC.....415 898-9022
505 Alexis Ct NAPA (94558) *(G-16684)*
Guardsmark LLC.....510 562-7606
100 Hegenberger Rd # 130 Oakland (94621) *(G-16685)*
Guardsmark LLC.....818 841-0288
101 S 1st St Ste 408 Burbank (91502) *(G-16686)*
Guardsmark LLC.....800 238-5878
4970 El Camino Real Los Altos (94022) *(G-16687)*
Guardsmark LLC.....858 499-0025
5095 Murphy Canyon Rd # 301 San Diego (92123) *(G-16688)*
Guardsmark LLC.....559 243-1217
600 W Shaw Ave Ste 200 Fresno (93704) *(G-16689)*
Guardsmark LLC.....818 841-0288
101 S 1st St Ste 408 Burbank (91502) *(G-16690)*
Guardsmark LLC.....415 898-9020
505 Alexis Ct NAPA (94558) *(G-16691)*
Guardsmark LLC.....831 769-8981
30 E San Joaquin St # 204 Salinas (93901) *(G-16692)*
Guardsmark LLC.....760 328-8320
77725 Enfield Ln Ste 170 Palm Desert (92211) *(G-16693)*
Guardsmark LLC.....650 685-2400
533 Airport Blvd Ste 303 Burlingame (94010) *(G-16694)*
Guardsmark LLC.....661 325-5906
5300 Lennox Ave Ste 102 Bakersfield (93309) *(G-16695)*
Guardsmark LLC.....310 225-3977
1225 W 190th St Ste 280 Gardena (90248) *(G-16696)*
Guardsmark LLC.....650 652-9130
1601 Bayshore Hwy Ste 350 Burlingame (94010) *(G-16697)*
Guardsmark LLC.....818 841-0288
101 S 1st St Ste 408 Burbank (91502) *(G-16698)*
Guardsmark LLC.....909 989-5345
2900 Adams St Ste C10a Riverside (92504) *(G-16699)*
Guavus Inc (PA).....650 243-3400
1800 Gateway Dr Ste 160 San Mateo (94404) *(G-15684)*
Gudgel Roofing Inc.....916 387-6900
5321 84th St Sacramento (95826) *(G-3177)*
Guerra Nut Shelling Company.....831 637-4471
190 Hillcrest Rd Hollister (95023) *(G-544)*
Guidance Software Inc (PA).....626 229-9191
1055 E Colo Blvd Ste 400 Pasadena (91106) *(G-15685)*
Guidance Solutions Inc.....310 754-4000
4134 Del Rey Ave Marina Del Rey (90292) *(G-16242)*
Guide Dogs For Blind Inc (PA).....415 499-4000
350 Los Ranchitos Rd San Rafael (94903) *(G-639)*
Guidebook Inc.....650 319-7233
1 Zoe St San Francisco (94107) *(G-15217)*
Guided Discoveries Inc.....951 659-6062
26800 Saunders Meadows Rd Idyllwild (92549) *(G-13464)*
Guidewire Software Inc (PA).....650 357-9100
1001 E Hillsdale Blvd # 800 Foster City (94404) *(G-15686)*
Guild Mortgage Company (PA).....800 283-8823
5898 Copley Dr Fl 4 San Diego (92111) *(G-9852)*
Guild Mortgage Company.....916 486-6257
3626 Fair Oaks Blvd Sacramento (95864) *(G-9928)*
Guild, The, Hawthorne *Also called Los Angeles Guild LLC (G-27511)*
Guinn Corporation.....661 325-6109
6533 Rosedale Hwy Bakersfield (93308) *(G-3431)*
Gulf- California Broadcast Co.....760 773-0342
31276 Dunham Way Thousand Palms (92276) *(G-5866)*
Gulfstream Aerospace Corp GA.....562 420-1818
4150 E Donald Douglas Dr Long Beach (90808) *(G-25846)*
Gumbiner & Savett Inc.....310 828-9798
1723 Cloverfield Blvd Santa Monica (90404) *(G-10993)*
Gumbiner, Savett, Finkel, Fing, Santa Monica *Also called Gumbiner & Savett Inc (G-10993)*
Gunderson Dettmer Stough Ville (PA).....650 321-2400
1200 Seaport Blvd Redwood City (94063) *(G-23294)*
Gursey Schneider & Co LLC (PA).....310 552-0960
1888 Century Park E # 900 Los Angeles (90067) *(G-26362)*
Guru Denim Inc (HQ).....323 266-3072
1888 Rosecrans Ave # 1000 Manhattan Beach (90266) *(G-8385)*
Guru Knits Inc.....323 235-9424
225 W 38th St Los Angeles (90037) *(G-17204)*
Gustine Mini Storage, Gustine *Also called Anderson Nut Company (G-509)*
Guthy-Renker Direct, Santa Monica *Also called Guthy-Renker LLC (G-8119)*
Guthy-Renker LLC (PA).....760 773-9022
3340 Ocean Park Blvd # 3055 Santa Monica (90405) *(G-8118)*
Guthy-Renker LLC.....949 454-1400
25892 Towne Centre Dr Foothill Ranch (92610) *(G-17205)*
Guthy-Renker LLC.....310 581-6250
3340 Ocean Park Blvd Fl 2 Santa Monica (90405) *(G-8119)*
Guy George.....831 728-2410
315 2nd St Ste A Watsonville (95076) *(G-114)*
Guy Yocom Construction Inc (PA).....951 284-3456
3299 Horseless Carriage R Norco (92860) *(G-3272)*
Guzmans Painting.....707 428-3727
2772 Bay Tree Dr Fairfield (94533) *(G-2453)*
Gva Enterprises Inc (PA).....213 484-0510
316 S Westlake Ave Los Angeles (90057) *(G-21258)*
Gva Enterprises Inc.....213 484-0784
415 S Union Ave Los Angeles (90017) *(G-21259)*
Gwf Power Systems LP.....925 933-7000
225 Lennon Ln Ste 120 Walnut Creek (94598) *(G-6287)*
Gyneclgic Onclogy Plvic Srgery, Los Gatos *Also called Sutter Health (G-25361)*
Gypsum Contractors Inc.....949 340-9100
23785 El Toro Rd Ste 135 Lake Forest (92630) *(G-2906)*
H & C Headwear Inc (PA).....310 324-5263
17145 Margay Ave Carson (90746) *(G-8344)*
H & D Construction, El Cajon *Also called Steve Duich Inc (G-3337)*
H & D Electric.....916 332-0794
5237 Walnut Ave Ste 100 Sacramento (95841) *(G-2602)*
H & F Grain Farms LLC.....805 754-4449
1181 S Wolff Rd Oxnard (93033) *(G-27938)*
H & H Transportation LLC.....951 817-2300
300 El Sobrante Rd Corona (92879) *(G-4193)*
H & H Truck Terminal, Victorville *Also called Hartwick & Hand Inc (G-4023)*
H & K Abouaf Corporation.....310 393-1282
9100 S Sepulveda Blvd # 1 Los Angeles (90045) *(G-22449)*
H & N Fish Company, Vernon *Also called H & N Foods International Inc (G-8633)*
H & N Foods International Inc (HQ).....323 586-9300
5580 S Alameda St Vernon (90058) *(G-8633)*
H & Q Asia Pacific Ltd.....650 838-8088
228 Hamilton Ave Fl 3 Palo Alto (94301) *(G-10150)*
H & R Accounts Inc.....619 819-8844
3131 Camino Del Rio N San Diego (92108) *(G-15218)*
H & R Block, Banning *Also called Akamai Holding Inc (G-13718)*
H & R Block, Los Angeles *Also called H&R Block Inc (G-13723)*
H & R Block Inc.....415 441-2666
1745 Van Ness Ave San Francisco (94109) *(G-23295)*
H & R Block Inc.....805 349-9266
401 N Broadway Ste B Santa Maria (93454) *(G-13721)*
H & R Block Inc.....707 643-1856
4300 Sonoma Blvd Ste 600 Vallejo (94589) *(G-13722)*
H & R Gunlund Ranches Inc.....559 864-8186
3510 W Saginaw Ave Caruthers (93609) *(G-157)*
H - Investment Company.....650 872-0500
450 B St Ste 1900 San Diego (92101) *(G-6926)*
H A Bowen Electric Inc.....510 483-0500
2055 Williams St San Leandro (94577) *(G-2603)*
H and H Drug Stores Inc.....209 931-5200
4692 E Waterloo Rd Stockton (95215) *(G-8120)*
H B, San Francisco *Also called Hassard Bonnington LLP (G-23303)*
H B A, Santa Monica *Also called Hirsch Bedner Associates (G-17220)*
H B J Corporation.....707 333-7066
5806 Frontier Way Carmichael (95608) *(G-2907)*
H C C S Inc.....916 454-5752
4700 Elvas Ave Sacramento (95819) *(G-20641)*
H C I, Norco *Also called Hci Inc (G-1937)*
H C Olsen Cnstr Co Inc.....626 359-8900
710 Los Angeles Ave Monrovia (91016) *(G-1433)*
H C S, Newport Beach *Also called Healthcare Cost Solutions Inc (G-26367)*
H C T Inc.....619 224-1234
1441 Quivira Rd San Diego (92109) *(G-12681)*
H D G Associates.....805 963-0744
1111 E Cabrillo Blvd Santa Barbara (93103) *(G-12682)*
H D R, Pasadena *Also called HDR Architecture Inc (G-25852)*
H D S I Managment.....323 231-1104
3460 S Broadway Los Angeles (90007) *(G-10994)*
H D Smith LLC.....310 641-1885
1370 E Victoria St Carson (90746) *(G-8260)*
H E L P Inc.....951 922-2305
53 S 6th St Banning (92220) *(G-23999)*
H F Cox Inc (PA).....661 366-3236
118 Cox Transport Way Bakersfield (93307) *(G-4194)*
H H M I, Stanford *Also called Howard Hughes Medical Inst (G-26530)*
H L Moe Co Inc (PA).....818 572-2100
526 Commercial St Glendale (91203) *(G-2242)*
H M C, Chula Vista *Also called Heartland Meat Company Inc (G-8670)*
H M H Engineers.....408 487-2200
1570 Oakland Rd San Jose (95131) *(G-25847)*
H M S, National City *Also called Hyperbaric MGT Systems Inc (G-19566)*
H Naraghi Farms, Escalon *Also called Noralco Inc (G-570)*
H O K, San Francisco *Also called Hellmuth Obata & Kassabaum Inc (G-26199)*
H P Sears Co Inc.....661 325-5981
2000 18th St Bakersfield (93301) *(G-17206)*
H Rauvel Inc (PA).....310 604-0060
1710 E Sepulveda Blvd Carson (90745) *(G-4566)*
H T V, Studio City *Also called High Technology Video Inc (G-18230)*
H U S D Maintenance Operation.....510 784-2666
24400 Amador St Hayward (94544) *(G-14318)*
H V Welker Co Inc.....408 263-4400
970 S Milpitas Blvd Milpitas (95035) *(G-3115)*

ALPHABETIC

H&E Equipment Services Inc ... 714 522-6590
14241 Alondra Blvd La Mirada (90638) ***(G-14544)***
H&R Block Inc ... 323 292-8836
4038 S Western Ave Los Angeles (90062) ***(G-13723)***
H.G. Fenton Company, San Diego *Also called Fenton Scripps Landing LLC* ***(G-11130)***
H/S Development Company LLC ... 661 327-0912
4800 Stockdale Hwy # 205 Bakersfield (93309) ***(G-1560)***
H2 Wellness Incorporated ... 310 362-1888
1801 Century Park E # 480 Los Angeles (90067) ***(G-15687)***
Ha-Le Aloha Convalescent Hosp, Ceres *Also called Mark One Corporation* ***(G-21308)***
Haaker Equipment Company (PA) ... 909 542-0800
2070 N White Ave La Verne (91750) ***(G-6679)***
Haas Factory Outlet, Anaheim *Also called Machining Time Savers Inc* ***(G-7858)***
Habenicht & Howlett A Corp ... 415 824-7040
25 Patterson St San Francisco (94124) ***(G-3411)***
Habitat For Humanity of Greate ... 310 323-4663
8739 Artesia Blvd Bellflower (90706) ***(G-24925)***
Habitat Rstration Sciences Inc (PA) ... 760 479-4210
1217 Distribution Way Vista (92081) ***(G-865)***
Habitat Rstration Sciences Inc ... 916 408-2990
3888 Cincinnati Ave Rocklin (95765) ***(G-866)***
Hacienda De Monterey, Palm Desert *Also called Atria Senior Living Group Inc* ***(G-24560)***
Hacienda Golf Club ... 562 694-1081
718 East Rd La Habra Heights (90631) ***(G-18958)***
Hacienda Health Care, Hanford *Also called Hacienda Rehabilitation & Heal* ***(G-20642)***
Hacienda Involved Parent Staff ... 408 535-6259
1290 Kimberly Dr San Jose (95118) ***(G-25269)***
Hacienda Rehabilitation & Heal ... 559 582-9221
361 E Grangeville Blvd Hanford (93230) ***(G-20642)***
Hackett Group Inc ... 310 842-8444
8522 National Blvd # 101 Culver City (90232) ***(G-16395)***
Hackney Electric Inc (PA) ... 949 264-4000
23286 Arroyo Vis Rcho STA Marg (92688) ***(G-2604)***
Hadco Metal Trading Co LLC ... 562 404-4040
14088 Borate St Santa Fe Springs (90670) ***(G-7373)***
Hagen Streiff Newton & Oshiro ... 415 982-4704
300 Montgomery St Ste 500 San Francisco (94104) ***(G-26363)***
Hagen Streiff Newton Oshiro ... 925 941-1050
1990 N Calif Blvd Ste 320 Walnut Creek (94596) ***(G-26364)***
Haggin Marketing Inc (PA) ... 415 289-1110
100 Shoreline Hwy A200 Mill Valley (94941) ***(G-13857)***
Haggin Oaks Golf Shop, Sacramento *Also called Morton Golf LLC* ***(G-18763)***
Hahn & Hahn LLP ... 626 796-9123
301 E Colo Blvd Ste 900 Pasadena (91101) ***(G-23296)***
Haider Spine Ctr Med Group Inc ... 951 413-0200
6276 River Crest Dr Ste A Riverside (92507) ***(G-19544)***
Haight Brown & Bonesteel LLP (PA) ... 213 542-8000
555 S Flower St Ste 4500 Los Angeles (90071) ***(G-23297)***
Haight Gdnr Holland & Knight, San Francisco *Also called Holland & Knight LLP* ***(G-23310)***
Hailwood Inc ... 805 487-4981
5755 Valentine Rd Ste 203 Ventura (93003) ***(G-10995)***
Hair Fashion Inc ... 310 274-0851
348 N Beverly Dr Beverly Hills (90210) ***(G-13678)***
Haircutters ... 562 690-2217
1230 W Imperial Hwy Ste A La Habra (90631) ***(G-13699)***
Hakes Sash & Door Inc ... 951 674-2414
31945 Corydon St Lake Elsinore (92530) ***(G-3052)***
Hal Hays Construction Inc (PA) ... 951 369-1008
4181 Latham St Riverside (92501) ***(G-1434)***
Hal-Mar-Jac Enterprises ... 415 467-1470
6271 3rd St San Francisco (94124) ***(G-16700)***
Halbert Brothers Inc ... 626 913-1800
17400 Chestnut St City of Industry (91748) ***(G-4349)***
Halcore Group Inc ... 626 575-0880
10941 Weaver Ave South El Monte (91733) ***(G-3802)***
Haldeman Inc ... 323 726-7011
2937 Tanager Ave Commerce (90040) ***(G-7739)***
Haldeman Inc ... 323 726-7011
2937 Tanager Ave Commerce (90040) ***(G-2243)***
Haleakala Ranch LLC ... 530 529-6651
9923 Tyler Rd Gerber (96035) ***(G-466)***
Half Moon Bay Golf Links, Half Moon Bay *Also called Ocean Links Corporation* ***(G-18767)***
Half Moon Bay Golf Links, Half Moon Bay *Also called Ocean Colony Partners LLC* ***(G-11992)***
Half Moon Fruit & Produce Co (PA) ... 530 662-1727
211 Court St Woodland (95695) ***(G-72)***
Hall AG Enterprises Inc ... 559 846-7360
759 S Madera Ave Kerman (93630) ***(G-665)***
Hall AG Services, Kerman *Also called Hall AG Enterprises Inc* ***(G-665)***
Hall Ambulance Service Inc ... 661 322-8741
2001 O St O Bakersfield (93301) ***(G-3803)***
Hall Company ... 209 364-0070
44328 W Nees Ave Firebaugh (93622) ***(G-363)***
Hall Management Corp ... 559 846-7382
759 S Madera Ave Kerman (93630) ***(G-27050)***
Hall Windsor ... 213 383-1547
1415 James M Wood Blvd Los Angeles (90015) ***(G-24675)***
Hall Wines LLC ... 707 967-2626
401 Saint Helena Hwy S Saint Helena (94574) ***(G-9105)***
Halliburton Energy Svcs Inc ... 760 353-2710
801 S 2nd St El Centro (92243) ***(G-1079)***
Halliburton Energy Svcs Inc ... 661 393-8111
34722 7th Standard Rd Bakersfield (93314) ***(G-1080)***
Halliburton Service Division, El Centro *Also called Halliburton Energy Svcs Inc* ***(G-1079)***
Hallmark Channel, Studio City *Also called Crown Media United States LLC* ***(G-5983)***
Hallmark Channel, The, Calabasas *Also called Crown Media Holdings Inc* ***(G-5849)***
Hallmark Distributing, Indio *Also called Triangle Distributing Co* ***(G-9089)***
Hallmark Inn, Davis *Also called Davis Hallmark Partnership* ***(G-12565)***
Hallmark Rehabilitation GP LLC ... 949 282-5900
27442 Portola Pkwy # 200 El Toro (92610) ***(G-24000)***
Halo ... 925 473-4642
4916 Chism Way Antioch (94531) ***(G-25539)***
Halo Business Intelligence, San Diego *Also called Iq4bis Software Incorporated* ***(G-7147)***
Halo Unlimted Inc ... 714 692-2270
1867 California Ave # 101 Corona (92881) ***(G-22966)***
Halstead Partnership ... 916 830-8000
2860 Gateway Oaks Dr # 300 Sacramento (95833) ***(G-10996)***
Halyard Health Inc ... 800 448-3569
43 Discovery Ste 100 Irvine (92618) ***(G-22967)***
Halyard Irvine, Irvine *Also called Halyard Health Inc* ***(G-22967)***
Hamann Construction ... 619 440-7424
1000 Pioneer Way El Cajon (92020) ***(G-1435)***
Hamblin's Auto & Body Shop, Riverside *Also called Hamblins Bdy Pnt Frame Sp Inc* ***(G-17800)***
Hamblins Bdy Pnt Frame Sp Inc ... 951 689-8440
7590 Cypress Ave Riverside (92503) ***(G-17800)***
Hamburger Home (PA) ... 323 876-0550
7120 Franklin Ave Los Angeles (90046) ***(G-24676)***
Hamburger Home ... 213 637-5000
3701 Wilshire Blvd # 900 Los Angeles (90010) ***(G-1188)***
Hamilton and Dillon Elc Inc ... 209 529-6292
1128 Reno Ave Modesto (95351) ***(G-2605)***
Hamilton Brwart Insur Agcy LLC ... 909 920-3250
1282 W Arrow Hwy Upland (91786) ***(G-10734)***
Hamilton Families ... 415 409-2100
1631 Hayes St San Francisco (94117) ***(G-24001)***
Hamilton Family Ranch ... 760 728-1358
2562 Doville Ranch Rd Fallbrook (92028) ***(G-218)***
Hamilton Partners ... 650 347-8800
1301 Shoreway Rd Ste 250 Burlingame (94010) ***(G-27457)***
Hamlow Ranches Inc ... 209 632-2873
4018 Swanson Rd Denair (95316) ***(G-234)***
Hammel Green & Abrahamson Inc ... 916 787-5100
1200 R St Ste 100 Sacramento (95811) ***(G-26194)***
Hammel Green & Abrahamson Inc ... 310 557-7600
1918 Main St Fl 3 Santa Monica (90405) ***(G-26195)***
Hammer Down Davila Cnstr ... 559 864-2001
2338 W Erie St Caruthers (93609) ***(G-1312)***
Hammonds Ranch Inc ... 209 364-6185
47375 W Dakota Ave Firebaugh (93622) ***(G-364)***
Hampstead Lafayette Hotel LLC ... 619 296-2101
2223 El Cajon Blvd San Diego (92104) ***(G-12683)***
Hampton Inn, San Diego *Also called Boykin Mgt Co Ltd Lblty Co* ***(G-12459)***
Hampton Inn, Elk Grove *Also called Dominion International Inc* ***(G-12586)***
Hampton Inn, Santa Ana *Also called Pacifica Hiorange LP* ***(G-13063)***
Hampton Inn, Garden Grove *Also called Stonebridge McWhinney LLC* ***(G-13306)***
Hampton Inn, Aliso Viejo *Also called Sunstone Hotel Properties Inc* ***(G-13326)***
Hampton Inn Norco Corona North ... 951 279-1111
1530 Hamner Ave Norco (92860) ***(G-12684)***
Hampton Inn San Diego-Downtown, San Diego *Also called Dimension Development Two LLC* ***(G-12571)***
Hampton Products Intl Corp (PA) ... 949 472-4256
50 Icon Foothill Ranch (92610) ***(G-7685)***
Hana Financial Inc (PA) ... 213 240-1234
1000 Wilshire Blvd Fl 20 Los Angeles (90017) ***(G-14545)***
Hancock Pk Rhblitation Ctr LLC ... 323 937-4860
505 N La Brea Ave Los Angeles (90036) ***(G-20643)***
Handford Community Center, Hanford *Also called Adventist Health System/West* ***(G-22649)***
Handlery Hotels Inc ... 415 781-7800
351 Geary St San Francisco (94102) ***(G-12685)***
Handlery Hotels Inc ... 415 781-4550
950 Hotel Cir N San Diego (92108) ***(G-12686)***
Handlery Union Square Hotel, San Francisco *Also called Handlery Hotels Inc* ***(G-12685)***
Hands-On Mobile Americas Inc (PA) ... 415 580-6400
208 Utah St Ste 300 San Francisco (94103) ***(G-15956)***
Handyman Connection, Orange *Also called Omnigen* ***(G-1228)***
Hanergy Holding America Inc ... 650 288-3722
1350 Bayshore Hwy Ste 825 Burlingame (94010) ***(G-6137)***
Hanes & Associates Inc ... 661 723-0779
43917 Division St Lancaster (93535) ***(G-3053)***
Hanford Adult School, Hanford *Also called Hanford Joint Un High Schl Dst* ***(G-24002)***
Hanford Community Hospital (HQ) ... 559 582-9000
450 Greenfield Ave Hanford (93230) ***(G-21589)***
Hanford Hotels Inc ... 714 957-6951
3131 Bristol St Costa Mesa (92626) ***(G-12687)***
Hanford Hotels LLC ... 714 210-0400
17542 17th St Ste 450 Tustin (92780) ***(G-12688)***
Hanford Joint Un High Schl Dst ... 559 583-5905
905 Campus Dr Hanford (93230) ***(G-24002)***
Hanford Nursing Rehabilitation, Hanford *Also called Mission Medical Entps Inc* ***(G-20792)***
Hangtown Knnel CLB Plcrvlle CA ... 530 622-4867
100 Placerville Dr Placerville (95667) ***(G-640)***
Hanil Development Inc ... 213 387-0111
3680 Wilshire Blvd B01 Los Angeles (90010) ***(G-12032)***
Hanjin Global Logistics, Carson *Also called Hanjin Transportation Co Ltd* ***(G-5092)***
Hanjin Transportation Co Ltd ... 310 522-5030
1111 E Watson Center Rd C Carson (90745) ***(G-5092)***
Hank Fisher Properties Inc ... 916 447-4444
2701 Capitol Ave Sacramento (95816) ***(G-24677)***
Hank Fisher Properties Inc ... 916 921-1970
641 Feature Dr Apt 233 Sacramento (95825) ***(G-21260)***
Hankey Group, Los Angeles *Also called Nowcom Corporation* ***(G-16440)***
Hanks Inc ... 909 350-8365
13866 Slover Ave Fontana (92337) ***(G-4022)***
Hanley Wood Mkt Intelligence (HQ) ... 714 540-8500
555 Anton Blvd Ste 950 Costa Mesa (92626) ***(G-26672)***

ALPHABETIC SECTION
Harris Mycfo Inc

Hanley Wood Mkt Intelligence (PA) 714 540-8500
555 Anton Blvd Ste 950 Costa Mesa (92626) ***(G-27939)***

Hanmi Bank (HQ) 213 382-2200
3660 Wilshire Blvd Ph A Los Angeles (90010) ***(G-9500)***

Hanna Brophy Mac Lean Mc Ale (PA) 510 839-1180
1956 Webster St Ste 450 Oakland (94612) ***(G-23298)***

Hannam Chain Super 1 Market, Los Angeles *Also called Hannam Chain USA Inc* ***(G-7217)***

Hannam Chain USA Inc (PA) 213 382-2922
2740 W Olympic Blvd Los Angeles (90006) ***(G-7217)***

Hannam Chain USA Inc 714 670-0670
5301 Beach Blvd Buena Park (90621) ***(G-11567)***

Hanover Builders Inc 818 706-2279
141 Duesenberg Dr Ste 6 Westlake Village (91362) ***(G-2606)***

Hans Technologies Inc 510 464-8018
1300 Clay St Ste 600 Oakland (94612) ***(G-2055)***

Hansen Bros Enterprises (PA) 530 273-3100
11727 La Barr Meadows Rd Grass Valley (95949) ***(G-1105)***

Hansen Icc LLC 760 268-7299
2111 Palomar Airport Rd Carlsbad (92011) ***(G-26365)***

Hansen Information Tech, Rancho Cordova *Also called Infor Public Sector Inc* ***(G-15701)***

Hansen Information Tech, Rancho Cordova *Also called Infor (us) Inc* ***(G-15700)***

Hansen Quality Loan Svcs Inc 858 909-4300
9339 Carroll Park Dr # 100 San Diego (92121) ***(G-11568)***

Hansen Ranches 559 992-3111
7124 Whitley Ave Corcoran (93212) ***(G-365)***

Hansol Goldpoint LLC 714 594-5073
12792 Valley View St # 211 Garden Grove (92845) ***(G-5093)***

Hanson Bridgett LLP 916 442-3333
500 Capitol Mall Ste 1500 Sacramento (95814) ***(G-23299)***

Hanson Bridgett LLP (PA) 415 543-2055
425 Market St Fl 26 San Francisco (94105) ***(G-23300)***

Hanson Distributing Company (PA) 626 224-9800
975 W 8th St Azusa (91702) ***(G-6736)***

Hanson Distributing Company 626 357-5241
975 W 8th St Azusa (91702) ***(G-6737)***

Hapag-Lloyd (america) LLC 510 251-8405
180 Grand Ave Ste 1535 Oakland (94612) ***(G-5094)***

Happy Camp Chamber Commerce 530 493-2900
35 Davis Rd Happy Camp (96039) ***(G-25089)***

Happy Pet Co 707 586-8660
5813 Skylane Blvd Windsor (95492) ***(G-619)***

Hara Software Inc, San Mateo *Also called Tunari Corp Inc* ***(G-15511)***

Haralambos Beverage Company 909 307-1777
26717 Palmetto Ave Redlands (92374) ***(G-9060)***

Haralambos Beverage Company (PA) 562 347-4300
2300 Pellissier Pl City of Industry (90601) ***(G-9061)***

Harbin Hot Springs, Middletown *Also called Heart Consciousness Church* ***(G-13493)***

Harbor Bay Club Inc 510 521-5414
200 Packet Landing Rd Alameda (94502) ***(G-18639)***

Harbor Building Services 310 320-2966
2701 Plaza Del Amo # 706 Torrance (90503) ***(G-14319)***

Harbor Corporate Park, Santa Ana *Also called Kaiser Foundation Hospitals* ***(G-19646)***

Harbor Department, San Pedro *Also called City of Los Angeles* ***(G-4746)***

Harbor Developmental Disabilit 310 540-1711
21231 Hawthorne Blvd Torrance (90503) ***(G-24926)***

Harbor Diesel and Eqp Inc 562 591-5665
537 W Anaheim St Long Beach (90813) ***(G-7847)***

Harbor Distributing LLC (HQ) 714 933-2400
5901 Bolsa Ave Huntington Beach (92647) ***(G-9062)***

Harbor Distributing LLC 310 538-5483
16407 S Main St Gardena (90248) ***(G-9063)***

Harbor Distributing Co, Gardena *Also called Harbor Distributing LLC* ***(G-9063)***

Harbor Freight Tools, Camarillo *Also called Central Purchasing LLC* ***(G-7928)***

Harbor Freight Tools Usa Inc 760 631-0347
820 Civic Center Dr Vista (92084) ***(G-5218)***

Harbor Freight Tools Usa Inc 760 336-0532
1750 N Imperial Ave El Centro (92243) ***(G-5095)***

Harbor Freight Tools Usa Inc 209 386-0829
1330 W Olive Ave Merced (95348) ***(G-5219)***

Harbor Freight Tools Usa Inc 925 757-8435
4403 Century Blvd Pittsburg (94565) ***(G-5220)***

Harbor Freight Tools Usa Inc 661 799-4907
23314 Valencia Blvd Valencia (91355) ***(G-5096)***

Harbor Freight Tools Usa Inc 951 304-2714
40516 Mrreta Hot Sprng Rd Murrieta (92563) ***(G-5097)***

Harbor Generating Station, Wilmington *Also called City of Los Angeles* ***(G-6114)***

Harbor Glen Care Center 626 963-7531
1033 E Arrow Hwy Glendora (91740) ***(G-20644)***

Harbor Health Care Inc 562 866-7054
16917 Clark Ave Bellflower (90706) ***(G-24678)***

Harbor Health Systems LLC 949 273-7020
3501 Jamboree Rd Ste 3000 Newport Beach (92660) ***(G-22968)***

Harbor Industrial Services 310 522-1193
211 N Marine Ave Wilmington (90744) ***(G-14483)***

Harbor Island Hotel Group LP 805 658-1212
1050 Schooner Dr Ventura (93001) ***(G-12689)***

Harbor Post Accute Care Center, Torrance *Also called Geri Care Inc* ***(G-20597)***

Harbor Regional Center, Torrance *Also called Harbor Developmental Disabilit* ***(G-24926)***

Harbor Ucla Med Foundation, Torrance *Also called Harbor-Ucla Med Foundation Inc* ***(G-27051)***

Harbor View Community Svcs Ctr, Long Beach *Also called Sunbridge Healthcare LLC* ***(G-21115)***

Harbor View Hotel Ventures LLC 619 239-6800
1646 Front St San Diego (92101) ***(G-12690)***

Harbor View Hotels Inc 650 340-8500
600 Airport Blvd Burlingame (94010) ***(G-12691)***

Harbor View House, San Pedro *Also called Healthview Inc* ***(G-24688)***

Harbor View Inn, Santa Barbara *Also called Beach Motel Partners Ltd* ***(G-12429)***

Harbor View Rehabilitation Ctr, Long Beach *Also called Sunbridge Harbor View* ***(G-20942)***

Harbor Villa Care Center 714 635-8131
861 S Harbor Blvd Anaheim (92805) ***(G-21261)***

Harbor Village II, Costa Mesa *Also called Independent Options* ***(G-24024)***

Harbor-Cla Med Ctr Dept Srgery 310 222-2700
1000 W Carson St 25 Torrance (90502) ***(G-21590)***

Harbor-Ucla Med Foundation Inc (PA) 310 222-5015
21840 S Norm Ave Ste 100 Torrance (90502) ***(G-27051)***

Harbor-Ucla Medical Center 310 222-2345
1000 W Carson St 2 Torrance (90502) ***(G-21591)***

Hard Rock Hotel, San Diego *Also called T-12 Three LLC* ***(G-13338)***

Hard Rock Hotel Palm Springs, Palm Springs *Also called Kittridge Hotels & Resorts LLC* ***(G-12889)***

Hardage Group of Companies 714 579-3200
3100 E Imperial Hwy Brea (92821) ***(G-12692)***

Hardage Investments Inc 510 795-1200
39150 Cedar Blvd Newark (94560) ***(G-10997)***

Hardcore Skateparks Inc 909 949-1601
285 N Benson Ave Upland (91786) ***(G-18823)***

Hardesty LLC (PA) 949 407-6625
19800 Macar Boule Ste 820 Irvine (92612) ***(G-14668)***

Harding & Associates, San Jose *Also called Harding Mktg Cmmunications Inc* ***(G-14148)***

Harding Mktg Cmmunications Inc (PA) 408 345-4545
377 S Daniel Way San Jose (95128) ***(G-14148)***

Hardisty Construction Administ 619 245-6828
410 W 30th St Ste A National City (91950) ***(G-1561)***

Hardrock Tile & Marble Inc 714 282-1766
23151 Verdugo Dr Ste 111 Laguna Hills (92653) ***(G-2817)***

Hardy & Harper Inc 714 444-1851
1312 E Warner Ave Santa Ana (92705) ***(G-1798)***

Hardy Diagnostics (PA) 805 346-2766
1430 W Mccoy Ln Santa Maria (93455) ***(G-7267)***

Haringa Inc (PA) 800 499-9991
14422 Best Ave Santa Fe Springs (90670) ***(G-17207)***

Harley Ellis Devereaux Corp 510 268-3800
417 Montgomery St Ste 400 San Francisco (94104) ***(G-26196)***

Harley Ellis Devereaux Corp 213 542-4500
601 Suth Fgroa St Ste 500 Los Angeles (90017) ***(G-26197)***

Harley Ellis Devereuax, Los Angeles *Also called Harley Ellis Devereaux Corp* ***(G-26197)***

Harmatz Entertaintment Corp 760 941-1032
435 W Vista Way Vista (92083) ***(G-18522)***

Harmonium Inc (PA) 858 684-3080
9245 Activity Rd Ste 200 San Diego (92126) ***(G-24466)***

Harmonium Inc 858 271-4000
8450 Mira Mesa Blvd San Diego (92126) ***(G-13465)***

Harmony Escrow Inc 949 474-1134
17100 Gillette Ave Irvine (92614) ***(G-11569)***

Harmony Home Health LLC 916 933-9777
2500 Ranch Rd Ste 104 Placerville (95667) ***(G-22450)***

Harmony Homecare, Placerville *Also called Harmony Home Health LLC* ***(G-22450)***

Haro & Haro Enterprises Inc 209 334-2035
115 W Walnut St Ste 4 Lodi (95240) ***(G-666)***

Harold E Nutter Inc 916 334-4343
5934 Rosebud Ln Sacramento (95841) ***(G-2607)***

Harold Jones Landscape Inc 805 582-7443
40 W Cochran St Ste 206 Simi Valley (93065) ***(G-770)***

Harold L Karpman MD, Beverly Hills *Also called Cardivsclr Mdcl Grp of Sthrn* ***(G-19403)***

Harper Construction Co Inc (PA) 619 233-7900
2241 Kettner Blvd Ste 300 San Diego (92101) ***(G-1562)***

Harper Mechanical Contrs LLC 619 543-1296
1011 Camino Del Rio S San Diego (92108) ***(G-7218)***

Harpo Entertainment Group, West Hollywood *Also called Harpo Productions Inc* ***(G-18090)***

Harpo Inc 312 633-1000
1041 N Formosa Ave West Hollywood (90046) ***(G-18396)***

Harpo Productions Inc 312 633-1000
1041 N Formosa Ave West Hollywood (90046) ***(G-18090)***

Harpo Studios, West Hollywood *Also called Harpo Inc* ***(G-18396)***

Harrington Industrial Plas LLC (HQ) 909 597-8641
14480 Yorba Ave Chino (91710) ***(G-7722)***

Harris & Associates Inc 949 655-3900
22 Executive Park Ste 200 Irvine (92614) ***(G-25848)***

Harris & Associates Inc (PA) 925 827-4900
1401 Wllw Pca Rd 500 Concord (94520) ***(G-25849)***

Harris & Associates Cnstr MGT, Concord *Also called Harris & Associates Inc* ***(G-25849)***

Harris & Ruth Painting Contg (PA) 626 960-4004
2107 W San Bernardino Rd West Covina (91790) ***(G-2454)***

Harris & Sloan Consulting 916 921-2800
2295 Gateway Oaks Dr # 165 Sacramento (95833) ***(G-27940)***

Harris Construction Co Inc 559 251-0301
5286 E Home Ave Fresno (93727) ***(G-1563)***

Harris Corporation 626 584-4527
1400 S Shamrock Ave Monrovia (91016) ***(G-25850)***

Harris Direct 818 357-2040
21250 Califa St Ste 114 Woodland Hills (91367) ***(G-17208)***

Harris Farm Horse Division, Coalinga *Also called Harris Farms Inc* ***(G-366)***

Harris Farms Inc 559 884-2203
27366 W Oakland Ave Coalinga (93210) ***(G-366)***

Harris Farms Inc 559 935-0717
24505 W Dorris Ave Coalinga (93210) ***(G-367)***

Harris Farms Inc 559 884-2477
23300 W Oakland Ave Coalinga (93210) ***(G-368)***

Harris Freeman & Co Inc (PA) 714 765-1190
3110 E Miraloma Ave Anaheim (92806) ***(G-8850)***

Harris L Woods Elec Contr 562 945-8751
9214 Norwalk Blvd Santa Fe Springs (90670) ***(G-2608)***

Harris Moran, Davis *Also called Hmclause Inc* ***(G-26529)***

Harris Mycfo Inc 480 348-7725
2200 Geng Rd Ste 100 Palo Alto (94303) ***(G-27458)***

ALPHABETIC

Harris Stockwell (PA) ALPHABETIC SECTION

Harris Stockwell (PA) ... 310 277-6669
3580 Wilshire Blvd Fl 19 Los Angeles (90010) *(G-23301)*

Harris Tea Company, Anaheim *Also called Harris Freeman & Co Inc (G-8850)*

Harris Woolf Almonds ... 559 884-1040
26060 Colusa Ave Coalinga (93210) *(G-545)*

Harris Woolf California Almond, Coalinga *Also called Harris Woolf Almonds (G-545)*

Harrison Iyke ... 909 463-8409
7611 Etiwanda Ave Rancho Cucamonga (91739) *(G-16886)*

Harrison Drywall Inc ... 415 821-9584
447 10th St San Francisco (94103) *(G-2908)*

Harrison Nichols Co Ltd ... 626 337-5020
501 W Foothill Blvd Azusa (91702) *(G-4350)*

Harrison, E J & Sons Recycling, Ventura *Also called E J Harrison & Sons Inc (G-6473)*

Harry Group Inc ... 310 631-9646
2839 E El Presidio St Carson (90810) *(G-5098)*

Harry's Auto Collision, Los Angeles *Also called Harrys Auto Body Inc (G-17757)*

Harry's Berries, Oxnard *Also called Iwamoto & Gean Farm (G-74)*

Harrys Auto Body Inc ... 323 933-4600
1013 S La Brea Ave Los Angeles (90019) *(G-17757)*

Hart Howerton Ltd (PA) ... 415 439-2200
1 Union St Fl 3 San Francisco (94111) *(G-771)*

Hart King Coldren A Prof Corp ... 714 432-8700
4 Hutton Cntre Dr Ste 900 Santa Ana (92707) *(G-23302)*

Harte Hanks Inc ... 210 829-9000
2337 W Commonwealth Ave Fullerton (92833) *(G-16138)*

Harte-Hanks Direct Mail/Califo ... 714 738-5478
2337 W Commonwealth Ave Fullerton (92833) *(G-14073)*

Harte-Hanks Mkt Intelligence (PA) ... 858 450-1667
15015 Ave Of Science # 110 San Diego (92128) *(G-16139)*

Hartford Casualty Insurance Co ... 415 836-4800
595 Market St Ste 500 San Francisco (94105) *(G-10427)*

Hartford Fire Insurance Co ... 916 294-1000
12009 Foundation Pl # 100 Gold River (95670) *(G-10735)*

Hartford Fire Insurance Co ... 213 452-5179
777 S Figueroa St Ste 700 Los Angeles (90017) *(G-10736)*

Hartman Industries ... 909 428-0114
14933 Whittram Ave Fontana (92335) *(G-7374)*

Hartmann Studios Incorporated ... 510 232-5060
70 W Ohio Ave Ste H Richmond (94804) *(G-17209)*

Hartwick & Hand Inc (PA) ... 760 245-1666
16953 N D St Victorville (92394) *(G-4023)*

Harvard Grand Inv Inc A Cal ... 310 513-7560
2 Civic Plaza Dr Carson (90745) *(G-12312)*

Harvest Facility Holdings LP ... 909 793-8691
10 Terracina Blvd Ofc Redlands (92373) *(G-11139)*

Harvest Food Distributors, National City *Also called Harvest Meat Company Inc (G-8669)*

Harvest Landscape Entps Inc ... 714 283-4298
1290 N Hancock St Ste 202 Anaheim (92807) *(G-867)*

Harvest Landscape Maintenance, Anaheim *Also called Harvest Landscape Entps Inc (G-867)*

Harvest Management Sub LLC ... 805 543-0187
1299 Briarwood Dr San Luis Obispo (93401) *(G-24679)*

Harvest Meat Company Inc (HQ) ... 619 477-0185
1022 Bay Marina Dr # 106 National City (91950) *(G-8669)*

Harvest of The Sea, Los Angeles *Also called Ore-Cal Corp (G-8642)*

Harvest Sensations LLC (PA) ... 213 895-6968
3030 E Washington Blvd Los Angeles (90023) *(G-8740)*

Harvest Technical Service Inc ... 925 937-4874
1839 Ygnacio Valley Rd # 390 Walnut Creek (94598) *(G-14669)*

Harvest V Citizens Patrol ... 951 926-9763
25098 Avenida Valencia Homeland (92548) *(G-16701)*

Harvey Inc ... 858 769-4000
9455 Ridgehaven Ct # 200 San Diego (92123) *(G-1564)*

Harvey Apartments, Los Angeles *Also called C M I Management Inc (G-11105)*

Harvey General Contracting, San Diego *Also called Harvey Inc (G-1564)*

Harveys Industries Inc ... 714 277-4700
1918 E Glenwood Pl Santa Ana (92705) *(G-8386)*

Hasc, Los Angeles *Also called Hospital Assn Southern Cal (G-24928)*

Haskell & White (PA) ... 949 450-6200
300 Spectrum Center Dr # 300 Irvine (92618) *(G-26366)*

Haskell Company (inc) ... 925 960-1815
478 Lindbergh Ave Livermore (94551) *(G-1436)*

Hassard Bonnington LLP (PA) ... 415 288-9800
275 Battery St Ste 1600 San Francisco (94111) *(G-23303)*

Hat Creek Cnstr & Mtls Inc (PA) ... 530 335-5501
24339 State Highway 89 Burney (96013) *(G-2056)*

Hatch Animation & Prod Studios ... 973 454-8654
1171 S Robertson Blvd Los Angeles (90035) *(G-18468)*

Hatch Mott Macdonald Group Inc ... 925 469-8010
4301 Hacienda Dr Ste 300 Pleasanton (94588) *(G-25851)*

Hatchbeauty Products LLC (PA) ... 310 396-7070
10951 W Pico Blvd Ste 300 Los Angeles (90064) *(G-8261)*

Hathaway Children and Family, Pacoima *Also called Hathaway-Sycamores Chld Fam Sv (G-24680)*

Hathaway Dinwiddie Cnstr Co ... 415 986-2718
565 Laurelwood Rd Santa Clara (95054) *(G-10998)*

Hathaway Dinwiddie Cnstr Co ... 415 986-2718
275 Battery St Ste 300 San Francisco (94111) *(G-1565)*

Hathaway Dinwiddie Cnstr Group ... 408 988-4200
565 Laurelwood Rd Santa Clara (95054) *(G-10999)*

Hathaway Dinwiddie Cnstr Group (PA) ... 415 352-1501
275 Battery St Ste 300 San Francisco (94111) *(G-1566)*

Hathaway Resource Center ... 323 837-0838
5701 S Eastrn Ave Ste 550 Los Angeles (90040) *(G-24003)*

Hathaway-Sycamores Chld Fam Sv ... 818 897-1766
12502 Van Nuys Blvd # 120 Pacoima (91331) *(G-24680)*

Hathaway-Sycamores Chld Fam Sv ... 323 257-9600
840 N Avenue 66 Los Angeles (90042) *(G-24681)*

Hathaway-Sycamores Chld Fam Sv ... 661 942-5749
44738 Sierra Hwy Lancaster (93534) *(G-24682)*

Hathaway-Sycamores Chld Fam Sv ... 323 733-0322
1968 W Adams Blvd Los Angeles (90018) *(G-24683)*

Hathaway-Sycamores Chld Fam Sv (PA) ... 626 844-1677
210 S De Lacey Ave # 110 Pasadena (91105) *(G-24684)*

Haulaway Storage Cntrs Inc ... 800 826-9040
11292 Western Ave Stanton (90680) *(G-4567)*

Havas Edge LLC (PA) ... 760 929-1357
2386 Faraday Ave Ste 200 Carlsbad (92008) *(G-13858)*

Havas Formula LLC ... 619 234-0345
1215 Cushman Ave San Diego (92110) *(G-27750)*

Havasu Landing Casino (PA) ... 760 858-5380
1 Main St Needles (92363) *(G-12693)*

Hawaiian Airlines Inc ... 310 417-1677
200 World Way Ste 9 Los Angeles (90045) *(G-4804)*

Hawaiian Gardens Casino (PA) ... 562 860-5887
21520 Pioneer Blvd # 305 Hawaiian Gardens (90716) *(G-19220)*

Hawaiian Gardens Casino ... 562 860-5887
11871 Carson St Hawaiian Gardens (90716) *(G-19221)*

Hawaiian Hotels & Resorts Inc ... 805 480-0052
2830 Borchard Rd Newbury Park (91320) *(G-12694)*

Hawk Transportation Inc ... 800 709-4295
15238 Arrow Blvd Fontana (92335) *(G-4195)*

Hawker Pacific Aerospace ... 818 765-6201
11240 Sherman Way Sun Valley (91352) *(G-17978)*

Haworth Inc ... 408 262-6400
931 Cadillac Ct Milpitas (95035) *(G-6817)*

Hawthorn Suites, Anaheim *Also called Sunstone Hotel Investors LLC (G-13321)*

Hawthorne Convalescent Center, Hawthorne *Also called Wilshire Hlth & Cmnty Svcs Inc (G-21424)*

Hawthorne Healthcare ... 310 679-9732
11630 Grevillea Ave Hawthorne (90250) *(G-20645)*

Hawthorne Lift Systems, Coachella *Also called Naumann/Hobbs Mtl Hdlg Corp II (G-7778)*

Hawthorne Lift Systems, Fontana *Also called Naumann/Hobbs Material (G-7868)*

Hawthorne Lift Systems, San Marcos *Also called Naumann/Hobbs Material (G-7869)*

Hawthorne Machinery Co (PA) ... 858 674-7000
16945 Camino San Bernardo San Diego (92127) *(G-14484)*

Hawthorne Machinery Co (HQ) ... 858 674-7000
16945 Camino San Bernardo San Diego (92127) *(G-14485)*

Hawthorne Machinery Co ... 858 674-7000
16945 Camino San Bernardo San Diego (92127) *(G-17801)*

Hawthorne Machinery Co ... 858 974-6800
8050 Othello Ave San Diego (92111) *(G-7770)*

Hay House Inc (PA) ... 760 431-7695
2776 Loker Ave W Carlsbad (92010) *(G-9165)*

Hay Kuhn Inc ... 760 353-0124
1880 Jeffrey Rd El Centro (92243) *(G-9270)*

Hayday Farms Inc ... 760 922-4713
15500 S Commercial St Blythe (92225) *(G-25)*

Hayes Mansion Conference Ctr ... 408 226-3200
200 Edenvale Ave San Jose (95136) *(G-12695)*

Hayes Welding Inc ... 760 246-4878
12522 Violet Rd Adelanto (92301) *(G-17954)*

Haynes and Boone LLP ... 650 687-8800
525 University Ave # 400 Palo Alto (94301) *(G-23304)*

Haynes Building Service LLC ... 626 359-6100
16027 Arrow Hwy Ste I Baldwin Park (91706) *(G-14320)*

Haynes Family Programs Inc ... 909 593-2581
233 Baseline Rd La Verne (91750) *(G-24685)*

Hayward Active Club, Hayward *Also called 24 Hour Fitness Usa Inc (G-18600)*

Hayward Area Recreation Pkdist ... 510 881-6700
1099 E St Hayward (94541) *(G-20295)*

Hayward Area Recreation Pkdist ... 510 317-2300
1401 Golf Course Rd Hayward (94541) *(G-18744)*

Hayward Area Recreation Pkdist ... 510 881-6750
1099 E St Rear Hayward (94541) *(G-4568)*

Hayward Baker Inc ... 805 933-1331
1780 E Lemonwood Dr Santa Paula (93060) *(G-3528)*

Hayward Convalescent Hospital, Hayward *Also called Hillsdale Group LP (G-21270)*

Hayward Hills Health Care Ctr, Hayward *Also called Mariner Health Care Inc (G-20766)*

Hayward Police Officers Assn ... 510 293-7207
300 W Winton Ave Hayward (94544) *(G-25172)*

Hayward Sisters Hospital (HQ) ... 510 264-4000
27200 Calaroga Ave Hayward (94545) *(G-21592)*

Hazard Construction Company ... 858 587-3600
6465 Marindustry Dr San Diego (92121) *(G-1893)*

Hazel Creek Assisted Living, Orangevale *Also called Summerville At Hazel Creek LLC (G-24824)*

Hazel Hawkins Memorial Hosp, Hollister *Also called San Benito Health Care Dst (G-21844)*

Hazens Investment LLC ... 310 642-1111
6101 W Century Blvd Los Angeles (90045) *(G-12696)*

HB Healthcare Associates LLC ... 714 887-0144
18811 Florida St Huntington Beach (92648) *(G-20646)*

HB Orchards Co Inc ... 530 743-5121
9909 State Highway 70 Marysville (95901) *(G-235)*

HB Parkco Construction Inc (PA) ... 714 444-1441
3190 Arprt Loop Dr Ste F Costa Mesa (92626) *(G-3273)*

Hba Incorporated ... 714 635-8602
421 E Cerritos Ave Anaheim (92805) *(G-2818)*

Hba International, Santa Monica *Also called Hirsch/Bedner Intl Inc (G-17221)*

Hbe Rental, Grass Valley *Also called Hansen Bros Enterprises (G-1105)*

HBO Indpendent Productions Inc (HQ) ... 310 382-3000
2500 Broadway Ste 400 Santa Monica (90404) *(G-18091)*

HCA Inc ... 408 729-2801
225 N Jackson Ave San Jose (95116) *(G-21593)*

HCA Inc ... 818 676-4000
7300 Medical Center Dr West Hills (91307) *(G-21594)*

ALPHABETIC

ALPHABETIC SECTION

HCA Inc..949 496-1122
  654 Camino De Los Mares San Clemente (92673) *(G-21595)*
HCC Investors LLC...858 759-7200
  18550 Seven Bridges Rd Rancho Santa Fe (92091) *(G-18959)*
HCC Surety Group, Los Angeles *Also called American Contrs Indemnity Co* *(G-10565)*
Hci Inc (HQ)...951 520-4202
  3166 Hrseless Carriage Rd Norco (92860) *(G-1937)*
Hci Systems Inc (PA)...909 628-7773
  1354 S Parkside Pl Ontario (91761) *(G-2609)*
Hcis, Ontario *Also called Hci Systems Inc* *(G-2609)*
Hcl America Inc (HQ)...408 733-0480
  330 Potrero Ave Sunnyvale (94085) *(G-16280)*
Hcl Finance Inc (PA)..408 845-9035
  2560 Mission College Blvd Santa Clara (95054) *(G-9853)*
Hco Holding I Corporation (HQ)...323 583-5000
  999 N Sepulveda Blvd El Segundo (90245) *(G-12068)*
Hcp Inc (PA)..949 407-0700
  1920 Main St Ste 1200 Irvine (92614) *(G-12248)*
Hcr Manorcare Med Svcs Fla LLC.......................................925 274-1325
  1975 Tice Valley Blvd Walnut Creek (94595) *(G-20647)*
Hcr Manorcare Med Svcs Fla LLC.......................................949 587-9000
  24962 Calle Aragon Aliso Viejo (92653) *(G-20648)*
Hcr Manorcare Med Svcs Fla LLC.......................................714 241-9800
  11680 Warner Ave Fountain Valley (92708) *(G-20649)*
Hcr Manorcare Med Svcs Fla LLC.......................................916 967-2929
  7807 Uplands Way Citrus Heights (95610) *(G-20650)*
Hcr Manorcare Med Svcs Fla LLC.......................................951 925-9171
  1717 W Stetson Ave Hemet (92545) *(G-20651)*
Hcr Manorcare Med Svcs Fla LLC.......................................408 735-7200
  1150 Tilton Dr Sunnyvale (94087) *(G-20652)*
Hcr Manorcare Med Svcs Fla LLC.......................................925 975-5000
  1226 Rossmoor Pkwy Walnut Creek (94595) *(G-20653)*
Hcr Manorcare Med Svcs Fla LLC.......................................760 944-0331
  944 Regal Rd Encinitas (92024) *(G-20654)*
Hd Supply Construction Supply..707 863-8282
  1995 W Cordelia Rd Fairfield (94534) *(G-7686)*
Hd Supply Construction Supply..408 428-2000
  595 Brennan St San Jose (95131) *(G-7687)*
Hdd Construction, Caruthers *Also called Hammer Down Davila Cnstr* *(G-1312)*
Hdl Companies, The, Diamond Bar *Also called Hdl Coren & Cone* *(G-27052)*
Hdl Coren & Cone..909 861-4335
  1340 Valley Vista Dr # 200 Diamond Bar (91765) *(G-27052)*
HDR Architecture Inc...626 584-1700
  251 S Lake Ave Ste 1000 Pasadena (91101) *(G-25852)*
HDR Architecture Inc...415 546-4242
  560 Mission St Ste 900 San Francisco (94105) *(G-25853)*
HDR Engineering Inc...714 730-2300
  3230 El Camino Real # 200 Irvine (92602) *(G-25854)*
HDR Engineering Inc...619 231-4865
  401 B St Ste 1110 San Diego (92101) *(G-25855)*
HDR Engineering Inc...858 712-8400
  8690 Balboa Ave Ste 200 San Diego (92123) *(G-27459)*
HDR Engineering Inc...626 584-1700
  251 S Lake Ave Ste 1000 Pasadena (91101) *(G-27460)*
HDR Engineering Inc...925 974-2500
  100 Pringle Ave Ste 400 Walnut Creek (94596) *(G-25856)*
HDR Engineering Inc...415 546-4200
  560 Mission St San Francisco (94105) *(G-27461)*
HDR Engineering Inc...916 564-4214
  2379 Gateway Oaks Dr # 200 Sacramento (95833) *(G-25857)*
HDR Engineering Inc...909 626-0967
  431 W Baseline Rd Claremont (91711) *(G-25858)*
HDR Engineering Inc...916 817-4700
  2365 Iron Point Rd # 300 Folsom (95630) *(G-27462)*
HDR Environmental Ope...858 712-8400
  8690 Balboa Ave Ste 200 San Diego (92123) *(G-26198)*
HDR/Cardno Entrix Joint Ventr..916 817-4700
  2365 Iron Point Rd # 300 Folsom (95630) *(G-25859)*
HEAD START, Quincy *Also called Sierra Cscade Fmly Opprtnities* *(G-24515)*
Head Start Program, Long Beach *Also called Charles Drew Univ Mdcine Scnce* *(G-24427)*
Headquarters, Los Angeles *Also called Nationwide Legal LLC* *(G-23463)*
Headstart, Watsonville *Also called Encompass Community Services* *(G-23960)*
Headstart Nursery Inc (PA)...408 842-3030
  4860 Monterey Rd Gilroy (95020) *(G-9192)*
Headstrong Corporation..408 732-8700
  150 Mathilda Pl Ste 200 Sunnyvale (94086) *(G-16396)*
Healdburg Senior Living Cmnty, Healdsburg *Also called Avalon Health Care Inc* *(G-20396)*
Healdsburg Dist Hosp Rehab Svc.......................................707 433-9150
  1540 Healdsburg Ave Healdsburg (95448) *(G-10279)*
Healdsburg District Hospital, Healdsburg *Also called North Sonoma County Hosp Dst* *(G-21760)*
Health & Human Services, San Diego *Also called County of San Diego* *(G-23896)*
Health & Human Services, Fallbrook *Also called County of San Diego* *(G-23897)*
Health & Human Services, Auburn *Also called County of Placer* *(G-23877)*
Health & Human Services, San Diego *Also called County of San Diego* *(G-23900)*
Health & Human Services, Auburn *Also called County of Placer* *(G-22707)*
Health & Human Services, San Diego *Also called County of San Diego* *(G-22057)*
Health & Rehabilitation Center..408 377-9275
  2065 Los Gatos Almaden Rd San Jose (95124) *(G-20655)*
Health Advocates LLC..818 995-9500
  14721 Califa St Van Nuys (91411) *(G-24927)*
Health and Human Service, Crescent City *Also called County of Del Norte* *(G-24904)*
Health and Human Service Agcy, San Diego *Also called County of San Diego* *(G-23898)*
Health and Human Services, Sacramento *Also called County of Sacramento* *(G-23891)*
Health and Human Services, San Diego *Also called County of San Diego* *(G-23903)*
Health and Human Services Agcy, San Diego *Also called County of San Diego* *(G-23902)*
Health and Social Services, Fairfield *Also called County of Solano* *(G-23920)*

Health By Design...916 974-3322
  2636 Fulton Ave Ste 100 Sacramento (95821) *(G-22451)*
Health Care Agency, Santa Ana *Also called County of Orange* *(G-22206)*
Health Care Developers, Hesperia *Also called Foremost Healthcare Centers* *(G-11132)*
Health Care Group, San Diego *Also called L C C H Associates Inc* *(G-21286)*
Health Care Investments Inc...310 323-3194
  1140 W Rosecrans Ave Gardena (90247) *(G-20656)*
Health Care Services Agency, San Leandro *Also called County of Alameda* *(G-23793)*
Health Care Workers Union (PA)..510 251-1250
  560 Thomas L Berkley Way Oakland (94612) *(G-11000)*
Health Comp Administrators (PA).......................................559 499-2450
  621 Santa Fe Ave Fresno (93721) *(G-10737)*
Health Department, Salinas *Also called County of Monterey* *(G-24908)*
Health Department, NAPA *Also called County of NAPA* *(G-22706)*
Health Dept, Los Angeles *Also called County of Los Angeles* *(G-22700)*
Health Educ Economic Devlpmnt..510 604-6143
  304 Coral Reef Rd Alameda (94501) *(G-27463)*
Health Educatn Psychiatry Offs, Los Angeles *Also called Kaiser Foundation Hospitals* *(G-22755)*
Health Entps Lf Long Plan...818 654-0330
  5805 Sepulveda Blvd Van Nuys (91411) *(G-22452)*
Health Entps Life-Long Plans, Van Nuys *Also called Health Entps Lf Long Plan* *(G-22452)*
Health Fitness America, Irvine *Also called Equinox-76th Street Inc* *(G-20318)*
Health Information Partners, Newport Beach *Also called US Healthcare Partners Inc* *(G-21404)*
Health Line Clinical Lab, Burbank *Also called Taurus West Inc* *(G-22289)*
Health Link Medi Van..310 981-9500
  6053 W Century Blvd # 900 Los Angeles (90045) *(G-5221)*
Health Net Inc...818 676-5603
  21271 Burbank Blvd Fl 2-5 Woodland Hills (91367) *(G-10280)*
Health Net Inc (HQ)...818 676-6000
  21650 Oxnard St Fl 25 Woodland Hills (91367) *(G-10281)*
Health Net Inc...818 543-9037
  101 N Brand Blvd Ste 1500 Glendale (91203) *(G-10282)*
Health Net Inc...510 465-9600
  155 Grand Ave Lbby Oakland (94612) *(G-10283)*
Health Net Inc...916 935-3520
  12033 Foundation Pl Gold River (95670) *(G-10284)*
Health Net California Inc...916 935-1600
  11971 Foundation Pl Gold River (95670) *(G-10285)*
Health Net California Inc (HQ)..818 676-6775
  21281 Burbank Blvd Fl 4 Woodland Hills (91367) *(G-10286)*
Health Net Cmnty Solutions Inc..800 675-6110
  11971 Foundation Pl Gold River (95670) *(G-19545)*
Health Net Community Solutions..818 676-6000
  21650 Oxnard St Fl 25 Woodland Hills (91367) *(G-10287)*
Health Net Federal Svcs LLC (HQ).....................................916 935-5000
  2025 Aerojet Rd Rancho Cordova (95742) *(G-10288)*
Health Net Life Insurance Co..800 865-6288
  21281 Burbank Blvd Woodland Hills (91367) *(G-10289)*
Health Net of California, Woodland Hills *Also called Health Net Inc* *(G-10280)*
Health Plan of San Joaquin...209 942-6300
  7751 S Manthey Rd French Camp (95231) *(G-10290)*
Health Plan of San Mateo, South San Francisco *Also called San Mateo Health Commission* *(G-23050)*
Health Pointe Medical Group (PA).....................................714 956-2663
  1717 E Lincoln Ave Anaheim (92805) *(G-19546)*
Health Quest, NAPA *Also called Back Street Fitness Inc* *(G-18606)*
Health Resources Corp...714 754-5454
  2701 S Bristol St Santa Ana (92704) *(G-21596)*
Health Services Advisory Group...818 409-9220
  700 N Brand Blvd Fl 1 Glendale (91203) *(G-22969)*
Health Services Dept, Palos Verdes Peninsu *Also called County of Los Angeles* *(G-21517)*
Health Services Dept, Los Angeles *Also called County of Los Angeles* *(G-21519)*
Health Services, Dept of, Acton *Also called County of Los Angeles* *(G-22131)*
Health Services, Dept of, Commerce *Also called County of Los Angeles* *(G-24906)*
Health Services, Dept of, Downey *Also called County of Los Angeles* *(G-22699)*
Health Services, Dept of, Los Angeles *Also called County of Los Angeles* *(G-21518)*
Health Services, Dept of, Los Angeles *Also called County of Los Angeles* *(G-22418)*
Health Services, Dept of, Los Angeles *Also called County of Los Angeles* *(G-19468)*
Health Services, Dept of, Los Angeles *Also called County of Los Angeles* *(G-22701)*
Health Services, Dept of, Torrance *Also called County of Los Angeles* *(G-8251)*
Health Services, Dept of, City of Industry *Also called County of Los Angeles* *(G-23844)*
Health Services, Dept of, Los Angeles *Also called County of Los Angeles* *(G-19471)*
Health Services, Dept of, Wilmington *Also called County of Los Angeles* *(G-19472)*
Health Services, Dept of, Los Angeles *Also called County of Los Angeles* *(G-19475)*
Health Source Staffing Inc..619 220-8044
  438 Camino Ste 101 San Diego (92108) *(G-22453)*
Health System, San Mateo *Also called County of San Mateo* *(G-22710)*
Health System Medical Network, Beverly Hills *Also called Cedars-Sinai Medical Center* *(G-21473)*
Health Trust (PA)...408 513-8700
  3180 Newberry Dr Ste 200 San Jose (95118) *(G-25136)*
Health Valley Foods Inc..626 334-3241
  16007 Cmino De La Cantera Irwindale (91702) *(G-8851)*
Healthcare Barton System..530 543-5575
  1111 Sierra At Tahoe Rd Twin Bridges (95735) *(G-17210)*
Healthcare Barton System (PA)..530 541-3420
  2170 South Ave South Lake Tahoe (96150) *(G-21597)*
Healthcare Barton System..530 543-5685
  2170 South Ave South Lake Tahoe (96150) *(G-21262)*
Healthcare California...559 243-9990
  5709 N West Ave Fresno (93711) *(G-22454)*
Healthcare Centre of Fresno, Fresno *Also called Fresno Skilled Nursing* *(G-20583)*

Healthcare Centre of Fresno 559 268-5361
1665 M St Fresno (93721) ***(G-20657)***
Healthcare Cost Solutions Inc 949 721-2795
1200 Newprt Cntr Dr 190 Newport Beach (92660) ***(G-26367)***
Healthcare Ctr of Downey LLC 562 869-0978
12023 Lakewood Blvd Downey (90242) ***(G-20658)***
Healthcare Group, Escondido *Also called Las Villas Del Norte* ***(G-20720)***
Healthcare Group 619 463-0281
5480 Marengo Ave Ste 619 La Mesa (91942) ***(G-24686)***
Healthcare MGT Partners LLC 949 263-8620
20 Executive Park Ste 155 Irvine (92614) ***(G-27053)***
Healthcare MGT Systems Inc (PA) 619 521-9641
900 Lane Ave Ste 190 Chula Vista (91914) ***(G-20659)***
Healthcare MGT Systems Inc 951 654-9347
980 W 7th St San Jacinto (92582) ***(G-20660)***
Healthcare Partners LLC 714 995-1000
1236 N Magnolia Ave Anaheim (92801) ***(G-22970)***
Healthcare Partners LLC 562 304-2100
3932 Long Beach Blvd Long Beach (90807) ***(G-19547)***
Healthcare Partners LLC 562 429-2473
4910 Airport Plaza Dr Long Beach (90815) ***(G-22971)***
Healthcare Partners LLC 562 988-7000
2600 Redondo Ave Ste 405 Long Beach (90806) ***(G-19548)***
Healthcare Partners LLC 626 444-0333
3144 Santa Anita Ave # 201 El Monte (91733) ***(G-19549)***
Healthcare Partners LLC 323 720-1144
2601 Via Campo Montebello (90640) ***(G-19550)***
Healthcare Partners LLC (HQ) 310 354-4200
2175 Park Pl El Segundo (90245) ***(G-19551)***
Healthcare Partners LLC 714 964-6229
3501 S Harbor Blvd # 100 Santa Ana (92704) ***(G-22972)***
Healthcare Partners Med Group, Long Beach *Also called Healthcare Partners LLC* ***(G-19547)***
Healthcare Partners Med Group, El Monte *Also called Healthcare Partners LLC* ***(G-19549)***
Healthcare Partners Med Group, Montebello *Also called Healthcare Partners LLC* ***(G-19550)***
Healthcare Partners Med Group, El Segundo *Also called Healthcare Partners LLC* ***(G-19551)***
Healthcare Pathways Management 831 373-1111
5 Mandeville Ct Monterey (93940) ***(G-22455)***
Healthcare Services, French Camp *Also called San Joaquin Hospital* ***(G-21850)***
Healthcare Services Group Inc 562 494-7939
5199 E Pacific Coast Hwy # 402 Long Beach (90804) ***(G-28133)***
Healthcare System 2000 714 899-2000
9191 Westminster Ave Garden Grove (92844) ***(G-19552)***
Healthcomp 559 499-2450
621 Santa Fe Ave Fresno (93721) ***(G-10738)***
Healthcomp Administrators, Fresno *Also called Healthcomp* ***(G-10738)***
Healthfusion Holdings Inc (HQ) 858 523-2120
100 N Rios Ave Solana Beach (92075) ***(G-12069)***
Healthline Systems LLC (HQ) 858 673-1700
17085 Camino San Bernardo San Diego (92127) ***(G-15688)***
Healthlink Staffing Inc 818 972-2140
4444 W Riverside Dr # 105 Burbank (91505) ***(G-14885)***
Healthpocket Inc 800 984-8015
444 Castro St Ste 710 Mountain View (94041) ***(G-10240)***
Healthright 360 408 934-1110
1340 Tully Rd Ste 304 San Jose (95122) ***(G-22741)***
Healthright 360 213 216-0484
2515 Camino Del Rio S San Diego (92108) ***(G-22742)***
Healthsmart Management Service 714 947-8600
10855 Bus Ctr Dr Ste C Cypress (90630) ***(G-10739)***
Healthsmart Pacific Inc (PA) 562 595-1911
20377 Sw Acacia St # 110 Newport Beach (92660) ***(G-21598)***
HealthSouth Corporation 714 832-9200
14851 Yorba St Tustin (92780) ***(G-22743)***
HealthSouth Corporation 661 323-5500
5001 Commerce Dr Bakersfield (93309) ***(G-24687)***
HealthSouth Corporation 916 929-9431
75 Scripps Dr Sacramento (95825) ***(G-22744)***
HealthSouth Corporation 510 547-2244
3875 Telegraph Ave Oakland (94609) ***(G-22143)***
HealthSouth Physicians, Bakersfield *Also called Physicians Plz Surgical Ctr LP* ***(G-19871)***
Healthsport Ltd A Ltd Partnr (PA) 707 822-3488
300 Dr Martin Luther Arcata (95521) ***(G-18640)***
Healthsport-Arcata, Arcata *Also called Healthsport Ltd A Ltd Partnr* ***(G-18640)***
Healthstream Inc 800 733-8737
17085 Camino San Bernardo San Diego (92127) ***(G-15689)***
Healthview Inc (PA) 310 547-3341
921 S Beacon St San Pedro (90731) ***(G-24688)***
Healthview Inc 562 468-0136
12750 Center Court Dr S # 410 Cerritos (90703) ***(G-24689)***
Healthy Beginnings French Camp 209 468-6147
500 W Hospital Rd French Camp (95231) ***(G-19553)***
Healtth Sanitation Services, Santa Maria *Also called Valley Garbage Rubbish Co Inc* ***(G-6592)***
Healy & Co 925 543-5700
268 Bush St 2704 San Francisco (94104) ***(G-28134)***
Hearsay Social Inc (PA) 888 990-3777
185 Berry St Ste 3800 San Francisco (94107) ***(G-15690)***
Hearst Communications Inc 805 375-3121
2323 Teller Rd Newbury Park (91320) ***(G-6005)***
Hearst Communications Inc 415 441-4444
900 Front St San Francisco (94111) ***(G-5867)***
Hearst Television Inc 831 422-8206
238 John St Salinas (93901) ***(G-5868)***
Heart Consciousness Church (PA) 707 987-2477
18424 Harbin Springs Rd Middletown (95461) ***(G-13493)***
Heartflow Inc (PA) 650 241-1221
1400 Seaport Blvd Bldg B Redwood City (94063) ***(G-15957)***
Hearthstone Inc 818 385-0005
24151 Ventura Blvd Calabasas (91302) ***(G-10151)***
Heartland Meat Company Inc 619 407-3668
3461 Main St Chula Vista (91911) ***(G-8670)***
Heartland Payment Systems Inc 650 678-2824
548 Shorebird Cir # 3101 Redwood City (94065) ***(G-17211)***
Heartland Payment Systems Inc 760 324-0133
510 Cerritos Way Cathedral City (92234) ***(G-17212)***
Heartland Payment Systems Inc 707 338-0510
1007 W College Ave Ste B Santa Rosa (95401) ***(G-17213)***
Heartland Payment Systems Inc 818 784-6665
4701 Petit Ave Encino (91436) ***(G-17214)***
Heartland Payment Systems Inc 415 518-4810
1460 Golden Gate Ave # 5 San Francisco (94115) ***(G-17215)***
Heartland Payment Systems Inc 916 844-9548
5325 Elkhorn Blvd Sacramento (95842) ***(G-17216)***
HEARTLAND PAYMENT SYSTEMS, INC., Redwood City *Also called Heartland Payment Systems Inc* ***(G-17211)***
HEARTLAND PAYMENT SYSTEMS, INC., Santa Rosa *Also called Heartland Payment Systems Inc* ***(G-17213)***
HEARTLAND PAYMENT SYSTEMS, INC., Encino *Also called Heartland Payment Systems Inc* ***(G-17214)***
HEARTLAND PAYMENT SYSTEMS, INC., San Francisco *Also called Heartland Payment Systems Inc* ***(G-17215)***
HEARTLAND PAYMENT SYSTEMS, INC., Sacramento *Also called Heartland Payment Systems Inc* ***(G-17216)***
Heat Ventures LLC, San Francisco *Also called Hvsf Transition LLC* ***(G-13860)***
Heather Ann Creations, Costa Mesa *Also called Alfreds Pictures Frames Inc* ***(G-16978)***
Heavenly Construction Inc 408 723-4954
370 Umbarger Rd Ste A San Jose (95111) ***(G-3529)***
Heavenly Greens, San Jose *Also called Heavenly Construction Inc* ***(G-3529)***
Heaviland Enterprises Inc 760 598-7065
2180 La Mirada Dr Vista (92081) ***(G-868)***
Hebrew Home For Aged Disabled 415 334-2500
302 Silver Ave San Francisco (94112) ***(G-20661)***
Heffernan Group, San Francisco *Also called Heffernan Insurance Brokers* ***(G-10740)***
Heffernan Insurance Brokers 415 398-7733
180 Howard St Ste 200 San Francisco (94105) ***(G-10740)***
HEI Irvine LLC 949 553-8332
2120 Main St Irvine (92614) ***(G-12697)***
HEI Long Beach LLC 562 983-3400
701 W Ocean Blvd Long Beach (90831) ***(G-12698)***
HEI Mission Valley LP 619 299-2729
901 Camino Del Rio S San Diego (92108) ***(G-12699)***
Heidi Corporation 626 333-6317
15815 Amar Rd City of Industry (91744) ***(G-1313)***
Heidrick & Struggles Intl Inc 415 981-2854
1 California St Ste 2400 San Francisco (94111) ***(G-14670)***
Height Brown and Bonesteel 213 241-0900
555 S Flower St Ste 4500 Los Angeles (90071) ***(G-23305)***
Heilind Electronics Inc 559 651-0168
700 N Plaza Dr Visalia (93291) ***(G-7576)***
Heimark Distributing, Santa Fe Springs *Also called Triangle Distributing Co* ***(G-9088)***
Heinaman Contract Glazing Inc (PA) 949 587-0266
26981 Vista Ter Ste E Lake Forest (92630) ***(G-3530)***
Helen Evans Home For Children, Hacienda Heights *Also called Care Associates Inc* ***(G-24579)***
Helen Woodward Animal Center (PA) 858 756-4117
6461 El Apajo Rancho Santa Fe (92067) ***(G-25540)***
Helinet Aviation Services LLC (PA) 818 902-0229
16303 Waterman Dr Van Nuys (91406) ***(G-18092)***
Helio, Los Angeles *Also called Virgin Mobile Usa Inc* ***(G-5726)***
Heliopower (PA) 951 677-7755
25747 Jefferson Ave Murrieta (92562) ***(G-2244)***
Helios Healthcare LLC 916 482-0465
2540 Carmichael Way Carmichael (95608) ***(G-20662)***
Helios Healthcare LLC 831 449-1515
350 Iris Dr Salinas (93906) ***(G-20663)***
Helios Healthcare LLC 530 345-1306
587 Rio Lindo Ave Chico (95926) ***(G-21263)***
Helios Healthcare LLC 925 935-6630
1911 Oak Park Blvd Pleasant Hill (94523) ***(G-20664)***
Helios Healthcare LLC 707 644-7401
2200 Tuolumne St Vallejo (94589) ***(G-21264)***
Helix Healthcare Inc 619 465-4411
7050 Parkway Dr La Mesa (91942) ***(G-22073)***
Helix Water District 619 466-0585
1233 Vernon Way El Cajon (92020) ***(G-6354)***
Hellman & Friedman Capital IV 415 788-5111
1 Maritime Plz Ste 1200 San Francisco (94111) ***(G-12313)***
Hellmann Wrldwide Lgistics Inc 310 847-4600
2270 E 220th St Long Beach (90810) ***(G-5099)***
Hellmann Wrldwide Lgistics Inc 310 847-4600
2270 E 220th St Carson (90810) ***(G-5100)***
Hellmuth Obata & Kassabaum Inc (HQ) 415 243-0555
1 Bush St Ste 200 San Francisco (94104) ***(G-26199)***
Hellmuth Obata & Kassabaum Inc 310 838-9555
9530 Jefferson Blvd Culver City (90232) ***(G-26200)***
Hellosign, San Francisco *Also called Jn Projects Inc* ***(G-13772)***
Helm Management Co (PA) 619 589-6222
4668 Nebo Dr Ste A La Mesa (91941) ***(G-11570)***
Helm Technical Services, El Dorado Hills *Also called G R Helm Inc* ***(G-14881)***
Helm, The, La Mesa *Also called Helm Management Co* ***(G-11570)***
Helman Group Ltd (PA) 805 487-7772
1621 Beacon Pl Oxnard (93033) ***(G-7499)***

ALPHABETIC SECTION HEs Transportation Svcs Inc

Helmet House Inc (PA)........800 421-7247
26855 Malibu Hills Rd Calabasas Hills (91301) ***(G-8345)***
Help At Home Inc........916 933-9050
4535 Mcuri Flat Rd Ste 2h Placerville (95667) ***(G-24004)***
Help For The Hurting Inc........909 796-4222
2205 S Artesia St San Bernardino (92408) ***(G-24005)***
Help Group West (PA)........818 781-0360
13130 Burbank Blvd Sherman Oaks (91401) ***(G-22745)***
Help Hospitalized Veterans II........951 926-4500
36585 Penfield Ln Winchester (92596) ***(G-24006)***
Help Unlmted Personnel Svc Inc........805 962-4646
319 E Carrillo St Ste 102 Santa Barbara (93101) ***(G-22456)***
Helping Hands of Westminster, Westminster *Also called Helping Hands Sanctuary of Ida* ***(G-20666)***
Helping Hands Pantry, San Bernardino *Also called Help For The Hurting Inc* ***(G-24005)***
Helping Hands Sanctuary of Ida........805 687-6651
3880 Via Lucero Santa Barbara (93110) ***(G-20665)***
Helping Hands Sanctuary of Ida........714 892-6686
240 Hospital Cir Westminster (92683) ***(G-20666)***
Helping Hearts Foundation Inc........916 368-7200
3050 Fite Cir Ste 205 Sacramento (95827) ***(G-24690)***
Helpline Youth Counseling (PA)........562 273-0722
14181 Telegraph Rd Whittier (90604) ***(G-24007)***
Hemacare Corporation (PA)........818 986-3883
15350 Sherman Way Van Nuys (91406) ***(G-22973)***
Hemar & Rousso Attys At Law, Encino *Also called Hemar Rousso & Heald L L P* ***(G-23306)***
Hemar Rousso & Heald L L P........818 501-3800
15910 Ventura Blvd # 1201 Encino (91436) ***(G-23306)***
Hemet Valley Ambulance, Hemet *Also called American Medical Response Inc* ***(G-3761)***
Hemet Vly Med Center-Education........951 652-2811
1117 E Devonshire Ave Hemet (92543) ***(G-21599)***
Hemington Landscape Svcs Inc........530 677-9290
4170 Business Dr Cameron Park (95682) ***(G-869)***
Hemodialysis Inc (PA)........818 500-8736
710 W Wilson Ave Glendale (91203) ***(G-22628)***
Hemodialysis Inc........818 365-6961
14901 Rinaldi St Ste 100 Mission Hills (91345) ***(G-22629)***
Hendrickson Trucking Inc........916 387-9614
7080 Florin Perkins Rd Sacramento (95828) ***(G-4196)***
Henkel Corporation........925 458-8086
2850 Willow Pass Rd Bay Point (94565) ***(G-25860)***
Henkels & McCoy Inc........925 493-7800
2840 Ficus St Pomona (91766) ***(G-1938)***
Henley Enterprises Inc........714 990-1900
230 N Brea Blvd Brea (92821) ***(G-17217)***
Henry Avocado Corporation (PA)........760 745-6632
2355 E Lincoln Ave Escondido (92027) ***(G-256)***
Henry Broadcasting Co........415 285-1133
2277 Jerrold Ave San Francisco (94124) ***(G-5777)***
Henry Bros Electronics Inc........714 525-4350
1511 E Orangethorpe Ave A Fullerton (92831) ***(G-15958)***
Henry Hibino Farms........831 757-3081
106 Rico St Salinas (93907) ***(G-73)***
Henry J Kaiser Fmly Foundation (PA)........650 854-9400
2400 Sand Hill Rd Ste 200 Menlo Park (94025) ***(G-12157)***
Henry Mayo Newhall Hospital (PA)........661 253-8000
23845 Mcbean Pkwy Valencia (91355) ***(G-21600)***
Henry Mayo Newhall Mem Hlth........661 253-8000
23845 Mcbean Pkwy Valencia (91355) ***(G-21601)***
Henry Mayo Newhall Mem Hosp........661 253-8112
23845 Mcbean Pkwy Valencia (91355) ***(G-19554)***
Henry Mayo Newhall Mem Hosp........661 253-8227
23845 Mcbean Pkwy Santa Clarita (91355) ***(G-22974)***
Henry Wine Group LLC (HQ)........707 745-8500
4301 Industrial Way Benicia (94510) ***(G-9106)***
Henry Wine Group of C.A., The, Benicia *Also called Henry Wine Group LLC* ***(G-9106)***
Henry's Pub, Berkeley *Also called Hotel Durant A Ltd Partnership* ***(G-12787)***
Henrymayo Newhall Mem Hosp, Valencia *Also called Henry Mayo Newhall Mem Hlth* ***(G-21601)***
Hensel Phelps Construction Co........858 266-7979
5251 Viewridge Ct Ste 120 San Diego (92123) ***(G-1567)***
Hensel Phelps Construction Co........408 452-1800
226 Airport Pkwy Ste 150 San Jose (95110) ***(G-1568)***
Hensel Phelps Construction Co........619 544-6828
9404 Genesee Ave Ste 140 La Jolla (92037) ***(G-1569)***
Hensel Phlps Grnte Hngr JV........949 852-0111
18850 Von Kamon 100 Irvine (92612) ***(G-1570)***
Henson Recording Studio, Los Angeles *Also called Jim Henson Company Inc* ***(G-18097)***
Henwood Energy Services Inc (HQ)........916 955-6031
2379 Gateway Oaks Dr # 110 Sacramento (95833) ***(G-25861)***
Heppner Hardwoods Inc........626 969-7983
555 W Danlee St Azusa (91702) ***(G-6927)***
Herald Christian Health Center (PA)........626 286-8700
8841 Garvey Ave Rosemead (91770) ***(G-19555)***
Herb Thyme Farm Inc........603 542-3690
7909 Crossway Dr Pico Rivera (90660) ***(G-26)***
Herbalife Intl Amer Inc (HQ)........310 410-9600
800 W Olympic Blvd # 406 Los Angeles (90015) ***(G-8262)***
Herbalife Ltd Inc........310 410-9600
990 W 190th St Ste 650 Torrance (90502) ***(G-8989)***
Herbs Pool Service Inc........415 479-4040
3769 Redwood Hwy San Rafael (94903) ***(G-17218)***
Herc Rentals Inc........707 586-4444
5500 Commerce Blvd Rohnert Park (94928) ***(G-17677)***
Herc Rentals Inc........310 233-5000
22422 S Alameda St Carson (90810) ***(G-17678)***
Herc Rentals Inc........916 448-2228
1025 16th St Sacramento (95814) ***(G-17679)***
Herc Rentals Inc........661 392-3661
6315 Snow Rd Bakersfield (93308) ***(G-17680)***
Herc Rentals Inc........707 747-4444
5251 Industrial Way Benicia (94510) ***(G-17681)***
Herc Rentals Inc........510 633-2040
7727 Oakport St Oakland (94621) ***(G-17682)***
Herc Rentals Prosolutions, Oakland *Also called Herc Rentals Inc* ***(G-17682)***
Herca Construction Services, Perris *Also called Herca Telecomm Services Inc* ***(G-7771)***
Herca Telecomm Services Inc........951 940-5941
18610 Beck St Perris (92570) ***(G-7771)***
Hercules Fitness........510 724-2900
600 Alfred Nobel Dr Hercules (94547) ***(G-18641)***
Here Films........310 806-4288
10990 Wilshire Blvd Los Angeles (90024) ***(G-27941)***
Here Media Inc (PA)........310 943-5858
10990 Wilshire Blvd Fl 18 Los Angeles (90024) ***(G-5628)***
Heritage 1 Window and Building........916 481-5030
4300 Jetway Ct North Highlands (95660) ***(G-6928)***
Heritage Bank of Commerce (HQ)........408 947-6900
150 Almaden Blvd Lbby San Jose (95113) ***(G-9501)***
Heritage California Aco, Northridge *Also called Regal Medical Group Inc* ***(G-25153)***
Heritage Community Credit Un (PA)........916 364-1700
10399 Old Placerville Rd Sacramento (95827) ***(G-9604)***
Heritage Community Credit Un........916 364-1700
10399 Old Clasaville Rd Rancho Cordova (95670) ***(G-9605)***
Heritage Conalescent Hospital, Sacramento *Also called Horizon West Inc* ***(G-20675)***
Heritage Construction........714 573-2223
18001 Irvine Blvd Tustin (92780) ***(G-1799)***
Heritage Estates-Livermore, Livermore *Also called Leisure Care LLC* ***(G-11156)***
Heritage Gardens Hlth Care Ctr, Loma Linda *Also called Heritage Health Care Inc* ***(G-20667)***
Heritage Golf Group Inc........949 369-6226
990 Avenida Talega San Clemente (92673) ***(G-18745)***
Heritage Golf Group Inc........661 254-4401
27330 Tourney Rd Valencia (91355) ***(G-18746)***
Heritage Health Care, Lancaster *Also called High Desert Med Corp A Med Grp* ***(G-19557)***
Heritage Health Care Inc........909 796-0216
25271 Barton Rd Loma Linda (92354) ***(G-20667)***
Heritage House, Camarillo *Also called Wilshire Health and Cmnty Svcs* ***(G-24858)***
Heritage Indemnity Company........303 987-5500
23 Pasteur Irvine (92618) ***(G-10428)***
Heritage Inn, Ridgecrest *Also called Great Western Hotels Corp* ***(G-12676)***
Heritage Interests LLC (PA)........916 481-5030
4300 Jetway Ct North Highlands (95660) ***(G-3054)***
Heritage Land Company Inc........209 444-1700
111 N Zuckerman Rd Stockton (95206) ***(G-288)***
Heritage Landscape Inc........818 999-2041
7949 Deering Ave Canoga Park (91304) ***(G-772)***
Heritage Manor Inc........626 573-3141
610 N Garfield Ave Monterey Park (91754) ***(G-20668)***
Heritage Medical Group........760 956-1286
12370 Hesperia Rd Ste 6 Victorville (92395) ***(G-22975)***
Heritage Medical Group (PA)........661 327-4411
4580 California Ave Bakersfield (93309) ***(G-19556)***
Heritage One Carpentry Inc........530 345-6622
2107 Forest Ave Ste 100 Chico (95928) ***(G-6929)***
Heritage One Door and Building........916 481-5030
4300 Jetway Ct North Highlands (95660) ***(G-6930)***
Heritage Pointe, Mission Viejo *Also called Jewish Home For The Aged of or* ***(G-24698)***
Heritage Psychiatric Health, Oakland *Also called Telecare Corporation* ***(G-22109)***
HERITAGE, THE, San Francisco *Also called San Francisco Ladies Protecti* ***(G-24802)***
Herman Health Care Center........408 269-0701
2295 Plummer Ave San Jose (95125) ***(G-20669)***
Herman Sanitarium........408 269-0701
2295 Plummer Ave San Jose (95125) ***(G-20670)***
Herman Weissker Inc (HQ)........951 826-8800
1645 Brown Ave Riverside (92509) ***(G-1939)***
Hermitage Health Care........707 823-1238
7025 Corline Ct Sebastopol (95472) ***(G-22144)***
Hermitage Hlthcr Mnkn Mnr........410 651-0011
400 Circle Dr Angwin (94508) ***(G-21265)***
Hero, San Diego *Also called Renovate America Inc* ***(G-15414)***
Herren Enterprises Inc........949 951-1666
23091 Terra Dr Laguna Hills (92653) ***(G-3804)***
Herrero Builders Incorporated (PA)........415 824-7675
2100 Oakdale Ave San Francisco (94124) ***(G-1437)***
Herrick Hospital, Berkeley *Also called Surgery Center of Alta Bates* ***(G-20076)***
Herring Broadcasting Company........858 270-6900
4757 Morena Blvd San Diego (92117) ***(G-5869)***
Herring Networks Inc........858 270-6900
4757 Morena Blvd San Diego (92117) ***(G-5870)***
Herritage Bank of Commerce, San Jose *Also called Heritage Bank of Commerce* ***(G-9501)***
Hertz, Carson *Also called Herc Rentals Inc* ***(G-17678)***
Hertz, Bakersfield *Also called Herc Rentals Inc* ***(G-17680)***
Hertz Claim Management Corp........626 296-4760
2923 Bradley St Ste 190 Pasadena (91107) ***(G-17683)***
Hertz Corporation........818 997-0414
2627 N Hollywood Way # 8 Burbank (91505) ***(G-17684)***
Hertz Corporation........408 450-6025
1000 Walsh Ave Santa Clara (95050) ***(G-17685)***
Hertz Corporation........925 680-0316
30 S Buchanan Cir Pacheco (94553) ***(G-17686)***
Hertz Corporation........650 624-6391
177 S Airport Blvd South San Francisco (94080) ***(G-17687)***
Hertz Corporation........818 569-6900
3111 N Kenwood St Burbank (91505) ***(G-17688)***
HEs Transportation Svcs Inc........510 783-6100
3623 Munster St Hayward (94545) ***(G-4024)***

ALPHABETIC

Hesperia Senior Living LLC.....760 244-5579
17581 Sultana St Hesperia (92345) **(G-27942)**
Hetrosys LLC.....408 270-0240
3858 Carrera Ct San Jose (95148) **(G-27943)**
Hewitt and Canfield Cnstr Inc.....805 522-4426
495 E Easy St Ste A Simi Valley (93065) **(G-3055)**
HEWLETT FOUNDATION, Menlo Park *Also called Hewlett Wlliam Flora Fndation* **(G-25541)**
Hewlett Packard.....650 857-1501
3000 Hanover St Palo Alto (94304) **(G-15219)**
Hewlett Packard Enterprise Co (PA).....650 857-5817
3000 Hanover St Palo Alto (94304) **(G-15691)**
Hewlett Wlliam Flora Fndation.....650 234-4500
2121 Sand Hill Rd Menlo Park (94025) **(G-25541)**
Hff Inc.....310 407-2100
1999 Avenue Of The Stars # 1200 Los Angeles (90067) **(G-9854)**
Hff Inc.....949 253-8800
18300 Von Karman Ave # 900 Irvine (92612) **(G-9855)**
Hfrm II Inc (PA).....530 242-2010
2051 Hilltop Dr Ste A18 Redding (96002) **(G-11001)**
HFS North America LLC (PA).....530 758-8253
231 G St Ste 4 Davis (95616) **(G-27944)**
HG Fenton Company.....619 400-0120
7577 Mission Valley Rd # 200 San Diego (92108) **(G-11140)**
Hga Architects and Engineers, Sacramento *Also called Hammel Green & Abrahamson Inc* **(G-26194)**
Hggc LLC (PA).....650 321-4910
1950 University Ave # 350 East Palo Alto (94303) **(G-12314)**
Hgt, Stockton *Also called Hub Group Trucking Inc* **(G-4025)**
Hgt, Ontario *Also called Hub Group Trucking Inc* **(G-4026)**
HHC Trs Portsmouth LLC.....760 322-6000
888 E Tahquitz Canyon Way Palm Springs (92262) **(G-12700)**
Hhlp San Diego Lessee LLC.....619 446-3000
530 Broadway San Diego (92101) **(G-12701)**
HHS Communications Inc.....909 230-5170
2042 S Grove Ave Ontario (91761) **(G-2610)**
Hhsa Data Center, Sacramento *Also called Califrnia Hlth Humn Srvcs Agcy* **(G-16106)**
Hl Desert Hospital, Lancaster *Also called County of Los Angeles* **(G-19470)**
Hl Fresno Hospitality LLC.....559 233-6650
1055 Van Ness Ave Fresno (93721) **(G-12702)**
Hl Lo Motel, Edgewood *Also called Siskiyou Development Company* **(G-13259)**
Hi-Desert Medical Center, Joshua Tree *Also called Hi-Desert Mem Hlth Care Dst* **(G-21602)**
Hi-Desert Mem Hlth Care Dst (PA).....760 366-3711
6601 White Feather Rd Joshua Tree (92252) **(G-21602)**
Hi-TEC Garments, Chatsworth *Also called Acme Laundry Products Inc* **(G-6840)**
Hi-TEC Sports Usa Inc (HQ).....209 545-1111
4801 Stoddard Rd Modesto (95356) **(G-8436)**
Hibshman Trading Corporation.....909 581-1800
9843 6th St Ste 103 Rancho Cucamonga (91730) **(G-8387)**
Hidden Valley Companies Inc.....760 466-7100
1218 Pacific Oaks Pl Escondido (92029) **(G-5101)**
Hidden Valley Golf Course, Hidden Valley Lake *Also called Hidden Valley Lake Association* **(G-25270)**
Hidden Valley Lake Association (PA).....707 987-3146
18174 Hidden Valley Rd Hidden Valley Lake (95467) **(G-25270)**
Hidden Valley Mvg & Stor Inc (PA).....602 252-7800
1218 Pacific Oaks Pl Escondido (92029) **(G-4351)**
Hidden Villa Ranch, Norco *Also called Luberski Inc* **(G-8600)**
Higard Farms LLC.....831 753-5982
6 Quail Run Cir Salinas (93907) **(G-369)**
Higgs Fletcher & Mack Llp.....619 236-1551
401 W A St Ste 2600 San Diego (92101) **(G-23307)**
High Adrenaline Enterprises.....925 687-7742
1150 Concord Ave Ste 100 Concord (94520) **(G-6680)**
High Caliber Line, Irwindale *Also called Calibre International LLC* **(G-27737)**
High Desert, Victorville *Also called Southern California Edison Co* **(G-6241)**
High Desert Mavericks Inc.....760 246-6287
12000 Stadium Rd Adelanto (92301) **(G-18548)**
High Desert Med Corp A Med Grp (PA).....661 945-5984
43839 15th St W Lancaster (93534) **(G-19557)**
High Desert Phoenix.....661 547-5630
42980 Staffordshire Dr Lancaster (93534) **(G-19222)**
High Dsert Ptent Care Svcs LLC.....760 956-4150
17095 Main St Hesperia (92345) **(G-19558)**
High End Development Inc.....925 687-2540
5600 Imhoff Dr Ste E Concord (94520) **(G-3531)**
High Haven, Los Angeles *Also called Broadview Inc* **(G-20421)**
High Performance Wall Systems, Redding *Also called Redding Drywall Systems Inc* **(G-2964)**
High Plains Ranch LLC (PA).....559 583-1277
2911 Hanford Armona Rd Hanford (93230) **(G-427)**
High Ridge Wind LLC.....888 903-6926
15445 Innovation Dr San Diego (92128) **(G-6138)**
High Road Sports.....805 545-7940
423 Oconnor Way San Luis Obispo (93405) **(G-27464)**
High St Car Wash Lube & Oil, Oakland *Also called High Street Hand Car Wash Inc* **(G-17883)**
High Street Hand Car Wash Inc.....510 536-4333
569 High St Oakland (94601) **(G-17883)**
High Summit LLC.....925 605-2900
6909 Las Positas Rd Ste D Livermore (94551) **(G-17822)**
High Technology Video Inc.....323 969-8822
10900 Ventura Blvd Studio City (91604) **(G-18230)**
High Tide and Green Grass Inc.....805 981-8722
2401 W Vineyard Ave Oxnard (93036) **(G-18747)**
High Valley Lodge, Sunland *Also called P R N Convalescent Hospital* **(G-20832)**
High-Light Electric Inc.....951 352-9646
7000 Jurupa Ave Riverside (92504) **(G-2611)**

Highcom Security Services.....510 893-7600
1900 Webster St Ste B Oakland (94612) **(G-16702)**
Highland Care Center Redlands, Redlands *Also called AG Redlands LLC* **(G-21127)**
Highland Head Start, Highland *Also called County of San Bernardino* **(G-24451)**
Highland Hospitality Corp.....760 322-6000
888 E Tahquitz Canyon Way Palm Springs (92262) **(G-12703)**
Highland Lumber Sales Inc.....714 778-2293
300 E Santa Ana St Anaheim (92805) **(G-6931)**
HIGHLAND PALMS HEALTHCARE CENT, Highland *Also called Cedar Holdings LLC* **(G-20442)**
Highland Park Skilled Nursing.....323 254-6125
5125 Monte Vista St Los Angeles (90042) **(G-20671)**
Highlands Inn Investors II LP.....831 624-3801
120 Highland Dr Carmel (93923) **(G-12704)**
Highmark Capital Management.....800 582-4734
350 California St Fl 22 San Francisco (94104) **(G-10152)**
Highpoint Productions Inc.....818 728-7600
13400 Rverside Dr Ste 300 Sherman Oaks (91423) **(G-18093)**
Hightail Inc (PA).....408 879-9118
1919 S Bascom Ave Ste 600 Campbell (95008) **(G-5629)**
Highway Patrol, Woodland Hills *Also called West Valley Area Squad Club* **(G-24997)**
Hignell Companies.....530 345-1965
1836 Laburnum Ave Chico (95926) **(G-11141)**
Hikvision USA Inc (HQ).....909 895-0400
908 Canada Ct City of Industry (91748) **(G-16887)**
Hikvision Usa, Inc., City of Industry *Also called Hikvision USA Inc* **(G-16887)**
Hilary A Brodie MD PHD.....916 734-3744
2521 Stockton Blvd 7200 Sacramento (95817) **(G-19559)**
Hilbers Inc.....530 673-2947
1210 Stabler Ln Yuba City (95993) **(G-1571)**
HILBERS CONTRACTORS & ENGINEER, Yuba City *Also called Hilbers Inc* **(G-1571)**
Hildreth Farm Incorporated.....707 462-0648
1520 Rddick Cunningham Rd Ukiah (95482) **(G-236)**
Hill & Knowlton Strategies LLC.....415 281-7120
60 Green St San Francisco (94111) **(G-27751)**
Hill Brothers Chemical Company (PA).....714 998-8800
1675 N Main St Orange (92867) **(G-8990)**
Hill Cress Home, San Bernardino *Also called Care Tech Inc* **(G-20436)**
Hill Farrer & Burrill.....213 620-0460
300 S Grand Ave Fl 37 Los Angeles (90071) **(G-23308)**
Hill Physicians Med Group Inc (PA).....800 445-5747
2409 Camino Ramon San Ramon (94583) **(G-19560)**
Hillcrest AC & Shtmtl, Bakersfield *Also called Hillcrest Sheet Metal Inc* **(G-3178)**
Hillcrest Care Inc.....909 882-2965
4280 Cypress Dr San Bernardino (92407) **(G-21266)**
Hillcrest Cnvalescent Hosp Inc.....323 636-3462
3401 Cedar Ave Long Beach (90807) **(G-21267)**
Hillcrest Contracting Inc.....951 273-9600
1467 Circle City Dr Corona (92879) **(G-1800)**
Hillcrest Country Club.....310 553-8911
10000 W Pico Blvd Los Angeles (90064) **(G-18960)**
Hillcrest Manor Sanitarium, National City *Also called Imaginative Horizons Inc* **(G-20682)**
Hillcrest Sheet Metal Inc.....661 335-1500
2324 Perseus Ct Bakersfield (93308) **(G-3178)**
Hilldale Habilitation Center, La Mesa *Also called Razavi Corporation* **(G-20864)**
Hillendale Home Care, Walnut Creek *Also called Caswell Bay Inc* **(G-22400)**
Hillhaven Convalescent Hosp, Burlingame *Also called Kindred Healthcare Operating* **(G-22149)**
Hillman Holdings LLC (PA).....559 685-6100
116 W Cedar Ave Tulare (93274) **(G-546)**
Hills Flat Lumber Co (PA).....530 273-6171
380 Railroad Ave Grass Valley (95945) **(G-2612)**
Hills Wldg & Engrg Contr Inc.....661 746-5400
22038 Stockdale Hwy Bakersfield (93314) **(G-1081)**
Hillsborough, Modesto *Also called Woodside Group Inc* **(G-9908)**
Hillsdale Group LP.....818 623-2170
12750 Riverside Dr North Hollywood (91607) **(G-21268)**
Hillsdale Group LP.....650 742-9150
1201 Broadway Ofc Millbrae (94030) **(G-21269)**
Hillsdale Group LP.....510 538-3866
1832 B St Hayward (94541) **(G-21270)**
Hillshire Brands Company.....510 276-1300
2411 Baumann Ave San Lorenzo (94580) **(G-8671)**
Hillshire Brands Company.....562 903-9260
10715 Springdale Ave # 5 Santa Fe Springs (90670) **(G-8852)**
Hillside Auto Salvage, Riverside *Also called Team Truck Dismantling Inc* **(G-6797)**
Hillside Care Center, San Rafael *Also called Cal-Coast Healthcare Inc* **(G-20431)**
Hillside Contractor, Santa Ana *Also called South Coast Stone Paving* **(G-1863)**
Hillside Enterprises, Long Beach *Also called Association For Retarded* **(G-24310)**
Hillside Hospital, San Diego *Also called San Miguel Hospital Assn* **(G-21852)**
Hillside House Inc.....805 687-4818
1235 Veronica Springs Rd Santa Barbara (93105) **(G-21084)**
Hillside Mem Pk & Mortuary, Los Angeles *Also called Temple Israel of Hollywood* **(G-13717)**
Hillsides.....323 254-2274
940 Avenue 64 Pasadena (91105) **(G-24691)**
Hilltop Commons Senior Living, Grass Valley *Also called Ray Stone Incorporated* **(G-24148)**
Hilltop Family YMCA, Richmond *Also called YMCA of East Bay* **(G-25409)**
Hilltop Manor, Auburn *Also called Horizon West Healthcare Inc* **(G-21272)**
Hilltop Ranch Inc.....209 874-1875
13890 Looney Rd Ballico (95303) **(G-547)**
Hilltop Securities Inc.....800 765-2200
8350 Wilshire Blvd Beverly Hills (90211) **(G-10011)**
Hilltown Packing Co Inc.....831 784-1931
9 Harris Pl A Salinas (93901) **(G-548)**
Hillview Acres.....714 694-2828
23091 Mill Creek Dr Laguna Hills (92653) **(G-24692)**

Hillview Acres Childrens Home, Laguna Hills *Also called Hillview Acres (G-24692)*
Hillview Convalescent Hospital....................408 779-3633
530 W Dunne Ave Morgan Hill (95037) *(G-20672)*
Hillview Mental Health Center....................818 363-7813
12450 Van Nuys Blvd # 200 Pacoima (91331) *(G-22074)*
Hilton, Santa Barbara *Also called Hilton Worldwide Inc (G-12715)*
Hilton, San Diego *Also called Ww San Diego Harbor Island LLC (G-13433)*
Hilton, San Diego *Also called Hilton Worldwide Inc (G-12717)*
Hilton, San Francisco *Also called Hilton Worldwide Inc (G-12718)*
Hilton, Sacramento *Also called Shri Sidhi Vinayaka Hotel Inc (G-13252)*
Hilton, Oakland *Also called Hilton Worldwide Inc (G-12719)*
Hilton, La Jolla *Also called Hilton Worldwide Inc (G-12720)*
Hilton, Pasadena *Also called Hilton Worldwide Inc (G-12723)*
Hilton, Mountain View *Also called Camino Real Group LLC (G-12483)*
Hilton, Ontario *Also called Hilton Worldwide Inc (G-12732)*
Hilton, Redding *Also called Win River Hotel Corporation (G-13412)*
Hilton, Emeryville *Also called Rljhgn Emeryville Lessee LP (G-13163)*
Hilton, Costa Mesa *Also called Hilton Worldwide Inc (G-12735)*
Hilton, Long Beach *Also called Merritt Hospitality LLC (G-12990)*
Hilton, San Diego *Also called Bay Rosie Hotel LLP (G-12425)*
Hilton, Oxnard *Also called T M Mian & Associates Inc (G-13337)*
Hilton, Huntington Beach *Also called Waterfront Hotel LLC (G-13395)*
Hilton, Monterey *Also called Ocean Park Hotels Inc (G-13034)*
Hilton, Los Angeles *Also called Hilton Worldwide Inc (G-12739)*
Hilton, Valencia *Also called Ocean Park Hotels Inc (G-13035)*
Hilton, Sacramento *Also called Shri Laxmi Naryan Hsptlty Grp (G-13251)*
Hilton Checkers Los Angeles, Los Angeles *Also called Chsp Trs Los Angeles LLC (G-12518)*
Hilton Concord, Concord *Also called Vwi Concord LLC (G-13383)*
Hilton El Segundo LLC....................310 726-0100
2100 E Mariposa Ave El Segundo (90245) *(G-12705)*
Hilton Garded, San Diego *Also called SD Stadium Hotel LLC (G-13225)*
Hilton Garden Hotel, Foster City *Also called Hilton Garden In San Mateo (G-12706)*
Hilton Garden In San Mateo....................650 522-9000
2000 Bridgepointe Pkwy Foster City (94404) *(G-12706)*
Hilton Garden Inn....................510 346-5533
510 Lewelling Blvd San Leandro (94579) *(G-12707)*
Hilton Garden Inn Calabasas, Calabasas *Also called T M Mian & Associates Inc (G-13336)*
Hilton Garden Inn Carlsbad Bch, Carlsbad *Also called Interstate Hotels Resorts Inc (G-27068)*
Hilton Garden Inn Emeryville, Emeryville *Also called Rlj Hgn Emeryville Lessee LP (G-13497)*
Hilton Garden Inn Monterey, Monterey *Also called 1000 Aguajito Op Co LLC (G-12356)*
Hilton Garden Inn Palo Alto, Palo Alto *Also called Palmetto Hospitality (G-13073)*
Hilton Garden Inn Pismo, Pismo Beach *Also called Castlblack Pismo Bch Owner LLC (G-12499)*
Hilton Garden Inn Sacremento, Sacramento *Also called Apple Hospitality Reit Inc (G-12393)*
Hilton Garden Inn San, South San Francisco *Also called Larkspur Hsptality Dev MGT LLC (G-12906)*
Hilton Garden Inns MGT LLC....................760 476-0800
6450 Carlsbad Blvd Carlsbad (92011) *(G-12708)*
Hilton Garden Inns MGT LLC....................310 726-0100
2100 E Mariposa Ave El Segundo (90245) *(G-12709)*
Hilton Garden Inns MGT LLC....................925 292-2000
2801 Constitution Dr Fl 2 Livermore (94551) *(G-12710)*
Hilton Hotel Long Beach, Long Beach *Also called Hlb Funding LLC (G-12744)*
Hilton Hotels, Long Beach *Also called HEI Long Beach LLC (G-12698)*
Hilton Hotels, Ontario *Also called Hilton Worldwide Inc (G-12722)*
Hilton Irvine, Irvine *Also called Equistar Irvine Company LLC (G-12621)*
Hilton Irvne/Orange Cnty Arprt, Irvine *Also called Interstate Hotels Resorts Inc (G-27072)*
Hilton Los Angles Universal Cy....................818 506-2500
555 Unversal Hollywood Dr Universal City (91608) *(G-12711)*
Hilton Los Angls/Nversal Cy Ht, Universal City *Also called Sun Hill Properties Inc (G-13308)*
Hilton Newark Sremont, Monrovia *Also called SM Broadway Corp (G-12273)*
Hilton Pasadena, Pasadena *Also called Amstar/Davidson Robles LLC (G-12385)*
Hilton Port Los Angls-San Pdro, San Pedro *Also called Meristar San Pedro Hilton LLC (G-12989)*
Hilton Resort In Palm Spring, Palm Springs *Also called Walters Family Partnership (G-13391)*
Hilton Resort Palm Springs....................760 320-6868
400 E Tahquitz Canyon Way Palm Springs (92262) *(G-17219)*
Hilton Sacramento Arden West, Sacramento *Also called Whgca LLC (G-13411)*
Hilton Sacramento Arden West, Sacramento *Also called Interstate Hotels Resorts Inc (G-12853)*
Hilton San Diego/Del Mar, Del Mar *Also called Ws Hdm LLC (G-13430)*
Hilton San Diego/Del Mar, Del Mar *Also called Ws Hdm LLC (G-13431)*
Hilton San Francisco, Burlingame *Also called Harbor View Hotels Inc (G-12691)*
Hilton Santa Clara, Santa Clara *Also called Ontario Airport Hotel Corp (G-13047)*
Hilton Santa Cruz/Scotts Vly, Scotts Valley *Also called Inn At Scotts Valley LLC (G-12837)*
Hilton Suites Inc....................714 938-1111
400 N State College Blvd Orange (92868) *(G-12712)*
Hilton Universal Hotel....................818 506-2500
555 Unversal Hollywood Dr Universal City (91608) *(G-12713)*
Hilton Wdlnd Hlls / Los Angles, Woodland Hills *Also called Canoga Hotel Corporation (G-12485)*
Hilton Woodland Hills & Towers....................818 595-1000
6360 Canoga Ave Woodland Hills (91367) *(G-12714)*
Hilton Worldwide Inc....................805 564-4333
633 E Cabrillo Blvd Santa Barbara (93103) *(G-12715)*
Hilton Worldwide Inc....................408 942-0400
901 E Calaveras Blvd Milpitas (95035) *(G-12716)*
Hilton Worldwide Inc....................619 276-4010
1775 E Mission Bay Dr San Diego (92109) *(G-12717)*
Hilton Worldwide Inc....................415 771-1400
333 Ofarrell St San Francisco (94102) *(G-12718)*
Hilton Worldwide Inc....................510 635-5000
1 Hegenberger Rd Oakland (94621) *(G-12719)*
Hilton Worldwide Inc....................858 450-4569
10950 N Torrey Pines Rd La Jolla (92037) *(G-12720)*
Hilton Worldwide Inc....................707 253-9540
1075 California Blvd NAPA (94559) *(G-12721)*
Hilton Worldwide Inc....................909 980-3420
700 N Haven Ave Ontario (91764) *(G-12722)*
Hilton Worldwide Inc....................626 577-1000
168 S Los Robles Ave Pasadena (91101) *(G-12723)*
Hilton Worldwide Inc....................415 392-8000
55 Cyril Magnin St San Francisco (94102) *(G-12724)*
Hilton Worldwide Inc....................626 915-3441
1211 E Garvey St Covina (91724) *(G-12725)*
Hilton Worldwide Inc....................310 415-3340
9876 Wilshire Blvd Beverly Hills (90210) *(G-12726)*
Hilton Worldwide Inc....................530 543-2126
4130 Lake Tahoe Blvd South Lake Tahoe (96150) *(G-12727)*
Hilton Worldwide Inc....................650 342-4600
150 Anza Blvd Burlingame (94010) *(G-12728)*
Hilton Worldwide Inc....................626 445-8525
211 E Huntington Dr Arcadia (91006) *(G-12729)*
Hilton Worldwide Inc....................562 861-1900
8425 Firestone Blvd Downey (90241) *(G-12730)*
Hilton Worldwide Inc....................714 739-5600
7762 Beach Blvd Buena Park (90620) *(G-12731)*
Hilton Worldwide Inc....................909 980-0400
700 N Haven Ave Ontario (91764) *(G-12732)*
Hilton Worldwide Inc....................626 270-2700
225 W Valley Blvd San Gabriel (91776) *(G-12733)*
Hilton Worldwide Inc....................949 553-8332
2120 Main St Irvine (92614) *(G-12734)*
Hilton Worldwide Inc....................714 540-7000
3050 Bristol St Costa Mesa (92626) *(G-12735)*
Hilton Worldwide Inc....................858 431-2116
4550 La Jolla Village Dr San Diego (92122) *(G-12736)*
Hilton Worldwide Inc....................415 499-9222
101 Mcinnis Pkwy San Rafael (94903) *(G-12737)*
Hilton Worldwide Inc....................415 771-1400
333 Ofarrell St San Francisco (94102) *(G-12738)*
Hilton Worldwide Inc....................310 410-4000
5711 W Century Blvd Los Angeles (90045) *(G-12739)*
Hilton Worldwide Inc....................714 632-1221
3100 E Frontera St Anaheim (92806) *(G-12740)*
Hilton Worldwide Inc....................650 589-3400
250 Gateway Blvd South San Francisco (94080) *(G-12741)*
Hilton Worldwide Inc....................530 541-6122
901 Ski Run Blvd South Lake Tahoe (96150) *(G-12742)*
HILTON WORLDWIDE, INC., San Francisco *Also called Hilton Worldwide Inc (G-12738)*
Hiltonm Grdn Inn Lax El Sgundo, El Segundo *Also called Hilton El Segundo LLC (G-12705)*
Hinds Hospice (PA)....................559 248-8579
2490 W Shaw Ave Ste 100a Fresno (93711) *(G-22457)*
Hinds Hospice Home, Fresno *Also called Hinds Hospice (G-22457)*
Hinerfeld-Ward Inc....................310 842-7929
8931 Ellis Ave Ste B1 Los Angeles (90034) *(G-1189)*
Hines Gs Properties Inc....................415 982-6200
101 California St # 1000 San Francisco (94111) *(G-11973)*
Hines Horticulture Inc....................760 723-1500
2500 Rainbow Valley Blvd Fallbrook (92028) *(G-9193)*
Hines Nurseries LLC....................602 254-2831
22941 Mill Creek Dr Laguna Hills (92653) *(G-9194)*
Hino Motors Mfg USA Inc....................951 727-0286
4550 Wineville Ave Mira Loma (91752) *(G-6738)*
Hinode, Woodland *Also called Sunfoods LLC (G-8528)*
Hinttech Inc....................415 874-3200
505 Montgomery St Fl 11 San Francisco (94111) *(G-27945)*
Hired Hand....................707 575-4700
2901 Cleveland Ave # 203 Santa Rosa (95403) *(G-22458)*
Hired Hands Inc....................707 265-6400
1754 2nd St Ste D NAPA (94559) *(G-14671)*
Hireforces, San Jose *Also called Incline Incorporated (G-14682)*
Hireright, Irvine *Also called Corporate Risk Hldings III Inc (G-17096)*
Hireright LLC (HQ)....................949 428-5800
3349 Michelson Dr Ste 150 Irvine (92612) *(G-16243)*
Hirsch Bedner Associates (PA)....................310 829-9087
3216 Nebraska Ave Santa Monica (90404) *(G-17220)*
Hirsch Electronics LLC....................949 250-8888
1900 Carnegie Ave Ste B Santa Ana (92705) *(G-7577)*
Hirsch/Bedner Intl Inc (PA)....................310 829-9087
3216 Nebraska Ave Santa Monica (90404) *(G-17221)*
Hirsh Inc....................213 622-9441
860 S Los Angeles St # 900 Los Angeles (90014) *(G-1082)*
HIS KIDS RANCH, Potrero *Also called Rancho De Sus Ninos Inc (G-24777)*
His Manna Inc....................831 423-5515
150 Felker St Ste B Santa Cruz (95060) *(G-27465)*
His Passion Inc....................800 760-6389
17195 Newhope St Ste 201 Fountain Valley (92708) *(G-22459)*
Hispanic Business Student Assn....................209 769-7279
5245 N Bcker Ave M/S Pd 7 Fresno (93740) *(G-25137)*
Historic Tours of America, San Diego *Also called Old Town Trlley Turs San Diego (G-4997)*
Historical Properties Inc (PA)....................619 230-8417
311 Island Ave San Diego (92101) *(G-12743)*
Historical Soc Centinela Vly....................310 649-6272
7634 Midfield Ave Los Angeles (90045) *(G-25022)*

ALPHABETIC

Hitachi America Ltd 650 827-6240
1000 Marina Blvd Ste 500 Brisbane (94005) *(G-7848)*
Hitachi Data Systems Corp 858 537-3000
15231 Ave Of Science # 100 San Diego (92128) *(G-7140)*
Hitachi Data Systems Corp (HQ) 408 970-1000
2845 Lafayette St Santa Clara (95050) *(G-7141)*
Hitachi High Tech Amer Inc 925 218-2800
5960 Inglewood Dr Ste 200 Pleasanton (94588) *(G-7578)*
Hkf Inc (PA) 323 225-1318
5983 Smithway St Commerce (90040) *(G-7740)*
Hks Architects Inc 415 356-3800
500 Howard St Fl 4 San Francisco (94105) *(G-26201)*
Hlb Funding LLC 562 983-3400
701 W Ocean Blvd Long Beach (90831) *(G-12744)*
Hlm Venture Partners II LP 415 814-6110
201 Mission St Ste 2240 San Francisco (94105) *(G-10153)*
HLT Operate Dtwc LLC 619 297-5466
7450 Hazard Center Dr San Diego (92108) *(G-12745)*
Hlw Corp 310 838-7100
11166 Venice Blvd Culver City (90232) *(G-17843)*
Hmbl LLC 323 656-8090
8400 W Sunset Blvd Ste 3a West Hollywood (90069) *(G-12746)*
HMC Architects, Ontario *Also called HMC Group (G-26202)*
HMC Group (PA) 909 989-9979
3546 Concours Ontario (91764) *(G-26202)*
HMC Group 909 980-8058
2930 Inland Empire Blvd # 100 Ontario (91764) *(G-26203)*
Hmclause Inc (HQ) 530 747-3700
555 Codoni Ave Modesto (95357) *(G-289)*
Hmclause Inc 530 747-3235
9241 Mace Blvd Davis (95618) *(G-26529)*
Hmclause Inc 530 713-5838
42 Glenshire Ln Chico (95973) *(G-290)*
Hmh Builders, Sacramento *Also called Swinerton Builders Hc (G-1683)*
Hmi Associates Inc 818 887-6800
6800 Owensmouth Ave # 330 Canoga Park (91303) *(G-16703)*
Hmointerfacecom LLC 310 251-4861
1601 N Sepulveda Blvd Manhattan Beach (90266) *(G-15220)*
HMS Agricultural Corporation 760 347-2335
46247 Arabia St Indio (92201) *(G-11571)*
HMS Construction Inc (PA) 760 727-9808
2885 Scott St Vista (92081) *(G-3357)*
Hmt Electric Inc 858 458-9771
2340 Meyers Ave Escondido (92029) *(G-2613)*
Hmwc Cpas & Business Advisors 714 505-9000
17501 17th St Ste 100 Tustin (92780) *(G-26368)*
Hntb Corporation 213 403-1000
601 W 5th St Ste 1000 Los Angeles (90071) *(G-25862)*
Hntb Corporation 415 963-6700
49 Stevenson St Ste 600 San Francisco (94105) *(G-26204)*
Hntb Corporation 714 460-1600
200 Sandpointe Ave # 200 Santa Ana (92707) *(G-25863)*
Hntb Corporation 949 460-1700
36 Executive Park Ste 200 Irvine (92614) *(G-25864)*
Hntb Gerwick Water Solutions 714 460-1600
200 Sandpointe Ave Santa Ana (92707) *(G-25865)*
Hntb-Gerwick JV 510 839-8972
1300 Clay St Fl 7 Oakland (94612) *(G-26205)*
Hoag Family Cancer Institute 949 764-7777
1190 Baker St Ste 103 Costa Mesa (92626) *(G-22976)*
Hoag Memorial Hospital Presbt (PA) 949 764-4624
1 Hoag Dr Newport Beach (92663) *(G-21603)*
Hoag Memorial Hospital Presbt 949 764-4624
16200 Sand Canyon Ave Irvine (92618) *(G-21604)*
Hob Entertainment LLC 714 778-2583
1350 S Disneyland Dr Anaheim (92802) *(G-18469)*
Hob Entertainment LLC 323 848-5100
8430 W Sunset Blvd West Hollywood (90069) *(G-18470)*
Hob Entertainment LLC 619 299-2583
1055 5th Ave San Diego (92101) *(G-18471)*
Hob Entertainment LLC (HQ) 323 769-4600
7060 Hollywood Blvd Los Angeles (90028) *(G-18472)*
Hoban Management, El Cajon *Also called Thomas J Hoban (G-11874)*
Hobbs Herder Advertising 800 999-6090
419 Main St Huntington Beach (92648) *(G-13859)*
Hobbs/Herder Training, Huntington Beach *Also called Hobbs Herder Advertising (G-13859)*
Hobby Lobby Stores Inc 909 393-8727
4635 Chino Hills Pkwy Chino Hills (91709) *(G-17222)*
Hobby Lobby Stores Inc 661 513-0005
26565 Bouquet Canyon Rd Santa Clarita (91350) *(G-17223)*
Hobby Lobby Stores Inc 909 307-0135
27651 San Bernardino Ave # 140 Redlands (92374) *(G-12217)*
Hobby Shack (PA) 714 964-0827
18480 Bandilier Cir Fountain Valley (92708) *(G-8044)*
Hodges Electric Inc 559 298-5533
1239 Hoblitt Ave Clovis (93612) *(G-2614)*
Hoem & Associates Inc 650 871-5194
951 Linden Ave South San Francisco (94080) *(G-3116)*
Hoffman Concrete Company Inc 951 372-8333
102 E Grand Blvd Corona (92879) *(G-3274)*
Hoffman Farms, Tulare *Also called Nielsens Creamery (G-436)*
Hoffman Hospice of The Valley 661 410-1010
8501 Brimhall Rd Bldg 100 Bakersfield (93312) *(G-21271)*
Hoffman Southwest Corp 714 630-0404
1183 N Kraemer Pl Anaheim (92806) *(G-17979)*
Hoffman Southwest Corp 909 397-0567
8930 Center Ave Rancho Cucamonga (91730) *(G-17980)*
Hoffman Texas Inc 661 257-9200
24971 Avenue Stanford Valencia (91355) *(G-17981)*
Hoffmann House, Citrus Heights *Also called Paradise Oaks Youth Services (G-24121)*

Hok Group Inc 415 243-0555
1 Bush St Ste 200 San Francisco (94104) *(G-26206)*
Hok Group Inc 310 838-9555
9530 Jefferson Blvd Culver City (90232) *(G-26207)*
Hokto Kinoko Company (HQ) 760 774-8453
2033 Marilyn Ln San Marcos (92069) *(G-333)*
Holbrook Construction Inc 714 523-1150
9814 Norwalk Blvd Ste 200 Santa Fe Springs (90670) *(G-1572)*
Holdrege Kull Consultimg Engr 530 894-2487
48 Bellarmine Ct Ste 40 Chico (95928) *(G-25866)*
Holiday Garden SF Corp 714 533-3555
1700 S Clementine St Anaheim (92802) *(G-12747)*
Holiday Inn, Los Angeles *Also called Packard Realty Inc (G-13070)*
Holiday Inn, La Mirada *Also called Sunstone Hotel Investors LLC (G-13318)*
Holiday Inn, Burbank *Also called JP Allen Extended Stay (G-12870)*
Holiday Inn, Marina Del Rey *Also called Washington Inn LLC (G-13393)*
Holiday Inn, San Diego *Also called Sunstone Hotel Investors Inc (G-13313)*
Holiday Inn, San Francisco *Also called Intercontinental Hotels Group (G-12843)*
Holiday Inn, Los Angeles *Also called Six Continents Hotels Inc (G-13263)*
Holiday Inn, Stockton *Also called Hospitality Solutions LLC (G-12759)*
Holiday Inn, Torrance *Also called Hpt Trs Ihg 2 Inc (G-12795)*
Holiday Inn, Anaheim *Also called Conestoga Hotel (G-12540)*
Holiday Inn, Sacramento *Also called Atrium Hotels LP (G-12401)*
Holiday Inn, Torrance *Also called Six Continents Hotels Inc (G-13264)*
Holiday Inn, San Francisco *Also called Intercntnntal Ht Group Rsurces (G-12840)*
Holiday Inn, Goleta *Also called Hpt Trs Ihg 2 Inc (G-12796)*
Holiday Inn, Anaheim *Also called Hpt Trs Ihg-2 Inc (G-12798)*
Holiday Inn, San Diego *Also called Jck Hotels LLC (G-12864)*
Holiday Inn, Valencia *Also called Ocean Park Hotels Mmex LLC (G-13036)*
Holiday Inn, Bakersfield *Also called Newport Hospitality Group Inc (G-13021)*
Holiday Inn, San Diego *Also called Narven Enterprises Inc (G-13014)*
Holiday Inn, San Diego *Also called Win Time Ltd (G-13413)*
Holiday Inn, Laguna Hills *Also called Laguna Hills Hotel Dev Ventr (G-12900)*
Holiday Inn, Visalia *Also called Grosvenor Visalia Associates (G-12680)*
Holiday Inn, San Francisco *Also called Todays Hotel Corporation (G-13347)*
Holiday Inn, Anaheim *Also called Dkn Hotel LLC (G-12580)*
Holiday Inn, Palmdale *Also called Palmdale Resort Inc (G-13072)*
Holiday Inn, Buena Park *Also called Uniwell Corporation (G-13367)*
Holiday Inn, Willows *Also called Kumar Hotels Inc (G-12892)*
Holiday Inn, Santa Maria *Also called Santa Maria Hotel Corp (G-13216)*
Holiday Inn, National City *Also called Six Continents Hotels Inc (G-13268)*
Holiday Inn, San Diego *Also called Narven Enterprises Inc (G-13015)*
Holiday Inn, Fresno *Also called HI Fresno Hospitality LLC (G-12702)*
Holiday Inn & Suites Annaheim 714 535-0300
1240 S Walnut St Anaheim (92802) *(G-12748)*
Holiday Inn - San Diego-On Bay, San Diego *Also called Six Continents Hotels Inc (G-13265)*
Holiday Inn Bay Bridge, Oakland *Also called Atrium Hotels LP (G-12400)*
Holiday Inn Concord, Concord *Also called Montclair Hotels Mb LLC (G-13005)*
Holiday Inn Diamond Bar, Diamond Bar *Also called Oak Creek LP (G-13031)*
Holiday Inn Dublin, Dublin *Also called Trevi Partners A Calif LP (G-13356)*
Holiday Inn Express and Suites, San Francisco *Also called Intercontinental Hotels Group (G-12845)*
Holiday Inn Express and Suites, West Hollywood *Also called Hmbl LLC (G-12746)*
Holiday Inn Express Merced 209 383-0333
730 Motel Dr Merced (95341) *(G-12749)*
Holiday Inn Express Sacramento, San Diego *Also called Manas Hospitality LLC (G-12939)*
Holiday Inn Hotel Torrance 310 781-9100
19800 S Vermont Ave Torrance (90502) *(G-12750)*
Holiday Inn Lax, Los Angeles *Also called Brisam Lax (de) LLC (G-12467)*
Holiday Inn Long Beach Airport, Long Beach *Also called Yhb Long Beach LLC (G-13445)*
Holiday Inn Northeast 916 338-5800
5321 Date Ave Sacramento (95841) *(G-12751)*
Holiday Inn Oceanside Marina, Oceanside *Also called Ocean Holiday LP (G-13033)*
Holiday Inn Orange Cnty Arprt, Santa Ana *Also called S W K Properties LLC (G-13184)*
Holiday Inn Rncho Bernardo LLC 858 485-6530
17065 W Bernardo Dr San Diego (92127) *(G-12752)*
Holiday Inn Scp, Sacramento *Also called Atrium Hotels LP (G-12402)*
Holiday Inn Select 714 739-8500
14299 Firestone Blvd La Mirada (90638) *(G-12753)*
Holiday Inn Universal Studios, North Hollywood *Also called Rio Vista Development Company (G-13152)*
Holiday Inn Van Nuys, Van Nuys *Also called Six Continents Hotels Inc (G-13262)*
Holiday Inn Victorville, Victorville *Also called Victorvlle Trsure Holdings LLC (G-13379)*
Holiday Inn Woodland Hills, Beverly Hills *Also called Ggwh LLC (G-12665)*
Holiday Manor, Canoga Park *Also called Sela Healthcare Inc (G-20903)*
Holiday Manor Care Center, Upland *Also called Sela Healthcare Inc (G-20902)*
Holiday Manor Nursitarium, Canoga Park *Also called C P Holiday Manor Inc (G-21172)*
Holiday Meat & Provision Corp 310 674-0541
405 Centinela Ave Inglewood (90302) *(G-8672)*
Holistic Approach HM Hlth Care, Stockton *Also called Holistic Approach Inc (G-14672)*
Holistic Approach Inc 209 956-7050
4505 Precissi Ln Ste B Stockton (95207) *(G-14672)*
Holland & Knight LLP 213 896-2400
400 S Hope St Ste 800 Los Angeles (90071) *(G-23309)*
Holland & Knight LLP 415 743-6900
50 California St Ste 2800 San Francisco (94111) *(G-23310)*
Holland America Flowers LLC 805 343-4004
808 Albert Way Arroyo Grande (93420) *(G-291)*
Holland Flower Market Inc (PA) 213 627-9900
755 Wall St Ste 7g Los Angeles (90014) *(G-9195)*

Hollandia Dairy Inc (PA).......760 744-3222
622 E Mission Rd San Marcos (92069) ***(G-428)***
Hollandia Produce LP.......805 684-8739
1545 Santa Monica Rd Carpinteria (93013) ***(G-334)***
HOLLENBECK HOME FOR THE AGED, Newhall *Also called Hollenbeck Palms* ***(G-24693)***
Hollenbeck Palms.......323 263-6195
24431 Lyons Ave Apt 336 Newhall (91321) ***(G-24693)***
Holliday Rock Co Inc (PA).......909 982-1553
1401 N Benson Ave Upland (91786) ***(G-6988)***
Hollingshead Management, Los Angeles *Also called Proland Property Managment LLC* ***(G-11770)***
Hollins Schechter A Prof Corp.......714 558-9119
1851 E 1st St Ste 600 Santa Ana (92705) ***(G-23311)***
Hollister Process Service.......831 634-1479
341 Tres Pinos Rd Ste 201 Hollister (95023) ***(G-17224)***
Hollyway Cleaners, Los Angeles *Also called Valetor Inc* ***(G-13589)***
Hollywood Cmnty Hosp Hollywood, Los Angeles *Also called Hollywood Community Hospital M* ***(G-21605)***
Hollywood Community Hospital M.......323 462-2271
6245 De Longpre Ave Los Angeles (90028) ***(G-21605)***
Hollywood Health System Inc.......323 662-3731
4640 Lankershim Blvd # 100 North Hollywood (91602) ***(G-22460)***
Hollywood Hills, Los Angeles *Also called Forest Lawn Memorial-Park Assn* ***(G-12030)***
Hollywood Home Health Services, North Hollywood *Also called Hollywood Health System Inc* ***(G-22460)***
Hollywood Medical Center LP.......213 413-3000
1300 N Vermont Ave Los Angeles (90027) ***(G-21606)***
Hollywood Mental Health Center.......323 769-6100
1224 Vine St Los Angeles (90038) ***(G-22746)***
Hollywood Presbyterian Med Ctr, Los Angeles *Also called Hollywood Medical Center LP* ***(G-21606)***
HOLLYWOOD PRESBYTERIAN MEDICAL, Los Angeles *Also called Cha Hollywood Medical Ctr LP* ***(G-21479)***
Hollywood Rntals Prod Svcs LLC (PA).......818 407-7800
12800 Foothill Blvd Sylmar (91342) ***(G-18231)***
Hollywood Roosevelt Hotel, Los Angeles *Also called Roosevelt Hotel LLC* ***(G-13165)***
Hollywood Spa Inc.......323 464-0445
5636 Vineland Ave North Hollywood (91601) ***(G-18642)***
Hollywood Spa, The, North Hollywood *Also called Hollywood Spa Inc* ***(G-18642)***
Hollywood Sports Park LLC.......562 867-9600
9030 Somerset Blvd Bellflower (90706) ***(G-17225)***
Hollywood Standard LLC.......323 822-3111
8300 W Sunset Blvd Los Angeles (90069) ***(G-12754)***
Holman Family Counseling Inc (PA).......818 704-1444
9451 Corbin Ave Ste 100 Northridge (91324) ***(G-20320)***
Holman Group, The, Northridge *Also called Holman Family Counseling Inc* ***(G-20320)***
Holmes & Narver Inc (HQ).......714 567-2400
999 W Town And Country Rd Orange (92868) ***(G-25867)***
Holmes Body Shop Inc (PA).......626 795-6447
1095 E Colorado Blvd Pasadena (91106) ***(G-17758)***
Holt CA, Pleasant Grove *Also called Holt of California* ***(G-7772)***
Holt of California (HQ).......916 991-8200
7310 Pacific Ave Pleasant Grove (95668) ***(G-7772)***
Holt of California.......916 373-4100
3850 Channel Dr West Sacramento (95691) ***(G-7773)***
Holt of California.......209 623-1149
526 10th St Modesto (95354) ***(G-7849)***
Holt of California.......209 462-3660
1234 W Charter Way Stockton (95206) ***(G-7774)***
Holthouse Carlin Van Trigt LLP.......626 243-5100
350 W Colo Blvd Fl 5 Pasadena (91105) ***(G-26369)***
Holthouse Carlin Van Trigt LLP.......805 374-8555
400 W Ventura Blvd # 250 Camarillo (93010) ***(G-26370)***
Holthouse Carlin Van Trigt LLP.......818 849-3140
15760 Ventura Blvd # 1700 Encino (91436) ***(G-26371)***
Holthouse Carlin Van Trigt LLP.......714 361-7600
555 Anton Blvd Ste 700 Costa Mesa (92626) ***(G-26372)***
Holthouse Carlin Van Trigt LLP (PA).......310 477-5551
11444 W Olympic Blvd # 11 Los Angeles (90064) ***(G-26373)***
Holy Cross Cemetary & Masoleum, Culver City *Also called Roman Cath Arch of Los Angels* ***(G-13712)***
Holy Cross Cemetery, Daly City *Also called Roman Catholic Archdiocese of* ***(G-12035)***
Holzmueller Corporation.......415 826-8383
1000 25th St San Francisco (94107) ***(G-14546)***
Holzmueller Productions, San Francisco *Also called Holzmueller Corporation* ***(G-14546)***
Home Away Inc.......559 642-3121
54432 Road 432 Bass Lake (93604) ***(G-12755)***
Home Box Office Inc.......310 382-3000
2500 Broadway Ste 400 Santa Monica (90404) ***(G-6006)***
Home Building, Corona *Also called Ryland Hmes Inlnd Empire Cstmr* ***(G-1249)***
Home Capital Group.......626 331-4213
948 N Grand Ave Covina (91724) ***(G-9856)***
Home Care America-San Marino, Pasadena *Also called Home Care of America Inc* ***(G-22461)***
Home Care of America Inc.......626 309-7696
750 E Green St Ste 303 Pasadena (91101) ***(G-22461)***
Home Carpet Investment Inc (PA).......619 262-8040
730 Design Ct Ste 401 Chula Vista (91911) ***(G-3117)***
Home Comfort USA, Anaheim *Also called Ken Starr Inc* ***(G-2266)***
Home Community Lending, Santa Clara *Also called Hcl Finance Inc* ***(G-9853)***
Home Depot USA Inc.......951 361-1235
11650 Venture Dr Mira Loma (91752) ***(G-4569)***
Home Depot USA Inc.......408 971-4890
2181 Monterey Hwy San Jose (95125) ***(G-4570)***
Home Depot USA Inc.......209 858-9243
18300 S Harlan Rd Lathrop (95330) ***(G-4571)***
Home Depot USA Inc.......209 835-5133
1400 E Pescadero Ave Tracy (95304) ***(G-4572)***
Home Depot, The, Mira Loma *Also called Home Depot USA Inc* ***(G-4569)***
Home Depot, The, San Jose *Also called Home Depot USA Inc* ***(G-4570)***
Home Depot, The, Lathrop *Also called Home Depot USA Inc* ***(G-4571)***
Home Depot, The, Tracy *Also called Home Depot USA Inc* ***(G-4572)***
Home Dining Restaurant Guide, San Francisco *Also called Waiters On Wheels Inc* ***(G-4090)***
Home Entertainment Div, Los Angeles *Also called Fox Inc* ***(G-5862)***
Home For Jewish Parents.......925 964-2062
4000 Camino Tassajara Danville (94506) ***(G-24008)***
Home Guiding Hands Corporation (PA).......619 938-2850
1825 Gillespie Way # 200 El Cajon (92020) ***(G-24694)***
Home Health Brownsville, Brownsville *Also called Sutter North Med Foundation* ***(G-20121)***
Home Health Care Management.......530 226-0120
1398 Ridgewood Dr Chico (95973) ***(G-22462)***
Home Health Plus, Santa Clara *Also called In Home Health Inc* ***(G-22481)***
Home Health Plus, West Covina *Also called In Home Health Inc* ***(G-22482)***
Home Helpers, Redding *Also called Thom Sharon & G Enterprises* ***(G-22581)***
Home Helpers San Mateo County.......650 532-3122
655 Miramontes St Half Moon Bay (94019) ***(G-22463)***
Home Improvement Company Inc.......760 744-4840
1585 Creek St San Marcos (92078) ***(G-3532)***
Home Instead Senior Care, San Jose *Also called South Bay Senior Solutions Inc* ***(G-22568)***
Home Instead Senior Care, Vista *Also called Sherpaul Corporation* ***(G-22563)***
Home Instead Senior Care, Palm Desert *Also called Ambiente Enterprises Inc* ***(G-22357)***
Home Instead Senior Care, Long Beach *Also called Coastal Cmnty Senior Care LLC* ***(G-23766)***
Home Instead Senior Care, Torrance *Also called Burdette De Cock Inc* ***(G-22384)***
Home Instead Senior Care, Long Beach *Also called Beach Cities Eldercare Inc* ***(G-22376)***
Home Instead Senior Care, Azusa *Also called Seracada* ***(G-22559)***
Home Instead Senior Care, Santa Barbara *Also called S B C Senior Care Inc* ***(G-22552)***
Home Instead Senior Care, Victorville *Also called Branlyn Prominence Inc* ***(G-23693)***
Home Instead Senior Care, Rancho Cucamonga *Also called Branlyn Prominence Inc* ***(G-22380)***
Home Instead Senior Care.......858 277-3722
9665 Gran Rdge Dr Ste 250 San Diego (92123) ***(G-22464)***
Home Instead Senior Care.......916 920-2273
11160 Sun Center Dr Rancho Cordova (95670) ***(G-22465)***
Home Instead Senior Care.......805 577-0926
1720 E Los Angeles Ave H Simi Valley (93065) ***(G-22466)***
Home Instead Senior Care.......619 460-6222
5360 Jackson Dr Ste 120 La Mesa (91942) ***(G-22467)***
Home Instead Senior Care.......707 678-2005
405 Court St Woodland (95695) ***(G-22468)***
Home Instead Senior Care.......510 686-9940
303 W Joaquin Ave Ste 230 San Leandro (94577) ***(G-22469)***
Home Instead Senior Care.......949 347-6767
28570 Marguerite Pkwy # 221 Mission Viejo (92692) ***(G-22470)***
Home Lenders, San Diego *Also called Nine-Twenty Inc* ***(G-11708)***
Home Port Inc.......408 377-4134
5030 Union Ave San Jose (95124) ***(G-11235)***
HOMEBOY BAKERY, Los Angeles *Also called Homeboy Industries* ***(G-24009)***
Homeboy Industries (PA).......323 526-1254
130 Bruno St Los Angeles (90012) ***(G-24009)***
Homebridge Inc.......415 255-2079
1035 Market St Ste L1 San Francisco (94103) ***(G-24010)***
Homecare Professionals Inc.......925 215-1214
1849 Willow Pass Rd # 305 Concord (94520) ***(G-22471)***
Homefrst Svcs Santa Clara Cnty.......408 539-2100
507 Valley Way Milpitas (95035) ***(G-24011)***
Homegaincom Inc.......888 542-0800
12667 Alcosta Blvd # 200 San Ramon (94583) ***(G-11572)***
Homegrown Natural Foods Inc.......510 558-7500
1610 5th St Berkeley (94710) ***(G-8485)***
Homeguard Incorporated (PA).......408 993-1900
510 Madera Ave San Jose (95112) ***(G-14186)***
Homeland Security Services Inc.......714 956-2200
31805 Temecula Pkwy Temecula (92592) ***(G-16888)***
Homelegance Inc.......510 933-6888
48200 Fremont Blvd Fremont (94538) ***(G-6818)***
Homeless Prenatal Program.......415 546-6756
33 Middle Point Rd San Francisco (94124) ***(G-24012)***
Homeowners Association, Helendale *Also called Silver Lakes Association* ***(G-25350)***
Homepointe Property Management, Sacramento *Also called Ram Commercial Enterprises Inc* ***(G-11785)***
Homeq Servicing Corporation (HQ).......916 339-6192
4837 Watt Ave North Highlands (95660) ***(G-9857)***
Homerun.com, San Francisco *Also called Demand Chain Inc* ***(G-7119)***
Homes By Shabbir Kazi.......714 524-4131
19631 Yorba Linda Blvd B Yorba Linda (92886) ***(G-1190)***
Homestar Systems Inc.......415 694-6000
230 California St Ste 510 San Francisco (94111) ***(G-16397)***
Homestead of Fair Oaks, Fair Oaks *Also called Eskaton Properties Inc* ***(G-20551)***
Homestore Apartments & Rentals, Westlake Village *Also called Move Sales Inc* ***(G-13780)***
Homestreet Bank.......626 339-9663
650 S Grand Ave Ste 105 Glendora (91740) ***(G-9502)***
Hometown Buffet, Los Angeles *Also called Ocb Restaurant Company LLC* ***(G-13782)***
Hometown Buffet 261, Cerritos *Also called Hometown Buffet Inc* ***(G-13764)***
Hometown Buffet 269, Fresno *Also called Ocb Restaurant Company LLC* ***(G-13781)***
Hometown Buffet Inc.......562 402-8307
11471 South St Cerritos (90703) ***(G-13764)***
Homewatch Caregivers, Carlsbad *Also called North Coast Home Care Inc* ***(G-22514)***
Homewatch Caregivers, Los Angeles *Also called South Bay Senior Services Inc* ***(G-22567)***
Homewood Care Center, San Jose *Also called Ocadian Care Centers LLC* ***(G-20823)***

ALPHABETIC

Homewood Suites Anaheim Resort, Anaheim *Also called Npl Anaheim Investments LLC* ***(G-13029)***
Homewood Suites Hilton Sfo, Brisbane *Also called Sage Hospitality Resources LLC* ***(G-13189)***
Homewood Suites Libery Station, San Diego *Also called Liberty Station Hhg Hotel LP* ***(G-12921)***
Homewood Suites Management LLC..........510 663-2700
1103 Embarcadero Oakland (94606) ***(G-12756)***
Honda Financial Services, Torrance *Also called American Honda Finance Corp* ***(G-9737)***
Honda Performance Dev Inc..........661 294-7300
25145 Anza Dr Santa Clarita (91355) ***(G-17884)***
Honda R&D Americas Inc..........818 345-7922
7514 Reseda Blvd Reseda (91335) ***(G-26673)***
Honey Lake Hospice Inc..........530 257-3137
60 S Lassen St Susanville (96130) ***(G-7268)***
Honeybook Inc..........770 403-9234
539 Bryant St Ste 200 San Francisco (94107) ***(G-15221)***
Honeyflower Holdings LLC..........951 351-2800
3688 Nye Ave Riverside (92505) ***(G-20673)***
Honeymoon Real Estate LP..........310 277-5221
9400 W Olympic Blvd Beverly Hills (90212) ***(G-12757)***
Honeyville Inc..........909 980-9500
11600 Dayton Dr Rancho Cucamonga (91730) ***(G-4482)***
Honeywell, Lompoc *Also called Kbrwyle Tech Solutions LLC* ***(G-6078)***
Honeywell, Torrance *Also called Friction Materials LLC* ***(G-25819)***
Honeywell International Inc..........714 562-8713
22 Centerpointe Dr # 100 La Palma (90623) ***(G-16889)***
Honeywell International Inc..........714 796-7500
514 S Lyon St Santa Ana (92701) ***(G-7741)***
Honeywell International Inc..........714 562-9003
22 Centerpointe Dr # 100 La Palma (90623) ***(G-25868)***
Honeywell International Inc..........714 562-3114
6 Center Pt Ste 300 La Palma (90623) ***(G-27054)***
Honeywell International Inc..........714 283-0110
1635 N Batavia St Orange (92867) ***(G-7445)***
Honeywell International Inc..........408 962-2000
1349 Moffett Park Dr Sunnyvale (94089) ***(G-7579)***
Honeywell International Inc..........408 986-8200
487 Mathew St Santa Clara (95050) ***(G-7580)***
Honeywell International Inc..........858 679-4140
13475 Danielson St # 100 Poway (92064) ***(G-25869)***
Hong Kong & Shanghai Banking..........213 626-2460
770 Wilshire Blvd Ste 800 Los Angeles (90017) ***(G-9700)***
Hong Kong & Shanghai Hotels..........310 551-2888
9882 Santa Monica Blvd Beverly Hills (90212) ***(G-12758)***
Hong Kong Bank, Los Angeles *Also called Hong Kong & Shanghai Banking* ***(G-9700)***
Honolulu Freight Service (PA)..........323 887-6777
1400 Date St Montebello (90640) ***(G-5102)***
Honor Rancho Station, Valencia *Also called Southern California Gas Co* ***(G-6280)***
Hood & Strong LLP (PA)..........415 781-0793
100 1st St Fl 14 San Francisco (94105) ***(G-26374)***
Hoopa Modular Building Entp..........530 244-2421
4415 Dogwood Ln Apt C Redding (96003) ***(G-1368)***
Hope Contra Costa, Pittsburg *Also called Lincoln Child Center Inc* ***(G-24711)***
Hope Hse For Mltpl-Handicapped (PA)..........626 443-1313
4215 Peck Rd El Monte (91732) ***(G-24695)***
Hope of Valley Mission..........661 673-5951
19379 Soledad Canyon Rd Santa Clarita (91351) ***(G-22747)***
Hope of Valley Rescue Mission..........818 392-0020
8165 San Fernando Rd Sun Valley (91352) ***(G-24013)***
Hope Services..........831 455-4940
19055 Portola Dr Salinas (93908) ***(G-24348)***
Hope Services (PA)..........408 284-2850
30 Las Colinas Ln San Jose (95119) ***(G-24349)***
Hopkins & Carley A Law Corp (PA)..........408 286-9800
70 S 1st St San Jose (95113) ***(G-23312)***
Hopland Band Pomo Indians Inc..........707 744-1395
13101 Nokomis Rd Hopland (95449) ***(G-19223)***
Hopland Band Pomo Indians Inc (PA)..........707 472-2100
3000 Shanel Rd Hopland (95449) ***(G-25542)***
Hopland Sho-Ka-Wah Casino, Hopland *Also called Shokawah Casino* ***(G-13249)***
Horizon Actuarial Services LLC..........818 691-2000
5200 Lankershim Blvd North Hollywood (91601) ***(G-27466)***
Horizon Beverage Company..........510 465-2212
8380 Pardee Dr Oakland (94621) ***(G-9064)***
Horizon Beverage Company LP..........510 465-2212
8380 Pardee Dr Oakland (94621) ***(G-8853)***
Horizon Dental Grp, El Cajon *Also called Anthony P Garofalo A Dental* ***(G-20246)***
Horizon For Hmwners Asscations, Mammoth Lakes *Also called Horizons 4 Condominiums Inc* ***(G-25271)***
Horizon Government Svcs Inc..........916 760-7913
4600 Northgate Blvd # 120 Sacramento (95834) ***(G-14673)***
Horizon Media Inc..........310 282-0909
1940 Century Park E Fl 3 Los Angeles (90067) ***(G-13996)***
Horizon Solar Power Inc..........844 765-2780
3570 W Florida Ave Hemet (92545) ***(G-2245)***
Horizon Systems, Sunnyvale *Also called Horizon Technologies Inc* ***(G-15222)***
Horizon Technologies Inc..........408 733-1530
1270 Oakmead Pkwy Ste 115 Sunnyvale (94085) ***(G-15222)***
Horizon Technology..........949 454-4614
1 Rancho Cir Lake Forest (92630) ***(G-7142)***
Horizon West, Monterey *Also called Monterey Pines Sklld Nursg Fac* ***(G-20797)***
Horizon West Inc..........916 488-8601
3529 Walnut Ave Carmichael (95608) ***(G-20674)***
Horizon West Inc..........916 331-4590
5255 Hemlock St Sacramento (95841) ***(G-20675)***
Horizon West Inc..........530 889-8122
3388 Bell Rd Auburn (95603) ***(G-26858)***
Horizon West Healthcare Inc..........916 782-1238
1161 Cirby Way Roseville (95661) ***(G-22145)***
Horizon West Healthcare Inc (HQ)..........916 624-6230
4020 Sierra College Blvd # 190 Rocklin (95677) ***(G-20676)***
Horizon West Healthcare Inc..........530 885-7511
12225 Shale Ridge Ln Auburn (95602) ***(G-21272)***
Horizon West Healthcare Inc..........707 462-1436
1162 S Dora St Ukiah (95482) ***(G-20677)***
Horizons 4 Condominiums Inc..........760 934-6779
2113 Meridan Blvd Mammoth Lakes (93546) ***(G-25271)***
Horizons Adult Day Health Care..........619 474-1822
1035 Harbison Ave National City (91950) ***(G-22977)***
Hornberger Worstell Assoc Inc..........415 391-1080
170 Maiden Ln Ste 600 San Francisco (94108) ***(G-26208)***
Hornberger, Mark R, San Francisco *Also called Hornberger Worstell Assoc Inc* ***(G-26208)***
Hornblower Cruises & Event, San Francisco *Also called Hornblower Yachts LLC* ***(G-4737)***
Hornblower Cruises & Events, San Diego *Also called Hornblower Yachts Inc* ***(G-4736)***
Hornblower Yachts Inc..........619 686-8700
2825 5th Ave San Diego (92103) ***(G-4736)***
Hornblower Yachts Inc..........619 234-8687
2825 5th Ave San Diego (92103) ***(G-27467)***
Hornblower Yachts LLC..........916 446-1185
200 Marina Blvd Berkeley (94710) ***(G-13765)***
Hornblower Yachts LLC (PA)..........415 788-8866
On The Embarcadero Pier 3 St Pier San Francisco (94111) ***(G-4737)***
Horner-Galleher Holding Co (PA)..........562 944-8885
9303 Greenleaf Ave Santa Fe Springs (90670) ***(G-6867)***
Hornitos Telephone Co..........608 831-1000
2896 Bear Vly Hornitos (95325) ***(G-5630)***
Horrigan Cole Enterprises, Murrieta *Also called National Mentor Holdings Inc* ***(G-24742)***
Horsemen Inc..........714 847-4243
16911 Algonquin St Huntington Beach (92649) ***(G-16704)***
Hort Tech Inc..........760 360-9000
78355 Darby Rd Bermuda Dunes (92203) ***(G-870)***
Horton Grand Hotel, San Diego *Also called Historical Properties Inc* ***(G-12743)***
Hortonworks Inc..........408 916-4121
5470 Great America Pkwy Santa Clara (95054) ***(G-15692)***
Hoshall Corporation..........916 987-1995
6608 Folsom Auburn Rd # 4 Folsom (95630) ***(G-13679)***
Hoshall Designer Group, Folsom *Also called Hoshall Corporation* ***(G-13679)***
Hospice & Home Health of E Bay..........510 632-4390
333 Hegenberger Rd # 700 Oakland (94621) ***(G-22472)***
Hospice By Bay (PA)..........415 927-2273
17 E Sir Francis Drake Bl Larkspur (94939) ***(G-22473)***
Hospice Caring Project of Sant..........831 430-3000
940 Disc Dr Scotts Valley (95066) ***(G-22474)***
Hospice Cheers..........626 799-2727
625 Fair Oaks Ave Ste 229 South Pasadena (91030) ***(G-22475)***
Hospice of Foothills (PA)..........530 272-5739
11270 Rough And Ready Hwy Grass Valley (95945) ***(G-22476)***
HOSPICE OF MARIN, Larkspur *Also called Hospice By Bay* ***(G-22473)***
Hospice of Owens Valley..........760 872-4663
162 E Line St Ste C Bishop (93514) ***(G-22477)***
Hospice of San Joaquin..........209 957-3888
3888 Pacific Ave Stockton (95204) ***(G-20678)***
Hospice Touch Inc..........310 574-5750
3401 W Sunflower Ave # 100 Santa Ana (92704) ***(G-22478)***
Hospital Assn Southern Cal (PA)..........213 347-2002
515 S Figueroa St # 1300 Los Angeles (90071) ***(G-24928)***
Hospital Business Services Inc..........909 235-4400
3300 E Guasti Rd Ontario (91761) ***(G-17226)***
Hospital Housekeeping..........323 913-4820
1300 N Vermont Ave Los Angeles (90027) ***(G-14321)***
Hospital of Barstow Inc..........760 256-1761
820 E Mountain View St Barstow (92311) ***(G-21607)***
Hospital of Community (HQ)..........831 624-5311
23625 Holman Hwy Monterey (93940) ***(G-22146)***
Hospitality Solutions LLC..........209 474-3301
111 E March Ln Stockton (95207) ***(G-12759)***
Hospitlity Fcsed Solutions Inc..........562 424-1720
3229 E Spring St Ste 200 Long Beach (90806) ***(G-26209)***
Host Hotels & Resorts Inc..........415 775-7555
1250 Columbus Ave San Francisco (94133) ***(G-12760)***
Host Hotels & Resorts Inc..........619 232-1234
1 Market Pl San Diego (92101) ***(G-12761)***
Host Hotels & Resorts LP..........949 640-4000
900 Newport Center Dr Newport Beach (92660) ***(G-12762)***
Host Hotels & Resorts LP..........619 692-3800
8757 Rio San Diego Dr San Diego (92108) ***(G-12763)***
Host Hotels & Resorts LP..........650 347-1234
1333 Bayshore Hwy Burlingame (94010) ***(G-12764)***
Host Hotels & Resorts LP..........408 988-1500
2700 Mission College Blvd Santa Clara (95054) ***(G-12765)***
Host Hotels & Resorts LP..........760 341-2211
74855 Country Club Dr Palm Desert (92260) ***(G-12766)***
Host Hotels & Resorts LP..........310 417-3807
201 World Way Los Angeles (90045) ***(G-12767)***
Host Hotels & Resorts LP..........619 291-2900
1380 Harbor Island Dr San Diego (92101) ***(G-12768)***
Host Hotels & Resorts LP..........415 896-1600
55 4th St San Francisco (94103) ***(G-12769)***
Host Hotels & Resorts LP..........714 957-1100
500 Anton Blvd Costa Mesa (92626) ***(G-12770)***
Host Hotels & Resorts LP..........949 854-4500
500 Bayview Cir Newport Beach (92660) ***(G-12771)***
Host Hotels & Resorts LP..........650 692-9100
1800 Old Bayshore Hwy Burlingame (94010) ***(G-12772)***
Host Hotels & Resorts LP..........310 823-1700
4375 Admiralty Way Venice (90292) ***(G-12773)***

Host Hotels & Resorts LP.....310 216-5858
5400 W Century Blvd Los Angeles (90045) ***(G-12774)***
Host Hotels & Resorts LP.....310 546-7511
1400 Park View Ave Manhattan Beach (90266) ***(G-12775)***
Host Hotels & Resorts LP.....310 301-3000
4100 Admiralty Way Marina Del Rey (90292) ***(G-12776)***
Host Hotels & Resorts LP.....310 216-5858
5400 W Century Blvd Los Angeles (90045) ***(G-12777)***
Host International Inc.....408 294-1702
1661 Airport Blvd Ste 3e San Jose (95110) ***(G-12778)***
Host International Inc.....619 231-5100
3835 N Harbor Dr San Diego (92101) ***(G-12779)***
Hostmark Investors Ltd Partnr.....408 330-0001
4949 Great America Pkwy Santa Clara (95054) ***(G-27055)***
Hot Dogger Tours Inc.....714 449-6888
223 Imperial Hwy Ste 165 Fullerton (92835) ***(G-3903)***
Hot Line Construction Inc.....925 634-9333
9020 Brentwood Blvd Ste H Brentwood (94513) ***(G-2615)***
Hotbox, Campbell *Also called Streamray Inc* ***(G-18500)***
Hotchkis Wiley Capitl MGT LLC (PA).....213 430-1000
725 S Figueroa St # 3900 Los Angeles (90017) ***(G-27056)***
Hotdoodle.com, Fremont *Also called Metabyte Inc* ***(G-16431)***
Hotel Adagio, San Francisco *Also called SC Hotel Partners LLC* ***(G-13224)***
Hotel Adventures LLC.....714 730-7717
17662 Irvine Blvd Ste 4 Tustin (92780) ***(G-12780)***
Hotel Bel-Air, Los Angeles *Also called Kava Holdings Inc* ***(G-12876)***
Hotel Bel-Air.....310 472-1211
701 Stone Canyon Rd Los Angeles (90077) ***(G-12781)***
Hotel Britton, San Francisco *Also called Reneson Hotels Inc* ***(G-13145)***
Hotel Casa Del Mar, Santa Monica *Also called Et Whitehall Seascape LLC* ***(G-12625)***
Hotel Circle Inn & Suites.....619 851-6800
2201 Hotel Cir S San Diego (92108) ***(G-12782)***
Hotel Circle Property LLC.....619 291-7131
500 Hotel Cir N San Diego (92108) ***(G-12783)***
Hotel Contracting Services Inc.....916 865-4204
2140 Prof Dr Ste 150 Roseville (95661) ***(G-12784)***
Hotel De Anza, San Jose *Also called Saratoga Capital Inc* ***(G-13220)***
Hotel Del Coronado LP.....619 522-8011
1500 Orange Ave Coronado (92118) ***(G-12785)***
Hotel Diamond.....530 893-3100
220 W 4th St Chico (95928) ***(G-12786)***
Hotel Durant A Ltd Partnership.....510 845-8981
2600 Durant Ave Berkeley (94704) ***(G-12787)***
Hotel Griffon, San Francisco *Also called Embarcadero Inn Associates* ***(G-12616)***
Hotel Hanford, The, Costa Mesa *Also called Hanford Hotels Inc* ***(G-12687)***
Hotel Healdsburg (PA).....707 431-2800
25 Matheson St Healdsburg (95448) ***(G-12788)***
Hotel Indigo San Diego, San Diego *Also called Intercntnntal Ht Group Rsurces* ***(G-12839)***
Hotel Kabuki, San Francisco *Also called Bre/Japantown Owner LLC* ***(G-12464)***
Hotel La Jolla.....858 459-0261
7955 La Jolla Shores Dr La Jolla (92037) ***(G-12789)***
Hotel Laguna, Laguna Beach *Also called Andersen Hotels Inc* ***(G-12391)***
Hotel Mac Restaurant Inc.....510 233-0576
50 Washington Ave Richmond (94801) ***(G-12790)***
Hotel Managers Group Llc.....858 673-1534
11590 W Bernardo Ct # 211 San Diego (92127) ***(G-27057)***
Hotel Marmonte, Santa Barbara *Also called H D G Associates* ***(G-12682)***
Hotel Maya, Long Beach *Also called Queensbay Hotel LLC* ***(G-13118)***
Hotel Menage, Anaheim *Also called Newage Anaheim Inn LLC* ***(G-13019)***
Hotel Moneco, San Francisco *Also called Kimpton Hotel & Rest Group LLC* ***(G-27095)***
Hotel Nikko San Francisco Inc.....415 394-1111
222 Mason St San Francisco (94102) ***(G-12791)***
Hotel On Huntington Beach, Huntington Beach *Also called R C Hotels Inc* ***(G-13119)***
Hotel Pacific, Monterey *Also called Coastal Hotel Group Inc* ***(G-12532)***
Hotel Palomar, Los Angeles *Also called Behringer Harvard Wilshire Blv* ***(G-12432)***
Hotel Portofino, Redondo Beach *Also called Portofino Hotel Partners LP* ***(G-13106)***
Hotel Rex, San Francisco *Also called Rex Rising L P* ***(G-13151)***
Hotel Sfitel San Francisco Bay, Redwood City *Also called French Redwood Inc* ***(G-12653)***
Hotel Sofitel, Redwood City *Also called Accor Bus & Leisure N Amer Inc* ***(G-12372)***
Hotel Solamar, San Diego *Also called Souldriver Lessee Inc* ***(G-13273)***
Hotel Tonight Inc.....800 208-2949
901 Market St Ste 310 San Francisco (94103) ***(G-12792)***
Hotel Vitale, San Francisco *Also called Mission Stuart Ht Partners LLC* ***(G-12999)***
Hotel Whitcomb.....415 626-8000
1231 Market St San Francisco (94103) ***(G-12793)***
Hotpads Com.....563 289-7368
225 Bush St Ste 1100 San Francisco (94104) ***(G-13766)***
Hotrollergirl Productions.....530 521-2745
11890 Silver Spur St Ojai (93023) ***(G-18549)***
Hotwire Inc.....415 645-7350
655 Montgomery St Ste 600 San Francisco (94111) ***(G-5631)***
Houalla Enterprises Ltd.....949 515-4350
2610 Avon St Newport Beach (92663) ***(G-1573)***
Houchin Blood Services.....661 327-8541
11515 Bolthouse Dr Bakersfield (93311) ***(G-22978)***
Houdini Inc.....714 228-4406
6311 Knott Ave Buena Park (90620) ***(G-4573)***
Houlihan Lokey Inc (PA).....310 553-8871
10250 Constellation Blvd # 5 Los Angeles (90067) ***(G-10012)***
House Ear Clinic Inc (PA).....213 483-9930
2100 W 3rd St Ste 111 Los Angeles (90057) ***(G-19561)***
House of Air LLC.....415 345-9675
926 Mason St San Francisco (94129) ***(G-19224)***
House of Blues, Los Angeles *Also called Hob Entertainment LLC* ***(G-18472)***
House of Blues Concerts Inc (HQ).....323 769-4977
6255 W Sunset Blvd Fl 16 Los Angeles (90028) ***(G-18473)***
House of Prayer.....916 410-3349
701 2nd St Modesto (95351) ***(G-12158)***
House of Seven Gables Re (PA).....714 731-3777
12651 Newport Ave Tustin (92780) ***(G-11573)***
House of Tudor, Vista *Also called Baked In Sun* ***(G-8803)***
Housing Athrty of The Cnty of.....831 454-9455
2931 Mission St Santa Cruz (95060) ***(G-11574)***
Housing Auth Cnty Monterey, Salinas *Also called The Housing Authority of* ***(G-13456)***
Housing Authority Division, Alhambra *Also called Community Development Comm* ***(G-11450)***
Housing Division, Sunnyvale *Also called City of Sunnyvale* ***(G-13490)***
Housing Services, San Luis Obispo *Also called Cal Poly Corporation* ***(G-13449)***
Houston Salem Inc.....310 719-7004
217 E 157th St Gardena (90248) ***(G-8346)***
Houweling Nurseries Oxnard Inc.....805 488-8832
645 Laguna Rd Camarillo (93012) ***(G-8486)***
Houweling's Tomatoes, Camarillo *Also called Houweling Nurseries Oxnard Inc* ***(G-8486)***
Houzz Inc (PA).....650 326-3000
285 Hamilton Ave Fl 4 Palo Alto (94301) ***(G-15223)***
Hovlid Skilled Nursing.....530 846-9065
240 Spruce St Gridley (95948) ***(G-20679)***
Howard John.....562 425-4232
7681 Carson Blvd Long Beach (90808) ***(G-12794)***
Howard CDM.....562 427-4124
3750 Long Beach Blvd Long Beach (90807) ***(G-1191)***
Howard Construction, Long Beach *Also called Howard CDM* ***(G-1191)***
Howard Contracting Inc.....562 596-2969
12354 Carson St Hawaiian Gardens (90716) ***(G-3432)***
Howard Fischer Associates Inc.....408 374-0580
254 E Hacienda Ave Campbell (95008) ***(G-14674)***
Howard Hughes Medical Inst.....650 725-8252
279 Campus Dr Rm B202 Stanford (94305) ***(G-26530)***
Howard Hughes Medical Inst.....415 476-9668
1550 4th St Rm 190 San Francisco (94143) ***(G-26531)***
Howard Johnson, Anaheim *Also called Northwest Hotel Corporation* ***(G-13028)***
Howard Roofing Company Inc.....909 622-5598
245 N Mountain View Ave Pomona (91767) ***(G-3179)***
Howard Training Center (PA).....209 538-2431
1424 Stonum Rd Modesto (95351) ***(G-24350)***
HOWARD, FRANK R MEMORIAL HOSPI, Willits *Also called Willits Hospital Inc* ***(G-22033)***
Howards Appliances Inc.....626 288-4010
5102 Industry Ave Pico Rivera (90660) ***(G-4574)***
Howards Warehouse & Svc Ctr, Pico Rivera *Also called Howards Appliances Inc* ***(G-4574)***
Howe Community Center.....916 927-3802
2201 Cottage Way Sacramento (95825) ***(G-19225)***
Howe Electric Construction Inc.....559 255-8992
4682 E Olive Ave Fresno (93702) ***(G-2616)***
Howrey LLP.....650 798-3300
1950 University Ave # 400 East Palo Alto (94303) ***(G-23313)***
Howroyd-Wright Emplymnt Agcy (HQ).....818 240-8688
327 W Broadway Glendale (91204) ***(G-14675)***
Howroyd-Wright Emplymnt Agcy.....818 240-8688
327 W Broadway Glendale (91204) ***(G-14676)***
Hoyu America Co.....714 230-3000
6265 Phyllis Dr Cypress (90630) ***(G-8263)***
HP Communications Inc.....951 572-1200
13341 Temescal Canyon Rd Corona (92883) ***(G-1940)***
HP Enterprise Services LLC.....916 636-1000
3215 Prospect Park Dr Rancho Cordova (95670) ***(G-16140)***
HP Enterprise Services LLC.....619 817-3851
3990 Sherman St San Diego (92110) ***(G-16141)***
HP Enterprise Services LLC.....310 331-1074
1 Hornet Way El Segundo (90245) ***(G-16142)***
HP Inc.....310 255-3000
2525 Colorado Ave Ste 310 Santa Monica (90404) ***(G-15224)***
HP Inc.....650 265-5448
4209 Technology Dr Fremont (94538) ***(G-15693)***
HP Inc.....408 886-3200
20400 Stevens Creek Blvd Cupertino (95014) ***(G-16890)***
HP Inc.....714 432-6588
575 Anton Blvd Ste 300 Costa Mesa (92626) ***(G-15959)***
HP Inc.....858 655-4100
16399 W Bernardo Dr # 66 San Diego (92127) ***(G-7581)***
HP Inc.....650 857-4946
1501 Page Mill Rd Palo Alto (94304) ***(G-26532)***
HP Inc.....650 857-1501
481 Cottonwood Dr Milpitas (95035) ***(G-4575)***
HP Inc.....916 449-9553
980 9th St Fl 16 Sacramento (95814) ***(G-15960)***
HP Inc.....818 227-5033
6320 Canoga Ave Ste 1500 Woodland Hills (91367) ***(G-15961)***
HP Inc.....650 857-1501
130 Lytton Ave Palo Alto (94301) ***(G-16298)***
HP Inc.....650 617-3330
250 University Ave Lbby Palo Alto (94301) ***(G-15694)***
HP Pavillion At San Jose, San Jose *Also called San Jose Sharks LLC* ***(G-18563)***
HP Sears Co., Bakersfield *Also called H P Sears Co Inc* ***(G-17206)***
Hpa-USA, Compton *Also called Hydroprocessing Associates LLC* ***(G-17230)***
HPM Construction LLC.....949 474-9170
17911 Mitchell S Irvine (92614) ***(G-1574)***
Hps Mechanical Inc (PA).....661 397-2121
3100 E Belle Ter Bakersfield (93307) ***(G-2246)***
Hps Plumbing Service Inc.....661 324-2121
3100 E Belle Ter Bakersfield (93307) ***(G-1941)***
Hpt Trs Ihg 2 Inc.....310 781-9100
19800 S Vermont Ave Torrance (90502) ***(G-12795)***
Hpt Trs Ihg 2 Inc.....805 964-6241
5650 Calle Real Goleta (93117) ***(G-12796)***

ALPHABETIC

Hpt Trs Ihg-2 Inc.....408 241-9305
481 El Camino Real Santa Clara (95050) **(G-12797)**
Hpt Trs Ihg-2 Inc.....714 748-7777
1915 S Manchester Ave Anaheim (92802) **(G-12798)**
Hpt Trs Ihg-2 Inc.....310 642-7500
5985 W Century Blvd Los Angeles (90045) **(G-12799)**
Hpt Trs Ihg-2 Inc.....310 318-8888
300 N Harbor Dr Redondo Beach (90277) **(G-12800)**
Hpt Trs Ihg-2 Inc.....408 745-1515
900 Hamlin Ct Sunnyvale (94089) **(G-12801)**
Hqp, San Diego *Also called Community Clinics Hlth Netwrk* **(G-25130)**
Hr Mission Commons Fc 5183.....909 793-8691
10 Terracina Blvd Redlands (92373) **(G-24696)**
Hrd Aero Systems Inc.....661 295-0670
25555 Avenue Stanford Valencia (91355) **(G-17982)**
Hrd Aero Systems Inc (PA).....661 295-0670
25555 Avenue Stanford Valencia (91355) **(G-17983)**
Hrd Oxygens, Valencia *Also called Hrd Aero Systems Inc* **(G-17982)**
Hrl Laboratories LLC.....310 317-5000
3011 Malibu Canyon Rd Malibu (90265) **(G-26769)**
Hrn Services, Citrus Heights *Also called Accountable Health Staff Inc* **(G-14830)**
Hronis Inc A California Corp (PA).....661 725-2503
10443 Hronis Rd Delano (93215) **(G-219)**
Hronopoulos.....619 237-6161
110 W A St Ste 900 San Diego (92101) **(G-27058)**
Hsbc Bank USA NA, Los Angeles *Also called Hsbc Business Credit (usa)* **(G-9784)**
Hsbc Business Credit (usa).....213 553-8089
660 S Figueroa St # 1030 Los Angeles (90017) **(G-9784)**
Hsbc Finance Corporation.....408 796-3600
1420 El Paseo De Saratoga San Jose (95130) **(G-9751)**
Hsbc Finance Corporation.....909 623-3355
931 Corporate Center Dr Pomona (91768) **(G-9752)**
Hsbc Finance Corporation.....818 999-9175
21801 Ventura Bouelvard Woodland Hills (91364) **(G-9858)**
Hsbc Finance Corporation.....213 628-8167
725 N Broadway Los Angeles (90012) **(G-9753)**
Hsf Programme, San Francisco *Also called San Francisco Health Authority* **(G-25155)**
Hsn LLC.....909 349-2600
13423 Santa Ana Ave Fontana (92337) **(G-4576)**
Hssc, Santa Rosa *Also called Sonoma County Humane Society* **(G-645)**
Hst Lessee Boston LLC.....619 692-2255
1380 Harbor Island Dr San Diego (92101) **(G-12802)**
Hst Lessee San Diego LP.....619 291-2900
1380 Harbor Island Dr San Diego (92101) **(G-11575)**
HSU FOUNDATION, Arcata *Also called Humboldt State University Spon* **(G-27946)**
Htec Groupinc.....650 949-4880
222 Kearny St Ste 800 San Francisco (94108) **(G-15225)**
Huawei Enterprise USA Inc.....408 394-4295
20400 Stevens Creek Blvd Cupertino (95014) **(G-5632)**
Hub Construction Spc Inc (PA).....909 235-4100
379 S I St San Bernardino (92410) **(G-14547)**
Hub Construction Spc Inc.....909 947-4669
1856 S Bon View Ave Ontario (91761) **(G-7775)**
Hub Construction Sups & Eqp, San Bernardino *Also called Hub Construction Spc Inc* **(G-14547)**
Hub Group Trucking Inc.....209 943-6975
4221 E Mariposa Rd Stockton (95215) **(G-4025)**
Hub Group Trucking Inc.....951 693-9813
3801 E Guasti Rd Ontario (91761) **(G-4026)**
Hub Intrntional Insur Svcs Inc.....916 974-7800
3636 American River Dr # 200 Sacramento (95864) **(G-10741)**
Hub Intrntional Insur Svcs Inc.....805 682-2571
40 E Alamar Ave Santa Barbara (93105) **(G-10742)**
HUB-LIMITED WORKSHOP, Los Angeles *Also called Mid Cities Assn Retarded Ctzns* **(G-24366)**
Hubb Systems LLC.....510 865-9100
2021 Challenger Dr Alameda (94501) **(G-15962)**
Hubbard Dianetics Foundation.....323 953-3206
4833 Fountain Ave Los Angeles (90029) **(G-25543)**
Hubbard Iron Doors Inc.....323 724-6500
7407 Telegraph Rd Montebello (90640) **(G-7375)**
Hubzone-Cw Driver Joint Ventr.....909 484-0933
9300 Santa Anita Ave Rancho Cucamonga (91730) **(G-17227)**
Hudson Gardens, Pasadena *Also called Aah Hudson LP* **(G-11080)**
Hudson Pacific Properties Inc (PA).....310 445-5700
11601 Wilshire Blvd Fl 6 Los Angeles (90025) **(G-12249)**
Hudson Ranch Power I LLC.....858 509-0150
409 W Mcdonald St Calipatria (92233) **(G-6139)**
Hudson Tchmart Cmmerce Ctr LLC.....408 451-4440
5201 Great America Pkwy Santa Clara (95054) **(G-11002)**
Hudson, H Claude Cmplte Hlth, Los Angeles *Also called County of Los Angeles* **(G-19469)**
HUG Company.....510 887-0340
2557 Barrington Ct Hayward (94545) **(G-8487)**
Hugo Alonso Inc.....619 660-5395
2820 Via Orange Way Ste J Spring Valley (91978) **(G-1438)**
Huitt - Zollars Inc.....949 988-5815
2603 Main St Ste 400 Irvine (92614) **(G-26275)**
Hulk Construction.....714 701-9458
4352 Lakeview Ave Yorba Linda (92886) **(G-3456)**
Hulu LLC (PA).....310 571-4700
2500 Broadway Fl 2 Santa Monica (90404) **(G-5871)**
Human Options Inc.....949 757-3635
1901 Newport Blvd Ste 240 Costa Mesa (92627) **(G-24014)**
Human Potential Cons LLC.....310 756-1560
373 Van Ness Ave Ste 160 Torrance (90501) **(G-27792)**
Human Resources, Anaheim *Also called Interstate Electronics Corp* **(G-27483)**
Human Resources, Santa Barbara *Also called Santa Barbara County of* **(G-24191)**
Human Resources Department, Redwood City *Also called County of San Mateo* **(G-26994)**
Human Resources Department, Redwood City *Also called County of San Mateo* **(G-26995)**
Human Resources Department, Covina *Also called Citrus Valley Medical Ctr Inc* **(G-21489)**
Human Resources Department, Redwood City *Also called County of San Mateo* **(G-26996)**
Human Services Agency, Belmont *Also called County of San Mateo* **(G-23915)**
Human Services Association (PA).....562 806-5400
6800 Florence Ave Bell (90201) **(G-24015)**
Human Services Department, Yreka *Also called County of Siskiyou* **(G-23919)**
Human Services Dept, Oakland *Also called City of Oakland* **(G-23756)**
Human Services Dept, Delano *Also called County of Kern* **(G-23818)**
Human Services Dept, Bakersfield *Also called County of Kern* **(G-24905)**
Human Services Projects Inc.....209 951-9625
5361 N Pershing Ave Ste H Stockton (95207) **(G-24697)**
Human Services Systems, San Bernardino *Also called County of San Bernardino* **(G-23892)**
Human Services Systems, San Bernardino *Also called County of San Bernardino* **(G-24450)**
Human Touch LLC.....562 426-8700
3030 Walnut Ave Long Beach (90807) **(G-6819)**
Human Touch Home Health.....424 247-8165
3629 N Sepulveda Blvd Manhattan Beach (90266) **(G-22479)**
Humane Society Silicon Valley.....408 262-2133
901 Ames Ave Milpitas (95035) **(G-641)**
Humanitycom Inc.....415 230-0108
235 Montgomery St Ste 500 San Francisco (94104) **(G-15226)**
Humble Hustle Incorporated.....951 444-0263
1101 California Ave # 100 Corona (92881) **(G-27468)**
Humboldt Commnty Accss Resrc.....707 444-9631
415 7th St Eureka (95501) **(G-24016)**
Humboldt County Mental Health, Eureka *Also called County of Humboldt* **(G-22697)**
Humboldt Home Health Services, Orange *Also called St Joseph Prof Svcs Entps Inc* **(G-23581)**
Humboldt Open Door Clinic, Arcata *Also called Open Door Community Hlth Ctrs* **(G-22783)**
Humboldt Senior Resource Ctr (PA).....707 443-9747
1910 California St Eureka (95501) **(G-24017)**
Humboldt State University Spon.....707 826-4189
1 Harpst St Arcata (95521) **(G-27946)**
Humboldt Yacht Club.....707 443-1469
2479 Wrigley Rd Eureka (95503) **(G-18961)**
Hume Lake Christian Camps Inc.....559 305-7770
64144 Hume Lake Rd Ofc Miramonte (93628) **(G-13466)**
Humetrix Inc.....858 259-8987
1155 Camino Del Mar Ste 5 Del Mar (92014) **(G-27469)**
Humnit Hotel At Lax LLC.....424 702-1234
6225 W Century Blvd Los Angeles (90045) **(G-12803)**
Humphrey Plumbing Inc.....209 634-4626
880 S Kilroy Rd Turlock (95380) **(G-2247)**
Humphreys Half Moon Inn, San Diego *Also called Bartell Hotels* **(G-12417)**
Hunsaker & Assoc Irvine Inc (PA).....949 583-1010
3 Hughes Irvine (92618) **(G-25870)**
Hunt Ortmann Palffy Nieves.....626 440-5200
301 N Lake Ave Fl 7 Pasadena (91101) **(G-23314)**
Hunt Convenience Stores LLC.....916 383-4868
5750 S Watt Ave Sacramento (95829) **(G-27059)**
Hunt Enterprises Inc.....310 325-1496
2270 Sepulveda Blvd # 50 Torrance (90501) **(G-11576)**
Hunter Advertising Mail Co, San Leandro *Also called Kp LLC* **(G-14078)**
Hunter Easterday Corporation.....714 238-3400
1475 N Hundley St Anaheim (92806) **(G-14322)**
Hunter Industries Incorporated (PA).....800 383-4747
1940 Diamond St San Marcos (92078) **(G-7967)**
Hunter Mc Clellan Inc.....626 397-2700
120 W Bellevue Dr Ste 200 Pasadena (91105) **(G-26210)**
Hunter Realty Inc.....805 346-8688
2605 S Miller St Ste 101 Santa Maria (93455) **(G-11577)**
Hunter-La Purisima Corp.....661 616-0600
5060 California Ave # 640 Bakersfield (93309) **(G-27947)**
Hunting Energy Services Inc.....661 633-4272
4900 California Ave 100a Bakersfield (93309) **(G-1083)**
Hunting-Vinson, Bakersfield *Also called Hunting Energy Services Inc* **(G-1083)**
Huntington Ambltry Surg Ctr.....626 229-8999
625 S Fair Oaks Ave Pasadena (91105) **(G-19562)**
Huntington Bch Cnvlescent Hosp.....714 847-3515
18811 Florida St Huntington Beach (92648) **(G-20680)**
Huntington Beach Cmnty Clinic, Huntington Beach *Also called Huntington Beach Commnty Clinc* **(G-19563)**
Huntington Beach Commnty Clinc.....714 847-4222
8041 Newman Ave Huntington Beach (92647) **(G-19563)**
Huntington Beach Hospital, Huntington Beach *Also called Prime Hlthcare Hntngton Bch* **(G-21816)**
Huntington Care LLC.....877 405-6990
2555 E Colo Blvd Ste 400h Pasadena (91107) **(G-22480)**
Huntington Care, Inc., Pasadena *Also called Huntington Care LLC* **(G-22480)**
Huntington Child Care Center, Los Angeles *Also called Casa Dscanso Convalescent Hosp* **(G-27777)**
Huntington Extended Care Ctr, Pasadena *Also called Pasadena Hospital Assn Ltd* **(G-20843)**
Huntington Hospital.....626 397-5000
100 W California Blvd Pasadena (91105) **(G-21608)**
Huntington Hotel Company.....858 756-1131
5951 Linea Del Cielo Rancho Santa Fe (92067) **(G-12804)**
Huntington Med Pathology Group, Pasadena *Also called Pasadena Cyto Pathology Lab* **(G-22252)**
Huntington Med Res Institutes.....626 397-5804
734 Fairmount Ave Pasadena (91105) **(G-26770)**
HUNTINGTON MEMORIAL HOSPITAL, Pasadena *Also called Pasadena Hospital Assn Ltd* **(G-21787)**
Huntington Memory Care Cmnty, Alhambra *Also called Silverado Senior Living Inc* **(G-21374)**

ALPHABETIC

ALPHABETIC SECTION

Huntington Otptent Surgery Ctr 626 535-2434
  625 S Fair Oaks Ave # 380 Pasadena (91105) *(G-19564)*
Huntington Park Nursing Center, Huntington Park *Also called Covenant Care California LLC (G-20492)*
HUNTINGTON PARK POLICE DEPARTM, Huntington Park *Also called Huntington Pk Police League (G-24018)*
Huntington Pk Police League 323 584-6254
  6542 Miles Ave Huntington Park (90255) *(G-24018)*
Huntington Reprodctve Ctr Inc (PA) 626 440-9161
  333 S Arroyo Pkwy Pasadena (91105) *(G-19565)*
Huntington Rsdntial Rtrment Ht, Torrance *Also called Longwood Management Inc (G-24716)*
HUNTINGTON VALLEY HEALTHCARE C, Huntington Beach *Also called Douglas Fir Holdings LLC (G-20521)*
Huntleigh USA Corporation 619 231-8111
  3707 N Harbor Dr A-110 San Diego (92101) *(G-4921)*
Huntley Hotel Santa Monica Bch, Santa Monica *Also called Second Street Corporation (G-13230)*
Hunton & Williams LLP 415 975-3700
  575 Market St Ste 3700 San Francisco (94105) *(G-23315)*
Hunton & Williams LLP 213 532-2000
  550 S Hope St Ste 2000 Los Angeles (90071) *(G-23316)*
Huntsman Architectural Group (PA) 415 394-1212
  50 California St Fl 7 San Francisco (94111) *(G-26211)*
Huoyen International Inc 714 635-9000
  1500 S Raymond Ave Fullerton (92831) *(G-12805)*
Huppe Landscape Company Inc (HQ) 916 784-7666
  9350 Viking Pl Roseville (95747) *(G-773)*
Hurley Construction Inc 916 446-7599
  1801 I St Ste 200 Sacramento (95811) *(G-1314)*
Huron Development Inc 949 863-9789
  19800 Macarthur Blvd Irvine (92612) *(G-12315)*
Huskies Lessee LLC 415 392-7755
  450 Powell St San Francisco (94102) *(G-12806)*
Hussmann Services Corporation 916 920-4993
  120 Main Ave Ste A1 Sacramento (95838) *(G-17922)*
Hustle Digital Inc 310 882-2680
  12777 W Jefferson Blvd Los Angeles (90066) *(G-17228)*
Hustler Casino, Gardena *Also called El Dorado Enterprises Inc (G-12613)*
Hutchinson & Bloodgood LLP (PA) 818 637-5000
  550 N Brand Blvd Fl 14 Glendale (91203) *(G-26375)*
Hutchison Corporation 310 763-7991
  6107 Obispo Ave Long Beach (90805) *(G-1575)*
Huttig Building Products Inc 916 383-3721
  8120 Pwr Rdge Rd Bldg 100 Sacramento (95826) *(G-6932)*
Huttig Sash & Door Co, Sacramento *Also called Huttig Building Products Inc (G-6932)*
Hv, Escondido *Also called Hidden Valley Companies Inc (G-5101)*
Hvi Cat Canyon Inc 805 621-5800
  2617 E Clark Ave Santa Maria (93455) *(G-1084)*
Hvsf Transition LLC 415 477-1999
  1100 Sansome St San Francisco (94111) *(G-13860)*
Hwe Mechanical, Bakersfield *Also called Hills Wldg & Engrg Contr Inc (G-1081)*
Hwn Mariposa Associates LLC 310 478-8757
  11150 Santa Monica Blvd # 760 Los Angeles (90025) *(G-1369)*
Hy-Lond Hlth Care Cnter-Merced, Merced *Also called Avalon Care Cntr Merced Hy (G-20391)*
Hy-Lond Hlth Care Cntr-Modesto, Modesto *Also called Avalon Health Care Inc (G-20395)*
Hy-Tech Tile Inc 951 788-0550
  1355 Palmyrita Ave Riverside (92507) *(G-3118)*
Hyatt Corporation 323 656-1234
  8401 W Sunset Blvd Los Angeles (90069) *(G-12807)*
Hyatt Corporation 530 562-3900
  4001 Northstar Dr Truckee (96161) *(G-12808)*
Hyatt Corporation 312 750-1234
  6225 W Century Blvd Los Angeles (90045) *(G-12809)*
Hyatt Corporation 909 240-9526
  3500 Market St Riverside (92501) *(G-12810)*
Hyatt Corporation 415 848-6050
  345 Stockton St San Francisco (94108) *(G-12811)*
Hyatt Corporation 415 788-1234
  50 Drumm St San Francisco (94111) *(G-12812)*
Hyatt Corporation 925 743-1882
  2323 San Ramon Vly Blvd San Ramon (94583) *(G-12813)*
Hyatt Corporation 562 432-0161
  200 S Pine Ave Long Beach (90802) *(G-12814)*
Hyatt Corporation 831 372-1234
  1 Old Golf Course Rd Monterey (93940) *(G-12815)*
Hyatt Corporation 949 975-1234
  17900 Jamboree Rd Irvine (92614) *(G-12816)*
Hyatt Corporation 714 750-1234
  11999 Harbor Blvd Garden Grove (92840) *(G-12817)*
Hyatt Corporation 760 341-1000
  44600 Indian Wells Ln Indian Wells (92210) *(G-12818)*
Hyatt Corporation 949 729-1234
  1107 Jamboree Rd Newport Beach (92660) *(G-12819)*
Hyatt Corporation 408 453-3006
  55 E Brokaw Rd San Jose (95112) *(G-12820)*
Hyatt Corporation 415 788-1234
  5 Embarcadero Ctr San Francisco (94111) *(G-12821)*
Hyatt Corporation 619 849-1234
  600 F St San Diego (92101) *(G-12822)*
Hyatt Corporation 805 557-1234
  880 S Westlake Blvd Westlake Village (91361) *(G-12823)*
Hyatt Equities LLC 408 993-1234
  1740 N 1st St San Jose (95112) *(G-12824)*
Hyatt Fisherman's Wharf, San Francisco *Also called Chsp Trs Fisherman Wharf LLC (G-12517)*
Hyatt Grand Champion Resort, Indian Wells *Also called Hyatt Corporation (G-12818)*
Hyatt Hotel, Monterey *Also called Classic Riverdale Inc (G-12527)*
Hyatt Hotel, Carmel *Also called Highlands Inn Investors II LP (G-12704)*
Hyatt Hotel, Los Angeles *Also called Hyatt Corporation (G-12807)*
Hyatt Hotel, San Francisco *Also called Hyatt Corporation (G-12812)*
Hyatt Hotel, Long Beach *Also called Hyatt Corporation (G-12814)*
Hyatt Hotel, San Jose *Also called Hyatt Equities LLC (G-12824)*
Hyatt Hotel, Irvine *Also called Hyatt Corporation (G-12816)*
Hyatt Hotel, Newport Beach *Also called Hyatt Corporation (G-12819)*
Hyatt Hotel, Los Angeles *Also called Jwmcc Limited Partnership (G-12873)*
Hyatt Hotel, Monterey *Also called Classic Rsdence Mgt Ltd Partnr (G-12528)*
Hyatt Hotel, San Diego *Also called Manchester Grand Resorts LP (G-12940)*
Hyatt Hotel, Westlake Village *Also called Hyatt Corporation (G-12823)*
Hyatt Hotels Corporation 831 372-1234
  1 Old Golf Course Rd Monterey (93940) *(G-12825)*
Hyatt Hotels Management Corp 661 799-1234
  24500 Town Center Dr Valencia (91355) *(G-12826)*
Hyatt Hotels Management Corp 858 552-1234
  3777 Lajolla Village Dr San Diego (92122) *(G-12827)*
Hyatt Hotels Management Corp 760 322-9000
  285 N Palm Canyon Dr Palm Springs (92262) *(G-12828)*
Hyatt Hotels Management Corp 650 352-1234
  4219 El Camino Real Palo Alto (94306) *(G-12829)*
Hyatt House Rancho Cordova, Rancho Cordova *Also called Select Hotels Group LLC (G-13232)*
Hyatt House San Ramon, San Ramon *Also called Hyatt Corporation (G-12813)*
Hyatt Los Angeles Airport, Los Angeles *Also called Hyatt Corporation (G-12809)*
Hyatt Pl Fremont/Silicon Vly, Fremont *Also called Select Hotels Group LLC (G-13231)*
Hyatt Place San Jose Hotel, San Jose *Also called West San Crlos Ht Partners LLC (G-13401)*
Hyatt Regency Century Plaza 310 228-1234
  2025 Avenue Of The Stars Los Angeles (90067) *(G-12830)*
Hyatt Regency Mission Bay Spa, San Diego *Also called H C T Inc (G-12681)*
Hyatt Regency Monterey, Monterey *Also called Hyatt Corporation (G-12815)*
Hyatt Regency Orange County, Garden Grove *Also called Hyatt Corporation (G-12817)*
Hyatt Regency Sacramento, Sacramento *Also called Capitol Regency LLC (G-12487)*
Hyatt Regency San Francisco Ht, San Francisco *Also called Hyatt Corporation (G-12821)*
Hyatt Regency Santa Clara 408 200-1234
  5101 Great America Pkwy Santa Clara (95054) *(G-12831)*
Hyatt Rgency Suites Palm Sprng, Palm Springs *Also called Rbd Hotel Palm Springs LLC (G-13130)*
Hyatt Rgncy San Frncisco Arprt, Burlingame *Also called Host Hotels & Resorts LP (G-12764)*
Hyatt Vacation Ownership Inc 310 285-0990
  9615 Brighton Way M180 Beverly Hills (90210) *(G-11578)*
Hyatt Vineyard Creek Ht & Spa, Santa Rosa *Also called Noble Aew Vineyard Creek LLC (G-13024)*
Hyatt Westlake Plaza Hotel, Westlake Village *Also called Sky Court USA Inc (G-13269)*
Hybrid Apparel, Cypress *Also called Hybrid Promotions LLC (G-8347)*
Hybrid Promotions LLC (PA) 714 952-3866
  10711 Walker St Cypress (90630) *(G-8347)*
Hyde & Hyde Inc (PA) 951 279-5239
  300 El Sobrante Rd Corona (92879) *(G-17229)*
Hyde Park Convalescent Hosp 323 753-1354
  6520 West Blvd Los Angeles (90043) *(G-20681)*
Hydraulx, Gardena *Also called Avongard Products USa Ltd (G-18215)*
Hydro Chem Industrial Services, Pittsburg *Also called Hydrochem LLC (G-14323)*
Hydro Power Service, Sacramento *Also called HDR Engineering Inc (G-25857)*
Hydro Tek Systems Inc 909 799-9222
  2353 Almond Ave Redlands (92374) *(G-7968)*
Hydro-Pressure Systems, North Hollywood *Also called Woods Maintenance Services Inc (G-3606)*
Hydrochem LLC 925 432-1749
  901 Loveridge Rd 592 Pittsburg (94565) *(G-14323)*
Hydroprocessing Associates LLC 310 667-6456
  19122 S Santa Fe Ave Compton (90221) *(G-17230)*
Hydrox Properties Xii LLC 510 262-7200
  3170 Hilltop Mall Rd Richmond (94806) *(G-11003)*
Hyland Software Inc 949 242-3100
  2355 Main St Ste 100 Irvine (92614) *(G-15227)*
Hylton Security Inc 916 442-1000
  1015 2nd St Fl 2 Sacramento (95814) *(G-16705)*
Hyperbaric MGT Systems Inc 619 336-2022
  3224 Hoover Ave National City (91950) *(G-19566)*
Hypercel Corporation 661 310-1000
  28385 Constellation Rd Valencia (91355) *(G-7582)*
Hyperloop One 213 800-3270
  2161 Sacramento St Los Angeles (90021) *(G-5222)*
Hypermedia Systems Inc 213 908-2214
  700 S Flower St Ste 3210 Los Angeles (90017) *(G-16398)*
Hyrian LLC 212 590-2567
  2355 Westwood Blvd Los Angeles (90064) *(G-14677)*
Hytrust Inc (PA) 650 681-8100
  1975 W El Camino Real # 203 Mountain View (94040) *(G-15695)*
Hyundai ABS Funding LLC 949 732-2697
  3161 Michelson Dr Irvine (92612) *(G-10013)*
Hyundai Atver TImtics Amer Inc 949 381-6000
  10550 Talbert Ave Fl 2 Fountain Valley (92708) *(G-15228)*
Hyundai Capital America (HQ) 714 965-3000
  3161 Michelson Dr # 1900 Irvine (92612) *(G-9754)*
Hyundai Finance, Irvine *Also called Hyundai Capital America (G-9754)*
Hyve Solutions Corporation 864 349-4415
  44201 Nobel Dr Fremont (94538) *(G-16143)*
I A C, Poway *Also called Intelligent Automation Corp (G-25883)*
I A C, Irvine *Also called Irvine APT Communities LP (G-11144)*
I B S, Roseville *Also called Ibs Enterprise Usa Inc (G-15230)*

I C A Nn, Los Angeles *Also called Internet Corp For Assigned Nam* ***(G-15969)***
I C Class Components Corp (PA) 310 539-5500
23605 Telo Ave Torrance (90505) ***(G-7583)***
I C M, Los Angeles *Also called International Creative Mgt Inc* ***(G-18398)***
I C M, Los Angeles *Also called International Creative MGT Inc* ***(G-18399)***
I C S, San Francisco *Also called Integrated Clg Solutions Inc* ***(G-14325)***
I C S I, Berkeley *Also called Interntional Cmpt Science Inst* ***(G-26773)***
I C W, San Diego *Also called Insurance Company of West* ***(G-10430)***
I Cypress Company 831 647-7500
2700 17 Mile Dr Pebble Beach (93953) ***(G-12832)***
I D Property Corporation 213 625-0100
1001 Wilshire Blvd # 100 Los Angeles (90017) ***(G-11579)***
I G F, Long Beach *Also called International Garment Finisher* ***(G-13632)***
I Heart Media Inc 559 243-4300
83 E Shaw Ave Ste 150 Fresno (93710) ***(G-5778)***
I Hot Leads 714 960-8028
19671 Beach Blvd Ste 204 Huntington Beach (92648) ***(G-16144)***
I I D, Imperial *Also called Imperial Irrigation District* ***(G-6140)***
I L S West Inc 714 505-7530
17501 17th St Ste 100 Tustin (92780) ***(G-26376)***
I Lan Systems Inc 626 304-9021
237 S Raymond Ave Alhambra (91801) ***(G-15963)***
I M T, Sherman Oaks *Also called Investors MGT Tr RE Group Inc* ***(G-11143)***
I Mean It Creative Inc 310 287-1000
10000 Venice Blvd Culver City (90232) ***(G-13861)***
I N C Builders Inc 760 352-4200
1560 Ocotillo Dr Ste L El Centro (92243) ***(G-14886)***
I N G, Compton *Also called Newport Apparel Corporation* ***(G-8405)***
I P I, Los Angeles *Also called Imperial Parking Industries* ***(G-17723)***
I P S, Mentone *Also called International Paving Svcs Inc* ***(G-1801)***
I P S Services Inc 909 305-0250
627 E Foothill Blvd San Dimas (91773) ***(G-22748)***
I PCA L P 310 395-3332
1707 4th St Santa Monica (90401) ***(G-12833)***
I Pwlc Inc 760 630-0231
408 Olive Ave Vista (92083) ***(G-774)***
I S A, Van Nuys *Also called Interviewing Service Amer Inc* ***(G-26675)***
I S D, Los Angeles *Also called IDS Real Estate Group* ***(G-11581)***
I S E, Los Angeles *Also called ISE Corporation* ***(G-26539)***
I T C, Citrus Heights *Also called Itc Service Group Inc* ***(G-27956)***
I T S, Long Beach *Also called International Trnsp Svc* ***(G-4747)***
I Wmi 562 977-4906
17100 Pioneer Blvd # 230 Artesia (90701) ***(G-1576)***
I2c Inc 650 480-5222
1300 Island Dr Ste 105 Redwood City (94065) ***(G-7143)***
I3pl LLC 909 839-2600
218 Machlin Ct Walnut (91789) ***(G-5103)***
Iaba, Los Angeles *Also called Institute For Applied Behavior* ***(G-20323)***
Iaba, Camarillo *Also called Institute For Applied Behavior* ***(G-20324)***
IAC Search & Media Inc (HQ) 510 985-7400
555 12th St Ste 500 Oakland (94607) ***(G-16244)***
Iaccess Technologies Inc 714 922-9158
1251 E Dyer Rd Ste 160 Santa Ana (92705) ***(G-25871)***
Iap West Inc 310 667-9720
20036 S Via Baron Rancho Dominguez (90220) ***(G-6739)***
Iap World Services Inc 650 604-0451
567 Dugan South Akron Rd Mountain View (94035) ***(G-27793)***
Iap World Services Inc 760 380-6772
510 S Loop 1st St Bldg T Fort Irwin (92310) ***(G-27794)***
Iapmo Research and Testing Inc (PA) 909 472-4100
5001 E Philadelphia St Ontario (91761) ***(G-25090)***
Ias Administrations Inc 323 953-3490
1311 N New Hampshire Ave Los Angeles (90027) ***(G-24929)***
Ibackup.com, Calabasas *Also called Idrive Inc* ***(G-16400)***
Ibaset Inc 949 598-5200
27442 Portola Pkwy # 300 Foothill Ranch (92610) ***(G-27948)***
Ibaset Federal Services LLC (PA) 949 598-5200
27442 Portola Pkwy # 300 Foothill Ranch (92610) ***(G-16399)***
Ibi Group (us) Inc (HQ) 949 477-5030
18401 Von Karman Ave # 110 Irvine (92612) ***(G-25872)***
Ibis Biosciences Inc 760 476-3200
2251 Faraday Ave Ste 150 Carlsbad (92008) ***(G-26533)***
Ibisworld Inc (HQ) 800 330-3772
11755 Wilshire Blvd # 1100 Los Angeles (90025) ***(G-26674)***
IBM, Agoura Hills *Also called International Bus Mchs Corp* ***(G-15968)***
IBM, San Jose *Also called International Bus Mchs Corp* ***(G-15248)***
IBM, San Francisco *Also called International Bus Mchs Corp* ***(G-7055)***
IBM, Costa Mesa *Also called International Bus Mchs Corp* ***(G-16408)***
IBM, Santa Clara *Also called International Bus Mchs Corp* ***(G-15249)***
IBM, Foster City *Also called International Bus Mchs Corp* ***(G-16409)***
IBM, Emeryville *Also called International Bus Mchs Corp* ***(G-15250)***
IBM, San Jose *Also called International Bus Mchs Corp* ***(G-7056)***
IBM, San Jose *Also called International Bus Mchs Corp* ***(G-26538)***
IBM, San Ramon *Also called International Bus Mchs Corp* ***(G-27481)***
Iboss Inc 877 742-6832
4110 Campus Point Ct San Diego (92121) ***(G-15229)***
Iboss Security, San Diego *Also called Iboss Inc* ***(G-15229)***
Ibs Enterprise Usa Inc (HQ) 916 542-2820
915 Highland Pointe Dr # 250 Roseville (95678) ***(G-15230)***
Ibuypower, City of Industry *Also called American Future Tech Corp* ***(G-7091)***
Ic BP III Holdings Xii LLC 415 549-5054
1 Sansome St Ste 1500 San Francisco (94104) ***(G-11580)***
Ic BP III Holdings Xv LLC 415 273-4250
1 Sansome St Fl 15 San Francisco (94104) ***(G-11256)***

Ic Compliance LLC (PA) 650 378-4150
1065 E Hillsdale Blvd # 300 Foster City (94404) ***(G-15231)***
Icallfirst 808 557-9299
18141 Beach Blvd Ste 290 Huntington Beach (92648) ***(G-5633)***
ICC, Fontana *Also called Inland Cc Inc* ***(G-3275)***
ICC Networking, Riverside *Also called Interntnal Communications Corp* ***(G-15970)***
ICC-NEXERGY, INC., Irvine *Also called Inventus Power Inc* ***(G-24036)***
Icci, Anaheim *Also called Interntnal Circuits Components* ***(G-7587)***
Ice, Brea *Also called Intercontinental Exchange Inc* ***(G-10109)***
Ice Center Enterprises LLC 510 604-8878
10123 N Wolfe Rd Ste 1020 Cupertino (95014) ***(G-19226)***
Ice Center, The, Cupertino *Also called Ice Center Enterprises LLC* ***(G-19226)***
Ice Delivery Systems Inc 408 640-4625
6920 Santa Teresa Blvd # 206 San Jose (95119) ***(G-4027)***
Ice Station Valencia L L C 661 775-8686
27745 Smyth Dr Valencia (91355) ***(G-19227)***
Icf Consulting Group Inc 703 934-3000
101 Lucas Valley Rd # 249 San Rafael (94903) ***(G-27470)***
Icf Jones & Stokes Inc 949 333-6600
1 Ada Ste 100 Irvine (92618) ***(G-27471)***
Icf Jones & Stokes Inc (HQ) 916 737-3000
630 K St Ste 400 Sacramento (95814) ***(G-27949)***
ICI Enterprises Inc 562 989-7715
790 E Willow St Ste 150 Long Beach (90806) ***(G-24351)***
ICI Services Corporation 805 988-3210
1000 Town Center Dr # 225 Oxnard (93036) ***(G-25873)***
Ickler Electric Corporation 858 486-1585
12175 Dearborn Pl Poway (92064) ***(G-2617)***
Icom Mechanical Inc 408 292-4968
477 Burke St San Jose (95112) ***(G-2248)***
Icon Exposure Inc 323 933-1666
5450 Wilshire Blvd Los Angeles (90036) ***(G-16950)***
Icon Media Direct Inc (PA) 818 995-6400
5910 Lemona Ave Van Nuys (91411) ***(G-13997)***
Icon Professional Services, Foster City *Also called Ic Compliance LLC* ***(G-15231)***
Ics Integrated Comm Systems 408 491-6000
550 Parrott St Ste 40 San Jose (95112) ***(G-2618)***
Ics Professional Services Inc 714 868-3900
7755 Center Ave Fl 11 Huntington Beach (92647) ***(G-3119)***
Ics-CA North, Roseville *Also called Industrial Container Services* ***(G-7936)***
Ictp, Anaheim *Also called Ray W Choi* ***(G-27609)***
Icu Eyewear Inc 510 848-4700
1900 Shelton Dr Hollister (95023) ***(G-8121)***
Icw Group Holdings Inc (PA) 858 350-2400
11455 El Camino Real San Diego (92130) ***(G-10429)***
Icw Valencia LLC 858 350-2600
11455 El Camino Real San Diego (92130) ***(G-11004)***
Icygen LLC 510 540-7122
940 Dwight Way Ste 13b Berkeley (94710) ***(G-15964)***
ID Analytics LLC 858 312-6200
15253 Ave Of Science San Diego (92128) ***(G-16891)***
Idc Technologies Inc 408 376-0212
1851 Mccarthy Blvd # 116 Milpitas (95035) ***(G-14678)***
Idea Bits LLC 818 736-5361
19749 Dearborn St Chatsworth (91311) ***(G-16951)***
Idea Travel Company 650 948-0207
13145 Byrd Ln Ste 101 Los Altos Hills (94022) ***(G-4962)***
Ideal Equipment Rental Inc 714 237-9232
14241 Alondra Blvd La Mirada (90638) ***(G-14548)***
Ideal Home Sales, Lafayette *Also called Rate Is Low* ***(G-9892)***
Ideal Living Management LLC 818 217-2000
14724 Ventura Blvd Fl 200 Sherman Oaks (91403) ***(G-27060)***
Ideal Transit Inc 626 448-2690
2301 Troy Ave South El Monte (91733) ***(G-3655)***
Idealab Holdings LLC (PA) 626 585-6900
130 W Union St Pasadena (91103) ***(G-12316)***
Idec Corporation (HQ) 408 747-0550
1175 Elko Dr Sunnyvale (94089) ***(G-7584)***
Identity Theft Recovery & Moni 888 269-2314
1990 N Calif Blvd Fl 8 Walnut Creek (94596) ***(G-13767)***
Identrus, San Francisco *Also called Efinance Corporation* ***(G-17145)***
Ideo LP 650 289-3400
780 High St Palo Alto (94301) ***(G-17231)***
Ideo LP (PA) 650 289-3400
150 Forest Ave Palo Alto (94301) ***(G-14149)***
Ideo LP 415 615-5000
The Embarcadero Pier 28 St Pier San Francisco (94105) ***(G-17232)***
Idexx Reference Labs Inc 949 477-2840
1370 Reynolds Ave Ste 109 Irvine (92614) ***(G-22225)***
Idexx Reference Labs Inc 916 372-4200
2825 Kovr Dr West Sacramento (95605) ***(G-22226)***
Idg California, La Palma *Also called Idg Usa LLC* ***(G-7935)***
Idg Usa LLC 714 994-6960
6842 Walker St La Palma (90623) ***(G-7935)***
Idle Acres Convalescent Hosp, El Monte *Also called Sabu Enterprises Inc* ***(G-21364)***
Idrive Inc 818 594-5972
26115 Mureau Rd Ste A Calabasas (91302) ***(G-16400)***
IDS, Pasadena *Also called Interprsnal Dvlpmntal Fclttors* ***(G-24035)***
IDS Real Estate Group (PA) 213 627-9937
515 S Figueroa St Fl 16 Los Angeles (90071) ***(G-11581)***
Idun Pharmaceuticals Inc 858 622-3000
9380 Judicial Dr San Diego (92121) ***(G-26771)***
IEC, Commerce *Also called Interstate Electric Co Inc* ***(G-7219)***
Iehp, Rancho Cucamonga *Also called Inland Empire Health Plan* ***(G-10241)***
Ies Engineering, Bakersfield *Also called Innovative Engrg Systems Inc* ***(G-25879)***
Iest Family Farms 559 674-9417
14576 Avenue 14 Madera (93637) ***(G-429)***
Ifly San Diego, San Diego *Also called Skygroup Investments LLC* ***(G-19284)***

ALPHABETIC

Ifncom Inc (PA)...213 452-1505
9841 Airport Blvd Fl 9 Los Angeles (90045) ***(G-5634)***
Ifwe Inc (PA)...415 946-1850
848 Battery St San Francisco (94111) ***(G-15696)***
Igate Corporation...415 836-8800
1 Market Plz Ste 1800 San Francisco (94105) ***(G-14679)***
Ignite Health LLC (PA)...949 861-3200
7535 Irvine Center Dr # 200 Irvine (92618) ***(G-13862)***
Ignited LLC (PA)...310 773-3100
2150 Park Pl Ste 100 El Segundo (90245) ***(G-13863)***
Ignition Creative LLC...310 315-6300
12959 Coral Tree Pl Los Angeles (90066) ***(G-18094)***
Igo Medical Group A Med Corp (PA)...858 455-7520
9339 Genesee Ave Ste 220 San Diego (92121) ***(G-19567)***
Igt Global Solutions Corp...562 946-9922
10415 Slusher Dr Ste 1 Santa Fe Springs (90670) ***(G-19228)***
Iheartcommunications Inc...415 975-5555
340 Townsend St Fl 4 San Francisco (94107) ***(G-5779)***
Iheartcommunications Inc...951 684-1992
2030 Iowa Ave Ste A Riverside (92507) ***(G-5780)***
Iheartcommunications Inc...559 222-4302
4880 N 1st St Fresno (93726) ***(G-5872)***
Iheartcommunications Inc...858 522-5547
9660 Gran Rdge Dr Ste 100 San Diego (92123) ***(G-5781)***
Iheartcommunications Inc...858 292-2000
9660 Gran Rdge Dr Ste 200 San Diego (92123) ***(G-5782)***
Iheartcommunications Inc...818 846-0029
3400 W Olive Ave Ste 550 Burbank (91505) ***(G-5873)***
Iheartcommunications Inc...916 929-5325
1545 River Park Dr # 500 Sacramento (95815) ***(G-5783)***
Iheartcommunications Inc...661 942-1268
352 E Avenue K4 Lancaster (93535) ***(G-5784)***
Iheartcommunications Inc...916 929-5325
1440 Ethan Way Sacramento (95825) ***(G-5785)***
Iheartcommunications Inc...858 565-6006
5745 Kearny Villa Rd M San Diego (92123) ***(G-5786)***
Iheartcommunications Inc...559 230-4300
83 E Shaw Ave Ste 150 Fresno (93710) ***(G-5787)***
Ihg Management (maryland) LLC...310 642-7500
5985 W Century Blvd Los Angeles (90045) ***(G-12834)***
Ihi, Roseville *Also called Intercare Holdings Insur Svcs* ***(G-10746)***
Ihms (sf) LLC...415 781-5555
340 Stockton St San Francisco (94108) ***(G-12835)***
Ihr Grnbuck Rncho Ccmnga Ventr, Rancho Cucamonga *Also called Aloft Ontario-Rancho Cucamonga* ***(G-12381)***
Ihs, Redding *Also called Redding Rancheria* ***(G-23039)***
IHSS Consortium, The, San Francisco *Also called Homebridge Inc* ***(G-24010)***
Ikano Communications Inc (PA)...801 924-0900
9221 Corbin Ave Ste 260 Northridge (91324) ***(G-16145)***
IKEA Purchasing Svcs US Inc...818 841-3500
600 N San Fernando Blvd Burbank (91502) ***(G-27061)***
Ikes Landscaping & Maintenance...530 758-1698
2700 Tiber Ave Davis (95616) ***(G-871)***
Ilanguagecom Inc...310 899-6800
901 Wilshire Blvd Ste 300 Santa Monica (90401) ***(G-17233)***
Illumina-Redwood City, Redwood City *Also called Verinata Health Inc* ***(G-26634)***
Illumio Inc...669 800-5000
160 San Gabriel Dr Sunnyvale (94086) ***(G-15232)***
Ilm Group, The, Ontario *Also called Industrial Labor MGT Group Inc* ***(G-14684)***
Ilwu Local 46, Port Hueneme *Also called Interntional Longshore Whse Un* ***(G-14687)***
Ima Europe Mwr Single Fund...210 466-1376
420 Montgomery St San Francisco (94104) ***(G-27062)***
Image 1st, Gardena *Also called Image First Healthcre Lndry Sp* ***(G-13631)***
Image Entertainment Inc (HQ)...818 407-9100
6320 Canoga Ave Ste 790 Woodland Hills (91367) ***(G-18275)***
Image First Healthcre Lndry Sp...310 819-1463
17818 S Figueroa St Gardena (90248) ***(G-13631)***
Image IV Systems Inc (PA)...323 849-3049
512 S Varney St Burbank (91502) ***(G-7053)***
Image Options...949 586-7665
80 Icon Foothill Ranch (92610) ***(G-13998)***
Imageologist, Inglewood *Also called Gelshmal Enterprises LLC* ***(G-7033)***
Imagescan Inc...626 844-2050
390 S Fair Oaks Ave Pasadena (91105) ***(G-16146)***
Imagestat Corporation...310 392-1100
2950 28th St Santa Monica (90405) ***(G-7144)***
Imageware Systems Inc (PA)...858 673-8600
10815 Rncho Brnrdo Rd 3 Ste 310 San Diego (92127) ***(G-15697)***
Imaginative Horizons Inc...619 477-1176
1889 National City Blvd National City (91950) ***(G-20682)***
Imaging Hlthcare Spcalists LLC...619 229-2299
6386 Alvarado Ct San Diego (92120) ***(G-26859)***
Imaging Technologies Group LLC...310 638-2500
5220 Pacific Concourse Dr Los Angeles (90045) ***(G-8169)***
Imarc, Laguna Hills *Also called Investors Mortgage Asset Recov* ***(G-9862)***
Imax Corporation...310 255-5500
12582 Millennium Los Angeles (90094) ***(G-18232)***
IMC, Canoga Park *Also called Interamerican Motor Corp* ***(G-6740)***
Imca Capital, Los Angeles *Also called Imperial Mridian Companies Inc* ***(G-14549)***
Imerys Filtration Minerals, Lompoc *Also called Imerys Minerals California Inc* ***(G-1113)***
Imerys Filtration Minerals Inc (HQ)...805 562-0200
1732 N 1st St Ste 450 San Jose (95112) ***(G-1115)***
Imerys Minerals California Inc...805 736-1221
2500 Miguelito Canyon Rd Lompoc (93436) ***(G-1113)***
Imerys Minerals California Inc (HQ)...805 736-1221
2500 San Miguelito Rd Lompoc (93436) ***(G-1116)***
IMG (PA)...714 974-1700
4560 Dorinda Rd Yorba Linda (92887) ***(G-17234)***
Immanuel Baptist Cruch...909 862-6641
28355 Baseline St Highland (92346) ***(G-24467)***
Immanuel Baptist Day School, Highland *Also called Immanuel Baptist Cruch* ***(G-24467)***
Immersion Medical Inc...408 467-1900
50 Rio Robles San Jose (95134) ***(G-23317)***
Immigration Voice...408 204-2200
3561 Homestead Rd 375 Santa Clara (95051) ***(G-12175)***
Imobile LLC...209 833-6757
2613 Naglee Rd Tracy (95304) ***(G-5399)***
Imobile LLC...909 599-8822
875 W Arrow Hwy San Dimas (91773) ***(G-5635)***
Imp, Los Angeles *Also called International Marine Pdts Inc* ***(G-8635)***
Imp Foods Inc...510 429-4600
1650 Delta Ct Hayward (94544) ***(G-8634)***
Impac Companies...949 475-3933
19500 Jamboree Rd Irvine (92612) ***(G-12070)***
Impac Mortgage Corp...949 475-3600
19500 Jamboree Rd Irvine (92612) ***(G-9859)***
Impac Mortgage Holdings Inc (PA)...949 475-3600
19500 Jamboree Rd Irvine (92612) ***(G-12250)***
Impac Mortgage Holdings Inc...949 475-3781
19500 Jamboree Rd Irvine (92612) ***(G-12251)***
Impac Secured Assets Corp...949 475-3600
19500 Jamboree Rd Irvine (92612) ***(G-12176)***
Impact Assessment Inc...858 459-0142
2166 Avenida De La Playa F La Jolla (92037) ***(G-26534)***
Impact Business Service, Redwood City *Also called Community Gatepath* ***(G-23773)***
IMPACT DRUG & ALCOHOL TREATMEN, Pasadena *Also called Principles Inc* ***(G-22810)***
Impact Lighting & Production, Richmond *Also called Hartmann Studios Incorporated* ***(G-17209)***
Impact Logistics...909 937-9035
1155 S Milliken Ave Ste I Ontario (91761) ***(G-14680)***
Impact Mktg Specialists Inc...949 348-2292
19781 Pauling Foothill Ranch (92610) ***(G-17235)***
Impact Solutions LLC...760 231-0450
3604 Ocean Ranch Blvd Oceanside (92056) ***(G-14681)***
Impec Group Inc...408 330-9350
3350 Scott Blvd Bldg 8 Santa Clara (95054) ***(G-14324)***
Imperial Capital Group LLC (PA)...310 246-3700
2000 Ave Of The Los Angeles (90067) ***(G-10014)***
Imperial Capital LLC (PA)...310 246-3700
2000 Avenue Of The Stars 900s Los Angeles (90067) ***(G-10015)***
Imperial Care Center, Studio City *Also called Longwood Management Corp* ***(G-21298)***
Imperial Cfs Inc...310 768-8188
1000 Francisco St Torrance (90502) ***(G-4687)***
Imperial Contracting...949 333-6460
30 Waterworks Way Irvine (92618) ***(G-1315)***
Imperial Convalescent, La Mirada *Also called Life Care Centers America Inc* ***(G-20729)***
Imperial County Behavioral HLT...760 482-2149
2695 S 4th St El Centro (92243) ***(G-22749)***
Imperial County Mental Health, El Centro *Also called County of Imperial* ***(G-22698)***
Imperial County Probation Off, El Centro *Also called County of Imperial* ***(G-23813)***
Imperial Crest Healthcare Ctr, Hawthorne *Also called Longwood Management Corp* ***(G-20741)***
Imperial Irrgtion Dst Wtr Dept, Imperial *Also called Imperial Irrigation District* ***(G-6644)***
Imperial Irrigation District (PA)...800 303-7756
333 E Barioni Blvd Imperial (92251) ***(G-6140)***
Imperial Irrigation District...760 339-9220
333 E Barioni Blvd Imperial (92251) ***(G-6644)***
Imperial Irrigation District...760 398-5811
81600 58th Ave La Quinta (92253) ***(G-6303)***
Imperial Irrigation District...760 339-9800
2151 W Adams Ave El Centro (92243) ***(G-6288)***
Imperial Marking Systems, Cerritos *Also called Best Label Company Inc* ***(G-7824)***
Imperial Mridian Companies Inc...310 447-3460
11901 Santa Monica Blvd # 338 Los Angeles (90025) ***(G-14549)***
Imperial Parking (us) LLC...415 495-3909
325 5th St San Francisco (94107) ***(G-17718)***
Imperial Parking (us) LLC...650 871-5423
195 N Access Rd South San Francisco (94080) ***(G-17719)***
Imperial Parking (us) LLC...650 877-0430
790 Mcdonnell Rd San Francisco (94128) ***(G-17720)***
Imperial Parking (us) LLC...650 724-4309
360 Oak Rd Ste 1 Stanford (94305) ***(G-17721)***
Imperial Parking (us) LLC...510 382-2140
7801 Earhart Rd Oakland (94621) ***(G-17722)***
Imperial Parking Industries (PA)...323 651-5588
6404 Wilshire Blvd # 1250 Los Angeles (90048) ***(G-17723)***
Imperial Pipe & Supply, Shafter *Also called Bakersfield Pipe and Sup Inc* ***(G-7360)***
Imperial Project Inc...310 671-3263
4721 Laurel Canyon Blvd # 100 Valley Village (91607) ***(G-18474)***
Imperva Inc (PA)...650 345-9000
3400 Bridge Pkwy Ste 200 Redwood City (94065) ***(G-15233)***
Import Collection (PA)...818 782-3060
7885 Nelson Rd Panorama City (91402) ***(G-9271)***
Import Direct, Van Nuys *Also called E & S International Entps Inc* ***(G-7494)***
Import Whl Univ Fund Raising, Los Angeles *Also called Gdf Parent LLC* ***(G-17183)***
Importers Software, Santa Clara *Also called Laxmi Group Inc* ***(G-15273)***
Impossible Foods Inc...650 461-4385
525 Chesapeake Dr Redwood City (94063) ***(G-8488)***
IMS, Sacramento *Also called Innovative Maint Solutions Inc* ***(G-2251)***
IMS, Marina Del Rey *Also called International Mgt Systems* ***(G-27954)***
IMS, Woodland Hills *Also called Innovative Merch Solutions LLC* ***(G-27478)***
IMS Recycling Services Inc (PA)...619 231-2521
2697 Main St San Diego (92113) ***(G-8073)***
In & Out Car Wash Inc...619 316-8492
3615 Monte Real Escondido (92029) ***(G-17844)***

ALPHABETIC

In Home Health Inc — 408 986-8160
2005 De La Cruz Blvd # 271 Santa Clara (95050) *(G-22481)*
In Home Health Inc — 419 254-7841
1000 Lakes Dr Ste 200 West Covina (91790) *(G-22482)*
In Home Supportive Services, Chula Vista *Also called San Diego County Adult Support (G-24173)*
In Shape Health Club — 760 381-1200
14601 Valley Center Dr Victorville (92395) *(G-22979)*
In Shape Health Clubs, Stockton *Also called In Shape Management Company (G-18643)*
In Shape Management Company — 209 472-2231
6 S El Dorado St Stockton (95202) *(G-18643)*
IN TOUCH LEADERSHIP PROJECT, Los Angeles *Also called Saint Justin Education Fu (G-24972)*
In-Roads Creative Programs — 909 989-9944
9057 Arrow Rte Ste 120 Rancho Cucamonga (91730) *(G-24019)*
In-Roads Creative Programs — 909 947-9142
1951 E Saint Andrews Dr Ontario (91761) *(G-24020)*
In-Roads Creative Programs — 951 672-1800
26900 Cherry Hills Blvd Sun City (92586) *(G-24021)*
In-Shape City, Stockton *Also called In-Shape Health Clubs LLC (G-18644)*
In-Shape Health Clubs LLC (PA) — 209 472-2231
6 S El Dorado St Ste 700 Stockton (95202) *(G-18644)*
In-Shape Health Clubs LLC — 209 836-2504
101 S Tracy Blvd Tracy (95376) *(G-18645)*
In2vision Programs LLC — 562 789-8888
13601 Whittier Blvd Whittier (90605) *(G-24022)*
Inamar, San Diego *Also called Ace Usa Inc (G-10583)*
Inapp — 650 424-0496
999 Commercial St Ste 210 Palo Alto (94303) *(G-17236)*
Incare Dme — 818 582-1016
15446 Sherman Way Apt 319 Van Nuys (91406) *(G-22980)*
Inclin Inc — 650 961-3422
2000 Alameda De Las Pulga San Mateo (94403) *(G-26535)*
Incline Incorporated — 408 454-1140
560 S Winchester Blvd # 500 San Jose (95128) *(G-14682)*
Inclusion Services LLC — 562 945-2000
13225 Philadelphia St E Whittier (90601) *(G-24023)*
Inclusive Cmnty Resources LLC — 510 981-8115
2855 Telegraph Ave Ste Ll Berkeley (94705) *(G-24352)*
Incom Mechanical Inc — 707 586-0511
975 Transport Way Ste 5 Petaluma (94954) *(G-2249)*
Indemnity Company California (HQ) — 949 263-3300
17771 Cowan Ste 100 Irvine (92614) *(G-10494)*
Independa Inc — 800 815-7829
11455 El Camino Real # 365 San Diego (92130) *(G-15965)*
Independence At Home Iah, Long Beach *Also called Senior Care (G-10379)*
Independent Construction Co, Concord *Also called D A McCosker Construction Co (G-1761)*
Independent Electric Sup Inc (HQ) — 520 908-7900
2001 Marina Blvd San Leandro (94577) *(G-7446)*
Independent Options — 714 434-1175
2532 Santa Catalina Dr # 104 Costa Mesa (92626) *(G-24024)*
Independent Physician MGT LLC — 562 981-9500
1100 E Willow St Signal Hill (90755) *(G-19568)*
Independent Quality Care Inc — 415 479-1230
40 Professional Ctr Pkwy San Rafael (94903) *(G-21273)*
Independent Quality Care Inc (PA) — 925 855-0881
3 Crow Canyon Ct San Ramon (94583) *(G-21274)*
Independent Quality Care Inc — 925 284-5544
3721 Mt Diablo Blvd Lafayette (94549) *(G-21275)*
Independent Quality Care Inc — 707 578-3226
2300 Bethards Dr Santa Rosa (95405) *(G-21276)*
Independent Trading Company, San Clemente *Also called Brad Rambo & Associates Inc (G-8335)*
Indepndnt Asstd Lvng & Memory, Arcadia *Also called Arcadia Gardens MGT Corp (G-21066)*
Index Fresh Inc (PA) — 909 877-0999
3880 Lemon St Ste 210 Riverside (92501) *(G-549)*
Indian Health Council — 760 749-1410
50100 Golsh Rd Valley Center (92082) *(G-25091)*
Indian Health Service — 760 572-0217
1 Indian Hill Rd Winterhaven (92283) *(G-21609)*
Indian Hills Golf Club, Riverside *Also called Banquet Facilities (G-13736)*
Indian River Transport Co — 209 664-0456
5100 Taylor Ct Turlock (95382) *(G-4197)*
Indian Valley Golf Club Inc — 415 897-1118
3035 Novato Blvd Novato (94947) *(G-18748)*
Indian Valley Health Care Dist — 530 284-7191
184 Hot Springs Rd Greenville (95947) *(G-21610)*
Indian Valley Hospital, Greenville *Also called Indian Valley Health Care Dist (G-21610)*
Indian Wells Country Club, Indian Wells *Also called Iw Golf Club Inc (G-18964)*
Indian Wells Golf Resort, Indian Wells *Also called Troon Golf LLC (G-27260)*
Indian Wells Resort Hotel — 760 345-6466
76661 Us Highway 111 Indian Wells (92210) *(G-12836)*
Indian Wells Vly Surgery Ctr, Ridgecrest *Also called Drummond Medical Group Inc (G-19509)*
Indiana Adhc, Los Angeles *Also called Community Care Health Centers (G-19451)*
Indigo Hospitality Management — 310 787-7595
1817 N Sepulveda Blvd Manhattan Beach (90266) *(G-27472)*
Indigo Hotels, Manhattan Beach *Also called Indigo Hospitality Management (G-27472)*
Indio Family Care Center, Indio *Also called County of Riverside (G-19481)*
Indio Hlthcare Wllness Ctr LLC — 760 347-6000
82262 Valencia Ave Indio (92201) *(G-20683)*
Indio Medical Offices, Indio *Also called Kaiser Foundation Hospitals (G-19621)*
Indium Software Inc — 408 501-8844
1250 Oakmead Pkwy Ste 210 Sunnyvale (94085) *(G-15698)*
Individuals Now — 707 544-3299
2447 Summerfield Rd Santa Rosa (95405) *(G-24025)*

Indosys Corporation — 408 705-1953
3315 San Felipe Rd Ste 37 San Jose (95135) *(G-14683)*
Inductors Inc — 949 623-2460
140 Technology Dr Ste 500 Irvine (92618) *(G-7585)*
Indus Light & Magic (vanco) LL — 415 292-4671
1110 Gorgas Ave San Francisco (94129) *(G-17984)*
Indus Technology Inc — 619 299-2555
2243 San Diego Ave # 200 San Diego (92110) *(G-25874)*
Industrial Coml Systems Inc — 760 300-4094
1165 Joshua Way Vista (92081) *(G-2250)*
Industrial Container Services — 916 781-2775
749 Galleria Blvd Roseville (95678) *(G-7936)*
Industrial Labor MGT Group Inc — 323 582-4100
647 E E St Ste 105 Ontario (91764) *(G-14684)*
Industrial Masonry Inc — 951 284-0251
3299 Horse Carri Rd Ste H Norco (92860) *(G-2819)*
Industrial Metal Supply Co, Sun Valley *Also called Norman Industrial Mtls Inc (G-7386)*
Industrial Metal Supply Co Eba, San Diego *Also called Norman Industrial Mtls Inc (G-7387)*
Industrial Parts Depot LLC (HQ) — 310 530-1900
23231 Normandie Ave Torrance (90501) *(G-7850)*
Industrial Pharmacy MGT LLC — 949 777-3100
3198 Arprt Loop Dr Ste F Costa Mesa (92626) *(G-27063)*
Industrial Stitchtech Inc — 818 361-6319
520 Library St San Fernando (91340) *(G-17237)*
Industrial Support Systems, Fontana *Also called Fontana Resources At Work (G-24341)*
Industry Events — 310 834-3422
25501 Narbonne Ave Lomita (90717) *(G-18804)*
Industry Station, City of Industry *Also called Southern California Gas Co (G-6276)*
Indvls — 949 339-0575
401 Rockefeller B1407 Irvine (92612) *(G-27473)*
Indyme Solutions LLC — 858 268-0717
8295 Aero Pl Ste 260 San Diego (92123) *(G-28135)*
Indyne — 805 606-0664
300 W Point Ave El Granada (94018) *(G-25138)*
Indyne Inc — 805 606-7225
105 13thstbld6525rma 7 Bldg 6525 Vandenberg Afb (93437) *(G-27795)*
Inegrated Care Communities, Moreno Valley *Also called Integrted Care Communities Inc (G-20687)*
Infant Hring Scrning Spcalists, Corona *Also called Halo Unlimted Inc (G-22966)*
Infant/Toddler Consort, Oakland *Also called California Child Care Resourc (G-23698)*
Infantino, San Diego *Also called Blue Box Opco LLC (G-8039)*
Infertlity Gynclogy Obstetrics, San Diego *Also called Igo Medical Group A Med Corp (G-19567)*
Infineon Raceway, Sonoma *Also called Speedway Sonoma LLC (G-18576)*
Infinite Computer Group LLC — 800 922-8075
21300 Superior St Chatsworth (91311) *(G-16299)*
Infinite Home Health Inc — 818 888-7772
22151 Ventura Blvd # 102 Woodland Hills (91364) *(G-22483)*
Infinite Technologies Inc (PA) — 916 987-3261
2140 E Bidwell St Ste 100 Folsom (95630) *(G-25875)*
Infinity Broadcasting Corp Cal — 323 936-5784
5670 Wilshire Blvd # 200 Los Angeles (90036) *(G-5788)*
Infinity Care of East LA — 323 261-8108
101 S Fickett St Los Angeles (90033) *(G-20684)*
Infinity Drywall Contg Inc — 714 634-2255
225 S Loara St Anaheim (92802) *(G-2909)*
Infinity Metals Inc — 562 697-8826
2001 Emery Ave La Habra (90631) *(G-3477)*
Infinity Nurses Care Inc — 510 713-8892
39159 Paseo Padre Pkwy # 111 Fremont (94538) *(G-14887)*
Infinity Staffing Service — 831 638-0360
710 Kirkpatric Ct Hollister (95023) *(G-14888)*
Inflection LLC — 650 618-9910
555 Twin Dolphin Dr # 200 Redwood City (94065) *(G-16147)*
Info Plus International, San Mateo *Also called Ip International Inc (G-16413)*
Infoblox Inc (PA) — 408 986-4000
3111 Coronado St Santa Clara (95054) *(G-16148)*
Infogain Corporation (PA) — 408 355-6000
485 Alberto Way Ste 100 Los Gatos (95032) *(G-16401)*
Infogroup Inc — 650 389-0700
951 Mariners Island Blvd # 130 San Mateo (94404) *(G-14074)*
Infonet Services Corporation — 310 335-2600
1320 E Franklin Ave El Segundo (90245) *(G-4577)*
Infonet Services Corporation (HQ) — 310 335-2859
2160 E Grand Ave El Segundo (90245) *(G-5636)*
Infor (us) Inc — 678 319-8000
26250 Entp Way Ste 220 Lake Forest (92630) *(G-15699)*
Infor (us) Inc — 916 921-0883
11000 Olson Dr Ste 201 Rancho Cordova (95670) *(G-15700)*
Infor Public Sector Inc (HQ) — 916 921-0883
11092 Sun Center Dr Rancho Cordova (95670) *(G-15701)*
Informa Research Services Inc (HQ) — 818 880-8877
26250 Agoura Rd Ste 300 Calabasas (91302) *(G-27474)*
Informatica LLC (HQ) — 650 385-5000
2100 Seaport Blvd Redwood City (94063) *(G-15702)*
Information & Referral Fed Los — 626 350-1841
526 W Las Tunas Dr San Gabriel (91776) *(G-13768)*
Information Management Svcs, Downey *Also called Rancho Los Amigos Nationa (G-24144)*
Information Resources Inc — 415 227-4500
525 Market St Fl 24 San Francisco (94105) *(G-15703)*
Information Services, Santa Cruz *Also called Santa Cruz County of (G-16182)*
Information Services Dept, Fresno *Also called Community Medical Centers (G-21501)*
Information Services Dept, Redwood City *Also called County of San Mateo (G-28125)*
Information Systems & Services, Sonora *Also called County of Tuolumne (G-16117)*
Information Systems Department, Santa Rosa *Also called County of Sonoma (G-16116)*
Information Systems Labs Inc (PA) — 858 535-9680
10070 Barnes Canyon Rd San Diego (92121) *(G-25876)*

Information Technology, Los Angeles *Also called Los Angeles Unified School Dst* ***(G-16301)***
Information Technology Agency, Los Angeles *Also called Los Angeles Unified School Dst* ***(G-16153)***
Informative Research (PA)....714 638-2855
13030 Euclid St Ste 209 Garden Grove (92843) ***(G-14061)***
Infosys Limited....510 742-3000
7707 Gateway Blvd Ste 110 Newark (94560) ***(G-15234)***
Infotech Consulting, San Francisco *Also called Infotech Global Services* ***(G-27475)***
Infotech Global Services....415 986-5400
301 Battery St Fl 2 San Francisco (94111) ***(G-27475)***
Infrascale Inc....310 878-2621
999 N Sepulveda Blvd # 100 El Segundo (90245) ***(G-15704)***
Infrastructure Engrg Corp....760 529-0795
301 Mission Ave Ste 202 Oceanside (92054) ***(G-25877)***
Ingenio Inc....415 248-4000
182 Howard St 826 San Francisco (94105) ***(G-5637)***
Ingenio LLC....415 992-8220
201 Mission St Ste 200 San Francisco (94105) ***(G-17238)***
Ingenium Technologies Corp....858 227-4422
5665 Oberlin Dr Ste 202 San Diego (92121) ***(G-25878)***
Ingenue Inc....323 726-8084
6114 Scott Way Commerce (90040) ***(G-459)***
Inglewood Child Dev Ctr, Inglewood *Also called Inglewood Unified School Dst* ***(G-24468)***
Inglewood Meadows Kbs LP....310 820-4888
1 S Locust St Inglewood (90301) ***(G-11142)***
Inglewood Unified School Dst....310 419-2691
401 S Inglewood Ave Inglewood (90301) ***(G-24468)***
Ingram Micro Inc (PA)....714 566-1000
3351 Michelson Dr Ste 100 Irvine (92612) ***(G-7145)***
Ingram Publisher Services Inc....510 528-1444
1700 4th St Berkeley (94710) ***(G-9166)***
Inhouseit Inc....949 660-5655
3193 Red Hill Ave Costa Mesa (92626) ***(G-16300)***
Inhouselender.com, Santa Ana *Also called Affiliated Funding Corporation* ***(G-9911)***
Initial Security, Santa Fe Springs *Also called Alliedbarton Security Svcs LLC* ***(G-16863)***
Inkling Systems Inc....415 975-4420
343 Sansome St 8 San Francisco (94104) ***(G-27476)***
Inko Industrial Corporation....408 830-1040
695 Vaqueros Ave Sunnyvale (94085) ***(G-16149)***
Inland Behaviour and Hlth Svcs, San Bernardino *Also called Westside Counseling Center* ***(G-22187)***
Inland Bhavioral Hlth Svcs Inc (PA)....909 881-6146
1963 N E St San Bernardino (92405) ***(G-22981)***
Inland Business Machines Inc (HQ)....916 928-0770
1326 N Market Blvd Sacramento (95834) ***(G-17985)***
Inland Cc Inc....909 355-1318
13820 Slover Ave Fontana (92337) ***(G-3275)***
Inland Christian Home Inc....909 395-9322
1950 S Mountain Ave Ofc Ontario (91762) ***(G-20685)***
Inland Cnties Regional Ctr Inc (PA)....909 890-3000
1365 S Waterman Ave San Bernardino (92408) ***(G-27064)***
Inland Cold Storage, Bloomington *Also called Lineage Logistics Holdings LLC* ***(G-4360)***
Inland Empire Chapter-Assn of....512 478-9000
4200 Concours Ste 360 Ontario (91764) ***(G-25544)***
Inland Empire Hauling, Corona *Also called USA Waste of California Inc* ***(G-6577)***
Inland Empire Health Plan....866 228-4347
805 W 2nd St Ste C San Bernardino (92410) ***(G-10291)***
Inland Empire Health Plan (PA)....909 890-2000
10801 6th St Ste 120 Rancho Cucamonga (91730) ***(G-10241)***
Inland Empire RE Solutions....909 476-1000
8794 19th St Alta Loma (91701) ***(G-11582)***
Inland Empire Real Estate....909 944-2070
8010 Haven Ave Rancho Cucamonga (91730) ***(G-11583)***
INLAND EMPIRE SURF SOCCER CLUB, San Bernardino *Also called Alliance Fc* ***(G-25487)***
Inland Empire Therapy Provider (PA)....909 985-7905
1150 N Mountain Ave # 214 Upland (91786) ***(G-20321)***
Inland Empire Utilities Agency....909 993-1755
12811 6th St Rancho Cucamonga (91739) ***(G-6355)***
Inland Empire Utilities Agency (PA)....909 993-1600
6075 Kimball Ave Chino (91708) ***(G-6356)***
Inland Empire Utilities Agency....909 357-0241
9400 Cherry Ave Fontana (92335) ***(G-6357)***
Inland Empre 66ers Bsebll CLB....909 888-9922
280 S E St San Bernardino (92401) ***(G-18550)***
Inland Erosion Control Svcs....951 301-8334
42181 Avenida Alvarado A Temecula (92590) ***(G-3433)***
Inland Eye Inst Med Group Inc (PA)....909 825-3425
1900 E Washington St Colton (92324) ***(G-19569)***
Inland Family Health Wellness....909 475-2300
400 N Pepper Ave Fl 6 Colton (92324) ***(G-21611)***
Inland Hand Therapy & Rehab, Upland *Also called Mountain View Physical Therapy* ***(G-20333)***
Inland Hlth Org of So Cal (HQ)....909 335-7171
1980 Orange Tree Ln # 200 Redlands (92374) ***(G-19570)***
Inland Kenworth (us) Inc (HQ)....909 823-9955
9730 Cherry Ave Fontana (92335) ***(G-6681)***
Inland Kenworth (us) Inc....619 328-1600
500 N Johnson Ave El Cajon (92020) ***(G-6682)***
Inland Medical Enterprises....323 732-0350
3551 W Olympic Blvd Los Angeles (90019) ***(G-20686)***
Inland Pacific Ballet, Montclair *Also called Foundation For Dance Education* ***(G-18393)***
Inland Regional Center, San Bernardino *Also called Inland Cnties Regional Ctr Inc* ***(G-27064)***
Inland Star Dist Ctrs Inc (PA)....559 237-2052
3146 S Chestnut Ave Fresno (93725) ***(G-4578)***
Inland Valley Business and Com....951 378-5316
40335 Winchester Rd Temecula (92591) ***(G-25545)***
INLAND VALLEY CARE & REHAB CTR, Pomona *Also called Inland Valley Partners LLC* ***(G-20322)***
Inland Valley Cnstr Co Inc....909 875-2112
18382 Slover Ave Bloomington (92316) ***(G-1370)***
Inland Valley Drug & Alcohol (PA)....909 932-1069
916 N Mountain Ave Ste A Upland (91786) ***(G-24026)***
Inland Valley Partners LLC....909 623-7100
250 W Artesia St Pomona (91768) ***(G-20322)***
Inland Vly Rgional Med Ctr Inc (HQ)....951 677-1111
36485 Inland Valley Dr Wildomar (92595) ***(G-21612)***
Inland-Metro Services Inc....909 373-6810
1059 W 14th St Upland (91786) ***(G-17239)***
Inman Spinosa & Buchan Inc....310 519-1080
28901 S Wstn Ave Ste 101 Rancho Palos Verdes (90275) ***(G-11584)***
Inn At Rancho Santa Fe, The, Rancho Santa Fe *Also called Huntington Hotel Company* ***(G-12804)***
Inn At Scotts Valley LLC....831 440-1000
6001 La Madrona Dr Scotts Valley (95060) ***(G-12837)***
Inner Circle Entertainment....415 693-0777
420 Mason St San Francisco (94102) ***(G-8622)***
Inner City Broadcasting Corp....415 284-1029
55 Hawthorne St Ste 900 San Francisco (94105) ***(G-5789)***
Inner City Struggle, Los Angeles *Also called Community Partners* ***(G-23776)***
Inner Space Constructors Div, Long Beach *Also called Hutchison Corporation* ***(G-1575)***
Inner-City Express, San Jose *Also called Ice Delivery Systems Inc* ***(G-4027)***
Innocean Wrldwide Americas LLC (PA)....714 861-5200
180 5th St Ste 200 Huntington Beach (92648) ***(G-13864)***
Innopath Software Inc (PA)....408 962-9200
333 W El Camino Real # 230 Sunnyvale (94087) ***(G-15235)***
Innotas....415 263-9800
111 Sutter St Ste 300 San Francisco (94104) ***(G-27477)***
Innova Solutions Inc....408 889-2020
4633 Old Ironsides Dr # 320 Santa Clara (95054) ***(G-16402)***
Innovasystems Intl LLC....619 955-5890
850 Beech St Unit 1006 San Diego (92101) ***(G-15236)***
Innovasystems Intl LLC (PA)....619 756-6500
2385 Northside Dr Ste 300 San Diego (92108) ***(G-15237)***
Innovated Packaging Company....510 713-3560
38505 Cherry St Ste C Newark (94560) ***(G-17240)***
Innovative Artists Talent Agny (PA)....310 656-0400
1505 10th St Santa Monica (90401) ***(G-18397)***
Innovative Bus Partnerships....760 243-2229
17191 Jasmine St Victorville (92395) ***(G-21277)***
Innovative Cnstr Solutions....714 893-6366
4011 W Chandler Ave Santa Ana (92704) ***(G-27796)***
Innovative Drywall Systems Inc....760 743-0331
116 Market Pl Escondido (92029) ***(G-2910)***
Innovative Education MGT Inc....530 295-3566
1166 Broadway Ste Q Placerville (95667) ***(G-27065)***
Innovative Engrg Systems Inc....661 381-7800
8800 Crippen St Bakersfield (93311) ***(G-25879)***
Innovative Eyewear, Simi Valley *Also called Revolution Eyewear Inc* ***(G-7337)***
Innovative Maint Solutions Inc....916 568-1400
125 Main Ave Sacramento (95838) ***(G-2251)***
Innovative Medical Solutions....714 505-7070
3002 Dow Ave Ste 110 Tustin (92780) ***(G-17986)***
Innovative Merch Solutions LLC....818 936-7800
21215 Burbank Blvd Woodland Hills (91367) ***(G-27478)***
Innovative Silicon Inc....408 572-8700
4800 Great America Pkwy # 500 Santa Clara (95054) ***(G-17241)***
Innovative Sleep Centers Inc....415 927-4990
1050 Northgate Dr Ste 250 San Rafael (94903) ***(G-19571)***
Innovative Staffing Resources, Tustin *Also called Innovtive Scntfic Slutions Inc* ***(G-14685)***
Innovative Surgical Products....714 836-4474
2761 Walnut Ave Tustin (92780) ***(G-7269)***
Innovel Solutions Inc....707 748-1940
521 Stone Rd Benicia (94510) ***(G-5104)***
Innovel Solutions Inc....661 721-5910
1700 Schuster Rd Delano (93215) ***(G-5105)***
Innovel Solutions Inc....909 605-1400
5691 E Philadelphia St # 125 Ontario (91761) ***(G-5106)***
Innovo Azteca Apparel Inc....323 837-3700
5901 S Eastern Ave 104 Commerce (90040) ***(G-8313)***
Innovtive Emplyee Slutions Inc....858 715-5100
9665 Gran Rdge Dr Ste 420 San Diego (92123) ***(G-26377)***
Innovtive Scntfic Slutions Inc....714 508-8620
17581 Irvine Blvd Ste 202 Tustin (92780) ***(G-14685)***
Inns of Monterey, Monterey *Also called Coastal Hotel Group Inc* ***(G-12531)***
Innsuites Hotels, San Diego *Also called Hampstead Lafayette Hotel LLC* ***(G-12683)***
Inovative Packaging, Newark *Also called Integrated Pkg & Crating Svcs* ***(G-5201)***
Inoxpa USA Inc....707 585-3900
3721 Santa Rosa Ave B4 Santa Rosa (95407) ***(G-7851)***
Inreach Internet LLC (HQ)....888 467-3224
4635 Georgetown Pl Stockton (95207) ***(G-5638)***
Insco Dico Group , The, Irvine *Also called Developers Surety Indemnity Co* ***(G-10491)***
Insco Insurance Services Inc (HQ)....949 797-9243
17771 Cowan Ste 100 Irvine (92614) ***(G-10743)***
Inside Outdoors Foundation....714 708-3885
8755 Santiago Canyon Rd Silverado (92676) ***(G-24027)***
Inside Source Inc (PA)....650 508-9101
985 Industrial Rd Ste 101 San Carlos (94070) ***(G-6820)***
Inside Source/Young, San Carlos *Also called Inside Source Inc* ***(G-6820)***
Inside Track Inc....415 243-4440
1620 Montgomery St # 230 San Francisco (94111) ***(G-27950)***
Insideview Technologies Inc....415 728-9309
444 De Haro St Ste 210 San Francisco (94107) ***(G-7146)***
Insight Environmental Wstn LLC....714 678-6700
3010 E Miraloma Ave Anaheim (92806) ***(G-25880)***
Insight Envmtl Engrg Cnstr Inc (PA)....714 678-6700
2749 Saturn St Brea (92821) ***(G-25881)***

ALPHABETIC

Insight Investments LLC (HQ) ... 714 939-2300
611 Anton Blvd Ste 700 Costa Mesa (92626) ***(G-16284)***

Insight Systems Exchange, Costa Mesa *Also called Insight Investments LLC* ***(G-16284)***

Insignia/Esg Ht Partners Inc (HQ) ... 310 765-2600
11150 Santa Monica Blvd # 220 Los Angeles (90025) ***(G-11005)***

Insikt Inc ... 415 391-2431
225 Bush St Ste 1840 San Francisco (94104) ***(G-17242)***

Insituform Technologies LLC ... 714 724-2324
19000 Macarthur Blvd Irvine (92612) ***(G-1942)***

Insomniac Inc ... 323 874-7020
9441 W Olympic Blvd Beverly Hills (90212) ***(G-18475)***

Inspection and Testing, Anaheim *Also called Emery Smith Laboratories Inc* ***(G-25785)***

Insperity Inc ... 909 569-1000
1440 Bridgegate Dr # 200 Diamond Bar (91765) ***(G-27479)***

Inspira Inc ... 408 247-9500
4125 Blackford Ave # 255 San Jose (95117) ***(G-15238)***

Inspiria Inc (PA) ... 949 206-0606
25741 Atl Ocn Dr Ste A Lake Forest (92630) ***(G-25882)***

Installmonetizer, San Jose *Also called Big Bulb Ideas Inc* ***(G-15053)***

Instant Systems Inc ... 510 657-8100
40211 Dolerita Ave Fremont (94539) ***(G-15705)***

Instantly, Encino *Also called Survey Sampling Intl LLC* ***(G-26709)***

Instantsys, Fremont *Also called Instant Systems Inc* ***(G-15705)***

Instart Labs, Palo Alto *Also called Instart Logic Inc* ***(G-15239)***

Instart Logic Inc ... 888 418-5044
450 Lambert Ave Palo Alto (94306) ***(G-15239)***

Instill Corporation ... 650 645-2600
777 Mariners Island Blvd # 400 San Mateo (94404) ***(G-15240)***

Institute Applied Bhvior Anlis, Tarzana *Also called Institute For Applied Behavior* ***(G-20325)***

Institute For Applied Behavior (PA) ... 310 649-0499
5777 W Century Blvd # 675 Los Angeles (90045) ***(G-20323)***

Institute For Applied Behavior ... 805 987-5886
2301 E Daily Dr Ste 201 Camarillo (93010) ***(G-20324)***

Institute For Applied Behavior ... 818 881-1933
19510 Ventura Blvd # 204 Tarzana (91356) ***(G-20325)***

Institute For Eductl Therapy ... 831 457-1207
1007 University Ave Berkeley (94710) ***(G-24353)***

Institute For Health & Healing ... 415 600-3503
2300 California St # 101 San Francisco (94115) ***(G-20326)***

Institute For Humn Social Dev (PA) ... 650 871-5613
155 Bovet Rd Ste 300 San Mateo (94402) ***(G-24469)***

Institute For La Jolla ... 858 752-6500
9420 Athena Cir La Jolla (92037) ***(G-26772)***

Institute For Mltcltrl Cnslng ... 213 381-1239
3580 Wilshire Blvd # 2000 Los Angeles (90010) ***(G-27951)***

Institute For One World Health ... 650 392-2510
25 Taylor St 209 San Francisco (94102) ***(G-18646)***

Institute LLC ... 408 782-7101
14830 Foothill Ave Morgan Hill (95037) ***(G-18749)***

Institute On Aging ... 415 600-2690
3698 California St San Francisco (94118) ***(G-24028)***

Institute On Aging (PA) ... 415 750-4101
3575 Geary Blvd San Francisco (94118) ***(G-24029)***

Institutional Financing Svcs, Benicia *Also called Americas Lemonade Stand Inc* ***(G-16988)***

Insulectro (PA) ... 949 587-3200
20362 Windrow Dr Ste 100 Lake Forest (92630) ***(G-7586)***

Insulfoam, Dixon *Also called Carlisle Construction Mtls Inc* ***(G-7011)***

Insurance Answer Center, Encino *Also called Answer Financial Inc* ***(G-16994)***

Insurance Auto Auctions Inc ... 818 487-2222
7245 Laurel Canyon Blvd # 5 North Hollywood (91605) ***(G-6683)***

Insurance Company of West (HQ) ... 858 350-2400
15025 Innovation Dr San Diego (92128) ***(G-10430)***

Insurance Dentists Amer Idoa, Campbell *Also called Dentistat Inc* ***(G-27408)***

Insurance Services Amercn LLC ... 805 981-2220
300 E Esplanade Dr # 2100 Oxnard (93036) ***(G-10744)***

Insurance Services Office Inc ... 415 874-4361
388 Market St Ste 750 San Francisco (94111) ***(G-16245)***

Insure Express Insurance Svc, Calabasas *Also called Cartel Marketing Inc* ***(G-10665)***

Intake Initiatives Inc ... 800 788-9637
999 Bayhill Dr Ste 200 San Bruno (94066) ***(G-8264)***

Intapp Inc (PA) ... 650 852-0400
200 Portage Ave Palo Alto (94306) ***(G-15706)***

Intech Mechanical Company Inc ... 916 797-4900
7501 Galilee Rd Roseville (95678) ***(G-2252)***

Intech Mechanical Company LLC ... 916 797-4900
7501 Galilee Rd Roseville (95678) ***(G-2253)***

Integra Lifesciences Corp ... 949 595-8710
2 Goodyear Ste A Irvine (92618) ***(G-26536)***

Integra Telecom Inc ... 408 758-7700
101 Metro Dr San Jose (95110) ***(G-17243)***

Integra Telecom Inc ... 707 284-4000
3700 Old Redwood Hwy # 100 Santa Rosa (95403) ***(G-17244)***

Integral Development Corp (PA) ... 650 424-4500
3400 Hillview Ave Palo Alto (94304) ***(G-15707)***

Integral Engineering, Palo Alto *Also called Integral Development Corp* ***(G-15707)***

Integral Senior Living LLC ... 858 484-3801
12979 Rncho Pnsqitos Blvd San Diego (92129) ***(G-467)***

Integral Senior Living LLC (PA) ... 760 547-2863
2333 State St Ste 300 Carlsbad (92008) ***(G-27066)***

Integrated Clg Solutions Inc ... 415 821-6757
3043 Mission St San Francisco (94110) ***(G-14325)***

Integrated Data Services Inc (PA) ... 310 647-3439
2141 Rosecrans Ave # 2050 El Segundo (90245) ***(G-15241)***

Integrated Decision Systems ... 310 954-5530
11150 W Olympic Blvd # 600 Los Angeles (90064) ***(G-15966)***

Integrated Dynmc Solutions Inc ... 818 707-8797
31194 La Baya Dr Ste 203 Westlake Village (91362) ***(G-15242)***

Integrated Mech Systems Inc ... 626 446-1854
2390 Bateman Ave Duarte (91010) ***(G-2254)***

Integrated Medical Specialists, San Diego *Also called Genesis Healthcare Partners PC* ***(G-22733)***

Integrated Pkg & Crating Svcs ... 510 494-1622
38505 Cherry St Ste C Newark (94560) ***(G-5201)***

Integrated Trnsp Svcs Inc ... 310 553-6060
9740 W Pico Blvd Los Angeles (90035) ***(G-3805)***

Integrex Innovations, Tustin *Also called Integrium LLC* ***(G-26537)***

Integrien Corporation ... 323 810-6870
3401 Hillview Ave Palo Alto (94304) ***(G-15243)***

Integrits Corporation (PA) ... 858 300-1600
5205 Kearny Villa Way # 200 San Diego (92123) ***(G-16403)***

Integrity Hlthcare Sltions Inc (PA) ... 858 576-9501
5625 Ruffin Rd Ste 225 San Diego (92123) ***(G-22484)***

Integrity Hlthcare Sltions Inc ... 760 432-9811
425 W 5th Ave Ste 101 Escondido (92025) ***(G-22485)***

Integrity Management Entps, San Diego *Also called Gerwend Enterprises Inc* ***(G-27790)***

Integrity Management Svcs Inc ... 805 238-0905
141 W Dana St Ste 100 Nipomo (93444) ***(G-14326)***

Integrity Mrtg Solutions Inc ... 310 643-8700
2321 Rosecrans Ave # 4210 El Segundo (90245) ***(G-9860)***

Integrity Rebar Placers ... 951 696-6843
1345 Nandina Ave Perris (92571) ***(G-3383)***

Integrium LLC (PA) ... 714 541-5591
14351 Myford Rd Ste A Tustin (92780) ***(G-26537)***

Integro USA Inc ... 626 795-9000
115 N El Molino Ave Pasadena (91101) ***(G-10745)***

Integrted Care Communities Inc ... 951 243-3837
11751 Davis St Moreno Valley (92557) ***(G-20687)***

Integrus LLC ... 714 547-9500
1430 Village Way Ste K Santa Ana (92705) ***(G-7054)***

Intel Media Inc ... 408 765-0063
2200 Mission College Blvd Santa Clara (95054) ***(G-6007)***

Intelex Systems Inc ... 818 518-1100
7728 Ducor Ave West Hills (91304) ***(G-15244)***

Intell Set, Long Beach *Also called Intelsat Corporation* ***(G-6076)***

Intellectsoft LLC ... 650 300-4335
721 Colorado Ave Ste 101 Palo Alto (94303) ***(G-15245)***

Intellicus Tech Pvt Ltd ... 408 213-3314
720 University Ave # 130 Los Gatos (95032) ***(G-15967)***

Intelligent Automation Corp ... 858 679-4140
13475 Danielson St # 100 Poway (92064) ***(G-25883)***

Intelliguard Security Services ... 510 547-7656
4663 Harbord Dr Oakland (94618) ***(G-16706)***

Intellipro Group Inc ... 408 200-9891
2905 Stender Way Ste 42 Santa Clara (95054) ***(G-16404)***

Intellirisk Management Corp ... 818 575-5400
31229 Cedar Valley Dr Westlake Village (91362) ***(G-14035)***

Intelliswift Software Inc (PA) ... 510 490-9240
2201 Walnut Ave Ste 180 Fremont (94538) ***(G-16405)***

Intellisync Corporation (HQ) ... 650 625-2185
313 Fairchild Dr Mountain View (94043) ***(G-15246)***

Intelpeer Cloud Cmmnctions LLC ... 650 525-9200
177 Bovet Rd Ste 400 San Mateo (94402) ***(G-5639)***

Intelsat Corporation ... 310 525-5500
1600 Forbes Way Long Beach (90810) ***(G-6076)***

Inter Act Pmti Inc (PA) ... 805 658-5600
4567 Telephone Rd Ste 203 Ventura (93003) ***(G-25884)***

Inter Community Hospital, Covina *Also called Citrus Valley Medical Ctr Inc* ***(G-21491)***

Inter Community Hospital, Covina *Also called Citrus Vly Hlth Partners Inc* ***(G-26968)***

Inter Con Security Inc ... 619 523-0291
2801 Camino Del Rio S 300h San Diego (92108) ***(G-27480)***

Inter Con Systems, Pasadena *Also called Inter-Con Investigators Inc* ***(G-16707)***

Inter-City Cleaners ... 650 875-9200
438 S Airport Blvd South San Francisco (94080) ***(G-13582)***

Inter-Con Investigators Inc ... 626 535-2200
210 S De Lacey Ave Pasadena (91105) ***(G-16707)***

Inter-Con Security Systems Inc (PA) ... 626 535-2200
210 S De Lacey Ave # 200 Pasadena (91105) ***(G-16708)***

Inter-Rail Trnspt Nshville LLC ... 510 231-2744
861 Wharf St Richmond (94804) ***(G-5223)***

Inter-Rail Trnspt Nshville LLC ... 707 746-1695
3800 Industrial Way Benicia (94510) ***(G-5224)***

Inter-Valley Health Plan Inc ... 909 623-6333
300 S Park Ave Ste 300 Pomona (91766) ***(G-10292)***

Inter/Media Advertising, Woodland Hills *Also called Inter/Media Time Buying Corp* ***(G-13865)***

Inter/Media Time Buying Corp (PA) ... 818 995-1455
22120 Clarendon St # 300 Woodland Hills (91367) ***(G-13865)***

Interactivate Inc ... 619 814-1999
707 Broadway Ste 1000 San Diego (92101) ***(G-16406)***

Interactive Data Corporation ... 510 266-6000
3955 Point Eden Way Hayward (94545) ***(G-10196)***

Interactive Data Corporation ... 310 664-2500
2901 28th St Ste 300 Santa Monica (90405) ***(G-15247)***

Interactive Media Holdings (PA) ... 949 861-8888
4 Park Plz Ste 1500 Irvine (92614) ***(G-13866)***

Interactive Medical Specialist ... 415 472-4204
454 Las Gallinas Ave # 287 San Rafael (94903) ***(G-14889)***

Interactive Solutions Inc (HQ) ... 510 214-9002
283 4th St Ste 301 Oakland (94607) ***(G-15708)***

Interamerican Motor Corp (HQ) ... 818 678-6571
8901 Canoga Ave Canoga Park (91304) ***(G-6740)***

Interbake Foods LLC ... 213 484-8161
1910 W Temple St Los Angeles (90026) ***(G-8854)***

Intercare Holdings Insur Svcs, Rocklin *Also called Pacific Secured Equities Inc* ***(G-27579)***

Intercare Holdings Insur Svcs ... 916 677-2500
3010 Lava Ridge Ct # 110 Roseville (95661) ***(G-10746)***

Intercare Therapy Inc 323 866-1880
4221 Wilshire Blvd 300a Los Angeles (90010) *(G-20327)*
Intercntnntal Clement Monterey 831 375-4500
750 Cannery Row Ste 100 Monterey (93940) *(G-12838)*
Intercntnntal Ht Group Rsurces 619 727-4000
509 9th Ave San Diego (92101) *(G-12839)*
Intercntnntal Ht Group Rsurces 415 771-9000
1300 Columbus Ave San Francisco (94133) *(G-12840)*
Intercntnntal Ht Group Rsurces 949 863-1999
17941 Von Karman Ave Irvine (92614) *(G-12841)*
Intercommunity Care Centers 562 427-8915
2626 Grand Ave Long Beach (90815) *(G-20688)*
Intercommunity Child 562 692-0383
10155 Colima Rd Whittier (90603) *(G-24030)*
Intercommunity Dialysis Center, Whittier *Also called Intercommunity Dialysis Svcs (G-22630)*
Intercommunity Dialysis Svcs 562 696-1841
12291 Washington Blvd # 410 Whittier (90606) *(G-22630)*
Intercontinental Exchange Inc (HQ) 770 857-4700
1415 Moonstone Brea (92821) *(G-10109)*
Intercontinental Hotels Group 949 863-1999
17941 Von Karman Ave Irvine (92614) *(G-12842)*
Intercontinental Hotels Group 415 626-6103
50 8th St San Francisco (94103) *(G-12843)*
Intercontinental Hotels Group 415 398-8900
480 Sutter St San Francisco (94108) *(G-12844)*
Intercontinental Hotels Group 415 409-4600
550 N Point St San Francisco (94133) *(G-12845)*
Intercontinental Hotels Group 909 930-5555
2280 S Haven Ave Ontario (91761) *(G-12846)*
Intercontinental Hotels Group 415 616-6500
888 Howard St San Francisco (94103) *(G-12847)*
Intercontinental Mark Hopkins, San Francisco *Also called One Nob Hill Associates LLC (G-13046)*
Intercontinental San Francisco, San Francisco *Also called Cdc San Francisco LLC (G-12504)*
Intercontinental San Francisco, San Francisco *Also called Intercontinental Hotels Group (G-12847)*
Intercontntl Hotels Grp Resour, Los Angeles *Also called Crowne Plaza Lax LLC (G-12556)*
Interdent Inc (HQ) 310 765-2400
9800 S La Cienega Blvd # 800 Inglewood (90301) *(G-20256)*
Interdent Service Corporation (HQ) 310 765-2400
9800 S La Cienega Blvd # 800 Inglewood (90301) *(G-20257)*
Interdependent Pictures LLC 310 779-2119
124 S Camden Dr Apt C Beverly Hills (90212) *(G-18095)*
INTERFACE CHILDREN FAMILY SERV, Camarillo *Also called Interface Community (G-24031)*
Interface Community (PA) 805 485-6114
4001 Mission Oaks Blvd I Camarillo (93012) *(G-24031)*
Interface Masters Tech Inc 408 441-9341
150 E Brokaw Rd San Jose (95112) *(G-27952)*
Interface Rehab Inc 714 646-8300
774 S Placentia Ave # 200 Placentia (92870) *(G-20328)*
Intergraded Media Systems Ctr, Los Angeles *Also called University Southern California (G-22004)*
Intergro Rehab Service 714 901-4200
1922 N Broadway Santa Ana (92706) *(G-20329)*
Interhealth Corporation (PA) 562 698-0811
12401 Washington Blvd Whittier (90602) *(G-21613)*
Interhealth Services Inc (HQ) 562 698-0811
12401 Washington Blvd Whittier (90602) *(G-22486)*
Interim Inc 831 754-3838
339 Pajaro St Ste B Salinas (93901) *(G-28136)*
Interim Assisited Care of Nort 530 722-1530
373 Smile Pl Redding (96001) *(G-22487)*
Interim Hlthcare San Dego Cnty, San Diego *Also called Integrity Hlthcare Sltions Inc (G-22484)*
Interim Services, Bakersfield *Also called Rncmba Inc (G-14938)*
Interim Services, Redding *Also called Interim Assisited Care of Nort (G-22487)*
Interim Services, Salinas *Also called Interim Inc (G-28136)*
Interior Electric Incorporated 714 771-9098
747 N Main St Orange (92868) *(G-2619)*
Interior Experts General Bldrs 909 203-4922
4534 Carter Ct Chino (91710) *(G-2911)*
Interior Office Solutions Inc (PA) 949 724-9444
17800 Mitchell N Irvine (92614) *(G-17245)*
Interior Office Solutions Inc 310 726-9067
444 S Flower St Ste 200 Los Angeles (90071) *(G-17246)*
Interior Rmoval Specialist Inc 323 357-6900
8990 Atlantic Ave South Gate (90280) *(G-3457)*
Interior Specialists Inc (HQ) 760 929-6700
1630 Faraday Ave Carlsbad (92008) *(G-3120)*
Interior Specialists Inc 530 885-0632
9300 Hubbard Rd Auburn (95602) *(G-3121)*
Interiors By Linda 760 341-9651
49585 Brian Ct La Quinta (92253) *(G-17247)*
Interlab Inc 619 302-3095
636 Broadway Ste 322 San Diego (92101) *(G-7343)*
Interlink 310 734-1499
10940 Wilshire Blvd Los Angeles (90024) *(G-9801)*
Interlink Company The, Los Angeles *Also called Interlink (G-9801)*
Intermedia Holdings Inc (PA) 650 641-4000
825 E Middlefield Rd Mountain View (94043) *(G-16407)*
Internal Associates Med Group, Culver City *Also called Gardner Neurologic Orthopedic (G-27033)*
Internal Mdcine Rsdncy Affairs 916 734-7080
4150 V St Ste 3116 Sacramento (95817) *(G-25139)*
Internal Services Dept, Los Angeles *Also called County of Los Angeles (G-17098)*

International Advisors LLC 497 961-7988
31248 Oak Crest Dr Westlake Village (91361) *(G-27953)*
International Alliance Thea 805 898-0442
P.O. Box 413 Santa Barbara (93102) *(G-25173)*
International Almond Exchange 831 728-4534
144 W Lake Ave Watsonville (95076) *(G-202)*
INTERNATIONAL ASSOCIATION OF P, Ontario *Also called Iapmo Research and Testing Inc (G-25090)*
International Bay Clubs LLC (PA) 949 645-5000
1221 W Coast Hwy Ste 145 Newport Beach (92663) *(G-18962)*
International Brthrhd of Elctr (PA) 707 452-2700
30 Orange Tree Cir Vacaville (95687) *(G-25174)*
International Bus Mchs Corp 914 499-1900
30501 Agoura Rd Ste 100 Agoura Hills (91301) *(G-15968)*
International Bus Mchs Corp 408 463-2000
555 Bailey Ave San Jose (95141) *(G-15248)*
International Bus Mchs Corp 415 545-4747
425 Market St San Francisco (94105) *(G-7055)*
International Bus Mchs Corp 714 327-3501
1540 Scenic Ave Costa Mesa (92626) *(G-16408)*
International Bus Mchs Corp 408 850-8999
2350 Mission College Blvd Santa Clara (95054) *(G-15249)*
International Bus Mchs Corp 800 426-4968
1001 E Hillsdale Blvd Foster City (94404) *(G-16409)*
International Bus Mchs Corp 510 652-6700
1480 64th St Ste 200 Emeryville (94608) *(G-15250)*
International Bus Mchs Corp 408 452-4800
2077 Gateway Pl San Jose (95110) *(G-7056)*
International Bus Mchs Corp 408 927-1080
650 Harry Rd San Jose (95120) *(G-26538)*
International Bus Mchs Corp 925 277-5000
4000 Executive Pkwy # 300 San Ramon (94583) *(G-27481)*
International Code Council 562 699-0541
3060 Saturn St Ste 100 Brea (92821) *(G-25140)*
International Creative Mgt Inc (HQ) 310 550-4000
10250 Constellation Blvd Los Angeles (90067) *(G-18398)*
International Creative MGT Inc 310 550-4000
10250 Constellation Blvd # 1 Los Angeles (90067) *(G-18399)*
International Delicacies 510 669-2444
2100 Atlas Rd Ste F Richmond (94806) *(G-8855)*
International Design Services 323 662-3963
2437 Micheltorena St Los Angeles (90039) *(G-25885)*
International Fmly Entrmt Inc (HQ) 818 560-1000
3800 W Alameda Ave Burbank (91505) *(G-6008)*
International Garment Finisher 562 983-7400
2144 W Gaylord St Long Beach (90813) *(G-13632)*
International Home Mortgage 562 945-7753
13601 Whittier Blvd # 411 Whittier (90605) *(G-9861)*
International House 510 642-9490
2299 Piedmont Ave Ste 535 Berkeley (94720) *(G-13452)*
International Industrial Park 858 623-9000
5440 Morehouse Dr # 4000 San Diego (92121) *(G-12140)*
International Inst Los Angeles (PA) 323 224-3800
3845 Selig Pl Los Angeles (90031) *(G-24032)*
International Lease Fin Corp (HQ) 310 788-1999
10250 Constellation Blvd Los Angeles (90067) *(G-14550)*
International Litigation Svcs 888 313-4457
65 Enterprise Aliso Viejo (92656) *(G-7057)*
International Longshoremens 209 464-1827
22 N Union St Stockton (95205) *(G-25175)*
International Marine Pdts Inc (HQ) 213 680-0190
500 E 7th St Los Angeles (90014) *(G-8635)*
International Media Group Inc 310 478-1818
1990 S Bundy Dr Ste 850 Los Angeles (90025) *(G-5874)*
International Medical Corps (PA) 310 826-7800
12400 Wilshire Blvd # 1500 Los Angeles (90025) *(G-24033)*
International Mgt Systems 310 822-2022
4640 Admiralty Way # 500 Marina Del Rey (90292) *(G-27954)*
International Missing Persons 714 827-1947
609 S Broder St Anaheim (92804) *(G-13769)*
International Mrtg Corp Assn 626 339-9094
1037 Park View Dr Ste 200 Covina (91724) *(G-9929)*
International Network Corp 858 794-2610
124 Via De La Vlle Unit 3 Solana Beach (92075) *(G-15251)*
International Paper, Livermore *Also called Veritiv Operating Company (G-7902)*
International Paper, La Mirada *Also called Veritiv Operating Company (G-8220)*
International Paving Svcs Inc 909 794-2101
1199 Opal Ave Mentone (92359) *(G-1801)*
International Rectifier Corp 310 726-8000
222 Kansas St El Segundo (90245) *(G-26378)*
International SEC Svcs Inc 925 634-1935
3350 Scott Blvd Bldg 36a Santa Clara (95054) *(G-16709)*
International Speedway Inc 949 492-9933
3103 S El Camino Real San Clemente (92672) *(G-18551)*
International Thermoproducts 619 562-7001
11015 Mission Park Ct Santee (92071) *(G-7852)*
International Toy Inc 949 333-3777
17682 Cowan Irvine (92614) *(G-8045)*
International Trnsp Svc (HQ) 562 435-7781
1281 Pier G Way Long Beach (90802) *(G-4747)*
Internationl TV Media Wireless, Bay Point *Also called Caribbean South Amercn Council (G-4959)*
Internet Applications Group, Palo Alto *Also called Inapp (G-17236)*
Internet Archive 415 561-6767
300 Funston Ave San Francisco (94118) *(G-16246)*
Internet Blueprint Inc 714 673-6000
1177 Warner Ave Tustin (92780) *(G-15252)*
Internet Booking Agencycom Inc 949 673-7707
232 Via Eboli Newport Beach (92663) *(G-14686)*

ALPHABETIC

Internet Brands Inc (PA) 310 280-4000
909 N Sepulveda Blvd # 11 El Segundo (90245) *(G-16150)*
Internet Corp For Assigned Nam (PA) 310 823-9358
12025 Waterfront Dr # 300 Los Angeles (90094) *(G-15969)*
Internet Marketing Assn Inc 949 443-9300
10 Mar Del Rey San Clemente (92673) *(G-27482)*
Internet Security Systems Inc 661 296-5752
28350 Tamarack Ln Santa Clarita (91390) *(G-15253)*
Internet-Journals Inc 510 665-1200
2100 Milvia St 300 Berkeley (94704) *(G-16410)*
Interntional Cmpt Science Inst 510 643-9153
1947 Center St Ste 600 Berkeley (94704) *(G-26773)*
Interntional Disposal Corp Cal 408 945-2802
1601 Dixon Landing Rd Milpitas (95035) *(G-6491)*
Interntional Longshore Whse Un 805 488-2944
Bldng 608 Port Heneme Hbr Port Hueneme (93041) *(G-14687)*
Interntional Pet Sups Dist Inc 858 453-7845
10850 Via Frontera San Diego (92127) *(G-9272)*
Interntional Un Oper Engineers 626 792-2519
150 Corson St Pasadena (91103) *(G-25176)*
Interntional Un Oper Engineers (PA) 916 444-6880
1121 L St Ste 401 Sacramento (95814) *(G-25177)*
Interntnal Ch of Frsqare Gospl 925 964-9044
4 Crow Canyon Ct San Ramon (94583) *(G-9503)*
Interntnal Circuits Components 714 572-1900
3701 E Miraloma Ave Anaheim (92806) *(G-7587)*
Interntnal Communications Corp 951 934-0531
11801 Pierce St Fl 2 Riverside (92505) *(G-15970)*
Interntnal Hse At U C Berkeley, Berkeley *Also called International House* *(G-13452)*
Interntnal Prnsrance Assoc LLC 415 223-5548
504 Redwood Blvd Ste 240e Novato (94947) *(G-10747)*
Interntnal Pvment Slutions Inc 909 794-2101
1209 Van Buren St Ste 3 Thermal (92274) *(G-3276)*
Interntnal Rscue Committee Inc 619 641-7510
5348 University Ave # 205 San Diego (92105) *(G-24034)*
Interntonal Win Treatments Inc (PA) 562 236-2120
12301 Hawkins St Santa Fe Springs (90670) *(G-6868)*
Intero Real Estate Services 408 848-8400
790 1st St Gilroy (95020) *(G-11585)*
Intero Real Estate Svcs Inc 408 741-1600
12900 Saratoga Ave Saratoga (95070) *(G-11586)*
Intero Real Estate Svcs Inc 562 861-7242
8255 Firestone Blvd # 200 Downey (90241) *(G-11587)*
Intero Real Estate Svcs Inc 510 489-8989
32145 Alvarado Niles Rd # 101 Union City (94587) *(G-11588)*
Intero Real Estate Svcs Inc 408 574-5000
5890 Silver Creek Vly Rd San Jose (95138) *(G-11589)*
Intero Real Estate Svcs Inc 408 558-3600
1900 Camden Ave San Jose (95124) *(G-11590)*
Intero Silicon Valley, San Jose *Also called Intero Real Estate Svcs Inc* *(G-11590)*
Interpac Distribution Center, Woodland *Also called Interpac Technologies Inc* *(G-17248)*
Interpac Technologies Inc 530 662-6363
260 N Pioneer Ave Woodland (95776) *(G-17248)*
Interpoltex, Jamul *Also called Poltex Company Inc* *(G-15391)*
Interprsnal Dvlpmntal Fclttors 626 793-8967
891 Worcester Ave Apt 3 Pasadena (91104) *(G-24035)*
Interpublic Group of Companies, Los Angeles *Also called Dailey & Associates* *(G-13830)*
Interquantum LLC 818 455-4434
22120 Clarendon St # 160 Woodland Hills (91367) *(G-10016)*
Interstate Btry San Diego Inc 858 790-8244
9345 Cabot Dr San Diego (92126) *(G-6741)*
Interstate Con Pmpg Co Inc 209 983-3092
11180 Vallejo Ct French Camp (95231) *(G-3277)*
Interstate Distributor Co 909 349-3400
10131 Redwood Ave Fontana (92335) *(G-4198)*
Interstate Electric Co Inc (PA) 323 724-0420
2240 Yates Ave Commerce (90040) *(G-7219)*
Interstate Electronics Corp 714 758-0500
708 E Vermont Ave Anaheim (92805) *(G-27483)*
Interstate Electronics Corp 858 552-9500
3033 Science Park Rd San Diego (92121) *(G-15971)*
Interstate Foods 323 264-4024
310 S Long Beach Blvd Compton (90221) *(G-8598)*
Interstate Fuel Systems Inc 916 457-6572
8221 Alpine Ave Sacramento (95826) *(G-9023)*
Interstate Hotels Resorts Inc 949 783-2500
4685 Macarthur Ct Ste 480 Newport Beach (92660) *(G-27067)*
Interstate Hotels Resorts Inc 415 362-5500
2500 Mason St San Francisco (94133) *(G-12848)*
Interstate Hotels Resorts Inc 213 617-1133
333 S Figueroa St Los Angeles (90071) *(G-12849)*
Interstate Hotels Resorts Inc 760 476-0800
6450 Carlsbad Blvd Carlsbad (92011) *(G-27068)*
Interstate Hotels Resorts Inc 213 624-1000
404 S Figueroa St 418a Los Angeles (90071) *(G-12850)*
Interstate Hotels Resorts Inc 760 322-7000
67 967 Vst Chno At Lndau Palm Springs (92263) *(G-27069)*
Interstate Hotels Resorts Inc 925 934-2500
1345 Treat Blvd Walnut Creek (94597) *(G-27070)*
Interstate Hotels Resorts Inc 510 843-3000
41 Tunnel Rd Berkeley (94705) *(G-12851)*
Interstate Hotels Resorts Inc 510 489-2200
32083 Alvarado Niles Rd Union City (94587) *(G-12852)*
Interstate Hotels Resorts Inc 916 922-4700
2200 Harvard St Sacramento (95815) *(G-12853)*
Interstate Hotels Resorts Inc 805 966-2285
901 E Cabrillo Blvd Santa Barbara (93103) *(G-27071)*
Interstate Hotels Resorts Inc 949 833-9999
18800 Macarthur Blvd Irvine (92612) *(G-27072)*

Interstate Meat & Provision 323 838-9400
6114 Scott Way Commerce (90040) *(G-8554)*
Interstate Plastics, Sacramento *Also called Dongalen Enterprises Inc* *(G-8969)*
Interstate Protective Services 818 995-6664
16200 Ventura Blvd # 210 Encino (91436) *(G-16710)*
Interstate Rhbltation Svcs LLC (PA) 818 244-5656
333 E Glenoaks Blvd # 204 Glendale (91207) *(G-20330)*
Interstate Truck Center LLC (PA) 209 944-5821
2110 S Sinclair Ave Stockton (95215) *(G-6684)*
Intertek Caleb Brett, Signal Hill *Also called Intertek USA Inc* *(G-17250)*
Intertek Testing Svcs NA Inc 949 448-4100
25800 Commercentre Dr Lake Forest (92630) *(G-26860)*
Intertek Testing Svcs NA Inc 949 349-1684
25791 Commercentre Dr Lake Forest (92630) *(G-17249)*
Intertek USA Inc 562 494-4999
1941 Freeman Ave Ste A Signal Hill (90755) *(G-17250)*
Intertrend Communications Inc 562 733-1888
228 E Broadway Long Beach (90802) *(G-13867)*
Intervec Phoenix Travel Club 828 728-5287
1456 Seacoast Dr Unit 4a Imperial Beach (91932) *(G-18963)*
Interviewing Service Amer Inc (PA) 818 989-1044
15400 Sherman Way Fl 4 Van Nuys (91406) *(G-26675)*
Interviewing Service Amer Inc 626 979-4140
200 S Grfield Ave Ste 302 Alhambra (91801) *(G-26676)*
Intervision Systems Tech Inc (PA) 408 980-8550
2270 Martin Ave Santa Clara (95050) *(G-15972)*
Interwall Dev Systems Inc 949 553-9102
17401 Armstrong Ave Irvine (92614) *(G-2912)*
Interwest Insurance Svcs Inc (PA) 916 488-3100
3636 American River Dr # 2 Sacramento (95864) *(G-10748)*
Interwest Insurance Svcs Inc 530 895-1010
1357 E Lassen Ave Ste 100 Chico (95973) *(G-10749)*
Interwoven Inc (HQ) 312 580-9100
1140 Enterprise Way Sunnyvale (94089) *(G-15709)*
Intex Recreation Corp 310 549-1846
4001 Via Oro Ave Ste 210 Long Beach (90810) *(G-6821)*
Intex Recreation Corp (PA) 310 549-5400
4001 Via Oro Ave Ste 210 Long Beach (90810) *(G-8021)*
Intex Recreation Corp 310 549-5400
1665 Hughes Way Long Beach (90810) *(G-11006)*
Intouch Health, Goleta *Also called Intouch Technologies Inc* *(G-15710)*
Intouch Technologies Inc 805 562-8686
6330 Hollister Ave Goleta (93117) *(G-15710)*
Intratek Computer Inc 949 334-4200
9950 Irvine Center Dr Irvine (92618) *(G-16411)*
Intravas Inc 760 650-4040
5840 El Camino Real Carlsbad (92008) *(G-27484)*
Intrepid Healthcare Svcs Inc (HQ) 888 447-2362
4605 Lankershim Blvd North Hollywood (91602) *(G-19572)*
Intrepid Security Solutions 855 379-2223
1999 S Bascom Ave Ste 700 Campbell (95008) *(G-16892)*
Intrinsik Envmtl Sciences Inc 310 392-6462
1608 Pacific Ave Ste 201 Venice (90291) *(G-27955)*
Intuit Financial Services, Redwood City *Also called Digital Insight Corporation* *(G-16228)*
Intuit Inc 818 436-7800
21215 Burbank Blvd Woodland Hills (91367) *(G-26379)*
Intuit Inc (PA) 650 944-6000
2700 Coast Ave Mountain View (94043) *(G-15711)*
Intuit Inc 650 944-6000
2700 Coast Ave Bldg 7 Mountain View (94043) *(G-15712)*
Intuit Inc 650 944-6000
2535 Garcia Ave Mountain View (94043) *(G-15713)*
Intuit Inc 650 944-2840
141 Corona Way Portola Valley (94028) *(G-15714)*
Intuit Inc 650 944-6000
180 Jefferson Dr Menlo Park (94025) *(G-15715)*
Intuit Inc 858 215-8000
7535 Torrey Santa Fe Rd San Diego (92129) *(G-15716)*
Invensys Processs Systems Inc 949 727-3200
26561 Rancho Pkwy S Lake Forest (92630) *(G-15254)*
Inventus Power Inc 949 553-0097
17672 Armstrong Ave Irvine (92614) *(G-24036)*
Inveserve Corporation 626 458-3435
123 S Chapel Ave Alhambra (91801) *(G-11591)*
Invesmart Inc 408 961-2800
55 Almaden Blvd Ste 800 San Jose (95113) *(G-10750)*
Investment Banking, Los Angeles *Also called J Alexander Investments Inc* *(G-12141)*
Investment Tech Group Inc 310 216-6777
400 Crprate Pinte Ste 855 Culver City (90230) *(G-10017)*
Investors Capital MGT Group 310 553-5175
10390 Santa Monica Blvd Los Angeles (90025) *(G-27073)*
Investors MGT Tr RE Group Inc (PA) 818 784-4700
15303 Ventura Blvd # 200 Sherman Oaks (91403) *(G-11143)*
Investors Mortgage Asset Recov 657 859-6200
23282 Mill Creek Dr # 370 Laguna Hills (92653) *(G-9862)*
Invitae Corporation (PA) 415 374-7782
458 Brannan St San Francisco (94107) *(G-26861)*
Invitation Homes 805 372-2900
6320 Canoga Ave Ste 150 Woodland Hills (91367) *(G-11007)*
Invuity Inc 415 665-2100
444 De Haro St Ste 100 San Francisco (94107) *(G-7270)*
Inyo Sheriff Office, Independence *Also called Sheriffs Offices* *(G-23566)*
Iogear, Irvine *Also called Aten Technology Inc* *(G-7096)*
Ion Media Networks Inc 818 953-7193
2600 W Olive Ave Ste 900 Burbank (91505) *(G-5875)*
Ionics Altrpure Wtr Crparation 562 948-2188
7777 Industry Ave Pico Rivera (90660) *(G-8856)*
Ip Access International 949 655-1000
31831 Cmno Capistrno 300a Ste 300 A San Juan Capistrano (92675) *(G-16412)*

ALPHABETIC

Ip Infusion Inc (HQ).......408 400-1900
3965 Freedom Cir Ste 200 Santa Clara (95054) ***(G-15973)***
Ip International Inc.......650 403-7800
1510 Fashion Island Blvd # 104 San Mateo (94404) ***(G-16413)***
Ipac Inc.......925 556-5530
7600 Dublin Blvd Ste 240 Dublin (94568) ***(G-17251)***
Ipass Inc.......650 232-4100
15241 Laguna Canyon Rd # 100 Irvine (92618) ***(G-15974)***
Ipass Inc (PA).......650 232-4100
3800 Bridge Pkwy Redwood City (94065) ***(G-5640)***
Ipayment Holdings Inc (HQ).......310 436-5294
30721 Russell Ranch Rd # 200 Westlake Village (91362) ***(G-17252)***
IPC (usa) Inc (HQ).......949 648-5600
4 Hutton Cntre Dr Ste 700 Santa Ana (92707) ***(G-9024)***
Ipd, Torrance *Also called Industrial Parts Depot LLC* ***(G-7850)***
Ipitek Inc (PA).......760 438-1010
2461 Impala Dr Carlsbad (92010) ***(G-2620)***
Ipolipo Inc.......408 916-5290
440 N Wolfe Rd Sunnyvale (94085) ***(G-15717)***
Ips, Encino *Also called Interstate Protective Services* ***(G-16710)***
Ips Group Inc (PA).......858 404-0607
5601 Oberlin Dr Ste 100 San Diego (92121) ***(G-6077)***
Ips Inc.......909 428-2647
14413 Glenoak Pl Fontana (92337) ***(G-16711)***
Ipsos Public Affairs Inc.......559 451-2820
3402 N Blackstone Ave Fresno (93726) ***(G-26677)***
Ipsy, San Mateo *Also called Personlized Buty Discovery Inc* ***(G-13684)***
Iq Pipeline LLC.......858 483-7400
1550 Hotel Cir N Ste 270 San Diego (92108) ***(G-14890)***
Iq4bis Software Incorporated.......858 565-4238
4885 Greencraig Ln 200 San Diego (92123) ***(G-7147)***
Iqa Solutions Inc.......562 420-1000
4089 E Conant St Long Beach (90808) ***(G-25886)***
Iqms (PA).......805 227-1122
2231 Wisteria Ln Paso Robles (93446) ***(G-15255)***
Ir Hussman, Sacramento *Also called Hussmann Services Corporation* ***(G-17922)***
Ira Services Inc.......650 593-2221
1160 Industrial Rd Ste 1 San Carlos (94070) ***(G-12177)***
Irby Construction Company.......760 344-4478
100 W Keystone Rd Brawley (92227) ***(G-1943)***
Irdeto Usa Inc (HQ).......760 268-7299
3255 Scott Blvd Ste 3-101 Santa Clara (95054) ***(G-15256)***
Irell & Manella LLP (PA).......310 277-1010
1800 Avenue Of The Stars # 900 Los Angeles (90067) ***(G-23318)***
Irell & Manella LLP.......949 760-0991
840 Nwport Ctr Dr Ste 400 Newport Beach (92660) ***(G-23319)***
Irell & Manella LLP.......213 620-1555
1800 Avenue Of The Stars # 900 Los Angeles (90067) ***(G-23320)***
Irene Swindell's Adult Day Car, San Francisco *Also called Institute On Aging* ***(G-24028)***
Irhythm Tech Inc Orange Cnty, Cypress *Also called Irhythm Technologies Inc* ***(G-26774)***
Irhythm Technologies Inc.......714 855-4030
11085 Knott Ave Cypress (90630) ***(G-26774)***
Irise (PA).......800 556-0399
2381 Rosecrans Ave # 100 El Segundo (90245) ***(G-15257)***
Irish Communication Company (HQ).......626 288-6170
2649 Stingle Ave Rosemead (91770) ***(G-1944)***
Irish Construction (HQ).......626 288-8530
2641 River Ave Rosemead (91770) ***(G-1945)***
Irish Construction.......408 612-8440
19490 Monterey St Morgan Hill (95037) ***(G-1946)***
Irish Construction.......209 576-8766
1028 Marchy Ln Ceres (95307) ***(G-1947)***
Irish Construction.......619 713-1991
1329 Sweetwater Ln Spring Valley (91977) ***(G-1948)***
Irma Colen Health Center, Culver City *Also called Venice Family Clinic* ***(G-20188)***
Iron Horse Insurance Co.......925 842-1000
6001 Bollinger Canyon Rd San Ramon (94583) ***(G-1045)***
Iron Law Inc (PA).......844 476-6529
663 S Rancho Santa Fe Rd San Marcos (92078) ***(G-23321)***
Iron Mechanical Inc.......916 341-3530
721 N B St Ste 100 Sacramento (95811) ***(G-2255)***
Iron Mntin/Pacific Rec MGT Inc.......916 924-1558
711 Striker Ave Sacramento (95834) ***(G-4688)***
Iron Mountain Assurance Corp, Milpitas *Also called Iron Mountain Fulfillment* ***(G-14075)***
Iron Mountain Fulfillment (HQ).......408 945-1600
565 Sinclair Frontage Rd Milpitas (95035) ***(G-14075)***
Iron Mountain Incorporated.......661 775-9008
28751 Witherspoon Pkwy Valencia (91355) ***(G-4689)***
Iron Mountain Incorporated.......909 484-4333
8595 Milliken Ave Ste 102 Rancho Cucamonga (91730) ***(G-4690)***
Iron Mountain Incorporated.......562 345-6900
P.O. Box 7877 Newport Beach (92658) ***(G-4691)***
Iron Mountain Info MGT LLC.......714 526-0916
12958 Midway Pl Cerritos (90703) ***(G-4692)***
Iron Workers Local 433.......909 884-5500
252 Hillcrest Ave San Bernardino (92408) ***(G-12178)***
Ironclad Security Services Inc.......408 773-2800
3561 Homestead Rd Ste 600 Santa Clara (95051) ***(G-16712)***
Ironworkers Union, Pasadena *Also called Ironwrker Emplyees Beneft Corp* ***(G-12179)***
Ironwrker Emplyees Beneft Corp.......626 792-7337
131 N El Molino Ave # 330 Pasadena (91101) ***(G-12179)***
Irp Lax Hotel LLC.......310 645-4600
9750 Airport Blvd Los Angeles (90045) ***(G-12854)***
Irri-Scape Construction Inc.......951 694-6936
20182 Carancho Rd Temecula (92590) ***(G-872)***
Irvine APT Communities LP (HQ).......949 720-5600
110 Innovation Dr Irvine (92617) ***(G-11144)***
Irvine Company LLC.......949 653-5300
1 Golf Club Dr Irvine (92618) ***(G-25546)***
Irvine Company LLC.......949 720-4400
111 Innovation Dr Irvine (92617) ***(G-11974)***
Irvine Company Office Property, Newport Beach *Also called Irvine Eastgate Office II LLC* ***(G-12252)***
Irvine Eastgate Office II LLC.......949 720-2000
550 Newport Center Dr Newport Beach (92660) ***(G-12252)***
Irvine Medical Center, Orange *Also called University California Irvine* ***(G-22003)***
Irvine Pharmaceutical Svcs Inc (PA).......949 951-4425
10 Vanderbilt Irvine (92618) ***(G-26862)***
Irvine Police Department, Irvine *Also called City of Irvine* ***(G-25129)***
Irvine Ranch Water District (PA).......949 453-5300
15600 Sand Canyon Ave Irvine (92618) ***(G-6358)***
Irvine Ranch Water District.......949 453-5300
3512 Michelson Dr Irvine (92612) ***(G-6359)***
Irvine Regional Hospital, Anaheim *Also called Tenet Healthsystem Medical* ***(G-21964)***
Irvine Technology Corporation.......714 445-2624
17900 Von Karman Ave # 100 Irvine (92614) ***(G-27485)***
Irvine Unified School Distict.......949 936-5300
100 Nightmist Irvine (92618) ***(G-3939)***
Irvine Valencia Growers.......949 936-8000
11501 Jeffrey Rd Irvine (92602) ***(G-257)***
Irwin Industries Inc (HQ).......310 233-3000
1580 W Carson St Long Beach (90810) ***(G-2057)***
Irwin Industries Inc.......805 874-3050
610 W Hueneme Rd Oxnard (93033) ***(G-2058)***
Irwin Naturals.......310 306-3636
5310 Beethoven St Los Angeles (90066) ***(G-8265)***
Irwindale 6000, Irwindale *Also called Southern California Edison Co* ***(G-6226)***
Isaac Fair Corporation.......858 369-8000
3661 Valley Centre Dr San Diego (92130) ***(G-15258)***
Iscs Inc.......408 362-3000
100 Great Oaks Blvd # 100 San Jose (95119) ***(G-15259)***
ISE Corporation.......858 413-1720
12302 Kerran St Los Angeles (90064) ***(G-26539)***
ISE Labs Inc.......510 687-2500
46800 Bayside Pkwy Fremont (94538) ***(G-26863)***
ISE Labs Inc (HQ).......510 687-2500
46800 Bayside Pkwy Fremont (94538) ***(G-26864)***
Isearch Media LLC.......415 358-0882
1710 S Amphlett Blvd # 320 San Mateo (94402) ***(G-13868)***
Iserve Residential Lending LLC.......858 486-4169
15015 Ave Of Science # 250 San Diego (92128) ***(G-9863)***
Ishares, San Francisco *Also called Blackrock Instnl Tr Nat Assn* ***(G-12106)***
Isheriff Inc.......650 412-4300
555 Twin Dolphin Dr Redwood City (94065) ***(G-15260)***
ISI Inspection Services Inc (PA).......415 243-3265
1798 University Ave Berkeley (94703) ***(G-17253)***
Islamic Relief USA.......714 676-1300
6131 Orangethorpe Ave # 450 Buena Park (90620) ***(G-24037)***
Island Hospitality MGT LLC.......408 720-1000
750 Lakeway Dr Sunnyvale (94085) ***(G-12855)***
Island Hospitality MGT LLC.......650 574-4700
2000 Winward Way San Mateo (94404) ***(G-12856)***
Island Hospitality MGT LLC.......408 720-8893
1080 Stewart Dr Sunnyvale (94085) ***(G-12857)***
Island Hospitality MGT LLC.......909 937-6788
2025 Convention Ctr Way Ontario (91764) ***(G-12858)***
Island Hospitality MGT LLC.......650 591-8600
400 Concourse Dr Belmont (94002) ***(G-12859)***
Islands Restaurant & Lounge, San Diego *Also called Crown Plaza SD* ***(G-12555)***
ISO Services Inc.......415 434-4599
388 Market St Ste 800 San Francisco (94111) ***(G-28137)***
Isolutecom Inc (PA).......805 498-6259
9 Northam Ave Newbury Park (91320) ***(G-15718)***
Isotis Orthobiologics Inc.......949 595-8710
2 Goodyear Ste A Irvine (92618) ***(G-26540)***
Ispace Inc.......310 563-3800
2381 Rosecrans Ave # 110 El Segundo (90245) ***(G-16414)***
Israel Discount Bank New York.......213 861-6440
888 S Figueroa St Ste 550 Los Angeles (90017) ***(G-9504)***
Israel Pops Orchestra.......818 343-6450
4841 Alonzo Ave Encino (91316) ***(G-18476)***
ISS Facility Services Inc.......650 593-9774
541 Taylor Way Ste 5 San Carlos (94070) ***(G-14327)***
Ists Worldwide Inc.......510 794-1400
2201 Walnut Ave Ste 210 Fremont (94538) ***(G-16415)***
Isuzu Truck Services, Santa Ana *Also called Toms Truck Center Inc* ***(G-17654)***
Isyndicate Inc.......415 896-1900
455 9th St San Francisco (94103) ***(G-16247)***
Isys Solutions Inc.......714 521-7656
2601 Saturn St Ste 302 Brea (92821) ***(G-27486)***
It Is Written, Riverside *Also called Adventist Media Center Inc* ***(G-18366)***
Ita Group Inc.......415 277-3200
350 Sansome St San Francisco (94104) ***(G-27487)***
Italee Optics Inc (PA).......213 385-8805
2641 W Olympic Blvd Los Angeles (90006) ***(G-7332)***
Italfoods Inc.......650 873-2640
205 Shaw Rd South San Francisco (94080) ***(G-8857)***
Italian Concepts, Pasadena *Also called Najarian Furniture Company Inc* ***(G-6826)***
Itc Nexus Holding Company, San Diego *Also called Accriva Dgnostics Holdings Inc* ***(G-12048)***
Itc Service Group Inc (PA).......877 370-4482
7777 Greenback Ln Ste 201 Citrus Heights (95610) ***(G-27956)***
Itco Solutions Inc.......650 367-0514
1003 Whitehall Ln Redwood City (94061) ***(G-16416)***
Itd Print Solutions, Los Angeles *Also called Imaging Technologies Group LLC* ***(G-8169)***
Itek Services Inc.......949 770-4835
25501 Arctic Ocean Dr Lake Forest (92630) ***(G-16417)***

A L P H A B E T I C

Itera Software, Irvine *Also called Vision Solutions Inc* ***(G-16523)***
Ito Farms, Westminster *Also called B & E Farms Inc* ***(G-104)***
Ito Packing Co Inc.....559 638-2531
1592 11th St Ste H Reedley (93654) ***(G-550)***
Itrenew Inc (PA).....510 795-1591
8356 Central Ave Newark (94560) ***(G-6492)***
Itron Inc.....510 844-2800
1111 Broadway Ste 1800 Oakland (94607) ***(G-2621)***
Its Technologies Logistics LLC.....209 460-6023
6540 Austin Rd Stockton (95215) ***(G-5225)***
Itseez Inc.....832 781-7169
548 Market St 82363 San Francisco (94104) ***(G-15261)***
Itson Inc.....650 517-2780
3 Lagoon Dr Ste 230 Redwood City (94065) ***(G-7588)***
Iunlimited Incorporated.....916 218-6198
7801 Folsom Blvd Ste 203 Sacramento (95826) ***(G-16713)***
IVBCF, Temecula *Also called Inland Valley Business and Com* ***(G-25545)***
Ivie McNeill Wyatt A Prof Law.....213 489-0028
444 S Flower St Ste 1800 Los Angeles (90071) ***(G-23322)***
Ivo Wall Experts Inc.....323 246-4026
5359 Sheila St Commerce (90040) ***(G-2913)***
Ivy Realty.....213 386-8888
611 S Wilton Pl Los Angeles (90005) ***(G-11592)***
Iw Golf Club Inc.....760 345-2561
46000 Club Dr Indian Wells (92210) ***(G-18964)***
Iw Group (PA).....310 289-5500
8687 Melrose Ave Ste G540 West Hollywood (90069) ***(G-13869)***
Iwamoto & Gean Farm.....805 659-4568
2064 Olga St Oxnard (93036) ***(G-74)***
Iwf Half Moon Bay LP.....650 726-9000
2400 Cabrillo Hwy S Half Moon Bay (94019) ***(G-12860)***
Iworks Us Inc.....323 278-8363
2501 S Malt Ave Commerce (90040) ***(G-3384)***
Ixia, Santa Clara *Also called Net Optics Inc* ***(G-15770)***
IXL Learning Inc.....650 357-6976
777 Mariners Island Blvd # 600 San Mateo (94404) ***(G-24470)***
Ixonos USA Limited.....949 278-1354
85 2nd St San Francisco (94105) ***(G-15975)***
Ixos Software Inc (PA).....949 784-8000
8717 Research Dr Irvine (92618) ***(G-7148)***
Ixsystems Inc.....408 943-4100
2490 Kruse Dr San Jose (95131) ***(G-15719)***
Izmocars, San Francisco *Also called Homestar Systems Inc* ***(G-16397)***
Izt Mortgage Inc (PA).....925 946-1858
3011 Citrus Cir Ste 202 Walnut Creek (94598) ***(G-9930)***
J & D Meat Company.....559 445-1123
4586 E Commerce Ave Fresno (93725) ***(G-8858)***
J & J Acoustics Inc.....408 275-9255
2260 De La Cruz Blvd Santa Clara (95050) ***(G-2914)***
J & J Air Conditioning Inc.....408 920-0662
1086 N 11th St San Jose (95112) ***(G-2256)***
J & J Farms.....559 659-1457
36245 W Ashlan Ave Firebaugh (93622) ***(G-370)***
J & J Maintenance Inc.....707 423-7453
100 Hangar Ave Bldg 785 Fairfield (94535) ***(G-14328)***
J & J Productions Incorporated.....714 535-0951
1775 E Lincoln Ave # 205 Anaheim (92805) ***(G-17254)***
J & L Collections Services Inc.....800 481-6006
651 N Cherokee Ln Ste B2 Lodi (95240) ***(G-14036)***
J & M Inc.....510 782-3434
3826 Depot Rd Hayward (94545) ***(G-1949)***
J & M Inc.....925 724-0300
6700 National Dr Livermore (94550) ***(G-1950)***
J & P Financial Inc (PA).....760 738-9000
330 W Felicita Ave Ste E1 Escondido (92025) ***(G-9931)***
J & P Solari.....209 931-1765
6302 Foppiano Ln Stockton (95212) ***(G-237)***
J & S Farm.....559 308-0294
803 W Kimball Ave Visalia (93277) ***(G-371)***
J A Contracting Inc.....559 733-4865
2209 W Tulare Ave Visalia (93277) ***(G-667)***
J Alexander Investments Inc (PA).....213 687-8400
922 S Barrington Ave A Los Angeles (90049) ***(G-12141)***
J and J Wall Baking Co Inc.....916 381-1410
8806 Fruitridge Rd Sacramento (95826) ***(G-8555)***
J B A, Pasadena *Also called B Jacqueline and Assoc Inc* ***(G-15048)***
J B Bostick Company Inc (PA).....714 238-2121
2870 E La Cresta Ave Anaheim (92806) ***(G-1802)***
J B C, Clovis *Also called John Birdsell Construction Inc* ***(G-3059)***
J B Company.....916 929-3003
1825 Bell St Ste 100 Sacramento (95825) ***(G-1577)***
J B Hunt Transport Inc.....909 466-5361
11559 Jersey Blvd Rancho Cucamonga (91730) ***(G-4199)***
J B J Distributing, Fullerton *Also called Veg-Land Inc* ***(G-4484)***
J B Laquindanum & Associates.....707 648-0501
2608 Springs Rd Vallejo (94591) ***(G-13724)***
J Baron Inc.....949 451-1200
5299 Alton Pkwy Irvine (92604) ***(G-11593)***
J C C, San Rafael *Also called Bernard Osher Marin Jewish Com* ***(G-23682)***
J C Entertainment Ltg Svcs Inc.....818 252-7481
5435 W San Fernando Rd Los Angeles (90039) ***(G-18400)***
J C French & Company.....909 596-1423
2984 1st St Ste L La Verne (91750) ***(G-2455)***
J C SALES, Vernon *Also called Shims Bargain Inc* ***(G-9302)***
J C Towing Inc.....619 429-1492
2501 Faivre St Chula Vista (91911) ***(G-17885)***
J Crecelius Inc.....209 883-4826
5043 N Montpelier Rd Denair (95316) ***(G-372)***

ALPHABETIC

J D L Motor Express.....619 232-6136
1250 Delevan Dr San Diego (92102) ***(G-4028)***
J G Boswell Company.....559 992-2141
710 Bainum Ave Corcoran (93212) ***(G-551)***
J G Boswell Company.....661 327-7721
21101 Bear Mountain Blvd Bakersfield (93311) ***(G-12)***
J G Boswell Company.....559 992-5141
28001 S Dairy Ave Corcoran (93212) ***(G-13)***
J G CONSTRUCTION, Chino *Also called June A Grothe Construction Inc* ***(G-1587)***
J G Golfing Enterprises Inc.....909 885-2414
1494 S Waterman Ave San Bernardino (92408) ***(G-18750)***
J Gelt Corporation.....619 424-8181
1424 30th St Ste C San Diego (92154) ***(G-24038)***
J Ginger Masonry LP (PA).....951 688-5050
8188 Lincoln Ave Ste 100 Riverside (92504) ***(G-2820)***
J Goodman & Associates.....310 828-5040
14544 Central Ave Chino (91710) ***(G-8556)***
J H Maddocks Photography.....818 842-7150
40 E Verdugo Ave Burbank (91502) ***(G-16952)***
J H Synder Co LLC.....323 857-5546
5757 Wilshire Blvd Ph 30 Los Angeles (90036) ***(G-11594)***
J Hellman Produce Inc.....213 627-1093
1601 E Olympic Blvd # 200 Los Angeles (90021) ***(G-8741)***
J I Miller, Granada Hills *Also called James I Miller* ***(G-620)***
J I T Supply, Paso Robles *Also called JIT Corporation* ***(G-7589)***
J I T Transportation, San Jose *Also called Dga Services Inc* ***(G-4341)***
J L S Concrete Pumping Inc.....805 643-0766
2055 N Ventura Ave Ventura (93001) ***(G-3278)***
J M A, San Mateo *Also called Judy Madrigal & Associates Inc* ***(G-19578)***
J M C International LLC.....559 256-1300
1470 W Herndon Ave # 100 Fresno (93711) ***(G-1578)***
J M Carden Sprinkler Co Inc.....323 258-8300
2909 Fletcher Dr Los Angeles (90065) ***(G-2257)***
J M Electric, Salinas *Also called Jensco Inc* ***(G-2624)***
J M Equipment Company Inc (PA).....209 522-3271
321 Spreckels Ave Manteca (95336) ***(G-14551)***
J M Equipment Company Inc.....559 233-0187
3751 E Calwa Ave Fresno (93725) ***(G-7776)***
J M J Enterprises Intl.....951 343-2323
10759 Magnolia Ave Ste F Riverside (92505) ***(G-25141)***
J M K C Express, Carson *Also called Harry Group Inc* ***(G-5098)***
J M Telford Farms.....559 875-4955
3280 N Academy Ave Sanger (93657) ***(G-373)***
J M V B Inc.....714 288-9797
12118 Severn Way Riverside (92503) ***(G-2456)***
J Marchini & Son Inc.....559 665-9710
8736 Minturn Rd Le Grand (95333) ***(G-75)***
J P Allen Co (PA).....818 848-1952
924 W Glenoaks Blvd Glendale (91202) ***(G-2258)***
J P Carroll Co Inc.....323 660-9230
5707 Milton Ave Whittier (90601) ***(G-2457)***
J P Consulting.....707 747-4800
4690 E 2nd St Ste 3 Benicia (94510) ***(G-27488)***
J P H Consulting Inc (PA).....323 934-5660
1101 Crenshaw Blvd Los Angeles (90019) ***(G-20689)***
J P H Consulting Inc.....323 934-5660
4515 Huntington Dr S Los Angeles (90032) ***(G-20690)***
J P Original Corp (PA).....626 839-4300
19101 E Walnut Dr N City of Industry (91748) ***(G-8437)***
J P Witherow Roofing Company.....619 297-4701
10176 Riverford Rd Lakeside (92040) ***(G-3180)***
J Paul Getty Trust.....310 440-7325
1200 Getty Center Dr # 400 Los Angeles (90049) ***(G-26678)***
J Perez Associates Inc (PA).....562 801-5397
10833 Valley View St # 200 Cypress (90630) ***(G-3533)***
J R Industries, Westlake Village *Also called Jri Inc* ***(G-7591)***
J R Pierce Plumbing Company.....510 483-5473
14481 Wicks Blvd San Leandro (94577) ***(G-2259)***
J R Roberts Corp (HQ).....916 729-5600
7745 Greenback Ln Ste 300 Citrus Heights (95610) ***(G-1579)***
J R Roberts Enterprises Inc.....916 729-5600
7745 Greenback Ln Ste 300 Citrus Heights (95610) ***(G-1580)***
J Redfern Inc.....925 371-3300
164 N L St Livermore (94550) ***(G-873)***
J Rivera Associates Inc.....415 617-5660
139 S Guild Ave Lodi (95240) ***(G-28138)***
J Robert Echter.....760 436-0188
1150 Quail Gardens Dr Encinitas (92024) ***(G-292)***
J Robert Scott Inc (PA).....310 659-4910
500 N Oak St Inglewood (90302) ***(G-8314)***
J T R Company Inc.....408 293-3272
1102 S 3rd St San Jose (95112) ***(G-4579)***
J Vineyards & Winery, Healdsburg *Also called E & J Gallo Winery* ***(G-153)***
J Vitale Landscape & Maint.....619 938-2435
8801 Cottonwood Ave Santee (92071) ***(G-874)***
J W Floor Covering Inc (PA).....858 536-8565
9881 Carroll Centre Rd San Diego (92126) ***(G-3122)***
J W Leavy Inc.....707 579-3805
3100 Dutton Ave Ste 126 Santa Rosa (95407) ***(G-2915)***
J Walter Thompson USA LLC.....415 268-5555
303 2nd St San Francisco (94107) ***(G-13870)***
J Waters Inc.....831 424-1946
75 San Miguel Ave Ste 5 Salinas (93901) ***(G-16714)***
J&L Teamworks, Lodi *Also called J & L Collections Services Inc* ***(G-14036)***
J&M Keystone Inc.....619 466-9876
2709 Via Orange Way Ste A Spring Valley (91978) ***(G-13599)***
J&R Fleet Services LLC.....909 820-7000
18244 Valley Blvd Bloomington (92316) ***(G-17802)***
J. Perez & Associates, Cypress *Also called J Perez Associates Inc* ***(G-3533)***

J2 Cloud Services Inc (HQ)....323 860-9200
6922 Hollywood Blvd # 500 Los Angeles (90028) **(G-5743)**
J2 Global Inc (PA)....323 860-9200
6922 Hollywood Blvd # 500 Los Angeles (90028) **(G-5744)**
J5th LLC....619 487-1200
356 6th Ave San Diego (92101) **(G-12861)**
Ja Automation & Control LLC....619 661-2591
6965 Cmino Mqladora Ste H San Diego (92154) **(G-7853)**
Jabez Building Services Inc....714 776-7705
2094 Orange Ave Costa Mesa (92627) **(G-14329)**
Jack Engle & Co (PA)....323 589-8111
8440 S Alameda St Los Angeles (90001) **(G-8074)**
Jack H Caldwell & Sons Inc....323 589-4008
4035 E 52nd St Maywood (90270) **(G-8742)**
Jack I Kaiser....415 833-8152
2238 Geary Blvd San Francisco (94115) **(G-25272)**
Jack Jones Trucking Inc....909 456-2500
1090 E Belmont St Ontario (91761) **(G-4352)**
Jack Morton Worldwide Inc....310 967-2400
8687 Melrose Ave Ste G700 West Hollywood (90069) **(G-13871)**
Jack Nadel Inc (PA)....310 815-2600
8701 Bellanca Ave Los Angeles (90045) **(G-27489)**
Jack Nadel International, Los Angeles *Also called Jack Nadel Inc* **(G-27489)**
Jack Neal & Son Inc....707 963-7303
360 Lafata St Saint Helena (94574) **(G-158)**
Jack P Selman....714 639-9860
144 N Orange St Orange (92866) **(G-26212)**
Jack Parker Corp....760 770-5000
4200 E Palm Canyon Dr Palm Springs (92264) **(G-12862)**
Jackie Hoofring....818 961-7272
3390 Auto Mall Dr Westlake Village (91362) **(G-14688)**
Jackoway Tyreman Wertheimer Au....310 553-0305
1925 Century Park E # 1500 Los Angeles (90067) **(G-23323)**
Jackson Demarco Tidus Peter (PA)....949 752-8585
2030 Main St Ste 1200 Irvine (92614) **(G-23324)**
Jackson & Blanc....858 831-7900
7929 Arjons Dr San Diego (92126) **(G-2260)**
Jackson Construction (PA)....916 381-8113
155 Cadillac Dr Sacramento (95825) **(G-1439)**
Jackson Family Wines Inc....415 819-0301
1190 Kittyhawk Blvd Ste A Santa Rosa (95403) **(G-9107)**
Jackson National Life Insur Co....310 899-7900
401 Wilshire Blvd # 1200 Santa Monica (90401) **(G-10210)**
Jackson Rancheria Casino & Ht....209 223-1677
12222 New York Ranch Rd Jackson (95642) **(G-19229)**
Jackson Rncheria Casino Resort, Jackson *Also called Jackson Rancheria Casino & Ht* **(G-19229)**
Jackson Shrub Supply Inc....818 982-0100
11505 Vanowen St North Hollywood (91605) **(G-18233)**
Jackson Tull Chrtred Engineers....310 658-2132
550 Continental Blvd # 195 El Segundo (90245) **(G-15976)**
Jacksons Hardware Inc....415 454-3740
62 Woodland Ave San Rafael (94901) **(G-7688)**
Jacmar Companies, The, Alhambra *Also called Pacific Ventures Ltd* **(G-27155)**
Jacmar Ddc LLC....916 372-9795
3057 Promenade St West Sacramento (95691) **(G-8859)**
Jacmar Food Service Dist, West Sacramento *Also called Jacmar Ddc LLC* **(G-8859)**
Jacob Health Care Center, San Diego *Also called Premier Management Company* **(G-22538)**
Jacobs Center For Nghbrhood (PA)....619 527-6161
404 Euclid Ave Ste 101 San Diego (92114) **(G-27490)**
Jacobs Civil Inc....310 847-2500
1500 Hughes Way Ste B400 Long Beach (90810) **(G-25887)**
Jacobs Consultancy Inc....650 579-7722
555 Airport Blvd Ste 300 Burlingame (94010) **(G-27957)**
Jacobs Cshman San Diego Fd Bnk....858 527-1419
9850 Distribution Ave San Diego (92121) **(G-24039)**
Jacobs Engineering Company....626 449-2171
1111 S Arroyo Pkwy Pasadena (91105) **(G-25888)**
Jacobs Engineering Group Inc....661 393-3922
3451 Unicorn Rd Bakersfield (93308) **(G-25889)**
Jacobs Engineering Group Inc....949 224-7585
3161 Michelson Dr Ste 500 Irvine (92612) **(G-25890)**
Jacobs Engineering Group Inc....661 275-5685
37528 Morning Cir Palmdale (93550) **(G-25891)**
Jacobs Engineering Group Inc....858 793-0461
420 Stevens Ave Ste 150 Solana Beach (92075) **(G-25892)**
Jacobs Engineering Group Inc....925 356-3900
2300 Clayton Rd Concord (94520) **(G-25893)**
Jacobs Engineering Group Inc....310 847-2500
1500 Hughes Way Ste B400 Long Beach (90810) **(G-25894)**
Jacobs Engineering Group Inc (PA)....626 578-3500
155 N Lake Ave Pasadena (91101) **(G-25895)**
Jacobs Engineering Group Inc....619 795-8872
404 Camino Del Rio S San Diego (92108) **(G-25896)**
Jacobs Engineering Group Inc....909 974-2700
3257 E Guasti Rd Ste 130 Ontario (91761) **(G-25897)**
Jacobs Engineering Group Inc....916 273-5500
1050 20th St Ste 200 Sacramento (95811) **(G-25898)**
Jacobs Engineering Group Inc....916 929-3323
1050 20th St Ste 200 Sacramento (95811) **(G-25899)**
Jacobs Engineering Group Inc....408 995-3257
95 S Market St Ste 300 San Jose (95113) **(G-25900)**
Jacobs Engineering Group Inc....213 362-4336
600 Wilshire Blvd # 1000 Los Angeles (90017) **(G-25901)**
Jacobs Engineering Group Inc....626 578-3500
1111 S Arroyo Pkwy Pasadena (91105) **(G-2059)**
Jacobs Engineering Inc (HQ)....626 578-3500
155 N Lake Ave Pasadena (91101) **(G-25902)**
Jacobs Facilities Inc....925 423-7564
4435 First St Pmb 338 Livermore (94551) **(G-1581)**
Jacobs Farm/Del Cabo Inc....650 827-1133
390 Swift Ave Ste 8 South San Francisco (94080) **(G-374)**
Jacobs Farm/Del Cabo Inc....831 460-3500
144 Holm Rd Spc 42 Watsonville (95076) **(G-4029)**
Jacobs Field Svcs N Amer Inc....949 224-7585
3161 Michelson Dr Ste 500 Irvine (92612) **(G-2060)**
Jacobs International Ltd Inc....626 578-3500
155 N Lake Ave Pasadena (91101) **(G-25903)**
Jacobs Project Management Co....949 224-7695
3161 Michelson Dr Ste 500 Irvine (92612) **(G-25904)**
Jacobs Project Management Co....510 457-2436
300 Frank H Ogawa Plz Oakland (94612) **(G-27491)**
Jacobs Technology Inc....760 446-7084
1550 N Norma St Ridgecrest (93555) **(G-25905)**
Jacobs Technology Inc....650 604-3784
Room 117a Bldg 227 Mountain View (94035) **(G-2061)**
Jacobs Technology Inc....650 604-5946
M S 213 15 Mountain View (94035) **(G-25906)**
Jacobs Technology Inc....760 446-1549
1550 N Norma St Ridgecrest (93555) **(G-25907)**
Jacobs Tree Specialist Inc....559 639-7138
2209 W Tulare Ave Visalia (93277) **(G-668)**
Jacobsson Engrg Cnstr Inc....760 345-8700
77590 Enfield Ln Palm Desert (92211) **(G-1803)**
Jacobus Consulting Inc....949 713-2101
15375 Barranca Pkwy B202 Irvine (92618) **(G-27492)**
Jade Global Inc....408 899-7200
1731 Tech Dr Ste 350 San Jose (95110) **(G-15977)**
Jade Inc....818 365-7137
11126 Sepulveda Blvd B Mission Hills (91345) **(G-2916)**
Jag Framing Inc....818 822-7110
16741 Los Alimos St Granada Hills (91344) **(G-3056)**
Jag Professional Services Inc....310 945-5648
2008 Walnut Ave Manhattan Beach (90266) **(G-27958)**
Jag Software Inc....408 262-0572
2235 Skyline Dr Milpitas (95035) **(G-7149)**
Jagpreet Enterprises Inc....510 336-8376
25823 Clawiter Rd Hayward (94545) **(G-8860)**
Jaguar Computer Systems Inc....951 273-7950
4135 Indus Way Riverside (92503) **(G-7150)**
Jake Hey Incorporated (PA)....323 856-5255
257 S Lake St Burbank (91502) **(G-16953)**
Jakes Crawfish & Seafood, Sacramento *Also called Pacific Sea Food Co Inc* **(G-8646)**
Jakks Sales Corporation....424 268-9444
2951 28th St Ste 51 Santa Monica (90405) **(G-8046)**
Jakov P Dulcich & Sons....661 792-6360
31956 Peterson Rd Mc Farland (93250) **(G-159)**
Jal Berry Farms LLC....831 763-7200
1767 San Juan Rd Aromas (95004) **(G-115)**
Jalux Americas Inc (HQ)....310 524-1000
390 N Sepulveda Blvd # 2000 El Segundo (90245) **(G-14552)**
JAM Industries Inc....310 254-0300
2101 E Via Arado Compton (90220) **(G-4580)**
Jam Warehouse, Compton *Also called JAM Industries Inc* **(G-4580)**
Jamboor Medical Corporation....760 241-8063
12675 Hesperia Rd Victorville (92395) **(G-22631)**
Jamboree Management, Laguna Hills *Also called Jamboree Realty Corp* **(G-11595)**
Jamboree Realty Corp (PA)....949 380-0300
22982 Mill Creek Dr Laguna Hills (92653) **(G-11595)**
Jamcracker Inc....408 496-5500
4677 Old Ironsides Dr # 450 Santa Clara (95054) **(G-5641)**
James B Branch Inc (PA)....818 765-3521
4367 Clybourn Ave Toluca Lake (91602) **(G-4353)**
James C Jenkins Insur Svc Inc....925 798-3334
1390 Willow Pass Rd # 800 Concord (94520) **(G-10751)**
James D Tate MD....530 225-8710
2888 Eureka Way Ste 200 Redding (96001) **(G-19573)**
James E Roberts-Obayashi Corp....925 820-0600
20 Oak Ct Danville (94526) **(G-1316)**
James Fedor Masonry Inc....760 772-3036
54859 Bodine Dr Thermal (92274) **(G-2821)**
James G Parker Insurance Assoc (PA)....559 222-7722
1753 E Fir Ave Fresno (93720) **(G-10752)**
James H Cowan & Associates Inc....310 457-2574
29243 Pacific Coast Hwy Malibu (90265) **(G-875)**
James Hardie Building Pdts Inc (HQ)....949 348-1800
26300 La Alameda Ste 400 Mission Viejo (92691) **(G-6933)**
James Hardie Building Pdts Inc....909 355-6500
10901 Elm Ave Fontana (92337) **(G-6934)**
James I Miller....818 363-7444
17659 Chatsworth St Granada Hills (91344) **(G-620)**
James J Stevinson A Corp (PA)....209 632-1681
25079 River Rd Stevinson (95374) **(G-430)**
James M Stewart Inc....707 374-6369
195 Edgewater Dr Rio Vista (94571) **(G-27)**
James Mathewson MD, San Diego *Also called Childrens Assoc Medical Group* **(G-19429)**
James McCutcheon....661 867-1810
17521 Walker Basin Rd Caliente (93518) **(G-1317)**
James McMinn Inc....909 514-1231
21801 Barton Rd Ste B Grand Terrace (92313) **(G-1804)**
James R Glidewell Dental....800 411-9723
2181 Dupont Dr Irvine (92612) **(G-22308)**
James R Glidewell Dental (PA)....949 440-2600
4141 Macarthur Blvd Newport Beach (92660) **(G-22309)**
James-Timec International....707 642-2222
155 Corporate Pl Vallejo (94590) **(G-2062)**
Jameshardie, Mission Viejo *Also called James Hardie Building Pdts Inc* **(G-6933)**
Jameson Properties Co Inc....213 487-3770
3530 Wilshire Blvd # 600 Los Angeles (90010) **(G-11008)**

ALPHABETIC

ALPHABETIC SECTION

Jamison Childrens Home..................................661 334-3500
  1010 Shalimar Dr Bakersfield (93306) *(G-24040)*
Jamm Management LLC.................................510 437-5200
  2447 Stanford Way Antioch (94531) *(G-6742)*
Jan, North Hollywood Also called Japanese Assistance Netwrk Inc *(G-17255)*
Jan Marini Skin Research Inc..........................408 620-3600
  5883 Rue Ferrari Ste 175 San Jose (95138) *(G-8266)*
Jan Pro Clg Systems Sthern Cal........................714 220-0500
  2401 E Katella Ave # 525 Anaheim (92806) *(G-14330)*
Jane McClurg..559 834-3080
  4584 E Floral Ave Selma (93662) *(G-160)*
Janet Hilton..310 851-7200
  990 W 190th St Ste 300 Torrance (90502) *(G-10753)*
Janet K Hartzler MD.......................................760 340-3937
  72057 Dinah Shore Dr D Rancho Mirage (92270) *(G-19574)*
Jangho Curtain Wall Americas.........................650 588-9688
  2181 Meyers Ave Ste C Escondido (92029) *(G-26213)*
Janico Building Maintenance..........................714 444-4339
  3001 Red Hill Ave 2-221 Costa Mesa (92626) *(G-14331)*
Janitorial, Santa Barbara Also called Master Clean USA Inc *(G-14351)*
Janitorial Equipment Svcs Inc.........................951 205-8937
  11752 Garden Grove Blvd # 100 Garden Grove (92843) *(G-14332)*
Jans Towing Inc (PA).....................................626 334-1383
  1045 W Kirkwald Rd Azusa (91702) *(G-17886)*
Janssen Alzheimer Immunothera.....................650 794-2500
  700 Gateway Blvd South San Francisco (94080) *(G-26541)*
Janus Corporation (PA)..................................925 969-9200
  1081 Shary Cir Concord (94518) *(G-3534)*
Janus Corporation...951 479-0700
  2025 Tandem Norco (92860) *(G-3535)*
Janus Et Cie (PA)...310 601-2958
  12310 Greenstone Ave Santa Fe Springs (90670) *(G-6822)*
Janus of Santa Cruz.......................................831 462-1060
  200 7th Ave Ste 150 Santa Cruz (95062) *(G-24041)*
Japan Airlines Co Ltd....................................310 607-2305
  300 Continental Blvd # 620 El Segundo (90245) *(G-4963)*
Japanese Assistance Netwrk Inc.....................818 505-6080
  11135 Magnolia Blvd # 140 North Hollywood (91601) *(G-17255)*
Japanese Cmnty Youth Council (PA)..............415 202-7905
  2012 Pine St San Francisco (94115) *(G-24930)*
Japanese Retirement Home, Los Angeles Also called Senior Keiro Health Care *(G-24808)*
Jarka Enterprises Inc....................................916 491-6180
  1059 Vine St Ste 108 Sacramento (95811) *(G-3536)*
Jaroth Inc..925 553-3650
  2001 Crow Canyon Rd # 200 San Ramon (94583) *(G-2622)*
Jarrow Formulas Inc (PA).............................310 204-6936
  1824 S Robertson Blvd Los Angeles (90035) *(G-8267)*
JAS Pacific..909 605-7777
  201 N Euclid Ave Ste A Upland (91786) *(G-25908)*
Jason Proctor Trnsp Co................................559 992-1767
  2375 Dairy Ave Corcoran (93212) *(G-3806)*
Jass & Associates Inc..................................408 436-1624
  2099 Gateway Pl Ste 304 San Jose (95110) *(G-16418)*
Javelin Logistics Corporation (PA).................510 795-7287
  7447 Morton Ave Ste A Newark (94560) *(G-4354)*
Jay Fisher Farms Inc...................................805 735-1598
  2251 W Central Ave Lompoc (93436) *(G-76)*
Jay Nolan Community Svcs Inc....................323 937-0094
  3699 Wilshire Blvd # 530 Los Angeles (90010) *(G-24354)*
Jay's Catering, Garden Grove Also called Mastroianni Family Entps Ltd *(G-13775)*
Jaycor Inc...858 720-4000
  3394 Carmel Mountain Rd San Diego (92121) *(G-26775)*
Jaylaneentertainment Corp..........................707 820-2773
  585 Fernando Dr Novato (94945) *(G-13970)*
Jaynes Corporation California.....................619 233-4080
  111 Elm St Fl 4 San Diego (92101) *(G-1582)*
Jazzercise Inc (PA)...................................760 476-1750
  2460 Impala Dr Carlsbad (92010) *(G-18647)*
JB Dental Supply Co Inc (PA)...................310 202-8855
  17000 Kingsview Ave Carson (90746) *(G-7271)*
JB Finish Inc..760 342-6300
  82750 Atlantic St Indio (92203) *(G-3057)*
JB Hunt Transport Svcs Inc.......................619 230-0054
  1620 5th Ave San Diego (92101) *(G-5226)*
JB Partners Group Inc..............................818 668-8201
  18375 Ventura Blvd Tarzana (91356) *(G-11596)*
JB Upland Ltd Liability Co........................909 944-5456
  9087 Arrow Rte Ste 140 Rancho Cucamonga (91730) *(G-27493)*
Jbhunt Transport, San Diego Also called JB Hunt Transport Svcs Inc *(G-5226)*
Jbs International Inc..............................650 373-4900
  555 Airport Blvd Ste 400 Burlingame (94010) *(G-26776)*
Jbwo Inc..916 239-7013
  3955 Kingsbarns Dr Roseville (95747) *(G-27074)*
JC Foodservice Inc (PA).........................626 299-3800
  415 S Atlantic Blvd Monterey Park (91754) *(G-7220)*
JC Party Rentals Inc..............................818 765-4819
  11562 Vanowen St North Hollywood (91605) *(G-14553)*
JC Penney, Buena Park Also called JC Penney Corporation Inc *(G-4581)*
JC Penney Corporation Inc......................714 523-6558
  6800 Valley View St Buena Park (90620) *(G-4581)*
JC Resorts Inn.......................................858 487-0700
  17550 Bernardo Oaks Dr San Diego (92128) *(G-12863)*
JC Resorts LLC......................................949 376-2579
  1555 S Coast Hwy Laguna Beach (92651) *(G-27075)*
JC Resorts LLC......................................760 944-1936
  1275 Quail Gardens Dr Encinitas (92024) *(G-27076)*
JC Sales, Commerce Also called Shims Bargain Inc *(G-1463)*
Jck Hotels LLC.....................................858 635-5566
  9888 Mira Mesa Blvd San Diego (92131) *(G-12864)*

Jct Company LLC................................949 589-2021
  29736 Avenida&Bandera Rancho Santa Margari (92688) *(G-2261)*
Jcv Inc...714 871-2007
  1118 W Orangethorpe Ave Fullerton (92833) *(G-2917)*
JD Food, Fresno Also called J & D Meat Company *(G-8858)*
JD Group, San Diego Also called Brokerage Lgstics Slutions Inc *(G-5036)*
JD Miller Construction Inc....................951 471-3513
  506 W Graham Ave Ste 202 Lake Elsinore (92530) *(G-2458)*
JD Power and Associates (PA)...............714 621-6200
  3200 Park Center Dr Fl 13 Costa Mesa (92626) *(G-26679)*
JD Wesson & Associates Inc...............707 255-8667
  3212 Jefferson St Ste 206 NAPA (94558) *(G-17256)*
Jdf Construction Inc............................714 526-1120
  1114 E Truslow Ave Fullerton (92831) *(G-1192)*
Jean Mart Inc....................................323 752-7775
  6700 Avalon Blvd Los Angeles (90003) *(G-8388)*
Jeanne Jugan, A Residence, San Pedro Also called Little Sisters The Poor of La *(G-20738)*
Jeep Gear, Irvine Also called Alcone Marketing Group Inc *(G-13816)*
Jeeva Corporation..............................909 238-4073
  750 E E St Unit B Ontario (91764) *(G-2623)*
Jeff Boldt Farms, Kingsburg Also called Jeff W Boldt Farms *(G-238)*
Jeff Carpenter Inc............................951 657-5115
  1380 W Oleander Ave Perris (92571) *(G-3434)*
Jeff Kerber Pool Plst Inc....................909 465-0677
  10735 Kadota Ave Montclair (91763) *(G-3537)*
Jeff Stover Inc..................................530 345-9427
  260 Cohasset Rd Ste 190 Chico (95926) *(G-18648)*
Jeff Tracy Inc..................................949 582-0877
  15375 Barranca Pkwy A110 Irvine (92618) *(G-2262)*
Jeff W Boldt Farms...........................559 897-0859
  12725 S Smith Ave Kingsburg (93631) *(G-238)*
Jeffco Painting & Coating Inc............707 562-1900
  1260 Railroad Ave Vallejo (94592) *(G-2459)*
Jeffer Mngels Btlr Mtchell LLP (PA)...310 203-8080
  1900 Avenue Of The Stars Los Angeles (90067) *(G-23325)*
Jeffer Mngels Btlr Mtchell LLP...........415 398-8080
  2 Embarcadero Ctr Fl 5 San Francisco (94111) *(G-23326)*
Jefferies LLC....................................310 445-1199
  11100 Santa Monica Blvd # 12 Los Angeles (90025) *(G-10018)*
Jefferson California Congress............760 331-5500
  6225 El Camino Real Carlsbad (92009) *(G-25273)*
Jeffrey Pine Holdings LLC.................619 442-0544
  622 S Anza St El Cajon (92020) *(G-20691)*
Jeffrey Rome & Associates................949 760-3929
  131 Innovation Dr Ste 100 Irvine (92617) *(G-26214)*
Jelani House Inc..............................415 822-5977
  1601 Quesada Ave San Francisco (94124) *(G-24042)*
Jeld-Wen Inc..................................760 597-4201
  2760 Progress St Ste B Vista (92081) *(G-6935)*
Jeld-Wen Windows, Vista Also called Jeld-Wen Inc *(G-6935)*
Jemtown Inc....................................916 315-0555
  6818 Five Star Blvd Rocklin (95677) *(G-17845)*
Jenco Productions Inc (PA)..............909 381-9453
  401 S J St San Bernardino (92410) *(G-17257)*
Jencor Door and Trim Inc.................661 251-8161
  26845 Oak Ave Ste 12 Canyon Country (91351) *(G-3058)*
Jenkins Gales & Martinez Inc...........310 645-0561
  6033 W Century Blvd # 601 Los Angeles (90045) *(G-27077)*
Jenny Craig Inc (HQ)......................760 696-4000
  5770 Fleet St Carlsbad (92008) *(G-13770)*
Jenny Craig Wght Loss Ctrs Inc (HQ)..760 696-4000
  5770 Fleet St Carlsbad (92008) *(G-13771)*
Jensco Inc.....................................831 422-7819
  400 Griffin St Salinas (93901) *(G-2624)*
Jensen Corp Landscape Contr..........408 446-4881
  1983 Concourse Dr San Jose (95131) *(G-876)*
Jensen Corp Landscape Contrs, San Jose Also called Jensen Landscape Services Inc *(G-878)*
Jensen Corporate Holdings Inc (PA)..408 446-1118
  1983 Concourse Dr San Jose (95131) *(G-877)*
Jensen Design & Survey Inc.............805 654-6977
  1672 Donlon St Ventura (93003) *(G-25909)*
Jensen Enterprises Inc...................916 992-8301
  5400 Raley Blvd Sacramento (95838) *(G-7024)*
Jensen Landscape Services Inc.......408 446-1118
  1983 Concourse Dr San Jose (95131) *(G-878)*
Jensen Meat Company Inc..............619 754-6450
  2550 Britannia Blvd # 101 San Diego (92154) *(G-8673)*
Jensen Precast, Sacramento Also called Jensen Enterprises Inc *(G-7024)*
Jeopardy Productions Inc...............310 244-8855
  10202 Washington Blvd Culver City (90232) *(G-18096)*
Jeppesen Dataplan Inc..................408 961-2825
  225 W Santa Clara St # 1600 San Jose (95113) *(G-16248)*
Jerry Leigh Entertainment AP, Van Nuys Also called Leigh Jerry California Inc *(G-8395)*
Jerry Melton & Sons Cnstr, Taft Also called Jerry Melton & Sons Cnstr *(G-1085)*
Jerry Melton & Sons Cnstr.............661 765-5546
  100 Jamison Ln Taft (93268) *(G-1085)*
Jerry S Powell MD........................916 734-5959
  4501 X St Sacramento (95817) *(G-19575)*
Jerry Thompson & Sons Pntg Inc..415 454-1500
  3 Simms St San Rafael (94901) *(G-2460)*
Jesse Lee Group Inc....................510 351-3700
  300 Crprate Pinte Ste 550 Culver City (90230) *(G-27078)*
Jesse Lee Group Inc....................209 832-2273
  2586 Buthmann Ave Tracy (95376) *(G-27079)*
Jessica Cosmetics Intl Inc............818 759-1050
  13209 Saticoy St North Hollywood (91605) *(G-8268)*
Jessica's Cosmetics, North Hollywood Also called Jessica Cosmetics Intl Inc *(G-8268)*

Jessie Lord Bakery LLC 310 328-7738
21100 S Western Ave Torrance (90501) *(G-8557)*
Jesus A Nava Farm Labor 760 344-8084
1698 Jones St Ste 1 Brawley (92227) *(G-669)*
Jet Advertising, El Segundo *Also called Your Man Tours Inc (G-5004)*
Jet Airways of India Inc 650 762-2345
111 Anza Blvd Ste 300 Burlingame (94010) *(G-4805)*
Jet Sets, North Hollywood *Also called M Gaw Inc (G-3548)*
Jet Source Inc 760 438-1042
2056 Palomar Airport Rd # 103 Carlsbad (92011) *(G-5227)*
Jetblue Airways Corporation 718 286-7900
2627 N Hollywood Way Burbank (91505) *(G-4806)*
Jetblue Airways Corporation 510 381-1369
130 Alan Shepard Way M Oakland (94621) *(G-4807)*
Jetblue Airways Corporation 619 725-0807
3835 N Harbor Dr Ste 108 San Diego (92101) *(G-4808)*
Jetmore International, South El Monte *Also called Jetworld Inc (G-6685)*
Jetmore Wind LLC 888 903-6926
15445 Innovation Dr San Diego (92128) *(G-6141)*
Jetro Cash and Carry Entps LLC 916 492-2305
1275 Vine St Sacramento (95811) *(G-8489)*
Jetro Cash and Carry Entps LLC 714 666-8211
1265 N Kraemer Blvd Anaheim (92806) *(G-8558)*
Jetro Cash and Carry Entps LLC 415 920-2888
2045 Evans Ave San Francisco (94124) *(G-8674)*
Jetro Cash and Carry Entps LLC 323 964-1200
5333 W Jefferson Blvd Los Angeles (90016) *(G-9065)*
Jetsuite Inc 949 892-4300
18952 Macarthur Blvd # 200 Irvine (92612) *(G-4881)*
Jett Pro Line Maintenance Inc (PA) 909 944-7035
2910 Inland Empire Blvd # 102 Ontario (91764) *(G-4922)*
Jetworld Inc 626 448-0150
2656 Chico Ave South El Monte (91733) *(G-6685)*
Jewis Vocational & Counseling 415 391-3600
225 Bush St Ste 400 San Francisco (94104) *(G-24355)*
Jewish Cmnty Fndn of (PA) 323 761-8700
6505 Wilshire Blvd Los Angeles (90048) *(G-25274)*
Jewish Community Ctr Long Bch 562 426-7601
3801 E Willow St Long Beach (90815) *(G-24043)*
Jewish Community Fedrtn San Fr (PA) 415 777-0411
121 Steuart St Fl 7 San Francisco (94105) *(G-24931)*
Jewish Family and Chld Svcs (PA) 415 449-1200
2150 Post St San Francisco (94115) *(G-24044)*
Jewish Family and Chld Svcs 650 688-3030
200 Channing Ave Palo Alto (94301) *(G-24045)*
Jewish Family Svc Los Angeles (PA) 323 761-8800
6505 Wilshire Blvd # 715 Los Angeles (90048) *(G-24046)*
Jewish Family Svc Los Angeles 818 984-0276
12821 Victory Blvd North Hollywood (91606) *(G-24047)*
Jewish Family Svc Los Angeles 323 937-5900
330 N Fairfax Ave Los Angeles (90036) *(G-24048)*
Jewish Free Loan Association, Los Angeles *Also called Jewish Family Svc Los Angeles (G-24046)*
Jewish Home For The Aged, San Francisco *Also called Hebrew Home For Aged Disabled (G-20661)*
Jewish Home For The Aged of or 949 364-0010
27356 Bellogente Apt 221 Mission Viejo (92691) *(G-24698)*
Jewish Senior Living Group 415 562-2600
302 Silver Ave San Francisco (94112) *(G-11145)*
Jewish Student Union 310 229-9006
9831 W Pico Blvd Ste 101 Los Angeles (90035) *(G-24049)*
Jewish Vocational Services (PA) 323 761-8888
6505 Wilshire Blvd # 200 Los Angeles (90048) *(G-24356)*
Jezowski & Markel Contrs Inc 714 978-2222
749 N Poplar St Orange (92868) *(G-3279)*
JF Shea Construction Inc 530 246-4292
17400 Clear Creek Rd Redding (96001) *(G-1193)*
JF Shea Construction Inc 949 526-8792
2 Ada Ste 200 Irvine (92618) *(G-1194)*
JF Shea Construction Inc 909 594-0998
675 Brea Canyon Rd Ste 8 Walnut (91789) *(G-1195)*
JF Shea Construction Inc 408 225-1475
6130 Monterey Hwy Ofc San Jose (95138) *(G-1196)*
JF Shea Construction Inc 925 245-3660
2580 Shea Center Dr Livermore (94551) *(G-1197)*
Jfc International Inc (HQ) 323 721-6100
7101 E Slauson Ave Commerce (90040) *(G-8861)*
Jfe Shoji Trade America Inc (HQ) 562 637-3500
301 E Ocean Blvd Ste 1750 Long Beach (90802) *(G-7376)*
Jfm, Lakeside *Also called Johnson Finch & McClure Cnstr (G-3539)*
Jfp Company, Norco *Also called Anna Corporation (G-2427)*
JH Bryant Jr Inc (PA) 310 532-1840
17217 S Broadway Gardena (90248) *(G-1440)*
Jh Capital Partners LP 415 364-0300
451 Jackson St San Francisco (94111) *(G-12317)*
Jhc Investment Inc 714 751-2400
7 Hutton Centre Dr Santa Ana (92707) *(G-12865)*
Jiangsu Juwang Info Tech Co 510 967-3729
901 Tasman Dr Santa Clara (95054) *(G-15262)*
Jifflenow, Sunnyvale *Also called Ipolipo Inc (G-15717)*
Jiffy Lube, Los Alamitos *Also called Alamitos Enterprises LLC (G-17870)*
Jill Taylor Macari 781 315-2597
17 Hemway Ter San Francisco (94117) *(G-27959)*
Jillians San Francisco CA 415 369-6100
101 4th St Ste 170 San Francisco (94103) *(G-17258)*
Jim & Doug Carters Automotive 818 842-5702
2612 N Hollywood Way Burbank (91505) *(G-17724)*
Jim Aartman Inc (PA) 209 599-5066
805 S Locust Ave Ripon (95366) *(G-4030)*
Jim Aartman Milk Transport, Ripon *Also called Jim Aartman Inc (G-4030)*
Jim Couch 415 381-2800
1 Kearny St Ste 1450 San Francisco (94108) *(G-5642)*
Jim Henson Company Inc (PA) 323 856-6680
1416 N La Brea Ave Los Angeles (90028) *(G-18097)*
Jim Murphy & Associates, Santa Rosa *Also called Murphy-True Inc (G-1616)*
Jimmy Kimmel Live, Los Angeles *Also called ABC Cable Networks Group (G-5746)*
Jimmys Fashions 818 790-8932
3135 Chadney Dr Glendale (91206) *(G-17259)*
Jims Supply Co Inc (PA) 661 324-6514
3530 Buck Owens Blvd Bakersfield (93308) *(G-7377)*
Jipc Management Inc 949 916-2000
22342 Avenida Empresa # 220 Rcho STA Marg (92688) *(G-27080)*
Jirbo Inc 310 775-8085
11440 San Vicente Blvd # 100 Los Angeles (90049) *(G-15263)*
JIT Corporation 805 238-5000
1610 Commerce Way Paso Robles (93446) *(G-7589)*
Jive Software Inc (PA) 650 319-1920
325 Lytton Ave Ste 200 Palo Alto (94301) *(G-15720)*
Jj Grand Hotel 213 383-3000
620 S Harvard Blvd Los Angeles (90005) *(G-12866)*
JJ Mac Intyre Co Inc (PA) 951 898-4300
4160 Temescal Canyon Rd Corona (92883) *(G-14037)*
JJ Rios Farm Services Inc 209 333-7467
4890 E Acampo Rd Acampo (95220) *(G-670)*
Jj Valencia Harvesting Inc 805 525-8467
15433 W Telegraph Rd Santa Paula (93060) *(G-495)*
Jjj Floor Covering Inc (PA) 562 692-9008
4831 Passons Blvd Ste A Pico Rivera (90660) *(G-3123)*
JJR Enterprises Inc (PA) 916 363-2666
10491 Old Placerville Rd # 150 Sacramento (95827) *(G-17936)*
Jk Consultants 209 532-7772
1257 Sanguinetti Rd Sonora (95370) *(G-27960)*
Jk Imaging Ltd 310 667-4898
17239 S Main St Gardena (90248) *(G-7034)*
JKB Corporation 562 905-3477
561 S Walnut St La Habra (90631) *(G-3280)*
Jkf Auto Service Inc 916 315-0555
6818 Five Star Blvd Rocklin (95677) *(G-17846)*
Jla Home, Woodland *Also called E & E Co Ltd (G-1169)*
Jla Home, Fremont *Also called E & E Co Ltd (G-6857)*
Jlg Harvesting Inc 831 422-7871
27 Zabala Rd Salinas (93908) *(G-552)*
Jlp Landscape Contracting 707 526-6285
901 7th St Santa Rosa (95404) *(G-879)*
Jls Environmental Services Inc 916 660-1525
3460 Swetzer Rd Loomis (95650) *(G-27797)*
JM Driver LLC 858 663-6226
10620 Treena St Ste 230 San Diego (92131) *(G-15264)*
JM Roofing Company Inc 805 966-3696
534 E Ortega St Santa Barbara (93103) *(G-3181)*
Jma Investments Ltd 916 685-1355
9265 Beatty Dr Sacramento (95826) *(G-880)*
Jmac Lending Inc 949 390-2688
16782 Von Karman Ave # 12 Irvine (92606) *(G-9755)*
JMB Construction Inc 650 267-5300
132 S Maple Ave South San Francisco (94080) *(G-1951)*
Jmbm, Los Angeles *Also called Jeffer Mngels Btlr Mtchell LLP (G-23325)*
Jme Inc (PA) 201 896-8600
527 Prk Ave San Fernando San Fernando (91340) *(G-7447)*
Jmg Security Systems Inc 714 545-8882
17150 Newhope St Ste 109 Fountain Valley (92708) *(G-2625)*
JMJ Financial Group (PA) 949 340-6336
26800 Aliso Viejo Pkwy # 200 Aliso Viejo (92656) *(G-9864)*
Jmp Securities LLC (HQ) 415 835-8900
600 Montgomery St # 1100 San Francisco (94111) *(G-10019)*
Jn Projects Inc 415 766-0273
944 Market St Ste 400 San Francisco (94102) *(G-13772)*
Jnr Inc 949 476-2788
19900 Macarthur Blvd # 700 Irvine (92612) *(G-27494)*
Joan Kroc Center, San Diego *Also called St Vincent De Paul Vlg Inc (G-25586)*
Joan Young Co Realtors, Westlake Village *Also called Young Realtors (G-11932)*
Job Options Incorporated 909 890-4612
1110 S Washington Ave San Bernardino (92408) *(G-13654)*
Jobs Plus, Chico *Also called Caminar (G-22670)*
Jobs Plus, San Ramon *Also called Plus Group Inc (G-14729)*
Jobvite Inc 650 376-7200
1300 S El Camino Real # 400 San Mateo (94402) *(G-27495)*
Joe & Mary Mottino YMCA, Oceanside *Also called YMCA of San Diego County (G-25426)*
Joe Canpagna 619 222-0555
2830 Shelter Island Dr San Diego (92106) *(G-11597)*
Joe Heidrick Enterprises Inc 530 662-2339
36826 County Road 24 Woodland (95695) *(G-7)*
Joe L Coelho Inc 209 667-2676
18637 E Bradbury Rd Turlock (95380) *(G-4200)*
Joe Lunardi Electric Inc 707 823-2129
5334 Sebastopol Rd Santa Rosa (95407) *(G-2626)*
Joe Muller and Sons 530 662-0105
15810 County Road 95 Woodland (95695) *(G-1)*
Joe Pucci & Sons Seafoods, Hayward *Also called Blue River Seafood Inc (G-8629)*
Joe's Auto Parks, Los Angeles *Also called L and R Auto Parks Inc (G-17725)*
Joerns LLC (HQ) 800 966-6662
19748 Dearborn St Chatsworth (91311) *(G-7272)*
Joes Sweeping Inc 562 929-4344
11914 Front St Norwalk (90650) *(G-3538)*
Johann B Garovi 415 898-1801
109 Pinheiro Cir Novato (94945) *(G-1894)*
Johannes Flowers Inc 805 684-5686
4990 Foothill Rd Carpinteria (93013) *(G-293)*

ALPHABETIC

John A Maida Enterprises
ALPHABETIC SECTION

John A Maida Enterprises 408 254-3100
P.O. Box 6144 San Jose (95150) ***(G-8170)***
John Aguilar & Company Inc 209 546-0171
1505 Navy Dr Stockton (95206) ***(G-4031)***
John Alden Life Insurance Co 818 595-7600
20950 Warner Center Ln A Woodland Hills (91367) ***(G-10211)***
John Benward Company Inc 707 996-7809
21750 8th St E Ste B Sonoma (95476) ***(G-1805)***
John Birdsell Construction Inc 559 834-6212
284 W Lester Ave Clovis (93619) ***(G-3059)***
John Brink General Contractor 530 583-2005
1760 W Lake Blvd Ste 3 Tahoe City (96145) ***(G-1806)***
John C Fremont Healthcare Dst 209 966-3631
5189 Hospital Rd Mariposa (95338) ***(G-21614)***
John Collins Co Inc 818 227-2190
5155 Cedarwood Rd Mgr Bonita (91902) ***(G-11146)***
John Deere Authorized Dealer, Fresno *Also called Vucovich Inc* ***(G-7814)***
John Deere Authorized Dealer, Manteca *Also called J M Equipment Company Inc* ***(G-14551)***
John Deere Authorized Dealer, Poway *Also called Bay City Equipment Inds Inc* ***(G-7418)***
John Deere Authorized Dealer, Firebaugh *Also called Thomason Tractor Co California* ***(G-7811)***
John Deere Authorized Dealer, Long Beach *Also called Harbor Diesel and Eqp Inc* ***(G-7847)***
John Deere Authorized Dealer, Lakeside *Also called Rdo Construction Equipment Co* ***(G-14496)***
John Deere Authorized Dealer, Colton *Also called A-Z Bus Sales Inc* ***(G-6657)***
John Deere Authorized Dealer, Sacramento *Also called Pape Machinery Inc* ***(G-7779)***
John Deere Authorized Dealer, Riverside *Also called Complete Coach Works* ***(G-17879)***
John Deere Authorized Dealer, Carson *Also called Buswest LLC* ***(G-3891)***
John Deere Authorized Dealer, Riverside *Also called Rdo Construction Equipment Co* ***(G-7786)***
John F Kennedy Memorial Hosp 760 347-6191
47111 Monroe St Indio (92201) ***(G-21615)***
John F Knnedy Mem Hosp Emrgncy, Indio *Also called John F Kennedy Memorial Hosp* ***(G-21615)***
John F Otto Inc 916 441-6870
1717 2nd St Sacramento (95811) ***(G-1583)***
John G Shipley 714 626-2000
100 W Valencia Mesa Dr # 201 Fullerton (92835) ***(G-11598)***
John Gore Organization Inc 650 340-0469
255 S B St San Mateo (94401) ***(G-18401)***
John Grizzle Farming 760 356-4381
1395 Bonds Corner Rd Holtville (92250) ***(G-375)***
John H Kautz Farms 209 334-4786
5490 Bear Creek Rd Lodi (95240) ***(G-480)***
John Hancock, Irvine *Also called Signature Resources Ins/Fncl* ***(G-10872)***
John Hancock Life Insur Co USA (HQ) 213 689-0813
865 S Figueroa St # 3320 Los Angeles (90017) ***(G-17260)***
John J Maguire DDS 213 740-6462
39340 Fremont Blvd Fremont (94538) ***(G-20258)***
John Jackson Masonry 916 381-8021
5691 Power Inn Rd Ste B Sacramento (95824) ***(G-2822)***
John Jory Corporation (PA) 714 279-7901
1894 N Main St Orange (92865) ***(G-2918)***
John Kennedy Masonry, Carlsbad *Also called Kennedy Masonry Inc* ***(G-2824)***
John Kenney Construction Inc 805 884-1579
619 E Montecito St Santa Barbara (93103) ***(G-3281)***
John L Ginger Masonry Inc 951 688-5050
8188 Lincoln Ave Ste 100 Riverside (92504) ***(G-2823)***
John M Adams Jr MD 310 829-2663
1301 20th St Ste 150 Santa Monica (90404) ***(G-19576)***
John M Frank Construction Inc 714 210-3600
913 E 4th St Santa Ana (92701) ***(G-1584)***
John M Frank Service Group, Santa Ana *Also called John M Frank Construction Inc* ***(G-1584)***
John Muir Behavioral Hlth Ctr 925 674-4100
2740 Grant St Concord (94520) ***(G-22075)***
John Muir Health 925 692-5600
5003 Commercial Cir Concord (94520) ***(G-21616)***
John Muir Health 925 952-2887
380 Civic Dr Ste 100 Pleasant Hill (94523) ***(G-21617)***
John Muir Health (PA) 925 939-3000
1601 Ygnacio Valley Rd Walnut Creek (94598) ***(G-21618)***
John Muir Health 925 947-5300
1981 N Broadway Ste 180 Walnut Creek (94596) ***(G-21619)***
John Muir Health 925 939-3000
1601 Ygnacio Valley Rd Walnut Creek (94598) ***(G-21620)***
John Muir Health 925 682-8200
2540 East St Concord (94520) ***(G-21621)***
John Muir Med Ctr Cncord Cmpus, Concord *Also called John Muir Health* ***(G-21621)***
John Muir Medical Center, Walnut Creek *Also called John Muir Physician Network* ***(G-21626)***
John Muir Medical Center, Walnut Creek *Also called John Muir Health* ***(G-21620)***
John Muir Physician Network 925 952-2701
112 La Casa Via Ste 300 Walnut Creek (94598) ***(G-21622)***
John Muir Physician Network 925 685-0843
91 Gregory Ln Ste 15 Pleasant Hill (94523) ***(G-21623)***
John Muir Physician Network 925 682-8200
2540 East St Concord (94520) ***(G-21624)***
John Muir Physician Network 925 939-3000
1601 Ygnacio Valley Rd Walnut Creek (94598) ***(G-21625)***
John Muir Physician Network (PA) 925 296-9700
1450 Treat Blvd Walnut Creek (94597) ***(G-21626)***
John Muir Physician Network 925 838-4633
1505 Saint Alphonsus Way Alamo (94507) ***(G-19577)***
John Muir Physician Network 925 674-2200
2720 Grant St Concord (94520) ***(G-21627)***
John Plane Construction Inc 415 468-0555
661 Hayne Rd Hillsborough (94010) ***(G-1585)***

John S Meek Company Inc 310 830-6323
14732 S Maple Ave Gardena (90248) ***(G-2063)***
John Shannon Mc Gee Co Inc 562 789-1777
8190 Byron Rd Whittier (90606) ***(G-7448)***
John Stewart Company 707 676-5660
191 Heritage Ln Dixon (95620) ***(G-11599)***
John Stewart Company 213 787-2700
888 S Figueroa St Ste 700 Los Angeles (90017) ***(G-11600)***
John Stewart Company (PA) 213 833-1860
1388 Sutter St Ste 1100 San Francisco (94109) ***(G-11601)***
John Stewart Company 626 967-3734
642 S 2nd Ave Covina (91723) ***(G-23327)***
John Tillman Company, Compton *Also called Blake H Brown Inc* ***(G-7826)***
John Wayne Airport, Costa Mesa *Also called County of Orange* ***(G-4913)***
John Wayne Institute For Ctr 310 449-5253
2200 Santa Monica Blvd Santa Monica (90404) ***(G-26777)***
John's Incredible Pizza Co, Rcho STA Marg *Also called Jipc Management Inc* ***(G-27080)***
John's Pet Products, San Jose *Also called Johns Dog Food Distributing* ***(G-8862)***
Johnre Care LLC 951 658-6374
461 E Johnston Ave Hemet (92543) ***(G-20692)***
Johns Dog Food Distributing 408 275-1943
1633 Monterey Hwy San Jose (95112) ***(G-8862)***
Johnsen Construction Inc 530 642-2123
6448 Capitol Ave Diamond Springs (95619) ***(G-3282)***
Johnson & Johnson Pistaccios 818 242-7853
1720 Ben Lomond Dr Glendale (91202) ***(G-28)***
Johnson & Turner Painting Co 714 828-8282
8241 Electric Ave Stanton (90680) ***(G-2461)***
Johnson Air, Clovis *Also called Ladell Inc* ***(G-2274)***
Johnson Controls Inc 805 522-5555
1757 Tapo Canyon Rd # 120 Simi Valley (93063) ***(G-7590)***
Johnson Controls Inc 707 546-3042
2226 Northpoint Pkwy Santa Rosa (95407) ***(G-25910)***
Johnson Fain Inc 323 224-6000
1201 N Broadway Los Angeles (90012) ***(G-26215)***
Johnson Finch & McClure Cnstr (PA) 619 938-9727
9749 Cactus St Lakeside (92040) ***(G-3539)***
Johnson La Follette 714 558-7008
2677 N Main St Ste 901 Santa Ana (92705) ***(G-23328)***
Johnson Machinery Co (PA) 951 686-4560
800 E La Cadena Dr Riverside (92507) ***(G-7777)***
Johnson Ranch Racquet Club, Roseville *Also called Spare-Time Inc* ***(G-19088)***
Johnson Western Gunite Company (PA) 510 568-8112
940 Doolittle Dr San Leandro (94577) ***(G-3283)***
Johnson/Johnson, Glendale *Also called Johnson & Johnson Pistaccios* ***(G-28)***
Johnston Farms 661 366-3201
13031 E Packinghouse Rd Edison (93220) ***(G-20)***
Johnston Vacuum Tank Service, Taft *Also called Watkins Construction Co Inc* ***(G-2015)***
Joie, Vernon *Also called Dutch LLC* ***(G-8379)***
Joie, Vernon *Also called Dutch LLC* ***(G-8378)***
Joie De Vivre Hospitality LLC 408 335-1700
210 E Main St Los Gatos (95030) ***(G-2627)***
Joie De Vivre Hospitality LLC (PA) 415 835-0300
530 Bush St Ste 501 San Francisco (94108) ***(G-27081)***
Joie De Vivre Hospitality LLC 415 986-2000
386 Geary St San Francisco (94102) ***(G-27082)***
Joie De Vivre Hospitality LLC 650 879-1100
2001 Rossi Rd Pescadero (94060) ***(G-27083)***
Joie De Vivre Hospitality Inc 408 738-0500
910 E Fremont Ave Sunnyvale (94087) ***(G-12867)***
Joint Corp 714 294-2846
3713 S Bristol St Santa Ana (92704) ***(G-20296)***
Joint Labor Mgmt Coop Committe 925 828-6322
6300 Village Pkwy Ste 200 Dublin (94568) ***(G-2628)***
Joint Labor MGT Retirement Tr 503 454-3800
1640 S Loop Rd Alameda (94502) ***(G-10242)***
Jolly Roger Inn, Anaheim *Also called Edward Thomas Companies* ***(G-12610)***
Jomar Industries Inc 323 770-0505
1500 W 139th St Gardena (90249) ***(G-17261)***
Jon K Takata Corporation (PA) 510 315-5400
4142 Point Eden Way Hayward (94545) ***(G-24050)***
Jon Wayne Construction, Vista *Also called Jwc Construction Inc* ***(G-1318)***
Jonair Services LLC 310 529-5482
9800 S Sepulveda Blvd Los Angeles (90045) ***(G-4882)***
Jonathan Beach Club, Santa Monica *Also called Jonathan Club* ***(G-18965)***
Jonathan Club (PA) 213 624-0881
545 S Figueroa St Los Angeles (90071) ***(G-25275)***
Jonathan Club 310 393-9245
850 Palisades Beach Rd Santa Monica (90403) ***(G-18965)***
Jonbec Care Incorporated (PA) 909 798-4003
1711 Plum Ln Redlands (92374) ***(G-21085)***
Jonce Thomas Construction Co 510 657-7171
3390 Seldon Ct Fremont (94539) ***(G-3060)***
Jones & Jones MGT Group Inc 818 594-0019
8220 Topanga Canyon Blvd Canoga Park (91304) ***(G-11147)***
Jones Covey Group, Rancho Cucamonga *Also called Jones/Covey Group Incorporated* ***(G-3540)***
Jones Day Limited Partnership 213 489-3939
555 S Flower St Fl 50 Los Angeles (90071) ***(G-17262)***
Jones Day Limited Partnership 858 314-1200
12265 El Cmino Real 200 San Diego (92130) ***(G-23329)***
Jones Day Limited Partnership 650 320-8412
1755 Embarcadero Rd # 101 Palo Alto (94303) ***(G-23330)***
Jones Day Limited Partnership 949 851-3939
3161 Michelson Dr Ste 800 Irvine (92612) ***(G-23331)***
Jones John 760 275-4168
72700 Bel Air Rd Palm Desert (92260) ***(G-3182)***

ALPHABETIC

Jones Lang La Salle..............................213 239-6000
515 S Flower St Fl 13 Los Angeles (90071) *(G-12253)*
Jones Lang Lasalle Inc..............................415 395-4900
4444 Mkt St Ste 1100 San Francisco (94111) *(G-11602)*
Jones Lang Lsalle Americas Inc..............................949 296-3600
2211 Michelson Dr Irvine (92612) *(G-10154)*
Jones Sign Co Inc..............................858 569-1400
9025 Balboa Ave Ste 150 San Diego (92123) *(G-7221)*
Jones Valley Resorts, Redding *Also called Shasta Lake Resorts LP (G-19281)*
Jones/Covey Group Incorporated..............................888 972-7581
9595 Lucas Ranch Rd # 100 Rancho Cucamonga (91730) *(G-3540)*
Joni and Friends (PA)..............................818 707-5664
30009 Ladyface Ct Agoura (91301) *(G-24051)*
Jonset Corporation..............................949 551-5151
16251 Construction Cir W Irvine (92606) *(G-6630)*
Jopari Solutions Inc..............................925 459-5200
1855 Gateway Blvd Ste 500 Concord (94520) *(G-17263)*
Jordana Cosmetics Corporation..............................323 585-4859
2035 E 49th St Vernon (90058) *(G-8269)*
Jordano's Food Service, Santa Barbara *Also called Jordanos Inc (G-9066)*
Jordanos Inc (PA)..............................805 964-0611
550 S Patterson Ave Santa Barbara (93111) *(G-9066)*
Jorge Pimental Diaz..............................661 344-5139
348 Manzanita Dr Delano (93215) *(G-671)*
Jorgensen & Co, Fresno *Also called Jorgensen & Sons Inc (G-8122)*
Jorgensen & Sons Inc (PA)..............................559 268-6241
2691 S East Ave Fresno (93706) *(G-8122)*
Jose Corona..............................909 606-3168
5572 Edison Ave Chino (91710) *(G-1198)*
Jose Vramontes..............................209 810-5384
14345 N Highway 88 Lodi (95240) *(G-376)*
Joseph C Sansone Company (PA)..............................818 226-3400
21300 Victory Blvd # 300 Woodland Hills (91367) *(G-23332)*
Joseph Dipuzo..............................760 325-1200
601 E Tahquitz Canyon Way # 120 Palm Springs (92262) *(G-13509)*
Joseph Fan..............................909 860-5440
21725 Gateway Center Dr Diamond Bar (91765) *(G-12868)*
Joseph Farms Cheese, Atwater *Also called Gallo Cattle Co A Ltd Partnr (G-426)*
Joseph J Albanese Inc..............................408 727-5700
851 Martin Ave Santa Clara (95050) *(G-3284)*
Joseph Jensen Filtration Plant, Granada Hills *Also called Metropolitan Water District (G-6376)*
Joseph T Ryerson & Son Inc..............................323 267-6000
4310 Bandini Blvd Vernon (90058) *(G-7378)*
Josephine's Personnel Services, San Jose *Also called Josephines Prof Staffing (G-14689)*
Josephines Prof Staffing (PA)..............................408 943-0111
2158 Ringwood Ave San Jose (95131) *(G-14689)*
Joshua House, Newport Beach *Also called National Therapeutic Svcs Inc (G-22778)*
Joshua J Bodenstadt CPA A Prof..............................858 642-5050
4225 Executive Sq Ste 900 La Jolla (92037) *(G-26380)*
Joshua Tree Center For Change, San Diego *Also called Mental Health Systems Inc (G-22774)*
Journal Broadcast Group Inc..............................760 568-3636
72920 Parkview Dr Palm Desert (92260) *(G-5876)*
Joyous Management Inc..............................805 278-2200
2101 W Vineyard Ave Oxnard (93036) *(G-12869)*
JP Allen Extended Stay..............................818 841-4770
150 E Angeleno Ave Burbank (91502) *(G-12870)*
JP Allen Extended Stay (PA)..............................818 956-0202
450 Pioneer Dr Glendale (91203) *(G-12871)*
JP Morgan Securities LLC..............................949 467-3900
660 Nwport Ctr Dr Ste 750 Newport Beach (92660) *(G-10020)*
JP Morgan Securities LLC..............................310 201-2693
14061 Mercado Dr Del Mar (92014) *(G-10021)*
JP Motorsports Inc..............................818 381-8313
11067 Olinda St Sun Valley (91352) *(G-3807)*
Jpa Landscape & Cnstr Inc..............................925 960-9602
256 Boeing Ct Livermore (94551) *(G-881)*
Jpi Development Group Inc..............................951 973-7680
41205 Golden Gate Cir Murrieta (92562) *(G-2263)*
Jpmorgan Chase & Co..............................209 460-2888
400 E Main St Fl 2 Stockton (95202) *(G-9571)*
Jpmorgan Chase Bank Nat Assn..............................707 864-4700
5095 Business Center Dr Fairfield (94534) *(G-9572)*
Jpmorgan Chase Bank Nat Assn..............................949 429-6071
20 Hallcrest Dr Ladera Ranch (92694) *(G-17264)*
Jpmorgan Chase Bank Nat Assn..............................626 795-5177
860 E Colorado Blvd Pasadena (91101) *(G-9573)*
Jpmorgan Chase Bank Nat Assn..............................805 482-2902
502 Las Posas Rd Camarillo (93010) *(G-17265)*
Jpmorgan Chase Bank Nat Assn..............................818 763-7343
12051 Ventura Blvd Studio City (91604) *(G-9574)*
Jpmorgan Chase Bank Nat Assn..............................626 919-3129
100 S Vincent Ave Fl 1 West Covina (91790) *(G-9575)*
Jpmorgan Chase Bank Nat Assn..............................858 605-3300
10790 Rancho Bernardo Rd San Diego (92127) *(G-17266)*
Jpmorgan Chase Bank Nat Assn..............................619 424-8197
1100 Palm Ave Imperial Beach (91932) *(G-9576)*
Jpmorgan Xign Corporation..............................925 469-9446
7077 Koll Center Pkwy Pleasanton (94566) *(G-26381)*
Jr Construction Inc..............................858 505-4760
8123 Engineer Rd San Diego (92111) *(G-1586)*
JR Filanc Cnstr Co Inc (PA)..............................760 941-7130
740 N Andreasen Dr Escondido (92029) *(G-1952)*
JR Perce Plbg Inc Sacramento..............................916 434-9554
3610 Cincinnati Ave Rocklin (95765) *(G-2264)*
JR Simplot Company..............................559 439-3900
3265 W Figarden Dr Fresno (93711) *(G-408)*
JR Simplot Company..............................559 659-2033
35836 W Bullard Ave Firebaugh (93622) *(G-475)*
Jra Landscape Inc..............................559 276-1726
1010 W Whites Bridge Ave Fresno (93706) *(G-882)*
Jri Inc..............................818 706-2424
31280 La Baya Dr Westlake Village (91362) *(G-7591)*
JS Homen Trucking Inc..............................209 723-9559
4224 Turlock Rd Snelling (95369) *(G-4032)*
Js Hospitality Group LLC..............................805 988-3600
600 E Esplanade Dr Oxnard (93036) *(G-12872)*
JS International Shipg Corp (PA)..............................650 697-3963
1535 Rollins Rd Ste B Burlingame (94010) *(G-5107)*
JS Real Estate Prpts Inc..............................310 856-6868
146 W 168th St Gardena (90248) *(G-3385)*
Js Tamers Inc..............................323 609-4101
468 N Camden Dr Ste 200 Beverly Hills (90210) *(G-11603)*
Jsi Shipping, Burlingame *Also called JS International Shipg Corp (G-5107)*
Jsl Technologies Inc..............................805 985-7700
1701 Pacific Ave Ste 270 Oxnard (93033) *(G-25911)*
Jst Fontana..............................909 854-4062
16730 Arrow Blvd Fontana (92335) *(G-14690)*
JT Wimsatt Contg Co Inc (PA)..............................661 775-8090
28064 Avenue Stanford B Valencia (91355) *(G-3285)*
Jt2 Integrated Resources (PA)..............................925 556-7012
519 17th St Oakland (94612) *(G-27084)*
Jt3 LLC..............................661 277-4900
190 S Wolfe Ave Bldg 1260 Edwards (93524) *(G-25912)*
Jtb Americas Ltd (HQ)..............................310 303-3750
19700 Mariner Ave Torrance (90503) *(G-4964)*
Juan Lopez..............................619 428-3138
3065 Beyer Blvd Ste B106 San Diego (92154) *(G-1199)*
Judianne Chew Lcsw..............................916 734-6629
3671 Business Dr Ste 100 Sacramento (95820) *(G-22750)*
Judy Madrigal & Associates Inc..............................650 873-3444
2000 Alameda De Las Pulga San Mateo (94403) *(G-19578)*
Judy Spiegel..............................650 596-5400
580 El Camino Real San Carlos (94070) *(G-11604)*
Julie Coleman Enterprises Inc..............................707 746-6067
3690 Sprig Dr Ste A Benicia (94510) *(G-6493)*
Julio Gonzalez..............................310 310-4055
1417 S Fairfax Ave Apt 4 Los Angeles (90019) *(G-27961)*
Julius Steve Construction Inc..............................949 369-7820
230 Calle Pintoresco San Clemente (92672) *(G-1441)*
Jump Dance Convention, North Hollywood *Also called Break Floor Productions LLC (G-18373)*
June A Grothe Construction Inc..............................909 993-9400
15632 El Prado Rd Chino (91710) *(G-1587)*
June Group LLC..............................858 450-4290
9444 Waples St Ste 100 San Diego (92121) *(G-14891)*
Jungle Fun & Adventure, Concord *Also called Leisure Planet (G-19235)*
Juniper Networks Inc..............................949 584-4591
600 Anton Blvd Fl 11 Costa Mesa (92626) *(G-15978)*
Juniper Networks Inc..............................916 503-1518
1215 K St Fl 17 Sacramento (95814) *(G-15979)*
Juno Healthcare Registry Inc..............................323 937-7210
4401 Wilshire Blvd # 230 Los Angeles (90010) *(G-14691)*
Jurlique Hlistic Skin Care Inc..............................310 899-1923
1230 Montana Ave Ste 105 Santa Monica (90403) *(G-13680)*
Jurlique Hlistic Skin Care Inc (PA)..............................914 998-8800
1411 5th St Ste 501 Santa Monica (90401) *(G-13681)*
Jurlique Wellness Day Spa, Santa Monica *Also called Jurlique Hlistic Skin Care Inc (G-13680)*
Jurupa Stadium Cinema 14, Riverside *Also called Edwards Theatres Circuit Inc (G-18321)*
Just Desserts, Fairfield *Also called New Desserts Inc (G-8891)*
Just Mortgage Inc..............................562 908-5000
8577 Haven Ave Ste 306 Rancho Cucamonga (91730) *(G-9865)*
Justice California Department..............................916 324-5039
1300 I St Ste 720 Sacramento (95814) *(G-27962)*
Justman Packaging & Display..............................323 728-8888
5819 Telegraph Rd Commerce (90040) *(G-8195)*
Juvenile Hall, Indio *Also called County of Riverside (G-24614)*
Juvenile Justice Division Cal..............................805 485-7951
3100 Wright Rd Camarillo (93010) *(G-27085)*
Jvc Americas Corp..............................714 527-7500
5665 Corporate Ave Cypress (90630) *(G-17909)*
Jvc Americas Corp..............................562 463-8110
11925 Pike St Santa Fe Springs (90670) *(G-17910)*
Jvc Company of America, Cypress *Also called Jvc Americas Corp (G-17909)*
Jvc Service & Engineering, Santa Fe Springs *Also called Jvc Americas Corp (G-17910)*
Jvckenwood USA Corporation (HQ)..............................310 639-9000
2201 E Dominguez St Long Beach (90810) *(G-7500)*
JVSLA, Los Angeles *Also called Jewish Vocational Services (G-24356)*
JW Marriott Desert, Palm Desert *Also called Host Hotels & Resorts LP (G-12766)*
Jwc Construction Inc (PA)..............................760 727-2494
2580 Fortune Way Vista (92081) *(G-1318)*
Jwc Construction Inc..............................949 252-2107
4570 Campus Dr Newport Beach (92660) *(G-1319)*
Jwch Institute Inc..............................562 867-7999
14371 Clark Ave Bellflower (90706) *(G-22982)*
Jwch Institute Inc..............................323 562-5813
6912 Ajax Ave Bell (90201) *(G-26778)*
Jwch Institute Inc..............................562 281-0306
12360 Firestone Blvd Norwalk (90650) *(G-26779)*
JWdangelo Company Inc..............................562 690-1000
601 S Harbor Blvd La Habra (90631) *(G-7969)*
Jwmcc Limited Partnership..............................310 277-1234
2151 Avenue Of The Stars Los Angeles (90067) *(G-12873)*

Jyg Concrete Construction Inc..661 607-0337
24841 Avenue Tibbitts Valencia (91355) *(G-3286)*
K & P Janitorial Services..310 540-8878
412 S Pacific Coast Hwy # 200 Redondo Beach (90277) *(G-14333)*
K & S Air Conditioning Inc..714 685-0077
143 E Meats Ave Orange (92865) *(G-2265)*
K & S Auto, Truck & Tractor, Bay Point *Also called K & S Towing & Transport (G-27496)*
K & S Towing & Transport..925 709-0759
2780 Willow Pass Rd Bay Point (94565) *(G-27496)*
K A Associates Inc..310 556-2721
1800 Avenue Of The Stars # 200 Los Angeles (90067) *(G-10022)*
K A R Construction Inc..909 988-5054
1306 Brooks St Ontario (91762) *(G-3287)*
K B Home Coastal..310 231-4000
10990 Wilshire Blvd Fl 7 Los Angeles (90024) *(G-1371)*
K B I, Anaheim *Also called Kinsbursky Bros Supply Inc (G-8075)*
K C C, El Segundo *Also called Carson Kurtzman Consultants (G-23146)*
K E, Irvine *Also called Kite Electric Inc (G-2632)*
K E M A, Oakland *Also called Kema Inc (G-27964)*
K E S, San Diego *Also called Koam Engineering Systems Inc (G-15980)*
K G O T V News Bureau..510 451-4772
520 3rd St Ste 200 Oakland (94607) *(G-5790)*
K G S Electronics, Arcadia *Also called Gar Enterprises (G-7135)*
K G Walters Cnstr Co Inc..707 527-9968
195 Concourse Blvd Ste A Santa Rosa (95403) *(G-2064)*
K Hovnanian, Irvine *Also called K Hovnanian Companies Cal Inc (G-1200)*
K Hovnanian Companies Cal Inc (PA)..949 222-7700
400 Exchange Ste 200 Irvine (92602) *(G-1200)*
K K R, Menlo Park *Also called Kohlberg Kravis Roberts Co LP (G-12320)*
K K W Trucking Inc (PA)..909 869-1200
3100 Pomona Blvd Pomona (91768) *(G-4201)*
K Line America Inc..714 861-5000
17011 Beach Blvd Ste 1100 Huntington Beach (92647) *(G-4716)*
K Love (klqv)..619 235-0600
600 W Broadway Ste 2150 San Diego (92101) *(G-5791)*
K N Properties Inc..650 726-4419
210 San Mateo Rd Half Moon Bay (94019) *(G-4770)*
K O X R, Oxnard *Also called Koxr Spanish Radio (G-5797)*
K P B S, San Diego *Also called San Diego State University (G-5820)*
K P F F Consulting Engineers, Los Angeles *Also called Kpff Inc (G-25926)*
K R Anderson Inc (PA)..408 825-1800
18330 Sutter Blvd Morgan Hill (95037) *(G-8991)*
K R G, Valencia *Also called Krg Technologies Inc (G-15270)*
K S B W- T V, Salinas *Also called Hearst Television Inc (G-5868)*
K S Fabrication & Machine Inc..661 617-1700
6205 District Blvd Bakersfield (93313) *(G-1953)*
K S I, Bakersfield *Also called KS Industries LP (G-1958)*
K S S C - F M, Los Angeles *Also called Entravsion Communications Corp (G-5856)*
K S S J Radio-101.9 FM City, Sacramento *Also called Entercom Communications Corp (G-5771)*
K T A Construction Inc..619 562-9464
1920 Cordell Ct Ste 105 El Cajon (92020) *(G-1954)*
K T Lucky Co Inc..626 579-7272
10925 Schmidt Rd El Monte (91733) *(G-8863)*
K T T V-Fox 11, Los Angeles *Also called Fox Television Stations LLC (G-5864)*
K T W Productions Inc..714 685-0428
6303 E Cedarbrooks Rd Orange (92867) *(G-6869)*
K Tech Security & Protect Svc..619 858-5832
665 Alvin St San Diego (92114) *(G-16715)*
K W P H Enterprises..559 443-5900
2911 E Tulare St Fresno (93721) *(G-3808)*
K X T V - T V Channel 10, Stockton *Also called Kxtv Inc (G-5892)*
K X T V Channel 10, Sacramento *Also called Kxtv Inc (G-5893)*
K Y L D, San Francisco *Also called Iheartcommunications Inc (G-5779)*
K&B Engineering..951 808-9501
290 Corporate Terrace Cir Corona (92879) *(G-25913)*
K&L Gates LLP..415 882-8200
55 2nd St Ste 1700 San Francisco (94105) *(G-23333)*
K&L Gates LLP..310 552-5000
10100 Santa Monica Blvd # 700 Los Angeles (90067) *(G-23334)*
K&L Gates LLP..949 756-0210
1 Park Plz Ste 1200 Irvine (92614) *(G-23335)*
K&L Gates LLP..415 249-1000
4 Embarcadero Ctr Fl 10 San Francisco (94111) *(G-23336)*
K&M Construction..831 643-2819
642 Pine Ave Pacific Grove (93950) *(G-1320)*
K&S, Orange *Also called K & S Air Conditioning Inc (G-2265)*
K-Fed Mutual Holding Company..626 339-9663
1359 N Grand Ave Covina (91724) *(G-12043)*
K-Love 102, San Diego *Also called K Love (klqv) (G-5791)*
K-Love Radio Network, Rocklin *Also called Educational Media Foundation (G-5766)*
K-Micro Inc..310 442-3200
1618 Stanford St Ste A Santa Monica (90404) *(G-7151)*
K/B Realty Advisors, Newport Beach *Also called Koll Investment Management (G-10157)*
K/P LLC..510 614-7800
13947 Washington Ave San Leandro (94578) *(G-14076)*
Ka Management Inc..858 404-6080
5820 Oberlin Dr Ste 201 San Diego (92121) *(G-27086)*
Kaa Design Group Inc..310 821-1400
4201 Redwood Ave Los Angeles (90066) *(G-26216)*
Kabafusion LLC..562 863-0555
17777 Center Court Dr N # 550 Cerritos (90703) *(G-8270)*
Kabam Inc (PA)..415 391-0817
795 Folsom St Fl 6 San Francisco (94107) *(G-15265)*
Kabc 790 Talk Radio, Los Angeles *Also called Citadel Broadcasting Corp (G-5764)*
Kabler Construction Svcs Inc..415 888-8812
467 Miller Ave Mill Valley (94941) *(G-27497)*
Kad Engineering, Yucaipa *Also called Kad Paving Company (G-1807)*
Kad Paving Company..909 790-3366
32147 Dunlap Blvd Ste K Yucaipa (92399) *(G-1807)*
Kadena Pacific Inc..951 990-7865
3421 Gato Ct Ste A Riverside (92507) *(G-1588)*
Kaercher Campbell Associate In..310 556-1900
600 Corporate Pointe # 1010 Culver City (90230) *(G-10754)*
Kagan Capital Management Inc..831 624-1536
126 Clock Tower Pl Carmel (93923) *(G-10155)*
Kaimanu Outrigger Canoe Club..510 895-0435
13424 Doolittle Dr San Leandro (94577) *(G-19230)*
Kainos Home & Training Ctr..650 361-1355
2761 Fair Oaks Ave Ste A Redwood City (94063) *(G-24052)*
Kainos Work Activity Ctr, Redwood City *Also called Kainos Home & Training Ctr (G-24052)*
Kaiser Engineering, Corona *Also called Kaiser Foundation Hospitals (G-25914)*
Kaiser Foundation Health Plan, San Diego *Also called Southern Cal Prmnnte Med Group (G-10381)*
Kaiser Foundation Health Plan, Union City *Also called Kaiser Foundation Hospitals (G-10293)*
Kaiser Foundation Health Plan, San Francisco *Also called Kaiser Foundation Hospitals (G-10294)*
Kaiser Foundation Health Plan, Pasadena *Also called Kaiser Foundation Hospitals (G-10295)*
Kaiser Foundation Health Plan, Vallejo *Also called Kaiser Foundation Hospitals (G-10296)*
Kaiser Foundation Health Plan, Los Angeles *Also called Kaiser Foundation Hospitals (G-10297)*
Kaiser Foundation Health Plan, Cupertino *Also called Kaiser Foundation Hospitals (G-10298)*
Kaiser Foundation Health Plan, Oakland *Also called Kaiser Foundation Hospitals (G-10299)*
Kaiser Foundation Health Plan, Fresno *Also called Kaiser Foundation Hospitals (G-10300)*
Kaiser Foundation Health Plan, Elk Grove *Also called Kaiser Foundation Hospitals (G-10301)*
Kaiser Foundation Health Plan, Victorville *Also called Kaiser Foundation Hospitals (G-10302)*
Kaiser Foundation Health Plan, San Diego *Also called Kaiser Foundation Hospitals (G-10303)*
Kaiser Foundation Health Plan, San Diego *Also called Kaiser Foundation Hospitals (G-10304)*
Kaiser Foundation Health Plan, Hayward *Also called Kaiser Foundation Hospitals (G-10305)*
Kaiser Foundation Health Plan, Panorama City *Also called Kaiser Foundation Hospitals (G-10306)*
Kaiser Foundation Health Plan, Temecula *Also called Kaiser Foundation Hospitals (G-10307)*
Kaiser Foundation Health Plan, Mission Hills *Also called Kaiser Foundation Hospitals (G-10308)*
Kaiser Foundation Health Plan, Mission Viejo *Also called Kaiser Foundation Hospitals (G-10309)*
Kaiser Foundation Health Plan, Los Angeles *Also called Kaiser Foundation Hospitals (G-10310)*
Kaiser Foundation Health Plan, San Rafael *Also called Kaiser Foundation Hospitals (G-10311)*
Kaiser Foundation Health Plan, Anaheim *Also called Kaiser Foundation Hospitals (G-10312)*
Kaiser Foundation Health Plan, Walnut Creek *Also called Kaiser Foundation Hospitals (G-10314)*
Kaiser Foundation Health Plan, Campbell *Also called Kaiser Foundation Hospitals (G-19672)*
Kaiser Foundation Health Plan, Clovis *Also called Kaiser Foundation Hospitals (G-10315)*
Kaiser Foundation Health Plan, Woodland Hills *Also called Kaiser Foundation Hospitals (G-10316)*
Kaiser Foundation Health Plan, Roseville *Also called Kaiser Foundation Hospitals (G-10317)*
Kaiser Foundation Health Plan, Oakhurst *Also called Kaiser Foundation Hospitals (G-10318)*
Kaiser Foundation Health Plan, Ontario *Also called Kaiser Foundation Hospitals (G-10319)*
Kaiser Foundation Health Plan, Ventura *Also called Kaiser Foundation Hospitals (G-10320)*
Kaiser Foundation Health Plan, Santa Ana *Also called Kaiser Foundation Hospitals (G-10321)*
Kaiser Foundation Health Plan, San Bernardino *Also called Kaiser Foundation Hospitals (G-10322)*
Kaiser Foundation Health Plan, Corona *Also called Kaiser Foundation Hospitals (G-22983)*
Kaiser Foundation Health Plan, Chino *Also called Kaiser Foundation Hospitals (G-10323)*
Kaiser Foundation Health Plan, Daly City *Also called Kaiser Foundation Hospitals (G-10324)*
Kaiser Foundation Health Plan, Union City *Also called Kaiser Foundation Hospitals (G-10325)*
Kaiser Foundation Health Plan, San Bruno *Also called Kaiser Foundation Hospitals (G-10326)*
Kaiser Foundation Health Plan, Santa Rosa *Also called Kaiser Foundation Hospitals (G-10327)*
Kaiser Foundation Health Plan, Santa Rosa *Also called Kaiser Foundation Hospitals (G-10328)*
Kaiser Foundation Health Plan, Modesto *Also called Kaiser Foundation Hospitals (G-10329)*
Kaiser Foundation Health Plan, Rohnert Park *Also called Kaiser Foundation Hospitals (G-10330)*
Kaiser Foundation Health Plan, Alameda *Also called Kaiser Foundation Hospitals (G-10331)*
Kaiser Foundation Health Plan, Oakland *Also called Kaiser Foundation Hospitals (G-10332)*
Kaiser Foundation Health Plan, Bellflower *Also called Kaiser Foundation Hospitals (G-10333)*
Kaiser Foundation Health Plan, Selma *Also called Kaiser Foundation Hospitals (G-10334)*
Kaiser Foundation Health Plan, Orange *Also called Kaiser Foundation Hospitals (G-10335)*

ALPHABETIC SECTION | Kaiser Foundation Hospitals

Kaiser Foundation Health Plan, Palm Springs *Also called Kaiser Foundation Hospitals* ***(G-10336)***
Kaiser Foundation Health Plan, Torrance *Also called Kaiser Foundation Hospitals* ***(G-10337)***
Kaiser Foundation Health Plan, Simi Valley *Also called Kaiser Foundation Hospitals* ***(G-10338)***
Kaiser Foundation Health Plan, San Juan Capistrano *Also called Kaiser Foundation Hospitals* ***(G-10339)***
Kaiser Foundation Health Plan, Fontana *Also called Kaiser Foundation Hospitals* ***(G-10340)***
Kaiser Foundation Health Plan, Downey *Also called Kaiser Foundation Hospitals* ***(G-10341)***
Kaiser Foundation Health Plan, Palm Desert *Also called Kaiser Foundation Hospitals* ***(G-10343)***
Kaiser Foundation Health Plan, Tracy *Also called Kaiser Foundation Hospitals* ***(G-10344)***
Kaiser Foundation Health Plan, Thousand Oaks *Also called Kaiser Foundation Hospitals* ***(G-10345)***
Kaiser Foundation Health Plan, San Jose *Also called Kaiser Foundation Hospitals* ***(G-10346)***
Kaiser Foundation Health Plan, Roseville *Also called Kaiser Foundation Hospitals* ***(G-10347)***
Kaiser Foundation Health Plan, North Hollywood *Also called Kaiser Foundation Hospitals* ***(G-21670)***
Kaiser Foundation Health Plan, Los Angeles *Also called Kaiser Foundation Hospitals* ***(G-21673)***
Kaiser Foundation Health Plan, Fresno *Also called Kaiser Foundation Hospitals* ***(G-21674)***
Kaiser Foundation Health Plan, Modesto *Also called Kaiser Foundation Hospitals* ***(G-10348)***
Kaiser Foundation Health Plan, Orange *Also called Kaiser Foundation Hospitals* ***(G-10349)***
Kaiser Foundation Health Plan, San Bruno *Also called Kaiser Foundation Hospitals* ***(G-10350)***

Kaiser Foundation Hospital 510 752-6295
4501 Broadway Oakland (94611) ***(G-22488)***
Kaiser Foundation Hospitals 760 591-4276
400 Craven Rd San Marcos (92078) ***(G-21628)***
Kaiser Foundation Hospitals 714 279-4675
411 N Lakeview Ave Anaheim (92807) ***(G-19579)***
Kaiser Foundation Hospitals 949 262-5780
6 Willard Irvine (92604) ***(G-21629)***
Kaiser Foundation Hospitals 510 675-5777
30116 Eigenbrodt Way Union City (94587) ***(G-10293)***
Kaiser Foundation Hospitals 619 662-5107
4650 Palm Ave San Diego (92154) ***(G-12180)***
Kaiser Foundation Hospitals 408 361-2100
50 Great Oaks Blvd San Jose (95119) ***(G-22489)***
Kaiser Foundation Hospitals 949 425-3150
24502 Pacific Park Dr Aliso Viejo (92656) ***(G-19580)***
Kaiser Foundation Hospitals 619 542-7210
8889 Rio San Diego Dr San Diego (92108) ***(G-19581)***
Kaiser Foundation Hospitals 916 746-3937
1680 E Roseville Pkwy Roseville (95661) ***(G-21630)***
Kaiser Foundation Hospitals 707 393-4000
401 Bicentennial Way Santa Rosa (95403) ***(G-19582)***
Kaiser Foundation Hospitals 619 528-5888
4647 Zion Ave San Diego (92120) ***(G-12181)***
Kaiser Foundation Hospitals 818 719-2000
5601 De Soto Ave Woodland Hills (91367) ***(G-21631)***
Kaiser Foundation Hospitals 925 813-6500
4501 Sand Creek Rd Antioch (94531) ***(G-19583)***
Kaiser Foundation Hospitals 661 726-2500
43112 15th St W Lancaster (93534) ***(G-21632)***
Kaiser Foundation Hospitals 714 741-3448
12100 Euclid St Garden Grove (92840) ***(G-19584)***
Kaiser Foundation Hospitals 323 783-4011
4867 W Sunset Blvd Los Angeles (90027) ***(G-21633)***
Kaiser Foundation Hospitals 925 906-2380
320 Lennon Ln Walnut Creek (94598) ***(G-21634)***
Kaiser Foundation Hospitals 415 833-2616
2350 Geary Blvd Fl 2 San Francisco (94115) ***(G-10294)***
Kaiser Foundation Hospitals 925 295-4145
710 S Broadway Walnut Creek (94596) ***(G-22751)***
Kaiser Foundation Hospitals 626 851-1011
1011 Baldwin Park Blvd Baldwin Park (91706) ***(G-21635)***
Kaiser Foundation Hospitals 925 372-1000
200 Muir Rd Martinez (94553) ***(G-12182)***
Kaiser Foundation Hospitals 562 657-9000
9333 Imperial Hwy Downey (90242) ***(G-21636)***
Kaiser Foundation Hospitals 510 752-1000
3600 Broadway Oakland (94611) ***(G-19585)***
Kaiser Foundation Hospitals 415 833-2000
2425 Geary Blvd San Francisco (94115) ***(G-19586)***
Kaiser Foundation Hospitals (HQ) 510 271-6611
1 Kaiser Plz Oakland (94612) ***(G-21637)***
Kaiser Foundation Hospitals 626 405-5000
393 E Walnut St Pasadena (91188) ***(G-10295)***
Kaiser Foundation Hospitals 562 461-3000
9400 Rosecrans Ave Bellflower (90706) ***(G-19587)***
Kaiser Foundation Hospitals 510 752-1000
280 W Macarthur Blvd Oakland (94611) ***(G-21638)***
Kaiser Foundation Hospitals 951 270-1220
1850 California Ave Corona (92881) ***(G-25914)***
Kaiser Foundation Hospitals 707 645-2720
1761 Broadway St Ste 210 Vallejo (94589) ***(G-10296)***
Kaiser Foundation Hospitals 909 394-2530
1255 W Arrow Hwy San Dimas (91773) ***(G-21639)***
Kaiser Foundation Hospitals 714 672-5100
1900 E Lambert Rd Brea (92821) ***(G-19588)***
Kaiser Foundation Hospitals 415 444-2000
99 Montecillo Rd San Rafael (94903) ***(G-19589)***
Kaiser Foundation Hospitals 619 528-2583
4405 Vandever Ave Fl 5 San Diego (92120) ***(G-21640)***
Kaiser Foundation Hospitals 510 307-1500
901 Nevin Ave Richmond (94801) ***(G-19590)***
Kaiser Foundation Hospitals 323 857-2000
6041 Cadillac Ave Los Angeles (90034) ***(G-19591)***
Kaiser Foundation Hospitals 818 375-2000
13651 Willard St Panorama City (91402) ***(G-21641)***
Kaiser Foundation Hospitals 909 609-3800
17284 Slover Ave Fontana (92337) ***(G-19592)***
Kaiser Foundation Hospitals 888 750-0036
1301 California St Redlands (92374) ***(G-19593)***
Kaiser Foundation Hospitals 408 972-6010
280 Hospital Pkwy San Jose (95119) ***(G-21642)***
Kaiser Foundation Hospitals 408 972-7000
250 Hospital Pkwy San Jose (95119) ***(G-19594)***
Kaiser Foundation Hospitals 800 954-8000
1550 W Manchester Ave Los Angeles (90047) ***(G-10297)***
Kaiser Foundation Hospitals 408 366-4247
19000 Homestead Rd Cupertino (95014) ***(G-10298)***
Kaiser Foundation Hospitals 510 752-7864
255 W Macarthur Blvd Oakland (94611) ***(G-10299)***
Kaiser Foundation Hospitals 559 448-4555
4785 N 1st St Fresno (93726) ***(G-10300)***
Kaiser Foundation Hospitals 916 544-6000
10305 Promenade Pkwy Elk Grove (95757) ***(G-10301)***
Kaiser Foundation Hospitals 888 750-0036
14011 Park Ave Victorville (92392) ***(G-10302)***
Kaiser Foundation Hospitals 619 528-5000
17140 Bernardo Center Dr San Diego (92128) ***(G-10303)***
Kaiser Foundation Hospitals 619 528-5000
5893 Copley Dr San Diego (92111) ***(G-10304)***
Kaiser Foundation Hospitals 510 454-1000
27303 Sleepy Hollow Ave S Hayward (94545) ***(G-10305)***
Kaiser Foundation Hospitals 818 375-2028
8001 Ventura Canyon Ave Panorama City (91402) ***(G-10306)***
Kaiser Foundation Hospitals 866 984-7483
27309 Madison Ave Temecula (92590) ***(G-10307)***
Kaiser Foundation Hospitals 888 778-5000
11001 Sepulveda Blvd Mission Hills (91345) ***(G-10308)***
Kaiser Foundation Hospitals 888 988-2800
Maquina Mission Viejo (92691) ***(G-10309)***
Kaiser Foundation Hospitals 800 954-8000
5620 Mesmer Ave Los Angeles (90230) ***(G-10310)***
Kaiser Foundation Hospitals 707 624-4000
1 Quality Dr Vacaville (95688) ***(G-19595)***
Kaiser Foundation Hospitals 209 839-3200
2185 W Grant Line Rd Tracy (95377) ***(G-19596)***
Kaiser Foundation Hospitals 510 675-4010
3555 Whipple Rd Union City (94587) ***(G-19597)***
Kaiser Foundation Hospitals 888 750-0036
10850 Arrow Rte Rancho Cucamonga (91730) ***(G-19598)***
Kaiser Foundation Hospitals 888 988-2800
5475 E La Palma Ave Anaheim (92807) ***(G-19599)***
Kaiser Foundation Hospitals 877 524-7373
3733 San Dimas St Bakersfield (93301) ***(G-19600)***
Kaiser Foundation Hospitals 888 988-2800
3460 E La Palma Ave Anaheim (92806) ***(G-19601)***
Kaiser Foundation Hospitals 661 395-3000
2615 Chester Ave Bakersfield (93301) ***(G-21643)***
Kaiser Foundation Hospitals 877 524-7373
2531 Chester Ave Bakersfield (93301) ***(G-19602)***
Kaiser Foundation Hospitals 661 337-7160
2620 Chester Ave Bakersfield (93301) ***(G-19603)***
Kaiser Foundation Hospitals 877 524-7373
1200 Discovery Dr Bakersfield (93309) ***(G-19604)***
Kaiser Foundation Hospitals 800 823-4040
10820 183rd St Cerritos (90703) ***(G-19605)***
Kaiser Foundation Hospitals 888 515-3500
2620 Las Posas Rd Camarillo (93010) ***(G-19606)***
Kaiser Foundation Hospitals 877 524-7373
8800 Ming Ave Bakersfield (93311) ***(G-19607)***
Kaiser Foundation Hospitals 562 463-4377
12801 Crossroads Pkwy S City of Industry (91746) ***(G-19608)***
Kaiser Foundation Hospitals 800 823-4040
9449 Imperial Hwy Downey (90242) ***(G-19609)***
Kaiser Foundation Hospitals 442 281-5000
2185 Citracado Pkwy Escondido (92029) ***(G-19610)***
Kaiser Foundation Hospitals 800 780-1277
1336 Bridgegate Dr Diamond Bar (91765) ***(G-19611)***
Kaiser Foundation Hospitals 760 739-3000
555 E Valley Pkwy Escondido (92025) ***(G-19612)***
Kaiser Foundation Hospitals 800 823-4040
9353 Imperial Hwy Downey (90242) ***(G-19613)***
Kaiser Foundation Hospitals 707 427-4000
1550 Gateway Blvd Fairfield (94533) ***(G-19614)***
Kaiser Foundation Hospitals 800 922-2000
26882 Towne Centre Dr # 1 Foothill Ranch (92610) ***(G-19615)***
Kaiser Foundation Hospitals 866 205-3595
9310 Sierra Ave Fontana (92335) ***(G-19616)***
Kaiser Foundation Hospitals 916 986-4178
285 Palladio Pkwy Folsom (95630) ***(G-19617)***
Kaiser Foundation Hospitals 800 780-1230
18600 S Figueroa St Gardena (90248) ***(G-19618)***
Kaiser Foundation Hospitals 818 832-7200
10605 Balboa Blvd Ste 330 Granada Hills (91344) ***(G-19619)***
Kaiser Foundation Hospitals 800 954-8000
501 N Orange St Glendale (91203) ***(G-19620)***
Kaiser Foundation Hospitals 866 984-7483
46900 Monroe St Indio (92201) ***(G-19621)***
Kaiser Foundation Hospitals 661 949-5000
1600 W Avenue J Lancaster (93534) ***(G-21644)***

ALPHABETIC

Kaiser Foundation Hospitals ALPHABETIC SECTION

Kaiser Foundation Hospitals 619 528-5000
3875 Avocado Blvd La Mesa (91941) ***(G-19622)***
Kaiser Foundation Hospitals 916 543-5153
1900 Dresden Dr Lincoln (95648) ***(G-19623)***
Kaiser Foundation Hospitals 661 951-0070
44444 20th St W Lancaster (93534) ***(G-19624)***
Kaiser Foundation Hospitals 310 325-6542
2081 Palos Verdes Dr N Lomita (90717) ***(G-19625)***
Kaiser Foundation Hospitals 415 444-2000
750 Redwood Hwy Frontage # 1206 Mill Valley (94941) ***(G-19626)***
Kaiser Foundation Hospitals 424 251-7000
2040 Pacific Coast Hwy Lomita (90717) ***(G-22752)***
Kaiser Foundation Hospitals 310 604-5700
3830 Martin Luther King Lynwood (90262) ***(G-19627)***
Kaiser Foundation Hospitals 209 735-5000
4601 Dale Rd Modesto (95356) ***(G-19628)***
Kaiser Foundation Hospitals 888 778-5000
5250 Lankershim Blvd North Hollywood (91601) ***(G-19629)***
Kaiser Foundation Hospitals 209 735-5000
4125 Bangs Ave Modesto (95356) ***(G-19630)***
Kaiser Foundation Hospitals 562 807-6100
12501 Imperial Hwy Norwalk (90650) ***(G-19631)***
Kaiser Foundation Hospitals 909 724-5000
2295 S Vineyard Ave Ontario (91761) ***(G-19632)***
Kaiser Foundation Hospitals 800 780-1277
1550 Town Center Dr Montebello (90640) ***(G-19633)***
Kaiser Foundation Hospitals 888 515-3500
2200 E Gonzales Rd Oxnard (93036) ***(G-19634)***
Kaiser Foundation Hospitals 800 777-1256
73733 Fred Waring Dr Palm Desert (92260) ***(G-19635)***
Kaiser Foundation Hospitals 805 988-6300
2103 E Gonzales Rd Oxnard (93036) ***(G-19636)***
Kaiser Foundation Hospitals 510 243-4000
1301 Pinole Valley Rd Pinole (94564) ***(G-19637)***
Kaiser Foundation Hospitals 866 984-7483
University Park Ctr Palm Desert (92211) ***(G-19638)***
Kaiser Foundation Hospitals 951 248-4000
5225 Canyon Crest Dr Riverside (92507) ***(G-19639)***
Kaiser Foundation Hospitals 866 984-7483
14305 Meridian Pkwy Riverside (92518) ***(G-19640)***
Kaiser Foundation Hospitals 858 847-3500
3851 Shaw Ridge Rd San Diego (92130) ***(G-19641)***
Kaiser Foundation Hospitals 858 502-1350
4510 Viewridge Ave San Diego (92123) ***(G-19642)***
Kaiser Foundation Hospitals 650 358-7000
1000 Franklin Pkwy San Mateo (94403) ***(G-19643)***
Kaiser Foundation Hospitals 858 573-0090
7035 Convoy Ct San Diego (92111) ***(G-22753)***
Kaiser Foundation Hospitals 510 454-1000
2500 Merced St San Leandro (94577) ***(G-19644)***
Kaiser Foundation Hospitals 925 244-7600
2300 Camino Ramon San Ramon (94583) ***(G-19645)***
Kaiser Foundation Hospitals 714 223-2606
3601 S Harbor Blvd Santa Ana (92704) ***(G-19646)***
Kaiser Foundation Hospitals 888 778-5000
26415 Carl Boyer Dr Santa Clarita (91350) ***(G-19647)***
Kaiser Foundation Hospitals 661 222-2000
27201 Tourney Rd Santa Clarita (91355) ***(G-22754)***
Kaiser Foundation Hospitals 888 515-3500
145 Hodencamp Rd Thousand Oaks (91360) ***(G-19648)***
Kaiser Foundation Hospitals 408 851-1000
1263 E Arques Ave Sunnyvale (94085) ***(G-19649)***
Kaiser Foundation Hospitals 888 515-3500
322 E Thousand Oaks Blvd Thousand Oaks (91360) ***(G-19650)***
Kaiser Foundation Hospitals 888 988-2800
2521 Michelle Dr Tustin (92780) ***(G-19651)***
Kaiser Foundation Hospitals 925 598-2799
5820 Owens Dr Bldg E-2 Pleasanton (94588) ***(G-21645)***
Kaiser Foundation Hospitals 415 444-3522
820 Las Gallinas Ave San Rafael (94903) ***(G-10311)***
Kaiser Foundation Hospitals 510 481-8575
1440 168th Ave San Leandro (94578) ***(G-22147)***
Kaiser Foundation Hospitals 916 973-5000
1650 Response Rd Sacramento (95815) ***(G-21646)***
Kaiser Foundation Hospitals 909 427-5000
9961 Sierra Ave Fontana (92335) ***(G-19652)***
Kaiser Foundation Hospitals 323 881-5516
5119 Pomona Blvd Los Angeles (90022) ***(G-12183)***
Kaiser Foundation Hospitals 310 325-5111
25825 Vermont Ave Harbor City (90710) ***(G-19653)***
Kaiser Foundation Hospitals 925 295-4000
1425 S Main St Walnut Creek (94596) ***(G-19654)***
Kaiser Foundation Hospitals 650 299-2000
1100 Veterans Blvd Redwood City (94063) ***(G-19655)***
Kaiser Foundation Hospitals 650 903-3000
555 Castro St Fl 3 Mountain View (94041) ***(G-21647)***
Kaiser Foundation Hospitals 916 784-4000
1001 Riverside Ave Roseville (95678) ***(G-19656)***
Kaiser Foundation Hospitals 714 284-6634
1011 S East St Fl 1 Anaheim (92805) ***(G-10312)***
Kaiser Foundation Hospitals 925 906-2000
501 Lennon Ln Walnut Creek (94598) ***(G-21648)***
Kaiser Foundation Hospitals 925 847-5000
7601 Stoneridge Dr Pleasanton (94588) ***(G-21649)***
Kaiser Foundation Hospitals 951 601-6174
12815 Heacock St Moreno Valley (92553) ***(G-12184)***
Kaiser Foundation Hospitals 951 353-2000
36450 Inland Valley Dr # 204 Wildomar (92595) ***(G-21650)***
Kaiser Foundation Hospitals 714 562-3420
5 Centerpointe Dr La Palma (90623) ***(G-19657)***
Kaiser Foundation Hospitals 818 552-3000
444 W Glenoaks Blvd Glendale (91202) ***(G-19658)***
Kaiser Foundation Hospitals 714 685-3520
22550 Savi Ranch Pkwy Yorba Linda (92887) ***(G-19659)***
Kaiser Foundation Hospitals 619 528-5000
1630 E Main St El Cajon (92021) ***(G-21651)***
Kaiser Foundation Hospitals 858 573-0299
7060 Clairemont Mesa Blvd San Diego (92111) ***(G-19660)***
Kaiser Foundation Hospitals 323 562-6400
7825 Atlantic Ave Cudahy (90201) ***(G-21652)***
Kaiser Foundation Hospitals 619 528-5000
250 Travelodge Dr El Cajon (92020) ***(G-21653)***
Kaiser Foundation Hospitals 619 528-5000
732 N Broadway Escondido (92025) ***(G-19661)***
Kaiser Foundation Hospitals 866 319-4269
1249 S Sunset Ave West Covina (91790) ***(G-21654)***
Kaiser Foundation Hospitals 310 325-5111
3900 E Pacific Coast Hwy Long Beach (90804) ***(G-21655)***
Kaiser Foundation Hospitals 310 517-2956
15446 S Western Ave Gardena (90249) ***(G-21656)***
Kaiser Foundation Hospitals 818 592-3100
21263 Erwin St Woodland Hills (91367) ***(G-21657)***
Kaiser Foundation Hospitals 916 631-3088
10725 International Dr Rancho Cordova (95670) ***(G-21658)***
Kaiser Foundation Hospitals 707 765-3900
3900 Lakeville Hwy Petaluma (94954) ***(G-21659)***
Kaiser Foundation Hospitals 415 899-7400
97 San Marin Dr Novato (94945) ***(G-21660)***
Kaiser Foundation Hospitals 510 678-4000
27400 Hesperian Blvd Hayward (94545) ***(G-19662)***
Kaiser Foundation Hospitals 626 583-2200
3280 E Foothill Blvd Pasadena (91107) ***(G-19663)***
Kaiser Foundation Hospitals 909 886-6711
1717 E Date Pl San Bernardino (92404) ***(G-19664)***
Kaiser Foundation Hospitals 530 757-7100
1955 Cowell Blvd Davis (95618) ***(G-19665)***
Kaiser Foundation Hospitals 707 624-4000
1 Quality Dr Vacaville (95688) ***(G-10313)***
Kaiser Foundation Hospitals 510 987-1000
1950 Franklin St Oakland (94612) ***(G-19666)***
Kaiser Foundation Hospitals 619 641-4663
10990 San Dego Mission Rd San Diego (92108) ***(G-21661)***
Kaiser Foundation Hospitals 619 528-5000
8080 Parkway Dr La Mesa (91942) ***(G-21662)***
Kaiser Foundation Hospitals 661 398-5011
3501 Stockdale Hwy Bakersfield (93309) ***(G-21663)***
Kaiser Foundation Hospitals 408 945-2900
770 E Calaveras Blvd Milpitas (95035) ***(G-19667)***
Kaiser Foundation Hospitals 510 891-3400
2000 Brdwy Oakland (94612) ***(G-21664)***
Kaiser Foundation Hospitals 661 334-2020
5055 California Ave # 110 Bakersfield (93309) ***(G-21665)***
Kaiser Foundation Hospitals 925 926-3000
25 N Via Monte Walnut Creek (94598) ***(G-10314)***
Kaiser Foundation Hospitals 650 742-2000
1200 El Camino Real South San Francisco (94080) ***(G-19668)***
Kaiser Foundation Hospitals 323 298-3300
5105 W Goldleaf Cir Los Angeles (90056) ***(G-22755)***
Kaiser Foundation Hospitals 916 688-2000
6600 Bruceville Rd Sacramento (95823) ***(G-19669)***
Kaiser Foundation Hospitals 925 779-5000
3400 Delta Fair Blvd Antioch (94509) ***(G-22756)***
Kaiser Foundation Hospitals 510 248-3000
39400 Paseo Padre Pkwy Fremont (94538) ***(G-19670)***
Kaiser Foundation Hospitals 707 258-2500
3285 Claremont Way NAPA (94558) ***(G-12185)***
Kaiser Foundation Hospitals 707 651-1000
975 Sereno Dr Vallejo (94589) ***(G-21666)***
Kaiser Foundation Hospitals 213 580-7200
765 W College St Los Angeles (90012) ***(G-22076)***
Kaiser Foundation Hospitals 916 817-5200
2155 Iron Point Rd Folsom (95630) ***(G-19671)***
Kaiser Foundation Hospitals 408 871-6500
220 E Hacienda Ave Campbell (95008) ***(G-19672)***
Kaiser Foundation Hospitals 562 907-3510
12470 Whittier Blvd Whittier (90602) ***(G-21667)***
Kaiser Foundation Hospitals 661 222-2323
27107 Tourney Rd Santa Clarita (91355) ***(G-19673)***
Kaiser Foundation Hospitals 559 324-5100
2071 Herndon Ave Clovis (93611) ***(G-10315)***
Kaiser Foundation Hospitals 888 515-3500
21263 Erwin St Woodland Hills (91367) ***(G-10316)***
Kaiser Foundation Hospitals 916 784-4050
1001 Riverside Ave Roseville (95678) ***(G-10317)***
Kaiser Foundation Hospitals 559 658-8388
40595 Westlake Dr Oakhurst (93644) ***(G-10318)***
Kaiser Foundation Hospitals 951 247-3183
10800 Magnolia Ave Riverside (92505) ***(G-19674)***
Kaiser Foundation Hospitals 909 427-5521
789 E Cooley Dr Colton (92324) ***(G-12186)***
Kaiser Foundation Hospitals 408 972-3000
250 Hospital Pkwy Bldg D San Jose (95119) ***(G-19675)***
Kaiser Foundation Hospitals 415 833-2000
2425 Geary Blvd San Francisco (94115) ***(G-12187)***
Kaiser Foundation Hospitals 951 243-0811
27300 Iris Ave Moreno Valley (92555) ***(G-19676)***
Kaiser Foundation Hospitals 209 825-3700
1777 W Yosemite Ave Manteca (95337) ***(G-21668)***
Kaiser Foundation Hospitals 888 750-0036
2295 S Vineyard Ave Ontario (91761) ***(G-10319)***

ALPHABETIC

Kaiser Foundation Hospitals 888 515-3500
888 S Hill Rd Ventura (93003) *(G-10320)*
Kaiser Foundation Hospitals 888 988-2800
3401 S Harbor Blvd Santa Ana (92704) *(G-10321)*
Kaiser Foundation Hospitals 888 750-0036
1717 Date Pike San Bernardino (92404) *(G-10322)*
Kaiser Foundation Hospitals 866 984-7483
2055 Kellogg Ave Corona (92879) *(G-22983)*
Kaiser Foundation Hospitals 888 750-0036
11911 Central Ave Chino (91710) *(G-10323)*
Kaiser Foundation Hospitals 650 301-5860
395 Hickey Blvd Daly City (94015) *(G-10324)*
Kaiser Foundation Hospitals 510 675-2170
3553 Whipple Rd Union City (94587) *(G-10325)*
Kaiser Foundation Hospitals 650 742-2100
901 El Camino Real San Bruno (94066) *(G-10326)*
Kaiser Foundation Hospitals 707 571-3835
3554 Round Barn Blvd Santa Rosa (95403) *(G-10327)*
Kaiser Foundation Hospitals 707 393-4033
3925 Old Redwood Hwy Santa Rosa (95403) *(G-10328)*
Kaiser Foundation Hospitals 855 268-4096
1320 Standiford Ave Modesto (95350) *(G-10329)*
Kaiser Foundation Hospitals 707 206-3000
5900 State Farm Dr # 100 Rohnert Park (94928) *(G-10330)*
Kaiser Foundation Hospitals....510 752-1190
2417 Central Ave Alameda (94501) *(G-10331)*
Kaiser Foundation Hospitals 510 251-0121
969 Broadway Oakland (94607) *(G-10332)*
Kaiser Foundation Hospitals 562 461-3084
9333 Rosecrans Ave Bellflower (90706) *(G-10333)*
Kaiser Foundation Hospitals 559 898-6000
2651 Highland Ave Selma (93662) *(G-10334)*
Kaiser Foundation Hospitals 714 748-7622
4201 W Chapman Ave Orange (92868) *(G-10335)*
Kaiser Foundation Hospitals 866 370-1942
1717 E Vista Chino Ste B2 Palm Springs (92262) *(G-10336)*
Kaiser Foundation Hospitals 800 780-1230
20790 Madrona Ave Torrance (90503) *(G-10337)*
Kaiser Foundation Hospitals 888 515-3500
3900 Alamo St Simi Valley (93063) *(G-10338)*
Kaiser Foundation Hospitals 888 988-2800
30400 Camino Capistrano San Juan Capistrano (92675) *(G-10339)*
Kaiser Foundation Hospitals 909 427-3910
9961 Sierra Ave Fontana (92335) *(G-10340)*
Kaiser Foundation Hospitals 562 622-4190
12200 Bellflower Blvd Downey (90242) *(G-10341)*
Kaiser Foundation Hospitals 805 482-0707
5259 Mission Oaks Blvd Camarillo (93012) *(G-10342)*
Kaiser Foundation Hospitals 760 360-1475
42575 Washington St Palm Desert (92211) *(G-10343)*
Kaiser Foundation Hospitals 209 832-6339
2417 Naglee Rd Tracy (95304) *(G-10344)*
Kaiser Foundation Hospitals 888 515-3500
365 E Hillcrest Dr Thousand Oaks (91360) *(G-10345)*
Kaiser Foundation Hospitals 619 409-6405
3955 Bonita Rd Bonita (91902) *(G-21669)*
Kaiser Foundation Hospitals 408 972-3376
5755 Cottle Rd San Jose (95123) *(G-10346)*
Kaiser Foundation Hospitals 916 784-4190
1840 Sierra Gardens Dr Roseville (95661) *(G-10347)*
Kaiser Foundation Hospitals 818 503-7082
11666 Sherman Way North Hollywood (91605) *(G-21670)*
Kaiser Foundation Hospitals 408 972-6700
275 Hospital Pkwy 765a San Jose (95119) *(G-21671)*
Kaiser Foundation Hospitals 310 419-3303
110 N La Brea Ave Inglewood (90301) *(G-19677)*
Kaiser Foundation Hospitals 626 440-5659
1055 E Colo Blvd Ste 100 Pasadena (91106) *(G-21672)*
Kaiser Foundation Hospitals 916 784-4000
1600 Eureka Rd Roseville (95661) *(G-19678)*
Kaiser Foundation Hospitals 800 954-8000
4867 W Sunset Blvd Los Angeles (90027) *(G-21673)*
Kaiser Foundation Hospitals 559 448-4500
7300 N Fresno St Fresno (93720) *(G-21674)*
Kaiser Foundation Hospitals 559 448-4500
7300 N Fresno St Fresno (93720) *(G-19679)*
Kaiser Foundation Hospitals 888 750-0036
250 W San Jose Ave Claremont (91711) *(G-21675)*
Kaiser Foundation Hospitals 916 525-6300
7300 Wyndham Dr Sacramento (95823) *(G-21676)*
Kaiser Foundation Hospitals 310 513-6707
23621 Main St Carson (90745) *(G-22757)*
Kaiser Foundation Hospitals 209 476-3101
7373 West Ln Stockton (95210) *(G-21677)*
Kaiser Foundation Hospitals 760 931-4228
6860 Avenida Encinas Carlsbad (92011) *(G-19680)*
Kaiser Foundation Hospitals 209 557-1000
1625 I St Modesto (95354) *(G-10348)*
Kaiser Foundation Hospitals 888 988-2800
200 N Lewis St Fl 1 Orange (92868) *(G-10349)*
Kaiser Foundation Hospitals 408 851-1000
710 Lawrence Expy Santa Clara (95051) *(G-21678)*
Kaiser Foundation Hospitals 650 742-2000
801 Traeger Ave Ste 217 San Bruno (94066) *(G-10350)*
Kaiser Foundation Hospitals 866 984-7483
182 Granite St Corona (92879) *(G-12188)*
Kaiser Foundation Hospitals 949 932-5000
6640 Alton Pkwy Irvine (92618) *(G-12189)*
Kaiser Foundation Hospitals 714 967-4700
1900 E 4th St Santa Ana (92705) *(G-21679)*

Kaiser Fundation Hlth Plan Inc (PA) 510 271-5800
1 Kaiser Plz Oakland (94612) *(G-10351)*
Kaiser Fundation Hlth Plan Inc 510 752-7644
3801 Howe St Oakland (94611) *(G-10352)*
Kaiser Fundation Hlth Plan Inc 510 271-5800
4460 Hacienda Dr Pleasanton (94588) *(G-10353)*
Kaiser Fundation Hlth Plan Inc 510 987-2255
1950 Franklin St Fl 3 Oakland (94612) *(G-10354)*
Kaiser Group Holdings Inc 510 419-6000
2101 Webster St Ste 1000 Oakland (94612) *(G-25915)*
Kaiser Hlth Plan Asset MGT Inc 510 271-5910
1 Kaiser Plz Ste 1333 Oakland (94612) *(G-27087)*
Kaiser Manteca Medical Office 209 825-3700
1721 W Yosemite Ave Manteca (95337) *(G-22227)*
Kaiser Med Clinic 650 903-2103
555 Castro St Mountain View (94041) *(G-19681)*
Kaiser Med Security Services 415 833-3683
2241 Geary Blvd San Francisco (94115) *(G-16716)*
Kaiser Mental Health Center, Los Angeles *Also called Kaiser Foundation Hospitals (G-22076)*
Kaiser Permanente, San Jose *Also called Kaiser Foundation Hospitals (G-22489)*
Kaiser Permanente, San Diego *Also called Southern Cal Prmnnte Med Group (G-20021)*
Kaiser Permanente, San Diego *Also called Kaiser Foundation Hospitals (G-12181)*
Kaiser Permanente, Woodland Hills *Also called Kaiser Foundation Hospitals (G-21631)*
Kaiser Permanente, Lancaster *Also called Kaiser Foundation Hospitals (G-21632)*
Kaiser Permanente, Garden Grove *Also called Kaiser Foundation Hospitals (G-19584)*
Kaiser Permanente, Los Angeles *Also called Kaiser Foundation Hospitals (G-21633)*
Kaiser Permanente, Walnut Creek *Also called Kaiser Foundation Hospitals (G-22751)*
Kaiser Permanente, Baldwin Park *Also called Kaiser Foundation Hospitals (G-21635)*
Kaiser Permanente, Oakland *Also called Kaiser Foundation Hospitals (G-21637)*
Kaiser Permanente, Bellflower *Also called Kaiser Foundation Hospitals (G-19587)*
Kaiser Permanente, Oakland *Also called Kaiser Foundation Hospitals (G-21638)*
Kaiser Permanente, San Dimas *Also called Kaiser Foundation Hospitals (G-21639)*
Kaiser Permanente, Brea *Also called Kaiser Foundation Hospitals (G-19588)*
Kaiser Permanente, San Rafael *Also called Kaiser Foundation Hospitals (G-19589)*
Kaiser Permanente, Pasadena *Also called Southern Cal Prmnnte Med Group (G-10382)*
Kaiser Permanente, San Diego *Also called Kaiser Foundation Hospitals (G-21640)*
Kaiser Permanente, Richmond *Also called Kaiser Foundation Hospitals (G-19590)*
Kaiser Permanente, Panorama City *Also called Kaiser Foundation Hospitals (G-21641)*
Kaiser Permanente, Redlands *Also called Kaiser Foundation Hospitals (G-19593)*
Kaiser Permanente, San Jose *Also called Kaiser Foundation Hospitals (G-19594)*
Kaiser Permanente, Sacramento *Also called Kaiser Foundation Hospitals (G-21646)*
Kaiser Permanente, Fontana *Also called Kaiser Foundation Hospitals (G-19652)*
Kaiser Permanente, Los Angeles *Also called Kaiser Foundation Hospitals (G-12183)*
Kaiser Permanente, Harbor City *Also called Kaiser Foundation Hospitals (G-19653)*
Kaiser Permanente, Walnut Creek *Also called Kaiser Foundation Hospitals (G-19654)*
Kaiser Permanente, Redwood City *Also called Kaiser Foundation Hospitals (G-19655)*
Kaiser Permanente, Walnut Creek *Also called Kaiser Foundation Hospitals (G-21648)*
Kaiser Permanente, Pleasanton *Also called Kaiser Foundation Hospitals (G-21649)*
KAISER PERMANENTE, Oakland *Also called Kaiser Hlth Plan Asset MGT Inc (G-27087)*
Kaiser Permanente, West Covina *Also called Kaiser Foundation Hospitals (G-21654)*
Kaiser Permanente, Bakersfield *Also called Kaiser Foundation Hospitals (G-21665)*
Kaiser Permanente, South San Francisco *Also called Kaiser Foundation Hospitals (G-19668)*
Kaiser Permanente, Antioch *Also called Kaiser Foundation Hospitals (G-22756)*
Kaiser Permanente, Fremont *Also called Kaiser Foundation Hospitals (G-19670)*
Kaiser Permanente, NAPA *Also called Kaiser Foundation Hospitals (G-12185)*
Kaiser Permanente, Whittier *Also called Kaiser Foundation Hospitals (G-21667)*
Kaiser Permanente, Santa Clarita *Also called Kaiser Foundation Hospitals (G-19673)*
Kaiser Permanente, Riverside *Also called Kaiser Foundation Hospitals (G-19674)*
Kaiser Permanente, Colton *Also called Kaiser Foundation Hospitals (G-12186)*
Kaiser Permanente, San Jose *Also called Kaiser Foundation Hospitals (G-19675)*
Kaiser Permanente, San Francisco *Also called Kaiser Foundation Hospitals (G-12187)*
Kaiser Permanente, Inglewood *Also called Kaiser Foundation Hospitals (G-19677)*
Kaiser Permanente, Pasadena *Also called Kaiser Foundation Hospitals (G-21672)*
Kaiser Permanente, Downey *Also called Southern Cal Prmnnte Med Group (G-23061)*
Kaiser Permanente, Roseville *Also called Kaiser Foundation Hospitals (G-19678)*
Kaiser Permanente, Fresno *Also called Kaiser Foundation Hospitals (G-19679)*
Kaiser Permanente, Claremont *Also called Kaiser Foundation Hospitals (G-21675)*
Kaiser Permanente, Carson *Also called Kaiser Foundation Hospitals (G-22757)*
Kaiser Permanente, Stockton *Also called Kaiser Foundation Hospitals (G-21677)*
Kaiser Permanente, Santa Ana *Also called Kaiser Foundation Hospitals (G-21679)*
Kaiser Permanente 707 393-4000
401 Bicentennial Way Santa Rosa (95403) *(G-19682)*
Kaiser Permanente 909 427-3910
9985 Sierra Ave Fontana (92335) *(G-21680)*
Kaiser Permanente Advice, Sacramento *Also called Kaiser Foundation Hospitals (G-21676)*
Kaiser Permanente Division RES, Oakland *Also called Kaiser Foundation Hospitals (G-21664)*
Kaiser Permanente Eye, Roseville *Also called Kaiser Foundation Hospitals (G-21630)*
Kaiser Permanente Kearny, San Diego *Also called Kaiser Foundation Hospitals (G-19642)*
Kaiser Permanente Medical Cen, San Marcos *Also called Kaiser Foundation Hospitals (G-21628)*
Kaiser Permanente Member Svcs, Palm Desert *Also called Kaiser Foundation Hospitals (G-19635)*
Kaiser Permanente Moreno, Moreno Valley *Also called Kaiser Foundation Hospitals (G-19676)*
Kaiser Permanente Post Acute, San Leandro *Also called Kaiser Foundation Hospitals (G-22147)*
Kaiser Permanente San, San Francisco *Also called Kaiser Foundation Hospitals (G-19586)*

ALPHABETIC

Kaiser Permanente San, San Mateo *Also called Kaiser Foundation Hospitals* ***(G-19643)***
Kaiser Permanente San, San Leandro *Also called Kaiser Foundation Hospitals* ***(G-19644)***
Kaiser Permanente San, San Jose *Also called Kaiser Foundation Hospitals* ***(G-21671)***
Kaiser Permanente Santa, Santa Rosa *Also called Kaiser Foundation Hospitals* ***(G-19582)***
Kaiser Permanente Santa, Santa Clara *Also called Kaiser Foundation Hospitals* ***(G-21678)***
Kaiser Permanente South, Sacramento *Also called Kaiser Foundation Hospitals* ***(G-19669)***
Kaiser Permanente West, Los Angeles *Also called Kaiser Foundation Hospitals* ***(G-19591)***
Kaiser Permements....951 270-1888
1830 California Ave Corona (92881) ***(G-19683)***
Kaiser Perminente, Folsom *Also called Kaiser Foundation Hospitals* ***(G-19671)***
Kaiser Prmanente Internet Svcs, Pleasanton *Also called Kaiser Foundation Hospitals* ***(G-21645)***
Kaiser Prmnente Downey Med Ctr, Downey *Also called Kaiser Foundation Hospitals* ***(G-21636)***
Kaiser Prmnnte Antioch Med Ctr, Antioch *Also called Kaiser Foundation Hospitals* ***(G-19583)***
Kaiser Prmnnte Hayward Med Ctr, Hayward *Also called Kaiser Foundation Hospitals* ***(G-19662)***
Kaiser Prmnnte Manteca Med Ctr, Manteca *Also called Kaiser Foundation Hospitals* ***(G-21668)***
Kaiser Prmnnte Psadena Med Off, Pasadena *Also called Kaiser Foundation Hospitals* ***(G-19663)***
Kaiser Prmnnte Vallejo Med Ctr, Vallejo *Also called Kaiser Foundation Hospitals* ***(G-21666)***
Kaiser Radiology....559 448-5541
7300 N Fresno St Fresno (93720) ***(G-22228)***
Kaiserair Inc (PA)....510 569-9622
8735 Earhart Rd Oakland (94621) ***(G-9025)***
Kaizen Staffing, San Diego *Also called Payrollingcom Corp* ***(G-26421)***
Kajima Construction Svcs Inc....323 269-0020
250 E 1st St Ste 400 Los Angeles (90012) ***(G-1442)***
Kajima International, Los Angeles *Also called Kajima Construction Svcs Inc* ***(G-1442)***
Kal Tool Co, Baldwin Park *Also called G K Tool Corp* ***(G-7684)***
Kaleidioscope Stadium Cinema, Mission Viejo *Also called Edwards Theatres Circuit Inc* ***(G-18324)***
Kallidus Inc....877 554-2176
425 Market St Ste 2200 San Francisco (94105) ***(G-15266)***
Kalpana LLC....619 543-9000
901 Camino Del Rio S San Diego (92108) ***(G-12874)***
Kaman Industrial Tech Corp....909 390-7919
910 S Wanamaker Ave Ontario (91761) ***(G-7937)***
Kamiya, Kenneth M Insurance, Torrance *Also called Charles M Kamiya and Sons Inc* ***(G-10667)***
Kamps Company....209 823-8924
1262 Dupont Ct Manteca (95336) ***(G-14892)***
Kan-Di-Ki LLC....818 549-1880
2820 N Ontario St Burbank (91504) ***(G-22229)***
Kana Pipeline Inc....714 986-1400
1639 E Miraloma Ave Placentia (92870) ***(G-1955)***
Kana Software Inc (HQ)....650 614-8300
2550 Walsh Ave Ste 120 Santa Clara (95051) ***(G-15721)***
Kandarian Agri Enterprises....559 834-1501
116 W Adams Ave Fowler (93625) ***(G-161)***
Kane & Finkel LLC....415 777-4990
534 4th St San Francisco (94107) ***(G-13872)***
Kane Fnkle Hlthcare Cmmnctions, San Francisco *Also called Kane & Finkel LLC* ***(G-13872)***
Kaney Foods, San Luis Obispo *Also called Amk Foodservices Inc* ***(G-8456)***
Kang Family Partners LLC....805 688-1000
555 Mcmurray Rd Buellton (93427) ***(G-12875)***
Kanopy Insurance Center LLC....877 513-2434
545 N Mountain Ave # 205 Upland (91786) ***(G-10571)***
Kapco Global, Brea *Also called Kirkhill Aircraft Parts Co* ***(G-7996)***
Kapl Inc....714 991-9543
1126 N Brookhurst St Anaheim (92801) ***(G-26542)***
Kapstone Container Corporation....510 569-2616
8511 Blaine St Oakland (94621) ***(G-8196)***
Karam Bath....559 864-3868
1673 W Kamm Ave Caruthers (93609) ***(G-162)***
Karcher Environmental Inc (PA)....714 385-1490
2300 E Orangewood Ave Anaheim (92806) ***(G-3541)***
Karcher Environmental Inc....510 297-0180
1718 Fairway Dr San Leandro (94577) ***(G-3542)***
Karma Inc....209 239-1222
410 Eastwood Ave Manteca (95336) ***(G-20693)***
Karpe Real Estate Center, Bakersfield *Also called Elmer F Karpe Inc* ***(G-11491)***
Karsyn Construction Inc....559 271-2900
2740 N Sunnyside Ave Fresno (93727) ***(G-1589)***
Kasdan Smnds Riley Vaughan LLP (PA)....949 851-9000
19900 Macarthur Blvd # 850 Irvine (92612) ***(G-23337)***
Kash Apparel LLC....213 747-8885
1929 Hooper Ave Los Angeles (90011) ***(G-8389)***
Kaspick & Co LLC (HQ)....650 585-4100
203 Redwood Shores Pkwy # 300 Redwood City (94065) ***(G-27498)***
Katch....310 219-6200
2381 Rosecrans Ave # 400 El Segundo (90245) ***(G-13873)***
Kate Somerville Holdings LLC....323 655-4170
144 S Beverly Dr Ste 500 Beverly Hills (90212) ***(G-8271)***
Kate Somerville Skincare LLC (HQ)....323 655-7546
144 S Beverly Dr Ste 500 Beverly Hills (90212) ***(G-8272)***
Kate Summerville, Beverly Hills *Also called Skin Health Experts Medic* ***(G-22832)***
Katella Properties....562 596-5561
3902 Katella Ave Los Alamitos (90720) ***(G-20694)***
Katella Property Solutions Inc....909 896-4489
10801 6th St Ste 212 Rancho Cucamonga (91730) ***(G-1201)***
Katherine Bousson....510 582-1166
1015 Palisade St Hayward (94542) ***(G-19231)***
Katten Muchin Rosenman LLP....714 386-5708
100 Spectrum Center Dr # 1050 Irvine (92618) ***(G-23338)***
Katten Muchin Rosenman LLP....310 788-4498
515 S Flower St Los Angeles (90071) ***(G-23339)***
Katten Muchin Rosenman LLP....415 360-5444
1999 Harrison St Ste 700 Oakland (94612) ***(G-23340)***
Katten Muchin Rosenman LLP....310 788-4400
2029 Century Park E # 2600 Los Angeles (90067) ***(G-23341)***
Katz Media Group Inc....323 966-5000
5700 Wilshire Blvd # 100 Los Angeles (90036) ***(G-27963)***
Katzkin Leather Inc (PA)....323 725-1243
6868 W Acco St Montebello (90640) ***(G-9273)***
Kaufman & Broad, Los Angeles *Also called Kaufman and Broad Limited* ***(G-1372)***
Kaufman & Broad San Antonio....310 231-4000
10990 Wilshire Blvd 7th Los Angeles (90024) ***(G-11605)***
Kaufman and Broad Limited....310 231-4000
10990 Wilshire Blvd Fl 7 Los Angeles (90024) ***(G-1372)***
Kaufman Properties, Woodland Hills *Also called 7410 Woodman Avenue LLC* ***(G-11078)***
Kautz Ironstone Vineyards, Murphys *Also called Kautz Vineyards Inc* ***(G-163)***
Kautz Vineyards Inc (PA)....209 728-1251
1894 6 Mile Rd Murphys (95247) ***(G-163)***
Kava Holdings Inc (PA)....310 472-1211
701 Stone Canyon Rd Los Angeles (90077) ***(G-12876)***
Kavaliro, Petaluma *Also called AB Closing Corporation* ***(G-14596)***
Kawahara Nursery Inc....408 779-2400
698 Burnett Ave Morgan Hill (95037) ***(G-294)***
Kawai America Corporation (HQ)....310 631-1771
2055 E University Dr Compton (90220) ***(G-8123)***
Kawasaki Motors Corp USA (HQ)....949 837-4683
26972 Burbank Foothill Ranch (92610) ***(G-6686)***
KAWEAH DELTA DISTRICT HOSPITAL, Visalia *Also called Kaweah Dlta Hlth Care Dst Gild* ***(G-21681)***
Kaweah Dlta Hlth Care Dst Gild....559 624-3100
4945 W Cypress Ave Visalia (93277) ***(G-22984)***
Kaweah Dlta Hlth Care Dst Gild....559 592-7300
1014 San Juan Ave Ste A Exeter (93221) ***(G-22985)***
Kaweah Dlta Hlth Care Dst Gild....559 592-7128
1014 San Juan Ave Exeter (93221) ***(G-19684)***
Kaweah Dlta Hlth Care Dst Gild (PA)....559 624-2000
400 W Mineral King Ave Visalia (93291) ***(G-21681)***
Kaweah Manor Convalescent Hosp, Visalia *Also called Moyles Health Care Inc* ***(G-21322)***
Kawela One LLC....650 843-5000
3000 El Camino Real Palo Alto (94306) ***(G-23342)***
Kay Automotive Distrs Inc (PA)....818 781-6850
14650 Calvert St Van Nuys (91411) ***(G-6743)***
Kaye Scholer LLP....650 319-4500
3000 El Camino Real 2-400 Palo Alto (94306) ***(G-23343)***
Kaye Scholer LLP....310 788-1000
1999 Ave Of Stars # 1500 Los Angeles (90067) ***(G-23344)***
Kayne Anderson Rudni....310 229-9260
1800 Avenue Of The Stars # 200 Los Angeles (90067) ***(G-12118)***
Kayne Andrson Cpitl Advsors LP....800 231-7414
1800 Avenue Of The Stars 2nd Los Angeles (90067) ***(G-10156)***
Kaza Azteca America Inc....818 241-5400
1139 Grand Central Ave Glendale (91201) ***(G-5877)***
Kazarian/Jewett Inc....562 594-5927
6621 Pcf Cast Hwy Ste 120 Long Beach (90803) ***(G-1443)***
Kazeon Systems Inc....650 641-8100
2841 Mission College Blvd Santa Clara (95054) ***(G-15267)***
KB Home (PA)....310 231-4000
10990 Wilshire Blvd Fl 5 Los Angeles (90024) ***(G-1373)***
KB Home Grater Los Angeles Inc (HQ)....310 231-4000
10990 Wilshire Blvd # 700 Los Angeles (90024) ***(G-1202)***
KB Home South Bay Inc....925 983-2500
5000 Executive Pkwy # 125 San Ramon (94583) ***(G-1321)***
Kbak TV Channel 29 CBS....661 327-7955
1901 Westwind Dr Bakersfield (93301) ***(G-5878)***
Kbaktv, Bakersfield *Also called Fisher Communications Inc* ***(G-5861)***
Kbl Group International Ltd....562 699-9995
9142 9150 Norwalk Blvd Santa Fe Springs (90670) ***(G-8390)***
Kbl International, Santa Fe Springs *Also called Kbl Group International Ltd* ***(G-8390)***
Kbm Fclity Sltons Holdings LLC, San Diego *Also called Kbm Fclity Sltons Holdings LLC* ***(G-14334)***
Kbm Fclity Sltons Holdings LLC....858 467-0202
7976 Engineer Rd Ste 200 San Diego (92111) ***(G-14334)***
Kbos Radio B, Fresno *Also called I Heart Media Inc* ***(G-5778)***
Kbrwyle Tech Solutions LLC....760 255-8322
850 E Main St Barstow (92311) ***(G-25916)***
Kbrwyle Tech Solutions LLC....805 734-2982
Vanonbrg Air Frc Bldg 660 Lompoc (93438) ***(G-6078)***
Kbzt Broadcasting, San Diego *Also called Abe Entercom Holdings LLC* ***(G-5747)***
Kc Services, Buena Park *Also called Korean Community Services Inc* ***(G-24059)***
Kcb Builders, Long Beach *Also called Kazarian/Jewett Inc* ***(G-1443)***
Kcb Towers Inc....909 862-0322
27260 Meines St Highland (92346) ***(G-3386)***
Kcba Fox TV 35, Salinas *Also called Cowles California Media Co* ***(G-5848)***
Kcbs News Radio 74....415 765-4112
865 Battery St San Francisco (94111) ***(G-5792)***
Kcetlink (PA)....747 201-5000
2900 W Alameda Ave # 600 Burbank (91505) ***(G-5879)***
Kci Environmental Inc....805 543-3311
207 Suburban Rd Ste 6 San Luis Obispo (93401) ***(G-28139)***
Kcrw FM Radio, Santa Monica *Also called Kcrw Foundation Inc* ***(G-24932)***
Kcrw Foundation Inc....310 450-5183
1900 Pico Blvd Santa Monica (90405) ***(G-24932)***
KCS Electric Inc....623 551-1500
1585 N Harmony Cir Anaheim (92807) ***(G-2629)***
Kcsm TV & Radio, San Mateo *Also called San Mateo County Community* ***(G-5909)***

ALPHABETIC

Kdc Construction, West Sacramento *Also called Cirks Construction Inc (G-1527)*
Kdc Inc (HQ) 714 828-7000
4462 Corporate Center Dr Los Alamitos (90720) *(G-2630)*
Kdc Systems, Los Alamitos *Also called Kdc Inc (G-2630)*
KDI Elements 760 345-9933
79431 Country Club Dr Bermuda Dunes (92203) *(G-3016)*
Kdk Management Inc 818 786-1700
15215 Keswick St Van Nuys (91405) *(G-8864)*
Kds Marketing 818 240-7000
965 N Todd Ave Azusa (91702) *(G-17267)*
Kds Printing and Packaging Inc 909 770-5400
13397 Marlay Ave Ste A Fontana (92337) *(G-17268)*
Kdtv, San Francisco *Also called Univision Television Group Inc (G-5922)*
Kearn Alternative Care Inc (PA) 661 631-2036
2029 21st St Bakersfield (93301) *(G-22490)*
Kearny Mesa Convalescent Hosp, San Diego *Also called Linda Vista Manor Inc (G-20737)*
Kearny Villa Hotel Venture LLC 858 573-0700
8651 Spectrum Center Blvd San Diego (92123) *(G-12877)*
Keating Dental Arts Inc 949 955-2100
16881 Hale Ave Ste A Irvine (92606) *(G-22310)*
Keb Keb Magic Clown 916 369-6054
637 Germaine Dr Galt (95632) *(G-19232)*
Kec Engineering 951 734-3010
200 N Sherman Ave Corona (92882) *(G-1808)*
Keck Graduate Institute (PA) 909 621-8000
535 Watson Dr Claremont (91711) *(G-26780)*
Keck Hospital of Usc 800 872-2273
1500 San Pablo St Los Angeles (90033) *(G-19685)*
Kedren Acute Psychia Hospit An, Los Angeles *Also called Kedren Community Hlth Ctr Inc (G-22077)*
Kedren Community Hlth Ctr Inc 562 335-9601
231 W Vernon Ave Los Angeles (90037) *(G-24053)*
Kedren Community Hlth Ctr Inc (PA) 323 233-0425
4211 Avalon Blvd Los Angeles (90011) *(G-22077)*
Kedren Community Hlth Ctr Inc 323 524-0634
3800 S Figueroa St Los Angeles (90037) *(G-24054)*
Keeco LLC (PA) 510 324-8800
30736 Wiegman Rd Hayward (94544) *(G-6870)*
Keefe Plumbing Services, Glendale *Also called H L Moe Co Inc (G-2242)*
Keen Account, Union City *Also called Buffalo Distribution (G-8422)*
Keenan & Associates 650 306-0616
1791 Broadway St Ste 200 Redwood City (94063) *(G-10755)*
Keenan & Associates (PA) 310 212-3344
2355 Crenshaw Blvd # 200 Torrance (90501) *(G-10756)*
Keenan & Associates 707 268-1616
626 H St Eureka (95501) *(G-10757)*
Keenan & Associates 916 858-2981
2868 Prospect Park Dr # 600 Rancho Cordova (95670) *(G-10758)*
Keenan & Associates 951 788-0330
3550 Vine St Ste 200 Riverside (92507) *(G-10759)*
Keenan & Associates 408 441-0754
1740 Tech Dr Ste 300 San Jose (95110) *(G-10760)*
Keenan & Associates 949 940-1760
901 Calle Amanecer # 200 San Clemente (92673) *(G-10761)*
Keenan Farms Inc 559 945-1400
31510 Plymouth Ave Kettleman City (93239) *(G-203)*
Keenan Hopkins Suder & Stowell (PA) 714 695-3670
5109 E La Palma Ave Ste A Anaheim (92807) *(G-2919)*
Keenan Hopkins Suder & Stowell 714 695-3670
5109 E La Palma Ave Ste A Anaheim (92807) *(G-1590)*
Keeney Truck Lines Inc 323 589-3231
3500 Fruitland Ave Maywood (90270) *(G-4033)*
Keesal Young Logan A Prof Corp (PA) 562 436-2000
400 Oceangate Ste 1400 Long Beach (90802) *(G-23345)*
Kehe Distributors LLC 714 255-4600
6 Pointe Dr Ste 300 Brea (92821) *(G-8865)*
Keiro Senior Health Care, Los Angeles *Also called Keiro Services (G-27088)*
Keiro Services 213 873-5700
420 E 3rd St Ste 1000 Los Angeles (90013) *(G-27088)*
Keisers Holdings LLC 559 265-4700
411 S West Ave Fresno (93706) *(G-18649)*
Keith Development Corporation 707 528-8703
2777 Cleveland Ave # 109 Santa Rosa (95403) *(G-11975)*
Keith T Kusunis MD 909 469-9494
91767 N Orange Grv Ave Ste 101 Pomona (91767) *(G-22758)*
Keker and Van Nest LLP 415 391-5400
633 Battery St Bsmt 91 San Francisco (94111) *(G-23346)*
Keller William Realty, Visalia *Also called Beethoven Holdings Inc (G-11317)*
Keller Williams 805 389-1919
770 Paseo Camarillo # 100 Camarillo (93010) *(G-11606)*
Keller Williams Realtors, Visalia *Also called Keller Williams Realty Inc (G-11611)*
Keller Williams Realtors, Auburn *Also called East Hall Investors Inc (G-12301)*
Keller Williams Realtors, Carmel Valley *Also called Keller Williams Realty (G-11607)*
Keller Williams Realtors, Covina *Also called Keller Williams Realty (G-11608)*
Keller Williams Realtors, Torrance *Also called Keller Williams Realty (G-11609)*
Keller Williams Realtors, Victorville *Also called Keller Williams Realty (G-11610)*
Keller Williams Realtors, Auburn *Also called Keller Williams Realty Inc (G-11612)*
Keller Williams Realtors, Corona *Also called Pro Group Inc (G-11763)*
Keller Williams Realtors, Chino Hills *Also called Ch Market Center Inc (G-11384)*
Keller Williams Realtors, Camarillo *Also called Keller Williams (G-11606)*
Keller Williams Realty 831 622-6200
39 Calle De Los Ositos Carmel Valley (93924) *(G-11607)*
Keller Williams Realty 626 384-2803
100 N Citrus Ave Covina (91723) *(G-11608)*
Keller Williams Realty 310 375-3511
23670 Hawthorne Blvd # 100 Torrance (90505) *(G-11609)*
Keller Williams Realty 760 951-5242
12530 Hesperia Rd Ste 110 Victorville (92395) *(G-11610)*
Keller Williams Realty Inc 559 636-1235
400 E Main St Visalia (93291) *(G-11611)*
Keller Williams Realty Inc 530 328-1900
400 Auburn Folsom Rd Auburn (95603) *(G-11612)*
Keller Wllams Rlty Bvrly Hills 310 432-6400
439 N Canon Dr Ste 300 Beverly Hills (90210) *(G-11613)*
Kelley Drye & Warren LLP 310 712-6100
10100 Santa Monica Blvd Los Angeles (90067) *(G-23347)*
Kelleyamerit Fleet Services, Walnut Creek *Also called Kelleyamerit Holdings Inc (G-27089)*
Kelleyamerit Holdings Inc 877 512-6374
1331 N Calif Blvd Ste 150 Walnut Creek (94596) *(G-27089)*
Kellogg Andlson Accntancy Corp (PA) 818 971-5100
21700 Oxnard St Ste 800 Woodland Hills (91367) *(G-26382)*
Kellogg Sales Company 916 787-0414
300 Harding Blvd Ste 215 Roseville (95678) *(G-8866)*
Kellwood Company LLC 626 934-4133
1307 E Temple Ave City of Industry (91746) *(G-8348)*
Kellwood Company LLC 626 934-4155
13085 Temple Ave City of Industry (91746) *(G-8391)*
Kelly Moses Floors 951 296-5147
27430 Bostik Ct Ste 101 Temecula (92590) *(G-3017)*
Kelly Paper Company (HQ) 909 859-8200
288 Brea Canyon Rd Walnut (91789) *(G-8153)*
Kelly Pipe Co LLC (HQ) 562 868-0456
11680 Bloomfield Ave Santa Fe Springs (90670) *(G-7379)*
Kelly Slater Wave Company LLC 310 202-9283
3300 La Cienega Pl Los Angeles (90016) *(G-26680)*
Kellytoy Worldwide Inc 323 923-1300
4811 S Alameda St Vernon (90058) *(G-8047)*
Kelomar Inc 760 344-5253
3949 Austin Rd Brawley (92227) *(G-77)*
Kelpien Health Care, Montebello *Also called Beverly Community Hosp Assn (G-21466)*
Kelvin Hildebrand Inc 831 768-9104
6 Lewis Rd Royal Oaks (95076) *(G-4034)*
Kema Inc 510 891-0446
155 Grand Ave Ste 500 Oakland (94612) *(G-27964)*
Kemeera Incorporated 510 281-9000
315 Jefferson St Oakland (94607) *(G-7152)*
Kemp Bros Construction Inc 562 236-5000
10135 Geary Ave Santa Fe Springs (90670) *(G-1444)*
Kemper Insurance, Woodland Hills *Also called Venbrook Insurance Svcs LLC (G-10923)*
Kemper Insurance, Glendale *Also called Arthur J Gallagher & Co (G-10624)*
Kemper Insurance, Petaluma *Also called Wells Fargo Insur Svcs USA Inc (G-10928)*
Kemper Insurance, Visalia *Also called Mitchell Buckman Inc (G-10787)*
Kemper Insurance, Kingsburg *Also called Van Beurden Insurance Svcs Inc (G-10921)*
Kemper Insurance, Los Angeles *Also called Grosslight Insurance Inc (G-10732)*
Kemper Insurance, Irvine *Also called USI South Coast (G-10919)*
Kemper Insurance, Pasadena *Also called United Agencies Inc (G-10913)*
Kemper Insurance, Sacramento *Also called Interwest Insurance Svcs Inc (G-10748)*
Kemper Insurance, Lafayette *Also called Arthur J Gallagher & Co (G-10627)*
Ken Blanchard Companies, The, Escondido *Also called Blanchard Training and Dev Inc (G-27349)*
Ken Grody Ford, Buena Park *Also called Ted Ford Jones Inc (G-17817)*
Ken Real Estate Lease Ltd 714 778-1700
900 S Disneyland Dr Anaheim (92802) *(G-12878)*
Ken Starr Inc 714 632-8789
3154 E La Palma Ave Ste B Anaheim (92806) *(G-2266)*
Kenan Advantage Group Inc 323 582-3778
2709 E 37th St Vernon (90058) *(G-4202)*
Kenco Group Inc 909 356-1635
7875 Hemlock Ave Fontana (92336) *(G-5228)*
Kenco Group Inc 909 483-1199
740 Vintage Ave Ontario (91764) *(G-5229)*
Kendal Floral Supply LLC (PA) 760 431-4910
1960 Kellogg Ave Carlsbad (92008) *(G-9196)*
Kendal North Bouquet Co, Carlsbad *Also called Kendal Floral Supply LLC (G-9196)*
Kendall Farms LP 760 731-0681
4230 White Lilac Rd Fallbrook (92028) *(G-295)*
Kendo Brands Inc 415 284-3700
525 Market St Fl 15 San Francisco (94105) *(G-27090)*
Kendrick Co The, Seal Beach *Also called Kendrick Construction Services (G-1445)*
Kendrick Construction Services 562 546-0200
3010 Old Ranch Pkwy # 470 Seal Beach (90740) *(G-1445)*
Kenedco Inc 951 699-9339
29363 Rancho Cal Rd Temecula (92591) *(G-17269)*
Kenmore Residence Club, San Francisco *Also called Monroe Residence Club (G-11170)*
Kennedy Care Center, Los Angeles *Also called BV General Inc (G-21171)*
Kennedy Care Center 323 651-0043
619 N Fairfax Ave Los Angeles (90036) *(G-21278)*
Kennedy Care Ctr Kosher Certif, Los Angeles *Also called Kennedy Care Center (G-21278)*
Kennedy Club Fitness 805 781-3488
188 Tank Farm Rd San Luis Obispo (93401) *(G-18650)*
Kennedy Masonry Inc 760 931-2671
7533 Navigator Cir Carlsbad (92011) *(G-2824)*
Kennedy Pipeline Company 949 380-8363
61 Argonaut Laguna Hills (92656) *(G-1956)*
Kennedy-Wilson Inc (PA) 310 887-6400
151 El Camino Dr Beverly Hills (90212) *(G-11614)*
Kennedy/Jenks Consultants Inc (PA) 415 243-2150
303 2nd St Ste 300s San Francisco (94107) *(G-25917)*
Kenneth Brdwick Intr Dsgns Inc 310 274-9999
1801 Century Park E # 1200 Los Angeles (90067) *(G-17270)*
Kenneth Corp 714 537-5160
12601 Garden Grove Blvd Garden Grove (92843) *(G-21682)*

ALPHABETIC

Kenneth Norris Cancer Hospital, Los Angeles *Also called Tenet Health Systems Norris* ***(G-22181)***
Kenneth P Slaught Inc....805 962-8989
200 E Carrillo St Ste 200 Santa Barbara (93101) ***(G-11615)***
Kenny Pabst....562 439-2147
248 Redondo Ave Long Beach (90803) ***(G-11616)***
Kenshoo Inc....877 536-7462
22 4th St Fl 7 San Francisco (94103) ***(G-27499)***
Kensington Agency Inc....619 280-6993
8469 La Mesa Blvd La Mesa (91942) ***(G-14893)***
Kensington Nursing Agency, La Mesa *Also called Kensington Agency Inc* ***(G-14893)***
Kensington Place, Walnut Creek *Also called Argonaut Kensington Associates* ***(G-23668)***
Kent Daniels & Associates Inc....626 859-5018
100 N Citrus St Ste 435 West Covina (91791) ***(G-14692)***
Kentfield Rehabilitation Hosp, Kentfield *Also called 1125 Sir Francis Drake Bouleva* ***(G-22112)***
Kentina, Temecula *Also called Sft Realty Galway Downs LLC* ***(G-11840)***
Kentmaster Mfg Co Inc (PA)....626 359-8888
1801 S Mountain Ave Monrovia (91016) ***(G-7854)***
Kenwood Service Center West, Cerritos *Also called Usaco Service Corp* ***(G-17948)***
Kenyon Construction Inc....925 371-8102
63 Trevarno Rd D Livermore (94551) ***(G-3288)***
Kenyon Construction Inc....559 277-5645
4667 N Blythe Ave Fresno (93722) ***(G-2920)***
Kenyon Construction Inc....916 514-9502
3223 E St North Highlands (95660) ***(G-2921)***
Kenyon Plastering, North Highlands *Also called Kenyon Construction Inc* ***(G-2921)***
Kenyon Plastream, Livermore *Also called Kenyon Construction Inc* ***(G-3288)***
Keolis Transit America Inc (HQ)....310 981-9500
6053 W Century Blvd # 900 Los Angeles (90045) ***(G-3809)***
Kerber Bros Inc....562 921-3447
14006 Gracebee Ave Norwalk (90650) ***(G-3543)***
Kerlan-Jobe Orthopedic Clinic (PA)....310 665-7200
6801 Park Ter Ste 500 Los Angeles (90045) ***(G-19686)***
Kerman Telephone Co....559 846-4868
811 S Madera Ave Kerman (93630) ***(G-5643)***
Kermantelnet Internet Service....559 842-2223
811 S Madera Ave Kerman (93630) ***(G-5644)***
Kern 2008 Cmnty Partners LP....559 651-3559
1219 N Plaza Dr Visalia (93291) ***(G-1322)***
Kern Alternative Care Inc....661 631-2036
2029 21st St Bakersfield (93301) ***(G-22491)***
Kern Around Clock Foundation....661 395-5800
5251 Office Park Dr # 400 Bakersfield (93309) ***(G-27091)***
Kern Cnty Mntal Hlth Child Sys....661 868-8300
1111 Columbus St Ste 3000 Bakersfield (93305) ***(G-21086)***
Kern County Water Agency....661 634-1512
811 Nadine Ln Bakersfield (93308) ***(G-6360)***
Kern Direct Marketing, Woodland Hills *Also called Kern Organization Inc* ***(G-13874)***
Kern Family Helathcare, Bakersfield *Also called Kern Health Systems Inc* ***(G-19687)***
Kern Federal Credit Union, Bakersfield *Also called Kern Member Insurance Services* ***(G-10762)***
Kern Federal Credit Union....661 327-9461
1717 Truxtun Ave Bakersfield (93301) ***(G-9606)***
Kern Health Systems Inc....661 664-5000
9700 Stockdale Hwy Bakersfield (93311) ***(G-19687)***
Kern Member Insurance Services....661 327-9461
1717 Truxtun Ave Bakersfield (93301) ***(G-10762)***
Kern Organization Inc....818 703-8775
20955 Warner Center Ln Woodland Hills (91367) ***(G-13874)***
Kern Rdlgy Imaging Systems Inc (PA)....661 326-9600
2301 Bahamas Dr Bakersfield (93309) ***(G-22230)***
Kern Regional Center (PA)....661 327-8531
3200 N Sillect Ave Bakersfield (93308) ***(G-24055)***
Kern Ridge Growers LLC....661 854-3141
25429 Barbara St Arvin (93203) ***(G-553)***
Kern River Adventures....760 376-3648
721 W Graaf Ave Ridgecrest (93555) ***(G-4738)***
Kern River Co Generation Co....661 392-2663
Sw China Grade Loop Bakersfield (93308) ***(G-6142)***
KERN RIVER HEALTH CENTER, Bakersfield *Also called Clinica Sierra Vista* ***(G-19446)***
Kern River Outfitters, Bayside *Also called O A Outfitting Inc* ***(G-19252)***
Kern River Tours Inc....760 379-4616
2712 Mayfair Rd Lake Isabella (93240) ***(G-19233)***
Kern Schools Federal Credit Un (PA)....661 833-7900
9500 Ming Ave Bakersfield (93311) ***(G-9607)***
Kern Security Corporation....661 363-6874
2701 Fruitvale Ave Bakersfield (93308) ***(G-16893)***
Kern Security Systems, Bakersfield *Also called Kern Security Corporation* ***(G-16893)***
Kern Steel Fabrication Inc (PA)....661 327-9588
627 Williams St Bakersfield (93305) ***(G-3387)***
Kern Valley Hosp Foundation (PA)....760 379-2681
6412 Laurel Ave Lake Isabella (93240) ***(G-21683)***
Kernen Construction....707 826-8686
2350 Glendale Dr McKinleyville (95519) ***(G-1446)***
Kerria, Auburn *Also called Westview Healh Care Center* ***(G-21036)***
Kerry McCaffrey Cnstr Inc....916 645-1388
3720 Wally Allen Rd Lincoln (95648) ***(G-1203)***
Kertel Communications Inc (HQ)....559 432-5800
7600 N Palm Ave Ste 101 Fresno (93711) ***(G-2631)***
Kesari Hospitality LLC....619 298-1291
445 Hotel Cir S San Diego (92108) ***(G-12879)***
Kesq TV, Thousand Palms *Also called Gulf- California Broadcast Co* ***(G-5866)***
Ketchum Incorporated....415 984-6100
1050 Battery St San Francisco (94111) ***(G-27752)***
Ketchum Inc....310 295-3300
12555 W Jefferson Blvd # 250 Los Angeles (90066) ***(G-27753)***
Ketchum Sheppard Inc....310 584-8300
340 Main St 100 Venice (90291) ***(G-27500)***

ALPHABETIC

Ketchum YMCA, Los Angeles *Also called Young Mens Chrstn Assn of La* ***(G-25470)***
Kevala International LLC....210 767-3324
5349 Zambrano St Commerce (90040) ***(G-8867)***
Kevcomp Inc....562 423-3028
4300 Long Beach Blvd # 720 Long Beach (90807) ***(G-25918)***
Kevcomp Engineering, Long Beach *Also called Kevcomp Inc* ***(G-25918)***
Kevin Holubowski LLC....310 908-6542
7462 Denrock Ave Los Angeles (90045) ***(G-24933)***
Kevin Persons Inc....805 371-8746
2977 Los Feliz Dr Thousand Oaks (91362) ***(G-775)***
Key Air Cnditioning Contrs Inc....562 941-2233
10905 Laurel Ave Santa Fe Springs (90670) ***(G-2267)***
Key Environmental Services, Los Angeles *Also called The Teecor Group Inc* ***(G-3589)***
Key Inn Ltd....714 832-3220
1611 El Camino Real Tustin (92780) ***(G-12880)***
Key Inn & Suites, Tustin *Also called Key Inn Ltd* ***(G-12880)***
Key Largo Casino, Newport Beach *Also called Ambassador Gaming Inc* ***(G-19134)***
Keynote Systems, San Mateo *Also called Sigos LLC* ***(G-16187)***
Keypoint Credit Union (PA)....408 731-4100
2805 Bowers Ave Ste 105 Santa Clara (95051) ***(G-9670)***
Keypoint Credit Union....408 562-7011
2805 Bowers Ave Ste 105 Santa Clara (95051) ***(G-9671)***
Keystone Marketing Specialists, Irvine *Also called Ksm Marketing Inc* ***(G-17279)***
Keystone NPS LLC (HQ)....909 633-6354
11980 Mount Vernon Ave Grand Terrace (92313) ***(G-24934)***
Keystone PCF Property MGT Inc (PA)....949 833-2600
16775 Von Karman Ave # 100 Irvine (92606) ***(G-11617)***
Keystone Schools-Ramona, Grand Terrace *Also called Keystone NPS LLC* ***(G-24934)***
Keystone Towing, Van Nuys *Also called United Road Towing Inc* ***(G-17903)***
Keyt Television, Santa Barbara *Also called Smith Broadcasting Group Inc* ***(G-5911)***
Kf Bella Vista Health Care, Ontario *Also called Bella Vista Healthcare Center* ***(G-20409)***
Kf Community Care LLC....626 357-3207
2335 Mountain Ave Duarte (91010) ***(G-21279)***
Kf Ontario Healthcare LLC....909 984-6713
1661 S Euclid Ave Ontario (91762) ***(G-21280)***
Kf Sunray LLC....323 734-2171
3210 W Pico Blvd Los Angeles (90019) ***(G-21281)***
Kfco Inc....310 441-2483
12100 W Washington Blvd Los Angeles (90066) ***(G-4035)***
Kfi....415 956-9812
1 Sansome St Fl 32 San Francisco (94104) ***(G-27092)***
Kfjc FM, Los Altos Hills *Also called Footh-De Anza Commun Colleg Di* ***(G-5776)***
Kforce Inc....858 550-1645
4510 Executive Dr Ste 325 San Diego (92121) ***(G-14693)***
Kfox, Los Angeles *Also called FM Seoul Bang Song Inc* ***(G-5775)***
Kfsn Television LLC....559 442-1170
1777 G St Fresno (93706) ***(G-5880)***
Kftv....559 222-2121
601 W Univision Plz Fresno (93704) ***(G-5881)***
KG Berry Farms LLC....805 680-6751
1660 Philbric Rd Santa Maria (93454) ***(G-377)***
Kgb, San Diego *Also called Iheartcommunications Inc* ***(G-5786)***
Kgi, Claremont *Also called Keck Graduate Institute* ***(G-26780)***
Kgo 810am, San Francisco *Also called San Francisco Radio Assets LLC* ***(G-5821)***
Kgo Television Inc....415 954-7777
900 Front St San Francisco (94111) ***(G-5882)***
Kgtv, San Diego *Also called EW Scripps Company* ***(G-5860)***
Khan Academy Inc....650 336-5426
1200 Villa St Ste 200 Mountain View (94041) ***(G-15722)***
Khatri Inc....209 576-1481
1608 Sunrise Ave Ste 6 Modesto (95350) ***(G-12881)***
Khatri Properties, Modesto *Also called Khatri Inc* ***(G-12881)***
KHEIR, Los Angeles *Also called Korean Health Education* ***(G-24060)***
Khop, Stockton *Also called Citadel Broadcasting Corp* ***(G-5765)***
Khorrami Shawn Law Office....818 947-5111
14550 Haynes St Van Nuys (91411) ***(G-23348)***
Khp II San Diego Hotel LLC....619 515-3000
1047 5th Ave San Diego (92101) ***(G-12882)***
Khp III Goleta LLC....805 964-6241
5650 Calle Real Goleta (93117) ***(G-12883)***
Khs & S Contractors, Anaheim *Also called Keenan Hopkins Suder & Stowell* ***(G-2919)***
Khsl TV, Chico *Also called Catamount Broadcasting of Chic* ***(G-5838)***
Khss Contractors, Anaheim *Also called Keenan Hopkins Suder & Stowell* ***(G-1590)***
Kicu TV 36, San Jose *Also called TV 36* ***(G-5918)***
KID HELPING KIDS, Santa Barbara *Also called San Marcos Kids Helpng Kids FN* ***(G-25335)***
Kid Iq 24 Hr Childcare....310 492-3037
4451 E Sierra Madre Ave Fresno (93726) ***(G-24471)***
Kid Stock Inc....415 753-3737
1539 Funston Ave San Francisco (94122) ***(G-18402)***
Kidango Inc....408 297-9044
730 Empey Way San Jose (95128) ***(G-22986)***
Kidder Mathews LLC....858 509-1200
12230 El Camino Real # 400 San Diego (92130) ***(G-11618)***
Kidney Center Inc....805 433-7777
50 Moreland Rd Simi Valley (93065) ***(G-22632)***
Kidney Dialysis Center Verdugo, Simi Valley *Also called Kidney Center Inc* ***(G-22632)***
Kids First Foundation....760 631-7550
1025 Service Pl Ste 103 Vista (92084) ***(G-24699)***
Kids First Foundation....760 631-7550
993 S Santa Fe Ave Ste C Vista (92083) ***(G-24700)***
Kids Klub Care Centers Inc (PA)....626 795-2501
380 S Raymond Ave Pasadena (91105) ***(G-24472)***
Kids Klub Pasadena, Pasadena *Also called Kids Klub Care Centers Inc* ***(G-24472)***
Kids Overcoming LLC....415 748-8052
40029 St Ste 204 Oakland (94609) ***(G-22492)***
Kids World Preschool, Temecula *Also called McCusker Enterprises Inc* ***(G-24482)***

Kids' Club YMCA Oxford School, Berkeley *Also called The Young Mens Chris Assoc of* ***(G-25378)***
Kidspace A Prticipatory Museum 626 449-9144
480 N Arroyo Blvd Pasadena (91103) ***(G-25023)***
Kie Con, Antioch *Also called Kiewit Pacific Co* ***(G-1813)***
Kie-Con Inc 925 754-9494
3551 Wilbur Ave Antioch (94509) ***(G-1591)***
Kieckhafer Schiffer & Co LLP (PA) 949 250-3900
6201 Oak Cyn Ste 200 Irvine (92618) ***(G-26383)***
Kier & Wright Civil ENGrs&srvy 925 245-8788
2850 Collier Canyon Rd Livermore (94551) ***(G-26276)***
Kiewit Corporation 707 439-7300
4650 Business Center Dr Fairfield (94534) ***(G-1592)***
Kiewit Corporation 858 208-4285
12700 Stowe Dr Ste 180 Poway (92064) ***(G-1593)***
Kiewit Corporation 907 222-9350
10704 Shoemaker Ave Santa Fe Springs (90670) ***(G-1594)***
Kiewit Infrastructure West Co 360 693-1478
12700 Stowe Dr Ste 180 Poway (92064) ***(G-1895)***
Kiewit Infrastructure West Co 510 452-1400
1111 Broadway Oakland (94607) ***(G-1809)***
Kiewit Infrastructure West Co 925 462-1088
3200 Busch Rd Pleasanton (94566) ***(G-1810)***
Kiewit Infrastructure West Co 562 946-1816
10704 Shoemaker Ave Santa Fe Springs (90670) ***(G-1811)***
Kiewit Infrastructure West Co 858 486-3410
12700 Stowe Dr Ste 180 Poway (92064) ***(G-1812)***
Kiewit Pacific Co 925 754-9494
3551 Wilbur Ave Antioch (94509) ***(G-1813)***
Kifm Smooth Jazz 981 Inc 619 297-3698
1615 Murray Canyon Rd San Diego (92108) ***(G-5793)***
Kiid, Roseville *Also called Walt Disney Company* ***(G-5829)***
Kilcrew Productions 619 564-2080
32811 Wesley St Wildomar (92595) ***(G-17271)***
Kilpatrick Twnsend Stckton LLP 925 472-5000
2175 N California Blvd Walnut Creek (94596) ***(G-23349)***
Kilpatrick Twnsend Stckton LLP 650 326-2595
1080 Marshall Rd Menlo Park (94025) ***(G-23350)***
Kilroy Realty LP 949 788-1200
2211 Michelson Dr Ste 330 Irvine (92612) ***(G-11619)***
Kilroy Realty LP 415 243-8803
100 1st St Ste 250 San Francisco (94105) ***(G-11620)***
Kilroy Realty Corporation (PA) 310 481-8400
12200 W Olympic Blvd # 200 Los Angeles (90064) ***(G-12254)***
Kim Chong 323 581-4700
2419 E 28th St Vernon (90058) ***(G-17272)***
Kim Wilson 619 741-1548
3322 Sweetwater Spg Spring Valley (91977) ***(G-22493)***
Klma W Medical Center 530 625-4114
1200 Airport Rd Hoopa (95546) ***(G-22759)***
Kimball Tirey & St John LLP (PA) 619 234-1690
7676 Hazard Center Dr # 900 San Diego (92108) ***(G-23351)***
Kimberlite Corporation 209 948-2551
3728 Imperial Way Stockton (95215) ***(G-16894)***
Kimberlite Corporation (PA) 559 264-9730
3621 W Beechwood Ave Fresno (93711) ***(G-16895)***
Kimberly Care Center Inc 805 925-8877
820 W Cook St Santa Maria (93458) ***(G-20695)***
Kimco Staffing Services Inc 925 256-3132
1801 Oakland Blvd Ste 220 Walnut Creek (94596) ***(G-22987)***
Kimley-Horn and Associates Inc 619 234-9411
517 4th Ave Ste 301 San Diego (92101) ***(G-25919)***
Kimpton Hotel & Rest Group LLC 415 885-2500
405 Taylor St San Francisco (94102) ***(G-12884)***
Kimpton Hotel & Rest Group LLC (HQ) 415 397-5572
222 Kearny St Ste 200 San Francisco (94108) ***(G-27093)***
Kimpton Hotel & Rest Group LLC 415 561-1100
425 N Point St San Francisco (94133) ***(G-12885)***
Kimpton Hotel & Rest Group LLC 415 394-0500
342 Grant Ave San Francisco (94108) ***(G-27094)***
Kimpton Hotel & Rest Group LLC 415 292-0100
501 Geary St San Francisco (94102) ***(G-27095)***
Kincaid Industries Inc 760 343-5457
31065 Plantation Dr Thousand Palms (92276) ***(G-2268)***
Kinder Mrgan Enrgy Partners LP 310 518-7700
2000 E Sepulveda Blvd Carson (90810) ***(G-4693)***
Kinder Mrgan Enrgy Partners LP 909 873-1553
2319 S Riverside Ave Bloomington (92316) ***(G-4951)***
Kinder Mrgan Lqds Trminals LLC 415 467-8107
950 Tunnel Ave Brisbane (94005) ***(G-4694)***
Kinder Mrgan Lqds Trminals LLC 619 283-6511
9950 San Diego Mission Rd San Diego (92108) ***(G-4695)***
Kinder Mrgan Lqds Trminals LLC 408 435-7399
2150 Kruse Dr San Jose (95131) ***(G-4696)***
Kindercare Education LLC 925 824-0267
3280 Crow Canyon Rd San Ramon (94583) ***(G-24473)***
Kindercare Learning Ctrs LLC 562 961-8882
5251 E Las Lomas St Long Beach (90815) ***(G-24474)***
Kindred Healthcare Inc 661 324-1232
5001 E Commercecenter Dr Bakersfield (93309) ***(G-22988)***
Kindred Healthcare Inc 760 241-7044
17290 Jasmine St Ste 104 Victorville (92395) ***(G-21087)***
Kindred Healthcare Inc 408 871-9860
901 Campisi Way Ste 205 Campbell (95008) ***(G-22989)***
Kindred Healthcare Inc 909 887-6391
1805 Medical Center Dr San Bernardino (92411) ***(G-22990)***
Kindred Healthcare Inc 951 436-3535
2224 Medical Center Dr Perris (92571) ***(G-21684)***
Kindred Healthcare Inc 408 297-2078
2055 Gateway Pl Ste 600 San Jose (95110) ***(G-21088)***
Kindred Healthcare Inc 858 380-4491
5095 Murphy Canyon Rd # 240 San Diego (92123) ***(G-22494)***
Kindred Healthcare Inc 619 546-9653
1503 30th St San Diego (92102) ***(G-21685)***
Kindred Healthcare Oper Inc 925 692-5886
1800 Adobe St Concord (94520) ***(G-20696)***
Kindred Healthcare Oper Inc 916 454-5752
4700 Elvas Ave Sacramento (95819) ***(G-20697)***
Kindred Healthcare Oper Inc 916 457-6521
3500 Folsom Blvd Sacramento (95816) ***(G-21282)***
Kindred Healthcare Oper Inc 714 529-6842
875 N Brea Blvd Brea (92821) ***(G-20698)***
Kindred Healthcare Oper Inc 805 487-7840
2641 S C St Oxnard (93033) ***(G-21283)***
Kindred Healthcare Oper Inc 909 862-0611
7534 Palm Ave Highland (92346) ***(G-20699)***
Kindred Healthcare Oper Inc 502 596-7300
1940 El Cajon Blvd San Diego (92104) ***(G-22148)***
Kindred Healthcare Oper Inc 650 962-6000
145 E Dana St Mountain View (94041) ***(G-21686)***
Kindred Healthcare Oper Inc 925 443-1800
76 Fenton St Livermore (94550) ***(G-20700)***
Kindred Healthcare Oper Inc 510 357-8300
2800 Benedict Dr San Leandro (94577) ***(G-21687)***
Kindred Healthcare Oper Inc 760 471-2986
1586 W San Marcos Blvd San Marcos (92078) ***(G-20701)***
Kindred Healthcare Oper Inc 831 424-8072
720 E Romie Ln Salinas (93901) ***(G-20702)***
Kindred Healthcare Oper Inc 415 922-5085
2121 Pine St San Francisco (94115) ***(G-20703)***
Kindred Healthcare Oper Inc 415 566-1200
1575 7th Ave San Francisco (94122) ***(G-21688)***
Kindred Healthcare Oper Inc 909 391-0333
550 N Monterey Ave Ontario (91764) ***(G-21689)***
Kindred Healthcare Operating 650 697-1865
1609 Trousdale Dr Burlingame (94010) ***(G-22149)***
Kindred Healthcare Operating 661 872-2121
2211 Mount Vernon Ave Bakersfield (93306) ***(G-20704)***
Kindred Healthcare Operating 916 351-9151
223 Fargo Way Folsom (95630) ***(G-20705)***
Kindred Healthcare Operating 310 642-0325
5525 W Slauson Ave Los Angeles (90056) ***(G-21690)***
Kindred Healthcare Operating 951 688-8200
9020 Garfield St Riverside (92503) ***(G-21284)***
Kindred Hospital, San Leandro *Also called Kindred Healthcare Oper Inc* ***(G-21687)***
Kindred Hospital - Brea, Brea *Also called Kindred Healthcare Oper Inc* ***(G-20698)***
Kindred Hospital - Rancho, Rancho Cucamonga *Also called Knd Development 55 LLC* ***(G-21693)***
Kindred Hospital La Mirada, La Mirada *Also called Southern Cal Spcialty Care Inc* ***(G-22177)***
Kindred Hospital La Mirata, West Covina *Also called Southern Cal Spcialty Care Inc* ***(G-21903)***
Kindred Hospital Orange County, Santa Ana *Also called Southern Cal Spcialty Care Inc* ***(G-21904)***
Kindred Hospital San Diego 619 543-4500
1940 El Cajon Blvd San Diego (92104) ***(G-22760)***
KINDRED HOSPITAL- SOUTH BAY, Gardena *Also called Knd Development 53 LLC* ***(G-22150)***
Kindred Hospital-Westminster 714 372-3014
200 Hospital Cir Westminster (92683) ***(G-21691)***
Kindred Nrsing Hlthcre- Bybrry, Concord *Also called Kindred Healthcare Oper Inc* ***(G-20696)***
Kindred Nursing, San Francisco *Also called Kindred Healthcare Oper Inc* ***(G-20703)***
Kindred Nursing and Reha, San Rafael *Also called Kindred Nursing Centers W LLC* ***(G-20707)***
Kindred Nursing Centers W LLC 510 521-5600
516 Willow St Alameda (94501) ***(G-20706)***
Kindred Nursing Centers W LLC 415 456-7170
1601 5th Ave San Rafael (94901) ***(G-20707)***
Kindred Nursing Centers W LLC 530 243-6317
2120 Benton Dr Redding (96003) ***(G-20708)***
Kindred Nursing Centers W LLC 209 957-4539
1517 Knickerbocker Dr Stockton (95210) ***(G-20709)***
Kindred Nursing Centers W LLC 415 673-8405
1359 Pine St San Francisco (94109) ***(G-22761)***
Kindred Nursng & Healthcare, Livermore *Also called Kindred Healthcare Oper Inc* ***(G-20700)***
Kindred Transitional, Stockton *Also called Kindred Nursing Centers W LLC* ***(G-20709)***
Kindred Transitional Care, Alameda *Also called Kindred Nursing Centers W LLC* ***(G-20706)***
Kindred Transitional Care, Redding *Also called Kindred Nursing Centers W LLC* ***(G-20708)***
Kindred Transitional Care, San Francisco *Also called Kindred Nursing Centers W LLC* ***(G-22761)***
Kinecta Alternative Fin 323 269-3929
2750 E 1st St Los Angeles (90033) ***(G-14077)***
Kinecta Alternative Fin (PA) 310 538-2242
1440 Rosecrans Ave Manhattan Beach (90266) ***(G-9720)***
Kinecta Federal Credit Union (PA) 310 643-5400
1440 Rosecrans Ave Manhattan Beach (90266) ***(G-9608)***
Kinemed Inc 510 655-6525
40 Lincoln Ave Piedmont (94611) ***(G-26543)***
Kinemetrics Inc (HQ) 626 795-2220
222 Vista Ave Pasadena (91107) ***(G-25920)***
Kinetic Systems Inc 949 770-7364
7 Marconi Irvine (92618) ***(G-2269)***
Kineticom Inc (PA) 619 330-3100
701 B St Ste 1350 San Diego (92101) ***(G-14694)***
Kinetics Mechanical Svc Inc 925 245-6200
6691 Brisa St Livermore (94550) ***(G-2270)***
King & Spalding LLP 415 318-1200
101 2nd St Ste 2300 San Francisco (94105) ***(G-23352)***

King Equipment LLC.........909 986-5300
1690 Ashley Way Colton (92324) *(G-14554)*
King George Cabbage, Watsonville *Also called Guy George (G-114)*
King Harbor Sports Center, Redondo Beach *Also called Sport Center Fitness Inc (G-18695)*
King Janitorial Equipment Svcs, Garden Grove *Also called Janitorial Equipment Svcs Inc (G-14332)*
King Monster Inc.........661 253-3000
25129 The Old Rd Ste 100 Stevenson Ranch (91381) *(G-11621)*
King Relocation Services, Santa Fe Springs *Also called Van King & Storage Inc (G-4088)*
King Relocation Services, Santa Fe Springs *Also called Van King & Storage Inc (G-4653)*
King Security Services Inc.........415 556-5464
1159 7th St Novato (94945) *(G-16717)*
King Supply Company LLC.........714 670-8980
6340 Valley View St Buena Park (90620) *(G-3544)*
King Taco, Pasadena *Also called La Restaurant Management Inc (G-27106)*
King Ventures.........805 544-4444
285 Bridge St San Luis Obispo (93401) *(G-11976)*
King's Caps, Carson *Also called H & C Headwear Inc (G-8344)*
King-Reynolds Ventures LLC.........650 879-2136
2001 Rossi Rd Pescadero (94060) *(G-17273)*
Kingdom Express Inc.........310 258-0900
18640 Crenshaw Blvd Torrance (90504) *(G-4355)*
Kingledon Inc.........805 643-6000
2055 Harbor Blvd Ventura (93001) *(G-12886)*
Kings Arena Ltd Partnership.........916 928-0000
1 Sports Pkwy Sacramento (95834) *(G-18552)*
Kings Casino Management Corp.........916 560-4405
6510 Antelope Rd Citrus Heights (95621) *(G-19234)*
Kings Community Action O (PA).........559 582-4386
1130 N 11th Ave Hanford (93230) *(G-24056)*
Kings County Probation Dept., Hanford *Also called County of Kings (G-23820)*
Kings County Truck Lines (HQ).........559 686-2857
754 S Blackstone St Tulare (93274) *(G-4203)*
Kings Credit Services.........559 322-2550
96 Shaw Ave Ste 221 Clovis (93612) *(G-14038)*
Kings Inn Hotel & Grille, San Diego *Also called Valley Ho Hotels Inc (G-13374)*
Kings Jewelry and Loan, Los Angeles *Also called Kings Pawnshop (G-9932)*
Kings Nrsing Rhabilitaion Hosp, Hanford *Also called Wilshire Hlth & Cmnty Svcs Inc (G-21425)*
Kings Nrsing Rhabilitation Ctr, Hanford *Also called Mission Medical Entps Inc (G-20793)*
Kings Pawnshop.........213 383-5555
800 S Vermont Ave Los Angeles (90005) *(G-9932)*
Kings Rehabilitation Center (PA).........559 582-9234
490 E Hanford Armona Rd Hanford (93230) *(G-24057)*
Kings River Conservation Dst.........559 237-5567
4886 E Jensen Ave Fresno (93725) *(G-28140)*
Kings Seafood Company LLC.........909 803-1280
12427 N Mainstreet Rancho Cucamonga (91739) *(G-8636)*
Kings Seafood Company LLC.........714 793-1177
7691 Edinger Ave Huntington Beach (92647) *(G-8637)*
Kings Seafood Company LLC.........714 771-6655
1521 W Katella Ave Orange (92867) *(G-8638)*
Kings View.........209 357-0321
100 Airpark Rd Atwater (95301) *(G-24357)*
Kings View.........559 582-9307
289 E 8th St Hanford (93230) *(G-22762)*
Kings View Work Experience Ctr.........209 826-8118
703 I St Los Banos (93635) *(G-10243)*
Kingsburg Apple Packers Inc.........559 897-5132
10363 Davis Ave Kingsburg (93631) *(G-8743)*
Kingsburg Apple Partners LP.........559 897-5132
10363 Davis Ave Kingsburg (93631) *(G-239)*
Kingsburg Center, Kingsburg *Also called Sunbridge Care Entps W LLC (G-20941)*
Kingsburg Center, Kingsburg *Also called Sunbridge Care Entps W Inc (G-20940)*
Kingsburg Hospital District Bd.........559 897-5841
1200 Smith St Kingsburg (93631) *(G-21692)*
Kingsburg Medical Center, Kingsburg *Also called Kingsburg Hospital District Bd (G-21692)*
Kingsburg Orchards, Kingsburg *Also called Kingsburg Apple Packers Inc (G-8743)*
Kingsley Apartments.........323 666-8862
1345 N Kingsley Dr Los Angeles (90027) *(G-11148)*
Kingsley Court Apartments, Los Angeles *Also called Kingsley Apartments (G-11148)*
Kingsley Manor, Los Angeles *Also called Front Porch Communities (G-20584)*
Kingsoft Office Software Inc.........408 806-0998
530 Lytton Ave Fl 2 Palo Alto (94301) *(G-15268)*
Kingsview Corp.........209 533-6245
2 S Green St Sonora (95370) *(G-22763)*
Kinnser Software Inc.........949 478-0890
11 Calle Portofino San Clemente (92673) *(G-15269)*
Kinsale Holdings Inc.........415 400-2600
475 Sansome St Ste 700 San Francisco (94111) *(G-8273)*
Kinsbursky Bros Supply Inc (PA).........714 738-8516
125 E Commercial St Ste A Anaheim (92801) *(G-8075)*
Kinship Center.........714 979-2365
18302 Irvine Blvd Ste 300 Tustin (92780) *(G-24058)*
Kintera Inc (HQ).........858 795-3000
9605 Scranton Rd Ste 200 San Diego (92121) *(G-15723)*
Kintetsu Enterprises.........213 687-2000
328 E 1st St Los Angeles (90012) *(G-27096)*
Kintetsu Enterprises Co Amer, Torrance *Also called Kintetsu Enterprises Co Amer (G-12887)*
Kintetsu Enterprises Co Amer (HQ).........310 782-9300
21241 S Wstn Ave Ste 100 Torrance (90501) *(G-12887)*
Kintetsu Enterprises Co Amer.........213 617-2000
328 E 1st St Los Angeles (90012) *(G-12888)*
Kintetsu Intl Ex USA Inc.........310 525-1650
879 W 190th St Ste 720 Gardena (90248) *(G-4965)*
Kio Networks, San Diego *Also called Castle Access Inc (G-5571)*
Kion News Talk 1460.........831 633-1460
903 N Main St Salinas (93906) *(G-5794)*
Kiosked.........310 392-2470
220 Main St Ste C Venice (90291) *(G-16419)*
Kipp Foundation.........415 399-1556
135 Main St Ste 1700 San Francisco (94105) *(G-24935)*
Kirkhill Aircraft Parts Co (PA).........714 223-5400
3120 Enterprise St Brea (92821) *(G-7996)*
Kirkhill Aircraft Parts Co.........714 223-5400
3101 Enterprise St Brea (92821) *(G-7997)*
Kirkland & Ellis LLP.........650 852-9131
3330 Hillview Ave Palo Alto (94304) *(G-23353)*
Kirkland & Ellis LLP.........415 439-1400
555 California St # 2700 San Francisco (94104) *(G-23354)*
Kirkland & Ellis LLP.........213 680-7480
333 S Hope St Ste 3000 Los Angeles (90071) *(G-23355)*
Kirkpatrick Ldscpg Svcs Inc.........760 347-6926
43752 Jackson St Indio (92201) *(G-883)*
Kirkwood Assisted Living, Orange *Also called Begroup (G-20407)*
Kirschenman Enterprises Inc.........661 366-5736
10100 Digiorgio Rd Bakersfield (93307) *(G-378)*
Kirschenman Enterprises Sls LP.........661 366-5736
12826 Edison Hwy Edison (93220) *(G-17274)*
Kirschenman Packing Inc.........661 366-5736
12826 Edison Hwy Edison (93220) *(G-554)*
Kisco Senior Living LLC.........415 664-6264
1601 19th Ave Ofc San Francisco (94122) *(G-27097)*
Kisco Senior Living LLC.........415 491-1935
275 Los Ranchitos Rd San Rafael (94903) *(G-11149)*
Kisco Senior Living LLC.........714 778-5100
1731 W Medical Center Dr Anaheim (92801) *(G-11150)*
Kisco Senior Living LLC.........559 449-8070
1100 E Spruce Ave Ofc Fresno (93720) *(G-27098)*
Kisco Senior Living LLC.........949 888-2250
21952 Buena Suerte Rcho STA Marg (92688) *(G-27099)*
Kisco Senior Living LLC.........707 585-1800
1350 Oak View Cir Rohnert Park (94928) *(G-27100)*
Kisco Senior Living LLC.........650 948-7337
1174 Los Altos Ave Ofc Los Altos (94022) *(G-27101)*
Kissito Health Care Inc.........510 582-8311
442 Sunset Blvd Hayward (94541) *(G-22495)*
Kissito Health Case Inc.........925 689-9222
3318 Willow Pass Rd Concord (94519) *(G-22496)*
Kissito Health Case Inc.........510 357-4015
368 Juana Ave San Leandro (94577) *(G-22497)*
Kissito Health Case Inc.........209 524-4817
1310 W Granger Ave Modesto (95350) *(G-20710)*
Kit Carson Nursing & Rehab, Jackson *Also called Tutera Group Inc (G-24838)*
Kitayama Bros Inc.........831 722-2912
481 San Andreas Rd Watsonville (95076) *(G-296)*
Kitayama Brothers Inc.........831 722-8118
481 San Andreas Rd Watsonville (95076) *(G-297)*
Kitayama Flowers, Watsonville *Also called Kitayama Brothers Inc (G-297)*
Kite Electric Inc.........949 380-7471
2 Thomas Irvine (92618) *(G-2632)*
Kite Pharma Inc (PA).........310 824-9999
2225 Colorado Ave Santa Monica (90404) *(G-26544)*
Kitson Landscape MGT Inc.........805 681-9460
5787 Thornwood Dr Goleta (93117) *(G-884)*
Kittridge Gardens, Reseda *Also called G & K Management Co Inc (G-11549)*
Kittridge Hotels & Resorts LLC.........760 325-9676
150 S Indian Canyon Dr Palm Springs (92262) *(G-12889)*
Kiwanis International Inc.........209 578-1448
3201 Canterbury Ct Modesto (95350) *(G-25276)*
Kixeye Inc (PA).........415 956-3413
333 Bush St Fl 19 San Francisco (94104) *(G-8048)*
Kjc Operating Company.........760 762-5562
41100 Us Highway 395 Boron (93516) *(G-6143)*
Kkzz 1590.........805 289-1400
2284 S Victoria Ave 2g Ventura (93003) *(G-5795)*
Kl Cutting Service Inc.........213 742-9001
2250 Maple Ave Los Angeles (90011) *(G-13655)*
Klassen Development Inc (PA).........661 327-0875
2021 Westwind Dr Bakersfield (93301) *(G-1595)*
Klax Radio Station, Los Angeles *Also called Spanish Brdcstg Sys of Cal (G-5822)*
Klein Denatale Goldner Et Al (PA).........661 401-7755
4550 California Ave Fl 2 Bakersfield (93309) *(G-23356)*
Klein Denatale Goldner Cooper, Bakersfield *Also called Klein Denatale Goldner Et Al (G-23356)*
Klein Foods Inc.........707 431-1533
11455 Old Redwood Hwy Healdsburg (95448) *(G-164)*
Klein-Testan-Brundo.........714 245-8888
1851 E 1st St Ste 100 Santa Ana (92705) *(G-23357)*
Kleinfelder Inc (HQ).........619 831-4600
550 W C St Ste 1200 San Diego (92101) *(G-25921)*
Kleinfelder Inc.........559 486-0750
5125 N Gates Ave Ste 102 Fresno (93722) *(G-25922)*
Kleinfelder Inc.........925 484-1700
6700 Koll Center Pkwy # 120 Pleasanton (94566) *(G-25923)*
Kleinfelder Inc.........951 801-3681
3880 Lemon St Ste 300 Riverside (92501) *(G-27965)*
Kleinfelder Inc.........916 366-1701
2882 Prospect Park Dr # 200 Rancho Cordova (95670) *(G-25924)*
Kleinfelder Associates.........619 831-4600
550 W C St Ste 1200 San Diego (92101) *(G-27966)*
Kleinpartners Capital Corp.........310 426-2055
400 Continental Blvd # 600 El Segundo (90245) *(G-12318)*
Klh Consulting Inc.........707 575-9986
2235 Mercury Way Ste 210 Santa Rosa (95407) *(G-27967)*

ALPHABETIC

Klingbeil Company...415 398-0106
615 Front St San Francisco (94111) *(G-11977)*
Klink Citrus Association...559 798-1881
32921 Road 159 Ivanhoe (93235) *(G-555)*
Klink Citrus Exchange, Ivanhoe *Also called Klink Citrus Association (G-555)*
Klm Management Company...626 330-3479
14120 Valley Blvd City of Industry (91746) *(G-8586)*
Klm Orthotic Laboratories Inc...661 295-2600
28280 Alta Vista Ave Valencia (91355) *(G-7273)*
Kloeckner Metals Corporation...562 906-2020
9804 Norwalk Blvd Ste 8 Santa Fe Springs (90670) *(G-7380)*
Kloeckner Metals Corporation...562 906-2020
9804 Norwalk Blvd Santa Fe Springs (90670) *(G-7381)*
Kloeckner Metals Corporation...559 688-7980
2000 S O St Tulare (93274) *(G-7382)*
Kls Air Express Inc (PA)...916 373-3353
2851 Gold Tailings Ct Rancho Cordova (95670) *(G-5108)*
Klx Inc...559 684-1037
3645 S K St Tulare (93274) *(G-4204)*
Klx Inc...310 604-0228
1351 Charles Willard St Carson (90746) *(G-7998)*
Km Fresno Investors LLC...323 556-6600
6222 Wilshire Blvd # 650 Los Angeles (90048) *(G-12319)*
Km Industrial Inc...562 786-6200
2375 W Esther St Long Beach (90813) *(G-14335)*
KMA Emergency Services Inc...510 614-1420
14275 Wicks Blvd San Leandro (94577) *(G-3810)*
Kmart Corporation...909 390-4515
5600 E Airport Dr Ontario (91761) *(G-4582)*
Kmart Corporation...951 727-3200
3100 Milliken Ave Mira Loma (91752) *(G-4583)*
Kmax TV, West Sacramento *Also called Sacramento Television Stns Inc (G-5908)*
KMD Architects (PA)...415 398-5191
222 Vallejo St San Francisco (94111) *(G-26217)*
Kmir-Tv6, Palm Desert *Also called Journal Broadcast Group Inc (G-5876)*
Kmph Fox 26...559 255-2600
5111 E Mckinley Ave Fresno (93727) *(G-5883)*
Kms Fishermans Wharf LP...415 561-1100
425 N Point St San Francisco (94133) *(G-12890)*
Knax Country 98...559 490-9800
1071 W Shaw Ave Fresno (93711) *(G-5796)*
Knd Development 53 LLC...310 323-5330
1246 W 155th St Gardena (90247) *(G-22150)*
Knd Development 55 LLC...909 581-6400
10841 White Oak Ave Rancho Cucamonga (91730) *(G-21693)*
Knet TV...323 469-5638
5757 Wilshire Blvd # 470 Los Angeles (90036) *(G-5884)*
Kniesels Auto Collision Center...916 315-8888
4680 Pacific St Rocklin (95677) *(G-6744)*
Knight Port Services, Compton *Also called Knight Transportation Inc (G-4205)*
Knight Transportation Inc...888 549-7802
2960 E Victoria St Compton (90221) *(G-4205)*
Knight Transportation Inc...559 685-9838
4450 S Blackstone St Tulare (93274) *(G-4036)*
Knight-Calabasas LLC (PA)...818 222-3200
4515 Park Entrada Calabasas (91302) *(G-18966)*
Knight-Calabasas LLC...415 453-4940
333 Biscayne Dr San Rafael (94901) *(G-18967)*
Knights of Columbus...408 262-6609
871 Founders Ln Milpitas (95035) *(G-25547)*
Knights of Columbus...408 371-1531
2211 Shamrock Dr Campbell (95008) *(G-25277)*
Knights of Columbus...805 525-7810
1344 Magnolia Dr Santa Paula (93060) *(G-25278)*
Kno Inc...408 844-8120
2200 Mission College Blvd Santa Clara (95054) *(G-15724)*
Knobbe Martens Olson Bear LLP (PA)...949 760-0404
2040 Main St Fl 14 Irvine (92614) *(G-23358)*
Knolls Convalescent Hospital (PA)...760 245-5361
16890 Green Tree Blvd Victorville (92395) *(G-20711)*
Knolls Convalescent Hospital...760 245-6477
14973 Hesperia Rd Victorville (92395) *(G-20712)*
Knolls West Enterprise...760 245-0107
16890 Green Tree Blvd Victorville (92395) *(G-24701)*
Knolls West Post Acute LLC...760 245-5361
16890 Green Tree Blvd Victorville (92395) *(G-21285)*
Knolls West Residential Care, Victorville *Also called Knolls West Enterprise (G-24701)*
Knollwood Center, Riverside *Also called Knollwood Psychiatric and Chem (G-22078)*
Knollwood Psychiatric and Chem...951 275-8400
5900 Brockton Ave Riverside (92506) *(G-22078)*
KNOLLWOOD PSYCHIATRIC CENTER, Riverside *Also called Behavioral Health Resources (G-22044)*
Knott Avenue Care Center...714 826-2330
9021 Knott Ave Buena Park (90620) *(G-20713)*
Knott's Berry Farm Hotel, Buena Park *Also called Knotts Berry Farm LLC (G-12891)*
Knotts Berry Farm LLC...714 995-1111
7675 Crescent Ave Buena Park (90620) *(G-12891)*
Knova Software Inc (HQ)...408 863-5800
10201 Torre Ave Ste 350 Cupertino (95014) *(G-15725)*
Knowledge Folk, Riverside *Also called Paul Kittle (G-27585)*
Knox Attorney Service Inc (PA)...619 233-9700
2250 4th Ave Ste 200 San Diego (92101) *(G-14122)*
Knox Copy Centers, San Diego *Also called Knox Attorney Service Inc (G-14122)*
Knudtson Building Maint Svc, Sherman Oaks *Also called Adhei Enterprises Inc (G-14213)*
Koam Engineering Systems Inc...858 292-0922
7807 Convoy Ct Ste 200 San Diego (92111) *(G-15980)*
Kobelco Compressors Amer Inc (HQ)...951 739-3030
1450 W Rincon St Corona (92880) *(G-1957)*
Kobey Corporation Inc (PA)...619 523-2700
3740 Sports Arena Blvd # 2 San Diego (92110) *(G-17275)*
Kobey Swap Meet At Spt Arena, San Diego *Also called Kobey Corporation Inc (G-17275)*
Koce-TV Foundation...714 241-4100
3080 Bristol St Ste 400 Costa Mesa (92626) *(G-5885)*
Koch-Armstrong General Engrg...619 561-2005
15315 Olde Highway 80 El Cajon (92021) *(G-25925)*
Kodiak Roofing & Waterproofing, Roseville *Also called Dwayne Nash Industries Inc (G-3167)*
Koeller Nbker Crlson Hluck LLP (PA)...949 864-3400
3 Park Plz Ste 1500 Irvine (92614) *(G-23359)*
Koffler Elec Mech Apprts Repai...510 567-0630
527 Whitney St San Leandro (94577) *(G-7449)*
Kogoam, San Diego *Also called Iheartcommunications Inc (G-5781)*
Kohlberg Kravis Roberts Co LP...650 233-6560
2800 Sand Hill Rd Ste 200 Menlo Park (94025) *(G-12320)*
Koi Design LLC...310 828-0055
1757 Stanford St Santa Monica (90404) *(G-8392)*
Koit, San Francisco *Also called Bonneville International Corp (G-5751)*
Kojenov Arkadi Nilovich...916 718-1790
5335 Hackberry Ln Sacramento (95841) *(G-5109)*
Kole Imports...310 834-0004
24600 Main St Carson (90745) *(G-9274)*
Koll Company LLC (PA)...562 948-5296
17755 Sky Park Cir # 100 Irvine (92614) *(G-1596)*
Koll Investment Management...949 833-3030
620 Newport Center Dr # 1300 Newport Beach (92660) *(G-10157)*
Koll Management Services Inc...949 833-3030
4343 Von Karman Ave # 150 Newport Beach (92660) *(G-11622)*
Kollstar Golf Company, Newport Beach *Also called Kollwood Golf Operating LP (G-18751)*
Kollwood Golf Operating LP...949 833-3025
4343 Von Karman Ave # 150 Newport Beach (92660) *(G-18751)*
Kolonaki (PA)...415 554-8000
1216 Broadway Plz Walnut Creek (94596) *(G-8393)*
Kommonwealth Inc...310 278-7328
6420 Wilshire Blvd Los Angeles (90048) *(G-8438)*
Kona Kai Resort Hotel, San Diego *Also called Westgroup Kona Kai LLC (G-19125)*
Konami Digital Entrmt Inc...310 220-8100
2381 Rosecrans Ave # 200 El Segundo (90245) *(G-15726)*
Kone Inc...858 578-5100
9850 Businesspark Ave San Diego (92131) *(G-17987)*
Konica Minolta Business Soluti...909 824-2000
1831 Commercenter W San Bernardino (92408) *(G-7058)*
Konocti Harbor Resort & Spa, Kelseyville *Also called Ua Local 38 Bonbelsent Tr Fund (G-13364)*
Konoike-Pacific California Inc (HQ)...310 518-1000
1420 Coil Ave Wilmington (90744) *(G-4496)*
Koos Manufacturing Inc...323 249-1000
2741 Seminole Ave South Gate (90280) *(G-17276)*
Kopy Kat Attorney Service, Brea *Also called V A Anderson Enterprises Inc (G-17580)*
Kor Hotel Groups Inc...310 309-8066
530 Pico Blvd Santa Monica (90405) *(G-27102)*
Kore1 Inc...949 706-6990
47 Discovery Ste 210 Irvine (92618) *(G-16420)*
Korean Air Lines Co Ltd...310 646-4866
380 World Way Ste S4 Los Angeles (90045) *(G-4809)*
Korean Airlines...310 417-5294
380 World Way Los Angeles (90045) *(G-4810)*
Korean Airlines...650 375-7123
800 Airport Blvd Ste 506 Burlingame (94010) *(G-4811)*
Korean Airlines Co Ltd...310 410-2000
6101 W Imperial Hwy Los Angeles (90045) *(G-4812)*
Korean Airlines Co Ltd...213 484-1900
1813 Wilshire Blvd # 400 Los Angeles (90057) *(G-4813)*
Korean Arln Crgo Reservations, Los Angeles *Also called Korean Airlines Co Ltd (G-4812)*
Korean Community Services Inc...714 527-6561
8633 Knott Ave Buena Park (90620) *(G-24059)*
Korean Health Education (PA)...213 427-4000
3727 W 6th St Ste 210 Los Angeles (90020) *(G-24060)*
KORN FERRY, Los Angeles *Also called Korn/Ferry International (G-27501)*
Korn/Ferry International (PA)...310 552-1834
1900 Avenue Stars Los Angeles (90067) *(G-27501)*
Kosan Biosciences Incorporated...510 732-8400
3832 Bay Center Pl Hayward (94545) *(G-26545)*
Kositch Enterprises Inc...510 657-4460
5700 Boscell Cmn Fremont (94538) *(G-2633)*
Kosmix Corporation...605 938-2300
444 Castro St Ste 109 Mountain View (94041) *(G-5645)*
Koury Engrg Tstg & Insptn...310 851-8685
14280 Euclid Ave Chino (91710) *(G-17277)*
Kovel/Fuller LLC...310 841-4444
9925 Jefferson Blvd Culver City (90232) *(G-13875)*
Koxr Spanish Radio...805 487-0444
200 S A St Ste 400 Oxnard (93030) *(G-5797)*
Kozuki Farming Inc...559 646-2652
16518 E Adams Ave Parlier (93648) *(G-240)*
Kp LLC...510 346-0729
13951 Washington Ave San Leandro (94578) *(G-14078)*
Kp LLC...510 614-7800
13951 Washington Ave San Leandro (94578) *(G-14079)*
Kpac, Wilmington *Also called Konoike-Pacific California Inc (G-4496)*
Kpc Healthcare Inc...661 229-4009
1800 30th St Ste 340 Bakersfield (93301) *(G-22991)*
Kpc Healthcare Inc...714 800-1919
2701 S Bristol St Santa Ana (92704) *(G-21694)*
Kpff Inc...310 665-1536
6080 Center Dr Ste 300 Los Angeles (90045) *(G-25926)*

ALPHABETIC

Kpff Inc ALPHABETIC SECTION

Kpff Inc 562 437-9100
400 Oceangate Ste 500 Long Beach (90802) *(G-25927)*
Kpff Inc 415 989-1004
45 Fremont St Fl 28 San Francisco (94105) *(G-25928)*
Kpff Consulting Engineers, San Francisco *Also called Kpff Inc (G-25928)*
Kpisoft Inc 415 439-5228
50 California St Ste 1500 San Francisco (94111) *(G-15727)*
Kpmg LLP 310 273-2770
9171 Wilshire Blvd # 500 Beverly Hills (90210) *(G-26384)*
Kpmg LLP 858 750-7100
4747 Executive Dr Ste 600 San Diego (92121) *(G-26385)*
Kpmg LLP 415 963-5100
55 2nd St Ste 1400 San Francisco (94105) *(G-26386)*
Kpmg LLP 212 758-9700
550 S Hope St Ste 1500 Los Angeles (90071) *(G-26387)*
Kpmg LLP 916 448-4700
500 Capitol Mall Ste 2100 Sacramento (95814) *(G-26388)*
Kpmg LLP 925 946-1300
2175 N Calif Blvd # 1000 Walnut Creek (94596) *(G-26389)*
Kpmg LLP 818 227-6900
21700 Oxnard St Ste 1800 Woodland Hills (91367) *(G-26390)*
Kpower Sup McRswitch Inverters, Irvine *Also called Zippy Usa Inc (G-7486)*
Kprs Construction Services Inc (PA) 714 672-0800
2850 Saturn St Ste 110 Brea (92821) *(G-1597)*
Kpwr, Burbank *Also called Emmis Radio LLC (G-5768)*
Kpwr Inc 818 953-4200
2600 W Olive Ave Ste 850 Burbank (91505) *(G-5798)*
Kpwr Power 106, Burbank *Also called Kpwr Inc (G-5798)*
Kpxn-TV, Burbank *Also called Ion Media Networks Inc (G-5875)*
Kqed Inc (PA) 415 864-2000
2601 Mariposa St San Francisco (94110) *(G-5886)*
KQED PUBLIC MEDIA, San Francisco *Also called Kqed Inc (G-5886)*
Kradjian Importing Company Inc (PA) 818 502-1313
5018 San Fernando Rd Glendale (91204) *(G-8868)*
Kraft & Kennedy Inc 415 956-4000
1 Post St Ste 2600 San Francisco (94104) *(G-15981)*
Kraft Heinz Foods Company 925 469-0057
5000 Hopyard Rd Ste 235 Pleasanton (94588) *(G-8869)*
Kraft Heinz Foods Company 559 499-5300
1055 E North Ave Fresno (93725) *(G-8870)*
Kramer-Wilson Company Inc (PA) 818 760-0880
6345 Balboa Blvd Ste 190 Encino (91316) *(G-10431)*
Kranem Corporation 650 319-6743
560 S Winchester Blvd San Jose (95128) *(G-15728)*
Kranz & Assoc Holdings LLC 650 854-4400
830 Menlo Ave Ste 100 Menlo Park (94025) *(G-26391)*
Kratos Public Safety & Securit (HQ) 858 812-7300
4820 Estgate Mall Ste 200 San Diego (92121) *(G-16896)*
Kratos Tech Trning Sltions Inc (HQ) 858 812-7300
4820 Estgate Mall Ste 200 San Diego (92121) *(G-15729)*
Kravitz Investment Svcs Inc 818 995-6100
16030 Ventura Blvd # 200 Encino (91436) *(G-10158)*
Krayden, Morgan Hill *Also called K R Anderson Inc (G-8991)*
Krazan & Associates (PA) 559 348-2200
215 W Dakota Ave Clovis (93612) *(G-27968)*
Krbs FM 107.1, Oroville *Also called Bird Street Media Project (G-5749)*
KRC Builders Incorporated 916 417-1200
6141 W 4th St Rio Linda (95673) *(G-3061)*
KRC Equipment LLC 760 744-1036
700 N Twin Oaks Valley Rd San Marcos (92069) *(G-7803)*
KRC Los Altos, Los Altos *Also called Kisco Senior Living LLC (G-27101)*
KRC Santa Margarita, Rcho STA Marg *Also called Kisco Senior Living LLC (G-27099)*
Krca Television Inc 818 563-5722
1845 W Empire Ave Burbank (91504) *(G-5887)*
Krca Tv-62, Burbank *Also called Krca Television Inc (G-5887)*
Krcr TV, Redding *Also called California Oregon Broadcasting (G-5837)*
Krcx 99 9 FM Tricolor, Sacramento *Also called Entravsion Communications Corp (G-5772)*
Kreger Inc 559 884-2585
3520 W Howard Ave Visalia (93277) *(G-672)*
Kretek International Inc (PA) 805 531-8888
5449 Endeavour Ct Moorpark (93021) *(G-9234)*
Kretschmar & Smith Inc 951 361-1405
6293 Pedley Rd Riverside (92509) *(G-2825)*
Krg Technologies Inc 661 257-9967
25000 Ave Stnford Ste 243 Valencia (91355) *(G-15270)*
Krikorian Premiere Theatre LLC 626 305-7469
410 S Myrtle Ave Monrovia (91016) *(G-1598)*
Krikorian Premiere Theatre LLC 760 945-7469
25 Main St Vista (92083) *(G-18337)*
Krikorian Premiere Theatre LLC 562 205-3456
8540 Whittier Blvd Pico Rivera (90660) *(G-18403)*
Krishnmrti Foundation of Amer (PA) 805 646-2726
134 Besant Rd Ojai (93023) *(G-12159)*
Kristine Nickel 707 443-9332
721 E St Eureka (95501) *(G-22498)*
Krlh-AM 590-AM, Glendale *Also called Salem Media Group Inc (G-5818)*
Krm Risk Management Svcs Inc 559 277-4800
4270 W Richert Ave # 101 Fresno (93722) *(G-27103)*
Kroeker Inc 559 237-3764
4627 S Chestnut Ave Fresno (93725) *(G-3458)*
Kron-TV, San Francisco *Also called Chronicle Broadcasting Co (G-5846)*
Kron-TV, San Francisco *Also called Young Brdcstg of San Francisco (G-5931)*
Kron-TV, San Francisco *Also called Hearst Communications Inc (G-5867)*
Kronick Moskovitz Tiedemann (PA) 916 321-4500
400 Capitol Mall Fl 27 Sacramento (95814) *(G-23360)*
Kronos Foods Corp 559 674-4445
2401 W Almond Ave Madera (93637) *(G-8871)*
Kronos Incorporated 800 580-7374
50 Corporate Park Irvine (92606) *(G-15730)*
Kropa Realty 925 937-4040
3093 Citrus Cir Ste 150 Walnut Creek (94598) *(G-11623)*
Kros-Wise 619 223-1980
4250 Pacific Hwy Ste 205 San Diego (92110) *(G-27969)*
Krth Radio 101 FM, Los Angeles *Also called Infinity Broadcasting Corp Cal (G-5788)*
Krty Ltd A Cal Ltd Partnr 408 293-8030
750 Story Rd San Jose (95122) *(G-5799)*
Krzr 103 7 FM, Fresno *Also called Iheartcommunications Inc (G-5787)*
KS Fabrication & Machine, Bakersfield *Also called K S Fabrication & Machine Inc (G-1953)*
KS Industries LP (PA) 661 617-1700
6205 District Blvd Bakersfield (93313) *(G-1958)*
Ksby Communications Inc 805 541-6666
1772 Calle Joaquin San Luis Obispo (93405) *(G-18098)*
Kscf 1037 FM 858 560-1037
8033 Linda Vista Rd San Diego (92111) *(G-5800)*
Ksee-TV 24, Fresno *Also called Nexstar Broadcasting Group Inc (G-5902)*
Kseg-FM, Sacramento *Also called Entercom Communications Corp (G-5769)*
Ksfcu, Bakersfield *Also called Kern Schools Federal Credit Un (G-9607)*
Ksi Corp (PA) 650 952-0815
839 Mitten Rd San Bruno (94066) *(G-5110)*
Ksi Corp 650 952-0815
839 Mitten Rd Burlingame (94010) *(G-17278)*
Ksi Engineering Inc 661 617-1700
6205 District Blvd Bakersfield (93313) *(G-25929)*
Ksl II Mngement Operations LLC 760 564-8000
50905 Avenida Bermudas La Quinta (92253) *(G-27104)*
KSL Media Inc 212 468-3395
15910 Ventura Blvd # 900 Encino (91436) *(G-13999)*
Ksm Healthcare Inc 818 242-1183
1400 W Glenoaks Blvd Glendale (91201) *(G-20714)*
Ksm Marketing Inc 949 597-2222
10 Holland Irvine (92618) *(G-17279)*
Kst Data Inc 213 384-9555
3699 Wilshire Blvd # 680 Los Angeles (90010) *(G-15271)*
Ksts Channel 48, San Jose *Also called Telemundo of Northern Cal (G-5914)*
Kswb, Los Angeles *Also called Bonneville International Corp (G-5750)*
Kswb Inc 858 492-9269
7191 Engineer Rd San Diego (92111) *(G-5888)*
Ktbo-TV, Tustin *Also called Trinity Brdcstg Netwrk Inc (G-5916)*
Ktff, Brisbane *Also called Lincoln Television Inc (G-5895)*
Ktgy Group Inc 510 463-2097
580 2nd St Ste 200 Oakland (94607) *(G-26218)*
Ktgy Group Inc (PA) 949 851-2133
17911 Von Karman Ave # 250 Irvine (92614) *(G-26219)*
Ktgy Group Inc 310 394-2625
12555 W Jefferson Blvd # 100 Los Angeles (90066) *(G-26220)*
Ktsf Channel 26 415 467-6397
100 Valley Dr Brisbane (94005) *(G-5889)*
Ktvu Partnership Inc 510 834-1212
2 Jack London Sq Oakland (94607) *(G-5890)*
Ktvu Television Fox 2, Oakland *Also called Ktvu Partnership Inc (G-5890)*
Ktxl-Fox 40, Sacramento *Also called Channel 40 Inc (G-5845)*
Ku Kyoung 510 582-2765
19960 Santa Maria Ave Castro Valley (94546) *(G-20715)*
Kubota Tractor Corporation (HQ) 310 370-3370
3401 Del Amo Blvd Torrance (90503) *(G-7804)*
Kuehne + Nagel Inc 510 785-0555
2660 W Winton Ave Hayward (94545) *(G-4584)*
Kuehne + Nagel Inc 415 656-4100
150 W Hill Pl Brisbane (94005) *(G-5111)*
Kuehne + Nagel Inc 909 574-2300
9425 Nevada St Redlands (92374) *(G-4585)*
Kuic Inc 707 446-0200
555 Mason St Ste 245 Vacaville (95688) *(G-5801)*
Kuic-FM, Vacaville *Also called Kuic Inc (G-5801)*
Kumar Hotels Inc 530 934-8900
545 N Humboldt Ave Willows (95988) *(G-12892)*
Kunde Estate Winery, Kenwood *Also called Arthur Kunde & Sons Inc (G-693)*
Kurt Meiswinkel Inc 650 344-7200
1407 E 3rd Ave San Mateo (94401) *(G-2922)*
Kushner & Associates, Calabasas *Also called Custom Tours Inc (G-5007)*
Kusumoto Farms 408 927-8348
6535 Stonehill Dr San Jose (95120) *(G-116)*
Kutir Corporation 510 402-4526
37600 Central Ct Ste 280 Newark (94560) *(G-15982)*
Kvea-Tv-Channel 52, Burbank *Also called Estrella Communications Inc (G-5859)*
Kvie Inc (PA) 916 929-5843
2030 W El Camino Ave # 100 Sacramento (95833) *(G-5891)*
KVIE CHANNEL 6, Sacramento *Also called Kvie Inc (G-5891)*
Kvl Holdings Inc (PA) 831 678-2132
37700 Foothill Rd Soledad (93960) *(G-165)*
Kw International Inc 310 747-1380
18511 S Broadwick St Rancho Dominguez (90220) *(G-5112)*
Kw International Inc 213 703-6914
18724 S Broadwick St Rancho Dominguez (90220) *(G-5113)*
Kwan Wo Ironworks Inc 415 822-9628
31628 Hayman St Hayward (94544) *(G-3388)*
Kwik Wash Laundries, Union City *Also called Coinmach Corporation (G-13575)*
Kxtv Inc 209 463-8471
400 Broadway Stockton (95205) *(G-5892)*
Kxtv Inc (HQ) 916 441-2345
400 Broadway Sacramento (95818) *(G-5893)*
Kya Services LLC 714 659-6476
1522 Brookhollow Dr Ste 3 Santa Ana (92705) *(G-3124)*
Kyakamena Sklled Nrsing Fcilty, Berkeley *Also called Sanhyd Inc (G-20895)*

Kyocera Dcment Sltons Amer Inc 925 849-3300
1855 Gateway Blvd Ste 400 Concord (94520) **(G-7059)**
Kyocera International Inc (HQ) 858 576-2600
8611 Balboa Ave San Diego (92123) **(G-7035)**
Kyocera International Inc 714 428-3600
3565 Cadillac Ave Costa Mesa (92626) **(G-7592)**
Kyocera International Inc 310 647-2805
222 N Sepulveda Blvd El Segundo (90245) **(G-7036)**
Kyocera Technology Development, Concord *Also called Kyocera Dcment Sltons Amer Inc* **(G-7059)**
Kyolic, Mission Viejo *Also called Wakunaga of America Co Ltd* **(G-8306)**
Kyoto Grand Hotel, Los Angeles *Also called 120 South Los Angeles Street H* **(G-12357)**
Kyoto Grand Hotel and Gardens, Los Angeles *Also called Crestline Hotels & Resorts Inc* **(G-12553)**
Kyriba Corp (HQ) 858 210-3560
9620 Towne Cntre Dr 200 San Diego (92121) **(G-27502)**
Kzsu 90.1 FM, Stanford *Also called Leland Stanford Junior Univ* **(G-5805)**
L & J Farms Caraccioli LLC 831 675-7901
27905 Corda Rd Gonzales (93926) **(G-379)**
L & L Logic and Logistics LP 707 795-2475
6 Hamilton Landing # 250 Novato (94949) **(G-8439)**
L & L Nursery Supply Inc (PA) 909 591-0461
5350 G St San Bernardino (92407) **(G-9138)**
L & O Aliso Viejo LLC 949 643-6700
50 Enterprise Aliso Viejo (92656) **(G-18651)**
L & R Distributors Inc 909 980-3807
9292 9th St Rancho Cucamonga (91730) **(G-8315)**
L & S Investment Co Inc 760 245-3461
14173 Green Tree Blvd Victorville (92395) **(G-12893)**
L & T Meat Co 323 262-2815
3050 E 11th St Los Angeles (90023) **(G-8559)**
L & W Supply Corporation 858 627-0811
7750 Convoy Ct San Diego (92111) **(G-6989)**
L & W Supply Corporation 510 429-8003
31625 Hayman St Hayward (94544) **(G-6990)**
L A Care Health Plan, Los Angeles *Also called Local Initiative Health Author* **(G-10356)**
L A County Hospital, Torrance *Also called County of Los Angeles* **(G-19467)**
L A Family Housing Corp 818 503-3908
7843 Lankershim Blvd North Hollywood (91605) **(G-24702)**
L A Fitness Intl LLC 805 289-9907
1760 S Victoria Ave Ventura (93003) **(G-18652)**
L A Fitness Sports Clubs, Ventura *Also called L A Fitness Intl LLC* **(G-18652)**
L A Fitness Sports Clubs, San Diego *Also called Fitness International LLC* **(G-18634)**
L A Girl, Ontario *Also called Beauty 21 Cosmetics Inc* **(G-8236)**
L A Hearne Company (PA) 831 385-5441
512 Metz Rd King City (93930) **(G-9139)**
L A Inflight Service Company, Gardena *Also called World Service West* **(G-4947)**
L A P F C U, Van Nuys *Also called Los Angeles Police Credit Un* **(G-9672)**
L A Party Rents Inc 818 989-4300
13520 Saticoy St Van Nuys (91402) **(G-14555)**
L A Philharmonic, Los Angeles *Also called Los Angeles Philharmonic Assn* **(G-18480)**
L A S Transportation Inc 559 264-6583
250 E Belmont Ave Fresno (93701) **(G-4206)**
L A Services Inc 310 838-0408
9405 Jefferson Blvd Culver City (90232) **(G-2271)**
L A Swikard Inc 858 408-3700
9520 Candida St San Diego (92126) **(G-885)**
L A U S D, Pico Rivera *Also called Los Angeles Unified School Dst* **(G-17302)**
L A U S D Program 323 962-9560
5210 Clinton St Los Angeles (90004) **(G-24703)**
L and R Auto Parks Inc 213 629-3263
990 W 8th St Ste 600 Los Angeles (90017) **(G-17725)**
L B C Holdings U S A Corp (PA) 650 873-0750
362 E Grand Ave South San Francisco (94080) **(G-4966)**
L B Construction, Roseville *Also called Lancaster Burns Cnstr Inc* **(G-2923)**
L B I Holdings I Inc (PA) 818 563-5722
1845 W Empire Ave Burbank (91504) **(G-5802)**
L Barrios & Associates Inc 626 960-2934
302 E Fthill Blvd Ste 101 San Dimas (91773) **(G-886)**
L C C H Associates Inc 858 565-4424
4311 3rd Ave B San Diego (92103) **(G-21286)**
L E Cooke Co 559 732-9146
26333 Road 140 Visalia (93292) **(G-298)**
L E Coppersmith Inc (PA) 310 607-8000
525 S Douglas St Ste 100 El Segundo (90245) **(G-5114)**
L E Coppersmith Inc 310 607-8000
525 S Douglas St El Segundo (90245) **(G-5115)**
L E G, Los Angeles *Also called Levity Entertainment Group LLC* **(G-27509)**
L I Metal Systems 562 948-5950
9041 Bermudez St Pico Rivera (90660) **(G-3183)**
L J Kruse Co 510 644-0260
920 Pardee St Berkeley (94710) **(G-2272)**
L J T Flowers Inc 805 488-0879
4279 E Hueneme Rd Oxnard (93033) **(G-9140)**
L J Trucking USA 323 469-9663
120 S Anderson St Los Angeles (90033) **(G-4207)**
L L V A R E, Redlands *Also called Loma Linda Vet Association For* **(G-25288)**
L Lyon Distributing Inc 909 798-7129
254 W Stuart Ave Redlands (92374) **(G-17280)**
L P A, Irvine *Also called LPA Inc* **(G-26225)**
L R G, Irvine *Also called Lifted Research Group Inc* **(G-8350)**
L R Investment Company 213 627-8211
515 S Flower St Ste 3200 Los Angeles (90071) **(G-17726)**
L Ruhland 415 435-5992
1877 Centro West St Belvedere Tiburon (94920) **(G-26392)**
L S A Associates Inc (PA) 949 553-0666
20 Executive Park Ste 200 Irvine (92614) **(G-27970)**

L Tech Network Services Inc 562 222-1121
9926 Pioneer Blvd Ste 101 Santa Fe Springs (90670) **(G-2634)**
L W Roth Insurance Agency 916 721-6273
6060 Sunrise Vista Dr # 1180 Citrus Heights (95610) **(G-10763)**
L&G Cable Construction 714 630-6174
2776 E Miraloma Ave Anaheim (92806) **(G-3545)**
L&H Airco LLC 916 677-1000
2530 Warren Dr Rocklin (95677) **(G-2273)**
L&L Foods Holdings LLC 714 254-1430
333 N Euclid Way Anaheim (92801) **(G-5202)**
L&T Staffing Inc 323 727-9056
2122 W Whittier Blvd Montebello (90640) **(G-14894)**
L'Auberge Del Mar, Del Mar *Also called Lhoberge Lessee Inc* **(G-12919)**
L'Ermitage Hotel, Beverly Hills *Also called Raffles Lrmitage Beverly Hills* **(G-13124)**
L-3 Applied Technologies Inc 510 577-7100
2700 Merced St San Leandro (94577) **(G-26546)**
L-3 Communications Corporation 858 623-6513
10770 Wtridge Cir Ste 200 San Diego (92121) **(G-6079)**
L-3 Communications Corporation 760 375-0390
117 S Gold Canyon St Ridgecrest (93555) **(G-15983)**
L-3 Communications Maripro Inc 805 683-3881
1522 Cook Pl Goleta (93117) **(G-25930)**
L-O Coronado Hotel Inc 619 435-6611
1500 Orange Ave Coronado (92118) **(G-12894)**
L-O Soma Hotel Inc 415 974-6400
50 3rd St San Francisco (94103) **(G-12895)**
L.A. Cold Storage, Los Angeles *Also called Standard-Southern Corporation* **(G-4502)**
L.A. Gay & Lesbian Center, Los Angeles *Also called Los Angeles Lgbt Center* **(G-24940)**
La Asociacion Nacional Pro Per 213 202-5900
1452 W Temple St Ste 100 Los Angeles (90026) **(G-24061)**
La Belle Days Spas and Salons, Palo Alto *Also called Beauty Bazar Inc* **(G-13667)**
La Boulange, San Francisco *Also called Bay Bread LLC* **(G-8806)**
La Boxing Franchise Corp 714 668-0911
1241 E Dyer Rd Ste 100 Santa Ana (92705) **(G-12218)**
La Canada Flintridge Cntry CLB 818 790-0611
5500 Godbey Dr La Canada (91011) **(G-18968)**
La Cantina Doors Inc 888 221-0141
1875 Ord Way Oceanside (92056) **(G-7025)**
La Casa Mental Health Center, Long Beach *Also called Telecare Corporation* **(G-22099)**
La Casa Mhrc, Long Beach *Also called Telecare Corporation* **(G-22098)**
La Cienega Associates 310 854-0071
8500 Beverly Blvd Ste 501 Los Angeles (90048) **(G-11624)**
La City Tours.com, Malibu *Also called Las Vegas Intmtnl Tours* **(G-17289)**
La Clinica De La Raza Inc 707 556-8100
243 Georgia St Vallejo (94590) **(G-19688)**
La Clinica De La Raza Inc 510 535-4700
3050 E 16th St Oakland (94601) **(G-20259)**
La Clinica De La Raza Inc 510 535-6200
1601 Fruitvale Ave Oakland (94601) **(G-22764)**
La Clinica De La Raza Inc 925 431-1250
337 E Leland Rd Pittsburg (94565) **(G-20260)**
La Costa Glen, Carlsbad *Also called Continuing Lf Communities LLC* **(G-10679)**
La Costa Limousine (PA) 760 438-4455
2770 Loker Ave W Carlsbad (92010) **(G-3811)**
La Costa Resort & Spa, Carlsbad *Also called Lc Trs Inc* **(G-12911)**
La County High Desert Hlth Sys 661 945-8461
44900 60th St W Lancaster (93536) **(G-19689)**
LA COUNTY MUSEUM OF ART, Los Angeles *Also called Museum Associates* **(G-25027)**
La County Probation, Whittier *Also called County of Los Angeles* **(G-23838)**
La Cumbre Country Club 805 687-2421
4015 Via Laguna Santa Barbara (93110) **(G-18969)**
La Curacao, Vernon *Also called Adir International LLC* **(G-1397)**
La Familia Counseling Center 916 452-3601
5523 34th St Sacramento (95820) **(G-24062)**
La Flor De Mexico Inc (PA) 626 334-0716
5121 Commerce Dr Baldwin Park (91706) **(G-8872)**
La Flor De Mexico Bakery, Baldwin Park *Also called La Flor De Mexico Inc* **(G-8872)**
La Follette Johnson De Haas (PA) 213 426-3600
865 S Figueroa St # 3200 Los Angeles (90017) **(G-23361)**
La Grande Farm 530 473-5923
P.O. Box 370 Williams (95987) **(G-78)**
La Habra Villa 714 529-1697
220 Newport Center Dr # 11 Newport Beach (92660) **(G-24704)**
La Hotel Venture LLC 213 617-1133
333 S Figueroa St Los Angeles (90071) **(G-12896)**
LA Hydro-Jet Rooter Svc Inc 818 768-4225
10639 Wixom St Sun Valley (91352) **(G-17988)**
La Hydrojet, Sun Valley *Also called LA Hydro-Jet Rooter Svc Inc* **(G-17988)**
LA Impact 323 869-6874
5700 S Eastern Ave Commerce (90040) **(G-17281)**
La Inc Convention Vistors Bur 213 236-2301
333 S Hope St Ste 1800 Los Angeles (90071) **(G-17282)**
La Joie Construction, San Mateo *Also called La Joie Jerry* **(G-27105)**
La Joie Jerry 650 375-1808
418 Sonora Dr San Mateo (94402) **(G-27105)**
La Jolla Bch & Tennis CLB Inc (PA) 858 454-7126
2000 Spindrift Dr La Jolla (92037) **(G-12897)**
La Jolla Bch & Tennis CLB Inc 858 459-8271
8110 Camino Del Oro La Jolla (92037) **(G-12898)**
La Jolla Country Club Inc 858 454-9601
7301 High Ave La Jolla (92037) **(G-18970)**
La Jolla Cove Hotel & Motel 858 459-2621
1155 Coast Blvd La Jolla (92037) **(G-11151)**
La Jolla Cove Motel, La Jolla *Also called La Jolla Cove Hotel & Motel* **(G-11151)**
La Jolla Group Inc (PA) 949 428-2800
14350 Myford Rd Irvine (92606) **(G-17283)**
La Jolla Group Inc 949 428-2800
14350 Myford Rd Irvine (92606) **(G-17284)**

ALPHABETIC

La Jolla Nrsing Rhbltation Ctr, La Jolla *Also called Covenant Care La Jolla LLC* ***(G-20503)***
La Jolla Nurses Home Care......858 454-9339
2223 Avenida De La Playa La Jolla (92037) ***(G-14695)***
La Jolla Orthopaedic......858 657-0055
4120 La Jolla Village Dr La Jolla (92037) ***(G-19690)***
La Jolla Pharmaceutical Co (PA)......858 207-4264
10182 Telesis Ct Ste 600 San Diego (92121) ***(G-26547)***
La Jolla Playhouse, La Jolla *Also called Theat and Arts Found of San Di* ***(G-25381)***
La Jolla Village Towers 500......858 646-7700
8515 Costa Verde Blvd Ofc San Diego (92122) ***(G-20716)***
La Jolla YMCA, La Jolla *Also called YMCA of San Diego County* ***(G-25415)***
La Laser Center Pc Cpmc......310 446-4400
10884 Santa Monica Blvd # 300 Los Angeles (90025) ***(G-19691)***
La Live Properties LLC......213 763-7700
800 W Olympic Blvd # 305 Los Angeles (90015) ***(G-18404)***
La Maestra Community Clinic, San Diego *Also called La Maestra Family Clinic Inc* ***(G-19693)***
La Maestra Community Hlth Ctrs, San Diego *Also called La Maestra Family Clinic Inc* ***(G-24063)***
La Maestra Family Clinic Inc......619 280-1105
165 S 1st St El Cajon (92019) ***(G-19692)***
La Maestra Family Clinic Inc......619 280-4213
4060 Fairmount Ave San Diego (92105) ***(G-19693)***
La Maestra Family Clinic Inc......619 501-1235
4305 University Ave # 120 San Diego (92105) ***(G-19694)***
La Maestra Family Clinic Inc (PA)......619 584-1612
4060 Fairmount Ave San Diego (92105) ***(G-24063)***
La Mancha Development, Los Angeles *Also called A M S Partnership* ***(G-11944)***
La Mesa Disposal, Signal Hill *Also called Edco Disposal Corporation Inc* ***(G-6478)***
La Mesa Health Care Center......619 465-1313
3780 Massachusetts Ave La Mesa (91941) ***(G-21287)***
La Mesa Internal Medical Group, La Mesa *Also called La Mesa Intrnl Mdc Mdcl Gr* ***(G-19695)***
La Mesa Intrnl Mdc Mdcl Gr......619 460-4050
5111 Garfield St La Mesa (91941) ***(G-19695)***
La Mesa Lions Club......619 469-9988
4387 Summit Dr La Mesa (91941) ***(G-25279)***
La Mesa Medical Offices, La Mesa *Also called Kaiser Foundation Hospitals* ***(G-21662)***
La Metro Hauling, Long Beach *Also called USA Waste of California Inc* ***(G-6584)***
LA Metropolitan Medical Ctr......323 730-7300
2231 Southwest Dr Los Angeles (90043) ***(G-21695)***
La Mirada Country Club, La Mirada *Also called American Golf Corporation* ***(G-18871)***
La Mirage, San Diego *Also called Regency Hill Associates* ***(G-11195)***
La Palma Care Center......714 772-7480
1130 W La Palma Ave Anaheim (92801) ***(G-20717)***
La Palma Farms Inc......805 928-2333
3130 Skyway Dr Ste 405 Santa Maria (93455) ***(G-9141)***
La Palma Hospital Medical Ctr......714 670-7400
7901 Walker St La Palma (90623) ***(G-21696)***
La Palma Intercommunity Hosp, La Palma *Also called La Palma Hospital Medical Ctr* ***(G-21696)***
La Palma Medical Offices, La Palma *Also called Kaiser Foundation Hospitals* ***(G-19657)***
La Palma Nursing Center, Long Beach *Also called 1130 W La Palma Ave Inc* ***(G-20363)***
La Palma Nursing Center, Anaheim *Also called La Palma Care Center* ***(G-20717)***
La Paz Geropsychiatric Center, Paramount *Also called Telecare Corporation* ***(G-22107)***
La Peer Health Systems, Beverly Hills *Also called La Peer Surgery Center LLC* ***(G-19696)***
La Peer Surgery Center LLC......310 360-9119
8920 Wilshire Blvd # 101 Beverly Hills (90211) ***(G-19696)***
La Petite Baleen Inc......650 588-7665
434 San Mateo Ave San Bruno (94066) ***(G-18653)***
La Petite Baleen Swim School, San Bruno *Also called La Petite Baleen Inc* ***(G-18653)***
La Posta Band Mission Indians, Boulevard *Also called La Posta Casino* ***(G-12899)***
La Posta Casino......619 824-4100
777 Crestwood Rd Boulevard (91905) ***(G-12899)***
La Provence Inc......760 736-3299
1370 W San Marcos Blvd # 130 San Marcos (92078) ***(G-8873)***
La Provence Bakery, San Marcos *Also called La Provence Inc* ***(G-8873)***
La Puerta......619 696-3466
560 4th Ave San Diego (92101) ***(G-25280)***
La Quinta Country Club......760 564-4151
77750 Avenue 50 La Quinta (92253) ***(G-18971)***
La Quinta Inn, Los Angeles *Also called Lq Management LLC* ***(G-12931)***
La Quinta Inn, San Francisco *Also called Mile Post Properties LLC* ***(G-12995)***
La Quinta Resort & Club, La Quinta *Also called Lqr Property LLC* ***(G-12932)***
La Radio LLC......310 840-4900
3321 S La Cienega Blvd Los Angeles (90016) ***(G-5803)***
La Restaurant Management Inc......626 792-0405
45 N Arroyo Pkwy Pasadena (91103) ***(G-27106)***
La Rinconada Country Club Inc (PA)......408 395-4181
14595 Clearview Dr Los Gatos (95032) ***(G-18972)***
LA RINCONADA GOLF AND COUNTRY, Los Gatos *Also called La Rinconada Country Club Inc* ***(G-18972)***
La Salette Rehab Convlesc Hos, Stockton *Also called Mariner Health Care Inc* ***(G-20772)***
La Salle Apartments......415 647-0607
30 Whitfield Ct Ste 1 San Francisco (94124) ***(G-11152)***
La Salle Preservation, San Francisco *Also called La Salle Apartments* ***(G-11152)***
LA Specialty Produce Co (PA)......562 741-2200
13527 Orden Dr Santa Fe Springs (90670) ***(G-8744)***
La Steel Services Inc......951 393-2013
1760 California Ave # 201 Corona (92881) ***(G-3389)***
La Tavola LLC (PA)......707 257-3358
2655 Napa Valley Corp Dr NAPA (94558) ***(G-13550)***
La Tortilla Factory Inc (PA)......707 586-4000
3300 Westwind Blvd Santa Rosa (95403) ***(G-8874)***
La Verne Nursery Inc......805 521-0111
3653 Center St Piru (93040) ***(G-299)***

La Vida Del Mar Associates, Solana Beach *Also called Senior Resource Group LLC* ***(G-11200)***
La Vida Mltispecialty Med Ctrs......213 765-7500
1400 S Grand Ave Los Angeles (90015) ***(G-19697)***
La Voie & Sons Construction......916 408-6900
1061 Nichols Ct Rocklin (95765) ***(G-27107)***
La Works, Irwindale *Also called East San Gbriel Vly Consortium* ***(G-3785)***
Laaco Ltd (PA)......213 622-1254
431 W 7th St Los Angeles (90014) ***(G-11257)***
Laaco Ltd......310 823-4567
4469 Admiralty Way Marina Del Rey (90292) ***(G-18973)***
Laapoa, Los Angeles *Also called Los Angeles Airport Peace Offc* ***(G-25290)***
Lab Italee, Los Angeles *Also called Italee Optics Inc* ***(G-7332)***
Labelle Fmly Rtreat Orgnzation......310 527-1883
269 S Beverly Dr 1257 Beverly Hills (90212) ***(G-24705)***
Labite, Los Angeles *Also called Kfco Inc* ***(G-4035)***
Labmed Partners......949 242-9925
5000 Birch St Newport Beach (92660) ***(G-27503)***
Labor Finders Staffing, Fresno *Also called Labor Fnders of The Palm Bches* ***(G-14895)***
Labor Fnders of The Palm Bches......559 221-2023
4325 N Blackstone Ave Fresno (93726) ***(G-14895)***
Labor Ready, Yuba City *Also called Trueblue Inc* ***(G-14963)***
Labor Ready, Santa Barbara *Also called Trueblue Inc* ***(G-14964)***
Labor Ready Southwest Inc......760 433-4980
1405 S El Camno Real 51 Oceanside (92054) ***(G-14896)***
Laboratory Corp Amer Holdings......818 361-7089
14901 Rinaldi St Ste 203 Mission Hills (91345) ***(G-22231)***
Laboratory Corp Amer Holdings......818 908-3600
19951 Mariner Ave Ste 150 Torrance (90503) ***(G-22232)***
Laboratory Corp Amer Holdings......510 635-4555
10930 Bigge St San Leandro (94577) ***(G-22233)***
Laboratory Specialty Gases......619 234-6060
2506 Market St San Diego (92102) ***(G-8992)***
Laborers Funds Administrative (PA)......707 864-2800
220 Campus Ln Fairfield (94534) ***(G-10553)***
Laborers Trust Funds Nthrn Cal, Fairfield *Also called Laborers Funds Administrative* ***(G-10553)***
Labratory, San Francisco *Also called Permanente Medical Group Inc* ***(G-19841)***
Labrent.com, Santa Clara *Also called Everett Basham* ***(G-5598)***
Lac Basketball Club Inc......213 742-7500
1111 S Figueroa St # 1100 Los Angeles (90015) ***(G-18553)***
Lac Club, Los Angeles *Also called Los Angles Clippers Foundation* ***(G-27512)***
Lac Usc Medical Center......323 226-7858
1200 N State St Rm 5250 Los Angeles (90033) ***(G-21697)***
LACERA, Pasadena *Also called Los Angeles Cnty Emp Retiremnt* ***(G-10555)***
Laclinica, Pittsburg *Also called La Clinica De La Raza Inc* ***(G-20260)***
Lacma, Los Angeles *Also called Los Angeles Cnty Mseum of Art* ***(G-25026)***
Lacmta, Los Angeles *Also called Los Angeles County MTA* ***(G-3668)***
Laco Associates (PA)......707 443-5054
21 W 4th St Eureka (95501) ***(G-25931)***
Lacolina Jr High CA Congress O......805 967-4506
4025 Foothill Rd Santa Barbara (93110) ***(G-25281)***
Laconstructora Co Inc......760 439-7686
2030 Broadway Oceanside (92054) ***(G-1204)***
Lacuesta Farming Inc......805 349-1940
1141 Tama Ln Santa Maria (93455) ***(G-117)***
Lacumbre Senior Living, Santa Barbara *Also called Helping Hands Sanctuary of Ida* ***(G-20665)***
Ladas & Parry LLP......323 934-2300
5670 Wilshire Blvd # 2100 Los Angeles (90036) ***(G-23362)***
Ladd Construction Co, Redding *Also called Roy E Ladd Inc* ***(G-1854)***
Ladell Inc......559 650-2000
605 N Halifax Ave Clovis (93611) ***(G-2274)***
Ladwp, Independence *Also called Los Angeles Dept Wtr & Pwr* ***(G-6366)***
Ladwp, Los Angeles *Also called Los Angeles Dept Wtr & Pwr* ***(G-6367)***
Laec Incorporated......818 840-9063
480 W Riverside Dr Burbank (91506) ***(G-642)***
Lafaltte Rhbilitation Care Ctr......209 466-2066
537 E Fulton St Stockton (95204) ***(G-20718)***
Lafayette Car Wash, Lafayette *Also called Prestige Car Wash Lafayette LP* ***(G-17860)***
Lafayette Textile Inds LLC......323 264-2212
2051 E 55th St Vernon (90058) ***(G-8316)***
Laguna Bch Golf Bnglow Vlg LLC......949 499-2271
31106 Coast Hwy Laguna Beach (92651) ***(G-468)***
Laguna Bch Golf Bnglow Vlg LLC......949 499-2271
31106 Coast Hwy Laguna Beach (92651) ***(G-18752)***
Laguna Country Mart Ltd Inc......310 826-5635
12410 Santa Monica Blvd Los Angeles (90025) ***(G-11009)***
Laguna Creek Racquet Club, Elk Grove *Also called Spare-Time Inc* ***(G-19091)***
Laguna Hills Hotel Dev Ventr......949 586-5000
25205 La Paz Rd Laguna Hills (92653) ***(G-12900)***
Laguna Hills Surgery Center, Laguna Hills *Also called Cirrus Health II LP* ***(G-19438)***
Laguna Niguel Racquet Club, Laguna Niguel *Also called Spearman Clubs Inc* ***(G-19286)***
Laguna Playhouse (PA)......949 497-2787
606 Laguna Canyon Rd Laguna Beach (92651) ***(G-18405)***
Laguna Woods Golf Club......949 597-4336
24112 Moulton Pkwy Laguna Hills (92637) ***(G-18753)***
Laguna Woods Village......949 597-4267
24351 El Toro Rd Laguna Beach (92653) ***(G-11625)***
Lahontan Golf Club......530 550-2400
12700 Lodgetrail Dr Truckee (96161) ***(G-18974)***
Laidlaw Education Services, San Bernardino *Also called First Student Inc* ***(G-3931)***
Laidlaw Education Services, Santa Ana *Also called First Student Inc* ***(G-3880)***
Laidlaw Educational Services, Palm Springs *Also called First Student Inc* ***(G-3929)***

ALPHABETIC

Laidlaw International Inc.....707 545-8064
959 Sebastopol Rd Santa Rosa (95407) *(G-3940)*
Laidlaw International Inc.....707 994-3384
9055 Hwy 53 Lower Lake (95457) *(G-3941)*
Laidlaw Transit Services, Madera *Also called First Student Inc (G-3794)*
Lake Almanor Clinic, Chester *Also called Seneca Healthcare District (G-21878)*
Lake Arrowhead Cmnty Svcs Dst.....909 337-6395
6727 Arrowhead Lake Rd Hesperia (92345) *(G-24936)*
Lake Arrwhead Rsort Oprtor Inc (PA).....909 744-3012
27984 Hwy 189 Lake Arrowhead (92352) *(G-12901)*
Lake Balboa Care Center, Van Nuys *Also called Van Nuys Care Center Inc (G-21409)*
Lake Bowl, Folsom *Also called Folsom Recreation Corp (G-18518)*
Lake Cnty Trbal Hlth Cnsortium.....707 263-8382
925 Bevins Ct Lakeport (95453) *(G-20261)*
Lake County Home Loans.....707 462-4000
350 E Gobbi St Ukiah (95482) *(G-9866)*
Lake County Public Health Svcs, Lakeport *Also called County Lake Health Services (G-22924)*
Lake Elsinore Unified Schl Dst.....951 253-7830
21641 Bundy Canyon Rd Wildomar (92595) *(G-3942)*
Lake Elsn SC Trans, Wildomar *Also called Lake Elsinore Unified Schl Dst (G-3942)*
Lake Forest Ll Master Homeown.....949 586-0860
24752 Toledo Ln Lake Forest (92630) *(G-25282)*
Lake Forest Nursing Center, Lake Forest *Also called Life Care Centers America Inc (G-20728)*
Lake Hemet Municipal Wtr Dst (PA).....951 927-1816
26385 Fairview Ave Hemet (92544) *(G-6361)*
Lake Merced Golf & Country CLB.....650 755-2233
2300 Junipero Serra Blvd Daly City (94015) *(G-18975)*
Lake Merritt Hotel Associates.....510 832-2300
1800 Madison St Oakland (94612) *(G-1323)*
Lake Mission Viejo Association.....949 770-1313
22555 Olympiad Rd Mission Viejo (92692) *(G-25283)*
Lake Natoma Inn, Folsom *Also called Lake Natoma Lodging LP (G-12902)*
Lake Natoma Lodging LP.....916 351-1500
702 Gold Lake Dr Folsom (95630) *(G-12902)*
Lake of The Pines Association.....530 268-1141
11665 Lakeshore N Auburn (95602) *(G-25284)*
Lake of The Pines Homeowners, Auburn *Also called Lake of The Pines Association (G-25284)*
Lake Oroville Country Retireme.....530 533-7857
55 Concordia Ln Apt 309 Oroville (95966) *(G-24706)*
Lake Park Retirment Residence, Oakland *Also called Califrnia-Nevada Methdst Homes (G-21176)*
Lake Piru Marina, Valencia *Also called Pyramid Enterprises Inc (G-19263)*
Lake San Marcos Resort, San Marcos *Also called Citizens Development Corp (G-18917)*
Lake Tahoe Resort Hotel, South Lake Tahoe *Also called Roppongi-Tahoe Lp A Californi (G-13166)*
Lake Tahoe Secret Witness.....530 541-6800
1051 Al Tahoe Blvd South Lake Tahoe (96150) *(G-16718)*
Lake Wildwood Association.....530 432-1152
11255 Cottontail Way Penn Valley (95946) *(G-25285)*
LAKE WILDWOOD GOLF COURSE., Penn Valley *Also called Lake Wildwood Association (G-25285)*
Lakenor Auto Salvage, Santa Fe Springs *Also called Cadnchev Inc (G-6795)*
Lakes Country Club Assn Inc (PA).....760 568-4321
161 Old Ranch Rd Palm Desert (92211) *(G-18976)*
Lakeside Clubhouse, Daly City *Also called Olympic Club (G-25305)*
Lakeside Fire Protection Dst.....619 390-2350
12216 Lakeside Ave Lakeside (92040) *(G-17285)*
Lakeside Golf Club.....818 984-0601
4500 W Lakeside Dr Burbank (91505) *(G-18977)*
Lakeside Grill, The, Yountville *Also called Vintners Golf Club (G-18797)*
Lakeside Medical Systems, Northridge *Also called Lakeside Systems Inc (G-27108)*
Lakeside Systems Inc.....866 654-3471
8510 Balboa Blvd Ste 150 Northridge (91325) *(G-27108)*
Lakeview Medical Offices, Anaheim *Also called Kaiser Foundation Hospitals (G-19579)*
Lakeview Ter Special Care Ctr, Newport Beach *Also called Ghc of Lakeview Terrace LLC (G-20598)*
Lakewood Cerritos Dental Ctr.....562 860-0388
5819 Adenmoor Ave Lakewood (90713) *(G-20262)*
Lakewood Country Club, Lakewood *Also called American Golf Corporation (G-18711)*
Lakewood Healthcare Center, Downey *Also called Healthcare Ctr of Downey LLC (G-20658)*
Lakewood Manor North Inc.....213 380-9175
831 S Lake St Los Angeles (90057) *(G-20719)*
Lakewood Mem Pk Fnrl Svcs Inc.....209 883-4465
900 Santa Fe Ave Hughson (95326) *(G-12033)*
Lakewood Memorial Pk & Fnrl HM, Hughson *Also called Alderwoods (delaware) Inc (G-12027)*
Lakewood Memorial Pk & Fnrl HM, Hughson *Also called Lakewood Mem Pk Fnrl Svcs Inc (G-12033)*
Lakewood Park Health Center, Downey *Also called Mental Hlth Cnvlscent Svcs Inc (G-20788)*
Lakewood Park Health Center (PA).....562 869-0978
12023 Lakewood Blvd Downey (90242) *(G-17286)*
Lakewood Regional Medical Ctr, Lakewood *Also called Tenet Healthsystem Medical (G-20131)*
Lakewood South Car Wash LLC.....562 430-4975
11031 Alamitos Ave Los Alamitos (90720) *(G-17847)*
Lakewood Y M C A Gymnastics, Lakewood *Also called Young Mens Chrstn Assc Gr L B (G-25457)*
Lakin Tire of Calif, Santa Fe Springs *Also called Lakin Tire West Incorporated (G-6787)*
Lakin Tire West Incorporated (PA).....562 802-2752
15305 Spring Ave Santa Fe Springs (90670) *(G-6787)*
Lamanuzzi & Pantaleo LLC (PA).....559 432-3170
11767 Road 27 1/2 Madera (93637) *(G-166)*
Lambda Lambda Sigma LLC.....310 558-8555
3434 Overland Ave Los Angeles (90034) *(G-13951)*
Lamesa City Public Works, La Mesa *Also called City of La Mesa (G-1750)*
Lamon Construction Company Inc.....530 671-1370
871 Von Geldern Way Yuba City (95991) *(G-1599)*
Lamp Liter Associates.....559 733-4328
3130 W Main St Ste A Visalia (93291) *(G-12903)*
Lamp Liter Inn, Visalia *Also called Lamp Liter Associates (G-12903)*
Lamson Investment Corp.....707 253-7461
806 W Imola Ave NAPA (94559) *(G-12321)*
Lanahan & Reilley LLP (PA).....415 856-4700
600 Bicentennial Way # 300 Santa Rosa (95403) *(G-23363)*
Lancashire Group Incorporated.....510 792-9384
37053 Cherry St Ste 210 Newark (94560) *(G-27504)*
Lancaster Burns Cnstr Inc.....916 624-8404
8655 Washington Blvd Roseville (95678) *(G-2923)*
Lancaster Comm Svcs Fndtn.....661 723-6230
46008 7th St W Lancaster (93534) *(G-17803)*
Lancaster Community Hospital.....661 947-3300
520 W Palmdale Blvd Ste Q Palmdale (93551) *(G-22499)*
Lancaster Crdlgy Med Group Inc (PA).....661 726-3058
43847 Heaton Ave Ste B Lancaster (93534) *(G-19698)*
Lancaster Health Care Center, Lancaster *Also called Five Star Quality Care Inc (G-20574)*
Lancaster Jethawks.....661 726-5400
45116 Valley Central Way Lancaster (93536) *(G-18978)*
Land & Personnel Management, Kerman *Also called Hall Management Corp (G-27050)*
Land Design Consultants Inc.....626 578-7000
2700 E Foothill Blvd # 200 Pasadena (91107) *(G-27971)*
Land Disposition Company, Irvine *Also called NRLL LLC (G-12332)*
Land Forms Landscape Cnstr, Irvine *Also called Jeff Tracy Inc (G-2262)*
Land Home Financial Svcs Inc (PA).....925 676-7038
1355 Willow Way Ste 250 Concord (94520) *(G-9867)*
Land Scapes, Costa Mesa *Also called Dwiw Inc (G-846)*
Land Services Landscape Contrs.....510 656-8101
901 Brown Rd Fremont (94539) *(G-887)*
Landcare Logic, San Diego *Also called Shoreline Land Care Inc (G-953)*
Landcare USA LLC.....949 559-7771
216 N Clara St Santa Ana (92703) *(G-888)*
Landcare USA LLC.....760 747-1174
770 Metcalf St Escondido (92025) *(G-889)*
Landcare USA LLC.....805 520-9394
1196 Patricia Ave Simi Valley (93065) *(G-890)*
Landcare USA LLC.....707 836-1460
930 Shiloh Rd Bldg 44-B Windsor (95492) *(G-891)*
Landcare USA LLC.....714 245-1465
216 N Clara St Santa Ana (92703) *(G-776)*
Landcare USA LLC.....310 719-1008
1315 W 130th St Gardena (90247) *(G-892)*
Landcare USA LLC.....310 354-1520
4134 Temple City Blvd Rosemead (91770) *(G-893)*
Landcare USA LLC.....858 252-0658
5248 Governor Dr San Diego (92122) *(G-894)*
Landcare USA LLC.....310 354-1520
1323 W 130th St Gardena (90247) *(G-895)*
Landcare USA LLC.....916 635-0936
3213 Fitzgerald Rd Rancho Cordova (95742) *(G-896)*
Landcare USA LLC.....858 453-1755
5248 Governor Dr San Diego (92122) *(G-897)*
Landcare USA LLC.....818 346-7552
7755 Deering Ave Canoga Park (91304) *(G-898)*
Landcare USA LLC.....408 727-4099
85 Old Tully Rd San Jose (95111) *(G-899)*
Landco.....818 612-0118
7333 Clybourn Ave Sun Valley (91352) *(G-900)*
Landesign Cnstr & Maint Inc.....707 578-2657
1328 Airport Blvd Santa Rosa (95403) *(G-901)*
Landforce Express Corporation.....760 843-7839
17201 N D St Victorville (92394) *(G-4208)*
Landmark Entertainment Group.....818 952-6292
466 Foothill Blvd La Canada (91011) *(G-17287)*
Landmark Event Staffing.....714 293-4248
4790 Irvine Blvd Ste 105 Irvine (92620) *(G-16719)*
Landmark Event Staffing.....510 632-9000
7700 Edgewater Dr Ste 555 Oakland (94621) *(G-14897)*
Landmark Healthcare Svcs Inc (PA).....800 638-4557
1610 Arden Way Ste 280 Sacramento (95815) *(G-20297)*
Landmark Hotels LLC.....949 640-5040
312 Broadway St Ste 204 Laguna Beach (92651) *(G-12904)*
Landmark Medical Center, Pomona *Also called Landmark Medical Services Inc (G-22079)*
Landmark Medical Services Inc.....909 593-2585
2030 N Garey Ave Pomona (91767) *(G-22079)*
Landmark Princess, Laguna Beach *Also called Landmark Hotels LLC (G-12904)*
Landmark Protection Inc.....408 293-6300
675 N 1st St Ste 620 San Jose (95112) *(G-8349)*
Landmark Realty Center, Rancho Palos Verdes *Also called Inman Spinosa & Buchan Inc (G-11584)*
Landmark Services Inc.....714 547-6308
410 N Fairview St Santa Ana (92703) *(G-14336)*
Landmark Theatres, Los Angeles *Also called Silver Cinemas Acquisition Co (G-18352)*
Landor Associates Intl Ltd (HQ).....415 365-1700
1001 Front St San Francisco (94111) *(G-14150)*
Landsberg Los Angeles Div 1001, Montebello *Also called Orora North America (G-8205)*
Landsberg Orora, Buena Park *Also called Orora Packaging Solutions (G-8211)*
Landsberg San Diego Div 1007, San Marcos *Also called Orora North America (G-8208)*

ALPHABETIC

Landscape Center, Riverside *Also called B & B Nurseries Inc* ***(G-9178)***
Landscape Development Inc (PA) 661 295-1970
28447 Witherspoon Pkwy Valencia (91355) ***(G-902)***
Lane Stuart Company LLC 805 553-9562
740 Lucille Ct Moorpark (93021) ***(G-11626)***
Lane Framing Systems Inc 714 630-7686
1038 E Bastanchury Rd # 606 Fullerton (92835) ***(G-3062)***
Lang Richert & Patch 559 228-6700
5200 N Palm Ave Ste 401 Fresno (93704) ***(G-23364)***
Lange Trucking Inc (PA) 510 836-1105
2226 Campbell St Oakland (94607) ***(G-4209)***
Langetwins Inc 209 339-4055
1298 E Jahant Rd Acampo (95220) ***(G-167)***
Langham Hotels International, Pasadena *Also called Langham Hotels Pacific Corp* ***(G-12905)***
Langham Hotels Pacific Corp 617 451-1900
1401 S Oak Knoll Ave Pasadena (91106) ***(G-12905)***
Language Weaver Inc 310 437-7300
6060 Center Dr Ste 150 Los Angeles (90045) ***(G-15272)***
Lani, Irvine *Also called Loan Administration Netwrk Inc* ***(G-14697)***
Lansing Mall Ltd Partnership 510 782-3527
1 Southland Mall Hayward (94545) ***(G-11010)***
Lansing Mall Ltd Partnership 818 885-9700
9301 Tampa Ave Ofc Northridge (91324) ***(G-11011)***
Lanting Hay Dealer Inc 909 563-5601
9032 Merrill Ave Ontario (91762) ***(G-9142)***
Lantz Security Systems Inc 805 496-5775
101 N Westlake Blvd # 200 Westlake Village (91362) ***(G-16720)***
Lantz Security Systems Inc 818 871-0193
4111 Las Virgenes Rd # 202 Calabasas (91302) ***(G-16897)***
Lantz Security Systems Inc (PA) 661 949-3565
43440 Sahuayo St Lancaster (93535) ***(G-16721)***
Lanwave Technology Inc 408 253-3883
20111 Stevens Creek Blvd Cupertino (95014) ***(G-25932)***
Lanza Vineyards Inc 707 864-0730
4756 Suisun Valley Rd Fairfield (94534) ***(G-168)***
Lapham Company Inc 510 531-6000
4844 Telegraph Ave Oakland (94609) ***(G-11627)***
Lapham Company Management, Oakland *Also called Lapham Company Inc* ***(G-11627)***
LARC RANCH, Santa Clarita *Also called Los Angeles Resdntl Cmmnty Fdn* ***(G-24719)***
Larchmont Radiology Med Group 213 483-5953
2010 Wilshire Blvd # 409 Los Angeles (90057) ***(G-19699)***
Laren D Tan MD 909 558-4444
11234 Anderson St Loma Linda (92354) ***(G-19700)***
Largo Concrete Inc 909 981-7844
1690 W Foothill Blvd B Upland (91786) ***(G-3289)***
Largo Concrete Inc 408 874-2500
891 W Hamilton Ave Campbell (95008) ***(G-3290)***
Largo Concrete Inc 619 356-2142
1650 Hotel Cir N San Diego (92108) ***(G-1205)***
Lark Avenue Car Wash 408 371-2565
5005 Almaden Expy San Jose (95118) ***(G-17848)***
LARK Industries Inc (PA) 714 701-4200
4900 E Hunter Ave Anaheim (92807) ***(G-17288)***
Larkin Leasing Inc 714 528-3232
674 N Batavia St Orange (92868) ***(G-1959)***
Larkspur Hsptality Dev MGT LLC 650 872-1515
670 Gateway Blvd South San Francisco (94080) ***(G-12906)***
Larrabee Brothrs Distribtng Co 805 922-2108
815 S Blosser Rd Santa Maria (93458) ***(G-9067)***
Larry Blair Realtor 650 991-5267
2488 Junipero Serra Blvd Daly City (94015) ***(G-11628)***
Larry Jacinto Construction Inc 909 794-2151
9555 N Wabash Ave Redlands (92374) ***(G-1814)***
Larsen Supply Co (PA) 562 698-0731
12055 Slauson Ave Santa Fe Springs (90670) ***(G-7723)***
Larson, Drake Sales, Thermal *Also called Drake Larson Ranchs* ***(G-152)***
Larsons Studios, Los Angeles *Also called Lgh Digital Media Inc* ***(G-18276)***
Las Brisas, San Luis Obispo *Also called Harvest Management Sub LLC* ***(G-24679)***
Las Cumbres Observatory Global 805 880-1600
6740 Cortona Dr Ste 102 Goleta (93117) ***(G-26781)***
Las Flores Convalescent Hosp, Gardena *Also called Gardena Flores Inc* ***(G-20592)***
Las Islas Family Med Group PC 805 385-8662
325 W Chnnel Islands Blvd Oxnard (93033) ***(G-19701)***
Las Posas Club Inc 805 482-1811
230 Ramona Pl Camarillo (93010) ***(G-18979)***
Las Posas Country Club 805 482-4518
955 Fairway Dr Camarillo (93010) ***(G-18980)***
Las Posas Road Medical Offices, Camarillo *Also called Kaiser Foundation Hospitals* ***(G-19606)***
Las Vegas / LA Express Inc (PA) 909 972-3100
1000 S Cucamonga Ave Ontario (91761) ***(G-4210)***
Las Vegas Intrntnl Tours 310 581-0718
18147 Coastline Dr Apt 1 Malibu (90265) ***(G-17289)***
Las Villas De Carlsbad, Carlsbad *Also called Villas De Carlsbad Ltd A Cali* ***(G-24850)***
Las Villas Del Norte 760 741-1047
1325 Las Villas Way Escondido (92026) ***(G-20720)***
Las Virgenes Municipal Wtr Dst 818 251-2100
4232 Las Virgenes Rd Lbby Calabasas (91302) ***(G-6362)***
Lasaltte Hlth Rhbilitation Ctr, Stockton *Also called Five Star Quality Care Inc* ***(G-20572)***
Lasco, Santa Fe Springs *Also called Larsen Supply Co* ***(G-7723)***
Laserfiche Document Imaging, Long Beach *Also called Compulink Management Ctr Inc* ***(G-15627)***
Lasertech Computer Distr Inc 626 435-2800
139 N Sunset Ave City of Industry (91744) ***(G-7153)***
Lash-San Francisco Office, San Bruno *Also called Intake Initiatives Inc* ***(G-8264)***
Lassen Canyon Nursery Inc 530 938-4720
14735 Big Springs Rd Weed (96094) ***(G-118)***
Lassen Canyon Nursery Inc 209 599-7777
11651 Palm Ln Ripon (95366) ***(G-119)***
Lassen Canyon Nursery Inc (PA) 530 223-1075
1300 Salmon Creek Rd Redding (96003) ***(G-120)***
Lassen Hse Assisted Living LLC 530 529-2900
705 Luther Rd Red Bluff (96080) ***(G-24707)***
Lassen Land Co 530 865-7676
320 E South St Orland (95963) ***(G-706)***
Lassen Medical Group Inc (PA) 530 527-0414
2450 Sster Mary Clumba Dr Red Bluff (96080) ***(G-19702)***
Lassley Enterprises Inc 559 226-4300
1289 E Shaw Ave Fresno (93710) ***(G-11153)***
Last Frontier Healthcare Dst 530 233-7036
228 W Mcdowell Ave Alturas (96101) ***(G-21698)***
Lastline Inc 805 456-7075
6950 Hollister Ave # 101 Goleta (93117) ***(G-15731)***
Latara Enterprise Inc (PA) 909 623-9301
1716 W Holt Ave Pomona (91768) ***(G-22234)***
Latara Enterprise Inc 661 665-9780
9610 Stockdale Hwy Bakersfield (93311) ***(G-22235)***
Latara Enterprise Inc 760 256-3450
705 E Virginia Way Ste D Barstow (92311) ***(G-22236)***
Latara Enterprise Inc 951 272-9420
817 S Main St Corona (92882) ***(G-22237)***
Lateral Designs Inc 415 847-6618
639 Front St Fl 3 San Francisco (94111) ***(G-14151)***
Latham & Watkins LLP 650 328-4600
140 Scott Dr Menlo Park (94025) ***(G-23365)***
Latham & Watkins LLP 714 755-8288
1722 Skyhill Way Santa Ana (92705) ***(G-23366)***
Latham & Watkins LLP 619 236-1234
12670 High Bluff Dr # 100 San Diego (92130) ***(G-23367)***
Latham & Watkins LLP 818 753-5000
111 Univrsal Hllywd 257 Universal City (91608) ***(G-23368)***
Latham & Watkins LLP (PA) 213 485-1234
355 S Grand Ave Ste 1000 Los Angeles (90071) ***(G-23369)***
Latham & Watkins LLP 213 891-7108
555 W 5th St Ste 800 Los Angeles (90013) ***(G-23370)***
Latham & Watkins LLP 714 540-1235
650 Town Center Dr # 2000 Costa Mesa (92626) ***(G-23371)***
Latham & Watkins LLP 415 391-0600
505 Montgomery St # 1900 San Francisco (94111) ***(G-23372)***
Latham & Watkins LLP 213 891-1200
520 S Grand Ave Ste 200 Los Angeles (90071) ***(G-23373)***
Lathrop & Gage LLP 310 789-4600
1888 Century Park E # 1000 Los Angeles (90067) ***(G-23374)***
Latino Commission 650 244-0304
301 Grand Ave Ste 301 South San Francisco (94080) ***(G-22765)***
Lattice Engines Inc (PA) 877 460-0010
1820 Gateway Dr Ste 200 San Mateo (94404) ***(G-16421)***
Laughlin Falbo Levy Moresi LLP (PA) 510 628-0496
555 12th St Ste 1900 Oakland (94607) ***(G-23375)***
Launch Media Inc (HQ) 310 593-6152
25 Taylor St San Francisco (94102) ***(G-5646)***
Launchpad Communications, Anaheim *Also called Consumer Resource Network LLC* ***(G-27388)***
Lauras House 949 361-3775
999 Corporate Dr Ste 225 Mission Viejo (92694) ***(G-24064)***
Laurel Convelescent Center, Fontana *Also called Sun Mar Management Services* ***(G-27236)***
Laurel Labor Services Inc 805 928-0113
727 Richmind Ct Santa Maria (93455) ***(G-14696)***
Laurel Park, Pomona *Also called Sunbridge Braswell Entps Inc* ***(G-20937)***
Laurels Medical Services 408 898-6360
5120 Manzanita Ave # 140 Carmichael (95608) ***(G-3864)***
Laurence-Hovenier Inc 951 736-2990
179 N Maple St Corona (92880) ***(G-3063)***
Lav Hotel Corp 858 454-0771
1132 Prospect St La Jolla (92037) ***(G-12907)***
Lava Beds National Monuments 530 667-2282
1 Indian Wells Hqtrs Tulelake (96134) ***(G-25548)***
Lavante Inc 408 754-0505
5285 Hellyer Ave Ste 200 San Jose (95138) ***(G-26393)***
Lavine Lofgren Morris & Enge 858 455-1200
4180 La Jolla Village Dr # 315 La Jolla (92037) ***(G-26394)***
Law Enforcement Officers Inc 855 477-3536
24000 Alicia Pkwy 17-229 Mission Viejo (92691) ***(G-16898)***
Law Office of Curtis O Barnes 866 477-8222
390 W Cerritos Ave Anaheim (92805) ***(G-23376)***
Law Offices Berglund & Johnson (PA) 951 276-4783
21550 Oxnard St Ste 900 Woodland Hills (91367) ***(G-23377)***
Law Offices of Thomas W 858 883-2000
14286 Danielson St # 103 Poway (92064) ***(G-23378)***
Law School Financial Inc 626 243-1800
175 S Lake Ave Unit 200 Pasadena (91101) ***(G-9732)***
Law School Loans, Pasadena *Also called Law School Financial Inc* ***(G-9732)***
Lawinfocom Inc 760 510-3000
5901 Priestly Dr Ste 200 Carlsbad (92008) ***(G-15732)***
Lawndle Hlthcare & Wellnss Cen 310 679-3344
15100 Prairie Ave Lawndale (90260) ***(G-20721)***
Lawnman II Inc 916 739-1420
4300 82nd St Ste C Sacramento (95826) ***(G-903)***
Lawrence B Bonas Company 714 668-5250
3197 Arprt Loop Dr Ste C Costa Mesa (92626) ***(G-2462)***
Lawrence Berkeley National Lab, Emeryville *Also called Energy Berkeley Office US Dept* ***(G-26756)***
Lawrence Berkeley National Lab, Brea *Also called Energy Berkeley Office US Dept* ***(G-26757)***
Lawrence Berkeley National Lab, Albany *Also called Energy Berkeley Office US Dept* ***(G-26758)***

ALPHABETIC

ALPHABETIC SECTION
Legacy Partners Limited Inc

Lawrence Berkeley National Lab, Berkeley *Also called Energy Berkeley Office US Dept* ***(G-26759)***
Lawrence Berkeley National Lab, Berkeley *Also called United States Dept of Energy* ***(G-26815)***
Lawrence Berkeley National Lab, Alameda *Also called Energy Berkeley Office US Dept* ***(G-26760)***
Lawrence Berkeley National Lab, Berkeley *Also called Energy Berkeley Office US Dept* ***(G-26761)***
Lawrence Berkeley National Lab 510 486-6792
1 Cyclotron Rd Berkeley (94720) ***(G-22238)***
Lawrence Family Jewish Commu (PA) 858 362-1144
4126 Executive Dr La Jolla (92037) ***(G-24937)***
Lawrence Livermore Nat Lab, San Francisco *Also called Energy Livermore Off US Dept* ***(G-26762)***
Lawrence Livermore Nat Lab, San Jose *Also called Energy Livermore Off US Dept* ***(G-26763)***
Lawrence Livermore Nat Lab, Livermore *Also called United States Dept of Energy* ***(G-26627)***
Lawson Mechanical Contractors (PA) 916 381-6704
6090 S Watt Ave Sacramento (95829) ***(G-2275)***
Lawson Roofing Co Inc 415 285-1661
1495 Tennessee St San Francisco (94107) ***(G-3184)***
Lawyers Title Company 858 650-3900
4542 Ruffner St Ste 200 San Diego (92111) ***(G-10529)***
Lawyers Title Company (HQ) 818 767-0425
7530 N Glenoaks Blvd Burbank (91504) ***(G-10530)***
Lawyers Title Insurance Corp 949 223-5575
18551 Von Karman Ave # 100 Irvine (92612) ***(G-10531)***
Lax Hospitality LP 310 670-9000
6225 W Century Blvd Los Angeles (90045) ***(G-12908)***
Lax Hotel Ventures LLC 310 645-4600
9750 Airport Blvd Los Angeles (90045) ***(G-12909)***
Lax International Service Ctr 310 337-8764
5800 W Century Blvd Los Angeles (90009) ***(G-17290)***
Lax Plaza Hotel 310 902-2202
6333 Bristol Pkwy Culver City (90230) ***(G-12910)***
LAX Wheel Refinishing Inc 323 269-1484
1520 Spence St Los Angeles (90023) ***(G-6745)***
Lax-C Inc 323 343-9000
1100 N Main St Los Angeles (90012) ***(G-8490)***
Laxmi Group Inc 408 329-7733
4699 Old Ironsides Dr # 100 Santa Clara (95054) ***(G-15273)***
Layfield USA Corporation (HQ) 619 562-1200
2500 Sweetwater Spgs Spring Valley (91978) ***(G-3546)***
Laz Parking Ltd 858 587-8888
9333 Genesee Ave Ste 220 San Diego (92121) ***(G-17727)***
Lazar Landscape Design & Cnstr 510 444-5195
2884 Ettie St Oakland (94608) ***(G-904)***
Lazer Electric Inc 714 777-4233
4701 E Hunter Ave Anaheim (92807) ***(G-2635)***
Laztrans Inc 661 833-3783
5200 District Blvd Bakersfield (93313) ***(G-4211)***
Lb Hills Golf Club LLC 760 775-2000
84000 Terra Lago Pkwy Indio (92203) ***(G-18754)***
Lba Realty Fund III - III LLC 949 833-0400
3347 Michelson Dr Ste 200 Irvine (92612) ***(G-12255)***
Lba Realty LLC (PA) 949 833-0400
3347 Michelson Dr Ste 200 Irvine (92612) ***(G-11629)***
Lba Rlty Fund I-Company IV LLC 949 955-9321
3347 Michelson Dr Ste 950 Irvine (92612) ***(G-12256)***
LBC Inc 805 581-1068
1881 Duncan St Simi Valley (93065) ***(G-3185)***
LBC Mundial Corporation (HQ) 650 873-0750
3563 Inv Blvd Ste 3 Hayward (94545) ***(G-4867)***
Lbf Travel Inc 858 429-7599
4545 Murphy Canyon Rd # 210 San Diego (92123) ***(G-4967)***
Lbi Media Inc 818 729-5316
1845 W Empire Ave Burbank (91504) ***(G-5804)***
Lbs Financial Credit Union 714 893-5111
1401 Quail St Ste 130 Newport Beach (92660) ***(G-9733)***
Lbs Financial Credit Union (PA) 714 893-5111
5505 Garden Grove Blvd # 500 Westminster (92683) ***(G-9734)***
Lc Trs Inc 760 438-9111
2100 Costa Del Mar Rd Carlsbad (92009) ***(G-12911)***
Ld Products Inc 562 986-6940
3700 Cover St Long Beach (90808) ***(G-7154)***
LDI Mechanical Inc 916 361-3925
3760 Happy Ln Sacramento (95827) ***(G-2276)***
LDI Mechanical Inc (PA) 951 340-9685
1587 E Bentley Dr Corona (92879) ***(G-2277)***
LDI Transportation Inc 909 620-7001
200 Erie St Pomona (91768) ***(G-4356)***
Ldla Clothing LLC 323 312-2805
1515 E 15th St Los Angeles (90021) ***(G-8394)***
Le Bleu Chateau Inc 818 843-3141
1900 Grismer Ave Burbank (91504) ***(G-24708)***
Le Courier, Burbank *Also called Tidavater Inc* ***(G-17531)***
Le Merdien Dlfina Santa Monica, Santa Monica *Also called Blue Devils Lessee LLC* ***(G-12454)***
Le Meridian Hotel, San Francisco *Also called Chesapeake Lodging Trust* ***(G-12511)***
Le Merigot, Santa Monica *Also called Cwgp Limited Partnership* ***(G-12560)***
Le Montrose Hotel 310 855-1115
900 Hammond St Apt 434 West Hollywood (90069) ***(G-12912)***
Le Montrose Suite Hotel, West Hollywood *Also called Le Montrose Hotel* ***(G-12912)***
Le Parc Suite Hotel, West Hollywood *Also called Ols Hotels & Resorts LP* ***(G-13040)***
Le Parker Meridien Palm Sprng, Palm Springs *Also called Jack Parker Corp* ***(G-12862)***
Le Technology Inc 310 845-5838
3553 N 1st St San Jose (95134) ***(G-7593)***
Le Vecke Corporation (PA) 951 681-8600
10810 Inland Ave Mira Loma (91752) ***(G-9068)***
Le Vecke Group, Mira Loma *Also called Le Vecke Corporation* ***(G-9068)***
Lead Staffing Corporation 800 928-5561
216 S Citrus St Ste 397 West Covina (91791) ***(G-14898)***
Leader Drug Store, Torrance *Also called Little Company Mary Hospital* ***(G-21707)***
Leader Emergency Vehicles, South El Monte *Also called Leader Industries Inc* ***(G-3812)***
Leader Industries Inc 626 575-0880
10941 Weaver Ave South El Monte (91733) ***(G-3812)***
Leading Edge Aviation Servs 760 246-1651
13640 Phantom St Victorville (92394) ***(G-4923)***
League of California Cities (PA) 916 341-0140
1400 K St Fl 4 Sacramento (95814) ***(G-27754)***
League of Wmen Voters Whittier 562 947-5818
10011 Melgar Dr Whittier (90603) ***(G-25481)***
Lear Capital Inc 310 571-0190
1990 S Bundy Dr Ste 600 Los Angeles (90025) ***(G-10023)***
Learn, Whittier *Also called Rio Hondo Education Consortium* ***(G-24159)***
Learning Services Corporation 408 848-4379
10855 De Bruin Way Gilroy (95020) ***(G-22766)***
Learning Services Corporation 760 746-3223
2335 Bear Valley Pkwy Escondido (92027) ***(G-22767)***
Learning Services Northern Cal, Gilroy *Also called Learning Services Corporation* ***(G-22766)***
Learning Tree Pre-School, Tujunga *Also called Crescenta-Canada YMCA* ***(G-25247)***
Leasing Equipment, San Francisco *Also called Atel Capital Group* ***(G-9794)***
Leavitt Group Enterprises Inc 707 465-6508
785 E Washington Blvd # 4 Crescent City (95531) ***(G-27109)***
Leavy Brothers Incorporated 916 773-5636
4117 Elverta Rd Ste 102 Antelope (95843) ***(G-2924)***
Led Global LLC 917 921-4315
1010 Wilshire Blvd Los Angeles (90017) ***(G-2278)***
Ledcor CMI Inc 602 595-3017
6405 Mira Mesa Blvd # 100 San Diego (92121) ***(G-1447)***
Ledcor Management Services Inc 858 527-6400
6405 Mira Mesa Blvd Ste 1 San Diego (92121) ***(G-27110)***
Ledcor Technical Services Inc 858 527-6400
6405 Mira Mesa Blvd San Diego (92121) ***(G-2636)***
Ledesma & Meyer Cnstr Co Inc 909 297-1100
9441 Haven Ave Rancho Cucamonga (91730) ***(G-1600)***
Ledesma & Meyer Dev Inc 909 476-0590
9441 Haven Ave Rancho Cucamonga (91730) ***(G-27111)***
Ledra Brands Inc 714 259-9959
15774 Gateway Cir Tustin (92780) ***(G-6871)***
Ledson Winery & Vineyards, Santa Rosa *Also called Steven N Ledson* ***(G-1263)***
Lee Burkhart Liu Inc (PA) 310 829-2249
5510 Lincoln Blvd Ste 250 Playa Vista (90094) ***(G-26221)***
Lee Hong Degerman Kang 949 250-9954
3501 Jamboree Rd Ste 6000 Newport Beach (92660) ***(G-23379)***
Lee & Assoc Comm Real Est Svcs 909 989-7771
3535 Inland Empire Blvd Ontario (91764) ***(G-11630)***
Lee & Associates Coml RE Svcs, Ontario *Also called Lee & Assoc Comm Real Est Svcs* ***(G-11630)***
Lee & Associates Coml RE Svcs (PA) 949 727-1200
7700 Irvine Center Dr # 600 Irvine (92618) ***(G-11631)***
Lee & Associates Realty Group 949 724-1000
100 Bayview Cir Ste 600 Newport Beach (92660) ***(G-11632)***
Lee & Ro Inc (PA) 626 912-3391
1199 Fullerton Rd City of Industry (91748) ***(G-25933)***
Lee Bros Foodservices Inc (PA) 408 275-0700
660 E Gish Rd San Jose (95112) ***(G-8491)***
Lee Industrial Catering, San Jose *Also called Lee Bros Foodservices Inc* ***(G-8491)***
Lee Johnson 858 481-4411
14750 El Camino Real Del Mar (92014) ***(G-21288)***
Lee Mar Aquarium & Pet Sups, Vista *Also called Lee-Mar Aquarium & Pet Sups* ***(G-9275)***
LEE& Associates, Newport Beach *Also called Lee & Associates Realty Group* ***(G-11632)***
Lee-Mar Aquarium & Pet Sups 760 727-1300
2459 Dogwood Way Vista (92081) ***(G-9275)***
Lee-Victorville Hotel Corp 760 245-3461
14173 Green Tree Blvd Victorville (92395) ***(G-12913)***
Leeco, San Jose *Also called Le Technology Inc* ***(G-7593)***
Leed International LLC 650 861-7883
1583 Shanghai Cir San Jose (95131) ***(G-27972)***
Leekilpatrick Management Inc 818 500-9631
412 W Broadway Fl 3 Glendale (91204) ***(G-27505)***
Leemah Electronics Inc 415 394-1288
1080 Sansome St San Francisco (94111) ***(G-6144)***
Leerink Partners LLC 800 778-1164
255 California St Fl 12 San Francisco (94111) ***(G-10024)***
Lees Maintenance Service Inc 818 988-6644
14740 Keswick St Van Nuys (91405) ***(G-14337)***
Legacy Farms LLC 714 736-1800
6625 Caballero Blvd Buena Park (90620) ***(G-8745)***
Legacy Frames 310 537-4210
11220 Wright Rd Lynwood (90262) ***(G-7594)***
Legacy Global Logistics Svcs, San Jose *Also called Legacy Transportation Svcs Inc* ***(G-4357)***
Legacy Inmate Communications, Cypress *Also called Legacy Long Distance Intl Inc* ***(G-5647)***
Legacy Long Distance Intl Inc 800 670-0015
10833 Valley View St # 150 Cypress (90630) ***(G-5647)***
Legacy Marketing Group (PA) 707 778-8638
2090 Marina Ave Petaluma (94954) ***(G-27506)***
Legacy Mech & Enrgy Svcs Inc 925 820-6938
3130 Crow Canyon Pl # 410 San Ramon (94583) ***(G-2279)***
Legacy Partners Hollywood 949 930-7706
1600 Vine St Los Angeles (90028) ***(G-11154)***
Legacy Partners Limited Inc 760 747-2711
738 W Washington Ave A Escondido (92025) ***(G-1815)***

A L P H A B E T I C

Legacy Paving, Escondido *Also called Legacy Partners Limited Inc* ***(G-1815)***
Legacy Prtners Coml Capitl Inc...949 863-0390
2050 Main St Ste 830 Irvine (92614) ***(G-11978)***
Legacy Prtners Residential Inc (HQ)...650 571-2250
4000 E 3rd Ave Ste 600 Foster City (94404) ***(G-27112)***
Legacy Transportation Svcs Inc (PA)...408 294-9800
935 Mclaughlin Ave San Jose (95122) ***(G-4357)***
Legacy Vulcan Corp...909 875-1150
2400 W Highland Ave San Bernardino (92407) ***(G-1106)***
Legacy Vulcan Corp...858 547-9459
5745 Mission Center Rd San Diego (92108) ***(G-1107)***
Legacy Vulcan Corp...925 373-1802
501 El Charro Rd Pleasanton (94588) ***(G-1108)***
Legal Enterprise, Calabasas *Also called Litigtion Rsrces of America-CA* ***(G-17296)***
Legal Recovery Law Offices Inc...619 275-4001
5030 Camino De La Siesta San Diego (92108) ***(G-23380)***
Legal Solutions Holdings Inc...800 244-3495
955 Overland Ct Ste 200 San Dimas (91773) ***(G-23381)***
Legal Support Network LLC...213 975-9850
1533 Wilshire Blvd Los Angeles (90017) ***(G-17291)***
Legally Yours LLC...909 396-7200
750 N Diamond Bar Blvd # 224 Diamond Bar (91765) ***(G-23382)***
Legalmatchcom...415 946-0800
395 Oyster Point Blvd South San Francisco (94080) ***(G-23383)***
Legalstaff of San Diego, San Diego *Also called Allen Lee Rose Inc* ***(G-14604)***
Legend Merchant Group Inc...415 957-9555
201 Mission St Ste 230 San Francisco (94105) ***(G-17292)***
Legend Transpotation, Yuba City *Also called New Legend Inc* ***(G-4234)***
Legend3d Inc...858 793-4420
1017 Cole Ave Los Angeles (90038) ***(G-18099)***
Leggett & Platt Incorporated...510 487-8063
30955 Huntwood Ave Hayward (94544) ***(G-14000)***
Legions Protective Svcs LLC...310 819-8881
17201 S Figueroa St Gardena (90248) ***(G-16722)***
Legislative Counsel Tstg Off, Sacramento *Also called Office of The Legislative Coun* ***(G-28008)***
Legislative Data Center, Sacramento *Also called Office of The Legislative Coun* ***(G-5406)***
Legoland California LLC...760 918-5346
1 Legoland Dr Carlsbad (92008) ***(G-18824)***
Legoland Florida, Carlsbad *Also called Merlin Entertainments* ***(G-18826)***
Legrande Affaire, Santa Clara *Also called Restivo Enterprises* ***(G-3833)***
Legrande Affaire Inc...408 988-4884
651 Aldo Ave Santa Clara (95054) ***(G-3813)***
Lehar Sales Co...510 465-3255
150 Chestnut St Oakland (94607) ***(G-8599)***
Lehman Brothers, Los Angeles *Also called Barclays Capital Inc* ***(G-9964)***
Lei AG Seattle, Los Angeles *Also called Lowe Enterprises Inc* ***(G-11638)***
LEICHTAG ASSISTED LIVING, Encinitas *Also called San Diego Hebrew Homes* ***(G-20888)***
Leidos Inc...858 826-5552
4035 Hancock St San Diego (92110) ***(G-16422)***
Leidos Inc...805 546-0307
1411 Marsh St San Luis Obispo (93401) ***(G-26548)***
Leidos Inc...310 791-9671
1874 S Pacific Coast Hwy Redondo Beach (90277) ***(G-26549)***
Leidos Inc...858 535-4499
9455 Towne Centre Dr # 200 San Diego (92121) ***(G-17293)***
Leidos Inc...858 826-7670
1550 N Norma St Ridgecrest (93555) ***(G-16151)***
Leidos Inc...714 257-6400
590 W Central Ave Ste I Brea (92821) ***(G-26550)***
Leidos Inc...805 563-9597
3700 State St Ste 300 Santa Barbara (93105) ***(G-26551)***
Leidos Inc...310 524-3134
300 N Sepulveda Blvd # 3000 El Segundo (90245) ***(G-26552)***
Leidos Inc...858 826-6616
10740 Thornmint Rd San Diego (92127) ***(G-26553)***
Leidos Inc...559 935-2305
139 N 5th St Coalinga (93210) ***(G-26554)***
Leidos Inc...510 428-2550
2000 Powell St Ste 1090 Emeryville (94608) ***(G-26555)***
Leidos Inc...858 826-6000
1299 Prospect St La Jolla (92037) ***(G-15984)***
Leidos Inc...858 826-6000
4065 Hancock St San Diego (92110) ***(G-26556)***
Leidos Inc...408 364-4700
475 14th St Oakland (94612) ***(G-26557)***
Leidos Inc...858 826-7129
10010 Campus Point Dr San Diego (92121) ***(G-26558)***
Leidos Inc...910 574-4597
N Depo Rd Bldg 4530 Fort Irwin (92310) ***(G-26559)***
Leidos Engineering LLC...714 257-6400
590 W Central Ave Ste I Brea (92821) ***(G-25934)***
Leidos Engineering LLC...408 364-4700
1671 Dell Ave Ste 100 Campbell (95008) ***(G-25935)***
Leidos Engineering LLC...858 826-6000
4161 Campus Point Ct E San Diego (92121) ***(G-25936)***
Leidos Engrg & Sciences LLC...619 542-3130
1330 30th St Ste A San Diego (92154) ***(G-26560)***
Leigh Jerry California Inc (PA)...818 909-6200
7860 Nelson Rd Van Nuys (91402) ***(G-8395)***
Leight Sales Co Inc...310 223-1000
1611 S Catalina Ave L45 Redondo Beach (90277) ***(G-7689)***
Leighton & Associates, Irvine *Also called Gradient Engineers Inc* ***(G-25845)***
Leighton and Associates Inc (PA)...949 250-1421
17781 Cowan Irvine (92614) ***(G-27973)***
Leighton Group Inc...760 776-4192
75450 Gerald Ford Dr Palm Desert (92211) ***(G-25142)***
Leisure Care, Livermore *Also called Livermore Snior Lving Assoc LP* ***(G-12072)***
Leisure Care Inc...949 645-6833
1455 Superior Ave Newport Beach (92663) ***(G-11155)***
Leisure Care LLC...818 713-0900
8138 Woodlake Ave Canoga Park (91304) ***(G-21089)***
Leisure Care LLC...925 371-2300
800 E Stanley Blvd Livermore (94550) ***(G-11156)***
Leisure Care LLC...714 974-1616
380 S Anaheim Hills Rd Anaheim (92807) ***(G-24709)***
Leisure Care LLC...559 434-1237
9525 N Fort Washington Rd Fresno (93730) ***(G-24710)***
Leisure Court Nursing Center, Anaheim *Also called 1135 N Leisure Ct Inc* ***(G-20364)***
Leisure Glen Convalescent Ctr, Glendale *Also called Buena Ventura Care Center Inc* ***(G-21168)***
Leisure Planet...925 687-4386
1975 Diamond Blvd Concord (94520) ***(G-19235)***
Leisure Sports Inc...925 942-6301
4670 Willow Rd Ste 100 Pleasanton (94588) ***(G-12071)***
Leisure Sports Inc...925 938-3058
2805 Jones Rd Walnut Creek (94597) ***(G-12914)***
Leisure Sports Inc...510 226-8500
46650 Landing Pkwy Fremont (94538) ***(G-18654)***
Leisure Sports Inc...925 934-4050
7090 Johnson Dr Pleasanton (94588) ***(G-19236)***
Leisure Village Association...805 484-2861
200 Leisure Village Dr Camarillo (93012) ***(G-25286)***
Leisure World Pharmacy, Seal Beach *Also called Tenet Healthsystem Medical* ***(G-20133)***
Leisure World Resales, Laguna Hills *Also called Professional Cmnty MGT Cal Inc* ***(G-11768)***
LEK Consulting LLC...310 209-9800
1100 Glendon Ave Ste 2100 Los Angeles (90024) ***(G-27507)***
Leland House, San Francisco *Also called Catholic Chrts Cyo Archdiocs* ***(G-23716)***
Leland Stanford Junior Univ...650 723-6254
1070 Arastradero Rd # 100 Palo Alto (94304) ***(G-26681)***
Leland Stanford Junior Univ...650 725-4868
551 Srra Mall Mem Adtrium Memorial Auditorium Stanford (94305) ***(G-5805)***
Leland Stanford Junior Univ...650 723-7863
1201 Welch Rd Stanford (94305) ***(G-19703)***
Leland Stanford Junior Univ...650 723-5548
3373 Hillview Ave Palo Alto (94304) ***(G-22992)***
Leland Stanford Junior Univ...650 723-2997
328 Lomita Dr Palo Alto (94305) ***(G-21699)***
Leland Stanford Junior Univ...650 723-2021
326 Galvez St Stanford (94305) ***(G-25287)***
Leland Stanford Junior Univ...650 723-7546
476 Lomita Mall Palo Alto (94305) ***(G-26682)***
Leland Stanford Junior Univ...650 723-4150
Melcode 4020 Bldg 540 Stanford (94305) ***(G-26782)***
Leland Stanford Junior Univ...650 723-9633
711 Serra St Stanford (94305) ***(G-2637)***
Leland Stanford Junior Univ...650 725-2377
820 Quarry Rd Palo Alto (94304) ***(G-21700)***
Leland Stanford Junior Univ...650 723-4000
2680 Hanover St Palo Alto (94304) ***(G-21701)***
Leland Stanford Junior Univ...650 723-0107
450 Via Palou Mall Stanford (94305) ***(G-26783)***
Leland Stanford Junior Univ...650 724-8899
397 Panama Mall Ste 360 Stanford (94305) ***(G-26784)***
Leland Stanford Junior Univ...650 725-4416
211 Quarry Rd N229 Palo Alto (94304) ***(G-19704)***
Leland Stanford Junior Univ...650 497-8000
725 Welch Rd Palo Alto (94304) ***(G-22151)***
Leland Stanford Junior Univ...650 725-4617
1000 Welch Rd Palo Alto (94304) ***(G-21702)***
Leland Stanford Junior Univ...650 725-2386
473 Via Ortega Stanford (94305) ***(G-21703)***
Leland Stanford Junior Univ...650 725-6127
243 Panama St Stanford (94305) ***(G-21704)***
Leland Stanford Junior Univ...650 723-0821
870 Campus Dr Stanford (94305) ***(G-19705)***
Leland Stanford Junior Univ...650 723-4000
300 Pasteur Dr Stanford (94305) ***(G-21705)***
Leland Stanford Junior Univ...650 723-4733
1201 Welch Rd Palo Alto (94305) ***(G-26785)***
Lemans Corporation...909 428-2424
11070 Mulberry Ave Ste A Fontana (92337) ***(G-4586)***
Lemo USA Inc...707 206-3700
635 Park Ct Rohnert Park (94928) ***(G-7595)***
Lemore Transportation Inc (PA)...925 689-6444
1420 Royal Industrial Way Concord (94520) ***(G-4212)***
Lender Processing Services Inc...626 808-9000
3100 New York Dr Ste 200 Pasadena (91107) ***(G-16152)***
Lendingclub Corporation (PA)...415 632-5600
71 Stevenson St Ste 300 San Francisco (94105) ***(G-9785)***
Lendlease US Construction Inc...213 430-4660
800 W 6th St Ste 1600 Los Angeles (90017) ***(G-27113)***
Lendup, San Francisco *Also called Flurish Inc* ***(G-9748)***
Lenexa Hotel LP...310 475-8711
10740 Wilshire Blvd Los Angeles (90024) ***(G-12915)***
Lenlyn Limited Which Will Do B (HQ)...310 417-3432
6151 W Century Blvd Los Angeles (90045) ***(G-9721)***
Lennar, Rancho Santa Fe *Also called HCC Investors LLC* ***(G-18959)***
Lennar Builders, Aliso Viejo *Also called Lennar Homes California Inc* ***(G-1206)***
Lennar Corporation...949 349-8000
25 Enterprise Ste 400 Aliso Viejo (92656) ***(G-1374)***
Lennar Homes California Inc (HQ)...949 349-8000
25 Enterprise Ste 400 Aliso Viejo (92656) ***(G-1206)***
Lennar Homes Inc...916 517-4950
3788 Edington Dr Rancho Cordova (95742) ***(G-1375)***
Lennar Homes Inc...951 739-0267
980 Montecito Dr 302 Corona (92879) ***(G-1376)***

ALPHABETIC

Lennar Multi Family Community, Aliso Viejo *Also called LMC Hollywood Highland* ***(G-1602)***
Lennar Partners of Los Angeles (PA).....949 885-8500
4350 Von Karman Ave # 200 Newport Beach (92660) ***(G-17294)***
Lennox Industries Inc.....951 241-8966
1790 Iowa Ave Riverside (92507) ***(G-7742)***
Lennox Industries Inc.....818 739-1616
19801 Nordhoff Pl Ste 109 Chatsworth (91311) ***(G-7743)***
Lenore John & Co (PA).....619 232-6136
1250 Delevan Dr San Diego (92102) ***(G-8875)***
Lenox Financial Mortgage Corp.....949 428-5100
200 Sandpointe Ave # 800 Santa Ana (92707) ***(G-9868)***
Leo A Daly Company, Sacramento *Also called Leo A Daly Company* ***(G-26224)***
Leo A Daly Company.....213 627-9300
550 S Hope St Ste 2700 Los Angeles (90071) ***(G-26222)***
Leo A Daly Company.....213 533-8855
550 S Hope St Ste 2700 Los Angeles (90071) ***(G-26223)***
Leo A Daly Company.....916 564-3259
2150 River Plaza Dr Sacramento (95833) ***(G-26224)***
Leo Chesney Fccf, Live Oak *Also called Geo Group Inc* ***(G-27788)***
Leo Daly Company, Los Angeles *Also called Leo A Daly Company* ***(G-26222)***
Leo J Ryan Child Care Ctr, South San Francisco *Also called Peninsula Family Service* ***(G-24130)***
Leon Chien Corp.....626 964-8302
17843 Colima Rd City of Industry (91748) ***(G-9869)***
Leonard Anthony Valenti Inc.....408 848-9688
9110 Marcella Ave Gilroy (95020) ***(G-905)***
Leonard Chaidez Inc.....714 279-8173
2298 N Batavia St Orange (92865) ***(G-994)***
Leonard Chaidez Tree Service, Orange *Also called Leonard Chaidez Inc* ***(G-994)***
Leonards Carpet Service Inc.....858 453-9525
6767 Nancy Ridge Dr San Diego (92121) ***(G-3291)***
Lereta LLC (PA).....626 543-1765
1123 Park View Dr Covina (91724) ***(G-10025)***
Leroy Durbin.....562 531-2001
14620 Lakewood Blvd Bellflower (90706) ***(G-11633)***
Leroy Haynes Center, La Verne *Also called Haynes Family Programs Inc* ***(G-24685)***
Les Kelley Family Health Ctr.....310 319-4700
1920 Colorado Ave Santa Monica (90404) ***(G-19706)***
Lesbro Company, Long Beach *Also called Ventura Transfer Company* ***(G-4299)***
Lesconcierges Inc (PA).....415 905-6088
200 Pine St Fl 2 San Francisco (94104) ***(G-14899)***
Lescure Company Inc.....925 283-2528
3667 Mt Diablo Blvd Lafayette (94549) ***(G-2280)***
Lesley Foundation.....650 726-4888
701 Arnold Way Bldg A Half Moon Bay (94019) ***(G-27974)***
Level 10 Construction LP.....408 747-5000
1050 Entp Way Ste 250 Sunnyvale (94089) ***(G-1601)***
Level 3 Communications Inc.....510 887-8920
23965 Connecticut St Hayward (94545) ***(G-6080)***
Level 9 Security Services.....562 949-7180
9020 Slauson Ave Ste 206 Pico Rivera (90660) ***(G-16723)***
Level Four Business MGT LLC.....310 914-1600
11812 San Vicente Blvd # 400 Los Angeles (90049) ***(G-27975)***
Level Studios Inc (HQ).....805 781-0546
4800 Morabito Pl San Luis Obispo (93401) ***(G-27508)***
Levin and Simes.....415 426-3000
353 Sacramento St Fl 20 San Francisco (94111) ***(G-23384)***
Levin-Richmond Terminal Corp.....510 232-4422
402 Wright Ave Richmond (94804) ***(G-4748)***
Levinson Law Group, Carlsbad *Also called Gordon R Levinson A Prof Corp* ***(G-23280)***
Levity Entertainment Group LLC.....310 417-4861
6701 Center Dr W Fl 11 Los Angeles (90045) ***(G-27509)***
Levy Cncessions At Staples Ctr, Los Angeles *Also called Levy Prmium Fdsrvice Ltd Prtnr* ***(G-1448)***
Levy Prmium Fdsrvice Ltd Prtnr.....213 742-7867
1111 S Figueroa St Los Angeles (90015) ***(G-1448)***
Lewis & Taylor LLC.....415 781-3496
440 Bryant St San Francisco (94107) ***(G-14338)***
Lewis & Taylor Bldg Svc Contrs, San Francisco *Also called Lewis & Taylor LLC* ***(G-14338)***
Lewis Brsbois Bsgard Smith LLP.....213 250-1800
633 W 5th St Ste 4000 Los Angeles (90071) ***(G-23385)***
Lewis Brsbois Bsgard Smith LLP.....951 252-6150
28765 Single Oak Dr Ste 1 Temecula (92590) ***(G-23386)***
Lewis Brsbois Bsgard Smith LLP (PA).....213 250-1800
633 W 5th St Ste 4000 Los Angeles (90071) ***(G-23387)***
Lewis Brsbois Bsgard Smith LLP.....619 233-1006
701 B St Ste 1900 San Diego (92101) ***(G-23388)***
Lewis Brsbois Bsgard Smith LLP.....714 545-6015
650 Town Center Dr # 1400 Costa Mesa (92626) ***(G-23389)***
Lewis Brsbois Bsgard Smith LLP.....415 362-2580
333 Bush St San Francisco (94104) ***(G-23390)***
Lewis Brsbois Bsgard Smith LLP.....909 387-1130
650 E Hospitality Ln # 600 San Bernardino (92408) ***(G-23391)***
Lewis Companies (PA).....909 985-0971
1156 N Mountain Ave Upland (91786) ***(G-1377)***
Lewis Family Playhouse.....909 477-2775
12505 Cultural Center Dr Rancho Cucamonga (91739) ***(G-25549)***
Lewis Marenstein Wicke Sherwin.....818 703-6000
20750 Ventura Blvd # 400 Woodland Hills (91364) ***(G-23392)***
Lewis P C Jackson.....415 394-9400
50 California St Fl 9 San Francisco (94111) ***(G-23393)***
Lewis P C Jackson.....213 689-0404
725 S Figueroa St # 2500 Los Angeles (90017) ***(G-23394)***
Lewis PR Inc (PA).....415 432-2400
575 Market St Ste 1200 San Francisco (94105) ***(G-27755)***
Lewis-Goetz and Company Inc.....916 366-9340
10182 Croydon Way Sacramento (95827) ***(G-7938)***
Lexani Wheel Corporation.....951 808-4220
2380 Railroad St Ste 101 Corona (92880) ***(G-6746)***
Lexington Group International (PA).....310 385-1071
9200 W Sunset Blvd # 700 West Hollywood (90069) ***(G-20722)***
Lexington Scenery & Props Inc.....818 768-5768
12800 Rangoon St Arleta (91331) ***(G-3064)***
Lexisnexis, Los Angeles *Also called Relx Inc* ***(G-16256)***
Lexisnexis Courtlink Inc.....425 974-5000
2101 K St Sacramento (95816) ***(G-25143)***
Lexmar Distribution Inc.....909 620-7001
200 Erie St Pomona (91768) ***(G-4358)***
Lexxiom Inc.....909 481-2536
7945 Cartilla Ave A Rancho Cucamonga (91730) ***(G-27114)***
Lg Display America Inc.....760 692-0900
2791 Loker Ave W Carlsbad (92010) ***(G-7596)***
Lg Display America Inc (HQ).....408 350-0190
2540 N 1st St Ste 400 San Jose (95131) ***(G-7597)***
Lg Elctrnics Mbilecomm USA Inc (HQ).....858 635-5300
10225 Willow Creek Rd San Diego (92131) ***(G-7598)***
Lg Infocomm U.S.A., San Diego *Also called Lg Elctrnics Mbilecomm USA Inc* ***(G-7598)***
Lge Electrical Sales Inc.....408 379-8568
7866 Convoy Ct San Diego (92111) ***(G-7450)***
Lgh Digital Media Inc.....323 469-3986
6520 W Sunset Blvd Los Angeles (90028) ***(G-18276)***
Lh Indian Wells Operating LLC.....760 341-2200
4500 Indian Wells Ln Indian Wells (92210) ***(G-12916)***
Lh Universal Operating LLC.....818 980-1212
333 Unversal Hollywood Dr Universal City (91608) ***(G-12917)***
Lho Santa Cruz One Lesse Inc.....831 475-5600
1 Chaminade Ln Santa Cruz (95065) ***(G-12918)***
Lhoberge Lessee Inc.....858 259-1515
1540 Camino Del Mar Del Mar (92014) ***(G-12919)***
Liberman Broadcasting Inc (PA).....818 729-5300
1845 W Empire Ave Burbank (91504) ***(G-5806)***
Liberty Ambulance LLC.....562 741-6230
9441 Washburn Rd Downey (90242) ***(G-3814)***
Liberty American Mortgage Corp (PA).....916 780-3000
193 Blue Ravine Rd # 240 Folsom (95630) ***(G-9933)***
Liberty Dental Plan Cal Inc.....949 223-0007
340 Commerce Ste 100 Irvine (92602) ***(G-10355)***
Liberty Energy, South Lake Tahoe *Also called Algonquin Power and Utilities* ***(G-2514)***
Liberty Energy, South Lake Tahoe *Also called Liberty Utlties Clpeco Elc LLC* ***(G-6145)***
Liberty Hardware Mfg Corp.....909 605-2300
5555 Jurupa St Ontario (91761) ***(G-7690)***
Liberty Healthcare of Oklahoma.....408 532-7677
4463 San Felipe Rd Ofc San Jose (95135) ***(G-20723)***
Liberty Landscaping Inc.....951 683-2999
5212 El Rivino Rd Riverside (92509) ***(G-906)***
Liberty Mutual Insurance Co.....310 316-9428
222 N Sepulveda Blvd # 2300 El Segundo (90245) ***(G-10432)***
Liberty Mutual Insurance Co.....415 957-1175
101 Mission St Ste 740 San Francisco (94105) ***(G-10433)***
Liberty Mutual Insurance Co.....916 294-9518
13405 Folsom Blvd Ste 200 Folsom (95630) ***(G-10434)***
Liberty Mutual Insurance Co.....909 476-6688
3633 Inland Empire Blvd # 500 Ontario (91764) ***(G-10435)***
Liberty Mutual Insurance Co.....714 937-1400
790 The City Dr S Ste 200 Orange (92868) ***(G-10436)***
Liberty Mutual Insurance Co.....559 435-2144
7600 N Palm Ave Ste 202 Fresno (93711) ***(G-10437)***
Liberty Mutual Insurance Co.....916 564-1792
1750 Howe Ave Ste 450 Sacramento (95825) ***(G-10438)***
Liberty Packing Company LLC (PA).....209 826-7100
724 Main St Woodland (95695) ***(G-8746)***
Liberty Station Hhg Hotel LP.....619 221-1900
2592 Laning Rd San Diego (92106) ***(G-12920)***
Liberty Station Hhg Hotel LP.....619 222-0500
2576 Laning Rd San Diego (92106) ***(G-12921)***
Liberty Utilities Pk Wtr Corp (HQ).....562 923-0711
9750 Washburn Rd Downey (90241) ***(G-6363)***
Liberty Utlties Clpeco Elc LLC.....530 543-5288
933 Eloise Ave South Lake Tahoe (96150) ***(G-6145)***
Libsource LLC.....323 852-1083
10390 Santa Monica Blvd Los Angeles (90025) ***(G-27115)***
Licensale Inc.....604 681-6888
900 Bush St Apt 205 San Francisco (94109) ***(G-12219)***
Lieberman RES Worldwide Inc (PA).....310 553-7721
1900 Ave Of The Sts 160 Ste 1600 Los Angeles (90067) ***(G-26683)***
Lieff Cabraser Heimann & (PA).....415 788-0245
275 Battery St Fl 29 San Francisco (94111) ***(G-23395)***
Life Alert Emergency Response (PA).....800 247-0000
16027 Ventura Blvd # 400 Encino (91436) ***(G-16899)***
Life Care Center of Bellflower, Bellflower *Also called Life Care Centers America Inc* ***(G-20730)***
Life Care Center of La Habra, La Habra *Also called Life Care Centers America Inc* ***(G-20724)***
Life Care Center of Norwalk, Norwalk *Also called Life Care Centers America Inc* ***(G-20731)***
Life Care Center San Gabriel, San Gabriel *Also called Life Care Centers of America* ***(G-20732)***
Life Care Centers America Inc.....562 690-0852
1233 W La Habra Blvd La Habra (90631) ***(G-20724)***
Life Care Centers America Inc.....760 724-8222
304 N Melrose Dr Vista (92083) ***(G-21289)***
Life Care Centers America Inc.....562 947-8691
12200 La Mirada Blvd La Mirada (90638) ***(G-20725)***
Life Care Centers America Inc.....562 943-7156
11926 La Mirada Blvd La Mirada (90638) ***(G-20726)***
Life Care Centers America Inc.....760 741-6109
1980 Felicita Rd Escondido (92025) ***(G-20727)***
Life Care Centers America Inc.....949 380-9380
25652 Old Trabuco Rd Lake Forest (92630) ***(G-20728)***

ALPHABETIC

Life Care Centers America Inc ... 562 943-7156
  11926 La Mirada Blvd La Mirada (90638) *(G-20729)*
Life Care Centers America Inc ... 562 867-1761
  16910 Woodruff Ave Bellflower (90706) *(G-20730)*
Life Care Centers America Inc ... 562 921-6624
  12350 Rosecrans Ave Norwalk (90650) *(G-20731)*
Life Care Centers of America ... 626 289-5365
  909 W Santa Anita Ave San Gabriel (91776) *(G-20732)*
Life Care Centers of Escondido, Escondido Also called Life Care Centers America Inc *(G-20727)*
Life Cycle Engineering Inc ... 619 785-5990
  2535 Camino Del Rio S # 250 San Diego (92108) *(G-14339)*
Life Enchancing Therapies, Upland Also called Inland Empire Therapy Provider *(G-20321)*
Life Gnerations Healthcare LLC ... 619 449-5555
  8778 Cuyamaca St Santee (92071) *(G-21290)*
Life Gnerations Healthcare LLC ... 619 460-2330
  7800 Parkway Dr La Mesa (91942) *(G-20733)*
Life Ivf Center, Irvine Also called Frank D Yelian MD PC *(G-19527)*
Life Steps Foundation Inc ... 562 436-0751
  500 E 4th St Long Beach (90802) *(G-24065)*
Lifecare Assurance Company, Woodland Hills Also called 21st Century Lf & Hlth Co Inc *(G-10230)*
Lifecare Assurance Company ... 818 887-4436
  21600 Oxnard St Fl 16 Woodland Hills (91367) *(G-10244)*
Lifecare Health, Cerritos Also called Healthview Inc *(G-24689)*
Lifecare Solutions, Pasadena Also called Founders Healthcare LLC *(G-22440)*
Lifecare Systems Inc ... 310 540-7676
  4101 Torrance Blvd Torrance (90503) *(G-20734)*
Lifeline Ambulance, Montebello Also called Eastwestproto Inc *(G-3786)*
Lifeline Medical Transport, Ventura Also called Ojai Ambulance Inc *(G-3823)*
Lifelong Learning ADM Corp ... 661 272-1225
  177 Holston Dr Lancaster (93535) *(G-27116)*
Lifelong Medical Care ... 510 981-4100
  3260 Sacramento St Berkeley (94702) *(G-19707)*
Lifelong Medical Care (PA) ... 510 704-6010
  2344 6th St Berkeley (94710) *(G-19708)*
Lifemoves (PA) ... 650 685-5880
  181 Constitution Dr Menlo Park (94025) *(G-24066)*
Lifeproof, San Diego Also called Treefrog Developments Inc *(G-8144)*
Liferay Inc (PA) ... 877 543-3729
  1400 Montefino Ave # 100 Diamond Bar (91765) *(G-15985)*
Lifespan Care Management Agcy, Santa Cruz Also called Lifespan Inc *(G-24938)*
Lifespan Inc ... 831 469-4900
  600 Frederick St Santa Cruz (95062) *(G-24938)*
Lifestream, San Bernardino Also called Blood Bank of San Bernardino A *(G-22897)*
Lifestreet Corporation ... 650 508-2220
  981 Industrial Rd Ste F San Carlos (94070) *(G-9276)*
Lifestreet Media, San Carlos Also called Lifestreet Corporation *(G-9276)*
Lifestyle Solutions Inc (PA) ... 510 249-9301
  5555 Auto Mall Pkwy Fremont (94538) *(G-6823)*
Lifestyles Senior Housing Man ... 916 714-3755
  9325 E Stockton Blvd Elk Grove (95624) *(G-24067)*
Lifetime Entrmt Svcs LLC ... 310 556-7500
  2049 Century Park E # 840 Los Angeles (90067) *(G-5894)*
Lifetime TV Network, Los Angeles Also called Lifetime Entrmt Svcs LLC *(G-5894)*
Lifetouch ... 916 535-7733
  7916 Alta Sunrise Ln Citrus Heights (95610) *(G-13660)*
Lifetouch Nat Schl Studios Inc ... 530 345-3993
  2860 Fair St Chico (95928) *(G-13661)*
Lifetouch Nat Schl Studios Inc ... 510 293-1818
  30351 Huntwood Ave Hayward (94544) *(G-13662)*
Lifetouch Nat Schl Studios Inc ... 909 985-3532
  2122 Porter Field Way Upland (91786) *(G-13663)*
Lifetouch Portrait Studios Inc ... 858 693-9197
  9770 Carroll Centre Rd C San Diego (92126) *(G-13664)*
Liffey Thames Group LLC ... 415 392-2900
  465 California St Fl 14 San Francisco (94104) *(G-16423)*
Liftech Elevator Services Inc ... 562 997-3639
  1901 E 29th St Signal Hill (90755) *(G-28141)*
Lifted Research Group Inc (PA) ... 949 581-1144
  7 Holland Irvine (92618) *(G-8350)*
Light & Sound Design Inc ... 818 260-6260
  9111 Sunland Blvd Sun Valley (91352) *(G-18406)*
Light House Group, The, Pacific Palisades Also called Lighthouse Capital Funding *(G-12322)*
Lightbeam Power Company Gridle ... 800 696-7114
  100 Century Center Ct # 100 San Jose (95112) *(G-1960)*
Lightbeam Pwr Gridley Main LLC ... 800 696-7114
  100 Century Center Ct # 100 San Jose (95112) *(G-1961)*
Lightbend Inc ... 877 989-7372
  625 Market St Ste 1000 San Francisco (94105) *(G-15274)*
Lightbrdge Hspice Plltive Care, San Diego Also called Lightbridge Hospice LLC *(G-22152)*
Lightbridge Hospice LLC ... 858 458-2992
  6155 Cornerstone Ct E San Diego (92121) *(G-22152)*
Lightcrest LLC ... 888 320-8495
  12424 Wilshire Blvd Ste 9 Los Angeles (90025) *(G-15986)*
Lighthouse Capital Funding ... 310 230-8335
  15332 Antioch St Ste 540 Pacific Palisades (90272) *(G-12322)*
Lighthouse Healthcare Ctr LLC ... 323 564-4461
  2222 Santa Ana Blvd Los Angeles (90059) *(G-20735)*
Lighting Department, Burbank Also called Walt Disney Company *(G-5926)*
Lighting DOT Com.com, Commerce Also called American De Rosa Lamparts LLC *(G-7412)*
Lightwaves 2020 Inc ... 408 503-8888
  1323 Great Mall Dr Milpitas (95035) *(G-26561)*
Lilien LLC (HQ) ... 415 389-7500
  17 E Sir Francis Dr # 110 Larkspur (94939) *(G-15987)*

Lily Holdings LLC ... 559 222-4807
  3510 E Shields Ave Fresno (93726) *(G-20736)*
Limbach Company LP ... 714 653-7000
  12442 Knott St Garden Grove (92841) *(G-2281)*
Liminex Inc ... 310 963-3031
  200 N Sepulveda Blvd Ste Hermosa Beach (90254) *(G-15275)*
Limited Editions, Chatsworth Also called Atlantic Optical Co Inc *(G-7330)*
Limoneira Company (PA) ... 805 525-5541
  1141 Cummings Rd Ofc Santa Paula (93060) *(G-556)*
Lincoln Child Center ... 510 531-3111
  1266 14th St Oakland (94607) *(G-25550)*
Lincoln Child Center Inc (PA) ... 510 273-4700
  1266 14th St Oakland (94607) *(G-22768)*
Lincoln Child Center Inc ... 925 521-1270
  51 Marina Blvd Pittsburg (94565) *(G-24711)*
Lincoln Glen Manor ... 408 267-1492
  2671 Plummer Ave Ste A San Jose (95125) *(G-21291)*
LINCOLN GLEN SKILLED NURSING, San Jose Also called Lincoln Glen Manor *(G-21291)*
Lincoln Hills Golf Club ... 916 543-9200
  1005 Sun City Ln Lincoln (95648) *(G-18755)*
Lincoln Mariners Assoc Ltd ... 619 225-1473
  4392 W Point Loma Blvd San Diego (92107) *(G-11157)*
Lincoln Medical Offices, Lincoln Also called Kaiser Foundation Hospitals *(G-19623)*
Lincoln Plaza Hotel Inc ... 626 571-8818
  123 S Lincoln Ave Monterey Park (91755) *(G-12922)*
Lincoln Products, City of Industry Also called Ferguson Enterprises Inc *(G-7712)*
Lincoln School Bus Trnsp ... 209 953-8596
  6749 Harrisburg Pl Stockton (95207) *(G-3881)*
Lincoln Television Inc ... 415 468-2626
  100 Valley Dr Brisbane (94005) *(G-5895)*
Lincoln Trainin ... 626 442-0621
  2643 Loma Ave South El Monte (91733) *(G-24358)*
Lincoln Witt Mercury ... 760 233-3333
  728 N Escondido Blvd Escondido (92025) *(G-17804)*
Linda Beach Coop Pre-School ... 510 547-4432
  400 Highland Ave Piedmont (94611) *(G-24475)*
Linda Loma Univ Hlth Care (HQ) ... 909 558-2806
  11370 Anderson St # 3900 Loma Linda (92350) *(G-21706)*
Linda Loma Univ Hlth Care ... 909 558-2851
  11370 Anderson St # 2100 Loma Linda (92354) *(G-19709)*
Linda Loma Univ Hlth Care (PA) ... 909 558-4985
  11175 Campus St Loma Linda (92350) *(G-19710)*
Linda Loma Univ Hlth Care ... 909 558-2840
  11370 Anderson St # 3950 Loma Linda (92350) *(G-19711)*
Linda Mar Care Center, Pacifica Also called Pacifica Linda Mar Inc *(G-20835)*
Linda Placentia-Yorba ... 714 985-8775
  1301 E Orangethorpe Ave Placentia (92870) *(G-4587)*
Linda Terra Farms (PA) ... 559 867-3473
  5494 W Mount Whitney Ave Riverdale (93656) *(G-415)*
Linda Valley Care Center, Loma Linda Also called Chancellor Hlth Care Cal I Inc *(G-21183)*
LINDA VISTA HEALTH CARE CENTER, San Diego Also called San Diego Family Care *(G-19939)*
Linda Vista Manor Inc ... 858 278-8121
  7675 Family Cir San Diego (92111) *(G-20737)*
Linda Yorba Water District (PA) ... 714 701-3000
  1717 E Miraloma Ave Placentia (92870) *(G-6364)*
Lindamood-Bell Lrng Processes (PA) ... 805 541-3836
  406 Higuera St Ste 120 San Luis Obispo (93401) *(G-22769)*
Lindbergh Parking Inc ... 619 291-1508
  3705 N Harbor Dr San Diego (92101) *(G-17728)*
Lindburgh Child Development, Costa Mesa Also called Orange Cnty Sprntndent Schools *(G-24493)*
Linden Center ... 213 251-8226
  812 N Fairfax Ave Los Angeles (90046) *(G-22080)*
LINDEN CENTER BUSINESS OFC, Los Angeles Also called Linden Center *(G-22080)*
Linden Crest Surgery Center ... 310 601-3900
  9735 Wilshire Blvd # 100 Beverly Hills (90212) *(G-19712)*
Linden Lab, San Francisco Also called Linden Research Inc *(G-15276)*
Linden Nut, Stockton Also called Pearl Crop Inc *(G-573)*
Linden Optometry A Prof Corp ... 323 681-5678
  477 E Colorado Blvd Pasadena (91101) *(G-20300)*
Linden Research Inc (PA) ... 415 243-9000
  945 Battery St San Francisco (94111) *(G-15276)*
Lindhurst Dental Clinic ... 530 743-4614
  4941 Olivehurst Ave Olivehurst (95961) *(G-20263)*
Lindhurst Family Health Center, Olivehurst Also called Ampla Health *(G-19343)*
Lindo Hanna & Abbott, Chico Also called Interwest Insurance Svcs Inc *(G-10749)*
Lindquist LLP (PA) ... 925 277-9100
  5000 Executive Pkwy # 400 San Ramon (94583) *(G-26395)*
Lindsay Fruit Company LLC ... 559 562-1327
  247 N Mount Vernon Ave Lindsay (93247) *(G-17295)*
Lindsay Transportation ... 707 374-6800
  180 River Rd Rio Vista (94571) *(G-7855)*
Lindsay Trnsp Solutions, Rio Vista Also called Lindsay Transportation *(G-7855)*
Lindsay Wildlife Museum ... 925 935-1978
  1931 1st Ave Walnut Creek (94597) *(G-25024)*
Line Hotel The, Los Angeles Also called Sydell Hotels LLC *(G-13333)*
Line Pipe International, Santa Fe Springs Also called Kelly Pipe Co LLC *(G-7379)*
Lineage Logistics LLC (HQ) ... 800 678-7271
  17911 Von Karman Ave # 400 Irvine (92614) *(G-4497)*
Lineage Logistics LLC ... 951 360-7970
  3251 De Forest Cir Ste C Mira Loma (91752) *(G-4498)*
Lineage Logistics Holdings LLC (PA) ... 800 678-7271
  17911 Von Karman Ave # 400 Irvine (92614) *(G-4499)*
Lineage Logistics Holdings LLC ... 909 433-3100
  17911 Von Karman Ave # 400 Irvine (92614) *(G-4359)*
Lineage Logistics Holdings LLC ... 909 874-1200
  2551 S Lilac Ave Bloomington (92316) *(G-4360)*

Linear Industries Ltd (PA)...626 303-1130
1850 Enterprise Way Monrovia (91016) ***(G-7939)***
Liner LLP (PA)...310 500-3500
1100 Glendon Ave Fl 14 Los Angeles (90024) ***(G-23396)***
Ling's, South El Monte *Also called Out of Shell LLC* ***(G-1456)***
Ling-Su Chinn Inc...310 396-1102
1653 12th St Santa Monica (90404) ***(G-8396)***
Link Canada Distribution, Davis *Also called HFS North America LLC* ***(G-27944)***
Linkedin Corporation (PA)...650 687-3600
2029 Stierlin Ct Ste 200 Mountain View (94043) ***(G-16249)***
Linksys LLC...310 751-5100
12045 Waterfront Dr Playa Vista (90094) ***(G-7599)***
Linksys LLC (HQ)...949 270-8500
131 Theory Irvine (92617) ***(G-7600)***
Linkus Enterprises LLC...559 256-6600
5595 W San Madele Ave Fresno (93722) ***(G-1962)***
Linkus Enterprises LLC (PA)...530 229-9197
18631 Lloyd Ln Anderson (96007) ***(G-1963)***
Linnco LLC...661 616-3900
5201 Truxtun Ave Bakersfield (93309) ***(G-1046)***
Linquest Corporation (PA)...323 924-1600
5140 W Goldleaf Cir # 400 Los Angeles (90056) ***(G-25937)***
Linwood Grdns Convalescent Ctr, Visalia *Also called Far West Inc* ***(G-20566)***
Lion Brothers Farms-Newstone, Madera *Also called Lion Raisins Inc* ***(G-380)***
Lion Creek Crossing V, Oakland *Also called Lion Creek Senior Housing Part* ***(G-11634)***
Lion Creek Senior Housing Part...510 878-9120
6710 Lion Way Oakland (94621) ***(G-11634)***
Lion Raisins Inc...559 662-8686
12555 Road 9 Madera (93637) ***(G-380)***
Lion-Vallen Ltd Partnership...760 385-4885
22 Area Aven A Bldg 2234 Camp Pendleton (92055) ***(G-27117)***
Lionakis...949 955-1919
20371 Irvine Ave Ste 120 Newport Beach (92660) ***(G-25938)***
Lionakis (PA)...916 558-1901
1919 19th St Sacramento (95811) ***(G-25939)***
Lions Club House...530 661-3104
417 Lincoln Ave Woodland (95695) ***(G-24068)***
Lions Gate Entertainment Inc (HQ)...310 449-9200
2700 Colorado Ave Ste 200 Santa Monica (90404) ***(G-18100)***
Lions Gate Films Inc...310 449-9200
2700 Colorado Ave Ste 200 Santa Monica (90404) ***(G-18101)***
Lionsgate Ht & Conference Ctr...916 643-6222
3410 Westover St McClellan (95652) ***(G-12923)***
Lionsgate Productions...310 255-3937
2700 Colorado Ave Ste 200 Santa Monica (90404) ***(G-18277)***
Lipman Insur Admnistrators Inc (PA)...510 796-4676
39420 Liberty St Ste 260 Fremont (94538) ***(G-10554)***
Liquid Investments Inc (PA)...858 509-8510
3840 Via De La Valle # 300 Del Mar (92014) ***(G-9069)***
Liquidate Direct LLC...800 750-7617
2929 Washington Blvd Fl 2 Marina Del Rey (90292) ***(G-15988)***
Liquidity Services Inc...714 738-6446
741 E Ball Rd Ste 200 Anaheim (92805) ***(G-8351)***
Lisi Inc (PA)...650 348-4131
1600 W Hillsdale Blvd # 100 San Mateo (94402) ***(G-10764)***
Lisi Inc...714 460-5153
2677 N Main St Ste 350 Santa Ana (92705) ***(G-10572)***
Lite Solar Corp...562 256-1249
3553 Atlantic Ave Long Beach (90807) ***(G-2282)***
Lite-On Inc (HQ)...408 946-4873
720 S Hillview Dr Milpitas (95035) ***(G-7601)***
Lite-On Sales and Dist Inc...510 687-1800
42000 Christy St Fremont (94538) ***(G-7155)***
Lite-On U S A, Milpitas *Also called Lite-On Inc* ***(G-7601)***
Litewave US LLC...888 399-6710
9107 Wilshire Blvd # 450 Beverly Hills (90210) ***(G-3547)***
Lithchem, Anaheim *Also called Retriev Technologies Inc* ***(G-6540)***
Lithia Motors Inc...209 956-1930
3077 E Hammer Ln Stockton (95212) ***(G-17805)***
Lithium Technologies Inc (PA)...510 653-6800
225 Bush St Fl 15 San Francisco (94104) ***(G-15733)***
Litigtion Rsrces of America-CA (PA)...818 878-9227
4232-1 Las Virgenes Rd Calabasas (91302) ***(G-17296)***
Little Citizens Schools Inc...323 732-1212
4256 S Western Ave Los Angeles (90062) ***(G-24476)***
Little Co Mary Hosp Pavilion, Torrance *Also called Providence Health System* ***(G-12198)***
Little Co Mary- San Pedro Hosp, San Pedro *Also called San Pedro Peninsula Hospital* ***(G-21853)***
Little Company Mary Hospital...310 540-7676
4101 Torrance Blvd Torrance (90503) ***(G-21707)***
Little Company Mary Svc Area, Torrance *Also called Providence Little Co of Mary* ***(G-27181)***
Little Company of Mary, Torrance *Also called Providence Health & Services* ***(G-23030)***
Little Giant Bldg Maint Inc...415 508-0282
15 Brooks Pl Pacifica (94044) ***(G-14340)***
Little Mary Amblatory Care Ctr, Torrance *Also called Del AMO Diagnostic Center* ***(G-22719)***
Little Peoples...951 849-1959
39514 Brookside Ave Cherry Valley (92223) ***(G-24712)***
Little Peoples World Inc...951 845-8367
39514 Brookside Ave Cherry Valley (92223) ***(G-24713)***
Little River Inn Inc...707 937-5942
7901 N Highway 1 Little River (95456) ***(G-12924)***
Little River Inn and Golf Crse, Little River *Also called Little River Inn Inc* ***(G-12924)***
Little Sister's Truck Wash, Fallbrook *Also called Little Sisters Truck Wash Inc* ***(G-17853)***
Little Sisters of Poor...415 751-6510
300 Lake St San Francisco (94118) ***(G-24714)***
Little Sisters The Poor of La...310 548-0625
2100 S Western Ave San Pedro (90732) ***(G-20738)***
Little Sisters Truck Wash Inc...760 343-3448
72189 Varner Rd Thousand Palms (92276) ***(G-17849)***
Little Sisters Truck Wash Inc...760 947-4448
8899 Three Flags Ave Oak Hills (92344) ***(G-17850)***
Little Sisters Truck Wash Inc...760 253-2277
2960 Lenwood Rd Barstow (92311) ***(G-17851)***
Little Sisters Truck Wash Inc...909 549-1862
14264 Valley Blvd Fontana (92335) ***(G-17852)***
Little Sisters Truck Wash Inc (PA)...760 731-3170
25 Rolling View Ln Fallbrook (92028) ***(G-17853)***
Littler Mendelson PC (PA)...415 433-1940
333 Bush St Fl 34 San Francisco (94104) ***(G-23397)***
Liva Distributors Inc (HQ)...619 423-9997
3173 Iris Ave San Diego (92173) ***(G-8492)***
Live International, Santa Monica *Also called Artisan Pictures Inc* ***(G-8105)***
Live Love Laugh Global...310 362-1783
8306 Wilshire Blvd # 350 Beverly Hills (90211) ***(G-25551)***
Live Media LLC...951 279-8877
1580 Magnolia Ave Corona (92879) ***(G-18477)***
Live Nation Entertainment Inc...323 468-1160
6255 W Sunset Blvd Fl 16 Los Angeles (90028) ***(G-17297)***
Live Nation Entertainment Inc...213 639-6178
7060 Hollywood Blvd Ste 2 Los Angeles (90028) ***(G-18407)***
Live Nation Entertainment Inc...323 462-4785
151 El Camino Dr Fl 3 Beverly Hills (90212) ***(G-17298)***
Live Nation Entertainment Inc...323 464-1330
7083 Hollywood Blvd Fl 2 Los Angeles (90028) ***(G-18478)***
Live Nation Entertainment Inc (PA)...310 867-7000
9348 Civic Center Dr Lbby Beverly Hills (90210) ***(G-18408)***
Live Nation Merchandise Inc (HQ)...415 247-7400
450 Mission St Ste 300 San Francisco (94105) ***(G-9277)***
Live Nation Worldwide Inc...415 371-5500
260 5th St San Francisco (94103) ***(G-18409)***
Live Nation Worldwide Inc...323 966-5066
6500 Wilshire Blvd # 200 Los Angeles (90048) ***(G-18410)***
Live Nation Worldwide Inc...949 860-2070
8808 Irvine Center Dr Irvine (92618) ***(G-18411)***
Live Oak Rehab, San Gabriel *Also called Longwood Management Corp* ***(G-21300)***
Live Pos, La Jolla *Also called CSS Holdings Inc* ***(G-15116)***
Livefyre Inc (PA)...415 800-0900
360 3rd St Ste 700 San Francisco (94107) ***(G-15277)***
Liveoffice LLC...877 253-2793
900 Corporate Pointe Culver City (90230) ***(G-15734)***
Liveops Inc (PA)...650 453-2700
555 Twin Dolphin Dr # 400 Redwood City (94065) ***(G-14900)***
Liver and Pancreatic Center, Torrance *Also called Providence Health & Services* ***(G-19888)***
Livermore Area Rcration Pk Dst...925 373-5700
71 Trevarno Rd Livermore (94551) ***(G-19237)***
Livermore Area Rcration Pk Dst (PA)...925 373-5700
4444 East Ave Livermore (94550) ***(G-19238)***
Livermore Casino, Livermore *Also called Sidjon Corporation* ***(G-13253)***
Livermore Snior Lving Assoc LP...925 371-2300
900 E Stanley Blvd # 383 Livermore (94550) ***(G-12072)***
Livermore Travel, Livermore *Also called Livermore World Travel Inc* ***(G-4994)***
Livermore VA Medical Center, Livermore *Also called Veterans Health Administration* ***(G-20214)***
Livermore Valley Tennis Club...925 443-7700
2000 Arroyo Rd Livermore (94550) ***(G-18655)***
Livermore World Travel Inc...925 373-2400
1453 1st St Ste A Livermore (94550) ***(G-4994)***
Livescribe Inc...510 777-0071
1 Twin Dolphin Dr Redwood City (94065) ***(G-7156)***
Livetime Software Inc...415 905-4009
276 Avocado St Apt C102 Costa Mesa (92627) ***(G-15735)***
Livevox Inc (PA)...415 671-6000
655 Montgomery St # 1190 San Francisco (94111) ***(G-27976)***
Liveworld Inc (PA)...408 564-6286
4340 Stevens Creek Blvd San Jose (95129) ***(G-5648)***
Livhome Inc (PA)...800 807-5854
5670 Wilshire Blvd # 500 Los Angeles (90036) ***(G-24069)***
Living Centers, Vallejo *Also called Empres Financial Services LLC* ***(G-20535)***
Living Colors Inc...818 893-5068
16026 Rayen St North Hills (91343) ***(G-2463)***
Living Desert...760 346-5694
47900 Portola Ave Palm Desert (92260) ***(G-25064)***
Living Doll, Los Angeles *Also called Ldla Clothing LLC* ***(G-8394)***
Living Opportunities MGT Co...323 589-5956
6900 Seville Ave Huntington Park (90255) ***(G-11158)***
Livingston Community Health...209 394-7913
1140 Main St Livingston (95334) ***(G-19713)***
Livingston Health Center, Livingston *Also called Livingston Community Health* ***(G-19713)***
Livingston Mem Vna Hlth Corp...805 642-0239
1996 Eastman Ave Ste 101 Ventura (93003) ***(G-27118)***
Livingston Mem Vst Nrs Associa, Ventura *Also called Livingston Mem Vna Hlth Corp* ***(G-27118)***
Livingston Ranch, Livingston *Also called E & J Gallo Winery* ***(G-697)***
Lizhang Enterprises Corp...714 734-6683
58 Paisley Pl Irvine (92620) ***(G-12073)***
Lj Distributors Inc...562 229-7660
12840 Leyva St Norwalk (90650) ***(G-8747)***
LJ Walch Co Inc...925 449-9252
6600 Preston Ave Livermore (94551) ***(G-7999)***
LJC Construction Inc...209 668-2700
712 W Harding Rd Turlock (95380) ***(G-3186)***
Ljg, Irvine *Also called La Jolla Group Inc* ***(G-17283)***
LL Frank Work Center, Los Angeles *Also called Abilityfirst* ***(G-23640)***
Llieche, Loma Linda *Also called Loma Linda - Inland Empire C* ***(G-21710)***

ALPHABETIC

Lloyd Pest Control Co 951 232-9687
19161 Newhall St North Palm Springs (92258) *(G-14187)*
Lloyd Pest Control Co 714 979-6021
566 E Dyer Rd Santa Ana (92707) *(G-14188)*
LLP Locke Lord 415 318-8800
44 Montgomery St Ste 4100 San Francisco (94104) *(G-23398)*
LLP Locke Lord 213 485-1500
300 S Grand Ave Ste 2600 Los Angeles (90071) *(G-23399)*
LLP Locke Lord 949 423-2100
660 Nwport Ctr Dr Ste 900 Newport Beach (92660) *(G-23400)*
LLP Locke Lord 310 860-8700
1901 Avenue Of The Stars Los Angeles (90067) *(G-23401)*
LLP Mayer Brown 650 331-2000
2 Palo Alto Sq Ste 300 Palo Alto (94306) *(G-23402)*
LLP Mayer Brown 213 229-9500
350 S Grand Ave Ste 2500 Los Angeles (90071) *(G-23403)*
LLP Moss Adams 916 503-8100
3100 Zinfandel Dr Ste 500 Rancho Cordova (95670) *(G-26396)*
LLP Moss Adams 818 577-1822
21700 Oxnard St Ste 300 Woodland Hills (91367) *(G-26397)*
LLP Moss Adams 209 955-6100
3121 W March Ln Ste 100 Stockton (95219) *(G-26398)*
LLP Moss Adams 415 956-1500
101 2nd St Ste 900 San Francisco (94105) *(G-26399)*
LLP Moss Adams 408 369-2400
635 Campbell Tech Pkwy # 100 Campbell (95008) *(G-26400)*
LLP Moss Adams 310 278-5850
10960 Wilshire Blvd # 1100 Los Angeles (90024) *(G-26401)*
LLP Moss Adams 858 627-1400
4747 Executive Dr # 1300 San Diego (92121) *(G-26402)*
LLP Moss Adams 949 221-4000
2040 Main St Ste 900 Irvine (92614) *(G-26403)*
LLP Robins Kaplan 310 552-0130
2049 Century Park E # 3400 Los Angeles (90067) *(G-23404)*
Llu Advntist Hlth Sciences Ctr 909 558-4386
101 E Redlands Blvd San Bernardino (92408) *(G-19714)*
Llu Center For Fertility, Loma Linda *Also called Linda Loma Univ Hlth Care (G-19711)*
LLUMC, Loma Linda *Also called Loma Linda University Med Ctr (G-21712)*
LMC Hollywood Highland 949 448-1600
95 Enterprise Ste 200 Aliso Viejo (92656) *(G-1602)*
LMC West Inc 209 869-0144
5300 Claus Rd Riverbank (95367) *(G-7856)*
LMD Intgrted Lgistics Svcs Inc 310 605-5100
3136 E Victoria St Compton (90221) *(G-4588)*
Lmno Cable Group, Encino *Also called Lmno Productions Inc (G-18102)*
Lmno Productions Inc 818 995-5555
15821 Ventura Blvd # 320 Encino (91436) *(G-18102)*
LMS Corporation 310 641-4222
300 Crprate Pinte Ste 301 Culver City (90230) *(G-17299)*
LMS Intellibound Inc 562 602-2217
14900 Garfield Ave Paramount (90723) *(G-4589)*
LN Curtis and Sons (PA) 510 839-5111
1800 Peralta St Oakland (94607) *(G-7970)*
Lo Bue Bros Inc 559 562-6367
713 E Hermosa St Lindsay (93247) *(G-557)*
Lo Bue Bros East, Lindsay *Also called Lo Bue Bros Inc (G-557)*
Loan Administration Netwrk Inc 949 752-5246
18952 Macarthur Blvd # 315 Irvine (92612) *(G-14697)*
Loan Depot Group, Woodland Hills *Also called Realty Alliance Inc (G-9947)*
Loandepotcom LLC (PA) 949 474-1322
26642 Towne Centre Dr Foothill Ranch (92610) *(G-9870)*
Loangeniecom Inc 949 788-6161
25 Technology Dr Ste B100 Irvine (92618) *(G-9934)*
Loanmart, Beverly Hills *Also called Colateral Lender Inc (G-9798)*
Lobel Financial Corporation (PA) 714 995-3333
1150 N Magnolia Ave Anaheim (92801) *(G-9756)*
Local 250 Health Care Wkrs Un, Oakland *Also called Health Care Workers Union (G-11000)*
Local 442, Santa Barbara *Also called International Alliance Thea (G-25173)*
Local Corporation (PA) 949 784-0800
7555 Irvine Center Dr Irvine (92618) *(G-13876)*
Local Initiative Health Author 213 694-1250
1055 W 7th St Fl 11 Los Angeles (90017) *(G-10356)*
Local Media of America LLC 858 888-7000
6160 Cornerstone Ct E # 150 San Diego (92121) *(G-5807)*
Local.com, Irvine *Also called Local Corporation (G-13876)*
Location Labs, Emeryville *Also called Waze Market Inc (G-15541)*
Locator Services Inc 619 229-6100
4616 Mission Gorge Pl San Diego (92120) *(G-16724)*
Lockheed Martin Astronautics, Lompoc *Also called Lockheed Martin Corporation (G-4924)*
Lockheed Martin Corporation 408 734-4980
2770 De La Cruz Blvd Santa Clara (95050) *(G-15989)*
Lockheed Martin Corporation 415 402-0406
275 Battery St Ste 750 San Francisco (94111) *(G-25940)*
Lockheed Martin Corporation 650 424-2000
3251 Hanover St Bldg 245 Palo Alto (94304) *(G-26562)*
Lockheed Martin Corporation 626 296-7977
505 W Woodbury Rd Altadena (91001) *(G-15278)*
Lockheed Martin Corporation 858 740-5100
10325 Meanley Dr San Diego (92131) *(G-15279)*
Lockheed Martin Corporation 831 425-6375
16020 Empire Grade Santa Cruz (95060) *(G-17300)*
Lockheed Martin Corporation 760 446-1700
1121 W Reeves Ave Ridgecrest (93555) *(G-25941)*
Lockheed Martin Corporation 303 971-4631
Bldg 8401 Lompoc (93437) *(G-4924)*
Lockheed Martin Government Ser 323 721-6979
500 N Via Val Verde Montebello (90640) *(G-16424)*
Lockheed Martin Naval, Ridgecrest *Also called Lockheed Martin Corporation (G-25941)*
Lockheed Martin Orincon 858 455-5530
10325 Meanley Dr San Diego (92131) *(G-15280)*
Lockheed Martin Orincon Corp (HQ) 858 455-5530
10325 Meanley Dr San Diego (92131) *(G-15281)*
Lockheed Martin Space Sys, Santa Cruz *Also called Lockheed Martin Corporation (G-17300)*
Lockton Companies Llc-Pacific 415 568-4000
2 Embarcadero Ctr # 1700 San Francisco (94111) *(G-10765)*
Lockton Companies Llc-Pacific (HQ) 213 689-0500
725 S Figueroa St Fl 35 Los Angeles (90017) *(G-10766)*
Lockton Companies Llc-Pacific 858 587-3100
4275 Executive Sq Ste 600 San Diego (92121) *(G-10767)*
Lockton Insurance Brokers, San Francisco *Also called Lockton Companies Llc-Pacific (G-10765)*
Lockton Insurance Brokers, Los Angeles *Also called Lockton Companies Llc-Pacific (G-10766)*
Lockton Insurance Brokers, San Diego *Also called Lockton Companies Llc-Pacific (G-10767)*
Loda Mem Hosp Occpational Hlth, Lodi *Also called Lodi Memorial Hosp Assn Inc (G-22994)*
Lodge At Tiburon, The, Belvedere Tiburon *Also called Tiburon Hotel LLC (G-13343)*
Lodge At Torrey Pines Partners 858 550-3908
998 W Mission Bay Dr San Diego (92109) *(G-12925)*
Lodge Inn and Health Center, Chico *Also called Terraces Retirement Community (G-24834)*
Lodgen Lacher Golditch Sard 818 783-0570
16530 Ventura Blvd # 305 Encino (91436) *(G-26404)*
Lodi Development Inc 209 367-7600
1420 S Mills Ave Ste A Lodi (95242) *(G-11979)*
Lodi Memorial Hosp Assn Inc 209 334-8520
1235 W Vine St Ste 22 Lodi (95240) *(G-22993)*
Lodi Memorial Hosp Assn Inc 209 339-7441
975 S Fairmont Ave Ste 8 Lodi (95240) *(G-22994)*
Lodi Memorial Hosp Assn Inc (PA) 209 334-3411
975 S Fairmont Ave Lodi (95240) *(G-21708)*
Lodi Memorial Hosp Assn Inc 209 339-7583
1200 W Vine St Lodi (95240) *(G-21709)*
Lodi Memorial Hosp Assn Inc 209 333-3100
800 S Lower Sacramento Rd Lodi (95242) *(G-19715)*
Lodi Unified School District 209 331-7181
1305 E Vine St Lodi (95240) *(G-14341)*
Lodi Unified School District 209 331-7169
820 S Cuff Ave Lodi (95240) *(G-3943)*
Loeb & Loeb LLP (PA) 310 282-2000
10100 Santa Monica Blvd # 2200 Los Angeles (90067) *(G-23405)*
Loews Coronado Bay Resort, Coronado *Also called 51st St & 8th Ave Corp (G-12365)*
Loews Corporation 619 424-4000
4000 Coronado Bay Rd Coronado (92118) *(G-23406)*
Loews Hollywood Hotel LLC 323 450-2235
1755 N Highland Ave Hollywood (90028) *(G-12926)*
Loews Regency San Francisco, San Francisco *Also called San Francisco Hotel Group LLC (G-13202)*
Loews Santa Monica Beach Hotel, Santa Monica *Also called Dtrs Santa Monica LLC (G-12602)*
Loewy Enterprises 323 726-3838
500 Burning Tree Rd Fullerton (92833) *(G-8748)*
Logicmonitor Inc 805 617-3884
12 E Carrillo St Santa Barbara (93101) *(G-16250)*
Logicor 949 260-2260
17752 Mitchell N Ste H Irvine (92614) *(G-15282)*
Logictier Inc 650 235-6600
7 41st Ave 76 San Mateo (94403) *(G-16425)*
Login Consulting Services Inc 310 607-9091
300 Continental Blvd # 530 El Segundo (90245) *(G-16426)*
Logistic Air Inc 925 465-0400
231 Market Pl Ste 203 San Ramon (94583) *(G-4883)*
Logistical Support LLC 818 341-3344
20409 Prairie St Chatsworth (91311) *(G-8000)*
Logistics Team, Walnut *Also called Amerifreight Inc (G-4522)*
Logistics Team, Walnut *Also called I3pl LLC (G-5103)*
Logitech Ice At San Jose 408 279-6000
1500 S 10th St San Jose (95112) *(G-19239)*
Logix Development Corporation 888 505-6449
473 Post St Camarillo (93010) *(G-15283)*
Logix Federal Credit Union 818 709-3896
10324 Mason Ave Chatsworth (91311) *(G-9609)*
Logix Federal Credit Union (PA) 888 718-5328
2340 N Hollywood Way Burbank (91505) *(G-9610)*
Loglogic Inc 408 215-5900
110 Rose Orchard Way San Jose (95134) *(G-15284)*
Logo Design Pros, San Francisco *Also called Lateral Designs Inc (G-14151)*
Logo Expressions, Ontario *Also called Dennis Foland Inc (G-8112)*
Logomark Inc 714 675-6100
1201 Bell Ave Tustin (92780) *(G-9278)*
Lois Lauer Realty 909 748-7000
1998 Orange Tree Ln Redlands (92374) *(G-11635)*
Lok Petaluma Marina Ht Co LLC 707 283-2888
745 Baywood Dr Petaluma (94954) *(G-12927)*
Lolapps Inc 415 243-0749
122 2nd Ave Ste 201 San Mateo (94401) *(G-15285)*
Loma Cleaning Service, San Carlos *Also called ISS Facility Services Inc (G-14327)*
Loma Linda - Inland Empire C 909 651-5832
11175 Campus St Csp 11006 11006 Csp Loma Linda (92354) *(G-21710)*
Loma Linda Catering Center, Loma Linda *Also called Loma Linda University Med Ctr (G-21713)*
Loma Linda Community Hospital, Loma Linda *Also called Loma Linda University Med Ctr (G-21715)*
Loma Linda Faculty Med Group, Loma Linda *Also called Linda Loma Univ Hlth Care (G-19709)*

ALPHABETIC

Loma Linda Healthcare Sys 605, Loma Linda *Also called Veterans Health Administration (G-20215)*
Loma Linda University.....909 558-4934
1686 Barton Rd Ste E Redlands (92373) ***(G-20331)***
Loma Linda University.....909 558-6422
1911 W Park Ave Redlands (92373) ***(G-19716)***
Loma Linda University Med Ctr.....909 558-2100
11370 Anderson St 2100 Loma Linda (92350) ***(G-21711)***
Loma Linda University Med Ctr (HQ).....909 558-4000
11234 Anderson St Loma Linda (92354) ***(G-21712)***
Loma Linda University Med Ctr.....909 558-8244
11175 Campus St Loma Linda (92350) ***(G-21713)***
Loma Linda University Med Ctr.....909 558-9275
1710 Barton Rd Redlands (92373) ***(G-21714)***
Loma Linda University Med Ctr.....909 558-3096
11265 Mountain View Ave E Loma Linda (92354) ***(G-22500)***
Loma Linda University Med Ctr.....909 796-0167
25333 Barton Rd Loma Linda (92350) ***(G-21715)***
Loma Linda Vet Association For.....909 583-6250
710 Brookside Ave Ste 2 Redlands (92373) ***(G-25288)***
Loma Riviera Community Assn.....619 224-1313
9610 Waples St San Diego (92121) ***(G-25289)***
Loma Sola House.....909 931-7534
1291 Loma Sola Ave Upland (91786) ***(G-21292)***
Loma Vista Nursery.....714 779-5583
18272 Bastanchury Rd Yorba Linda (92886) ***(G-9197)***
Loma Vista Nursery 2, Yorba Linda *Also called Loma Vista Nursery (G-9197)*
Lomas Santa Fe Country Club, Solana Beach *Also called American Golf Corporation (G-18851)*
Lombardo Diamnd Core Drlg Inc.....408 727-7922
2225 De La Cruz Blvd Santa Clara (95050) ***(G-3292)***
Lombardy Holdings Inc (PA).....951 808-4550
3166 Hrseless Carriage Rd Norco (92860) ***(G-1964)***
LOMITA CARE CENTER, Lomita *Also called Lomita Verde Inc (G-21293)*
Lomita Logistics LLC.....310 784-8485
3541 Lomita Blvd Torrance (90505) ***(G-14080)***
Lomita Medical Offices, Lomita *Also called Kaiser Foundation Hospitals (G-19625)*
Lomita Verde Inc.....310 325-1970
1955 Lomita Blvd Lomita (90717) ***(G-21293)***
Lompoc Convlsnt Care Ctr, Lompoc *Also called Lompoc Valley Medical Center (G-21294)*
Lompoc Family YMCA, Lompoc *Also called Channel Islands Young Mens Ch (G-25231)*
Lompoc Skilled Care Center, Lompoc *Also called Lompoc Valley Medical Center (G-21716)*
Lompoc Skilled Nrsng & Rehab, Lompoc *Also called Ghc of Lompoc LLC (G-22734)*
Lompoc Valley Medical Center.....805 735-9229
1111 E Ocean Ave Ste 2 Lompoc (93436) ***(G-19717)***
Lompoc Valley Medical Center (PA).....805 737-3300
1515 E Ocean Ave Lompoc (93436) ***(G-21716)***
Lompoc Valley Medical Center.....805 736-3466
216 N 3rd St Lompoc (93436) ***(G-21294)***
Lone Cypress Company LLC.....831 624-3811
17 Mile Dr Pebble Beach (93953) ***(G-12928)***
Lone Cypress Company LLC.....831 625-8507
1567 Cypress Dr Pebble Beach (93953) ***(G-18981)***
Lone Oak Farms.....559 583-1277
13866 4th Ave Hanford (93230) ***(G-381)***
Lone Tree Convalescent Hosp.....925 754-0470
4001 Lone Tree Way Antioch (94509) ***(G-20739)***
LONE TREE GOLF COURSE, Antioch *Also called Antioch Public Golf Corp (G-18714)*
Long & Levit LLP.....415 397-2222
465 California St Ste 500 San Francisco (94104) ***(G-23407)***
Long Bch Convention Entrmt Ctr, Long Beach *Also called City of Long Beach (G-17076)*
Long Bch Museum Art Foundation.....562 439-2119
2300 E Ocean Blvd Long Beach (90803) ***(G-25025)***
Long Bch Unfied Schl Dst Lbusd, Long Beach *Also called Long Beach Unified School Dst (G-14698)*
Long Beach Airport, Long Beach *Also called City of Long Beach (G-4907)*
LONG BEACH CAP, Long Beach *Also called Long Beach Cmnty Action Partnr (G-24939)*
Long Beach Care Center Inc.....562 426-6141
2615 Grand Ave Long Beach (90815) ***(G-20740)***
Long Beach City College Whse, Long Beach *Also called Long Beach Cmnty College Dst (G-4590)*
Long Beach City Fleet Services, Long Beach *Also called City of Long Beach (G-17788)*
Long Beach Cmnty Action Partnr.....562 216-4600
117 W Victoria St Long Beach (90805) ***(G-24939)***
Long Beach Cmnty College Dst.....562 938-4291
1855 Walnut Ave Long Beach (90806) ***(G-4590)***
Long Beach Convention Center, Long Beach *Also called Smg Holdings Inc (G-11051)*
Long Beach Cty Flt Svc Ofc, Long Beach *Also called City of Long Beach (G-23152)*
Long Beach Day Nursery.....562 421-1488
3965 N Bellflower Blvd Long Beach (90808) ***(G-24477)***
Long Beach Golden Sails Inc.....562 795-5241
6285 E Pacific Coast Hwy Long Beach (90803) ***(G-12929)***
Long Beach Hilton, The, Long Beach *Also called World Trade Ctr Ht Assoc Ltd (G-13429)*
Long Beach Investment Group.....562 595-7277
2041 Pacific Coast Hwy Lomita (90717) ***(G-9871)***
Long Beach Marriott, Long Beach *Also called Ruffin Hotel Corp of Cal (G-13180)*
Long Beach Medical Offices, Long Beach *Also called Kaiser Foundation Hospitals (G-21655)*
Long Beach Memorial Med Ctr (HQ).....562 933-2000
2801 Atlantic Ave Fl 2 Long Beach (90806) ***(G-21717)***
Long Beach Mental Health Ctr, Long Beach *Also called Long Beach Mntl Hlth Srvcs (G-19718)*
Long Beach Mntl Hlth Srvcs.....562 218-4001
1975 Long Beach Blvd Long Beach (90806) ***(G-19718)***
Long Beach Pain Center, Newport Beach *Also called Healthsmart Pacific Inc (G-21598)*
Long Beach Public Transit, Long Beach *Also called Long Beach Public Trnsp Co (G-3657)*
Long Beach Public Trnsp Co.....562 591-2301
1300 Gardenia Ave Long Beach (90813) ***(G-3656)***
Long Beach Public Trnsp Co (PA).....562 591-8753
1963 E Anaheim St Long Beach (90813) ***(G-3657)***
Long Beach Public Trnsp Co.....562 591-8753
1963 E Anaheim St Long Beach (90813) ***(G-3658)***
Long Beach Stadium Cinemas 26, Long Beach *Also called Edwards Theatres Circuit Inc (G-18328)*
Long Beach Unified School Dist.....562 997-7550
2425 Webster Ave Long Beach (90810) ***(G-14342)***
Long Beach Unified School Dst.....562 491-1281
999 Atlantic Ave Fl 3 Long Beach (90813) ***(G-14698)***
Long Beach Unified School Dst.....562 426-6176
2700 Pine Ave Long Beach (90806) ***(G-3944)***
Long Beach Unified School Dst.....562 493-3596
3351 Val Verde Ave Long Beach (90808) ***(G-17301)***
Long Beach Yacht Club.....562 598-9401
6201 E Appian Way Long Beach (90803) ***(G-18982)***
Long Dragon Financial Service, Arcadia *Also called Long Dragon Realty Co Inc (G-11636)*
Long Dragon Realty Co Inc.....626 309-7999
2633 S Baldwin Ave Arcadia (91007) ***(G-11636)***
Long Point Development LLC.....310 265-2800
100 Terranea Way Rancho Palos Verdes (90275) ***(G-12930)***
Long Swimming Pool Steel Inc.....714 524-8172
3920 E Coronado St # 205 Anaheim (92807) ***(G-3390)***
Long-Lok Fasteners Corporation.....310 667-4200
20501 Belshaw Ave Carson (90746) ***(G-7691)***
LONGSHOREMEN'S & WAREHOUSEMENS, Stockton *Also called International Longshoremens (G-25175)*
Longust Distributing Inc.....480 820-6244
1206 N Miller St Unit A Anaheim (92806) ***(G-6872)***
Longwood Management, San Dimas *Also called San Dimas Retirement Center (G-11199)*
Longwood Management Corp.....310 679-1461
11834 Inglewood Ave Hawthorne (90250) ***(G-20741)***
Longwood Management Corp.....323 735-5146
2000 W Washington Blvd Los Angeles (90018) ***(G-21295)***
Longwood Management Corp.....818 246-7174
605 W Broadway Glendale (91204) ***(G-21296)***
Longwood Management Corp.....818 881-7414
7836 Reseda Blvd Reseda (91335) ***(G-21718)***
Longwood Management Corp.....818 781-6348
6728 Sepulveda Blvd Van Nuys (91411) ***(G-11159)***
Longwood Management Corp.....562 693-5240
7716 Pickering Ave Whittier (90602) ***(G-21719)***
Longwood Management Corp.....818 360-1864
17922 San Frnando Msn Granada Hills (91344) ***(G-20742)***
Longwood Management Corp.....626 280-2293
8101 Hill Dr Rosemead (91770) ***(G-20743)***
Longwood Management Corp.....626 280-4820
8035 Hill Dr Rosemead (91770) ***(G-20744)***
Longwood Management Corp.....323 737-7778
2190 W Adams Blvd Los Angeles (90018) ***(G-21297)***
Longwood Management Corp.....818 980-8200
11429 Ventura Blvd Studio City (91604) ***(G-21298)***
Longwood Management Corp.....213 382-8461
1240 S Hoover St Los Angeles (90006) ***(G-21299)***
Longwood Management Corp.....818 884-7100
895 E Pasadena St Pomona (91767) ***(G-11160)***
Longwood Management Corp.....323 933-1560
1900 S Longwood Ave Los Angeles (90016) ***(G-20745)***
Longwood Management Corp.....626 289-3763
537 W Live Oak St San Gabriel (91776) ***(G-21300)***
Longwood Management Corp.....714 962-5531
9925 La Alameda Ave Fountain Valley (92708) ***(G-24715)***
Longwood Management Corp.....562 432-5751
1913 E 5th St Long Beach (90802) ***(G-21301)***
Longwood Management Inc.....310 370-5828
20920 Earl St Ofc Torrance (90503) ***(G-24716)***
Longwood Manor.....323 935-1157
4853 W Washington Blvd Los Angeles (90016) ***(G-20746)***
Longwood Manor Convalescent HM, Los Angeles *Also called Longwood Manor (G-20746)*
Loofs Lite A Line.....562 436-2978
2500 Long Beach Blvd Long Beach (90806) ***(G-18805)***
Lookout Productions LLC.....310 408-5687
3748 W 9th St Apt 403 Los Angeles (90019) ***(G-18103)***
Loomis Armored Us Inc.....408 273-1101
897 Wrigley Way Milpitas (95035) ***(G-16725)***
Loomis Armored Us LLC.....510 233-1055
3200 Regatta Blvd Ste B Richmond (94804) ***(G-16726)***
Loomis Armored Us LLC.....619 232-5106
3555 Aero Ct San Diego (92123) ***(G-16727)***
Loomis Armored Us LLC.....916 441-1091
315 12th St Sacramento (95814) ***(G-16728)***
Loomworks Apparel, Irvine *Also called Delta Galil USA Inc (G-8377)*
Looney Bins Inc (PA).....818 485-8200
12153 Montague St Pacoima (91331) ***(G-6494)***
Lopez & Associates Engineers, El Monte *Also called R and L Lopez Associates Inc (G-26028)*
Lopez Canyon Landfill.....818 834-5122
11950 Lopez Canyon Rd Sylmar (91342) ***(G-6495)***
Lopez Harvesting.....559 568-2553
24079 Avenue 196 Strathmore (93267) ***(G-496)***
Lorber Greenfield & Polito LLP (PA).....858 486-6757
13985 Stowe Dr Poway (92064) ***(G-23408)***
LOreal Usa Inc.....510 548-0130
1848 4th St Berkeley (94710) ***(G-8274)***
Loretta Lima Trnsp Corp.....626 330-5517
240 S 6th Ave City of Industry (91746) ***(G-4213)***
Loring Ward, San Jose *Also called Lwi Financial Inc (G-27515)*

A L P H A B E T I C

Loring Ward Advisor Services....408 260-3109
10 Almaden Blvd Ste 1500 San Jose (95113) ***(G-10159)***
Los Alamitos Hemo Dialysis Ctr, Los Alamitos *Also called Los Almtos Hmodialysis Ctr Inc* ***(G-22633)***
Los Alamitos Medical Ctr Inc (HQ)....714 826-6400
3751 Katella Ave Los Alamitos (90720) ***(G-21720)***
Los Almtos Hmodialysis Ctr Inc....562 426-8881
3810 Katella Ave Los Alamitos (90720) ***(G-22633)***
Los Altos Center, Los Altos *Also called Palo Alto Medical Foundation* ***(G-19815)***
Los Altos Food Products Inc....626 330-6555
450 Baldwin Park Blvd City of Industry (91746) ***(G-8587)***
Los Altos Golf and Country CLB....650 947-3100
1560 Country Club Dr Los Altos (94024) ***(G-18983)***
Los Altos YMCA, Long Beach *Also called Young Mens Chrstn Assc Gr L B* ***(G-25458)***
Los Alts Sub-Acute Rhbltn, Los Altos *Also called Covenant Care California LLC* ***(G-20501)***
Los Amigos Country Club Inc....562 923-9696
7295 Quill Dr Downey (90242) ***(G-18984)***
Los Amigos Golf Course, Downey *Also called Los Amigos Country Club Inc* ***(G-18984)***
Los Angeles 2024....310 407-0204
10960 Wilshire Blvd Fl 16 Los Angeles (90024) ***(G-25552)***
Los Angeles 2024 Exploratory....310 407-0539
10960 Wilshire Blvd Los Angeles (90024) ***(G-18985)***
Los Angeles Airport Peace Offc....310 242-5218
6080 Center Dr Fl 6 Los Angeles (90045) ***(G-25290)***
Los Angeles Angels of Anaheim, Anaheim *Also called Angels Baseball LP* ***(G-18535)***
Los Angeles Athletic Club Inc....213 625-2211
431 W 7th St Los Angeles (90014) ***(G-18656)***
Los Angeles Auto Auction, Rosemead *Also called Cox Automotive Inc* ***(G-6668)***
Los Angeles Bio Med RES Inst....310 222-3604
1124 W Carson St Rm 5l2 Torrance (90502) ***(G-26684)***
Los Angeles Branch, Los Angeles *Also called Federal Rsrve Bnk San Frncisco* ***(G-9316)***
Los Angeles Branch, Los Angeles *Also called First Republic Bank* ***(G-9551)***
Los Angeles Cardiology Assoc (PA)....213 977-0419
1245 Wilshire Blvd # 703 Los Angeles (90017) ***(G-19719)***
Los Angeles Chmber Orchstra....213 622-7001
350 S Figueroa St Ste 183 Los Angeles (90071) ***(G-18479)***
Los Angeles Christn Hlth Ctrs (HQ)....213 893-1960
311 Winston St Los Angeles (90013) ***(G-19720)***
Los Angeles Clippers, Los Angeles *Also called Lac Basketball Club Inc* ***(G-18553)***
Los Angeles Cnty Dev Svc Fndtn....213 383-1300
3303 Wilshire Blvd # 700 Los Angeles (90010) ***(G-22995)***
Los Angeles Cnty Economic Dev, Los Angeles *Also called Economic Dev Corp of La County* ***(G-27907)***
Los Angeles Cnty Emp Retiremnt (PA)....626 564-6000
300 N Lake Ave Ste 720 Pasadena (91101) ***(G-10555)***
Los Angeles Cnty Mseum of Art....323 857-6000
5905 Wilshire Blvd Los Angeles (90036) ***(G-25026)***
Los Angeles Cnty Mtro Trnspt, Los Angeles *Also called Los Angeles County MTA* ***(G-3663)***
Los Angeles Cold Storage, Los Angeles *Also called Standard-Southern Corporation* ***(G-4503)***
Los Angeles Cold Storage Co, Los Angeles *Also called Standard-Southern Corporation* ***(G-4501)***
Los Angeles Community Hospital, Los Angeles *Also called Alta Hospitals System LLC* ***(G-21445)***
Los Angeles Convention and Exh....213 741-1151
1201 S Figueroa St Los Angeles (90015) ***(G-11012)***
Los Angeles Convention Center, Los Angeles *Also called AEG Management Lacc LLC* ***(G-26912)***
Los Angeles Country Club....310 276-6104
10101 Wilshire Blvd Los Angeles (90024) ***(G-18986)***
Los Angeles County, Pacoima *Also called County of Los Angeles* ***(G-19473)***
Los Angeles County Apprentices....323 221-5881
6023 Garfield Ave Commerce (90040) ***(G-12160)***
Los Angeles County Bar Assn (PA)....213 627-2727
1055 W 7th St Ste 2700 Los Angeles (90017) ***(G-25144)***
Los Angeles County Fair Assn (PA)....909 623-3111
1101 W Mckinley Ave Pomona (91768) ***(G-19240)***
Los Angeles County Health Svc....310 763-2244
1108 N Oleander Ave Compton (90222) ***(G-19721)***
Los Angeles County Hospital, Los Angeles *Also called Lac Usc Medical Center* ***(G-21697)***
Los Angeles County MTA....213 922-6308
9201 Canoga Ave Chatsworth (91311) ***(G-3659)***
Los Angeles County MTA....213 922-5887
900 Lyon St Los Angeles (90012) ***(G-3660)***
Los Angeles County MTA....213 922-6301
1130 E 6th St Los Angeles (90021) ***(G-3661)***
Los Angeles County MTA....213 922-6203
630 W Avenue 28 Los Angeles (90065) ***(G-3662)***
Los Angeles County MTA....213 922-6202
1 Gateway Plz Los Angeles (90012) ***(G-3663)***
Los Angeles County MTA (PA)....323 466-3876
1 Gateway Plz Fl 25 Los Angeles (90012) ***(G-3664)***
Los Angeles County MTA....213 922-6207
8800 Santa Monica Blvd Los Angeles (90069) ***(G-3665)***
Los Angeles County MTA....213 922-6215
11900 Branford St Sun Valley (91352) ***(G-3666)***
Los Angeles County MTA....213 533-1506
720 E 15th St Los Angeles (90021) ***(G-3667)***
Los Angeles County MTA....213 922-5012
470 Bauchet St Los Angeles (90012) ***(G-3668)***
Los Angeles County MTA....310 392-8636
100 Sunset Ave Venice (90291) ***(G-3669)***
Los Angeles County MTA....213 244-6783
818 W 7th St Ste 500 Los Angeles (90017) ***(G-3670)***
Los Angeles County MTA....213 626-4455
320 S Santa Fe Ave Los Angeles (90013) ***(G-3671)***
Los Angeles County Pub Works, South Gate *Also called County of Los Angeles* ***(G-22933)***
Los Angeles Cy of Dept Wtr Pwr, Los Angeles *Also called Los Angeles Dept Wtr & Pwr* ***(G-6146)***
Los Angeles Dept Wtr & Pwr....213 367-1342
11801 Sheldon St Sun Valley (91352) ***(G-6365)***
Los Angeles Dept Wtr & Pwr....760 878-2156
201 S Webster St Independence (93526) ***(G-6366)***
Los Angeles Dept Wtr & Pwr (PA)....213 367-4043
111 N Hope St Rm 1063 Los Angeles (90012) ***(G-6367)***
Los Angeles Dept Wtr & Pwr....213 367-4211
111 N Hope St 743 Los Angeles (90012) ***(G-6146)***
Los Angeles Dept Wtr & Pwr....213 367-5706
1141 W 2nd St Bldg D Los Angeles (90012) ***(G-6368)***
Los Angeles Dept Wtr & Pwr....310 524-8500
12700 Vista Del Mar Playa Del Rey (90293) ***(G-6304)***
Los Angeles Deseret Industries, Los Angeles *Also called Corp of Church of Christ Ld St* ***(G-17951)***
Los Angeles District Office, Glendale *Also called State Compensation Insur Fund* ***(G-10472)***
Los Angeles Dr-In Theatre Co, Montclair *Also called Mission Drive-In Theatre Co* ***(G-18360)***
Los Angeles Engineering Inc....626 869-1400
633 N Barranca Ave Covina (91723) ***(G-3459)***
Los Angeles Federal Credit Un (PA)....818 242-8640
300 S Glendale Ave # 100 Glendale (91205) ***(G-9611)***
Los Angeles Free Clinic (PA)....323 653-8622
8405 Beverly Blvd Los Angeles (90048) ***(G-27510)***
Los Angeles Free Clinic....323 653-8622
8405 Beverly Blvd Los Angeles (90048) ***(G-19722)***
Los Angeles Freightliner, Fontana *Also called Los Angeles Truck Centers LLC* ***(G-6687)***
Los Angeles Guild LLC....323 733-5033
3437 W El Segundo Blvd Hawthorne (90250) ***(G-27511)***
Los Angeles Hospice, Burbank *Also called Silverado Senior Living Inc* ***(G-21109)***
Los Angeles Job Corps....213 748-0135
1020 S Olive St Los Angeles (90015) ***(G-24359)***
Los Angeles Junction Rlwy Co....323 277-2004
4433 Exchange Ave Vernon (90058) ***(G-3628)***
Los Angeles Lakers Inc....310 426-6000
555 N Nash St El Segundo (90245) ***(G-18554)***
Los Angeles Lawyer Magazine, Los Angeles *Also called Los Angeles County Bar Assn* ***(G-25144)***
Los Angeles Lgbt Center (PA)....323 993-7618
1625 Schrader Blvd Los Angeles (90028) ***(G-24940)***
Los Angeles Magazine Inc....323 801-0100
5900 Wilshire Blvd Fl 10 Los Angeles (90036) ***(G-9167)***
Los Angeles Marriott Downtown, Los Angeles *Also called La Hotel Venture LLC* ***(G-12896)***
Los Angeles Orphan Asylum Inc....323 283-9311
7600 Graves Ave Rosemead (91770) ***(G-24717)***
Los Angeles Orphans Home Soc (HQ)....323 463-2119
815 N El Centro Ave Los Angeles (90038) ***(G-24718)***
Los Angeles Philharmonic Assn (PA)....213 972-7300
151 S Grand Ave Los Angeles (90012) ***(G-18480)***
Los Angeles Police Command....877 275-5273
100 W 1st St Los Angeles (90012) ***(G-25553)***
Los Angeles Police Credit Un (PA)....818 787-6520
16150 Sherman Way Van Nuys (91406) ***(G-9672)***
Los Angeles Rams LLC (PA)....314 982-7267
29899 Agoura Rd Agoura Hills (91301) ***(G-18555)***
Los Angeles Regional Food Bank....323 234-3030
1734 E 41st St Vernon (90058) ***(G-24070)***
Los Angeles Regional Office, Brea *Also called International Code Council* ***(G-25140)***
Los Angeles Regional Office, Pasadena *Also called Employee Benefits Security ADM* ***(G-10552)***
Los Angeles Resdntl Cmmnty Fdn....661 296-8636
29890 Bouquet Canyon Rd Santa Clarita (91390) ***(G-24719)***
Los Angeles Residential Comm F....661 296-8636
29890 Bouquet Canyon Rd Santa Clarita (91390) ***(G-24720)***
Los Angeles Royal Vista Golf C....909 595-7471
20055 Colima Rd Walnut (91789) ***(G-18987)***
Los Angeles Rubber Company (PA)....323 263-4131
2915 E Washington Blvd Los Angeles (90023) ***(G-7451)***
Los Angeles Senior Citizen....310 271-9670
1425 S Wooster St Los Angeles (90035) ***(G-11161)***
Los Angeles South Bay Dst Off, Long Beach *Also called Rehabilitation California Dept* ***(G-24153)***
Los Angeles Terminal, Los Angeles *Also called El Pas-Los Angles Lmsne Ex Inc* ***(G-3901)***
Los Angeles Truck Centers LLC....909 510-4000
13800 Valley Blvd Fontana (92335) ***(G-6687)***
Los Angeles Turf Club Inc....626 574-6330
285 W Huntington Dr Arcadia (91007) ***(G-18570)***
Los Angeles Unified School Dst....323 227-4400
2011 N Soto St Los Angeles (90032) ***(G-3961)***
Los Angeles Unified School Dst....818 997-2640
6651 Balboa Blvd Van Nuys (91406) ***(G-22770)***
Los Angeles Unified School Dst....818 365-9645
11450 Sharp Ave Mission Hills (91345) ***(G-24360)***
Los Angeles Unified School Dst....213 485-3691
200 N Main St Ste 1400 Los Angeles (90012) ***(G-16301)***
Los Angeles Unified School Dst....213 847-6911
200 N Main St Ste 1400 Los Angeles (90012) ***(G-16153)***
Los Angeles Unified School Dst....323 753-3175
816 W 51st St Los Angeles (90037) ***(G-25291)***
Los Angeles Unified School Dst....323 939-7322
1212 Queen Anne Pl Los Angeles (90019) ***(G-24478)***
Los Angeles Unified School Dst....213 739-5600
1157 S Berendo St Los Angeles (90006) ***(G-24071)***
Los Angeles Unified School Dst....310 258-2000
8810 Emerson Ave Los Angeles (90045) ***(G-24072)***
Los Angeles Unified School Dst....562 654-9007
8525 Rex Rd Pico Rivera (90660) ***(G-17302)***

ALPHABETIC

Los Angeles Unified School Dst 310 808-1500
17729 S Figueroa St Gardena (90248) ***(G-14343)***

Los Angeles Unified School Dst 310 518-1128
1468 N Marine Ave Wilmington (90744) ***(G-24073)***

Los Angeles World Airports (PA) 310 646-7911
6320 W 96th St Los Angeles (90045) ***(G-4925)***

Los Angeles Ambulatory Care Ctr, Los Angeles *Also called Veterans Health Administration* ***(G-20220)***

Los Angles Arbretum Foundation 626 821-3222
301 N Baldwin Ave Arcadia (91007) ***(G-25065)***

Los Angles Area Chmber Cmmerce 213 580-7500
350 S Bixel St Los Angeles (90017) ***(G-25092)***

Los Angles Arprt Hilton Towers, Los Angeles *Also called Fortuna Enterprises LP* ***(G-12643)***

Los Angles Child Gdance Clinic (PA) 323 766-2360
3031 S Vermont Ave Los Angeles (90007) ***(G-24074)***

Los Angles Clippers Foundation 213 742-7555
1111 S Figueroa St # 1100 Los Angeles (90015) ***(G-27512)***

Los Angles Cllege Chiropractic, Whittier *Also called S CA University Hlth Sciences* ***(G-20298)***

Los Angles Cnsrvtion Corps Inc (PA) 213 362-9000
605 W Olympic Blvd # 450 Los Angeles (90015) ***(G-14901)***

Los Angles Cnty Cntl Jail Hosp, Los Angeles *Also called County of Los Angeles* ***(G-21520)***

Los Angles Cnty Employees Assn 213 368-8660
1545 Wilshire Blvd Los Angeles (90017) ***(G-25178)***

Los Angles Dst Off Policy Svcs, Monterey Park *Also called State Compensation Insur Fund* ***(G-10477)***

Los Angles Homecare Pediatrics, Los Angeles *Also called Maxim Healthcare Services Inc* ***(G-22505)***

Los Angles Jewish HM For Aging (PA) 818 774-3000
7150 Tampa Ave Reseda (91335) ***(G-20747)***

Los Angles Jewish HM For Aging 818 774-3000
18855 Victory Blvd Reseda (91335) ***(G-20748)***

Los Angles Kings Hockey CLB LP 310 535-4502
555 N Nash St El Segundo (90245) ***(G-18556)***

Los Angles Ryal Vsta Golf Crse, Walnut *Also called Los Angeles Royal Vista Golf C* ***(G-18987)***

Los Angles Trism Convention Bd (PA) 213 624-7300
333 S Hope St Ste 1800 Los Angeles (90071) ***(G-17303)***

Los Angles Universal Preschool 213 416-1200
888 S Figueroa St Ste 800 Los Angeles (90017) ***(G-24479)***

Los Banos Nursing and Rehab, Los Banos *Also called Para & Palli Inc* ***(G-20839)***

Los Banos School District, Los Banos *Also called Facilities Operation and Trnsp* ***(G-3926)***

Los Coyotes Pro Shop, Buena Park *Also called McAuley Lcx Corporation* ***(G-18994)***

Los Defensores Inc 310 519-4050
1010 S Cabrillo Ave San Pedro (90731) ***(G-13877)***

Los Dos Valles Harvstg & Pkg 805 739-1688
2365 Westgate Rd Santa Maria (93455) ***(G-497)***

Los Gatos Meadows, Los Gatos *Also called Episcopal Senior Communities* ***(G-24646)***

Los Padres Bank, Solvang *Also called Pacific Western Bank* ***(G-9580)***

Los Palos Convalescent Hosp, San Pedro *Also called San Pedro Convalescent Home* ***(G-20893)***

Los Posadas Service Center, Camarillo *Also called Telecare Corporation* ***(G-22104)***

Los Prietos Boys Camp 805 692-1750
3900 Paradise Rd Santa Barbara (93105) ***(G-24721)***

Los Robles Bank 805 373-6763
33 W Thousand Oaks Blvd Thousand Oaks (91360) ***(G-9505)***

Los Serranos Golf & Cntry CLB, Chino Hills *Also called Los Serranos Golf Club* ***(G-18756)***

Los Serranos Golf Club 909 597-1769
15656 Yorba Ave Chino Hills (91709) ***(G-18756)***

Los Verdes Golf Course, Rancho Palos Verdes *Also called American Golf Corporation* ***(G-18867)***

Los Verdes Golf Curse, Rancho Palos Verdes *Also called Los Verdes MNS Golf Cntry CLB* ***(G-18757)***

Los Verdes MNS Golf Cntry CLB 310 377-7370
7000 Los Verdes Dr Ste 1 Rancho Palos Verdes (90275) ***(G-18757)***

Loss and Risk Advisors, San Diego *Also called Barney & Barney Inc* ***(G-10642)***

Lost Canyons Golf Course, Simi Valley *Also called Big Sky Country Club LLC* ***(G-18716)***

Lotus Communications Corp (PA) 323 512-2225
3301 Barham Blvd Ste 200 Los Angeles (90068) ***(G-5808)***

Lotus Interworks Inc 310 442-3330
10801 National Blvd # 500 Los Angeles (90064) ***(G-27513)***

Lou Bozigian 661 948-4737
5900 Alleppo Ln Palmdale (93551) ***(G-11637)***

Louie Almeida & Settler (PA) 818 461-9559
303 N Glenoaks Blvd Fl 4 Burbank (91502) ***(G-23409)***

Louis Luskin & Sons Inc 323 938-5142
6004 Venice Blvd Los Angeles (90034) ***(G-2283)***

Louis Wurth and Company (HQ) 714 529-1771
895 Columbia St Brea (92821) ***(G-7692)***

Lovazzano Mechanical Inc 650 367-6216
189 Constitution Dr Menlo Park (94025) ***(G-2284)***

Lovco Construction Inc 562 595-1601
1300 E Burnett St Signal Hill (90755) ***(G-3435)***

Lovely Living Homecare 909 625-7999
112 Harvard Ave Claremont (91711) ***(G-22501)***

Loves Travel Stops 661 823-1484
2000 E Tehachapi Blvd Tehachapi (93561) ***(G-4968)***

Low Ball & Lynch A Prof Corp 831 655-8822
2 Lower Ragsdale Dr # 120 Monterey (93940) ***(G-23410)***

Low Ball & Lynch A Prof Corp (PA) 415 981-6630
505 Montgomery St Fl 7 San Francisco (94111) ***(G-23411)***

Low Cost Insurance, Northridge *Also called 1-800-4-insure Insurance Svcs* ***(G-10574)***

Lowcom LLC 213 408-0080
818 W 7th St Ste 700 Los Angeles (90017) ***(G-13878)***

Lowe Enterprises Inc (PA) 310 820-6661
11777 San Vicente Blvd # 900 Los Angeles (90049) ***(G-11638)***

Lowe Enterprises Coml Group 310 820-6661
11777 San Vicente Blvd # 900 Los Angeles (90049) ***(G-11980)***

Lowe Enterprises Inc 310 820-6661
11777 San Vincente Blvd S Ste 900 Los Angeles (90049) ***(G-11981)***

Lowenstein Sandler LLP 650 433-5800
390 Lytton Ave Palo Alto (94301) ***(G-23412)***

Lowepro, Petaluma *Also called Daymen US Inc* ***(G-7031)***

Lowermybills Inc (HQ) 310 348-6800
12181 Bluff Creek Dr Playa Vista (90094) ***(G-16251)***

Lowermybills.com, Playa Vista *Also called Lowermybills Inc* ***(G-16251)***

Lowes Home Centers LLC 209 513-9560
Luce Ave Bldg 512 Stockton (95203) ***(G-4591)***

Lowes Home Centers LLC 951 601-2230
16850 Heacock St Moreno Valley (92551) ***(G-4592)***

Loyal Svc Unt Spec Team, La Puente *Also called Michael McCarthy* ***(G-16736)***

Loyal3 Holdings Inc 415 981-0700
150 California St Ste 400 San Francisco (94111) ***(G-17304)***

Loyalton At Rancho Solano 707 425-3588
3350 Cherry Hills Ct Ofc Fairfield (94534) ***(G-24722)***

Loyola Marymount University 310 338-2866
1 Lmu Dr Ste 100 Los Angeles (90045) ***(G-5809)***

Lozano Car Wash, Mountain View *Also called Lozano Inc* ***(G-17854)***

Lozano Inc 650 941-0590
2690 W El Camino Real Mountain View (94040) ***(G-17854)***

Lozano Smith A Prof Corp (PA) 559 431-5600
7404 N Spalding Ave Fresno (93720) ***(G-23413)***

LPA Inc (PA) 949 261-1001
5161 California Ave # 100 Irvine (92617) ***(G-26225)***

LPA Inc 408 780-7200
60 S Market St Ste 150 San Jose (95113) ***(G-26226)***

Lpa Insurance Agency Inc 916 286-7850
4030 Truxel Rd Ste B Sacramento (95834) ***(G-15736)***

Lpas Inc 916 443-0335
2484 Natomas Park Dr # 100 Sacramento (95833) ***(G-26227)***

LPC West, San Diego *Also called 600b Ag-Lo Owner L P* ***(G-11269)***

Lpcc, Camarillo *Also called Las Posas Country Club* ***(G-18980)***

Lpl Financial Holdings Inc 310 823-4999
8055 W Manchester Ave # 350 Playa Del Rey (90293) ***(G-10160)***

Lpl Holdings Inc (HQ) 858 450-9606
4707 Executive Dr San Diego (92121) ***(G-10026)***

Lq Management LLC 310 645-2200
5249 W Century Blvd Los Angeles (90045) ***(G-12931)***

Lqr Property LLC 760 564-4111
49499 Eisenhower Dr La Quinta (92253) ***(G-12932)***

Lres Corporation (PA) 714 520-5737
765 The City Dr S Ste 300 Orange (92868) ***(G-11639)***

Lrn Corporation (PA) 310 209-5400
1100 Glendon Ave Ste 800 Los Angeles (90024) ***(G-23414)***

Lrw Investments LLC 310 337-1944
9700 Bellanca Ave Los Angeles (90045) ***(G-17729)***

LS Farms LLC 661 792-3192
29794 Schuster Rd Mc Farland (93250) ***(G-382)***

Ltl Ex Inc 951 255-1222
11081 Cherry Ave Fontana (92337) ***(G-5116)***

LTS, San Diego *Also called Ledcor Technical Services Inc* ***(G-2636)***

Luberski Inc 951 271-3866
1811 Mountain Ave Norco (92860) ***(G-8600)***

Lubert-Dler Mnagement-West Inc 310 496-4130
1401 Ocean Ave Ste 350 Santa Monica (90401) ***(G-12257)***

Lucas and Mercier Cnstr Inc 949 589-4480
29712 Ave De Las Bandera Rcho STA Marg (92688) ***(G-3065)***

Lucasfilm Coml Productions, San Francisco *Also called Lucasfilm Ltd LLC* ***(G-18104)***

Lucasfilm Ltd LLC (HQ) 415 623-1000
1110 Gorgas Ave Bldg C-Hr San Francisco (94129) ***(G-18104)***

Lucasfilm Ltd LLC 415 662-1800
5858 Lucas Valley Rd Nicasio (94946) ***(G-18105)***

Lucich Santos Farms 209 892-6500
12631 Rogers Rd Patterson (95363) ***(G-383)***

Lucid Design Group Inc 510 907-0400
304 12th St Ste 3c Oakland (94607) ***(G-15990)***

Lucile Packard Childrens Hosp, Palo Alto *Also called Leland Stanford Junior Univ* ***(G-22151)***

Lucile Packard Childrens Hosp 650 736-4089
1520 Page Mill Rd Palo Alto (94304) ***(G-22153)***

Lucile Salter Packard Chil 925 277-7550
5601 Norris Canyon Rd # 230 San Ramon (94583) ***(G-19723)***

Lucile Salter Packard Chil 650 724-0503
4100 Bohannon Dr Menlo Park (94025) ***(G-22154)***

Lucile Salter Packard Chil (PA) 650 736-7398
725 Welch Rd Palo Alto (94304) ***(G-22155)***

Lucile Salter Packard Chil 650 723-5791
300 Pasteur Dr Stanford (94305) ***(G-22156)***

Lucile Salter Packard Chil 650 736-4030
725 Welch Rd Palo Alto (94304) ***(G-28142)***

Lucky Chances Inc 650 758-2237
1700 Hillside Blvd Colma (94014) ***(G-19241)***

Lucky Chances Casino, Colma *Also called Lucky Chances Inc* ***(G-19241)***

Lucky Derby Casino 916 727-2727
7433 Greenback Ln Ste C Citrus Heights (95610) ***(G-19242)***

Lucky Farms Inc 909 799-6688
1194 E Brier Dr San Bernardino (92408) ***(G-79)***

Lucky Installations 562 948-5950
9041 Bermudez St Pico Rivera (90660) ***(G-3187)***

Lucky Lady Card Room, San Diego *Also called California Club Lucky Lady* ***(G-19157)***

Lucky Pacific LLC 650 330-0263
2000 Broadway St 102 Redwood City (94063) ***(G-27514)***

Lucky Strike Del AMO, Torrance *Also called Lucky Strike Entertainment LLC* ***(G-18524)***

Lucky Strike Entertainment LLC 818 933-3752
6801 Hollywood Blvd # 143 Los Angeles (90028) ***(G-7344)***

Lucky Strike Entertainment LLC.....818 933-0872
15260 Ventura Blvd # 1110 Sherman Oaks (91403) *(G-18523)*
Lucky Strike Entertainment LLC.....310 802-7010
3525 W Carson St Ste 77 Torrance (90503) *(G-18524)*
Lucky Strike Entertainment LLC.....248 374-3420
20 City Blvd W Ste G2 Orange (92868) *(G-18525)*
Lufkin Industries LLC.....661 746-0030
31127 Coberly Rd Shafter (93263) *(G-7857)*
Lufthnsa Crgo Aktngesellschaft.....310 242-2590
5721 W Imperial Hwy Los Angeles (90045) *(G-4814)*
Luis Esparza Services Inc.....661 766-2344
183 Hwy 33 Maricopa (93252) *(G-14699)*
Lukenbill Enterprises.....916 454-2400
3600 Power Inn Rd Ste H Sacramento (95826) *(G-4815)*
Lumberyard Plaza Mall, Los Angeles *Also called Laguna Country Mart Ltd Inc (G-11009)*
Lumenis Inc (HQ).....408 764-3000
2033 Gateway Pl Ste 200 San Jose (95110) *(G-7274)*
Lumens (PA).....916 444-5585
2020 L St Ste Ll10 Sacramento (95811) *(G-7452)*
Lumens Light & Living, Sacramento *Also called Lumens (G-7452)*
Lumetra Healthcare Solutions.....415 677-2000
550 Kearny St Ste 300 San Francisco (94108) *(G-27977)*
Lumina At Home, Los Angeles *Also called Lumina Healthcare LLC (G-22502)*
Lumina Healthcare LLC (PA).....888 958-6462
5220 Pacific Concourse Dr Los Angeles (90045) *(G-22502)*
Luminous Consumer Services Inc.....661 993-1475
25322 Rye Canyon Rd # 106 Valencia (91355) *(G-11640)*
Lunares, San Francisco *Also called Sunday Bazaar Inc (G-6888)*
Lund Construction Co.....916 344-5800
5302 Roseville Rd North Highlands (95660) *(G-25942)*
Lund Equipment LP.....916 344-5800
5302 Roseville Rd North Highlands (95660) *(G-1816)*
Lundblade Builders, Eureka *Also called Fred H Lundblade Jr (G-10985)*
Lundstrom & Associates Inc.....619 641-5900
4804 Sunrise Hills Dr El Cajon (92020) *(G-25943)*
Luppen and Hawley Inc.....916 456-7831
6330 N Point Way Sacramento (95831) *(G-2285)*
Lupton Excavation Inc.....916 387-1104
8467 Florin Rd Sacramento (95828) *(G-3436)*
Lusamerica Foods Inc (PA).....408 294-6622
16480 Railroad Ave Morgan Hill (95037) *(G-8639)*
Lusardi Construction Co.....925 829-1114
6376 Clark Ave Dublin (94568) *(G-1603)*
Lusive Decor.....323 227-9207
3400 Medford St Los Angeles (90063) *(G-27978)*
Luth Research Inc (PA).....619 234-5884
1365 4th Ave San Diego (92101) *(G-26685)*
Luther Burbank Mem Foundation.....707 546-3600
50 Mark West Springs Rd Santa Rosa (95403) *(G-18412)*
Luther Burbank Savings Corp (HQ).....707 578-9216
500 3rd St Santa Rosa (95401) *(G-9586)*
Lutheran Health Facility, Burbank *Also called Front Porch Communities & Svcs (G-21224)*
Lutheran Health Facility, The, Alhambra *Also called Front Porch Communities & Svcs (G-21225)*
Lutrel Trucking Inc.....661 397-9756
12856 Old River Rd Bakersfield (93311) *(G-5117)*
Luxar Tech Inc.....408 835-2551
42840 Christy St Ste 101 Fremont (94538) *(G-5649)*
Luxe City Center, Los Angeles *Also called Emerik Hotel Corp (G-12618)*
Luxe Sunset Boulevard Hotel, Los Angeles *Also called E H Summit Inc (G-12604)*
Luxera Inc.....510 456-7690
39300 Civic Center Dr # 140 Fremont (94538) *(G-14344)*
Luxn Inc.....408 213-7437
580 Maude Ct Sunnyvale (94085) *(G-6081)*
Luxor Cabs Inc.....415 282-4141
2230 Jerrold Ave San Francisco (94124) *(G-3865)*
Luxury Link LLC.....310 215-8060
5510 Lincoln Blvd Ste 275 Playa Vista (90094) *(G-12933)*
Luxury Link Travel Group, Playa Vista *Also called Luxury Link LLC (G-12933)*
LVI Facility Services, Hayward *Also called Northstar Contg Group Inc (G-3559)*
Lwi Financial Inc.....408 260-3100
3055 Olin Ave Ste 2000 San Jose (95128) *(G-27119)*
Lwi Financial Inc.....408 217-8886
10 Almaden Blvd San Jose (95113) *(G-27515)*
Lydia C Gonzalez.....650 299-4707
1400 Veterans Blvd Redwood City (94063) *(G-24075)*
Lyft Inc.....415 230-2905
185 Berry St Ste 5000 San Francisco (94107) *(G-3815)*
Lyle Company.....916 266-7000
3140 Gold Camp Dr Ste 30 Rancho Cordova (95670) *(G-27979)*
Lyles Mechanical Co.....559 237-2200
5014 E University Ave # 101 Fresno (93727) *(G-2286)*
Lynberg & Watkins A Prof Corp (PA).....213 624-8700
888 S Figueroa St # 1600 Los Angeles (90017) *(G-23415)*
Lynberg & Watkins Attys At Law, Los Angeles *Also called Lynberg & Watkins A Prof Corp (G-23415)*
Lynch Ambulance Service, Anaheim *Also called Filyn Corporation (G-3791)*
Lynch Creek Medical Management, Petaluma *Also called Crocodile Bay Lodge (G-13451)*
Lynch Gilardi & Grummer LLP.....415 397-2800
170 Columbus Ave Fl 5 San Francisco (94133) *(G-23416)*
Lynup Corporation.....858 207-4610
16875 W Bernardo Dr # 110 San Diego (92127) *(G-27516)*
Lynwood Developmental Care.....310 764-2023
14925 S Atlantic Ave Compton (90221) *(G-21302)*
Lynwood Medical Offices, Lynwood *Also called Kaiser Foundation Hospitals (G-19627)*
Lynx Software Technologies Inc (PA).....408 979-3900
855 Embedded Way San Jose (95138) *(G-15737)*
Lyon & Associates Realtors, Sacramento *Also called William L Lyon & Assoc Inc (G-11922)*
Lyon Promenade LLC.....949 252-9101
4901 Birch St Newport Beach (92660) *(G-1378)*
Lyon Real Estate.....916 355-7000
150 Natoma Station Dr # 300 Folsom (95630) *(G-11641)*
Lyon Realtors, Fair Oaks *Also called William L Lyon & Assoc Inc (G-11923)*
Lyon Realty.....916 784-1500
2220 Douglas Blvd Ste 100 Roseville (95661) *(G-11642)*
Lyon Realty.....916 481-3840
2580 Fair Oaks Blvd # 20 Sacramento (95825) *(G-11643)*
Lyon Realty.....916 962-0111
8814 Madison Ave Fair Oaks (95628) *(G-11644)*
Lyon Realty.....916 787-7700
851 Pleasant Grove Blvd # 150 Roseville (95678) *(G-11645)*
Lyon Realty.....530 295-4444
4330 Golden Center Dr C Kelsey (95667) *(G-11258)*
Lyon Realty.....916 939-5300
3900 Park Dr El Dorado Hills (95762) *(G-11646)*
Lyon Realty (PA).....916 574-8800
2280 Del Paso Rd Ste 100 Sacramento (95834) *(G-11647)*
Lyons Security Service Inc.....714 401-4850
P.O. Box 18955 Anaheim (92817) *(G-16900)*
LYTTON GARDEN I, Palo Alto *Also called Community Housing Inc (G-24603)*
Lytton Gardens Inc (PA).....650 328-3300
437 Webster St Palo Alto (94301) *(G-20749)*
Lytton Gardens Inc.....650 328-3300
656 Lytton Ave Palo Alto (94301) *(G-20750)*
Lytton Gardens Inc.....650 321-0400
330 Everett Ave Palo Alto (94301) *(G-20751)*
Lytton Gardens Health Care Ctr, Palo Alto *Also called Lytton Gardens Inc (G-20750)*
Lytton Rancheria.....510 215-7888
13255 San Pablo Ave San Pablo (94806) *(G-19243)*
Lyttont Gardens 3, Palo Alto *Also called Lytton Gardens Inc (G-20751)*
M & A Mortgage Inc.....714 560-1970
1600 N Broadway Ste 1020 Santa Ana (92706) *(G-9935)*
M & C, Los Angeles *Also called Murchison & Cumming LLP (G-23458)*
M & G Jewelers Inc.....909 989-2929
10823 Edison Ct Rancho Cucamonga (91730) *(G-17950)*
M & H Realty Partners LP.....415 693-9000
353 Sacramento St Fl 21 San Francisco (94111) *(G-12323)*
M & L Plumbing Co Inc.....559 291-5525
3540 N Duke Ave Fresno (93727) *(G-2287)*
M & M Distributors, Los Angeles *Also called Wiemar Distributors Inc (G-8790)*
M & M Electric, Sacramento *Also called May-Han Electric Inc (G-2643)*
M & M Interiors Inc.....951 279-9535
3410 La Sierra Ave Ste F Riverside (92503) *(G-1604)*
M & M Plumbing Inc.....951 354-5388
6782 Columbus St Riverside (92504) *(G-2288)*
M & M Stone Inc.....209 478-1791
5250 Claremont Ave Stockton (95207) *(G-11648)*
M & R Co.....209 941-2631
33 E Tokay St Lodi (95240) *(G-8749)*
M & R Joint Venture Electrical.....909 598-7700
231 Benton Ct Walnut (91789) *(G-2638)*
M & R Wood Products Inc.....909 460-1865
13312 Ranchero Rd 150 Oak Hills (92344) *(G-1207)*
M & S Acquisition Corporation (PA).....213 385-1515
707 Wilshire Blvd # 5200 Los Angeles (90017) *(G-11649)*
M & S Security Services Inc.....661 397-9616
2900 L St Bakersfield (93301) *(G-16729)*
M & S Trading Inc.....714 241-7190
15778 Gateway Cir Tustin (92780) *(G-8352)*
M & T Calf Ranch.....559 686-7663
14998 Avenue 192 Tulare (93274) *(G-411)*
M A A C Project, Chula Vista *Also called Metropolitan Area Advisory Com (G-24363)*
M A C, Northridge *Also called Mikuni American Corporation (G-6749)*
M A O F, Commerce *Also called Mexican Amrcn Oprtnty Fndation (G-24086)*
M Arthur Gensler Jr Assoc Inc.....408 885-8100
225 W Santa Clara St San Jose (95113) *(G-26228)*
M Arthur Gensler Jr Assoc Inc.....408 858-8100
225 S 1st St San Jose (95113) *(G-26229)*
M Arthur Gensler Jr Assoc Inc (PA).....415 433-3700
2 Harrison St Fl 4 San Francisco (94105) *(G-26230)*
M Arthur Gensler Jr Assoc Inc.....510 625-7400
2101 Webster St Ste 2000 Oakland (94612) *(G-26231)*
M Arthur Gensler Jr Assoc Inc.....213 927-3600
500 S Figueroa St Los Angeles (90071) *(G-26232)*
M Arthur Gensler Jr Assoc Inc.....949 863-9434
4675 Macarthur Ct Ste 100 Newport Beach (92660) *(G-26233)*
M B M, Pleasanton *Also called Meadowbrook Meat Company Inc (G-8561)*
M Bar C Construction Inc.....760 744-4131
674 Rancheros Dr San Marcos (92069) *(G-3391)*
M Block & Sons Inc.....909 335-6684
26875 Pioneer Ave Redlands (92374) *(G-4593)*
M C, Los Angeles *Also called Muir-Chase Plumbing Co Inc (G-2298)*
M C Builder Corp.....760 323-8010
1251 Montalvo Way Ste L Palm Springs (92262) *(G-2464)*
M C C, Brea *Also called Mercury Casualty Company (G-10439)*
M C M Harvesters Inc.....805 659-6833
1585 Lirio Ave Ventura (93004) *(G-14700)*
M Caratan Inc.....661 725-1777
33787 Cecil Ave Delano (93215) *(G-169)*
M Channel Inc.....310 231-5124
2015 S Westgate Ave Los Angeles (90025) *(G-13971)*
M D S I, Chowchilla *Also called Madera Disposal Systems Inc (G-6497)*
M E Nollkamper Inc (PA).....951 737-9300
940 Manor Way Corona (92882) *(G-27517)*
M F Commercial Landscape Svcs.....949 660-8655
1821 Reynolds Ave Irvine (92614) *(G-777)*

M F Maher Inc....707 552-2774
490 Ryder St Vallejo (94590) *(G-1817)*
M F Salta Co Inc (PA)....562 421-2512
20 Executive Park Ste 150 Irvine (92614) *(G-27518)*
M Gaw Inc....818 503-7997
6910 Farmdale Ave North Hollywood (91605) *(G-3548)*
M H Deyoung Memorial, San Francisco *Also called Corportion of Fine Arts Mseums (G-25015)*
M I G, Berkeley *Also called Moore Iacofano Goltsman Inc (G-27993)*
M I I, Bakersfield *Also called Mechanical Industries Inc (G-3392)*
M J D Concrete Works, Agoura Hills *Also called Mjd Construction Corp (G-1225)*
M K H Inc....818 882-9274
8870 Tampa Ave Northridge (91324) *(G-17855)*
M K S Construction Inc....916 446-2521
471 Bannon St Sacramento (95811) *(G-1208)*
M K Technical Services Inc....408 528-0401
4349 San Felipe Rd San Jose (95135) *(G-14902)*
M L Stern & Co LLC (HQ)....323 658-4400
8350 Wilshire Blvd Fl 1 Beverly Hills (90211) *(G-10027)*
M M C, Covina *Also called Magan Medical Clinic Inc (G-19725)*
M M Direct Marketing Inc....714 265-4100
14271 Corporate Dr Garden Grove (92843) *(G-14081)*
M M Fab Inc....310 763-3800
2300 E Gladwick St Compton (90220) *(G-8317)*
M Network Television Inc....818 756-5150
6007 Sepulveda Blvd Van Nuys (91411) *(G-5896)*
M O C Insurance Services, San Francisco *Also called Maroevich OShea & Coghlan (G-10771)*
M O Dion & Sons Inc (PA)....714 540-5535
1543 W 16th St Long Beach (90813) *(G-9026)*
M P Environmental Services, Bakersfield *Also called M P Vacuum Truck Service (G-6496)*
M P M & Associates Inc....818 708-9676
19625 Ventura Blvd # 100 Tarzana (91356) *(G-1605)*
M P O Inc (HQ)....562 628-1007
3760 Kilroy Airport Way # 5 Long Beach (90806) *(G-8275)*
M P S, Redding *Also called Mission Provider Services Inc (G-21317)*
M P Vacuum Truck Service (PA)....661 393-1151
3400 Manor St Bakersfield (93308) *(G-6496)*
M R S, American Canyon *Also called Medical Receivables Solutions (G-27537)*
M S, Pleasant Hill *Also called Mark Scott Construction Inc (G-1608)*
M S E Enterprises Inc (PA)....818 223-3500
23622 Calabasas Rd # 200 Calabasas (91302) *(G-11650)*
M S International Inc (PA)....714 685-7500
2095 N Batavia St Orange (92865) *(G-6991)*
M Squared Consulting, San Francisco *Also called Collabrus Inc (G-26314)*
M T C, Los Angeles *Also called Mutual Trading Co Inc (G-8881)*
M T C, San Francisco *Also called Metropolitan Trnsp Comm (G-3673)*
M T C, City of Industry *Also called Micro-Technology Concepts Inc (G-7163)*
M T C Holdings (HQ)....912 651-4000
3 Embarcadero Ctr Ste 550 San Francisco (94111) *(G-4749)*
M T D, Santa Barbara *Also called Santa Barbara Metro Trnst Dst (G-3713)*
M T M & M Inc....626 445-2922
3333 Peck Rd Monrovia (91016) *(G-14486)*
M T R, Newark *Also called Membrane Technology & RES Inc (G-26566)*
M V E, Modesto *Also called Mve Inc (G-25978)*
M V Transportation....831 373-1395
1375 Britain Ave Salinas (93901) *(G-5230)*
M V Transportation....760 255-3330
1612 State St Barstow (92311) *(G-5231)*
M X R, San Diego *Also called Merry X-Ray Chemical Corp (G-7280)*
M Z T, Santa Ana *Also called Macro-Z-Technology Company (G-1818)*
M&C Hotel Interests Inc....310 399-9344
530 Pico Blvd Santa Monica (90405) *(G-12934)*
M&G Duravent Inc....800 835-4429
877 Cotting Ct Vacaville (95688) *(G-4594)*
M&M Asseet Management Gnl....310 769-6669
2936 W El Segundo Blvd Gardena (90249) *(G-11162)*
M&R, Lodi *Also called M & R Co (G-8749)*
M+w US Inc....415 621-1199
1453 Mission St Fl 2 San Francisco (94103) *(G-25944)*
M-E Engineers Inc....310 842-8700
10113 Jefferson Blvd Culver City (90232) *(G-25945)*
M-N-Z Janitorial Services Inc....323 851-4115
2109 W Burbank Blvd Burbank (91506) *(G-14345)*
M4 Wind Services Inc....562 981-7797
4020 Long Beach Blvd Fl 2 Long Beach (90807) *(G-28143)*
MA Laboratories Inc....626 820-8988
18725 San Jose Ave City of Industry (91748) *(G-26563)*
MA Labs, City of Industry *Also called MA Laboratories Inc (G-26563)*
MA Steiner Construction Inc....916 988-6300
8999 Greenback Ln Fl 2 Orangevale (95662) *(G-1449)*
Maac Project, Chula Vista *Also called Metropolitan Area Advisory Com (G-24365)*
Maac Project Cwbh, San Diego *Also called Metropolitan Area Advisory Com (G-24364)*
Maap, Sacramento *Also called Mexican Amrcn Alcoholism Progr (G-24084)*
Mabie Marketing Group Inc....858 279-5585
8352 Clairemont Mesa Blvd San Diego (92111) *(G-17305)*
Mac Kenzie Warehouse, San Francisco *Also called S F Auto Parts Whse Inc (G-6760)*
Mac Pro Inc....562 623-4300
12300 Washington Blvd R Whittier (90606) *(G-13773)*
Macarthur Transit Community....415 989-1111
345 Spear St Ste 700 San Francisco (94105) *(G-1209)*
Maccarthy House, San Jose *Also called Momentum For Mental Health (G-24943)*
Macdonald Housing Partners LP....510 620-0865
350 Macdonald Ave Ste 100 Richmond (94801) *(G-11651)*
Macdonald Mott Group Inc....323 903-4100
3699 Crenshaw Blvd Los Angeles (90016) *(G-25946)*
Macdonald Mott LLC....408 321-5900
3103 N 1st St Bldg B San Jose (95134) *(G-25947)*
Macdonald Mott LLC....916 399-0580
2495 Natomas Park Dr # 530 Sacramento (95833) *(G-25948)*
Macdonald-Bedford LLC....510 436-4020
2100 Embarcadero Oakland (94606) *(G-27519)*
Macerich Company (PA)....310 394-6000
401 Wilshire Blvd Ste 700 Santa Monica (90401) *(G-12258)*
Macerich Company....310 474-6255
10800 W Pico Blvd Ste 312 Los Angeles (90064) *(G-11013)*
Macerich Company....562 861-9233
251 Stonewood St Downey (90241) *(G-11014)*
Macerich Company....310 474-5940
10800 W Pico Blvd Ste 312 Los Angeles (90064) *(G-11652)*
Machado & Sons Cnstr Inc....209 632-5260
1000 S Kilroy Rd Turlock (95380) *(G-1210)*
Machine Tools Supply, Costa Mesa *Also called Mt Supply Inc (G-7942)*
Machinima Inc....323 872-5300
3500 W Olive Ave Burbank (91505) *(G-16427)*
Machining Time Savers Inc....714 635-7373
1338 S State College Pkwy Anaheim (92806) *(G-7858)*
Machintel Corporation....617 517-3090
4225 Executive Sq La Jolla (92037) *(G-13879)*
Macias Gini & OConnell LLP (PA)....916 928-4600
3000 S St Ste 300 Sacramento (95816) *(G-26405)*
Mackay Smps Cvil Engineers Inc (PA)....925 416-1790
5142 Franklin Dr Ste C Pleasanton (94588) *(G-25949)*
Mackenzie Landscape A Cal Corp....951 679-5477
33380 Bailey Park Blvd Menifee (92584) *(G-907)*
Macmurray Pacific, San Francisco *Also called Wildenradt-Mcmurray Inc (G-7704)*
Macqurie Arcft Lsg Svcs US Inc....415 829-6600
2 Embarcadero Ctr Ste 200 San Francisco (94111) *(G-14556)*
Macro-Pro Inc (PA)....562 595-0900
2400 Grand Ave Long Beach (90815) *(G-17306)*
Macro-Pro Inc....510 483-2679
14764 Wicks Blvd San Leandro (94577) *(G-17307)*
Macro-Z-Technology Company (PA)....714 564-1130
841 E Washington Ave Santa Ana (92701) *(G-1818)*
Macronix America Inc (HQ)....408 262-8887
680 N Mccarthy Blvd # 200 Milpitas (95035) *(G-7602)*
Macrovision, San Jose *Also called Rovi Corporation (G-15430)*
Macsei Industries Corporation....323 233-7864
1784 E Vernon Ave Vernon (90058) *(G-8675)*
Macys Inc....916 373-0333
6200 Franklin Blvd Sacramento (95824) *(G-4697)*
Mad Dog Express Inc (PA)....650 588-1900
299 Lawrence Ave South San Francisco (94080) *(G-4037)*
Mad Dogg Athletics Inc (PA)....310 823-7008
2111 Narcissus Ct Venice (90291) *(G-8397)*
Mad River Community Hospital, Arcata *Also called American Hospital Mgt Corp (G-21448)*
Madden Corporation....714 922-1670
733 W Taft Ave Orange (92865) *(G-17308)*
Maddox Dairy LLC....559 867-3545
3899 W Davis Ave Riverdale (93656) *(G-431)*
Maddox Dairy A Ltd Partnership (PA)....559 867-3545
3899 W Davis Ave Riverdale (93656) *(G-432)*
Maddox Dairy A Ltd Partnership....559 867-4457
7285 W Davis Ave Riverdale (93656) *(G-433)*
Maddox Dairy A Ltd Partnership....559 866-5624
12863 W Kamm Ave Riverdale (93656) *(G-434)*
Made In USA Foundation Inc....310 623-3872
11950 San Vicente Blvd # 220 Los Angeles (90049) *(G-25292)*
Mader News Inc....818 551-5000
913 Ruberta Ave Glendale (91201) *(G-9168)*
Madera Cnty Bhvioral Hlth Svcs....559 673-3508
209 E 7th St Madera (93638) *(G-22771)*
Madera Community Hospital....559 675-5530
1210 E Almond Ave Ste A Madera (93637) *(G-19724)*
Madera Community Hospital....559 665-3768
285 Hospital Dr Chowchilla (93610) *(G-21721)*
Madera Community Hospital (PA)....559 675-5555
1250 E Almond Ave Madera (93637) *(G-21722)*
Madera Convalescent Hospital (PA)....559 673-9228
517 S A St Madera (93638) *(G-20752)*
Madera Convalescent Hospital....209 723-8814
1255 B St Merced (95341) *(G-22081)*
Madera Convalescent Hospital....209 723-2911
510 W 26th St Merced (95340) *(G-21303)*
Madera Convalescent Hospital....530 885-7051
260 Racetrack St Auburn (95603) *(G-21304)*
Madera County Probation Dept, Madera *Also called County of Los Angeles (G-23861)*
Madera County Road Department, Madera *Also called County of Madera (G-17880)*
Madera Disposal Systems Inc (HQ)....559 665-3099
21739 Road 19 Chowchilla (93610) *(G-6497)*
Madera Private Security Patrol....559 662-1546
910 W Yosemite Ave Madera (93637) *(G-16730)*
Madera Quality Nut, Madera *Also called Ready Roast Nut Company LLC (G-577)*
Maderas Golf Club....858 451-8100
17750 Old Coach Rd Poway (92064) *(G-18988)*
Madison Care Center LLC....619 444-1107
1391 E Madison Ave El Cajon (92021) *(G-20753)*
Madison Club Owners Assn....760 777-9320
53035 Meriwether Way La Quinta (92253) *(G-18758)*
Madison Club, The, La Quinta *Also called Madison Club Owners Assn (G-18758)*
Madison Materials....714 664-0159
1035 E 4th St Santa Ana (92701) *(G-6498)*
Madison Radiology Med Group....626 793-8189
65 N Madison Ave Ste M250 Pasadena (91101) *(G-22239)*
Madison Square Building, Oakland *Also called San Francisco Bay Area Rapid (G-3708)*

ALPHABETIC

Madrigal Vineyards, Calistoga *Also called Madrigal Vineyard Management* ***(G-17309)***
Madrigal Vineyard Management 707 942-8691
3718 Saint Helena Hwy Calistoga (94515) ***(G-17309)***
Madrona Mnr Wine Cntry Inn 707 433-4231
1001 Westside Rd Healdsburg (95448) ***(G-12935)***
Madrone Vineyard Management, Sonoma *Also called Clarbec Inc* ***(G-147)***
Maersk Inc 714 428-5500
555 Anton Blvd Ste 300 Costa Mesa (92626) ***(G-5118)***
Maersk Line, Costa Mesa *Also called Maersk Inc* ***(G-5118)***
Mafab Inc (PA) 714 893-0551
1925 Century Park E # 650 Los Angeles (90067) ***(G-12074)***
Magagnini, Fremont *Also called Intelliswift Software Inc* ***(G-16405)***
Magan Medical Clinic Inc (PA) 626 331-6411
420 W Rowland St Covina (91723) ***(G-19725)***
Magan Medical Clinic Inc 909 592-9712
330 W Covina Blvd San Dimas (91773) ***(G-19726)***
Magana Labor Services 805 524-0446
2896 W Telegraph Rd Fillmore (93015) ***(G-14701)***
Magarro Farms 949 859-6506
3 Sterling Irvine (92618) ***(G-558)***
Magave Tequila Inc 415 515-3536
6 Park Pl Belvedere Tiburon (94920) ***(G-9108)***
Magdalena Ecke Family YMCA, Encinitas *Also called YMCA of San Diego County* ***(G-25417)***
Magento Commerce, Campbell *Also called Xcommerce Inc* ***(G-15553)***
Maggiora Brosdrilling Inc (PA) 831 724-1338
595 Airport Blvd Watsonville (95076) ***(G-3358)***
Magic 92.5, San Diego *Also called Local Media of America LLC* ***(G-5807)***
Magic International, Santa Monica *Also called Mens Apparel Guild In Cal Inc* ***(G-25093)***
Magic Mountain LLC 661 255-4100
26101 Magic Mountain Pkwy Valencia (91355) ***(G-18413)***
Magic Workforce Solutions LLC 310 246-6153
9100 Wilsh Blvd Ste 700e Beverly Hills (90212) ***(G-27756)***
Magma Consulting Group LLC 415 315-9364
830 Traction Ave 3a Los Angeles (90013) ***(G-16428)***
Magma Design Automation Inc (HQ) 408 565-7500
1650 Tech Dr Ste 100 San Jose (95110) ***(G-15286)***
Magmalabs, Los Angeles *Also called Magma Consulting Group LLC* ***(G-16428)***
Magnell Associate Inc 626 271-1420
9997 Rose Hills Rd Whittier (90601) ***(G-4595)***
Magnell Associate Inc (HQ) 562 695-8823
17560 Rowland St City of Industry (91748) ***(G-7157)***
Magnell Associate Inc 626 271-1580
18045 Rowland St City of Industry (91748) ***(G-7158)***
Magnesite Specialties Inc 858 578-4186
8686 Production Ave Ste A San Diego (92121) ***(G-3125)***
Magnet In Sand Inc 623 703-5650
17011 Beach Blvd Ste 900 Huntington Beach (92647) ***(G-16154)***
Magnetic Imaging Affilates 510 204-1820
5730 Telegraph Ave Oakland (94609) ***(G-22240)***
Magnetika Inc (PA) 310 527-8100
2041 W 139th St Gardena (90249) ***(G-7453)***
Magnolia Convalescent Hospital, Riverside *Also called Magnolia Rhblttion Nursing Ctr* ***(G-21305)***
Magnolia Grdns Convalescent HM, Granada Hills *Also called Longwood Management Corp* ***(G-20742)***
Magnolia of Millbrae Inc 650 697-7700
201 Chadbourne Ave Millbrae (94030) ***(G-24723)***
Magnolia Rhblttion Nursing Ctr 951 688-4321
8133 Magnolia Ave Riverside (92504) ***(G-21305)***
Magnolia Special Care Center 619 442-8826
635 S Magnolia Ave El Cajon (92020) ***(G-21090)***
Magnolia Ventures Ltd 213 389-6900
4032 Wilshire Blvd Fl 6 Los Angeles (90010) ***(G-17310)***
Magnum Drywall Inc 510 979-0420
42027 Boscell Rd Fremont (94538) ***(G-2925)***
Magnum USA, Modesto *Also called Hi-TEC Sports Usa Inc* ***(G-8436)***
Magnus Security 619 546-7789
2667 Camino Del Rio S San Diego (92108) ***(G-16731)***
Magnus Tech Solutions Inc 650 320-0073
2600 Ei Camino Real Ste 601 Palo Alto (94306) ***(G-15287)***
Magnussens Dodge Crysler Jeep 530 885-2900
1901 Grass Valley Hwy Auburn (95603) ***(G-17806)***
Maguire Aviation, Van Nuys *Also called 16700 Roscoe Associates LLC* ***(G-18840)***
Maguire Aviation Group LLC 818 989-2300
7155 Valjean Ave Van Nuys (91406) ***(G-4884)***
Maguire Properties Twr 17 LLC 310 857-1100
1733 Ocean Ave Fl 4 Santa Monica (90401) ***(G-12259)***
Maher M F Concrete Cnstr, Vallejo *Also called M F Maher Inc* ***(G-1817)***
Mahler Enterprises Inc 760 537-7690
2121 E Tahquitz Canyon Wa Palm Springs (92262) ***(G-14903)***
MAI Construction Inc 408 434-9880
50 Bonaventura Dr San Jose (95134) ***(G-1211)***
MAI Systems, Lake Forest *Also called Infor (us) Inc* ***(G-15699)***
Maida Specialties Co, San Jose *Also called John A Maida Enterprises* ***(G-8170)***
Mail Boxes Etc, San Diego *Also called UPS Store Inc* ***(G-17577)***
Mailmark Enterprises LLC 818 407-0660
8587 Canoga Ave Canoga Park (91304) ***(G-14082)***
Main Electric Supply Co (PA) 949 833-3052
3600 W Segerstrom Ave Santa Ana (92704) ***(G-7454)***
Main Electric Supply Co 951 784-2900
461 Main St Riverside (92501) ***(G-7455)***
Main Frame Construction, Santa Clarita *Also called Santa Clarita Valley Bldrs Inc* ***(G-3086)***
Main Hospital, San Jose *Also called HCA Inc* ***(G-21593)***
Main Source Group Inc 213 387-1001
3255 Wilshire Blvd # 1806 Los Angeles (90010) ***(G-14346)***
Main Street Fibers Inc 909 986-6310
608 E Main St Ontario (91761) ***(G-6499)***
Main Street Specialty Surgery 714 704-1900
280 S Mn St Ste 100 Orange (92868) ***(G-21723)***
Mainfreight Inc (HQ) 310 900-1974
1400 Glenn Curtiss St Carson (90746) ***(G-5119)***
Mainline Equipment Inc 800 444-2288
20917 Higgins Ct Torrance (90501) ***(G-17937)***
Maintech Incorporated 714 921-8000
2401 N Glassell St Orange (92865) ***(G-15288)***
Maintenance, Long Beach *Also called Long Beach Unified School Dist* ***(G-14342)***
Maintenance & Operation Dept, Montebello *Also called Montebello Unified School Dst* ***(G-14363)***
Maintenance & Operations, Lodi *Also called Lodi Unified School District* ***(G-14341)***
Maintenance & Trnsp Fcilty, Irvine *Also called Irvine Unified School Distict* ***(G-3939)***
Maintenance Department, Petaluma *Also called Transportation California Dept* ***(G-1876)***
Maintenance Department, Fresno *Also called Fresno Unified School District* ***(G-14304)***
Maintenance Dept, Gardena *Also called Los Angeles Unified School Dst* ***(G-14343)***
Maintenance Dept, Brea *Also called City of Brea* ***(G-27778)***
Maintenance Service For The Cy 510 865-3778
1616 Fortmann Way Alameda (94501) ***(G-14347)***
Maintenance Staff Inc 562 493-3982
122 W 8th St Long Beach (90813) ***(G-14348)***
Maintenance Unit, San Diego *Also called San Diego Unified School Dst* ***(G-14417)***
Majestic Industry Hills LLC 626 810-4455
1 Industry Hills Pkwy City of Industry (91744) ***(G-12936)***
Majestic Roofing Inc 661 588-6120
3124 Patton Way Bakersfield (93308) ***(G-3188)***
Majesty One Properties Inc 909 980-8000
6249 Quartz St Rancho Cucamonga (91701) ***(G-11653)***
Major Transportation Svcs Inc 559 485-5949
3342 N Weber Ave Fresno (93722) ***(G-4214)***
Makar Anaheim LLC 714 740-4431
777 W Convention Way Anaheim (92802) ***(G-12937)***
Maker Studios Inc (HQ) 310 606-2182
3562 Eastham Dr Culver City (90232) ***(G-18481)***
Making Waves Education Program (PA) 510 237-3434
3220 Blume Dr Ste 250 San Pablo (94806) ***(G-12190)***
Makita USA Inc (HQ) 714 522-8088
14930 Northam St La Mirada (90638) ***(G-7693)***
Makkunis Inc 310 328-1999
2808 Oregon Ct Ste L10 Torrance (90503) ***(G-8124)***
Malaysia Airlines, Cerritos *Also called Malaysian Airline System* ***(G-5011)***
Malaysian Airline System 310 535-9288
17215 Studebaker Rd # 120 Cerritos (90703) ***(G-5011)***
Malco Maintenance Inc 714 630-0194
3703 E Melville Way Anaheim (92806) ***(G-3549)***
Malco Services, Anaheim *Also called Malco Maintenance Inc* ***(G-3549)***
Malco Services Inc 714 630-0194
3703 E Melville Way Anaheim (92806) ***(G-27520)***
Malcolm & Cisneros A Law Corp 949 252-1039
2112 Business Center Dr # 200 Irvine (92612) ***(G-23417)***
Malcolm Cisneros, Irvine *Also called Malcolm & Cisneros A Law Corp* ***(G-23417)***
Malcolm Drilling Company Inc (PA) 415 901-4400
92 Natoma St Ste 400 San Francisco (94105) ***(G-3550)***
Malibu Beach Inn, Malibu *Also called Mbipch LLC* ***(G-12985)***
Malibu Canyon Ldscp & Maint 805 523-2676
2046 Tierra Rejada Rd Moorpark (93021) ***(G-778)***
Malibu Castle, Aliso Viejo *Also called Apex Parks Group LLC* ***(G-19139)***
Malibu Castle 210 341-6663
27061 Aliso Creek Rd # 100 Aliso Viejo (92656) ***(G-18825)***
Malibu Conference Center Inc 818 889-6440
327 Latigo Canyon Rd Malibu (90265) ***(G-11015)***
Malibu Country Club, Malibu *Also called California Fuji International* ***(G-18719)***
Malibu Design Group 323 271-1700
5445 Jillson St Commerce (90040) ***(G-8398)***
Malibu Grand Prix 51, Newport Beach *Also called Festival Fun Parks LLC* ***(G-18821)***
Malibu Lagoon Museum, Malibu *Also called Parks and Recreation Cal Dept* ***(G-25036)***
Malibu Limousine Service, Marina Del Rey *Also called Executive Network Entps Inc* ***(G-3790)***
Malikco LLC 925 974-3555
2121 N Calif Blvd Ste 290 Walnut Creek (94596) ***(G-15738)***
Malka Communications Group 818 528-6894
15736 Hartsook St Encino (91436) ***(G-5400)***
Malka Communications Group Inc 818 990-0278
15260 Ventura Blvd # 1430 Sherman Oaks (91403) ***(G-28144)***
Malka Vrs, Encino *Also called Malka Communications Group* ***(G-5400)***
Mallcraft Inc 626 765-9100
2225 Windsor Ave Altadena (91001) ***(G-1606)***
Malloy Orchards Inc 530 695-1861
925 Koch Ln Live Oak (95953) ***(G-241)***
Maloof Sport Entertainment, Sacramento *Also called Kings Arena Ltd Partnership* ***(G-18552)***
Mamco Inc (PA) 951 776-9300
764 Ramona Expy Ste C Perris (92571) ***(G-1819)***
Mammoet Western Inc 626 444-4942
1419 Potrero Ave El Monte (91733) ***(G-4215)***
Mammography Center, Lompoc *Also called Lompoc Valley Medical Center* ***(G-19717)***
Mammoth Hospital, Mammoth Lakes *Also called Southern Mono Healthcare Dst* ***(G-21908)***
Mammoth Mountain Lake Corp 760 934-2571
10001 Minaret Rd Mammoth Lakes (93546) ***(G-13467)***
Mammoth Mountain Ski Area LLC (HQ) 760 934-2571
10001 Minaret Rd Mammoth Lakes (93546) ***(G-12938)***
Mamone James M, Roseville *Also called Sutter Health* ***(G-20080)***
Managed Care Systems Kern Cnty 661 716-7100
5251 Office Park Dr # 405 Bakersfield (93309) ***(G-10768)***
Managed Health Network 714 934-5519
7755 Center Ave Ste 700 Huntington Beach (92647) ***(G-10357)***
Managed Health Network (HQ) 415 460-8168
2370 Kerner Blvd San Rafael (94901) ***(G-10358)***

ALPHABETIC

Managed Health Network 510 620-6143
2370 Kerner Blvd San Rafael (94901) ***(G-10359)***
Managed Homecare Inc 951 341-0782
2520 Redhill Ave Santa Ana (92705) ***(G-22503)***
Managed Network Services LLC 650 232-4287
3800 Bridge Pkwy Redwood City (94065) ***(G-16155)***
Management Applied Programming (PA) 562 463-5000
13191 Crossroads Pkwy N # 205 City of Industry (91746) ***(G-16156)***
Management Associates, Saint Helena *Also called Silverado Orchards* ***(G-11204)***
Management Consulting Group, San Rafael *Also called McG Services Corporation* ***(G-14905)***
Management Success, Glendale *Also called Leekilpatrick Management Inc* ***(G-27505)***
Management Tech Consulting LLC 323 851-5008
7738 Skyhill Dr Los Angeles (90068) ***(G-27980)***
Management Trust Assn Inc 805 496-5514
100 E Thousand Oaks Blvd Thousand Oaks (91360) ***(G-12191)***
Management Trust Assn Inc 858 547-4373
9815 Carroll Canyon Rd San Diego (92131) ***(G-12192)***
Management Trust Assn Inc 951 694-1758
4160 Temescal Canyon Rd # 202 Corona (92883) ***(G-12193)***
Management Trust Assn Inc (PA) 714 285-2626
15661 Red Hill Ave # 201 Tustin (92780) ***(G-12194)***
Management Trust Assn Inc 562 926-3372
12607 Hiddencreek Way R Cerritos (90703) ***(G-27521)***
Management Trust, The, Tustin *Also called Management Trust Assn Inc* ***(G-12194)***
Manas Hospitality LLC 619 298-1291
445 Hotel Cir S San Diego (92108) ***(G-12939)***
Manatt Phelps & Phillips LLP 310 312-4249
11355 W Olympic Blvd Fl 2 Los Angeles (90064) ***(G-23418)***
Manatt Phelps & Phillips LLP 714 371-2500
695 Town Center Dr # 1400 Costa Mesa (92626) ***(G-23419)***
Manchester Band Pomo Indians 707 882-2788
24 Mamie Laiwa Dr Point Arena (95468) ***(G-24076)***
Manchester Center, Fresno *Also called US Property Group Inc* ***(G-11066)***
Manchester Grand Resorts LP 619 232-1234
1 Market Pl Fl 33 San Diego (92101) ***(G-12940)***
Manchester Point Arena, Point Arena *Also called Manchester Band Pomo Indians* ***(G-24076)***
Manchster Mnor Cnvlescent Hosp 323 753-1789
837 W Manchester Ave Los Angeles (90044) ***(G-21306)***
Mandalay Baseball Properties, Los Angeles *Also called Mandalay Sports Entrmt LLC* ***(G-18557)***
Mandalay Sports Entrmt LLC (PA) 323 549-4300
4751 Wilshire Blvd Fl 3 Los Angeles (90010) ***(G-18557)***
Manduka LLC (HQ) 310 426-1495
2121 Park Pl Ste 250 El Segundo (90245) ***(G-8022)***
Maneri Traffic Control Inc 951 695-5104
47423 Rainbow Canyon Rd Temecula (92592) ***(G-1820)***
Mangan Inc (PA) 310 835-8080
3901 Via Oro Ave Long Beach (90810) ***(G-25950)***
Mangold Property Management 831 372-1338
575 Calle Principal Monterey (93940) ***(G-11654)***
Mangrove Lab & X-Ray, Chico *Also called Mangrove Medical Group* ***(G-19727)***
Mangrove Medical Group 530 345-0064
1040 Mangrove Ave Chico (95926) ***(G-19727)***
Manhattan Beach Marriott, Manhattan Beach *Also called Host Hotels & Resorts LP* ***(G-12775)***
Manhattan Country Club, Manhattan Beach *Also called 1334 Partners LP* ***(G-18839)***
Manheim Riverside Auto Auction, Riverside *Also called Cox Automotive Inc* ***(G-6671)***
Manheim San Diego, Oceanside *Also called Cox Automotive Inc* ***(G-6672)***
Manhole Adjusting Contrs Inc 323 725-1387
9500 Beverly Rd Pico Rivera (90660) ***(G-1821)***
Maniflo Money Exchange Inc (PA) 619 434-7200
1442 Highland Ave National City (91950) ***(G-9722)***
Mann Lake Ltd 530 662-4061
500 Santa Anita Dr Woodland (95776) ***(G-9143)***
Mann Packing Co Inc (PA) 831 422-7405
1333 Schilling Pl Salinas (93901) ***(G-559)***
Mann's Theatres, Los Angeles *Also called Weststar Cinemas Inc* ***(G-18354)***
Manning Gardens Inc 559 834-2586
2113 E Manning Ave Fresno (93725) ***(G-21307)***
Manning Gardens Care Ctr Inc 559 834-2586
2113 E Manning Ave Fresno (93725) ***(G-20754)***
Manning Grdns Cnvalescent Hosp, Fresno *Also called Manning Gardens Inc* ***(G-21307)***
Manning Kass Ellrod Ram Trestr (PA) 213 624-6900
801 S Figueroa St Fl 15 Los Angeles (90017) ***(G-23420)***
Mannkind Corporation (PA) 661 775-5300
25134 Rye Canyon Loop # 300 Valencia (91355) ***(G-26564)***
MANOR AT SANTA TERESITA HOSPIT, Duarte *Also called Santa Teresita Inc* ***(G-21864)***
Manor Bell L P 707 526-9782
790 Sonoma Ave Santa Rosa (95404) ***(G-1379)***
Manor Care, Fountain Valley *Also called Hcr Manorcare Med Svcs Fla LLC* ***(G-20649)***
Manor Care, Citrus Heights *Also called Hcr Manorcare Med Svcs Fla LLC* ***(G-20650)***
Manor Care, Sunnyvale *Also called Hcr Manorcare Med Svcs Fla LLC* ***(G-20652)***
Manorcare Health Services, Walnut Creek *Also called Hcr Manorcare Med Svcs Fla LLC* ***(G-20647)***
Manorcare Health Services, Aliso Viejo *Also called Hcr Manorcare Med Svcs Fla LLC* ***(G-20648)***
Manorcare Health Svcs Hemet, Hemet *Also called Hcr Manorcare Med Svcs Fla LLC* ***(G-20651)***
Manorcare Health Svcs Rossmoor, Walnut Creek *Also called Hcr Manorcare Med Svcs Fla LLC* ***(G-20653)***
Manorcare Hlth Svcs Encinitas, Encinitas *Also called Hcr Manorcare Med Svcs Fla LLC* ***(G-20654)***
Manpower, San Diego *Also called United States Dept of Navy* ***(G-14967)***
Mansion Hospitality Services 916 643-6222
3410 Westover St McClellan (95652) ***(G-27522)***
Manteca Care Rhabilitation Ctr, Manteca *Also called Karma Inc* ***(G-20693)***
Mantech International Corp 310 765-9324
615 N Nash St Ste 200 El Segundo (90245) ***(G-15991)***
Mantech International Corp 858 492-9938
8328 Clairemont Mesa Blvd San Diego (92111) ***(G-15992)***
Mantech Systems Engrg Corp 858 292-9000
8328 Clairemont Mesa Blvd # 100 San Diego (92111) ***(G-27981)***
Manual Arts Svc Ctr Studnt Bdy 323 732-0153
3721 W Washington Blvd Los Angeles (90018) ***(G-18657)***
Manufacturers Bank (HQ) 213 489-6200
515 S Figueroa St Ste 400 Los Angeles (90071) ***(G-9506)***
Manufacturing Facility, Davis *Also called Schilling Robotics LLC* ***(G-26056)***
MAOF, Montebello *Also called Mexican Amrcn Oprtnty Fndation* ***(G-24085)***
Map Cargo Global Logistics (PA) 310 297-8300
2501 Santa Fe Ave Redondo Beach (90278) ***(G-5120)***
Maple Dairy LP 661 396-9600
15857 Bear Mountain Blvd Bakersfield (93311) ***(G-435)***
Mapr Technologies Inc (PA) 408 428-9472
350 Holger Way San Jose (95134) ***(G-15289)***
Mapr Technology, San Jose *Also called Mapr Technologies Inc* ***(G-15289)***
Maqui Holdings LLC 530 877-9316
1633 Cypress Ln Paradise (95969) ***(G-20755)***
Mar-Kell Seal, Irvine *Also called Quadion LLC* ***(G-10176)***
Marathon General Inc 760 738-9714
1728 Mission Rd Escondido (92029) ***(G-1822)***
Marathon Industries Inc 661 286-1520
25597 Springbrook Ave Santa Clarita (91350) ***(G-6688)***
Marathon Land Inc (PA) 805 488-3585
2599 E Hueneme Rd Oxnard (93033) ***(G-300)***
Marathon Truck Bodies, Santa Clarita *Also called Marathon Industries Inc* ***(G-6688)***
Maravilla Foundation (PA) 323 721-4162
5729 Union Pacific Ave Commerce (90022) ***(G-25293)***
Marbella Country Club 949 248-3700
30800 Golf Club Dr San Juan Capistrano (92675) ***(G-18989)***
Marbella Golf & Country Club 949 248-3700
30800 Golf Club Dr San Juan Capistrano (92675) ***(G-18990)***
Marblewest Inc 714 847-6472
7421 Vincent Cir Huntington Beach (92648) ***(G-3018)***
Marbleworks, Huntington Beach *Also called Marblewest Inc* ***(G-3018)***
Marborg Industries (PA) 805 963-1852
728 E Yanonali St Santa Barbara (93103) ***(G-6500)***
Marc, San Diego *Also called Mscsoftware Corporation* ***(G-15765)***
March International Inc 909 821-5128
1249 S Dmnd Bar Blvd 20 Diamond Bar (91765) ***(G-2065)***
Marchbrook Building Co 209 473-6084
3255 W March Ln Ste 400 Stockton (95219) ***(G-1212)***
Marco Crane & Rigging Co 619 938-8080
10168 Channel Rd Lakeside (92040) ***(G-14487)***
Marco Roofing, Fremont *Also called Milan Corporation* ***(G-3192)***
Marcolin USA Inc 415 383-6348
6 Janet Way Apt 116 Belvedere Tiburon (94920) ***(G-7333)***
Marcor Environmental-West 562 921-2733
16027 Carmenita Rd Cerritos (90703) ***(G-3551)***
Marcos Auto Body Inc (PA) 626 286-5691
1390 E Palm St Altadena (91001) ***(G-17759)***
Marcum LLP 415 543-6900
303 2nd St Ste 950 San Francisco (94107) ***(G-26406)***
Marcum LLP 310 432-7400
2049 Century Park E # 300 Los Angeles (90067) ***(G-26407)***
Marcus & Millichap Capitl Corp 650 494-1400
777 S California Ave Palo Alto (94304) ***(G-11655)***
Marcus Millichap Reis Nev Inc 650 494-1400
23975 Park Sorrento # 400 Calabasas (91302) ***(G-11656)***
Marcus Mllchap RE Inv Svcs Inc 415 391-9220
750 Battery St Fl 5 San Francisco (94111) ***(G-11657)***
Mardx Diagnostics Inc 760 929-0500
5919 Farnsworth Ct Carlsbad (92008) ***(G-7275)***
Mare Island Outpatient Clinic, Vallejo *Also called Veterans Health Administration* ***(G-20195)***
Marelich Mechanical Co Inc (HQ) 510 785-5500
24041 Amador St Hayward (94544) ***(G-2289)***
Margate Construction Inc 310 830-8610
25007 Figueroa St Carson (90745) ***(G-1965)***
Marguerite Gardens, Alhambra *Also called California Peo Home* ***(G-24578)***
Mariadb Usa Inc 847 562-9000
350 Bay St Ste 100-319 San Francisco (94133) ***(G-7159)***
Mariak Industries Inc 310 661-4400
575 W Manville St Rancho Dominguez (90220) ***(G-6873)***
Mariak Window Fashion, Rancho Dominguez *Also called Mariak Industries Inc* ***(G-6873)***
Marian Extended Care Cntr, Santa Maria *Also called Dignity Health* ***(G-20520)***
Marian Home Care and Hospice, Santa Maria *Also called Dignity Health* ***(G-22424)***
Marian Hospital Homecare, Arroyo Grande *Also called Dignity Health* ***(G-22423)***
Marian Regional Medical Center, Santa Maria *Also called Dignity Health* ***(G-21533)***
Marian West, Santa Maria *Also called Dignity Health* ***(G-22720)***
Mariani Nut Company 530 662-3311
709 Dutton St Winters (95694) ***(G-560)***
Mariani Nut Company Inc (PA) 530 795-3311
709 Dutton St Winters (95694) ***(G-204)***
Mariani Nut Company Inc 530 795-1272
1709 Deutton Winters (95694) ***(G-205)***
Mariani Nut Company Inc 530 795-2225
12 Baker St Winters (95694) ***(G-206)***
Mariani Packing Co Inc (PA) 707 452-2800
500 Crocker Dr Vacaville (95688) ***(G-561)***
Marianis Inn & Restaurant 408 243-0312
2500 El Camino Real Santa Clara (95051) ***(G-12941)***

ALPHABETIC

Marianne Frostig Center (PA)....626 791-1255
971 N Altadena Dr Pasadena (91107) ***(G-25145)***
Maricopa Packers, Bakersfield *Also called Sun Pacific Maricopa* ***(G-588)***
Marie Cllender Wholesalers Inc....951 737-6760
170 E Rincon St Corona (92879) ***(G-8560)***
Marika Group Inc....858 537-5300
8960 Carroll Way San Diego (92121) ***(G-8399)***
Marin Airporter Inc....415 884-2878
1455 N Hamilton Pkwy Novato (94949) ***(G-3882)***
Marin Cnvlscent Rhbltion Hosp....415 435-4554
30 Hacienda Dr Belvedere Tiburon (94920) ***(G-20756)***
Marin Community Clinic....415 448-1500
1177 Francisco Blvd E B San Rafael (94901) ***(G-19728)***
Marin Community Clinics, San Rafael *Also called Marin Community Clinic* ***(G-19728)***
Marin Country Club Inc....415 382-6700
500 Country Club Dr Novato (94949) ***(G-18991)***
Marin County Sart Program....415 892-1628
655 Canyon Rd Novato (94947) ***(G-22082)***
Marin County Welfare Dept, San Rafael *Also called County of Marin* ***(G-23863)***
Marin General Hospital....415 925-7000
250 Bon Air Rd Greenbrae (94904) ***(G-21724)***
Marin Horizon School Inc....415 388-8408
305 Montford Ave Mill Valley (94941) ***(G-24480)***
Marin Humane Society....415 883-4621
171 Bel Marin Keys Blvd Novato (94949) ***(G-25554)***
Marin Industrial Distributors, San Rafael *Also called Jacksons Hardware Inc* ***(G-7688)***
Marin Labor Services....805 525-7730
277 Country View Ct Santa Paula (93060) ***(G-673)***
Marin Municipal Water District (PA)....415 945-1455
220 Nellen Ave Corte Madera (94925) ***(G-6369)***
Marin Resource Recovery Center, San Rafael *Also called Marin Sanitary Service* ***(G-6501)***
Marin Sanitary Service (PA)....415 456-2601
1050 Andersen Dr San Rafael (94901) ***(G-6501)***
Marin Software Incorporated (PA)....415 399-2580
123 Mission St Fl 27 San Francisco (94105) ***(G-16157)***
Marina Auto Body Shop Inc....310 822-6615
4095 Redwood Ave Los Angeles (90066) ***(G-17760)***
Marina Autobody, Los Angeles *Also called Williamson Enterprises Inc* ***(G-17776)***
Marina Breeze, San Leandro *Also called Vasona Management Inc* ***(G-11219)***
Marina Care Center, Culver City *Also called D K Fortune & Associates Inc* ***(G-21205)***
Marina City Club LP A Cali....310 822-0611
4333 Admiralty Way Marina Del Rey (90292) ***(G-11163)***
Marina Convalescent Center, Fremont *Also called C J Health Services Inc* ***(G-20428)***
Marina Del Rey Hospital....310 823-8911
4650 Lincoln Blvd Marina Del Rey (90292) ***(G-21725)***
Marina International Hotel, Venice *Also called Outrigger Hotels Hawaii* ***(G-13050)***
Marina International Hotel, Marina Del Rey *Also called Al Anwa USA Incorporated* ***(G-12377)***
Marine Avenue Adult Center, Wilmington *Also called Los Angeles Unified School Dst* ***(G-24073)***
Marine Band San Diego....619 524-1754
1400 Russell Ave San Diego (92140) ***(G-18482)***
Marine Corps United States....760 725-1304
Camp Pendleton Oceanside (92055) ***(G-22157)***
Marine Corps United States....760 430-4709
A St Bldg 1341 Camp Pendleton (92055) ***(G-12942)***
Marine Corps United States....760 725-7144
Bldg 632044 Camp Pendleton (92055) ***(G-24361)***
Marine Corps Community Svcs, San Diego *Also called Business and Support Services* ***(G-19155)***
Marine Mammal Center (PA)....415 339-0430
2000 Bunker Rd Sausalito (94965) ***(G-621)***
Marine Technical Services Inc....310 549-8030
211 N Marine Ave Wilmington (90744) ***(G-17311)***
Marine World/Africa USA, Vallejo *Also called City of Vallejo* ***(G-18815)***
Mariner, San Jose *Also called Health & Rehabilitation Center* ***(G-20655)***
Mariner Health Care Inc....310 371-4628
4109 Emerald St Torrance (90503) ***(G-20757)***
Mariner Health Care Inc....510 792-3743
39022 Presidio Way Fremont (94538) ***(G-20758)***
Mariner Health Care Inc....408 842-9311
8170 Murray Ave Gilroy (95020) ***(G-20759)***
Mariner Health Care Inc....916 422-4825
7400 24th St Sacramento (95822) ***(G-20760)***
Mariner Health Care Inc....408 298-3950
2065 Forest Ave San Jose (95128) ***(G-20761)***
Mariner Health Care Inc....510 232-5945
13484 San Pablo Ave San Pablo (94806) ***(G-27120)***
Mariner Health Care Inc....323 665-1185
3032 Rowena Ave Los Angeles (90039) ***(G-20762)***
Mariner Health Care Inc....530 756-1800
1850 E 8th St Davis (95616) ***(G-20763)***
Mariner Health Care Inc....818 246-5677
430 N Glendale Ave Glendale (91206) ***(G-20764)***
Mariner Health Care Inc....831 475-6323
675 24th Ave Santa Cruz (95062) ***(G-20765)***
Mariner Health Care Inc....510 538-4424
1768 B St Hayward (94541) ***(G-20766)***
Mariner Health Care Inc....510 785-2880
19700 Hesperian Blvd Hayward (94541) ***(G-20767)***
Mariner Health Care Inc....562 942-7019
8925 Mines Ave Pico Rivera (90660) ***(G-20768)***
Mariner Health Care Inc....415 479-3610
45 Professional Ctr Pkwy San Rafael (94903) ***(G-20769)***
Mariner Health Care Inc....408 377-9275
2065 Los Gatos Almaden Rd San Jose (95124) ***(G-20770)***
Mariner Health Care Inc....510 261-5200
3025 High St Oakland (94619) ***(G-20771)***
Mariner Health Care Inc....209 466-2066
537 E Fulton St Stockton (95204) ***(G-20772)***
Mariner Health Care Inc....818 985-5990
13000 Victory Blvd North Hollywood (91606) ***(G-20773)***
Mariner Health Care Inc....818 957-0850
3050 Montrose Ave La Crescenta (91214) ***(G-20774)***
Mariner Health Care Inc....916 481-5500
3400 Alta Arden Expy Sacramento (95825) ***(G-20775)***
Mariner Square Athletic Inc....510 523-8011
2227 Mariner Square Loop Alameda (94501) ***(G-18658)***
Mariner Systems Inc (PA)....305 266-7255
114 C Ave Coronado (92118) ***(G-17312)***
Mariner's Point Golf Course, Foster City *Also called Vb Golf LLC* ***(G-27274)***
Mariners Cove Apartments, San Diego *Also called Lincoln Mariners Assoc Ltd* ***(G-11157)***
Marines Memorial Association....415 673-6672
609 Sutter St San Francisco (94102) ***(G-25294)***
MARINES' MEMORIAL CLUB & HOTEL, San Francisco *Also called Marines Memorial Association* ***(G-25294)***
Marinow Harry MD Facs Inc....562 430-3561
3742 Katella Ave Ste 401 Los Alamitos (90720) ***(G-19729)***
Mariposa Horticultural Entps, Irwindale *Also called Mariposa Landscapes Inc* ***(G-908)***
Mariposa Landscapes Inc (PA)....623 463-2200
15529 Arrow Hwy Irwindale (91706) ***(G-908)***
Maritime Hotel Associates LP....415 563-0800
495 Jefferson St San Francisco (94109) ***(G-12943)***
Maritzcx Research LLC....310 783-4300
20285 S Wstn Ave Ste 101 Torrance (90501) ***(G-4995)***
Maritzcx Research LLC....310 525-1300
3901 Via Oro Ave Ste 200 Long Beach (90810) ***(G-26686)***
Mariz Berry Farms....805 981-9908
1650 E Gonzales Rd Oxnard (93036) ***(G-121)***
Mark 1 Mortgage Corporation....562 924-6173
19147 Bloomsville Ave Cerritos (90703) ***(G-9872)***
Mark 1 Mortgage Corporation (PA)....714 752-5700
1428 E Chapman Ave Orange (92866) ***(G-9936)***
Mark Diversified Inc....916 923-6275
650 Howe Ave Ste 1045 Sacramento (95825) ***(G-1607)***
Mark E Jacobson M D....707 571-4022
1260 N Dutton Ave Ste 230 Santa Rosa (95401) ***(G-19730)***
Mark Garcia....707 446-4529
5131 Ellsworth Rd Ste B Vacaville (95688) ***(G-14349)***
Mark H Leibenhaut MD....916 454-6600
2800 L St Ste 110 Sacramento (95816) ***(G-19731)***
Mark Herzog & Company Inc....818 762-4640
4640 Lankershim Blvd North Hollywood (91602) ***(G-18106)***
Mark Hopkins IHC....415 616-6991
999 California St San Francisco (94108) ***(G-12944)***
Mark III Construction Inc....916 381-8080
5101 Florin Perkins Rd Sacramento (95826) ***(G-2639)***
Mark III Dvlpers Dsgn/Builders, Sacramento *Also called Mark III Construction Inc* ***(G-2639)***
Mark Land Electric Inc....818 883-5110
7876 Deering Ave Canoga Park (91304) ***(G-2640)***
Mark One Corporation....209 537-4581
1711 Richland Ave Ceres (95307) ***(G-21308)***
Mark R Eggen Construction Inc....949 661-2674
3910 Calle Andalucia San Clemente (92673) ***(G-1213)***
Mark Roberts, Santa Ana *Also called Celmol Inc* ***(G-9251)***
Mark Scott Construction Inc....209 982-0502
241 Frank West Cir # 200 Stockton (95206) ***(G-1324)***
Mark Scott Construction Inc (PA)....925 944-0502
2835 Contra Costa Blvd Pleasant Hill (94523) ***(G-1608)***
Mark Twain Conv. Hospital, San Andreas *Also called Avalon Health Care Inc* ***(G-20397)***
Mark Twain Medical Center (HQ)....209 754-3521
768 Mountain Ranch Rd San Andreas (95249) ***(G-21726)***
Mark Twain Medical Center....209 754-1487
768 Mountain Ranch Rd San Andreas (95249) ***(G-21727)***
Mark Twain St Josephs Hospital, San Andreas *Also called Dignity Health* ***(G-19502)***
Mark Twain St Josephs Hospital, San Andreas *Also called Mark Twain Medical Center* ***(G-21726)***
Markel Corp....818 595-0600
21600 Oxnard St Ste 900 Woodland Hills (91367) ***(G-10769)***
Markel West Inc....818 595-0600
21600 Oxnard St Ste 400 Woodland Hills (91367) ***(G-10770)***
Marker Hotel, The, San Francisco *Also called Geary Darling Lessee Inc* ***(G-12661)***
Market Centre, Livermore *Also called Unified Grocers Inc* ***(G-8543)***
Market Hall Foods, Oakland *Also called Pasta Shop* ***(G-8898)***
Market Metrix, Larkspur *Also called Clarabridge Inc* ***(G-16335)***
Market Motive....831 706-2369
10 Victor Sq Ste 250 Scotts Valley (95066) ***(G-27523)***
Market Scan Info Systems Inc (PA)....805 823-4258
811 Camarillo Springs Rd B Camarillo (93012) ***(G-15290)***
Market Smart Inc....925 846-6237
6900 Koll Center Pkwy # 406 Pleasanton (94566) ***(G-8493)***
Market Tech Media Corporation....661 257-4745
27220 Turnberry Ln # 190 Valencia (91355) ***(G-14152)***
Marketing Department, San Francisco *Also called Morrison & Foerster LLP* ***(G-23451)***
Marketing Professionals Inc....714 578-0500
5100 E La Palma Ave # 116 Anaheim (92807) ***(G-27524)***
Marketing Sales & Dist Div, Fontana *Also called Weyerhaeuser Company* ***(G-6970)***
Marketlinx Inc....714 250-6751
4 First American Way Santa Ana (92707) ***(G-15739)***
Marketlive Inc....707 780-1600
617 2nd St Ste B Petaluma (94952) ***(G-16158)***
Marketo Inc (HQ)....650 376-2300
901 Mariners Island Blvd San Mateo (94404) ***(G-15291)***
Marketshare Inc (PA)....408 262-0677
2001 Tarob Ct Milpitas (95035) ***(G-13952)***

ALPHABETIC

ALPHABETIC SECTION
Martin Associates Group Inc (PA)

Marketshare Partners LLC (HQ)..............................310 914-5677
11150 Santa Monica Blvd # 500 Los Angeles (90025) *(G-26687)*
Marketwatch Inc (HQ)..............................415 439-6400
201 California St Fl 13 San Francisco (94111) *(G-16948)*
Marketwire Inc (HQ)..............................310 765-3200
100 N Sepulveda Blvd El Segundo (90245) *(G-16949)*
Marklogic Corporation (PA)..............................650 655-2300
999 Skyway Rd Ste 200 San Carlos (94070) *(G-15292)*
Markmonitor Holdings Inc..............................415 278-8400
425 Market St Ste 500 San Francisco (94105) *(G-15293)*
Markmonitor Inc (HQ)..............................415 278-8400
425 Market St Ste 500 San Francisco (94105) *(G-16429)*
Markstein Bev Co Sacramento..............................916 920-3911
60 Main Ave Sacramento (95838) *(G-9070)*
Markstein Beverage Co..............................760 744-9100
505 S Pacific St San Marcos (92078) *(G-9071)*
Markstein Beverage Company, Sacramento *Also called Markstein Bev Co Sacramento (G-9070)*
Markwins Beauty Products Inc..............................909 595-8898
22067 Ferrero City of Industry (91789) *(G-8276)*
Marland Co LP..............................213 614-6171
444 S Flower St Ste 1200 Los Angeles (90071) *(G-220)*
Marlin Equity Partners LLC (PA)..............................310 364-0100
338 Pier Ave Hermosa Beach (90254) *(G-10161)*
Marlinda Imperial Hospital, Pasadena *Also called Two Palms Nursing Center Inc (G-21396)*
Marlinda Management Inc (PA)..............................310 638-6691
3351 E Imperial Hwy Lynwood (90262) *(G-21309)*
Marlora Investments LLC..............................562 494-3311
3801 E Anaheim St Long Beach (90804) *(G-20776)*
Marlora Post Accute, Long Beach *Also called Marlora Investments LLC (G-20776)*
Marmalade LLC..............................310 317-4242
3894 Cross Creek Rd Malibu (90265) *(G-17313)*
Marmalade Cafes, Malibu *Also called Marmalade LLC (G-17313)*
Marmol Radziner..............................310 826-6222
12210 Nebraska Ave Los Angeles (90025) *(G-26234)*
Marna Health Services Inc..............................909 882-2965
4280 Cypress Dr San Bernardino (92407) *(G-22996)*
Marne Construction Inc..............................714 935-0995
749 N Poplar St Orange (92868) *(G-3293)*
Maroevich OShea & Coghlan..............................415 957-0600
44 Montgomery St Ste 1700 San Francisco (94104) *(G-10771)*
Marotto Corporation..............................818 775-0320
9620 Topanga Canyon Pl D Chatsworth (91311) *(G-14350)*
Marques Pipeline Inc..............................916 923-3434
7225 26th St Rio Linda (95673) *(G-25951)*
Marquez Brothers Advg Agcy..............................408 960-2700
5801 Rue Ferrari San Jose (95138) *(G-17314)*
Marquez Brothers Entps Inc..............................626 330-3310
15480 Valley Blvd City of Industry (91746) *(G-8494)*
Marquez Brothers Intl Inc..............................323 722-8103
1328 W Colegrove Ave Montebello (90640) *(G-8495)*
Marquez Brothers Intl Inc..............................559 584-8000
179 S 11th Ave Hanford (93230) *(G-8496)*
Marrakesh Golf Shop..............................760 568-2688
47000 Marrakesh Dr Palm Desert (92260) *(G-18992)*
Marrakesh Management, Palm Desert *Also called Marrakesh Golf Shop (G-18992)*
Marrakesh Management Corp..............................760 568-2688
47000 Marrakesh Dr Palm Desert (92260) *(G-11658)*
Marriot Courtyard..............................415 775-1103
580 Beach St San Francisco (94133) *(G-12945)*
Marriott, Riverside *Also called Sunstone Hotel Management Inc (G-13322)*
Marriott, San Diego *Also called Host Hotels & Resorts LP (G-12763)*
Marriott, San Jose *Also called Host International Inc (G-12778)*
Marriott, San Diego *Also called Hhlp San Diego Lessee LLC (G-12701)*
Marriott, NAPA *Also called Sunstone Hotel Investors Inc (G-13314)*
Marriott, Burbank *Also called Shc Burbank II LLC (G-13239)*
Marriott, Los Angeles *Also called Host Hotels & Resorts LP (G-12767)*
Marriott, Newport Beach *Also called Host Hotels & Resorts LP (G-12771)*
Marriott, Santa Monica *Also called Windsor Capital Group Inc (G-13418)*
Marriott, Fullerton *Also called Merritt Hospitality LLC (G-12991)*
Marriott, Oakland *Also called Cim/Oakland City Center LLC (G-12521)*
Marriott, Baldwin Park *Also called Ols Hotels & Resorts LP (G-13041)*
Marriott, Marina Del Rey *Also called Host Hotels & Resorts LP (G-12776)*
Marriott, Riverside *Also called Windsor Capital Group Inc (G-13424)*
Marriott, Walnut Creek *Also called Windsor Capital Group Inc (G-13425)*
Marriott..............................760 720-9898
3140 El Camino Real Carlsbad (92008) *(G-12946)*
Marriott..............................949 380-3000
10 Morgan Irvine (92618) *(G-12947)*
Marriott Burbank, Burbank *Also called AWH Burbank Hotel LLC (G-12408)*
Marriott Burbank, Burbank *Also called Spire Concessions LLC (G-13280)*
Marriott Fisherman's Wharf, San Francisco *Also called Host Hotels & Resorts Inc (G-12760)*
Marriott Foundation For People..............................510 834-4700
1970 Broadway Ste 1000 Oakland (94612) *(G-24362)*
Marriott Grand Residence..............................530 542-8400
1001 Heavenly Village Way South Lake Tahoe (96150) *(G-12948)*
Marriott Hotels & Resorts..............................510 451-4000
1001 Broadway Oakland (94607) *(G-12949)*
Marriott International Inc..............................760 431-9399
5835 Owens Ave Carlsbad (92008) *(G-12950)*
Marriott International Inc..............................714 209-6586
4381 Myra Ave Cypress (90630) *(G-12951)*
Marriott International Inc..............................310 337-2800
9620 Airport Blvd Los Angeles (90045) *(G-12952)*
Marriott International Inc..............................858 523-1700
11966 El Camino Real San Diego (92130) *(G-12953)*
Marriott International Inc..............................310 641-5700
5855 W Century Blvd Los Angeles (90045) *(G-12954)*
Marriott International Inc..............................415 947-0700
299 2nd St San Francisco (94105) *(G-12955)*
Marriott International Inc..............................619 831-0225
900 Bayfront Ct San Diego (92101) *(G-12956)*
Marriott International Inc..............................949 724-3606
18000 Von Karman Ave Irvine (92612) *(G-12957)*
Marriott International Inc..............................510 413-3700
46100 Landing Pkwy Fremont (94538) *(G-12958)*
Marriott International Inc..............................858 587-1414
4240 La Jolla Village Dr La Jolla (92037) *(G-12959)*
Marriott International Inc..............................858 587-1770
5852 Stadium St San Diego (92122) *(G-12960)*
Marriott International Inc..............................760 776-0050
38305 Cook St Palm Desert (92211) *(G-12961)*
Marriott International Inc..............................310 333-0888
2135 E El Segundo Blvd El Segundo (90245) *(G-12962)*
Marriott International Inc..............................858 278-2100
5400 Kearny Mesa Rd San Diego (92111) *(G-12963)*
Marriott International Inc..............................562 425-5210
4700 Airport Plaza Dr Long Beach (90815) *(G-12964)*
Marriott International Inc..............................909 937-6788
2025 Convention Ctr Way Ontario (91764) *(G-12965)*
Marriott International Inc..............................818 887-4800
21850 Oxnard St Woodland Hills (91367) *(G-12966)*
Marriott International Inc..............................951 371-0107
1015 Montecito Dr Corona (92879) *(G-12967)*
Marriott International Inc..............................310 322-0700
2000 E Mariposa Ave El Segundo (90245) *(G-12968)*
Marriott International Inc..............................310 725-9696
14400 Aviation Blvd Hawthorne (90250) *(G-12969)*
Marriott International Inc..............................408 252-9100
10605 N Wolfe Rd Cupertino (95014) *(G-12970)*
Marriott International Inc..............................415 989-3500
905 California St San Francisco (94108) *(G-12971)*
Marriott International Inc..............................510 657-4600
39802 Cedar Blvd Newark (94560) *(G-12972)*
Marriott International Inc..............................562 595-0909
4111 E Willow St Long Beach (90815) *(G-12973)*
Marriott International Inc..............................707 935-6600
1325 Broadway Sonoma (95476) *(G-12974)*
Marriott International Inc..............................714 545-5261
3130 S Harbor Blvd # 550 Santa Ana (92704) *(G-12975)*
Marriott International Inc..............................925 689-1010
700 Ellinwood Way Pleasant Hill (94523) *(G-12976)*
Marriott International Inc (PA)..............................415 929-2030
500 Post St San Francisco (94102) *(G-12977)*
Marriott International Inc..............................213 284-3862
900 W Olympic Blvd Los Angeles (90015) *(G-12978)*
Marriott International Inc..............................650 692-9100
1800 Old Bayshore Hwy Burlingame (94010) *(G-12979)*
Marriott International Inc..............................925 866-1228
18090 San Ramon Vly Blvd San Ramon (94583) *(G-12980)*
Marriott International Inc..............................619 831-0224
900 Bayfront Ct San Diego (92101) *(G-12981)*
Marriott Los Angeles Downtown, Los Angeles *Also called Interstate Hotels Resorts Inc (G-12849)*
Marriott San Dego Gslamp Qrter, San Diego *Also called San Diego Hotel Company LLC (G-13197)*
Marriotts Newport Coast Villa..............................949 464-6000
23000 Newport Coast Dr Newport Beach (92657) *(G-12982)*
Marrow Meadows, Walnut *Also called M & R Joint Venture Electrical (G-2638)*
Mars & Co Consulting LLC..............................415 288-6970
600 Montgomery St # 4200 San Francisco (94111) *(G-27525)*
Marsh & McLennan Agency LLC..............................949 544-8460
101 Enterprise Ste 330 Aliso Viejo (92656) *(G-10772)*
Marsh & McLennan Agency LLC..............................415 243-4160
Steuart Towe 1market San Francisco (94105) *(G-10773)*
Marsh & McLennan Agency LLC..............................510 273-8888
1340 Treat Blvd Ste 250 Walnut Creek (94597) *(G-10774)*
Marsh & McLennan Agency LLC..............................858 457-3414
9171 Towne Centre Dr # 500 San Diego (92122) *(G-10775)*
Marsh Risk & Insurance Svcs, San Jose *Also called Marsh USA Inc (G-10778)*
Marsh Risk & Insurance Svcs (HQ)..............................213 624-5555
777 S Figueroa St # 2200 Los Angeles (90017) *(G-10776)*
Marsh USA Inc..............................415 743-8000
345 California St # 1300 San Francisco (94104) *(G-10777)*
Marsh USA Inc..............................408 467-5600
1735 Tech Dr Ste 790 San Jose (95110) *(G-10778)*
Marshall Hospital, Placerville *Also called Marshall Medical Center (G-21729)*
Marshall Medical Center..............................916 933-2273
1100 Marshall Way El Dorado Hills (95762) *(G-21728)*
Marshall Medical Center (PA)..............................530 622-1441
1100 Marshall Way Placerville (95667) *(G-21729)*
Marshall Medical Center..............................530 626-2920
1095 Marshall Way Placerville (95667) *(G-19732)*
Marshall S Ezralow & Assoc, Calabasas *Also called M S E Enterprises Inc (G-11650)*
Marshall, Spector MD, San Gabriel *Also called Facey Medical Foundation (G-22961)*
Martech Medical Products Inc..............................215 256-8833
565 Clara Nofal Rd Calexico (92231) *(G-19733)*
Marthas Village & Kitchen..............................760 347-4741
83791 Date Ave Indio (92201) *(G-24077)*
Marticus Electric Inc..............................916 368-2186
9266 Beatty Dr D Sacramento (95826) *(G-2641)*
Martin AC Partners Inc..............................213 683-1900
444 S Flower St Ste 1200 Los Angeles (90071) *(G-26235)*
Martin Associates Group Inc (PA)..............................213 483-6490
950 S Grand Ave Fl 4 Los Angeles (90015) *(G-25952)*

ALPHABETIC

Employee Codes: A=Over 500 employees, B=251-500
C=101-250, D=51-100, E=45-50
2017 Directory of California
Wholesalers and Services Companies
© Mergent Inc. 1-800-342-5647
1459

Martin Bros/Marcowall Inc (PA) 310 532-5335
17104 S Figueroa St Gardena (90248) ***(G-2926)***
Martin Brothers Construction (PA) 916 381-0911
20 Light Sky Ct Sacramento (95828) ***(G-1823)***
Martin De Porres House, San Francisco *Also called MD P Foundation Inc* ***(G-24079)***
Martin Integrated Systems 714 998-9100
2330 N Pacific St Orange (92865) ***(G-2927)***
Martin Lther King/Drew Med Ctr 310 773-4926
1670 E 120th St Los Angeles (90059) ***(G-19734)***
Martin Lthr Kng Chldr Ctr, Pittsburg *Also called State Preschool* ***(G-24520)***
Martin Media Inc (PA) 415 913-7446
415 Brannan St San Francisco (94107) ***(G-13880)***
Martin, John A & Associates, Los Angeles *Also called Martin Associates Group Inc* ***(G-25952)***
Martin-Brower Company LLC 209 466-2980
4704 Fite Ct Stockton (95215) ***(G-8497)***
Martina Landscape Inc 408 871-8800
811 Camden Ave Campbell (95008) ***(G-909)***
Martinez Cert 925 228-0911
129 Midhill Rd Martinez (94553) ***(G-25555)***
Martinez Farms Inc 619 661-6571
2440 Cactus Rd San Diego (92154) ***(G-301)***
Martinez Medical Offices, Martinez *Also called Kaiser Foundation Hospitals* ***(G-12182)***
Martini Inc 209 389-4566
12006 Le Grand Rd Le Grand (95333) ***(G-207)***
Martini Media Network, San Francisco *Also called Martin Media Inc* ***(G-13880)***
Martins Achievement Place 916 338-1001
5240 Jackson St North Highlands (95660) ***(G-24724)***
Martrac, Fresno *Also called UPS Ground Freight Inc* ***(G-4285)***
Marty Franich Leasing Co 831 724-2463
555 Auto Center Dr Watsonville (95076) ***(G-17702)***
Marty's Cutting Service, Vernon *Also called Martys Cutting Inc* ***(G-17315)***
Martys Cutting Inc 323 582-5758
2615 Fruitland Ave Vernon (90058) ***(G-17315)***
Maruchan Inc 949 789-2300
15800 Laguna Canyon Rd Irvine (92618) ***(G-4596)***
Marvel Studios LLC 310 727-2700
1600 Rosecrans Ave Manhattan Beach (90266) ***(G-14153)***
Mary and Friends 562 691-1575
1101 Farrington Dr La Habra (90631) ***(G-24725)***
Mary Grahams Childrens Shelter, French Camp *Also called County of San Joaquin* ***(G-23907)***
Mary Hlth SCK Cnvlscnt &NRsng 805 498-3644
2929 Theresa Dr Newbury Park (91320) ***(G-20777)***
Marycrest Manor 310 838-2778
10664 Saint James Dr Culver City (90230) ***(G-21310)***
Marymount Villa LLC 510 895-5007
345 Davis St Ofc San Leandro (94577) ***(G-21091)***
Marysville Care Center, Marysville *Also called Marysvlle Nrsing Rehab Ctr LLC* ***(G-20778)***
Marysville Post-Acute, Marysville *Also called Melon Holdings LLC* ***(G-20787)***
Marysvlle Nrsing Rehab Ctr LLC 530 742-7311
1617 Ramirez St Marysville (95901) ***(G-20778)***
Maryvale 626 280-6510
7600 Graves Ave Rosemead (91770) ***(G-24726)***
Maryvale Day Care Center 626 357-1514
2502 Huntington Dr Duarte (91010) ***(G-24481)***
Maryvale Edcatn Fmly Rsrce Ctr, Duarte *Also called Maryvale Day Care Center* ***(G-24481)***
Masa Trucking Co 310 329-1567
231 W 135th St Los Angeles (90061) ***(G-4361)***
Masa's, San Francisco *Also called San Francisco Hotel Associates* ***(G-13201)***
Masada Homes, Gardena *Also called Counseling and Research Assoc* ***(G-24607)***
Masada Homes Foster Fmly Agcy, Lancaster *Also called Counseling and Research Assoc* ***(G-24608)***
Masco, San Jose *Also called Topbuild Services Group Corp* ***(G-3590)***
Mashburn Trnsp Svcs Inc 661 763-5724
1423 Kern St Taft (93268) ***(G-4216)***
Masker Painting, Oakland *Also called George E Masker Inc* ***(G-2448)***
Mason Street Opco LLC 415 772-5000
950 Mason St San Francisco (94108) ***(G-12983)***
Mason-Mcduffie Real Estate Inc 510 705-8611
2095 Rose St Ste 100 Berkeley (94709) ***(G-11659)***
Mason-Mcduffie Real Estate Inc 925 932-1000
2051 Mt Diablo Blvd Walnut Creek (94596) ***(G-11660)***
Mason-Mcduffie Real Estate Inc 925 837-4281
630 San Ramon Valley Blvd # 100 Danville (94526) ***(G-11661)***
Mason-Mcduffie Real Estate Inc 925 254-0440
89 Davis Rd Ste 100 Orinda (94563) ***(G-11662)***
Mason-Mcduffie Real Estate Inc 925 776-2740
5887 Lone Tree Way Ste A Antioch (94531) ***(G-11663)***
Mason-Mcduffie Real Estate Inc 510 886-7511
21060 Redwood Rd Ste 100 Castro Valley (94546) ***(G-11664)***
Mason-Mcduffie Real Estate Inc 510 834-2010
3320 Grand Ave Oakland (94610) ***(G-11665)***
Mason-Mcduffie Real Estate Inc 925 734-5000
5950 Stoneridge Dr Pleasanton (94588) ***(G-11666)***
Mason-West Inc 619 226-8253
3910 Chapman St Ste D San Diego (92110) ***(G-7859)***
Masonic Home For Adults, Union City *Also called Masonic Homes of California* ***(G-24728)***
Masonic Homes of California (PA) 415 776-7000
1111 California St San Francisco (94108) ***(G-24727)***
Masonic Homes of California 510 441-3700
34400 Mission Blvd Union City (94587) ***(G-24728)***
Masonic Homes of California 626 251-2200
1650 E Old Badillo St Covina (91724) ***(G-24729)***
Masonry Concepts Inc 562 802-3700
15408 Cornet St Santa Fe Springs (90670) ***(G-2826)***

ALPHABETIC

Masonry Group Nevada Inc 951 509-5300
8188 Lincoln Ave Ste 99 Riverside (92504) ***(G-2827)***
Mass Electric Construction Co 800 933-6322
1925 Wright Ave Ste D La Verne (91750) ***(G-2642)***
Mass Precision Inc 408 451-0929
2371 Paragon Dr San Jose (95131) ***(G-17761)***
Massachusetts Mutl Lf Insur Co 323 951-0131
8383 Wilshire Blvd # 600 Beverly Hills (90211) ***(G-10212)***
Massage Place 310 204-3004
2516 Overland Ave Los Angeles (90064) ***(G-13774)***
Massdrop Inc 415 340-2999
100 Bush St Ste 1000 San Francisco (94104) ***(G-27982)***
Massmutual, Beverly Hills *Also called Massachusetts Mutl Lf Insur Co* ***(G-10212)***
Massnexus, Studio City *Also called Dpr Holdings LLC* ***(G-12059)***
Master Clean USA Inc 805 681-0950
5511 Ekwill St Ste D Santa Barbara (93111) ***(G-14351)***
Master Design Drywall Inc 760 480-9001
360 S Spruce St Escondido (92025) ***(G-2928)***
Master Disposal Co 626 444-6789
1980 S Reservoir St Pomona (91766) ***(G-6502)***
Master Drywall Inc 707 448-8659
6727 Bucktown Ln Vacaville (95688) ***(G-2929)***
Master Lightning SEC Solutions 310 419-2915
1509 W Cameron Ave # 230 West Covina (91790) ***(G-16732)***
Master Roofing Systems Inc 415 407-4450
52 S Linden Ave South San Francisco (94080) ***(G-3189)***
Master-Chef's Linen Rental, Los Angeles *Also called American Textile Maint Co* ***(G-13522)***
Master-Sort Inc 714 258-7678
245 W Carl Karcher Way Anaheim (92801) ***(G-17316)***
Masters Electric Telcom, Riverside *Also called T S J Elec Communications Inc* ***(G-2765)***
Masterserv Inc 818 356-4602
560 Library St San Fernando (91340) ***(G-2290)***
Mastersev, San Fernando *Also called Masterserv Inc* ***(G-2290)***
Mastroianni Family Entps Ltd 310 952-1700
10581 Garden Grove Blvd Garden Grove (92843) ***(G-13775)***
Masudas Landscape Services 408 379-7100
423 Salmar Ave Campbell (95008) ***(G-779)***
Matagrano Inc 650 829-4829
440 Forbes Blvd South San Francisco (94080) ***(G-9072)***
Matched Care Gvrs Cntns Care, Atherton *Also called Matched Caregivers Inc* ***(G-22504)***
Matched Caregivers Inc 408 560-2382
1800 El Camino Real Ste B Atherton (94027) ***(G-22504)***
Mater Misericordiae Hospital (PA) 209 564-5000
333 Mercy Ave Merced (95340) ***(G-21730)***
Material Handling Supply Inc (HQ) 562 921-7715
12900 Firestone Blvd Santa Fe Springs (90670) ***(G-7860)***
Material Transport, Sacramento *Also called Pacific Coast Trnsp Svcs Inc* ***(G-5233)***
Materials Marketing 949 729-9881
250 Baker St E Ste 100 Costa Mesa (92626) ***(G-27526)***
Maternal Child Clinic, Alhambra *Also called Nca Program* ***(G-19765)***
Matheny Sars Linkert Jaime LLP 916 978-3434
3638 American River Dr Sacramento (95864) ***(G-23421)***
Matheson Fast Freight Inc 209 342-0184
9785 Goethe Rd Sacramento (95827) ***(G-4217)***
Matheson Fast Freight Inc (HQ) 916 686-4600
9780 Dino Dr Elk Grove (95624) ***(G-4218)***
Matheson Postal Services Inc 916 685-2330
9785 Goethe Rd Sacramento (95827) ***(G-4038)***
Matheson Trucking Inc (PA) 916 685-2330
9785 Goethe Rd Sacramento (95827) ***(G-4219)***
Mathews & Clark Communications, Sunnyvale *Also called Positea Inv & Pub Relations* ***(G-27763)***
Matich Corporation (PA) 909 382-7400
1596 E Harry Shepard Blvd San Bernardino (92408) ***(G-1824)***
Matix Clothing Company, Costa Mesa *Also called Dvs Shoe Co Inc* ***(G-8431)***
Matomy USA Inc 408 400-2401
2900 Gordon Ave Santa Clara (95051) ***(G-5650)***
Matrix Aviation Services Inc 310 337-3037
200 World Way Ste 6 Los Angeles (90045) ***(G-5012)***
Matrix Environmental Inc 562 236-2704
2330 E Cherry Indl Cir Long Beach (90805) ***(G-3552)***
Matrix Group International Inc 626 960-6205
1520 W Cameron Ave West Covina (91790) ***(G-1214)***
Matrix Industries Inc 562 236-2700
2330 E Cherry Indus Cir Long Beach (90805) ***(G-3553)***
Matrix Service Inc 714 289-4419
500 W Collins Ave Orange (92867) ***(G-1966)***
Matrix Surfaces Inc 714 696-5449
5449 E La Palma Ave Anaheim (92807) ***(G-3019)***
Matson Navigation Company Inc (HQ) 510 628-4000
555 12th St Oakland (94607) ***(G-4718)***
Matsui Nursery Inc (PA) 831 422-6433
1645 Old Stage Rd Salinas (93908) ***(G-302)***
Matsushita International Corp (PA) 949 498-1000
1141 Via Callejon San Clemente (92673) ***(G-12324)***
Matt Construction Corporation (PA) 562 903-2277
9814 Norwalk Blvd Ste 100 Santa Fe Springs (90670) ***(G-27527)***
Matt-Colombo A Joint Venture 562 903-2277
9814 Norwalk Blvd Ste 100 Santa Fe Springs (90670) ***(G-1609)***
Mattel Inc 310 227-8230
909 N Sepulveda Blvd # 540 El Segundo (90245) ***(G-15294)***
Mattel Toy Company 310 252-2357
333 Continental Blvd El Segundo (90245) ***(G-8049)***
Matthew Burns 209 676-4940
617 Flower Dr Folsom (95630) ***(G-1610)***
Mattress Liqidation, Rancho Cucamonga *Also called Hibshman Trading Corporation* ***(G-8387)***

ALPHABETIC SECTION McCormick Barstow, Fresno

Maud Booth Family Center, North Hollywood *Also called Volunteers of Amer Los Angeles (G-24282)*
Maui Fresh International LLC 213 688-0880
 1601 E Olympic Blvd # 509 Los Angeles (90021) *(G-8750)*
Mavenir Intl Holdings Inc 408 855-2900
 2890 Zanker Rd Ste 207 San Jose (95134) *(G-15295)*
Mavent Inc 949 223-6424
 3 Park Plz Ste 700 Irvine (92614) *(G-15993)*
Maverick Entertainment, Burbank *Also called Maverick Records LLC (G-17317)*
Maverick Hotel Partners LLC 415 655-9526
 466 Green St Ste 302 San Francisco (94133) *(G-27121)*
Maverick Records LLC 212 275-2000
 3300 Warner Blvd Burbank (91505) *(G-17317)*
Max Group Corporation (PA) 626 935-0050
 17011 Green Dr City of Industry (91745) *(G-7160)*
Max Leather 310 841-6990
 8533 Washington Blvd Culver City (90232) *(G-9279)*
Max Sommers Real Estate 310 560-1499
 615 Esplanade Unit 312 Redondo Beach (90277) *(G-11667)*
Max/Mr Imaging Inc 818 382-2220
 17530 Ventura Blvd # 105 Encino (91316) *(G-22241)*
Maxco Supply Inc 559 646-6700
 8419 Di Giorgio Rd Lamont (93241) *(G-8197)*
Maxim Crane Works LP 209 464-7635
 2373 E Mariposa Rd Stockton (95205) *(G-14488)*
Maxim Healthcare Services Inc 805 278-4593
 500 E Esplanade Dr Oxnard (93036) *(G-28145)*
Maxim Healthcare Services Inc 323 937-9410
 4221 Wilshire Blvd # 394 Los Angeles (90010) *(G-22505)*
Maxim Healthcare Services Inc 951 684-4148
 1845 Bus Ctr Dr Ste 112 San Bernardino (92408) *(G-14904)*
Maxim Planning Group 818 425-4343
 1214 E Colorado Blvd Pasadena (91106) *(G-27983)*
Maximum Fitness LLC 707 447-0606
 135 Dobbins St Vacaville (95688) *(G-18659)*
Maximus Inc 916 673-2175
 625 Coolidge Dr Ste 100 Folsom (95630) *(G-27528)*
Maximus Inc 916 364-6610
 3130 Kilgore Rd Ste 100 Rancho Cordova (95670) *(G-22506)*
Maximus Inc 916 673-4162
 625 Coolidge Dr Ste 100 Folsom (95630) *(G-27529)*
Maximus CA Healthy Family, Folsom *Also called Maximus Inc (G-27528)*
Maxon Lift Corporation 562 464-0099
 11921 Slauson Ave Santa Fe Springs (90670) *(G-7861)*
Maxonic Inc 408 777-6825
 2041 Mission College Blvd # 140 Santa Clara (95054) *(G-16430)*
Maxson Young Assoc Inc 415 228-6400
 180 Montgomery St # 2100 San Francisco (94104) *(G-10779)*
Maxus USA 323 202-4650
 6300 Wilshire Blvd # 720 Los Angeles (90048) *(G-28146)*
Maxwell Hotel, The, San Francisco *Also called Joie De Vivre Hospitality LLC (G-27082)*
Maxwell Petersen Associates 714 230-3150
 13950 Milton Ave Ste 200 Westminster (92683) *(G-27530)*
Maxx Metals Inc 650 654-1500
 355 Quarry Rd San Carlos (94070) *(G-7383)*
May-Han Electric Inc 916 929-0150
 1600 Auburn Blvd Sacramento (95815) *(G-2643)*
Mayacama Golf Club LLC 707 569-2915
 1240 Mayacama Club Dr Santa Rosa (95403) *(G-18993)*
Mayekawa Manufacturing Company, Torrance *Also called Mayekawa USA Inc (G-7755)*
Mayekawa USA Inc 310 618-3170
 19475 Gramercy Pl Torrance (90501) *(G-7755)*
Mayer Associates 310 274-5553
 9090 Wilshire Blvd Fl 3 Beverly Hills (90211) *(G-11164)*
Mayer Brown & Platt, Los Angeles *Also called LLP Mayer Brown (G-23403)*
Mayesh Wholesale Florist Inc (PA) 310 342-0980
 5401 W 104th St Los Angeles (90045) *(G-9198)*
Mayfair Hotel 213 484-9789
 1430 Amherst Ave Apt 5 Los Angeles (90025) *(G-12984)*
Mayfield Robotics, Redwood City *Also called Robert Bosch Start-Up Platf (G-15427)*
Mayflower Gardens Health Facil 661 943-2832
 6705 Columbia Way Lancaster (93536) *(G-20779)*
Mayflwer Grdns Cnvlescent Hosp, Lancaster *Also called Mayflower Gardens Health Facil (G-20779)*
Maynard Cooper & Gale PC 415 704-7433
 600 Montgomery St # 2600 San Francisco (94111) *(G-23422)*
Mayor Office, Pasadena *Also called City of Pasadena (G-14249)*
Mayoral Bros 707 693-9111
 420 Hillcrest Cir Dixon (95620) *(G-674)*
Maywood Acres Health Care Ctr, Oxnard *Also called Kindred Healthcare Oper Inc (G-21283)*
Maywood Halthcare Wellness Ctr 323 560-0720
 6025 Pine Ave Maywood (90270) *(G-20780)*
Mazar Corp 909 292-8269
 3200 E Guasti Rd Ste 100 Ontario (91761) *(G-16733)*
Mazda Research & Dev of N Amer 949 852-8898
 1421 Reynolds Ave Irvine (92614) *(G-25953)*
Mazzetti Inc (PA) 415 362-3266
 220 Montgomery St Ste 650 San Francisco (94104) *(G-25954)*
Mazzetti GBA, San Francisco *Also called Mazzetti Inc (G-25954)*
MB Coatings Inc 714 625-2118
 571 N Poplar St Ste G Orange (92868) *(G-17318)*
MB Herzog Electric Inc 562 531-2002
 15709 Illinois Ave Paramount (90723) *(G-2644)*
MB Landscaping & Nursery Inc 310 965-1923
 20300 Figueroa St Carson (90745) *(G-9199)*
Mbari, Moss Landing *Also called Monterey Bay Aquarium RES Inst (G-26570)*
MBC Systems, Santa Ana *Also called Medical Network Inc (G-27125)*
Mbe, Pasadena *Also called Ttg Engineers (G-26107)*

Mbh Architects Inc 510 865-8663
 960 Atlantic Ave Alameda (94501) *(G-26236)*
Mbh Enterprises Inc 510 302-6680
 1430 Franklin St Ste 201 Oakland (94612) *(G-7161)*
MBI, Stockton *Also called Midstate Barrier Inc (G-1827)*
Mbipch LLC 310 456-6444
 22878 Pacific Coast Hwy Malibu (90265) *(G-12985)*
Mbit Wireless Inc 949 205-4559
 4340 Von Karman Ave # 140 Newport Beach (92660) *(G-5401)*
MBK Laguna, Irvine *Also called MBK Real Estate Companies (G-11668)*
MBK Real Estate Companies 949 789-8300
 4 Park Plz Ste 1000 Irvine (92614) *(G-11668)*
MBK Real Estate Ltd A Calfor 831 438-7533
 100 Lockewood Ln Scotts Valley (95066) *(G-11165)*
MBK Real Estate Ltd A Calfor (HQ) 949 789-8300
 4 Park Plz Ste 850 Irvine (92614) *(G-11982)*
MBK Real Estate Ltd A Califor 310 399-3227
 2107 Ocean Ave Ofc Santa Monica (90405) *(G-11166)*
MBK Senior Living LLC 951 506-5555
 41780 Btterfield Stage Rd Temecula (92592) *(G-21311)*
MBK Senior Living LLC (PA) 949 242-1400
 4 Park Plz Ste 400 Irvine (92614) *(G-24078)*
Mblox Incorporated (HQ) 408 617-3700
 1901 S Bascom Ave Ste 400 Campbell (95008) *(G-15296)*
Mbm, Riverside *Also called Meadowbrook Meat Company Inc (G-4221)*
Mbp Land LLC 619 291-5720
 595 Hotel Cir S San Diego (92108) *(G-12986)*
Mbs Equipment Company (PA) 310 558-3100
 4060 Ince Blvd Culver City (90232) *(G-18234)*
Mc Clintock Enterprises 619 579-5300
 795 Gable Way El Cajon (92020) *(G-3894)*
Mc Consultants Inc (PA) 760 930-9966
 2055 Corte Del Nogal Carlsbad (92011) *(G-25955)*
Mc Graw Commercial Insur Svc 714 939-9875
 8185 E Kaiser Blvd Anaheim (92808) *(G-10780)*
Mc Graw Commercial Insur Svc (PA) 650 780-4800
 3601 Haven Ave Menlo Park (94025) *(G-10781)*
Mc Graw Insurance Services Co 650 780-4800
 2200 Geng Rd Ste 200 Palo Alto (94303) *(G-10782)*
Mc Laughlin Mine, Lower Lake *Also called Barrick Gold Corporation (G-1021)*
Mc Namara Dodge Ney Beatt (PA) 925 939-5330
 1211 Newell Ave Walnut Creek (94596) *(G-23423)*
Mc Painting (PA) 760 599-8000
 2525 Ramona Dr Vista (92084) *(G-2465)*
MCA Logistics-Stockton, Stockton *Also called Mike Campbell & Associates Ltd (G-4039)*
MCA Music, Universal City *Also called Universal Studios Inc (G-18179)*
McAfee Inc 858 967-2342
 6707 Barnhurst Dr San Diego (92117) *(G-15740)*
McAfee Inc (HQ) 408 346-3832
 2821 Mission College Blvd Santa Clara (95054) *(G-15741)*
McAfee Security LLC 866 622-3911
 2821 Mission College Blvd Santa Clara (95054) *(G-15742)*
McAlister Institute For Treat 760 726-4451
 3923 Waring Rd Oceanside (92056) *(G-22772)*
MCASD, La Jolla *Also called Museum Cntmprary Art San Diego (G-25028)*
McAuley Lcx Corporation 714 994-7788
 8888 Los Coyotes Dr Buena Park (90621) *(G-18994)*
MCB-Cjs LLC 714 230-3600
 5312 Bolsa Ave Huntington Beach (92649) *(G-27531)*
McCain Inc (PA) 760 727-8100
 2365 Oak Ridge Way Vista (92081) *(G-7862)*
McCampbell Analytical Inc 925 252-9262
 1534 Willow Pass Rd Pittsburg (94565) *(G-26865)*
McCandless, Harrison MD, Torrance *Also called Torrence Family Practice (G-20139)*
McCann World Group Inc (PA) 415 262-5500
 653 Front St San Francisco (94111) *(G-13881)*
McCann-Erickson Corporation (HQ) 415 348-5600
 135 Main St Fl 21 San Francisco (94105) *(G-13882)*
McCann-Erickson Usa Inc 415 262-5600
 600 Battery St Fl 1 San Francisco (94111) *(G-26688)*
McCarthy Bldg Companies Inc 949 851-8383
 20401 Sw Birch St Ste 200 Newport Beach (92660) *(G-1611)*
McCarthy Bldg Companies Inc 949 851-8383
 20401 Sw Birch St Ste 300 Newport Beach (92660) *(G-1612)*
McCarthy Construction, Lawndale *Also called McCarthy Framing Construction (G-3066)*
McCarthy Framing Construction 310 219-3038
 15133 Grevillea Ave Lawndale (90260) *(G-3066)*
McClatchy Company 916 321-1941
 2100 Q St Sacramento (95816) *(G-28147)*
McClatchy Newspapers Inc 209 238-4636
 1325 H St Modesto (95354) *(G-17319)*
McClellan Business Park LLC 916 965-7100
 3140 Peacekeeper Way McClellan (95652) *(G-27532)*
McClellan Facilities Svcs LLC 916 965-7100
 3140 Peacekeeper Way McClellan (95652) *(G-11016)*
McClellan Hospitality Svcs LLC 916 965-7100
 3140 Peacekeeper Way McClellan (95652) *(G-12987)*
McClenahan Pest Control Inc 650 326-8781
 1 Arastradero Rd Portola Valley (94028) *(G-14189)*
McClenahan S P Co Tree Service, Portola Valley *Also called SP McClenahan Co (G-998)*
McClier Corporation 714 835-8923
 999 W Town And Country Rd Orange (92868) *(G-26237)*
McClone Construction Company 703 433-9406
 4340 Product Dr Cameron Park (95682) *(G-1215)*
McCollisters Trnsp Group Inc 909 428-5700
 10672 Jasmine St Fontana (92337) *(G-4220)*
McCormack Roofng Constrctn & E 714 777-4040
 1260 N Hancock St Ste 108 Anaheim (92807) *(G-3190)*
McCormick Barstow, Fresno *Also called McCormick Barstow Shepprd Wayt (G-23424)*

McCormick Barstow Shepprd Wayt (PA) 559 433-1300
7647 N Fresno St Fresno (93720) ***(G-23424)***
McCoy's Patrol Service, San Francisco *Also called Hal-Mar-Jac Enterprises* ***(G-16700)***
McCusker Enterprises Inc 951 676-5445
29879 Santiago Rd Temecula (92592) ***(G-24482)***
McCutcheon Enterprises Inc 559 864-3200
604 W Nebraska Ave Fresno (93706) ***(G-170)***
McDermott Will & Emery LLP Inc 310 277-4110
2049 Century Park E Fl 38 Los Angeles (90067) ***(G-23425)***
McDermott Will & Emery LLP Inc 949 757-7165
4 Park Plz Ste 1700 Irvine (92614) ***(G-23426)***
McDonald's, NAPA *Also called Lamson Investment Corp* ***(G-12321)***
McDonald's, Los Angeles *Also called Garco Enterprises Inc* ***(G-27930)***
McDonald's, Los Angeles *Also called D Bailey Management Comp* ***(G-27001)***
McDonough-Western Rim JV 619 749-5339
8942 Creekford Dr Lakeside (92040) ***(G-2066)***
McElvany Inc 209 826-1102
13343 Johnson Rd Los Banos (93635) ***(G-1967)***
McEvoy of Marin LLC 707 778-2307
5935 Red Hill Rd Petaluma (94952) ***(G-9280)***
McEvoy Ranch, Petaluma *Also called McEvoy of Marin LLC* ***(G-9280)***
McFadden Farm 707 743-1122
16000 Powerhouse Rd Potter Valley (95469) ***(G-5)***
McG Services Corporation 415 721-1444
1010 B St Ste 425 San Rafael (94901) ***(G-14905)***
McGee Company, Whittier *Also called John Shannon Mc Gee Co Inc* ***(G-7448)***
McGrath Rentcorp 925 453-3312
5700 Las Positas Rd Livermore (94551) ***(G-14557)***
McGrath Rentcorp 877 221-2813
5700 Las Positas Rd Livermore (94551) ***(G-14558)***
McGrath Rentcorp (PA) 925 606-9200
5700 Las Positas Rd Livermore (94551) ***(G-14559)***
McGraw Insurance Services, Anaheim *Also called Mc Graw Commercial Insur Svc* ***(G-10780)***
McGreever and Danlee Very, Azusa *Also called Morris National Inc* ***(G-8623)***
McGuire and Hester (PA) 510 632-7676
9009 Railroad Ave Oakland (94603) ***(G-1968)***
McGuire Contracting Inc 909 357-1200
16579 Slover Ave Fontana (92337) ***(G-3294)***
McGuire Talent Inc 909 527-7006
8608 Utica Ave Ste 220 Rancho Cucamonga (91730) ***(G-18414)***
McGuirewoods LLP 310 315-8200
1800 Century Park E Fl 8 Los Angeles (90067) ***(G-23427)***
Mch, Madera *Also called Madera Community Hospital* ***(G-21722)***
Mch Electric Inc (PA) 209 835-9755
7693 Longard Rd Livermore (94551) ***(G-2645)***
Mch Electric Inc 209 835-9755
4923 W 11th St Tracy (95304) ***(G-13776)***
McHc, Ukiah *Also called Mendocino Cmnty Hlth Clnic Inc* ***(G-19745)***
McHenry Bowl Inc 209 571-2695
3700 Mchenry Ave Modesto (95356) ***(G-18526)***
McHenry Medical Group Inc 209 577-3388
1541 Florida Ave Ste 200 Modesto (95350) ***(G-19735)***
MCI Communications Svcs Inc 323 460-5178
1957 N Bronson Ave # 106 Los Angeles (90068) ***(G-5651)***
MCI Communications Svcs Inc 213 625-1005
700 S Flower St Ste 1600 Los Angeles (90017) ***(G-5652)***
McIntyre Vineyards, Carmel *Also called Monterey Pacific Inc* ***(G-710)***
McKann World Group, San Francisco *Also called McCann-Erickson Usa Inc* ***(G-26688)***
McKee Electric, Bakersfield *Also called Surgener Electric Inc* ***(G-2761)***
McKesson Corporation 650 952-8400
395 Oyster Point Blvd # 500 South San Francisco (94080) ***(G-8277)***
McKesson Corporation 951 686-3575
6969 Brockton Ave Ste B Riverside (92506) ***(G-8278)***
McKesson Corporation 510 666-0854
3000 Colby St Berkeley (94705) ***(G-7276)***
McKesson Corporation 562 463-2100
9501 Norwalk Blvd Santa Fe Springs (90670) ***(G-8279)***
McKesson Corporation 916 372-3655
3775 Seaport Blvd West Sacramento (95691) ***(G-8280)***
McKesson Corporation (PA) 415 983-8300
1 Post St Fl 18 San Francisco (94104) ***(G-8281)***
McKesson Drug, Santa Fe Springs *Also called McKesson Corporation* ***(G-8279)***
McKesson Drug, West Sacramento *Also called McKesson Corporation* ***(G-8280)***
McKesson Medical-Surgical Inc 800 767-6339
16043 El Prado Rd Chino (91708) ***(G-7277)***
McKesson Medical-Surgical Inc 805 375-8800
1525 Rnch Conejo Blvd # 104 Newbury Park (91320) ***(G-7278)***
McKesson Technologies Inc 559 455-4000
5110 E Clinton Way # 101 Fresno (93727) ***(G-17320)***
McKinley Childrens Center Inc (PA) 909 599-1227
762 Cypress St San Dimas (91773) ***(G-24730)***
McKinley Equipment Corporation (PA) 800 770-6094
17611 Armstrong Ave Irvine (92614) ***(G-7863)***
McKinley Home Foundation 909 599-1227
762 Cypress St San Dimas (91773) ***(G-24941)***
McKinley Park Care Center 916 452-3592
3700 H St Sacramento (95816) ***(G-21731)***
McKinley Plaza LLC 619 405-6307
2401 E Division St National City (91950) ***(G-27122)***
McKinnon Publishing Company 858 571-5151
4575 Viewridge Ave San Diego (92123) ***(G-5897)***
McKinsey & Company Inc 424 249-1000
2000 Avenue Of The Stars # 800 Los Angeles (90067) ***(G-27533)***
McKinsey & Company Inc 415 981-0250
555 California St # 4800 San Francisco (94104) ***(G-27534)***
McKinsey & Company Inc 650 494-6262
3075 Hansen Way Bldg A Palo Alto (94304) ***(G-27535)***
McKool Smith Hennigan 213 694-1200
300 S Grand Ave Ste 2900 Los Angeles (90071) ***(G-23428)***
McKowskis Maint Systems Inc 619 269-4600
10979 San Dego Mission Rd San Diego (92108) ***(G-14352)***
McLane Company Inc 209 221-7500
800 E Pescadero Ave Tracy (95304) ***(G-8498)***
McLane/Pacific Inc 209 725-2500
3876 E Childs Ave Merced (95341) ***(G-8499)***
McLane/Southern California Inc 909 887-7500
4472 Georgia Blvd San Bernardino (92407) ***(G-8500)***
MCM Construction Inc (PA) 916 334-1221
6413 32nd St North Highlands (95660) ***(G-1896)***
MCM Construction Inc 909 875-0533
19010 Slover Ave Bloomington (92316) ***(G-1897)***
McM Partners Inc 925 463-9500
6111 Johnson Ct Ste 110 Pleasanton (94588) ***(G-11669)***
McManis Faulkner A Prof Corp 408 279-8700
50 W San Fernando St # 1000 San Jose (95113) ***(G-23429)***
McMillan Bros Electric Inc 415 826-5100
1950 Cesar Chavez San Francisco (94124) ***(G-2646)***
McMillan Data Cmmnications Inc 415 826-5100
1950 Cesar Chavez San Francisco (94124) ***(G-2647)***
McMillan Farm Management 951 676-2045
29379 Rancho California R Temecula (92591) ***(G-27123)***
McMillin Communities Inc 951 506-3303
41687 Temeku Dr Temecula (92591) ***(G-1216)***
McMillin Communities Inc (PA) 619 561-5275
2750 Womble Rd Ste 200 San Diego (92106) ***(G-12325)***
McMillin Companies LLC (PA) 619 477-4117
2750 Womble Rd Ste 200 San Diego (92106) ***(G-12326)***
McMillin Construction Svcs LP 619 477-4170
2750 Womble Rd San Diego (92106) ***(G-1217)***
McMillin Homes, San Diego *Also called McMillin Companies LLC* ***(G-12326)***
McMillin Homes, San Diego *Also called McMillin Management Svcs LP* ***(G-12119)***
McMillin Management Svcs LP (HQ) 619 477-4117
2750 Womble Rd Ste 200 San Diego (92106) ***(G-12119)***
McMillin RE & Mrtg Co Inc 619 422-4500
320 E H St Chula Vista (91910) ***(G-11670)***
McMillin Realty, San Diego *Also called McMillin Communities Inc* ***(G-12325)***
McMurray Stern Inc 562 623-3000
15511 Carmenita Rd Santa Fe Springs (90670) ***(G-6824)***
MCP Industries Inc 562 944-5511
10039 Norwalk Blvd Santa Fe Springs (90670) ***(G-8993)***
MCS, Bakersfield *Also called Managed Care Systems Kern Cnty* ***(G-10768)***
McWong Envmtl & Enrgy Group 916 371-8080
1921 Arena Blvd Sacramento (95834) ***(G-27984)***
MD Care Inc 562 344-3400
1640 E Hill St Signal Hill (90755) ***(G-10245)***
MD Care Healthplan, Signal Hill *Also called MD Care Inc* ***(G-10245)***
MD Imaging Inc A Prof Med Corp 530 243-1249
2020 Court St Redding (96001) ***(G-19736)***
MD P Foundation Inc 415 552-0240
225 Potrero Ave San Francisco (94103) ***(G-24079)***
Md7 LLC (PA) 858 799-7850
10590 W Ocean Air Dr # 300 San Diego (92130) ***(G-17321)***
Mda US Systems LLC (HQ) 626 296-1373
1250 Lincoln Ave Ste 100 Pasadena (91103) ***(G-25956)***
Mda US Systems LLC 626 296-1373
1250 Lincoln Ave Ste 100 Pasadena (91103) ***(G-25957)***
Mda US Systems LLC 626 296-1373
4398 Corporate Center Dr Los Alamitos (90720) ***(G-25958)***
Mdcc, Covina *Also called Mohan Dialysis Ctr of Covina* ***(G-22635)***
Mddr Inc 714 792-1993
555 Vanguard Way Brea (92821) ***(G-2291)***
MDE Electric Company Inc 408 738-8600
152 Commercial St Sunnyvale (94086) ***(G-2648)***
Mdr Inc 707 750-5376
100 Oak Rd Benicia (94510) ***(G-25959)***
Mds Consulting (PA) 949 251-8821
17320 Red Hill Ave # 350 Irvine (92614) ***(G-25960)***
ME and ME Inc 818 891-0197
14536 Roscoe Blvd Ste 112 Van Nuys (91402) ***(G-14906)***
ME Fox & Company Inc 408 435-8510
128 Component Dr San Jose (95131) ***(G-9073)***
Mea Digital Worx LLC 619 238-8923
530 B St Ste 1900 San Diego (92101) ***(G-13883)***
Meadow Club 415 453-3274
1001 Bolinas Rd Fairfax (94930) ***(G-18995)***
Meadow View Manor Inc 530 272-2273
396 Dorsey Dr Grass Valley (95945) ***(G-20781)***
Meadowbrook Bhavioral Hlth Ctr, Los Angeles *Also called Genesis Healthcare Corporation* ***(G-20595)***
Meadowbrook Convalescent Hosp 951 658-2293
461 E Johnston Ave Hemet (92543) ***(G-24731)***
Meadowbrook Meat Company Inc 909 484-6100
3051 N Church St Rancho Cucamonga (91730) ***(G-8676)***
Meadowbrook Meat Company Inc 252 985-7200
5675 Sunol Blvd Pleasanton (94566) ***(G-8561)***
Meadowbrook Meat Company Inc 951 686-1200
1050 Palmyrita Ave Riverside (92507) ***(G-4221)***
Meadowbrook Senior Living 818 991-3544
5217 Chesebro Rd Agoura Hills (91301) ***(G-24080)***
Meadowood Care Center, Stockton *Also called Meadowood Hlth Rehabilitation* ***(G-20782)***
Meadowood Hlth Rehabilitation 209 956-3444
3110 Wagner Heights Rd Stockton (95209) ***(G-20782)***
Meadowood Nursing Center, Clearlake *Also called Vindra Inc* ***(G-21015)***
Meadows Nappa Valley Care Ctr, NAPA *Also called California Odd Fellows* ***(G-11111)***
Meadows of NAPA Valley, NAPA *Also called California Odd Fellows* ***(G-11110)***

A L P H A B E T I C

Meadows Senior Living, The, Elk Grove *Also called Lifestyles Senior Housing Man* ***(G-24067)***
Meals On Wheels-The Health Tr......408 961-9870
1400 Parkmoor Ave Ste 230 San Jose (95126) ***(G-24081)***
Meals On Whels San Frncsco Inc......415 920-1111
1375 Fairfax Ave San Francisco (94124) ***(G-24082)***
Meany Wilson L P......415 905-5300
4 Embarcadero Ctr # 3330 San Francisco (94111) ***(G-11983)***
Mearsk, San Pedro *Also called APM Terminals Pacific LLC* ***(G-5029)***
Measure of Excellence Cabinets, Poway *Also called Kiewit Corporation* ***(G-1593)***
Meathead Movers......805 496-1416
300 Rolling Oaks Dr Thousand Oaks (91361) ***(G-4222)***
Meathead Movers......805 349-8000
101 W Canon Perdido St Santa Maria (93454) ***(G-4223)***
Meathead Movers Inc......805 541-4285
964 Johnson Ave San Luis Obispo (93401) ***(G-4224)***
Meathead Movers Inc (PA)......805 544-6328
3600 S Higuera St San Luis Obispo (93401) ***(G-4225)***
Meathead Movers Inc......805 437-5100
331 Dawson Dr Camarillo (93012) ***(G-4226)***
Meathead Movers Inc......805 966-6328
1524 State St Santa Barbara (93101) ***(G-4227)***
Mec International......415 866-4497
1932 Gauguin Pl Davis (95618) ***(G-25961)***
Mechanical Drives and Belting, Los Angeles *Also called Los Angeles Rubber Company* ***(G-7451)***
Mechanical Industries Inc......661 634-9477
314 Yampa St Bakersfield (93307) ***(G-3392)***
Mechanics Bank (HQ)......800 797-6324
1111 Civic Dr Ste 333 Walnut Creek (94596) ***(G-9507)***
Mechanics Bank......949 270-9700
18400 Von Karman Ave Irvine (92612) ***(G-9508)***
Mechanics Bank......510 741-7545
725 Alfred Nobel Dr Hercules (94547) ***(G-4597)***
Mechanics Bank Atm, Walnut Creek *Also called Mechanics Bank* ***(G-9507)***
Mecs Inc......925 313-0681
1778 Monsanto Way Martinez (94553) ***(G-17322)***
Med Focus/California Radiology, Santa Monica *Also called Stephen B Meisel MD A Med Corp* ***(G-20068)***
Med Staffing LLC......510 795-0114
39039 Paseo Padre Pkwy # 208 Fremont (94538) ***(G-14907)***
Med-Data Incorporated......916 771-1362
3741 Douglas Blvd Ste 170 Roseville (95661) ***(G-26408)***
Med-Life Ambulance Services......818 242-1785
4304 Alger St Los Angeles (90039) ***(G-3816)***
Med-Link Nursing Services Inc......951 279-6333
1307 W 6th St Ste 121 Corona (92882) ***(G-14702)***
Medallia Inc (PA)......650 321-3000
395 Page Mill Rd Ste 100 Palo Alto (94306) ***(G-15743)***
Medallion Cnstr Clean-Up, Mountain View *Also called Service By Medallion* ***(G-14425)***
Medallion Landscape MGT Inc (PA)......408 782-7500
10 San Bruno Ave Morgan Hill (95037) ***(G-780)***
Medamerica Billing Svcs Inc (HQ)......209 491-7710
1601 Cummins Dr Ste D Modesto (95358) ***(G-26409)***
Medasend Biomedical Inc (PA)......800 200-3581
1402 Daisy Ave Long Beach (90813) ***(G-22997)***
Medata Inc (HQ)......714 918-1310
2741 Walnut Ave Fl 2 Irvine (92606) ***(G-15744)***
Medcath Incorporated......704 815-7700
3001 Sillect Ave Bakersfield (93308) ***(G-22158)***
Medeanalytics Inc (PA)......510 647-1300
5858 Horton St Ste 170 Emeryville (94608) ***(G-27124)***
Medex Pratice Solutions Inc......209 845-1346
4725 Enterprise Way Ste 1 Modesto (95356) ***(G-26410)***
Medfocus Radiology Network, Santa Monica *Also called Stephen B Meisel MD PC* ***(G-20067)***
Medi-Flight Northern Cal, Modesto *Also called Sutter Central Vly Hospitals* ***(G-4888)***
Medi-Van Ambulette, Los Angeles *Also called Health Link Medi Van* ***(G-5221)***
Media All Stars Inc......858 300-9600
8525 Gibbs Dr Ste 206 San Diego (92123) ***(G-17323)***
Media Arts Lab, Los Angeles *Also called Tbwa Worldwide Inc* ***(G-13927)***
Media Design Group, Los Angeles *Also called Revenue Frontier LLC* ***(G-14009)***
Media Link LLC......646 722-3632
1901 Avenue Of The Stars # 1775 Los Angeles (90067) ***(G-27985)***
MEDIA SERVICES, Los Angeles *Also called Oberman Tivoli Miller Pickert* ***(G-16022)***
Media Temple Inc......877 578-4000
6060 Center Dr Fl 5 Los Angeles (90045) ***(G-5653)***
Media Vntures Entrmt Group LLC......310 260-3171
1547 14th St Santa Monica (90404) ***(G-18107)***
Mediabrands Worldwide Inc......323 370-8000
5700 Wilshire Blvd # 400 Los Angeles (90036) ***(G-14001)***
Mediaplatform Inc......310 909-8410
8383 Wilshire Blvd # 460 Beverly Hills (90211) ***(G-18108)***
Mediaplex Inc (HQ)......818 575-4500
30699 Russell Ranch Rd # 250 Westlake Village (91362) ***(G-13884)***
Mediashift Inc......949 407-8488
600 N Brand Blvd Ste 230 Glendale (91203) ***(G-13972)***
Medic Ambulance Service Inc (PA)......707 644-1761
506 Couch St Vallejo (94590) ***(G-3817)***
Medical and Dental Clinics, Bellflower *Also called Universal Care Inc* ***(G-22859)***
Medical Billing Services, Monrovia *Also called California Business Bureau Inc* ***(G-14021)***
Medical Care Professionals......650 583-9898
363 El Cmino Real Ste 215 South San Francisco (94080) ***(G-20783)***
Medical Center, San Diego *Also called University Cal San Diego* ***(G-21992)***
Medical Center, San Bernardino *Also called Far West Inc* ***(G-20568)***
Medical Center, Ventura *Also called County of Ventura* ***(G-23934)***
Medical Centre, Sacramento *Also called University California Davis* ***(G-21999)***
Medical Couriers Inc......650 872-1144
1282 Montgomery Ave San Bruno (94066) ***(G-4416)***
Medical Diagnostic......714 841-2273
17682 Beach Blvd Ste 103 Huntington Beach (92647) ***(G-21312)***
Medical Ex Courier Systems, Orange *Also called Mx Courier Systems Inc* ***(G-17346)***
Medical Examiner Forensic Ctr, San Diego *Also called County of San Diego* ***(G-22936)***
Medical Eye Services Inc......714 619-4660
345 Baker St E Costa Mesa (92626) ***(G-10783)***
Medical Group Bverly Hills Inc (PA)......310 385-3200
200 N Robertson Blvd Beverly Hills (90211) ***(G-19737)***
Medical Group Bverly Hills Inc......310 247-4646
250 N Robertson Blvd # 603 Beverly Hills (90211) ***(G-19738)***
Medical Hill Rehabilitation, Oakland *Also called Ocadian Care Centers LLC* ***(G-20820)***
Medical HM Care Professionals, Redding *Also called Medical Home Specialists Inc* ***(G-14908)***
Medical Home Specialists Inc......530 226-5577
2115 Churn Creek Rd Redding (96002) ***(G-14908)***
Medical Inst of Little Co Mary, Torrance *Also called Lifecare Systems Inc* ***(G-20734)***
Medical Insurance Exchange Cal......510 596-4935
6250 Claremont Ave Oakland (94618) ***(G-10784)***
Medical Investment Co......818 360-1003
16553 Rinaldi St Granada Hills (91344) ***(G-21313)***
Medical Linen Services Inc......650 873-1221
290 S Maple Ave South San Francisco (94080) ***(G-13551)***
Medical Management Cons Inc......858 587-0609
6046 Cornerstone Ct W San Diego (92121) ***(G-27536)***
Medical Management Cons Inc (PA)......310 659-3835
8150 Beverly Blvd Los Angeles (90048) ***(G-14909)***
Medical Network Inc......949 863-0022
1809 E Dyer Rd Ste 311 Santa Ana (92705) ***(G-27125)***
Medical Receivables Solutions......707 980-6733
101 W American Canyon Rd American Canyon (94503) ***(G-27537)***
Medical Specialties Managers......714 571-5000
1 City Blvd W Ste 1100 Orange (92868) ***(G-27538)***
Medical Specialty Billing, Orange *Also called Medical Specialties Managers* ***(G-27538)***
Medical Support Services, Los Angeles *Also called MSS Nurses Registry Inc* ***(G-14913)***
Medical Support Services......323 860-7994
6660 W Sunset Blvd Ste J Los Angeles (90028) ***(G-14910)***
Medical Technologies Intl......760 837-4778
75145 Saint Charles Pl B Palm Desert (92211) ***(G-26565)***
Medical Transcription Billing......800 869-3700
405 Kenyon St Ste 300 San Diego (92110) ***(G-15745)***
Medicl Imgng Ctr of Southrn CA......310 829-9788
2811 Wilshire Blvd # 100 Santa Monica (90403) ***(G-19739)***
Medicl-Srgcal Nrsing Cnference, San Francisco *Also called University of San Francisco* ***(G-17574)***
Medico Professional Linen Svc, Los Angeles *Also called American Textile Maint Co* ***(G-13520)***
Medicrest of California 1......909 626-1294
5119 Bandera St Montclair (91763) ***(G-20784)***
Medidata Solutions Inc......415 295-4300
343 Sansome St Ste 1400 San Francisco (94104) ***(G-26786)***
Medimpact Hlthcare Systems Inc (HQ)......858 566-2727
10181 Scripps Gateway Ct San Diego (92131) ***(G-25146)***
Medimpact Holdings Inc (PA)......858 790-6646
10181 Scripps Gateway Ct San Diego (92131) ***(G-12327)***
Medina Construction, Riverside *Also called Bens Asphalt & Maint Co Inc* ***(G-1741)***
Mediscan Diagnostic Svcs Inc, Woodland Hills *Also called Mediscan Diagnostic Svcs LLC* ***(G-22998)***
Mediscan Diagnostic Svcs LLC......818 758-4224
21050 Califa St Ste 100 Woodland Hills (91367) ***(G-22998)***
Mediscan, Inc., Woodland Hills *Also called New Mediscan II LLC* ***(G-23006)***
Meditab Software Inc......510 632-2021
333 Hegenberger Rd # 800 Oakland (94621) ***(G-15746)***
Medley Communications Inc......760 294-4579
255 N Ash St Escondido (92027) ***(G-2649)***
Medley Communications Inc (PA)......951 245-5200
41531 Date St Murrieta (92562) ***(G-2650)***
Medlin Development......909 825-5296
320 Tropicana Ranch Rd Colton (92324) ***(G-910)***
Medmark Services Inc......559 264-2700
1310 M St Fresno (93721) ***(G-22159)***
Medpharm Communications......858 412-6848
1734 Caminito Ardiente La Jolla (92037) ***(G-27539)***
Medpoint Management Inc......818 702-0100
6400 Canoga Ave Ste 163 Woodland Hills (91367) ***(G-19740)***
Medric, Burlingame *Also called Acumen LLC* ***(G-15896)***
Medrio Inc......415 963-3700
345 California St Ste 325 San Francisco (94104) ***(G-15747)***
Medsphere Systems Corporation (PA)......760 692-3700
1903 Wright Pl Ste 120 Carlsbad (92008) ***(G-27540)***
Medstar LLC......916 669-0550
20 Busneca Pk Way Ste 100 Sacramento (95828) ***(G-3818)***
Medstop Medical, North Hollywood *Also called Morigon Technologies LLC* ***(G-7283)***
Medusind Solutions Inc......949 240-8895
31103 Rancho Viejo Rd San Juan Capistrano (92675) ***(G-17324)***
Mee Industries Inc......626 359-4550
16021 Adelante St Irwindale (91702) ***(G-476)***
Meebo Inc (PA)......650 253-0000
1600 Amphitheatre Pkwy Mountain View (94043) ***(G-5654)***
Meek's, Rocklin *Also called Cha-Dor Realty* ***(G-6914)***
Meeting Services Inc......858 348-0100
10895 Thornmint Rd Ste A San Diego (92127) ***(G-14560)***
Mef Realty LLC......951 687-2900
2900 Adams St Ste B30-6 Riverside (92504) ***(G-11671)***
Mega Appraisers Inc......818 246-7370
14724 Ventura Blvd # 800 Sherman Oaks (91403) ***(G-17325)***

ALPHABETIC

Mega Builders, Chatsworth *Also called A I T Development Corp* ***(G-1119)***
Mega Farm Labor Services Inc ... 661 229-8077
110 S Montclair St # 103 Bakersfield (93309) ***(G-14703)***
Mega Mail Mall Inc ... 888 998-6245
128 Avenida Del Mar San Clemente (92672) ***(G-11017)***
Mega Professional Intl ... 408 946-1500
995 Montague Expy Ste 121 Milpitas (95035) ***(G-15297)***
Megapath, Pleasanton *Also called Gtt Communications (mp) Inc* ***(G-5627)***
Megapath Cloud Company LLC (PA) ... 925 201-2500
6800 Koll Center Pkwy Pleasanton (94566) ***(G-5655)***
Megapath Group Inc (HQ) ... 408 952-6400
2510 Zanker Rd San Jose (95131) ***(G-5656)***
Megapath Group Inc ... 408 324-1353
2510 Zanker Rd San Jose (95131) ***(G-5657)***
Mehrdad Razavi, San Rafael *Also called Innovative Sleep Centers Inc* ***(G-19571)***
Meiko America Inc ... 951 360-0281
12300 Riverside Dr Mira Loma (91752) ***(G-4598)***
Mejico Express Inc (PA) ... 714 690-8300
14849 Firestone Blvd Fl 1 La Mirada (90638) ***(G-4868)***
Mek Escondido LLC ... 760 747-0430
421 E Mission Ave Escondido (92025) ***(G-20785)***
Mek Norwood Pines LLC ... 916 922-7177
500 Jessie Ave Sacramento (95838) ***(G-20786)***
Meks's Auto Body, Concord *Also called Mike Roses Auto Body Inc* ***(G-17762)***
Mekwus Solar Energy ... 510 731-4134
20283 Santa Maria Ave # 2103 Castro Valley (94546) ***(G-6289)***
Mel Bernie and Company Inc ... 818 841-1928
3000 W Empire Ave Burbank (91504) ***(G-8400)***
Melano Enterprises, Oceanside *Also called Mellano & Co* ***(G-9201)***
Melissa & Doug LLC ... 209 830-7900
4718 Newcastle Rd Stockton (95215) ***(G-17326)***
Melissa Bradley RE Inc ... 415 388-5113
206 E Blithedale Ave Mill Valley (94941) ***(G-11672)***
Melissa Bradley RE Inc ... 707 258-3900
3249 Browns Valley Rd NAPA (94558) ***(G-11673)***
Melissa Bradley RE Inc ... 707 536-0888
1401 4th St Santa Rosa (95404) ***(G-11674)***
Melissa Bradley RE Inc ... 415 435-2705
1690 Tiburon Blvd Belvedere Tiburon (94920) ***(G-11675)***
Melissa Bradley RE Inc ... 415 209-1000
1701 Novato Blvd Ste 100 Novato (94947) ***(G-11676)***
Melissa Bradley RE Inc ... 415 485-4300
44 Bolinas Rd Fairfax (94930) ***(G-11677)***
Melissa Sweitzer PHD Inc ... 714 974-8727
17853 Santiago Blvd Villa Park (92861) ***(G-22083)***
Melissa's Produce, Vernon *Also called World Variety Produce Inc* ***(G-8792)***
Mellano & Co (PA) ... 213 622-0796
766 Wall St Los Angeles (90014) ***(G-9200)***
Mellano & Co ... 760 433-9550
734 Wilshire Rd Oceanside (92057) ***(G-9201)***
Mellano Enterprises, Los Angeles *Also called Mellano & Co* ***(G-9200)***
Mellennia Holdings, Los Angeles *Also called Millennia Holdings Inc* ***(G-27550)***
Mellmo Inc (HQ) ... 858 847-3272
120 S Sierra Ave Solana Beach (92075) ***(G-15298)***
Mellon Capital Management Corp (HQ) ... 415 905-5448
50 Fremont St Ste 3900 San Francisco (94105) ***(G-10162)***
Mellor, Anna B MD, Torrance *Also called South Bay Family Medical Group* ***(G-20010)***
Melmet Steven J Law Ofc ... 949 263-1000
2912 Daimler St Santa Ana (92705) ***(G-23430)***
Melo Concrete Construction ... 408 842-3484
5820 Obata Way Gilroy (95020) ***(G-3295)***
Melon Holdings LLC ... 530 742-7311
1617 Ramirez St Marysville (95901) ***(G-20787)***
Melos Plst Lthg & Drywall ... 559 237-0028
2038 E Jensen Ave Fresno (93706) ***(G-2930)***
Meltwater News US Inc (HQ) ... 415 829-5900
225 Bush St Ste 1000 San Francisco (94104) ***(G-27541)***
Melvin T Wheeler & Sons ... 209 526-9770
5301 Woodland Ave Modesto (95358) ***(G-562)***
Membrane Technology & RES Inc (PA) ... 650 328-2228
39630 Eureka Dr Newark (94560) ***(G-26566)***
Memeged Tevuot Shemesh (PA) ... 866 575-1211
6711 Valjean Ave Van Nuys (91406) ***(G-2292)***
Memo Scaffolding Inc ... 562 404-8600
12722 Carmenita Rd Santa Fe Springs (90670) ***(G-3554)***
Memon Aamir ... 818 339-8810
20832 Roscoe Blvd Ste 207 Winnetka (91306) ***(G-16734)***
Memor Ortho Surgic Group A M ... 562 424-6666
2760 Atlantic Ave Long Beach (90806) ***(G-19741)***
Memorex Products Inc ... 562 653-2800
17777 Center Court Dr N S Cerritos (90703) ***(G-7501)***
MEMORIAL CARE MEDICAL CENTERS, Laguna Hills *Also called Saddleback Memorial Med Ctr* ***(G-21836)***
MEMORIAL CARE MEDICAL CENTERS, Long Beach *Also called Long Beach Memorial Med Ctr* ***(G-21717)***
Memorial Counseling Assoc Inc ... 562 961-0155
4525 E Atherton St Long Beach (90815) ***(G-19742)***
Memorial Healthtec Labratories ... 714 962-4677
9920 Talbert Ave Fountain Valley (92708) ***(G-26567)***
Memorial Hospital of Gardena, Gardena *Also called Gardena Hospital LP* ***(G-21574)***
Memorial Hospital of Gardena ... 323 268-5514
4060 Woody Blvd Los Angeles (90023) ***(G-21732)***
Memorial Medical Center, Modesto *Also called Sutter Central Vly Hospitals* ***(G-21941)***
Memorial Psychiatric Hlth Svcs ... 562 494-9243
4525 E Atherton St Long Beach (90815) ***(G-19743)***
Memorial Surgical Group ... 562 424-6666
2760 Atlantic Ave Long Beach (90806) ***(G-19744)***
Memorialcare Med Foundation (PA) ... 714 389-5353
2742 Dow Ave Tustin (92780) ***(G-25295)***
Memory To Go ... 310 446-0111
10801 National Blvd # 101 Los Angeles (90064) ***(G-7162)***
Menchies Group Inc ... 818 708-0316
17555 Ventura Blvd # 200 Encino (91316) ***(G-8588)***
Mendelsohn/Zien Advg LLC ... 310 444-1990
11901 Santa Monica Blvd # 618 Los Angeles (90025) ***(G-13885)***
Mendes Calf Ranch ... 559 688-4708
13356 Avenue 168 Tipton (93272) ***(G-409)***
Mendicino Cast Otptent Surgery, Fort Bragg *Also called Mendocino Coast District Hosp* ***(G-21734)***
Mendocino Cmnty Hlth Clnic Inc (PA) ... 707 468-1010
333 Laws Ave Ukiah (95482) ***(G-19745)***
Mendocino Coast Clinics Inc ... 707 964-1251
205 South St Fort Bragg (95437) ***(G-22773)***
Mendocino Coast District Hosp (PA) ... 707 961-1234
700 River Dr Fort Bragg (95437) ***(G-21733)***
Mendocino Coast District Hosp ... 707 961-4736
700 River Dr Fort Bragg (95437) ***(G-21734)***
Mendocino Forest Pdts Co LLC ... 707 468-1431
850 Hollow Tree Rd Ukiah (95482) ***(G-6936)***
Mendocino Forest Pdts Co LLC ... 707 485-6800
6375 N State St Calpella (95418) ***(G-6937)***
Mendocino Forest Pdts Co LLC ... 707 620-2961
6500 Durable Mill Rd Calpella (95418) ***(G-8125)***
Mendocino Hotel & Resort Corp ... 707 937-0511
45080 Main St Mendocino (95460) ***(G-12988)***
Mendocino Railway ... 530 666-9646
341 Industrial Way Woodland (95776) ***(G-5121)***
Mendocino Transit Authority ... 707 462-1422
111 Boatyard Dr Fort Bragg (95437) ***(G-3672)***
Mendoza Farms Inc ... 805 352-1070
527 W Fesler St Apt A Santa Maria (93458) ***(G-122)***
Menifee Lakes Country Club ... 951 672-4824
3200 E Guasti Rd Ste 100 Ontario (91761) ***(G-18996)***
Menifee Valley Hospital Center, Sun City *Also called Physicians For Healthy Hospita* ***(G-21798)***
Menlo Charity Horse Show Inc ... 650 858-0202
2470 El Camino Real Palo Alto (94306) ***(G-19244)***
Menlo Circus Club ... 650 322-4616
190 Park Ln Atherton (94027) ***(G-18997)***
Menlo Gateway Inc ... 650 356-2900
303 Vintage Park Dr # 250 Foster City (94404) ***(G-11236)***
Menlo Med Clinic A Med Corp ... 650 498-6500
1300 Crane St Menlo Park (94025) ***(G-19746)***
Menlo Park VA Medical Center, Menlo Park *Also called Veterans Health Administration* ***(G-20216)***
Mens Apparel Guild In Cal Inc ... 310 857-7500
2901 28th St Ste 100 Santa Monica (90405) ***(G-25093)***
Mental Health Amer Los Angeles ... 562 437-6717
456 Elm Ave Long Beach (90802) ***(G-24083)***
Mental Health Assn Orange Cnty, Orange *Also called Orange County Association* ***(G-22786)***
Mental Health California Dept ... 707 449-6504
1600 California Dr Vacaville (95696) ***(G-22084)***
Mental Health Department, Oakland *Also called La Clinica De La Raza Inc* ***(G-22764)***
Mental Health Dept, Van Nuys *Also called Los Angeles Unified School Dst* ***(G-22770)***
Mental Health Dept of, Arcadia *Also called County of Los Angeles* ***(G-23848)***
Mental Health Dept of, Artesia *Also called County of Los Angeles* ***(G-22702)***
Mental Health Dept of, Long Beach *Also called County of Los Angeles* ***(G-19474)***
Mental Health Services, Stockton *Also called County of San Joaquin* ***(G-22708)***
Mental Health Services, Red Bluff *Also called County of Tehama* ***(G-23928)***
Mental Health Systems Inc (PA) ... 858 573-2600
9465 Farnham St San Diego (92123) ***(G-22774)***
Mental Hlth Cnvlscent Svcs Inc ... 562 869-0978
12023 Lakewood Blvd Downey (90242) ***(G-20788)***
Mental Hlth Sbstnce Abuse Svcs, Auburn *Also called County of Placer* ***(G-23879)***
Mental Hlth Svcs For Kngs Cnty, Hanford *Also called Kings View* ***(G-22762)***
Mentor Media (usa) Sup ... 909 930-0800
3768 Milliken Ave Ste A Eastvale (91752) ***(G-27126)***
Mentor Worldwide LLC ... 805 681-6000
5425 Hollister Ave Santa Barbara (93111) ***(G-7279)***
Mera Software Services Inc ... 650 703-7226
2350 Mission College Blvd # 340 Santa Clara (95054) ***(G-15299)***
Merabi & Sons LLC ... 818 817-0006
14545 Friar St Ste 101 Van Nuys (91411) ***(G-12260)***
Meraki Inc ... 415 632-5800
500 Terry A Francois Blvd San Francisco (94158) ***(G-15300)***
Mercado Latino Inc (PA) ... 626 333-6862
245 Baldwin Park Blvd City of Industry (91746) ***(G-8501)***
Mercado Latino Inc ... 510 475-5500
33430 Western Ave Union City (94587) ***(G-8502)***
Merced Convalescent Hospital, Merced *Also called Madera Convalescent Hospital* ***(G-21303)***
Merced Irrigation District (PA) ... 209 722-5761
744 W 20th St Merced (95340) ***(G-6147)***
Merced Irrigation District ... 209 722-2719
3321 Franklin Rd Merced (95348) ***(G-6645)***
Merced School Employees F C U (PA) ... 209 383-5550
1021 Olivewood Dr Merced (95348) ***(G-9612)***
Merced Transportation Company ... 209 384-2575
300 Grogan Ave Merced (95341) ***(G-3945)***
Mercedes Diaz Homes Inc ... 562 698-7479
7239 Washington Ave # 100 Whittier (90602) ***(G-1218)***
Mercedes-Benz RE ... 310 549-7600
4035 Via Oro Ave Long Beach (90810) ***(G-26568)***
Mercer (us) Inc ... 213 346-2200
777 S Figueroa St # 2000190 Los Angeles (90017) ***(G-27542)***

Mercer (us) Inc.....415 743-8700
4 Embarcadero Ctr Fl 4 San Francisco (94111) ***(G-27543)***
Mercer (us) Inc.....949 222-1300
17901 Von Karman Ave # 1100 Irvine (92614) ***(G-27544)***
Mercer Advisors Inc (PA).....805 565-1681
1801 E Cabrillo Blvd Santa Barbara (93108) ***(G-10163)***
Mercer Consulting, Irvine *Also called Mercer (us) Inc* ***(G-27544)***
Mercer Global Securities LLC.....805 565-1681
1801 E Cabrillo Blvd A Santa Barbara (93108) ***(G-10028)***
Mercer Health & Benefits LLC.....415 743-8751
3 Embarcadero Ctr San Francisco (94111) ***(G-27545)***
Merchant of Tennis Inc.....310 855-1946
1118 S La Cienega Blvd Los Angeles (90035) ***(G-17327)***
Merchant of Tennis Inc.....909 923-3388
1625 Proforma Ave Ontario (91761) ***(G-17328)***
Merchant Services, Irvine *Also called Universal Card Inc* ***(G-17568)***
Merchant Services Inc (PA).....817 725-0900
1 S Van Ness Ave Fl 5 San Francisco (94103) ***(G-16159)***
Merchants Bank California N A.....310 549-4350
1 Civic Plaza Dr Ste 100 Carson (90745) ***(G-9400)***
Merchants Building Maint Co.....714 973-9272
1639 E Edinger Ave Ste C Santa Ana (92705) ***(G-14353)***
Merchants Building Maint Co (PA).....323 881-6701
1190 Monterey Pass Rd Monterey Park (91754) ***(G-14354)***
Merchants Building Maint Co.....909 622-8260
1995 W Holt Ave Pomona (91768) ***(G-14355)***
Merchants Building Maint Co.....323 881-8902
606 Monterey Paca Rd 20 Ste 202 Monterey Park (91754) ***(G-14356)***
Merchants Building Maint Co.....800 560-6700
1190 Monterey Pass Rd Los Angeles (90065) ***(G-14357)***
Mercury Air Cargo Inc (HQ).....310 258-6100
6040 Avion Dr Ste 200 Los Angeles (90045) ***(G-4926)***
Mercury Casualty Company (HQ).....323 937-1060
555 W Imperial Hwy Brea (92821) ***(G-10439)***
Mercury Defense Systems Inc (HQ).....714 898-8200
10855 Bus Ctr Dr Bldg A Cypress (90630) ***(G-25962)***
Mercury General Corporation (PA).....323 937-1060
4484 Wilshire Blvd Los Angeles (90010) ***(G-10440)***
Mercury Insurance Broker, Santa Monica *Also called Mercury Insurance Company* ***(G-10443)***
Mercury Insurance Company.....714 671-6700
555 W Imperial Hwy Brea (92821) ***(G-10441)***
Mercury Insurance Company.....916 353-4859
104 Woodmere Rd Folsom (95630) ***(G-10442)***
Mercury Insurance Company.....310 451-4943
1433 Santa Monica Blvd Santa Monica (90404) ***(G-10443)***
Mercury Insurance Company.....714 255-5000
1700 Greenbriar Ln Brea (92821) ***(G-10444)***
Mercury Insurance Company (HQ).....323 937-1060
4484 Wilshire Blvd Los Angeles (90010) ***(G-10445)***
Mercury Insurance Company.....858 694-4100
9635 Gran Rdge Dr Ste 200 San Diego (92123) ***(G-10446)***
Mercury Insurance Company.....661 291-6470
27200 Tourney Rd Ste 400 Valencia (91355) ***(G-10447)***
Mercury Insurance Group, Folsom *Also called Mercury Insurance Company* ***(G-10442)***
Mercury Insurance Services LLC.....323 937-1060
4484 Wilshire Blvd Los Angeles (90010) ***(G-10448)***
Mercury Interactive LLC (HQ).....650 857-1501
3000 Hanover St Palo Alto (94304) ***(G-15748)***
Mercury Mailing Systems Inc.....323 730-0307
2727 Exposition Blvd Los Angeles (90018) ***(G-14083)***
Mercury Messenger Service Inc.....818 989-3115
16735 Saticoy St Ste 104 Van Nuys (91406) ***(G-17329)***
Mercury Systems, Cypress *Also called Mercury Defense Systems Inc* ***(G-25962)***
Mercury Technology Group Inc.....949 417-0260
6430 Oak Cyn Ste 100 Irvine (92618) ***(G-16160)***
Mercury World Cargo, Los Angeles *Also called Mercury Air Cargo Inc* ***(G-4926)***
Mercy Air Tri-County LLC.....909 829-1051
1670 Miro Way Rialto (92376) ***(G-4885)***
Mercy Foundation North.....530 247-3424
2625 Edith Ave Ste E Redding (96001) ***(G-22999)***
Mercy General Hospital, Sacramento *Also called Mercy HM Svcs A Cal Ltd Partnr* ***(G-21742)***
Mercy General Hospital, Sacramento *Also called Mercy Healthcare Sacramento* ***(G-22242)***
Mercy General Hospital Bus Off, Sacramento *Also called C H W Mercy Healthcare* ***(G-21467)***
Mercy Healthcare Sacramento.....916 537-5151
6501 Coyle Ave Fl 6 Carmichael (95608) ***(G-21735)***
Mercy Healthcare Sacramento.....916 537-5000
6501 Coyle Ave Carmichael (95608) ***(G-21736)***
Mercy Healthcare Sacramento (HQ).....916 379-2871
3400 Data Dr Rancho Cordova (95670) ***(G-21737)***
Mercy Healthcare Sacramento.....916 851-3800
11391 Sunrise Gold Cir # 100 Rancho Cordova (95742) ***(G-4599)***
Mercy Healthcare Sacramento.....916 983-7400
1650 Creekside Dr Folsom (95630) ***(G-21738)***
Mercy Healthcare Sacramento.....916 453-4453
4001 J St Sacramento (95819) ***(G-22242)***
Mercy HM Svcs A Cal Ltd Partnr.....661 632-5234
2215 Truxtun Ave Bakersfield (93301) ***(G-21739)***
Mercy HM Svcs A Cal Ltd Partnr (HQ).....530 225-6000
2175 Rosaline Ave Ste A Redding (96001) ***(G-21740)***
Mercy HM Svcs A Cal Ltd Partnr.....530 225-6000
2175 Rosaline Ave Ste A Redding (96001) ***(G-19747)***
Mercy HM Svcs A Cal Ltd Partnr.....530 926-6111
914 Pine St Mount Shasta (96067) ***(G-21741)***
Mercy HM Svcs A Cal Ltd Partnr.....916 453-4545
4001 J St Sacramento (95819) ***(G-21742)***
Mercy HM Svcs A Cal Ltd Partnr.....209 564-4200
2740 M St Merced (95340) ***(G-19748)***
Mercy HM Svcs A Cal Ltd Partnr.....530 245-4070
1544 Market St Redding (96001) ***(G-22507)***
Mercy Hospital, Bakersfield *Also called Dignity Health* ***(G-21543)***
Mercy Housing Calif Xxv, Sacramento *Also called Mercy Housing California Xxvi* ***(G-11678)***
Mercy Housing California Xxvi.....916 414-4400
2512 River Plaza Dr Sacramento (95833) ***(G-11678)***
Mercy Hsing California Xxxiv.....415 503-0816
66 9th St San Francisco (94103) ***(G-11167)***
Mercy Medical, Red Bluff *Also called Lassen Medical Group Inc* ***(G-19702)***
Mercy Medical Center, Merced *Also called Mercy HM Svcs A Cal Ltd Partnr* ***(G-19748)***
Mercy Medical Center Nampa.....209 485-1380
315 Merced Mall Merced (95348) ***(G-21743)***
Mercy Medical Center - Redding, Redding *Also called Mercy HM Svcs A Cal Ltd Partnr* ***(G-21740)***
Mercy Medical Center Merced, Merced *Also called Mater Misericordiae Hospital* ***(G-21730)***
Mercy Medical Center Redding, Redding *Also called Dignity Health* ***(G-19499)***
Mercy Medical Group Inc.....831 475-1111
1595 Soquel Dr Ste 140 Santa Cruz (95065) ***(G-25296)***
Mercy Methodist Hospital (PA).....916 423-6063
7500 Hospital Dr Sacramento (95823) ***(G-21744)***
Mercy Methodist Hospital.....916 681-1600
7601 Hospital Dr Ste 103 Sacramento (95823) ***(G-19749)***
Mercy Methodist Hospital.....916 379-2996
3400 Data Dr Rancho Cordova (95670) ***(G-21745)***
Mercy Retirement and Care Ctr.....510 534-8540
3431 Foothill Blvd Oakland (94601) ***(G-24732)***
Mercy San Juan Hospital, Carmichael *Also called Mercy Healthcare Sacramento* ***(G-21735)***
Mercy San Juan Hospital, Rancho Cordova *Also called Mercy Healthcare Sacramento* ***(G-21737)***
Mercy San Juan Medical Center, Carmichael *Also called Mercy Healthcare Sacramento* ***(G-21736)***
Meredith Baer & Associates, South Gate *Also called Meribear Productions Inc* ***(G-17330)***
Meribear Productions Inc.....323 588-7421
4100 Ardmore Ave South Gate (90280) ***(G-17330)***
Merical LLC (PA).....714 238-7225
2995 E Miraloma Ave Anaheim (92806) ***(G-17331)***
Meridian Gold Inc.....209 785-3222
4461 Rock Creek Rd Copperopolis (95228) ***(G-1023)***
Meridian Holdings.....805 539-2752
2580 El Camino Real Atascadero (93422) ***(G-7724)***
Meridian Industrial Trust.....415 281-3900
455 Market St Ste 1700 San Francisco (94105) ***(G-12261)***
Meridian Management Group.....415 434-9700
1145 Bush St San Francisco (94109) ***(G-11168)***
Meridian Medical Offices, Riverside *Also called Kaiser Foundation Hospitals* ***(G-19640)***
Meridian Project Systems Inc (HQ).....916 294-2000
1720 Pririe Cy Rd Ste 120 Folsom (95630) ***(G-15749)***
Meridian Rack & Pinion Inc.....858 587-8777
6740 Cobra Way Ste 200 San Diego (92121) ***(G-6747)***
Meridian Systems, Folsom *Also called Meridian Project Systems Inc* ***(G-15749)***
Meridian Textiles Inc (PA).....323 869-5700
6415 Canning St Commerce (90040) ***(G-8318)***
Meridian Vineyards, Paso Robles *Also called Treasury Wine Estates Americas* ***(G-190)***
Meristar San Pedro Hilton LLC.....310 514-3344
2800 Via Cabrillo Marina San Pedro (90731) ***(G-12989)***
Merit Companies The, Irvine *Also called Merit Property Management Inc* ***(G-11679)***
Merit Integrated Logistics LLC.....949 481-0685
29122 Rancho Viejo Rd # 211 San Juan Capistrano (92675) ***(G-5122)***
Merit Property Management Inc (HQ).....949 448-6000
15241 Laguna Canyon Rd Irvine (92618) ***(G-11679)***
Merit Technologies LLC.....858 623-9800
10509 Vista Sorrento Pkwy # 100 San Diego (92121) ***(G-27546)***
Meritage Group LP.....415 399-5330
The Embarcad Pier 5 St Pier San Francisco (94111) ***(G-27127)***
Meritage Homes Corporation.....661 829-6739
15937 Cusano Pl Bakersfield (93314) ***(G-1219)***
Meritage Resort and Spa.....707 259-0633
875 Bordeaux Way NAPA (94558) ***(G-18660)***
Meriwest Credit Union (PA).....408 363-3200
5615 Chesbro Ave Ste 100 San Jose (95123) ***(G-9613)***
Merle Norman Cosmetics Inc.....818 362-3235
15180 Bledsoe St Sylmar (91342) ***(G-8282)***
Merli Concrete Pumping, Gardena *Also called Stefan Merli Plastering Co Inc* ***(G-3336)***
Merlin Entertainments.....877 350-5346
1 Legoland Dr Carlsbad (92008) ***(G-18826)***
Merlin Global Services LLC.....904 305-9559
380 Stevens Ave Ste 305 Solana Beach (92075) ***(G-4886)***
Merlin Securities LLC.....415 848-0269
45 Fremont St Ste 3000 San Francisco (94105) ***(G-10029)***
Merlot Film Productions Inc.....323 575-2906
7800 Beverly Blvd Los Angeles (90036) ***(G-18109)***
Meroform Systems USA, Tustin *Also called Absolute Exhibits Inc* ***(G-16965)***
Merridian Neuro Care.....949 263-6630
18a Journey Ste 200 Aliso Viejo (92656) ***(G-19750)***
Merrill Gardens.....510 790-1645
2860 Country Dr Ofc Fremont (94536) ***(G-11237)***
Merrill Gardens At Bankers Hl, San Diego *Also called Merrill Gardens LLC* ***(G-11683)***
Merrill Gardens LLC.....707 447-7496
799 Yellowstone Dr Vacaville (95687) ***(G-11680)***
Merrill Gardens LLC.....707 553-2698
350 Locust Dr Apt L215 Vallejo (94591) ***(G-11681)***
Merrill Gardens LLC.....707 585-7878
4855 Snyder Ln Apt 152 Rohnert Park (94928) ***(G-11682)***
Merrill Gardens LLC.....619 961-4990
2567 2nd Ave San Diego (92103) ***(G-11683)***
Merrill Gardens LLC.....714 842-6569
17200 Goldenwest St # 101 Huntington Beach (92647) ***(G-11684)***

ALPHABETIC

Merrill Gardens LLC...408 370-6431
2115 Winchester Blvd Campbell (95008) *(G-11685)*
Merrill Gardens LLC...760 414-9880
3500 Lake Blvd Oceanside (92056) *(G-11686)*
Merrill Gardens LLC...805 310-4102
1220 Suey Rd Bldg A Santa Maria (93454) *(G-21314)*
Merrill Gardens LLC...707 996-7101
800 Oregon St Sonoma (95476) *(G-24733)*
Merrill Gardens LLC...209 823-0164
430 N Union Rd Manteca (95337) *(G-24734)*
Merrill Gardens LLC...562 693-0505
13250 Philadelphia St Ofc Whittier (90601) *(G-24735)*
Merrill Gardns At Chateau Whit, Whittier *Also called Merrill Gardens LLC (G-24735)*
Merrill Lynch Pierce Fenner...650 473-7888
333 Middlefield Rd Menlo Park (94025) *(G-10030)*
Merrill Lynch Pierce Fenner...818 528-7809
16830 Ventura Blvd # 601 Encino (91436) *(G-10031)*
Merrill Lynch Pierce Fenner...310 858-1500
9560 Wilshire Blvd Fl 3 Beverly Hills (90212) *(G-10032)*
Merrill Lynch Pierce Fenner...818 528-7800
16830 Ventura Blvd # 601 Encino (91436) *(G-10164)*
Merrill Lynch Pierce Fenner...650 842-2440
3075b Hansen Way Palo Alto (94304) *(G-10033)*
Merrill Lynch Pierce Fenner...661 802-0764
730 Patricia Dr San Luis Obispo (93405) *(G-10034)*
Merrill Lynch Pierce Fenner...949 467-3760
520 Newport Center Dr Newport Beach (92660) *(G-10035)*
Merrill Lynch Pierce Fenner...800 964-5182
300 E Esplanade Dr Oxnard (93036) *(G-10036)*
Merrill Lynch Pierce Fenner...650 473-7888
333 Middlefield Rd # 202 Menlo Park (94025) *(G-10037)*
Merrill Lynch Pierce Fenner...619 699-3700
701 B St Ste 2350 San Diego (92101) *(G-10038)*
Merrill Lynch Pierce Fenner...415 955-3700
555 California St Fl 9 San Francisco (94104) *(G-10039)*
Merrill Lynch Pierce Fenner...714 257-4400
145 S State College Blvd # 300 Brea (92821) *(G-10106)*
Merrill Lynch Pierce Fenner...310 407-3900
2049 Century Park E # 1100 Los Angeles (90067) *(G-10040)*
Merrill Lynch Pierce Fenner...510 208-3800
1111 Broadway Ste 2200 Oakland (94607) *(G-10107)*
Merrill Lynch Pierce Fenner...408 283-3000
50 W San Fernando St 16 San Jose (95113) *(G-10041)*
Merrill Lynch Pierce Fenner...925 945-4800
1331 N Calif Blvd Ste 400 Walnut Creek (94596) *(G-10042)*
Merrill Lynch Pierce Fenner...415 274-7000
101 California St Fl 24 San Francisco (94111) *(G-10043)*
Merrill Lynch Pierce Fenner...626 844-8500
800 E Colo Blvd Ste 400 Pasadena (91101) *(G-10108)*
Merrill Lynch Pierce Fenner...858 381-8112
16912 Via De Santa Fe Rancho Santa Fe (92091) *(G-10044)*
Merrill Lynch Pierce Fenner...949 859-2900
100 Spectrum Center Dr # 1100 Irvine (92618) *(G-10045)*
Merrill Lynch Pierce Fenner...858 456-3600
7825 Fay Ave Ste 300 La Jolla (92037) *(G-10046)*
Merritt Hawkins & Assoc LLC (HQ)...858 792-0711
12400 High Bluff Dr San Diego (92130) *(G-14911)*
Merritt Hospitality LLC...562 983-3400
701 W Ocean Blvd Long Beach (90831) *(G-12990)*
Merritt Hospitality LLC...714 738-7800
2701 Nutwood Ave Fullerton (92831) *(G-12991)*
Merritt Hospitality LLC...707 523-7555
3555 Round Barn Blvd Santa Rosa (95403) *(G-12992)*
Merritt Mnor Convalescent Hosp, Tulare *Also called Moyles Health Care Inc (G-21320)*
Merry X-Ray Chemical Corp (PA)...858 565-4472
4444 Viewridge Ave A San Diego (92123) *(G-7280)*
Merry X-Ray Corporation...858 565-4472
4444 Viewridge Ave San Diego (92123) *(G-7281)*
Meruelo Enterprises, Downey *Also called Cantamar Property MGT Inc (G-11340)*
Mesa Cnsld Wtr Dst Imprv Corp (PA)...949 631-1200
1965 Placentia Ave Costa Mesa (92627) *(G-6370)*
Mesa Cold Strg 4145, Fullerton *Also called US Foods Inc (G-8948)*
Mesa Contracting Corporation...714 974-7300
22845 Savi Ranch Pkwy D Yorba Linda (92887) *(G-1825)*
Mesa Distributing Coinc (HQ)...858 452-2300
3840 Via De La Valle # 300 Del Mar (92014) *(G-9074)*
Mesa Energy Systems Inc (HQ)...949 460-0460
2 Cromwell Irvine (92618) *(G-2293)*
Mesa Energy Systems Inc...559 277-7900
4668 N Sonora Ave Ste 102 Fresno (93722) *(G-2294)*
Mesa Energy Systems Inc...818 756-0500
16130 Sherman Way Van Nuys (91406) *(G-2295)*
Mesa Management Inc...949 851-0995
1451 Quail St Ste 201 Newport Beach (92660) *(G-11687)*
Mesa Pointe Stadium 12, Costa Mesa *Also called Edwards Theatres Circuit Inc (G-18322)*
Mesa Verde Country Club...714 549-0377
3000 Club House Rd Costa Mesa (92626) *(G-18998)*
Mesa Verde Partners...714 540-7500
1701 Golf Course Dr Costa Mesa (92626) *(G-18759)*
Mesa Vineyard Management Inc...805 925-7200
2570 Prell Rd Santa Maria (93454) *(G-707)*
Mesa Vineyard Management Inc (PA)...805 434-4100
110 Gibson Rd Templeton (93465) *(G-708)*
Mesa Vrde Cnvalescent Hosp Inc...949 548-5584
661 Center St Costa Mesa (92627) *(G-20789)*
Mesa Water District, Costa Mesa *Also called Mesa Cnsld Wtr Dst Imprv Corp (G-6370)*
Mesquite Golf & Country Club...760 323-9377
2700 E Mesquite Ave Ofc Palm Springs (92264) *(G-19245)*
Message Broadcastcom LLC...949 428-3111
4685 Macarthur Ct Ste 250 Newport Beach (92660) *(G-17332)*
Message Center Communication...858 974-7419
6779 Mesa Ridge Rd # 100 San Diego (92121) *(G-17333)*
Messagesolution Inc...408 383-0100
1851 Mccarthy Blvd # 105 Milpitas (95035) *(G-16161)*
Messenger Express (PA)...213 614-0475
5435 Cahuenga Blvd Ste C North Hollywood (91601) *(G-4417)*
Messenger Express...858 550-1400
10671 Roselle St Ste 200 San Diego (92121) *(G-4418)*
Meta Company...844 638-2266
2855 Campus Dr Ste 300 San Mateo (94403) *(G-15301)*
Metabyte Inc...510 494-9700
39350 Civic Center Dr # 200 Fremont (94538) *(G-16431)*
Metagenics Inc (HQ)...949 366-0818
25 Enterprise Ste 200 Aliso Viejo (92656) *(G-8283)*
Metagenics Inc...800 692-9400
100 Avenida Lapata Sacramento (94203) *(G-8284)*
Metamor Entp Solutions LLC...866 565-4746
18350 Mount Langley St # 1 Fountain Valley (92708) *(G-16432)*
Metaswitch Networks...415 513-1500
1751 Harbor Bay Pkwy Alameda (94502) *(G-15302)*
Method Studios LLC...310 434-6500
3401 Exposition Blvd Santa Monica (90404) *(G-18110)*
Methodist Hosp Southern Cal (PA)...626 898-8000
300 W Huntington Dr Arcadia (91007) *(G-21746)*
Methodist Hospital of S CA...626 574-3755
300 W Huntington Dr Arcadia (91007) *(G-21747)*
Methodist Hospital Sacramento, Sacramento *Also called Dignity Health (G-19503)*
Metier Ltd...707 546-9300
1083 Vine St Ste 511 Healdsburg (95448) *(G-16433)*
MetLife, San Francisco *Also called Metropolitan Life Insur Co (G-10785)*
Metric Equipment Sales Inc...510 264-0887
25841 Industrial Blvd # 200 Hayward (94545) *(G-7603)*
Metrick Property Management, San Francisco *Also called Blackrock Holdco 2 Inc (G-11325)*
Metricstream Inc (PA)...650 620-2900
2600 E Bayshore Rd Palo Alto (94303) *(G-15750)*
Metricus Inc...650 328-2500
P.O. Box 458 Palo Alto (94302) *(G-17334)*
Metro Bldrs & Engineers Group, Newport Beach *Also called Houalla Enterprises Ltd (G-1573)*
Metro Building Maintenance, Los Angeles *Also called US Metro Group Inc (G-14460)*
Metro City, Sherman Oaks *Also called Metro Home Loan Inc (G-9873)*
Metro Home Loan Inc...818 461-9840
15301 Ventura Blvd D300 Sherman Oaks (91403) *(G-9873)*
Metro Networks, Los Angeles *Also called Westwoodone (G-18443)*
Metro One Telecom Inc...626 337-8100
4900 Rivergrade Rd B210 Irwindale (91706) *(G-13886)*
Metro Pcs, Los Angeles *Also called Richards Group Inc (G-13912)*
Metro Service South Inc...310 995-8950
3605 Cahuenga Blvd W Los Angeles (90068) *(G-14358)*
Metro-Gldwyn-Mayer Studios Inc...310 449-3620
245 N Beverly Dr Beverly Hills (90210) *(G-18111)*
Metro-Gldwyn-Mayer Studios Inc...310 449-3000
245 N Beverly Dr Beverly Hills (90210) *(G-18112)*
Metro-Goldwyn-Mayer Inc (HQ)...310 449-3000
245 N Beverly Dr Beverly Hills (90210) *(G-18113)*
Metrocell Construction Inc...909 627-1502
4711 Chino Ave Chino (91710) *(G-1969)*
Metrolink, Los Angeles *Also called Southern Cal Rgional Rail Auth (G-3721)*
Metrolux 14 Theatres, Los Angeles *Also called Metrolux Theatres (G-18278)*
Metrolux Theatres...310 858-2800
8727 W 3rd St Los Angeles (90048) *(G-18278)*
Metromile Inc (PA)...888 244-1702
690 Folsom St Ste 200 San Francisco (94107) *(G-10449)*
Metron Incorporated...858 792-8904
12250 El Camino Real # 260 San Diego (92130) *(G-27547)*
Metropcs-Fremont, Fremont *Also called T-Mobile Usa Inc (G-5414)*
Metropcs-Modesto, Modesto *Also called T-Mobile Usa Inc (G-5415)*
Metropcs-Roseville, Roseville *Also called T-Mobile Usa Inc (G-5413)*
Metropcs-Van Ness, San Francisco *Also called T-Mobile Usa Inc (G-5416)*
Metroplex Theatres LLC...310 856-1270
2275 W 190th St Ste 201 Torrance (90504) *(G-18338)*
Metroplitan Oakland Intl Arprt, Oakland *Also called Port Dept City of Oakland (G-4931)*
Metropolitan Area Advisory Com (PA)...619 426-3595
1355 3rd Ave Chula Vista (91911) *(G-24363)*
Metropolitan Area Advisory Com...619 255-7284
1102 Cesar E Chavez Pkwy San Diego (92113) *(G-24364)*
Metropolitan Area Advisory Com...619 420-8981
1355 3rd Ave Chula Vista (91911) *(G-24365)*
Metropolitan Automotive Whse (PA)...909 885-2886
535 Tennis Court Ln San Bernardino (92408) *(G-6748)*
Metropolitan Club...415 673-0600
640 Sutter St San Francisco (94102) *(G-25297)*
Metropolitan Dst Private SEC...661 942-3999
44262 Division St Ste A Lancaster (93535) *(G-16735)*
Metropolitan Elec Cnstr Inc...415 642-3000
2400 3rd St San Francisco (94107) *(G-2651)*
Metropolitan Life Insur Co...415 536-1065
425 Market St Ste 960 San Francisco (94105) *(G-10785)*
Metropolitan Trnsp Comm (PA)...510 817-5700
375 Beale St San Francisco (94105) *(G-3673)*
Metropolitan Van and Stor Inc (PA)...707 745-1150
5400 Industrial Way Benicia (94510) *(G-4228)*
Metropolitan Waste Disposal, Paramount *Also called Calmet Inc (G-6453)*
Metropolitan Water District...213 217-6000
700 N Alameda St Ste 1 Los Angeles (90012) *(G-6371)*
Metropolitan Water District...909 890-3776
1820 Commercenter Cir San Bernardino (92408) *(G-6372)*

ALPHABETIC

Metropolitan Water District....951 688-5672
18250 La Sierra Ave Riverside (92503) *(G-6373)*
Metropolitan Water District....714 528-7231
3972 Valley View Ave Yorba Linda (92886) *(G-6374)*
Metropolitan Water District....760 663-4911
Gene Cp Parker Dam (92267) *(G-6375)*
Metropolitan Water District....818 368-3731
13100 Balboa Blvd Granada Hills (91344) *(G-6376)*
Metropolitan Water District....909 593-7474
700 Moreno Ave La Verne (91750) *(G-6377)*
Metropolitan Water District....213 217-6667
700 N Alameda St Ste 1 Los Angeles (90012) *(G-6646)*
Metropolitan Water District....951 926-7095
33752 Newport Rd Winchester (92596) *(G-6378)*
Metropolitan Water District....951 780-1511
550 E Alessandro Blvd Riverside (92508) *(G-6379)*
Metropolitan Water District....310 832-6106
2300 Palos Verdes Dr N Rllng HLS Est (90274) *(G-6647)*
Metropolitan Water District....951 926-1501
33740 Borel Rd Winchester (92596) *(G-6380)*
Metropolitan Water Lavern, La Verne *Also called Metropolitan Water District (G-6377)*
Metropower Inc....562 305-9617
941 Grand Ave Long Beach (90804) *(G-2652)*
Metropro Road Services Inc (PA)....714 556-7600
2550 S Garnsey St Santa Ana (92707) *(G-17887)*
Meus, Cypress *Also called Mitsubishi Electric Us Inc (G-7605)*
Mexican Amrcn Alcoholism Progr (PA)....916 394-2320
4241 Florin Rd Ste 110 Sacramento (95823) *(G-24084)*
Mexican Amrcn Oprtnty Fndation (PA)....323 890-9600
401 N Garfield Ave Montebello (90640) *(G-24085)*
Mexican Amrcn Oprtnty Fndation....323 588-7320
2650 Zoe Ave Fl 3 Huntington Park (90255) *(G-24483)*
Mexican Amrcn Oprtnty Fndation....323 890-1555
5657 E Washington Blvd Commerce (90040) *(G-24086)*
Meyer Coatings Inc....714 467-4600
606 N Eckhoff St Orange (92868) *(G-2466)*
Meyer Corporation US....707 399-2100
2001 Meyer Way Fairfield (94533) *(G-6874)*
Meyers Nave Riback Silver & (PA)....510 351-4300
555 12th St Ste 1500 Oakland (94607) *(G-23431)*
Meyers Earthwork Inc....530 365-8858
4150 Fig Tree Ln Redding (96002) *(G-3437)*
Meyers Farming, Firebaugh *Also called Oxford Farms Inc (G-712)*
Meyers Group, Costa Mesa *Also called Hanley Wood Mkt Intelligence (G-26672)*
Mf Daily Oxnard Ranch Partnr....805 646-5633
1033 E Ojai Ave Ojai (93023) *(G-18760)*
Mf Services Company LLC (HQ)....949 474-5800
4350 Von Karman Ave # 400 Newport Beach (92660) *(G-27548)*
Mfw Partners....858 454-8857
1120 Silverado St La Jolla (92037) *(G-11018)*
Mg Computers Inc....831 970-3231
436 S Dawes Ave Stockton (95215) *(G-16302)*
Mg Restaurants Inc....415 296-8222
475 Sansome St Ste 100s San Francisco (94111) *(G-27128)*
MGA Entertainment Inc (PA)....818 894-2525
16300 Roscoe Blvd Ste 150 Van Nuys (91406) *(G-8050)*
MGA Healthcare California Inc....310 324-5591
879 W 190th St Ste 260 Gardena (90248) *(G-14912)*
Mgb Construction Inc....951 342-0303
91 Commercial Ave Riverside (92507) *(G-1826)*
Mge Underground Inc....805 238-3510
816 26th St Paso Robles (93446) *(G-1970)*
Mggb Inc....714 226-0520
10841 Noel St Ste 110 Los Alamitos (90720) *(G-25963)*
Mgh Corporation....323 754-1408
1202 W 101st St Los Angeles (90044) *(G-24736)*
Mgi, Newark *Also called Mickwee Group Inc (G-17335)*
MGM, Beverly Hills *Also called Metro-Gldwyn-Mayer Studios Inc (G-18111)*
MGM, Beverly Hills *Also called Metro-Gldwyn-Mayer Studios Inc (G-18112)*
MGM, Beverly Hills *Also called Metro-Goldwyn-Mayer Inc (G-18113)*
MGM Drywall Inc....408 292-4085
1165 Peach Ct San Jose (95116) *(G-2931)*
Mgr Services Inc....909 981-4466
1425 W Foothill Blvd # 300 Upland (91786) *(G-11688)*
MGT Industries Inc....310 324-3152
19034 S Vermont Ave Gardena (90248) *(G-27129)*
Mhh Holdings Inc....949 651-9903
5653 Alton Pkwy Irvine (92618) *(G-8876)*
Mhh Holdings Inc....626 744-9370
415 S Lake Ave Ste 108 Pasadena (91101) *(G-8877)*
Mhm Services Inc....805 904-6678
230 Station Way Arroyo Grande (93420) *(G-22775)*
Mhm Services Inc....415 416-6992
350 Brannan St San Francisco (94107) *(G-22776)*
Mhm Services Inc....707 623-9080
2380 Professional Dr Santa Rosa (95403) *(G-22777)*
Mhn Government Services Inc....916 294-4941
2370 Kerner Blvd San Rafael (94901) *(G-24087)*
Mhn Services....415 460-8300
2370 Kerner Blvd San Rafael (94901) *(G-10360)*
MHRP Resort Inc....760 249-5808
24510 Highway 2 Wrightwood (92397) *(G-12993)*
MHS Customer Service Inc....858 695-2151
7586 Trade St Ste C San Diego (92121) *(G-14704)*
Mias Fashion Mfg Co Inc....562 906-1060
12623 Cisneros Ln Santa Fe Springs (90670) *(G-8401)*
Michael A Meczka....310 670-4824
5757 W Century Blvd # 120 Los Angeles (90045) *(G-26689)*
Michael B Mayock Inc....415 456-9306
1945 Francisco Blvd E # 31 San Rafael (94901) *(G-2932)*
Michael Baker Jr Inc....805 383-3373
5051 Verdugo Way Ste 300 Camarillo (93012) *(G-25964)*
Michael Baker Intl Inc....510 879-0950
1 Kaiser Plz Ste 1150 Oakland (94612) *(G-25965)*
Michael Baker Intl Inc....916 361-8384
2729 Prospect Park Dr # 220 Rancho Cordova (95670) *(G-27986)*
Michael Baker Intl Inc....858 453-3602
6020 Cornerstone Ct W San Diego (92121) *(G-27987)*
Michael Baker Intl Inc....909 974-4900
3300 E Guasti Rd Ste 100 Ontario (91761) *(G-27988)*
Michael Bruington....831 663-1772
9 Soledad Dr Ste E Monterey (93940) *(G-1220)*
Michael Dusi Trucking Inc....805 237-9499
3230 Rverside Ave Ste 220 Paso Robles (93446) *(G-4362)*
Michael G Fortaanasce Phys....323 254-6000
920 Lohman Ln South Pasadena (91030) *(G-20332)*
Michael Grove....909 883-5398
3260 N E St Ste C San Bernardino (92405) *(G-13777)*
Michael Jon Designs, Vernon *Also called Morgan Fabrics Corporation (G-8320)*
Michael Madden Co Inc....800 834-6248
2815 Warner Ave Irvine (92606) *(G-8198)*
Michael Maguire & Associates....714 435-7500
611 Anton Blvd Ste 900 Costa Mesa (92626) *(G-10786)*
Michael McCarthy....310 800-5367
211 S Shiplan Ave La Puente (91744) *(G-16736)*
Michael P Byko DDS A Prof Corp (PA)....909 888-7817
164 W Hospitality Ln # 14 San Bernardino (92408) *(G-20264)*
Michael SD Nagatini....559 738-7502
5400 W Hillsdale Ave Visalia (93291) *(G-19751)*
Michael W Morgan....760 344-5253
3949 Austin Rd Brawley (92227) *(G-80)*
Michael-Antonio Studio, Montclair *Also called E M S Trading Inc (G-8432)*
Michaels Stores Inc....661 951-3500
3501 W Avenue H Lancaster (93536) *(G-9281)*
Michaels Trnsp Svc Inc....707 674-6013
140 Yolano Dr Vallejo (94589) *(G-3895)*
Michaelson Connor & Boul (PA)....714 846-6099
5312 Bolsa Ave Ste 200 Huntington Beach (92649) *(G-27549)*
Micheli Farms Inc....530 695-9022
6005 Highway 99 Live Oak (95953) *(G-242)*
Michelle Alexander, Fresno *Also called Xtreme Zone Inc (G-19311)*
Michelle Pasternak, Los Angeles *Also called SM 10000 Property LLC (G-12012)*
Michelson Laboratories Inc (PA)....562 928-0553
6280 Chalet Dr Commerce (90040) *(G-26866)*
Mickey Wall Painting Inc....209 669-0557
2470 Acme Ct Turlock (95380) *(G-2467)*
Mickwee Group Inc....510 651-5527
5600 Mowry School Rd # 230 Newark (94560) *(G-17335)*
Micon Construction Cal Inc....714 666-0203
1616 Sierra Madre Cir Placentia (92870) *(G-1613)*
Micro Dental Laboratories (HQ)....925 829-3611
5601 Arnold Rd Fl 100 Dublin (94568) *(G-22311)*
Micro Holding Corp....415 788-5111
1 Maritime Plz Fl 12 San Francisco (94111) *(G-16162)*
Micro-Mechanics Inc....408 779-2927
465 Woodview Ave Morgan Hill (95037) *(G-7604)*
Micro-Pro Microfilming Svcs, Long Beach *Also called Macro-Pro Inc (G-17306)*
Micro-Technology Concepts Inc....626 839-6800
17837 Rowland St City of Industry (91748) *(G-7163)*
Microbial Diseases Laboratory, Richmond *Also called Department Health Care Svcs (G-22208)*
Microconstants Inc....858 652-4600
9050 Camino Santa Fe San Diego (92121) *(G-27989)*
Microfinancial Incorporated....805 367-8900
2801 Townsgate Rd Westlake Village (91361) *(G-14561)*
Microlease, Hayward *Also called Metric Equipment Sales Inc (G-7603)*
Microsoft Corporation....650 964-7200
1065 La Avenida St Mountain View (94043) *(G-5658)*
Microsoft Corporation....619 849-5872
7007 Friars Rd San Diego (92108) *(G-15751)*
Microsoft Corporation....650 693-1009
1020 Entp Way Bldg B Sunnyvale (94089) *(G-15752)*
Microsoft Corporation....949 263-3000
3 Park Plz Ste 1800 Irvine (92614) *(G-15753)*
Microsoft Corporation....213 806-7300
13031 W Jefferson Blvd # 200 Playa Vista (90094) *(G-15754)*
Microsoft Corporation....415 972-6400
555 California St Ste 200 San Francisco (94104) *(G-15755)*
Microsoft Corporation....408 987-9608
2045 Lafayette St Santa Clara (95050) *(G-15756)*
Microtek Lab Inc (HQ)....310 687-5823
13337 South St Cerritos (90703) *(G-7060)*
Microtel Computer Systems Inc....626 839-6038
5545 Daniels St Chino (91710) *(G-16434)*
Mid Century Insurance Company....323 932-7116
4680 Wilshire Blvd Los Angeles (90010) *(G-10450)*
Mid Cities Assn Retarded Ctzns (PA)....310 537-4510
14208 Towne Ave Los Angeles (90061) *(G-24366)*
Mid Coast Builders Supply Inc....805 484-3157
624 Calle Plano Camarillo (93012) *(G-1221)*
MID PENN HOUSING, Saratoga *Also called Saratoga Court Inc (G-11241)*
Mid State Steel Erection (PA)....209 464-9497
1916 Cherokee Rd Stockton (95205) *(G-3393)*
Mid Valley Packaging & Sup Co, Fowler *Also called Gahvejian Enterprises Inc (G-8192)*
Mid Valley Plastering Inc....209 858-9766
15300 Mckinley Ave Lathrop (95330) *(G-2933)*

ALPHABETIC

Mid Vlley Racquetball Athc CLB ALPHABETIC SECTION

Mid Vlley Racquetball Athc CLB..............................818 705-6500
18420 Hart St Reseda (91335) ***(G-18999)***
Mid Wilshire Health Care Ctr..............................213 483-9921
676 S Bonnie Brae St Los Angeles (90057) ***(G-20790)***
Mid-Peninsula Roofing Inc..............................650 375-7850
1326 Marsten Rd Burlingame (94010) ***(G-3191)***
Mid-Valley Athletic Club, Reseda *Also called Mid Vlley Racquetball Athc CLB* ***(G-18999)***
Mid-Valley Labor Services Inc..............................559 661-6390
19358 Avenue 18 1/2 Madera (93637) ***(G-14705)***
Mid-Valley Y M C A, Van Nuys *Also called Young Mens Chrstn Assn of La* ***(G-25464)***
Mida Industries Inc..............................562 616-1020
6101 Obispo Ave Long Beach (90805) ***(G-14359)***
Midas Express Los Angeles Inc..............................310 609-0366
11854 Alameda St Lynwood (90262) ***(G-4698)***
Midas Muffler, Santa Barbara *Also called Freeman Investments Inc* ***(G-17778)***
Midland Credit Management Inc..............................877 240-2377
3111 Camino Del Rio N San Diego (92108) ***(G-9786)***
Midnight Auto Recycling LLC..............................909 884-5308
434 E 6th St San Bernardino (92410) ***(G-8076)***
Midnight Mission (PA)..............................213 624-9258
601 S San Pedro St Los Angeles (90014) ***(G-25298)***
Midnight Snack LP..............................310 202-1470
4182 Irving Pl Culver City (90232) ***(G-27130)***
Midnite Air Corp..............................310 330-2300
8801 Bellanca Ave Los Angeles (90045) ***(G-4869)***
Midnite Air Corp (HQ)..............................310 330-2300
2132 Michelson Dr Irvine (92612) ***(G-4870)***
Midokura USA Inc..............................888 512-0460
235 Montgomery St Ste 850 San Francisco (94104) ***(G-15303)***
Midori Landscape Inc..............................714 751-8792
3231 S Main St Santa Ana (92707) ***(G-911)***
Midori Landscaping, Santa Ana *Also called Midori Landscape Inc* ***(G-911)***
MIDPEN HOUSING, Foster City *Also called Menlo Gateway Inc* ***(G-11236)***
MIDPEN HOUSING, San Jose *Also called Vivente 1 Inc* ***(G-11242)***
Midpen Housing Corporation..............................650 356-2900
303 Vintage Park Dr # 250 Foster City (94404) ***(G-11984)***
Midpen Resident Services Corp..............................650 356-2965
303 Vintage Park Dr # 250 Foster City (94404) ***(G-11238)***
Midpeninsul Rgnl Opn Sp..............................650 691-1200
330 Distel Cir Los Altos (94022) ***(G-28148)***
Midstate Barrier Inc..............................209 944-9565
3291 S Highway 99 Stockton (95215) ***(G-1827)***
Midstate Construction Corp..............................707 762-3200
1180 Holm Rd Ste A Petaluma (94954) ***(G-1222)***
Midway Car Rental, North Hollywood *Also called Midway Rent A Car Inc* ***(G-17703)***
Midway Clinic Cars, Los Angeles *Also called Midway Rent A Car Inc* ***(G-17689)***
Midway International Inc..............................562 802-0800
13131 166th St Cerritos (90703) ***(G-9282)***
Midway Rent A Car Inc..............................818 985-9770
4201 Lankershim Blvd North Hollywood (91602) ***(G-17703)***
Midway Rent A Car Inc..............................310 445-4355
1800 S Sepulveda Blvd Los Angeles (90025) ***(G-17689)***
Midwest Enviromental Control..............................661 255-0722
22430 13th St Santa Clarita (91321) ***(G-26569)***
Mig Management Services LLC..............................949 474-5800
660 Newport Center Dr # 1300 Newport Beach (92660) ***(G-27131)***
Mighty Enterprises Inc..............................310 516-7478
19706 Normandie Ave Torrance (90502) ***(G-7864)***
Mighty Leaf Tea..............................415 491-2650
100 Smith Ranch Rd # 120 San Rafael (94903) ***(G-8878)***
Mighty USA, Torrance *Also called Mighty Enterprises Inc* ***(G-7864)***
Miguel Ramos..............................831 761-9941
196 San Andreas Rd Watsonville (95076) ***(G-469)***
Miguelito Manpower Inc..............................323 582-3376
23295 Buckland Ln Lake Forest (92630) ***(G-4229)***
Mikado Best Western Hotel, North Hollywood *Also called Mikado Hotels Inc* ***(G-12994)***
Mikado Hotels Inc..............................818 763-9141
12600 Riverside Dr North Hollywood (91607) ***(G-12994)***
Mikaelian & Sons Inc..............................559 591-6324
10368 Avenue 400 Dinuba (93618) ***(G-81)***
Mike Brown Electric Co..............................707 792-8100
561a Mercantile Dr Cotati (94931) ***(G-2653)***
Mike Campbell & Associates Ltd (PA)..............................626 369-3981
13031 Temple Ave City of Industry (91746) ***(G-4500)***
Mike Campbell & Associates Ltd..............................209 234-7920
2121 Boeing Way Stockton (95206) ***(G-4039)***
Mike Campbell Assoc Logictics, City of Industry *Also called Mike Campbell & Associates Ltd* ***(G-4500)***
Mike Champlin..............................925 961-1004
4374 Contractors Cmn Livermore (94551) ***(G-2468)***
Mike Champlin Painting, Livermore *Also called Mike Champlin* ***(G-2468)***
Mike Jensen Farms..............................559 897-4192
13138 S Bethel Ave Kingsburg (93631) ***(G-243)***
Mike McCall Landscape Inc..............................925 363-8100
4749 Clayton Rd Concord (94521) ***(G-912)***
Mike Parker Landscape, Santa Ana *Also called Mpl Enterprises Inc* ***(G-916)***
Mike Roses Auto Body Inc..............................925 686-1739
2001 Fremont St Concord (94520) ***(G-17762)***
Mike Rovner Construction Inc..............................949 458-1562
22600 Lambert St Lake Forest (92630) ***(G-27132)***
Mike Rovner Construction Inc..............................408 453-4061
1758 Junction Ave Ste C San Jose (95112) ***(G-1223)***
Miken Clothing, Commerce *Also called Miken Sales Inc* ***(G-8402)***
Miken Sales Inc (PA)..............................323 266-2560
7230 Oxford Way Commerce (90040) ***(G-8402)***
Mikes Bopps Ranches, Fresno *Also called Mikes Vineyard Spray Inc* ***(G-14190)***
Mikes Vineyard Spray Inc..............................559 269-7109
5156 W Minarets Ave Fresno (93722) ***(G-14190)***

Mikuni American Corporation (HQ)..............................310 676-0522
8910 Mikuni Ave Northridge (91324) ***(G-6749)***
Milan Corporation..............................510 656-6400
43230 Osgood Rd Fremont (94539) ***(G-3192)***
Milauskas Eye Institute, Rancho Mirage *Also called Outpatnt Eye Srgry Ctr of Dsrt* ***(G-19802)***
Milbank Global Securities, Los Angeles *Also called Milbank Tweed Hdley McCloy LLP* ***(G-23432)***
Milbank Tweed Hdley McCloy LLP..............................213 892-4000
2029 Century Park E # 3300 Los Angeles (90067) ***(G-23432)***
Milco Constructors Inc..............................562 595-1977
3930b Cherry Ave Long Beach (90807) ***(G-2067)***
Mile Post Properties LLC..............................415 673-4711
1050 Van Ness Ave San Francisco (94109) ***(G-12995)***
Mile Square Golf Course..............................714 962-5541
10401 Warner Ave Fountain Valley (92708) ***(G-18761)***
Milen, Seal Beach *Also called P2f Holdings* ***(G-9284)***
Miles Construction Group Inc..............................951 260-2504
27226 Via Industria Temecula (92590) ***(G-1450)***
Milestone Health Care Center, Costa Mesa *Also called Newport Sbacute Healthcare Ctr* ***(G-21327)***
Milestone Hospice..............................310 782-1177
1500 Crenshaw Blvd # 200 Torrance (90501) ***(G-23000)***
Milestone Technologies Inc (PA)..............................510 651-2454
3101 Skyway Ct Fremont (94539) ***(G-15994)***
Milestones Adult Dev Ctr..............................707 644-0464
1 Florida St Vallejo (94590) ***(G-24088)***
Milestones of Development Inc..............................707 644-0496
1 Florida St Vallejo (94590) ***(G-21092)***
Milhous Childrens Services Inc..............................530 265-9057
24077 State Highway 49 Nevada City (95959) ***(G-21093)***
Milhous Feed..............................530 292-3242
24077 State Highway 49 Nevada City (95959) ***(G-9144)***
Milken Family Foundation..............................310 570-4800
1250 4th St Fl 1 Santa Monica (90401) ***(G-24089)***
Milken Institute..............................310 570-4600
1250 4th St Fl 2 Santa Monica (90401) ***(G-26787)***
Mill Creek Manor, Mentone *Also called Nice Avenue LLC* ***(G-20807)***
Mill Valley Medical Offices, Mill Valley *Also called Kaiser Foundation Hospitals* ***(G-19626)***
Mill Valley Parks & Recreation, Mill Valley *Also called City of Mill Valley* ***(G-19175)***
Mill Valley Refuse Service Inc..............................415 457-2287
112 Front St San Rafael (94901) ***(G-6503)***
Millbrae Racquet Club..............................650 583-4345
301 Santa Paula Ave Millbrae (94030) ***(G-19000)***
Millbrae Serra Sanitarium..............................650 697-8386
150 Serra Ave Millbrae (94030) ***(G-21315)***
Millbrae Srra Cnvalescent Hosp, Millbrae *Also called Millbrae Serra Sanitarium* ***(G-21315)***
Millbrae Wcp Hotel I LLC..............................415 397-7000
335 Powell St San Francisco (94102) ***(G-12996)***
Millbrae Wcp Hotel II LLC..............................650 443-5500
401 E Millbrae Ave Millbrae (94030) ***(G-12997)***
Millenia Development..............................951 660-5691
929 Bettina Way San Jacinto (92582) ***(G-1224)***
Millenium Athletic Club LLc..............................805 562-3845
170 Los Carneros Way Goleta (93117) ***(G-18661)***
Millennia Holdings Inc..............................213 252-1230
3731 Wilshire Blvd # 618 Los Angeles (90010) ***(G-27550)***
Millennia Stainless Inc..............................562 946-3545
10016 Romandel Ave Santa Fe Springs (90670) ***(G-7940)***
Millennium Biltmore Hotel, Los Angeles *Also called Whb Corporation* ***(G-13410)***
Millennium Engrg Integration..............................703 413-7750
350 N Akron Rd Bldg 19 Moffett Field (94035) ***(G-25966)***
Millennium Health LLC (PA)..............................877 451-3534
16981 Via Tazon Ste F San Diego (92127) ***(G-26867)***
Millennium Partners Sports C..............................415 243-0492
747 Market St San Francisco (94103) ***(G-18662)***
Millennium Transportation Inc..............................714 956-7882
3164 E La Palma Ave Ste D Anaheim (92806) ***(G-5123)***
Miller Starr & Regalia A Pro (PA)..............................925 935-9400
1331 N Calif Blvd Ste 500 Walnut Creek (94596) ***(G-23433)***
Miller & Associates LLP..............................310 315-1100
2530 Wilshire Blvd Fl 1 Santa Monica (90403) ***(G-23434)***
Miller Environmental Inc..............................714 385-0099
1130 W Trenton Ave Orange (92867) ***(G-3460)***
Miller Milling Company LLC..............................510 536-9555
2201 E 7th St Oakland (94606) ***(G-563)***
Millers Custom Work Inc..............................530 257-4207
471-825 Diane Dr Susanville (96130) ***(G-1828)***
Millers Progressive Care, Riverside *Also called Wilmon Corporation* ***(G-21043)***
Millie and Severson Inc..............................562 493-3611
3601 Serpentine Dr Los Alamitos (90720) ***(G-1451)***
Milliman Inc..............................415 403-1333
650 California St Fl 17 San Francisco (94108) ***(G-28149)***
Millmens Local 1496..............................559 275-8676
6190 N Cecelia Ave Fresno (93722) ***(G-25179)***
Mills Corporation..............................909 484-8300
1 Mills Cir Ste 1 Ontario (91764) ***(G-11019)***
Mills-Peninsula Health HM Care, San Mateo *Also called Alliance Hospital Services* ***(G-22350)***
Mills-Peninsula Health Svcs (HQ)..............................650 696-5400
1501 Trousdale Dr Burlingame (94010) ***(G-21748)***
Mills-Peninsula Hospitals, Burlingame *Also called Mills-Peninsula Health Svcs* ***(G-21748)***
Millsap Degnan & Assoc Inc..............................415 472-4244
4280 Redwood Hwy Ste 10 San Rafael (94903) ***(G-1325)***
Millward Brown LLC..............................310 309-3352
2425 Olympic Blvd 240e Santa Monica (90404) ***(G-26690)***
Millward Brown LLC..............................323 966-5770
6500 Wilshire Blvd # 460 Los Angeles (90048) ***(G-26691)***
Millward Brown International, Los Angeles *Also called Millward Brown LLC* ***(G-26691)***
Millwork Holdings, Irvine *Also called Alton Irvine Inc* ***(G-6802)***

ALPHABETIC

Milo Wind Project LLC 888 903-6926
15445 Innovation Dr San Diego (92128) *(G-6148)*
Milpitas Medical Offices, Milpitas *Also called Kaiser Foundation Hospitals (G-19667)*
Milspec Industries Inc (HQ) 213 680-9690
5825 Greenwood Ave Commerce (90040) *(G-7694)*
Milt & Michael Master Dry Clrs, Burbank *Also called Shadkor Inc (G-13586)*
Miltenyi Biotec Inc (HQ) 530 745-2800
2303 Lindbergh St Auburn (95602) *(G-7282)*
Mimg Medical Management LLC 949 282-1600
26522 La Alameda Ste 120 Mission Viejo (92691) *(G-27133)*
Minami Tamaki LLP 415 788-9000
360 Post St Fl 8 San Francisco (94108) *(G-23435)*
Mind Dragon Inc 877 367-6060
36002 Pansy St Winchester (92596) *(G-27990)*
Mind Over Eye, El Segundo *Also called Source Interlink Media LLC (G-15472)*
Mind Research Institute 949 345-8700
111 Academy Ste 100 Irvine (92617) *(G-26788)*
Mindbody Inc (PA) 877 755-4279
4051 Broad St Ste 220 San Luis Obispo (93401) *(G-15757)*
Mindfull Body 415 931-2639
2876 California St San Francisco (94115) *(G-19246)*
Mindjet LLC (HQ) 415 229-4344
275 Battery St Ste 1000 San Francisco (94111) *(G-15758)*
Mindless Entertainment, North Hollywood *Also called 51 Minds Entertainment LLC (G-18449)*
Mindring Productions LLC 323 466-9200
5200 Lankershim Blvd # 200 North Hollywood (91601) *(G-18114)*
Mindsource Inc 650 314-6400
555 Clyde Ave Ste 100 Mountain View (94043) *(G-15304)*
Mindwave Software, San Diego *Also called Isaac Fair Corporation (G-15258)*
Mindworks Press, Costa Mesa *Also called Amen Clinics Inc A Med Corp (G-22189)*
Mine Fashion, Los Angeles *Also called Edgemine Inc (G-8380)*
Minegar Contracting Inc 760 598-5001
925 Poinsettia Ave Ste 10 Vista (92081) *(G-3296)*
Minerva Networks Inc (PA) 800 806-9594
2150 Gold St Alviso (95002) *(G-15305)*
Mineta San Jose Intl Arprt, San Jose *Also called City of San Jose (G-4910)*
Ming Medical Offices, Bakersfield *Also called Kaiser Foundation Hospitals (G-19607)*
Minilec Service Inc 818 341-1125
9207 Deering Ave Ste A Chatsworth (91311) *(G-17911)*
Minilec Service-Los Angeles BR, Chatsworth *Also called Minilec Service Inc (G-17911)*
Minimalisms Inc 415 309-3108
49 Missouri St Apt 10 San Francisco (94107) *(G-17336)*
Minka Group, Corona *Also called Minka Lighting Inc (G-7456)*
Minka Lighting Inc (PA) 951 735-9220
1151 Bradford Cir Corona (92882) *(G-7456)*
Minneapolis Radio Assets LLC 612 617-4000
3800 W Alameda Ave 17 Burbank (91505) *(G-5810)*
Minor League Baseball, Adelanto *Also called High Desert Mavericks Inc (G-18548)*
Minority Aids Project Inc 323 936-4949
5147 W Jefferson Blvd Los Angeles (90016) *(G-24090)*
Minshew Brothers Stl Cnstr Inc 619 561-5700
12578 Vigilante Rd Lakeside (92040) *(G-1452)*
Mintie Corporation (PA) 323 225-4111
1114 N San Fernando Rd Los Angeles (90065) *(G-14360)*
Mintie Technologies, Los Angeles *Also called Mintie Corporation (G-14360)*
Mintz Levin Cohn Ferris GL 858 314-1500
3580 Carmel Mountain Rd # 300 San Diego (92130) *(G-23436)*
Mira Mesa Stadium 18, San Diego *Also called Edwards Theatres Circuit Inc (G-18325)*
Mira Vista Golf and Cntry CLB 510 233-7550
7901 Cutting Blvd El Cerrito (94530) *(G-19001)*
Mirabella Farms Inc 559 237-4495
5551 S Orange Ave Fresno (93725) *(G-171)*
Miracle Home Health Agency 562 653-0668
13146 Mungo Ct Rancho Cucamonga (91739) *(G-22508)*
Mirada, Los Angeles *Also called Motion Theory Inc (G-14155)*
Mirada Hills Rehabilitation 562 947-8691
12200 La Mirada Blvd La Mirada (90638) *(G-21316)*
Mirada Hills Rehb & Conva, La Mirada *Also called Life Care Centers America Inc (G-20725)*
Miramar Ford Truck Sales Inc 858 450-0707
6066 Miramar Rd San Diego (92121) *(G-6689)*
Miramar Transportation Inc 858 693-0071
9340 Cabot Dr Ste I San Diego (92126) *(G-5124)*
Miramar Truck Center, San Diego *Also called Transwest San Diego LLC (G-4383)*
Miramax Film Ny LLC 310 409-4321
2450 Colorado Ave Ste 10 Santa Monica (90404) *(G-18115)*
Miramed Global Services Inc 805 277-1017
199 E Thsand Oaks Blvd Thousand Oaks (91360) *(G-27991)*
Miramnte High Schl Parents CLB 925 280-3965
750 Moraga Way Orinda (94563) *(G-24942)*
Mirion Technologies Gds Inc (HQ) 949 419-1000
2652 Mcgaw Ave Irvine (92614) *(G-26868)*
Mirnavseh Inc 858 335-2470
8436 Florissant Ct San Diego (92129) *(G-15306)*
Miro Technologies Inc 858 677-2100
5643 Copley Dr San Diego (92111) *(G-15995)*
Mirum Inc 619 237-5552
350 10th Ave Ste 1200 San Diego (92101) *(G-14154)*
MIS International Inc 310 320-4546
370 Crenshaw Blvd E206 Torrance (90503) *(G-4040)*
Mis Sciences Corp 818 847-0213
2550 N Hollywood Way Burbank (91505) *(G-5659)*
Mishima Foods USA Inc (PA) 310 787-1533
2340 Plaza Del Amo # 105 Torrance (90501) *(G-8503)*
Mission Ambulance Inc 951 272-2300
1055 E 3rd St Corona (92879) *(G-3819)*
Mission Bargain Center, Oxnard *Also called Rescue Mission Alliance (G-25570)*
Mission Bay Aquatic Center, San Diego *Also called Associated Students San Diego (G-25492)*
Mission Beverage Co (HQ) 323 266-6238
550 S Mission Rd Los Angeles (90033) *(G-9075)*
Mission Car Wash 707 537-2040
59 Mission Cir Santa Rosa (95409) *(G-17856)*
Mission Car Wash & Quik Lube, Santa Rosa *Also called Mission Car Wash (G-17856)*
MISSION CARE CENTER, Riverside *Also called Riverside Equities LLC (G-20876)*
Mission Care Center, Rosemead *Also called Ensign Group Inc (G-20543)*
Mission Cmmons Rtrment Rsdence, Redlands *Also called Harvest Facility Holdings LP (G-11139)*
Mission Community Hospital, Panorama City *Also called Deanco Healthcare LLC (G-22067)*
Mission Courier Inc 916 484-1992
3204 Orange Grove Ave North Highlands (95660) *(G-17337)*
Mission Critical Tech Inc 310 246-4455
2041 Rosecrans Ave # 220 El Segundo (90245) *(G-15307)*
Mission Crmchael Halthcare Ctr, Carmichael *Also called SSC Carmichael Operating Co LP (G-20924)*
Mission De La Casa, San Jose *Also called Careage Inc (G-20438)*
Mission Drive-In Theatre Co 909 465-9219
4407 State St Montclair (91763) *(G-18360)*
MISSION ELECTRIC COMPANY, Fremont *Also called Kositch Enterprises Inc (G-2633)*
Mission Energy Holding Company 949 752-5588
2600 Michelson Dr # 1700 Irvine (92612) *(G-12075)*
Mission Federal Services LLC (PA) 800 500-6328
5785 Oberlin Dr Ste 333 San Diego (92121) *(G-9614)*
Mission Hills Country Club 760 324-9400
34600 Mission Hills Dr Rancho Mirage (92270) *(G-19002)*
Mission Hills Healthcare Ctr, San Diego *Also called Mission Hills Healthcare Inc (G-20791)*
Mission Hills Healthcare Inc 619 297-4086
4033 6th Ave San Diego (92103) *(G-20791)*
Mission Hills Mortgage Bankers, Irvine *Also called Mission Hills Mortgage Corp (G-9937)*
Mission Hills Mortgage Corp (HQ) 714 972-3832
18500 Von Karman Ave # 1100 Irvine (92612) *(G-9937)*
Mission Hosp Regional Med Ctr (PA) 949 364-1400
27700 Medical Center Rd Mission Viejo (92691) *(G-21749)*
Mission Internal Med Group Inc 949 364-3570
26800 Crown Valley Pkwy # 103 Mission Viejo (92691) *(G-19752)*
Mission Internal Med Group Inc 949 364-6559
26800 Crown Valley Pkwy # 103 Mission Viejo (92691) *(G-19753)*
Mission Internal Med Group Inc 949 364-3605
27882 Forbes Rd Ste 110 Laguna Niguel (92677) *(G-19754)*
Mission Landscape Service 909 947-7290
952 E Francis St Ontario (91761) *(G-913)*
Mission Ldscp Companies Inc 714 545-9962
536 E Dyer Rd Santa Ana (92707) *(G-914)*
Mission Linen & Uniform Svc, Oceanside *Also called Mission Linen Supply (G-13552)*
Mission Linen & Uniform Svc, Sacramento *Also called Mission Linen Supply (G-13554)*
Mission Linen & Uniform Svc, Salinas *Also called Mission Linen Supply (G-13555)*
Mission Linen & Uniform Svc, Fresno *Also called Mission Linen Supply (G-13556)*
Mission Linen & Uniform Svc, Oxnard *Also called Mission Linen Supply (G-13558)*
Mission Linen & Uniform Svc, Union City *Also called Mission Linen Supply (G-13559)*
Mission Linen & Uniform Svc, Salinas *Also called Mission Linen Supply (G-13633)*
Mission Linen & Uniform Svc, Santa Barbara *Also called Mission Linen Supply (G-13560)*
Mission Linen & Uniform Svc, Chico *Also called Mission Linen Supply (G-13561)*
Mission Linen & Uniform Svc, Pacific Grove *Also called Mission Linen Supply (G-13562)*
Mission Linen & Uniform Svc, Lancaster *Also called Mission Linen Supply (G-13563)*
Mission Linen & Uniform Svc, Sacramento *Also called Mission Linen Supply (G-13564)*
Mission Linen & Uniform Svc, Santa Maria *Also called Mission Linen Supply (G-13565)*
Mission Linen & Uniform Svc, Chino *Also called Mission Linen Supply (G-13566)*
Mission Linen Supply 760 757-9099
2727 Industry St Oceanside (92054) *(G-13552)*
Mission Linen Supply 805 772-4451
399 Errol St Morro Bay (93442) *(G-13553)*
Mission Linen Supply 916 423-3179
7520 Reese Rd Sacramento (95828) *(G-13554)*
Mission Linen Supply 831 424-1707
315 Kern St Salinas (93905) *(G-13555)*
Mission Linen Supply 559 268-0647
2555 S Orange Ave Fresno (93725) *(G-13556)*
Mission Linen Supply 707 443-8681
1401 Summer St Eureka (95501) *(G-13557)*
Mission Linen Supply 805 485-6794
505 Maulhardt Ave Oxnard (93030) *(G-13558)*
Mission Linen Supply 510 429-7305
30305 Union City Blvd Union City (94587) *(G-13559)*
Mission Linen Supply 831 424-1753
435 W Market St Salinas (93901) *(G-13633)*
Mission Linen Supply 805 962-7687
712 E Montecito St Santa Barbara (93103) *(G-13560)*
Mission Linen Supply 530 342-4110
1340 W 7th St Chico (95928) *(G-13561)*
Mission Linen Supply 831 375-2491
801 Sunset Dr Pacific Grove (93950) *(G-13562)*
Mission Linen Supply 661 948-5051
619 W Avenue I Lancaster (93534) *(G-13563)*
Mission Linen Supply 916 423-3135
7524 Reese Rd Sacramento (95828) *(G-13564)*
Mission Linen Supply 805 922-3579
602 S Western Ave Santa Maria (93458) *(G-13565)*
Mission Linen Supply 909 393-5589
5400 Alton Way Chino (91710) *(G-13566)*
Mission Linen Supply & Svcs, Eureka *Also called Mission Linen Supply (G-13557)*

Mission Medical Entps Inc 559 582-2871
1007 W Lacey Blvd Hanford (93230) ***(G-20792)***
Mission Medical Entps Inc 559 582-4414
851 Leslie Ln Hanford (93230) ***(G-20793)***
Mission Neighborhood Hlth Ctr (PA) 415 552-3870
240 Shotwell St San Francisco (94110) ***(G-19755)***
Mission Oaks Hospital, Los Gatos *Also called Good Samaritan Hospital LP* ***(G-21585)***
Mission Pines Apts, Martinez *Also called Braddock & Logan Inc* ***(G-11099)***
Mission Produce Inc 805 981-3650
3803 Dufau Rd Oxnard (93033) ***(G-8751)***
Mission Provider Services Inc 530 222-5633
2970 Innsbruck Dr Ste C Redding (96003) ***(G-21317)***
Mission Ranch Inc 831 624-6436
26270 Dolores St Carmel (93923) ***(G-12998)***
Mission Security and Patrol 805 899-3039
27 W Anapamu St Ste 141 Santa Barbara (93101) ***(G-16737)***
Mission Skilled Nursing Home, Santa Clara *Also called Covenant Care California LLC* ***(G-20488)***
Mission Stuart Ht Partners LLC 415 278-3700
8 Mission St San Francisco (94105) ***(G-12999)***
Mission Terrace, Santa Barbara *Also called Cliff View Terrace Inc* ***(G-24601)***
Mission Trail Wste Systems Inc 408 727-5365
1060 Richard Ave Santa Clara (95050) ***(G-4041)***
Mission Truck Sales 408 436-2920
780 E Brokaw Rd San Jose (95112) ***(G-17704)***
Mission Valley, San Diego *Also called Boykin Mgt Co Ltd Lblty Co* ***(G-12461)***
Mission Valley Bancorp 818 394-2300
9116 Sunland Blvd Sun Valley (91352) ***(G-12044)***
Mission Valley Ht Operator Inc 619 291-5720
595 Hotel Cir S San Diego (92108) ***(G-13000)***
Mission Valley Hts Surgery Ctr 619 291-3737
7485 Mission Valley Rd # 106 San Diego (92108) ***(G-19756)***
Mission Valley Truck Center, San Jose *Also called Mission Truck Sales* ***(G-17704)***
Mission Valley V A, San Diego *Also called Veterans Health Administration* ***(G-20205)***
Mission Valley YMCA, San Diego *Also called YMCA of San Diego County* ***(G-25424)***
Mission Viejo Country Club 949 582-1550
26200 Country Club Dr Mission Viejo (92691) ***(G-19003)***
Mission Viejo Pateadores Inc 949 350-5590
7 El Corzo Rcho STA Marg (92688) ***(G-18558)***
Mission View Health Center, San Luis Obispo *Also called Compass Health Inc* ***(G-21189)***
Mission Villa LLC 650 756-1995
995 E Market St Daly City (94014) ***(G-24737)***
Mission Vlla Alzhmers Rsidence 408 559-8301
3333 S Bascom Ave Campbell (95008) ***(G-24738)***
Mission Vly Rock Asp & Rdymx, San Diego *Also called Legacy Vulcan Corp* ***(G-1107)***
Mistras Group Inc 661 829-1192
21215 Kratzmeyer Rd A Bakersfield (93314) ***(G-25967)***
Mistras Group Inc 562 597-3932
2230 E Artesia Blvd Long Beach (90805) ***(G-25968)***
Mistras Group Inc 323 583-1653
8427 Atlantic Ave Cudahy (90201) ***(G-25969)***
Mistras Group Inc 707 746-5870
6170 Egret Ct Benicia (94510) ***(G-26869)***
Mistras Impro, Bakersfield *Also called Mistras Group Inc* ***(G-25967)***
Mitch Brown Construction Inc 559 781-6389
14200 Road 284 Porterville (93257) ***(G-2068)***
Mitchell Buckman Inc (PA) 559 733-1181
500 N Santa Fe St Visalia (93292) ***(G-10787)***
Mitchell Concrete, Rancho Cordova *Also called Mitchell Jones Concrete Inc* ***(G-3297)***
Mitchell Engineering 415 227-1040
1395 Evans Ave San Francisco (94124) ***(G-3438)***
Mitchell International Inc (HQ) 858 368-7000
6220 Greenwich Dr San Diego (92122) ***(G-15308)***
Mitchell Jones Concrete Inc 916 638-6870
3185 Fitzgerald Rd Rancho Cordova (95742) ***(G-3297)***
Mitchell Silberberg Knupp LLP (PA) 310 312-2000
11377 W Olympic Blvd Fl 2 Los Angeles (90064) ***(G-23437)***
Mitchell Vineyard Management, Saint Helena *Also called Mitchell Vineyards LLC* ***(G-709)***
Mitchell Vineyards LLC 707 963-7050
1831 Sarahs Way Saint Helena (94574) ***(G-709)***
Mitchells Group Home, Los Angeles *Also called Mgh Corporation* ***(G-24736)***
Mitek Systems Inc (PA) 858 309-1700
8911 Balboa Ave Ste B San Diego (92123) ***(G-15759)***
Mitsuba Corporation 909 374-2631
2509 Reata Pl Diamond Bar (91765) ***(G-7164)***
Mitsubishi Electric Us Inc (HQ) 714 220-2500
5900 Katella Ave Ste A Cypress (90630) ***(G-7605)***
Mitsubishi Electric Us Inc 714 934-5300
7345 Orangewood Ave Garden Grove (92841) ***(G-7606)***
Mitsubishi Materials USA Corp (HQ) 714 352-6100
11250 Slater Ave Fountain Valley (92708) ***(G-7941)***
Mitsubishi Motors Cr Amer Inc (HQ) 714 799-4730
6400 Katella Ave Cypress (90630) ***(G-9757)***
Mitsubishi Warehouse Cal Corp 310 886-5500
3040 E Victoria St Compton (90221) ***(G-4600)***
Mitsui & Co (usa) Inc 213 896-1100
601 S Figueroa St # 2650 Los Angeles (90017) ***(G-7384)***
Mitsui USA, Los Angeles *Also called Mitsui & Co (usa) Inc* ***(G-7384)***
Mitzel Company, Santa Ana *Also called Ralph D Mitzel Inc* ***(G-14495)***
Mixpanel Inc 415 528-2827
405 Howard St Fl 2 San Francisco (94105) ***(G-15309)***
Miyako Hotels 213 617-2000
328 E 1st St Ste 510 Los Angeles (90012) ***(G-13001)***
Miyamoto International Inc (PA) 916 373-1995
1450 Halyard Dr Ste 1 West Sacramento (95691) ***(G-25970)***
Mizuho Corporate Bank Cal (HQ) 213 612-2848
350 S Grand Ave Ste 1500 Los Angeles (90071) ***(G-9509)***
Mizuho Securities USA Inc 415 268-5500
3 Embarcadero Ctr # 1620 San Francisco (94111) ***(G-10047)***
Mj Brothers Trucking 559 686-4413
20969 Road 52 Tulare (93274) ***(G-4230)***
Mj Star-Lite Inc 818 717-0834
9232 Independence Ave Chatsworth (91311) ***(G-2654)***
MJB Partners LLC 909 623-2481
651 N Main St Pomona (91768) ***(G-20794)***
Mjd Construction Corp 818 575-9864
28244 Dorothy Dr Agoura Hills (91301) ***(G-1225)***
Mkni, Visalia *Also called Morgan Kleppe & Nash* ***(G-10790)***
ML Electricworks Inc 951 687-5078
11325 Magnolia Ave Riverside (92505) ***(G-2655)***
ML Prior Inc 626 653-5160
955 Berrand Ct Ste 200 San Dimas (91773) ***(G-23438)***
Mladen Buntich Cnstr Co Inc 909 920-9977
1500 W 9th St Upland (91786) ***(G-1971)***
Mlim Holdings LLC 619 299-3131
350 Camino De La Reina San Diego (92108) ***(G-12076)***
Mlslistings Inc 408 874-0200
350 Oakmead Pkwy Ste 200 Sunnyvale (94085) ***(G-27551)***
Mm Advertising, Garden Grove *Also called Money Mailer LLC* ***(G-14084)***
Mma Renewable Ventures LLC 415 229-8817
44 Montgomery St Ste 2200 San Francisco (94104) ***(G-7725)***
MMC, San Diego *Also called Medical Management Cons Inc* ***(G-27536)***
MMC, Los Angeles *Also called Marsh Risk & Insurance Svcs* ***(G-10776)***
MMC, Los Angeles *Also called Medical Management Cons Inc* ***(G-14909)***
Mmi Services Inc 661 589-9366
4042 Patton Way Bakersfield (93308) ***(G-1086)***
MNS Engineers Inc (PA) 805 692-6921
201 N Calle Cesar Santa Barbara (93103) ***(G-25971)***
MNX, Irvine *Also called Midnite Air Corp* ***(G-4870)***
Mob Scene LLC 323 648-7200
8447 Wilshire Blvd # 100 Beverly Hills (90211) ***(G-13887)***
Mob Scene Creative Productions, Beverly Hills *Also called Mob Scene LLC* ***(G-13887)***
Mobica US Inc 650 450-6654
2570 N 1st St Fl 2 San Jose (95131) ***(G-15996)***
Mobile Application, Santa Clara *Also called Soundhound Inc* ***(G-15471)***
Mobile Line Cmmunications Corp 877 247-2544
1402 Morgan Cir Tustin (92780) ***(G-7607)***
Mobile Messenger Americas Inc (PA) 310 957-3300
6601 Center Dr W Ste 700 Los Angeles (90045) ***(G-17338)***
Mobile Modular, Livermore *Also called McGrath Rentcorp* ***(G-14558)***
Mobile Programming LLC 310 584-6300
30300 Agoura Rd Ste 140 Agoura Hills (91301) ***(G-15310)***
Mobileiron Inc (PA) 650 919-8100
415 E Middlefield Rd Mountain View (94043) ***(G-15760)***
Mobilenet Services Inc (PA) 949 951-4444
18 Morgan Ste 200 Irvine (92618) ***(G-25972)***
Mobileum Inc (PA) 408 844-6600
2880 Lakeside Dr Ste 135 Santa Clara (95054) ***(G-6082)***
Mobility Plus Trnsp LLC 925 957-9841
4961 Pacheco Blvd Martinez (94553) ***(G-3674)***
Mobilityware Inc 949 788-9900
440 Exchange Ste 100 Irvine (92602) ***(G-15311)***
Mobillcash, San Francisco *Also called Boku Inc* ***(G-15061)***
Mobilona LLC 213 260-3200
601 S Figueroa St # 4050 Los Angeles (90017) ***(G-11689)***
Mobilygen Corporation 408 601-1000
160 Rio Robles San Jose (95134) ***(G-7608)***
Mobis Parts America LLC (HQ) 786 515-1101
10550 Talbert Ave Fl 4 Fountain Valley (92708) ***(G-6690)***
Mobis Wholesale, Carpinteria *Also called Ocean Breeze International* ***(G-306)***
Mobitv Inc (PA) 510 981-1303
6425 Christie Ave Fl 5 Emeryville (94608) ***(G-5660)***
Mobley Enterprises Inc 209 726-9185
1771 Grogan Ave Merced (95341) ***(G-14361)***
Mobpartner Inc 415 813-1202
625 2nd St Ste 280 San Francisco (94107) ***(G-13953)***
Mobsoc Media LLC 415 974-5429
855 Folsom St Apt 523 San Francisco (94107) ***(G-15761)***
Moc Products Company Inc 510 635-1230
9840 Kitty Ln Oakland (94603) ***(G-17888)***
Moc Products Company Inc (PA) 818 794-3500
12306 Montague St Pacoima (91331) ***(G-8994)***
Mocana Corporation 415 617-0055
20 California St Ste 400 San Francisco (94111) ***(G-16163)***
Mocean, Burbank *Also called Cmp Film & Design Burbank LLC* ***(G-27742)***
Mocean LLC 310 481-0808
2440 S Sepulveda Blvd # 150 Los Angeles (90064) ***(G-16164)***
Mocha, Oakland *Also called Museum of Childrens Art* ***(G-19249)***
Mocse Federal Credit Union 209 572-3600
3600 Coffee Rd Modesto (95355) ***(G-9615)***
Mod Vid Film, Glendale *Also called Modern Videofilm Inc* ***(G-18236)***
Modani Furniture, West Hollywood *Also called Modani Los Angeles LLC* ***(G-6825)***
Modani Los Angeles LLC 310 652-2323
8873 W Sunset Blvd West Hollywood (90069) ***(G-6825)***
Mode Media Corporation (PA) 650 244-4000
2000 Sierra Point Pkwy # 10 Brisbane (94005) ***(G-13973)***
Modern Alloys Inc 714 893-0551
1925 Century Park E # 650 Los Angeles (90067) ***(G-7026)***
Modern Alloys Inc 714 893-0551
1925 Century Park E # 650 Los Angeles (90067) ***(G-12077)***
Modern Building Inc 530 891-4533
3083 Southgate Ln Chico (95928) ***(G-1453)***
Modern Button Company of Cal 213 747-7431
3957 S Hill St Los Angeles (90037) ***(G-8319)***

ALPHABETIC

Modern Concepts Medical Group 323 728-6070
1217 W Whittier Blvd Montebello (90640) ***(G-19757)***
Modern Dev Co A Ltd Partnr 949 646-6400
7900 All America City Way Paramount (90723) ***(G-17339)***
Modern Hr Inc 310 270-9800
9000 W Sunset Blvd # 900 West Hollywood (90069) ***(G-13725)***
Modern Parking Inc 310 821-1081
14110 Palawan Way Marina Del Rey (90292) ***(G-17730)***
Modern Videofilm (PA) 818 840-1700
2300 W Empire Ave Burbank (91504) ***(G-18235)***
Modern Videofilm Inc 818 637-6800
1733 Flower St Glendale (91201) ***(G-18236)***
Modesto Court Room Inc 209 577-1060
2012 Mchenry Ave Modesto (95350) ***(G-19004)***
Modesto Hospitality Lessee LLC 209 526-6000
1150 9th St Ste C Modesto (95354) ***(G-13002)***
Modesto Imaging Center, Modesto *Also called Radnet Management Inc* ***(G-27190)***
Modesto Industrial Elec Co Inc (PA) 209 495-1597
1417 Coldwell Ave Modesto (95350) ***(G-2656)***
Modesto Irrigation District 209 526-7563
1231 11th St Modesto (95354) ***(G-6149)***
Modesto Irrigation District (PA) 209 526-7337
1231 11th St Modesto (95354) ***(G-6150)***
Modesto Irrigation District 209 526-7373
929 Woodland Ave Modesto (95351) ***(G-6151)***
Modesto Medical Offices, Modesto *Also called Kaiser Foundation Hospitals* ***(G-19628)***
Modesto Wstewater Trtmnt Plant 209 577-5300
1221 Sutter Ave Modesto (95351) ***(G-6504)***
Modoc County ADM Svcs, Alturas *Also called County of Modoc* ***(G-23866)***
Modoc Medical Center, Alturas *Also called Last Frontier Healthcare Dst* ***(G-21698)***
Modular Systems Inc 805 963-9350
800 Garden St Ste K Santa Barbara (93101) ***(G-11690)***
Moduslink Corporation 951 571-8300
2111 Eastridge Ave Riverside (92507) ***(G-15762)***
Moffatt & Nichol 925 944-5411
2185 N Calif Blvd Ste 500 Walnut Creek (94596) ***(G-25973)***
Moffatt & Nichol 562 426-9551
3780 Kilroy Arprt Way # 600 Long Beach (90806) ***(G-25974)***
Moffitt H C Hospital 415 476-1000
505 Parnassus Ave San Francisco (94143) ***(G-21750)***
Mofo, San Francisco *Also called Morrison & Foerster LLP* ***(G-23450)***
MOG Inc 510 883-7100
2607 7th St Ste C Berkeley (94710) ***(G-15312)***
Mogl Loyalty Services Inc 858 436-7036
9645 Scranton Rd Ste 110 San Diego (92121) ***(G-13778)***
Mohan Dialysis Center Industry 626 333-3801
15757 E Valley Blvd City of Industry (91744) ***(G-22634)***
Mohan Dialysis Ctr of Covina 626 859-2522
158 W College St Covina (91723) ***(G-22635)***
Mohler Nixon & Williams Accoun (PA) 408 369-2400
635 Campbell Tech Pkwy # 100 Campbell (95008) ***(G-26411)***
Mojo Networks Inc (PA) 650 961-1111
339 Bernardo Ave Ste 200 Mountain View (94043) ***(G-16901)***
Mola Inc 323 582-0088
2957 E 46th St Vernon (90058) ***(G-8403)***
Mold Testing and Inspection 760 643-1834
4785 Sequoia Pl Oceanside (92057) ***(G-17340)***
Molecular Bioproducts Inc (HQ) 858 453-7551
9389 Waples St San Diego (92121) ***(G-6505)***
Molecular Bioproducts Inc 707 762-6689
2200 S Mcdowell Blvd Ext Petaluma (94954) ***(G-7345)***
Molina Healthcare Inc 858 614-1580
9275 Sky Park Ct Ste 400 San Diego (92123) ***(G-23001)***
Molina Healthcare Inc 909 546-7116
790 E Foothill Blvd Rialto (92376) ***(G-19758)***
Molina Healthcare Inc (PA) 562 435-3666
200 Oceangate Ste 100 Long Beach (90802) ***(G-19759)***
Molina Healthcare of Californi 562 435-3666
200 Oceangate Ste 100 Long Beach (90802) ***(G-10246)***
Molina Information Systems LLC 562 435-3666
200 Oceangate Ste 100 Long Beach (90802) ***(G-19760)***
Molly Maid, La Verne *Also called Steve and Beth Chaput* ***(G-14439)***
Molly Maid 949 367-8000
24412 Muirlands Blvd A Lake Forest (92630) ***(G-14362)***
Momentous Insurance Brkg Inc 818 933-2700
5990 Sepulvda Blvd # 550 Van Nuys (91411) ***(G-10788)***
Momentum For Mental Health 408 261-7777
2001 The Alameda San Jose (95126) ***(G-24943)***
Moms Orange County 714 972-2610
1128 W Santa Ana Blvd Santa Ana (92703) ***(G-22509)***
Monarch Bay Golf Resort 510 895-2162
13800 Monarch Bay Dr San Leandro (94577) ***(G-19005)***
Monarch Beach Golf Links (HQ) 949 240-8247
50 Monarch Beach Resort N Dana Point (92629) ***(G-18762)***
Monarch E & S Insurance Svcs 559 226-0200
2540 Foothill Blvd # 101 La Crescenta (91214) ***(G-10789)***
Monarch Healthcare A Medical (HQ) 949 923-3200
11 Technology Dr Irvine (92618) ***(G-19761)***
Monarch Nut Company LLC 661 725-6458
786 Road 188 Delano (93215) ***(G-564)***
Monarch Place Piedmont LLC 510 658-9266
4500 Gilbert St Oakland (94611) ***(G-24739)***
Monarchy Diamond Inc 213 924-1161
550 S Hill St Ste 1088 Los Angeles (90013) ***(G-1117)***
Monark LP 310 769-6669
2804 W El Segundo Blvd Gardena (90249) ***(G-11169)***
Mondelez Global LLC 909 605-0140
5815 Clark St Ontario (91761) ***(G-8879)***
Mondrian Hotel, Los Angeles *Also called Morgans Hotel Group MGT LLC* ***(G-13008)***
Money Mailer LLC (HQ) 714 889-3800
12131 Western Ave Garden Grove (92841) ***(G-14084)***
Moneyline Lending Services, Irvine *Also called Genpact Mortgage Services Inc* ***(G-9844)***
Monique Suraci 951 677-8111
41885 Ivy St Murrieta (92562) ***(G-18663)***
Monitise Americas Inc 415 526-7000
1 Embrcdero Cntre Fl 9 San Francisco (94111) ***(G-15313)***
Monitor Company Group GP LLC 415 932-5300
555 Mission St Ste 1400 San Francisco (94105) ***(G-27552)***
Mono Nation 559 877-2450
58288 Road 225 North Fork (93643) ***(G-24091)***
Mono Wind Casino 559 855-4350
37302 Rancheria Ln Auberry (93602) ***(G-13003)***
Monoprice Inc 909 989-6887
11701 6th St Rancho Cucamonga (91730) ***(G-8126)***
Monoprice.com, Rancho Cucamonga *Also called Monoprice Inc* ***(G-8126)***
Monroe Residence Club 415 771-9119
1499 Sutter St San Francisco (94109) ***(G-11170)***
Monrovia Convalescent Hospital 626 359-6618
1220 Huntington Dr Duarte (91010) ***(G-21318)***
Monrovia Growes, Azusa *Also called Monrovia Nursery Company* ***(G-303)***
Monrovia Health Center 626 256-1600
330 W Maple Ave Monrovia (91016) ***(G-19762)***
Monrovia Memorial Hospital, Monrovia *Also called Alakor Healthcare LLC* ***(G-21441)***
Monrovia Nursery Company (PA) 626 334-9321
817 E Monrovia Pl Azusa (91702) ***(G-303)***
Monrovia Ranch Market, Victorville *Also called E & T Foods Inc* ***(G-465)***
Monrovia Service Center, Monrovia *Also called Southern California Edison Co* ***(G-6213)***
Monsanto, Woodland *Also called Seminis Vegetable Seeds Inc* ***(G-9152)***
Monsanto Company 530 669-6224
37437 State Highway 16 Woodland (95695) ***(G-8752)***
Monster Inc (PA) 415 840-2000
455 Valley Dr Brisbane (94005) ***(G-8127)***
Monster Energy Company (HQ) 951 739-6200
1 Monster Way Corona (92879) ***(G-8880)***
Monster Mechanical Inc 408 727-8362
90 Railway Ave Campbell (95008) ***(G-2296)***
Monster Products, Brisbane *Also called Monster Inc* ***(G-8127)***
Montage Beverly Hills, Beverly Hills *Also called Montage Hotels & Resorts LLC* ***(G-13004)***
Montage Hotels & Resorts LLC 310 499-4199
225 N Canon Dr Beverly Hills (90210) ***(G-13004)***
Montage Hotels & Resorts LLC (PA) 949 715-5002
1 Ada Ste 250 Irvine (92618) ***(G-11691)***
Montage Laguna Beach, Irvine *Also called Montage Hotels & Resorts LLC* ***(G-11691)***
Montalvo Association 408 961-5800
15400 Montalvo Rd Saratoga (95070) ***(G-25066)***
Montana Investigation, San Francisco *Also called Black Bear Security Services* ***(G-16575)***
Montavista Software LLC (HQ) 408 572-8000
2315 N 1st St Fl 4 San Jose (95131) ***(G-15314)***
Montclair Hospital Medical Ctr, Montclair *Also called Prime Healthcare Svcs III LLC* ***(G-21814)***
Montclair Hotels Mb LLC 925 687-5500
1050 Burnett Ave Concord (94520) ***(G-13005)***
Montclair Mnor Cnvlescent Hosp, Montclair *Also called Medicrest of California 1* ***(G-20784)***
Montclair Physical Therapy, Claremont *Also called Pomona Valley Hospital Med Ctr* ***(G-21804)***
Monte Vista Grove Homes 626 796-6135
2889 San Pasqual St Pasadena (91107) ***(G-24740)***
Monte Vista Retirement Lodge 619 465-1331
6458 Lake Tahoe Ct San Diego (92119) ***(G-11171)***
Monte Vista School, Redding *Also called County of Shasta* ***(G-24452)***
Monte Vista Village, San Diego *Also called Monte Vista Retirement Lodge* ***(G-11171)***
Monte Vsta Mem Schlrship Assoc 831 722-8178
2 School Way Watsonville (95076) ***(G-27992)***
Montebello Medical Offices, Montebello *Also called Kaiser Foundation Hospitals* ***(G-19633)***
Montebello School Transportion 323 887-7900
505 S Greenwood Ave Montebello (90640) ***(G-3946)***
Montebello Transit 323 887-4600
400 S Taylor Ave Montebello (90640) ***(G-3675)***
Montebello Unified School Dst 323 887-2140
500 Hendricks St Fl 2 Montebello (90640) ***(G-14363)***
Montecito Country Club Inc 805 969-0800
920 Summit Rd Santa Barbara (93108) ***(G-19006)***
Montecito Family YMCA, Santa Barbara *Also called Channel Islands Young Mens Ch* ***(G-25234)***
Montecito Fire Protection Dst 805 969-7762
595 San Ysidro Rd Santa Barbara (93108) ***(G-25299)***
Montecito Retirement Assn 805 969-8011
300 Hot Springs Rd Santa Barbara (93108) ***(G-20795)***
Montecito Sequoia Inc 559 565-3388
8000 Generals Hwy Kings Canyon Nationa (93633) ***(G-13006)***
Montecito Sequoia Lodge, Kings Canyon Nationa *Also called Montecito Sequoia Inc* ***(G-13006)***
Montego Heights Lodge, Walnut Creek *Also called Atria Senior Living Group Inc* ***(G-11089)***
Montenay Pacific Power, Long Beach *Also called Veolia Es Waste-To-Energy Inc* ***(G-6593)***
Monterey Bay Acadamy Laundry 831 728-1481
675 Beach Dr Watsonville (95076) ***(G-13504)***
Monterey Bay Aqar Foundation (PA) 831 648-4800
886 Cannery Row Monterey (93940) ***(G-25067)***
Monterey Bay Aquarium RES Inst 831 775-1700
7700 Sandholdt Rd Moss Landing (95039) ***(G-26570)***
Monterey Bay Bouquet Acquisit 831 786-2700
481 San Andreas Rd Watsonville (95076) ***(G-9202)***
Monterey Bay Masonry Inc 408 289-8295
333 Phelan Ave San Jose (95112) ***(G-2828)***
Monterey Beach Hotel, Monterey *Also called Zhg Inc* ***(G-13447)***

Monterey Construction Company, Salinas — ALPHABETIC SECTION

Monterey Construction Company, Salinas Also called Reegs Inc *(G-1336)*
Monterey Country Club, Palm Desert Also called American Golf Corporation *(G-18870)*
Monterey County Office Educatn 831 755-0324
 901 Blanco Cir Salinas (93901) *(G-26692)*
Monterey County Public Works, Salinas Also called County of Monterey *(G-1760)*
Monterey County Sheriffs Dept, Salinas Also called County of Monterey *(G-25520)*
Monterey Credit Union (PA) 831 647-1000
 501 E Franklin St Monterey (93940) *(G-9673)*
Monterey Dental Group 831 373-3068
 333 El Dorado St Monterey (93940) *(G-20265)*
Monterey Financial Svcs Inc (PA) 760 639-3500
 4095 Avenida De La Plata Oceanside (92056) *(G-9758)*
Monterey Healthcare & Wellness 626 280-3220
 1267 San Gabriel Blvd Rosemead (91770) *(G-20796)*
Monterey Inst of Intl Studies 831 647-4100
 460 Pierce St Monterey (93940) *(G-26789)*
Monterey Marriott, Monterey Also called San Carlos Associates Ltd *(G-13194)*
Monterey Mechanical Co (PA) 510 632-3173
 8275 San Leandro St Oakland (94621) *(G-2069)*
Monterey Mushrooms Inc 408 779-4191
 642 Hale Ave Morgan Hill (95037) *(G-335)*
Monterey Mushrooms Inc (PA) 831 763-5300
 260 Westgate Dr Watsonville (95076) *(G-336)*
Monterey Mushrooms Inc 831 728-8300
 777 Maher Ct Royal Oaks (95076) *(G-337)*
Monterey Mushrooms-Morgan Hill, Morgan Hill Also called Monterey Mushrooms Inc *(G-335)*
Monterey Pacific Inc (PA) 831 678-4845
 169 The Crossroads Blvd Carmel (93923) *(G-710)*
Monterey Park Hospital, Monterey Park Also called Monterey Park Hospital *(G-21751)*
Monterey Park Hospital 626 570-9000
 900 S Atlantic Blvd Monterey Park (91754) *(G-21751)*
Monterey Peninsula Country CLB 831 373-1556
 3000 Club Rd Pebble Beach (93953) *(G-19007)*
Monterey Peninsula Dntl Group 831 373-3068
 333 El Dorado St Monterey (93940) *(G-20266)*
Monterey Peninsula Hospital 831 373-0924
 576 Hartnell St Ste 260 Monterey (93940) *(G-21752)*
Monterey Pines Sklld Nursg Fac 831 373-3716
 1501 Skyline Dr Monterey (93940) *(G-20797)*
Monterey Pk Convalescent Hosp 626 280-0280
 416 N Garfield Ave Monterey Park (91754) *(G-21319)*
Monterey Plaza Hotel & Spa, Monterey Also called Monterey Plaza Ht Ltd Partnr *(G-13007)*
Monterey Plaza Ht Ltd Partnr 800 334-3999
 400 Cannery Row Monterey (93940) *(G-13007)*
Monterey Pnnsula Hrtclture Inc 310 884-5911
 7909 Crosswhite Drve Pico Rivera (90660) *(G-29)*
Monterey Rgional Waste MGT Dst 831 384-5313
 14201 Del Monte Blvd Marina (93933) *(G-6506)*
Monterey-Salinas Transit Corp 831 754-2804
 1375 Burton Ave Salinas (93901) *(G-3883)*
Monterrey The Natural Choice, San Diego Also called Mpci Holdings Inc *(G-8677)*
Montessori On The Lake, Lake Forest Also called Environments For Learning Inc *(G-24459)*
Montetisea Framing, Denair Also called J Crecelius Inc *(G-372)*
Montgomery Tank Lines, South Gate Also called Quality Carriers Inc *(G-4248)*
Montpelier Orchards MGT Co Inc 209 883-4079
 4931 S Montpelier Rd Denair (95316) *(G-244)*
Montrenes Financial Svcs Inc 562 795-0450
 27 Montpellier Newport Beach (92660) *(G-14062)*
Montrose Envmtl Group Inc 925 680-4300
 2825 Verne Roberts Cir Antioch (94509) *(G-26870)*
Montrose Travel, Montrose Also called Sara Enterprises Inc *(G-4973)*
Monument Construction Inc 408 778-1350
 16200 Vineyard Blvd # 100 Morgan Hill (95037) *(G-915)*
Monument Security Inc 510 430-3540
 7700 Edgewater Dr Ste 630 Oakland (94621) *(G-16738)*
Monument Security Inc 562 944-2666
 12016 Telg Rd Ste 201 Santa Fe Springs (90670) *(G-16739)*
Monument Security Inc (PA) 916 564-4234
 4926 43rd St Ste 10 McClellan (95652) *(G-16740)*
Moodys Wall St Analytics Inc 650 266-9660
 395 Oyster Point Blvd # 215 South San Francisco (94080) *(G-15315)*
Moog Inc 650 210-9000
 2581 Leghorn St Mountain View (94043) *(G-25975)*
Moon Mountain Farms LLC 805 521-1742
 3846 E Telegraph Rd Fillmore (93015) *(G-384)*
Mooney Farms 530 899-2661
 1220 Fortress St Chico (95973) *(G-565)*
Moonlight Companies, Reedley Also called Moonlight Packing Corporation *(G-8753)*
Moonlight Packing Corporation (PA) 559 638-7799
 17719 E Huntsman Ave Reedley (93654) *(G-8753)*
Moonstone Hotel Properties, Cambria Also called Moonstone Management Corp *(G-11692)*
Moonstone Management Corp (PA) 805 927-4200
 2905 Burton Dr Cambria (93428) *(G-11692)*
Moor Products, Mission Viejo Also called Greenleaf Paper Products *(G-8194)*
Moore Business Forms, Walnut Creek Also called RR Donnelley & Sons Company *(G-3615)*
Moore Business Forms, Temecula Also called RR Donnelley & Sons Company *(G-8178)*
Moore Document Solutions, San Ramon Also called R R Donnelley & Sons Company *(G-8177)*
Moore Iacofano Goltsman Inc (PA) 510 845-7549
 800 Hearst Ave Berkeley (94710) *(G-27993)*
Moore Law Group A Prof Corp 714 431-2000
 3710 S Susan St Ste 210 Santa Ana (92704) *(G-23439)*
Moore Twining Associates Inc (PA) 559 268-7021
 2527 Fresno St Fresno (93721) *(G-26871)*
Mooretown Rancheria 530 533-3885
 3 Alverda Dr Oroville (95966) *(G-18806)*

Mooretown Rancheria (PA) 530 533-3625
 1 Alverda Dr Oroville (95966) *(G-19247)*
Moorpark Active Adult Center, Moorpark Also called City of Moorpark *(G-23755)*
Moose Family Center 545, Santa Cruz Also called Moose International Inc *(G-25300)*
Moose International Inc 831 438-1817
 2470 El Rancho Dr Santa Cruz (95060) *(G-25300)*
Moov Corporation 877 666-8932
 123 Mission St Ste 1000 San Francisco (94105) *(G-15316)*
Moovweb, San Francisco Also called Moov Corporation *(G-15316)*
Mopar Enterprises 858 492-1123
 1710 Dornoch Ct Ste A San Diego (92154) *(G-14085)*
Morada Produce Company LP 209 546-0426
 500 N Jack Tone Rd Stockton (95215) *(G-566)*
Moraga Cntry CLB Hmowners Assn 925 376-2200
 1600 Saint Andrews Dr Moraga (94556) *(G-19008)*
Morale Welfare Recreation Fund 831 242-6631
 4260 Gigling Rd Seaside (93955) *(G-24944)*
More Truck Lines Inc 951 371-6673
 1776 All American Way Corona (92879) *(G-4042)*
MORE WORKSHOP, Placerville Also called Mother Lode Rehabilit *(G-24741)*
Moreland PCF Snoqualmie LLC 661 322-1081
 5060 California Ave # 1150 Bakersfield (93309) *(G-11985)*
Moreno & Associates Inc 408 924-0353
 1260 Birchwood Dr Sunnyvale (94089) *(G-14364)*
Moreno General Engineering, Van Nuys Also called Moreno-Menco Pacific JV *(G-1614)*
Moreno Valley Family Hlth Ctr, Moreno Valley Also called Community Health Systems Inc *(G-19454)*
Moreno Valley Heacock Med Offs, Moreno Valley Also called Kaiser Foundation Hospitals *(G-12184)*
Moreno-Menco Pacific JV 760 747-4405
 15110 Keswick St Van Nuys (91405) *(G-1614)*
Morgan Lewis & Bockius LLP 415 393-2000
 1 Market St Ste 500 San Francisco (94105) *(G-23440)*
Morgan Lewis & Bockius LLP 650 843-4000
 1400 Page Mill Rd Palo Alto (94304) *(G-23441)*
Morgan Lewis & Bockius LLP 949 399-7000
 600 Anton Blvd Ste 1800 Costa Mesa (92626) *(G-23442)*
Morgan Lewis & Bockius LLP 650 858-2400
 1117 S California Ave Palo Alto (94304) *(G-23443)*
Morgan Lewis & Bockius LLP 213 612-2500
 300 S Grand Ave Ste 2200 Los Angeles (90071) *(G-23444)*
Morgan Lewis & Bockius LLP 415 442-1000
 1 Market Plz Lbby 1 San Francisco (94105) *(G-23445)*
Morgan Lewis & Bockius LLP 213 680-6400
 355 S Grand Ave Fl 44 Los Angeles (90071) *(G-23446)*
Morgan Fabrics Corporation (PA) 323 583-9981
 4265 Exchange Ave Vernon (90058) *(G-8320)*
Morgan Farm LLC 831 726-5120
 201 Vista Dr Watsonville (95076) *(G-123)*
Morgan Kleppe & Nash 559 732-3436
 600 W Acequia Ave Visalia (93291) *(G-10790)*
Morgan Linen Service, Los Angeles Also called Morgan Services Inc *(G-13567)*
Morgan Services Inc 213 485-9666
 905 Yale St Los Angeles (90012) *(G-13567)*
Morgan Stanley, San Francisco Also called TransMontaigne PDT Svcs LLC *(G-5247)*
Morgan Stanley 949 760-2440
 800 Nwport Ctr Dr Ste 500 Newport Beach (92660) *(G-10165)*
Morgan Stanley 626 405-9313
 55 S Lake Ave Ste 800 Pasadena (91101) *(G-10048)*
Morgan Stanley 858 597-7777
 4350 La Jolla Village Dr # 1000 San Diego (92122) *(G-10049)*
Morgan Stanley 949 809-1200
 1901 Main St Ste 700 Irvine (92614) *(G-10050)*
Morgan Stanley & Co LLC 916 444-8041
 407 Capitol Mall Ste 1900 Sacramento (95814) *(G-10051)*
Morgan Stanley & Co LLC 559 431-5900
 5250 N Palm Ave Ste 321 Fresno (93704) *(G-10052)*
Morgan Stanley & Co LLC 714 836-5181
 2677 N Main St Fl 10 Santa Ana (92705) *(G-10053)*
Morgan Stanley & Co LLC 619 236-1331
 101 W Broadway Ste 1800 San Diego (92101) *(G-10054)*
Morgan Stanley & Co LLC 661 663-8100
 9100 Ming Ave Ste 205 Bakersfield (93311) *(G-10055)*
Morgan Stanley & Co LLC 510 839-8080
 1999 Harrison St Ste 2200 Oakland (94612) *(G-10056)*
Morgan Stanley & Co LLC 650 340-6550
 216 Lorton Ave Burlingame (94010) *(G-10057)*
Morgan Stanley & Co LLC 408 947-2200
 225 W Santa Clara St # 900 San Jose (95113) *(G-10058)*
Morgan Stanley & Co LLC 310 285-4800
 335 N Maple Dr Ste 150 Beverly Hills (90210) *(G-10059)*
Morgan Stanley & Co LLC 310 319-5200
 1453 3rd St Ste 200 Santa Monica (90401) *(G-10060)*
Morgan Stanley & Co LLC 415 693-6000
 101 California St Fl 3 San Francisco (94111) *(G-10061)*
Morgans Hotel Group MGT LLC 323 650-8999
 8440 W Sunset Blvd Los Angeles (90069) *(G-13008)*
Morgans Hotel Group MGT LLC 415 775-4700
 495 Geary St San Francisco (94102) *(G-13009)*
Morigon Technologies LLC 818 764-8880
 7621 Fulton Ave North Hollywood (91605) *(G-7283)*
Morley Construction, Santa Monica Also called MSC Service Co *(G-26412)*
Morley Construction Company (HQ) 310 399-1600
 3330 Ocean Park Blvd Santa Monica (90405) *(G-3298)*
Morning Star Company The, Woodland Also called Liberty Packing Company LLC *(G-8746)*
Morningside Community Assn 760 328-3323
 82 Mayfair Dr Rancho Mirage (92270) *(G-25301)*

Morningside Corecare Assoc LP..........650 854-5600
2180 Sand Hill Rd Ste 200 Menlo Park (94025) ***(G-20798)***
Morningside of Fullerton, Fullerton *Also called Corecare I I I* ***(G-24606)***
Morphosis Architects..........310 453-2247
3440 Wesley St Culver City (90232) ***(G-26238)***
Morphotrak LLC (HQ)..........714 238-2000
5515 E La Palma Ave # 100 Anaheim (92807) ***(G-15997)***
Morris Distributing Inc..........707 769-7294
3800a Lakeville Hwy Petaluma (94954) ***(G-9076)***
Morris Grritano Insur Agcy Inc..........805 543-6887
1122 Laurel Ln San Luis Obispo (93401) ***(G-10791)***
Morris National Inc (HQ)..........626 385-2000
760 N Mckeever Ave Azusa (91702) ***(G-8623)***
Morris Polich & Purdy LLP (PA)..........213 891-9100
1055 W 7th St Ste 2400 Los Angeles (90017) ***(G-23447)***
Morrison & Foerster LLP..........213 892-5200
707 Wilshire Blvd # 6000 Los Angeles (90017) ***(G-23448)***
Morrison & Foerster LLP..........858 720-5100
12531 High Bluff Dr # 100 San Diego (92130) ***(G-23449)***
Morrison & Foerster LLP (PA)..........415 268-7000
425 Market St Fl 30 San Francisco (94105) ***(G-23450)***
Morrison & Foerster LLP..........415 268-7178
425 Market St Fl 32 San Francisco (94105) ***(G-23451)***
Morrison & Foerster LLP..........650 813-5600
755 Page Mill Rd Ste A100 Palo Alto (94304) ***(G-23452)***
Morrison & Foerster LLP..........925 295-3300
425 Market St Fl 32 San Francisco (94105) ***(G-23453)***
Morrison & Foerster - Library, Palo Alto *Also called Morrison & Foerster LLP* ***(G-23452)***
Morrison Concrete Inc..........562 802-1450
14114 Rosecrans Ave Ste C Santa Fe Springs (90670) ***(G-3299)***
Morrison Health Care, Palm Springs *Also called Morrison MGT Specialists Inc* ***(G-27134)***
Morrison Landscaping Inc..........714 571-0455
1225 E Wakeham Ave Santa Ana (92705) ***(G-7410)***
Morrison MGT Specialists, Fresno *Also called Morrison MGT Specialists Inc* ***(G-23002)***
Morrison MGT Specialists Inc..........559 459-6449
2823 Fresno St Fresno (93721) ***(G-23002)***
Morrison MGT Specialists Inc..........760 323-6296
1150 N Indian Canyon Dr Palm Springs (92262) ***(G-27134)***
Morrison MGT Specialists Inc..........530 332-7557
1531 Esplanade Chico (95926) ***(G-27135)***
Morrison MGT Specialists Inc..........818 364-4219
14445 Olive View Dr Sylmar (91342) ***(G-27136)***
Morro Bay Public Works..........805 772-6261
955 Shasta Ave Morro Bay (93442) ***(G-1829)***
Morrow-Meadows Corporation (PA)..........858 974-3650
231 Benton Ct City of Industry (91789) ***(G-2657)***
Morrow-Meadows Corporation..........510 562-1980
1050 Bing St San Carlos (94070) ***(G-2658)***
Morse Court Apartments, Sunnyvale *Also called Mp Morse Court Associates* ***(G-11239)***
Mortgage & Realty Prof Svc, San Diego *Also called Mrp Real Estate Services Inc* ***(G-9940)***
Mortgage Capital Assoc Inc..........310 477-6877
11150 W Olympic Blvd # 1160 Los Angeles (90064) ***(G-9938)***
Mortgage Capital Partners Inc..........310 295-2900
12400 Wilshire Blvd # 900 Los Angeles (90025) ***(G-9874)***
Mortgage Corp America Inc..........805 582-2220
2315 Kuehner Dr Ste 115 Simi Valley (93063) ***(G-9939)***
Mortgage Corp of America, Simi Valley *Also called Mortgage Corp America Inc* ***(G-9939)***
Mortgage Fax Inc..........714 899-2656
18685 Main St Ste 101 Huntington Beach (92648) ***(G-14063)***
Mortgage Works Financial, Redlands *Also called Mountain West Financial Inc* ***(G-9875)***
Mortgage X L..........925 830-8951
3130 Crow Canyon Pl # 325 San Ramon (94583) ***(G-10062)***
Morton & Pitalo Inc (PA)..........916 984-7621
75 Iron Point Cir Ste 120 Folsom (95630) ***(G-25976)***
Morton Bakar Center, Alameda *Also called Garfield Nursing Home Inc* ***(G-20593)***
Morton Bakar Center, Hayward *Also called Telecare Corporation* ***(G-22101)***
Morton Golf LLC..........916 481-4653
3645 Fulton Ave Sacramento (95821) ***(G-18763)***
Mosaic..........858 397-2261
10991 Via Banco San Diego (92126) ***(G-27137)***
Mosaic Quest, San Diego *Also called Mosaic* ***(G-27137)***
Moschip Semiconductor Tech USA..........408 737-7141
840 N Hillview Dr Milpitas (95035) ***(G-7609)***
Moskow, Lonnie J MD, Laguna Hills *Also called South County Orthopedic Specia* ***(G-20012)***
Moss & Company Inc (PA)..........310 453-0911
15300 Ventura Blvd # 418 Sherman Oaks (91403) ***(G-11693)***
Moss Landing Marine Labs..........831 771-4400
8272 Moss Landing Rd Moss Landing (95039) ***(G-22243)***
Motech Americas LLC..........302 451-7500
1300 Valley Vista Dr # 207 Diamond Bar (91765) ***(G-26571)***
Motel 6 Operating LP..........310 419-1234
5101 W Century Blvd Inglewood (90304) ***(G-13010)***
Mother Lode Rehabilit..........530 622-4848
399 Placerville Dr Placerville (95667) ***(G-24741)***
Motherlode Investors LLC..........209 736-8112
711 Mccauley Ranch Rd Angels Camp (95222) ***(G-18764)***
Motion Pcture Hlth Wlfare Fund..........818 769-0007
11365 Ventura Blvd # 300 Studio City (91604) ***(G-10556)***
Motion Picture and TV Fund (PA)..........818 876-1777
23388 Mulholland Dr # 200 Woodland Hills (91364) ***(G-21753)***
Motion Picture and TV Fund..........310 231-3000
1950 Sawtelle Blvd # 130 Los Angeles (90025) ***(G-21754)***
Motion Picture Assn Amer In, Sherman Oaks *Also called Motion Picture Assn Amer Inc* ***(G-25094)***
Motion Picture Assn Amer Inc..........818 995-6600
15301 Ventura Blvd Bldg E Sherman Oaks (91403) ***(G-25094)***
Motion Picture Industry Plans..........818 769-0007
11365 Ventura Blvd # 300 Studio City (91604) ***(G-10557)***

Motion Solutions, Aliso Viejo *Also called Bearing Engineers Inc* ***(G-7925)***
Motion Theory Inc..........310 396-9433
4235 Redwood Ave Los Angeles (90066) ***(G-14155)***
Motivational Fulfillment, Chino *Also called Motivational Marketing Inc* ***(G-17341)***
Motivational Marketing Inc..........909 517-2200
15820 Euclid Ave Chino (91708) ***(G-17341)***
Motivational Systems Inc (PA)..........619 474-8246
2200 Cleveland Ave National City (91950) ***(G-14156)***
Motive Energy Inc (PA)..........714 888-2525
125 E Coml St Bldg B Anaheim (92801) ***(G-7457)***
Motive Nation, Downey *Also called Rockview Dairies Inc* ***(G-8913)***
Motoir Ltd..........949 552-6552
23272 Mill Creek Dr Laguna Hills (92653) ***(G-6648)***
Motorola Irrigation, Laguna Hills *Also called Motoir Ltd* ***(G-6648)***
Motorola Mobility LLC..........858 455-1500
6450 Sequence Dr San Diego (92121) ***(G-7610)***
Moulton Logistics Management (PA)..........818 997-1800
7850 Ruffner Ave Van Nuys (91406) ***(G-17342)***
Moulton Niguel Water (PA)..........949 831-2500
27500 La Paz Rd Laguna Niguel (92677) ***(G-6381)***
Mount Diablo Medical Center, Concord *Also called John Muir Physician Network* ***(G-21624)***
Mount Hermon Association Inc..........805 472-9201
2500 Smith Rd Bradley (93426) ***(G-13468)***
Mount Hermon Association Inc (PA)..........831 335-4466
37 Conference Dr Mount Hermon (95041) ***(G-13469)***
Mount Miguel Covenant Village, Spring Valley *Also called Evangelical Covenant Church* ***(G-24654)***
Mount Rbdoux Convalescent Hosp..........951 681-2200
6401 33rd St Riverside (92509) ***(G-20799)***
Mount San Jcnto Winter Pk Corp..........760 325-1449
1 Tramway Rd Palm Springs (92262) ***(G-19248)***
Mount Shasta Resort, Mount Shasta *Also called Siskiyou Lake Golf Resort Inc* ***(G-18788)***
Mount View Hotel, Calistoga *Also called Mv Hospitality Inc* ***(G-18666)***
Mount View Spa, Calistoga *Also called Spa Partners Inc* ***(G-18687)***
Mount Woodson Country Club, Ramona *Also called Spe Go Holdings Inc* ***(G-19092)***
Mount Zion Hospital & Med Ctr, San Francisco *Also called Regents of The Univ of Cal* ***(G-22086)***
Mountain Comm Hlth Cre Dist..........530 623-5541
410 N Taylor St Weaverville (96093) ***(G-21755)***
Mountain Comm Hlth Cre Dist (PA)..........530 623-5541
60 Easter Ave Weaverville (96093) ***(G-21756)***
Mountain Gate Country Club, Los Angeles *Also called American Golf Corporation* ***(G-18862)***
Mountain Gear Corporation..........626 851-2488
4889 4th St Irwindale (91706) ***(G-8353)***
Mountain High Resort Assoc LLC..........760 249-5808
24512 Highway 2 Wrightwood (92397) ***(G-11694)***
Mountain High Ski Resort, Wrightwood *Also called MHRP Resort Inc* ***(G-12993)***
Mountain Lakes Senior Living, Redding *Also called Northstar Senior Living Inc* ***(G-27148)***
Mountain Meadow Mushrooms Inc..........760 749-1201
26948 N Broadway Escondido (92026) ***(G-338)***
Mountain Mining Incorporated..........530 342-6059
3097 Southgate Ln Chico (95928) ***(G-6507)***
Mountain Play Association..........415 383-1100
1556 4th St B San Rafael (94901) ***(G-18415)***
Mountain Retreat Incorporated..........925 838-7780
111 Deerwood Rd Ste 100 San Ramon (94583) ***(G-11986)***
Mountain Shadows Cmnty Homes, Escondido *Also called Mountain Shadows Support Group* ***(G-21094)***
Mountain Shadows Support Group (PA)..........760 743-3714
2067 W El Norte Pkwy Escondido (92026) ***(G-21094)***
Mountain Springs Kirkwood LLC..........209 258-6000
1501 Kirkwood Meadows Dr Kirkwood (95646) ***(G-13011)***
Mountain Valley Express Co Inc (PA)..........209 823-2168
6750 Longe St Ste 100 Stockton (95206) ***(G-4231)***
Mountain Valley Express Co Inc..........562 630-5500
7701 Rosecrans Ave Paramount (90723) ***(G-5125)***
Mountain View AG Services Inc..........559 528-6004
13281 Avenue 416 Orosi (93647) ***(G-675)***
Mountain View Child Care Inc..........818 252-5863
10716 La Tuna Canyon Rd Sun Valley (91352) ***(G-24484)***
Mountain View Child Care Inc (PA)..........909 796-6915
1720 Mountain View Ave Loma Linda (92354) ***(G-21757)***
Mountain View Cnvalescent Hosp..........818 367-1033
13333 Fenton Ave Sylmar (91342) ***(G-20800)***
Mountain View Healthcare Ctr, Mountain View *Also called Balboa Enterprises Inc* ***(G-20404)***
Mountain View Physical Therapy..........909 949-6235
299 W Fthill Blvd Ste 200 Upland (91786) ***(G-20333)***
Mountain View Sport Club, Mountain View *Also called 24 Hour Fitness Usa Inc* ***(G-18598)***
Mountain West Financial Inc (PA)..........909 793-1500
1209 Nevada St Ste 200 Redlands (92374) ***(G-9875)***
Mountains Commu..........909 336-3651
29101 Hospital Rd Lake Arrowhead (92352) ***(G-21758)***
Mountasia Family Fun Center, Saugus *Also called Mountasia of Santa Clarita* ***(G-13779)***
Mountasia Family Fun Center..........661 253-4386
21516 Golden Triangle Rd Santa Clarita (91350) ***(G-18827)***
Mountasia of Santa Clarita..........661 253-4386
21516 Golden Triangle Rd Saugus (91350) ***(G-13779)***
Mounting Systems Inc..........916 374-8872
820 Riverside Pkwy West Sacramento (95605) ***(G-2297)***
Movaris Inc..........408 213-3400
1901 S Bascom Ave Ste 500 Campbell (95008) ***(G-15763)***
Move Inc..........818 701-0012
8428 Calvin Ave Northridge (91324) ***(G-11695)***
Move Inc (HQ)..........408 558-7100
3315 Scott Blvd Santa Clara (95054) ***(G-11696)***
Move Co..........805 557-2300
30700 Russell Ranch Rd # 100 Westlake Village (91362) ***(G-11697)***

ALPHABETIC

Move Sales Inc (HQ)......805 557-2300
30700 Russell Ranch Rd # 100 Westlake Village (91362) ***(G-13780)***
Mover Services Inc......310 868-5143
721 E Compton Blvd Rancho Dominguez (90220) ***(G-4363)***
Movie Movers, West Hollywood *Also called Quixote Mm LLC* ***(G-18249)***
Movieclips.com, Venice *Also called Zefr Inc* ***(G-18208)***
Moving Picture Company, Culver City *Also called Mpc La* ***(G-18116)***
Moving Solutions Inc......408 920-0110
376 Martin Ave Santa Clara (95050) ***(G-4364)***
Movoto LLC......888 766-8686
1900 S Norfolk St Ste 310 San Mateo (94403) ***(G-11698)***
Mowery Thomason Inc......714 666-1717
1225 N Red Gum St Anaheim (92806) ***(G-2934)***
Moya Farm Labor Services, Reedley *Also called Moya Juan Farm Labor Services* ***(G-676)***
Moya Juan Farm Labor Services......559 638-9498
7919 S Alta Ave Reedley (93654) ***(G-676)***
Moyes Custom Furniture Inc......714 729-0234
3431 E La Palma Ave Ste 3 Anaheim (92806) ***(G-17952)***
Moyles Central Vly Hlth Care (PA)......559 688-0288
999 N M St Tulare (93274) ***(G-20801)***
Moyles Central Vly Hlth Care......559 782-1509
1100 W Morton Ave Porterville (93257) ***(G-20802)***
Moyles Health Care Inc......559 686-1601
604 E Merritt Ave Tulare (93274) ***(G-21320)***
Moyles Health Care Inc......661 725-2501
729 Browning Rd Delano (93215) ***(G-21321)***
Moyles Health Care Inc......559 732-2244
37110 W Tulare Ave Visalia (93277) ***(G-21322)***
Mozilla Corporation (HQ)......650 903-0800
331 E Evelyn Ave Ste 100 Mountain View (94041) ***(G-15998)***
Mozingo Construction Inc......209 848-0160
751 Wakefield Ct Oakdale (95361) ***(G-3439)***
Mp Aero LLC......818 901-9828
7701 Woodley Ave Van Nuys (91406) ***(G-3555)***
Mp Environmental Services Inc (PA)......800 458-3036
3400 Manor St Bakersfield (93308) ***(G-6508)***
Mp Holdings, McClellan *Also called McClellan Business Park LLC* ***(G-27532)***
Mp Morse Court Associates......408 734-9442
825 Morse Ave Sunnyvale (94085) ***(G-11239)***
Mp Shoreline Assoc Ltd Partnr......650 966-1327
460 N Shoreline Blvd Mountain View (94043) ***(G-11172)***
Mp Tice Oaks Associates A CA......650 356-2976
2150 Valley Blvd Walnut Creek (94595) ***(G-11699)***
Mpc La......310 526-5800
8921 Lindblade St Culver City (90232) ***(G-18116)***
MPCC, Pebble Beach *Also called Monterey Peninsula Country CLB* ***(G-19007)***
Mpci Holdings Inc (PA)......619 294-2222
7850 Waterville Rd San Diego (92154) ***(G-8677)***
Mpic, Milpitas *Also called Mega Professional Intl* ***(G-15297)***
Mpl Enterprises Inc......714 545-1717
2302 S Susan St Santa Ana (92704) ***(G-916)***
Mpower Communications Corp (HQ)......213 213-3000
515 S Flower St Los Angeles (90071) ***(G-5661)***
Mpp Brea Div 6079, Brea *Also called Orora North America* ***(G-8202)***
Mpp Fullerton Div 6061, Fullerton *Also called Orora North America* ***(G-8207)***
Mpp San Diego Div 6064, San Marcos *Also called Orora North America* ***(G-8203)***
MPS Security, Murrieta *Also called National Bus Invstigations Inc* ***(G-17347)***
Mr Clean Maintenance Systems, Bloomington *Also called Chiro Inc* ***(G-7965)***
Mr Cool, Fresno *Also called Donald P Dick AC Inc* ***(G-2207)***
Mr Copy Inc (HQ)......858 573-6300
5657 Copley Dr San Diego (92111) ***(G-7061)***
Mr Mailer, Baldwin Park *Also called All Direct Mail Services Inc* ***(G-14065)***
Mr Rooter, Fremont *Also called Growith Inc* ***(G-2241)***
Mr Rooter, Ventura *Also called D S R Inc* ***(G-17970)***
Mrc, Smart Tech Solutions, San Diego *Also called Mr Copy Inc* ***(G-7061)***
Mrp Real Estate Services Inc......858 362-6005
925 Fort Stockton Dr San Diego (92103) ***(G-9940)***
MS Industrial Shtmtl Inc......951 272-6610
1731 Pomona Rd Corona (92880) ***(G-3193)***
Msas Cargo International, Brisbane *Also called Exel Inc* ***(G-5067)***
MSC Chatsworth......818 718-7696
9324 Corbin Ave Northridge (91324) ***(G-8128)***
MSC Metalworking, City of Industry *Also called Rutland Tool & Supply Co* ***(G-7950)***
MSC Service Co......310 399-1600
3330 Ocean Park Blvd # 101 Santa Monica (90405) ***(G-26412)***
Mscsoftware Corporation (HQ)......714 540-8900
4675 Macarthur Ct Ste 900 Newport Beach (92660) ***(G-15764)***
Mscsoftware Corporation......858 546-4414
4370 La Jolla Village Dr San Diego (92122) ***(G-15765)***
Mscsoftware Corporation......714 540-8900
4675 Macarthur Ct Ste 900 Newport Beach (92660) ***(G-15999)***
MSEFCU, Merced *Also called Merced School Employees F C U* ***(G-9612)***
Msg Networks Inc......310 330-7300
333 W Florence Ave Inglewood (90301) ***(G-18559)***
Mshift Inc......408 437-2740
39899 Balentine Dr # 235 Newark (94560) ***(G-15317)***
MSI, Santa Barbara *Also called Modular Systems Inc* ***(G-11690)***
MSI, Orange *Also called M S International Inc* ***(G-6991)***
MSI Computer Corp (HQ)......626 913-0828
901 Canada Ct City of Industry (91748) ***(G-7165)***
MSI Invntory Srvce-Los Angeles, Covina *Also called Accu-Count Inventory Svcs Inc* ***(G-16968)***
MSI PRODUCTION SERVICES, San Diego *Also called Meeting Services Inc* ***(G-14560)***
Msj Healthcare LLC......818 244-8446
2555 E Colorado Blvd Fl 4 Pasadena (91107) ***(G-22510)***

Msl Electric Inc......714 693-4837
4938 E La Palma Ave Anaheim (92807) ***(G-2659)***
Msla Management LLC......626 824-6020
1294 E Colorado Blvd Pasadena (91106) ***(G-27994)***
Msr Hotels & Resorts Inc......408 496-6400
2885 Lakeside Dr Santa Clara (95054) ***(G-13012)***
MSS Nurses Registry Inc......323 467-5717
6660 W Sunset Blvd Ste J Los Angeles (90028) ***(G-14913)***
Mssp, San Francisco *Also called Institute On Aging* ***(G-24029)***
Mt Diablo Heart Health Center, Concord *Also called John Muir Physician Network* ***(G-21627)***
Mt Diablo Medical Center, Walnut Creek *Also called John Muir Physician Network* ***(G-21625)***
Mt Eden Nursery Co Inc (PA)......408 213-5777
2124 Bering Dr San Jose (95131) ***(G-11259)***
Mt Miquel Covenant Village......619 479-4790
325 Kempton St Spring Valley (91977) ***(G-21323)***
Mt Rubidoux Convalescent Hosp, San Bernardino *Also called Waterman Convalescent Hospital* ***(G-21025)***
Mt Sinai Mem Pk & Mortuary, Los Angeles *Also called Sinai Temple* ***(G-13715)***
Mt Supply Inc......714 434-4748
3505 Cadillac Ave Ste K2 Costa Mesa (92626) ***(G-7942)***
Mt View Apartments LLC......925 866-8429
3170 Crow Canyon Pl # 165 San Ramon (94583) ***(G-11173)***
MT&i, Oceanside *Also called Mold Testing and Inspection* ***(G-17340)***
Mtc, Temecula *Also called Maneri Traffic Control Inc* ***(G-1820)***
Mtc Financial Inc......949 252-8300
17100 Gillette Ave Irvine (92614) ***(G-12195)***
Mtc Worldwide Corp......626 839-6800
17837 Rowland St City of Industry (91748) ***(G-7166)***
Mthuron Inc......925 932-4101
1903 Rutan Dr Livermore (94551) ***(G-3020)***
MTI, San Diego *Also called Merit Technologies LLC* ***(G-27546)***
Mtm & Thomasville Co......626 934-1112
16035 Phoenix Dr City of Industry (91745) ***(G-1615)***
Mtv Networks, Santa Monica *Also called Viacom Networks* ***(G-18282)***
Muehlhan Certifed Coatings Inc......707 639-4414
2320 Cordelia Rd Fairfield (94534) ***(G-3556)***
Mueller Grooming & Pet Sups, Sacramento *Also called Mueller Pet Medical Center* ***(G-622)***
Mueller Pet Medical Center......916 428-9202
7625 Freeport Blvd Sacramento (95832) ***(G-622)***
Mufg Union Bank Na (HQ)......212 782-6800
400 California St San Francisco (94104) ***(G-9401)***
Mufg Union Bank Na......213 972-5500
120 S San Pedro St Los Angeles (90012) ***(G-9402)***
Mufg Union Bank Na......805 969-5091
20 E Carrillo St Santa Barbara (93101) ***(G-9403)***
Mufg Union Bank Na......310 550-6522
9460 Wilshire Blvd # 200 Beverly Hills (90212) ***(G-9404)***
Mufg Union Bank Na......213 312-4500
900 S Main St Los Angeles (90015) ***(G-9405)***
Mufg Union Bank Na......619 230-4666
530 B St Ste 2400 San Diego (92101) ***(G-9406)***
Mufg Union Bank Na......310 354-4700
15800 S Western Ave Gardena (90247) ***(G-9407)***
Mufg Union Bank Na......661 799-8529
23620 Lyons Ave Fl 2 Santa Clarita (91321) ***(G-9408)***
Mufg Union Bank Na......831 449-7251
1890 N Main St Salinas (93906) ***(G-9409)***
Mufg Union Bank Na......510 891-2495
460 Hegenberger Rd Fl 3 Oakland (94621) ***(G-9410)***
Mufg Union Bank Na......805 541-6100
995 Higuera St San Luis Obispo (93401) ***(G-9411)***
Mufg Union Bank Na......831 638-3350
300 Tres Pinos Rd Hollister (95023) ***(G-9412)***
Mufg Union Bank Na......619 533-7612
9885 Towne Centre Dr San Diego (92121) ***(G-9413)***
Muir Labs......925 947-3335
1601 Ygnacio Valley Rd Walnut Creek (94598) ***(G-22244)***
Muir Orthopedic Specialists......925 939-8585
2405 Shadelands Dr # 210 Walnut Creek (94598) ***(G-19763)***
Muir Senior Care......925 228-8383
1790 Muir Rd Martinez (94553) ***(G-24092)***
Muir-Chase Plumbing Co Inc......818 500-1940
4530 Brazil St Ste 1 Los Angeles (90039) ***(G-2298)***
Muirlab, Walnut Creek *Also called Muir Labs* ***(G-22244)***
Mulesoft Inc (PA)......415 229-2009
77 Geary St Fl 400 San Francisco (94108) ***(G-15318)***
Mulhearn......562 860-2443
11306 183rd St Ste 101 Cerritos (90703) ***(G-11700)***
Mulhearn Group, Hacienda Heights *Also called Berkshire Hattaway Home Servcs* ***(G-11320)***
Mulhearn Realtors Inc......562 462-1055
11642 Firestone Blvd Norwalk (90650) ***(G-11701)***
Mulholland SEC & Patrol Inc......818 755-0202
11454 San Vicente Blvd Fl Los Angeles (90049) ***(G-16741)***
Mullahey Chevrolet Inc......714 871-2545
11899 Woodruff Ave Downey (90241) ***(G-17763)***
Mullen & Henzell LLP......805 966-1501
112 E Victoria St Santa Barbara (93101) ***(G-23454)***
Muller Taj LLC......949 470-9840
23521 Paseo De Valencia # 200 Laguna Hills (92653) ***(G-11020)***
Muller-Ing-Gateway LLC......951 687-2900
23521 Paseo De Valencia # 206 Laguna Hills (92653) ***(G-11021)***
Mulligan Family Fun Center, Murrieta *Also called Mulligan Ltd A Cal Ltd Partnr* ***(G-18828)***
Mulligan Ltd A Cal Ltd Partnr......951 696-9696
24950 Madison Ave Murrieta (92562) ***(G-18828)***
Mullikin Medical Center, Stockton *Also called Caremark Rx LLC* ***(G-19406)***
Mullin TBG Insur Agcy Svcs LLC (HQ)......310 203-8770
100 N Sepulveda Blvd El Segundo (90245) ***(G-10792)***
Mullintbg, El Segundo *Also called Mullin TBG Insur Agcy Svcs LLC* ***(G-10792)***

ALPHABETIC

Multi Mechanical Inc 714 632-7404
1210 N Barsten Way Anaheim (92806) *(G-2299)*
Multi Specialty Group Practice, Yuba City *Also called Sutter North Med Foundation (G-20119)*
Multi Specialty Medical Svc, Visalia *Also called Visalia Medical Clinic Inc (G-20226)*
Multimodal Esquer Inc 619 710-0477
8856 Siempre Viva Rd San Diego (92154) *(G-4232)*
Multipoint Wireless LLC 714 262-4172
2549 Eastbluff Dr Ste 474 Newport Beach (92660) *(G-25977)*
Multiquip Inc (HQ) 310 537-3700
18910 Wilmington Ave Carson (90746) *(G-7458)*
Multiven Inc 408 828-2715
303 Twin Dolphin Dr # 600 Redwood City (94065) *(G-16435)*
Multivision Inc (HQ) 510 740-5600
66 Franklin St Fl 3 Oakland (94607) *(G-17343)*
Munger Tolles & Olson LLP 213 683-9100
355 S Grand Ave Fl 35 Los Angeles (90071) *(G-23455)*
Munger Bros LLC 661 721-0390
786 Road 188 Delano (93215) *(G-258)*
Munger Farm, Delano *Also called Munger Bros LLC (G-258)*
Munger Farms, Delano *Also called Monarch Nut Company LLC (G-564)*
Munger Tolles Olson Foundation (PA) 213 683-9100
355 S Grand Ave Ste 3500 Los Angeles (90071) *(G-23456)*
Munger Tolles Olson Foundation 415 512-4000
560 Mission St Fl 27 San Francisco (94105) *(G-23457)*
Muni-Fed Energy Inc 714 321-3346
192 N Marina Dr Long Beach (90803) *(G-2300)*
Municipal Svcs Agency, Sacramento *Also called County of Sacramento (G-1888)*
Muniservices LLC (HQ) 800 800-8181
7625 N Palm Ave Ste 108 Fresno (93711) *(G-27553)*
Muranaka Farm 805 529-0201
11018 W Los Angeles Ave Moorpark (93021) *(G-82)*
Murata Rockey Landscaping 562 921-3210
15417 Cornet St Santa Fe Springs (90670) *(G-781)*
Murchison & Cumming LLP (PA) 213 623-7400
801 S Grand Ave Ste 900 Los Angeles (90017) *(G-23458)*
Murcor Inc 909 623-4001
740 Corp Ctr Dr Pomona (91768) *(G-11702)*
Murphy (PA) 415 788-1900
88 Kearny St Fl 10 San Francisco (94108) *(G-23459)*
Murphy McKay & Associates Inc 925 283-9555
3468 Mt Diablo Blvd B108 Lafayette (94549) *(G-16436)*
Murphy OBrien Inc 310 453-2539
11444 W Olympic Blvd # 600 Los Angeles (90064) *(G-27757)*
Murphy-True Inc 707 576-7337
464 Kenwood Ct Ste B Santa Rosa (95407) *(G-1616)*
Murray Company, E Rncho Dmngz *Also called Murray Plumbing and Htg Corp (G-2302)*
Murray Entps Staffing Svcs 530 409-5703
23250 Lawrence Rd Fiddletown (95629) *(G-14914)*
Murray Plumbing and Htg Corp 858 952-8795
8520 Production Ave San Diego (92121) *(G-2301)*
Murray Plumbing and Htg Corp (PA) 310 637-1500
18414 S Santa Fe Ave E Rncho Dmngz (90221) *(G-2302)*
Murrieta Day Spa, Murrieta *Also called Monique Suraci (G-18663)*
Murrieta Gardens Senior Living 951 600-7676
18878 E Armstead St Azusa (91702) *(G-21095)*
Murrietta Circuits 714 970-2430
5000 E Landon Dr Anaheim (92807) *(G-2660)*
Murtaugh Myer Nlson Trglia LLP 949 794-4000
2603 Main St Irvine (92614) *(G-23460)*
Muscle Improvement Inc 310 374-5522
200 N Harbor Dr Redondo Beach (90277) *(G-18664)*
Musclebound Inc 805 496-9331
197 N Moorpark Rd Thousand Oaks (91360) *(G-18665)*
Muscolino Inventory Svc Inc 209 576-8469
1620 N Carptr Rd Ste D50 Modesto (95351) *(G-17344)*
Muse Concrete Contractors Inc 530 226-5151
8599 Commercial Way Redding (96002) *(G-1830)*
Museum Associates 323 857-6172
5905 Wilshire Blvd Los Angeles (90036) *(G-25027)*
Museum Cntmprary Art San Diego 858 454-3541
700 Prospect St La Jolla (92037) *(G-25028)*
Museum of Childrens Art 510 465-8770
1625 Clay St Ste 100 Oakland (94612) *(G-19249)*
Museum of Contemporary Art (PA) 213 626-6222
250 S Grand Ave Los Angeles (90012) *(G-25029)*
Museum of Latin American Art 562 437-1689
628 Alamitos Ave Long Beach (90802) *(G-25030)*
Music Center, Los Angeles *Also called Performing Arts Center of La C (G-18423)*
Music Center Unified Fund, Los Angeles *Also called The Music Ctr of La Cty Inc (G-24985)*
Music Collective LLC 818 508-3303
12711 Ventura Blvd # 110 Studio City (91604) *(G-18237)*
Music Hall LLC 415 885-0750
859 Ofarrell St San Francisco (94109) *(G-18416)*
Music Intllgnce Neuro Dev Inst, Irvine *Also called Mind Research Institute (G-26788)*
Musick Peeler & Garrett LLP (PA) 213 629-7600
624 S Grand Ave Ste 2000 Los Angeles (90017) *(G-23461)*
Musicmatch Inc 858 485-4300
16935 W Bernardo Dr # 270 San Diego (92127) *(G-15766)*
Muth Development Co Inc 714 527-2239
11100 Beach Blvd Stanton (90680) *(G-11022)*
Mutual Propane Inc 310 515-0553
17117 S Broadway Gardena (90248) *(G-8995)*
Mutual Trading Co Inc (PA) 213 626-9458
431 Crocker St Los Angeles (90013) *(G-8881)*
Mv Hospitality Inc 707 942-6877
1457 Lincoln Ave Calistoga (94515) *(G-18666)*
Mv Medical Management 323 257-7637
1860 Colo Blvd Ste 200 Los Angeles (90041) *(G-27554)*
Mv Transportation Inc 323 666-0856
13690 Vaughn St San Fernando (91340) *(G-3676)*
Mv Transportation Inc 949 553-1639
16721 Hale Ave Irvine (92606) *(G-3677)*
Mv Transportation Inc 510 351-1603
1944 Williams St San Leandro (94577) *(G-3820)*
Mv Transportation Inc 818 409-3387
1242 Los Angeles St Glendale (91204) *(G-3678)*
Mv Transportation Inc 209 547-7879
1250 S Wilson Way Ste A1 Stockton (95205) *(G-3679)*
Mv Transportation Inc 209 339-1972
24 S Sacramento St Lodi (95240) *(G-3680)*
Mv Transportation Inc 805 557-7372
265 S Rancho Rd Thousand Oaks (91361) *(G-3681)*
Mv Transportation Inc 408 292-3600
705 Tully Rd San Jose (95111) *(G-24093)*
Mv Transportation Inc 707 446-5573
827 Missouri St Ste 6 Fairfield (94533) *(G-3904)*
Mv Transportation Inc 562 790-8642
7231 Rosecrans Ave Paramount (90723) *(G-3682)*
Mve Inc (PA) 209 526-4214
1117 L St Modesto (95354) *(G-25978)*
Mve + Partners Inc (PA) 949 809-3388
1900 Main St Ste 800 Irvine (92614) *(G-26239)*
Mventix Inc 661 263-1768
25129 The Old Rd Ste 112 Stevenson Ranch (91381) *(G-17345)*
Mvf World Wide Services, Burbank *Also called Modern Videofilm (G-18235)*
Mvp Partners, Santa Ana *Also called Colton Real Estate Group (G-11250)*
Mw U.S., San Francisco *Also called M+w US Inc (G-25944)*
Mw2 Consulting LLC 408 573-6310
981 Manor Way Los Altos (94024) *(G-27555)*
MWH Americas Inc 805 683-2409
437 2nd St Solvang (93463) *(G-25979)*
MWH Americas Inc 925 627-4500
2121 N Calif Blvd Ste 600 Walnut Creek (94596) *(G-25980)*
MWH Americas Inc 626 386-1100
750 Royal Oaks Dr Ste 100 Monrovia (91016) *(G-26872)*
MWH Americas Inc 949 328-2400
19800 Macarthur Blvd # 550 Irvine (92612) *(G-25981)*
MWH Americas Inc 626 796-9141
300 N Lake Ave 4001040 Pasadena (91101) *(G-25982)*
MWH Americas Inc 916 924-8844
3301 C St Ste 1900 Sacramento (95816) *(G-25983)*
MWH Americas Inc 415 430-1800
44 Montgomery St Ste 1400 San Francisco (94104) *(G-25984)*
MWH Americas Inc 626 796-9141
618 Michillinda Ave # 200 Arcadia (91007) *(G-25985)*
Mws Precision Wire Inds Inc 818 991-8553
31200 Cedar Valley Dr Westlake Village (91362) *(G-7385)*
Mws Wire Industries, Westlake Village *Also called Mws Precision Wire Inds Inc (G-7385)*
Mx Courier Systems Inc 714 288-8622
990 N Tustin St Orange (92867) *(G-17346)*
Mxic, Milpitas *Also called Macronix America Inc (G-7602)*
My Choice Inhome Care LLC 951 244-8770
31610 Rr Cyn Rd Ste 4 Canyon Lake (92587) *(G-22511)*
My Display Work, Irvine *Also called Comwork (G-17090)*
My Express Freight, Beverly Hills *Also called G Katen Partners Ltd Lblty Co (G-5082)*
My Eye Media LLC 818 559-7200
2211 N Hollywood Way Burbank (91505) *(G-15767)*
My Office Inc 858 549-6700
6060 Nncy Rdge Dr Ste 100 San Diego (92121) *(G-3557)*
My Points.com, San Francisco *Also called Mypointscom LLC (G-13888)*
My Wireless, Santa Ana *Also called B-Per Electronic Inc (G-5277)*
Myconvoy, San Francisco *Also called Convoy Inc (G-16290)*
Myers & Sons Construction LP 916 283-9950
4600 Northgate Blvd # 100 Sacramento (95834) *(G-1831)*
Myers Capital Partners LLC 626 568-1398
450 S Marengo Ave Pasadena (91101) *(G-10063)*
Mygrant Glass Company Inc (PA) 510 785-4360
3271 Arden Rd Hayward (94545) *(G-6750)*
Myinternetservicescom LLC 213 256-0575
1010 E Union St Ste 125 Pasadena (91106) *(G-5662)*
Myoscience Inc 510 933-1500
46400 Fremont Blvd Fremont (94538) *(G-27995)*
Mypointscom LLC (HQ) 415 615-1100
44 Montgomery St Ste 250 San Francisco (94104) *(G-13888)*
Myra Investment and Dev Corp 209 834-2343
47 W 6th St Tracy (95376) *(G-12262)*
Myriad Flowers International 805 684-8079
4601 Foothill Rd Carpinteria (93013) *(G-304)*
Mystic Inc (PA) 213 746-8538
2444 Porter St Los Angeles (90021) *(G-8404)*
N & S Tractor Co (PA) 209 383-5888
600 S St 59 Merced (95341) *(G-17989)*
N A Aricent Inc 408 324-1800
2580 N 1st St Ste 480 San Jose (95131) *(G-15319)*
N A C O, Groveland *Also called Thousand Trails Inc (G-13484)*
N A Citibank 415 627-6000
1 Sansome St Fl 28 San Francisco (94104) *(G-9787)*
N A T C, Pleasanton *Also called North American Title Co Inc (G-10532)*
N Compass International Inc 323 785-1700
8223 Santa Monica Blvd West Hollywood (90046) *(G-27556)*
N F L Alumni 650 366-3659
1311 Madison Ave Redwood City (94061) *(G-25556)*
N G I, Brea *Also called The Nevell Group Inc (G-1691)*
N H A, San Diego *Also called Neighborhood House Association (G-24095)*
N I D, Grass Valley *Also called Nevada Irrigation District (G-6649)*

A L P H A B E T I C

N Model Inc (PA).....650 610-4600
1600 Seaport Blvd Ste 400 Redwood City (94063) **(G-15320)**
N N R, Carson *Also called Nnr Global Logistics USA Inc* **(G-5134)**
N Qiagen Amercn Holdings Inc (HQ).....661 702-3000
27220 Turnberry Ln # 200 Valencia (91355) **(G-8285)**
N S B N Investments Llc.....310 273-2501
9454 Wilshire Blvd Fl 4 Beverly Hills (90212) **(G-12328)**
N T S, Calabasas *Also called NTS Technical Systems* **(G-26880)**
N Th Degree, Foothill Ranch *Also called Nth Degree Inc* **(G-17371)**
N V H, San Leandro *Also called N V Heathorn Inc* **(G-2303)**
N V Heathorn Inc.....510 569-9100
1155 Beecher St San Leandro (94577) **(G-2303)**
N V Landscape Inc.....661 286-8888
24400 Walnut St Ste D Newhall (91321) **(G-917)**
N-U Enterprise, Irvine *Also called Ancca Corporation* **(G-2855)**
Nabisco, Ontario *Also called Mondelez Global LLC* **(G-8879)**
Nabors Well Services Co.....805 641-0390
2567 N Ventura Ave C Ventura (93001) **(G-1087)**
Nabors Well Services Co.....661 588-6140
1025 Earthmover Ct Bakersfield (93314) **(G-1060)**
Nabors Well Services Co.....661 589-3970
7515 Rosedale Hwy Bakersfield (93308) **(G-1088)**
Nabors Well Services Co.....310 639-7074
19431 S Santa Fe Ave Compton (90221) **(G-1089)**
Nadavon Capital Partners LLC.....714 427-1000
3333 W Coast Hwy Ste 300 Newport Beach (92663) **(G-12078)**
Nadel Inc (PA).....310 826-2100
1990 S Bundy Dr Ste 400 Los Angeles (90025) **(G-26240)**
Nafithat Alsharq, La Mesa *Also called Abbood Zeyad* **(G-25608)**
NAFTA Distributors.....909 605-7515
5120 Santa Ana St Ontario (91761) **(G-8504)**
Nafta Shoes Inc.....626 369-9681
14632 Nelson Ave City of Industry (91744) **(G-13701)**
Nagarro Inc (PA).....408 436-6170
2001 Gateway Pl Ste 100w San Jose (95110) **(G-16000)**
Nagra, San Francisco *Also called Opentv Inc* **(G-15784)**
Nagra Usa Inc.....310 335-5225
485 Clyde Ave Mountain View (94043) **(G-7865)**
Nagra Usa Inc (HQ).....310 335-5225
841 Apollo St Ste 300 El Segundo (90245) **(G-7866)**
Naht Care At, San Diego *Also called Neighborhood House Association* **(G-24096)**
Nail Emporium.....714 779-9889
1221 N Lakeview Ave Anaheim (92807) **(G-7971)**
Nail Emporium Beauty Supply, Anaheim *Also called Nail Emporium* **(G-7971)**
Nailagio.....818 222-6633
23677 Calabasas Rd Calabasas (91302) **(G-13682)**
Nailissimo, Calabasas *Also called Nailagio* **(G-13682)**
Najarian Furniture Company Inc.....626 839-8700
265 N Euclid Ave Pasadena (91101) **(G-6826)**
Nakase Brothers Wholesale Nurs (PA).....949 855-4388
9441 Krepp Dr Huntington Beach (92646) **(G-9203)**
Nakase Brothers Wholesale Nurs.....949 855-4388
20621 Lake Forest Dr Lake Forest (92630) **(G-9204)**
Naked Infusions LLC.....818 239-9058
23679 Calabasas Rd 305 Calabasas (91302) **(G-8882)**
Nalco Company LLC.....925 957-9720
1320 Arnold Dr Ste 246 Martinez (94553) **(G-8996)**
Nallatech Inc.....805 383-8997
741 Flynn Rd Camarillo (93012) **(G-7611)**
Namasta Inc.....650 591-3639
2313 Hastings Dr Belmont (94002) **(G-19009)**
Namecheap Inc.....310 259-3259
11400 W Olympic Blvd Los Angeles (90064) **(G-5663)**
Namm, Carlsbad *Also called National Assn Mus Mrchants Inc* **(G-25095)**
Nan Fang Dist Group Inc.....510 297-5382
2100 Williams St San Leandro (94577) **(G-7867)**
Nan McKay and Associates Inc.....619 258-1855
1810 Gillespie Way # 202 El Cajon (92020) **(G-27557)**
Nanas Stern Biers Neinstein Co, Los Angeles *Also called Nsbn LLP* **(G-26414)**
Nancy Smith Construction Inc.....510 923-1671
47 Yorkshire Dr Oakland (94618) **(G-1326)**
Nanolab Technologies Inc (PA).....408 433-3320
1708 Mccarthy Blvd Milpitas (95035) **(G-26873)**
Nanosys Inc.....408 240-6700
233 S Hillview Dr Milpitas (95035) **(G-26790)**
Nantmobile LLC.....310 883-7888
9920 Jefferson Blvd Culver City (90232) **(G-15321)**
Nantworks LLC (PA).....310 405-7539
9920 Jefferson Blvd Culver City (90232) **(G-16001)**
NAPA Ambulance Service Inc.....707 224-3123
1820 Pueblo Ave NAPA (94558) **(G-3821)**
NAPA Auto Parts, NAPA *Also called County of NAPA* **(G-23868)**
NAPA County Juvenile Probation, NAPA *Also called County of NAPA* **(G-23869)**
NAPA Golf Associates LLC.....707 257-1900
2555 Jamieson Canyon Rd NAPA (94558) **(G-19010)**
NAPA Nursing Center Inc.....707 257-0931
3275 Villa Ln NAPA (94558) **(G-20803)**
NAPA Sanitation District.....707 254-9231
1515 Soscol Ferry Rd NAPA (94558) **(G-6412)**
NAPA Solano Cmnty Blood Ctr, Fairfield *Also called Blood Centers of Pacific* **(G-22899)**
NAPA State Hospital, NAPA *Also called Califrnia Dept State Hospitals* **(G-22048)**
NAPA Sunrise Rotary Club Inc.....707 257-9564
P.O. Box 5324 NAPA (94581) **(G-25302)**
NAPA Valley Country Club.....707 252-1111
3385 Hagen Rd NAPA (94558) **(G-19011)**
NAPA Valley Lodge LP.....707 875-3525
103 Coast Highway 1 Bodega Bay (94923) **(G-13013)**
NAPA VALLEY MEDICAL CENTER, NAPA *Also called Queen of Valley Medical Center* **(G-21827)**
NAPA Valley PSI Inc.....707 255-0177
651 Trabajo Ln NAPA (94559) **(G-24367)**
NAPA Valley Railroad Co, NAPA *Also called NAPA Valley Wine Train Inc* **(G-19250)**
NAPA Valley Wine Train Inc (HQ).....707 253-2160
1275 Mckinstry St NAPA (94559) **(G-19250)**
NAPA West, Five Points *Also called ATI Machinery Inc* **(G-7799)**
Napastyle Inc (PA).....707 251-5100
360 Industrial Ct Ste A NAPA (94558) **(G-13974)**
Narven Enterprises Inc (PA).....619 239-2261
1430 7th Ave Ste B San Diego (92101) **(G-13014)**
Narven Enterprises Inc.....619 232-2261
1430 7th Ave Ste B San Diego (92101) **(G-13015)**
Nasco Healthcare Inc.....209 545-1600
4825 Stoddard Rd Modesto (95356) **(G-9145)**
Nasdaq Information Tech Ctr.....805 982-2707
1000 23rd Ave Bldg 2 Port Hueneme (93043) **(G-16165)**
Nasser Company Inc (PA).....714 279-2100
22720 Savi Ranch Pkwy Yorba Linda (92887) **(G-8505)**
Nasser Company of Arizona, Yorba Linda *Also called Nasser Company Inc* **(G-8505)**
Nat Sim Corp.....818 705-3131
7405 Woodley Ave Van Nuys (91406) **(G-8171)**
Natera Inc (PA).....650 249-9090
201 Industrial Rd Ste 410 San Carlos (94070) **(G-22245)**
National Air Inc.....619 299-2500
2053 Kurtz St San Diego (92110) **(G-2304)**
National Air and Energy, San Diego *Also called National Air Inc* **(G-2304)**
National Air Cargo Inc.....310 662-4766
222 N Sepulveda Blvd # 2000 El Segundo (90245) **(G-5126)**
National Apartment Flooring.....800 773-6904
3205 Ocean Park Blvd # 180 Santa Monica (90405) **(G-3126)**
National Assn For Hispanic, Los Angeles *Also called La Asociacion Nacional Pro Per* **(G-24061)**
National Assn Ltr Carriers.....805 543-7329
4251 S Higuera St San Luis Obispo (93401) **(G-25557)**
National Assn Ltr Carriers.....415 362-0214
2310 Mason St Fl 4 San Francisco (94133) **(G-25558)**
National Assn Ltr Crrers BR 52, San Luis Obispo *Also called National Assn Ltr Carriers* **(G-25557)**
National Assn Mus Mrchants Inc.....760 438-8001
5790 Armada Dr Carlsbad (92008) **(G-25095)**
National Association For Self, Citrus Heights *Also called L W Roth Insurance Agency* **(G-10763)**
National Builder Services Inc.....714 634-7800
3835 E Thousand Oaks Blvd R Westlake Village (91362) **(G-14915)**
National Bus Invstigations Inc.....951 677-3500
25020 Las Brisas Rd Ste A Murrieta (92562) **(G-17347)**
National Business Group Inc (PA).....818 221-6000
15319 Chatsworth St Mission Hills (91345) **(G-14489)**
National Cble Cmmnications LLC.....310 231-0745
11150 Santa Monica Blvd # 900 Los Angeles (90025) **(G-14002)**
National Cement, Duarte *Also called United Hauling Corp* **(G-17656)**
National Center For The Pres.....213 625-0414
369 E 1st St Los Angeles (90012) **(G-25031)**
National Center On Deafness.....818 677-2054
18111 Nordhoff St Northridge (91330) **(G-24094)**
National City Floor Covering.....619 477-7000
132 W 8th St National City (91950) **(G-3127)**
National Cmnty Renaissance Cal (PA).....909 483-2444
9421 Haven Ave Ste 100 Rancho Cucamonga (91730) **(G-11987)**
National Cnstr Rentals Inc (HQ).....818 221-6000
15319 Chatsworth St Mission Hills (91345) **(G-14490)**
National Commercial Services.....818 701-4400
6644 Valjean Ave Ste 100 Van Nuys (91406) **(G-14039)**
National Community Renaissance (PA).....909 483-2444
9421 Haven Ave Ste 100 Rancho Cucamonga (91730) **(G-13494)**
National Construction & Maint.....909 888-7042
1955 W 9th St San Bernardino (92411) **(G-1617)**
National Council Negro Women.....415 564-4153
784 Cole St San Francisco (94117) **(G-25559)**
National Crdtors Cnnection Inc.....949 461-7540
14 Orchard Ste 100 Lake Forest (92630) **(G-10793)**
National Credit Industries Inc.....626 967-4355
1100 Via Verde San Dimas (91773) **(G-9941)**
National Custom Packing Inc.....831 724-2026
13526 Blackie Rd Castroville (95012) **(G-567)**
National Distribution Agcy Inc (HQ).....510 487-6226
7025 Central Ave Newark (94560) **(G-4601)**
National Distribution Centers.....909 390-5696
5140 Santa Ana St Ontario (91761) **(G-14003)**
National Distribution Services.....951 739-2400
340 N Grant Ave Corona (92882) **(G-8129)**
National Economic RES Assoc.....213 346-3000
777 S Figueroa St # 1950 Los Angeles (90017) **(G-27996)**
National Employee Benefits LLC.....877 778-8330
3200 E Guasti Rd Ste 100 Ontario (91761) **(G-27558)**
National Everclean Svcs Inc.....877 532-5326
28632 Roadside Dr Ste 275 Agoura Hills (91301) **(G-26874)**
National Fail Safe Inc.....562 493-5447
6442 Industry Way Westminster (92683) **(G-2661)**
National Fail-Safe SEC Systems, Westminster *Also called National Fail Safe Inc* **(G-2661)**
National Film Laboratories.....323 466-0281
900 Glenneyre St Laguna Beach (92651) **(G-18238)**
National Fitness Testing, Los Angeles *Also called Young Mens Chrstn Assn of La* **(G-24296)**
National Fncl Srvcs Cnsrtm LLC.....650 572-2872
3161 Los Prados St San Mateo (94403) **(G-27559)**

A L P H A B E T I C

National General Insurance Co...909 944-8085
3633 Inland Empire Blvd # 700 Ontario (91764) *(G-10451)*
National Genetics Institute...310 996-6610
2440 S Sepulveda Blvd # 235 Los Angeles (90064) *(G-22246)*
National Golf Properties Inc...415 488-4030
5800 Sir Francis Drake San Geronimo (94963) *(G-19012)*
National Hospitality LLC...805 688-8000
400 Alisal Rd Solvang (93463) *(G-13016)*
National Hot Rod Association (PA)...626 914-4761
2035 E Financial Way Glendora (91741) *(G-18571)*
National Instruments Corp...408 610-6800
4600 Patrick Henry Dr Santa Clara (95054) *(G-15768)*
NATIONAL LEAGUE, Covina *Also called Assistance League Covina Vly (G-24874)*
National Lgal Studies Inst Inc...951 653-4240
23962 Alssndro Blvd Ste P Moreno Valley (92553) *(G-17348)*
National Link Incorporated...909 670-1900
2235 Auto Centre Dr Glendora (91740) *(G-7062)*
National Liquidators...949 631-6715
2715 W Coast Hwy Newport Beach (92663) *(G-8023)*
National Maintenance Inc...805 680-6779
355 Foxen Ln Los Alamos (93440) *(G-14365)*
National Marine Fisheries Svc...858 546-7081
8604 La Jolla Shores Dr La Jolla (92037) *(G-26572)*
National Mentor Inc...909 483-2505
9166 Anaheim Pl Ste 200 Rancho Cucamonga (91730) *(G-24368)*
National Mentor Holdings Inc...951 677-1453
30033 Technology Dr Murrieta (92563) *(G-24742)*
National Mentor Holdings Inc...818 366-8389
19640 Bermuda St Chatsworth (91311) *(G-24743)*
National Monitoring Center, Lake Forest *Also called Advanced Protection Inds Inc (G-16861)*
National Notary Association...818 739-4071
9350 De Soto Ave Chatsworth (91311) *(G-25147)*
National Nurses United, Oakland *Also called California Nurses Association (G-25122)*
National Organization of...800 489-0210
18663 Ventura Blvd Tarzana (91356) *(G-23003)*
National Parking & Valet, Monterey *Also called National Parking Corporation (G-6631)*
National Parking Corporation...831 646-0426
2560 Garden Rd Ste 109 Monterey (93940) *(G-6631)*
National Paving Company Inc...951 369-1332
4361 Fort Dr Riverside (92509) *(G-1832)*
National Planning Corporation...800 881-7174
100 N Sepulveda Blvd # 1800 El Segundo (90245) *(G-9759)*
National Product Services LLC...562 594-8206
1005 Marvista Ave Seal Beach (90740) *(G-27758)*
National Promotions & Advg, Los Angeles *Also called Lambda Lambda Sigma LLC (G-13951)*
National Public Safety...619 401-9431
490 N Magnolia Ave El Cajon (92020) *(G-16742)*
National Railroad Pass Corp...925 335-5180
601 Marina Vista Ave Martinez (94553) *(G-3613)*
National Railroad Pass Corp...619 239-9989
1050 Kettner Blvd Ste 1 San Diego (92101) *(G-3614)*
National Real Estate Solutions...805 496-1084
299 W Hillcrest Dr # 117 Thousand Oaks (91360) *(G-14366)*
National Rent A Car, Oakland *Also called National Rental (us) Inc (G-17690)*
National Rent A Car, Santa Clara *Also called National Rental (us) Inc (G-17691)*
National Rental (us) Inc...510 877-4507
7600 Earhart Rd Ste 4 Oakland (94621) *(G-17690)*
National Rental (us) Inc...408 492-0501
2752 De La Cruz Blvd Santa Clara (95050) *(G-17691)*
National Research Group Inc...323 817-2000
6255 W Sunset Blvd Fl 19 Los Angeles (90028) *(G-26693)*
National Retail Trnsp Inc...310 605-3777
355 W Carob St Compton (90220) *(G-4233)*
National Riverside Co, Rancho Cucamonga *Also called Scheu Manufacturing Co (G-249)*
National Rtrement Partners Inc (PA)...949 488-8726
34700 Pacific Coast Hwy Capistrano Beach (92624) *(G-10794)*
National Safe, Fullerton *Also called Henry Bros Electronics Inc (G-15958)*
National Safety Services...714 679-9118
3400 Avenue Of The Arts Costa Mesa (92626) *(G-27997)*
National Security, San Diego *Also called Leidos Inc (G-26556)*
National Security Industries...916 779-0640
1217 Del Paso Blvd Ste A Sacramento (95815) *(G-16902)*
National Security Tech LLC...925 960-2500
161 S Vasco Rd Ste A Livermore (94551) *(G-25986)*
National Security Tech LLC...805 681-2488
5520 Ekwill St Ste B Santa Barbara (93111) *(G-16743)*
National Shopping Service, Rocklin *Also called Business Index Group Inc (G-26647)*
National Surety Corporation...415 899-2000
1465 N Mcdowell Blvd # 100 Petaluma (94954) *(G-10495)*
National Technical Systems Inc...909 382-2360
3505 E 3rd St San Bernardino (92408) *(G-26875)*
National Technical Systems Inc...714 998-4351
1536 E Valencia Dr Fullerton (92831) *(G-26876)*
National Technical Systems Inc...661 259-8184
20970 Centre Pointe Pkwy Santa Clarita (91350) *(G-26877)*
National Technical Systems Inc...310 671-6488
5320 W 104th St Los Angeles (90045) *(G-26878)*
National Teleconsultants Inc (PA)...818 265-4400
550 N Brand Blvd Fl 17 Glendale (91203) *(G-25987)*
National Therapeutic Svcs Inc (PA)...949 650-4334
4343 Von Karman Ave # 100 Newport Beach (92660) *(G-22778)*
National Tube & Steel, Mission Hills *Also called National Business Group Inc (G-14489)*
National Veterinary Associates (PA)...805 777-7722
29229 Canwood St Ste 100 Agoura Hills (91301) *(G-623)*
National Vision Inc...760 365-7350
58501 29 Palms Hwy Yucca Valley (92284) *(G-20301)*
NationaLease, San Diego *Also called Miramar Ford Truck Sales Inc (G-6689)*
Nationbuilder, Los Angeles *Also called 3dna Corp (G-14989)*
Nationl Medcl Assn Comp Health...619 231-9300
3177 Ocean View Blvd San Diego (92113) *(G-22779)*
Nations Capital Group LLC...818 793-2050
5353 Balboa Blvd Ste 300 Encino (91316) *(G-9788)*
Nations Direct Lender & In...800 969-7779
160 S Old Springs Rd # 260 Anaheim (92808) *(G-17349)*
Nations Petroleum Cal LLC...661 387-6402
9600 Ming Ave Ste 300 Bakersfield (93311) *(G-1065)*
Nations Surgery Center, Encino *Also called Nations Capital Group LLC (G-9788)*
Nationwide Environmental Svcs, Norwalk *Also called Joes Sweeping Inc (G-3538)*
Nationwide Funding LLC...949 679-3600
5520 Trabuco Rd Ste 100 Irvine (92620) *(G-9802)*
Nationwide Guard Services Inc...909 608-1112
299 W Fthill Blvd Ste 124 Upland (91786) *(G-16744)*
Nationwide Legal LLC...916 443-4400
716 10th St Ste 102 Sacramento (95814) *(G-23462)*
Nationwide Legal LLC (PA)...213 249-9999
1609 James M Wood Blvd Los Angeles (90015) *(G-23463)*
Nationwide SEC & Bldg Svcs Inc (PA)...800 804-0059
9045 Imperial Hwy Downey (90242) *(G-17990)*
Nationwide Theatres Corp (HQ)...310 657-8420
120 N Robertson Blvd Fl 3 Los Angeles (90048) *(G-18361)*
Nationwide Theatres Corp...562 421-8448
2500 Carson St Lakewood (90712) *(G-18527)*
Nationwide Trans Inc (PA)...909 355-3211
1633 S Campus Ave Ontario (91761) *(G-5127)*
Native American Health Ctr Inc (PA)...510 535-4400
2950 International Blvd Oakland (94601) *(G-19764)*
Native Sons Landscaping Inc...925 837-8175
25 Beta Ct Ste L San Ramon (94583) *(G-918)*
Natividad Hospital Inc...831 755-4111
1441 Constitution Blvd Salinas (93906) *(G-21759)*
Natividad Medical Center, Salinas *Also called County of Monterey (G-21522)*
Natomas Marketplace 16, Sacramento *Also called Regal Cinemas Inc (G-18348)*
Natomas Racquet Club, Sacramento *Also called Spare-Time Inc (G-19090)*
Natrol LLC (HQ)...818 739-6000
21411 Prairie St Chatsworth (91311) *(G-8286)*
Natural History Museum of Los...213 763-3442
900 Exposition Blvd Los Angeles (90007) *(G-25032)*
Natural Rsrces Def Council Inc...310 434-2300
1314 2nd St Santa Monica (90401) *(G-25303)*
Naturebridge...415 332-5771
1033 Fort Cronkhite Sausalito (94965) *(G-25560)*
Natures Best Distribution LLC...714 255-4600
6 Pointe Dr Ste 300 Brea (92821) *(G-8883)*
Natures Image Inc...949 680-4400
20361 Hermana Cir Lake Forest (92630) *(G-782)*
Natures Produce Company...323 235-4343
3305 Bandini Blvd Vernon (90058) *(G-8754)*
Naumann/Hobbs Material...909 427-0125
8575 Cherry Ave Fontana (92335) *(G-7868)*
Naumann/Hobbs Material...858 207-2800
1600 E Mission Rd San Marcos (92069) *(G-7869)*
Naumann/Hobbs Mtl Hdlg Corp II...866 266-2244
86998 Avenue 52 Coachella (92236) *(G-7778)*
Naumes Inc...530 743-2055
3792 Feather River Blvd Olivehurst (95961) *(G-305)*
Naval Coating Inc...619 234-8366
3475 E St San Diego (92102) *(G-2469)*
Naval Dental Center, San Diego *Also called United States Dept of Navy (G-20158)*
Naval Fac Eng Cmmd SW Wrkng CA...619 532-1158
1220 Pacific Hwy San Diego (92132) *(G-25988)*
Naval Hospital Lemoore, Lemoore *Also called United States Dept of Navy (G-21982)*
Naval Medical Center, San Diego *Also called United States Dept of Navy (G-21984)*
Naval Medical Clinic, Port Hueneme *Also called United States Dept of Navy (G-20161)*
Naval Research, San Diego *Also called United States Dept of Navy (G-26628)*
Naval Research Lab, Monterey *Also called United States Dept of Navy (G-26629)*
Navfac-Southwest General Funds, San Diego *Also called United States Dept of Navy (G-26117)*
Navigant Consulting Inc...213 452-4516
300 S Grand Ave Ste 3850 Los Angeles (90071) *(G-27560)*
Navis Corporation...510 267-5000
55 Harrison St Oakland (94607) *(G-4750)*
Navis Holdings LLC...510 267-5000
55 Harrison St Oakland (94607) *(G-15322)*
Navisite LLC...408 965-9000
2720 Zanker Rd San Jose (95134) *(G-5664)*
Navitas LLC...415 883-8116
15 Pamaron Way Novato (94949) *(G-8884)*
Navitas Naturals, Novato *Also called Navitas LLC (G-8884)*
Navmedwest, San Diego *Also called United States Dept of Navy (G-20162)*
Navtrak LLC...410 548-2337
20 Enterprise Ste 100 Aliso Viejo (92656) *(G-16903)*
Navy Bachelor Quarters, Ridgecrest *Also called Navy Exchange Service Command (G-13495)*
Navy Exchange, San Diego *Also called Nex Coronado Nab (G-27565)*
Navy Exchange Service Command...760 939-8681
1395 Hussey Rd Ridgecrest (93555) *(G-13495)*
Navy Exchange Service Command...909 517-2640
4250 Eucalyptus Ave Chino (91710) *(G-4602)*
Navy Federal Credit Union...888 842-6328
2040 Harbison Dr Vacaville (95687) *(G-9616)*
Navy Hospital, Lemoore *Also called United States Dept of Navy (G-21981)*
Naws Children Center...760 939-2653
1 Administration Cir Ridgecrest (93555) *(G-24485)*
Nazareth House, Fresno *Also called Congregation of Poor Sisters (G-24604)*

ALPHABETIC

Nazareth House, San Rafael *Also called Sisters of Nazareth* ***(G-21379)***
Nazareth House, San Diego *Also called Poor Sisters of Nazareth of SA* ***(G-24770)***
Naztech, Valencia *Also called Hypercel Corporation* ***(G-7582)***
Nazzareno Electric Co Inc......714 712-4744
1250 E Gene Autry Way Anaheim (92805) ***(G-2662)***
Nb Enterprises & Dist Inc......866 216-1515
603 Wilshire Blvd Los Angeles (90017) ***(G-27138)***
NBBJ LP......213 243-3333
523 W 6th St Ste 300 Los Angeles (90014) ***(G-26241)***
NBC 7/Channel 39, San Diego *Also called Station Venture Operations LP* ***(G-5912)***
NBC Studios Inc (HQ)......818 777-1000
100 Universal City Plz Universal City (91608) ***(G-18417)***
NBC Subsidiary (knbc-Tv) LLC......818 684-5746
100 Universal City Plz Universal City (91608) ***(G-5898)***
NBC Suite Hotel......310 640-3600
1440 E Imperial Ave El Segundo (90245) ***(G-13017)***
NBC Universal Inc......818 260-5746
3000 W Alameda Ave Burbank (91523) ***(G-5899)***
NBC Universal Inc (HQ)......818 777-1000
100 Universal City Plz Universal City (91608) ***(G-18117)***
NBC Universal Inc......415 995-6800
55 Hawthorne St Ste 1100 San Francisco (94105) ***(G-5811)***
NBC Universal Inc......818 840-4395
3000 W Alameda Ave Rm 320 Burbank (91523) ***(G-5900)***
Nbccat Corp......209 858-0283
1044 Madruga Rd Lathrop (95330) ***(G-17823)***
Nbcuniversal Media LLC......818 526-7000
3000 W Alameda Ave Burbank (91523) ***(G-18118)***
Nbcuniversal Media LLC......818 777-1000
100 Universal City Plz Universal City (91608) ***(G-5812)***
NC Interactive LLC......650 393-2200
1900 S Norfolk St Ste 125 San Mateo (94403) ***(G-15769)***
Nca Program......323 226-5068
1000 S Fremont Ave Unit 1 Alhambra (91803) ***(G-19765)***
Nca,, Los Angeles *Also called National Cble Cmmnications LLC* ***(G-14002)***
Ncc Group Inc (HQ)......415 268-9300
123 Mission St Ste 1020 San Francisco (94105) ***(G-16437)***
Ncca Diagnostics Medical Group, Sacramento *Also called Northern California Cardiology* ***(G-19783)***
Ncci, Lake Forest *Also called National Crdtors Cnnection Inc* ***(G-10793)***
Ncircle Network Security Inc (HQ)......415 625-5900
101 2nd St Ste 400 San Francisco (94105) ***(G-15323)***
Ncire, San Francisco *Also called Northern California Institute* ***(G-24949)***
NCM, San Bernardino *Also called National Construction & Maint* ***(G-1617)***
Ncompass International, West Hollywood *Also called N Compass International Inc* ***(G-27556)***
Ncpa, Roseville *Also called Northern California Power Agcy* ***(G-6152)***
Ncpa- Plant 1, Middletown *Also called Northern California Power Agcy* ***(G-6153)***
Nctd, Oceanside *Also called North County Transit District* ***(G-3683)***
ND Systems Inc......408 776-0085
5750 Hellyer Ave San Jose (95138) ***(G-14004)***
Ndga, Santa Clara *Also called Bandai Namco Entrmt Amer Inc* ***(G-8038)***
Ndn, Palo Alto *Also called News Distribution Network Inc* ***(G-15776)***
Nds Americas Inc (HQ)......714 434-2100
3500 Hyland Ave Costa Mesa (92626) ***(G-6009)***
Nds Surgical Imaging LLC......408 776-0085
5750 Hellyer Ave San Jose (95138) ***(G-7284)***
Ndti, Ridgecrest *Also called New Directions Tech Inc* ***(G-16011)***
Neal Electric Corp (HQ)......858 513-2525
2790 Business Park Dr Vista (92081) ***(G-2663)***
Neal Trucking Inc......951 685-5048
9749 Bellegrave Ave Riverside (92509) ***(G-4043)***
Neals Janitorial Service......408 271-9944
1588 Calco Creek Dr San Jose (95127) ***(G-14367)***
Near N Entrmt Insurances L L C......310 556-1900
1840 Century Park E # 1100 Los Angeles (90067) ***(G-10795)***
Neardata Inc......818 249-2469
4502 Dyer St Ste 103 La Crescenta (91214) ***(G-27561)***
Neardata Systems, La Crescenta *Also called Neardata Inc* ***(G-27561)***
Nebula Inc......650 539-9900
215 Castro St Fl 3 Mountain View (94041) ***(G-26573)***
Nebula Systems, Mountain View *Also called Nebula Inc* ***(G-26573)***
Nec Corporation of America......916 636-5740
10850 Gold Center Dr # 200 Rancho Cordova (95670) ***(G-15324)***
Necam, Rancho Cordova *Also called Nec Corporation of America* ***(G-15324)***
Ned E Dunphy......661 395-1000
4550 California Ave Fl 2 Bakersfield (93309) ***(G-23464)***
Ned L Webster Concrete Cnstr......805 529-4900
8800 Grimes Canyon Rd Moorpark (93021) ***(G-3300)***
Nederlander of California Inc......323 468-1700
6233 Hollywood Blvd Fl 2 Los Angeles (90028) ***(G-11023)***
Neese Inc......707 544-4444
588 Roseland Ave Santa Rosa (95407) ***(G-3866)***
Nefab Packaging West LLC......408 678-2516
8477 Central Ave Newark (94560) ***(G-17350)***
Neff Construction, Ontario *Also called Southtown Industrial Park* ***(G-11056)***
Nehemiah Construction Inc......707 746-6815
12150 Tributary Ln P Rancho Cordova (95670) ***(G-1833)***
Nehemiah Progressive Housing D......916 231-1999
424 N 7th St Ste 250 Sacramento (95811) ***(G-11988)***
Neighborhood Healthcare......951 225-6400
41840 Enterprise Cir N Temecula (92590) ***(G-23004)***
Neighborhood Healthcare......619 390-9975
10039 Vine St Ste A Lakeside (92040) ***(G-23005)***
Neighborhood Healthcare (PA)......760 520-8372
425 N Date St Ste 203 Escondido (92025) ***(G-19766)***
Neighborhood Healthcare......760 737-7896
1001 E Grand Ave Escondido (92025) ***(G-19767)***
Neighborhood Healthcare......619 440-2751
855 E Madison Ave El Cajon (92020) ***(G-19768)***
Neighborhood Healthcare......760 737-2000
460 N Elm St Escondido (92025) ***(G-19769)***
Neighborhood House Association (PA)......858 715-2642
5660 Copley Dr San Diego (92111) ***(G-24095)***
Neighborhood House Association......619 527-1287
4425 Federal Blvd Ste 24 San Diego (92102) ***(G-24096)***
Neighborhood House Association......619 263-7761
841 S 41st St San Diego (92113) ***(G-24097)***
Neighborhood Hse Assoc Fmily, San Diego *Also called Neighborhood House Association* ***(G-24097)***
Neighborhood Legal Svcs LLC......626 572-9330
9354 Telstar Ave El Monte (91731) ***(G-23465)***
Neighborhood Preservation Div, Stockton *Also called County of San Joaquin* ***(G-24910)***
Neil Dymott Frank McFall......619 238-1712
1010 2nd Ave Ste 2500 San Diego (92101) ***(G-23466)***
Neil Bassetti Farms......831 674-2040
41715 Espinosa Rd Greenfield (93927) ***(G-83)***
Neil Dymott Perkins Brown, San Diego *Also called Neil Dymott Frank McFall* ***(G-23466)***
Neilson Marketing Services, Laguna Hills *Also called Nms Data Inc* ***(G-28002)***
Neiman Marcus Group LLC......562 463-9333
2500 Workman Mill Rd City of Industry (90601) ***(G-4603)***
Neiman Marcus W Coast Svc Ctr, City of Industry *Also called Neiman Marcus Group LLC* ***(G-4603)***
Nek Services Inc......858 277-8760
2280 Historic Decatur Rd San Diego (92106) ***(G-25989)***
Nelson Shelton & Associates......310 271-2229
355 N Canon Dr Beverly Hills (90210) ***(G-11703)***
Nelson & Associates Inc......562 921-4423
12816 Leffingwell Ave Santa Fe Springs (90670) ***(G-7459)***
Nelson Moving & Storage Inc......949 582-0380
25742 Atlantic Ocean Dr Lake Forest (92630) ***(G-4365)***
Nelson North American, Lake Forest *Also called Nelson Moving & Storage Inc* ***(G-4365)***
Nelson, Jeffrey Do, Pasadena *Also called Huntington Reprodctve Ctr Inc* ***(G-19565)***
Nelson, Shelton, & Associates, Beverly Hills *Also called Nelson Shelton & Associates* ***(G-11703)***
Neogenomics Inc......239 768-0600
5 Jenner Ste 100 Irvine (92618) ***(G-26574)***
Neogov, El Segundo *Also called Governmentjobscom Inc* ***(G-15682)***
Neostyle Eyewear Corporation......760 305-4004
2651 La Mirada Dr Ste 150 Vista (92081) ***(G-7334)***
Neovia Logistics Dist LP......626 358-8025
600 Live Oak Ave Baldwin Park (91706) ***(G-5128)***
Neovia Logistics Dist LP......626 359-4500
600 Live Oak Ave Irwindale (91706) ***(G-5129)***
Nep Group Inc......412 423-1354
7635 Airport Bus Pkwy Van Nuys (91406) ***(G-18119)***
Neps Worldwide, La Mirada *Also called Northeast Protective Svcs Inc* ***(G-16749)***
Neptune Management Corporation......310 832-6923
150 W 6th St Ste 100 San Pedro (90731) ***(G-13707)***
Neptune Management Corporation......510 797-2269
4065 Mowry Ave Fremont (94538) ***(G-13708)***
Neptune Management Corporation......916 771-5300
9650 Fairway Dr 120 Roseville (95678) ***(G-13709)***
Nest Labs Inc (HQ)......650 331-1127
3400 Hillview Ave Palo Alto (94304) ***(G-7612)***
Nestle Dreyers Ice Cream Co......909 595-0677
351 Cheryl Ln Walnut (91789) ***(G-8589)***
Nestle Ice Cream Company......661 398-3500
7301 District Blvd Bakersfield (93313) ***(G-8590)***
Nestle Waters North Amer Inc......714 532-6220
619 N Main St Orange (92868) ***(G-8885)***
Nestle Waters North Amer Inc......626 443-3236
4250 Baldwin Ave El Monte (91731) ***(G-8886)***
Nestle Waters North Amer Inc......213 763-1380
1544 E Washington Blvd Los Angeles (90021) ***(G-8887)***
Nestle Waters North Amer Inc......925 294-7720
7480 Las Positas Rd Livermore (94551) ***(G-8888)***
Nestle Waters North Amer Inc......714 792-2100
3230 E Imperial Hwy # 100 Brea (92821) ***(G-8889)***
Nestor Enterprises LLC......209 727-5711
13852 E Peltier Rd Acampo (95220) ***(G-172)***
Nestwise LLC......855 444-6378
9785 Towne Centre Dr San Diego (92121) ***(G-17351)***
Net Express......510 887-4395
32 Snyder Way Fremont (94536) ***(G-16002)***
Net Optics Inc......408 737-7777
5303 Betsy Ross Dr Santa Clara (95054) ***(G-15770)***
Net4site LLC......408 427-3004
3350 Scott Blvd Bldg 34b Santa Clara (95054) ***(G-27562)***
Netafim Irrigation Inc (HQ)......559 453-6800
5470 E Home Ave Fresno (93727) ***(G-7805)***
Netapp Inc......949 754-6600
300 Spectrum Center Dr # 900 Irvine (92618) ***(G-16003)***
Netapp Inc......408 822-3402
1299 Orleans Dr Sunnyvale (94089) ***(G-16004)***
Netapp Inc......818 227-5025
6320 Canoga Ave Ste 1500 Woodland Hills (91367) ***(G-16005)***
Netapp Inc......408 419-5301
1345 Crossman Ave Sunnyvale (94089) ***(G-16006)***
Netapp Inc......408 822-3803
3334 Meadowlands Ln San Jose (95135) ***(G-16007)***
Netapp Inc......310 426-1700
222 N Sepulveda Blvd El Segundo (90245) ***(G-16008)***

ALPHABETIC

Netball America Inc 949 307-4455
4686 Oceano Cir Huntington Beach (92649) ***(G-17352)***
Netbase Solutions Inc (PA) 650 810-2100
3960 Freedom Cir 201 Santa Clara (95054) ***(G-27563)***
Netcontinuum Inc 408 961-5600
1454 Almaden Valley Dr San Jose (95120) ***(G-16904)***
Netcube Systems Inc 650 862-7858
1275 Arbor Ave Los Altos (94024) ***(G-15771)***
Netfortris Corporation 888 469-5100
455 Market St Ste 620 San Francisco (94105) ***(G-6083)***
Netline Corporation (PA) 408 374-4200
750 University Ave # 200 Los Gatos (95032) ***(G-5665)***
Netlinx Publishing Solutions, Sacramento *Also called System Integrators Inc* ***(G-16062)***
Netnow 408 370-0425
41 Heritage Village Ln Campbell (95008) ***(G-5666)***
Netpace Inc 925 543-7760
12657 Alcosta Blvd # 410 San Ramon (94583) ***(G-15325)***
Netpolarity Inc 408 971-1100
900 E Campbell Ave Campbell (95008) ***(G-14706)***
Netronix Integration Inc 408 573-1444
2170 Paragon Dr San Jose (95131) ***(G-2664)***
Netskope Inc 800 979-6988
270 3rd St Los Altos (94022) ***(G-15326)***
Netsource Inc 415 831-3681
5955 Geary Blvd San Francisco (94121) ***(G-14707)***
Netsuite Inc (PA) 650 627-1000
2955 Campus Dr Ste 100 San Mateo (94403) ***(G-15772)***
Netversant - Silicon Vly Inc (PA) 510 771-1200
47811 Warm Springs Blvd Fremont (94539) ***(G-2665)***
Network Affiliates Inc 415 291-2914
600 Montgomery St San Francisco (94111) ***(G-10064)***
Network Automation Inc 213 738-1700
3530 Wilshire Blvd # 1800 Los Angeles (90010) ***(G-15773)***
Network Capital Funding Corp (PA) 949 442-0060
5 Park Plz Ste 800 Irvine (92614) ***(G-9876)***
Network Global Logistics LLC 888 285-7447
13479 Valley Blvd Fontana (92335) ***(G-4871)***
Network Intgrtion Partners Inc 909 919-2800
11981 Jack Benny Dr # 103 Rancho Cucamonga (91739) ***(G-16009)***
Network Management Group Inc (PA) 323 263-2632
1100 S Flower St Ste 3110 Los Angeles (90015) ***(G-27139)***
Network Medical Management Inc 818 370-9125
14120 Victory Blvd Van Nuys (91401) ***(G-27140)***
Network Physics Inc 240 497-3000
333 S Grand Ave Ste 4070 Los Angeles (90071) ***(G-16010)***
Networked Insurance Agents LLC 800 682-8476
443 Crown Point Cir Ste A Grass Valley (95945) ***(G-10796)***
Networkfleet Inc 858 450-3245
9868 Scranton Rd Ste 1000 San Diego (92121) ***(G-15327)***
Netzero Inc (HQ) 805 418-2000
21301 Burbank Blvd Fl 3 Woodland Hills (91367) ***(G-15328)***
Neubauer-Jennison Inc 760 934-2511
53 Sierra Manor Rd Mammoth Lakes (93546) ***(G-1618)***
Neudesic LLC (PA) 949 754-4500
100 Spectrum Center Dr # 1200 Irvine (92618) ***(G-16438)***
Neuro Drinks, Burbank *Also called Neurobrands LLC* ***(G-8890)***
Neurobrands LLC 310 393-6444
2550 N Hollywood Way # 100 Burbank (91505) ***(G-8890)***
Neuropace Inc 650 237-2700
455 Bernardo Ave Mountain View (94043) ***(G-26575)***
Nevada Cancer Institute, Oakland *Also called Regents of The University Cal* ***(G-21830)***
Nevada County Behavioral Hlth 530 265-1450
500 Crown Point Cir # 120 Grass Valley (95945) ***(G-22780)***
Nevada Irrigation District (PA) 530 273-6185
1036 W Main St Grass Valley (95945) ***(G-6649)***
Nevada Republic Electric N Inc 916 294-0140
11855 White Rock Rd Rancho Cordova (95742) ***(G-2666)***
Never Ignore Kids Education 310 984-6847
2785 Pacific Coast Hwy # 356 Torrance (90505) ***(G-24945)***
Neversoft Entertainment Inc 818 610-4100
21255 Burbank Blvd # 600 Woodland Hills (91367) ***(G-15329)***
Neville Alleyne MD, Oceanside *Also called Tri City Orthopedic Sgy & Mdcl* ***(G-20142)***
Nevin Levy LLP A Partnership 415 800-5770
50 California St Ste 1500 San Francisco (94111) ***(G-11704)***
Nevins Adams Properties, Santa Barbara *Also called Nevins-Adams Properties Inc* ***(G-11024)***
Nevins-Adams Properties Inc (PA) 805 963-2884
920 Garden St Ste A Santa Barbara (93101) ***(G-11024)***
New Advances For People Disabi 661 327-0188
1120 21st St Bakersfield (93301) ***(G-24946)***
New Age Electric Inc 408 279-8787
1085 N 11th St San Jose (95112) ***(G-2667)***
New American Funding, Encinitas *Also called Broker Solutions Inc* ***(G-9776)***
New American Funding, Tustin *Also called Broker Solutions Inc* ***(G-27360)***
New Bi US Gaming LLC 858 592-2472
10920 Via Frontera # 420 San Diego (92127) ***(G-15774)***
New Bridge Foundation Inc 510 548-7270
2323 Hearst Ave Berkeley (94709) ***(G-24098)***
New Bridge Foundation Inc 510 548-7270
1820 Scenic Ave Berkeley (94709) ***(G-22160)***
New Bthny Rsdntl CRE&sklld 209 827-8933
1441 Berkeley Dr Los Banos (93635) ***(G-24744)***
New CAM Commerce Solutions LLC 714 241-9241
17075 Newhope St Ste A Fountain Valley (92708) ***(G-17353)***
New Century Media Corp 562 695-1000
2727 Pellissier Pl City of Industry (90601) ***(G-8130)***
New Century Science & Tech 626 581-5500
18031 Cortney Ct City of Industry (91748) ***(G-8024)***
New Cingular Wireless Svcs Inc 562 924-0000
P.O. Box 68055 Artesia (90702) ***(G-5667)***
New Cingular Wireless Svcs Inc 323 588-9348
6408 Pacific Blvd Huntington Park (90255) ***(G-6084)***
New Cingular Wireless Svcs Inc 562 941-6422
9830 Norwalk Blvd Ste 100 Santa Fe Springs (90670) ***(G-5402)***
New Civic Company Ltd 415 986-1668
870 Market St Ste 1168 San Francisco (94102) ***(G-12329)***
New Covenant Care Cal Inc 925 930-7733
130 Tampico Walnut Creek (94598) ***(G-20804)***
NEW COVENANT CARE CENTER OF DI, Dinuba *Also called New Covenant Care of Dinuba* ***(G-20805)***
New Covenant Care of Dinuba 559 591-3300
1730 S College Ave Dinuba (93618) ***(G-20805)***
New Crew Production Corp 323 234-8880
200 W 138th St Los Angeles (90061) ***(G-17354)***
New Day Staffing Inc 619 481-5400
5920 Friars Rd Ste 104 San Diego (92108) ***(G-14916)***
New Deal Studios Inc 310 578-9929
1812 W Burbank Blvd Burbank (91506) ***(G-18239)***
New Desserts Inc 415 780-6860
5000 Fulton Dr Fairfield (94534) ***(G-8891)***
New Directions Inc (PA) 310 914-4045
1529 E 1st St 12 Long Beach (90802) ***(G-24099)***
New Directions For Veterans, Long Beach *Also called New Directions Inc* ***(G-24099)***
New Directions Tech Inc (PA) 760 384-2444
137 Drummond Ave Ste A Ridgecrest (93555) ***(G-16011)***
New Discovery Inc 925 783-6613
1475 Clubhouse Dr Byron (94505) ***(G-19013)***
New Discovery Inc 925 634-0505
2600 Cherry Hills Dr Byron (94505) ***(G-18765)***
New Dream Network LLC (PA) 626 644-9466
135 S State College Blvd Brea (92821) ***(G-5668)***
New Dream Network LLC 323 375-3842
707 Wilshire Blvd # 5050 Los Angeles (90017) ***(G-5669)***
New Earth Enterprises Inc 760 942-1298
3790 Manchester Ave Encinitas (92024) ***(G-919)***
New Economics For Women (PA) 213 483-2060
303 Loma Dr Los Angeles (90017) ***(G-24100)***
New England Financial, Woodland Hills *Also called Russon Financial Services Inc* ***(G-27629)***
New England Shtmtl Works Inc 559 268-7375
2731 S Cherry Ave Fresno (93706) ***(G-25990)***
New Figueroa Hotel Inc 213 627-8971
1000 S Hope St Apt 201 Los Angeles (90015) ***(G-13018)***
New Global Telecom Inc 213 489-3708
624 S Grand Ave Ste 2900 Los Angeles (90017) ***(G-17355)***
New Haven Youth Fmly Svcs Inc 760 630-4060
P.O. Box 1199 Vista (92085) ***(G-24101)***
New Home Company Inc (PA) 949 382-7800
85 Enterprise Ste 450 Aliso Viejo (92656) ***(G-1380)***
New Home Professionals 925 556-1555
6500 Dublin Blvd Ste 201 Dublin (94568) ***(G-11705)***
New Hope Care Center, Tracy *Also called Jesse Lee Group Inc* ***(G-27079)***
New Horizons Worldwide Inc 818 894-9301
15917 Chase St North Hills (91343) ***(G-22512)***
New Image Landscape Company 510 226-9191
3250 Darby Cmn Fremont (94539) ***(G-920)***
New Inspiration Brdcstg Co Inc 805 987-0400
4880 Santa Rosa Rd Camarillo (93012) ***(G-5813)***
New Legend Inc 530 674-3100
1235 Oswald Rd Yuba City (95991) ***(G-4234)***
New Mediscan II LLC 818 462-0000
21050 Califa St 100 Woodland Hills (91367) ***(G-23006)***
New Mid Coast Builders, Camarillo *Also called Mid Coast Builders Supply Inc* ***(G-1221)***
New Ngc Inc 510 234-6745
1040 Canal Blvd Richmond (94804) ***(G-8077)***
New Paradigm Productions Inc (PA) 415 924-8000
39 Mesa St Ste 212 San Francisco (94129) ***(G-18120)***
New Port Orthopedic Institute 949 722-5071
19582 Beach Blvd Ste 118 Huntington Beach (92648) ***(G-19770)***
New Pride Corporation 310 631-7000
2757 E Del Amo Blvd Compton (90221) ***(G-17780)***
New Regency Productions Inc (PA) 310 369-8300
10201 W Pico Blvd Bldg 12 Los Angeles (90064) ***(G-18121)***
New Relic Inc (PA) 650 777-7600
188 Spear St Ste 1200 San Francisco (94105) ***(G-15775)***
New Solar Incorporated 888 886-0103
1525 Mccarthy Blvd Milpitas (95035) ***(G-27141)***
New Start Home Health Care Inc 818 665-7898
21515 Vanowen St Ste 205 Canoga Park (91303) ***(G-24102)***
New Stockton Poultry Inc 209 466-1952
302 S San Joaquin St Stockton (95203) ***(G-8601)***
New View Landscape Inc 818 222-8972
24860 Calabasas Rd Calabasas (91302) ***(G-921)***
New Visa Health Services Inc 760 723-0053
3414 Preakness Ct Fallbrook (92028) ***(G-21324)***
New Vista Health Services 310 477-5501
1516 Sawtelle Blvd Los Angeles (90025) ***(G-21325)***
New Vista Health Services 818 352-1421
8647 Fenwick St Sunland (91040) ***(G-21326)***
New Vista Pst Act Care Cntr, Los Angeles *Also called New Vista Health Services* ***(G-21325)***
New Vsta Nrsing Rhbltation Ctr, Sunland *Also called New Vista Health Services* ***(G-21326)***
New Wave Entertainment, Burbank *Also called NW Entertainment Inc* ***(G-18123)***
New Wave Transport, Long Beach *Also called Gold Tree Inc* ***(G-27451)***
New Way Landscape & Tree Svcs 858 505-8300
7485 Ronson Rd San Diego (92111) ***(G-922)***
New Way LLC 925 688-1520
1130 Burnett Ave Ste G Concord (94520) ***(G-24745)***

ALPHABETIC

New West Partitions...916 456-8365
2550 Sutterville Rd Sacramento (95820) *(G-2935)*
New York Life Insurance Co...650 571-1220
1300 S El Cmno Real 400 San Mateo (94402) *(G-10797)*
New York Life Insurance Co...925 809-7020
191 Sand Creek Rd Ste 200 Brentwood (94513) *(G-10213)*
New York Life Insurance Co...714 672-0236
675 Placentia Ave Ste 250 Brea (92821) *(G-10798)*
New York Life Insurance Co...805 898-7625
3757 State St Ste 310 Santa Barbara (93105) *(G-10214)*
New York Life Insurance Co...818 662-7500
801 N Brand Blvd Ste 1400 Glendale (91203) *(G-10215)*
New York Life Insurance Co...408 392-9782
1731 Tech Dr Ste 400 San Jose (95110) *(G-10799)*
New York Life Insurance Co...559 447-3900
5329 Office Center Ct # 223 Bakersfield (93309) *(G-10800)*
New York Life Insurance Co...949 797-2400
2020 Main St Ste 1200 Irvine (92614) *(G-10801)*
New York Life Insurance Co...951 354-2094
4204 Riverwalk Pkwy # 200 Riverside (92505) *(G-10216)*
New York Life Insurance Co...415 393-6060
425 Market St Fl 16 San Francisco (94105) *(G-10802)*
New York Life Insurance Co...909 902-1027
901 Corporate Center Dr Pomona (91768) *(G-10803)*
New York Life Insurance Co...916 774-6200
2999 Douglas Blvd Ste 350 Roseville (95661) *(G-10804)*
New York Life Insurance Co...858 623-8600
4365 Executive Dr Ste 800 San Diego (92121) *(G-10805)*
New York Life Insurance Co...415 999-9576
2633 Camino Ramon Ste 525 San Ramon (94583) *(G-10217)*
New York Life Insurance Co...805 656-4598
300 E Esplanade Dr # 2050 Oxnard (93036) *(G-10806)*
New York Life Insurance Co...323 782-3000
6300 Wilshire Blvd # 1900 Los Angeles (90048) *(G-10807)*
New York Life Insurance Co...559 447-3900
7112 N Fresno St Ste 100 Fresno (93720) *(G-10808)*
New York Life Insurance Co...909 305-6500
140 Via Verde Ste 200 San Dimas (91773) *(G-10809)*
New-Jack Industries Inc...310 297-3605
2613 Manhattan Beach Blvd # 100 Redondo Beach (90278) *(G-16745)*
Newage Anaheim Inn LLC...714 758-0900
1221 S Harbor Blvd Anaheim (92805) *(G-13019)*
Newark Courtyard By Marriott...510 792-5200
34905 Newark Blvd Newark (94560) *(G-13020)*
Neway Packaging Corp (PA)...602 454-9000
1973 E Via Arado Rancho Dominguez (90220) *(G-8199)*
Newco Distributors Inc...909 291-2240
9060 Rochester Ave Rancho Cucamonga (91730) *(G-9146)*
Newcomb Academy, Long Beach *Also called Long Beach Unified School Dst (G-17301)*
Newland Group Inc (PA)...858 455-7503
4790 Eastgate Mall # 150 San Diego (92121) *(G-11989)*
Newland Northwest, San Diego *Also called Newland Group Inc (G-11989)*
Newland Real Estate Group LLC (HQ)...858 455-7503
4790 Eastgate Mall # 150 San Diego (92121) *(G-10166)*
Newma Garris Gilmo + Partne I...949 756-0818
3100 Bristol St Ste 400 Costa Mesa (92626) *(G-26242)*
Newmark & Company RE Inc...714 667-8252
1551 N Tustin Ave Ste 300 Santa Ana (92705) *(G-27564)*
Newmark & Company RE Inc...949 608-2000
4675 Macarthur Ct # 1600 Newport Beach (92660) *(G-11706)*
Newmark Grubb Knight Frank, Santa Ana *Also called Newmark & Company RE Inc (G-27564)*
Newmark Grubb Knight Frank, Newport Beach *Also called Newmark & Company RE Inc (G-11706)*
Newmeyer & Dillion LLP (PA)...949 854-7000
895 Dove St Fl 5 Newport Beach (92660) *(G-23467)*
Newport Apparel Corporation (PA)...310 605-1900
1215 W Walnut St Compton (90220) *(G-8405)*
Newport Bay Hospital, Newport Beach *Also called Beacon Healthcare Services (G-22042)*
Newport Bch Marriott Ht & Spa, Newport Beach *Also called Host Hotels & Resorts LP (G-12762)*
Newport Beach Country Club Inc...949 644-9550
1 Clubhouse Dr Newport Beach (92660) *(G-19014)*
Newport Beach Dialysis Center, Newport Beach *Also called Riverside Research Institute (G-26803)*
Newport Beach Fbo LLC...949 851-0049
19711 Campus Dr Ste 100 Santa Ana (92707) *(G-14917)*
Newport Beach Medspa...949 631-2800
2131 Westcliff Dr Ste 100 Newport Beach (92660) *(G-19771)*
Newport Beach Orthopedic Inst...949 722-7038
22 Corporate Plaza Dr Newport Beach (92660) *(G-19772)*
Newport Beach Surgery Ctr LLC...949 631-0988
361 Hospital Rd Ste 124 Newport Beach (92663) *(G-19773)*
Newport Diagnostic Center Inc (PA)...949 760-3025
1605 Avocado Ave Newport Beach (92660) *(G-22247)*
Newport Diversified Inc...562 921-4359
13963 Alondra Blvd Santa Fe Springs (90670) *(G-17356)*
Newport Diversified Inc...619 449-7800
1286 Fletcher Pkwy El Cajon (92020) *(G-17357)*
Newport Diversified Inc...619 448-3147
1280 Fletcher Pkwy El Cajon (92020) *(G-17358)*
Newport Fmly Mdcne/A Med Group...949 644-1025
520 Superior Ave Newport Beach (92663) *(G-19774)*
Newport Group Inc (PA)...925 328-4540
1350 Treat Blvd Ste 300 Walnut Creek (94597) *(G-27142)*
Newport Harbor Radiology Assoc...949 721-8191
360 San Miguel Dr # 105106 Newport Beach (92660) *(G-19775)*
Newport Hospitality Group Inc...661 323-1900
801 Truxtun Ave Bakersfield (93301) *(G-13021)*
Newport Imaging Center, Newport Beach *Also called Newport Harbor Radiology Assoc (G-19775)*
Newport Mesa Memory Care Cmnty, Costa Mesa *Also called Silverado Senior Living Inc (G-21373)*
Newport Radio Surgery Center, Newport Beach *Also called Newport Diagnostic Center Inc (G-22247)*
Newport Sbacute Healthcare Ctr...949 642-1974
2570 Newport Blvd Costa Mesa (92627) *(G-21327)*
Newport Specialty Hospital, Los Angeles *Also called Tustin Hospital and Med Ctr (G-21974)*
Newport Television LLC...559 761-0243
4880 N 1st St Fresno (93726) *(G-18418)*
Newport Television LLC...661 283-1700
2120 L St Bakersfield (93301) *(G-5901)*
News Distribution Network Inc...773 426-5938
437 Lytton Ave Ste 200 Palo Alto (94301) *(G-15776)*
Newstar Fresh Foods LLC...831 758-7800
126 Sun St Salinas (93901) *(G-568)*
Newstar Fresh Foods LLC (PA)...831 758-7800
850 Work St Ste 101 Salinas (93901) *(G-569)*
Newsways Distributors, Los Angeles *Also called Newsways Services Inc (G-9169)*
Newsways Services Inc...323 258-6000
1324 Cypress Ave Los Angeles (90065) *(G-9169)*
Newton Softed Inc...949 396-6192
30 Corporate Park Ste 101 Irvine (92606) *(G-27998)*
Newwest Funding, Downey *Also called Newwest Mortgage Company (G-9942)*
Newwest Mortgage Company...562 861-8393
8255 Firestone Blvd # 101 Downey (90241) *(G-9942)*
Nex Coronado Nab...619 522-7403
3632 Guadalcanal Rd San Diego (92155) *(G-27565)*
Nexa Technologies Inc (HQ)...972 590-8669
18552 Macarthur Blvd # 100 Irvine (92612) *(G-15330)*
Nexant Inc (PA)...415 369-1000
101 2nd St Ste 1000 San Francisco (94105) *(G-27999)*
Nexcare Collaborative (PA)...818 907-0322
15477 Ventura Blvd Sherman Oaks (91403) *(G-24103)*
Nexenta Systems Inc...408 791-3341
451 El Cmino Real Ste 201 Santa Clara (95050) *(G-15777)*
Nexgenix Inc (PA)...714 665-6240
2 Peters Canyon Rd # 200 Irvine (92606) *(G-15331)*
Nexgrill Industries Inc...909 598-8799
14050 Laurelwood Pl Chino (91710) *(G-6875)*
Nexinfo Solutions Inc...714 368-1452
8502 E Chapman Ave # 364 Orange (92869) *(G-7167)*
Nexsentio...408 392-9249
3071 Muirdrum Pl San Jose (95148) *(G-14368)*
Nexsentio Inc...408 392-9249
1346 Ridder Park Dr San Jose (95131) *(G-14369)*
Nexstar Broadcasting Group Inc...559 222-2411
5035 E Mckinley Ave Fresno (93727) *(G-5902)*
Next Door Sltons To Dom Vlence...408 279-2962
234 E Gish Rd Ste 200 San Jose (95112) *(G-24947)*
Next Image Medical Inc (PA)...858 847-9185
3390 Carmel Mountain Rd # 150 San Diego (92121) *(G-27566)*
Next Management LLC...323 782-0038
8447 Wilshire Blvd # 301 Beverly Hills (90211) *(G-27567)*
Next Management Co, Beverly Hills *Also called Next Management LLC (G-27567)*
Next Venture Inc...818 637-2888
560 Rverdale Drv Glendale Glendale (91204) *(G-1619)*
Nextdoorcom Inc...415 236-0000
760 Market St Ste 300 San Francisco (94102) *(G-24948)*
Nextel Communications Inc...323 290-2400
1810 W Slauson Ave Ste G Los Angeles (90047) *(G-5403)*
Nextel Communications Inc...925 682-2355
272 Sun Valley Mall Concord (94520) *(G-5404)*
Nextel Communications Inc...949 727-1400
16 Technology Dr Irvine (92618) *(G-5405)*
Nextivity Inc...858 485-9442
12230 World Trade Dr # 250 San Diego (92128) *(G-7613)*
Nextpoint Inc (PA)...310 360-5904
8750 Wilshire Blvd 300e Beverly Hills (90211) *(G-5670)*
Nfl Network, Culver City *Also called Nfl Properties LLC (G-18419)*
Nfl Properties LLC...310 840-4635
10950 Wash Blvd Ste 100 Culver City (90232) *(G-18419)*
Nfp Advisors, Simi Valley *Also called Nfp Property & Casualty Svcs (G-27568)*
Nfp Property & Casualty Svcs...805 579-1900
2450 Tapo St Simi Valley (93063) *(G-27568)*
Ngi Construction, NAPA *Also called Nova Group Inc (G-2072)*
NGL, Fontana *Also called Network Global Logistics LLC (G-4871)*
NGS Fish House, Rancho Cucamonga *Also called Kings Seafood Company LLC (G-8636)*
Ngs Group Inc...323 735-1700
4152 W Washington Blvd Los Angeles (90018) *(G-8892)*
Nguyen, Myhanh MD, Sunnyvale *Also called Sutter Health (G-20101)*
Nhca Inc...310 519-8200
601 S Palos Verdes St San Pedro (90731) *(G-13022)*
Nhic Corp...530 332-1168
402 Otterson Dr Chico (95928) *(G-10810)*
Nhr Newco Holdings LLC (PA)...800 230-6638
6500 Hollister Ave # 210 Santa Barbara (93117) *(G-7168)*
Nhra, Glendora *Also called National Hot Rod Association (G-18571)*
Ni Ki Cruz LLC...408 332-7616
5255 Stevens Creek Blvd Santa Clara (95051) *(G-17359)*
Ni Microwave Components, Santa Clara *Also called National Instruments Corp (G-15768)*
Nia Healthcare Services Inc...559 251-1526
5265 E Huntington Ave Fresno (93727) *(G-20806)*
Niacc-Avitech Technologies Inc (PA)...559 291-2500
245 W Dakota Ave Clovis (93612) *(G-17991)*
Nibbelink Masonry Cnstr Corp...661 948-7859
2010 W Avenue K Lancaster (93536) *(G-2829)*

ALPHABETIC

Nibbi Bros Associates Inc......415 863-1820
180 Hubbell St San Francisco (94107) ***(G-1327)***
Nibbi Bros Concrete, San Francisco *Also called Nibbi Bros Associates Inc* ***(G-1327)***
Nic Partners, Rancho Cucamonga *Also called Network Intgrtion Partners Inc* ***(G-16009)***
Nice Avenue LLC......909 794-1189
2278 Nice Ave Mentone (92359) ***(G-20807)***
Nicholas B Macy Dvm......831 475-5400
2585 Soquel Dr Santa Cruz (95065) ***(G-624)***
Nicholas Grant Corporation......619 390-3900
12570 Highway 67 Lakeside (92040) ***(G-1834)***
Nicholas Lane Contractors Inc......714 630-7630
1157 N Red Gum St Anaheim (92806) ***(G-1226)***
Nichols Inst Reference Labs (HQ)......949 728-4000
33608 Ortega Hwy San Juan Capistrano (92675) ***(G-22248)***
Nichols Lumber & Hardware Co......626 960-4802
13470 Dalewood St Baldwin Park (91706) ***(G-6938)***
Nick and MO, Irwindale *Also called Wor International Inc* ***(G-8366)***
Nicola International Inc......818 767-1133
11119 Dora St Sun Valley (91352) ***(G-8893)***
Nicolaides Fink Tho......415 745-3778
601 California St Fl 3 San Francisco (94108) ***(G-23468)***
Nicole Pttrson Crt Rprting LLC......559 400-2407
545 E Alluvial Ave # 109 Fresno (93720) ***(G-23469)***
Nidek Incorporated......510 226-5700
47651 Westinghouse Dr Fremont (94539) ***(G-7335)***
Nielsen Claritas Inc......858 622-0800
9444 Waples St Ste 280 San Diego (92121) ***(G-15332)***
Nielsen Company (us) LLC......323 817-2000
6255 W Sunset Blvd Fl 20 Los Angeles (90028) ***(G-26694)***
Nielsen Company (us) LLC......858 677-9542
5375 Mira Sorrento Pl # 400 San Diego (92121) ***(G-26695)***
Nielsen Company (us) LLC......323 462-0050
6255 W Sunset Blvd Fl 19 Los Angeles (90028) ***(G-18483)***
Nielsen Media Research, Los Angeles *Also called Nielsen Company (us) LLC* ***(G-26694)***
Nielsen Mobile LLC (HQ)......917 435-9301
1010 Battery St San Francisco (94111) ***(G-17360)***
Nielsens Creamery (PA)......559 686-4744
21346 Road 140 Tulare (93274) ***(G-436)***
Nieves Landscape Inc......714 835-7332
1629 E Edinger Ave Santa Ana (92705) ***(G-923)***
NIFTY THRIFT, Lafayette *Also called Futures Explored Inc* ***(G-23990)***
Nightingale Vantagemed Corp (HQ)......916 638-4744
10670 White Rock Rd Rancho Cordova (95670) ***(G-15778)***
Nightrider Overnite Copy Svc, San Francisco *Also called Ricoh Usa Inc* ***(G-7068)***
Nightrider Overnite Copy Svc, Los Angeles *Also called Ricoh Usa Inc* ***(G-14125)***
Nightrider Overnite Copy Svc, Oakland *Also called Ricoh Usa Inc* ***(G-14126)***
Nihon Kohden America Inc (HQ)......949 580-1555
15353 Barranca Pkwy Irvine (92618) ***(G-7285)***
Nijjar Realty Inc (PA)......626 575-0062
4900 Santa Anita Ave 2b El Monte (91731) ***(G-11707)***
Nikewoman......408 942-6457
447 Great Mall Dr Milpitas (95035) ***(G-8440)***
Nikken Global Inc (HQ)......949 789-2000
2 Corporate Park Ste 100 Irvine (92606) ***(G-7972)***
Nikon Precision Inc (HQ)......650 508-4674
1399 Shoreway Rd Belmont (94002) ***(G-7870)***
Nine-Twenty Inc......619 497-4900
1040 University Ave B211 San Diego (92103) ***(G-11708)***
Nines Restaurant......925 516-3413
100 Summerset Dr Brentwood (94513) ***(G-27569)***
Ninos Latino Unidos FSA......562 801-5454
10016 Pioneer Blvd # 123 Santa Fe Springs (90670) ***(G-24746)***
Ninth House Inc......612 339-0927
1 Montgomery St Ste 2200 San Francisco (94104) ***(G-24369)***
Ninth House Network, San Francisco *Also called Ninth House Inc* ***(G-24369)***
Ninyo & AMP Moore Geotechnical, Irvine *Also called Ninyo & Moore Geotechnical* ***(G-28001)***
Ninyo & Moore Geotechnical (PA)......858 576-1000
5710 Ruffin Rd San Diego (92123) ***(G-28000)***
Ninyo & Moore Geotechnical......949 753-7070
475 Goddard Ste 200 Irvine (92618) ***(G-28001)***
Nipomo Dial A Ride......805 929-2881
179 Cross St San Luis Obispo (93401) ***(G-3884)***
Nippon Ex Nec Lgstics Amer Inc......310 604-6100
18615 S Ferris Pl Rancho Dominguez (90220) ***(G-4044)***
Nippon Express USA Inc......310 532-6300
970 Francisco St Torrance (90502) ***(G-5130)***
Nippon Express USA Inc......310 532-6300
300 Westmont Dr San Pedro (90731) ***(G-5131)***
Nippon Express USA Inc......310 535-7200
2233 E Grand Ave El Segundo (90245) ***(G-5132)***
Nippon Travel Agency Amer Inc......310 768-1817
1025 W 190th St Ste 301 Gardena (90248) ***(G-4969)***
Nippon Travel Agency PCF Inc (HQ)......310 768-0017
1025 W 190th St Ste 300 Gardena (90248) ***(G-4970)***
Nissan North America Inc......714 433-3700
1683 Sunflower Ave Costa Mesa (92626) ***(G-6691)***
Nissan North America Inc......916 920-4712
3939 N Freeway Blvd Sacramento (95834) ***(G-4604)***
Nissen Vineyard Services Inc......707 963-3480
1226 Spring St Saint Helena (94574) ***(G-711)***
Nissho of California Inc......760 727-9719
89055 64th Ave Thermal (92274) ***(G-245)***
Nissin Intl Trnspt USA Inc (HQ)......310 222-8500
1540 W 190th St Torrance (90501) ***(G-5133)***
Nitai Partners Inc......855 879-2847
1761 Reichert Way Chula Vista (91913) ***(G-15333)***
Nitro Software Inc......415 632-4894
225 Bush St Ste 700 San Francisco (94104) ***(G-15779)***
Nittany Lion Landscaping Inc......714 635-1788
14770 Firestone Blvd # 203 La Mirada (90638) ***(G-924)***
Nitto Denko Technical Corp......760 435-7011
501 Via Del Monte Oceanside (92058) ***(G-26696)***
Nix Check Cashing Service, Manhattan Beach *Also called Kinecta Alternative Fin* ***(G-9720)***
Nixon Inc (PA)......760 944-0900
701 S Coast Highway 101 Encinitas (92024) ***(G-8100)***
Nixon Peabody LLP......415 984-8200
1 Embarcadero Ctr # 1800 San Francisco (94111) ***(G-23470)***
Nixon Peabody LLP......213 629-6000
555 W 5th St Fl 30 Los Angeles (90013) ***(G-23471)***
Nixon Watches, Encinitas *Also called Nixon Inc* ***(G-8100)***
Nl Services, La Mirada *Also called Nittany Lion Landscaping Inc* ***(G-924)***
NLc Enterprises Incorporated......562 693-3590
15710 Leffingwell Rd Whittier (90604) ***(G-17361)***
Nliven, San Diego *Also called Defenseweb Technologies Inc* ***(G-16353)***
Nlsi, Moreno Valley *Also called National Lgal Studies Inst Inc* ***(G-17348)***
Nlyte Software Americas Ltd (HQ)......650 561-8200
2800 Campus Dr Ste 135 San Mateo (94403) ***(G-15334)***
Nmc Group Inc......909 451-2290
2755 Thompson Creek Rd Pomona (91767) ***(G-7943)***
Nmi Holdings Inc......855 530-6642
2100 Powell St Fl 12th Emeryville (94608) ***(G-10496)***
Nmms Twin Peaks LLC......818 710-6100
5850 Canoga Ave Ste 650 Woodland Hills (91367) ***(G-11709)***
Nmn Constr Solana Generating......714 389-2104
3002 Dow Ave Ste 526 Tustin (92780) ***(G-1620)***
NMN Construction Inc......707 763-6981
1077 Lakeville St Petaluma (94952) ***(G-3301)***
Nms Data Inc......949 472-2700
23172 Plaza Pointe Dr # 205 Laguna Hills (92653) ***(G-28002)***
Nms Management Inc......619 425-0440
155 W 35th St Ste A National City (91950) ***(G-14370)***
Nms Properties Inc......310 475-7600
1430 5th St Ste 101 Santa Monica (90401) ***(G-11710)***
NMWD, Novato *Also called North Marin Water District* ***(G-6382)***
Nna Insurance Services, Chatsworth *Also called Nna Services LLC* ***(G-10811)***
Nna Services, Chatsworth *Also called National Notary Association* ***(G-25147)***
Nna Services LLC (PA)......818 739-4071
9350 De Soto Ave Chatsworth (91311) ***(G-10811)***
Nnj Services Inc......858 550-7900
9610 Waples St San Diego (92121) ***(G-11711)***
Nnncc Ranch......559 626-4890
7602 Monson Ave Orange Cove (93646) ***(G-17362)***
Nnr Global Logistics USA Inc......310 357-2100
21023 Main St Ste D Carson (90745) ***(G-5134)***
No Barriers......707 451-1947
479 Mason St Ste 325 Vacaville (95688) ***(G-24104)***
No More Dirt Inc......415 821-6757
1699 Valencia St San Francisco (94110) ***(G-7973)***
No Ordinary Moments Inc......714 848-3800
16742 Gothard St Ste 115 Huntington Beach (92647) ***(G-22513)***
No Shnacks Inc......909 293-8747
7480 Harvard Ct Fontana (92336) ***(G-27143)***
Noah Concrete Corporation......408 842-7211
5900 Rossi Ln Gilroy (95020) ***(G-3302)***
Nob Hill Properties Inc......415 474-5400
1075 California St San Francisco (94108) ***(G-13023)***
Noble Aew Vineyard Creek LLC......707 284-1234
170 Railroad St Santa Rosa (95401) ***(G-13024)***
Noble Americas Enrgy Solutions, San Diego *Also called Noble Amrcas Enrgy Sltions LLC* ***(G-6290)***
Noble Amrcas Enrgy Sltions LLC (HQ)......877 273-6772
401 W A St Ste 500 San Diego (92101) ***(G-6290)***
Noble Energy, Seal Beach *Also called Samedan Oil Corporation* ***(G-1050)***
Noble Rents Inc......855 767-4424
8314 Slauson Ave Pico Rivera (90660) ***(G-14491)***
Noble Tower Preservation LP......510 444-5228
1515 Lakeside Dr Oakland (94612) ***(G-11712)***
Noble/Utah Long Beach LLC......562 436-3000
333 E Ocean Blvd Long Beach (90802) ***(G-13025)***
Noblesse Oblige Inc......760 353-3336
2015 Silsbee Rd El Centro (92243) ***(G-498)***
Nohl Ranch Inn, Anaheim *Also called Leisure Care LLC* ***(G-24709)***
Noiro West LLC......619 819-6620
701 A St San Diego (92101) ***(G-13026)***
Nolan Hamerly Etienne & Hoss, Salinas *Also called Gold Valley Properties* ***(G-23277)***
Nolte Associates, Sacramento *Also called Nv5 Inc* ***(G-25994)***
Nolte, George S & Associates, San Diego *Also called Nv5 Inc* ***(G-25995)***
Nominum Inc (PA)......650 381-6000
800 Bridge Pkwy Ste 100 Redwood City (94065) ***(G-15335)***
Nomura Securities Intl Inc......415 445-3831
425 California St # 2600 San Francisco (94104) ***(G-10065)***
Nongshim America Inc (HQ)......909 481-3698
12155 6th St Rancho Cucamonga (91730) ***(G-8506)***
Nor Thowds, Alhambra *Also called Pacific Snow Valley Resort LLC* ***(G-13062)***
Nor-Cal Beverage Co Inc (PA)......916 372-0600
2150 Stone Blvd West Sacramento (95691) ***(G-9077)***
Nor-Cal Beverage Co Inc......714 526-8600
1226 N Olive St Anaheim (92801) ***(G-17363)***
Nor-Cal Medical Temps, Belvedere Tiburon *Also called Pharmacy Temps Inc* ***(G-14923)***
Nor-Cal Moving Services (PA)......510 371-4942
3129 Corporate Pl Hayward (94545) ***(G-4366)***
Nor-Cal Moving Services......408 954-1175
560 E Trimble Rd San Jose (95131) ***(G-4367)***
Nor-Cal Pipeline Services......530 673-3886
5050 Bus Center Dr 200 Fairfield (94534) ***(G-17992)***

Nor-Cal Produce Inc....916 373-0830
2995 Oates St West Sacramento (95691) *(G-8755)*
Nora Lighting Inc....800 686-6672
6505 Gayhart St Commerce (90040) *(G-7460)*
Noralco Inc....209 551-4545
20001 Mchenry Ave Escalon (95320) *(G-570)*
Norcal Ambulance Services, Oakland *Also called North Star Emergency Svcs Inc (G-3822)*
Norcal Beverage Co, Anaheim *Also called Nor-Cal Beverage Co Inc (G-17363)*
Norcal Care Centers Inc....925 757-8787
1210 A St Antioch (94509) *(G-21328)*
Norcal Gold Inc....916 984-8778
2340 E Bidwell St Folsom (95630) *(G-11713)*
Norcal Inc....714 224-3949
1400 Moonstone Brea (92821) *(G-3067)*
Norcal Mutual Insurance Co (PA)....415 397-9703
560 Davis St Fl 2 San Francisco (94111) *(G-10812)*
Norcal Painters Inc....415 566-6800
60 29th St 241 San Francisco (94110) *(G-2470)*
Norco Auto Wash, Fountain Valley *Also called Norco Hills Car Wash (G-17857)*
Norco Delivery Service Inc....818 558-4810
3082 N Lima St Burbank (91504) *(G-17364)*
Norco Fire Department....951 737-8097
3902 Hillside Ave Norco (92860) *(G-10558)*
Norco Hills Car Wash....951 279-4398
18020 Magnolia St Fountain Valley (92708) *(G-17857)*
Norco Ranch Inc (HQ)....951 737-6735
12005 Cabernet Dr Fontana (92337) *(G-447)*
Norco Ranch Inc., Fontana *Also called Norco Ranch Inc (G-447)*
Nordic Industries Inc....530 742-7124
1437 Furneaux Rd Olivehurst (95961) *(G-2070)*
Nordic Security Services, Newport Beach *Also called Dansk Enterprises Inc (G-16622)*
Nordman Cormany Hair & Compton....805 485-1000
1000 Town Center Dr Fl 6 Oxnard (93036) *(G-23472)*
Nordstrom, South Gate *Also called Rick Studer (G-4252)*
Nordstrom Inc....909 390-1040
1600 S Milliken Ave Ontario (91761) *(G-4605)*
Nordstrom Inc....510 794-5440
37599 Filbert St Newark (94560) *(G-4606)*
Noritsu America Corporation (HQ)....714 521-9040
6900 Noritsu Ave Buena Park (90620) *(G-7037)*
Noritz America Corporation (HQ)....714 433-2905
11160 Grace Ave Fountain Valley (92708) *(G-7744)*
Norland Group....408 855-8255
3350 Scott Blvd Ste 6502 Santa Clara (95054) *(G-16439)*
Norlyn Builders Newport Beach, Newport Beach *Also called Leisure Care Inc (G-11155)*
Norman Charter, Santa Fe Springs *Also called Norman International Inc (G-6876)*
Norman Industrial Mtls Inc (PA)....818 729-3333
8300 San Fernando Rd Sun Valley (91352) *(G-7386)*
Norman Industrial Mtls Inc....858 277-8200
7550 Ronson Rd San Diego (92111) *(G-7387)*
Norman International Inc....562 946-0420
12301 Hawkins St Santa Fe Springs (90670) *(G-6876)*
Norman S Wright Mech Eqp Corp (PA)....415 467-7600
99 S Hill Dr Ste A Brisbane (94005) *(G-7745)*
Normand/Wlshire Rtrment Ht Inc....818 373-5429
6700 Sepulveda Blvd Van Nuys (91411) *(G-11174)*
Normandie Casino & Showroom, Gardena *Also called Normandie Club LP (G-19251)*
Normandie Club LP....310 352-3486
1045 W Rosecrans Ave Gardena (90247) *(G-19251)*
Normandin Auto Brokers....408 266-2824
900 Cptl Expy Aut Mall San Jose (95136) *(G-6692)*
Normandin Chrysler Jeep, San Jose *Also called Normandins (G-17807)*
Normandins....877 330-0391
900 Cptl Expy Aut Mall San Jose (95136) *(G-17807)*
Normans Nursery Inc (PA)....626 285-9795
8665 Duarte Rd San Gabriel (91775) *(G-9205)*
Normans Nursery Inc....209 887-2033
6250 N Escalon Bellota Rd Linden (95236) *(G-9206)*
Norogachi Construction Inc/CA....916 236-4201
600 Industrial Dr Ste 100 Galt (95632) *(G-2936)*
Norrise Institute of Training....510 229-6545
5938 Clement Ave San Pablo (94806) *(G-24105)*
Norse Corp....650 513-2881
104 La Mesa Dr Portola Valley (94028) *(G-16905)*
Norse Dairy Systems, Los Angeles *Also called Interbake Foods LLC (G-8854)*
Nortech Waste LLC....916 645-5230
3033 Fiddyment Rd Roseville (95747) *(G-6509)*
North Amercn Science Assoc Inc....949 951-3110
9 Morgan Irvine (92618) *(G-26879)*
North America Marine Serveyers, Fremont *Also called American Dept of Inspections (G-16986)*
North American Acceptance Corp....714 868-3195
3191 Red Hill Ave Ste 100 Costa Mesa (92626) *(G-9760)*
North American Cinemas Inc....707 571-1412
409 Aviation Blvd Santa Rosa (95403) *(G-18339)*
North American Health Care....530 662-9193
625 Cottonwood St Woodland (95695) *(G-27144)*
North American Health Care Inc (PA)....949 240-2423
32836 Pacific Coast Hwy Dana Point (92629) *(G-27145)*
North American Med MGT Cal Inc (HQ)....909 605-8012
3281 E Guasti Rd Fl 7 Ontario (91761) *(G-27146)*
North American Pet Products, Corona *Also called Pet Partners Inc (G-9292)*
North American Security Inc....310 630-4840
550 E Carson St P Carson (90745) *(G-16746)*
North American Studio Alliance, Belmont *Also called Namasta Inc (G-19009)*
North American Title Co Inc....925 399-3000
6612 Owens Dr 100 Pleasanton (94588) *(G-10532)*
North American Van Lines, Garden Grove *Also called South Coast Logistics (G-4376)*
North American Van Lines, Santa Clara *Also called Moving Solutions Inc (G-4364)*
North Amrcn SEC Invstgtons Inc....323 634-1911
550 E Carson Plaza Dr Carson (90746) *(G-16747)*
North Area Cmmnty Mntl Hlth CN, Sacramento *Also called Terkensha Associates Inc (G-24248)*
North Bay Construction Inc....707 283-0093
431 Payran St Petaluma (94952) *(G-1835)*
North Bay Construction Inc....707 836-8500
930 Shiloh Rd Bldg 46 Windsor (95492) *(G-3303)*
North Bay Developmental (PA)....707 256-1224
10 Executive Ct Ste A NAPA (94558) *(G-24370)*
North Bay Distribution Inc....707 450-1219
2029 E Monte Vista Ave Vacaville (95688) *(G-8354)*
North Bay Distribution Inc (PA)....707 452-9984
2050 Cessna Dr Vacaville (95688) *(G-8355)*
North Bay Drywall & Plst Inc....707 763-6819
715 Southpoint Blvd Ste B Petaluma (94954) *(G-2937)*
North Bay Eye Assoc A Med Corp....707 206-0849
50 Professional Center Dr # 210 Rohnert Park (94928) *(G-19776)*
North Bay Eye Assoc Med Group, Rohnert Park *Also called North Bay Eye Assoc A Med Corp (G-19776)*
North Bay Pool and Spa, Monrovia *Also called Vivopools LLC (G-17599)*
North Bay Regional Center, NAPA *Also called North Bay Developmental (G-24370)*
North Brook Nursing and Rehab, Willits *Also called Ensign Willits LLC (G-21212)*
North Coast Fabricators, Arcata *Also called Aquatic Desigining Inc (G-1400)*
North Coast Home Care Inc....760 260-8700
5845 Avenida Encinas S129 Carlsbad (92008) *(G-22514)*
North Coast Presbyterian Ch....760 753-2535
1831 S El Camino Real Encinitas (92024) *(G-24486)*
North Coast Surgery Center....760 940-0997
3903 Waring Rd Oceanside (92056) *(G-22781)*
North Counties Drywall Inc....707 996-0198
20563 Broadway Sonoma (95476) *(G-2938)*
North County Health Prj Inc (PA)....760 736-6755
150 Valpreda Rd Frnt San Marcos (92069) *(G-19777)*
North County Serenity Hse Inc (PA)....760 233-4533
240 S Hickory St Ste 210 Escondido (92025) *(G-24747)*
North County Services, San Marcos *Also called North County Health Prj Inc (G-19777)*
North County Transit District (PA)....760 966-6500
810 Mission Ave Oceanside (92054) *(G-3683)*
North Federal, Portola Valley *Also called Norse Corp (G-16905)*
North Hollywood Medical Offs, North Hollywood *Also called Kaiser Foundation Hospitals (G-19629)*
North Island Credit Union, San Diego *Also called North Island Financial Cr Un (G-9674)*
North Island Financial Cr Un (PA)....619 656-6525
5898 Copley Dr Ste 100 San Diego (92111) *(G-9674)*
North Island Hispanic Assn....619 545-6156
1878 Port Albans Chula Vista (91913) *(G-25561)*
North La County Regional Ctr (PA)....818 778-1900
15400 Sherman Way Ste 170 Van Nuys (91406) *(G-28003)*
North La County Regional Ctr....661 945-6761
43210 Gingham Ave Ste 6 Lancaster (93535) *(G-28004)*
North Main Branch, Salinas *Also called Mufg Union Bank Na (G-9409)*
North Marin Water District (PA)....415 897-4133
999 Rush Creek Pl Novato (94945) *(G-6382)*
North Modesto Kiwanis Club, Modesto *Also called Kiwanis International Inc (G-25276)*
North Orange Cnty Fmly Y M C A, Fullerton *Also called YMCA of North Orange County (G-25413)*
North Orange Coast Pntg Inc....951 279-2694
3969 Sierra Ave Norco (92860) *(G-2471)*
North Orange County Svc Ctr, Fullerton *Also called Southern California Edison Co (G-6220)*
North Pt Hlth Wellness Ctr LLC....559 320-2200
668 E Bullard Ave Fresno (93710) *(G-20808)*
North Ranch Country Club....818 889-3531
4761 Valley Spring Dr Westlake Village (91362) *(G-19015)*
North Ridge Country Club....916 967-5716
7600 Madison Ave Fair Oaks (95628) *(G-19016)*
North River Ranch LLC....714 556-6244
3601 W Pendleton Ave Santa Ana (92704) *(G-124)*
North Shore Greenhouses Inc....760 397-0400
82900 Johnson St Thermal (92274) *(G-339)*
North Shore Investment Inc....707 464-6151
1280 Marshall St Crescent City (95531) *(G-20809)*
North Shore Living Herbs, Thermal *Also called North Shore Greenhouses Inc (G-339)*
North Sonoma County Hosp Dst....707 431-6500
1375 University St Healdsburg (95448) *(G-21760)*
North Star Building Maint Inc....805 518-0417
2828 Cochran St Ste 214 Simi Valley (93065) *(G-14371)*
North Star Emergency Svcs Inc....510 452-3400
2537 Willow St Oakland (94607) *(G-3822)*
North Star Video Duplicators, Ventura *Also called Northstar Duplicators Inc (G-18240)*
North State Elec Contrs Inc....916 572-0571
11415 Sunrise Gold Cir # 1 Rancho Cordova (95742) *(G-2668)*
North State Imaging, Chico *Also called North State Radiology (G-19778)*
North State Radiology....530 898-0504
1702 Esplanade Chico (95926) *(G-19778)*
North State Security Inc....530 243-0295
1242 Oregon St Redding (96001) *(G-16748)*
North Valley Construction Inc....925 373-1246
4010 Raymond Rd Livermore (94551) *(G-3558)*
North Valley Nursing Center, Tujunga *Also called Sun Mar Management Services (G-27238)*
North Valley Occupational Ctr, Mission Hills *Also called Los Angeles Unified School Dst (G-24360)*
North West Learning Center....559 228-3057
3542 W Gettysburg Ave Fresno (93722) *(G-24487)*

A
L
P
H
A
B
E
T
I
C

Northbay Healthcare Corp (PA) 707 646-5000
1200 B Gale Wilson Blvd Fairfield (94533) *(G-21761)*
Northbay Healthcare Group (PA) 707 646-5000
1200 B Gale Wilson Blvd Fairfield (94533) *(G-21762)*
Northbay Healthcare System, Fairfield *Also called Northbay Healthcare Corp (G-21761)*
NORTHBAY MEDICAL CENTER, Fairfield *Also called Northbay Healthcare Group (G-21762)*
Northbound LLC 408 245-6500
2870 Zanker Rd Ste 210 San Jose (95134) *(G-27570)*
Northcoast Childrens Services 530 629-2283
730 Hwy 96 Willow Creek (95573) *(G-24106)*
Northcountry Clinic 707 822-2481
785 18th St Arcata (95521) *(G-19779)*
Northeast Protective Svcs Inc 800 577-0899
16040 Peppertree Ln La Mirada (90638) *(G-16749)*
Northeast Valley Health Corp 818 340-3570
7107 Remmet Ave Canoga Park (91303) *(G-23007)*
Northeast Valley Health Corp 661 673-8888
26974 Rainbow Glen Dr Canyon Country (91351) *(G-23008)*
Northeast Valley Health Corp 818 432-4400
7223 Fair Ave Sun Valley (91352) *(G-23009)*
Northeast Valley Health Corp (PA) 818 898-1388
1172 N Maclay Ave San Fernando (91340) *(G-24107)*
Northeast Valley Health Corp 818 365-8086
1600 San Fernando Rd San Fernando (91340) *(G-19780)*
Northeast Valley Health Corp 818 896-0531
12756 Van Nuys Blvd Pacoima (91331) *(G-19781)*
Northeastern Rur Hlth Clinics (PA) 530 251-5000
1850 Spring Ridge Dr Susanville (96130) *(G-19782)*
Northern CA Cngrgtnl Rtmt 831 624-1281
8545 Carmel Valley Rd Carmel (93923) *(G-21329)*
Northern CA Retiredd Ofcrs 707 432-1200
2600 Estates Dr Fairfield (94533) *(G-24748)*
Northern Cal Rehabilitation, Redding *Also called Ocadian Care Centers LLC (G-20818)*
Northern Cal Ret Clks-Emp Fund 925 746-7530
190 N Wiget Ln Ste 110 Walnut Creek (94598) *(G-12196)*
Northern California Cardiology (PA) 916 733-1788
5301 F St Ste 117 Sacramento (95819) *(G-19783)*
Northern California Hlth Care 530 223-2332
16201 Plateau Cir Redding (96001) *(G-22515)*
Northern California Inalliance (PA) 916 381-1300
6950 21st Ave Sacramento (95820) *(G-24371)*
Northern California Institute 415 750-6954
4150 Clement St San Francisco (94121) *(G-24949)*
Northern California Power Agcy (PA) 916 781-3636
651 Commerce Dr Roseville (95678) *(G-6152)*
Northern California Power Agcy 707 987-2381
12000 Ridge Rd Middletown (95461) *(G-6153)*
Northern California Presbyteri 415 464-1767
501 Via Casitas Ofc Greenbrae (94904) *(G-21330)*
Northern California Presbyteri 415 673-2352
1400 Geary Blvd San Francisco (94109) *(G-11175)*
Northern California Presbyteri 415 922-9700
1400 Geary Blvd San Francisco (94109) *(G-20810)*
Northern California Region, San Mateo *Also called Securitas SEC Svcs USA Inc (G-16919)*
Northern California Region, Stockton *Also called Securitas SEC Svcs USA Inc (G-16786)*
Northern California Region, Fresno *Also called Securitas SEC Svcs USA Inc (G-16788)*
Northern California Region, Redding *Also called Securitas SEC Svcs USA Inc (G-16791)*
Northern California Region, Petaluma *Also called Securitas SEC Svcs USA Inc (G-16796)*
Northern California Region, Eureka *Also called Securitas SEC Svcs USA Inc (G-16798)*
Northern California Region, Palm Desert *Also called Securitas SEC Svcs USA Inc (G-16801)*
Northern California Region, Salinas *Also called Securitas SEC Svcs USA Inc (G-16802)*
Northern California Region, Oakland *Also called Securitas SEC Svcs USA Inc (G-16803)*
Northern California Regional, Sacramento *Also called Granite Construction Company (G-2054)*
Northern California Rehab 530 246-9000
2801 Eureka Way Redding (96001) *(G-21763)*
Northern Cnstr & Operations, Escondido *Also called San Diego Gas & Electric Co (G-6307)*
Northern Division, Pittsburg *Also called Arb Inc (G-4524)*
Northern Hydro, Big Creek *Also called Southern California Edison Co (G-6212)*
Northern Inyo Cty Hospital Dst 760 873-5811
150 Pioneer Ln Bishop (93514) *(G-21764)*
Northern Inyo Hospital, Bishop *Also called Northern Inyo Cty Hospital Dst (G-21764)*
Northern Mono Chamber Commerce 530 208-6078
115281 Us Highway 395 Topaz (96133) *(G-25096)*
Northern Queen Inc 530 265-4492
400 Railroad Ave Nevada City (95959) *(G-13027)*
Northern Queen Inn, Nevada City *Also called Northern Queen Inc (G-13027)*
Northern Reg. Sub Base, Bakersfield *Also called Southern California Gas Co (G-6263)*
Northern Rfrigerated Trnsp Inc (PA) 209 664-3800
2700 W Main St Turlock (95380) *(G-4235)*
Northern Rfrigerated Trnsp Inc 559 241-7350
3261 N Marks Ave Fresno (93722) *(G-4236)*
Northern Sheets LLC 916 437-2800
4841 Urbani Ave Ste D McClellan (95652) *(G-17365)*
Northern Valley Catholic Socia 530 241-0552
2400 Washington Ave Redding (96001) *(G-24108)*
Northern Vly Indian Hlth Inc 530 896-9400
845 W East Ave Chico (95926) *(G-20267)*
Northern Vly Indian Hlth Inc 530 529-2567
2500 Main St Red Bluff (96080) *(G-20268)*
Northgate Branch, San Rafael *Also called Bank of Marin (G-9471)*
Northgate Care Center 415 479-1230
40 Professional Ctr Pkwy San Rafael (94903) *(G-21331)*
Northgate Convalescent Hosp, San Rafael *Also called Independent Quality Care Inc (G-21273)*
Northgate Gonzalez Inc 714 957-2529
1120 S Bricol St Santa Ana (92704) *(G-17366)*
Northgate Market 11, Santa Ana *Also called Northgate Gonzalez Inc (G-17366)*
Northgate Ter Cmnty Partner LP 510 465-9346
550 24th St Oakland (94612) *(G-11714)*
Northgate Terrace Apts 530 671-2026
1290 Northgate Dr Apt 48 Yuba City (95991) *(G-11176)*
Northland Control Systems Inc (PA) 510 403-7600
44150 S Grimmer Blvd Fremont (94538) *(G-2669)*
Northpoint Day Treatment Sch, Northridge *Also called Child and Family Guidance Ctr (G-22682)*
Northpointe Apartment Homes, Long Beach *Also called Parwood Preservation LP (G-11741)*
Northpointe Healthcare Centre, Fresno *Also called North Pt Hlth Wellness Ctr LLC (G-20808)*
Northridge 07 A LLC 818 505-6777
12411 Ventura Blvd Studio City (91604) *(G-11025)*
Northridge Fashion Center, Northridge *Also called Lansing Mall Ltd Partnership (G-11011)*
Northridge Fashion Center 10, Northridge *Also called Pacific Theaters (G-18290)*
Northridge Nursing Center, Reseda *Also called Longwood Management Corp (G-21718)*
Northrop Grmmn Spce & Mssn Sys (HQ) 703 280-2900
6377 San Ignacio Ave San Jose (95119) *(G-16012)*
Northrop Grmmn Spce & Mssn Sys 858 592-3000
1 Rancho Carmel Dr San Diego (92128) *(G-26576)*
Northrop Grmmn Spce & Mssn Sys 310 764-3000
1762 Glenn Curtiss St Carson (90746) *(G-15336)*
Northrop Grmmn Spce & Mssn Sys 855 737-8364
1 Space Park Blvd Redondo Beach (90278) *(G-28005)*
Northrop Grmmn Spce & Mssn Sys 909 382-6800
862 E Hospitality Ln San Bernardino (92408) *(G-16013)*
Northrop Grmmn Spce & Mssn Sys 858 514-9000
9326 Spectrum Center Blvd San Diego (92123) *(G-15337)*
Northrop Grmmn Spce & Mssn Sys 909 382-6800
862 E Hospitality Ln San Bernardino (92408) *(G-26577)*
Northrop Grumman Enterprise Mg 760 380-4268
806 S Loop Rd Fort Irwin (92310) *(G-27147)*
Northrop Grumman Federal Cr Un (PA) 310 808-4000
879 W 190th St Ste 800 Gardena (90248) *(G-9617)*
Northrop Grumman Systems Corp 310 556-4911
6411 W Imperial Hwy Los Angeles (90045) *(G-17367)*
Northrop Grumman Systems Corp 858 514-0400
9326 Spectrum Center Blvd San Diego (92123) *(G-15338)*
Northrop Grumman Systems Corp 650 604-6056
P.O. Box 81 Moffett Field (94035) *(G-16014)*
Northrop Grumman Systems Corp 805 987-9739
5161 Verdugo Way Camarillo (93012) *(G-16015)*
Northrop Grumman Systems Corp 650 604-5381
243 Ames Res Ctr Bldg N Mountain View (94035) *(G-15339)*
Northstar, Irvine *Also called Custom Business Solutions Inc (G-7051)*
Northstar Contg Group Inc 714 639-7600
13320 Cambridge St Santa Fe Springs (90670) *(G-3461)*
Northstar Contg Group Inc (HQ) 510 491-1300
31500 Hayman St Hayward (94544) *(G-3559)*
Northstar Dem & Remediation LP (HQ) 714 672-3500
404 N Berry St Brea (92821) *(G-3462)*
Northstar Duplicators Inc 805 984-3888
5198 Colt St Ste B Ventura (93003) *(G-18240)*
Northstar Media Packg Svcs LLC 805 650-0990
5776 Lindero Canyon Rd D Westlake Village (91362) *(G-18241)*
Northstar Senior Living Inc 530 242-8300
2334 Washington Ave Ste A Redding (96001) *(G-27148)*
Northstar-At-Tahoe, Truckee *Also called Trimont Land Company (G-11883)*
Northstate Plastering Inc 707 207-0950
2210 Cordelia Rd Fairfield (94534) *(G-3304)*
Northwest Circuits Corp 619 661-1701
8660 Avenida Costa Blanca San Diego (92154) *(G-25991)*
Northwest Correctnl Med Grp 831 649-8994
2511 Garden Rd Ste A160 Monterey (93940) *(G-22782)*
Northwest Excavating Inc 818 349-5861
18201 Napa St Northridge (91325) *(G-14492)*
Northwest Hotel Corporation (PA) 714 776-6120
1380 S Harbor Blvd Anaheim (92802) *(G-13028)*
Northwest Insurance Agency 707 573-1300
418 B St Ste 100 Santa Rosa (95401) *(G-10813)*
Northwest Landscape Maint Co 408 298-6489
283 Kinney Dr San Jose (95112) *(G-925)*
Northwest Medical Group Inc 559 271-6302
7355 N Palm Ave Ste 100 Fresno (93711) *(G-19784)*
Northwest Medical Pharmacy, Fresno *Also called Northwest Physicians Med Group (G-19785)*
Northwest Physicians Med Group 559 271-6370
7355 N Palm Ave Ste 100 Fresno (93711) *(G-19785)*
Northwest Staffing Resources 916 960-2668
701 University Ave # 120 Sacramento (95825) *(G-14708)*
Northwest Vntr Partners VII LP 650 321-8000
525 University Ave # 800 Palo Alto (94301) *(G-12330)*
Northwestern Bell Telephones, City of Industry *Also called Unical Enterprises Inc (G-7207)*
Northwestern Mutl Fincl Netwrk (PA) 619 234-3111
4225 Executive Sq La Jolla (92037) *(G-10066)*
Norton Simon Museum 626 449-6840
411 W Colorado Blvd Pasadena (91105) *(G-25033)*
Norwalk Community Hospital 562 863-4763
13222 Bloomfield Ave Norwalk (90650) *(G-21765)*
Norwalk Marriott Hotel, Paramount *Also called Goldenpark LLC (G-12669)*
Norwalk Meadows Nursing Ctr LP 562 864-2541
10625 Leffingwell Rd Norwalk (90650) *(G-20811)*
Norwalk Medical Offices, Norwalk *Also called Kaiser Foundation Hospitals (G-19631)*
Norwalk Transit System 562 929-5550
12650 Imperial Hwy Norwalk (90650) *(G-3684)*
Norwest Venture Partners VI LP 650 289-2243
525 University Ave # 800 Palo Alto (94301) *(G-12331)*

ALPHABETIC

ALPHABETIC SECTION

Nossaman LLP (PA)...........................213 612-7800
  777 S Figueroa St # 3400 Los Angeles (90017) *(G-23473)*
Nossaman LLP...........................415 398-3600
  50 California St Ste 3400 San Francisco (94111) *(G-23474)*
Nossaman LLP...........................949 833-7800
  18101 Von Karman Ave # 1800 Irvine (92612) *(G-23475)*
Notellage Corporation...........................323 257-8151
  4681 Eagle Rock Blvd Los Angeles (90041) *(G-21332)*
Notthoff Engineering, Huntington Beach Also called AMG Huntington Beach LLC *(G-25656)*
Nourmand & Associates...........................310 274-4000
  421 N Beverly Dr Ste 200 Beverly Hills (90210) *(G-11715)*
Nova Brink A Joint Venture...........................707 265-1100
  185 Devlin Rd NAPA (94558) *(G-2071)*
Nova Commercial Company Inc (PA)...........................510 728-7000
  24683 Oneil Ave Hayward (94544) *(G-14372)*
Nova Container Freight Station, Carson Also called H Rauvel Inc *(G-4566)*
Nova Development, Calabasas Also called Avanquest North America Inc *(G-15044)*
Nova Group Inc...........................707 257-3200
  185 Devlin Rd NAPA (94558) *(G-1972)*
Nova Group Inc...........................707 265-1100
  185 Devlin Rd NAPA (94558) *(G-2072)*
Nova Grp Inc -Obayashi Corp A...........................707 265-1116
  185 Devlin Rd NAPA (94558) *(G-1973)*
Nova Lane Constructors A JV...........................707 265-1100
  185 Devlin Rd NAPA (94558) *(G-2073)*
Nova Ortho-Med Inc...........................310 352-3600
  1470 Beachey Pl Carson (90746) *(G-7286)*
Nova Plumbing Inc...........................714 556-6682
  3111 W Central Ave Santa Ana (92704) *(G-2305)*
Nova-Cpf Inc...........................707 257-3200
  7411 Napa Vallejo Hwy NAPA (94558) *(G-1974)*
Novaeon Inc...........................858 503-1588
  9665 Chesapeake Dr # 430 San Diego (92123) *(G-24109)*
Novariant Inc (HQ)...........................510 933-4800
  46610 Landing Pkwy Fremont (94538) *(G-25992)*
Novastar Post Inc...........................323 467-5020
  23466 Hatteras St Woodland Hills (91367) *(G-18122)*
Novatime Technology Inc (PA)...........................909 895-8100
  1440 Bridgegate Dr # 300 Diamond Bar (91765) *(G-14709)*
Novato Community Hospital, Novato Also called Sutter West Bay Hospitals *(G-21956)*
Novato Fire Protection Dist...........................415 878-2690
  95 Rowland Way Novato (94945) *(G-17368)*
Novato Healthcare Center LLC...........................415 897-6161
  1565 Hill Rd Novato (94947) *(G-20812)*
Novato Medical Offices, Novato Also called Kaiser Foundation Hospitals *(G-21660)*
Novitex Entp Solutions Inc...........................415 528-2960
  71 Park Ln Brisbane (94005) *(G-14123)*
Novo Construction Inc (PA)...........................650 701-1500
  1460 Obrien Dr Menlo Park (94025) *(G-1621)*
Novo Construction Inc...........................650 701-1500
  608 Folsom St San Francisco (94107) *(G-1622)*
Novo Engineering Inc (PA)...........................760 598-6686
  1350 Specialty Dr Ste A Vista (92081) *(G-25993)*
Novo Nordisk Biotech, Davis Also called Novozymes Inc *(G-26697)*
Novogradac and Co LLP...........................415 356-8000
  246 1st St Ste 500 San Francisco (94105) *(G-26413)*
Novozymes Inc (HQ)...........................530 757-8100
  1445 Drew Ave Davis (95618) *(G-26697)*
Novozymes Us Inc...........................530 757-8100
  1445 Drew Ave Davis (95618) *(G-12079)*
Now Medical Services Inc...........................310 479-4520
  1641 1/2 Westwood Blvd Los Angeles (90024) *(G-14918)*
Nowcom Corporation...........................323 938-6449
  4751 Wilshire Blvd # 205 Los Angeles (90010) *(G-16440)*
Nowher Partners LLC...........................818 857-3566
  26767 Agoura Rd Ste A Calabasas (91302) *(G-8894)*
Npario Inc...........................650 461-9696
  350 Cambridge Ave Ste 330 Palo Alto (94306) *(G-15340)*
Nph Medical Services...........................530 899-2255
  2639 Forest Ave Ste 110 Chico (95928) *(G-14710)*
Nphase LLC...........................312 577-1650
  6195 Lusk Blvd Ste 200 San Diego (92121) *(G-6085)*
Npl Anaheim Investments LLC...........................714 750-2010
  2010 S Harbor Blvd Anaheim (92802) *(G-13029)*
NPS Marketing...........................916 941-5510
  3381 Sage Rose Ln Placerville (95667) *(G-27571)*
Nr 2 Group Inc...........................626 251-6681
  1561 Chapin Unit C Baldwin Park (91706) *(G-4045)*
NRC Environmental Services Inc...........................562 432-1304
  3777 N Long Beach Blvd Long Beach (90807) *(G-6510)*
NRC Environmental Services Inc (HQ)...........................510 749-1390
  1605 Ferry Pt Ste 200 Alameda (94501) *(G-6632)*
Nrea-TRC 711 LLC...........................213 486-6500
  700 S Flower St Ste 2600 Los Angeles (90017) *(G-13030)*
NRG California South LP...........................909 899-7241
  8996 Etiwanda Ave Rancho Cucamonga (91739) *(G-6154)*
NRG El Segundo Operations Inc...........................310 615-6344
  301 Vista Del Mar El Segundo (90245) *(G-6155)*
NRG Energy Inc...........................415 255-8105
  455 Golden Gate Ave San Francisco (94102) *(G-6156)*
NRG Energy Inc...........................913 689-3904
  3201 Wilbur Ave Antioch (94509) *(G-6157)*
NRG Power Inc...........................714 424-6484
  3011 S Shannon St Santa Ana (92704) *(G-2670)*
Nrhc, Susanville Also called Northeastern Rur Hlth Clinics *(G-19782)*
Nri Distribution, Los Angeles Also called Nri Usa LLC *(G-5135)*
Nri Secure Technologies Ltd...........................949 537-2957
  26 Executive Park Ste 150 Irvine (92614) *(G-16441)*

Nri Usa LLC...........................323 345-6456
  13200 S Broadway Los Angeles (90061) *(G-5135)*
NRLL LLC...........................949 768-7777
  1 Mauchly Irvine (92618) *(G-12332)*
Nrp Holding Co Inc (PA)...........................949 583-1000
  1 Mauchly Irvine (92618) *(G-12080)*
Nrt, Concord Also called Goldman Avram *(G-27042)*
Nrt Commercial Utah LLC...........................626 449-5222
  42 S Pasadena Ave Pasadena (91105) *(G-11716)*
Nsbn LLP (PA)...........................310 273-2501
  1925 Century Park E Fl 16 Los Angeles (90067) *(G-26414)*
Nsg Technology Inc (HQ)...........................408 547-8700
  1705 Junction Ct Ste 200 San Jose (95112) *(G-17938)*
Nsw Real Estate Holdings LLC...........................415 467-7600
  99 S Hill Dr Ste A Brisbane (94005) *(G-17369)*
Nt Sunset Inc...........................510 420-3772
  2220 Livingston St # 201 Oakland (94606) *(G-26791)*
Nta America, Gardena Also called Nippon Travel Agency Amer Inc *(G-4969)*
Nta Pacific, Gardena Also called Nippon Travel Agency PCF Inc *(G-4970)*
Ntent Inc...........................760 930-7600
  1808 Aston Ave Ste 170 Carlsbad (92008) *(G-15341)*
Nth Connect Telecom Inc...........................408 922-0800
  2371 Bering Dr San Jose (95131) *(G-17370)*
Nth Degree Inc...........................714 734-4155
  27092 Burbank Foothill Ranch (92610) *(G-17371)*
NTN Buzztime Inc (PA)...........................760 438-7400
  2231 Rutherford Rd # 200 Carlsbad (92008) *(G-5903)*
Ntrepid Corporation...........................800 921-2414
  10201 Wtridge Cir Ste 300 San Diego (92121) *(G-27149)*
Ntrust Infotech Inc...........................562 207-1600
  230 Commerce Ste 180 Irvine (92602) *(G-15780)*
Ntrust Infotech Private Ltd...........................562 207-1610
  2700 N Main St Ste 300 Santa Ana (92705) *(G-15342)*
NTS It Care Inc...........................408 480-4083
  1605 S Main St Ste 125 Milpitas (95035) *(G-15343)*
NTS Technical Systems, Fullerton Also called National Technical Systems Inc *(G-26876)*
NTS Technical Systems, Los Angeles Also called National Technical Systems Inc *(G-26878)*
NTS Technical Systems (PA)...........................818 591-0776
  24007 Ventura Blvd # 200 Calabasas (91302) *(G-26880)*
Ntt Data Inc...........................213 228-2500
  1000 Corporate Center Dr # 140 Monterey Park (91754) *(G-16016)*
Ntt Data Inc...........................310 301-7835
  4553 Glencoe Ave Ste 350 Marina Del Rey (90292) *(G-16017)*
Nty Franchise Company LLC...........................714 964-3488
  18645 Brookhurst St Fountain Valley (92708) *(G-246)*
Nu Flow America Inc (PA)...........................619 275-9130
  7710 Kenamar Ct San Diego (92121) *(G-2306)*
Nu Horizons Electronics Corp...........................408 946-4154
  890 N Mccarthy Blvd San Jose (95131) *(G-7614)*
Nu Image Inc (PA)...........................310 388-6900
  6423 Wilshire Blvd Los Angeles (90048) *(G-18288)*
Nu Image Holdings, Los Angeles Also called Nu Image Inc *(G-18288)*
Nuance Communications Inc...........................408 245-5358
  1198 E Arques Ave Sunnyvale (94085) *(G-15781)*
Nuance Communications Inc...........................650 847-0000
  1005 Hamilton Ct Menlo Park (94025) *(G-15344)*
Nuerology Dept, Santa Rosa Also called Kaiser Permanente *(G-19682)*
Nuevo Amnecer Latino Chld Svcs (PA)...........................323 720-9951
  5400 Pomona Blvd Los Angeles (90022) *(G-24749)*
Nugget Market Inc...........................530 662-5479
  157 Main St Woodland (95695) *(G-4607)*
Nugget Mkts Pharmacy, Woodland Also called Nugget Market Inc *(G-4607)*
Nulaid Foods Inc (PA)...........................209 599-2121
  200 W 5th St Ripon (95366) *(G-8602)*
Numero Uno Market...........................323 231-9403
  4373 S Vermont Ave Los Angeles (90037) *(G-12333)*
Numero Uno Market...........................213 381-1734
  9127 S Figueroa St Los Angeles (90003) *(G-12334)*
Numonyx Inc...........................916 458-3888
  2235 Iron Point Rd Folsom (95630) *(G-7169)*
Nuna Health, San Francisco Also called Nuna Incorporated *(G-15345)*
Nuna Incorporated...........................650 390-7745
  650 Townsend St Ste 425 San Francisco (94103) *(G-15345)*
Nunes Company Inc (PA)...........................831 751-7510
  925 Johnson Ave Salinas (93901) *(G-8756)*
Nunes Cooling Inc...........................831 751-7510
  925 Johnson Ave Salinas (93901) *(G-571)*
Nurlogic Design Inc (HQ)...........................858 455-7570
  5580 Morehouse Dr San Diego (92121) *(G-16018)*
Nurse Providers Inc...........................650 992-8559
  355 Gellert Blvd Ste 110 Daly City (94015) *(G-14711)*
Nursecore Management Svcs...........................805 938-7660
  1010 S Broadway Santa Maria (93454) *(G-24750)*
Nursefinders Inc (PA)...........................800 445-0459
  12400 High Bluff Dr San Diego (92130) *(G-14919)*
Nursefinders LLC...........................909 890-2286
  1832 Commercenter Cir B San Bernardino (92408) *(G-14712)*
Nursefinders LLC (HQ)...........................858 314-7427
  12400 High Bluff Dr San Diego (92130) *(G-14713)*
Nurses & Prof Hlth Care, Chico Also called Nph Medical Services *(G-14710)*
Nurses Tuch HM Hlth Prvder Inc...........................818 500-4877
  135 S Jackson St Ste 100 Glendale (91205) *(G-22516)*
Nursing & Rehab At Home...........................650 286-4272
  1660 S Amphlett Blvd # 112 San Mateo (94402) *(G-22517)*
Nursing Registry, Daly City Also called Nurse Providers Inc *(G-14711)*
Nushake Inc...........................209 239-8616
  319 S Parallel Ave Ripon (95366) *(G-3194)*
Nushake Roofing, Ripon Also called Nushake Inc *(G-3194)*

Nutanix Inc (PA)....408 216-8360
1740 Tech Dr Ste 150 San Jose (95110) *(G-16019)*
Nutec Enterprises Inc....661 287-3200
24200 Magic Mountain Pkwy # 105 Valencia (91355) *(G-11717)*
Nutra-Figs, Fresno *Also called San Joaquin Figs Inc (G-582)*
Nutricion Fundamental Inc....916 922-0150
811 Grand Ave Sacramento (95838) *(G-20334)*
Nutririon Services, Santa Ana *Also called Santa Ana Unified School Dst (G-23052)*
Nutrition Service Division, Long Beach *Also called Women Infant & Children (G-24293)*
Nuvi Global....559 306-2646
518 W Henderson Ave Apt 9 Porterville (93257) *(G-7287)*
Nuvision Fincl Federal Cr Un (PA)....714 375-8000
7812 Edinger Ave Ste 100 Huntington Beach (92647) *(G-9675)*
Nuvo TV, Glendale *Also called Sitv Inc (G-5910)*
Nuvoton Technology Corp Amer....408 544-1718
2727 N 1st St San Jose (95134) *(G-7615)*
Nuworld Business Systems, Cerritos *Also called Young Systems Corporation (G-7079)*
Nv5 Inc (HQ)....916 641-9100
2525 Natomas Park Dr # 300 Sacramento (95833) *(G-25994)*
Nv5 Inc....858 385-0500
15092 Avenue Of Science # 200 San Diego (92128) *(G-25995)*
Nv5 Inc....916 641-9100
2495 Natomas Park Dr # 300 Sacramento (95833) *(G-25996)*
Nvision Laser Eye Centers....949 951-1457
24022 Calle De La Plata Laguna Hills (92653) *(G-20335)*
NW Entertainment Inc (PA)....818 295-5000
2660 W Olive Ave Burbank (91505) *(G-18123)*
NW Manor Community Partners LP....714 662-5565
17782 Sky Park Cir Irvine (92614) *(G-11990)*
NW Packaging LLC (PA)....909 706-3627
1201 E Lexington Ave Pomona (91766) *(G-9283)*
Nwp Services Corporation (HQ)....949 253-2500
535 Anton Blvd Ste 1100 Costa Mesa (92626) *(G-15782)*
NY Transport Inc....909 355-9832
14998 Washington Dr Fontana (92335) *(G-4237)*
Nygard Inc....310 776-8900
14401 S San Pedro St Gardena (90248) *(G-8406)*
Nylon Molding Corporation, Pomona *Also called Nmc Group Inc (G-7943)*
O & R, Glendale *Also called Rev Enterprises (G-16772)*
O & S Holdings LLC....310 207-8600
11611 San Vicente Blvd Los Angeles (90049) *(G-11991)*
O A Outfitting Inc....707 498-2917
6602 Wofford Heights Blvd Bayside (95524) *(G-19252)*
O C Jones & Sons Inc (PA)....510 526-3424
1520 4th St Berkeley (94710) *(G-1836)*
O C Jones & Sons Inc....510 663-6911
155 Filbert St Ste 209 Oakland (94607) *(G-28006)*
O C McDonald Co Inc....408 295-2182
1150 W San Carlos St San Jose (95126) *(G-2307)*
O C P T, Orange *Also called Orange Children & Parents (G-24492)*
O C Sailing Club Inc....510 843-4200
1 Spinnaker Way Berkeley (94710) *(G-19253)*
O D U, Camarillo *Also called Odu-Usa Inc (G-7616)*
O E C, Santa Maria *Also called Oilfield Envmtl Compliance Inc (G-26881)*
O E C Shipg Los Angeles Inc....562 926-7186
13100 Alondra Blvd # 100 Cerritos (90703) *(G-5136)*
O H I, Irvine *Also called European Hotl Invstrs of CA (G-11127)*
O P I Products Inc (HQ)....818 759-8688
13034 Saticoy St North Hollywood (91605) *(G-7974)*
O'Connor Wound Care Clinic, San Jose *Also called OConnor Hospital (G-21767)*
O'Neill Vintners & Distillers, Larkspur *Also called ONeill Beverages Co LLC (G-174)*
O.H. Kruse Grain and Milling, Goshen *Also called Western Milling LLC (G-9155)*
O1 Communications Inc....888 444-1111
4359 Town Center Blvd # 217 El Dorado Hills (95762) *(G-5671)*
O2 Micro Inc....408 987-5920
3118 Patrick Henry Dr Santa Clara (95054) *(G-16020)*
O2a, Paso Robles *Also called Omega 2 Alpha Services LLC (G-27572)*
Oak Creek LP....909 860-5440
21725 Gateway Center Dr Diamond Bar (91765) *(G-13031)*
Oak Creek Apartments....650 327-1600
1600 Sand Hill Rd Palo Alto (94304) *(G-11177)*
Oak Creek Golf Club, Irvine *Also called Irvine Company LLC (G-25546)*
Oak Distribution, Los Angeles *Also called Oak Paper Products Co Inc (G-8200)*
Oak Grove Center, Murrieta *Also called Oak Grove Inst Foundation Inc (G-19786)*
Oak Grove Inst Foundation Inc (PA)....951 677-5599
24275 Jefferson Ave Murrieta (92562) *(G-19786)*
Oak Harbor Freight Lines Inc....510 608-8841
6700 Smith Ave Newark (94560) *(G-4238)*
Oak Harbor Freight Lines Inc....916 371-3960
832 F St West Sacramento (95605) *(G-4239)*
Oak Hill Capital Partners LP....650 234-0500
2775 Sand Hill Rd Ste 220 Menlo Park (94025) *(G-22518)*
Oak Knoll Convalescent Center....707 778-8686
450 Hayes Ln Petaluma (94952) *(G-20813)*
Oak Paper Products Co Inc (PA)....323 268-0507
3686 E Olympic Blvd Los Angeles (90023) *(G-8200)*
Oak Ridge Winery LLC....209 369-4768
6100 E Hwy 12 Victor Rd Lodi (95240) *(G-173)*
Oak River Rehabilitation....530 365-0025
3300 Franklin St Anderson (96007) *(G-20814)*
Oak Springs Nursery Inc....818 367-5832
13761 Eldridge Ave Sylmar (91342) *(G-6650)*
Oak Street Physical Therapy, Lomita *Also called Kaiser Foundation Hospitals (G-22752)*
Oak Valley Golf Club, Beaumont *Also called California Oak Valley Golf (G-18909)*
Oak Valley Hospital District (HQ)....209 847-3011
350 S Oak Ave Oakdale (95361) *(G-21766)*
Oak View Snoma Hlls Apartments, Rohnert Park *Also called Kisco Senior Living LLC (G-27100)*
Oakdale Golf and Country Club....209 847-2984
243 N Stearns Rd Oakdale (95361) *(G-19017)*
Oakdale Heights MGT Corp (PA)....530 222-6797
250 Hemsted Dr Ste 100 Redding (96002) *(G-11178)*
Oakdale Heights Senior Living....661 663-9671
3209 Brookside Dr Bakersfield (93311) *(G-20815)*
Oakdale Irrgtion Dst Fing Corp....209 847-0341
1205 E F St Oakdale (95361) *(G-6383)*
Oakdale Memorial Park (PA)....626 335-0281
1401 S Grand Ave Glendora (91740) *(G-12034)*
Oakhurst Country Club, Clayton *Also called American Golf Corporation (G-18864)*
Oakhurst Healthcare, Oakhurst *Also called Oakhurst Skilled Nursing Welln (G-20816)*
Oakhurst Industries Inc....510 265-2400
3265 Investment Blvd Hayward (94545) *(G-8507)*
Oakhurst Skilled Nursing Welln....559 683-2244
40131 Highway 49 Oakhurst (93644) *(G-20816)*
Oakland Athletics, Oakland *Also called Athletics Investment Group LLC (G-18537)*
Oakland District Office, Oakland *Also called State Compensation Insur Fund (G-10463)*
Oakland Healthcare & Wellness....323 330-6572
3030 Webster St Oakland (94609) *(G-20817)*
Oakland Ice Center, Oakland *Also called City of Oakland (G-19178)*
Oakland Medical Center, Oakland *Also called Kaiser Foundation Hospitals (G-19585)*
Oakland Mrtime Spport Svcs Inc....510 868-1005
11 Burma Rd Oakland (94607) *(G-4771)*
Oakland Museum of California....510 318-8519
1000 Oak St Oakland (94607) *(G-25034)*
Oakland Pallet Company Inc....707 746-0100
4245 Industrial Way Benicia (94510) *(G-6939)*
Oakland Pallet Company Inc (PA)....510 278-1291
2500 Grant Ave San Lorenzo (94580) *(G-6940)*
Oakland Private Industry Counc....510 768-4400
1212 Broadway Ste 300 Oakland (94612) *(G-24372)*
Oakland Public Education Fund....510 221-6968
1000 Broadway Ste 300 Oakland (94607) *(G-12161)*
Oakland Shops/Annex, Oakland *Also called San Francisco Bay Area Rapid (G-3706)*
Oakland Unified School Dst....510 535-2717
955 High St Oakland (94601) *(G-14373)*
Oakland V A Outpatient Clinic, Oakland *Also called Veterans Health Administration (G-20202)*
Oakland Zoo In Knowland Park, Oakland *Also called East Bay Btncal Zoological Soc (G-19201)*
Oakmont Country Club....818 542-4260
3100 Country Club Dr Glendale (91208) *(G-19018)*
Oakmont Gardens, Santa Rosa *Also called Retirement Project-Oakmont (G-11196)*
Oakmont Golf Club Inc (PA)....707 538-2454
7025 Oakmont Dr Santa Rosa (95409) *(G-18766)*
Oakridge Care Center, Oakland *Also called A T Associates Inc (G-21122)*
Oakridge Landscape Inc (PA)....661 295-7228
28064 Avenue Stanford K Valencia (91355) *(G-481)*
Oaks Diagnostics Inc (PA)....310 855-0035
6310 San Vicente Blvd Los Angeles (90048) *(G-19787)*
Oaks, The, Petaluma *Also called Oak Knoll Convalescent Center (G-20813)*
Oaktree Capital Management LP (HQ)....213 830-6300
333 S Grand Ave Ste 2800 Los Angeles (90071) *(G-10167)*
Oaktree Holdings Inc....213 830-6300
333 S Grand Ave Ste 2800 Los Angeles (90071) *(G-12335)*
Oaktree Real Estate Opportunit....213 830-6300
333 S Grand Ave Fl 28 Los Angeles (90071) *(G-11718)*
Oaktree Strategic Income LLC....213 830-6300
333 S Grand Ave Fl 28 Los Angeles (90071) *(G-17372)*
Oakview Convalescent Hospital....818 352-4426
9166 Tujunga Canyon Blvd Tujunga (91042) *(G-21333)*
Oakville Produce Partners LLC....415 647-2991
453 Valley Dr Brisbane (94005) *(G-8757)*
Oakwood Apartments, Woodland Hills *Also called R & B Realty Group (G-11192)*
Oakwood Apts, Marina Del Rey *Also called R & B Realty Group (G-11193)*
Oakwood Athletic Club, Lafayette *Also called Clubsport San Ramon LLC (G-18621)*
Oakwood Corporate Housing Inc (PA)....310 478-1021
2222 Corinth Ave Los Angeles (90064) *(G-13453)*
Oakwood Garden Apts, Los Angeles *Also called R & B Realty Group (G-11191)*
Oakwood Gardens Care Center, Fresno *Also called Lily Holdings LLC (G-20736)*
Oakwood Village, Auburn *Also called Horizon West Inc (G-26858)*
Oakwood Worldwide, Los Angeles *Also called R & B Realty Group LP (G-11782)*
Oasis Brands Inc....540 658-2830
6700 Artesia Blvd Buena Park (90620) *(G-8201)*
Oasis Country Club, Palm Desert *Also called Oasis Palm Dsert Hmowners Assn (G-19019)*
Oasis IPA, Palm Springs *Also called Desert Medical Group Inc (G-19491)*
Oasis Mental Health Trtmnt Ctr....760 863-8609
47915 Oasis St Indio (92201) *(G-22085)*
Oasis Palm Dsert Hmowners Assn....760 345-5661
42330 Casbah Way Palm Desert (92211) *(G-19019)*
Oasis Repower LLC....888 903-6926
15445 Innovation Dr San Diego (92128) *(G-6158)*
Oasis Technology Inc....805 445-4833
601 E Daily Dr Ste 226 Camarillo (93010) *(G-16021)*
Oates Buzz Enterprises....916 381-3600
555 Capitol Mall Fl 9 Sacramento (95814) *(G-11026)*
Oatey Supply Chain Svcs Inc....510 797-4677
6600 Smith Ave Newark (94560) *(G-7726)*
Oberman Tivoli Miller Pickert....310 440-9600
500 S Sepulveda Blvd # 500 Los Angeles (90049) *(G-16022)*
Obey Clothing, Irvine *Also called One 3 Two Inc (G-8407)*
Objective Systems Integrators (HQ)....916 467-1500
35 Iron Point Cir Ste 250 Folsom (95630) *(G-15346)*

ALPHABETIC

Oblong Industries Inc (PA)....213 683-8863
923 E 3rd St Ste 111 Los Angeles (90013) *(G-15347)*
OBryant Electric Inc....818 407-1986
9314 Eton Ave Chatsworth (91311) *(G-2671)*
Obscura Digital Incorporated....415 227-9979
729 Tennessee St San Francisco (94107) *(G-13975)*
Observatories of The Carnegie, Pasadena *Also called Carnegie Institution Wash (G-26746)*
OC Communications Inc....916 686-3700
2204 Kausen Dr Ste 100 Elk Grove (95758) *(G-6010)*
Oc Engineering....714 667-3212
300 N Flower St Santa Ana (92703) *(G-25997)*
Oc IV A California LP....925 734-5800
4511 Willow Rd Ste 1 Pleasanton (94588) *(G-17808)*
Oc Lighthouse Construction....949 797-0151
1901 Carnegie Ave Ste 1j Santa Ana (92705) *(G-1328)*
OC Special Events SEC Inc....714 541-4111
1232 Village Way Ste K Santa Ana (92705) *(G-16750)*
Oc Waste & Recycling, Santa Ana *Also called County of Orange (G-6470)*
Ocadian Care Centers LLC....530 246-9000
2801 Eureka Way Redding (96001) *(G-20818)*
Ocadian Care Centers LLC....925 939-5820
1449 Ygnacio Valley Rd Walnut Creek (94598) *(G-20819)*
Ocadian Care Centers LLC....510 832-3222
475 29th St Oakland (94609) *(G-20820)*
Ocadian Care Centers LLC....415 461-9700
1220 S Eliseo Dr Greenbrae (94904) *(G-20821)*
Ocadian Care Centers LLC....415 499-1000
1550 Silveira Pkwy San Rafael (94903) *(G-20822)*
Ocadian Care Centers LLC....408 295-2665
75 N 13th St San Jose (95112) *(G-20823)*
Ocb Restaurant Company LLC....559 271-1927
3617 W Shaw Ave Fresno (93711) *(G-13781)*
Ocb Restaurant Company LLC....310 216-9208
8629 S Sepulveda Blvd # 310 Los Angeles (90045) *(G-13782)*
Ocb Riverside, Riverside *Also called American Reprographics Co LLC (G-14105)*
Occidental Area Health Center, Guerneville *Also called West County Health Centers Inc (G-20234)*
Occidental Cnty Sanitation Dst....707 547-1900
404 Aviation Blvd Santa Rosa (95403) *(G-6413)*
Occupational Health Services, Mountain View *Also called El Camino Hospital (G-22140)*
Occupational Medicine, Salinas *Also called Natividad Hospital Inc (G-21759)*
Occupational Therapy Training, Torrance *Also called Special Service For Groups Inc (G-24981)*
Occupnl Urgnt Care Hlth Syst....916 374-4600
750 Riverpoint Dr West Sacramento (95605) *(G-23010)*
Ocean Avenue LLC....310 576-7777
101 Wilshire Blvd Santa Monica (90401) *(G-13032)*
Ocean Blue Envmtl Svcs Inc (PA)....562 624-4120
925 W Esther St Long Beach (90813) *(G-4046)*
Ocean Breeze International....805 684-1747
3910 Via Real Carpinteria (93013) *(G-306)*
Ocean Breeze Manufacturing....323 586-8760
1961 Hawkins Cir Los Angeles (90001) *(G-17373)*
Ocean Colony Partners LLC....650 726-5764
2450 Cabrillo Hwy S # 200 Half Moon Bay (94019) *(G-11992)*
Ocean Dream, Commerce *Also called Malibu Design Group (G-8398)*
Ocean Fresh Fish Seafood Mktg, Los Angeles *Also called Ocean Group Inc (G-8640)*
Ocean Group Inc (PA)....213 622-3677
1100 S Santa Fe Ave Los Angeles (90021) *(G-8640)*
Ocean Holiday LP....760 231-7000
1401 Carmelo Dr Oceanside (92054) *(G-13033)*
Ocean House Retirement Inn, Santa Monica *Also called MBK Real Estate Ltd A Califor (G-11166)*
Ocean Knight Shipping Inc....310 885-3388
19516 S Susana Rd # 101 Compton (90221) *(G-5137)*
Ocean Links Corporation....650 726-1800
2 Miramontes Point Rd Half Moon Bay (94019) *(G-18767)*
Ocean Mist Farming Company (PA)....831 633-2144
10855 Ocean Mist Pkwy A Castroville (95012) *(G-84)*
Ocean Mist Farms, Castroville *Also called California Artichoke & Vegetab (G-517)*
Ocean Mist Farms, Castroville *Also called Ocean Mist Farming Company (G-84)*
Ocean Park Community Center....310 828-6717
1447 16th St Santa Monica (90404) *(G-28007)*
Ocean Park Community Center....310 450-0650
1751 Cloverfield Blvd Santa Monica (90404) *(G-24110)*
Ocean Park Health Center....415 753-8100
1351 24th Ave San Francisco (94122) *(G-19788)*
Ocean Park Hotels Inc....831 373-6141
1000 Aguajito Rd Monterey (93940) *(G-13034)*
Ocean Park Hotels Inc....661 284-3200
27710 The Old Rd Valencia (91355) *(G-13035)*
Ocean Park Hotels Mmex LLC....661 284-2101
27513 Wayne Mills Pl Valencia (91355) *(G-13036)*
Ocean Queen 87 Inc....323 585-1200
4511 Everett Ave Vernon (90058) *(G-8641)*
Ocean Service, San Diego *Also called Overseas Service Corporation (G-28152)*
Ocean View Flowers LLC....800 736-5608
1105 Union Sugar Ave Lompoc (93436) *(G-307)*
Ocean View Manor LP....805 781-3088
3533 Empleo St San Luis Obispo (93401) *(G-11260)*
Ocean View Manor Apartments, San Luis Obispo *Also called Ocean View Manor LP (G-11260)*
Oceans Eleven Casino....760 439-6988
121 Brooks St Oceanside (92054) *(G-19254)*
Oceanside Hlthcare Stffing Inc....213 503-5649
2216 El Camino Rela 211 Santa Clarita (91350) *(G-23011)*
Oceanside Laundry LLC....831 722-4358
675 Beach Dr Watsonville (95076) *(G-13576)*
Oceanside Lifeguards....760 435-4500
300 N Coast Hwy Oceanside (92054) *(G-19255)*
Oceanview Produce Company....805 488-6401
3000 E Hueneme Rd Oxnard (93033) *(G-85)*
Ocj Group, The, Woodland Hills *Also called Brenner Info Tech Staffing Inc (G-14616)*
Ocm Real Estate Opportunities....213 830-6300
333 S Grand Ave Fl 28 Los Angeles (90071) *(G-12336)*
Ocmban, Irvine *Also called Ocmbc Inc (G-9877)*
Ocmbc Inc....714 479-0999
19000 Macarthur Blvd # 200 Irvine (92612) *(G-9877)*
OConnell Landscape Maint Inc....760 630-4963
4600 Leisure Village Way Oceanside (92056) *(G-926)*
OConner Woods A California....209 956-3400
3400 Wagner Heights Rd Stockton (95209) *(G-11179)*
OConnor Hospital (PA)....408 947-2500
2105 Forest Ave San Jose (95128) *(G-21767)*
OConnor Hospital....408 947-2990
2105 Forest Ave San Jose (95128) *(G-19789)*
Oconnor Hospital Radiology....408 947-2992
2105 Forest Ave San Jose (95128) *(G-19790)*
Oconnor Imaging Medical Group, San Jose *Also called Oconnor Hospital Radiology (G-19790)*
OConnor Woods Housing Corp....209 956-3400
3400 Wagner Heights Rd Stockton (95209) *(G-11180)*
Octa, Orange *Also called Orange County Trnsp Auth (G-3688)*
Odc....415 863-9834
3153 17th St San Francisco (94110) *(G-18364)*
Odd Fellow-Rebekah Chld HM Cal (PA)....408 846-2100
290 I O O F Ave Gilroy (95020) *(G-24751)*
Odd Fellow-Rebekah Chld HM Cal....831 775-0348
1260 S Main St Ste 101 Salinas (93901) *(G-24752)*
Odd Fellows Home California....408 741-7100
14500 Fruitvale Ave # 3000 Saratoga (95070) *(G-24753)*
Oddworld Inhabitants Inc....805 503-3000
869 Monterey St San Luis Obispo (93401) *(G-15783)*
Odesk Corporation....650 853-4100
441 Logue Ave Mountain View (94043) *(G-14714)*
Odona Central Security Inc....323 728-8818
71 N San Gabriel Blvd Pasadena (91107) *(G-16751)*
ODonnell & Shaeffer LLP....213 627-3769
550 S Hope St Ste 2000 Los Angeles (90071) *(G-23476)*
Ods Technologies LP....310 242-9400
6701 Center Dr W Ste 160 Los Angeles (90045) *(G-5904)*
Odu-Usa Inc (HQ)....805 484-0540
4010 Adolfo Rd Camarillo (93012) *(G-7616)*
Odyssey Environmental Services, Lodi *Also called Odyssey Landscaping Co Inc (G-3305)*
Odyssey Healthcare Inc....714 245-7420
525 Cabrillo Park Dr # 150 Santa Ana (92701) *(G-20824)*
Odyssey Healthcare Inc....408 626-4868
1500 E Hamilton Ave # 212 Campbell (95008) *(G-20825)*
Odyssey Healthcare Inc....858 565-2499
9444 Balboa Ave Ste 290 San Diego (92123) *(G-22519)*
Odyssey Healthcare Inc....760 674-0066
74350 Country Club Dr Palm Desert (92260) *(G-21334)*
Odyssey Healthcare Inc....760 241-7044
17290 Jasmine St Ste 104 Victorville (92395) *(G-22520)*
Odyssey Healthcare Bakersfield, Bakersfield *Also called Kindred Healthcare Inc (G-22988)*
Odyssey Landscaping Co Inc....209 369-6197
5400 W Highway 12 Lodi (95242) *(G-3305)*
Odyssey Telecorp Inc....650 470-7550
550 Lytton Ave Fl 2 Palo Alto (94301) *(G-5672)*
Oec Group, Cerritos *Also called O E C Shipg Los Angeles Inc (G-5136)*
Oel/Hhh Inc....818 246-6050
1833 Victory Blvd Glendale (91201) *(G-26243)*
Oerlikon USA Inc....949 863-1857
18881 Von Karman Ave # 200 Irvine (92612) *(G-16166)*
OES Equipment LLC (PA)....510 284-1900
37421 Centralmont Pl Fremont (94536) *(G-14562)*
Office Cmnty Inv Infrstructure, San Francisco *Also called Successor To San Francisco (G-28063)*
Office Depot Inc....916 927-0171
4720 Northgate Blvd Sacramento (95834) *(G-8172)*
Office Movers Inc....408 254-5010
4020 Nelson Ave Ste 200 Concord (94520) *(G-4368)*
Office of Child Development....310 842-4230
10800 Farragut Dr Culver City (90230) *(G-24488)*
Office of Inspector General, Los Angeles *Also called Los Angeles County MTA (G-3670)*
Office of Nutritional Services, Visalia *Also called Visalia Unified School Dst (G-24279)*
Office of Special Services....510 524-9559
8633 Arbor Dr El Cerrito (94530) *(G-17374)*
Office of The Legislative Coun....916 341-8708
1100 J St Fl 7 Sacramento (95814) *(G-5406)*
Office of The Legislative Coun....916 445-3796
925 L St Ste 900 Sacramento (95814) *(G-28008)*
Office On Aging, ADRC Of River, Riverside *Also called County of Riverside (G-23888)*
Office Star Products, Ontario *Also called Blumenthal Distributing Inc (G-6807)*
Office Team, Menlo Park *Also called Robert Half International Inc (G-14768)*
Office Team, San Ramon *Also called Robert Half International Inc (G-14773)*
OfficeMax Incorporated....951 485-9353
7300 Chapman Ave Garden Grove (92841) *(G-4608)*
Officeteam, Irvine *Also called Robert Half International Inc (G-14769)*
Officeworks Inc....951 784-2534
11801 Pierce St Fl 2 Riverside (92505) *(G-14715)*
Official Police Garage Assn of....805 624-0572
67 W Boulder Creek Rd Simi Valley (93065) *(G-4767)*
Offshore Crane & Service Co (PA)....805 648-3348
1375 N Olive St Ste A Ventura (93001) *(G-14493)*

ALPHABETIC

Offshore Service Vessels LLC......619 237-1314
757 Emory St Pm565 Imperial Beach (91932) ***(G-4751)***
Ofi Markesa International, Vernon *Also called Orient Fisheries Inc **(G-8643)***
Ofjcc......650 223-8600
3921 Fabian Way Palo Alto (94303) ***(G-24111)***
Ogilvy & Mather Worldwide Inc......310 280-2200
2425 Olympic Blvd 2200w Santa Monica (90404) ***(G-13889)***
Ogilvy Pub Rltons Wrldwide Inc......916 231-7700
1530 J St Sacramento (95814) ***(G-27759)***
OGrady Paving Inc......650 966-1926
2513 Wyandotte St Mountain View (94043) ***(G-1837)***
OHagin Manufacturing LLC......707 872-3620
210 Classic Ct Ste 100 Rohnert Park (94928) ***(G-2308)***
OHagins Inc......707 303-3660
210 Classic Ct Ste 100 Rohnert Park (94928) ***(G-2309)***
Ohana Partners Inc (PA)......408 856-3232
454 S Abbott Ave Milpitas (95035) ***(G-14563)***
Ohanians Drywall Inc......559 277-2946
4655 W Jacquelyn Ave Fresno (93722) ***(G-2939)***
Ohi Resort Hotels LLC......714 867-5555
12021 Harbor Blvd Garden Grove (92840) ***(G-13037)***
Ohl, Redlands *Also called Geodis Logistics LLC **(G-4559)***
Oil Changers, Pleasanton *Also called Oc IV A California LP **(G-17808)***
Oil Well Service Company (PA)......562 612-0600
10840 Norwalk Blvd Santa Fe Springs (90670) ***(G-1090)***
Oilfield Electric & Motor, Ventura *Also called Oilfield Electric Company **(G-2672)***
Oilfield Electric Company......805 648-3131
1801 N Ventura Ave Ventura (93001) ***(G-2672)***
Oilfield Envmtl Compliance Inc......805 922-4772
307 Roemer Way Ste 300 Santa Maria (93454) ***(G-26881)***
Oj Insulation LP......408 842-6315
5820 Obata Way Unit B Gilroy (95020) ***(G-2940)***
Oj Insulation LP......760 839-3200
2061 Albergrov Ave Escondido (92029) ***(G-2941)***
Oj Insulation LP......760 200-4343
78 015 Wildcat Dr Ste 105 Palm Desert (92211) ***(G-2942)***
Oj Insulation LP (PA)......626 812-6070
600 S Vincent Ave Azusa (91702) ***(G-2943)***
Oj Insulation & Fireplaces, Escondido *Also called Oj Insulation LP **(G-2941)***
Ojai Ambulance Inc......805 653-9111
632 E Thompson Blvd Ventura (93001) ***(G-3823)***
Ojai Raptor Center......805 649-6884
370 Baldwin Rd Ojai (93023) ***(G-643)***
Ojai Valley Community Hospital......805 646-1401
1306 Maricopa Hwy Ojai (93023) ***(G-21768)***
Ojai Valley Inn & Spa, Ojai *Also called Ovis Llc **(G-13052)***
Ojai Valley Inn Golf Course......805 646-2420
905 Country Club Rd Ojai (93023) ***(G-13038)***
Ojai Valley Spa, Ojai *Also called Ojai Valley Inn Golf Course **(G-13038)***
OK Produce, Fresno *Also called Charlies Enterprises **(G-8704)***
Okabe International Inc (PA)......415 921-0808
1739 Buchanan St Ste B San Francisco (94115) ***(G-4996)***
Okta Inc (PA)......415 494-8029
301 Brannan St Fl 1 San Francisco (94107) ***(G-15348)***
Olam Americas Inc (HQ)......559 447-1390
25 Union Pl Ste 3 Fresno (93720) ***(G-572)***
Olam Spices & Vegetables Inc......408 846-3200
1350 Pacheco Pass Hwy Gilroy (95020) ***(G-8758)***
Old Dominion Freight Line Inc......323 725-3400
1225 Washington Blvd Montebello (90640) ***(G-4240)***
Old Fishermans Grotto......831 375-4604
39 Fishermans Wharf Monterey (93940) ***(G-11993)***
Old Globe Theatre......619 234-5623
1363 Old Globe Way San Diego (92101) ***(G-18420)***
Old Republic Construction Prog......626 683-5200
225 S Lake Ave Ste 900 Pasadena (91101) ***(G-10814)***
Old Republic HM Protection Inc......925 866-1500
2 Annabel Ln Ste 112 San Ramon (94583) ***(G-10815)***
Old Republic Title Company......818 240-1936
101 N Brand Blvd Ste 1400 Glendale (91203) ***(G-10533)***
Old Republic Title Company......831 757-8051
584 S Main St Salinas (93901) ***(G-10534)***
Old Town Fmly Hospitality Corp......619 246-8010
4962 Concannon Ct San Diego (92130) ***(G-13039)***
Old Town Gallery of Fine Art, Auburn *Also called Auburn Old Town Gallery **(G-19145)***
Old Town Trlley Turs San Diego......619 298-8687
2115 Kurtz St San Diego (92110) ***(G-4997)***
Olde Thompson Inc......805 983-0388
3250 Camino Del Sol Oxnard (93030) ***(G-6877)***
Oldenkamp Trucking Inc (PA)......661 833-3400
13535 S Union Ave Bakersfield (93307) ***(G-4047)***
Older Adult Health Services, Long Beach *Also called Dignity Health **(G-23945)***
Older Adults Care Management (PA)......650 329-1411
881 Fremont Ave Ste A2 Los Altos (94024) ***(G-24112)***
Oldtimers Housing Dev Corp III......562 924-6509
18750 Clarkdale Ave Artesia (90701) ***(G-24113)***
Ole Health......707 254-1770
1100 Trancas St Ste 300 NAPA (94558) ***(G-19791)***
Oleander Holdings LLC......916 331-4590
5255 Hemlock St Sacramento (95841) ***(G-20826)***
Olen Commercial Realty Corp......949 644-6536
7 Corporate Plaza Dr Newport Beach (92660) ***(G-11027)***
Olen Companies, The, Newport Beach *Also called Olen Residential Realty Corp **(G-1329)***
Olen Residential Realty, Newport Beach *Also called Olen Commercial Realty Corp **(G-11027)***
Olen Residential Realty Corp (HQ)......949 644-6536
7 Corporate Plaza Dr Newport Beach (92660) ***(G-1329)***
Olive Crest......760 341-8507
73700 Dinah Shore Dr # 101 Palm Desert (92211) ***(G-24754)***
Olive Crest (PA)......714 543-5437
2130 E 4th St Ste 200 Santa Ana (92705) ***(G-24755)***
Olive Crest......562 216-8841
917 Pine Ave Long Beach (90813) ***(G-24756)***
Olive Crest Op, Long Beach *Also called Olive Crest **(G-24756)***
Olive Grove Retirement Resort......951 687-2241
7858 California Ave Riverside (92504) ***(G-11181)***
Olive Hill Greenhouses......760 728-4596
3508 Olive Hill Rd Fallbrook (92028) ***(G-308)***
Olive Knolls Christian School......661 393-3566
6201 Fruitvale Ave Bakersfield (93308) ***(G-24489)***
Olive Ridge Post Acute Care, Oroville *Also called Evergreen At Oroville LLC **(G-20557)***
Olive View-Ucla Medical Center (PA)......818 364-1555
14445 Olive View Dr Sylmar (91342) ***(G-19792)***
Olive View/Ucla Education &......818 364-3434
14445 Olive View Dr Sylmar (91342) ***(G-26792)***
Olive Vista, Center, Pomona *Also called Sunbridge Braswell Entps Inc **(G-20938)***
Olivenhain Municipal Water Dst......760 753-6466
1966 Olivenhain Rd Encinitas (92024) ***(G-6384)***
Oliver & Company Inc......510 412-9090
1300 S 51st St Richmond (94804) ***(G-1623)***
Olivermcmillan LLC (PA)......619 321-1111
733 8th Ave San Diego (92101) ***(G-11994)***
Olivet International Inc (PA)......951 681-8888
11015 Hopkins St Mira Loma (91752) ***(G-8131)***
Olivieri Enterprises LP......916 791-7857
210 Estates Dr Ste 200 Roseville (95678) ***(G-3068)***
Ols Hotels & Resorts LP......310 855-1115
733 W Knoll Dr West Hollywood (90069) ***(G-13040)***
Ols Hotels & Resorts LP......626 962-6000
14635 Bldwin Pk Towne Ctr Baldwin Park (91706) ***(G-13041)***
Olson & Assoc......714 878-6649
3448 Lupine Cir Ste 102 Costa Mesa (92626) ***(G-16442)***
Olson Company LLC (PA)......562 596-4770
3010 Old Ranch Pkwy # 100 Seal Beach (90740) ***(G-1227)***
Olson Company, The, Seal Beach *Also called Olson Urban Housing LLC **(G-11995)***
Olson Homes, Seal Beach *Also called Olson Company LLC **(G-1227)***
Olson Urban Housing LLC......562 596-4770
3010 Old Ranch Pkwy # 100 Seal Beach (90740) ***(G-11995)***
Oltmans Construction Co (PA)......562 948-4242
10005 Mission Mill Rd Whittier (90601) ***(G-1454)***
Oltmans Investment Company......562 948-4242
10005 Mission Mill Rd Whittier (90601) ***(G-11028)***
Oltmans Property Management, Whittier *Also called Oltmans Investment Company **(G-11028)***
Olvera, Robert MD, Costa Mesa *Also called St Jude Hospital Yorba Linda **(G-20061)***
Olympia Convalescent Hospital......213 487-3000
1100 S Alvarado St Los Angeles (90006) ***(G-21335)***
Olympia Health Care LLC......323 938-3161
5900 W Olympic Blvd Los Angeles (90036) ***(G-21769)***
Olympic Circle Sailing Club, Berkeley *Also called O C Sailing Club Inc **(G-19253)***
Olympic Club......415 676-1412
665 Sutter St San Francisco (94102) ***(G-19020)***
Olympic Club (PA)......415 345-5100
524 Post St San Francisco (94102) ***(G-25304)***
Olympic Club......415 404-4300
599 Skyline Dr Daly City (94015) ***(G-25305)***
Olympic Construction, Roseville *Also called Olivieri Enterprises LP **(G-3068)***
Olympic Frt & Vegatable Distr, Los Angeles *Also called Coast Citrus Distributors **(G-8708)***
Olympic Investors Ltd......925 322-8996
1908 Olympic Blvd Walnut Creek (94596) ***(G-19021)***
Olympic Security, Bellflower *Also called Advent Securities Investments **(G-9957)***
Olympus Adhc Inc......310 572-7272
11613 Washington Pl Los Angeles (90066) ***(G-24490)***
Olympus Adult Day Hlthcare Ctr, Los Angeles *Also called Olympus Adhc Inc **(G-24490)***
Olympus America Inc......949 466-3548
23342 Madero Mission Viejo (92691) ***(G-7288)***
Olympus America Inc......408 935-5000
2400 Ringwood Ave San Jose (95131) ***(G-7289)***
OLYMPUS AMERICA INC., Mission Viejo *Also called Olympus America Inc **(G-7288)***
Olympus Power LLC......661 393-6885
34759 Lencioni Ave Bakersfield (93308) ***(G-6159)***
Omega 2 Alpha Services LLC......805 610-2249
935 Riverside Ave Ste 23 Paso Robles (93446) ***(G-27572)***
Omega Insurance Services......714 973-0311
721 S Parker St Ste 300 Orange (92868) ***(G-10816)***
Omega Management Services, Corning *Also called Omega Waste Management Inc **(G-27573)***
Omega Moulding West LLC......323 261-3510
5500 Lindbergh Ln Bell (90201) ***(G-6878)***
Omega Security Services & Cons......818 831-1100
10611 Garden Grove Ave # 2 Northridge (91326) ***(G-16752)***
Omega Walnut Inc......530 865-0136
7233 County Road 24 Orland (95963) ***(G-24114)***
Omega Waste Management Inc......530 824-1890
957 Colusa St Corning (96021) ***(G-27573)***
Omega/Cinema Props Inc......323 466-8201
5857 Santa Monica Blvd Los Angeles (90038) ***(G-18242)***
OMelveny & Myers LLP (PA)......213 430-6000
400 S Hope St Fl 19 Los Angeles (90071) ***(G-23477)***
OMelveny & Myers LLP......949 760-9600
610 Nwport Ctr Dr Fl 17 Newport Beach (92660) ***(G-23478)***
OMelveny & Myers LLP......310 553-6700
1999 Avenue Of The Stars # 600 Los Angeles (90067) ***(G-23479)***
OMelveny & Myers LLP......650 473-2600
2765 Sand Hill Rd Menlo Park (94025) ***(G-23480)***
OMelveny & Myers LLP......415 984-8700
2 Embarcadero Ctr Fl 28 San Francisco (94111) ***(G-23481)***

ALPHABETIC

Omni Consulting Group LLP....................530 750-5199
3531 Mono Pl Ste 100 Davis (95618) ***(G-27574)***
Omni Family Health....................661 764-5211
277 E Front St Buttonwillow (93206) ***(G-23012)***
Omni Family Health (PA)....................661 459-1900
4900 California Ave 400b Bakersfield (93309) ***(G-19793)***
Omni Hotels Corporation....................760 568-2727
41000 Bob Hope Dr Rancho Mirage (92270) ***(G-13042)***
Omni Hotels Corporation....................619 231-6664
675 L St San Diego (92101) ***(G-13043)***
Omni Hotels Corporation....................415 677-9494
500 California St San Francisco (94104) ***(G-13044)***
Omni Hotels Corporation....................213 617-3300
251 S Olive St Fl 1 Los Angeles (90012) ***(G-13045)***
Omni Research Group, Davis *Also called Omni Consulting Group LLP* ***(G-27574)***
Omni Ventures Group Llc....................510 384-1033
300 Pasadena Ave South Pasadena (91030) ***(G-12081)***
Omni Womens Hlth Med Group Inc....................559 441-4271
2550 Merced St Fresno (93721) ***(G-19794)***
Omnia Italian Design Inc....................909 393-4400
4900 Edison Ave Chino (91710) ***(G-6827)***
Omnicare Inc....................510 293-9663
20967 Cabot Blvd Hayward (94545) ***(G-8287)***
Omnigen....................714 288-0077
1740 W Katella Ave Ste G Orange (92867) ***(G-1228)***
Omnikron Systems Inc....................818 591-7890
20920 Warner Center Ln A Woodland Hills (91367) ***(G-16443)***
Omninet Twin Towers Gp LLC....................310 300-4118
9420 Wilshire Blvd # 400 Beverly Hills (90212) ***(G-11719)***
Omninet Twin Towers LP....................310 300-4110
9420 Wilshire Blvd # 400 Beverly Hills (90212) ***(G-11720)***
Omniteam Inc....................562 923-9660
9300 Hall Rd Downey (90241) ***(G-7756)***
Omnitek Information Systems....................949 581-5895
24081 Lindley St Mission Viejo (92691) ***(G-15349)***
Omnitrans....................909 383-1680
234 S I St San Bernardino (92410) ***(G-24757)***
Omnitrans....................909 379-7100
4748 Arrow Hwy Montclair (91763) ***(G-3685)***
Omnitrans Access, San Bernardino *Also called Omnitrans* ***(G-24757)***
Omnitrol Networks Inc....................408 919-1100
4580 Auto Mall Pkwy # 121 Fremont (94538) ***(G-16023)***
Omniupdate Inc....................805 484-9400
1320 Flynn Rd Ste 100 Camarillo (93012) ***(G-15350)***
On Assignment Inc (PA)....................818 878-7900
26745 Malibu Hills Rd Calabasas (91301) ***(G-14920)***
On Call Consulting, Thousand Oaks *Also called Miramed Global Services Inc* ***(G-27991)***
On Call Employee Solutions Inc....................949 955-4994
895 Dove St Ste 300 Newport Beach (92660) ***(G-14921)***
On Central Realty Inc....................323 543-8500
1648 Colorado Blvd Los Angeles (90041) ***(G-11721)***
On Link Technologies Inc....................650 477-5000
2207 Bridgepointe Pkwy Foster City (94404) ***(G-17375)***
On Lok Inc....................415 292-8888
1333 Bush St San Francisco (94109) ***(G-19795)***
On Lok Life Ways, Fremont *Also called On Lok Senior Health Services* ***(G-10362)***
On Lok Lifeways, San Francisco *Also called On Lok Senior Health Services* ***(G-10361)***
On Lok Senior Health Services (PA)....................415 292-8888
1333 Bush St San Francisco (94109) ***(G-10361)***
On Lok Senior Health Services....................510 249-2700
159 Washington Blvd Fremont (94539) ***(G-10362)***
On The Move....................707 251-9432
780 Lincoln Ave NAPA (94558) ***(G-24950)***
On Trac Overhead Door Co Inc....................909 799-8555
1430 Richardson St San Bernardino (92408) ***(G-3069)***
On-Scene Security Services Inc....................661 263-2343
P.O. Box 800147 Santa Clarita (91380) ***(G-16753)***
On-Site Manager Inc (PA)....................866 266-7483
307 Orchard Cy Dr Ste 110 Campbell (95008) ***(G-17376)***
On-Time AC & Htg Inc (PA)....................925 444-4444
7020 Commerce Dr Ste C Pleasanton (94588) ***(G-2310)***
On24 Inc (PA)....................877 202-9599
201 3rd St Fl 3 San Francisco (94103) ***(G-5673)***
Ona, Irvine *Also called Canon Solutions America Inc* ***(G-7830)***
Oncor Insurance Services LLC....................916 932-3210
870 Glenn Dr Folsom (95630) ***(G-10817)***
One 3 Two Inc....................949 596-8400
17353 Derian Ave Irvine (92614) ***(G-8407)***
One California Plaza, Los Angeles *Also called Hill Farrer & Burrill* ***(G-23308)***
One Call Medical Inc....................818 346-8700
8501 Fllbrook Ave Ste 100 Canoga Park (91304) ***(G-27575)***
ONE EAPP, Oakland *Also called Center To Promote Healthcare A* ***(G-22914)***
One Embarcadero Center Venture....................415 772-0700
4 Embarcadero Ctr Ste 1 San Francisco (94111) ***(G-12263)***
One Generation (PA)....................818 708-6625
17400 Victory Blvd Van Nuys (91406) ***(G-24115)***
One K Studios LLC....................818 531-3800
3400 W Olive Ave Ste 300 Burbank (91505) ***(G-14157)***
One Legal Inc....................213 617-1212
350 S Figueroa St Ste 385 Los Angeles (90071) ***(G-17377)***
One Medical Group, San Francisco *Also called 1life Healthcare Inc* ***(G-22869)***
One Medical Group Inc (PA)....................415 578-3100
130 Sutter St Fl 2 San Francisco (94104) ***(G-19796)***
One Medical Group Inc....................415 529-4522
3885 24th St San Francisco (94114) ***(G-19797)***
One Medical Group Inc....................415 291-0480
130 Sutter St Fl 6 San Francisco (94104) ***(G-19798)***
One Nob Hill Associates LLC....................415 392-3434
999 California St San Francisco (94108) ***(G-13046)***

One Planet Ops Inc (PA)....................925 983-3400
12667 Alcosta Blvd # 200 San Ramon (94583) ***(G-13890)***
One Stop Program, Los Angeles *Also called Uaw-Lbor Emplyment Trning Corp* ***(G-14810)***
One Work Place, San Francisco *Also called One Workplace L Ferrari LLC* ***(G-27798)***
One Workplace L Ferrari, San Francisco *Also called One Workplace L Ferrari LLC* ***(G-6828)***
One Workplace L Ferrari LLC....................415 357-2200
475 Brannan St San Francisco (94107) ***(G-6828)***
One Workplace L Ferrari LLC....................415 357-2200
475 Brannan St Ste 210 San Francisco (94107) ***(G-27798)***
Onebill Software Inc....................844 462-7638
3080 Olcott St Ste D230 Santa Clara (95054) ***(G-15351)***
Onebody Inc....................510 285-2000
2000 Powell St Ste 555 Emeryville (94608) ***(G-22521)***
Onehealth Solutions Inc....................858 947-6333
420 Stevens Ave Ste 200 Solana Beach (92075) ***(G-16444)***
ONeil Data Systems LLC....................310 448-6400
12655 Beatrice St Los Angeles (90066) ***(G-7871)***
ONeill Beverages Co LLC (PA)....................844 825-6600
101 Larkspur Landing Cir Larkspur (94939) ***(G-174)***
Onelegacy (PA)....................213 625-0665
221 S Figueroa St Ste 500 Los Angeles (90012) ***(G-23013)***
Onesource Distributors LLC (HQ)....................760 966-4500
3951 Oceanic Dr Oceanside (92056) ***(G-7461)***
Onesource Distributors LLC....................714 523-1012
12101 Western Ave Garden Grove (92841) ***(G-7462)***
Oneunited Bank....................323 295-3381
3683 Crenshaw Blvd Los Angeles (90016) ***(G-9510)***
Oneunited Bank....................323 290-4848
3910 W Martin Luther King Los Angeles (90008) ***(G-9511)***
Onewest Bank NA....................562 433-0971
3500 E 7th St Long Beach (90804) ***(G-9577)***
Online Communications Inc....................916 652-7253
3291 Swetzer Rd Loomis (95650) ***(G-2673)***
Online Energy LLC....................510 583-0091
20885 Redwood Rd Unit 405 Castro Valley (94546) ***(G-7872)***
Online Energy Uv Systems, Castro Valley *Also called Online Energy LLC* ***(G-7872)***
Onrad Inc....................800 848-5876
1770 Iowa Ave Ste 280 Riverside (92507) ***(G-27150)***
Onrad Medical Group, Riverside *Also called Onrad Inc* ***(G-27150)***
Onsite Clims Apprisal Tech Inc....................805 474-0893
255 Piedra Springs Rd Arroyo Grande (93420) ***(G-10818)***
Onsite Consulting LLC....................323 401-3190
5042 Wilshire Blvd # 135 Los Angeles (90036) ***(G-28009)***
Onsite-Cat, Arroyo Grande *Also called Onsite Clims Apprisal Tech Inc* ***(G-10818)***
Ontario Airport Hotel Corp....................408 562-6709
4949 Great America Pkwy Santa Clara (95054) ***(G-13047)***
Ontario Community Hospital, Ontario *Also called Kindred Healthcare Oper Inc* ***(G-21689)***
Ontario Convention Center, Ontario *Also called Smg Food and Beverage LLC* ***(G-17492)***
Ontario Convention Center Corp....................909 937-3000
2000 E Convention Ctr Way Ontario (91764) ***(G-17378)***
Ontario Distribution Center, Ontario *Also called National Distribution Centers* ***(G-14003)***
Ontario Health Educatn Co Inc....................951 817-8553
3130 Sedona Ct Ontario (91764) ***(G-22522)***
Ontario Healthcare Center, Ontario *Also called Kf Ontario Healthcare LLC* ***(G-21280)***
Ontario Mills Shopping Center, Ontario *Also called Mills Corporation* ***(G-11019)***
Ontario Montclar Sch Dist Food....................909 930-6360
1525 S Bon View Ave Ontario (91761) ***(G-23014)***
Ontario Refrigeration Svc Inc (PA)....................909 984-2771
635 S Mountain Ave Ontario (91762) ***(G-2311)***
Ontario Refrigeration,, Ontario *Also called Ontario Refrigeration Svc Inc* ***(G-2311)***
Ontario Vineyard Medical Offs, Ontario *Also called Kaiser Foundation Hospitals* ***(G-19632)***
Ontario-Don, Ontario *Also called Synnex Corporation* ***(G-4643)***
Ontel Security Services Inc....................209 521-0200
708 L St Modesto (95354) ***(G-16906)***
Ontic Engineering and Mfg Inc....................818 678-6555
20400 Plummer St Chatsworth (91311) ***(G-8001)***
Ontrac, Santa Maria *Also called Express Messenger Systems Inc* ***(G-4405)***
Ontrac, Fresno *Also called Express Messenger Systems Inc* ***(G-4843)***
Oocl (usa) Inc....................408 576-6543
2700 Zanker Rd Ste 200 San Jose (95134) ***(G-5138)***
Oocl (usa) Inc....................562 499-2600
111 W Ocean Blvd Ste 1800 Long Beach (90802) ***(G-5139)***
Oocl (usa) Inc....................562 499-2600
17777 Center Court Dr N # 500 Cerritos (90703) ***(G-5140)***
Ooma Inc....................650 566-6600
1880 Embarcadero Rd Palo Alto (94303) ***(G-5674)***
Ooyala Inc (HQ)....................650 961-3400
4750 Patrick Henry Dr Santa Clara (95054) ***(G-15352)***
Opal Fry and Son....................661 858-2523
Maricopa Hwy Bakersfield (93307) ***(G-86)***
Opal Soft Inc....................408 267-2211
1288 Kifer Rd Ste 201 Sunnyvale (94086) ***(G-16445)***
Opallios Inc....................408 769-4594
3211 Scott Blvd Ste 205 Santa Clara (95054) ***(G-28010)***
Opalsoft, Sunnyvale *Also called Opal Soft Inc* ***(G-16445)***
Oparc....................909 598-8055
355 S Lemon Ave Ste J Walnut (91789) ***(G-24116)***
Oparc (PA)....................909 982-4090
9029 Vernon Ave Montclair (91763) ***(G-24373)***
Open Door Community Hlth Ctrs....................707 826-8610
770 10th St Arcata (95521) ***(G-22783)***
Open Door Community Hlth Ctrs (PA)....................707 826-8642
670 9th St Ste 203cfo Arcata (95521) ***(G-22784)***
Open Harbor Inc....................650 413-4200
1123 Industrial Rd San Francisco (94111) ***(G-27576)***
Opentable Inc (HQ)....................415 344-4200
1 Montgomery St Ste 700 San Francisco (94104) ***(G-17379)***

ALPHABETIC

Opentv Inc (HQ)...415 962-5000
275 Sacramento St Ste Sl1 San Francisco (94111) *(G-15784)*
Openwave Mobility Inc...650 480-7200
400 Seaport Ct Ste 104 Redwood City (94063) *(G-15785)*
Openx Technologies Inc (HQ)...855 673-6948
888 E Walnut St Fl 2 Pasadena (91101) *(G-13891)*
Opera San Jose Inc...408 437-4450
2149 Paragon Dr San Jose (95131) *(G-18421)*
Operating Engineers Funds Inc (PA)...626 792-8900
100 Corson St Ste 222 Pasadena (91103) *(G-12197)*
Operating Engneers Local Un 3...408 995-5095
798 N 1st St B San Jose (95112) *(G-9618)*
Operating Engneers Local Un 3 (PA)...925 454-4000
250 N Canyons Pkwy Livermore (94551) *(G-25180)*
Operation Samahan Inc...619 477-4451
2835 Highland Ave Ste C National City (91950) *(G-28011)*
Operation Technology Inc (PA)...949 462-0100
17 Goodyear Ste 100 Irvine (92618) *(G-15353)*
Operations, Los Angeles *Also called Wells Fargo Bank National Assn (G-11069)*
Operations Center, Hercules *Also called Mechanics Bank (G-4597)*
Operations Control Center, Oakland *Also called San Francisco Bay Area Rapid (G-3701)*
Operations/Risk Group, Pasadena *Also called Parsons Constructors Inc (G-27159)*
Operatix Inc...408 332-5796
111 N Market St Ste 300 San Jose (95113) *(G-17380)*
Opex Communications Inc...562 968-5420
3777 Long Beach Blvd # 300 Long Beach (90807) *(G-5675)*
Oplv Inc...310 672-1012
301 Centinela Ave Inglewood (90302) *(G-20827)*
Opower Inc...415 848-4700
680 Folsom St Ste 300 San Francisco (94107) *(G-15786)*
Oprah Winfrey Network, West Hollywood *Also called Own LLC (G-6011)*
Opsec Specialized Protection...661 942-3999
44262 Division St Ste A Lancaster (93535) *(G-16754)*
Optec Displays Inc...626 369-7188
1700 S De Soto Pl Ste A Ontario (91761) *(G-7222)*
Opterra Energy Services Inc (HQ)...844 678-3772
500 12th St Ste 300 Oakland (94607) *(G-25998)*
Optics East Inc (PA)...831 763-6931
180 Westgate Dr Watsonville (95076) *(G-7336)*
Optics Laboratory Inc...626 350-1926
9480 Telstar Ave Ste 3 El Monte (91731) *(G-22249)*
Optima Building Services Maint...707 586-6640
210 Mountain View Ave Santa Rosa (95407) *(G-14374)*
Optima Mortgage Corporation...714 389-4650
2081 Bus Ctr Dr Ste 230 Irvine (92612) *(G-9878)*
Optima Network Services Inc (HQ)...305 599-1800
15345 Fairfield Ranch Rd # 225 Chino Hills (91709) *(G-28150)*
Optima Tax Relief LLC...714 361-4636
3100 S Harbor Blvd # 250 Santa Ana (92704) *(G-13726)*
Optimal Health Services Inc...661 393-4483
1315 Boughton Dr Bakersfield (93308) *(G-22523)*
Optimal Hospice Care, Bakersfield *Also called Optmial Hospice Foundation (G-22524)*
Optimal Hospice Care, Santa Clara *Also called Optmial Hospice Foundation (G-22525)*
Optimizely Inc (PA)...415 376-4598
631 Howard St Ste 100 San Francisco (94105) *(G-15354)*
Optimum Design Associates Inc (PA)...925 401-2004
1075 Serpentine Ln Ste A Pleasanton (94566) *(G-25999)*
Optimum Solutions Group LLC (HQ)...415 954-7100
419 Ponderosa Ct Lafayette (94549) *(G-15787)*
Optimus Ventures LLC...888 881-5969
2608 Spring St Redwood City (94063) *(G-7617)*
Option One Home Med Eqp Inc...909 478-5413
1220 Research Dr Ste A Redlands (92374) *(G-14475)*
Options Family of Services...805 462-8544
5755 Valentina Ave Atascadero (93422) *(G-22785)*
Options For Learning...626 308-2411
2001 Elm St Alhambra (91803) *(G-24491)*
Optisource Technologies Inc...714 288-0825
1855 W Katella Ave # 170 Orange (92867) *(G-14124)*
Optmial Hospice Foundation...562 494-7687
3200 E 19th St Signal Hill (90755) *(G-21096)*
Optmial Hospice Foundation...661 716-4000
1675 Chester Ave Ste 401 Bakersfield (93301) *(G-22524)*
Optmial Hospice Foundation...408 207-9222
3375 Scott Blvd Ste 410 Santa Clara (95054) *(G-22525)*
Optumrx Inc...760 804-2399
2858 Loker Ave E Ste 100 Carlsbad (92010) *(G-10363)*
Optumrx Inc (HQ)...714 825-3600
2300 Main St Irvine (92614) *(G-10364)*
Opus Bank...714 578-7500
200 W Commonwealth Ave Fullerton (92832) *(G-9578)*
Opus Bank...909 599-0871
2100 Foothill Blvd Ste B La Verne (91750) *(G-9512)*
Opus Inspection Inc...714 999-6727
1410 S Acacia Ave Ste A Fullerton (92831) *(G-15355)*
Oracle America Inc...408 276-4300
4220 Network Cir Santa Clara (95054) *(G-15356)*
Oracle America Inc...408 276-3331
4120 Network Cir Santa Clara (95054) *(G-15357)*
Oracle America Inc...408 635-3072
80 Railroad Ave Milpitas (95035) *(G-16446)*
Oracle America Inc...800 633-0584
500 Oracle Pkwy Redwood City (94065) *(G-7170)*
Oracle Corp...650 506-7000
17901 Von Karman Ave # 800 Irvine (92614) *(G-28151)*
Oracle Corporation...713 654-0919
279 Barnes Rd Tustin (92782) *(G-15788)*
Oracle Corporation...650 607-5402
214 Clarence Ave Sunnyvale (94086) *(G-15789)*
Oracle Corporation...650 678-3612
1408 Antigua Ln Foster City (94404) *(G-15790)*
Oracle Corporation...408 421-2890
1490 Newhall St Santa Clara (95050) *(G-15791)*
Oracle Corporation...408 276-5552
231 Kerry Dr Santa Clara (95050) *(G-15792)*
Oracle Corporation...408 276-3822
3084 Thurman Dr San Jose (95148) *(G-15793)*
Oracle Corporation...858 587-5374
9515 Towne Centre Dr San Diego (92121) *(G-15794)*
Oracle Corporation...650 506-9864
3532 Eastin Pl Santa Clara (95051) *(G-15795)*
Oracle Corporation...408 390-8623
372 Calero Ave San Jose (95123) *(G-15796)*
Oracle Corporation...415 402-7200
475 Sansome St Fl 15 San Francisco (94111) *(G-15797)*
Oracle Corporation...916 435-8342
6224 Hummingbird Ln Rocklin (95765) *(G-15798)*
Oracle Corporation...877 767-2253
5805 Owens Dr Pleasanton (94588) *(G-15799)*
Oracle Corporation...925 694-6258
3925 Emerald Isle Ln San Jose (95135) *(G-15800)*
Oracle Corporation...510 471-6971
5863 Carmel Way Union City (94587) *(G-15801)*
Oracle Corporation...310 258-7500
5750 Hannum Ave Ste 200 Culver City (90230) *(G-15802)*
Oracle Corporation...310 343-7405
200 N Sepulveda Blvd # 400 El Segundo (90245) *(G-15803)*
Oracle Corporation...916 315-3500
1001 Sunset Blvd Rocklin (95765) *(G-15804)*
Oracle Corporation (PA)...650 506-7000
500 Oracle Pkwy Redwood City (94065) *(G-15805)*
Oracle Systems Corporation...818 817-2900
15760 Ventura Blvd # 1400 Encino (91436) *(G-15806)*
Oracle Systems Corporation...650 506-8648
102 Santa Barbara Ave Daly City (94014) *(G-15358)*
Oracle Systems Corporation...650 506-4060
17527 Via Sereno Monte Sereno (95030) *(G-15359)*
Oracle Systems Corporation...650 654-7606
301 Island Pkwy Belmont (94002) *(G-16024)*
Oracle Systems Corporation...650 506-6780
500 Oracle Pwky San Mateo (94403) *(G-15360)*
Oracle Systems Corporation...650 506-0300
10 Twin Dolphin Dr Redwood City (94065) *(G-15807)*
Oracle Systems Corporation (HQ)...650 506-7000
500 Oracle Pkwy Redwood City (94065) *(G-15808)*
Oracle Systems Corporation...925 694-3000
5840 Owens Dr Pleasanton (94588) *(G-15809)*
Oracle Systems Corporation...949 224-1000
2010 Main St Ste 450 Irvine (92614) *(G-15361)*
Oracle Systems Corporation...949 623-9460
17901 Von Karman Ave # 800 Irvine (92614) *(G-15810)*
Oracle Usa Inc...650 506-7000
500 Oracle Pkwy Redwood City (94065) *(G-15811)*
Orange Belt Adventures, Visalia *Also called Orange Belt Stages (G-3905)*
Orange Belt Stages (PA)...559 733-4408
2134 E Mineral King Ave Visalia (93292) *(G-3905)*
Orange Cast Title Southern Cal (PA)...714 558-2836
640 N Tustin Ave Ste 106 Santa Ana (92705) *(G-17381)*
Orange Children & Parents...714 639-4000
1063 N Glassell St Orange (92867) *(G-24492)*
Orange Cnty Conservation Corps...714 451-1301
1853 N Raymond Ave Anaheim (92801) *(G-24374)*
Orange Cnty George M Raymond N, Orange *Also called Raymond Group (G-27195)*
Orange Cnty Sprntndent Schools...949 650-2506
220 23rd St Costa Mesa (92627) *(G-24493)*
Orange Coast Building Services...714 453-6300
2191 S Dupont Dr Anaheim (92806) *(G-1455)*
Orange Coast Masonry Acquisit...714 538-4386
601 N Batavia St Orange (92868) *(G-2830)*
Orange Coast Service Center, Westminster *Also called Southern California Edison Co (G-6236)*
Orange Coast Title Company...714 822-3211
2411 W La Palma Ave # 300 Anaheim (92801) *(G-11938)*
Orange Cost Cntr For Surg Care...714 369-1070
18111 Brookhurst St # 3200 Fountain Valley (92708) *(G-21770)*
Orange County Association (PA)...714 547-7559
822 W Town And Country Rd Orange (92868) *(G-22786)*
Orange County Child Abuse...714 543-4333
2390 E Orangewood Ave # 300 Anaheim (92806) *(G-24117)*
Orange County Cncl Bsa (PA)...714 546-4990
1211 E Dyer Rd Ste 100 Santa Ana (92705) *(G-25306)*
Orange County Dept Education...714 730-7301
300 S C St Tustin (92780) *(G-27151)*
Orange County Employees Retir...714 558-6200
2223 S Wellington Ave Santa Ana (92701) *(G-12120)*
Orange County Global Med Ctr...714 953-3500
1001 N Tustin Ave Santa Ana (92705) *(G-21771)*
Orange County Head Start (PA)...714 241-8920
2501 Pullman St Ste 100 Santa Ana (92705) *(G-24494)*
Orange County Head Start...714 761-4967
9200 W Pacific Pl Anaheim (92804) *(G-24495)*
Orange County Health Auth...714 246-8500
505 City Pkwy W Orange (92868) *(G-25148)*
Orange County Internet Xchange...714 450-7109
2001 E Dyer Rd Ste 102 Santa Ana (92705) *(G-5676)*
Orange County One Stop Center...714 241-4900
5405 Grdn Rd Blvd Ste 100 Westminster (92683) *(G-14716)*
Orange County Plst Co Inc...714 957-1971
3191 Arprt Loop Dr Ste B1 Costa Mesa (92626) *(G-2944)*

ALPHABETIC

Orange County Produce LLC ALPHABETIC SECTION

Orange County Produce LLC 949 451-0880
11405 Jeffrey Rd Irvine (92602) ***(G-125)***

Orange County Royale Convlscnt 949 458-6346
23228 Madero Mission Viejo (92691) ***(G-21336)***

Orange County Royale Convlscnt (PA) 714 546-6450
1030 W Warner Ave Santa Ana (92707) ***(G-21337)***

Orange County Sanitation (PA) 714 962-2411
10844 Ellis Ave Fountain Valley (92708) ***(G-6511)***

Orange County Sanitation 714 962-2411
22212 Brookhurst St Huntington Beach (92646) ***(G-6414)***

Orange County Service Center, San Clemente *Also called San Diego Gas & Electric Co* ***(G-6293)***

Orange County Services Inc 714 541-9753
3022 N Hesperian St Santa Ana (92706) ***(G-2312)***

ORANGE COUNTY TRANSIT DISTRICT, Orange *Also called Orange County Trnsp Auth* ***(G-3687)***

Orange County Trnsp Auth 714 560-6282
11790 Cardinal Cir Garden Grove (92843) ***(G-3686)***

Orange County Trnsp Auth (PA) 714 636-7433
550 S Main St Orange (92868) ***(G-3687)***

Orange County Trnsp Auth 714 999-1726
600 S Main St Ste 910 Orange (92868) ***(G-3688)***

Orange County-Irvine Med Ctr, Irvine *Also called Kaiser Foundation Hospitals* ***(G-12189)***

Orange Countys Credit Union (PA) 714 755-5900
1721 E Saint Andrew Pl Santa Ana (92705) ***(G-9676)***

Orange Courier Inc 714 384-3600
3731 W Warner Ave Santa Ana (92704) ***(G-17382)***

Orange Cove Health Center, Orange Cove *Also called United Health Ctrs San Joaquin* ***(G-22857)***

Orange Healthcare & Wellness 714 633-3568
920 W La Veta Ave Orange (92868) ***(G-20828)***

Orange Labs, San Francisco *Also called France Telecom RES & Dev LLC* ***(G-26663)***

Orange Pacific Plumbing Inc 714 992-4547
801 Panorama Rd Fullerton (92831) ***(G-2313)***

Orange Silicon Valley 415 243-1500
60 Spear St Ste 1100 San Francisco (94105) ***(G-28012)***

Orangetree Convalescent Hosp 951 785-6060
4000 Harrison St Riverside (92503) ***(G-21772)***

Orangewood Chld Foundation 714 480-2300
1575 E 17th St Santa Ana (92705) ***(G-25562)***

Orbital Sciences Corporation 703 406-5000
2401 E El Segundo Blvd # 200 El Segundo (90245) ***(G-26578)***

Orchard - Post Acute Care Ctr 562 693-7701
12385 Washington Blvd Whittier (90606) ***(G-20829)***

Orchard Holdings Group Inc 949 502-8300
1 Venture Ste 300 Irvine (92618) ***(G-11722)***

Orchard Hospital 530 846-5671
240 Spruce St Gridley (95948) ***(G-21773)***

Orchard Hotel, San Francisco *Also called Orchard International Group* ***(G-13048)***

Orchard International Group (PA) 415 362-8878
665 Bush St San Francisco (94108) ***(G-13048)***

Orchard Medical Offices, Downey *Also called Kaiser Foundation Hospitals* ***(G-19609)***

Orchard Park, Clovis *Also called Regent Assisted Living Inc* ***(G-24785)***

Orchard Supply Company LLC 408 269-1550
1375 Blossom Hill Rd # 24 San Jose (95118) ***(G-8132)***

Orchid MPS 714 549-9203
3233 W Harvard St Santa Ana (92704) ***(G-7290)***

Orco Block, Stanton *Also called Muth Development Co Inc* ***(G-11022)***

Ore-Cal Corp (PA) 213 623-8493
634 Crocker St Los Angeles (90021) ***(G-8642)***

Oregon PCF Bldg Pdts Calif Inc 916 381-8051
8185 Signal Ct Ste A Sacramento (95824) ***(G-6941)***

Oregon PCF Bldg Pdts Maple Inc 909 627-4043
2401 E Philadelphia St Ontario (91761) ***(G-6942)***

Oren's Replay, Van Nuys *Also called Factory 2-U Import Export Inc* ***(G-8383)***

Orenda Center 707 565-7450
1430 Neotomas Ave Santa Rosa (95405) ***(G-24951)***

Orepac Building Products, Sacramento *Also called Oregon PCF Bldg Pdts Calif Inc* ***(G-6941)***

Orepac Millwork Products, Ontario *Also called Oregon PCF Bldg Pdts Maple Inc* ***(G-6942)***

Oreq Corporation 951 296-5076
42306 Remington Ave Temecula (92590) ***(G-27152)***

Organic Inc 310 543-4600
390 Amapola Ave Ste 8 Torrance (90501) ***(G-16447)***

Organic Inc (HQ) 415 581-5300
600 California St Fl 8 San Francisco (94108) ***(G-16448)***

Organic & Sustainable Buty Inc 310 815-8201
5933 Bowcroft St Los Angeles (90016) ***(G-13683)***

Organic Affinity LLC 801 870-7433
3980 Hopevale Dr Sherman Oaks (91403) ***(G-7618)***

Organic Holdings Inc 415 581-5300
600 California St Fl 8 San Francisco (94108) ***(G-13892)***

Organic On, San Francisco *Also called Organic Holdings Inc* ***(G-13892)***

Organic Pastures Dairy Co LLC 559 846-9732
7221 S Jameson Ave Fresno (93706) ***(G-437)***

Organicgirl LLC 831 758-7800
900 Work St Salinas (93901) ***(G-8759)***

Organztion Amrcn Kdaly Edctors 310 441-3555
10801 National Blvd # 590 Los Angeles (90064) ***(G-25563)***

Orient Fisheries Inc 323 588-4185
1912 E Vernon Ave Ste 110 Vernon (90058) ***(G-8643)***

Oriental Motor U S A Corp (HQ) 310 715-3300
1001 Knox St Torrance (90502) ***(G-7463)***

Origaudio, Huntington Beach *Also called Forty Four Group LLC* ***(G-13851)***

Origin Systems Inc 650 628-1500
209 Redwood Shores Pkwy Redwood City (94065) ***(G-15362)***

Original Mowbrays Tree Svc Inc 559 798-0530
17332 Millwood Dr Visalia (93292) ***(G-995)***

Original Petes Pizza Inc 916 442-6770
2001 J St Sacramento (95811) ***(G-12220)***

Original Retro Brands, Commerce *Also called Wildcat Retro Brands LLC* ***(G-8416)***

Original Seatbeltbag , The, Santa Ana *Also called Harveys Industries Inc* ***(G-8386)***

Original Sid Blackman Plbg Inc 760 352-3632
1160 S 2nd St El Centro (92243) ***(G-2314)***

Orinda Convalescent Hospital 925 254-6500
11 Altarinda Rd Orinda (94563) ***(G-21338)***

Orinda Country Club 925 254-4313
315 Camino Sobrante Orinda (94563) ***(G-19022)***

Orion Construction Corporation 760 597-9660
2185 La Mirada Dr Vista (92081) ***(G-1975)***

Orion Security, San Jose *Also called Yosh Enterprises Inc* ***(G-16857)***

Ormat Nevada Inc 760 353-8200
947 Dogwood Rd Heber (92249) ***(G-6305)***

Ormesa LLC 760 356-3020
3300 E Evan Hewes Hwy Holtville (92250) ***(G-6160)***

Orohealth Corporation 530 534-9183
900 Oro Dam Blvd E Oroville (95965) ***(G-19799)***

Orora North America 714 984-2300
3200 Enterprise St Brea (92821) ***(G-8202)***

Orora North America 760 510-7170
664 N Twin Oaks Valley Rd San Marcos (92069) ***(G-8203)***

Orora North America 510 487-1211
33463 Western Ave Union City (94587) ***(G-8204)***

Orora North America 323 832-2000
1640 S Greenwood Ave Montebello (90640) ***(G-8205)***

Orora North America 626 284-9524
3201 W Mission Rd Alhambra (91803) ***(G-8206)***

Orora North America 714 278-6000
1901 E Rosslynn Ave Fullerton (92831) ***(G-8207)***

Orora North America 760 510-7000
664 N Twin Oaks Valley Rd San Marcos (92069) ***(G-8208)***

Orora North America 714 773-0124
1911 E Rosslynn Ave Fullerton (92831) ***(G-8209)***

Orora North America 714 562-6002
6200 Caballero Blvd Buena Park (90620) ***(G-8210)***

Orora Packaging Solutions (HQ) 714 562-6000
6600 Valley View St Buena Park (90620) ***(G-8211)***

Oroville Hosp Post Acute Ctr, Oroville *Also called 1000 Executive Parkway LLC* ***(G-20362)***

Oroville Hospital, Oroville *Also called Orohealth Corporation* ***(G-19799)***

Oroville Hospital (PA) 530 533-8500
2767 Olive Hwy Oroville (95966) ***(G-21774)***

Oroville Hospital 530 538-8700
2353 Myers St Ste B Oroville (95966) ***(G-20336)***

Oroville Internal Meds Group 530 538-3171
2721 Olive Hwy Ste 12 Oroville (95966) ***(G-19800)***

Oroweat Foods, Anaheim *Also called Bimbo Bakeries Usa Inc* ***(G-8808)***

Orrick Hrrington Sutcliffe LLP (PA) 415 773-5700
405 Howard St San Francisco (94105) ***(G-23482)***

Orrick Hrrington Sutcliffe LLP 650 614-7454
1020 Marsh Rd Menlo Park (94025) ***(G-23483)***

Orrick Hrrington Sutcliffe LLP 650 614-7400
1000 Marsh Rd Menlo Park (94025) ***(G-23484)***

Orrick Hrrington Sutcliffe LLP 213 629-2020
777 S Figueroa St # 3200 Los Angeles (90017) ***(G-23485)***

Orrick Hrrington Sutcliffe LLP 916 447-9200
400 Capitol Mall Ste 3000 Sacramento (95814) ***(G-23486)***

Ortega Elementary Pto 650 738-6670
1283 Terra Nova Blvd Pacifica (94044) ***(G-25307)***

Orthocad, San Jose *Also called Cadent Inc* ***(G-15912)***

Orthopaedic Hospital (PA) 213 742-1000
403 W Adams Blvd Los Angeles (90007) ***(G-21775)***

Orthopaedic Inst For Children, Los Angeles *Also called Orthopaedic Hospital* ***(G-21775)***

Orthopedic Consultants (PA) 818 788-7343
16311 Ventura Blvd # 800 Encino (91436) ***(G-19801)***

Orthopedics Department, Los Angeles *Also called Southern Cal Prmnnte Med Group* ***(G-20029)***

Ortiz Asphalt Paving Inc 951 966-7060
382 E Orange Show Rd San Bernardino (92408) ***(G-1838)***

Ortiz Enterprises Incorporated (PA) 949 753-1414
6 Cushing Ste 200 Irvine (92618) ***(G-1839)***

Orwick Fresh Foods Inc 909 985-5604
7940 Cherry Ave Ste 203 Fontana (92336) ***(G-8895)***

Osata Enterprises Inc 310 297-1550
225 S Aviation Blvd El Segundo (90245) ***(G-8441)***

Osborne Organization, The, Modesto *Also called Capax Management and Services* ***(G-10662)***

Oscar Valero 530 668-4342
1685 Jones St Woodland (95776) ***(G-385)***

Oshman Family Jewish Cmnty Ctr, Palo Alto *Also called Ofjcc* ***(G-24111)***

Oshman Family Jewish Cmnty Ctr 650 223-8700
3921 Fabian Way Palo Alto (94303) ***(G-24118)***

Oshyn Inc 213 483-1770
200 Pine Ave Ste 503 Long Beach (90802) ***(G-16167)***

OSI, Folsom *Also called Objective Systems Integrators* ***(G-15346)***

OSI Consulting Inc 949 724-8300
2525 Main St Ste 350 Irvine (92614) ***(G-16449)***

OSI Software, San Leandro *Also called Osisoft LLC* ***(G-15812)***

Osisoft LLC (PA) 510 297-5800
777 Davis St Ste 250 San Leandro (94577) ***(G-15812)***

Osram Opto Semiconductors Inc 408 588-3800
1150 Kifer Rd Ste 100 Sunnyvale (94086) ***(G-7619)***

Osram Opto Semiconductors Inc (HQ) 408 588-3800
1150 Kifer Rd Ste 100 Sunnyvale (94086) ***(G-7620)***

Osscim Inc 714 680-0015
172 E Orangethorpe Ave Placentia (92870) ***(G-3195)***

Ost Crane Service, Ventura *Also called Ost Trucks and Cranes Inc* ***(G-17383)***

ALPHABETIC

Ost Trucks and Cranes Inc 805 643-9963
2951 N Ventura Ave Ventura (93001) *(G-17383)*
Ostcs, Covina *Also called Outsource Testing Inc (G-28013)*
Ostendo Technologies Inc (PA) 760 710-3003
6185 Paseo Del Norte # 200 Carlsbad (92011) *(G-26579)*
Osterhout Design Group, San Francisco *Also called Osterhout Group Inc (G-17384)*
Osterhout Group Inc 415 644-4000
153 Townsend St Ste 570 San Francisco (94107) *(G-17384)*
Otay Lakes Road Branch, Chula Vista *Also called Citibank National Association (G-9375)*
Otay Mesa Medical Offices, San Diego *Also called Kaiser Foundation Hospitals (G-12180)*
Otay Water District 619 670-2222
2554 Swetwater Sprng Blvd Spring Valley (91978) *(G-6385)*
Otb Acquisition LLC 520 458-0540
770 S Brea Blvd Ste 227 Brea (92821) *(G-13049)*
Otis Elevator Company 323 342-4500
2701 Media Center Dr # 2 Los Angeles (90065) *(G-7873)*
Otis Elevator Company 714 758-9593
711 E Ball Rd Ste 200 Anaheim (92805) *(G-17993)*
Otis Elevator Company 415 546-0880
444 Spear St Ste 100 San Francisco (94105) *(G-3478)*
Otis Elevator Intl Inc 510 874-5129
1358 14th St Oakland (94607) *(G-3479)*
Otis Spunkmeyer, San Leandro *Also called Aryzta LLC (G-8799)*
Otis Spunkmeyer, San Leandro *Also called Aryzta LLC (G-8800)*
Otismed Corporation 510 786-3171
1600 Harbor Bay Pkwy # 200 Alameda (94502) *(G-7291)*
Otto Cap, Ontario *Also called Otto International Inc (G-8356)*
OTTO CONSTRUCTION, Sacramento *Also called John F Otto Inc (G-1583)*
Otto International Inc (PA) 909 937-1998
3550 Jurupa St Ste A Ontario (91761) *(G-8356)*
Otx Corporation (HQ) 310 736-3400
10567 Jefferson Blvd Culver City (90232) *(G-27577)*
Ouch Systems, West Sacramento *Also called Occupnl Urgnt Care Hlth Syst (G-23010)*
Oum & Co LLP (PA) 415 434-3744
465 California St Ste 700 San Francisco (94104) *(G-26415)*
Our Alchemy LLC 310 893-6289
5900 Wilshire Blvd Fl 18 Los Angeles (90036) *(G-18289)*
Our House, Vallejo *Also called Crestwood Behavioral Hlth Inc (G-22063)*
Our House Residential Care Ctr 559 674-8670
109 E Central Ave Madera (93638) *(G-21339)*
Our Lady of Fatima Villa Inc 408 741-2950
20400 Srtoga Los Gatos Rd Saratoga (95070) *(G-20830)*
Our Lady of Grace P T G 619 466-0055
2766 Navajo Rd El Cajon (92020) *(G-17385)*
Our Watch 714 897-1022
12832 Valley View St # 211 Garden Grove (92845) *(G-22526)*
Our Way, Oceanside *Also called E R I T Inc (G-24639)*
Out of Shell LLC 626 401-1923
9658 Remer St South El Monte (91733) *(G-1456)*
Outcast Agency LLC 415 392-8282
100 Montgomery St # 1200 San Francisco (94104) *(G-27760)*
Outdoor Systems Advertising 323 222-7171
1731 Workman St Los Angeles (90031) *(G-13954)*
Outfront Media Inc 657 221-2760
2100 W Orangewood Ave Orange (92868) *(G-13955)*
Outfront Media LLC 510 527-3350
1695 Eastshore Hwy Berkeley (94710) *(G-13956)*
Outlook Amusements Inc 818 433-3800
2900 W Alameda Ave # 400 Burbank (91505) *(G-16450)*
Outpatient Rehabilitation Svcs, Walnut Creek *Also called John Muir Health (G-21619)*
Outpatnt Eye Srgry Ctr of Dsrt 760 340-3937
72057 Dinah Shore Dr D1 Rancho Mirage (92270) *(G-19802)*
Outreach & Escort Inc (PA) 408 436-2865
2221 Oakland Rd Ste 200 San Jose (95131) *(G-3689)*
Outrigger Hotels Hawaii 310 301-2000
4200 Admiralty Way Venice (90292) *(G-13050)*
Outrigger Hotels Hawaii 323 491-9015
8462 W Sunset Blvd West Hollywood (90069) *(G-13051)*
Outside Lines Inc 714 637-4747
20331 Irvine Ave Ste E7 Newport Beach (92660) *(G-783)*
Outsource Testing Inc 909 592-8898
1278 Center Court Dr Covina (91724) *(G-28013)*
Ovations Fanfare 714 708-1880
88 Fair Dr Costa Mesa (92626) *(G-27153)*
Over 60 Health Center, Berkeley *Also called Lifelong Medical Care (G-19707)*
Over 60 Health Center, Berkeley *Also called Lifelong Medical Care (G-19708)*
OVERAA CONSTRUCTION, Richmond *Also called C Overaa & Co (G-1409)*
Overhead Door Corporation 714 680-0600
1617 N Orangethorpe Way Anaheim (92801) *(G-3070)*
Overland Pacific & Cutler (PA) 562 429-9391
3750 Schaufele Ave # 150 Long Beach (90808) *(G-17386)*
Overseas Service Corporation 858 408-0751
8221 Arjons Dr Ste B2 San Diego (92126) *(G-28152)*
Overseenet (PA) 213 408-0080
550 S Hope St Ste 200 Los Angeles (90071) *(G-13893)*
Overton Security Services Inc 510 791-7380
39300 Civic Center Dr # 370 Fremont (94538) *(G-16907)*
Ovis Llc 805 646-5511
905 Country Club Rd Ojai (93023) *(G-13052)*
Owen & Company 916 993-2700
1455 Response Rd Ste 260 Sacramento (95815) *(G-10819)*
Owen Dunn Insurance Services 916 443-0200
1455 Response Rd Ste 260 Sacramento (95815) *(G-10820)*
Owens & Minor Inc 909 944-2100
5125 Ontario Mills Pkwy Ontario (91764) *(G-7292)*
Owens & Minor Inc 209 833-4600
18520 Stanford Rd Tracy (95377) *(G-7293)*
Owens Corning Sales LLC 408 235-1351
960 Central Expy Santa Clara (95050) *(G-7013)*
Owens Health Care 530 246-1075
2247 Court St Redding (96001) *(G-22527)*
Owens Valley Inter Agency 760 873-2405
351 Pacu Ln Bishop (93514) *(G-25097)*
Owl Education and Training 949 797-2000
2465 Campus Dr Irvine (92612) *(G-24375)*
Own LLC 323 602-5500
1041 N Formosa Ave West Hollywood (90046) *(G-6011)*
Ownit Mortgage Solutions Inc 513 872-6922
4360 Park Terrace Dr # 100 Westlake Village (91361) *(G-9879)*
Oxford Farms Inc 559 659-3033
901 N St Ste 103 Firebaugh (93622) *(G-712)*
Oxford Palace 213 382-7756
745 S Oxford Ave Los Angeles (90005) *(G-13053)*
Oxford Suites Chico, Chico *Also called Baney Corporation (G-12415)*
Oxnard 2103 East Gonzales Road, Oxnard *Also called Kaiser Foundation Hospitals (G-19636)*
Oxnard 2200 East Gonzales, Oxnard *Also called Kaiser Foundation Hospitals (G-19634)*
Oxnard Beach Hotel LP 805 488-6560
350 E Port Hueneme Rd Port Hueneme (93041) *(G-13054)*
Oxnard City Corps 805 385-8081
555 S A St Ste 200 Oxnard (93030) *(G-24376)*
Oxnard Family Circle Adhc, Oxnard *Also called Family Circle Inc (G-23968)*
Oxnard Manor LP 805 983-0324
1400 W Gonzales Rd Oxnard (93036) *(G-20831)*
OXNARD MANOR HEALTHCARE CENTER, Oxnard *Also called Oxnard Manor LP (G-20831)*
Oxnard Perfrmn Arts & Convtn 805 486-2424
800 Hobson Way Oxnard (93030) *(G-17387)*
Oxnard Veterans Center, Oxnard *Also called Veterans Health Administration (G-20211)*
OXY USA Inc 661 869-8000
9600 Ming Ave Ste 300 Bakersfield (93311) *(G-1047)*
Oxyheal Medical Systems Inc 619 336-2022
3224 Hoover Ave National City (91950) *(G-17994)*
Ozoo Inc 323 585-4383
4662 E 49th St Vernon (90058) *(G-17388)*
P & D Consultants Inc (HQ) 714 835-4447
999 W Town And Country Rd Orange (92868) *(G-26000)*
P & P Agrilabor 831 679-2307
Highway 101 Floretta Rd Chualar (93925) *(G-14717)*
P & R Paper Supply Co Inc (PA) 909 389-1811
1898 E Colton Ave Redlands (92374) *(G-8212)*
P A C E, Los Angeles *Also called Pacific Asian Consortm Emplymn (G-24377)*
P A T H, Los Angeles *Also called People Assisting Homeless (G-24132)*
P B C Pavers Inc 714 278-0488
1560 W Lambert Rd Brea (92821) *(G-2472)*
P B I, Long Beach *Also called Pbi-Birkenwald Market Eqp Inc (G-7223)*
P C A, Livermore *Also called Pen-Cal Administrators Inc (G-27162)*
P C A Farm Management LLC 661 720-2400
1901 S Lexington St Delano (93215) *(G-713)*
P C I & Associates, San Diego *Also called PCI Collections Inc (G-14040)*
P C M, Foothill Ranch *Also called Professional Community MGT Cal (G-11769)*
P C S, Concord *Also called Patriot Contract Services LLC (G-4717)*
P C Vericare 858 454-3610
4715 Vewridge Ave Ste 230 San Diego (92123) *(G-20337)*
P D Rabbit Messenger Service, Los Angeles *Also called Pete Helling (G-17410)*
P E I, Tracy *Also called Petz Enterprises Inc (G-15377)*
P H B Contracting Inc 760 347-7290
43180 Sunburst St Indio (92201) *(G-2945)*
P H Ranch Inc 209 358-5111
6335 Oakdale Rd Winton (95388) *(G-438)*
P H S, Northridge *Also called Progressive Health Care System (G-19880)*
P H S Management Group (PA) 714 547-7551
721 N Eckhoff St Orange (92868) *(G-27578)*
P J J Enterprises Inc 619 232-6136
1250 Delevan Dr San Diego (92102) *(G-14564)*
P J Video Services Inc 714 705-6088
200 N Tustin Ave Ste 120 Santa Ana (92705) *(G-18124)*
P J'S Construction Supplies, Fremont *Also called PJs Lumber Inc (G-6948)*
P L D S, Fremont *Also called Philips & Lite-On Digital (G-7346)*
P M B, San Diego *Also called Pacific Medical Buildings LP (G-11725)*
P M C A, Burlingame *Also called Provident Mrtg Cpitl Assoc Inc (G-9889)*
P Monterey LP 831 250-6159
200 Glenwood Cir Ste A50 Monterey (93940) *(G-24758)*
P Murphy & Associates Inc 818 841-2002
2301 W Olive Ave Burbank (91506) *(G-15363)*
P R N Convalescent Hospital 818 352-3158
7912 Topley Ln Sunland (91040) *(G-20832)*
P R P, Costa Mesa *Also called Profit Recovery Partners LLC (G-28023)*
P T C, San Jose *Also called Ptc Inc (G-15401)*
P W C, San Dimas *Also called Pacific W Space Cmmnctions Inc (G-1977)*
P& JP Brokerage LLC 310 801-9707
15301 Ventura Blvd Ste P2 Sherman Oaks (91403) *(G-5141)*
P-Cove Enterprises Inc 818 341-1101
8745 Remmet Ave Canoga Park (91304) *(G-16025)*
P-Wave Holdings LLC 310 209-3010
10877 Wilshire Blvd Los Angeles (90024) *(G-12337)*
P2f Holdings 562 296-1055
1760 Apollo Ct Seal Beach (90740) *(G-9284)*
P2s Commissioning, Long Beach *Also called P2s Engineering Inc (G-26001)*
P2s Engineering Inc 562 497-2999
5000 E Spring St Ste 800 Long Beach (90815) *(G-26001)*
P8ge Consulting Inc 310 666-2301
8406 Beverly Blvd Los Angeles (90048) *(G-28014)*

ALPHABETIC

Paat & Kimmel Development Inc 909 315-8074
5450 Riverside Dr Chino (91710) *(G-1624)*
Pac West Land Care Inc 760 630-0231
408 Olive Ave Vista (92083) *(G-927)*
Pac-12 Enteprises LLC 415 580-4200
360 3rd St Ste 300 San Francisco (94107) *(G-13976)*
Pacbell, San Francisco *Also called Pacific Bell Telephone Company (G-5677)*
Paccar Leasing Corporation 559 268-4344
2892 E Jensen Ave Fresno (93706) *(G-17642)*
Pace Inc 925 602-0900
2301 Arnold Industrial Wa Concord (94520) *(G-2946)*
Pace Administrator To Work, Los Angeles *Also called Pacific Asian Consortm Emplymn (G-24119)*
Pace Drywall, Concord *Also called Pace Inc (G-2946)*
Pace Supply Corp (PA) 707 303-0320
6000 State Farm Dr # 200 Rohnert Park (94928) *(G-7727)*
Pacer, Commerce *Also called Xpo Cartage Inc (G-4095)*
Pachinko World Inc 714 895-7772
5912 Bolsa Ave Ste 108 Huntington Beach (92649) *(G-18807)*
Pachulski Stang Zehl Jones LLP (PA) 310 277-6910
10100 Santa Monica Blvd # 1100 Los Angeles (90067) *(G-23487)*
Pacific Advnced Cvil Engrg Inc (PA) 714 481-7300
17520 Newhope St Ste 200 Fountain Valley (92708) *(G-26002)*
Pacific Airworks Group LLC 909 815-7012
255 S Leland Norton Way San Bernardino (92408) *(G-26003)*
Pacific Ambulance Inc 949 470-2355
5550 Oberlin Dr Ste A San Diego (92121) *(G-3824)*
Pacific American Fish Co Inc (PA) 323 319-1551
5525 S Santa Fe Ave Vernon (90058) *(G-8644)*
Pacific Aquascape Inc 714 481-7260
17520 Newhope St Ste 120 Fountain Valley (92708) *(G-3560)*
Pacific Arspc Rsurces Tech LLC 760 530-1767
18200 Phantom W Victorville (92394) *(G-17995)*
Pacific Asian Consortm Emplymn 213 989-3228
1055 Wilshire Blvd # 1475 Los Angeles (90017) *(G-24119)*
Pacific Asian Consortm Emplymn (PA) 213 353-3982
1055 Wilshire Blvd Ste 14 Los Angeles (90017) *(G-24377)*
Pacific Aviation Corporation (PA) 310 646-4015
380 World Way Ste S31 Los Angeles (90045) *(G-4927)*
Pacific Bay Properties (PA) 949 440-7200
4041 Macarthur Blvd # 500 Newport Beach (92660) *(G-1229)*
Pacific Bell Telephone Company (HQ) 415 542-9000
430 Bush St Fl 3 San Francisco (94108) *(G-5677)*
Pacific Bonding Corporation (PA) 760 431-9911
1959 Palomar Oaks Way # 200 Carlsbad (92011) *(G-17389)*
Pacific Boring Incorporated 559 864-9444
1985 W Mountain View Ave Caruthers (93609) *(G-3359)*
Pacific Building Care, Fresno *Also called Pbc Solution One Inc (G-3567)*
Pacific Building Group 858 552-0600
13541 Stoney Creek Rd San Diego (92129) *(G-2947)*
Pacific Building Group (PA) 858 552-0600
9752 Aspen Creek Ct # 100 San Diego (92126) *(G-1625)*
Pacific Building Maint Inc (PA) 805 642-0214
1601 Ives Ave Ste E Oxnard (93033) *(G-14375)*
Pacific Bulk Trnsp Co Inc 714 521-2399
6250 Caballero Blvd Buena Park (90620) *(G-4369)*
Pacific Cambria Inc 805 927-6114
2905 Burton Dr Cambria (93428) *(G-13055)*
Pacific Capital Companies LLC 800 583-3015
11620 Wilshire Blvd Los Angeles (90025) *(G-9803)*
Pacific Care Inc 562 494-6500
1903 Redondo Ave Long Beach (90755) *(G-22528)*
Pacific Cast CLB Vndenburg Afb 805 734-4375
758 Nebraska Ave Lompoc (93437) *(G-25308)*
Pacific Cast Sightseeing Tours, Anaheim *Also called Coach Usa Inc (G-4991)*
Pacific Centrex Services Inc 818 623-2300
28001 Dorothy Dr Agoura Hills (91301) *(G-5678)*
Pacific Cheese Co Inc (PA) 510 784-8800
21090 Cabot Blvd Hayward (94545) *(G-8591)*
Pacific Chemical Dist Corp (HQ) 714 521-7161
6250 Caballero Blvd Buena Park (90620) *(G-4699)*
Pacific Choice Seafood Company 707 442-2981
1 Commercial St Eureka (95501) *(G-8645)*
Pacific Cities Management Inc (PA) 916 348-1188
6056 Rutland Dr Ste 1 Carmichael (95608) *(G-11723)*
Pacific City Bank 714 263-1800
13140 Yale Ave Irvine (92620) *(G-9554)*
Pacific Civil & Strl Cons LLC 916 421-1000
7415 Greenhaven Dr # 100 Sacramento (95831) *(G-26004)*
Pacific Cleaning Service Inc 949 829-8790
3334 Pacific Coast Hwy # 205 Corona Del Mar (92625) *(G-14376)*
Pacific Clinics 562 942-8256
11741 Telegraph Rd Ste G Santa Fe Springs (90670) *(G-22787)*
Pacific Clinics 562 949-8455
11721 Telegraph Rd Ste A Santa Fe Springs (90670) *(G-22788)*
Pacific Club (PA) 949 955-1123
4110 Macarthur Blvd Newport Beach (92660) *(G-19023)*
Pacific Coast Bankers Bank 415 399-1900
1676 N Calif Blvd Ste 300 Walnut Creek (94596) *(G-9513)*
Pacific Coast Care Center, Salinas *Also called Kindred Healthcare Oper Inc (G-20702)*
Pacific Coast Companies Inc 916 631-6500
10600 White Rock Rd # 100 Rancho Cordova (95670) *(G-17390)*
Pacific Coast Container Inc (PA) 510 346-6100
432 Estudillo Ave Ste 1 San Leandro (94577) *(G-5232)*
Pacific Coast Drum Company 626 443-3096
2200 Rosemead Blvd 2204 El Monte (91733) *(G-7944)*
Pacific Coast Ldscp MGT Inc 925 513-2310
3960 Holway Dr Byron (94514) *(G-784)*
Pacific Coast Manor, Capitola *Also called Covenant Care LLC (G-20483)*

Pacific Coast Mines Inc 661 287-5400
26877 Tourney Rd Valencia (91355) *(G-1112)*
Pacific Coast Produce Inc 805 240-3385
950 Mountain View Ave # 1 Oxnard (93030) *(G-8760)*
Pacific Coast Producers 209 365-9982
650 S Guild Ave Lodi (95240) *(G-17391)*
Pacific Coast Services Inc 209 956-2532
1919 Grand Canal Blvd C3 Stockton (95207) *(G-22529)*
Pacific Coast Supply LLC 916 481-2220
4290 Roseville Rd North Highlands (95660) *(G-6943)*
Pacific Coast Supply LLC (HQ) 916 971-2301
4290 Roseville Rd North Highlands (95660) *(G-6944)*
Pacific Coast Sweeping, Rancho Santa Margari *Also called Wendt Landscape Services Inc (G-979)*
Pacific Coast Trnsp Svcs Inc 916 266-5300
7500 San Joaquin St Sacramento (95820) *(G-5233)*
Pacific Coast Warehouse Co, Newark *Also called National Distribution Agcy Inc (G-4601)*
Pacific Communications Assoc 925 634-1203
761 2nd St Brentwood (94513) *(G-28015)*
Pacific Communities Bldr Inc 949 660-8988
1000 Dove St Ste 100 Newport Beach (92660) *(G-11996)*
Pacific Compensation Insur Co 818 575-8500
1 Baxter Way Ste 170 Westlake Village (91362) *(G-10452)*
Pacific Concept Laundry, Los Angeles *Also called E & C Fashion Inc (G-17138)*
Pacific Concept Laundry Inc 323 980-3800
1370 Esperanza St Los Angeles (90023) *(G-13577)*
Pacific Concrete Specialties 209 358-0741
101 Business Park Way Atwater (95301) *(G-3306)*
Pacific Contours Corporation (PA) 714 693-1260
5340 E Hunter Ave Anaheim (92807) *(G-8002)*
Pacific Couriers Inc 714 278-6100
1706 W Orangethorpe Ave Fullerton (92833) *(G-4419)*
Pacific Crane Maint Co LP (PA) 562 432-8066
250 W Wardlow Rd Long Beach (90807) *(G-17996)*
Pacific Crossing LLC 949 679-2588
95 Argonaut Ste 100 Aliso Viejo (92656) *(G-16026)*
Pacific Cycle Inc 909 481-5613
9282 Pittsburgh Ave Rancho Cucamonga (91730) *(G-4609)*
Pacific Cycle P Finished Goods, Rancho Cucamonga *Also called Pacific Cycle Inc (G-4609)*
Pacific Dental Services Inc (PA) 714 845-8500
17000 Red Hill Ave Irvine (92614) *(G-20269)*
Pacific Design Directions Inc 714 685-7766
8171 E Kaiser Blvd Anaheim (92808) *(G-1230)*
Pacific Diagnostic Labs LLC 805 653-5443
64 N Brent St Ventura (93003) *(G-22250)*
Pacific Dining Food Svc MGT, Fremont *Also called Page Front Catering (G-7975)*
Pacific Eagle Holdings Corp 415 398-2473
353 Sacramento St Ste 360 San Francisco (94111) *(G-11029)*
Pacific Earth Resources (PA) 805 986-8277
305 Hueneme Rd Camarillo (93012) *(G-309)*
Pacific Eastern Intl Pdts 714 538-3434
12551 Barrett Ln Santa Ana (92705) *(G-9285)*
Pacific Eastern Intl Pdts I, Santa Ana *Also called Pacific Eastern Intl Pdts (G-9285)*
Pacific Echo Inc 310 539-1822
23540 Telo Ave Torrance (90505) *(G-7945)*
Pacific Energy Fuels Company 415 973-8200
77 Beale St Ste 100 San Francisco (94105) *(G-6270)*
Pacific Engineering Builders 650 557-1238
1009 Terra Nova Blvd Pacifica (94044) *(G-1626)*
Pacific Equities Captl 310 477-5300
1640 S Sepulveda Blvd # 308 Los Angeles (90025) *(G-11261)*
Pacific Event Productions Inc (PA) 858 458-9908
6989 Corte Santa Fe San Diego (92121) *(G-17392)*
Pacific Excavation Inc 916 686-2800
9796 Kent St Elk Grove (95624) *(G-3440)*
Pacific Exteriors, Garden Grove *Also called Quail Engineering Inc (G-1847)*
Pacific Exteriors Inc 714 265-1998
13911 Enterprise Dr Ste B Garden Grove (92843) *(G-2948)*
Pacific Eye Associated Inc 415 923-3007
2100 Webster St Ste 214 San Francisco (94115) *(G-19803)*
Pacific Fire Safety, Pomona *Also called Ferguson Fire Fabrication Inc (G-7719)*
Pacific Foods & Dist Inc 714 547-0787
3431 W Carriage Dr Santa Ana (92704) *(G-8896)*
Pacific Fresh Sea Food Company (HQ) 916 419-5500
1420 National Dr Sacramento (95834) *(G-8562)*
Pacific Fresh Seafood Company, Wilmington *Also called Pacific Sea Food Co Inc (G-8647)*
Pacific Frnsic Psychlogy Assoc 925 253-3111
9261 Folsom Blvd Ste 300 Sacramento (95826) *(G-22789)*
Pacific Gardens, Santa Clara *Also called Community Home Partners LLC (G-21071)*
Pacific Gardens Hlth Care Ctr, Fresno *Also called Covenant Care California LLC (G-20493)*
Pacific Gas and Electric Co 415 973-7000
425 Beck Ave Fairfield (94533) *(G-6161)*
Pacific Gas and Electric Co (HQ) 415 973-7000
77 Beale St San Francisco (94105) *(G-6162)*
Pacific Gas and Electric Co 916 375-5005
885 Embarcadero Dr West Sacramento (95605) *(G-6163)*
Pacific Gas and Electric Co 530 742-3251
530 E St Marysville (95901) *(G-6164)*
Pacific Gas and Electric Co 510 450-5744
4525 Hollis St Oakland (94608) *(G-6165)*
Pacific Gas and Electric Co 510 784-3253
24300 Clawiter Rd Hayward (94545) *(G-6271)*
Pacific Gas and Electric Co 650 592-9411
1970 Industrial Way Belmont (94002) *(G-6166)*
Pacific Gas and Electric Co 800 756-7243
111 Stony Cir Santa Rosa (95401) *(G-6167)*
Pacific Gas and Electric Co 530 894-4739
460 Rio Lindo Ave Chico (95926) *(G-6272)*

Pacific Gas and Electric Co. 530 892-4519
  15449 Humbug Rd Magalia (95954) *(G-6168)*
Pacific Gas and Electric Co. 530 477-3245
  788 Taylorville Rd Grass Valley (95949) *(G-6169)*
Pacific Gas and Electric Co. 707 765-5118
  210 Corona Rd Petaluma (94954) *(G-6170)*
Pacific Gas and Electric Co. 559 268-2868
  650 O St Fresno (93721) *(G-6171)*
Pacific Gas and Electric Co. 805 506-5280
  9 Mi Nw Of Avila Bch Avila Beach (93424) *(G-6172)*
Pacific Gas and Electric Co. 530 365-7672
  3600 Meadow View Dr Redding (96002) *(G-6173)*
Pacific Gas and Electric Co. 415 973-0778
  303 2nd Ave San Francisco (94118) *(G-6174)*
Pacific Gas and Electric Co. 925 676-0948
  4690 Evora Rd Concord (94520) *(G-6175)*
Pacific Gas and Electric Co. 925 674-6305
  1850 Gateway Blvd Ste 800 Concord (94520) *(G-6176)*
Pacific Gas and Electric Co. 707 444-0700
  1000 King Salmon Ave Eureka (95503) *(G-6177)*
Pacific Gas and Electric Co. 650 755-1236
  450 Eastmoor Ave Daly City (94015) *(G-6178)*
Pacific Gas and Electric Co. 209 576-6636
  1524 N Carpenter Rd Modesto (95351) *(G-6179)*
Pacific Gas and Electric Co. 209 942-1787
  3136 Boeing Way Stockton (95206) *(G-6180)*
Pacific Gas and Electric Co. 707 468-3954
  776 S State St Ste 103 Ukiah (95482) *(G-6181)*
Pacific Gas and Electric Co. 805 773-6109
  800 Price Canyon Rd Pismo Beach (93449) *(G-6182)*
Pacific Gas and Electric Co. 916 386-5204
  5555 Florin Perkins Rd Sacramento (95826) *(G-6183)*
Pacific Gas and Electric Co. 831 648-3231
  2311 Garden Rd Monterey (93940) *(G-6184)*
Pacific Gas and Electric Co. 510 770-2025
  42105 Boyce Rd Fremont (94538) *(G-6185)*
Pacific Gas and Electric Co. 559 855-6112
  33755 Old Mill Rd Auberry (93602) *(G-6186)*
Pacific Gas and Electric Co. 925 373-2623
  3797 1st St Livermore (94551) *(G-6187)*
Pacific Gas and Electric Co. 530 757-5803
  316 L St Davis (95616) *(G-6188)*
Pacific Gas and Electric Co. 415 695-3513
  2180 Harrison St San Francisco (94110) *(G-6189)*
Pacific Gas and Electric Co. 408 945-6215
  66 Ranch Dr Milpitas (95035) *(G-6190)*
Pacific Gas and Electric Co. 209 295-2651
  28570 Tiger Creek Rd Pioneer (95666) *(G-6191)*
Pacific Gas and Electric Co. 661 398-5918
  4201 Arrow St Bakersfield (93308) *(G-6192)*
Pacific Gas and Electric Co. 805 434-4418
  160 Cow Meadow Pl Templeton (93465) *(G-6193)*
Pacific Gas and Electric Co. 415 973-8089
  245 Market St Ste 104 San Francisco (94105) *(G-6194)*
Pacific Gas Turbine Center LLC 858 877-2910
  7007 Consolidated Way San Diego (92121) *(G-17997)*
Pacific Golf & Country Club 949 498-6604
  200 Avenida La Pata San Clemente (92673) *(G-19024)*
Pacific Grain & Foods LLC (PA) 559 276-2580
  4067 W Shaw Ave Ste 116 Fresno (93722) *(G-8961)*
Pacific Grain and Foods, Fresno Also called Pacific Grain & Foods LLC *(G-8961)*
Pacific Groservice Inc 408 727-4826
  567 Cinnabar St San Jose (95110) *(G-9235)*
Pacific Grove Aslmar Oper Corp 831 372-8016
  800 Asilomar Blvd Pacific Grove (93950) *(G-13056)*
Pacific Grove Cnvalescnet Hosp 831 375-2695
  200 Lighthouse Ave Pacific Grove (93950) *(G-21340)*
Pacific Grove Hospital, Riverside Also called Vista Behavioral Health Inc *(G-22111)*
Pacific Growth Equities LLC 415 274-6800
  1 Bush St Ste 1700 San Francisco (94104) *(G-10067)*
Pacific Gtwy Wrkfrce Prtnr Inc 562 570-3700
  3447 Atlantic Ave Long Beach (90807) *(G-14718)*
Pacific Haven Convalescent HM, Garden Grove Also called Pacific Haven Convalescent HM *(G-21341)*
Pacific Haven Convalescent HM 714 534-1942
  12072 Trask Ave Garden Grove (92843) *(G-21341)*
Pacific Hills Manor, Morgan Hill Also called Covenant Care LLC *(G-20484)*
Pacific Home Works Inc 310 781-3012
  20725 S Wstn Ave Ste 100 Torrance (90501) *(G-3561)*
Pacific Homecare Services, Stockton Also called Pacific Coast Services Inc *(G-22529)*
Pacific Homes Foundation 818 729-8106
  303 N Lennox Glenoaks1000 # 1000 Burbank (91502) *(G-21342)*
Pacific Hotel Dev Ventr LP 650 347-8260
  625 El Camino Real Palo Alto (94301) *(G-13057)*
Pacific Hotel Management LLC 510 547-7888
  1603 Powell St Emeryville (94608) *(G-13058)*
Pacific Hotel Management LLC 510 262-0700
  3150 Garrity Way Richmond (94806) *(G-13059)*
Pacific Hotel Management LLC 650 328-2800
  625 El Camino Real Palo Alto (94301) *(G-13060)*
Pacific Hotel Management Inc 949 608-1091
  4545 Macarthur Blvd Newport Beach (92660) *(G-13061)*
Pacific Housing Management (PA) 714 508-1777
  945 Katella St Laguna Beach (92651) *(G-11724)*
Pacific Hydrotech Corporation 951 943-8803
  314 E 3rd St Perris (92570) *(G-26005)*
Pacific Indemnity Company 213 622-2334
  555 S Flower St Ste 300 Los Angeles (90071) *(G-10821)*
Pacific Inn, The, Seal Beach Also called Saga Seal Co Ltd *(G-13187)*

Pacific Inptient Med Group Inc 415 485-8824
  9 Jeffrey Ct Novato (94945) *(G-19804)*
Pacific Insulation, Commerce Also called Farwest Insulation Contracting *(G-2896)*
Pacific Interior Design, Anaheim Also called Pacific Design Directions Inc *(G-1230)*
Pacific Interior Medicine, San Francisco Also called Arlene Keller MD *(G-19356)*
PACIFIC INTERNATIONAL MARKETIN, Salinas Also called Pacific Intl Vgetable Mktg Inc *(G-8761)*
Pacific Intl Vgetable Mktg Inc (PA) 831 422-3745
  740 Airport Blvd Salinas (93901) *(G-8761)*
Pacific Investment MGT Co LLC (HQ) 949 720-6000
  650 Nwport Ctr Dr Ste 100 Newport Beach (92660) *(G-10168)*
Pacific Labor Services Inc 805 488-4625
  5690 Cypress Rd Oxnard (93033) *(G-13454)*
Pacific Lath & Plaster, Escondido Also called Master Design Drywall Inc *(G-2928)*
Pacific Legal Foundation (PA) 916 419-7111
  930 G St Sacramento (95814) *(G-23488)*
Pacific Leisure Management, San Francisco Also called Okabe International Inc *(G-4996)*
Pacific Life & Annuity Company 949 219-3011
  700 Newport Center Dr Newport Beach (92660) *(G-10218)*
Pacific Lighting Manufacturer 310 327-7711
  2329 E Pacifica Pl Compton (90220) *(G-7464)*
Pacific Line Clean-Up Inc 949 348-0245
  27601 Forbes Rd Ste 29 Laguna Niguel (92677) *(G-3562)*
Pacific Lodge Boy's Home, Woodland Hills Also called Pacific Lodge Youth Services *(G-24759)*
Pacific Lodge Youth Services 818 347-1577
  4900 Serrania Ave Woodland Hills (91364) *(G-24759)*
Pacific Logistics Corp (PA) 562 478-4700
  7255 Rosemead Blvd Pico Rivera (90660) *(G-5142)*
Pacific Maintenance Company, Santa Clara Also called Pyramid Building Maint Corp *(G-14398)*
Pacific Maintenance Svcs Inc 909 793-7111
  1902 Verde Vista Dr Redlands (92373) *(G-14377)*
Pacific Marine Credit Union (PA) 760 430-7511
  1278 Rocky Point Dr Oceanside (92056) *(G-9619)*
Pacific Marine Development 858 674-6642
  16870 W Bernardo Dr San Diego (92127) *(G-26006)*
Pacific Maritime Freight Inc 562 590-8188
  1512 Pier C St Long Beach (90813) *(G-4768)*
Pacific Medical Inc (PA) 800 726-9180
  1700 N Chrisman Rd Tracy (95304) *(G-17393)*
Pacific Medical Buildings LP 858 794-1900
  3394 Carmel Mountain Rd # 200 San Diego (92121) *(G-11725)*
Pacific Mercantile Bank (HQ) 714 438-2500
  949 S Coast Dr Ste 300 Costa Mesa (92626) *(G-9514)*
Pacific Metro Electric Inc 209 939-3222
  3150 E Fremont St Stockton (95205) *(G-2674)*
Pacific Metro LLC (PA) 408 201-5000
  235 Pine St Ste 1150 San Francisco (94104) *(G-9286)*
Pacific Monarch Resorts Inc 949 228-1396
  7 Grenada St Laguna Niguel (92677) *(G-11726)*
Pacific Monarch Resorts Inc 951 905-5377
  981 Iowa Ave Ste C Riverside (92507) *(G-11727)*
Pacific Monarch Resorts Inc (PA) 949 609-2400
  4000 Macarthur Blvd # 600 Newport Beach (92660) *(G-11728)*
Pacific Mortgage Resources, Walnut Creek Also called Diablo Realty Inc *(G-11470)*
Pacific Nursing Services, La Jolla Also called Care Health Services of Fla *(G-22388)*
Pacific Occptnal Medicine Svcs 562 997-2290
  2776 Pacific Ave Long Beach (90806) *(G-21776)*
Pacific Outdoor Living, Sun Valley Also called Pro Ponds West Inc *(G-789)*
Pacific Outdoor Living, Sun Valley Also called Pacific Pavingstone Inc *(G-3307)*
Pacific Palms Healthcare LLC 562 433-6791
  1020 Termino Ave Long Beach (90804) *(G-22530)*
Pacific Park, Santa Monica Also called Santa Monica Amusements LLC *(G-18831)*
Pacific Park Management (PA) 415 434-4400
  465 California St Ste 473 San Francisco (94104) *(G-17731)*
Pacific Parts International, Canoga Park Also called Richard Huetter Inc *(G-6759)*
Pacific Pavingstone Inc 818 244-4000
  8309 Tujunga Ave Unit 201 Sun Valley (91352) *(G-3307)*
Pacific Pharma Inc 714 246-4600
  18600 Von Karman Ave Irvine (92612) *(G-8288)*
Pacific Pioneer Insur Group, Cypress Also called Pacific Pioneer Insur Group *(G-10822)*
Pacific Pioneer Insur Group (PA) 714 228-7888
  6363 Katella Ave Cypress (90630) *(G-10822)*
Pacific Plms Conference Resort, City of Industry Also called Majestic Industry Hills LLC *(G-12936)*
Pacific Premier Bank (HQ) 714 431-4000
  17901 Von Karman Ave Irvine (92614) *(G-11729)*
Pacific Preservation Services, Thousand Oaks Also called National Real Estate Solutions *(G-14366)*
Pacific Process Systems Inc (PA) 661 321-9681
  7401 Rosedale Hwy Bakersfield (93308) *(G-1091)*
Pacific Production Plumbing (PA) 951 509-3100
  1584 Pioneer Way El Cajon (92020) *(G-2315)*
Pacific Program/Design Managem 626 440-2000
  100 W Walnut St Pasadena (91124) *(G-27154)*
Pacific Properties Realty, Hawthorne Also called Argon Enterprises Inc *(G-11305)*
Pacific Protection Services 818 313-9369
  22144 Clarendon St # 110 Woodland Hills (91367) *(G-16755)*
Pacific Pulmonary Services Co, Novato Also called Braden Partners LP A Calif *(G-22379)*
Pacific Racing Association 510 559-7300
  1100 Eastshore Hwy Albany (94710) *(G-18572)*
Pacific Rebar Inc 909 984-7199
  501 S Oaks Ave Ontario (91762) *(G-3394)*
Pacific Rehabilitation & Wel 707 443-9767
  2211 Harrison Ave Eureka (95501) *(G-20833)*

Pacific Relocation Consultants, Long Beach *Also called Overland Pacific & Cutler* ***(G-17386)***
Pacific Restoration Group Inc....951 940-6069
325 E Ellis Ave Perris (92570) ***(G-785)***
Pacific Retirement Svcs Inc....530 753-1450
1515 Shasta Dr Ofc Davis (95616) ***(G-24760)***
Pacific Rim Contractors Inc....714 641-7380
1315 E Saint Andrew Pl B Santa Ana (92705) ***(G-2949)***
Pacific Rim Mech Contrs Inc....714 285-2600
1701 E Edinger Ave Ste F2 Santa Ana (92705) ***(G-2316)***
Pacific Rim Mech Contrs Inc (PA)....858 974-6500
7655 Convoy Ct San Diego (92111) ***(G-2317)***
Pacific Rim Realty Group....805 553-9562
740 Lucille Ct Moorpark (93021) ***(G-11730)***
Pacific Rim Recycling, Benicia *Also called Julie Coleman Enterprises Inc* ***(G-6493)***
Pacific Rim Rsrces Search Agcy....714 638-0307
14148 Brookhurst St Garden Grove (92843) ***(G-14719)***
Pacific Royal Group....510 200-2993
5500 Stewart Ave Ste 113 Fremont (94538) ***(G-9287)***
Pacific Sd/Pcfic Arbor Nrsries, Camarillo *Also called Pacific Earth Resources* ***(G-309)***
Pacific Sea Food Co Inc....916 419-5500
1420 National Dr Sacramento (95834) ***(G-8646)***
Pacific Sea Food Co Inc....310 835-4343
605 Flint Ave Wilmington (90744) ***(G-8647)***
Pacific Seafood Sacramento, Sacramento *Also called Pacific Fresh Sea Food Company* ***(G-8562)***
Pacific Secured Equities Inc (PA)....916 677-2500
6020 W Oaks Blvd Ste 100 Rocklin (95765) ***(G-27579)***
Pacific Service Credit Union (PA)....888 858-6878
3000 Clayton Rd Concord (94519) ***(G-9677)***
Pacific Shores Masonry....951 371-8550
1369 Walker Ln Corona (92879) ***(G-2831)***
Pacific Shores Med Group Inc (PA)....562 590-0345
1043 Elm Ave Ste 104 Long Beach (90813) ***(G-19805)***
Pacific Slope Tree Coop Inc....415 663-1300
11201 State Rte One 201 Point Reyes Station (94956) ***(G-996)***
Pacific Snow Valley Resort LLC....626 588-2889
1427 W Valley Blvd # 201 Alhambra (91803) ***(G-13062)***
Pacific Southwest, Long Beach *Also called Foss Maritime Company* ***(G-4715)***
Pacific Southwest Cnstr & Eqp....619 445-5190
2308 Shaylene Way Alpine (91901) ***(G-1976)***
Pacific Southwest Instruments, Corona *Also called Pacwest Instrument Labs* ***(G-17998)***
Pacific Spanish Network Inc....619 427-6323
296 H St Ste 300 Chula Vista (91910) ***(G-5814)***
Pacific Specialty Insurance Co....650 780-4800
2200 Geng Rd Ste 200 Palo Alto (94303) ***(G-10823)***
Pacific State Bancorp....209 870-3214
1899 W March Ln Stockton (95207) ***(G-9579)***
Pacific States Industries Inc....408 779-7354
10 Madrone Ave Morgan Hill (95037) ***(G-6945)***
Pacific States Investors....650 326-0990
1551 Emerson St Palo Alto (94301) ***(G-12082)***
Pacific Sterling Properties....949 222-9911
2101 Bus Ctr Dr Ste 140 Irvine (92612) ***(G-11030)***
Pacific Sthwest Structures Inc....619 469-2323
7845 Lemon Grove Way A Lemon Grove (91945) ***(G-3308)***
Pacific Structures Inc....415 367-9399
953 Mission St Ste 200 San Francisco (94103) ***(G-3309)***
Pacific Structures Cnstr Inc....740 480-4133
101 State Pl Ste E Escondido (92029) ***(G-3310)***
Pacific Sttes Envmtl Cntrs Inc....925 803-4333
11555 Dublin Blvd Dublin (94568) ***(G-1627)***
Pacific Suites Hotel, Santa Monica *Also called Windsor Capital Group Inc* ***(G-13415)***
Pacific Supply, Santa Ana *Also called Beacon Sales Acquisition Inc* ***(G-7008)***
Pacific Symphony....714 876-2301
3631 S Harbor Blvd # 100 Santa Ana (92704) ***(G-18484)***
Pacific Systems Interiors Inc....310 436-6820
1612 W 139th St Gardena (90249) ***(G-2950)***
Pacific Tank Lines Inc....951 680-1900
5230 Wilson St Ste A Riverside (92509) ***(G-6260)***
Pacific Telemanagement Svcs, San Ramon *Also called Jaroth Inc* ***(G-2622)***
Pacific Terrace, San Diego *Also called Bartell Hotels* ***(G-12419)***
Pacific Terrace Inn, Coronado *Also called El Cordova Hotel* ***(G-12612)***
Pacific Theaters....818 501-5121
9400 Shirley Ave Northridge (91324) ***(G-18290)***
Pacific Theaters Inc (PA)....310 657-8420
120 N Robertson Blvd Fl 3 Los Angeles (90048) ***(G-18340)***
Pacific Theaters Inc....310 607-0007
831 S Nash St El Segundo (90245) ***(G-18341)***
Pacific Theaters Inc....562 634-1183
4821 Del Amo Blvd Lakewood (90712) ***(G-18342)***
Pacific Theatres Entrmt Corp (HQ)....310 657-8420
120 N Robertson Blvd Fl 3 Los Angeles (90048) ***(G-27580)***
Pacific Thtres Cmmerce Theatre, Commerce *Also called Commerce Center Theatres* ***(G-18318)***
Pacific Towboat & Salvage Co....562 435-0171
Berth 35 Pier D Long Beach (90802) ***(G-4769)***
Pacific Towing, Stockton *Also called Covey Auto Express Inc* ***(G-17881)***
Pacific Toxicology Labs....818 598-3110
9348 De Soto Ave Chatsworth (91311) ***(G-22251)***
Pacific Trellis Fruit LLC (PA)....559 255-5437
5108 E Clinton Way # 108 Fresno (93727) ***(G-8762)***
Pacific Unified Pd Inc....310 817-3346
678 S Indian Hill Blvd Claremont (91711) ***(G-16908)***
Pacific Unified Railroad Co, Claremont *Also called Pacific Unified Pd Inc* ***(G-16908)***
Pacific Union Club....415 775-1234
1000 California St San Francisco (94108) ***(G-25309)***
Pacific Union Co....415 474-6600
1699 Van Ness Ave San Francisco (94109) ***(G-11731)***
Pacific Union Financial LLC....714 918-0799
3 Macarthur Pl Ste 500 Santa Ana (92707) ***(G-10169)***
Pacific Union Homes Inc (PA)....925 314-3800
675 Hartz Ave Ste 300 Danville (94526) ***(G-11997)***
Pacific Union RE Group (HQ)....415 929-7100
1 Letterman Dr Ste 300 San Francisco (94129) ***(G-11732)***
Pacific Union Residental Brkg....510 339-6460
1900 Mountain Blvd # 102 Oakland (94611) ***(G-11733)***
Pacific Utlity Instllation Inc....714 970-6430
1585 N Harmony Cir Anaheim (92807) ***(G-2675)***
Pacific Ventures Ltd....626 576-0737
2200 W Valley Blvd Alhambra (91803) ***(G-27155)***
Pacific View Companies, La Mesa *Also called Pvcc Inc* ***(G-11035)***
Pacific Vision Services Inc....909 824-6090
1900 E Washington St Colton (92324) ***(G-20302)***
Pacific W Space Cmmnctions Inc....909 592-4321
900 W Gladstone St San Dimas (91773) ***(G-1977)***
Pacific West Corporation (PA)....515 270-8181
10369 Regis Ct Rancho Cucamonga (91730) ***(G-16451)***
Pacific West Lath & Plaster....916 329-9028
6853 Mccomber St Sacramento (95828) ***(G-2951)***
Pacific West Security Inc....801 748-1034
1587 Schallenberger Rd San Jose (95131) ***(G-16909)***
Pacific West Tree Service, Vista *Also called Pac West Land Care Inc* ***(G-927)***
Pacific Western Bank....760 432-1350
900 Canterbury Pl Ste 300 Escondido (92025) ***(G-9414)***
Pacific Western Bank....310 996-9100
11150 W Olympic Blvd # 100 Los Angeles (90064) ***(G-9415)***
Pacific Western Bank....760 918-2469
5900 La Place Ct Ste 200 Carlsbad (92008) ***(G-9416)***
Pacific Western Bank....619 562-6400
9955 Mission Gorge Rd Santee (92071) ***(G-9515)***
Pacific Western Bank....858 436-3500
12481 High Bluff Dr # 350 San Diego (92130) ***(G-9417)***
Pacific Western Bank....760 432-1100
900 Cantebury Pl Ste 300 Escondido (92025) ***(G-9418)***
Pacific Western Bank....805 688-6644
610 Alamo Pintado Rd Solvang (93463) ***(G-9580)***
Pacific Western Sales....714 572-6730
2980 Enterprise St Ste A Brea (92821) ***(G-9288)***
Pacific Wine Distributors Inc....626 471-9997
15751 Tapia St Irwindale (91706) ***(G-4048)***
Pacific Ygnacio Corporation....925 939-3275
500 Ygnacio Valley Rd # 340 Walnut Creek (94596) ***(G-11262)***
Pacifica Care Center....650 355-5622
385 Esplanade Ave Pacifica (94044) ***(G-20834)***
Pacifica Companies LLC (PA)....619 296-9000
1775 Hancock St Ste 200 San Diego (92110) ***(G-12264)***
Pacifica Crossroads, San Ramon *Also called Pacifica Reflections* ***(G-1381)***
Pacifica Health and Medical....619 688-1848
2650 Cmino Del Rio N 21 San Diego (92108) ***(G-13783)***
Pacifica Hiorange LP....714 556-3838
2720 Hotel Ter Santa Ana (92705) ***(G-13063)***
Pacifica Home Loans Inc....949 417-1063
7505 Irvine Center Dr Irvine (92618) ***(G-9880)***
Pacifica Hospital of Valley, Sun Valley *Also called Pacifica of Valley Corporation* ***(G-21777)***
Pacifica Host Inc....916 444-8000
700 16th St Sacramento (95814) ***(G-13064)***
Pacifica Hosts Inc....310 670-9000
6225 W Century Blvd Los Angeles (90045) ***(G-13065)***
Pacifica Hotel & Conference Ce....310 649-1776
6161 W Centinela Ave Culver City (90230) ***(G-13066)***
Pacifica Hotel Company....619 221-8000
1551 Shelter Island Dr San Diego (92106) ***(G-13067)***
Pacifica Hotel Company (HQ)....805 957-0095
1933 Cliff Dr Ste 1 Santa Barbara (93109) ***(G-11734)***
Pacifica Hotel Company....650 726-9000
2400 Cabrillo Hwy S Half Moon Bay (94019) ***(G-13068)***
Pacifica Katie Avenue LLC....619 296-9000
1775 Hancock St Ste 100 San Diego (92110) ***(G-26698)***
Pacifica Linda Mar Inc....650 359-4800
751 San Pedro Terrace Rd Pacifica (94044) ***(G-20835)***
Pacifica Nursing & Rehab Ctr, Pacifica *Also called Pacifica Care Center* ***(G-20834)***
Pacifica of Valley Corporation....818 767-3310
9449 San Fernando Rd Sun Valley (91352) ***(G-21777)***
Pacifica Reflections....925 275-9800
405 Reflections Cir San Ramon (94583) ***(G-1381)***
Pacifica San Jose LP....619 296-9000
1775 Hancock St Ste 100 San Diego (92110) ***(G-13069)***
Pacifica Services Inc....626 405-0131
106 S Mentor Ave Ste 200 Pasadena (91106) ***(G-26007)***
Pacificare, Concord *Also called United Behavioral Health* ***(G-10385)***
Pacificare Dental....661 631-8613
3110 W Lake Center Dr Santa Ana (92704) ***(G-10365)***
Pacificare Health Plan Admin (HQ)....714 825-5200
3120 W Lake Center Dr Santa Ana (92704) ***(G-10366)***
Pacificare Health Systems, Huntington Beach *Also called Unitedhealth Group Inc* ***(G-10386)***
Pacificare Health Systems, Cypress *Also called Unitedhealth Group Inc* ***(G-10387)***
Pacificare Health Systems LLC (HQ)....714 952-1121
5995 Plaza Dr Cypress (90630) ***(G-10367)***
Pacificare of California, Cypress *Also called Uhc of California* ***(G-10384)***
Pacificdental Benefits Inc (PA)....925 363-6000
2300 Clayton Rd Ste 1000 Concord (94520) ***(G-10368)***
Pacificore Construction Inc....657 859-4500
1342 Bell Ave Ste 3a Tustin (92780) ***(G-1628)***
Paciolan Inc....949 476-2050
5171 California Ave # 200 Irvine (92617) ***(G-15813)***
Pacira Pharmaceuticals Inc....858 625-2424
10578 Science Center Dr San Diego (92121) ***(G-8289)***

ALPHABETIC

Pack & Crate Services Inc......760 737-6893
238 N Quince St Escondido (92025) *(G-4370)*
Packaging Innovators Corp......925 371-2000
6650 National Dr Livermore (94550) *(G-8213)*
Packaging Manufacturing Inc......619 498-9199
9295 Siempre Viva Rd C San Diego (92154) *(G-9289)*
Packard Childrens Hlth Aliance......650 723-0439
725 Welch Rd Palo Alto (94304) *(G-19806)*
Packard Hospitality Group LLC......858 277-4305
9555 Chesapeake Dr # 202 San Diego (92123) *(G-27156)*
Packard Medical Group Inc......650 724-3637
770 Welch Rd Palo Alto (94304) *(G-19807)*
Packard Realty Inc......310 649-5151
9901 S La Cienega Blvd Los Angeles (90045) *(G-13070)*
Packet Design Inc......408 490-1000
1 Almaden Blvd Ste 1150 San Jose (95113) *(G-15364)*
Packetvideo Corporation......310 526-5200
1901 Avenue Of The Stars # 390 Los Angeles (90067) *(G-15365)*
Packetvideo Corporation (HQ)......858 731-5300
10350 Science Center Dr San Diego (92121) *(G-15366)*
PacLease, Fresno *Also called Paccar Leasing Corporation (G-17642)*
Paclo, Pico Rivera *Also called Pacific Logistics Corp (G-5142)*
Pactron......408 329-5500
3000 Patrick Henry Dr Santa Clara (95054) *(G-16452)*
Pacwest Instrument Labs......951 737-0790
1721 Railroad St Corona (92880) *(G-17998)*
Padi Americas Inc......949 858-7234
30151 Tomas Rcho STA Marg (92688) *(G-25149)*
Padi Worldwide Corp (HQ)......949 858-7234
30151 Tomas Rcho STA Marg (92688) *(G-25150)*
Padilla Construction Company......714 685-8500
1130 W Trenton Ave Orange (92867) *(G-2952)*
Padilla Farm Labor Inc......559 562-1166
20486 Road 196 Lindsay (93247) *(G-221)*
Padilla Landscape Inc......925 513-9353
181 Sand Creek Rd Ste B Brentwood (94513) *(G-928)*
Padre Associates Inc......661 829-2686
3500 Coffee Rd Ste B Bakersfield (93308) *(G-26008)*
Padre Dam Municipal Water Dst (PA)......619 258-4617
9300 Fanita Pkwy Santee (92071) *(G-6386)*
Padres LP......619 795-5000
100 Pk Blvd Petco Park Petco Pk San Diego (92101) *(G-18560)*
Pafco, Vernon *Also called Pacific American Fish Co Inc (G-8644)*
Paganini Companies, San Francisco *Also called Paganini Electric Corporation (G-2676)*
Paganini Electric Corporation......415 575-3900
190 Hubbell St Ste 200 San Francisco (94107) *(G-2676)*
Page Front Catering......408 406-8487
34793 Ardentech Ct Fremont (94555) *(G-7975)*
Pagerduty Inc......650 989-2965
600 Townsend St Ste 200e San Francisco (94103) *(G-6086)*
Paglia & Associates Cnstr......714 982-5151
2651 Saturn St Brea (92821) *(G-1231)*
Pahc Apartments Inc......650 321-9709
725 Alma St Palo Alto (94301) *(G-11182)*
Pain Management Specialists PC......805 544-7246
1551 Bishop St Ste 230 San Luis Obispo (93401) *(G-19808)*
Paint Sundries Solutions Inc......818 843-2382
2930 N San Fernando Blvd Burbank (91504) *(G-9238)*
Painted Hills Power......760 406-1771
15234 Painted Hills Rd Whitewater (92282) *(G-1840)*
Paiute Palace Casino, Bishop *Also called Bishop Paiute Gaming Corp (G-19151)*
Pajaro Valley Greenhouses (PA)......831 722-2773
90 Hecker Pass Rd Watsonville (95076) *(G-9207)*
Pajaro Valley Prevntn & Studen......831 728-6445
335 E Lake Ave Watsonville (95076) *(G-24120)*
Pak West Paper & Packaging, Santa Ana *Also called Blower-Dempsay Corporation (G-8151)*
Paklab, Chino *Also called Universal Packg Systems Inc (G-4648)*
Pala Band of Mission Indians......760 207-2603
3478 Sunset Dr Fallbrook (92028) *(G-18485)*
Pala Casino Spa & Resort......760 510-5100
35008 Pala Temecula Rd Pala (92059) *(G-18667)*
Pala Mesa Limited Partnership......760 728-5881
2001 Old Highway 395 Fallbrook (92028) *(G-13071)*
Pala Mesa Resort, Fallbrook *Also called Pala Mesa Limited Partnership (G-13071)*
Palace Entertainment Inc (HQ)......949 261-0404
4590 Macarthur Blvd # 400 Newport Beach (92660) *(G-19256)*
Palace of The Legion Honor, San Francisco *Also called Corportion of Fine Arts Mseums (G-25014)*
Palace Park, Irvine *Also called Festival Fun Parks LLC (G-19211)*
Paladin Eastside Services Inc......323 890-0180
111 S Grfield Ave Ste 101 Montebello (90640) *(G-24761)*
Paladin Private Security, North Highlands *Also called Paladin Prtction Spcalists Inc (G-16910)*
Paladin Prtction Spcalists Inc......916 331-3175
4741 Watt Ave Ste B North Highlands (95660) *(G-16910)*
Palantir Technologies Inc (PA)......650 815-0200
100 Hamilton Ave Ste 300 Palo Alto (94301) *(G-15367)*
Palantir Usg Inc......650 815-0240
635 Waverley St Palo Alto (94301) *(G-15368)*
Palcare Inc......650 340-1289
945 California Dr Burlingame (94010) *(G-24496)*
Palecek Imports Inc (PA)......510 236-7730
601 Parr Blvd Richmond (94801) *(G-6829)*
Palisades Interactive, Santa Monica *Also called Palisades Media Group Inc (G-14005)*
Palisades Media Group Inc (PA)......310 564-5400
1620 26th St Ste 200s Santa Monica (90404) *(G-14005)*
Palisades Optimist Foundation......310 454-4111
15312 Whitfield Ave Pacific Palisades (90272) *(G-25310)*
Pall Fortebio Corp......650 322-1360
1360 Willow Rd Ste 201 Menlo Park (94025) *(G-26580)*
Palm Canyon Resort & Spa......760 866-1800
2800 S Palm Canyon Dr Palm Springs (92264) *(G-18668)*
Palm Desert Community Assn, Palm Desert *Also called Sun City Palm Dsert Cmnty Assn (G-25354)*
Palm Desert Greens Association......760 346-8005
73750 Country Club Dr Palm Desert (92260) *(G-25311)*
Palm Desert Medical Offices, Palm Desert *Also called Kaiser Foundation Hospitals (G-19638)*
Palm Desert Town Center, Palm Desert *Also called West Ville Palm Desert (G-11071)*
Palm Drive Healthcare District, Sebastopol *Also called County of Sonoma (G-21524)*
Palm Dsert Rcrtl Fclities Corp......760 346-0015
38995 Desert Willow Dr Palm Desert (92260) *(G-19025)*
Palm Garden Hotel, Thousand Oaks *Also called Ventu Park LLC (G-13376)*
Palm Grdns Rsdntial Care Fclty......530 661-0574
240 Palm Ave Woodland (95695) *(G-24762)*
Palm Grove Health Care, Torrance *Also called Unified Inv Programs Inc (G-23077)*
Palm Harbor Residency LP......562 595-4551
3501 Cedar Ave Long Beach (90807) *(G-21343)*
Palm Haven Care Center, Manteca *Also called Palm Haven Nursing & Rehab LLC (G-20836)*
Palm Haven Nursing & Rehab LLC......209 823-2782
469 E North St Manteca (95336) *(G-20836)*
Palm Springs Aerial Tramway, Palm Springs *Also called Mount San Jcnto Winter Pk Corp (G-19248)*
Palm Springs Art Museum Inc......760 322-4800
101 N Museum Dr Palm Springs (92262) *(G-25035)*
Palm Springs Convention Center, Palm Springs *Also called Smg Holdings Inc (G-27652)*
Palm Springs Disposal Services......760 327-1351
4690 E Mesquite Ave Palm Springs (92264) *(G-6512)*
Palm Springs Health Care Ctr, Palm Springs *Also called Five Star Quality Care Inc (G-27025)*
Palm Springs Hotel, Palm Springs *Also called Highland Hospitality Corp (G-12703)*
Palm Springs Renaissance, Palm Springs *Also called Remington Hotel Corporation (G-13138)*
Palm Sprng Riviera Resorts Spa, Palm Springs *Also called Riviera Reincarnate LLC (G-13160)*
Palm Ter Hlth Care Rhblitation, Laguna Hills *Also called Gate Three Healthcare LLC (G-24667)*
PALM TERRACE CARE CENTER, Riverside *Also called T C H P Inc (G-21389)*
Palmcrest Grand Care Ctr Inc......562 595-4551
3501 Cedar Ave Long Beach (90807) *(G-20837)*
Palmcrest Medallion Convalesc......562 595-4336
3355 Pacific Pl Long Beach (90806) *(G-20838)*
Palmcrest North Convalescent, Long Beach *Also called Palm Harbor Residency LP (G-21343)*
Palmdale Area, Lancaster *Also called Granite Construction Company (G-1781)*
Palmdale Center For Pain MGT......661 267-6876
819 Auto Center Dr Palmdale (93551) *(G-19809)*
Palmdale Med Mental Hlth Svcs, Santa Clarita *Also called American Health Services LLC (G-19339)*
Palmdale Regional Medical Ctr......661 382-5000
38600 Medical Center Dr Palmdale (93551) *(G-19810)*
Palmdale Resort Inc......661 947-8055
38630 5th St W Palmdale (93551) *(G-13072)*
Palmdale Water District......661 947-4111
2029 E Avenue Q Palmdale (93550) *(G-6387)*
Palmdale Womans Club......661 266-3008
2141 E Avenue Q Palmdale (93550) *(G-13784)*
Palmetto Hospitality......650 843-0795
4216 El Camino Real Palo Alto (94306) *(G-13073)*
Palms Assistd Lvng & Mmry Cre......916 786-7200
100 Sterling Ct Ofc Roseville (95661) *(G-24763)*
Palo Alpo Medical Foudation, Palo Alto *Also called Sutter Health (G-20104)*
Palo Alto Clinic, Palo Alto *Also called Palo Alto Medical Foundation (G-19814)*
Palo Alto Commons......650 494-0760
4075 El Camino Way Palo Alto (94306) *(G-24764)*
Palo Alto Community Child Care......650 855-9828
890 Escondido Rd Stanford (94305) *(G-24497)*
Palo Alto Egg and Food Svc Co......510 456-2420
6691 Clark Ave Newark (94560) *(G-8508)*
Palo Alto Family Y M C A......650 856-9622
3412 Ross Rd Palo Alto (94303) *(G-25312)*
Palo Alto Food Company, Newark *Also called Palo Alto Egg and Food Svc Co (G-8508)*
Palo Alto Hills Golf An......650 948-1800
3000 Alexis Dr Palo Alto (94304) *(G-13785)*
Palo Alto Med Fndtion STA Cruz......831 458-5670
2025 Soquel Ave Santa Cruz (95062) *(G-19811)*
Palo Alto Medical Clinic......650 321-4121
795 El Camino Real Palo Alto (94301) *(G-19812)*
Palo Alto Medical Foundation......650 934-3565
2350 W El Cmino Real Fl 4 Mountain View (94040) *(G-19813)*
Palo Alto Medical Foundation (HQ)......650 321-4121
795 El Camino Real Palo Alto (94301) *(G-19814)*
Palo Alto Medical Foundation......650 254-5200
370 Distel Cir Los Altos (94022) *(G-19815)*
Palo Alto Medical Foundation......408 730-4321
535 Oakmead Pkwy Sunnyvale (94085) *(G-19816)*
Palo Alto Medical Foundation......408 730-4390
201 Old San Francisco Rd Sunnyvale (94086) *(G-19817)*
Palo Alto Medical Foundation......408 524-5900
323 N Mathilda Ave Sunnyvale (94085) *(G-19818)*
Palo Alto Medical Foundation......408 739-6000
701 E El Camino Real Mountain View (94040) *(G-19819)*

ALPHABETIC

Palo Alto Medical Foundation....................650 326-8120
795 El Camino Real Palo Alto (94301) *(G-26581)*
Palo Alto Nursing Center, Palo Alto *Also called Covenant Care California LLC (G-20487)*
Palo Alto Research Center Inc....................650 812-4000
3333 Coyote Hill Rd Palo Alto (94304) *(G-26582)*
Palo Alto VA Medical Center, Palo Alto *Also called Veterans Health Administration (G-20201)*
Palo Alto Vineyard MGT LLC....................707 996-7725
50 Adobe Canyon Rd Kenwood (95452) *(G-677)*
Palo Alto Vterans Inst For RES....................650 858-3970
3801 Miran Ave Bldg 101a Palo Alto (94304) *(G-26793)*
Palo Verde Health Care Dst....................760 922-4115
250 N 1st St Blythe (92225) *(G-21778)*
Palo Verde Hospital, Blythe *Also called Palo Verde Health Care Dst (G-21778)*
Palo Verde Hospital Assn....................760 922-4115
250 N 1st St Blythe (92225) *(G-25151)*
Palo Verde Irrigation District....................760 922-3144
180 W 14th Ave Blythe (92225) *(G-6651)*
Palomar Gem & Mineral Club....................760 743-0809
2120 Mission Rd Ste 260 Escondido (92029) *(G-19026)*
Palomar Health....................858 675-5360
555 E Valley Pkwy 6 Escondido (92025) *(G-23015)*
Palomar Health (PA)....................442 281-5000
456 E Grand Ave Escondido (92025) *(G-21779)*
Palomar Health....................760 739-3000
2185 Citracado Pkwy Escondido (92029) *(G-21780)*
Palomar Health....................858 613-4000
15615 Pomerado Rd Poway (92064) *(G-21781)*
Palomar Health....................760 739-2243
150 W Crest St Escondido (92025) *(G-27581)*
Palomar Health....................858 613-4000
15615 Pomerado Rd Poway (92064) *(G-22312)*
Palomar Health Downtown Campus, Escondido *Also called Kaiser Foundation Hospitals (G-19612)*
Palomar Medical Center, Escondido *Also called Palomar Health (G-21779)*
Palomar Medical Center, Escondido *Also called Kaiser Foundation Hospitals (G-19610)*
Palomar Medical Center, Escondido *Also called Palomar Health (G-21780)*
Palomar San Diego, San Diego *Also called Khp II San Diego Hotel LLC (G-12882)*
PALOMAR VISTA HEALTHCARE CENTE, Escondido *Also called West Escondido Healthcare LLC (G-21031)*
Palomar Vista Healthcare Ctr, Escondido *Also called Ensign Group Inc (G-20541)*
Palomino Db Inc....................775 572-8854
222 8th St San Francisco (94103) *(G-16453)*
Paloras Corporation....................650 440-7663
228 Hamilton Ave Fl 3 Palo Alto (94301) *(G-27582)*
Palos Verdes Beach & Athc CLB....................310 375-8777
389 Paseo Del Mar Palos Verdes Estates (90274) *(G-19027)*
Palos Verdes Bowl, Torrance *Also called Crenshaw Bowling (G-18517)*
Palp Inc....................562 599-5841
2230 Lemon Ave Long Beach (90806) *(G-1841)*
Pam's Delivery Svc & Nat Msgnr, Orange *Also called Madden Corporation (G-17308)*
Pama Management Co....................951 929-0340
123 N Inez St Ste 16 Hemet (92543) *(G-27157)*
Pamc Ltd....................323 343-9460
4837 Huntington Dr N Los Angeles (90032) *(G-19820)*
Pamc Ltd (PA)....................213 624-8411
531 W College St Los Angeles (90012) *(G-21782)*
Pamc Health Foundation, Los Angeles *Also called Pamc Ltd (G-21782)*
Pamco Construction Services....................951 279-1962
211 Granite St Ste H Corona (92879) *(G-1629)*
Pamona Valley Physical Therapy, Claremont *Also called Pomona Valley Hospital Med Ctr (G-20342)*
Pamona Vallley Hospital, Pomona *Also called Pomona Valley Hospital Med Ctr (G-22161)*
Pan American Agriculture Corp....................805 524-1489
583 Ojai St Fillmore (93015) *(G-30)*
Pan American Body Shop Inc....................408 289-8745
555 Burke St San Jose (95112) *(G-17764)*
Pan Pacific Petroleum Co Inc....................661 589-3200
1850 Coffee Rd Bakersfield (93308) *(G-4241)*
Pan Pacific Petroleum Co Inc (PA)....................562 928-0100
9302 Garfield Ave South Gate (90280) *(G-4242)*
Pan Pacific San Diego, San Diego *Also called Pan Pcfic Htels Rsrts Amer Inc (G-13074)*
Pan Pcfic Htels Rsrts Amer Inc....................619 239-4500
400 W Broadway San Diego (92101) *(G-13074)*
Pan-Pacific Mechanical LLC (PA)....................949 474-9170
18250 Euclid St Fountain Valley (92708) *(G-2318)*
Pan-Pacific Mechanical LLC....................650 561-8810
1205 Chrysler Dr Menlo Park (94025) *(G-2319)*
Pan-Pacific Mechanical LLC....................858 764-2464
11622 El Camino Real San Diego (92130) *(G-2320)*
Pan-Pacific Plumbing & Mech, San Diego *Also called Pan-Pacific Mechanical LLC (G-2320)*
Pana-Pacific, Fresno *Also called Brix Group Inc (G-7534)*
Pana-Pacific OEM Division, Fresno *Also called Brix Group Inc (G-7535)*
Panalpina Inc....................650 873-1390
401 E Grand Ave South San Francisco (94080) *(G-5143)*
Panalpina Inc....................310 819-4060
19900 S Vermont Ave Ste A Torrance (90502) *(G-5144)*
Panama-Buena Vista Un Schl Dst....................661 397-2205
5901 Schirra Ct Bakersfield (93313) *(G-14378)*
Panama-Buena Vista Un Schl Dst....................661 831-7879
4200 Ashe Rd Bakersfield (93313) *(G-4610)*
Panaroma Gardens, Panorama City *Also called Ensign Group Inc (G-20538)*
Panasas Inc (PA)....................408 215-6800
969 W Maude Ave Sunnyvale (94085) *(G-15369)*
Panasonic....................949 581-0661
26160 Enterprise Way Lake Forest (92630) *(G-7502)*
Panasonic Broadcast TV Systems, Los Angeles *Also called Panasonic Corp North America (G-7503)*
Panasonic Corp North America....................323 436-3500
3330 Chnga Blvd W Ste 505 Los Angeles (90068) *(G-7503)*
Panasonic Corp North America....................201 348-7000
2033 Gateway Pl Ste 200 San Jose (95110) *(G-7504)*
Panasonic Corp North America....................408 861-3900
10900 N Tantau Ave 200 Cupertino (95014) *(G-26583)*
Panasonic Corp North America....................619 661-1134
2055 Sanyo Ave San Diego (92154) *(G-7505)*
Panattoni Development Co Inc (PA)....................916 381-1561
20411 Sw Birch St Ste 200 Newport Beach (92660) *(G-11735)*
Panavision Group, Woodland Hills *Also called Panavision Inc (G-14565)*
Panavision Inc (PA)....................818 316-1000
6101 Variel Ave Woodland Hills (91367) *(G-14565)*
Pancan, Manhattan Beach *Also called Pancreatic Cancr Actn Netwrk I (G-23016)*
Pancreatic Cancr Actn Netwrk I (PA)....................310 725-0025
1500 Rosecrans Ave # 200 Manhattan Beach (90266) *(G-23016)*
Pandol & Sons....................661 725-3755
401 Road 192 Delano (93215) *(G-175)*
Pandora Media Inc....................424 653-6803
3000 Ocean Park Blvd # 3050 Santa Monica (90405) *(G-5815)*
Pangea Corporation....................949 443-0666
34145 Pacific Coast Hwy Dana Point (92629) *(G-28153)*
Panorama Community Hospital....................818 787-2222
14850 Roscoe Blvd Panorama City (91402) *(G-21783)*
Panorama Madows Nursing Ctr LP....................818 894-5707
14857 Roscoe Blvd Panorama City (91402) *(G-21344)*
Panorama Park Apts....................661 325-4047
401 W Columbus St Apt 64 Bakersfield (93301) *(G-11183)*
Panther Custom Wheels, Chino *Also called Prestige Autotech Corporation (G-6755)*
Panzura Inc....................408 457-8504
695 Campbell Tech Pkwy Campbell (95008) *(G-16027)*
Pape Machinery Inc....................916 922-7181
2850 El Centro Rd Sacramento (95833) *(G-7779)*
Pape Material Handling Inc....................510 651-8200
47132 Kato Rd Fremont (94538) *(G-7874)*
Paper Company, The, Irvine *Also called Michael Madden Co Inc (G-8198)*
Paper Mart Indus & Ret Packg, Orange *Also called Frick Paper Company (G-8191)*
Papercraft Los Angeles, Cerritos *Also called Bunzl Usa Inc (G-8186)*
Papich Construction Co Inc (PA)....................805 473-3016
800 Farroll Rd Grover Beach (93433) *(G-1842)*
Pappas Telecasting Company, Fresno *Also called Kmph Fox 26 (G-5883)*
Papyrus, Fairfield *Also called Schurman Fine Papers (G-8215)*
Papyrus, San Jose *Also called Schurman Fine Papers (G-17479)*
Par Electrical Contractors Inc....................760 291-1192
525 Corporate Dr Escondido (92029) *(G-2677)*
Par Electrical Contractors Inc....................909 854-2880
11276 5th St Ste 100 Rancho Cucamonga (91730) *(G-2678)*
Par Electrical Contractors Inc....................707 693-1237
1416 Midway Rd Vacaville (95688) *(G-2679)*
Par Services, Culver City *Also called Exceptional Chld Foundation (G-24338)*
Par Services, Culver City *Also called Exceptional Chld Foundation (G-24339)*
Par Services, Culver City *Also called Exceptional Chld Foundation (G-24340)*
Para & Palli Inc....................209 826-0790
931 Idaho Ave Los Banos (93635) *(G-20839)*
Para Los Ninos....................213 623-3942
845 E 6th St Los Angeles (90021) *(G-24498)*
Paracelsus Los Angeles Comm....................323 267-0477
4081 E Olympic Blvd Los Angeles (90023) *(G-21784)*
Paradigm A Tlent Literary Agcy (PA)....................310 288-8000
360 N Crescent Dr Beverly Hills (90210) *(G-18422)*
Paradigm Industries Inc....................310 965-1900
13344 S Main St Ste C Los Angeles (90061) *(G-17394)*
Paradigm Information Services....................858 693-6115
10755 F Scrps Pwy Pkwy424 San Diego (92131) *(G-28154)*
Paradigm Staffing Solutions....................510 663-7860
1970 Broadway Ste 615 Oakland (94612) *(G-14720)*
Paradise Ambulance Service....................530 879-5520
333 Huss Dr Chico (95928) *(G-3825)*
Paradise Building Services....................909 399-0707
9664 Hermosa Ave Rancho Cucamonga (91730) *(G-14379)*
Paradise Electric Inc....................619 449-4141
697 Greenfield Dr El Cajon (92021) *(G-2680)*
Paradise Oaks Youth Services....................916 725-7182
7806 Uplands Way A Citrus Heights (95610) *(G-24121)*
Paradise Point Resort, San Diego *Also called Westgroup San Diego Associates (G-13403)*
Paradise Point Resort & Spa, San Diego *Also called San Diego Paradise Pt Resort (G-13199)*
PARADISE RIDGE FAMILY RESOURCE, Paradise *Also called Youth For Change (G-24299)*
Paradise Ridge Post-Acute, Paradise *Also called Maqui Holdings LLC (G-20755)*
Paradise Solid Waste, Paradise *Also called USA Waste of California Inc (G-6586)*
Paradise Valley Estates, Fairfield *Also called Northern CA Retiredd Ofcrs (G-24748)*
Paradise Valley Hospital (PA)....................619 470-4100
2400 E 4th St National City (91950) *(G-21785)*
Paradise Valley Hospital Inc....................619 472-7500
180 Otay Lakes Rd Ste 100 Bonita (91902) *(G-22531)*
Paradise Vly Hlth Care Ctr Inc....................619 470-6700
2575 E 8th St National City (91950) *(G-20840)*
Paragon Coml Bldg Maint Inc....................916 334-8801
6731 32nd St Ste J North Highlands (95660) *(G-14380)*
Paragon Health & Rehab CT....................559 638-3578
1090 E Dinuba Ave Reedley (93654) *(G-22790)*
Paragon Partners Ltd (PA)....................714 379-3376
5762 Bolsa Ave Ste 201 Huntington Beach (92649) *(G-28016)*
Paragon Personel Services, Brea *Also called Sunshine Clearing Corporation (G-14798)*
Paragon Plastics Co Div, Chino *Also called Consolidated Plastics Corp (G-8968)*

ALPHABETIC

Paragon Real Estate Group......415 738-7000
1400 Van Ness Ave San Francisco (94109) ***(G-11736)***
Paragon Real Estate Group......415 292-2384
1400 Van Ness Ave San Francisco (94109) ***(G-11737)***
Paragon Textiles Inc......310 323-7500
13003 S Figueroa St Los Angeles (90061) ***(G-8408)***
Paramount, San Francisco *Also called Third & Mission Associates LLC* ***(G-11873)***
Paramount Bldg Solutions LLC......951 272-4001
2045 California Ave Corona (92881) ***(G-14381)***
Paramount Bldg Solutions LLC......916 564-4102
4741 Pell Dr Sacramento (95838) ***(G-1630)***
Paramount Citrus, Delano *Also called Wonderful Company LLC* ***(G-225)***
Paramount Citrus, Mc Farland *Also called Wonderful Citrus Packing LLC* ***(G-607)***
Paramount Citrus Packing Co, Delano *Also called Wonderful Citrus Packing LLC* ***(G-605)***
Paramount Convalescent Group......562 634-6895
8558 Rosecrans Ave Paramount (90723) ***(G-21345)***
Paramount Equity Mortgage LLC......916 290-9999
10888 White Rock Rd Rancho Cordova (95670) ***(G-9881)***
Paramount Equity Mortgage LLC......916 290-9999
22 Executive Park Ste 100 Irvine (92614) ***(G-9882)***
Paramount Equity Mortgage LLC......916 290-9999
4200 Douglas Blvd Granite Bay (95746) ***(G-9883)***
Paramount Farming, Shafter *Also called Wonderful Orchards LLC* ***(G-210)***
Paramount Meadows Nursing Ctr, Paramount *Also called Paramunt Madows Nursing Ctr LP* ***(G-27158)***
Paramount Pictures, Los Angeles *Also called Paramount Television Service* ***(G-18126)***
Paramount Pictures Corporation (HQ)......323 956-5000
5555 Melrose Ave Los Angeles (90038) ***(G-18125)***
Paramount Properties, Beverly Hills *Also called Rodeo Realty Inc* ***(G-11819)***
Paramount Properties, Woodland Hills *Also called Rodeo Realty Inc* ***(G-11821)***
Paramount Properties Encino BR, Encino *Also called Rodeo Realty Inc* ***(G-11817)***
Paramount Studios, Los Angeles *Also called Paramount Pictures Corporation* ***(G-18125)***
Paramount Swap Meet, Paramount *Also called Modern Dev Co A Ltd Partnr* ***(G-17339)***
Paramount Television Service......323 956-5000
5555 Melrose Ave Los Angeles (90038) ***(G-18126)***
Paramount Theatre of Arts Inc......510 893-2300
2025 Broadway Oakland (94612) ***(G-11031)***
Paramount Trnsp Systems Inc (PA)......760 510-7979
1350 Grand Ave San Marcos (92078) ***(G-5145)***
Paramout Farms, Lost Hills *Also called Roll Properties Intl Inc* ***(G-12341)***
Paramunt Contrs Developers Inc......323 464-7050
6464 W Sunset Blvd # 700 Los Angeles (90028) ***(G-11738)***
Paramunt Madows Nursing Ctr LP......562 531-0990
7039 Alondra Blvd Paramount (90723) ***(G-27158)***
Parasec Incorporated (PA)......916 576-7000
2804 Gateway Oaks Dr # 200 Sacramento (95833) ***(G-23489)***
Parasoft Corporation (PA)......626 305-0041
101 E Huntington Dr Fl 2 Monrovia (91016) ***(G-7171)***
Paratransit Incorporated (PA)......916 429-2009
2501 Florin Rd Sacramento (95822) ***(G-3826)***
Paratransit Incorporated......209 522-2300
3300 Tully Rd Modesto (95350) ***(G-3827)***
Paray Development Corp......760 685-2462
2030 Ardath Ave Escondido (92027) ***(G-1232)***
Parc, Palo Alto *Also called Palo Alto Research Center Inc* ***(G-26582)***
Parc 55 Hotel, San Francisco *Also called Rp/Kinetic Parc 55 Owner LLC* ***(G-13174)***
Parc Management LLC......925 609-1364
1950 Waterworld Pkwy Concord (94520) ***(G-19257)***
Parc Specialty Contractors......916 992-5405
1400 Vinci Ave Sacramento (95838) ***(G-3563)***
Parca, Burlingame *Also called Peninsula Assoc For Retarded* ***(G-24127)***
Parchment Inc......480 719-1646
3000 Lava Ridge Ct # 210 Roseville (95661) ***(G-17395)***
Pardee Homes......858 259-6390
12220 El Camino Real # 300 San Diego (92130) ***(G-11998)***
Pardee Homes (HQ)......310 955-3100
177 E Colo Blvd Ste 550 Pasadena (91105) ***(G-11999)***
Pardee Tree Nursery......760 630-5400
30970 Via Puerta Del Sol Oceanside (92057) ***(G-9208)***
Parent Child Development Ctr (PA)......510 452-0492
690 18th St Oakland (94612) ***(G-24499)***
Parenthood of Planned (PA)......619 881-4500
1075 Camino Del Rio S # 100 San Diego (92108) ***(G-22791)***
Parenthood of Planned (PA)......805 963-2445
518 Garden St Santa Barbara (93101) ***(G-22792)***
Parenthood of Planned......951 222-3101
12900 Frederick St Ste C Moreno Valley (92553) ***(G-22793)***
Parents Place, Palo Alto *Also called Jewish Family and Chld Svcs* ***(G-24045)***
Parents United, San Jose *Also called Giarretto Institute* ***(G-23993)***
Pareto Networks Inc......877 727-8020
1183 Bordeaux Dr Ste 22 Sunnyvale (94089) ***(G-5679)***
Parexel International Corp......818 254-7076
1560 E Chevy Chase Dr # 140 Glendale (91206) ***(G-26584)***
Pariveda Solutions Inc......415 946-6100
100 Pine St Ste 375 San Francisco (94111) ***(G-16028)***
Park and Recreation, San Diego *Also called City of San Diego* ***(G-22129)***
Park and Recreation, Folsom *Also called City of Folsom* ***(G-19170)***
Park Central Hotel Fresno, Fresno *Also called Park Inn By Readisson Fresno* ***(G-13076)***
Park Cleaners Inc (PA)......626 281-5942
419 Mcgroarty St San Gabriel (91776) ***(G-13568)***
Park Cntl Care Rhblitation Ctr......510 797-5300
2100 Parkside Dr Fremont (94536) ***(G-24765)***
Park Disposal Service, Buena Park *Also called Edco Disposal Corporation Inc* ***(G-6479)***
Park Hyatt Aviara Resort, Carlsbad *Also called Aviara Resort Associates* ***(G-12407)***
Park Inn, Anaheim *Also called Badalian Enterprises Inc* ***(G-12412)***
Park Inn By Radisson......559 226-2200
3737 N Blackstone Ave Fresno (93726) ***(G-13075)***
Park Inn By Readisson Fresno......559 226-2200
3737 N Blackstone Ave Fresno (93726) ***(G-13076)***
Park Labrea Management, Los Angeles *Also called Plb Management LLC* ***(G-11188)***
Park Landscape Maint 1-2-3-4, Rcho STA Marg *Also called Park Landscape Maintenance* ***(G-930)***
Park Landscape Maintenance......760 317-2550
529 W 4th Ave Escondido (92025) ***(G-929)***
Park Landscape Maintenance (PA)......949 546-8300
22421 Gilberto Ste A Rcho STA Marg (92688) ***(G-930)***
Park Lane A Classic Residenc, Monterey *Also called Classic Park Lane Partnership* ***(G-11116)***
Park Lane, The, Monterey *Also called P Monterey LP* ***(G-24758)***
Park Maintenance, Torrance *Also called City of Torrance* ***(G-19182)***
Park Management Corp......707 643-6722
1001 Fairgrounds Dr Vallejo (94589) ***(G-18829)***
Park Manor Suites, San Diego *Also called Gentry Associates LLC* ***(G-12662)***
Park Marino Convalescent Ctr......626 463-4105
2585 E Washington Blvd Pasadena (91107) ***(G-21346)***
Park Newport Apartments, Newport Beach *Also called Park Newport Ltd* ***(G-11184)***
Park Newport Ltd (PA)......949 644-1900
1 Park Newport Newport Beach (92660) ***(G-11184)***
PARK PASEO, Glendale *Also called Cal Southern Presbt Homes* ***(G-11108)***
Park Place Ford LLC......909 946-5555
555 W Foothill Blvd Upland (91786) ***(G-17809)***
Park Plaza Hotel......510 635-5300
150 Hegenberger Rd Oakland (94621) ***(G-13077)***
Park Regency Inc......818 363-6116
10146 Balboa Blvd Granada Hills (91344) ***(G-11739)***
Park Shadelands Medical Offs, Walnut Creek *Also called Kaiser Foundation Hospitals* ***(G-21634)***
Park Uniform Rentals, San Gabriel *Also called Park Cleaners Inc* ***(G-13568)***
Park View Gardens, Santa Rosa *Also called Ensign Group Inc* ***(G-20540)***
Park Vista At Morningside, Fullerton *Also called Corecare V A Cal Ltd Partnr* ***(G-20472)***
Park West Rescom Inc......949 546-8300
22421 Gilberto Rcho STA Marg (92688) ***(G-931)***
Parkco Building Company......714 444-1441
3190 Airport Loop Dr F Costa Mesa (92626) ***(G-1631)***
Parker Landscape Dev Inc......916 383-4071
6251 Sky Creek Dr Ste A Sacramento (95828) ***(G-786)***
Parker Milliken Clark OHar......818 784-8087
555 S Flower St Fl 30 Los Angeles (90071) ***(G-23490)***
Parker Stanbury LLP (PA)......619 528-1259
444 S Flower St Ste 1900 Los Angeles (90071) ***(G-23491)***
Parkers Retirement Residence, Fountain Valley *Also called Longwood Management Corp* ***(G-24715)***
Parkhouse Tire Service Inc......909 428-1415
13655 Santa Ana Ave Fontana (92337) ***(G-6788)***
Parkhurst Terrace......831 685-0800
100 Parkhurst Cir Aptos (95003) ***(G-1330)***
Parking Co Amer Universal Inc......562 862-2118
11101 Lakewood Blvd Downey (90241) ***(G-17732)***
Parking Concepts Inc......949 752-5558
18601 Airport Way Ste 7 Santa Ana (92707) ***(G-17396)***
Parking Concepts Inc......714 836-6009
601 S Ross St Santa Ana (92701) ***(G-17397)***
Parking Concepts Inc......310 208-1611
1036 Broxton Ave Los Angeles (90024) ***(G-17733)***
Parking Concepts Inc......213 746-5764
1801 Georgia St Los Angeles (90015) ***(G-17734)***
Parking Concepts Inc......310 821-1081
14110 Palawan Way Venice (90292) ***(G-17735)***
Parking Concepts Inc......213 623-2661
800 Wilshire Blvd Los Angeles (90017) ***(G-17736)***
Parking Concepts Inc......310 322-5008
12001 Vista Del Mar Playa Del Rey (90293) ***(G-17737)***
Parking Network Inc......213 613-1500
350 S Figueroa St Ste 420 Los Angeles (90071) ***(G-3564)***
Parking Spot, The, Los Angeles *Also called Prg Parking Century LLC* ***(G-17740)***
Parking Spot, The, Los Angeles *Also called Tps Parking Management LLC* ***(G-17744)***
Parkinsons Institute......800 786-2958
675 Almanor Ave Ste 101 Sunnyvale (94085) ***(G-26794)***
Parkman Agents......310 860-7757
468 N Camden Dr Beverly Hills (90210) ***(G-12121)***
Parkmerced Investors LLC......877 243-5544
3711 19th Ave San Francisco (94132) ***(G-14566)***
Parks & Recreation, Commerce *Also called City of Commerce* ***(G-19167)***
Parks & Recreation Dept, Los Angeles *Also called City of Los Angeles* ***(G-25011)***
Parks & Recreation Dept, Spring Valley *Also called County of San Diego* ***(G-23901)***
Parks & Recreation Dept, Los Angeles *Also called City of Los Angeles* ***(G-13462)***
Parks & Recreation Dept, Los Angeles *Also called City of Los Angeles* ***(G-23754)***
Parks and Recreation Cal Dept......209 763-5121
2000 Camanche Rd Ofc Ione (95640) ***(G-19258)***
Parks and Recreation Cal Dept......310 456-8432
23200 Pacific Coast Hwy Malibu (90265) ***(G-25036)***
Parks and Recreation Dept, Pomona *Also called County of Los Angeles* ***(G-18727)***
Parks Department, Redwood City *Also called County of San Mateo* ***(G-13479)***
Parks Recreation Libraries, Orange *Also called City of Orange* ***(G-19179)***
Parks-Rcreation-Community Svcs, Irvine *Also called City of Irvine* ***(G-19174)***
Parkside Lending LLC......415 771-3700
1130 Howard St San Francisco (94103) ***(G-10068)***
Parkside Special Care Center......619 442-7744
444 W Lexington Ave El Cajon (92020) ***(G-20841)***
Parkview Cmnty Hosp Med Ctr......951 354-7404
3865 Jackson St Riverside (92503) ***(G-21786)***

ALPHABETIC

Parkview Jlian Cnvlescent Hosp 661 831-9150
1801 Julian Ave Bakersfield (93304) ***(G-20842)***
Parkway Apartments LLC 925 866-8429
3170 Crow Canyon Pl # 165 San Ramon (94583) ***(G-11185)***
Parkwest Apartments 650 856-0930
562 Kendall Ave Palo Alto (94306) ***(G-11186)***
Parkwood Landscape Maint Inc 818 988-9677
16443 Hart St Van Nuys (91406) ***(G-932)***
Parma Management Co Inc 858 457-4999
6390 Greenwich Dr Ste 150 San Diego (92122) ***(G-11740)***
Parole Unit Office, Eureka *Also called Correctons Rhbltation Cal Dept* ***(G-23788)***
Parpro Holdings Co Ltd 619 498-9004
9355 Airway Rd Ste 4 San Diego (92154) ***(G-12083)***
Pars Publishing Corp 818 280-0540
4485 Runway St Simi Valley (93063) ***(G-14158)***
Parsec Inc 323 268-5011
4940 Sheila St Commerce (90040) ***(G-5234)***
Parsec Inc 323 276-3116
750 Lamar St Los Angeles (90031) ***(G-5235)***
Parsons Airgas Inc 858 278-2050
9010 Clairemont Mesa Blvd San Diego (92123) ***(G-7875)***
Parsons Brinckerhoff Inc 714 973-4880
505 S Main St Ste 900 Orange (92868) ***(G-26009)***
Parsons Brinckerhoff Inc 212 465-5000
444 S Flower St Ste 800 Los Angeles (90071) ***(G-26010)***
Parsons Brinckerhoff Inc 415 243-4600
425 Market St Fl 17 San Francisco (94105) ***(G-26011)***
Parsons Brinckerhoff Inc 650 697-1869
1818 Gilbreth Rd Burlingame (94010) ***(G-27583)***
Parsons Brinckerhoff Inc 909 888-1106
451 E Vanderbilt Way # 200 San Bernardino (92408) ***(G-26012)***
Parsons Constructors Inc 626 440-2000
100 W Walnut St Pasadena (91124) ***(G-27159)***
Parsons Corporation (PA) 626 440-2000
100 W Walnut St Pasadena (91124) ***(G-2074)***
Parsons Corporation 714 736-6826
1 Centerpointe Dr La Palma (90623) ***(G-2075)***
Parsons Corporation 626 440-2000
100 W San Fernando St # 450 San Jose (95113) ***(G-1843)***
Parsons Engrg Science Inc (HQ) 626 440-2000
100 W Walnut St Pasadena (91124) ***(G-26013)***
Parsons Global Services Inc., Pasadena *Also called Parsons Gvrnment Svcs Intl Inc* ***(G-1632)***
Parsons Government Svcs Inc (HQ) 626 440-2000
100 W Walnut St Pasadena (91124) ***(G-26014)***
Parsons Government Svcs Inc 925 313-3217
2000 Marina Vista Ave Martinez (94553) ***(G-26015)***
Parsons Government Svcs Inc (HQ) 949 768-8161
25531 Commercentre Dr Lake Forest (92630) ***(G-26585)***
Parsons Gvrnment Svcs Intl Inc 626 440-6000
100 W Walnut St Pasadena (91124) ***(G-1632)***
Parsons Project Services Inc 626 440-4000
100 W Walnut St Pasadena (91124) ***(G-1457)***
Parsons Technical Services Inc 626 440-3998
100 W Walnut St Pasadena (91124) ***(G-26016)***
Parsons Wtr Infrastructure Inc 626 440-7000
100 W Walnut St Pasadena (91124) ***(G-26017)***
Part Time Day Care Center, Ridgecrest *Also called Naws Children Center* ***(G-24485)***
Parthenon DCS Holdings LLC 925 960-4800
4 Embarcadero Ctr San Francisco (94111) ***(G-27160)***
Participant Media LLC 310 550-5100
331 Foothill Rd Fl 3 Beverly Hills (90210) ***(G-18127)***
Partitions Installation Inc 562 207-9868
13021 Leffingwell Ave Santa Fe Springs (90670) ***(G-3565)***
Partner Assessment Corporation (PA) 800 419-4923
2154 Torrance Blvd # 200 Torrance (90501) ***(G-26018)***
Partner Engineering & Science, Torrance *Also called Partner Assessment Corporation* ***(G-26018)***
Partner Hero Inc 888 968-2767
1001 Avenida Pico C260 San Clemente (92673) ***(G-17398)***
Partners Capital Group Inc 949 916-3900
201 Sandpointe Ave Santa Ana (92707) ***(G-17399)***
Partners Capital Group Inc (PA) 949 916-3900
65 Enterprise Ste 455 Aliso Viejo (92656) ***(G-17400)***
Partners For Community Access 510 558-6700
708 Gilman St Berkeley (94710) ***(G-24122)***
Partners In Leadership Interme (PA) 951 506-6878
27555 Ynez Rd Temecula (92591) ***(G-27584)***
Partners Information Tech Inc (HQ) 714 736-4487
7101 Village Dr Buena Park (90621) ***(G-16454)***
Partnership Health Plan Cal 707 863-4100
4665 Business Center Dr Fairfield (94534) ***(G-10369)***
Partos Company 310 458-7800
227 Broadway Ste 204 Santa Monica (90401) ***(G-17401)***
Partos Company, The, Santa Monica *Also called Partos Company* ***(G-17401)***
Parts 916 371-3115
2445 Evergreen Ave West Sacramento (95691) ***(G-17643)***
Parts Unlimited, Fontana *Also called Lemans Corporation* ***(G-4586)***
Parts Warehouse Distrs Inc 650 616-4988
449 Littlefield Ave South San Francisco (94080) ***(G-6751)***
Partschannel Inc 562 654-3400
8905 Rex Rd Pico Rivera (90660) ***(G-6752)***
Party Pantry Garden Room 714 899-0626
12777 Knott St Garden Grove (92841) ***(G-13786)***
Parwood Preservation LP 562 531-7880
5441 N Paramount Blvd Long Beach (90805) ***(G-11741)***
Paryroll Department, Redwood City *Also called Verity Health System Cal Inc* ***(G-22015)***
Pasadena Baking Co 626 796-5093
70 W Pal Meto Ave Pasadena (91105) ***(G-8897)***
Pasadena Billing Associates 626 795-6596
225 S Lake Ave Ste 535 Pasadena (91101) ***(G-26416)***
Pasadena Center Operating Co 626 795-9311
300 E Green St Pasadena (91101) ***(G-17402)***
Pasadena Child Dev Assoc Inc 626 793-7350
620 N Lake Ave Pasadena (91101) ***(G-22794)***
Pasadena Child Development Ass 626 793-7350
620 N Lake Ave Pasadena (91101) ***(G-24123)***
Pasadena Chld Training Soc 626 798-0853
2933 El Nido Dr Altadena (91001) ***(G-24766)***
PASADENA CONVENTION CENTER, Pasadena *Also called Pasadena Center Operating Co* ***(G-17402)***
Pasadena Cyto Pathology Lab 626 397-8616
100 W Calif Blvd Fl 3 Pasadena (91105) ***(G-22252)***
Pasadena Hospital Assn Ltd (PA) 626 397-5000
100 W California Blvd Pasadena (91105) ***(G-21787)***
Pasadena Hospital Assn Ltd 626 397-3322
716 S Fair Oaks Ave Pasadena (91105) ***(G-20843)***
Pasadena Hotel Dev Ventr LP 626 449-4000
303 Cordova St Pasadena (91101) ***(G-13078)***
Pasadena Humane Society 626 792-7151
361 S Raymond Ave Pasadena (91105) ***(G-25564)***
Pasadena Madows Nursing Ctr LP 626 796-1103
150 Bellefontaine St Pasadena (91105) ***(G-20844)***
Pasadena Model Railroad Club 323 222-1718
5458 Alhambra Ave Los Angeles (90032) ***(G-19028)***
Pasadena Rbles Acquisition LLC 626 577-1000
168 S Los Robles Ave Pasadena (91101) ***(G-13079)***
Pasadena Rehabilitation Inst, Pasadena *Also called Algos Inc A Medical Corp* ***(G-22653)***
Pasadena Residential Care Ctr, Los Angeles *Also called Robincrost Care Corporation* ***(G-20880)***
Pasadena Sport Club, Pasadena *Also called 24 Hour Fitness Usa Inc* ***(G-18585)***
Pasadena Vision, Pasadena *Also called Linden Optometry A Prof Corp* ***(G-20300)***
Pasadena Water & Power, Pasadena *Also called City of Pasadena* ***(G-6302)***
Paseo Vlg Hsing Partners LP 714 991-9172
1115 N Citron St Anaheim (92801) ***(G-11742)***
Pasha Distribution Svcs LLC 714 889-2460
5882 Bolsa Ave Ste 200 Huntington Beach (92649) ***(G-5146)***
Pasha Freight, San Rafael *Also called Pasha Group* ***(G-5147)***
Pasha Group (PA) 415 927-6400
4040 Civic Center Dr # 350 San Rafael (94903) ***(G-5147)***
Pasha Group 310 735-0952
19020 S Dminguez Hills Dr Compton (90220) ***(G-5148)***
Pasha Stevedoring Terminals LP 310 233-2006
802 S Fries Ave Wilmington (90744) ***(G-4752)***
Pasha Stevedoring Terminals LP 415 927-6353
802 S Fries Ave Wilmington (90744) ***(G-4719)***
Paso Robles Hotel, Paso Robles *Also called Paso Robles Inn LLC* ***(G-13080)***
Paso Robles Inn LLC 805 238-2660
1103 Spring St Paso Robles (93446) ***(G-13080)***
Paso Robles Tank (PA) 805 227-1641
825 26th St Paso Robles (93446) ***(G-3395)***
Passages, Malibu *Also called Grasshopper House LLC* ***(G-22738)***
Passco Companies LLC (PA) 949 442-1000
2050 Main St Ste 650 Irvine (92614) ***(G-11743)***
Passport Acceptance Facility 562 494-2296
2300 Redondo Ave Long Beach (90809) ***(G-17403)***
Passport To Learning Inc 661 538-9200
41319 12th St W Palmdale (93551) ***(G-7294)***
Passprt Accept Fclty Los Angel 323 460-4811
1425 N Cherokee Ave Los Angeles (90093) ***(G-17404)***
Pasta Shop (PA) 510 250-6005
5655 College Ave Ste 201 Oakland (94618) ***(G-8898)***
Patelco Credit Union 925 785-9487
310 Hartz Ave Danville (94526) ***(G-9620)***
Patelco Credit Union (PA) 800 358-8228
5050 Hopyard Rd Pleasanton (94588) ***(G-9621)***
Patenaude & Felix A Prof Corp (PA) 702 952-2031
4545 Murphy Canyon Rd # 3 San Diego (92123) ***(G-23492)***
Pater Digintas Inc 831 624-1875
23795 Holman Hwy Monterey (93940) ***(G-20845)***
Pathfinder Health Inc 714 636-5649
10051 Lampson Ave Garden Grove (92840) ***(G-22532)***
Pathpoint 805 782-8890
11491 Los Osos Valley Rd San Luis Obispo (93405) ***(G-24378)***
Pathway Capital Management LP (PA) 949 622-1000
2211 Michelson Dr Ste 900 Irvine (92612) ***(G-27161)***
Pathway Inc 909 890-1070
287 W Orange Show Ln San Bernardino (92408) ***(G-24124)***
Pathway Society 408 244-1834
102 S 11th St San Jose (95112) ***(G-22795)***
Pathway To Choices Inc 510 724-9044
751 Belmont Way Pinole (94564) ***(G-24125)***
Pathways, Oakland *Also called Hospice & Home Health of E Bay* ***(G-22472)***
Pathways Home Health 650 634-0133
395 Oyster Point Blvd # 128 South San Francisco (94080) ***(G-23017)***
Pathways La (PA) 213 427-2700
3325 Wilshire Blvd # 1100 Los Angeles (90010) ***(G-24126)***
Patient Accounting, Sunnyvale *Also called Palo Alto Medical Foundation* ***(G-19816)***
Patient Business Services, Escondido *Also called Palomar Health* ***(G-23015)***
Patientpop Inc 310 260-3968
1221 2nd St Santa Monica (90401) ***(G-15814)***
Patients Hospital 530 225-8700
2900 Eureka Way Redding (96001) ***(G-21788)***
Patientsafe Solutions Inc (PA) 858 746-3100
5375 Mira Sorrento Pl San Diego (92121) ***(G-15370)***
Patric Communications Inc (PA) 619 579-2898
1488 Pioneer Way Ste 4 El Cajon (92020) ***(G-2681)***

ALPHABETIC

Patrick Dean Bryan.....530 273-5484
12481 Lttle Deer Creek Ln Nevada City (95959) *(G-3566)*
Patrick Industries Inc.....909 350-4440
13414 Slover Ave Fontana (92337) *(G-6992)*
Patrick K Willis and Co Inc.....800 398-6480
5118 Rbert J Mathews Pkwy El Dorado Hills (95762) *(G-17405)*
Patricks Construction Clean-Up.....916 452-5495
7851 14th Ave Sacramento (95826) *(G-2076)*
Patriot Contract Services LLC.....925 296-2000
1320 Willow Pass Rd # 485 Concord (94520) *(G-4717)*
Patrol Masters Inc.....714 426-2526
1651 E 4th St Ste 150 Santa Ana (92701) *(G-16756)*
Pattern Energy Group LP (PA).....415 283-4000
Bay 3 Pier 1 San Francisco (94111) *(G-6195)*
Patterson Dental 426, El Segundo *Also called Patterson Dental Supply Inc (G-7295)*
Patterson Dental 454, Roseville *Also called Patterson Dental Supply Inc (G-7296)*
Patterson Dental 590, Dinuba *Also called Patterson Dental Supply Inc (G-7297)*
Patterson Dental Supply Inc.....310 426-3100
185 S Douglas St Ste 100 El Segundo (90245) *(G-7295)*
Patterson Dental Supply Inc.....916 780-5100
1030 Winding Creek Rd # 150 Roseville (95678) *(G-7296)*
Patterson Dental Supply Inc.....559 595-1450
800 Monte Vista Dr Dinuba (93618) *(G-7297)*
Patterson Dental Supply Inc.....818 435-1368
9200 Eton Ave Chatsworth (91311) *(G-15371)*
Patterson Dental Supply Inc.....408 773-0776
5087 Commercial Cir Concord (94520) *(G-7298)*
Patterson Ritner Lockwood (PA).....818 241-8001
620 N Brand Blvd Fl 3 Glendale (91203) *(G-23493)*
Patton Air Conditioning, Fresno *Also called Patton Sheet Metal Works Inc (G-3196)*
Patton Sheet Metal Works Inc.....559 486-5222
272 N Palm Ave Fresno (93701) *(G-3196)*
Patton State Hospital, Patton *Also called Califrnia Dept State Hospitals (G-22049)*
Paul Calvo and Company.....626 814-8000
1619 W Garvey Ave N # 201 West Covina (91790) *(G-11744)*
Paul Graham Drilling & Svc Co.....707 374-5123
2500 Airport Rd Rio Vista (94571) *(G-1061)*
Paul Hastings LLP.....858 458-3000
4747 Executive Dr # 1200 San Diego (92121) *(G-23494)*
Paul Hastings LLP.....714 668-6200
695 Town Center Dr # 120 Costa Mesa (92626) *(G-23495)*
Paul Hastings LLP (PA).....213 683-6000
515 S Flower St Fl 25 Los Angeles (90071) *(G-23496)*
Paul Hastings LLP.....415 856-7000
55 2nd St Fl 24 San Francisco (94105) *(G-23497)*
Paul Hastings LLP.....650 320-1800
1117 S California Ave Palo Alto (94304) *(G-23498)*
Paul Kagan Associates, Carmel *Also called Kagan Capital Management Inc (G-10155)*
Paul Kittle.....951 684-0918
4495 Mt Vernon Ave Riverside (92507) *(G-27585)*
Paul Maurer Company.....714 231-8241
16081 Warren Ln Huntington Beach (92649) *(G-19259)*
Paul Maurer Shows, Huntington Beach *Also called Paul Maurer Company (G-19259)*
Paul Mitchell John Systems (PA).....661 298-0400
20705 Centre Pointe Pkwy Santa Clarita (91350) *(G-8290)*
Paul P Ortner DDS.....530 934-4603
249 N Humboldt Ave Willows (95988) *(G-13081)*
Paul Pietrzyk.....209 726-5034
1142 Acapulco Ct Merced (95348) *(G-2953)*
Paul Trucking, Watsonville *Also called Amar Transportation Inc (G-4105)*
Paul Williams Tile Co Inc.....760 772-7440
77570 Springfield Ln K Palm Desert (92211) *(G-3021)*
Pauley Construction Inc.....760 347-7608
81529 Industrial Pl Indio (92201) *(G-1978)*
Pauls Drywall, Merced *Also called Paul Pietrzyk (G-2953)*
Pauls Tv LLC (PA).....949 596-8800
900 Glenneyre St Laguna Beach (92651) *(G-7506)*
Paulus Engineering Inc.....714 632-3322
2871 E Coronado St Anaheim (92806) *(G-1979)*
Pauma Band of Mission Indians.....760 742-2177
777 Pauma Reservation Rd Pauma Valley (92061) *(G-13082)*
Pauma Valley Country Club.....760 742-1230
15835 Pauma Valley Dr Pauma Valley (92061) *(G-19029)*
Pave-Tech Inc.....760 727-8700
2231 La Mirada Dr Vista (92081) *(G-1844)*
Pavement Recycling Systems Inc (PA).....951 682-1091
10240 San Sevaine Way Jurupa Valley (91752) *(G-8078)*
Pavex Construction Company, Redwood City *Also called Granite Rock Co (G-1793)*
Pavigym America Corp.....858 414-8624
1902 Wright Pl Fl 2 Carlsbad (92008) *(G-6879)*
Pavir, Palo Alto *Also called Palo Alto Vterans Inst For RES (G-26793)*
Pavletich Elc Cmmnications Inc (PA).....661 589-9473
6308 Seven Seas Ave Bakersfield (93308) *(G-2682)*
Pax Labs Inc.....510 828-8174
660 Alabama St Fl 2 San Francisco (94110) *(G-18)*
Paxata Inc.....650 542-7897
305 Walnut St Fl 2 Redwood City (94063) *(G-15815)*
Paxvax Inc.....858 450-9595
3985 Sorrento Valley Blvd A San Diego (92121) *(G-26586)*
Paychex Inc.....559 432-1100
9 E River Park Pl E # 210 Fresno (93720) *(G-26417)*
Paychex Inc.....858 547-2920
10150 Meanley Dr Ste 200 San Diego (92131) *(G-26418)*
Paychex Inc.....310 338-7900
300 Crprate Pinte Ste 150 Culver City (90230) *(G-26419)*
Paychex Inc.....951 682-6100
1420 Iowa Ave Ste 100 Riverside (92507) *(G-26420)*
Paychex Benefit Tech Inc.....800 322-7292
2385 Northside Dr Ste 100 San Diego (92108) *(G-5680)*
Paycycle Inc.....866 729-2925
210 Portage Ave Palo Alto (94306) *(G-5681)*
Payden and Rygel (PA).....213 625-1900
333 S Grand Ave Ste 3200 Los Angeles (90071) *(G-10170)*
Paylocity Holding Corporation.....847 956-4850
2107 Livingston St Oakland (94606) *(G-15816)*
Payment Resources Intl.....949 729-1400
620 Newport Center Dr # 150 Newport Beach (92660) *(G-17406)*
Payne & Fears LLP (PA).....949 851-1101
4 Park Plz Ste 1100 Irvine (92614) *(G-23499)*
Payne Brothers Ranches.....530 662-2354
13330 County Road 102 Woodland (95776) *(G-87)*
Payne, E L Company, Los Angeles *Also called E L Payne Heating Company (G-2212)*
Payoff Inc.....949 430-0630
3200 Park Center Dr # 800 Costa Mesa (92626) *(G-9761)*
Paypal Inc (HQ).....877 981-2163
2211 N 1st St San Jose (95131) *(G-5682)*
Payroll Dept., Chico *Also called Enloe Medical Center (G-19515)*
Payrollingcom Corp.....858 866-2626
4626 Albuquerque St Uppr San Diego (92109) *(G-26421)*
Paysys, Los Angeles *Also called Citadel Group Solutions LLC (G-15921)*
Pb Car Movers.....310 283-2741
5510 W 120th St Hawthorne (90250) *(G-17407)*
Pbc Companies, Brea *Also called Peterson Bros Contruction Inc (G-3313)*
Pbc Solution One Inc.....559 348-0019
2695 N Fowler Ave Ste 110 Fresno (93727) *(G-3567)*
Pbi-Birkenwald Market Eqp Inc (PA).....562 595-4785
2667 Gundry Ave Long Beach (90755) *(G-7223)*
PBM Maintenance Corp.....818 771-1100
8523 Lankershim Blvd Sun Valley (91352) *(G-14382)*
Pbms Inc.....213 386-2552
1909 Wilshire Blvd Los Angeles (90057) *(G-14383)*
Pbp Hotel LLC.....619 881-6900
1515 Hotel Cir S San Diego (92108) *(G-12000)*
PBR Twin Peaks, Woodland Hills *Also called Nmms Twin Peaks LLC (G-11709)*
PBS SOCAL, Costa Mesa *Also called Koce-TV Foundation (G-5885)*
PC Mechanical Inc.....805 925-2888
2803 Industrial Pkwy Santa Maria (93455) *(G-1092)*
PC World Corp (PA).....240 855-8988
2017 Merkley Ave West Sacramento (95691) *(G-5683)*
PCA, Los Angeles *Also called Beres Consulting (G-25076)*
Pcamp, Downey *Also called Parking Co Amer Universal Inc (G-17732)*
PCC Northwest, San Leandro *Also called Pacific Coast Container Inc (G-5232)*
Pcg Technology Consulting, Sacramento *Also called Public Consulting Group Inc (G-27601)*
Pcgs, Santa Ana *Also called Professional Coin Grading Svc (G-17431)*
PCHA, Palo Alto *Also called Packard Childrens Hlth Aliance (G-19806)*
PCI, San Diego *Also called Project Concern International (G-25100)*
PCI Collections Inc.....619 595-3114
402 W Broadway Fl 4 San Diego (92101) *(G-14040)*
PCL Construction Services Inc.....818 246-3481
500 N Brand Blvd Ste 1500 Glendale (91203) *(G-1633)*
PCL Industrial Services Inc.....661 832-3995
1500 S Union Ave Bakersfield (93307) *(G-1458)*
Pcm, Laguna Woods *Also called Professional Cmnty MGT Cal Inc (G-11766)*
Pcm, Foothill Ranch *Also called Professional Cmnty MGT Cal Inc (G-11240)*
Pcs Link Inc.....949 655-5000
12424 Wilshire Blvd # 1030 Los Angeles (90025) *(G-28017)*
Pcs Property Managment LLC.....310 231-1000
11859 Wilshire Blvd # 600 Los Angeles (90025) *(G-11745)*
Pcs1, Agoura Hills *Also called Pacific Centrex Services Inc (G-5678)*
Pcv Murcor Real Estate Svcs, Pomona *Also called Murcor Inc (G-11702)*
Pcw Contracting Services.....949 548-9969
981 W 18th St Ste D Costa Mesa (92627) *(G-3568)*
Pcwc, Ontario *Also called Chino-Pacific Warehouse Corp (G-4535)*
Pd Hotel Associates LLC.....916 922-2020
500 Leisure Ln Sacramento (95815) *(G-13083)*
Pd Liquidation Inc.....818 772-0100
21350 Lassen St Chatsworth (91311) *(G-9290)*
PDC Capital Group LLC.....866 500-8550
250 Fischer Ave Costa Mesa (92626) *(G-12001)*
PDM Steel Service Centers.....408 988-3000
3500 Bassett St Santa Clara (95054) *(G-7388)*
PDM Steel Service Centers.....559 442-1410
4005 E Church Ave Fresno (93725) *(G-7389)*
PDM Steel Service Centers (HQ).....209 943-0555
3535 E Myrtle St Stockton (95205) *(G-7390)*
PDM Steel Service Centers.....209 234-0548
936 Performance Dr Stockton (95206) *(G-7391)*
PDQ Automatic Transm Parts Inc.....916 870-6543
8380 Tiogawoods Dr Sacramento (95828) *(G-6753)*
Pdrfc, Palm Desert *Also called Palm Dsert Rcrtl Fclities Corp (G-19025)*
Pds, Irvine *Also called Pacific Dental Services Inc (G-20269)*
Pds Tech Inc.....408 916-4848
1798 Tech Dr Ste 130 San Jose (95110) *(G-14721)*
Pds Tech Inc.....805 418-9862
370 N Wstlake Blvd Stw120 Stw Westlake Village (91362) *(G-16455)*
Pds Tech Inc.....214 647-9600
3100 S Harbor Blvd # 135 Santa Ana (92704) *(G-14722)*
Peace Keepers Private Security.....925 978-4140
2734b Delta Fair Blvd Antioch (94509) *(G-16757)*
Peace Officrs For A Grn Envirn.....909 798-1122
21800 Barton Rd Ste 108 Grand Terrace (92313) *(G-3569)*
Peaceful Hearts Home Care Inc.....951 541-9343
387 Magnolia Ave Ste 103 Corona (92879) *(G-22533)*
Peach Inc.....323 654-2333
1311 N Highland Ave Los Angeles (90028) *(G-4420)*

ALPHABETIC

Peach Tree Healthcare 530 749-3242
  5730 Packard Ave Ste 500 Marysville (95901) *(G-19821)*
Peachwood Medical Group Clovis 559 324-6200
  275 W Herndon Ave Clovis (93612) *(G-19822)*
Peacock Gap Golf & Country CLB, San Rafael Also called Knight-Calabasas LLC *(G-18967)*
Peacock Stes Resort Ltd Partnr 714 535-8255
  1745 S Anaheim Blvd Anaheim (92805) *(G-13084)*
Peak Broadcasting, Fresno Also called Knax Country 98 *(G-5796)*
Pearce Services LLC 805 237-7480
  90 Wellsona Rd Paso Robles (93446) *(G-1980)*
Pearl Crop Inc (PA) 209 808-7575
  1550 Industrial Dr Stockton (95206) *(G-573)*
Pearlman Borska & Wax LLP (PA) 818 501-4343
  15910 Ventura Blvd Fl 18 Encino (91436) *(G-23500)*
Pearson Dental Supplies Inc (PA) 818 362-2600
  13161 Telfair Ave Sylmar (91342) *(G-7299)*
Pearson English Corporation (HQ) 650 246-6000
  2000 Sierra Point Pkwy # 300 Brisbane (94005) *(G-5684)*
Pearson Surgical Supply Co, Sylmar Also called Pearson Dental Supplies Inc *(G-7299)*
Pebble Bch Resrt Co DBA Lone C (PA) 831 647-7500
  2700 17 Mile Dr Pebble Beach (93953) *(G-13085)*
Pebble Beach Co A Ltd Partnr (PA) 831 647-7500
  2700 17 Mile Dr Pebble Beach (93953) *(G-13086)*
Pebble Beach Company, Pebble Beach Also called I Cypress Company *(G-12832)*
Pebble Beach Resorts, Pebble Beach Also called Pebble Bch Resrt Co DBA Lone C *(G-13085)*
Pechanga Development Corp 951 695-4655
  45000 Pechanga Pkwy Temecula (92592) *(G-13087)*
Pechanga Resort & Casino, Temecula Also called Pechanga Development Corp *(G-13087)*
Peci, San Francisco Also called Clearesult Consulting Inc *(G-27882)*
Peck & Hiller Company 707 258-8800
  870 Napa Vally Corp Way Ste A NAPA (94558) *(G-3311)*
Pecs, Rancho Cucamonga Also called Professnal Elec Cnstr Svcs Inc *(G-2690)*
Pedi Center, Bakersfield Also called Dignity Health *(G-21542)*
Pediatric & Family Medical Ctr 213 342-3325
  1530 S Olive St Los Angeles (90015) *(G-22796)*
Pediatric Cancer Research, Orange Also called Childrens Healthcare Cal *(G-19431)*
Pediatric Physical Rehab Clnc 559 353-6130
  9300 Valley Childrens Pl Madera (93636) *(G-22797)*
Pediatric Therapy Network 310 328-0275
  1815 W 213th St Ste 100 Torrance (90501) *(G-22798)*
Peed Equipment Company 951 657-0900
  1480 Nandina Ave Perris (92571) *(G-14494)*
Peel Technologies Inc 650 204-7977
  321 Castro St Mountain View (94041) *(G-7172)*
Peerless Building Maint Co, Chatsworth Also called Tuttle Family Enterprises Inc *(G-14449)*
Peerless Building Maint Inc 530 222-6369
  4665 Mountain Lakes Blvd Redding (96003) *(G-14384)*
Peerless Maintenance Service 714 871-3380
  1100 S Euclid St La Habra (90631) *(G-14385)*
Peeters Transportation Co 800 356-5877
  451 Eccles Ave South San Francisco (94080) *(G-4371)*
Peeters/Mayflower, South San Francisco Also called Peeters Transportation Co *(G-4371)*
Pegasus Building Svcs Co Inc 858 457-8201
  7554 Trade St San Diego (92121) *(G-14386)*
Pegasus Building Svcs Co Inc (PA) 562 961-1998
  2343 Mira Mar Ave Long Beach (90815) *(G-14387)*
Pegasus Home Health Care A CA 818 551-1932
  132 N Maryland Ave Glendale (91206) *(G-22534)*
Pegasus Home Health Services, Glendale Also called Pegasus Home Health Care A CA *(G-22534)*
Pegasus Maritime Inc 714 728-8565
  535 N Brand Blvd Ste 400 Glendale (91203) *(G-5149)*
Pegasus Risk Management Inc (PA) 209 574-2800
  642 Galaxy Way Modesto (95356) *(G-10824)*
Peggs Company Inc (PA) 253 584-9548
  4851 Felspar St Riverside (92509) *(G-17999)*
Peking Handicraft Inc (PA) 650 871-3788
  1388 San Mateo Ave South San Francisco (94080) *(G-6880)*
Pelomar Family YMCA, Escondido Also called YMCA of San Diego County *(G-25419)*
Peloria Bridge Bay LLC 530 275-3021
  10300 Bridge Bay Rd Redding (96003) *(G-13088)*
Pemer Packing Co Inc 831 758-8586
  20260 Spence Rd Salinas (93908) *(G-14723)*
Pen-Cal Administrators Inc 925 251-3400
  7633 Suthfront Rd Ste 120 Livermore (94551) *(G-27162)*
Pena Grading & Demolition Inc 818 768-5202
  11253 Vinedale St Sun Valley (91352) *(G-1845)*
Pena Trucking, Sun Valley Also called Pena Grading & Demolition Inc *(G-1845)*
Pena's Recycling Center, Cutler Also called Penas Disposal Inc *(G-6513)*
Penas Disposal Inc 559 528-3909
  12094 Avenue 408 Cutler (93615) *(G-6513)*
Pendleton Farms 760 754-2359
  307 Wilshire Rd Oceanside (92057) *(G-126)*
Penguin Computing Inc (PA) 415 954-2800
  45800 Northport Loop W Fremont (94538) *(G-7173)*
Penhall Company 510 357-8810
  13750 Catalina St San Leandro (94577) *(G-3463)*
Penhall Company (HQ) 714 772-6450
  320 N Crescent Way Anaheim (92801) *(G-2832)*
Penhall International Corp (HQ) 714 772-6450
  320 N Crescent Way Anaheim (92801) *(G-3464)*
Penhall San Leandro 153, San Leandro Also called Penhall Company *(G-3463)*
Peninou French Ldry & Clrs Inc (PA) 800 392-2532
  101 S Maple Ave South San Francisco (94080) *(G-13656)*
Peninsula Assoc For Retarded 650 312-0730
  800 Airport Blvd Ste 320 Burlingame (94010) *(G-24127)*
Peninsula Beverly Hill's, Beverly Hills Also called Belvedere Hotel Partnership *(G-12434)*
Peninsula Beverly Hills, The, Beverly Hills Also called Belvedere Partnership *(G-12435)*
Peninsula Community Foundation 650 358-9369
  1700 S El Camino Real # 300 San Mateo (94402) *(G-12162)*
Peninsula Crrdor Jint Pwers Bd 650 508-6200
  1250 San Carlos Ave San Carlos (94070) *(G-3690)*
Peninsula Custom Homes Inc 650 574-0241
  1401 Old County Rd San Carlos (94070) *(G-1233)*
Peninsula Family Service 650 325-8719
  260 Van Buren Rd Menlo Park (94025) *(G-24128)*
Peninsula Family Service (PA) 650 403-4300
  24 2nd Ave San Mateo (94401) *(G-24129)*
Peninsula Family Service 650 952-6848
  1200 Miller Ave South San Francisco (94080) *(G-24130)*
Peninsula Family YMCA Sunshine, San Diego Also called YMCA of San Diego County *(G-25421)*
Peninsula Humane Soc & Spca 650 340-7022
  1450 Rollins Rd Burlingame (94010) *(G-25565)*
Peninsula Jewish Community Ctr 650 212-7522
  800 Foster City Blvd Foster City (94404) *(G-24131)*
Peninsula Pathology Associates, South San Francisco Also called Pennisula Pthlogists Med Group *(G-22253)*
Peninsula Regent, The, San Mateo Also called Bay Area Senior Services Inc *(G-23677)*
Peninsula Womens Health (PA) 650 692-3818
  1828 El Camino Real Ste 8 Burlingame (94010) *(G-19823)*
Peninsula YMCA, San Mateo Also called Young Mens Christian Assoc SF *(G-25449)*
Penney Lawn Service Inc 661 366-3777
  4000 Allen Rd Bakersfield (93314) *(G-933)*
Pennisula Pthlogists Med Group 650 616-2940
  393 E Grand Ave Ste I South San Francisco (94080) *(G-22253)*
Pennmar, El Monte Also called San Gbriel Vly Cnvlescent Hosp *(G-22090)*
Penny Lane Centers (PA) 818 892-3423
  15305 Rayen St North Hills (91343) *(G-24952)*
Penny Lane Centers 818 892-3423
  15317 Rayen St North Hills (91343) *(G-24953)*
Penny Lane Centers 818 892-3423
  15317 Rayen St North Hills (91343) *(G-24954)*
Penny Lane Centers 562 903-4135
  10330 Pioneer Blvd # 290 Santa Fe Springs (90670) *(G-24955)*
Penny Lane Centers 818 892-3423
  15331 Rayen St North Hills (91343) *(G-24956)*
Penny Lane Centers 818 894-9162
  15305 Ranch St North Hills (91343) *(G-24957)*
Penny Lane Centers 818 892-1112
  15302 Rayen St North Hills (91343) *(G-24958)*
Penny Lane Centers 818 892-3423
  15256 Acre St North Hills (91343) *(G-24959)*
Penny Lane Centers 818 892-3423
  1020 E Palmdale Blvd Palmdale (93550) *(G-24960)*
Penny Lane Centers 323 318-9960
  2450 S Atl Blvd Ste 101 Commerce (90040) *(G-24961)*
Penny Lane Centers 661 274-0770
  43520 Division St Lancaster (93535) *(G-24962)*
Penny Lane Centers 818 892-3423
  44248 44258 Cedar Ave Lancaster (93534) *(G-24963)*
Penny Lawn Service, Bakersfield Also called Penney Lawn Service Inc *(G-933)*
Penny Roofing Company 323 731-5424
  2501 Exposition Blvd Los Angeles (90018) *(G-3197)*
Pennymac, Agoura Hills Also called Private Nat Mrtg Accptance LLC *(G-9887)*
Pennymac Corp 818 878-8416
  27001 Agoura Rd Agoura Hills (91301) *(G-9943)*
Pennymac Financial Svcs Inc 818 224-7442
  6101 Condor Dr Moorpark (93021) *(G-9884)*
Penske Automotive Group Inc 415 492-1922
  17 Woodland Ave San Rafael (94901) *(G-17644)*
Penske Automotive Group Inc 408 293-7688
  803 S 1st St San Jose (95110) *(G-17645)*
Penske Leasing 714 522-3330
  15050 Northam St La Mirada (90638) *(G-14567)*
Penske Logistics LLC 800 529-6531
  2090 Etiwanda Ave Ontario (91761) *(G-4243)*
Penske Truck Leasing Co LP 213 628-1255
  2300 E Olympic Blvd Los Angeles (90021) *(G-17646)*
Penske Truck Leasing Co LP 310 327-3116
  19646 Figueroa St Long Beach (90745) *(G-17647)*
Penske Truck Leasing Co LP 559 486-7000
  3080 E Malaga Ave Fresno (93725) *(G-17648)*
Penske Truck Rental Inc 818 718-2536
  11200 Peoria St Sun Valley (91352) *(G-17649)*
Pentair Technical Products 858 740-2400
  7328 Trade St San Diego (92121) *(G-9291)*
Pentel of America Ltd (HQ) 310 320-3831
  2715 Columbia St Torrance (90503) *(G-8173)*
Pentel of America Ltd 909 975-2200
  4000 E Airport Dr Ste C Ontario (91761) *(G-8174)*
Penterman Farming Co Inc 707 967-9977
  3851 Chiles Pope Vly Rd Saint Helena (94574) *(G-714)*
Pentron Clinical Tech LLC 203 265-7397
  1717 W Collins Ave Orange (92867) *(G-22254)*
Penwal Industries Inc 909 466-1555
  10611 Acacia St Rancho Cucamonga (91730) *(G-1634)*
People Assisting Homeless 323 644-2216
  340 N Madison Ave Los Angeles (90004) *(G-24132)*
People Creating Success Inc 661 225-9700
  1607 E Palmdale Blvd H Palmdale (93550) *(G-24133)*
People Creating Success Inc 805 644-9480
  380 Arneill Rd Camarillo (93010) *(G-19824)*
People Creating Success Inc 805 692-5290
  5350 Hollister Ave Ste I Santa Barbara (93111) *(G-24134)*

People Onesource, Long Beach *Also called Covenant Industries Inc* ***(G-14630)***
People Science Inc....888 924-1004
951 Mariners Island Blvd San Mateo (94404) ***(G-14724)***
People's Place, Torrance *Also called Topwin Corporation* ***(G-8362)***
Peoplefluent Inc....805 730-1450
201 N Calle Cesar Chavez # 100 Santa Barbara (93103) ***(G-15372)***
Peoples Care Inc....760 962-1900
13901 Amargosa Rd Ste 101 Victorville (92392) ***(G-22535)***
Peoples Care Inc....562 320-0174
7355 Greenleaf Ave Whittier (90602) ***(G-24500)***
Peoples Choice Home (PA)....949 494-6167
7515 Irvine Center Dr Irvine (92618) ***(G-9885)***
Peoples Choice Staffing Inc....951 735-0550
4218 Green River Rd # 101 Corona (92880) ***(G-14725)***
Peopleware Technical Resources....310 640-2406
302 W Grand Ave Ste 4 El Segundo (90245) ***(G-14726)***
Pep Boys Manny Moe Jack of Cal....562 908-4400
11456 Washington Blvd Whittier (90606) ***(G-17810)***
Pepper Tree Inn....530 583-3711
645 N Lake Blvd Tahoe City (96145) ***(G-13089)***
Pepperjam LLC....760 585-7150
408 Cassidy St Ste 101 Oceanside (92054) ***(G-15373)***
Peppermill Casinos Inc....925 671-7711
4021 Port Chicago Hwy Concord (94520) ***(G-13090)***
Peppermint Ridge (PA)....951 273-7320
825 Magnolia Ave Corona (92879) ***(G-24767)***
Pepsi-Cola Metro Btlg Co Inc....707 535-4560
3029 Coffey Ln Santa Rosa (95403) ***(G-8899)***
Pepsi-Cola Metro Btlg Co Inc....707 746-5404
4701 Park Rd Benicia (94510) ***(G-4611)***
Pepsi-Cola Metro Btlg Co Inc....909 885-0741
6659 Sycamore Canyon Blvd Riverside (92507) ***(G-8900)***
Pepsi-Cola Metro Btlg Co Inc....209 557-5100
200 River Rd Modesto (95351) ***(G-4612)***
Pepsi-Cola Metro Btlg Co Inc....626 338-5531
4416 Azusa Canyon Rd Baldwin Park (91706) ***(G-8901)***
Pepsi-Cola Metro Btlg Co Inc....818 898-3829
1200 Arroyo St San Fernando (91340) ***(G-8902)***
Pepsi-Cola Metro Btlg Co Inc....415 206-7400
200 Jennings St San Francisco (94124) ***(G-8903)***
Pepsi-Cola Metro Btlg Co Inc....951 697-3200
6659 Sycamore Canyon Blvd Riverside (92507) ***(G-7757)***
Pepsico Inc....626 338-5531
4416 Azusa Canyon Rd Baldwin Park (91706) ***(G-8624)***
Peralta Service Corporation....510 535-5027
1900 Fruitvale Ave Ste 2a Oakland (94601) ***(G-24379)***
Pereira & ODell LLC (PA)....415 284-9916
215 2nd St Ste 100 San Francisco (94105) ***(G-13894)***
Perennial Engrg & Cnstr Inc....714 771-2103
2907 Tech Ctr Santa Ana (92705) ***(G-1234)***
Perez Contracting LLC....661 399-2700
12620 Snow Rd Bakersfield (93314) ***(G-715)***
Perfect Bar LLC....866 628-8548
5360 Eastgate Mall Ste A San Diego (92121) ***(G-8904)***
Perfect Foods, San Diego *Also called Perfect Bar LLC* ***(G-8904)***
Perfection Glass Inc....951 674-0240
554 3rd St Lake Elsinore (92530) ***(G-3412)***
Perficient Inc....877 654-0033
2000 Alameda De Las Pulga San Mateo (94403) ***(G-15374)***
Performance Building Services....949 364-4364
22642 Lambert St Ste 409 Lake Forest (92630) ***(G-14388)***
Performance Cleanroom Services, Lake Forest *Also called Performance Building Services* ***(G-14388)***
Performance Designed Pdts LLC (HQ)....323 234-9911
2300 W Empire Ave # 600 Burbank (91504) ***(G-8051)***
Performance Food Group Inc....909 673-1780
3790 Jurupa St Ontario (91761) ***(G-8905)***
Performance Food Group Inc....714 535-2111
16639 Gale Ave City of Industry (91745) ***(G-8906)***
Performance Food Group Inc....831 462-4400
1047 17th Ave Santa Cruz (95062) ***(G-8509)***
Performance Sheets LLC....626 333-0195
440 Baldwin Park Blvd City of Industry (91746) ***(G-3198)***
Performance Team Frt Sys Inc....562 741-1300
12816 Shoemaker Ave Santa Fe Springs (90670) ***(G-4613)***
Performance Team Frt Sys Inc....801 301-1732
1898 Marigold Ave Redlands (92374) ***(G-17408)***
Performance Team Frt Sys Inc....310 241-4100
401 Westmont Dr San Pedro (90731) ***(G-4614)***
Performance Team Frt Sys Inc....562 345-2200
1331 Torrance Blvd Torrance (90501) ***(G-5150)***
Performance Team Frt Sys Inc (PA)....562 345-2200
2240 E Maple Ave El Segundo (90245) ***(G-5151)***
Performance Tech Partners LLC....916 307-5669
11341 Gold Ex Dr Ste 160 Gold River (95670) ***(G-16456)***
Performant Financial Corp (PA)....925 960-4800
333 N Canyons Pkwy # 100 Livermore (94551) ***(G-16252)***
Performant Recovery Inc....209 858-3500
17080 S Harlan Rd Lathrop (95330) ***(G-14041)***
Performant Recovery Inc (HQ)....209 858-3994
333 N Canyons Pkwy # 100 Livermore (94551) ***(G-14042)***
Performant Technologies Inc....925 960-4800
333 N Canyons Pkwy # 100 Livermore (94551) ***(G-10171)***
Performing Arts Center of La C....213 972-7211
135 N Grand Ave Los Angeles (90012) ***(G-18423)***
Performnce Foodservice Ledyard, Santa Cruz *Also called Performance Food Group Inc* ***(G-8509)***
Perkins Coie LLP....415 725-1313
3150 Porter Dr Palo Alto (94304) ***(G-23501)***
Perkins Coie LLP....310 788-9900
1620 26th St Ste 600s Santa Monica (90404) ***(G-23502)***
Perkins Coie LLP....415 344-7000
505 Howard St Ste 1000 San Francisco (94105) ***(G-23503)***
Perkowitz & Ruth Architects, Long Beach *Also called Ruth Perkowitz Inc* ***(G-26249)***
Perkstreet Financial Inc....978 801-1177
1100 La Avenida St Ste A Mountain View (94043) ***(G-27586)***
Perlegen Sciences Inc....650 625-4500
35473 Dumbarton Ct Newark (94560) ***(G-26587)***
Permanente Federation LLC....510 625-6920
1800 Harrison St Fl 22 Oakland (94612) ***(G-27587)***
Permanente Kaiser Intl....323 857-2000
6041 Cadillac Ave Fl 4 Los Angeles (90034) ***(G-19825)***
Permanente Kaiser Intl....707 258-4541
3285 Claremont Way NAPA (94558) ***(G-20338)***
Permanente Kaiser Intl....650 299-3888
910 Maple St Redwood City (94063) ***(G-19826)***
Permanente Kaiser Intl....925 813-6500
4501 Sand Creek Rd Antioch (94531) ***(G-19827)***
Permanente Kaiser Intl....619 409-6050
3955 Bonita Rd Bldg B Bonita (91902) ***(G-21789)***
Permanente Kaiser Intl....805 374-7433
365 E Hillcrest Dr Thousand Oaks (91360) ***(G-19828)***
Permanente Kaiser Intl....909 427-5000
9961 Sierra Ave Fontana (92335) ***(G-21790)***
Permanente Kaiser Intl....916 979-3531
2829 Watt Ave Ste 150 Sacramento (95821) ***(G-19829)***
Permanente Kaiser Intl....510 454-1000
2500 Merced St San Leandro (94577) ***(G-19830)***
Permanente Kaiser Intl....310 517-2645
25965 Normandie Ave Fl 3 Harbor City (90710) ***(G-21791)***
Permanente Kaiser Intl....760 739-3000
555 E Valley Pkwy Escondido (92025) ***(G-21792)***
Permanente Kaiser Intl....408 236-6400
710 Lawrence Expy Santa Clara (95051) ***(G-19831)***
Permanente Kaiser Intl....619 641-4300
10990 San Dego Mission Rd San Diego (92108) ***(G-23018)***
Permanente Kaiser Intl....951 662-8194
156 Acacia Glen Dr Riverside (92506) ***(G-24964)***
Permanente Kaiser Intl....951 358-2600
10917 Magnolia Ave Riverside (92505) ***(G-22536)***
Permanente Kaiser Intl....626 960-4844
1511 W Garvey Ave N West Covina (91790) ***(G-19832)***
Permanente Kaiser Intl....818 705-5500
18040 Sherman Way Reseda (91335) ***(G-19833)***
Permanente Kaiser Intl....310 737-4800
5620 Mesmer Ave Culver City (90230) ***(G-21793)***
Permanente Kaiser Intl....707 453-5197
3700 New Horizons Way Vacaville (95688) ***(G-21794)***
Permanente Medical Group, Mountain View *Also called Kaiser Foundation Hospitals* ***(G-21647)***
Permanente Medical Group Inc....510 248-3000
39400 Paseo Padre Pkwy Fremont (94538) ***(G-19834)***
Permanente Medical Group Inc....650 299-2000
1150 Veterans Blvd Redwood City (94063) ***(G-19835)***
Permanente Medical Group Inc (HQ)....866 858-2226
1950 Franklin St Fl 18th Oakland (94612) ***(G-23019)***
Permanente Medical Group Inc....707 765-3930
1617 Broadway St Vallejo (94590) ***(G-19836)***
Permanente Medical Group Inc....559 448-4500
7300 N Fresno St Fresno (93720) ***(G-19837)***
Permanente Medical Group Inc....916 688-2055
6600 Bruceville Rd Sacramento (95823) ***(G-19838)***
Permanente Medical Group Inc....650 742-2100
901 El Camino Real San Bruno (94066) ***(G-19839)***
Permanente Medical Group Inc....707 393-4000
3558 Round Barn Blvd Santa Rosa (95403) ***(G-19840)***
Permanente Medical Group Inc....415 833-2000
2425 Geary Blvd San Francisco (94115) ***(G-19841)***
Permanente Medical Group Inc....408 972-6883
275 Hospital Pkwy Ste 470 San Jose (95119) ***(G-19842)***
Permanente Medical Group Inc....925 372-1000
200 Muir Rd Martinez (94553) ***(G-19843)***
Permanente Medical Group Inc....510 752-1000
3779 Piedmont Ave Oakland (94611) ***(G-19844)***
Permanente Medical Group Inc....510 752-1190
235 W Macarthur Blvd Oakland (94611) ***(G-19845)***
Permanente Medical Group Inc....408 945-2900
770 E Calaveras Blvd Milpitas (95035) ***(G-19846)***
Permanente Medical Group Inc....925 813-6149
4501 Sand Creek Rd Antioch (94531) ***(G-19847)***
Permanente Medical Group Inc....650 827-6495
220 Oyster Point Blvd South San Francisco (94080) ***(G-19848)***
Permanente Medical Group Inc....650 299-2015
910 Marshall St Redwood City (94063) ***(G-19849)***
Permanente Medical Group Inc....510 231-5406
914 Marina Way S Richmond (94804) ***(G-19850)***
Permanente Medical Group Inc....650 598-2852
900 Veterans Blvd Ste 400 Redwood City (94063) ***(G-19851)***
Permanente Medical Group Inc....510 454-1000
2500 Merced St San Leandro (94577) ***(G-19852)***
Permanente Medical Group Inc....415 444-2000
99 Montecillo Rd San Rafael (94903) ***(G-19853)***
Permanente Medical Group Inc....925 906-2000
320 Lennon Ln Walnut Creek (94598) ***(G-19854)***
Permanente Medical Group Inc....415 209-2444
100 Rowland Way Ste 125 Novato (94945) ***(G-19855)***
Permanente Medical Group Inc....209 476-3737
7373 West Ln Stockton (95210) ***(G-19856)***

Permanente Medical Group Inc..........510 559-5119
1725 Eastshore Hwy Berkeley (94710) *(G-21795)*
Permanente Medical Group Inc..........415 899-7400
97 San Marin Dr Novato (94945) *(G-19857)*
Permanente Medical Group Inc..........916 784-4000
1600 Eureka Rd Roseville (95661) *(G-19858)*
Permanente Medical Group Inc..........415 833-2000
2238 Geary Blvd San Francisco (94115) *(G-19859)*
Permanente Medical Group Inc..........510 559-5338
1750 2nd St Berkeley (94710) *(G-19860)*
Permanente Medical Group Inc..........707 765-3900
3900 Lakeville Hwy Petaluma (94954) *(G-19861)*
Permanente Medical Group Inc..........707 427-4000
1550 Gateway Blvd Fairfield (94533) *(G-21796)*
Permanente Medical Group Inc..........209 476-2000
1305 Tommydon St Stockton (95210) *(G-19862)*
Permanente Medical Group Inc..........510 675-4010
3555 Whipple Rd Union City (94587) *(G-19863)*
Permanente Medical Group Inc..........925 243-2600
3000 Las Positas Rd Livermore (94551) *(G-19864)*
Permanente Medical Group Inc..........916 631-3000
10725 International Dr Rancho Cordova (95670) *(G-19865)*
Permanente Medical Group Inc..........650 301-5860
395 Hickey Blvd Fl 1 Daly City (94015) *(G-19866)*
Permanente Medical Group Inc..........650 358-7000
1000 Franklin Pkwy San Mateo (94403) *(G-19867)*
Permanente Medical Group Inc..........209 735-5000
4601 Dale Rd Modesto (95356) *(G-19868)*
Permanentee Medical Group, Roseville *Also called Kaiser Foundation Hospitals (G-19656)*
Permits Today LLC..........626 585-2931
140 S Lake Ave Ste 323 Pasadena (91101) *(G-17409)*
Pernixdata Inc..........408 724-8413
1745 Tech Dr Ste 800 San Jose (95110) *(G-15375)*
Perona Langer Beck A Prof Corp..........562 426-6155
300 E San Antonio Dr Long Beach (90807) *(G-23504)*
Perot Systems Corporation..........310 342-3200
6701 Center Dr W Ste 1000 Los Angeles (90045) *(G-16281)*
Perr & Knight Inc (PA)..........310 230-9339
401 Wilshire Blvd Ste 300 Santa Monica (90401) *(G-10825)*
Perris Valley Cmnty Hosp LLC..........909 581-6400
10841 White Oak Ave Rancho Cucamonga (91730) *(G-21797)*
Perry & Shaw Inc..........619 390-6500
9029 Park Plaza Dr # 104 La Mesa (91942) *(G-26019)*
Perry Coast Construction Inc..........951 774-0677
6770 Central Ave Ste B Riverside (92504) *(G-1635)*
Perry Floor Systems Inc..........909 949-1211
261 Industry Way Upland (91786) *(G-3312)*
Perry, Joseph Allen, Glendale *Also called J P Allen Co (G-2258)*
Persistent Systems Inc (HQ)..........408 216-7010
2055 Laurelwood Rd # 210 Santa Clara (95054) *(G-15376)*
Personalis Inc..........650 752-1300
1330 Obrien Dr Menlo Park (94025) *(G-26588)*
Personlized Buty Discovery Inc..........888 769-4526
201 Baldwin Ave Fl 2 San Mateo (94401) *(G-13684)*
Personlzed Hmcare Hmmaker Agcy..........916 979-4975
4700 Northgate Blvd Sacramento (95834) *(G-22537)*
Personnel Preference Inc..........530 938-3909
150 Boles St Ste A Weed (96094) *(G-14922)*
Perterman, San Jose *Also called Durham School Services (G-28128)*
Perverted Jstice Fundation Inc..........310 910-9380
703 Pier Ave Ste B154 Hermosa Beach (90254) *(G-12163)*
Pescadero Conservation Aliance..........650 879-1441
4100 Cabrillo Hwy Pescadero (94060) *(G-25313)*
Pestana Construction, San Jose *Also called Ernest E Pestana Inc (G-1929)*
Pet Partners Inc (PA)..........951 279-9888
450 N Sheridan St Corona (92880) *(G-9292)*
Pet Pourri, Milpitas *Also called Humane Society Silicon Valley (G-641)*
Petalon Landscape MGT Inc..........408 453-3998
1766 Rogers Ave San Jose (95112) *(G-934)*
Petaluma Creamery, Petaluma *Also called Spring Hill Jersey Cheese Inc (G-8592)*
Petaluma Health Center Inc..........707 559-7500
1179 N Mcdowell Blvd A Petaluma (94954) *(G-19869)*
Petaluma Jint Un High Schl Dst..........707 778-4677
333 Casa Grande Rd Petaluma (94954) *(G-11746)*
Petaluma Medical Offices, Petaluma *Also called Kaiser Foundation Hospitals (G-21659)*
Petaluma Valley Hospital, Petaluma *Also called Srm Alliance Hospital Services (G-21912)*
Petaluma Valley Hospital, Petaluma *Also called St Joseph Health System (G-21918)*
Petco Animal Supplies Inc (HQ)..........858 453-7845
10850 Via Frontera San Diego (92127) *(G-644)*
Pete Helling..........310 390-2710
11600 Wash Pl Ste 117 Los Angeles (90066) *(G-17410)*
Pete Santellan..........559 564-3748
176 S Valencia Blvd Ste C Woodlake (93286) *(G-678)*
Peter H Mattson & Co Inc..........650 356-2500
383 Vintage Park Dr Foster City (94404) *(G-26589)*
Peter J Wolk MD..........530 534-6517
2721 Olive Hwy Oroville (95966) *(G-19870)*
Peter Kiewit Sons Inc..........909 962-6001
1925 Wright Ave Ste C La Verne (91750) *(G-1846)*
Peter Wylan DDS..........562 925-3765
10318 Rosecrans Ave Bellflower (90706) *(G-20270)*
Petersen Auto Mseum Foundation..........323 930-2277
6060 Wilshire Blvd Los Angeles (90036) *(G-25037)*
Petersen Builders Inc..........707 838-3035
7706 Bell Rd Ste A Windsor (95492) *(G-1235)*
Petersen-Dean Inc..........661 254-3322
21616 Golden Triangle Rd # 101 Santa Clarita (91350) *(G-3199)*
Petersen-Dean Inc..........707 469-7470
1705 Enterprise Dr Fairfield (94533) *(G-3200)*
Petersen-Dean Inc..........714 629-9670
2210 S Dupont Dr Anaheim (92806) *(G-3201)*
Petersen-Dean Inc..........510 494-9982
39300 Civic Center Dr # 300 Fremont (94538) *(G-3202)*
Petersen-Dean Commercial Inc..........707 469-7470
1705 Enterprise Dr Fairfield (94533) *(G-3203)*
Petersendean, Fairfield *Also called Petersen-Dean Commercial Inc (G-3203)*
Petersendean, Santa Clarita *Also called Petersen-Dean Inc (G-3199)*
Petersendean, Anaheim *Also called Petersen-Dean Inc (G-3201)*
Petersendean, Fremont *Also called Petersen-Dean Inc (G-3202)*
Peterson Bros Construction, Brea *Also called P B C Pavers Inc (G-2472)*
Peterson Bros Contruction Inc..........714 278-0488
1560 W Lambert Rd Brea (92821) *(G-3313)*
Peterson Cat, San Leandro *Also called Peterson Machinery Co (G-17939)*
Peterson Family Inc..........559 897-5064
38694 Road 16 Kingsburg (93631) *(G-247)*
Peterson Machinery Co..........541 302-9199
955 Marina Blvd San Leandro (94577) *(G-17939)*
Peterson Painting Inc..........925 455-5864
5750 La Ribera St Livermore (94550) *(G-2473)*
Petes Connection Inc..........909 373-6414
280 N Benson Ave Ste 78 Upland (91786) *(G-6012)*
Petes Connection Inc..........760 723-1972
407 Ranger Rd Fallbrook (92028) *(G-6013)*
Petit Ermitage, West Hollywood *Also called Valadon Hotel LLC (G-13373)*
Petra Risk Solutions..........800 466-8951
5927 Priestly Dr Ste 112 Carlsbad (92008) *(G-10826)*
Petrelli Electric Inc..........661 268-7312
11615 Davenport Rd Agua Dulce (91390) *(G-2683)*
Petrochem Insulation Inc..........310 638-6663
19010 S Alameda St Compton (90221) *(G-2954)*
Petrol Advertising Inc..........323 644-3720
443 N Varney St Burbank (91502) *(G-13895)*
Petroleum Sales Inc..........415 945-1309
2066 Redwood Hwy Greenbrae (94904) *(G-1048)*
Petroquip, Santa Ana *Also called G W Maintenance Inc (G-7932)*
Pets Unlimited..........415 563-6700
2343 Fillmore St San Francisco (94115) *(G-25566)*
Petti Kohn Ingrassia & L PR Co..........310 649-5772
11622 El Camino Real San Diego (92130) *(G-23505)*
Petz Enterprises Inc (PA)..........209 835-1360
7575 W Linne Rd Tracy (95304) *(G-15377)*
Pf West LLC..........415 479-9600
101 Lucas Valley Rd # 150 San Rafael (94903) *(G-18669)*
Pfitech, Costa Mesa *Also called Precise Fit Limited One LLC (G-14731)*
Pfl Security, Rancho Mirage *Also called Protect-For-Less Security Svcs (G-16913)*
Pfs Investments Inc..........707 435-9507
1955 W Texas St Ste 1 Fairfield (94533) *(G-10827)*
Pfyffer Associates Inc..........831 423-8572
2611 Mission St Santa Cruz (95060) *(G-88)*
PG&e, Fairfield *Also called Pacific Gas and Electric Co (G-6161)*
PG&e, San Francisco *Also called Pacific Gas and Electric Co (G-6162)*
PG&e, West Sacramento *Also called Pacific Gas and Electric Co (G-6163)*
PG&e, Marysville *Also called Pacific Gas and Electric Co (G-6164)*
PG&e, Hayward *Also called Pacific Gas and Electric Co (G-6271)*
PG&e, Chico *Also called Pacific Gas and Electric Co (G-6272)*
PG&e, Magalia *Also called Pacific Gas and Electric Co (G-6168)*
PG&e, Grass Valley *Also called Pacific Gas and Electric Co (G-6169)*
PG&e, Petaluma *Also called Pacific Gas and Electric Co (G-6170)*
PG&e, Fresno *Also called Pacific Gas and Electric Co (G-6171)*
PG&e, Avila Beach *Also called Pacific Gas and Electric Co (G-6172)*
PG&e, Redding *Also called Pacific Gas and Electric Co (G-6173)*
PG&e, San Francisco *Also called Pacific Gas and Electric Co (G-6174)*
PG&e, Concord *Also called Pacific Gas and Electric Co (G-6175)*
PG&e, Concord *Also called Pacific Gas and Electric Co (G-6176)*
PG&e, San Francisco *Also called Pacific Energy Fuels Company (G-6270)*
PG&e, Eureka *Also called Pacific Gas and Electric Co (G-6177)*
PG&e, Daly City *Also called Pacific Gas and Electric Co (G-6178)*
PG&e, Modesto *Also called Pacific Gas and Electric Co (G-6179)*
PG&e, Stockton *Also called Pacific Gas and Electric Co (G-6180)*
PG&e, Ukiah *Also called Pacific Gas and Electric Co (G-6181)*
PG&e, Pismo Beach *Also called Pacific Gas and Electric Co (G-6182)*
PG&e, Sacramento *Also called Pacific Gas and Electric Co (G-6183)*
PG&e, Monterey *Also called Pacific Gas and Electric Co (G-6184)*
PG&e, Fremont *Also called Pacific Gas and Electric Co (G-6185)*
PG&e, Auberry *Also called Pacific Gas and Electric Co (G-6186)*
PG&e, Livermore *Also called Pacific Gas and Electric Co (G-6187)*
PG&e, Davis *Also called Pacific Gas and Electric Co (G-6188)*
PG&e, San Francisco *Also called Pacific Gas and Electric Co (G-6189)*
PG&e, Milpitas *Also called Pacific Gas and Electric Co (G-6190)*
PG&e, Pioneer *Also called Pacific Gas and Electric Co (G-6191)*
PG&e, Bakersfield *Also called Pacific Gas and Electric Co (G-6192)*
PG&e, Templeton *Also called Pacific Gas and Electric Co (G-6193)*
PG&e, San Francisco *Also called Pacific Gas and Electric Co (G-6194)*
PG&e Capital LLC..........415 321-4600
1 Market San Francisco (94105) *(G-27588)*
PG&e Corporation (PA)..........415 973-1000
77 Beale St San Francisco (94105) *(G-6291)*
Pgande..........209 942-1745
10901 E Highway 120 Manteca (95336) *(G-25098)*
Pgs Subsidiary II Company..........626 440-2000
100 W Walnut St Pasadena (91124) *(G-26020)*

ALPHABETIC

Phacil Inc 415 901-1600
601 California St # 1710 San Francisco (94108) *(G-15378)*
Phamatech Incorporated 858 643-5555
15175 Innovation Dr San Diego (92128) *(G-26882)*
Pharmacy Temps Inc 415 459-5211
2125 Paradise Dr Belvedere Tiburon (94920) *(G-14923)*
Pharmatek Laboratories Inc 858 805-6383
7330 Carroll Rd Ste 200 San Diego (92121) *(G-26883)*
Phase 1 Tele-Team 562 746-8734
1119 Electric St Gardena (90248) *(G-14727)*
Phase 3 Communications Inc 408 946-9011
224 N 27th St Ste B San Jose (95116) *(G-16029)*
Phase 3 Inc 209 848-0290
8191 Laughlin Rd Oakdale (95361) *(G-4928)*
Phelan & Taylor Produce Co 805 489-2413
1860 Pacific Coast Hwy Oceano (93445) *(G-574)*
Phelps Group 310 752-4400
12121 W Bluff Dr Ste 200 Los Angeles (90094) *(G-13896)*
Phenomenon Mktg & Entrmt Inc (PA) 323 648-4035
5900 Wilshire Blvd Fl 28 Los Angeles (90036) *(G-27589)*
PHF II Burbank LLC 818 843-6000
2500 N Hollywood Way Burbank (91505) *(G-13091)*
PHF Ruby LLC 415 885-4700
2620 Jones St San Francisco (94133) *(G-13092)*
Phfe, City of Industry *Also called Public Hlth Fndation Entps Inc* *(G-27185)*
Phfe Wic Program 626 856-6650
12871 Schabarum Ave Irwindale (91706) *(G-24135)*
PHI Delta Theta Inc 818 885-9940
17740 Halsted St Northridge (91325) *(G-13496)*
Phifactor Technologies LLC 424 234-9494
6415 Surfside Way Malibu (90265) *(G-22255)*
Phihong USA Corp (HQ) 510 445-0100
47800 Fremont Blvd Fremont (94538) *(G-7174)*
Philharmonia Baroque Orchestra 415 252-1288
414 Mason St Ste 606 San Francisco (94102) *(G-18486)*
Philip DAmato Racing LLC 949 830-7027
28202 Palmada Mission Viejo (92692) *(G-18573)*
Philippine Airlines 310 646-1981
11001 Aviation Blvd Los Angeles (90045) *(G-4816)*
Philippine Airlines Inc 415 217-3100
447 Sutter St Ste 200 San Francisco (94108) *(G-4817)*
Philips & Lite-On Digital (HQ) 510 824-9690
42000 Christy St Fremont (94538) *(G-7346)*
Philips Hlthcare Infrmtics Inc (HQ) 650 293-2300
4100 E 3rd Ave Ste 101 Foster City (94404) *(G-15379)*
Philips Medical Systems Clevel 949 699-2300
1 Marconi Irvine (92618) *(G-7300)*
Phillips & Assoc Law Offs PC 510 464-8040
1300 Clay St Ste 600 Oakland (94612) *(G-23506)*
Phillips Farms 559 798-1871
33771 Road 156 Visalia (93292) *(G-248)*
Phillips Pet Food and Supplies (PA) 916 373-7300
3885 Seaport Blvd Ste 10 West Sacramento (95691) *(G-8907)*
Phillips Plywood Co Inc 818 897-7736
13599 Desmond St Pacoima (91331) *(G-6946)*
Phillips Steel Company 562 435-7571
1368 W Anaheim St Long Beach (90813) *(G-7392)*
Philmont Management Inc 213 380-0159
3450 Wilshire Blvd # 850 Los Angeles (90010) *(G-1636)*
Philotic Inc 510 730-1740
524 3rd St San Francisco (94107) *(G-15380)*
Phoenix American Incorporated (PA) 415 485-4500
2401 Kerner Blvd San Rafael (94901) *(G-6014)*
Phoenix Engineering Co Inc 310 532-1134
20630 Leapwood Ave Ste B Carson (90746) *(G-14924)*
Phoenix Home Lf Mutl Insur Co, Hemet *Also called Anka Behavioral Health Inc* *(G-10604)*
Phoenix Hospice, Willits *Also called Adventist Health System/West* *(G-22341)*
Phoenix House Orange County 714 953-9373
1207 E Fruit St Santa Ana (92701) *(G-24768)*
Phoenix Houses Los Angeles Inc 818 686-3000
11600 Eldridge Ave Lake View Terrace (91342) *(G-24769)*
PHOENIX HSE FNDTN, INC. & AF, Lake View Terrace *Also called Phoenix Houses Los Angeles Inc* *(G-24769)*
Phoenix International, Torrance *Also called CH Robinson Freight Svcs Ltd* *(G-5045)*
Phoenix Intl Holdings Inc 619 207-0871
127 Press Ln Chula Vista (91910) *(G-17411)*
Phoenix Lounge and Casino 916 334-4225
5948 Auburn Blvd Ste M Citrus Heights (95621) *(G-13093)*
Phoenix Personnel, Carson *Also called Phoenix Engineering Co Inc* *(G-14924)*
Phoenix RE Investment Co 408 213-8600
1754 Tech Dr Ste 108 San Jose (95110) *(G-11747)*
Phoenix Satellite TV US Inc 626 388-1188
3810 Durbin St Baldwin Park (91706) *(G-5905)*
Phoenix Textile Inc 213 239-9640
910 S Los Angeles St Los Angeles (90015) *(G-17412)*
Phone App Company, The, Hermosa Beach *Also called Southbay Website Design LLC* *(G-16192)*
Phone Ware Inc 858 530-8550
8902 Activity Rd Ste A San Diego (92126) *(G-17413)*
Phonepower, Northridge *Also called Quality Speaks LLC* *(G-16254)*
Photo TLC Inc 415 462-0010
3925 Cypress Dr Petaluma (94954) *(G-16954)*
Photocenter Imaging, Burbank *Also called J H Maddocks Photography* *(G-16952)*
Phs / Mwa (HQ) 950 695-1008
42355 Rio Nedo Temecula (92590) *(G-4929)*
Phs Staffing, Los Angeles *Also called Premier Healthcare Svcs LLC* *(G-14733)*
Phs/Mwa Aviation Services, Temecula *Also called Phs / Mwa* *(G-4929)*

Physical Optics Corporation (PA) 310 320-3088
1845 W 205th St Torrance (90501) *(G-26590)*
Physical Rehabilitation Netwrk 408 570-0510
2833 Junction Ave Ste 206 San Jose (95134) *(G-20339)*
Physical Rehabilitation Netwrk (PA) 760 931-8310
5962 La Place Ct Ste 170 Carlsbad (92008) *(G-20340)*
Physical Therapy Hand Ctrs Inc 760 233-9655
1815 E Valley Pkwy Ste 5 Escondido (92027) *(G-20341)*
Physical/Occupational Therapy, Madera *Also called Pediatric Physical Rehab Clnc* *(G-22797)*
Physician Assoc San Gabriel 626 817-8300
199 S Los Robles Ave Pasadena (91101) *(G-10370)*
Physician Management Group Inc 858 309-6300
3860 Calle Fortunada # 210 San Diego (92123) *(G-27163)*
Physician Office Support Svcs, Torrance *Also called Torrance Health Assn Inc* *(G-21968)*
Physician Weblink of Cal (HQ) 949 923-3201
7 Technology Dr Irvine (92618) *(G-27164)*
Physicians Automated Lab, Taft *Also called Physicians Automated Lab Inc* *(G-26884)*
Physicians Automated Lab Inc (PA) 661 325-0744
820 34th St Ste 102 Bakersfield (93301) *(G-22256)*
Physicians Automated Lab Inc 661 765-4522
107 Adkisson Way Taft (93268) *(G-26884)*
Physicians Choice LLC 818 340-9988
21860 Burbank Blvd # 120 Woodland Hills (91367) *(G-26422)*
Physicians For Healthy Hospita 951 679-8888
28400 Mccall Blvd Sun City (92585) *(G-21798)*
Physicians For Healthy Hospita 951 652-2811
1280 S Buena Vista St San Jacinto (92583) *(G-21799)*
Physicians Plz Surgical Ctr LP 661 322-4744
6000 Physicians Blvd # 205 Bakersfield (93301) *(G-19871)*
Physicians Referral Service, Lancaster *Also called Lancaster Crdlgy Med Group Inc* *(G-19698)*
Piano Disc, Sacramento *Also called Burgett Incorporated* *(G-8107)*
Piazza Trucking, South Gate *Also called Samuel J Piazza & Son Inc* *(G-4374)*
Piccadilly Hospitality LLC 559 348-5520
2305 W Shaw Ave Fresno (93711) *(G-13094)*
Piccadilly Inn, Fresno *Also called Regent Corp* *(G-13790)*
Piccadilly Inn Airport, Fresno *Also called Art Piccadilly Shaw LLC* *(G-12397)*
Piccadilly Inn Shaw, Fresno *Also called Piccadilly Hospitality LLC* *(G-13094)*
Pick Pull Auto Dismantling Inc (HQ) 916 689-2000
10850 Gold Center Dr # 325 Rancho Cordova (95670) *(G-8079)*
Pick-A-Part, Monrovia *Also called M T M & M Inc* *(G-14486)*
Pick-A-Part Auto Wrecking 559 485-3071
9445 Cambridge St Cypress (90630) *(G-8080)*
Pickford Realty Inc 805 782-6000
1015 Nipomo St Ste 100 San Luis Obispo (93401) *(G-11748)*
Pickford Realty Inc 858 793-6106
11120 E Ocean Air Dr # 103 San Diego (92130) *(G-11749)*
Pickford Realty Inc 619 294-3113
2365 Northside Dr Ste 200 San Diego (92108) *(G-11750)*
Pickford Realty Inc 619 435-8722
101 Orange Ave Coronado (92118) *(G-11751)*
Pickwick Hotel The, San Francisco *Also called Yhb San Francisco LLC* *(G-13446)*
Pico Cleaner Inc (PA) 310 274-2431
9150 W Pico Blvd Los Angeles (90035) *(G-13583)*
Pico Party Rents, Los Angeles *Also called Pico Rents Inc* *(G-14568)*
Pico Rents Inc 310 275-9431
13414 S Figueroa St Los Angeles (90061) *(G-14568)*
PICO WOOSTER SENIOR HOUSING, Los Angeles *Also called Los Angeles Senior Citizen* *(G-11161)*
Picture It On Canvas Inc 858 679-1200
12525 Stowe Dr Poway (92064) *(G-16955)*
Pie Town Productions Inc 818 255-9300
5433 Laurel Canyon Blvd North Hollywood (91607) *(G-18128)*
Piedmont Cncil Boy Scouts Amer 510 547-4493
10 Highland Way Piedmont (94611) *(G-25314)*
Piedmont Gardens, Oakland *Also called American Baptist Homes of West* *(G-24547)*
Piedmont Transfer & Storage 408 288-5600
1555 S 7th St Ste A San Jose (95112) *(G-4244)*
Piege Co (PA) 818 727-9100
20120 Plummer St Chatsworth (91311) *(G-8409)*
Piehl, Joel J DDS, Hawthorne *Also called Schnierow Dental Care* *(G-20276)*
Pier 2620 Ht Fishermans Wharf, San Francisco *Also called PHF Ruby LLC* *(G-13092)*
Pier 39 Limited Partnership (PA) 415 705-5500
Beach Embarcadero Level 3 San Francisco (94133) *(G-11032)*
Pier Pont Hotel LP 805 643-6144
550 San Jon Rd Ventura (93001) *(G-13095)*
Pier Restaurant, San Francisco *Also called Blue and Gold Fleet* *(G-4731)*
Pierce Brothers (HQ) 818 763-9121
10621 Victory Blvd North Hollywood (91606) *(G-13710)*
Pierce Enterprises, El Monte *Also called Wgg Enterprises Inc* *(G-3001)*
Piercey Automotive Group, Irvine *Also called Piercey Management Svcs Inc* *(G-27165)*
Piercey Management Svcs Inc (PA) 949 379-3701
16901 Millikan Ave Irvine (92606) *(G-27165)*
Pierre Landscape Inc 818 373-0023
5455 2nd St Irwindale (91706) *(G-787)*
Pigeon & Poodle, Baldwin Park *Also called Ardmore Home Design Inc* *(G-6843)*
Pih Health, Whittier *Also called Interhealth Corporation* *(G-21613)*
PIH HOME HEALTH SERVICES, Downey *Also called Downey Regional Medical* *(G-21547)*
PIH HOME HEALTH SERVICES, Whittier *Also called Presbyterian Intrcmmnty Hosptl* *(G-21805)*
Pilgrim Haven Retirement Home, Los Altos *Also called American Baptist Homes of West* *(G-21138)*
Pilgrim Place Beauty Salon, Claremont *Also called Pilgrim Place In Claremont* *(G-13685)*
Pilgrim Place In Claremont (PA) 909 399-5500
625 Mayflower Rd Claremont (91711) *(G-21347)*

ALPHABETIC

Pilgrim Place In Claremont ... 909 621-9581
721 Harrison Ave Claremont (91711) *(G-13685)*
Pillsbury Winthrop Shaw ... 415 983-1000
4 Embarcadero Ctr Fl 22 San Francisco (94111) *(G-23507)*
Pillsbury Winthrop Shaw ... 213 488-7100
725 S Figueroa St # 2800 Los Angeles (90017) *(G-23508)*
Pillsbury Winthrop Shaw ... 415 983-1865
29 Eucalyptus Rd Berkeley (94705) *(G-23509)*
Pillsbury Winthrop Shaw ... 415 983-1075
50 Fremont St Ste 522 San Francisco (94105) *(G-23510)*
Pillsbury Winthrop Shaw ... 650 233-4500
2550 Hanover St Palo Alto (94304) *(G-23511)*
Pilot Automotive, City of Industry *Also called Pilot Inc (G-6754)*
Pilot Freight Services, San Diego *Also called Miramar Transportation Inc (G-5124)*
Pilot Inc (PA) ... 800 237-7560
13000 Temple Ave City of Industry (91746) *(G-6754)*
Pilot Painting & Construction ... 714 229-5900
5555 Corporate Ave Cypress (90630) *(G-2474)*
Pimco, Newport Beach *Also called Pacific Investment MGT Co LLC (G-10168)*
Pimco Funds Distribution Co ... 949 720-4761
840 Nwport Ctr Dr Ste 100 Newport Beach (92660) *(G-12122)*
Pina Vineyard Management LLC ... 707 944-2229
7960 Silverado Trl NAPA (94558) *(G-716)*
Pinamar LLC ... 925 243-8979
6909 Las Positas Rd Ste D Livermore (94551) *(G-14569)*
Pinasco Mechinical, Stockton *Also called Pinasco Plumbing & Heating Inc (G-2321)*
Pinasco Plumbing & Heating Inc ... 209 463-7793
2145 E Taylor St Stockton (95205) *(G-2321)*
Pindler & Pindler Inc (PA) ... 805 531-9090
11910 Poindexter Ave Moorpark (93021) *(G-8321)*
Pine & Powell Partners LLC ... 415 989-3500
905 California St San Francisco (94108) *(G-13096)*
Pine Company, Culver City *Also called Pine Data Processing Inc (G-16168)*
Pine Crest, Maywood *Also called Maywood Halthcare Wellness Ctr (G-20780)*
Pine Data Processing Inc ... 310 815-5700
10559 Jefferson Blvd Culver City (90232) *(G-16168)*
Pine Grove Healthcare ... 626 285-3131
126 N San Gabriel Blvd San Gabriel (91775) *(G-20846)*
PINE KNOLL PUBLICATIONS, Redlands *Also called Study Tapes (G-18162)*
Pine Mountain Lake Association ... 209 962-4080
19228 Pine Mountain Dr Groveland (95321) *(G-25315)*
Pine Tree Lumber Company LP (PA) ... 760 745-0411
707 N Andreasen Dr Escondido (92029) *(G-6947)*
Pine View Center, Paradise *Also called Sunbridge Paradise Rhblttn Ctr (G-20944)*
Pinedridge Care Ctr, San Rafael *Also called Mariner Health Care Inc (G-20769)*
Pinegrove Hlthcare Wllness Ctr, San Gabriel *Also called Fernview Convalescent Hospital (G-20569)*
Pinelands Preservation Inc ... 609 703-0359
4501 Auburn Blvd Ste 201 Sacramento (95841) *(G-935)*
Piner's Medical Supply, NAPA *Also called Piners Nursing Home Inc (G-20847)*
Piner's NAPA Ambulance Service, NAPA *Also called NAPA Ambulance Service Inc (G-3821)*
Piners Nursing Home Inc ... 707 224-7925
1800 Pueblo Ave NAPA (94558) *(G-20847)*
Pinery LLC ... 858 675-3575
13701 Highland Valley Rd Escondido (92025) *(G-1012)*
Pines At Plcrvlle Hlthcare Ctr, Placerville *Also called Gladiolus Holdings LLC (G-20599)*
Pink Diamonds, Vernon *Also called Stone Blue Inc (G-13643)*
Pinnacle 1617 LLC ... 619 239-9600
1617 1st Ave San Diego (92101) *(G-13097)*
Pinnacle Builders Inc ... 916 372-5000
1911 Douglas Blvd Ste 85 Roseville (95661) *(G-1236)*
Pinnacle Communication Svcs, Glendale *Also called Pinnacle Networking Svcs Inc (G-2684)*
Pinnacle Contracting Corp ... 818 888-6548
21800 Burbank Blvd # 210 Woodland Hills (91367) *(G-1637)*
Pinnacle Document Systems (PA) ... 925 417-8400
470 Boulder Ct Ste 100 Pleasanton (94566) *(G-7063)*
Pinnacle Electrical Svcs Inc ... 818 241-6009
730 Fairmont Ave Ste 100 Glendale (91203) *(G-28018)*
Pinnacle Escrow Company, Northridge *Also called Pinnacle Estate Properties (G-11752)*
Pinnacle Estate Properties (PA) ... 818 993-4707
9137 Reseda Blvd Northridge (91324) *(G-11752)*
Pinnacle Funding Group Inc ... 925 552-5302
2092 Omega Rd Ste H San Ramon (94583) *(G-9944)*
Pinnacle Hotels Usa Inc ... 858 974-8201
8369 Vickers St Ste 101 San Diego (92111) *(G-13098)*
Pinnacle Networking Services, Glendale *Also called Pinnacle Electrical Svcs Inc (G-28018)*
Pinnacle Networking Svcs Inc ... 818 241-6009
730 Fairmont Ave Glendale (91203) *(G-2684)*
Pinnacle Rvrside Hspitality LP ... 951 784-8000
3400 Market St Riverside (92501) *(G-13099)*
Pinnacle Telecom Inc ... 916 426-1032
7066 Las Positas Rd Livermore (94551) *(G-16030)*
Pinnacle Telecom Inc (PA) ... 916 426-1000
4242 Forcum Ave Ste 200 McClellan (95652) *(G-16031)*
Pinner Construction Co Inc (PA) ... 714 490-4000
1255 S Lewis St Anaheim (92805) *(G-1638)*
Pinole Assisted Living Cmnty ... 510 758-1122
2850 Estates Ave Pinole (94564) *(G-21348)*
Pinole Medical Offices, Pinole *Also called Kaiser Foundation Hospitals (G-19637)*
Pinole Senior Center ... 510 724-9800
2500 Charles St Pinole (94564) *(G-24136)*
Pinole Senior Village, Pinole *Also called Pinole Assisted Living Cmnty (G-21348)*
Pinsetters Inc ... 916 488-7545
2600 Watt Ave Sacramento (95821) *(G-18528)*
Pinterest Inc ... 415 400-4645
808 Brannan St San Francisco (94103) *(G-14006)*
Pinterest Inc (PA) ... 650 561-5407
808 Brannan St San Francisco (94103) *(G-16253)*
Pioneer Electronics (usa) Inc (HQ) ... 310 952-2000
1925 E Dominguez St Long Beach (90810) *(G-7507)*
Pioneer Electronics Service (HQ) ... 213 746-6337
1925 E Dominguez St Long Beach (90810) *(G-7508)*
Pioneer Health Care Services ... 925 631-9100
1640 School St Ste 100 Moraga (94556) *(G-27166)*
PIONEER HOUSE, Sacramento *Also called Cathedral Pioneer Church Homes (G-20441)*
Pioneer Medical Group Inc ... 562 862-2775
11411 Brookshire Ave # 108 Downey (90241) *(G-19872)*
Pioneer Medical Group Inc ... 562 597-4181
2220 Clark Ave Long Beach (90815) *(G-19873)*
Pioneer Medical Group Inc ... 562 229-0902
16510 Bloomfield Ave Cerritos (90703) *(G-23020)*
Pioneer Square Hotel Company ... 415 346-2323
1940 Fillmore St San Francisco (94115) *(G-13100)*
Pioneer Theatres Inc ... 310 532-8183
2500 Redondo Beach Blvd Torrance (90504) *(G-17414)*
Pioneer Towers Rhf Partners LP ... 916 443-6548
515 P St Ofc Sacramento (95814) *(G-11187)*
Pioneers Mem Healthcare Dst (PA) ... 760 351-3333
207 W Legion Rd Brawley (92227) *(G-21800)*
Pioneers Memorial Hospital, Brawley *Also called Pioneers Mem Healthcare Dst (G-21800)*
Pipe Dream Products, Chatsworth *Also called Pd Liquidation Inc (G-9290)*
Pipe Restoration Inc ... 714 564-7600
3122 W Alpine St Santa Ana (92704) *(G-2322)*
Pipeline Plumbing, Norco *Also called F J Hoover Plumbing Inc (G-2222)*
Pircher Nichols & Meeks (PA) ... 310 201-0132
1925 Century Park E # 1700 Los Angeles (90067) *(G-23512)*
Pismo Beach Athletic Club ... 805 773-3011
1751 Price St Pismo Beach (93449) *(G-18670)*
Pismo Coast Village Inc ... 805 773-5649
165 S Dolliver St Pismo Beach (93449) *(G-13101)*
Piston Agency, San Diego *Also called Mea Digital Worx LLC (G-13883)*
Pit River Casino, Burney *Also called Pit River Tribal Council (G-19260)*
Pit River Health Service Inc (PA) ... 530 335-5090
36977 Park Ave Burney (96013) *(G-23021)*
Pit River Health Services, Burney *Also called Pit River Tribal Council (G-19874)*
Pit River Tribal Council ... 530 335-3651
36977 Park Ave Burney (96013) *(G-19874)*
Pit River Tribal Council ... 530 335-2334
20265 Tamarack Ave Burney (96013) *(G-19260)*
Pitco Foods, San Jose *Also called Pacific Groservice Inc (G-9235)*
Pitco Foods ... 916 372-7772
1670 Overland Ct West Sacramento (95691) *(G-8510)*
Pitney Bowes Presort Svcs Inc ... 310 763-4615
18550 S Broadwick St Compton (90220) *(G-17415)*
Pitney Bowes Presort Svcs Inc ... 415 468-1660
125 Valley Dr Brisbane (94005) *(G-17416)*
Pitts & Bachmann Realtors Inc ... 805 963-1391
1436 State St Santa Barbara (93101) *(G-11753)*
Pittsburg Care Center Ltd ... 925 432-3831
535 School St Pittsburg (94565) *(G-20848)*
Pittsburg Pre School, Pittsburg *Also called Pittsburg Pre-School & C (G-24501)*
Pittsburg Pre-School & C ... 925 439-2061
1760 Chester Dr Pittsburg (94565) *(G-24501)*
Pittsburg Skilled Nursing ... 925 808-6540
535 School St Pittsburg (94565) *(G-20849)*
Piveg Inc ... 858 436-3070
10455 Sorrento Valley Rd # 101 San Diego (92121) *(G-8511)*
Pivot Interiors Inc ... 949 988-5400
3200 Park Center Dr # 100 Costa Mesa (92626) *(G-2685)*
Pivot Systems Inc ... 408 435-1000
4320 Stevens Creek Blvd San Jose (95129) *(G-15381)*
Pivot Technology Solutions Ltd ... 647 788-2034
11988 El Camino Real San Diego (92130) *(G-16457)*
Pivotal Software Inc (HQ) ... 650 846-1600
3495 Deer Creek Rd Palo Alto (94304) *(G-15382)*
Pivotcloud Inc ... 408 475-6090
1230 Midas Way Ste 210 Sunnyvale (94085) *(G-15383)*
Pixar ... 510 922-3000
1200 Park Ave Emeryville (94608) *(G-18129)*
Pixar Animation Studios, Emeryville *Also called Pixar (G-18129)*
Pixelmags Inc ... 310 598-7303
1800 Century Park E # 600 Los Angeles (90067) *(G-15384)*
Pixim Inc ... 650 934-0550
1730 N 1st St San Jose (95112) *(G-16032)*
Pixior LLC (PA) ... 323 721-2221
5901 S Eastern Ave Commerce (90040) *(G-17417)*
PJs Lumber Inc ... 510 743-5300
45055 Fremont Blvd Fremont (94538) *(G-6948)*
Pk Autobody Inc ... 559 298-9691
361 N Minnewawa Ave Clovis (93612) *(G-17765)*
Pk Management LLC ... 818 808-0600
15301 Ventura Blvd # 570 Sherman Oaks (91403) *(G-27167)*
Pk Nevada LLC ... 310 255-0025
1317 5th St Fl 2 Santa Monica (90401) *(G-11754)*
Pkf Certif Pub Accts A Prof (PA) ... 818 630-7630
550 N Brand Blvd Ste 950 Glendale (91203) *(G-26423)*
Pkl Services Inc ... 858 679-1755
14265 Danielson St C1 Poway (92064) *(G-18000)*
Place Asian Amrcn Rcovery Svcs, San Jose *Also called Asian Amercn Recovery Svcs Inc (G-22114)*
Placentia Linda Hospital, Placentia *Also called Tenet Healthsystem Medical (G-22182)*
Placer County ADM Svcs ... 530 886-5401
2962 Richardson Dr Auburn (95603) *(G-28155)*

Placer County Water Agency (PA)...530 823-4850
144 Ferguson Rd Auburn (95603) *(G-6196)*
Placer County- Adult Sys Care...530 886-2974
11533 C Ave Auburn (95603) *(G-22799)*
Placer Insurance, Roseville *Also called Premiere Agency of California (G-10834)*
Placervlle Pnes Cnvlscent Hosp...530 622-3400
1040 Marshall Way Placerville (95667) *(G-21349)*
Plan Member Financial Corp...805 684-1199
6187 Carpinteria Ave Carpinteria (93013) *(G-10172)*
Plan-It Life Inc...951 742-7561
5729 Vista Del Caballero Riverside (92509) *(G-24137)*
Planet, San Diego *Also called Kscf 1037 FM (G-5800)*
Planet Fitness, San Rafael *Also called Pf West LLC (G-18669)*
Planet Labs Inc...415 829-3313
346 9th St San Francisco (94103) *(G-16169)*
Planet Technologies Inc...631 269-6140
1215 K St Fl 17 Sacramento (95814) *(G-16033)*
Planetout Inc (HQ)...415 834-6500
795 Folsom St Fl 1 San Francisco (94107) *(G-5685)*
Planetpro Inc (PA)...925 277-0727
2410 Camino Ramon Ste 275 San Ramon (94583) *(G-14728)*
Plangrid Inc...415 349-7440
2111 Mission St Ste 400 San Francisco (94110) *(G-15817)*
Planmember Services, Carpinteria *Also called Plan Member Financial Corp (G-10172)*
Planned Parenthood...909 890-5511
1873 Commercenter W San Bernardino (92408) *(G-22800)*
Planned Parenthood Federation...949 548-8830
601 W 19th St Ste B Costa Mesa (92627) *(G-22801)*
Planned Parenthood Federation...619 262-3941
220 Euclid Ave Ste 40 San Diego (92114) *(G-22802)*
Planned Parenthood Federation...916 446-5247
555 Capitol Mall Ste 510 Sacramento (95814) *(G-22803)*
Planned Parenthood Los Angeles (PA)...213 284-3200
400 W 30th St Los Angeles (90007) *(G-22804)*
Planned Parenthood Shasta-Paci, Concord *Also called Planned Prnthod Shst-Dblo Inc (G-22805)*
Planned Prnthod Shst-Dblo Inc (PA)...925 676-0300
2185 Pacheco St Concord (94520) *(G-22805)*
Planned Prnthod Shst-Dblo Inc...707 317-2111
600 Nut Tree Rd Ste 340 Vacaville (95687) *(G-19875)*
Planned Prnthood Mar Monte Inc...408 287-7529
1691 The Alameda San Jose (95126) *(G-22806)*
Planned Prnthood Mar Monte Inc (PA)...408 287-7532
1691 The Alameda San Jose (95126) *(G-22807)*
Planned Prnthood Mar Monte Inc...949 768-3643
26302 La Paz Rd 200 Mission Viejo (92691) *(G-22808)*
Planning and Public Works Agcy, Willows *Also called County of Glenn (G-1755)*
Plant Maintenance Inc...925 228-3285
1330 Arnold Dr Ste 147 Martinez (94553) *(G-14925)*
Plant Sciences Inc...530 398-4042
234 Juniper Knoll Rd Macdoel (96058) *(G-9209)*
Plant Source Inc...760 743-7743
2029 Sycamore Dr San Marcos (92069) *(G-310)*
Plantasia Inc...310 375-0387
2550 Via Tejon Ste 3f Palos Verdes Estates (90274) *(G-936)*
Plantasia Landscaping, Palos Verdes Estates *Also called Plantasia Inc (G-936)*
Plantation Golf Club Inc...760 775-3688
50994 Monroe St Indio (92201) *(G-19030)*
Planters Hay Inc...760 344-0620
1295 E St 78 Brawley (92227) *(G-9147)*
Plas-Tal Manufacturing Co, Santa Fe Springs *Also called Brunton Enterprises Inc (G-3369)*
Plasma Collection Centers Inc...323 441-7720
2410 Lillyvale Ave Los Angeles (90032) *(G-23022)*
Plastiflex Company Inc (HQ)...619 662-8792
601 E Palomar St Ste 424 Chula Vista (91911) *(G-17418)*
Platinum Clg Indianapolis LLC...310 584-8000
1522 2nd St Santa Monica (90401) *(G-14389)*
Platinum Construction Inc...714 527-0700
865 S East St Anaheim (92805) *(G-1639)*
Platinum Equity, Beverly Hills *Also called Finn Holding Corporation (G-4722)*
Platinum Equity Partners Inc...714 444-3100
3131 S Standard Ave Santa Ana (92705) *(G-17766)*
Platinum Facilities Services...408 998-9004
1530 Oakland Rd Ste 120 San Jose (95112) *(G-14390)*
Platinum Group Companies Inc (PA)...818 721-3800
8407 Fllbrook Ave Ste 250 Canoga Park (91304) *(G-12084)*
Platinum Home Mortgage Corp...209 955-2200
3031 W March Ln Ste 239 Stockton (95219) *(G-10173)*
Platinum Landscape Inc...760 200-3673
50885 Washington St # 110 La Quinta (92253) *(G-788)*
Platinum Protection Group Inc...800 824-1097
8018 E Santa Ana Cyn Rd Anaheim (92808) *(G-16758)*
Platinum Roofing Inc...408 280-5028
1900 Dobbin Dr San Jose (95133) *(G-3204)*
Platinum Strands Salon...714 532-2633
3443 E Chapman Ave Orange (92869) *(G-13686)*
Platinum Visual Systems, Corona *Also called ABC School Equipment Inc (G-7338)*
Platt Security Services, Long Beach *Also called Platt Security Systems Inc (G-16759)*
Platt Security Systems Inc...562 986-4484
3275 E Grant St Ste D Long Beach (90755) *(G-16759)*
Playa Vista Medical Offices, Culver City *Also called Permanente Kaiser Intl (G-21793)*
Playboy Enterprises Inc (HQ)...310 424-1800
9346 Civic Center Dr # 200 Beverly Hills (90210) *(G-18130)*
Playboy Entrmt Group Inc (HQ)...323 276-4000
2300 W Empire Ave Burbank (91504) *(G-18131)*
Playboy Magazine, Beverly Hills *Also called Playboy Enterprises Inc (G-18130)*
Playhaven LLC...310 308-9668
1447 2nd St Ste 200 Santa Monica (90401) *(G-15385)*
Playmar Inc...408 324-1930
2502 Channing Ave San Jose (95131) *(G-6993)*
Playphone Inc (PA)...408 261-6200
345 S B St Fl 2 San Mateo (94401) *(G-15386)*
Playtika Santa Monica LLC...310 622-7380
2120 Colorado Ave Ste 400 Santa Monica (90404) *(G-18808)*
Playworks...510 893-4180
380 Washington St Oakland (94607) *(G-25316)*
Playworks Education Energized (PA)...510 893-4180
380 Washington St Oakland (94607) *(G-19261)*
Playwrights Foundation Inc...415 626-2176
1616 16th St Ste 350 San Francisco (94103) *(G-18424)*
Plaza De La Raza Child Develop...323 224-1788
225 N Avenue 25 Los Angeles (90031) *(G-24502)*
Plaza De La Raza Child Develop...562 695-1070
6411 Norwalk Blvd Whittier (90606) *(G-24503)*
Plaza De La Raza Child Develop (PA)...562 776-1301
8337 Telegraph Rd Ste 300 Pico Rivera (90660) *(G-24504)*
Plaza Hand Carwash Inc...951 697-4420
23100 Alssndro Blvd Ste B Moreno Valley (92553) *(G-17858)*
Plaza Home Mortgage Inc (PA)...858 346-1200
4820 Eastgate Mall # 100 San Diego (92121) *(G-9886)*
Plaza Home Mortgage Inc...408 573-7880
2001 Gateway Pl Ste 650w San Jose (95110) *(G-10069)*
Plaza Home Mortgage Inc...714 508-6406
420 Exchange Ste 200 Irvine (92602) *(G-10070)*
Plaza Manor Preservation LP...619 475-2125
2615 E Plaza Blvd National City (91950) *(G-11755)*
Plaza Suites...408 748-9800
3100 Lakeside Dr Santa Clara (95054) *(G-13102)*
Plb Management LLC...323 549-5400
6200 W 3rd St Los Angeles (90036) *(G-11188)*
PLD Enterprises Inc...213 626-4444
440 Stanford Ave Los Angeles (90013) *(G-8648)*
Plda Inc...408 273-4528
2570 N 1st St 218 San Jose (95131) *(G-11263)*
Pleasant Canyon Hotel Inc...925 847-0535
11920 Dublin Canyon Rd Pleasanton (94588) *(G-13103)*
Pleasant Care, Alameda *Also called Emmanuel Cnvlscent Hosp Almeda (G-21210)*
Pleasant Care of Vista...760 945-3033
247 E Bobier Dr Vista (92084) *(G-20850)*
Pleasant Hawaiian Holiday, Westlake Village *Also called Pleasant Holidays LLC (G-4998)*
Pleasant Hl Byshore Dspsal Inc...925 685-4711
441 N Buchanan Cir Pacheco (94553) *(G-6514)*
Pleasant Holidays LLC (HQ)...818 991-3390
2404 Townsgate Rd Westlake Village (91361) *(G-4998)*
Pleasant Valley Flowers Inc...805 986-2776
3132 E Pleasant Valley Rd Oxnard (93033) *(G-340)*
Pleasant View Convalescent Hos...408 253-9034
22590 Voss Ave Cupertino (95014) *(G-21350)*
Pleasanton Asphalt Sand & Grav, Pleasanton *Also called Legacy Vulcan Corp (G-1108)*
Pleasanton Hilton Hotel, Pleasanton *Also called American Property Management (G-12383)*
Pleasanton Marriott, Pleasanton *Also called Pyramid Advisors LLC (G-13114)*
Pleasanton Unified School Dst...925 462-5500
4665 Bernal Ave Pleasanton (94566) *(G-14159)*
Pleasantview Industries Inc...661 296-6700
27921 Urbandale Ave Saugus (91350) *(G-22809)*
Plex Systems Inc...248 391-8001
4305 Hacienda Dr Ste 500 Pleasanton (94588) *(G-16170)*
Plexicor Inc (PA)...714 918-8700
3598 Cadillac Ave Costa Mesa (92626) *(G-16911)*
Plh Aviation Services Corp...310 417-0124
7251 World Way W Los Angeles (90045) *(G-4930)*
Plivo Inc...415 758-3659
340 Pine St Ste 503 San Francisco (94104) *(G-5686)*
Plivo US, San Francisco *Also called Plivo Inc (G-5686)*
Plott Family Care Center, Riverside *Also called Mount Rbdoux Convalescent Hosp (G-20799)*
Plott Family Care Centers, Riverside *Also called Orangetree Convalescent Hosp (G-21772)*
Plott Family Home Care, San Bernardino *Also called Plott Management Co (G-20851)*
Plott Management Co...909 883-0288
264 E 18th St San Bernardino (92404) *(G-20851)*
Plowboy Landscapes Inc...805 643-4966
2190 N Ventura Ave Ventura (93001) *(G-937)*
Plug Connection Inc...760 631-0992
2627 Ramona Dr Vista (92084) *(G-311)*
Plum Healthcare Group LLC...909 793-2609
1620 W Fern Ave Redlands (92373) *(G-17419)*
Plum Healthcare Group LLC...408 998-8447
1990 Fruitdale Ave San Jose (95128) *(G-20852)*
Plum Healthcare Group LLC (PA)...760 471-0388
100 E San Marcos Blvd San Marcos (92069) *(G-20853)*
Plum Healthcare Group LLC...619 873-2500
1391 E Madison Ave El Cajon (92021) *(G-20854)*
Plumas District Hospital (PA)...530 283-2121
1065 Bucks Lake Rd Quincy (95971) *(G-21801)*
Plumas District Hospital...530 283-0650
1045 Bucks Lake Rd Quincy (95971) *(G-19876)*
Plumas Rural Services...530 283-2725
711 E Main St Quincy (95971) *(G-24138)*
Plumb Tech Inc...310 322-4925
1242 E Maple Ave El Segundo (90245) *(G-2323)*
Plumbing, San Jose *Also called Aqualine Piping Inc (G-2148)*
Plumbing Limited Inc...559 453-0690
5270 E Pine Ave Fresno (93727) *(G-2324)*
Plumbing Piping & Cnstr Inc...714 821-0490
5950 Lakeshore Dr Cypress (90630) *(G-2325)*
Plumgrid Inc...408 800-7586
5155 Old Ironsides Dr # 100 Santa Clara (95054) *(G-15818)*

ALPHABETIC

Plummer Vlg Preservation LP 818 891-0646
15450 Plummer St North Hills (91343) *(G-11189)*
Plumpjack The, Olympic Valley Also called Cncml A California Ltd Partnr *(G-12530)*
Plus Group Inc 925 831-8551
2551 Sn Rmn Vlly Blvd 2 Ste 201 San Ramon (94583) *(G-14729)*
Ply Gem Pacific Windows Corp 951 272-1300
235 Radio Rd Corona (92879) *(G-6949)*
Plymouth Square, Stockton Also called Stockton Congregational Home *(G-24823)*
Plymouth Square, Stockton Also called Retirement Housing Foundation *(G-11812)*
Plymouth Village, Redlands Also called American Baptist Homes of West *(G-21136)*
Pm2net, Irvine Also called Newton Softed Inc *(G-27998)*
Pmbc, Costa Mesa Also called Pacific Mercantile Bank *(G-9514)*
Pmd Industries Inc 949 222-0999
703 Randolph Ave Costa Mesa (92626) *(G-2686)*
Pmk-Bnc Inc (PA) 310 854-0455
8687 Melrose Ave Fl 8th Los Angeles (90069) *(G-27761)*
Pmk-Bnc Inc 310 854-4800
8687 Melrose Ave Fl 8th Los Angeles (90069) *(G-27762)*
PNC, San Francisco Also called Esurance Inc *(G-10702)*
Pnc Inc 619 713-2278
2533 Folex Way Spring Valley (91978) *(G-8678)*
PNC Realty Investors Inc 818 880-3300
26901 Agoura Rd Ste 200 Calabasas (91301) *(G-27590)*
PNC Realty Investors Inc 626 432-4500
2 N Lake Ave Ste 440 Pasadena (91101) *(G-9419)*
PNC Realty Investors Inc 626 351-2211
465 N Halstead St Ste 160 Pasadena (91107) *(G-9420)*
Point Blue Cnservation Science, Petaluma Also called Point Reyes Bird Observator *(G-25567)*
Point Loma Convalescent Hosp 619 224-4141
3202 Duke St San Diego (92110) *(G-20855)*
Point Loma Post Acute Care Ctr, San Diego Also called Point Loma Rhblitation Ctr LLC *(G-20856)*
Point Loma Rhblitation Ctr LLC 619 224-4141
3202 Duke St San Diego (92110) *(G-20856)*
Point of View Inc 909 860-0705
947 N Del Sol Ln Diamond Bar (91765) *(G-15387)*
Point Reyes Bird Observator 415 868-0371
3820 Cypress Dr Ste 11 Petaluma (94954) *(G-25567)*
Point Reyes Bird Observatory 707 781-2555
3820 Cypress Dr Ste 11 Petaluma (94954) *(G-26795)*
Point-Walker, Citrus Heights Also called Lucky Derby Casino *(G-19242)*
Point360 .... 310 481-7000
12421 W Olympic Blvd Los Angeles (90064) *(G-18243)*
Point360 .... 818 556-5700
1133 N Hollywood Way Burbank (91505) *(G-18244)*
Point360 (PA) 818 565-1400
2701 Media Center Dr Los Angeles (90065) *(G-18245)*
Pointdirect Transport Inc 909 371-0837
10858 Almond Ave Fontana (92337) *(G-5152)*
Pointspeed Inc 650 638-3720
135 Wyndham Dr Portola Valley (94028) *(G-16458)*
Poison Spyder Customs Inc 951 849-5911
1177 W Lincoln St Ste 100 Banning (92220) *(G-17889)*
Polar Air Cargo LP 310 568-4551
100 Oceangate Fl 15 Long Beach (90802) *(G-4818)*
Polar Tankers Inc (HQ) 562 388-1400
300 Oceangate Long Beach (90802) *(G-4720)*
Polarion Software Inc 877 572-4005
1001 Marina Village Pkwy # 403 Alameda (94501) *(G-15819)*
Polaris Building Maintenance 650 964-9400
2580 Wyandotte St Ste E Mountain View (94043) *(G-14391)*
Polaris Networks Incorporated 408 625-7273
14856 Holden Way San Jose (95124) *(G-15388)*
Polaris Research & Development 415 777-3229
390 4th St Fl 1 San Francisco (94107) *(G-28019)*
Polaris Wireless Inc 408 492-8900
301 N Whisman Rd Mountain View (94043) *(G-15389)*
Polestar Labs Inc 760 480-2600
1223 Pacific Oaks Pl # 102 Escondido (92029) *(G-7301)*
Polexis Inc 858 812-7300
4820 Eastgate Mall San Diego (92121) *(G-15390)*
Police Department, Oakland Also called San Francisco Bay Area Rapid *(G-3707)*
Police Department, Berkeley Also called City of Berkeley *(G-26311)*
Policeone Academy, San Francisco Also called Praetorian Group *(G-16460)*
Poliseek Ais Insur Sltions Inc 866 480-7335
17785 Center Court Dr N # 250 Cerritos (90703) *(G-10828)*
Pollard Crnert Crwford Stevens 626 793-4440
35 N Lake Ave Ste 500 Pasadena (91101) *(G-23513)*
Polsinelli PC 310 556-1801
2049 Century Park E Los Angeles (90067) *(G-23514)*
Poltex Company Inc 619 669-1846
14748 Wild Colt Pl Jamul (91935) *(G-15391)*
Polycom Inc (PA) 408 586-6000
6001 America Center Dr San Jose (95002) *(G-27168)*
Polycomp Administrative Svcs 916 773-3480
3000 Lava Ridge Ct # 130 Roseville (95661) *(G-10829)*
Polymer Technology Group, The, Berkeley Also called DSM Biomedical Inc *(G-26505)*
Polypeptide Laboratories Inc (HQ) 310 782-3569
365 Maple Ave Torrance (90503) *(G-22257)*
Polyvore Inc 650 968-1195
701 First Ave Sunnyvale (94089) *(G-9293)*
Pomerado Hospital, Poway Also called Palomar Health *(G-21781)*
Pomerado Hospital, Poway Also called Palomar Health *(G-22312)*
Pomerado Operations LLC 858 487-6242
12696 Monte Vista Rd Poway (92064) *(G-20857)*
Pomeroy Rcrtion Rhbltation Ctr (PA) 415 665-4100
207 Skyline Blvd San Francisco (94132) *(G-24139)*

Pomona City Refuse Collection, Pomona Also called City of Pomona *(G-6460)*
Pomona College 909 607-8650
150 E 8th St Claremont (91711) *(G-18487)*
Pomona College 909 621-8000
333 N College Way Claremont (91711) *(G-14086)*
Pomona Housing Partners LP 909 622-1010
1731 W Holt Ave Pomona (91768) *(G-11756)*
Pomona Intergenerational, Pomona Also called Pomona Housing Partners LP *(G-11756)*
Pomona Valley Hospital Med Ctr (PA) 909 865-9500
1798 N Garey Ave Pomona (91767) *(G-21802)*
Pomona Valley Hospital Med Ctr 909 865-9104
1601 Monte Vista Ave Claremont (91711) *(G-21803)*
Pomona Valley Hospital Med Ctr 909 865-9700
1798 N Garey Ave Pomona (91767) *(G-22161)*
Pomona Valley Hospital Med Ctr 909 621-7956
1775 Monte Vista Ave Claremont (91711) *(G-20342)*
Pomona Valley Hospital Med Ctr 909 865-9977
1601 Monte Vista Ave # 270 Claremont (91711) *(G-21804)*
Pomona Vista Alzheimers Center, Pomona Also called Trinity Health Systems *(G-20995)*
Pomona Vista Care Center, Pomona Also called MJB Partners LLC *(G-20794)*
Pomwonderful LLC (HQ) 310 966-5800
4805 Centennial Ste 100 Bakersfield (93301) *(G-8908)*
Ponderosa Builders Inc 714 434-9494
3300 W Macarthur Blvd Santa Ana (92704) *(G-14392)*
Ponderosa Electric Inc 949 253-3100
17155 Von Karman Ave # 101 Irvine (92614) *(G-2687)*
Ponderosa Homes Inc 925 460-8900
6130 Stoneridge Mall Rd # 185 Pleasanton (94588) *(G-12002)*
Ponderosa Mobile Estates, San Francisco Also called Marcus Mllchap RE Inv Svcs Inc *(G-11657)*
Ponte Vineyard Inn 951 587-6688
35001 Rancho Cal Rd Temecula (92591) *(G-13104)*
Ponto Nursery Inc 760 724-6003
2545 Ramona Dr Vista (92084) *(G-9210)*
Pool Pals Division, Temecula Also called Oreq Corporation *(G-27152)*
Poolmaster Inc 916 567-9800
770 Del Paso Rd Sacramento (95834) *(G-8025)*
Poor Sisters of Nazareth of SA 619 563-0480
6333 Rancho Mission Rd San Diego (92108) *(G-24770)*
Pop Media Networks LLC (HQ) 323 856-4000
5510 Lincoln Blvd Ste 400 Playa Vista (90094) *(G-18488)*
Pop-Tent Inc 949 313-7160
34221 Golden Lantern St # 202 Dana Point (92629) *(G-13897)*
Poppy Hills Inc 831 625-1513
3200 Lopez Rd Pebble Beach (93953) *(G-18768)*
Poppy Ridge Golf Course, Livermore Also called Poppy Ridge Inc *(G-18769)*
Poppy Ridge Inc 925 456-8229
4280 Greenville Rd Livermore (94550) *(G-18769)*
Poppy State Express, Fresno Also called Northern Rfrigerated Trnsp Inc *(G-4236)*
Poppy State Express Inc (PA) 209 664-3950
2700 W Main St Turlock (95380) *(G-4245)*
POPS, Manhattan Beach Also called Puttin On Productions Corp *(G-18136)*
Por La Mar Nursery, Santa Barbara Also called W J Griffin Inc *(G-324)*
Porchlight Inc 562 989-5100
3800 Kilroy Airport Way Long Beach (90806) *(G-21351)*
Porrey Pines Bank Inc 510 899-7500
1951 Webster St Oakland (94612) *(G-9421)*
Port Dept City of Oakland (PA) 510 627-1100
530 Water St Fl 3 Oakland (94607) *(G-4753)*
Port Dept City of Oakland 510 563-3300
1 Airport Dr Ste 45 Oakland (94621) *(G-4931)*
Port Logistics Group Inc 310 669-2551
19801 S Santa Fe Ave Compton (90221) *(G-5236)*
Port Logistics Group Inc 626 330-1300
15530 Salt Lake Ave City of Industry (91745) *(G-5153)*
Port of Long Bch Employees CLB 562 590-4102
4801 Airport Plaza Dr Long Beach (90815) *(G-25181)*
Port of Los Angeles, Wilmington Also called City of Los Angeles *(G-3955)*
Port of Oakland, Oakland Also called Port Dept City of Oakland *(G-4753)*
Port of Sacramento, West Sacramento Also called Sacramento-Yolo Port District *(G-4755)*
Port of San Diego, San Diego Also called San Diego Unified Port Dst *(G-4757)*
Port of Stockton, Stockton Also called Stockton Port District *(G-4762)*
Portal Insurance Agency Inc 925 937-8787
1277 Treat Blvd Ste 650 Walnut Creek (94597) *(G-10830)*
Portellus Inc 949 250-9600
2522 Chambers Rd Ste 100 Tustin (92780) *(G-15820)*
Porter Construction Co Inc 831 455-3020
18931 Portola Dr Ste A Salinas (93908) *(G-1237)*
Porter Crispin & LLC Bogusky 305 859-2070
2110 Colorado Ave Ste 200 Santa Monica (90404) *(G-13898)*
Porter Ranch Development Co 323 655-7330
8383 Wilshire Blvd # 1000 Beverly Hills (90211) *(G-1382)*
Porter Valley Catering, Northridge Also called Porter Valley Country Club *(G-19031)*
Porter Valley Country Club 818 360-1071
19216 Singing Hills Dr Northridge (91326) *(G-19031)*
Portermatt Electric Inc 714 596-8788
5431 Production Dr Huntington Beach (92649) *(G-2688)*
Porterville Convalescent Hosp, Porterville Also called Moyles Central Vly Hlth Care *(G-20802)*
Porterville Developmental Ctr, Porterville Also called Developmental Svcs Cal Dept *(G-20519)*
Porterville Sheltered Workshop 559 684-9168
1853 E Cross Ave Tulare (93274) *(G-7302)*
Portfolio Hotels & Resorts LLC 831 375-2411
700 Munras Ave Monterey (93940) *(G-13105)*
Porto Vista Hotel, San Diego Also called 1835 Columbia Street LP *(G-12360)*

Portofino Hotel Partners LP 310 379-8481
260 Portofino Way Redondo Beach (90277) *(G-13106)*
Portofino Inn & Suites Anaheim 714 782-7600
1831 S Harbor Blvd Anaheim (92802) *(G-13107)*
Portola Hotel & Spa, Monterey *Also called Custom House Hotel LP (G-12559)*
Ports America Inc 510 749-7400
1601 Harbor Bay Pkwy # 150 Alameda (94502) *(G-4754)*
Ports America Group 310 241-1742
389 Terminal Way San Pedro (90731) *(G-5154)*
Portsmouth Square Inc 310 889-2500
10940 Wilshire Blvd Los Angeles (90024) *(G-12003)*
Posada Royale Hotel & Suites 805 584-6300
1775 Madera Rd Simi Valley (93065) *(G-13108)*
Posh Bagel Inc (PA) 408 980-8451
445 Nelo St Santa Clara (95054) *(G-8909)*
Posh Bakery Inc 408 980-8451
445 Nelo St Santa Clara (95054) *(G-8910)*
Positea Inv & Pub Relations 408 736-1120
710 Lakeway Dr Sunnyvale (94085) *(G-27763)*
Positive Choice Wellness Ctr, San Diego *Also called Kaiser Foundation Hospitals (G-22753)*
Positive Solution Staffing LLC 909 606-7512
15949 Oak Hill Dr Chino Hills (91709) *(G-14730)*
Post Alarm Systems (PA) 626 446-7159
47 E Saint Joseph St Arcadia (91006) *(G-16912)*
Post Alarm Systems Patrol Svcs, Arcadia *Also called Post Alarm Systems (G-16912)*
Post Factory, Santa Ana *Also called P J Video Services Inc (G-18124)*
Post Group Inc (PA) 323 462-2300
1415 N Cahuenga Blvd Los Angeles (90028) *(G-18246)*
Post Modern Edit LLC 310 396-7375
4551 Glencoe Ave Ste 210 Marina Del Rey (90292) *(G-18132)*
Post Modern Edit LLC (PA) 949 608-8700
2941 Alton Pkwy Irvine (92606) *(G-18133)*
Post Street Renaissance 415 563-0303
545 Post St San Francisco (94102) *(G-13109)*
Post Surgical Recovery Center, Huntington Beach *Also called Friedman Professional Mgt Co (G-19531)*
Postaer Rubin and Associates (PA) 310 394-4000
2525 Colorado Ave Ste 100 Santa Monica (90404) *(G-13899)*
Postmates Inc (PA) 800 882-6106
425 Market St Fl 8 San Francisco (94105) *(G-5237)*
Potential Industries Inc (PA) 310 807-4466
922 E E St Wilmington (90744) *(G-6515)*
Potter Roemer LLC (PA) 626 855-4890
17451 Hurley St City of Industry (91744) *(G-6950)*
Pottery Barn Inc 310 545-1906
3200 N Sepulveda Blvd B1 Manhattan Beach (90266) *(G-6881)*
Pottery Barn Inc 415 924-1391
1822 Redwood Hwy Corte Madera (94925) *(G-6882)*
Poumtjack Hotels, NAPA *Also called Carneros Inn LLC (G-12493)*
Pounce Consulting Inc 714 774-3500
6080 Center Dr Ste 600 Los Angeles (90045) *(G-16459)*
Poundex Associates Corporation (PA) 909 444-5874
21490 Baker Pkwy City of Industry (91789) *(G-6830)*
Power 106 Radio 818 953-4200
2600 W Olive Ave Fl 8 Burbank (91505) *(G-5816)*
Power Acoustik Electronics, Montebello *Also called Epsilon Electronics Inc (G-7496)*
Power Engineers Incorporated 714 507-2700
731 E Ball Rd Ste 100 Anaheim (92805) *(G-26021)*
Power Engineers Incorporated 925 372-9284
218 Loreto Ct Martinez (94553) *(G-26022)*
Power Logistics, Stockton *Also called Exel N Amercn Logistics Inc (G-4494)*
Power Plant, Glendale *Also called City of Glendale (G-6113)*
Power Plus, Perris *Also called SR Bray LLC (G-14581)*
Power Plus, Anaheim *Also called SR Bray LLC (G-2742)*
Power Plus LLC 714 507-1881
1210 N Red Gum St Anaheim (92806) *(G-7465)*
Power Plus Solutions Corp 714 507-1881
1210 N Red Gum St Anaheim (92806) *(G-2689)*
Power Studios Inc 310 314-2800
300 Rose Ave Venice (90291) *(G-18134)*
Powerhouse Building Inc 415 446-0188
4320 Redwood Hwy Ste 200 San Rafael (94903) *(G-3314)*
Powerhouse Realty Inc 323 562-7777
3452 E Florence Ave Huntington Park (90255) *(G-11757)*
Powerlight, Richmond *Also called Sunpower Corporation Systems (G-2389)*
Powerplant Mint Spcialists Inc 714 427-6900
2900 Bristol St Ste H202 Costa Mesa (92626) *(G-2077)*
Powerreviews Oc LLC 415 315-9208
180 Montgomery St # 1800 San Francisco (94104) *(G-15392)*
Ppc Enterprises Inc 951 354-5402
5920 Rickenbacker Ave Riverside (92504) *(G-2326)*
Ppic, San Francisco *Also called Public Policy Institute Cal (G-25101)*
Ppm Real Estate Inc 510 758-5636
3575 San Pablo Dam Rd El Sobrante (94803) *(G-11758)*
Ppmc, Corona *Also called Primary Provider MGT Co Inc (G-27172)*
Pponext Inc 888 446-6098
1501 Hughes Way Ste 400 Long Beach (90810) *(G-23023)*
Pps Parking Inc 949 223-8707
1800 E Garry Ave Ste 107 Santa Ana (92705) *(G-13787)*
Practice Fusion Inc (PA) 415 346-7700
731 Market St Ste 400 San Francisco (94103) *(G-15393)*
Practice Wares Inc 916 526-2674
2377 Gold Meadow Way Gold River (95670) *(G-7303)*
Practicewares Dental Supply, Gold River *Also called Practice Wares Inc (G-7303)*
Praetorian Event Services, Petaluma *Also called Praetorian USA (G-13788)*
Praetorian Group 415 962-8310
200 Green St Ste 200 San Francisco (94111) *(G-16460)*
Praetorian USA 707 780-8020
925 Lakeville St 129 Petaluma (94952) *(G-13788)*
Pragiti Inc 408 891-7423
2560 N 1st St Ste 210 San Jose (95131) *(G-28020)*
Prajin 1 Stop Distributors Inc (PA) 323 395-5302
5701 Pacific Blvd 5711 Huntington Park (90255) *(G-8133)*
Prajin Discount Distributors, Huntington Park *Also called Prajin 1 Stop Distributors Inc (G-8133)*
Pramira Inc 800 678-1169
1422 Edinger Ave Ste 250 Tustin (92780) *(G-16461)*
Prana Living LLC 866 915-6457
3209 Lionshead Ave Carlsbad (92010) *(G-8357)*
Praxair Inc 562 983-2100
2300 E Pacific Coast Hwy Wilmington (90744) *(G-8997)*
Praxair Inc 562 427-0099
2677 Signal Pkwy Long Beach (90755) *(G-7876)*
Praxair Distribution Inc 310 371-1254
19200 Hawthorne Blvd Torrance (90503) *(G-6283)*
PRBO, Petaluma *Also called Point Reyes Bird Observatory (G-26795)*
PRC Builders Inc 949 529-7011
26616 Mission St San Juan Capistrano (92675) *(G-1331)*
Prdctions N Fremantle Amer Inc (HQ) 818 748-1100
2900 W Alameda Ave 8 Burbank (91505) *(G-18425)*
Pre Con Industries Inc 805 928-3397
4340 Viewridge Ave Ste B San Diego (92123) *(G-2955)*
Pre Con Industries Inc 805 345-3147
725 Oak St Santa Maria (93454) *(G-3071)*
Pre Con Industries Inc 760 499-6176
917 W Inyokern Rd Ste C Ridgecrest (93555) *(G-2956)*
Pre Con Industries Inc 805 345-3147
514 Work St Salinas (93901) *(G-27169)*
Pre-Employcom 800 300-1821
3655 Meadow View Dr Redding (96002) *(G-16760)*
Pre-Employcom Inc 530 378-7680
2301 Balls Ferry Rd Anderson (96007) *(G-16761)*
Precept Inc (HQ) 949 955-1430
130 Theory Ste 200 Irvine (92617) *(G-10831)*
Precept Group The, Irvine *Also called Precept Inc (G-10831)*
Precidio YMCA, San Francisco *Also called Young Mens Christian Assnsf (G-25442)*
Precise Air Systems Inc 818 240-1737
5467 W San Fernando Rd Los Angeles (90039) *(G-2327)*
Precise Auto Protection, Azusa *Also called Precise Enterprises LLC (G-27591)*
Precise Distribution Inc 951 367-1037
12215 Holly St Riverside (92509) *(G-4615)*
Precise Enterprises LLC 818 599-6450
751 W 9th St Azusa (91702) *(G-27591)*
Precise Fit Limited One LLC 310 824-1800
959 Suth Cast Dr Ste 200 Costa Mesa (92626) *(G-14731)*
Precision Auto Body, Reseda *Also called Auto Body Management Inc (G-17748)*
Precision Auto Detailing LLC 650 992-9775
700 Serramonte Blvd Colma (94014) *(G-17859)*
Precision Framing Inc 916 791-7464
1504 Eureka Rd Ste 160 Roseville (95661) *(G-3072)*
Precision Ideo Inc 650 688-3400
150 Forest Ave Palo Alto (94301) *(G-17420)*
Precision Inspection Co Inc (PA) 209 862-9511
1247 Main St Newman (95360) *(G-17421)*
Precision Relocation Inc 714 690-9344
16055 Heron Ave Ste B La Mirada (90638) *(G-17422)*
Precision Television Inc 925 825-5296
2820 Broadmoor Ave Concord (94520) *(G-17912)*
Precision Toxicology LLC 858 274-4813
3030 Bunker Hill St San Diego (92109) *(G-22258)*
Precision TV, Concord *Also called Precision Television Inc (G-17912)*
Predentials, Oakland *Also called Mason-Mcduffie Real Estate Inc (G-11665)*
Preferred Brokers Inc (PA) 661 836-2345
9100 Ming Ave Ste 100 Bakersfield (93311) *(G-11759)*
Preferred Care West Inc 619 291-5270
3520 4th Ave San Diego (92103) *(G-20858)*
Preferred Construction Co Inc 714 630-3004
5199 E Pacific Coast Hwy Long Beach (90804) *(G-1640)*
Preferred Employers Insur Co 619 688-3900
9797 Aero Dr Ste 200 San Diego (92123) *(G-10832)*
Preferred Financial, San Ramon *Also called A D Bilich Inc (G-9809)*
Preferred Hlthcare Rgistry Inc 800 462-1896
9089 Clairemont Mesa Blvd # 200 San Diego (92123) *(G-14926)*
Preferred Plumbing and Drain, North Highlands *Also called AAA Drain Patrol (G-2104)*
Preferred Produce, Salinas *Also called Elioco Produce Inc (G-657)*
Preferred Valet Parking LLC 619 233-7275
2568 Violet St San Diego (92105) *(G-17738)*
Prellis Group Inc 818 363-1717
11011 Balboa Blvd Granada Hills (91344) *(G-11760)*
Prellis Mortgage Company, Granada Hills *Also called Prellis Group Inc (G-11760)*
Premier America Credit Union (PA) 818 772-4000
19867 Prairie St Lbby Chatsworth (91311) *(G-9678)*
Premier Auto W Covina LLC 626 858-7202
298 N Azusa Ave West Covina (91791) *(G-17811)*
Premier Building Maint Svcs, Los Angeles *Also called Pbms Inc (G-14383)*
Premier Business Centers, Irvine *Also called Premier Office Centers LLC (G-17424)*
Premier Care Center For Palm, Palm Springs *Also called Ensign Palm I LLC (G-20544)*
Premier Commercial Bancorp 714 978-2400
2400 E Katella Ave # 125 Anaheim (92806) *(G-9516)*
Premier Commercial Painting 714 546-3692
17150 Newhope St Ste 405 Fountain Valley (92708) *(G-2475)*
Premier Dealer Services Inc 858 810-1700
9449 Balboa Ave Ste 300 San Diego (92123) *(G-10833)*
Premier Disp & Exhibits Inc (PA) 562 431-2731
11261 Warland Dr Cypress (90630) *(G-17423)*

ALPHABETIC

Premier Drywall, Salinas *Also called Pre Con Industries Inc* ***(G-27169)***
Premier Drywall, Santa Maria *Also called Pre Con Industries Inc* ***(G-3071)***
Premier Drywall....805 928-3397
725 Oak St Santa Maria (93454) ***(G-2957)***
Premier Exec Solutions Inc....310 989-9925
269 S Beverly Dr Ste 981 Beverly Hills (90212) ***(G-28021)***
Premier Golf Properties LP....619 442-9891
3121 Willow Glen Dr El Cajon (92019) ***(G-18770)***
Premier Healthcare Svcs LLC....619 491-0300
2020 Camino Del Rio N # 600 San Diego (92108) ***(G-14732)***
Premier Healthcare Svcs LLC (PA)....626 204-7930
815 Colorado Blvd Ste 400 Los Angeles (90041) ***(G-14733)***
Premier Hlthcare Solutions Inc....858 569-8629
12225 El Camino Real San Diego (92130) ***(G-27170)***
Premier IMS Insurance Services, San Diego *Also called Premier Hlthcare Solutions Inc* ***(G-27170)***
Premier Insite Group Inc....562 741-5018
111 W Ocean Blvd Ste 400 Long Beach (90802) ***(G-14734)***
Premier Management Company....619 582-5168
4075 54th St San Diego (92105) ***(G-22538)***
Premier Meat Company, Vernon *Also called Wayne Provision Co Inc* ***(G-8689)***
Premier Medical Transport Inc....888 353-9556
530 N Puente St Brea (92821) ***(G-5155)***
Premier Medical Trnsp Inc....909 433-3939
575 Maple Ct Ste A Colton (92324) ***(G-3828)***
Premier Mushrooms LP (PA)....530 458-2700
2880 Niagara Ave Colusa (95932) ***(G-341)***
Premier Mushrooms LP....530 458-2700
2847 Niagara Ave Colusa (95932) ***(G-342)***
Premier Office Centers LLC (PA)....949 253-4147
2102 Bus Ctr Dr Ste 130 Irvine (92612) ***(G-17424)***
Premier Packaging/Assembly, Santa Fe Springs *Also called Haringa Inc* ***(G-17207)***
Premier Plumbing Company, Riverside *Also called Ppc Enterprises Inc* ***(G-2326)***
Premier Pools and Spas LP (PA)....916 852-0223
11250 Pyrites Way Gold River (95670) ***(G-3570)***
Premier Silica LLC....949 728-0171
31302 Ortega Hwy San Juan Capistrano (92675) ***(G-1110)***
Premier Source LLC....415 349-2010
999 Bayhill Dr Fl 3 San Bruno (94066) ***(G-26796)***
Premier Tile & Marble....310 516-1712
15000 S Main St Gardena (90248) ***(G-3022)***
Premiere Agency of California....916 784-1008
5 Sierra Gate Plz Fl 2nd Roseville (95678) ***(G-10834)***
Premiere Financial....760 518-5034
6498 Willow Pl Carlsbad (92011) ***(G-10174)***
Premiere Packing, Shafter *Also called Grimmway Enterprises Inc* ***(G-361)***
Premiere Properties, Carlsbad *Also called Premiere Financial* ***(G-10174)***
Premiere Rack Solutions Inc....909 605-6300
4502 Brickell Privado St Ontario (91761) ***(G-6831)***
Premiere Radio Network Inc (HQ)....818 377-5300
15260 Ventura Blvd # 400 Sherman Oaks (91403) ***(G-18426)***
Premiere Valet Service Inc....310 652-4647
6601 Santa Monica Blvd Los Angeles (90038) ***(G-17739)***
Premium Harvesting, Salinas *Also called Premium Packing Inc* ***(G-499)***
Premium Packing Inc....831 443-6855
449 Harrison Rd Salinas (93907) ***(G-499)***
Premium Rock Drywall Inc....818 676-3350
31348 Via Colinas Ste 103 Westlake Village (91362) ***(G-2958)***
Prentice Hall Legal Fincl Svcs, Sacramento *Also called Corporation Service Company* ***(G-14265)***
Presbyterian Inter Cmnty Hosp, Whittier *Also called Interhealth Services Inc* ***(G-22486)***
Presbyterian Intrcmmnty Hosptl (PA)....562 698-0811
12401 Washington Blvd Whittier (90602) ***(G-21805)***
Presbyterian Intrcmmnty Hosptl....562 904-5482
11500 Brookshire Ave Downey (90241) ***(G-21806)***
Preschool Service, San Bernardino *Also called County of San Bernardino* ***(G-24449)***
Prescott Communications Inc....818 898-2352
10640 Sepulveda Blvd # 1 Mission Hills (91345) ***(G-28022)***
Prescott Companies (PA)....760 634-4700
5950 La Place Ct Ste 200 Carlsbad (92008) ***(G-11761)***
Prescott Hotel, The, San Francisco *Also called Post Street Renaissance* ***(G-13109)***
Prescription Solutions, Carlsbad *Also called Optumrx Inc* ***(G-10363)***
Prescription Solutions, Irvine *Also called Optumrx Inc* ***(G-10364)***
Prescription Solutions....760 804-2370
2858 Loker Ave E Ste 100 Carlsbad (92010) ***(G-27592)***
Preserve Golf Club Inc....831 620-6871
1 Rancho San Carlos Rd Carmel (93923) ***(G-18771)***
Presidian Hotel, Visalia *Also called Viscamar LLC* ***(G-13381)***
Presidio Community YMCA, San Francisco *Also called Young Mens Christian Assnsf* ***(G-25440)***
Presidio Hotel Group LLC....916 631-7500
10713 White Rock Rd Rancho Cordova (95670) ***(G-13110)***
Presidio Surgerycenter....415 346-1218
1635 Divisadero St # 200 San Francisco (94115) ***(G-21807)***
Presidio Wealth Management LLC....415 449-2500
101 California St # 1200 San Francisco (94111) ***(G-10175)***
Presido YMCA, San Francisco *Also called Young Mens Christian Assnsf* ***(G-25441)***
Presort Center, The, Fresno *Also called Central Valley Presort Inc* ***(G-14067)***
Press Enterprise, The, Santa Ana *Also called Freedom Cmmnctons Holdings Inc* ***(G-12062)***
Prestige Asstd Lvng in Chico, Chico *Also called Caldwell Ventures LLC* ***(G-20432)***
Prestige Auto Collision Inc....949 470-6031
23726 Via Fabricante Mission Viejo (92691) ***(G-17767)***
Prestige Autotech Corporation....909 627-6411
4975 Edison Ave Chino (91710) ***(G-6755)***
Prestige Car Wash Lafayette LP....925 283-1190
3319 Mt Diablo Blvd Lafayette (94549) ***(G-17860)***
Prestige Concrete....858 679-2772
13507 Midland Rd Poway (92064) ***(G-3315)***
Prestige Gunite California Inc....909 276-9096
18300 Wood Edge Ln Riverside (92504) ***(G-3316)***
Prestige Protection, San Ramon *Also called Universal Protection Svc LP* ***(G-16840)***
Prestige Sales II LLC....714 632-8020
1038 E Bastanchury Rd Fullerton (92835) ***(G-8911)***
Prestige Security Service Inc....310 670-5999
5855 Green Valley Cir # 207 Culver City (90230) ***(G-16762)***
Prestige Too Auto Body Inc....310 787-8852
11899 Woodruff Ave Downey (90241) ***(G-17768)***
Preston Pipelines Inc (PA)....408 262-1418
133 Bothelo Ave Milpitas (95035) ***(G-1981)***
Preston Pipelines Inc A Cal....408 262-6989
133 Bothelo Ave Milpitas (95035) ***(G-1982)***
Preston Wynne Spa Inc....408 741-1750
14567 Big Basin Way A2 Saratoga (95070) ***(G-18671)***
Prevent Life Safety Svcs Inc....925 667-2088
1410 Stealth St Livermore (94551) ***(G-17425)***
Prevention Institute....510 444-4133
221 Oak St Ste A Oakland (94607) ***(G-27593)***
Prg (california) Inc....818 252-2600
1245 Aviation Pl San Fernando (91340) ***(G-18135)***
Prg Lighting....818 252-1268
1245 Aviation Pl San Fernando (91340) ***(G-14570)***
Prg Parking Century LLC....310 642-0947
5701 W Century Blvd Los Angeles (90045) ***(G-17740)***
Prh Pro Inc....714 510-7226
13089 Peyton Dr Ste C362 Chino Hills (91709) ***(G-7946)***
PRI Medical Technologies Inc (HQ)....818 394-2800
10939 Pendleton St Sun Valley (91352) ***(G-7304)***
Pribuss Engineering Inc....650 588-0447
523 Mayfair Ave South San Francisco (94080) ***(G-2328)***
Price Associates....818 995-9216
15760 Ventura Blvd # 1100 Encino (91436) ***(G-13900)***
Price Law Group A Prof Corp (PA)....818 995-4540
15760 Ventura Blvd # 800 Encino (91436) ***(G-23515)***
Price Postel and Parma LLP....805 962-0011
200 E Carrillo St Ste 400 Santa Barbara (93101) ***(G-23516)***
Price, Stuart, Encino *Also called Price Associates* ***(G-13900)***
Pricemetrix Usa Inc....714 357-6192
3 Bridgeport Rd Newport Coast (92657) ***(G-16171)***
Pricewaterhousecoopers LLP....949 437-5200
2020 Main St Ste 400 Irvine (92614) ***(G-26424)***
Pricewaterhousecoopers LLP....408 817-3700
488 Almaden Blvd Ste 1800 San Jose (95110) ***(G-26425)***
Pricewaterhousecoopers LLP....858 677-2400
5375 Mira Sorrento Pl San Diego (92121) ***(G-26426)***
Pricewaterhousecoopers LLP....916 930-8100
400 Capitol Mall Ste 600 Sacramento (95814) ***(G-26427)***
Pricewaterhousecoopers LLP....415 498-5000
3 Embarcadero Ctr Fl 20 San Francisco (94111) ***(G-26428)***
Pride Auto Body, Van Nuys *Also called Pride Collision Centers Inc* ***(G-17769)***
Pride Collision Centers Inc (PA)....818 909-0660
7950 Haskell Ave Van Nuys (91406) ***(G-17769)***
Pride Industries (PA)....916 788-2100
10030 Foothills Blvd Roseville (95747) ***(G-4700)***
Pride Industries....805 985-8481
Cbc Base Bldg 19 43rd St Port Hueneme (93041) ***(G-1332)***
Pride Industries....530 888-0331
13080 Earhart Ave Auburn (95602) ***(G-24380)***
Pride Industries....530 477-1832
12451 Loma Rica Dr Grass Valley (95945) ***(G-24381)***
Pride Industries....916 334-5415
3608 Madison Ave Ste 43 North Highlands (95660) ***(G-24382)***
Pride Industries....916 649-9499
1281 National Dr Sacramento (95834) ***(G-28156)***
Prima Royale, Pasadena *Also called Prima Royale Enterprises Ltd* ***(G-8442)***
Prima Royale Enterprises Ltd....626 960-8388
150 S Los Robles Ave # 100 Pasadena (91101) ***(G-8442)***
Primary Care Assod Med Group (PA)....760 471-7505
1635 Lake San Marcos Dr # 105 San Marcos (92078) ***(G-27171)***
Primary Color Systems Corp....310 841-0250
401 Coral Cir El Segundo (90245) ***(G-14132)***
Primary Critical Care Medical....818 847-9950
620 N Brand Blvd Ste 500 Glendale (91203) ***(G-19877)***
Primary Eyecare Network, Alameda *Also called Abb/Con-Cise Optical Group LLC* ***(G-7328)***
Primary Provider MGT Co Inc (PA)....951 280-7700
2115 Compton Ave Ste 301 Corona (92881) ***(G-27172)***
Prime Administration LLC....323 549-7155
357 S Curson Ave Los Angeles (90036) ***(G-12265)***
Prime Focus North America Inc (HQ)....323 461-7887
5750 Hannum Ave Ste 100 Culver City (90230) ***(G-18247)***
Prime Focus World, Culver City *Also called Prime Focus North America Inc* ***(G-18247)***
Prime Group, Los Angeles *Also called Prime Administration LLC* ***(G-12265)***
Prime Halthcare Foundation Inc....909 235-4400
3300 E Guasti Rd Fl 3 Ontario (91761) ***(G-19878)***
Prime Health Care Svcs Grdn Gr....714 537-5160
12601 Garden Grove Blvd Garden Grove (92843) ***(G-21808)***
Prime Healthcare Anaheim LLC....714 827-3000
3033 W Orange Ave Anaheim (92804) ***(G-21809)***
Prime Healthcare Centinela LLC....310 673-4660
555 E Hardy St Inglewood (90301) ***(G-21810)***
Prime Healthcare Services, Ontario *Also called Bio-Med Services Inc* ***(G-22893)***
Prime Healthcare Services....530 244-5400
1100 Butte St Redding (96001) ***(G-21811)***
Prime Healthcare Servs Sh....530 244-5458
1450 Liberty St Redding (96001) ***(G-21812)***

ALPHABETIC SECTION
Probation Dept, Auburn

Prime Healthcare Svcs II LLC..........818 981-7111
4929 Van Nuys Blvd Sherman Oaks (91403) *(G-21813)*
Prime Healthcare Svcs III LLC (HQ)..........909 625-5411
5000 San Bernardino St Montclair (91763) *(G-21814)*
Prime Healthcare-San Dimas LLC..........909 599-6811
1350 W Covina Blvd San Dimas (91773) *(G-21815)*
Prime Hlthcare Hntngton Bch..........714 843-5000
17772 Beach Blvd Huntington Beach (92647) *(G-21816)*
Prime International Security..........310 670-4565
1630 Centinela Ave # 209 Inglewood (90302) *(G-16763)*
Prime Marketing Holdings LLC..........888 991-6412
11620 Wilshire Blvd B Los Angeles (90025) *(G-17426)*
Prime Security, Inglewood *Also called Prime International Security (G-16763)*
Prime Stop, Moreno Valley *Also called Plaza Hand Carwash Inc (G-17858)*
Prime Tech Cabinets Inc..........714 558-4837
2652 White Rd Irvine (92614) *(G-3073)*
Prime Time Athletic Club Inc..........650 204-3662
1730 Rollins Rd Burlingame (94010) *(G-18672)*
PRIME TIME INTERNATIONAL, Coachella *Also called Sun and Sands Enterprises LLC (G-96)*
Prime-Line Products Company (PA)..........909 887-8118
26950 San Bernardino Ave Redlands (92374) *(G-7695)*
Primecare Quality HM Care Inc..........949 681-3515
2372 Morse Ave Irvine (92614) *(G-1238)*
Primeco Painting & Cnstr..........760 967-8278
1107 S Cleveland St Oceanside (92054) *(G-2476)*
Primed MGT Consulting Svcs Inc..........925 327-6710
2409 Camino Ramon San Ramon (94583) *(G-27173)*
Primerica Financial Svcs Inc..........951 695-4325
27470 Jefferson Ave 5a Temecula (92590) *(G-10835)*
Primerica Life Insurance Co..........650 323-2554
260 Sheridan Ave Ste B42 Palo Alto (94306) *(G-10836)*
Primerica Life Insurance Co..........661 947-9070
41307 12th St W Ste 200 Palmdale (93551) *(G-10837)*
Primerica Life Insurance Co..........951 652-6190
175 N Cawston Ave Hemet (92545) *(G-10838)*
Primetime International Inc..........760 399-4166
86705 Avenue 54 Ste A Coachella (92236) *(G-8763)*
Primetime Nutrition, Sacramento *Also called Nutricion Fundamental Inc (G-20334)*
Primex Clinical Labs Inc (PA)..........818 779-0496
16742 Stagg St Ste 120 Van Nuys (91406) *(G-22259)*
Primitive Logic Inc..........415 391-8080
704 Sansome St San Francisco (94111) *(G-16034)*
Primitive Shoes Inc..........818 639-3690
9223 Eton Ave Chatsworth (91311) *(G-8443)*
Primitive Skate, Chatsworth *Also called Primitive Shoes Inc (G-8443)*
Primm Valley Golf Club..........702 679-5509
1 Yates Wells Rd Nipton (92364) *(G-18772)*
Primoris Services Corporation..........949 598-9242
26000 Commercentre Dr Lake Forest (92630) *(G-1983)*
Primrose Alzheimers Living (PA)..........707 568-4355
726 College Ave Santa Rosa (95404) *(G-24771)*
Primrose Alzheimers Living..........707 578-8360
2080 Guerneville Rd Santa Rosa (95403) *(G-24772)*
Primrose Alzheimers Living..........916 392-3510
7707 Rush River Dr Sacramento (95831) *(G-24773)*
Primrose Sacramento, Sacramento *Also called Primrose Alzheimers Living (G-24773)*
Primus Group Inc (PA)..........805 922-0055
2810 Industrial Pkwy Santa Maria (93455) *(G-27594)*
Primus Labs, Santa Maria *Also called Primus Group Inc (G-27594)*
Princess Cruise Lines Ltd (HQ)..........661 753-0000
24305 Town Center Dr Santa Clarita (91355) *(G-4725)*
Princess Cruise Lines Ltd..........661 753-2291
P.O. Box 966 Santa Clarita (91380) *(G-4726)*
Princess Cruise Lines Ltd..........661 753-0000
24300 Town Center Dr # 100 Valencia (91355) *(G-4727)*
Princess Cruise Lines Ltd..........661 753-0000
24300 Town Center Dr # 100 Valencia (91355) *(G-4728)*
Princess Cruise Lines Ltd..........661 753-0000
24305 Town Center Dr Valencia (91355) *(G-4729)*
Princess Cruises, Santa Clarita *Also called Princess Cruise Lines Ltd (G-4725)*
Princess Cruises, Santa Clarita *Also called Princess Cruise Lines Ltd (G-4726)*
Princess Cruises, Valencia *Also called Princess Cruise Lines Ltd (G-4728)*
Princess Cruises and Tours Inc (HQ)..........206 336-6000
24305 Town Center Dr # 200 Valencia (91355) *(G-19262)*
Principal Financial Group Inc..........408 273-7500
2590 N 1st St Ste 350 San Jose (95131) *(G-10219)*
Principal Financial Group Inc..........818 243-7141
500 N Brand Blvd Ste 1800 Glendale (91203) *(G-10220)*
Principal Financial Group Inc..........559 261-2000
1350 E Spruce Ave Ste 100 Fresno (93720) *(G-10221)*
Principles Inc (PA)..........323 681-2575
1680 N Fair Oaks Ave Pasadena (91103) *(G-22810)*
Prindle Decker & Amaro LLP (PA)..........562 436-3946
310 Golden Shore Fl 4 Long Beach (90802) *(G-23517)*
Printing Inds Assn Suthern Cal..........323 728-9500
5800 S Eastrn Ave Ste 400 Commerce (90040) *(G-25099)*
Printing Technology Inc..........818 576-9220
21001 Nordhoff St Chatsworth (91311) *(G-7947)*
Printrak International Inc (HQ)..........714 238-2000
1250 N Tustin Ave Anaheim (92807) *(G-16303)*
Priority Building Services LLC..........714 255-2940
521 Mercury Ln Brea (92821) *(G-14393)*
Priority Cooling, Firebaugh *Also called Tri-State AG Inc (G-6641)*
Priority Dispatch Service Inc..........408 400-3860
309 Laurelwood Rd Ste 10 Santa Clara (95054) *(G-4421)*
Priority Landscape Services, Brea *Also called Priority Building Services LLC (G-14393)*
Priority One Med Trnspt Inc (PA)..........909 948-4400
9327 Fairway View Pl # 300 Rancho Cucamonga (91730) *(G-3829)*
Priority One Support, Irvine *Also called Alorica Inc (G-16981)*
Prism Electronics Corp (PA)..........408 778-7050
900 Lightpost Way 100 Morgan Hill (95037) *(G-7621)*
Prison Industry Authority-Pia..........559 386-6060
1 Kings Way Avenal (93204) *(G-23518)*
Pritchett Rapf and Associates..........310 456-6771
23732 Malibu Rd Malibu (90265) *(G-11762)*
Private Label Pc LLC..........626 965-8686
748 Epperson Dr Ste B City of Industry (91748) *(G-7175)*
Private Medical-Care Inc..........562 924-8311
12898 Towne Center Dr Cerritos (90703) *(G-10371)*
Private Nat Mrtg Accptance LLC (PA)..........818 224-7401
6101 Condor Dr Agoura Hills (91301) *(G-9887)*
Privilege International Inc..........323 585-0777
2323 Firestone Blvd South Gate (90280) *(G-6832)*
Prize Proz..........909 509-8600
1500 S Hellman Ave Ontario (91761) *(G-27595)*
Prn LLC (HQ)..........415 805-2525
600 Montgomery St Fl 18 San Francisco (94111) *(G-15394)*
Prn Ambulance LLC..........818 810-3600
8928 Sepulveda Blvd North Hills (91343) *(G-3830)*
Prn Radio Networks, Sherman Oaks *Also called Premiere Radio Network Inc (G-18426)*
Pro Act LLC..........831 655-4250
40 Ragsdale Dr Ste 200 Monterey (93940) *(G-8764)*
Pro America Premium Tools, Baldwin Park *Also called American Kal Enterprises Inc (G-7670)*
Pro Building Maintenance Inc..........951 279-3386
149 N Maple St Ste H Corona (92880) *(G-14394)*
Pro Care 2000 Home Health Care, Long Beach *Also called Pacific Care Inc (G-22528)*
Pro Document Solutions Inc..........559 719-1281
90 W Poplar Ave Porterville (93257) *(G-8175)*
Pro Group Inc..........951 271-3000
4160 Temescal Canyon Rd # 500 Corona (92883) *(G-11763)*
Pro Iron Workshop, Pomona *Also called F & B Inc (G-17953)*
Pro Pacific Fresh, Durham *Also called Chico Produce Inc (G-8705)*
Pro Ponds West Inc..........818 244-4000
8309 Tujunga Ave Unit 201 Sun Valley (91352) *(G-789)*
Pro Scape Inc..........760 480-1544
510 Venture St Escondido (92029) *(G-938)*
Pro Specialties Group Inc..........858 541-1100
4863 Shawline St Ste D San Diego (92111) *(G-9294)*
Pro TEC Manufacturing, Canoga Park *Also called T M P Inc (G-8361)*
Pro Unlimited Inc..........650 344-1099
1350 Bayshore Hwy Ste 350 Burlingame (94010) *(G-27174)*
Pro-Craft Construction Inc..........909 389-7990
31597 Outer Highway 10 B Redlands (92373) *(G-2329)*
Pro-Med Hlth Care Admnistrator..........909 932-1045
4150 Concours Ste 100 Ontario (91764) *(G-27175)*
Pro-Tech Design & Mfg Inc..........562 207-1680
14561 Marquardt Ave Santa Fe Springs (90670) *(G-17427)*
Pro-Tek Consulting (PA)..........805 807-5571
21300 Victory Blvd # 240 Woodland Hills (91367) *(G-16462)*
Pro-Wash Inc..........323 756-6000
9117 S Main St Los Angeles (90003) *(G-13505)*
Proactiv, Santa Monica *Also called Guthy-Renker LLC (G-8118)*
Proactive Bus Solutions Inc..........510 302-0120
428 13th St Fl 5 Oakland (94612) *(G-27176)*
Probation, Red Bluff *Also called County of Tehama (G-23929)*
Probation Department, Fresno *Also called County of Fresno (G-23805)*
Probation Department, Pasadena *Also called County of Los Angeles (G-23821)*
Probation Department, Lancaster *Also called County of Los Angeles (G-23824)*
Probation Department, Redwood City *Also called County of San Mateo (G-23910)*
Probation Department, San Mateo *Also called County of San Mateo (G-23911)*
Probation Department, San Mateo *Also called County of San Mateo (G-23912)*
Probation Department, Fresno *Also called County of Fresno (G-23806)*
Probation Department, Sacramento *Also called Sacramento County Off Educatn (G-24164)*
Probation Department, Los Angeles *Also called County of Los Angeles (G-23836)*
Probation Department, East Palo Alto *Also called County of San Mateo (G-23913)*
Probation Department, Downey *Also called County of Los Angeles (G-23856)*
Probation Department, Downey *Also called County of Los Angeles (G-23857)*
Probation Department, San Mateo *Also called County of San Mateo (G-23916)*
Probation Department, Redwood City *Also called County of San Mateo (G-23917)*
Probation Department Roseville, Auburn *Also called County of Placer (G-23878)*
Probation Dept, Sylmar *Also called County of Los Angeles (G-24609)*
Probation Dept, San Diego *Also called County of San Diego (G-23899)*
Probation Dept, Anaheim *Also called County of Orange (G-23871)*
Probation Dept, Westminster *Also called County of Orange (G-23872)*
Probation Dept, Orange *Also called County of Orange (G-23873)*
Probation Dept, Los Angeles *Also called County of Los Angeles (G-23839)*
Probation Dept, Santa Barbara *Also called Santa Barbara County of (G-24187)*
Probation Dept, Santa Maria *Also called Santa Barbara County of (G-24188)*
Probation Dept, Rancho Cucamonga *Also called County of San Bernardino (G-23893)*
Probation Dept, Arcadia *Also called County of Los Angeles (G-23845)*
Probation Dept, Van Nuys *Also called County of Los Angeles (G-23847)*
Probation Dept, Santa Monica *Also called County of Los Angeles (G-23849)*
Probation Dept, Los Angeles *Also called County of Los Angeles (G-23850)*
Probation Dept, Los Angeles *Also called County of Los Angeles (G-23853)*
Probation Dept, Compton *Also called County of Los Angeles (G-23854)*
Probation Dept, Pasadena *Also called County of Los Angeles (G-23855)*
Probation Dept, San Jose *Also called Santa Clara County of (G-24193)*
Probation Dept, Auburn *Also called County of Placer (G-23880)*

ALPHABETIC

Employee Codes: A=Over 500 employees, B=251-500
C=101-250, D=51-100, E=45-50
2017 Directory of California
Wholesalers and Services Companies

1509

Probation Dept, Santa Barbara *Also called Santa Barbara County of* ***(G-24190)***
Probation Dept-Juvenile, Bakersfield *Also called County of Kern* ***(G-23814)***
Probation Dept-Juvenile Div, Morgan Hill *Also called Santa Clara County of* ***(G-24804)***
Probation Office, Pomona *Also called County of Los Angeles* ***(G-23822)***
Probe Information Services Inc...916 676-1826
6375 Auburn Blvd Citrus Heights (95621) ***(G-16764)***
Prober & Raphael A Law Corp...818 227-0100
20750 Ventura Blvd # 100 Woodland Hills (91364) ***(G-23519)***
Prober & Raphael, ALC, Woodland Hills *Also called Prober & Raphael A Law Corp* ***(G-23519)***
Probuild Company LLC...619 440-7711
1262 E Main St El Cajon (92021) ***(G-6951)***
Probuild Company LLC...619 425-6660
3450 Highland Ave National City (91950) ***(G-6952)***
Probuild Company LLC...858 755-0246
663 Lomas Santa Fe Dr Solana Beach (92075) ***(G-6953)***
Procall Solutions Inc...800 733-9675
20 Ragsdale Dr Ste 100 Monterey (93940) ***(G-17428)***
Procel Temporary Services Inc...310 372-0560
222 W 6th St Ste 370 San Pedro (90731) ***(G-14927)***
Procera Networks Inc (HQ)...510 230-2777
47448 Fremont Blvd Fremont (94538) ***(G-15395)***
Processing Office, Corcoran *Also called J G Boswell Company* ***(G-551)***
Processweaver Inc...888 932-8373
5201 Great America Pkwy # 300 Santa Clara (95054) ***(G-15396)***
Procida Landscape Inc...916 387-5296
8465 Specialty Cir Sacramento (95828) ***(G-939)***
Procore Technologies Inc...866 477-6267
6309 Carpinteria Ave # 100 Carpinteria (93013) ***(G-15397)***
Procter & Gamble Distrg LLC...209 538-3987
1992 Rockefeller Dr Ceres (95307) ***(G-8998)***
Procter & Gamble Distrg LLC...925 867-4900
2400 Camino Ramon Ste 300 San Ramon (94583) ***(G-8999)***
Prodata Research, San Diego *Also called Soleil Communications LLC* ***(G-26707)***
Prodege LLC (PA)...310 294-9599
100 N Sepulveda Blvd Fl 8 El Segundo (90245) ***(G-5687)***
Produce Company...310 508-7760
16809 Bellflower Blvd # 32 Bellflower (90706) ***(G-8765)***
Produce Exchange Incorporated (HQ)...925 454-8700
7407 Southfront Rd Livermore (94551) ***(G-8766)***
Producer -Writers Guild...818 846-1015
2900 W Alameda Ave # 1100 Burbank (91505) ***(G-10559)***
Producers Dairy Foods Inc (PA)...559 264-6583
250 E Belmont Ave Fresno (93701) ***(G-8563)***
Produces Dairy, Fresno *Also called L A S Transportation Inc* ***(G-4206)***
Product Development Corp (PA)...831 333-1100
20 Ragsdale Dr Ste 100 Monterey (93940) ***(G-17429)***
Product Partners, Santa Monica *Also called Beachbody LLC* ***(G-13959)***
Product Quality Partners Inc...925 484-6491
450 Main St Ste 207 Pleasanton (94566) ***(G-16463)***
Product Slingshot Inc...760 929-9380
2221 Rutherford Rd Carlsbad (92008) ***(G-17430)***
Production Delivery Svcs Inc...562 777-0060
12133 Greenstone Ave Santa Fe Springs (90670) ***(G-4246)***
Production Framing Inc...916 978-2843
2000 Opportunity Dr # 140 Roseville (95678) ***(G-3074)***
Production Framing Systems Inc (PA)...916 978-2888
2000 Opportunity Dr # 140 Roseville (95678) ***(G-3075)***
Production Plus Plumbing Inc...760 597-0235
2472 Grand Ave Vista (92081) ***(G-2330)***
Production Special Events Svcs...818 831-5326
17326 Devonshire St Northridge (91325) ***(G-18427)***
Production Transport, Santa Fe Springs *Also called Production Delivery Svcs Inc* ***(G-4246)***
Productos Chata, Chula Vista *Also called Culinary Hispanic Foods Inc* ***(G-8827)***
Products & Services Inc...949 583-1681
2600 Michelson Dr # 1700 Irvine (92612) ***(G-7509)***
Profed Mortgage, Rancho Cucamonga *Also called Provident Savings Bank* ***(G-9890)***
Professional Building Maint, Sun Valley *Also called PBM Maintenance Corp* ***(G-14382)***
Professional Bureau of Collect...916 685-3399
9675 Elk Grv Florin Rd Elk Grove (95624) ***(G-14571)***
Professional Cir Staffing Inc (PA)...323 930-2333
5900 Wilshire Blvd # 1100 Los Angeles (90036) ***(G-14735)***
Professional Cmnty MGT Cal Inc...949 597-4359
2335 Avenida Sevilla Laguna Woods (92637) ***(G-11764)***
Professional Cmnty MGT Cal Inc...951 845-2191
850 Country Club Dr Banning (92220) ***(G-11765)***
Professional Cmnty MGT Cal Inc...949 206-0580
24351 El Toro Rd Laguna Woods (92637) ***(G-11766)***
Professional Cmnty MGT Cal Inc...949 768-7261
27051 Towne Centre Dr # 200 Foothill Ranch (92610) ***(G-11240)***
Professional Cmnty MGT Cal Inc...949 268-2271
24351 El Toro Rd Laguna Hills (92637) ***(G-11767)***
Professional Cmnty MGT Cal Inc...949 597-4200
23522 Paseo De Valencia Laguna Hills (92653) ***(G-11768)***
Professional Coin Grading Svc...949 567-1246
1921 E Alton Ave Ste 100 Santa Ana (92705) ***(G-17431)***
Professional Community MGT Cal (PA)...800 369-7260
27051 Towne Centre Dr # 200 Foothill Ranch (92610) ***(G-11769)***
Professional Construction Svcs, Rancho Cucamonga *Also called Rwc Enterprises Inc* ***(G-26046)***
Professional Exchange Svc...559 229-6249
4747 N 1st St Ste 140 Fresno (93726) ***(G-17432)***
Professional Golf MGT LLC...760 564-0804
49155 Vista Estrella La Quinta (92253) ***(G-27177)***
Professional Health Tech...858 449-1599
8131 Calle Del Cielo La Jolla (92037) ***(G-19879)***
Professional Healthcare At HM, Campbell *Also called Kindred Healthcare Inc* ***(G-22989)***
Professional Healthcare At HM...925 363-7876
395 Taylor Blvd Ste 118 Pleasant Hill (94523) ***(G-22539)***
Professional Hospital Sup Inc (HQ)...951 699-5000
42500 Winchester Rd Temecula (92590) ***(G-7305)***
Professional Hospital Sup Inc...707 720-0164
2100 Courage Dr Fairfield (94533) ***(G-7306)***
Professional Insur Assoc Inc (PA)...650 592-7333
1100 Industrial Rd Ste 3 San Carlos (94070) ***(G-10839)***
Professional Janitorial Svc...310 410-1452
234 Eucalyptus Dr B El Segundo (90245) ***(G-14395)***
Professional Maint Systems, San Diego *Also called Professional Maint Systems Inc* ***(G-14396)***
Professional Maint Systems Inc...619 276-1150
4912 Naples St San Diego (92110) ***(G-14396)***
Professional Produce...323 277-1550
2570 E 25th St Los Angeles (90058) ***(G-8767)***
Professional Security Cons (PA)...310 207-7729
11454 San Vicente Blvd # 2 Los Angeles (90049) ***(G-16765)***
Professional Services Company, San Francisco *Also called Shenyang Zhong Yi Tin-Plating* ***(G-11044)***
Professional Staffing, Granada Hills *Also called PS National Inc* ***(G-14739)***
Professional Staffing Associat, Downey *Also called Rancho Los Amigos Nationa* ***(G-24145)***
Professional Svcs Med Group, Huntington Park *Also called All Care Medical Group Inc* ***(G-19329)***
Professnal Elec Cnstr Svcs Inc...909 373-4100
9112 Santa Anita Ave Rancho Cucamonga (91730) ***(G-2690)***
Professnal Ldscp Solutions Inc...916 424-3815
6108 27th St Ste C Sacramento (95822) ***(G-790)***
Professnal Rgistry Netwrk Corp...714 394-4071
20132 Canyon Dr Yorba Linda (92886) ***(G-14736)***
Professonal Technical SEC Svcs...415 243-2100
625 Market St Fl 9 San Francisco (94105) ***(G-16766)***
Professonal Tele Answering Svc, Chatsworth *Also called Seven One Inc* ***(G-17488)***
Professsional Insurance, San Carlos *Also called Professional Insur Assoc Inc* ***(G-10839)***
Proficient LLC...310 519-8200
601 S Palos Verdes St San Pedro (90731) ***(G-13111)***
Profil Inst For Clncal RES Inc...619 427-1300
855 3rd Ave Ste 4400 Chula Vista (91911) ***(G-26591)***
Profile of Santa Cruz...831 479-0393
2045 40th Ave Ste B Capitola (95010) ***(G-14737)***
Profit Recovery Partners LLC...949 851-2777
2995 Red Hill Ave Ste 200 Costa Mesa (92626) ***(G-28023)***
Progauge Technologies Inc...661 392-9600
2331 Cepheus Ct Bakersfield (93308) ***(G-7877)***
Progenity Inc (PA)...855 293-2639
4330 La Jolla Village Dr # 200 San Diego (92122) ***(G-22260)***
Progress Advocates Group LLC...800 279-9319
3100 Bristol St Ste 300 Costa Mesa (92626) ***(G-13789)***
Progress Foundation...415 553-3100
52 Dore St San Francisco (94103) ***(G-25317)***
Progress Glass Co Inc (PA)...415 824-7040
25 Patterson St San Francisco (94124) ***(G-3413)***
Progress Rail Services Corp...916 645-6006
3909 Cincinnati Ave Rocklin (95765) ***(G-5238)***
Progress Van Guard, Rocklin *Also called Progress Rail Services Corp* ***(G-5238)***
Progressin Drywall, Lancaster *Also called Excel Contractors Inc* ***(G-1172)***
Progressive Floor Covering Inc...714 213-8805
924 S Highland Ave Fullerton (92832) ***(G-3128)***
Progressive Health Care System...818 707-9603
8510 Balboa Blvd Ste 150 Northridge (91325) ***(G-19880)***
Progressive Management Systems, West Covina *Also called RM Galicia Inc* ***(G-14044)***
Progressive Marketing Group, Commerce *Also called Progressive Produce Lcc* ***(G-8768)***
Progressive Power Group Inc...714 899-2300
12552 Western Ave Garden Grove (92841) ***(G-2331)***
Progressive Produce Lcc (HQ)...323 890-8100
5790 Peachtree St Commerce (90040) ***(G-8768)***
Progressive Solutions, San Jose *Also called Sarpa-Feldman Enterprises Inc* ***(G-17476)***
Progressive Sub-Acute Care...408 378-8875
13425 Sousa Ln Saratoga (95070) ***(G-22162)***
Progressive Trnsp Svcs Inc...510 268-3776
19500 S Alameda St Compton (90221) ***(G-7948)***
Progressive West Insurance Co...916 864-6000
10940 White Rock Rd Rancho Cordova (95670) ***(G-10840)***
Project Air Force, Santa Monica *Also called Air Force US Dept of* ***(G-26730)***
Project Boat Holdings LLC...310 712-1850
360 N Crescent Dr Bldg S Beverly Hills (90210) ***(G-12085)***
Project Concern International (PA)...858 279-9690
5151 Murphy Canyon Rd # 320 San Diego (92123) ***(G-25100)***
Project Consulting Specialists...650 265-2400
425 N Whisman Rd Ste 600 Mountain View (94043) ***(G-28024)***
Project Design Consultants...619 235-6471
701 B St Ste 800 San Diego (92101) ***(G-28025)***
Project Frog Inc...415 814-8500
99 Green St Ste 200 San Francisco (94111) ***(G-1333)***
Project Go Incorporated...916 782-3443
801 Vernon St Roseville (95678) ***(G-3571)***
Project Management Institute...760 458-6198
8895 Towne Centre Dr San Diego (92122) ***(G-27178)***
Project Open Hand (PA)...415 292-3400
730 Polk St Fl 3 San Francisco (94109) ***(G-24140)***
Project Six...818 781-0360
13130 Burbank Blvd Sherman Oaks (91401) ***(G-17433)***
Project Y, Brisbane *Also called Mode Media Corporation* ***(G-13973)***
Projistics, San Jose *Also called Nagarro Inc* ***(G-16000)***
Proland Property Managment LLC (PA)...213 738-8175
2510 W 7th St Fl 2 Los Angeles (90057) ***(G-11770)***
Prolifics Inc (HQ)...212 267-7722
24025 Park Sorrento # 450 Calabasas (91302) ***(G-16464)***
Prolifics Testing Inc...925 485-9535
4637 Chabot Dr Ste 210 Pleasanton (94588) ***(G-15398)***

ALPHABETIC

ALPHABETIC SECTION
Provident Bank, Riverside

Prolinx Services Inc...408 689-5777
2033 Gateway Pl Ste 500 San Jose (95110) *(G-14738)*
Prologic Rdmption Slutions Inc (PA)...310 322-7774
2121 Rosecrans Ave El Segundo (90245) *(G-17434)*
Prologis Inc (PA)...415 394-9000
Bay 1 Pier 1 San Francisco (94111) *(G-12266)*
Prologis LP (HQ)...415 394-9000
Bay 1 Pier 1 San Francisco (94111) *(G-12267)*
Promab Biotechnologies Inc...510 860-4615
2600 Hilltop Dr San Pablo (94806) *(G-26592)*
Promed Hlth Care Admnistrators...909 932-1045
9302 Pttsbrgh Ave Ste 220 Rancho Cucamonga (91730) *(G-19881)*
Promesa Behavioral Health...209 725-3114
2815 G St Merced (95340) *(G-24774)*
Prometheus RE Group Inc (PA)...650 931-3400
1900 S Norfolk St Ste 150 San Mateo (94403) *(G-11771)*
Promise Hosp E Los Angeles LP...323 261-0432
16453 Colorado Ave Paramount (90723) *(G-21817)*
Promise Hospital of San Diego, San Diego *Also called Quantum Properties LP (G-21825)*
Promise Technology Inc...408 228-1400
580 Cottonwood Dr Milpitas (95035) *(G-7176)*
Prommis Solutions LLC...619 590-9200
525 E Main St El Cajon (92020) *(G-10071)*
Promo Shop Inc (PA)...208 333-0881
5420 Mcconnell Ave Los Angeles (90066) *(G-27596)*
Proofpoint Inc (PA)...408 517-4710
892 Ross Dr Sunnyvale (94089) *(G-15399)*
Proove Medical Labs Inc...949 427-5303
15326 Elton Pkwy Irvine (92618) *(G-22261)*
Propane Transport Service Inc...209 823-8005
903 W Center St Ste 7 Manteca (95337) *(G-4049)*
Propel Software Corporation...408 571-6300
1010 Rincon Cir San Jose (95131) *(G-16465)*
Property I D, Los Angeles *Also called I D Property Corporation (G-11579)*
Property Insight...909 876-6505
1007 E Cooley Dr Colton (92324) *(G-11033)*
Property Management Assoc Inc (PA)...323 295-2000
6011 Bristol Pkwy Culver City (90230) *(G-11772)*
Prophet Brand Strategy (PA)...415 677-0909
1 Bush St Fl 7 San Francisco (94104) *(G-27597)*
Propulsion Controls Engrg (PA)...619 235-0961
1620 Rigel St San Diego (92113) *(G-18001)*
Pros Incorporated...661 589-5400
3400 Patton Way Bakersfield (93308) *(G-1093)*
Proscape Landscape, Signal Hill *Also called Fenderscape Inc (G-853)*
Prosearch Strategies Inc...213 355-1260
3250 Wilshire Blvd # 301 Los Angeles (90010) *(G-26699)*
Proskauer Rose LLP...310 557-2900
2049 Century Park E # 3200 Los Angeles (90067) *(G-23520)*
Prosoft Technology Inc (PA)...661 716-5100
9201 Camino Media Ste 200 Bakersfield (93311) *(G-6087)*
Prospect Enterprises Inc (PA)...213 599-5700
625 Kohler St Los Angeles (90021) *(G-8649)*
Prospect Medical Group Inc (HQ)...714 796-5900
1920 E 17th St Ste 200 Santa Ana (92705) *(G-27179)*
Prospect Medical Holdings Inc (PA)...310 943-4500
3415 S Sepulveda Blvd # 9 Los Angeles (90034) *(G-19882)*
Prospect Medical Systems Inc (HQ)...714 667-8156
600 City Pkwy W Ste 800 Orange (92868) *(G-27180)*
Prospect Mortgage LLC (PA)...818 981-0606
15301 Ventura Blvd D300 Sherman Oaks (91403) *(G-9945)*
Prosper Marketplace Inc (PA)...415 593-5400
221 Main St Fl 3 San Francisco (94105) *(G-9946)*
Prostavar Rx, Los Angeles *Also called Superbalife International LLC (G-8297)*
Prosum Inc (PA)...310 404-1545
2321 Rosecrans Ave # 4225 El Segundo (90245) *(G-16172)*
Prosum Technology Services, El Segundo *Also called Prosum Inc (G-16172)*
Protean Health Services Inc...510 536-6512
1833 10th Ave Oakland (94606) *(G-21352)*
Protec Association Services (PA)...858 569-1080
10180 Willow Creek Rd San Diego (92131) *(G-14397)*
Protec Building Services, San Diego *Also called Protec Association Services (G-14397)*
Protech, San Francisco *Also called Professonal Technical SEC Svcs (G-16766)*
Protech Construction, Brea *Also called Paglia & Associates Cnstr (G-1231)*
Protect-For-Less Security Svcs...760 343-1192
72877 Dinah Shore Dr Rancho Mirage (92270) *(G-16913)*
Protected Outcomes Corporation...203 545-9565
9663 Santa Monica Blvd Beverly Hills (90210) *(G-16767)*
Protection One Inc...925 251-9088
6691 Owens Dr Pleasanton (94588) *(G-16914)*
Protection Specialists...818 503-1306
6841 Whitsett Ave Apt 104 North Hollywood (91605) *(G-16768)*
Protege Builders Inc...916 825-8478
4306 Pinell St Sacramento (95838) *(G-3076)*
Proteus Inc...661 721-5800
1816 Cecil Ave Delano (93215) *(G-24141)*
Prothena Biosciences Inc...650 837-8550
650 Gateway Blvd South San Francisco (94080) *(G-26797)*
Protiviti Inc...415 402-3663
2613 Camino Ramon San Ramon (94583) *(G-26429)*
Protiviti Inc (HQ)...650 234-6000
2884 Sand Hill Rd Ste 200 Menlo Park (94025) *(G-27598)*
Protiviti Inc...213 327-1400
400 S Hope St Ste 900 Los Angeles (90071) *(G-27599)*
Protosource Corporation...559 490-8600
2511 W Shaw Ave Ste 102 Fresno (93711) *(G-16173)*
Prototypes Centers For Innov...909 624-1233
845 E Arrow Hwy Pomona (91767) *(G-24142)*
Prototypes Women's Center, Pomona *Also called Prototypes Centers For Innov (G-24142)*

Protravel International LLC...310 271-9566
9171 Wilshire Blvd # 428 Beverly Hills (90210) *(G-4971)*
Providence All Saints Subacute, San Leandro *Also called Providnce All STS Subacute LLC (G-20859)*
Providence Health & Services...818 847-4999
181 S Buena Vista St # 300 Burbank (91505) *(G-19883)*
Providence Health & Services...818 881-0800
18321 Clark St Tarzana (91356) *(G-23024)*
Providence Health & Services...310 355-0100
13355 Hawthorne Blvd Hawthorne (90250) *(G-23025)*
Providence Health & Services...818 841-0112
2601 W Alameda Ave # 212 Burbank (91505) *(G-23026)*
Providence Health & Services...310 835-6627
21501 Avalon Blvd Carson (90745) *(G-23027)*
Providence Health & Services...310 370-5895
5315 Torrance Blvd Torrance (90503) *(G-22540)*
Providence Health & Services...310 540-1334
21311 Madrona Ave Torrance (90503) *(G-23028)*
Providence Health & Services...323 298-2530
4314 W Slauson Ave Los Angeles (90043) *(G-23029)*
Providence Health & Services...562 865-4600
17315 Studebaker Rd # 310 Cerritos (90703) *(G-22541)*
Providence Health & Services...310 792-3440
21135 Hawthorne Blvd Torrance (90503) *(G-22811)*
Providence Health & Services...818 401-4173
5359 Balboa Blvd Encino (91316) *(G-20343)*
Providence Health & Services...310 831-0371
1360 W 6th St Ste 100 San Pedro (90732) *(G-22262)*
Providence Health & Services...310 618-8217
20911 Earl St Ste 380 Torrance (90503) *(G-20344)*
Providence Health & Services...818 344-3143
18360 Burbank Blvd Tarzana (91356) *(G-19884)*
Providence Health & Services...661 257-9999
27875 Smyth Dr Santa Clarita (91355) *(G-28157)*
Providence Health & Services...310 792-5050
21311 Madrona Ave Ste D Torrance (90503) *(G-19885)*
Providence Health & Services...818 898-4445
11570 Indian Hills Rd Mission Hills (91345) *(G-20271)*
Providence Health & Services...310 545-6627
1101 N Sepulveda Blvd Manhattan Beach (90266) *(G-19886)*
Providence Health & Services...310 937-1980
20929 Hawthorne Blvd Torrance (90503) *(G-23030)*
Providence Health & Services...661 294-1030
27875 Smyth Dr Ste 100 Valencia (91355) *(G-7307)*
Providence Health & Services...310 831-9482
1499 W 1st St 2 San Pedro (90732) *(G-19887)*
Providence Health & Services...310 793-4263
20911 Earl St Torrance (90503) *(G-19888)*
Providence Health & Services F...818 843-5111
501 S Buena Vista St Burbank (91505) *(G-24965)*
Providence Health & Services S...310 832-3311
1300 W 7th St San Pedro (90732) *(G-21818)*
Providence Health & Svcs - Ore...510 444-0839
540 23rd St Oakland (94612) *(G-21819)*
Providence Health & Svcs - Ore...818 365-8051
15031 Rinaldi St Mission Hills (91345) *(G-21820)*
Providence Health System...818 898-4530
15031 Rinaldi St Mission Hills (91345) *(G-19889)*
Providence Health System...818 898-4561
15031 Rinaldi St Mission Hills (91345) *(G-21821)*
Providence Health System...310 376-9474
20929 Hawthorne Blvd Torrance (90503) *(G-19890)*
Providence Health System...818 843-5111
501 S Buena Vista St Burbank (91505) *(G-21822)*
Providence Health System...310 543-5900
4320 Maricopa St Torrance (90503) *(G-12198)*
Providence Health System...310 540-7676
4101 Torrance Blvd Torrance (90503) *(G-19891)*
Providence Health System...310 370-5895
3551 Voyager St Ste 201 Torrance (90503) *(G-12199)*
Providence Health System...310 378-8587
3620 Lomita Blvd Torrance (90505) *(G-12200)*
Providence Health System...818 846-8141
511 S Buena Vista St Burbank (91505) *(G-12201)*
Providence Health System...310 530-3800
2601 Airport Dr Ste 230 Torrance (90505) *(G-21823)*
Providence Holy Cross (PA)...818 365-8051
15031 Rinaldi St Mission Hills (91345) *(G-21824)*
PROVIDENCE HOLY CROSS FOUNDATI, Burbank *Also called Providence Health & Services F (G-24965)*
Providence Holy Cross Med Ctr, Mission Hills *Also called Providence Health System (G-21821)*
Providence Holy Cross Med Ctr, Mission Hills *Also called Providence Health & Svcs - Ore (G-21820)*
Providence Little Co Mary Hosp, Torrance *Also called Providence Health System (G-19891)*
Providence Little Co of Mary (HQ)...310 540-7676
4101 Torrance Blvd Torrance (90503) *(G-27181)*
Providence Little Co of Mary...310 303-6970
4101 Torrance Blvd Torrance (90503) *(G-27182)*
Providence Little Company of M, San Pedro *Also called Providence Health & Services S (G-21818)*
Providence Seminars Inc...760 827-2100
6349 Palomar Oaks Ct Carlsbad (92011) *(G-27600)*
Providence Speech Hearing Ctr...714 639-4990
1301 W Providence Ave Orange (92868) *(G-22812)*
Providence Tarzana Medical Ctr...818 881-0800
18321 Clark St Tarzana (91356) *(G-19892)*
Provident Bank, Riverside *Also called Providnt Svngs Bank Chrtble FN (G-9517)*

ALPHABETIC

Provident Bank, Riverside *Also called Provident Savings Bank (G-9581)*
Provident Bank, Riverside *Also called Provident Savings Bank (G-9582)*
Provident Care Inc 209 526-5160
100 Sycamore Ave Ste 100 Modesto (95354) *(G-22542)*
Provident Credit Union (PA) 650 508-0300
303 Twin Dolphin Dr # 303 Redwood City (94065) *(G-9679)*
Provident Financial Management 310 282-0477
2850 Ocean Park Blvd # 300 Santa Monica (90405) *(G-27183)*
Provident Funding Assoc LP (PA) 650 652-1300
851 Traeger Ave Ste 100 San Bruno (94066) *(G-9888)*
Provident Group Crown Pnte LLC 951 737-7482
737 Magnolia Ave Ofc Corona (92879) *(G-11190)*
Provident Mrtg Cpitl Assoc Inc 650 652-1300
1633 Bayshore Hwy Ste 155 Burlingame (94010) *(G-9889)*
Provident Savings Bank (HQ) 951 782-6177
3756 Central Ave Riverside (92506) *(G-9581)*
Provident Savings Bank 951 686-6060
6674 Brockton Ave Riverside (92506) *(G-9582)*
Provident Savings Bank 909 484-6286
10370 Commerce Center Dr # 200 Rancho Cucamonga (91730) *(G-9890)*
Providian Staffing Corporation 909 456-7529
1801 Excise Ave Ste 112 Ontario (91761) *(G-14928)*
Providnce All STS Subacute LLC 510 481-3200
1652 Mono Ave San Leandro (94578) *(G-20859)*
Providnt Svngs Bank Chrtble FN 951 686-6060
3756 Central Ave Riverside (92506) *(G-9517)*
Proview Advanced Solutions Inc 949 752-2484
130 Theory Ste 200 Irvine (92617) *(G-10841)*
Prowall Lath and Plaster 760 480-9001
360 S Spruce St Escondido (92025) *(G-2959)*
Prs/Roebbelen JV 916 641-0324
4811 Tunis Rd Sacramento (95835) *(G-1641)*
Prsi, Jurupa Valley *Also called Pavement Recycling Systems Inc (G-8078)*
Prudential, Encino *Also called Burkshire Has A Way Home Servc (G-11332)*
Prudential, Pleasanton *Also called McM Partners Inc (G-11669)*
Prudential, San Diego *Also called Joe Canpagna (G-11597)*
Prudential, San Luis Obispo *Also called Pickford Realty Inc (G-11748)*
Prudential, Thousand Oaks *Also called Gemmm Corp (G-11553)*
Prudential, Berkeley *Also called Mason-Mcduffie Real Estate Inc (G-11659)*
Prudential, Walnut Creek *Also called Mason-Mcduffie Real Estate Inc (G-11660)*
Prudential, Santa Maria *Also called Hunter Realty Inc (G-11577)*
Prudential, Danville *Also called Mason-Mcduffie Real Estate Inc (G-11661)*
Prudential, Irvine *Also called Brer Affiliates Inc (G-12211)*
Prudential, Chula Vista *Also called Coronado Financial Corp (G-11459)*
Prudential, Antioch *Also called Mason-Mcduffie Real Estate Inc (G-11663)*
Prudential, Modesto *Also called Stone Real Estate Inc (G-11859)*
Prudential, Rancho Cucamonga *Also called Empire Estates Inc (G-11492)*
Prudential, San Diego *Also called Pickford Realty Inc (G-11750)*
Prudential, Norwalk *Also called Mulhearn Realtors Inc (G-11701)*
Prudential, Irvine *Also called Brookfield Relocation Inc (G-12212)*
Prudential, Coronado *Also called Pickford Realty Inc (G-11751)*
Prudential, Valencia *Also called Nutec Enterprises Inc (G-11717)*
Prudential 24 Hour Real Estate 562 861-7257
8635 Florence Ave Ste 101 Downey (90240) *(G-11773)*
Prudential CA Realty 510 487-6088
39275 Mssion Blvd Ste 103 Fremont (94539) *(G-11774)*
Prudential California Realty 818 993-8900
9003 Reseda Blvd Ste 105 Northridge (91324) *(G-11775)*
Prudential California Realty 949 888-2300
29947 Ave De Las Bndra # 150 Rcho STA Marg (92688) *(G-11776)*
Prudential California Realty 415 664-9400
677 Portola Dr San Francisco (94127) *(G-11777)*
Prudential California Realty 858 487-3520
976 Main St Ste A Ramona (92065) *(G-11778)*
Prudential Cleanroom Services, Milpitas *Also called Prudential Overall Supply (G-13637)*
Prudential Cleanroom Services, Commerce *Also called Prudential Overall Supply (G-13638)*
Prudential Dust Control, Riverside *Also called Prudential Overall Supply (G-13636)*
Prudential Insur Co of Amer 949 440-5300
3333 Michelson Dr Ste 820 Irvine (92612) *(G-10842)*
Prudential Insur Co of Amer 415 398-7310
4 Embarcadero Ctr # 2700 San Francisco (94111) *(G-10843)*
Prudential Insur Co of Amer 818 990-2122
15303 Ventura Blvd # 1550 Sherman Oaks (91403) *(G-10844)*
Prudential Insur Co of Amer 415 486-3050
180 Montgomery St # 1900 San Francisco (94104) *(G-10845)*
Prudential Insur Co of Amer 818 901-0028
5990 Sepulvda Blvd # 300 Van Nuys (91411) *(G-10846)*
Prudential Malibu Realty, Malibu *Also called Terra Coastal Properties Inc (G-11869)*
Prudential Norcal Realty, Carmichael *Also called Diez & Leis RE Group Inc (G-11471)*
Prudential Overall Supply 323 724-4888
6920 Bandini Blvd Commerce (90040) *(G-13634)*
Prudential Overall Supply (PA) 949 250-4855
1661 Alton Pkwy Irvine (92606) *(G-13635)*
Prudential Overall Supply 951 687-0440
6997 Jurupa Ave Riverside (92504) *(G-13636)*
Prudential Overall Supply 408 719-0886
1437 N Milpitas Blvd Milpitas (95035) *(G-13637)*
Prudential Overall Supply 323 722-0636
6948 Bandini Blvd Commerce (90040) *(G-13638)*
Prudential Overall Supply 559 264-8231
1260 E North Ave Fresno (93725) *(G-13639)*
Prudential Overall Supply 760 717-6803
16901 Aston Irvine (92606) *(G-13640)*
Prudential Overall Supply 805 529-0833
5300 Gabbert Rd Moorpark (93021) *(G-13641)*
Prudential Overall Supply Inc 760 727-7163
2485 Ash St Vista (92081) *(G-13642)*
Prudential Realty Corp 415 566-9800
1430 Taraval St San Francisco (94116) *(G-11779)*
Prudential Security Services, Los Angeles *Also called Eastside Group Corporation (G-16631)*
Pruitthealth Corporation 626 810-5567
1982 Camwood Ave City of Industry (91748) *(G-21353)*
Prutel Joint Venture 949 240-2000
1 Ritz Carlton Dr Dana Point (92629) *(G-13112)*
Pryor Cashman LLP 310 556-9608
1801 Century Park E # 2419 Los Angeles (90067) *(G-23521)*
PS Arts 310 586-1017
6701 Center Dr W Ste 550 Los Angeles (90045) *(G-28026)*
PS Business Parks Inc (PA) 818 244-8080
701 Western Ave Glendale (91201) *(G-12268)*
PS Business Parks LP 818 244-8080
701 Western Ave Glendale (91201) *(G-11780)*
PS Development Corporation 818 340-0965
21625 Prairie St Chatsworth (91311) *(G-2691)*
PS Environmental Svcs Inc 310 373-6259
23775 Madison St Torrance (90505) *(G-17435)*
PS National Inc 818 366-1300
17645 Chatsworth St Granada Hills (91344) *(G-14739)*
PS Partners III Ltd 818 244-8080
701 Western Ave Ste 200 Glendale (91201) *(G-4616)*
Ps2 (PA) 310 243-2980
17903 S Hobart Blvd Gardena (90248) *(G-2477)*
Psav, Cerritos *Also called Audio Visual Headquarters (G-14514)*
Psav Holdings LLC 562 366-0138
111 W Ocean Blvd Ste 1110 Long Beach (90802) *(G-14572)*
PSC Industrial Outsourcing LP 562 997-6000
1661 E 32nd St Long Beach (90807) *(G-6516)*
PSC Industrial Outsourcing LP 831 635-0220
1802 Shelton Dr Hollister (95023) *(G-6633)*
PSC Industrial Outsourcing LP 831 627-2595
62117 Railroad Ave San Ardo (93450) *(G-4050)*
PSI Fire 408 842-9308
820 Eschenburg Dr Gilroy (95020) *(G-15400)*
PSI Group 415 468-1660
125 Valley Dr Brisbane (94005) *(G-14087)*
Psinapse Technology Ltd 925 225-0400
5820 Stnrge Mall Rd # 212 Pleasanton (94588) *(G-14740)*
Pslq Inc 951 795-4260
28910 Rancho California R Temecula (92590) *(G-1334)*
Psomas 714 751-7373
3 Hutton Cntre Dr Ste 200 Santa Ana (92707) *(G-26277)*
Psomas 760 843-5700
14369 Park Ave Ste 101b Victorville (92392) *(G-26278)*
Psomas (PA) 310 954-3700
555 S Flower St Ste 4300 Los Angeles (90071) *(G-26279)*
Psomas 916 788-8122
1075 Crkside Rdg Dr # 200 Roseville (95678) *(G-26023)*
Psomas & Associates, Santa Ana *Also called Psomas (G-26277)*
Pss World Medical Inc 714 459-4000
1938 W Malvern Ave Fullerton (92833) *(G-7308)*
Psychemedics Corporation 310 216-7776
5832 Uplander Way Culver City (90230) *(G-22263)*
Psychiatric Ctrs At San Diego (PA) 619 528-4600
6153 Fairmount Ave # 140 San Diego (92120) *(G-19893)*
Psychiatric Health Facility, Placerville *Also called County of El Dorado (G-22056)*
Psychiatric Solutions Inc 626 286-1191
4619 Rosemead Blvd Rosemead (91770) *(G-22813)*
Psychiatric Solutions Inc 916 288-0300
8001 Bruceville Rd Sacramento (95823) *(G-19894)*
Psychiatric Solutions Inc 916 489-3336
4250 Auburn Blvd Sacramento (95841) *(G-19895)*
Psychiatric Solutions Inc 510 796-1100
39001 Sundale Dr Fremont (94538) *(G-19896)*
Psychiatric Solutions Inc 951 789-4405
17241 Van Buren Blvd Riverside (92504) *(G-19897)*
Psynergy Programs Inc 408 776-0422
18225 Hale Ave Morgan Hill (95037) *(G-24775)*
Pszyjw, Los Angeles *Also called Pachulski Stang Zehl Jones LLP (G-23487)*
Pt Gaming LLC 323 260-5060
970 W 190th St Ste 400 Torrance (90502) *(G-13113)*
Pt Logistics Inc 831 728-4535
144 W Lake Ave Ste B Watsonville (95076) *(G-4051)*
Pta CA Congress of Parents 818 340-6700
5014 Serrania Ave Woodland Hills (91364) *(G-25318)*
Pta California Cong P A S Elem 925 606-4700
5280 Irene Way Livermore (94550) *(G-25319)*
Pta California Congress of Par 310 328-3100
21514 Halldale Ave Torrance (90501) *(G-25320)*
Pta California Congress of Par 408 928-7900
13901 Nordyke Dr San Jose (95127) *(G-25321)*
Ptac Carmel Valley Mid School 858 481-8221
3800 Mykonos Ln San Diego (92130) *(G-25322)*
Ptac Rail Ranch Elem School 951 696-1404
25030 Via Santee Murrieta (92563) *(G-25323)*
Ptc Inc 408 434-8500
2550 N 1st St Ste 500 San Jose (95131) *(G-15401)*
Pti, Chatsworth *Also called Printing Technology Inc (G-7947)*
Pti Solutions, Livermore *Also called Pinnacle Telecom Inc (G-16030)*
Pti Solutions, McClellan *Also called Pinnacle Telecom Inc (G-16031)*
Ptr Group Inc 951 965-1822
652 S Joyce Ave Rialto (92376) *(G-27184)*
Pts Staffing Solutions 949 268-4000
9960 Research Dr Ste 200 Irvine (92618) *(G-26024)*

Ptsa 31st Dst Creative Kids....818 996-2668
17445 Cantlay St Van Nuys (91406) ***(G-24505)***
Ptsi Managed Services Inc....626 440-3118
100 W Walnut St Pasadena (91124) ***(G-26025)***
Pub Works/Community Dev, Santa Barbara *Also called Santa Barbara City of* ***(G-17474)***
Public Bell Inc....818 396-1675
9755 Garden Grove Blvd Garden Grove (92844) ***(G-15402)***
Public Communications Svcs Inc....310 231-1000
11859 Wilshire Blvd # 600 Los Angeles (90025) ***(G-5688)***
Public Consulting Group Inc....916 565-8090
2150 River Plaza Dr # 380 Sacramento (95833) ***(G-27601)***
Public Counsel....213 385-2977
610 S Ardmore Ave Los Angeles (90005) ***(G-23522)***
Public Defender, Fullerton *Also called County of Orange* ***(G-23179)***
Public Defender, Compton *Also called County of Los Angeles* ***(G-23176)***
Public Defender Administration, Los Angeles *Also called County of Los Angeles* ***(G-23175)***
Public Defender's Office, Fresno *Also called County of Fresno* ***(G-23170)***
Public Defender's Office, Sacramento *Also called County of Sacramento* ***(G-23181)***
Public Defender- Main Office, Riverside *Also called County of Riverside* ***(G-23180)***
Public Defenders Office, Los Angeles *Also called County of Los Angeles* ***(G-23172)***
Public Employees Retirement....916 795-3400
400 Q St Sacramento (95811) ***(G-10560)***
Public Employees Retirement....916 326-3065
400 P St 3260 Sacramento (95814) ***(G-10561)***
Public Health California Dept....213 620-6160
320 W 4th St Ste 830 Los Angeles (90013) ***(G-19898)***
Public Health California Dept....661 835-4668
2400 Wible Rd Ste 14 Bakersfield (93304) ***(G-19899)***
Public Health California Dept....510 412-1502
850 Marina Bay Pkwy F175 Richmond (94804) ***(G-19900)***
Public Health Department, El Centro *Also called County of Imperial* ***(G-22926)***
Public Health Dept, San Francisco *Also called City & County of San Francisco* ***(G-21493)***
Public Health Dept, Santa Barbara *Also called Santa Barbara County of* ***(G-23053)***
Public Health Dept, San Jose *Also called Santa Clara County of* ***(G-19954)***
Public Health Institute....916 285-1231
1825 Bell St Ste 203 Sacramento (95825) ***(G-23031)***
Public Health Institute (PA)....510 285-5500
555 12th St Ste 1050 Oakland (94607) ***(G-26798)***
Public Health Nursing Service, Sacramento *Also called County of Sacramento* ***(G-20481)***
Public Hlth Fndation Entps Inc....626 856-6600
12781 Schabarum Ave Irwindale (91706) ***(G-23032)***
Public Hlth Fndation Entps Inc....323 261-6388
3648 E Olympic Blvd Los Angeles (90023) ***(G-23033)***
Public Hlth Fndation Entps Inc....562 801-2323
8666 Whittier Blvd Pico Rivera (90660) ***(G-23034)***
Public Hlth Fndation Entps Inc....323 263-0262
277 S Atlantic Blvd Los Angeles (90022) ***(G-25324)***
Public Hlth Fndation Entps Inc....323 733-9381
1649 W Washington Blvd Los Angeles (90007) ***(G-23035)***
Public Hlth Fndation Entps Inc....310 320-5215
1640 W Carson St Ste G Torrance (90501) ***(G-25325)***
Public Hlth Fndation Entps Inc....310 518-2835
125 E Anaheim St Wilmington (90744) ***(G-23036)***
Public Hlth Fndation Entps Inc....626 856-6618
12781 Shama Rd El Monte (91732) ***(G-23037)***
Public Hlth Fndation Entps Inc (PA)....562 692-4643
12801 Crossrds Pkwy S 200 City of Industry (91746) ***(G-27185)***
Public Policy Institute Cal (PA)....415 291-4400
500 Washington St Ste 600 San Francisco (94111) ***(G-25101)***
Public Security Inc....323 293-9884
3860 Crenshaw Blvd # 223 Los Angeles (90008) ***(G-16915)***
Public Service Yard, Glendale *Also called City of Glendale* ***(G-6325)***
Public Services, Coronado *Also called City of Coronado* ***(G-6285)***
Public Social Service, Norco *Also called County of Riverside* ***(G-23881)***
Public Social Services, Moreno Valley *Also called County of Riverside* ***(G-19478)***
Public Social Services, Lake Elsinore *Also called County of Riverside* ***(G-23883)***
Public Social Services, Lake Elsinore *Also called County of Riverside* ***(G-23884)***
Public Social Services, Canyon Country *Also called County of Los Angeles* ***(G-10549)***
Public Social Services, Los Angeles *Also called County of Los Angeles* ***(G-23841)***
Public Social Services, Norwalk *Also called County of Los Angeles* ***(G-23851)***
Public Stor Coml Prpts Group....818 244-8080
701 Western Ave Glendale (91201) ***(G-11034)***
Public Storage (PA)....818 244-8080
701 Western Ave Glendale (91201) ***(G-12269)***
Public Storage Prpts IV Ltd....818 244-8080
701 Western Ave Glendale (91201) ***(G-4617)***
Public Storage Prpts Xviii Inc....818 244-8080
701 Western Ave Ste 200 Glendale (91201) ***(G-12086)***
Public Works, Imperial *Also called County of Imperial* ***(G-1756)***
Public Works, Corona *Also called City of Corona* ***(G-6301)***
Public Works Department, Morgan Hill *Also called City of Morgan Hill* ***(G-27880)***
Public Works Department, Woodland *Also called City of Woodland* ***(G-27779)***
Public Works Department, Woodland *Also called City of Woodland* ***(G-25744)***
Public Works Dept, Los Angeles *Also called City of Los Angeles* ***(G-25740)***
Public Works Dept, Hayward *Also called County of Alameda* ***(G-1753)***
Public Works Dept, Palmdale *Also called City of Palmdale* ***(G-14248)***
Public Works Engineering Div, Daly City *Also called City of Daly City* ***(G-25738)***
Public Works Office, Vacaville *Also called City of Vacaville* ***(G-25743)***
Public Works Operations, Modesto *Also called County of Stanislaus* ***(G-6625)***
Public Works Superintendent, Alameda *Also called Maintenance Service For The Cy* ***(G-14347)***
Public Works, Dept of, Alhambra *Also called County of Los Angeles* ***(G-6335)***
Public Works, Dept of, Palmdale *Also called County of Los Angeles* ***(G-1757)***
Public Works, Dept of, Los Angeles *Also called County of Los Angeles* ***(G-1758)***

Publicis & Hal Riney (HQ)....415 981-0950
2001 The Embarcadero San Francisco (94133) ***(G-13901)***
Publis Works, Lomita *Also called City of Lomita* ***(G-6327)***
Publishers Group Incorporated (HQ)....510 528-1444
1700 4th St Berkeley (94710) ***(G-9170)***
Publishers Group West, Berkeley *Also called Publishers Group Incorporated* ***(G-9170)***
Pubmatic Inc (PA)....650 351-9162
305 Main St Fl 1 Redwood City (94063) ***(G-13902)***
Puente Hills Landfill, Whittier *Also called Sanitation District* ***(G-6560)***
Pulmonary Medicine Assoc....916 733-5040
2801 K St Ste 500 Sacramento (95816) ***(G-19901)***
Pulp Studio Incorporated (PA)....310 815-4999
2100 W 139th St Gardena (90249) ***(G-14160)***
Pulse Secure LLC (HQ)....408 372-9600
2700 Zanker Rd Ste 200 San Jose (95134) ***(G-15403)***
Pulse-Link Inc....760 496-2136
2730 Loker Ave W Carlsbad (92010) ***(G-26593)***
Pulte Home Corporation....925 249-3200
6210 Stoneridge Mall Rd Pleasanton (94588) ***(G-1239)***
Punch Studio LLC (PA)....310 390-9900
6025 W Slauson Ave Culver City (90230) ***(G-8176)***
Pupil Transportation, Whittier *Also called County of Los Angeles* ***(G-3917)***
Puratos Bakery Supply, Rancho Cucamonga *Also called Puratos Corporation* ***(G-4483)***
Puratos Corporation....909 484-1312
11167 White Birch Dr Rancho Cucamonga (91730) ***(G-4483)***
Purcell-Murray Company Inc (PA)....415 468-6620
185 Park Ln Brisbane (94005) ***(G-7728)***
Purchasing & Warehouse, Bakersfield *Also called Panama-Buena Vista Un Schl Dst* ***(G-4610)***
Purchasing 411 Inc....818 717-9980
12670 Paxton St Pacoima (91331) ***(G-7976)***
Purchasing Department, Redlands *Also called City of Redlands* ***(G-6461)***
Purchasing Department, Ventura *Also called Community Mem HSP/Sn Benua* ***(G-21508)***
Pure Beauty-A Freeman Company, Union City *Also called Purebeauty Inc* ***(G-7977)***
Pure Luxury Limousine Service....800 626-5466
4246 Petaluma Blvd N Petaluma (94952) ***(G-3831)***
Pure Luxury Worldwide Trnsp, Petaluma *Also called Pure Luxury Limousine Service* ***(G-3831)***
Purebeauty Inc....510 477-7950
32920 Alvarado Niles Rd # 220 Union City (94587) ***(G-7977)***
PUREGEAR, Baldwin Park *Also called Superior Communications Inc* ***(G-7642)***
Purelife LLC....877 777-3303
201 Santa Monica Blvd # 400 Santa Monica (90401) ***(G-7309)***
Purolator International Inc....650 871-7075
775 W Manville St Compton (90220) ***(G-5156)***
Puronics Retail Services Inc....925 456-7000
5775 Las Positas Rd Livermore (94551) ***(G-2332)***
Puronics Water Systems Inc....925 456-7000
5775 Las Positas Rd Livermore (94551) ***(G-7729)***
Purosil Division, Santa Fe Springs *Also called MCP Industries Inc* ***(G-8993)***
Puttin On Productions Corp....310 546-5544
2010 N Sepulveda Blvd A Manhattan Beach (90266) ***(G-18136)***
Pv Acquisition Bank....559 438-2002
255 E Rver Pk Cir Ste 180 Fresno (93720) ***(G-9555)***
Pvcc Inc (PA)....619 463-4040
8100 La Mesa Blvd Ste 101 La Mesa (91942) ***(G-11035)***
Pvhmc, Pomona *Also called Pomona Valley Hospital Med Ctr* ***(G-21802)***
PW Gillibrand Co Inc....805 526-2195
4537 Ish Dr Simi Valley (93063) ***(G-1111)***
Pw Jade LLC....707 843-5192
1111 Sonoma Ave Ste 324 Santa Rosa (95405) ***(G-22543)***
PW Stephens Envmtl Inc....510 782-9600
3478 Investment Blvd Hayward (94545) ***(G-6634)***
PW Stephens Envmtl Inc....510 651-9506
4047 Clipper Ct Fremont (94538) ***(G-3572)***
PWC STRategy& (us) LLC....281 685-8325
2141 Rosecrans Ave # 5100 El Segundo (90245) ***(G-27602)***
PWC STRategy& (us) LLC....415 391-1900
101 California St # 3300 San Francisco (94111) ***(G-27603)***
Pws Inc (HQ)....323 721-8832
12020 Garfield Ave South Gate (90280) ***(G-7978)***
PWS Holdings LLC....323 721-8832
6500 Flotilla St Commerce (90040) ***(G-7979)***
Pyj V A California Ltd Partnr....805 495-8437
4812 Lakeview Canyon Rd Westlake Village (91361) ***(G-18773)***
Pyramid Advisors LLC....925 847-6000
11950 Dublin Canyon Rd Pleasanton (94588) ***(G-13114)***
Pyramid Building Maint Corp (PA)....408 727-9393
2175 Martin Ave Santa Clara (95050) ***(G-14398)***
Pyramid Building Maint Corp....707 454-2020
600 Eubanks Ct Ste C Vacaville (95688) ***(G-14399)***
Pyramid Enterprises Inc (PA)....661 702-1420
28368 Constellation Rd # 380 Valencia (91355) ***(G-19263)***
Pyramid Flowers Inc....805 382-8070
3813 Doris Ave Oxnard (93030) ***(G-312)***
Pyramid Logistics Services Inc (PA)....714 903-2600
14650 Hoover St Westminster (92683) ***(G-4247)***
Pyramid Painting Inc....650 903-9791
2925 Bayview Dr Fremont (94538) ***(G-2478)***
Pyramid Peak Corporation....949 769-8600
450 Nwport Ctr Dr Ste 650 Newport Beach (92660) ***(G-12338)***
Pyramid Produce Inc....661 366-5736
12826 Edison Hwy Bakersfield (93307) ***(G-679)***
Pyro Spectaculars Inc....510 632-4516
1438 141st Ave San Leandro (94578) ***(G-19264)***
Pyro-Comm Systems Inc (PA)....714 902-8000
15531 Container Ln Huntington Beach (92649) ***(G-2692)***

Q Analysts LLC (PA) 408 907-8500
5201 Great America Pkwy # 238 Santa Clara (95054) ***(G-27604)***
Q B C, Los Angeles *Also called Qualified Blling Cllctions LLC* ***(G-14043)***
Q C Poultry, Commerce *Also called Ingenue Inc* ***(G-459)***
Q L P Inc 805 579-0440
2285 Ward Ave Simi Valley (93065) ***(G-7466)***
Q S H Properties Inc 714 957-9200
2701 Hotel Ter Santa Ana (92705) ***(G-13115)***
Q S I, South San Francisco *Also called Quality Systems Installations* ***(G-3573)***
Q S San Luis Obispo LP 805 541-5001
1631 Monterey St San Luis Obispo (93401) ***(G-13116)***
Q T C, Diamond Bar *Also called Qtc Management Inc* ***(G-23038)***
Q-See, Anaheim *Also called Digital Periph Solutions Inc* ***(G-16879)***
Qad Inc (PA) 805 566-6000
100 Innovation Pl Santa Barbara (93108) ***(G-15821)***
Qal Affiliate Inc 408 238-5111
2680 S White Rd Ste 150 San Jose (95148) ***(G-11781)***
Qantas Vctons Nwmans Vacations, Los Angeles *Also called Stella Travel Services USA Inc* ***(G-4974)***
Qasource, Pleasanton *Also called Raico Inc* ***(G-15406)***
Qbe First Insurance Agency Inc 949 206-6200
9800 Muirlands Blvd Irvine (92618) ***(G-10847)***
Qc (us) International Inc 559 447-1390
205 E Rver Pk Cir Ste 310 Fresno (93720) ***(G-27186)***
Qc Wall Systems, Rancho Murieta *Also called Energy Store of California Inc* ***(G-2219)***
Qct LLC 510 270-6111
1010 Rincon Cir San Jose (95131) ***(G-16035)***
Qlm Consulting Inc 415 331-9292
2400 Bridgeway Ste 290 Sausalito (94965) ***(G-27605)***
Qmadix Inc 818 988-4300
14350 Arminta St Panorama City (91402) ***(G-7622)***
Qre Operating LLC 213 225-5900
707 Wilshire Blvd # 4600 Los Angeles (90017) ***(G-1066)***
Qtc Management Inc (HQ) 909 396-6902
21700 Copley Dr Ste 200 Diamond Bar (91765) ***(G-23038)***
Quad Knopf Inc (PA) 559 733-0440
901 E Main St Visalia (93292) ***(G-26026)***
Quad/Graphics Inc 916 371-9500
1201 Shore St West Sacramento (95691) ***(G-13903)***
Quad/Graphics Inc 949 930-5400
15342 Graham St Huntington Beach (92649) ***(G-18248)***
Quadion LLC 714 546-0994
17651 Armstrong Ave Irvine (92614) ***(G-10176)***
Quadra Productions Inc 310 244-1234
10202 Washington Blvd Culver City (90232) ***(G-18137)***
Quadrant Components Inc 510 656-9988
46567 Fremont Blvd Fremont (94538) ***(G-7177)***
Quadrix Information Tech Inc 424 603-2140
10736 Jefferson Blvd # 132 Culver City (90230) ***(G-28027)***
Quadrixit, Culver City *Also called Quadrix Information Tech Inc* ***(G-28027)***
Quagga Corporation 916 357-5129
90 Blue Ravine Rd 200a Folsom (95630) ***(G-1984)***
Quail Engineering Inc 714 636-0612
11372 Trask Ave Ste 110 Garden Grove (92843) ***(G-1847)***
Quail H Farms LLC 209 394-8001
5301 Robin Ave Livingston (95334) ***(G-31)***
Quail Hill Investments Inc 408 978-9000
1124 Meridian Ave San Jose (95125) ***(G-12270)***
Quail Lodge Inc 831 624-1581
8205 Valley Greens Dr Carmel (93923) ***(G-13117)***
Quail Park 559 624-3500
4520 W Cypress Ave Visalia (93277) ***(G-21097)***
Quail Park Retirement Village, Visalia *Also called Quail Park* ***(G-21097)***
Quail Ridge Senior Living, Grass Valley *Also called Grass Valley LLC* ***(G-24673)***
Quails Inn Motel, San Marcos *Also called San Marcos Caterers Inc* ***(G-13206)***
Quailty Inn of Barstow, Barstow *Also called Darensburg Roghair & Renier* ***(G-12563)***
QUAKER GARDENS, Stanton *Also called California Friends Homes* ***(G-24577)***
Quaker Oats Company 714 526-8800
2501 E Orangethorpe Ave Fullerton (92831) ***(G-4618)***
Quaker Pet Group Inc 415 721-7400
160 Mitchell Blvd San Rafael (94903) ***(G-9295)***
Qualcomm Innovation Center Inc (HQ) 858 587-1121
4365 Executive Dr # 1100 San Diego (92121) ***(G-15822)***
Qualcomm International Inc (HQ) 858 587-1121
5775 Morehouse Dr San Diego (92121) ***(G-12221)***
Qualfax Inc 562 988-1272
3605 Long Beach Blvd # 428 Long Beach (90807) ***(G-17436)***
Qualified Benefits Inc 818 594-4900
21021 Ventura Blvd # 100 Woodland Hills (91364) ***(G-10848)***
Qualified Blling Cllctions LLC 323 556-3470
4601 Wilshire Blvd Fl 3 Los Angeles (90010) ***(G-14043)***
Quality Auto Craft Inc 925 426-0120
3295 Bernal Ave Ste B Pleasanton (94566) ***(G-17812)***
Quality Carriers Inc 800 282-2031
5042 Cecelia St South Gate (90280) ***(G-4248)***
Quality Childrens Services, Fallbrook *Also called Quality Childrens Services* ***(G-24506)***
Quality Childrens Services 760 723-3228
710 S Stage Coach Ln Fallbrook (92028) ***(G-24506)***
Quality Claims Management Corp 619 450-8600
2763 Camino Del Rio S San Diego (92108) ***(G-10849)***
Quality Coast Incorporated 619 443-9192
2462 Main St Ste H Chula Vista (91911) ***(G-14400)***
Quality Conservation Svcs Inc 650 266-9490
264 Michelle Ct South San Francisco (94080) ***(G-28158)***
Quality Construction, Tarzana *Also called Zohar Construction Inc* ***(G-1288)***
Quality Electrical Services, Costa Mesa *Also called Edward Straling* ***(G-2580)***
Quality Group Homes Inc 916 930-0066
250 Dos Rios St Ste A1 Sacramento (95811) ***(G-1240)***
Quality Home Loans 818 206-6600
27001 Agoura Rd Ste 200 Agoura Hills (91301) ***(G-9891)***
Quality Hotel Airport, Arcadia *Also called Goodrich Lax A Cal Ltd Partnr* ***(G-12670)***
Quality In-Hmecare Specialists 530 303-3477
1166 Broadway Ste T Placerville (95667) ***(G-22544)***
Quality Inn, San Diego *Also called San Diego Farah Partners* ***(G-13195)***
Quality Investment Santa Clara 408 844-6000
2807 Mission College Blvd Santa Clara (95054) ***(G-16174)***
Quality Laminating, Pacoima *Also called Phillips Plywood Co Inc* ***(G-6946)***
Quality Loan Service Corp 619 645-7711
411 Ivy St San Diego (92101) ***(G-12202)***
Quality Long Term Care Nev Inc 818 361-0191
14122 Hubbard St Sylmar (91342) ***(G-20860)***
Quality Management, Stanford *Also called Stanford Health Care* ***(G-21931)***
Quality Marine, Los Angeles *Also called Allaquaria LLC* ***(G-9243)***
Quality Planning Corporation 415 369-0707
388 Market St Ste 750 San Francisco (94111) ***(G-27606)***
Quality Plumbing Associates 831 775-0655
28 Quail Run Cir Ste F Salinas (93907) ***(G-2333)***
Quality Plus Auto Parts Inc 619 424-9991
1333 30th St Ste C San Diego (92154) ***(G-6756)***
Quality Production Svcs Inc 310 406-3350
3730 Skypark Dr Torrance (90505) ***(G-2960)***
Quality Reinforcing Inc 858 748-8400
13275 Gregg St Poway (92064) ***(G-3396)***
Quality Speaks LLC 818 264-4400
9221 Corbin Ave Ste 260 Northridge (91324) ***(G-16254)***
Quality Suites Hotel, Santa Ana *Also called Q S H Properties Inc* ***(G-13115)***
Quality Systems Inc (PA) 949 255-2600
18111 Von Karman Ave # 700 Irvine (92612) ***(G-15823)***
Quality Systems Installations 650 875-9000
212 Shaw Rd Ste 3 South San Francisco (94080) ***(G-3573)***
Quality Techniques Engrg Cnstr, Rocklin *Also called Quality Telecom Consultants* ***(G-1985)***
Quality Telecom Consultants (PA) 916 315-0500
3740 Cincinnati Ave Rocklin (95765) ***(G-1985)***
Quality Temp Staffing, Granada Hills *Also called Siracusa Enterprises Inc* ***(G-14786)***
Quality Towing, Ontario *Also called United Road Towing Inc* ***(G-17904)***
Quality Wall Systems Inc 951 739-4409
104 S Maple St Corona (92880) ***(G-2961)***
Qualstaff Resources, San Diego *Also called June Group LLC* ***(G-14891)***
Qualys Inc (PA) 650 801-6100
1600 Bridge Pkwy Ste 201 Redwood City (94065) ***(G-15404)***
Quanta Computer Usa Inc (HQ) 510 226-1371
45630 Northport Loop E Fremont (94538) ***(G-7178)***
Quantcast Corporation (PA) 415 738-4755
201 3rd St Ste 2 San Francisco (94103) ***(G-14007)***
Quantos Payroll, Los Angeles *Also called Film Payroll Services Inc* ***(G-26350)***
Quantum Properties LP 619 582-3800
5550 University Ave San Diego (92105) ***(G-21825)***
Quantum Secure Inc 408 453-1008
100 Century Center Ct # 800 San Jose (95112) ***(G-16036)***
Quantum Solutions Inc 818 577-4555
5146 Douglas Fir Rd # 205 Calabasas (91302) ***(G-16466)***
Quantum Technologies Inc 949 399-4500
25242 Arctic Ocean Dr Lake Forest (92630) ***(G-1049)***
Quantumscape Corporation 408 452-2051
1730 Technology Dr San Jose (95110) ***(G-27607)***
Quarry At La Quinta Inc (PA) 760 777-1100
41865 Boardwalk Ste 214 Palm Desert (92211) ***(G-18774)***
Quarry Collection, Huntington Beach *Also called GBI Tile & Stone Inc* ***(G-6985)***
Quartus Engineering Inc (PA) 858 875-6000
10251 Vista Sorrento Pkwy # 250 San Diego (92121) ***(G-26027)***
Qubera Solutions Inc 650 294-4460
676 Gail Ave Apt 26 Sunnyvale (94086) ***(G-16467)***
Quechan Gaming Commission, Winterhaven *Also called Quechan Indian Tribe* ***(G-19265)***
Quechan Indian Tribe 760 572-2413
350 Picacho Rd Winterhaven (92283) ***(G-19265)***
Queen Anne Early Education Ctr, Los Angeles *Also called Los Angeles Unified School Dst* ***(G-24478)***
Queen Mary Hotel, Long Beach *Also called RMS Foundation Inc* ***(G-13164)***
Queen Mary, The, Long Beach *Also called Save Queen LLC* ***(G-13221)***
Queen of Angels Hollywood Pres 213 413-3000
1300 N Vermont Ave Los Angeles (90027) ***(G-21826)***
Queen of The Valley Campus, West Covina *Also called Citrus Vly Hlth Partners Inc* ***(G-19439)***
Queen of The Valley Hospital, West Covina *Also called Citrus Valley Medical Ctr Inc* ***(G-21490)***
Queen of Valley Hospital 626 962-4011
1115 S Sunset Ave West Covina (91790) ***(G-25152)***
Queen of Valley Medical Center (HQ) 707 252-4411
1000 Trancas St NAPA (94558) ***(G-21827)***
Queensbay Hotel LLC 562 481-3910
700 Queensway Dr Long Beach (90802) ***(G-13118)***
Queenscare Fmly Clinics-Eastsd, Los Angeles *Also called Queenscare Health Centers* ***(G-19902)***
Queenscare Health Centers 323 780-4510
4816 E 3rd St Los Angeles (90022) ***(G-19902)***
Queenscare Health Centers 323 644-6180
4618 Fountain Ave Los Angeles (90029) ***(G-19903)***
Quercus Ranch, Kelseyville *Also called BT Holdings Inc* ***(G-229)***
Quest Components Inc 626 333-5858
14711 Clark Ave City of Industry (91745) ***(G-7623)***
Quest Dgnstics Clncal Labs Inc 408 975-1015
2369 Bering Dr San Jose (95131) ***(G-22264)***
Quest Dgnstics Clncal Labs Inc 661 964-6582
26081 Avenue Hall 150 Valencia (91355) ***(G-22265)***

Quest Diagn Nichols Inst Valen, Valencia *Also called Specialty Laboratories Inc* ***(G-22286)***
Quest Diagnostics, West Hills *Also called Unilab Corporation* ***(G-22292)***
Quest Diagnostics Incorporated....925 687-2514
401 Gregory Ln Ste 146 Pleasant Hill (94523) ***(G-22266)***
Quest Diagnostics Incorporated....949 728-4235
33608 Ortega Hwy Mission Viejo (92675) ***(G-22267)***
Quest Diagnostics Incorporated....559 438-2893
1275 E Spruce Ave Ste 102 Fresno (93720) ***(G-22268)***
Quest Discovery Services Inc....310 769-5557
1515 W 190th St Ste 410 Gardena (90248) ***(G-14929)***
Quest Group (PA)....949 585-0111
2621 White Rd Irvine (92614) ***(G-8134)***
Quest Intl Monitor Svc Inc (PA)....949 581-9900
65 Parker Irvine (92618) ***(G-16304)***
Quest Media & Supplies Inc (PA)....916 338-7070
5822 Roseville Rd Sacramento (95842) ***(G-16037)***
Quest Transportation Inc....805 545-8400
241b Prado Rd San Luis Obispo (93401) ***(G-27764)***
Questus Inc (PA)....415 677-5700
675 Davis St San Francisco (94111) ***(G-16175)***
Quetico LLC....909 628-6200
5521 Schaefer Ave Chino (91710) ***(G-9296)***
Quick Quack Car Wash (PA)....888 772-2792
6505 Fair Oaks Blvd Carmichael (95608) ***(G-27187)***
Quick-N-Ezee Indian Foods, Hayward *Also called Jagpreet Enterprises Inc* ***(G-8860)***
Quickhealth Inc....650 286-1986
9 41st Ave San Mateo (94403) ***(G-27188)***
Quicksilver Delivery Inc....415 431-1600
129 Kissling St San Francisco (94103) ***(G-17437)***
Quicksilver Delivery Service, San Francisco *Also called Quicksilver Delivery Inc* ***(G-17437)***
Quicksort Inc (PA)....925 820-8272
100 Ryan Industrial Ct San Ramon (94583) ***(G-17438)***
Quicksort Bus Mailing Svcs, San Ramon *Also called Quicksort Inc* ***(G-17438)***
Quigly-Simpson Heppelwhite Inc....818 444-3450
11601 Wilshire Blvd Los Angeles (90025) ***(G-13904)***
Quik Pick Express LLC....310 763-3000
1021 E 233rd St Carson (90745) ***(G-5157)***
Quiksilver Inc....714 893-5187
15202 Graham St Huntington Beach (92649) ***(G-8358)***
Quincy Family Medicine, Quincy *Also called Plumas District Hospital* ***(G-19876)***
Quinn Company....562 463-4000
3500 Shepherd Dr City of Industry (90601) ***(G-7878)***
Quinn Company....818 767-7171
13275 Golden State Rd Sylmar (91342) ***(G-7780)***
Quinn Company....661 393-5800
2200 Pegasus Dr Bakersfield (93308) ***(G-7781)***
Quinn Company....805 485-2171
801 Del Norte Blvd Oxnard (93030) ***(G-7782)***
Quinn Company....805 925-8611
1655 Carlotti Dr Santa Maria (93454) ***(G-7783)***
Quinn Emanuel Urquhart....415 875-6600
50 California St Fl 22 San Francisco (94111) ***(G-23523)***
Quinn Emanuel Urquhart....650 801-5000
555 Twin Dolphin Dr Fl 5 Redwood City (94065) ***(G-23524)***
Quinn Emanuel Urquhart (PA)....213 443-3000
865 S Figueroa St Fl 10 Los Angeles (90017) ***(G-23525)***
Quinn Group Inc....805 485-2171
801 Del Norte Blvd Oxnard (93030) ***(G-7806)***
Quinn Group Inc....661 393-5800
2200 Pegasus Dr Bakersfield (93308) ***(G-7807)***
Quinn Group Inc....831 758-8461
1300 Abbott St Salinas (93901) ***(G-7784)***
Quinn Lift Inc....831 758-4086
1300 Abbott St Salinas (93901) ***(G-7879)***
Quinn Shepherd Machinery....562 463-6000
10006 Rose Hills Rd City of Industry (90601) ***(G-7785)***
Quinstreet Inc (PA)....650 578-7700
950 Tower Ln Ste 600 Foster City (94404) ***(G-17439)***
Quintiles Pacific Incorporated (HQ)....650 567-2000
448 E Middlefield Rd Mountain View (94043) ***(G-26700)***
Quiring Corporation....559 432-2800
5118 E Clinton Way # 201 Fresno (93727) ***(G-1642)***
Quiring General LLC....559 432-2800
5118 E Clinton Way # 201 Fresno (93727) ***(G-1643)***
Quiringeneral, Fresno *Also called Quiring Corporation* ***(G-1642)***
Quixote Mm LLC....323 851-5030
1011 N Fuller Ave Ste B West Hollywood (90046) ***(G-18249)***
Quixote Production Vehicles, West Hollywood *Also called Quixote Studios LLC* ***(G-14573)***
Quixote Studios LLC (PA)....323 851-5030
1011 N Fuller Ave West Hollywood (90046) ***(G-14573)***
Quixote Studios LLC....818 252-7722
11473 Penrose St Sun Valley (91352) ***(G-17707)***
Qumu Inc....650 396-8530
1100 Grundy Ln Ste 110 San Bruno (94066) ***(G-15824)***
Quora Inc....650 485-2464
261 Hamilton Ave Ste 212 Palo Alto (94301) ***(G-16255)***
Quotient Technology Inc (PA)....650 605-4600
400 Logue Ave Mountain View (94043) ***(G-14008)***
Quova Inc....650 965-2898
401 Castro St Fl 3 Mountain View (94041) ***(G-28028)***
Quovera Inc (PA)....650 691-0114
788 Stone Ln Palo Alto (94303) ***(G-28029)***
Quovera Inc....949 224-3825
19800 Macarthur Blvd Irvine (92612) ***(G-28030)***
Qupid Shoe, Walnut *Also called East Lion Corporation* ***(G-8433)***
Quri Inc....888 886-8423
475 Brannan St Ste 400 San Francisco (94107) ***(G-26701)***
Qw Media International LLC....949 200-4616
620 Newport Center Dr # 11 Newport Beach (92660) ***(G-13977)***
Qwest Corporation....213 612-0193
624 S Grand Ave Ste 315 Los Angeles (90017) ***(G-5689)***
Qwest Corporation....925 974-4908
1350 Treat Blvd Ste 200 Walnut Creek (94597) ***(G-5690)***
R & A Painting Inc....916 688-3955
11730 Sheldon Lake Dr Elk Grove (95624) ***(G-2479)***
R & B Realty Group....323 851-3450
3600 Barham Blvd Los Angeles (90068) ***(G-11191)***
R & B Realty Group....818 710-5400
22122 Victory Blvd Woodland Hills (91367) ***(G-11192)***
R & B Realty Group....310 751-4545
4111 Via Marina Marina Del Rey (90292) ***(G-11193)***
R & B Realty Group LP....310 478-1021
2222 Corinth Ave Los Angeles (90064) ***(G-11782)***
R & B Reinforcing Steel Corp....909 591-1726
13581 5th St Chino (91710) ***(G-3397)***
R & B Wholesale Distrs Inc (PA)....909 230-5400
2350 S Milliken Ave Ontario (91761) ***(G-7510)***
R & D Leasing Inc....559 924-1276
19101 Kent Ave Lemoore (93245) ***(G-14574)***
R & G Enterprises....559 781-1351
155 N D St Porterville (93257) ***(G-500)***
R & N Packing Co....209 364-6101
47920 W Nees Ave Firebaugh (93622) ***(G-575)***
R & R Electric....310 785-0288
2029 Century Park E A4 Los Angeles (90067) ***(G-2693)***
R & R Maher Cnstr Co Inc....707 552-0330
1324 Lemon St Vallejo (94590) ***(G-1848)***
R & R Mechanical Contrs Inc....619 449-9900
9330 Stevens Rd Ste A Santee (92071) ***(G-2334)***
R & R Profession....760 754-9020
2216 S El Camino Real # 211 Oceanside (92054) ***(G-20345)***
R & S Floor Covering, Riverside *Also called R&S Carpet Services Inc* ***(G-6883)***
R & V Management Corporation....619 429-3305
768 Hollister St San Diego (92154) ***(G-27189)***
R A F LP....714 633-1442
1702 Fairhaven Ave Santa Ana (92705) ***(G-13711)***
R A Greene Corporation....760 747-0810
1234 Industrial Ave Escondido (92029) ***(G-2962)***
R A Schreiber Plumbing....619 659-3101
2358 Tavern Rd Alpine (91901) ***(G-2335)***
R and L Lopez Associates Inc (PA)....626 336-9655
3649 Tyler Ave El Monte (91731) ***(G-26028)***
R and R Labor Inc....831 638-0290
710 Kirkpatric Ct Hollister (95023) ***(G-680)***
R and R Prof Hlthcare Staffing, Santa Clarita *Also called Oceanside Hlthcare Stffing Inc* ***(G-23011)***
R and R Professional Medical, Oceanside *Also called R & R Profession* ***(G-20345)***
R B Spencer Inc....530 674-8307
1188 Hassett Ave Yuba City (95991) ***(G-2336)***
R C H, San Francisco *Also called Pomeroy Rcrtion Rhbltation Ctr* ***(G-24139)***
R C Hotels Inc....714 891-0123
7667 Center Ave Huntington Beach (92647) ***(G-13119)***
R C I Enterprises Inc....310 370-5900
3848 Del Amo Blvd Ste 301 Torrance (90503) ***(G-7347)***
R C I Image Systems, Torrance *Also called R C I Enterprises Inc* ***(G-7347)***
R C O Reforesting Inc....530 842-7647
1332 Fairlane Rd Ste A Yreka (96097) ***(G-1016)***
R C Roberts & Co (PA)....415 456-8600
801 A St San Rafael (94901) ***(G-11245)***
R D S Unlimited Inc....619 443-0221
14372 Olde Highway 80 E El Cajon (92021) ***(G-3077)***
R DS For Healthcare....209 333-2115
1420 W Kettleman Ln N5 Lodi (95242) ***(G-20346)***
R E Cuddie Co....408 998-1250
1751 Junction Ave San Jose (95112) ***(G-3129)***
R E Maher Inc....707 642-3907
4545 Hess Rd American Canyon (94503) ***(G-3317)***
R F Macdonald Co (PA)....510 784-0110
25920 Eden Landing Rd Hayward (94545) ***(G-7880)***
R F R Corporation....800 346-7663
3310 Verdugo Rd Los Angeles (90065) ***(G-12004)***
R Fellen Inc....559 233-6248
2939 S Peach Ave Fresno (93725) ***(G-20861)***
R G Canning Enterprises Inc....323 560-7469
4515 E 59th Pl Maywood (90270) ***(G-17440)***
R G Vanderweil Engineers LLP....562 256-8623
3760 Kilroy Airport Way # 230 Long Beach (90806) ***(G-26029)***
R H D, Corona *Also called Ranch House Doors Inc* ***(G-6954)***
R H Framing Incorporated....831 759-8860
1000 Pajaro St Ste Bb Salinas (93901) ***(G-3078)***
R H O Capital Partners Inc....650 463-0300
525 University Ave # 1350 Palo Alto (94301) ***(G-12339)***
R H Phillips Inc (HQ)....530 757-5557
26836 County Road 12a Esparto (95627) ***(G-176)***
R H Phillips Vineyard, Esparto *Also called R H Phillips Inc* ***(G-176)***
R Haupt Roofing Construction....310 515-9709
1305 W 132nd St Fl 2 Gardena (90247) ***(G-3205)***
R J Dailey Construction Co....650 948-5196
401 1st St Los Altos (94022) ***(G-1241)***
R J M Construction Inc....909 794-8853
224 Donna Dr Redlands (92374) ***(G-1644)***
R K I, Union City *Also called Rki Instruments Inc* ***(G-7884)***
R K Properties, Long Beach *Also called Rance King Properties Inc* ***(G-11194)***
R L G, San Mateo *Also called Research Libraries Group Inc* ***(G-16258)***
R L Jones-San Diego Inc (PA)....760 357-3177
1778 Zinetta Rd Ste A Calexico (92231) ***(G-5158)***
R L Jones-San Diego Inc....760 357-0140
1778 Zinetta Rd Ste A1 Calexico (92231) ***(G-5159)***

A L P H A B E T I C

R L Klein & Associates ALPHABETIC SECTION

R L Klein & Associates 562 427-5577
3553 Atlantic Ave Ste A Long Beach (90807) ***(G-14930)***
R L Safety Inc 408 557-0887
2157 Cherrystone Dr San Jose (95128) ***(G-24143)***
R L T, Redding *Also called Redding Lumber Transport Inc* ***(G-4372)***
R M A Group Inc (PA) 909 980-6096
12130 Santa Margarita Ct Rancho Cucamonga (91730) ***(G-26030)***
R M B Packaging Co Inc 818 998-0658
9667 Canoga Ave Chatsworth (91311) ***(G-9297)***
R M B SEC Cnslting Invstgtions, Fountain Valley *Also called Bell Private Security Inc* ***(G-16574)***
R M Harris Company Inc 925 335-3000
1000 Howe Rd Ste 200 Martinez (94553) ***(G-1898)***
R M S Car Movers Corp 310 325-2192
24632 Maple Ln Harbor City (90710) ***(G-4052)***
R Marchini' Enterprises, Le Grand *Also called Martini Inc* ***(G-207)***
R Mc Closkey Insurance Agency 949 223-8100
4001 Macarthur Blvd # 300 Newport Beach (92660) ***(G-10850)***
R Mora Farm Labor 661 746-2858
930 5th St Wasco (93280) ***(G-681)***
R N D Enterprises, Lancaster *Also called BDR Industries Inc* ***(G-5935)***
R Navarro Landscape Services 562 690-6414
359 West Rd La Habra Heights (90631) ***(G-940)***
R P Direct, Santa Monica *Also called Postaer Rubin and Associates* ***(G-13899)***
R P S Resort Corp 760 327-8311
1600 N Indian Canyon Dr Palm Springs (92262) ***(G-13120)***
R Q Construction Inc 760 477-1199
3194 Lionshead Ave Carlsbad (92010) ***(G-1459)***
R Q Construction LLC 760 631-7707
3194 Lionshead Ave Carlsbad (92010) ***(G-1460)***
R R Donnelley & Sons Company 925 901-5300
5000 Executive Pkwy Ste 2 San Ramon (94583) ***(G-8177)***
R R Donnelley Coml Press Plant, San Diego *Also called RR Donnelley & Sons Company* ***(G-8154)***
R Ranch Market 714 573-1182
1112 Walnut Ave Tustin (92780) ***(G-470)***
R S A Laboratories, Santa Clara *Also called Rsa Security LLC* ***(G-15431)***
R S I Insurance Brokers Inc (PA) 714 546-6616
2801 Bristol St Ste 200 Costa Mesa (92626) ***(G-10851)***
R S Investments LLC 415 591-2700
1 Bush St Fl 9 San Francisco (94104) ***(G-10177)***
R S P, Commerce *Also called Rolled Steel Products Corp* ***(G-7399)***
R S Software India Limited 408 382-1200
1900 Mccarthy Blvd # 103 Milpitas (95035) ***(G-16468)***
R Stanley Security Service 661 634-9283
403 18th St Bakersfield (93301) ***(G-16769)***
R Systems Inc (HQ) 916 939-9696
5000 Windplay Dr Ste 5 El Dorado Hills (95762) ***(G-16469)***
R T A, Riverside *Also called Riverside Transit Agency* ***(G-3692)***
R T Framing Corporation 805 496-3985
299 W Hillcrest Dr # 212 Thousand Oaks (91360) ***(G-3079)***
R T I, Sunnyvale *Also called Real-Time Innovations Inc* ***(G-15410)***
R W Garcia Co Inc (PA) 408 275-1597
521 Parrott St San Jose (95112) ***(G-8625)***
R W Lyall & Company Inc (HQ) 951 270-1500
2665 Research Dr Corona (92882) ***(G-1067)***
R W Zant Co (PA) 323 980-5457
1470 E 4th St Los Angeles (90033) ***(G-8679)***
R&S Carpet Services Inc 909 740-6645
1485 Spruce St Ste C106 Riverside (92507) ***(G-6883)***
R-Bros Painting Inc 408 291-6820
707 W Hedding St San Jose (95110) ***(G-2480)***
R2c Group, San Francisco *Also called Respond 2 LLC* ***(G-18143)***
R2g Enterprises Inc 510 489-6218
31154 San Benito St Hayward (94544) ***(G-3206)***
R3 Strategic Support Group Inc 800 418-2040
1050 B Ave Ste A Coronado (92118) ***(G-27608)***
Ra Hughes Enterprises Inc 619 390-4880
9316 Abraham Way Santee (92071) ***(G-2337)***
RABBIT HAVEN THE, Scotts Valley *Also called Ava The Rabbit Haven Inc* ***(G-27843)***
Rabin Worldwide Inc 415 522-5700
21 Locust Ave 2a Mill Valley (94941) ***(G-17441)***
Rabobank National Association 831 422-6642
301 Main St Salinas (93901) ***(G-9518)***
Race Street Fish & Poultry, San Jose *Also called Race Street Foods Inc* ***(G-8603)***
Race Street Foods Inc (PA) 408 294-6161
1130 Olinder Ct San Jose (95122) ***(G-8603)***
Racelegal Com 619 265-8159
315 4th Ave Chula Vista (91910) ***(G-25568)***
Racquet Club of Irvine 949 786-3000
5 Ethel Coplen Way Ste 5 Irvine (92612) ***(G-19032)***
Racquetball World, Canoga Park *Also called Bay Clubs Inc* ***(G-18884)***
Radar Medical Systems Inc 440 337-9521
1510 Cotner Ave Los Angeles (90025) ***(G-28159)***
Radford Alexander Corporation 310 523-2555
14700 S Avalon Blvd Gardena (90248) ***(G-4053)***
Radford Studio Center Inc 818 655-5000
4024 Radford Ave Studio City (91604) ***(G-18428)***
Radiabeam Technologies LLC 310 822-5845
1717 Stuart St Santa Clara (95054) ***(G-26799)***
Radiant Logic Inc (PA) 415 209-6800
75 Rowland Way Ste 300 Novato (94945) ***(G-15405)***
Radiant Services Corp (PA) 310 327-6300
651 W Knox St Gardena (90248) ***(G-13506)***
Radica Enterprises Ltd 310 252-2000
333 Continental Blvd El Segundo (90245) ***(G-8052)***
Radica USA, El Segundo *Also called Radica Enterprises Ltd* ***(G-8052)***
Radio Disney, Burbank *Also called Walt Disney Company* ***(G-5830)***
Radio Disney Kdiz AM, Burbank *Also called Minneapolis Radio Assets LLC* ***(G-5810)***
Radio Station, Los Angeles *Also called Loyola Marymount University* ***(G-5809)***
RADIO STATION KFBS, La Mirada *Also called Far East Broadcasting Co Inc* ***(G-5774)***
Radiology Department Cal Hosp 213 742-5840
1338 S Hope St Fl 4 Los Angeles (90015) ***(G-19904)***
Radiometer America Inc (HQ) 800 736-0600
250 S Kraemer Blvd Brea (92821) ***(G-7310)***
Radison Hotel Newport Beach, Newport Beach *Also called Pacific Hotel Management Inc* ***(G-13061)***
Radisson Hotel La Westside, Culver City *Also called Pacifica Hotel & Conference Ce* ***(G-13066)***
Radisson Hotel Sacramento, Sacramento *Also called Pd Hotel Associates LLC* ***(G-13083)***
Radisson Hotel Santa Maria, Santa Maria *Also called Santa Maria Airport Regency* ***(G-13215)***
Radisson Hotel Whittier, Whittier *Also called Greenleaf Hotel Inc* ***(G-12678)***
Radisson Ht Fishermans Wharf 415 392-6700
250 Beach St San Francisco (94133) ***(G-13121)***
Radisson Inn, Los Angeles *Also called Pacifica Hosts Inc* ***(G-13065)***
Radisson Inn, Berkeley *Also called Boykin Mgt Co Ltd Lblty Co* ***(G-12460)***
Radisson Inn, Sunnyvale *Also called S R H H Inc* ***(G-13183)***
Radisson Inn, San Diego *Also called Rancho Bernardo Partners Ltd* ***(G-13127)***
Radisson Inn, Union City *Also called Interstate Hotels Resorts Inc* ***(G-12852)***
Radisson Inn, Agoura Hills *Also called Ww Lbv Inc* ***(G-13432)***
Radisson Inn, Los Angeles *Also called Lax Hospitality LP* ***(G-12908)***
Radisson Inn, Los Angeles *Also called Radlax Gateway Hotel LLC* ***(G-13123)***
Radisson Inn, San Bernardino *Also called First Hotels International Inc* ***(G-12636)***
Radisson Plaza Hotel Inn, San Jose *Also called Silicon Valley Hwang LLC* ***(G-13255)***
Radisson Suites Hotel Buena Pk 714 739-5600
7762 Beach Blvd Buena Park (90620) ***(G-13122)***
Radiumone Inc (PA) 415 418-2840
55 2nd St Ste 1800 San Francisco (94105) ***(G-27765)***
Radix Textile Inc 213 623-6006
819 Towne Ave Los Angeles (90021) ***(G-8322)***
Radlax Gateway Hotel LLC 310 670-9000
6225 W Century Blvd Los Angeles (90045) ***(G-13123)***
Radleys 310 765-2223
3780 Wilshire Blvd Los Angeles (90010) ***(G-18138)***
Radnet Inc 562 216-5137
2708 E Willow St Signal Hill (90755) ***(G-19905)***
Radnet Inc (PA) 310 445-2800
1510 Cotner Ave Los Angeles (90025) ***(G-22269)***
Radnet Management Inc 209 524-6800
157 E Coolidge Ave Modesto (95350) ***(G-27190)***
Radnet Management Inc 323 549-3000
8750 Wilshire Blvd # 100 Beverly Hills (90211) ***(G-27191)***
Radonich Corp 408 275-8888
886 Faulstich Ct San Jose (95112) ***(G-2694)***
Rady Childrens Hosp & Hlth Ctr (PA) 858 576-1700
3020 Childrens Way San Diego (92123) ***(G-22163)***
Rady Chld Hospital-San Diego 858 966-6795
8001 Frost St San Diego (92123) ***(G-22164)***
Rady Chld Hospital-San Diego (PA) 858 576-1700
3020 Childrens Way San Diego (92123) ***(G-22165)***
Rady Chld Hospital-San Diego 858 966-5833
8022 Birmingham Dr # 22 San Diego (92123) ***(G-27192)***
Rady Chld Hospital-San Diego 858 576-5803
3020 Childrens Way San Diego (92123) ***(G-22166)***
Rady Chld Physcn MGT Svcs Inc 619 262-3415
292 Euclid Ave San Diego (92114) ***(G-19906)***
Rafael Convalescent Hospital 415 479-3450
234 N San Pedro Rd San Rafael (94903) ***(G-21354)***
Raffles Lrmitage Beverly Hills 310 278-3344
9291 Burton Way Beverly Hills (90210) ***(G-13124)***
Raging Waters San Dimas 703, San Dimas *Also called Festival Fun Parks LLC* ***(G-8018)***
Raging Wire, Sacramento *Also called Ragingwire Data Centers Inc* ***(G-16282)***
Ragingwire Data Centers Inc (HQ) 916 286-3000
1200 Striker Ave Sacramento (95834) ***(G-16282)***
Rahmati Consulting Group, Newport Beach *Also called Rcg International* ***(G-28036)***
Rai Care Ctrs Nthrn Cal II LLC 415 206-9775
1750 Cesar Chavez Ste A San Francisco (94124) ***(G-22636)***
Rai Csar Chvez St-San Frncisco, San Francisco *Also called Rai Care Ctrs Nthrn Cal II LLC* ***(G-22636)***
Raico Inc 925 271-5555
73 Ray St Pleasanton (94566) ***(G-15406)***
Rail Delivery Services Inc 909 355-4100
8600 Banana Ave Fontana (92335) ***(G-4054)***
Railex LLC 661 370-4300
2121 S Browning Rd Delano (93215) ***(G-5160)***
Railpros Inc (PA) 714 734-8765
1 Ada Ste 200 Irvine (92618) ***(G-26031)***
Railpros Field Services 877 315-0513
1 Ada Ste 200 Irvine (92618) ***(G-17442)***
Railroad Technology, Sacramento *Also called Macdonald Mott LLC* ***(G-25948)***
Rain Creek Baking, Madera *Also called Kronos Foods Corp* ***(G-8871)***
Rainbow - Brite Indus Svcs LLC 559 925-2580
16998 Kent Ave Lemoore (93245) ***(G-14401)***
Rainbow Camp Inc 310 456-3066
26619 Marigold Ct Calabasas (91302) ***(G-19266)***
Rainbow Childrens Academy Inc 310 672-2400
1213 Centinela Ave Inglewood (90302) ***(G-24507)***
Rainbow Disposal Co Inc (HQ) 714 847-3581
17121 Nichols Ln Huntington Beach (92647) ***(G-6517)***
Rainbow Farms, Denair *Also called Valley Fresh Foods Inc* ***(G-449)***
Rainbow Home Care Services 714 544-8070
202 Fashion Ln Ste 118 Tustin (92780) ***(G-22545)***
Rainbow Municipal Water Dst 760 728-1178
3707 Old Highway 395 Fallbrook (92028) ***(G-6388)***

ALPHABETIC

Rainbow Networking.....650 377-0913
688 Matsonia Dr Foster City (94404) *(G-16176)*
Rainbow Properties Inc.....323 562-0730
4812 Ostrom Ave Lakewood (90713) *(G-11783)*
Rainbow Ranches Inc.....661 858-2266
13650 Copus Rd Bakersfield (93313) *(G-386)*
Rainbow Realty Corporation.....949 770-9626
24221 Paseo De Valencia Laguna Woods (92637) *(G-11784)*
Rainbow Refuse Recycling, Huntington Beach *Also called Rainbow Disposal Co Inc (G-6517)*
Rainbow Transfer Recycling.....714 847-5818
17121 Nichols Ln Huntington Beach (92647) *(G-6518)*
Rainbow Wtrprofing Restoration.....415 641-1578
600 Treat Ave San Francisco (94110) *(G-3574)*
Raines Law Group LLP.....310 440-4100
9720 Wilshire Blvd Fl 5 Beverly Hills (90212) *(G-23526)*
Rainier Financial Group LLC.....310 335-9200
2321 Rosecrans Ave # 4270 El Segundo (90245) *(G-17443)*
Rainmaker Systems Inc.....408 659-1800
1821 S Bascom Ave 385 Campbell (95008) *(G-27193)*
Raintree Convalescent Hospital, Fresno *Also called Nia Healthcare Services Inc (G-20806)*
Raintree Systems Inc.....951 252-9400
27307 Via Industria Temecula (92590) *(G-15407)*
Raiser Senior Services LLC.....650 342-4106
601 Laurel Ave Apt 903 San Mateo (94401) *(G-24776)*
Raison D'Etre Bakery, South San Francisco *Also called Ashbury Market Inc (G-8802)*
Rakon America LLC.....847 930-5100
7600 Dublin Blvd Dublin (94568) *(G-7624)*
Rakstar Production, Los Angeles *Also called Entertainment & Sports Today (G-5854)*
Raleigh Enterprises Inc.....323 466-3111
5300 Melrose Ave Fl 3 Los Angeles (90038) *(G-18250)*
Raleigh Enterprises Inc (PA).....310 899-8900
5300 Melrose Ave Fl 4 Los Angeles (90038) *(G-13125)*
Raleigh Holdings, Los Angeles *Also called Raleigh Enterprises Inc (G-13125)*
Raleigh Studios, Los Angeles *Also called Raleigh Enterprises Inc (G-18250)*
Ralis Services Corp.....844 347-2547
1 City Blvd W Ste 600 Orange (92868) *(G-17444)*
Ralph Collazo Packing Inc.....760 353-0856
72 E Main St Ste A Heber (92249) *(G-17445)*
Ralph D Mitzel Inc.....714 554-4745
1520 N Fairview St Santa Ana (92706) *(G-14495)*
Ralph S Distribution Center, Riverside *Also called Ralphs Grocery Company (G-4620)*
Ralph Wilson Plastics, Santa Fe Springs *Also called Wilsonart LLC (G-4671)*
Ralphs 00131, Huntington Beach *Also called Ralphs Grocery Company (G-4627)*
Ralphs 00134, Glendale *Also called Ralphs Grocery Company (G-4619)*
Ralphs 00173, Downey *Also called Ralphs Grocery Company (G-4625)*
Ralphs 00664, Ventura *Also called Ralphs Grocery Company (G-4624)*
Ralphs 6, Encino *Also called Ralphs Grocery Company (G-4623)*
Ralphs 96, Pasadena *Also called Ralphs Grocery Company (G-4626)*
Ralphs Grocery Company.....818 549-0035
211 N Glendale Ave Glendale (91206) *(G-4619)*
Ralphs Grocery Company.....310 884-9000
1500 Eastridge Ave Riverside (92507) *(G-4620)*
Ralphs Grocery Company.....310 637-1101
4841-45 San Fernando W Los Angeles (90039) *(G-4621)*
Ralphs Grocery Company.....562 633-0830
13525 Lakewood Blvd Downey (90242) *(G-4622)*
Ralphs Grocery Company.....818 345-6882
17840 Ventura Blvd Encino (91316) *(G-4623)*
Ralphs Grocery Company.....805 650-0239
1776 S Victoria Ave Ventura (93003) *(G-4624)*
Ralphs Grocery Company.....562 869-2042
9200 Lakewood Blvd Downey (90240) *(G-4625)*
Ralphs Grocery Company.....626 793-7480
160 N Lake Ave Pasadena (91101) *(G-4626)*
Ralphs Grocery Company.....714 377-0024
5241 Warner Ave Huntington Beach (92649) *(G-4627)*
Ram Commercial Enterprises Inc.....916 429-1205
5896 S Land Park Dr Sacramento (95822) *(G-11785)*
Ram Mechanical Inc.....209 531-9155
3506 Moore Rd Ceres (95307) *(G-2338)*
Ram-Mar Painting Inc.....760 949-4844
11768 Mariposa Rd Hesperia (92345) *(G-18002)*
Ramada Clock Tower Inn, Ventura *Also called Clocktower Inn (G-12529)*
Ramada Inn, Fresno *Also called Fresno Hotel Partners LP (G-12655)*
Ramada Inn, Sunnyvale *Also called Executive Inn Inc (G-12628)*
Ramada Inn, San Diego *Also called Royal Hospitality Incorporated (G-13172)*
Ramada Inn, San Diego *Also called Trigild International Inc (G-13360)*
Ramada Inn, Hawthorne *Also called Calhot Illinios LLC (G-12480)*
Ramada Inn, Redondo Beach *Also called D & W LLC (G-12562)*
Ramada Inn, Santa Ana *Also called East Katella Partnership (G-12606)*
Ramada Inn Fresno Airport, Fresno *Also called Fresno Airport Hotels LLC (G-12654)*
Ramada Inn University, Fresno *Also called Shaw Hospitality Group Inc (G-13238)*
Ramada Plaza Ht Anaheim Resort.....714 991-6868
515 W Katella Ave Anaheim (92802) *(G-13126)*
Ramada Plz Ht San Dego/ Ht Cir, San Diego *Also called G5 Global Partners Ix LLC (G-12656)*
Ramboll Environ US Corporation.....949 798-3604
18100 Von Karman Ave # 600 Irvine (92612) *(G-28031)*
Ramboll Environ US Corporation.....510 655-7400
2200 Powell St Ste 700 Emeryville (94608) *(G-28032)*
Ramboll Environ US Corporation.....949 261-5151
18100 Von Karman Ave # 600 Irvine (92612) *(G-28033)*
Ramcar Batteries Inc.....323 726-1212
2700 Carrier Ave Commerce (90040) *(G-6757)*
Ramco Employment Services, Oxnard *Also called Ramco Enterprises LP (G-576)*
Ramco Enterprises LP.....805 922-9888
325 Plaza Dr Ste 1 Santa Maria (93454) *(G-14741)*
Ramco Enterprises LP.....831 722-3370
585 Auto Center Dr Watsonville (95076) *(G-14742)*
Ramco Enterprises LP.....805 486-9328
520 E 3rd St Ste B Oxnard (93030) *(G-576)*
Ramkade Insurance Services.....818 444-1340
21550 Oxnard St Ste 500 Woodland Hills (91367) *(G-10852)*
Ramona Care Center Inc.....626 442-5721
11900 Ramona Blvd El Monte (91732) *(G-20862)*
Ramona Community Services Corp (HQ).....951 658-9288
890 W Stetson Ave Ste A Hemet (92543) *(G-22546)*
Ramona Rehabilitation and Post.....951 652-0011
485 W Johnston Ave Hemet (92543) *(G-20863)*
Ramona Vna & Hospice, Hemet *Also called Ramona Community Services Corp (G-22546)*
Ramos Oil Co Inc (PA).....916 371-2570
1515 S River Rd West Sacramento (95691) *(G-9008)*
Ramos Orchards.....530 795-4748
9192 Boyce Rd Winters (95694) *(G-208)*
Rams, San Francisco *Also called Richmond Area Mlt-Services Inc (G-22816)*
Rams Hill Country Club.....760 767-4259
1881 Rams Hill Rd Borrego Springs (92004) *(G-19033)*
Ramsell Public Health Rx LLC.....510 587-2600
200 Webster St Ste 300 Oakland (94607) *(G-10853)*
Ramsey-Shilling Residential RE.....323 851-5512
3360 Barham Blvd Los Angeles (90068) *(G-11786)*
Ramsgate Engineering Inc.....661 392-0050
2331 Cepheus Ct Bakersfield (93308) *(G-26032)*
Rance King Properties Inc (PA).....562 240-1000
3737 E Broadway Long Beach (90803) *(G-11194)*
Ranch At Laguna Beach, The, Laguna Beach *Also called Laguna Bch Golf Bnglow Vlg LLC (G-468)*
Ranch At Little Hills, The, San Ramon *Also called Concessionaires Urban Park (G-19191)*
Ranch Golf Club.....408 270-0557
4601 Hill Top View Ln San Jose (95138) *(G-18775)*
Ranch Hand Entertainment Inc.....612 396-2632
11333 Moorpark St Pmb 441 Studio City (91602) *(G-18139)*
Ranch House Doors Inc.....951 278-2884
1527 Pomona Rd Corona (92880) *(G-6954)*
Ranch Winery The, Saint Helena *Also called E & J Gallo Winery (G-27900)*
Ranching Shop, Corcoran *Also called J G Boswell Company (G-13)*
Rancho Bernardo Golf Club.....858 487-1134
17550 Bernardo Oaks Dr San Diego (92128) *(G-19034)*
Rancho Bernardo Partners Ltd.....858 451-6600
11520 W Bernardo Ct San Diego (92127) *(G-13127)*
Rancho California Landscaping.....310 768-1680
13801 S Western Ave Gardena (90249) *(G-941)*
Rancho California Water Dst (PA).....951 296-6900
42135 Winchester Rd Temecula (92590) *(G-1986)*
Rancho Ccamonga Cmnty Hosp LLC.....909 581-6400
10841 White Oak Ave Rancho Cucamonga (91730) *(G-21828)*
Rancho Clinic Rancho San Diego, La Mesa *Also called Scripps Health (G-19973)*
Rancho Cordova Medical Offices, Rancho Cordova *Also called Kaiser Foundation Hospitals (G-21658)*
Rancho Cucamonga Family YMCA, Rancho Cucamonga *Also called West End Yung MNS Christn Assn (G-25402)*
Rancho Cucamonga Medical Offs, Rancho Cucamonga *Also called Kaiser Foundation Hospitals (G-19598)*
Rancho Cucamonga Sport Club, Rancho Cucamonga *Also called 24 Hour Fitness Usa Inc (G-18586)*
Rancho De Sus Ninos Inc.....619 661-9232
P.O. Box 360 Potrero (91963) *(G-24777)*
Rancho Del Oro Ldscp Maint Inc.....760 726-0215
4167 Avenida De La Plata Oceanside (92056) *(G-791)*
Rancho Foods Inc.....323 585-0503
2528 E 37th St Vernon (90058) *(G-8680)*
Rancho Jurupa Park.....951 684-7032
4800 Crestmore Rd Riverside (92509) *(G-19267)*
Rancho La Quinta Country Club, La Quinta *Also called TD Desert Dev Ltd Partnr (G-12018)*
Rancho Laguna Farms Inc.....805 925-7805
2410 W Main St Santa Maria (93458) *(G-387)*
Rancho Leonero Resort.....760 438-2905
5671 Palmer Way Ste E Carlsbad (92010) *(G-13128)*
Rancho Los Amigos Nationa.....562 401-7111
7601 Imperial Hwy Downey (90242) *(G-24144)*
Rancho Los Amigos Nationa.....562 401-7111
7601 Imperial Hwy Downey (90242) *(G-24145)*
Rancho Los Amigos Nationa.....310 940-7266
12852 Erickson Ave Downey (90242) *(G-24146)*
Rancho Los Amigos Nationa (PA).....562 401-7111
7601 Imperial Hwy Downey (90242) *(G-24147)*
Rancho Murieta Country Club.....916 354-2400
7000 Alameda Dr Rancho Murieta (95683) *(G-19035)*
Rancho Niguel Dental Group.....949 249-4180
30140 Town Center Dr Laguna Niguel (92677) *(G-20272)*
Rancho Pacific Electric Inc.....909 476-1022
201 W State St Ontario (91762) *(G-2695)*
Rancho Penasquitos Sport Club, San Diego *Also called 24 Hour Fitness Usa Inc (G-18599)*
Rancho Physical Therapy Inc.....760 752-1011
277 Rancheros Dr San Marcos (92069) *(G-20347)*
Rancho Physical Therapy Inc (PA).....951 696-9353
24630 Washington Ave # 200 Murrieta (92562) *(G-20348)*
Rancho Research Institute.....562 401-8111
7601 Imperial Hwy Downey (90242) *(G-26800)*
Rancho Salinas Packing Inc.....831 758-3624
2376 Alisal Rd Salinas (93908) *(G-682)*
Rancho San Antonio Boys HM Inc (PA).....818 882-6400
21000 Plummer St Chatsworth (91311) *(G-24778)*

Rancho San Antonio Medical Ctr, Rancho Cucamonga *Also called San Antonio Community Hospital* ***(G-21843)***
Rancho San Antonio Retirement 650 265-2637
23500 Cristo Rey Dr Cupertino (95014) ***(G-24779)***
Rancho San Diego Cinema 16, El Cajon *Also called Edwards Theatres Circuit Inc* ***(G-18323)***
Rancho San Diego Medical Offs, La Mesa *Also called Kaiser Foundation Hospitals* ***(G-19622)***
Rancho San Joaquin Golf Course, Irvine *Also called American Golf Corporation* ***(G-18853)***
Rancho Santa Ana Botanic Grdn 909 625-8767
1500 N College Ave Claremont (91711) ***(G-25068)***
Rancho Santa Fe Association A 858 756-1182
5827 Viadelacumere Rancho Santa Fe (92067) ***(G-19036)***
Rancho Santa Fe Protective Svc 760 433-8887
1991 Village Park Way # 100 Encinitas (92024) ***(G-16770)***
Rancho Sante Fe Golf Club, Rancho Santa Fe *Also called Rancho Santa Fe Association A* ***(G-19036)***
Rancho Speciality Hospital, Rancho Cucamonga *Also called Rancho Ccamonga Cmnty Hosp LLC* ***(G-21828)***
Rancho Springs Medical Center, Murrieta *Also called Southwest Healthcare Sys Aux* ***(G-21910)***
Rancho Valencia Resort 858 756-1123
5921 Valencia Cir Rancho Santa Fe (92067) ***(G-13129)***
Rancho Vista Health Center 760 941-1480
760 E Bobier Dr Vista (92084) ***(G-21098)***
Rancho West Landscape 951 301-3979
39140 Pala Vista Dr Temecula (92591) ***(G-942)***
Rancho Wholesale, Chino *Also called Redwood Products Chino Inc* ***(G-6955)***
Ranchwood Contractors Inc 209 826-6200
923 E Pacheco Blvd Los Banos (93635) ***(G-1645)***
Rancon Real Estate Corporation (PA) 951 677-1800
27740 Jefferson Ave # 100 Temecula (92590) ***(G-11787)***
Rand Medical Billing Inc 805 578-8300
1633 Erringer Rd Fl 1 Simi Valley (93065) ***(G-26430)***
Rand Technology LLC (PA) 949 255-5700
15225 Alton Pkwy Unit 100 Irvine (92618) ***(G-7625)***
Randall Foods Inc 323 587-2383
2905 E 50th St Bldg 12 Vernon (90058) ***(G-8604)***
Randall Mc-Anany Company 310 822-3344
4935 Mcconnell Ave Ste 20 Los Angeles (90066) ***(G-2481)***
Randall-Bold Wtr Trtmnt Plant, Oakley *Also called Contra Costa Water District* ***(G-6334)***
Randazzo Enterprises Inc 831 633-4420
13550 Blackie Rd Castroville (95012) ***(G-3465)***
Rando AAA Hvac Inc 408 293-4717
1712 Stone Ave Ste 1 San Jose (95125) ***(G-2339)***
Random Holdings Inc 949 722-7103
1599 Superior Ave Ste A1 Costa Mesa (92627) ***(G-27194)***
Randstad Finance & Accounting, Burlingame *Also called Randstad Professionals Us LP* ***(G-14744)***
Randstad North America Inc 559 297-0054
7014 N Cedar Ave Fresno (93720) ***(G-14743)***
Randstad North America Inc 559 582-2700
106 E 7th St Hanford (93230) ***(G-14931)***
Randstad North America Inc 559 592-6700
1110 W Visalia Rd Ste 116 Exeter (93221) ***(G-14932)***
Randstad North America Inc 415 397-3384
27 Maiden Ln Ste 202 San Francisco (94108) ***(G-14933)***
Randstad Professionals Us LP 650 343-5111
111 Anza Blvd Ste 202 Burlingame (94010) ***(G-14744)***
Randstad Technologies LP 619 798-7300
8880 Rio San Diego Dr # 107 San Diego (92108) ***(G-16470)***
Range Generation Next LLC 310 647-9438
105 13th St Bldg 6525 Vandenberg Afb (93437) ***(G-26033)***
Range Generation Next LLC 310 647-9438
Pillar Point Air Sta El Granada (94018) ***(G-28034)***
Rangel Drywall Inc 209 525-9490
1401 S 7th St Modesto (95351) ***(G-2963)***
Ranger Pipelines Incorporated 415 822-3700
1790 Yosemite Ave San Francisco (94124) ***(G-1987)***
Ranker Inc 323 782-1448
6420 Wilshire Blvd # 880 Los Angeles (90048) ***(G-13905)***
Ranscapes Inc 866 883-9297
30 Hughes Ste 209 Irvine (92618) ***(G-14402)***
Ransome Company 510 686-9900
1933 Williams St San Leandro (94577) ***(G-1646)***
Raphaels Party Rentals Inc (PA) 858 444-1692
8606 Miramar Rd San Diego (92126) ***(G-14575)***
Rapid Armada SEC Svcs Rass LLC 909 609-4370
6774 Kaiser Ave Fontana (92336) ***(G-16771)***
Rapid Product Dev Group Inc 760 703-5770
300 W Grand Ave Escondido (92025) ***(G-28035)***
Rapid Solutions Consulting LLC 801 755-7828
1900 S Norfolk St Ste 350 San Mateo (94403) ***(G-15408)***
Rapp Worldwide Inc 310 563-7200
12777 W Jefferson Blvd Los Angeles (90066) ***(G-13906)***
Raptor Pharmaceutical Corp (PA) 415 408-6200
7 Hamilton Landing # 100 Novato (94949) ***(G-26801)***
Ras, Sacramento *Also called Mark H Leibenhaut MD* ***(G-19731)***
Ras Management Inc (PA) 510 727-1800
4545 Crow Canyon Pl Castro Valley (94552) ***(G-4628)***
Rashman Corporation 818 993-3030
8600 Wilbur Ave Northridge (91324) ***(G-7980)***
Ratcliff Architects 510 899-6400
5856 Doyle St Emeryville (94608) ***(G-26244)***
Rate Is Low 925 299-9364
3744 Mt Diablo Blvd # 205 Lafayette (94549) ***(G-9892)***
Raul Acevedo 559 791-1304
1638 W Castle Ave Porterville (93257) ***(G-997)***
Rava Ranches Inc 831 385-3285
700 Airport Rd King City (93930) ***(G-471)***
Raven Biotechnologies Inc 650 624-2600
1 Corporate Dr South San Francisco (94080) ***(G-26594)***
Ravenswood Family Health, East Palo Alto *Also called South Cnty Cmnty Hlth Ctr Inc* ***(G-23060)***
Ravenswood Solutions Inc 650 241-3661
3065 Skyway Ct Fremont (94539) ***(G-16038)***
Rawitser Golf Shop Mike 408 441-4653
1560 Oakland Rd San Jose (95131) ***(G-18776)***
Rawlings Mechanical Corp (PA) 323 875-2040
11615 Pendleton St Sun Valley (91352) ***(G-2340)***
Rax Inc 858 715-2500
12220 Parkway Centre Dr Poway (92064) ***(G-8026)***
Ray A Morgan Company 925 400-4160
7042 Commerce Cir Ste A Pleasanton (94588) ***(G-15409)***
Ray Stone, Sacramento *Also called Brunswick Corner Partnership* ***(G-11330)***
Ray Stone Incorporated 530 272-5274
131 Eureka St Grass Valley (95945) ***(G-24148)***
Ray W Choi 714 783-1000
731 E Ball Rd Ste 100 Anaheim (92805) ***(G-27609)***
Rayco Electric, Rancho Cordova *Also called Rci Electric Inc* ***(G-2697)***
Raycon Construction Inc 805 525-5256
1795 E Lemonwood Dr Santa Paula (93060) ***(G-2833)***
Raycon Environmental Cnstr 805 955-0900
882 Patriot Dr Ste G Moorpark (93021) ***(G-3575)***
Raylee Electric 916 408-7556
1202 Tarapin Ln Lincoln (95648) ***(G-2696)***
Raymond Brown Company, San Francisco *Also called Walter E McGuire RE Inc* ***(G-11908)***
Raymond Group (PA) 714 771-7670
520 W Walnut Ave Orange (92868) ***(G-27195)***
Raymond Handling Concepts Corp (PA) 510 745-7500
41400 Boyce Rd Fremont (94538) ***(G-18003)***
Raymond Handling Solutions Inc (HQ) 562 944-8067
9939 Norwalk Blvd Santa Fe Springs (90670) ***(G-7881)***
Raymond Handling Solutions Inc 909 930-9399
1945 Burgundy Pl Ontario (91761) ***(G-7882)***
Rayner Equipment Systems, Sacramento *Also called California Pavement Maint Inc* ***(G-1745)***
Raytheon Command and Control 714 446-3232
2000 E El Segundo Blvd El Segundo (90245) ***(G-7626)***
Raytheon Company 626 304-1007
300 N Lake Ave Ste 1120 Pasadena (91101) ***(G-17940)***
Raytheon Company 858 455-9741
9985 Pcf Hts Blvd Ste 200 San Diego (92121) ***(G-26034)***
Raytheon Company 310 647-9438
2000 E El Segundo Blvd El Segundo (90245) ***(G-26035)***
Raytheon Company 805 562-2941
75 Coromar Dr Goleta (93117) ***(G-17446)***
Raytheon Company 760 386-2572
988 Inner Loop Rd Fort Irwin (92310) ***(G-17941)***
Razavi Corporation 619 465-8010
7979 La Mesa Blvd La Mesa (91942) ***(G-20864)***
Razor USA LLC (PA) 562 345-6000
12723 166th St Cerritos (90703) ***(G-8027)***
Razorgator Inc (PA) 310 481-3400
4094 Glencoe Ave Ste A Marina Del Rey (90292) ***(G-19268)***
RB Anglers Club 858 487-6484
12578 Cresta Pl San Diego (92128) ***(G-19037)***
Rbb Architects Inc (PA) 310 479-1473
10980 Wilshire Blvd Los Angeles (90024) ***(G-26245)***
Rbc Wealth Management 310 273-7600
9665 Wilshire Blvd Fl 4 Beverly Hills (90212) ***(G-10072)***
Rbd Hotel Palm Springs LLC 760 322-1383
285 N Palm Canyon Dr Palm Springs (92262) ***(G-13130)***
Rbf Consulting 951 676-8042
40810 County Center Dr # 100 Temecula (92591) ***(G-26036)***
RC Construction Services, Rialto *Also called Robert Clapper Cnstr Svcs Inc* ***(G-1653)***
RC Packing LLC 831 675-0308
26769 El Camino Real Gonzales (93926) ***(G-501)***
RC Wendt Painting Inc 714 960-2700
21612 Surveyor Cir Huntington Beach (92646) ***(G-2482)***
RCA Properties, Paso Robles *Also called RE Max Parkside Real Estate* ***(G-11790)***
Rcac, West Sacramento *Also called Rural Cmnty Assistance Corp* ***(G-24161)***
Rcb Corporation (PA) 916 567-2600
2485 Natomas Park Dr # 100 Sacramento (95833) ***(G-9519)***
Rcc Facility Incorporated 510 658-2041
210 40th Street Way Oakland (94611) ***(G-21355)***
Rcg International 714 956-7027
4570 Campus Dr Ste 100 Newport Beach (92660) ***(G-28036)***
Rci, Irvine *Also called Racquet Club of Irvine* ***(G-19032)***
Rci Electric Inc 916 858-8000
3144 Fitzgerald Rd Rancho Cordova (95742) ***(G-2697)***
RCM Capital Management LLC (HQ) 415 954-5400
555 Mission St Ste 1700 San Francisco (94105) ***(G-10073)***
RCM Capital Management LLC 415 364-2327
555 Mission St Ste 1700 San Francisco (94105) ***(G-10178)***
Rcr Companies, Riverside *Also called Rcr Plumbing and Mech Inc* ***(G-2341)***
Rcr Plumbing and Mech Inc (PA) 951 371-5000
12620 Magnolia Ave Riverside (92503) ***(G-2341)***
Rcs World Travel, Ventura *Also called Registration Ctrl Systems Inc* ***(G-17449)***
Rcsn Inc 714 965-0244
10221 Slater Ave Ste 214 Fountain Valley (92708) ***(G-14745)***
Rcwd, Temecula *Also called Rancho California Water Dst* ***(G-1986)***
Rdi Engineering, Monterey Park *Also called Roque Development and Inv Inc* ***(G-26044)***
Rdl Reference Laboratory, Los Angeles *Also called Rheumatology Diagnostics Lab* ***(G-22274)***
RDM Electric Co Inc 909 591-0990
13867 Redwood Ave Chino (91710) ***(G-2698)***

ALPHABETIC

Rdo Construction Equipment Co.....619 443-3758
10108 Riverford Rd Lakeside (92040) *(G-14496)*
Rdo Construction Equipment Co.....951 778-3700
20 Iowa Ave Riverside (92507) *(G-7786)*
Rdo Vermeer LLC.....916 643-0999
3980 Research Dr Sacramento (95838) *(G-7787)*
Rdp Acquisition Company.....510 652-8187
5929 College Ave Oakland (94618) *(G-26702)*
Rdr Builders LP.....209 368-7561
1806 W Kettleman Ln Ste F Lodi (95242) *(G-1335)*
Rdr Production Builders, Lodi *Also called Rdr Builders LP (G-1335)*
RE Barren Ridge 1 LLC.....415 675-1500
300 California St Fl 7 San Francisco (94104) *(G-6197)*
RE Infolink, Sunnyvale *Also called Mlslistings Inc (G-27551)*
RE La Mesa LLC.....415 675-1500
300 California St Fl 8 San Francisco (94104) *(G-2078)*
RE Max 2000 Realty, City of Industry *Also called Leon Chien Corp (G-9869)*
RE Max Advantage.....800 247-4200
648 Yerington Ln Lincoln (95648) *(G-11788)*
RE Max All Cities Lk Arrowhead.....909 337-6111
28200 Highway 189 Lake Arrowhead (92352) *(G-11789)*
RE Max Parkside Real Estate.....805 239-3310
711 12th St Paso Robles (93446) *(G-11790)*
RE Max Westlake Investments, Daly City *Also called Casbn Investment Inc (G-11345)*
RE Milano Plumbing Corp.....925 500-1372
4881 Sunrise Dr Ste B Martinez (94553) *(G-2342)*
RE Mohican LLC.....415 675-1500
300 California St Fl 8 San Francisco (94104) *(G-2079)*
RE Santa Clara LLC.....415 675-1500
300 California St Fl 8 San Francisco (94104) *(G-2080)*
Re/Max, Westlake Village *Also called Remax Olson (G-11808)*
Re/Max, Los Alamitos *Also called College Park Realty Inc (G-11441)*
Re/Max, San Diego *Also called Remax Ranch Beach (G-11809)*
Re/Max, Sacramento *Also called Remax Gold (G-11806)*
Re/Max, Yorba Linda *Also called Yorba Properties Corp (G-11930)*
Re/Max, Irvine *Also called J Baron Inc (G-11593)*
Re/Max, Ventura *Also called Evans/Sipes Inc (G-11497)*
Re/Max, Lincoln *Also called RE Max Advantage (G-11788)*
Re/Max, Cypress *Also called Riphagen & Bullerdick Inc (G-11814)*
Re/Max, Winnetka *Also called Clayton Place Associates Inc (G-11396)*
Re/Max, Folsom *Also called Norcal Gold Inc (G-11713)*
Re/Max, Costa Mesa *Also called Remax Metro Inc (G-11807)*
Re/Max.....661 616-4040
201 New Stine Rd Ste 300 Bakersfield (93309) *(G-11791)*
Re/Max LLC.....303 770-5531
1071 E 16th St Upland (91784) *(G-11792)*
Re/Max Beach Cities Realty Mar.....310 376-2225
400 S Sepulveda Blvd # 100 Manhattan Beach (90266) *(G-11793)*
Re/Max Magic.....661 616-4040
11420 Ming Ave Ste 530 Bakersfield (93311) *(G-11794)*
Re/Max Plos Vrdes Rlty / Exces.....310 541-5224
450 Silver Spur Rd Rancho Palos Verdes (90275) *(G-11795)*
Re/Maxcc, Walnut Creek *Also called C C Connection Inc (G-11335)*
Reach Fitness Club.....650 327-3224
1235 Radio Rd Ste 120 Redwood City (94065) *(G-18673)*
Reach Removal Inc.....916 447-9679
8989 Elder Creek Rd Sacramento (95829) *(G-3207)*
Reaching For Independence Inc.....707 725-9010
609 14th St Fortuna (95540) *(G-24966)*
Reachlocal Inc (HQ).....818 274-0260
21700 Oxnard St Ste 1600 Woodland Hills (91367) *(G-13907)*
Reading and Beyond.....559 840-1068
4670 E Butler Ave Fresno (93702) *(G-25326)*
Reading Entertainment Inc (HQ).....213 235-2226
500 Citadel Dr Ste 300 Commerce (90040) *(G-18343)*
Reading International Inc.....951 696-7045
41090 California Oaks Rd Murrieta (92562) *(G-18344)*
Reading International Inc.....858 207-2606
11620 Carmel Mountain Rd San Diego (92128) *(G-18345)*
Reading International Inc.....916 442-0985
2508 Land Park Dr Sacramento (95818) *(G-18346)*
Reading International Inc (PA).....213 235-2240
6100 Center Dr Ste 900 Los Angeles (90045) *(G-18347)*
Reading Partners (PA).....510 444-9800
180 Grand Ave Ste 800 Oakland (94612) *(G-25569)*
Reading Partners.....408 945-5720
600 Valley Way Milpitas (95035) *(G-24149)*
Ready Roast Nut Company LLC (PA).....559 661-1696
2805 Falcon Dr Madera (93637) *(G-577)*
Readylink Healthcare.....760 343-7000
72030 Metroplex Dr Thousand Palms (92276) *(G-14746)*
Real Branding LLC.....415 522-1516
77 Maiden Ln Fl 4 San Francisco (94108) *(G-13908)*
Real Estate California Dept.....951 715-0130
3737 Main St Ofc Riverside (92501) *(G-11796)*
Real Estate Digital LLC.....800 234-2139
27081 Aliso Creek Rd # 200 Aliso Viejo (92656) *(G-17447)*
Real Estate Image.....714 502-3900
1415 S Acacia Ave Fullerton (92831) *(G-14088)*
Real Estate Law Center PC.....213 201-6384
695 S Vt Ave Ste 1100 Los Angeles (90005) *(G-11036)*
Real Property Systems Inc.....760 243-1143
1443 E Washington Blvd Pasadena (91104) *(G-11797)*
Real Software Systems LLC (PA).....818 313-8000
21255 Burbank Blvd # 220 Woodland Hills (91367) *(G-15825)*
Real Time Logic Inc.....858 812-7300
4820 Estgate Mall Ste 200 San Diego (92121) *(G-16039)*
Real Time Staffing Services.....805 882-2200
3820 State St Ste A Santa Barbara (93105) *(G-14747)*
Real-Time Innovations Inc.....408 990-7400
232 E Java Dr Sunnyvale (94089) *(G-15410)*
Really Likeable People Inc.....760 431-5577
2251 Las Palmas Dr Carlsbad (92011) *(G-8444)*
Realogy Holdings Corp.....707 284-1111
3554 Round Barn Blvd Santa Rosa (95403) *(G-11798)*
Realtor Sfr Green.....858 488-4090
4090 Mission Blvd San Diego (92109) *(G-11799)*
Realty Alliance Inc.....818 610-0080
20812 Ventura Blvd # 101 Woodland Hills (91364) *(G-9947)*
Realty Executives, Escondido *Also called J & P Financial Inc (G-9931)*
Realty Income Corporation (PA).....858 284-5000
11995 El Camino Real San Diego (92130) *(G-12271)*
Realty One Group Inc.....951 565-8105
19322 Jesse Ln Riverside (92508) *(G-11800)*
Realty One Group Solution, Stevenson Ranch *Also called King Monster Inc (G-11621)*
Realty World, Wheatland *Also called Wheatland School District (G-11920)*
Reaume and Associates Inc.....310 398-5768
11527 W Washington Blvd Los Angeles (90066) *(G-26037)*
Reaume, E M & Associates, Los Angeles *Also called Reaume and Associates Inc (G-26037)*
Rebar Engineering Inc.....562 946-2461
10706 Painter Ave Santa Fe Springs (90670) *(G-3398)*
Rebecca Terley.....562 925-4252
9028 Rose St Bellflower (90706) *(G-20865)*
Rebekah Children's Services, Gilroy *Also called Odd Fellow-Rebekah Chld HM Cal (G-24751)*
Rebekah Children's Services, Salinas *Also called Odd Fellow-Rebekah Chld HM Cal (G-24752)*
Rec Center.....415 831-6818
501 Stanyan St San Francisco (94117) *(G-8028)*
Rec Solar Commercial Corp.....844 732-7652
3450 Broad St Ste 105 San Luis Obispo (93401) *(G-1988)*
Reche Canyon Convalescent Ctr.....909 370-4411
1350 Reche Canyon Rd Colton (92324) *(G-21356)*
Reche Cyn Regional Rehab Ctr, Colton *Also called Reche Cyn Rhblitation Hlth Ctr (G-20866)*
Reche Cyn Rhabilation Hlth Ctr, Colton *Also called Reche Canyon Convalescent Ctr (G-21356)*
Reche Cyn Rhblitation Hlth Ctr.....909 370-4411
1350 Reche Canyon Rd Colton (92324) *(G-20866)*
Recology Cleanscapes.....415 626-5685
2265 Revere Ave San Francisco (94124) *(G-14403)*
Recology Inc (PA).....415 875-1000
50 California St Fl 24 San Francisco (94111) *(G-6519)*
Recology Inc.....415 330-1300
Tunnel Ave And Beatty Rd San Francisco (94134) *(G-6520)*
Recology Inc.....916 379-3300
245 N 1st St Dixon (95620) *(G-6521)*
Recology Inc.....415 970-1582
100 Cargo Way San Francisco (94124) *(G-6522)*
Recology Inc.....530 533-5868
2720 S 5th Ave Oroville (95965) *(G-6523)*
Recology Inc.....415 330-1400
501 Tunnel Ave San Francisco (94134) *(G-6524)*
Recology Inc., Sun Valley *Also called Recology Los Angeles (G-6526)*
Recology Los Altos.....650 961-8044
650 Martin Ave Santa Clara (95050) *(G-6525)*
Recology Los Angeles.....415 875-1140
9189 De Garmo Ave Sun Valley (91352) *(G-6526)*
Recology San Francisco.....415 468-1752
501 Tunnel Ave San Francisco (94134) *(G-6527)*
Recology San Mateo County.....650 595-3900
225 Shoreway Rd San Carlos (94070) *(G-6528)*
Recology South Bay.....408 725-4020
650 Martin Ave Santa Clara (95050) *(G-6529)*
Recology South Valley (HQ).....408 842-3358
1351 Pacheco Pass Hwy Gilroy (95020) *(G-6530)*
Recology Sunset Scavenger, San Francisco *Also called Sunset Scavenger Company (G-6566)*
Recology Sustainable Crushing, San Francisco *Also called Recology Inc (G-6522)*
Recology Vacaville Solano.....707 448-2945
1 Town Sq Ste 200 Vacaville (95688) *(G-6531)*
Recology Vallejo.....707 552-3110
2021 Broadway St Vallejo (94589) *(G-6532)*
Recology Yuba-Sutter.....530 743-6933
3001 N Levee Rd Marysville (95901) *(G-6533)*
Recon Environmental Inc (PA).....520 325-9977
1927 5th Ave Ste 200 San Diego (92101) *(G-28037)*
Records Center/Storage, Oakland *Also called San Francisco Bay Area Rapid (G-3702)*
Recovery Place Inc.....954 200-8308
5000 E Spring St Ste 650 Long Beach (90815) *(G-22167)*
Recovery Solutions Santa Ana, Santa Ana *Also called CRC Health Corporate (G-22717)*
Recp Cy Oxnard LLC.....805 604-7527
600 E Esplanade Dr Oxnard (93036) *(G-13131)*
Recp Rl Oxnard LLC.....805 278-2200
2101 W Vineyard Ave Oxnard (93036) *(G-13132)*
Recp/Wndsor Scramento Ventr LP.....916 455-6800
4422 Y St Sacramento (95817) *(G-13133)*
Recreation Complex, South Lake Tahoe *Also called City of South Lake Tahoe (G-19181)*
Recreation Dept, Coronado *Also called City of Coronado (G-19169)*
Recreation Park Golf Course 18, Long Beach *Also called American Golf Corporation (G-18858)*
Recreational Equipment Inc.....650 969-1938
2450 Charleston Rd Mountain View (94043) *(G-7224)*
Recreational Equipment Inc.....760 479-0128
1590 Leucadia Blvd Encinitas (92024) *(G-7225)*

ALPHABETIC

Recreational Equipment Inc
ALPHABETIC SECTION

Recreational Equipment Inc ... 909 646-8360
12218 Foothill Blvd Rancho Cucamonga (91739) *(G-7226)*
Recreational Equipment Inc ... 209 957-9479
5757 Pacific Ave Ste A105 Stockton (95207) *(G-7227)*
Recurrent Energy LLC (HQ) ... 415 956-3168
300 California St Fl 7 San Francisco (94104) *(G-2343)*
Recurrent Engy Dev Hldngs LLC (HQ) ... 415 675-1500
300 California St Fl 7 San Francisco (94104) *(G-12340)*
Recurve Inc ... 510 540-4860
220 Montgomery St Ste 820 San Francisco (94104) *(G-17923)*
Recycle Waste, Santa Clara *Also called Mission Trail Wste Systems Inc (G-4041)*
Recycled Wood Products, Pomona *Also called Rwp Transfer Inc (G-8137)*
Recycler Core Company Inc ... 951 276-1687
2727 Kansas Ave Riverside (92507) *(G-6758)*
Recycling Industries Inc ... 916 452-3961
4741 Watt Ave North Highlands (95660) *(G-6534)*
Red and White Fleet, San Francisco *Also called Golden Gate Scnic Stmship Corp (G-4735)*
Red Blossom Farms, Salinas *Also called Red Blossom Sales Inc (G-388)*
Red Blossom Sales Inc ... 805 349-9404
865 Black Rd Santa Maria (93458) *(G-127)*
Red Blossom Sales Inc ... 831 751-9169
9 Harris Pl Salinas (93901) *(G-388)*
Red Bull Distribution Co Inc (HQ) ... 916 515-3501
1740 Stewart St Santa Monica (90404) *(G-8912)*
Red Carpet Car Wash, Visalia *Also called Bowie Enterprises (G-17831)*
Red Carpet Car Wash, Fresno *Also called Bowie Enterprises (G-17832)*
Red Carpet Car Wash, Clovis *Also called Bowie Enterprises (G-17833)*
Red Carpet Car Wash, Fresno *Also called Bowie Enterprises (G-17876)*
Red Chamber Co (PA) ... 323 234-9000
1912 E Vernon Ave Vernon (90058) *(G-8650)*
Red Condor Inc ... 707 569-7419
1300 Valley House Dr # 115 Rohnert Park (94928) *(G-15411)*
Red Door Interactive Inc (PA) ... 619 398-2670
350 10th Ave Ste 100 San Diego (92101) *(G-13909)*
Red Earth Casino, Thermal *Also called Torres-Martinez (G-13349)*
Red Earth Casino ... 760 395-1200
3089 Norm Niver Rd Thermal (92274) *(G-13134)*
Red Hawk Casino, Placerville *Also called Shingle Sprng Trbal Gming Auth (G-19282)*
Red Hawk Fire & SEC CA Inc ... 510 438-1300
4384 Enterprise Pl Fremont (94538) *(G-2699)*
Red Hawk Fire & SEC CA Inc ... 714 685-8100
1640 N Batavia St Orange (92867) *(G-2700)*
Red Hawk Fire & SEC CA Inc (HQ) ... 818 683-1500
2705 Media Center Dr Los Angeles (90065) *(G-2701)*
Red Hawk Fire & SEC CA Inc ... 760 233-9787
920 S Andreasen Dr # 102 Escondido (92029) *(G-2702)*
Red Hill Country Club ... 909 982-1358
8358 Red Hl Cntry Clb Dr Rancho Cucamonga (91730) *(G-19038)*
Red Lion Hotel Anaheim, Anaheim *Also called Red Lion Hotels Corporation (G-13135)*
Red Lion Hotel Eureka, Eureka *Also called Rl Eureka LLC (G-13161)*
Red Lion Hotel Redding, Redding *Also called Rl Redding LLC (G-13162)*
Red Lion Hotels Corporation ... 714 750-2801
1850 S Harbor Blvd Anaheim (92802) *(G-13135)*
Red Oak Technologies Inc ... 408 200-3500
2001 Gateway Pl Ste 150w San Jose (95110) *(G-16471)*
Red One - PSI Joint Ventr LLC ... 559 772-8264
310 W Murray Ave Visalia (93291) *(G-1647)*
Red Peak Group LLC ... 818 222-7762
23975 Park Sorrento # 365 Calabasas (91302) *(G-27610)*
Red Pointe Roofing LP ... 818 998-3857
9542 Topanga Canyon Blvd Chatsworth (91311) *(G-3208)*
Red Road Sobriety House ... 408 512-8474
10 Kirk Ave San Jose (95127) *(G-13455)*
Red Sky Interactive ... 415 430-3200
201 Mission St Fl 8 San Francisco (94105) *(G-13910)*
Red Storm, San Francisco *Also called Ubisoft Holdings Inc (G-15514)*
Red Tail Golf Assoc, Rancho Santa Fe *Also called Farms Golf Club Inc (G-18949)*
Red Top Rice Growers ... 530 868-5975
3200 8th St Biggs (95917) *(G-578)*
Redbarn Pet Products Inc ... 562 495-7315
3229 E Spring St Ste 310 Long Beach (90806) *(G-9298)*
Redbarn Premium Pet Products, Long Beach *Also called Redbarn Pet Products Inc (G-9298)*
Redbull Distribution Co Colo, Santa Monica *Also called Red Bull Distribution Co Inc (G-8912)*
Redding Aero Enterprises Inc ... 530 224-2300
3775 Flight Ave Ste 100 Redding (96002) *(G-3691)*
Redding Bank of Commerce (HQ) ... 530 224-7355
1951 Churn Creek Rd Redding (96002) *(G-9556)*
Redding District Office, Redding *Also called State Compensation Insur Fund (G-10465)*
Redding Drywall Systems Inc ... 530 222-8767
3092 Crossroads Dr Redding (96003) *(G-2964)*
Redding Family Medicine Assoc ... 530 244-4907
2510 Airpark Dr Ste 201 Redding (96001) *(G-19907)*
Redding Jet Center, Redding *Also called Redding Aero Enterprises Inc (G-3691)*
Redding Lumber Transport Inc ... 530 241-8193
4301 Eastside Rd Redding (96001) *(G-4372)*
Redding Medical Group, Redding *Also called David Civalier MD Inc (G-19486)*
Redding Medical Home Care, Redding *Also called Tenet Healthsystem Medical (G-22579)*
Redding Pathologists Lab (PA) ... 530 225-8050
1725 Gold St Redding (96001) *(G-19908)*
Redding Pathologists Lab ... 530 225-8050
2036 Railroad Ave Redding (96001) *(G-22270)*
Redding Rancheria (PA) ... 530 225-8979
2000 Redding Rancheria Rd Redding (96001) *(G-13136)*
Redding Rancheria ... 530 224-2700
1441 Liberty St Redding (96001) *(G-23039)*
Redding Specialty Hospital, Redding *Also called Tenet Healthsystem Medical (G-24247)*
Redding Tree Growers Corp ... 559 594-9299
18985 Avenue 256 Apt A Exeter (93221) *(G-1017)*
Redding V A Outpatient Clinic, Redding *Also called Veterans Health Administration (G-20200)*
Redding Veterans Home, The, Redding *Also called Veterans Affairs Cal Dept (G-21006)*
Redevelopment Agency of The Ci ... 707 421-7309
701 Civic Center Blvd Suisun City (94585) *(G-28038)*
Redgate Memorial Hospital, Long Beach *Also called Behavioral Health Services Inc (G-23680)*
Redhill Group Inc ... 949 752-5900
18010 Sky Park Cir # 275 Irvine (92614) *(G-26703)*
Redhill Towing & Autobody ... 415 456-8943
428 Irwin St San Rafael (94901) *(G-17890)*
Redhorse Constructors Inc ... 415 492-2020
36 Professional Ctr Pkwy San Rafael (94903) *(G-1242)*
Redhorse Corporation (PA) ... 619 241-4609
1370 India St Ste 200 San Diego (92101) *(G-27611)*
Redhorse Technical Services, San Diego *Also called Redhorse Corporation (G-27611)*
Redis Labs Inc ... 415 930-9666
700 E El Camino Real # 170 Mountain View (94040) *(G-15412)*
Redlands Cmnty Hosp Foundation ... 909 793-1382
1875 Barton Rd Redlands (92373) *(G-21357)*
Redlands Community Hospital, Redlands *Also called RHS Corp (G-27201)*
Redlands Community Hospital (PA) ... 909 335-5500
350 Terracina Blvd Redlands (92373) *(G-22168)*
Redlands Country Club ... 909 793-2661
1749 Garden St Redlands (92373) *(G-19039)*
Redlands Division, Redlands *Also called American Med (G-3742)*
Redlands Employment Services ... 951 688-0083
4295 Jurupa St Ste 110 Ontario (91761) *(G-14748)*
Redlands Foothill Groves ... 909 793-2164
304 9th St Redlands (92374) *(G-579)*
Redlands Ford Inc ... 909 793-3211
1121 W Colton Ave Redlands (92374) *(G-17770)*
Redlands Health Care Group, Redlands *Also called Plum Healthcare Group LLC (G-17419)*
Redlands Healthcare Center, Redlands *Also called Ash Holdings LLC (G-20384)*
Redlands Recycling, Riverside *Also called Riverside Scrap Ir & Met Corp (G-8081)*
Redlands Staffing Services, Ontario *Also called Redlands Employment Services (G-14748)*
Redman Container, Carson *Also called Calko Transport Company Inc (G-4333)*
Redrocks Fumigation, San Jose *Also called Homeguard Incorporated (G-14186)*
Redseal Inc ... 408 641-2200
940 Stewart Dr Ste 101 Sunnyvale (94085) *(G-15826)*
Redstone Print & Mail Inc ... 916 318-6450
910 Riverside Pkwy Ste 40 West Sacramento (95605) *(G-27612)*
Redwood, Culver City *Also called Woven Digital Inc (G-6101)*
Redwood Bridge Club ... 619 296-4274
3111 6th Ave San Diego (92103) *(G-19040)*
Redwood Building Maint Co ... 707 782-9100
1364 N Mcdowell Blvd B Petaluma (94954) *(G-14404)*
Redwood Coast Regional ... 707 445-0893
525 2nd St Ste 300 Eureka (95501) *(G-24150)*
Redwood Coast Regional Center, Eureka *Also called Redwood Coast Regional (G-24150)*
Redwood Coast Seniors Inc ... 707 964-0443
490 N Harold St Fort Bragg (95437) *(G-24151)*
Redwood Convalescent Hospital ... 510 537-8848
22103 Redwood Rd Castro Valley (94546) *(G-21358)*
Redwood Credit Union ... 800 479-7928
1129 S Cloverdale Blvd A Cloverdale (95425) *(G-9762)*
Redwood Credit Union (PA) ... 707 545-4000
3033 Cleveland Ave # 100 Santa Rosa (95403) *(G-9763)*
Redwood Elderlink & Homelink, Escondido *Also called Redwood Elderlink Scph (G-24780)*
Redwood Elderlink Scph ... 760 480-1030
710 W 13th Ave Escondido (92025) *(G-24780)*
Redwood Electric Group Inc (PA) ... 707 451-7348
2775 Northwestern Pkwy Santa Clara (95051) *(G-2703)*
Redwood Empir ... 707 586-5533
3400 Standish Ave Santa Rosa (95407) *(G-6535)*
Redwood Empire Addctons Prgram, Santa Rosa *Also called Drug Abuse Alternatives Center (G-22722)*
Redwood Empire Packing Inc ... 707 462-5521
8801 Old River Rd Ukiah (95482) *(G-580)*
Redwood Empire Vineyard Mgt ... 707 857-3401
22000 Geyserville Ave Geyserville (95441) *(G-717)*
Redwood Empire Whl Lbr Pdts, Morgan Hill *Also called Pacific States Industries Inc (G-6945)*
Redwood Health Club (PA) ... 707 468-0441
3101 S State St Ukiah (95482) *(G-18674)*
Redwood Healthcare Staffing ... 619 238-4180
600 B St Ste 1570 San Diego (92101) *(G-14934)*
Redwood Memorial Hospital Inc (PA) ... 707 725-7327
3300 Renner Dr Fortuna (95540) *(G-21829)*
Redwood Painting Co Inc ... 925 432-4500
620 W 10th St Pittsburg (94565) *(G-2483)*
Redwood Products Chino Inc ... 909 923-5656
9301 Remington Ave Chino (91710) *(G-6955)*
Redwood Regional Medical Group, Santa Rosa *Also called Sotoyome Medical Building LLC (G-11053)*
Redwood Regional Medical Group ... 707 546-4062
3555 Round Barn Cir Santa Rosa (95403) *(G-22271)*
Redwood Regional Medical Group ... 707 463-3636
1165 S Dora St Bldg H Ukiah (95482) *(G-19909)*
Redwood Regional Medical Group (PA) ... 707 525-4080
990 Sonoma Ave Ste 15 Santa Rosa (95404) *(G-22272)*
Redwood Regional Oncology Ctr, Santa Rosa *Also called Redwood Regional Medical Group (G-22272)*

A L P H A B E T I C

Redwood Senior Homes & Svcs, Escondido *Also called Cal Southern Presbt Homes (G-24575)*
Redwood Town Court, Escondido *Also called Cal Southern Presbt Homes (G-24576)*
Redwood Toxicology Lab Inc....707 577-7958
3650 Westwind Blvd Santa Rosa (95403) *(G-22273)*
Redwood Trust Inc (PA)....415 389-7373
1 Belvedere Pl Ste 300 Mill Valley (94941) *(G-12272)*
Redwood Valley Industrial Park....707 485-8766
8800 West Rd Redwood Valley (95470) *(G-4629)*
Redwoods, The, Mill Valley *Also called The Redwoods A Cmnty Seniors (G-24835)*
Reed Brothers Security, Oakland *Also called Security Central Inc (G-18014)*
Reed Smith LLP....415 659-5964
2 Embarcadero Ctr Fl 20 San Francisco (94111) *(G-23527)*
Reed Smith LLP....213 457-8000
355 S Grand Ave Ste 2900 Los Angeles (90071) *(G-23528)*
Reed Smith LLP....415 543-8700
101 2nd St Ste 1800 San Francisco (94105) *(G-23529)*
Reed Smith LLP....415 543-8700
2 Embarcadero Ctr Fl 21 San Francisco (94111) *(G-23530)*
Reed Thomas Company Inc....714 558-7691
1025 N Santiago St Santa Ana (92701) *(G-3441)*
Reef, Carlsbad *Also called South Cone Inc (G-8446)*
Reegs Inc....831 455-7931
88 Monterey Salinas Hwy A Salinas (93908) *(G-1336)*
Reel Fx Inc....310 264-6440
2115 Colorado Ave Santa Monica (90404) *(G-18140)*
Reeve Trucking Company Inc (PA)....209 948-4061
5050 Carpenter Rd Stockton (95215) *(G-4249)*
Reeve-Knight Construction Inc....916 786-5112
128 Ascot Dr Roseville (95661) *(G-1648)*
Reeves Tractor Service Inc....714 692-4020
5455 Blue Ridge Dr Yorba Linda (92887) *(G-1849)*
Referral Realty Cupertino, Cupertino *Also called Z & M Assciates Inc (G-11933)*
Referral Realty Inc....408 996-8100
1601 S De Anza Blvd # 150 Cupertino (95014) *(G-11801)*
Reflections and Enclave Hoa, Irvine *Also called Keystone PCF Property MGT Inc (G-11617)*
Refrigeration Hdwr Sup Corp....818 768-3636
9021 Norris Ave Sun Valley (91352) *(G-7758)*
Refugee Resettlement, San Diego *Also called Catholic Charities Diocese San (G-23709)*
Regal Cinemas Inc....916 419-0205
3561 Truxel Rd Sacramento (95834) *(G-18348)*
Regal Cinemas Inc....310 544-3042
550 Deep Valley Dr # 339 Rllng HLS Est (90274) *(G-18349)*
Regal Medical Group Inc (PA)....818 654-3400
8510 Balboa Blvd Ste 275 Northridge (91325) *(G-25153)*
Regency, San Jose *Also called Liberty Healthcare of Oklahoma (G-20723)*
Regency Caterers By Hyatt, San Diego *Also called Hyatt Hotels Management Corp (G-12827)*
Regency Centers LP....760 724-9795
40 Main St Vista (92083) *(G-20867)*
Regency Enterprises, Los Angeles *Also called New Regency Productions Inc (G-18121)*
Regency Enterprises Inc (PA)....818 901-0255
9261 Jordan Ave Chatsworth (91311) *(G-7467)*
Regency Fire Protection Inc....818 982-0126
7651 Densmore Ave Van Nuys (91406) *(G-2344)*
Regency Health Services, Covina *Also called Covina Rehabilitation Center (G-20504)*
Regency Hill Associates....619 281-5200
6560 Ambrosia Dr San Diego (92124) *(G-11195)*
Regency Inn, Bakersfield *Also called Bakersfield Rodeway Inn Inc (G-12413)*
Regency Inn, Costa Mesa *Also called US Hotel and Resort MGT Inc (G-13371)*
Regency Lighting, Chatsworth *Also called Regency Enterprises Inc (G-7467)*
Regency Oaks Care Center....562 498-3368
3850 E Esther St Long Beach (90804) *(G-20868)*
Regency Park, Pasadena *Also called Zenith Health Care (G-11934)*
Regency Park El Molino, Pasadena *Also called Regency Park Senior Living Inc (G-11802)*
Regency Park Oak Knoll, Pasadena *Also called Regency Park Senior Living Inc (G-24781)*
Regency Park Senior Living Inc....626 396-4911
255 S Oak Knoll Ave Pasadena (91101) *(G-24781)*
Regency Park Senior Living Inc....626 578-0460
245 S El Molino Ave Pasadena (91101) *(G-11802)*
Regency Theatres Inc....818 224-3825
26901 Agoura Rd Ste 150 Agoura Hills (91301) *(G-18350)*
Regenesis Bioremediation Pdts (PA)....949 366-8000
1011 Calle Sombra San Clemente (92673) *(G-28039)*
Regent Assisted Living Inc....626 332-3344
150 S Grand Ave Ofc West Covina (91791) *(G-24782)*
Regent Assisted Living Inc....661 663-8400
8100 Westwold Dr Ofc Bakersfield (93311) *(G-24783)*
Regent Assisted Living Inc....209 491-0800
2325 St Pauls Way Modesto (95355) *(G-792)*
Regent Assisted Living Inc....831 459-8400
80 Front St Santa Cruz (95060) *(G-24784)*
Regent Assisted Living Inc....559 325-8400
675 W Alluvial Ave Ofc Clovis (93611) *(G-24785)*
Regent At Laurel Springs, Bakersfield *Also called Regent Assisted Living Inc (G-24783)*
Regent Corp....559 226-3850
2305 W Shaw Ave Fresno (93711) *(G-13790)*
Regent Court, Modesto *Also called Regent Assisted Living Inc (G-792)*
Regent Senior Living W Covina, West Covina *Also called Regent Assisted Living Inc (G-24782)*
Regent Worldwide Sales LLC....310 806-4288
10990 Wilshire Blvd Los Angeles (90024) *(G-18141)*
Regents of The Univ of Cal....415 476-9000
1600 Divisadero St San Francisco (94143) *(G-22086)*
Regents of The Univ of Cal....510 987-0700
616 Forbes Blvd San Francisco (94143) *(G-17448)*
Regents of The University Cal....619 543-3713
1111 Franklin St Oakland (94607) *(G-21830)*
Regents of Uc....310 827-3700
4560 Admiralty Way # 100 Marina Del Rey (90292) *(G-19910)*
Regents Point, Irvine *Also called Cal Southern Presbt Homes (G-11106)*
Regional Center, Chico *Also called Far Northern Coordinating Coun (G-23976)*
Regional Center For Devlpmtnly, Lancaster *Also called North La County Regional Ctr (G-28004)*
Regional Center of E Bay Inc (PA)....510 383-1200
7677 Oakport St Ste 300 Oakland (94621) *(G-24152)*
Regional Connector Constrs....951 368-6400
1995 Agua Mansa Rd Riverside (92509) *(G-1243)*
Regional Investment & MGT LLC....310 821-1945
4640 Admiralty Way # 1050 Marina Del Rey (90292) *(G-1337)*
Regional Office, Redlands *Also called Southern California Gas Co (G-6275)*
Regional Youth Svcs N Vly Schl, Victor *Also called Victor Treatment Centers Inc (G-24846)*
Regis Corporation....310 274-8791
9403 Santa Monica Blvd Beverly Hills (90210) *(G-13687)*
Registrar of Voters, Santa Ana *Also called County of Orange (G-25480)*
Registration Ctrl Systems Inc (PA)....805 654-0171
1833 Portola Rd Unit B Ventura (93003) *(G-17449)*
Registry Monitoring Ins Srvcs....818 933-6350
5388 Sterling Center Dr Westlake Village (91361) *(G-10854)*
Regulus Group LLC (HQ)....707 259-7100
860 Latour Ct NAPA (94558) *(G-16177)*
Regulus West, NAPA *Also called Regulus Group LLC (G-16177)*
Rehab Associates, Long Beach *Also called Eric D Feldman MD Inc (G-19517)*
Rehab West Inc....619 518-3710
277 Rancheros Dr Ste 190 San Marcos (92069) *(G-10855)*
Rehabilitation California Dept....562 422-8325
4300 Long Beach Blvd # 200 Long Beach (90807) *(G-24153)*
Rehabilitation Center, Lodi *Also called Lodi Memorial Hosp Assn Inc (G-19715)*
Rehabltion Cntre of Bvrly Hlls....323 782-1500
580 S San Vicente Blvd Los Angeles (90048) *(G-20869)*
Rehabltion Cntre of Bkrsfield, Bakersfield *Also called Bakersfield Healthcare (G-20403)*
Rehabworks At Freedom Village, Lake Forest *Also called Freedom Village Healthcare Ctr (G-20581)*
Rei, Stockton *Also called Recreational Equipment Inc (G-7227)*
Rei Rancho Cucamonga, Rancho Cucamonga *Also called Recreational Equipment Inc (G-7226)*
Reichardt Duck Farm Inc....707 762-6314
3770 Middle Two Rock Rd Petaluma (94952) *(G-460)*
Reichert Lengfeld Ltd Partnr....510 845-1077
725 Folger Ave Albany (94710) *(G-13137)*
Reid & Helly....951 682-1771
3880 Lemon St Fl 5 Riverside (92501) *(G-23531)*
Reign Accessories Inc....310 297-6400
4000 Redondo Beach Ave Redondo Beach (90278) *(G-27196)*
Reilly Worldwide Inc....310 449-4065
3000 Olympic Blvd Santa Monica (90404) *(G-18142)*
Reinhardt Roofing Inc....510 713-7014
19258 Donna Ct Morgan Hill (95037) *(G-3209)*
Reiter Affl Companies LLC....805 925-8577
124 Carmen Ln Ste A Santa Maria (93458) *(G-128)*
Reiter Affl Companies LLC....831 786-4244
140 Westridge Dr Watsonville (95076) *(G-129)*
Reiter Berry Watsonville, Watsonville *Also called Reiter Affl Companies LLC (G-129)*
Relational Investors LLC....858 704-3333
12400 High Bluff Dr # 600 San Diego (92130) *(G-10179)*
Relationedge LLC....858 227-2955
1917 Palomar Oaks Way # 310 Carlsbad (92008) *(G-26038)*
Reliable Building Maint Co, Redwood City *Also called Reliable International Svcs (G-14405)*
Reliable Caregivers Inc....415 436-0100
1700 California St # 400 San Francisco (94109) *(G-22547)*
Reliable Carriers Inc....818 252-6400
9122 Glenoaks Blvd Sun Valley (91352) *(G-4250)*
Reliable Co, Glendale *Also called Coinmach Corporation (G-13574)*
Reliable Concepts Corporation....408 271-6655
954 Chestnut St San Jose (95110) *(G-793)*
Reliable Container, Santa Fe Springs *Also called Georgia-Pacific LLC (G-8193)*
Reliable Energy Management Inc....562 984-5511
7201 Rosecrans Ave Paramount (90723) *(G-2345)*
Reliable Gardens Inc....818 904-9801
7837 Burnet Ave Van Nuys (91405) *(G-943)*
Reliable Graphics, Van Nuys *Also called ARC Document Solutions Inc (G-14111)*
Reliable Health Care Svcs Inc....310 397-2229
5705 Sepulveda Blvd Culver City (90230) *(G-14935)*
Reliable Interiors Inc....951 371-3390
104 S Maple St Corona (92880) *(G-27197)*
Reliable International Svcs....760 772-1377
P.O. Box 12249 Palm Desert (92255) *(G-14405)*
Reliable Nursing Solutions....760 946-9191
16057 Kamana Rd Ste B Apple Valley (92307) *(G-14749)*
Reliable Wholesale Lumber Inc (PA)....714 848-8222
7600 Redondo Cir Huntington Beach (92648) *(G-6956)*
Reliance Company, Los Angeles *Also called Zastrow Construction Inc (G-1354)*
Reliance Intermodal Inc....209 946-0200
1919 Martin Luther King Ste A Stockton (95210) *(G-8512)*
Reliance Media Works Vfx Inc....818 557-7333
1800 Vine St Los Angeles (90028) *(G-18251)*
Reliance Steel & Aluminum Co (PA)....213 687-7700
350 S Grand Ave Ste 5100 Los Angeles (90071) *(G-7393)*
Reliance Steel & Aluminum Co....510 476-4400
33201 Western Ave Union City (94587) *(G-7394)*
Reliance Steel & Aluminum Co....562 695-0467
9351 Norwalk Blvd Santa Fe Springs (90670) *(G-7395)*

ALPHABETIC

Reliance Steel & Aluminum Co ... 714 736-4800
  15090 Northam St La Mirada (90638) *(G-7396)*
Reliance Steel & Aluminum Co ... 323 583-6111
  2537 E 27th St Vernon (90058) *(G-7397)*
Reliance Steel & Aluminum Co ... 562 777-9672
  12034 Greenstone Ave Santa Fe Springs (90670) *(G-7398)*
Reliance Steel Company, Vernon Also called Reliance Steel & Aluminum Co *(G-7397)*
Reliant Immediate Care ... 310 215-6020
  9601 S Sepulveda Blvd Los Angeles (90045) *(G-23040)*
Reliant Travel LLC ... 847 509-0097
  2000 Mandela Pkwy Oakland (94607) *(G-3962)*
Relibale Carries, Sun Valley Also called Reliable Carriers Inc *(G-4250)*
Religious Technology Center ... 323 663-3258
  1710 Ivar Ave Ste 1100 Los Angeles (90028) *(G-12222)*
Reloaded Games Inc ... 714 333-1420
  17011 Beach Blvd Ste 320 Huntington Beach (92647) *(G-15827)*
Rels LLC ... 949 214-1000
  40 Pacifica Ste 900 Irvine (92618) *(G-11803)*
Rels Valuation, Irvine Also called Rels LLC *(G-11803)*
Reltio Inc ... 855 360-3282
  100 Marine Pkwy Ste 275 Redwood City (94065) *(G-15413)*
Relx Inc ... 213 627-1130
  555 W 5th St Ste 4500 Los Angeles (90013) *(G-16256)*
REM Eye Wear, Sun Valley Also called REM Optical Company Inc *(G-7348)*
REM Optical Company Inc ... 818 504-3950
  10941 La Tuna Canyon Rd Sun Valley (91352) *(G-7348)*
Remax Active Realty ... 510 505-1660
  4056 Decoto Rd Fremont (94555) *(G-11804)*
Remax Active Teal State, Fremont Also called Remax Active Realty *(G-11804)*
Remax All Stars Realty ... 951 739-4000
  765 N Main St Corona (92880) *(G-11805)*
Remax Champions Real Estate, Upland Also called Re/Max LLC *(G-11792)*
Remax College Park Realty, Long Beach Also called College Park Realty Inc *(G-11442)*
Remax Estate Properties, Rancho Palos Verdes Also called Re/Max Plos Vrdes Rlty / Exces *(G-11795)*
Remax Gold ... 916 609-2800
  3620 Fair Oaks Blvd # 300 Sacramento (95864) *(G-11806)*
Remax Legends, Alta Loma Also called Inland Empire RE Solutions *(G-11582)*
Remax Metro Inc ... 714 557-2544
  150 Paularino Ave Ste 125 Costa Mesa (92626) *(G-11807)*
Remax Olson ... 805 267-4929
  30699 Russell Ranch Rd Westlake Village (91362) *(G-11808)*
Remax Ranch Beach ... 858 391-5800
  16787 Bernardo Center Dr # 6 San Diego (92128) *(G-11809)*
Remax Value Properties, San Jose Also called Quail Hill Investments Inc *(G-12270)*
Remax VIP, Bell Gardens Also called Auchante Inc *(G-11309)*
Remcon, Oakdale Also called Remediation Constructors Inc *(G-1850)*
Remediation Constructors Inc ... 209 847-9186
  751 Wakefield Ct Oakdale (95361) *(G-1850)*
Remedy Intelligent Staffing, Aliso Viejo Also called Remedytemp Inc *(G-14936)*
Remedytemp Inc (HQ) ... 949 425-7600
  101 Enterprise Ste 100 Aliso Viejo (92656) *(G-14936)*
Remington Club I & II, San Diego Also called Five Star Quality Care Inc *(G-20576)*
Remington Hotel Corporation ... 760 322-6000
  888 E Tahquitz Canyon Way Palm Springs (92262) *(G-13138)*
Remington Ldging Hsptality LLC ... 877 932-5333
  6526 Yount St Yountville (94599) *(G-13139)*
Remitware Payments Inc ... 650 843-9192
  2600 El Camino Real Palo Alto (94306) *(G-13911)*
Renaissance Inc ... 559 320-0048
  2615 W Dudley Ave Fresno (93728) *(G-2965)*
Renaissance Clubsport, Walnut Creek Also called Leisure Sports Inc *(G-12914)*
Renaissance Hotel Clubsport ... 949 643-6700
  50 Enterprise Aliso Viejo (92656) *(G-13140)*
Renaissance Hotel Holdings Inc ... 707 935-6600
  1325 Broadway Sonoma (95476) *(G-13141)*
Renaissance Hotel Operating Inc ... 760 773-4444
  44400 Indian Wells Ln Indian Wells (92210) *(G-13142)*
Renaissance Indian Wells, Indian Wells Also called Renaissance Hotel Operating Co *(G-13142)*
Renaissance Palm Springs, Palm Springs Also called HHC Trs Portsmouth LLC *(G-12700)*
Renaissance Palm Springs Hotel, Palm Springs Also called Crestline Hotels & Resorts LLC *(G-12554)*
Renaissance Total Comfort, Fresno Also called Renaissance Inc *(G-2965)*
Renaissnce Clbsport Aliso Vejo, Aliso Viejo Also called L & O Aliso Viejo LLC *(G-18651)*
Renaissnce Esmralda Resort Spa ... 760 773-4444
  44400 Indian Wells Ln Indian Wells (92210) *(G-13143)*
Renal Center, Orange Also called St Joseph Hospital of Orange *(G-21922)*
Renal Treatment Centers Inc (HQ) ... 310 536-2400
  601 Hawaii St El Segundo (90245) *(G-26802)*
Renal Treatment Ctrs - Cal Inc ... 949 930-6882
  15271 Laguna Canyon Rd Irvine (92618) *(G-22637)*
Renal Trtmnt Cntrs-Clfrnia Inc ... 714 990-0110
  595 Tamarack Ave Ste A Brea (92821) *(G-22638)*
Renesas Electronics Amer Inc (HQ) ... 408 588-6000
  2801 Scott Blvd Santa Clara (95050) *(G-7627)*
Renesas Technology America Inc ... 408 588-6000
  2801 Scott Blvd Santa Clara (95050) *(G-7628)*
Reneson Hotels Inc (PA) ... 650 449-5353
  2700 Junipero Serra Blvd Daly City (94015) *(G-13144)*
Reneson Hotels Inc ... 415 621-7001
  112 7th St San Francisco (94103) *(G-13145)*
Renn Transportation Inc ... 408 842-3545
  8845 Forest St Gilroy (95020) *(G-4251)*
Reno Tenco, Boron Also called Rio Tinto Minerals Inc *(G-1026)*

Renova Energy Corp ... 760 568-3413
  75181 Mediterranean Palm Desert (92211) *(G-2346)*
Renovate America Inc ... 858 605-5333
  15073 Ave Of Science # 200 San Diego (92128) *(G-15414)*
Renovo Solutions LLC ... 714 599-7969
  4 Executive Cir Ste 185 Irvine (92614) *(G-18004)*
Rent.com, Los Angeles Also called Viva Group Inc *(G-11226)*
Renteria Santiago J Farm Labo ... 661 792-0052
  137 W Kern Ave Mc Farland (93250) *(G-14750)*
Rentjuice Corporation ... 415 376-0369
  225 Bush St Ste 1100 San Francisco (94104) *(G-5691)*
Rentokil North America Inc ... 562 802-2238
  15415 Marquardt Ave Santa Fe Springs (90670) *(G-9148)*
Rentpayment.com, Walnut Creek Also called Yapstone Inc *(G-17635)*
Renty LLC ... 858 560-0066
  8025 Clairemont Mesa Blvd San Diego (92111) *(G-3832)*
Renwood Realtytrac LLC ... 949 502-8300
  1 Venture Ste 300 Irvine (92618) *(G-11810)*
Renzenberger Inc ... 909 888-8858
  433 S Sierra Way San Bernardino (92408) *(G-17692)*
REO Vista Healthcare Center ... 619 475-2211
  6061 Banbury St San Diego (92139) *(G-20870)*
REO World Inc ... 949 478-8000
  170 Nwport Ctr Dr Ste 150 Newport Beach (92660) *(G-12123)*
Replanet LLC ... 909 980-1203
  9910 6th St Rancho Cucamonga (91730) *(G-6536)*
Reprints Desk Inc ... 310 477-0354
  5435 Balboa Blvd Ste 202 Encino (91316) *(G-16257)*
Reproductive Science Center ... 925 867-1800
  100 Park Pl Ste 200 San Ramon (94583) *(G-19911)*
Reproductive Science Ctr Bay, San Ramon Also called Reproductive Science Center *(G-19911)*
Republic Electric Inc ... 916 294-0140
  3820 Happy Ln Sacramento (95827) *(G-2704)*
Republic Electric West Inc ... 916 294-0140
  3820 Happy Ln Sacramento (95827) *(G-2705)*
Republic Indemnity Co Amer ... 415 981-3200
  100 Pine St Ste 1400 San Francisco (94111) *(G-10453)*
Republic Indemnity Co Amer (HQ) ... 818 990-9860
  15821 Ventura Blvd # 370 Encino (91436) *(G-10454)*
Republic Indemnity Company Cal ... 818 990-9860
  15821 Ventura Blvd # 370 Encino (91436) *(G-10455)*
Republic Master Chefs Textile, Long Beach Also called American Textile Maint Co *(G-6842)*
Republic Services, Salinas Also called BFI Waste Systems N Amer Inc *(G-6441)*
Republic Services Inc ... 909 370-3377
  2059 E Steel Rd Colton (92324) *(G-6537)*
Republic Services Inc ... 310 527-6980
  1449 W Rosecrans Ave Gardena (90249) *(G-6538)*
Republic Services Inc ... 805 385-8060
  111 S Del Norte Blvd Oxnard (93030) *(G-6539)*
Republic Uniform, Long Beach Also called American Textile Maint Co *(G-13521)*
Reputation Impression LLC ... 858 633-4500
  9245 Activity Rd Ste 106 San Diego (92126) *(G-27613)*
Reputation Management Cons Inc ... 949 682-7906
  1720 E Garry Ave Ste 103 Santa Ana (92705) *(G-27614)*
Reputationcom Inc (PA) ... 650 381-3056
  1001 Marshall St Fl 2 Redwood City (94063) *(G-16916)*
RES-Care Inc ... 800 707-8781
  17291 Irvine Blvd Ste 150 Tustin (92780) *(G-22548)*
RES-Care Inc ... 818 637-7727
  611 S Central Ave Glendale (91204) *(G-21099)*
RES-Care California Inc ... 626 334-7861
  200 W Paramount St Azusa (91702) *(G-21100)*
Res.net, Lake Forest Also called US Real Estate Services Inc *(G-11893)*
Rescom Services Inc ... 760 930-3900
  2575 Fortune Way Ste E Vista (92081) *(G-944)*
Rescue Children Inc ... 559 268-1123
  335 G St Fresno (93706) *(G-24154)*
Rescue Concrete Inc ... 916 852-2400
  9275 Beatty Dr Sacramento (95826) *(G-3318)*
Rescue Mission Alliance (PA) ... 805 487-1234
  315 N A St Oxnard (93030) *(G-25570)*
Rescue Mission Alliance ... 805 201-4341
  125 S Harrison Ave Oxnard (93030) *(G-23041)*
Rescue Rooter, Hayward Also called American Residential Svcs LLC *(G-2136)*
Rescue Rooter, Orange Also called American Residential Svcs LLC *(G-2137)*
Rescue Rooter, Sylmar Also called American Residential Svcs LLC *(G-2138)*
Rescue Rooter Bay Area North, Burlingame Also called American Residential Svcs LLC *(G-2135)*
Rescue Rooter Bay Area South, San Jose Also called American Residential Svcs LLC *(G-17960)*
Rescue Rotter, Riverside Also called American Residential Svcs LLC *(G-2134)*
Research, San Diego Also called Sun Pharmaceuticals Inc *(G-26613)*
Research & Dev & Mfg Site, San Diego Also called Pacira Pharmaceuticals Inc *(G-8289)*
Research Affiliates Capital LP ... 949 325-8700
  620 Nwport Ctr Dr Ste 900 Newport Beach (92660) *(G-10180)*
Research Affiliates LLC ... 949 325-8700
  620 Nwport Ctr Dr Ste 900 Newport Beach (92660) *(G-10181)*
Research Libraries Group Inc ... 650 288-1288
  777 Mariners Island Blvd # 550 San Mateo (94404) *(G-16258)*
Research Management Cons Inc (PA) ... 805 987-5538
  816 Camarillo Springs Rd J Camarillo (93012) *(G-28040)*
Research of America ... 916 443-4722
  1232 Q St Ste 100 Sacramento (95811) *(G-16178)*
Research Triangle Institute ... 510 849-4942
  2150 Shattuck Ave Ste 800 Berkeley (94704) *(G-27615)*
Reserve At Spanos Park, The, Stockton Also called American Golf Corporation *(G-18861)*

Reserve Club...760 674-2222
49400 Desert Butte Trl Indian Wells (92210) ***(G-19041)***
Residence In Anaheim, Anaheim *Also called Holiday Garden SF Corp* ***(G-12747)***
Residence Inn By Mariott, San Diego *Also called J5th LLC* ***(G-12861)***
Residence Inn By Marriot Lax/C, Los Angeles *Also called Svi Lax LLC* ***(G-13329)***
Residence Inn By Marriott, Oxnard *Also called Windsor Capital Group Inc* ***(G-13414)***
Residence Inn By Marriott, Pleasanton *Also called Pleasant Canyon Hotel Inc* ***(G-13103)***
Residence Inn By Marriott, San Diego *Also called Marriott International Inc* ***(G-12981)***
Residence Inn By Marriott, San Diego *Also called Marriott International Inc* ***(G-12960)***
Residence Inn By Marriott, San Mateo *Also called Island Hospitality MGT LLC* ***(G-12856)***
Residence Inn By Marriott, Ontario *Also called Island Hospitality MGT LLC* ***(G-12858)***
Residence Inn By Marriott, Palm Desert *Also called Marriott International Inc* ***(G-12961)***
Residence Inn By Marriott, El Segundo *Also called Marriott International Inc* ***(G-12962)***
Residence Inn By Marriott, San Diego *Also called Marriott International Inc* ***(G-12963)***
Residence Inn By Marriott, Ontario *Also called Marriott International Inc* ***(G-12965)***
Residence Inn By Marriott, Corona *Also called Marriott International Inc* ***(G-12967)***
Residence Inn By Marriott, Los Angeles *Also called Sunstone Hotel Properties Inc* ***(G-13324)***
Residence Inn By Marriott, Manhattan Beach *Also called Sunstone Hotel Properties Inc* ***(G-13325)***
Residence Inn By Marriott, Pleasant Hill *Also called Marriott International Inc* ***(G-12976)***
Residence Inn By Marriott, Los Angeles *Also called Beverly Sunstone Hills LLC* ***(G-12447)***
Residence Inn By Marriott, La Mirada *Also called B S A Partners* ***(G-12411)***
Residence Inn By Marriott...559 222-8900
5322 N Diana St Fresno (93710) ***(G-13146)***
Residence Inn By Marriott...714 533-3555
1700 S Clementine St Anaheim (92802) ***(G-13147)***
Residence Inn By Marriott...858 673-1900
11002 Rancho Carmel Dr San Diego (92128) ***(G-13148)***
Residence Inn By Marriott...714 996-0555
700 W Kimberly Ave Placentia (92870) ***(G-13149)***
Residence Inn La Lax El Segndo, El Segundo *Also called ARC Hospitality Portfolio* ***(G-12396)***
Residence Mutual Insurance Co...949 724-9402
2172 Dupont Dr Ste 220 Irvine (92612) ***(G-10456)***
Resident Group Services Inc (PA)...714 630-5300
1156 N Grove St Anaheim (92806) ***(G-945)***
Residential Design Service, Anaheim *Also called LARK Industries Inc* ***(G-17288)***
Residential Fire Systems Inc...714 666-8450
8085 E Crystal Dr Anaheim (92807) ***(G-2347)***
Residential Mortgage Ctr 39, El Segundo *Also called City National Bank* ***(G-9388)***
Residential Wall Systems, Corona *Also called Quality Wall Systems Inc* ***(G-2961)***
Residnce Inn By Mrriott Oxnard, Oxnard *Also called Recp Rl Oxnard LLC* ***(G-13132)***
Residnce Inn By Mrrott Stckton, Stockton *Also called Castlehill Properties Inc* ***(G-12500)***
Residnce Inn Oxnard Rver Ridge, Oxnard *Also called Joyous Management Inc* ***(G-12869)***
Residncy Prgram Natividad Hosp, Salinas *Also called County of Monterey* ***(G-21521)***
Residntial Alzheimers Care Inc...858 565-4424
9619 Chesapeake Dr # 103 San Diego (92123) ***(G-27198)***
Resmae Financial Corporation...714 577-4577
3350 E Birch St Ste 102 Brea (92821) ***(G-9948)***
Resolve Systems LLC (PA)...949 325-0120
2302 Martin Ste 300 Irvine (92612) ***(G-15415)***
Resonate Inc (PA)...408 545-5500
16360 Monterey St Ste 260 Morgan Hill (95037) ***(G-15416)***
Resort At Pelican Hill LLC...949 467-6800
22701 Pelican Hill Rd S Newport Coast (92657) ***(G-13150)***
Resort At Squaw Creek, Alpine Meadows *Also called Squaw Creek Associates LLC* ***(G-13282)***
Resort Campground Intl, Lytle Creek *Also called Burlingame Industries Inc* ***(G-13476)***
Resort Parking Services Inc...760 328-4041
68364 Commercial Rd A Cathedral City (92234) ***(G-17741)***
Resort Procomm Inc...858 866-6280
9550 Waples St Ste 105 San Diego (92121) ***(G-27616)***
Resortime.com, Carlsbad *Also called Grand Pacific Resorts Inc* ***(G-17198)***
Resource Collection Inc...310 219-3272
3771 W 242nd St Ste 205 Torrance (90505) ***(G-14406)***
Resource Connection of Amador (PA)...209 754-3114
444 E Saint Charles St San Andreas (95249) ***(G-24967)***
Resource Connection of Amador...209 223-7685
430 Sutter Hill Rd Sutter Creek (95685) ***(G-24155)***
RESOURCE CONNECTION, THE, San Andreas *Also called Resource Connection of Amador* ***(G-24967)***
Resource Management Group Inc (PA)...858 677-0884
4686 Mercury St San Diego (92111) ***(G-28041)***
Resource Rfrral Child Care Dev...559 673-9173
1225 Gill Ave Madera (93637) ***(G-24156)***
Resource Staffing Group, Sacramento *Also called Northwest Staffing Resources* ***(G-14708)***
Resources Connection Inc (PA)...714 430-6400
17101 Armstrong Ave Irvine (92614) ***(G-27617)***
Resources Connection LLC (HQ)...714 430-6400
17101 Armstrong Ave Irvine (92614) ***(G-14751)***
Resources Global Professionals, Irvine *Also called Resources Connection LLC* ***(G-14751)***
RESPITE SERVICE, Yuba City *Also called Tri County Respite Care Svc* ***(G-24258)***
Respond 2 LLC...415 398-4200
727 Ansome St San Francisco (94111) ***(G-18143)***
Response 1 Medical Staffing...916 932-0430
1101 Inv Blvd Ste 140 El Dorado Hills (95762) ***(G-14752)***
Responselink LLC...650 864-9801
60 S Market St Ste 1500 San Jose (95113) ***(G-19912)***
Responselogix Inc...408 220-6505
2001 Gateway Pl Ste 750w San Jose (95110) ***(G-27199)***
Responsible Med Solutions Corp...951 308-0024
41715 Winchester Rd # 101 Temecula (92590) ***(G-19913)***
Responsys Inc (HQ)...650 745-1700
1100 Grundy Ln Ste 300 San Bruno (94066) ***(G-15417)***
Responsys.com, San Bruno *Also called Responsys Inc* ***(G-15417)***
Restaurant Depot, Sacramento *Also called Jetro Cash and Carry Entps LLC* ***(G-8489)***
Restaurant Depot, San Francisco *Also called Jetro Cash and Carry Entps LLC* ***(G-8674)***
Restaurant Depot...714 378-3535
10850 Spencer St Fountain Valley (92708) ***(G-8513)***
Restaurant Depot LLC...714 666-9205
1265 N Kraemer Blvd Anaheim (92806) ***(G-9078)***
Restaurant Depot LLC...626 744-0204
180 N San Gabriel Blvd Pasadena (91107) ***(G-8564)***
Restaurant Depot LLC...310 516-7400
19901 Hamilton Ave Ste A Torrance (90502) ***(G-9079)***
Restaurant Depot LLC...415 920-2888
2045 Evans Ave San Francisco (94124) ***(G-9080)***
Restaurant Depot LLC...323 964-1220
5333 W Jefferson Blvd Los Angeles (90016) ***(G-9081)***
Restaurant Depot LLC...510 628-0600
400 High St Oakland (94601) ***(G-8565)***
Restaurant Depot LLC...714 378-3535
10850 Spencer St Fountain Valley (92708) ***(G-8566)***
Restaurant Depot LLC...562 634-6771
2300 E 68th St Long Beach (90805) ***(G-8567)***
Restaurant Depot LLC...818 376-7687
15853 Strathern St Van Nuys (91406) ***(G-9082)***
Restaurant Depot LLC...408 344-0107
520 Brennan St San Jose (95131) ***(G-8568)***
Restaurant In A Box Llc...800 676-1281
3191 Red Hill Ave Costa Mesa (92626) ***(G-15418)***
Restec Contractors Inc...510 670-0100
22955 Kidder St Hayward (94545) ***(G-3576)***
Restivo Enterprises...408 988-4884
2590 Lafayette St Santa Clara (95050) ***(G-3833)***
Restoration Management Company, Hayward *Also called Jon K Takata Corporation* ***(G-24050)***
Restoration Resources, Rocklin *Also called Sierra View Landscape Inc* ***(G-954)***
Restoration Resources Hrs, Rocklin *Also called Habitat Rstration Sciences Inc* ***(G-866)***
Result Group Inc...480 777-7130
2603 Main St Ste 710 Irvine (92614) ***(G-16040)***
Retail Pro International LLC...916 605-7200
400 Plaza Dr Ste 200 Folsom (95630) ***(G-15419)***
Retail Pro Software, Folsom *Also called Retail Pro International LLC* ***(G-15419)***
Retailnext Inc (PA)...408 884-2162
60 S Market St Ste 1000 San Jose (95113) ***(G-15420)***
Retailnext Inc...408 298-2585
845 Market St Ste 450 San Francisco (94103) ***(G-26704)***
Retinal Consultants Inc...530 899-2251
19 Ilahee Ln Chico (95973) ***(G-28042)***
Retinal Consultants Inc (PA)...916 454-4861
3939 J St Ste 106 Sacramento (95819) ***(G-19914)***
Retirement Housing Foundation (PA)...562 257-5100
911 N Studebaker Rd # 100 Long Beach (90815) ***(G-11811)***
Retirement Housing Foundation...530 823-6131
750 Auburn Ravine Rd Auburn (95603) ***(G-24786)***
Retirement Housing Foundation...209 466-4341
1319 N Madison St Ofc Stockton (95202) ***(G-11812)***
Retirement Lf Care Communities...510 505-0555
3800 Walnut Ave Apt 401 Fremont (94538) ***(G-24787)***
Retirement Project-Oakmont...707 538-1914
301 White Oak Dr Apt 293 Santa Rosa (95409) ***(G-11196)***
Retirement System, Fresno *Also called City of Fresno* ***(G-12138)***
Retreat & Conference Center...707 252-3810
4401 Redwood Rd NAPA (94558) ***(G-13791)***
Retriev Technologies Inc (PA)...714 738-8516
125 E Commercial St Ste A Anaheim (92801) ***(G-6540)***
Retronix International Inc...949 388-6930
65 Enterprise Aliso Viejo (92656) ***(G-18005)***
Retronix Semiconductors, Aliso Viejo *Also called Retronix International Inc* ***(G-18005)***
Rett Inc...619 231-0403
402 W Broadway Ste 400 San Diego (92101) ***(G-14167)***
Reuben H Fleet Science Center...619 238-1233
1875 El Prado San Diego (92101) ***(G-25038)***
Reutlinger Community, Danville *Also called Home For Jewish Parents* ***(G-24008)***
Rev Enterprises...818 551-7111
417 Arden Ave Ste 103 Glendale (91203) ***(G-16772)***
Revchem Composites Inc (PA)...909 877-8477
2720 S Willow Ave B Bloomington (92316) ***(G-7014)***
Revchem Plastics, Bloomington *Also called Revchem Composites Inc* ***(G-7014)***
Revel Travel At Altour, Beverly Hills *Also called Revel Travel Service Inc* ***(G-4972)***
Revel Travel Service Inc...310 553-5555
449 S Beverly Dr Ste 101 Beverly Hills (90212) ***(G-4972)***
Revenue Frontier LLC...310 584-9200
6922 Hollywood Blvd 2 Los Angeles (90028) ***(G-14009)***
Revenue, Dept of, San Jose *Also called Santa Clara County of* ***(G-14046)***
Review Boost, Carlsbad *Also called Intravas Inc* ***(G-27484)***
REVIVALS THRIFT STORES, Palm Springs *Also called Desert Aids Project* ***(G-23940)***
Revlon Professional, San Diego *Also called Creative Nail Design Inc* ***(G-13671)***
Revo Payments, Venice *Also called Globalex Corporation* ***(G-15680)***
Revolt Media and Tv LLC...323 645-3000
1800 N Highland Ave Fl 7 Los Angeles (90028) ***(G-5906)***
Revolution Eyewear Inc...818 989-2020
997 Flower Glen St Simi Valley (93065) ***(G-7337)***
Rew Inc...805 541-1308
973 Higuera St Ste A San Luis Obispo (93401) ***(G-10372)***
Rex Moore Group Inc...916 372-1300
6001 Outfall Cir Sacramento (95828) ***(G-2706)***
Rex More Elec Contrs Engineers (PA)...916 372-1300
6001 Outfall Cir Sacramento (95828) ***(G-2707)***
Rex More Elec Contrs Engineers...559 294-1300
5803 E Harvard Ave Fresno (93727) ***(G-2708)***

Rex More Elec Contrs Engineers..........................510 785-1300
  6001 Outfall Cir Sacramento (95828) *(G-2709)*
Rex Rising L P..415 273-9790
  562 Sutter St San Francisco (94102) *(G-13151)*
Rey Con Construction Inc.......................................805 525-8134
  1795 E Lemonwood Dr Santa Paula (93060) *(G-3319)*
Rey-Crest Roofg Waterproofing, Los Angeles Also called Rey-Crest Roofg Waterproofing *(G-3577)*
Rey-Crest Roofg Waterproofing................................323 257-9329
  3065 Verdugo Rd Los Angeles (90065) *(G-3577)*
Reyes Holdings LLC...714 445-3392
  1625 S Lewis St Anaheim (92805) *(G-27200)*
Reyes Holdings LLC...858 452-2300
  8870 Liquid Ct San Diego (92121) *(G-10074)*
Reynen & Bardis Construction (PA)...........................916 366-3665
  10630 Mather Blvd Mather (95655) *(G-1244)*
Reynolds Buick/GMC Trucks....................................626 966-4461
  345 N Citrus St West Covina (91791) *(G-17705)*
Reynolds Cleaning Services Inc.................................650 599-0202
  1472 Oddstad Dr Redwood City (94063) *(G-14407)*
Reynolds Health Industries..562 591-7621
  1201 Walnut Ave Long Beach (90813) *(G-21359)*
Reynolds Leasing Co, West Covina Also called Reynolds Buick/GMC Trucks *(G-17705)*
RFI Communications SEC Systems, San Jose Also called RFI Enterprises Inc *(G-2710)*
RFI Enterprises Inc (PA)...408 298-5400
  360 Turtle Creek Ct San Jose (95125) *(G-2710)*
Rfj Corporation...415 824-6890
  930 Innes Ave San Francisco (94124) *(G-2966)*
Rfj Meiswinkel, San Francisco Also called Rfj Corporation *(G-2966)*
Rfxcel Corporation...925 824-0300
  12667 Alcosta Blvd # 375 San Ramon (94583) *(G-7179)*
Rgis LLC..858 653-0355
  9663 Tierra Grande St # 205 San Diego (92126) *(G-17450)*
Rgis LLC..916 387-9692
  8801 Folsom Blvd Ste 173 Sacramento (95826) *(G-17451)*
Rgis LLC..248 651-2511
  500 E Olive Ave Ste 240 Burbank (91501) *(G-17452)*
Rgis LLC..925 829-2875
  7567 Amador Valley Blvd Dublin (94568) *(G-17453)*
Rgis LLC..619 624-9882
  6153 Fairmount Ave San Diego (92120) *(G-17454)*
Rgis LLC..661 702-8987
  25115 Avenue Stanford Valencia (91355) *(G-17455)*
Rgis LLC..530 898-1015
  20 Landing Cir Ste 100 Chico (95973) *(G-17456)*
Rgis LLC..626 974-4841
  1041 W Badillo St Covina (91722) *(G-17457)*
Rgis LLC..714 541-1431
  2000 E 4th St Ste 350 Santa Ana (92705) *(G-17458)*
Rgis LLC..650 757-6770
  2171 Junipero Serra Blvd # 400 Daly City (94014) *(G-17459)*
Rgis LLC..661 827-9195
  5500 Ming Ave Ste 185 Bakersfield (93309) *(G-17460)*
Rgis LLC..805 644-0454
  1787 Mesa Verde Ave Ventura (93003) *(G-17461)*
Rgis LLC..408 243-9141
  4320 Stevens Creek Blvd San Jose (95129) *(G-17462)*
Rgis LLC..559 224-5898
  1322 E Shaw Ave Ste 170 Fresno (93710) *(G-17463)*
Rgis LLC..909 605-1893
  876 N Mountain Ave # 103 Upland (91786) *(G-17464)*
Rgnext, Vandenberg Afb Also called Range Generation Next LLC *(G-26033)*
Rgnext, El Granada Also called Range Generation Next LLC *(G-28034)*
Rgs Services, Anaheim Also called Resident Group Services Inc *(G-945)*
Rh, Alamo Also called Round Hill Country Club *(G-19049)*
Rhc Equipment LLC..530 892-1918
  5237 Mallard Estates Rd Chico (95973) *(G-1649)*
Rheumatology Diagnostics Lab..................................310 253-5455
  10755 Venice Blvd Los Angeles (90034) *(G-22274)*
Rhf Plymouth Tower...951 248-0456
  3401 Lemon St Ofc Riverside (92501) *(G-24788)*
Rhino Building Services Inc.....................................858 455-1440
  6650 Flanders Dr Ste K San Diego (92121) *(G-14408)*
Rhino Ready Mix Trucking Inc (PA)...........................661 679-3643
  3701 Pegasus Dr Ste 126 Bakersfield (93308) *(G-4055)*
Rhinodox, Livermore Also called Access Info MGT Shred Svcs LLC *(G-16214)*
RHO Chem LLC (HQ)..323 776-6234
  425 Isis Ave Inglewood (90301) *(G-6635)*
RHODA GOLDMAN PLAZA, San Francisco Also called Scott Street Senior Housing Co *(G-21102)*
Rhodes Retail Services Inc.......................................916 714-9233
  8603 Excelsior Rd Elk Grove (95624) *(G-27618)*
RHS Corp...909 335-5500
  350 Terracina Blvd Redlands (92373) *(G-27201)*
Rhythm & Hues Studios, El Segundo Also called Rhythm and Hues Inc *(G-18144)*
Rhythm and Hues Inc (PA)......................................310 448-7500
  2100 E Grand Ave Ste A El Segundo (90245) *(G-18144)*
Rhythmone LLC...650 961-9024
  800 W El Camino Real Mountain View (94040) *(G-15421)*
Rhythmone LLC (HQ)..415 655-1450
  1 Market St Ste 1810 San Francisco (94105) *(G-5692)*
Ria Financial Service, Buena Park Also called Continental Exch Solutions Inc *(G-17094)*
Riad Adoumie MD..310 373-6864
  23560 Madison St Ste 110 Torrance (90505) *(G-19915)*
Rialto Bioenergy Facility LLC...................................760 436-8870
  5780 Fleet St Ste 310 Carlsbad (92008) *(G-26039)*
RICA, Encino Also called Republic Indemnity Company Cal *(G-10455)*

Rice Drywall Inc..714 543-5400
  919 E 6th St Santa Ana (92701) *(G-2967)*
Richard Bagdasarian Inc...760 396-2168
  65500 Lincoln St Mecca (92254) *(G-177)*
Richard Brady & Associates Inc.................................657 204-9124
  18837 Brookhurst St Fountain Valley (92708) *(G-26040)*
Richard Burns MD..951 296-9300
  41637 Margarita Rd # 100 Temecula (92591) *(G-19916)*
Richard De Benedetto..559 665-1712
  26393 Road 22 1/2 Chowchilla (93610) *(G-718)*
Richard De Benedetto..559 665-1712
  26393 Road 22 1/2 Chowchilla (93610) *(G-719)*
Richard Finn..951 274-3506
  4444 Magnolia Ave Riverside (92501) *(G-19917)*
Richard Heath & Associates Inc.................................858 514-4025
  7847 Convoy Ct Ste 102 San Diego (92111) *(G-27619)*
Richard Huetter Inc..818 700-8001
  21050 Osborne St Canoga Park (91304) *(G-6759)*
Richard Iest Dairy, Madera Also called Iest Family Farms *(G-429)*
Richard Iest Dairy Inc..559 673-2635
  13507 Road 17 Madera (93637) *(G-32)*
Richard J Mendoza Inc..415 644-0180
  501 2nd St Ste 330 San Francisco (94107) *(G-10457)*
Richard J Metz MD Inc...310 553-3189
  2080 Century Park E # 1609 Los Angeles (90067) *(G-19918)*
Richard K Newman and Assoc Inc (PA).....................661 634-1130
  121 Monterey St Bakersfield (93305) *(G-13584)*
Richard M Gonzalez..559 591-2207
  11450 Avenue 388 Cutler (93615) *(G-14753)*
Richard Realty Group Inc..760 603-8377
  2792 Gateway Rd Ste 103 Carlsbad (92009) *(G-11813)*
Richard Shames MD...415 388-0456
  25 Mitchell Blvd Ste 8 San Rafael (94903) *(G-19919)*
Richard Swanson Inc...209 632-3883
  17659 Swanson Rd Delhi (95315) *(G-209)*
Richard Wilson Wellington...626 812-7881
  1025 N Todd Ave Azusa (91702) *(G-313)*
Richards Watson & Gershon PC (PA)........................213 626-8484
  355 S Grand Ave Fl 40 Los Angeles (90071) *(G-23532)*
Richards Group Inc...214 891-5700
  888 S Figueroa St # 1400 Los Angeles (90017) *(G-13912)*
Richards Grove Saralees Vinyrd.................................707 837-9200
  1998 Jones Rd Windsor (95492) *(G-178)*
Richardson A Clark...760 496-3714
  2701 Loker Ave W Ste 145 Carlsbad (92010) *(G-26041)*
Richmond American Homes.......................................818 908-3267
  16600 Sherman Way Ste 180 Van Nuys (91406) *(G-1245)*
Richmond American Homes.......................................949 467-2600
  5171 California Ave # 120 Irvine (92617) *(G-1246)*
Richmond Area Mlt-Services Inc................................415 668-5998
  4020 Balboa St San Francisco (94121) *(G-20349)*
Richmond Area Mlt-Services Inc................................415 392-4453
  720 Sacramento St San Francisco (94108) *(G-22814)*
Richmond Area Mlt-Services Inc................................415 800-0699
  3120 Mission St San Francisco (94110) *(G-22815)*
Richmond Area Mlt-Services Inc................................415 800-0699
  639 14th Ave San Francisco (94118) *(G-22816)*
Richmond Area Mlt-Services Inc................................415 689-5662
  1375 Mission St San Francisco (94103) *(G-22817)*
Richmond Area Mlt-Services Inc (PA).........................415 668-5955
  3626 Balboa St San Francisco (94121) *(G-22087)*
Richmond Country Club..510 231-2241
  1 Markovich Ln Richmond (94806) *(G-19042)*
Richmond District YMCA, San Francisco Also called Young Mens Christian Assoc SF *(G-25451)*
Richmond Dst Neighborhood Ctr................................415 750-8554
  600 32nd Ave T3 San Francisco (94121) *(G-24157)*
Richmond Peak Quality, Richmond Also called Richmond Wholesale Meat Co *(G-8681)*
Richmond Plastering Inc...562 924-4202
  12102 Centralia Rd Ste B Hawaiian Gardens (90716) *(G-2968)*
Richmond Repair Shop, Richmond Also called San Francisco Bay Area Rapid *(G-3703)*
Richmond Rescue Mission (PA).................................510 215-4555
  2114 Macdonald Ave Richmond (94801) *(G-24158)*
Richmond Sanitary Service Inc (HQ)..........................510 262-7100
  3260 Blume Dr Ste 100 Richmond (94806) *(G-6636)*
Richmond Village Beacon, San Francisco Also called Richmond Dst Neighborhood Ctr *(G-24157)*
Richmond Wholesale Meat Co..................................510 233-5111
  2920 Regatta Blvd Richmond (94804) *(G-8681)*
Richmond Yard Tower, Richmond Also called San Francisco Bay Area Rapid *(G-5241)*
Richter Bros Inc..530 735-6721
  22474 Karnak Rd Knights Landing (95645) *(G-89)*
Rick Berry Inc..559 875-1460
  1300 Commerce Way Sanger (93657) *(G-3023)*
Rick Engineering Company, San Diego Also called Glenn A Rick Engrg & Dev Co *(G-25843)*
Rick H Hitch Plastering Inc......................................916 334-3591
  3306 Orange Grove Ave North Highlands (95660) *(G-2969)*
Rick Hamm Construction Inc...................................714 532-0815
  201 W Carleton Ave Orange (92867) *(G-1851)*
Rick Solomon Enterprises Inc (PA)...........................310 280-3700
  8460 Higuera St Culver City (90232) *(G-8359)*
Rick Studer..323 357-1720
  2610 Wisconsin Ave South Gate (90280) *(G-4252)*
Rick Weiss New Hope Apartments..............................310 395-1026
  1637 Appian Way Santa Monica (90401) *(G-11197)*
Ricochet Television, Los Angeles Also called Alaska Experiment Inc *(G-2512)*
Ricoh Business Solutions, Huntington Beach Also called Ricoh Usa Inc *(G-7066)*
Ricoh Usa Inc..916 638-3333
  3046 Prospect Park Dr # 100 Rancho Cordova (95670) *(G-15422)*

Ricoh Usa Inc 415 733-5600
333 Bush St Ste 2500 San Francisco (94104) *(G-7064)*
Ricoh Usa Inc 818 294-8601
9430 Topanga Canyon Blvd # 100 Chatsworth (91311) *(G-7065)*
Ricoh Usa Inc 714 396-0568
17011 Beach Blvd Ste 1000 Huntington Beach (92647) *(G-7066)*
Ricoh Usa Inc 213 629-1838
6330 Variel Ave Woodland Hills (91367) *(G-7067)*
Ricoh Usa Inc 415 392-6850
333 Bush St Ste 2500 San Francisco (94104) *(G-7068)*
Ricoh Usa Inc 213 489-1700
333 S Hope St Ste E200 Los Angeles (90071) *(G-14125)*
Ricoh Usa Inc 818 703-0265
21820 Burbank Blvd # 229 Woodland Hills (91367) *(G-7069)*
Ricoh Usa Inc 510 839-6399
1300 Clay St Ste 165 Oakland (94612) *(G-14126)*
Ricoh Usa Inc 925 988-4000
1320 Willow Pass Rd Concord (94520) *(G-7070)*
Ricoh Usa Inc 925 938-2049
390 N Wiget Ln Walnut Creek (94598) *(G-7071)*
Ricoh Usa Inc 949 225-2300
16715 Von Karman Ave # 100 Irvine (92606) *(G-7072)*
RIDE ON TRANSPORTATION, San Luis Obispo *Also called United Cerebral Palsy Assoc of (G-24990)*
Rideout Memorial Hospital (HQ) 530 749-4416
726 4th St Marysville (95901) *(G-21831)*
Ridgecrest Healthcare Inc (PA) 323 344-0601
1131 N China Lake Blvd Ridgecrest (93555) *(G-20871)*
Ridgecrest Regional Hospital 760 446-3551
1081 N China Lake Blvd Ridgecrest (93555) *(G-21832)*
Ridgeside Construction Inc 909 218-7593
4345 E Lowell St Ste A Ontario (91761) *(G-1247)*
Ridgeside Finishing, Ontario *Also called Ridgeside Construction Inc (G-1247)*
Ridgway, Santa Rosa *Also called Finley Swim Center (G-19214)*
Right At Home, Santa Rosa *Also called Pw Jade LLC (G-22543)*
Right At Home, Pasadena *Also called Good Works LLC (G-22446)*
Right At Home 310 313-0600
3435 Ocean Park Blvd # 110 Santa Monica (90405) *(G-22549)*
Right Choice A Health Care 626 335-1318
620 S Glendora Ave Ste A Glendora (91740) *(G-14754)*
Right Choice In-Home Care Inc 818 836-6001
7104 Owensmouth Ave Canoga Park (91303) *(G-22550)*
Right Stuff Health Club, The, San Jose *Also called SIM Investment Corporation (G-18681)*
Rightscale Inc 805 500-4164
402 E Gutierrez St Santa Barbara (93101) *(G-15423)*
Rightsourcing Inc (HQ) 800 660-9544
1150 Iron Point Rd # 100 Folsom (95630) *(G-14937)*
Rika Corporation 949 830-9050
332 W Brenna Ln Orange (92867) *(G-3399)*
Riley & Powell MD 650 328-0511
1900 University Ave 101e East Palo Alto (94303) *(G-19920)*
Rim Architects California Inc 415 247-0400
639 Front St Fl 2 San Francisco (94111) *(G-26246)*
Rinaldi Convalescent Hospital, Granada Hills *Also called Medical Investment Co (G-21313)*
Rinaldi Tile & Marble, Royal Oaks *Also called Gino Rinaldi Inc (G-3014)*
Rincon Pacific LLC 805 986-8806
1312 Del Norte Rd Camarillo (93010) *(G-130)*
Ringadoc, San Francisco *Also called Practice Fusion Inc (G-15393)*
Ringcentral Inc (PA) 650 472-4100
20 Davis Dr Belmont (94002) *(G-15828)*
Rinks Anaheim Ice, The, Anaheim *Also called Anaheim Ice (G-19136)*
Rio Bravo Ranch Shop 661 872-5050
15701 Highway 178 Bakersfield (93306) *(G-472)*
Rio Bravo Rocklin, Lincoln *Also called Rocklin Power Investors LP (G-6198)*
Rio Hndo Sbcute Nrsing Ctr LLC 323 838-5915
273 E Beverly Blvd Montebello (90640) *(G-20872)*
Rio Hondo Community Dev Corp 626 401-2784
11706 Ramona Blvd Ste 107 El Monte (91732) *(G-24968)*
Rio Hondo Convalescent Hosp, Montebello *Also called Rio Hndo Sbcute Nrsing Ctr LLC (G-20872)*
Rio Hondo Education Consortium 562 945-0150
7200 Greenleaf Ave # 300 Whittier (90602) *(G-24159)*
Rio Mesa Farms LLC 831 728-1965
75 Sakata Ln Watsonville (95076) *(G-131)*
Rio Seo, San Diego *Also called Riosoft Holdings Inc (G-15424)*
Rio Tinto Minerals Inc 760 762-7121
14486 Borax Rd Boron (93516) *(G-1026)*
Rio Vista Development Company (PA) 818 980-8000
4222 Vineland Ave North Hollywood (91602) *(G-13152)*
Rio Vista Ventures LLC (PA) 760 480-8502
15651 Old Milky Way Escondido (92027) *(G-8514)*
Rio Vista Ventures LLC 559 897-6730
3646 Avenue 416 Reedley (93654) *(G-8515)*
Riolo Transportation Inc 760 729-4405
2725 Jefferson St Ste 2d Carlsbad (92008) *(G-5239)*
Rios Farming Company LLC 707 965-2587
3851 Chiles Pope Vly Rd Saint Helena (94574) *(G-179)*
Riosoft Holdings Inc 858 529-5005
9255 Towne Centre Dr San Diego (92121) *(G-15424)*
Riot Games Inc (HQ) 310 828-7953
12333 W Olympic Blvd Los Angeles (90064) *(G-15425)*
Riphagen & Bullerdick Inc 714 763-2100
5925 Ball Rd Cypress (90630) *(G-11814)*
Rls Electrical Contrs Inc 951 688-8049
7330 Sycamore Canyon Blvd # 1 Riverside (92508) *(G-2711)*
Risk Management, San Bernardino *Also called Llu Advntist Hlth Sciences Ctr (G-19714)*
Risk Management Solutions Inc (HQ) 510 505-2500
7575 Gateway Blvd Newark (94560) *(G-12223)*
Risk Management Strategies Inc 619 281-1100
8530 La Mesa Blvd Ste 200 La Mesa (91942) *(G-28043)*
Riskalyze Inc 530 748-1660
373 Elm Ave Auburn (95603) *(G-16472)*
Ritchie Plumbing Inc 949 709-7575
11320 Lombardy Ln Moreno Valley (92557) *(G-2348)*
Rite of Pass Athletic Trng Ctr 209 736-4500
10400 Fricot City Rd San Andreas (95249) *(G-24789)*
Rite Way Enterprises 818 376-6960
7131 Valjean Ave Van Nuys (91406) *(G-5161)*
Rite-Way Meat Packers Inc 323 826-2144
5151 Alcoa Ave Vernon (90058) *(G-8682)*
Ritz Carlton, Rancho Mirage *Also called Ritz-Carlton Hotel Company LLC (G-13154)*
Ritz Carlton Rancho Mirage, Rancho Mirage *Also called Ritz-Carlton Hotel Company LLC (G-13157)*
Ritz Companies, Irvine *Also called Savoy Contractors Group Inc (G-1251)*
Ritz-Carlton Halfmoon Bay, Half Moon Bay *Also called Bre Diamond Hotel LLC (G-12463)*
Ritz-Carlton Hotel Company LLC 415 781-9000
690 Market St San Francisco (94104) *(G-13153)*
Ritz-Carlton Hotel Company LLC 760 321-8282
68900 Frank Sinatra Dr Rancho Mirage (92270) *(G-13154)*
Ritz-Carlton Hotel Company LLC 949 240-5020
1 Ritz Carlton Dr Dana Point (92629) *(G-13155)*
Ritz-Carlton Hotel Company LLC 415 773-6168
600 Stockton St San Francisco (94108) *(G-13156)*
Ritz-Carlton Hotel Company LLC 760 321-8282
68900 Frank Sinatra Dr Rancho Mirage (92270) *(G-13157)*
Ritz-Carlton Ht Marina Del Rey, Venice *Also called Host Hotels & Resorts LP (G-12773)*
Ritz-Carlton Laguna Niguel, Dana Point *Also called Prutel Joint Venture (G-13112)*
Ritz-Carlton Marina Del Rey 310 823-1700
4375 Admiralty Way Marina Del Rey (90292) *(G-13158)*
Ritz-Carlton San Francisco, San Francisco *Also called Ritz-Carlton Hotel Company LLC (G-13156)*
River Bend Nursing Home Inc 916 371-1890
2215 Oakmont Way West Sacramento (95691) *(G-20873)*
River City Auto Recovery Inc 916 851-1100
3401 Fitzgerald Rd Rancho Cordova (95742) *(G-17465)*
River City Bank, Sacramento *Also called Rcb Corporation (G-9519)*
River City Bank (HQ) 916 567-2600
2485 Natomas Park Dr # 100 Sacramento (95833) *(G-9520)*
River Cy Geoprofessionals Inc 916 372-1434
3050 Industrial Blvd West Sacramento (95691) *(G-26042)*
River Island Country Club Inc 559 781-2917
31989 River Island Dr Porterville (93257) *(G-19043)*
River Oak Center For Children 916 226-2800
9412 Big Horn Blvd Ste 6 Elk Grove (95758) *(G-20350)*
River Oak Center For Children (PA) 916 609-5100
5445 Laurel Hills Dr Sacramento (95841) *(G-22088)*
River Oak Center For Children 916 550-5600
5445 Laurel Hills Dr Sacramento (95841) *(G-21360)*
River Ranch Fresh Foods LLC (HQ) 831 758-1390
911 Blanco Cir Ste B Salinas (93901) *(G-8769)*
River Ridge Farms Inc 805 647-6880
3135 Los Angeles Ave Oxnard (93036) *(G-314)*
River Ridge Golf Club, Oxnard *Also called High Tide and Green Grass Inc (G-18747)*
River Ridge Golf Club 805 981-8724
2401 W Vineyard Ave Oxnard (93036) *(G-19044)*
River Ridge Gulf Course, Oxnard *Also called City of Oxnard (G-18724)*
River Rock Casino, Geyserville *Also called River Rock Entertainment Auth (G-13159)*
River Rock Entertainment Auth 707 857-2777
3250 Highway 128 Geyserville (95441) *(G-13159)*
River Rock Equipment LLC 916 791-1609
216 Kenroy Ln Roseville (95678) *(G-12087)*
River Side Cmnty Hosp Fd Svcs 951 788-3121
4445 Magnolia Ave Riverside (92501) *(G-21833)*
Rivera Sanitarium Inc 562 949-2591
7246 Rosemead Blvd Pico Rivera (90660) *(G-20874)*
Riverside Auto Auction, Anaheim *Also called Califrnia Auto Dalers Exch LLC (G-6666)*
Riverside Bhvral Heathcare Ctr, Riverside *Also called Riverside Sanitarium LLC (G-20878)*
Riverside Care Inc 951 683-7111
4301 Caroline Ct Riverside (92506) *(G-20875)*
Riverside Cmnty Hlth Systems (HQ) 951 788-3000
4445 Magnolia Ave Fl 6 Riverside (92501) *(G-21834)*
Riverside Cnty Probation Dept, Riverside *Also called County of Riverside (G-23889)*
Riverside Community Hospital, Riverside *Also called Riverside Healthcare System LP (G-21835)*
Riverside Companion Services, San Bernardino *Also called Maxim Healthcare Services Inc (G-14904)*
Riverside Convention Center, Riverside *Also called Entrepreneurial Hospitality (G-17151)*
Riverside Convention Center, Riverside *Also called City of Riverside (G-17078)*
Riverside Dialysis Center 951 682-2700
4361 Latham St Ste 100 Riverside (92501) *(G-22639)*
Riverside District Office, Riverside *Also called State Compensation Insur Fund (G-10474)*
Riverside Equities LLC 951 688-2222
8487 Magnolia Ave Riverside (92504) *(G-20876)*
Riverside Health Care Corp 209 523-5667
1611 Scenic Dr Modesto (95355) *(G-21361)*
Riverside Health Care Corp (PA) 530 897-5100
1469 Humboldt Rd Ste 175 Chico (95928) *(G-21362)*
Riverside Health Care Corp 916 446-2506
1090 Rio Ln Sacramento (95822) *(G-20877)*
Riverside Healthcare System LP 951 788-3000
4445 Magnolia Ave Riverside (92501) *(G-21835)*
Riverside Marriott, Riverside *Also called Pinnacle Rvrside Hspitality LP (G-13099)*
Riverside Med Clnic Ptient Ctr, Riverside *Also called Riverside Medical Clinic Inc (G-19923)*

Riverside Medical Clinic
ALPHABETIC SECTION

Riverside Medical Clinic ... 951 360-5260
6250 Clay Mira Loma (91752) ***(G-19921)***

Riverside Medical Clinic Inc ... 951 683-6370
7117 Brockton Ave Riverside (92506) ***(G-19922)***

Riverside Medical Clinic Inc (PA) ... 951 683-6370
3660 Arlington Ave Riverside (92506) ***(G-19923)***

Riverside Nursery & Ldscp Inc ... 559 275-1891
5215 N Golden State Blvd Fresno (93722) ***(G-9211)***

Riverside Research Institute ... 949 631-0107
3333 W Coast Hwy Ste 101 Newport Beach (92663) ***(G-26803)***

Riverside Sanitarium LLC ... 951 684-7701
4580 Palm Ave Riverside (92501) ***(G-20878)***

Riverside Scrap Ir & Met Corp (PA) ... 951 686-2120
2993 6th St Riverside (92507) ***(G-8081)***

Riverside Transit Agency (PA) ... 951 565-5000
1825 3rd St Riverside (92507) ***(G-3692)***

Riverside-San Bernardino (PA) ... 951 849-4761
11555 1/2 Potrero Rd Banning (92220) ***(G-22818)***

Riverside-San Bernardino ... 951 654-0803
607 Donna Way San Jacinto (92583) ***(G-19924)***

Riverview Golf and Country CLB ... 530 224-2254
4200 Bechelli Ln Redding (96002) ***(G-19045)***

Riverwalk PST-Cute Rhblitation, Mission Viejo *Also called Rock Canyon Healthcare Inc* ***(G-21363)***

Riviera Health Care Center, Pico Rivera *Also called Riviera Nursing & Conva* ***(G-20879)***

Riviera Nursing & Conva ... 562 806-2576
8203 Telegraph Rd Pico Rivera (90660) ***(G-20879)***

Riviera Partners LLC (PA) ... 877 748-4372
141 10th St San Francisco (94103) ***(G-27620)***

Riviera Reincarnate LLC ... 760 327-8311
1600 N Indian Canyon Dr Palm Springs (92262) ***(G-13160)***

Rivio Inc ... 408 653-4400
2500 Augustine Dr Ste 100 Santa Clara (95054) ***(G-5693)***

Rizal Community Center, Sacramento *Also called Southgate Recreation & Pk Dst* ***(G-24223)***

RJ Allen Inc ... 714 539-1022
10392 Stanford Ave Garden Grove (92840) ***(G-14497)***

RJ Noble Company (PA) ... 714 637-1550
15505 E Lincoln Ave Orange (92865) ***(G-1852)***

Rjb Enterprises Inc ... 714 484-3101
2579 W Woodland Dr Anaheim (92801) ***(G-2712)***

Rjc Architects Inc ... 619 239-9292
320 Laurel St San Diego (92101) ***(G-26247)***

Rjms Corporation (PA) ... 510 675-0500
31010 San Antonio St Hayward (94544) ***(G-7883)***

RJN Investigations Inc ... 951 686-7638
360 E 1st St Ste 696 Tustin (92780) ***(G-16773)***

RJP Construction & Painting (PA) ... 949 707-5449
22600 Lambert St Ste 807 Lake Forest (92630) ***(G-2484)***

RJS & Associates Inc ... 510 670-9111
1675 Sabre St Hayward (94545) ***(G-3320)***

RK Electric Inc ... 510 580-2850
42021 Osgood Rd Fremont (94539) ***(G-2713)***

Rk Logistics Goup, The, Fremont *Also called Rk Logistics Group Inc* ***(G-5162)***

Rk Logistics Group Inc ... 408 942-8107
41707 Christy St Fremont (94538) ***(G-5162)***

Rki Instruments Inc (PA) ... 510 441-5656
33248 Central Ave Union City (94587) ***(G-7884)***

Rl Eureka LLC ... 707 268-8341
1929 4th St Eureka (95501) ***(G-13161)***

Rl Properties, Albany *Also called Reichert Lengfeld Ltd Partnr* ***(G-13137)***

Rl Redding LLC ... 530 221-8700
1830 Hilltop Dr Redding (96002) ***(G-13162)***

Rlh Fire Protection, Bakersfield *Also called CMA Fire Protection* ***(G-2183)***

Rlj Hgn Emeryville Lessee LP ... 510 658-9300
1800 Powell St Emeryville (94608) ***(G-13497)***

Rljhgn Emeryville Lessee LP ... 510 658-9300
1800 Powell St Emeryville (94608) ***(G-13163)***

Rm Esop Inc ... 831 783-3140
340 El Camino Real S # 36 Salinas (93901) ***(G-9299)***

Rm Esop Inc ... 805 483-5331
1051 S Rose Ave Oxnard (93030) ***(G-7808)***

RM Galicia Inc ... 626 813-6200
1521 W Cameron Ave # 100 West Covina (91790) ***(G-14044)***

RMA - Ecc A Joint Venture LLC ... 714 985-2888
2707 Saturn St Brea (92821) ***(G-1650)***

RMA Group, Rancho Cucamonga *Also called R M A Group Inc* ***(G-26030)***

RMC Painting & Restoration, Burlingame *Also called Robert Meuschke Company Inc* ***(G-2485)***

RMC Transport, Riverside *Also called Bledsoe Masonry Inc* ***(G-2804)***

Rmci, Camarillo *Also called Research Management Cons Inc* ***(G-28040)***

Rmi International Inc ... 310 781-6768
1919 Torrance Blvd Torrance (90501) ***(G-16774)***

Rmis, Westlake Village *Also called Registry Monitoring Ins Srvcs* ***(G-10854)***

Rmkr, Campbell *Also called Rainmaker Systems Inc* ***(G-27193)***

RMR Construction Company ... 415 647-0884
2424 Oakdale Ave San Francisco (94124) ***(G-1651)***

RMR Inc (PA) ... 805 928-4013
2311 S Oakley Ave Ste C Santa Maria (93455) ***(G-3321)***

RMS Foundation Inc ... 562 435-3511
1126 Queens Hwy Long Beach (90802) ***(G-13164)***

RMS Group Inc ... 714 373-4882
17802 Mitchell N Irvine (92614) ***(G-1652)***

Rmt Landscape Contractors Inc ... 510 568-3208
421 Pendleton Way Oakland (94621) ***(G-946)***

Rnc Capital Management LLC ... 310 477-6543
11601 Wilshire Blvd Ph Los Angeles (90025) ***(G-10182)***

Rnc Genter Capital Management, Los Angeles *Also called Rnc Capital Management LLC* ***(G-10182)***

Rncmba Inc ... 661 395-1700
4801 Truxtun Ave Bakersfield (93309) ***(G-14938)***

Road Dept, San Andreas *Also called County of Calaveras* ***(G-23800)***

Road Safety Inc ... 916 543-4600
4335 Pacific St Ste A Rocklin (95677) ***(G-17466)***

Roadex America Inc ... 310 878-9800
1515 W 178th St Gardena (90248) ***(G-5163)***

Roadium Open Air Market, Torrance *Also called Pioneer Theatres Inc* ***(G-17414)***

Roadrunner Shuttle, Camarillo *Also called Airport Connection Inc* ***(G-3633)***

Roadstar Trucking Inc ... 510 487-2404
30527 San Antonio St Hayward (94544) ***(G-4253)***

Roambi, Solana Beach *Also called Mellmo Inc* ***(G-15298)***

Robany Inc ... 818 721-2150
21550 Oxnard St Fl 3 Woodland Hills (91367) ***(G-27621)***

Robbins Geller Rudman Dowd LLP (PA) ... 619 231-1058
655 W Broadway Ste 1900 San Diego (92101) ***(G-23533)***

Robert A Bothman Inc (PA) ... 408 279-2277
2690 Scott Blvd Santa Clara (95050) ***(G-3322)***

Robert A Hall ... 707 837-8564
9769 Dawn Way Windsor (95492) ***(G-14939)***

Robert Alves Farms Inc ... 559 896-3309
10642 E Dinuba Ave Selma (93662) ***(G-180)***

Robert B Diemer Trtmnt Plant, Yorba Linda *Also called Metropolitan Water District* ***(G-6374)***

Robert Ballard Rehab Hospital (HQ) ... 909 473-1200
1760 W 16th St San Bernardino (92411) ***(G-20351)***

Robert Bosch Healthcare ... 650 690-9100
2400 Geng Rd Ste 200 Palo Alto (94303) ***(G-15426)***

Robert Bosch Start-Up Platf ... 248 876-6430
400 Convention Way Redwood City (94063) ***(G-15427)***

Robert C Davis MD ... 510 893-2820
400 Estudillo Ave Ste 100 San Leandro (94577) ***(G-19925)***

Robert C Hamilton ... 626 794-4103
1760 N Fair Oaks Ave Pasadena (91103) ***(G-24790)***

Robert Cecchini Inc ... 925 634-4400
5301 Orwood Rd Brentwood (94513) ***(G-90)***

Robert Clapper Cnstr Svcs Inc ... 909 829-3688
2223 N Locust Ave Rialto (92377) ***(G-1653)***

Robert Consl Englekirk Strctrl (PA) ... 323 733-6673
2116 Arlington Ave Lbby Los Angeles (90018) ***(G-26043)***

Robert Half International Inc ... 408 961-2975
10 Almaden Blvd Ste 900 San Jose (95113) ***(G-14755)***

Robert Half International Inc ... 213 270-6731
865 S Figueroa St # 2600 Los Angeles (90017) ***(G-14756)***

Robert Half International Inc ... 415 434-2429
50 California St Fl 10 San Francisco (94111) ***(G-14757)***

Robert Half International Inc ... 510 744-6486
39141 Civic Center Dr # 205 Fremont (94538) ***(G-14758)***

Robert Half International Inc ... 831 241-9042
4 Lower Ragsdale Dr # 101 Monterey (93940) ***(G-14759)***

Robert Half International Inc ... 714 450-9838
1 City Blvd W Ste 1115 Orange (92868) ***(G-14760)***

Robert Half International Inc (PA) ... 650 234-6000
2884 Sand Hill Rd Ste 200 Menlo Park (94025) ***(G-14940)***

Robert Half International Inc ... 562 356-1031
17871 Park Plaza Dr # 100 Cerritos (90703) ***(G-14761)***

Robert Half International Inc ... 951 779-9081
2280 Market St Ste 220 Riverside (92501) ***(G-14762)***

Robert Half International Inc ... 916 852-1705
3100 Zinfandel Dr Ste 260 Rancho Cordova (95670) ***(G-14763)***

Robert Half International Inc ... 925 930-7766
3000 Oak Rd Ste 625 Walnut Creek (94597) ***(G-14764)***

Robert Half International Inc ... 408 293-8611
10 Almaden Blvd Ste 900 San Jose (95113) ***(G-14941)***

Robert Half International Inc ... 888 744-9202
4225 Executive Sq Ste 300 La Jolla (92037) ***(G-14942)***

Robert Half International Inc ... 415 434-1900
50 California St Fl 10 San Francisco (94111) ***(G-14765)***

Robert Half International Inc ... 650 574-8200
1850 Gateway Dr Ste 200 San Mateo (94404) ***(G-14943)***

Robert Half International Inc ... 650 234-6000
2884 Sand Hill Rd Ste 200 Menlo Park (94025) ***(G-14766)***

Robert Half International Inc ... 650 234-6000
2884 Sand Hill Rd Ste 200 Menlo Park (94025) ***(G-14767)***

Robert Half International Inc ... 650 234-6000
2884 Sand Hill Rd Ste 200 Menlo Park (94025) ***(G-14768)***

Robert Half International Inc ... 949 476-3199
18200 Von Karman Ave # 800 Irvine (92612) ***(G-14769)***

Robert Half International Inc ... 626 463-2037
790 E Colo Blvd Ste 650 Pasadena (91101) ***(G-14770)***

Robert Half International Inc ... 310 719-1400
990 W 190th St Ste 290 Torrance (90502) ***(G-14771)***

Robert Half International Inc ... 650 812-9790
3600 W Byshore Rd Ste 103 Palo Alto (94303) ***(G-14772)***

Robert Half International Inc ... 925 913-1000
2613 Camino Ramon San Ramon (94583) ***(G-14773)***

Robert Half MGT Resources ... 510 271-0910
1999 Harrison St Ste 1100 Oakland (94612) ***(G-27622)***

Robert Heely Inc ... 559 935-0570
236 W Forest Ave Coalinga (93210) ***(G-1989)***

Robert Heely Construction, Coalinga *Also called Robert Heely Inc* ***(G-1989)***

Robert J Echter Foxpoint Farms, Encinitas *Also called J Robert Echter* ***(G-292)***

Robert Kaufman Co Inc ... 310 538-3482
135 W 132nd St Los Angeles (90061) ***(G-8323)***

Robert Meuschke Company Inc ... 650 342-3993
1039 Edwards Rd Burlingame (94010) ***(G-2485)***

Robert Moreno Insurance Svcs ... 714 525-5168
22860 Savi Ranch Pkwy Yorba Linda (92887) ***(G-10856)***

Robert Morken Construction ... 530 386-1512
1300 Regency Way Ste 59 Kings Beach (96143) ***(G-1248)***

ALPHABETIC

Robert Quintero Labor Contg......559 732-6954
1827 S Bardo St Visalia (93277) *(G-14774)*
Robert Sknner Filtration Plant, Winchester *Also called Metropolitan Water District (G-6380)*
Robert Young Family Ltd Partnr......707 433-3228
4950 Red Winery Rd Geyserville (95441) *(G-720)*
Robert Young Vineyards, Geyserville *Also called Robert Young Family Ltd Partnr (G-720)*
Robert's Lumber, Bloomington *Also called Roberts Lumber Sales Inc (G-6957)*
Robertas Labor Contracting......831 678-8176
137 Main St Soledad (93960) *(G-14775)*
Roberts & Associates Inc......951 727-4357
8175 Limonite Ave Ste A1 Riverside (92509) *(G-22551)*
Roberts Lumber Sales Inc......909 350-9164
2661 S Lilac Ave Bloomington (92316) *(G-6957)*
Roberts Outdoor Advertising, Los Angeles *Also called Outdoor Systems Advertising (G-13954)*
Robertson Piper Management LLC......650 625-8333
963 Fremont Ave Los Altos (94024) *(G-27623)*
Robin K......323 235-5152
4731 Fruitland Ave Vernon (90058) *(G-8410)*
Robincrost Care Corporation......323 934-3515
636 S Plymouth Blvd Los Angeles (90005) *(G-20880)*
Robinsn Clgne Rsn Shpr Dvs Inc......619 338-4060
620 Nwport Ctr Dr Ste 700 San Diego (92101) *(G-23534)*
Robinson & Sons......530 265-5844
293 Lower Grass Valley Rd # 201 Nevada City (95959) *(G-412)*
Robinson and Enterprises, Nevada City *Also called Robinson & Sons (G-412)*
Robinson and Wood Inc......408 298-7120
227 N 1st St San Jose (95113) *(G-23535)*
Robinson Company Contrs Inc......619 697-6040
8871 Troy St Spring Valley (91977) *(G-2349)*
Robinson Electric, Spring Valley *Also called Robinson Company Contrs Inc (G-2349)*
Robinson Pharma Inc......714 241-0235
1683 Sunflower Ave # 103 Costa Mesa (92626) *(G-8291)*
Robinson Ranch Golf LLC......818 885-0599
27734 Sand Canyon Rd Santa Clarita (91387) *(G-18777)*
Roboca Technology......561 501-3999
245 E Main St Ste 115 Alhambra (91801) *(G-15428)*
Rocha Transportation, Modesto *Also called Ed Rocha Livestock Trnsp Inc (G-4145)*
Rocha, Jill B MD, Ventura *Also called West Ventura Family Care Ctr (G-20236)*
Roche Molecular Systems Inc......510 814-2800
1145 Atlantic Ave Ste 100 Alameda (94501) *(G-26595)*
Roche Molecular Systems Inc (HQ)......925 730-8000
4300 Hacienda Dr Pleasanton (94588) *(G-26596)*
Rock Cancer CARE Inc......888 251-0620
5402 Ruffin Rd Ste 205 San Diego (92123) *(G-24160)*
Rock Canyon Healthcare Inc......949 487-9500
27101 Puerta Real Ste 450 Mission Viejo (92691) *(G-21363)*
Rock Paper Scissors LLC......310 586-0600
2308 Broadway Santa Monica (90404) *(G-18145)*
Rock-It Cargo USA LLC......310 455-1900
120 N Topanga Canyon Blvd Topanga (90290) *(G-5164)*
Rockefeller Group Dev Corp......949 468-1800
4 Park Plz Ste 840 Irvine (92614) *(G-12005)*
Rocket Ems Inc......408 727-3700
2950 Patrick Henry Dr Santa Clara (95054) *(G-2714)*
Rocket Farms Inc (PA)......831 442-2400
360 Espinosa Rd Salinas (93907) *(G-315)*
Rocket Farms Inc......760 439-6515
297 Wilshire Rd Oceanside (92057) *(G-33)*
Rocket Farms Herbs Inc......562 205-1900
7909 Crossway Dr Pico Rivera (90660) *(G-389)*
Rocket Fuel Inc (PA)......650 595-1300
1900 Seaport Blvd Redwood City (94063) *(G-13913)*
Rocket Smog Inc......310 390-7664
11413 W Washington Blvd Los Angeles (90066) *(G-17891)*
Rockin Jump Inc......925 401-7200
5875 Arnold Rd Ste 100 Dublin (94568) *(G-19269)*
Rockland Footware, Ontario *Also called Rockland Intl Trading Inc (G-8445)*
Rockland Intl Trading Inc......909 923-8061
760 E Francis St Ste T Ontario (91761) *(G-8445)*
Rocklin Power Investors LP......916 645-3383
3100 Thunder Valley Ct Lincoln (95648) *(G-6198)*
Rockport ADM Svcs LLC......323 223-3441
4585 N Figueroa St Los Angeles (90065) *(G-20881)*
Rockport ADM Svcs LLC (PA)......323 330-6500
5900 Wilshire Blvd # 1600 Los Angeles (90036) *(G-27624)*
Rockport Healthcare Services, Los Angeles *Also called Rockport ADM Svcs LLC (G-27624)*
Rockstar San Diego......760 929-0700
2200 Faraday Ave Ste 200 Carlsbad (92008) *(G-16179)*
Rockview Dairies Inc (PA)......562 927-5511
7011 Stewart And Gray Rd Downey (90241) *(G-8913)*
Rocky Coast Builders Inc......760 489-7770
135 Market Pl Escondido (92029) *(G-3080)*
Rocky Packaging Solutions Inc......909 591-3331
13980 Mountain Ave Chino (91710) *(G-9300)*
Rocky Point Care Center, Lakeport *Also called Windflower Holdings LLC (G-21044)*
Rockyou Inc (PA)......415 580-6400
303 2nd St Ste S600 San Francisco (94107) *(G-16259)*
Rocology South Bay, Santa Clara *Also called Recology Los Altos (G-6525)*
Rodbat Security Services, Torrance *Also called Rmi International Inc (G-16774)*
Rodda Electric Inc (PA)......925 240-6024
380 Carrol Ct Ste L Brentwood (94513) *(G-2350)*
Roddy Ranch Pbc LLC......925 978-4653
1 Tour Way Antioch (94531) *(G-19046)*
Rodeo Realty Inc......818 986-7300
15300 Ventura Blvd # 101 Sherman Oaks (91403) *(G-11815)*
Rodeo Realty Inc......310 873-0100
11940 San Vicente Blvd Los Angeles (90049) *(G-11816)*
Rodeo Realty Inc......818 285-3700
17501 Ventura Blvd Encino (91316) *(G-11817)*
Rodeo Realty Inc......818 308-8273
12345 Ventura Blvd Ste A Studio City (91604) *(G-11818)*
Rodeo Realty Inc (PA)......818 349-9997
9171 Wilshire Blvd # 321 Beverly Hills (90210) *(G-11819)*
Rodeo Realty Inc......818 349-9997
9338 Reseda Blvd Ste 102 Northridge (91324) *(G-11820)*
Rodeo Realty Inc......818 999-2030
21031 Ventura Blvd # 100 Woodland Hills (91364) *(G-11821)*
Rodeway Inn, Tahoe City *Also called Pepper Tree Inn (G-13089)*
Rodgers Trucking Co, San Leandro *Also called Frank Ghiglione Inc (G-4020)*
Rodin & Co Inc......818 358-3427
7411 Laurel Canyon Blvd # 10 North Hollywood (91605) *(G-2486)*
Rodney Strong Vineyards, Healdsburg *Also called Klein Foods Inc (G-164)*
Roe Holdings LLC......310 559-9222
8437 Warner Dr Culver City (90232) *(G-13914)*
Roebbelen Construction Inc......916 939-4000
1241 Hawks Flight Ct El Dorado Hills (95762) *(G-1654)*
Roebbelen Contracting Inc......916 939-4000
1241 Hawks Flight Ct El Dorado Hills (95762) *(G-1655)*
Rogan Building Services Inc......951 248-1261
1531 7th St Riverside (92507) *(G-14409)*
Roger L Crumley MD Inc......714 456-5750
101 City Dr S Bldg 56 5 Orange (92868) *(G-19926)*
Rogers & Cowan (HQ)......310 854-8100
8687 Melrose Ave Ste G700 West Hollywood (90069) *(G-27766)*
Rogers Joseph ODonnell A Pro (PA)......415 956-2828
311 California St Fl 10 San Francisco (94104) *(G-23536)*
Rogers Poultry Co (PA)......323 585-0802
2020 E 67th St Los Angeles (90001) *(G-8605)*
Rogers Trucking, San Leandro *Also called Frank Ghiglione Inc (G-4021)*
Roi Communications Inc (PA)......831 430-0170
5274 Scotts Valley Dr # 107 Scotts Valley (95066) *(G-28044)*
Roisman Leon D DMD Inc......626 795-6855
310 S Lake Ave Ste B1 Pasadena (91101) *(G-20273)*
Roku Inc (PA)......408 556-9040
150 Winchester Cir Los Gatos (95032) *(G-6015)*
Roland Corporation US (HQ)......323 890-3700
5100 S Eastern Ave Los Angeles (90040) *(G-8135)*
Roland Dga Corporation (HQ)......949 727-2100
15363 Barranca Pkwy Irvine (92618) *(G-7180)*
Roll Properties Intl Inc......661 797-6500
13646 Highway 33 Lost Hills (93249) *(G-12341)*
Rolled Steel Products Corp (PA)......323 723-8836
2187 Garfield Ave Commerce (90040) *(G-7399)*
Rolling Hills Casino......530 528-3500
2655 Everett Freeman Way Corning (96021) *(G-19270)*
Rolling Hills Club, Novato *Also called Tennis Everyone Incorporated (G-19104)*
Rolling Hills Estates City of, Rllng HLS Est *Also called Rolling Hlls Esttes Tennis CLB (G-19271)*
Rolling Hlls Esttes Tennis CLB......310 541-4585
25851 Hawthorne Blvd Rllng HLS Est (90275) *(G-19271)*
Rolling Willow LLC......916 961-6171
5555 Mariposa Ave Citrus Heights (95610) *(G-18675)*
Rolo Logistics, Pico Rivera *Also called Rolo Transportation Company (G-4056)*
Rolo Transportation Company......562 463-1440
9935 Beverly Blvd Pico Rivera (90660) *(G-4056)*
Roma Food Enterprises Inc......800 233-6211
6211 Las Positas Rd Livermore (94551) *(G-8914)*
Roma of Northern California, Livermore *Also called Roma Food Enterprises Inc (G-8914)*
Romach LLC......805 378-1174
2956 Sparrow Dr Fullerton (92835) *(G-7468)*
Roman Cath Arch of Los Angels......310 836-5500
5835 W Slauson Ave Culver City (90230) *(G-13712)*
Roman Cath Arch of Los Angels......805 687-8811
199 N Hope Ave Santa Barbara (93110) *(G-13713)*
Roman Catholic Archdiocese of......650 756-2060
1500 Old Mission Rd Daly City (94014) *(G-12035)*
Roman Cthlic Bshp of Snta Rosa......707 528-8712
987 Airway Ct Santa Rosa (95403) *(G-24969)*
Roman Services, Pico Rivera *Also called Romans Transportation Inc (G-4630)*
Romans Transportation Inc......562 463-1433
9935 Beverly Blvd Pico Rivera (90660) *(G-4630)*
Romark Logistics of California......909 356-5600
13521 Santa Ana Ave Ste A Fontana (92337) *(G-4631)*
Romeo Cecylia K Beauty Salon......858 946-0179
11740 Carmel Mountain Rd # 198 San Diego (92128) *(G-13688)*
Romeo & Layla Warehousing Inc......909 947-9055
1041 Mildred St Ontario (91761) *(G-4632)*
ROMERO CONSTRUCTION, Escondido *Also called Romero General Cnstr Corp (G-1853)*
Romero General Cnstr Corp......760 489-8412
2150 N Centre City Pkwy Escondido (92026) *(G-1853)*
Ron D & Shelley N Horn......559 834-2118
3719 E Floral Ave Fresno (93725) *(G-181)*
Ron Faulkner Trucking......559 684-8536
24134 Road 208 Lindsay (93247) *(G-4057)*
Ron Filice Enterprises Inc......408 294-0477
738 N 1st St Ste 202 San Jose (95112) *(G-10857)*
Ron Nurss Inc......916 631-9761
11290 Sunrise Park Dr B Rancho Cordova (95742) *(G-3323)*
Ron's Pharmacy Services, San Diego *Also called Belville Enterprises Inc (G-19373)*
Ronald J Lemieux Assoc Law Off......562 375-0095
4195 N Viking Way Ste E Long Beach (90808) *(G-23537)*
Ronald L Wolfe & Assoc Inc......805 964-6770
173 Chapel St Santa Barbara (93111) *(G-11822)*
Ronald Reagan Building, Los Angeles *Also called Ucla Health System (G-20151)*

ALPHABETIC

Ronald Reagan Ucla Medical Ctr, Los Angeles *Also called University Cal Los Angeles (G-21991)*
Ronco Inventions LLC (PA) ... 800 486-1806
21344 Superior St Chatsworth (91311) ***(G-6884)***
Rongcheng Trading LLC ... 626 338-1090
19319 Arenth Ave City of Industry (91748) ***(G-8683)***
Ronsin Photocopy Inc (PA) ... 909 594-5995
215 Lemon Creek Dr Walnut (91789) ***(G-17467)***
Roofing Constructors Inc ... 415 648-6472
15002 Wicks Blvd San Leandro (94577) ***(G-3210)***
Roofing Supply Group LLC ... 424 269-7330
14128 Kornblum Ave Hawthorne (90250) ***(G-7015)***
Roofing Wholesale Co Inc ... 619 287-7600
8674 Jamacha Rd Spring Valley (91977) ***(G-7016)***
Roofing Wholesale Co Inc ... 909 825-8440
118 Commercial Rd San Bernardino (92408) ***(G-7017)***
Roofline Sup Delivery-Burbank, Burbank *Also called SRS Distribution Inc (G-7019)*
Room & Board Inc ... 415 252-9280
685 7th St San Francisco (94103) ***(G-11198)***
Roosevelt Hotel LLC ... 323 466-7000
7000 Hollywood Blvd Los Angeles (90028) ***(G-13165)***
Roosevelt Wind Holdings LLC ... 888 903-6926
15445 Innovation Dr San Diego (92128) ***(G-6199)***
Roost, Sausalito *Also called Gate Five Group LLC (G-6863)*
Rooster Run Golf Club Inc ... 707 778-1211
2301 E Washington St Petaluma (94954) ***(G-18778)***
Rope Partner Inc ... 831 460-9448
125 Mcpherson St Ste B Santa Cruz (95060) ***(G-7949)***
Ropers Majeski Kohn & Bentley, Redwood City *Also called Ropers Majeski Kohn Bentley (G-23538)*
Ropers Majeski Kohn Bentley (PA) ... 650 364-8200
1001 Marshall St Fl 3 Redwood City (94063) ***(G-23538)***
Ropes & Gray LLP ... 415 315-6300
3 Embarcadero Ctr Ste 300 San Francisco (94111) ***(G-23539)***
Ropes & Gray LLP ... 650 617-4000
1900 University Ave # 600 East Palo Alto (94303) ***(G-23540)***
Roppongi-Tahoe Lp A Californi ... 530 544-5400
4130 Lake Tahoe Blvd South Lake Tahoe (96150) ***(G-13166)***
Roque Development and Inv Inc ... 626 427-9077
227 E Pomona Blvd Ste B Monterey Park (91755) ***(G-26044)***
Rore Inc (PA) ... 858 404-7393
5151 Shoreham Pl Ste 260 San Diego (92122) ***(G-1461)***
Rory V Parker ... 510 595-5543
818 27th St Ste 101 Oakland (94607) ***(G-16775)***
Rosanna Inc ... 714 751-5100
3350 Avenue Of The Arts Costa Mesa (92626) ***(G-13167)***
Rosano Partners ... 213 802-0300
700 S Flower St Ste 2526 Los Angeles (90017) ***(G-11823)***
Rosary Academy Parent Council ... 714 879-6302
1340 N Acacia Ave Fullerton (92831) ***(G-25327)***
Roscoe Real Estate Ltd Partnr ... 310 260-7500
1819 Ocean Ave Santa Monica (90401) ***(G-13168)***
Rose & Kindel Grayling ... 916 441-1034
1414 K St Ste 220 Sacramento (95814) ***(G-24970)***
Rose & Shore Inc ... 323 826-2144
5151 Alcoa Ave Vernon (90058) ***(G-17468)***
Rose Bowl Aquatics Center ... 626 564-0330
360 N Arroyo Blvd Pasadena (91103) ***(G-19047)***
Rose Brand Wipers Inc ... 818 505-6290
10616 Lanark St Sun Valley (91352) ***(G-18429)***
Rose Garden Convalescent Ctr, Pasadena *Also called David Ross Inc (G-20511)*
Rose Hills Co, Whittier *Also called Rose Hills Mortuary Inc (G-13714)*
Rose Hills Company (HQ) ... 562 699-0921
3888 Workman Mill Rd Whittier (90601) ***(G-12036)***
Rose Hills Holdings Corp (PA) ... 562 699-0921
3888 Workman Mill Rd Whittier (90601) ***(G-12037)***
Rose Hills Mem Pk & Mortuary, Whittier *Also called Rose Hills Company (G-12036)*
Rose Hills Mem Pk & Mortuary, Whittier *Also called Rose Hills Holdings Corp (G-12037)*
Rose Hills Mortuary Inc ... 562 699-0921
3888 Workman Mill Rd Whittier (90601) ***(G-13714)***
Rose International Inc ... 636 812-4000
450 N Brand Blvd Fl 6 Glendale (91203) ***(G-15429)***
Rose International Inc ... 636 812-4000
4000 Executive Pkwy # 150 San Ramon (94583) ***(G-28045)***
Rose International Inc ... 636 812-4000
18952 Macarthur Blvd # 440 Irvine (92612) ***(G-28046)***
Rose Ox Inc (HQ) ... 619 239-4111
402 W Broadway Ste 1600 San Diego (92101) ***(G-14168)***
Rose Thompson Company ... 760 736-6020
949 Cassou Rd San Marcos (92069) ***(G-316)***
Rosecrans Care Center, Gardena *Also called Health Care Investments Inc (G-20656)*
Rosemary Childrens Services (PA) ... 626 844-3033
36 S Kinneloa Ave 200 Pasadena (91107) ***(G-24791)***
Rosen Electronics LLC ... 951 898-9808
1120 California Ave Corona (92881) ***(G-8136)***
Rosen Electronics, L.P., Corona *Also called Rosen Electronics LLC (G-8136)*
Rosendin Electric Inc (PA) ... 408 286-2800
880 Mabury Rd San Jose (95133) ***(G-2715)***
Rosendin Electric Inc ... 408 321-2200
2698 Orchard Pkwy San Jose (95134) ***(G-2716)***
Rosendin Electric Inc ... 415 495-9300
2121 Oakdale Ave San Francisco (94124) ***(G-2717)***
Rosendin Electric Inc ... 415 495-9300
1001 Potrero Ave San Francisco (94110) ***(G-2718)***
Rosenthal & Company LLC ... 415 884-1100
75 Rowland Way Ste 250 Novato (94945) ***(G-27625)***
Rosenthal Group, The, Venice *Also called Trg Inc (G-11881)*
Roseryan Inc ... 510 456-3056
35473 Dumbarton Ct Newark (94560) ***(G-26431)***

Roses Maid Service, Quail Valley *Also called Francois Annanie (G-14302)*
Rosetta LLC ... 408 275-7117
60 S Market St Ste 750 San Jose (95113) ***(G-27626)***
Rosetta LLC ... 347 332-7659
4800 Morabito Pl San Luis Obispo (93401) ***(G-27627)***
ROSEVILLE CARE CENTER, Roseville *Also called Crocus Holdings LLC (G-20508)*
Roseville Convalescent Hosp, Roseville *Also called Horizon West Healthcare Inc (G-22145)*
Roseville Foothils and Jct, Roseville *Also called Wells Fargo Bank National Assn (G-9442)*
Roseville Imaging, Roseville *Also called Sutter Health (G-20105)*
Roseville Sportworld Inc ... 916 783-8550
1009 Orlando Ave Roseville (95661) ***(G-19272)***
Roseville Towne Place Suites ... 916 782-2232
10569 Fairway Dr Roseville (95678) ***(G-13169)***
Rosewood Care Center, Pleasant Hill *Also called Helios Healthcare LLC (G-20664)*
Rosewood Convalescent Hospital, Pleasant Hill *Also called Dreamctchers Empwerment Netwrk (G-24635)*
Rosewood Hotels & Resorts LLC ... 650 561-1500
2825 Sand Hill Rd Menlo Park (94025) ***(G-13170)***
Rosewood Rehabilitation, Carmichael *Also called Carmichael Care Inc (G-20439)*
Rosewood Retirement Community, Bakersfield *Also called American Baptist Homes of West (G-21135)*
Rosewood Sand Hill Hotel, Menlo Park *Also called Rosewood Hotels & Resorts LLC (G-13170)*
Ross F Carroll Inc ... 209 848-5959
8873 Warnerville Rd Oakdale (95361) ***(G-26045)***
Ross Hospital ... 415 258-6900
1111 Sir Francis Dr Kentfield (94904) ***(G-22169)***
Ross Valley Homes Inc ... 415 461-2300
501 Via Casitas Greenbrae (94904) ***(G-21101)***
Rossi Hamerslough Reishchl & ... 408 244-4570
1960 The Alameda Ste 200 San Jose (95126) ***(G-23541)***
Rossmoor, Walnut Creek *Also called Golden Rain Foundation (G-11557)*
Rossmoor Carwash, Los Alamitos *Also called Lakewood South Car Wash LLC (G-17847)*
Rostami Nejat Medical Group ... 213 413-2700
2007 Wilshire Blvd # 215 Los Angeles (90057) ***(G-19927)***
Rotary Club, Palo Cedro *Also called Rotary International (G-25328)*
ROTARY CLUB OF NAPA SUNRISE OF, NAPA *Also called NAPA Sunrise Rotary Club Inc (G-25302)*
Rotary Club San Rafael Fund ... 415 457-4284
851 Irwin St Ste 202 San Rafael (94901) ***(G-19048)***
Rotary International ... 530 547-5272
9839 Meadowlark Way Palo Cedro (96073) ***(G-25328)***
Rotex, Gardena *Also called Rotor Exchange (G-6796)*
Roth Capital Partners LLC (PA) ... 800 678-9147
888 San Clemente Dr # 400 Newport Beach (92660) ***(G-10075)***
Roth Staffing Companies LP (PA) ... 714 939-8600
450 N State College Blvd Orange (92868) ***(G-14944)***
Rothfleisch Ranches Inc ... 760 344-1819
129 S El Cerrito Dr Brawley (92227) ***(G-721)***
Roto Rooter Plumbing & Drain S ... 951 658-8541
796 N State St Hemet (92543) ***(G-18006)***
Roto-Rooter, Anaheim *Also called Hoffman Southwest Corp (G-17979)*
Roto-Rooter, Rancho Cucamonga *Also called Hoffman Southwest Corp (G-17980)*
Roto-Rooter Services Company ... 650 322-2366
220 Demeter St East Palo Alto (94303) ***(G-18007)***
Rotor Exchange ... 310 323-5710
14010 S Western Ave Gardena (90249) ***(G-6796)***
Rotorcraft Support Inc ... 818 997-8060
16425 Hart St Van Nuys (91406) ***(G-8003)***
Rouche O Edgar DDS, Riverside *Also called American Dntl Partners of Cal (G-20244)*
Round Hill Country Club ... 925 934-8211
3169 Roundhill Rd Alamo (94507) ***(G-19049)***
Round Hill Enterprises ... 925 934-8211
3169 Roundhill Rd Alamo (94507) ***(G-19050)***
Round Hill Golf & Country Club, Alamo *Also called Round Hill Enterprises (G-19050)*
Round Valley Indian Health Ctr ... 707 983-6182
Hwy 162 Biggar Ln Covelo (95428) ***(G-19928)***
Roundabout Entertainment Inc ... 818 842-9300
217 S Lake St Burbank (91502) ***(G-18146)***
Rounseville Rehabilitation Ctr, Oakland *Also called Rcc Facility Incorporated (G-21355)*
Rountree Plumbing and Htg Inc ... 650 298-0300
1659c Industrial Rd San Carlos (94070) ***(G-2351)***
Roux Associates Inc ... 562 446-8600
5150 E Pacific Coast Hwy # 450 Long Beach (90804) ***(G-28047)***
Rovi Corporation ... 408 445-8100
150 Menard Dr San Jose (95138) ***(G-15430)***
Rovi Corporation (PA) ... 408 562-8400
2 Circle Star Way San Carlos (94070) ***(G-15829)***
Row Management Ltd Inc ... 310 887-3671
499 N Canon Dr Beverly Hills (90210) ***(G-11824)***
Rowan Incorporated ... 760 692-0700
2778 Loker Ave W Carlsbad (92010) ***(G-2719)***
Rowan Electric, Carlsbad *Also called Rowan Incorporated (G-2719)*
Rowland Convalescent Hosp Inc ... 626 967-2741
330 W Rowland St Covina (91723) ***(G-20882)***
Rowland, The, Covina *Also called Rowland Convalescent Hosp Inc (G-20882)*
Roxbury Management Company ... 310 274-4142
P.O. Box 1345 Beverly Hills (90213) ***(G-11825)***
Roy C Shannon MD, Oroville *Also called Oroville Internal Meds Group (G-19800)*
Roy E Ladd Inc ... 530 241-6102
3724 Sunlight Ct Redding (96001) ***(G-1854)***
Roy E Whitehead Inc ... 951 682-1490
2245 Via Cerro Riverside (92509) ***(G-3081)***
Roy Jorgensen Associates Inc ... 310 468-2478
19001 S Western Ave Torrance (90501) ***(G-14410)***

Roy Miller Freight Lines LLC (PA) 714 632-5511
3165 E Coronado St Anaheim (92806) *(G-4058)*
Royal Airline Linen Inc 310 677-9885
125 N Ash Ave Inglewood (90301) *(G-13507)*
Royal Ambulance Inc 510 568-6161
14472 Wicks Blvd San Leandro (94577) *(G-3834)*
Royal Care Skilled Nursing Ctr, Long Beach *Also called Covenant Care California LLC (G-20490)*
Royal Coach Tours (PA) 408 279-4801
630 Stockton Ave San Jose (95126) *(G-3693)*
Royal Crest Building Maint 714 562-5034
8601 Roland St Ste E Buena Park (90621) *(G-14411)*
Royal Crest Healthcare, Covina *Also called Cruz Hoffstetter LLC (G-17108)*
Royal Crown Enterprises Inc (PA) 626 854-8080
780 Epperson Dr City of Industry (91748) *(G-8915)*
Royal Express Inc (PA) 559 272-3500
3545 E Date Ave Fresno (93725) *(G-4373)*
Royal Glass Company Inc 408 969-0444
3200 De La Cruz Blvd Santa Clara (95054) *(G-3414)*
Royal Gorge Crss Cntry Ski Rst, Soda Springs *Also called Royal Gorge Nordic Ski Resort (G-13171)*
Royal Gorge Nordic Ski Resort (PA) 530 426-3871
9411 Hillside Rd Soda Springs (95728) *(G-13171)*
Royal Hospitality Incorporated 858 278-0800
5550 Kearny Mesa Rd San Diego (92111) *(G-13172)*
Royal Investigation Patrol Inc 510 352-6800
2950 Merced St Ste 108 San Leandro (94577) *(G-16776)*
Royal Laundry, South San Francisco *Also called American Etc Inc (G-13499)*
Royal Medjool Date Garden 760 572-0524
1203 Perez Rd Bard (92222) *(G-259)*
Royal Mountain King, Copperopolis *Also called Meridian Gold Inc (G-1023)*
Royal Oaks, Duarte *Also called Cal Southern Presbt Homes (G-11109)*
Royal Oaks Enterprises Inc 408 779-2362
15480 Watsonville Rd Morgan Hill (95037) *(G-343)*
Royal Oaks Manor, Duarte *Also called Begroup (G-20408)*
Royal Oaks Mushroom, Morgan Hill *Also called Royal Oaks Enterprises Inc (G-343)*
Royal Packing Dcf 559 945-2537
32839 S Lassen Ave Huron (93234) *(G-91)*
Royal Paper Corp (PA) 562 903-9030
10232 Palm Dr Santa Fe Springs (90670) *(G-8214)*
Royal Plywood Company LLC 916 386-9873
6003 88th St Ste 100 Sacramento (95828) *(G-6958)*
Royal Plywood Company LLC (PA) 562 404-2989
14171 Park Pl Cerritos (90703) *(G-6959)*
Royal Poultry, Vernon *Also called Golden West Trading Inc (G-8668)*
Royal Ridge Frt Cold Stor LLC 925 600-0224
790 San Rmon Blvd Ste 200 Danville (94526) *(G-8916)*
Royal Roofing & Cnstr Co 714 764-1100
1144 N Armando St Anaheim (92806) *(G-3211)*
Royal Roofing Construction Co, Placentia *Also called Osscim Inc (G-3195)*
Royal Scandinavian Inn, Solvang *Also called National Hospitality LLC (G-13016)*
Royal Specialty Undwrt Inc 818 922-6700
15303 Ventura Blvd # 500 Sherman Oaks (91403) *(G-10458)*
Royal Terrace Healthcare 626 256-4654
1340 Highland Ave Duarte (91010) *(G-20883)*
Royal Truck Body, Paramount *Also called Fortress Resources LLC (G-17791)*
Royal Trucking, Concord *Also called Lemore Transportation Inc (G-4212)*
Royal West Drywall Inc 951 271-4600
2008 2nd St Norco (92860) *(G-2970)*
Royale Hlth Care Mission Viejo, Mission Viejo *Also called Orange County Royale Convlscnt (G-21336)*
Royalty Tours 408 279-4801
630 Stockton Ave San Jose (95126) *(G-4999)*
Rp Realty Partners LLC 310 207-6990
990 W 8th St Ste 600 Los Angeles (90017) *(G-11037)*
Rp Scs Wsd Hotel LLC 619 398-3020
421 W B St San Diego (92101) *(G-13173)*
Rp/Kinetic Parc 55 Owner LLC 415 392-8000
55 Cyril Magnin St San Francisco (94102) *(G-13174)*
RPC Old Town Avenue Owner LLC 619 299-7400
3900 Old Town Ave San Diego (92110) *(G-13175)*
RPC Old Town Jefferson 619 725-4221
2435 Jefferson St San Diego (92110) *(G-13176)*
Rpd Hotels 18 LLC (PA) 213 746-1531
2361 Rosecrans Ave # 150 El Segundo (90245) *(G-13177)*
RPM Consolidated Services Inc (PA) 714 388-3500
1901 Raymer Ave Fullerton (92833) *(G-4633)*
RPM Mechanical - A Joint Ventr 858 565-4131
2919 E Victoria St Compton (90221) *(G-2352)*
RPM Mortgage Inc (PA) 925 295-9300
3240 Stone Valley Rd W Alamo (94507) *(G-9893)*
RPM Mortgage Inc 925 627-7100
1777 Botelho Dr Ste 200 Walnut Creek (94596) *(G-9894)*
RPM Transportation Inc (HQ) 714 388-3500
1901 Raymer Ave Fullerton (92833) *(G-4254)*
Rpx Corporation (PA) 866 779-7641
1 Market Plz Ste 800 San Francisco (94105) *(G-12224)*
Rqc, Carlsbad *Also called R Q Construction LLC (G-1460)*
RR Donnelley & Sons Company 310 784-8485
3541 Lomita Blvd Torrance (90505) *(G-14089)*
RR Donnelley & Sons Company 858 693-6662
8925 Carroll Way San Diego (92121) *(G-17469)*
RR Donnelley & Sons Company 925 951-1320
1646 N Calif Blvd Ste 510 Walnut Creek (94596) *(G-3615)*
RR Donnelley & Sons Company 951 296-2890
40610 County Center Dr Temecula (92591) *(G-8178)*
RR Donnelley & Sons Company 619 527-4600
955 Gateway Center Way San Diego (92102) *(G-8154)*

RRI, Downey *Also called Rancho Research Institute (G-26800)*
Rrm Design Group (PA) 805 439-0442
3765 S Higuera St Ste 102 San Luis Obispo (93401) *(G-26248)*
Rromeo Corporation 714 640-3800
535 Anton Blvd Ste 200 Costa Mesa (92626) *(G-27202)*
Rs Calibration Services Inc 925 462-4217
1047 Serpentine Ln # 500 Pleasanton (94566) *(G-18008)*
Rs Investment Management LP (PA) 415 591-2700
1 Bush St Ste 900 San Francisco (94104) *(G-12124)*
Rsa Security LLC 650 529-9992
2831 Mission College Blvd Santa Clara (95054) *(G-15431)*
Rse, Sacramento *Also called Runyon Saltzman Einhorn Inc (G-13916)*
Rsf Protective Services, Encinitas *Also called Rancho Santa Fe Protective Svc (G-16770)*
RSI Professional Cab Solutions 909 614-2900
11350 Riverside Dr Frnt Mira Loma (91752) *(G-3082)*
RSM US LLP 415 848-5300
44 Montgomery St Ste 3900 San Francisco (94104) *(G-26432)*
RSM US LLP 949 255-6500
18401 Von Karman Ave # 500 Irvine (92612) *(G-26433)*
RSM US LLP 408 572-4440
100 W San Fernando St San Jose (95113) *(G-26434)*
Rsui Group, Sherman Oaks *Also called Royal Specialty Undwrt Inc (G-10458)*
Rt Pasad Hotel Partners LP 626 403-7600
180 N Fair Oaks Ave Pasadena (91103) *(G-13178)*
Rt/Dt Inc 925 757-1981
1777 Vineyard Dr Antioch (94509) *(G-2353)*
RTC, Los Angeles *Also called Religious Technology Center (G-12222)*
RTC Aerospace, Chatsworth *Also called Logistical Support LLC (G-8000)*
RTC Brea, Brea *Also called Renal Trtmnt Cntrs-Clfrnia Inc (G-22638)*
Rte Enterprises Inc 818 999-5300
21530 Roscoe Blvd Canoga Park (91304) *(G-2487)*
Rte Welding, Fontana *Also called Tikos Tanks Inc (G-17955)*
Ruan 209 634-4928
830 W Glenwood Ave Turlock (95380) *(G-4059)*
Ruann Dairy, Riverdale *Also called Maddox Dairy A Ltd Partnership (G-433)*
Rubicon B Hacienda LLC 424 290-5555
475 N Sepulveda Blvd El Segundo (90245) *(G-13179)*
Rubicon Corporation America 818 765-2001
10425 Oklahoma Ave Chatsworth (91311) *(G-11826)*
Rubicon Enterprises Inc 510 235-1516
2500 Bissell Ave Richmond (94804) *(G-14412)*
RUBICON PROGRAMS, Richmond *Also called Rubicon Enterprises Inc (G-14412)*
Rubicon Programs Incorporated (PA) 510 235-1516
2500 Bissell Ave Richmond (94804) *(G-14413)*
Rubicon Project Inc (PA) 310 207-0272
12181 Bluff Creek Dr Fl 4 Los Angeles (90094) *(G-13915)*
Rubicon Realty, Chatsworth *Also called Rubicon Corporation America (G-11826)*
Rubidoux Family Care Center, Riverside *Also called County of Riverside (G-19477)*
Ruby Creek Resources 212 671-0404
1835 W Olympic Blvd Los Angeles (90006) *(G-27628)*
Ruby Hill Golf Club LLC 925 417-5840
3400 W Ruby Hill Dr Pleasanton (94566) *(G-19051)*
Ruby Sky, San Francisco *Also called Inner Circle Entertainment (G-8622)*
Ruckus Wireless Inc (HQ) 650 265-4200
350 W Java Dr Sunnyvale (94089) *(G-5694)*
Ruder, Michael MD, Palo Alto *Also called Cardic Arithmias (G-19401)*
Rudolph and Sletten Inc (HQ) 650 216-3600
1600 Seaport Blvd Ste 350 Redwood City (94063) *(G-1656)*
Rudolph Foods Company Inc 909 383-7463
145 Hillcrest Ave San Bernardino (92408) *(G-8516)*
Rudolph Foods West, San Bernardino *Also called Rudolph Foods Company Inc (G-8516)*
Rudy Carrillo Drywall Inc 818 841-2011
1913 W Magnolia Blvd Burbank (91506) *(G-2971)*
Ruffin Hotel Corp of Cal 562 425-5210
4700 Airport Plaza Dr Long Beach (90815) *(G-13180)*
Rugby Laboratories Inc (HQ) 951 270-1400
311 Bonnie Cir Corona (92880) *(G-8292)*
Rugged Engineered Pdts Sector, San Diego *Also called Epsilon Systems Solutions Inc (G-25800)*
Ruiz Janitorial Co Inc 650 361-1303
446 Heller St Redwood City (94063) *(G-14414)*
Running Creek Casino 707 275-9209
635 E State Highway 20 Upper Lake (95485) *(G-13181)*
Runyon Saltzman Einhorn Inc 916 446-9900
2020 L St Ste 100 Sacramento (95811) *(G-13916)*
Rural Cmnty Assistance Corp (PA) 916 447-2854
3120 Freeboard Dr Ste 201 West Sacramento (95691) *(G-24161)*
Rural/Metro Corporation 510 266-0885
2364 W Winton Ave Hayward (94545) *(G-3835)*
Rural/Metro Corporation 888 876-0740
1345 Vander Way San Jose (95112) *(G-3836)*
Rural/Metro San Diego Inc 619 280-6060
10405 San Diego Mission R San Diego (92108) *(G-3837)*
Rush Enterprises Inc 800 776-3647
15463 Valley Blvd Fontana (92335) *(G-4060)*
Russell Fisher Partnership 714 842-4453
16061 Beach Blvd Huntington Beach (92647) *(G-17861)*
Russell Mechanical Inc 916 635-2522
3251 Monier Cir Ste A Rancho Cordova (95742) *(G-2354)*
Russian River Health Center 707 869-2849
16319 3rd St Guerneville (95446) *(G-19929)*
Russian River Sportsman Club 707 865-9429
25150 Steelhead Blvd Duncans Mills (95430) *(G-19052)*
Russon Financial Services Inc 818 999-2800
19935 Ventura Blvd # 100 Woodland Hills (91364) *(G-27629)*
Rutan & Tucker LLP (PA) 714 641-5100
611 Anton Blvd Ste 1400 Costa Mesa (92626) *(G-23542)*

A L P H A B E T I C

Ruth Barajas....415 977-6949
965 Mission St Ste 520 San Francisco (94103) *(G-24162)*
Ruth Perkowitz Inc (PA)....562 628-8000
111 W Ocean Blvd Ste 21 Long Beach (90802) *(G-26249)*
Rutherford Co Inc (PA)....323 666-5284
2905 Allesandro St Los Angeles (90039) *(G-2972)*
Rutland Tool & Supply Co (HQ)....562 566-5000
2225 Workman Mill Rd City of Industry (90601) *(G-7950)*
Rutledge Claims Management Inc....858 888-2000
14286 Danielson St # 103 Poway (92064) *(G-14045)*
Ruuhwa Dann and Associates Inc....909 467-4800
1541 Brooks St Ontario (91762) *(G-7181)*
Rvtlzation Anaheim II Partners....714 520-4041
1515 S Calle Del Mar Anaheim (92802) *(G-11827)*
RW Lynch Co Inc (PA)....925 837-3877
2333 San Ramon Valley Blv San Ramon (94583) *(G-13917)*
RW&g, Los Angeles *Also called Richards Watson & Gershon PC (G-23532)*
Rwc Enterprises Inc....909 373-4100
9130 Santa Anita Ave Rancho Cucamonga (91730) *(G-26046)*
Rwp Transfer Inc....909 868-6882
1313 E Phillips Blvd Pomona (91766) *(G-8137)*
Rx Pro Health LLC....858 369-4050
12400 High Bluff Dr San Diego (92130) *(G-14945)*
Ryan Herco Flow Solutions, Burbank *Also called Ryan Herco Products Corp (G-7730)*
Ryan Herco Products Corp (PA)....818 841-1141
3010 N San Fernando Blvd Burbank (91504) *(G-7730)*
Ryan Partnership, Los Angeles *Also called D L Ryan Companies LLC (G-27744)*
Ryans Express Trnsp Svcs Inc (PA)....702 795-7021
19500 Mariner Ave Torrance (90503) *(G-5000)*
Ryde Hotel LLC....916 776-1318
14340 State Highway 160 Walnut Grove (95690) *(G-13182)*
Ryde Motel, Walnut Grove *Also called Ryde Hotel LLC (G-13182)*
Rydek Eletronics LLC....310 641-9800
898 N Sepulveda Blvd # 475 El Segundo (90245) *(G-14776)*
Ryder Integrated Logistics Inc....818 701-9332
19133 Parthenia St Northridge (91324) *(G-17650)*
Ryder Truck Rental Inc....415 285-0756
2700 3rd St San Francisco (94107) *(G-17651)*
Ryder Truck Rental Inc....562 921-0033
13630 Firestone Blvd Santa Fe Springs (90670) *(G-17652)*
Ryder Truck Rental Inc....909 980-5084
9608 Santa Anita Ave Rancho Cucamonga (91730) *(G-17653)*
Rye Electric Inc....949 441-0545
3940 Electric Ave Laguna Hills (92653) *(G-2720)*
Ryland Hmes Inlnd Empire Cstmr....951 273-3473
1250 Corona Pointe Ct # 100 Corona (92879) *(G-1249)*
Ryland Homes, Carlsbad *Also called Calatlantic Group Inc (G-1359)*
Ryland Homes of Texas Inc....805 367-3800
15360 Barranca Pkwy Irvine (92618) *(G-1383)*
Ryte Professionals, Cypress *Also called Sws2 Inc (G-14799)*
S & J, Los Angeles *Also called Sam Jung USA Inc (G-8324)*
S & J Ranches LLC....559 437-2600
39639 Avenue 10 Madera (93636) *(G-722)*
S & L Specialty Contracting....619 264-3771
4514 Federal Blvd Ste C San Diego (92102) *(G-2973)*
S & M Moving Systems, Santa Fe Springs *Also called Van Torrance & Storage Company (G-4387)*
S & M Moving Systems....510 497-2300
48551 Warm Springs Blvd Fremont (94539) *(G-4255)*
S & S Construction Co, Beverly Hills *Also called Shapell Industries LLC (G-12008)*
S & S Construction Services, El Monte *Also called S & S Rent-A-Fence Inc (G-14577)*
S & S Portable Services Inc....626 967-9300
4511 Rowland Ave El Monte (91731) *(G-14576)*
S & S Ranch Inc....559 655-3491
904 S Lyon Ave Mendota (93640) *(G-482)*
S & S Rent-A-Fence Inc....818 896-7710
4511 Rowland Ave El Monte (91731) *(G-14577)*
S & S Tool & Supply Inc (PA)....925 335-4000
2700 Maxwell Way Fairfield (94534) *(G-7951)*
S A Cali-U Acoustics Inc....805 376-9300
1111 Rancho Conejo Blvd # 501 Thousand Oaks (91320) *(G-2974)*
S A Camp Companies (PA)....661 399-4451
17876 Zerker Rd Bakersfield (93308) *(G-7809)*
S A Camp Pump Company....661 399-2976
17876 Zerker Rd Bakersfield (93308) *(G-18009)*
S A S, Pacheco *Also called Bay Alarm Company (G-2528)*
S A S, Millbrae *Also called Trans World Maintenance Inc (G-2498)*
S and S Supplies and Solutions, Fairfield *Also called S & S Tool & Supply Inc (G-7951)*
S B C, Fresno *Also called AT&T Services Inc (G-5531)*
S B C, Monterey *Also called AT&T Services Inc (G-5534)*
S B C Senior Care Inc....805 560-6995
101 W Anapamu St Ste C Santa Barbara (93101) *(G-22552)*
S B COMMUNICATIONS, Hawthorne *Also called South Bay Rgonal Pub Comm Auth (G-6089)*
S B M, McClellan *Also called Sbm Site Services LLC (G-14421)*
S C A, Victorville *Also called Southern California AVI LLC (G-4938)*
S C A G, Los Angeles *Also called Cal Southern Assn Governments (G-27861)*
S C L, Gardena *Also called Schumacher Cargo Logistics Inc (G-5166)*
S C P M G, Fontana *Also called Southern Cal Prmnnte Med Group (G-21902)*
S C P M G, Colton *Also called Southern Cal Prmnnte Med Group (G-20030)*
S C P M G, El Cajon *Also called Southern Cal Prmnnte Med Group (G-20032)*
S C P M G, Anaheim *Also called Southern Cal Prmnnte Med Group (G-20033)*
S C P M G, San Juan Capistrano *Also called Southern Cal Prmnnte Med Group (G-20034)*
S C P M G, Yorba Linda *Also called Southern Cal Prmnnte Med Group (G-20035)*
S C P M G, Santa Ana *Also called Southern Cal Prmnnte Med Group (G-20036)*
S C P M G, San Diego *Also called Southern Cal Prmnnte Med Group (G-20037)*
S C P M G, Escondido *Also called Southern Cal Prmnnte Med Group (G-20038)*
S C P M G, Cudahy *Also called Southern Cal Prmnnte Med Group (G-20039)*
S C P M G, Woodland Hills *Also called Southern Cal Prmnnte Med Group (G-20040)*
S C P M G, Santa Clarita *Also called Southern Cal Prmnnte Med Group (G-20041)*
S C P M G, San Diego *Also called Southern Cal Prmnnte Med Group (G-20042)*
S C P M G, San Dimas *Also called Southern Cal Prmnnte Med Group (G-20043)*
S C S, North Highlands *Also called Security Contractor Svcs Inc (G-7027)*
S C Security Inc....661 251-6999
26752 Oak Ave Ste C Santa Clarita (91351) *(G-16777)*
S CA University Hlth Sciences....562 947-8755
P.O. Box 1166 Whittier (90609) *(G-20298)*
S D I, Lakeside *Also called Standard Drywall Inc (G-2983)*
S D O A, San Diego *Also called San Diego Orthopaedic Associat (G-19940)*
S D Property Management Inc....323 658-7990
14937 Delano St Van Nuys (91411) *(G-11828)*
S D Y S, San Diego *Also called San Diego Youth Services Inc (G-24176)*
S E C C Corporation....760 246-6218
16224 Koala Rd Adelanto (92301) *(G-1990)*
S E C C Corporation....805 578-3596
900 W Los Angeles Ave Simi Valley (93065) *(G-26047)*
S E O P Inc....949 682-7906
1720 E Garry Ave Ste 103 Santa Ana (92705) *(G-27630)*
S E Pipe Line Construction Co....562 868-9771
11832 Bloomfield Ave Santa Fe Springs (90670) *(G-1991)*
S F Auto Parts Whse Inc....415 255-0115
6000 3rd St San Francisco (94124) *(G-6760)*
S F Broadcasting of Wisconsin....310 586-2410
2425 Olympic Blvd Santa Monica (90404) *(G-5907)*
S G D Enterprises....818 782-3455
14937 Delano St Van Nuys (91411) *(G-947)*
S G S Produce, Los Angeles *Also called Shapiro-Gilman-Shandler Co (G-8775)*
S H E, Visalia *Also called Self Help Enterprises (G-25346)*
S I J Inc....951 304-9444
26035 Jefferson Ave Murrieta (92562) *(G-3083)*
S J Amoroso Cnstr Co Inc (PA)....650 654-1900
390 Bridge Pkwy Redwood City (94065) *(G-1657)*
S J General Building Maint....408 392-0800
919 Berryessa Rd Ste 10 San Jose (95133) *(G-14415)*
S J S Link International Inc (PA)....310 860-7666
468 N Camden Dr Ste 311 Beverly Hills (90210) *(G-8569)*
S J W, San Jose *Also called San Jose Water Company (G-6397)*
S K & A Information Svcs Inc (HQ)....949 476-2051
2601 Main St Ste 650 Irvine (92614) *(G-26705)*
S L G G Consulting Group LLC (PA)....310 477-3924
10960 Wilshire Blvd # 1100 Los Angeles (90024) *(G-26435)*
S L H C C Inc....916 457-6521
3500 Folsom Blvd Sacramento (95816) *(G-20884)*
S L S Hotel, Los Angeles *Also called Sbehg 465 S La Cienega LLC (G-13222)*
S M C, Simi Valley *Also called Smart Living Company (G-9303)*
S M G, San Francisco *Also called Smg Holdings Inc (G-11050)*
S M U D, Sacramento *Also called Sacramento Municpl Utility Dst (G-6200)*
S N S West LLC....909 350-8118
10700 Business Dr Fontana (92337) *(G-4701)*
S O S Club, Modesto *Also called Sportsmen of Stanislaus Inc (G-18696)*
S P R E Inc....510 222-8340
3223 Blume Dr Richmond (94806) *(G-11829)*
S P Richards Company....916 564-5891
2190 Hanson Way Woodland (95776) *(G-8179)*
S P Richards Company....951 681-3114
10235 San Sevaine Way # 120 Mira Loma (91752) *(G-8180)*
S Patterson Construction Inc....661 391-9939
3335 Pegasus Dr Apt 308 Bakersfield (93308) *(G-2975)*
S R H H Inc....408 247-0800
1085 E El Camino Real Sunnyvale (94087) *(G-13183)*
S R I C B I....650 859-4865
333 Ravenswood Ave Menlo Park (94025) *(G-28048)*
S R J, San Clemente *Also called Julius Steve Construction Inc (G-1441)*
S R Mutual Funds, City of Industry *Also called California Country Club (G-18906)*
S R S M Inc....310 952-9000
945 E Church St Riverside (92507) *(G-6885)*
S S 8, Milpitas *Also called Ss8 Networks Inc (G-6091)*
S S F, South San Francisco *Also called Ssf Imported Auto Parts LLC (G-6773)*
S S I, Oxnard *Also called Synectic Solutions Inc (G-16491)*
S S W Mechanical Cnstr Inc....760 327-1481
670 S Oleander Rd Palm Springs (92264) *(G-2355)*
S Stamoules Inc....559 655-9777
904 S Lyon Ave Mendota (93640) *(G-581)*
S Surabian & Sons....559 591-5215
225 W Tulare St Dinuba (93618) *(G-222)*
S T L, Sacramento *Also called Sacramento Theatrical Ltg Ltd (G-18430)*
S Taylor Construction Inc....310 291-4505
23905 Clinton Keith Rd Wildomar (92595) *(G-1250)*
S V M, Santa Clara *Also called Silicon Vly McRelectronics Inc (G-7632)*
S W Construction Inc....714 978-7871
1145 E Stanford Ct Anaheim (92805) *(G-3084)*
S W K Properties LLC....714 481-6300
2726 S Grand Ave Lbby Santa Ana (92705) *(G-13184)*
S W K Properties LLC (PA)....213 383-9204
3807 Wilshire Blvd # 1226 Los Angeles (90010) *(G-27203)*
S W P T X Inc....714 564-7900
1682 Langley Ave Irvine (92614) *(G-2488)*
S&B Surgery Center II, Rllng HLS Est *Also called Spalding Srgcl Ctr of Bvrly Hl (G-20048)*
S&F Management Company Inc (PA)....310 385-1090
9200 W Sunset Blvd # 700 West Hollywood (90069) *(G-20885)*
S&P Global Inc....831 393-6044
1566 Moffett St Salinas (93905) *(G-10183)*

ALPHABETIC

ALPHABETIC SECTION
Saehan Bank (PA)

S.p Richards, Mira Loma *Also called S P Richards Company* ***(G-8180)***
S1 Corporation....818 992-3299
8501 Fllbrook Ave Ste 200 Canoga Park (91304) ***(G-16041)***
SA Camp Pump and Drilling Co, Bakersfield *Also called S A Camp Pump Company* ***(G-18009)***
SA Photonics Inc....408 560-3500
120 Knowles Dr Los Gatos (95032) ***(G-28049)***
SA Recycling LLC....559 237-6677
3489 S Chestnut Ave Fresno (93725) ***(G-6541)***
SA Recycling LLC....619 238-6740
3055 Commercial St San Diego (92113) ***(G-6542)***
SA Recycling LLC....323 564-5601
10313 S Alameda St Los Angeles (90002) ***(G-6543)***
SA Recycling LLC....805 483-0512
780 E Easy St Simi Valley (93065) ***(G-6544)***
SA Recycling LLC....714 667-7898
2006 W 5th St Santa Ana (92703) ***(G-6545)***
SA Recycling LLC....323 875-2520
9754 San Fernando Rd Sun Valley (91352) ***(G-6546)***
SA Recycling LLC....559 688-0271
2525 S K St Tulare (93274) ***(G-6547)***
SA Recycling LLC....626 359-5815
2495 Buena Vista St Irwindale (91010) ***(G-6548)***
SA Recycling LLC....323 723-8327
1540 S Greenwood Ave Montebello (90640) ***(G-6549)***
SA Recycling LLC....909 899-1767
8822 Etiwanda Ave Rancho Cucamonga (91739) ***(G-6550)***
SA Recycling LLC....661 327-3559
2000 E Brundage Ln Bakersfield (93307) ***(G-6551)***
SA Recycling LLC....626 444-9530
12301 Valley Blvd El Monte (91732) ***(G-6552)***
SA Recycling LLC....760 391-5591
48100 Harrison St Coachella (92236) ***(G-6553)***
SA Recycling LLC....909 622-3337
11614 Eastend Ave Chino (91710) ***(G-6554)***
SA Recycling LLC (PA)....714 632-2000
2411 N Glassell St Orange (92865) ***(G-8082)***
SA Recycling LLC....661 723-1383
42353 8th St E Lancaster (93535) ***(G-6555)***
SA Recycling LLC....909 825-1662
790 E M St Colton (92324) ***(G-6556)***
SA Recycling LLC....714 632-2000
3202 Main St San Diego (92113) ***(G-6557)***
Sa-Tech, Oxnard *Also called Systems Application & Tech Inc* ***(G-26083)***
Saa Sierra Programs LLC....530 541-1244
130 Fallen Leaf Rd South Lake Tahoe (96150) ***(G-25329)***
Saab Sensis Corporation....315 445-0550
1700 Dell Ave Campbell (95008) ***(G-15432)***
Saalex Corp (PA)....805 482-1070
811 Camarillo Springs Rd A Camarillo (93012) ***(G-26048)***
Saalex Solutions, Camarillo *Also called Saalex Corp* ***(G-26048)***
Saama Technologies Inc (PA)....408 371-1900
900 E Hamilton Ave Campbell (95008) ***(G-15433)***
Saarman Construction Ltd....415 749-2700
683 Mcallister St San Francisco (94102) ***(G-1338)***
Saatchi & Saatchi N Amer Inc....310 437-2500
13031 W Jefferson Blvd Los Angeles (90094) ***(G-13918)***
Saatchi & Saatchi North Amer....310 214-6000
3501 Sepulveda Blvd Torrance (90505) ***(G-14010)***
Sab Pacific, San Diego *Also called All Stars* ***(G-3488)***
Saba Software Inc (HQ)....650 581-2500
2400 Bridge Pkwy Redwood City (94065) ***(G-15830)***
Sabah International Inc (PA)....925 734-5750
5925 Stoneridge Dr Pleasanton (94588) ***(G-2721)***
Sabal Financial Group LP....626 351-6859
465 N Halstead St Ste 105 Pasadena (91107) ***(G-27631)***
Saban Brands LLC (HQ)....310 557-5230
10100 Santa Monica Blvd # 500 Los Angeles (90067) ***(G-27632)***
Saban Capital Group, Los Angeles *Also called Saban Music Group Inc* ***(G-12143)***
Saban Capital Group Inc....310 557-5100
10100 Santa Monica Blvd Los Angeles (90067) ***(G-12142)***
SABAN COMMUNITY CLINIC, Los Angeles *Also called Los Angeles Free Clinic* ***(G-27510)***
Saban Music Group Inc (PA)....310 557-5100
10100 Santa Monica Blvd # 1050 Los Angeles (90067) ***(G-12143)***
Saber Plumbing Inc....760 480-5716
325 Market Pl Escondido (92029) ***(G-2356)***
Sabu Enterprises Inc....626 443-1351
5044 Buffington Rd El Monte (91732) ***(G-21364)***
Sac Health System (PA)....909 382-7100
1455 3rd Ave San Bernardino (92408) ***(G-20274)***
Sac International Steel Inc (PA)....323 232-2467
6130 Avalon Blvd Los Angeles (90003) ***(G-7400)***
Sac River Outfitters....530 275-3500
1403 Edgewood Dr Redding (96003) ***(G-19273)***
Sac Val Waste Disposal, Sacramento *Also called USA Waste of California Inc* ***(G-4080)***
Saccani Distributing Company....916 441-0213
2600 5th St Sacramento (95818) ***(G-9083)***
Sackett National Holdings Inc....866 834-6242
2605 Camino Del Rio S # 400 San Diego (92108) ***(G-27633)***
Sacramento, Sacramento *Also called Nationwide Legal LLC* ***(G-23462)***
Sacramento 49er, Sacramento *Also called Sacramnto Forty Niner Trvl Plz* ***(G-13186)***
Sacramento Area Sewer District (PA)....916 876-6000
10060 Goethe Rd Sacramento (95827) ***(G-6558)***
Sacramento Childrens Home....916 927-5059
1217 Del Paso Blvd Ste B Sacramento (95815) ***(G-24792)***
Sacramento Childrens Home (PA)....916 452-3981
2750 Sutterville Rd Sacramento (95820) ***(G-24793)***
Sacramento Chinese Community S....916 442-4228
420 I St Ste 5 Sacramento (95814) ***(G-24163)***
Sacramento County Off Educatn....916 875-0312
9750 Bus Park Dr Ste 220 Sacramento (95827) ***(G-24164)***
Sacramento County Water Agency....916 874-6851
827 7th St Ste 301 Sacramento (95814) ***(G-6389)***
Sacramento Credit Union (PA)....916 444-6070
800 H St Ste 100 Sacramento (95814) ***(G-9680)***
Sacramento Cy Unified Schl Dst (PA)....916 643-7400
5735 47th Ave Sacramento (95824) ***(G-25330)***
Sacramento District Office, Sacramento *Also called State Compensation Insur Fund* ***(G-10471)***
Sacramento Div, West Sacramento *Also called Quad/Graphics Inc* ***(G-13903)***
Sacramento Ear Nose & Throat (PA)....916 736-3399
1111 Expo Blvd Ste 700 Sacramento (95815) ***(G-19930)***
Sacramento Employement & Train....916 263-3800
925 Del Paso Blvd Ste 100 Sacramento (95815) ***(G-24383)***
Sacramento Employement & Train (PA)....916 263-3800
925 Del Paso Blvd Ste 100 Sacramento (95815) ***(G-24384)***
Sacramento GF Div, Sacramento *Also called Amerisourcebergen Corporation* ***(G-8232)***
Sacramento Harness Association....916 239-4040
1600 Exposition Blvd Sacramento (95815) ***(G-18574)***
Sacramento Heart and Cardiovas (PA)....916 830-2000
500 University Ave Sacramento (95825) ***(G-19931)***
Sacramento Hotel Partners LLC....916 326-5000
100 Capitol Mall Sacramento (95814) ***(G-13185)***
Sacramento Kenworth, Sacramento *Also called Ssmb Pacific Holding Co Inc* ***(G-6697)***
Sacramento Loaves & Fishes (PA)....916 446-0874
1351 N C St Ste 22 Sacramento (95811) ***(G-24165)***
Sacramento Mental Hlth Clinic, Mather *Also called Veterans Health Administration* ***(G-20198)***
Sacramento Municpl Utility Dst (PA)....916 452-3211
6201 S St Sacramento (95817) ***(G-6200)***
Sacramento Municpl Utility Dst....916 452-3211
6201 S St Sacramento (95817) ***(G-6201)***
Sacramento Municpl Utility Dst....916 452-3211
6201 S St Sacramento (95817) ***(G-17824)***
Sacramento Municpl Utility Dst....916 732-5155
6301 S St Sacramento (95817) ***(G-6202)***
Sacramento Municpl Utility Dst....916 732-5616
6201 S St Sacramento (95817) ***(G-6203)***
Sacramento Municpl Utility Dst....530 644-2013
7540 Hwy 50 Pacific House (95726) ***(G-6204)***
Sacramento Operating Co LP....916 422-4825
7400 24th St Sacramento (95822) ***(G-20886)***
Sacramento Post-Acute, Sacramento *Also called Oleander Holdings LLC* ***(G-20826)***
Sacramento Prestige Gunite Inc....916 723-0404
8634 Antelope North Rd Antelope (95843) ***(G-3324)***
Sacramento Reg Co Sanit Dist (PA)....916 876-6000
10060 Goethe Rd Sacramento (95827) ***(G-6637)***
Sacramento Reg Co Sanit Dist....916 875-9000
8521 Laguna Station Rd Elk Grove (95758) ***(G-6415)***
Sacramento Regional Trnst Dist (PA)....916 726-2877
1400 29th St Sacramento (95816) ***(G-3694)***
Sacramento River Cats Baseball....916 376-4700
400 Ball Park Dr West Sacramento (95691) ***(G-18561)***
Sacramento Suburban Water Dst....916 972-7171
3701 Marconi Ave Ste 100 Sacramento (95821) ***(G-6390)***
Sacramento Suburban Water Dst....916 972-7171
3701 Marconi Ave Ste 100 Sacramento (95821) ***(G-6391)***
Sacramento Television Stns Inc (HQ)....916 374-1452
2713 Kovr Dr West Sacramento (95605) ***(G-5908)***
Sacramento Theatrical Ltg Ltd....916 447-3258
950 Richards Blvd Sacramento (95811) ***(G-18430)***
Sacramento V A Medical Center, Mather *Also called Veterans Health Administration* ***(G-20213)***
Sacramento Yolo Cnty Mosquito....916 685-1022
8631 Bond Rd Elk Grove (95624) ***(G-6638)***
Sacramento Zoological Society....916 808-5888
3930 W Land Park Dr Sacramento (95822) ***(G-25069)***
Sacramento-Yolo Port District....916 371-8000
1110 W Capitol Ave West Sacramento (95691) ***(G-4755)***
Sacramnto Forty Niner Trvl Plz....916 927-4774
2828 El Centro Rd Sacramento (95833) ***(G-13186)***
Sacramnto Hsing Rdvlpment Agcy....916 440-1376
630 I St Fl 3 Sacramento (95814) ***(G-10858)***
Sacramnto Ntiv Amercn Hlth Ctr....916 341-0575
2020 J St Sacramento (95811) ***(G-19932)***
Sacromento Eductn Readng Lions....916 228-2219
10461 Old Plza Vlle 130 Ste 130 Ville Sacramento (95827) ***(G-25331)***
Sada Systems Inc....818 766-2400
5250 Lankershim Blvd # 620 North Hollywood (91601) ***(G-16473)***
Sadaf Foods, Vernon *Also called Soofer Co Inc* ***(G-8922)***
Saddle Back Valley YMCA, Mission Viejo *Also called Young Mens Chrstn Assn Orange* ***(G-25474)***
Saddle Creek Corporation....619 229-2200
3010 Saddle Creek Rd San Diego (92120) ***(G-4634)***
Saddleback Dialysis, Laguna Hills *Also called Dva Renal Healthcare Inc* ***(G-22625)***
Saddleback Memorial Hospital, San Clemente *Also called San Clemente Medical Ctr LLC* ***(G-21845)***
Saddleback Memorial Med Ctr (HQ)....949 837-4500
24451 Health Center Dr Laguna Hills (92653) ***(G-21836)***
Saddleback Valley Service Ctr, Irvine *Also called Southern California Edison Co* ***(G-6234)***
Saddleback Vly....949 586-1234
25631 Peter A Hartman Way Mission Viejo (92691) ***(G-19053)***
Saddlemen, Compton *Also called Bst Enterprises Inc* ***(G-6719)***
Sadie Rose Baking Co....858 831-0290
8926 Ware Ct San Diego (92121) ***(G-8917)***
Saehan Bank (PA)....213 368-7700
3200 Wilshire Blvd # 700 Los Angeles (90010) ***(G-9521)***

ALPHABETIC

Safari Harvstg & Farming LLC....805 925-2600
313 Plaza Dr Ste B12 Santa Maria (93454) *(G-390)*
Safc Carlsbad Inc....760 918-0007
6211 El Camino Real Carlsbad (92009) *(G-26804)*
Safe Credit Union (PA)....916 979-7233
2295 Iron Point Rd # 100 Folsom (95630) *(G-9681)*
Safe Credit Union....916 979-7233
2295 Iron Point Rd # 100 Folsom (95630) *(G-9682)*
Safe Credit Union....916 979-7233
9055 Woodcreek Oaks Blvd # 150 Roseville (95747) *(G-9949)*
Safe Harbor Intl Relief....949 858-6786
30615 Avnida De Las Flres Rancho Santa Margari (92688) *(G-24971)*
Safe Harbor Treatment Cen....949 645-1026
1966 Maple Ave Costa Mesa (92627) *(G-22819)*
Safe Refuge....562 987-5722
1041 Redondo Ave Long Beach (90804) *(G-24794)*
Safe Security Inc....925 830-4777
2440 Camino Ramon Ste 200 San Ramon (94583) *(G-16917)*
Safeco Door & Hardware Inc....510 429-4768
31054 San Antonio St Hayward (94544) *(G-3415)*
Safeco Glass, Hayward *Also called Safeco Door & Hardware Inc (G-3415)*
Safeco Insurance Company Amer....818 956-4250
330 N Brand Blvd Ste 680 Glendale (91203) *(G-10859)*
Safeguard Business Systems Inc....805 486-9769
414 N A St Oxnard (93030) *(G-8181)*
Safeguard Health Enterprises (HQ)....949 425-4300
95 Enterprise Ste 100 Aliso Viejo (92656) *(G-10373)*
Safelite Autoglass, Sacramento *Also called Safelite Fulfillment Inc (G-17782)*
Safelite Fulfillment Inc....916 442-4715
261 Richards Blvd Sacramento (95811) *(G-17782)*
Safety Dynamics, Oakland *Also called Intelliguard Security Services (G-16706)*
Safety Security Patrol LLC....909 888-7778
560 N Arrowhead Ave 3b San Bernardino (92401) *(G-16778)*
Safetypark Corporation....310 399-1499
100 Venice Way Venice (90291) *(G-17742)*
Safeway Inc....323 889-4240
3415 Boxford Ave Commerce (90040) *(G-4635)*
Safeway Inc....209 833-4700
16900 W Schulte Rd Tracy (95377) *(G-4636)*
Safeway Inc....916 373-3900
2935 Ramco St Ste 10 West Sacramento (95691) *(G-4637)*
Safran, Anaheim *Also called Morphotrak LLC (G-15997)*
Safway Services LP....650 652-9255
1660 Gilbreth Rd Burlingame (94010) *(G-7788)*
Safway Services LP....707 745-2000
4072b Teal Ct Benicia (94510) *(G-7789)*
Sag- Aftra Federal....818 562-3400
134 N Kenwood St Burbank (91505) *(G-9622)*
Sag-Aftra....818 954-9400
3601 W Olive Ave Fl 2 Burbank (91505) *(G-10562)*
Sag-Aftra....323 954-1600
5757 Wilshire Blvd Fl 7 Los Angeles (90036) *(G-18489)*
Saga Seal Co Ltd....562 493-7501
600 Marina Dr Seal Beach (90740) *(G-13187)*
Sage Behavior Services Inc....714 773-0077
505 E Commonwealth Ave Fullerton (92832) *(G-22089)*
Sage Electric Company....818 718-9080
9144 Owensmouth Ave Chatsworth (91311) *(G-2722)*
Sage Hospitality Resources LLC....626 357-5211
700 W Huntington Dr Monrovia (91016) *(G-13188)*
Sage Hospitality Resources LLC....650 589-1600
2000 Shoreline Ct Brisbane (94005) *(G-13189)*
Sage Software Inc....650 579-3628
1380 Tatan Trail Rd Burlingame (94010) *(G-15831)*
Sage Software Holdings Inc (HQ)....866 530-7243
6561 Irvine Center Dr Irvine (92618) *(G-15832)*
Sager Electrical Supply Co Inc....714 962-8666
3611 S Harbor Blvd # 205 Santa Ana (92704) *(G-7629)*
Sager Electronics, Santa Ana *Also called Sager Electrical Supply Co Inc (G-7629)*
Sahara, Artesia *Also called South Asian Help Referral Agcy (G-24218)*
Sahargun Mechanical, Stockton *Also called Sahargun Plumbing Inc (G-2357)*
Sahargun Plumbing Inc....209 474-2611
2216 Stewart St Stockton (95205) *(G-2357)*
Saia Inc....916 483-8331
1508 Wyant Way Sacramento (95864) *(G-4256)*
Saia Motor Freight Line LLC....916 690-8417
9119 Elkmont Dr Elk Grove (95624) *(G-4257)*
Saia Motor Freight Line LLC....323 277-2880
2550 E 28th St Vernon (90058) *(G-4258)*
Saia Motor Freight Line Inc....510 347-6890
1755 Aurora Dr San Leandro (94577) *(G-4259)*
Saia S Reno Barbara K, Sacramento *Also called Saia Inc (G-4256)*
Saic, San Diego *Also called Science Applications Intl Corp (G-16045)*
Saic, San Diego *Also called Science Applications Intl Corp (G-16046)*
Saic, Oakland *Also called Leidos Inc (G-26557)*
Saic Government Solutions, San Diego *Also called Science Applications Intl Corp (G-16475)*
Saiful/Bouquet Con Stru Eng (PA)....626 304-2616
155 N Lake Ave Fl 6 Pasadena (91101) *(G-26049)*
Saint Agnes HM Hlth & Hospice, Fresno *Also called Trinity Home Health Svcs Inc (G-22583)*
Saint Agnes Med Providers Inc....559 450-7200
1105 E Spruce Ave Ste 201 Fresno (93720) *(G-23042)*
Saint Agnes Medical Center (HQ)....559 450-3000
1303 E Herndon Ave Fresno (93720) *(G-21837)*
Saint Baldricks Foundation, Simi Valley *Also called Vickie Lobello (G-25595)*
SAINT BARNABAS SENIOR SERVICES, Los Angeles *Also called St Barnabas Senior Center of L (G-24227)*
Saint Claires Nursing Center....916 392-4440
6248 66th Ave Sacramento (95823) *(G-20887)*
Saint Franceis Fmly Hlth, Huntington Park *Also called St Francis Medical Ce (G-20052)*
Saint Francis Memorial Hosp (HQ)....415 353-6000
900 Hyde St San Francisco (94109) *(G-21838)*
Saint Helena Hosp Clearlake, Clearlake *Also called Adventist Health Clearlake (G-21430)*
Saint Jhns Hlth Ctr Foundation....310 315-6111
2200 Santa Monica Blvd Santa Monica (90404) *(G-19933)*
Saint Jhns Hlth Ctr Foundation....310 829-8921
1339 20th St Santa Monica (90404) *(G-24508)*
Saint Jhns Hlth Ctr Foundation....310 829-8970
2020 Santa Monica Blvd 3rdfl3 Santa Monica (90404) *(G-21839)*
Saint John's Well Child Center, Los Angeles *Also called St Johns Well Child (G-20278)*
Saint Johns Child Fmly Dev Ctr, Santa Monica *Also called Saint Jhns Hlth Ctr Foundation (G-24508)*
Saint Joseph Center Volunteer, Venice *Also called St Joseph Center (G-24228)*
Saint Joseph Hlth Sys HM Hlth, Anaheim *Also called St Joseph Home Health Network (G-22572)*
Saint Joseph Hlth Sys Hospice, Anaheim *Also called St Joseph Hospice (G-24229)*
Saint Joseph Home Care Network....707 206-9124
1165 Montgomery Dr Santa Rosa (95405) *(G-24795)*
Saint Justin Education Fu....323 221-3400
2415 Shoredale Ave Los Angeles (90031) *(G-24972)*
Saint Louise Hospital....408 848-2000
9400 N Name Uno Gilroy (95020) *(G-21840)*
Saint Mary Medical Center, Long Beach *Also called Dignity Health (G-21536)*
Saint Nicolas Vineyard, Soledad *Also called Kvl Holdings Inc (G-165)*
Saint-Joseph Home Health....408 244-5488
1525 Mccarthy Blvd # 208 Milpitas (95035) *(G-23043)*
Sajahtera Inc....310 276-2251
9641 Sunset Blvd Beverly Hills (90210) *(G-13190)*
Sakata Seed America Inc (HQ)....408 778-7758
18095 Serene Dr Morgan Hill (95037) *(G-9149)*
Sakura Finetek USA Inc (HQ)....310 972-7800
1750 W 214th St Torrance (90501) *(G-7311)*
Salad Time Farms, Baldwin Park *Also called Tanimura & Antle Inc (G-595)*
Saladinos Inc (PA)....559 271-3700
3325 W Figarden Dr Fresno (93711) *(G-8517)*
Salas OBrien Engineers Inc (PA)....408 282-1500
305 S 11th St San Jose (95112) *(G-26050)*
Salazar Labor Contracting....760 746-0805
957 Sugarloaf Dr Escondido (92026) *(G-683)*
Salem Lutheran Home Associatio....510 769-2700
1301 Marina Vil Pkwy 21 # 210 Alameda (94501) *(G-24796)*
Salem Media Group Inc (PA)....818 956-0400
4880 Santa Rosa Rd Camarillo (93012) *(G-5817)*
Salem Media Group Inc....818 956-5254
701 N Brand Blvd Ste 550 Glendale (91203) *(G-5818)*
Salesforcecom Inc (PA)....415 901-7000
1 Market Ste 300 San Francisco (94105) *(G-15833)*
Salesforcecom Foundation....800 667-6389
The Landmark One St The Landma San Francisco (94105) *(G-5695)*
Salesian Boys and Girls Club....415 397-3068
680 Filbert St San Francisco (94133) *(G-19054)*
Salestar LLC (PA)....510 637-4700
300 Lakeside Dr Fl 11 Oakland (94612) *(G-7182)*
Salimar Inc....661 327-9651
2620 Buck Owens Blvd Bakersfield (93308) *(G-13191)*
Salinas Disposal Service, Hayward *Also called USA Waste of California Inc (G-6591)*
Salinas Disposal Service, Salinas *Also called USA Waste of California Inc (G-6587)*
Salinas Med Mngt Srvcs Org Inc....831 751-7070
355 Abbott St Ste 100 Salinas (93901) *(G-23044)*
Salinas Urgent Care, Salinas *Also called Salinas Valley Memorial Hlthca (G-19936)*
Salinas Valley Memorial Hlthca....831 759-3236
440 E Romie Ln Salinas (93901) *(G-19934)*
Salinas Valley Memorial Hlthca....831 884-5048
5 Lower Ragsdle Dr 102 Monterey (93940) *(G-19935)*
Salinas Valley Memorial Hlthca....831 759-1995
120 Wilgart Way Salinas (93901) *(G-24166)*
Salinas Valley Memorial Hlthca (PA)....831 757-4333
450 E Romie Ln Salinas (93901) *(G-21841)*
Salinas Valley Memorial Hlthca....831 755-7880
558 Abbott St Salinas (93901) *(G-19936)*
SALINAS VALLEY MEMORIAL HOSPIT, Salinas *Also called Salinas Valley Memorial Hlthca (G-21841)*
Salinas Valley Prime Care Med, Salinas *Also called Salinas Med Mngt Srvcs Org Inc (G-23044)*
Salomon Smith Barney, El Segundo *Also called Citigroup Global Markets Inc (G-9975)*
Salomon Smith Barney, Sacramento *Also called Citigroup Global Markets Inc (G-9976)*
Salomon Smith Barney, Fresno *Also called Citigroup Global Markets Inc (G-9981)*
Salon Lujon Inc....714 738-1882
216 N Harbor Blvd Fullerton (92832) *(G-13689)*
Salon Technique....714 871-4247
101 N Harbor Blvd Fullerton (92832) *(G-13792)*
Salon-Salon....209 571-3500
1700 Mchenry Ave Ste 29 Modesto (95350) *(G-13690)*
Salson Logistics Inc....310 328-6906
1331 Torrance Blvd Torrance (90501) *(G-5240)*
Salt Catering, Los Angeles *Also called Salt of Earth Productions Inc (G-17470)*
Salt Lake Hotel Associates LP (PA)....415 397-5572
222 Kearny St Ste 200 San Francisco (94108) *(G-13192)*
Salt of Earth Productions Inc....818 399-1860
1437 S Robertson Blvd Los Angeles (90035) *(G-17470)*
Saltzburg Ray & Bergman LLP....310 481-6700
12121 Wilshire Blvd # 600 Los Angeles (90025) *(G-23543)*
Salu Beauty Inc....916 475-1400
11344 Coloma Rd Ste 725 Gold River (95670) *(G-25154)*
Salu.net, Gold River *Also called Salu Beauty Inc (G-25154)*

ALPHABETIC

Salud Para La Gente..............831 728-0222
195 Aviation Way Ste 200 Watsonville (95076) *(G-19937)*
Salud Para La Gnte Hlth Clinic, Watsonville *Also called Salud Para La Gente (G-19937)*
Salutary Sports Clubs Inc..............530 677-5705
4242 Sports Club Dr Shingle Springs (95682) *(G-18676)*
Salvador Martinez..............559 781-5150
2049 N Newcomb St Porterville (93257) *(G-684)*
Salvation Army..............323 254-9015
809 E 5th St Los Angeles (90013) *(G-22170)*
Salvation Army..............213 484-0772
2737 W Sunset Blvd Los Angeles (90026) *(G-24167)*
Salvation Army..............661 325-8626
200 19th St Bakersfield (93301) *(G-22820)*
Salvation Army..............209 466-3871
1247 S Wilson Way Stockton (95205) *(G-22821)*
Salvation Army..............858 279-1100
2799 Health Center Dr San Diego (92123) *(G-24797)*
Salvation Army..............909 889-9604
363 S Doolittle Ave San Bernardino (92408) *(G-22822)*
Salvation Army..............858 279-1100
2799 Health Center Dr San Diego (92123) *(G-24798)*
Salvation Army..............415 643-8000
1500 Valencia St San Francisco (94110) *(G-24799)*
Salvation Army..............619 269-1404
6845 University Ave San Diego (92115) *(G-18677)*
Salvation Army..............916 563-3700
3755 N Freeway Blvd Sacramento (95834) *(G-24973)*
Salvation Army Glden State Div (PA)..............415 553-3500
832 Folsom St Fl 6 San Francisco (94107) *(G-24168)*
Salvation Army Residences Inc..............213 553-3273
900 James M Wood Blvd Los Angeles (90015) *(G-24169)*
Salvation Army Residences Inc..............707 433-3334
200 Lytton Springs Rd Healdsburg (95448) *(G-24800)*
Sam Freitas Trucking Inc..............209 474-0294
2420 E Eight Mile Rd Stockton (95210) *(G-4061)*
Sam Hill & Sons Inc..............805 620-0828
2627 Beene Rd Ventura (93003) *(G-1992)*
Sam Jung USA Inc..............323 231-0811
843 E 31st St Los Angeles (90011) *(G-8324)*
Sam Kholi Transport, Fontana *Also called Defenders Trnsp Svcs Inc (G-5054)*
Sam Trans, South San Francisco *Also called San Mateo County Transit Dst (G-3712)*
Sam Trans, San Carlos *Also called San Mateo County Transit Dst (G-3963)*
Samaritan Village Inc..............209 883-3212
7700 Fox Rd Hughson (95326) *(G-24170)*
Samarkand Retirement Community, Santa Barbara *Also called Evangelical Covenant Church (G-24655)*
Samba TV, San Francisco *Also called Free Stream Media Corp (G-9266)*
Sambazon Inc (PA)..............877 726-2296
1160 Calle Cordillera San Clemente (92673) *(G-8770)*
Sambreel Services LLC..............760 266-5090
5857 Owens Ave Ste 300 Carlsbad (92008) *(G-15434)*
Samedan Oil Corporation..............661 319-5038
1360 Landing Ave Seal Beach (90740) *(G-1050)*
Samiyatex, Los Angeles *Also called Paragon Textiles Inc (G-8408)*
Samrod Corporation..............661 945-3602
28425 Calex Dr Valencia (91354) *(G-26051)*
Samsung..............925 380-6523
2603 Camino Ramon Ste 350 San Ramon (94583) *(G-7469)*
Samsung Electronics Amer Inc..............310 537-7000
18600 S Broadwick St Rancho Dominguez (90220) *(G-7511)*
Samsung Electronics Amer Inc..............650 210-1000
665 Clyde Ave Mountain View (94043) *(G-27634)*
Samsung Research America Inc (HQ)..............408 544-5700
665 Clyde Ave Mountain View (94043) *(G-26597)*
Samsung SDS America Inc..............408 638-8800
1732 N 1st St Ste 100 San Jose (95112) *(G-15435)*
Samsung Semiconductor Inc (HQ)..............408 544-4000
3655 N 1st St San Jose (95134) *(G-7630)*
Samsung Sns Central Valley Off, San Ramon *Also called Samsung (G-7469)*
Samuel J Piazza & Son Inc (PA)..............323 357-1999
9001 Rayo Ave South Gate (90280) *(G-4374)*
Samuel Son & Co Inc..............323 722-0300
6415 Corvette St Commerce (90040) *(G-7401)*
Samy Co, Cypress *Also called Hoyu America Co (G-8263)*
San Andreas Regional Center (PA)..............408 374-9960
300 Orchard Cy Dr Ste 170 Campbell (95008) *(G-24171)*
San Antnio Cmnty Hosp Dntl Ctr, Rancho Cucamonga *Also called Assistance League Foothill Com (G-24875)*
San Antonio Community Hospital (PA)..............909 985-2811
999 San Bernardino Rd Upland (91786) *(G-21842)*
San Antonio Community Hospital..............909 948-8000
7777 Milliken Ave Ste A Rancho Cucamonga (91730) *(G-21843)*
San Benito Bank, Hollister *Also called Mufg Union Bank Na (G-9412)*
San Benito Health Care Dst (PA)..............831 637-5711
911 Sunset Dr Ste A Hollister (95023) *(G-21844)*
San Benito Htg & Shtmtl Inc..............831 637-1112
1771 San Felipe Rd Hollister (95023) *(G-2358)*
San Bernabe Vineyards..............831 385-4897
53001 Oasis Rd King City (93930) *(G-182)*
San Bernandino Medical Offices, San Bernardino *Also called Kaiser Foundation Hospitals (G-19664)*
San Bernardino California City..............909 384-5111
300 N D St Fl 3 San Bernardino (92418) *(G-26052)*
San Bernardino City Unf School..............909 388-6100
956 W 9th St San Bernardino (92411) *(G-14416)*
San Bernardino City Unf School..............909 388-6307
303 S K St San Bernardino (92410) *(G-24509)*
San Bernardino City Unf School..............909 881-8000
1257 Northpark Blvd San Bernardino (92407) *(G-23045)*
San Bernardino County Museum, Redlands *Also called County of San Bernardino (G-25018)*
San Bernardino Family YMCA, San Bernardino *Also called YMCA of East Valley (G-25411)*
San Bernardino Golf Club, San Bernardino *Also called J G Golfing Enterprises Inc (G-18750)*
San Bernardino Hilton (HQ)..............909 889-0133
285 E Hospitality Ln San Bernardino (92408) *(G-13193)*
San Bernardino Med Group Inc (PA)..............909 883-8611
1700 N Waterman Ave San Bernardino (92404) *(G-19938)*
San Bernardino Mtns Wildlife..............909 226-6189
29450 Pine Ridge Dr Cedar Glen (92321) *(G-462)*
San Bernardino Parole Unit 14, San Bernardino *Also called Correctons Rhbltation Cal Dept (G-23789)*
San Bernardino Symphony Assn..............909 381-5388
198 N Arrowhead Ave 2b San Bernardino (92408) *(G-18490)*
San Brnrdino Pub Emplyees Assn..............909 386-1260
433 N Sierra Way San Bernardino (92410) *(G-25182)*
San Carlos Associates Ltd..............831 649-4234
350 Calle Principal Monterey (93940) *(G-13194)*
San Clemente Medical Ctr LLC..............949 496-1122
654 Camino De Los Mares San Clemente (92673) *(G-21845)*
San Clemente Villas By Sea..............949 489-3400
660 Camino De Los Mares San Clemente (92673) *(G-24801)*
San Dego Cnty Rgnal Arprt Auth (PA)..............619 400-2400
3225 N Harbor Dr Fl 3 San Diego (92101) *(G-4932)*
San Dego Cnvntion Ctr Corp Inc (PA)..............619 525-5000
111 W Harbor Dr San Diego (92101) *(G-11038)*
San Dego Mission Vly Hilton Ht, San Diego *Also called Kalpana LLC (G-12874)*
San Dego Ntural History Museum, San Diego *Also called San Dego Soc of Ntural History (G-25039)*
San Dego Soc of Ntural History..............619 232-3821
1788 El Prado San Diego (92101) *(G-25039)*
San Dego State Univ Foundation..............888 999-6897
9210 Sky Park Ct Ste 150 San Diego (92123) *(G-24172)*
San Dego State Univ Foundation..............619 594-1515
5200 Campanile Dr San Diego (92182) *(G-5819)*
San Diego Aerospace Museum..............619 258-1221
335 Kenney St El Cajon (92020) *(G-25040)*
San Diego Arcft Carier Museum..............619 544-9600
910 N Harbor Dr San Diego (92101) *(G-25041)*
San Diego Bay Area Elc Inc..............858 748-2060
13100 Kirkham Way Ste 205 Poway (92064) *(G-2723)*
San Diego Blood Bank (PA)..............619 296-6393
3636 Gtwy Ctr Ave Ste 100 San Diego (92102) *(G-23046)*
San Diego Blood Bank..............619 441-1804
776 Arnele Ave El Cajon (92020) *(G-23047)*
San Diego Blood Bnk Foundation, San Diego *Also called San Diego Blood Bank (G-23046)*
San Diego Center For Children (PA)..............858 277-9550
3002 Armstrong St San Diego (92111) *(G-21365)*
San Diego Chargers, San Diego *Also called Chargers Football Company LLC (G-18541)*
San Diego Choices, San Diego *Also called Telecare Corporation (G-22103)*
San Diego CLD Stg 4140, National City *Also called US Foods Inc (G-8952)*
San Diego Coastl Med Group Inc..............760 901-5259
2201 Mission Ave Oceanside (92058) *(G-23048)*
San Diego Community Hsing Corp..............619 527-4633
230 Catania St San Diego (92113) *(G-28050)*
San Diego Correctional Fcilty, San Diego *Also called Corrections Corp America (G-27781)*
San Diego Country Club Inc..............619 422-8895
88 L St Chula Vista (91911) *(G-19055)*
San Diego Country Estates Assn..............760 789-3788
24157 San Vicente Rd Ramona (92065) *(G-25332)*
San Diego County Adult Support..............619 476-6300
780 Bay Blvd Ste 200 Chula Vista (91910) *(G-24173)*
San Diego County Credit Union (PA)..............858 453-2112
6545 Sequence Dr San Diego (92121) *(G-9683)*
San Diego County Employees Ret..............619 515-6800
2275 Rio Bonito Way # 200 San Diego (92108) *(G-10860)*
San Diego County Water Auth (PA)..............858 522-6600
4677 Overland Ave San Diego (92123) *(G-6392)*
San Diego County Water Auth..............760 480-1991
610 W 5th Ave Escondido (92025) *(G-6393)*
San Diego Courtyard Central, San Diego *Also called AV Courtyard SD Spectrum (G-12405)*
San Diego Creative Community S..............619 250-3394
1501 Front St Unit 509 San Diego (92101) *(G-24174)*
San Diego Data Proc Corp Inc..............858 581-9600
202 C St Fl 3 San Diego (92101) *(G-16180)*
San Diego District Office, San Diego *Also called State Compensation Insur Fund (G-10466)*
San Diego Family Care (PA)..............858 279-0925
6973 Linda Vista Rd San Diego (92111) *(G-19939)*
San Diego Family Housing LLC..............858 874-8100
3360 Murray Ridge Rd San Diego (92123) *(G-25571)*
San Diego Farah Partners..............619 239-2261
1430 7th Ave Ste B San Diego (92101) *(G-13195)*
San Diego Fish Market, San Diego *Also called Top of Market (G-27254)*
San Diego Gas & Electric Co (HQ)..............619 696-2000
8326 Century Park Ct San Diego (92123) *(G-6292)*
San Diego Gas & Electric Co..............760 432-2508
2300 Harveson Pl Escondido (92029) *(G-2724)*
San Diego Gas & Electric Co..............800 411-7343
990 Bay Blvd Chula Vista (91911) *(G-6254)*
San Diego Gas & Electric Co..............949 361-8090
662 Camino De Los Mares San Clemente (92673) *(G-6293)*
San Diego Gas & Electric Co..............760 438-6200
5016 Carlsbad Blvd Carlsbad (92008) *(G-6306)*
San Diego Gas & Electric Co..............760 432-5885
571 Enterprise St Escondido (92029) *(G-6307)*
San Diego Gas & Electric Co..............619 699-1018
701 33rd St San Diego (92102) *(G-6308)*

ALPHABETIC

San Diego Harbor Excursion, Coronado *Also called Star & Crescent Boat Company* ***(G-4740)***
San Diego Hbr Excursions Inc 619 234-4111
1050 N Harbor Dr San Diego (92101) ***(G-2081)***
San Diego Hebrew Homes (PA) 760 942-2695
211 Saxony Rd Encinitas (92024) ***(G-20888)***
San Diego Homecare 858 457-1520
6181 Arnoldson Pl San Diego (92122) ***(G-22553)***
San Diego Hospice 619 688-1600
2400 Historic Decatur Rd # 107 San Diego (92106) ***(G-22554)***
San Diego Hospice & Institute, San Diego *Also called San Diego Hospice* ***(G-22554)***
San Diego Hotel Cir Owner LLC 619 881-6900
1515 Hotel Cir S San Diego (92108) ***(G-13196)***
San Diego Hotel Company LLC 619 696-0234
660 K St San Diego (92101) ***(G-13197)***
San Diego Hotel Lease LLC 619 446-3000
530 Broadway San Diego (92101) ***(G-13198)***
San Diego Imaging - Chula Vist (PA) 858 565-0950
8745 Aero Dr Ste 200 San Diego (92123) ***(G-22275)***
San Diego Land Systems 858 558-0542
8720 Miramar Pl San Diego (92121) ***(G-794)***
San Diego Lesbian Gay Bisexu 619 692-2077
3909 Centre St San Diego (92103) ***(G-24175)***
San Diego Med Svcs Entp LLC 619 280-6060
10405 Sn Diego Mn Rd 20 Ste 201 San Diego (92108) ***(G-3838)***
San Diego Messenger Inc 858 514-8866
4848 Ronson Ct Ste G San Diego (92111) ***(G-4422)***
San Diego Metro Trnst Sys 619 231-1466
1255 Imperial Ave # 1000 San Diego (92101) ***(G-3695)***
San Diego Metropolitan Cr Un (PA) 619 297-4835
9212 Balboa Ave San Diego (92123) ***(G-9684)***
San Diego Mission Vly Hilton, San Diego *Also called HEI Mission Valley LP* ***(G-12699)***
San Diego Mortgage & RE 619 334-7779
9461 Grsmnt Smt Dr Ste D La Mesa (91941) ***(G-11830)***
San Diego Museum of Art 619 696-1971
1450 El Prado San Diego (92101) ***(G-25042)***
San Diego Old Town, San Diego *Also called RPC Old Town Jefferson* ***(G-13176)***
San Diego Opera Association (PA) 619 232-7636
233 A St Ste 500 San Diego (92101) ***(G-18431)***
San Diego Orthopaedic Associat 619 299-8500
4060 4th Ave Ste 700 San Diego (92103) ***(G-19940)***
San Diego Padres, San Diego *Also called Padres LP* ***(G-18560)***
San Diego Paradise Pt Resort 858 274-4630
1404 Vacation Rd San Diego (92109) ***(G-13199)***
San Diego Private Bank 619 437-1000
801 Orange Ave Ste 101 Coronado (92118) ***(G-9522)***
San Diego Recyling Inc 619 287-7555
6670 Federal Blvd Lemon Grove (91945) ***(G-6559)***
San Diego Region, San Diego *Also called Water Resources Control Bd Cal* ***(G-25109)***
San Diego Regional Ctr For Dev, National City *Also called San Diego-Imperial* ***(G-24178)***
San Diego Regional Teen Center, San Diego *Also called Harmonium Inc* ***(G-13465)***
San Diego Rescue Mission Inc (PA) 619 819-1880
120 Elm St San Diego (92101) ***(G-24974)***
San Diego Sheraton Corporation 619 291-6400
1590 Harbor Island Dr San Diego (92101) ***(G-13200)***
San Diego State University 619 265-6438
5200 Campanile Dr San Diego (92182) ***(G-5820)***
San Diego Supercomputer Center, La Jolla *Also called University Cal San Diego* ***(G-16206)***
San Diego Symphony Orchestra 619 235-0800
1245 7th Ave San Diego (92101) ***(G-18491)***
San Diego Testing Engineers 858 715-5800
7895 Convoy Ct Ste 18 San Diego (92111) ***(G-26053)***
San Diego Theatres Inc 619 615-4000
1100 3rd Ave San Diego (92101) ***(G-11039)***
San Diego Tourism Authority (PA) 619 232-3101
750 B St Ste 1500 San Diego (92101) ***(G-17471)***
San Diego Transit Corporation (PA) 619 238-0100
100 16th St San Diego (92101) ***(G-3696)***
San Diego Transit Corporation 619 238-0100
100 16th St San Diego (92101) ***(G-3697)***
San Diego Trolley Inc 619 595-4933
1341 Commercial St San Diego (92113) ***(G-3698)***
San Diego Unified Hbr Police, San Diego *Also called San Diego Unified Port Dst* ***(G-4756)***
San Diego Unified Port Dst 619 686-6585
3380 N Harbor Dr San Diego (92101) ***(G-4756)***
San Diego Unified Port Dst (PA) 619 686-6200
3165 Pacific Hwy San Diego (92101) ***(G-4757)***
San Diego Unified Port Dst 619 683-8966
1140 N Harbor Dr Ste 147 San Diego (92101) ***(G-8004)***
San Diego Unified School Dst 858 627-7130
4860 Ruffner St San Diego (92111) ***(G-14417)***
San Diego Urban League Inc 619 266-6247
4305 University Ave # 360 San Diego (92105) ***(G-25333)***
San Diego Welders Supply, San Diego *Also called Westair Gases & Equipment Inc* ***(G-7906)***
San Diego Wholesale Electric, Oceanside *Also called Onesource Distributors LLC* ***(G-7461)***
SAN DIEGO WILD ANIMAL PARK, San Diego *Also called Zoological Society San Diego* ***(G-25071)***
San Diego Wild Animal Park, Escondido *Also called Zoological Society San Diego* ***(G-25072)***
San Diego Youth Services Inc (PA) 619 221-8600
3255 Wing St Ste 550 San Diego (92110) ***(G-24176)***
San Diego Zoo, San Diego *Also called Zoological Society San Diego* ***(G-25073)***
San Diego-Imperial 760 736-1200
1370 W Sn Mrcos Blvd # 100 San Marcos (92078) ***(G-24177)***
San Diego-Imperial 619 336-6600
2727 Hoover Ave National City (91950) ***(G-24178)***
San Diego-Imperial Counties De (PA) 858 576-2996
4355 Ruffin Rd Ste 110 San Diego (92123) ***(G-24179)***
San Dimas Bushnell Building, Rosemead *Also called Southern California Edison Co* ***(G-6228)***
San Dimas Community Hospital, San Dimas *Also called Prime Healthcare-San Dimas LLC* ***(G-21815)***
San Dimas Golf Inc 909 599-8486
1400 Avenida Entrada San Dimas (91773) ***(G-19056)***
San Dimas Luggage Company 909 510-8820
2095 S Archibald Ave Ontario (91761) ***(G-8138)***
San Dimas Medical Group Inc 661 663-4800
100 Old River Rd Bakersfield (93311) ***(G-19941)***
San Dimas Retirement Center (PA) 909 599-8441
834 W Arrow Hwy San Dimas (91773) ***(G-11199)***
San Fernando City of Inc 818 832-2400
10605 Balboa Blvd Ste 100 Granada Hills (91344) ***(G-22823)***
San Fernando Health Center, San Fernando *Also called Northeast Valley Health Corp* ***(G-19780)***
San Fernando Juvenile Hall, Sylmar *Also called County of Los Angeles* ***(G-24611)***
San Fernando Valley Community (PA) 818 901-4830
16360 Roscoe Blvd Ste 210 Van Nuys (91406) ***(G-22824)***
San Fernando Valley Interfaith, Van Nuys *Also called County of Los Angeles* ***(G-23843)***
San Francisco City & County 415 695-5660
1520 Oakdale Ave San Francisco (94124) ***(G-24180)***
San Francisco City & County 415 753-4439
2400 Hillcrest Dr NAPA (94558) ***(G-24181)***
San Francisco City & County 415 557-3013
455 Golden Gate Ave Fl 1 San Francisco (94102) ***(G-21846)***
San Francisco 49ers, Santa Clara *Also called Forty Niners Football Co LLC* ***(G-18544)***
San Francisco Aids Foundation (PA) 415 487-3000
1035 Market St Ste 400 San Francisco (94103) ***(G-24182)***
San Francisco Ballet Assn 415 865-2000
455 Franklin St San Francisco (94102) ***(G-18432)***
San Francisco Bay, San Francisco *Also called Charolais Care V Inc* ***(G-22404)***
San Francisco Bay AR Tran Assn 510 501-5318
915 San Antonio Ave Alameda (94501) ***(G-25572)***
SAN FRANCISCO BAY AREA COUNCIL, San Leandro *Also called San Francisco-Bay Cncl Bsa* ***(G-25334)***
San Francisco Bay Area Rapid 510 441-2278
2000 Bart Way Fremont (94538) ***(G-3699)***
San Francisco Bay Area Rapid 510 464-6000
1330 Broadway Oakland (94612) ***(G-3700)***
San Francisco Bay Area Rapid 510 834-1297
800 Madison St Oakland (94607) ***(G-3701)***
San Francisco Bay Area Rapid 510 464-6126
300 Lakeside Dr 23 Oakland (94612) ***(G-3702)***
San Francisco Bay Area Rapid 510 233-6848
1101 13th St Richmond (94801) ***(G-3703)***
San Francisco Bay Area Rapid 510 441-2278
699 B St Hayward (94541) ***(G-3704)***
San Francisco Bay Area Rapid (PA) 510 464-6000
300 Lakeside Dr Oakland (94604) ***(G-3705)***
San Francisco Bay Area Rapid 510 233-7444
1101 13th St Richmond (94801) ***(G-5241)***
San Francisco Bay Area Rapid 510 286-2893
101 8th St Oakland (94607) ***(G-3706)***
San Francisco Bay Area Rapid 510 464-7000
800 Madison St Oakland (94607) ***(G-3707)***
San Francisco Bay Area Rapid 510 464-6000
300 Lakeside Dr Fl 17 Oakland (94612) ***(G-3708)***
San Francisco City & County 415 356-2700
617 Mission St San Francisco (94105) ***(G-24183)***
San Francisco City & County 415 356-2700
617 Mission St San Francisco (94105) ***(G-24184)***
San Francisco City & County 415 550-4600
1800 Jerrold Ave Ste A San Francisco (94124) ***(G-17825)***
San Francisco City Clinic 415 487-5500
356 7th St San Francisco (94103) ***(G-22825)***
San Francisco Federal Cr Un (PA) 415 775-5377
770 Golden Gate Ave Fl 1 San Francisco (94102) ***(G-9685)***
San Francisco Fertility Ctrs 415 834-3000
55 Francisco St Ste 300 San Francisco (94133) ***(G-19942)***
San Francisco Food Bank 415 286-3614
900 Pennsylvania Ave San Francisco (94107) ***(G-24185)***
San Francisco Forty Niners 408 562-4949
4949 Mrie P Debartolo Way Santa Clara (95054) ***(G-12088)***
San Francisco Forty Niners (PA) 408 562-4949
4949 Mrie P Debartolo Way Santa Clara (95054) ***(G-18562)***
San Francisco Foundation 415 733-8500
1 Embarcadero Ctr # 4150 San Francisco (94111) ***(G-17472)***
San Francisco General Hospital, San Francisco *Also called Gastroenterology Division* ***(G-19534)***
San Francisco General Hospital, San Francisco *Also called City & County of San Francisco* ***(G-21492)***
San Francisco Health Authority (PA) 415 615-4407
50 Beale St Fl 12 San Francisco (94105) ***(G-25155)***
San Francisco Herb Natural Fd (PA) 510 770-1215
47444 Kato Rd Fremont (94538) ***(G-8918)***
San Francisco Herb Tea & Spice, Fremont *Also called San Francisco Herb Natural Fd* ***(G-8918)***
San Francisco Hotel Associates 415 392-4666
650 Bush St San Francisco (94108) ***(G-13201)***
San Francisco Hotel Group LLC 415 276-9888
222 Sansome St San Francisco (94104) ***(G-13202)***
San Francisco Hq, Mill Valley *Also called Telecommunictns Cmmnctns Srvcs* ***(G-6092)***
San Francisco Ladies Protecti 415 931-3136
3400 Laguna St San Francisco (94123) ***(G-24802)***
San Francisco Marriott Marquis, San Francisco *Also called Host Hotels & Resorts LP* ***(G-12769)***

San Francisco Marriott Un Sq, San Francisco *Also called Intercontinental Hotels Group* ***(G-12844)***
San Francisco Medical Group......415 221-0665
1 Shrader St Ste 650 San Francisco (94117) ***(G-19943)***
San Francisco Meritime N H P......415 561-7000
Fort Myson Ctr Bldg E265 San Francisco (94123) ***(G-25043)***
San Francisco Museum Modrn Art (PA)......415 357-4035
151 3rd St San Francisco (94103) ***(G-25044)***
San Francisco Opera Assn......415 861-4008
301 Van Ness Ave San Francisco (94102) ***(G-18433)***
San Francisco Public Schools, San Francisco *Also called San Francisco City & County* ***(G-24180)***
San Francisco Radio Assets LLC (HQ)......415 216-1300
750 Battery St Fl 2 San Francisco (94111) ***(G-5821)***
San Francisco Reinsurance Co......415 899-2000
1465 N Mcdowell Blvd Petaluma (94954) ***(G-10247)***
San Francisco Residential Care, San Francisco *Also called Self-Help For Elderly* ***(G-24201)***
San Francisco Sightseeing, San Francisco *Also called Franciscan Lines Inc* ***(G-3796)***
San Francisco Symphony Inc (PA)......415 552-8000
201 Van Ness Ave San Francisco (94102) ***(G-18492)***
San Francisco Tennis Club......415 777-9000
645 5th St San Francisco (94107) ***(G-18678)***
San Francisco Towers, San Francisco *Also called Episcopal Senior Communities* ***(G-24649)***
San Francisco Travel Assn......415 974-6900
1 Front St Ste 2900 San Francisco (94111) ***(G-17473)***
San Francisco Vamc, San Francisco *Also called Veterans Health Administration* ***(G-20203)***
San Francisco Zoological Soc......415 753-7080
1 Zoo Rd San Francisco (94132) ***(G-19274)***
San Francisco-Bay Cncl Bsa......510 577-9000
1001 Davis St San Leandro (94577) ***(G-25334)***
San Fransisco Speciality Prod, Santa Fe Springs *Also called LA Specialty Produce Co* ***(G-8744)***
San Frncsco Conservation Corps......415 928-7417
102 Fort Mason San Francisco (94123) ***(G-23049)***
San Frncsco Econ Oprtnty Cncil......415 749-3798
1426 Fillmore St Ste 301 San Francisco (94115) ***(G-24975)***
San Frncsco North/Petaluma KOA......707 763-1492
20 Rainsville Rd Petaluma (94952) ***(G-13482)***
San Frnndo Vly Intrfith Cuncil......818 885-5220
8956 Vanalden Ave Northridge (91324) ***(G-24976)***
San Gabriel Ambulatory Sugery......626 300-5300
207 S Santa Anita St G16 San Gabriel (91776) ***(G-19944)***
San Gabriel Childrens Ctr Inc......626 859-2089
4740 N Grand Ave Covina (91724) ***(G-24803)***
San Gabriel Convalescent Ctr, Rosemead *Also called Longwood Management Corp* ***(G-20744)***
San Gabriel Country Club......626 287-9671
350 E Hermosa Dr San Gabriel (91775) ***(G-19057)***
San Gabriel Nursery and Flor (PA)......626 286-0787
632 S San Gabriel Blvd San Gabriel (91776) ***(G-317)***
San Gabriel Transit Inc......626 430-3650
14913 Ramona Blvd Baldwin Park (91706) ***(G-3867)***
San Gabriel Transit Inc (PA)......626 258-1310
3650 Rockwell Ave El Monte (91731) ***(G-3709)***
San Gabriel Transit Inc......818 771-0374
7955 San Fernando Rd Sun Valley (91352) ***(G-3868)***
San Gabriel Valley Cab Co, El Monte *Also called San Gabriel Transit Inc* ***(G-3709)***
San Gabriel Valley Water Assn......626 815-1305
725 N Azusa Ave Azusa (91702) ***(G-6394)***
San Gabriel Valley Water Co (PA)......626 448-6183
11142 Garvey Ave El Monte (91733) ***(G-6395)***
San Gabriel Valley Water Co......909 822-2201
8440 Nuevo Ave Fontana (92335) ***(G-6396)***
SAN GABRIEL/POMONA REGIONAL CE, Pomona *Also called San Gabriel/Pomona Valleys* ***(G-24186)***
San Gabriel/Pomona Valleys......909 620-7722
75 Rancho Camino Dr Pomona (91766) ***(G-24186)***
San Gbriel Vly Cnvlescent Hosp......626 401-1557
3938 Cogswell Rd El Monte (91732) ***(G-22090)***
San Gbriel Vly Med Ctr Fndtion......626 289-5454
438 W Las Tunas Dr San Gabriel (91776) ***(G-21847)***
San Geronimo Golf Course, San Geronimo *Also called National Golf Properties Inc* ***(G-19012)***
San Gorgonio Memorial Hospital (PA)......951 845-1121
600 N Highland Sprng Ave Banning (92220) ***(G-21848)***
San Jacinto Unified School......951 654-7769
905 Industrial Way San Jacinto (92582) ***(G-11264)***
San Joaquin Beverage, Stockton *Also called Dbi Beverage San Joaquin* ***(G-9052)***
San Joaquin Beverage Inc......209 320-2400
3121 W March Ln Ste 100 Stockton (95219) ***(G-9084)***
San Joaquin Community Hospital, Bakersfield *Also called Kaiser Foundation Hospitals* ***(G-21643)***
San Joaquin Community Hospital (PA)......661 395-3000
2615 Chester Ave Bakersfield (93301) ***(G-21849)***
San Joaquin Country Club......559 439-3483
3484 W Bluff Ave Fresno (93711) ***(G-19058)***
San Joaquin County Adult Svcs, Stockton *Also called County of San Joaquin* ***(G-23906)***
San Joaquin Figs Inc......559 224-4492
3564 N Hazel Ave Fresno (93722) ***(G-582)***
San Joaquin Gardens, Fresno *Also called American Baptist Homes of West* ***(G-24546)***
San Joaquin General Hospital......209 468-6000
500 W Hospital Rd French Camp (95231) ***(G-19945)***
San Joaquin Hills Transporttn (PA)......949 754-3400
125 Pacifica Ste 100 Irvine (92618) ***(G-1855)***
San Joaquin Hospital......209 468-6000
500 W Hospital Rd French Camp (95231) ***(G-21850)***
San Joaquin Regional Trnst Dst......209 948-5566
421 E Weber Ave Stockton (95202) ***(G-3710)***
San Joaquin Valley A P C D......559 230-6000
1990 E Gettysburg Ave Fresno (93726) ***(G-28051)***
San Joaquin Valley Intergrp......559 856-0559
6048 E Cimarron Ave Fresno (93727) ***(G-25573)***
San Joaquin Valley Railroad Co......559 592-1857
221 N F St Exeter (93221) ***(G-3616)***
San Joaquin Valley Rehabili (HQ)......559 436-3600
7173 N Sharon Ave Fresno (93720) ***(G-22826)***
San Joaquin Vly Dialysis Ctr, Fresno *Also called Bio Mdcal Applications Fla Inc* ***(G-22618)***
San Jose Airport Garden Hotel, San Jose *Also called San Jose Airport Hotel LLC* ***(G-13204)***
San Jose Airport Garden Hotel......408 793-3300
1740 N 1st St San Jose (95112) ***(G-13203)***
San Jose Airport Hotel LLC......408 793-3939
1740 N 1st St San Jose (95112) ***(G-13204)***
San Jose Arena Management LLC......510 623-7200
44388 Old Warm Sprng Blvd Fremont (94538) ***(G-27204)***
San Jose Bluprt Svc & Sup Co (PA)......408 295-5770
821 Martin Ave Santa Clara (95050) ***(G-14127)***
San Jose Chld Discovery Museum......408 298-5437
180 Woz Way San Jose (95110) ***(G-25045)***
San Jose Conservation Corps......408 283-7171
2650 Senter Rd San Jose (95111) ***(G-24385)***
San Jose Construction Co Inc (PA)......408 986-8711
1210 Coleman Ave Santa Clara (95050) ***(G-1658)***
San Jose Country Club......408 258-3636
15571 Alum Rock Ave San Jose (95127) ***(G-19059)***
San Jose District Office, San Jose *Also called State Compensation Insur Fund* ***(G-10464)***
San Jose Fairmont Lessee LLC......408 998-1900
170 S Market St Lbby San Jose (95113) ***(G-13205)***
San Jose Foothill Family Comm......408 729-4290
2670 Suite 200 San Jose (95127) ***(G-19946)***
San Jose Hilton and Towers, San Jose *Also called West Hotel Partners LP* ***(G-13399)***
San Jose Hlthcare Wellness Ctr, San Jose *Also called San Joses Healthcare & Well* ***(G-20889)***
San Jose Jet Center Inc......408 297-7552
1250 Aviation Ave Ste 235 San Jose (95110) ***(G-4933)***
San Jose Medical Clinic Inc (PA)......408 278-3000
400 Race St San Jose (95126) ***(G-19947)***
San Jose Medical Clinic Inc......408 278-3000
2585 Samaritan Dr Ste 101 San Jose (95124) ***(G-19948)***
San Jose Medical Group, San Jose *Also called San Jose Medical Clinic Inc* ***(G-19947)***
San Jose Medical Group, San Jose *Also called San Jose Medical Clinic Inc* ***(G-19948)***
San Jose Municipal Golf Course, San Jose *Also called Rawitser Golf Shop Mike* ***(G-18776)***
San Jose Museum of Art Assn......408 271-6840
110 S Market St San Jose (95113) ***(G-25046)***
San Jose Redevelopment Agency......408 535-8500
200 E Santa Clara St 14th San Jose (95113) ***(G-28052)***
San Jose Sharks LLC......408 287-6655
525 W Santa Clara St San Jose (95113) ***(G-18563)***
San Jose Silicon Valley Cham......408 291-5250
101 W Santa Clara St San Jose (95113) ***(G-25102)***
San Jose State University......408 924-1000
1 Washington Sq San Jose (95112) ***(G-19949)***
San Jose Surgical Supply Inc (PA)......408 293-9033
902 S Bascom Ave San Jose (95128) ***(G-7312)***
San Jose Water Company (HQ)......408 288-5314
110 W Taylor St San Jose (95110) ***(G-6397)***
San Jose Water Company......408 298-0364
1221 S Bascom Ave San Jose (95128) ***(G-6398)***
San Joses Healthcare & Well......408 295-2665
75 N 13th St San Jose (95112) ***(G-20889)***
San Juan Golf Inc......949 493-1167
32120 San Juan Creek Rd San Juan Capistrano (92675) ***(G-18779)***
San Juan Hill Country Club, San Juan Capistrano *Also called San Juan Golf Inc* ***(G-18779)***
San Juan Oaks LLC......831 636-6113
3825 Union Rd Hollister (95023) ***(G-18780)***
San Juan Oaks Golf Club, Hollister *Also called San Juan Oaks LLC* ***(G-18780)***
San Judas Medical Group Inc......213 483-1902
2005 Wilshire Blvd # 207 Los Angeles (90057) ***(G-19950)***
San Leandro Healthcare Center, San Leandro *Also called Kissito Health Case Inc* ***(G-22497)***
San Leandro Healthcare Center......510 357-4015
368 Juana Ave San Leandro (94577) ***(G-20890)***
San Leandro Hospital LP......510 357-6500
13855 E 14th St San Leandro (94578) ***(G-21851)***
San Leandro Surgery Center Lt......510 276-2800
15035 E 14th St San Leandro (94578) ***(G-19951)***
San Lndro Care Rhblitation Ctr, San Leandro *Also called Sunbridge Healthcare LLC* ***(G-21117)***
San Lorenzo 0119, San Lorenzo *Also called Wells Fargo Bank National Assn* ***(G-9452)***
San Lorenzo Village Shopg Ctr, San Mateo *Also called David D Bohannon Organization* ***(G-10973)***
San Luis Ambulance Service Inc......805 543-2626
3546 S Higuera St San Luis Obispo (93401) ***(G-3839)***
San Luis Care Center, Newman *Also called Avalon Care Ctr - Newman LLC* ***(G-20394)***
San Luis Dlta-Mendota Wtr Auth......209 835-2593
15990 Kelso Rd Byron (94514) ***(G-6652)***
San Luis Obispo Golf......805 543-3400
255 Country Club Dr San Luis Obispo (93401) ***(G-19060)***
San Luis Obispo Quality Suites, San Luis Obispo *Also called Q S San Luis Obispo LP* ***(G-13116)***
San Luis Obispo VA Cboc, San Luis Obispo *Also called Veterans Health Administration* ***(G-20197)***
San Manuel Indian Bingo Casino, Highland *Also called San Manuel Indian Bingo Casino* ***(G-19275)***

ALPHABETIC

San Manuel Indian Bingo Casino (PA) 909 864-5050
777 San Manuel Blvd Highland (92346) ***(G-19275)***
San Mar Properties Inc (PA) 559 439-5500
6356 N Fresno St Ste 101 Fresno (93710) ***(G-11831)***
San Marcos Caterers Inc 760 744-0120
1025 La Bonita Dr San Marcos (92078) ***(G-13206)***
San Marcos Country Club 760 744-9385
1750 San Pablo Dr San Marcos (92078) ***(G-13793)***
San Marcos Kids Helpng Kids FN 800 659-6411
4750 Hollister Ave Santa Barbara (93110) ***(G-25335)***
San Marcos Mechanical, Vista *Also called Industrial Coml Systems Inc* ***(G-2250)***
San Marcos Operating Co LP 760 471-2986
1586 W Square Marcos Blvd San Marcos (92078) ***(G-20891)***
San Marcos Stadium Cinema 18, San Marcos *Also called Edwards Theatres Circuit Inc* ***(G-18329)***
San Marcos Unified School Dst 760 752-1252
255 Pico Ave Ste 250 San Marcos (92069) ***(G-24510)***
San Marino Manor 626 446-5263
6812 Oak Ave San Gabriel (91775) ***(G-21366)***
San Marino Plastering Inc 714 693-7840
4501 E La Palma Ave # 200 Anaheim (92807) ***(G-2976)***
San Mateo Cnty Expo Fair Assn 650 574-3247
2495 S Delaware St San Mateo (94403) ***(G-19276)***
San Mateo Cnty Pub Hlth Clinic 650 301-8600
380 90th St Daly City (94015) ***(G-22827)***
San Mateo County Community 650 574-6586
1700 W Hillsdale Blvd San Mateo (94402) ***(G-5909)***
SAN MATEO COUNTY EXPO CENTER, San Mateo *Also called San Mateo Cnty Expo Fair Assn* ***(G-19276)***
San Mateo County Transit Dst (PA) 650 508-6200
1250 San Carlos Ave San Carlos (94070) ***(G-3711)***
San Mateo County Transit Dst 650 588-4860
301 N Access Rd South San Francisco (94080) ***(G-3712)***
San Mateo County Transit Dst 650 508-6412
501 Pico Blvd San Carlos (94070) ***(G-3963)***
San Mateo Credit Union (PA) 650 363-1725
350 Convention Way # 300 Redwood City (94063) ***(G-9686)***
San Mateo Credit Union 650 363-1725
1515 S El Camino Real # 100 San Mateo (94402) ***(G-9687)***
SAN MATEO HEAD START PROGRAM, San Mateo *Also called Institute For Humn Social Dev* ***(G-24469)***
San Mateo Health Commission 650 616-0050
701 Gateway Blvd South San Francisco (94080) ***(G-23050)***
San Mateo Healthcare & Wellnes 650 692-3758
1100 Trousdale Dr Burlingame (94010) ***(G-20892)***
San Mateo Sport Club, Burlingame *Also called 24 Hour Fitness Usa Inc* ***(G-18593)***
San Miguel Hospital Assn 619 297-2251
1940 El Cajon Blvd San Diego (92104) ***(G-21852)***
San Miguel Produce Inc 805 488-6461
4444 Navalair Rd Oxnard (93033) ***(G-92)***
SAN MIGUEL VILLA, Concord *Also called Tranquility Incorporated* ***(G-21392)***
San Mrco Nrsing Rhbltation Ctr, Walnut Creek *Also called New Covenant Care Cal Inc* ***(G-20804)***
San Onfre Nclear Gnerating Stn, San Clemente *Also called Southern California Edison Co* ***(G-6221)***
San Pablo Lodge 43 ....707 642-1391
342 Georgia St Vallejo (94590) ***(G-25336)***
San Pblo Hlthcare Wellness Ctr 510 235-3720
13328 San Pablo Ave San Pablo (94806) ***(G-23051)***
San Pedro Convalescent Home 310 519-0359
1430 W 6th St San Pedro (90732) ***(G-20893)***
San Pedro Court House 562 519-6023
9537 Pettswood Dr Huntington Beach (92646) ***(G-11832)***
San Pedro Hospital Pavilion, San Pedro *Also called San Pedro Peninsula Hospital* ***(G-21854)***
San Pedro Peninsula Hospital (PA) 310 832-3311
1300 W 7th St San Pedro (90732) ***(G-21853)***
San Pedro Peninsula Hospital 310 514-5270
1322 W 6th St San Pedro (90732) ***(G-21854)***
San Pedro Peninsula Hospital 310 370-5895
4101 Torrance Blvd Torrance (90503) ***(G-22555)***
San Psqual Band Mssion Indians 760 291-5500
16300 Nyemii Pass Rd Valley Center (92082) ***(G-13207)***
San Psqual Csino Dev Group Inc 760 291-5500
16300 Nyemii Pass Rd Valley Center (92082) ***(G-13208)***
San Rafael Rock Quarry Inc (HQ) 415 459-7740
1000 Point San Pedro Rd San Rafael (94901) ***(G-1102)***
San Ramon Medical Offices, San Ramon *Also called Kaiser Foundation Hospitals* ***(G-19645)***
San Ramon Regional Med Ctr Inc 925 275-0634
6001 Norris Canyon Rd San Ramon (94583) ***(G-21855)***
San Salvador Pre-School, Colton *Also called Colton Joint Unified Schl Dst* ***(G-24441)***
San Tomas Convalescent Hosp, San Jose *Also called Aquinas Corporation* ***(G-20380)***
San Val Alarm System, Thousand Palms *Also called San Val Corp* ***(G-795)***
San Val Corp (PA) 760 346-3999
72203 Adelaid St Thousand Palms (92276) ***(G-795)***
San Vicente Hospital 323 930-1040
6000 San Vicente Blvd Los Angeles (90036) ***(G-21856)***
San Vicente Inn & Golf Club, Ramona *Also called San Diego Country Estates Assn* ***(G-25332)***
San Vincente Labor LLC 831 755-0955
1140 Abbott St Ste C Salinas (93901) ***(G-8771)***
San Ysidro Bb Property LLC 805 969-5046
900 San Ysidro Ln Santa Barbara (93108) ***(G-13209)***
San Ysidro Health Center, San Ysidro *Also called Centro De Salud De La* ***(G-22680)***
San-Joaquin Helicopters Inc 661 725-2682
15216 County Line Rd Delano (93215) ***(G-26054)***
San-Mar Construction Co Inc 714 693-5400
4875 E La Palma Ave # 601 Anaheim (92807) ***(G-3085)***

A L P H A B E T I C

Sanborn Theatres Inc 909 296-9728
41090 Calif Oaks Rd Murrieta (92562) ***(G-18351)***
Sanco Pipelines Incorporated 408 377-2793
727 University Ave Los Gatos (95032) ***(G-1993)***
Sanctuary, The, Redwood City *Also called Western Athletic Clubs Inc* ***(G-18705)***
Sand Canyon Corporation (HQ) 949 727-9425
7595 Irvine Center Dr # 100 Irvine (92618) ***(G-9950)***
Sand Canyon LLC 949 551-2560
11 Strawberry Farm Rd Irvine (92612) ***(G-18781)***
Sand Dollar Holdings Inc (PA) 619 477-0185
1022 Bay Marina Dr # 106 National City (91950) ***(G-8684)***
Sandbar Solar and Electric, Santa Cruz *Also called Santa Cruz Westside Elc Inc* ***(G-2725)***
Sandcraft Inc 925 253-8311
3003 Bunker Hill Ln # 101 Santa Clara (95054) ***(G-26598)***
Sanderlings, Aptos *Also called Seascape Resort Ltd A Calif* ***(G-13228)***
Sanders & Wohrman Corporation 714 919-0446
709 N Poplar St Orange (92868) ***(G-2489)***
Sandhurst Convales Grp Ltd A 310 675-3304
13922 Cerise Ave Hawthorne (90250) ***(G-20894)***
Sandis Civil Engineers (PA) 408 636-0900
1700 Winchester Blvd Campbell (95008) ***(G-26280)***
Sandisk Corporation 408 801-1000
951 Sandisk Dr Milpitas (95035) ***(G-27635)***
Sandoval Brothers Inc 831 678-1465
36503 Mile End Rd Soledad (93960) ***(G-14777)***
Sandoval Labor Contractor, Williams *Also called Elvira Sandoval* ***(G-14647)***
Sandrini Farms 661 792-3192
29794 Schuster Rd Mc Farland (93250) ***(G-183)***
Sands Rv Resort, San Rafael *Also called R C Roberts & Co* ***(G-11245)***
Sandwich Spot (PA) 916 492-2613
1630 18th St Sacramento (95811) ***(G-13210)***
Sanford Burnham Prebys Medical (PA) 858 795-5000
10901 N Torrey Pines Rd La Jolla (92037) ***(G-26805)***
Sangiacomo Vineyards, Sonoma *Also called V Sangiacomo & Sons* ***(G-191)***
Sanhyd Inc 510 843-2131
2131 Carleton St Berkeley (94704) ***(G-20895)***
Sanitary Fill, San Francisco *Also called Recology Inc* ***(G-6524)***
Sanitation, Simi Valley *Also called Golden State Water Company* ***(G-6353)***
Sanitation District 562 699-5204
2800 Workman Mill Rd Whittier (90601) ***(G-6560)***
Sanitation District 310 638-1161
920 S Alameda St Compton (90221) ***(G-6639)***
Sanitation Districts 562 908-4288
1955 Workman Mill Rd Whittier (90601) ***(G-6561)***
Sankara Eye Foundation USA 408 456-0555
1900 Mccarthy Blvd # 302 Milpitas (95035) ***(G-25574)***
Sanrise Inc 925 560-3900
7950 Dublin Blvd Ste 101 Dublin (94568) ***(G-16181)***
Sansa Technology LLC 866 204-3710
6232 Murdock Way San Ramon (94582) ***(G-26599)***
Sansei Gardens Inc 510 226-9191
3250 Darby Cmn Fremont (94539) ***(G-948)***
Sanspan Corporation 619 435-6611
1500 Orange Ave Coronado (92118) ***(G-13211)***
Sansum Clinic (PA) 805 681-7700
470 S Patterson Ave Santa Barbara (93111) ***(G-19952)***
Sansum Clinic 805 682-6507
509 E Montecito St # 200 Santa Barbara (93103) ***(G-22556)***
Santa Ana City of 714 565-2600
1000 E Santa Ana Blvd # 108 Santa Ana (92701) ***(G-14778)***
Santa Ana Country Club 714 556-3000
20382 Newport Blvd Santa Ana (92707) ***(G-19061)***
Santa Ana District Office, Santa Ana *Also called State Compensation Insur Fund* ***(G-10461)***
Santa Ana Police Officers Assn 714 836-1211
1607 N Sycamore St Santa Ana (92701) ***(G-25337)***
Santa Ana Radiology Center 714 835-6055
1100 N Tustin Ave Ste A Santa Ana (92705) ***(G-19953)***
Santa Ana Unified School Dst 714 431-1900
1749 Carnegie Ave Santa Ana (92705) ***(G-23052)***
Santa Anita Associates (PA) 626 447-2764
405 S Santa Anita Ave Arcadia (91006) ***(G-18782)***
Santa Anita Convalescent Hospi 626 579-0310
5522 Gracewood Ave Temple City (91780) ***(G-21367)***
Santa Anita Family Young 626 359-9244
501 S Mountain Ave Monrovia (91016) ***(G-24386)***
Santa Anita Golf Course, Arcadia *Also called Santa Anita Associates* ***(G-18782)***
Santa Anita Park, Arcadia *Also called Los Angeles Turf Club Inc* ***(G-18570)***
Santa Barbara Airbus 805 964-7759
750 Technology Dr Goleta (93117) ***(G-3840)***
Santa Barbara Athletic CLB Inc 805 966-6147
520 Castillo St Santa Barbara (93101) ***(G-19062)***
Santa Barbara City of 805 564-5485
630 Garden St Santa Barbara (93101) ***(G-17474)***
Santa Barbara Cnty Social Svcs, Santa Maria *Also called Santa Barbra Cttge Hsptl* ***(G-21858)***
Santa Barbara Convalescent Ctr, Santa Barbara *Also called California Convalescent Hosp* ***(G-21173)***
Santa Barbara Cottage Care Ctr, Santa Barbara *Also called Cottage Care Center* ***(G-21513)***
Santa Barbara Cottage Hospital (PA) 805 682-7111
400 W Pueblo St Santa Barbara (93105) ***(G-21857)***
Santa Barbara County of 805 882-3700
117 E Carrillo St Santa Barbara (93101) ***(G-24187)***
Santa Barbara County of 805 614-1550
1410 S Broadway Ste L Santa Maria (93454) ***(G-24188)***
Santa Barbara County of 805 681-5100
345 Camino Del Remedio Santa Barbara (93110) ***(G-23053)***
Santa Barbara County of 805 737-7080
1100 W Laurel Ave Lompoc (93436) ***(G-24189)***

Santa Barbara County of...805 346-7540
312 E Cook St Ste D Santa Maria (93454) ***(G-23544)***
Santa Barbara County of...805 884-1600
429 N San Antonio Rd Santa Barbara (93110) ***(G-24190)***
Santa Barbara County of...866 901-3212
4 E Carrillo St Santa Barbara (93101) ***(G-24191)***
Santa Barbara Fabricare Inc...805 963-6677
14 W Gutierrez St Santa Barbara (93101) ***(G-13585)***
Santa Barbara Family YMCA, Santa Barbara *Also called Channel Islands Young Mens Ch* ***(G-25233)***
Santa Barbara Farms LLC (PA)...805 736-9776
1200 Union Sugar Ave Lompoc (93436) ***(G-93)***
Santa Barbara Inn, Santa Barbara *Also called Interstate Hotels Resorts Inc* ***(G-27071)***
Santa Barbara Metro Trnst Dst (PA)...805 963-3364
550 Olive St Santa Barbara (93101) ***(G-3713)***
Santa Barbara Museum...805 682-4711
2559 Puesta Del Sol Santa Barbara (93105) ***(G-25047)***
Santa Barbara Museum of Art (PA)...805 963-4364
1130 State St Santa Barbara (93101) ***(G-25048)***
Santa Barbara PC Users Group...805 964-5411
462 S San Marcos Rd Santa Barbara (93111) ***(G-17475)***
Santa Barbara San Luis Obispo...800 421-2560
4050 Calle Real Santa Barbara (93110) ***(G-10248)***
Santa Barbara Service Center, Goleta *Also called Southern California Edison Co* ***(G-6230)***
Santa Barbara Trnsp Corp (HQ)...805 681-8355
6414 Hollister Ave Goleta (93117) ***(G-3947)***
Santa Barbara Trnsp Corp...805 928-0402
1331 Jason Way Santa Maria (93455) ***(G-3948)***
Santa Barbra Cttge Hsptl...805 569-7367
400 W Pueblo St Santa Barbara (93105) ***(G-22276)***
Santa Barbra Cttge Hsptl...805 569-7224
400 W Pueblo St Santa Barbara (93105) ***(G-22277)***
Santa Barbra Cttge Hsptl...805 346-7135
2125 Centerpointe Pkwy Santa Maria (93455) ***(G-21858)***
Santa Brbara Zlgcal Foundation...805 962-1673
500 Ninos Dr Santa Barbara (93103) ***(G-25070)***
Santa Catalina Island Company...310 510-7410
1 Descanso Beach Way Avalon (90704) ***(G-19063)***
Santa Catalina Island Company (PA)...310 510-2000
150 Metropole Ave Avalon (90704) ***(G-5001)***
Santa Clara County of...408 435-2000
2314 N 1st St San Jose (95131) ***(G-24192)***
Santa Clara Arques Med Offs, Sunnyvale *Also called Kaiser Foundation Hospitals* ***(G-19649)***
Santa Clara Cnty Fderal Cr Un (PA)...408 282-0700
1641 N 1st St Ste 245 San Jose (95112) ***(G-9623)***
Santa Clara County of...408 792-2704
3180 Newberry Dr Ste 150 San Jose (95118) ***(G-23545)***
Santa Clara County of...408 201-7600
19050 Malaguerra Ave Morgan Hill (95037) ***(G-24804)***
Santa Clara County of...408 885-7200
2325 Enborg Ln Fl 4 San Jose (95128) ***(G-26436)***
Santa Clara County of...408 993-4700
2310 N 1st St Ste 200 San Jose (95131) ***(G-14418)***
Santa Clara County of...408 885-6818
2325 Enborg Ln Ste 380 San Jose (95128) ***(G-21859)***
Santa Clara County of...408 355-2200
298 Garden Hill Dr Los Gatos (95032) ***(G-19277)***
Santa Clara County of...408 282-3200
1555 Berger Dr Fl 1 San Jose (95112) ***(G-14046)***
Santa Clara County of...408 435-2111
2314 N 1st St San Jose (95131) ***(G-24193)***
Santa Clara County of...408 792-5680
976 Lenzen Ave Ste 1800 San Jose (95126) ***(G-19954)***
Santa Clara County of...408 885-7354
751 S Bascom Ave Fl 4 San Jose (95128) ***(G-26437)***
Santa Clara Hilton, The, Santa Clara *Also called Hostmark Investors Ltd Partnr* ***(G-27055)***
Santa Clara Marriott Hotel, Santa Clara *Also called Host Hotels & Resorts LP* ***(G-12765)***
Santa Clara Tenant Corp...408 496-6400
2885 Lakeside Dr Santa Clara (95054) ***(G-13212)***
Santa Clara Valley Corporation...408 947-1100
715 N 1st St Ste 27 San Jose (95112) ***(G-14419)***
Santa Clara Valley Health & Ho, San Jose *Also called Santa Clara County of* ***(G-21859)***
Santa Clara Valley Medical Ctr...408 885-6300
2400 Moorpark Ave San Jose (95128) ***(G-19955)***
Santa Clara Valley Medical Ctr...408 792-5586
976 Lenzen Ave San Jose (95126) ***(G-19956)***
Santa Clara Valley Medical Ctr...408 885-5730
2220 Moorpark Ave San Jose (95128) ***(G-23054)***
Santa Clara Valley Medical Ctr (PA)...408 885-5000
751 S Bascom Ave San Jose (95128) ***(G-21860)***
Santa Clara Valley Trnsp Auth...408 321-5555
3331 N 1st St San Jose (95134) ***(G-3885)***
Santa Clara Valley Water (PA)...408 265-2600
5750 Almaden Expy San Jose (95118) ***(G-6399)***
Santa Clara Valley Water...408 395-8121
400 More Ave Los Gatos (95032) ***(G-6400)***
Santa Clara Valley Water Dst, San Jose *Also called Santa Clara Valley Water* ***(G-6399)***
Santa Clara Vlly Health/Hosptl, San Jose *Also called Santa Clara County of* ***(G-26437)***
Santa Clara Vly Job Career Ctr...805 933-8300
725 E Main St Ste 101 Santa Paula (93060) ***(G-14779)***
Santa Clara Vngard Booster CLB...408 727-5532
1795 Space Park Dr Santa Clara (95054) ***(G-25338)***
Santa Clara Woman's Club Adobe, Santa Clara *Also called Santa Clara Womens Club* ***(G-19064)***
Santa Clara Womens Club...408 246-8000
3260 The Alameda Santa Clara (95050) ***(G-19064)***
Santa Clarita City of...661 294-1287
28250 Constellation Rd Santa Clarita (91355) ***(G-3886)***
Santa Clarita City of...661 284-1423
23920 Valencia Blvd # 300 Santa Clarita (91355) ***(G-19278)***
Santa Clarita Athletic Club...661 255-3365
23942 Lyons Ave Ste 106 Newhall (91321) ***(G-18679)***
Santa Clarita Concrete...661 252-2012
16164 Sierra Hwy Santa Clarita (91390) ***(G-3325)***
Santa Clarita Convalescent HM, Newhall *Also called Valencia Health Care Inc* ***(G-21406)***
Santa Clarita Executive Plaza, Santa Clarita *Also called Kaiser Foundation Hospitals* ***(G-22754)***
Santa Clarita Hauling/Blue, Santa Clarita *Also called USA Waste of California Inc* ***(G-6589)***
Santa Clarita Health Care Assn (PA)...661 253-8000
23845 Mcbean Pkwy Santa Clarita (91355) ***(G-27205)***
Santa Clarita Health Care Ctr, Santa Clarita *Also called Henry Mayo Newhall Mem Hosp* ***(G-22974)***
Santa Clarita Interiors Inc...661 253-0861
25682 Springbrook Ave # 130 Santa Clarita (91350) ***(G-3400)***
Santa Clarita Medical Group...661 255-6802
25775 Mcbean Pkwy Ste 209 Valencia (91355) ***(G-19957)***
Santa Clarita Valley Bldrs Inc...661 295-6722
24307 Magic Mountain Pkwy # 122 Santa Clarita (91355) ***(G-3086)***
SANTA CLARITA VALLEY SENIOR CE, Santa Clarita *Also called Santa Clarita Vlly Cmmtt Aging* ***(G-24194)***
Santa Clarita Vlly Cmmtt Aging...661 259-9444
22900 Market St Santa Clarita (91321) ***(G-24194)***
Santa Cruz Biotechnology Inc...831 457-3800
2145 Delaware Ave Santa Cruz (95060) ***(G-26600)***
Santa Cruz County of...831 763-8400
1430 Freedom Blvd Ste D Watsonville (95076) ***(G-19958)***
Santa Cruz County of...831 454-2030
701 Ocean St Rm 530 Santa Cruz (95060) ***(G-16182)***
Santa Cruz County Symphony...831 462-0553
307 Church St Santa Cruz (95060) ***(G-18493)***
Santa Cruz Hotel Associates...831 426-4330
175 W Cliff Dr Santa Cruz (95060) ***(G-13213)***
Santa Cruz Medical Foundation (HQ)...831 458-5537
2025 Soquel Ave Santa Cruz (95062) ***(G-19959)***
Santa Cruz Metro...831 426-6080
135 Aviation Way Ste 2 Watsonville (95076) ***(G-3887)***
Santa Cruz Metro Trnst Dst...831 469-1954
110 Vernon St Ste B Santa Cruz (95060) ***(G-3888)***
Santa Cruz Montessori School...831 476-1646
6230 Soquel Dr Aptos (95003) ***(G-24511)***
Santa Cruz Seaside Company (PA)...831 423-5590
400 Beach St Santa Cruz (95060) ***(G-18830)***
Santa Cruz Seaside Company...831 427-3400
201 W Cliff Dr Santa Cruz (95060) ***(G-13214)***
Santa Cruz Westside Elc Inc...831 469-8888
2119 Delaware Ave Santa Cruz (95060) ***(G-2725)***
Santa Fe Pacific Pipeline, Bloomington *Also called Kinder Mrgan Enrgy Partners LP* ***(G-4951)***
Santa Fe Plaster...760 747-9950
620 Alpine Way Escondido (92029) ***(G-2977)***
Santa For Hire.com, Newport Beach *Also called Internet Booking Agencycom Inc* ***(G-14686)***
Santa Lucia Preserve Company...831 620-6760
1 Rancho San Carlos Rd Carmel (93923) ***(G-19065)***
Santa Margarita Water District (PA)...949 459-6400
26111 Antonio Pkwy Rcho STA Marg (92688) ***(G-6401)***
Santa Margarita Water District...949 459-6400
26101 Antonio Pkwy Rcho STA Marg (92688) ***(G-6402)***
Santa Margarita YMCA Garrison, Oceanside *Also called YMCA of San Diego County* ***(G-25427)***
Santa Maria Airport Regency...805 928-8000
3455 Skyway Dr Santa Maria (93455) ***(G-13215)***
SANTA MARIA CARE CENTER, Santa Maria *Also called Kimberly Care Center Inc* ***(G-20695)***
Santa Maria Cinema 10, Santa Maria *Also called Edwards Theatres Circuit Inc* ***(G-18336)***
Santa Maria Hotel Corp...805 928-6000
2100 N Broadway Santa Maria (93454) ***(G-13216)***
Santa Maria Valley YMCA...805 937-8521
3400 Skyway Dr Santa Maria (93455) ***(G-25339)***
Santa Mnica Mntins Trils Cncil...818 222-4531
24735 Mulholland Hwy Woodland Hills (91302) ***(G-25340)***
Santa Mnica Wlshire Imging LLC...323 549-3055
5455 Wilshire Blvd Los Angeles (90036) ***(G-22278)***
Santa Monica Amusements LLC...310 451-9641
380 Santa Monica Pier Santa Monica (90401) ***(G-18831)***
Santa Monica Bay Physcians...310 459-2363
881 Alma Real Dr Ste 214 Pacific Palisades (90272) ***(G-19960)***
Santa Monica Bay Physicians He (PA)...310 417-5900
5767 W Century Blvd Los Angeles (90045) ***(G-19961)***
Santa Monica Bay Womens Club...310 395-1308
1210 4th St Santa Monica (90401) ***(G-25575)***
Santa Monica Big Blue Bus, Santa Monica *Also called City of Santa Monica* ***(G-3877)***
Santa Monica City of...310 399-5865
2802 4th St Santa Monica (90405) ***(G-24512)***
Santa Monica City of...310 451-5444
1660 7th St Santa Monica (90401) ***(G-3714)***
Santa Monica City of...310 458-8551
1855 Main St Santa Monica (90401) ***(G-11040)***
Santa Monica Express Inc...310 458-6000
12424 Wilshire Blvd # 740 Los Angeles (90025) ***(G-4062)***
Santa Monica Family YMCA...310 451-7387
1332 6th St Santa Monica (90401) ***(G-25341)***
Santa Monica Hsr Ltd Partnr...310 395-3332
1707 4th St Santa Monica (90401) ***(G-13217)***
Santa Monica Municpl Bus Line, Santa Monica *Also called Santa Monica City of* ***(G-3714)***
Santa Monica Orthopedic (PA)...310 315-2018
2020 Santa Monica Blvd # 230 Santa Monica (90404) ***(G-19962)***

ALPHABETIC

Santa Monica Outpatient Center, Santa Monica *Also called Childrens Hospital Los Angeles* ***(G-19434)***
Santa Monica Seafood Company 310 393-5244
1000 Wilshire Blvd Santa Monica (90401) ***(G-8651)***
Santa Monica Sport Club, Santa Monica *Also called 24 Hour Fitness Usa Inc* ***(G-18591)***
Santa Monica Ucla Medical Ctr, Santa Monica *Also called University Cal Los Angeles* ***(G-21990)***
Santa Paula Berry Farms LLC....805 981-1469
1650 E Gonzales Rd Oxnard (93036) ***(G-132)***
Santa Paula Hospital, Santa Paula *Also called Ventura County Medical Center* ***(G-20191)***
Santa Paula Water Works Ltd....562 923-0711
9750 Washburn Rd Downey (90241) ***(G-12089)***
Santa Rosa City of 707 543-3040
100 Santa Rosa Ave Santa Rosa (95404) ***(G-23546)***
Santa Rosa & Sonoma Co Real Es 707 524-1124
1057 College Ave Santa Rosa (95404) ***(G-11833)***
Santa Rosa Clinic, Santa Rosa *Also called Veterans Health Administration* ***(G-20212)***
Santa Rosa Community Hlth Ctrs (PA) 707 547-2222
3569 Round Barn Cir Santa Rosa (95403) ***(G-24195)***
Santa Rosa Convalescent Hosp, Santa Rosa *Also called Ashley Ltc Inc* ***(G-20385)***
Santa Rosa Dental Group....707 545-0944
1820 Sonoma Ave Ste 80 Santa Rosa (95405) ***(G-20275)***
Santa Rosa Golf & Country Club....707 546-3485
333 Country Club Dr Santa Rosa (95401) ***(G-19066)***
Santa Rosa Memorial Hospital (HQ)....707 546-3210
1165 Montgomery Dr Santa Rosa (95405) ***(G-21861)***
Santa Rosa Memorial Hospital....707 542-2771
1165 Montgomery Dr Santa Rosa (95405) ***(G-20896)***
Santa Rosa Radiology Med Group (PA) 707 546-4062
121 Sotoyome St Santa Rosa (95405) ***(G-22279)***
Santa Rosa Rnchria Gaming Comm....559 924-6948
17225 Jersey Ave Lemoore (93245) ***(G-18494)***
Santa Rosa Surgery Center LP....707 578-4100
1111 Sonoma Ave Ste 308 Santa Rosa (95405) ***(G-21862)***
Santa Teresa Conv Hospital....562 948-1961
9140 Verner St Pico Rivera (90660) ***(G-21863)***
Santa Teresa Golf Center, San Jose *Also called Santa Teresa Golf Club* ***(G-18783)***
Santa Teresa Golf Club....408 225-2650
260 Bernal Rd San Jose (95119) ***(G-18783)***
Santa Teresita Inc (PA) 626 359-3243
819 Buena Vista St Duarte (91010) ***(G-21864)***
Santa Ynez Valley Cottage Hosp 805 688-6431
2050 Viborg Rd Solvang (93463) ***(G-21865)***
Santa Ynez Valley Marriott, Buellton *Also called Kang Family Partners LLC* ***(G-12875)***
Santaluz Club Inc....858 759-3120
8170 Caminito Santaluz E San Diego (92127) ***(G-19067)***
Santana Concrete....909 421-2218
18241 Slover Ave Bloomington (92316) ***(G-3326)***
Santana Row Hotel Partners LP 408 551-0010
355 Santana Row San Jose (95128) ***(G-13218)***
Sante Community Physicians, Fresno *Also called Sante Health System Inc* ***(G-19963)***
Sante Health System Inc 559 228-5400
7370 N Palm Ave Ste 101 Fresno (93711) ***(G-19963)***
Santee Systems Services II....323 445-0044
229 E Gage Ave Los Angeles (90003) ***(G-24196)***
Santee Systems Services II LL 323 445-0044
229 E Gage Ave Los Angeles (90003) ***(G-18680)***
Santellan Farm Labor Contr, Woodlake *Also called Pete Santellan* ***(G-678)***
Santen Incorporated....415 268-9100
2100 Powell St Fl 16 Emeryville (94608) ***(G-26806)***
Sants Clair Alcohol Meth Prog, San Jose *Also called Central Valley Clinic Inc* ***(G-22677)***
Sanwa Jutaku Co Ltd....562 861-1900
8425 Firestone Blvd Downey (90241) ***(G-13219)***
Sanyo Denki America Inc (HQ) 310 783-5400
468 Amapola Ave Torrance (90501) ***(G-7183)***
Sanyo Foods Corp America 714 730-1611
12442 Tustin Ranch Rd Tustin (92782) ***(G-19068)***
Sanzaru Games Inc....650 312-1000
1065 E Hillsdale Blvd Foster City (94404) ***(G-15436)***
Sap America Inc 760 603-8034
2121 Palomar Airport Rd # 350 Carlsbad (92011) ***(G-15437)***
Sap Labs LLC 650 849-4129
3475 Deer Creek Rd Palo Alto (94304) ***(G-15438)***
Sap Labs LLC (HQ) 650 849-4000
3410 Hillview Ave Palo Alto (94304) ***(G-15439)***
Sap, Oracle, Service Provider, West Sacramento *Also called PC World Corp* ***(G-5683)***
SARA, Cypress *Also called Scientific Applications & RES* ***(G-26601)***
Sara Enterprises Inc (HQ)....818 553-3200
2349 Honolulu Ave Montrose (91020) ***(G-4973)***
Sara Lee, San Lorenzo *Also called Hillshire Brands Company* ***(G-8671)***
Sarabian Farms, Sanger *Also called Virginia Sarabian* ***(G-251)***
Sarah Elizabeth Treusdell....661 949-0131
921 W Avenue J Ste C Lancaster (93534) ***(G-22828)***
Saratoga Capital Inc....408 286-1000
233 W Santa Clara St San Jose (95113) ***(G-13220)***
Saratoga Court Inc....408 866-1392
18855 Cox Ave Saratoga (95070) ***(G-11241)***
Saratoga Retirement Community, Saratoga *Also called Odd Fellows Home California* ***(G-24753)***
Saroyan Lumber and Moulding Co, Huntington Park *Also called Saroyan Lumber Company Inc* ***(G-6960)***
Saroyan Lumber Company Inc (PA)....800 624-9309
6230 S Alameda St Huntington Park (90255) ***(G-6960)***
Sarpa-Feldman Enterprises Inc....408 982-1790
650 N King Rd San Jose (95133) ***(G-17476)***
Sas Institute Inc....949 250-9999
1148 N Lemon St Orange (92867) ***(G-15834)***

Sat, Sacramento *Also called Lpa Insurance Agency Inc* ***(G-15736)***
Sat Corporation (HQ) 402 208-9200
3200 Patrick Henry Dr # 150 Santa Clara (95054) ***(G-15440)***
Satellite Dialysis, Modesto *Also called Satellite Healthcare Inc* ***(G-22640)***
Satellite Dialysis Centers, San Jose *Also called Satellite Healthcare Inc* ***(G-22641)***
Satellite Healthcare Inc....209 578-0691
3500 Coffee Rd Ste 21 Modesto (95355) ***(G-22640)***
Satellite Healthcare Inc (PA)....650 404-3600
300 Santana Row Ste 300 San Jose (95128) ***(G-22641)***
Satellite Healthcare Inc....408 258-8720
2121 Alexian Dr Ste 118 San Jose (95116) ***(G-22642)***
Satellite Management Co (PA)....714 558-2411
1010 E Chestnut Ave Santa Ana (92701) ***(G-11834)***
Satellite Office, Van Nuys *Also called Southern Cal Orthpd Inst LP* ***(G-20015)***
Satellite Pros, Ontario *Also called Jeeva Corporation* ***(G-2623)***
Sather Installation, Murrieta *Also called SI Inc* ***(G-3089)***
Saticoy Country Club....805 647-1153
4450 Clubhouse Dr Somis (93066) ***(G-19069)***
Saticoy Fruit Exchange, Santa Paula *Also called Saticoy Lemon Association* ***(G-583)***
Saticoy Fruit Exchange, Ventura *Also called Saticoy Lemon Association* ***(G-223)***
Saticoy Lemon Association (PA) 805 654-6500
103 N Peck Rd Santa Paula (93060) ***(G-583)***
Saticoy Lemon Association....805 654-6500
7560 Bristol Rd Ventura (93003) ***(G-223)***
Saticoy Lemon Association....805 654-6543
600 E 3rd St Oxnard (93030) ***(G-584)***
Satmetrix Systems Inc (PA)....650 227-8300
3 Twin Dolphin Dr Ste 225 Redwood City (94065) ***(G-15441)***
Saturn Electric Inc....858 271-4100
7552 Trade St Ste A San Diego (92121) ***(G-2726)***
Sauce Labs Inc 415 946-1117
539 Bryant St Ste 303 San Francisco (94107) ***(G-16042)***
Saugus Division, Santa Clarita *Also called National Technical Systems Inc* ***(G-26877)***
Saugus Union School District....661 298-3240
26501 Ruether Ave Santa Clarita (91350) ***(G-3949)***
Savant Construction Inc....909 614-4300
13830 Mountain Ave Chino (91710) ***(G-1659)***
Save Our Sunol 925 862-2263
2934 Kilkare Rd Sunol (94586) ***(G-25342)***
Save Queen LLC....562 435-3511
429 Shoreline Village Dr I Long Beach (90802) ***(G-13221)***
Savings Bank Mendocino County (PA)....707 462-6613
200 N School St Ukiah (95482) ***(G-9523)***
Savoy Contractors Group Inc 949 753-1919
8905 Research Dr Irvine (92618) ***(G-1251)***
Savvis Communications Corp 408 884-6269
2101 Tasman Dr Ste 100 Santa Clara (95054) ***(G-16260)***
Savvis Communications Corp 310 726-1166
200 N Nash St El Segundo (90245) ***(G-16043)***
Savvius Inc (PA) 925 937-3200
1340 Treat Blvd Ste 500 Walnut Creek (94597) ***(G-15442)***
Sawmill, Ukiah *Also called Mendocino Forest Pdts Co LLC* ***(G-6936)***
Sawyers Heating & AC....209 416-7700
5272 Jerusalem Ct Ste D Modesto (95356) ***(G-2359)***
Saxco International LLC....707 422-9999
1855 Gateway Blvd Ste 400 Concord (94520) ***(G-9301)***
Saylor Lane Healthcare Center, Sacramento *Also called Kindred Healthcare Oper Inc* ***(G-21282)***
Saylor Lane Healthcare Center, Sacramento *Also called S L H C C Inc* ***(G-20884)***
Sb Freight, City of Industry *Also called Shipbycom LLC* ***(G-4063)***
Sb Group Us Inc 650 562-8110
1 Circle Star Way Fl 1 San Carlos (94070) ***(G-10184)***
Sbb Roofing Inc (PA)....323 254-2888
3310 Verdugo Rd Los Angeles (90065) ***(G-3212)***
SBC, San Diego *Also called AT&T Services Inc* ***(G-5525)***
SBC, San Ramon *Also called AT&T Services* ***(G-5515)***
SBC, Monterey *Also called AT&T Services Inc* ***(G-5527)***
SBC, Modesto *Also called AT&T Services Inc* ***(G-5529)***
SBC, Jackson *Also called AT&T Services Inc* ***(G-5530)***
SBC, Paso Robles *Also called AT&T Services Inc* ***(G-5533)***
SBC, San Diego *Also called AT&T Services Inc* ***(G-5535)***
SBC, Anaheim *Also called AT&T Services Inc* ***(G-5536)***
SBC, Mountain View *Also called AT&T Services Inc* ***(G-5537)***
SBC, Bakersfield *Also called AT&T Services Inc* ***(G-27840)***
SBC, Glendale *Also called AT&T Services Inc* ***(G-1906)***
SBC, Los Angeles *Also called AT&T Services Inc* ***(G-5538)***
SBC, Anaheim *Also called AT&T Services Inc* ***(G-5542)***
SBC, Santa Rosa *Also called AT&T Services Inc* ***(G-5544)***
SBC, Los Angeles *Also called AT&T Services Inc* ***(G-5546)***
SBC, San Francisco *Also called AT&T Services Inc* ***(G-5547)***
SBC, Fremont *Also called AT&T Services Inc* ***(G-5548)***
SBC, Buena Park *Also called AT&T Services Inc* ***(G-5550)***
SBC, Concord *Also called AT&T Services Inc* ***(G-5551)***
SBC, Sacramento *Also called AT&T Services Inc* ***(G-5553)***
SBC, Oceanside *Also called AT&T Services Inc* ***(G-5521)***
SBC, Sacramento *Also called AT&T Services* ***(G-5522)***
SBC, Concord *Also called AT&T Services Inc* ***(G-5554)***
SBC, San Diego *Also called AT&T Services Inc* ***(G-5555)***
SBC, Escondido *Also called AT&T Services Inc* ***(G-5556)***
SBC, Alhambra *Also called AT&T Services Inc* ***(G-5559)***
SBC, San Jose *Also called AT&T Services Inc* ***(G-5560)***
SBC Communications, Rancho Cordova *Also called AT&T Services Inc* ***(G-5540)***
SBC West, Bakersfield *Also called AT&T Services Inc* ***(G-5543)***

ALPHABETIC

SBE Hotel Group LLC ... 323 655-8000
8000 Beverly Blvd Los Angeles (90048) ***(G-12342)***

Sbehg 465 S La Cienega LLC ... 310 247-0400
465 S La Cienega Blvd Los Angeles (90048) ***(G-13222)***

Sbm Management Services LP ... 866 855-2211
5241 Arnold Ave McClellan (95652) ***(G-14420)***

Sbm Site Services LLC (PA) ... 916 922-7600
5241 Arnold Ave McClellan (95652) ***(G-14421)***

Sbmc, Ukiah *Also called Savings Bank Mendocino County* ***(G-9523)***

SBP, La Jolla *Also called Sanford Burnham Prebys Medical* ***(G-26805)***

SBPEA, San Bernardino *Also called San Brnrdino Pub Emplyees Assn* ***(G-25182)***

Sbrm Inc (PA) ... 760 480-0208
2342 Meyers Ave Escondido (92029) ***(G-14422)***

Sbrpstc, San Jose *Also called South Bay Regl Public Safety T* ***(G-24388)***

SBSA, Redwood City *Also called Silicon Valley Clean Water* ***(G-6416)***

SC Builders Inc (PA) ... 408 328-0688
910 Thompson Pl Sunnyvale (94085) ***(G-1660)***

SC Fuels, Orange *Also called Southern Counties Oil Co* ***(G-9009)***

SC Harp El Segundo LLC ... 310 322-0999
1985 E Grand Ave El Segundo (90245) ***(G-13223)***

SC Hotel Partners LLC ... 415 775-5000
550 Geary St San Francisco (94102) ***(G-13224)***

SC Wright Construction Inc ... 619 698-6909
3838 Camino Del Rio Nth S Ste 370 San Diego (92108) ***(G-26055)***

Sca Enterprises Inc (PA) ... 818 845-7621
3817 W Magnolia Blvd Burbank (91505) ***(G-17477)***

Scalematrix Holdings Inc ... 888 349-9994
5775 Kearny Villa Rd San Diego (92123) ***(G-16474)***

Scan, Long Beach *Also called Porchlight Inc* ***(G-21351)***

Scan Health Plan, Long Beach *Also called Senior Care* ***(G-10378)***

Scan Health Plan (PA) ... 562 989-5100
3800 Kilroy Airport Way # 100 Long Beach (90806) ***(G-10374)***

Scan Health Plan ... 818 550-4900
500 N Central Ave Ste 350 Glendale (91203) ***(G-10375)***

Scan Health Plan ... 805 658-0365
6633 Telephone Rd Ste 100 Ventura (93003) ***(G-10376)***

Scan-Vino LLC (PA) ... 209 931-3570
5463 Cherokee Rd Stockton (95215) ***(G-4260)***

Scandia Amusement Park, Ontario *Also called Scandia Recreation Centers* ***(G-18809)***

Scandia Family Fun Center, Sacramento *Also called Scandia Sports Inc* ***(G-19279)***

Scandia Recreation Centers ... 909 390-3092
1155 S Wanamaker Ave Ontario (91761) ***(G-18809)***

Scandia Sports Inc ... 916 331-5757
5070 Hillsdale Blvd Sacramento (95842) ***(G-19279)***

Scantibodies Clinical Lab Inc ... 866 249-1212
9236 Abraham Way Santee (92071) ***(G-22280)***

Scarborough Farms Inc ... 805 483-9113
731 Pacific Ave Oxnard (93030) ***(G-94)***

Scat Enterprises Inc ... 310 370-5501
1400 Kingsdale Ave Redondo Beach (90278) ***(G-6761)***

Scattergood Generation Plant, Playa Del Rey *Also called Los Angeles Dept Wtr & Pwr* ***(G-6304)***

SCC Acquisitions Inc ... 949 777-4000
2392 Morse Ave Irvine (92614) ***(G-12006)***

SCC ESA Dept of Risk Mgmt ... 408 441-4207
2310 N 1st St Ste 202 San Jose (95131) ***(G-10861)***

SCCH Inc ... 562 494-5188
1880 Dawson Ave Signal Hill (90755) ***(G-27206)***

Scci, Santa Maria *Also called Spiess Construction Co Inc* ***(G-1998)***

SCE Eastern Hydro Division ... 760 873-0767
4000 Bishop Creek Rd Bishop (93514) ***(G-6205)***

SCE FCU, Baldwin Park *Also called SCE Federal Credit Union* ***(G-9624)***

SCE Federal Credit Union (PA) ... 626 960-6888
12701 Schabarum Ave Baldwin Park (91706) ***(G-9624)***

Scene7 Inc ... 415 506-6000
6 Hamilton Landing # 150 Novato (94949) ***(G-15443)***

Scenic Circle Care Center, Modesto *Also called Riverside Health Care Corp* ***(G-21361)***

Scenic Route Inc ... 818 896-6006
13516 Desmond St Pacoima (91331) ***(G-3578)***

Scga Golf Course MGT Inc ... 951 677-7446
39500 Robrt Trnt Jnes Pkw Murrieta (92563) ***(G-18784)***

Schaefer Ambulance Service Inc (PA) ... 323 469-1473
4627 Beverly Blvd Los Angeles (90004) ***(G-3841)***

Schaefer Ambulance Service Inc ... 714 545-8486
2215 S Bristol St Santa Ana (92704) ***(G-14476)***

Schaefer Ambulance Service Inc ... 760 353-3380
905 S Imperial Ave El Centro (92243) ***(G-3842)***

Schaefer Ambulance Service Inc ... 626 333-4533
324 N Towne Ave Pomona (91767) ***(G-3843)***

Schaefer Mary-Judith ... 562 634-3164
7202 Petterson Ln Paramount (90723) ***(G-3579)***

Schaefer Parking Lot Service, Paramount *Also called Schaefer Mary-Judith* ***(G-3579)***

Schafer Bros Trnsf Pano Movers (PA) ... 310 835-7231
1981 E 213th St Carson (90810) ***(G-4638)***

Schafer Logistics, Carson *Also called Schafer Bros Trnsf Pano Movers* ***(G-4638)***

Schaper Construction Inc (PA) ... 408 437-0337
1177 N 15th St San Jose (95112) ***(G-2490)***

Schaper Construction Inc ... 951 808-1140
211 Granite St Ste G Corona (92879) ***(G-2491)***

Scharp's Oasis House, Los Angeles *Also called South Cntl Heatlh & Rehab Prog* ***(G-22837)***

Scheid Vineyards Cal Inc ... 831 385-4801
305 Hilltown Rd Salinas (93908) ***(G-184)***

Scheid Vineyards Inc ... 310 545-4757
1201 Morningside Dr Ste 1 Manhattan Beach (90266) ***(G-185)***

Scheid Vineyards Inc (PA) ... 310 301-1555
305 Hilltown Rd Salinas (93908) ***(G-186)***

Scheid Vineyards Inc ... 707 433-1858
373 Healdsburg Ave Healdsburg (95448) ***(G-187)***

Schenker Inc ... 650 745-3000
380 Littlefield Ave South San Francisco (94080) ***(G-5165)***

Scherzer International Corp (PA) ... 818 227-2770
6351 Owensmouth Ave # 213 Woodland Hills (91367) ***(G-17478)***

Schetter Electric, Sacramento *Also called M K S Construction Inc* ***(G-1208)***

Schetter Electric Inc (PA) ... 916 446-2521
471 Bannon St Sacramento (95811) ***(G-2727)***

Scheu Manufacturing Co ... 909 981-5343
8855 Baker Ave Rancho Cucamonga (91730) ***(G-249)***

Schick Moving & Storage Co (PA) ... 714 731-5500
2721 Michelle Dr Tustin (92780) ***(G-4375)***

Schilling Paradise Corp ... 619 449-4141
697 Greenfield Dr El Cajon (92021) ***(G-1994)***

Schilling Robotics LLC ... 530 753-6718
260 Cousteau Pl Ste 200 Davis (95618) ***(G-26056)***

Schindler Elevator Corporation ... 310 785-9775
2000 Avenue Of The Stars Los Angeles (90067) ***(G-7885)***

Schirmer Fire Protection Eng ... 213 630-2020
707 Wilshire Blvd # 2600 Los Angeles (90017) ***(G-10862)***

Schlumberger Technology Corp ... 661 864-4750
2841 Pegasus Dr Bakersfield (93308) ***(G-1094)***

Schlumberger Technology Corp ... 714 379-7332
12131 Industry St Garden Grove (92841) ***(G-1095)***

Schlumberger Well Services, Bakersfield *Also called Schlumberger Technology Corp* ***(G-1094)***

Schmidt Fire Protection Co Inc ... 858 279-6122
4760 Murphy Canyon Rd # 100 San Diego (92123) ***(G-2360)***

Schmidt Phyllis MD Corporation ... 213 613-1163
711 W College St Los Angeles (90012) ***(G-21866)***

Schneider Electric 600, Pleasanton *Also called Schneider Electric Usa Inc* ***(G-7470)***

Schneider Electric 650, Diamond Bar *Also called Schneider Electric Usa Inc* ***(G-7471)***

Schneider Electric Sftwr LLC (PA) ... 949 727-3200
26561 Rancho Pkwy S Lake Forest (92630) ***(G-16044)***

Schneider Electric Usa Inc ... 925 462-0986
6160 Stoneridge Mall Rd # 200 Pleasanton (94588) ***(G-7470)***

Schneider Electric Usa Inc ... 909 612-5400
21680 Gateway Center Dr # 300 Diamond Bar (91765) ***(G-7471)***

Schneider National Inc ... 661 858-1031
4193 Industrial Pkwy Dr Lebec (93243) ***(G-4261)***

Schneider National Inc ... 909 574-2165
14392 Valley Blvd Fontana (92335) ***(G-4262)***

Schnierow Dental Care ... 310 377-6453
13450 Hawthorne Blvd Hawthorne (90250) ***(G-20276)***

Schnitzer Steel Industries Inc ... 510 444-3919
1101 Embarcadero W Oakland (94607) ***(G-7402)***

Scholastic Book Fairs Inc ... 714 237-1100
2890 E White Star Ave Anaheim (92806) ***(G-9171)***

Scholastic Book Fairs Inc ... 510 771-1700
42001 Christy St Fremont (94538) ***(G-9172)***

Scholls, Bloomington *Also called Distribution Alternatives Inc* ***(G-4543)***

School Innovations Achievement (PA) ... 916 933-2290
5200 Golden Foothill Pkwy El Dorado Hills (95762) ***(G-15835)***

School of Hope, San Bernardino *Also called Assoc For Retarded Citizens* ***(G-24309)***

School Portraits By Kranz ... 714 545-1775
9992 Center Dr Villa Park (92861) ***(G-13665)***

Schools Financial Credit Union (PA) ... 916 569-5400
1485 Response Rd Ste 126 Sacramento (95815) ***(G-9688)***

Schoolsfirst Federal Credit Un (PA) ... 714 258-4000
2115 N Broadway Santa Ana (92706) ***(G-9625)***

Schoolsfirst Federal Credit Un ... 714 258-4000
15442 Newport Ave Tustin (92780) ***(G-9557)***

Schramsberg Vineyards Company ... 707 942-4558
1400 Schramsberg Rd Calistoga (94515) ***(G-188)***

Schrimp, Roger Attorney, Oakdale *Also called Damrell Nelson Schrimp Pall* ***(G-23194)***

Schryver Med Sls & Mktg LLC ... 303 371-0073
526 Mccormick St San Leandro (94577) ***(G-22281)***

Schryver Med Sls & Mktg LLC ... 303 459-8160
8545 Arjons Dr San Diego (92126) ***(G-22282)***

Schryver Med Sls & Mktg LLC ... 303 459-8160
1845 N Case St Orange (92865) ***(G-22283)***

Schryver Med Sls & Mktg LLC ... 303 459-8150
310 N Cluff Ave Ste 212 Lodi (95240) ***(G-22284)***

Schuff Steel Company ... 209 938-0869
2324 Navy Dr Stockton (95206) ***(G-3401)***

Schulte Ranches ... 805 563-0821
Rr 1 Box 228 Goleta (93117) ***(G-391)***

Schumacher Cargo Logistics Inc (PA) ... 310 324-1365
550 W 135th St Gardena (90248) ***(G-5166)***

Schurman Fine Papers (PA) ... 707 425-8006
500 Chadbourne Rd Fairfield (94534) ***(G-8215)***

Schurman Fine Papers ... 408 971-8843
1002 S 2nd St San Jose (95112) ***(G-17479)***

Schwager Davis Inc ... 408 281-9300
198 Hillsdale Ave San Jose (95136) ***(G-2082)***

Schwartz Msl LLC ... 415 817-2500
100 California St Fl 9 San Francisco (94111) ***(G-27767)***

Schwarz Paper Company LLC ... 909 476-2457
8449 Milliken Ave Ste 102 Rancho Cucamonga (91730) ***(G-8216)***

Schweizer Rena ... 818 501-7100
15720 Ventura Blvd # 100 Encino (91436) ***(G-11835)***

SCI, North Hollywood *Also called Pierce Brothers* ***(G-13710)***

SCI, Corona Del Mar *Also called Service Corp International* ***(G-11839)***

SCI, Oceanside *Also called Service Corp International* ***(G-12038)***

Sci Inc ... 951 245-7511
18501 Collier Ave B106 Lake Elsinore (92530) ***(G-3327)***

Scico, Avalon *Also called Santa Catalina Island Company* ***(G-5001)***

Scicon Technologies Corp (PA) ... 661 295-8630
27525 Newhall Ranch Rd # 2 Valencia (91355) ***(G-26057)***

ALPHABETIC

Employee Codes: A=Over 500 employees, B=251-500
C=101-250, D=51-100, E=45-50
2017 Directory of California
Wholesalers and Services Companies
© Mergent Inc. 1-800-342-5647
1539

Scicon Technologies Corp.......................................949 252-1341
1300 Quail St Ste 208 Newport Beach (92660) ***(G-26058)***
Science Applications Intl Corp.......................................703 676-4300
4015 Hancock St Ste 1000 San Diego (92110) ***(G-16475)***
Science Applications Intl Corp.......................................858 826-3061
4015 Hancock St San Diego (92110) ***(G-16045)***
Science Applications Intl Corp.......................................858 826-6000
4242 Campus Point Ct San Diego (92121) ***(G-16046)***
Scientific Applications & RES (PA).......................................714 828-1465
6300 Gateway Dr Cypress (90630) ***(G-26601)***
Scientific Concepts Inc.......................................650 578-1142
303 Vintage Park Dr # 220 Foster City (94404) ***(G-18010)***
SCIHP, Santa Rosa *Also called Sonoma County Indian Health PR* ***(G-20008)***
Scils, Petaluma *Also called Sonoma Cnty Ind Living Skills* ***(G-24816)***
Scion, Torrance *Also called Toyota Motor Sales USA Inc* ***(G-9804)***
Sciots Tract Association.......................................530 753-5219
937 Chestnut Ln Davis (95616) ***(G-25343)***
Scl Company Inc.......................................818 993-4758
19545 Parthenia St Northridge (91324) ***(G-17826)***
Sclarc, Los Angeles *Also called South Central Los* ***(G-24980)***
SCM Advisors LLC.......................................415 486-6500
909 Montgomery St Fl 5 San Francisco (94133) ***(G-10185)***
Scmg, San Diego *Also called Sharp Community Medical Group* ***(G-25156)***
Scmh, Whittier *Also called Southern California Mtl Hdlg* ***(G-7891)***
SCMS, Aptos *Also called Santa Cruz Montessori School* ***(G-24511)***
Scope Industries (PA).......................................310 458-1574
2811 Wilshire Blvd # 410 Santa Monica (90403) ***(G-6562)***
Scope Products, Santa Monica *Also called Scope Industries* ***(G-6562)***
Scope Seven LLC.......................................310 220-3939
2201 Park Pl Ste 100 El Segundo (90245) ***(G-8139)***
Scorpio Enterprises.......................................562 946-9464
12556 Mccann Dr Santa Fe Springs (90670) ***(G-2361)***
Scorpion Athc Booster CLB Inc.......................................805 482-2005
300 E Esplanade Dr # 250 Oxnard (93036) ***(G-25344)***
Scorpion Design LLC.......................................661 702-0100
28480 Ave Stnford Ste 140 Valencia (91355) ***(G-27636)***
Scott A Porter Prof Corp.......................................916 929-1481
350 University Ave # 200 Sacramento (95825) ***(G-23547)***
Scott J Witlin Atty, Los Angeles *Also called Proskauer Rose LLP* ***(G-23520)***
Scott Jacks DDS Inc.......................................323 564-2444
4444 Tweedy Blvd South Gate (90280) ***(G-20277)***
Scott Place Associates.......................................650 345-8222
60 31st Ave San Mateo (94403) ***(G-11836)***
Scott Silva Concrete Inc.......................................916 859-0593
11374 Gold Dredge Way Rancho Cordova (95742) ***(G-3328)***
Scott Street Senior Housing Co.......................................415 345-5083
2180 Post St San Francisco (94115) ***(G-21102)***
Scott Valley Bank (HQ).......................................530 623-2732
2544 Westside Rd Yreka (96097) ***(G-9524)***
Scott's Glass Service, Carson *Also called Scotts Labor Leasing Co Inc* ***(G-14780)***
Scottel Voice & Data Inc.......................................310 737-7300
6100 Center Dr Ste 720 Los Angeles (90045) ***(G-17942)***
Scottish American Insurance (PA).......................................714 550-5050
2002 E Mcfadden Ave # 100 Santa Ana (92705) ***(G-10863)***
Scotts Labor Leasing Co Inc.......................................310 835-8388
22560 Lucerne St Carson (90745) ***(G-14780)***
Scotts Montessori Valley Inc.......................................831 439-9313
123 S Navarra Dr Scotts Valley (95066) ***(G-24513)***
Scotts Plant Service Co.......................................209 545-0903
6206 Carver Rd Modesto (95356) ***(G-949)***
SCR, Costa Mesa *Also called South Coast Repertory Inc* ***(G-18435)***
SCR, Irvine *Also called Redhill Group Inc* ***(G-26703)***
Scrape Certified Welding Inc.......................................760 728-1308
2525 Old Highway 395 Fallbrook (92028) ***(G-3402)***
Screen Actors Guild-Producers, Burbank *Also called Sag-Aftra* ***(G-10562)***
Screen Gems-EMI Music Inc.......................................310 586-2700
2700 Colorado Ave Ste 100 Santa Monica (90404) ***(G-17480)***
Screen Spe Usa LLC (HQ).......................................408 523-9140
820 Kifer Rd Ste B Sunnyvale (94086) ***(G-7631)***
Screenworks LLC.......................................951 279-8877
1580 Magnolia Ave Corona (92879) ***(G-14161)***
Scribd Inc.......................................415 896-9890
333 Bush St Ste 2400 San Francisco (94104) ***(G-16261)***
Scrip Advantage Inc.......................................559 320-0052
4273 W Richert Ave # 110 Fresno (93722) ***(G-17481)***
Scripps Ambulatory Surgery Ctr, Encinitas *Also called Scripps Health* ***(G-19968)***
Scripps Aquarium, La Jolla *Also called Birch Aquarium At Scripps* ***(G-25059)***
Scripps Clinic.......................................858 794-1250
12395 El Camino Real San Diego (92130) ***(G-19964)***
Scripps Clinic - Encinatas, Encinitas *Also called Scripps Health* ***(G-19975)***
Scripps Clinic Carmel Valley.......................................858 554-8096
10666 N Torrey Pines Rd La Jolla (92037) ***(G-19965)***
Scripps Clinic Foundation.......................................858 554-9000
12395 El Camino Real San Diego (92130) ***(G-27207)***
Scripps Clinic Medical Group.......................................858 554-9606
10666 N Torrey Pines Rd La Jolla (92037) ***(G-19966)***
Scripps Del Mar, San Diego *Also called Scripps Health* ***(G-22830)***
Scripps Dialasys Inc (PA).......................................619 453-9070
9870 Genesee Ave La Jolla (92037) ***(G-19967)***
Scripps Dialysis Center, La Jolla *Also called Scripps Dialasys Inc* ***(G-19967)***
Scripps Green Hospital, La Jolla *Also called Scripps Health* ***(G-21869)***
Scripps Health.......................................760 753-8413
320 Santa Fe Dr Ste 310 Encinitas (92024) ***(G-19968)***
Scripps Health.......................................858 622-9076
10140 Campus Point Dr San Diego (92121) ***(G-19969)***
Scripps Health.......................................619 294-8111
4077 5th Ave San Diego (92103) ***(G-20897)***
Scripps Health.......................................619 862-6600
237 Church Ave Chula Vista (91910) ***(G-19970)***
Scripps Health.......................................858 678-6966
10010 Campus Point Dr San Diego (92121) ***(G-25345)***
Scripps Health.......................................858 657-4218
10790 Rancho Bernardo Rd San Diego (92127) ***(G-20898)***
Scripps Health.......................................858 271-9770
15004 Innovation Dr San Diego (92128) ***(G-22829)***
Scripps Health.......................................619 245-2350
7565 Mission Valley Rd # 200 San Diego (92108) ***(G-23055)***
Scripps Health.......................................760 479-3900
477 N El Camino Real A208 Encinitas (92024) ***(G-19971)***
Scripps Health.......................................760 901-5070
4318 Mission Ave Oceanside (92057) ***(G-19972)***
Scripps Health.......................................858 554-4100
10670 John J Hopkins Dr San Diego (92121) ***(G-20352)***
Scripps Health.......................................619 670-5400
10862 Calle Verde La Mesa (91941) ***(G-19973)***
Scripps Health.......................................760 753-6501
354 Santa Fe Dr Encinitas (92024) ***(G-21867)***
Scripps Health.......................................619 691-7000
435 H St Chula Vista (91910) ***(G-21868)***
Scripps Health (PA).......................................858 678-7000
4275 Campus Point Ct San Diego (92121) ***(G-20899)***
Scripps Health.......................................858 292-4211
7910 Frost St Ste 320 San Diego (92123) ***(G-19974)***
Scripps Health.......................................858 455-9100
10666 N Torrey Pines Rd La Jolla (92037) ***(G-21869)***
Scripps Health.......................................619 294-8111
4077 Fifth Ave San Diego (92103) ***(G-21870)***
Scripps Health.......................................858 764-3000
3811 Valley Centre Dr San Diego (92130) ***(G-22557)***
Scripps Health.......................................760 633-6915
310 Santa Fe Dr Ste 200 Encinitas (92024) ***(G-19975)***
Scripps Health.......................................800 727-4777
10666 N Torrey Pines Rd La Jolla (92037) ***(G-21871)***
Scripps Health.......................................760 737-7373
488 E Valley Pkwy Ste 411 Escondido (92025) ***(G-19976)***
Scripps Health.......................................858 458-5100
9834 Genesee Ave Ste 311 La Jolla (92037) ***(G-19977)***
Scripps Health.......................................858 626-5200
9850 Genesee Ave Ste 620 La Jolla (92037) ***(G-19978)***
Scripps Health.......................................858 626-6150
9888 Genesee Ave La Jolla (92037) ***(G-21872)***
Scripps Health.......................................858 554-8892
10666 N Torrey Pines Rd La Jolla (92037) ***(G-19979)***
Scripps Health.......................................858 554-9489
10666 N Torrey Pines Rd La Jolla (92037) ***(G-19980)***
Scripps Health.......................................760 901-5200
3998 Vista Way Ste E Oceanside (92056) ***(G-19981)***
Scripps Health.......................................858 626-4123
9888 Genesee Ave La Jolla (92037) ***(G-21873)***
Scripps Health.......................................858 784-5888
10790 Rancho Bernardo Rd San Diego (92127) ***(G-19982)***
Scripps Health.......................................858 652-5504
11025 N Torrey Pines Rd # 200 La Jolla (92037) ***(G-26602)***
Scripps Health.......................................858 794-0160
3811 Valley Centre Dr San Diego (92130) ***(G-22830)***
Scripps Mem Hosp - Encinitas, Encinitas *Also called Scripps Health* ***(G-21867)***
Scripps Mem Hosp - La Jolla, La Jolla *Also called Scripps Health* ***(G-21873)***
Scripps Mem Hospital-La Jolla, La Jolla *Also called Scripps Health* ***(G-21872)***
Scripps Memorial Hospitals.......................................858 450-4481
9834 Genesee Ave Ste 328 La Jolla (92037) ***(G-21874)***
Scripps Mercy Hospital, San Diego *Also called Scripps Health* ***(G-20897)***
Scripps Mercy Hospital, San Diego *Also called Scripps Health* ***(G-21870)***
Scripps Mercy Hospital.......................................619 294-8111
4077 5th Ave Mer35 San Diego (92103) ***(G-21875)***
Scripps Mercy Hospitals, Chula Vista *Also called Scripps Health* ***(G-21868)***
Scripps Rancho Bernardo, San Diego *Also called Scripps Health* ***(G-22829)***
Scripps Research Institute (PA).......................................858 784-1000
10550 N Torrey Pines Rd La Jolla (92037) ***(G-26807)***
Scripps Shared Services, San Diego *Also called Scripps Health* ***(G-20898)***
Scripps Torrey Pines, La Jolla *Also called Scripps Health* ***(G-21871)***
Scripps Whttier Dbetes Program, San Diego *Also called Scripps Health* ***(G-19969)***
Script To Screen Inc.......................................714 558-3287
200 N Tustin Ave Ste 200 Santa Ana (92705) ***(G-18147)***
Scripto, Ontario *Also called Calico Brands* ***(G-9250)***
Scst Inc (PA).......................................619 280-4321
6280 Riverdale St San Diego (92120) ***(G-26885)***
Scvmc, San Jose *Also called Santa Clara Valley Medical Ctr* ***(G-21860)***
Scwa, Sacramento *Also called Sacramento County Water Agency* ***(G-6389)***
Scyence Inc.......................................510 481-8614
2401 Grant Ave Lot B San Lorenzo (94580) ***(G-950)***
SD Deacon Corp (PA).......................................916 969-0900
7745 Greenback Ln Ste 250 Citrus Heights (95610) ***(G-1661)***
SD Deacon Corp.......................................949 222-9060
17880 Fitch Irvine (92614) ***(G-1662)***
SD Sports MDCne&fmly Hlth Cntr.......................................619 229-3910
6699 Alvarado Rd Ste 2100 San Diego (92120) ***(G-19983)***
SD Stadium Hotel LLC.......................................858 278-9300
3805 Murphy Canyon Rd San Diego (92123) ***(G-13225)***
Sdcraa, San Diego *Also called San Dego Cnty Rgnal Arprt Auth* ***(G-4932)***
Sdg Enterprises.......................................805 777-7978
822 Hampshire Rd Ste H Westlake Village (91361) ***(G-2362)***
Sdi Media USA, Los Angeles *Also called SDI Media USA Inc* ***(G-18252)***
SDI Media USA Inc (HQ).......................................323 602-5455
6060 Center Dr Ste 100 Los Angeles (90045) ***(G-18252)***

ALPHABETIC

ALPHABETIC SECTION

Sdj General Partnership....................805 582-3200
2125 N Madera Rd Ste C Simi Valley (93065) *(G-11041)*
Sdl, Los Angeles *Also called Language Weaver Inc (G-15272)*
SDS, San Diego *Also called Strategic Data Systems (G-16060)*
SE San Diego Hotel LLC....................619 515-3000
1047 5th Ave San Diego (92101) *(G-13226)*
SE Scher Corporation....................408 844-0772
1585 The Alameda San Jose (95126) *(G-14946)*
SE Scher Corporation....................858 546-8300
2525 Camino Del Rio S San Diego (92108) *(G-14781)*
SE Scher Corporation....................916 632-1363
6731 Five Star Blvd Ste C Rocklin (95677) *(G-14782)*
Sea & Sand Inn, Santa Cruz *Also called Santa Cruz Seaside Company (G-13214)*
Sea Breeze Collision, Tustin *Also called Sterling Collision Center LLC (G-17775)*
Sea Breeze Financial Services (PA)....................949 223-9700
18191 Von Karman Ave # 150 Irvine (92612) *(G-9895)*
Sea Breeze Health Care Inc....................714 847-9671
7781 Garfield Ave Huntington Beach (92648) *(G-20900)*
Sea Breeze Mortgage Services, Irvine *Also called Sea Breeze Financial Services (G-9895)*
Sea Catch Seafoods, Anaheim *Also called Atlanta Seafoods LLC (G-8628)*
Sea Cliff Health Care, Huntington Beach *Also called Huntington Bch Cnvlescent Hosp (G-20680)*
Sea Cliff Healthcare Center, Huntington Beach *Also called HB Healthcare Associates LLC (G-20646)*
Sea Lodge Hotel, La Jolla *Also called La Jolla Bch & Tennis CLB Inc (G-12897)*
Sea View Medical Group Inc....................805 373-5781
1901 Solar Dr Ste 265 Oxnard (93036) *(G-23056)*
Sea Win Inc....................213 688-2899
526 Stanford Ave Los Angeles (90013) *(G-8652)*
Sea World LLC....................619 226-3842
500 Sea World Dr San Diego (92109) *(G-18832)*
Sea World of California, San Diego *Also called Sea World LLC (G-18832)*
Sea-Air International Inc....................310 338-0778
11222 S La Cienega Blvd # 100 Inglewood (90304) *(G-5167)*
Seaboard Produce Distrs Inc....................805 981-8001
710 Del Norte Blvd Oxnard (93030) *(G-7810)*
Seabreeze Management Comp, Aliso Viejo *Also called Glenwood Village Cmnty Assn (G-25264)*
Seabreeze Management Company (PA)....................949 855-1800
39 Argonaut Ste 100 Aliso Viejo (92656) *(G-27208)*
Seabury & Smith Delaware Inc....................213 346-5000
777 S Figueroa St # 2400 Los Angeles (90017) *(G-10864)*
Seacastle Inc....................925 480-3000
4000 Executive Pkwy # 240 San Ramon (94583) *(G-14578)*
Seacliff Country Club, Huntington Beach *Also called American Golf Corporation (G-18856)*
Seacliff Inn Inc....................831 661-4671
7500 Old Dominion Ct Aptos (95003) *(G-13227)*
Seacoast Commerce Bank (PA)....................858 432-7000
11939 Rancho Bernardo Rd # 200 San Diego (92128) *(G-9558)*
Seacrest Convalescent Hosp Inc....................310 833-3526
1416 W 6th St San Pedro (90732) *(G-20901)*
Seafus Corporation....................415 584-6100
439 Eccles Ave South San Francisco (94080) *(G-14423)*
Seagate Services....................510 903-7100
6121 I C 365 Ste 2 Emeryville (94608) *(G-16047)*
Seal Electric Inc....................619 449-7323
1162 Greenfield Dr El Cajon (92021) *(G-2728)*
Sealant Systems International....................805 489-0490
125 Venture Dr Ste 210 San Luis Obispo (93401) *(G-6789)*
Sealaska Envmtl Svcs LLC....................619 564-8329
3838 Camino Del Rio N # 240 San Diego (92108) *(G-28053)*
Seaman Nurseries Inc....................559 665-1860
336 Robertson Blvd Ste A Chowchilla (93610) *(G-483)*
Sean P OConnor....................949 851-7323
1900 Main St Ste 700 Irvine (92614) *(G-23548)*
Sean's Embroidery, Vernon *Also called Kim Chong (G-17272)*
Seaport Fish Company, Wilmington *Also called Star Fisheries (G-8657)*
Seaport Meat Company, Spring Valley *Also called Pnc Inc (G-8678)*
Search Agency Inc (PA)....................310 582-5706
11150 W Olym Blvd Ste 600 Los Angeles (90064) *(G-13919)*
Search Engine Optimization Inc....................760 929-0039
5841 Edison Pl Ste 140 Carlsbad (92008) *(G-17482)*
Search Optics LLC (PA)....................858 678-0707
5770 Oberlin Dr San Diego (92121) *(G-27637)*
Sears, Benicia *Also called Innovel Solutions Inc (G-5104)*
Sears, Delano *Also called Innovel Solutions Inc (G-5105)*
Sears, Ontario *Also called Innovel Solutions Inc (G-5106)*
Sears Roebuck and Co....................951 719-3528
40680 Winchester Rd Temecula (92591) *(G-17892)*
Sears Roebuck and Co....................530 751-4628
1235 Colusa Ave Yuba City (95991) *(G-17893)*
Sears Roebuck and Co....................714 256-7328
100 Brea Mall Brea (92821) *(G-18011)*
Sears Roebuck and Co....................909 390-4210
5691 E Philadelphia St Ontario (91761) *(G-18012)*
Sears Roebuck and Co....................559 244-6214
3365 W Sussex Way Fresno (93722) *(G-18013)*
Sears Auto Center, Yuba City *Also called Sears Roebuck and Co (G-17893)*
Sears Home Imprv Pdts Inc....................858 790-7721
9586 Dist Ave Ste F San Diego (92121) *(G-1252)*
Sears Service and Parts Center, Fresno *Also called Sears Roebuck and Co (G-18013)*
Seascape Golf Club, Aptos *Also called American Golf Corporation (G-18869)*
Seascape Resort Ltd A Calif....................831 662-7120
19 Seascape Vlg Aptos (95003) *(G-13228)*
Seasholtz John....................559 659-3805
1355 M St Firebaugh (93622) *(G-95)*

Seaside Hotel Lessee Inc....................310 260-7500
1819 Ocean Ave Santa Monica (90401) *(G-17483)*
Seaside Laguna Inn & Suites....................949 494-9717
1661 S Coast Hwy Laguna Beach (92651) *(G-13229)*
Season Produce Co Inc....................213 689-0008
1601 E Olympic Blvd # 315 Los Angeles (90021) *(G-8772)*
Seasons....................562 691-1200
200 W Whittier Blvd La Habra (90631) *(G-24805)*
Seatech Consulting Group Inc....................310 356-6828
609 Deep Valley Dr # 200 Rllng HLS Est (90274) *(G-16476)*
Seaver International....................707 291-4929
4169 Green Valley Schl Rd Sebastopol (95472) *(G-16477)*
Seaview Hlthcre & Rehab Ctr LL....................707 443-5668
6400 Purdue Dr Eureka (95503) *(G-24806)*
Seaview Industries....................714 957-5073
2501 Harbor Blvd Costa Mesa (92626) *(G-17484)*
Sebastian, Kerman *Also called Kerman Telephone Co (G-5643)*
Sebastian, Fresno *Also called Kertel Communications Inc (G-2631)*
Sebastopol Rifle & Pistol Club....................707 824-0184
343 Flynn St Sebastopol (95472) *(G-19070)*
SEC Pac Inc....................925 938-9200
1555 Riviera Ave Ste E Walnut Creek (94596) *(G-11837)*
Seca Eqp Removal & Dismantle....................209 543-1600
684 Bitritto Ct Modesto (95356) *(G-3466)*
Seca Eqp Removal & Dismantling, Modesto *Also called Seca Eqp Removal & Dismantle (G-3466)*
Secom International (PA)....................310 641-1290
9610 Bellanca Ave Los Angeles (90045) *(G-16048)*
Second Harvest Food....................949 653-2900
8014 Marine Way Irvine (92618) *(G-24197)*
Second Harvest Food Bank (PA)....................408 266-8866
750 Curtner Ave San Jose (95125) *(G-24198)*
Second Image National LLC....................909 445-8080
700 E Bonita Ave Pomona (91767) *(G-14133)*
Second Image National LLC (PA)....................800 229-7477
170 E Arrow Hwy San Dimas (91773) *(G-23549)*
Second Opinion Med Grp Inc....................805 496-4315
2876 Sycamore Dr Ste 305 Simi Valley (93065) *(G-10377)*
Second Street Corporation....................310 394-5454
1111 2nd St Santa Monica (90403) *(G-13230)*
Secova Inc....................714 384-0530
5000 Birch St Ste 1400 Newport Beach (92660) *(G-27638)*
Secova Eservices Inc (HQ)....................714 384-0655
5000 Birch St Newport Beach (92660) *(G-27639)*
Secrom Inc....................310 830-4010
345 E Carson St Carson (90745) *(G-21368)*
Sectek Inc....................650 604-1785
Bldg 15 Mountain View (94035) *(G-16918)*
Sectran Armored Truck Service, Pico Rivera *Also called Sectran Security Incorporated (G-16779)*
Sectran Security Incorporated (PA)....................562 948-1446
7633 Industry Ave Pico Rivera (90660) *(G-16779)*
Secure Data Recovery Services, Los Angeles *Also called World Acceptance Group Corp (G-16271)*
Secure Net Protection....................818 848-4900
217 E Alameda Ave Ste 301 Burbank (91502) *(G-16780)*
Secure Nursing Service Inc....................213 736-6771
3333 Wilshire Blvd # 625 Los Angeles (90010) *(G-14783)*
Secure One Data Solutions LLC....................562 924-7056
11090 Artesia Blvd Ste D Cerritos (90703) *(G-16183)*
Secure Transportation Co Inc....................858 790-3958
9557 Candida St San Diego (92126) *(G-5242)*
Secure Transportation Company....................951 737-7300
12785 Magnolia Ave # 102 Riverside (92503) *(G-3844)*
Secureauth Corporation (PA)....................949 777-6959
8845 Irvine Center Dr # 200 Irvine (92618) *(G-15444)*
Secured Shuttle Service Inc....................909 594-9054
20475 Yellow Brick Rd 3a Walnut (91789) *(G-3845)*
Securematics Inc....................408 970-8566
2540 Gateway Rd Carlsbad (92009) *(G-7184)*
Securitas Critical Infrastruct....................858 560-0448
3914 Murphy Canyon Rd A120 San Diego (92123) *(G-16781)*
Securitas Critical Infrastruct....................310 817-2177
19701 Hamilton Ave # 180 Torrance (90502) *(G-16782)*
Securitas Critical Infrastruct....................310 426-3300
360 N Sepulveda Blvd El Segundo (90245) *(G-16783)*
Securitas Critical Infrastruct....................805 685-1100
Rm 117 Bldg 7525 Vandenberg Afb (93437) *(G-16784)*
Securitas SEC Svcs USA Inc....................805 650-6285
5700 Ralston St Ste 105 Ventura (93003) *(G-16785)*
Securitas SEC Svcs USA Inc....................650 358-1556
1650 Borel Pl Ste 227 San Mateo (94402) *(G-16919)*
Securitas SEC Svcs USA Inc....................209 943-1401
3115 W March Ln Ste A Stockton (95219) *(G-16786)*
Securitas SEC Svcs USA Inc....................916 564-2009
2045 Hurley Way Sacramento (95825) *(G-16787)*
Securitas SEC Svcs USA Inc....................559 221-2302
155 E Shaw Ave Ste 315 Fresno (93710) *(G-16788)*
Securitas SEC Svcs USA Inc....................571 321-0913
750 Terrado Plz Ste 107 Covina (91723) *(G-16789)*
Securitas SEC Svcs USA Inc....................510 568-6818
425 Bush St Ste 400 San Francisco (94108) *(G-16790)*
Securitas SEC Svcs USA Inc....................530 245-0256
407 Lake Blvd Redding (96003) *(G-16791)*
Securitas SEC Svcs USA Inc....................760 353-8177
2344 S 2nd St Ste C El Centro (92243) *(G-16792)*
Securitas SEC Svcs USA Inc....................909 974-3160
402 S Milliken Ave Ste Gh Ontario (91761) *(G-16793)*

Securitas SEC Svcs USA Inc 619 641-0049
1550 Hotel Cir N Ste 440 San Diego (92108) *(G-16794)*
Securitas SEC Svcs USA Inc 818 706-4909
4330 Park Terrace Dr Westlake Village (91361) *(G-16795)*
Securitas SEC Svcs USA Inc 707 586-1393
1304 Sthpint Blvd Ste 110 Petaluma (94954) *(G-16796)*
Securitas SEC Svcs USA Inc 805 967-8987
5276 Hollister Ave # 204 Goleta (93111) *(G-16797)*
Securitas SEC Svcs USA Inc 707 445-5463
1606 Koster St Ste A Eureka (95501) *(G-16798)*
Securitas SEC Svcs USA Inc 916 569-4500
2045 Hurley Way Ste 175 Sacramento (95825) *(G-16799)*
Securitas SEC Svcs USA Inc 951 676-3954
27450 Ynez Rd Ste 315 Temecula (92591) *(G-16800)*
Securitas SEC Svcs USA Inc 760 779-0728
43 100 Cook St Ste 204 Palm Desert (92211) *(G-16801)*
Securitas SEC Svcs USA Inc 831 444-9607
1611 Bunker Hill Way # 100 Salinas (93906) *(G-16802)*
Securitas SEC Svcs USA Inc 925 746-0552
7677 Oakport St Ste 725 Oakland (94621) *(G-16803)*
Securitas SEC Svcs USA Inc 909 865-4356
1101 W Mckinley Ave Pomona (91768) *(G-16804)*
Securitas SEC Svcs USA Inc 323 832-9074
6055 E Wash Blvd Ste 155 Commerce (90040) *(G-16805)*
Securitas SEC Svcs USA Inc 213 217-7489
3325 Wilshire Blvd # 11000 Los Angeles (90010) *(G-16806)*
Securitas SEC Svcs USA Inc 213 580-8825
1055 Wilshire Blvd Los Angeles (90017) *(G-16807)*
Securitas SEC Svcs USA Inc 562 427-2737
1500 W Carson St Ste 109 Long Beach (90810) *(G-16808)*
Securitas SEC Svcs USA Inc 714 385-9745
2099 S State College Blvd Anaheim (92806) *(G-16809)*
Securitas SEC Svcs USA Inc 310 787-0747
400 Crenshaw Blvd Ste 200 Torrance (90503) *(G-16810)*
Securitas SEC Svcs USA Inc 760 245-1915
15428 Civic Dr Ste 305 Victorville (92392) *(G-16811)*
Securitas SEC Svcs USA Inc 818 891-0458
16909 Parthenia St # 202 Northridge (91343) *(G-16812)*
Securitas SEC Svcs USA Inc 818 706-6800
4330 Park Terrace Dr Westlake Village (91361) *(G-16813)*
Securitas Security Svcs USA 909 974-3160
402 S Milliken Ave Ste Gh Ontario (91761) *(G-16814)*
Securitech Security Services 213 387-5050
3550 Wilshire Blvd # 920 Los Angeles (90010) *(G-16920)*
Security Alarm Fing Entps Inc 925 830-4777
2440 Camino Ramon Ste 200 San Ramon (94583) *(G-16921)*
Security America Inc 310 532-0121
18105 La Salle Ave Gardena (90248) *(G-16815)*
Security California Bancorp 951 368-2265
3403 10th St Ste 830 Riverside (92501) *(G-12045)*
Security Central Inc 510 652-2477
4432 Telegraph Ave Oakland (94609) *(G-18014)*
Security Company, Burbank *Also called Secure Net Protection (G-16780)*
Security Contractor Svcs Inc (PA) 916 338-4200
5339 Jackson St North Highlands (95660) *(G-7027)*
Security Indust Spcialists Inc (PA) 310 215-5100
6071 Bristol Pkwy Culver City (90230) *(G-16816)*
Security Nat Mstr Holdg Co LLC (PA) 707 442-2818
323 5th St Eureka (95501) *(G-9896)*
Security Officers & Investigat 817 386-6947
21 Orinda Way Ste 145c Orinda (94563) *(G-16817)*
Security On-Demand Inc 858 563-5655
12121 Scripps Summit Dr # 320 San Diego (92131) *(G-16049)*
Security On-Site Services Inc 916 988-6500
8999 Greenback Ln Fl 2 Orangevale (95662) *(G-16922)*
Security One Inc 800 778-3017
1859 Streiff Ln Santa Rosa (95403) *(G-16818)*
Security Pacific Home Loans, Westlake Village *Also called Ownit Mortgage Solutions Inc (G-9879)*
Security Pacific RE Brkg, Richmond *Also called S P R E Inc (G-11829)*
Security Pacific RE Brkg 510 245-9901
292 Violet Rd Hercules (94547) *(G-11838)*
Security Pacific Real Estate, Walnut Creek *Also called SEC Pac Inc (G-11837)*
Security Paving Company Inc 818 362-9200
13170 Telfair Ave Sylmar (91342) *(G-1856)*
Security Signal Devices Inc (PA) 714 888-6230
1740 N Lemon St Anaheim (92801) *(G-16923)*
Security Specialists, San Fernando *Also called Tyan Inc (G-16837)*
Securonix Inc 310 641-1000
5777 W Century Blvd # 838 Los Angeles (90045) *(G-16050)*
Secuto Music, Burbank *Also called Roundabout Entertainment Inc (G-18146)*
Sedgwick Claims Mgt Svcs 714 245-7800
701 S Parker St Ste 5000 Orange (92868) *(G-10865)*
Sedgwick Claims MGT Svcs Inc 626 568-1415
3280 E Foothill Blvd # 350 Pasadena (91107) *(G-10866)*
Sedgwick Claims MGT Svcs Inc 818 782-8820
5990 Sepulvda Blvd # 500 Sherman Oaks (91411) *(G-10867)*
Sedgwick Claims MGT Svcs Inc 818 591-9444
24025 Park Sorrento # 200 Calabasas (91302) *(G-10868)*
Sedgwick Claims MGT Svcs Inc 510 302-3000
2101 Webster St Oakland (94612) *(G-10869)*
Sedgwick Claims MGT Svcs Inc 916 568-7394
1851 Heritage Ln Sacramento (95815) *(G-10870)*
Sedgwick LLP (PA) 415 781-7900
333 Bush St Fl 30 San Francisco (94104) *(G-23550)*
Sedgwick LLP 213 426-6900
801 S Figueroa St # 1800 Los Angeles (90017) *(G-23551)*
Sedgwick LLP 949 852-8200
2020 Main St Ste 1100 Irvine (92614) *(G-23552)*
Sedgwick LLP 415 537-3000
135 Main St Fl 14 San Francisco (94105) *(G-23553)*
Sedona Surgical Center Inc 760 413-8056
39700 Bob Hope Dr Ste 301 Rancho Mirage (92270) *(G-19984)*
See Grins Rv's and Farm Land, Gilroy *Also called See-Grins Inc (G-473)*
See's Candies, Long Beach *Also called Sees Candy Shops Incorporated (G-4702)*
See-Grins Inc 408 683-4652
7900 Arroyo Cir Gilroy (95020) *(G-473)*
Seecon Built Homes Inc 925 671-7711
4021 Port Chicago Hwy Concord (94520) *(G-12007)*
Seed Dynamics Inc 831 424-1177
1081b Harkins Rd Salinas (93901) *(G-585)*
Seeds of Change Inc 310 764-7700
2555 S Dominguez Hills Dr Rancho Dominguez (90220) *(G-9150)*
Seeley Brothers, Brea *Also called Norcal Inc (G-3067)*
Seeley Brothers 714 224-3949
1400 Moonstone Brea (92821) *(G-3087)*
Seems Plumbing Co Inc 310 297-4969
5400 W Rosecrans Ave Lowr Hawthorne (90250) *(G-2363)*
Seepeedee Inc (PA) 562 868-3751
13100 Studebaker Rd Norwalk (90650) *(G-21876)*
Sees Candy Shops Incorporated 310 559-4911
20600 S Alameda St Long Beach (90810) *(G-4702)*
Sega Entertainment USA Inc 909 987-4263
4541 Mills Cir Ontario (91764) *(G-18810)*
Sega of America Inc 415 701-6000
350 Rhode Island St # 400 San Francisco (94103) *(G-7185)*
Seguin Mreau NAPA Coperage Inc 707 252-3408
151 Camino Dorado NAPA (94558) *(G-7952)*
Segura Enterprises Inc 805 349-0550
1011 W Mccoy Ln Santa Maria (93455) *(G-16924)*
Segura Security Services, Santa Maria *Also called Segura Enterprises Inc (G-16924)*
Seidner-Miller Automotive Inc 909 394-3500
1253 S Lone Hill Ave Glendora (91740) *(G-17813)*
Seiler LLP (PA) 650 365-4646
3 Lagoon Dr Ste 400 Redwood City (94065) *(G-26438)*
Seirra Telephone, Oakhurst *Also called Sierra Tel Cmmunications Group (G-5699)*
SEIU Local 1021 ....510 350-9811
447 29th St Oakland (94609) *(G-685)*
Seiu Local 2015 ....213 985-0463
2910 Beverly Blvd Los Angeles (90057) *(G-25183)*
Seiu Local 721 ....213 368-8660
1545 Wilshire Blvd # 100 Los Angeles (90017) *(G-24199)*
Seiu Uhw-West, Commerce *Also called Seiu United Healthcare Workers (G-25185)*
Seiu Ultcw 213 985-0463
2910 Beverly Blvd Los Angeles (90057) *(G-24807)*
Seiu United Healthcare Workers (PA) 510 251-1250
560 Thomas L Berkley Way Oakland (94612) *(G-25184)*
Seiu United Healthcare Workers 323 734-8399
5480 Ferguson Dr Commerce (90022) *(G-25185)*
Sela Healthcare Inc (PA) 909 985-1981
867 E 11th St Upland (91786) *(G-20902)*
Sela Healthcare Inc 818 341-9800
20554 Roscoe Blvd Canoga Park (91306) *(G-20903)*
Select Data Inc 714 577-1000
4155 E La Palma Ave # 250 Anaheim (92807) *(G-15445)*
Select Harvest Usa LLC 209 668-2471
14827 W Harding Rd Turlock (95380) *(G-8965)*
Select Home Care 805 777-3855
660 Hampshire Rd Ste 100 Westlake Village (91361) *(G-22558)*
Select Hotels Group LLC 510 623-6000
3101 W Warren Ave Fremont (94538) *(G-13231)*
Select Hotels Group LLC 916 638-4141
11260 Point East Dr Rancho Cordova (95742) *(G-13232)*
Select Personnel Services, Santa Barbara *Also called Select Temporaries LLC (G-14784)*
Select Staffing, Santa Barbara *Also called Real Time Staffing Services (G-14747)*
Select Staffing, Santa Barbara *Also called Employbridge LLC (G-14873)*
Select Temporaries LLC (HQ) 805 882-2200
3820 State St Santa Barbara (93105) *(G-14784)*
Selecta Products Inc (PA) 661 823-7050
1200 E Tehachapi Blvd Tehachapi (93561) *(G-7472)*
Selecta Switch, Tehachapi *Also called Selecta Products Inc (G-7472)*
Selectforce Inc, Irvine *Also called Accurate Background LLC (G-16215)*
Selectquote Insurance Services (PA) 415 543-7338
595 Market St Fl 10 San Francisco (94105) *(G-10871)*
Selex Inc 707 836-8836
930 Shiloh Rd Windsor (95492) *(G-3580)*
Self Help Enterprises (PA) 559 651-1000
8445 W Elowin Ct Visalia (93291) *(G-25346)*
Self Serve Auto Dismantlers (PA) 714 630-8901
3200 E Frontera St Anaheim (92806) *(G-8083)*
Self-Aid Workshop, Glendale *Also called Camble Center (G-24319)*
Self-Help For Elderly 415 391-3843
777 Stockton St Ste 110 San Francisco (94108) *(G-24200)*
Self-Help For Elderly (PA) 415 677-7600
731 Sansome St Ste 100 San Francisco (94111) *(G-24201)*
Self-Help For Elderly 408 873-1183
940 S Stelling Rd Cupertino (95014) *(G-24202)*
Selig Construction Corp 530 893-5898
337 Huss Dr Chico (95928) *(G-1253)*
Selligent Inc (HQ) 650 421-4200
1300 Island Dr Ste 200 Redwood City (94065) *(G-16051)*
Selma Community Hospital Inc 559 891-1000
1141 Rose Ave Selma (93662) *(G-21877)*
Selma Portuguese Azorian Assn 559 896-2508
1245 Nebraska Ave Selma (93662) *(G-24203)*
Seltzer Caplan McMahon (PA) 619 685-3003
750 B St Ste 2100 San Diego (92101) *(G-23554)*

ALPHABETIC

Selvi-Vidovich LP 408 720-8500
865 W El Camino Real Sunnyvale (94087) *(G-13233)*
Selzer Home Loans, Ukiah *Also called Lake County Home Loans (G-9866)*
SEMA, Diamond Bar *Also called Specialty Equipment Mkt Assn (G-25105)*
Sema Construction Inc 949 330-4300
6 Orchard Ste 150 Irvine (92618) *(G-1899)*
Semafone 925 855-7400
496 Quail Glen Dr Oakley (94561) *(G-17485)*
Semans Communications (PA) 650 529-9984
112 Stonegate Rd Portola Vally (94028) *(G-2729)*
Semantic Research Inc (PA) 619 222-4050
4922 N Harbor Dr San Diego (92106) *(G-16052)*
Semiconductor Eqp & Mtls Intl (PA) 408 943-6900
3081 Zanker Rd San Jose (95134) *(G-25103)*
Semifreddi's Bakery, Alameda *Also called Semifreddis Inc (G-8919)*
Semifreddis Inc (PA) 510 596-9930
1980 N Loop Rd Alameda (94502) *(G-8919)*
Seminis Inc 831 623-4554
500 Lucy Brown Rd San Juan Bautista (95045) *(G-26603)*
Seminis Inc (HQ) 805 485-7317
2700 Camino Del Sol Oxnard (93030) *(G-26604)*
Seminis Vegetable Seeds Inc (HQ) 855 733-3834
2700 Camino Del Sol Oxnard (93030) *(G-9151)*
Seminis Vegetable Seeds Inc 530 669-6903
37437 State Highway 16 Woodland (95695) *(G-9152)*
Sempra Energy (PA) 619 696-2000
488 8th Ave San Diego (92101) *(G-6298)*
Sempra Energy Global Entps 619 696-2000
101 Ash St San Diego (92101) *(G-6273)*
Sempra Energy International (HQ) 619 696-2000
101 Ash St San Diego (92101) *(G-6206)*
Sempra Energy Utilities, San Diego *Also called Sempra Energy International (G-6206)*
Sempra Natural Gas, San Diego *Also called Sempra US Gas & Power LLC (G-6255)*
Sempra US Gas & Power LLC (HQ) 877 736-7721
488 8th Ave San Diego (92101) *(G-6255)*
Sendgrid Inc 888 985-7363
814 W Chapman Ave Orange (92868) *(G-16184)*
Sendmail Inc (HQ) 510 594-5400
892 Ross Dr Sunnyvale (94089) *(G-5696)*
Sendme Inc 415 978-9504
150 Spear St Ste 1400 San Francisco (94105) *(G-5697)*
Sendmemobile.com, San Francisco *Also called Sendme Inc (G-5697)*
Seneca Center, Fremont *Also called Seneca Family of Agencies (G-24204)*
Seneca Family of Agencies 510 226-6180
40950 Chapel Way Fremont (94538) *(G-24204)*
Seneca Healthcare District 530 258-2151
130 Brentwood Dr Chester (96020) *(G-19985)*
Seneca Healthcare District 530 258-1977
199 Reynolds Rd Chester (96020) *(G-19986)*
Seneca Healthcare District (PA) 530 258-2151
130 Brentwood Dr Chester (96020) *(G-21878)*
Seneca Hospital Almanor Clinic, Chester *Also called Seneca Healthcare District (G-19986)*
Senegence International, Irvine *Also called Sgii Inc (G-8293)*
Senior Assist of Peninsula LLC 650 652-9791
1720 Marco Polo Way Ste E Burlingame (94010) *(G-24205)*
Senior Assisted Living Comm Ch, Pleasant Hill *Also called Carlton Senior Living (G-22398)*
Senior Care (PA) 562 989-5100
3800 Kilroy Airport Way Long Beach (90806) *(G-10378)*
Senior Care 562 492-9878
2501 Cherry Ave Ste 380 Long Beach (90755) *(G-10379)*
Senior Care Inc 619 817-8855
3423 Channel Way San Diego (92110) *(G-21103)*
Senior Care Inc 619 928-5644
4960 Mills St La Mesa (91942) *(G-21104)*
Senior Care Inc 818 275-9717
2640 Honolulu Ave Montrose (91020) *(G-21105)*
Senior Companions At Home 650 364-1265
650 El Camino Real Ste E Redwood City (94063) *(G-24206)*
Senior Connection, The, Carmichael *Also called Eskaton Properties Inc (G-23962)*
Senior Helpers South Coast, Fountain Valley *Also called His Passion Inc (G-22459)*
Senior Keiro Health Care 323 263-9651
325 S Boyle Ave Los Angeles (90033) *(G-24808)*
Senior Living Solutions LLC 408 385-1835
1725 S Bascom Ave Apt 105 Campbell (95008) *(G-21106)*
SENIOR NUTRITION, Fort Bragg *Also called Redwood Coast Seniors Inc (G-24151)*
Senior Prdcrs In Rtrmnt TV 760 773-9525
75895 Altamira Dr Indian Wells (92210) *(G-18148)*
Senior Resource Group LLC 858 519-0890
850 Del Mar Downs Rd # 338 Solana Beach (92075) *(G-11200)*
Senior Services, Oxnard *Also called City of Oxnard (G-23758)*
Senior TV, Indian Wells *Also called Senior Prdcrs In Rtrmnt TV (G-18148)*
Senomyx Inc 858 646-8300
4767 Nexus Center Dr San Diego (92121) *(G-26605)*
Sensity Systems Inc (PA) 408 774-9492
1237 E Arques Ave Sunnyvale (94085) *(G-28054)*
Sentek Consulting Inc 619 543-9550
2811 Nimitz Blvd Ste G San Diego (92106) *(G-16478)*
Sentek Global, San Diego *Also called Sentek Consulting Inc (G-16478)*
Sentient Technologies USA LLC 415 422-9886
1 California St Ste 2300 San Francisco (94111) *(G-15446)*
Sentinel Monitoring Corp 949 453-1550
220 Technology Dr Ste 200 Irvine (92618) *(G-16925)*
Sentinel Offender Services LLC (PA) 949 453-1550
201 Technology Dr Irvine (92618) *(G-16926)*
Sepulveda Ambulatory Care, North Hills *Also called Veterans Health Administration (G-20206)*
Sequel Contractors Inc 562 802-7227
13546 Imperial Hwy Santa Fe Springs (90670) *(G-1857)*
Sequenom Inc (HQ) 858 202-9000
3595 John Hopkins Ct San Diego (92121) *(G-26606)*
Sequenom Center For Molecular 858 202-9051
3595 John Hopkins Ct San Diego (92121) *(G-22285)*
Sequenom Laboratories, San Diego *Also called Sequenom Center For Molecular (G-22285)*
Sequoia Adrc LP 650 364-5504
650 Main St Redwood City (94063) *(G-24207)*
Sequoia Alchol DRG Rcovery Ctr, Redwood City *Also called Sequoia Adrc LP (G-24207)*
Sequoia Beverage 559 651-2444
2122 N Plaza Dr Visalia (93291) *(G-9085)*
Sequoia Bnefits Insur Svcs LLC 650 369-0200
1850 Gateway Dr Ste 600 San Mateo (94404) *(G-27640)*
Sequoia Capital Operations LLC 650 854-3927
2800 Sand Hill Rd Ste 100 Menlo Park (94025) *(G-12343)*
Sequoia Concepts Inc 818 409-6000
28632 Roadside Dr Ste 110 Agoura Hills (91301) *(G-14047)*
Sequoia Enterprises Inc 559 592-9455
150 W Pine St Exeter (93221) *(G-8773)*
Sequoia Financial Services, Agoura Hills *Also called Sequoia Concepts Inc (G-14047)*
Sequoia Green 310 753-0728
P.O. Box 67517 Los Angeles (90067) *(G-15447)*
Sequoia Health Services (HQ) 650 369-5811
170 Alameda De Las Pulgas Redwood City (94062) *(G-21879)*
Sequoia Hospital, Redwood City *Also called Sequoia Health Services (G-21879)*
Sequoia Insurance Company (HQ) 831 655-9612
31 Upper Ragsdale Dr Monterey (93940) *(G-10459)*
Sequoia Orange, Exeter *Also called Sequoia Enterprises Inc (G-8773)*
Sequoia Regional Cancer Center 559 624-3000
602 W Willow Ave Visalia (93291) *(G-22171)*
Sequoia Residential Funding 415 389-7373
1 Belvedere Pl Ste 330 Mill Valley (94941) *(G-9789)*
Sequoia Retail Systems Inc (HQ) 650 237-9000
660 W Dana St Mountain View (94041) *(G-15448)*
Sequoia Senior Solutions Inc 707 763-6600
1372 N Mcdowell Blvd S Petaluma (94954) *(G-24208)*
Sequoia Surgical Center LP 925 935-6700
2405 Shadelands Dr # 200 Walnut Creek (94598) *(G-19987)*
Sequoia Surgical Pavilion, Walnut Creek *Also called Sequoia Surgical Center LP (G-19987)*
Sequoia Wood Country Club 209 795-1000
1000 Cypress Point Dr Arnold (95223) *(G-19071)*
Sequoias, The, San Francisco *Also called Northern California Presbyteri (G-11175)*
Sequos-San Frncsco Residential, San Francisco *Also called Northern California Presbyteri (G-20810)*
Ser Jobs For Progress Inc San 559 452-0881
255 N Fulton St Ste 106 Fresno (93701) *(G-24209)*
Seracada 626 486-0800
709 E Lavender Way Azusa (91702) *(G-22559)*
Serco Inc 858 569-8979
9350 Waxie Way Ste 400 San Diego (92123) *(G-26059)*
Serec Entertainment LLC 626 893-0600
1671 N Rocky Rd Upland (91784) *(G-7696)*
Serimian M S D L Ranch 559 896-1517
10463 S Del Rey Ave Selma (93662) *(G-392)*
Serpico Landscaping Inc 510 293-0341
1764 National Ave Hayward (94545) *(G-951)*
Serra Community Med Clinic Inc 818 768-8882
9375 San Fernando Rd Sun Valley (91352) *(G-19988)*
Serra Medical Clinic Inc 818 768-3000
9375 San Fernando Rd Sun Valley (91352) *(G-19989)*
Serrania Charter Elementary, Woodland Hills *Also called Pta CA Congress of Parents (G-25318)*
Serrano Associates LLC 916 933-5005
5005 Serrano Pkwy El Dorado Hills (95762) *(G-19072)*
Serrano Country Club, El Dorado Hills *Also called Serrano Associates LLC (G-19072)*
Serrano Country Club Inc 916 933-5005
5005 Serrano Pkwy P El Dorado Hills (95762) *(G-19073)*
Serrano Covalescent Hospital 323 465-2106
5401 Fountain Ave Los Angeles (90029) *(G-20904)*
Serrano Electric Inc 408 986-1570
1705 Russell Ave Santa Clara (95054) *(G-2730)*
Serrano Hotel, San Francisco *Also called Kimpton Hotel & Rest Group LLC (G-12884)*
Serrato-Mcdermott Inc 510 656-6233
43815 S Grimmer Blvd Fremont (94538) *(G-6762)*
Servi-Tech Controls Inc (PA) 559 264-6679
2480 S Cherry Ave Fresno (93706) *(G-2364)*
Servi-Tek Inc 858 638-7735
3970 Sorrento Valley Blvd San Diego (92121) *(G-14424)*
Servi-Tek Janitorial Services, San Diego *Also called Servi-Tek Inc (G-14424)*
Service 1st Electrical Svcs 714 630-9699
1092 N Armando St Anaheim (92806) *(G-2731)*
Service By Medallion 650 625-1010
455 National Ave Mountain View (94043) *(G-14425)*
Service Champions, Pleasanton *Also called On-Time AC & Htg Inc (G-2310)*
Service Cleaning and Maint, Los Angeles *Also called Service Parking Corporation (G-17743)*
Service Container Company LLC 310 223-1666
1754 Carr Rd Ste 204 Calexico (92231) *(G-17486)*
Service Contractors Network, Tustin *Also called Heritage Construction (G-1799)*
Service Corp International 949 644-2700
3500 Pacific View Dr Corona Del Mar (92625) *(G-11839)*
Service Corp International 760 754-6600
1999 S El Camino Real Oceanside (92054) *(G-12038)*
Service Employee Intl Un, Los Angeles *Also called Los Angles Cnty Employees Assn (G-25178)*
Service Employees Intl Union, San Jose *Also called Service Workers Local 715 (G-25186)*
Service First Contrs Netwrk 714 573-2200
2510 N Grand Ave Ste 110 Santa Ana (92705) *(G-1663)*

ALPHABETIC

Service King Paint & Body LLC ALPHABETIC SECTION

Service King Paint & Body LLC 925 829-5571
6080 Dublin Blvd Dublin (94568) *(G-17771)*
Service Lathing Company 510 483-9732
1090 139th Ave San Leandro (94578) *(G-2978)*
Service Master Industries Inc 760 480-0208
2342 Meyers Ave Escondido (92029) *(G-17487)*
Service Parking Corporation 323 851-2416
3800 Barham Blvd Ste P1 Los Angeles (90068) *(G-17743)*
Service Partners Supply LLC (HQ) 916 379-2290
8321 Demetre Ave Sacramento (95828) *(G-7018)*
Service Pro Security Inc 707 746-6532
342 Acacia St Fairfield (94533) *(G-10197)*
Service Quality, Concord *Also called Customer Loyalty Builders Inc (G-27403)*
Service Solutions Group LLC 626 960-9390
5367 2nd St Irwindale (91706) *(G-17943)*
Service Workers Local 715 (PA) 408 678-3300
2302 Zanker Rd San Jose (95131) *(G-25186)*
ServiceMaster, South San Francisco *Also called Seafus Corporation (G-14423)*
ServiceMaster, Long Beach *Also called Aramark MGT Svcs Ltd Partnr (G-14234)*
ServiceMaster, Merced *Also called Mobley Enterprises Inc (G-14361)*
ServiceMaster, Merced *Also called Culver-Melin Enterprises (G-2808)*
ServiceMaster, Santa Maria *Also called Skylstad-Schoelen Co Inc (G-14433)*
ServiceMaster Company LLC 760 298-7001
1003 Hi Point St Los Angeles (90035) *(G-14426)*
ServiceMaster Company LLC 714 245-1465
216 N Clara St Santa Ana (92703) *(G-14427)*
Servicemax Inc (PA) 925 965-7859
4450 Rosewood Dr Ste 200 Pleasanton (94588) *(G-15449)*
Servicesource Intl Inc (PA) 415 901-6030
760 Market St Fl 4 San Francisco (94102) *(G-27641)*
Servicmster Clean By Integrity, Oxnard *Also called Pacific Building Maint Inc (G-14375)*
Servicmster Cmplete Rstoration, Escondido *Also called Sbrm Inc (G-14422)*
Servico Building Maint Co 707 935-1224
13732b Carmel Ave Glen Ellen (95442) *(G-14428)*
Servicon Systems Inc 310 970-0700
3329 Jack Northrop Ave Hawthorne (90250) *(G-3329)*
Serving Seniors LLC 916 372-9640
2764 Rogue River Cir West Sacramento (95691) *(G-22560)*
SES, San Diego *Also called Superior Envmtl Svcs Inc (G-14441)*
Ses LLC 949 727-3200
26561 Rancho Pkwy S Lake Forest (92630) *(G-15450)*
Sesloc Federal Credit Union (PA) 805 543-1816
11491 Los Osos Valley Rd San Luis Obispo (93405) *(G-9626)*
Set A Head Start Westside, Sacramento *Also called Sacramento Employement & Train (G-24383)*
Set Free Services Inc 530 243-3373
3300 Veda St Redding (96001) *(G-27642)*
Seta, Sacramento *Also called Sacramento Employement & Train (G-24384)*
Sethi Management Inc 760 692-5288
6100 Innovation Way Carlsbad (92009) *(G-27209)*
Sethi Management Inc 760 652-4010
183 Calle Magdalena # 101 Encinitas (92024) *(G-13234)*
Seti Institute 650 961-6633
189 Bernardo Ave 100 Mountain View (94043) *(G-26808)*
Seti Institute, The, Mountain View *Also called Seti Institute (G-26808)*
Seton Medical Center (HQ) 650 992-4000
1900 Sullivan Ave Daly City (94015) *(G-21880)*
Seton Medical Center 650 728-5521
600 Marine Blvd Moss Beach (94038) *(G-21881)*
Seton Medical Center 650 992-4000
1784 Sullivan Ave Ste 200 Daly City (94015) *(G-21882)*
Seton Medical Center Coastside, Moss Beach *Also called Seton Medical Center (G-21881)*
Setton Pstchio Terra Bella Inc (HQ) 559 535-6050
9370 Road 234 Terra Bella (93270) *(G-8920)*
Seven Hospitality, Irvine *Also called State Group LLC (G-27666)*
Seven Lakes Hm Assn Cntry CLB 760 328-2695
1 Desert Lakes Dr Palm Springs (92264) *(G-19074)*
Seven Licensing Company LLC 323 881-0308
801 S Figueroa St # 2500 Los Angeles (90017) *(G-8411)*
Seven Oaks Country Club 661 664-6404
2000 Grand Lakes Ave Bakersfield (93311) *(G-19075)*
Seven One Inc (PA) 818 904-3435
21540 Prairie St Ste E Chatsworth (91311) *(G-17488)*
Seven Resorts Inc (PA) 949 588-7100
9771 Irvine Center Dr # 100 Irvine (92618) *(G-19280)*
Seven Seas Associates LLC 619 291-1300
411 Hotel Cir S San Diego (92108) *(G-13235)*
Seven Seas Best Western, San Diego *Also called Seven Seas Associates LLC (G-13235)*
Seven7 Brands, Los Angeles *Also called Seven Licensing Company LLC (G-8411)*
Severson & Werson A Prof Corp 415 283-4911
1 Embarcadero Ctr Fl 26 San Francisco (94111) *(G-23555)*
Severson Group Incorporated (PA) 562 493-3611
3601 Serpentine Dr Los Alamitos (90720) *(G-1664)*
Seville Construction Svcs Inc 626 204-0800
199 S Hudson Ave Pasadena (91101) *(G-27643)*
Sexy Hair Concepts 800 848-3383
9232 Eton Ave Chatsworth (91311) *(G-8325)*
Seyfarth Shaw LLP 213 270-9600
333 S Hope St Ste 3900 Los Angeles (90071) *(G-23556)*
Seyfarth Shaw LLP 310 277-7200
2029 Century Park E # 3400 Los Angeles (90067) *(G-23557)*
Seyfarth Shaw LLP 415 397-2823
560 Mission St Fl 31 San Francisco (94105) *(G-23558)*
Seymour Gale & Associates 213 622-5361
4501 Cedros Ave Unit 118 Sherman Oaks (91403) *(G-8412)*
Sezzo Labs Inc 408 562-0081
2336 Walsh Ave Ste A Santa Clara (95051) *(G-16053)*
Sf-Marin Food Bank, San Francisco *Also called San Francisco Food Bank (G-24185)*
Sf-Potrero Hill, San Francisco *Also called Citibank National Association (G-9374)*
Sfadia Inc 323 622-1930
10011 Pioneer Blvd Santa Fe Springs (90670) *(G-2732)*
Sfcu, Palo Alto *Also called Stanford Federal Credit Union (G-9629)*
Sfd Partners LLC 415 392-7755
450 Powell St San Francisco (94102) *(G-13236)*
SFF, Sacramento *Also called Sierra Forever Families (G-24210)*
Sfi 2365 Iron Point LLC 415 395-9701
260 California St Ste 300 San Francisco (94111) *(G-11042)*
Sfi Carlsbad LLC 415 395-9701
260 California St Ste 300 San Francisco (94111) *(G-11043)*
Sfi Pleasanton LLC 415 395-0960
260 California St # 1100 San Francisco (94111) *(G-12344)*
SFMC, Lynwood *Also called St Francis Medical Center (G-20053)*
Sfmoma Museum Store, San Francisco *Also called San Francisco Museum Modrn Art (G-25044)*
Sfn Group Inc 949 727-8500
114 Pacifica Ste 210 Irvine (92618) *(G-14947)*
Sfn Group Inc 530 222-3434
3050 Bictor Ave Ste A Redding (96002) *(G-14948)*
Sfo Airporter Inc (PA) 650 246-2775
160 S Linden Ave Ste 300 South San Francisco (94080) *(G-3715)*
Sfo Airporter Inc 415 495-3909
325 5th St San Francisco (94107) *(G-3716)*
Sfo Shuttle Bus Company, San Francisco *Also called Imperial Parking (us) LLC (G-17720)*
Sfo Shuttle Bus Company, Stanford *Also called Imperial Parking (us) LLC (G-17721)*
Sfo Shuttle Bus Company, Oakland *Also called Imperial Parking (us) LLC (G-17722)*
Sfo Shuttle Bus Inc 650 877-0430
San Francisco Intl Arprt San Francisco (94128) *(G-3717)*
Sfo-3 - San Francisco Full Svc, Brisbane *Also called Expeditors Intl Wash Inc (G-5068)*
Sfpp LP (HQ) 714 560-4400
1100 W Town And Country R Orange (92868) *(G-4950)*
Sft Realty Galway Downs LLC 951 232-1880
38801 Los Porralitos Temecula (92592) *(G-11840)*
Sfusd Building Ground 415 695-5508
834 Toland St San Francisco (94124) *(G-14429)*
Sfusd Jrotc Brigade 415 242-2546
2162 24th Ave San Francisco (94116) *(G-15451)*
SGF Produce Holding Corp 714 630-2170
701 W Kimberly Ave # 210 Placentia (92870) *(G-8774)*
Sgii Inc 949 521-6161
9211 Irvine Blvd Irvine (92618) *(G-8293)*
Sgokc, Beale Afb *Also called US Dept of the Air Force (G-20175)*
SGS Accutest Inc 408 588-0200
2105 Lundy Ave San Jose (95131) *(G-26886)*
Shade Structures Inc 714 427-6981
1085 N Main St Ste C Orange (92867) *(G-3581)*
Shadkor Inc 818 953-4627
4021 W Alameda Ave Burbank (91505) *(G-13586)*
Shadow Animation LLC 323 466-7771
940 N Mansfield Ave Los Angeles (90038) *(G-18149)*
Shadow Hlls Cnvlscent Hosp Inc 818 352-4438
10158 Sunland Blvd Sunland (91040) *(G-20905)*
Shadow Mnt Rsort/Rcqut CL Tns, Palm Desert *Also called Destination Resort MGT Inc (G-12567)*
Shadowbrook Health Care Inc 530 534-1353
1 Gilmore Ln Oroville (95966) *(G-20906)*
Shady Canyon Golf Club Inc 949 856-7000
100 Shady Canyon Dr Irvine (92603) *(G-19076)*
Shake Smart Inc 661 993-7383
4640 Cass St Unit 90488 San Diego (92169) *(G-16956)*
Shaklee Corporation 510 887-5000
1992 Alpine Way Hayward (94545) *(G-8294)*
Shalev Senior Living 818 780-4808
6245 Matilija Ave Van Nuys (91401) *(G-24809)*
Shamrock Center, Burbank *Also called Shamrock Plus Inc (G-10076)*
Shamrock Companies, The, Anaheim *Also called Shamrock Supply Company Inc (G-7697)*
Shamrock Plus Inc 818 845-4444
4444 W Lakeside Dr Lbby Burbank (91505) *(G-10076)*
Shamrock Supply Company Inc (PA) 714 575-1800
3366 E La Palma Ave Anaheim (92806) *(G-7697)*
Shamrock-Hostmark Palm Desrt 760 340-6600
74700 Highway 111 Palm Desert (92260) *(G-13237)*
Shannon Ranches Inc 707 998-9656
12601 E Highway 20 Clearlake Oaks (95423) *(G-27644)*
Shapell Inc 925 735-4253
9000 S Gale Ridge Rd San Ramon (94582) *(G-18785)*
Shapell Industries LLC (HQ) 323 655-7330
8383 Wilshire Blvd # 700 Beverly Hills (90211) *(G-12008)*
Shapell Industries LLC 818 366-1132
11280 Corbin Ave Northridge (91326) *(G-1254)*
Shapell's Home Center, Northridge *Also called Shapell Industries LLC (G-1254)*
Shapiro Ben Basat Painting, Van Nuys *Also called C B B Z S Inc (G-2433)*
Shapiro-Gilman-Shandler Co (PA) 213 593-1200
739 Decatur St Los Angeles (90021) *(G-8775)*
Shapp International Trdg Inc 818 348-3000
6000 Reseda Blvd Tarzana (91356) *(G-6961)*
Shapp Internatioonal, Tarzana *Also called Shapp International Trdg Inc (G-6961)*
Shared Services, Torrance *Also called Securitas SEC Svcs USA Inc (G-16810)*
Sharedata Inc 408 490-2500
2465 Augustine Dr Santa Clara (95054) *(G-15836)*
Sharedta/E Trade Bus Solutions, Santa Clara *Also called Sharedata Inc (G-15836)*
Sharethis Inc (PA) 650 641-0191
4005 Miranda Ave Ste 100 Palo Alto (94304) *(G-13920)*
Sharf Woodward & Associates 818 989-2200
5900 Sepulvda Blvd # 104 Van Nuys (91411) *(G-14785)*
Shark's Ice, San Jose *Also called Logitech Ice At San Jose (G-19239)*

ALPHABETIC

Sharks Sports & Entrmt LLC..........408 287-7070
525 W Santa Clara St San Jose (95113) *(G-18564)*
Sharon Care Center LLC..........323 655-2023
8167 W 3rd St Los Angeles (90048) *(G-20907)*
Sharon Crest Apts..........650 854-5130
680 Sharon Park Dr Apt 25 Menlo Park (94025) *(G-11201)*
Sharp Chula Vista Medical Ctr, Chula Vista *Also called Sharp Chula Vista Medical Ctr (G-21883)*
Sharp Chula Vista Medical Ctr..........619 502-5800
751 Medical Center Ct Chula Vista (91911) *(G-21883)*
Sharp Chula Vista Medical Ctr..........858 499-5150
8695 Spectrum Center Blvd San Diego (92123) *(G-21884)*
Sharp Community Medical Group..........858 499-4525
8695 Spectrum Center Blvd San Diego (92123) *(G-25156)*
Sharp Grossmont, La Mesa *Also called Team Health Holdings Inc (G-20129)*
Sharp Guard Services Inc..........213 739-1900
3450 Wilshire Blvd # 1000 Los Angeles (90010) *(G-16819)*
Sharp Health Care, San Diego *Also called Sharp Healthcare (G-21886)*
Sharp Health Plan..........858 499-8300
8520 Tech Way Ste 200 San Diego (92123) *(G-10380)*
Sharp Healthcare..........619 398-2988
7910 Frost St Ste 280 San Diego (92123) *(G-19990)*
Sharp Healthcare..........858 621-4090
10670 Wexford St San Diego (92131) *(G-19991)*
Sharp Healthcare..........858 939-5434
8008 Frost St Ste 106 San Diego (92123) *(G-19992)*
Sharp Healthcare (PA)..........858 499-4000
8695 Spectrum Center Blvd San Diego (92123) *(G-21885)*
Sharp Healthcare..........619 446-1575
300 Fir St San Diego (92101) *(G-20908)*
Sharp Healthcare..........619 688-3543
2929 Health Center Dr San Diego (92123) *(G-19993)*
Sharp Healthcare..........858 653-6100
8901 Activity Rd San Diego (92126) *(G-19994)*
Sharp Healthcare..........858 627-5152
3554 Ruffin Rd Ste Soca San Diego (92123) *(G-21886)*
Sharp Healthcare..........760 901-5100
3230 Waring Ct Ste P Oceanside (92056) *(G-19995)*
Sharp Healthcare..........760 806-5600
130 Cedar Rd Vista (92083) *(G-21887)*
Sharp Healthcare..........858 541-4850
8080 Dagget St Ste 200 San Diego (92111) *(G-22561)*
Sharp Healthcare..........858 499-2000
751 Medical Center Ct Chula Vista (91911) *(G-20909)*
Sharp Healthcare..........858 616-8411
2020 Genesee Ave Fl 2 San Diego (92123) *(G-19996)*
Sharp Healthcare..........858 621-4010
10670 Wexford St San Diego (92131) *(G-21888)*
Sharp Healthcare..........800 827-4277
4510 Viewridge Ave San Diego (92123) *(G-19997)*
Sharp Healthcare..........619 460-6200
8860 Center Dr Ste 450 La Mesa (91942) *(G-19998)*
Sharp Healthcare..........858 541-4896
9765 Clairemont Mesa Blvd San Diego (92124) *(G-22562)*
Sharp Healthcare..........858 616-8200
2020 Genesee Ave San Diego (92123) *(G-19999)*
Sharp Home Care, San Diego *Also called Sharp Healthcare (G-22561)*
Sharp Home Health, San Diego *Also called Sharp Healthcare (G-22562)*
Sharp Mary Birch H..........858 939-3400
3003 Health Center Dr San Diego (92123) *(G-21889)*
Sharp Memorial Hospital (HQ)..........858 939-3636
7901 Frost St San Diego (92123) *(G-21890)*
Sharp Memorial Hospital..........858 278-4110
7850 Vista Hill Ave San Diego (92123) *(G-22091)*
Sharp Mesa Vista Hospital, San Diego *Also called Sharp Memorial Hospital (G-22091)*
Sharp Mission Park Medical Ctr, Vista *Also called Sharp Healthcare (G-21887)*
Sharp Reece Stealy Med Group, San Diego *Also called Sharp Healthcare (G-19997)*
Sharp Rees-Stealy, San Diego *Also called Sharp Healthcare (G-19992)*
Sharp Rees-Stealy Div, San Diego *Also called Sharp Healthcare (G-20908)*
Sharp Rees-Stealy Pharmacy, San Diego *Also called Sharp Healthcare (G-21885)*
Sharp Rees-Stealy Pharmacy, San Diego *Also called Sharp Healthcare (G-19993)*
Sharper Future..........415 297-6767
870 Market St Ste 1265 San Francisco (94102) *(G-20000)*
Shartsis Friese LLP..........415 421-6500
1 Maritime Plz Fl 18 San Francisco (94111) *(G-23559)*
Shason Inc (PA)..........323 269-6666
4940 Triggs St Ste B Commerce (90022) *(G-8326)*
SHASTA BLOOD CENTER, San Francisco *Also called Blood Centers of Pacific (G-22898)*
Shasta Cattle Women, Cottonwood *Also called County of Shasta (G-25243)*
Shasta Convalescent Center..........530 222-3630
3550 Churn Creek Rd Redding (96002) *(G-21369)*
Shasta Convalescent Hospital, Redding *Also called Shasta Convalescent Center (G-21369)*
Shasta County Calworks, Redding *Also called County of Shasta (G-10550)*
Shasta County Head Start Child (PA)..........530 241-1036
375 Lake Blvd Ste 100 Redding (96003) *(G-24514)*
Shasta Lake Resorts LP..........209 785-3300
22300 Jones Vly Marina Dr Redding (96003) *(G-19281)*
Shasta Landscaping Inc..........760 744-6551
1340 Descanso Ave San Marcos (92069) *(G-952)*
Shasta Livestock Auction Yard..........530 347-3793
3917 Main St Cottonwood (96022) *(G-8962)*
Shasta Medical Associates..........530 243-3231
1555 East St Ste 210 Redding (96001) *(G-20001)*
Shasta Produce Co, South San Francisco *Also called Andrighetto Produce Inc (G-3491)*
Shasta Regional Med Ctr Srmc, Redding *Also called Prime Healthcare Services (G-21811)*
Shasta-Trinity Ranger Unit, Redding *Also called Forestry and Fire Protection (G-1015)*
Shattuck Healthcare, Berkeley *Also called Elmwood LNG TRM& Tran Care (G-20534)*
Shaw Construction, Fresno *Also called Shaws Strctures Unlimited Inc (G-1462)*
Shaw Envmtl & Infrastructure..........916 928-3300
1326 N Market Blvd Sacramento (95834) *(G-26060)*
Shaw Group Inc..........925 288-2011
4005 Port Chicago Hwy Concord (94520) *(G-26887)*
Shaw Group Inc..........949 261-6441
18100 Von Karman Ave # 450 Irvine (92612) *(G-26888)*
Shaw Hospitality Group Inc..........559 224-4040
324 E Shaw Ave Fresno (93710) *(G-13238)*
Shawmut Design and Cnstr, Los Angeles *Also called Shawmut Woodworking & Sup Inc (G-1665)*
Shawmut Woodworking & Sup Inc..........323 602-1000
11390 W Olympic Blvd Fl 2 Los Angeles (90064) *(G-1665)*
Shaws Strctures Unlimited Inc..........559 275-3475
2573 W Cambridge Ave Fresno (93705) *(G-1462)*
Shc Burbank II LLC..........818 843-6000
2500 N Hollywood Way Burbank (91505) *(G-13239)*
Shc Reference Laboratory, Palo Alto *Also called Stanford Health Care (G-21934)*
Shea Convalescent Hospital, Whittier *Also called Longwood Management Corp (G-21719)*
Shea Family Care Mission Hlth..........619 297-4484
3680 Reynard Way San Diego (92103) *(G-22831)*
Shea Family Care Somerset, El Cajon *Also called Somerset Special Care Center (G-21111)*
Shea Homes, Irvine *Also called JF Shea Construction Inc (G-1194)*
Shea Homes, Rio Vista *Also called Trilogy Rio Vista (G-1476)*
Shea Homes, San Jose *Also called JF Shea Construction Inc (G-1196)*
Shea Homes, Livermore *Also called JF Shea Construction Inc (G-1197)*
Shea Homes Arizona Ltd Partnr..........909 594-9500
655 Brea Canyon Rd Walnut (91789) *(G-11841)*
Shea Homes At Montage LLC..........909 594-9500
655 Brea Canyon Rd Walnut (91789) *(G-1255)*
Shea Homes Lmtd Partnership A (HQ)..........909 594-9500
655 Brea Canyon Rd Walnut (91789) *(G-1256)*
Shea Homes Ltd Prtnershp, Walnut *Also called Vistancia Marketing LLC (G-27715)*
Shea Homes Vantis LLC..........909 594-9500
655 Brea Canyon Rd Walnut (91789) *(G-1339)*
Shea Labagh Dobberstein Cpa (PA)..........415 731-0100
505 Montgomery St Ste 500 San Francisco (94111) *(G-26439)*
Shea Properties LLC..........949 389-7000
130 Vantis Ste 200 Aliso Viejo (92656) *(G-11842)*
Shea Properties MGT Co Inc..........949 389-7000
130 Vantis Ste 200 Aliso Viejo (92656) *(G-11843)*
Shed Media US Inc..........323 904-4680
3800 Barham Blvd Ste 410 Los Angeles (90068) *(G-13978)*
Sheedy Drayage Co (PA)..........415 648-7171
1215 Michigan St San Francisco (94107) *(G-14498)*
Sheehan Construction Inc..........707 603-2610
477 Devlin Rd Ste 108 NAPA (94558) *(G-1257)*
Shekinah Inc..........714 475-5460
7755 Center Ave Ste 1000 Huntington Beach (92647) *(G-23560)*
Sheldon Mechanical Corporation..........661 286-1361
26015 Avenue Hall Santa Clarita (91355) *(G-2365)*
Sheldon Ranches..........559 562-3978
25140 Burr Dr Lindsay (93247) *(G-393)*
Shell Vacations LLC..........415 441-7100
501 Post St San Francisco (94102) *(G-27210)*
Shelter Inc..........925 335-0698
1333 Willow Pass Rd # 206 Concord (94520) *(G-28055)*
Shelter Point Hotel & Marina, San Diego *Also called Pacifica Hotel Company (G-13067)*
Shelter Pointe Hotel & Marina, San Diego *Also called Shelter Pointe LLC (G-4772)*
Shelter Pointe LLC..........619 221-8000
1551 Shelter Island Dr San Diego (92106) *(G-4772)*
Shelton Construction Company..........714 903-7853
5628 Spinnaker Bay Dr Long Beach (90803) *(G-1858)*
Shen Zhen New World II LLC..........818 980-1212
333 Unversal Hollywood Dr Universal City (91608) *(G-13240)*
Shenyang Zhong Yi Tin-Plating..........415 788-2280
870 Market St Ste 950 San Francisco (94102) *(G-11044)*
Shepard Eye Center..........805 925-2637
1418 E Main St Ste 110 Santa Maria (93454) *(G-20002)*
Sheplace Design Center, San Francisco *Also called Bay West Shwplace Invstors LLC (G-10962)*
Sheppard Mullin Richter (PA)..........213 620-1780
333 S Hope St Fl 43 Los Angeles (90071) *(G-23561)*
Sheppard Mullin Richter..........619 338-6500
12275 El Camino R Ste 200 San Diego (92130) *(G-23562)*
Sheppard Mullin Richter..........415 434-9100
4 Embarcadero Ctr # 1700 San Francisco (94111) *(G-23563)*
Sheppard Mullin Richter..........310 228-3700
1901 Avenue Of The Stars # 1600 Los Angeles (90067) *(G-23564)*
Sheppard Mullin Richter..........714 513-5100
650 Town Center Dr Fl 4 Costa Mesa (92626) *(G-23565)*
Sheppard Mullin, Los Angeles *Also called Sheppard Mullin Richter (G-23561)*
Sheraton, San Francisco *Also called Interstate Hotels Resorts Inc (G-12848)*
Sheraton, Los Angeles *Also called Hazens Investment LLC (G-12696)*
Sheraton, Santa Monica *Also called M&C Hotel Interests Inc (G-12934)*
Sheraton, Emeryville *Also called Pacific Hotel Management LLC (G-13058)*
Sheraton, San Diego *Also called Dimension Development Two LLC (G-12572)*
Sheraton, Pasadena *Also called Dallas Union Hotel Inc (G-12242)*
Sheraton, San Diego *Also called Hst Lessee Boston LLC (G-12802)*
Sheraton, San Diego *Also called 8110 Aero Holding LLC (G-12369)*
Sheraton, La Jolla *Also called Bartell Hotels (G-12421)*
Sheraton, Palo Alto *Also called Pacific Hotel Management LLC (G-13060)*
Sheraton Carlsbad Resort & Spa, Carlsbad *Also called Grand Pacific Carlsbad Ht LP (G-12672)*
Sheraton Corporation..........415 362-5500
2500 Mason St San Francisco (94133) *(G-13241)*

ALPHABETIC

Sheraton Corporation...310 642-1111
6101 W Century Blvd Los Angeles (90045) *(G-13242)*
Sheraton Corporation...916 447-1700
1230 J St 13th Sacramento (95814) *(G-13243)*
Sheraton Corporation...909 204-6100
11960 Foothill Blvd Rancho Cucamonga (91739) *(G-13244)*
Sheraton Corporation...925 463-3330
5990 Stoneridge Mall Rd Pleasanton (94588) *(G-13245)*
Sheraton Downtown Los Angeles, Los Angeles *Also called Nrea-TRC 711 LLC (G-13030)*
Sheraton Fisherman's Wharf, San Francisco *Also called Capstar San Francisco Co LLC (G-12488)*
Sheraton Grand Sacramento Ht, Sacramento *Also called Sheraton Corporation (G-13243)*
Sheraton Grand Sacramento Ht, Sacramento *Also called Cim/J Street Ht Sacramento Inc (G-12520)*
Sheraton Hotel Sunnyvale, Sunnyvale *Also called Sunnyvale Sof-X Owner L P (G-13310)*
Sheraton Hotel Sunnyvale, Sunnyvale *Also called W2005 New Cntury Ht Prtflio LP (G-13388)*
Sheraton Htl San Diego Msn Vly...619 321-4602
1433 Camino Del Rio S San Diego (92108) *(G-27645)*
Sheraton Los Angeles, Los Angeles *Also called 711 Hope LP (G-12368)*
Sheraton Ontario Airport Hotel, Los Angeles *Also called S W K Properties LLC (G-27203)*
Sheraton Palo Alto, Palo Alto *Also called Pacific Hotel Dev Ventr LP (G-13057)*
Sheraton Pasadena, Pasadena *Also called Pasadena Hotel Dev Ventr LP (G-13078)*
Sheraton Pk Ht At Anheim Rsort, Anaheim *Also called Anaheim Hotel LLC (G-12387)*
Sheraton Pk Ht At Anheim Rsort...714 750-1811
1855 S Harbor Blvd Anaheim (92802) *(G-13246)*
Sheraton San Diego Ht & Marina, San Diego *Also called Hst Lessee San Diego LP (G-11575)*
Sheraton San Diego Ht & Marina, San Diego *Also called Host Hotels & Resorts LP (G-12768)*
Sheraton San Diego Mission Vly, San Diego *Also called Sheraton Htl San Diego Msn Vly (G-27645)*
Sheraton Sn Diego Htl Msn Vly, San Diego *Also called Ashford Trs Nickel LLC (G-26928)*
Sheraton Sonoma County Hotel, Petaluma *Also called Lok Petaluma Marina Ht Co LLC (G-12927)*
Sheraton Suites San Diego, San Diego *Also called Noiro West LLC (G-13026)*
Sheraton Universal Hotel, Universal City *Also called Shen Zhen New World II LLC (G-13240)*
Sheraton Universal Hotel, North Hollywood *Also called SLC Operating Ltd Partnership (G-13795)*
Sheraton Universal Hotel, Universal City *Also called Lh Universal Operating LLC (G-12917)*
Sheriff's Dept, Elk Grove *Also called County of Sacramento (G-27784)*
Sheriff's Dept, San Francisco *Also called City & County of San Francisco (G-23748)*
Sheriffs Fndtion For Pub Sfety, Fresno *Also called County of Fresno (G-25519)*
Sheriffs Offices...760 878-0383
550 S Clay St Independence (93526) *(G-23566)*
Sherman Oaks Health System...818 981-7111
4929 Van Nuys Blvd Sherman Oaks (91403) *(G-21891)*
Sherman Oaks Hospital, Sherman Oaks *Also called Prime Healthcare Svcs II LLC (G-21813)*
Sherman Security...909 941-4167
7218 Hermosa Ave Rancho Cucamonga (91701) *(G-16820)*
Sherman Terrace, Reseda *Also called Permanente Kaiser Intl (G-19833)*
Sherman Village Hlth Care Ctr, North Hollywood *Also called Hillsdale Group LP (G-21268)*
Sherman Village Hlth Care Ctr, North Hollywood *Also called Coldwater Care Center LLC (G-20464)*
Shermn-Lehr Cstm Tile Wrks Inc...916 386-0417
5691 Power Inn Rd Ste A Sacramento (95824) *(G-3024)*
Sherpaul Corporation...760 639-6472
901 Hacienda Dr B Vista (92081) *(G-22563)*
Sherton Grdn Grove Anheim S Ht...714 703-8400
12221 Harbor Blvd Garden Grove (92840) *(G-13247)*
Sherwood Country Club...805 496-3036
320 W Stafford Rd Thousand Oaks (91361) *(G-19077)*
Sherwood Guest Home, Lynwood *Also called Marlinda Management Inc (G-21309)*
Sherwood Healthcare Center, Sacramento *Also called H C C S Inc (G-20641)*
Sherwood Mechanical Inc...858 679-3000
6630 Top Gun St San Diego (92121) *(G-2366)*
Sherwood Oaks Enterprises...707 964-6333
130 Dana St Fort Bragg (95437) *(G-20910)*
Sherwood Oaks Health Center, Fort Bragg *Also called Sherwood Oaks Enterprises (G-20910)*
Sherwood Valley Rancheria...707 459-7330
100 Kawi Pl Willits (95490) *(G-13248)*
Sherwood Vllley Rnchria Casino, Willits *Also called Sherwood Valley Rancheria (G-13248)*
Shibui Apartments, Torrance *Also called Hunt Enterprises Inc (G-11576)*
Shield Security Inc (HQ)...714 210-1501
1551 N Tustin Ave Ste 650 Santa Ana (92705) *(G-16821)*
Shield Security Inc...818 239-5800
21110 Vanowen St Canoga Park (91303) *(G-16822)*
Shield Security Inc...562 283-1100
150 E Wardlow Rd Long Beach (90807) *(G-16823)*
Shield Security Inc...909 920-1173
265 N Euclid Ave Upland (91786) *(G-16824)*
Shields For Families (PA)...323 242-5000
11601 S Western Ave Los Angeles (90047) *(G-22172)*
Shields Nursing Centers Inc (PA)...510 724-9911
606 Alfred Nobel Dr Hercules (94547) *(G-20911)*
Shields Nursing Centers Inc...510 525-3212
3230 Carlson Blvd El Cerrito (94530) *(G-20912)*
Shift Technologies Inc...415 800-2038
2500 Market St San Francisco (94114) *(G-6693)*
Shih Yu-Lang Central YMCA, San Francisco *Also called Young Mens Christian Assoc SF (G-25453)*
Shii LLC...909 354-8000
8300 Utica Ave Ste 300 Rancho Cucamonga (91730) *(G-11844)*
Shilpark Paint Automotive, Los Angeles *Also called Shilpark Paint Corporation (G-9239)*
Shilpark Paint Corporation (PA)...323 732-7093
1640 S Vermont Ave Los Angeles (90006) *(G-9239)*
Shimadzu Medical Systems Div, Long Beach *Also called Shimadzu Precision Instrs Inc (G-8005)*
Shimadzu Precision Instrs Inc (HQ)...562 420-6226
3645 N Lakewood Blvd Long Beach (90808) *(G-8005)*
Shimadzu Precision Instrs Inc...310 217-8855
20101 S Vermont Ave Torrance (90502) *(G-7313)*
Shimano American Corporation (HQ)...949 951-5003
1 Holland Irvine (92618) *(G-8029)*
Shimmick Construction Co Inc...510 777-5000
16481 Scientific Bldg 2 Irvine (92618) *(G-1258)*
Shimmick Construction Co Inc...925 862-1901
6535 Calaveras Rd Sunol (94586) *(G-1259)*
Shimmick Construction Co Inc (PA)...510 777-5000
8201 Edgewater Dr Ste 202 Oakland (94621) *(G-2083)*
Shims Bargain Inc (PA)...323 881-0099
2600 S Soto St Vernon (90058) *(G-9302)*
Shims Bargain Inc...323 726-8800
7030 E Slauson Ave Commerce (90040) *(G-1463)*
Shinazy Enterprises Inc...415 673-4700
1270 Bush St San Francisco (94109) *(G-17772)*
Shine and Bright Hand Car Wash, Culver City *Also called Hlw Corp (G-17843)*
Shingle Sprng Trbal Gming Auth...530 677-7000
1 Red Hawk Pkwy Placerville (95667) *(G-19282)*
Shipbycom LLC...626 271-9800
900 Turnbull Canyon Rd City of Industry (91745) *(G-4063)*
Shipco Transport Inc...562 295-2900
100 W Victoria St Long Beach (90805) *(G-4723)*
Shipito, Hawthorne *Also called Eastbiz Corporation (G-19204)*
Shiva-Shakthi, San Diego *Also called Marika Group Inc (G-8399)*
Shn Cnslting Engnrs-Geologists, Eureka *Also called Shn Consulting Engin (G-26061)*
Shn Consulting Engin (PA)...707 441-8855
812 W Wabash Ave Eureka (95501) *(G-26061)*
Sho-Air International Inc (PA)...949 476-9111
5401 Argosy Ave Ste 102 Huntington Beach (92649) *(G-5168)*
Shoe Metro, San Diego *Also called Ebuys Inc (G-8434)*
Shoei Foods USA Inc...530 742-7866
1900 Feather River Blvd Olivehurst (95961) *(G-8518)*
Shokawah Casino...707 744-1395
13101 Nokomis Rd Hopland (95449) *(G-13249)*
Shook & Waller Cnstr Inc...707 578-3933
7677 Bell Rd Ste 101 Windsor (95492) *(G-3088)*
Shook Hardy & Bacon LLP...415 544-1900
1 Montgomery St Ste 2700 San Francisco (94104) *(G-23567)*
Shooter & Butts Inc...925 460-5155
3768 Old Santa Rita Rd Pleasanton (94588) *(G-796)*
Shopkick Inc...650 763-8727
900 Middlefield Rd Ste 3 Redwood City (94063) *(G-15452)*
Shopper Inc...805 527-6700
3987 Heritage Oak Ct Simi Valley (93063) *(G-7228)*
Shopping Center Mgt Corp...650 617-8234
660 Stanford Shopping Ctr Palo Alto (94304) *(G-11045)*
Shoppingcom Inc...650 616-6500
8000 Marina Blvd Ste 500 Brisbane (94005) *(G-16185)*
Shopzilla.com, Los Angeles *Also called Connexity Inc (G-5581)*
Shore Hotel...310 458-1515
1515 Ocean Ave Santa Monica (90401) *(G-13250)*
Shorebreeze Apartments, Mountain View *Also called Mp Shoreline Assoc Ltd Partnr (G-11172)*
Shorecliff Properties, Pismo Beach *Also called T I C Hotels Inc (G-13335)*
Shoreline Care Center, Oxnard *Also called Covenant Care California LLC (G-20491)*
Shoreline Holdings Inc (PA)...562 498-6444
2505 Mira Mar Ave Long Beach (90815) *(G-2733)*
Shoreline Land Care Inc...858 560-8555
7348 Trade St Ste B San Diego (92121) *(G-953)*
Shoreline S Intermediate Care...510 523-8857
430 Willow St Alameda (94501) *(G-21107)*
Shorenstein Company LLC...415 772-8209
235 Montgomery St Fl 15 San Francisco (94104) *(G-11046)*
Shorenstein Properties LLC (PA)...415 772-7000
235 Montgomery St Fl 16 San Francisco (94104) *(G-11047)*
Shores Restaurant, La Jolla *Also called La Jolla Bch & Tennis CLB Inc (G-12898)*
Shoreview Preservation LP...415 647-6922
35 Lillian Ct San Francisco (94124) *(G-11202)*
Shoring & Excavating, Santa Fe Springs *Also called Shoring Engineers (G-3582)*
Shoring Engineers...562 944-9331
12645 Clark St Santa Fe Springs (90670) *(G-3582)*
Show Call Productions Inc...619 602-0656
3605 Hemlock St San Diego (92113) *(G-18434)*
Showcase Installations, Santa Fe Springs *Also called Partitions Installation Inc (G-3565)*
Shri Laxmi Naryan Hsptlty Grp...916 922-8041
1401 Arden Way Sacramento (95815) *(G-13251)*
Shri Sidhi Vinayaka Hotel Inc...855 922-5252
500 Leisure Ln Sacramento (95815) *(G-13252)*
Shriner's Hospital, Los Angeles *Also called Shriners Hspitals For Children (G-22173)*
Shriners Hspitals For Children...213 388-3151
3160 Geneva St Los Angeles (90020) *(G-22173)*
Shriners Hspitals For Children...916 453-2050
2425 Stockton Blvd Sacramento (95817) *(G-22174)*
Shriners Hspitals For Children...916 453-2000
2425 Stockton Blvd Sacramento (95817) *(G-22175)*
Shud Wcv Inc...650 692-7380
855 Malcolm Rd Burlingame (94010) *(G-13587)*
Shuler, Kurt MD, Davis *Also called Sutter Health (G-20111)*
Shusters Transportation Inc...707 459-4131
750 E Valley St Willits (95490) *(G-4064)*

ALPHABETIC

Shutterfly Inc (PA)..........650 610-5200
2800 Bridge Pkwy Ste 100 Redwood City (94065) ***(G-16957)***
Shutters On The Beach, Santa Monica *Also called By The Blue Sea LLC* ***(G-12476)***
Shutters On The Beach, Santa Monica *Also called Edward Thomas Hospitality Corp* ***(G-12611)***
Shuttleport California, San Jose *Also called Veolia Transportation Svcs Inc* ***(G-3732)***
SI Inc..........951 304-9444
26035 Jefferson Ave Murrieta (92562) ***(G-3089)***
Sia Engineering (usa) Inc..........310 693-7108
7001 W Imperial Hwy Los Angeles (90045) ***(G-26062)***
Sideman & Bancroft LLP..........415 392-1960
1 Embarcadero Ctr Fl 22 San Francisco (94111) ***(G-23568)***
Sidjon Corporation..........925 606-6135
3571 1st St Livermore (94551) ***(G-13253)***
Sidley Austin LLP..........650 565-7000
1001 Page Mill Rd Bldg 1 Palo Alto (94304) ***(G-23569)***
Sidley Austin LLP..........415 772-1200
555 California St Fl 20 San Francisco (94104) ***(G-23570)***
Siemens AG..........650 969-9112
685 E Middlefield Rd Mountain View (94043) ***(G-26063)***
Siemens Government Tech Inc..........619 656-4740
1675 Brandywine Ave Ste F Chula Vista (91911) ***(G-18015)***
Siemens Industry Inc..........510 783-6000
25821 Industrial Blvd # 300 Hayward (94545) ***(G-26064)***
Siemens Industry Inc..........510 783-6000
25821 Industrial Blvd # 300 Hayward (94545) ***(G-7886)***
Siemens Industry Inc..........858 693-8711
9835 Carroll Ctre Rd 10 Ste 100 San Diego (92126) ***(G-7887)***
Siemens Industry Inc..........916 371-2600
1585 Parkway Blvd West Sacramento (95691) ***(G-17944)***
Siemens Med Solutions USA Inc..........650 694-5747
685 E Middlefield Rd Mountain View (94043) ***(G-7314)***
Siemens PLM Software, Cypress *Also called Siemens Product Life Mgmt Sftw* ***(G-15453)***
Siemens Product Life Mgmt Sftw..........714 952-6500
10824 Hope St Cypress (90630) ***(G-15453)***
Sierra At Taho Ski Resorts..........530 659-7519
1111 Sierra At Tahoe Rd Twin Bridges (95735) ***(G-13254)***
Sierra Aviation, Oakdale *Also called Phase 3 Inc* ***(G-4928)***
Sierra Bancorp..........559 449-8145
7029 N Ingram Ave Ste 101 Fresno (93650) ***(G-9559)***
Sierra Bay Contractors Inc..........925 671-7711
4021 Port Chicago Hwy # 150 Concord (94520) ***(G-1464)***
Sierra Bookkeeping & Tax Svc..........916 349-7610
5777 Madison Ave Ste 615 Sacramento (95841) ***(G-26440)***
Sierra Care Rehabilitation Ctr..........916 782-3188
310 Oak Ridge Dr Roseville (95661) ***(G-20913)***
Sierra Cascade Blueberries..........530 894-8728
12753 Doe Mill Rd Forest Ranch (95942) ***(G-133)***
Sierra Central Credit Union (PA)..........530 671-3009
1351 Harter Pkwy Yuba City (95993) ***(G-9689)***
Sierra Club (PA)..........415 977-5500
2101 Webster St Ste 1300 Oakland (94612) ***(G-25347)***
Sierra Club Angeles Chapter, Los Angeles *Also called Friends of Angeles Chapter* ***(G-25533)***
Sierra Club Books, Oakland *Also called Sierra Club* ***(G-25347)***
Sierra Cscade Fmly Opprtnities (PA)..........530 283-1242
424 N Mill Creek Rd Quincy (95971) ***(G-24515)***
Sierra Disposal Service, South Lake Tahoe *Also called South Tahoe Refuse Co* ***(G-6565)***
Sierra Electric Co, San Francisco *Also called Stadtner Co Inc* ***(G-2746)***
Sierra Entertainment..........530 666-9646
341 Industrial Way Woodland (95776) ***(G-3617)***
Sierra Equipment Leasing Inc..........925 676-7300
1140 Suncast Ln El Dorado Hills (95762) ***(G-14579)***
Sierra Family Health Center, Colton *Also called Inland Family Health Wellness* ***(G-21611)***
Sierra Forever Families..........916 368-5114
8928 Volunteer Ln Ste 100 Sacramento (95826) ***(G-24210)***
Sierra Gold Nurseries Inc..........530 674-1145
5320 Garden Hwy Yuba City (95991) ***(G-318)***
Sierra Group, Glendale *Also called Next Venture Inc* ***(G-1619)***
Sierra Health Services LLC..........209 956-7725
2423 W March Ln Ste 100 Stockton (95207) ***(G-26441)***
Sierra Hills Care Center Inc..........916 782-7007
1139 Cirby Way Roseville (95661) ***(G-21108)***
Sierra International McHy LLC..........661 327-7073
1620 E Brundage Ln Frnt Bakersfield (93307) ***(G-8084)***
Sierra La Verne Cntry CLB Inc..........909 596-2100
6300 Country Club Dr La Verne (91750) ***(G-19078)***
Sierra Lakes Golf Club..........909 350-2500
16600 Clubhouse Dr Fontana (92336) ***(G-18786)***
Sierra Landscape & Maint Inc..........530 895-0263
3760 Morrow Ln Ste A Chico (95928) ***(G-797)***
Sierra Lathing Company Inc..........909 421-0211
1189 Leiske Dr Rialto (92376) ***(G-2979)***
Sierra Lobo Inc..........626 510-6340
465 N Halstead St Ste 130 Pasadena (91107) ***(G-26065)***
Sierra Lodge 788, Oakhurst *Also called Sierra Masonic Association* ***(G-25348)***
Sierra Lumber & Decking, San Jose *Also called Sierra Lumber Co* ***(G-3090)***
Sierra Lumber Co..........408 286-7071
1711 Senter Rd San Jose (95112) ***(G-3090)***
Sierra Manor Apts, Chico *Also called Hignell Companies* ***(G-11141)***
Sierra Masonic Association..........559 683-7713
2166 Hwy 49 Oakhurst (93644) ***(G-25348)***
Sierra Mountain Express, El Dorado Hills *Also called Sierra Equipment Leasing Inc* ***(G-14579)***
Sierra Nevada Corporation..........408 395-2004
985 University Ave Ste 4 Los Gatos (95032) ***(G-26066)***
Sierra Nevada Home Care, Grass Valley *Also called Sierra Nevada Memorial Hm Care* ***(G-22564)***
Sierra Nevada Memorial Hm Care..........530 274-6350
1020 Mccourtney Rd Ste A Grass Valley (95949) ***(G-22564)***
Sierra Oaks Senior Living..........530 241-5100
1520 Collyer Dr Redding (96003) ***(G-24810)***
Sierra Pacific 4117, Modesto *Also called US Foods Inc* ***(G-8949)***
Sierra Pacific Development..........559 256-1300
1470 W Herndon Ave # 100 Fresno (93711) ***(G-12009)***
Sierra Pacific Farms Inc (PA)..........951 699-9980
43406 Business Park Dr Temecula (92590) ***(G-723)***
Sierra Pacific Htg & Air-Solar, Rancho Cordova *Also called Sierra PCF HM & Comfort Inc* ***(G-7746)***
Sierra Pacific Mortgage Co Inc..........805 489-6060
104 Traffic Way Arroyo Grande (93420) ***(G-9897)***
Sierra Pacific Mortgage Co Inc (PA)..........916 932-1700
1180 Iron Point Rd # 200 Folsom (95630) ***(G-9898)***
Sierra Pacific Ortho..........559 256-5200
1630 E Herndon Ave Fresno (93720) ***(G-20003)***
Sierra Pacific West Inc..........760 599-0755
2125 La Mirada Dr Vista (92081) ***(G-1666)***
Sierra PCF HM & Comfort Inc..........916 638-0543
2550 Mercantile Dr Ste D Rancho Cordova (95742) ***(G-7746)***
Sierra Recycling & Dem Inc..........661 327-7073
1620 E Brundage Ln Frnt Bakersfield (93307) ***(G-3467)***
Sierra Tel Business Systems, Oakhurst *Also called Sierra Tel Cmmunications Group* ***(G-5698)***
Sierra Tel Cmmunications Group..........559 683-7777
40044 Highway 49 Ste C2 Oakhurst (93644) ***(G-5698)***
Sierra Tel Cmmunications Group (PA)..........559 683-4611
49150 Road 426 Oakhurst (93644) ***(G-5699)***
Sierra Telephone Company Inc..........559 683-4611
49150 Crane Valley Rd 426 Oakhurst (93644) ***(G-5700)***
Sierra Transport Inc..........661 836-3166
12856 Old River Rd Bakersfield (93311) ***(G-4065)***
Sierra Valley Rehab Center..........559 784-7375
301 W Putnam Ave Porterville (93257) ***(G-21370)***
SIERRA VIEW CARE CENTER, Baldwin Park *Also called Sierra View Care Holdings LLC* ***(G-20914)***
Sierra View Care Holdings LLC..........626 960-1971
14318 Ohio St Baldwin Park (91706) ***(G-20914)***
Sierra View Country Club..........916 782-3741
105 Alta Vista Ave Roseville (95678) ***(G-19079)***
Sierra View District Hospital, Porterville *Also called Sierra View Local Hospital Dst* ***(G-20004)***
Sierra View District Hospital, Porterville *Also called Sierra View Local Hospital Dst* ***(G-21892)***
Sierra View Homes..........559 637-2256
1155 E Springfield Ave Reedley (93654) ***(G-20915)***
SIERRA VIEW HOMES RESIDENTIAL, Reedley *Also called Sierra View Homes* ***(G-20915)***
Sierra View Landscape Inc..........916 408-2990
3888 Cincinnati Ave Rocklin (95765) ***(G-954)***
Sierra View Local Hospital Dst (PA)..........559 784-1110
465 W Putnam Ave Porterville (93257) ***(G-20004)***
Sierra View Local Hospital Dst..........559 781-7877
283 Pearson Dr Porterville (93257) ***(G-21892)***
Sierra Vista Extended Stay, Brea *Also called Otb Acquisition LLC* ***(G-13049)***
Sierra Vista Family Medical..........805 582-4000
1227 E Los Angeles Ave Simi Valley (93065) ***(G-23057)***
Sierra Vista Hospital, Sacramento *Also called Psychiatric Solutions Inc* ***(G-19894)***
Sierra Vista Hospital Inc (HQ)..........805 546-7600
1010 Murray Ave San Luis Obispo (93405) ***(G-21893)***
Sierra Vista Memory Care Cmnty, Azusa *Also called Silverado Senior Living Inc* ***(G-21372)***
Sierra Vista Regional Med Ctr, San Luis Obispo *Also called Sierra Vista Hospital Inc* ***(G-21893)***
Sierra Waste Transport Inc..........916 386-9937
6956 Florin Perkins Rd Sacramento (95828) ***(G-5243)***
Sierra Weatherization Co Inc..........408 354-1900
43 E Main St Ste B Los Gatos (95030) ***(G-13921)***
Sierra West Construction Inc..........530 268-7614
24744 Connie Ct Auburn (95602) ***(G-3091)***
Sierra West Home Care, Santa Monica *Also called Right At Home* ***(G-22549)***
Sierra Wireless America Inc..........760 444-5650
2738 Loker Ave W Ste A Carlsbad (92010) ***(G-5407)***
Sierra-Cascade Nursery Inc (PA)..........530 254-6867
472-715 Johnson Rd Susanville (96130) ***(G-319)***
Sigma Investment Holdings LLC..........626 398-3098
2288 Villa Heights Rd Pasadena (91107) ***(G-2084)***
Sigma Kappa Sorority..........510 540-9142
2409 Warring St Berkeley (94704) ***(G-13498)***
Sigma Networks Inc..........408 876-4002
2191 Zanker Rd San Jose (95131) ***(G-5701)***
Sigma Services Inc (PA)..........805 642-8377
2140 Eastman Ave Ste 200 Ventura (93003) ***(G-1667)***
Sigmanet Inc (HQ)..........909 230-7500
4290 E Brickell St Ontario (91761) ***(G-7186)***
Sigmaways Inc..........510 573-4208
39737 Paseo Padre Pkwy Fremont (94538) ***(G-27646)***
Sign of Dove..........916 786-3277
707 Sunrise Ave Ofc Roseville (95661) ***(G-11203)***
Signal Pharmaceuticals LLC..........858 795-4700
10300 Campus Point Dr # 100 San Diego (92121) ***(G-8295)***
Signaldemand Inc..........415 356-0800
101 Montgomery St Ste 400 San Francisco (94104) ***(G-15454)***
Signalfx Inc..........888 958-5950
60 E 3rd Ave Ste 400 San Mateo (94401) ***(G-16186)***
Signature Athletic Club The, Carmichael *Also called Wenmat Inc* ***(G-25597)***
Signature Building Maint Inc..........408 377-8066
1330 White Oaks Rd Campbell (95008) ***(G-14430)***
Signature Consultants LLC..........310 229-5731
8560 W Sunset Blvd Los Angeles (90069) ***(G-28056)***

Signature Consultants LLC 415 544-7510
44 Montgomery St Ste 1450 San Francisco (94104) ***(G-28160)***
Signature Flight Support Corp 559 981-2490
3050 N Winery Ave Fresno (93703) ***(G-4934)***
Signature Flight Support Corp 650 877-6800
1052 N Access Rd San Francisco (94128) ***(G-4935)***
Signature Flight Support Corp 818 464-9500
7240 Hayvenhurst Ave Van Nuys (91406) ***(G-4936)***
Signature Flight Support Corp 562 997-0700
3333 E Spring St Ste 205 Long Beach (90806) ***(G-4937)***
Signature Flooring Inc 714 558-9200
701 N Hariton St Orange (92868) ***(G-3130)***
Signature Floors, Orange *Also called Signature Flooring Inc* ***(G-3130)***
Signature Interiors Inc 951 340-2200
1587 E Bentley Dr Ste 101 Corona (92879) ***(G-1260)***
Signature Painting & Cnstr Inc 925 287-0444
1565 3rd Ave Walnut Creek (94597) ***(G-1859)***
Signature Properties Inc 925 463-1122
4670 Willow Rd Ste 200 Pleasanton (94588) ***(G-12010)***
Signature Resources Ins/Fncl 949 794-0800
16755 Von Karman Ave # 200 Irvine (92606) ***(G-10872)***
Signature Services 949 851-9391
4425 Jamboree Rd Ste 250 Newport Beach (92660) ***(G-11048)***
Signatures Sni, San Francisco *Also called Live Nation Merchandise Inc* ***(G-9277)***
Signet Armorlite Inc (HQ) 760 744-4000
5803 Newton Dr Ste A Carlsbad (92008) ***(G-23058)***
Signet Testing Labs Inc (HQ) 510 887-8484
3526 Breakwater Ct Hayward (94545) ***(G-17489)***
Significant Cleaning Svcs LLC 408 559-5959
1855 Hamilton Ave Ste 104 San Jose (95125) ***(G-14431)***
Signon San Diego, San Diego *Also called Copley Press Inc* ***(G-15629)***
Sigos LLC (HQ) 650 376-3033
777 Mariners Island Blvd San Mateo (94404) ***(G-16187)***
Sigue Corporation (PA) 818 837-5939
13190 Telfair Ave Sylmar (91342) ***(G-17490)***
Silent Valley Club Inc 951 849-4501
46305 Poppet Flats Rd Banning (92220) ***(G-13483)***
Silicatec Rentals Inc 209 234-1500
800 Mossdale Rd Lathrop (95330) ***(G-14580)***
Silicon Prime Technologies Inc 310 279-0222
4154 W 172nd St Torrance (90504) ***(G-15455)***
Silicon Space Inc 858 751-0200
8765 Aero Dr Ste 226 San Diego (92123) ***(G-15456)***
Silicon Valley Bank 408 654-7730
3005 Jasmine Dr Pleasanton (94588) ***(G-9422)***
Silicon Valley Bank 818 382-2600
15260 Ventura Blvd # 1800 Sherman Oaks (91403) ***(G-9423)***
Silicon Valley Bank 415 610-4855
58 Commercial St Sunnyvale (94085) ***(G-9560)***
Silicon Valley Bank (HQ) 408 654-7400
3003 Tasman Dr Santa Clara (95054) ***(G-9561)***
Silicon Valley Clean Water 650 591-7121
1400 Radio Rd Redwood City (94065) ***(G-6416)***
Silicon Valley Hwang LLC 408 452-0200
1471 N 4th St San Jose (95112) ***(G-13255)***
Silicon Valley Mechanical Inc 408 943-0380
2115 Ringwood Ave San Jose (95131) ***(G-2367)***
Silicon Valley Monterey Bay Co 209 965-3432
29211 Highway 108 Long Barn (95335) ***(G-13470)***
Silicon Valley Office, Menlo Park *Also called Winston & Strawn LLP* ***(G-23630)***
Silicon Valley Power, Santa Clara *Also called City of Santa Clara* ***(G-6116)***
Silicon Vly Cmnty Foundation 650 450-5400
2440 W El Camin Mountain View (94040) ***(G-25349)***
Silicon Vly Educatn Foundation 408 790-9400
1400 Parkmoor Ave Ste 200 San Jose (95126) ***(G-24977)***
Silicon Vly McRelectronics Inc (PA) 408 844-7100
2985 Kifer Rd Santa Clara (95051) ***(G-7632)***
Silicon Vly SEC & Patrol Inc (PA) 408 267-1539
1131 Luchessi Dr Ste 2 San Jose (95118) ***(G-16825)***
Siliconexpert Technologies 408 330-7575
2975 Scott Blvd Ste 100 Santa Clara (95054) ***(G-16188)***
Siliconsystems Inc 949 900-9400
26840 Aliso Viejo Pkwy # 1 Aliso Viejo (92656) ***(G-7473)***
Siliconware Usa Inc (HQ) 408 573-5500
1735 Tech Dr Ste 300 Fl 3 San Jose (95110) ***(G-7633)***
Silk Botanica Inc 415 594-0888
304 Shaw Rd South San Francisco (94080) ***(G-9212)***
Silla Automotive LLC 818 902-0334
7336 Laurel Canyon Blvd North Hollywood (91605) ***(G-6763)***
Silla Automotive LLC (PA) 800 624-1499
1217 W Artesia Blvd Compton (90220) ***(G-6764)***
Silla Automotive LLC 916 929-2646
1554 Juliesse Ave C-D Sacramento (95815) ***(G-6765)***
Silla Automotive LLC 323 733-5027
2833 W Pico Blvd Los Angeles (90006) ***(G-6766)***
Silla Automotive LLC 619 424-7752
1616 Industrial Blvd Chula Vista (91911) ***(G-6767)***
Silla Automotive LLC 661 392-8880
1901 Mineral Ct Ste C Bakersfield (93308) ***(G-6768)***
Silla Automotive LLC 909 624-2801
5199 Brooks St Ste G Montclair (91763) ***(G-6769)***
Silla Automotive LLC 209 577-5089
1295 N Emerald Ave Ste H Modesto (95351) ***(G-6770)***
Silla Automotive LLC 559 457-0711
2695 S Cherry Ave Ste 118 Fresno (93706) ***(G-6771)***
Silla Cooling System, Compton *Also called Silla Automotive LLC* ***(G-6764)***
Sillcrest Nursing Home, San Bernardino *Also called Marna Health Services Inc* ***(G-22996)***
Silliker Labs Group Inc 714 226-0000
6360 Gateway Dr Cypress (90630) ***(G-26889)***

Silman Construction, San Leandro *Also called Silman Venture Corporation* ***(G-1465)***
Silman Venture Corporation (PA) 510 347-4800
1600 Factor Ave San Leandro (94577) ***(G-1465)***
Silv Communication Inc 213 381-7999
3460 Wilshire Blvd # 1100 Los Angeles (90010) ***(G-28057)***
Silva Farms, Gonzales *Also called Ed Silva* ***(G-61)***
Silva Trucking Inc 209 982-1114
36 W Mathews Rd French Camp (95231) ***(G-4066)***
Silver Cinemas Acquisition Co (PA) 310 473-6701
2222 S Barrington Ave Los Angeles (90064) ***(G-18352)***
Silver Creek Home Owners 408 559-1977
1935 Dry Creek Rd Ste 203 Campbell (95008) ***(G-27211)***
Silver Creek Industries Inc 951 943-5393
2830 Barrett Ave Perris (92571) ***(G-1668)***
Silver Creek Vly Cntry CLB Inc 408 239-5775
5460 Country Club Pkwy San Jose (95138) ***(G-19080)***
Silver Crk Vlly Ctry CLB HM Ow, Campbell *Also called Silver Creek Home Owners* ***(G-27211)***
Silver Fredman A Prof Law Corp 310 556-2356
2029 Century Park E # 1900 Los Angeles (90067) ***(G-23571)***
Silver Lake Financial, San Francisco *Also called Silver Lake Partners II LP* ***(G-12146)***
Silver Lake Medical Center, Los Angeles *Also called Success Healthcare 1 LLC* ***(G-22574)***
Silver Lake Partners LP (PA) 650 233-8120
2775 Sand Hill Rd Ste 100 Menlo Park (94025) ***(G-12144)***
Silver Lake Partners II LP 408 454-4732
10080 N Wolfe Rd Sw3190 Cupertino (95014) ***(G-12145)***
Silver Lake Partners II LP 415 293-4355
1 Market Plz San Francisco (94105) ***(G-12146)***
Silver Lakes Association 760 245-1606
15273 Orchard Hill Ln Helendale (92342) ***(G-25350)***
Silver Oak Wine Cellars LP 707 857-3562
1183 Dunaweal Ln Calistoga (94515) ***(G-9109)***
Silver Rock Resort Golf Club 760 777-8884
79179 Ahmanson Ln La Quinta (92253) ***(G-18787)***
Silver Saddle Ranch & Club Inc 760 373-8617
20751 Aristotle Dr California City (93505) ***(G-12011)***
Silver Service, San Andreas *Also called Mark Twain Medical Center* ***(G-21727)***
Silver Spring Networks Inc (PA) 669 770-4000
230 W Tasman Dr San Jose (95134) ***(G-6088)***
Silver Spur Christian Camp 209 928-4248
17301 Silver Spur Dr Tuolumne (95379) ***(G-13471)***
Silver Strand 818 701-9707
8945 Fullbright Ave Chatsworth (91311) ***(G-3092)***
Silverado Contractors Inc (PA) 510 658-9960
2855 Mandela Pkwy Fl 2 Oakland (94608) ***(G-3468)***
Silverado Country CLB & Resort 707 257-0200
1303 Jefferson St 300a NAPA (94559) ***(G-19081)***
Silverado Energy Company 949 752-5588
18101 Von Karman Ave Irvine (92612) ***(G-6207)***
Silverado Orchards (PA) 707 963-1461
601 Pope St Ofc Saint Helena (94574) ***(G-11204)***
Silverado Rsort Svcs Group LLC 707 257-0200
1600 Atlas Peak Rd NAPA (94558) ***(G-13256)***
Silverado Senior Living Inc 424 257-6418
514 N Prospect Ave # 120 Redondo Beach (90277) ***(G-20916)***
Silverado Senior Living Inc (PA) 949 240-7200
6400 Oak Cyn Ste 200 Irvine (92618) ***(G-21371)***
Silverado Senior Living Inc 818 848-4048
601 S Glenoaks Blvd # 201 Burbank (91502) ***(G-21109)***
Silverado Senior Living Inc 626 650-9891
125 W Sierra Madre Ave Azusa (91702) ***(G-21372)***
Silverado Senior Living Inc 949 945-0189
350 W Bay St Costa Mesa (92627) ***(G-21373)***
Silverado Senior Living Inc 626 872-3941
1118 N Stoneman Ave Alhambra (91801) ***(G-21374)***
Silverado Senior Living Inc 760 456-5137
1500 Borden Rd Escondido (92026) ***(G-21375)***
Silverado Senior Living Inc 760 270-9917
335 Saxony Rd Encinitas (92024) ***(G-21376)***
Silverado Senior Living Inc 657 888-5752
240 E 3rd St Tustin (92780) ***(G-24811)***
Silverado Senior Living Inc 323 984-7313
330 N Hayworth Ave Los Angeles (90048) ***(G-21377)***
Silvergate San Marcos, San Marcos *Also called Americare Hlth Retirement Inc* ***(G-10958)***
Silverline Construction Inc 310 464-8314
1421 W 132nd St Gardena (90249) ***(G-1669)***
Silverscreen Healthcare Inc 909 793-1382
1875 Barton Rd Redlands (92373) ***(G-21378)***
Silverscreen Healthcare Inc 818 763-8247
10830 Oxnard St North Hollywood (91606) ***(G-20917)***
Silverwood Landscape Cnstr Inc 714 427-6134
2209 S Lyon St Santa Ana (92705) ***(G-955)***
Silvestri Studio Inc 323 277-0800
8830 Miner St Los Angeles (90002) ***(G-7229)***
SIM Investment Corporation 408 445-3310
1329 Blossom Hill Rd San Jose (95118) ***(G-18681)***
Simas Floor Co Inc (PA) 916 452-4933
3550 Power Inn Rd Sacramento (95826) ***(G-3131)***
Simas Floor Co Design Center, Sacramento *Also called Simas Floor Co Inc* ***(G-3131)***
Simbol Inc (PA) 925 226-7400
6920 Koll Center Pkwy # 216 Pleasanton (94566) ***(G-26607)***
Simbol Materials, Pleasanton *Also called Simbol Inc* ***(G-26607)***
Simco Electronics (PA) 408 734-9750
3131 Jay St Ste 100 Santa Clara (95054) ***(G-26890)***
Simi Hills Golf Course, Simi Valley *Also called American Golf Corporation* ***(G-18872)***
Simi Radiology & Imaging 805 522-5978
4100 Guardian St Ste 205 Simi Valley (93063) ***(G-27647)***
Simi Valley Family YMCA, Simi Valley *Also called Young Mens Christian Asso* ***(G-19312)***
Simi Valley Plaza 10, Simi Valley *Also called Edwards Theatres Circuit Inc* ***(G-18335)***
Simi Vly Care & Rehabilitation, Simi Valley *Also called Chase Group Llc* ***(G-27379)***

ALPHABETIC SECTION

Simi Vly Hosp & Hlth Care Svcs (HQ) 805 955-6000
2975 Sycamore Dr Simi Valley (93065) *(G-20353)*
Simi West Inc 805 583-2000
999 Enchanted Way Simi Valley (93065) *(G-13257)*
Simmons Construction Inc 661 636-1321
19252 Flypath Way Bakersfield (93308) *(G-1670)*
Simon and Gladstone A Prof, Marina Del Rey *Also called Berger Kahn (G-23110)*
Simon Mrtn-Vgue Wnklstein Mris, San Francisco *Also called A Smwm California Corporation (G-26159)*
Simone Fruit Co Inc 559 275-1368
8008 W Shields Ave Fresno (93723) *(G-586)*
Simoni & Massoni Farms 925 634-2304
2510 Taylor Ln Byron (94514) *(G-8)*
Simonich Corporation (HQ) 925 830-1500
3130 Crow Canyon Pl # 300 San Ramon (94583) *(G-9951)*
Simons Wholesale Bakery Inc 714 259-0855
1901 Ritchey St Santa Ana (92705) *(G-8921)*
Simora Trading, Torrance *Also called Makkunis Inc (G-8124)*
Simple Luxuries LLC 310 627-6514
1560 N Sycamore Ave Rialto (92376) *(G-3330)*
Simplehuman LLC (PA) 310 436-2250
19850 Magellan Dr Torrance (90502) *(G-6886)*
Simplexgrinnell LP 805 642-0366
1868 Palma Dr Ventura (93003) *(G-2368)*
Simplexgrinnell LP 562 405-3817
12728 Shoemaker Ave Santa Fe Springs (90670) *(G-16927)*
Simplexgrinnell LP 707 578-3212
3077 Wiljan Ct Ste B Santa Rosa (95407) *(G-2369)*
Simplexgrinnell LP 760 336-0109
1099 Industry Way El Centro (92243) *(G-7474)*
Simplot Growers Solutions, Firebaugh *Also called JR Simplot Company (G-475)*
Simpson & Simpson 213 736-6664
633 W 5th St Ste 3320 Los Angeles (90071) *(G-27212)*
Simpson Delmore and Greene LLP (PA) 619 515-1194
600 W Broadway Ste 400 San Diego (92101) *(G-23572)*
Simpson Gumpertz & Heger Inc 415 495-3700
100 Pine St Ste 1600 San Francisco (94111) *(G-26067)*
Simpson Gumpertz & Heger Inc 510 835-0705
500 12th St Oakland (94607) *(G-26068)*
Simpson Strong-Tie Intl Inc 925 560-9000
5956 W Las Positas Blvd Pleasanton (94588) *(G-7403)*
Simpson Thacher & Bartlett LLP 650 251-5000
2475 Hanover St Palo Alto (94304) *(G-23573)*
Sims Group USA Corporation 408 494-4242
1900 Monterey Hwy San Jose (95112) *(G-8085)*
Sims Group USA Corporation (HQ) 510 412-5300
600 S 4th St Richmond (94804) *(G-8086)*
Sims Group USA Corporation 510 236-0606
600 S 4th St Richmond (94804) *(G-8087)*
Sims/LMC Recyclers, San Jose *Also called Sims Group USA Corporation (G-8085)*
Simsmetal America, Richmond *Also called Sims Group USA Corporation (G-8086)*
Sinai Temple 323 469-6000
5950 Forest Lawn Dr Los Angeles (90068) *(G-13715)*
Sinanian Development Inc 818 996-9666
18980 Ventura Blvd # 200 Tarzana (91356) *(G-1671)*
Sinclair Companies 619 238-1818
1055 2nd Ave San Diego (92101) *(G-13258)*
Sinclair Concrete 916 663-0303
7205 Church St Penryn (95663) *(G-3331)*
Singapore Airlines Cargo Pte 650 876-7363
710 Mcdonald Rd San Francisco (94128) *(G-4819)*
Singapore Airlines Limited 310 647-1922
222 N Sepulveda Blvd # 1600 El Segundo (90245) *(G-4820)*
Singerlewak LLP (PA) 310 477-3924
10960 Wilshire Blvd Los Angeles (90024) *(G-26442)*
Singerlewak LLP 949 261-8600
2050 Main St Ste 700 Irvine (92614) *(G-26443)*
Singerlewak LLP 818 999-3924
21550 Oxnard St Ste 1000 Woodland Hills (91367) *(G-26444)*
Singley Enterprises (PA) 916 427-4573
2901 Duluth St West Sacramento (95691) *(G-6962)*
Sintex Security Services Inc 510 208-0474
650 W 20th St Merced (95340) *(G-28161)*
Sion & Shamoneil Fmly Partner, Vernon *Also called Bobco Metals LLC (G-7361)*
Sioux City Ht & Conference Ctr, Escondido *Also called Choa Hope LLC (G-12515)*
Sippi Anne Riverside Ranch LLP 661 871-9697
18200 Highway 178 Bakersfield (93306) *(G-24812)*
Sir Francis Drake Hotel, San Francisco *Also called Huskies Lessee LLC (G-12806)*
Sir Francis Drake Hotel, San Francisco *Also called Sfd Partners LLC (G-13236)*
Siracusa Enterprises Inc 818 831-1130
17737 Chtswrth St Ste 200 Granada Hills (91344) *(G-14786)*
Sirva Inc 925 824-3109
2010 Crow Canyon Pl San Ramon (94583) *(G-4263)*
Sisa, Mountain View *Also called Samsung Research America Inc (G-26597)*
Sisco Family Connection, Milpitas *Also called Bright Horizons Chld Ctrs LLC (G-24418)*
Siskiyou Development Company 530 938-2731
88 S Weed Blvd Edgewood (96094) *(G-13259)*
Siskiyou Hospital Inc 530 842-4121
444 Bruce St Yreka (96097) *(G-21894)*
Siskiyou Lake Golf Resort Inc 530 926-3030
1000 Siskiyou Lake Blvd Mount Shasta (96067) *(G-18788)*
Siskiyou Opportunity Center 530 842-4110
321 N Gold St Yreka (96097) *(G-14787)*
Siskiyou Opportunity Center (PA) 530 926-4698
1516 S Mount Shasta Blvd Mount Shasta (96067) *(G-24387)*
Sissc, Ridgecrest *Also called Leidos Inc (G-16151)*
Sisters of Nazareth 415 479-8282
245 Nova Albion Way San Rafael (94903) *(G-21379)*
Sisters of Nzareth Los Angeles 310 839-2361
3333 Manning Ave Los Angeles (90064) *(G-24813)*
Sisters of St Joseph Orange 707 257-4124
980 Trancas St Ste 9 NAPA (94558) *(G-22565)*
Sita Ram LLC 209 223-0211
200 S State Highway 49 Jackson (95642) *(G-13260)*
Site 210, Pacheco *Also called Pleasant Hl Byshore Dspsal Inc (G-6514)*
Site 910, Santa Barbara *Also called BFI Waste Systems N Amer Inc (G-6440)*
Site 916, Fremont *Also called BFI Waste Systems N Amer Inc (G-6442)*
Site Crew Inc 714 668-0100
3185 Airway Ave Ste G Costa Mesa (92626) *(G-14432)*
Site L69, Milpitas *Also called Interntional Disposal Corp Cal (G-6491)*
Site R45, Milpitas *Also called Browning-Ferris Industries Inc (G-6446)*
Site R46, San Carlos *Also called Browning-Ferris Inds Cal Inc (G-6445)*
Sitelite Holdings Inc 949 265-6200
111 Theory Fl 2 Irvine (92617) *(G-16479)*
Sitestuff Yardi Systems I 805 966-3666
430 S Fairview Ave Goleta (93117) *(G-27648)*
Sitoa 916 444-0008
6900 Airport Blvd Sacramento (95837) *(G-3869)*
Sitrick Brincko Group LLC 310 788-2850
1840 Century Park E # 800 Los Angeles (90067) *(G-27649)*
Situs Holdings LLC 415 374-2820
2 Embarcadero Ctr # 1300 San Francisco (94111) *(G-12345)*
Sitv Inc 323 317-9534
700 N Central Ave Ste 600 Glendale (91203) *(G-5910)*
Six Continents Hotels Inc 310 371-8525
19901 Prairie Ave Torrance (90503) *(G-13261)*
Six Continents Hotels Inc 818 989-5010
8244 Orion Ave Van Nuys (91406) *(G-13262)*
Six Continents Hotels Inc 213 748-1291
1020 S Figueroa St Los Angeles (90015) *(G-13263)*
Six Continents Hotels Inc 310 781-9100
19800 S Vermont Ave Torrance (90502) *(G-13264)*
Six Continents Hotels Inc 619 232-3861
1355 N Harbor Dr San Diego (92101) *(G-13265)*
Six Continents Hotels Inc 925 847-6000
11950 Dublin Canyon Rd # 609 Pleasanton (94588) *(G-13266)*
Six Continents Hotels Inc 619 795-4000
1110 A St San Diego (92101) *(G-13267)*
Six Continents Hotels Inc 619 474-2800
700 National City Blvd National City (91950) *(G-13268)*
Six Flags Discovery Kingdom, Vallejo *Also called Six Flags Entertainment Corp (G-18833)*
Six Flags Discovery Kingdom, Vallejo *Also called Park Management Corp (G-18829)*
Six Flags Entertainment Corp 707 644-6000
2001 Fairgrounds Dr Vallejo (94589) *(G-18833)*
Six Flags Entertainment Corp 916 924-3747
1600 Exposition Blvd Sacramento (95815) *(G-18834)*
Six Flags Magic Mountain, Valencia *Also called Magic Mountain LLC (G-18413)*
Six Per Cent Management 310 399-2611
2800 Neilson Way Apt 601 Santa Monica (90405) *(G-27213)*
Six Point Harness 323 462-3344
1759 Glendale Blvd Los Angeles (90026) *(G-18253)*
Six Rivers National Bank (HQ) 707 443-8400
402 F St Eureka (95501) *(G-9424)*
Six Rivers Planned Parenthood 707 442-5700
3225 Timber Fall Ct Eureka (95503) *(G-24978)*
SJ Distributors Inc (PA) 888 988-2328
625 Vista Way Milpitas (95035) *(G-8570)*
Sj Hotel Manager LLC 401 946-4600
350 W Santa Clara St San Jose (95113) *(G-27214)*
SJHS SONOMA COUNTY, Santa Rosa *Also called Santa Rosa Memorial Hospital (G-21861)*
Sjsu Foundation 408 924-1410
210 N 4th St Ste 300 San Jose (95112) *(G-25576)*
Sjvi, Fresno *Also called San Joaquin Valley Intergrp (G-25573)*
SJW Corp (PA) 408 279-7800
110 W Taylor St San Jose (95110) *(G-6403)*
Sk Hynix America Inc (HQ) 408 232-8000
3101 N 1st St San Jose (95134) *(G-7634)*
Sk Hynix Memory Solutions Inc 408 514-3500
3103 N 1st St San Jose (95134) *(G-16480)*
Sk Sanctuary Day Spa Salon LLC 858 459-2400
6919 La Jolla Blvd La Jolla (92037) *(G-18682)*
SK&a, Irvine *Also called S K & A Information Svcs Inc (G-26705)*
Skadden Arps Slate Meagher & F 213 687-5000
300 S Grand Ave Ste 3400 Los Angeles (90071) *(G-23574)*
Skanska Rocky Mountain Dst, Riverside *Also called Skanska USA Civil West Rocky M (G-2085)*
Skanska USA Civil West Rocky M (HQ) 970 565-8000
1995 Agua Mansa Rd Riverside (92509) *(G-2085)*
Skanska USA Cvil W Cal Dst Inc (HQ) 951 684-5360
1995 Agua Mansa Rd Riverside (92509) *(G-1860)*
Skanska USA Cvil W Cal Dst Inc 760 342-8004
88200 Fargo Cnyn Rd Coachella (92236) *(G-1861)*
Skanska-Rados A Joint Venture 213 978-0600
11390 W Olympic Blvd Los Angeles (90064) *(G-1862)*
Skate Enterprises Inc 562 924-0911
12356 Central Ave Chino (91710) *(G-19283)*
Skatetown, Roseville *Also called Roseville Sportworld Inc (G-19272)*
Skava, San Francisco *Also called Kallidus inc (G-15266)*
Skeffington Enterprises Inc 714 540-1700
2200 S Yale St Santa Ana (92704) *(G-12090)*
Skidmore Owings & Merrill LLP 415 981-1555
1 Front St Ste 2500 San Francisco (94111) *(G-26250)*
Skidmore Owings & Merrill LLP 310 651-9924
10100 Santa Monica Blvd Beverly Hills (90210) *(G-26251)*
Skidmore Owings & Merrill LLP 213 996-8366
555 W 5th St Fl 30 Los Angeles (90013) *(G-26252)*

Skilled Healthcare LLC.......................................323 663-3951
5154 W Sunset Blvd Los Angeles (90027) ***(G-20918)***
Skilled Nursing Facility, Taft *Also called West Side District Hospital* ***(G-22029)***
Skin Health Experts Medic.......................................310 623-6869
144 S Beverly Dr Ste 500 Beverly Hills (90212) ***(G-22832)***
Skirball Cultural Center.......................................310 440-4500
2701 N Sepulveda Blvd Los Angeles (90049) ***(G-25577)***
Skire Inc.......................................650 289-2600
500 Oracle Pkwy Redwood City (94065) ***(G-15457)***
Skitch, Redwood City *Also called Evernote Corporation* ***(G-5599)***
Skoll Foundation.......................................650 331-1031
250 University Ave Lbby Palo Alto (94301) ***(G-25578)***
Skunk Train, The, Woodland *Also called Mendocino Railway* ***(G-5121)***
Sky Chefs Inc.......................................650 652-7886
1845 Rollins Rd Burlingame (94010) ***(G-4639)***
Sky Court USA Inc.......................................805 497-9991
880 S Westlake Blvd Westlake Village (91361) ***(G-13269)***
Sky King, Sacramento *Also called Lukenbill Enterprises* ***(G-4815)***
Sky Park Gardens Assisted.......................................916 422-5650
5510 Sky Pkwy Ofc Sacramento (95823) ***(G-24814)***
Sky Scan Satelite Systems.......................................909 322-1393
9994 Willowbrook Rd Riverside (92509) ***(G-6016)***
Sky West Golf Course, Hayward *Also called Hayward Area Recreation Pkdist* ***(G-18744)***
Skyblue Sewing Manufacturing.......................................415 777-9978
960 Mission St Fl 2 San Francisco (94103) ***(G-17491)***
Skygroup Investments LLC.......................................619 432-4359
2385 Camino Del Rio N San Diego (92108) ***(G-19284)***
Skyhigh Networks Inc.......................................408 564-0278
900 E Hamilton Ave # 400 Campbell (95008) ***(G-16928)***
Skyhill Financial Inc.......................................714 657-3938
7071 Warner Ave Ste F378 Huntington Beach (92647) ***(G-11845)***
Skylar Film Studios LLC.......................................424 653-8902
13589 Mindanao Way # 11 Marina Del Rey (90292) ***(G-18254)***
Skyles Insurance Agency.......................................916 361-9585
9840 Business Park Dr Sacramento (95827) ***(G-10873)***
Skylight Convalescent Center, Long Beach *Also called Reynolds Health Industries* ***(G-21359)***
Skylight Halthcare Systems Inc.......................................858 523-3700
10935 Vista Sorrento Pkwy # 350 San Diego (92130) ***(G-27650)***
Skyline Coml Interiors Inc (PA).......................................415 908-1020
731 Sansome St Fl 4 San Francisco (94111) ***(G-1672)***
Skyline Construction, San Francisco *Also called Skyline Coml Interiors Inc* ***(G-1672)***
Skyline Consulting Group.......................................650 529-3455
13186 Skyline Blvd Woodside (94062) ***(G-27651)***
Skyline Flwr Growers Shippers, Oxnard *Also called L J T Flowers Inc* ***(G-9140)***
Skyline Health Care Center, San Jose *Also called Mariner Health Care Inc* ***(G-20761)***
Skyline Health Care Ctr, Los Angeles *Also called Mariner Health Care Inc* ***(G-20762)***
Skyline Healthcare & Wellness.......................................323 665-1185
3032 Rowena Ave Los Angeles (90039) ***(G-20919)***
Skyline Healthcare Center, Los Angeles *Also called Skyline Healthcare & Wellness* ***(G-20919)***
Skyline Place, Sonora *Also called Sonora Retirement Center Inc* ***(G-24817)***
Skylstad-Schoelen Co Inc.......................................805 349-0503
3130 Skyway Dr Ste 701 Santa Maria (93455) ***(G-14433)***
Skyone Federal Credit Union (PA).......................................310 491-7500
14600 Aviation Blvd Hawthorne (90250) ***(G-9627)***
Skypark Inc.......................................650 875-6655
1000 San Mateo Ave San Bruno (94066) ***(G-13794)***
Skype Inc.......................................650 493-7900
1 Microsoft Way Redmond Palo Alto (94304) ***(G-5702)***
Skyva Construction Inc.......................................916 726-4999
5781 Old Antelope N Rd Antelope (95843) ***(G-1261)***
Skywest Airlines Inc.......................................951 926-9511
32128 Chagall Ct Winchester (92596) ***(G-4821)***
Skywest Airlines Inc.......................................951 600-9181
26818 Bahama Way Murrieta (92563) ***(G-4822)***
Slack Technologies Inc.......................................415 373-8825
155 5th St Fl 6 San Francisco (94103) ***(G-15837)***
Slade Gorton & Co Inc.......................................714 676-4200
1 Centerpointe Dr Ste 311 La Palma (90623) ***(G-8653)***
Slade Industrial Landscape Inc.......................................818 885-1916
8838 Zelzah Ave Sherwood Forest (91325) ***(G-798)***
Slakey Brothers Inc.......................................408 494-0460
1480 Nicora Ave San Jose (95133) ***(G-7747)***
Slant, South San Francisco *Also called Formation Brands LLC* ***(G-6861)***
Slate Creek Wind Project LLC.......................................888 903-6926
15445 Innovation Dr San Diego (92128) ***(G-6208)***
Slater Inc.......................................909 822-6800
11045 Rose Ave Fontana (92337) ***(G-2086)***
Slauson Plaza Med Group, Pico Rivera *Also called Altamed Health Services Corp* ***(G-22882)***
SLC Operating Ltd Partnership.......................................818 980-1212
333 Unversal Hollywood Dr North Hollywood (91608) ***(G-13795)***
Slch Inc (PA).......................................626 798-0558
1920 N Fair Oaks Ave Pasadena (91103) ***(G-20920)***
Sleepy Giant Entertainment Inc.......................................949 464-7986
4 San Joaquin Plz Ste 200 Newport Beach (92660) ***(G-15458)***
Sleepy Giant Entertainment Inc.......................................714 460-4113
3501 Jamboree Rd Ste 5000 Newport Beach (92660) ***(G-18495)***
Slide Go, Redlands *Also called Prime-Line Products Company* ***(G-7695)***
Slideco Recreation Inc.......................................530 246-9550
151 N Boulder Dr Redding (96003) ***(G-18835)***
Sling Media Inc (HQ).......................................650 293-8000
1051 E Hillsdale Blvd # 500 Foster City (94404) ***(G-5408)***
Slipgatte Ironworks, San Mateo *Also called Gazillion Inc* ***(G-15675)***
SLM Services, Simi Valley *Also called Specialized Landscape MGT Svcs* ***(G-958)***
SLO TRANSITIONS, San Luis Obispo *Also called Transitions - Mental Hlth Assn* ***(G-24257)***
SM 10000 Property LLC.......................................305 374-5700
10000 Santa Monica Blvd Los Angeles (90067) ***(G-12012)***
SM Broadway Corp.......................................626 301-1198
710 S Myrtle Ave Ste 285 Monrovia (91016) ***(G-12273)***
SM International, Fremont *Also called S & M Moving Systems* ***(G-4255)***
SM Uni Inc.......................................213 626-2557
8307 Elsmore Dr Rosemead (91770) ***(G-8654)***
SMA America, Rocklin *Also called SMA Solar Technology Amer LLC* ***(G-7635)***
SMA Builders Inc.......................................818 994-8306
16134 Leadwell St Van Nuys (91406) ***(G-1262)***
SMA Solar Technology Amer LLC (HQ).......................................916 625-0870
6020 W Oaks Blvd Rocklin (95765) ***(G-7635)***
Smachines, Santa Clara *Also called Soft Machines Inc* ***(G-16054)***
Smart & Final Holdings LLC.......................................310 843-1900
10205 Constellation Blvd Los Angeles (90067) ***(G-8519)***
Smart Choice Investments Inc.......................................310 944-6985
23332 Hawthorne Blvd # 203 Torrance (90505) ***(G-14788)***
Smart Energy Solar Inc.......................................951 273-9595
1641 Comm St Corona (92880) ***(G-2370)***
Smart Energy Systems LLC (PA).......................................909 703-9609
19900 Macarthur Blvd Irvine (92612) ***(G-15459)***
Smart Energy Systems LLC.......................................909 703-9609
Michelson Dr Ste 3370 Irvine (92612) ***(G-15460)***
Smart Energy USA, Corona *Also called Smart Energy Solar Inc* ***(G-2370)***
Smart Living Company (PA).......................................805 578-5500
4100 Guardian St Simi Valley (93063) ***(G-9303)***
Smart Management & Companies.......................................916 392-3000
1501 Corp Way Ste 200 Sacramento (95831) ***(G-27215)***
Smart Systems Technologies (PA).......................................949 367-9375
9 Goodyear Irvine (92618) ***(G-6209)***
Smartcues Inc, Mountain View *Also called Spotcues Inc* ***(G-7194)***
Smartdrive Systems Inc.......................................866 933-9930
9450 Carroll Park Dr San Diego (92121) ***(G-8140)***
Smartplay, Inc., San Jose *Also called N A Aricent Inc* ***(G-15319)***
Smartrecruiters Inc.......................................415 508-3755
56 Tehama St San Francisco (94105) ***(G-14789)***
Smartrevenuecom Inc.......................................203 733-9156
101 Cooper St Ste 205 Santa Cruz (95060) ***(G-26706)***
Smartzip Analytics Inc.......................................925 218-1900
6210 Stoneridge Mall Rd # 100 Pleasanton (94588) ***(G-11846)***
Smashon Inc.......................................855 762-7466
1754 Tech Dr Ste 234 San Jose (95110) ***(G-16481)***
SMC Corporation of America.......................................408 943-9600
2841 Junction Ave Ste 110 San Jose (95134) ***(G-7888)***
SMC Networks Inc (HQ).......................................949 679-8000
20 Mason Irvine (92618) ***(G-7187)***
Smci, Costa Mesa *Also called Software Management Cons Inc* ***(G-15464)***
Smci, Glendale *Also called Software Management Cons Inc* ***(G-16484)***
Smf Clinical Lab, Sacramento *Also called Sutter Health* ***(G-25364)***
Smg.......................................310 432-2893
225 E Broadway 312 Glendale (91205) ***(G-11049)***
Smg Food and Beverage LLC (PA).......................................909 937-3000
2000 E Convention Ctr Way Ontario (91764) ***(G-17492)***
Smg Holdings Inc.......................................650 738-8737
747 Howard St San Francisco (94103) ***(G-11050)***
Smg Holdings Inc.......................................559 445-8100
848 M St Fl 2nd Fresno (93721) ***(G-17493)***
Smg Holdings Inc.......................................760 325-6611
277 N Avenida Caballeros Palm Springs (92262) ***(G-27652)***
Smg Holdings Inc.......................................562 436-3636
300 E Ocean Blvd Long Beach (90802) ***(G-11051)***
Smg Management Facility, Ontario *Also called Ontario Convention Center Corp* ***(G-17378)***
Smg Stone Company Inc.......................................818 767-0000
8460 San Fernando Rd Sun Valley (91352) ***(G-2834)***
Smile Brands Group Inc (PA).......................................714 668-1300
100 Spectrum Center Dr # 1500 Irvine (92618) ***(G-27216)***
Smile Housing Corporation.......................................805 772-6066
800 Quintana Rd Ste 2c Morro Bay (93442) ***(G-22833)***
Smile Keepers, Inglewood *Also called Interdent Inc* ***(G-20256)***
Smile Wide Dental, Irvine *Also called Universal Care Inc* ***(G-22858)***
Smisc Holdings.......................................707 938-8448
Hwy 121 Sonoma (95476) ***(G-18575)***
Smith & Sons Investment Co.......................................949 646-9648
735 Ohms Way Costa Mesa (92627) ***(G-11847)***
Smith Barney, Los Angeles *Also called Citigroup Global Markets Inc* ***(G-9973)***
Smith Barney, Torrance *Also called Citigroup Global Markets Inc* ***(G-9978)***
Smith Barney, Irvine *Also called Citigroup Global Markets Inc* ***(G-9979)***
Smith Barney, La Jolla *Also called Citigroup Global Markets Inc* ***(G-9980)***
Smith Barney, Rllng HLS Est *Also called Citigroup Global Markets Inc* ***(G-9982)***
Smith Barneys, Menlo Park *Also called Citigroup Global Markets Inc* ***(G-9984)***
Smith Broadcasting Group Inc (PA).......................................805 965-0400
2315 Red Rose Way Santa Barbara (93109) ***(G-27217)***
Smith Broadcasting Group Inc.......................................805 882-3933
730 Miramonte Dr Santa Barbara (93109) ***(G-5911)***
Smith Brothers Restaurant Inc.......................................626 577-2400
100 Corson St Lbby Pasadena (91103) ***(G-27218)***
Smith Coleman Inc.......................................310 671-8271
707 N La Brea Ave Inglewood (90302) ***(G-11848)***
Smith Electric Service, Santa Maria *Also called Brannon Inc* ***(G-1408)***
Smith Micro Software Inc (PA).......................................949 362-5800
51 Columbia Aliso Viejo (92656) ***(G-15838)***
Smith Packing Inc.......................................805 343-0329
680 S Simas Rd Santa Maria (93455) ***(G-9304)***
Smith Ranch.......................................530 695-2521
1671 Campbell Rd Live Oak (95953) ***(G-250)***
Smith Residential Care Fcilty (PA).......................................559 584-8451
318 E 4th St Hanford (93230) ***(G-22566)***

ALPHABETIC

ALPHABETIC SECTION
Softworks, Huntington Beach

Smith River Lucky 7 Casino....707 487-7777
350 N Indian Rd Smith River (95567) ***(G-13270)***
Smith-Emery Company (PA)....213 745-5312
781 E Washington Blvd Los Angeles (90021) ***(G-27653)***
Smith-Emery San Francisco Inc....415 642-7326
1940 Oakdale Ave San Francisco (94124) ***(G-17494)***
Smithgroup California, San Francisco *Also called Smithgroupjjr Inc* ***(G-26253)***
Smithgroupjjr Inc....313 442-8351
301 Battery St Fl 7 San Francisco (94111) ***(G-26253)***
Smitty Transportation, Lake Forest *Also called Miguelito Manpower Inc* ***(G-4229)***
SMK America Group, Chula Vista *Also called SMK Electronics Corp USA* ***(G-7475)***
SMK Electronics Corp USA (HQ)....619 216-6400
1055 Tierra Del Rey Chula Vista (91910) ***(G-7475)***
Smoke Tree Inc....760 327-1221
1850 Smoke Tree Ln Palm Springs (92264) ***(G-13271)***
Smoke Tree Ranch, Palm Springs *Also called Smoke Tree Inc* ***(G-13271)***
SMS Transportation....310 527-9200
18516 S Broadway Gardena (90248) ***(G-23575)***
SMS Transportation Svcs Inc....213 489-5367
865 S Figueroa St # 2750 Los Angeles (90017) ***(G-3718)***
Smud Energy Services, Sacramento *Also called Sacramento Municpl Utility Dst* ***(G-6202)***
Smuk Inc....323 904-4680
3800 Barham Blvd Ste 410 Los Angeles (90068) ***(G-18150)***
Snackademic, San Francisco *Also called Cesar Chavez Student Center* ***(G-10970)***
Snap Inc....310 745-0632
579 Toyopa Dr Pacific Palisades (90272) ***(G-15839)***
Snap Inc (PA)....310 399-3339
63 Market St Venice (90291) ***(G-15840)***
Snap Technologies Inc....626 585-6900
130 W Union St Pasadena (91103) ***(G-27654)***
Snap-On Incorporated....626 965-0668
19220 San Jose Ave City of Industry (91748) ***(G-7698)***
Snap-On Tools, City of Industry *Also called Snap-On Incorporated* ***(G-7698)***
Snapchat, Venice *Also called Snap Inc* ***(G-15840)***
Snapdragon Place 1 LP....805 659-3791
702 County Square Dr Ventura (93003) ***(G-11205)***
Snapnrack Inc....877 732-2860
775 Fiero Ln Ste 200 San Luis Obispo (93401) ***(G-7731)***
Sneary Construction Inc....909 982-1833
1182 Monte Vista Ave # 2 Upland (91786) ***(G-2980)***
Snell & Wilmer LLP....714 427-7000
600 Anton Blvd Ste 1400 Costa Mesa (92626) ***(G-23576)***
Snelling Employment LLC....510 769-4400
2203 Harvbor Bay Pkwy Alameda (94502) ***(G-14790)***
Snf Management....310 385-1090
9200 W Sunset Blvd # 700 West Hollywood (90069) ***(G-27219)***
Snoozie Shavings Inc (HQ)....707 464-6186
525 Elk Valley Rd Crescent City (95531) ***(G-4264)***
Snow Creek Resort, Mammoth Lakes *Also called Snowcreek Property Management* ***(G-11849)***
Snow Summit Mountain Resort, Big Bear City *Also called Snow Summit Ski Corporation* ***(G-19285)***
Snow Summit Ski Corporation (PA)....909 866-5766
880 Summit Blvd Big Bear Lake (92315) ***(G-13272)***
Snow Summit Ski Corporation....909 585-2517
43101 Goldmine Dr Big Bear City (92314) ***(G-19285)***
Snowbounders Ski Club....714 892-4897
5402 Tattershall Ave Westminster (92683) ***(G-19082)***
Snowcreek Property Management....760 934-3333
1254 Old Mammoth Rd Mammoth Lakes (93546) ***(G-11849)***
Snowline Hspc Eldorado Cnty....530 647-2703
3550 Carson Rd Camino (95709) ***(G-21110)***
Snowline Hspice El Dorado Cnty....530 621-7820
6520 Pleasant Valley Rd Diamond Springs (95619) ***(G-24979)***
Snyder Langston, Irvine *Also called Snyder Langston L P* ***(G-1673)***
Snyder Langston L P....949 863-9200
17962 Cowan Irvine (92614) ***(G-1673)***
So CA Edison, Rosemead *Also called Southern California Edison Co* ***(G-6242)***
So Cal Sandbags Inc....951 277-3404
12620 Bosley Ln Corona (92883) ***(G-7953)***
So Cal Ship Services....310 519-8411
971 S Seaside Ave San Pedro (90731) ***(G-4739)***
So Cal Truck Management....858 759-1964
1742 Burgundy Rd Encinitas (92024) ***(G-4067)***
So Calif Stone Center, Encino *Also called Southern Cal Stone Ctr LLC* ***(G-20045)***
So California Ventures Ltd....714 524-0021
1101 Richfield Rd Placentia (92870) ***(G-1674)***
So-Cal Strl Stl Fbrication Inc....909 877-1299
130 S Spruce Ave Rialto (92376) ***(G-3403)***
So-Cal Truck Management, Encinitas *Also called So Cal Truck Management* ***(G-4067)***
Soaprojects Inc (PA)....650 960-9900
495 N Whisman Rd Ste 100 Mountain View (94043) ***(G-27655)***
Soasta Inc....650 210-4941
444 Castro St Ste 400 Mountain View (94041) ***(G-16482)***
Sobaliving Llc....800 595-3803
22669 Pacific Coast Hwy Malibu (90265) ***(G-23059)***
Sobel Ross H Law Offices....310 788-8995
1875 Century Park E Los Angeles (90067) ***(G-23577)***
Sobel, Ross Howell, Los Angeles *Also called Sobel Ross H Law Offices* ***(G-23577)***
Soboba Band Luiseno Indians....951 665-1000
23333 Soboba Rd San Jacinto (92583) ***(G-17495)***
Soboba Casino, San Jacinto *Also called Soboba Band Luiseno Indians* ***(G-17495)***
Soboba Indian Health Clinic, San Jacinto *Also called Riverside-San Bernardino* ***(G-19924)***
Sobol Philip A MD P C Inc....310 649-5894
8618 S Sepulveda Blvd # 130 Los Angeles (90045) ***(G-20005)***
Sobriety House, Long Beach *Also called Safe Refuge* ***(G-24794)***
Soc/General Services/Bpm....415 703-5341
455 Golden Gate Ave # 2600 San Francisco (94102) ***(G-27220)***
Socal Auto Supply Inc....302 360-8373
21418 Osborne St Canoga Park (91304) ***(G-13569)***
Socal Coatings Inc....619 660-5395
2820 Via Orange Way Ste J Spring Valley (91978) ***(G-2492)***
Socal Home Care-Givers Svcs, Tustin *Also called RES-Care Inc* ***(G-22548)***
Socal Janitoral, Pacoima *Also called Purchasing 411 Inc* ***(G-7976)***
Socal Services Inc....858 453-1331
6336 Greenwich Dr Ste 100 San Diego (92122) ***(G-14791)***
Socal Sportsnet LLC....619 795-5000
100 Park Blvd San Diego (92101) ***(G-18496)***
Socal Staffing, San Diego *Also called Therastaff Inc* ***(G-14959)***
Socal Uniform Rental, San Gabriel *Also called Cal Southern Services* ***(G-13540)***
Sociable Labs Inc....415 225-8740
25 Division St San Mateo (94402) ***(G-16189)***
Social Advocates For Youth, Santa Rosa *Also called Individuals Now* ***(G-24025)***
Social Advocates For Youth....858 974-3603
87550 Drive San Diego (92117) ***(G-24211)***
Social Advocates For Youth....619 283-9624
4275 El Cajon Blvd # 101 San Diego (92105) ***(G-24212)***
Social Finance Inc....415 697-2078
1 Letterman Dr San Francisco (94129) ***(G-9952)***
Social Hblttion Rlpse Prvntion, San Francisco *Also called Sharper Future* ***(G-20000)***
Social Science Service Center....909 421-7120
18612 Santa Ana Ave Bloomington (92316) ***(G-22176)***
Social Services Agency, Santa Ana *Also called County of Orange* ***(G-23875)***
Social Services Agency, Orange *Also called County of Orange* ***(G-23876)***
Social Services Dept, Lompoc *Also called Santa Barbara County of* ***(G-24189)***
Social Services, Department of, Ukiah *Also called County of Mendocino* ***(G-23864)***
Social Services, Dept of, Lancaster *Also called County of Los Angeles* ***(G-23827)***
Social Studies School Service....310 839-2436
10200 Jefferson Blvd Culver City (90232) ***(G-7349)***
Social Vocational Services Inc....818 831-1321
8550 Balboa Blvd Ste 218 Northridge (91325) ***(G-22834)***
Social Vocational Services Inc....310 793-9600
2772 Artesia Blvd Ste 204 Redondo Beach (90278) ***(G-24213)***
Social Vocational Services Inc....661 323-0533
3601 Union Ave Bakersfield (93305) ***(G-14949)***
Socialize Inc....415 529-4019
450 Townsend St 102 San Francisco (94107) ***(G-15841)***
Socie of Saint Vince De PA....323 224-6280
210 N Avenue 21 Los Angeles (90031) ***(G-24214)***
Society For Info Display....408 399-6000
236 N Santa Cruz Ave Los Gatos (95030) ***(G-25579)***
Society For San Francisco....415 554-3000
201 Alabama St San Francisco (94103) ***(G-25580)***
Society of St Vincent (PA)....510 638-7600
9235 San Leandro St Oakland (94603) ***(G-25581)***
Society of St Vincent De Paul (PA)....323 224-6214
210 N Avenue 21 Los Angeles (90031) ***(G-25582)***
Society of St Vincent De Paul....650 589-9039
344 Grand Ave South San Francisco (94080) ***(G-24215)***
Society6 LLC....310 394-6400
1655 26th St Santa Monica (90404) ***(G-16190)***
Sodexo Inc....818 952-2201
1812 Verdugo Blvd Fl 1 Glendale (91208) ***(G-27656)***
Sodexo Management Inc....925 325-9657
851 Howard St San Francisco (94103) ***(G-27221)***
Sodexo Management Inc....209 667-3634
1 University Cir Turlock (95382) ***(G-27222)***
Sodexo Operations LLC....831 582-3838
100 Campus Ctr Bldg 16 Seaside (93955) ***(G-27223)***
Sodexo Operations LLC....619 429-5692
1325 Iris Ave Bldg 181 Imperial Beach (91932) ***(G-14434)***
Soex Group, Vernon *Also called Soex West Usa LLC* ***(G-8360)***
Soex West Usa LLC....323 264-8300
3294 E 26th St Vernon (90058) ***(G-8360)***
Soffietti Co....909 907-2277
236 W Orange Show San Bernardino (92408) ***(G-7699)***
Soffront Software Inc....510 413-9000
45437 Warm Springs Blvd Fremont (94539) ***(G-15461)***
Sofitel, Los Angeles *Also called Beverly Blvd Leaseco LLC* ***(G-12445)***
Sofitel Los Angeles, Los Angeles *Also called Accor Corp* ***(G-12373)***
Soft Machines Inc....408 969-0215
3920 Freedom Cir Santa Clara (95054) ***(G-16054)***
Softhq....858 658-9200
6494 Weathers Pl Ste 200 San Diego (92121) ***(G-16483)***
Softline Home Fashions Inc....310 630-4848
13122 S Normandie Ave Gardena (90249) ***(G-8327)***
Softscript Inc....310 451-2110
2215 Campus Dr El Segundo (90245) ***(G-14169)***
Softsol Resources Inc (HQ)....510 824-2000
46755 Fremont Blvd Fremont (94538) ***(G-15462)***
Software Ag Inc....408 490-5300
2901 Tasman Dr Ste 219 Santa Clara (95054) ***(G-15842)***
Software AG of Virginia, Santa Clara *Also called Software Ag Inc* ***(G-15842)***
Software AG Usa Inc....703 860-5050
1198 E Arques Ave Sunnyvale (94085) ***(G-15463)***
Software Dynamics, Canoga Park *Also called S1 Corporation* ***(G-16041)***
Software Dynamics Incorporated....818 992-3299
8501 Fllbrook Ave Ste 200 Canoga Park (91304) ***(G-16055)***
Software Management Cons Inc....714 662-1841
959 S Coast Dr Ste 415 Costa Mesa (92626) ***(G-15464)***
Software Management Cons Inc (PA)....818 240-3177
500 Nth Brn Blvd Ste 1100 Glendale (91203) ***(G-16484)***
Softworks, Huntington Beach *Also called EMC Corporation* ***(G-15654)***

ALPHABETIC

Sohnen Enterprises Inc (PA)...562 903-4957
8945 Dice Rd Santa Fe Springs (90670) *(G-17913)*
Soiree Valet Parking Service...415 284-9700
1470 Howard St San Francisco (94103) *(G-13796)*
Sol Republic Inc...877 400-0310
1000 Van Ness Ave San Francisco (94109) *(G-7636)*
Sol Transportation Inc...310 800-8069
1555 S Coast Hwy Ste 120 Oceanside (92054) *(G-3846)*
Solag Inc...949 728-1206
31641 Ortege Hwy San Juan Capistrano (92675) *(G-6563)*
Solairus Aviation, Petaluma *Also called Sunset Aviation LLC (G-4887)*
Solano County Mental Health...707 428-1131
2101 Courage Dr Fairfield (94533) *(G-24216)*
Solano County Probation Dept, Fairfield *Also called County of Solano (G-23921)*
Solano Family & Chld Council...707 863-3950
421 Executive Ct N Fairfield (94534) *(G-24516)*
Solano Garbage Company Inc...707 437-8900
2901 Industrial Ct Fairfield (94533) *(G-6564)*
Solano Irrigation District...707 448-6847
810 Vaca Valley Pkwy # 201 Vacaville (95688) *(G-6653)*
Solano Pacific Corporation...707 745-6000
900 1st St Benicia (94510) *(G-11850)*
Solano Regional Medical Group (PA)...707 426-3911
1234 Empire St Fairfield (94533) *(G-20006)*
Solar Company Inc...510 888-9488
20861 Wilbeam Ave Ste 1 Castro Valley (94546) *(G-2371)*
Solar Energy LLC...818 449-5816
21600 Oxnard St Ste 1200 Woodland Hills (91367) *(G-2372)*
Solar Link International Inc...909 605-7789
4652 E Brickell St Ste A Ontario (91761) *(G-7954)*
Solar Millennium LLC...510 524-4517
1111 Broadway Ste 400 Oakland (94607) *(G-2087)*
Solar Service Center Inc...951 928-3300
34859 Frederick St # 113 Wildomar (92595) *(G-2373)*
Solar Service Center Inc (PA)...888 760-7652
1622 Illinois Ave Ste 18 Perris (92571) *(G-2374)*
Solarcity Corporation...888 765-2489
249 E Avenue K8 Ste 111 Lancaster (93535) *(G-2375)*
Solarcity Corporation (PA)...650 638-1028
3055 Clearview Way San Mateo (94402) *(G-2376)*
Solari Enterprises Inc...714 282-2520
1507 W Yale Ave Orange (92867) *(G-11052)*
Solaris Paper Inc...562 376-9717
13415 Carmenita Rd Santa Fe Springs (90670) *(G-8088)*
Solartis, Manhattan Beach *Also called Hmointerfacecom LLC (G-15220)*
Solarworld Americas LLC (HQ)...503 844-3400
4650 Adohr Ln Camarillo (93012) *(G-7476)*
Solcom Inc...510 940-2490
24801 Huntwood Ave Hayward (94544) *(G-1995)*
Solcom Communications Inc, Hayward *Also called Solcom Inc (G-1995)*
Solcom Group Inc...510 940-2490
28835 Mack St Hayward (94545) *(G-1996)*
Solecon Industrial Contrs Inc...209 572-7390
1401 Mcwilliams Way Modesto (95351) *(G-2377)*
Soledad Cmnty Hlth Care Dst...831 678-2462
612 Main St Soledad (93960) *(G-20921)*
SOLEDAD MEDICAL GROUP, Soledad *Also called Soledad Cmnty Hlth Care Dst (G-20921)*
Soleeva Energy Inc...408 396-4954
448 Kato Ter Fremont (94539) *(G-2378)*
Soleil Communications LLC...619 624-2888
2655 Camino Dl Rio N 11 Ste 110 San Diego (92108) *(G-26707)*
Solex Contracting Inc...951 308-1706
42146 Remington Ave Temecula (92590) *(G-1997)*
Solheim Lutheran Home...323 257-7518
2236 Merton Ave Los Angeles (90041) *(G-24815)*
Soli-Bond Inc...661 631-1633
4230 Foster Ave Bakersfield (93308) *(G-1096)*
Solid Commerce, Marina Del Rey *Also called Liquidate Direct LLC (G-15988)*
Solid Drywall, Antelope *Also called Leavy Brothers Incorporated (G-2924)*
Solid Waste Services, San Marcos *Also called Edco Waste & Recycl Svcs Inc (G-6480)*
Solidcore Systems Inc (HQ)...408 387-8400
3965 Freedom Cir Santa Clara (95054) *(G-15465)*
Soligent Distribution LLC (HQ)...707 992-3100
1500 Valley House Dr # 210 Rohnert Park (94928) *(G-7637)*
Solimar Farms Inc...805 986-8806
1312 Del Norte Rd Camarillo (93010) *(G-134)*
Solimar Systems Inc (PA)...619 849-2800
1515 2nd Ave San Diego (92101) *(G-15466)*
Solix Technologies Inc (PA)...408 654-6400
4701 Patrick Henry Dr # 2001 Santa Clara (95054) *(G-15467)*
Solo W-2 Inc...925 680-0200
3478 Buskirk Ave Ste 1000 Pleasant Hill (94523) *(G-27657)*
Solo Workforce, Pleasant Hill *Also called Solo W-2 Inc (G-27657)*
Solomon Ward Sdnwurm Smith LLP...619 231-0303
401 B St Ste 1200 San Diego (92101) *(G-23578)*
Solopoint Solutions Inc...714 708-3639
150 Paularino Ave Ste 282 Costa Mesa (92626) *(G-26069)*
Solpac Inc...619 296-6247
2424 Congress St San Diego (92110) *(G-1675)*
Solpac Construction Inc...619 296-6247
2424 Congress St San Diego (92110) *(G-27224)*
Soltek Pacific, San Diego *Also called Solpac Inc (G-1675)*
Soltek Pacific Construction Co, San Diego *Also called Solpac Construction Inc (G-27224)*
Soltis Golf Incorporated...909 822-7000
8579 Cottonwood Ave Fontana (92335) *(G-2088)*
Solugenix Corporation (PA)...866 749-7658
601 Valencia Ave Brea (92823) *(G-28058)*
Solugenix Corporation...866 749-7658
225 N Barranca St West Covina (91791) *(G-16485)*

A
L
P
H
A
B
E
T
I
C

Solution One Industries Inc...254 702-7329
Ave G St Bldg 934 Fort Irwin (92310) *(G-4640)*
Solution Set LLC...415 367-6300
100 Montgomery St # 1500 San Francisco (94104) *(G-13922)*
Solutions 2 Go LLC...949 825-7700
111 Theory Ste 250 Irvine (92617) *(G-8053)*
Solve All Facility Services, Oceanside *Also called Bergensons Property Svcs Inc (G-14237)*
Solver Inc...310 691-5300
10780 Santa Monica Blvd # 370 Los Angeles (90025) *(G-7188)*
Soma Surgicenter...415 641-6889
1580 Valencia St San Francisco (94110) *(G-20007)*
Somansa Technologies Inc...408 297-1234
3003 N 1st St 301 San Jose (95134) *(G-7189)*
Somerford Place, Fresno *Also called Fresno Heritage Partners (G-24665)*
Somerford Place Encinitas, Encinitas *Also called Five Star Quality Care Inc (G-24658)*
Somerford Place Fresno, Fresno *Also called Five Star Quality Care Inc (G-20577)*
Somerford Place Stockton, Stockton *Also called Five Star Quality Care Inc (G-22439)*
Somerset Special Care Center...619 442-0245
151 Claydelle Ave El Cajon (92020) *(G-21111)*
Somis Pacific AG Management, Temecula *Also called Sierra Pacific Farms Inc (G-723)*
Sonata Software North Amer Inc (HQ)...510 791-7220
2201 Walnut Ave Ste 180 Fremont (94538) *(G-15468)*
Sonic Boom Wellness Inc...760 438-1600
5963 La Place Ct Ste 100 Carlsbad (92008) *(G-15469)*
Sonic Industries Inc...310 532-8382
20030 Normandie Ave Torrance (90502) *(G-26070)*
Sonicboomwellness.com, Carlsbad *Also called Sonic Boom Wellness Inc (G-15469)*
Sonicocom Inc...213 291-0475
2202 S Figueroa St Los Angeles (90007) *(G-16486)*
Sonics Inc (PA)...408 457-2800
2570 N 1st St Ste 100 San Jose (95131) *(G-16056)*
Sonicwall LLC (HQ)...800 509-1265
5455 Great America Pkwy Santa Clara (95054) *(G-16057)*
Sonifi Solutions Inc...650 752-1980
1065 E Hillsdale Blvd # 228 Foster City (94404) *(G-6017)*
Sonim Technologies Inc (PA)...650 378-8100
1825 S Grant St Ste 200 San Mateo (94402) *(G-5409)*
Sonitrol, San Jose *Also called Pacific West Security Inc (G-16909)*
Sonitrol Security Systems, Fresno *Also called Kimberlite Corporation (G-16895)*
Sonoma Cnty Ind Living Skills...707 765-8444
1799 Pepper Rd Petaluma (94952) *(G-24816)*
Sonoma County Airport Express...707 837-8700
5807 Old Redwood Hwy Santa Rosa (95403) *(G-3719)*
Sonoma County Data Processing, Santa Rosa *Also called County of Sonoma (G-16115)*
Sonoma County Humane Society...707 542-0882
5345 Highway 12 Santa Rosa (95407) *(G-645)*
Sonoma County Indian Health PR (PA)...707 521-4545
144 Stony Point Rd Santa Rosa (95401) *(G-20008)*
Sonoma County Water Agency...707 526-5370
404 Aviation Blvd Ste 0 Santa Rosa (95403) *(G-6404)*
Sonoma Grapevines Inc (PA)...707 542-5521
1919 Dennis Ln Santa Rosa (95403) *(G-9213)*
Sonoma Life Support, Santa Rosa *Also called American Med Resp Amblnc Svc (G-3748)*
Sonoma Technology Inc...707 665-9900
1450 N Mcdowell Blvd Petaluma (94954) *(G-28059)*
Sonoma Valley Health Care Dst (PA)...707 935-5000
347 Andrieux St Sonoma (95476) *(G-21895)*
SONOMA VALLEY HOSPITAL, Sonoma *Also called Sonoma Valley Health Care Dst (G-21895)*
Sonoma Valley Womans Club...707 938-8313
574 1st St E Sonoma (95476) *(G-25351)*
Sonoma Vly Cnty Sanitation Dst...707 547-1900
404 Aviation Blvd Santa Rosa (95403) *(G-6417)*
Sonoma West Medical Center...707 823-8511
501 Petaluma Ave Sebastopol (95472) *(G-20009)*
Sonoma West Medical Center...707 823-8511
501 Petaluma Ave Sebastopol (95472) *(G-21896)*
Sonora Regional Medical Center (HQ)...209 532-5000
1000 Greenley Rd Sonora (95370) *(G-21897)*
Sonora Retirement Center Inc...209 588-0373
12877 Sylva Ln Ofc Sonora (95370) *(G-24817)*
Sonora Trade Company Inc...619 878-5848
2127 Olympic Pkwy Chula Vista (91915) *(G-9305)*
Sonoran Roofing Inc (PA)...916 624-1080
4161 Citrus Ave Rocklin (95677) *(G-3213)*
Sonshine Auto Body, Victorville *Also called Sonshine Collision Services (G-17773)*
Sonshine Collision Services...760 243-3185
17200 Jasmine St Victorville (92395) *(G-17773)*
Sonshine North Autobody...760 245-3183
17200 Jasmine St Victorville (92395) *(G-17774)*
Sonsray Machinery LLC (HQ)...323 319-1900
23935 Madison St Torrance (90505) *(G-14499)*
Sonsray Machinery LLC...909 355-1075
10062 Live Oak Ave Fontana (92335) *(G-7790)*
Sony Corporation of America...650 655-8000
2207 Bridgepointe Pkwy Foster City (94404) *(G-15470)*
Sony Electronics Inc...714 508-7634
14450 Myford Rd Irvine (92606) *(G-18151)*
Sony Electronics Inc...415 833-4796
835 Howard St San Francisco (94103) *(G-18152)*
Sony Electronics Inc...310 835-6121
2201 E Carson St Carson (90810) *(G-7512)*
Sony Interactive Entrmt LLC (HQ)...310 981-1500
6080 Center Dr Fl 10 Los Angeles (90045) *(G-17496)*
Sony Interactve Entertnmnt Net, Los Angeles *Also called Sony Interactive Entrmt LLC (G-17496)*
Sony Intrctive Entrmt Amer LLC...858 824-5501
10075 Barnes Canyon Rd San Diego (92121) *(G-8054)*

Sony Intrctive Entrtmt Amer LLC (HQ)....650 655-8000
2207 Bridgepointe Pkwy Foster City (94404) ***(G-8055)***
Sony Logistics, Carson *Also called Sony Electronics Inc* ***(G-7512)***
Sony Media Cloud Services....310 244-4000
10202 Washington Blvd Culver City (90232) ***(G-18153)***
Sony Music Entertainment Inc....310 272-2555
9830 Wilshire Blvd Beverly Hills (90212) ***(G-8141)***
SONY PICTURES ENTERTAINMENT, INC., Culver City *Also called Sony Pictures Entrmt Inc* ***(G-18497)***
Sony Pictures Entrmt Inc....310 840-8000
9050 Washington Blvd Culver City (90232) ***(G-18497)***
Sony Pictures Entrmt Inc....310 202-1234
9336 Washington Blvd Culver City (90232) ***(G-18498)***
Sony Pictures Entrmt Inc....310 244-3558
6527 W 82nd St Los Angeles (90045) ***(G-18499)***
Sony Pictures Entrmt Inc (HQ)....310 244-4000
10202 Washington Blvd Culver City (90232) ***(G-18154)***
Sony Pictures Imageworks Inc....310 840-8000
9050 Washington Blvd Culver City (90232) ***(G-16191)***
Sony Pictures Studios, Culver City *Also called Sony Pictures Entrmt Inc* ***(G-18154)***
Sony Pictures Studios Inc....310 244-4000
1250 S Beverly Glen Blvd # 112 Los Angeles (90024) ***(G-18155)***
Sony Pictures Television Inc (HQ)....310 244-7625
10202 Washington Blvd Culver City (90232) ***(G-18156)***
Sony Publishers, Beverly Hills *Also called Sony Music Entertainment Inc* ***(G-8141)***
Soofer Co Inc....323 234-6666
2828 S Alameda St Vernon (90058) ***(G-8922)***
Sophia Lyn Convalescent Hosp, Pasadena *Also called Slch Inc* ***(G-20920)***
Soren McAdam Christianson LLP....909 798-2222
2068 Orange Tree Ln # 100 Redlands (92374) ***(G-26445)***
Soroptomist Intl Tahoe Sierra....530 573-1657
3050 Lake Tahoe Blvd South Lake Tahoe (96150) ***(G-25583)***
Sorrento Therapeutics Inc (PA)....858 210-3700
9380 Judicial Dr San Diego (92121) ***(G-26608)***
SOS Hosting, El Segundo *Also called Infrascale Inc* ***(G-15704)***
SOS Metals Inc (HQ)....310 217-8848
201 E Gardena Blvd Gardena (90248) ***(G-8089)***
SOS Security Incorporated....310 392-9600
2601 Ocean Park Blvd # 208 Santa Monica (90405) ***(G-16826)***
SOS Security Incorporated....510 782-4900
26250 Industrial Blvd # 48 Hayward (94545) ***(G-16827)***
SOS Security LLC....310 859-8248
331 N Beverly Dr Ste 3 Beverly Hills (90210) ***(G-16828)***
Sosa Granite & Marble Inc....925 373-7675
7701 Marathon Dr Livermore (94550) ***(G-3025)***
Sosa Tile Co, Livermore *Also called Sosa Granite & Marble Inc* ***(G-3025)***
Sothebys Intl Rlty Inc....310 456-6431
23405 Pacific Coast Hwy Malibu (90265) ***(G-11851)***
Soto Company Inc....949 493-9403
34275 Camino Capistrano A Capistrano Beach (92624) ***(G-956)***
Soto Food Service, Alhambra *Also called Soto Provision Inc* ***(G-6887)***
Soto Provision Inc....626 458-4600
949 S Meridian Ave Alhambra (91803) ***(G-6887)***
Sotoyome Medical Building LLC....707 525-4000
990 Sonoma Ave Ste 15 Santa Rosa (95404) ***(G-11053)***
Soulcycle Inc....310 973-7685
3874 Cross Creek Rd Malibu (90265) ***(G-18683)***
Souldriver Lessee Inc....619 819-9500
435 6th Ave San Diego (92101) ***(G-13273)***
Soule Park Golf Course, Ojai *Also called Mf Daily Oxnard Ranch Partnr* ***(G-18760)***
Sound Technologies Inc....760 918-9626
5810 Van Allen Way Carlsbad (92008) ***(G-7315)***
Sound-Crete Contracting....760 291-1240
530 Opper St Ste A Escondido (92029) ***(G-7791)***
Sound-Eklin, Carlsbad *Also called Sound Technologies Inc* ***(G-7315)***
Soundhound Inc (PA)....408 441-3200
3979 Freedom Cir Ste 400 Santa Clara (95054) ***(G-15471)***
Source 44 LLC....877 916-6337
1921 Palomar Oaks Way # 205 Carlsbad (92008) ***(G-28060)***
Source Intelligence, Carlsbad *Also called Source 44 LLC* ***(G-28060)***
Source Interlink Media LLC....310 531-9394
2221 Rosecrans Ave # 195 El Segundo (90245) ***(G-15472)***
Source Refrigeration....714 578-2300
800 E Orangethorpe Ave Anaheim (92801) ***(G-7759)***
Source Rfrgn & Hvac Inc (PA)....714 578-2300
800 E Orangethorpe Ave Anaheim (92801) ***(G-2379)***
Sourcebits Inc....650 433-7920
2191 E Byshore Rd Ste 200 Palo Alto (94303) ***(G-15473)***
Sourcewise....408 350-3200
2115 The Alameda San Jose (95126) ***(G-24217)***
South Asian Help Referral Agcy....562 402-4132
17100 Pioneer Blvd # 260 Artesia (90701) ***(G-24218)***
South Bay Airport Shuttle....408 225-4444
14420 Union Ave San Jose (95124) ***(G-3720)***
South Bay Auto Auction....310 719-2000
13210 S Normandie Ave Gardena (90249) ***(G-6694)***
South Bay Community Services....619 420-3620
430 F St Chula Vista (91910) ***(G-24219)***
South Bay Construction Company, Campbell *Also called B C S Inc* ***(G-1495)***
South Bay Ctr For Counseling....310 414-2090
540 N Marine Ave Wilmington (90744) ***(G-24220)***
South Bay Drive In Theatre, San Diego *Also called De Anza Land & Leisure Corp* ***(G-18359)***
South Bay Family Medical Group....310 378-2234
3105 Lomita Blvd Torrance (90505) ***(G-20010)***
South Bay Historical RR Soc....408 243-3969
1005 Railroad Ave Santa Clara (95050) ***(G-25584)***
SOUTH BAY PACKAGING & ASSEMBLY, Carson *Also called South Bay Vocational Center* ***(G-24389)***
South Bay Power Plant, Chula Vista *Also called San Diego Gas & Electric Co* ***(G-6254)***
South Bay Regl Public Safety T....408 270-6494
3095 Yerba Buena Rd San Jose (95135) ***(G-24388)***
South Bay Rgonal Pub Comm Auth....310 973-1802
4440 W Broadway Hawthorne (90250) ***(G-6089)***
South Bay Sand Blasting and Ta....619 238-8338
326 W 30th St National City (91950) ***(G-18016)***
South Bay Senior Services Inc....310 338-7558
8939 S Sepulveda Blvd # 330 Los Angeles (90045) ***(G-22567)***
South Bay Senior Solutions Inc....408 370-6360
1660 Hamilton Ave Ste 204 San Jose (95125) ***(G-22568)***
South Bay Vlla Preservation LP....310 516-7325
13111 S San Pedro St Los Angeles (90061) ***(G-11206)***
South Bay Vocational Center....310 784-2032
20706 Main St Carson (90745) ***(G-24389)***
South Baylo Acupuncture Clinic, Los Angeles *Also called South Baylo University* ***(G-22835)***
South Baylo University....213 387-2414
2727 W 6th St Los Angeles (90057) ***(G-22835)***
South Capitol Cottage....951 662-3026
15054 Daisy Rd Adelanto (92301) ***(G-28061)***
South Central Family Hlth Ctr....323 908-4200
4425 S Central Ave Los Angeles (90011) ***(G-20011)***
South Central Los (PA)....213 744-7000
2500 S Western Ave Los Angeles (90018) ***(G-24980)***
South China Sheet Metal Inc....323 225-1522
1740 Albion St Los Angeles (90031) ***(G-2380)***
South Cntl Heatlh & Rehab Prog....310 667-4070
2620 Industry Way Lynwood (90262) ***(G-22836)***
South Cntl Heatlh & Rehab Prog....323 751-2677
5201 S Vermont Ave Los Angeles (90037) ***(G-22837)***
South Cnty Cmnty Hlth Ctr Inc (PA)....650 330-7407
1885 Bay Rd East Palo Alto (94303) ***(G-23060)***
South Coast Auto Insurance, Cypress *Also called Freeway Insurance* ***(G-10722)***
South Coast Childrens Soc Inc....714 966-8650
27261 Las Ramblas Ste 220 Mission Viejo (92691) ***(G-24221)***
South Coast Community Services, Mission Viejo *Also called South Coast Childrens Soc Inc* ***(G-24221)***
South Coast Concrete Cnstr....951 351-7777
6770 Central Ave Ste B Riverside (92504) ***(G-3332)***
South Coast Fencing Center....714 549-2946
3518 W Lake Center Dr C Santa Ana (92704) ***(G-3583)***
South Coast Logistics....714 894-4744
12572 Western Ave Garden Grove (92841) ***(G-4376)***
South Coast Mechanical Inc....714 738-6644
2283 E Via Burton Anaheim (92806) ***(G-2381)***
South Coast Medical Center (PA)....949 364-1770
2100 Douglas Blvd Roseville (95661) ***(G-21898)***
South Coast Plaza LLC (PA)....714 546-0110
3333 Bristol St Ofc Costa Mesa (92626) ***(G-11054)***
South Coast Plaza LLC....714 435-2000
3333 Bristol St Ofc Costa Mesa (92626) ***(G-11055)***
South Coast Plaza Mall, Costa Mesa *Also called South Coast Plaza LLC* ***(G-11055)***
South Coast Plaza Village, Costa Mesa *Also called South Coast Plaza LLC* ***(G-11054)***
South Coast Repertory Inc....714 708-5500
655 Town Center Dr Costa Mesa (92626) ***(G-18435)***
South Coast Stone Paving....714 835-0258
2618 N Baker St Santa Ana (92706) ***(G-1863)***
South Coast Village, Santa Ana *Also called Edwards Theatres Circuit Inc* ***(G-18326)***
South Coast Westin Hotel Co....714 540-2500
686 Anton Blvd Costa Mesa (92626) ***(G-13274)***
South Cone Inc....760 431-2300
5935 Darwin Ct Carlsbad (92008) ***(G-8446)***
South County Housing Corp (PA)....510 582-1460
16500 Monterey St Ste 120 Morgan Hill (95037) ***(G-11852)***
South County Orthopedic Specia....949 586-3200
24331 El Toro Rd Ste 200 Laguna Hills (92637) ***(G-20012)***
South Gate Care Centers, South Gate *Also called Far West Inc* ***(G-20567)***
South Gate Dental Group, South Gate *Also called Castle Dental* ***(G-20248)***
South Hills Country Club....626 339-1231
2655 S Citrus St West Covina (91791) ***(G-19083)***
South of Market Child Care....415 820-3500
790 Folsom St San Francisco (94107) ***(G-24517)***
South Pacific Financial Corp....760 353-1080
2299 W Adams Ave Ste 113 El Centro (92243) ***(G-27658)***
South Pasadena San Marino YMCA, South Pasadena *Also called Young Mens Chrstn Assn of La* ***(G-25465)***
South San Jquin Irrigation Dst....209 249-4600
11011 E Highway 120 Manteca (95336) ***(G-6654)***
South Seas Imports, Compton *Also called M M Fab Inc* ***(G-8317)***
South Tahoe Public Utility Dst....530 544-6474
1275 Meadow Crest Dr South Lake Tahoe (96150) ***(G-6418)***
South Tahoe Refuse Co....530 541-5105
2140 Ruth Ave South Lake Tahoe (96150) ***(G-6565)***
South Valley Almond Co LLC....661 391-9000
15443 Beech Ave Wasco (93280) ***(G-8966)***
South Valley Farms, Wasco *Also called South Valley Almond Co LLC* ***(G-8966)***
South Valley Plumbing Inc....408 265-5566
3750 Charter Park Dr F San Jose (95136) ***(G-2382)***
South Valley School District, Fountain Valley *Also called Fountain Valley School Dst* ***(G-14301)***
South West Sun Solar Inc....714 582-3909
5871 Westminster Blvd C Westminster (92683) ***(G-7732)***
Southbay Sndblst & Tank Clg....619 238-8338
3589 Dalbergia St San Diego (92113) ***(G-18017)***
Southbay Teen Challenge, Santa Clara *Also called Teen Challenge Norwestcal Nev* ***(G-24246)***
Southbay Website Design LLC....310 370-4043
1601 Pcf Cast Hwy Ste 290 Hermosa Beach (90254) ***(G-16192)***

A L P H A B E T I C

Southbourne Inc ALPHABETIC SECTION

Southbourne Inc...415 781-5555
340 Stockton St San Francisco (94108) ***(G-13275)***
Southcoast Dyeing & Finishing, Santa Ana *Also called Chroma Systems* ***(G-13593)***
Southcoast Heating and Air, Vista *Also called ARS American Residential* ***(G-2151)***
Southeast Area Social Services...562 946-2237
10400 Pioneer Blvd Ste 8 Santa Fe Springs (90670) ***(G-24222)***
SOUTHEAST INDUSTRIES, Downey *Also called Association For Retarded Citzn* ***(G-24311)***
Southeastern Westminster, Westminster *Also called Southern California Edison Co* ***(G-6233)***
Southern Building & Con Inc...760 337-8932
2303 Weakley St El Centro (92243) ***(G-3333)***
Southern Building Maint Inc...213 598-7071
836 Crenshaw Blvd Ste 102 Los Angeles (90005) ***(G-14435)***
Southern CA Hlth & Rhbltn Prg...310 631-8004
2610 Industry Way Ste A Lynwood (90262) ***(G-20013)***
Southern Cal Appraisal Co, Burbank *Also called Sca Enterprises Inc* ***(G-17477)***
Southern Cal Blldog Rescue Inc...714 547-5725
2219 N Spurgeon St Santa Ana (92706) ***(G-25585)***
Southern Cal Halthcare Sys Inc...310 943-4500
3415 S Sepulveda Blvd # 9 Los Angeles (90034) ***(G-21899)***
Southern Cal Hosp At Culver Cy (HQ)...310 836-7000
3828 Delmas Ter Culver City (90232) ***(G-21900)***
Southern Cal Maid Svc Crpt Clg...310 675-0585
14909 Crenshaw Blvd # 209 Gardena (90249) ***(G-14436)***
Southern Cal Orthopedics, Anaheim *Also called Health Pointe Medical Group* ***(G-19546)***
Southern Cal Orthpd Inst LP...805 497-7015
375 Rolling Oaks Dr Thousand Oaks (91361) ***(G-20014)***
Southern Cal Orthpd Inst LP...818 901-6600
6815 Noble Ave Frnt Frnt Van Nuys (91405) ***(G-20015)***
Southern Cal Orthpd Inst LP...818 901-6600
6815 Noble Ave Ste 112 Westlake Village (91361) ***(G-20016)***
Southern Cal Orthpd Inst LP (PA)...818 901-6600
6815 Noble Ave Van Nuys (91405) ***(G-20017)***
Southern Cal Pipe Trades, Los Angeles *Also called Defined Contribution Trust Fun* ***(G-12172)***
Southern Cal Pipe Trades ADM, Los Angeles *Also called Southern Cal Pipe Trades ADM* ***(G-12203)***
Southern Cal Pipe Trades ADM (PA)...213 385-6161
501 Shatto Pl Ste 500 Los Angeles (90020) ***(G-12203)***
Southern Cal Prmnnte Med Group...949 262-5780
6 Willard Irvine (92604) ***(G-20018)***
Southern Cal Prmnnte Med Group...800 272-3500
13652 Cantara St Panorama City (91402) ***(G-20019)***
Southern Cal Prmnnte Med Group...858 974-1000
5855 Copley Dr Ste 250 San Diego (92111) ***(G-10381)***
Southern Cal Prmnnte Med Group...661 398-5085
3501 Stockdale Hwy Bakersfield (93309) ***(G-20020)***
Southern Cal Prmnnte Med Group...619 528-5000
4647 Zion Ave San Diego (92120) ***(G-20021)***
Southern Cal Prmnnte Med Group...310 604-5700
3830 Martin L King Jr Blv Lynwood (90262) ***(G-20022)***
Southern Cal Prmnnte Med Group...661 290-3100
26415 Carl Boyer Dr Santa Clarita (91350) ***(G-21901)***
Southern Cal Prmnnte Med Group...323 857-2000
6041 Cadillac Ave Los Angeles (90034) ***(G-20023)***
Southern Cal Prmnnte Med Group...800 780-1230
25825 Vermont Ave Harbor City (90710) ***(G-20024)***
Southern Cal Prmnnte Med Group...909 427-5000
9961 Sierra Ave Fontana (92335) ***(G-21902)***
Southern Cal Prmnnte Med Group...888 778-5000
5250 Lankershim Blvd North Hollywood (91601) ***(G-20025)***
Southern Cal Prmnnte Med Group...323 783-5455
4841 Hollywood Blvd Los Angeles (90027) ***(G-20026)***
Southern Cal Prmnnte Med Group...626 960-4844
1511 W Garvey Ave N West Covina (91790) ***(G-20027)***
Southern Cal Prmnnte Med Group...714 734-4500
17542 17th St Ste 300 Tustin (92780) ***(G-20028)***
Southern Cal Prmnnte Med Group...323 783-4893
4760 W Sunset Blvd Los Angeles (90027) ***(G-20029)***
Southern Cal Prmnnte Med Group (PA)...626 405-5704
393 Walnut Dr Pasadena (91107) ***(G-10382)***
Southern Cal Prmnnte Med Group...909 370-2501
789 E Cooley Dr Colton (92324) ***(G-20030)***
Southern Cal Prmnnte Med Group...714 841-7293
18081 Beach Blvd Huntington Beach (92648) ***(G-20031)***
Southern Cal Prmnnte Med Group...619 528-5000
1630 E Main St El Cajon (92021) ***(G-20032)***
Southern Cal Prmnnte Med Group...714 279-4675
411 N Lakeview Ave Anaheim (92807) ***(G-20033)***
Southern Cal Prmnnte Med Group...949 234-2139
30400 Camino Capistrano San Juan Capistrano (92675) ***(G-20034)***
Southern Cal Prmnnte Med Group...714 685-3520
22550 Savi Ranch Pkwy Yorba Linda (92887) ***(G-20035)***
Southern Cal Prmnnte Med Group...714 967-4760
1900 E 4th St Santa Ana (92705) ***(G-20036)***
Southern Cal Prmnnte Med Group...619 516-6000
4405 Vandever Ave San Diego (92120) ***(G-20037)***
Southern Cal Prmnnte Med Group...760 839-7200
732 N Broadway Escondido (92025) ***(G-20038)***
Southern Cal Prmnnte Med Group...323 562-6459
7825 Atlantic Ave Cudahy (90201) ***(G-20039)***
Southern Cal Prmnnte Med Group...818 592-3038
21263 Erwin St Woodland Hills (91367) ***(G-20040)***
Southern Cal Prmnnte Med Group...661 222-2150
27107 Tourney Rd Santa Clarita (91355) ***(G-20041)***
Southern Cal Prmnnte Med Group...619 528-5000
17140 Bernardo Center Dr San Diego (92128) ***(G-20042)***
Southern Cal Prmnnte Med Group...909 394-2505
1255 W Arrow Hwy San Dimas (91773) ***(G-20043)***
Southern Cal Prmnnte Med Group...619 528-5000
6860 Avenida Encinas Carlsbad (92011) ***(G-20354)***
Southern Cal Prmnnte Med Group...562 657-2200
9353 Imperial Hwy Downey (90242) ***(G-23061)***
Southern Cal Prmnnte Med Group...949 376-8619
23781 Maquina Mission Viejo (92691) ***(G-23062)***
Southern Cal Prmnnte Med Group...661 334-2020
5055 California Ave Bakersfield (93309) ***(G-20044)***
Southern Cal Rgional Rail Auth (PA)...213 452-0200
1 Gateway Plz Fl 12 Los Angeles (90012) ***(G-3721)***
Southern Cal Spcialty Care Inc...626 339-5451
845 N Lark Ellen Ave West Covina (91791) ***(G-21903)***
Southern Cal Spcialty Care Inc...714 564-7800
1901 College Ave Santa Ana (92706) ***(G-21904)***
Southern Cal Spcialty Care Inc (HQ)...562 944-1900
14900 Imperial Hwy La Mirada (90638) ***(G-22177)***
Southern Cal Stone Ctr LLC...818 784-8975
5400 Balboa Blvd Ste 111 Encino (91316) ***(G-20045)***
Southern Calif Mtl Hdlg Co, Northridge *Also called Southern California Mtl Hdlg* ***(G-7889)***
Southern California / Hawa Reg, El Centro *Also called Securitas SEC Svcs USA Inc* ***(G-16792)***
Southern California / Hawa Reg, Goleta *Also called Securitas SEC Svcs USA Inc* ***(G-16797)***
Southern California / Hawa Reg, Pomona *Also called Securitas SEC Svcs USA Inc* ***(G-16804)***
Southern California / Hawa Reg, Commerce *Also called Securitas SEC Svcs USA Inc* ***(G-16805)***
Southern California / Hawa Reg, Los Angeles *Also called Securitas SEC Svcs USA Inc* ***(G-16806)***
Southern California / Hawa Reg, Los Angeles *Also called Securitas SEC Svcs USA Inc* ***(G-16807)***
Southern California / Hawa Reg, Long Beach *Also called Securitas SEC Svcs USA Inc* ***(G-16808)***
Southern California / Hawa Reg, Victorville *Also called Securitas SEC Svcs USA Inc* ***(G-16811)***
Southern California Alcohol An (PA)...562 923-4545
11500 Paramount Blvd Downey (90241) ***(G-22838)***
Southern California AVI LLC...760 523-5057
18438 Readiness St Victorville (92394) ***(G-4938)***
Southern California Car Transf...858 586-0006
11139 Roxboro Rd San Diego (92131) ***(G-5244)***
Southern California Cen, Long Beach *Also called Memor Ortho Surgic Group A M* ***(G-19741)***
Southern California Edison Co (HQ)...626 302-1212
2244 Walnut Grove Ave Rosemead (91770) ***(G-6210)***
Southern California Edison Co...626 543-8081
4900 Rivergrade Rd 2b1 Irwindale (91706) ***(G-6211)***
Southern California Edison Co...559 893-3611
54205 Mt Poplar Ave Big Creek (93605) ***(G-6212)***
Southern California Edison Co...626 303-8480
1440 S California Ave Monrovia (91016) ***(G-6213)***
Southern California Edison Co...559 685-3742
2425 S Blackstone St Tulare (93274) ***(G-6214)***
Southern California Edison Co...760 873-0715
4000 Bishop Creek Rd Bishop (93514) ***(G-6215)***
Southern California Edison Co...714 934-0838
14799 Chestnut St Westminster (92683) ***(G-6216)***
Southern California Edison Co...559 893-2037
55481 Mt Poplar Big Creek (93605) ***(G-6217)***
Southern California Edison Co...626 302-5101
8380 Klingerman St Rosemead (91770) ***(G-6218)***
Southern California Edison Co...626 543-6093
4900 Rivergrade Rd Baldwin Park (91706) ***(G-6219)***
Southern California Edison Co...714 870-3225
1851 W Valencia Dr Fullerton (92833) ***(G-6220)***
Southern California Edison Co...949 368-2881
14300 Mesa Rd San Clemente (92672) ***(G-6221)***
Southern California Edison Co...626 302-1212
2131 Walnut Grove Ave Rosemead (91770) ***(G-6222)***
Southern California Edison Co...559 893-3646
54205 Mountain Poplar Rd Big Creek (93605) ***(G-6223)***
Southern California Edison Co...714 973-5481
1241 S Grand Ave Santa Ana (92705) ***(G-6224)***
Southern California Edison Co...818 999-1880
3589 Foothill Dr Thousand Oaks (91361) ***(G-6225)***
Southern California Edison Co...626 815-7296
6000 N Irwindale Ave A Irwindale (91702) ***(G-6226)***
Southern California Edison Co...909 469-0251
265 N East End Ave Pomona (91767) ***(G-6227)***
Southern California Edison Co...714 895-0488
1515 Walnut Grove Ave Rosemead (91770) ***(G-6228)***
Southern California Edison Co...310 608-5029
1924 E Cashdan St Compton (90220) ***(G-6229)***
Southern California Edison Co...805 683-5291
103 Love Pl Goleta (93117) ***(G-6230)***
Southern California Edison Co...714 636-2166
10231 Woodbury Rd Apt B Garden Grove (92843) ***(G-6231)***
Southern California Edison Co...714 973-5574
1444 E Mcfadden Ave Santa Ana (92705) ***(G-6232)***
Southern California Edison Co...714 895-0420
7300 Fenwick Ln Westminster (92683) ***(G-6233)***
Southern California Edison Co...949 587-5416
14155 Bake Pkwy Irvine (92618) ***(G-6234)***
Southern California Edison Co...626 633-3070
6042a N Irwindale Ave Irwindale (91702) ***(G-6235)***
Southern California Edison Co...714 895-0163
7333 Bolsa Ave Westminster (92683) ***(G-6236)***
Southern California Edison Co...626 814-4212
13025 Los Angeles St Irwindale (91706) ***(G-6237)***
Southern California Edison Co...909 592-3757
800 W Cienega Ave San Dimas (91773) ***(G-6238)***

ALPHABETIC

Southern California Edison Co.....562 903-3191
9901 Geary Ave Santa Fe Springs (90670) ***(G-6239)***
Southern California Edison Co.....562 491-3803
125 Elm Ave Long Beach (90802) ***(G-6240)***
Southern California Edison Co.....760 951-3242
12353 Hesperia Rd Victorville (92395) ***(G-6241)***
Southern California Edison Co.....626 302-0530
1515 Walnut Grove Ave Rosemead (91770) ***(G-6242)***
Southern California Fleet Svc.....951 272-8655
6726 Nicolett St Riverside (92504) ***(G-17814)***
Southern California Gas Co (HQ).....213 244-1200
555 W 5th St Fl 31 Los Angeles (90013) ***(G-6274)***
Southern California Gas Co.....310 605-7800
701 S Bullis Rd Compton (90221) ***(G-6261)***
Southern California Gas Co.....714 634-7221
1 Liberty Aliso Viejo (92656) ***(G-6262)***
Southern California Gas Co.....661 399-4431
1510 N Chester Ave Bakersfield (93308) ***(G-6263)***
Southern California Gas Co.....213 244-1200
1801 S Atlantic Blvd Monterey Park (91754) ***(G-27225)***
Southern California Gas Co.....909 335-7802
1981 W Lugonia Ave Redlands (92374) ***(G-6275)***
Southern California Gas Co.....213 244-1200
920 S Stimson Ave City of Industry (91745) ***(G-6276)***
Southern California Gas Co.....213 244-1200
25200 Trumble Rd Romoland (92585) ***(G-6277)***
Southern California Gas Co.....323 881-3587
333 E Main St Ste J Alhambra (91801) ***(G-6278)***
Southern California Gas Co.....562 803-3341
6738 Bright Ave Whittier (90601) ***(G-6264)***
Southern California Gas Co.....310 823-7945
8141 Gulana Ave Venice (90293) ***(G-6256)***
Southern California Gas Co.....909 335-7941
155 S G St San Bernardino (92410) ***(G-6265)***
Southern California Gas Co.....213 244-1200
1600 Corporate Center Dr Monterey Park (91754) ***(G-6266)***
Southern California Gas Co.....562 803-7453
9240 Firestone Blvd Downey (90241) ***(G-6279)***
Southern California Gas Co.....909 305-8297
1050 Overland Ct San Dimas (91773) ***(G-6257)***
Southern California Gas Co.....800 427-2200
23130 Valencia Blvd Valencia (91355) ***(G-6280)***
Southern California Gas Co.....800 427-0018
3 Mi S Newberry Springs (92365) ***(G-6267)***
Southern California Gas Co.....818 701-2592
9400 Oakdale Ave Chatsworth (91311) ***(G-6258)***
Southern California Gas Tower (HQ).....213 244-1200
555 W 5th St Ste 1700 Los Angeles (90013) ***(G-6281)***
Southern California Golf Assn (PA).....818 980-3630
3740 Cahuenga Blvd North Hollywood (91604) ***(G-25104)***
Southern California Mar Assn.....714 850-4004
3333 Fairview Rd Costa Mesa (92626) ***(G-17815)***
Southern California Mkt Area, Los Angeles *Also called Veritiv Operating Company* ***(G-8221)***
Southern California Mkt Area, Commerce *Also called Veritiv Operating Company* ***(G-8222)***
Southern California Mtl Hdlg.....805 650-6000
19755 Bahama St Northridge (91324) ***(G-7889)***
Southern California Mtl Hdlg.....818 349-1220
8124 Deering Ave Canoga Park (91304) ***(G-7890)***
Southern California Mtl Hdlg (HQ).....562 949-1006
12393 Slauson Ave Whittier (90606) ***(G-7891)***
Southern California Physicia.....858 824-7000
6760 Top Gun St Ste 100 San Diego (92121) ***(G-27226)***
Southern California Regional, Indio *Also called Granite Construction Company* ***(G-1779)***
Southern Clfrn Edsn - Prvt CHR, Rosemead *Also called Southern California Edison Co* ***(G-6222)***
Southern Contracting Company.....760 744-0760
559 N Twin Oaks Valley Rd San Marcos (92069) ***(G-2734)***
Southern Counties Oil Co (PA).....714 744-7140
1800 W Katella Ave # 400 Orange (92867) ***(G-9009)***
Southern Fresh Prod Provs Inc.....562 236-2784
11954 Washington Blvd Whittier (90606) ***(G-8776)***
Southern Fresh Produce Inc.....562 236-2784
11954 Washington Blvd Whittier (90606) ***(G-8777)***
Southern Hmbldt Cmnty Dst Hosp.....707 923-3921
733 Cedar St Garberville (95542) ***(G-21905)***
Southern Humboldt Cmnty Clinic, Garberville *Also called Southern Hmbldt Cmnty Dst Hosp* ***(G-21905)***
Southern Indian Health Council (PA).....619 445-1188
4058 Willows Rd Alpine (91901) ***(G-20046)***
Southern Inyo Healthcare Dst.....760 876-5501
501 E Locust St Lone Pine (93545) ***(G-20922)***
Southern Mnterey Cnty Mem Hosp (PA).....831 385-7100
300 Canal St King City (93930) ***(G-21906)***
Southern Mnterey Cnty Mem Hosp.....831 674-0112
467 El Camino Real Greenfield (93927) ***(G-21907)***
Southern Mntrey Cnty Labor Sup, Greenfield *Also called Southern Mntrrey Cnty Lbor Sup* ***(G-686)***
Southern Mntrrey Cnty Lbor Sup.....831 674-2727
44 El Camino Real Unit A Greenfield (93927) ***(G-686)***
Southern Mono Healthcare Dst.....760 934-3311
85 Sierra Park Rd Mammoth Lakes (93546) ***(G-21908)***
Southern Oregon Goodwill Inds.....530 842-6627
1202 S Main St Yreka (96097) ***(G-24390)***
Southern Pacific Railroad, Bakersfield *Also called Union Pacific Railroad Company* ***(G-3627)***
Southern Pacific Trnsp.....415 541-2589
1 Market Plz San Francisco (94105) ***(G-3618)***
SOUTHERN SIERRA MEDICAL CLINIC, Ridgecrest *Also called Ridgecrest Regional Hospital* ***(G-21832)***
Southern Wine & Spirits Amrca.....951 274-2420
723 Palmyrita Ave Riverside (92507) ***(G-9110)***
Southern Wine & Spirits Amrca.....858 537-3912
10730 Scripps Ranch Blvd San Diego (92131) ***(G-9111)***
Southern Wine & Spirits Amrca.....408 750-3540
2320 Kruse Dr San Jose (95131) ***(G-9112)***
Southern Wine & Spirits Amrca.....562 926-2000
17101 Valley View Ave Cerritos (90703) ***(G-9113)***
Southgate Recreation & Pk Dst.....916 421-7275
7320 Florin Mall Dr Sacramento (95823) ***(G-24223)***
Southland Car Counters, Orange *Also called Field Data Services* ***(G-27922)***
Southland Care, Mission Viejo *Also called Ensign Southland LLC* ***(G-20546)***
Southland Credit Union (PA).....562 862-6831
10701 Los Alamitos Blvd Los Alamitos (90720) ***(G-9690)***
Southland Credit Union.....562 862-6831
8545 Florence Ave Downey (90240) ***(G-9691)***
Southland Electric Inc (PA).....858 634-5050
4950 Greencraig Ln San Diego (92123) ***(G-2735)***
Southland Health Center, Santa Ana *Also called Vietnamese Cmnty Orange Cnty* ***(G-24995)***
Southland Industries (PA).....800 613-6240
7390 Lincoln Way Garden Grove (92841) ***(G-2383)***
Southland Industries.....714 901-5800
7421 Orangewood Ave Garden Grove (92841) ***(G-2384)***
Southland Lutheran Home, Norwalk *Also called Front Porch Communities & Svcs* ***(G-21226)***
Southland Mall, Hayward *Also called Lansing Mall Ltd Partnership* ***(G-11010)***
Southland Paving Inc.....760 747-6895
361 N Hale Ave Escondido (92029) ***(G-3334)***
Southland Steel, Newport Beach *Also called Fallon Land Company Inc* ***(G-7370)***
Southland Technology Inc.....858 694-0932
8053 Vickers St San Diego (92111) ***(G-7190)***
Southland Transit Inc.....661 726-4225
44110 Yucca Ave Lancaster (93534) ***(G-3722)***
Southland Transit Co, Baldwin Park *Also called San Gabriel Transit Inc* ***(G-3867)***
Southtown Industrial Park.....909 947-3768
1701 S Bon View Ave 104 Ontario (91761) ***(G-11056)***
Southwest Airlines Co.....510 563-1000
1 Airport Dr Ste 25 Oakland (94621) ***(G-4823)***
Southwest Airlines Co.....619 231-7345
3665 N Harbor Dr Ste 216 San Diego (92101) ***(G-4824)***
Southwest Airlines Co.....310 665-5700
100 World Way Ste 328 Los Angeles (90045) ***(G-4825)***
Southwest Airlines Co.....510 563-1234
10 Alan Shepard Way Oakland (94621) ***(G-4826)***
Southwest Construction Co Inc.....760 728-4460
2909 Rainbow Valley Blvd Fallbrook (92028) ***(G-3335)***
Southwest Convalesant, Hawthorne *Also called Windsor Gardens* ***(G-21048)***
Southwest Correctional Medical.....831 641-3298
2511 Garden Rd Ste A160 Monterey (93940) ***(G-22839)***
Southwest Express LLC.....949 474-5038
1720 E Garry Ave Ste 107 Santa Ana (92705) ***(G-4068)***
Southwest Fsheries Science Ctr, La Jolla *Also called National Marine Fisheries Svc* ***(G-26572)***
Southwest General Contrs Inc.....760 480-8747
912 S Andreasen Dr # 101 Escondido (92029) ***(G-7792)***
Southwest Healthcare Sys Aux.....800 404-6627
38977 Sky Canyon Dr # 200 Murrieta (92563) ***(G-21909)***
Southwest Healthcare Sys Aux (HQ).....951 696-6000
25500 Medical Center Dr Murrieta (92562) ***(G-21910)***
Southwest Hospital Dev Group.....951 943-4555
2224 Medical Center Dr Perris (92571) ***(G-21911)***
Southwest Inspection and Tstg.....562 941-2990
441 Commercial Way La Habra (90631) ***(G-17497)***
Southwest Inspection Testing, La Habra *Also called Southwest Inspection and Tstg* ***(G-17497)***
Southwest Landscape Inc.....714 545-1084
2205 S Standard Ave Santa Ana (92707) ***(G-957)***
Southwest Material Hdlg Inc (PA).....951 727-0477
3725 Nobel Ct Mira Loma (91752) ***(G-7892)***
Southwest Rgnal Cncil Crpnters (PA).....213 385-1457
533 S Fremont Ave Fl 10 Los Angeles (90071) ***(G-25187)***
Southwest Toyota Lift, Mira Loma *Also called Southwest Material Hdlg Inc* ***(G-7892)***
Southwest Traders Incorporated.....209 462-1607
4747 Frontier Way Stockton (95215) ***(G-8520)***
Southwest Traders Incorporated (PA).....951 699-7800
27565 Diaz Rd Temecula (92590) ***(G-8521)***
Southwest Transportation Agcy, Caruthers *Also called Fresno Cnty Supt Schools Cent* ***(G-3938)***
Southwest YMCA, Saratoga *Also called YMCA of Silicon Valley* ***(G-25602)***
Southwestern Artists Assn.....619 232-3522
1770 Vlg Pl Gallery 23 23 Gallery San Diego (92101) ***(G-25049)***
Southwestern Orthpd Med Corp.....562 803-0600
15901 Hawthorne Blvd Lawndale (90260) ***(G-20047)***
Southwestern Yacht Club Inc.....619 222-0438
2702 Qualtrough St San Diego (92106) ***(G-19084)***
Southwind Foods LLC (PA).....323 262-8222
20644 S Fordyce Ave Carson (90810) ***(G-8655)***
Southwire Company LLC.....909 989-2888
9199 Cleveland Ave # 100 Rancho Cucamonga (91730) ***(G-7477)***
Sovereign Capital MGT Group, San Diego *Also called Sovereign Capitl MGT Group Inc* ***(G-11853)***
Sovereign Capitl MGT Group Inc.....619 294-8989
750 B St Ste 2620 San Diego (92101) ***(G-11853)***
Sovereign Health of California, Los Angeles *Also called Dual Diagnosis Trtmnt Ctr Inc* ***(G-22211)***
Sovereign Health of California, San Clemente *Also called Dual Diagnosis Trtmnt Ctr Inc* ***(G-22723)***

A L P H A B E T I C

SP McClenahan Co 650 326-8781
1 Arastradero Rd Portola Valley (94028) ***(G-998)***
Sp Plus Corporation 213 488-3100
3470 Wilshire Blvd # 400 Los Angeles (90010) ***(G-3584)***
Spa At Club Sport, San Ramon *Also called Clubsport San Ramon LLC* ***(G-18622)***
Spa Blue, Del Mar *Also called Spa Gregories LLC* ***(G-13691)***
Spa Cas Palmas 760 836-3106
41000 Bob Hope Dr Rancho Mirage (92270) ***(G-18684)***
Spa Dreams 818 298-1120
6419 Hesperia Ave Reseda (91335) ***(G-18685)***
Spa Gregories LLC 858 481-6672
2710 Via De Vly Ste B Del Mar (92014) ***(G-13691)***
Spa Havens LP 760 945-2055
29402 Spa Haven Way Vista (92084) ***(G-18686)***
Spa Las Palmas of Marriot Intl, Rancho Mirage *Also called Spa Cas Palmas* ***(G-18684)***
Spa Partners Inc 707 942-5789
1457 Lincoln Ave Calistoga (94515) ***(G-18687)***
Spa Resort Casino, Palm Springs *Also called Agua Clnte Band Chilla Indians* ***(G-12375)***
Spa Resort Casino (PA) 760 883-1000
401 E Amado Rd Palm Springs (92262) ***(G-13276)***
Spa Resort Casino 760 883-1034
100 N Indian Canyon Dr Palm Springs (92262) ***(G-13277)***
Space Age Metal Products Inc 310 539-5500
23605 Telo Ave Torrance (90505) ***(G-7191)***
Space Components Division, San Diego *Also called Atk Space Systems Inc* ***(G-26737)***
Space Dvson-Integrated Systems, Pasadena *Also called Mda US Systems LLC* ***(G-25957)***
Space Systems/Loral LLC 650 852-4000
1140 Hamilton Ct Menlo Park (94025) ***(G-4641)***
Spacetone Acoustics Inc 925 931-0749
1051 Serpentine Ln # 300 Pleasanton (94566) ***(G-2981)***
Spad Holdings LLC 805 496-9978
966 S Westlake Blvd Ste 4 Westlake Village (91361) ***(G-18688)***
Spad Holdings LLC 661 286-0229
24245 Magic Mountain Pkwy Valencia (91355) ***(G-18689)***
Spad Holdings LLC 714 993-6003
860 N Rose Dr Placentia (92870) ***(G-18690)***
Spad Holdings LLC 949 733-0473
14280 Culver Dr Ste B Irvine (92604) ***(G-18691)***
Spad Holdings LLC 818 710-7606
6100 Topanga Canyon Blvd # 1310 Woodland Hills (91367) ***(G-18692)***
Spad Holdings LLC 818 772-8900
19456 Nordhoff St Northridge (91324) ***(G-18693)***
Spad Holdings LLC 818 552-2027
601 N Brand Blvd Glendale (91203) ***(G-18694)***
Spalding Srgcl Ctr of Bvrly Hl 310 385-7755
27520 Hawthorne Blvd # 176 Rllng HLS Est (90274) ***(G-20048)***
Span Construction & Engrg Inc (PA) 559 661-1111
1841 Howard Rd Madera (93637) ***(G-1676)***
Spanish Brdcstg Sys of Cal 310 203-0900
7007 Nw 77th Ave Los Angeles (90064) ***(G-5822)***
Spanish Hills Country Club (PA) 805 389-1644
999 Crestview Ave Camarillo (93010) ***(G-19085)***
Spanish Trils Girl Scout Cncil 909 627-2609
5007 Center St Chino (91710) ***(G-24224)***
Spare-Time Inc 916 983-9180
820 Halidon Way Folsom (95630) ***(G-19086)***
Spare-Time Inc 916 859-5910
11344 Coloma Rd Ste 350 Gold River (95670) ***(G-19087)***
Spare-Time Inc 916 782-2600
2501 Eureka Rd Roseville (95661) ***(G-19088)***
Spare-Time Inc 209 371-0241
429 W Lockeford St Lodi (95240) ***(G-18529)***
Spare-Time Inc 916 638-7001
2201 Gold Rush Dr Gold River (95670) ***(G-19089)***
Spare-Time Inc 916 649-0909
2450 Natomas Park Dr Sacramento (95833) ***(G-19090)***
Spare-Time Inc 916 859-5910
9570 Racquet Ct Elk Grove (95758) ***(G-19091)***
Spark Networks Inc (PA) 310 893-0550
11150 Santa Monica Blvd # 600 Los Angeles (90025) ***(G-13797)***
Spark Unlimited Inc 818 788-1005
15000 Ventura Blvd # 202 Sherman Oaks (91403) ***(G-15474)***
Sparkle Uniform & Linen Svc, Bakersfield *Also called Richard K Newman and Assoc Inc* ***(G-13584)***
Sparkletts, Van Nuys *Also called Ds Services of America Inc* ***(G-8829)***
Sparkletts, Irwindale *Also called Ds Services of America Inc* ***(G-8830)***
Sparta Consulting Inc 916 985-0300
111 Woodmere Rd Ste 200 Folsom (95630) ***(G-16487)***
Spc Building Services, Riverside *Also called J M V B Inc* ***(G-2456)***
Spe Go Holdings Inc 858 638-0672
16422 N Woodson Dr Ramona (92065) ***(G-19092)***
Spear Management Company 323 963-7515
1642 N Cahuenga Blvd Los Angeles (90028) ***(G-16829)***
Spearman Clubs Inc (PA) 949 496-2070
23500 Clubhouse Dr Laguna Niguel (92677) ***(G-19286)***
Spec Personnel LLC 408 727-8000
1900 La Fytte St Unit 125 Santa Clara (95050) ***(G-14792)***
Spec Services Inc 714 963-8077
10540 Talbert Ave 100e Fountain Valley (92708) ***(G-26071)***
Spec Services Inc (PA) 714 963-8077
10540 Talbert Ave 100e Fountain Valley (92708) ***(G-26072)***
Special Dispatch Cal Inc 510 713-0300
8328 Central Ave Newark (94560) ***(G-4265)***
Special Dispatch Cal Inc (PA) 602 296-8860
16330 Phoebe Ave La Mirada (90638) ***(G-4377)***
Special Events, Livermore *Also called Pinamar LLC* ***(G-14569)***
Special Events, Livermore *Also called High Summit LLC* ***(G-17822)***
Special Events Staffing 626 296-6771
1015 N Lake Ave Ste 202 Pasadena (91104) ***(G-14793)***
Special Home Needs 408 985-8666
1440 Jackson St Santa Clara (95050) ***(G-21112)***
Special Needs Network 323 291-7100
4401 Crenshaw Blvd # 215 Los Angeles (90043) ***(G-22178)***
Special Service Contrs Inc 805 227-1081
3580 Airport Rd Paso Robles (93446) ***(G-3585)***
Special Service For Groups Inc 310 323-6887
19401 S Vt Ave Ste A200 Torrance (90502) ***(G-24981)***
Special Service For Groups Inc (PA) 213 368-1888
905 E 8th St Unit 1 Los Angeles (90021) ***(G-24391)***
Special Service For Groups Inc 213 620-5713
470 E 3rd St Ste D Los Angeles (90013) ***(G-24982)***
Specialized Landscape MGT Svcs 805 520-7590
4212 Peast Los Angeles Simi Valley (93063) ***(G-958)***
Specialized Laundry Svcs Inc 510 487-8297
33483 Western Ave Union City (94587) ***(G-13657)***
Specialty Construction Inc 805 543-1706
645 Clarion Ct San Luis Obispo (93401) ***(G-2736)***
Specialty Equipment Mkt Assn (PA) 909 396-0289
1575 Valley Vista Dr Diamond Bar (91765) ***(G-25105)***
Specialty Laboratories Inc (HQ) 661 799-6543
27027 Tourney Rd Valencia (91355) ***(G-22286)***
Specialty Minerals Inc 760 248-5300
6565 Meridian Rd Lucerne Valley (92356) ***(G-1100)***
Specialty Produce, San Diego *Also called Tomatoes Extraordinaire Inc* ***(G-8937)***
Specialty Risk Services Inc 714 674-1000
1 Pointe Dr Ste 220 Brea (92821) ***(G-10874)***
Specialty Risk Services Inc 877 809-9478
6140 Stoneridge Mall Rd # 245 Pleasanton (94588) ***(G-10875)***
Specialty Services, Arcadia *Also called Andover Maintenance Inc* ***(G-14230)***
Specialty Solid Waste & Recycl, Santa Clara *Also called Bay Counties Waste Svcs Inc* ***(G-6436)***
Specialty Steel Service, Stockton *Also called PDM Steel Service Centers* ***(G-7390)***
Specialty Steel Service Co Inc (HQ) 916 771-4737
3300 Douglas Blvd Ste 128 Roseville (95661) ***(G-7404)***
Specialty Surgical Centers 949 341-3499
15825 Laguna Canyon Rd # 200 Irvine (92618) ***(G-20049)***
Specialty Team Plastering Inc 805 966-3858
4652 Vintage Ranch Ln Santa Barbara (93110) ***(G-2982)***
Specialty Textile Services LLC 619 476-8750
1333 30th St Ste A San Diego (92154) ***(G-8328)***
Specilzed Foster Care Pasadena, Pasadena *Also called County of Los Angeles* ***(G-22930)***
Specimen Contracting, Sunland *Also called Brightview Tree Company* ***(G-1007)***
Spectacor Management Group 562 436-3636
300 E Ocean Blvd Long Beach (90802) ***(G-11057)***
Spectra, Santa Clara *Also called Spec Personnel LLC* ***(G-14792)***
Spectra Company 909 599-0760
2510 Supply St Pomona (91767) ***(G-2835)***
Spectra I California 310 835-0808
21818 S Wilmington Ave # 402 Carson (90810) ***(G-2737)***
Spectra Industrial Electric, Carson *Also called Spectra I California* ***(G-2737)***
Spectra Premium (usa) Corp 951 653-0640
14530 Innovation Dr Riverside (92518) ***(G-6772)***
Spectrum Abatement, Orange *Also called United Spectrum Inc* ***(G-3594)***
Spectrum Brands Inc 949 672-4003
19701 Da Vinci Foothill Ranch (92610) ***(G-13798)***
Spectrum Brands Hhi, Foothill Ranch *Also called Spectrum Brands Inc* ***(G-13798)***
Spectrum Care Landscaping, Laguna Hills *Also called Spectrum Care Landscpe Mngmnt* ***(G-959)***
Spectrum Care Landscpe Mngmnt 949 454-6900
23282 Del Lago Dr Laguna Hills (92653) ***(G-959)***
Spectrum Communications Cablin 951 371-0549
310 S Maple St Ste F Corona (92880) ***(G-6090)***
Spectrum Construction Inc 760 631-3450
427 College Blvd Oceanside (92057) ***(G-1677)***
Spectrum Credit Union 510 251-6000
500 12th St Ste 200 Oakland (94607) ***(G-9628)***
Spectrum Hotel Group LLC 949 471-8888
90 Pacifica Irvine (92618) ***(G-13278)***
Spectrum Hotel Group LLC 949 471-8888
90 Pacifica Irvine (92618) ***(G-13279)***
Spectrum Information Services (PA) 949 752-7070
16 Technology Dr Ste 107 Irvine (92618) ***(G-14090)***
Spectrum MGT Holdg Co LLC 661 947-3130
41551 10th St W Palmdale (93551) ***(G-6018)***
Spectrum MGT Holdg Co LLC 714 657-1040
6021 Katella Ave Ste 100 Cypress (90630) ***(G-6019)***
Spectrum MGT Holdg Co LLC 951 260-3143
4077 W Stetson Ave Hemet (92545) ***(G-6020)***
Spectrum MGT Holdg Co LLC 323 657-0899
3550 Wilshire Blvd Los Angeles (90010) ***(G-6021)***
Spectrum MGT Holdg Co LLC 562 372-4008
350 Stonewood St Downey (90241) ***(G-6022)***
Spectrum MGT Holdg Co LLC 310 417-4260
6695 Green Valley Cir Culver City (90230) ***(G-6023)***
Spectrum MGT Holdg Co LLC 714 657-1060
6021 Katella Ave Ste 100 Cypress (90630) ***(G-6024)***
Spectrum MGT Holdg Co LLC 714 903-4000
7441 Chapman Ave Garden Grove (92841) ***(G-6025)***
Spectrum MGT Holdg Co LLC 760 340-2225
41725 Cook St Palm Desert (92211) ***(G-6026)***
Spectrum MGT Holdg Co LLC 714 414-1431
3430 E Miraloma Ave Anaheim (92806) ***(G-6027)***
Spectrum Prof Staffing Inc 800 644-1150
13520 Evening Creek Dr N # 300 San Diego (92128) ***(G-14950)***

ALPHABETIC

Spectrum Services Group Inc...916 760-7913
4600 Northgate Blvd # 120 Sacramento (95834) ***(G-28062)***
Spectrum Sttlment Recovery LLC...415 392-5900
100 Shrline Hwy Ste B-125 San Francisco (94111) ***(G-27659)***
Speedway Sonoma LLC...707 938-8448
Hwy 37 N Sonoma (95476) ***(G-18576)***
Speedy Locksmith...760 439-5000
429 Avnida De La Estrella San Clemente (92672) ***(G-18018)***
Spell Control, Bakersfield *Also called Advanced Cleanup Tech Inc* ***(G-3972)***
Spencer Building Maintenance...916 922-1900
1336 Dixieanne Ave Sacramento (95815) ***(G-14437)***
Sperry Van Ness Intl Corp...310 979-0800
11999 San Vicente Blvd # 215 Los Angeles (90049) ***(G-11854)***
Sph-Irvine LLC...949 833-1432
18952 Macarthur Blvd # 103 Irvine (92612) ***(G-20050)***
Spherion Staffing Group, Redding *Also called Sfn Group Inc* ***(G-14948)***
Spicers Paper Inc (HQ)...562 698-1199
12310 Slauson Ave Santa Fe Springs (90670) ***(G-8155)***
Spidercloud Wireless Inc...408 567-9165
475 Sycamore Dr Milpitas (95035) ***(G-5703)***
Spiess Construction Co Inc...805 937-5859
1110 E Clark Ave Ste 210 Santa Maria (93455) ***(G-1998)***
Spigit Inc...855 774-4480
275 Battery St San Francisco (94111) ***(G-7192)***
Spilo Worldwide Inc...213 687-8600
2950 E Vernon Ave Vernon (90058) ***(G-7981)***
Spinacom Inc...510 270-2669
42808 Christy St Ste 201 Fremont (94538) ***(G-7193)***
Spinecare Medical Group Inc...650 985-7500
455 Hickey Blvd Ste 310 Daly City (94015) ***(G-20051)***
Spiniello Companies...909 629-1000
1441 E 9th St Pomona (91766) ***(G-1999)***
Spinning, Venice *Also called Mad Dogg Athletics Inc* ***(G-8397)***
Spinning Spur Wind Three LLC...858 521-3319
15445 Innovation Dr San Diego (92128) ***(G-6243)***
Spira-Loc, El Cajon *Also called University Mechanical &* ***(G-2403)***
Spiral Technology Inc...661 723-3148
229 E Avenue K8 Ste 105 Lancaster (93535) ***(G-26073)***
Spiraledge Inc (PA)...800 691-4065
1919 S Bascom Ave Fl 3 Campbell (95008) ***(G-15843)***
Spire Concessions LLC...818 843-6000
2500 N Hollywood Way Burbank (91505) ***(G-13280)***
Spirit of Woman of California...559 233-4353
327 W Belmont Ave Fresno (93728) ***(G-22840)***
Spiritual Direction...650 952-9456
164 San Luis Ave San Bruno (94066) ***(G-24225)***
Splash Entertainment LLC...818 999-0062
21300 Oxnard St Ste 100 Woodland Hills (91367) ***(G-18157)***
Splash Swim School Inc...925 838-7946
2411 Old Crow Canyon Rd San Ramon (94583) ***(G-19287)***
Splunk Inc (PA)...415 848-8400
250 Brannan St San Francisco (94107) ***(G-15844)***
Sport Center Fitness Inc...310 376-9443
819 N Harbor Dr Redondo Beach (90277) ***(G-18695)***
Sport Chalet LLC...818 781-4000
7541 Woodman Pl Van Nuys (91405) ***(G-8030)***
Sports Basement...408 732-0300
1590 Bryant St San Francisco (94103) ***(G-8031)***
Sports Club La The, San Francisco *Also called Millennium Partners Sports C* ***(G-18662)***
Sports Club of El Dorado, Shingle Springs *Also called Salutary Sports Clubs Inc* ***(G-18676)***
Sports Office, Oakland *Also called City of Oakland* ***(G-19177)***
Sportsmen of Stanislaus Inc...209 578-5801
819 Sunset Ave Modesto (95351) ***(G-18696)***
Sportsmens Lodge Hotel LLC...818 769-4700
12825 Ventura Blvd Studio City (91604) ***(G-13281)***
Sportvision Inc...510 736-2925
6657 Kaiser Dr Fremont (94555) ***(G-18158)***
Spot Free Car Wash, Escondido *Also called In & Out Car Wash Inc* ***(G-17844)***
Spotcues Inc...408 435-2700
1975 W El Cmno Real 301 Mountain View (94040) ***(G-7194)***
Spotlight 29 Casino, Coachella *Also called 29 Palms Enterprises Corp* ***(G-19129)***
Spreadtrum Cmmncations USA Inc...858 546-0895
10180 Telesis Ct Ste 500 San Diego (92121) ***(G-26609)***
Sprig Electric Co...415 947-0138
65 Oak Grove St San Francisco (94107) ***(G-2738)***
Sprig Electric Co (PA)...408 298-3134
1860 S 10th St San Jose (95112) ***(G-2739)***
Sprin Nonpr Consu Credi Manag...951 684-3168
1605 Spruce St Ste 100 Riverside (92507) ***(G-13799)***
Spring Break 83 Production LLC...323 871-4466
650 N Bronson Ave Los Angeles (90004) ***(G-18159)***
Spring Hill Jersey Cheese Inc...707 762-3446
621 Western Ave Petaluma (94952) ***(G-8592)***
Spring Hl Mnor Cnvlescent Hosp, Grass Valley *Also called Springhill Manor Rehabilitatio* ***(G-21380)***
Spring Lake Village, Santa Rosa *Also called Episcopal Senior Communities* ***(G-24648)***
Spring Valley Lake Country CLB...760 245-5356
13229 Spring Valley Pkwy Victorville (92395) ***(G-19093)***
Spring Valley Post Acute LLC...760 245-6477
14973 Hesperia Rd Victorville (92395) ***(G-20923)***
Springhill Manor Rehabilitatio...530 273-7247
355 Joerschke Dr Grass Valley (95945) ***(G-21380)***
Springhill Suites, San Diego *Also called Marriott International Inc* ***(G-12956)***
Springhill Suites Oceanside, Oceanside *Also called Gfp Oceanside Block 21 LLC* ***(G-12664)***
Springhuse Manor Care Hlth Svc...714 671-7898
285 W Central Ave Ofc Brea (92821) ***(G-24818)***
Springs Ambulance Service Inc...760 883-5000
1111 Montalvo Way Palm Springs (92262) ***(G-3847)***
Springs Club Inc...760 328-0254
1 Duke Dr Rancho Mirage (92270) ***(G-19094)***
Springs Country Club, The, Rancho Mirage *Also called Springs Club Inc* ***(G-19094)***
Sprint Communications Co LP...818 755-7100
111 Unversal Hollywood Dr Universal City (91608) ***(G-5704)***
Sprint Communications Co LP...909 382-6030
1505 E Enterprise Dr San Bernardino (92408) ***(G-5705)***
Sprint Corporation...949 748-3353
6591 Irvine Center Dr # 100 Irvine (92618) ***(G-5410)***
Sprint Spectrum LP...323 473-5454
3733 W Sunset Blvd Los Angeles (90026) ***(G-2740)***
Sprint Spectrum LP...424 372-2500
11201 National Blvd Los Angeles (90064) ***(G-2741)***
Sprouts Farmers Market Inc...661 414-1109
24235 Magic Mountain Pkwy Valencia (91355) ***(G-8522)***
Sprouts Farmers Market Inc...951 766-6746
1295 S State St Hemet (92543) ***(G-8523)***
Sprouts Farmers Market Inc...310 500-1192
1751 Westwood Blvd Los Angeles (90024) ***(G-8524)***
Sprouts Farmers Market Inc...858 350-7900
659 Lomas Santa Fe Dr Solana Beach (92075) ***(G-8525)***
Sprouts Farmers Market Inc...714 572-3535
17482 Yorba Linda Blvd Yorba Linda (92886) ***(G-8526)***
Sprouts Farmers Market Inc...714 751-6399
3030 Harbor Blvd Ste D Costa Mesa (92626) ***(G-8527)***
Spruce Technology Inc...925 415-8160
3516 Browntail Way San Ramon (94582) ***(G-15475)***
Spurr Co., Paso Robles *Also called Dave Spurr Excavating Inc* ***(G-3426)***
Spus7 235 Pine LP...231 683-4200
235 Pine St Ste 125 San Francisco (94104) ***(G-12147)***
Spus7 Miami Acc LP...213 683-4200
515 S Flower St Ste 3100 Los Angeles (90071) ***(G-12148)***
Spycher Brothers, Turlock *Also called Select Harvest Usa LLC* ***(G-8965)***
Spyglass Hill Community Assn...949 855-1800
39 Argonaut Ste 100 Aliso Viejo (92656) ***(G-25352)***
Sqa Services Inc...310 544-6888
550 Silver Spur Rd # 300 Rllng HLS Est (90275) ***(G-27660)***
Squab Producers Calif Inc...209 537-4744
409 Primo Way Modesto (95358) ***(G-8606)***
Squar Milner Peterson Miran (PA)...949 222-2999
4100 Nwport Pl Dr Ste 300 Newport Beach (92660) ***(G-26446)***
Square Inc (PA)...415 375-3176
1455 Market St Ste 600 San Francisco (94103) ***(G-15845)***
Square Enix Inc...310 846-0400
999 N Sepulveda Blvd Fl 3 El Segundo (90245) ***(G-7195)***
Squaretrade Inc (PA)...415 541-1000
360 3rd St Fl 6 San Francisco (94107) ***(G-10876)***
Squaw Creek Associates LLC...530 581-6624
400 Squaw Creek Rd Alpine Meadows (96146) ***(G-13282)***
Squaw Valley Development Co (HQ)...530 583-6985
1960 Squaw Valley Rd Olympic Valley (96146) ***(G-13283)***
Squaw Valley Ski, Olympic Valley *Also called Squaw Valley Development Co* ***(G-13283)***
Squaw Valley Ski Corporation (HQ)...530 583-6985
1960 Squaw Valley Rd Olympic Valley (96146) ***(G-13284)***
Squire Patton Boggs (us) LLP...415 954-0334
275 Battery St Ste 2600 San Francisco (94111) ***(G-23579)***
Squire Sanders (us) LLP...213 624-2500
555 S Flower St Fl 31 Los Angeles (90071) ***(G-23580)***
SR Bray LLC...951 436-2920
2750 N Perris Blvd Perris (92571) ***(G-14581)***
SR Bray LLC (PA)...714 765-7551
1210 N Red Gum St Anaheim (92806) ***(G-2742)***
SR Freeman Inc...408 364-2200
89 Dillon Ave Ste A Campbell (95008) ***(G-3093)***
Sra Oss Inc...408 855-8200
5201 Great America Pkwy # 419 Santa Clara (95054) ***(G-15846)***
Srcsd, Sacramento *Also called Sacramento Reg Co Sanit Dist* ***(G-6637)***
Srd Engineering Inc...714 630-2480
3578 E Enterprise Dr Anaheim (92807) ***(G-2000)***
Srg Management LLC...858 792-9300
500 Stevens Ave Ste 100 Solana Beach (92075) ***(G-27227)***
Srht Property Mgmt Co...213 683-0522
1317 E 7th St Los Angeles (90021) ***(G-27228)***
SRI International (PA)...650 859-2000
333 Ravenswood Ave Menlo Park (94025) ***(G-26809)***
SRI International...805 542-9330
4111 Broad St Ste 220 San Luis Obispo (93401) ***(G-26810)***
SRK Global Consulting...310 295-2524
7225 Crescent Park W # 255 Los Angeles (90094) ***(G-16488)***
Srm Alliance Hospital Services (PA)...707 778-1111
400 N Mcdowell Blvd Petaluma (94954) ***(G-21912)***
Srm Contracting & Paving, San Diego *Also called Superior Ready Mix Concrete LP* ***(G-1871)***
SRS Consulting Inc...510 252-0625
39465 Paseo Padre P Ste 1100 Fremont (94538) ***(G-16489)***
SRS Distribution Inc...818 840-8851
700 N Victory Blvd Burbank (91502) ***(G-7019)***
SRS Protection Inc...805 744-7122
4464 Mcgrath St Ste 103 Ventura (93003) ***(G-16830)***
Ss Skikos Incorporated...707 575-3000
1289 Sebastopol Rd Santa Rosa (95407) ***(G-4378)***
Ss Travel, San Francisco *Also called San Francisco Travel Assn* ***(G-17473)***
Ss8 Networks Inc (PA)...408 894-8400
750 Tasman Dr Milpitas (95035) ***(G-6091)***
Ssa Containers Inc...206 623-0304
1521 Pier J Ave Long Beach (90802) ***(G-4758)***
Ssa Marine Inc...562 983-1001
1521 Pier J Ave Long Beach (90802) ***(G-4759)***
Ssa Pacific Inc...916 374-1866
2895 Industrial Blvd # 100 West Sacramento (95691) ***(G-4760)***

Ssa Pacific Inc 310 833-9606
Outer Harbor Berth 54 55 San Pedro (90731) ***(G-4761)***
SSC Carmichael Operating Co LP 916 485-4793
3630 Mission Ave Carmichael (95608) ***(G-20924)***
SSC Construction Inc 951 278-1177
2073 Railroad St Corona (92880) ***(G-26074)***
SSC Newport Beach Oper Co LP 949 642-8044
466 Flagship Rd Newport Beach (92663) ***(G-20925)***
SSC Oakland Excell Oper Co LP 510 261-5200
3025 High St Oakland (94619) ***(G-20926)***
SSC Pittsburg Operating Co LP 925 427-4444
2351 Loveridge Rd Pittsburg (94565) ***(G-21381)***
SSC San Jose Operating Co LP 408 249-0344
340 Northlake Dr San Jose (95117) ***(G-20927)***
Ssd Systems, Anaheim *Also called Security Signal Devices Inc* ***(G-16923)***
SSE Merchandise, San Jose *Also called Sharks Sports & Entrmt LLC* ***(G-18564)***
Ssf Imported Auto Parts LLC (PA) 800 203-9287
466 Forbes Blvd South San Francisco (94080) ***(G-6773)***
Ssf Imported Auto Parts LLC 310 782-8859
21175 Main St Ste A Carson (90745) ***(G-6774)***
SSG ADMINISTRATIVE OFFICES, Los Angeles *Also called Special Service For Groups Inc* ***(G-24391)***
Ssg Hop Sp 323 432-4399
5811 S San Pedro St Los Angeles (90011) ***(G-28162)***
Ssi, Rocklin *Also called Surveillance Systems* ***(G-7643)***
Ssi, Valley Center *Also called Survival Systems Intl Inc* ***(G-18020)***
Ssi, San Luis Obispo *Also called Sealant Systems International* ***(G-6789)***
Ssi-Turlock Dairy Division 209 668-2100
2600 Spengler Way Turlock (95380) ***(G-8593)***
Ssinfotek Inc 949 732-3100
15615 Alton Pkwy Ste 450 Irvine (92618) ***(G-16058)***
Ssjid, Manteca *Also called South San Jquin Irrigation Dst* ***(G-6654)***
Ssmb Pacific Holding Co Inc (PA) 510 836-6100
1755 Adams Ave San Leandro (94577) ***(G-6695)***
Ssmb Pacific Holding Co Inc 530 222-1212
20769 Industry Rd Anderson (96007) ***(G-6696)***
Ssmb Pacific Holding Co Inc 916 371-3372
707 Display Way Sacramento (95838) ***(G-6697)***
SSMC, Vallejo *Also called Sutter Solano Medical Center* ***(G-21954)***
SSPCA, Sacramento *Also called The For Sacramento Society* ***(G-25589)***
Ssw, Palm Springs *Also called S S W Mechanical Cnstr Inc* ***(G-2355)***
St Andrews Children Center 949 651-0198
4400 Barranca Pkwy Irvine (92604) ***(G-24518)***
St Andrews Health Care, Los Angeles *Also called Washington Enterprises 3 LLC* ***(G-21024)***
ST ANNE'S HOME, San Francisco *Also called Little Sisters of Poor* ***(G-24714)***
St Annes Maternity Home 213 381-2931
155 N Occidental Blvd Los Angeles (90026) ***(G-24819)***
St Anthony Foundation (PA) 415 241-2600
150 Golden Gate Ave San Francisco (94102) ***(G-24226)***
St Baldricks Foundation Inc (PA) 626 792-8247
1333 S Mayflower Ave Monrovia (91016) ***(G-25157)***
St Barnabas Senior Center of L 213 388-4444
675 S Carondelet St Los Angeles (90057) ***(G-24227)***
St Denis Electric Inc 805 343-9999
734 Ralcoa Way Arroyo Grande (93420) ***(G-2743)***
St Edna Sbcute Cnvalescent Ctr, Santa Ana *Also called Covenant Care California LLC* ***(G-20500)***
St Elizabeth Community Hosp (HQ) 530 529-7760
2550 Sster Mary Clumba Dr Red Bluff (96080) ***(G-21913)***
St Francis Electric Inc 510 639-0639
975 Carden St San Leandro (94577) ***(G-2744)***
St Francis Electric LLC 510 750-8271
975 Carden St San Leandro (94577) ***(G-2745)***
St Francis Extended Care Inc 510 785-3630
718 Bartlett Ave Hayward (94541) ***(G-21382)***
St Francis Heights Convales 650 755-9515
35 Escuela Dr Daly City (94015) ***(G-21383)***
St Francis Medical Ce 323 588-8558
2700 E Slauson Ave # 200 Huntington Park (90255) ***(G-20052)***
St Francis Medical Center, Redwood City *Also called Verity Health System Cal Inc* ***(G-22013)***
St Francis Medical Center 310 900-8900
3630 E Imperial Hwy Lynwood (90262) ***(G-20053)***
St Francis Medical Center of (PA) 310 900-8900
3630 E Imperial Hwy Lynwood (90262) ***(G-21914)***
St Francis Pavillion, Daly City *Also called Forte Enterprises Inc* ***(G-27028)***
St Francis Yacht Club 415 563-6363
700 Marina Blvd San Francisco (94123) ***(G-19095)***
St Helena Hospital Clearlake, Clearlake *Also called Advintist Hlth Clearlake Hosp* ***(G-21435)***
St Helena Hospital (PA) 707 963-1882
10 Woodland Rd Saint Helena (94574) ***(G-21915)***
St Helena Hospital Clearlake, Clearlake *Also called Adventist Health System/West* ***(G-19324)***
St John's Health Centre, Santa Monica *Also called Saint Jhns Hlth Ctr Foundation* ***(G-21839)***
St Johns Health Center 310 829-5511
2121 Santa Monica Blvd Santa Monica (90404) ***(G-23063)***
St Johns Regional Medical Ctr, Oxnard *Also called Dignity Health* ***(G-21541)***
St Johns Retirement Village (PA) 530 662-9674
135 Woodland Ave Woodland (95695) ***(G-21384)***
St Johns Retirement Village 530 662-9674
135 Woodland Ave Woodland (95695) ***(G-21916)***
St Johns Well Child (PA) 323 541-1600
808 W 58th St Los Angeles (90037) ***(G-20278)***
St Joseph Center 310 396-6468
204 Hampton Dr Venice (90291) ***(G-24228)***
St Joseph Community Home Care 209 478-9547
7400 Shoreline Dr Ste 4 Stockton (95219) ***(G-22569)***
St Joseph Health System 714 992-3000
101 E Valencia Mesa Dr Fullerton (92835) ***(G-21917)***
St Joseph Health System 707 443-9371
2280 Harrison Ave Ste B Eureka (95501) ***(G-20054)***
St Joseph Health System (HQ) 949 381-4000
3345 Michelson Dr Ste 100 Irvine (92612) ***(G-22570)***
St Joseph Health System 707 778-2505
400 N Mcdowell Blvd Fl 1 Petaluma (94954) ***(G-21918)***
St Joseph Heritage Med Group (PA) 714 633-1011
2212 E 4th St Ste 201 Santa Ana (92705) ***(G-20055)***
St Joseph Home Health Network (HQ) 714 712-9500
200 W Center St Promenade Anaheim (92805) ***(G-22571)***
St Joseph Home Health Network 714 712-9559
200 W Center St Promenade Anaheim (92805) ***(G-22572)***
St Joseph Hospice 714 712-7100
200 W Center St Promenade Anaheim (92805) ***(G-24229)***
St Joseph Hospital (PA) 707 445-8121
2700 Dolbeer St Eureka (95501) ***(G-21919)***
St Joseph Hospital 707 268-0190
2700 Dolbeer St Eureka (95501) ***(G-14951)***
St Joseph Hospital of Eureka 707 445-8121
2700 Dolbeer St Eureka (95501) ***(G-21920)***
St Joseph Hospital of Orange (HQ) 714 633-9111
1100 W Stewart Dr Orange (92868) ***(G-21921)***
St Joseph Hospital of Orange 714 771-8037
1100 W Stewart Dr Orange (92868) ***(G-21922)***
St Joseph Prof Svcs Entps Inc 714 347-7500
440 S Batavia St Orange (92868) ***(G-23581)***
St Joseph Surgery Center LP 209 467-6316
1800 N California St # 1 Stockton (95204) ***(G-20056)***
St Josephs Med Ctr Stockton 209 943-2000
1800 N California St Stockton (95204) ***(G-21923)***
St Josephs Medical Center 209 943-2000
1800 N California St Stockton (95204) ***(G-21924)***
St Jude Heritage Medical Group 714 528-4211
4300 Rose Dr Yorba Linda (92886) ***(G-20057)***
St Jude Hospital (HQ) 714 871-3280
101 E Valencia Mesa Dr Fullerton (92835) ***(G-21925)***
St Jude Hospital 714 578-8500
279 Imperial Hwy Ste 770 Fullerton (92835) ***(G-21926)***
St Jude Hospital 714 992-3057
101 E Valencia Mesa Dr Fullerton (92835) ***(G-20058)***
St Jude Hospital Yorba Linda 714 665-1797
11420 Warner Ave Fountain Valley (92708) ***(G-20059)***
St Jude Hospital Yorba Linda 949 365-2492
27800 Medical Center Rd Mission Viejo (92691) ***(G-20060)***
St Jude Hospital Yorba Linda 714 557-6300
722 Baker St Costa Mesa (92626) ***(G-20061)***
St Jude Hospital Yorba Linda (PA) 714 449-4800
251 Imperial Hwy Ste 481 Fullerton (92835) ***(G-27661)***
St Jude Medical Center, Fullerton *Also called St Jude Hospital* ***(G-21925)***
St Jude Medical Ctr Purch Dept, Fullerton *Also called St Jude Hospital* ***(G-20058)***
St Louis Rams, Agoura Hills *Also called Los Angeles Rams LLC* ***(G-18555)***
St Luke Hlthcr & Rehab Ctr LL 707 725-4467
2321 Newburg Rd Fortuna (95540) ***(G-20928)***
St Lukes Hospital (HQ) 415 600-3959
2351 Clay St San Francisco (94115) ***(G-21927)***
St Madeleine Sophies Center 619 442-5129
2119 E Madison Ave El Cajon (92019) ***(G-24392)***
St Mary Medical Center (HQ) 562 491-9000
1050 Linden Ave Long Beach (90813) ***(G-21928)***
St Mary's School of Nursing, Long Beach *Also called St Mary Medical Center* ***(G-21928)***
St Marys Med Ctr Foundation 415 668-1000
450 Stanyan St San Francisco (94117) ***(G-21929)***
St Michael Convalescent Hosp 510 782-8424
25919 Gading Rd Hayward (94544) ***(G-20929)***
St Paul's Towers, Oakland *Also called Episcopal Senior Communities* ***(G-24645)***
St Paul's Villa, National City *Also called St Pauls Episcopal Home Inc* ***(G-24822)***
St Pauls Episcopal Home Inc 619 239-8687
235 Nutmeg St San Diego (92103) ***(G-24820)***
St Pauls Episcopal Home Inc 619 239-2097
2635 2nd Ave Ofc San Diego (92103) ***(G-24821)***
St Pauls Episcopal Home Inc 619 232-2996
2700 E 4th St National City (91950) ***(G-24822)***
St Regis Resort Monarch Beach, Dana Point *Also called Cph Monarch Hotel LLC* ***(G-12551)***
ST ROSE HOSPITAL, Hayward *Also called Hayward Sisters Hospital* ***(G-21592)***
St Vincent De Paul, Oakland *Also called District Council DC* ***(G-23946)***
St Vincent De Paul of La, Los Angeles *Also called Society of St Vincent De Paul* ***(G-25582)***
St Vincent De Paul Society 916 485-3482
3100 Norris Ave Sacramento (95821) ***(G-24230)***
St Vincent De Paul Vlg Inc 619 233-8500
1501 Imperial Ave San Diego (92101) ***(G-25586)***
St Vincent Health Care, Pasadena *Also called Vincent Hayley Enterprises* ***(G-21414)***
St Vincent Medical Center 213 484-7111
2131 W 3rd St Los Angeles (90057) ***(G-21930)***
St Vincent Senior Citizn Nutr (PA) 213 484-7775
2131 W 3rd St Los Angeles (90057) ***(G-25158)***
St. Francis Medical Center, Lynwood *Also called Verity Health System Cal Inc* ***(G-22018)***
St. Johns Pleasant Valley Hosp, Camarillo *Also called Dignity Health* ***(G-21540)***
STA, Thousand Palms *Also called Sunline Transit Agency* ***(G-3889)***
STA Barbara Cnty Air Pltn Cntr, Santa Barbara *Also called Air Pollution Control District* ***(G-27822)***
STA Clara Valley Medical Ctr 408 885-2334
751 S Bascom Ave San Jose (95128) ***(G-20062)***
Staccato Communications Inc 858 812-0981
6195 Lusk Blvd Ste 200 San Diego (92121) ***(G-17498)***
Stadtner Co Inc 415 752-2850
3112 Geary Blvd San Francisco (94118) ***(G-2746)***
Staff Pro Inc 619 544-1774
675 Convention Way San Diego (92101) ***(G-16831)***

ALPHABETIC SECTION

Star One Credit Union (PA)

Staff Pro Inc (PA) 714 230-7200
15272 Jason Cir Huntington Beach (92649) *(G-16929)*

Staff Today Incorporated 800 928-5561
212 E Rowland St 313 Covina (91723) *(G-14952)*

Staffchex Inc 818 709-6100
20537 Devonshire St Chatsworth (91311) *(G-14794)*

Staffing Home Care, San Bruno *Also called Staffing Specialists Intl (G-22573)*

Staffing Solutions, Montebello *Also called L&T Staffing Inc (G-14894)*

Staffing Solutions Inc 408 980-9000
2142 Bering Dr San Jose (95131) *(G-14795)*

Staffing Specialists Intl 650 737-0777
2598 Olympic Dr San Bruno (94066) *(G-22573)*

Stafford-King-Wiese Architects 916 930-5900
622 20th St Sacramento (95811) *(G-26254)*

Stage II Design & Production, Belvedere Tiburon *Also called Stage II Inc (G-17499)*

Stage II Inc 415 285-8400
1100 Mar West St Ste F Belvedere Tiburon (94920) *(G-17499)*

Stage Right Production Svcs, Agoura *Also called Up Stage Inc (G-18186)*

Stagecoach Vineyards 707 255-5459
1345 Hestia Way NAPA (94558) *(G-189)*

Stagnaro Brothers Seafood Inc 831 423-1188
320 Washington St Santa Cruz (95060) *(G-8656)*

Stalker Software Inc 415 569-2280
1100 Larkspur Landing Cir # 355 Larkspur (94939) *(G-15847)*

Stamoules Produce Co, Mendota *Also called S Stamoules Inc (G-581)*

Stamoules Produce Company, Mendota *Also called S & S Ranch Inc (G-482)*

Stampscom Inc (PA) 310 482-5800
1990 E Grand Ave El Segundo (90245) *(G-14091)*

Stan Tashman & Associates Inc 310 460-7600
8675 Wash Blvd Ste 203 Culver City (90232) *(G-27229)*

Stan Winston Inc 818 782-0870
340 Parkside Dr San Fernando (91340) *(G-18255)*

Stan Winston Studio, San Fernando *Also called Stan Winston Inc (G-18255)*

Standard Chartered Bank 626 639-8000
601 S Figueroa St # 2775 Los Angeles (90017) *(G-9525)*

Standard Drywall Inc (HQ) 619 443-7034
9902 Channel Rd Lakeside (92040) *(G-2983)*

Standard Hotel, The, Los Angeles *Also called 550 Flower St Operations LLC (G-12366)*

Standard Industries Inc 209 242-5000
3301 Navone Rd Stockton (95215) *(G-7020)*

Standard Industries Inc 661 387-1110
6505 S Zerker Rd Shafter (93263) *(G-7021)*

Standard Iron & Metals Co 510 535-0222
4525 San Leandro St Oakland (94601) *(G-8090)*

Standard Pacific Capital LLC 415 352-7100
101 California St Fl 36 San Francisco (94111) *(G-10077)*

Standard Pacific Homes, Carlsbad *Also called Calatlantic Group Inc (G-1146)*

Standard Pacific Homes, Irvine *Also called Calatlantic Group Inc (G-1300)*

Standard Pacific of Texas Inc 949 789-1621
15360 Barranca Pkwy Irvine (92618) *(G-1384)*

Standard Poors Fincl Svcs LLC 415 371-5000
1 California St Fl 31 San Francisco (94111) *(G-10186)*

Standard Register Inc 925 449-3700
5775 Brisa St Livermore (94550) *(G-4703)*

Standard The, Los Angeles *Also called Hollywood Standard LLC (G-12754)*

Standard-Southern Corporation 213 624-1831
400 S Central Ave Los Angeles (90013) *(G-4501)*

Standard-Southern Corporation 213 624-1831
440 S Central Ave Los Angeles (90013) *(G-4502)*

Standard-Southern Corporation 213 624-1831
715 E 4th St Los Angeles (90013) *(G-4503)*

Standardaero Bus AVI Svcs LLC 310 568-3700
6201 W Imperial Hwy Los Angeles (90045) *(G-4939)*

Standardbearer Insur Co Ltd 949 487-9500
27101 Puerta Real Ste 450 Mission Viejo (92691) *(G-20930)*

Stanford 650 799-3773
450 Serra Mall Stanford (94305) *(G-20063)*

STANFORD & LATHROP MEMORIAL HO, Sacramento *Also called Stanford Youth Solutions (G-24983)*

Stanford Alumni Association, Stanford *Also called Leland Stanford Junior Univ (G-25287)*

Stanford Cancer Center S Bay, San Jose *Also called Stanford Health Care (G-21932)*

Stanford Court Hotel, San Francisco *Also called Pine & Powell Partners LLC (G-13096)*

Stanford Court Nursing Center, La Mesa *Also called Life Gnerations Healthcare LLC (G-20733)*

Stanford Crt Nrsing Cntr-Sntee, Santee *Also called Life Gnerations Healthcare LLC (G-21290)*

Stanford Federal Credit Union (PA) 650 725-1000
1860 Embarcadero Rd # 200 Palo Alto (94303) *(G-9629)*

Stanford Fmly Prctc-Blake Wilb 650 723-6963
211 Quarry Rd Fl 3 Palo Alto (94304) *(G-20064)*

Stanford Health Care 650 723-4000
300 Pasteur Dr Stanford (94305) *(G-21931)*

Stanford Health Care 408 426-4900
2589 Samaritan Dr San Jose (95124) *(G-21932)*

Stanford Health Care (HQ) 650 723-4000
300 Pasteur Dr Stanford (94305) *(G-21933)*

Stanford Health Care 650 736-7844
3375 Hillview Ave Palo Alto (94304) *(G-21934)*

Stanford Health Services, Palo Alto *Also called Stanford Fmly Prctc-Blake Wilb (G-20064)*

Stanford Hospital and Clinics 650 213-8360
1510 Page Mill Rd Ste 2 Palo Alto (94304) *(G-21935)*

Stanford Hospitals and Clinics, Palo Alto *Also called Leland Stanford Junior Univ (G-21700)*

Stanford Hotels Corporation 415 398-3333
433 California St Ste 700 San Francisco (94104) *(G-13285)*

STANFORD LINEAR ACCELERATOR CE, Stanford *Also called Stanford Univ Med Ctr Aux (G-24231)*

Stanford Management Company 650 721-2200
635 Knight Way Stanford (94305) *(G-27230)*

Stanford Medical Center, Stanford *Also called Stanford Health Care (G-21933)*

Stanford Medical Center, Palo Alto *Also called Leland Stanford Junior Univ (G-21701)*

Stanford Park Hotel 650 322-1234
100 El Camino Real Menlo Park (94025) *(G-13286)*

Stanford Sierra Camp & Lodge, South Lake Tahoe *Also called Saa Sierra Programs LLC (G-25329)*

Stanford Univ Earth Secinces, Stanford *Also called Leland Stanford Junior Univ (G-26784)*

Stanford Univ Med Ctr Aux 650 723-6636
300 Pasteur Dr Stanford (94305) *(G-24231)*

Stanford University, Stanford *Also called Leland Stanford Junior Univ (G-21703)*

Stanford University, Stanford *Also called Leland Stanford Junior Univ (G-21704)*

Stanford University Med Ctr, Palo Alto *Also called Leland Stanford Junior Univ (G-21702)*

Stanford University Medical, Stanford *Also called Leland Stanford Junior Univ (G-21705)*

Stanford Youth Solutions (PA) 916 344-0199
8912 Volunteer Ln Sacramento (95826) *(G-24983)*

Stanislaus Consol Fire Prot 209 549-8404
321 E St Waterford (95386) *(G-17500)*

Stanislaus County Police 209 529-9121
1325 Beverly Dr Modesto (95351) *(G-24232)*

Stanislaus Farm Supply Company (PA) 860 678-5160
624 E Service Rd Modesto (95358) *(G-9153)*

Stanislaus Medical Center, Modesto *Also called County of Stanislaus (G-21525)*

Stanislaus Recovery Center 209 541-2121
1904 Richland Ave Ceres (95307) *(G-22841)*

Stanislaus Surgical Center, Modesto *Also called Stanislaus Surgical Hosp LLC (G-21936)*

Stanislaus Surgical Hosp LLC (PA) 209 572-2700
1421 Oakdale Rd Modesto (95355) *(G-21936)*

Stanisluas County Mental Hlth, Modesto *Also called County of Stanislaus (G-22713)*

Stanley M Kirkpatrick MD 858 966-5855
3020 Childrens Way San Diego (92123) *(G-20065)*

Stanley R Klein MD Facs Inc 310 373-6864
23451 Madison St Ste 300 Torrance (90505) *(G-20066)*

Stanley Steemer Carpet Cleaner, San Diego *Also called Colt Services Inc (G-13596)*

Stanley Steemer of Los Angles (PA) 626 791-9400
841 W Foothill Blvd Azusa (91702) *(G-13600)*

Stansbury Hm Preservation Assn 530 895-3848
307 W 5th St Chico (95928) *(G-25050)*

Stantec Arch & Engrg PC 415 882-9500
100 California St # 1000 San Francisco (94111) *(G-26075)*

Stantec Arch & Engrg PC 949 923-6000
38 Technology Dr Ste 100 Irvine (92618) *(G-26076)*

Stantec Architecture Inc 949 923-6000
38 Technology Dr Ste 100 Irvine (92618) *(G-26255)*

Stantec Architecture Inc 925 941-1400
1340 Treat Blvd Ste 300 Walnut Creek (94597) *(G-26256)*

Stantec Architecture Inc 415 882-9500
100 California St # 1000 San Francisco (94111) *(G-26077)*

Stantec Consulting Svcs Inc 916 773-8100
3875 Atherton Rd Rocklin (95765) *(G-26257)*

Stantec Consulting Svcs Inc 949 474-1000
46 Discovery Ste 250 Irvine (92618) *(G-26281)*

Stantec Consulting Svcs Inc 805 963-9532
111 E Victoria St Santa Barbara (93101) *(G-26282)*

Stantec Consulting Svcs Inc 949 923-6000
38 Technology Dr Ste 100 Irvine (92618) *(G-26258)*

Stantec Consulting Svcs Inc 415 882-9500
100 California St # 1000 San Francisco (94111) *(G-26078)*

Stantec Energy & Resources Inc (HQ) 661 396-3770
5500 Ming Ave Ste 300 Bakersfield (93309) *(G-26283)*

Stantec Holdings Del III Inc (PA) 661 396-3770
5500 Ming Ave Ste 300 Bakersfield (93309) *(G-12091)*

Stanton Holdings Americas 714 689-9551
6595 Fairlynn Blvd Yorba Linda (92886) *(G-17501)*

Stantru Reinforcing Steel, Fontana *Also called Stantru Resources Inc (G-1466)*

Stantru Resources Inc 909 587-1441
11175 Redwood Ave Fontana (92337) *(G-1466)*

Star & Crescent Boat Company (PA) 619 234-4111
1311 1st St Coronado (92118) *(G-4740)*

Star - Lite Electric, Chatsworth *Also called Mj Star-Lite Inc (G-2654)*

Star Brite Building Maint 562 988-2829
2688 Dawson Ave Long Beach (90755) *(G-14438)*

Star Electric 626 422-9227
517 E Baseline Rd San Dimas (91773) *(G-2747)*

Star Estate, Aliso Viejo *Also called Tyson Investments Inc (G-11890)*

Star Fisheries 310 549-4992
841 Watson Ave Wilmington (90744) *(G-8657)*

Star H-R 707 265-9911
1822 Jefferson St NAPA (94559) *(G-14796)*

Star H-R 707 894-4404
105 E 1st St Cloverdale (95425) *(G-14797)*

Star Inc 916 632-8407
4145 Delmar Ave Ste 1 Rocklin (95677) *(G-24233)*

Star Lax LLC 310 642-4500
150 S Doheny Dr Beverly Hills (90211) *(G-17693)*

Star Nail International, Valencia *Also called Star Nail Products Inc (G-8296)*

Star Nail Products Inc 661 257-3376
29120 Avenue Paine Valencia (91355) *(G-8296)*

Star Nail Products Inc 661 257-7827
29120 Avenue Paine Valencia (91355) *(G-7982)*

Star of California 805 379-1401
299 W Hillcrest Dr Thousand Oaks (91360) *(G-23064)*

Star of California (PA) 805 644-7823
4880 Market St Ventura (93003) *(G-23065)*

Star One Credit Union (PA) 408 543-5202
1306 Bordeaux Dr Sunnyvale (94089) *(G-9630)*

ALPHABETIC

Star Real Estate.......714 500-3300
19440 Goldenwest St Huntington Beach (92648) ***(G-11855)***
Star Real Estate South County.......949 389-0004
26711 Aliso Creek Rd 200a Aliso Viejo (92656) ***(G-11856)***
Star Scrap Metal Company Inc.......562 921-5045
1509 S Bluff Rd Montebello (90640) ***(G-8091)***
Star View Adolescent Center.......310 373-4556
4025 W 226th St Torrance (90505) ***(G-22092)***
Star View Chldrn Fmly Srvcs.......310 868-5379
1085 W Victoria St Compton (90220) ***(G-24234)***
Starbucks Corporation.......818 565-3510
2950 N Hollywood Way # 175 Burbank (91505) ***(G-27662)***
Starbucks Corporation.......714 378-1107
17700 Newhope St Ste 200 Fountain Valley (92708) ***(G-27663)***
Starbucks Corporation.......626 203-1862
1451 Francis Ave Upland (91786) ***(G-27664)***
Starbucks Corporation.......415 537-7170
60 Spear St Ste 700 San Francisco (94105) ***(G-27665)***
Stargate Digital, South Pasadena *Also called Stargate Films Inc* ***(G-18160)***
Stargate Films Inc.......626 403-8403
1001 El Centro St South Pasadena (91030) ***(G-18160)***
Stark Services.......818 985-2003
12444 Victory Blvd # 300 North Hollywood (91606) ***(G-16193)***
Starlight Educational Center, Westminster *Also called Westview Services Inc* ***(G-24406)***
Starlight Management Group.......408 334-7456
1355 N 4th St San Jose (95112) ***(G-13287)***
Starline Tours Hollywood Inc.......323 463-3333
6801 Hollywood Blvd # 221 Los Angeles (90028) ***(G-19288)***
Starline Tours Hollywood Inc (PA).......323 262-1114
2130 S Tubeway Ave Commerce (90040) ***(G-19289)***
Starlink Freight Sys Sfo Inc (PA).......650 589-2575
206 Utah Ave South San Francisco (94080) ***(G-5169)***
Starpoint Property MGT LLC.......310 247-0550
450 N Roxbury Dr Ste 1050 Beverly Hills (90210) ***(G-11857)***
Starpoint Surgery Center, Irvine *Also called Sph-Irvine LLC* ***(G-20050)***
Starr Investment Holdings LLC.......415 216-4000
101 2nd St Ste 2500 San Francisco (94105) ***(G-12149)***
Stars, San Leandro *Also called Subacute Trtmnt Adolescnt Reha* ***(G-20933)***
Stars Recreation Center LP.......707 455-7827
155 Browns Valley Pkwy Vacaville (95688) ***(G-18530)***
Startel Corporation (PA).......949 863-8700
16 Goodyear B-125 Irvine (92618) ***(G-15476)***
Startup Farms Intl LLC.......510 440-0110
45690 Northport Loop E Fremont (94538) ***(G-15477)***
Starvista.......650 591-9623
610 Elm St Ste 212 San Carlos (94070) ***(G-24235)***
Starwest Botanicals Inc (PA).......916 638-8100
161 Main Ave Ste A Sacramento (95838) ***(G-8923)***
Starwood Hotel.......310 641-7740
5990 Green Valley Cir Culver City (90230) ***(G-13288)***
Starwood Hotels & Resorts, San Francisco *Also called W Hotel* ***(G-13384)***
Starwood Hotels & Resorts, Costa Mesa *Also called South Coast Westin Hotel Co* ***(G-13274)***
Starwood Hotels & Resorts, San Diego *Also called San Diego Sheraton Corporation* ***(G-13200)***
Starwood Hotels & Resorts, Millbrae *Also called Western Host Inc* ***(G-13402)***
Starwood Hotels & Resorts, Culver City *Also called Starwood Hotel* ***(G-13288)***
Starwood Hotels & Resorts, Santa Rosa *Also called Merritt Hospitality LLC* ***(G-12992)***
Starwood Hotels & Resorts.......909 484-2018
10480 4th St Rancho Cucamonga (91730) ***(G-13289)***
Starwood Hotels & Resorts.......310 208-8765
930 Hilgard Ave Los Angeles (90024) ***(G-13290)***
Starwood Hotels & Resorts.......916 447-1700
1230 J St Sacramento (95814) ***(G-13291)***
Starwood Hotels & Resorts.......714 258-4575
15621 Red Hill Ave # 100 Tustin (92780) ***(G-13292)***
Starwood Hotels & Resorts.......415 777-5300
181 3rd St San Francisco (94103) ***(G-13293)***
Starwood Hotels & Resorts.......213 624-1000
404 S Figueroa St Los Angeles (90071) ***(G-13294)***
Starwood Hotels & Resorts.......415 479-8800
1010 Northgate Dr San Rafael (94903) ***(G-13295)***
Starwood Hotels & Resorts.......650 692-6363
401 E Millbrae Ave Millbrae (94030) ***(G-13296)***
Starwood Hotels & Resorts.......760 328-5955
71333 Dinah Shore Dr Rancho Mirage (92270) ***(G-13297)***
Starwood Hotels & Resorts.......415 284-4049
125 3rd St San Francisco (94103) ***(G-13298)***
Starwood Hotels & Resorts.......415 512-1111
2 New Montgomery St San Francisco (94105) ***(G-13299)***
Starwood Hotels & Resorts.......415 284-4000
125 3rd St San Francisco (94103) ***(G-13300)***
Starwood Hotels & Resorts.......619 239-2200
910 Broadway Cir San Diego (92101) ***(G-13301)***
Starwood Hotels & Resorts.......323 798-1300
6250 Hollywood Blvd Los Angeles (90028) ***(G-13302)***
Starwood Hotels & Resorts.......909 622-2220
601 W Mckinley Ave Pomona (91768) ***(G-13303)***
Starwood Hotels & Resorts.......619 239-9600
1617 1st Ave San Diego (92101) ***(G-13304)***
State Bar of California (PA).......415 538-2000
180 Howard St Fl Grnd San Francisco (94105) ***(G-25159)***
State Bar of California.......213 765-1000
845 S Figueroa St Los Angeles (90017) ***(G-25160)***
State Compensation Insur Fund (PA).......888 782-8338
333 Bush St Fl 8 San Francisco (94104) ***(G-10460)***
State Compensation Insur Fund.......714 565-5000
1750 E 4th St Fl 3 Santa Ana (92705) ***(G-10461)***
State Compensation Insur Fund.......661 664-4000
9801 Camino Media Ste 101 Bakersfield (93311) ***(G-10462)***
State Compensation Insur Fund.......510 577-3000
2955 Peralta Oaks Ct Oakland (94605) ***(G-10463)***
State Compensation Insur Fund.......888 782-8338
333 W San Carlos St # 950 San Jose (95110) ***(G-10464)***
State Compensation Insur Fund.......888 782-8338
364 Knollcrest Dr Redding (96002) ***(G-10465)***
State Compensation Insur Fund.......888 782-8338
10105 Pacific Hgts Blvd San Diego (92121) ***(G-10466)***
State Compensation Insur Fund.......559 433-2700
10 E Rver Pk Pl E Ste 110 Fresno (93720) ***(G-10467)***
State Compensation Insur Fund.......213 576-7335
655 N Central Ave Ste 200 Glendale (91203) ***(G-10468)***
State Compensation Insur Fund.......888 782-8338
3247 W March Ln Ste 110 Stockton (95219) ***(G-10469)***
State Compensation Insur Fund.......323 266-5551
655 N Central Ave Ste 200 Glendale (91203) ***(G-10470)***
State Compensation Insur Fund.......916 924-5100
2275 Gateway Oaks Dr Sacramento (95833) ***(G-10471)***
State Compensation Insur Fund.......888 782-8338
655 N Central Ave Ste 200 Glendale (91203) ***(G-10472)***
State Compensation Insur Fund.......707 443-9721
800 W Harris St Ste 37 Eureka (95503) ***(G-10473)***
State Compensation Insur Fund.......888 782-8338
6301 Day St Riverside (92507) ***(G-10474)***
State Compensation Insur Fund.......888 782-8338
2901 N Ventura Rd Ste 100 Oxnard (93036) ***(G-10249)***
State Compensation Insur Fund.......925 523-5000
5880 Owens Dr Pleasanton (94588) ***(G-10475)***
State Compensation Insur Fund.......888 782-8338
5890 Owens Dr Pleasanton (94588) ***(G-10476)***
State Compensation Insur Fund.......323 266-5000
900 Corporate Center Dr Monterey Park (91754) ***(G-10477)***
State Farm Fire and Cslty Co.......559 625-4330
5127 W Walnut Ave Visalia (93277) ***(G-10877)***
State Farm Fire and Cslty Co.......707 588-6011
6400 State Farm Dr Rohnert Park (94928) ***(G-10878)***
State Farm Insurance, Los Angeles *Also called State Farm Mutl Auto Insur Co* ***(G-10879)***
State Farm Insurance, Encino *Also called State Farm Mutl Auto Insur Co* ***(G-10880)***
State Farm Insurance, Visalia *Also called State Farm Fire and Cslty Co* ***(G-10877)***
State Farm Insurance, Santa Fe Springs *Also called State Farm Mutl Auto Insur Co* ***(G-10881)***
State Farm Insurance, Bakersfield *Also called State Farm Mutl Auto Insur Co* ***(G-10882)***
State Farm Insurance, Los Altos *Also called State Farm Mutl Auto Insur Co* ***(G-10883)***
State Farm Insurance, Culver City *Also called State Farm Mutl Auto Insur Co* ***(G-10884)***
State Farm Insurance, Agoura Hills *Also called State Farm Mutl Auto Insur Co* ***(G-10885)***
State Farm Insurance, Long Beach *Also called State Farm Mutl Auto Insur Co* ***(G-10886)***
State Farm Insurance, Fontana *Also called State Farm Mutl Auto Insur Co* ***(G-10887)***
State Farm Insurance, Bakersfield *Also called State Farm Mutl Auto Insur Co* ***(G-10888)***
State Farm Insurance, San Mateo *Also called State Farm Mutl Auto Insur Co* ***(G-10889)***
State Farm Insurance, Culver City *Also called State Farm Mutl Auto Insur Co* ***(G-10890)***
State Farm Insurance, Irvine *Also called State Farm Mutl Auto Insur Co* ***(G-10891)***
State Farm Insurance, Oakhurst *Also called State Farm Mutl Auto Insur Co* ***(G-10892)***
State Farm Insurance, Woodland Hills *Also called State Farm Mutl Auto Insur Co* ***(G-10893)***
State Farm Insurance, Pacific Palisades *Also called State Farm Mutl Auto Insur Co* ***(G-10894)***
State Farm Insurance, Los Angeles *Also called State Farm Mutl Auto Insur Co* ***(G-10895)***
State Farm Insurance, Bakersfield *Also called State Farm Mutl Auto Insur Co* ***(G-10896)***
State Farm Insurance, Pinole *Also called State Farm Mutl Auto Insur Co* ***(G-10897)***
State Farm Insurance, Rohnert Park *Also called State Farm Fire and Cslty Co* ***(G-10878)***
State Farm Insurance, Bakersfield *Also called State Farm Mutl Auto Insur Co* ***(G-10898)***
State Farm Mutl Auto Insur Co.......309 766-2311
12122 S Halldale Ave # 200 Los Angeles (90047) ***(G-10879)***
State Farm Mutl Auto Insur Co.......818 849-5126
16656 Ventura Blvd # 203 Encino (91436) ***(G-10880)***
State Farm Mutl Auto Insur Co.......562 903-2800
10350 Hritg Pk Dr Ste 202 Santa Fe Springs (90670) ***(G-10881)***
State Farm Mutl Auto Insur Co.......661 663-1921
900 Old River Rd Bakersfield (93311) ***(G-10882)***
State Farm Mutl Auto Insur Co.......650 694-6767
5050 El Camino Real # 108 Los Altos (94022) ***(G-10883)***
State Farm Mutl Auto Insur Co.......310 568-5824
200 Corporate Pointe # 210 Culver City (90230) ***(G-10884)***
State Farm Mutl Auto Insur Co.......818 597-4300
30125 Agoura Rd Ste 200 Agoura Hills (91301) ***(G-10885)***
State Farm Mutl Auto Insur Co.......310 632-9810
1705 E 10th St Apt 201 Long Beach (90813) ***(G-10886)***
State Farm Mutl Auto Insur Co.......909 349-2050
17122 Slover Ave Ste 106 Fontana (92337) ***(G-10887)***
State Farm Mutl Auto Insur Co.......661 324-4077
2019 24th St Bakersfield (93301) ***(G-10888)***
State Farm Mutl Auto Insur Co.......650 345-3571
2555 Flores St Ste 175 San Mateo (94403) ***(G-10889)***
State Farm Mutl Auto Insur Co.......310 568-5200
300 Crprate Pinte Ste 200 Culver City (90230) ***(G-10890)***
State Farm Mutl Auto Insur Co.......309 766-2311
3351 Michelson Dr Ste 200 Irvine (92612) ***(G-10891)***
State Farm Mutl Auto Insur Co.......559 683-3467
40315 Junction Dr Ste A Oakhurst (93644) ***(G-10892)***
State Farm Mutl Auto Insur Co.......818 887-1060
5345 Fallbrook Ave Woodland Hills (91367) ***(G-10893)***
State Farm Mutl Auto Insur Co.......310 454-0349
845 Via De La Paz Ste 12 Pacific Palisades (90272) ***(G-10894)***
State Farm Mutl Auto Insur Co.......323 852-6868
7944 W 3rd St Los Angeles (90048) ***(G-10895)***
State Farm Mutl Auto Insur Co.......661 664-9663
4600 Ashe Rd Ste 308 Bakersfield (93313) ***(G-10896)***

ALPHABETIC SECTION Stewart Painting Inc

State Farm Mutl Auto Insur Co....510 222-1102
1558 Fitzgerald Dr Pinole (94564) *(G-10897)*
State Farm Mutl Auto Insur Co....661 663-1313
900 Old River Rd Bakersfield (93311) *(G-10898)*
State Fund, San Francisco *Also called State Compensation Insur Fund (G-10460)*
State Fund Office, Glendale *Also called State Compensation Insur Fund (G-10468)*
State Group LLC....949 612-2879
36 Umbria Irvine (92618) *(G-27666)*
State Pipe & Supply Inc....909 356-5670
2180 N Locust Ave Rialto (92377) *(G-2001)*
State Pipe & Supply Inc (HQ)....909 877-9999
183 S Cedar Ave Rialto (92376) *(G-7405)*
State Preschool, Alhambra *Also called Options For Learning (G-24491)*
State Preschool....661 940-4535
831 E Avenue K2 Lancaster (93535) *(G-24519)*
State Preschool....925 473-4380
950 El Pueblo Ave Pittsburg (94565) *(G-24520)*
State Roofing Systems Inc....510 317-1477
15444 Hesperian Blvd San Leandro (94578) *(G-3214)*
States Drawer Box Spc LLC....714 744-4247
1482 N Batavia St Orange (92867) *(G-6963)*
States Logistics Services Inc....714 523-1276
7221 Cate Dr Buena Park (90621) *(G-5170)*
States Logistics Services Inc (PA)....714 521-6520
5650 Dolly Ave Buena Park (90621) *(G-4642)*
Statewide, Sacramento *Also called Domus Construction & Design (G-1168)*
Statewide Enterprises Inc....818 709-4434
8151 Reseda Blvd Apt 101 Reseda (91335) *(G-11207)*
Station Venture Operations LP....619 578-0233
225 Broadway 100-300 San Diego (92101) *(G-5912)*
Stations Group LLC....818 247-0400
1139 Grand Central Ave Glendale (91201) *(G-5913)*
Status Medical Management, Modesto *Also called Pegasus Risk Management Inc (G-10824)*
Staybrdge Sites By Holiday Inn, Torrance *Also called Six Continents Hotels Inc (G-13261)*
Staybridge Suites, San Diego *Also called Six Continents Hotels Inc (G-13267)*
Staybridge Suites, Sunnyvale *Also called Hpt Trs Ihg-2 Inc (G-12801)*
STC Netcom Inc (PA)....951 685-8181
11611 Industry Ave Fontana (92337) *(G-2748)*
Steadfast Management Co Inc....714 542-2229
15520 Tustin Village Way Tustin (92780) *(G-11208)*
Stearns Lending LLC....760 776-5555
44875 Deep Canyon Rd Palm Desert (92260) *(G-9764)*
Stearns Lending LLC....831 471-1977
317 Soquel Ave Santa Cruz (95062) *(G-9953)*
Stearns Lending LLC (PA)....714 513-7777
555 Anton Blvd Ste 300 Costa Mesa (92626) *(G-9899)*
Stearns Lending LLC....657 999-4915
1601 E Orangewood Ave Anaheim (92805) *(G-9954)*
Steel House Inc....310 773-3331
3644 Eastham Dr Culver City (90232) *(G-13923)*
Steele Canyon Golf Club Corp....619 441-6900
3199 Stonefield Dr Jamul (91935) *(G-18789)*
Steele Cis Inc....415 692-5000
1 Sansome St Ste 3500 San Francisco (94104) *(G-23582)*
Steele Corp SEC Advisory Svcs, San Francisco *Also called Steele International Inc (G-16832)*
Steele International Inc....415 781-4300
1350 Treat Blvd Ste 250 Walnut Creek (94597) *(G-27667)*
Steele International Inc (PA)....415 781-4300
1 Sansome St Ste 3500 San Francisco (94104) *(G-16832)*
Steelkiwi Inc....415 449-8696
1025 Alameda De Las Ste 535 Belmont (94002) *(G-16059)*
Steelpoint Capital Partners LP....858 764-8700
437 S Highway 101 Ste 212 Solana Beach (92075) *(G-10187)*
Steelriver Infrastructure Fund (HQ)....415 848-5448
1 Letterman Dr Ste 500 San Francisco (94129) *(G-6282)*
Steelriver Infrasturcture Part (PA)....415 512-1515
1 Letterman Dr San Francisco (94129) *(G-12092)*
Steeltech Construction Svcs....714 630-2890
4081 E La Palma Ave Ste G Anaheim (92807) *(G-1467)*
Steelwave Inc (PA)....650 571-2200
4000 E 3rd Ave Ste 600 Foster City (94404) *(G-12013)*
Steelwave LLC....650 571-2200
4000 E 3rd Ave Ste 500 Foster City (94404) *(G-12014)*
Steelwedge Software Inc (PA)....925 460-1700
3875 Hopyard Rd Ste 300 Pleasanton (94588) *(G-15848)*
Steelwrkers Old Tmers Fndation....323 582-6090
3355 E Gage Ave Huntington Park (90255) *(G-24236)*
Stefan Merli Plastering Co Inc (PA)....310 323-0404
1230 W 130th St Gardena (90247) *(G-3336)*
Steger Inc....714 974-4383
1938 N Batavia St Ste L Orange (92865) *(G-2493)*
Stein & Lubin LLP....415 981-0550
600 Montgomery St Fl 14 San Francisco (94111) *(G-23583)*
Steinberg Architects (PA)....408 295-5446
125 S Market St Ste 110 San Jose (95113) *(G-26259)*
Steinberg Group Architects, San Jose *Also called Steinberg Architects (G-26259)*
Steinhart & Falconer LLP....415 836-2500
153 Townsend St Ste 800 San Francisco (94107) *(G-23584)*
Steiny and Company Inc (PA)....626 962-1055
221 N Ardmore Ave Los Angeles (90004) *(G-2749)*
Steiny and Company Inc....707 552-6900
27 Sheridan St Vallejo (94590) *(G-2750)*
Steiny and Company Inc....213 382-2331
221 N Ardmore Ave Los Angeles (90004) *(G-2751)*
Stella Travel Services USA Inc....310 535-1000
6171 W Century Blvd # 160 Los Angeles (90045) *(G-4974)*
Stellar Distributing Inc....559 664-8400
21801 Avenue 16 Madera (93637) *(G-8778)*
Stellar Group Incorporated....209 549-0899
1035 Reno Ave Modesto (95351) *(G-7760)*
Stellar Microelectronics Inc....661 775-3500
28454 Livingston Ave Valencia (91355) *(G-7638)*
Stellartech Research Corp (PA)....408 331-3134
560 Cottonwood Dr Milpitas (95035) *(G-26610)*
Steno Employment Services Inc....909 476-1404
8560 Vineyard Ave Ste 208 Rancho Cucamonga (91730) *(G-14953)*
Step, Sacramento *Also called Stratgies To Empwer People Inc (G-21113)*
Step House Recovery, Fountain Valley *Also called Stephouse Recovery Center (G-24237)*
Stephen B Meisel MD PC....310 828-8843
2811 Wilshire Blvd # 900 Santa Monica (90403) *(G-20067)*
Stephen B Meisel MD A Med Corp (HQ)....310 828-8843
2811 Wilshire Blvd # 900 Santa Monica (90403) *(G-20068)*
Stephouse Recovery Center....714 394-3494
10529 Slater Ave Fountain Valley (92708) *(G-24237)*
Stepping Stn Grwth Ctr Fr Chld....510 568-3331
311 Macarthur Blvd San Leandro (94577) *(G-24393)*
Steptoe & Johnson LLP....213 439-9400
633 W 5th St Fl 7 Los Angeles (90071) *(G-23585)*
Steren Electronics Intl LLC (PA)....800 266-3333
6920 Carroll Rd Ste 100 San Diego (92121) *(G-7639)*
Steren Shop, San Diego *Also called Steren Electronics Intl LLC (G-7639)*
Stereo D LLC....818 861-3100
3355 W Empire Ave Fl 1 Burbank (91504) *(G-18256)*
Stereod, Burbank *Also called Stereo D LLC (G-18256)*
Stereomax, Mill Valley *Also called Haggin Marketing Inc (G-13857)*
Stericycle Comm Solutions Inc....888 370-6711
2255 Watt Ave Ste 50 Sacramento (95825) *(G-17502)*
Stericycle Comm Solutions Inc....714 991-9595
612 S Harbor Blvd Anaheim (92805) *(G-17503)*
Sterling Asset Management, Fairfield *Also called Community Housing Opport (G-26979)*
Sterling Brand, San Francisco *Also called Sterling Consulting Group LLC (G-27668)*
Sterling Building Services, Anaheim *Also called Danlil Enterprise Inc (G-14282)*
Sterling Collision Center LLC (PA)....714 259-1111
1111 Bell Ave Ste A Tustin (92780) *(G-17775)*
Sterling Construction....209 984-5594
17661 Greenwood Way Jamestown (95327) *(G-1340)*
Sterling Consulting Group LLC....415 248-7900
55 Union St Fl 3 San Francisco (94111) *(G-27668)*
Sterling Court, San Mateo *Also called Fifty Peninsula Partners (G-11131)*
Sterling Dry Cleaners, Los Angeles *Also called Sterling Westwood Inc (G-13588)*
Sterling Hsa Inc....800 617-4729
475 14th St Ste 120 Oakland (94612) *(G-17504)*
Sterling Inn, Victorville *Also called Sterling-Ase Ltd Partnership (G-11209)*
Sterling Mktg & Fincl Corp....209 593-1140
4660 Spyres Way Ste 1 Modesto (95356) *(G-27669)*
Sterling Pacific Meat Company, Commerce *Also called Interstate Meat & Provision (G-8554)*
Sterling Plumbing Inc....714 641-5480
3111 W Central Ave Santa Ana (92704) *(G-2385)*
Sterling Senior Communities, Temecula *Also called MBK Senior Living LLC (G-21311)*
Sterling Westwood Inc....310 287-2431
3405 Overland Ave Los Angeles (90034) *(G-13588)*
Sterling-Ase Ltd Partnership....760 951-9507
17738 Francesca Rd Victorville (92395) *(G-11209)*
Steve and Beth Chaput....909 596-9994
1025 Sentinel Dr Ste 103 La Verne (91750) *(G-14439)*
Steve Beattie Inc....310 454-1786
1766 Westridge Rd Los Angeles (90049) *(G-2494)*
Steve Beattie Painting, Los Angeles *Also called Steve Beattie Inc (G-2494)*
Steve Duich Inc....619 444-6118
1369 N Magnolia Ave El Cajon (92020) *(G-3337)*
Steve Manning Construction Inc....530 222-0810
5211 Churn Creek Rd Redding (96002) *(G-1864)*
Steve Roberson....562 927-2626
7825 Florence Ave Downey (90240) *(G-11858)*
Steve Silver Productions Inc....415 421-4284
678 Green St Ste 2 San Francisco (94133) *(G-18436)*
Steven Engineering Inc....650 588-9200
230 Ryan Way South San Francisco (94080) *(G-7955)*
Steven G Fogg MD....559 449-5010
1360 E Herndon Ave # 401 Fresno (93720) *(G-20069)*
Steven Global Freight Services, Redondo Beach *Also called Stevens Global Logistics Inc (G-5171)*
Steven N Ledson....707 537-3810
7335 Sonoma Hwy Santa Rosa (95409) *(G-1263)*
Steven Rubinstein MD, Sunnyvale *Also called Palo Alto Medical Foundation (G-19817)*
Steven Snyder, Hollister *Also called Hollister Process Service (G-17224)*
Stevens Creek Quarry Inc (PA)....408 253-2512
12100 Stevens Canyon Rd Cupertino (95014) *(G-1865)*
Stevens Global Logistics Inc (PA)....310 216-5645
3700 Redondo Beach Ave Redondo Beach (90278) *(G-5171)*
Stevinson Ranch Golf Club, Stevinson *Also called Stevinson Ranch-Savannah GP (G-18790)*
Stevinson Ranch-Savannah GP....209 668-8200
2700 Van Clief Rd Stevinson (95374) *(G-18790)*
Stewardship Company LLC....831 620-6700
1 Rancho San Carlos Rd Carmel (93923) *(G-27231)*
Stewart Brothers, Rio Vista *Also called James M Stewart Inc (G-27)*
Stewart Enterprises Inc....858 453-2121
5600 Carroll Canyon Rd San Diego (92121) *(G-13716)*
Stewart Information Svcs Corp....805 677-6915
6477 Telephone Rd Ste 8 Ventura (93003) *(G-11939)*
Stewart Information Svcs Corp....805 899-7700
3888 State St Ste 201 Santa Barbara (93105) *(G-11940)*
Stewart Painting Inc....650 968-3706
1351 Brookdale Ave Mountain View (94040) *(G-2495)*

ALPHABETIC

Stewart Title California Inc (HQ) 818 291-9145
525 N Brand Blvd Ste 100 Glendale (91203) **(G-10535)**
Stewart, John Attorney At Law, Covina *Also called John Stewart Company* **(G-23327)**
Stidham Trucking Inc 530 842-4161
321 Payne Ln Yreka (96097) **(G-4266)**
Stila Styles, Mira Loma *Also called Geodis Logistics LLC* **(G-4561)**
Stitches Inc 323 622-0175
2838 Vail Ave Commerce (90040) **(G-17505)**
Stjohn God Rtirement Care Ctr 323 731-0641
2468 S St Andrews Pl Los Angeles (90018) **(G-20931)**
Stk International Inc 310 720-1277
6160 Peach Tree St Compton (90220) **(G-8056)**
Stmicroelectronics Inc 408 452-8585
2755 Great America Way Santa Clara (95054) **(G-7640)**
Stockbridge/Sbe Holdings LLC 323 655-8000
5900 Wilshire Blvd # 3100 Los Angeles (90036) **(G-13305)**
Stockcross Financial Services (PA) 800 225-6196
9464 Wilshire Blvd Beverly Hills (90212) **(G-10078)**
Stockdale Country Club 661 832-0310
7001 Stockdale Hwy Bakersfield (93309) **(G-19096)**
Stockdale Medical Offices, Bakersfield *Also called Kaiser Foundation Hospitals* **(G-21663)**
Stocker & Allaire Inc 831 375-1890
21 Mandeville Ct Monterey (93940) **(G-1264)**
Stockham Construction Inc 707 664-0945
475 Portal St Ste F Cotati (94931) **(G-3094)**
Stockmar Industrial, Long Beach *Also called Elite Craftsman* **(G-14288)**
Stockton Cardiology Medical Gr 209 824-1555
1148 Norman Dr Ste 3 Manteca (95336) **(G-20070)**
Stockton Cardiology Medical Gr (PA) 209 754-1012
415 E Harding Way Ste D Stockton (95204) **(G-20071)**
Stockton Congregational Home 209 466-4341
1319 N Madison St Ofc Stockton (95202) **(G-24823)**
Stockton District Office, Stockton *Also called State Compensation Insur Fund* **(G-10469)**
Stockton Edson Healthcare Corp 209 948-8762
1630 N Edison St Stockton (95204) **(G-21385)**
Stockton Orthpd Med Group Inc 209 948-1641
2545 W Hammer Ln Stockton (95209) **(G-20072)**
Stockton Port District 209 946-0246
2201 W Washington St # 13 Stockton (95203) **(G-4762)**
Stockton Scavengers Assn, Stockton *Also called USA Waste of California Inc* **(G-4082)**
Stockton Unlimited Company 209 464-2200
2481 E Main St Stockton (95205) **(G-17506)**
Stoke, San Jose *Also called Mavenir Intl Holdings Inc* **(G-15295)**
Stollwood Convalescent Hosp, Woodland *Also called St Johns Retirement Village* **(G-21916)**
STOLLWOOD CONVALESCENT HOSPITA, Woodland *Also called St Johns Retirement Village* **(G-21384)**
Stomper Co Inc 510 574-0570
7799 Enterprise Dr Newark (94560) **(G-3469)**
Stone & Youngberg LLC (PA) 415 445-2300
1 Ferry Plz San Francisco (94111) **(G-10079)**
Stone Blue Inc 323 277-0008
2501 E 28th St Vernon (90058) **(G-13643)**
Stone Bros. & Associates, Stockton *Also called M & M Stone Inc* **(G-11648)**
Stone Entertainment, Costa Mesa *Also called Volcom LLC* **(G-17600)**
Stone Land Company (PA) 559 947-3185
28521 Nevada Ave Stratford (93266) **(G-14)**
Stone Publishing Inc (PA) 408 450-7910
2549 Scott Blvd Santa Clara (95050) **(G-27232)**
Stone Ranch, Stratford *Also called Stone Land Company* **(G-14)**
Stone Real Estate Inc (PA) 209 847-1230
1101 Sylvan Ave Ste B25 Modesto (95350) **(G-11859)**
Stone Tree Landscape Corp 323 965-0944
5757 Wilshire Blvd # 505 Los Angeles (90036) **(G-960)**
Stonebrae LP 510 728-7878
222 Country Club Dr Hayward (94542) **(G-19097)**
Stonebridge McWhinney LLC 714 703-8800
11747 Harbor Blvd Garden Grove (92840) **(G-13306)**
Stonebrook Convalescent Center 925 689-7457
4367 Concord Blvd Concord (94521) **(G-20932)**
Stonebrook Health Care Center, Concord *Also called Stonebrook Convalescent Center* **(G-20932)**
Stonehouse Restaurant, Santa Barbara *Also called San Ysidro Bb Property LLC* **(G-13209)**
Stoneland, North Hollywood *Also called Arriaga Usa Inc* **(G-3005)**
Stoneridge Country Club 858 487-2117
17166 Stonerdge Cntry Poway (92064) **(G-19098)**
Stoneridge Creek Pleasanton, Pleasanton *Also called Conti Life Comm Plea LLC* **(G-17093)**
Stoneriver Fsc, Inc., Agoura Hills *Also called Vertafore Fsc Inc* **(G-15526)**
Stonetree Golf LLC 415 209-6744
9 Stonetree Ln Novato (94945) **(G-18791)**
Stonetree Management, Novato *Also called Stonetree Golf LLC* **(G-18791)**
Stonewood Ctr Mall Office, Downey *Also called Macerich Company* **(G-11014)**
Stop Hop Center, Carson *Also called Anschutz So Calif Sports Compl* **(G-18536)**
Stopirsdebtcom Inc 323 857-5809
10100 Santa Monica Blvd Los Angeles (90067) **(G-13727)**
Storage West, Los Angeles *Also called Laaco Ltd* **(G-11257)**
Store 17, Moorpark *Also called Prudential Overall Supply* **(G-13641)**
Storer Transportation 209 644-5100
1909 S Argonaut St Stockton (95206) **(G-3723)**
Storer Transportation Service 661 288-0400
21429 Centre Pointe Pkwy Santa Clarita (91350) **(G-5245)**
Storer Transportation Service (PA) 209 521-8250
3519 Mcdonald Ave Modesto (95358) **(G-3896)**
Storer Travel Service, Modesto *Also called Storer Transportation Service* **(G-3896)**
Story Teller, Universal City *Also called Amblin/Reliance Holding Co LLC* **(G-18041)**
Storybook Productions Inc 323 468-5050
6230 W Sunset Blvd Los Angeles (90028) **(G-18437)**

Stout & Burg Electric Inc 714 544-5066
17256 Red Hill Ave Irvine (92614) **(G-2752)**
Stradling Yocca Carlson & Raut (PA) 949 725-4000
660 Newport Center Dr # 1600 Newport Beach (92660) **(G-23586)**
Stradling Yocca Carlson & Raut 916 449-2350
500 Capitol Mall Ste 1120 Sacramento (95814) **(G-23587)**
Straight Edge, Windsor *Also called Robert A Hall* **(G-14939)**
Straight Lander Inc 323 337-9075
8335 W Sunset Blvd # 320 Los Angeles (90069) **(G-27233)**
Straight Line Roofing & Cnstr 530 672-9995
3811 Dividend Dr Ste A Shingle Springs (95682) **(G-3215)**
Strand Energy Company 562 944-9580
10350 Heritage Park Dr Santa Fe Springs (90670) **(G-1051)**
Strands Finance, San Mateo *Also called Strands Labs Inc* **(G-15479)**
Strands Inc A Delaware Corp 541 753-4426
999 Baker Way Ste 430 San Mateo (94404) **(G-15478)**
Strands Labs Inc 415 398-4333
999 Baker Way Ste 430 San Mateo (94404) **(G-15479)**
Strata Information Group Inc 619 296-0170
3935 Harney St Ste 203 San Diego (92110) **(G-16490)**
Stratacare Llc 949 743-1200
17838 Gillette Ave Ste D Irvine (92614) **(G-15480)**
Stratcitycom LLC 408 858-0006
1317 Monterosso St Danville (94506) **(G-15849)**
Strategic Bus Insights Inc (PA) 650 859-4600
333 Ravenswood Ave Menlo Park (94025) **(G-27670)**
Strategic Data Systems 619 546-7200
610 W Ash St Ste 1100 San Diego (92101) **(G-16060)**
Strategic Enlace Inc 714 256-8648
281 N Puente St Brea (92821) **(G-27671)**
Strategic Financial Group 949 622-7200
18191 Von Karman Ave # 100 Irvine (92612) **(G-10899)**
Strategic Mechanical Inc 559 291-1952
4661 E Commerce Ave Fresno (93725) **(G-2386)**
Strategic Property Management 619 295-2211
2055 3rd Ave Ste 200 San Diego (92101) **(G-11860)**
Strategic Secuirty Services, Fremont *Also called Strategic Security Services* **(G-10198)**
Strategic Security Services 510 623-2355
48521 Warm Springs Blvd # 302 Fremont (94539) **(G-10198)**
Strategy Companion Corp 714 460-8398
3240 El Camino Real # 120 Irvine (92602) **(G-15850)**
Strategy For Water & Land Reso 949 572-3034
49 Donovan Irvine (92620) **(G-26611)**
Stratford, San Mateo *Also called Raiser Senior Services LLC* **(G-24776)**
Stratford School Inc 408 371-3020
220 Kensington Way Los Gatos (95032) **(G-24521)**
Stratgies To Empwer People Inc (PA) 916 679-1527
2330 Glendale Ln Sacramento (95825) **(G-21113)**
Stratham Homes Inc 949 833-1554
2201 Dupont Dr Ste 300 Irvine (92612) **(G-1341)**
Straub - Brutoco A Joint Ventr 760 414-9000
202 W College St Ste 201 Fallbrook (92028) **(G-1385)**
Straub Distributing Co Ltd (PA) 714 779-4000
4633 E La Palma Ave Anaheim (92807) **(G-9086)**
Strawberry Farms Golf Club, Irvine *Also called Sand Canyon LLC* **(G-18781)**
Strawberry Farms Golf Club LLC 949 551-2560
11 Strawberry Farm Rd Irvine (92612) **(G-19099)**
Streamline Finishes Inc 949 600-8964
26429 Rancho Pkwy S # 140 Lake Forest (92630) **(G-1678)**
Streamray Inc 408 745-5449
910 E Hamilton Ave Fl 6 Campbell (95008) **(G-18500)**
Strech Plastics Inc 951 922-2224
900 John St Ste J Banning (92220) **(G-8006)**
Street Maintenance Department, Encinitas *Also called City of Encinitas* **(G-1749)**
Street Sidewalks St Tree Maint, Chino *Also called City of Chino* **(G-6621)**
Streets Street Tree Inquiries, Oxnard *Also called City of Oxnard* **(G-18814)**
Stress Relief Services 760 241-7472
12603 Mariposa Rd Victorville (92395) **(G-13307)**
Strevus Inc 415 704-8182
455 Market St Ste 1670 San Francisco (94105) **(G-15851)**
Stria, Bakersfield *Also called Technosocialworkcom LLC* **(G-16199)**
Strikes Unlimited Inc 916 626-3600
5681 Lonetree Blvd Rocklin (95765) **(G-18531)**
Stripe Payments Company 888 963-8955
3180 18th St Ste 100 San Francisco (94110) **(G-17507)**
Strlng Path Medcl Corp 562 799-8900
3030 Old Ranch Pkwy # 430 Seal Beach (90740) **(G-17894)**
Strocal Inc (PA) 209 948-4646
4651 Quail Lakes Dr Stockton (95207) **(G-3404)**
Stronghold Engineering Inc (PA) 951 684-9303
2000 Market St Riverside (92501) **(G-1866)**
Stroock & Stroock & Lavan LLP 310 556-5800
2029 Century Park E # 1800 Los Angeles (90067) **(G-23588)**
Structural Integrity Assoc Inc (PA) 408 978-8200
5215 Hellyer Ave Ste 210 San Jose (95138) **(G-26079)**
Structure Cast, Bakersfield *Also called Golden Empire Concrete Pdts* **(G-3266)**
Structure Cnstr & Dev Inc 619 846-2555
4420 Hotel Circle Ct San Diego (92108) **(G-1265)**
Structure Cnstr & Rmdlg Co, San Diego *Also called Structure Cnstr & Dev Inc* **(G-1265)**
Structures West Inc 760 737-2349
300 W Grand Ave Ste 201 Escondido (92025) **(G-3338)**
Stu Segall Productions Inc 858 974-8988
4705 Ruffin Rd San Diego (92123) **(G-18161)**
Stuart C. Gildred Family YMCA, Santa Ynez *Also called Channel Islands Young Mens Ch* **(G-25236)**
Stuart Lovett 510 444-0790
350 30th St Ste 208 Oakland (94609) **(G-20073)**
Stuart Rental Company, Milpitas *Also called Ohana Partners Inc* **(G-14563)**

A L P H A B E T I C

Stubhub Inc (HQ)...415 222-8400
199 Fremont St Fl 4 San Francisco (94105) *(G-16194)*
Stubhub.com, San Francisco *Also called Stubhub Inc (G-16194)*
Stucco Works Inc...916 383-6699
5900 Warehouse Way Sacramento (95826) *(G-2984)*
Student Advocates, Costa Mesa *Also called Progress Advocates Group LLC (G-13789)*
Student Government Associat...949 824-5547
D200 Student Center Irvine (92697) *(G-4975)*
Student Health Services, San Jose *Also called San Jose State University (G-19949)*
Student Movers Inc...303 296-0600
825 Chalcedony St San Diego (92109) *(G-4379)*
Student Transportation America, San Jose *Also called Student Trnsp Amer Inc (G-3848)*
Student Transportation America, Santa Maria *Also called Santa Barbara Trnsp Corp (G-3948)*
Student Trnsp Amer Inc...818 982-1663
12560 Raymer St North Hollywood (91605) *(G-3906)*
Student Trnsp Amer Inc...408 998-8275
1540 S 7th St San Jose (95112) *(G-3848)*
Student Trnsp Amer Inc...951 940-0300
2935 Indian Ave Perris (92571) *(G-3950)*
Student Un San Jose State Univ...408 924-6405
211 S. 9th Street San Jose (95192) *(G-25587)*
Student Union Building, San Jose *Also called Student Un San Jose State Univ (G-25587)*
Student Works Painting, Irvine *Also called S W P T X Inc (G-2488)*
Student Works Painting Inc...714 564-7900
1682 Langley Ave Irvine (92614) *(G-2496)*
Students of Associated...916 278-6216
6000 J St Sacramento (95819) *(G-24522)*
Studio 13...310 837-8107
800 S Pacific Coast Hwy # 8 Redondo Beach (90277) *(G-13924)*
Studio 71 LP...323 370-1500
8383 Wilshire Blvd Ste 10 Beverly Hills (90211) *(G-13979)*
Studio By Clubsport, The, Danville *Also called 2 G Fitness LLC (G-18577)*
Study Tapes...909 792-0111
1341 Pine Knoll Cres Redlands (92373) *(G-18162)*
Study US Research Inst Inc...213 840-9575
1335 N La Brea Ave 2-205 Los Angeles (90028) *(G-26811)*
Stumbaugh & Associates Inc (PA)...818 240-1627
3303 N San Fernando Blvd Burbank (91504) *(G-3586)*
Sturgeon & Son, Bakersfield *Also called Sturgeon Services Intl Inc (G-12093)*
Sturgeon Services Intl, Santa Maria *Also called Sturgeon Son Grading & Pav Inc (G-26080)*
Sturgeon Services Intl Inc (PA)...661 322-4408
3511 Gilmore Ave Bakersfield (93308) *(G-12093)*
Sturgeon Son Grading & Pav Inc (PA)...661 322-4408
3511 Gilmore Ave Bakersfield (93308) *(G-3442)*
Sturgeon Son Grading & Pav Inc...805 938-0618
6516 Cat Canyon Rd Santa Maria (93454) *(G-26080)*
Stv Architects Inc...213 482-9444
1055 W 7th St Ste 3150 Los Angeles (90017) *(G-26260)*
Stx Wireless Operations LLC...858 882-6000
5887 Copley Dr San Diego (92111) *(G-5411)*
Sub-Acute Saratoga Hospital, Saratoga *Also called Progressive Sub-Acute Care (G-22162)*
Subacute Childrens Hosp of Cal...408 558-3644
3777 S Bascom Ave Campbell (95008) *(G-22179)*
Subacute Trtmnt Adolescnt Reha (PA)...510 352-9200
545 Estudillo Ave San Leandro (94577) *(G-20933)*
Success Factors, South San Francisco *Also called Successfactors Inc (G-15481)*
Success Healthcare 1 LLC (PA)...213 989-6100
1711 W Temple St Los Angeles (90026) *(G-22574)*
Success Healthcare 1 LLC...626 288-1160
7500 Hellman Ave Rosemead (91770) *(G-20074)*
Success Strategies Inst Inc...888 866-3377
6 Executive Cir Ste 250 Irvine (92614) *(G-24394)*
Successfactors Inc (HQ)...800 845-0395
1 Tower Pl Fl 11 South San Francisco (94080) *(G-15481)*
Successor To San Francisco...415 749-2400
1 S Van Ness Ave Fl 5 San Francisco (94103) *(G-28063)*
Suddath Relo Sys of No CA...408 288-3030
2055 S 7th St San Jose (95112) *(G-4267)*
Sudhakar Company International...909 879-2933
1450 N Fitzgerald Ave Rialto (92376) *(G-1867)*
Suds Car Wash Inc...916 673-6300
4620 Post St El Dorado Hills (95762) *(G-17862)*
Suffolk Construction Co Inc...949 453-9400
550 S Hope St Los Angeles (90071) *(G-1679)*
Sufi, Fremont *Also called Startup Farms Intl LLC (G-15477)*
Sugar Bowl Corporation...530 426-9000
629 Sugar Bowl Rd Norden (95724) *(G-19290)*
Sugar Foods Corporation...818 768-7900
9500 El Dorado Ave Sun Valley (91352) *(G-17508)*
Sugar Foods Corporation...818 768-7900
9500 El Dorado Ave Sun Valley (91352) *(G-17509)*
Sugar Transport of The NW...209 931-3587
5463 Cherokee Rd Stockton (95215) *(G-4069)*
Sugar Workers Local 1...510 787-1676
641 Loring Ave Crockett (94525) *(G-25188)*
Sugarcrm Inc (PA)...408 454-6900
10050 N Wolfe Rd Sw2130 Cupertino (95014) *(G-15482)*
Sugarfish, Los Angeles *Also called Sushi Nozawa LLC (G-15484)*
Suissa Miller Advertising LLC...310 392-9666
8687 Melrose Ave West Hollywood (90069) *(G-13925)*
SUISUN REDEVELOPMENT AGENCY, Suisun City *Also called Redevelopment Agency of The Ci (G-28038)*
Suja Juice, San Diego *Also called Suja Life LLC (G-8924)*
Suja Life LLC...855 879-7852
8380 Camino Santa Fe San Diego (92121) *(G-8924)*
Sukut Construction LLC...714 540-5351
4010 W Chandler Ave Santa Ana (92704) *(G-1868)*
Sukut Construction Inc (PA)...714 540-5351
4010 W Chandler Ave Santa Ana (92704) *(G-3443)*
Sullinovo...619 260-1432
2750 Womble Rd Ste 100 San Diego (92106) *(G-6640)*
Sullivan & Cromwell LLP...310 712-6600
1888 Century Park E # 2100 Los Angeles (90067) *(G-23589)*
Sullivan Gj & Associates Inc (PA)...213 626-1000
800 W 6th St Ste 1800 Los Angeles (90017) *(G-10900)*
Sullivan Group, The, Los Angeles *Also called Sullivan Gj & Associates Inc (G-10900)*
Sullivan Moving & Storage (PA)...858 874-2600
5704 Copley Dr San Diego (92111) *(G-4268)*
Sullivancurtismonroe Insurance (PA)...800 427-3253
1920 Main St Ste 600 Irvine (92614) *(G-27672)*
Sully-Miller Contracting Co (HQ)...714 578-9600
135 Sstate College Ste 400 Brea (92821) *(G-1869)*
Sulphur Springs Union Pta...661 252-2725
16628 Lost Canyon Rd Canyon Country (91387) *(G-25353)*
Suma Fruit Intl USA Inc...559 875-5000
1810 Academy Ave Sanger (93657) *(G-587)*
Sumitomo Elc USA Holdings Inc...310 792-6016
21250 Hawthorne Blvd # 730 Torrance (90503) *(G-27234)*
Sumitomo Electric Device Innov...408 232-9500
2355 Zanker Rd San Jose (95131) *(G-7641)*
Sumitomo Mitsui Tr Bnk USA Inc...213 955-0800
601 S Figueroa St # 1800 Los Angeles (90017) *(G-9526)*
Sumitomo Rubber North Amer Inc (HQ)...909 466-1116
8656 Haven Ave Rancho Cucamonga (91730) *(G-6790)*
Summer Crest Apartments, National City *Also called Plaza Manor Preservation LP (G-11755)*
Summer Systems Inc...661 257-4419
28942 Hancock Pkwy Valencia (91355) *(G-1680)*
Summerfield Suites By Hyatt, Belmont *Also called Island Hospitality MGT LLC (G-12859)*
Summerhill Construction Co...925 244-7520
3000 Executive Pkwy # 450 San Ramon (94583) *(G-1266)*
Summerhill Homes, San Ramon *Also called Summerhill Construction Co (G-1266)*
Summerville At Hazel Creek LLC...916 988-7901
6125 Hazel Ave Orangevale (95662) *(G-24824)*
Summerville Senior Living Inc...562 943-3724
10615 Jordan Rd Whittier (90603) *(G-24825)*
Summerville Senior Living Inc...818 341-2552
20801 Devonshire St Chatsworth (91311) *(G-24826)*
Summit Electric, Santa Rosa *Also called Summit Technology Group Inc (G-2754)*
Summit Electric Inc...707 542-4773
2450 Bluebell Dr Ste C Santa Rosa (95403) *(G-2753)*
Summit Entertainment LLC (HQ)...310 309-8400
2700 Colorado Ave Ste 200 Santa Monica (90404) *(G-18291)*
Summit Funding Inc (PA)...916 571-3000
2241 Harvard St Ste 200 Sacramento (95815) *(G-9900)*
Summit Hr Worldwide Inc...408 884-7100
220 Main St Ste 208a San Jose (95112) *(G-27673)*
Summit Technology Group Inc...707 542-4773
2450c Bluebell Dr Ste C Santa Rosa (95403) *(G-2754)*
Summitpointe Golf Club, Milpitas *Also called American Golf Corporation (G-18865)*
Summitview Child Treatment...530 621-9800
670 Placerville Dr Ste 1b Placerville (95667) *(G-24238)*
Summitview Child Treatment Ctr...530 644-2412
5036 Sunrey Rd Placerville (95667) *(G-24827)*
Sun & Sail Club, Lake Forest *Also called Lake Forest Ll Master Homeown (G-25282)*
Sun America, Los Angeles *Also called American Intl Group Inc (G-10596)*
Sun America Housing Fund...310 772-6000
1999 Avenue Of The Stars Los Angeles (90067) *(G-11058)*
Sun and Sands Enterprises LLC (PA)...760 399-4278
86705 Avenue 54 Ste A Coachella (92236) *(G-96)*
Sun Chlorella USA Corp...310 891-0600
3305 Kashiwa St Torrance (90505) *(G-8925)*
Sun City Gardens, Sun City *Also called Sun City Rhf Housing Inc (G-24828)*
Sun City Palm Dsert Cmnty Assn (PA)...760 200-2100
38180 Del Webb Blvd Palm Desert (92211) *(G-25354)*
Sun City Rhf Housing Inc...951 679-2391
28500 Bradley Rd Sun City (92586) *(G-24828)*
Sun City Rsvlle Cmnty Assn Inc (PA)...916 774-3880
7050 Del Webb Blvd Roseville (95747) *(G-18792)*
Sun Coast Gen Insur Agcy Inc...949 768-1132
23042 Mill Creek Dr Laguna Hills (92653) *(G-10901)*
Sun Coast Merchandise Corp...323 720-9700
6315 Bandini Blvd Commerce (90040) *(G-8142)*
Sun Diego Charter, National City *Also called Sureride Charter Inc (G-3907)*
Sun Edison LLC (HQ)...650 453-5600
600 Clipper Dr Belmont (94002) *(G-6244)*
Sun Electric LP...714 210-3744
2101 S Yale St Ste B Santa Ana (92704) *(G-2755)*
Sun Express, Fontana *Also called Hanks Inc (G-4022)*
Sun Garden Date Growers LP...760 957-0396
1455 Hagberg Rd Bard (92222) *(G-260)*
Sun Haven Care Inc...714 578-2794
201 E Bastanchury Rd Fullerton (92835) *(G-20934)*
Sun Healthcare Group Inc (HQ)...949 255-7100
18831 Von Karman Ave # 400 Irvine (92612) *(G-20075)*
Sun Hill Properties Inc (HQ)...818 506-2500
555 Unversal Hollywood Dr Universal City (91608) *(G-13308)*
Sun Innovations Inc...510 573-3913
43241 Osgood Rd Fremont (94539) *(G-26612)*
Sun Lakes Cntry Club Hmeownrs...951 845-2135
850 Country Club Dr Banning (92220) *(G-19100)*
Sun Lakes Country Club, Banning *Also called Professional Cmnty MGT Cal Inc (G-11765)*
Sun Light & Power...510 845-2997
1035 Folger Ave Berkeley (94710) *(G-17510)*
Sun Maid Growers, Kingsburg *Also called Sun-Maid Growers California (G-8928)*

ALPHABETIC

Sun Mar Health Care, Rosemead *Also called Sun Mar Management Services* ***(G-27237)***
Sun Mar Management Service, Monterey Park *Also called Monterey Pk Convalescent Hosp* ***(G-21319)***
Sun Mar Management Services, Anaheim *Also called Sun Mar Nursing Center Inc* ***(G-21386)***
Sun Mar Management Services 714 827-9263
501 S Beach Blvd Anaheim (92804) ***(G-27235)***
Sun Mar Management Services 909 822-8066
7509 Laurel Ave Fontana (92336) ***(G-27236)***
Sun Mar Management Services 626 288-8353
3136 Del Mar Ave Rosemead (91770) ***(G-27237)***
Sun Mar Management Services 818 352-1454
7660 Wyngate St Tujunga (91042) ***(G-27238)***
Sun Mar Management Services 951 687-3842
8171 Magnolia Ave Riverside (92504) ***(G-20935)***
Sun Mar Nursing Center Inc 714 776-1720
1720 W Orange Ave Anaheim (92804) ***(G-21386)***
Sun Microsystems, Santa Clara *Also called Oracle America Inc* ***(G-15356)***
Sun Microsystems, Milpitas *Also called Oracle America Inc* ***(G-16446)***
Sun Pacific Cold Storage, Bakersfield *Also called Exeter Packers Inc* ***(G-4495)***
Sun Pacific Farming, Bakersfield *Also called 7th Standard Ranch Company* ***(G-139)***
Sun Pacific Farming, Bakersfield *Also called Sun Pacific Marketing Coop Inc* ***(G-8779)***
Sun Pacific Farming Coop Inc (PA) 559 592-7121
1250 E Myer Ave Exeter (93221) ***(G-724)***
Sun Pacific Maricopa 661 847-1015
31452 Old River Rd Bakersfield (93311) ***(G-588)***
Sun Pacific Marketing Coop Inc 661 847-1015
31452 Old River Rd Bakersfield (93311) ***(G-8779)***
Sun Pacific Packers, Exeter *Also called Exeter Packers Inc* ***(G-529)***
Sun Pacific Trucking Inc 310 830-4528
512 E C St Wilmington (90744) ***(G-4269)***
Sun Pharmaceuticals Inc 858 380-8865
13718 Sorbonne Ct San Diego (92128) ***(G-26613)***
Sun Rich Fresh Foods USA Inc (HQ) 951 735-3800
515 E Rincon St Corona (92879) ***(G-589)***
Sun Ten Labs Liquidation Co 949 587-0509
9250 Jeronimo Rd Irvine (92618) ***(G-8926)***
Sun Valley Dairy, Sun Valley *Also called Svd Inc* ***(G-8594)***
Sun Valley Group Inc (PA) 707 822-2885
3160 Upper Bay Rd Arcata (95521) ***(G-320)***
Sun Villa Inc 559 784-6644
350 N Villa St Porterville (93257) ***(G-20936)***
Sun West Wild Rice Facility 530 868-5188
Vance Ave Biggs (95917) ***(G-6)***
Sun World International Inc (PA) 661 392-5000
16351 Driver Rd Bakersfield (93308) ***(G-590)***
Sun World International LLC 661 392-5000
5701 Truxtun Ave Ste 200 Bakersfield (93309) ***(G-394)***
Sun World International Inc 760 398-9300
52200 Industrial Way Coachella (92236) ***(G-591)***
Sun-Air Convalescent Hospital, Panorama City *Also called Panorama Madows Nursing Ctr LP* ***(G-21344)***
Sun-Maid Growers California (PA) 559 897-6235
13525 S Bethel Ave Kingsburg (93631) ***(G-8927)***
Sun-Maid Growers California 559 897-8900
15628 E Nebraska Ave Kingsburg (93631) ***(G-8928)***
SunAmerica Annuity Lf Asrn Co (HQ) 310 772-6000
1 Sun America Ctr Los Angeles (90067) ***(G-10222)***
SunAmerica Hsng Fnd 1071 ....310 772-6000
1 Sun America Ctr Fl 36 Los Angeles (90067) ***(G-11059)***
SunAmerica Inc (HQ) 310 772-6000
1 Sun America Ctr Fl 38 Los Angeles (90067) ***(G-9704)***
SunAmerica Investments Inc (HQ) 310 772-6000
1 Sun America Ctr Fl 37 Los Angeles (90067) ***(G-27239)***
SunAmerica Investments Inc 310 772-6000
1 Sun America Ctr Fl 38 Los Angeles (90067) ***(G-12125)***
Sunbelt Controls Inc 626 610-2340
735 N Todd Ave Azusa (91702) ***(G-2387)***
Sunbelt Controls Inc 925 660-3900
4511 Willow Rd Ste 4 Pleasanton (94588) ***(G-17924)***
Sunbelt Controls Inc (HQ) 818 244-6571
6265 San Fernando Rd Glendale (91201) ***(G-2756)***
Sunbelt Towing Inc (PA) 619 297-8697
4370 Pacific Hwy San Diego (92110) ***(G-17895)***
Sunbrdge Care Ctr - Bellflower, Bellflower *Also called Rebecca Terley* ***(G-20865)***
Sunbridge Braswell Entps Inc 909 622-1069
1425 Laurel Ave Pomona (91768) ***(G-20937)***
Sunbridge Braswell Entps Inc 909 628-6024
2335 S Towne Ave Pomona (91766) ***(G-20938)***
Sunbridge Brittany Rehab Centr 916 484-1393
3900 Garfield Ave Carmichael (95608) ***(G-20939)***
Sunbridge Care Ctr - Grnd Ter, Grand Terrace *Also called Grand Terrace Care Center* ***(G-20634)***
Sunbridge Care Ctr For Downey, Downey *Also called Sunbridge Healthcare LLC* ***(G-21116)***
Sunbridge Care Entps W Inc 559 897-5881
1101 Stroud Ave Kingsburg (93631) ***(G-20940)***
Sunbridge Care Entps W LLC 559 897-5881
1101 Stroud Ave Kingsburg (93631) ***(G-20941)***
Sunbridge Elmhaven Care Center, Stockton *Also called Sunbridge Healthcare LLC* ***(G-20943)***
Sunbridge Harbor View 562 989-9907
490 W 14th St Long Beach (90813) ***(G-20942)***
Sunbridge Healthcare LLC 209 477-4817
6940 Pacific Ave Stockton (95207) ***(G-20943)***
Sunbridge Healthcare LLC 530 934-2834
320 N Crawford St Willows (95988) ***(G-21114)***
Sunbridge Healthcare LLC 562 981-9392
850 E Wardlow Rd Long Beach (90807) ***(G-21115)***
Sunbridge Healthcare LLC 562 869-2567
9300 Telegraph Rd Downey (90240) ***(G-21116)***
Sunbridge Healthcare LLC 510 352-2211
14766 Washington Ave San Leandro (94578) ***(G-21117)***
Sunbridge Paradise Rhblttn Ctr 530 872-3200
8777 Skyway Paradise (95969) ***(G-20944)***
Suncrest Nurseries Inc 831 728-2595
400 Casserly Rd Watsonville (95076) ***(G-9214)***
Sundance Construction Inc 714 437-0802
3500 W Lake Center Dr B Santa Ana (92704) ***(G-3095)***
Sundance Financial Inc 619 298-9877
2505 Congress St Ste 220 San Diego (92110) ***(G-12015)***
Sundance Natural Foods Company 760 945-9898
2231 Willowbrook Dr Oceanside (92056) ***(G-261)***
Sunday Bazaar Inc 415 621-0764
495 Barneveld Ave San Francisco (94124) ***(G-6888)***
Sundt Construction, Sacramento *Also called Halstead Partnership* ***(G-10996)***
Sunfood Corporation 619 596-7979
1830 Gillespie Way # 101 El Cajon (92020) ***(G-8929)***
Sunfood Superfoods, El Cajon *Also called Sunfood Corporation* ***(G-8929)***
Sunfoods LLC (HQ) 530 661-0578
1620 E Kentucky Ave Woodland (95776) ***(G-8528)***
Sungard Bi-Tech Inc (HQ) 530 891-5281
890 Fortress St Chico (95973) ***(G-15483)***
Sungevity Inc (PA) 510 496-5500
66 Franklin St Ste 310 Oakland (94607) ***(G-2388)***
Sunharbor Management LLC 760 356-1262
708 E 5th St Holtville (92250) ***(G-24829)***
Suning Cmmerce R D Ctr USA Inc 650 834-9800
845 Page Mill Rd Palo Alto (94304) ***(G-26708)***
Sunkist Enterprises 650 347-3900
1308 Rollins Rd Burlingame (94010) ***(G-7700)***
Sunkist Growers Inc (PA) 818 986-4800
27770 N Entertainment Dr # 120 Valencia (91355) ***(G-8780)***
Sunkist Growers Inc 909 983-9811
531 W Poplar Ave Tipton (93272) ***(G-592)***
Sunkist Growers Inc 559 752-4256
531 W Poplar Ave Tipton (93272) ***(G-593)***
Sunline Transit Agency 760 972-4059
790 Vine Ave Coachella (92236) ***(G-3849)***
Sunline Transit Agency (PA) 760 343-3456
32505 Harry Oliver Trl Thousand Palms (92276) ***(G-3889)***
Sunlit Gardens, Murrieta *Also called Alta Loma Assisted Living LLC* ***(G-23653)***
Sunny Cal Adhc Inc 626 307-7772
8450 Valley Blvd Ste 121b Rosemead (91770) ***(G-24239)***
Sunny Retirement Home 408 454-5600
22445 Cupertino Rd Cupertino (95014) ***(G-21387)***
Sunny TV Productions Inc 310 840-7440
8660 Hayden Pl Fl 2 Culver City (90232) ***(G-18163)***
Sunny View Care Center, Los Angeles *Also called Longwood Management Corp* ***(G-21295)***
Sunnyside Convalescent Hosp, Fresno *Also called R Fellen Inc* ***(G-20861)***
Sunnyside Country Club 559 255-8926
5704 E Butler Ave Fresno (93727) ***(G-19101)***
Sunnyside Farms, Turlock *Also called Ssi-Turlock Dairy Division* ***(G-8593)***
Sunnyside Gardens 408 730-4070
1025 Carson Dr Sunnyvale (94086) ***(G-24830)***
Sunnyside Resort 530 583-7200
1850 W Lake Blvd Tahoe City (96145) ***(G-13309)***
Sunnyside Rhblttion Nrsing Ctr 310 320-4130
22617 S Vermont Ave Torrance (90502) ***(G-20945)***
Sunnyslope Tree Farm Inc 714 532-1440
4025 E La Palma Ave # 203 Anaheim (92807) ***(G-9215)***
Sunnyslope Trees, Anaheim *Also called Sunnyslope Tree Farm Inc* ***(G-9215)***
Sunnyvale Fluid Sys Tech Inc 510 933-2500
3393 W Warren Ave Fremont (94538) ***(G-7956)***
Sunnyvale Health Care, Sunnyvale *Also called Sunnyvale Healthcare Center* ***(G-20946)***
Sunnyvale Healthcare Center 408 245-8070
1291 S Bernardo Ave Sunnyvale (94087) ***(G-20946)***
Sunnyvale Sof-X Owner L P 408 542-8264
1100 N Mathilda Ave Sunnyvale (94089) ***(G-13310)***
Sunol Valley Golf Course, Sunol *Also called Sunol Vly Golf & Recreation Co* ***(G-18793)***
Sunol Vly Golf & Recreation Co 925 862-2404
6900 Mission Rd Sunol (94586) ***(G-18793)***
Sunplus HM Care - Pleasant Hl, Pleasant Hill *Also called Accentcare Home Health Cal Inc* ***(G-22324)***
Sunplus HM Hlth - Newport Bch, Newport Beach *Also called Accentcare Home Health Cal Inc* ***(G-22330)***
Sunplus Home Care - Ontario, Ontario *Also called Accentcare Home Health Cal Inc* ***(G-22326)***
Sunplus Home Care - San Diego, San Diego *Also called Accentcare Home Health Cal Inc* ***(G-22328)***
Sunplus Home Care - W Covina, Covina *Also called Accentcare Home Health Cal Inc* ***(G-22329)***
Sunplus Home Hlth - San Marino, San Marino *Also called Accentcare Home Health Cal Inc* ***(G-22327)***
Sunpower Corporation Systems (HQ) 510 260-8200
1414 Harbour Way S # 1901 Richmond (94804) ***(G-2389)***
Sunpro Solar Inc 951 678-7733
34859 Frederick St # 101 Wildomar (92595) ***(G-3480)***
Sunray Healthcare Center, Los Angeles *Also called Kf Sunray LLC* ***(G-21281)***
Sunridge Care & Rehabilitation, Salinas *Also called Helios Healthcare LLC* ***(G-20663)***
Sunridge Farms, Royal Oaks *Also called Falcon Trading Company* ***(G-8834)***
Sunridge Nurseries Inc 661 363-8463
441 Vineland Rd Bakersfield (93307) ***(G-484)***
Sunrise Assistd Lving of Wlnt, Walnut Creek *Also called Sunrise Senior Living LLC* ***(G-20968)***

ALPHABETIC

ALPHABETIC SECTION
Sunstone Hotel Investors Inc

Sunrise Asssted Lving San Mteo, San Mateo *Also called Sunrise Senior Living Inc* **(G-20952)**
Sunrise At Alta Loma, Rancho Cucamonga *Also called Sunrise Senior Living Inc* **(G-20947)**
Sunrise At Bonita, Chula Vista *Also called Sunrise Senior Living LLC* **(G-20973)**
Sunrise At La Costa, Carlsbad *Also called Sunrise Senior Living LLC* **(G-20972)**
Sunrise At Raincross Village, Riverside *Also called Sunrise Senior Living LLC* **(G-20986)**
Sunrise At Sterling Canyon, Valencia *Also called Sunrise Senior Living Inc* **(G-20961)**
Sunrise At Wood Ranch, Simi Valley *Also called Sunrise Senior Living Inc* **(G-20949)**
Sunrise Convalescent Hospital, Pasadena *Also called D & C Care Center Inc* **(G-21204)**
Sunrise Delivery Service Inc....323 464-5121
13351 Riverside Dr 672d Sherman Oaks (91423) **(G-4423)**
Sunrise Desert Partners....760 404-1280
300 Eagle Cir Palm Desert (92211) **(G-12016)**
Sunrise Farms LLC....707 778-6450
395 Liberty Rd Petaluma (94952) **(G-8607)**
Sunrise Food Ministry....916 965-5431
5901 San Juan Ave Citrus Heights (95610) **(G-24240)**
Sunrise Growers Inc (HQ)....714 630-2170
701 W Kimberly Ave # 210 Placentia (92870) **(G-8781)**
Sunrise Growers-Frozsun Foods, Placentia *Also called Sunrise Growers Inc* **(G-8781)**
Sunrise Merger Sub, LLC, Agoura Hills *Also called Arpi Reit LLC* **(G-12238)**
Sunrise of Belmont, Belmont *Also called Sunrise Senior Living Inc* **(G-20955)**
Sunrise of Beverly Hills, Beverly Hills *Also called Sunrise Senior Living Inc* **(G-20960)**
Sunrise of Carmichael, Carmichael *Also called Sunrise Senior Living Inc* **(G-20965)**
Sunrise of Danville, Danville *Also called Sunrise Senior Living LLC* **(G-24241)**
Sunrise of Fresno, Fresno *Also called Sunrise Senior Living LLC* **(G-20979)**
Sunrise of Hemet, Hemet *Also called Sunrise Senior Living LLC* **(G-20983)**
Sunrise of Hermosa Beach, Hermosa Beach *Also called Sunrise Senior Living LLC* **(G-20971)**
Sunrise of La Palma, La Palma *Also called Sunrise Senior Living LLC* **(G-24832)**
Sunrise of Mission Viejo, Mission Viejo *Also called Sunrise Senior Living LLC* **(G-20970)**
Sunrise of Monterey, Monterey *Also called Sunrise Senior Living Inc* **(G-20966)**
Sunrise of Oakland Hills, Moraga *Also called Sunrise Senior Living Inc* **(G-20950)**
Sunrise of Palm Springs, Palm Springs *Also called Sunrise Senior Living LLC* **(G-20980)**
Sunrise of Palo Alto, Beverly Hills *Also called Sunrise Senior Living Inc* **(G-20957)**
Sunrise of Petaluma, Petaluma *Also called Sunrise Senior Living Inc* **(G-20951)**
Sunrise of Petaluma....707 776-2885
815 Wood Sorrel Dr Petaluma (94954) **(G-24831)**
Sunrise of Playa Vista, Los Angeles *Also called Sunrise Senior Living Inc* **(G-20959)**
Sunrise of Rocklin, Rocklin *Also called Sunrise Senior Living LLC* **(G-20984)**
Sunrise of Sacramento, Sacramento *Also called Sunrise Senior Living LLC* **(G-20974)**
Sunrise of Santa Rosa, Santa Rosa *Also called Sunrise Senior Living Inc* **(G-20967)**
Sunrise of Studio City, Studio City *Also called Sunrise Senior Living LLC* **(G-20978)**
Sunrise of Sunnyvale, Sunnyvale *Also called Sunrise Senior Living LLC* **(G-20975)**
Sunrise of Westlake Village, Westlake Village *Also called Sunrise Senior Living LLC* **(G-20977)**
Sunrise of Woodland Hills, Encino *Also called Sunrise Senior Living Inc* **(G-20954)**
Sunrise Plumbing & Mech Inc....562 424-0332
5259 Cherry Ave Long Beach (90805) **(G-2390)**
Sunrise Produce Company, Fullerton *Also called Loewy Enterprises* **(G-8748)**
Sunrise Ranch....805 488-0813
3623 Etting Rd Oxnard (93033) **(G-321)**
Sunrise Retirement Villa, Roseville *Also called Sign of Dove* **(G-11203)**
Sunrise Retirement Villa....916 786-3277
707 Sunrise Ave Ofc Roseville (95661) **(G-11210)**
Sunrise Senior Living Inc....909 941-3001
9519 Baseline Rd Rancho Cucamonga (91730) **(G-20947)**
Sunrise Senior Living Inc....760 340-5999
72201 Country Club Dr Palm Desert (92210) **(G-20948)**
Sunrise Senior Living Inc....805 584-8881
136 Tierra Rejada Rd Simi Valley (93065) **(G-20949)**
Sunrise Senior Living Inc....510 531-7190
1600 Canyon Rd 103 Moraga (94556) **(G-20950)**
Sunrise Senior Living Inc....707 776-2885
815 Wood Sorrel Dr Petaluma (94954) **(G-20951)**
Sunrise Senior Living Inc....650 558-8555
955 S El Camino Real San Mateo (94402) **(G-20952)**
Sunrise Senior Living Inc....562 594-5788
3840 Lampson Ave Seal Beach (90740) **(G-20953)**
Sunrise Senior Living Inc....818 346-9046
5501 Newcastle Ave # 130 Encino (91316) **(G-20954)**
Sunrise Senior Living Inc....650 508-0400
1010 Almeda De Las Pulgas Belmont (94002) **(G-20955)**
Sunrise Senior Living Inc....949 248-8855
31741 Rancho Viejo Rd San Juan Capistrano (92675) **(G-20956)**
Sunrise Senior Living Inc....650 326-1108
201 N Crescent Dr Apt 503 Beverly Hills (90210) **(G-20957)**
Sunrise Senior Living Inc....949 234-3000
25421 Sea Bluffs Dr Dana Point (92629) **(G-20958)**
Sunrise Senior Living Inc....310 437-7178
5555 Playa Vista Dr Los Angeles (90094) **(G-20959)**
Sunrise Senior Living Inc....310 274-4479
201 N Crescent Dr Beverly Hills (90210) **(G-20960)**
Sunrise Senior Living Inc....661 253-3551
25815 Mcbean Pkwy Ofc Valencia (91355) **(G-20961)**
Sunrise Senior Living Inc....415 664-6264
1601 19th Ave San Francisco (94122) **(G-20962)**
Sunrise Senior Living Inc....408 223-1312
4855 San Felipe Rd San Jose (95135) **(G-20963)**
Sunrise Senior Living Inc....949 581-6111
24552 Paseo De Valencia Laguna Hills (92653) **(G-20964)**
Sunrise Senior Living Inc....916 485-4500
5451 Fair Oaks Blvd Carmichael (95608) **(G-20965)**
Sunrise Senior Living Inc....831 643-2400
1110 Carmelo St Monterey (93940) **(G-20966)**
Sunrise Senior Living Inc....707 575-7503
3250 Chanate Rd Ofc Santa Rosa (95404) **(G-20967)**
Sunrise Senior Living LLC....925 309-4178
1027 Diablo Rd Danville (94526) **(G-24241)**
Sunrise Senior Living LLC....925 932-3500
2175 Ygnacio Valley Rd Walnut Creek (94598) **(G-20968)**
Sunrise Senior Living LLC....818 886-1616
17650 Devonshire St Northridge (91325) **(G-20969)**
Sunrise Senior Living LLC....949 582-2010
26151 Country Club Dr Mission Viejo (92691) **(G-20970)**
Sunrise Senior Living LLC....310 937-0959
1837 Pacific Coast Hwy Hermosa Beach (90254) **(G-20971)**
Sunrise Senior Living LLC....760 930-0060
7020 Manzanita St Carlsbad (92011) **(G-20972)**
Sunrise Senior Living LLC....619 470-2220
3302 Bonita Rd Chula Vista (91910) **(G-20973)**
Sunrise Senior Living LLC....916 486-0200
345 Munroe St Sacramento (95825) **(G-20974)**
Sunrise Senior Living LLC....408 749-8600
633 S Knickerbocker Dr # 263 Sunnyvale (94087) **(G-20975)**
Sunrise Senior Living LLC....303 410-0500
530 Water St Fl 5 Oakland (94607) **(G-20976)**
Sunrise Senior Living LLC....805 557-1100
3101 Townsgate Rd Westlake Village (91361) **(G-20977)**
Sunrise Senior Living LLC....818 505-8484
4610 Coldwater Canyon Ave Studio City (91604) **(G-20978)**
Sunrise Senior Living LLC....559 325-8170
7444 N Cedar Ave Fresno (93720) **(G-20979)**
Sunrise Senior Living LLC....760 322-3444
1780 E Baristo Rd Palm Springs (92262) **(G-20980)**
Sunrise Senior Living LLC....714 739-8111
5321 La Palma Ave Fl 2 La Palma (90623) **(G-24832)**
Sunrise Senior Living LLC....650 654-9700
1301 Ralston Ave Ste A Belmont (94002) **(G-20981)**
Sunrise Senior Living LLC....805 388-8086
6000 Santa Rosa Rd Ofc Camarillo (93012) **(G-20982)**
Sunrise Senior Living LLC....951 929-5988
1177 S Palm Ave Hemet (92543) **(G-20983)**
Sunrise Senior Living LLC....916 632-3003
6100 Sierra College Blvd Rocklin (95677) **(G-20984)**
Sunrise Senior Living LLC....760 346-5420
41505 Carlotta Dr Palm Desert (92211) **(G-20985)**
Sunrise Senior Living LLC....951 785-1200
5232 Central Ave Riverside (92504) **(G-20986)**
Sunrise Villa Ctr Head Start, Wasco *Also called Community Action Partnr Kern* **(G-24442)**
Sunrize Staging Inc....760 743-2043
2210 Meyers Ave Ste 6b Escondido (92029) **(G-11861)**
Sunrun Installation Svcs Inc....408 746-3062
2300 Zanker Rd Ste F San Jose (95131) **(G-2391)**
Sunrun Installation Svcs Inc (HQ)....805 528-9705
775 Fiero Ln Ste 200 San Luis Obispo (93401) **(G-2757)**
Sunset Aviation LLC (PA)....707 775-2786
201 1st St Ste 307 Petaluma (94952) **(G-4887)**
Sunset Building Maintance Inc....408 727-3408
1920 Lafayette St Ste E Santa Clara (95050) **(G-14440)**
Sunset Building Maintenance, Santa Clara *Also called Sunset Building Maintance Inc* **(G-14440)**
Sunset Development Company, San Ramon *Also called Annabel Investment Company* **(G-11948)**
Sunset Hills Country Club, Thousand Oaks *Also called American Golf Corporation* **(G-18852)**
Sunset Landscape Maintenance....949 455-4636
27201 Burbank El Toro (92610) **(G-961)**
Sunset Linen Service, Santa Rosa *Also called City Towel & Dust Service Inc* **(G-13546)**
Sunset Manor Convalescent Hosp, El Monte *Also called Gibralter Convalescent Hosp* **(G-21234)**
Sunset Neighborhood Beacon Ctr, San Francisco *Also called Aspiranet* **(G-24554)**
Sunset Property Services, Irvine *Also called Jonset Corporation* **(G-6630)**
Sunset Scavenger Company....415 330-1300
250 Executive Park Blvd # 2100 San Francisco (94134) **(G-6566)**
Sunset Station, Los Angeles *Also called Passprt Accept Fclty Los Angel* **(G-17404)**
Sunset Tower Hotel LLC....323 654-7100
8358 W Sunset Blvd Los Angeles (90069) **(G-13311)**
Sunshine Child Care & Lrng Ctr, Valencia *Also called Sunshine Day Camp Inc* **(G-24523)**
Sunshine Clearing Corporation....714 829-0273
1215 W Imperial Hwy # 210 Brea (92821) **(G-14798)**
Sunshine Communications Inc....619 448-7600
350 Cypress Ln Ste D El Cajon (92020) **(G-2758)**
Sunshine Day Camp Inc....661 254-6855
23720 Wiley Canyon Rd Valencia (91355) **(G-24523)**
Sunshine Floral Inc....805 684-1177
4595 Foothill Rd Carpinteria (93013) **(G-9216)**
Sunshine Floral LLC....805 982-8822
1070 S Rice Ave Ste 1 Oxnard (93033) **(G-9217)**
Sunshine Metal Clad Inc....661 366-0575
7201 Edison Hwy Bakersfield (93307) **(G-2985)**
Sunshine Villa Assisted Living, Santa Cruz *Also called Regent Assisted Living Inc* **(G-24784)**
Sunstone Center Crt Lessee Inc....949 382-4000
120 Vantis Ste 350 Aliso Viejo (92656) **(G-13312)**
Sunstone Hotel Investors Inc....619 239-6171
1617 1st Ave Ste 16 San Diego (92101) **(G-13313)**
Sunstone Hotel Investors Inc....707 253-8600
3425 Solano Ave NAPA (94558) **(G-13314)**
Sunstone Hotel Investors Inc....310 215-1000
9801 Airport Blvd Los Angeles (90045) **(G-13315)**

ALPHABETIC

Sunstone Hotel Investors Inc (PA).....949 330-4000
120 Vantis Ste 350 Aliso Viejo (92656) *(G-12274)*
Sunstone Hotel Investors Inc.....949 476-2001
4500 Macarthur Blvd Newport Beach (92660) *(G-13316)*
Sunstone Hotel Investors Inc.....310 649-1400
6161 W Century Blvd Los Angeles (90045) *(G-13317)*
Sunstone Hotel Investors LLC.....714 739-8500
14299 Firestone Blvd La Mirada (90638) *(G-13318)*
Sunstone Hotel Investors LLC.....661 267-6587
39375 5th St W Palmdale (93551) *(G-13319)*
Sunstone Hotel Investors LLC.....310 830-9200
2 Civic Plaza Dr Carson (90745) *(G-13320)*
Sunstone Hotel Investors LLC (HQ).....949 330-4000
120 Vantis Ste 350 Aliso Viejo (92656) *(G-12346)*
Sunstone Hotel Investors LLC.....714 635-5000
1752 S Clementine St Anaheim (92802) *(G-13321)*
Sunstone Hotel Management Inc.....951 784-8000
3400 Market St Riverside (92501) *(G-13322)*
Sunstone Hotel Management Inc (PA).....949 297-4183
120 Vantis Ste 350 Aliso Viejo (92656) *(G-13323)*
Sunstone Hotel Properties Inc.....310 228-4100
1177 S Beverly Dr Los Angeles (90035) *(G-13324)*
Sunstone Hotel Properties Inc.....310 546-7627
1700 N Sepulveda Blvd Manhattan Beach (90266) *(G-13325)*
Sunstone Hotel Properties Inc (HQ).....949 330-4000
120 Vantis Ste 350 Aliso Viejo (92656) *(G-13326)*
Sunstone Ocean Lessee Inc.....949 382-4000
120 Vantis Ste 350 Aliso Viejo (92656) *(G-13327)*
Sunstone Top Gun LLC.....858 453-0400
4550 La Jolla Village Dr San Diego (92122) *(G-13328)*
Suntreat Pkg Shipg A Ltd Prtnr.....559 562-4991
391 Oxford Ave Lindsay (93247) *(G-5203)*
Sunwater Solar, San Diego *Also called Adroit Energy Inc (G-2107)*
Sunwest Bank (HQ).....714 730-4441
2050 Main St Fl 3 Irvine (92614) *(G-9527)*
Sunwest Electric Inc.....714 630-8700
3064 E Miraloma Ave Anaheim (92806) *(G-2759)*
Super 8 Motel, San Francisco *Also called Chirag Hospitality Inc (G-12514)*
Super Center Concepts Inc.....323 223-3878
133 W Avenue 45 Los Angeles (90065) *(G-17511)*
Super Color Labs, West Hollywood *Also called Super Photo Laboratory Inc (G-16958)*
Super Garden Centers Inc.....818 348-9266
7659 Topanga Canyon Blvd Canoga Park (91304) *(G-9218)*
Super Photo Laboratory Inc.....323 512-0247
979 N La Brea Ave West Hollywood (90038) *(G-16958)*
Super Shuttle, Sun Valley *Also called Arcadia Transit Inc (G-3635)*
Super Store Industries.....209 858-2010
16888 Mckinley Ave Lathrop (95330) *(G-8930)*
Super Talent Technology Corp.....408 957-8133
2077 N Capitol Ave San Jose (95132) *(G-7196)*
Superbalife International LLC.....310 553-7400
1171 S Robertson Blvd # 525 Los Angeles (90035) *(G-8297)*
Superclean America, Palm Springs *Also called Joseph Dipuzo (G-13509)*
Superco Specialty Products, Valencia *Also called Cns Industries Inc (G-8984)*
Superior Automatic Sprnklr Co.....408 946-7272
4378 Enterprise St Fremont (94538) *(G-2392)*
Superior Berry Farms LLC.....805 483-1000
730 S A St Oxnard (93030) *(G-135)*
Superior Coffee & Foods, Santa Fe Springs *Also called Hillshire Brands Company (G-8852)*
Superior Communications Inc (PA).....626 388-2573
5027 Irwindale Ave # 900 Baldwin Park (91706) *(G-7642)*
Superior Construction Inc.....951 808-8780
265 N Joy St Ste 100 Corona (92879) *(G-1267)*
Superior Court Unit, Fresno *Also called County of Fresno (G-23169)*
Superior Elec Mech & Plbg Inc.....909 357-9400
8613 Helms Ave Rancho Cucamonga (91730) *(G-2760)*
Superior Envmtl Svcs Inc.....619 462-7079
6383 Lake Arrowhead Dr San Diego (92119) *(G-14441)*
Superior Foods Inc.....831 728-3691
275 Westgate Dr Watsonville (95076) *(G-8571)*
Superior Foods Companies, The, Watsonville *Also called Superior Foods Inc (G-8571)*
Superior Grocers, Los Angeles *Also called Super Center Concepts Inc (G-17511)*
Superior Gunite (PA).....818 896-9199
12306 Van Nuys Blvd Sylmar (91342) *(G-3339)*
Superior Home Design Inc.....213 455-8972
1800 E 50th St Los Angeles (90058) *(G-6889)*
Superior Machining Mfg Co Inc.....714 529-6000
322 Oak Pl Brea (92821) *(G-7893)*
Superior Marine Solutions LLC.....619 773-7800
2700 Hoover Ave Ste A National City (91950) *(G-18019)*
Superior Masonry Walls Ltd.....909 370-1800
300 W Olive St Ste A Colton (92324) *(G-2836)*
Superior Mobile Medics Inc.....619 299-3926
7480 Mission Valley Rd # 101 San Diego (92108) *(G-23066)*
Superior Paving Company Inc.....951 739-9200
1880 N Delilah St Corona (92879) *(G-1870)*
Superior Pntg Drywall Fnshings, Carmichael *Also called H B J Corporation (G-2907)*
Superior Ready Mix Concrete LP.....619 265-0955
7192 Mission Gorge Rd San Diego (92120) *(G-1871)*
Superior Seafood Co, Los Angeles *Also called PLD Enterprises Inc (G-8648)*
Superior Services, Oceanside *Also called Superior Support Services Inc (G-27240)*
Superior Sod I LP.....909 923-5068
17821 17th St Ste 165 Tustin (92780) *(G-322)*
Superior Support Services Inc.....559 458-0507
702 Civic Center Dr Oceanside (92054) *(G-27240)*
Superior Tile Co, San Leandro *Also called TRM Corporation (G-3026)*
Superior Vision Services Inc (PA).....916 859-6218
11101 White Rock Rd # 150 Rancho Cordova (95670) *(G-10383)*

Supermedia Sales Inc.....805 278-3400
300 E Esplanade Dr # 600 Oxnard (93036) *(G-14011)*
Supershuttle International Inc.....909 944-2606
9559 Center Ave Ste F Rancho Cucamonga (91730) *(G-3724)*
Supershuttle International Inc.....916 648-2500
3100 Northgate Blvd Sacramento (95833) *(G-3725)*
Supershuttle Los Angeles Inc.....310 222-5500
531 Van Ness Ave Torrance (90501) *(G-3726)*
Supershuttle Orange County.....310 222-5500
531 Van Ness Ave Torrance (90501) *(G-3727)*
Supershuttle Sacramento, Sacramento *Also called Supershuttle International Inc (G-3725)*
Supertex Inc.....408 222-8880
71 Vista Montana San Jose (95134) *(G-26891)*
Supply Change Services, Sacramento *Also called Sacramento Municpl Utility Dst (G-6203)*
Support Associates Inc.....949 595-4379
22901 Mill Creek Dr Laguna Hills (92653) *(G-27799)*
Support For Home Inc.....530 792-8484
1333 Howe Ave Ste 206 Sacramento (95825) *(G-1268)*
Supportcom Inc (PA).....650 556-9440
900 Chesapeake Dr Fl 2 Redwood City (94063) *(G-16195)*
Supreme Court United States.....619 557-7149
101 W Broadway Ste 700 San Diego (92101) *(G-24242)*
Sure Forming Systems Inc.....562 598-6348
10602 Humbolt St Los Alamitos (90720) *(G-3340)*
Sure Haven.....949 467-9213
2900 Bristol St Ste B300 Costa Mesa (92626) *(G-22180)*
Sure Haven Addic, Costa Mesa *Also called Sure Haven (G-22180)*
Surecraft Supply Inc.....760 737-2120
2875 Executive Pl Escondido (92029) *(G-3096)*
Sureride Charter Inc.....619 336-9200
522 W 8th St National City (91950) *(G-3907)*
Surety West Logistics Inc.....800 761-2551
980 9th St Fl 16 Sacramento (95814) *(G-5172)*
Surety West Transportation, Sacramento *Also called Surety West Logistics Inc (G-5172)*
Surewest Telephone, Roseville *Also called Cal Consoldated Communications (G-5566)*
Surf Sand Hotel, Laguna Beach *Also called JC Resorts LLC (G-27075)*
Surface Pumps Inc (PA).....661 393-1545
3301 Unicorn Rd Bakersfield (93308) *(G-7894)*
Surfside Race Place At Del Mar, Del Mar *Also called Del Mar Thoroughbred Club (G-18569)*
Surgener Electric Inc.....661 399-3321
1406 N Chester Ave Bakersfield (93308) *(G-2761)*
Surgery Center of Alta Bates (HQ).....510 204-4444
2450 Ashby Ave Berkeley (94705) *(G-21937)*
Surgery Center of Alta Bates.....510 204-4411
2001 Dwight Way Berkeley (94704) *(G-20076)*
Surgery Center of Alta Bates.....510 204-1591
2001 Dwight Way Berkeley (94704) *(G-22842)*
Surgery Center of Health South, Oakland *Also called EBSC LP (G-19510)*
Surgical Care Affiliate.....916 529-4590
2450 Venture Oaks Way # 120 Sacramento (95833) *(G-26447)*
Surgical Staff Inc.....916 444-4424
1523 G St Sacramento (95814) *(G-14954)*
Surplus Line Association Cal.....415 434-4900
50 California St Fl 18 San Francisco (94111) *(G-25106)*
Surprise Valley Hlth Care Dst.....530 279-6111
741 N Main St Cedarville (96104) *(G-21938)*
Surveillance Systems.....800 508-6981
4465 Granite Dr Ste 700 Rocklin (95677) *(G-7643)*
Survey Sampling Intl LLC.....866 872-4006
16501 Ventura Blvd # 300 Encino (91436) *(G-26709)*
Surveysavvy.com, San Diego *Also called Luth Research Inc (G-26685)*
Survival Insurance Inc.....818 565-1584
2550 N Hollywood Way # 120 Burbank (91505) *(G-10902)*
Survival Insurance Brkg A Cal, Burbank *Also called Survival Insurance Inc (G-10902)*
Survival Systems Intl Inc (PA).....760 749-6800
34140 Valley Center Rd Valley Center (92082) *(G-18020)*
Survivalcave Inc.....800 719-7650
10620 Treena St Ste 230 San Diego (92131) *(G-8931)*
Susan S Reishchl, San Jose *Also called Rossi Hamerslough Reishchl & (G-23541)*
Sushi Nozawa LLC.....310 963-7377
11628 Santa Monica Blvd Los Angeles (90025) *(G-15484)*
Sustainable Agriculture, Rancho Dominguez *Also called Seeds of Change Inc (G-9150)*
Sutherland Asbill Brennan LLP.....916 241-0500
500 Capitol Mall Ste 2500 Sacramento (95814) *(G-23590)*
Sutherland Halthcare Solutions.....310 464-5000
9841 Arprt Blvd Ste 1414 Los Angeles (90045) *(G-27241)*
Sutra Lounge, Costa Mesa *Also called Random Holdings Inc (G-27194)*
Sutta Company Incorporated (PA).....510 873-8777
1221 3rd St Oakland (94607) *(G-8092)*
Sutter Alhambra Surgery Center, Sacramento *Also called Sutter Health (G-20090)*
Sutter Amador Hospital (HQ).....209 223-7500
200 Mission Blvd Jackson (95642) *(G-21939)*
Sutter Amador Hospital Lab, Jackson *Also called Sutter Hlth Scrmnto Sierra Reg (G-20115)*
Sutter Auburn Faith Hospital, Auburn *Also called Sutter Health (G-22844)*
Sutter Bay Hospitals (HQ).....415 600-6000
633 Folsom St Fl 7 San Francisco (94107) *(G-21940)*
SUTTER C H S, Castro Valley *Also called Eden Township Hospital Dst (G-21550)*
SUTTER C H S, Sacramento *Also called Sutter Health (G-21945)*
SUTTER C H S, Crescent City *Also called Sutter Coast Hospital (G-21942)*
Sutter Central Vly Hospitals (HQ).....209 526-4500
1700 Coffee Rd Modesto (95355) *(G-21941)*
Sutter Central Vly Hospitals.....209 526-4500
1700 Coffee Rd Modesto (95355) *(G-4888)*
Sutter Club Inc.....916 442-0456
1220 9th St Sacramento (95814) *(G-25355)*
Sutter Coast Hospital (HQ).....707 464-8511
800 E Washington Blvd Crescent City (95531) *(G-21942)*

Sutter Connect LLC (HQ)....916 854-6600
10470 Old Placrvl Rd # 100 Sacramento (95827) ***(G-27674)***
Sutter Davis Hospital, Davis *Also called Sutter Hlth Scrmnto Sierra Reg* ***(G-21948)***
Sutter Delta Medical Ctr Aux....925 779-7200
3901 Lone Tree Way Antioch (94509) ***(G-21943)***
Sutter East Bay Hospitals....510 204-1609
2420 Ashby Ave Berkeley (94705) ***(G-21944)***
Sutter Elk Grove Surgery Ctr, Elk Grove *Also called Sutter Health* ***(G-25359)***
Sutter Gould Med Foundation (PA)....209 948-5940
600 Coffee Rd Modesto (95355) ***(G-20077)***
Sutter Health, Santa Rosa *Also called Santa Rosa Surgery Center LP* ***(G-21862)***
Sutter Health....530 747-0389
2068 John Jones Rd # 100 Davis (95616) ***(G-20078)***
Sutter Health....916 733-1025
1625 Stockton Blvd # 102 Sacramento (95816) ***(G-20079)***
Sutter Health....916 797-4725
3 Medical Plaza Dr # 110 Roseville (95661) ***(G-20080)***
Sutter Health....707 586-0440
1400 Medical Center Dr Cotati (94928) ***(G-20081)***
Sutter Health....650 853-2975
795 El Camino Real Palo Alto (94301) ***(G-25356)***
Sutter Health....916 733-9588
1020 29th St Ste 600 Sacramento (95816) ***(G-20082)***
Sutter Health....408 524-5952
2734 El Camino Real Santa Clara (95051) ***(G-20083)***
Sutter Health....530 757-5111
2000 Sutter Pl Davis (95616) ***(G-20084)***
Sutter Health....415 600-3311
633 Folsom St Fl 5 San Francisco (94107) ***(G-27675)***
Sutter Health....707 526-1800
510 Doyle Park Dr Santa Rosa (95405) ***(G-23067)***
Sutter Health....415 345-0100
3468 California St San Francisco (94118) ***(G-20085)***
Sutter Health....209 366-2007
1335 S Fairmont Ave Lodi (95240) ***(G-23068)***
Sutter Health....415 731-6300
595 Buckingham Way # 515 San Francisco (94132) ***(G-20086)***
Sutter Health....209 223-5445
100 Mission Blvd Jackson (95642) ***(G-20087)***
Sutter Health....415 600-0110
1375 Sutter St San Francisco (94109) ***(G-20088)***
Sutter Health....916 797-4715
3 Medical Plaza Dr Roseville (95661) ***(G-23069)***
Sutter Health....831 458-6310
1301 Mission St Santa Cruz (95060) ***(G-25357)***
Sutter Health....916 691-5900
8170 Laguna Blvd Ste 210 Elk Grove (95758) ***(G-20089)***
Sutter Health....916 455-8137
1201 Alhambra Blvd # 110 Sacramento (95816) ***(G-20090)***
Sutter Health....415 600-1020
2340 Clay St Rm 121 San Francisco (94115) ***(G-26081)***
Sutter Health....707 263-6885
5196 Hill Rd E Ste 300 Lakeport (95453) ***(G-20091)***
Sutter Health....916 566-4819
2880 Gateway Oaks Dr # 220 Sacramento (95833) ***(G-23070)***
Sutter Health....831 458-6272
2950 Research Park Dr Soquel (95073) ***(G-25358)***
Sutter Health....916 544-5423
8200 Laguna Blvd Elk Grove (95758) ***(G-25359)***
Sutter Health....209 827-4866
502 Washington Ave Los Banos (93635) ***(G-25360)***
Sutter Health....415 600-4280
2015 Steiner St Fl 1 San Francisco (94115) ***(G-27242)***
Sutter Health....415 897-8495
100 Rowland Way Ste 210 Novato (94945) ***(G-23071)***
Sutter Health....408 523-3900
360 Dardanelli Ln Ste 2d Los Gatos (95032) ***(G-25361)***
Sutter Health....916 646-8300
1500 Expo Pkwy Sacramento (95815) ***(G-20092)***
Sutter Health....510 547-2244
3875 Telegraph Ave Oakland (94609) ***(G-20093)***
Sutter Health (PA)....916 733-8800
2200 River Plaza Dr Sacramento (95833) ***(G-21945)***
Sutter Health....530 406-5600
475 Pioneer Ave Ste 400 Woodland (95776) ***(G-24243)***
Sutter Health....209 524-1211
600 Coffee Rd Modesto (95355) ***(G-20094)***
Sutter Health....916 434-1224
965 Orchard Creek Ln Lincoln (95648) ***(G-20355)***
Sutter Health....510 869-8777
3000 Telegraph Ave Oakland (94609) ***(G-22287)***
Sutter Health....916 454-8200
3707 Schriever Ave Mather (95655) ***(G-20987)***
Sutter Health....530 406-5600
475 Pioneer Ave Ste 100 Woodland (95776) ***(G-20095)***
Sutter Health....209 538-1733
2516 E Whitmore Ave Ceres (95307) ***(G-20096)***
Sutter Health....209 522-0146
3612 Dale Rd Modesto (95356) ***(G-20097)***
Sutter Health....916 691-5900
8170 Laguna Blvd Ste 220 Elk Grove (95758) ***(G-20098)***
Sutter Health....650 262-4262
50 S San Mateo Dr Ste 470 San Mateo (94401) ***(G-20099)***
Sutter Health....510 204-1591
2001 Dwight Way Berkeley (94704) ***(G-22288)***
Sutter Health....916 733-8133
5151 F St Sacramento (95819) ***(G-22843)***
Sutter Health....805 966-1600
25 W Micheltorena St Santa Barbara (93101) ***(G-20100)***
Sutter Health....831 477-3600
2880 Soquel Ave Ste 10 Santa Cruz (95062) ***(G-21946)***
Sutter Health....408 733-4380
325 N Mathilda Ave Sunnyvale (94085) ***(G-20101)***
Sutter Health....707 545-2255
4702 Hoen Ave Santa Rosa (95405) ***(G-20102)***
Sutter Health....707 263-6885
5196 Hill Rd E Ste 300 Lakeport (95453) ***(G-20103)***
Sutter Health....650 853-2904
795 El Camino Real Palo Alto (94301) ***(G-20104)***
Sutter Health....916 784-2277
1640 E Roseville Pkwy Roseville (95661) ***(G-20105)***
Sutter Health....916 451-3344
3161 L St Sacramento (95816) ***(G-20106)***
Sutter Health....916 453-5955
1020 29th St Ste 570b Sacramento (95816) ***(G-20107)***
Sutter Health....415 647-8600
3555 Cesar Chavez San Francisco (94110) ***(G-20108)***
Sutter Health....530 749-3585
969 Plumas St Ste 103116 Yuba City (95991) ***(G-20109)***
Sutter Health....916 797-4700
3 Medical Plaza Dr # 100 Roseville (95661) ***(G-20988)***
Sutter Health....408 241-3801
2734 El Camino Real Santa Clara (95051) ***(G-20110)***
Sutter Health....831 458-5500
2880 Soquel Ave Santa Cruz (95062) ***(G-25362)***
Sutter Health....707 523-7253
2449 Summerfield Rd Santa Rosa (95405) ***(G-25363)***
Sutter Health....530 750-5888
2030 Sutter Pl Ste 1300 Davis (95616) ***(G-20111)***
Sutter Health....916 262-9456
2725 Capitol Ave Dept 404 Sacramento (95816) ***(G-20112)***
Sutter Health....530 888-4500
11815 Education St Auburn (95602) ***(G-22844)***
Sutter Health....916 551-9550
2715 K St Ste A Sacramento (95816) ***(G-25364)***
Sutter Health At Work....916 565-8607
1014 N Market Blvd Ste 20 Sacramento (95834) ***(G-20113)***
Sutter Hlth At Work - Natomas, Sacramento *Also called Sutter Health At Work* ***(G-20113)***
Sutter Hlth Rhabilitation Svcs....916 733-3040
2801 L St Fl 3 Sacramento (95816) ***(G-24244)***
Sutter Hlth Scrmnto Sierra Reg....530 747-5010
2030 Sutter Pl Ste 2000 Davis (95616) ***(G-20114)***
Sutter Hlth Scrmnto Sierra Reg....209 223-7540
100 Mission Blvd Jackson (95642) ***(G-20115)***
Sutter Hlth Scrmnto Sierra Reg....916 733-7080
701 Howe Ave Ste F20 Sacramento (95825) ***(G-23072)***
Sutter Hlth Scrmnto Sierra Reg (HQ)....916 733-8800
2200 River Plaza Dr Sacramento (95833) ***(G-21947)***
Sutter Hlth Scrmnto Sierra Reg....530 756-6440
2000 Sutter Pl Davis (95616) ***(G-21948)***
Sutter Hlth Scrmnto Sierra Reg....916 446-3100
1234 U St Sacramento (95818) ***(G-24245)***
Sutter Hlth Scrmnto Sierra Reg....916 781-1000
1 Medical Plaza Dr Roseville (95661) ***(G-21949)***
Sutter Hlth Scrmnto Sierra Reg....916 733-3095
2800 L St Sacramento (95816) ***(G-23073)***
Sutter Hlth Scrmnto Sierra Reg....530 406-5616
475 Pioneer Ave Ste 100 Woodland (95776) ***(G-20116)***
Sutter Lakeside Hospital (HQ)....707 262-5000
5176 Hill Rd E Lakeport (95453) ***(G-21950)***
Sutter Maternity & Surgery Ctr....831 477-2200
2900 Chanticleer Ave Santa Cruz (95065) ***(G-21951)***
Sutter Med Group of Redwoods, Santa Rosa *Also called Sutter Health* ***(G-23067)***
Sutter Med Group of Redwoods....707 546-2788
3883 Airway Dr Ste 202 Santa Rosa (95403) ***(G-20117)***
Sutter Medical Center, Sacramento *Also called Sutter Hlth Scrmnto Sierra Reg* ***(G-23073)***
Sutter Medical Center, Woodland *Also called Sutter Hlth Scrmnto Sierra Reg* ***(G-20116)***
Sutter Medical Ctr Sacramento, Sacramento *Also called Sutter Hlth Rhabilitation Svcs* ***(G-24244)***
Sutter Medical Foundation....916 924-7764
1014 N Market Blvd Ste 20 Sacramento (95834) ***(G-20356)***
Sutter Medical Group, Cotati *Also called Sutter Health* ***(G-20081)***
Sutter Memorial Hospital, Sacramento *Also called Sutter Hlth Scrmnto Sierra Reg* ***(G-21947)***
Sutter N Med Group A Prof Corp (PA)....530 749-3661
969 Plumas St Ste 205 Yuba City (95991) ***(G-20118)***
Sutter North Med Foundation (PA)....530 741-1300
969 Plumas St Yuba City (95991) ***(G-20119)***
Sutter North Med Foundation....530 749-3635
480 Plumas Blvd Yuba City (95991) ***(G-20120)***
Sutter North Med Foundation....530 675-1245
16911 Willow Glen Rd Brownsville (95919) ***(G-20121)***
Sutter North Med Foundation....530 749-3450
400 Plumas Blvd Ste 115 Yuba City (95991) ***(G-20122)***
Sutter Occupational Hlth Svcs, Roseville *Also called Sutter Health* ***(G-20988)***
Sutter Pacific Med Foundation, San Francisco *Also called Sutter Health* ***(G-20088)***
Sutter Pacific Med Foundation, Santa Rosa *Also called Sutter Health* ***(G-20102)***
Sutter Pacific Med Foundation, Lakeport *Also called Sutter Health* ***(G-20103)***
Sutter Physician Services, Sacramento *Also called Sutter Connect LLC* ***(G-27674)***
Sutter Regional Med Foundation....707 551-3616
127 Hospital Dr Ste 102 Vallejo (94589) ***(G-25365)***
Sutter Regional Med Foundation....707 374-6833
2720 Low Ct Fairfield (94534) ***(G-20123)***
Sutter Regional Med Foundation....707 454-5800
770 Mason St Vacaville (95688) ***(G-20124)***
Sutter Roseville Medical Ctr, Roseville *Also called Sutter Hlth Scrmnto Sierra Reg* ***(G-21949)***
Sutter Roseville Medical Ctr....916 781-1000
1 Medical Plaza Dr Roseville (95661) ***(G-21952)***

ALPHABETIC

ALPHABETIC SECTION

Sutter Rsvlle Med Ctr Fndation...................916 781-1000
  1 Medical Plaza Dr Roseville (95661) *(G-21953)*
Sutter Senior Care, Sacramento Also called Sutter Hlth Scrmnto Sierra Reg *(G-24245)*
Sutter Solano Medical Center (HQ)...................707 554-4444
  300 Hospital Dr Vallejo (94589) *(G-21954)*
Sutter Surgical Hospital N Vly...................530 749-5700
  455 Plumas Blvd Yuba City (95991) *(G-21955)*
Sutter Vsiting Nurse Assn Hosp, Concord Also called Sutter Vsting Nrse Assn Hspice *(G-22577)*
Sutter Vsting Nrse Assn Hspice...................415 600-6200
  1625 Van Ness Ave San Francisco (94109) *(G-22575)*
Sutter Vsting Nrse Assn Hspice (HQ)...................866 652-9178
  1900 Powell St Ste 300 Emeryville (94608) *(G-22576)*
Sutter Vsting Nrse Assn Hspice...................510 618-5277
  1651 Alvarado St San Leandro (94577) *(G-20989)*
Sutter Vsting Nrse Assn Hspice...................925 677-4250
  1900 Bates Ave Ste A Concord (94520) *(G-22577)*
Sutter West Bay Hospitals (HQ)...................415 209-1300
  180 Rowland Way Novato (94945) *(G-21956)*
Sutter West Foundation, Davis Also called Sutter Hlth Scrmnto Sierra Reg *(G-20114)*
Sutter Yuba Mental Health Svcs, Yuba City Also called County of Sutter *(G-22714)*
Suttter North Home Health, Yuba City Also called Sutter North Med Foundation *(G-20122)*
Svb Financial Group (PA)...................408 654-7400
  3003 Tasman Dr Santa Clara (95054) *(G-9528)*
Svcf, Mountain View Also called Silicon Vly Cmnty Foundation *(G-25349)*
Svd Inc...................818 504-1775
  8088 San Fernando Rd Sun Valley (91352) *(G-8594)*
SVDPLA, Los Angeles Also called Socie of Saint Vince De PA *(G-24214)*
Svi Lax LLC...................310 281-0300
  5933 W Century Blvd Los Angeles (90045) *(G-13329)*
Swa Group (PA)...................415 332-5100
  2200 Bridgeway Sausalito (94965) *(G-799)*
Swagbucks, El Segundo Also called Prodege LLC *(G-5687)*
Swagelok Northern California, Fremont Also called Sunnyvale Fluid Sys Tech Inc *(G-7956)*
Swaminatha Mahadevan MD...................650 723-6576
  701 Welch Rd Bldg C Palo Alto (94304) *(G-20125)*
Swander Pace Capital LLC...................415 477-8500
  101 Mission St Ste 1900 San Francisco (94105) *(G-27676)*
Swann Communications USA Inc...................562 777-2551
  12636 Clark St Santa Fe Springs (90670) *(G-7197)*
Swanson Farms...................209 667-2002
  5213 W Main St Turlock (95380) *(G-453)*
Swanton Berry Farms Inc...................831 425-8919
  25 Swanton Rd Davenport (95017) *(G-395)*
Sward Trucking Inc...................209 847-4210
  1657 Merritt St Turlock (95380) *(G-4270)*
Swayzer A-1 Sanitizing, Carson Also called Swayzers Incorporated *(G-14442)*
Swayzers Incorporated...................323 979-7223
  1663 E Del Amo Blvd Carson (90746) *(G-14442)*
Swca Incorporated...................626 240-0587
  150 S Arroyo Pkwy Fl 2 Pasadena (91105) *(G-28064)*
Swca Environmental Consultants, Pasadena Also called Swca Incorporated *(G-28064)*
Sweda Company LLC...................626 357-9999
  17411 E Valley Blvd City of Industry (91744) *(G-8101)*
Sweetbrier Development...................831 722-5577
  151 Silliman Rd Watsonville (95076) *(G-413)*
Sweetwater Authority (PA)...................619 422-8395
  505 Garrett Ave Chula Vista (91910) *(G-6405)*
Sweetwater Gardens Inc...................707 937-4140
  955 Ukiah Mendocino (95460) *(G-18697)*
Sweis Inc (PA)...................310 375-0558
  23760 Hawthorne Blvd Torrance (90505) *(G-7983)*
Swenson Developers and Contrs, San Jose Also called Santa Clara Valley Corporation *(G-14419)*
Swenson, Barry Builder, San Jose Also called Green Valley Corporation *(G-1558)*
Swh Mimis Cafe LLC...................714 544-5522
  17231 17th St Tustin (92780) *(G-8685)*
Swift Courier Service, Concord Also called Swift Worldwide Inc *(G-4274)*
Swift Transportation Company...................209 858-1630
  901 Darcy Pkwy Lathrop (95330) *(G-4271)*
Swift Transportation Company...................559 441-0340
  2797 S Orange Ave Fresno (93725) *(G-4272)*
Swift Transportation Company...................951 360-0130
  11888 Mission Blvd Mira Loma (91752) *(G-4273)*
Swift Worldwide Inc (PA)...................510 351-7949
  1390 Willow Pass Rd # 420 Concord (94520) *(G-4274)*
Swimoutlet.com, Campbell Also called Spiraledge Inc *(G-15843)*
Swinerton Bldrs Pacific R...................619 954-8011
  16798 W Bernardo Dr San Diego (92127) *(G-1681)*
Swinerton Builders (HQ)...................415 421-2980
  260 Townsend St San Francisco (94107) *(G-1468)*
Swinerton Builders...................213 896-3400
  865 S Figueroa St # 3000 Los Angeles (90017) *(G-1682)*
Swinerton Builders...................858 622-4040
  16798 W Bernardo Dr San Diego (92127) *(G-1469)*
Swinerton Builders Hc...................916 383-4825
  15 Business Park Way # 101 Sacramento (95828) *(G-1683)*
Swinerton Builders Inc...................925 602-6400
  2300 Clayton Rd Ste 800 Concord (94520) *(G-1269)*
Swinerton Incorporated...................925 689-2536
  2300 Clayton Rd Ste 800 Concord (94520) *(G-1342)*
Swinerton Incorporated (PA)...................415 421-2980
  260 Townsend St San Francisco (94107) *(G-1684)*
Swinerton MGT & Consulting, San Francisco Also called Swinerton Builders *(G-1468)*
Swinford Electric Inc...................714 578-8888
  1150 E Elm Ave Fullerton (92831) *(G-2762)*
Swiss Dairy, City of Industry Also called Dean Socal LLC *(G-8583)*

Swiss Hotel Group Inc...................707 938-2884
  18 W Spain St Sonoma (95476) *(G-13330)*
Swiss Port Corp...................310 417-0258
  11001 Aviation Blvd Los Angeles (90045) *(G-27800)*
Swiss RE America Holding Corp...................858 485-5018
  27412 Carino Cir Mission Viejo (92692) *(G-10223)*
Swissport, Los Angeles Also called Swiss Port Corp *(G-27800)*
Swissport Cargo Services LP...................310 910-9541
  11001 Aviation Blvd Los Angeles (90045) *(G-4940)*
Swissport Fueling Inc...................510 562-1701
  1 Edward White Way Oakland (94621) *(G-9027)*
Swissport Usa Inc...................310 345-1986
  7025 W Imperial Hwy Los Angeles (90045) *(G-4941)*
Swissport Usa Inc...................650 821-6220
  San Francisco Intl Arprt San Francisco (94128) *(G-4942)*
Swissport Usa Inc...................571 214-7068
  Delta Cargo Bldg 612 San Francisco (94128) *(G-4943)*
Swissport Usa Inc...................310 910-9560
  11001 Aviation Blvd Los Angeles (90045) *(G-4944)*
Swisstex California Inc (PA)...................310 516-6800
  13660 S Figueroa St Los Angeles (90061) *(G-17512)*
Switchfly Inc (PA)...................415 541-9100
  601 Montgomery St Fl 17 San Francisco (94111) *(G-7198)*
Sws2 Inc...................714 821-6699
  4141 Ball Rd Ste 517 Cypress (90630) *(G-14799)*
Swt Stockton, Temecula Also called Southwest Traders Incorporated *(G-8521)*
Swvp Del Mar Hotel LLC...................858 481-5900
  11915 El Camino Real San Diego (92130) *(G-13331)*
Syar Industries Inc...................707 643-3261
  885 Lake Herman Rd Vallejo (94591) *(G-1101)*
Syar Industries Inc...................707 433-3366
  13666 Healdsburg Ave Healdsburg (95448) *(G-6994)*
Sybase 365 LLC...................925 236-5000
  1 Sybase Dr Dublin (94568) *(G-5412)*
Sycamore Cc Inc...................760 451-3700
  3742 Flowerwood Ln Fallbrook (92028) *(G-19102)*
Sycamore Cogeneration Co (PA)...................661 615-4630
  1546 China Grade Loop Bakersfield (93308) *(G-6245)*
Sycamore Mineral Spring Resort...................805 595-7302
  1215 Avila Beach Dr San Luis Obispo (93405) *(G-13332)*
Sycamore Park Care Center LLC...................323 223-3441
  4585 N Figueroa St Los Angeles (90065) *(G-21388)*
SYCAMORE PARK CONVALESCENT HOSPITAL, Los Angeles Also called Sycamore Park Care Center LLC *(G-21388)*
Sycamores School, Altadena Also called Pasadena Chld Training Soc *(G-24766)*
Syconex Corporation...................213 386-7383
  3200 Wilshire Blvd # 601 Los Angeles (90010) *(G-7895)*
Sycuan Casino...................619 445-6002
  5459 Casino Way El Cajon (92019) *(G-19291)*
Sycuan Resort and Casino, El Cajon Also called Sycuan Casino *(G-19291)*
Sydell Hotels LLC...................213 381-7411
  3515 Wilshire Blvd Los Angeles (90010) *(G-13333)*
Sygma Network Inc...................661 723-0405
  46905 47th St W Lancaster (93536) *(G-8932)*
Sygma Network Inc...................209 932-5300
  3741 Gold River Ln Stockton (95215) *(G-8529)*
Sygma Network, The, Sun Valley Also called Sugar Foods Corporation *(G-17508)*
Sylmar Hlth Rehabilitation Ctr, Sylmar Also called Sylmar Hlth Rehabilitation Ctr *(G-22093)*
Sylmar Hlth Rehabilitation Ctr, Sylmar Also called Golden State Health Ctrs Inc *(G-22071)*
Sylmar Hlth Rehabilitation Ctr...................818 834-5082
  12220 Foothill Blvd Sylmar (91342) *(G-22093)*
Sylmark Group, Van Nuys Also called Sylmark Inc *(G-27243)*
Sylmark Inc (PA)...................818 217-2000
  7821 Orion Ave Ste 200 Van Nuys (91406) *(G-27243)*
Sylvester Roofing Company Inc...................760 743-0048
  2593 Auto Park Way Escondido (92029) *(G-3216)*
Symantec Corporation (PA)...................650 527-8000
  350 Ellis St Mountain View (94043) *(G-15852)*
Symitar Systems Inc...................619 542-6700
  8985 Balboa Ave San Diego (92123) *(G-15485)*
Symtech Industries Inc (PA)...................626 683-7555
  800 E Colorado Blvd Pasadena (91101) *(G-27244)*
Symtech Industries Inc...................626 683-7555
  100 N Lake Ave Pasadena (91101) *(G-27245)*
Synagro West LLC...................650 652-6531
  1499 Bayshore Hwy Ste 111 Burlingame (94010) *(G-28065)*
Synarc's, Newark Also called Bioclinca *(G-26488)*
Synectic Solutions Inc (PA)...................805 483-4800
  1701 Pacific Ave Ste 260 Oxnard (93033) *(G-16491)*
Synergex International Corp...................916 635-7300
  2330 Gold Meadow Way Gold River (95670) *(G-15853)*
Synergy Companies, Hayward Also called Eagle Systems Intl Inc *(G-2213)*
Synergy Environmental, Hayward Also called American Synergy Asbestos Remo *(G-3489)*
Synergy Health Ast LLC (HQ)...................858 586-1166
  9020 Activity Rd Ste D San Diego (92126) *(G-27677)*
Synergy Health North Amer Inc...................562 428-5858
  2240 E Artesia Blvd Long Beach (90805) *(G-13570)*
Synergy Labs...................415 291-8080
  135 Townsend St Ste 608 San Francisco (94107) *(G-16492)*
Synermed...................213 626-4556
  711 W College St Fl 4 Los Angeles (90012) *(G-27246)*
Synermed...................216 406-2845
  1200 Corp Ctr Dr Ste 200 Monterey Park (91754) *(G-20126)*
Syngenta Seeds Inc...................408 847-4242
  5653 Monterey Frontage Rd Gilroy (95020) *(G-9154)*
Syniverse Technologies LLC...................408 324-1830
  181 Metro Dr Ste 450 San Jose (95110) *(G-16493)*

Synnex Corporation....909 923-8900
3655 E Philadelphia St Ontario (91761) *(G-4643)*
Synnexxus LLC....714 933-4500
20251 Sw Acacia St # 200 Newport Beach (92660) *(G-23591)*
Synopsys Inc (PA)....650 584-5000
690 E Middlefield Rd Mountain View (94043) *(G-15486)*
Synopsys Inc....626 795-9101
199 S Los Robles Ave # 400 Pasadena (91101) *(G-15854)*
Synoptek LLC (PA)....949 241-8600
19520 Jamboree Rd Ste 110 Irvine (92612) *(G-16494)*
Synplicity Inc (HQ)....408 215-6000
600 W California Ave Sunnyvale (94086) *(G-15855)*
Syntelesys Inc....323 859-2160
2550 Corp Pl Ste C108 Monterey Park (91754) *(G-17914)*
Synteracthcr Inc (HQ)....760 268-8200
5759 Fleet St Ste 100 Carlsbad (92008) *(G-26614)*
Synteracthcr Corporation (HQ)....760 268-8200
5759 Fleet St Ste 100 Carlsbad (92008) *(G-26615)*
Synteracthcr Holdings Corp (PA)....760 268-8200
5759 Fleet St Ste 100 Carlsbad (92008) *(G-26616)*
Synthetic Genomics Inc (HQ)....858 754-2900
11149 N Torrey Pines Rd La Jolla (92037) *(G-26617)*
Sypartners LLC (HQ)....415 536-6600
475 Brannan St Ste 100 San Francisco (94107) *(G-28066)*
Sysco Central California Inc....209 527-7700
136 Mariposa Rd Modesto (95354) *(G-8530)*
Sysco Los Angeles Inc....909 595-9595
20701 Currier Rd Walnut (91789) *(G-8531)*
Sysco Newport Meat Company....949 399-4200
16691 Hale Ave Irvine (92606) *(G-8686)*
Sysco Riverside Inc....951 601-5300
15750 Meridian Pkwy Riverside (92518) *(G-8532)*
Sysco Sacramento Inc....916 275-2714
7062 Pacific Ave Pleasant Grove (95668) *(G-8533)*
Sysco San Diego Inc....858 513-7300
12180 Kirkham Rd Poway (92064) *(G-8534)*
Sysco San Francisco Inc (HQ)....510 226-3000
5900 Stewart Ave Fremont (94538) *(G-8535)*
Sysco San Francisco Inc....831 771-5000
1622 Moffett St Salinas (93905) *(G-8536)*
Sysco Ventura Inc....805 205-7000
3100 Sturgis Rd Oxnard (93030) *(G-8537)*
Sysintelli Inc....858 271-1600
9466 Black Mountain Rd # 200 San Diego (92126) *(G-15487)*
Syska & Hennessy Engineers Inc....310 312-0200
800 Crprate Pinte Ste 200 Culver City (90230) *(G-26082)*
Sysorex USA (HQ)....415 389-7500
17 E Sir Francis Drake Larkspur (94939) *(G-16061)*
Syspro Impact Software Inc....714 437-1000
959 S Coast Dr Ste 100 Costa Mesa (92626) *(G-7199)*
Systech Integrators Inc....408 441-2700
2050 Gateway Pl San Jose (95110) *(G-16495)*
Systechs, Orange *Also called Cruz Modular Inc (G-4338)*
System Integrators Inc (HQ)....916 830-2400
1740 N Market Blvd Sacramento (95834) *(G-16062)*
System One Holdings LLC....310 483-7800
21221 S Wstn Ave Ste 110 Torrance (90501) *(G-17513)*
System Solding (usa) Inc....310 608-5588
2301 E Del Amo Blvd Compton (90220) *(G-26710)*
Systems and Software Entps LLC (HQ)....714 854-8600
2929 E Imperial Hwy # 170 Brea (92821) *(G-15488)*
Systems Application & Tech Inc....805 487-7373
1000 Town Center Dr # 110 Oxnard (93036) *(G-26083)*
Systems Paving Inc (PA)....714 957-5776
1570 Brookhollow Dr Santa Ana (92705) *(G-2837)*
Syzygy Technologies Inc....619 297-0970
12526 High Bluff Dr San Diego (92130) *(G-26084)*
T & P Farms....530 476-3038
1241 Putnam Way Arbuckle (95912) *(G-2)*
T & R Painting Construction....818 779-3800
7116 Valjean Ave Van Nuys (91406) *(G-2497)*
T & T Solutions Inc....818 676-1786
7018 Owensmouth Ave # 201 Canoga Park (91303) *(G-16496)*
T & T Truck & Crane Service, Ventura *Also called Offshore Crane & Service Co (G-14493)*
T & T Trucking Inc (PA)....800 692-3457
11396 N Hwy 99 Lodi (95240) *(G-4275)*
T - Y Nursery Inc....760 742-2151
15335 Highway 76 Pauma Valley (92061) *(G-9219)*
T and M Agricultural Svcs LLC....707 963-3330
493 Dowdell Ln Saint Helena (94574) *(G-725)*
T and W Farms....661 396-7203
18000 Old River Rd Bakersfield (93311) *(G-726)*
T B Penick & Sons Inc....951 719-1492
41892 Enterprise Cir S Temecula (92590) *(G-1270)*
T B Penick & Sons Inc (PA)....858 558-1800
15435 Innovation Dr # 100 San Diego (92128) *(G-1470)*
T Boyer Company....949 642-2431
1656 Babcock St Costa Mesa (92627) *(G-2763)*
T C Construction Company Inc....619 448-4560
10540 Prospect Ave Santee (92071) *(G-2002)*
T C H P Inc....951 687-7330
11162 Palm Terrace Ln Riverside (92505) *(G-21389)*
T C I, Redondo Beach *Also called Transportation Concept Inc (G-3730)*
T C P, Santa Monica *Also called Tennenbaum Capitl Partners LLC (G-12150)*
T C R Limited Partnership....310 645-1881
5440 W Century Blvd Los Angeles (90045) *(G-17694)*
T C W Realty Fund VI....213 683-4200
515 S Flower St Fl 31 Los Angeles (90071) *(G-12275)*
T D R, Turlock *Also called Turlock Dairy & Rfrgn Inc (G-7813)*
T F Louderback Inc (PA)....510 965-6120
700 National Ct Richmond (94804) *(G-9087)*
T G Construction....310 321-5900
139 Nevada St El Segundo (90245) *(G-1343)*
T G T Enterprises Inc....858 413-0300
12650 Danielson Ct Poway (92064) *(G-14092)*
T I C Hotels Inc....619 238-7577
555 W Ash St San Diego (92101) *(G-13334)*
T I C Hotels Inc....805 773-4671
2555 Price St Pismo Beach (93449) *(G-13335)*
T I D, Turlock *Also called Turlock Irrigation District (G-6247)*
T I D, Turlock *Also called Turlock Irrigation District (G-6655)*
T L Fabrications LP....562 802-3980
2921 E Coronado St Anaheim (92806) *(G-3405)*
T M B, San Fernando *Also called Jme Inc (G-7447)*
T M Cobb Company....916 381-7330
8490 Rovana Cir Sacramento (95828) *(G-6964)*
T M I, San Diego *Also called Toward Maximum Independence (G-24253)*
T M Mian & Associates Inc....818 591-2300
24150 Park Sorrento Calabasas (91302) *(G-13336)*
T M Mian & Associates Inc....805 983-8600
2000 Solar Dr Oxnard (93036) *(G-13337)*
T M P Inc....818 718-1222
21051 Osborne St Canoga Park (91304) *(G-8361)*
T M S, Campbell *Also called Telecmmnctons MGT Slutions Inc (G-2769)*
T McGee Electric Inc....909 591-6461
2390 S Reservoir St Pomona (91766) *(G-2764)*
T Mobile Santa Ana, Santa Ana *Also called T-Mobile Usa Inc (G-17945)*
T Points Inc....323 846-9176
350 W Mrtn Lthr King Jr Los Angeles (90037) *(G-13658)*
T R L, Rancho Cucamonga *Also called TRL Systems Incorporated (G-2776)*
T Royal Management (PA)....559 447-9887
7419 N Cedar Ave Ste 102 Fresno (93720) *(G-11862)*
T S D, Berkeley *Also called Two Star Dog Inc (G-8364)*
T S J Elec Communications Inc....951 785-0921
7490 Jurupa Ave Riverside (92504) *(G-2765)*
T T Miyasaka Inc....831 722-3871
209 Riverside Rd Watsonville (95076) *(G-136)*
T U D, Sonora *Also called Tuolumne Utilities District (G-6406)*
T W R Framing....951 279-2000
1661 Railroad St Corona (92880) *(G-14800)*
T Y Lin International (HQ)....415 291-3700
345 California St Fl 23 San Francisco (94104) *(G-26085)*
T Y R, Seal Beach *Also called Tyr Sport Inc (G-8415)*
T&C Roofing Inc....925 513-8463
2155 Elkins Way Ste H Brentwood (94513) *(G-3217)*
T-12 Three LLC....619 702-3000
207 5th Ave San Diego (92101) *(G-13338)*
T-Force Inc (PA)....949 208-1527
4695 Macarthur Ct Newport Beach (92660) *(G-28067)*
T-Mobile Usa Inc....626 261-7359
307 E 1st St Ste 1e Santa Ana (92701) *(G-17945)*
T-Mobile Usa Inc....916 786-3339
1420 E Roseville Pkwy Roseville (95661) *(G-5413)*
T-Mobile Usa Inc....510 797-8290
4095 Mowry Ave Fremont (94538) *(G-5414)*
T-Mobile Usa Inc....209 529-0539
2225 Plaza Pkwy Ste I1b Modesto (95350) *(G-5415)*
T-Mobile Usa Inc....415 440-5370
900 Van Ness Ave Ste 1 San Francisco (94109) *(G-5416)*
T-N-T Grading, Escondido *Also called TNT Grading Inc (G-1874)*
T-Netix Telecom Svcs, Grass Valley *Also called Evercom Systems Inc (G-5597)*
T.C.A.H, Sonora *Also called Watch Resources Inc (G-24285)*
T.S.c, Altadena *Also called Tom Sawyer Camps Inc (G-24526)*
T25cl Entertainment LLC....951 308-2040
1074 55th St Oakland (94608) *(G-18164)*
T3 Direct, Modesto *Also called Sterling Mktg & Fincl Corp (G-27669)*
Ta-Kai Home Care Inc....714 393-4586
22343 La Palma Ave # 128 Yorba Linda (92887) *(G-22578)*
Tabak Steven William M MD....310 278-3400
414 N Camden Dr Ste 1100 Beverly Hills (90210) *(G-20127)*
Taber Company Inc....714 543-7100
1442 Ritchey St Santa Ana (92705) *(G-6965)*
Table Community Foudation....209 951-1753
3201 W Benjamin Holt Dr Stockton (95219) *(G-25366)*
Table Mountain Casino....559 822-2485
8184 Table Mountain Rd Friant (93626) *(G-19292)*
Tabletops Unlimited Inc (PA)....310 549-6000
23000 Avalon Blvd Carson (90745) *(G-6890)*
Tabula Inc....408 986-9140
1100 La Avenida St Ste A Mountain View (94043) *(G-7644)*
TAC Rbo, Sacramento *Also called Surgical Care Affiliate (G-26447)*
Tacer, Van Nuys *Also called Town & Country Event Rentals (G-14584)*
Tachi Palace Hotel & Casino....559 924-7751
17225 Jersey Ave Lemoore (93245) *(G-13339)*
Tachyon Inc....858 882-8108
9339 Carroll Park Dr # 150 San Diego (92121) *(G-5706)*
Tacit Knowledge Inc....415 694-4322
27 Maiden Ln Fl 4 San Francisco (94108) *(G-16497)*
Tacori Enterprises....818 863-1536
1736 Gardena Ave Glendale (91204) *(G-8102)*
Tactical Engrg & Analis Inc (PA)....858 573-9869
6050 Santo Rd Ste 250 San Diego (92124) *(G-16498)*
Tactical Lgistic Solutions Inc....909 464-2813
13799 Monte Vista Ave Chino (91710) *(G-4644)*
Tactical Telesolutions Inc....415 788-8808
550 Kearny St Ste 210 San Francisco (94108) *(G-17514)*

ALPHABETIC

Employee Codes: A=Over 500 employees, B=251-500
C=101-250, D=51-100, E=45-50
2017 Directory of California
Wholesalers and Services Companies
© Mergent Inc. 1-800-342-5647
1569

Tadin Inc...213 406-8880
3345 E Slauson Ave Vernon (90058) ***(G-8933)***
Tadin Herb & Tea Co., Vernon *Also called Tadin Inc* ***(G-8933)***
Taft Broadcasting Company LLC...951 413-2337
23755 Z St March ARB (92518) ***(G-18165)***
Taft College Children Center...661 763-7850
29 Emmons Park Dr Taft (93268) ***(G-24524)***
Taft Correctional Institution, Taft *Also called Geo Group Inc* ***(G-27787)***
Taft Electric Company (PA)...805 642-0121
1694 Eastman Ave Ventura (93003) ***(G-2766)***
Taft Electric Company...661 729-2581
42209 5th St E Lancaster (93535) ***(G-2767)***
Taft Production Company...661 765-7194
950 Petroleum Club Rd Taft (93268) ***(G-1027)***
Tahoe Beach & Ski Club...530 541-6220
3601 Lake Tahoe Blvd South Lake Tahoe (96150) ***(G-13340)***
Tahoe Donner Association...530 587-9437
12790 Northwoods Blvd Truckee (96161) ***(G-25367)***
Tahoe Donner Golf Course Inc...530 587-9455
11509 Northwoods Blvd Truckee (96161) ***(G-18794)***
Tahoe Forest Hospital District...530 582-3277
10956 Donner Paca Rd Ste 230 Truckee (96161) ***(G-21957)***
Tahoe Forest Hospital District (PA)...530 587-6011
10121 Pine Ave Truckee (96161) ***(G-21958)***
Tahoe Lake Partners LLC...707 255-9890
855 Bordeaux Way Ste 200 NAPA (94558) ***(G-12017)***
Tahoe Seasons Resort Time Inte...530 541-6700
3901 Saddle Rd South Lake Tahoe (96150) ***(G-11863)***
Tahoe Workx, Truckee *Also called Tahoe Forest Hospital District* ***(G-21957)***
Tahoe-Truckee Sanitation Agcy...530 587-2525
13720 Butterfield Dr Truckee (96161) ***(G-6419)***
Tai Seng Entertainment, South San Francisco *Also called U-2 Home Entertainment Inc* ***(G-7650)***
Tailored Living Choices LLC...707 259-0526
1957 Sierra Ave NAPA (94558) ***(G-3587)***
Taisei Construction Corp (HQ)...714 886-1530
970 W 190th St Ste 920 Torrance (90502) ***(G-1471)***
Tait Environmental Svcs Inc (PA)...714 560-8200
701 Parkcenter Dr Santa Ana (92705) ***(G-3588)***
Taj Mahal Building, Laguna Hills *Also called Muller Taj LLC* ***(G-11020)***
TAJ Marketing Llc...213 232-0150
3550 Wilshire Blvd Los Angeles (90010) ***(G-27678)***
Takara Bio Usa Inc...650 237-5700
1290 Terra Bella Ave Mountain View (94043) ***(G-26618)***
Take Care Employer Solutions, San Leandro *Also called Advantage Medical Group Inc* ***(G-19317)***
Takeda California Inc...858 622-8528
10410 Science Center Dr San Diego (92121) ***(G-26812)***
Talbot Insurance & Fincl Svcs, Santa Barbara *Also called Caesar and Seider Insur Svcs* ***(G-10655)***
Talco Plastics Inc (PA)...951 531-2000
1000 W Rincon St Corona (92880) ***(G-6567)***
Talega Golf Club, San Clemente *Also called Heritage Golf Group Inc* ***(G-18745)***
Talend Inc (HQ)...650 539-3200
800 Bridge Pkwy Ste 200 Redwood City (94065) ***(G-16063)***
Talent Space Inc...408 330-1900
2570 N 1st St Ste 400 San Jose (95131) ***(G-14801)***
Talentburst Inc...415 813-4011
575 Market St Ste 3025 San Francisco (94105) ***(G-17515)***
Talentscale LLC...951 744-0053
31805 Temecula Pkwy 204 Temecula (92592) ***(G-26086)***
Taleo Corporation...925 452-3000
4140 Dublin Blvd Ste 400 Dublin (94568) ***(G-15856)***
Talix Inc...415 281-3100
660 3rd St San Francisco (94107) ***(G-15857)***
Talkmex California Corporation...323 479-3279
1221 W 3rd St Los Angeles (90017) ***(G-5707)***
Tall Pony Productions Inc...310 456-7495
300 Loma Metisse Rd Malibu (90265) ***(G-18166)***
Talley & Associates, Santa Fe Springs *Also called Talley Inc* ***(G-7645)***
Talley Farms...805 489-2508
2900 Lopez Dr Arroyo Grande (93420) ***(G-594)***
Talley Inc (PA)...562 906-8000
12976 Sandoval St Santa Fe Springs (90670) ***(G-7645)***
Talley Transportation...559 673-9013
12325 Road 29 Madera (93638) ***(G-4070)***
Talon Executive Services Inc...714 434-7476
151 Kalmus Dr Ste A103 Costa Mesa (92626) ***(G-16930)***
Tama Trading Company...213 748-8262
1920 E 20th St Vernon (90058) ***(G-8934)***
Tamal Pais, Greenbrae *Also called Northern California Presbyteri* ***(G-21330)***
TAMALPAIS, Greenbrae *Also called Ross Valley Homes Inc* ***(G-21101)***
Tamalpais Creek, Novato *Also called Atria Senior Living Group Inc* ***(G-24559)***
Tamarack Bch Condo Owners Assn...760 729-3500
3200 Carlsbad Blvd Carlsbad (92008) ***(G-25368)***
Tammi R James MD...916 383-6783
7273 14th Ave Ste 120b Sacramento (95820) ***(G-20128)***
Tamtron Corporation (HQ)...408 323-3303
6203 San Ignacio Ave # 110 San Jose (95119) ***(G-15489)***
Tan Jay-Nygard Outlet Store, Gardena *Also called Nygard Inc* ***(G-8406)***
Tanaka Farms...949 653-2100
5380 University Dr Irvine (92612) ***(G-8935)***
Tang E TSE Inc...714 957-4000
3001 S Croddy Way Santa Ana (92704) ***(G-16499)***
Tangoe Inc...858 452-6800
9920 Pcf Hts Blvd Ste 200 San Diego (92121) ***(G-15858)***
Tanimura & Antle Inc...831 424-6100
4401 Foxdale St Baldwin Park (91706) ***(G-595)***
Tanimura & Antle Inc...805 483-2358
761 Commercial Ave Oxnard (93030) ***(G-4645)***
Tanimura Antle Fresh Foods Inc (PA)...831 455-2950
1 Harris Rd Salinas (93908) ***(G-97)***
Tanimura Brothers...831 424-0841
81 Hitchcock Rd Salinas (93908) ***(G-10080)***
Tanner Mainstain Blatt & Gly...310 446-2700
10866 Wilshire Blvd Fl 10 Los Angeles (90024) ***(G-26448)***
Tano Capital LLC...650 212-0330
1 Franklin Pkwy San Mateo (94403) ***(G-12347)***
Tantra Lake Partners LP...949 756-5959
18802 Bardeen Ave Irvine (92612) ***(G-11211)***
Tao Mechanical Ltd...925 447-5220
4023 1st St Livermore (94551) ***(G-2393)***
Taos Mountain Inc...888 826-7686
1 Market St Fl 36 San Francisco (94105) ***(G-14955)***
Taos Mountain LLC (PA)...408 324-2800
121 Daggett Dr San Jose (95134) ***(G-16500)***
Tap Operating Co LLC...310 900-5500
400 W Artesia Blvd Compton (90220) ***(G-6775)***
Tap Ram Reinforcing Inc...562 484-0859
11658 Excelsior Dr Norwalk (90650) ***(G-3406)***
Tap Worldwide LLC...619 216-1444
2360 Boswell Rd Chula Vista (91914) ***(G-17516)***
Tap Worldwide LLC (PA)...310 900-5500
400 W Artesia Blvd Compton (90220) ***(G-6776)***
Tapestry Solutions Inc (HQ)...858 503-1990
5643 Copley Dr San Diego (92111) ***(G-15490)***
Tapia Brothers Co, Maywood *Also called Tapia Enterprises Inc* ***(G-8538)***
Tapia Enterprises Inc (PA)...323 560-7415
6067 District Blvd Maywood (90270) ***(G-8538)***
Tapia Farms...661 256-4401
8425 W Ave 8 Rosamond (93560) ***(G-396)***
Tapjoy Inc (PA)...415 766-6900
111 Sutter St Fl 13 San Francisco (94104) ***(G-13926)***
Tarbell Realtors, Murrieta *Also called F M Tarbell Co* ***(G-11503)***
Tarbell Financial Corporation...909 335-0750
1440 Industrial Park Ave Redlands (92374) ***(G-11864)***
Tarbell Financial Corporation (PA)...714 972-0988
1403 N Tustin Ave Ste 380 Santa Ana (92705) ***(G-9955)***
Tarbell Realtors, Anaheim *Also called F M Tarbell Co* ***(G-11504)***
Tarbell Realtors, Anaheim *Also called F M Tarbell Co* ***(G-11505)***
Tarbell Realtors, Santa Ana *Also called F M Tarbell Co* ***(G-11506)***
Tarbell Realtors, Corona *Also called F M Tarbell Co* ***(G-11507)***
Tarbell Realtors, Laguna Hills *Also called F M Tarbell Co* ***(G-11508)***
Tarbell Realtors, Menifee *Also called F M Tarbell Co* ***(G-11509)***
Tarbell Realtors, Temecula *Also called F M Tarbell Co* ***(G-11510)***
Tarbell Realtors, Diamond Bar *Also called F M Tarbell Co* ***(G-11511)***
Tarbell Realtors, San Clemente *Also called F M Tarbell Co* ***(G-11512)***
Tarbell Realtors, Santa Ana *Also called F M Tarbell Co* ***(G-11514)***
Tarbell Realtors, Irvine *Also called F M Tarbell Co* ***(G-11515)***
Tarbell Realtors, Upland *Also called F M Tarbell Co* ***(G-11517)***
Target Corporation...530 666-3705
2050 E Beamer St Woodland (95776) ***(G-4704)***
Target Corporation...559 431-0104
7600 N Blackstone Ave Fresno (93720) ***(G-4705)***
Target Cw, San Diego *Also called Wmbe Payrolling Inc* ***(G-14820)***
Target Specialty Products, Santa Fe Springs *Also called Rentokil North America Inc* ***(G-9148)***
Target Specialty Products, Santa Fe Springs *Also called Western Exterminator Company* ***(G-14196)***
Targetsolutions Inc (HQ)...858 592-6880
10805 Rancho Bernardo Rd # 200 San Diego (92127) ***(G-28068)***
Targus International LLC (PA)...714 765-5555
1211 N Miller St Anaheim (92806) ***(G-9306)***
Tariff Building Associates LP (PA)...415 397-5572
222 Kearny St Ste 200 San Francisco (94108) ***(G-11060)***
Tarpy Heating and Air...619 820-4580
9723 Roe Dr Santee (92071) ***(G-2394)***
Tarpy Plumbing Heating and Air, Santee *Also called Tarpy Heating and Air* ***(G-2394)***
Tarra Landscape, Oakland *Also called Tree Sculpture Group* ***(G-964)***
Tarrant Apparel Group...323 780-8250
801 S Figueroa St # 2500 Los Angeles (90017) ***(G-8413)***
Tarsadia Hotels, Newport Beach *Also called Uka LLC* ***(G-13365)***
Tarsco Inc (HQ)...562 231-5400
11905 Regentview Ave Downey (90241) ***(G-18021)***
Tarzana Treatment Centers Inc...818 654-3815
422 W Rancho Vista Blvd C280 Palmdale (93551) ***(G-22845)***
Tarzana Treatment Centers Inc (PA)...818 996-1051
18646 Oxnard St Tarzana (91356) ***(G-22846)***
Tarzana Treatment Centers Inc...562 428-4111
5190 Atlantic Ave Lakewood (90805) ***(G-22847)***
Tarzana Treatment Centers Inc...562 218-1868
2101 Magnolia Ave Long Beach (90806) ***(G-22848)***
Tarzana Treatment Centers Inc...661 726-2630
44447 10th St W Lancaster (93534) ***(G-22849)***
Tarzana Treatment Ctr, Lancaster *Also called Tarzana Treatment Centers Inc* ***(G-22849)***
Tarzana Trtmnt Ctrs LNG Bch O, Lakewood *Also called Tarzana Treatment Centers Inc* ***(G-22847)***
Tasc, San Diego *Also called Engility Corporation* ***(G-25788)***
Task Force For Reg Autostaff, El Monte *Also called Trap* ***(G-17542)***
Taskus Inc...888 400-8275
3233 Donald Santa Monica (90405) ***(G-16196)***
Taslimi Construction Co Inc...310 447-3000
1805 Colorado Ave Santa Monica (90404) ***(G-1685)***

ALPHABETIC

Tasq Technology Inc...916 632-7600
8875 Washington Blvd A Roseville (95678) *(G-9723)*
Tata America Intl Corp...408 569-5845
5201 Great America Pkwy # 522 Santa Clara (95054) *(G-16501)*
Tata Communications Amer Inc...650 262-0004
700 Airport Blvd Ste 100 Burlingame (94010) *(G-17517)*
Tata Consulting Services, Santa Clara *Also called Tata America Intl Corp (G-16501)*
Tate Neurological Surgery, Redding *Also called James D Tate MD (G-19573)*
Taulia Inc (PA)...415 376-8280
201 Mssion St Fl9 Ste 900 San Francisco (94105) *(G-15491)*
Taurus West Inc (HQ)...818 954-0202
1903 W Empire Ave Burbank (91504) *(G-22289)*
Tavant Technologies Inc (PA)...408 519-5400
3965 Freedom Cir Ste 750 Santa Clara (95054) *(G-15492)*
Tawa Services Inc (PA)...714 521-8899
6281 Regio Ave Fl 2 Buena Park (90620) *(G-8936)*
Tax and Financial Group, Newport Beach *Also called R Mc Closkey Insurance Agency (G-10850)*
Tax Compliance Inc...858 547-4100
10089 Willow Creek Rd # 300 San Diego (92131) *(G-15493)*
Tax Problem Center, Los Angeles *Also called Authority Tax Services LLC (G-17010)*
Tax Resolution Services, Co, Encino *Also called Danerica Enterprises Inc (G-13754)*
Taxaudit.com, Citrus Heights *Also called Taxresources Inc (G-26449)*
Taxresources Inc (PA)...877 369-7827
7803 Madison Ave Ste 100 Citrus Heights (95610) *(G-26449)*
Taylor & Assoc Architects Inc...949 574-1325
17850 Fitch Irvine (92614) *(G-26261)*
Taylor Bailey Inc...707 967-8090
355 Lafata St Ste E Saint Helena (94574) *(G-1686)*
Taylor Design, Irvine *Also called Taylor & Assoc Architects Inc (G-26261)*
Taylor Farms California Inc (HQ)...831 754-0471
150 Main St Ste 500 Salinas (93901) *(G-596)*
Taylor Fresh Foods Inc (PA)...831 676-9023
150 Main St Ste 400 Salinas (93901) *(G-597)*
Taylor Structures Inc...707 499-6870
905 Cotting Ln Ste 100 Vacaville (95688) *(G-1687)*
Taylored Services Holdings LLC...909 628-5300
1495 E Locust St Ontario (91761) *(G-5173)*
TBG Insurance Services Corp...310 203-8770
100 N Sepulveda Blvd # 500 El Segundo (90245) *(G-10903)*
Tbwa Chiat/Day Inc...310 305-5000
5353 Grosvenor Blvd Los Angeles (90066) *(G-17518)*
Tbwa Worldwide Inc...310 305-4400
12539 Beatrice St Los Angeles (90066) *(G-13927)*
Tc Property Mgt A Californi...530 666-5799
1224 Cottonwood St Ofc Woodland (95695) *(G-12348)*
Tc3 Health Inc (HQ)...949 943-8700
1901 E Alton Ave Ste 100 Santa Ana (92705) *(G-28069)*
Tcal, San Diego *Also called Takeda California Inc (G-26812)*
Tcb Industrial Inc (PA)...209 571-0569
2955 Farrar Ave Modesto (95354) *(G-1472)*
Tccsc, Los Angeles *Also called Tessie Clvland Cmnty Svcs Corp (G-24250)*
Tcg Builders Inc...408 321-6450
890 N Mccarthy Blvd # 100 Milpitas (95035) *(G-1688)*
Tcg Software Services Inc...714 665-6200
320 Commerce Ste 200 Irvine (92602) *(G-15494)*
TCI Aluminum/North Inc...510 786-3750
2353 Davis Ave Hayward (94545) *(G-7406)*
Tcm Group LLC...909 527-8580
3130 Inland Empire Blvd Ontario (91764) *(G-27247)*
Tcmi Inc (PA)...650 614-8200
528 Ramona St Palo Alto (94301) *(G-12349)*
Tcp Global Corporation (PA)...858 909-2110
6695 Rasha St San Diego (92121) *(G-9240)*
Tct Circuit Supply Inc...714 644-9700
1200 N Van Buren St Ste A Anaheim (92807) *(G-7957)*
Tcv Management 2004 LLC...650 614-8200
528 Ramona St Palo Alto (94301) *(G-27248)*
Tcw Absolute Return Credit LLC...213 244-0000
865 S Figueroa St # 2100 Los Angeles (90017) *(G-10188)*
Tcw Funds Management Inc...213 244-0000
865 S Figueroa St # 2100 Los Angeles (90017) *(G-10081)*
Tcw Group Inc (HQ)...213 244-0000
865 S Figueroa St # 2100 Los Angeles (90017) *(G-9529)*
Tcw Specialized Cash Mgt Ltd...213 244-0000
865 S Figueroa St # 1800 Los Angeles (90017) *(G-27249)*
Tcw Value Added Ltd Partnr...213 244-0000
865 S Figueroa St Los Angeles (90017) *(G-12204)*
TD Desert Dev Ltd Partnr (HQ)...760 777-1001
81570 Carboneras La Quinta (92253) *(G-12018)*
Td Service Company...714 543-8372
4000 W Metro Dr Ste 400 Orange (92868) *(G-17519)*
TD Service Financial Corp (PA)...714 543-8372
4000 W Metro Dr Ste 400 Orange (92868) *(G-14048)*
Tdic, Sacramento *Also called Dentists Insurance Company (G-10688)*
TDS, Hornitos *Also called Hornitos Telephone Co (G-5630)*
Teac Aerospace Tech Inc...323 837-2700
2727 E Imperial Hwy Brea (92821) *(G-7646)*
Teale Data Center, Rancho Cordova *Also called Technology Services Cal Dept (G-16198)*
Tealium Inc...858 779-1344
11085 Torreyana Rd Fl 2 San Diego (92121) *(G-16197)*
Team Companies Inc (PA)...818 558-3261
901 W Alameda Ave Ste 100 Burbank (91506) *(G-26450)*
Team Dykspra (PA)...951 898-6482
2315 California Ave Corona (92881) *(G-17863)*
Team Finish Inc...714 671-9190
155 Arovista Cir Ste A Brea (92821) *(G-3341)*
Team Ghilotti Inc...707 763-8700
2531 Petaluma Blvd S Petaluma (94952) *(G-1872)*
Team Health Holdings Inc...619 740-4401
5555 Grossmont Center Dr La Mesa (91942) *(G-20129)*
Team Makena LLC (PA)...949 474-1753
17461 Derian Ave Ste 200 Irvine (92614) *(G-7316)*
Team Mobile...949 567-6800
2008 Mcgaw Ave Irvine (92614) *(G-5417)*
Team One, Los Angeles *Also called Team-One Emplyment Spclsts LLC (G-14802)*
Team Post-Op Inc (HQ)...949 253-5500
17256 Red Hill Ave Irvine (92614) *(G-7317)*
Team Power Forklift, Fair Oaks *Also called Clarklift-West Inc (G-7835)*
Team San Jose...408 295-9600
408 Almaden Blvd San Jose (95110) *(G-17520)*
Team Services, Burbank *Also called Team Companies Inc (G-26450)*
Team Spirit Realty Inc...714 562-0404
6301 Beach Blvd Ste 225 Buena Park (90621) *(G-11865)*
Team Superstores, Vallejo *Also called Teamross Inc (G-17816)*
Team Tomato, Norwalk *Also called Lj Distributors Inc (G-8747)*
Team Truck Dismantling Inc...951 685-6744
3760 Pyrite St Riverside (92509) *(G-6797)*
Team West Contracting Corp...951 340-3426
1611 Jenks Dr Corona (92880) *(G-2089)*
Team-One Emplyment Spclsts LLC...310 481-4482
2999 Overland Ave Ste 212 Los Angeles (90064) *(G-14802)*
Teamross Inc...707 643-9000
301 Auto Mall Pkwy Vallejo (94591) *(G-17816)*
Tech Flex Package...323 241-1800
12624 Daphne Ave Hawthorne (90250) *(G-14162)*
Tech Knowledge Associates LLC...714 735-3810
1 Centerpointe Dr Ste 200 La Palma (90623) *(G-18022)*
Tech Mahindra (americas) Inc...949 462-0640
23461 S Pointe Dr Ste 370 Laguna Hills (92653) *(G-15495)*
Tech Museum of Innovation (PA)...408 795-6116
201 S Market St San Jose (95113) *(G-25051)*
Tech Soup Spock, San Francisco *Also called Techsoup Global (G-25369)*
Tech Systems Inc...714 523-5404
7372 Walnut Ave Ste J Buena Park (90620) *(G-7647)*
Tech-Ed Networks Inc...916 784-2005
10000 Allantown Dr # 175 Roseville (95678) *(G-16502)*
Techaisle LLC...408 253-4416
5053 Doyle Rd Ste 105 San Jose (95129) *(G-26711)*
Techcon, Morgan Hill *Also called Monument Construction Inc (G-915)*
Techexcel Inc (PA)...925 871-3900
3675 Mt Diablo Blvd # 330 Lafayette (94549) *(G-15496)*
Technclor Crative Svcs USA Inc (HQ)...818 260-3800
6040 W Sunset Blvd Los Angeles (90028) *(G-18257)*
Technclor Crative Svcs USA Inc...323 467-1244
6040 W Sunset Blvd Los Angeles (90028) *(G-18258)*
Technclor Vdocassette Mich Inc (HQ)...805 445-1122
3233 Mission Oaks Blvd Camarillo (93012) *(G-18259)*
Technical Services, Mountain View *Also called Northrop Grumman Systems Corp (G-16014)*
Technical Temps Inc...408 956-8256
1096 Pecten Ct Milpitas (95035) *(G-14803)*
Technicolor Inc...818 260-4577
2255 N Ontario St Ste 180 Burbank (91504) *(G-16959)*
Technicolor - Funimation Ent, Calexico *Also called Technicolor HM Entrmt Svcs Inc (G-18260)*
Technicolor HM Entrmt Svcs Inc...760 357-3372
1778 Zinetta Rd Ste F Calexico (92231) *(G-18260)*
Technicolor HM Entrmt Svcs Inc...909 974-2016
5491 E Philadelphia St Ontario (91761) *(G-18261)*
Technicolor HM Entrmt Svcs Inc (HQ)...805 445-1122
3233 Mission Oaks Blvd Camarillo (93012) *(G-18262)*
Technicolor Hollywood, Los Angeles *Also called Technicolor Thomson Group (G-18263)*
Technicolor Lab, Burbank *Also called Technicolor Inc (G-16959)*
Technicolor New Media Inc...818 480-5100
250 E Olive Ave Ste 300 Burbank (91502) *(G-18167)*
Technicolor Thomson Group...323 817-6600
6040 W Sunset Blvd Los Angeles (90028) *(G-18263)*
Technicolor Thomson Group...818 260-3600
2255 N Ontario St Ste 100 Burbank (91504) *(G-18264)*
Technicolor Thomson Group...909 974-2222
5491 E Philadelphia St Ontario (91761) *(G-18265)*
Technicolor Thomson Group...805 445-1122
3301 Mission Oaks Blvd Camarillo (93012) *(G-18266)*
Technicolor Video Service, Camarillo *Also called Technclor Vdocassette Mich Inc (G-18259)*
Technicolor Video Services, Camarillo *Also called Technicolor HM Entrmt Svcs Inc (G-18262)*
Technicon Design Corporation...949 218-1300
32238 Paseo Adelanto A San Juan Capistrano (92675) *(G-17521)*
Technip Usa Inc...909 447-3600
555 W Arrow Hwy Claremont (91711) *(G-26087)*
Techno Coatings Inc...714 774-4671
795 Debra St Anaheim (92805) *(G-1689)*
Technocel, Simi Valley *Also called Foreign Trade Corporation (G-7567)*
Technologent, Irvine *Also called Thomas Gallaway Corporation (G-15501)*
Technology Associates EC Inc...760 765-5275
3115 Melrose Dr Ste 110 Carlsbad (92010) *(G-27679)*
Technology Credit Union...408 467-2382
1562 S Bascom Ave San Jose (95125) *(G-9692)*
Technology Credit Union...408 467-2385
43848 Pcf Commons Blvd Fremont (94538) *(G-9693)*
Technology Credit Union (PA)...408 451-9111
2010 N 1st St Ste 200 San Jose (95131) *(G-9694)*
Technology Credit Union...650 326-6445
490 S California Ave Palo Alto (94306) *(G-9695)*
Technology Crossover Ventures, Palo Alto *Also called Tcmi Inc (G-12349)*

ALPHABETIC

ALPHABETIC SECTION

Technology Resource Center Inc 714 542-1004
2101 E 4th St Ste 130a Santa Ana (92705) *(G-16503)*
Technology Services Cal Dept 916 464-3747
10860 Gold Center Dr # 100 Rancho Cordova (95670) *(G-16198)*
Technology Services Cal Dept (HQ) 916 319-9223
1325 J St Ste 1600 Sacramento (95814) *(G-16504)*
Technosocialworkcom LLC 661 617-6601
4300 Resnik Ct Unit 103 Bakersfield (93313) *(G-16199)*
Techsoup Global 415 633-9325
435 Brannan St Ste 100 San Francisco (94107) *(G-25369)*
Tecolote Research Inc 310 640-4700
2120 E Grand Ave Ste 200 El Segundo (90245) *(G-27680)*
Tecom Industries Incorporated 818 341-4010
375 Conejo Ridge Ave Thousand Oaks (91361) *(G-7648)*
Tecta America Southern Cal Inc (HQ) 714 973-6233
1217 E Wakeham Ave Santa Ana (92705) *(G-3218)*
Tectura Corporation (PA) 650 273-4249
951 Old County Rd 2-317 Belmont (94002) *(G-16505)*
Ted Cooper/Cooper Industries 408 358-3060
P.O. Box 36007 San Jose (95158) *(G-962)*
Ted Ford Jones Inc (PA) 714 521-3110
6211 Beach Blvd Buena Park (90621) *(G-17817)*
Ted Jacob Engrg Group Inc (PA) 510 763-4880
1763 Broadway Oakland (94612) *(G-26088)*
Ted Levine Drum Co (PA) 626 579-1084
1817 Chico Ave South El Monte (91733) *(G-18023)*
Teen Challenge Norwestcal Nev 408 703-2001
390 Mathew St Santa Clara (95050) *(G-24246)*
TEEN TRIUMPH, Stockton Also called Human Services Projects Inc *(G-24697)*
Teg Staffing Inc 619 584-3444
2604 El Camino Real Ste B Carlsbad (92008) *(G-14956)*
Tegged.com, San Francisco Also called Ifwe Inc *(G-15696)*
Tegile Systems Inc 510 791-7900
7999 Gateway Blvd Ste 120 Newark (94560) *(G-26619)*
Tegp Inc 619 584-3408
2375 Northside Dr Ste 360 San Diego (92108) *(G-14957)*
Tegsco LLC 415 865-8200
450 7th St San Francisco (94103) *(G-17896)*
Tegtmeier Associates Inc 530 872-7700
6701 Clark Rd Paradise (95969) *(G-11061)*
Tehachapi Recycling Center 661 822-6421
416 N Dennison Rd Tehachapi (93561) *(G-6568)*
Tehachapi Vly Hosp Hlthcre Dis (PA) 661 823-3000
115 W E St Tehachapi (93561) *(G-21959)*
Tehama Golf Club LLC 831 622-2200
4 Tehama Carmel (93923) *(G-19103)*
Teichert Construction, Sacramento Also called A Teichert & Son Inc *(G-6971)*
Teixeira Farms Inc 805 928-3801
2600 Bonita Lateral Rd Santa Maria (93458) *(G-98)*
Tejon Marketing Company 661 248-3000
4436 Lebec Rd Lebec (93243) *(G-27681)*
Tejon Ranch Co (PA) 661 248-3000
4436 Lebec Rd Lebec (93243) *(G-11866)*
Tekever Corporation 408 730-2617
5201 Great America Pkwy Santa Clara (95054) *(G-15859)*
Tektetco 707 822-9000
5251 Ericson Way Arcata (95521) *(G-1473)*
Tekworks Inc (PA) 858 668-1705
13000 Gregg St Ste B Poway (92064) *(G-17522)*
Tel Tech Plus Inc 760 510-1323
393 Enterprise St San Marcos (92078) *(G-2768)*
Telacu, Commerce Also called East Los Angeles Community Un *(G-9781)*
Telacu Industries Inc (HQ) 323 721-1655
5400 E Olympic Blvd # 300 Commerce (90022) *(G-9901)*
Telacu NW Five Inc (PA) 323 721-1655
5400 E Olympic Blvd Commerce (90022) *(G-11062)*
Telaflora LLC 310 231-9199
11444 W Olympic Blvd Fl 4 Los Angeles (90064) *(G-9220)*
Teldata, Santee Also called Catania Hijar Corporation *(G-1917)*
Tele Car, Los Angeles Also called Doma Laszlo *(G-4397)*
Tele-Car Courier Service, Los Angeles Also called Tele-Car Couriers Inc *(G-4424)*
Tele-Car Couriers Inc 877 910-1313
4035 Eagle Rock Blvd Los Angeles (90065) *(G-4424)*
Tele-Direct Communications 916 348-2170
4741 Madison Ave Ste 200 Sacramento (95841) *(G-17523)*
Tele-Interpreters LLC 800 811-7881
1 Lower Ragsdale Dr # 2 Monterey (93940) *(G-17524)*
Telecare Corporation 714 361-6760
275 Baker St E Costa Mesa (92626) *(G-22094)*
Telecare Corporation 510 895-5502
2050 Fairmont Dr San Leandro (94578) *(G-22095)*
Telecare Corporation 760 245-8837
16460 Victor St Victorville (92395) *(G-22096)*
Telecare Corporation 619 275-8000
1675 Morena Blvd Ste 100 San Diego (92110) *(G-22097)*
Telecare Corporation 562 630-8672
6060 N Paramount Blvd Long Beach (90805) *(G-22098)*
Telecare Corporation 562 634-9534
6060 N Paramount Blvd Long Beach (90805) *(G-22099)*
Telecare Corporation 510 261-9191
1451 28th Ave Oakland (94601) *(G-22100)*
Telecare Corporation 510 582-7676
494 Blossom Way Hayward (94541) *(G-22101)*
Telecare Corporation 510 352-9690
15200 Foothill Blvd San Leandro (94578) *(G-22102)*
Telecare Corporation 619 692-8225
3851 Rosecrans St San Diego (92110) *(G-22103)*
Telecare Corporation 805 383-3669
1756 S Lewis Rd Camarillo (93012) *(G-22104)*
Telecare Corporation 650 367-1890
200 Edmonds Rd Redwood City (94062) *(G-22105)*
Telecare Corporation 510 337-7950
1080 Marina Village Pkwy # 100 Alameda (94501) *(G-22106)*
Telecare Corporation 562 633-5111
8835 Vans St Paramount (90723) *(G-22107)*
Telecare Corporation 650 817-9070
300 Harbor Blvd E Belmont (94002) *(G-22108)*
Telecare Corporation 510 535-5115
2633 E 27th St Oakland (94601) *(G-22109)*
Telecare La Step Down 562 216-4900
4335 Atlantic Ave Long Beach (90807) *(G-22850)*
Telecare Las Posadas 805 383-3669
1756 S Lewis Rd Camarillo (93012) *(G-22851)*
Telecmmnctons MGT Slutions Inc 408 866-5495
570 Division St Campbell (95008) *(G-2769)*
Telecom Evolutions LLC 818 264-4400
9221 Corbin Ave Ste 260 Northridge (91324) *(G-17525)*
Telecom Inc 510 873-8283
2201 Broadway Ste 103 Oakland (94612) *(G-17526)*
Telecom Technology Svcs Inc 925 224-7812
7901 Stoneridge Dr # 500 Pleasanton (94588) *(G-28070)*
Telecommunications Dept, Salinas Also called County of Monterey *(G-17100)*
Telecommunications Division, Sacramento Also called General Services Cal Dept *(G-25835)*
Telecommunictns Cmmnctns Srvcs 415 869-9000
21 Locust Ave Mill Valley (94941) *(G-6092)*
Telecontact Resource Services, Riverbank Also called Econtactlive Inc *(G-17141)*
Teledyne Imaging Sensors, Thousand Oaks Also called Teledyne Scentific Imaging LLC *(G-26621)*
Teledyne Scentific Imaging LLC 805 373-4979
5212 Verdugo Way Camarillo (93012) *(G-26620)*
Teledyne Scentific Imaging LLC (HQ) 805 373-4545
1049 Camino Dos Rios Thousand Oaks (91360) *(G-26621)*
Telegraph Hill Partners Invest 415 765-6980
360 Post St Ste 601 San Francisco (94108) *(G-27682)*
Telemarketing, Fresno Also called Fowler Packing Company Inc *(G-534)*
Telemundo of Northern Cal 408 432-6221
2450 N 1st St San Jose (95131) *(G-5914)*
Telenet Voip Inc 310 253-9000
850 N Park View Dr El Segundo (90245) *(G-17946)*
Telepacific Communications, Los Angeles Also called US Telepacific Corp *(G-5714)*
Telepictures, Burbank Also called Warner Bros Transatlantic Inc *(G-18287)*
Teleplan Service Solutions Inc 916 677-4619
8875 Washington Blvd B Roseville (95678) *(G-16305)*
Telesign Holdings Inc 310 742-8228
13274 Fiji Way Ste 600 Marina Del Rey (90292) *(G-15860)*
Telesis Community Credit Union (PA) 818 885-1226
9301 Winnetka Ave Chatsworth (91311) *(G-9631)*
Telesis Onion Co 559 884-2441
21484 S Colusa Five Points (93624) *(G-598)*
Telestar Consulting Inc 310 748-0008
519 N Alta Dr Beverly Hills (90210) *(G-27683)*
Telesys Software 650 522-9922
1900 S Norfolk St Ste 221 San Mateo (94403) *(G-15497)*
Teletrac Inc (HQ) 714 897-0877
7391 Lincoln Way Garden Grove (92841) *(G-6093)*
Television Academy, North Hollywood Also called Academy TV Arts & Sciences *(G-25113)*
Television Games Network, Los Angeles Also called Ods Technologies LP *(G-5904)*
Telfer Oil Company (PA) 925 228-1515
211 Foster St Martinez (94553) *(G-1873)*
Telisimo International Corp 619 325-1593
2330 Shelter Island Dr 210a San Diego (92106) *(G-5708)*
Tell Steel Inc 562 435-4826
2345 W 17th St Long Beach (90813) *(G-7407)*
Telmate LLC 415 300-4314
655 Montgomery St # 1800 San Francisco (94111) *(G-17527)*
Telogis Inc (HQ) 949 389-5500
20 Enterprise Ste 100 Aliso Viejo (92656) *(G-16200)*
Telstar Instruments (PA) 925 671-2888
1717 Solano Way Ste 34 Concord (94520) *(G-2770)*
Temalpakh Inc 760 770-5778
979 S Gene Autry Trl Palm Springs (92264) *(G-1690)*
Temarry Recycling Inc 619 270-9453
476 Tecate Rd Tecate (91980) *(G-6569)*
Temco, Laguna Beach Also called C & B Delivery Services *(G-4528)*
Temecula 24 Hour Care, Temecula Also called Responsible Med Solutions Corp *(G-19913)*
Temecula Stadium Cinemas 15, Temecula Also called Edwards Theatres Circuit Inc *(G-18331)*
Temecula Valley Drywall Inc 951 600-1742
41228 Raintree Ct Murrieta (92562) *(G-2986)*
Temecula Vly Unified Schl Dst 951 695-7110
40516 Roripaugh Rd Temecula (92591) *(G-3951)*
Temecula Vly Unified Schl Dst 951 302-5140
33125 Regina Dr Temecula (92592) *(G-25370)*
Temeku Hills, Temecula Also called McMillin Communities Inc *(G-1216)*
Temp Unlimited LLC 562 860-3340
11306 183rd St Ste 301 Cerritos (90703) *(G-14958)*
Tempest Telecom Solutions LLC (PA) 805 879-4800
136 W Canon Perdido St A Santa Barbara (93101) *(G-28071)*
Temple City Convalescent Hosp, Temple City Also called Fran-Jom Inc *(G-21217)*
Temple City Youth Dev Fund 626 548-5085
6415 N Muscatel Ave San Gabriel (91775) *(G-25371)*
Temple Community Hospital, Los Angeles Also called Temple Hospital Corporation *(G-21960)*
Temple Garden Homes Inc 626 286-6408
5746 Loma Ave Temple City (91780) *(G-24833)*
Temple Hospital Corporation 213 355-3200
242 N Hoover St Los Angeles (90004) *(G-21960)*

Temple Israel of Hollywood (PA)....323 876-8330
7300 Hollywood Blvd Los Angeles (90046) *(G-13717)*
Temple Park Convalescent Hosp....213 380-2035
2411 W Temple St Los Angeles (90026) *(G-21390)*
Templeton Franklin Intl Tr....650 312-2000
1 Franklin Pkwy San Mateo (94403) *(G-12126)*
Templo Calvario Cmnty Dev Corp....714 543-3711
2501 W 5th St Santa Ana (92703) *(G-24984)*
Templton Fgn Smaller Companies, San Mateo *Also called Templeton Franklin Intl Tr (G-12126)*
Temporary Plant Cleaners, Martinez *Also called Plant Maintenance Inc (G-14925)*
Ten Enthusiast Network LLC (HQ)....310 531-9900
831 S Douglas St Ste 100 El Segundo (90245) *(G-9173)*
Ten The Enthusiast Network LLC....714 709-9021
1821 E Dyer Rd Ste 150 Santa Ana (92705) *(G-9174)*
Ten-X LLC....800 793-6107
1301 Shoreway Rd Ste 425 Belmont (94002) *(G-11867)*
Ten-X LLC (PA)....949 859-2777
1 Mauchly Irvine (92618) *(G-11868)*
Tenderloin Housing Clinic Inc....415 771-2427
472 Turk St San Francisco (94102) *(G-23074)*
Tenergy Corporation....510 687-0388
436 Kato Ter Fremont (94539) *(G-7478)*
TENET, Tarzana *Also called Amisub of California Inc (G-21451)*
TENET, Fountain Valley *Also called Fountain Valley Regl Hospl (G-21568)*
Tenet, Palm Springs *Also called Desert Regional Med Ctr Inc (G-22137)*
Tenet Health System Hospital, Manteca *Also called Tenet Healthsystem Medical (G-21963)*
Tenet Health Systems Norris....323 865-3000
1441 Eastlake Ave Los Angeles (90089) *(G-22181)*
Tenet Healthsystem Desert Inc, Palm Springs *Also called Desert Regional Med Ctr Inc (G-21529)*
Tenet Healthsystem Medical....714 966-8191
13032 Earlham St Santa Ana (92705) *(G-21961)*
Tenet Healthsystem Medical....925 275-8303
414 Cliffside Dr Danville (94526) *(G-20130)*
Tenet Healthsystem Medical....562 531-2550
3700 South St Lakewood (90712) *(G-20131)*
Tenet Healthsystem Medical....562 531-2550
16331 Arthur St Cerritos (90703) *(G-21962)*
Tenet Healthsystem Medical....619 426-6310
330 Moss St Chula Vista (91911) *(G-22110)*
Tenet Healthsystem Medical....209 823-3111
1205 E North St Manteca (95336) *(G-21963)*
Tenet Healthsystem Medical....714 428-6800
1400 S Duglaca Rd Ste 250 Anaheim (92806) *(G-21964)*
Tenet Healthsystem Medical....530 222-1992
475 Knollcrest Dr Redding (96002) *(G-22579)*
Tenet Healthsystem Medical....805 546-7698
3751 Katella Ave Los Alamitos (90720) *(G-20132)*
Tenet Healthsystem Medical....714 993-2000
1301 N Rose Dr Placentia (92870) *(G-22182)*
Tenet Healthsystem Medical....562 493-9581
1661 Golden Rain Rd Seal Beach (90740) *(G-20133)*
Tenet Healthsystem Medical....408 378-6131
815 Pollard Rd Los Gatos (95032) *(G-21965)*
Tenet Healthsystem Medical....530 246-9000
2801 Eureka Way Redding (96001) *(G-24247)*
Tenet Healthsystem Medical....626 300-5500
1000 S Fremont Ave Unit 1 Alhambra (91803) *(G-20134)*
Tenex Greenhouse Ventures LLC....650 375-7021
533 Airport Blvd Ste 400 Burlingame (94010) *(G-12350)*
Tennant Health Systems....626 300-3500
1000 S Fremont Ave Unit 2 Alhambra (91803) *(G-20135)*
Tennenbaum Capitl Partners LLC (PA)....310 396-5451
2951 28th St Ste 1000 Santa Monica (90405) *(G-12150)*
Tennis Channel Inc (HQ)....310 392-1920
2850 Ocean Park Blvd # 150 Santa Monica (90405) *(G-18438)*
Tennis Everyone Incorporated....415 897-2185
351 San Andreas Dr Novato (94945) *(G-19104)*
Tennis Pro Shop....209 529-2446
819 Sunset Ave Modesto (95351) *(G-18698)*
Tennyson Electric Inc....925 606-1038
7275 National Dr Livermore (94550) *(G-2771)*
Tenpo Hardware, Ontario *Also called Ameriwest Industries Inc (G-7671)*
Tensilica Inc (HQ)....408 986-8000
3393 Octavius Dr Santa Clara (95054) *(G-12225)*
Teraburst Networks Inc....408 400-4100
1289 Anvilwood Ave Sunnyvale (94089) *(G-6094)*
Teradata Corporation....650 232-4400
999 Skyway Rd Ste 100 San Carlos (94070) *(G-15498)*
Teris LLC....619 231-3282
600 W Broadway Ste 300 San Diego (92101) *(G-16201)*
Teris-Bay Area LLC....650 213-9922
2455 Faber Pl Ste 200 Palo Alto (94303) *(G-23592)*
Terix Computer Service, Sunnyvale *Also called Tusa Inc (G-16308)*
Terkensha Associates Inc....916 922-9868
811 Grand Ave Ste D Sacramento (95838) *(G-24248)*
Terminix Intl Co Ltd Partnr....818 972-2037
3055 N California St Burbank (91504) *(G-14191)*
Terminix Intl Co Ltd Partnr....909 332-2479
649 S Waterman Ave Ste A San Bernardino (92408) *(G-14192)*
Terminix Intl Co Ltd Partnr....925 460-5063
6678 Owens Dr Ste 100 Pleasanton (94588) *(G-14193)*
Terra Coastal Properties Inc....310 457-2534
23405 Pacific Coast Hwy Malibu (90265) *(G-11869)*
Terra Firma Farm Corp....530 795-2473
4713 Baker Rd Winters (95694) *(G-99)*
Terra Firma Farms, Winters *Also called Terra Firma Farm Corp (G-99)*
Terra Firma Landscape Company, San Diego *Also called L A Swikard Inc (G-885)*
Terra Linda Farms 1....559 867-3400
17625 S Marks Ave Riverdale (93656) *(G-397)*
Terra Nova Counseling (PA)....916 344-0249
5750 Sunrise Blvd Ste 100 Citrus Heights (95610) *(G-24249)*
Terra Pacific Landscape (PA)....714 567-0177
1627 E Wilshire Ave Santa Ana (92705) *(G-800)*
Terra Vista Management, San Diego *Also called Terra Vista Management Inc (G-11870)*
Terra Vista Management Inc....858 581-4200
2211 Pacific Beach Dr San Diego (92109) *(G-11870)*
Terracare Associates LLC....925 374-0060
921 Arnold Dr Martinez (94553) *(G-27684)*
Terrace View Care Center, Fullerton *Also called Sun Haven Care Inc (G-20934)*
Terraces At Par Marino, Pasadena *Also called Diversified Health Svcs Del (G-24632)*
Terraces of Los Gatos Agei, Los Gatos *Also called American Baptist Homes of West (G-21139)*
Terraces of Roseville, The, Roseville *Also called Westmont Living Inc (G-24854)*
Terraces Retirement Community....530 894-1010
2850 Sierra Sunrise Ter Chico (95928) *(G-24834)*
Terracina Meadows Apts....916 419-0925
4500 Tynebourne St F105 Sacramento (95834) *(G-11212)*
Terranea Resort, Rancho Palos Verdes *Also called Long Point Development LLC (G-12930)*
Terranomics, Burlingame *Also called Cushman & Wakefield Inc (G-11462)*
Terranova Ranch Inc....559 866-5644
16729 W Floral Ave Helm (93627) *(G-398)*
Terravia Holdings Inc (PA)....650 780-4777
225 Gateway Blvd South San Francisco (94080) *(G-26622)*
Terre Du Soleil Ltd....707 963-1211
180 Rutherford Hill Rd Rutherford (94573) *(G-13341)*
Terry Hines & Assoc, Burbank *Also called GL Nemirow Inc (G-13854)*
Terry Hines & Assoicates, Burbank *Also called GL Newmirow Inc (G-13855)*
Terry Meyer....408 723-3300
1712 Meridian Ave Ste C San Jose (95125) *(G-11871)*
Terry Tuell Concrete Inc....559 431-0812
287 W Fallbrook Ave # 105 Fresno (93711) *(G-3342)*
Tesancia La Jlla Ht Spa Resort, La Jolla *Also called Destination Residences LLC (G-13756)*
Tesi Investment Company LLC....619 224-3254
5005 N Harbor Dr San Diego (92106) *(G-13342)*
Tessie Clvland Cmnty Svcs Corp....323 586-7333
8019 Compton Ave Ste 219 Los Angeles (90001) *(G-24250)*
Test America, San Bruno *Also called Emlab P&K LLC (G-26850)*
Test-Rite Products Corp (HQ)....909 605-9899
1900 Burgundy Pl Ontario (91761) *(G-6891)*
Testamerica Laboratories Inc....949 261-1022
17461 Derian Ave Ste 100 Irvine (92614) *(G-26892)*
Testamerica Laboratories Inc....916 373-5600
880 Riverside Pkwy West Sacramento (95605) *(G-26893)*
Testing and Selection, Sacramento *Also called Justice California Department (G-27962)*
Testing Engineers San Diego, San Diego *Also called San Diego Testing Engineers (G-26053)*
Teter LLP (PA)....559 437-0887
7535 N Palm Ave Ste 201 Fresno (93711) *(G-26089)*
Tetra Tech Inc....619 525-7188
1230 Columbia St Ste 1000 San Diego (92101) *(G-27685)*
Tetra Tech Inc....805 739-2600
3201 Airpark Dr Ste 108 Santa Maria (93455) *(G-28072)*
Tetra Tech Inc....949 263-0846
17885 Von Karman Ave # 500 Irvine (92614) *(G-26090)*
Tetra Tech Inc....949 809-5000
17885 Von Karman Ave # 500 Irvine (92614) *(G-26091)*
Tetra Tech Bas Inc (HQ)....909 860-7777
1360 Valley Vista Dr Diamond Bar (91765) *(G-26092)*
Tetra Tech Dpk, San Francisco *Also called Dpk Consulting (G-27414)*
Tetra Tech Ec Inc....619 234-8690
1230 Columbia St Ste 750 San Diego (92101) *(G-28073)*
Tetra Tech Ec Inc....916 852-8300
2969 Prospect Park Dr # 100 Rancho Cordova (95670) *(G-28074)*
Tetra Tech Engrg & Arch Svcs, Irvine *Also called Tetra Tech Inc (G-26091)*
Tetra Tech Executive Svcs Inc....626 470-2400
3475 E Foothill Blvd Pasadena (91107) *(G-14804)*
Tetra Tech Nus Inc....412 921-7090
3475 E Foothill Blvd Pasadena (91107) *(G-28075)*
Tetra Tech Technical Services....626 351-4664
3475 E Foothill Blvd Fl 3 Pasadena (91107) *(G-26093)*
Teutonic Holdings LLC....818 264-4400
9221 Corbin Ave Ste 260 Northridge (91324) *(G-16262)*
Teva Pharmaceuticals Usa Inc....949 457-2828
19 Hughes Irvine (92618) *(G-8298)*
Texaco Inc....661 654-7000
9525 Camino Media Bakersfield (93311) *(G-11872)*
Texas Home Health America LP (PA)....972 201-3800
1455 Auto Center Dr # 200 Ontario (91761) *(G-20357)*
Texas Instruments Sunnyvale....408 541-9900
165 Gibraltar Ct Sunnyvale (94089) *(G-17528)*
Textainer Equipment Mgt US Ltd (HQ)....415 434-0551
650 California St Fl 16 San Francisco (94108) *(G-14582)*
Textainer Group Holdings Ltd (HQ)....415 434-0551
650 California St Fl 16 San Francisco (94108) *(G-27250)*
Textaner Eqp Income Fund II LP....415 434-0551
650 California St Fl 16 San Francisco (94108) *(G-14583)*
Textplus Inc....424 272-0296
13160 Mindanao Way # 217 Marina Del Rey (90292) *(G-5418)*
Texture Specialties Inc....559 904-6047
295 Mccreary Ave Hanford (93230) *(G-3407)*
Tf Courier Inc....916 379-0708
8331 Demetre Ave Sacramento (95828) *(G-4425)*
Tf Courier Inc....858 271-0021
7130 Miramar Rd Ste 400 San Diego (92121) *(G-4426)*

A L P H A B E T I C

Tf Courier Inc............714 888-1452
2051 Raymer Ave Ste A Fullerton (92833) ***(G-4427)***
Tf Courier Inc............214 560-9000
21760 Garcia Ln City of Industry (91789) ***(G-4428)***
TFC Holding Company............626 363-9708
18605 Gale Ave Ste 238 City of Industry (91748) ***(G-9425)***
Tgcon Inc (HQ)............925 449-5764
50 Contractors St Livermore (94551) ***(G-26094)***
Tgic Wine Imp & Wholesaler, Woodland Hills *Also called Guarachi Wine Partners Inc* ***(G-9104)***
Thales-Raytheon Systems Co LLC (HQ)............714 446-3118
1801 Hughes Dr Fullerton (92833) ***(G-7649)***
Tharp Truck Rental Inc (PA)............559 782-5800
15243 Road 192 Porterville (93257) ***(G-18024)***
Tharpe & Howell (PA)............714 437-4900
15250 Ventura Blvd Fl 9 Sherman Oaks (91403) ***(G-23593)***
The Bay Club Hotel and Marina, San Diego *Also called Bay Club Hotel and Marina A C* ***(G-12424)***
The Boardwalk, El Cajon *Also called Newport Diversified Inc* ***(G-17357)***
The Boston Cnsulting Group Inc............213 621-2772
355 S Grand Ave Ste 3300 Los Angeles (90071) ***(G-27686)***
The Broadmoore, San Francisco *Also called Broadmoor Hotel* ***(G-11100)***
The Central Valley Trnsp Auth............559 305-7037
675 W Manning Ave Reedley (93654) ***(G-3728)***
The Charles Schwab Trust Co (HQ)............415 371-0518
425 Market St Fl 7 San Francisco (94105) ***(G-12205)***
The David Lcile Pckard Fndtion............650 917-7167
300 2nd St Los Altos (94022) ***(G-25588)***
The Designory Inc (HQ)............562 624-0200
211 E Ocean Blvd Ste 100 Long Beach (90802) ***(G-14163)***
The Eberly Company, Beverly Hills *Also called Charles & Cynthia Eberly Inc* ***(G-11114)***
The For Califo Cente............760 839-4138
340 N Escondido Blvd Escondido (92025) ***(G-25052)***
The For Hospital Committee (HQ)............925 847-3000
5555 W Las Positas Blvd Pleasanton (94588) ***(G-21966)***
The For Sacramento Society............916 383-7387
6201 Florin Perkins Rd Sacramento (95828) ***(G-25589)***
The For Work Training Center............530 534-1112
1811 Kusel Rd Oroville (95966) ***(G-24395)***
The Golf Club of California, Fallbrook *Also called Sycamore Cc Inc* ***(G-19102)***
The Goodwin Company, Garden Grove *Also called Goodwin Ammonia Company* ***(G-4563)***
The Gray-Line Tours Company............323 463-3333
6541 Hollywood Blvd Los Angeles (90028) ***(G-3908)***
The Housing Authority of............831 449-7268
1112 Parkside St Salinas (93906) ***(G-13456)***
The Lodge At Torrey Pines, La Jolla *Also called Bh Partn A Calif Limit Partne* ***(G-12449)***
The Messenger Company, San Diego *Also called San Diego Messenger Inc* ***(G-4422)***
The Music Ctr of La Cty Inc............213 972-8007
135 N Grand Ave Ste 201 Los Angeles (90012) ***(G-24985)***
The National Food Lab LLC............925 828-1440
365 N Canyons Pkwy # 201 Livermore (94551) ***(G-26813)***
The Nevell Group Inc (PA)............714 579-7501
3001 Entp St Ste 200 Brea (92821) ***(G-1691)***
The Newly Wed, Culver City *Also called Avoca Productions Inc* ***(G-18048)***
The Palms, Roseville *Also called Palms Assistd Lvng & Mmry Cre* ***(G-24763)***
The Peninsula Beverly Hills, Beverly Hills *Also called Hong Kong & Shanghai Hotels* ***(G-12758)***
The Pines Ltd............619 447-1880
1423 E Washington Ave El Cajon (92019) ***(G-11213)***
The Redwoods A Cmnty Seniors............415 383-2741
40 Camino Alto Ofc Mill Valley (94941) ***(G-24835)***
The Residence, Encino *Also called Actual Reality Pictures Inc* ***(G-11275)***
The Sterling Hotel, Sacramento *Also called Elizabethan Inn Associates LP* ***(G-12615)***
The Teecor Group Inc............213 632-2350
1450 S Burlington Ave Los Angeles (90006) ***(G-3589)***
The Tristaff Group, San Diego *Also called Garich Inc* ***(G-14660)***
The Valley Club of Montecito............805 969-2215
1901 E Valley Rd Santa Barbara (93108) ***(G-19105)***
The Valley Inn, Holtville *Also called Sunharbor Management LLC* ***(G-24829)***
The Villa Florence Hotel, San Francisco *Also called Florence Villa Hotel* ***(G-12639)***
The War At Home Series, Burbank *Also called Warner Bros Entertainment Inc* ***(G-18197)***
The Woodbridge Golf Cntry CLB............209 369-2371
800 E Woodbridge Rd Woodbridge (95258) ***(G-19106)***
The Young Mens Chris Assoc of............510 841-4152
1222 University Ave Berkeley (94702) ***(G-25372)***
The Young Mens Chris Assoc of............925 687-8900
350 Civic Dr Pleasant Hill (94523) ***(G-25373)***
The Young Mens Chris Assoc of............510 601-8674
4727 San Pablo Ave Emeryville (94608) ***(G-25374)***
The Young Mens Chris Assoc of............510 486-8400
2111 Mrtn Lthr King Jr Wa Berkeley (94704) ***(G-25375)***
The Young Mens Chris Assoc of............510 848-9092
2009 10th St Berkeley (94710) ***(G-25376)***
The Young Mens Chris Assoc of............510 848-9622
2001 Allston Way Berkeley (94704) ***(G-25377)***
The Young Mens Chris Assoc of............510 526-2146
1130 Oxford St Berkeley (94707) ***(G-25378)***
The Young Mens Chris Assoc of............510 848-6800
2001 Allston Way Berkeley (94704) ***(G-25379)***
The Young Mens Chris Assoc of............510 559-2090
1422 San Pablo Ave Berkeley (94702) ***(G-25380)***
Theat and Arts Found of San Di............858 623-3366
2910 La Jolla Village Dr La Jolla (92093) ***(G-25381)***
Thefloorstore/Flor Stor, Laguna Hills *Also called Tom Ray Industries Inc* ***(G-6894)***
Thera Home Care, Redwood City *Also called Zb Rehab Staffing Inc* ***(G-14987)***
Therapak LLC (HQ)............909 267-2000
651 Wharton Dr Claremont (91711) ***(G-7318)***
Therapy For Kids Inc............714 870-6116
233 Orangefair Mall Fullerton (92832) ***(G-20358)***
Therapy In Your Home O TP TS............408 358-0201
147 Vista Del Monte Los Gatos (95030) ***(G-22580)***
Therastaff Inc............858 569-7555
2355 Northside Dr Ste 140 San Diego (92108) ***(G-14959)***
Therm Pacific, Commerce *Also called Hkf Inc* ***(G-7740)***
Thermal Air, Anaheim *Also called General Engineering Wstn Inc* ***(G-2235)***
Thermal Club............760 674-0088
86030 62nd Ave Thermal (92274) ***(G-19107)***
Thermal Mechanical Inc............408 988-8744
425 Aldo Ave Santa Clara (95054) ***(G-2395)***
Thermalair Inc (HQ)............714 630-3200
1140 N Red Gum St Anaheim (92806) ***(G-2396)***
Thermasource LLC (PA)............707 523-2960
235 Pine St Ste 1150 San Francisco (94104) ***(G-26095)***
Thermasource LLC............530 476-3333
333 S Grand Ave Ste 4070 Los Angeles (90071) ***(G-26096)***
Thermo Fisher Scientific............408 894-9835
355 River Oaks Pkwy San Jose (95134) ***(G-7350)***
Thermo Fisher Scientific Inc............650 876-1949
200 Oyster Point Blvd South San Francisco (94080) ***(G-7351)***
Thermo Power Industries............562 799-0087
10570 Humbolt St Los Alamitos (90720) ***(G-2987)***
Thermofinnegan, San Jose *Also called Thermo Fisher Scientific* ***(G-7350)***
Thetradedesk, Ventura *Also called Trade Desk Inc* ***(G-13929)***
Thiara Sukhwant............530 673-1581
1537 Atkinson Ct Yuba City (95993) ***(G-485)***
Thiara Orchards, Yuba City *Also called Thiara Sukhwant* ***(G-485)***
Think Passenger Inc (PA)............323 556-5400
12100 Wilshire Blvd # 1950 Los Angeles (90025) ***(G-15499)***
Think Together............562 236-3835
12016 Telegraph Rd Santa Fe Springs (90670) ***(G-18699)***
Think Together............626 373-2311
1730 W Cameron Ave West Covina (91790) ***(G-24525)***
Thinkom Solutions Inc............310 371-5486
4881 W 145th St Hawthorne (90250) ***(G-6095)***
Thinkwell Group Inc............818 333-3444
2710 Media Center Dr Los Angeles (90065) ***(G-18439)***
Third & Mission Associates LLC............415 341-8457
680 Mission St San Francisco (94105) ***(G-11873)***
Thirdwave Technology Services............310 563-2160
4054 Del Rey Ave Ste 207 Marina Del Rey (90292) ***(G-16306)***
Thismoment Inc............415 200-4730
221 Kearny St Fl 4 San Francisco (94108) ***(G-15500)***
Thoits Insurance Service Inc............408 792-5400
444 Castro St Ste 200 Mountain View (94041) ***(G-10904)***
Thom Sharon & G Enterprises............530 226-8350
2620 Larkspur Ln Ste N Redding (96002) ***(G-22581)***
Thoma Electric Co, San Luis Obispo *Also called Thoma Electric Inc* ***(G-2772)***
Thoma Electric Inc............805 543-3850
3562 Empleo St Ste C San Luis Obispo (93401) ***(G-2772)***
Thomas Crane and Trckg Co Inc............562 592-2837
18851 Stewart Ln Huntington Beach (92648) ***(G-2090)***
Thomas Doll & Company, Walnut Creek *Also called Thomas Wirig Doll & Co Cpas* ***(G-26451)***
Thomas Gallaway Corporation (PA)............949 716-9500
100 Spectrum Center Dr # 700 Irvine (92618) ***(G-15501)***
Thomas J Hoban (PA)............619 442-1665
215 W Lexington Ave El Cajon (92020) ***(G-11874)***
Thomas Kinkade Company, The, San Francisco *Also called Pacific Metro LLC* ***(G-9286)***
Thomas M Obinson Jr............559 432-6200
7480 N Palm Ave Ste 101 Fresno (93711) ***(G-11875)***
Thomas Mark & Company Inc (PA)............408 453-5373
2290 N 1st St Ste 304 San Jose (95131) ***(G-26097)***
Thomas P Cox Architects Inc............949 862-0270
19782 Macarthur Blvd # 300 Irvine (92612) ***(G-26262)***
Thomas Plumbing, Antioch *Also called Rt/Dt Inc* ***(G-2353)***
Thomas Weisel Partners LLC (HQ)............415 364-2500
1 Montgomery St Ste 3700 San Francisco (94104) ***(G-10082)***
Thomas Wirig Doll & Co Cpas............925 939-2500
165 Lennon Ln Ste 200 Walnut Creek (94598) ***(G-26451)***
Thomason Tractor Co California............559 659-2039
985 12th St Firebaugh (93622) ***(G-7811)***
Thompson & Colegate LLP............951 682-5550
3610 14th St Lowr Riverside (92501) ***(G-23594)***
Thompson & Rich Crane Service............209 465-3161
2373 E Mariposa Rd Stockton (95205) ***(G-17529)***
Thompson Builders Corporation............415 456-8972
250 Bel Marin Keys Blvd A Novato (94949) ***(G-1344)***
Thompson Building Materials, Orange *Also called Valori Sand & Gravel Company* ***(G-6998)***
Thompson Building Materials, Fontana *Also called Valori Sand & Gravel Company* ***(G-6999)***
Thompson Building Mtls Inc............619 287-9410
6618 Federal Blvd Lemon Grove (91945) ***(G-6995)***
Thompson Coburn LLP............310 282-2500
2029 Century Park E # 1900 Los Angeles (90067) ***(G-23595)***
Thompson Family Farms LLC............714 848-7536
16478 Beach Blvd Ste 391 Westminster (92683) ***(G-399)***
Thompson Hysell Engineers............209 521-8986
1016 12th St Modesto (95354) ***(G-26098)***
Thompson/Brooks Inc............415 581-2600
151 Vermont St Ste 9 San Francisco (94103) ***(G-1271)***
Thomson Financial Services............213 955-5902
633 W 5th St Los Angeles (90071) ***(G-28076)***
Thomson Reuters (legal) Inc............650 210-1900
2440 W El Camino Real Mountain View (94040) ***(G-28077)***
Thomson Reuters (legal) Inc............415 344-6000
50 California St Ste 200 San Francisco (94111) ***(G-28078)***
Thomson Reuters (markets) LLC............415 677-2500
1 Sansome St Ste 3650 San Francisco (94104) ***(G-17530)***

ALPHABETIC

ALPHABETIC SECTION Time Warner Cable Inc

Thomson Reuters Corporation.....408 524-4628
800 W California Ave # 100 Sunnyvale (94086) ***(G-15502)***
Thomson Rters Tax Accnting Inc.....510 452-6900
1300 Clay St Ste 810 Oakland (94612) ***(G-13728)***
Thoreau Janitorial Svcs Inc.....310 822-8017
5301 Beethoven St Ste 109 Los Angeles (90066) ***(G-14443)***
Thoreau Services Nationwide, Los Angeles *Also called Thoreau Janitorial Svcs Inc* ***(G-14443)***
Thorkelson Ranches.....209 892-9111
13218 Elm Ave Patterson (95363) ***(G-100)***
Thornton Tomasetti Inc.....415 365-6900
650 California St Fl 14 San Francisco (94108) ***(G-26099)***
Thorpe Design Inc.....925 634-0787
410 Beatrice St Ct Ste A Brentwood (94513) ***(G-2397)***
Thorsens Inc.....209 524-5296
2310 N Walnut Rd Turlock (95382) ***(G-3219)***
Thorsens Plumbing & AC, Turlock *Also called Thorsens Inc* ***(G-3219)***
Thorsnes Bartolotta & McGuire.....619 236-9363
2550 5th Ave Ste 1100 San Diego (92103) ***(G-23596)***
Thosand Oaks 145 Hodencamp, Thousand Oaks *Also called Kaiser Foundation Hospitals* ***(G-19648)***
Thoughtful Asia Limited, Sherman Oaks *Also called Thoughtful Media Group Inc* ***(G-13980)***
Thoughtful Media Group Inc.....818 465-7500
14724 Ventura Blvd # 1110 Sherman Oaks (91403) ***(G-13980)***
Thousand Oaks 322 E Thousand, Thousand Oaks *Also called Kaiser Foundation Hospitals* ***(G-19650)***
Thousand Oaks Health Care Ctr, Thousand Oaks *Also called Five Star Quality Care Inc* ***(G-20575)***
Thousand Oaks Service Center, Thousand Oaks *Also called Southern California Edison Co* ***(G-6225)***
Thousand Oaks Surgical Hosp LP.....805 777-7750
401 Rolling Oaks Dr Thousand Oaks (91361) ***(G-21967)***
Thousand Trails Inc.....209 962-0100
31191 Hardin Flat Rd Groveland (95321) ***(G-13484)***
Thousandeyes Inc.....415 513-4526
301 Howard St Ste 1700 San Francisco (94105) ***(G-15861)***
Thousands Oaks Mecial Offices, Thousand Oaks *Also called Permanente Kaiser Intl* ***(G-19828)***
Threatmetrix Inc.....408 200-5700
160 W Santa Clara St # 1400 San Jose (95113) ***(G-16506)***
Three D Electric, Benicia *Also called Western Sun Enterprises Inc* ***(G-2794)***
Three Rivers Golf Course, Lawndale *Also called Alondra Golf Course Inc* ***(G-18710)***
Three Rvers Prvider Netwrk Inc.....619 230-0508
910 Hale Pl Ste 101 Chula Vista (91914) ***(G-16064)***
Three Sons Inc.....562 801-4100
5201 Industry Ave Pico Rivera (90660) ***(G-8687)***
Three Way, Fremont *Also called Triple Play Services Inc* ***(G-5179)***
Three Way Inc.....408 748-6902
2940 Mead Ave Santa Clara (95051) ***(G-4380)***
Threshold Digital Research Lab.....310 452-8885
1649 11th St Santa Monica (90404) ***(G-27687)***
Threshold Technologies Inc.....909 606-1666
8352 Kimball Ave Bldg F35 Chino (91708) ***(G-4945)***
Thrifty Car Rental, Newport Beach *Also called Thrifty Rent-A-Car System Inc* ***(G-17696)***
Thrifty Car Rental, San Carlos *Also called Thrifty Rent-A-Car System Inc* ***(G-17697)***
Thrifty Car Rental, Los Angeles *Also called T C R Limited Partnership* ***(G-17694)***
Thrifty Car Rental.....415 788-8111
780 Mcdonnell Rd Ste 1 San Francisco (94128) ***(G-17695)***
Thrifty Rent-A-Car System Inc.....949 757-0659
3500 Irvine Ave Newport Beach (92660) ***(G-17696)***
Thrifty Rent-A-Car System Inc.....650 737-8084
780 Mcdonald Rd San Carlos (94070) ***(G-17697)***
Thrive Support Services Inc.....510 292-5058
324 G St Antioch (94509) ***(G-28163)***
Thunder Group Inc (PA).....626 935-1605
780 Nogales St Ste C City of Industry (91748) ***(G-6892)***
Thunder Valley Casino, Lincoln *Also called United Auburn Indian Community* ***(G-13366)***
Thunderbird Country Club.....760 328-2161
70737 Country Club Dr Rancho Mirage (92270) ***(G-19108)***
Thurston Martin H DDS Ms.....858 676-5010
11616 Iberia Pl San Diego (92128) ***(G-20279)***
Thyssenkrupp Elevator Corp.....510 476-1900
14400 Catalina St San Leandro (94577) ***(G-7896)***
Thyssenkrupp Elevator Corp.....510 476-1900
30984 Santana St Hayward (94544) ***(G-7897)***
Thyssenkrupp Elevator Corp.....323 278-9888
6087 Triangle Dr Commerce (90040) ***(G-18025)***
Tibco Finance Technology Inc.....650 461-3000
3375 Hillview Ave Palo Alto (94304) ***(G-16065)***
Tibco Software Inc (PA).....650 846-1000
3303 Hillview Ave Palo Alto (94304) ***(G-15503)***
Tiburcio Vasquez Hlth Ctr Inc (PA).....510 471-5880
33255 9th St Union City (94587) ***(G-20136)***
Tiburcio Vasquez Hlth Ctr Inc.....510 471-5907
22331 Mission Blvd Hayward (94541) ***(G-20137)***
Tiburon Inc.....858 799-7000
9477 Waples St Ste 100 San Diego (92121) ***(G-16066)***
Tiburon Hotel LLC.....415 435-5996
1651 Tiburon Blvd Belvedere Tiburon (94920) ***(G-13343)***
Tiburon Peninsula Club Inc.....415 789-7900
1600 Mar West St Belvedere Tiburon (94920) ***(G-19109)***
Tic, Panorama City *Also called Import Collection* ***(G-9271)***
Tic Hotels Inc.....619 238-7577
555 W Ash St San Diego (92101) ***(G-13344)***
Tic World-Wide Corp.....619 233-7500
555 W Ash St San Diego (92101) ***(G-13345)***
Tic Worldwide, San Diego *Also called Tic Hotels Inc* ***(G-13344)***
Tice Oaks Apartments, Walnut Creek *Also called Mp Tice Oaks Associates A CA* ***(G-11699)***
Tickco, Marina Del Rey *Also called Razorgator Inc* ***(G-19268)***
Ticketmaster Entertainment LLC.....800 653-8000
8800 W Sunset Blvd West Hollywood (90069) ***(G-18440)***
Ticketmob LLC.....800 927-0939
11833 Mississippi Ave Los Angeles (90025) ***(G-27251)***
Ticketweb LLC.....415 901-0210
685 Market St Ste 200 San Francisco (94105) ***(G-19293)***
Ticor Title Company California.....951 509-0211
4210 Riverwalk Pkwy # 200 Riverside (92505) ***(G-10536)***
Ticor Title Insurance Company (HQ).....616 302-3121
131 N El Molino Ave Pasadena (91101) ***(G-10537)***
Tidavater Inc.....818 848-4151
2107 W Alameda Ave Burbank (91506) ***(G-17531)***
Tidebreak Inc.....650 289-9869
958 San Leandro Ave # 500 Mountain View (94043) ***(G-7200)***
Tides Inc (PA).....415 561-6400
1014 Torney Ave Ste 1 San Francisco (94129) ***(G-24986)***
Tides Center.....415 359-9401
124 Turk St San Francisco (94102) ***(G-13346)***
Tides Center.....415 673-0234
520 Jones St San Francisco (94102) ***(G-24987)***
Tides Network.....415 561-6400
The Prsdio 1014 Trney Ave San Francisco (94129) ***(G-24988)***
TIDES SHARED SPACES, San Francisco *Also called Tides Inc* ***(G-24986)***
Tidwell Excav Acquisition Inc.....805 647-4707
1691 Los Angeles Ave Ventura (93004) ***(G-3444)***
Tierra Del Oro Girl Scout Cnsl.....916 452-9174
6601 Elvas Ave Sacramento (95819) ***(G-25382)***
Tierra Del Sol Foundation (PA).....818 352-1419
9919 Sunland Blvd Sunland (91040) ***(G-24836)***
Tierra Del Sol Foundation.....909 626-8301
250 W 1st St Ste 120 Claremont (91711) ***(G-19294)***
Tierra Del Soul, Claremont *Also called Tierra Del Sol Foundation* ***(G-19294)***
Tierra Oaks Golf Club Inc.....530 275-0795
19700 La Crescenta Dr Redding (96003) ***(G-19110)***
Tierra Rejada Golf Course, Moorpark *Also called Donovan Bros Golf LLC* ***(G-18735)***
Tifanny Mulhearn Realtors, Cerritos *Also called Mulhearn* ***(G-11700)***
Tiffany Dale Inc (PA).....714 739-2700
14765 Firestone Blvd La Mirada (90638) ***(G-6893)***
Tiger Analytics LLC.....408 508-4430
2701 Patrick Henry Dr Bldg 16 Santa Clara (95054) ***(G-26712)***
Tiger Electric Inc (PA).....714 529-8061
650 N Berry St Brea (92821) ***(G-2773)***
Tiger Financial Management LLC.....626 448-2400
11000 Lower Azusa Rd El Monte (91731) ***(G-9724)***
Tiger Lines LLC (HQ).....209 334-4100
927 Black Diamond Way Lodi (95240) ***(G-4276)***
Tigertext Inc.....310 401-1820
2110 Bradway Santa Monica Santa Monica (90404) ***(G-16507)***
Tikos Tanks Inc.....951 757-8014
14561 Hawthorne Ave Fontana (92335) ***(G-17955)***
Tiller Constructors Partnr Inc.....714 771-5600
306 W Katella Ave Ste A Orange (92867) ***(G-1692)***
Tillster Inc (PA).....858 784-0800
5959 Cornerstone Ct W # 100 San Diego (92121) ***(G-16508)***
Tim Brown.....408 717-2575
1096 Blossom Hill Rd # 200 San Jose (95123) ***(G-11876)***
Tim Hofer Inc.....559 732-6676
148 N Akers St Visalia (93291) ***(G-14444)***
Tim Paxins Pacific Excavation.....916 686-2800
9796 Kent St Elk Grove (95624) ***(G-3445)***
Timber Creek Golf Course, Roseville *Also called Sun City Rsvlle Cmnty Assn Inc* ***(G-18792)***
Timber Works Construction Inc.....916 786-6666
7031 Roseville Rd Ste A Sacramento (95842) ***(G-1272)***
Timberlake Painting, Murrieta *Also called Temecula Valley Drywall Inc* ***(G-2986)***
Timbre Technologies Inc.....510 624-3300
3100 W Warren Ave Fremont (94538) ***(G-15504)***
Timco, Newport Beach *Also called Allianz Globl Invstors Amer LP* ***(G-10113)***
Time and Alarm Systems (PA).....951 685-1761
3828 Wacker Dr Mira Loma (91752) ***(G-2774)***
Time Financial Services, Woodland Hills *Also called Ramkade Insurance Services* ***(G-10852)***
Time Inc.....415 982-5000
2 Embarcadero Ctr # 1900 San Francisco (94111) ***(G-13981)***
Time Inc.....310 268-7200
11766 Wilshire Blvd # 1700 Los Angeles (90025) ***(G-13982)***
Time Warner, Palmdale *Also called Spectrum MGT Holdg Co LLC* ***(G-6018)***
Time Warner, Cypress *Also called Spectrum MGT Holdg Co LLC* ***(G-6024)***
Time Warner, Garden Grove *Also called Spectrum MGT Holdg Co LLC* ***(G-6025)***
Time Warner, Anaheim *Also called Spectrum MGT Holdg Co LLC* ***(G-6027)***
Time Warner Cable Entps LLC.....818 972-0808
3500 W Olive Ave Ste 1000 Burbank (91505) ***(G-18168)***
Time Warner Cable Entps LLC.....323 993-7076
1438 N Gower St Los Angeles (90028) ***(G-6028)***
Time Warner Cable Entps LLC.....818 972-0328
5432 W 100 2nd St Los Angeles (90045) ***(G-5915)***
Time Warner Cable Entps LLC.....469 665-7735
550 Continental Blvd # 250 El Segundo (90245) ***(G-6029)***
Time Warner Cable Entps LLC.....818 953-3283
3300 Warner Blvd Burbank (91505) ***(G-6030)***
Time Warner Cable Inc.....619 346-4573
3051 Clairemont Dr San Diego (92117) ***(G-6031)***
Time Warner Cable Inc.....888 892-2253
118 N 8th St Santa Paula (93060) ***(G-6032)***
Time Warner Cable Inc.....805 214-1353
2323 Teller Rd Newbury Park (91320) ***(G-6033)***
Time Warner Cable Inc.....626 857-1075
1041 E Route 66 Glendora (91740) ***(G-6034)***

ALPHABETIC

Time Warner Cable Inc ALPHABETIC SECTION

Time Warner Cable Inc...951 587-8660
27555 Ynez Rd Ste 203 Temecula (92591) ***(G-6035)***
Time Warner Cable Inc...909 918-6972
1078 E Hospitality Ln D San Bernardino (92408) ***(G-6036)***
Time Warner Cable Inc...213 599-7968
5120 W Goldleaf Cir Los Angeles (90056) ***(G-6037)***
Time Warner Cable Inc...562 677-0228
17777 Center Court Dr N Cerritos (90703) ***(G-6038)***
Time Warner Cable Inc...951 682-6180
12763 Mitchell Ave Los Angeles (90066) ***(G-6039)***
Time Warner Cable Inc...858 695-3220
10450 Pacific Center Ct San Diego (92121) ***(G-6040)***
Time Warner Cable Inc...714 709-3617
19780 Hawthorne Blvd # 102 Torrance (90503) ***(G-5419)***
Time Warner Cable Inc...951 306-3117
660 W Acacia Ave Hemet (92543) ***(G-6041)***
Time Warner Cable Inc...619 684-6106
5865 Friars Rd San Diego (92110) ***(G-6042)***
Time Warner Cable Inc...714 871-2643
1565 S Harbor Blvd Fullerton (92832) ***(G-6043)***
Time Warner Cable Inc...818 700-6126
9260 Topanga Canyon Blvd Chatsworth (91311) ***(G-6044)***
Time Warner Cable Inc...424 529-6011
500 Lakewood Center Mall Lakewood (90712) ***(G-6045)***
Time Warner Cable Inc...626 705-7482
15255 Salt Lake Ave City of Industry (91745) ***(G-6046)***
Time Warner Cable Inc...760 256-3526
1881 W Main St Barstow (92311) ***(G-6047)***
Time Warner Cable Inc...323 993-8000
900 N Cahuenga Blvd Los Angeles (90038) ***(G-6048)***
Time Warner Cable Inc...310 647-3000
550 Continental Blvd # 250 El Segundo (90245) ***(G-6049)***
Time Warner Cable Inc...858 695-3110
8949 Ware Ct San Diego (92121) ***(G-6050)***
Time Warner Cable Inc...760 335-4800
313 N 8th St El Centro (92243) ***(G-6051)***
Time Warner Cable Inc...951 571-8738
12625 Frederick St F10 Moreno Valley (92553) ***(G-6052)***
Time Warner Inc...661 344-1546
2014 W Avenue K Lancaster (93536) ***(G-6053)***
Time Warner Inc...805 421-4467
2650 Tapo Canyon Rd Simi Valley (93063) ***(G-6054)***
Time Warner Media Sales, Cypress *Also called Spectrum MGT Holdg Co LLC* ***(G-6019)***
Timec Acquisitions Inc (HQ)...707 642-2222
155 Corporate Pl Vallejo (94590) ***(G-2091)***
Timec Companies Inc (HQ)...707 642-2222
155 Corporate Pl Vallejo (94590) ***(G-2092)***
Timelogic, Carlsbad *Also called Active Motif Inc* ***(G-26460)***
Timeshare Relief Inc...310 755-6434
2239 W 190th St Torrance (90504) ***(G-11941)***
Timesharerentorsell Com LLC...888 872-2517
1685 E Main St Ste 201 El Cajon (92021) ***(G-17532)***
Timmerman Starlite Trckg Inc...209 538-1706
3955 Starlite Dr Ceres (95307) ***(G-4071)***
Tinco Sheet Metal Inc...323 263-0511
958 N Eastern Ave Los Angeles (90063) ***(G-3220)***
Tintri Inc...650 810-8200
303 Ravendale Dr Mountain View (94043) ***(G-16263)***
Tire Centers LLC...909 854-1200
10516 Commerce Way # 875 Fontana (92337) ***(G-6791)***
Tireco Inc (PA)...310 767-7990
500 W 190th St Ste 100 Gardena (90248) ***(G-6792)***
Tishman Construction Corp Cal...213 542-6400
444 S Flower St Ste 2500 Los Angeles (90071) ***(G-27252)***
Tissue Repair Co, San Diego *Also called Cardium Biologics Inc* ***(G-26492)***
Titan Pulse Sciences Division, San Leandro *Also called Engility LLC* ***(G-25791)***
Titan Sheet Metal Inc...951 372-1362
180 Vander St Corona (92880) ***(G-3221)***
Titan Solar, Van Nuys *Also called Memeged Tevuot Shemesh* ***(G-2292)***
Title Records Inc...818 767-9610
8926 Sunland Blvd Sun Valley (91352) ***(G-11942)***
Tivo Solutions Inc (HQ)...408 519-9100
2160 Gold St Alviso (95002) ***(G-15505)***
Tj Cross Engineers Inc...661 831-8782
200 New Stine Rd Ste 270 Bakersfield (93309) ***(G-26100)***
Tjd LLC...209 357-3420
1685 Shaffer Rd Atwater (95301) ***(G-21391)***
Tk Carsites Inc...714 937-1239
2975 Red Hill Ave Ste 175 Costa Mesa (92626) ***(G-15506)***
Tka, La Palma *Also called Tech Knowledge Associates LLC* ***(G-18022)***
TLC of Bay Area Inc...408 988-7667
991 Clyde Ave Santa Clara (95054) ***(G-20990)***
Tlcs Inc...916 441-0123
650 Howe Ave Ste 400 Sacramento (95825) ***(G-24251)***
Tlg, Newark *Also called Lancashire Group Incorporated* ***(G-27504)***
Tm Financial Forensics LLC (PA)...415 692-6350
2 Embarcadero Ctr # 2510 San Francisco (94111) ***(G-28079)***
Tm Motion Picture Eqp Rentals, Culver City *Also called Mbs Equipment Company* ***(G-18234)***
Tmg Financial...925 989-0632
3478 Buskirk Ave Ste 1031 Pleasant Hill (94523) ***(G-27688)***
Tmp Worldwide Advertising & Co...818 539-2000
330 N Brand Blvd Ste 1050 Glendale (91203) ***(G-13928)***
TMT Industries Inc...909 770-8514
8978 Haven Ave Rancho Cucamonga (91730) ***(G-4277)***
Tmw Marketing, Brea *Also called Alta Resources Corp* ***(G-16983)***
Tnci Operating Company LLC (HQ)...800 800-8400
114 E Haley St Ste I Santa Barbara (93101) ***(G-5709)***
Tnppm North Stafford LLC...949 833-8252
1900 Main St Ste 700 Irvine (92614) ***(G-11063)***
TNT Express Worldwide, Los Angeles *Also called TNT USA Inc* ***(G-4872)***
TNT Grading Inc...760 736-4054
529 W 4th Ave B Escondido (92025) ***(G-1874)***
TNT Originals, Burbank *Also called Turner Broadcasting System Inc* ***(G-18173)***
TNT USA Inc...310 242-9700
8500 Osage Ave Los Angeles (90045) ***(G-4872)***
To Celerity Educational Group...323 231-7005
4501 Wadsworth Ave Los Angeles (90011) ***(G-28080)***
Toad 1350...951 369-1350
2030 Iowa Ave Ste A Riverside (92507) ***(G-5823)***
Tobin Lucks, Woodland Hills *Also called Joseph C Sansone Company* ***(G-23332)***
Todays Hotel Corporation (PA)...415 441-4000
1500 Van Ness Ave San Francisco (94109) ***(G-13347)***
Todays Vi LLC...909 980-2200
4760 Mills Cir Ontario (91764) ***(G-13348)***
Todd Plumbing Inc...559 651-5820
1701 Clancy Ct Visalia (93291) ***(G-2398)***
Tofasco of America Inc (PA)...909 392-8282
1661 Fairplex Dr La Verne (91750) ***(G-27253)***
Tog Landscaping Inc...323 549-3150
5057 W Washington Blvd Los Angeles (90016) ***(G-801)***
Toiyabe Indian Health Prj Inc (PA)...760 873-8461
250 N See Vee Ln Bishop (93514) ***(G-20280)***
Tokio Marine Management Inc...650 295-1180
1825 S Grant St Ste 570 San Mateo (94402) ***(G-10905)***
Tokio Marine Management Inc...626 568-7600
800 E Colorado Blvd Ste 8 Pasadena (91101) ***(G-10906)***
Toll Brothers Inc...925 855-0260
6800 Koll Center Pkwy # 320 Pleasanton (94566) ***(G-1273)***
Toll Brothers Division Office, Pleasanton *Also called Toll Brothers Inc* ***(G-1273)***
Toll Global Fwdg Americas...626 363-8600
780 Nogales St Ste D City of Industry (91748) ***(G-5246)***
Tollfreeforwarding.com, Los Angeles *Also called Ifncom Inc* ***(G-5634)***
Tollhouse Hotel, Los Gatos *Also called Trevi Partners A Calif LP* ***(G-13355)***
Tom Dreher Sales Inc...562 355-4074
2021 W 17th St Long Beach (90813) ***(G-7230)***
Tom Ferry Your Coach, Irvine *Also called Success Strategies Inst Inc* ***(G-24394)***
Tom Hom Investment Corp...858 456-5000
7660 Fay Ave Ste H La Jolla (92037) ***(G-11064)***
Tom Malloy Corporation (PA)...310 327-5554
636 E Rosecrans Ave Los Angeles (90059) ***(G-7793)***
Tom Ray, Sacramento *Also called T M Cobb Company* ***(G-6964)***
Tom Ray Industries Inc...949 380-8333
23052 Alcalde Dr Ste B Laguna Hills (92653) ***(G-6894)***
Tom Sawyer Camps Inc...626 794-1156
707 W Woodbury Rd Ste F Altadena (91001) ***(G-24526)***
Tomahawk Acquisition LLC...415 765-6500
150 California St Fl 19 San Francisco (94111) ***(G-12151)***
Tomarco Contractor Spc Inc (PA)...714 523-1771
14848 Northam St La Mirada (90638) ***(G-7701)***
Tomarco Fastening Systems, La Mirada *Also called Tomarco Contractor Spc Inc* ***(G-7701)***
Tomas Jewelry, Arcata *Also called Toucan Inc* ***(G-8103)***
Tomatoes Extraordinaire Inc...619 295-3172
1929 Hancock St Ste 150 San Diego (92110) ***(G-8937)***
Tommy Bahama Group Inc...805 482-8868
610 Ventura Blvd Ste 1340 Camarillo (93010) ***(G-17533)***
Tommy Bahama Group Inc...415 737-0400
1720 Redwood Hwy Spc A019 Corte Madera (94925) ***(G-17534)***
Tommy Bahama Group Inc...619 651-2200
4061 Camino De La Plz # 480 San Diego (92173) ***(G-17535)***
Tommy Gun Plastering Inc...909 795-9966
944 4th St Calimesa (92320) ***(G-2988)***
Tomra Recycling Network, Rancho Cucamonga *Also called Replanet LLC* ***(G-6536)***
Toms Truck Center Inc...714 835-1978
1008 E 4th St Santa Ana (92701) ***(G-17654)***
Toner Supply USA Inc...818 504-6540
8055 Lankershim Blvd # 11 North Hollywood (91605) ***(G-7201)***
Toni & Guy Hairdressing (PA)...949 721-1666
1177 Newport Center Dr Newport Beach (92660) ***(G-13692)***
Tonner Hills Hsing Partners LP...949 263-8676
17701 Cowan Ste 200 Irvine (92614) ***(G-1345)***
Tonopah Solar Energy LLC...310 315-2200
520 Broadway Fl 6 Santa Monica (90401) ***(G-2399)***
Tony Gomez Tree Service...619 593-1552
700 N Johnson Ave Ste H El Cajon (92020) ***(G-999)***
Tony La Russas Animal RES Fnd...925 256-1273
2890 Mitchell Dr Walnut Creek (94598) ***(G-625)***
Tony Marquez Pool Plst Inc...818 767-5177
14960 Foothill Blvd Sylmar (91342) ***(G-2989)***
Tony R Crisalli Inc...951 727-0110
3468 Campbell St Riverside (92509) ***(G-14500)***
Tonys Express Inc (PA)...909 427-8700
10613 Jasmine St Fontana (92337) ***(G-4278)***
Tonys Fine Foods (HQ)...916 374-4000
3575 Reed Ave West Sacramento (95605) ***(G-8688)***
Too Good Gourmet Inc...510 317-8150
2380 Grant Ave San Lorenzo (94580) ***(G-8938)***
Toolwire Inc (PA)...925 227-8500
7031 Koll Center Pkwy # 220 Pleasanton (94566) ***(G-15507)***
Toolworks Inc...510 649-1322
3075 Adeline St Ste 230 Berkeley (94703) ***(G-24252)***
Toolworks Inc (PA)...415 733-0990
25 Kearny St Ste 400 San Francisco (94108) ***(G-24396)***
Toot Sweets Fine Desserts, Berkeley *Also called Toot Sweets Ltd* ***(G-8939)***
Toot Sweets Ltd (PA)...510 526-0610
1277 Gilman St Berkeley (94706) ***(G-8939)***
Top Finance Company, Canoga Park *Also called Platinum Group Companies Inc* ***(G-12084)***
Top Notch Security...818 528-2875
4312 Woodman Ave Ste 202 Sherman Oaks (91423) ***(G-16833)***

ALPHABETIC

Top of Market...619 234-4867
750 N Harbor Dr San Diego (92101) *(G-27254)*
Top Priority Couriers Inc (PA)...951 781-1000
1257 Columbia Ave Ste D1 Riverside (92507) *(G-4429)*
Top Seed Tennis Academy Inc...818 222-2782
23400 Park Sorrento Calabasas (91302) *(G-19295)*
Top Tier Consulting...818 338-2121
21550 Oxnard St Fl 3 Woodland Hills (91367) *(G-27689)*
Topa Berkeley Ltd...310 203-9199
1800 Avenue Of The Stars Los Angeles (90067) *(G-11877)*
Topa Insurance Company (HQ)...310 201-0451
1800 Ave Of Stars # 1200 Los Angeles (90067) *(G-10573)*
Topa Management Company (PA)...310 203-9199
1800 Avenue Of The Stars # 1400 Los Angeles (90067) *(G-11065)*
Topanga Villas Company...818 884-8017
5807 Topanga Canyon Blvd Woodland Hills (91367) *(G-11214)*
Topbuild Services Group Corp...408 882-0411
1341 Old Oakland Rd San Jose (95112) *(G-3590)*
Topco Sales, Simi Valley *Also called Wsm Investments LLC (G-12231)*
Topdown Consulting Inc...888 644-8445
530 Divisadero St Ste 310 San Francisco (94117) *(G-27690)*
Topica Inc...415 344-0800
1 Post St Ste 875 San Francisco (94104) *(G-5710)*
Tops Auto Parks, Los Angeles *Also called Paramunt Contrs Developers Inc (G-11738)*
Topson Downs California Inc (PA)...310 558-0300
3840 Watseka Ave Culver City (90232) *(G-8414)*
Topstar Floral Inc...805 984-7972
4255 W Gonzales Rd Oxnard (93036) *(G-323)*
Topwin Corporation (PA)...310 325-2255
1808 Abalone Ave Torrance (90501) *(G-8362)*
Toro Enterprises Inc...805 483-4515
2101 E Ventura Blvd Oxnard (93036) *(G-1875)*
Toro Nursery Inc...310 715-1982
17585 Crenshaw Blvd Torrance (90504) *(G-9221)*
Torrance Care Center West Inc...310 370-4561
4333 Torrance Blvd Torrance (90503) *(G-20991)*
Torrance Health Assn Inc (PA)...310 325-9110
23550 Hawthorne Blvd Torrance (90505) *(G-21968)*
Torrance Hilton At South Bay, Torrance *Also called Ctc Group Inc (G-12055)*
Torrance Hospital IPA...310 784-0800
23600 Telo Ave Torrance (90505) *(G-21969)*
Torrance Marriott Hotel, Torrance *Also called Xld Group LLC (G-13444)*
Torrance Memorial Medical Ctr (HQ)...310 325-9110
3330 Lomita Blvd Torrance (90505) *(G-21970)*
Torrance Surgery Center LP...310 784-5880
23560 Crenshaw Blvd # 104 Torrance (90505) *(G-20138)*
Torrence Family Practice...310 542-0455
20911 Earl St Ste 440 Torrance (90503) *(G-20139)*
Torres Construction Corp (PA)...323 257-7460
7330 N Figueroa St Los Angeles (90041) *(G-1474)*
Torres Fence Co Inc...559 237-4141
2357 S Orange Ave Fresno (93725) *(G-3591)*
Torres General Inc...619 448-8900
9484 Mission Park Pl Santee (92071) *(G-1274)*
Torres-Martinez...760 395-1200
3089 Norm Niver Rd Thermal (92274) *(G-13349)*
Torrey Pines Bank (HQ)...858 523-4600
12220 El Camino Real # 200 San Diego (92130) *(G-9530)*
Torrey Pines Institute For MO...858 455-3803
3550 General Atomics Ct San Diego (92121) *(G-26814)*
Toscana, Palm Desert *Also called Sunrise Desert Partners (G-12016)*
Toscana Country Club, Palm Desert *Also called Toscana Homes LP (G-1346)*
Toscana Country Club Inc...760 404-1444
76009 Via Club Villa Indian Wells (92210) *(G-19111)*
Toscana Homes LP...760 772-7227
300 Eagle Dance Cir Palm Desert (92211) *(G-1346)*
Toscana Land LLC...760 772-7200
300 Eagle Dance Cir Palm Desert (92211) *(G-12019)*
Toshiba Amer Bus Solutions Inc (HQ)...949 462-6000
9740 Irvine Blvd Irvine (92618) *(G-7073)*
Toshiba Amer Med Systems Inc (HQ)...714 730-5000
2441 Michelle Dr Tustin (92780) *(G-7319)*
Toshiba Bus Solutions USA Inc (HQ)...949 462-6000
9740 Irvine Blvd Irvine (92618) *(G-17947)*
Toshiba Education Center...949 583-3000
9740 Irvine Blvd Irvine (92618) *(G-26713)*
Toshiba Medical Systems, Tustin *Also called Toshiba Amer Med Systems Inc (G-7319)*
Toshiba TEC America Retail Inf (HQ)...949 462-2850
2 Musick Irvine (92618) *(G-7074)*
Tosoh Bioscience Inc...650 615-4970
6000 Shoreline Ct Ste 101 South San Francisco (94080) *(G-7320)*
Tosoh USA, South San Francisco *Also called Tosoh Bioscience Inc (G-7320)*
Total Airport Services Inc...650 358-0144
3537 Branson Dr San Mateo (94403) *(G-4946)*
Total Building Care Inc...562 467-8333
21228 Norwalk Blvd Hawaiian Gardens (90716) *(G-1693)*
TOTAL CLEAN, La Verne *Also called Haaker Equipment Company (G-6679)*
Total Defense Inc...408 598-4299
100 W San Fernando St # 565 San Jose (95113) *(G-15862)*
Total Drywall Inc...951 279-0044
2867 Sampson Ave Corona (92879) *(G-2990)*
Total Education Solutions Inc (PA)...323 341-5580
625 Fair Oaks Ave Ste 300 South Pasadena (91030) *(G-28081)*
Total Immersion, Los Angeles *Also called Dfusion Software Inc (G-15135)*
Total Intermodal Services Inc (PA)...562 427-6300
2396 E Sepulveda Blvd Long Beach (90810) *(G-4763)*
Total Professional Network...213 382-5550
3275 Wilshire Blvd # 100 Los Angeles (90010) *(G-14805)*
Total Quality Maintenance Inc...650 846-4700
895 Commercial St Palo Alto (94303) *(G-14445)*
Total Quality Staffing Service, City of Industry *Also called Tq Inc (G-14806)*
Total Renal Care Inc...925 737-0120
5720 Stoneridge Mall Rd # 160 Pleasanton (94588) *(G-22643)*
Total Renal Care Inc...949 930-6882
15253 Bake Pkwy Irvine (92618) *(G-22644)*
Total Renal Care Inc...707 556-3637
125 Corporate Pl Ste C Vallejo (94590) *(G-22645)*
Total Renal Care Inc...760 947-7405
14135 Main St Ste 501 Hesperia (92345) *(G-22646)*
Total Source Enviromental Inc...619 822-8518
306 W El Norte Pkwy Ste 5 Escondido (92026) *(G-1347)*
Total Tire Recycling, Sacramento *Also called AAA Signs Inc (G-17779)*
Total Trnsp & Dist Inc...310 603-0467
1551 E Victoria St Carson (90746) *(G-4381)*
Total Trnsp Logistics Inc...951 360-9521
4325 Etiwanda Ave Ste A Mira Loma (91752) *(G-4279)*
Total Woman...714 993-6003
860 N Rose Dr Placentia (92870) *(G-18700)*
Total Woman - Glendale, Glendale *Also called Spad Holdings LLC (G-18694)*
Total Woman - Irvine, Irvine *Also called Spad Holdings LLC (G-18691)*
Total Woman - Northridge, Northridge *Also called Spad Holdings LLC (G-18693)*
Total Woman - Placentia, Placentia *Also called Spad Holdings LLC (G-18690)*
Total Woman - Warner Center, Woodland Hills *Also called Spad Holdings LLC (G-18692)*
Total Woman - Westlake Village, Westlake Village *Also called Spad Holdings LLC (G-18688)*
Total-Western Inc...661 589-5200
2811 Fruitvale Ave Ste A Bakersfield (93308) *(G-1348)*
Total-Western Inc (HQ)...562 220-1450
8049 Somerset Blvd Paramount (90723) *(G-1097)*
Totally Kids Rhbilitation Hosp, Loma Linda *Also called Mountain View Child Care Inc (G-21757)*
Totally Kids Spcalty Hlth Care, Sun Valley *Also called Mountain View Child Care Inc (G-24484)*
Totallyfreepagingcom Inc...310 845-8700
10000 Culver Blvd Culver City (90232) *(G-5420)*
Totten Tubes Inc (PA)...626 812-0220
500 W Danlee St Azusa (91702) *(G-7408)*
Toucan Inc (PA)...707 822-6662
1275 8th St Arcata (95521) *(G-8103)*
Touchstone Television Prod LLC (PA)...323 671-5116
500 S Buena Vista St Burbank (91521) *(G-18169)*
Tough2beat Auto Sales, Granada Hills *Also called Errama Trucking Company Inc (G-4146)*
Tour Master, Calabasas Hills *Also called Helmet House Inc (G-8345)*
Tourdates.com, San Francisco *Also called Launch Media Inc (G-5646)*
Toward Maximum Independence (PA)...858 467-0600
4740 Murphy Canyon Rd # 300 San Diego (92123) *(G-24253)*
Towbes Group Inc (PA)...805 962-2121
21 E Victoria St Ste 200 Santa Barbara (93101) *(G-12020)*
Tower Car Wash, San Francisco *Also called Vladigor Investment Inc (G-17865)*
Tower Energy Group (PA)...310 538-8000
1983 W 190th St Ste 100 Torrance (90504) *(G-9028)*
Tower Glass Inc...619 596-6199
9570 Pathway St Ste A Santee (92071) *(G-3416)*
Tower Hematology Oncology Medi...310 888-8680
9090 Wilshire Blvd # 200 Beverly Hills (90211) *(G-20140)*
Tower Park Marina, Lodi *Also called Westrec Marina Management Inc (G-4773)*
Tower St John Imaging, Los Angeles *Also called Santa Mnica Wlshire Imging LLC (G-22278)*
Towers Perrin, Los Angeles *Also called Towers Watson Pennsylvania Inc (G-27692)*
Towers Watson & Co...415 733-4100
345 California St Fl 15 San Francisco (94104) *(G-27691)*
Towers Watson Pennsylvania Inc...310 551-5600
300 S Grand Ave Ste 2000 Los Angeles (90071) *(G-27692)*
Towmaster Tire & Wheel, Anaheim *Also called Greenball Corp (G-6786)*
Town & Country Event Rentals (PA)...818 908-4211
7725 Airport Bus Pkwy Van Nuys (91406) *(G-14584)*
Town & Country Event Rentals...805 770-5729
1 N Calle Cesar Chavez # 7 Santa Barbara (93103) *(G-17536)*
Town & Country Manor of The Ch...714 547-7581
555 E Memory Ln Ofc Ofc Santa Ana (92706) *(G-20992)*
Town & Country Roofing, Brentwood *Also called T&C Roofing Inc (G-3217)*
Town Cats Morgan Hill Rescue...408 779-5761
195 San Pedro Ave Ste B Morgan Hill (95037) *(G-646)*
Town of Danville...925 314-3400
420 Front St Danville (94526) *(G-19296)*
Towne Inc...714 540-3095
3441 W Macarthur Blvd Santa Ana (92704) *(G-14093)*
Towne Advertising, Santa Ana *Also called Towne Inc (G-14093)*
Towne Construction Inc...619 390-4557
12115 Lakeside Ave Lakeside (92040) *(G-2991)*
TownePlace Suites...408 370-4510
700 E Campbell Ave Campbell (95008) *(G-13350)*
TownePlace Suites By Marriott, Campbell *Also called TownePlace Suites (G-13350)*
Towns End Studios LLC...415 802-7936
699 8th St San Francisco (94103) *(G-15508)*
Townsend and Townsend, Menlo Park *Also called Kilpatrick Twnsend Stckton LLP (G-23350)*
Toyo Tire USA Corp...562 431-6502
2151 S Vintage Ave Ontario (91761) *(G-6793)*
Toyon Research Corporation (PA)...805 968-6787
6800 Cortona Dr Goleta (93117) *(G-26101)*
Toyota Logistics Services...619 531-0157
1340 Cesar E Chavez Pkwy San Diego (92113) *(G-17897)*
Toyota Logistics Services (HQ)...310 618-5009
19001 S Western Ave Torrance (90501) *(G-17898)*
Toyota Logistics Services...562 437-6767
785 Edison Ave Long Beach (90813) *(G-17899)*

Toyota Logistics Services.......510 498-7817
45250 Fremont Blvd Fremont (94538) ***(G-17900)***
Toyota Material Hdlg Nthrn Cal, Hayward *Also called Rjms Corporation* ***(G-7883)***
Toyota Motor Credit Corp.......925 830-8200
4000 Executive Pkwy # 525 San Ramon (94583) ***(G-9765)***
Toyota Motor Sales USA Inc (HQ).......310 468-4000
19001 S Western Ave Torrance (90501) ***(G-9804)***
Toyota Motor Sales USA Inc.......310 468-7626
19340 Van Ness Ave Torrance (90501) ***(G-9805)***
Toyota-Sunnyvale Inc (PA).......408 245-6640
898 W El Camino Real Sunnyvale (94087) ***(G-17818)***
TP USA, Claremont *Also called Technip Usa Inc* ***(G-26087)***
Tp-Link USA Corporation.......562 528-7700
3760 Kilroy Airport Way Long Beach (90806) ***(G-7202)***
TPC Stonebrea, Hayward *Also called Stonebrae LP* ***(G-19097)***
Tpd Dell Dios.......760 741-2888
1817 Avenida Del Diablo Escondido (92029) ***(G-24254)***
Tpg La Commerce LLC.......401 946-4600
5757 Telegraph Rd Commerce (90040) ***(G-13351)***
Tpg Reflections II LLC.......213 613-1900
515 S Flower St Los Angeles (90071) ***(G-11215)***
Tpg/Calstrs, Los Angeles *Also called Tpg Reflections II LLC* ***(G-11215)***
Tps Aviation Inc (PA).......510 475-1010
1515 Crocker Ave Hayward (94544) ***(G-8007)***
Tps Parking Management LLC.......310 846-4747
9101 S Sepulveda Blvd Los Angeles (90045) ***(G-17744)***
Tq Inc (PA).......562 908-9655
13191 Crocaroad Pkwy N Ste 143 City of Industry (91746) ***(G-14806)***
Tr Warner Center LP.......818 887-4800
21850 Oxnard St Woodland Hills (91367) ***(G-13352)***
Trace3 Inc.......310 220-0164
2120 E Grand Ave Ste 145 El Segundo (90245) ***(G-27693)***
Trace3 Inc (PA).......949 333-1801
7565 Irvine Center Dr # 200 Irvine (92618) ***(G-27694)***
Tracy Dlta Solid Waste Mgt Inc.......209 835-0601
30703 S Macarthur Dr Tracy (95377) ***(G-6570)***
Tracy Industries, City of Industry *Also called Genuine Parts Distributors* ***(G-6733)***
Tracy Interfaith Ministries.......209 836-5424
311 W Grant Line Rd Tracy (95376) ***(G-24255)***
Tracy Medical Offices, Tracy *Also called Kaiser Foundation Hospitals* ***(G-19596)***
Tracy Sutter Community Hosp.......209 835-1500
1420 N Tracy Blvd Tracy (95376) ***(G-21971)***
Tracy Trujillo MD.......925 838-6511
200 Porter Dr Ste 300 San Ramon (94583) ***(G-20141)***
Trade Desk Inc (PA).......805 585-3434
42 N Chestnut St Ventura (93001) ***(G-13929)***
Trade Services E2002-031, El Monte *Also called Wells Fargo Bank National Assn* ***(G-9440)***
Tradebeam Inc.......650 653-4800
303 Twin Dolphin Dr # 600 Redwood City (94065) ***(G-16509)***
Tradecom Med Transcription Inc.......408 225-9200
363 Piercy Rd San Jose (95138) ***(G-7321)***
Tradeshift Holdings Inc (HQ).......800 381-3585
612 Howard St Ste 100 San Francisco (94105) ***(G-12094)***
Tradewind Seafood Inc.......805 483-8555
1505 Mountain View Ave Oxnard (93030) ***(G-8658)***
Tradewinds Lodge (PA).......707 964-4761
400 S Main St Fort Bragg (95437) ***(G-13353)***
Tradewinds Lodge Partnership, Sacramento *Also called Tradewinds Partnership* ***(G-13354)***
Tradewinds Partnership.......916 333-5239
2920 Arden Way Ste F1 Sacramento (95825) ***(G-13354)***
Tradeworld.com, Long Beach *Also called Wsc America* ***(G-5191)***
Trading America Corp.......786 842-7888
535 N Brand Blvd Ste 275 Glendale (91203) ***(G-27695)***
TRADITION GOLF CLUB, La Quinta *Also called Chapman Golf Development LLC* ***(G-18721)***
Tradition Golf Club Associates.......760 564-3355
78505 Avenue 52 La Quinta (92253) ***(G-19112)***
Traditions Golf LLC.......408 323-5200
23600 Mckean Rd San Jose (95141) ***(G-18795)***
Traffic Management Inc.......562 264-2353
1244 S Claudina St Anaheim (92805) ***(G-27255)***
Traffic Management Inc.......916 394-2200
5806 Perrin Ave McClellan (95652) ***(G-27256)***
Traffic Management Inc (PA).......562 595-4278
2435 Lemon Ave Signal Hill (90755) ***(G-17537)***
Traffic Tech Inc.......800 396-2531
910 Hale Pl Ste 100 Chula Vista (91914) ***(G-5174)***
Traffic Tech Inc (HQ).......514 343-0044
910 Hale Pl Ste 100 Chula Vista (91914) ***(G-5175)***
Trail Lines Inc.......562 758-6980
9415 Sorensen Ave Santa Fe Springs (90670) ***(G-4072)***
Trailblazer Technologies.......818 848-6500
4100 W Burbank Blvd Fl 3 Burbank (91505) ***(G-17538)***
Trailer Park Inc.......831 462-3271
4300 Soquel Dr Spc 90 Soquel (95073) ***(G-13485)***
Trailer Park Inc.......310 845-8400
6922 Hollywood Blvd # 1200 Los Angeles (90028) ***(G-13930)***
Trailer Park Inc (PA).......310 845-3000
6922 Hollywood Blvd Fl 12 Los Angeles (90028) ***(G-13931)***
Traina Dried Fruit Inc.......209 892-5472
337 1/2 Lemon Ave Patterson (95363) ***(G-8940)***
Traina Foods, Patterson *Also called Traina Dried Fruit Inc* ***(G-8940)***
Training Toward Self Reliance.......916 442-8877
620 Bercut Dr Sacramento (95811) ***(G-24256)***
Trams Inc (HQ).......310 641-8726
5777 W Century Blvd # 1200 Los Angeles (90045) ***(G-16067)***
Trandes Corp.......619 398-0464
4250 Pacific Hwy Ste 209 San Diego (92110) ***(G-26102)***
Trane US Inc.......916 577-1100
4145 Delmar Ave Ste 2 Rocklin (95677) ***(G-7748)***

Tranquility Incorporated.......925 825-4280
1050 San Miguel Rd Concord (94518) ***(G-21392)***
Trans West Investigations Inc.......213 381-1500
3255 Wilshire Blvd Los Angeles (90010) ***(G-16834)***
Trans World Maintenance Inc.......650 455-2450
1590 Rollins Rd Millbrae (94030) ***(G-2498)***
Trans-Pak Incorporated (PA).......408 254-0500
520 Marburg Way San Jose (95133) ***(G-17539)***
Trans-Pak Incorporated.......858 292-9094
8710 Avenida De La Fuente San Diego (92154) ***(G-5204)***
Trans-Pak Incorporated.......310 618-6937
2111 Abalone Ave Torrance (90501) ***(G-17540)***
Trans-West Security Svcs Inc.......661 381-2900
8503 Crippen St Bakersfield (93311) ***(G-16835)***
Transamerica Cbo I Inc.......415 983-4000
600 Montgomery St Fl 16 San Francisco (94111) ***(G-10189)***
Transamerica Finance Corp.......714 778-5100
1731 W Medical Center Dr Anaheim (92801) ***(G-10224)***
Transamerica Intl Holdings.......415 983-4000
600 Montgomery St Fl 16 San Francisco (94111) ***(G-12095)***
Transamerica Securities Sales.......213 741-7702
1150 S Olive St Ste T25 Los Angeles (90015) ***(G-10083)***
Transamerican Auto Parts, Banning *Also called Poison Spyder Customs Inc* ***(G-17889)***
Transbay Fire Protection Inc (PA).......925 846-9484
2182 Rheem Dr Pleasanton (94588) ***(G-3481)***
Transcription Company, The, Burbank *Also called Trailblazer Technologies* ***(G-17538)***
Transdev Services Inc.......951 943-1371
110 S G St Perris (92570) ***(G-3850)***
Transdev Services Inc.......626 357-7912
5640 Peck Rd Arcadia (91006) ***(G-3851)***
Transer America, Torrance *Also called Timeshare Relief Inc* ***(G-11941)***
Transforce Inc.......209 952-2573
965 E Yosemite Ave Ste 7 Manteca (95336) ***(G-14960)***
Transiris Corporation.......650 303-3495
900 Industrial Rd Ste B San Carlos (94070) ***(G-27696)***
Transit Air Cargo Inc.......714 571-0393
2204 E 4th St Santa Ana (92705) ***(G-5176)***
Transitamerica Services Inc.......760 430-0770
1 Coaster Way Camp Pendleton (92055) ***(G-3729)***
Transition Connection.......916 481-3470
2740 Fulton Ave Ste 101 Sacramento (95821) ***(G-17541)***
Transitional Assistance Dept, Yucca Valley *Also called County of San Bernardino* ***(G-23895)***
Transitions - Mental Hlth Assn.......805 614-4940
117 W Tunnell St Santa Maria (93458) ***(G-22852)***
Transitions - Mental Hlth Assn (PA).......805 540-6500
784 High St San Luis Obispo (93401) ***(G-24257)***
Transitworks, Irvine *Also called Gkk Works* ***(G-27038)***
Transmerica Fincl Advisors Inc.......213 741-7702
1150 S Olive St Ste T250 Los Angeles (90015) ***(G-10084)***
TransMontaigne PDT Svcs LLC.......415 576-2000
555 California St # 2100 San Francisco (94104) ***(G-5247)***
Transmrcan Mling Flfllment Inc.......760 745-5343
355 State Pl Escondido (92029) ***(G-14094)***
Transmrica Occidental Lf Insur (HQ).......213 742-2111
1150 S Olive St Fl 23 Los Angeles (90015) ***(G-10225)***
Transpac, Vacaville *Also called Valyria LLC* ***(G-6902)***
Transpac Inc.......707 452-0600
1050 Piper Dr Vacaville (95688) ***(G-6895)***
Transpacific Management Svc.......949 248-2822
647 Camino De Los Mares # 230 San Clemente (92673) ***(G-11878)***
Transpacific Management Svc.......714 285-2626
15661 Red Hill Ave # 205 Tustin (92780) ***(G-11879)***
Transpak Los Angeles, Torrance *Also called Trans-Pak Incorporated* ***(G-17540)***
Transport Drivers Inc.......800 497-6345
620 N Dmnd Bar Blvd Ste B Diamond Bar (91765) ***(G-14961)***
Transport Drivers Inc.......909 937-3312
2131 S Grove Ave Ste D Ontario (91761) ***(G-14962)***
Transport Express Inc.......310 898-2000
19801 S Santa Fe Ave Compton (90221) ***(G-4382)***
Transportation, Lodi *Also called Lodi Unified School District* ***(G-3943)***
Transportation Branch, Los Angeles *Also called Los Angeles Unified School Dst* ***(G-3961)***
Transportation Bureau, Los Angeles *Also called County of Los Angeles* ***(G-5216)***
Transportation California Dept.......707 762-6641
611 Payran St Petaluma (94952) ***(G-1876)***
Transportation California Dept.......530 225-3349
1490 George Dr Redding (96003) ***(G-963)***
Transportation California Dept.......562 692-0823
1940 Workman Mill Rd Whittier (90601) ***(G-1877)***
Transportation California Dept.......707 428-2031
2019 W Texas St Fairfield (94533) ***(G-1878)***
Transportation Chrtr Svcs Inc.......714 396-0346
1931 N Batavia St Orange (92865) ***(G-3909)***
Transportation Concept Inc.......323 268-2202
1521 Kingsdale Ave Redondo Beach (90278) ***(G-3730)***
Transportation Department, Berkeley *Also called Berkeley Unified School Dst* ***(G-3913)***
Transportation Department, Sacramento *Also called Elk Grove Unified School Dst* ***(G-3925)***
Transportation Department, Long Beach *Also called Long Beach Unified School Dst* ***(G-3944)***
Transportation Department, Santa Clarita *Also called Saugus Union School District* ***(G-3949)***
Transportation Dept, Ukiah *Also called County of Mendocino* ***(G-6624)***
Transportation Management LLC.......310 524-1555
880 Apollo St Ste 235 El Segundo (90245) ***(G-4073)***
Transprttion Corridor Agencies, Irvine *Also called San Joaquin Hills Transporttn* ***(G-1855)***
Transtar Automotive, Van Nuys *Also called Transtar Industries Inc* ***(G-6777)***
Transtar Industries Inc.......818 785-2000
15010 Calvert St Van Nuys (91411) ***(G-6777)***
Transwest San Diego LLC.......858 450-0707
6066 Miramar Rd San Diego (92121) ***(G-4383)***

ALPHABETIC

Transwestern Corp Pointe LLC....310 642-1001
600 Crprate Pinte Ste 250 Culver City (90230) ***(G-11880)***
Trap....626 572-5610
9040 Telstar Ave Ste 115 El Monte (91731) ***(G-17542)***
Trapac LLC (HQ)....310 513-1572
630 W Harry Bridges Blvd Wilmington (90744) ***(G-4764)***
Travana Inc....415 919-4140
600 Townsend St Fl 5 San Francisco (94103) ***(G-4976)***
Travel Store....805 987-3425
4980 Verdugo Way Camarillo (93012) ***(G-4977)***
Travel Store....714 529-1947
633 S Brea Blvd Brea (92821) ***(G-4978)***
Travel Store (PA)....310 575-5540
11601 Wilshire Blvd Los Angeles (90025) ***(G-4979)***
Travel Syndicate....818 297-9979
350 S Beverly Dr Ste 170 Beverly Hills (90212) ***(G-4980)***
Travelers Club Luggage Inc....714 523-8808
5911 Fresca Dr Ste B La Palma (90623) ***(G-8143)***
Travelers Indemnity Company....909 612-3000
21688 Gateway Center Dr # 300 Diamond Bar (91765) ***(G-10907)***
Travelers Insurance, Diamond Bar *Also called Travelers Indemnity Company* ***(G-10907)***
Travelers Insurance, Walnut Creek *Also called Travelers Property Cslty Corp* ***(G-10908)***
Travelers Insurance, Brea *Also called Travelers Property Cslty Corp* ***(G-10909)***
Travelers Property Cslty Corp....925 945-4000
205 Lennon Ln Walnut Creek (94598) ***(G-10908)***
Travelers Property Cslty Corp....714 671-8000
145 S State College Blvd # 240 Brea (92821) ***(G-10909)***
Travelmasters Inc....916 722-1648
8350 Auburn Blvd Ste 200 Citrus Heights (95610) ***(G-4981)***
Travelodge, Los Angeles *Also called Airport Century Inn* ***(G-12376)***
Travelstore, Camarillo *Also called Travel Store* ***(G-4977)***
Travelstore, Los Angeles *Also called Travel Store* ***(G-4979)***
Travelzoo Usa Inc....650 316-6956
800 W El Camino Re Mountain View (94040) ***(G-13983)***
Travers Tree Service Inc....310 545-5816
1811 Lomita Blvd Lomita (90717) ***(G-486)***
Travidia Inc (PA)....530 343-6400
265 Airpark Blvd Ste 500 Chico (95973) ***(G-15863)***
Travis Credit Union....707 449-4000
1300 E Covell Blvd Davis (95616) ***(G-9632)***
Travis Credit Union....800 877-8328
1796 Tuolumne St Vallejo (94589) ***(G-9633)***
Travis Credit Union....800 877-8328
1257 Willow Pass Rd Concord (94520) ***(G-9634)***
Travis Credit Union....800 877-8328
3263 Claremont Way NAPA (94558) ***(G-9635)***
Travis Credit Union (PA)....707 449-4000
1 Travis Way Vacaville (95687) ***(G-9636)***
Travis Credit Union....916 443-1446
1515 K St Sacramento (95814) ***(G-9637)***
Travis Credit Union....209 723-0732
1194 W Olive Ave Merced (95348) ***(G-9638)***
Travis Credit Union....925 777-0573
5819 Lone Tree Way Ste A Antioch (94531) ***(G-9639)***
Travis Credit Union....707 449-4000
11 Cernon St Vacaville (95688) ***(G-9640)***
Travis Credit Union....707 449-4000
2570 N Texas St Fairfield (94533) ***(G-9641)***
Travis Credit Union....800 877-8328
1372 E Main St Woodland (95776) ***(G-9642)***
Travis Credit Union....707 449-4000
2020 Harbison Dr Vacaville (95687) ***(G-9643)***
TRC Pleasanton Dialysis Cntr, Pleasanton *Also called Total Renal Care Inc* ***(G-22643)***
TRC Solutions Inc (HQ)....949 753-0101
9685 Research Dr Ste 100 Irvine (92618) ***(G-28082)***
Treadwell & Rollo Inc (HQ)....415 955-9040
555 Montgomery St # 1300 San Francisco (94111) ***(G-26103)***
Treasure Island Yacht Club....925 939-0230
2333 Lariat Ln Walnut Creek (94596) ***(G-19113)***
Treasurer/Tax Collector, Alturas *Also called County of Modoc* ***(G-17099)***
Treasury Wine Estates Americas....805 237-6000
7000 E Highway 46 Paso Robles (93446) ***(G-190)***
Tree Sculpture Group....510 562-4000
463 Roland Way Oakland (94621) ***(G-964)***
Treebeard Landscape Inc....619 697-8302
9917 Campo Rd Spring Valley (91977) ***(G-965)***
Treefrog Developments Inc....619 324-7755
15110 Ave Of Science San Diego (92128) ***(G-8144)***
Treeline and Associates....909 476-2757
9330 Baseline Rd Ste 106 Rancho Cucamonga (91701) ***(G-27697)***
Treepeople Inc....818 753-4600
12601 Mulholland Dr Beverly Hills (90210) ***(G-1000)***
Trees Apartments LLC....408 848-6400
7030 Eigleberry St Gilroy (95020) ***(G-11216)***
Trellisware Technologies Inc....858 753-1600
16516 Via Esprillo # 300 San Diego (92127) ***(G-5421)***
Trench Shoring Company, Los Angeles *Also called Tom Malloy Corporation* ***(G-7793)***
Trend Micro Incorporated....408 257-1500
10101 N De Anza Blvd Cupertino (95014) ***(G-7203)***
Trendex Corporation....818 407-9600
9353 Eton Ave Chatsworth (91311) ***(G-1694)***
Trendnet Inc (PA)....310 961-5500
20675 Manhattan Pl Torrance (90501) ***(G-7204)***
Trendnet Company, Torrance *Also called Trendnet Inc* ***(G-7204)***
Trendsettah Usa Inc....888 775-4881
25950 Acero Ste 210 Mission Viejo (92691) ***(G-8145)***
Trendshift LLC....866 644-8877
435 N Oakhurst Dr Beverly Hills (90210) ***(G-15509)***
Trendsource Inc....619 718-7467
4891 Pacific Hwy Ste 200 San Diego (92110) ***(G-26714)***
Trepco Imports & Dist Ltd....619 690-7999
1626 Frontage Rd Chula Vista (91911) ***(G-9236)***
Tressler LLP....949 336-1200
2 Park Plz Ste 1050 Irvine (92614) ***(G-23597)***
Trevi Partners A Calif LP....408 395-7070
140 S Santa Cruz Ave Los Gatos (95030) ***(G-13355)***
Trevi Partners A Calif LP (HQ)....925 828-7750
6680 Regional St Dublin (94568) ***(G-13356)***
Trevi Partners A Calif LP....831 624-1841
3665 Rio Rd Carmel (93923) ***(G-13357)***
Trevi Partners A Calif LP (PA)....925 225-4000
5955 Coronado Ln Pleasanton (94588) ***(G-13358)***
Trex Partners LLC....858 646-5300
10455 Pacific Center Ct San Diego (92121) ***(G-12096)***
Trg Inc....310 396-6750
1350 Abbot Kinney Blvd # 101 Venice (90291) ***(G-11881)***
Tri - Star Win Coverings Inc....818 718-3188
19555 Prairie St Northridge (91324) ***(G-6896)***
Tri Alpha Energy Inc....949 830-2117
27121 Towne Centre Dr # 150 Foothill Ranch (92610) ***(G-26623)***
Tri Ced Community Recycling, Union City *Also called Tri-City Economic Dev Corp* ***(G-6571)***
Tri City Emergency Med Group....760 439-1963
5050 Avenida Encinas # 200 Carlsbad (92008) ***(G-26452)***
Tri City Mental Health Center....909 784-3200
1900 Royalty Dr Pomona (91767) ***(G-22853)***
Tri City Orthopedic Sgy & Mdcl....760 724-9000
3905 Waring Rd Oceanside (92056) ***(G-20142)***
Tri Counties Bank (HQ)....530 898-0300
63 Constitution Dr Chico (95973) ***(G-9562)***
Tri Counties Bank....530 478-6001
305 Railroad Ave Ste 1 Nevada City (95959) ***(G-9563)***
Tri County Regional Center....805 485-3177
2220 E Gonzales Rd 210a Oxnard (93036) ***(G-20359)***
Tri County Respite Care Svc....530 755-3500
1215 Plumas St Ste 1600 Yuba City (95991) ***(G-24258)***
Tri Pointe Homes Inc (HQ)....949 438-1400
19520 Jamboree Rd Ste 300 Irvine (92612) ***(G-1386)***
Tri Valley Vegetable Harvstg....805 928-2727
123 N Depot St Santa Maria (93458) ***(G-502)***
Tri Valley Wholesale, Fairfield *Also called Tri-Valley Supply Inc* ***(G-7022)***
Tri-Ad Actuaries Inc....760 743-7555
221 W Crest St Ste 300 Escondido (92025) ***(G-10910)***
Tri-City Economic Dev Corp....510 429-8030
33377 Western Ave Union City (94587) ***(G-6571)***
Tri-City Health Center (PA)....510 770-8040
39500 Liberty St Fremont (94538) ***(G-20143)***
Tri-City Home Care Services....760 940-5800
2095 W Vista Way Ste 220 Vista (92083) ***(G-22582)***
Tri-City Hospital District (PA)....760 724-8411
4002 Vista Way Oceanside (92056) ***(G-21972)***
TRI-CITY MEDICAL CENTER, Oceanside *Also called Tri-City Hospital District* ***(G-21972)***
Tri-Counties Association F (PA)....805 962-7881
520 E Montecito St Santa Barbara (93103) ***(G-24259)***
Tri-Counties Association F....805 922-4640
1234 Fairway Dr A Santa Maria (93455) ***(G-24989)***
Tri-Counties Blood Bank, San Luis Obispo *Also called Blood Systems Inc* ***(G-22901)***
TRI-COUNTIES REGIONAL CENTER, Santa Barbara *Also called Tri-Counties Association F* ***(G-24259)***
Tri-Ed Distribution Inc....916 563-7560
855 National Dr Ste 103 Sacramento (95834) ***(G-7479)***
Tri-Marine Fish Company LLC....310 547-1144
220 Cannery St San Pedro (90731) ***(G-8659)***
Tri-Mountain, Irwindale *Also called Mountain Gear Corporation* ***(G-8353)***
Tri-Power Group Inc....925 583-8200
617 N Mary Ave Sunnyvale (94085) ***(G-6096)***
Tri-Signal Integration Inc (PA)....818 566-8558
15853 Monte St Ste 101 Sylmar (91342) ***(G-2775)***
Tri-Star Ccw Management L P....310 322-0999
1985 E Grand Ave El Segundo (90245) ***(G-13359)***
Tri-Star Drywall Lp....559 299-9858
2479 Burgan Ave Clovis (93611) ***(G-2992)***
Tri-State AG Inc....209 364-6185
47375 W Dakota Ave Firebaugh (93622) ***(G-6641)***
Tri-State Employment Svc Inc....310 521-9616
450 Westmont Dr San Pedro (90731) ***(G-14807)***
Tri-Tech Internet Services Inc....818 548-5400
3465 Ocean View Blvd Glendale (91208) ***(G-16264)***
Tri-Tech Restoration Co Inc....818 565-3900
3301 N San Fernando Blvd Burbank (91504) ***(G-1475)***
Tri-Union Seafoods LLC (HQ)....858 558-9662
9330 Scranton Rd Ste 500 San Diego (92121) ***(G-8660)***
Tri-Valley Supply Inc (PA)....707 469-7470
1705 Enterprise Dr Fairfield (94533) ***(G-7022)***
Tri-West Ltd (PA)....562 692-9166
12005 Pike St Santa Fe Springs (90670) ***(G-6897)***
Triad Broadcasting Company (PA)....831 655-6350
2511 Garden Rd Ste A104 Monterey (93940) ***(G-5824)***
Triad Homes Assoc....760 873-4273
873 N Main St Ste 150 Bishop (93514) ***(G-26104)***
Triad Systems International (PA)....818 222-6811
23801 Calabasas Rd # 2022 Calabasas (91302) ***(G-28083)***
Triad-Holmes Associates, Bishop *Also called Triad Homes Assoc* ***(G-26104)***
Triage Consulting Group (PA)....415 512-9400
221 Main St Ste 1100 San Francisco (94105) ***(G-27698)***
Triage Entertainment Inc....310 417-4800
6701 Center Dr W Ste 1111 Los Angeles (90045) ***(G-18170)***

ALPHABETIC

Triage Partners LLC 562 634-0058
15717 Texaco Ave Paramount (90723) ***(G-16510)***
Trialpay Inc (PA) 650 318-0000
800 California St Ste 300 Mountain View (94041) ***(G-16511)***
Triangle Distributing Co (PA) 562 699-3424
12065 Pike St Santa Fe Springs (90670) ***(G-9088)***
Triangle Distributing Co 760 347-4052
82851 Avenue 45 Indio (92201) ***(G-9089)***
Triangle T Ranch Inc 559 665-2964
4408 Hays Dr Chowchilla (93610) ***(G-15)***
Trianim Health Services Inc 818 362-6882
27201 Tourney Rd Ste 115 Valencia (91355) ***(G-23075)***
Trianz (HQ) 408 387-5800
3979 Freedom Cir Ste 210 Santa Clara (95054) ***(G-16512)***
Tribal Tektet, Arcata *Also called Tektetco* ***(G-1473)***
Tribeworx LLC 800 949-3432
4 San Joaquin Plz Ste 150 Newport Beach (92660) ***(G-15864)***
Tricor America Inc 310 676-0800
12441 Eucalyptus Ave 7 Hawthorne (90250) ***(G-5177)***
Tricor America Inc 714 701-9880
1465 N Brasher St Anaheim (92807) ***(G-4430)***
Tricor America Inc 916 371-1704
1690 Cebrian St West Sacramento (95691) ***(G-4431)***
Tricor America Inc 510 293-3960
3149 Diablo Ave Hayward (94545) ***(G-4873)***
Tricor California, West Sacramento *Also called Tricor America Inc* ***(G-4431)***
Tricor Entertainment Inc 626 282-5184
1613 Chelsea Rd San Marino (91108) ***(G-18171)***
Tricor International 650 877-3678
1320 San Mateo Ave South San Francisco (94080) ***(G-5178)***
Tricorp Construction Inc (PA) 916 779-8010
1030 G St Sacramento (95814) ***(G-1695)***
Tricorp Hearn Construction, Sacramento *Also called Tricorp Construction Inc* ***(G-1695)***
Trident Dental Labratories, Hawthorne *Also called Trident Labs Inc* ***(G-22313)***
Trident Labs Inc 310 915-9121
12000 Aviation Blvd Hawthorne (90250) ***(G-22313)***
Trifacta Inc 415 429-7570
575 Market St Fl 11 San Francisco (94105) ***(G-16202)***
Trigild International Inc 619 291-6500
2151 Hotel Cir S San Diego (92108) ***(G-13360)***
Trilar Management Group 951 925-2021
1025 S Gilbert St Hemet (92543) ***(G-27257)***
Trilink Biotechnologies Inc 858 546-0004
9955 Mesa Rim Rd San Diego (92121) ***(G-26624)***
Trilliant Networks Inc (PA) 650 204-5050
1100 Island Dr Ste 201 Redwood City (94065) ***(G-17543)***
Trilogy Day Spa, Manhattan Beach *Also called Trilogy Squaw Spa LLC* ***(G-13693)***
Trilogy Financial Services Inc 858 755-6696
12526 High Bluff Dr # 150 San Diego (92130) ***(G-17544)***
Trilogy Golf At La Quinta 760 771-0707
60151 Trilogy Pkwy La Quinta (92253) ***(G-18796)***
Trilogy Plumbing Inc (PA) 714 441-2952
1525 S Sinclair St Anaheim (92806) ***(G-2400)***
Trilogy Realty Group Inc 937 206-0725
2025 N Mantle Ln Santa Ana (92705) ***(G-11882)***
Trilogy Rio Vista 707 374-1100
1200 Clubhouse Dr Rio Vista (94571) ***(G-1476)***
Trilogy Squaw Spa LLC 310 760-0044
451 Manhattan Beach Blvd B108 Manhattan Beach (90266) ***(G-13693)***
Trim Tech Industries Inc 408 573-4514
1724 Ringwood Ave San Jose (95131) ***(G-6966)***
Trimarine Fish Group, San Pedro *Also called Trimarine Fishing MGT LLC* ***(G-27258)***
Trimarine Fishing MGT LLC 310 547-1144
220 Cannery St San Pedro (90731) ***(G-27258)***
Trimark Associates Inc 916 357-5970
2365 Iron Point Rd # 100 Folsom (95630) ***(G-28084)***
Trimark Raygal Inc 949 474-1000
2801 Mcgaw Ave Irvine (92614) ***(G-17545)***
TRIMARK UNITED EAST, Irvine *Also called Trimark Raygal Inc* ***(G-17545)***
Trimont Land Company (HQ) 530 562-2252
5001 Northstar Dr Truckee (96161) ***(G-11883)***
Trinchero Family Estates Inc 707 963-5928
18667 Jacob Brack Rd Lodi (95242) ***(G-17546)***
Trinet Group Inc (PA) 510 352-5000
1100 San Leandro Blvd # 300 San Leandro (94577) ***(G-14808)***
Trinet Hr Corporation 972 789-3900
1100 San Leandro Blvd # 300 San Leandro (94577) ***(G-27699)***
Trinity Brdcstg Netwrk Inc 714 832-2950
2442 Michelle Dr Tustin (92780) ***(G-5916)***
Trinity Broadcasting Network, Tustin *Also called Trinity Christian Center of SA* ***(G-5917)***
Trinity Building Services 650 873-2121
430 N Canal St Ste 2 South San Francisco (94080) ***(G-14446)***
Trinity Capital Corporation (HQ) 415 956-5174
475 Sansome St Fl 19 San Francisco (94111) ***(G-9806)***
Trinity Care & Nutria, Cerritos *Also called Trinitycare LLC* ***(G-22584)***
Trinity Christian Center of SA (PA) 714 665-3619
2442 Michelle Dr Tustin (92780) ***(G-5917)***
Trinity Fresh Distribution LLC 916 714-7368
8200 Berry Ave Ste 140 Sacramento (95828) ***(G-8941)***
Trinity Fruit Packing Company 559 743-3913
18700 E South Ave Reedley (93654) ***(G-599)***
Trinity Health Systems 818 983-0103
13400 Sherman Way North Hollywood (91605) ***(G-21393)***
Trinity Health Systems 562 437-2797
723 E 9th St Long Beach (90813) ***(G-20993)***
Trinity Health Systems (PA) 626 960-1971
14318 Ohio St Baldwin Park (91706) ***(G-20994)***
Trinity Health Systems 949 623-2481
651 N Main St Pomona (91768) ***(G-20995)***
Trinity Home Care, Torrance *Also called San Pedro Peninsula Hospital* ***(G-22555)***
Trinity Home Health Svcs Inc 559 450-5112
6729 N Willow Ave Ste 103 Fresno (93710) ***(G-22583)***
Trinity Hospital, Weaverville *Also called Mountain Comm Hlth Cre Dist* ***(G-21755)***
Trinity Hospital, Weaverville *Also called Mountain Comm Hlth Cre Dist* ***(G-21756)***
Trinity Plaza, Richmond *Also called Macdonald Housing Partners LP* ***(G-11651)***
Trinity Technology Group Inc 916 779-0201
2015 J St Ste 105 Sacramento (95811) ***(G-16068)***
Trinity Youth Services (PA) 909 825-5588
201 N Indian Hill Blvd # 201 Claremont (91711) ***(G-24837)***
Trinitycare LLC (PA) 818 709-4221
13030 Alondra Blvd Cerritos (90703) ***(G-22584)***
Trinus Corporation 818 246-1143
177 E Colorado Blvd 200 Pasadena (91105) ***(G-15510)***
Trio Consulting LLC 818 309-7919
15763 Kenneth Pl Santa Clarita (91387) ***(G-25590)***
Trio Vntura Cnty W Vly Chapter, Santa Clarita *Also called Trio Consulting LLC* ***(G-25590)***
Trion Worlds Inc (PA) 650 631-9800
1200 Bridge Pkwy Redwood City (94065) ***(G-15865)***
Triple A, Walnut Creek *Also called California State Automobile* ***(G-10408)***
Triple A Insurance, Roseville *Also called California State Automobile* ***(G-10409)***
Triple E Trucking 661 834-0071
1215 E White Ln Bakersfield (93307) ***(G-4074)***
Triple Play Services Inc (PA) 408 748-3929
42505 Christy St Fremont (94538) ***(G-5179)***
Triple R Transportation Inc 661 725-6494
978 Rd 192 Delano (93215) ***(G-3852)***
Triple Ring Technologies Inc 510 592-3000
39655 Eureka Dr Newark (94560) ***(G-27700)***
Triple-E Machinery Moving Inc 626 444-1137
3301 Gilman Rd El Monte (91732) ***(G-4280)***
Triplecurve LLC 855 874-2878
5716 Corsa Ave Ste 110 Westlake Village (91362) ***(G-27701)***
Tristaff Group, Fallbrook *Also called Garich Inc* ***(G-14661)***
Tristar Insurance Group Inc (PA) 562 495-6600
100 Oceangate Ste 700 Long Beach (90802) ***(G-10478)***
Tristar Risk Management 714 543-0700
203 N Golden Circle Dr # 200 Santa Ana (92705) ***(G-10911)***
Tristar Television Music Inc 310 244-4000
10202 Washington Blvd Culver City (90232) ***(G-18441)***
Tristart Risk Management, Long Beach *Also called Tristar Insurance Group Inc* ***(G-10478)***
Triton Consolidated Industries 323 852-0370
7710 Kester Ave Van Nuys (91405) ***(G-5180)***
Triton Cont Intl Inc N Amer (HQ) 415 956-6311
55 Green St Ste 500 San Francisco (94111) ***(G-14501)***
Triton Hotel, The, San Francisco *Also called Kimpton Hotel & Rest Group LLC* ***(G-27094)***
Triton Logistics Corporation 619 822-8832
706 Steffy Rd Ramona (92065) ***(G-5181)***
Triton Management Services LLC 760 431-9911
1000 Aviara Dr Ste 300 Carlsbad (92011) ***(G-27259)***
Triton Media Group LLC 661 294-9000
8935 Lindblade St Culver City (90232) ***(G-5825)***
Triton Structural Concrete Inc 858 866-2450
15435 Innovation Dr # 225 San Diego (92128) ***(G-1696)***
Triton Tower Inc (PA) 916 375-8546
3200 Jefferson Blvd West Sacramento (95691) ***(G-2003)***
Trius Trucking Inc 559 834-4000
4692 E Lincoln Ave Fowler (93625) ***(G-5182)***
Triways Inc 951 361-4840
11201 Iberia St Ste B Mira Loma (91752) ***(G-4384)***
TRL Systems Incorporated 909 390-8392
9531 Milliken Ave Rancho Cucamonga (91730) ***(G-2776)***
TRM Corporation (PA) 510 895-2700
2300 Polvorosa Ave San Leandro (94577) ***(G-3026)***
Trojan Professional Svcs Inc 714 816-7169
4410 Cerritos Ave Los Alamitos (90720) ***(G-16265)***
Troon Golf LLC 760 346-4653
44500 Indian Wells Ln Indian Wells (92210) ***(G-27260)***
Troop Real Estate Inc 805 402-3028
4165 E Thousand Oaks Blvd # 101 Westlake Village (91362) ***(G-11884)***
Troop Real Estate Inc (PA) 805 581-3200
3200 E Los Angeles Ave Simi Valley (93065) ***(G-11885)***
Trope & Trope, Los Angeles *Also called Trope and Trope LLP* ***(G-23598)***
Trope and Trope LLP 323 879-2726
12121 Wilshire Blvd # 801 Los Angeles (90025) ***(G-23598)***
Tropical Plaza Nursery Inc 714 998-4100
9642 Santiago Blvd Villa Park (92867) ***(G-966)***
Tropicana Gardens Holdings LLC 805 968-4319
6585 El Colegio Rd Santa Barbara (93117) ***(G-13361)***
Trotta Associates 310 306-6866
13160 Mindanao Way # 100 Marina Del Rey (90292) ***(G-26715)***
Troutman Sanders LLP 858 509-6000
11682 El Camino Real # 400 San Diego (92130) ***(G-23599)***
Troutman Sanders LLP 415 477-5700
580 California St # 1100 San Francisco (94104) ***(G-23600)***
Troy Lee Designs (PA) 951 371-5219
155 E Rincon St Corona (92879) ***(G-8032)***
Troyer Contracting Company Inc 562 944-6452
10122 Freeman Ave Santa Fe Springs (90670) ***(G-3592)***
Troygould PC 310 553-4441
1801 Century Park E # 1600 Los Angeles (90067) ***(G-23601)***
Trs Staffing Solutions, Aliso Viejo *Also called Fluor Corporation* ***(G-25811)***
Tru Green Landcare Inc 602 276-4311
5248 Governor Dr San Diego (92122) ***(G-967)***
Tru Green-Chemlawn, Fairfield *Also called Trugreen Limited Partnership* ***(G-968)***
Tru Green-Chemlawn, Riverside *Also called Trugreen Limited Partnership* ***(G-969)***
Truck Terminal, Bakersfield *Also called Pan Pacific Petroleum Co Inc* ***(G-4241)***

ALPHABETIC

Truck Underwriters Association (HQ).....323 932-3200
4680 Wilshire Blvd Los Angeles (90010) ***(G-23602)***
Truck Underwriters Association.....323 932-3200
6303 Owensmouth Ave Fl 1 Woodland Hills (91367) ***(G-10226)***
Truckee Dnner Rcreation Pk Dst.....530 582-7720
8924 Donner Pass Rd Truckee (96161) ***(G-19297)***
Truckee Donner Pub Utility Dst.....530 587-3896
11570 Donner Pass Rd Truckee (96161) ***(G-6246)***
TRUCKEE DONNER PUD, Truckee *Also called Truckee Donner Pub Utility Dst* ***(G-6246)***
True Air Mechanical Inc.....949 382-6337
4 Faraday Irvine (92618) ***(G-2401)***
True North Ar LLC.....916 369-9850
10971 Sun Center Dr 200 Rancho Cordova (95670) ***(G-14809)***
True Religion Brand Jeans, Manhattan Beach *Also called Guru Denim Inc* ***(G-8385)***
True Religion Sales LLC.....323 266-3072
1888 Rosecrans Ave # 1000 Manhattan Beach (90266) ***(G-8363)***
True Ultimate Standards.....415 520-3400
835 Market St Ste 800 San Francisco (94103) ***(G-16513)***
True Wrld Fods Los Angeles LLC.....323 846-3300
4200 S Alameda St Vernon (90058) ***(G-8661)***
True Wrld Fods San Frncsco LLC.....510 352-8140
1815 Williams St San Leandro (94577) ***(G-8662)***
Truebeck Construction (PA).....650 227-1957
201 Redwood Shores Pkwy # 125 Redwood City (94065) ***(G-1697)***
Trueblue Inc.....530 755-3291
1362 Colusa Hwy Yuba City (95993) ***(G-14963)***
Trueblue Inc.....805 963-5370
123 E Carrillo St Santa Barbara (93101) ***(G-14964)***
Truecar Inc.....415 821-8270
140 New Montgomery St # 2400 San Francisco (94105) ***(G-5711)***
Truecar Inc (PA).....800 200-2000
120 Broadway Ste 200 Santa Monica (90401) ***(G-6698)***
Truesdail Laboratories Inc.....714 730-6239
3337 Michelson Dr Irvine (92612) ***(G-26625)***
Truform Construction Corp.....714 630-7447
1041 N Shepard St Anaheim (92806) ***(G-3097)***
Trugreen, Santa Ana *Also called Landcare USA LLC* ***(G-888)***
Trugreen, Escondido *Also called Landcare USA LLC* ***(G-889)***
Trugreen, Simi Valley *Also called Landcare USA LLC* ***(G-890)***
Trugreen, Gardena *Also called Landcare USA LLC* ***(G-895)***
Trugreen, Rancho Cordova *Also called Landcare USA LLC* ***(G-896)***
Trugreen, San Diego *Also called Landcare USA LLC* ***(G-897)***
Trugreen, Canoga Park *Also called Landcare USA LLC* ***(G-898)***
Trugreen, San Jose *Also called Landcare USA LLC* ***(G-899)***
Trugreen Limited Partnership.....707 864-5594
393 Watt Dr Ste B Fairfield (94534) ***(G-968)***
Trugreen Limited Partnership.....951 683-0144
1130 Palmyrita Ave # 300 Riverside (92507) ***(G-969)***
Truitt Oilfield Maint Corp.....661 871-4099
1051 James Rd Bakersfield (93308) ***(G-1098)***
Trulia Inc (HQ).....415 648-4358
535 Mission St Fl 7 San Francisco (94105) ***(G-16203)***
Trust Automation Inc.....805 544-0761
143 Suburban Rd Ste 100 San Luis Obispo (93401) ***(G-26105)***
Trust Company of The West, Los Angeles *Also called Tcw Group Inc* ***(G-9529)***
Trust Company of West (HQ).....213 244-0000
865 S Figueroa St # 1800 Los Angeles (90017) ***(G-10085)***
Trust Employee ADM & MGT, La Mesa *Also called Risk Management Strategies Inc* ***(G-28043)***
Truste, San Francisco *Also called True Ultimate Standards* ***(G-16513)***
Truste.....415 520-3490
835 Market St San Francisco (94103) ***(G-5712)***
Trustee Corps, Irvine *Also called Mtc Financial Inc* ***(G-12195)***
Trustwave Corporation, Irvine *Also called TW Security Corp* ***(G-7205)***
Truxtun Radiology Med Group LP.....661 325-6200
3940 San Dimas St Bakersfield (93301) ***(G-22290)***
Tryad Service Corporation.....661 391-1524
5900 E Lerdo Hwy Shafter (93263) ***(G-1099)***
Trz Holdings II Inc.....213 955-7170
725 S Figueroa St # 1850 Los Angeles (90017) ***(G-11886)***
Tscm Corporation.....714 841-1988
17791 Jamestown Ln Huntington Beach (92647) ***(G-14447)***
TSE, Escondido *Also called Total Source Enviromental Inc* ***(G-1347)***
Tsg, San Diego *Also called Socal Services Inc* ***(G-14791)***
Tsi.....949 515-7800
789 W 20th St Costa Mesa (92627) ***(G-14448)***
Tsmc North America (HQ).....408 382-8000
2851 Junction Ave San Jose (95134) ***(G-27702)***
Tst Inc.....310 835-0115
11601 Etiwanda Ave Fontana (92337) ***(G-4075)***
Tst Inc.....909 590-1098
11601 Etiwanda Ave Fontana (92337) ***(G-8093)***
Tsu Corporate Services, North Hollywood *Also called Toner Supply USA Inc* ***(G-7201)***
Ttg Engineers.....714 490-5555
222 S Harbor Blvd Ste 800 Anaheim (92805) ***(G-26106)***
Ttg Engineers (PA).....626 463-2800
300 N Lake Ave Fl 14 Pasadena (91101) ***(G-26107)***
TTI, Milpitas *Also called Technical Temps Inc* ***(G-14803)***
Ttp-US, San Marcos *Also called Tel Tech Plus Inc* ***(G-2768)***
Tts, Pleasanton *Also called Telecom Technology Svcs Inc* ***(G-28070)***
TTSA, Truckee *Also called Tahoe-Truckee Sanitation Agcy* ***(G-6419)***
TTSR, Sacramento *Also called Training Toward Self Reliance* ***(G-24256)***
TTT West Coast Inc.....818 972-0500
1840 Victory Blvd Glendale (91201) ***(G-18172)***
Tubemogul Inc (PA).....510 653-0126
1250 53rd St Ste 2 Emeryville (94608) ***(G-15866)***
Tucker Distributors.....714 970-5742
5380 E Hunter Ave Anaheim (92807) ***(G-7749)***
Tucker Electric Corporation.....818 426-7645
3365 Chestnut Ln Santa Rosa Valley (93012) ***(G-2777)***
Tucker Electrical, Santa Rosa Valley *Also called Tucker Electric Corporation* ***(G-2777)***
Tucker Ellis LLP.....213 430-3400
1000 Wilshire Blvd # 1800 Los Angeles (90017) ***(G-23603)***
Tucker Sheet Metal Distr, Anaheim *Also called Tucker Distributors* ***(G-7749)***
Tucoemas Federal Credit Union.....559 429-7094
2300 W Whitendale Ave Visalia (93277) ***(G-9644)***
Tudor Cnstr & Restoration, Elk Grove *Also called Bennathon Corp* ***(G-1503)***
Tulare Cnty Chld Care Home Edu.....559 651-0247
7000 W Doe Ave Ste C Visalia (93291) ***(G-24527)***
Tulare Cty Trng Ctr Hndcpd.....559 651-3683
8929 W Goshen Ave Visalia (93291) ***(G-24397)***
Tulare Home Care, Tulare *Also called Tulare Local Health Care Dst* ***(G-21973)***
Tulare Local Health Care Dst.....559 685-3462
869 N Cherry St Tulare (93274) ***(G-21973)***
Tulare Nrsing Rhbilitation Ctr, Tulare *Also called Tulare Nrsing Rhblitation Hosp* ***(G-20996)***
Tulare Nrsing Rhblitation Hosp.....559 686-8581
680 E Merritt Ave Tulare (93274) ***(G-20996)***
Tulare Youth Service Bureau (PA).....559 685-8547
327 S K St Tulare (93274) ***(G-24260)***
Tulare Yth Sxl ABS Trtmnt Prgr, Tulare *Also called Tulare Youth Service Bureau* ***(G-24260)***
Tule River Indian Hlth Ctr Inc.....559 784-2316
380 N Reservation Rd Porterville (93257) ***(G-22854)***
Tuls Cattle, Tulare *Also called M & T Calf Ranch* ***(G-411)***
Tum Yeto Inc.....619 232-7523
2001 Commercial St San Diego (92113) ***(G-8033)***
Tumbleweed Day Camp, Los Angeles *Also called Tumbleweed Educational Entps* ***(G-19298)***
Tumbleweed Educational Entps.....310 444-3232
1024 Hanley Ave Los Angeles (90049) ***(G-19298)***
Tumi Inc.....408 244-6512
333 Santana Row Apt 230 San Jose (95128) ***(G-8146)***
Tunari Corp Inc.....650 249-6740
2755 Campus Dr Ste 300 San Mateo (94403) ***(G-15511)***
Tuolumne Cnty Bhvrl Hlth, Sonora *Also called Kingsview Corp* ***(G-22763)***
Tuolumne City Inv Grp II LP.....209 928-1567
18402 Tuolumne Rd Apt 31 Tuolumne (95379) ***(G-11217)***
Tuolumne Cy Senior Apartments, Tuolumne *Also called Tuolumne City Inv Grp II LP* ***(G-11217)***
Tuolumne Me-Wuk Indian.....209 928-5400
18880 Cherry Valley Blvd Tuolumne (95379) ***(G-20144)***
Tuolumne Me-Wuk Tribal Council.....707 319-3472
1182 24th St Ste 311 Oakland (94607) ***(G-25383)***
Tuolumne Mewuk Indian Health, Tuolumne *Also called Tuolumne Me-Wuk Indian* ***(G-20144)***
Tuolumne Utilities District.....209 532-5536
18885 Nugget Blvd Sonora (95370) ***(G-6406)***
Turbine Repair Services LLC (PA).....909 947-2256
1838 E Cedar St Ontario (91761) ***(G-18026)***
Turelk Inc.....858 633-8085
11622 El Camino Real # 100 San Diego (92130) ***(G-1698)***
Turelk San Diego, San Diego *Also called Turelk Inc* ***(G-1698)***
Turf Star Inc.....760 772-3575
79253 Country Club Dr Bermuda Dunes (92203) ***(G-7812)***
Turfstar, Bermuda Dunes *Also called Turf Star Inc* ***(G-7812)***
Turk & Eddy Associates LP.....415 474-6524
201 Eddy St San Francisco (94102) ***(G-11218)***
Turkey Creek Golf Club, Lincoln *Also called Clubcorp Usa Inc* ***(G-18726)***
Turlock Dairy & Rfrgn Inc.....209 667-6455
1819 S Walnut Rd Turlock (95380) ***(G-7813)***
Turlock Diagnostic Center, Turlock *Also called Emanuel Medical Center Inc* ***(G-21557)***
Turlock Irrigation District (PA).....209 883-8222
333 E Canal Dr Turlock (95380) ***(G-6247)***
Turlock Irrigation District.....209 883-8300
901 N Broadway Turlock (95380) ***(G-6655)***
Turlock Nrsing Rhabilation Ctr, Turlock *Also called Covenant Care California LLC* ***(G-20496)***
Turn Around Communications Inc.....626 443-2400
4400 Temple City Blvd El Monte (91731) ***(G-2004)***
Turn Inc (PA).....650 353-4399
901 Marshall St 200 Redwood City (94063) ***(G-14012)***
TURNABOUT SHOP, El Cerrito *Also called Berkeley Clinic Auxuillary* ***(G-25506)***
Turner Broadcasting System Inc.....818 977-5452
3500 W Olive Ave Ste 1500 Burbank (91505) ***(G-18173)***
Turner Broadcasting System Inc.....310 788-6767
1888 Century Park E # 1200 Los Angeles (90067) ***(G-5826)***
Turner Construction Company.....714 940-9000
1900 S State College Blvd # 200 Anaheim (92806) ***(G-7794)***
Turner Construction Company.....213 891-3000
555 S Flower St Ste 4220 Los Angeles (90071) ***(G-1275)***
Turner Construction Company.....916 444-4421
1211 H St Sacramento (95814) ***(G-1699)***
Turner Construction Company.....510 267-8100
300 Frank H Ogawa Plz # 510 Oakland (94612) ***(G-1700)***
Turner Construction Company.....415 705-8900
75 Hawthorne St Ste 2000 San Francisco (94105) ***(G-1701)***
Turner Construction Company.....858 320-4040
15378 Ave Of Science # 100 San Diego (92128) ***(G-1702)***
Turner Construction Company.....916 444-4421
1211 H St Sacramento (95814) ***(G-1703)***
Turner Duckworth LLC.....415 675-7777
831 Montgomery St San Francisco (94133) ***(G-14164)***
Turner Security Systems Inc.....559 486-3466
120 W Shields Ave Fresno (93705) ***(G-16836)***
Turner Techtronics Inc.....949 724-1339
17845 Sky Park Cir Irvine (92614) ***(G-16307)***
Turning Point Central Cal Inc.....559 664-9021
117 N R St Madera (93637) ***(G-24261)***

ALPHABETIC

Turning Point Central Cal Inc....559 627-1490
711 N Court St Visalia (93291) ***(G-24262)***
Turning Point For God....619 258-3600
10007 Riverford Rd Lakeside (92040) ***(G-18442)***
Turning Point Ministries, Lakeside *Also called Turning Point For God* ***(G-18442)***
Turning Pt Rvnue Cycle Sltions....800 360-2300
1255 Treat Blvd Ste 300 San Diego (92131) ***(G-14965)***
Turnstone Systems Inc....408 907-1400
2220 Central Expy Santa Clara (95050) ***(G-11887)***
Turnupseed Electric Service....559 686-1541
1580 S K St Tulare (93274) ***(G-2778)***
Turtle Bay Exploration Park....530 243-4282
1335 Arboretum Dr Ste A Redding (96003) ***(G-25053)***
Turtle Entertainment America....818 861-7315
1212 Chestnut St Burbank (91506) ***(G-13800)***
Turtle Rock Cdc, Irvine *Also called Child Development Incorporated* ***(G-24432)***
Tusa Inc (PA)....888 848-3749
388 Oakmead Pkwy Sunnyvale (94085) ***(G-16308)***
Tuscan and Pescatore, The, San Francisco *Also called Creedence Lessee LLC* ***(G-12552)***
Tuscan Inn, San Francisco *Also called Kms Fishermans Wharf LP* ***(G-12890)***
Tuscan Inn, San Francisco *Also called Kimpton Hotel & Rest Group LLC* ***(G-12885)***
Tuscan Inn, San Francisco *Also called 425 North Point Street LLC* ***(G-12361)***
Tustin Care Center Corp....714 832-6780
1051 Bryan Ave Tustin (92780) ***(G-21118)***
Tustin Hcnda Memory Care Cmnty, Tustin *Also called Silverado Senior Living Inc* ***(G-24811)***
Tustin Hospital and Med Ctr....714 619-7700
3699 Wilshire Blvd # 540 Los Angeles (90010) ***(G-21974)***
Tustin Ranch Golf Club, Tustin *Also called Crown Golf Properties LP* ***(G-27397)***
Tustin Ranch Golf Club, Tustin *Also called Sanyo Foods Corp America* ***(G-19068)***
Tustin Ranch Medical Offices, Tustin *Also called Kaiser Foundation Hospitals* ***(G-19651)***
Tutera Group Inc....209 223-2231
811 Court St Jackson (95642) ***(G-24838)***
TUTOR PERINI, Redwood City *Also called Rudolph and Sletten Inc* ***(G-1656)***
Tutor Perini Corporation (PA)....818 362-8391
15901 Olden St Sylmar (91342) ***(G-1704)***
Tutor Perini Corporation....818 362-8391
15901 Olden St Sylmar (91342) ***(G-1705)***
Tutor Perini Corporation....415 638-6941
530 Bush St San Francisco (94108) ***(G-1706)***
Tutor Perini/Zachry/Parsons....559 385-7025
1401 Fulton St Ste 400 Fresno (93721) ***(G-2093)***
Tutor-Saliba Corporation (HQ)....818 362-8391
15901 Olden St Sylmar (91342) ***(G-1707)***
Tuttle Family Enterprises Inc....818 534-2566
21020 Superior St Chatsworth (91311) ***(G-14449)***
Tuv Sud America Inc....858 546-3999
10040 Mesa Rim Rd San Diego (92121) ***(G-26894)***
TV 36....408 953-3636
2102 Commerce Dr San Jose (95131) ***(G-5918)***
TV Guide Networks, LLC, Playa Vista *Also called Pop Media Networks LLC* ***(G-18488)***
Tvb (usa) Inc (HQ)....562 345-9871
15411 Blackburn Ave Norwalk (90650) ***(G-6055)***
Tvddc EC Murrieta....951 566-5229
25150 Hancock Ave Ste 530 Murrieta (92562) ***(G-20145)***
Tvgla, Los Angeles *Also called Visionaire Group Inc* ***(G-13937)***
TW Security Corp (HQ)....949 932-1000
8845 Irvine Center Dr # 101 Irvine (92618) ***(G-7205)***
TW Services Inc....714 441-2400
2751 E Chapman Ave # 204 Fullerton (92831) ***(G-5248)***
Twain Harte Horsemen....209 601-5585
23580 View Ln Columbia (95310) ***(G-25384)***
TWC Aviation LLC....888 923-1001
16700 Roscoe Blvd Hngr C Van Nuys (91406) ***(G-4889)***
TWC Aviation LLC....408 286-3832
1162 Aviation Ave San Jose (95110) ***(G-4890)***
Twelve Bridges Golf Club, Lincoln *Also called Crstb Partners LLC* ***(G-18730)***
Twentieth Century Fox (HQ)....310 369-1000
10201 W Pico Blvd Los Angeles (90064) ***(G-18279)***
Twentieth Century Fox Home E (HQ)....310 369-1000
10201 W Pico Blvd Los Angeles (90064) ***(G-5919)***
Twentieth Century Fox In....310 369-1000
10201 W Pico Blvd Los Angeles (90064) ***(G-11888)***
Twentieth Cntury Fox Film Corp (HQ)....310 369-1000
10201 W Pico Blvd Los Angeles (90064) ***(G-18174)***
Twentieth Cntury Fox Film Corp....310 369-2582
2121 Avenue Of The Stars Los Angeles (90067) ***(G-18175)***
Twenty4seven Hotels Corp....949 734-6400
567 San Nicolas Dr # 100 Newport Beach (92660) ***(G-27261)***
TWI- Techno West Inc....714 635-4070
1391 S Allec St Anaheim (92805) ***(G-2499)***
Twilight Haven....559 251-8417
1717 S Winery Ave Fresno (93727) ***(G-20997)***
Twilio Inc (PA)....415 390-2337
645 Harrison St Fl 3 San Francisco (94107) ***(G-15867)***
Twilio Inc....877 889-4546
399 W El Camino Real Mountain View (94040) ***(G-15512)***
Twin Advantage Inc....951 445-4200
39755 Murrieta Hot S Ste G Murrieta (92563) ***(G-11889)***
Twin Cities Community Hosp Inc....805 434-3500
1100 Las Tablas Rd Templeton (93465) ***(G-20146)***
Twin Med LLC (PA)....323 582-9900
11333 Greenstone Ave Santa Fe Springs (90670) ***(G-7322)***
Twin Oaks Nrsing Rhbltion Ctr, Chico *Also called Evergreen Healthcare Inc* ***(G-20561)***
Twin Oaks Power LP (HQ)....619 696-2034
101 Ash St Hq10b San Diego (92101) ***(G-6248)***
Twining Labs Southern Cal Inc (PA)....562 426-3355
2883 E Spring St Ste 300 Long Beach (90806) ***(G-26895)***
Twitter Inc (PA)....415 222-9670
1355 Market St Ste 900 San Francisco (94103) ***(G-16266)***
Two Bunch Palms LLC....760 329-8791
67425 Two Bunch Palms Trl Desert Hot Springs (92240) ***(G-13362)***
Two Harbors Enterprises Inc....310 510-2000
150 Metropole Ave Avalon (90704) ***(G-3731)***
Two Jinn Inc....707 421-9600
325 Texas St Fairfield (94533) ***(G-17547)***
Two Jinn Inc (PA)....760 431-9911
1000 Aviara Dr Ste 300 Carlsbad (92011) ***(G-17548)***
Two Palms Nursing Center....323 681-4615
150 Bellefontaine St Pasadena (91105) ***(G-21394)***
Two Palms Nursing Center Inc (PA)....626 798-8991
2637 E Washington Blvd Pasadena (91107) ***(G-21395)***
Two Palms Nursing Center Inc....626 796-1103
150 Bellefontaine St Pasadena (91105) ***(G-21396)***
Two Rivers Demolition Inc....916 638-6775
2620 Mercantile Dr 100 Rancho Cordova (95742) ***(G-3470)***
Two Roads Prof Resources Inc....714 901-3804
5122 Bolsa Ave Ste 112 Huntington Beach (92649) ***(G-14966)***
Two Star Dog Inc....510 525-1100
1370 10th St Berkeley (94710) ***(G-8364)***
TWR Enterprises Inc....951 279-2000
1661 Railroad St Corona (92880) ***(G-3098)***
Ty Five Star Corporation....510 317-7360
27285 Sleepy Hollow Ave S # 204 Hayward (94545) ***(G-21975)***
Ty Investment Inc....619 448-4242
9200 Inwood Dr Santee (92071) ***(G-19114)***
TY Lin International Group (PA)....415 291-3700
345 California St Fl 23 San Francisco (94104) ***(G-26108)***
Tyan Inc....818 785-5831
1500 Glenoaks Blvd San Fernando (91340) ***(G-16837)***
Tyan Computer Corporation....510 651-8868
3288 Laurelview Ct Fremont (94538) ***(G-7206)***
Tyco Integrated Security LLC....818 428-6669
104 E Graham Pl Burbank (91502) ***(G-16931)***
Tyco Integrated Security LLC....951 787-0420
1120 Palmyrita Ave # 280 Riverside (92507) ***(G-16932)***
Tyco Integrated Security LLC....561 988-3600
3870 Murphy Canyon Rd # 140 San Diego (92123) ***(G-16933)***
Tyco Integrated Security LLC....916 565-2061
4650 Beloit Dr Sacramento (95838) ***(G-16934)***
Tyco Integrated Security LLC....650 634-9000
150 N Hill Dr Ste 3 Brisbane (94005) ***(G-16935)***
Tyco Integrated Security LLC....510 785-2912
3825 Bay Center Pl B Hayward (94545) ***(G-16936)***
Tyco Integrated Security LLC....209 574-2704
4725 Enterprise Way Ste 5 Modesto (95356) ***(G-16937)***
Tyco Integrated Security LLC....714 223-2300
7565 Irvine Center Dr # 100 Irvine (92618) ***(G-16938)***
Tyler Bluff Wind Project LLC....888 903-6926
15445 Innovation Dr San Diego (92128) ***(G-6249)***
Tyler Palmieri Wiener....949 851-9400
1900 Main St Ste 700 Irvine (92614) ***(G-23604)***
Tyme Maidu Tribe-Berry Creek....530 538-4560
4020 Olive Hwy Oroville (95966) ***(G-13363)***
Tyr Sport Inc....562 430-1380
1790 Apollo Ct Seal Beach (90740) ***(G-8415)***
Tyson Investments Inc....949 389-0004
26711 Aliso Creek Rd Aliso Viejo (92656) ***(G-11890)***
Tz Holdings LP....949 719-2200
567 San Nicolas Dr # 120 Newport Beach (92660) ***(G-15868)***
Tzippy Care Inc....323 737-7778
2190 W Adams Blvd Los Angeles (90018) ***(G-21397)***
U B C 1, San Diego *Also called Mufg Union Bank Na* ***(G-9406)***
U B C 102, Los Angeles *Also called Mufg Union Bank Na* ***(G-9402)***
U B C 103, Gardena *Also called Mufg Union Bank Na* ***(G-9407)***
U B C 200, Beverly Hills *Also called Mufg Union Bank Na* ***(G-9404)***
U B C 309, Los Angeles *Also called Mufg Union Bank Na* ***(G-9405)***
U C Health Systems, Sacramento *Also called U C Med Humn Rsrces Aplcat Svc* ***(G-21976)***
U C I Distribution Plus, Pasadena *Also called United Couriers Inc* ***(G-4838)***
U C L Incorporated (PA)....323 232-3469
620 S Hacienda Blvd City of Industry (91745) ***(G-4281)***
U C L A Dermatology, Los Angeles *Also called Gary Lask* ***(G-19533)***
U C Med Humn Rsrces Aplcat Svc....916 734-5916
2730 Stockton Blvd # 21002500 Sacramento (95817) ***(G-21976)***
U C P-UNITED CEREBAL PALSY ASS, Fresno *Also called United Crbrl Plsy of Cntrl CA* ***(G-24270)***
U C S F School of Dentistry....415 476-5609
100 Buchanan St San Francisco (94102) ***(G-20281)***
U C San Francisco Gynecology....415 885-7788
2356 Sutter St San Francisco (94115) ***(G-20147)***
U F C Pension Trust Fund, Cypress *Also called Cal Southern United Food* ***(G-10542)***
U P S, San Francisco *Also called Fritz Companies Inc* ***(G-5080)***
U S Army Corps of Engineers....916 557-7491
1645 Riverbank Rd West Sacramento (95605) ***(G-26109)***
U S Army Corps of Engineers....213 452-3139
300 N Los Angeles St Los Angeles (90012) ***(G-26110)***
U S Army Corps of Engineers....916 649-0133
2194 Ascot Ave Rio Linda (95673) ***(G-26111)***
U S Army Corps of Engineers....916 925-7001
3900 Roseville Rd North Highlands (95660) ***(G-26112)***
U S Army Corps of Engineers....415 289-3067
2100 Bridgeway Sausalito (94965) ***(G-26113)***
U S Army Corps of Engineers....213 452-3403
915 Wilshire Blvd Ste 930 Los Angeles (90017) ***(G-7795)***
U S Foods, La Mirada *Also called US Foods Inc* ***(G-8548)***
U S GOVERNMENT, Tulelake *Also called Lava Beds National Monuments* ***(G-25548)***

U S Merchant Services, Newport Beach *Also called Montrenes Financial Svcs Inc* ***(G-14062)***
U S Office & Industry Supply, Van Nuys *Also called Nat Sim Corp* ***(G-8171)***
U S Perma Inc...408 436-0600
1696 Rogers Ave San Jose (95112) ***(G-3027)***
U S Private Protection SEC Inc...310 301-0010
5555 Inglewood Blvd # 205 Culver City (90230) ***(G-16838)***
U S Xpress Inc...760 768-6707
363 Nina Lee Rd Calexico (92231) ***(G-4282)***
U T L A, Los Angeles *Also called United Teachers Los Angeles* ***(G-25191)***
U Turn Seven Corporation...323 662-1587
1802 N Vermont Ave Los Angeles (90027) ***(G-8539)***
U W G Northern California Div, Stockton *Also called Unified Grocers Inc* ***(G-8542)***
U W G Southern California Div, Los Angeles *Also called Unified Grocers Inc* ***(G-8595)***
U-2 Home Entertainment Inc...650 871-8118
170 S Spruce Ave Ste 200 South San Francisco (94080) ***(G-7650)***
U-Dub Productions, Palm Desert *Also called Desert Television LLC* ***(G-5851)***
U-Haul Co of California (HQ)...800 528-0463
44511 S Grimmer Blvd Fremont (94538) ***(G-17655)***
U. S. Grant Hotel, San Diego *Also called American Prprty-Mnagement Corp* ***(G-12384)***
U.S. Healthworks Medical Group, Valencia *Also called US Healthworks Inc* ***(G-20176)***
Ua Galaxy Los Cerritos...562 865-6499
4900 E 4th St Ontario (91764) ***(G-18353)***
Ua Galaxy Los Cerritos 33, Ontario *Also called Ua Galaxy Los Cerritos* ***(G-18353)***
Ua Local 38 Bonbelsent Tr Fund...707 279-4281
8727 Soda Bay Rd Ofc Kelseyville (95451) ***(G-13364)***
Uaw-Lbor Emplyment Trning Corp...323 730-7900
3965 S Vermont Ave Los Angeles (90037) ***(G-14810)***
Uber, Pasadena *Also called Citywide Limo Services Inc* ***(G-3863)***
Uber Technologies Inc (HQ)...415 986-2715
1455 Market St Fl 4 San Francisco (94103) ***(G-15869)***
Ubi Soft Entertainment...415 547-4000
625 3rd St Fl 3 San Francisco (94107) ***(G-18501)***
Ubics Inc...415 289-1400
1050 Bridgeway Sausalito (94965) ***(G-15513)***
Ubiquiti Networks Inc (PA)...408 942-3085
2580 Orchard Pkwy San Jose (95131) ***(G-16069)***
Ubisoft Holdings Inc (HQ)...415 547-4000
625 3rd St Fl 3 San Francisco (94107) ***(G-15514)***
UBS Financial Services Inc...213 972-1511
777 S Figueroa St # 5100 Los Angeles (90017) ***(G-10086)***
UBS Financial Services Inc...310 274-8441
131 S Rodeo Dr Ste 200 Beverly Hills (90212) ***(G-10087)***
UBS Financial Services Inc...415 954-6700
555 California St # 4650 San Francisco (94104) ***(G-10088)***
UBS Financial Services Inc...562 495-5500
3030 Old Ranch Pkwy # 300 Seal Beach (90740) ***(G-10089)***
UBS Financial Services Inc...949 760-5308
888 San Clemente Dr # 300 Newport Beach (92660) ***(G-10090)***
UBS Financial Services Inc...415 398-6400
555 California St # 4650 San Francisco (94104) ***(G-10091)***
UBS Financial Services Inc...951 684-6300
3801 University Ave # 300 Riverside (92501) ***(G-17549)***
UBS Financial Services Inc...858 454-9181
1200 Prospect St Ste 500 La Jolla (92037) ***(G-17550)***
UBS Financial Services Inc...626 449-1501
200 S Los Robles Ave # 600 Pasadena (91101) ***(G-10092)***
UBS Financial Services Inc...415 398-6400
555 California St # 4650 San Francisco (94104) ***(G-10093)***
UBS Financial Services Inc...310 556-0746
2029 Century Park E # 3000 Los Angeles (90067) ***(G-10094)***
UBS Securities LLC...415 352-5650
555 California St # 4650 San Francisco (94104) ***(G-10095)***
Uc David Home Care Services, Sacramento *Also called Ucd Mc Home Care Services* ***(G-27262)***
Uc Davies Caare Center, Sacramento *Also called Judianne Chew Lcsw* ***(G-22750)***
Uc Davis Health System (PA)...916 734-1000
4610 X St Sacramento (95817) ***(G-20148)***
Uc Davis Hlth Systm Fclts Dsgn...916 734-6570
4800 2nd Ave Ste 3010 Sacramento (95817) ***(G-20149)***
Uc Davis Medical Center, Sacramento *Also called University California Davis* ***(G-21998)***
Uc Davis Medical Center, Sacramento *Also called Uc Davis Hlth Systm Fclts Dsgn* ***(G-20149)***
Uc Davis Medical Center, Sacramento *Also called University California Davis* ***(G-22000)***
Uc Irvine Hlth Rgonal Burn Ctr, Orange *Also called University California Irvine* ***(G-20169)***
Uc Irvine Medical Center, Orange *Also called University California Irvine* ***(G-22002)***
Uc Irvine Recreation Center...949 824-5346
680 California Ave Irvine (92617) ***(G-19115)***
Uc Regents...310 301-8777
300 Medical Plaza Los Angeles (90095) ***(G-20150)***
Uca General Insurance, Cypress *Also called United Chinese American Genera* ***(G-10914)***
Ucc Direct Services Inc...818 662-4100
330 N Brand Blvd Ste 700 Glendale (91203) ***(G-16204)***
Uccr, Petaluma *Also called United Cmps Cnfrences Retreats* ***(G-13472)***
Ucd Mc Home Care Services...916 734-2458
3630 Business Dr Sacramento (95820) ***(G-27262)***
Ucd Recreation Hall...530 752-6071
1 Shields Ave Davis (95616) ***(G-19299)***
Ucdavis...530 757-3322
1820 Point Reyes Pl Davis (95616) ***(G-17551)***
Ucde - Center For Human Svcs...530 757-8538
1632 Da Vinci Ct Davis (95618) ***(G-28164)***
UCI Construction Inc...661 587-0192
3900 Fruitvale Ave Bakersfield (93308) ***(G-26114)***
UCI Family Health Center, Santa Ana *Also called University California Irvine* ***(G-20170)***
Ucla Assoc Stdnts Event Servs...310 206-0832
308 Westwood Plz Rm A262a Los Angeles (90095) ***(G-16939)***
Ucla Bookstore, Los Angeles *Also called Associated Students UCLA* ***(G-24877)***
Ucla Copy Services...310 794-6371
555 Westwood Plz Ste B Los Angeles (90095) ***(G-14128)***
Ucla Faculty Center Assn Inc...310 825-0877
480 Charles E Young Dr S Los Angeles (90095) ***(G-25161)***
Ucla Foundation...310 794-3193
10920 Wilshire Blvd # 200 Los Angeles (90024) ***(G-12164)***
Ucla Health System...310 393-5153
1250 15th St Ste 111 Santa Monica (90404) ***(G-17552)***
Ucla Health System...310 825-9111
757 Westwood Plz Los Angeles (90095) ***(G-20151)***
Ucla Health System Auxiliary...310 794-0500
10920 Wilshire Blvd # 1700 Los Angeles (90024) ***(G-22585)***
Ucla Healthcare...310 319-4560
1821 Wilshire Blvd Fl 6 Santa Monica (90403) ***(G-21977)***
Ucla Marina Center...310 825-3671
111 Deneve Dr Los Angeles (90095) ***(G-19300)***
Ucla Mdcn SC Phrmclgy, Los Angeles *Also called Associated Students UCLA* ***(G-19362)***
Ucla Medical Center, Los Angeles *Also called University Cal Los Angeles* ***(G-21988)***
Ucla Medical Center, Sylmar *Also called University Cal Los Angeles* ***(G-21989)***
Ucla Nrpsychtric Bhvioral Hlth, Los Angeles *Also called Uc Regents* ***(G-20150)***
Ucla Primary Care Westlake, Westlake Village *Also called University Cal Los Angeles* ***(G-20163)***
Ucla Radiation Oncology, Los Angeles *Also called University Cal Los Angeles* ***(G-21987)***
Ucla SC Theater Film & TV Eqp...310 825-6165
102 East Melnitz Los Angeles (90095) ***(G-17915)***
Ucp Dronfield North, Sylmar *Also called United Cerebral Palsy* ***(G-21398)***
Ucp Work Inc...805 962-6699
2040 Alameda Padre Serra Santa Barbara (93103) ***(G-25591)***
Ucp Work Inc (PA)...805 566-9000
5464 Carpinteria Ave B Carpinteria (93013) ***(G-24398)***
Ucr Botany and Plant Sciences...951 827-5133
3401 Watkins Dr Riverside (92507) ***(G-12165)***
Ucsd Healthcare...858 657-7105
355 Dickinson St 340 San Diego (92103) ***(G-23076)***
Ucsd Thornton Hospital, La Jolla *Also called University Cal San Diego* ***(G-21993)***
Ucsf Aids Health Project...415 476-3902
1930 Market St San Francisco (94102) ***(G-24263)***
UCSF BENIOFF CHILDREN'S HOSPIT, Oakland *Also called Childrens Hospotal & Research* ***(G-21485)***
Ucsf Medical Center, San Francisco *Also called University Cal San Francisco* ***(G-21994)***
Ucsf Medical Center, San Francisco *Also called University Cal San Francisco* ***(G-20164)***
Ucsf Medical Center At Mt Zion, San Francisco *Also called University Cal San Francisco* ***(G-21997)***
Ucsf Mmory Clnic Alzhimers Ctr, San Francisco *Also called University Cal San Francisco* ***(G-20166)***
Ucsf Vascular Laboratories, San Francisco *Also called University Cal San Francisco* ***(G-21995)***
UDC, Anaheim *Also called Universal Dust Collector* ***(G-1477)***
Udp USA...408 519-5774
3003 N 1st St Ste 324 San Jose (95134) ***(G-16940)***
Uesugi Farms Inc (PA)...408 842-1294
1020 State Highway 25 Gilroy (95020) ***(G-101)***
Ufcw Employers Benefit Plan (PA)...925 746-7530
2200 Prof Dr Ste 200 Roseville (95661) ***(G-12206)***
Ufcw Local 770, Los Angeles *Also called United Food and Commercial* ***(G-25190)***
UFS International LLC...714 713-6311
16871 Millikan Ave Irvine (92606) ***(G-17553)***
Ugm Citatah Inc (PA)...562 921-9549
13220 Cambridge St Santa Fe Springs (90670) ***(G-6996)***
Ugmc, Santa Fe Springs *Also called Ugm Citatah Inc* ***(G-6996)***
Uhc of California (HQ)...714 952-1121
5995 Plaza Dr Cypress (90630) ***(G-10384)***
Uhp Healthcare, Inglewood *Also called Watts Health Foundation Inc* ***(G-21119)***
UHS, Chino *Also called Canyon Ridge Hospital Inc* ***(G-22052)***
UHS Surgical Services, Sun Valley *Also called PRI Medical Technologies Inc* ***(G-7304)***
Uhs-Corona Inc (HQ)...951 737-4343
800 S Main St Corona (92882) ***(G-21978)***
Uhs-Corona Inc...951 736-7200
730 Magnolia Ave Corona (92879) ***(G-22855)***
Uiprojects, Irvine *Also called United Infrstrcture Prjcts Inc* ***(G-26115)***
Uka LLC...949 610-8000
620 Newport Center Dr # 1400 Newport Beach (92660) ***(G-13365)***
Ukiah Adventist Hospital (PA)...707 463-7346
275 Hospital Dr Ukiah (95482) ***(G-21979)***
Ukiah Adventist Hospital...707 462-3111
1120 S Dora St Ukiah (95482) ***(G-21980)***
Ukiah Convalescent Hospital, Ukiah *Also called Berryman Health Inc* ***(G-21154)***
Ukiah SC Transportation...707 463-5234
710 Maple Ave Ukiah (95482) ***(G-3952)***
UKIAH VALLEY MEDICAL CENTER, Ukiah *Also called Ukiah Adventist Hospital* ***(G-21979)***
Uline Inc...909 605-7090
2950 Jurupa St Ontario (91761) ***(G-8217)***
Ullmen Associates LLC...310 444-3915
22129 Martinez St Woodland Hills (91364) ***(G-28085)***
Ulta Salon Cosmt Fragrance Inc...909 592-5393
1229 S Lone Hill Ave Glendora (91740) ***(G-13694)***
Ulta Salon Cosmt Fragrance Inc...661 664-1402
9000 Ming Ave Bakersfield (93311) ***(G-13695)***
Ulta Salon Cosmt Fragrance Inc...209 664-1725
2841 Countryside Dr Turlock (95380) ***(G-13696)***
Ulta Salon Cosmt Fragrance Inc...760 744-0853
185 S Las Posas Rd San Marcos (92078) ***(G-13697)***
Ultimate Communication Systems, Anaheim *Also called Rjb Enterprises Inc* ***(G-2712)***
Ultimate Construction Inc...562 633-3389
8811 Alonzo Blvd Long Beach (90805) ***(G-3099)***

ALPHABETIC

ULTIMATE DEMO, Pomona *Also called Ultimate Removal Inc* ***(G-3471)***
Ultimate Landscape Mgt Co....714 502-9711
700 E Sycamore St Anaheim (92805) ***(G-970)***
Ultimate Landscaping MGT....714 502-9711
700 E Sycamore St Anaheim (92805) ***(G-971)***
Ultimate Maintenance Svcs Inc....310 542-1474
4237 Redondo Beach Blvd Lawndale (90260) ***(G-14450)***
Ultimate Removal Inc....909 524-0800
2168 Pomona Blvd Pomona (91768) ***(G-3471)***
Ultimate Staffing Services, Orange *Also called Roth Staffing Companies LP* ***(G-14944)***
Ultimo Software Solutions Inc....408 943-1490
2860 Zanker Rd Ste 203 San Jose (95134) ***(G-15515)***
Ultra Solutions LLC....909 628-1778
1137 E Philadelphia St Ontario (91761) ***(G-7323)***
Ultradot Media....562 906-0737
9908 Bell Ranch Dr Santa Fe Springs (90670) ***(G-13984)***
Ultraex LLC....510 723-3760
2633 Barrington Ct Hayward (94545) ***(G-4432)***
Ultraex Inc....800 882-1000
2633 Barrington Ct Hayward (94545) ***(G-4433)***
Ultralink LLC....714 427-5500
535 Anton Blvd Ste 200 Costa Mesa (92626) ***(G-10227)***
Ultrasigns Electrical Advg, San Diego *Also called Jones Sign Co Inc* ***(G-7221)***
Ultraviolet Devices Inc....661 295-8140
26145 Technology Dr Valencia (91355) ***(G-7750)***
Uma Enterprises Inc (PA)....310 631-1166
350 W Apra St Compton (90220) ***(G-6898)***
Umina Bros Inc (PA)....213 622-9206
1601 E Olympic Blvd # 403 Los Angeles (90021) ***(G-8782)***
Umpqua Bank....818 385-1362
16501 Ventura Blvd Encino (91436) ***(G-9426)***
Umpqua Bank....949 474-1020
4040 Macarthur Blvd # 100 Newport Beach (92660) ***(G-9564)***
Umpqua Bank....619 668-5159
7777 Alvarado Rd Ste 515 La Mesa (91942) ***(G-9531)***
Ums Banking, Glendale *Also called United Merchant Svcs Cal Inc* ***(G-7075)***
UNAC/UHCP, San Dimas *Also called Associations of United Nurses* ***(G-25166)***
Uncle Credit Union (PA)....925 447-5001
2100 Las Positas Ct Livermore (94551) ***(G-9696)***
Undc, Sacramento *Also called Universal Network Dev Corp* ***(G-28086)***
Underground Cnstr Co Inc....707 746-8800
5145 Industrial Way Benicia (94510) ***(G-6294)***
Underground Elephant Inc....800 466-4178
600 B St Ste 1300 San Diego (92101) ***(G-13932)***
Underwriters Laboratories Inc....248 427-5300
455 E Trimble Rd San Jose (95131) ***(G-26896)***
Underwriters Laboratories Inc....510 771-1000
47173 Benicia St Fremont (94538) ***(G-26897)***
Underwriters Laboratories Inc....408 754-6500
4510 Riding Club Ct Hayward (94542) ***(G-26898)***
Underwriters Laboratories Inc....408 493-9910
2191 Zanker Rd San Jose (95131) ***(G-26899)***
Unec Solutions Inc....510 851-2808
655 Lewelling Blvd San Leandro (94579) ***(G-16514)***
Unfi, Rocklin *Also called United Natural Foods West Inc* ***(G-8945)***
Unfi, Rocklin *Also called United Natural Foods Inc* ***(G-8944)***
Unger & Associates Inc....949 249-2800
29805 Weatherwood Ste 200 Laguna Niguel (92677) ***(G-27703)***
Unical Aviation Inc (PA)....626 813-1901
680 S Lemon Ave City of Industry (91789) ***(G-8008)***
Unical Enterprises Inc....626 965-5588
16960 Gale Ave City of Industry (91745) ***(G-7207)***
Unico Industrial Service Co (PA)....707 736-8787
945 Tyler St Benicia (94510) ***(G-18027)***
Unico Mechanical Corp....707 745-4540
1209 Polk St Benicia (94510) ***(G-7898)***
Unifax Insurance Systems Inc....818 591-9800
26050 Mureau Rd Fl 2 Calabasas (91302) ***(G-10912)***
Unified Aircraft Services Inc (PA)....909 877-0535
1571 S Lilac Ave Bloomington (92316) ***(G-5205)***
Unified Food Ingredients Inc....760 744-7225
145 Vallecitos De Oro # 208 San Marcos (92069) ***(G-8942)***
Unified Grocers Inc (PA)....323 264-5200
5200 Sheila St Commerce (90040) ***(G-8540)***
Unified Grocers Inc....323 232-6124
457 E Martin Luther King Los Angeles (90011) ***(G-8595)***
Unified Grocers Inc....323 373-1339
3626 11th Ave Los Angeles (90018) ***(G-8541)***
Unified Grocers Inc....209 931-1990
1990 Piccoli Rd Stockton (95215) ***(G-8542)***
Unified Grocers Inc....323 264-5200
455 N Canyons Pkwy Livermore (94551) ***(G-8543)***
Unified Inv Programs Inc (PA)....310 782-1878
2368 Torrance Blvd # 200 Torrance (90501) ***(G-23077)***
Unified Teldata Inc....415 888-8940
126 Neider Ln Mill Valley (94941) ***(G-7651)***
Unified Valet Parking Inc....818 822-5807
99 S Chester Ave Fl 2 Pasadena (91106) ***(G-13801)***
Unifirst Corporation....209 941-8364
819 N Hunter St Stockton (95202) ***(G-13644)***
Unifirst Corporation....916 929-3766
4630 Beloit Dr Ste 40 Sacramento (95838) ***(G-13571)***
Unifirst Corporation....619 263-6116
4041 Market St San Diego (92102) ***(G-13645)***
Unifirst Corporation....909 390-8670
700 Etiwanda Ave Ste C Ontario (91761) ***(G-13646)***
Unifirst Corporation....559 233-0400
4730 E Commerce Ave Fresno (93725) ***(G-13647)***
Unifirst Corporation....408 297-8101
2016 Zanker Rd San Jose (95131) ***(G-13648)***
UNIFORM ACCESSORIES, Northridge *Also called Rashman Corporation* ***(G-7980)***
Unify Financial Federal Cr Un (PA)....310 536-5000
1899 Western Way Ste 100 Torrance (90501) ***(G-9645)***
Unigro, San Bernardino *Also called L & L Nursery Supply Inc* ***(G-9138)***
Unilab Corporation....916 927-9900
3714 Northgate Blvd Sacramento (95834) ***(G-22291)***
Unilab Corporation (HQ)....818 737-6000
8401 Fallbrook Ave West Hills (91304) ***(G-22292)***
Unilab Corporation....408 927-8331
6475 Camden Ave Ste 104 San Jose (95120) ***(G-22293)***
Union Asphalt Inc....805 922-3551
1625 E Donovan Rd Santa Maria (93454) ***(G-4076)***
Union Bank Cal Foundation, Los Angeles *Also called Union Bank Foundation* ***(G-9532)***
Union Bank Data Processing Ctr, San Diego *Also called Mufg Union Bank Na* ***(G-9413)***
Union Bank Foundation (HQ)....213 236-5000
445 S Figueroa St Ste 710 Los Angeles (90071) ***(G-9532)***
Union Bank of California....213 236-6444
445 S Figueroa St Ste 710 Los Angeles (90071) ***(G-9533)***
Union Building Maintenance, Commerce *Also called Uniserve Facilities Svcs Corp* ***(G-14451)***
Union City Medical Offices, Union City *Also called Kaiser Foundation Hospitals* ***(G-19597)***
Union Environmental Inc....714 550-0005
1534 E Edinger Ave Ste 1 Santa Ana (92705) ***(G-3593)***
Union Pacific Corporation....916 789-5311
9451 Atkinson St Ste 100 Roseville (95747) ***(G-3619)***
Union Pacific Railroad Company....805 286-5851
999 Paso Robles St Paso Robles (93446) ***(G-3620)***
Union Pacific Railroad Company....559 443-2244
3135 N Weber Ave Fresno (93705) ***(G-3621)***
Union Pacific Railroad Company....909 685-2710
2000 S Sycamore Ave Bloomington (92316) ***(G-3622)***
Union Pacific Railroad Company....916 789-5930
9391 Atkinson St Ste 100 Roseville (95747) ***(G-3623)***
Union Pacific Railroad Company....213 446-1900
4341 E Washington Blvd Commerce (90023) ***(G-3624)***
Union Pacific Railroad Company....916 789-6055
10031 Fthlls Blvd Ste 200 Roseville (95747) ***(G-3625)***
Union Pacific Railroad Company....510 874-1174
224 Curtis Ave Milpitas (95035) ***(G-3626)***
Union Pacific Railroad Company....559 443-2277
1300 E Shaw Ave Fresno (93710) ***(G-3629)***
Union Pacific Railroad Company....661 321-4604
730 Sumner St Bakersfield (93305) ***(G-3627)***
Union Pan Asian Communities (PA)....619 232-6454
1031 25th St San Diego (92102) ***(G-24264)***
Union Sanitary District....510 477-7500
5072 Benson Rd Union City (94587) ***(G-6420)***
Union Station Homeless Svcs....626 240-4550
825 E Orange Grove Blvd Pasadena (91104) ***(G-24265)***
Union Supply Company, Rancho Dominguez *Also called Union Supply Group Inc* ***(G-8544)***
Union Supply Group Inc (PA)....310 603-8899
2301 E Pacifica Pl Rancho Dominguez (90220) ***(G-8544)***
Unipark LLC....510 724-0811
1511 Sycamore Ave Ste 2m Hercules (94547) ***(G-17745)***
Unique Carpets Ltd....951 352-8125
7360 Jurupa Ave Riverside (92504) ***(G-6899)***
Uniserve Facilities Svcs Corp (PA)....213 533-1000
2363 S Atlantic Blvd Commerce (90040) ***(G-14451)***
Uniserve Facilities Svcs Corp....310 440-6747
1200 Getty Center Dr Los Angeles (90049) ***(G-14452)***
Unish Corporation....408 708-9300
4300 Stevens Creek Blvd San Jose (95129) ***(G-16515)***
Unison Electric....714 375-5915
16652 Gemini Ln Huntington Beach (92647) ***(G-2779)***
Unisource Maint Sup Systems, La Palma *Also called Veritiv Operating Company* ***(G-8223)***
Unisource Packaging Inc....925 227-6000
4225 Hacienda Dr Ste A Pleasanton (94588) ***(G-8218)***
Unisource Solutions Inc (PA)....562 654-3500
8350 Rex Rd Pico Rivera (90660) ***(G-6833)***
Unisys Corporation....949 380-5000
9701 Jeronimo Rd Ste 100 Irvine (92618) ***(G-15516)***
Unitas Global LLC (PA)....213 785-6200
453 S Spring St Ste 201 Los Angeles (90013) ***(G-16205)***
Unitd Van Lines Agnt, Hayward *Also called Chipman Corporation* ***(G-4127)***
Unite Eurotherapy Inc....760 585-1800
1255 Keystone Way Ste 106 Vista (92081) ***(G-8299)***
United Administrative Services, San Jose *Also called Chelbay Schuler & Chelbay* ***(G-10547)***
United Administrative Services....408 288-4400
6800 Santa Teresa Blvd # 100 San Jose (95119) ***(G-10563)***
United Agencies Inc (PA)....626 564-2670
301 E Colo Blvd Ste 200 Pasadena (91101) ***(G-10913)***
United Agribusiness League (PA)....949 975-1424
54 Corporate Park Irvine (92606) ***(G-25107)***
UNITED AGRICULTURAL BENEFIT TR, Irvine *Also called United Agribusiness League* ***(G-25107)***
United Airlines Inc....650 634-4209
United Airlines Mnt Optnb San Francisco (94128) ***(G-4827)***
United Airlines Inc....408 294-4028
1661 Airport Blvd San Jose (95110) ***(G-4828)***
United Airlines Inc....650 634-2468
2435 Whitman Way San Bruno (94066) ***(G-4829)***
United Airlines Inc....916 877-3002
6850 Airport Blvd Ste 34 Sacramento (95837) ***(G-5013)***
United Airlines Inc....310 342-8086
6018 Avion Dr Los Angeles (90045) ***(G-4830)***
United Airlines Inc....650 634-7800
Maintenance Operation Ctr San Francisco (94128) ***(G-4831)***
United Airlines Inc....310 646-3107
700 World Way Ste I Los Angeles (90045) ***(G-4832)***

ALPHABETIC

ALPHABETIC SECTION United Parcel Service Inc OH

United Airlines Inc......619 692-3310
3835 N Harbor Dr Ste 115 San Diego (92101) *(G-4833)*
United Airlines Inc......310 258-3319
7300 World Way W Rm 144 Los Angeles (90045) *(G-4834)*
United Airlines Inc......650 634-4469
San Francisco Intl Arprt San Francisco (94128) *(G-4835)*
United Airlines Inc......760 778-5690
3400 E Tahquitz Cyn 17 Palm Springs (92262) *(G-4836)*
United Airlines Inc......650 634-2772
545 Mcdonald Rd 68305 San Francisco (94128) *(G-4837)*
United Artists Productions Inc......310 449-3000
10250 Constellation Blvd # 19 Los Angeles (90067) *(G-18280)*
United Auburn Indian Community......916 408-7777
1200 Athens Ave Lincoln (95648) *(G-13366)*
United Behavioral Health......925 246-1343
2300 Clayton Rd Ste 1000 Concord (94520) *(G-10385)*
United Behavioral Health......619 641-6800
3111 Cmino Del Rio N 50 Ste 500 San Diego (92108) *(G-27263)*
United Behavioral Health (HQ)......415 547-1403
425 Market St Fl 18 San Francisco (94105) *(G-27264)*
United Biosource LLC......415 293-1340
303 2nd St Ste 700 San Francisco (94107) *(G-727)*
United Blood Services Ventura, San Luis Obispo *Also called Blood Systems Inc (G-22900)*
United Brothers Concrete Inc......760 346-1013
41905 Boardwalk Ste K Palm Desert (92211) *(G-3343)*
United Building Maintenance......916 772-8101
8211 Sierra College Blvd # 420 Roseville (95661) *(G-14453)*
United Building Services, Santa Ana *Also called Ponderosa Builders Inc (G-14392)*
United California Glass & Door......415 824-8500
745 Cesar Chavez San Francisco (94124) *(G-18028)*
United California Realty Inc......760 949-4040
12829 Bear Valley Rd Victorville (92392) *(G-11891)*
United Care Homes, City of Industry *Also called Pruitthealth Corporation (G-21353)*
United Cargo Logistics, City of Industry *Also called U C L Incorporated (G-4281)*
United Cerebral Palsy......818 364-5911
13272 Dronfield Ave Sylmar (91342) *(G-21398)*
United Cerebral Palsy Assn San, Stockton *Also called United Cerebral Palsy Associat (G-22183)*
United Cerebral Palsy Assn San (PA)......858 495-3155
8525 Gibbs Dr Ste 209 San Diego (92123) *(G-25592)*
United Cerebral Palsy Assoc......949 333-6400
980 Roosevelt Ste 100 Irvine (92620) *(G-24266)*
United Cerebral Palsy Assoc (PA)......209 956-0290
333 W Benjamin Holt Dr # 1 Stockton (95207) *(G-24267)*
United Cerebral Palsy Assoc of......805 543-2039
3620 Sacramento Dr # 201 San Luis Obispo (93401) *(G-24990)*
United Cerebral Palsy Associat......209 956-0295
333 W Benjamin Holt Dr # 1 Stockton (95207) *(G-22183)*
United Chinese American Genera (PA)......714 228-7800
6363 Katella Ave Cypress (90630) *(G-10914)*
United Cmps Cnfrences Retreats (PA)......707 762-3220
1304 Sthpint Blvd Ste 200 Petaluma (94954) *(G-13472)*
United Com Serve......530 790-3000
1260 Williams Way Yuba City (95991) *(G-20998)*
United Consortium, Valencia *Also called CC Wellness LLC (G-8248)*
United Convalescent Facilities......626 629-6950
230 E Adams Blvd Los Angeles (90011) *(G-21399)*
United Couriers Inc (HQ)......213 383-3611
3280 E Foothill Blvd Pasadena (91107) *(G-4838)*
United Cp/S Chldrns Fndn La......805 494-1141
2170 N Westlake Blvd 22 Westlake Village (91362) *(G-24268)*
United Cp/S Chldrns Fndn La......818 998-8755
11051 Old Snta Susna Pass Chatsworth (91311) *(G-24839)*
United Cp/S Chldrns Fndn La......818 782-2211
6430 Independence Ave Woodland Hills (91367) *(G-21400)*
United Cp/S Chldrns Fndn La......323 737-0303
2628 Brighton Ave Los Angeles (90018) *(G-24269)*
United Cpitl Fncl Advisers LLC......949 999-8500
620 Nwport Ctr Dr Ste 500 Newport Beach (92660) *(G-10190)*
United Crbrl Plsy of Cntrl CA (PA)......559 221-8272
4224 N Cedar Ave Fresno (93726) *(G-24270)*
United Development Group Inc......858 244-0900
2805 Dickens St Ste 103 San Diego (92106) *(G-12021)*
United El Segundo Inc (PA)......310 323-3992
17311 S Main St Gardena (90248) *(G-9029)*
United Exchange Corp......562 977-4500
17211 Valley View Ave Cerritos (90703) *(G-8300)*
United Express Messengers Inc......310 261-2000
1801 Century Park E # 520 Los Angeles (90067) *(G-17554)*
United Fabricare Supply Inc (PA)......310 886-3790
1237 W Walnut St Compton (90220) *(G-7984)*
United Fabrics Intl Inc......213 749-8200
1723 S Central Ave Los Angeles (90021) *(G-8329)*
United Facilities Inc......209 839-8051
25451 Mountain House Pkwy Tracy (95377) *(G-4646)*
United Facilities Inc......951 685-7030
11618 Mulberry Ave Fontana (92337) *(G-4647)*
United Family Care Inc......909 822-1164
8110 Mango Ave Ste 104 Fontana (92335) *(G-20152)*
United Family Care Inc (PA)......909 874-1679
8110 Mango Ave Ste 104 Fontana (92335) *(G-20153)*
United Farm Workers America (PA)......661 822-5571
29700 Wdford Tehachapi Rd Keene (93531) *(G-25189)*
United Floral Exchange Inc......760 597-1940
2834 La Mirada Dr Ste B Vista (92081) *(G-9222)*
United Food and Commercial (PA)......213 487-7070
630 Shatto Pl Ste 300 Los Angeles (90005) *(G-25190)*
United General Title Insurance, Riverside *Also called First American Financial Corp (G-10516)*
United Hauling Corp......626 358-9417
2620 Buena Vista St Duarte (91010) *(G-17656)*
United Health Ctrs San Joaquin (PA)......559 646-6618
650 S Zediker Ave Bldg 3 Parlier (93648) *(G-22856)*
United Health Ctrs San Joaquin......559 626-4031
445 11th St Orange Cove (93646) *(G-22857)*
United Health Systems Inc......530 662-9161
124 Walnut St Woodland (95695) *(G-20999)*
United Imaging, Woodland Hills *Also called United Ribbon Company Inc (G-8182)*
United Independent Taxi Co......213 385-2227
900 N Alvarado St Los Angeles (90026) *(G-3870)*
United Indian Health Services (PA)......707 825-5000
1600 Weeot Way Arcata (95521) *(G-20154)*
United Infrstrcture Prjcts Inc......213 402-1232
9891 Irvine Center Dr # 200 Irvine (92618) *(G-26115)*
United Insurance Company......323 869-9381
5601 E Slauson Ave # 105 Commerce (90040) *(G-10915)*
United International, San Rafael *Also called Cellmark Inc (G-8108)*
United Landscape Resource Inc......530 671-1029
5411 Colusa Hwy Yuba City (95993) *(G-972)*
United Marble & Granite Inc......408 347-3300
2163 Martin Ave Santa Clara (95050) *(G-6997)*
United Medical Imaging Inc......310 943-8400
1762 Westwood Blvd # 230 Los Angeles (90024) *(G-20155)*
United Medical Management Inc......909 886-5291
1680 N Waterman Ave San Bernardino (92404) *(G-21401)*
United Merchant Svcs Cal Inc......818 246-6767
750 Fairmont Ave Ste 201 Glendale (91203) *(G-7075)*
United Mfg Assembly Inc......510 490-1065
44169 Fremont Blvd Fremont (94538) *(G-26900)*
United Natural Foods Inc......831 462-5870
2450 17th Ave Ste 250 Santa Cruz (95062) *(G-8943)*
United Natural Foods Inc......916 625-4100
1101 Sunset Blvd Rocklin (95765) *(G-8944)*
United Natural Foods West Inc (HQ)......401 528-8634
1101 Sunset Blvd Rocklin (95765) *(G-8945)*
United Oil, Gardena *Also called United El Segundo Inc (G-9029)*
United Pacific Services Inc......562 691-4600
251 Imperial Hwy Ste 450 South Gate (90280) *(G-973)*
United Pacific Waste......562 699-7600
4334 San Gbriel Rver Pkwy Pico Rivera (90660) *(G-6572)*
United Paradyne Corporation......805 734-2359
P.O. Box 5368 Santa Barbara (93150) *(G-27265)*
United Parcel Service Inc......760 241-5540
14592 Palmdale Rd Victorville (92392) *(G-17555)*
United Parcel Service Inc......800 742-5877
12745 Arroyo St Sylmar (91342) *(G-4434)*
United Parcel Service Inc......650 737-3737
657 Forbes Blvd South San Francisco (94080) *(G-4435)*
United Parcel Service Inc OH......760 325-1762
650 N Commercial Rd Palm Springs (92262) *(G-4436)*
United Parcel Service Inc OH......530 623-3938
716 Main St 1 Weaverville (96093) *(G-4437)*
United Parcel Service Inc OH......678 339-3171
3331 Industrial Dr Ste C Santa Rosa (95403) *(G-17556)*
United Parcel Service Inc OH......510 262-2338
1601 Atlas Rd Richmond (94806) *(G-4438)*
United Parcel Service Inc OH......800 742-5877
2800 W 227th St Torrance (90505) *(G-4439)*
United Parcel Service Inc OH......323 837-1220
2747 Vail Ave Commerce (90040) *(G-17557)*
United Parcel Service Inc OH......530 365-7850
6845 Eastside Rd Anderson (96007) *(G-4440)*
United Parcel Service Inc OH......760 872-7661
2915 N Sierra Hwy Bishop (93514) *(G-4441)*
United Parcel Service Inc OH......916 373-4076
1380 Shore St West Sacramento (95691) *(G-4442)*
United Parcel Service Inc OH......800 742-5877
1400 Hil Mor Dr Ceres (95307) *(G-4443)*
United Parcel Service Inc OH......707 864-8200
5000 W Cordelia Rd Fairfield (94534) *(G-4444)*
United Parcel Service Inc OH......760 752-7809
111 Bingham Dr San Marcos (92069) *(G-4445)*
United Parcel Service Inc OH......707 224-1205
2531 Napa Valley Corp Dr NAPA (94558) *(G-4446)*
United Parcel Service Inc OH......916 373-4089
128 Shore St Sacramento (95829) *(G-4447)*
United Parcel Service Inc OH......323 260-8957
3333 S Downey Rd Vernon (90058) *(G-4874)*
United Parcel Service Inc OH......310 217-2646
17115 S Western Ave Gardena (90247) *(G-4448)*
United Parcel Service Inc OH......209 463-1971
1532 N Broadway Ave Stockton (95205) *(G-4449)*
United Parcel Service Inc OH......408 291-2942
1999 S 7th St San Jose (95112) *(G-4450)*
United Parcel Service Inc OH......951 928-5221
25283 Sherman Rd Sun City (92585) *(G-4875)*
United Parcel Service Inc OH......209 944-5932
1724 Wawona St Manteca (95337) *(G-4876)*
United Parcel Service Inc OH......415 252-4564
2222 17th St San Francisco (94103) *(G-4451)*
United Parcel Service Inc OH......707 252-4560
1012 Sterling St Vallejo (94591) *(G-4452)*
United Parcel Service Inc OH......949 643-6595
22 Brookline Aliso Viejo (92656) *(G-4453)*
United Parcel Service Inc OH......909 974-7250
3221 E Jurupa Ontario (91764) *(G-17558)*
United Parcel Service Inc OH......310 474-0019
10690 Santa Monica Blvd Los Angeles (90025) *(G-4454)*

ALPHABETIC

United Parcel Service Inc OH.....858 455-8800
6060 Cornerstone Ct W San Diego (92121) ***(G-4455)***
United Parcel Service Inc OH.....909 974-7190
Ontario Airport Ontario (91758) ***(G-4877)***
United Parcel Service Inc OH.....404 828-6000
16000 Arminta St Van Nuys (91406) ***(G-4456)***
United Parcel Service Inc OH.....909 279-5111
7925 Ronson Rd San Diego (92111) ***(G-4457)***
United Parcel Service Inc OH.....559 651-0995
10609 W Goshen Ave 304 Visalia (93291) ***(G-4458)***
United Parcel Service Inc OH.....800 828-8264
290 W Avenue L Lancaster (93534) ***(G-4459)***
United Parcel Service Inc OH.....800 742-5877
1746 D St South Lake Tahoe (96150) ***(G-17559)***
United Parcel Service Inc OH.....562 404-3236
13233 Moore St Cerritos (90703) ***(G-4460)***
United Parcel Service Inc OH.....626 280-8012
201 W Garvey Ave Ste 102 Monterey Park (91754) ***(G-17560)***
United Parcel Service Inc OH.....707 468-5481
259 Cherry St Ukiah (95482) ***(G-4461)***
United Parcel Service Inc OH.....818 735-0945
4607 Lakeview Canyon Rd Westlake Village (91361) ***(G-17561)***
United Parcel Service Inc OH.....831 757-6294
6 Upper Ragsdale Dr Monterey (93940) ***(G-4462)***
United Parcel Service Inc OH.....619 443-3266
17370 Jasmine St Victorville (92395) ***(G-4463)***
United Parcel Service Inc OH.....801 973-3400
3601 Sacramento Dr San Luis Obispo (93401) ***(G-4464)***
United Parcel Service Inc OH.....650 952-5200
3860 Cypress Dr Petaluma (94954) ***(G-4465)***
United Parcel Service Inc OH.....805 964-7848
505 Pine Ave Goleta (93117) ***(G-4466)***
United Parcel Service Inc OH.....805 922-7851
309 Cooley Ln Santa Maria (93455) ***(G-4467)***
United Parcel Service Inc OH.....925 689-6584
1970 Olivera Rd Concord (94520) ***(G-4468)***
United Parcel Service Inc OH.....209 736-0878
2342 Gun Club Rd Angels Camp (95222) ***(G-4469)***
United Parcel Service Inc OH.....805 375-1832
1501 Rancho Conejo Blvd Newbury Park (91320) ***(G-4470)***
United Parcel Service Inc OH.....323 729-6762
3000 E Washington Blvd Los Angeles (90023) ***(G-4471)***
United Parcel Service Inc OH.....714 491-7000
2300 Boswell Ct Chula Vista (91914) ***(G-4472)***
United Parcel Service Inc OH.....559 651-7690
7401 W Sunnyview Ave Visalia (93291) ***(G-4473)***
United Parcel Service Inc OH.....831 425-1054
251 Sylvania Ave Santa Cruz (95060) ***(G-4474)***
United Parcel Service Inc OH.....909 974-7000
3140 Jurupa St Ontario (91761) ***(G-4475)***
United Parcel Service Inc OH.....800 833-9943
4500 Norris Canyon Rd San Ramon (94583) ***(G-4476)***
United Parcel Service Inc OH.....951 749-3400
11811 Landon Dr Mira Loma (91752) ***(G-17562)***
United Parcel Service Inc OH.....805 656-3442
2559 Palma Dr Ventura (93003) ***(G-4477)***
United Parcel Service Inc OH.....626 814-6216
1100 Baldwin Park Blvd Baldwin Park (91706) ***(G-4478)***
United Parcel Service Inc OH.....916 857-0311
3930 Kristi Ct Sacramento (95827) ***(G-4479)***
United Parcel Service Inc OH.....800 742-5877
48921 Warm Springs Blvd Fremont (94539) ***(G-17563)***
United Parcel Service Inc OH.....866 553-1069
91 W Easy St Simi Valley (93065) ***(G-17564)***
United Paving Company, Corona *Also called Superior Paving Company Inc* ***(G-1870)***
United Payment Services Inc.....866 886-4833
3537 Old Conejo Rd # 113 Newbury Park (91320) ***(G-17565)***
United Petrochemicals Inc.....949 629-8736
3000 W Macarthur Blvd # 300 Santa Ana (92704) ***(G-9000)***
United Power Contractors Inc.....760 735-8028
405 Maple St Ste A-103 Ramona (92065) ***(G-2005)***
United Pumping Service Inc.....626 961-9326
14000 Valley Blvd City of Industry (91746) ***(G-4077)***
United Refrigeration Inc.....310 204-2500
3573a Hayden Ave Culver City (90232) ***(G-7761)***
United Rentals North Amer Inc.....209 948-9500
2911 E Fremont St Stockton (95205) ***(G-14585)***
United Rentals North Amer Inc.....562 695-0748
3455 San Gbriel Rver Pkwy Pico Rivera (90660) ***(G-14586)***
United Ribbon Company Inc.....818 716-1515
21201 Oxnard St Woodland Hills (91367) ***(G-8182)***
United Riggers & Erectors Inc (PA).....909 978-0400
4188 Valley Blvd Walnut (91789) ***(G-3482)***
United Road Towing Inc.....909 923-6100
1516 S Bon View Ave Ontario (91761) ***(G-17901)***
United Road Towing Inc.....909 798-4863
945 W Brockton Ave Redlands (92374) ***(G-17902)***
United Road Towing Inc.....818 782-1996
7817 Woodley Ave Van Nuys (91406) ***(G-17903)***
United Road Towing Inc.....702 649-5711
1516 S Bon View Ave Ontario (91761) ***(G-17904)***
United Samples Inc.....949 251-1768
2590 Main St Irvine (92614) ***(G-8301)***
United Seal Coating Slurryseal.....805 563-4922
3463 State St Ste 522 Santa Barbara (93105) ***(G-1708)***
United Service Tech Inc.....714 224-1406
21801 Cactus Ave Ste A Riverside (92518) ***(G-18029)***
United Services Auto Assn.....760 757-1340
2178 Vista Way Ste E5 Oceanside (92054) ***(G-10479)***
United Site Services Cal Inc (PA).....626 462-9110
242 Live Oak Ave Irwindale (91706) ***(G-14587)***
United Site Services Cal Inc.....408 295-2263
3408 Hillcap Ave San Jose (95136) ***(G-14588)***
United Site Services Cal Inc.....707 747-2810
1 Oak Rd Benicia (94510) ***(G-6573)***
United Spectrum Inc.....714 283-1010
1910 N Lime St Orange (92865) ***(G-3594)***
United States Cold Storage.....661 832-2653
6501 District Blvd Bakersfield (93313) ***(G-4504)***
United States Cold Storage.....559 237-6145
2003 S Cherry Ave Fresno (93721) ***(G-4505)***
United States Cold Storage CA, Union City *Also called United States Cold Storage Inc* ***(G-4506)***
United States Cold Storage Cal, Bakersfield *Also called United States Cold Storage* ***(G-4504)***
United States Cold Storage Inc.....510 489-8300
33400 Dowe Ave Union City (94587) ***(G-4506)***
United States Cold Storage Inc.....559 686-1110
810 E Continental Ave Tulare (93274) ***(G-4507)***
United States Cold Storage Inc.....209 835-2653
1400 N Macarthur Dr Ste A Tracy (95376) ***(G-4508)***
United States Dept of Army.....916 557-5100
1325 J St Sacramento (95814) ***(G-26116)***
United States Dept of Energy.....510 486-4000
1 Cyclotron Rd Berkeley (94720) ***(G-26815)***
United States Dept of Energy.....510 486-4936
1 Cyclotron Rd Berkeley (94720) ***(G-26626)***
United States Dept of Energy.....925 422-1100
7000 East Ave Livermore (94550) ***(G-26627)***
United States Dept of Navy.....619 524-1069
32444 Echo Ln Fl 3 San Diego (92147) ***(G-14967)***
United States Dept of Navy.....559 998-4201
937 Vista Pl Lemoore (93245) ***(G-21981)***
United States Dept of Navy.....619 532-6397
8808 Balboa Ave San Diego (92123) ***(G-20156)***
United States Dept of Navy.....619 532-8953
34800 Bob Wilson Dr # 409 San Diego (92134) ***(G-20157)***
United States Dept of Navy.....619 556-8210
2310 Craven St San Diego (92136) ***(G-20158)***
United States Dept of Navy.....559 998-4481
Bldg 937 Franklin Ave Lemoore (93246) ***(G-21982)***
United States Dept of Navy.....619 532-2317
1220 Pacific Hwy San Diego (92132) ***(G-26117)***
United States Dept of Navy.....760 830-2190
Us Naval Hosp Bldg 1145 Twentynine Palms (92278) ***(G-21983)***
United States Dept of Navy.....805 982-6392
162 1st St Port Hueneme (93043) ***(G-20159)***
United States Dept of Navy.....619 532-6400
34800 Bob Wilson Dr San Diego (92134) ***(G-21984)***
United States Dept of Navy.....619 532-1897
937 N Harbor Dr San Diego (92132) ***(G-26628)***
United States Dept of Navy.....559 998-2894
937 Franklin Blvd Lemoore (93246) ***(G-21985)***
United States Dept of Navy.....619 532-7400
34730 Bob Wilson Dr San Diego (92134) ***(G-20160)***
United States Dept of Navy.....805 982-6370
162 1st St Bldg 1402 Port Hueneme (93043) ***(G-20161)***
United States Dept of Navy.....619 767-6592
4170 Norman Scott Rd San Diego (92136) ***(G-20162)***
United States Dept of Navy.....831 656-4613
7 Grace Hopper Ave Stop 2 Monterey (93943) ***(G-26629)***
United States Fdral Prbatn, San Jose *Also called Adminstrtive Office of US Crts* ***(G-23643)***
United States Fire Insur Co.....213 797-3100
777 S Figueroa St # 1500 Los Angeles (90017) ***(G-10916)***
United States Forest Service.....530 335-4103
17696 State Highway 89 Hat Creek (96040) ***(G-1018)***
United States Info Systems Inc.....845 353-9224
7621 Galilee Rd Roseville (95678) ***(G-2780)***
United States Marines Youth Fd.....805 967-7990
90 La Venta Dr Santa Barbara (93110) ***(G-25385)***
United States Pipe Fndry LLC.....510 441-5810
1295 Whipple Rd Union City (94587) ***(G-4952)***
United States Pony Clubs.....916 791-1223
7010 Hidden Valley Pl Granite Bay (95746) ***(G-19116)***
United States Probation Office, San Diego *Also called Adminstrtive Office of US Crts* ***(G-23644)***
United States Technical Svcs.....714 374-6300
16541 Gothard St Ste 214 Huntington Beach (92647) ***(G-16516)***
United Stationers, City of Industry *Also called Essendant Co* ***(G-8166)***
United Sttes Bowl Congress Inc.....530 527-9049
12895 Arbor Ln Red Bluff (96080) ***(G-25593)***
United Sttes Intrmdal Svcs LLC.....209 341-4045
502 E Whitmore Ave Modesto (95358) ***(G-5183)***
United Sttes Olympic Committee.....619 656-1500
2800 Olympic Pkwy Chula Vista (91915) ***(G-18565)***
United Svcs Amer Federal Cr Un (PA).....858 831-8100
9999 Willow Creek Rd San Diego (92131) ***(G-9646)***
United Talent Agency Inc.....310 385-2800
1880 Century Park E Los Angeles (90067) ***(G-27704)***
United Teachers Los Angeles.....213 487-5560
3303 Wilshire Blvd Fl 10 Los Angeles (90010) ***(G-25191)***
United Temp Services Inc.....408 472-4309
694 Albanese Cir San Jose (95111) ***(G-14811)***
United Transport Service Inc.....951 258-2262
6750 Black Forest Dr Corona (92880) ***(G-17566)***
United Van Lines, San Diego *Also called Sullivan Moving & Storage* ***(G-4268)***
United Van Lines, Fontana *Also called McCollisters Trnsp Group Inc* ***(G-4220)***
United Van Lines Agent.....909 946-7655
1450 N Benson Ave Upland (91786) ***(G-4283)***

ALPHABETIC

United Way Inc 661 874-4288
44907 10th St W Lancaster (93534) ***(G-24991)***
United Way Inc (PA) 213 808-6220
1150 S Olive St Ste T500 Los Angeles (90015) ***(G-24992)***
United Way Greater Los Angeles, Los Angeles *Also called United Way Inc* ***(G-24992)***
United Way of Bay Area (PA) 415 808-4300
550 Kearny St Ste 1000 San Francisco (94108) ***(G-24271)***
United Way, The, San Francisco *Also called United Way of Bay Area* ***(G-24271)***
United Westlabs Inc 661 254-0801
25751 Mcbean Pkwy Ste 200 Santa Clarita (91355) ***(G-22294)***
Unitedhealth Group Inc 714 969-9050
7891 Moonmist Cir Huntington Beach (92648) ***(G-10386)***
Unitedhealth Group Inc 952 936-1300
5701 Katella Ave Cypress (90630) ***(G-10387)***
Unitedhealth Group Inc 530 879-8251
2080 E 20th St Chico (95928) ***(G-10388)***
Unitek Inc 510 623-8544
47333 Warm Springs Blvd Fremont (94539) ***(G-16070)***
Unitek Information Systems Inc (PA) 510 249-1060
4670 Auto Mall Pkwy Fremont (94538) ***(G-16517)***
Unitek It Education, Fremont *Also called Unitek Information Systems Inc* ***(G-16517)***
Unity Courier Service Inc 510 568-8890
1132 Beecher St San Leandro (94577) ***(G-17567)***
Unity SEC & Protective Svc 323 695-7234
619 E Washington Blvd Pasadena (91104) ***(G-16839)***
Unity Software Inc 415 848-2533
30 3rd St San Francisco (94103) ***(G-15870)***
Unity Technologies, San Francisco *Also called Unity Software Inc* ***(G-15870)***
Univ of CA 831 459-5041
1156 High St Santa Cruz (95064) ***(G-26716)***
Univar USA Inc 323 727-7005
2600 Garfield Ave Commerce (90040) ***(G-9001)***
Univar USA Inc 408 435-8649
2256 Junction Ave San Jose (95131) ***(G-9002)***
Univers of Calif San Diego Hs 619 543-3713
200 W Arbor Dr 8201 San Diego (92103) ***(G-21986)***
Universal 909 882-5337
4632 Acacia Ave San Bernardino (92407) ***(G-14454)***
Universal Accounts Inc 626 356-7900
690 E Green St Ste 300 Pasadena (91101) ***(G-14049)***
Universal Asphalt Co Inc 562 941-0201
10610 Painter Ave Santa Fe Springs (90670) ***(G-1879)***
Universal Bank (PA) 626 854-2818
3455 S Nogales St Fl 2 West Covina (91792) ***(G-9583)***
Universal Bldg Svcs & Sup Co (PA) 510 527-1078
3120 Pierce St Richmond (94804) ***(G-14455)***
Universal Bldg Svcs & Sup Co 925 934-5533
421 N Buchanan Cir Pacheco (94553) ***(G-14456)***
Universal Bldg Svcs & Sup Co 408 995-5111
430 Roberson Ln San Jose (95112) ***(G-14457)***
Universal Building Maint LLC 714 619-9700
1551 N Tustin Ave Ste 650 Santa Ana (92705) ***(G-14458)***
Universal Card Inc 949 861-4000
9012 Research Dr Ste 200 Irvine (92618) ***(G-17568)***
Universal Care Inc (PA) 562 424-6200
19762 Macarthur Blvd # 100 Irvine (92612) ***(G-22858)***
Universal Care Inc 562 461-1179
17660 Lakewood Blvd Bellflower (90706) ***(G-22859)***
Universal City Studios Inc 310 865-5000
2220 Colorado Ave Santa Monica (90404) ***(G-18176)***
Universal City Studios LLC 818 777-1000
100 Universal City Plz Universal City (91608) ***(G-18177)***
Universal Custom Courier, San Fernando *Also called Universal Mail Delivery Svc* ***(G-4078)***
Universal Custom Farming Co, Tranquillity *Also called Don Gragnani Farms* ***(G-356)***
Universal Cylinder Exch Inc 714 744-1036
692 N Cypress St Ste B Orange (92867) ***(G-28165)***
Universal Dust Collector 714 630-8588
1041 N Kraemer Pl Anaheim (92806) ***(G-1477)***
Universal Framing Products, Santa Clarita *Also called Universal Wood Moulding Inc* ***(G-6900)***
Universal General Builders 650 591-3104
871 Industrial Rd Ste A San Carlos (94070) ***(G-26118)***
Universal Home Care Inc 323 653-9222
151 N San Vicente Blvd Beverly Hills (90211) ***(G-22586)***
Universal Limousine & Trnsp Co 916 361-5466
9944 Mills Station Rd C Sacramento (95827) ***(G-3853)***
Universal Mail Delivery Svc (PA) 818 997-7531
501 S Brand Blvd Ste 4 San Fernando (91340) ***(G-4078)***
Universal Mail Delivery Svc 310 884-5900
220 W Victoria St Compton (90220) ***(G-4079)***
Universal McCann, San Francisco *Also called McCann World Group Inc* ***(G-13881)***
Universal Mus Investments Inc (HQ) 818 577-4700
2220 Colorado Ave Santa Monica (90404) ***(G-17569)***
Universal Music Enterprises 310 865-7857
2220 Colorado Ave Santa Monica (90404) ***(G-12226)***
Universal Music Group Inc (HQ) 310 865-4000
2220 Colorado Ave Santa Monica (90404) ***(G-17570)***
Universal Music Group Inc 310 865-4000
2220 Colorado Ave Santa Monica (90404) ***(G-18502)***
Universal Music Group Inc 818 286-4000
10 Universal City Plz Universal City (91608) ***(G-17571)***
Universal Network Dev Corp (PA) 916 475-1200
2555 3rd St Ste 112 Sacramento (95818) ***(G-28086)***
Universal Network Exchange, Burbank *Also called Unx Inc A Delaware Corp* ***(G-15517)***
Universal Packg Systems Inc 909 517-2442
14570 Monte Vista Ave Chino (91710) ***(G-4648)***
Universal Pain MGT Med Corp (PA) 661 267-6876
819 Auto Center Dr Ste A Palmdale (93551) ***(G-27266)***
Universal Pictures Intl, Universal City *Also called Nbcuniversal Media LLC* ***(G-5812)***
Universal Protection Svc LP 805 496-4401
2415 San Ramon Vly Blvd San Ramon (94583) ***(G-16840)***
Universal Protection Svc LP 562 981-5700
340 Golden Shore Ste 100 Long Beach (90802) ***(G-16841)***
Universal Protection Svc LP 818 227-1240
21300 Victory Blvd # 230 Woodland Hills (91367) ***(G-16842)***
Universal Protection Svc LP (HQ) 714 619-9700
1551 N Tustin Ave Ste 650 Santa Ana (92705) ***(G-16843)***
Universal Protection Svc LP 415 759-5056
1208 Vicente St San Francisco (94116) ***(G-16844)***
Universal Self Storage 951 206-5263
25980 Barton Rd Loma Linda (92354) ***(G-4649)***
Universal Services America LP 831 751-3230
141 Auburn St Salinas (93901) ***(G-17572)***
Universal Services America LP 760 200-2865
77725 Enfield Ln Palm Desert (92211) ***(G-28166)***
Universal Services America LP (PA) 714 619-9700
1551 N Tustin Ave Santa Ana (92705) ***(G-16845)***
Universal Services America LP 408 993-1965
777 N 1st St Ste 150 San Jose (95112) ***(G-16941)***
Universal Site Services Inc 408 295-9688
760 E Capitol Ave Milpitas (95035) ***(G-14459)***
Universal Stdios HM Entrmt LLC 818 777-1000
100 Universal City Plz Universal City (91608) ***(G-18178)***
Universal Stdios Licensing Inc 818 762-6284
100 Universal City Plz Universal City (91608) ***(G-12227)***
Universal Studios Inc 818 622-4455
1000 Univ Studio Blvd 2 Universal City (91608) ***(G-18179)***
Universal Studios Inc (HQ) 818 777-1000
100 Universal City Plz North Hollywood (91608) ***(G-18180)***
Universal Studios Inc 818 777-1000
100 Universal City Plz # 3 Universal City (91608) ***(G-18181)***
Universal Studios Inc 818 262-4301
1295 Los Angeles St Ste 1 Glendale (91204) ***(G-18182)***
Universal Studios Inc 310 235-4749
2440 S Sepulveda Blvd # 100 Los Angeles (90064) ***(G-18183)***
Universal Studios Inc 818 753-0000
4123 Lankershim Blvd North Hollywood (91602) ***(G-18184)***
Universal Studios Inc 818 777-2351
3900 Lankershim Blvd Studio City (91604) ***(G-18185)***
Universal Studios Consmr Pdts, Universal City *Also called Universal Stdios Licensing Inc* ***(G-12227)***
Universal Studios Hollywood, Universal City *Also called Universal City Studios LLC* ***(G-18177)***
Universal Wood Moulding Inc (PA) 661 362-6262
21139 Centre Pointe Pkwy Santa Clarita (91350) ***(G-6900)***
Universe Holdings Dev Co LLC 310 785-0077
350 S Beverly Dr Ste 210 Beverly Hills (90212) ***(G-11892)***
UNIVERSITY BOOKSTORE, Los Angeles *Also called California State Univ Aux Svcs* ***(G-26954)***
University Cal Irvine Med Cent 714 456-5678
208 Giotto Irvine (92614) ***(G-23078)***
University Cal Los Angeles 805 494-6920
1250 Avanta Dr Ste 207 Westlake Village (91361) ***(G-20163)***
University Cal Los Angeles 310 825-9771
200 Medical Pl Ste B265 Los Angeles (90095) ***(G-21987)***
University Cal Los Angeles 310 825-0640
200 Ucla Medical Plz Los Angeles (90095) ***(G-21988)***
University Cal Los Angeles 818 364-1555
14445 Olive View Dr Sylmar (91342) ***(G-21989)***
University Cal Los Angeles 310 319-4000
1225 15th St Santa Monica (90404) ***(G-21990)***
University Cal Los Angeles 310 825-9111
757 Westwood Plz Los Angeles (90095) ***(G-21991)***
University Cal San Diego 619 543-6654
200 W Arbor Dr Frnt San Diego (92103) ***(G-21992)***
University Cal San Diego 858 534-5000
10100 Hopkins Dr La Jolla (92093) ***(G-16206)***
University Cal San Diego 858 657-7000
9300 Campus Point Dr La Jolla (92037) ***(G-21993)***
University Cal San Francisco 415 476-9000
500 Parnassus Ave San Francisco (94143) ***(G-26816)***
University Cal San Francisco 415 476-1000
185 Berry St Ste 2000 San Francisco (94107) ***(G-21994)***
University Cal San Francisco 415 476-1000
505 Parnassus Ave San Francisco (94143) ***(G-21995)***
University Cal San Francisco 415 476-7000
401 Parnassus Ave San Francisco (94143) ***(G-21996)***
University Cal San Francisco 415 476-2075
1855 Folsom St Ste 425 San Francisco (94103) ***(G-26453)***
University Cal San Francisco 415 353-3155
3330 Geary Blvd San Francisco (94118) ***(G-20164)***
University Cal San Francisco 415 567-6600
1600 Divisadero St San Francisco (94143) ***(G-21997)***
University Cal San Francisco 415 353-2573
505 Parnassus Ave L308 San Francisco (94143) ***(G-20165)***
University Cal San Francisco 415 476-6880
1500 Owens St Ste 320 San Francisco (94158) ***(G-20166)***
University California Davis 916 734-2011
2315 Stockton Blvd Sacramento (95817) ***(G-21998)***
University California Davis 916 734-2846
2315 Stockton Blvd # 6309 Sacramento (95817) ***(G-20167)***
University California Davis 916 734-3141
4400 V St Sacramento (95817) ***(G-21999)***
University California Davis 530 752-2300
Student House Ctr Davis (95616) ***(G-20168)***
University California Davis 916 734-2011
2450 48th St Ste 2401 Sacramento (95817) ***(G-22000)***
University California Davis 916 734-5113
4150 V St Ste 1200 Sacramento (95817) ***(G-22001)***

University California Irvine ALPHABETIC SECTION

University California Irvine....714 456-6170
101 The City Dr S Bldg 1a Orange (92868) *(G-20169)*
University California Irvine....714 480-2443
800 N Main St Santa Ana (92701) *(G-20170)*
University California Irvine....714 456-6011
101 The City Dr S Orange (92868) *(G-22002)*
University California Berkeley....510 642-2000
2222 Bancroft Way Berkeley (94720) *(G-20171)*
University California Irvine....949 646-2267
1640 Newport Blvd Ste 340 Costa Mesa (92627) *(G-20172)*
University California Irvine....714 456-5558
200 S Manchester Ave # 400 Orange (92868) *(G-22003)*
University Credit Union....310 477-6628
1500 S Sepulveda Blvd Los Angeles (90025) *(G-9697)*
University Head Neck Surgeons, Orange *Also called Roger L Crumley MD Inc (G-19926)*
University Health Services, Berkeley *Also called University California Berkeley (G-20171)*
University Healthcare Alliance....510 974-8281
7999 Gateway Blvd Ste 200 Newark (94560) *(G-22587)*
University Lease, Irvine *Also called California First National Bank (G-9546)*
University Marelich Mech Inc....714 632-2600
1000 N Kraemer Pl Anaheim (92806) *(G-2402)*
University Mechanical & (HQ)....619 956-2500
1168 Fesler St El Cajon (92020) *(G-2403)*
University of CA Office, Oakland *Also called C/O Uc San Francisco (G-26951)*
University of Pacific....209 946-2030
1040 E Stadium Dr Stockton (95204) *(G-19301)*
University of San Francisco....415 502-8600
3333 California St Ste 11 San Francisco (94118) *(G-17573)*
University of San Francisco....415 422-2028
275 S Airport Blvd San Francisco (94115) *(G-17574)*
University Park Healthcare Ctr, Los Angeles *Also called United Convalescent Facilities (G-21399)*
University Retirement Cmnty, Davis *Also called Pacific Retirement Svcs Inc (G-24760)*
University Sequoia, Fresno *Also called Sunnyside Country Club (G-19101)*
University Southern California....213 740-9790
3737 Watt Way Fl 3 Los Angeles (90089) *(G-22004)*
University Southern California....626 457-4240
1000 S Fremont Ave Unit 7 Alhambra (91803) *(G-26630)*
University Southern California....323 442-8500
1500 San Pablo St Los Angeles (90033) *(G-22005)*
University Southern California....213 743-5339
849 W 34th St Ste 208 Los Angeles (90089) *(G-20173)*
University Student Union Inc....323 343-2450
5151 State University Dr Los Angeles (90032) *(G-17575)*
University Student Union of CA....818 677-2251
18111 Nordhoff St Northridge (91330) *(G-25386)*
Univision 67, Monterey *Also called Entravsion Communications Corp (G-5855)*
Univision Communications Inc....916 927-2041
1710 Arden Way Sacramento (95815) *(G-5920)*
Univision Communications Inc....818 484-7399
655 N Central Ave # 2500 Glendale (91203) *(G-5827)*
Univision Radio Inc....559 430-8500
601 W Univision Plz Fresno (93704) *(G-5828)*
Univision Television Group Inc....559 222-2121
601 W Univision Plz Fresno (93704) *(G-5921)*
Univision Television Group Inc....415 538-8000
50 Fremont St Fl 41 San Francisco (94105) *(G-5922)*
Univision Television Group Inc....858 576-1919
5770 Ruffin Rd San Diego (92123) *(G-5923)*
Uniwell Corporation....714 522-7000
7000 Beach Blvd Buena Park (90620) *(G-13367)*
Uniwell Corporation....559 268-1000
2233 Ventura St Fresno (93721) *(G-12022)*
Uniwell Fresno Hotel LLC....559 268-1000
2233 Ventura St Fresno (93721) *(G-13368)*
Uniworld Boutique River Cruise, Encino *Also called Uniworld River Cruises Inc (G-5002)*
Uniworld River Cruises Inc....818 382-2322
17323 Ventura Blvd # 300 Encino (91316) *(G-5002)*
Unlimited Frontiers Inc....909 793-0142
45 N Lincoln St Redlands (92374) *(G-21402)*
Unlimited Security Specialist....877 310-4877
13636 Ventura Blvd # 206 Sherman Oaks (91423) *(G-16846)*
UNUM Life Insurance Co Amer....818 291-4739
655 N Central Ave Glendale (91203) *(G-10917)*
Unumprovident, Glendale *Also called UNUM Life Insurance Co Amer (G-10917)*
Unx Inc A Delaware Corp....818 333-3300
175 E Olive Ave Fl 2 Burbank (91502) *(G-15517)*
Unycom Inc....415 513-0316
2600 10th St Ste 622 Berkeley (94710) *(G-27267)*
Unycom Intellectual, Berkeley *Also called Unycom Inc (G-27267)*
Unyeway Inc....619 562-6330
11440 Riverside Dr Ste D Lakeside (92040) *(G-24399)*
Up Stage Inc....818 879-8781
30757 Canwood St Agoura (91301) *(G-18186)*
UPAC, San Diego *Also called Union Pan Asian Communities (G-24264)*
Upek Inc....510 868-0800
2000 Powell St Emeryville (94608) *(G-16071)*
Upham Hotel....805 962-0058
1404 De La Vina St # 93101 Santa Barbara (93101) *(G-13369)*
Upland Community Care Inc....909 985-1903
1221 E Arrow Hwy Upland (91786) *(G-21403)*
Upland Rehabilitation Care Ctr, Upland *Also called Upland Community Care Inc (G-21403)*
Upland Valley Fun Center, Upland *Also called Apex Parks Group LLC (G-19138)*
Upland Ymca-Valencia, Upland *Also called West End Yung MNS Christn Assn (G-25401)*
Uplift Family Services (PA)....408 379-3790
251 Llewellyn Ave Campbell (95008) *(G-24840)*
Uplift Family Services....408 379-3790
499 Loma Alta Ave Los Gatos (95030) *(G-22860)*
Uplift Family Services....916 366-6820
9343 Tech Center Dr # 200 Sacramento (95826) *(G-24272)*
Upload Demo Inc....818 983-2395
9663 Santa Monica Blvd Beverly Hills (90210) *(G-17576)*
UPS, Palm Springs *Also called United Parcel Service Inc OH (G-4436)*
UPS, Weaverville *Also called United Parcel Service Inc OH (G-4437)*
UPS, Santa Rosa *Also called United Parcel Service Inc OH (G-17556)*
UPS, Richmond *Also called United Parcel Service Inc OH (G-4438)*
UPS, Torrance *Also called United Parcel Service Inc OH (G-4439)*
UPS, Commerce *Also called United Parcel Service Inc OH (G-17557)*
UPS, Anderson *Also called United Parcel Service Inc OH (G-4440)*
UPS, Bishop *Also called United Parcel Service Inc OH (G-4441)*
UPS, West Sacramento *Also called United Parcel Service Inc OH (G-4442)*
UPS, Ceres *Also called United Parcel Service Inc OH (G-4443)*
UPS, Fairfield *Also called United Parcel Service Inc OH (G-4444)*
UPS, San Marcos *Also called United Parcel Service Inc OH (G-4445)*
UPS, NAPA *Also called United Parcel Service Inc OH (G-4446)*
UPS, Sacramento *Also called United Parcel Service Inc OH (G-4447)*
UPS, Vernon *Also called United Parcel Service Inc OH (G-4874)*
UPS, Gardena *Also called United Parcel Service Inc OH (G-4448)*
UPS, Stockton *Also called United Parcel Service Inc OH (G-4449)*
UPS, San Jose *Also called United Parcel Service Inc OH (G-4450)*
UPS, Sun City *Also called United Parcel Service Inc OH (G-4875)*
UPS, Manteca *Also called United Parcel Service Inc OH (G-4876)*
UPS, Vallejo *Also called United Parcel Service Inc OH (G-4452)*
UPS, Aliso Viejo *Also called United Parcel Service Inc OH (G-4453)*
UPS, Ontario *Also called United Parcel Service Inc OH (G-17558)*
UPS, Los Angeles *Also called United Parcel Service Inc OH (G-4454)*
UPS, San Diego *Also called United Parcel Service Inc OH (G-4455)*
UPS, Ontario *Also called United Parcel Service Inc OH (G-4877)*
UPS, Victorville *Also called United Parcel Service Inc (G-17555)*
UPS, Sylmar *Also called United Parcel Service Inc (G-4434)*
UPS, Van Nuys *Also called United Parcel Service Inc OH (G-4456)*
UPS, San Diego *Also called United Parcel Service Inc OH (G-4457)*
UPS, Visalia *Also called United Parcel Service Inc OH (G-4458)*
UPS, Lancaster *Also called United Parcel Service Inc OH (G-4459)*
UPS, South Lake Tahoe *Also called United Parcel Service Inc OH (G-17559)*
UPS, Cerritos *Also called United Parcel Service Inc OH (G-4460)*
UPS, Monterey Park *Also called United Parcel Service Inc OH (G-17560)*
UPS, Ukiah *Also called United Parcel Service Inc OH (G-4461)*
UPS, Westlake Village *Also called United Parcel Service Inc OH (G-17561)*
UPS, Monterey *Also called United Parcel Service Inc OH (G-4462)*
UPS, Victorville *Also called United Parcel Service Inc OH (G-4463)*
UPS, San Luis Obispo *Also called United Parcel Service Inc OH (G-4464)*
UPS, Petaluma *Also called United Parcel Service Inc OH (G-4465)*
UPS, Goleta *Also called United Parcel Service Inc OH (G-4466)*
UPS, Santa Maria *Also called United Parcel Service Inc OH (G-4467)*
UPS, Concord *Also called United Parcel Service Inc OH (G-4468)*
UPS, Angels Camp *Also called United Parcel Service Inc OH (G-4469)*
UPS, Newbury Park *Also called United Parcel Service Inc OH (G-4470)*
UPS, Los Angeles *Also called United Parcel Service Inc OH (G-4471)*
UPS, South San Francisco *Also called United Parcel Service Inc (G-4435)*
UPS, Chula Vista *Also called United Parcel Service Inc OH (G-4472)*
UPS, Visalia *Also called United Parcel Service Inc OH (G-4473)*
UPS, Santa Cruz *Also called United Parcel Service Inc OH (G-4474)*
UPS, Ontario *Also called United Parcel Service Inc OH (G-4475)*
UPS, San Ramon *Also called United Parcel Service Inc OH (G-4476)*
UPS, Mira Loma *Also called United Parcel Service Inc OH (G-17562)*
UPS, Ventura *Also called United Parcel Service Inc OH (G-4477)*
UPS, Baldwin Park *Also called United Parcel Service Inc OH (G-4478)*
UPS, Sacramento *Also called United Parcel Service Inc OH (G-4479)*
UPS, Fremont *Also called United Parcel Service Inc OH (G-17563)*
UPS, Simi Valley *Also called United Parcel Service Inc OH (G-17564)*
UPS Expedited Mail Svcs Inc....510 297-4600
3004 Alvarado St Ste G San Leandro (94577) *(G-14095)*
UPS Freight, Pico Rivera *Also called UPS Ground Freight Inc (G-4292)*
UPS Freight Services Inc....909 879-7400
2650 S Willow Ave Bloomington (92316) *(G-4284)*
UPS Ground Freight Inc....559 445-9010
4587 S Chestnut Ave Fresno (93725) *(G-4285)*
UPS Ground Freight Inc....661 395-9500
600 Williams St Bakersfield (93305) *(G-4286)*
UPS Ground Freight Inc....209 858-5095
1444 Lathrop Rd Lathrop (95330) *(G-4287)*
UPS Ground Freight Inc....951 361-1300
12455 Harvest Dr Mira Loma (91752) *(G-4288)*
UPS Ground Freight Inc....707 526-1910
7 College Ave Santa Rosa (95401) *(G-4289)*
UPS Ground Freight Inc....408 400-0595
925 Morse Ave Sunnyvale (94089) *(G-4290)*
UPS Ground Freight Inc....831 751-0262
20760 Spence Rd Salinas (93908) *(G-4291)*
UPS Ground Freight Inc....562 801-1300
7754 Paramount Blvd Pico Rivera (90660) *(G-4292)*
UPS Ground Freight Inc....916 371-9101
900 E St West Sacramento (95605) *(G-4293)*
UPS Ground Freight Inc....866 372-5619
650 S Acacia Ave Fullerton (92831) *(G-4294)*
UPS Store Inc (HQ)....858 455-8800
6060 Cornerstone Ct W San Diego (92121) *(G-17577)*

ALPHABETIC

UPS Supply Chain Solutions Gen 951 749-3134
11991 Landon Dr Mira Loma (91752) *(G-4480)*
UPS Supply Chain Solutions Inc 310 404-2719
19701 Hamilton Ave # 250 Torrance (90502) *(G-5184)*
UPS Supply Chain Solutions Inc 650 875-8300
455 Forbes Blvd South San Francisco (94080) *(G-4650)*
UPS Supply Chain Solutions Inc 650 635-2678
550-3 Accels Ave South San Francisco (94080) *(G-4651)*
UPS Supply Chain Solutions Inc 415 775-6644
601 Van Neca Ave Ste E San Francisco (94102) *(G-4652)*
UPS Worldwide Logistics Inc 310 673-7661
3600 W Century Blvd Inglewood (90303) *(G-5185)*
Uptowners Barber Shop 760 256-5813
134 E Main St Barstow (92311) *(G-13700)*
Upwind Blade Solutions Inc 866 927-3142
4863 Shawline St Ste A San Diego (92111) *(G-18030)*
Upwork Inc 650 316-7500
441 Logue Ave Mountain View (94043) *(G-14812)*
Upwork Inc (PA) 650 316-7500
441 Logue Ave Ste 150 Mountain View (94043) *(G-13933)*
Urata & Sons Cement Inc 916 638-5364
3430 Luyung Dr Rancho Cordova (95742) *(G-3344)*
Urban Bros Painting Inc 415 485-1130
40 Lisbon St San Rafael (94901) *(G-2500)*
Urban Corps of San Diego 619 235-6884
3127 Jefferson St San Diego (92110) *(G-24400)*
Urban Services YMCA, Oakland *Also called YMCA of East Bay (G-25407)*
Urban Sony Service Center, Irvine *Also called Sony Electronics Inc (G-18151)*
Urban Trading Software Inc 877 633-6171
21227 Foothill Blvd Hayward (94541) *(G-15871)*
Urgent Care-Selma Dst Hosp, Selma *Also called Selma Community Hospital Inc (G-21877)*
Uribe Trucking Inc 714 549-8696
605 S East St Anaheim (92805) *(G-4385)*
Urology Assoc of Cen Cal 559 321-2800
7014 N Whitney Ave Ste A Fresno (93720) *(G-20174)*
URS Energy & Consruction, San Francisco *Also called Aecom Global II LLC (G-25636)*
URS Group Inc 510 893-3600
1333 Broadway Ste 800 Oakland (94612) *(G-26119)*
URS Group Inc 415 896-5858
1 Montgomery St Ste 900 San Francisco (94104) *(G-26120)*
URS Group Inc 213 996-2200
915 Wilshire Blvd Ste 700 Los Angeles (90017) *(G-26121)*
URS Group Inc 909 980-4000
901 Via Piemonte Ste 500 Ontario (91764) *(G-26122)*
URS Group Inc 213 996-2200
915 Wilshire Blvd Ste 700 Los Angeles (90017) *(G-26123)*
URS Group Inc 925 446-3800
2300 Clayton Rd Ste 1400 Concord (94520) *(G-26124)*
URS Group Inc 619 294-9400
4225 Executive Sq # 1600 La Jolla (92037) *(G-26125)*
URS Group Inc 805 964-6010
130 Robin Hill Rd Ste 100 Santa Barbara (93117) *(G-26126)*
URS Group Inc 916 679-2000
2870 Gateway Oaks Dr # 150 Sacramento (95833) *(G-26127)*
URS Group Inc 408 297-9585
100 W San Fernando St # 200 San Jose (95113) *(G-26128)*
URS Group Inc 714 835-6886
999 W Town And Country Rd Orange (92868) *(G-26129)*
URS Group Inc 916 929-2346
2870 Gateway Oaks Dr # 300 Sacramento (95833) *(G-26130)*
URS Group Inc 415 896-5858
1 Montgomery St Ste 900 San Francisco (94104) *(G-26131)*
URS Holdings Inc (HQ) 415 774-2700
600 Montgomery St Fl 25 San Francisco (94111) *(G-26132)*
URS-Gei Joint Venture 510 874-3051
1333 Broadway Ste 800 Oakland (94612) *(G-26133)*
URS-Weston Joint Venture 714 433-7710
2020 E 1st St Ste 400 Santa Ana (92705) *(G-26134)*
Urs/Contrack-Pacer Forge JV 415 774-2700
600 Montgomery St Fl 26 San Francisco (94111) *(G-2094)*
US Advisor LLC 707 253-9953
600 Trancas St NAPA (94558) *(G-12276)*
US Airforce Band of Golden W 707 424-2263
551 Waldron St Bldg 240 Travis Afb (94535) *(G-18503)*
US Airways, Palm Springs *Also called American Airlines Inc (G-4790)*
US Airways, Los Angeles *Also called American Airlines Inc (G-4900)*
US Airways, Los Angeles *Also called American Airlines Inc (G-4792)*
US Army Corps of Engineers 916 557-7490
1325 J St Frnt Sacramento (95814) *(G-26135)*
US Army Corps of Engineers 213 452-3967
915 Wilshire Blvd Ste 930 Los Angeles (90017) *(G-26136)*
US Bank, Los Alamitos *Also called US Bank National Association (G-9902)*
US Bank, San Diego *Also called US Bank National Association (G-9427)*
US Bank National Association 562 795-7520
10021 Bloomfield St Los Alamitos (90720) *(G-9902)*
US Bank National Association 619 744-2140
1420 Kettner Blvd Ste 101 San Diego (92101) *(G-9427)*
US Bankcard Services Inc 888 888-8872
17171 Gale Ave Ste 110 City of Industry (91745) *(G-17578)*
US Best Repair Service Inc 888 750-2378
2004 Mcgaw Ave Irvine (92614) *(G-1276)*
US Best Repairs, Irvine *Also called US Best Repair Service Inc (G-1276)*
US Control Group Inc 888 500-7090
9157 W Sunset Blvd # 212 West Hollywood (90069) *(G-24273)*
US Credit Bancorp Inc 310 829-2112
851 20th St Santa Monica (90403) *(G-9903)*
US Data Management LLC (PA) 888 231-0816
1746 S Victoria Ave Ste F Ventura (93003) *(G-16518)*
US Dept of the Air Force 661 277-3030
35 N Wolfe Ave Edwards (93524) *(G-6097)*
US Dept of the Air Force 530 634-4839
15301 Warren Shingle Rd Marysville (95903) *(G-22006)*
US Dept of the Air Force 661 275-5410
10 E Saturn Dr Edwards (93524) *(G-26631)*
US Dept of the Air Force 310 363-1155
2420 Vela Way Ste 1467 El Segundo (90245) *(G-16072)*
US Dept of the Air Force 530 634-4738
15301 Warren Shingle Rd Beale Afb (95903) *(G-20175)*
US Family Care, Rialto *Also called Caremark Rx Inc (G-19404)*
US Family Care, Hesperia *Also called Caremark Rx LLC (G-19405)*
US Fhotc, Camp Pendleton *Also called Marine Corps United States (G-24361)*
US Foods Inc 951 256-2400
1283 Sherborn St Ste 102 Corona (92879) *(G-8545)*
US Foods Inc 760 599-6200
1201 Park Center Dr Vista (92081) *(G-9307)*
US Foods Inc 800 888-3147
1283 Sherborn St Ste 102 Corona (92879) *(G-8946)*
US Foods Inc 925 606-3525
300 Lawrence Dr Frnt Livermore (94551) *(G-8546)*
US Foods Inc 951 582-8500
1283 Sherborn St Ste 102 Corona (92879) *(G-8947)*
US Foods Inc 714 670-3500
15155 Northam St La Mirada (90638) *(G-8547)*
US Foods Inc 714 670-3500
15155 Northam St La Mirada (90638) *(G-8548)*
US Foods Inc 714 449-9990
700 S Raymond Ave Fullerton (92831) *(G-8948)*
US Foods Inc 209 572-2882
4300 Finch Rd Modesto (95357) *(G-8949)*
US Foods Inc 714 449-2880
1415 N Raymond Ave Anaheim (92801) *(G-8950)*
US Foods Inc 714 670-3500
15155 Northam St La Mirada (90638) *(G-8951)*
US Foods Inc 619 474-6525
1240 W 28th St National City (91950) *(G-8952)*
US Foods Inc 951 256-2400
1283 Sherborn St Ste 102 Corona (92879) *(G-8953)*
US Foods International LLC 310 515-2189
500 W 140th St Fl 2 Gardena (90248) *(G-8549)*
US Grant Hotel Ventures LLC 619 744-2007
326 Broadway San Diego (92101) *(G-13370)*
US Green Building Council - 818 621-4880
2879 Breezy Meadow Ln Corona (92883) *(G-12166)*
US GREEN BUILDING COUNCIL INLA, Corona *Also called US Green Building Council - (G-12166)*
US Growers Cold Storage Inc (PA) 323 583-3163
3141 E 44th St Vernon (90058) *(G-4509)*
US Growers Cold Storage Inc 323 583-3163
2045 E Vernon Ave Vernon (90058) *(G-4510)*
US Healthcare Partners Inc 949 261-5000
4041 Macarthur Blvd # 360 Newport Beach (92660) *(G-21404)*
US Healthworks Inc (HQ) 800 720-2432
25124 Springfield Ct Valencia (91355) *(G-20176)*
US Home, Corona *Also called US Home Corporation (G-1387)*
US Home Corporation 951 817-3500
980 Montecito Dr 302 Corona (92879) *(G-1387)*
US Hotel and Resort MGT Inc 949 650-2988
2544 Newport Blvd Costa Mesa (92627) *(G-13371)*
US Interactive Corp Delaware 408 863-7500
1270 Oakmead Pkwy Ste 318 Sunnyvale (94085) *(G-13934)*
US International Media LLC (PA) 310 482-6700
1201 Alta Loma Rd Los Angeles (90069) *(G-14013)*
US Interstate Distrg Inc 818 678-4592
21621 Nordhoff St Chatsworth (91311) *(G-5713)*
US Investmnt Cmrce Fisheries 714 823-5209
11067 Petal Ave Fountain Valley (92708) *(G-8663)*
US Lines LLC (HQ) 714 751-3333
3501 Jamboree Rd Ste 300 Newport Beach (92660) *(G-25108)*
US Loan Auditors LLC 916 248-8625
7485 Rush Rver Dr Ste 710 Sacramento (95831) *(G-26454)*
US Merchant Systems LLC 877 432-8871
48073 Fremont Blvd Fremont (94538) *(G-7652)*
US Merchants Fincl Group Inc 909 923-3388
1625 Proforma Ave Ontario (91761) *(G-17579)*
US Metro Group Inc 213 382-6435
605 S Wilton Pl Los Angeles (90005) *(G-14460)*
US Mktg Promotions Agcy Inc 310 754-3000
4721 Alla Rd Marina Del Rey (90292) *(G-26717)*
US Naval Medical Clinical Lab, Port Hueneme *Also called United States Dept of Navy (G-20159)*
US Outdoor, Los Angeles *Also called US International Media LLC (G-14013)*
US Probation, San Diego *Also called Supreme Court United States (G-24242)*
US Property Group Inc 559 227-1901
1901 E Shields Ave # 203 Fresno (93726) *(G-11066)*
US Real Estate Services Inc 949 598-9920
25520 Commercentre Dr # 1 Lake Forest (92630) *(G-11893)*
US Security Associates Inc 209 476-7062
555 W Benjamin Holt Dr # 222 Stockton (95207) *(G-16847)*
US Security Associates Inc 951 256-4601
495 E Rincon St Ste 207 Corona (92879) *(G-16848)*
US Skillserve Inc 909 621-4751
9620 Fremont Ave Montclair (91763) *(G-21000)*
US Small Cpitl Value Portfolio 310 395-8005
1299 Ocean Ave Ste 150 Santa Monica (90401) *(G-12127)*
US Telepacific Corp (HQ) 213 213-3000
515 S Flower St Fl 47 Los Angeles (90071) *(G-5714)*

ALPHABETIC

US Tournament Golf Ltd Lblty...909 987-6695
10808 Stamfield Dr Rancho Cucamonga (91730) ***(G-27705)***
USA Bouquet LLC...800 878-9909
2834 La Mirada Dr Ste B Vista (92081) ***(G-9223)***
USA Fact Inc (PA)...951 656-7800
6200 Box Springs Blvd Riverside (92507) ***(G-27706)***
USA Federal Credit Union, San Diego *Also called United Svcs Amer Federal Cr Un* ***(G-9646)***
USA Multifamily Management...916 773-6060
3200 Douglas Blvd Ste 200 Roseville (95661) ***(G-11894)***
USA Properties Fund Inc (PA)...916 773-6060
3200 Douglas Blvd Ste 200 Roseville (95661) ***(G-12023)***
USA Transport Inc...559 783-3563
12191 Violet Rd Adelanto (92301) ***(G-4386)***
USA Truck Inc...909 334-1406
5861 Pine Ave Ste A-2 Chino Hills (91709) ***(G-4295)***
USA Valet Parking LLC...916 792-1055
980 9th St Ste 1620 Sacramento (95814) ***(G-13802)***
USA Vily Group...323 457-6888
4301 Valley Blvd Ste D2 Los Angeles (90032) ***(G-16207)***
USA Waste of California Inc...559 741-1766
26951 Road 140 Visalia (93292) ***(G-6574)***
USA Waste of California Inc...916 379-0500
8491 Fruitridge Rd Sacramento (95826) ***(G-6575)***
USA Waste of California Inc (HQ)...916 387-1400
11931 Foundation Pl # 200 Gold River (95670) ***(G-6576)***
USA Waste of California Inc...916 379-2611
8761 Younger Creek Dr Sacramento (95828) ***(G-4080)***
USA Waste of California Inc...831 384-4860
11240 Commercial Pkwy Castroville (95012) ***(G-4081)***
USA Waste of California Inc...209 946-5721
1240 Navy Dr Stockton (95206) ***(G-4082)***
USA Waste of California Inc...800 423-9986
800 S Temescal St Corona (92879) ***(G-6577)***
USA Waste of California Inc...831 633-7878
11240 Commercial Pkwy Castroville (95012) ***(G-6578)***
USA Waste of California Inc...530 274-3090
13083 Grass Valley Ave Grass Valley (95945) ***(G-4083)***
USA Waste of California Inc...626 856-1285
13970 Live Oak Ave Baldwin Park (91706) ***(G-6579)***
USA Waste of California Inc...805 466-3636
8740 Pueblo Ave Ste B Atascadero (93422) ***(G-6580)***
USA Waste of California Inc...619 596-5117
1001 W Bradley Ave El Cajon (92020) ***(G-6581)***
USA Waste of California Inc...909 590-1793
13793 Redwood St Chino (91710) ***(G-6582)***
USA Waste of California Inc...559 834-9151
4333 E Jefferson Ave Fresno (93725) ***(G-6583)***
USA Waste of California Inc...310 830-7100
1970 E 213th St Long Beach (90810) ***(G-6584)***
USA Waste of California Inc...310 763-8500
407 E El Segundo Blvd Compton (90222) ***(G-6585)***
USA Waste of California Inc...530 877-2777
951 American Way Paradise (95969) ***(G-6586)***
USA Waste of California Inc...831 754-2500
1120 Madison Ln Salinas (93907) ***(G-6587)***
USA Waste of California Inc...559 834-4070
10725 W Goshen Ave Visalia (93291) ***(G-6588)***
USA Waste of California Inc...661 259-2398
25772 Springbrook Ave Santa Clarita (91350) ***(G-6589)***
USA Waste of California Inc...714 637-3010
1800 S Grand Ave Santa Ana (92705) ***(G-6590)***
USA Waste of California Inc...831 384-5000
29331 Pacific St Hayward (94544) ***(G-6591)***
Usaco Service Corp...562 483-8747
16205 Distribution Way Cerritos (90703) ***(G-17948)***
Usag Ansbach Financial MGT Div...210 466-1376
420 Montgomery St San Francisco (94104) ***(G-27268)***
Usag Rheinland Pfalz Fincl MGT...210 466-1376
420 Montgomery St San Francisco (94104) ***(G-27269)***
Usag Vicenza Italy Dmwr F M D...210 466-1376
420 Montgomery St San Francisco (94104) ***(G-27270)***
Usag Wiesbaden Fincl MGT Div...210 466-1376
420 Montgomery St San Francisco (94104) ***(G-27271)***
Usas Express International...310 645-2313
420 Hindry Ave Ste G Inglewood (90301) ***(G-5186)***
USB Solarcity Master Tenant...650 963-5693
393 Vintage Park Dr # 140 Foster City (94404) ***(G-12097)***
Usc Care Medical Group Inc...323 442-5100
1510 San Pablo St Ste 649 Los Angeles (90033) ***(G-22007)***
Usc Credit Union...213 821-7100
1025 W 34th St Los Angeles (90089) ***(G-9647)***
Usc Emergency Medicine Assoc...323 226-6667
1200 N State St Ste 1011 Los Angeles (90033) ***(G-20177)***
Usc Institute For Neuroimaging...323 442-7246
2001 N Soto St Ste 102 Los Angeles (90032) ***(G-20178)***
Usc MARk& Mary Steven Neuro, Los Angeles *Also called Usc Institute For Neuroimaging* ***(G-20178)***
Usc Shoah Fndn Inst For Visual...213 740-6001
650 W 35th St Ste 114 Los Angeles (90089) ***(G-25594)***
Usc Srgcal Edcatn RES Fndation, Los Angeles *Also called Usc Surgeons Incorporated* ***(G-20179)***
Usc Student Health Center, Los Angeles *Also called University Southern California* ***(G-20173)***
Usc Surgeons Incorporated...323 442-5910
1510 San Pablo St Ste 514 Los Angeles (90033) ***(G-20179)***
Usc University Hospital, Los Angeles *Also called University Southern California* ***(G-22005)***
Usc Verdugo Hills Hospital LLC...818 790-7100
1812 Verdugo Blvd Glendale (91208) ***(G-22008)***

Uscb Inc...213 387-6181
3535 Wilshire Blvd # 700 Los Angeles (90010) ***(G-14050)***
Uscb Inc (PA)...213 985-2111
3333 Wilshire Blvd Fl 7 Los Angeles (90010) ***(G-14051)***
Uscb America, Los Angeles *Also called Uscb Inc* ***(G-14051)***
Uscf Caps Department Medicine, San Francisco *Also called University Cal San Francisco* ***(G-26816)***
Usd, Union City *Also called Union Sanitary District* ***(G-6420)***
USDA Forest Service...951 680-1560
4955 Canyon Crest Dr Riverside (92507) ***(G-26632)***
USDA Forest Service...530 626-1546
100 Forni Rd Placerville (95667) ***(G-1019)***
Usdm, Ventura *Also called US Data Management LLC* ***(G-16518)***
User Zoom Inc...408 533-8619
10 Almaden Blvd Ste 250 San Jose (95113) ***(G-16073)***
USF Import FWD Wh 4150, Corona *Also called US Foods Inc* ***(G-8953)***
USF Reddaway Inc...562 923-0648
11937 Regentview Ave Downey (90241) ***(G-4296)***
USF-La Mirada 4150, La Mirada *Also called US Foods Inc* ***(G-8951)***
Usfi Inc...310 768-1937
110 W Walnut St 221 Gardena (90248) ***(G-8550)***
USG Enterprises Inc...310 827-2220
4325 Glencoe Ave Marina Del Rey (90292) ***(G-4741)***
USG Interiors LLC...209 466-4636
2575 Loomis Rd Stockton (95205) ***(G-6967)***
Ushio America Inc (HQ)...714 236-8600
5440 Cerritos Ave Cypress (90630) ***(G-7480)***
USI of Southern California Ins...818 251-3000
21700 Oxnard St Ste 1200 Woodland Hills (91367) ***(G-10918)***
USI South Coast...949 790-9200
29a Technology Dr 200 Irvine (92618) ***(G-10919)***
Usps, Long Beach *Also called Passport Acceptance Facility* ***(G-17403)***
USS Cal Builders Inc...714 828-4882
8051 Main St Stanton (90680) ***(G-1709)***
UST Development Inc...626 205-1123
2001 Elm Ct Ontario (91761) ***(G-5422)***
UST Global Inc (PA)...949 716-8757
5 Polaris Way Aliso Viejo (92656) ***(G-15518)***
UST Telecom, Ontario *Also called UST Development Inc* ***(G-5422)***
Usts, Huntington Beach *Also called United States Technical Svcs* ***(G-16516)***
Utah Pacific Construction Co...951 677-9876
40940 Eleanora Way Murrieta (92562) ***(G-2006)***
Utblo Inc...562 493-3664
11061 Los Alamitos Blvd Los Alamitos (90720) ***(G-12098)***
UTC Fire SEC Americas Corp Inc...949 737-7800
2955 Red Hill Ave Ste 100 Costa Mesa (92626) ***(G-15519)***
Utc, Mas, Costa Mesa *Also called UTC Fire SEC Americas Corp Inc* ***(G-15519)***
Utdi, Mill Valley *Also called Unified Teldata Inc* ***(G-7651)***
Uti Integrated Logistics LLC...909 427-1939
13230 San Bernardino Ave B Fontana (92335) ***(G-4706)***
Uti Integrated Logistics LLC...714 630-0110
3454 E Miraloma Ave Anaheim (92806) ***(G-5249)***
Uti Leak Seekers...323 724-0081
1398 Monterey Pass Rd Monterey Park (91754) ***(G-2007)***
Uti Underground Technology, Monterey Park *Also called Uti Leak Seekers* ***(G-2007)***
Uti United States Inc...650 588-9477
573 Forbes Blvd South San Francisco (94080) ***(G-5187)***
Utility Systems Science (PA)...714 542-1004
601 Parkcenter Dr Ste 209 Santa Ana (92705) ***(G-15520)***
Utility Trailer Sales of S CA (PA)...909 428-8300
15567 Valley Blvd Fontana (92335) ***(G-6699)***
Utility Tree Service Inc (HQ)...530 226-0330
1884 Keystone Ct Ste A Redding (96003) ***(G-1001)***
Utility Tree Services, Goleta *Also called Asplundh Tree Expert Co* ***(G-984)***
Utility Trlr Sls of Centl Cal...559 237-2001
2680 S East Ave Fresno (93706) ***(G-7899)***
Utopia Lighting, Compton *Also called Pacific Lighting Manufacturer* ***(G-7464)***
Uyeda Farm...831 722-6345
656 Lakeview Rd Watsonville (95076) ***(G-137)***
Uyematsu Inc...831 724-2200
1004 E Lake Ave Watsonville (95076) ***(G-138)***
V & L Produce Inc...323 589-3125
2550 E 25th St Vernon (90058) ***(G-8783)***
V A Anderson Enterprises Inc (PA)...714 990-6100
400 Atlas St Brea (92821) ***(G-17580)***
V A Anderson Enterprises Inc...925 866-6150
2680 Bishop Dr Ste 140 San Ramon (94583) ***(G-14129)***
V and V Farms, Lodi *Also called Jose Vramontes* ***(G-376)***
V B Z, Richgrove *Also called Vincent B Zaninovich Sons Inc* ***(G-192)***
V C Concrete, Atwater *Also called Vince Fucillo* ***(G-3348)***
V Development Inc...925 634-8890
550 Harvest Park Dr Ste A Brentwood (94513) ***(G-1349)***
V G Carelli International Corp...310 247-8410
1 Park Plz Ste 600 Irvine (92614) ***(G-17581)***
V G Pacific Equities, Los Angeles *Also called Pacific Equities Captl* ***(G-11261)***
V G S, Salinas *Also called Vegetable Growers Supply Co* ***(G-9308)***
V N A & Hospice Southern Calif, San Bernardino *Also called Vna Hospice & Pllatve Cre S CA* ***(G-22610)***
V P H, Van Nuys *Also called Valley Presbyterian Hospital* ***(G-22010)***
V P I, Camarillo *Also called Voice Print International Inc* ***(G-16210)***
V S N F Inc...916 452-6631
2120 Stockton Blvd Sacramento (95817) ***(G-21001)***
V S S, West Sacramento *Also called Vss International Inc* ***(G-1882)***
V Sangiacomo & Sons...707 938-5503
21543 Broadway Sonoma (95476) ***(G-191)***

V Troth Inc...661 948-4646
1801 W Avenue K Ste 101 Lancaster (93534) *(G-11895)*
V Vcc Havens, Vista *Also called Vista Valley Country Club* *(G-19123)*
V&V Farm Labor Contractor...209 599-4834
18396 S Wagner Ave Ripon (95366) *(G-400)*
V-Tek Systems Corporation...909 396-5355
21045 Ridge Park Dr Yorba Linda (92886) *(G-16074)*
VA Hospital, Fresno *Also called Veterans Health Administration* *(G-22019)*
VA HSR&d Center of Excellence, North Hills *Also called Veterans Health Administration* *(G-20217)*
Vacation and Holiday Benefit F...213 385-6161
501 Shatto Pl Ste 5 Los Angeles (90020) *(G-12207)*
Vacation Interval Realty, Newport Beach *Also called Pacific Monarch Resorts Inc* *(G-11728)*
Vacation Marketing Group, Riverside *Also called Pacific Monarch Resorts Inc* *(G-11727)*
Vacaville Medical Center, Vacaville *Also called Kaiser Foundation Hospitals* *(G-19595)*
Vacaville Psychiatric Program, Vacaville *Also called Mental Health California Dept* *(G-22084)*
Vacavlle Cnvalescent Rehab Ctr...707 449-8000
585 Nut Tree Ct Vacaville (95687) *(G-21405)*
Vaco Lajolla LLC...858 642-0000
4250 Executive Sq Ste 750 La Jolla (92037) *(G-14813)*
Vaco Technology, La Jolla *Also called Vaco Lajolla LLC* *(G-14813)*
Vadnais Trenchless Svcs Inc...858 550-1460
26000 Commercentre Dr Lake Forest (92630) *(G-2008)*
Vadnais Trenchless Svcs Inc...858 550-1460
2130 La Mirada Dr Vista (92081) *(G-2009)*
Vagabond Inn Corporation (HQ)...213 284-7533
2361 Rosecrans Ave # 150 El Segundo (90245) *(G-13372)*
Vagabond Inns, El Segundo *Also called Rpd Hotels 18 LLC* *(G-13177)*
Valadon Hotel LLC...310 854-1114
8822 Cynthia St West Hollywood (90069) *(G-13373)*
Valassis Communications Inc...714 751-4006
1575 Corporate Dr Costa Mesa (92626) *(G-14096)*
Valassis Direct Mail Inc...510 505-6500
6955 Mowry Ave Newark (94560) *(G-14097)*
Valco Construction, Bakersfield *Also called Gilliam & Sons Inc* *(G-3429)*
Vale Healthcare Center, San Pablo *Also called Mariner Health Care Inc* *(G-27120)*
Vale Healthcare Center, San Pablo *Also called Grancare LLC* *(G-20632)*
Valeant Biomedicals Inc (HQ)...949 461-6000
1 Enterprise Aliso Viejo (92656) *(G-9003)*
Valencia Bros Inc...760 353-2168
257 Maple Ave El Centro (92243) *(G-3345)*
Valencia Brothers Concrete, El Centro *Also called Valencia Bros Inc* *(G-3345)*
Valencia Country Club, Valencia *Also called Heritage Golf Group Inc* *(G-18746)*
Valencia Division, Valencia *Also called Amerisourcebergen Corporation* *(G-8229)*
Valencia Gardens Hlth Care Ctr, Riverside *Also called Riverside Care Inc* *(G-20875)*
Valencia Health Care Inc...661 254-2425
23801 Newhall Ave Newhall (91321) *(G-21406)*
Valencia Tree Landscape...805 965-4244
321 N Quarantina St Santa Barbara (93103) *(G-802)*
Valente Concrete...951 279-2221
255 Benjamin Dr Corona (92879) *(G-3346)*
Valentine Corporation...415 453-3732
111 Pelican Way San Rafael (94901) *(G-3595)*
Valero Labor, Woodland *Also called Oscar Valero* *(G-385)*
Valet Parking Svc A Cal Partnr (PA)...323 465-5873
6933 Hollywood Blvd Los Angeles (90028) *(G-17746)*
Valet Services, Bell Gardens *Also called Anitsa Inc* *(G-13500)*
Valetor Inc...323 654-1271
8359 Santa Monica Blvd Los Angeles (90069) *(G-13589)*
Valew Welding & Fabrication, Adelanto *Also called Hayes Welding Inc* *(G-17954)*
Valgenesis Inc...510 445-0505
42840 Christy St Ste 102 Fremont (94538) *(G-7208)*
Validant, San Francisco *Also called Kinsale Holdings Inc* *(G-8273)*
Validus Group Inc...949 457-7606
1 Orchard Ste 210 Lake Forest (92630) *(G-14814)*
Valin Corporation (PA)...408 730-9850
1941 Ringwood Ave San Jose (95131) *(G-7900)*
Valle Sanit and Flood Contr Di...707 644-8949
450 Ryder St Vallejo (94590) *(G-28087)*
Valle Verde Retirement Center, Santa Barbara *Also called American Baptist Homes of West* *(G-11085)*
Valle Vista Convalescent Hosp, Escondido *Also called Covenant Care California LLC* *(G-20499)*
Valle Vsta Cnvlescent Hosp Inc...760 745-1288
1025 W 2nd Ave Escondido (92025) *(G-21407)*
Vallejo Garbage & Recycling, Vallejo *Also called Recology Vallejo* *(G-6532)*
Valley Aggregate Transport Inc...530 821-2600
753 N George Wash Blvd Yuba City (95993) *(G-4084)*
Valley Agricultural Labor Svcs, Cutler *Also called Richard M Gonzalez* *(G-14753)*
Valley Base Materials, Sylmar *Also called Security Paving Company Inc* *(G-1856)*
Valley Bulk Inc...760 843-0574
17649 Turner Rd Victorville (92394) *(G-4297)*
Valley Can...916 273-4890
921 11th St Ste 220 Sacramento (95814) *(G-24993)*
VALLEY CARE CENTER, Porterville *Also called Wescordon Incorporated* *(G-21028)*
Valley Care Health System, The, Pleasanton *Also called The For Hospital Committee* *(G-21966)*
Valley Care Olive View Med Ctr, Sylmar *Also called Olive View-Ucla Medical Center* *(G-19792)*
Valley Center Municipal...760 735-4500
29300 Valley Center Rd Valley Center (92082) *(G-6407)*
Valley Child Guidance Clinic, Palmdale *Also called Child and Family Guidance Ctr* *(G-22681)*
Valley Childrens Healthcare...559 353-3000
9300 Valley Childrens Pl Madera (93636) *(G-20180)*
Valley Childrens Hospital...559 353-6425
9300 Valley Childrens Pl Madera (93636) *(G-20181)*
Valley Childrens Hospital (PA)...559 353-3000
9300 Valley Childrens Pl Madera (93636) *(G-22184)*
Valley Clark Plbg & Htg Co Inc (PA)...818 782-1047
7640 Gloria Ave Ste L Van Nuys (91406) *(G-2404)*
Valley Communications Inc (PA)...916 349-7300
6921 Roseville Rd Sacramento (95842) *(G-2781)*
Valley Community Health Center, Pleasanton *Also called Center Cnslng Edctn & Crisis* *(G-23721)*
Valley Community Healthcare...818 763-8836
6801 Coldwater Canyon Ave 1b North Hollywood (91605) *(G-20182)*
Valley Convalescent Hospital, Watsonville *Also called West Coast Hospitals Inc* *(G-21419)*
Valley Couriers Inc...714 541-0111
1111 W Twn And Cntry Rd # 28 Orange (92868) *(G-4085)*
Valley Couriers Inc (PA)...818 591-2212
646 N San Fernando Rd Los Angeles (90065) *(G-4086)*
Valley Demo Inc...661 900-4818
1016 Meredith Dr Bakersfield (93304) *(G-1880)*
Valley Detriot Diesel, Bakersfield *Also called Valley Power Systems Inc* *(G-7901)*
Valley Drive-In Theatre, Santa Maria *Also called Cal Gran Theatres LLC* *(G-18313)*
Valley Eye Center Group, Van Nuys *Also called George M Rajacich MD PC* *(G-19535)*
Valley Farm Management Inc...831 678-1592
37500 Foothill Rd Soledad (93960) *(G-728)*
Valley Fig Growers...559 237-3893
2028 S 3rd St Fresno (93702) *(G-600)*
Valley Floor Maintenance Inc...559 495-3083
1945 N Helm Ave Ste 102 Fresno (93727) *(G-14461)*
Valley Flowers Inc...805 684-6651
3920 Via Real Carpinteria (93013) *(G-9224)*
Valley Fresh Foods Inc...209 669-5600
3600 E Linwood Ave Turlock (95380) *(G-448)*
Valley Fresh Foods Inc...209 669-5510
1220 Hall Rd Denair (95316) *(G-449)*
Valley Garbage Rubbish Co Inc...805 614-1131
1850 W Betteravia Rd Santa Maria (93455) *(G-6592)*
Valley Health Care Systems Inc...916 669-0508
1401 El Cmino Ave Ste 510 Sacramento (95815) *(G-24274)*
Valley Healthcare, San Bernardino *Also called United Medical Management Inc* *(G-21401)*
Valley Healthcare Center LLC...559 251-7161
4840 E Tulare Ave Fresno (93727) *(G-21002)*
Valley Healthcare Center LLC...559 251-7161
4840 E Tulare Ave Fresno (93727) *(G-21003)*
Valley Ho Hotels Inc...619 297-2231
1333 Hotel Cir S San Diego (92108) *(G-13374)*
Valley Hospital Medical Center (HQ)...818 885-8500
18300 Roscoe Blvd Northridge (91325) *(G-22009)*
Valley House Care Center, Santa Clara *Also called TLC of Bay Area Inc* *(G-20990)*
Valley Hunt Club...626 793-7134
520 S Orange Grove Blvd Pasadena (91105) *(G-25387)*
Valley Industrial X-Ra...661 399-8497
3700 Pegasus Dr 100 Bakersfield (93308) *(G-26901)*
Valley Inventory Service Inc...707 422-6050
1180 Horizon Dr Ste B Fairfield (94533) *(G-17582)*
Valley Labor Service Inc...559 591-5591
39678 Road 84 Dinuba (93618) *(G-14815)*
Valley Landscaping & Maint Inc...209 334-3659
12900 N Lwer Scramento Rd Lodi (95242) *(G-974)*
Valley Light Industries Inc...626 337-6200
5360 Irwindale Ave Baldwin Park (91706) *(G-24401)*
Valley Management Services...626 333-1243
425 S Hacienda Blvd City of Industry (91745) *(G-27272)*
Valley Manor Convalescent Hosp, North Hollywood *Also called Golden Care Inc* *(G-21236)*
Valley Med Ctr Billing Dept, San Jose *Also called Santa Clara County of* *(G-26436)*
Valley Medical Group of Lompoc...805 736-1253
136 N 3rd St Lompoc (93436) *(G-20183)*
Valley Molding & Frame, North Hollywood *Also called Valley Wholesale Supply Corp* *(G-6901)*
Valley Mtn Regional Ctr Inc (PA)...209 473-0951
702 N Aurora St Stockton (95202) *(G-24275)*
Valley Mtn Regional Ctr Inc...209 529-2626
1620 Cummins Dr Modesto (95358) *(G-24841)*
Valley Northamerican, Concord *Also called Valley Relocation and Storage* *(G-4298)*
Valley Nurses...714 549-2512
1450 W 9th St Pomona (91766) *(G-20360)*
Valley Oak Dental Group...209 823-9341
1507 W Yosemite Ave Manteca (95337) *(G-20282)*
Valley Oaks Residential...209 239-3244
10623 E Highway 120 Manteca (95336) *(G-24276)*
Valley Ob Gyn Medical Group...909 580-6333
400 N Pepper Ave Fl 6 Colton (92324) *(G-20184)*
Valley of California, Inc., Concord *Also called Coldwell Bnkr Residential Brkg* *(G-11425)*
Valley of Sun Cosmetics LLC...310 327-9062
535 Patrice Pl Gardena (90248) *(G-8302)*
Valley of The Sun Labs, Gardena *Also called Valley of Sun Cosmetics LLC* *(G-8302)*
Valley Pacific Concrete Inc...951 672-6151
27580 Tabb Ln Menifee (92584) *(G-3347)*
Valley Pacific Petro Svcs Inc...661 746-7737
9521 Enos Ln Bakersfield (93314) *(G-9030)*
Valley Palms Convalescent Hosp, North Hollywood *Also called Trinity Health Systems* *(G-21393)*
Valley Peterbilt, Stockton *Also called Interstate Truck Center LLC* *(G-6684)*
Valley Physical Theraphy, Escondido *Also called Physical Therapy Hand Ctrs Inc* *(G-20341)*
Valley Pinte Nursing Rehab Ctr...510 538-8464
20090 Stanton Ave Castro Valley (94546) *(G-24842)*
Valley Plaza Doctors Hospital, Perris *Also called Southwest Hospital Dev Group* *(G-21911)*
Valley Point Nursing Center, Santa Rosa *Also called Independent Quality Care Inc* *(G-21276)*

Valley Power System, City of Industry *Also called Valley Management Services* ***(G-27272)***
Valley Power Systems Inc..........661 325-9001
4000 Rosedale Hwy Bakersfield (93308) ***(G-7901)***
Valley Presbyterian Hospital..........818 782-6600
15107 Vanowen St Van Nuys (91405) ***(G-22010)***
Valley Pride Inc..........760 398-1353
86120 Tyler Ln Coachella (92236) ***(G-503)***
Valley Pride Inc (PA)..........831 633-5883
10855 Ocean Mist Pkwy D Castroville (95012) ***(G-687)***
Valley Process Systems Inc..........408 261-1277
3567 Benton St Ste 341 Santa Clara (95051) ***(G-2405)***
Valley Productions Inc..........559 661-6121
17247 La Canada Rd Madera (93636) ***(G-17583)***
Valley Properties Inc..........818 360-3430
10324 Balboa Blvd Lbby Granada Hills (91344) ***(G-11067)***
Valley Radiology Consultants (PA)..........619 797-8248
6185 Paseo Del Norte # 110 Carlsbad (92011) ***(G-22295)***
Valley Relocation and Storage (PA)..........925 230-2025
5000 Marsh Dr Concord (94520) ***(G-4298)***
Valley Resource Center For Th (PA)..........951 657-0609
1285 N Santa Fe St Hemet (92543) ***(G-24402)***
Valley Rsrce Ctr For Retarded..........951 766-8659
1285 N Santa Fe St Hemet (92543) ***(G-24994)***
Valley Rubber & Gasket, Sacramento *Also called Lewis-Goetz and Company Inc* ***(G-7938)***
Valley Sanitary Supply, Fresno *Also called Valley Floor Maintenance Inc* ***(G-14461)***
Valley Sheet Metal Co, Marysville *Also called Frank M Booth Inc* ***(G-25818)***
Valley Shelter, North Hollywood *Also called L A Family Housing Corp* ***(G-24702)***
Valley Skilled Nursing Care, Sacramento *Also called V S N F Inc* ***(G-21001)***
Valley Stre Frnt Jwsh Fmly Svc, North Hollywood *Also called Jewish Family Svc Los Angeles* ***(G-24047)***
Valley Sun Mechanical Cnstr..........661 321-9070
4205 Atlas Ct Bakersfield (93308) ***(G-3596)***
Valley Teen Ranch..........559 437-1144
2610 W Shaw Ln Ste 105 Fresno (93711) ***(G-24843)***
Valley Toxicology Service Inc..........916 371-5440
2401 Port St West Sacramento (95691) ***(G-22296)***
Valley US Inc..........408 260-7342
888 Saratoga Ave Ste 201 San Jose (95129) ***(G-16519)***
Valley View Care Center, Riverbank *Also called Valley West Health Care Inc* ***(G-21005)***
Valley View Casino, Valley Center *Also called San Psqual Band Mssion Indians* ***(G-13207)***
Valley View Casino, Valley Center *Also called San Psqual Csino Dev Group Inc* ***(G-13208)***
Valley View Place Retirement, Long Beach *Also called Brookdale Senior Living Inc* ***(G-21165)***
Valley View Skilled Nursing, Ukiah *Also called Horizon West Healthcare Inc* ***(G-20677)***
Valley View Sklled Nursing Ctr..........707 462-1436
1162 S Dora St Ukiah (95482) ***(G-21004)***
Valley Village, Santa Clara *Also called Church of Vly Rtrment Hmes Inc* ***(G-24599)***
Valley Water Proofing Inc..........408 985-7701
825 Civic Center Dr Ste 6 Santa Clara (95050) ***(G-3597)***
Valley West Care Center, Williams *Also called Valley West Health Care Inc* ***(G-21408)***
Valley West Health Care Inc (PA)..........530 473-5321
1224 E St Williams (95987) ***(G-21408)***
Valley West Health Care Inc..........209 869-2569
2649 Topeka St Riverbank (95367) ***(G-21005)***
Valley Wholesale Drug Co LLC..........209 466-0131
1401 W Fremont St Stockton (95203) ***(G-8303)***
Valley Wholesale Supply Corp (PA)..........818 769-5656
10708 Vanowen St North Hollywood (91605) ***(G-6901)***
Valley Wide Beverage Company, Fresno *Also called Fresno Beverage Company Inc* ***(G-9057)***
Valley Wide Recreation Pk Dst (PA)..........951 654-1505
901 W Esplanade Ave San Jacinto (92582) ***(G-19302)***
Valley-HI Country Club..........916 684-2120
9595 Franklin Blvd Elk Grove (95758) ***(G-19117)***
Valleycare Health, Livermore *Also called Valleycare Hospital Corp* ***(G-20185)***
Valleycare Health System, Livermore *Also called For Hospital Committee* ***(G-27026)***
Valleycare Hospital Corp (HQ)..........925 447-7000
1111 E Stanley Blvd Livermore (94550) ***(G-20185)***
Valleycrest Golf Crse Mint Inc, Calabasas *Also called Brightview Golf Maint Inc* ***(G-2030)***
Valleycrest Ldscp Maint Vcc..........800 466-8510
24121 Ventura Blvd Calabasas (91302) ***(G-803)***
Valleywide Construction Inc..........559 834-6212
284 W Lester Ave Clovis (93619) ***(G-1277)***
Valleywide Maintenance, Fresno *Also called San Mar Properties Inc* ***(G-11831)***
Valor Communication Inc..........626 581-8085
18071 Arenth Ave City of Industry (91748) ***(G-7653)***
Valori Sand & Gravel Company (PA)..........714 637-0104
141 W Taft Ave Orange (92865) ***(G-6998)***
Valori Sand & Gravel Company..........909 350-3000
11027 Cherry Ave Fontana (92337) ***(G-6999)***
Vals Plumbing and Heating Inc..........831 424-1633
413 Front St Salinas (93901) ***(G-2406)***
Valtox Laboratories, West Sacramento *Also called Valley Toxicology Service Inc* ***(G-22296)***
Valuation Concepts LLC..........818 812-6233
16350 Ventura Blvd D140 Encino (91436) ***(G-11896)***
Value Options-V B H, Cypress *Also called Valueoptions of California* ***(G-10920)***
Valueoptions of California..........800 228-1286
10805 Holder St Ste 300 Cypress (90630) ***(G-10920)***
Valverde Construction Inc..........562 906-1826
10918 Shoemaker Ave Santa Fe Springs (90670) ***(G-2010)***
Valvoline Instant Oil Change, Santa Fe Springs *Also called Valvoline International Inc* ***(G-17905)***
Valvoline International Inc..........562 906-6200
9520 John St Santa Fe Springs (90670) ***(G-17905)***
Valyria LLC..........707 452-0600
1050 Aviator Dr Vacaville (95688) ***(G-6902)***

Van Acker Cnstr Assoc Inc..........415 383-5589
1060 Redwood Hwy Frntg Rd Mill Valley (94941) ***(G-1278)***
Van Beurden Insurance Svcs Inc (PA)..........559 634-7125
1600 Draper St Kingsburg (93631) ***(G-10921)***
Van Daele Development Corp..........951 354-6800
2900 Adams St Ste C25 Riverside (92504) ***(G-1388)***
Van Daele Homes, Riverside *Also called Van Daele Development Corp* ***(G-1388)***
Van De Pol Enterprises Inc (PA)..........209 944-9115
4895 S Airport Way Stockton (95206) ***(G-9031)***
Van De Pol Enterprises Inc..........559 860-4100
3081 E Hamilton Ave Fresno (93721) ***(G-9032)***
Van Dyk Tank Lines Inc..........951 682-5000
1800 S Riverside Ave Colton (92324) ***(G-4087)***
Van Etten Suzumoto Becket LLP..........310 315-8284
1620 26th St Ste 6000n Santa Monica (90404) ***(G-27707)***
Van Groningen & Sons Inc..........209 982-5248
15100 Jack Tone Rd Manteca (95336) ***(G-401)***
Van Grow Jack S MD..........714 564-3300
1140 W La Veta Ave # 640 Orange (92868) ***(G-20186)***
Van Horn Youth Center, Riverside *Also called County of Riverside* ***(G-23890)***
Van King & Storage Inc (PA)..........562 921-0555
13535 Larwin Cir Santa Fe Springs (90670) ***(G-4088)***
Van King & Storage Inc..........562 921-0555
13535 Larwin Cir Santa Fe Springs (90670) ***(G-4653)***
Van Ness Hotel Inc..........415 673-4711
1050 Van Ness Ave San Francisco (94109) ***(G-13375)***
Van Nuys Airport, Van Nuys *Also called City of Los Angeles* ***(G-4908)***
Van Nuys Care Center Inc..........818 343-0700
16955 Vanowen St Van Nuys (91406) ***(G-21409)***
Van Nuys Community Hospital, Van Nuys *Also called Alta Healthcare System LLC* ***(G-24862)***
Van Nuys Health Care Center, Van Nuys *Also called Five Star Quality Care Inc* ***(G-20573)***
Van Torrance & Storage Company (PA)..........562 567-2100
12128 Burke St Santa Fe Springs (90670) ***(G-4387)***
Vanalden Ave School, Reseda *Also called West Valley Family YMCA* ***(G-24531)***
Vance Corporation..........909 355-4333
2271 N Locust Ave Rialto (92377) ***(G-1881)***
Vancrest Construction Corp..........323 256-0011
7171 N Figueroa St Los Angeles (90042) ***(G-1710)***
Vandenberg Afb Child Care..........805 606-1555
Summersill Bldg 11613 Lompoc (93437) ***(G-24528)***
Vander Weerd General Cnstr..........559 688-1099
837 Commercial Ave Tulare (93274) ***(G-3446)***
Vandorpe Chou Associates Inc..........714 978-9780
1845 W Orangewood Ave # 210 Orange (92868) ***(G-26137)***
VANGUARD CADETS, Santa Clara *Also called Santa Clara Vngard Booster CLB* ***(G-25338)***
Vanguard Legato, San Leandro *Also called Vanguard Legato A Cal Corp* ***(G-6834)***
Vanguard Legato A Cal Corp..........510 351-3333
2121 Williams St San Leandro (94577) ***(G-6834)***
Vanguard Lgistics Svcs USA Inc (HQ)..........310 847-3000
5000 Airport Plaza Dr Long Beach (90815) ***(G-5188)***
Vanguard Lgistics Svcs USA Inc..........310 637-3700
2665 E Del Amo Blvd Compton (90221) ***(G-4654)***
Vanguard Resources Corp..........858 336-7147
13816 Fontanelle Pl San Diego (92128) ***(G-27801)***
Vanir Construction MGT Inc (PA)..........916 444-3700
4540 Duckhorn Dr Ste 300 Sacramento (95834) ***(G-27273)***
Vanpike Inc (PA)..........858 453-1331
6336 Greenwich Dr Ste 100 San Diego (92122) ***(G-14968)***
Vantage Company, Orange *Also called W Corporation* ***(G-28096)***
Vantage Oncology LLC (HQ)..........310 335-4000
1500 Rosecrans Ave # 400 Manhattan Beach (90266) ***(G-20187)***
Vantage Plaster & Drywall..........760 345-3622
79607 Country Club Dr Bermuda Dunes (92203) ***(G-2993)***
Vantagepoint Capital Partners, San Bruno *Also called Vantagepoint Management Inc* ***(G-12351)***
Vantagepoint Management Inc (PA)..........650 866-3100
1001 Bayhill Dr Ste 300 San Bruno (94066) ***(G-12351)***
Vantagepoint Venture Partners..........650 866-3100
1001 Bayhill Dr Ste 300 San Bruno (94066) ***(G-12128)***
Vaquero Energy Incorporated..........661 363-7240
15545 Hermosa Rd Bakersfield (93307) ***(G-1052)***
Vaquero Farms Inc..........559 659-2790
43405 W Panoche Rd Firebaugh (93622) ***(G-402)***
Varian Medical Systems Inc..........408 321-9400
660 N Mccarthy Blvd Milpitas (95035) ***(G-7324)***
Varis LLC..........916 294-0860
3915 Security Park Dr B Rancho Cordova (95742) ***(G-27708)***
Varmour Networks Inc..........650 564-5100
800 W El Cam Mountain View (94040) ***(G-15521)***
Varner Family Ltd Partnership (PA)..........661 399-1163
5900 E Lerdo Hwy Shafter (93263) ***(G-12208)***
Varsity Contractors Inc..........661 398-0275
5880 District Blvd Ste 1 Bakersfield (93313) ***(G-26263)***
Varsity Contractors Inc..........949 586-8283
24155 Laguna Hills Mall # 900 Laguna Hills (92653) ***(G-14462)***
Vasindas Around The Clock Care..........661 395-5820
5251 Office Park Dr # 403 Bakersfield (93309) ***(G-24844)***
Vasko Electric Inc..........916 568-7700
4300 Astoria St Sacramento (95838) ***(G-2782)***
Vasona Management Inc..........510 352-8728
13931 Doolittle Dr San Leandro (94577) ***(G-11219)***
Vasona Management Inc..........510 413-0091
37390 Central Mont Pl Fremont (94538) ***(G-1279)***
Vasonic Construction, Fremont *Also called Vasona Management Inc* ***(G-1279)***
Vasquez Brothers Inc..........831 678-8894
157 Kidder St Soledad (93960) ***(G-601)***
Vasto Valle Farms, Huron *Also called Dick Anderson & Sons Farming* ***(G-355)***
Vauche Bank Berkshire Mortgage, Irvine *Also called Berkshire Mortgage Fin Corp* ***(G-9822)***

Vavrinek Trine Day and Co LLP (PA)..........909 466-4410
10681 Fthill Blvd Ste 300 Rancho Cucamonga (91730) *(G-26455)*
Vaxaville Medical Offices, Vacaville *Also called Kaiser Foundation Hospitals (G-10313)*
Vaya, San Diego *Also called Vietnms-Mrcan Yuth Alance Corp (G-25396)*
Vayan Marketing Group LLC..........310 943-4990
10877 Wilshire Blvd Fl 12 Los Angeles (90024) *(G-27709)*
Vb Golf LLC..........650 573-7888
2401 E 3rd Ave Foster City (94404) *(G-27274)*
Vbp Orange, San Francisco *Also called Venables/Bell & Partners LLC (G-13935)*
VCA Animal Hospitals Inc..........916 652-5816
3901 Sierra College Blvd Loomis (95650) *(G-626)*
VCA Animal Hospitals Inc..........760 778-9999
4299 E Ramon Rd Palm Springs (92264) *(G-627)*
VCA Animal Hospitals Inc (HQ)..........310 571-6500
12401 W Olympic Blvd Los Angeles (90064) *(G-628)*
VCA Antech Inc..........310 207-0781
12401 W Olympic Blvd Los Angeles (90064) *(G-629)*
VCA Code Group..........714 363-4700
2200 W Orangewood Ave # 150 Orange (92868) *(G-26138)*
VCA Engineering, Orange *Also called Vandorpe Chou Associates Inc (G-26137)*
VCA Inc..........310 473-2951
1818 S Sepulveda Blvd Los Angeles (90025) *(G-630)*
VCA Inc..........530 224-2200
2505 Hilltop Dr Redding (96002) *(G-631)*
VCA Lmis Bsin Vterinary Clinic, Loomis *Also called VCA Animal Hospitals Inc (G-626)*
VCA TLC Animal Hospital, Los Angeles *Also called VCA Animal Hospitals Inc (G-628)*
VCA-Asher Animal Hospital, Redding *Also called VCA Inc (G-631)*
Vcall, Beverly Hills *Also called Mediaplatform Inc (G-18108)*
Vci Construction LLC (HQ)..........909 946-0905
1921 W 11th St Ste A Upland (91786) *(G-2011)*
Vci Event Technology Inc..........714 772-2002
1261 S Simpson Cir Anaheim (92806) *(G-14589)*
Veatch Carlson Grogan & Nelson..........213 381-2861
700 S Flower St Ste 2200 Los Angeles (90017) *(G-23605)*
Veba Administrators Inc..........310 577-1444
4640 Admiralty Way Fl 9 Marina Del Rey (90292) *(G-10922)*
Vector Resources Inc (PA)..........310 436-1000
3530 Voyager St Torrance (90503) *(G-2783)*
Vector Resources Inc..........858 546-1014
9808 Waples St San Diego (92121) *(G-26139)*
Vector Security Inc..........323 224-6700
5411 Valley Blvd Los Angeles (90032) *(G-2784)*
Vector USA, San Diego *Also called Vector Resources Inc (G-26139)*
Vectorusa, Torrance *Also called Vector Resources Inc (G-2783)*
Veeva Systems Inc (PA)..........925 452-6500
4280 Hacienda Dr Pleasanton (94588) *(G-15872)*
Veg-Fresh Farms LLC..........800 422-5535
1400 W Rincon St Corona (92880) *(G-8784)*
Veg-Land Inc..........714 871-6712
1518 E Valencia Dr Fullerton (92831) *(G-4484)*
Vegetable Growers Supply Co (PA)..........831 759-4600
1360 Merrill St Salinas (93901) *(G-9308)*
Vegiworks Inc..........415 643-8686
2101 Jerrold Ave San Francisco (94124) *(G-8785)*
Velazquez Packing Inc..........805 735-6477
124 N I St Lompoc (93436) *(G-688)*
Veldhuis Dairy, Winton *Also called P H Ranch Inc (G-438)*
Veldhuis North Dairy..........209 394-5117
12465 Lee Rd Ballico (95303) *(G-439)*
Velocitel Rf Inc..........949 809-4999
2415 Campus Dr Ste 200 Irvine (92612) *(G-26140)*
Velocity Arospc - Burbank Inc (HQ)..........818 246-8431
2840 N Ontario St Burbank (91504) *(G-18031)*
Velocity Commercial Capitl LLC..........818 532-3700
30699 Russell Ranch Rd Westlake Village (91362) *(G-11897)*
Velti Inc (PA)..........415 362-2077
150 California St Fl 10 San Francisco (94111) *(G-15873)*
Velti USA, San Francisco *Also called Velti Inc (G-15873)*
Venables/Bell & Partners LLC..........415 288-3300
201 Post St Fl 2 San Francisco (94108) *(G-13935)*
Venbrook Insurance Svcs LLC (PA)..........818 598-8900
6320 Canoga Ave Fl 12 Woodland Hills (91367) *(G-10923)*
Venco Western Inc (PA)..........805 981-2400
2400 Eastman Ave Oxnard (93030) *(G-975)*
Vencore Inc..........408 961-3250
1315 Dell Ave Campbell (95008) *(G-16075)*
Vencore Inc..........571 313-6000
1315 Dell Ave Campbell (95008) *(G-28088)*
Vencore Inc..........619 321-6000
1315 Dell Ave Campbell (95008) *(G-16076)*
Vencore Svcs & Solutions Inc..........408 961-3200
1315 Dell Ave Campbell (95008) *(G-16077)*
Vend Catering Supply Inc..........562 483-7337
14455 Industry Cir La Mirada (90638) *(G-7985)*
Vendavo Inc (HQ)..........650 960-4300
401 E Middlefield Rd Mountain View (94043) *(G-15874)*
Vendini Inc (PA)..........415 693-9611
660 Market St Ste 400 San Francisco (94104) *(G-15522)*
Vendor Direct Solutions LLC..........213 362-5622
515 S Figueroa St # 1900 Los Angeles (90071) *(G-27275)*
Vengroff Williams & Assoc Inc..........714 889-6200
2099 S State College Blvd # 300 Anaheim (92806) *(G-14052)*
Venice Family Clinic..........310 392-8636
4700 Inglewood Blvd # 102 Culver City (90230) *(G-20188)*
Venice Family Clinic (PA)..........310 664-7703
604 Rose Ave Venice (90291) *(G-20189)*
Venice Family Clinic..........310 392-8636
2509 Pico Blvd Santa Monica (90405) *(G-20190)*
Venida Packing Company..........559 592-2816
19823 Avenue 300 Exeter (93221) *(G-5206)*
Ventage Senior Housing..........949 631-3555
4000 Hilaria Way Newport Beach (92663) *(G-24845)*
Ventana Inn & Spa, Big Sur *Also called 48123 CA Investors LLC (G-12363)*
Ventas Inc..........949 718-4400
2050 Main St Ste 800 Irvine (92614) *(G-12024)*
Ventrum LLC..........510 304-0852
2033 Gateway Pl Ste 500 San Jose (95110) *(G-16520)*
Ventu Park LLC..........805 716-4200
495 N Ventu Park Rd Thousand Oaks (91320) *(G-13376)*
Ventura Beach Marriott Hotel, Ventura *Also called Kingledon Inc (G-12886)*
Ventura Cnty Council On Aging..........805 986-1424
4917 S Rose Ave Oxnard (93033) *(G-24277)*
Ventura Cnty Human Srvce, Oxnard *Also called County of Ventura (G-24453)*
Ventura County Credit Union (PA)..........805 477-4000
6026 Telephone Rd Ventura (93003) *(G-9698)*
Ventura County Fire Department..........805 389-9710
165 Durley Ave Camarillo (93010) *(G-25388)*
Ventura County Lemon Coops..........805 385-3345
P.O. Box 6986 Oxnard (93031) *(G-602)*
Ventura County Medical Center..........805 933-8600
845 N 10th St Ste 3 Santa Paula (93060) *(G-20191)*
Ventura County Medical Center (PA)..........805 652-6000
3291 Loma Vista Rd Ventura (93003) *(G-20192)*
Ventura County Medical Center..........805 652-6201
3291 Loma Vista Rd # 343 Ventura (93003) *(G-20193)*
Ventura County Office Educatn..........805 495-7037
1379 Oakridge Ct Thousand Oaks (91362) *(G-25389)*
Ventura Family YMCA, Ventura *Also called Channel Islands Young Mens Ch (G-25235)*
Ventura Hsptality Partners LLC..........805 648-2100
450 Harbor Blvd Ventura (93001) *(G-13377)*
Ventura Pacific Co, Ventura *Also called Ventura County Lemon Coops (G-602)*
Ventura Streets Dept..........805 652-4515
336 San Jon Rd Ventura (93001) *(G-1280)*
Ventura Transfer Company (PA)..........310 549-1660
2418 E 223rd St Long Beach (90810) *(G-4299)*
Ventura Yuth Crrctional Fcilty, Camarillo *Also called Juvenile Justice Division Cal (G-27085)*
Venture Design Services Inc (PA)..........714 765-3740
1051 S East St Anaheim (92805) *(G-26633)*
Venture Design Services Inc..........707 524-8368
451 Aviation Blvd Ste 215 Santa Rosa (95403) *(G-17584)*
Venture Lath and Plaster, North Highlands *Also called Rick H Hitch Plastering Inc (G-2969)*
Venture Pacific Tools Inc..........949 475-5505
17152 Daimler St Irvine (92614) *(G-7702)*
Venue Management Services Inc..........626 445-6000
500 N 1st Ave Ste 4 Arcadia (91006) *(G-28089)*
Venus Group Inc..........949 609-1299
25861 Wright Foothill Ranch (92610) *(G-6903)*
Venus Textiles, Foothill Ranch *Also called Venus Group Inc (G-6903)*
Venvest Ballard Inc..........951 276-9744
3030 Myers St Riverside (92503) *(G-2407)*
Veolia Es Industrial Svcs Inc..........707 745-1581
4501 California Ct Benicia (94510) *(G-18032)*
Veolia Es Industrial Svcs Inc..........707 745-0501
511 E Channel Rd Benicia (94510) *(G-14463)*
Veolia Es Waste-To-Energy Inc..........562 436-0636
100 Pier S Ave Long Beach (90802) *(G-6593)*
Veolia Transportation Svcs Inc..........408 277-3661
1601 Airport Blvd San Jose (95110) *(G-3732)*
Veolia Transportation Svcs Inc..........760 947-5719
17150 Smoketree St Hesperia (92345) *(G-3733)*
Veolia Transportation Svcs Inc..........661 294-2541
25663 Avenue Stanford Valencia (91355) *(G-3734)*
Veolia Transportation Svcs Inc..........530 342-6851
326 Huss Dr Chico (95928) *(G-3735)*
Veolia Transportation Svcs Inc..........925 455-7500
1362 Rutan Dr Ste 200 Livermore (94551) *(G-3736)*
Veolia Transportation Svcs Inc..........707 585-7516
355 W Robles Ave Santa Rosa (95407) *(G-3737)*
Ver Sales Inc (PA)..........818 567-3000
2509 N Naomi St Burbank (91504) *(G-7409)*
Vera Bradley Inc..........408 615-8370
356 Santana Row Ste 1020 San Jose (95128) *(G-17585)*
Veracyte Inc..........650 243-6300
6000 Shoreline Ct Ste 300 South San Francisco (94080) *(G-22297)*
Verance Corporation..........858 202-2800
10089 Willow Creek Rd San Diego (92131) *(G-26718)*
Verasa Management LLC..........707 257-1800
1314 Mckinstry St NAPA (94559) *(G-13378)*
Verdugo Hills Hosp Foundation (PA)..........818 790-7100
1812 Verdugo Blvd Glendale (91208) *(G-22011)*
Verdugo Hills Medical Assoc, Glendale *Also called Verdugo Hills Urgent Care Mg (G-20194)*
Verdugo Hills Urgent Care Mg..........818 241-4331
544 N Glendale Ave Glendale (91206) *(G-20194)*
Verdugo Hlls Vsting Nurse Assn..........949 263-4704
2826 E Foothill Blvd # 101 Pasadena (91107) *(G-22588)*
Verdugo Mental Health..........818 244-7257
1540 E Colorado St Glendale (91205) *(G-22861)*
Verdugo Vista Healthcare Ctr, La Crescenta *Also called Mariner Health Care Inc (G-20774)*
Verdugo Vly Convalescent Hosp, Montrose *Also called Great Wstn Cnvlescent Hosp Inc (G-21256)*
Vergence Labs Inc..........650 691-3009
333 Wshington Blvd Ste 50 Marina Del Rey (90292) *(G-22298)*
Verifaya Corporation..........408 566-0220
650 Castro St Ste 120-264 Mountain View (94041) *(G-15875)*
Verifi Inc..........323 655-5789
8391 Beverly Blvd Ste 310 Los Angeles (90048) *(G-27710)*

ALPHABETIC

Verifone Inc....916 408-4900
1401 Aviation Blvd Lincoln (95648) ***(G-4655)***
Verihealth Inc....707 303-8000
200 Montgomery Dr Ste D Santa Rosa (95404) ***(G-3854)***
Verinata Health Inc....650 632-1680
800 Saginaw Dr Redwood City (94063) ***(G-26634)***
Verint, Santa Clara *Also called Kana Software Inc* ***(G-15721)***
Verint Americas Inc....408 830-5400
2250 Walsh Ave Ste 120 Santa Clara (95050) ***(G-15523)***
Veritable Vegetable Inc....415 641-3500
1100 Cesar Chavez San Francisco (94124) ***(G-8786)***
Veritas Health Services Inc....909 464-8600
5451 Walnut Ave Chino (91710) ***(G-22012)***
Veritas Technologies LLC (HQ)....650 933-1000
500 E Middlefield Rd Mountain View (94043) ***(G-15524)***
Veritas US Inc (PA)....650 933-1000
500 E Middlefield Rd Mountain View (94043) ***(G-15525)***
Veritiv Operating Company....925 245-6075
7337 Las Positas Rd Livermore (94551) ***(G-7902)***
Veritiv Operating Company....559 268-0467
2325 S Cedar Ave Fresno (93725) ***(G-8219)***
Veritiv Operating Company....714 690-4000
15005 Northam St La Mirada (90638) ***(G-8220)***
Veritiv Operating Company....415 586-9160
345 Schwerin St San Francisco (94134) ***(G-8156)***
Veritiv Operating Company....310 527-3000
13217 S Figueroa St Los Angeles (90061) ***(G-8221)***
Veritiv Operating Company....323 725-3700
2600 Commerce Way Commerce (90040) ***(G-8222)***
Veritiv Operating Company....714 690-6600
20 Centerpointe Dr # 130 La Palma (90623) ***(G-8223)***
Verity Health System Cal Inc....310 900-8900
203 Redwood Shores Pkwy Redwood City (94065) ***(G-22013)***
Verity Health System Cal Inc....408 947-2762
2105 Forest Ave San Jose (95128) ***(G-22014)***
Verity Health System Cal Inc....650 551-6507
203 Redwood Shores Pkwy # 700 Redwood City (94065) ***(G-22015)***
Verity Health System Cal Inc....408 848-2000
9400 N Name Uno Gilroy (95020) ***(G-22016)***
Verity Health System Cal Inc....310 900-2000
3680 E Imperial Hwy # 306 Lynwood (90262) ***(G-22017)***
Verity Health System Cal Inc....650 551-6700
203 Redwood Shr Pkwy # 800 Redwood City (94065) ***(G-28167)***
Verity Health System Cal Inc....650 917-4500
3630 E Imperial Hwy Lynwood (90262) ***(G-22018)***
Verizon, Indio *Also called Frontier California Inc* ***(G-5605)***
Verizon, Torrance *Also called Cellco Partnership* ***(G-5286)***
Verizon, Livermore *Also called Cellco Partnership* ***(G-5287)***
Verizon, Lindsay *Also called GTE Corporation* ***(G-27937)***
Verizon, Oxnard *Also called GTE Corporation* ***(G-14667)***
Verizon, Costa Mesa *Also called Cellco Partnership* ***(G-5296)***
Verizon, Santa Monica *Also called GTE Corporation* ***(G-17203)***
Verizon, Roseville *Also called Cellco Partnership* ***(G-5298)***
Verizon, Santa Maria *Also called Frontier California Inc* ***(G-5606)***
Verizon, Irvine *Also called Cellco Partnership* ***(G-5299)***
Verizon, Barstow *Also called Frontier California Inc* ***(G-5607)***
Verizon, Capitola *Also called Cellco Partnership* ***(G-5304)***
Verizon, Bakersfield *Also called Cellco Partnership* ***(G-5305)***
Verizon, Carlsbad *Also called Cellco Partnership* ***(G-5306)***
Verizon, Corte Madera *Also called Cellco Partnership* ***(G-5307)***
Verizon, El Cajon *Also called Cellco Partnership* ***(G-5308)***
Verizon, Fresno *Also called Cellco Partnership* ***(G-5309)***
Verizon, Cerritos *Also called Cellco Partnership* ***(G-5310)***
Verizon, Chico *Also called Cellco Partnership* ***(G-5311)***
Verizon, Corona *Also called Cellco Partnership* ***(G-5312)***
Verizon, Brea *Also called Cellco Partnership* ***(G-5314)***
Verizon, Chula Vista *Also called Cellco Partnership* ***(G-5315)***
Verizon, San Fernando *Also called Frontier California Inc* ***(G-5608)***
Verizon, Manteca *Also called Frontier California Inc* ***(G-5609)***
Verizon, Folsom *Also called Cellco Partnership* ***(G-5354)***
Verizon, San Francisco *Also called Cellco Partnership* ***(G-5371)***
Verizon, Whittier *Also called Cellco Partnership* ***(G-5372)***
Verizon, Westlake Village *Also called Frontier California Inc* ***(G-7569)***
Verizon, Bakersfield *Also called GTE Corporation* ***(G-5624)***
Verizon, Hayward *Also called American Messaging Svcs LLC* ***(G-5458)***
Verizon, Laguna Niguel *Also called Cellco Partnership* ***(G-5376)***
Verizon, Ontario *Also called Frontier California Inc* ***(G-5610)***
Verizon, Westlake Village *Also called Frontier California Inc* ***(G-5611)***
Verizon, Exeter *Also called Frontier California Inc* ***(G-5612)***
Verizon, Dublin *Also called Cellco Partnership* ***(G-5382)***
Verizon, San Luis Obispo *Also called Cellco Partnership* ***(G-5383)***
Verizon, Tustin *Also called Cellco Partnership* ***(G-5385)***
Verizon, Fresno *Also called Frontier California Inc* ***(G-5397)***
Verizon Bus Netwrk Svcs Inc....916 779-5600
11080 White Rock Rd # 100 Rancho Cordova (95670) ***(G-5715)***
Verizon Bus Netwrk Svcs Inc....408 975-2244
55 S Market St Ste 1250 San Jose (95113) ***(G-5716)***
Verizon Bus Netwrk Svcs Inc....916 569-5999
1740 Creekside Oaks 200 Sacramento (95833) ***(G-5717)***
Verizon Bus Netwrk Svcs Inc....510 497-2500
4340 Solar Way Fremont (94538) ***(G-16283)***
Verizon Business, Los Angeles *Also called MCI Communications Svcs Inc* ***(G-5651)***
Verizon Business, Los Angeles *Also called MCI Communications Svcs Inc* ***(G-5652)***
Verizon Business Global LLC....415 606-3621
1516 Stillwell Rd Apt F San Francisco (94129) ***(G-5718)***
Verizon Business Global LLC....951 653-4482
6177 River Crest Dr Ste B Riverside (92507) ***(G-6056)***
Verizon Business Global LLC....408 222-2300
464 Oakmead Pkwy Sunnyvale (94085) ***(G-5719)***
Verizon Business Global LLC....909 466-5633
800 W 6th St Ste 1150 Los Angeles (90017) ***(G-5720)***
Verizon Communications Inc....626 858-1739
176 E Badillo St Covina (91723) ***(G-2785)***
Verizon Communications Inc....562 496-0288
5077 E Lew Davis St Long Beach (90808) ***(G-5721)***
Verizon Communications Inc....760 245-0409
16461 Mojave Dr Victorville (92395) ***(G-5722)***
Verizon Communications Inc....805 390-5417
2801 Townsgate Rd Ste 300 Westlake Village (91361) ***(G-17586)***
Verizon Communications Inc....916 568-0440
1417 Howe Ave Sacramento (95825) ***(G-5723)***
Verizon Communications Inc....818 438-1104
18442 Arminta St Reseda (91335) ***(G-17587)***
Verizon Communications Inc....562 804-0354
9900 Flower St Bellflower (90706) ***(G-6098)***
Verizon Communications Inc....909 421-5053
18850 Orange St Bloomington (92316) ***(G-17588)***
Verizon Communications Inc....213 330-2556
700 S Flower St Ste 1700 Los Angeles (90017) ***(G-17589)***
Verizon Communications Inc....805 445-8125
201 Flynn Rd Camarillo (93012) ***(G-18281)***
Verizon Communications Inc....818 388-8549
21306 Superior St Chatsworth (91311) ***(G-5724)***
Verizon Digital Media Svcs Inc....310 396-7400
13031 W Jefferson Blvd # 900 Los Angeles (90094) ***(G-16521)***
Verizon Networkfleet, San Diego *Also called Networkfleet Inc* ***(G-15327)***
Verizon New York Inc....909 481-7897
961 N Milliken Ave # 101 Ontario (91764) ***(G-7654)***
Verizon South Inc....805 681-8527
424 S Patterson Ave Goleta (93111) ***(G-5725)***
Verizon Wireless, Beaumont *Also called Cellco Partnership* ***(G-5284)***
Verizon Wireless, Temecula *Also called Cellco Partnership* ***(G-5285)***
Verizon Wireless, Monterey *Also called Cellco Partnership* ***(G-5288)***
Verizon Wireless, Orange *Also called Cellco Partnership* ***(G-5289)***
Verizon Wireless, Brentwood *Also called Cellco Partnership* ***(G-5290)***
Verizon Wireless, Riverside *Also called Cellco Partnership* ***(G-5291)***
Verizon Wireless, Fresno *Also called Cellco Partnership* ***(G-5295)***
Verizon Wireless, Mira Loma *Also called Cellco Partnership* ***(G-5297)***
Verizon Wireless, Watsonville *Also called Cellco Partnership* ***(G-5300)***
Verizon Wireless, La Habra *Also called Cellco Partnership* ***(G-5301)***
Verizon Wireless, Orange *Also called Cellco Partnership* ***(G-5302)***
Verizon Wireless, San Marcos *Also called Cellco Partnership* ***(G-5303)***
Verizon Wireless, Fremont *Also called Cellco Partnership* ***(G-5313)***
Verizon Wireless, Menifee *Also called Cellco Partnership* ***(G-5574)***
Verizon Wireless, San Diego *Also called Cellco Partnership* ***(G-5317)***
Verizon Wireless, Panorama City *Also called Cellco Partnership* ***(G-5319)***
Verizon Wireless, Ventura *Also called Cellco Partnership* ***(G-5320)***
Verizon Wireless, Encinitas *Also called Cellco Partnership* ***(G-5323)***
Verizon Wireless, Corona *Also called Cellco Partnership* ***(G-5324)***
Verizon Wireless, Santa Clarita *Also called Cellco Partnership* ***(G-5325)***
Verizon Wireless, Burbank *Also called Cellco Partnership* ***(G-5327)***
Verizon Wireless, Baldwin Park *Also called Cellco Partnership* ***(G-5328)***
Verizon Wireless, Gilroy *Also called Cellco Partnership* ***(G-5329)***
Verizon Wireless, Pasadena *Also called Cellco Partnership* ***(G-5330)***
Verizon Wireless, Sacramento *Also called Cellco Partnership* ***(G-5331)***
Verizon Wireless, Rancho Mirage *Also called Cellco Partnership* ***(G-5332)***
Verizon Wireless, Milpitas *Also called Cellco Partnership* ***(G-5333)***
Verizon Wireless, Lake Forest *Also called Cellco Partnership* ***(G-5334)***
Verizon Wireless, San Francisco *Also called Cellco Partnership* ***(G-5336)***
Verizon Wireless, Turlock *Also called Cellco Partnership* ***(G-5337)***
Verizon Wireless, Tustin *Also called Cellco Partnership* ***(G-5339)***
Verizon Wireless, Encino *Also called Cellco Partnership* ***(G-5340)***
Verizon Wireless, Los Angeles *Also called Cellco Partnership* ***(G-5342)***
Verizon Wireless, Sacramento *Also called Cellco Partnership* ***(G-5343)***
Verizon Wireless, Downey *Also called Cellco Partnership* ***(G-5346)***
Verizon Wireless, Hesperia *Also called Cellco Partnership* ***(G-5347)***
Verizon Wireless, Chula Vista *Also called Cellco Partnership* ***(G-5348)***
Verizon Wireless, Oakland *Also called Cellco Partnership* ***(G-5349)***
Verizon Wireless, Clovis *Also called Cellco Partnership* ***(G-5350)***
Verizon Wireless, Palmdale *Also called Cellco Partnership* ***(G-5351)***
Verizon Wireless, Huntington Beach *Also called Cellco Partnership* ***(G-5352)***
Verizon Wireless, Los Angeles *Also called Cellco Partnership* ***(G-5353)***
Verizon Wireless, Modesto *Also called Cellco Partnership* ***(G-5355)***
Verizon Wireless, Los Angeles *Also called Cellco Partnership* ***(G-5356)***
Verizon Wireless, Carson *Also called Cellco Partnership* ***(G-5357)***
Verizon Wireless, Hollywood *Also called Cellco Partnership* ***(G-5358)***
Verizon Wireless, West Hollywood *Also called Cellco Partnership* ***(G-5359)***
Verizon Wireless, San Francisco *Also called Cellco Partnership* ***(G-5360)***
Verizon Wireless, Union City *Also called Cellco Partnership* ***(G-5361)***
Verizon Wireless, Redding *Also called Cellco Partnership* ***(G-5362)***
Verizon Wireless, Valencia *Also called Cellco Partnership* ***(G-5363)***
Verizon Wireless, Cypress *Also called Cellco Partnership* ***(G-5364)***
Verizon Wireless, El Centro *Also called Cellco Partnership* ***(G-5365)***
Verizon Wireless, Simi Valley *Also called Cellco Partnership* ***(G-5366)***

ALPHABETIC

ALPHABETIC SECTION Via Embedded Store, Fremont

Verizon Wireless, Canoga Park *Also called Cellco Partnership (G-5367)*
Verizon Wireless, Santa Cruz *Also called Cellco Partnership (G-5368)*
Verizon Wireless, San Bernardino *Also called Cellco Partnership (G-5369)*
Verizon Wireless, Citrus Heights *Also called Cellco Partnership (G-5370)*
Verizon Wireless, San Diego *Also called Cellco Partnership (G-5373)*
Verizon Wireless, Chino *Also called Cellco Partnership (G-5374)*
Verizon Wireless, Yuba City *Also called Cellco Partnership (G-5375)*
Verizon Wireless, Santa Barbara *Also called Cellco Partnership (G-5378)*
Verizon Wireless, Santa Rosa *Also called Cellco Partnership (G-5379)*
Verizon Wireless, Palo Alto *Also called Cellco Partnership (G-5381)*
Verizon Wireless, Irvine *Also called 4g Wireless Inc (G-5252)*
Verizon Wireless, Santa Ana *Also called Cellco Partnership (G-5384)*
Verizon Wireless, Huntington Park *Also called Cellco Partnership (G-6064)*
Verizon Wireless, San Diego *Also called Cellco Partnership (G-5742)*
Verizon Wireless, Lancaster *Also called Cellco Partnership (G-5386)*
Verizon Wireless, Commerce *Also called Cellco Partnership (G-5388)*
Verizon Wireless, Pico Rivera *Also called Cellco Partnership (G-5389)*
Verizon Wireless Inc....805 928-7433
570 E Betteravia Rd Santa Maria (93454) ***(G-5423)***
Verizon Wireless Inc....408 354-6374
15 Montebello Way Los Gatos (95030) ***(G-5424)***
Verizon Wireless Inc....760 771-5587
78742 Highway 111 La Quinta (92253) ***(G-5425)***
Verizon Wireless Inc....909 592-5211
1331 S Lone Hill Ave # 170 Glendora (91740) ***(G-5426)***
Verizon Wireless Inc....707 399-0866
1586 Gateway Blvd Fairfield (94533) ***(G-5427)***
Verizon Wireless Inc....714 730-7790
13262 Jamboree Rd Irvine (92602) ***(G-5428)***
Verizon Wireless Inc....909 355-0725
16695 Sierra Lakes Pkwy Fontana (92336) ***(G-5429)***
Verizon Wireless Inc....916 784-6886
1208 Galleria Blvd Roseville (95678) ***(G-5430)***
Verizon Wireless Inc....707 442-8334
1122 Broadway Eureka (95501) ***(G-5431)***
Verizon Wireless Inc....925 224-9868
1460 Stoneridge Mall Rd Pleasanton (94588) ***(G-5432)***
Verizon Wireless Inc....661 836-3141
2350 White Ln Bakersfield (93304) ***(G-5433)***
Verizon Wireless Premium Ret, Carlsbad *Also called 4g Wireless Inc (G-5444)*
Verizon Wreless Authorized Ret, Bell *Also called 4g Wireless Inc (G-5439)*
Verizon Wreless Authorized Ret, Dublin *Also called 4g Wireless Inc (G-5440)*
Verizon Wreless Authorized Ret, Los Angeles *Also called 4g Wireless Inc (G-5441)*
Verizon Wreless Authorized Ret, Los Angeles *Also called 4g Wireless Inc (G-5442)*
Verizon Wreless Authorized Ret, Escondido *Also called 4g Wireless Inc (G-5443)*
Verizon Wreless Authorized Ret, Perris *Also called 4g Wireless Inc (G-5445)*
Verizon Wreless Authorized Ret, Redondo Beach *Also called 4g Wireless Inc (G-5446)*
Verizon Wreless Authorized Ret, Long Beach *Also called 4g Wireless Inc (G-5447)*
Verizon Wreless Authorized Ret, West Hollywood *Also called 4g Wireless Inc (G-5448)*
Vermeer Pacific, Sacramento *Also called Rdo Vermeer LLC (G-7787)*
VERMONT CARE CENTER, Torrance *Also called Geri-Care II Inc (G-21232)*
Vernon Autoparts Inc....323 249-7545
1559 W 134th St Gardena (90249) ***(G-17827)***
Vernon Central Warehouse Inc....323 234-2200
2050 E 38th St Vernon (90058) ***(G-4388)***
Vernon Security Inc....562 790-8993
15317 Parmnt Blvd Ste 201 Paramount (90723) ***(G-16942)***
Vernon Transportation Company, Stockton *Also called John Aguilar & Company Inc (G-4031)*
Vernon Truck Wash Inc....323 267-0706
3308 Bandini Blvd Vernon (90058) ***(G-17864)***
Vernon Warehouse Co, Vernon *Also called Vernon Central Warehouse Inc (G-4388)*
Versa Engineering & Tech Inc....925 405-4505
1320 Willow Pass Rd S500 Concord (94520) ***(G-26141)***
Versa Products Inc (PA)....310 353-7100
14105 Avalon Blvd Los Angeles (90061) ***(G-6835)***
Versacheck, San Diego *Also called G7 Productivity Systems (G-15673)*
Versatables.com, Los Angeles *Also called Versa Products Inc (G-6835)*
Vertafore Fsc Inc....800 433-2550
28038 Dorothy Dr Agoura Hills (91301) ***(G-15526)***
Vertex Coatings Inc....909 923-5795
1291 W State St Ontario (91762) ***(G-2501)***
Vertex Phrmctcals San Dego LLC (HQ)....858 404-6600
11010 Torreyana Rd San Diego (92121) ***(G-26635)***
Vertical Communications Inc (PA)....408 404-1600
3900 Freedom Cir Ste 110 Santa Clara (95054) ***(G-15876)***
Vertical Search Works Inc....212 967-9502
1808 Aston Ave Ste 170 Carlsbad (92008) ***(G-13936)***
Verticalresponse Inc....415 905-6880
50 Beale St Fl 10 San Francisco (94105) ***(G-27711)***
Vertis Ltc, Huntington Beach *Also called Quad/Graphics Inc (G-18248)*
Vertisystem Inc....510 794-8099
39300 Civic Center Dr # 230 Fremont (94538) ***(G-16078)***
Verve Music Group, Santa Monica *Also called Universal Music Group Inc (G-18502)*
Very Important Pet Vaccine Svc, Windsor *Also called Happy Pet Co (G-619)*
Vestek Systems Inc (HQ)....415 344-6000
425 Market St Fl 6 San Francisco (94105) ***(G-16267)***
Veterans Affairs Cal Dept....530 224-3300
3400 Knighton Rd Redding (96002) ***(G-21006)***
Veterans Affairs Cal Dept....916 653-2535
1227 O St Ste 105 Sacramento (95814) ***(G-28090)***
Veterans Affairs Testing Off, Sacramento *Also called Veterans Affairs Cal Dept (G-28090)*
Veterans Health Administration....858 552-7525
3350 La Jolla Village Dr San Diego (92161) ***(G-20283)***
Veterans Health Administration....707 562-8200
Walnut Ave Bldg 201 Vallejo (94589) ***(G-20195)***
Veterans Health Administration....310 478-3711
11301 Wilshire Blvd Los Angeles (90073) ***(G-20196)***
Veterans Health Administration....559 225-6100
2615 E Clinton Ave Fresno (93703) ***(G-22019)***
Veterans Health Administration....805 543-1233
1288 Morro St Ste 200 San Luis Obispo (93401) ***(G-20197)***
Veterans Health Administration....916 366-5427
10535 Hospital Way Mather (95655) ***(G-20198)***
Veterans Health Administration....559 225-6100
2615 E Clinton Ave Fresno (93703) ***(G-20199)***
Veterans Health Administration....530 226-7555
351 Hartnell Ave Redding (96002) ***(G-20200)***
Veterans Health Administration....650 493-5000
3801 Miranda Ave Bldg 101 Palo Alto (94304) ***(G-20201)***
Veterans Health Administration....510 267-7820
2221 Martin Luther King J Oakland (94612) ***(G-20202)***
Veterans Health Administration....415 750-2009
4150 Clement St 6205 San Francisco (94121) ***(G-20203)***
Veterans Health Administration....818 895-9311
16111 Plummer St North Hills (91343) ***(G-20204)***
Veterans Health Administration....619 400-5000
8810 Rio San Diego Dr San Diego (92108) ***(G-20205)***
Veterans Health Administration....818 891-7711
16111 Plummer St North Hills (91343) ***(G-20206)***
Veterans Health Administration....530 879-5000
280 Cohasset Rd Chico (95926) ***(G-20207)***
Veterans Health Administration....707 442-5335
727 E St Eureka (95501) ***(G-20208)***
Veterans Health Administration....619 409-1600
835 3rd Ave Chula Vista (91911) ***(G-20209)***
Veterans Health Administration....760 745-2000
815 E Pennsylvania Ave Escondido (92025) ***(G-20210)***
Veterans Health Administration....805 983-6384
250 Citrus Grove Ln # 250 Oxnard (93036) ***(G-20211)***
Veterans Health Administration....707 570-3800
3315 Chanate Rd Santa Rosa (95404) ***(G-20212)***
Veterans Health Administration....916 843-7000
10535 Hospital Way Mather (95655) ***(G-20213)***
Veterans Health Administration....925 447-2560
4951 Arroyo Rd Livermore (94550) ***(G-20214)***
Veterans Health Administration....909 825-7084
11201 Benton St Loma Linda (92357) ***(G-20215)***
Veterans Health Administration....650 614-9997
795 Willow Rd Menlo Park (94025) ***(G-20216)***
Veterans Health Administration....818 895-9449
16111 Plummer St North Hills (91343) ***(G-20217)***
Veterans Health Administration....714 780-5400
1801 W Romneya Dr Ste 303 Anaheim (92801) ***(G-20218)***
Veterans Health Administration....661 632-1871
1801 Westwind Dr Bakersfield (93301) ***(G-20219)***
Veterans Health Administration....213 253-2677
351 E Temple St Los Angeles (90012) ***(G-20220)***
Veterans Health Administration....661 323-8387
1110 Golden Valley Fwy Bakersfield (93301) ***(G-20221)***
Veterans Home Cal - Fresno....559 493-4400
2811 W California Ave Fresno (93706) ***(G-21007)***
Veterans Medical Research Fund....858 642-3080
3350 La Jolla Village Dr San Diego (92161) ***(G-26817)***
Veterans of Foreign Wars of US....951 202-3792
1525 W Oakland Ave Hemet (92543) ***(G-25390)***
Veterans of Foreign Wars of US....909 797-1898
12235 California St Yucaipa (92399) ***(G-25391)***
Veterans of Foreign Wars of US....916 786-7757
9136 Elk Grove Blvd # 100 Elk Grove (95624) ***(G-25392)***
Veterans of Foreign Wars of US....530 241-9168
1251 Oregon St Redding (96001) ***(G-25393)***
VETERANS VILLAGE OF SAN DIEGO, San Diego *Also called Vietnam Veterans of San Diego (G-25395)*
Veterinary Centers America VCA, Los Angeles *Also called Vicar Operating Inc (G-632)*
Veterinary Pet Insur Svcs Inc (HQ)....714 989-0555
1800 E Emperi Hwy Ste 145 Brea (92821) ***(G-10924)***
Veterinary Pharmaceuticals Inc....559 582-6800
13159 13th Rd W Hanford (93230) ***(G-8304)***
Veterinary Service Inc....951 328-4900
935 Palmyrita Ave Riverside (92507) ***(G-7325)***
Veterinary Surgical Associates....650 696-8196
251 N Amphlett Blvd San Mateo (94401) ***(G-20222)***
Veternary Med Srgcal Group Inc....805 339-2290
2199 Sperry Ave Ventura (93003) ***(G-14969)***
Vetronix Crpration/Bosch Group, Santa Barbara *Also called Vetronix Sales Corporation (G-6778)*
Vetronix Sales Corporation....805 966-2000
2030 Alameda Padre Serra Santa Barbara (93103) ***(G-6778)***
Vexillum Inc....916 218-3815
10636 Industrial Ave Roseville (95678) ***(G-6250)***
Vfs Fire Protection Services, Orange *Also called Bernel Inc (G-2164)*
VFW Post 6476....909 754-3828
1789 N 8th St Colton (92324) ***(G-25394)***
VI At Palo Alto, Palo Alto *Also called Cc-Palo Alto Inc (G-21069)*
Via Adventures Inc (PA)....209 384-1315
300 Grogan Ave Merced (95341) ***(G-3910)***
Via Care Cmnty Hlth Ctr Inc....323 268-9191
507 S Atlantic Blvd Los Angeles (90022) ***(G-20223)***
Via Charter Lines, Merced *Also called Via Adventures Inc (G-3910)*
Via Communications Inc....510 687-4650
940 Mission Ct Fremont (94539) ***(G-26636)***
Via Embedded Store, Fremont *Also called Via Technologies Inc (G-7655)*

ALPHABETIC

Via Magazine, San Francisco ALPHABETIC SECTION

Via Magazine, San Francisco *Also called CA Ste Atom Assoc Intr-Ins Bur* ***(G-10403)***
Via Technologies Inc....510 683-3300
940 Mission Ct Fremont (94539) ***(G-7655)***
Via Trading Corporation....877 202-3616
2520 Industry Way Lynwood (90262) ***(G-9309)***
Via Verde Country Club, San Dimas *Also called San Dimas Golf Inc* ***(G-19056)***
Viacom Consumer Products Inc....323 956-5634
5555 Melrose Ave Los Angeles (90038) ***(G-12228)***
Viacom Networks....310 453-4826
2600 Colorado Ave Santa Monica (90404) ***(G-18282)***
Viacyte Inc....858 455-3708
3550 General Atomics Ct B2-503 San Diego (92121) ***(G-26818)***
Viad Corp....562 370-1500
5560 Katella Ave Cypress (90630) ***(G-17590)***
Vian Enterprises Inc....530 885-1997
1501 Industrial Dr Auburn (95603) ***(G-17591)***
Viant, Irvine *Also called Interactive Media Holdings* ***(G-13866)***
Viaworld Advanced Products....408 597-7051
1002 S De Anza Blvd Ste 4 San Jose (95129) ***(G-7703)***
Vib Corp....760 352-5000
1498 W Main St El Centro (92243) ***(G-9534)***
Vibra Healthcare LLC....559 325-5601
1315 Shaw Ave Ste 102 Clovis (93612) ***(G-22020)***
Vibra Healthcare LLC....530 246-9000
2801 Eureka Way Redding (96001) ***(G-21008)***
Vibra Healthcare LLC....559 436-3600
7173 N Sharon Ave Fresno (93720) ***(G-22021)***
Vibra Healthcare LLC....619 260-8300
555 Washington St San Diego (92103) ***(G-22022)***
Vibra Hosp San Bernardino LLC....909 473-1233
1760 W 16th St San Bernardino (92411) ***(G-22023)***
Vibra Hospital Northern Cal, Redding *Also called Vibra Healthcare LLC* ***(G-21008)***
Vibra Hospital of San Diego, San Diego *Also called Vibra Healthcare LLC* ***(G-22022)***
Vibra Hospital Sacramento LLC....916 351-9151
330 Montrose Dr Folsom (95630) ***(G-22185)***
Vibra Hospital San Diego LLC....619 260-8300
555 Washington St San Diego (92103) ***(G-22024)***
Vicar Operating Inc (HQ)....310 571-6500
12401 W Olympic Blvd Los Angeles (90064) ***(G-632)***
Vicenti Lloyd & Stutzman....626 857-7300
2210 E Route 66 Ste 100 Glendora (91740) ***(G-26456)***
Viceroy Santa Monica, Santa Monica *Also called Seaside Hotel Lessee Inc* ***(G-17483)***
Vickie Lobello....805 750-2327
1333 S Mayflower Ave 40 Ste 400 Simi Valley (93063) ***(G-25595)***
Vicor Inc....510 621-2000
855 Marina Bay Pkwy # 100 Richmond (94804) ***(G-16079)***
Vicount Group, Los Angeles *Also called Viscount Petroleum LLC* ***(G-9033)***
Victor Cmnty Support Svcs Inc....530 273-2244
900 E Main St Ste 201 Grass Valley (95945) ***(G-28168)***
Victor Corsiglia MD....408 278-3210
625 Lincoln Ave San Jose (95126) ***(G-20224)***
Victor Treatment Centers Inc....209 340-7900
9150 E Hwy 12 Victor (95253) ***(G-24846)***
Victor Treatment Centers Inc....707 576-0171
341 Irwin Ln Santa Rosa (95401) ***(G-24847)***
VICTOR VALLEY GLOBAL MEDICAL C, Victorville *Also called Victor Vly Hosp Acqisition Inc* ***(G-10389)***
Victor Vly Hosp Acqisition Inc....760 245-8691
15248 Eleventh St Victorville (92395) ***(G-10389)***
Victoria Care Center....805 642-1736
5445 Everglades St Ventura (93003) ***(G-21009)***
Victoria Island Farms....209 465-5609
16021 E Hwy 4 Holt (95234) ***(G-403)***
Victoria Management, Palo Alto *Also called Parkwest Apartments* ***(G-11186)***
Victoria Post Acute Care....619 440-5005
654 S Anza St El Cajon (92020) ***(G-21410)***
Victorian Inn, Monterey *Also called Coastal Hotel Group Inc* ***(G-12533)***
Victorvlle Trsure Holdings LLC....760 245-6565
15494 Palmdale Rd Victorville (92392) ***(G-13379)***
Victory Foam Inc (PA)....949 474-0690
3 Holland Irvine (92618) ***(G-7958)***
Victory Studio, Burbank *Also called Warner Bros Entertainment Inc* ***(G-18195)***
Vid, Vista *Also called Vista Irrigation District* ***(G-6656)***
Vidal Sassoon Salon, Beverly Hills *Also called Regis Corporation* ***(G-13687)***
Vident....714 221-6700
22705 Savi Ranch Pkwy # 100 Yorba Linda (92887) ***(G-7326)***
Video Products Distributors, Folsom *Also called VPD IV Inc* ***(G-18283)***
Videocam, Anaheim *Also called Vci Event Technology Inc* ***(G-14589)***
Vidhwan Inc....408 521-0167
2 N Market St Ste 410 San Jose (95113) ***(G-15527)***
Viele & Sons Inc....714 446-1686
1820 E Valencia Dr Fullerton (92831) ***(G-8551)***
Viele & Sons Instnl Groc, Fullerton *Also called Viele & Sons Inc* ***(G-8551)***
Vienna Convalescent Hospital....209 368-7141
800 S Ham Ln Lodi (95242) ***(G-21411)***
Vietnam Veterans of San Diego (PA)....619 497-0142
4141 Pacific Hwy San Diego (92110) ***(G-25395)***
Vietnamese Cmnty Orange Cnty (PA)....714 558-6009
1618 W 1st St Santa Ana (92703) ***(G-24995)***
Vietnms-Mrcan Yuth Alance Corp....619 320-8292
7968 Arjons Dr Ste 109 San Diego (92126) ***(G-25396)***
View Heights Convalescent Hosp, Los Angeles *Also called Amada Enterprises Inc* ***(G-20377)***
View Park Convalescent Center, Los Angeles *Also called Burlington Convalescent Hosp* ***(G-20426)***
View Park Convalescent Center, Los Angeles *Also called Burlington Convalescent Hosp* ***(G-21170)***

Vignolo Farms Inc....661 391-0682
1270 E Riverside Shafter (93263) ***(G-16)***
Viharas Group Inc....310 537-6700
1919 W Artesia Blvd Compton (90220) ***(G-12129)***
Viking Asset Management LLC....415 981-5300
505 Sansome St Ste 1275 San Francisco (94111) ***(G-10191)***
Viking Demolition, Glendale *Also called Viking Equipment Corp* ***(G-3472)***
Viking Equipment Corp....818 500-9447
540 W Windsor Rd Glendale (91204) ***(G-3472)***
Viking Office Products Inc (HQ)....562 490-1000
3366 E Willow St Signal Hill (90755) ***(G-8183)***
Viking River Cruises Inc (HQ)....818 227-1234
5700 Canoga Ave Ste 200 Woodland Hills (91367) ***(G-4982)***
Villa Balboa Community Assoc....949 450-1515
22 Mauchly Irvine (92618) ***(G-25397)***
Villa Convalescent Hospital, Riverside *Also called Villa Health Care Center Inc* ***(G-21010)***
Villa De La Mar Inc....562 494-5001
5001 E Anaheim St Long Beach (90804) ***(G-21412)***
Villa Del Rey Retirement Inn, Escondido *Also called Emeritus Corporation* ***(G-11124)***
Villa Fairmont Mental Hlth Ctr, San Leandro *Also called Telecare Corporation* ***(G-22102)***
Villa Gardens, Pasadena *Also called Front Porch Communities & Svcs* ***(G-24666)***
Villa Health Care Center Inc....951 689-5788
8965 Magnolia Ave Riverside (92503) ***(G-21010)***
Villa La Esperanza LP....805 781-3088
3533 Empleo St San Luis Obispo (93401) ***(G-1389)***
Villa Las Plmas Healthcare Ctr, El Cajon *Also called Jeffrey Pine Holdings LLC* ***(G-20691)***
Villa Las Posas, Camarillo *Also called Atria Senior Living Group Inc* ***(G-24557)***
Villa Maria Care Center, Long Beach *Also called Trinity Health Systems* ***(G-20993)***
Villa Maria Care Center, Baldwin Park *Also called Trinity Health Systems* ***(G-20994)***
Villa Marin Homeowners Assn....415 499-8711
100 Thorndale Dr San Rafael (94903) ***(G-25398)***
VILLA MONTALVO, Saratoga *Also called Montalvo Association* ***(G-25066)***
Villa Mrin Rtrement Residences, San Rafael *Also called Villa Marin Homeowners Assn* ***(G-25398)***
Villa Oaks Convalescent Homes, Pasadena *Also called Voch Inc* ***(G-21418)***
Villa Pacific Contractors Inc....714 850-1640
3505 Cadillac Ave Ste L3 Costa Mesa (92626) ***(G-2838)***
Villa Paseo Palms, Paso Robles *Also called Villa Paseo Senior Residences* ***(G-11220)***
Villa Paseo Senior Residences....805 227-4588
2818 Ramada Dr Paso Robles (93446) ***(G-11220)***
Villa Rancho Bernardo Care Ctr, San Diego *Also called Villa Rancho Brno Hlth Cr LLC* ***(G-21011)***
Villa Rancho Brno Hlth Cr LLC....858 672-3900
15720 Bernardo Center Dr San Diego (92127) ***(G-21011)***
Villa Sclabrini Retirement Ctr, Sun Valley *Also called Fathers of St Charles* ***(G-11129)***
Villa Serra Corporation....831 754-5532
1320 Padre Dr Apt 103 Salinas (93901) ***(G-11221)***
Villa Siena....650 961-6484
1855 Miramonte Ave 117 Mountain View (94040) ***(G-21413)***
Villa Theresa Mobile Home Park, San Jose *Also called Barbaccia Properties* ***(G-11244)***
Villa Valencia Health Care Ctr, Laguna Hills *Also called Sunrise Senior Living Inc* ***(G-20964)***
Village 8, Westlake Village *Also called WF Cinema Holdings LP* ***(G-18355)***
Village At Granite Bay....916 789-0326
8550 Barton Rd Granite Bay (95746) ***(G-24848)***
Village At Northridge....818 514-4497
9222 Corbin Ave Northridge (91324) ***(G-24849)***
Village At Sydney Creek, San Luis Obispo *Also called Village Pacific Mgt Group* ***(G-21012)***
Village At Sydney Creek, San Luis Obispo *Also called Village Pacific Mgt Group* ***(G-21013)***
Village Club....619 425-3333
429 Broadway Chula Vista (91910) ***(G-19303)***
Village Family Services (PA)....818 755-8786
6736 Laurel Canyon Blvd # 200 North Hollywood (91606) ***(G-22862)***
Village Glen Apartments....626 963-4575
633 S Pasadena Ave Apt 45 Glendora (91740) ***(G-11222)***
Village Integrated Svc Agcy, Long Beach *Also called Mental Health Amer Los Angeles* ***(G-24083)***
Village Nurseries Whl LLC (PA)....714 279-3100
1589 N Main St Orange (92867) ***(G-9225)***
Village Nurseries Whl LLC....916 993-2292
6901 Bradshaw Rd Sacramento (95829) ***(G-9226)***
Village Nurseries Whl LLC....951 657-3940
20099 Santa Rosa Mine Rd Perris (92570) ***(G-9227)***
Village Pacific Mgt Group....805 543-2350
1234 Laurel Ln San Luis Obispo (93401) ***(G-21012)***
Village Pacific Mgt Group (PA)....805 543-2300
55 Broad St San Luis Obispo (93405) ***(G-21013)***
Village Square Healthcare Ctr, San Marcos *Also called San Marcos Operating Co LP* ***(G-20891)***
Village Square Nursing Center....760 471-2986
1586 W San Marcos Blvd San Marcos (92078) ***(G-21014)***
Village West Health Center, Riverside *Also called Air Force Village West Inc* ***(G-20372)***
Village West Yacht Club....209 478-8992
6633 Embarcadero Dr Stockton (95219) ***(G-19118)***
Villagecraft Quality Furn, Santa Monica *Also called Century Finance Incorporated* ***(G-9828)***
Villages Golf and Country Club....408 274-4400
5000 Cribari Ln San Jose (95135) ***(G-19119)***
Villages, The, San Jose *Also called Villages Golf and Country Club* ***(G-19119)***
Villageway Management Inc....949 450-1515
23041 Ave De La Carlta # 270 Laguna Hills (92653) ***(G-11898)***
Villageway Property Management, Laguna Hills *Also called Villageway Management Inc* ***(G-11898)***
Villagio Inn & Spa LLC....707 944-8877
6481 Washington St Yountville (94599) ***(G-18701)***
Villara Corporation (PA)....916 646-2700
4700 Lang Ave McClellan (95652) ***(G-2408)***

ALPHABETIC

Villara Corporation....916 364-9370
9828 Bus Park Dr Ste A1 Sacramento (95827) ***(G-2409)***
Villara Corporation....707 863-8222
499 Watt Dr Ste A Suisun City (94534) ***(G-3222)***
Villara Corporation....209 824-1082
332 E Wetmore St Manteca (95337) ***(G-2410)***
Villara Corporation....916 646-2222
4700 Lang Ave McClellan (95652) ***(G-2411)***
Villas De Carlsbad Ltd A Cali....760 434-7116
1088 Laguna Dr Carlsbad (92008) ***(G-24850)***
Vimark Inc....707 857-3588
19500 Geyserville Ave Geyserville (95441) ***(G-729)***
Vimark Vineyards, Geyserville *Also called Vimark Inc* ***(G-729)***
Vimo Inc....650 618-4600
1305 Terra Bella Ave Mountain View (94043) ***(G-28091)***
Vin Dibona Productions, Los Angeles *Also called Cara Communications Corp* ***(G-18059)***
Vin Lux LLC....707 265-4100
80 Technology Ct NAPA (94558) ***(G-4389)***
Vina Holdings Inc....714 622-5334
13800 Arizona St Westminster (92683) ***(G-22589)***
Vince Fucillo....209 358-9175
3564 Atwater Blvd Atwater (95301) ***(G-3348)***
Vincent B Zaninovich Sons Inc....661 720-9031
20715 Ave 8 Richgrove (93261) ***(G-192)***
Vincent Hayley Enterprises....626 398-8182
1810 N Fair Oaks Ave Pasadena (91103) ***(G-21414)***
Vincent Lozano Investigations....909 949-0179
P.O. Box 205 Upland (91785) ***(G-16849)***
Vincent V Zaninovich & Sons....661 849-2613
2480 E Washington St Earlimart (93219) ***(G-193)***
Vinculums Services Inc....949 783-3552
10 Pasteur Ste 100 Irvine (92618) ***(G-28092)***
Vindicia Inc....650 264-4700
303 Twin Dolphin Dr # 200 Redwood City (94065) ***(G-15877)***
Vindra Inc....707 994-7738
3805 Dexter Ln Clearlake (95422) ***(G-21015)***
Vine Transit, NAPA *Also called City of NAPA* ***(G-3876)***
Vineyard Plastering Inc....909 357-3701
10335 Vineyard Dr Fontana (92337) ***(G-2994)***
Vino Farms Inc....707 258-2729
1451 Stanley Ln NAPA (94559) ***(G-404)***
Vino Farms Inc (PA)....209 334-6975
1377 E Lodi Ave Lodi (95240) ***(G-730)***
Vino Farms Inc....707 433-8241
10651 Eastside Rd Healdsburg (95448) ***(G-731)***
Vino Farms Inc....916 775-4095
51375 S Netherlands Rd Clarksburg (95612) ***(G-405)***
Vino Farms LLC....209 334-6975
1377 E Lodi Ave Lodi (95240) ***(G-9114)***
Vinod Kumar MD....661 324-4100
5020 Commerce Dr Bakersfield (93309) ***(G-20225)***
Vinson & Elkins LLP....650 617-8400
1841 Page Mill Rd Fl 2 Palo Alto (94304) ***(G-23606)***
Vinson & Elkins LLP....415 979-6900
555 Mission St Ste 2000 San Francisco (94105) ***(G-23607)***
Vinson Chase Inc....209 577-4747
220 Standiford Ave Ste A Modesto (95350) ***(G-11899)***
Vintage Associates Inc....760 772-3673
78755 Darby Rd Bermuda Dunes (92203) ***(G-976)***
Vintage Club (PA)....760 341-1476
75001 Vintage Club Dr W Indian Wells (92210) ***(G-19120)***
Vintage Club Master Assn Inc....760 340-0500
75001 Vintage Dr W Indian Wells (92210) ***(G-25399)***
Vintage Design Inc (PA)....714 974-4822
5 Whatney Irvine (92618) ***(G-3132)***
Vintage Estates of Hayward, Hayward *Also called St Michael Convalescent Hosp* ***(G-20929)***
Vintage Faire Nrsng Rhbltn, Modesto *Also called Covenant Care California LLC* ***(G-21198)***
VINTAGE GARDENS, Fresno *Also called Central Cal Nikkei Foundation* ***(G-23725)***
Vintage Golden Gate, San Francisco *Also called Avalon Golden Gate LLC* ***(G-24562)***
Vintage Nursery, Bermuda Dunes *Also called Vintage Associates Inc* ***(G-976)***
Vintage Production California, Bakersfield *Also called California Resources Prod Corp* ***(G-1041)***
Vintage Senior Housing LLC....805 583-3500
5300 E Los Angeles Ave Simi Valley (93063) ***(G-11223)***
Vintage Senior Living Corp....949 364-6210
27783 Center Dr Mission Viejo (92692) ***(G-11224)***
Vintage Senior Management Inc....818 954-9500
2721 W Willow St Burbank (91505) ***(G-24278)***
Vintage Senior Management Inc....707 595-0009
91 Napa Rd Sonoma (95476) ***(G-11225)***
Vintage Silver Creek, San Jose *Also called Sunrise Senior Living Inc* ***(G-20963)***
Vintage Simi Hills, Simi Valley *Also called Vintage Senior Housing LLC* ***(G-11223)***
Vintners Golf Club....707 944-1992
7901 Solano Ave Yountville (94599) ***(G-18797)***
Vintners Inn....707 575-7350
4350 Barnes Rd Santa Rosa (95403) ***(G-13380)***
Vintrust Inc....877 846-8787
38 Keyes Ave Ste 200 San Francisco (94129) ***(G-4707)***
Vinwood Cellars Inc....707 857-4011
18700 Geyserville Ave Geyserville (95441) ***(G-9115)***
VIP Tours of California Inc....310 216-7507
9830 Bellanca Ave Los Angeles (90045) ***(G-5003)***
VIP Transport Inc....951 272-3700
2703 Wardlow Rd Corona (92882) ***(G-4300)***
Vipstore USA Co....626 934-7880
13674 Star Ruby Ave Corona (92880) ***(G-9310)***
Virco Inc (HQ)....310 533-0474
2027 Harpers Way Torrance (90501) ***(G-6836)***
Virgil Convalescent Hospital, Los Angeles *Also called Virgil Sntrium Cnvlescent Hosp* ***(G-21016)***
Virgil Sntrium Cnvlescent Hosp....323 665-5793
975 N Virgil Ave Los Angeles (90029) ***(G-21016)***
Virgin America Inc (PA)....877 359-8474
555 Airport Blvd Ste 400 Burlingame (94010) ***(G-4839)***
Virgin Fish Inc (PA)....310 391-6161
1000 Corporate Pointe # 150 Culver City (90230) ***(G-3855)***
Virgin Mobile Usa Inc....310 445-7000
10960 Wilshire Blvd Fl 5 Los Angeles (90024) ***(G-5726)***
Virginia Cntry CLB of Long Bch....562 427-0924
4602 N Virginia Rd Long Beach (90807) ***(G-19121)***
Virginia Hardwood Company (PA)....626 815-0540
1000 W Foothill Blvd Azusa (91702) ***(G-6968)***
Virginia Sarabian....559 493-2900
2816 S Leonard Ave Sanger (93657) ***(G-251)***
Virident Systems Inc....408 573-5000
1745 Tech Dr Ste 700 San Jose (95110) ***(G-26637)***
Virtual Instruments Corp....408 579-4000
25 Metro Dr San Jose (95110) ***(G-16522)***
Visa International Svc Assn....650 432-3579
3125 Clearview Way San Mateo (94402) ***(G-17592)***
Visa International Svc Assn (HQ)....650 432-3200
900 Metro Center Blvd Foster City (94404) ***(G-17593)***
Visa USA Inc (HQ)....650 432-3200
900 Metro Center Blvd Foster City (94404) ***(G-17594)***
Visalia Convention Center, Visalia *Also called City of Visalia* ***(G-17081)***
Visalia Country Club....559 734-3733
625 N Ranch St Visalia (93291) ***(G-19122)***
Visalia Medical Clinic Inc (PA)....559 733-5222
5400 W Hillsdale Ave Visalia (93291) ***(G-20226)***
Visalia Mrrott At Cnvntion Ctr, Visalia *Also called Welcome Group Management LLC* ***(G-13397)***
Visalia Unified School Dst....559 730-7871
801 N Mooney Blvd Visalia (93291) ***(G-24279)***
Visalia Youth Services, Visalia *Also called Turning Point Central Cal Inc* ***(G-24262)***
Visalus Inc....323 801-2400
6300 Wilshire Blvd # 610 Los Angeles (90048) ***(G-10925)***
Visalus Science, Los Angeles *Also called Visalus Inc* ***(G-10925)***
Viscamar LLC....559 636-1111
300 S Court St Visalia (93291) ***(G-13381)***
Viscira LLC....415 848-8010
200 Vallejo St San Francisco (94111) ***(G-7209)***
Viscount Petroleum LLC....213 382-1058
3699 Wilshire Blvd # 880 Los Angeles (90010) ***(G-9033)***
Visio Integ Profe LLC (HQ)....916 608-8320
80 Iron Point Cir Ste 100 Folsom (95630) ***(G-27712)***
Vision Care Center (PA)....559 486-2000
7075 N Sharon Ave Fresno (93720) ***(G-20227)***
Vision Care Center Central Cal, Fresno *Also called Vision Care Center* ***(G-20227)***
Vision Express/Wrag-Time Trnsp, Gardena *Also called Wragtime Air Freight Inc* ***(G-4306)***
Vision Fund International, Monrovia *Also called World Vision International* ***(G-25601)***
Vision Realty Managements, Beverly Hills *Also called Starpoint Property MGT LLC* ***(G-11857)***
Vision Service Plan (PA)....916 851-5000
3333 Quality Dr Rancho Cordova (95670) ***(G-10390)***
Vision Solutions Inc (HQ)....949 253-6500
15300 Barranca Pkwy # 100 Irvine (92618) ***(G-15528)***
Vision Solutions Inc....949 253-6500
15300 Barranca Pkwy # 100 Irvine (92618) ***(G-16523)***
Vision Tech Solutions LLC....310 656-3100
222 N Sepulveda Blvd El Segundo (90245) ***(G-5727)***
Visionaire Group Inc....310 823-1800
5340 Alla Rd Ste 100 Los Angeles (90066) ***(G-13937)***
Visionary Intgrtion Prfssonals, Folsom *Also called Visio Integ Profe LLC* ***(G-27712)***
Visioneering Studios Inc....949 417-5800
2050 Main St Ste 400 Irvine (92614) ***(G-13803)***
Visionfund International....626 303-8811
800 W Chestnut Ave Monrovia (91016) ***(G-17595)***
Visions Unlimited (PA)....916 394-0800
6833 Stockton Blvd # 485 Sacramento (95823) ***(G-22863)***
Visionstar Inc....213 387-3700
3435 Wilsh Blvd Ste 2120 Los Angeles (90010) ***(G-27713)***
Visit Anaheim, Anaheim *Also called Anaheim/Orange Cnty Visitor Bu* ***(G-16990)***
Visiting Angels, Chino *Also called Angels In Motion LLC* ***(G-22365)***
Visiting Angels, Redlands *Also called Angels Everyday Inc* ***(G-22364)***
Visiting Angels Riverside Cnty, Riverside *Also called Roberts & Associates Inc* ***(G-22551)***
Visiting Care & Companions Inc....805 690-6202
509 E Montecito St # 200 Santa Barbara (93103) ***(G-22590)***
Visiting Nrse Assn Orange Cnty (PA)....949 263-4700
2520 Redhill Ave Santa Ana (92705) ***(G-22591)***
Visiting Nurse & Hospice Care, Santa Barbara *Also called Visiting Nurse & Hospice Care* ***(G-25162)***
Visiting Nurse & Hospice Care (PA)....805 965-5555
509 E Montecito St # 200 Santa Barbara (93103) ***(G-25162)***
Visiting Nurse Associ....909 621-3961
150 W 1st St Ste 176 Claremont (91711) ***(G-22592)***
Visiting Nurse Association....831 385-1014
5 Lower Ragsdle Dr 102 Monterey (93940) ***(G-22593)***
Visiting Nurse Association of....209 736-2338
20100 Cedar Rd N Ste C Sonora (95370) ***(G-22594)***
Visiting Nurse Association of (HQ)....831 477-2600
2880 Soquel Ave Ste 10 Santa Cruz (95062) ***(G-22595)***
Visitng Nurse Assn Inlnd CNT (PA)....951 413-1200
6235 River Crest Dr Ste L Riverside (92507) ***(G-22596)***
Visitng Nurse Assn Inlnd CNT....760 346-3982
42600 Cook St Ste 202 Palm Desert (92211) ***(G-22597)***

ALPHABETIC

Visitng Nurse Assn Inlnd CNT ALPHABETIC SECTION

Visitng Nurse Assn Inlnd CNT 760 962-1966
12421 Hesperia Rd Ste 11 Victorville (92395) *(G-22598)*
Visitor Services & Facilities, San Jose *Also called City of San Jose (G-25061)*
Visiworks Software, El Dorado Hills *Also called Dorado Software Inc (G-15146)*
Vista Anglina Hsing Prtners LP 213 482-4718
418 E Edgeware Rd Los Angeles (90026) *(G-11900)*
Vista Behavioral Health Inc 800 992-0901
5900 Brockton Ave Riverside (92506) *(G-22111)*
Vista Care Group LLC (PA) 760 295-3900
1863 Devon Pl Vista (92084) *(G-24280)*
Vista Community Clinic (PA) 760 631-5000
1000 Vale Terrace Dr Vista (92084) *(G-20292)*
Vista Community Clinic 760 631-5030
134 Grapevine Rd Vista (92083) *(G-20293)*
Vista Cove Care Center 805 525-7134
250 March St Santa Paula (93060) *(G-21415)*
Vista Cove Care Center At Long 562 426-4461
3401 Cedar Ave Long Beach (90807) *(G-21017)*
Vista Cove Care Ctr - Rialto 909 877-1361
1471 S Riverside Ave Rialto (92376) *(G-21018)*
Vista Del Mar Child Fmly Svcs 310 836-1223
1533 Euclid St Santa Monica (90404) *(G-24851)*
Vista Del Mar Health Centers, Vista *Also called Life Care Centers America Inc (G-21289)*
VISTA DEL SOL CARE CENTER, Los Angeles *Also called Vista Del Sol Health Services (G-21416)*
Vista Del Sol Health Services 310 390-9045
11620 W Washington Blvd Los Angeles (90066) *(G-21416)*
Vista Entertainment Center, Vista *Also called Harmatz Entertaintment Corp (G-18522)*
Vista Equity Partners Fund Vi- 415 765-6500
4 Embarcadero Ctr Fl 20 San Francisco (94111) *(G-12130)*
Vista Gardens, Vista *Also called Vista Care Group LLC (G-24280)*
Vista Hill Foundation (PA) 585 514-5100
8910 Clairemont Mesa Blvd San Diego (92123) *(G-25163)*
Vista Hospital Riverside, Rancho Cucamonga *Also called Perris Valley Cmnty Hosp LLC (G-21797)*
Vista Hospital San Gabriel Vly, Baldwin Park *Also called Vista Specialty Hosp Cal LP (G-22025)*
Vista Investments LLC (PA) 213 284-7500
2361 Rosecrans Ave # 150 El Segundo (90245) *(G-13382)*
Vista Irrigation District 760 597-3100
1391 Engineer St Vista (92081) *(G-6656)*
Vista Knoll Inc 760 630-2273
2000 Westwood Rd Vista (92083) *(G-21019)*
Vista Knoll Spclzed Care Fclty, Vista *Also called Vista Woods Health Assoc LLC (G-21021)*
Vista Pacifica Enterprises Inc (PA) 951 682-4833
3674 Pacific Ave Riverside (92509) *(G-21020)*
Vista Pacifica Enterprises Inc 951 682-4867
3662 Pacific Ave Riverside (92509) *(G-21417)*
Vista Pcifica Convalescent Ctr, Riverside *Also called Vista Pacifica Enterprises Inc (G-21020)*
Vista Pcifica Convalescent Ctr, Riverside *Also called Vista Pacifica Enterprises Inc (G-21417)*
Vista Specialty Hosp Cal LP 626 388-2700
14148 Francisquito Ave Baldwin Park (91706) *(G-22025)*
Vista Steel Co Inc 805 653-1189
331 W Lewis St Ventura (93001) *(G-2095)*
Vista Valencia Group Inc 661 255-4600
25545 Via Paladar Valencia (91355) *(G-11901)*
Vista Valley Country Club 760 758-5275
29354 Vista Valley Dr Vista (92084) *(G-19123)*
Vista Verde Farms 661 720-9733
11251 Melcher Rd Delano (93215) *(G-8954)*
Vista Verde Farms Inc 559 992-3111
7124 Whitley Ave Corcoran (93212) *(G-487)*
Vista Woods Health Assoc LLC 760 630-2273
2000 Westwood Rd Vista (92083) *(G-21021)*
Vistage International Inc (PA) 858 523-6800
11452 El Camino Real # 400 San Diego (92130) *(G-27714)*
Vistancia Marketing LLC 909 594-9500
655 Brea Canyon Rd Walnut (91789) *(G-27715)*
Visual Concepts Entertainment 415 479-3634
10 Hamilton Landing Novato (94949) *(G-15529)*
Visually Handicapped, Los Angeles *Also called L A U S D Program (G-24703)*
Vit, San Bernardino *Also called Vocational Imprv Program Inc (G-7327)*
Vita North America, Yorba Linda *Also called Vident (G-7326)*
Vital Express Inc 330 777-5450
4000 Macarthur Blvd Ste 6 Newport Beach (92660) *(G-5250)*
Vitas Healthcare Corp Cal (HQ) 305 374-4143
7888 Mission Grove Pkwy S Riverside (92508) *(G-22599)*
Vitas Healthcare Corp Cal 408 964-6800
670 N Mccarthy Blcvd 220 Milpitas (95035) *(G-22600)*
Vitas Healthcare Corp Cal 916 925-7010
2710 Gateway Oaks Dr # 100 Sacramento (95833) *(G-22601)*
Vitas Healthcare Corp Cal 925 930-9373
365 Lennon Ln Ste 140 Walnut Creek (94598) *(G-22602)*
Vitas Healthcare Corp Cal 626 918-2273
1343 N Grand Ave Ste 100 Covina (91724) *(G-22603)*
Vitas Healthcare Corp Cal 310 324-2273
990 W 190th St Ste 550 Torrance (90502) *(G-22604)*
Vitas Healthcare Corp Cal 909 386-6000
7888 Mission Grove Pkwy S Riverside (92508) *(G-22605)*
Vitas Healthcare Corp Cal 818 760-2273
16830 Ventura Blvd # 315 Encino (91436) *(G-22606)*
Vitas Healthcare Corp Cal 619 680-4400
9655 Gran Rdge Dr Ste 300 San Diego (92123) *(G-22607)*
Vitas Healthcare Corporation 805 437-2100
333 N Lantana St Ste 124 Camarillo (93010) *(G-22608)*
Vitas Innovative Hospice Care, Milpitas *Also called Vitas Healthcare Corp Cal (G-22600)*
Vitas Innovative Hospice Care, Riverside *Also called Vitas Healthcare Corp Cal (G-22605)*
Vitas Innovative Hospice Care, Encino *Also called Vitas Healthcare Corp Cal (G-22606)*
Vitas Innovative Hospice Care, San Diego *Also called Vitas Healthcare Corp Cal (G-22607)*
Vitco Distributors Inc 909 355-1300
10660 Mulberry Ave Fontana (92337) *(G-8224)*
Vitco Food Service, Fontana *Also called Vitco Distributors Inc (G-8224)*
Vitesse LLC 650 543-4800
1601 Willow Rd Menlo Park (94025) *(G-16208)*
Vitran Logistics Inc 909 972-3100
1000 S Cucamonga Ave Ontario (91761) *(G-4656)*
Vitreo Retinal Medical Group, Chico *Also called Retinal Consultants Inc (G-28042)*
Vitro LLC 619 234-0408
2305 Historic Decatur Rd # 205 San Diego (92106) *(G-13938)*
Vitron Electronic Services Inc 408 251-1600
1901 Las Plumas Ave San Jose (95133) *(G-7481)*
Vitron Electronics Mfg & Svcs, San Jose *Also called Vitron Electronic Services Inc (G-7481)*
Vitrorobertson LLC 619 234-0408
2305 Historic Decatur Rd San Diego (92106) *(G-13939)*
Viva Group Inc 310 449-6400
11766 Wilshire Blvd # 300 Los Angeles (90025) *(G-11226)*
Viva International, Belvedere Tiburon *Also called Marcolin USA Inc (G-7333)*
Viva Life Science Inc 949 645-6100
350 Paularino Ave Costa Mesa (92626) *(G-8305)*
Viva Vina Inc 323 225-4984
2702 Media Center Dr Los Angeles (90065) *(G-17596)*
Vivente 1 Inc 408 279-2706
2400 Enborg Ln San Jose (95128) *(G-11242)*
Vivente 2 Inc 408 279-2706
5347 Dent Ave San Jose (95118) *(G-11243)*
Vivid Entertainment LLC 323 845-4557
3599 Cahuenga Blvd W Los Angeles (90068) *(G-18187)*
Vivid Solution 310 498-2559
5959 W Century Blvd Los Angeles (90045) *(G-17597)*
Vivopools Inc 818 952-2121
825 S Primrose Ave Ste H Monrovia (91016) *(G-17598)*
Vivopools LLC 888 702-8486
825 S Primrose Ave Ste H Monrovia (91016) *(G-17599)*
Vladigor Investment Inc 415 558-9274
1601 Mission St San Francisco (94103) *(G-17865)*
Vlot Brothers, Chowchilla *Also called Case Vlott Cattle (G-420)*
Vlot Brothers Dairy, Chowchilla *Also called Vlot Brothers Trucking Co Inc (G-440)*
Vlot Brothers Trucking Co Inc 559 665-7399
3197 Avenue 21 Chowchilla (93610) *(G-440)*
Vm International, Riverside *Also called S R S M Inc (G-6885)*
Vm Services Inc 714 678-5200
1051 S East St Anaheim (92805) *(G-15530)*
Vm Services Inc (HQ) 510 744-3720
6701 Mowry Ave Newark (94560) *(G-15531)*
Vm Ware 650 424-8193
3401 Hillview Ave Palo Alto (94304) *(G-15532)*
Vmbc, Aliso Viejo *Also called Voice Mail Broadcasting Corp (G-16209)*
Vmsg, Ventura *Also called Veternary Med Srgcal Group Inc (G-14969)*
Vmware Inc 650 427-2100
3400 Hillview Ave Lbby Palo Alto (94304) *(G-15533)*
Vmware Inc (HQ) 650 427-5000
3401 Hillview Ave Palo Alto (94304) *(G-15534)*
Vmware Inc 650 812-8200
3305 Hillview Ave Palo Alto (94304) *(G-15535)*
Vmware Inc 650 812-8200
3210 Porter Dr Palo Alto (94304) *(G-15536)*
Vn Home Health Care LP 408 998-0550
2528 Qume Dr Ste 7 San Jose (95131) *(G-22609)*
Vna Care, Pasadena *Also called Verdugo Hlls Vsting Nurse Assn (G-22588)*
Vna Home Health Systems, Santa Ana *Also called Visiting Nrse Assn Orange Cnty (G-22591)*
Vna Hospice & Pllatve Cre S CA 909 384-0737
412 E Vanderbilt Way San Bernardino (92408) *(G-22610)*
Vna Hospice & Pllatve Cre S CA (PA) 909 624-3574
150 W 1st St Ste 270 Claremont (91711) *(G-22611)*
Vna Private Duty Care, Claremont *Also called Visiting Nurse Associ (G-22592)*
Vna Private Duty Care, Claremont *Also called Vna Hospice & Pllatve Cre S CA (G-22611)*
Vnahnc, Emeryville *Also called Sutter Vsting Nrse Assn Hspice (G-22576)*
Vnaic, Riverside *Also called Visitng Nurse Assn Inlnd CNT (G-22596)*
Vocational Imprv Program Inc 909 478-7537
1310 Riverview Dr San Bernardino (92408) *(G-7327)*
Vocational Imprv Program Inc (PA) 909 483-5924
8675 Boston Pl Rancho Cucamonga (91730) *(G-24403)*
Vocational Visions 949 837-7280
26041 Pala Mission Viejo (92691) *(G-24404)*
Voch Inc 626 798-1111
1920 N Fair Oaks Ave Pasadena (91103) *(G-21418)*
Vodafone Americas Inc 925 210-3812
2999 Oak Rd Fl 5 Walnut Creek (94597) *(G-5434)*
Vodafone Americas Inc (HQ) 650 832-6600
1 Buccaneer Ln Redwood City (94065) *(G-5435)*
Voice Cnty Amer & Lrng For Lf 714 546-8558
1211 E Dyer Rd Santa Ana (92705) *(G-25400)*
Voice Mail Broadcasting Corp 714 437-0600
5 Columbia Aliso Viejo (92656) *(G-16209)*
Voice Print International Inc (PA) 805 389-5200
160 Camino Ruiz Camarillo (93012) *(G-16210)*
Voit Commercial Brokerage, Irvine *Also called Voit Development Manager Inc (G-12025)*
Voit Development Manager Inc 949 851-5110
2020 Main St Ste 100 Irvine (92614) *(G-12025)*
Voit Real Estate Services Lp 949 644-8648
101 Shipyard Way Ste A Newport Beach (92663) *(G-11902)*

ALPHABETIC

Volcano Communications Company (PA)...209 296-7502
20000 State Highway 88 Pine Grove (95665) ***(G-5728)***
Volcano Telephone Co., Pine Grove *Also called Volcano Vision Inc* ***(G-6057)***
Volcano Telephone Company, Pine Grove *Also called Volcano Communications Company* ***(G-5728)***
Volcano Vision Inc...209 296-2288
20000 State Highway 88 Pine Grove (95665) ***(G-6057)***
Volcom LLC...949 646-2175
1725 Monrovia Ave Costa Mesa (92627) ***(G-8365)***
Volcom LLC (HQ)...949 646-2175
1740 Monrovia Ave Costa Mesa (92627) ***(G-17600)***
Volk Enterprises Inc...209 632-3826
618 S Kilroy Rd Turlock (95380) ***(G-7903)***
Volt Information Sciences Inc...714 921-8000
2401 N Glassell St Orange (92865) ***(G-6295)***
Volt Management Corp...310 316-8523
19191 S Vt Ave Ste 950 Torrance (90502) ***(G-14970)***
Volt Management Corp...714 921-7460
2411 N Glassell St Orange (92865) ***(G-14971)***
Volt Management Corp...858 576-3140
7676 Hazard Center Dr # 1000 San Diego (92108) ***(G-14972)***
Volt Management Corp...858 578-0920
7676 Hazard Center Dr # 1000 San Diego (92108) ***(G-14973)***
Volt Management Corp...559 435-1255
7330 N Palm Ave Ste 105 Fresno (93711) ***(G-14974)***
Volt Management Corp...714 921-8800
2401 N Glassell St Orange (92865) ***(G-14975)***
Volt Management Corp...916 923-0454
3001 Lava Ridge Ct # 160 Roseville (95661) ***(G-14976)***
Volt Management Corp...951 789-8133
1650 Iowa Ave Ste 140 Riverside (92507) ***(G-14977)***
Volt Management Corp...209 952-5627
3558 Deer Park Dr 2 Stockton (95219) ***(G-14978)***
Volt Management Corp...805 485-0506
1701 Solar Dr Ste 145 Oxnard (93030) ***(G-14979)***
Volt Telecom Group, Corona *Also called Volt Telecom Group Inc* ***(G-28093)***
Volt Telecom Group, Corona *Also called Volt Telecom Group Inc* ***(G-28094)***
Volt Telecom Group Inc...727 571-2268
218 Helicopter Cir Corona (92880) ***(G-28093)***
Volt Telecom Group Inc...951 493-8900
218 Helicopter Cir Corona (92880) ***(G-28094)***
Volt Temporary Services, Orange *Also called Volt Management Corp* ***(G-14971)***
Volt Workforce Solutions, Torrance *Also called Volt Management Corp* ***(G-14970)***
Volt Workforce Solutions, San Diego *Also called Volt Management Corp* ***(G-14972)***
Volt Workforce Solutions, San Diego *Also called Volt Management Corp* ***(G-14973)***
Volt Workforce Solutions, Fresno *Also called Volt Management Corp* ***(G-14974)***
Volt Workforce Solutions, Orange *Also called Volt Management Corp* ***(G-14975)***
Volt Workforce Solutions, Roseville *Also called Volt Management Corp* ***(G-14976)***
Volt Workforce Solutions, Riverside *Also called Volt Management Corp* ***(G-14977)***
Volt Workforce Solutions, Stockton *Also called Volt Management Corp* ***(G-14978)***
Volt Workforce Solutions, Oxnard *Also called Volt Management Corp* ***(G-14979)***
Volume Services Inc...619 525-5800
111 W Harbor Dr San Diego (92101) ***(G-19304)***
Volume Services Inc...415 972-1500
24 Willie Mays Plz San Francisco (94107) ***(G-19305)***
Volume Services Inc...323 644-6038
5333 Zoo Dr Los Angeles (90027) ***(G-19306)***
Volume Services Inc...951 245-9995
500 Diamond Dr Lake Elsinore (92530) ***(G-19307)***
Volunteer Center Los Angeles...818 908-5151
1375 N St Andrews Pl Los Angeles (90028) ***(G-24281)***
Volunteer Center of La Alsc, Los Angeles *Also called Volunteer Center Los Angeles* ***(G-24281)***
Volunteers of Amer Los Angeles...818 506-0597
11243 Kittridge St North Hollywood (91606) ***(G-24282)***
Volunteers of America...714 426-9834
2100 N Broadway Ste 300 Santa Ana (92706) ***(G-24283)***
Volunteers of America Greater...916 265-3400
3434 Marconi Ave Ste A Sacramento (95821) ***(G-24284)***
Vons Companies Inc...626 350-8405
4300 N Shirley Ave El Monte (91731) ***(G-4657)***
Vons Meat Distribution Center, El Monte *Also called Vons Companies Inc* ***(G-4657)***
Vormetric Inc (HQ)...408 433-6000
2860 Junction Ave San Jose (95134) ***(G-16524)***
Vorwaller & Brooks Inc...760 262-6300
72182 Corporate Way Thousand Palms (92276) ***(G-17601)***
Voter Precinct Voter Reg Off, Norwalk *Also called County of Los Angeles* ***(G-16113)***
Votum Staffing Inc...310 499-4902
515 W Whittier Blvd Montebello (90640) ***(G-14816)***
Vox Network Solutions Inc...650 989-1000
8000 Marina Blvd Ste 130 Brisbane (94005) ***(G-28095)***
Voxify Inc...510 545-3011
1151 Marina Village Pkwy Alameda (94501) ***(G-15537)***
VPD IV Inc (PA)...916 605-1500
150 Parkshore Dr Folsom (95630) ***(G-18283)***
Vpl Inc...209 931-2682
11199 N Highway 99 Lodi (95240) ***(G-4089)***
Vpl Transport, Lodi *Also called Vpl Inc* ***(G-4089)***
Vpm Management Inc...949 863-1500
2400 Main St Ste 201 Irvine (92614) ***(G-27276)***
Vps Companies Inc (PA)...831 724-7551
310 Walker St Watsonville (95076) ***(G-8572)***
Vps Companies Inc...831 633-4011
13526 Blackie Rd Castroville (95012) ***(G-8573)***
Vsp Holding Company Inc...916 851-5000
3333 Quality Dr Rancho Cordova (95670) ***(G-10391)***
Vss International Inc (HQ)...916 373-1500
3785 Channel Dr West Sacramento (95691) ***(G-1882)***
Vss Monitoring Inc...408 585-6800
178 E Tasman Dr San Jose (95134) ***(G-5729)***
VT Milcom Inc...619 424-9024
2232 Verus St Ste A San Diego (92154) ***(G-26142)***
Vta Telephone Information...408 321-7127
3331 N 1st St San Jose (95134) ***(G-5730)***
Vtc Enterprises (PA)...805 928-5000
2445 A St Santa Maria (93455) ***(G-24405)***
Vubiquity Inc...818 526-5000
15301 Ventura Blvd Bldg E Sherman Oaks (91403) ***(G-18284)***
Vubiquity Holdings Inc (PA)...818 526-5000
15301 Ventura Blvd # 3000 Sherman Oaks (91403) ***(G-6058)***
Vucovich Inc (PA)...559 486-8020
4288 S Bagley Ave Fresno (93725) ***(G-7814)***
Vungle Inc...415 800-1400
185 Clara St Ste 100 San Francisco (94107) ***(G-13940)***
Vwi Concord LLC...925 827-2000
1970 Diamond Blvd Concord (94520) ***(G-13383)***
VWR International LLC...714 220-2615
6609 Mount Whitney Dr Buena Park (90620) ***(G-7352)***
VWR Scientific, Buena Park *Also called VWR International LLC* ***(G-7352)***
Vxi Global Solutions LLC (PA)...213 739-4720
220 W 1st St Fl 3 Los Angeles (90012) ***(G-17602)***
Vyborny Vineyard Management...707 944-9135
7327 Silverado Trl Rutherford (94573) ***(G-732)***
W A Rasic Cnstr Co Inc (PA)...562 928-6111
4150 Long Beach Blvd Long Beach (90807) ***(G-2012)***
W B Starr Inc...949 770-8835
20602 Canada Rd Lake Forest (92630) ***(G-977)***
W Bradley Electric Inc...650 701-1502
501 Seaport Ct Ste 103a Redwood City (94063) ***(G-2786)***
W Bradley Electric Inc (PA)...415 898-1400
90 Hill Rd Novato (94945) ***(G-2787)***
W Brown & Assc Property & Csu...949 851-2060
19000 Macarthur Blvd Irvine (92612) ***(G-10926)***
W C I, Hollister *Also called Woltcom Inc* ***(G-2796)***
W Corporation...949 861-2927
1643 W Orange Grove Ave Orange (92868) ***(G-28096)***
W Diamond Supply Co (HQ)...909 859-8939
19321 E Walnut Dr N City of Industry (91748) ***(G-6904)***
W F Hayward Co...530 303-3030
629 Main St Ste 101 Placerville (95667) ***(G-2995)***
W G A, Irvine *Also called Western Growers Association* ***(G-25110)***
W G B, Tustin *Also called Wood Gutmann Bogart Insur Brkg* ***(G-10944)***
W G Warranty and Insur Svcs, Calabasas *Also called All Motorists Insurance Agency* ***(G-10585)***
W H C Inc...916 927-9300
2240 Northrop Ave Sacramento (95825) ***(G-21022)***
W Hotel...415 777-5300
181 3rd St San Francisco (94103) ***(G-13384)***
W I C, Sutter Creek *Also called Resource Connection of Amador* ***(G-24155)***
W I S, Moreno Valley *Also called Washington Inventory Service* ***(G-17609)***
W I S, El Monte *Also called Washington Inventory Service* ***(G-17610)***
W J Griffin Inc...805 683-5639
905 S Patterson Ave Santa Barbara (93111) ***(G-324)***
W K G Company...530 345-1393
1400 W 3rd St Chico (95928) ***(G-11903)***
W L Butler Construction Inc (PA)...650 361-1270
204 Franklin St Redwood City (94063) ***(G-1711)***
W L Hickey Sons Inc...408 736-4938
190 Commercial St Sunnyvale (94085) ***(G-2412)***
W Los Angeles...310 208-8765
930 Hilgard Ave Los Angeles (90024) ***(G-13385)***
W M, Long Beach *Also called Windes McClghry Accntancy Corp* ***(G-26458)***
W M Klorman Construction Corp...818 591-5969
23047 Ventura Blvd Woodland Hills (91364) ***(G-1712)***
W M Lyles Co (HQ)...951 973-7393
1210 W Olive Ave Fresno (93728) ***(G-2013)***
W M Lyles Co...661 387-1600
2810 Unicorn Rd Bakersfield (93308) ***(G-26143)***
W O R K, Carpinteria *Also called Ucp Work Inc* ***(G-24398)***
W P Media Complex...310 477-1938
2323 Corinth Ave Los Angeles (90064) ***(G-17603)***
W R Hambrecht Co Inc (PA)...415 551-8600
Bay 3 Pier 1 San Francisco (94111) ***(G-10096)***
W S B & Associates Inc...510 444-6266
519 17th St Ste 230 Oakland (94612) ***(G-16850)***
W S B & Associates Inc (PA)...415 864-3510
1390 Market St Ste 314 San Francisco (94102) ***(G-16851)***
W San Diego Hotel, San Diego *Also called Rp Scs Wsd Hotel LLC* ***(G-13173)***
W Scott Bllard Dsign Arch Inc...323 386-4740
1800 Century Park E # 600 Los Angeles (90067) ***(G-17604)***
W W Grainger Inc...951 727-2300
4700 Hamner Ave Mira Loma (91752) ***(G-7986)***
W Why W Enterprises Inc...626 969-4292
2671 Pomona Blvd Pomona (91768) ***(G-4390)***
W-Bel Age LLC...310 854-1111
1020 N San Vicente Blvd West Hollywood (90069) ***(G-13386)***
W-Emerald LLC...619 239-4500
400 W Broadway San Diego (92101) ***(G-13387)***
W2005 New Cntury Ht Prtflio LP...408 745-6000
1100 N Mathilda Ave Sunnyvale (94089) ***(G-13388)***
W2005 Wyn Hotels LP...323 887-8100
5757 Telegraph Rd Commerce (90040) ***(G-13389)***
Wachovia A Division Wells F...415 571-2832
420 Montgomery St San Francisco (94104) ***(G-9428)***

Wad Productions Inc 818 260-5673
3500 W Olive Ave Ste 1000 Burbank (91505) *(G-18188)*
Waddell & Reed Inc 714 437-7510
695 Town Center Dr # 200 Costa Mesa (92626) *(G-10097)*
Wagan Corporation 800 231-5806
31088 San Clemente St Hayward (94544) *(G-6779)*
Wageworks Inc (PA) 650 577-5200
1100 Park Pl Fl 4 San Mateo (94403) *(G-27716)*
Waggoners Trucking 800 999-9097
801 Mcwane Blvd Port Hueneme (93043) *(G-4301)*
Wagner Financials, Manhattan Beach *Also called GBS Financial Corp (G-17182)*
Wagner Heights Nursing & Rehab, Stockton *Also called Covenant Care California LLC (G-21197)*
Wagner Jacobson Brokerage Inc 323 872-1636
16400 Ventura Blvd # 333 Encino (91436) *(G-11904)*
Wah Hung Intl McHy Inc 323 263-3513
800 Monterey Pass Rd Monterey Park (91754) *(G-6700)*
Waiters On Wheels Inc (PA) 415 452-6600
5425 Mission St San Francisco (94112) *(G-4090)*
Wakunaga of America Co Ltd (HQ) 949 855-2776
23501 Madero Mission Viejo (92691) *(G-8306)*
Wal-Mart Stores Inc 909 349-3600
13550 Valley Blvd Fontana (92335) *(G-4658)*
Wal-Mart Stores Inc 760 961-6300
21101 Johnson Rd Apple Valley (92307) *(G-4659)*
Wal-Mart Stores Inc 530 529-0916
10815 Highway 99w Red Bluff (96080) *(G-4660)*
Wal-Mart Stores Inc 951 681-7256
4250 Hamner Ave Mira Loma (91752) *(G-4661)*
Wal-Mart Stores Inc 559 783-1109
1300 S F St Porterville (93257) *(G-4662)*
Walgreen Arizona Drug Co 928 526-1400
17500 Perris Blvd Moreno Valley (92551) *(G-4663)*
Walgreen Co 530 406-7700
2370 E Main St Woodland (95776) *(G-4664)*
Walgreens, Woodland *Also called Walgreen Co (G-4664)*
Walgreens Home Care Inc 818 351-3000
9401 Chivers Ave Sun Valley (91352) *(G-22612)*
Walgreens Home Care Inc 650 551-7020
975 Industrial Rd Ste E San Carlos (94070) *(G-22613)*
Walk Through Video, McClellan *Also called Villara Corporation (G-2408)*
Walker & Dunlop Inc 949 660-1999
2603 Main St Ste 200 Irvine (92614) *(G-9904)*
Walker & Zanger Inc (PA) 818 280-8300
16719 Schoenborn St North Hills (91343) *(G-7000)*
Walker Advertising Inc 310 519-4050
1010 S Cabrillo Ave San Pedro (90731) *(G-13941)*
Walker Brothers McHy Mvg Inc (PA) 714 630-5957
3839 E Coronado St Anaheim (92807) *(G-17605)*
Walker Communications Inc 707 421-1300
521 Railroad Ave Suisun City (94585) *(G-2788)*
Walkme Inc 855 492-5563
22 4th St Fl 14 San Francisco (94103) *(G-15538)*
Walkup Mldia Klly Schoenberger 415 981-7210
650 California St Fl 26 San Francisco (94108) *(G-23608)*
Wall Systems Inc 805 523-9091
11975 Discovery Ct Moorpark (93021) *(G-2996)*
Wall Tech, Diamond Bar *Also called March International Inc (G-2065)*
Wallace-Kuhl & Associates, West Sacramento *Also called River Cy Geoprofessionals Inc (G-26042)*
Wallace-Kuhl Investments LLC (PA) 916 372-1434
3050 Industrial Blvd West Sacramento (95691) *(G-26144)*
Wallis Fashions Inc 510 763-8018
1100 8th Ave Oakland (94606) *(G-17606)*
Wally Park, Los Angeles *Also called Lrw Investments LLC (G-17729)*
Walmart, Fontana *Also called Wal-Mart Stores Inc (G-4658)*
Walmart, Apple Valley *Also called Wal-Mart Stores Inc (G-4659)*
Walmart, Red Bluff *Also called Wal-Mart Stores Inc (G-4660)*
Walmart, Mira Loma *Also called Wal-Mart Stores Inc (G-4661)*
Walmart, Porterville *Also called Wal-Mart Stores Inc (G-4662)*
Walnut Country, Concord *Also called Cowell Homeowners Association (G-25244)*
Walnut Creek Active Club, Walnut Creek *Also called 24 Hour Fitness Usa Inc (G-18597)*
Walnut Creek Spt & Fitnes CLB, Walnut Creek *Also called Olympic Investors Ltd (G-19021)*
Walnut Investment Corp 714 238-9240
2940 E White Star Ave Anaheim (92806) *(G-6969)*
Walnut Manor Care Center, Anaheim *Also called Front Porch Communities (G-21218)*
Walnut Valley Unified Schl Dst 909 444-3460
2975 Castle Rock Rd Diamond Bar (91765) *(G-24529)*
Walnut Valley Unified School 909 444-3415
880 S Lemon Ave Walnut (91789) *(G-25596)*
Walnut Valley Water District 909 595-7554
271 Brea Canyon Rd Walnut (91789) *(G-6408)*
Walnut Whtney Cnvalescent Hosp 916 488-8601
3529 Walnut Ave Carmichael (95608) *(G-21023)*
Walnut Whtney Convalecent Hosp, Carmichael *Also called Horizon West Inc (G-20674)*
Walong Marketing Inc (PA) 714 670-8899
6281 Regio Ave Fl 1 Buena Park (90620) *(G-8955)*
Walpert Center, Hayward *Also called ARC of Alameda County (G-24306)*
Walsh Vineyards Management Inc 707 255-1650
1125 Golden Gate Dr NAPA (94558) *(G-11905)*
Walsworth Franklin & Bevins, Orange *Also called Walswrth Frnklin Bevins McCall (G-23609)*
Walswrth Frnklin Bevins McCall (PA) 714 634-2522
1 City Blvd W Ste 500 Orange (92868) *(G-23609)*
Walt Disney Company 916 780-1470
8265 Sierra College Blvd # 21 Roseville (95661) *(G-5829)*
Walt Disney Company 818 544-5009
532 Paula Ave Glendale (91201) *(G-5924)*
Walt Disney Company 818 295-3134
914 N Victory Blvd Burbank (91502) *(G-5925)*
Walt Disney Company 818 560-1268
121 E Buena Vista Burbank (91521) *(G-5926)*
Walt Disney Company 818 567-5590
3900 W Alameda Ave Rm 845 Burbank (91505) *(G-18504)*
Walt Disney Company 972 448-3143
3800 W Alameda Ave # 1150 Burbank (91505) *(G-5830)*
Walt Disney Company 818 544-6500
1133 Flower St Glendale (91201) *(G-18836)*
Walt Disney Company 714 781-4532
1313 S Harbor Blvd Anaheim (92802) *(G-4665)*
Walt Disney Company 714 781-4278
1598 S Harbor Blvd Anaheim (92802) *(G-13390)*
Walt Disney Company 818 553-7333
650 S Buenavista St Burbank (91501) *(G-18837)*
Walt Disney Company 714 449-6600
501 S State College Blvd Fullerton (92831) *(G-18838)*
Walt Disney Company 818 460-6655
500 S Buena Vista St Burbank (91521) *(G-5927)*
Walt Disney Company 818 560-1000
500 S Buena Vista St Burbank (91521) *(G-5928)*
Walt Disney Company (PA) 818 560-1000
500 S Buena Vista St Burbank (91521) *(G-5929)*
Walt Disney Company 818 553-4222
601 Circle Seven Dr Glendale (91201) *(G-18189)*
Walt Disney Company 818 560-1000
350 S Buena Vista St Burbank (91521) *(G-5930)*
Walt Disney Family Museum 415 345-6800
104 Montgomery St San Francisco (94129) *(G-25054)*
Walt Disney Imagineering (HQ) 818 544-6500
1401 Flower St Glendale (91201) *(G-18267)*
Walt Disney Music Company (HQ) 818 560-1000
500 S Buena Vista St Burbank (91521) *(G-12229)*
Walt Disney Pictures and TV 818 560-1000
500 S Buena Vista St Burbank (91521) *(G-18292)*
Walt Disney Records Direct (HQ) 818 560-1000
500 S Buena Vista St Burbank (91521) *(G-18190)*
Walt Disney Studios, Burbank *Also called Walt Disney Company (G-5930)*
Walter & Wolf, Fremont *Also called Walters & Wolf Glass Company (G-3417)*
Walter Anderson Plumbing Inc 619 449-7646
1830 John Towers Ave El Cajon (92020) *(G-2413)*
Walter E McGuire RE Inc 650 348-0222
360 Primrose Rd Burlingame (94010) *(G-11906)*
Walter E McGuire RE Inc (PA) 415 929-1500
2001 Lombard St San Francisco (94123) *(G-11907)*
Walter E McGuire RE Inc 415 296-0123
17 Bluxome St San Francisco (94107) *(G-11908)*
Walter J Conn & Associates 213 683-0500
800 W 6th St Ste 600 Los Angeles (90017) *(G-26264)*
Walter N Coffman Inc 619 266-2642
5180 Naranja St San Diego (92114) *(G-2997)*
Walter Voss Cynthia RE Max 562 434-5980
6695 E Pacific Coast Hwy # 150 Long Beach (90803) *(G-11909)*
Walters & Wolf Glass Company (PA) 510 490-1115
41450 Boscell Rd Fremont (94538) *(G-3417)*
Walters & Wolf Interiors (PA) 415 243-9400
41450 Boscell Rd Fremont (94538) *(G-3100)*
Walters Family Partnership 760 320-6868
400 E Tahquitz Canyon Way Palm Springs (92262) *(G-13391)*
Walters Wholesale Electric Co (HQ) 562 988-3100
2825 Temple Ave Signal Hill (90755) *(G-7482)*
Walters Wholesale Electric Co 714 784-1900
200 N Berry St Brea (92821) *(G-7483)*
Walton Electric Corporation 909 981-5051
755 N Central Ave Upland (91786) *(G-2789)*
Walton Engineering Inc 916 372-1888
3900 Commerce Dr West Sacramento (95691) *(G-3598)*
Walz Group LLC (HQ) 951 491-6800
27398 Via Industria Temecula (92590) *(G-15539)*
Walz Postal Solutions, Temecula *Also called Walz Group LLC (G-15539)*
Wamc Company Inc (PA) 858 454-2753
7420 Clairemont Mesa Blvd San Diego (92111) *(G-11227)*
Wannajob Inc 562 426-5272
2710 Saint Louis Ave Signal Hill (90755) *(G-14980)*
War Memorial Prfrmg Art Ctr, San Francisco *Also called City & County of San Francisco (G-18382)*
Ward Enterprises 209 358-0445
2679 Buhach Rd Atwater (95301) *(G-14464)*
Ward, E B, Brisbane *Also called Edward B Ward & Company Inc (G-7736)*
Ware Disposal Inc (PA) 714 834-0234
1451 Manhattan Ave Fullerton (92831) *(G-6594)*
Ware Malcomb (PA) 949 660-9128
10 Edelman Irvine (92618) *(G-26265)*
Warehouse, Laguna Beach *Also called Pauls Tv LLC (G-7506)*
Warehouse, Lancaster *Also called Michaels Stores Inc (G-9281)*
Warehouse, El Segundo *Also called Infonet Services Corporation (G-4577)*
Warehouse and Distribution, Mira Loma *Also called Triways Inc (G-4384)*
Wargaming America Inc (HQ) 510 962-6747
1480 64th St Ste 300 Emeryville (94608) *(G-15878)*
Warmington Homes (PA) 714 434-4435
3090 Pullman St Costa Mesa (92626) *(G-1390)*
Warmington Homes 949 679-3100
15615 Alton Pkwy Ste 150 Irvine (92618) *(G-1391)*
Warmington Homes 925 866-6700
2400 Camino Ramon Ste 234 San Ramon (94583) *(G-1392)*
Warmington Residential Cal Inc 714 557-5511
3090 Pullman St Costa Mesa (92626) *(G-1281)*

ALPHABETIC

Warner Bros Accounting Dept, Burbank *Also called Warner Bros Entertainment Inc* ***(G-18199)***
Warner Bros Consumer Pdts Inc (HQ)....818 954-7980
4001 W Olive Ave Burbank (91505) ***(G-28097)***
Warner Bros Distributing Inc....818 954-6000
4000 Warner Blvd Bldg 154 Burbank (91522) ***(G-27277)***
Warner Bros Domestic TV Dist, Burbank *Also called Warner Bros Entertainment Inc* ***(G-18194)***
Warner Bros Entertainment Inc....818 954-1817
4000 Warner Blvd Burbank (91522) ***(G-18191)***
Warner Bros Entertainment Inc....818 954-7232
4000 Warner Blvd Burbank (91522) ***(G-18192)***
Warner Bros Entertainment Inc....818 954-3000
4000 Warner Blvd Burbank (91522) ***(G-18193)***
Warner Bros Entertainment Inc....818 954-5301
4000 Warner Blvd Bldg 118 Burbank (91522) ***(G-18194)***
Warner Bros Entertainment Inc (HQ)....818 954-6000
4000 Warner Blvd Burbank (91522) ***(G-18195)***
Warner Bros Entertainment Inc....818 954-6901
300 Tlvsion Plz Bldg 137 Burbank (91505) ***(G-17607)***
Warner Bros Entertainment Inc....818 954-3000
4000 Warner Blvd Burbank (91522) ***(G-18196)***
Warner Bros Entertainment Inc....818 954-7065
4000 Warner Blvd Bldg 137 Burbank (91522) ***(G-18197)***
Warner Bros Entertainment Inc....818 954-2181
4000 Warner Blvd Bldg 30 Burbank (91522) ***(G-18198)***
Warner Bros Entertainment Inc....818 954-2187
4000 Warner Blvd B-156 Burbank (91522) ***(G-18199)***
Warner Bros Entertainment Inc....818 954-6000
4000 Warner Blvd Bldg 30 Burbank (91522) ***(G-18200)***
Warner Bros Intl TV Dist Inc....818 954-6000
4000 Warner Blvd Burbank (91522) ***(G-18201)***
Warner Bros Records Inc (HQ)....818 953-3378
3300 Warner Blvd Burbank (91505) ***(G-17608)***
Warner Bros Studio Facilities, Burbank *Also called Warner Bros Entertainment Inc* ***(G-18193)***
Warner Bros Transatlantic Inc (HQ)....818 954-6000
4000 Warner Blvd Burbank (91522) ***(G-18285)***
Warner Bros Transatlantic Inc....818 977-6384
3300 W Olive Ave Unit 200 Burbank (91505) ***(G-18286)***
Warner Bros Transatlantic Inc....818 972-0777
3500 W Olive Ave Ste 1000 Burbank (91505) ***(G-18287)***
Warner Bros. Legal Department, Burbank *Also called Warner Bros Entertainment Inc* ***(G-18192)***
Warner Bros. Paint Department, Burbank *Also called Warner Bros Entertainment Inc* ***(G-18191)***
Warner Bros. Television, Burbank *Also called Warner Bros Entertainment Inc* ***(G-17607)***
Warner Brothers Studios....818 954-5000
4000 Warner Blvd Burbank (91522) ***(G-7038)***
Warner Center Marriott Hotel, Woodland Hills *Also called Tr Warner Center LP* ***(G-13352)***
Warner Films LLC....310 601-3184
468 N Camden Dr Beverly Hills (90210) ***(G-18202)***
Warner Mountain Group Hom....530 233-5200
250 Cnty Rd 82 Canby (96015) ***(G-24852)***
Warner Pacific Insur Svcs Inc (PA)....408 298-4049
32110 Agoura Rd Westlake Village (91361) ***(G-10927)***
Warner Villa, Woodland Hills *Also called Topanga Villas Company* ***(G-11214)***
Warrack Corporation....707 523-7271
3033 Cleveland Ave Santa Rosa (95403) ***(G-22026)***
Warrack Hospital, Santa Rosa *Also called Warrack Corporation* ***(G-22026)***
Warren Auto De Mexico LLC....858 794-7947
517 S Cedros Ave Solana Beach (92075) ***(G-9311)***
Warren Distributing Inc (PA)....562 789-3360
8737 Dice Rd Santa Fe Springs (90670) ***(G-6780)***
Warren Drye Kelley....310 712-6100
10100 Santa Monica Blvd # 1050 Los Angeles (90067) ***(G-23610)***
Warren E & P, Long Beach *Also called Warren E&P Inc* ***(G-9034)***
Warren E&P Inc....562 590-0909
400 Oceangate Ste 200 Long Beach (90802) ***(G-9034)***
Warren Security Systems Inc....415 456-7034
1305 Francisco Blvd E San Rafael (94901) ***(G-16943)***
Warrior Custom Golf Inc (PA)....949 699-2499
15 Mason Irvine (92618) ***(G-8034)***
Warrior Golf, Irvine *Also called Warrior Custom Golf Inc* ***(G-8034)***
Wartnick Chaber Harowitz....415 986-5566
100 1st St Ste 2500 San Francisco (94105) ***(G-23611)***
Wartnick Law Firm, San Francisco *Also called Wartnick Chaber Harowitz* ***(G-23611)***
Warwick California Corporation....415 992-3809
490 Geary St San Francisco (94102) ***(G-13392)***
Warwick Hotel San Francisco, San Francisco *Also called Warwick California Corporation* ***(G-13392)***
Wash Mltfmily Ldry Systems LLC (PA)....310 643-8491
100 N Sepulveda Blvd El Segundo (90245) ***(G-13578)***
Washington Enterprises 3 LLC....323 731-0861
2300 W Washington Blvd Los Angeles (90018) ***(G-21024)***
Washington Group, Del Mar *Also called Aecom Energy & Cnstr Inc* ***(G-1724)***
Washington Group, La Mirada *Also called Aecom Energy & Cnstr Inc* ***(G-25622)***
Washington Hosp Healthcare Sys....510 797-3342
2000 Mowry Ave Fremont (94538) ***(G-22027)***
Washington Inn LLC....310 821-4455
737 Washington Blvd Marina Del Rey (90292) ***(G-13393)***
Washington Inventory Service....951 653-1472
13800 Heacock St D135c Moreno Valley (92553) ***(G-17609)***
Washington Inventory Service....626 288-1200
9080 Telstar Ave Ste 313 El Monte (91731) ***(G-17610)***
Washington Inventory Service (HQ)....858 565-8111
9265 Sky Park Ct Ste 100 San Diego (92123) ***(G-17611)***
Washington Inventory Service....916 485-3427
3800 Watt Ave Ste 101 Sacramento (95821) ***(G-17612)***
Washington Inventory Service....619 461-8198
7150 El Cajon Blvd San Diego (92115) ***(G-17613)***
Washington Inventory Service....510 498-5979
43068 Christy St Fremont (94538) ***(G-17614)***
Washington Inventory Service....818 407-2680
19420 Business Center Dr Northridge (91324) ***(G-17615)***
Washington Iron Works, Gardena *Also called Washington Orna Ir Works Inc* ***(G-3599)***
Washington Mutual, Studio City *Also called Jpmorgan Chase Bank Nat Assn* ***(G-9574)***
Washington Orna Ir Works Inc (PA)....310 327-8660
17926 S Broadway Gardena (90248) ***(G-3599)***
Washington Otptent Surgery Ctr, Fremont *Also called Washington Outpatient* ***(G-20228)***
Washington Outpatient....510 791-5374
2299 Mowry Ave Fl 1 Fremont (94538) ***(G-20228)***
Wasser Filtration Inc....714 525-0630
1215 N Fee Ana St Anaheim (92807) ***(G-7904)***
Wasserman Comden & Casselman (PA)....323 872-0995
5567 Reseda Blvd Ste 330 Tarzana (91356) ***(G-23612)***
Wasserman Media Group LLC (PA)....310 407-0200
10960 Wilshire Blvd Los Angeles (90024) ***(G-27717)***
Waste Connections, Diamond Springs *Also called County of El Dorado* ***(G-6469)***
Waste Connections Cal Inc....408 752-8530
301 Carl Rd Sunnyvale (94089) ***(G-6595)***
Waste Connections Cal Inc (PA)....408 282-4400
1333 Oakland Rd San Jose (95112) ***(G-6596)***
Waste Management, Visalia *Also called USA Waste of California Inc* ***(G-6574)***
Waste Management, Gold River *Also called USA Waste of California Inc* ***(G-6576)***
Waste Management, Castroville *Also called Ajax Portable Services* ***(G-14509)***
Waste Management, Castroville *Also called USA Waste of California Inc* ***(G-6578)***
Waste Management, Baldwin Park *Also called USA Waste of California Inc* ***(G-6579)***
Waste Management, Atascadero *Also called USA Waste of California Inc* ***(G-6580)***
Waste Management, El Cajon *Also called USA Waste of California Inc* ***(G-6581)***
Waste Management, Chino *Also called USA Waste of California Inc* ***(G-6582)***
Waste Management Cal Inc (HQ)....877 836-6526
9081 Tujunga Ave Sun Valley (91352) ***(G-6597)***
Waste Management Cal Inc....619 596-5100
1001 W Bradley Ave El Cajon (92020) ***(G-6598)***
Waste Management Cal Inc....661 947-7197
1200 W City Ranch Rd Palmdale (93551) ***(G-6599)***
Waste Management Cal Inc....562 427-7277
15902 S Main St Gardena (90248) ***(G-4091)***
Waste Management Cal Inc....760 439-2824
2141 Oceanside Blvd Oceanside (92054) ***(G-6600)***
Waste Management Nevada County, Grass Valley *Also called USA Waste of California Inc* ***(G-4083)***
Waste Management Orange County, Santa Ana *Also called USA Waste of California Inc* ***(G-6590)***
Waste Managment, Corning *Also called Andersncttonwood Disposal Svcs* ***(G-3977)***
Waste MGT Collectn & Recycl....951 242-0421
17700 Indian St Moreno Valley (92551) ***(G-6601)***
Waste Mgt Collectn & Recycl....626 960-7551
5701 S Eastrn Ave Ste 300 Commerce (90040) ***(G-6602)***
Waste Mgt Collectn & Recycl....925 935-8900
2658 N Main St Walnut Creek (94597) ***(G-4092)***
Waste Mgt Collectn & Recycl (HQ)....714 282-0200
2050 N Glassell St Orange (92865) ***(G-6603)***
Waste Mgt Collectn & Recycl....831 768-9505
1340 W Beach St Watsonville (95076) ***(G-6604)***
Waste MGT Collectn & Recycl....707 462-0210
219 Pudding Creek Rd Fort Bragg (95437) ***(G-6605)***
Waste MGT Collectn & Recycl....949 451-2600
16122 Construction Cir E Irvine (92606) ***(G-6606)***
Waste MGT Collectn & Recycl....909 242-0421
17700 Indian St Moreno Valley (92551) ***(G-6607)***
Waste MGT Collectn & Recycl....707 462-0210
450 Orr Springs Rd Ukiah (95482) ***(G-6608)***
Waste MGT Collectn Recycl Inc....714 637-3010
1800 S Grand Ave Santa Ana (92705) ***(G-14502)***
Waste MGT of Alameda Cnty (HQ)....510 613-8710
172 98th Ave Oakland (94603) ***(G-6609)***
Waste MGT of Alameda Cnty....510 638-2303
2615 Davis St San Leandro (94577) ***(G-6610)***
Waste MGT of Alameda Cnty....909 280-5438
800 S Temescal St Corona (92879) ***(G-6611)***
Watch Resources Inc (PA)....209 533-0510
12801 Cabezut Rd Sonora (95370) ***(G-24285)***
Watchit Media Inc....702 740-1700
655 Montgomery St # 1000 San Francisco (94111) ***(G-18203)***
Water & Power Department, Long Beach *Also called County of Los Angeles* ***(G-6336)***
Water & Power Dept, Van Nuys *Also called City of Los Angeles* ***(G-6115)***
Water & Sewer Service....925 828-8524
7051 Dublin Blvd Dublin (94568) ***(G-2014)***
Water Course Way, Palo Alto *Also called Watercourse Way* ***(G-13804)***
Water Department, Lomita *Also called City of Lomita* ***(G-6326)***
Water Division, Fresno *Also called City of Fresno* ***(G-6324)***
Water Drops Express Carwash, Santa Monica *Also called Alisam Oxnard Operating* ***(G-10955)***
Water Emergency Dispatch, Long Beach *Also called City of Long Beach* ***(G-6328)***
Water Heaters Only Inc....650 368-9998
3620 Haven Ave Redwood City (94063) ***(G-7513)***
Water Quality Control Plant, Palo Alto *Also called City of Palo Alto* ***(G-17077)***
Water Resources Cal Dept....916 324-3812
1416 9th St Rm 1225 Sacramento (95814) ***(G-16268)***
Water Resources Control Bd Cal....619 521-3010
2375 Northside Dr Ste 100 San Diego (92108) ***(G-25109)***

ALPHABETIC

Water Resources Division, Livermore *Also called City of Livermore* ***(G-2041)***
Water Supply, Vacaville *Also called County of Solano* ***(G-6338)***
Water Svcs Operations & Repr, Oxnard *Also called City of Oxnard* ***(G-6329)***
Watercourse Way..................650 462-2000
165 Channing Ave Palo Alto (94301) ***(G-13804)***
Waterfall Resort..................805 879-3780
5951 Encina Rd Ste 207 Goleta (93117) ***(G-13394)***
Waterfront Hotel LLC..................714 845-8000
21100 Pacific Coast Hwy Huntington Beach (92648) ***(G-13395)***
Waterfront Plaza Hotel LLC..................510 836-3800
10 Washington St Oakland (94607) ***(G-13396)***
Waterhill Ltd..................626 369-6828
140 N Orange Ave City of Industry (91744) ***(G-6837)***
Waterhouse Management Corp..................916 772-4918
500 Giuseppe Ct Ste 2 Roseville (95678) ***(G-11246)***
Waterman Convalescent Hospital..................951 681-2200
6401 33rd St Riverside (92509) ***(G-22186)***
Waterman Convalescent Hospital (PA)..................909 882-1215
1850 N Waterman Ave San Bernardino (92404) ***(G-21025)***
Watermark Rtrment Cmmnties Inc..................760 346-5420
41505 Carlotta Dr Palm Desert (92211) ***(G-21026)***
Watermark Rtrment Cmmnties Inc..................858 597-8000
3890 Nobel Dr San Diego (92122) ***(G-11910)***
Waters Edge Lodge..................510 769-6264
801 Island Dr Apt 267 Alameda (94502) ***(G-24853)***
Waters Moving & Storage Inc..................925 372-0914
37 Bridgehead Rd Martinez (94553) ***(G-4391)***
Waterworks Park, Redding *Also called Slideco Recreation Inc* ***(G-18835)***
Waterworld USA, Concord *Also called Parc Management LLC* ***(G-19257)***
Waterworld USA, Sacramento *Also called Six Flags Entertainment Corp* ***(G-18834)***
Watg, Irvine *Also called Wimberly Allison Tong Goo Inc* ***(G-26269)***
Watkin & Bortolussi Inc..................415 453-4675
726 Alfred Nobel Dr Hercules (94547) ***(G-978)***
Watkins Construction Co Inc..................661 763-5395
112 E Cedar St Taft (93268) ***(G-2015)***
Watson Carton..................408 979-9618
4178 Ross Ave San Jose (95124) ***(G-24996)***
Watson Cogeneration Co Inc..................310 816-8100
22850 Wilmington Ave Carson (90745) ***(G-6251)***
Watson Contractors Inc..................916 481-6293
3185 Longview Dr Sacramento (95821) ***(G-1478)***
Watson ME Inc..................661 768-1717
26871 Henry Rd Fellows (93224) ***(G-1282)***
Watson Wyatt Worldwide 421, San Francisco *Also called Towers Watson & Co* ***(G-27691)***
Watsonville Coast Produce Inc..................831 722-3851
275 Kearney Ext Frnt Watsonville (95076) ***(G-8787)***
Watsonville Community Hospital..................831 724-4741
75 Neilson St Watsonville (95076) ***(G-22028)***
Watsonville Health Clinic, Watsonville *Also called Santa Cruz County of* ***(G-19958)***
Watsonville Nursing Center, Watsonville *Also called CF Watsonville East LLC* ***(G-20450)***
Watsonville Post Acute Center, Watsonville *Also called CF Watsonville LLC* ***(G-20449)***
Watsonville Post Acute Center, Watsonville *Also called CF Watsonville West LLC* ***(G-20451)***
Watt Commercial Properties, Santa Monica *Also called Watt Properties Inc* ***(G-11068)***
Watt Investment Partners LLC..................310 450-3802
2716 Ocean Park Blvd Santa Monica (90405) ***(G-11911)***
Watt Properties Inc (PA)..................310 314-2430
2716 Ocean Park Blvd # 2025 Santa Monica (90405) ***(G-11068)***
Watts Health Center, Los Angeles *Also called Watts Health Foundation Inc* ***(G-12209)***
Watts Health Foundation Inc (HQ)..................310 424-2220
3405 W Imperial Hwy # 304 Inglewood (90303) ***(G-21119)***
Watts Health Foundation Inc..................323 357-6688
10300 Compton Ave Los Angeles (90002) ***(G-12209)***
Watts Healthcare Corporation..................323 241-1780
700 W Imperial Hwy Los Angeles (90044) ***(G-20229)***
Watts Healthcare Corporation (PA)..................323 568-3059
10300 Compton Ave Los Angeles (90002) ***(G-20230)***
Wave Plastic Surgery Ctr Inc..................626 964-7788
18433 Colima Rd La Puente (91748) ***(G-20231)***
Wawanesa General Insurance Co..................619 285-6020
9050 Friars Rd Ste 200 San Diego (92108) ***(G-10480)***
Wawansea General Insurance, San Diego *Also called Wawanesa General Insurance Co* ***(G-10480)***
Wawona Packing Co LLC..................559 528-4000
12133 Avenue 408 Cutler (93615) ***(G-603)***
Wawona Packing Co LLC..................559 528-4699
12133 Avenue 408 Cutler (93615) ***(G-17616)***
Waxies Enterprises Inc..................925 454-2900
901 N Canyon Pkwy Livermore (94551) ***(G-7987)***
Way Cool Homecare Inc..................619 444-3200
450 Fletcher Pkwy Ste 216 El Cajon (92020) ***(G-22614)***
Way Forward Technology Inc..................661 286-2769
28738 The Old Rd Valencia (91355) ***(G-15540)***
Wayne E Swisher Cem Contr Inc..................925 757-3660
2620 E 18th St Antioch (94509) ***(G-3349)***
Wayne Maples Plumbing & Htg..................707 445-2500
317 W Cedar St Eureka (95501) ***(G-2414)***
Wayne Perry Inc (PA)..................714 826-0352
8281 Commonwealth Ave Buena Park (90621) ***(G-3600)***
Wayne Provision Co Inc (PA)..................323 277-5888
5030 Gifford Ave Vernon (90058) ***(G-8689)***
Wayne R Kidder..................805 967-6993
915 Via Los Padres Santa Barbara (93111) ***(G-20232)***
Waypoint Real Estate Group LLC..................510 250-2200
1999 Harrison St Fl 22nd Oakland (94612) ***(G-11912)***
Waze Market Inc (PA)..................510 469-3123
5980 Horton St Ste 675 Emeryville (94608) ***(G-15541)***
Wb Electric Inc..................408 842-7911
30611 Road 400 Coarsegold (93614) ***(G-2790)***
Wca, Los Angeles *Also called West Coast Ambulance Corp* ***(G-3856)***
Wcct Global LLC (PA)..................714 668-1500
3545 Howard Way Costa Mesa (92626) ***(G-26819)***
Wcg World, San Francisco *Also called Weisscomm Group Ltd* ***(G-28098)***
WCIRB, Oakland *Also called Workers Compensation* ***(G-10483)***
Wdc Explrtion Wells Holdg Corp..................916 419-6043
1300 National Dr Ste 140 Sacramento (95834) ***(G-2016)***
Wdi, Santa Fe Springs *Also called Warren Distributing Inc* ***(G-6780)***
Wdm Group, Carlsbad *Also called White Digital Media Inc* ***(G-9175)***
Wdpt Film Distribution LLC..................818 560-1000
500 S Buena Vista St Burbank (91521) ***(G-7656)***
We Care Day Care & Pre School..................209 832-4072
1790 Sequoia Blvd Tracy (95376) ***(G-24530)***
We Pack It All, Duarte *Also called Bershtel Enterprises LLC* ***(G-17029)***
Wealth Educators Inc..................310 623-9145
5209 Wilshire Blvd Los Angeles (90036) ***(G-27278)***
Wealthtv, San Diego *Also called Herring Broadcasting Company* ***(G-5869)***
Weatherford International LLC..................661 587-6930
21728 Rosedale Hwy Bakersfield (93314) ***(G-7796)***
Weave, Sacramento *Also called WEAVE Incorporated* ***(G-14981)***
WEAVE Incorporated (PA)..................916 448-2321
1900 K St Ste 200 Sacramento (95811) ***(G-14981)***
Web Spiders Inc..................415 230-2202
180 Snsome St Rocketspace San Francisco (94104) ***(G-15542)***
Web Traffic School, Oakland *Also called Interactive Solutions Inc* ***(G-15708)***
Webb Sunrise Inc..................619 220-7050
3320 Kemper St Ste 201 San Diego (92110) ***(G-9312)***
Webcor Builders, Alameda *Also called Webcor Construction LP* ***(G-1713)***
Webcor Construction LP (HQ)..................510 748-1900
1751 Harbor Bay Pkwy # 200 Alameda (94502) ***(G-1713)***
Weber Distribution Cwo, Rancho Cucamonga *Also called Weber Distribution Warehouses* ***(G-4666)***
Weber Distribution Warehouses..................909 481-1600
9345 Santa Anita Ave B Rancho Cucamonga (91730) ***(G-4666)***
Weber Distribution Warehouses..................619 423-8770
1366 30th St San Diego (92154) ***(G-4667)***
Weber Distribution Warehouses..................562 404-9996
15301 Shoemaker Ave Norwalk (90650) ***(G-4668)***
Weber Logistics, San Diego *Also called Weber Distribution Warehouses* ***(G-4667)***
Weber Shandwick..................415 262-5600
600 Battery St Fl 1 San Francisco (94111) ***(G-27768)***
Webers Quality Meats Inc..................510 635-9892
990 Carden St San Leandro (94577) ***(G-8690)***
Webex.com, Santa Clara *Also called Cisco Webex LLC* ***(G-17072)***
Webly Systems Inc..................888 444-6400
2603 Camino Ramon Ste 200 San Ramon (94583) ***(G-17617)***
Webpass Inc..................415 233-4100
267 8th St San Francisco (94103) ***(G-5731)***
Webster Investment Management, San Francisco *Also called Forward Management LLC* ***(G-10143)***
Webyog Inc..................408 512-1434
2900 Gordon Ave 100-7p Santa Clara (95051) ***(G-15543)***
Weckworth Construction Co Inc..................916 939-6636
3941 Park Dr Ste 20-373 El Dorado Hills (95762) ***(G-2791)***
Weckworth Electric Company, El Dorado Hills *Also called Weckworth Construction Co Inc* ***(G-2791)***
Weco - Us.ca. El Centro, El Centro *Also called Wilbur-Ellis Company LLC* ***(G-9158)***
Weco Aerospace Systems, Lincoln *Also called Weygandt & Associates* ***(G-18034)***
Weco Aerospace Systems, Lincoln *Also called Gdsa-Lincoln Inc* ***(G-17935)***
Wedbush Securities Inc (HQ)..................213 688-8000
1000 Wilshire Blvd # 900 Los Angeles (90017) ***(G-10098)***
Wedriveu Holdings Inc..................650 579-5800
700 Airport Blvd Ste 250 Burlingame (94010) ***(G-14817)***
WEI-Chuan USA Inc (PA)..................323 587-2101
6655 Garfield Ave Bell Gardens (90201) ***(G-8574)***
Weil Gotshal & Manges LLP..................650 802-3000
201 Redwood Shors Pkwy Ste 400 Redwood City (94065) ***(G-23613)***
Weinberg Roger & Resenfeld (PA)..................510 337-1001
1001 Marina Village Pkwy # 200 Alameda (94501) ***(G-23614)***
Weingart Center Association..................213 622-6359
566 S San Pedro St Los Angeles (90013) ***(G-24286)***
Weingart Center For Homeless, Los Angeles *Also called Weingart Center Association* ***(G-24286)***
Weingart-Lakewood Family YMCA, Lakewood *Also called Young Mens Chrstn Assc Gr L B* ***(G-25460)***
Weinstein Company LLC..................424 204-4800
9100 Wilshire Blvd 700w Beverly Hills (90212) ***(G-18204)***
Weinstein Construction Corp..................818 782-4000
15102 Raymer St Van Nuys (91405) ***(G-1714)***
Weintraub Tobin Chediak..................310 393-9500
201 Santa Monica Blvd # 300 Santa Monica (90401) ***(G-23615)***
Weintraub Tobin Chediak..................310 858-7888
9665 Wilshire Blvd # 900 Beverly Hills (90212) ***(G-23616)***
Weintraub Tobin Chediak (PA)..................916 558-6000
400 Capitol Mall Fl 11 Sacramento (95814) ***(G-23617)***
Weiss Associates, Emeryville *Also called Aguatierra Associates Inc* ***(G-27772)***
Weisscomm Group Ltd (PA)..................415 362-5018
50 Francisco St Ste 400 San Francisco (94133) ***(G-28098)***
Weisscomm Group Ltd..................415 362-5018
50 Francisco St Ste 400 San Francisco (94133) ***(G-27718)***
Weitz & Luxenberg PC..................310 247-0921
1880 Century Park E # 700 Los Angeles (90067) ***(G-23618)***
Welcome Baby, Anaheim *Also called Orange County Child Abuse* ***(G-24117)***
Welcome Group Management LLC..................310 378-6666
300 S Court St Visalia (93291) ***(G-13397)***
Welfare Administration, Oroville *Also called County of Butte* ***(G-23797)***

Welfare Department, Sonora *Also called County of Tuolumne* ***(G-23930)***
Welfare Dept, Pomona *Also called City of Pomona* ***(G-24890)***
Welfare Dept Warehouse, Oroville *Also called County of Butte* ***(G-23798)***
Welk Group Inc...619 516-7800
6150 Micaion Gorge Rd 1 Ste 140 San Diego (92120) ***(G-26719)***
Welk Group Inc (PA)...760 749-3000
8860 Lawrence Welk Dr Escondido (92026) ***(G-13398)***
Welk Music Group, Escondido *Also called Welk Group Inc* ***(G-13398)***
Welk Resort Center, San Marcos *Also called Welk Resort Group Inc* ***(G-11913)***
Welk Resort Group Inc (PA)...760 652-4913
300 Rancheros Dr Ste 450 San Marcos (92069) ***(G-11913)***
Welker Bros, Milpitas *Also called H V Welker Co Inc* ***(G-3115)***
Well Being Group Inc...559 432-3737
7075 N Howard St Ste 102 Fresno (93720) ***(G-22615)***
Well Within Spa...831 458-9355
417 Cedar St Santa Cruz (95060) ***(G-3601)***
Wellhead Electric Company Inc...916 447-5171
650 Bercut Dr Ste C Sacramento (95811) ***(G-6252)***
Wellington, The, Laguna Hills *Also called Birtcher/Aetna Laguna Hills* ***(G-11098)***
Wellmade Products, Merced *Also called WLMD* ***(G-3605)***
Wells & Bennett Realtors (PA)...510 531-7000
1451 Leimert Blvd Oakland (94602) ***(G-11914)***
Wells Fargo & Company (PA)...866 249-3302
420 Montgomery St Frnt San Francisco (94104) ***(G-9429)***
Wells Fargo & Company...801 246-1774
420 Montgomery St Ste 600 San Francisco (94104) ***(G-9565)***
Wells Fargo Advisors LLC...415 291-1200
555 California St # 2300 San Francisco (94104) ***(G-10099)***
Wells Fargo Advisors LLC...562 594-1220
3020 Old Ranch Pkwy # 190 Seal Beach (90740) ***(G-10100)***
Wells Fargo Advisors LLC...818 226-2222
5820 Canoga Ave Ste 100 Woodland Hills (91367) ***(G-10101)***
Wells Fargo Bank Ltd...213 253-6227
333 S Grand Ave Ste 500 Los Angeles (90071) ***(G-9535)***
Wells Fargo Bank National Assn...818 766-7172
10225 Riverside Dr Toluca Lake (91602) ***(G-9430)***
Wells Fargo Bank National Assn (HQ)...415 396-7392
464 California St San Francisco (94104) ***(G-9431)***
Wells Fargo Bank National Assn...415 396-6267
120 Kearny St Ste 1750 San Francisco (94108) ***(G-9432)***
Wells Fargo Bank National Assn...415 396-6161
1 Montgomery St Ste 200 San Francisco (94104) ***(G-9433)***
Wells Fargo Bank National Assn...209 578-6810
1120 K St Modesto (95354) ***(G-9434)***
Wells Fargo Bank National Assn...408 998-3714
2170 Tully Rd San Jose (95122) ***(G-9435)***
Wells Fargo Bank National Assn...858 622-6958
4365 Executive Dr Fl 18 San Diego (92121) ***(G-9436)***
Wells Fargo Bank National Assn...858 646-0550
4475 Executive Dr Ste 100 San Diego (92121) ***(G-9437)***
Wells Fargo Bank National Assn...707 259-5552
901 Main St NAPA (94559) ***(G-9438)***
Wells Fargo Bank National Assn...925 746-3718
1200 Montego Walnut Creek (94598) ***(G-9439)***
Wells Fargo Bank National Assn...626 312-3006
9000 Flair Dr Fl 3 El Monte (91731) ***(G-9440)***
Wells Fargo Bank National Assn...858 454-0362
7714 Girard Ave La Jolla (92037) ***(G-9441)***
Wells Fargo Bank National Assn...916 724-2982
5007 Foothills Blvd Roseville (95747) ***(G-9442)***
Wells Fargo Bank National Assn...408 378-8155
60 W Hamilton Ave Campbell (95008) ***(G-9443)***
Wells Fargo Bank National Assn...626 685-9900
350 W Colorado Blvd # 100 Pasadena (91105) ***(G-9444)***
Wells Fargo Bank National Assn...415 777-9497
100 Spear St Ste 100 San Francisco (94105) ***(G-9445)***
Wells Fargo Bank National Assn...916 774-2249
1620 E Roseville Pkwy Roseville (95661) ***(G-9446)***
Wells Fargo Bank National Assn...626 573-1338
3440 Flair Dr El Monte (91731) ***(G-9447)***
Wells Fargo Bank National Assn...310 831-0632
28350 S Western Ave Rancho Palos Verdes (90275) ***(G-9448)***
Wells Fargo Bank National Assn...818 673-1857
17945 Chatsworth St Granada Hills (91344) ***(G-9449)***
Wells Fargo Bank National Assn...925 463-1983
5798 Stoneridge Mall Rd Pleasanton (94588) ***(G-9450)***
Wells Fargo Bank National Assn...916 440-4570
2301 Watt Ave Sacramento (95825) ***(G-9451)***
Wells Fargo Bank National Assn...510 276-0875
16000 Hesperian Blvd San Lorenzo (94580) ***(G-9452)***
Wells Fargo Bank National Assn...510 792-3512
39265 Paseo Padre Pkwy Fremont (94538) ***(G-9453)***
Wells Fargo Bank National Assn...510 266-0595
950 Southland Dr Hayward (94545) ***(G-9454)***
Wells Fargo Bank National Assn...805 541-0143
665 Marsh St San Luis Obispo (93401) ***(G-9455)***
Wells Fargo Bank National Assn...415 394-4021
420 Montgomery St Fl 6 San Francisco (94104) ***(G-9456)***
Wells Fargo Bank National Assn...415 222-6834
455 Market Fremont (94536) ***(G-9457)***
Wells Fargo Bank National Assn...415 222-1360
420 Montgomery St San Francisco (94104) ***(G-9458)***
Wells Fargo Bank National Assn...510 530-3095
2220 Mountain Blvd # 160 Oakland (94611) ***(G-9459)***
Wells Fargo Bank National Assn...562 924-1616
18712 Gridley Rd Cerritos (90703) ***(G-9460)***
Wells Fargo Bank National Assn...213 628-2251
333 S Hope St Ste D100 Los Angeles (90071) ***(G-11069)***
Wells Fargo Bank National Assn...510 745-5025
3440 Walnut Ave Fl 3 Fremont (94538) ***(G-9461)***
Wells Fargo Bank National Assn...310 285-5817
433 N Camden Dr Ste 1200 Beverly Hills (90210) ***(G-9462)***
Wells Fargo Bank National Assn...714 571-2200
2525 N Main St Ste 100 Santa Ana (92705) ***(G-9463)***
Wells Fargo Capital Fin Inc (HQ)...310 453-7300
2450 Colo Ave 3000w 3rd 3000 3rd Santa Monica (90404) ***(G-17618)***
Wells Fargo Capital Fin LLC (HQ)...310 453-7300
2450 Colo Ave Ste 3000w Santa Monica (90404) ***(G-9807)***
Wells Fargo Coml Dist Fin LLC...916 636-2020
3100 Zinfandel Dr Ste 255 Rancho Cordova (95670) ***(G-9790)***
Wells Fargo Dealer Svcs Inc (HQ)...949 727-1002
23 Pasteur Irvine (92618) ***(G-9766)***
Wells Fargo Home Mortgage Inc...925 288-7100
1350 Montego Walnut Creek (94598) ***(G-9905)***
Wells Fargo Home Mortgage Inc...916 782-2221
3010 Lava Ridge Ct # 150 Roseville (95661) ***(G-9906)***
Wells Fargo Home Mortgage Inc...760 603-7000
5540 Fermi Ct Fl 2002 Carlsbad (92008) ***(G-9907)***
Wells Fargo Insur Svcs USA Inc...707 769-2900
1039 N Mcdowell Blvd A Petaluma (94954) ***(G-10928)***
Wells Fargo Insur Svcs USA Inc...559 228-6300
5200 N Palm Ave Ste 114 Fresno (93704) ***(G-10929)***
Wells Fargo Insur Svcs USA Inc...818 464-9300
15303 Ventura Blvd Fl 7 Sherman Oaks (91403) ***(G-10930)***
Wells Fargo Insur Svcs USA Inc...916 589-8000
10940 White Rock Rd Rancho Cordova (95670) ***(G-10931)***
Wells Fargo Insur Svcs USA Inc...650 413-4499
959 Skyway Rd Ste 200 San Carlos (94070) ***(G-10932)***
Wells Fargo Insur Svcs USA Inc...925 988-1700
1350 Treat Blvd Ste 550 Walnut Creek (94597) ***(G-10933)***
Wells Fargo Insurance Svcs Inc...916 231-3400
11017 Cobblerock Dr # 100 Rancho Cordova (95670) ***(G-10934)***
Wells Fargo Intl Bond CIT...415 396-4943
525 Market St Fl 10 San Francisco (94105) ***(G-12131)***
Wells Fargo Securities LLC...415 645-0800
600 California St Fl 17 San Francisco (94108) ***(G-10102)***
Wells Frgo Insur Svcs Minn Inc...909 481-3802
4141 Inland Empire Blvd Ontario (91764) ***(G-10935)***
Wells Hse Hspice Fundation Inc...714 952-3795
245 Cherry Ave Long Beach (90802) ***(G-21027)***
Wellspace Health (PA)...916 325-5556
1820 J St Sacramento (95811) ***(G-22864)***
Wendel Rosen Black & Dean LLP (PA)...510 834-6600
1111 Broadway Ste 24 Oakland (94607) ***(G-23619)***
Wendt Landscape Services Inc...949 589-8680
29714 Avenida De Las Rancho Santa Margari (92688) ***(G-979)***
Wenmat Inc...916 485-0714
6001 Fair Oaks Blvd Carmichael (95608) ***(G-25597)***
Wentworth Hauser & Violich Inc...415 981-6911
301 Battery St Fl 4 San Francisco (94111) ***(G-10192)***
Wenzlau Engineering Inc...310 604-3400
2950 E Harcourt St Compton (90221) ***(G-7657)***
WERM Investments LLC...213 627-8070
14242 Ventura Blvd # 212 Sherman Oaks (91423) ***(G-18505)***
Wermers Multi-Family Corp (PA)...858 535-1475
5120 Shoreham Pl Ste 150 San Diego (92122) ***(G-1350)***
Werner Enterprises Inc...909 823-5803
10251 Calabash Ave Fontana (92335) ***(G-4302)***
Wesco Aircraft, Valencia *Also called Falcon Aerospace Holdings LLC* ***(G-27023)***
Wesco Aircraft Hardware Corp (HQ)...661 775-7200
24911 Avenue Stanford Valencia (91355) ***(G-8009)***
Wescom Central Credit Union (PA)...888 493-7266
123 S Marengo Ave Pasadena (91101) ***(G-9699)***
Wescon Technology Inc...408 727-8818
4655 Old Ironsides Dr # 170 Santa Clara (95054) ***(G-16080)***
Wescordon Incorporated (PA)...559 784-8371
661 W Poplar Ave Porterville (93257) ***(G-21028)***
Weslar Inc...661 702-1362
28310 Constellation Rd Valencia (91355) ***(G-3101)***
Weslend Financial, Santa Ana *Also called Lenox Financial Mortgage Corp* ***(G-9868)***
Wesley Palms, San Diego *Also called Front Porch Communities & Svcs* ***(G-21223)***
West Air Inc...559 454-7843
5005 E Andersen Ave Fresno (93727) ***(G-4878)***
West Anaheim Care Center, Anaheim *Also called West Anaheim Extended Care* ***(G-21029)***
West Anaheim Extended Care...714 821-1993
645 S Beach Blvd Anaheim (92804) ***(G-21029)***
West Anaheim Medical Center, Anaheim *Also called Prime Healthcare Anaheim LLC* ***(G-21809)***
West Antlope Vly Hstorical Soc...661 945-5369
45026 11th St W Lancaster (93534) ***(G-25055)***
West Central Produce Inc...213 629-3600
12840 Leyva St Norwalk (90650) ***(G-8788)***
West Cntinela Vly Care Ctr Inc...310 674-3216
950 S Flower St Inglewood (90301) ***(G-21030)***
West Coast AC Co Inc...619 561-8000
1155 Pioneer Way Ste 101 El Cajon (92020) ***(G-2415)***
West Coast Aggregate Supply...760 342-7598
92500 Airport Blvd Thermal (92274) ***(G-1109)***
West Coast Air Conditioning, Oxnard *Also called Gmh Inc* ***(G-17921)***
West Coast Ambulance Corp...310 435-1862
6739 S Victoria Ave Los Angeles (90043) ***(G-3856)***
West Coast Arborists Inc...805 671-5092
11405 Nardo St Ventura (93004) ***(G-1002)***
West Coast Arborists Inc...858 566-4204
8524 Commerce Ave Ste B San Diego (92121) ***(G-1283)***
West Coast Arborists Inc...909 783-6544
21718 Walnut Ave Grand Terrace (92313) ***(G-1003)***
West Coast Aviation Svcs LLC (PA)...949 852-8340
19711 Campus Dr Ste 200 Santa Ana (92707) ***(G-27719)***

ALPHABETIC

West Coast Beauty Supply Co (HQ).......707 748-4800
5001 Industrial Way Benicia (94510) *(G-7988)*
West Coast Charters, Santa Ana *Also called West Coast Aviation Svcs LLC (G-27719)*
West Coast Childrens Center.......510 269-9030
545 Ashbury Ave El Cerrito (94530) *(G-20233)*
WEST COAST CONSTRUCTION, Riverside *Also called Perry Coast Construction Inc (G-1635)*
West Coast Consulting LLC (PA).......949 250-4102
9233 Research Dr Ste 200 Irvine (92618) *(G-15879)*
West Coast Contractors Inc.......541 267-7689
2320 Courage Dr Ste 111 Fairfield (94533) *(G-1715)*
West Coast Coupon Inc.......818 341-2400
9400 Oso Ave Chatsworth (91311) *(G-14014)*
West Coast Drywall & Co Inc.......951 778-3592
1610 W Linden St Riverside (92507) *(G-2998)*
West Coast Firestopping Inc.......714 935-1104
1130 W Trenton Ave Orange (92867) *(G-3602)*
West Coast Grape Farming Inc.......209 538-3131
800 E Keyes Rd Ceres (95307) *(G-733)*
West Coast Hospitals Inc.......831 722-3581
919 Freedom Blvd Watsonville (95076) *(G-21419)*
West Coast Interiors Inc.......951 778-3592
1610 W Linden St Riverside (92507) *(G-2502)*
West Coast Legal Service Inc.......408 938-6520
1245 S Winchester Blvd # 208 San Jose (95128) *(G-17619)*
West Coast Ltg & Enrgy Inc.......951 296-0680
18550 Minthorn St Lake Elsinore (92530) *(G-2792)*
West Coast Mailing & Dist, San Diego *Also called Mopar Enterprises (G-14085)*
West Coast Maintenance Inc.......310 324-2511
16312 S Main St Gardena (90248) *(G-14465)*
West Coast Materials, Buena Park *Also called West Coast Sand and Gravel Inc (G-7001)*
West Coast Painting, Riverside *Also called West Coast Interiors Inc (G-2502)*
West Coast Physical Therapy, Laguna Niguel *Also called Mission Internal Med Group Inc (G-19754)*
West Coast Prime Meats LLC.......714 255-8560
344 Cliffwood Park St Brea (92821) *(G-8691)*
West Coast Radiology Center, Santa Ana *Also called Santa Ana Radiology Center (G-19953)*
West Coast Rags, Long Beach *Also called Coastal Closeouts Inc (G-17087)*
West Coast Sand and Gravel Inc (PA).......714 522-0282
7282 Orangethorpe Ave Buena Park (90621) *(G-7001)*
West Coast Santa Cruz Hotel, Santa Cruz *Also called Santa Cruz Hotel Associates (G-13213)*
West Coast Ship Supply.......562 435-5245
2835 E Ana St Compton (90221) *(G-8147)*
West Coast Storm Inc (PA).......909 890-5700
9701 Wilshire Blvd # 1000 Beverly Hills (90212) *(G-27802)*
West Coast Turf (PA).......760 340-7300
42540 Melanie Pl Palm Desert (92211) *(G-325)*
West Coast Valet Services, Burlingame *Also called Shud Wcv Inc (G-13587)*
West Corporation.......310 481-7878
170 N Church Ln Los Angeles (90049) *(G-17620)*
West Corporation.......949 294-2801
3063 W Chapman Ave # 2353 Orange (92868) *(G-17621)*
West Cotton AG Management Inc.......559 945-2511
15900 W Dorris Huron (93234) *(G-734)*
West Countra Costa Youth Svcs (PA).......510 412-5647
263 S 20th St Richmond (94804) *(G-24287)*
West County Health Centers Inc.......707 869-2849
16312 3rd St Guerneville (95446) *(G-20234)*
West County Resource Recovery.......510 231-4200
101 Pittsburg Ave Richmond (94801) *(G-6612)*
West Covina Lanes, West Covina *Also called Bowlmor AMF Corp (G-18512)*
West Covina Medical Clinic Inc (PA).......626 960-8614
1500 W West Covina Pkwy West Covina (91790) *(G-20235)*
West Covina Physical Therapy, West Covina *Also called Doctors Hospital W Covina Inc (G-21544)*
West Dermatology Med MGT Inc.......909 793-3000
101 E Rdlnds Blvd Ste 212 Redlands (92373) *(G-10392)*
West End Yung MNS Christn Assn.......909 946-6120
1150 E Foothill Blvd Upland (91786) *(G-25401)*
West End Yung MNS Christn Assn.......909 477-2780
11200 Baseline Rd Rancho Cucamonga (91701) *(G-25402)*
West Escondido Healthcare LLC.......760 746-0303
201 N Fig St Escondido (92025) *(G-21031)*
West Flower Growers Inc.......805 488-0814
3623 Etting Rd Oxnard (93033) *(G-326)*
West Health Care, Bonita *Also called Paradise Valley Hospital Inc (G-22531)*
West Hills Construction Inc.......800 515-5270
423 Jenks Cir Ste 101 Corona (92880) *(G-1284)*
West Hills Golf Associates.......714 528-6400
1800 Carbon Canyon Rd Chino Hills (91709) *(G-19124)*
West Hills Hospital & Med Ctr, West Hills *Also called HCA Inc (G-21594)*
West Hollywood Sport Club, West Hollywood *Also called 24 Hour Fitness Usa Inc (G-18587)*
West Hotel Partners LP.......408 947-4450
300 Almaden Blvd San Jose (95110) *(G-13399)*
West Inn & Suites LLC.......760 448-4500
4970 Avenida Encinas Carlsbad (92008) *(G-13400)*
West Lake Touchless Car Wash.......650 992-5344
223 87th St Daly City (94015) *(G-17866)*
West Los Angeles V A Med Ctr, Los Angeles *Also called Veterans Health Administration (G-20196)*
West Medions, San Leandro *Also called KMA Emergency Services Inc (G-3810)*
West Oahu Mall Associates.......310 276-1290
1880 Century Park E # 810 Los Angeles (90067) *(G-12277)*
West Oakland Health Center, Oakland *Also called West Oakland Health Council (G-22865)*
West Oakland Health Council (PA).......510 465-1800
700 Adeline St Oakland (94607) *(G-22865)*
West Pacific Medical Lab, Santa Fe Springs *Also called California Lab Sciences LLC (G-26836)*
West Pico Foods Inc.......323 586-9050
5201 S Downey Rd Vernon (90058) *(G-8575)*
West Publishing Corporation.......424 243-2100
800 Crprate Pinte Ste 150 Culver City (90230) *(G-16081)*
West Riverside Veterinary Hosp.......951 686-2242
5488 Mission Blvd Riverside (92509) *(G-633)*
West San Crlos Ht Partners LLC.......408 998-0400
282 Almaden Blvd San Jose (95113) *(G-13401)*
West Side District Hospital.......805 763-4211
110 E North St Taft (93268) *(G-22029)*
West Side Rehab Corporation.......323 231-4174
1755 E M L King Jr Blvd Los Angeles (90058) *(G-11070)*
West States Skanska Inc.......970 565-4903
1995 Agua Mansa Rd Riverside (92509) *(G-2017)*
West Unfied Cmmnctons Svcs Inc.......925 988-7112
1676 N California Blvd Walnut Creek (94596) *(G-17622)*
West Valley Area Squad Club.......818 888-0980
5825 De Soto Ave Woodland Hills (91367) *(G-24997)*
West Valley Christian Academy, Tracy *Also called We Care Day Care & Pre School (G-24530)*
West Valley Cnstr Co Inc (PA).......408 371-5510
580 E Mcglincy Ln Campbell (95008) *(G-2018)*
West Valley Engineering Inc.......925 416-9707
3875 Hopyard Rd Ste 130 Pleasanton (94588) *(G-14818)*
West Valley Engineering Inc (PA).......408 735-1420
390 Potrero Ave Sunnyvale (94085) *(G-14982)*
West Valley Family YMCA.......818 774-2840
18810 Vanowen St Reseda (91335) *(G-24531)*
West Valley Jewish Cmnty Ctr.......818 348-0048
22622 Vanowen St Canoga Park (91307) *(G-19308)*
West Valley M R F, Fontana *Also called West Valley Mrf LLC (G-6613)*
West Valley Mrf LLC.......909 899-5501
13373 Napa St Fontana (92335) *(G-6613)*
West Valley Staffing Group, Sunnyvale *Also called West Valley Engineering Inc (G-14982)*
West Ventura Family Care Ctr.......805 641-5620
133 W Santa Clara St Ventura (93001) *(G-20236)*
West Ville Palm Desert.......760 346-2121
72840 Highway 111 Ste 115 Palm Desert (92260) *(G-11071)*
West Yost & Associates Inc (PA).......530 756-5905
2020 Res Pk Dr Ste 100 Davis (95618) *(G-26145)*
West-Spec Partners.......818 725-7000
20525 Nordhoff St Ste 42 Chatsworth (91311) *(G-7959)*
Westair Gas and Equipment, San Diego *Also called Laboratory Specialty Gases (G-8992)*
Westair Gases & Equipment Inc.......619 474-0079
2300 Haffley Ave National City (91950) *(G-7905)*
Westair Gases & Equipment Inc (PA).......866 937-8247
2506 Market St San Diego (92102) *(G-7906)*
Westak International Sales Inc (HQ).......408 734-8686
1116 Elko Dr Sunnyvale (94089) *(G-7658)*
Westamerica Bancorporation.......707 863-6029
4550 Mangels Blvd Suisun City (94534) *(G-9566)*
Westamerica Bank.......707 995-4140
15342 Lakeshore Dr Clearlake (95422) *(G-9536)*
Westar Capital Assoc II LLC.......714 481-5160
949 S Coast Dr Costa Mesa (92626) *(G-12352)*
Westar Manufacturing Inc.......562 633-0581
13217 Laureldale Ave Downey (90242) *(G-3603)*
Westar Marine Services, San Francisco *Also called Cross Link Inc (G-4766)*
Westar Transport.......559 834-3551
9220 E South Ave Selma (93662) *(G-4093)*
Westates Mechanical Corp Inc.......510 635-9830
734 Whitney St San Leandro (94577) *(G-2416)*
Westcal Management, Carmichael *Also called Pacific Cities Management Inc (G-11723)*
Westchester Emerson Cmnty, Los Angeles *Also called Los Angeles Unified School Dst (G-24072)*
Westcoast Childrens Clinic.......510 269-9030
3301 E 12th St Ste 259 Oakland (94601) *(G-22866)*
Westcoast Medial Imaging, Los Angeles *Also called Larchmont Radiology Med Group (G-19699)*
Westcoast Performance Pdts USA.......714 630-4411
3100 E Coronado St Anaheim (92806) *(G-12278)*
Westcoast Pipe Lining Div, Rialto *Also called State Pipe & Supply Inc (G-2001)*
Westcoast Warehousing LLC.......310 537-9958
100 W Manville St Rancho Dominguez (90220) *(G-4669)*
Westcoe Escrow Division, Riverside *Also called Westcoe Realtors Inc (G-11915)*
Westcoe Realtors Inc.......951 784-2500
7191 Magnolia Ave Riverside (92504) *(G-11915)*
Westcor Construction of Cal.......909 796-8900
2351 W Lugonia Ave Ste D Redlands (92374) *(G-1285)*
Westcore Croydon, San Diego *Also called Westcore Delta LLC (G-12353)*
Westcore Delta LLC.......858 625-4100
4435 Estgate Mall Ste 300 San Diego (92121) *(G-12353)*
Westech Systems Inc.......559 298-5237
827 Jefferson Ave Clovis (93612) *(G-2793)*
Wested.......510 302-4200
300 Lakeside Dr Fl 25th Oakland (94612) *(G-26820)*
Wested.......415 289-2300
180 Harbor Dr Ste 112 Sausalito (94965) *(G-26821)*
Wested (PA).......415 565-3000
730 Harrison St Ste 500 San Francisco (94107) *(G-26822)*
Wested.......415 565-3000
730 Harrison St Ste 500 San Francisco (94107) *(G-26823)*
Western Air & Refrigeration, Garden Grove *Also called Limbach Company LP (G-2281)*
Western Alliance Bank, Oakland *Also called Porrey Pines Bank Inc (G-9421)*
Western Alliance Bank.......408 423-8500
55 Almaden Blvd Ste 200 San Jose (95113) *(G-9537)*

ALPHABETIC

ALPHABETIC SECTION
Westin San Diego, San Diego

Western Alliance Bank....415 230-4834
455 Market St Ste 1050 San Francisco (94105) ***(G-9538)***

Western Alliance Bank....408 423-8500
55 Almaden Blvd Ste 200 San Jose (95113) ***(G-9539)***

Western Alliance Bank....916 851-6800
3035 Prospect Park Dr # 100 Rancho Cordova (95670) ***(G-9540)***

Western Alliance Bank....408 282-1670
1655 The Alameda San Jose (95126) ***(G-9541)***

Western Alliance Bank....408 423-8500
55 Almaden Blvd Ste 100 San Jose (95113) ***(G-9542)***

Western Alliance Bank....949 222-0855
7545 Irvine Center Dr # 200 Irvine (92618) ***(G-9543)***

Western Allied Mechanical Inc....650 326-8290
1180 Obrien Dr Menlo Park (94025) ***(G-2417)***

Western Allied Service Company....562 941-3243
12046 Florence Ave Santa Fe Springs (90670) ***(G-17925)***

Western America Properties LLC....310 374-4381
111 N Sepulveda Blvd # 330 Manhattan Beach (90266) ***(G-11916)***

Western Area Security Services, Burbank *Also called Callan Management Corporation* ***(G-16873)***

Western Asset Management Co (HQ)....626 844-9265
385 E Colorado Blvd # 250 Pasadena (91101) ***(G-10193)***

Western Asset Mrtg Capitl Corp....626 844-9400
385 E Colorado Blvd Pasadena (91101) ***(G-12279)***

Western Athletic Clubs Inc (HQ)....415 781-1874
1 Lombard St Lbby San Francisco (94111) ***(G-18702)***

Western Athletic Clubs Inc....415 945-3000
220 Corte Madera Town Ctr Corte Madera (94925) ***(G-18703)***

Western Athletic Clubs Inc....408 738-2582
3250 Central Expy Santa Clara (95051) ***(G-18704)***

Western Athletic Clubs Inc....650 593-1112
200 Redwood Shr Pkwy Redwood City (94065) ***(G-18705)***

Western Building Materials Co (PA)....559 454-8500
4620 E Olive Ave Fresno (93702) ***(G-2999)***

Western City Magazine, Sacramento *Also called League of California Cities* ***(G-27754)***

Western Communications, Newbury Park *Also called Hearst Communications Inc* ***(G-6005)***

Western Concrete Pumping Inc (PA)....760 598-7855
2181 La Mirada Dr Vista (92081) ***(G-3350)***

Western Convalescent Hospital, Los Angeles *Also called Tzippy Care Inc* ***(G-21397)***

Western Convelescence, Los Angeles *Also called Longwood Management Corp* ***(G-21297)***

Western Costume Leasing....818 760-0900
11041 Vanowen St North Hollywood (91605) ***(G-13805)***

Western Dental Services Inc....951 643-6104
3880 Chicago Ave Riverside (92507) ***(G-20284)***

Western Dental Services Inc....916 509-3350
8324 Elk Grove Florin Rd # 100 Sacramento (95829) ***(G-20285)***

Western Dental Services Inc....831 998-9427
921 S Main St Ste A Salinas (93901) ***(G-20286)***

Western Dental Services Inc (PA)....714 480-3000
530 S Main St Ste 600 Orange (92868) ***(G-20287)***

Western Division Regional Off, Long Beach *Also called Southern California Edison Co* ***(G-6240)***

Western Drug Medical Supply, Stockton *Also called H and H Drug Stores Inc* ***(G-8120)***

Western Drywall Inc....209 847-6401
4981 Salida Blvd Salida (95368) ***(G-3000)***

Western Energetix LLC....530 885-0401
2360 Lindbergh St Auburn (95602) ***(G-9010)***

Western Exterminator Company....310 274-9244
3333 W Temple St Los Angeles (90026) ***(G-14194)***

Western Exterminator Company....310 835-3513
1985 W Wardlow Rd Long Beach (90810) ***(G-14195)***

Western Exterminator Company....562 802-2238
15415 Marquardt Ave Santa Fe Springs (90670) ***(G-14196)***

Western General Agency Inc....818 766-6500
12200 Sylvan St Ste 140 North Hollywood (91606) ***(G-10936)***

Western General Holding Co (PA)....818 880-9070
5230 Las Virgenes Rd # 100 Calabasas (91302) ***(G-10481)***

Western General Insurance Co....818 880-9070
5230 Las Virgenes Rd Calabasas (91302) ***(G-10482)***

Western Growers Association (PA)....949 863-1000
15525 Sand Canyon Ave Irvine (92618) ***(G-25110)***

Western Health Advantage....916 567-1950
2349 Gateway Oaks Dr # 100 Sacramento (95833) ***(G-10250)***

Western Healthcare Center, Colton *Also called Western Healthcare Management* ***(G-21032)***

Western Healthcare Management....909 824-1530
1700 E Washington St Colton (92324) ***(G-21032)***

Western Hills Country Club, Chino Hills *Also called West Hills Golf Associates* ***(G-19124)***

Western Hills Golf & Cntry CLB, Chino *Also called Donovan Golf Courses MGT* ***(G-18736)***

Western Homes, Fresno *Also called Lassley Enterprises Inc* ***(G-11153)***

Western Host Inc (HQ)....650 692-3500
1 Old Bayshore Hwy Millbrae (94030) ***(G-13402)***

Western Insulfoam, Chino *Also called Carlisle Construction Mtls Inc* ***(G-7010)***

Western Magnesite Inc....818 255-1150
11927 Sherman Rd Unit 1 North Hollywood (91605) ***(G-3604)***

Western Meat Processors Inc....760 355-1175
502 E Barioni Blvd Imperial (92251) ***(G-414)***

Western Med Assoc Med Group (PA)....831 475-1111
1595 Soquel Dr Ste 330 Santa Cruz (95065) ***(G-20237)***

Western Med Center-Santa Ana, Santa Ana *Also called Western Medical Center Aux* ***(G-22030)***

Western Med Rhbltion Assoc LP....714 832-9200
14851 Yorba St Tustin (92780) ***(G-24288)***

Western Medical Center Aux (HQ)....714 835-3555
1301 N Tustin Ave Santa Ana (92705) ***(G-22030)***

Western Medical Center-Anaheim, Anaheim *Also called Anaheim Global Medical Center* ***(G-21452)***

Western Medical Management LLC....949 260-6575
3333 Michelson Dr Ste 735 Irvine (92612) ***(G-27279)***

Western Messenger Service Inc....415 487-4229
75 Columbia Sq San Francisco (94103) ***(G-4094)***

Western Milling LLC (HQ)....559 302-1000
31120 West St Goshen (93227) ***(G-9155)***

Western National Contractors....949 862-6200
8 Executive Cir Irvine (92614) ***(G-27280)***

Western National Properties (PA)....949 862-6200
8 Executive Cir Irvine (92614) ***(G-1351)***

Western National Securities (PA)....949 862-6200
8 Executive Cir Irvine (92614) ***(G-11917)***

Western Nevada Supply Co....530 582-5009
10990 Industrial Way A Truckee (96161) ***(G-8148)***

Western Oil & Spreading, Martinez *Also called Telfer Oil Company* ***(G-1873)***

Western Oilfields Supply Co (PA)....661 399-9058
3404 State Rd Bakersfield (93308) ***(G-14590)***

Western Operations, Rancho Cucamonga *Also called Gentex Corporation* ***(G-26526)***

Western Operations Center, Westlake Village *Also called Securitas SEC Svcs USA Inc* ***(G-16795)***

Western Overseas Corporation (PA)....562 985-0616
10731 Walker St Ste B Cypress (90630) ***(G-5189)***

Western Pacific Distrg LLC....714 974-6837
341 W Meats Ave Orange (92865) ***(G-7002)***

Western Pacific Packaging Inc....805 239-1188
2715 Adelaida Rd Paso Robles (93446) ***(G-17623)***

Western Paving Contractors Inc....626 338-7889
15533 Arrow Hwy Irwindale (91706) ***(G-1883)***

Western Precooling Systems....805 486-6371
761 Commercial Ave Oxnard (93030) ***(G-14591)***

Western Pump Inc (PA)....619 239-9988
3235 F St San Diego (92102) ***(G-18033)***

Western Region, Milpitas *Also called Xcerra Corporation* ***(G-7661)***

Western Regional Office, Rancho Cordova *Also called Ducks Unlimited Inc* ***(G-1020)***

Western Repacking Lllp....916 688-8443
8371 Carbide Ct Ste 200 Sacramento (95828) ***(G-17624)***

Western Rim Constructors Inc....760 489-4328
621 S Andreasen Dr Ste B Escondido (92029) ***(G-1884)***

Western Rim Pipeline, Lakeside *Also called A M Ortega Construction Inc* ***(G-2505)***

Western Roofing Service, San Leandro *Also called Roofing Constructors Inc* ***(G-3210)***

WESTERN SLOPE HEALTH CARE, Placerville *Also called Western Slope Health Center* ***(G-21033)***

Western Slope Health Center....530 622-6842
3280 Washington St Placerville (95667) ***(G-21033)***

Western Staffing Solutions LLC....951 545-4449
1235 Carbide Dr Corona (92881) ***(G-14819)***

Western Star Nurseries LLC....209 744-2552
9394 Robson Rd Galt (95632) ***(G-9228)***

Western State Design Inc (PA)....510 786-9271
2331 Tripaldi Way Hayward (94545) ***(G-7989)***

Western States Affiliate, Los Angeles *Also called American Heart Association Inc* ***(G-24868)***

Western States Fire Protection....562 731-2961
3720 Industry Ave Ste 107 Lakewood (90712) ***(G-2418)***

Western States Fire Protection....916 924-1631
4740 Northgate Blvd # 150 Sacramento (95834) ***(G-2419)***

Western States Info Netwrk Inc....916 263-1180
1825 Bell St Ste 205 Sacramento (95825) ***(G-26824)***

Western Sun Enterprises Inc....707 748-2542
4690 E 2nd St Ste 4 Benicia (94510) ***(G-2794)***

Western Tear-Off & Disposal....626 443-9984
10920 Grand Ave Temple City (91780) ***(G-3223)***

Western Towing, San Diego *Also called Sunbelt Towing Inc* ***(G-17895)***

Western Transit Systems Inc....949 515-0188
13591 Harbor Blvd Garden Grove (92843) ***(G-3871)***

Western United Insurance Co....800 959-9842
3349 Michelson Dr Ste 100 Irvine (92612) ***(G-10937)***

Western Waste Services, Temple City *Also called Western Tear-Off & Disposal* ***(G-3223)***

Western Wine Services Inc (PA)....707 645-4300
875 Hanna Dr American Canyon (94503) ***(G-4670)***

Western Youth Services....949 595-8610
26137 La Paz Rd Ste 230 Mission Viejo (92691) ***(G-24289)***

Westfield LLC (HQ)....813 926-4600
2049 Century Park E # 4100 Los Angeles (90067) ***(G-11072)***

Westfield America Inc (HQ)....310 478-4456
2049 Century Park E Fl 41 Los Angeles (90067) ***(G-11073)***

Westfield America Ltd Partnr....310 478-4456
2049 Century Park E Fl 41 Los Angeles (90067) ***(G-12026)***

Westfield America Ltd Partnr....310 277-3898
2049 Century Park E # 4100 Los Angeles (90067) ***(G-11074)***

Westgage Grdn Convalescent Ctr, Visalia *Also called Far West Inc* ***(G-21214)***

Westgate Gardens Care Center....559 733-0901
4525 W Tulare Ave Visalia (93277) ***(G-21034)***

Westgate Hotel, San Diego *Also called Sinclair Companies* ***(G-13258)***

Westgroup Kona Kai LLC....619 221-8000
1551 Shelter Island Dr San Diego (92106) ***(G-19125)***

Westgroup San Diego Associates....858 274-4630
1404 Vacation Rd San Diego (92109) ***(G-13403)***

Westin Bonaventure Ht & Suites, Los Angeles *Also called Interstate Hotels Resorts Inc* ***(G-12850)***

Westin Desert Willow....760 636-7003
75 Willow Ridge Palm Desert (92260) ***(G-13404)***

Westin Long Beach Hotel, The, Long Beach *Also called Noble/Utah Long Beach LLC* ***(G-13025)***

Westin Los Angeles Airport, Los Angeles *Also called Host Hotels & Resorts LP* ***(G-12774)***

Westin Los Angeles Airport, Los Angeles *Also called Host Hotels & Resorts LP* ***(G-12777)***

Westin Pasadena, The, Pasadena *Also called Brookfield Dtla Fund Office* ***(G-12471)***

Westin San Diego, San Diego *Also called Diamondrock San Dego Tnant LLC* ***(G-12570)***

Westin San Diego, San Diego *Also called W-Emerald LLC* ***(G-13387)***

ALPHABETIC

Westin Sfo, San Francisco *Also called Millbrae Wcp Hotel I LLC* ***(G-12996)***

Westlake Christian Terrace - E, Oakland *Also called Christian Church Homes* ***(G-11390)***

Westlake Development Group LLC (PA) ... 650 579-1010
520 S El Camino Real # 900 San Mateo (94402) ***(G-11075)***

Westlake Development Group LLC ... 650 579-1010
520 El Camino Real Fl 9 Belmont (94002) ***(G-27281)***

Westlake Financial Services, Los Angeles *Also called Westlake Services LLC* ***(G-9808)***

Westlake Health Care Center ... 805 494-1233
1101 Crenshaw Blvd Los Angeles (90019) ***(G-21035)***

Westlake Inn Hotel, Westlake Village *Also called Westlake Village Inn* ***(G-13405)***

Westlake Nail Spa ... 650 994-7777
233 Lake Merced Blvd Daly City (94015) ***(G-18706)***

Westlake Realty Group Inc (PA) ... 650 579-1010
520 S El Camino Real 9th San Mateo (94402) ***(G-11918)***

Westlake Services LLC ... 323 692-8800
4751 Wilshire Blvd # 100 Los Angeles (90010) ***(G-9808)***

Westlake Village Apartments, Daly City *Also called Gerson Baker & Associates* ***(G-11137)***

Westlake Village Golf Course, Westlake Village *Also called Pyj V A California Ltd Partnr* ***(G-18773)***

Westlake Village Inn ... 805 496-1667
31943 Agoura Rd Westlake Village (91361) ***(G-13405)***

Westland Floral, Carpinteria *Also called Westland Orchids Inc* ***(G-9229)***

Westland Hotel Corporation ... 209 931-3131
4219 E Waterloo Rd Stockton (95215) ***(G-13406)***

Westland Orchids Inc ... 805 684-1436
1400 Cravens Ln Carpinteria (93013) ***(G-9229)***

Westland Trailer Mfg, Lodi *Also called Bjj Company LLC* ***(G-4118)***

Westlink, Modesto *Also called Stanislaus Farm Supply Company* ***(G-9153)***

Westmed Ambulance ... 510 401-5420
14275 Wicks Blvd San Leandro (94577) ***(G-3857)***

Westmed Ambulance Inc ... 310 456-3830
3872 Las Flores Canyon Rd Malibu (90265) ***(G-3858)***

Westmed Ambulance Inc ... 310 219-1779
2537 Old San Pasqual Rd Escondido (92027) ***(G-3859)***

Westminster Gardens ... 626 359-2571
1420 Santo Domingo Ave Duarte (91010) ***(G-21420)***

Westminster Housing Parteners ... 714 891-3000
8140 13th St Westminster (92683) ***(G-11919)***

Westminster Presbyterian Ch ... 818 889-1491
32111 Watergate Rd Westlake Village (91361) ***(G-24532)***

Westminster Woods Camp & Confe ... 707 874-2426
6510 Bohemian Hwy Occidental (95465) ***(G-13473)***

Westmnster Prsbt Preschool Ctr, Westlake Village *Also called Westminster Presbyterian Ch* ***(G-24532)***

Westmont Living Inc ... 916 786-3277
707 Sunrise Ave Roseville (95661) ***(G-24854)***

Westmont Living Inc (PA) ... 858 456-1233
7660 Fay Ave Ste N La Jolla (92037) ***(G-24855)***

Weston Bnshf Rchfrt Rublcv & M ... 213 576-1000
333 S Hope St Fl 16 Los Angeles (90071) ***(G-23620)***

Weston Solutions Inc ... 760 795-6900
5817 Dryden Pl Ste 101 Carlsbad (92008) ***(G-26638)***

Westower Communications Inc ... 916 783-6400
2017 Opportunity Dr Ste 4 Roseville (95678) ***(G-28169)***

Westpac Materials, Orange *Also called Western Pacific Distrg LLC* ***(G-7002)***

Westpac Materials LLC ... 714 974-6837
341 W Meats Ave Orange (92865) ***(G-7003)***

Westpoint Marketing Intl Inc ... 323 233-0233
5901 Avalon Blvd Los Angeles (90003) ***(G-17625)***

Westport Capital Partners LLC ... 310 294-1234
2121 Rosecrans Ave # 4325 El Segundo (90245) ***(G-12354)***

Westport/Berger A Joint Ventr ... 626 447-2448
4333 E Live Oak Ave Arcadia (91006) ***(G-1479)***

Westpost Berkeley LLC ... 510 548-7920
200 Marina Blvd Berkeley (94710) ***(G-13407)***

Westrec Marina Management Inc ... 209 369-1041
14900 W Highway 12 Frnt Lodi (95242) ***(G-4773)***

Westridge Golf Inc ... 562 690-4200
1400 S La Habra Hills Dr La Habra (90631) ***(G-18798)***

Westrux International Inc ... 909 825-5121
2200 E Steel Rd Colton (92324) ***(G-5190)***

Westside Building Mtl Corp (PA) ... 714 385-1644
1111 E Howell Ave Anaheim (92805) ***(G-7004)***

Westside Childrens Center Inc ... 310 846-4100
5721 W Slauson Ave # 140 Culver City (90230) ***(G-24533)***

Westside Counseling Center ... 909 881-2425
1963 N E St San Bernardino (92405) ***(G-22187)***

Westside Health Center, Los Angeles *Also called Motion Picture and TV Fund* ***(G-21754)***

Westside Jewish Cmnty Ctr Inc (PA) ... 323 938-2531
5870 W Olympic Blvd Los Angeles (90036) ***(G-24998)***

Westside Lodge ... 415 864-1515
120 Page St San Francisco (94102) ***(G-24999)***

Westside Pavilion, Los Angeles *Also called Macerich Company* ***(G-11013)***

Westside Pump, Bakersfield *Also called Western Oilfields Supply Co* ***(G-14590)***

Westside Security Patrol, Bakersfield *Also called M & S Security Services Inc* ***(G-16729)***

Weststar Cinemas Inc ... 323 461-3331
6801 Hollywood Blvd # 335 Los Angeles (90028) ***(G-18354)***

Weststar Marine Services Inc ... 415 495-3191
50 Pier San Francisco (94158) ***(G-4776)***

Westview Cmnty Arts Program, Anaheim *Also called Westview Services Inc* ***(G-21037)***

Westview Healh Care Center ... 530 885-7511
12225 Shale Ridge Ln Auburn (95602) ***(G-21036)***

Westview Services Inc ... 714 956-4199
1701 S Euclid St Ste E Anaheim (92802) ***(G-21037)***

Westview Services Inc ... 714 418-2090
9421 Edinger Ave Westminster (92683) ***(G-24406)***

Westward Hospitality MGT ... 510 548-7920
200 Marina Blvd Berkeley (94710) ***(G-13408)***

Westwind Communications, Bakersfield *Also called Kbak TV Channel 29 CBS* ***(G-5878)***

Westwind Engineering Inc ... 310 831-3454
553 N Pcf Coastte B179 B Redondo Beach (90277) ***(G-26146)***

Westwind Media, Burbank *Also called Westwind Studios LLC* ***(G-18206)***

Westwind Media Inc ... 818 972-9000
100 W Alameda Ave Burbank (91502) ***(G-18205)***

Westwind Studios LLC ... 818 972-9000
100 W Alameda Ave Burbank (91502) ***(G-18206)***

Westwood Healthcare Center LP ... 310 826-0821
12121 Santa Monica Blvd Los Angeles (90025) ***(G-21038)***

Westwood Insurance Agency (HQ) ... 818 990-9715
8407 Fllbrook Ave Ste 200 Canoga Park (91304) ***(G-10938)***

Westwood Marquis Hotel & Grdns, Los Angeles *Also called W Los Angeles* ***(G-13385)***

Westwoodone ... 323 904-4660
5757 Wilshire Blvd # 660 Los Angeles (90036) ***(G-18443)***

Wet (PA) ... 818 769-6200
10847 Sherman Way Sun Valley (91352) ***(G-17626)***

Wetherby Asset Management ... 415 399-9159
580 California St Fl 8 San Francisco (94104) ***(G-10194)***

Wetzel & Sons Moving and Stor ... 818 890-0992
12400 Osborne St Pacoima (91331) ***(G-4392)***

Wetzel Trucking, Pacoima *Also called Wetzel & Sons Moving and Stor* ***(G-4392)***

Weyerhaeuser Company ... 562 983-6709
800 Pier T Ave Long Beach (90802) ***(G-1013)***

Weyerhaeuser Company ... 909 877-6100
17400 Slover Ave Fontana (92337) ***(G-6970)***

Weygandt & Associates ... 916 543-0431
1501 Avi Blvd Ste 100 Lincoln (95648) ***(G-18034)***

WF Cinema Holdings LP ... 805 379-8966
180 Promenade Way Ste R Westlake Village (91362) ***(G-18355)***

Wfc Holdings Corp (HQ) ... 415 396-7392
420 Montgomery St San Francisco (94104) ***(G-9464)***

Wfcf Technology E2040-030, Santa Monica *Also called Wells Fargo Capital Fin Inc* ***(G-17618)***

Wfg National Title Insur Co ... 408 560-3000
333 W Santa Clara St # 110 San Jose (95113) ***(G-11943)***

Wfg National Title Insur Co (PA) ... 818 476-4000
700 N Brand Blvd Ste 1100 Glendale (91203) ***(G-10538)***

Wfs, Los Angeles *Also called Worldwide Flight Services Inc* ***(G-4840)***

Wg, Santa Fe Springs *Also called Ethosenergy Field Services LLC* ***(G-1075)***

Wga West Inc ... 323 782-4512
7000 W 3rd St Los Angeles (90048) ***(G-13985)***

Wgg Enterprises Inc ... 626 442-5493
11340 Stewart St El Monte (91731) ***(G-3001)***

Whaling Bar & Grill, La Jolla *Also called Lav Hotel Corp* ***(G-12907)***

Whatever It Takes Inc ... 760 329-6000
10805 Palm Dr Desert Hot Springs (92240) ***(G-13409)***

Whatsapp Inc ... 650 336-3079
3561 Homestead Rd 416 Santa Clara (95051) ***(G-6099)***

Whb Corporation ... 213 624-1011
506 S Grand Ave Los Angeles (90071) ***(G-13410)***

Wheatland School District ... 530 633-3135
100 Wheatland Park Dr Wheatland (95692) ***(G-11920)***

Wheatland Wind Project LLC ... 888 903-6926
15445 Innovation Dr San Diego (92128) ***(G-6253)***

Wheel of Fortune, Culver City *Also called Quadra Productions Inc* ***(G-18137)***

Wheeler, M T Trucking & Custom, Modesto *Also called Melvin T Wheeler & Sons* ***(G-562)***

Whelan Security Co ... 310 343-8628
400 Continental Blvd El Segundo (90245) ***(G-16852)***

Whgca LLC ... 916 922-4700
2200 Harvard St Sacramento (95815) ***(G-13411)***

Whiskey Girl ... 619 236-1616
702 5th Ave San Diego (92101) ***(G-27282)***

Whispering Hope Care Center ... 209 473-3004
5320 Carrington Cir Stockton (95210) ***(G-21039)***

Whitaker Welness Institute In ... 949 851-1550
4321 Birch St Ste 100 Newport Beach (92660) ***(G-20238)***

White Nelson & Co Cpas LLP ... 714 978-1300
2875 Michelle Ste 300 Irvine (92606) ***(G-26457)***

White & Case LLP ... 213 687-9655
555 S Flower St Ste 2700 Los Angeles (90071) ***(G-23621)***

White Blossom Care Center, San Jose *Also called Plum Healthcare Group LLC* ***(G-20852)***

White Cap 24, Fairfield *Also called Hd Supply Construction Supply* ***(G-7686)***

White Cap 35, San Jose *Also called Hd Supply Construction Supply* ***(G-7687)***

White Cap Construction Supply ... 949 794-5300
1815 Ritchey St Santa Ana (92705) ***(G-7797)***

White Carnival LLC ... 310 914-1600
11812 San Vicente Blvd # 4 Los Angeles (90049) ***(G-27283)***

White Digital Media Inc ... 760 827-7800
5901 Priestly Dr Ste 300 Carlsbad (92008) ***(G-9175)***

White Hills Vineyard Ranc ... 805 934-1986
8385 Graciosa Rd Santa Maria (93455) ***(G-735)***

White House Properties, Encino *Also called Schweizer Rena* ***(G-11835)***

White House Sales, Sacramento *Also called Chem Quip Inc* ***(G-8014)***

White Memorial Med Group Inc (PA) ... 323 987-1300
1701 E Cesar E Chavez Ave # 510 Los Angeles (90033) ***(G-20239)***

White Memorial Medical Center (HQ) ... 323 268-5000
1720 E Cesar E Chavez Ave Los Angeles (90033) ***(G-22031)***

White Rabbit Partners Inc ... 310 975-1450
9000 W Sunset Blvd # 1500 West Hollywood (90069) ***(G-24856)***

White Sands of La Jolla Clinic, La Jolla *Also called Cal Southern Presbt Homes* ***(G-24574)***

Whitefield Medical Lab & Rdlgy, Pomona *Also called Whitefield Medical Lab Inc* ***(G-22299)***

Whitefield Medical Lab Inc (PA) ... 909 625-2114
764 Indigo Ct Ste A Pomona (91767) ***(G-22299)***

Whitegold Solutions Inc ... 415 456-4493
43 Fernwood Way Ste 210 San Rafael (94901) ***(G-16525)***

Whitehat Security Inc ... 408 343-8300
3970 Freedom Cir Santa Clara (95054) ***(G-16526)***

Whiting Concrete Construction, Rancho Murieta *Also called Whiting Construction Inc* **(G-3351)**
Whiting Construction Inc 916 354-2756
7281 Lone Pine Dr Rancho Murieta (95683) **(G-3351)**
Whiting-Turner Contracting Co 949 863-0800
250 Commerce Ste 150 Irvine (92602) **(G-1716)**
Whitmire Distribution, Valencia *Also called Cardinal Health Inc* **(G-8247)**
Whittier Active Club, Whittier *Also called 24 Hour Fitness Usa Inc* **(G-18596)**
Whittier City Community Svcs, Whittier *Also called City of Whittier* **(G-23760)**
Whittier Equipment Rentals 562 863-0641
11832 Bloomfield Ave Santa Fe Springs (90670) **(G-2019)**
Whittier Hills Health Care Ctr, Whittier *Also called Ensign Group Inc* **(G-20539)**
Whittier Hospital Med Ctr Inc 562 945-3561
9080 Colima Rd Whittier (90605) **(G-22032)**
Whittier Inst For Diabetes 877 944-8843
10140 Campus Point Dr San Diego (92121) **(G-26825)**
Whittier Service Center, Santa Fe Springs *Also called Southern California Edison Co* **(G-6239)**
Whole Child 562 692-0383
10155 Colima Rd Whittier (90603) **(G-24290)**
Whole Leaf Co LLC 831 755-2057
375 W Market St Salinas (93901) **(G-8789)**
Wholesale Air-Time Inc 951 693-1880
27515 Enterprise Cir W Temecula (92590) **(G-5732)**
Wholesale Fabrics, Moorpark *Also called Pindler & Pindler Inc* **(G-8321)**
Wholesale Fuels Inc 661 327-4900
2200 E Brundage Ln Bakersfield (93307) **(G-9035)**
Wl Spa LLC 213 487-2700
2700 Wilshire Blvd Los Angeles (90057) **(G-18707)**
Wic, Torrance *Also called Public Hlth Fndation Entps Inc* **(G-25325)**
Wic, Bakersfield *Also called Public Health California Dept* **(G-19899)**
Wic, El Monte *Also called Public Hlth Fndation Entps Inc* **(G-23037)**
Wic Prgram Admnstrative Office, San Diego *Also called San Dego State Univ Foundation* **(G-24172)**
Wicoro Inc (HQ) 626 962-4489
919 N Sunset Ave West Covina (91790) **(G-21421)**
Wideorbit Inc (PA) 415 675-6700
1160 Battery St Ste 300 San Francisco (94111) **(G-15544)**
Wiemar Distributors Inc 213 747-7036
1953 S Alameda St Los Angeles (90058) **(G-8790)**
Wier Construction Corporation 760 743-6776
16884 Old Survey Rd Escondido (92025) **(G-1717)**
Wightman Enterprises Inc 916 961-2959
8017 Sacramento St Fair Oaks (95628) **(G-14983)**
Wikia Inc 415 762-0780
360 3rd St Ste 750 San Francisco (94107) **(G-16269)**
Wikimedia Foundation Inc 415 839-6885
149 New Montgomery St # 6 San Francisco (94105) **(G-25598)**
Wilbur-Ellis Company LLC 559 866-5667
12550 S Colorado Ave Helm (93627) **(G-9156)**
Wilbur-Ellis Company LLC (HQ) 415 772-4000
345 California St Fl 27 San Francisco (94104) **(G-9157)**
Wilbur-Ellis Company LLC 760 352-2847
45 W Danenberg Rd El Centro (92243) **(G-9158)**
Wilbur-Ellis Company LLC 831 422-6473
1427 Abbott St Salinas (93901) **(G-9159)**
Wilco Imports Inc 650 204-7800
1811 Adrian Rd Burlingame (94010) **(G-9313)**
Wild Electric Incorporated 559 251-7770
4626 E Olive Ave Fresno (93702) **(G-2795)**
Wild Goose Storage Inc 530 846-7350
2780 W Liberty Rd Gridley (95948) **(G-6259)**
Wild Karma Inc 510 639-9088
400 Estudillo Ave Ste 100 San Leandro (94577) **(G-21040)**
Wild Palms Hotel & Bar, Sunnyvale *Also called Joie De Vivre Hospitality Inc* **(G-12867)**
Wild Side West (PA) 818 837-5000
311 Parkside Dr San Fernando (91340) **(G-14165)**
Wildcat Retro Brands LLC 213 572-0431
2701 Carrier Ave Commerce (90040) **(G-8416)**
Wilde & Guernsey Inc 805 646-7288
727 W Ojai Ave Ojai (93023) **(G-11921)**
Wildenradt-Mcmurray Inc 510 835-5500
568 7th St San Francisco (94103) **(G-7704)**
Wildhaven Ranch, Cedar Glen *Also called San Bernardino Mtns Wildlife* **(G-462)**
Wildlife International, Santa Clara *Also called Evans Analytical Group LLC* **(G-26853)**
Wildlife Waystation 818 899-5201
14831 Lttle Tjunga Cyn Rd Sylmar (91342) **(G-463)**
Wildomar Medical Offices, Wildomar *Also called Kaiser Foundation Hospitals* **(G-21650)**
Wildside, San Fernando *Also called Wild Side West* **(G-14165)**
Wildwood Express 559 805-3237
12416 Swanson Ave Kingsburg (93631) **(G-4303)**
Wiline Networks Inc (PA) 888 494-5463
1164 Triton Dr Foster City (94404) **(G-5733)**
Wilkie Masonry Inc 916 652-0118
4016 Hunter Oaks Ln Loomis (95650) **(G-2839)**
Will Perkins Inc 213 270-8400
617 W 7th St Fl 12 Los Angeles (90017) **(G-26266)**
Will Perkins Inc 415 896-0800
2 Bryant St Ste 300 San Francisco (94105) **(G-26267)**
Willamette Valley Trtmnt Ctr, Cupertino *Also called CRC Health Corporate* **(G-22718)**
Willdan Engineering 714 978-8200
2401 E Katella Ave # 300 Anaheim (92806) **(G-26147)**
Willdan Group Inc (PA) 800 424-9144
2401 E Katella Ave # 300 Anaheim (92806) **(G-26148)**
William Brammer 858 756-3088
9018 Artesian Rd San Diego (92127) **(G-8791)**
William C Arterberry 760 728-9096
40147 Calle Roxanne Fallbrook (92028) **(G-262)**
William E Heinselman 916 920-0220
3303 Luyung Dr Rancho Cordova (95742) **(G-26149)**
William F Kellogg Corporation 818 845-7455
475 W Riverside Dr 479dr Burbank (91506) **(G-8010)**
William H Warden III MD 562 424-6666
2760 Atlantic Ave Long Beach (90806) **(G-20240)**
William Hzmlhlch Archtects Inc 949 250-0607
2850 Redhill Ave Ste 200 Santa Ana (92705) **(G-26268)**
William L Lyon & Assoc Inc 916 447-7878
2801 J St Sacramento (95816) **(G-11922)**
William L Lyon & Assoc Inc 916 535-0356
8814 Madison Ave Fair Oaks (95628) **(G-11923)**
William Lettis & Associates 713 369-5400
1777 Botelho Dr Ste 262 Walnut Creek (94596) **(G-26826)**
William Love Swimming Pool, Compton *Also called City of Compton* **(G-19168)**
William Lyon Fin Services, Newport Beach *Also called Duxford Financial Inc* **(G-9837)**
William Lyon Homes (PA) 949 833-3600
4695 Macarthur Ct Ste 800 Newport Beach (92660) **(G-1393)**
William Morris Agency, Los Angeles *Also called William Morris Endeavor* **(G-18444)**
William Morris Consulting, Beverly Hills *Also called William Morris Endeavor* **(G-18445)**
William Morris Endeavor 310 285-9000
2624 Military Ave Los Angeles (90064) **(G-18444)**
William Morris Endeavor 310 285-9000
9601 Wilshire Blvd Fl 3 Beverly Hills (90210) **(G-18445)**
William Morris Endeavor Entert (PA) 310 285-9000
9601 Wilshire Blvd Fl 3 Beverly Hills (90210) **(G-18446)**
William Oneil & Co Inc 310 448-6800
12655 Beatrice St Los Angeles (90066) **(G-10103)**
William S Hart Pony & Softball 661 254-9780
23437 Valencia Blvd Valencia (91355) **(G-28099)**
William Warren Group Inc (PA) 310 451-2130
201 Wilshire Blvd Ste 102 Santa Monica (90401) **(G-17657)**
Williams & Sons Masonry Inc 619 443-1751
8531 Winter Gardens Blvd A Lakeside (92040) **(G-2840)**
Williams & Williams Home Care, Seal Beach *Also called Williams and Williams Homecare* **(G-14984)**
Williams and Williams Homecare 562 597-1006
4756 Hazelnut Ave Seal Beach (90740) **(G-14984)**
Williams Data Management, Vernon *Also called Williams Service Corporation* **(G-4708)**
Williams Service Corporation (PA) 323 234-3453
1925 E Vernon Ave Ste 4 Vernon (90058) **(G-4708)**
Williams Tank Lines (PA) 209 944-5613
1477 Tillie Lewis Dr Stockton (95206) **(G-4304)**
Williamson Enterprises Inc 310 822-6615
4095 Redwood Ave Los Angeles (90066) **(G-17776)**
Willis Allen Real Estate (PA) 858 459-4033
1131 Wall St La Jolla (92037) **(G-11924)**
Willis Allen Real Estate 858 756-2444
6024 Pasco Delicias Rancho Santa Fe (92067) **(G-11925)**
Willis Insurance Svcs Cal Inc 858 678-2000
4250 Executive Sq Ste 250 La Jolla (92037) **(G-10228)**
Willis Towers Watson, San Diego *Also called Wtw Delaware Holdings LLC* **(G-27724)**
Willits Hospital Inc 707 459-6801
1 Madrone St Willits (95490) **(G-22033)**
Willits Perpetual LLC 818 668-6800
21600 Oxnard St Woodland Hills (91367) **(G-17627)**
Willits Seniors Inc 707 459-6826
1501 Baechtel Rd Willits (95490) **(G-24291)**
Willmark Cmmnties Univ Vlg Inc (PA) 858 271-0582
9948 Hibert St Ste 210 San Diego (92131) **(G-11228)**
Willow Creek Care Center, Clovis *Also called Willow Creek Halthcare Ctr LLC* **(G-21042)**
Willow Creek Halthcare Ctr LLC 559 323-6200
650 W Alluvial Ave Clovis (93611) **(G-21041)**
Willow Creek Halthcare Ctr LLC 559 323-6200
650 W Alluvial Ave Clovis (93611) **(G-21042)**
Willow Creek Racquet Club, Citrus Heights *Also called Rolling Willow LLC* **(G-18675)**
Willow Creek Treatment Center, Santa Rosa *Also called Victor Treatment Centers Inc* **(G-24847)**
Willow Farms LLC 805 647-0720
9452 Telephone Rd Pmb 142 Ventura (93004) **(G-406)**
Willow Garage Inc 650 322-2584
921 E Charleston Rd Palo Alto (94303) **(G-26639)**
Willow Glen Hsing Partners LP 408 267-7252
465 Willow Glen Way # 100 San Jose (95125) **(G-11926)**
Willow Glen Villa, San Jose *Also called Atria Senior Living Group Inc* **(G-11090)**
Willow Glen Villa A 408 266-1660
1660 Gaton Dr San Jose (95125) **(G-11229)**
Willow Pass Healthcare Center, Concord *Also called Kissito Health Case Inc* **(G-22496)**
Willow Rock Center, San Leandro *Also called Telecare Corporation* **(G-22095)**
Willow Sprngs Alzhmrs Spcl Cr 530 242-0654
191 Churn Creek Rd Redding (96003) **(G-24857)**
Willow Tree Convalescent Hosp, Oakland *Also called Willow Tree Nursing Center* **(G-21422)**
Willow Tree Nursing Center, Oakland *Also called Covenant Care California LLC* **(G-20489)**
Willow Tree Nursing Center 510 261-2628
2124 57th Ave Oakland (94621) **(G-21422)**
Willows Care Rhabilitation Ctr, Willows *Also called Sunbridge Healthcare LLC* **(G-21114)**
Wilmark Development, San Diego *Also called Wilmark Management Services* **(G-11927)**
Wilmark Management Services (PA) 858 271-0583
9948 Hibert St Ste 210 San Diego (92131) **(G-11927)**
Wilmay Inc 805 524-2603
893 Oak Ave Fillmore (93015) **(G-17628)**
Wilmer Cutler Pick Hale Dorr 213 443-5300
350 S Grand Ave Ste 2100 Los Angeles (90071) **(G-23622)**
Wilmington Branch, Wilmington *Also called Banc of California Inc* **(G-9318)**

ALPHABETIC

Wilmington Schll Bys & Grls CL, Wilmington *Also called Boys and Girls Clubs of The La* ***(G-25215)***
Wilmon Corporation....951 685-7474
8951 Granite Hill Dr Riverside (92509) ***(G-21043)***
Wilmor & Sons Plumbing & Cnstr....916 381-9114
8510 Thys Ct Sacramento (95828) ***(G-2420)***
Wilner Klein Siegel....310 550-4595
9601 Wilshire Blvd # 700 Beverly Hills (90210) ***(G-23623)***
Wilshire Animal Hospital....310 828-4587
2421 Wilshire Blvd Santa Monica (90403) ***(G-634)***
Wilshire Associates Inc (PA)....310 451-3051
1299 Ocean Ave Ste 700 Santa Monica (90401) ***(G-27720)***
Wilshire Boulevard Temple....310 457-7861
11495 Pacific Coast Hwy Malibu (90265) ***(G-13474)***
Wilshire Center Dental Group....213 386-3336
3932 Wilshire Blvd # 102 Los Angeles (90010) ***(G-20288)***
Wilshire Consumer Credit....323 692-8585
4751 Wilshire Blvd Los Angeles (90010) ***(G-9767)***
Wilshire Country Club....323 934-6050
301 N Rossmore Ave Los Angeles (90004) ***(G-19126)***
Wilshire Health and Cmnty Svcs....805 434-3035
290 Heather Ct Templeton (93465) ***(G-21423)***
Wilshire Health and Cmnty Svcs....805 484-2777
903 Carmen Dr Camarillo (93010) ***(G-24858)***
Wilshire Hlth & Cmnty Svcs Inc....310 679-9732
11630 Grevillea Ave Hawthorne (90250) ***(G-21424)***
Wilshire Hlth & Cmnty Svcs Inc....559 582-4414
851 Leslie Ln Hanford (93230) ***(G-21425)***
Wilshire Insurance Company....661 940-7300
1206 W Avenue J Ste 100 Lancaster (93534) ***(G-10939)***
Wilshire Investments Corp....310 207-0704
12100 Wilshire Blvd # 1400 Los Angeles (90025) ***(G-11928)***
Wilshire Nursing & Rehab, Templeton *Also called Wilshire Health and Cmnty Svcs* ***(G-21423)***
Wilshire West LLC....310 828-2910
9595 Wilshire Blvd # 501 Beverly Hills (90212) ***(G-17867)***
Wilshire West Carwash, Beverly Hills *Also called Wilshire West LLC* ***(G-17867)***
Wilson Elser Moskowitz....213 443-5100
555 S Flower St Ste 2900 Los Angeles (90071) ***(G-23624)***
Wilson Hampton Pntg Contrs Inc....714 772-5091
1524 W Mable St Anaheim (92802) ***(G-2503)***
Wilson Sonsini Goodrich & Rosa....858 350-2300
12235 El Camino Real # 200 San Diego (92130) ***(G-23625)***
Wilson Sonsini Goodrich & Rosa (PA)....650 493-9300
650 Page Mill Rd Palo Alto (94304) ***(G-23626)***
Wilson Sonsini Goodrich & Rosa....415 947-2000
1 Market Plz Fl 33 San Francisco (94105) ***(G-23627)***
Wilson Stephen Construction Co, Anaheim *Also called S W Construction Inc* ***(G-3084)***
Wilson Supply, Compton *Also called Dnow LP* ***(G-4684)***
Wilson Turner Kosmo LLP....619 236-9600
550 W C St Ste 1050 San Diego (92101) ***(G-23628)***
Wilsonart LLC....562 921-7426
13911 Gannet St Santa Fe Springs (90670) ***(G-4671)***
Wimberly Allison Tong Goo Inc....949 574-8500
300 Spectrum Center Dr # 500 Irvine (92618) ***(G-26269)***
Wimer Construction....818 848-0400
10855 Wimer Country Rd Sunland (91040) ***(G-1718)***
Win River Casino Bingo, Redding *Also called Redding Rancheria* ***(G-13136)***
Win River Hotel Corporation....530 226-5111
5050 Bechelli Ln Redding (96002) ***(G-13412)***
Win Time Ltd (PA)....858 695-2300
9335 Kearny Mesa Rd San Diego (92126) ***(G-13413)***
Win-Dor Inc (PA)....714 576-2030
450 Delta Ave Brea (92821) ***(G-3102)***
Win-River Resort & Casino....530 243-3377
2100 Redding Rancheria Rd Redding (96001) ***(G-19309)***
Winbond Electronics Corp Amer (HQ)....408 943-6666
2727 N 1st St San Jose (95134) ***(G-7659)***
Wincere Inc....408 841-4355
2350 Mission College Blvd # 290 Santa Clara (95054) ***(G-16527)***
Winchester Mystery House LLC....408 247-2000
525 S Winchester Blvd San Jose (95128) ***(G-19310)***
Winchester Reo LLC....530 878-3000
3030 Legends Dr Meadow Vista (95722) ***(G-19127)***
Wind River Systems Inc (HQ)....510 748-4100
500 Wind River Way Alameda (94501) ***(G-15880)***
Wind River Systems Inc....858 824-3100
10505 Sorrento Valley Rd San Diego (92121) ***(G-26150)***
Windermere Real Estate East....760 568-2568
71691 Highway 111 Rancho Mirage (92270) ***(G-11929)***
Windes Mcclghry Accntancy Corp (PA)....562 435-1191
111 W Ocean Blvd Ste 22 Long Beach (90802) ***(G-26458)***
Windflower Holdings LLC....707 263-6101
625 16th St Lakeport (95453) ***(G-21044)***
Windham At Saint Agnes....559 449-8070
1100 E Spruce Ave Ofc Fresno (93720) ***(G-11230)***
Window Factory Inc....858 689-9737
7550 Miramar Rd Ste 220 San Diego (92126) ***(G-3103)***
Windrow Earth Transport Inc....909 355-5531
14032 Santa Ana Ave Fontana (92337) ***(G-2096)***
Windsor Capital Group Inc....805 988-0627
2101 W Vineyard Ave Oxnard (93036) ***(G-13414)***
Windsor Capital Group Inc....310 566-1100
3250 Ocean Park Blvd # 350 Santa Monica (90405) ***(G-13415)***
Windsor Capital Group Inc....310 566-1100
3250 Ocean Park Blvd # 350 Santa Monica (90405) ***(G-13416)***
Windsor Capital Group Inc....209 577-3825
3250 Ocean Park Blvd # 350 Santa Monica (90405) ***(G-13417)***
Windsor Capital Group Inc....209 577-3825
3250 Ocean Park Blvd # 350 Santa Monica (90405) ***(G-13418)***
Windsor Capital Group Inc....714 990-6000
900 E Birch St Brea (92821) ***(G-13419)***
Windsor Capital Group Inc....951 676-5656
29345 Rancho California Temecula (92591) ***(G-13420)***
Windsor Capital Group Inc....310 566-1100
3250 Ocean Park Blvd # 350 Santa Monica (90405) ***(G-13421)***
Windsor Capital Group Inc....310 566-1100
3250 Ocean Park Blvd # 350 Santa Monica (90405) ***(G-13422)***
Windsor Capital Group Inc....714 241-3800
1325 E Dyer Rd Santa Ana (92705) ***(G-13423)***
Windsor Capital Group Inc....951 276-1200
1510 University Ave Riverside (92507) ***(G-13424)***
Windsor Capital Group Inc....925 934-2000
2355 N Main St Walnut Creek (94596) ***(G-13425)***
Windsor Capital Holet Group, Sacramento *Also called Recp/Wndsor Scramento Ventr LP* ***(G-13133)***
Windsor Convalescent....925 689-2266
3806 Clayton Rd Concord (94521) ***(G-21045)***
Windsor Convalescent....831 424-0687
637 E Romie Ln Salinas (93901) ***(G-21046)***
Windsor Court/Stratford Place, Westminster *Also called Westminster Housing Parteners* ***(G-11919)***
Windsor Garden Conv Ctr Hwthrn, Hawthorne *Also called Sandhurst Convales Grp Ltd A* ***(G-20894)***
Windsor Gardens....562 422-9219
4333 Torrance Blvd Torrance (90503) ***(G-21047)***
Windsor Gardens....310 675-3304
13922 Cerise Ave Hawthorne (90250) ***(G-21048)***
Windsor Gardens (PA)....714 826-8950
3415 W Ball Rd Anaheim (92804) ***(G-21049)***
Windsor Gardens Convalescnt, National City *Also called Windsor Healthcare Management* ***(G-21052)***
Windsor Gardens Hea, North Hollywood *Also called Mariner Health Care Inc* ***(G-20773)***
Windsor Gardens Healthcare C....510 582-4636
1628 B St Hayward (94541) ***(G-21426)***
WINDSOR GARDENS OF FULLERTON, Fullerton *Also called Windsor Gardns Healthcare Cntr* ***(G-21050)***
Windsor Gardens of Long Beach, Torrance *Also called Windsor Gardens* ***(G-21047)***
WINDSOR GARDENS REHABILITATION CENTER OF SALINAS, Salinas *Also called Windsor Convalescent* ***(G-21046)***
Windsor Gardns Healthcare Cntr....714 871-6020
245 E Wilshire Ave Fullerton (92832) ***(G-21050)***
Windsor Golf Club Inc....707 838-7888
1340 19th Hole Dr Windsor (95492) ***(G-18799)***
Windsor Grdns Cnvalescent Hosp....323 937-5466
915 Crenshaw Blvd Los Angeles (90019) ***(G-21051)***
Windsor Grdns Cnvlescent Ctr A, Anaheim *Also called Windsor Gardens* ***(G-21049)***
Windsor Healthcare Management....619 474-6741
220 E 24th St National City (91950) ***(G-21052)***
Windsor Manor, Glendale *Also called Cal Southern Presbt Homes* ***(G-11107)***
Windsor Mnor Rhabilitation Ctr, Concord *Also called Windsor Convalescent* ***(G-21045)***
Windsor Monterey Care Ctr LLC....831 373-2731
1575 Skyline Dr Monterey (93940) ***(G-21427)***
Windsor Palms Care Ctr Artesia, Artesia *Also called Windsor Twin Palms Hlthcare* ***(G-21055)***
Windsor Rdge Rhblttion Ctr LLC....831 449-1515
350 Iris Dr Salinas (93906) ***(G-22867)***
Windsor Redding Care Ctr LLC....530 246-2586
2490 Court St Redding (96001) ***(G-21053)***
Windsor Redwoods LP....707 526-1020
790 Sonoma Ave Santa Rosa (95404) ***(G-17629)***
Windsor Skyline Care Ctr LLC....831 449-5496
348 Iris Dr Salinas (93906) ***(G-21054)***
Windsor Twin Palms Hlthcare....562 865-0271
11900 Artesia Blvd Artesia (90701) ***(G-21055)***
Windsor Vallejo Care Center, Vallejo *Also called Helios Healthcare LLC* ***(G-21264)***
Windwalker Security Patrol Inc....209 333-3953
23987 Nw Frontage Rd Acampo (95220) ***(G-16853)***
Wine Country Care Center....209 334-3760
321 W Turner Rd Lodi (95240) ***(G-21056)***
Wine Dept, Los Angeles *Also called Youngs Market Company LLC* ***(G-9121)***
Wine Warehouse, Commerce *Also called Ben Myerson Candy Co Inc* ***(G-9092)***
Wine Warehouse, Richmond *Also called Ben Myerson Candy Co Inc* ***(G-9093)***
Winegard Energy Inc....559 441-0243
2885 S Chestnut Ave Fresno (93725) ***(G-3002)***
Winegard Energy Inc....661 393-9467
2159 Zeus Ct Bakersfield (93308) ***(G-3003)***
Winegardner Masonry Inc....909 795-9711
32147 Dunlap Blvd Ste A Yucaipa (92399) ***(G-2841)***
Winfield Construction, Emeryville *Also called Alpha-Winfield Contractors Inc* ***(G-1124)***
Wing Lam Ha....626 462-0048
615 Las Tunas Dr Ste J Arcadia (91007) ***(G-21428)***
Wingert Grebing Brubaker & Jus....619 232-8151
600 W Broadway Ste 1200 San Diego (92101) ***(G-23629)***
Wingz Inc....415 420-2222
2800 3rd St San Francisco (94107) ***(G-5734)***
Winiarski Management Inc....707 944-2020
5766 Silverado Trl NAPA (94558) ***(G-9116)***
Winkler Advertising Inc....415 957-0242
301 Howard St Ste 2100 San Francisco (94105) ***(G-13942)***
Winmax Systems Corporation....408 894-9000
1551 Mccarthy Blvd # 101 Milpitas (95035) ***(G-15545)***
Winners Only Inc....760 599-0300
1365 Park Center Dr Vista (92081) ***(G-6838)***
Winning Performance Pdts Inc....818 367-1041
13010 Bradley Ave Sylmar (91342) ***(G-17630)***
Winnresidential Ltd Partnr....559 435-3434
2350 W Shaw Ave Ste 148 Fresno (93711) ***(G-17658)***

ALPHABETIC

Winsor House Compalessant 707 448-6458
101 S Orchard Ave Vacaville (95688) *(G-21057)*
Winsor House Convalescent Hosp, Vacaville *Also called Winsor House Compalessant (G-21057)*
Winston & Strawn LLP 650 858-6500
275 Middlefield Rd # 205 Menlo Park (94025) *(G-23630)*
Winston Retail Solutions LLC (PA) 415 558-9000
456 Montgomery St Lowr 5 San Francisco (94104) *(G-27721)*
Winter Care Center Sacramento 916 922-8855
501 Jessie Ave Sacramento (95838) *(G-21058)*
Winterthur U S Holdings Inc 213 228-0281
888 S Figueroa St Ste 570 Los Angeles (90017) *(G-10940)*
Winton Ireland Strom & Green (PA) 209 667-0995
627 E Canal Dr Turlock (95380) *(G-10941)*
Winton-Ireland, Strom and Gr, Turlock *Also called Winton Ireland Strom & Green (G-10941)*
Winward International (PA) 510 487-8686
31033 Huntwood Ave Hayward (94544) *(G-9230)*
Winward Silks, Hayward *Also called Winward International (G-9230)*
Winzler & Kelly 707 523-1010
2235 Mercury Way Ste 150 Santa Rosa (95407) *(G-26151)*
Wipfli LLP 510 768-0066
505 14th St Fl 5 Oakland (94612) *(G-27722)*
Wipli HFS Consultants, Oakland *Also called Wipfli LLP (G-27722)*
Wireless Lines, Los Angeles *Also called Cellular Palace Inc (G-7545)*
Wireless Store Inc 916 206-3600
11290 Point East Dr # 210 Rancho Cordova (95742) *(G-6100)*
Wirenetics Co, Valencia *Also called Circle W Enterprises Inc (G-7427)*
Wirtz Qulty Installations Inc 858 569-3816
7932 Armour St San Diego (92111) *(G-2842)*
Wirtz Tile & Stone Inc 858 569-3816
7932 Armour St San Diego (92111) *(G-3133)*
Wis, Sacramento *Also called Washington Inventory Service (G-17612)*
Wis, San Diego *Also called Washington Inventory Service (G-17613)*
Wis International 858 565-8111
9265 Sky Park Ct Ste 100 San Diego (92123) *(G-17631)*
Wisdom University 415 259-7122
35 Miller Ave Mill Valley (94941) *(G-25599)*
Wise Commerce Inc 855 469-4737
267 8th St San Francisco (94103) *(G-15546)*
Wish I Ah Care Center Inc 559 855-2211
1665 M St Fresno (93721) *(G-21059)*
Wish-Ah Skilled, Fresno *Also called Wish-I-Ah Skilled Nursing (G-21061)*
Wish-I-Ah Hlthcre & Wellness 559 855-2211
1665 M St Fresno (93721) *(G-21060)*
Wish-I-Ah Skilled Nursing 949 285-8859
1665 M St Fresno (93721) *(G-21061)*
Wismettac Asian Foods Inc (HQ) 562 802-1900
13409 Orden Dr Santa Fe Springs (90670) *(G-8956)*
Wismettac Fresh Fish, Santa Fe Springs *Also called Wismettac Asian Foods Inc (G-8956)*
Withrow Cattle 916 780-0364
5301 Pleasant Grove Rd Pleasant Grove (95668) *(G-441)*
Withrow Dairy, Pleasant Grove *Also called Withrow Cattle (G-441)*
Withrow Phrm & Hlth Spc Lab 323 721-4281
2235 Via Puerta Unit A Laguna Woods (92637) *(G-8307)*
Wjbradley Mortgage Capital, Newport Beach *Also called Emery Financial Inc (G-9921)*
WL Butler Inc 650 361-1270
204 Franklin St Redwood City (94063) *(G-1352)*
WLMD (PA) 209 723-9120
1715 Kibby Rd Merced (95341) *(G-3605)*
Wm B Saleh Co 559 255-2046
1364 N Jackson Ave Fresno (93703) *(G-2504)*
Wm Bolthouse Farms Inc (HQ) 661 366-7205
7200 E Brundage Ln Bakersfield (93307) *(G-102)*
Wm Healthcare Solutions Inc 713 328-7350
4280 Bandini Blvd Vernon (90058) *(G-6614)*
Wm Michael Stemler Inc (PA) 209 948-8483
3244 Brookside Rd Ste 200 Stockton (95219) *(G-10942)*
Wm Michael Stemler Inc 559 228-4144
7110 N Fresno St Ste 350 Fresno (93720) *(G-10943)*
Wm ONeill Lath and Plst Corp 408 329-1413
P.O. Box 60352 Sunnyvale (94088) *(G-1353)*
Wm Recycle America LLC 562 948-3888
8405 Loch Lomond Dr Pico Rivera (90660) *(G-6615)*
Wm S Hart Pony & Softball, Valencia *Also called William S Hart Pony & Softball (G-28099)*
Wm Vandergeest Landscape Care 714 545-8432
3342 W Castor St Santa Ana (92704) *(G-980)*
Wm Wireless Inc 562 633-9288
6723 N Paramount Blvd Long Beach (90805) *(G-5436)*
Wmbe Payrolling Inc 858 810-3000
9475 Chesapeake Dr Ste A San Diego (92123) *(G-14820)*
Wmi 562 977-4950
17100 Pioneer Blvd # 230 Artesia (90701) *(G-2421)*
Wmk Office San Diego LLC (PA) 858 569-4700
4780 Estgate Mall Ste 100 San Diego (92121) *(G-6839)*
Wmk Sacramento LLC 916 929-8855
2001 Point West Way Sacramento (95815) *(G-13426)*
WMS Transportation, Ventura *Also called Sam Hill & Sons Inc (G-1992)*
Wnc & Associates Inc 714 662-5565
17782 Sky Park Cir Irvine (92614) *(G-28100)*
Wnc Housing LP 714 662-5565
17782 Sky Park Cir Irvine (92614) *(G-12355)*
Wolf Firm A Law Corporation 949 720-9200
2955 Main St Ste 200 Irvine (92614) *(G-23631)*
Wolfe & Associates, Santa Barbara *Also called Ronald L Wolfe & Assoc Inc (G-11822)*
Wolfe Trucking Inc 818 376-6960
7131 Valjean Ave Van Nuys (91406) *(G-4305)*
Wolfsen Incorporated 209 827-7700
1269 W I St Los Banos (93635) *(G-17)*
Woltcom Inc 831 638-4900
2300 Tech Pkwy Ste 8 Hollister (95023) *(G-2796)*
Wolters Kluwer Corp Legal Svcs, Aliso Viejo *Also called Citizenhawk Inc (G-26967)*
Womans Alliance Woma 408 279-2962
234 E Gish Rd Ste 200 San Jose (95112) *(G-24292)*
Womans Thursday Club Fair Oak 916 967-7891
10625 Fair Oaks Blvd Fair Oaks (95628) *(G-25600)*
Women Infant & Children 562 570-4228
2525 Grand Ave Long Beach (90815) *(G-24293)*
Women' S Health, French Camp *Also called Healthy Beginnings French Camp (G-19553)*
Women's Health Center, Merced *Also called Golden Valley Health Centers (G-22736)*
Women's Imaging Center, Redding *Also called MD Imaging Inc A Prof Med Corp (G-19736)*
Womencom Networks Inc 650 378-6500
1820 Gateway Dr Ste 150 San Mateo (94404) *(G-16270)*
Womens Law Center 714 667-1038
950 W 17th St Ste D Santa Ana (92706) *(G-24294)*
Wonderful Citrus Packing LLC 805 525-3818
2707 W Telegraph Rd Fillmore (93015) *(G-224)*
Wonderful Citrus Packing LLC 661 720-2400
5286 S Del Rey Ave Del Rey (93616) *(G-604)*
Wonderful Citrus Packing LLC (HQ) 661 720-2400
1901 S Lexington St Delano (93215) *(G-605)*
Wonderful Citrus Packing LLC 559 798-3100
36445 Road 172 Visalia (93292) *(G-606)*
Wonderful Citrus Packing LLC 661 387-1288
13293 Famoso Rd Mc Farland (93250) *(G-607)*
Wonderful Citrus Packing LLC 805 988-1456
710 Del Norte Blvd Oxnard (93030) *(G-608)*
Wonderful Company LLC 661 720-2400
1901 S Lexington St Delano (93215) *(G-225)*
Wonderful Orchards LLC (PA) 661 399-4456
6801 E Lerdo Hwy Shafter (93263) *(G-210)*
Wonderful Orchards LLC 661 797-6400
13646 Highway 33 Lost Hills (93249) *(G-211)*
Wonderfulpistachiosandalmonds, Lost Hills *Also called Wonderful Orchards LLC (G-211)*
Wonderland Music Company Inc 818 840-1671
500 S Buena Vista St Burbank (91521) *(G-12230)*
Wondertreats Inc 209 521-8881
2200 Lapham Dr Modesto (95354) *(G-9314)*
Wonderware Corporation (HQ) 949 727-3200
26561 Rancho Pkwy S Lake Forest (92630) *(G-7210)*
Wood Bros Inc 559 924-7715
14147 18th Ave Lemoore (93245) *(G-2097)*
Wood Castle Construction Inc 626 966-8600
770 W Golden Grove Way Covina (91722) *(G-1286)*
Wood Gutmann Bogart Insur Brkg 714 505-7000
15901 Red Hill Ave # 100 Tustin (92780) *(G-10944)*
Wood Ranch Golf Club, Simi Valley *Also called American Golf Corporation (G-18712)*
Wood Rodgers Inc (PA) 916 341-7760
3301 C St Ste 100b Sacramento (95816) *(G-26152)*
Wood Smith Henning Berman LLP (PA) 310 481-7600
10960 Wilshire Blvd Fl 18 Los Angeles (90024) *(G-23632)*
Woodbridge Glass Inc 714 838-4444
14321 Myford Rd Tustin (92780) *(G-3418)*
Woodbridge Village Association 949 786-1800
31 Creek Rd Irvine (92604) *(G-25403)*
Woodcraft Rangers 213 749-3031
2111 Park Grove Ave Los Angeles (90007) *(G-25404)*
Wooden Valley Farms, Fairfield *Also called Lanza Vineyards Inc (G-168)*
Woodfin Suite Hotels LLC 858 314-7910
12555 High Bluff Dr # 330 San Diego (92130) *(G-13427)*
Woodfin Suites, Newark *Also called Hardage Investments Inc (G-10997)*
Woodfin Suites Hotel Brea, Brea *Also called Hardage Group of Companies (G-12692)*
Woodland Care Center LLC 818 881-4540
7120 Corbin Ave Reseda (91335) *(G-21429)*
Woodland Healthcare 530 756-2364
2660 W Covell Blvd Davis (95616) *(G-22034)*
Woodland Healthcare 530 668-2600
1207 Fairchild Ct Woodland (95695) *(G-22035)*
Woodland Jint Unified Schl Dst 530 662-0201
25 Matmor Rd Woodland (95776) *(G-3953)*
Woodland Lfyett Sklled Nursing, Lafayette *Also called Independent Quality Care Inc (G-21275)*
Woodland Lfytte Cnvlscent Hosp, San Ramon *Also called Independent Quality Care Inc (G-21274)*
Woodland Park Retirement Hotel, Pomona *Also called Longwood Management Corp (G-11160)*
Woodland Residential Services 530 419-0059
1381 E Gum Ave Woodland (95776) *(G-11231)*
Woodland Sklled Nursing Fcilty 530 668-1190
678 3rd St Woodland (95695) *(G-21062)*
Woodland Swim Team Bosters CLB 530 662-9783
155 West St Woodland (95695) *(G-25405)*
Woodley Lakes Golf Course 818 780-6886
6331 Woodley Ave Van Nuys (91406) *(G-18800)*
Woodmont Real Estate Svcs LP 707 569-0582
3883 Airway Dr Santa Rosa (95403) *(G-28170)*
Woodmont Realty Advisors Inc 650 592-3960
1050 Ralston Ave Belmont (94002) *(G-10564)*
Woodruff Spradlin & Smart 714 558-7000
555 Anton Blvd Ste 1200 Costa Mesa (92626) *(G-23633)*
Woodruff Convalescent Center, Bellflower *Also called Estrella Inc (G-20553)*
Woodruff-Sawyer & Co (PA) 415 391-2141
50 California St Fl 12 San Francisco (94111) *(G-10945)*
Woods C J Engineering Contrs, Yuba City *Also called Carl J Woods Construction Inc (G-2037)*
Woods Electric Company, Santa Fe Springs *Also called Harris L Woods Elec Contr (G-2608)*

ALPHABETIC

Woods Maintenance Services Inc 818 764-2515
7260 Atoll Ave North Hollywood (91605) *(G-3606)*
Woodside Group Inc 209 579-2030
3509 Coffee Rd Ste D10 Modesto (95355) *(G-9908)*
Woodside Healthcare Center, Sacramento *Also called W H C Inc (G-21022)*
Woodside Terrace, Redwood City *Also called Brookdale Lving Cmmunities Inc (G-20422)*
Woodspur Farming LLC 760 398-9464
52 200 Industrial Way Coachella (92236) *(G-10199)*
Woolf Enterprises, Huron *Also called California Valley Land Co Inc (G-477)*
Wor International Inc 626 812-8888
15612 1st St Irwindale (91706) *(G-8366)*
Word & Brown Insurance 714 567-4398
721 S Parker St Ste 200 Orange (92868) *(G-27284)*
Word and Brown, Orange *Also called Omega Insurance Services (G-10816)*
Word and Brown Hearing Ctr, Orange *Also called Providence Speech Hearing Ctr (G-22812)*
Wordsmart Corporation 858 565-8068
10025 Mesa Rim Rd San Diego (92121) *(G-15881)*
Work Force Services Inc 661 327-5019
300 Truxtun Ave Bakersfield (93301) *(G-14985)*
Work Force Staffing, Bakersfield *Also called Work Force Services Inc (G-14985)*
Workcare Inc 714 978-7488
300 S Harbor Blvd Ste 600 Anaheim (92805) *(G-27803)*
Workday Inc (PA) 925 951-9000
6230 Stoneridge Mall Rd Pleasanton (94588) *(G-15547)*
Workers Compensation (PA) 415 777-0777
1221 Broadway Ste 900 Oakland (94612) *(G-10483)*
Workflowone, Livermore *Also called Standard Register Inc (G-4703)*
Workforce, Santa Cruz *Also called His Manna Inc (G-27465)*
Workforce Development Bureau, Long Beach *Also called Career Transition Center (G-24320)*
Workforce Investment- Admin, Merced *Also called County of Merced (G-24330)*
Workforce Logic LLC 866 296-3343
19080 Lomita Ave Bldg 3 Sonoma (95476) *(G-27723)*
Workforce Resource Center, Santa Maria *Also called Employment Dev Cal Dept (G-14648)*
Workforcelogic 707 939-4300
425 California St San Francisco (94104) *(G-14821)*
Working Assets Long Distance, San Francisco *Also called Credo Mobile Inc (G-5584)*
Working Solutions Inc 818 366-5009
19360 Rinaldi St Ste 450 Northridge (91326) *(G-25111)*
Working With Autism 818 501-4240
16530 Ventura Blvd # 310 Encino (91436) *(G-22868)*
Workmens Auto Insurance Co 213 742-8700
714 W Olympic Blvd # 800 Los Angeles (90015) *(G-10484)*
Workrite Uniform Company Inc (HQ) 805 483-0175
1701 Lombard St Ste 200 Oxnard (93030) *(G-13649)*
Works Floor & Wall, The, Palm Springs *Also called Temalpakh Inc (G-1690)*
World Acceptance Group Corp (PA) 800 388-1266
8271 Melrose Ave Ste 205 Los Angeles (90046) *(G-16271)*
World Class Distribution Inc 909 574-4140
2121 Boeing Way Stockton (95206) *(G-4672)*
World Class Distribution Inc 909 574-4140
800 S Shamrock Ave Monrovia (91016) *(G-4673)*
World For US, San Diego *Also called Mirnavseh Inc (G-15306)*
World Gym Fitness Centers, Burbank *Also called Executive Fitness Management (G-18630)*
World Mark By Trend West, Oceanside *Also called World Mark of Oceanside (G-13428)*
World Mark of Oceanside 760 721-0890
1301 Carmelo Dr Oceanside (92054) *(G-13428)*
World Mark The Club, Palm Springs *Also called Wyndham Resort Dev Corp (G-17633)*
World Mark The Club, San Dimas *Also called Wyndham Resort Dev Corp (G-17634)*
World Private Security Inc 818 894-1800
16921 Parthenia St # 201 Northridge (91343) *(G-16854)*
World Service West 310 538-7000
1812 W 135th St Gardena (90249) *(G-4947)*
World Trade Ctr Ht Assoc Ltd 562 983-3400
701 W Ocean Blvd Long Beach (90831) *(G-13429)*
World Tuned Radio, Oceanside *Also called CK Enterprises Inc (G-17082)*
World Variety Produce Inc 323 588-0151
5325 S Soto St Vernon (90058) *(G-8792)*
World Vision International (HQ) 626 303-8811
800 W Chestnut Ave Monrovia (91016) *(G-25601)*
World Wide Technology Inc 310 537-8335
1165 W Walnut St Compton (90220) *(G-7211)*
Worldlink East, Los Angeles *Also called Worldlink LLC (G-17632)*
Worldlink LLC (PA) 323 866-5900
6100 Wilshire Blvd # 1400 Los Angeles (90048) *(G-17632)*
Worldmark Resort, Angels Camp *Also called Wyndham Resort Dev Corp (G-13442)*
Worldpac Inc (HQ) 510 742-8900
37137 Hickory St Newark (94560) *(G-6781)*
Worldsite.ws, Carlsbad *Also called Global Domains International (G-5616)*
Worldway Airmail Center, Los Angeles *Also called Lax International Service Ctr (G-17290)*
Worldwide Flight Services Inc 310 646-7510
5908 Avion Dr Los Angeles (90045) *(G-4948)*
Worldwide Flight Services Inc 310 342-7830
5758 W Century Blvd Los Angeles (90045) *(G-4840)*
Worldwide Ground Transportatio 408 727-0000
651 Aldo Ave Santa Clara (95054) *(G-3860)*
Worldwide Holdings Inc (PA) 213 236-4500
725 S Figueroa St # 1900 Los Angeles (90017) *(G-10946)*
Worldwide Intgrted Rsurces Inc 323 838-8938
7171 Telegraph Rd Montebello (90640) *(G-7990)*
Worldwide Produce, San Diego *Also called Green Farms Inc (G-8735)*
Worldwide Produce, Los Angeles *Also called Green Farms Inc (G-8736)*
Worldwide Security Associates (HQ) 310 743-3000
10311 S La Cienega Blvd Los Angeles (90045) *(G-16855)*
Worldwind Services LLC 661 822-4877
915 Tehachapi Wllw Spgs Tehachapi (93561) *(G-2797)*
Worleyparsons Group Inc 626 294-3300
125 W Huntington Dr Arcadia (91007) *(G-26153)*
Worleyparsons Group Inc 610 855-2000
721 Charles E Young Dr S Los Angeles (90095) *(G-26154)*
Worxsitehr Insur Solutions Inc 877 479-3591
5000 Parkway Calabasas # 302 Calabasas (91302) *(G-10947)*
Woundco Holdings Inc 310 551-0101
10877 Wilshire Blvd Los Angeles (90024) *(G-14477)*
Woven Digital Inc (PA) 310 488-8941
10381 Jefferson Blvd Culver City (90232) *(G-6101)*
Wow Party Rental Inc 714 367-3380
14575 Firestone Blvd La Mirada (90638) *(G-14592)*
Wp Electric Communications Inc 909 606-3510
14198 Albers Way Chino (91710) *(G-2798)*
Wpcs International Inc (PA) 707 421-1300
521 Railroad Ave Suisun City (94585) *(G-6102)*
Wpcs Intrntional-Suisun Cy Inc 916 624-1300
2208 Srra Madows Dr Ste B Rocklin (95677) *(G-2799)*
Wr Chavez Company, Poway *Also called Wr Chavez Construction Inc (G-1719)*
Wr Chavez Construction Inc 858 375-2100
12125 Kear Pl Ste A Poway (92064) *(G-1719)*
Wr Forde Associates 415 924-3072
984 Hensley St Richmond (94801) *(G-1885)*
Wragtime Air Freight Inc (PA) 800 586-9701
596 W 135th St Gardena (90248) *(G-4306)*
Wright Broadband Group Inc 858 362-0380
4413 La Jolla Village Dr San Diego (92122) *(G-28101)*
Wright Finley & Zak LLP 949 477-5050
4665 Macarthur Ct Ste 200 Newport Beach (92660) *(G-23634)*
Wrist Ship Supply, Compton *Also called West Coast Ship Supply (G-8147)*
Writers Guild America West Inc 323 951-4000
7000 W 3rd St Los Angeles (90048) *(G-25192)*
Writing Company, Culver City *Also called Social Studies School Service (G-7349)*
Wrns Studio 415 489-2268
501 2nd St Ste 402 San Francisco (94107) *(G-26270)*
Ws Hdm LLC 858 792-5200
15575 Jimmy Durante Blvd Del Mar (92014) *(G-13430)*
Ws Hdm LLC 858 792-5200
15575 Jimmy Durante Blvd Del Mar (92014) *(G-13431)*
Wsa Group Inc (PA) 310 743-3000
19208 S Vermont Ave 200 Gardena (90248) *(G-16856)*
Wsc America 562 367-4212
1 World Trade Ctr Ste 800 Long Beach (90831) *(G-5191)*
WSH&b, Los Angeles *Also called Wood Smith Henning Berman LLP (G-23632)*
Wsj Worldwide Inc 626 961-7380
16775 E Johnson Dr City of Industry (91745) *(G-6782)*
Wsm Investments LLC 818 332-4600
3990b Heritage Oak Ct Simi Valley (93063) *(G-12231)*
Wso2 Inc (PA) 650 745-4499
787 Castro St Mountain View (94041) *(G-15548)*
Wsp USA Corp 415 398-3833
405 Howard St Ste 500 San Francisco (94105) *(G-26155)*
Wtw Delaware Holdings LLC 858 523-5500
10955 Vista Sorrento Pkwy # 300 San Diego (92130) *(G-27724)*
Wu Yee Child Care Center, San Francisco *Also called Wu Yee Childrens Services (G-28171)*
Wu Yee Childrens Services 415 677-0100
880 Clay St San Francisco (94108) *(G-24534)*
Wu Yee Childrens Services 415 677-0100
831 Broadway San Francisco (94133) *(G-28171)*
Wulfsberg Reese Colving and 510 835-9100
300 Lakeside Dr Ste 2400 Oakland (94612) *(G-23635)*
Wurldtech Security Tech Ltd 604 669-6674
2623 Camino Ramon San Ramon (94583) *(G-7660)*
Wurms Janitorial Service Inc 951 582-0003
544 Bateman Cir Corona (92880) *(G-14466)*
Wurzel Landscape Maintenance 818 762-8653
3214 Oakdell Rd Studio City (91604) *(G-981)*
WW Grainger Inc 408 432-8200
2261 Ringwood Ave San Jose (95131) *(G-7484)*
Ww Lbv Inc 818 707-1220
30100 Agoura Rd Agoura Hills (91301) *(G-13432)*
Ww San Diego Harbor Island LLC 619 291-6700
1960 Harbor Island Dr San Diego (92101) *(G-13433)*
Wwl Vehicle Svcs Americas Inc 310 835-8806
500 E Water St Wilmington (90744) *(G-4674)*
Wyle Information Systems LLC 310 563-6694
1960 E Grand Ave Ste 900 El Segundo (90245) *(G-16211)*
Wyndgate Technologies 916 404-8400
4925 Robert J Mathews Pkw El Dorado Hills (95762) *(G-16528)*
Wyndham Anaheim Garden Grove, Garden Grove *Also called Ohi Resort Hotels LLC (G-13037)*
Wyndham Garden Hotel, San Jose *Also called Starlight Management Group (G-13287)*
Wyndham Garden Hotel, Commerce *Also called Wyndham International Inc (G-13438)*
Wyndham Garden Pierpont Inn, Ventura *Also called Fpl LLC (G-12651)*
Wyndham Hotels & Resorts, Carmel *Also called Wyndham International Inc (G-13437)*
Wyndham Hotels & Resorts, Fullerton *Also called Anaheim Park Hotel (G-12388)*
Wyndham Hotels & Resorts, Belmont *Also called Wyndham International Inc (G-13440)*
Wyndham Hotels & Resorts, San Jose *Also called Wyndham International Inc (G-13441)*
Wyndham International Inc 714 992-1700
222 W Houston Ave Fullerton (92832) *(G-13434)*
Wyndham International Inc 760 322-6000
888 E Tahquitz Canyon Way Palm Springs (92262) *(G-13435)*
Wyndham International Inc 619 239-4500
400 W Broadway San Diego (92101) *(G-13436)*
Wyndham International Inc 831 625-9500
1 Old Ranch Rd Carmel (93923) *(G-13437)*
Wyndham International Inc 323 887-4331
5757 Telegraph Rd Commerce (90040) *(G-13438)*

ALPHABETIC

ALPHABETIC SECTION Yancey Roofing, Sacramento

Wyndham International Inc 714 751-5100
3350 Ave Of The Arts Costa Mesa (92626) ***(G-13439)***
Wyndham International Inc 650 591-8600
400 Concourse Dr Belmont (94002) ***(G-13440)***
Wyndham International Inc 408 451-3050
1350 N 1st St San Jose (95112) ***(G-13441)***
Wyndham Irvn-Orange Cnty Arprt 949 863-1999
17941 Von Karman Ave Irvine (92614) ***(G-27285)***
Wyndham Resort Dev Corp 209 736-2999
123 Selkirk Ranch Rd Angels Camp (95222) ***(G-13442)***
Wyndham Resort Dev Corp 760 864-8726
1177 N Palm Canyon Dr Palm Springs (92262) ***(G-17633)***
Wyndham Resort Dev Corp 909 484-8500
140 Via Verde San Dimas (91773) ***(G-17634)***
Wyndham San Dego At Emrald Plz, San Diego *Also called Wyndham International Inc* ***(G-13436)***
Wyndham San Jose, San Diego *Also called Pacifica San Jose LP* ***(G-13069)***
Wynne Systems Inc (HQ) 949 224-6300
2603 Main St Ste 710 Irvine (92614) ***(G-15549)***
Wynwood At The Palms, Loma Linda *Also called Brookdale Snior Lving Cmmnties* ***(G-21167)***
X M G M, Lathrop *Also called Nbccat Corp* ***(G-17823)***
X Prize Foundation Inc 310 741-4880
800 Crprate Pinte Ste 350 Culver City (90230) ***(G-25000)***
X-Act Finish & Trim Inc 951 582-9229
248 Glider Cir Corona (92880) ***(G-3104)***
X3 Management Services Inc 760 597-9336
2128 Auto Park Way Escondido (92029) ***(G-28102)***
Xactly Corporation (PA) 408 977-3132
300 Park Ave Ste 1700 San Jose (95110) ***(G-15550)***
Xad Inc 650 386-6867
189 Bernardo Ave 100 Mountain View (94043) ***(G-27725)***
Xad Inc 415 480-6366
440 N Wolfe Rd Sunnyvale (94085) ***(G-13943)***
Xamarin Inc (PA) 855 926-2746
394 Pacific Ave Fl 4 San Francisco (94111) ***(G-15551)***
Xanterra Parks & Resorts Inc 760 786-2345
Hwy 190 Death Valley (92328) ***(G-13443)***
Xantrion Incorporated 510 272-4701
651 Thomas L Berkley Way Oakland (94612) ***(G-16529)***
Xap Corporation (PA) 310 743-0450
100 Crprate Pinte Ste 350 Culver City (90230) ***(G-15552)***
Xavient Info Systems Inc 805 955-4111
2125 N Madera Rd Ste B Simi Valley (93065) ***(G-15882)***
Xavor Corporation 949 529-7372
8925 Research Dr Irvine (92618) ***(G-16530)***
Xceed Financial Credit Union (PA) 800 932-8222
888 N Nash St El Segundo (90245) ***(G-9648)***
XCEL Mechanical Systems Inc 310 660-0090
1710 W 130th St Gardena (90249) ***(G-2422)***
Xcelmobility Inc 650 632-4210
2225 E Byshore Rd Ste 200 Palo Alto (94303) ***(G-15883)***
Xcerra Corporation 408 635-4300
1355 California Cir Milpitas (95035) ***(G-7661)***
Xcommerce Inc (PA) 310 954-8012
54 N Central Ave Ste 200 Campbell (95008) ***(G-15553)***
Xdbs Corporation 302 566-3006
3501 Jack Northrop Ave Hawthorne (90250) ***(G-26720)***
Xdbsb2b, Hawthorne *Also called Xdbs Corporation* ***(G-26720)***
Xdimensional Technologies Inc 714 672-8960
145 S State College Blvd # 160 Brea (92821) ***(G-16082)***
Xenos Fashion Inc 323 585-0088
1616 E 14th St Los Angeles (90021) ***(G-8417)***
Xerox Corporation 818 848-8676
914 S Victory Blvd Burbank (91502) ***(G-14130)***
Xerox Corporation 916 444-8100
560 J St Ste 300 Sacramento (95814) ***(G-7076)***
Xerox Corporation 626 294-3754
1218 S 5th Ave Monrovia (91016) ***(G-7077)***
Xerox Corporation 714 565-1100
1851 E 1st St Ste 200 Santa Ana (92705) ***(G-7078)***
Xerox Corporation 408 953-2700
2665 N 1st St Ste 200 San Jose (95134) ***(G-16309)***
Xerox Education Services LLC (HQ) 310 830-9847
2277 E 220th St Long Beach (90810) ***(G-16212)***
Xi Enterprise Inc 661 266-3200
2140 E Palmdale Blvd Palmdale (93550) ***(G-18708)***
Xl Construction Corporation 916 282-2900
9245 Laguna Springs Dr # 135 Elk Grove (95758) ***(G-1287)***
Xl Construction Corporation (PA) 408 240-6000
851 Buckeye Ct Milpitas (95035) ***(G-1720)***
Xl Specialty Insurance Corp 925 942-6142
1340 Treat Blvd Walnut Creek (94597) ***(G-10497)***
Xl Staffing Inc 619 579-0442
450 Fletcher Pkwy Ste 204 El Cajon (92020) ***(G-14822)***
Xld Group LLC 310 316-3636
3635 Fashion Way Torrance (90503) ***(G-13444)***
Xo Communications LLC 408 817-2800
1400 Parkmoor Ave San Jose (95126) ***(G-5735)***
Xojet Inc (PA) 650 594-6300
2000 Sierra Point Pkwy # 200 Brisbane (94005) ***(G-4949)***
Xoom Corporation (HQ) 415 777-4800
425 Market St Fl 12 San Francisco (94105) ***(G-9725)***
Xoriant Corporation (PA) 408 743-4427
1248 Reamwood Ave Sunnyvale (94089) ***(G-16531)***
Xoxo, City of Industry *Also called Kellwood Company LLC* ***(G-8348)***
Xoxo, City of Industry *Also called Kellwood Company LLC* ***(G-8391)***
Xp Systems Corporation (HQ) 805 532-9100
405 Science Dr Moorpark (93021) ***(G-16083)***
Xpo, Torrance *Also called Lomita Logistics LLC* ***(G-14080)***
Xpo Cartage Inc (HQ) 800 837-7584
5800 Sheila St Commerce (90040) ***(G-4095)***
Xpo Enterprise Services Inc 209 983-8285
5475 S Airport Way Stockton (95206) ***(G-4307)***
Xpo Enterprise Services Inc 858 569-8921
4965 Convoy St San Diego (92111) ***(G-4308)***
Xpo Enterprise Services Inc 408 435-3876
2171 Otoole Ave San Jose (95131) ***(G-4309)***
Xpo Enterprise Services Inc 559 485-1164
4195 E Central Ave Fresno (93725) ***(G-4310)***
Xpo Enterprise Services Inc 831 758-8874
787 Airport Blvd Salinas (93901) ***(G-4311)***
Xpo Enterprise Services Inc 818 890-2095
12466 Montague St Pacoima (91331) ***(G-4312)***
Xpo Enterprise Services Inc 714 282-7717
2102 N Batavia St Orange (92865) ***(G-4313)***
Xpo Enterprise Services Inc 916 399-8291
3516 Kiessig Ave Sacramento (95823) ***(G-4314)***
Xpo Enterprise Services Inc 949 581-9030
20697 Prism Pl Lake Forest (92630) ***(G-4315)***
Xpo Enterprise Services Inc 213 744-0664
1955 E Washington Blvd Los Angeles (90021) ***(G-4316)***
Xpo Enterprise Services Inc 760 922-8538
12555 Mesa Dr Blythe (92225) ***(G-4317)***
Xpo Enterprise Services Inc 707 584-0211
4095 S Moorland Ave Santa Rosa (95407) ***(G-4318)***
Xpo Enterprise Services Inc 916 399-8291
3810 Hill Rd Lakeport (95453) ***(G-4319)***
Xpo Enterprise Services Inc 510 785-6920
2200 Claremont Ct Hayward (94545) ***(G-4320)***
Xpo Enterprise Services Inc 951 685-1244
13364 Marlay Ave Fontana (92337) ***(G-4321)***
Xpo Enterprise Services Inc 562 946-8331
12903 Lakeland Rd Santa Fe Springs (90670) ***(G-4322)***
Xpo Logistics Supply Chain Inc 909 390-9799
5200b E Airport Dr Ontario (91761) ***(G-5192)***
Xpo Logistics Supply Chain Inc 559 408-7951
3825 S Willow Ave Fresno (93725) ***(G-5193)***
Xpo Logistics Supply Chain Inc 909 975-6300
5200a E Airport Dr Ontario (91761) ***(G-5194)***
Xqawesome Inc 949 929-9622
20 Mason Ln Ladera Ranch (92694) ***(G-24407)***
Xsolla (usa) Inc 818 435-6613
15260 Ventura Blvd # 2230 Sherman Oaks (91403) ***(G-5736)***
Xtra Department Inc 562 462-3800
12631 Imperial Hwy F106 Santa Fe Springs (90670) ***(G-27286)***
Xtraplus Corporation 510 897-1890
39889 Eureka Dr Newark (94560) ***(G-7212)***
Xtreme Zone Inc 559 474-6861
1740 E Shepherd Ave Fresno (93720) ***(G-19311)***
Xyka Inc 408 340-1923
5201 Great America Pkwy # 320 Santa Clara (95054) ***(G-15554)***
Xyratex Technology Ltd 916 375-8181
840 Embarcadero Dr Ste 80 West Sacramento (95605) ***(G-7213)***
Y & R, San Francisco *Also called Young & Rubicam Inc* ***(G-13944)***
Y & S Auto Body Shop, San Pedro *Also called Y & S Enterprises Inc* ***(G-17777)***
Y & S Enterprises Inc (PA) 310 548-1120
1441 N Gaffey St San Pedro (90731) ***(G-17777)***
Y M C A Childcare Resource Ser, Oceanside *Also called YMCA of San Diego County* ***(G-25414)***
Y M C A Los Cerritos, Bellflower *Also called Young Mens Chrstn Assc Gr L B* ***(G-25459)***
Y M C A Metro Clinic, Berkeley *Also called The Young Mens Chris Assoc of* ***(G-25375)***
Y M C A The, Long Beach *Also called Young Mens Chrstn Assc Gr L B* ***(G-25463)***
Y W C A of Sonoma County 707 546-9922
811 3rd St Ste 100 Santa Rosa (95404) ***(G-25406)***
Y, The, San Diego *Also called YMCA of San Diego County* ***(G-25416)***
Yagi Bros Inc 209 394-7311
5614 Lincoln Blvd Livingston (95334) ***(G-34)***
Yagi Bros Produce, Livingston *Also called Yagi Bros Inc* ***(G-34)***
Yahoo Inc 408 349-5080
3420 Central Expy Santa Clara (95051) ***(G-5737)***
Yahoo Inc (PA) 408 349-3300
701 First Ave Sunnyvale (94089) ***(G-16084)***
Yale/Chase Eqp & Svcs Inc (PA) 562 463-8000
2615 Pellissier Pl City of Industry (90601) ***(G-7907)***
Yaley Enterprises Inc 530 365-5252
7664 Avianca Dr Redding (96002) ***(G-8149)***
Yamaha Corporation of America (HQ) 714 522-9011
6600 Orangethorpe Ave Buena Park (90620) ***(G-8150)***
Yamaha Marine Division, Cypress *Also called Yamaha Motor Corporation USA* ***(G-7485)***
Yamaha Motor Corporation USA (HQ) 714 761-7300
6555 Katella Ave Cypress (90630) ***(G-8011)***
Yamaha Motor Corporation USA 714 761-7300
6555 Katella Ave Cypress (90630) ***(G-7485)***
Yamaha Motor Corporation USA 714 236-9754
6555 Katella Ave Cypress (90630) ***(G-7815)***
Yamaha Music Corporation U S A, Buena Park *Also called Yamaha Corporation of America* ***(G-8150)***
Yamamoto of Orient Inc (HQ) 909 594-7356
122 Voyager St Pomona (91768) ***(G-8957)***
Yamamotoyama of America, Pomona *Also called Yamamoto of Orient Inc* ***(G-8957)***
Yamas Controls Group Inc (PA) 916 357-6000
5030 Hillsdale Cir # 102 El Dorado Hills (95762) ***(G-7751)***
Yamazen Inc 800 882-8558
23700 Via Del Rio Ste C Yorba Linda (92887) ***(G-7908)***
Yammer Inc 415 796-7401
410 Townsend St San Francisco (94107) ***(G-16532)***
Yancey Roofing, Sacramento *Also called Gudgel Roofing Inc* ***(G-3177)***

ALPHABETIC

Yang C Park 408 260-8066
3703 Payne Ave San Jose (95117) ***(G-14823)***
Yang Ming America Corporation 626 782-9797
181 W Huntington Dr # 202 Monrovia (91016) ***(G-5195)***
Yapstone Inc (PA) 866 289-5977
2121 N Calif Blvd Ste 400 Walnut Creek (94596) ***(G-17635)***
Yardi Systems Inc (PA) 805 699-2040
430 S Fairview Ave Santa Barbara (93117) ***(G-15555)***
Yates & Associates, Santa Ana *Also called Scottish American Insurance* ***(G-10863)***
YC Cable Usa Inc (HQ) 510 824-2788
44061 Nobel Dr Fremont (94538) ***(G-17636)***
Ycg LLC 760 230-8016
566 Shanas Ln Encinitas (92024) ***(G-28103)***
Year Round Landscape Maint Inc 909 597-7734
15189 Sierra Bonita Ln Chino (91710) ***(G-982)***
Yee Yuen Linen Service, Los Angeles *Also called Yuen Yee Laundry & Cleaners* ***(G-13508)***
Yefllow Shttle Vtrans Sdan Svc, San Leandro *Also called A-Para Transit Corp* ***(G-3738)***
Yellow A Cab 650 344-2060
5 Aragon Blvd Ste 125 San Mateo (94402) ***(G-3872)***
Yellow Cab Company 925 779-9292
100 Willow St Pacheco (94553) ***(G-3873)***
Yellow Cab Company Penninsula 408 739-1234
1330 Memorex Dr Santa Clara (95050) ***(G-3874)***
Yellow Cab Cooperative Inc 415 333-3333
1200 Mississippi St San Francisco (94107) ***(G-3875)***
Yellow Cabs, Santa Clara *Also called Yellow Cab Company Penninsula* ***(G-3874)***
Yellow Radio Service, San Diego *Also called Administrative Services SD* ***(G-3862)***
Yellow Transportation, Hayward *Also called Yrc Inc* ***(G-4323)***
Yellow Transportation, Gardena *Also called Yrc Inc* ***(G-4324)***
Yellow Transportation, Tracy *Also called Yrc Inc* ***(G-5251)***
Yelp Inc (PA) 415 908-3801
140 New Montgomery St # 900 San Francisco (94105) ***(G-16272)***
Yes Videocom Inc (PA) 408 907-7600
2805 Bowers Ave Ste 130 Santa Clara (95051) ***(G-18207)***
Yeshiva Rau Isacsohn Academy 323 549-3170
540 N La Brea Ave Los Angeles (90036) ***(G-24535)***
Yeshivath Torath Emeth Academy, Los Angeles *Also called Yeshiva Rau Isacsohn Academy* ***(G-24535)***
Ygnacio Convalescent Hospital, Walnut Creek *Also called Ocadian Care Centers LLC* ***(G-20819)***
Yhb Long Beach LLC 562 597-4401
2640 N Lakewood Blvd Long Beach (90815) ***(G-13445)***
Yhb San Francisco LLC 415 421-7500
85 5th St San Francisco (94103) ***(G-13446)***
YMCA, Burbank *Also called Young Mens Christian* ***(G-25439)***
YMCA, Alhambra *Also called Young MN Chrstn Assc* ***(G-24297)***
YMCA, Los Angeles *Also called Young Mens Chrstn Assn of La* ***(G-25466)***
YMCA, San Francisco *Also called Young Mens Christian Assoc SF* ***(G-25452)***
YMCA, Fullerton *Also called Young Mens Chrstn Assn Orange* ***(G-25473)***
YMCA, San Francisco *Also called Bayview Hunters Point Y M C A* ***(G-25205)***
YMCA Child Care Resource Svcs, San Diego *Also called YMCA of San Diego County* ***(G-25422)***
YMCA Crescenta-Canada, La Canada *Also called Crescenta-Canada YMCA* ***(G-25246)***
YMCA Glb Grant, Long Beach *Also called Young Mens Chrstn Assc Gr L B* ***(G-25462)***
YMCA Head Start, Berkeley *Also called The Young Mens Chris Assoc of* ***(G-25376)***
YMCA Metro La Summit Park, Valencia *Also called Young Mens Chrstn Assn of La* ***(G-25468)***
YMCA Metro La-52nd St School, Los Angeles *Also called Los Angeles Unified School Dst* ***(G-25291)***
YMCA of East Bay 510 654-9622
3265 Market St Oakland (94608) ***(G-25407)***
YMCA of East Bay 510 412-5647
263 S 20th St Richmond (94804) ***(G-25408)***
YMCA of East Bay 510 222-9622
4300 Lakeside Dr Richmond (94806) ***(G-25409)***
YMCA of East Valley (PA) 909 798-9622
500 E Citrus Ave Redlands (92373) ***(G-25410)***
YMCA of East Valley 909 881-9622
808 E 21st St San Bernardino (92404) ***(G-25411)***
YMCA of East Valley 909 425-9622
7793 Central Ave Highland (92346) ***(G-25412)***
YMCA of North Orange County 714 879-9622
2000 Youth Way Fullerton (92835) ***(G-25413)***
YMCA of San Diego County 760 754-6042
1310 Union Plaza Ct # 200 Oceanside (92054) ***(G-25414)***
YMCA of San Diego County 858 453-3483
8355 Cliffridge Ave La Jolla (92037) ***(G-25415)***
YMCA of San Diego County (PA) 858 292-9622
3708 Ruffin Rd San Diego (92123) ***(G-25416)***
YMCA of San Diego County 858 292-4034
200 Saxony Rd Encinitas (92024) ***(G-25417)***
YMCA of San Diego County 619 464-1323
8881 Dallas St La Mesa (91942) ***(G-25418)***
YMCA of San Diego County 760 745-7490
1050 N Broadway Escondido (92026) ***(G-25419)***
YMCA of San Diego County 619 281-8313
2927 Meade Ave San Diego (92116) ***(G-25420)***
YMCA of San Diego County 619 226-8888
2150 Beryl St Ste 18 San Diego (92109) ***(G-25421)***
YMCA of San Diego County 619 521-3055
3333 Camino Del Rio S # 400 San Diego (92108) ***(G-25422)***
YMCA of San Diego County 760 765-0642
4761 Pine Hills Rd Julian (92036) ***(G-25423)***
YMCA of San Diego County 619 298-3576
5505 Friars Rd San Diego (92110) ***(G-25424)***
YMCA of San Diego County 619 449-9622
10123 Hoffman Ln Santee (92071) ***(G-25425)***

ALPHABETIC

YMCA of San Diego County 760 758-0808
4701 Mesa Dr Oceanside (92056) ***(G-25426)***
YMCA of San Diego County 760 757-8270
333 Garrison St Oceanside (92054) ***(G-25427)***
YMCA of San Diego County 619 422-8068
50 4th Ave Chula Vista (91910) ***(G-25428)***
YMCA of San Francisco, San Francisco *Also called Young Mens Christian Assoc SF* ***(G-25450)***
YMCA of San Joaquin County 209 472-9622
2105 W March Ln Ste 1 Stockton (95207) ***(G-25429)***
YMCA of Santa Clara Valley, San Jose *Also called YMCA of Silicon Valley* ***(G-25434)***
YMCA of Silicon Valley (PA) 408 351-6400
80 Saratoga Ave Santa Clara (95051) ***(G-25430)***
YMCA of Silicon Valley 650 493-9622
1922 The Alameda Ste 300 San Jose (95126) ***(G-25431)***
YMCA of Silicon Valley 408 298-1717
1717 The Alameda San Jose (95126) ***(G-25432)***
YMCA of Silicon Valley 650 969-9622
2400 Grant Rd Mountain View (94040) ***(G-25433)***
YMCA of Silicon Valley 408 226-9622
5632 Santa Teresa Blvd San Jose (95123) ***(G-25434)***
YMCA of Silicon Valley 408 370-1877
13500 Quito Rd Saratoga (95070) ***(G-25602)***
YMCA of Stanislaus County, Modesto *Also called Young Mens Chrstn Assn Stanis* ***(G-25475)***
YMCA of The Mid-Peninsula Inc 650 493-9622
1922 The Alameda Ste 300 San Jose (95126) ***(G-25435)***
YMCA of Westchester, Los Angeles *Also called Young Mens Chrstn Assn of La* ***(G-25467)***
YMCA Overnight Camp, Julian *Also called YMCA of San Diego County* ***(G-25423)***
YMCA Richmond Afterschool Ctr, San Francisco *Also called Young Mens Christian Assnsf* ***(G-25444)***
YMCA San Francisco-Marin Cnty, San Rafael *Also called Young Mens Christian Assnsf* ***(G-25446)***
YMCA Youth & Family Service, San Rafael *Also called Young Mens Christian Assnsf* ***(G-25443)***
YMCA Youth & Family Services, San Diego *Also called YMCA of San Diego County* ***(G-25420)***
YMCA Youth & Family Services 619 543-9850
4080 Centre St Ste 203 San Diego (92103) ***(G-25436)***
Yodlee Inc (HQ) 650 980-3600
3600 Bridge Pkwy Ste 200 Redwood City (94065) ***(G-27726)***
Yoga Works Inc (PA) 310 664-6470
2215 Main St Santa Monica (90405) ***(G-18709)***
Yogaworks, Santa Monica *Also called Yoga Works Inc* ***(G-18709)***
Yogibotanicals 310 275-9891
1616 Preuss Rd Los Angeles (90035) ***(G-8958)***
Yokohl Valley Packing, Lindsay *Also called Lindsay Fruit Company LLC* ***(G-17295)***
Yolo Hospice Inc (PA) 530 758-5566
1909 Galileo Ct Ste A Davis (95618) ***(G-22616)***
Yorba Linda Country Club, Yorba Linda *Also called American Golf Corporation* ***(G-18857)***
Yorba Linda Medical Offices, Yorba Linda *Also called Kaiser Foundation Hospitals* ***(G-19659)***
Yorba Park Medical Group, Santa Ana *Also called St Joseph Heritage Med Group* ***(G-20055)***
Yorba Properties Corp 714 777-5112
20459 Yorba Linda Blvd Yorba Linda (92886) ***(G-11930)***
York Hlthcare Wllness Cntre LP 323 254-3407
6071 York Blvd Los Angeles (90042) ***(G-21063)***
Yosan University 310 301-8115
13315 Washington Blvd Marina Del Rey (90292) ***(G-20361)***
Yosemite Capital Mangagement, Tustin *Also called Hmwc Cpas & Business Advisors* ***(G-26368)***
Yosemite Concession Services, Yosemite Ntpk *Also called DNC Prks Rsrts At Yosemite Inc* ***(G-12581)***
YOSEMITE CONSERVANCY, San Francisco *Also called Yosemite Foundation* ***(G-25437)***
Yosemite Farm Credit Aca (PA) 209 667-2366
806 W Monte Vista Ave Turlock (95382) ***(G-9735)***
Yosemite Foundation 415 434-1782
101 Montgomery St # 1700 San Francisco (94104) ***(G-25437)***
Yosemite Lakes Owners Assn 559 658-7466
30250 Yosemite Springs Pk Coarsegold (93614) ***(G-25438)***
Yosemite Meat Company Inc 209 524-5117
601 Zeff Rd Modesto (95351) ***(G-4511)***
Yosemite Waters, Irvine *Also called Bastanchury Waters Company Inc* ***(G-8805)***
Yosemite Waters, Los Angeles *Also called Aab Water Company Inc* ***(G-6309)***
Yosh Enterprises Inc 408 287-4411
675 E Gish Rd San Jose (95112) ***(G-16857)***
Yoshimura Research & Dev Amer 909 628-4722
5420 Daniels St Ste A Chino (91710) ***(G-6783)***
You Consulting Group, Encinitas *Also called Ycg LLC* ***(G-28103)***
Young & Rubicam Inc 415 882-0600
303 2nd St Ste N300 San Francisco (94107) ***(G-13944)***
Young & Rubicam Inc 415 591-4000
303 2nd St Ste N350 San Francisco (94107) ***(G-27769)***
Young Bae Fashions Inc 323 583-8684
4811 Hampton St Vernon (90058) ***(G-8418)***
Young Brdcstg of San Francisco 415 441-4444
900 Front St San Francisco (94111) ***(G-5931)***
Young Communications, San Francisco *Also called Young Electric Co* ***(G-2800)***
Young Dowlin L 760 397-4104
101 Clay St San Francisco (94111) ***(G-226)***
Young Electric Co 415 648-3355
195 Erie St San Francisco (94103) ***(G-2800)***
Young Estates 805 446-1800
971 S Westlke Blvd 100 Westlake Village (91361) ***(G-11931)***
Young Mens Christian (PA) 818 845-8551
321 E Magnolia Blvd Burbank (91502) ***(G-25439)***

ALPHABETIC SECTION Z57 Inc (HQ)

Young Mens Christian Assn, South Pasadena *Also called Young Mens Chrstn Assn of La (G-25471)*
Young Mens Christian Assnsf......415 447-9602
57 Post St San Francisco (94104) *(G-25440)*
Young Mens Christian Assnsf......415 447-9622
63 Funston Ave San Francisco (94129) *(G-25441)*
Young Mens Christian Assnsf......415 447-9645
Main Post Gym Bldg 63 San Francisco (94129) *(G-25442)*
Young Mens Christian Assnsf......415 459-9622
1115 3rd St San Rafael (94901) *(G-25443)*
Young Mens Christian Assnsf......415 752-0790
4545 Anza St San Francisco (94121) *(G-25444)*
Young Mens Christian Assnsf......415 421-5721
914 Clay St San Francisco (94108) *(G-25445)*
Young Mens Christian Assnsf......415 492-9622
1500 Los Gamos Dr San Rafael (94903) *(G-25446)*
Young Mens Christian Asso......805 583-5338
3200 Cochran St Simi Valley (93065) *(G-19312)*
Young Mens Christian Asso......805 523-7613
4031 N Moorpark Rd Thousand Oaks (91360) *(G-25447)*
Young Mens Christian Assoc SF......415 831-4093
680 18th Ave San Francisco (94121) *(G-25448)*
Young Mens Christian Assoc SF......650 286-9622
1877 S Grant St San Mateo (94402) *(G-25449)*
Young Mens Christian Assoc SF (PA)......415 777-9622
50 California St Ste 650 San Francisco (94111) *(G-25450)*
Young Mens Christian Assoc SF......415 666-9622
360 18th Ave San Francisco (94121) *(G-25451)*
Young Mens Christian Assoc SF......415 957-9622
169 Steuart St San Francisco (94105) *(G-25452)*
Young Mens Christian Assoc SF......415 885-0460
246 Eddy St San Francisco (94102) *(G-25453)*
Young Mens Christian Assoc SF......415 883-9622
3 Hamilton Landing # 140 Novato (94949) *(G-25454)*
Young Mens Christian Associat......562 624-2376
525 E 7th St Long Beach (90813) *(G-25455)*
Young Mens Christn Assn Orange......714 771-1287
146 N Grand St Orange (92866) *(G-25456)*
Young Mens Chrstn Assc Gr L B......562 272-4884
4116 South St Lakewood (90712) *(G-25457)*
Young Mens Chrstn Assc Gr L B......562 596-3394
1720 N Bellflower Blvd Long Beach (90815) *(G-25458)*
Young Mens Chrstn Assc Gr L B......562 925-1292
15530 Woodruff Ave Bellflower (90706) *(G-25459)*
Young Mens Chrstn Assc Gr L B......562 425-7431
5835 Carson St Lakewood (90713) *(G-25460)*
Young Mens Chrstn Assc Gr L B......562 423-0491
4949 Atlantic Ave Long Beach (90805) *(G-25461)*
Young Mens Chrstn Assc Gr L B......562 423-0491
4949 Atlantic Ave Long Beach (90805) *(G-25462)*
Young Mens Chrstn Assc Gr L B......562 633-0106
6125 Coke Ave Long Beach (90805) *(G-25463)*
Young Mens Chrstn Assn of La......818 989-3800
6901 Lennox Ave Van Nuys (91405) *(G-25464)*
Young Mens Chrstn Assn of La......626 799-9119
1605 Garfield Ave South Pasadena (91030) *(G-25465)*
Young Mens Chrstn Assn of La (PA)......213 351-2256
625 S New Hampshire Ave Los Angeles (90005) *(G-25466)*
Young Mens Chrstn Assn of La......310 216-9036
8015 S Sepulveda Blvd Los Angeles (90045) *(G-25467)*
Young Mens Chrstn Assn of La......661 253-3593
26147 Mcbean Pkwy Valencia (91355) *(G-25468)*
Young Mens Chrstn Assn of La......562 862-4201
11531 Downey Ave Downey (90241) *(G-24295)*
Young Mens Chrstn Assn of La......323 467-4161
1553 N Shrader Blvd Los Angeles (90028) *(G-24296)*
Young Mens Chrstn Assn of La......562 862-4201
11531 Downey Ave Downey (90241) *(G-25469)*
Young Mens Chrstn Assn of La......818 763-5126
5142 Tujunga Ave North Hollywood (91601) *(G-24536)*
Young Mens Chrstn Assn of La......213 624-2348
401 S Hope St Los Angeles (90071) *(G-25470)*
Young Mens Chrstn Assn of La......323 682-2147
1605 Garfield Ave South Pasadena (91030) *(G-25471)*
Young Mens Chrstn Assn Orange......949 642-9990
2300 University Dr Newport Beach (92660) *(G-25472)*
Young Mens Chrstn Assn Orange......714 879-9622
2000 Youth Way Fullerton (92835) *(G-25473)*
Young Mens Chrstn Assn Orange......949 859-9622
27341 Trabuco Cir Mission Viejo (92692) *(G-25474)*
Young Mens Chrstn Assn Stanis......209 578-9622
2700 Mchenry Ave Modesto (95350) *(G-25475)*
Young Mens Chrstn Assoc Gndl......818 484-8256
140 N Louise St Glendale (91206) *(G-25476)*
Young MN Chrstn Assc (PA)......626 576-0226
401 Corto St Alhambra (91801) *(G-24297)*
Young Realtors......805 497-0947
971 S Westlake Blvd # 100 Westlake Village (91361) *(G-11932)*
Young Systems Corporation......562 921-2256
13125 Midway Pl Cerritos (90703) *(G-7079)*
Young Womens Christian Associ......408 295-4011
375 S 3rd St San Jose (95112) *(G-25477)*
Young's Nursery, San Francisco *Also called Young Dowlin L (G-226)*
Youngs Holdings Inc (PA)......714 368-4615
14402 Franklin Ave Tustin (92780) *(G-9117)*
Youngs Market Company LLC (HQ)......714 368-4615
14402 Franklin Ave Tustin (92780) *(G-9118)*
Youngs Market Company LLC......408 782-3121
850 Jarvis Dr Morgan Hill (95037) *(G-9119)*
Youngs Market Company LLC......510 475-2200
5100 Franklin Dr Pleasanton (94588) *(G-9120)*
Youngs Market Company LLC......213 629-3929
500 S Central Ave Los Angeles (90013) *(G-9121)*
Youngs Market Company LLC......707 584-5170
256 Sutton Pl Ste 106 Santa Rosa (95407) *(G-9122)*
Youngs Market Company LLC......916 617-4402
3620 Industrial Blvd # 10 West Sacramento (95691) *(G-9123)*
Youngstown Grape Distrs Inc......916 635-2200
1625 G St Reedley (93654) *(G-609)*
Your Executive Solutions......562 388-4150
9054 Slauson Ave Pico Rivera (90660) *(G-14824)*
Your Man Tours Inc (HQ)......310 649-3820
100 N Sepulveda Blvd # 1700 El Segundo (90245) *(G-5004)*
Your Man Tours Inc......513 772-4411
100 N Sepulveda Blvd # 1700 El Segundo (90245) *(G-25603)*
Your Practice Online LLC......877 388-8569
18662 Macarthur Blvd # 200 Irvine (92612) *(G-5738)*
Your Way Fumigation Inc......951 699-9116
41880 Kalmia St Ste 170 Murrieta (92562) *(G-14197)*
Yourpeople Inc......415 798-9086
303 2nd St Ste 401 San Francisco (94107) *(G-10948)*
Youth For Change......530 605-1520
2400 Washington Ave Redding (96001) *(G-24298)*
Youth For Change (PA)......530 877-1965
7200 Skyway Paradise (95969) *(G-24299)*
Youth For Change......530 538-8347
2185 Baldwin Ave Oroville (95966) *(G-24300)*
Youth Homes Incorporated......925 933-2627
1159 Everett Ct Concord (94518) *(G-24859)*
Youth Treatment & Educatn Crt, NAPA *Also called San Francisco City & County (G-24181)*
Youth Uprising......510 777-9909
8711 Macarthur Blvd Oakland (94605) *(G-14986)*
Ypcom LLC (HQ)......818 937-5500
611 N Brand Blvd Fl 3 Glendale (91203) *(G-17637)*
Yrc Freight, Adelanto *Also called Yrc Inc (G-4712)*
Yrc Inc......510 783-7010
25555 Clawiter Rd Hayward (94545) *(G-4323)*
Yrc Inc......310 404-2221
15400 S Main St Gardena (90248) *(G-4324)*
Yrc Inc......760 246-0031
17401 Adelanto Rd Adelanto (92301) *(G-4712)*
Yrc Inc......916 371-4555
3210 52nd Ave Sacramento (95823) *(G-4325)*
Yrc Inc......209 833-1300
1535 E Pescadero Ave Tracy (95304) *(G-5251)*
Yrc Worldwide Inc......650 952-1112
201 Haskins Way South San Francisco (94080) *(G-4326)*
Yreka Employment Services, Yreka *Also called Siskiyou Opportunity Center (G-14787)*
Yreka Employment Services, Mount Shasta *Also called Siskiyou Opportunity Center (G-24387)*
Ytech, Monterey Park *Also called Syntelesys Inc (G-17914)*
Yti, San Pedro *Also called Yusen Terminals Inc (G-4765)*
Yuba City Nursing & Rehab LLC......530 671-0550
1220 Plumas St Yuba City (95991) *(G-21064)*
Yuba City Racquet Club Inc......530 673-6900
825 Jones Rd Yuba City (95991) *(G-19128)*
Yuba County Probation Dept, Marysville *Also called County of Yuba (G-23936)*
Yucaipa Companies LLC (PA)......310 789-7200
9130 W Sunset Blvd Los Angeles (90069) *(G-28104)*
Yucaipa Valley Water District (PA)......909 797-5117
12770 2nd St Yucaipa (92399) *(G-6409)*
Yucca Valley Fire Protection......760 365-3335
57485 Aviation Dr A Yucca Valley (92284) *(G-17638)*
Yuen SOO Benevolent Assn......209 464-3048
119 Chung Wah Ln Stockton (95202) *(G-25478)*
Yuen Yee Laundry & Cleaners......323 734-7205
2575 S Normandie Ave Los Angeles (90007) *(G-13508)*
Yuma Lakes Resort, Earp *Also called Colorado River Adventures Inc (G-13478)*
Yume Inc (PA)......650 591-9400
1204 Middlefield Rd Redwood City (94063) *(G-13945)*
Yuneec USA Inc......855 284-8888
5555 Ontario Mills Pkwy Ontario (91764) *(G-7662)*
Yupana LLC......925 482-0657
201 N Civic Dr Ste 180 Walnut Creek (94596) *(G-26156)*
Yusen Logistics Americas Inc......310 518-3008
2417 E Carson St Ste 100 Long Beach (90810) *(G-4675)*
Yusen Terminals Inc (HQ)......310 548-8000
701 New Dock St San Pedro (90731) *(G-4765)*
YWCA, Santa Rosa *Also called Y W C A of Sonoma County (G-25406)*
YWCA Contra Costa/Sacramento (PA)......925 372-4213
1320 Arnold Dr Ste 170 Martinez (94553) *(G-24301)*
YWCA of San Diego County (PA)......619 239-0355
1012 C St San Diego (92101) *(G-25479)*
Z & M Assciates Inc......408 996-8100
1601 S Danza Blvd Ste 150 Cupertino (95014) *(G-11933)*
Z Garcia Farm Labor, Arvin *Also called Edwardo Z Garcia (G-656)*
Z J'S Auto Body, Clovis *Also called Pk Autobody Inc (G-17765)*
Z Microsystems, San Diego *Also called Zmicro Inc (G-16086)*
Z The Fresno State Foundation, Fresno *Also called Calif Stat Univ Fres Foun (G-25510)*
Z Valet & Shuttle Service, Los Angeles *Also called Z Valet Inc (G-13806)*
Z Valet Inc......323 954-3700
4221 Wilshire Blvd 170-11 Los Angeles (90010) *(G-13806)*
Z-Best Concrete Inc......951 774-1870
2575 Main St Riverside (92501) *(G-3352)*
Z57 Inc (HQ)......858 623-5577
10045 Mesa Rim Rd San Diego (92121) *(G-13946)*

ALPHABETIC

Zabin Industries Inc (PA) — 213 749-1215
3957 S Hill St Ste A Los Angeles (90037) *(G-8330)*
Zact Mobile, Redwood City *Also called Itson Inc (G-7588)*
Zaharoni Holdings — 310 297-9722
5400 W Rosecrans Ave Lowr Hawthorne (90250) *(G-27287)*
Zanker Road Landfill, San Jose *Also called Zanker Road Resource MGT Ltd (G-6616)*
Zanker Road Resource MGT Ltd — 408 457-1189
675 Los Esteros Rd San Jose (95134) *(G-6616)*
Zantaz Inc (HQ) — 925 598-3000
5758 W Las Positas Blvd Pleasanton (94588) *(G-15556)*
Zantos Living Trust, Anaheim *Also called Westcoast Performance Pdts USA (G-12278)*
Zastrow Construction Inc — 323 478-1956
3267 Verdugo Rd Los Angeles (90065) *(G-1354)*
Zb National Association — 858 793-7400
11622 El Camino Real San Diego (92130) *(G-9465)*
Zb National Association — 310 258-9300
100 Crprate Pinte Ste 250 Culver City (90230) *(G-9466)*
Zb Rehab Staffing Inc — 650 396-2207
650 El Camino Real Ste M Redwood City (94063) *(G-14987)*
Zeeaero Inc — 650 964-4570
2700 Broderick Way Mountain View (94043) *(G-26157)*
Zeeto Media, San Diego *Also called Zeetogroup LLC (G-13947)*
Zeetogroup LLC — 888 771-9194
925 B St Fl 5 San Diego (92101) *(G-13947)*
Zefr Inc — 310 392-3555
1621 Abbot Kinney Blvd Venice (90291) *(G-18208)*
Zeiter Eye Medical Group Inc (PA) — 209 366-0446
255 E Weber Ave Stockton (95202) *(G-20241)*
Zelle Hofmann Voelbel Masn LLP — 415 693-0700
44 Montgomery St Ste 3400 San Francisco (94104) *(G-23636)*
Zellerbach Rehearsal Hall, San Francisco *Also called City & County of San Francisco (G-18381)*
Zelos Consulting LLC — 650 968-2881
2400 Wyandotte St B103 Mountain View (94043) *(G-28105)*
Zemarc Corporation (PA) — 323 721-5598
6431 Flotilla St Commerce (90040) *(G-7909)*
Zend Technologies Usa Inc — 408 253-8800
19200 Stevens Creek Blvd Cupertino (95014) *(G-15557)*
Zendesk Inc (PA) — 415 418-7506
1019 Market St San Francisco (94103) *(G-15884)*
Zenefits Ftw Insurance Svcs, San Francisco *Also called Yourpeople Inc (G-10948)*
Zenith A Fairfax Company, The, Woodland Hills *Also called Zenith Insurance Company (G-10485)*
Zenith Health Care — 626 578-0460
245 S El Molino Ave Pasadena (91101) *(G-11934)*
Zenith Infotech Limited — 510 687-1943
39675 Cedar Blvd Ste 240b Newark (94560) *(G-16085)*
Zenith Insurance Company (HQ) — 818 713-1000
21255 Califa St Woodland Hills (91367) *(G-10485)*
Zenith Insurance Company — 619 299-6252
7676 Hazard Center Dr # 1200 San Diego (92108) *(G-10486)*
Zenith Insurance Company — 925 460-0600
4460 Rosewood Dr Pleasanton (94588) *(G-10229)*
Zenith Talent Corporation — 844 467-2300
3315 San Felipe Rd Ste 37 San Jose (95135) *(G-14825)*
Zentek Corporation — 916 749-3610
3031 Stnfrd Rnch Rd 2 Rocklin (95765) *(G-15558)*
Zephyr Health Inc — 415 529-7649
450 Mission St Ste 201 San Francisco (94105) *(G-16213)*
Zephyr Real Estate, San Francisco *Also called Dppm Inc (G-11479)*
Zephyr River Expeditions Inc — 800 431-3636
22517 Parrotts Ferry Rd Columbia (95310) *(G-19313)*
Zephyr White Water Expeditions, Columbia *Also called Zephyr River Expeditions Inc (G-19313)*
Zerep Management Corporation — 626 961-6291
17445 Railroad St City of Industry (91748) *(G-6617)*
Zero Energy Contracting Inc — 626 701-3180
13850 Cerritos Corporate Cerritos (90703) *(G-2423)*
Zero Energy Contracting LLC — 626 701-3180
13850 Cerritos Corporate Cerritos (90703) *(G-2424)*
Zero Motorcycles Inc — 831 438-3500
380 El Pueblo Rd Scotts Valley (95066) *(G-6701)*
Zero Waste Solutions Inc — 925 270-3339
1850 Gateway Blvd # 1030 Concord (94520) *(G-27288)*
Zestfinance Inc — 323 450-3000
6636 Hollywood Blvd Los Angeles (90028) *(G-15559)*
Zettler Components Inc (PA) — 714 939-6699
1701 W Sequoia Ave Orange (92868) *(G-7663)*
Zhg Inc — 831 394-3321
2600 Sand Dunes Dr Monterey (93940) *(G-13447)*
Ziffren B B F G-L S&C Fnd — 310 552-3388
1801 Century Park W Los Angeles (90067) *(G-23637)*
Zignal Labs Inc — 415 683-7871
995 Market St Fl 2 San Francisco (94103) *(G-15560)*
Zikko Inc — 916 949-8989
6345 Auburn Blvd Ste C Citrus Heights (95621) *(G-4393)*
Zillionaire Empress Danielle B — 310 461-9923
8549 Wilshire Blvd # 817 Beverly Hills (90211) *(G-12132)*
Zim Industries Inc — 661 393-9661
7212 Fruitvale Ave Bakersfield (93308) *(G-3360)*
Zimmer Gnsul Frsca Partnr Amer, Los Angeles *Also called Zimmer Gunsul (G-26271)*
Zimmer Gunsul — 213 617-1901
515 S Flower St Ste 3700 Los Angeles (90071) *(G-26271)*
Zimmerman Roofing Inc — 916 454-3667
3675 R St Sacramento (95816) *(G-3224)*
Zinio Systems Inc — 415 494-2700
114 Sansome St Fl 4 San Francisco (94104) *(G-15885)*
Ziontech Solutions Inc — 408 434-6001
2665 N 1st St Ste 200 San Jose (95134) *(G-16533)*
Zippy Usa Inc — 949 366-9525
1 Morgan Irvine (92618) *(G-7486)*
Ziprealty Inc (HQ) — 510 735-2600
2000 Powell St Ste 300 Emeryville (94608) *(G-11935)*
Zipzoomfly, Newark *Also called Xtraplus Corporation (G-7212)*
ZI Technologies Inc — 408 240-8989
860 N Mccarthy Blvd Milpitas (95035) *(G-7214)*
ZMC Hotels LLC — 925 933-4000
1855 Olympic Blvd Ste 300 Walnut Creek (94596) *(G-13448)*
Zmicro Inc (PA) — 858 831-7000
9820 Summers Ridge Rd San Diego (92121) *(G-16086)*
Zmodo Technology Corp Ltd — 217 903-5673
17870 Castleton St # 200 City of Industry (91748) *(G-7664)*
Zodiac Inflight Innovations US, Brea *Also called Systems and Software Entps LLC (G-15488)*
Zoe Holding Company Inc — 415 421-4900
44 Montgomery St San Francisco (94104) *(G-28172)*
Zoel Holding Company Inc — 916 646-3100
2143 Hurley Way Sacramento (95825) *(G-14826)*
Zohar Construction Inc — 818 609-7473
4272 Pasadero Pl Tarzana (91356) *(G-1288)*
Zoic Inc — 310 838-0770
3582 Eastham Dr Culver City (90232) *(G-18209)*
Zoic Studios, Culver City *Also called Zoic Inc (G-18209)*
Zonare Medical Systems Inc (HQ) — 650 230-2800
420 Bernardo Ave Mountain View (94043) *(G-26827)*
Zonneveld Dairies Inc — 559 923-4546
1560 Cerini Ave Laton (93242) *(G-442)*
Zonneveld Farms — 559 923-4546
1560 Cerini Ave Laton (93242) *(G-443)*
Zoological Society San Diego (PA) — 619 231-1515
2920 Zoo Dr San Diego (92101) *(G-25071)*
Zoological Society San Diego — 760 747-8702
15500 San Pasqual Vly Rd Escondido (92027) *(G-25072)*
Zoological Society San Diego — 619 744-3325
2920 Zoo Dr San Diego (92101) *(G-25073)*
Zoosk Inc — 415 728-9543
989 Market St Fl 5 San Francisco (94103) *(G-5739)*
Zoove, Campbell *Also called Mblox Incorporated (G-15296)*
Zs Associates Inc — 805 413-5900
2535 W Hillcrest Dr # 100 Thousand Oaks (91320) *(G-27727)*
Zs Associates Inc — 650 762-7800
400 S El Camino Real # 1500 San Mateo (94402) *(G-17639)*
Zs Associates Inc — 858 677-2200
4365 Executive Dr # 1530 San Diego (92121) *(G-27728)*
Zscaler Inc — 408 533-0288
110 Rose Orchard Way San Jose (95134) *(G-15561)*
Zspace Inc — 408 498-4050
490 De Guigne Dr 200 Sunnyvale (94085) *(G-7487)*
Zubi Advertising Services Inc — 310 575-4839
11601 Wilshire Blvd Fl 5 Los Angeles (90025) *(G-13948)*
Zumwalt Construction Inc — 559 252-1000
5520 E Lamona Ave Fresno (93727) *(G-1721)*
Zuora Inc (PA) — 650 241-4508
1051 E Hillsdale Blvd # 600 Foster City (94404) *(G-5740)*
Zurich American Insurance Co — 213 270-0600
777 S Figueroa St Ste 400 Los Angeles (90017) *(G-10487)*
Zurich American Insurance Co — 415 538-7100
525 Market St Ste 2900 San Francisco (94105) *(G-10949)*
Zurich Financial Resources (PA) — 626 963-4398
1110 Kregmont Dr Glendora (91741) *(G-11936)*
Zvents Inc — 408 376-7346
199 Fremont St Fl 4 San Francisco (94105) *(G-13949)*
Zwicker & Associates PC — 925 689-7070
1320 Willow Paca Rd 730 Concord (94520) *(G-23638)*
Zws/ABS Joint Venture LLC — 510 461-1433
39899 Balentine Dr # 200 Newark (94560) *(G-14467)*
Zymax Envirotechnology Inc — 760 781-3338
600 S Andreasen Dr Escondido (92029) *(G-26902)*
Zymax Forensics, Escondido *Also called Zymax Envirotechnology Inc (G-26902)*
Zyme Solutions Inc (PA) — 650 585-2258
240 Twin Dolphin Dr Ste D Redwood City (94065) *(G-16273)*
Zymo Research Corp — 949 679-1190
17062 Murphy Ave Irvine (92614) *(G-26640)*
Zynga Inc (PA) — 855 449-9642
699 8th St San Francisco (94103) *(G-15886)*
Zynx Health Incorporated (HQ) — 310 954-1950
10880 Wilshire Blvd Los Angeles (90024) *(G-15562)*
Zyrion Inc — 408 524-7424
440 N Wolfe Rd Sunnyvale (94085) *(G-15887)*
Zyxel Communications Inc — 714 632-0882
1130 N Miller St Anaheim (92806) *(G-5741)*

COUNTY/CITY CROSS-REFERENCE INDEX

Alameda
Alameda
Albany
Berkeley
Castro Valley
Dublin
Emeryville
Fremont
Hayward
Livermore
Newark
Oakland
Piedmont
Pleasanton
San Leandro
San Lorenzo
Sunol
Union City

Alpine
Kirkwood

Amador
Fiddletown
Ione
Jackson
Pine Grove
Pioneer
Plymouth
Sutter Creek

Butte
Biggs
Chico
Durham
Forest Ranch
Gridley
Magalia
Oroville
Paradise

Calaveras
Angels Camp
Arnold
Bear Valley
Copperopolis
Murphys
San Andreas
Valley Springs

Colusa
Arbuckle
Colusa
Williams

Contra Costa
Alamo
Antioch
Bay Point
Brentwood
Byron
Clayton
Concord
Crockett
Danville
Diablo
El Cerrito
El Sobrante
Hercules
Lafayette
Martinez
Moraga
Oakley
Orinda
Pacheco
Pinole
Pittsburg
Pleasant Hill
Richmond
San Pablo
San Ramon
Walnut Creek

Del Norte
Crescent City
Smith River

El Dorado
Cameron Park
Camino
Diamond Springs
El Dorado
El Dorado Hills
Garden Valley
Kelsey
Lotus
Pacific House
Placerville
Shingle Springs
South Lake Tahoe
Twin Bridges

Fresno
Auberry
Big Creek
Caruthers
Clovis
Coalinga
Del Rey
Firebaugh
Five Points
Fowler
Fresno
Friant
Helm
Huron
Kerman
Kingsburg
Lakeshore
Laton
Mendota
Miramonte
Orange Cove
Parlier
Reedley
Riverdale
Sanger
Selma
Tollhouse
Tranquillity

Glenn
Orland
Willows

Humboldt
Arcata
Bayside
Blue Lake
Eureka
Fortuna
Garberville
Hoopa
Korbel
Loleta
McKinleyville
Petrolia
Trinidad
Willow Creek

Imperial
Bard
Brawley
Calexico
Calipatria
El Centro
Heber
Holtville
Imperial
Winterhaven

Inyo
Bishop
Death Valley
Independence
Little Lake
Lone Pine

Kern
Arvin
Bakersfield
Boron
Buttonwillow
Caliente
California City
Delano
Edison
Edwards
Edwards Afb
Fellows
Inyokern
Keene
Lake Isabella
Lamont
Lebec
Lost Hills
Maricopa
Mc Farland
Mc Kittrick
Mojave
Ridgecrest
Rosamond
Shafter
Taft
Tehachapi
Wasco

Kings
Avenal
Corcoran
Hanford
Kettleman City
Lemoore
Stratford

Lake
Clearlake
Clearlake Oaks
Hidden Valley Lake
Kelseyville
Lakeport
Lower Lake
Middletown
Upper Lake

Lassen
Herlong
Susanville

Los Angeles
Acton
Agoura
Agoura Hills
Agua Dulce
Alhambra
Altadena
Arcadia
Arleta
Artesia
Avalon
Azusa
Baldwin Park
Bell
Bell Gardens
Bellflower
Beverly Hills
Burbank
Calabasas
Calabasas Hills
Canoga Park
Canyon Country
Carson
Cerritos
Chatsworth
City of Industry
Claremont
Commerce
Compton
Covina
Cudahy
Culver City
Diamond Bar
Downey
Duarte
E Rncho Dmngz
El Monte
El Segundo
Encino
Gardena
Glendale
Glendora
Granada Hills
Hacienda Heights
Harbor City
Hawaiian Gardens
Hawthorne
Hermosa Beach
Hidden Hills
Hollywood
Huntington Park
Inglewood
Irwindale
La Canada
La Canada Flintridge
La Crescenta
La Mirada
La Puente
La Verne
Lake View Terrace
Lakewood
Lancaster
Lawndale
Littlerock
Llano
Lomita
Long Beach
Los Angeles
Lynwood
Malibu
Manhattan Beach
Marina Del Rey
Maywood
Mission Hills
Monrovia
Montebello
Monterey Park
Montrose
Newhall
North Hills
North Hollywood
Northridge
Norwalk
Pacific Palisades
Pacoima
Palmdale
Palos Verdes Estates
Palos Verdes Peninsu
Panorama City
Paramount
Pasadena
Pico Rivera
Playa Del Rey
Playa Vista
Pls Vrds Pnsl
Pomona
Porter Ranch
Rancho Dominguez
Rancho Palos Verdes
Redondo Beach
Reseda
Rlng HLS Est
Rosemead
San Dimas
San Fernando
San Gabriel
San Marino
San Pedro
Santa Clarita
Santa Fe Springs
Santa Monica
Saugus
Sherman Oaks
Sherwood Forest
Signal Hill
South El Monte
South Gate
South Pasadena
Stevenson Ranch
Studio City
Sun Valley
Sunland
Sylmar
Tarzana
Temple City
Toluca Lake

2017 Directory of California
Wholesalers and Services Companies

1615

COUNTY/CITY CROSS-REFERENCE

Topanga
Torrance
Tujunga
Universal City
Valencia
Valley Village
Van Nuys
Venice
Vernon
Walnut
West Covina
West Hills
West Hollywood
Whittier
Wilmington
Winnetka
Woodland Hills

Madera
Bass Lake
Chowchilla
Coarsegold
Madera
North Fork
Oakhurst

Marin
Belvedere Tiburon
Corte Madera
Fairfax
Greenbrae
Kentfield
Larkspur
Mill Valley
Nicasio
Novato
Point Reyes Station
San Geronimo
San Quentin
San Rafael
Sausalito

Mariposa
Hornitos
Mariposa
Yosemite Ntpk

Mendocino
Albion
Calpella
Caspar
Covelo
Fort Bragg
Hopland
Little River
Mendocino
Point Arena
Potter Valley
Redwood Valley
Ukiah
Willits

Merced
Atwater
Ballico
Delhi
Dos Palos
Gustine
Le Grand
Livingston
Los Banos
Merced
Snelling

Stevinson
Winton

Modoc
Alturas
Canby
Cedarville

Mono
Mammoth Lakes
Topaz

Monterey
Aromas
Big Sur
Bradley
Carmel
Carmel Valley
Castroville
Chualar
Gonzales
Greenfield
King City
Marina
Monterey
Moss Landing
Pacific Grove
Pebble Beach
Salinas
San Ardo
Seaside
Soledad

Napa
American Canyon
Angwin
Calistoga
NAPA
Rutherford
Saint Helena
Yountville

Nevada
Grass Valley
Nevada City
Norden
Penn Valley
Soda Springs
Truckee

Orange
Aliso Viejo
Anaheim
Brea
Buena Park
Capistrano Beach
Corona Del Mar
Costa Mesa
Cypress
Dana Point
El Toro
Foothill Ranch
Fountain Valley
Fullerton
Garden Grove
Huntington Beach
Irvine
La Habra
La Habra Heights
La Palma
Ladera Ranch
Laguna Beach
Laguna Hills

Laguna Niguel
Laguna Woods
Lake Forest
Los Alamitos
Mission Viejo
Newport Beach
Newport Coast
Orange
Placentia
Rancho Santa Margari
Rcho STA Marg
San Clemente
San Juan Capistrano
Santa Ana
Seal Beach
Silverado
Stanton
Trabuco Canyon
Tustin
Villa Park
Westminster
Yorba Linda

Placer
Alpine Meadows
Auburn
Granite Bay
Kings Beach
Lincoln
Loomis
Meadow Vista
Olympic Valley
Penryn
Rocklin
Roseville
Tahoe City

Plumas
Chester
Greenville
Portola
Quincy

Riverside
Anza
Banning
Beaumont
Bermuda Dunes
Blythe
Cabazon
Calimesa
Canyon Lake
Cathedral City
Cherry Valley
Coachella
Corona
Desert Hot Springs
Eastvale
Hemet
Homeland
Idyllwild
Indian Wells
Indio
Jurupa Valley
La Quinta
Lake Elsinore
March ARB
Mecca
Menifee
Mira Loma
Moreno Valley
Murrieta

Norco
North Palm Springs
Palm Desert
Palm Springs
Perris
Quail Valley
Rancho Mirage
Riverside
Romoland
San Jacinto
Sun City
Temecula
Thermal
Thousand Palms
Whitewater
Wildomar
Winchester

Sacramento
Antelope
Carmichael
Citrus Heights
Courtland
Elk Grove
Fair Oaks
Folsom
Galt
Gold River
Mather
McClellan
North Highlands
Orangevale
Rancho Cordova
Rancho Murieta
Rio Linda
Sacramento
Walnut Grove

San Benito
Hollister
San Juan Bautista

San Bernardino
Adelanto
Alta Loma
Apple Valley
Barstow
Big Bear City
Big Bear Lake
Bloomington
Blue Jay
Cedar Glen
Chino
Chino Hills
Colton
Earp
Etiwanda
Fontana
Fort Irwin
Grand Terrace
Helendale
Hesperia
Highland
Joshua Tree
Lake Arrowhead
Loma Linda
Lucerne Valley
Lytle Creek
Mentone
Montclair
Mountain Pass
Needles

Newberry Springs
Nipton
Oak Hills
Ontario
Parker Dam
Patton
Rancho Cucamonga
Redlands
Rialto
San Bernardino
Twentynine Palms
Upland
Victorville
Wrightwood
Yermo
Yucaipa
Yucca Valley

San Diego
Alpine
Bonita
Bonsall
Borrego Springs
Boulevard
Camp Pendleton
Campo
Carlsbad
Chula Vista
Coronado
Del Mar
El Cajon
Encinitas
Escondido
Fallbrook
Imperial Beach
Jamul
Julian
La Jolla
La Mesa
Lakeside
Lemon Grove
National City
Oceanside
Pala
Pauma Valley
Potrero
Poway
Ramona
Rancho Santa Fe
San Diego
San Marcos
San Ysidro
Santee
Solana Beach
Spring Valley
Tecate
Valley Center
Vista

San Francisco
San Francisco

San Joaquin
Acampo
Escalon
Farmington
French Camp
Holt
Lathrop
Linden
Lodi
Manteca

COUNTY/CITY CROSS-REFERENCE

Ripon
Stockton
Tracy
Victor
Woodbridge

San Luis Obispo
Arroyo Grande
Atascadero
Avila Beach
Cambria
Grover Beach
Los Osos
Morro Bay
Nipomo
Oceano
Paso Robles
Pismo Beach
San Luis Obispo
San Simeon
Shell Beach
Templeton

San Mateo
Atherton
Belmont
Brisbane
Burlingame
Colma
Daly City
El Granada
Foster City
Half Moon Bay
Hillsborough
Menlo Park
Millbrae
Moss Beach
Pacifica
Pescadero
Portola Valley
Portola Vally
Redwood City
San Bruno
San Carlos
San Francisco
San Mateo
South San Francisco
Woodside

Santa Barbara
Buellton
Carpinteria
Goleta
Guadalupe
Lompoc
Los Alamos
Santa Barbara
Santa Maria
Santa Ynez
Solvang
Vandenberg Afb

Santa Clara
Alviso
Campbell
Cupertino
East Palo Alto
Gilroy
Los Altos
Los Altos Hills
Los Gatos
Milpitas
Moffett Field
Monte Sereno
Morgan Hill
Mountain View
Palo Alto
San Jose
San Martin
Santa Clara
Saratoga
Stanford
Sunnyvale

Santa Cruz
Aptos
Boulder Creek
Capitola
Davenport
Felton
Mount Hermon
Royal Oaks
Santa Cruz
Scotts Valley
Soquel
Watsonville

Shasta
Anderson
Burney
Cottonwood
Hat Creek
Palo Cedro
Redding

Sierra
Loyalton

Siskiyou
Edgewood
Etna
Happy Camp
Macdoel
Mount Shasta
Tulelake
Weed
Yreka

Solano
Benicia
Dixon
Fairfield
Rio Vista
Suisun City
Travis Afb
Vacaville
Vallejo

Sonoma
Bodega Bay
Cazadero
Cloverdale
Cotati
Duncans Mills
Geyserville
Glen Ellen
Guerneville
Healdsburg
Kenwood
Occidental
Petaluma
Rohnert Park
Santa Rosa
Sebastopol
Sonoma
Windsor

Stanislaus
Ceres
Denair
Hickman
Hughson
Keyes
Modesto
Newman
Oakdale
Patterson
Riverbank
Salida
Turlock
Waterford

Sutter
Live Oak
Meridian
Pleasant Grove
Yuba City

Tehama
Corning
Gerber
Red Bluff
Vina

Trinity
Weaverville

Tulare
Cutler
Dinuba
Earlimart
Exeter
Goshen
Ivanhoe
Kings Canyon Nationa
Lindsay
Orosi
Porterville
Richgrove
Strathmore
Terra Bella
Tipton
Traver
Tulare
Visalia
Woodlake

Tuolumne
Columbia
Groveland
Jamestown
Long Barn
Pinecrest
Sonora
Tuolumne

Ventura
Agoura Hills
Camarillo
Fillmore
Moorpark
Newbury Park
Oak View
Ojai
Oxnard
Piru
Port Hueneme
Santa Paula
Santa Rosa Valley
Simi Valley
Somis
Thousand Oaks
Ventura
Westlake Village

Yolo
Brooks
Clarksburg
Davis
El Macero
Esparto
Knights Landing
West Sacramento
Winters
Woodland

Yuba
Beale Afb
Brownsville
Marysville
Olivehurst
Wheatland

GEOGRAPHIC SECTION

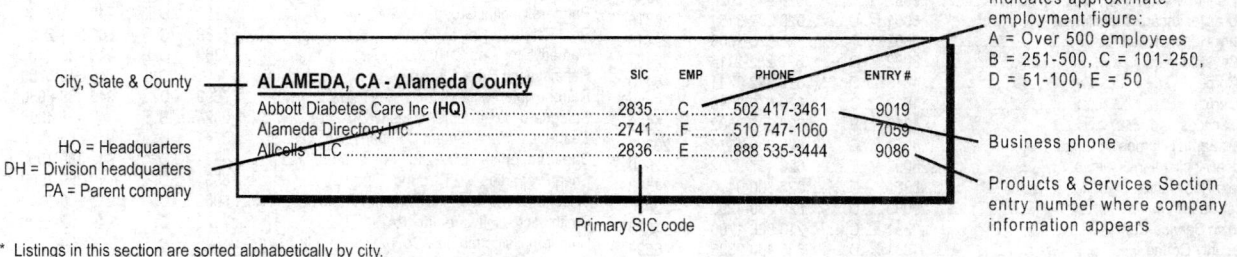

* Listings in this section are sorted alphabetically by city.
* Listings within each city are sorted alphabetically by company name.

	SIC	EMP	PHONE	ENTRY #
ACAMPO, CA - San Joaquin County				
JJ Rios Farm Services Inc	0761	D	209 333-7467	670
Langetwins Inc	0172	D	209 339-4055	167
Nestor Enterprises LLC	0172	E	209 727-5711	172
Windwalker Security Patrol Inc	7381	D	209 333-3953	16853
ACTON, CA - Los Angeles County				
County of Los Angeles	8069	D	661 223-8700	22131
Dedication & Everlasting Love	0752	D	661 269-4010	638
Delta Rescue Inc	8699	D	661 269-4010	25524
ADELANTO, CA - San Bernardino County				
Adelanto YWCA	8641	D	760 530-1850	25195
Commercial Wood Products Co	1751	C	760 246-4530	3038
Cwp Cabinets Inc	1751	C	760 246-4530	3040
General Atomic Aeron	8731	C	760 246-3660	26522
General Atomic Aeron	8734	C	760 246-3662	26855
Geo Group Inc	8741	D	760 246-1171	27034
Hayes Welding Inc	7692	D	760 246-4878	17954
High Desert Mavericks Inc	7941	D	760 246-6287	18548
S E C C Corporation	1623	C	760 246-6218	1990
South Capitol Cottage	8748	D	951 662-3026	28061
USA Transport Inc	4214	E	559 783-3563	4386
Yrc Inc	4231	D	760 246-0031	4712
AGOURA, CA - Los Angeles County				
Abraham Jsha Hschl Dy Schl Wst	8351	D	818 707-2365	24409
Joni and Friends **(PA)**	8322	D	818 707-5664	24051
Up Stage Inc	7812	E	818 879-8781	18186
AGOURA HILLS, CA - Los Angeles County				
Amcal Communities Inc	6552	E	818 706-0694	11946
American Homes 4 Rent **(PA)**	6798	D	805 413-5300	12234
Amh Portfolio One LLC	6798	B	480 921-4600	12237
Arpi Reit LLC	6798	D	805 413-5300	12238
Canon Solutions America Inc	5044	D	818 871-6700	7045
Davidson Hotel Partners Lp	7011	C	818 707-1220	12564
First Amrcn Mrtg Solutions LLC **(HQ)**	6163	D	800 333-4510	9925
First Student Inc	4151	D	818 707-2082	3935
International Bus Mchs Corp	7373	D	914 499-1900	15968
Los Angeles Rams LLC **(PA)**	7941	D	314 982-7267	18555
Meadowbrook Senior Living	8322	D	818 991-3544	24080
Mjd Construction Corp	1521	D	818 575-9864	1225
Mobile Programming LLC	7371	D	310 584-6300	15310
National Everclean Svcs Inc	8734	D	877 532-5326	26874
National Veterinary Associates **(PA)**	0742	C	805 677-7722	623
Pacific Centrex Services Inc	4813	D	818 623-2300	5678
Pennymac Corp	6163	A	818 878-8416	9943
Private Nat Mrtg Accptance LLC **(PA)**	6162	A	818 224-7401	9887
Quality Home Loans	6162	D	818 206-6600	9891
Regency Theatres Inc	7832	E	818 224-3825	18350
Sequoia Concepts Inc	7322	D	818 409-6000	14047
State Farm Mutl Auto Insur Co	6411	D	818 597-4300	10885
Vertafore Fsc Inc	7371	C	800 433-2550	15526
Ww Lbv Inc	7011	D	818 707-1220	13432
Coldwell Bankers Residential **(PA)**	6531	D	818 575-2660	11420
AGUA DULCE, CA - Los Angeles County				
Petrelli Electric Inc	1731	D	661 268-7312	2683
ALAMEDA, CA - Alameda County				
Abb/Con-Cise Optical Group LLC	5048	D	800 852-8089	7328
Abb/Con-Cise Optical Group LLC	5048	D	800 852-8089	7329
Absolutdata Technologies Inc	7389	D	510 748-9922	16964
Alameda Alliance For Health	6324	C	510 747-4555	10254

	SIC	EMP	PHONE	ENTRY #
Alameda Bureau Elec Imprv Corp **(PA)**	4911	D	510 748-3901	6106
Alameda Family Services	8351	D	510 629-6300	24414
Alameda Hlthcare & Wellnss Ctr	8051	D	510 523-8857	20373
American Cancer Soc Cal Div **(PA)**	8733	D	510 893-7900	26732
ARC Document Solutions Inc	7334	E	415 495-8700	14109
Bay View Rhbilitation Hosp LLC	8051	D	510 521-5600	20405
Bladium Inc **(PA)**	7997	D	510 814-4999	18896
Chipman Corporation **(PA)**	4214	E	510 748-8700	4334
City Alameda Health Care Corp **(PA)**	8062	D	510 522-3700	21494
City Alameda Health Care Corp	8741	B	510 814-4000	26970
Delphi Productions Inc **(PA)**	7389	C	510 748-7494	17120
Elder Care Alliance Camarillo	8361	D	510 769-2700	24642
Elder Care Alliance San Rafael	8051	D	510 769-2700	20530
Embarcadero Systems Corp	7371	D	510 749-7400	15162
Emmanuel Cnvlscent Hosp Almeda	8059	D	510 521-5765	21210
Energy Berkeley Office US Dept	8733	B	510 468-5662	26760
Family Stations Inc **(PA)**	4832	C	510 568-6200	5773
Frito-Lay North America Inc	5145	D	510 569-5000	8617
Garfield Nursing Home Inc	8051	D	510 582-7676	20593
Girl Scouts Northern Cal **(PA)**	8641	D	510 562-8470	25261
Global 360 Inc	8741	D	510 263-4800	27039
Harbor Bay Club Inc	7991	D	510 521-5414	18639
Health Educ Economic Devlpmnt	8742	D	510 604-6143	27463
Hubb Systems LLC	7373	D	510 865-9100	15962
Joint Labor MGT Retirement Tr	6321	E	503 454-3800	10242
Kaiser Foundation Hospitals	6324	D	510 752-1190	10331
Kindred Nursing Centers W LLC	8051	D	510 521-5600	20706
Maintenance Service For The Cy	7349	D	510 865-3778	14347
Mariner Square Athletic Inc	7991	D	510 523-8011	18658
Mbh Architects Inc	8712	C	510 865-8663	26236
Metaswitch Networks	7371	E	415 513-1500	15302
NRC Environmental Services Inc **(HQ)**	4959	D	510 749-1390	6632
Otismed Corporation	5047	D	510 786-3171	7291
Polarion Software Inc	7372	D	877 572-4005	15819
Ports America Inc	4491	C	510 749-7400	4754
Roche Molecular Systems Inc	8731	D	510 814-2800	26595
Salem Lutheran Home Associatio	8361	C	510 769-2700	24796
San Francisco Bay AR Tran Assn	8699	C	510 501-5318	25572
Semifreddis Inc **(PA)**	5149	D	510 596-9930	8919
Shoreline S Intermediate Care	8052	D	510 523-8857	21107
Snelling Employment LLC	7361	D	510 769-4400	14790
Telecare Corporation	8063	D	510 337-7950	22106
Voxify Inc	7371	D	510 545-3011	15537
Waters Edge Lodge	8361	E	510 769-6264	24853
Webcor Construction LP **(DH)**	1542	D	510 748-1900	1713
Weinberg Roger & Resenfeld **(PA)**	8111	D	510 337-1001	23614
Wind River Systems Inc **(HQ)**	7372	C	510 748-4100	15880
ALAMO, CA - Contra Costa County				
Cintas Corporation	7213	D	925 743-1745	13542
John Muir Physician Network	8011	E	925 838-4633	19577
Round Hill Country Club	7997	D	925 934-8211	19049
Round Hill Enterprises	7997	C	925 934-8211	19050
RPM Mortgage Inc **(PA)**	6162	D	925 295-9300	9893
ALBANY, CA - Alameda County				
Blize Healthcare Cal Inc	8082	D	800 343-2549	22378
Energy Berkeley Office US Dept	8733	A	510 701-1089	26758
Pacific Racing Association	7948	C	510 559-7300	18572
Reichert Lengfeld Ltd Partnr	7011	D	510 845-1077	13137
ALBION, CA - Mendocino County				
Albion River Inn Incorporated	7011	D	707 937-1919	12379

ALHAMBRA, CA

GEOGRAPHIC SECTION

	SIC	EMP	PHONE	ENTRY #
ALHAMBRA, CA - Los Angeles County				
Ahmc Healthcare	8062	C	626 570-0612	21437
Ahmc Healthcare Inc	8099	A	626 248-3452	22880
Ahmc Healthcare Inc **(PA)**	8062	C	626 943-7526	21438
Alhambra Healthcare & Wellness	8051	D	626 282-3151	20375
Alhambra Hospital Med Ctr LP	8062	C	626 570-1606	21443
Allied Physicians	8082	D	626 282-2116	22351
AT&T Corp	4813	D	626 382-0241	5470
AT&T Corp	4813	D	626 576-3616	5479
AT&T Services Inc	4813	B	626 308-8582	5559
Atherton Baptist Homes	8051	D	626 289-4178	20387
Bio-Mdcal Applications Cal Inc	8092	E	626 457-9002	22620
California Peo Home	8361	D	626 300-0400	24578
Care 1st Health Plan	8099	C	626 299-4299	22910
Chinatown Service Center	8331	C	213 808-1700	24323
City Security Co Inc	7381	D	626 458-2325	16599
Community Development Comm	8741	E	626 262-4511	26977
Community Development Comm	6531	C	626 262-4511	11450
County of Los Angeles	6324	C	626 299-5300	10275
County of Los Angeles	4941	B	626 458-3126	6335
County of Los Angeles	8322	C	626 308-5542	23859
Drew Chain Security Corp	7382	D	626 457-8626	16880
Eastern Los Angeles RE **(PA)**	8322	C	626 299-4700	23952
Evikecom Inc	5091	D	626 286-0360	8017
Front Porch Communities & Svcs	8059	C	626 289-6211	21225
I Lan Systems Inc	7373	D	626 304-9021	15963
Interviewing Service Amer Inc	8732	C	626 979-4140	26676
Inveserve Corporation	6531	D	626 458-3435	11591
Nca Program	8011	D	323 226-5068	19765
Options For Learning	8351	C	626 308-2411	24491
Orora North America	5113	D	626 284-9524	8206
Pacific Snow Valley Resort LLC	7011	E	626 588-2889	13062
Pacific Ventures Ltd	8741	C	626 576-0737	27155
Roboca Technology	7371	C	561 501-3999	15428
Silverado Senior Living Inc	8059	E	626 872-3941	21374
Soto Provision Inc	5023	D	626 458-4600	6887
Southern California Gas Co	4924	A	323 881-3587	6278
Tenet Healthsystem Medical	8011	B	626 300-5500	20134
Tennant Health Systems	8011	C	626 300-3500	20135
University Southern California	8731	D	626 457-4240	26630
Young MN Chrstn Assc **(PA)**	8322	D	626 576-0226	24297
ALISO VIEJO, CA - Orange County				
AAA Accounting Services	8721	D	949 791-7368	26285
Aliso Viejo Golf Club Inc	7997	C	949 598-9200	18845
All Hnds Crwash Dtail Ctr Lube	7542	D	949 716-3600	17828
Ambry Genetics Corporation **(PA)**	8734	D	949 900-5500	26831
American Zettler Inc **(HQ)**	5065	C	949 360-5830	7519
Apex Parks Group LLC **(PA)**	7996	C	949 349-8461	18811
Apex Parks Group LLC	7999	D	210 341-6663	19139
Basketball Marketing Co Inc	8742	E	866 866-1232	27340
Bearing Engineers Inc **(PA)**	5085	D	949 586-7442	7925
Blueyield Inc	7371	D	949 385-6219	15059
Citizenhawk Inc	8741	D	949 427-3002	26967
Clarient Diagnostic Svcs Inc	8071	D	888 443-3310	22200
Countryside Inn-Corona LP	7011	D	949 588-0131	12542
Covenant Care California LLC **(HQ)**	8051	E	949 349-1200	20498
Cox Communications Inc	4841	D	949 716-2020	5973
Cresse Mark School of Baseball	7999	D	714 892-6145	19194
Daniel J Edelman Inc	7313	D	949 330-6760	13964
Datallegro Inc	5045	D	949 680-3000	7118
Dell Software Inc **(DH)**	7373	A	949 754-8000	15931
Diageo North America Inc	5182	D	949 421-3974	9096
Facility Services Partners	8741	D	949 480-4090	27021
Fluor Corporation	8711	D	949 349-2000	25811
Fluor Daniel Construction Co **(DH)**	1622	B	949 349-2000	1891
Fluor Enterprises Inc	5082	C	949 349-2000	7769
Fluor Enterprises Inc	1799	D	469 398-7000	3521
Fluor Industrial Services Inc	7349	A	949 439-2000	14300
Fluor Plant Services Intl Inc **(HQ)**	8711	D	949 349-2000	25814
Fluoramec LLC **(HQ)**	8711	E	949 349-2000	25815
Gaikai Inc	7372	A	949 330-6850	15674
Geo Telecom	1623	E	949 362-0921	1934
Glenwood Village Cmnty Assn	8641	D	949 855-1800	25264
Hcr Manorcare Med Svcs Fla LLC	8051	C	949 587-9000	20648
International Litigation Svcs	5044	D	888 313-4457	7057
JMJ Financial Group **(PA)**	6162	D	949 340-6336	9864
Kaiser Foundation Hospitals	8011	C	949 425-3150	19580
L & O Aliso Viejo LLC	7991	D	949 643-6700	18651
Lennar Corporation	1531	D	949 349-8000	1374
Lennar Homes California Inc **(DH)**	1521	D	949 349-8000	1206
LMC Hollywood Highland	1542	B	949 448-1600	1602
Malibu Castle	7996	E	210 341-6663	18825
Marsh & McLennan Agency LLC	6411	D	949 544-8460	10772
Merridian Neuro Care	8011	E	949 263-6630	19750
Metagenics Inc **(DH)**	5122	C	949 366-0818	8283
Navtrak LLC	7382	D	410 548-2337	16903
New Home Company Inc **(PA)**	1531	C	949 382-7800	1380
Pacific Crossing LLC	7373	D	949 679-2588	16026
Partners Capital Group Inc **(PA)**	7389	D	949 916-3900	17409
Real Estate Digital LLC	7389	C	800 234-2139	17447
Remedytemp Inc **(DH)**	7363	D	949 425-7600	14936
Renaissance Hotel Clubsport	7011	D	949 643-6700	13140
Retronix International Inc	7699	D	949 388-6930	18005
Safeguard Health Enterprises **(HQ)**	6324	B	949 425-4300	10373
Seabreeze Management Company **(PA)**	8741	D	949 855-1800	27208
Shea Properties LLC	6531	D	949 389-7000	11842
Shea Properties MGT Co Inc	6531	D	949 389-7000	11843
Siliconsystems Inc	5063	D	949 900-9400	7473
Smith Micro Software Inc **(PA)**	7372	C	949 362-5800	15838
Southern California Gas Co	4923	D	714 634-7221	6262
Spyglass Hill Community Assn	8641	E	949 855-1800	25352
Star Real Estate South County	6531	C	949 389-0004	11856
Sunstone Center Crt Lessee Inc	7011	C	949 382-4000	13312
Sunstone Hotel Investors Inc **(PA)**	6798	E	949 330-4000	12274
Sunstone Hotel Investors LLC **(HQ)**	6799	D	949 330-4000	12346
Sunstone Hotel Management Inc **(PA)**	7011	E	949 297-4183	13323
Sunstone Hotel Properties Inc **(DH)**	7011	D	949 330-4000	13326
Sunstone Ocean Lessee Inc	7011	B	949 382-4000	13327
Telogis Inc **(DH)**	7374	C	949 389-5500	16200
Tyson Investments Inc	6531	D	949 389-0004	11890
United Parcel Service Inc OH	4215	C	949 643-6595	4453
UST Global Inc **(PA)**	7371	D	949 716-8757	15518
Valeant Biomedicals Inc **(DH)**	5169	D	949 461-6000	9003
Voice Mail Broadcasting Corp	7374	D	714 437-0600	16209
ALPINE, CA - San Diego County				
Abhe & Svoboda Inc	1542	D	619 659-1320	1482
Alpine Convalescent Center	8093	D	619 659-3120	22655
Pacific Southwest Cnstr & Eqp	1623	D	619 445-5190	1976
R A Schreiber Plumbing	1711	E	619 659-3101	2335
Southern Indian Health Council **(PA)**	8011	D	619 445-1188	20046
ALPINE MEADOWS, CA - Placer County				
Alpine Meadows Ski Area	7011	E	530 583-4232	12382
Squaw Creek Associates LLC	7011	A	530 581-6624	13282
ALTA LOMA, CA - San Bernardino County				
Expreal Inc	6531	D	909 373-4400	11501
Inland Empire RE Solutions	6531	D	909 476-1000	11582
ALTADENA, CA - Los Angeles County				
5 Acrs-The Bys Grls Aid Soc La	8361	B	626 798-6793	24538
Altadena Town and Country Club	7997	D	626 345-9088	18850
City of Hope	8999	B	626 256-4673	28123
Cutting Edge Protection I	7241	E	949 307-1596	13698
D C Golf A CA Partnership	7992	E	626 797-3821	18732
Lockheed Martin Corporation	7371	D	626 296-7977	15278
Mallcraft Inc	1542	E	626 765-9100	1606
Marcos Auto Body Inc **(PA)**	7532	D	626 286-5691	17759
Pasadena Chld Training Soc	8361	E	626 798-0853	24766
Tom Sawyer Camps Inc	8351	C	626 794-1156	24526
ALTURAS, CA - Modoc County				
Cellco Partnership	4812	D	530 233-2100	5322
County of Modoc	7389	C	530 233-6223	17099
County of Modoc	8322	D	530 233-6501	23865
County of Modoc	8051	D	530 233-3416	20480
County of Modoc	8322	D	530 233-6400	23866
Last Frontier Healthcare Dst	8062	C	530 233-7036	21698
ALVISO, CA - Santa Clara County				
Acme Building Maintenance Co **(HQ)**	7349	D	408 263-5911	14211
Bayscape Management Inc	8741	D	408 288-2940	26938
Minerva Networks Inc **(PA)**	7371	D	800 806-9594	15305
Tivo Solutions Inc **(HQ)**	7371	C	408 519-9100	15505
AMERICAN CANYON, CA - Napa County				
Biagi Bros Inc	4225	D	707 642-4412	4526
Comcast Corporation	4841	D	707 266-7584	5954
Eagle Vnes Vnyrds Golf CLB LLC	7997	D	707 257-4470	18943
Ghilotti Construction Co Inc	1611	D	707 556-9145	1774
Medical Receivables Solutions	8742	E	707 980-6733	27537
R E Maher Inc	1771	D	707 642-3907	3317
Western Wine Services Inc **(PA)**	4225	D	707 645-4300	4670
ANAHEIM, CA - Orange County				
1135 N Leisure Ct Inc	8051	C	714 772-1353	20364
24 Hour Fitness Usa Inc	7991	E	714 525-9924	18581
3067 Orange Avenue LLC	8051	C	714 827-2440	20365
5 Day Business Forms Mfg Inc	5112	D	714 632-8674	8157
A & R Wholesale Distrs Inc	5145	D	714 777-7742	8608
A S I Corporation	7311	D	714 526-5533	13809

Mergent email: customerrelations@mergent.com
2017 Directory of California Wholesalers and Services Companies
(P-0000) Products & Services Section entry number
(PA)=Parent Co (HQ)=Headquarters (DH)=Div Headquarters

GEOGRAPHIC SECTION ANAHEIM, CA

Company	SIC	EMP	PHONE	ENTRY #
Aat Kings Tours USA Inc	4725	D	714 456-0505	4983
Above Hlth HM Care Sltions LLC	8082	D	714 585-2185	22319
Advantage Mailing Inc (PA)	7331	C	714 538-3881	14064
Advantage-Crown Sls & Mktg LLC (DH)	5141	A	714 780-3000	8454
Adventure City Inc	7999	D	714 821-3311	19130
Aecom Global II LLC	8711	D	415 774-2700	25623
Agire Mortgage Corporation	6162	E	714 564-5821	9810
Air Mechanical Inc	1711	D	714 995-3947	2112
Albd Electric and Cable	1731	D	949 440-1216	2513
Alexanders Grand Salon	7231	D	714 282-6438	13666
Aliantel Inc	8748	D	800 274-7074	27823
Alix Technologies Inc	5122	C	714 630-6000	8226
Alsco Inc	7213	D	714 774-4165	13515
American Chem & Sani Sup Inc	4959	D	714 632-3010	6618
American Team Managers Inc	6411	E	714 414-1200	10599
Amisub (irvine Regional Hospi)	8062	A	949 916-7556	21450
Ampco Contracting Inc	4959	D	949 955-2255	6619
Anaheim Arena Management LLC	7941	C	714 704-2400	18534
Anaheim Arts Council	8412	C	714 868-6094	25001
Anaheim Ducks Hockey Club LLC	7997	D	714 940-2900	18873
Anaheim First Fmly Dntl Group	8741	D	714 999-5050	26921
Anaheim Global Medical Center	8062	B	714 533-6220	21452
Anaheim Harbor Medical Group (PA)	8011	E	714 533-4511	19344
Anaheim Hills Auto Body Inc	7532	D	714 632-8266	17747
Anaheim Hotel LLC	7011	C	714 750-1811	12387
Anaheim Ice	7999	D	714 518-3200	19136
Anaheim Medical Center	8011	D	714 774-1450	19345
Anaheim Park Inn and Camelot	7011	D	714 635-7275	12389
Anaheim Plaza Hotel Inc	7011	D	714 772-5900	12390
Anaheim Regional Medical Ctr	8011	D	714 999-3847	19346
Anaheim/Orange Cnty Visitor Bu (PA)	7389	D	714 765-8888	16990
Angels Baseball LP (PA)	7941	A	714 940-2000	18535
Ardcore Senior Living	8361	D	714 974-2226	24551
Arizona Tile LLC	5032	D	714 978-6403	6972
AT&T Corp	4812	D	714 284-3818	5260
AT&T Corp	7389	D	714 284-2878	17006
AT&T Corp	4813	C	714 940-9976	5499
AT&T Services Inc	4813	C	714 259-4441	5532
AT&T Services Inc	4813	C	210 886-4922	5536
AT&T Services Inc	4813	C	714 575-8320	5542
Atchesons Express Inc	4212	E	714 808-9199	3979
ATL Services	7349	B	714 712-4220	14235
Atlanta Seafoods LLC	5146	D	626 626-4900	8628
Avalon Building Maintenance (PA)	7349	D	714 693-2407	14236
B & B Specialties Inc	5072	D	714 985-3075	7675
Badalian Enterprises Inc	7011	D	714 635-4082	12412
Bally Total Fitness Corp	7991	E	714 952-3101	18611
Bcp Systems Inc	7378	D	714 202-3900	16287
Bell Pipe & Supply Co	5085	E	714 772-3200	7926
Benchmaster Furniture LLC	5021	B	714 414-0240	6805
Best Cheer Stone Inc (PA)	5032	E	714 399-1588	6974
Best Interiors Inc (PA)	1742	D	714 490-7999	2862
Best Western Stovalls Inn	7011	E	714 776-4800	12442
Best Western Stovalls Inn (PA)	7011	E	714 956-4430	12443
Bethesda University California	6732	D	714 517-1945	12154
Bimbo Bakeries Usa Inc	5149	D	714 634-8068	8808
Bomel Construction Co Inc (PA)	1541	D	714 921-1660	1407
Bpo Management Services Inc (PA)	7371	D	714 972-2670	15062
Brady Company/Los Angeles Inc	1742	D	714 533-9850	2865
Brendan Tours Inc	4725	C	818 428-6000	4988
Bridgford Marketing Company (DH)	5147	D	714 526-5533	8665
Brightview Landscape Dev Inc	0781	D	714 414-0914	747
Brownco Construction Co Inc	1542	D	714 935-9600	1512
Buena Vista Care Center Inc	8051	D	714 535-7264	20425
C and E Inc	7514	D	714 236-5790	17668
Cal-State Auto Parts Inc (PA)	5013	C	714 630-5954	6720
California Private Trnsp Co LP	4785	D	714 637-9191	5207
California Safety Agency	7381	E	866 996-6990	16590
Califrnia Auto Dalers Exch LLC	5012	D	714 996-2400	6666
Carmel Architectural Sales	1761	D	714 630-7221	3147
Carrington Mortgage Services	8741	C	888 267-0584	26960
Cbre Inc	6531	C	714 939-2100	11351
Challenger Industries Inc	8748	D	714 630-4344	27876
Cinderella Motel	7011	D	559 432-0118	12522
Cinema City Theaters	7832	E	714 970-0865	18315
Cintas Corporation No 2	5199	D	714 288-8400	9254
City of Anaheim	6512	B	714 704-2400	10971
Clinica Sagrado Corazon	8011	E	714 491-7777	19444
Clp Resources Inc	7363	D	714 300-0510	14860
Coach Usa Inc	4725	C	714 978-8855	4991
Coast West Plumbing Inc	1711	D	714 446-8686	2184
Comfort California Inc	7011	D	714 750-3131	12536
Command Security Corporation	7381	C	714 557-9355	16602
Conestoga Hotel	7011	D	714 535-0300	12540
Consolidated Design West Inc	7336	D	714 999-1476	14139
Construction Customer Service	1521	E	714 701-1858	1159
Consumer Resource Network LLC	8742	B	800 291-4794	27388
Contiki US Holdings Inc	4725	D	714 935-0808	4992
Control Air Conditioning Corp (PA)	1711	C	714 777-8600	2189
Control Air Conditioning Svc	1711	D	714 777-8600	2190
Coordnted Dlvry Instlltion Inc	4212	D	714 501-4040	3999
Country Villa Service Corp (PA)	8741	D	310 574-3733	26986
County of Orange	8322	D	714 937-4500	23871
Credit Union Southern Cal	6061	C	714 671-2700	9593
Crocker Group LLC	6531	D	714 221-5621	11461
Crossmark Inc	5141	D	714 464-6318	8470
CTS Cement Manufacturing Corp	5032	D	714 808-1945	6980
Cusa Pcstc LLC	8742	D	714 978-8855	27402
D Y U Inc	6719	C	714 239-2433	12057
D/K Mechanical Contractors Inc	1711	D	714 970-0180	2200
Danlil Enterprise Inc	7349	D	714 776-7705	14282
Danny Ryan Precision Contg Inc	1795	D	949 642-6664	3453
Development Resource Cons Inc (PA)	8711	D	714 685-6860	25768
Digital Periph Solutions Inc	7382	D	714 998-3440	16879
Disney Enterprises Inc	7011	B	714 817-7317	12573
Disney Enterprises Inc	7011	B	714 956-6425	12574
Disneyland International	7996	C	714 781-4000	18818
Disneyland International	7011	C	714 956-6746	12575
Disneyland International Inc	4222	C	714 999-4000	4492
Disneys Grand Californian Ht	7011	C	714 635-2300	12577
Diversified Clinical Services	8099	D	714 579-8400	22946
Dkn Hotel LLC	7011	D	714 535-0300	12580
Dma Greencare Contracting Inc	0782	E	714 630-9470	842
Dolphins Cove Resort Ltd	7011	D	714 980-0830	12585
Donahue Schriber Rlty Group LP	6512	D	714 283-3535	10977
Doubltree Suites By Hilton LLC	7011	D	714 750-3000	12601
Driver Spg	7389	E	626 351-8800	17134
E R A First Star Realty	6531	E	714 974-3111	11483
E&S Building Maintenance Inc	7349	D	714 961-8078	14285
Eastwood Insurance Services (PA)	6411	C	800 468-5377	10694
Econo Air Conditioning Inc	1711	E	714 630-3090	2214
Edge Mortgage Advisory Co LLC	8748	D	714 564-5800	27908
Edward Thomas Companies	7011	D	714 782-7500	12610
Emerald Landscape Services	0782	D	714 844-2200	848
Emercon Construction Inc (PA)	1521	E	714 630-9615	1171
Emery Smith Laboratories Inc	8711	D	714 238-6133	25785
Eps Corporate Holdings Inc	5074	D	714 635-3131	7709
Etherwan Systems Inc	7379	D	714 779-3800	16368
Evriholder Products LLC (PA)	5023	E	714 690-7878	6860
Exactax Inc (PA)	7291	D	714 284-4802	13720
Express Messenger Systems Inc	4215	D	949 235-1400	4404
F M Tarbell Co	6531	D	714 772-8990	11504
F M Tarbell Co	6531	C	714 637-7240	11505
Family Tree Produce Inc	5148	C	714 693-5688	8723
Fci Lender Services Inc	7322	D	714 974-1945	14031
Fedex Freight Corporation	4213	C	714 996-8720	4161
Fedex Ground Package Sys Inc	4213	C	714 879-0788	4175
Fenceworks Inc	1799	D	714 238-0091	3517
Filyn Corporation	4119	D	714 632-0225	3791
First Team RE - Orange Cnty	6531	D	714 974-9191	11538
Fjs Inc	7011	D	714 905-1050	12638
Fkc Partners A Cal Ltd Partnr	6531	E	714 528-9864	11540
Fortress Holding Group LLC	6719	E	714 202-8710	12061
Frank Gates Service Company	6331	D	800 994-4611	10422
Freeman Audio Visual Inc	7359	C	714 254-3400	14542
Freeman Expositions Inc	7389	D	714 254-3400	17174
Freight Management Inc	8742	D	714 632-1440	27441
Front Porch Communities	8059	C	714 776-7150	21218
G4s Secure Solutions (usa)	7381	D	714 939-4900	16654
GBS Linens Inc (PA)	7213	C	714 778-6448	13549
General Engineering Wstn Inc (PA)	1711	D	714 630-3200	2235
Golden State Water Company	4941	D	714 535-7711	6350
Greenball Corp (PA)	5014	D	714 782-3060	6786
Harbor Villa Care Center	8059	D	714 635-8131	21261
Harris Freeman & Co Inc (PA)	5149	B	714 765-1190	8850
Harvest Landscape Entps Inc	0782	C	714 283-4298	867
Hba Incorporated	1741	D	714 635-8602	2818
Health Pointe Medical Group (PA)	8011	D	714 956-2663	19546
Healthcare Partners LLC	8099	D	714 995-1000	22970
Highland Lumber Sales Inc	5031	D	714 778-2293	6931
Hilton Worldwide Inc	7011	D	714 632-1221	12740
Hob Entertainment LLC	7929	D	714 778-2583	18469
Hoffman Southwest Corp	7699	E	714 630-0404	17979
Holiday Garden SF Corp	7011	E	714 533-3555	12747
Holiday Inn & Suites Annaheim	7011	D	714 535-0300	12747
Hpt Trs Ihg-2 Inc	7011	D	714 748-7777	12798
Hunter Easterday Corporation	7349	C	714 238-3400	14322
Infinity Drywall Contg Inc	1742	D	714 634-2255	2909
Insight Environmental Wstn LLC	8711	D	714 678-6700	25880
International Missing Persons	7299	D	714 827-1947	13769

Employment Codes: A=Over 500 employees, B=251-500, C=101-250, D=51-100, E=45-50

2017 Directory of California Wholesalers and Services Companies

© Mergent Inc. 1-800-342-5647

1621

ANAHEIM, CA

Company	SIC	EMP	PHONE	ENTRY #
Interntnl Circuits Components	5065	C	714 572-1900	7587
Interstate Electronics Corp	8742	A	714 758-0500	27483
J & J Productions Incorporated	7389	E	714 535-0951	17254
J B Bostick Company Inc (PA)	1611	D	714 238-2121	1802
Jan Pro Clg Systems Sthern Cal	7349	E	714 220-0500	14330
Jetro Cash and Carry Entps LLC	5142	D	714 666-8211	8558
Kaiser Foundation Hospitals	8011	C	714 279-4675	19579
Kaiser Foundation Hospitals	8011	A	888 988-2800	19599
Kaiser Foundation Hospitals	8011	A	888 988-2800	19601
Kaiser Foundation Hospitals	6324	D	714 284-6634	10312
Kapl Inc	8731	B	714 991-9543	26542
Karcher Environmental Inc (PA)	1799	E	714 385-1490	3541
KCS Electric Inc	1731	D	623 551-1500	2629
Keenan Hopkins Suder & Stowell (PA)	1742	D	714 695-3670	2919
Keenan Hopkins Suder & Stowell	1542	D	714 695-3670	1590
Ken Real Estate Lease Ltd	7011	D	714 778-1700	12878
Ken Starr Inc	1711	D	714 632-8789	2266
Kinsbursky Bros Supply Inc (PA)	5093	D	714 738-8516	8075
Kisco Senior Living LLC	6513	D	714 778-5100	11150
L&G Cable Construction	1799	D	714 630-6174	3545
L&L Foods Holdings LLC	4783	C	714 254-1430	5202
La Palma Care Center	8051	D	714 772-7480	20717
LARK Industries Inc (PA)	7389	C	714 701-4200	17288
Law Office of Curtis O Barnes	8111	D	866 477-8222	23376
Lazer Electric Inc	1731	D	714 777-4233	2635
Leisure Care LLC	8361	E	714 974-1616	24709
Liquidity Services Inc	5136	D	714 738-6446	8351
Lobel Financial Corporation (PA)	6141	D	714 995-3333	9756
Long Swimming Pool Steel Inc	1791	E	714 524-8172	3390
Longust Distributing Inc	5023	E	480 820-6244	6872
Lyons Security Service Inc	7382	D	714 401-4850	16900
Machining Time Savers Inc	5084	D	714 635-7373	7858
Makar Anaheim LLC	7011	A	714 740-4431	12937
Malco Maintenance Inc	1799	D	714 630-0194	3549
Malco Services Inc	8742	D	714 630-0194	27520
Marketing Professionals Inc	8742	B	714 578-0500	27524
Master-Sort Inc	7389	C	714 258-7678	17316
Matrix Surfaces Inc	1743	C	714 696-5449	3019
Mc Graw Commercial Insur Svc	6411	D	714 939-9875	10780
McCormack Roofng Constrctn & E	1761	D	714 777-4040	3190
Merical LLC (PA)	7389	D	714 238-7225	17331
Millennium Transportation Inc	4731	D	714 956-7882	5123
Morphotrak LLC (DH)	7373	D	714 238-2000	15997
Motive Energy Inc (PA)	5063	D	714 888-2525	7457
Mowery Thomason Inc	1742	D	714 666-1717	2934
Moyes Custom Furniture Inc	7641	E	714 729-0234	17952
Msl Electric Inc	1731	D	714 693-4837	2659
Multi Mechanical Inc	1711	D	714 632-7404	2299
Murrietta Circuits	1731	D	714 970-2430	2660
Nail Emporium	5087	E	714 779-9889	7971
Nations Direct Lender & In	7389	C	800 969-7779	17349
Nazzareno Electric Co Inc	1731	D	714 712-4744	2662
Newage Anaheim Inn LLC	7011	C	714 758-0900	13019
Nicholas Lane Contractors Inc	1521	B	714 630-7630	1226
Nor-Cal Beverage Co Inc	7389	C	714 526-8600	17363
Northwest Hotel Corporation (PA)	7011	D	714 776-6120	13028
Npl Anaheim Investments LLC	7011	D	714 750-2010	13029
Orange Cnty Conservation Corps	8331	D	714 451-1301	24374
Orange Coast Building Services	1541	D	714 453-6300	1455
Orange Coast Title Company	6541	D	714 822-3211	11938
Orange County Child Abuse	8322	D	714 543-4333	24117
Orange County Head Start	8351	C	714 761-4967	24495
Otis Elevator Company	7699	E	714 758-9593	17993
Overhead Door Corporation	1751	D	714 680-0600	3070
Pacific Contours Corporation (PA)	5088	D	714 693-1260	8002
Pacific Design Directions Inc	1521	D	714 685-7766	1230
Pacific Utility Instllation Inc	1731	D	714 970-6430	2675
Paseo Vlg Hsing Partners LP	6531	D	714 991-9172	11742
Paulus Engineering Inc	1623	D	714 632-3322	1979
Peacock Stes Resort Ltd Partnr	7011	D	714 535-8255	13084
Penhall Company (DH)	1741	D	714 772-6450	2832
Penhall International Corp (HQ)	1795	C	714 772-6450	3464
Petersen-Dean Inc	1761	D	714 629-9670	3201
Pinner Construction Co (PA)	1542	D	714 490-4000	1638
Platinum Construction Inc	1542	D	714 527-0700	1639
Platinum Protection Group Inc	7381	D	800 824-1097	16758
Portofino Inn & Suites Anaheim	7011	A	714 782-7600	13107
Power Engineers Incorporated	8711	B	714 507-2700	26021
Power Plus LLC	5063	D	714 507-1881	7465
Power Plus Solutions Corp	1731	E	714 507-1881	2689
Premier Commercial Bancorp	6022	D	714 978-2400	9516
Prime Healthcare Anaheim LLC	8062	A	714 827-3000	21809
Printrak International Inc (DH)	7378	B	714 238-2000	16303
Ramada Plaza Ht Anaheim Resort	7011	A	714 991-6868	13126
Ray W Choi	8742	D	714 783-1000	27609
Red Lion Hotels Corporation	7011	D	714 750-2801	13135
Residence Inn By Marriott	7011	D	714 533-3555	13147
Resident Group Services Inc (PA)	0782	C	714 630-5300	945
Residential Fire Systems Inc	1711	D	714 666-8450	2347
Restaurant Depot LLC	5181	C	714 666-9205	9078
Retriev Technologies Inc (PA)	4953	D	714 738-8516	6540
Reyes Holdings LLC	8741	D	714 445-3392	27200
Rjb Enterprises Inc	1731	E	714 484-3101	2712
Roy Miller Freight Lines LLC (PA)	4212	D	714 632-5511	4058
Royal Roofing & Cnstr Co	1761	D	714 764-1100	3211
Rvtlzation Anaheim II Partners	6531	D	714 520-4041	11827
S W Construction Inc	1751	D	714 978-7871	3084
San Marino Plastering Inc	1742	A	714 693-7840	2976
San-Mar Construction Co Inc	1751	D	714 693-5400	3085
Scholastic Book Fairs Inc	5192	D	714 237-1100	9171
Securitas SEC Svcs USA Inc	7381	D	714 385-9745	16809
Security Signal Devices Inc (PA)	7382	E	714 888-6230	16923
Select Data Inc	7371	D	714 577-1000	15445
Self Serve Auto Dismantlers (PA)	5093	D	714 630-8901	8083
Service 1st Electrical Svcs	1731	E	714 630-9699	2731
Shamrock Supply Company Inc (PA)	5072	D	714 575-1800	7697
Sheraton Pk Ht At Anheim Rsort	7011	D	714 750-1811	13246
Source Refrigeration	5078	E	714 578-2300	7759
Source Rfrgn & Hvac Inc (PA)	1711	C	714 578-2300	2379
South Coast Mechanical Inc	1711	D	714 738-6644	2381
Southern Cal Prmnnte Med Group	8011	E	714 279-4675	20033
Spectrum MGT Holdg Co LLC	4841	D	714 414-1431	6027
SR Bray LLC (PA)	1731	E	714 765-7551	2742
Srd Engineering Inc	1623	D	714 630-2480	2000
St Joseph Home Health Network (DH)	8082	D	714 712-9500	22571
St Joseph Home Health Network	8082	D	714 712-9559	22572
St Joseph Hospice	8322	D	714 712-7100	24229
Stearns Lending LLC	6163	D	657 999-4915	9954
Steeltech Construction Svcs	1541	D	714 630-2890	1467
Stericycle Comm Solutions Inc	7389	E	714 991-9595	17503
Straub Distributing Co Ltd (PA)	5181	C	714 779-4000	9086
Sun Mar Management Services	8741	A	714 827-9263	27235
Sun Mar Nursing Center Inc	8059	D	714 776-1720	21386
Sunnyslope Tree Farm Inc	5193	D	714 532-1440	9215
Sunstone Hotel Investors LLC	7011	C	714 635-5000	13321
Sunwest Electric Inc	1731	D	714 630-8700	2759
T L Fabrications LP	1791	D	562 802-3980	3405
Targus International LLC (PA)	5199	C	714 765-5555	9306
Tct Circuit Supply Inc	5085	D	714 644-9700	7957
Techno Coatings Inc	1542	C	714 774-4671	1689
Tenet Healthsystem Medical	8062	A	714 428-6800	21964
Thermalair Inc (HQ)	1711	D	714 630-3200	2396
Traffic Management Inc	8741	D	562 264-2353	27255
Transamerica Finance Corp	6311	D	714 778-5100	10224
Tricor America Inc	4215	D	714 701-9880	4430
Trilogy Plumbing Inc (PA)	1711	C	714 441-2952	2400
Truform Construction Corp	1751	D	714 630-7447	3097
Ttg Engineers	8711	D	714 490-5555	26106
Tucker Distributors	5075	E	714 970-5742	7749
Turner Construction Company	5082	B	714 940-9000	7794
TWI- Techno West Inc	1721	D	714 635-4070	2499
Ultimate Landscape Mgt Co	0782	E	714 502-9711	970
Ultimate Landscaping MGT	0782	C	714 502-9711	971
Universal Dust Collector	1541	D	714 630-8588	1477
University Marelich Mech Inc	1711	D	714 632-2600	2402
Uribe Trucking Inc	4214	C	714 549-8696	4385
US Foods Inc	5149	C	714 449-2880	8950
Uti Integrated Logistics LLC	4789	D	714 630-0110	5249
Vci Event Technology Inc	7359	C	714 772-2002	14589
Vengroff Williams & Assoc Inc	7322	C	714 889-6200	14052
Venture Design Services Inc (PA)	8731	D	714 765-3740	26633
Veterans Health Administration	8011	D	714 780-5400	20218
Vm Services Inc	7371	E	714 678-5200	15530
Walker Brothers McHy Mvg Inc (PA)	7389	E	714 630-5957	17605
Walnut Investment Corp	5031	A	714 238-9240	6969
Walt Disney Company	4225	B	714 781-4532	4665
Walt Disney Company	7011	A	714 781-4278	13390
Wasser Filtration Inc	5084	D	714 525-0630	7904
West Anaheim Extended Care	8051	C	714 821-1993	21029
Westcoast Performance Pdts USA	6798	C	714 630-4411	12278
Westside Building Mtl Corp (PA)	5032	C	714 385-1644	7004
Westview Services Inc	8051	B	714 956-4199	21037
Willdan Engineering	8711	A	714 978-8200	26147
Willdan Group Inc (PA)	8711	C	800 424-9144	26148
Wilson Hampton Pntg Contrs Inc	1721	D	714 772-5091	2503
Windsor Gardens (PA)	8051	B	714 826-8950	21049
Workcare Inc	8744	C	714 978-7488	27803
Zyxel Communications Inc	4813	D	714 632-0882	5741

ANDERSON, CA - Shasta County

Company	SIC	EMP	PHONE	ENTRY #
Bettendorf Enterprises Inc	4213	D	530 365-1937	4115

	SIC	EMP	PHONE	ENTRY #
Davey Tree Surgery Company	0783	D	530 378-2674	990
Linkus Enterprises LLC (PA)	1623	C	530 229-9197	1963
Oak River Rehabilitation	8051	D	530 365-0025	20814
Pre-Employcom Inc	7381	D	530 378-7680	16761
Ssmb Pacific Holding Co Inc	5012	D	530 222-1212	6696
United Parcel Service Inc OH	4215	D	530 365-7850	4440

ANGELS CAMP, CA - Calaveras County

	SIC	EMP	PHONE	ENTRY #
Motherlode Investors LLC	7992	D	209 736-8112	18764
United Parcel Service Inc OH	4215	C	209 736-0878	4469
Wyndham Resort Dev Corp	7011	E	209 736-2999	13442

ANGWIN, CA - Napa County

	SIC	EMP	PHONE	ENTRY #
Hermitage Hlthcr Mnkn Mnr	8059	C	410 651-0011	21265

ANTELOPE, CA - Sacramento County

	SIC	EMP	PHONE	ENTRY #
Leavy Brothers Incorporated	1742	D	916 773-5636	2924
Sacramento Prestige Gunite Inc	1771	E	916 723-0404	3324
Skyva Construction Inc	1521	E	916 726-4999	1261

ANTIOCH, CA - Contra Costa County

	SIC	EMP	PHONE	ENTRY #
Antioch Public Golf Corp	7992	D	925 706-4220	18714
Antioch Rotary Club	7997	E	925 757-1800	18875
AT&T Corp	4813	D	925 776-1200	5512
Banister Electrical Inc	1731	D	925 778-7801	2526
Bay Area Credit Service LLC (PA)	7322	C	408 392-4425	14019
Better Homes and Gardens Mason	6531	D	925 776-2740	11321
Black Diamond Electric Inc	1731	D	925 777-3440	2534
Bond Manufacturing Co Inc	5083	E	925 252-1135	7800
City of Antioch	4959	D	925 779-6950	6620
Contra Costa ARC	8331	D	925 755-4925	24327
Contra Costa Newspapers Inc	5192	E	925 757-2525	9162
First Student Inc	4111	C	925 754-4878	3647
Freschi Air Systems Inc	1711	D	925 827-9761	2229
Halo	8699	E	925 473-4642	25539
Jamm Management LLC	5013	E	510 437-5200	6742
Kaiser Foundation Hospitals	8011	C	925 813-6500	19583
Kaiser Foundation Hospitals	8093	C	925 779-5000	22756
Kie-Con Inc	1542	D	925 754-9494	1591
Kiewit Pacific Co	1611	E	925 754-9494	1813
Lone Tree Convalescent Hosp	8051	C	925 754-0470	20739
Mason-Mcduffie Real Estate Inc	6531	D	925 776-2740	11663
Montrose Envmtl Group Inc	8734	B	925 680-4300	26870
Norcal Care Centers Inc	8059	D	925 757-8787	21328
NRG Energy Inc	4911	D	913 689-3904	6157
Peace Keepers Private Security	7381	D	925 978-4140	16757
Permanente Kaiser Intl	8011	A	925 813-6500	19827
Permanente Medical Group Inc	8011	B	925 813-6149	19847
Roddy Ranch Pbc LLC	7997	D	925 978-4653	19046
Rt/Dt Inc	1711	D	925 757-1981	2353
Sutter Delta Medical Ctr Aux	8062	D	925 779-7200	21943
Thrive Support Services Inc	8999	E	510 292-5058	28163
Travis Credit Union	6061	B	925 777-0573	9639
Wayne E Swisher Cem Contr Inc	1771	D	925 757-3660	3349

ANZA, CA - Riverside County

	SIC	EMP	PHONE	ENTRY #
Cahuilla Creek Rest & Casino	7999	C	951 763-1200	19156

APPLE VALLEY, CA - San Bernardino County

	SIC	EMP	PHONE	ENTRY #
8520 Western Ave Inc	8059	C	714 828-8222	21120
Alpha Connection Group Home	8631	D	760 247-6370	25164
Apple Valley Golf Club	7997	C	760 242-3653	18876
Apple Vlley/ Vctrvlle Cnsrtium	7299	D	760 240-7000	13733
AT&T Corp	4813	D	760 240-3592	5497
Automobile Club Southern Cal	6411	C	760 247-4110	10638
Bear Vly Fbrcators Stl Sup Inc	1541	D	760 247-5381	1404
Front Porch Communities & Svcs	8051	D	760 240-5051	20585
Reliable Nursing Solutions	7361	D	760 946-9191	14749
Wal-Mart Stores Inc	4225	B	760 961-6300	4659

APTOS, CA - Santa Cruz County

	SIC	EMP	PHONE	ENTRY #
Aegis Senior Communities LLC	8082	E	831 684-2700	22346
American Golf Corporation	7997	D	831 688-3213	18869
Cabrillo College Children Ctr	8351	D	831 479-6352	24421
Dignity Health Med Foundation	8099	D	831 535-1560	22940
Easter Seals Central Cal	8322	B	831 684-2166	23951
First Alarm (PA)	7382	C	831 476-1111	16885
Parkhurst Terrace	1522	D	831 685-0800	1330
Santa Cruz Montessori School	8351	E	831 476-1646	24511
Seacliff Inn Inc	7011	D	831 661-4671	13227
Seascape Resort Ltd A Calif	7011	E	831 662-7120	13228

ARBUCKLE, CA - Colusa County

	SIC	EMP	PHONE	ENTRY #
Alsco - Geyer Irrigation Inc	5083	D	530 476-2253	7798
T & P Farms	0111	D	530 476-3038	2

ARCADIA, CA - Los Angeles County

	SIC	EMP	PHONE	ENTRY #
Andover Maintenance Inc	7349	D	626 254-1651	14230
Arcadia Convalescent Hosp Inc (PA)	8059	C	323 681-1504	21143
Arcadia Gardens MGT Corp	8052	D	626 574-8571	21066
Arroyo Insurance Services Inc (PA)	6411	D	626 799-9532	10622
Aventra Real Estate Services	6531	E	626 357-7028	11311
Cathay General Bancorp	6022	B	626 574-9530	9481
Century 21 Ludecke Inc (PA)	6531	D	626 445-0123	11380
Childrens Hospital Los Angeles	8062	D	626 795-7177	21483
City of Arcadia	4111	D	626 574-5435	3638
Coldwell Banker Residential RE	6531	D	626 445-5500	11417
Commercial Roofing Systems Inc	1761	D	626 359-5354	3154
Community Housing Options	8322	D	626 359-3300	23774
Country Villa Service Corp	8051	D	626 445-2421	20478
County of Los Angeles	8322	D	626 350-4566	23845
County of Los Angeles	8322	E	626 821-5858	23848
Ego Inc	8721	C	626 447-0296	26334
Forta (PA)	8049	D	626 446-7027	20319
Fumai Industrial Inc	5065	D	626 272-1788	7572
Gar Enterprises (PA)	5045	D	626 574-1175	7135
George Fasching	7542	E	626 446-0654	17842
Goodrich Lax A Cal Ltd Partnr	7011	D	626 254-9988	12670
Hilton Worldwide Inc	7011	C	626 445-8525	12729
Long Dragon Realty Co Inc	6531	C	626 309-7999	11636
Los Angeles Turf Club Inc	7948	B	626 574-6330	18570
Los Angles Arbretum Foundation	8422	D	626 821-3222	25065
Methodist Hosp Southern Cal (PA)	8062	A	626 898-8000	21746
Methodist Hospital of S CA	8062	D	626 574-3755	21747
MWH Americas Inc	8711	D	626 796-9141	25985
Post Alarm Systems (PA)	7382	D	626 446-7159	16912
Santa Anita Associates (PA)	7992	C	626 447-2764	18782
Transdev Services Inc	4119	B	626 357-7912	3851
Venue Management Services Inc	8748	B	626 445-6000	28089
Westport/Berger A Joint Ventr	1541	C	626 447-2448	1479
Wing Lam Ha	8059	E	626 462-0048	21428
Worleyparsons Group Inc	8711	D	626 294-3300	26153

ARCATA, CA - Humboldt County

	SIC	EMP	PHONE	ENTRY #
American Hospital Mgt Corp (PA)	8062	B	707 822-3621	21448
Aquatic Designing Inc	1541	D	707 822-4629	1400
Danco Builders Inc	1522	D	707 822-9000	1306
Danco Builders Northwest	1542	D	707 822-9000	1536
Danco Communities	6552	D	707 822-9000	11961
Healthsport Ltd A Ltd Partnr (PA)	7991	C	707 822-3488	18640
Humboldt State University Spon	8748	E	707 826-4189	27946
Northcountry Clinic	8011	D	707 822-2401	19779
Open Door Community Hlth Ctrs	8093	E	707 826-8610	22783
Open Door Community Hlth Ctrs (PA)	8093	D	707 826-8642	22784
Sun Valley Group Inc (PA)	0181	B	707 822-2885	320
Tektetco	1541	D	707 822-9000	1473
Toucan Inc (PA)	5094	D	707 822-6662	8103
United Indian Health Services (PA)	8011	C	707 825-5000	20154

ARLETA, CA - Los Angeles County

	SIC	EMP	PHONE	ENTRY #
Lexington Scenery & Props Inc	1751	C	818 768-5768	3064

ARNOLD, CA - Calaveras County

	SIC	EMP	PHONE	ENTRY #
Sequoia Wood Country Club	7997	D	209 795-1000	19071

AROMAS, CA - Monterey County

	SIC	EMP	PHONE	ENTRY #
Driscoll Strawberry Assoc Inc	5148	E	831 763-5100	8719
Farmhill LLC	0171	D	831 726-1986	111
Granite Rock Co	1611	D	831 768-2330	1792
Granite Rock Co	5032	D	831 392-3780	6987
Granite Rock Co	1442	D	831 768-2300	1104
Jal Berry Farms LLC	0171	D	831 763-7200	115

ARROYO GRANDE, CA - San Luis Obispo County

	SIC	EMP	PHONE	ENTRY #
Ameri-Kleen	7349	C	805 546-0706	14224
Ball Tagawa Growers	0181	E	805 481-7526	266
Community Action Partnership	8111	A	805 489-4026	23160
Compass Health Inc	8059	C	805 489-8137	21191
Cypress Ridge Golf Course	7992	E	805 474-7979	18731
Dignity Health	8082	D	805 489-4261	22423
Dignity Health	8062	D	805 473-7626	21535
Greenheart Farms Inc (PA)	0182	D	805 481-2234	331
Holland America Flowers LLC	0181	D	805 343-4004	291
Mhm Services Inc	8093	C	805 904-6678	22775
Onsite Clims Apprisal Tech Inc	6411	D	805 474-0893	10818
Sierra Pacific Mortgage Co Inc	6162	D	805 489-6060	9897
St Denis Electric Inc	1731	E	805 343-9999	2743
Talley Farms	0723	C	805 489-2508	594

ARTESIA, CA - Los Angeles County

	SIC	EMP	PHONE	ENTRY #
Artesia Christian Home Inc	8059	D	562 865-5218	21145
County of Los Angeles	8093	E	562 402-0688	22702
E R G Home Health Provider	8082	D	562 403-1070	22429
Edwards Theatres Circuit Inc	7832	D	562 403-1133	18330
I Wmi	1542	B	562 977-4906	1576

ARTESIA, CA

Company	SIC	EMP	PHONE	ENTRY #
New Cingular Wireless Svcs Inc	4813	C	562 924-0000	5667
Oldtimers Housing Dev Corp III	8322	D	562 924-6509	24113
South Asian Help Referral Agcy	8322	E	562 402-4132	24218
Windsor Twin Palms Hlthcare	8051	C	562 865-0271	21055
Wmi	1711	D	562 977-4950	2421

ARVIN, CA - Kern County

Company	SIC	EMP	PHONE	ENTRY #
Arvin-Edison Water Storage Dst (PA)	4971	C	661 854-5573	6642
Edwardo Z Garcia	0761	C	661 854-5414	656
Evergreen Health Care LLC	8051	C	661 854-4475	20560
Granite Construction Company	1611	D	661 854-3051	1780
Grimmway Enterprises Inc	1541	D	661 854-6240	1432
Grimmway Enterprises Inc	0723	B	661 854-6250	539
Grimmway Enterprises Inc	0723	B	661 854-6200	540
Kern Ridge Growers LLC	0723	B	661 854-3141	553

ATASCADERO, CA - San Luis Obispo County

Company	SIC	EMP	PHONE	ENTRY #
AT&T Corp	4813	D	805 461-6400	5498
Atascadero Hotel Partners LLC	7011	D	805 462-3500	12399
Califrnia Dept State Hospitals	8063	A	805 468-2000	22050
Califrnia Department of State	8063	A	805 468-2501	22051
Compass Health Inc	8059	D	805 466-9254	21192
Meridian Holdings	5074	D	805 539-2752	7724
Options Family of Services	8093	E	805 462-8544	22785
USA Waste of California Inc	4953	D	805 466-3636	6580

ATHERTON, CA - San Mateo County

Company	SIC	EMP	PHONE	ENTRY #
Matched Caregivers Inc	8082	C	408 560-2382	22504
Menlo Circus Club	7997	D	650 322-4616	18997

ATWATER, CA - Merced County

Company	SIC	EMP	PHONE	ENTRY #
Bloss Memorial Health Care Dst (PA)	8011	D	209 381-2000	19375
Castle Family Health Ctrs Inc (PA)	8093	D	209 381-2000	22675
Central Counties	8734	D	209 356-0355	26837
Gallo Cattle Co A Ltd Partnr	0241	B	209 394-7984	426
Gino/Giuseppe Inc	1771	C	209 358-0556	3265
Kings View	8331	D	209 357-0321	24357
Pacific Concrete Specialties	1771	D	209 358-0741	3306
Tjd LLC	8059	C	209 357-3420	21391
Vince Fucillo	1771	D	209 358-9175	3348
Ward Enterprises	7349	B	209 358-0445	14464

AUBERRY, CA - Fresno County

Company	SIC	EMP	PHONE	ENTRY #
Mono Wind Casino	7011	D	559 855-4350	13003
Pacific Gas and Electric Co	4911	E	559 855-6112	6186

AUBURN, CA - Placer County

Company	SIC	EMP	PHONE	ENTRY #
American Medical Response Inc	4119	E	530 887-9440	3763
Andregg Geomatics	8713	D	530 885-7072	26272
Auburn Oaks Care Center	8051	D	650 949-7777	20389
Auburn Old Town Gallery	7999	D	530 887-9150	19145
Auburn Placer Disposal Service	4953	D	530 885-3735	6435
Century Lighting and Electric	5063	E	530 823-1004	7425
Chapa-De Indian Health (PA)	8011	D	530 887-2800	19426
Coldwell Bnkr Residential Brkg	6531	D	530 823-7653	11424
Congrgtnal Ch Retirement Cmnty	8399	D	530 823-6131	24901
County of Placer	8322	D	530 886-1870	23877
County of Placer	8322	D	530 889-7900	23878
County of Placer	8093	D	530 889-7215	22707
County of Placer	8322	C	530 823-4300	23879
County of Placer	8322	D	530 889-7900	23880
Decker Landscaping Inc	0782	D	916 652-1780	835
East Hall Investors Inc	6799	D	530 320-1900	12301
Foothill Oaks Care Center Inc	8051	D	530 888-6257	20578
Horizon West Inc	8734	D	530 889-8122	26858
Horizon West Healthcare Inc	8059	C	530 885-7511	21272
Interior Specialists Inc	1752	D	530 885-0632	3121
Keller Williams Realty Inc	6531	D	530 328-1900	11612
Lake of The Pines Association	8641	E	530 268-1141	25284
Madera Convalescent Hospital	8059	D	530 885-7051	21304
Magnussens Dodge Crysler Jeep	7538	D	530 885-2900	17806
Miltenyi Biotec Inc (HQ)	5047	D	530 745-2800	7282
Placer County ADM Svcs	8999	C	530 886-5401	28155
Placer County Water Agency (PA)	4911	D	530 823-4850	6196
Placer County- Adult Sys Care	8093	D	530 886-2974	22799
Pride Industries	8331	D	530 888-0331	24380
Retirement Housing Foundation	8361	C	530 823-6131	24786
Riskalyze Inc	7379	D	530 748-1660	16472
Sierra West Construction Inc	1751	E	530 268-7614	3091
Sutter Health	8093	A	530 888-4500	22844
Vian Enterprises Inc	7389	E	530 885-1997	17591
Western Energetix LLC	5171	D	530 885-0401	9010
Westview Healh Care Center	8051	C	530 885-7511	21036

AVALON, CA - Los Angeles County

Company	SIC	EMP	PHONE	ENTRY #
Catalina Business Entps Inc	7999	E	310 510-1600	19159
Catalina Glassbottom Boat Inc	4489	D	310 510-2888	4734
Santa Catalina Island Company	7997	D	310 510-7410	19063
Santa Catalina Island Company (PA)	4725	D	310 510-2000	5001
Two Harbors Enterprises Inc	4111	D	310 510-2000	3731

AVENAL, CA - Kings County

Company	SIC	EMP	PHONE	ENTRY #
Prison Industry Authority-Pia	8111	D	559 386-6060	23518

AVILA BEACH, CA - San Luis Obispo County

Company	SIC	EMP	PHONE	ENTRY #
Pacific Gas and Electric Co	4911	A	805 506-5280	6172

AZUSA, CA - Los Angeles County

Company	SIC	EMP	PHONE	ENTRY #
Applebee & Sheehan Inc (PA)	7349	D	800 200-8872	14231
Artistic Entrmt Svcs LLC	7929	D	626 334-9388	18456
Buena Vista Food Products Inc	5149	C	626 815-8859	8810
California Pediatric Fmly Svcs	8322	D	626 210-0055	23699
Cemex Cement Inc	5032	D	626 969-1747	6975
David L Amador Inc	1771	D	626 334-2011	3253
Direct Pack Inc	7389	D	626 380-2360	17125
Hanson Distributing Company (PA)	5013	C	626 224-9800	6736
Hanson Distributing Company	5013	D	626 357-5241	6737
Harrison Nichols Co Ltd	4214	C	626 337-5020	4350
Heppner Hardwoods Inc	5031	D	626 969-7983	6927
Jans Towing Inc (PA)	7549	D	626 334-1383	17886
Kds Marketing	7389	D	818 240-7000	17267
Monrovia Nursery Company (PA)	0181	A	626 334-9321	303
Morris National Inc (HQ)	5145	D	626 385-2000	8623
Murrieta Gardens Senior Living	8052	D	951 600-7676	21095
Oj Insulation LP (PA)	1742	C	626 812-6070	2943
Precise Enterprises LLC	8742	E	818 599-6450	27591
RES-Care California Inc	8052	E	626 334-7861	21100
Richard Wilson Wellington	0181	D	626 812-7881	313
San Gabriel Valley Water Assn	4941	D	626 815-1305	6394
Seracada	8082	E	626 486-0800	22559
Silverado Senior Living Inc	8059	D	626 650-9891	21372
Stanley Steemer of Los Angles (PA)	7217	D	626 791-9400	13600
Sunbelt Controls Inc	1711	D	626 610-2340	2387
Totten Tubes Inc (PA)	5051	D	626 812-0220	7408
Virginia Hardwood Company (PA)	5031	D	626 815-0540	6968

BAKERSFIELD, CA - Kern County

Company	SIC	EMP	PHONE	ENTRY #
7th Standard Ranch Company	0172	B	661 399-0416	139
A-C Electric Company	8711	D	661 633-5368	25607
ABM Jntrial Svcs - Sthwest Inc	7349	D	661 322-3280	14207
Accelerated Envmtl Svcs Inc	7349	D	661 765-4013	14209
Account Control Technology Inc	7322	E	661 395-5702	14015
Advance Beverage Co Inc	5181	D	661 833-3783	9037
Advanced Cleanup Tech Inc	4212	D	661 392-7765	3972
Aera Energy (HQ)	1381	A	661 665-5000	1053
Ag-Wise Enterprises Inc (PA)	0762	C	661 325-1567	689
Agape In Home Care Inc	8082	E	661 835-0364	22349
Agri-Mix Transport Inc	4212	C	661 833-6280	3974
Alaidandrew Corporation	8059	D	661 334-2200	21129
Alliance Health Inc	8999	B	661 325-6937	28112
Allpro Industry Solutions LLC	4731	E	661 854-3613	5026
American Baptist Homes of West	8059	C	661 834-0620	21135
Ameripride Services Inc	7213	C	661 324-7941	13526
AMF Bowling Centers Inc	7933	E	661 324-4966	18508
Anthony Vineyards Inc (PA)	0172	E	661 858-6211	141
Arrival Communications Inc (DH)	7389	D	661 322-7375	17002
Asbury Transportation Co	4213	C	661 327-2271	4112
AT&T Services	4813	B	661 327-6030	5516
AT&T Services Inc	4813	C	661 398-2000	5526
AT&T Services Inc	8748	C	661 324-2046	27840
AT&T Services Inc	4813	D	661 398-4650	5543
Automobile Club Southern Cal	8699	E	661 327-4661	25498
B & B Surplus Inc (PA)	5051	D	661 589-0381	7359
Baker Petrolite Corporation	1389	D	661 325-4138	1069
Bakersfield Assc Rrtd Ctzns	8331	C	661 834-2272	24312
Bakersfield Country Club	7997	D	661 871-4000	18880
Bakersfield Dialysis Center	8092	D	661 325-4741	22617
Bakersfield Family Med Group	7389	D	661 861-1835	17020
Bakersfield Healthcare	8051	D	661 872-2121	20403
Bakersfield Kitchen & Bath	1711	D	661 836-2284	2157
Bakersfield Memorial Hospital	8062	A	661 327-1792	21459
Bakersfield Rodeway Inn Inc	7011	D	661 324-6666	12413
Bakersfield Symphony Orch	7929	D	661 323-7928	18457
Baymarr Constructors Inc (PA)	1771	D	661 395-1676	3230
Bc Laboratories Inc	8734	D	661 327-4911	26833
Beautitudes Beauty Supply LLC	5087	D	800 830-6076	7964
Behavioral H Bakersfield	8063	D	661 398-1800	22043
Better Way Services	8322	D	661 326-6444	23683
Bic Real Estate Dev Corp	6153	A	661 847-9691	9773
Biomat Usa Inc	8099	D	661 863-0621	22896
Bolthouse Farms	0161	A	661 366-7205	41
Boys Girls CLB of Bakersfield	8641	C	661 325-3730	25216
Braden Partners LP A Calif	5047	D	661 632-1979	7247
Braun Electric Company Inc (HQ)	1731	E	661 633-1451	2536
Bright House Networks LLC	4841	D	661 634-2200	5936

GEOGRAPHIC SECTION

BAKERSFIELD, CA

Company	SIC	EMP	PHONE	ENTRY #
Brown Armstrong Accntancy Corp	8721	D	661 324-4971	26298
Burtch Trucking Inc	1611	D	661 399-1736	1744
Calcot Ltd (PA)	5159	D	661 327-5961	8964
California Physicians Service	6324	C	661 631-2277	10261
California Resources Corp	1311	C	661 395-8000	1037
California Resources Prod Corp (HQ)	1311	D	661 869-8000	1041
California Water Service Co	4941	D	661 396-2400	6320
Cameron West Coast Inc	5082	D	661 837-4980	7765
Castle & Cooke Inc	4953	E	661 664-6500	6456
Castle & Cooke Commercial CA	6552	D	661 665-1540	11958
Cbiz Southern California LLC	8721	E	661 325-7500	26308
Cellco Partnership	4812	D	661 827-8728	5305
Cellco Partnership	4899	D	661 663-9451	6063
Central Cardiology Med Clinic	8011	C	661 395-0000	19420
Centre For Neuro Skills (PA)	8093	D	661 872-3408	22679
Cintas Corporation No 3	7218	D	661 282-4300	13619
Citizens Business Bank	6022	D	661 281-0300	9486
City of Bakersfield	8322	C	661 852-7300	23750
CL Knox Inc	1389	D	661 837-0477	1071
Clifford & Brown A Prof Corp	8111	D	661 322-6023	23156
Clinica Sierra Vista	8099	E	661 326-6490	22921
Clinica Sierra Vista (PA)	8011	D	661 635-3050	19446
CMA Fire Protection (PA)	1711	D	661 322-9344	2183
Coastal Industrial Svcs Inc	7699	D	661 392-0001	17967
Community Action Partnr Kern	8399	D	661 336-0317	24886
Community Action Partnr Kern	8351	D	661 366-5953	24443
Community Action Partnr Kern (PA)	8322	E	661 336-5236	23771
Construction Specialty Svc Inc	1623	D	661 864-7573	1922
Contra Costa Electric Inc	1731	C	661 322-4036	2562
Core-Mark International Inc	5149	C	661 366-2673	8821
Core-Mark International Inc	5194	C	661 366-2673	9232
County of Kern	8322	A	661 868-4100	23814
County of Kern	8322	D	661 392-2010	23815
County of Kern	8322	D	661 336-6800	23816
County of Kern	8011	E	661 868-8360	19465
County of Kern	8062	A	661 326-2054	21515
County of Kern	7374	D	661 868-2000	16112
County of Kern	8399	A	661 631-6346	24905
County of Kern	8322	D	661 363-8910	23819
County of Kern	8111	D	661 868-2000	23171
Crestwood Behavioral Hlth Inc	8063	D	661 363-8127	22061
Crestwood Behavioral Hlth Inc	8069	C	661 363-6711	22135
Crystal Organic Farms LLC	0191	A	661 845-5200	352
Csub Nursing Class of 2006	7389	D	408 219-5914	17109
CW Welding Service Inc	5094	D	661 399-5422	8098
Delmart Cold Storage Co Inc	4222	D	661 849-8608	4491
Dennis Hyde Construction Inc	1521	D	661 393-1077	1166
Dhv Industries Inc	5085	D	661 392-8948	7931
Dignity Health	8351	D	661 832-8300	24456
Dignity Health	8082	E	661 663-6767	22425
Dignity Health	8062	C	661 632-5279	21542
Dignity Health	8062	D	661 632-5000	21543
Diversified Prj Svcs Intl Inc (PA)	8711	D	661 371-2800	25770
Diversified Utility Svcs Inc	1623	B	661 325-3212	1927
Don Kinzel Construction Inc	1542	D	661 322-9105	1544
Donald Valpredo Farming Inc	0161	D	661 858-2245	59
Doubletree LLC	7011	C	661 323-7111	12593
Downs Equipment Rentals Inc (PA)	7353	D	661 615-6119	14480
E & B Ntral Resources Mgt Corp (PA)	1311	D	661 679-1714	1043
Electrcal Instrumentation Intl	1731	B	661 836-9466	2583
Electrical & Instrumentation	1731	B	661 836-9466	2586
Elmer F Karpe Inc	6531	E	661 847-4800	11491
Elysium Jennings LLC	1381	C	661 679-1700	1057
Engineered Well Svc Intl Inc	1389	D	866 913-6283	1074
Esparza Enterprises Inc (PA)	7361	E	661 831-0002	14652
Esparza Enterprises Inc	7361	D	661 831-0002	14653
Esparza Enterprises Inc	4213	A	661 631-0347	4147
Esys Energy Control Company	5084	D	661 833-1902	7842
Evergreen At Lakeport LLC	8051	C	661 871-3133	20556
Excalibur Well Services Corp (PA)	1381	D	661 589-5338	1058
Exeter Packers Inc	4222	C	661 399-0416	4495
First Transit Inc	4111	B	661 391-3614	3651
Fisher Communications Inc	4833	D	661 327-7955	5861
Flyers Energy LLC	5172	B	661 321-9961	9019
Freeport-Mcmoran Oil & Gas LLC	1311	D	661 322-7600	1044
Fritch Eye Care Medical Center	8011	D	661 665-2020	19532
Frito-Lay North America Inc	5145	E	661 835-0347	8615
Frontier Mechanical Inc	1711	D	661 589-6203	2231
Frye Construction Inc	1742	D	661 588-8870	2900
G4s Secure Solutions (usa)	7381	C	661 834-3454	16649
Garcia Roofing Inc	1761	D	661 325-5736	3176
Garlic Company	0139	C	661 393-4212	23
Gentiva Hospice	8052	B	661 324-1232	21083
Geo Guidance Drilling Svcs Inc	1781	D	661 833-9999	3355
Gilliam & Sons Inc	1794	E	661 589-0913	3429
Giumarra Vineyards Corporation	0172	D	661 395-7071	155
Glenn E Porter	6331	E	661 615-1500	10423
Glenwood Gardens	8051	B	661 587-0221	20601
Golden Empire Concrete Pdts	1771	D	661 833-4490	3266
Golden Empire Mortgage (PA)	6162	D	661 328-1600	9848
Golden Empire Mortgage Inc (PA)	6162	D	661 328-1600	9849
Golden Empire Transit District (PA)	4111	C	661 869-2438	3654
Golden Living LLC	8051	D	661 323-2894	20609
Golden State Drilling Inc	1381	D	661 589-0730	1059
Good Samaritan Hospital (PA)	8062	D	661 399-4461	21582
Good Samaritan Hospital	8063	D	661 398-1800	22072
Goodwill Inds S Centl Cal	8331	D	661 377-0191	24344
Granite Construction Company	1611	D	661 399-3361	1778
Grant Construction Inc	1751	C	661 638-4586	3051
Grayson Service Inc	1389	C	661 589-5444	1078
Griffith Company	1611	D	661 831-7331	1795
Griffith Company	1611	D	661 392-6640	1797
Grimmway Enterprises Inc	0723	C	661 845-5200	541
GTE Corporation	4813	E	661 328-2226	5624
Guardsmark LLC	7381	C	661 325-5906	16695
Guinn Corporation	1794	D	661 325-6109	3431
H F Cox Inc (PA)	4213	D	661 366-3236	4194
H P Sears Co Inc	7389	D	661 325-5981	17206
H/S Development Company LLC	1542	D	661 327-0912	1560
Hall Ambulance Service Inc	4119	D	661 322-8741	3803
Halliburton Energy Svcs Inc	1389	D	661 393-8111	1080
HealthSouth Corporation	8361	D	661 323-5500	24687
Herc Rentals Inc	7514	C	661 392-3661	17680
Heritage Medical Group (PA)	8011	D	661 327-4411	19556
Hillcrest Sheet Metal Inc	1761	D	661 335-1500	3178
Hills Wldg & Engrg Contr Inc	1389	D	661 746-5400	1081
Hoffman Hospice of The Valley	8059	D	661 410-1010	21271
Houchin Blood Services	8099	D	661 327-8541	22978
Hps Mechanical Inc (PA)	1711	C	661 397-2121	2246
Hps Plumbing Service Inc	1623	D	661 324-2121	1941
Hunter-La Purisima Corp	8748	D	661 616-0600	27947
Hunting Energy Services Inc	1389	D	661 633-4272	1083
Innovative Engrg Systems Inc	8711	E	661 381-7800	25879
J G Boswell Company	0131	C	661 327-7721	12
Jacobs Engineering Group Inc	8711	D	661 393-3922	25889
Jamison Childrens Home	8322	D	661 334-3500	24040
Jims Supply Co Inc (PA)	5051	D	661 324-6514	7377
K S Fabrication & Machine Inc	1623	C	661 617-1700	1953
Kaiser Foundation Hospitals	8011	A	877 524-7373	19600
Kaiser Foundation Hospitals	8062	B	661 395-3000	21643
Kaiser Foundation Hospitals	8011	A	877 524-7373	19602
Kaiser Foundation Hospitals	8011	A	661 337-7160	19603
Kaiser Foundation Hospitals	8011	A	877 524-7373	19604
Kaiser Foundation Hospitals	8011	A	877 524-7373	19607
Kaiser Foundation Hospitals	8062	E	661 398-5011	21663
Kaiser Foundation Hospitals	8062	C	661 334-2020	21665
Kbak TV Channel 29 CBS	4833	D	661 327-7955	5878
Kearn Alternative Care Inc (PA)	8082	B	661 631-2036	22490
Kern Alternative Care Inc	8082	C	661 631-2036	22491
Kern Around Clock Foundation	8741	E	661 395-5800	27091
Kern Cnty Mntal Hlth Child Sys	8052	D	661 868-8300	21086
Kern County Water Agency	4941	D	661 634-1512	6360
Kern Federal Credit Union	6061	D	661 327-9461	9606
Kern Health Systems Inc	8011	D	661 664-5000	19687
Kern Member Insurance Services	6411	E	661 327-9461	10762
Kern Rdlgy Imaging Systems Inc (PA)	8071	D	661 326-9600	22230
Kern Regional Center (PA)	8322	C	661 327-8531	24055
Kern River Co Generation Co	4911	D	661 392-2663	6142
Kern Schools Federal Credit Un (PA)	6061	D	661 833-7900	9607
Kern Security Corporation	7382	D	661 363-6874	16893
Kern Steel Fabrication Inc (PA)	1791	D	661 327-9588	3387
Kindred Healthcare Inc	8099	C	661 324-1232	22988
Kindred Healthcare Operating	8051	C	661 872-6767	20704
Kirschenman Enterprises Inc	0191	D	661 366-5736	378
Klassen Development Inc (PA)	1542	D	661 327-0875	1595
Klein Denatale Goldner Et Al (PA)	8111	D	661 401-7755	23356
Kpc Healthcare Inc	8099	C	661 229-4009	22991
KS Industries LP (PA)	1623	A	661 617-1700	1958
Ksi Engineering Inc	8711	E	661 617-1700	25929
Latara Enterprise Inc	8071	D	661 665-9780	22235
Laztrans Inc	4213	E	661 833-3783	4211
Linnco LLC	1311	A	661 616-3900	1046
Lutrel Trucking Inc	4731	D	661 397-9756	5117
M & S Security Services Inc	7381	D	661 397-9616	16729
M P Vacuum Truck Service (PA)	4953	D	661 393-1151	6496
Majestic Roofing Inc	1761	D	661 588-6120	3188
Managed Care Systems Kern Cnty	6411	D	661 716-7100	10768
Maple Dairy LP	0241	D	661 396-9600	435
Mechanical Industries Inc	1791	E	661 634-9477	3392
Medcath Incorporated	8069	B	704 815-7700	22158

BAKERSFIELD, CA

Company	SIC	EMP	PHONE	ENTRY #
Mega Farm Labor Services Inc	7361	C	661 229-8077	14703
Mercy HM Svcs A Cal Ltd Partnr	8062	C	661 632-5234	21739
Meritage Homes Corporation	1521	D	661 829-6739	1219
Mistras Group Inc	8711	D	661 829-1192	25967
Mmi Services Inc	1389	C	661 589-9366	1086
Moreland PCF Snoqualmie LLC	6552	C	661 322-1081	11985
Morgan Stanley & Co LLC	6211	D	661 663-8100	10055
Mp Environmental Services Inc (PA)	4953	C	800 458-3036	6508
Nabors Well Services Co	1381	C	661 589-5416	1060
Nabors Well Services Co	1389	B	661 589-3970	1088
Nations Petroleum Cal LLC	1382	D	661 387-6402	1065
Ned E Dunphy	8111	D	661 395-1000	23464
Nestle Ice Cream Company	5143	A	661 398-3500	8590
New Advances For People Disabi	8399	D	661 327-0188	24946
New York Life Insurance Co	6411	D	559 447-3900	10800
Newport Hospitality Group Inc	7011	C	661 323-1900	13021
Newport Television LLC	4833	D	661 283-1700	5901
Oakdale Heights Senior Living	8051	E	661 663-9671	20815
Oldenkamp Trucking Inc (PA)	4212	D	661 833-3400	4047
Olive Knolls Christian School	8351	D	661 393-3566	24489
Olympus Power LLC	4911	C	661 393-6885	6159
Omni Family Health (PA)	8011	C	661 459-1900	19793
Opal Fry and Son	0161	E	661 858-2523	86
Optimal Health Services Inc	8082	C	661 393-4483	22523
Optmial Hospice Foundation	8082	C	661 716-4000	22524
OXY USA Inc	1311	C	661 869-8000	1047
Pacific Gas and Electric Co	4911	D	661 398-5918	6192
Pacific Process Systems Inc (PA)	1389	C	661 321-9681	1091
Padre Associates Inc	8711	D	661 829-2686	26008
Pan Pacific Petroleum Co Inc	4213	C	661 589-3200	4241
Panama-Buena Vista Un Schl Dst	7349	B	661 397-2205	14378
Panama-Buena Vista Un Schl Dst	4225	C	661 831-7879	4610
Panorama Park Apts	6513	C	661 325-4047	11183
Parkview Jlian Cnvlescent Hosp	8051	D	661 831-9150	20842
Pavletich Elc Cmmnications Inc (PA)	1731	D	661 589-9473	2682
PCL Industrial Services Inc	1541	B	661 832-3995	1458
Penney Lawn Service Inc	0782	D	661 366-3777	933
Perez Contracting LLC	0762	D	661 399-2700	715
Physicians Automated Lab Inc (PA)	8071	C	661 325-0744	22256
Physicians Plz Surgical Ctr LP	8011	E	661 322-4744	19871
Pomwonderful LLC (DH)	5149	C	310 966-5800	8908
Preferred Brokers Inc (PA)	6531	D	661 836-2345	11759
Progauge Technologies Inc	5084	E	661 392-9600	7877
Pros Incorporated	1389	D	661 589-5400	1093
Prosoft Technology Inc (PA)	4899	C	661 716-5100	6087
Public Health California Dept	8011	C	661 835-4668	19899
Pyramid Produce Inc	0761	C	661 366-5736	679
Quinn Company	5082	D	661 393-5800	7781
Quinn Group Inc	5083	D	661 393-5800	7807
R Stanley Security Service	7381	D	661 634-9283	16769
Rainbow Ranches Inc	0191	E	661 858-2266	386
Ramsgate Engineering Inc	8711	D	661 392-0050	26032
Re/Max	6531	E	661 616-4040	11791
Re/Max Magic	6531	E	661 616-4040	11794
Regent Assisted Living Inc	8361	E	661 663-8400	24783
Rgis LLC	7389	E	661 827-9195	17460
Rhino Ready Mix Trucking Inc (PA)	4212	E	661 679-3643	4055
Richard K Newman and Assoc Inc (PA)	7216	E	661 634-1130	13584
Rio Bravo Ranch Shop	0291	E	661 872-5050	472
Rncmba Inc	7363	C	661 395-1700	14938
S A Camp Companies (PA)	5083	E	661 399-4451	7809
S A Camp Pump Company	7699	D	661 399-2976	18009
S Patterson Construction Inc	1742	D	661 391-9939	2975
SA Recycling LLC	4953	D	661 327-3559	6551
Salimar Inc	7011	D	661 327-9651	13191
Salvation Army	8093	D	661 325-8626	22820
San Dimas Medical Group Inc	8011	D	661 663-4800	19941
San Joaquin Community Hospital (PA)	8062	A	661 395-3000	21849
Schlumberger Technology Corp	1389	D	661 864-4750	1094
Seven Oaks Country Club	7997	C	661 664-6404	19075
Sierra International McHy LLC	5093	D	661 327-7073	8084
Sierra Recycling & Dem Inc	1795	D	661 327-7073	3467
Sierra Transport Inc	4212	D	661 836-3166	4065
Silla Automotive LLC	5013	D	661 392-8880	6768
Simmons Construction Inc	1542	E	661 636-1321	1670
Sippi Anne Riverside Ranch LLP	8361	B	661 871-9697	24812
Social Vocational Services Inc	7363	D	661 323-0533	14949
Soli-Bond Inc	1389	E	661 631-1633	1096
Southern Cal Prmnnte Med Group	8011	D	661 398-5085	20020
Southern Cal Prmnnte Med Group	8011	D	661 334-2020	20044
Southern California Gas Co	4923	E	661 399-4431	6263
Stantec Energy & Resources Inc (HQ)	8713	C	661 396-3770	26283
Stantec Holdings Del III Inc (PA)	6719	C	661 396-3770	12091
State Compensation Insur Fund	6331	C	661 664-4000	10462
State Farm Mutl Auto Insur Co	6411	D	661 663-1921	10882
State Farm Mutl Auto Insur Co	6411	D	661 324-4077	10888
State Farm Mutl Auto Insur Co	6411	D	661 664-9663	10896
State Farm Mutl Auto Insur Co	6411	A	661 663-1313	10898
Stockdale Country Club	7997	D	661 832-0310	19096
Sturgeon Services Intl Inc (PA)	6719	E	661 322-4408	12093
Sturgeon Son Grading & Pav Inc (PA)	1794	C	661 322-4408	3442
Sun Pacific Maricopa	0723	B	661 847-1015	588
Sun Pacific Marketing Coop Inc	5148	A	661 847-1015	8779
Sun World International Inc (PA)	0723	A	661 392-5000	590
Sun World International LLC	0191	B	661 392-5000	394
Sunridge Nurseries Inc	0721	C	661 363-8463	484
Sunshine Metal Clad Inc	1742	D	661 366-0575	2985
Surface Pumps Inc (PA)	5084	D	661 393-1545	7894
Surgener Electric Inc	1731	D	661 399-3321	2761
Sycamore Cogeneration Co (PA)	4911	D	661 615-4630	6245
T and W Farms	0762	E	661 396-7203	726
Technosocialworkcom LLC	7374	D	661 617-6601	16199
Texaco Inc	6531	B	661 654-7000	11872
Tj Cross Engineers Inc	8711	C	661 831-8782	26100
Total-Western Inc	1522	D	661 589-5200	1348
Trans-West Security Svcs Inc	7381	B	661 381-2900	16835
Triple E Trucking	4212	D	661 834-0071	4074
Truitt Oilfield Maint Corp	1389	B	661 871-4099	1098
Truxtun Radiology Med Group LP	8071	C	661 325-6200	22290
UCI Construction Inc	8711	D	661 587-0192	26114
Ulta Salon Cosmt Fragrance Inc	7231	C	661 664-1402	13695
Union Pacific Railroad Company	4011	D	661 321-4604	3627
United States Cold Storage	4222	D	661 832-2653	4504
UPS Ground Freight Inc	4213	D	661 395-9500	4286
Valley Demo Inc	1611	D	661 900-4818	1880
Valley Industrial X-Ra	8734	C	661 399-8497	26901
Valley Pacific Petro Svcs Inc	5172	C	661 746-7737	9030
Valley Power Systems Inc	5084	E	661 325-9001	7901
Valley Sun Mechanical Cnstr	1799	D	661 321-9070	3596
Vaquero Energy Incorporated	1311	E	661 363-7240	1052
Varsity Contractors Inc	8712	C	661 398-0275	26263
Vasindas Around The Clock Care	8361	D	661 395-5820	24844
Verizon Wireless Inc	4812	C	661 836-3141	5433
Veterans Health Administration	8011	E	661 632-1871	20219
Veterans Health Administration	8011	B	661 323-8387	20221
Vinod Kumar MD	8011	D	661 324-4100	20225
W M Lyles Co	8711	E	661 387-1600	26143
Weatherford International LLC	5082	D	661 587-6930	7796
Western Oilfields Supply Co (PA)	7359	C	661 399-9058	14590
Wholesale Fuels Inc	5172	C	661 327-4900	9035
Winegard Energy Inc	1742	D	661 393-9467	3003
Wm Bolthouse Farms Inc (DH)	0161	A	661 366-7205	102
Work Force Services Inc	7363	C	661 327-5019	14985
Zim Industries Inc	1781	D	661 393-9661	3360

BALDWIN PARK, CA - Los Angeles County

Company	SIC	EMP	PHONE	ENTRY #
All Direct Mail Services Inc	7331	C	818 833-7773	14065
All Star Automotive Products	5013	D	626 960-5164	6703
American Kal Enterprises Inc (PA)	5072	C	626 338-7308	7670
American Mzhou Dngpo Group Inc	8741	D	626 820-9239	26918
Ardmore Home Design Inc	5023	E	626 939-1177	6843
Baldwin Hospitality LLC	7011	D	626 962-6000	12414
Cbre Inc	6531	B	626 814-7900	11352
Cedarwood-Young Company (PA)	5093	D	626 962-4047	8067
Cedarwood-Young Company	5093	D	626 962-4047	8068
Cellco Partnership	4812	D	626 472-6196	5328
CH Stone Plumbing Co Inc	1711	D	626 962-5001	2179
County of Los Angeles	8711	C	626 337-1277	25756
Crowner Sheet Metal Pdts Inc	1761	E	626 960-4971	3156
First Avenue Inc	1761	D	626 856-2076	3173
G K Tool Corp	5072	C	626 338-7300	7684
Garden View Care Center Inc	8051	D	626 962-7095	20591
Golden State Habilitation Conv (PA)	8051	C	626 962-3274	20628
Haynes Building Service LLC	7349	C	626 359-6100	14320
Kaiser Foundation Hospitals	8062	A	626 851-1011	21635
La Flor De Mexico Inc (PA)	5149	D	626 334-0716	8872
Neovia Logistics Dist LP	4731	D	626 358-8025	5128
Nichols Lumber & Hardware Co	5031	D	626 960-4802	6938
Nr 2 Group Inc	4212	E	626 251-6681	4045
Ols Hotels & Resorts LP	7011	A	626 962-6000	13041
Pepsi-Cola Metro Btlg Co Inc	5149	D	626 338-5531	8901
Pepsico Inc	5145	C	626 338-5531	8624
Phoenix Satellite TV US Inc	4833	E	626 388-1188	5905
San Gabriel Transit Inc	4121	D	626 430-3650	3867
SCE Federal Credit Union	6061	D	626 960-6888	9624
Sierra View Care Holdings LLC	8051	D	626 960-1971	20914
Southern California Edison Co	4911	D	626 543-6093	6219
Superior Communications Inc (PA)	5065	C	626 388-2573	7642
Tanimura & Antle Inc	0723	B	831 424-6100	595
Trinity Health Systems (PA)	8051	D	626 960-1971	20994
United Parcel Service Inc OH	4215	C	626 814-6216	4478

	SIC	EMP	PHONE	ENTRY #
USA Waste of California Inc	4953	D	626 856-1285	6579
Valley Light Industries Inc	8331	C	626 337-6200	24401
Vista Specialty Hosp Cal LP	8062	C	626 388-2700	22025

BALLICO, CA - Merced County

	SIC	EMP	PHONE	ENTRY #
Hilltop Ranch Inc	0723	C	209 874-1875	547
Veldhuis North Dairy	0241	E	209 394-5117	439

BANNING, CA - Riverside County

	SIC	EMP	PHONE	ENTRY #
Akamai Holding Inc	7291	D	951 922-2419	13718
Bho LLC	8361	E	951 845-2220	24566
Ferrees Group Home Inc	8361	E	951 849-1927	24657
Green Thumb Produce	5148	E	951 849-4711	8737
H E L P Inc	8322	D	951 922-2305	23999
Poison Spyder Customs Inc	7549	A	951 849-5911	17889
Professional Cmnty MGT Cal Inc	6531	E	951 845-2191	11765
Riverside-San Bernardino (PA)	8093	D	951 849-4761	22818
San Gorgonio Memorial Hospital (PA)	8062	C	951 845-1121	21848
Silent Valley Club Inc	7033	D	951 849-4501	13483
Strech Plastics Inc	5088	E	951 922-2224	8006
Sun Lakes Cntry Club Hmeownrs	7997	D	951 845-2135	19100

BARD, CA - Imperial County

	SIC	EMP	PHONE	ENTRY #
Royal Medjool Date Garden	0179	D	760 572-0524	259
Sun Garden Date Growers LP	0179	E	760 957-0396	260

BARSTOW, CA - San Bernardino County

	SIC	EMP	PHONE	ENTRY #
Barstow Redevelopment Agency	8748	C	760 256-3531	27847
Bnsf Railway Company	4011	C	760 255-7803	3608
Burrtec Waste Group Inc	4212	C	760 256-2730	3986
Darensburg Roghair & Renier	7011	E	760 256-6891	12563
Economy Inn	7011	E	760 256-5601	12609
Frontier California Inc	4813	C	760 256-3511	5607
Hospital of Barstow Inc	8062	C	760 256-1761	21607
Kbrwyle Tech Solutions LLC	8711	C	760 255-8322	25916
Latara Enterprise Inc	8071	C	760 256-3450	22236
Little Sisters Truck Wash Inc	7542	C	760 253-2277	17851
M V Transportation	4789	C	760 255-3330	5231
Time Warner Cable Inc	4841	D	760 256-3526	6047
Uptowners Barber Shop	7241	D	760 256-5813	13700

BASS LAKE, CA - Madera County

	SIC	EMP	PHONE	ENTRY #
Basslake LLC	7011	D	559 642-3121	12422
Home Away Inc	7011	D	559 642-3121	12755

BAY POINT, CA - Contra Costa County

	SIC	EMP	PHONE	ENTRY #
Ambrose Recreation & Park Dst	7999	D	925 458-1601	19135
Caribbean South Amercn Council	4724	E	925 709-3433	4959
Henkel Corporation	8711	C	925 458-8086	25860
K & S Towing & Transport	8742	D	925 709-0759	27496

BAYSIDE, CA - Humboldt County

	SIC	EMP	PHONE	ENTRY #
O A Outfitting Inc	7999	D	707 498-2917	19252

BEALE AFB, CA - Yuba County

	SIC	EMP	PHONE	ENTRY #
US Dept of the Air Force	8011	D	530 634-4738	20175

BEAR VALLEY, CA - Calaveras County

	SIC	EMP	PHONE	ENTRY #
Bear Valley Ski Co	7999	B	209 753-2301	19147

BEAUMONT, CA - Riverside County

	SIC	EMP	PHONE	ENTRY #
Anderson Chrnesky Strl Stl Inc	1791	D	951 769-5700	3362
Arrow USA	5087	D	951 845-6144	7963
Beaumont Unified School Dst	4151	A	951 845-3010	3912
California Oak Valley Golf	7997	E	951 769-9771	18909
Carpe Diem Enterprises Inc	5063	E	866 251-0852	7423
Cellco Partnership	4812	C	951 769-0985	5284
Charlee Family Care	8361	D	951 845-3588	24591
Childhelp Inc	8361	C	951 845-6737	24592

BELL, CA - Los Angeles County

	SIC	EMP	PHONE	ENTRY #
4g Wireless Inc	4813	D	562 928-2972	5439
Affiliated Temporary Help	7363	B	323 771-1383	14833
Bernard Perrin Supowitz Inc	5141	C	323 981-2800	8459
Bluprint Clothing Corp	5137	E	323 780-4347	8371
Briarcrest Nursing Center Inc	8051	C	562 927-2641	20416
City of Bell	8322	C	323 773-1596	23751
El Aviso Magazine	5192	D	323 586-9199	9164
Fam LLC	5136	E	323 888-7755	8340
Human Services Association (PA)	8322	C	562 806-5400	24015
Jwch Institute Inc	8733	D	323 562-5813	26778
Omega Moulding West LLC	5023	D	323 261-3510	6878

BELL GARDENS, CA - Los Angeles County

	SIC	EMP	PHONE	ENTRY #
Anitsa Inc	7211	C	213 237-0533	13500
Auchante Inc	6531	D	562 231-1880	11309
Bell Gardens Bicycle Club Inc	7999	A	562 806-4646	19148
Bicycle Casino LP	7011	D	562 806-4646	12450
C T and F Inc	1731	D	562 927-2339	2546

	SIC	EMP	PHONE	ENTRY #
Del Rio Sanitarium Inc	8051	C	562 927-6586	20515
Energized Distribution LLC	5149	C	562 319-0232	8833
WEI-Chuan USA Inc (PA)	5142	C	323 587-2101	8574

BELLFLOWER, CA - Los Angeles County

	SIC	EMP	PHONE	ENTRY #
Advent Securities Investments (PA)	6211	E	562 920-5467	9957
Bio-Mdcal Applications Cal Inc	8092	D	562 920-2070	22619
Empire Enterprises Inc	4119	C	562 529-2676	3788
Empire Transportation	4141	B	562 529-2676	3893
Estrella Inc	8051	C	562 925-6418	20553
Habitat For Humanity of Greate	8399	E	310 323-4663	24925
Harbor Health Care Inc	8361	C	562 866-7054	24678
Hollywood Sports Park LLC	7389	D	562 867-9600	17225
Jwch Institute Inc	8099	D	562 867-7999	22982
Kaiser Foundation Hospitals	8011	A	562 461-3000	19587
Kaiser Foundation Hospitals	6324	C	562 461-3084	10333
Leroy Durbin	6531	E	562 531-2001	11633
Life Care Centers America Inc	8051	D	562 867-1761	20730
Peter Wylan DDS	8021	D	562 925-3765	20270
Produce Company	5148	C	310 508-7760	8765
Rebecca Terley	8051	E	562 925-4252	20865
Universal Care Inc	8093	E	562 461-1179	22859
Verizon Communications Inc	4899	C	562 804-0354	6098
Young Mens Chrstn Assc Gr L B	8641	E	562 925-1292	25459

BELMONT, CA - San Mateo County

	SIC	EMP	PHONE	ENTRY #
Belmont Oaks Academy	8351	D	650 593-6175	24416
County of San Mateo	8322	C	650 802-6470	23915
Enmetric Systems Inc	7371	E	650 489-4441	15166
Island Hospitality MGT LLC	7011	E	650 591-8600	12859
Namasta Inc	7997	E	650 591-3639	19009
Nikon Precision Inc (DH)	5084	C	650 508-4674	7870
Oracle Systems Corporation	7373	B	650 654-7606	16024
Pacific Gas and Electric Co	4911	B	650 592-9411	6166
Ringcentral Inc (PA)	7372	C	650 472-4100	15828
Steelkiwi Inc	7373	D	415 449-8696	16059
Sun Edison LLC (HQ)	4911	D	650 453-5600	6244
Sunrise Senior Living Inc	8051	D	650 508-0400	20955
Sunrise Senior Living LLC	8051	D	650 654-9700	20981
Tectura Corporation (PA)	7379	D	650 273-4249	16505
Telecare Corporation	8063	D	650 817-9070	22108
Ten-X LLC	6531	C	800 793-6107	11867
Westlake Development Group LLC	8741	D	650 579-1010	27281
Woodmont Realty Advisors Inc	6371	D	650 592-3960	10564
Wyndham International Inc	7011	E	650 591-8600	13440

BELVEDERE TIBURON, CA - Marin County

	SIC	EMP	PHONE	ENTRY #
Accenture LLP	8742	C	415 537-5860	27296
Digital Foundry Inc	7371	E	415 789-1600	15139
L Ruhland	8721	E	415 435-5992	26392
Magave Tequila Inc	5182	E	415 515-3536	9108
Marcolin USA Inc	5048	E	415 383-6348	7333
Marin Cnvlscent Rhbltion Hosp	8051	E	415 435-4554	20756
Melissa Bradley RE Inc	6531	E	415 435-2705	11675
Pharmacy Temps Inc	7363	E	415 459-5211	14923
Stage II Inc	7389	E	415 285-8400	17499
Tiburon Hotel LLC	7011	E	415 435-5996	13343
Tiburon Peninsula Club Inc	7997	E	415 789-7900	19109

BENICIA, CA - Solano County

	SIC	EMP	PHONE	ENTRY #
1-800 Radiator & A/C (PA)	5013	D	707 747-7400	6702
All-Points Petroleum LLC	5172	D	707 745-1116	9011
American Civil Const	1622	C	707 746-8028	1887
American Civil Constrs LLC	1629	C	707 746-8028	2020
Americas Lemonade Stand Inc	7389	C	707 745-1274	16988
Anthony Trevino	1752	D	707 747-4776	3105
Benicia Plumbing Inc	1711	D	707 745-2930	2163
Biagi Bros Inc	4214	D	707 745-8115	4332
C E Toland & Son	1799	C	707 747-1000	3504
Califrnia Erectors Bay Area Inc	1791	C	707 746-1990	3373
Certifiedsafety Inc	8742	C	707 747-9400	27377
Clean Harbors Envmtl Svcs Inc	4953	C	707 747-6699	6464
Csu Holding Company	6719	E	707 746-0353	12054
DC Solar Solutions Inc	1711	E	925 203-1088	2203
F3 and Associates Inc (PA)	8713	D	707 748-4300	26274
Fairway Independent Mrtg Corp	6211	E	707 361-5342	9996
Flatiron West Inc	1622	C	707 742-6000	1889
Henry Wine Group LLC (HQ)	5182	B	707 745-8500	9106
Herc Rentals Inc	7514	C	707 747-4444	17681
Innovel Solutions Inc	4731	C	707 748-1940	5104
Inter-Rail Trnspt Nshville LLC	4789	D	707 746-1695	5224
J P Consulting	8742	D	707 747-4800	27488
Julie Coleman Enterprises Inc	4953	D	707 746-6067	6493
Mdr Inc	8711	D	707 750-5376	25959
Metropolitan Van and Stor Inc (PA)	4213	E	707 745-1150	4228
Mistras Group Inc	8734	C	707 746-5870	26869
Oakland Pallet Company Inc	5031	D	707 746-0100	6939

Employment Codes: A=Over 500 employees, B=251-500, C=101-250, D=51-100, E=45-50

BENICIA, CA

Company	SIC	EMP	PHONE	ENTRY #
Pepsi-Cola Metro Btlg Co Inc	4225	C	707 746-5404	4611
Safway Services LP	5082	E	707 745-2000	7789
Solano Pacific Corporation	6531	D	707 745-6000	11850
Underground Cnstr Co Inc	4931	C	707 746-8800	6294
Unico Industrial Service Co (PA)	7699	E	707 736-8787	18027
Unico Mechanical Corp	5084	E	707 745-4540	7898
United Site Services Cal Inc	4953	E	707 747-2810	6573
Veolia Es Industrial Svcs Inc	7699	D	707 745-1581	18032
Veolia Es Industrial Svcs Inc	7349	D	707 745-0501	14463
West Coast Beauty Supply Co (HQ)	5087	C	707 748-4800	7988
Western Sun Enterprises Inc	1731	C	707 748-2542	2794

BERKELEY, CA - Alameda County

Company	SIC	EMP	PHONE	ENTRY #
A T Associates Inc	8059	E	510 649-6670	21121
Altcare Cedar Creek LLC	8361	D	510 527-7282	24545
Amtel LLC	4812	D	510 529-3220	5254
Annies Homegrown Inc	5149	D	510 558-7500	8795
Backroads (PA)	4725	D	510 527-1555	4987
Barra LLC (HQ)	7372	B	510 548-5442	15595
Bayer Healthcare LLC	8731	A	510 705-7539	26486
Berkeley 75 Hsing Partners LP	6531	E	510 705-1488	11319
Berkeley Cement Inc	1771	C	510 525-8175	3233
Berkeley Repertory Theatre (PA)	7922	D	510 204-8901	18372
Berkeley Student Coop Inc	7041	D	510 848-1936	13488
Berkeley Symphony Orchestra	7929	E	510 841-2800	18459
Berkeley Unified School Dst	4151	E	510 644-6182	3913
Boykin Mgt Co Ltd Lblty Co	7011	B	510 548-7920	12460
California Shakespeare Theater	7922	A	510 548-3422	18376
Chaparral Foundation	8051	D	510 848-8774	20454
City of Berkeley	8721	A	510 981-6750	26311
Claremont Ht Prpts Ltd Partnr	7011	A	510 843-3000	12524
DSM Biomedical Inc	8731	A	510 841-8800	26505
Earth Island Institute Inc	8699	D	510 859-9100	25527
Elmwood LNG TRM& Tran Care	8051	D	510 665-2800	20534
Els	8748	E	510 549-2929	27910
Energy Berkeley Office US Dept	8733	A	510 642-1440	26759
Energy Berkeley Office US Dept	8733	A	510 486-4033	26761
Fmr LLC	6282	C	800 225-6447	10141
Griffin Motorwerke Inc	7538	A	510 524-7447	17798
Gtxcel Inc	7371	D	800 609-8994	15216
Homegrown Natural Foods Inc	5141	D	510 558-7500	8485
Hornblower Yachts LLC	7299	C	916 446-1185	13765
Hotel Durant A Ltd Partnership	7011	B	510 845-8981	12787
Icygen LLC	7373	D	510 540-7122	15964
Inclusive Cmnty Resources LLC	8331	C	510 981-8115	24352
Ingram Publisher Services Inc	5192	D	510 528-1444	9166
Institute For Eductl Therapy	8331	E	831 457-1207	24353
International House	7021	C	510 642-9490	13452
Internet-Journals Inc	7379	C	510 665-1200	16410
Interntional Cmpt Science Inst	8733	E	510 643-9153	26773
Interstate Hotels Resorts Inc	7011	E	510 843-3000	12851
ISI Inspection Services Inc (PA)	7389	D	415 243-3265	17253
L J Kruse Co	1711	A	510 644-0260	2272
Lawrence Berkeley National Lab	8071	A	510 486-6792	22238
Lifelong Medical Care	8011	E	510 981-4100	19707
Lifelong Medical Care (PA)	8011	E	510 704-6010	19708
LOreal Usa Inc	5122	C	510 548-0130	8274
Mason-Mcduffie Real Estate Inc	6531	D	510 705-8611	11659
McKesson Corporation	5047	D	510 666-0854	7276
MOG Inc	7371	B	510 883-7100	15312
Moore Iacofano Goltsman Inc (PA)	8748	D	510 845-7549	27993
New Bridge Foundation Inc	8322	D	510 548-7270	24098
New Bridge Foundation Inc	8069	D	510 548-7270	22160
O C Jones & Sons Inc (PA)	1611	C	510 526-3424	1836
O C Sailing Club Inc	7999	D	510 843-4200	19253
Outfront Media LLC	7312	D	510 527-3350	13956
Partners For Community Access	8322	D	510 558-6700	24122
Permanente Medical Group Inc	8062	D	510 559-5119	21795
Permanente Medical Group Inc	8011	D	510 559-5338	19860
Pillsbury Winthrop Shaw	8111	C	415 983-1865	23509
Publishers Group Incorporated (DH)	5192	C	510 528-1444	9170
Research Triangle Institute	8742	D	510 849-4942	27615
Sanhyd Inc	8051	D	510 843-2131	20895
Sigma Kappa Sorority	7041	D	510 540-9142	13498
Sun Light & Power	7389	D	510 845-2997	17510
Surgery Center of Alta Bates (HQ)	8062	A	510 204-4444	21937
Surgery Center of Alta Bates	8011	E	510 204-4411	20076
Surgery Center of Alta Bates	8093	D	510 204-1591	22842
Sutter East Bay Hospitals	8062	D	510 204-1609	21944
Sutter Health	8071	C	510 204-1591	22288
The Young Mens Chris Assoc of	8641	D	510 841-4152	25372
The Young Mens Chris Assoc of	8641	D	510 486-8400	25375
The Young Mens Chris Assoc of	8641	D	510 848-9092	25376
The Young Mens Chris Assoc of	8641	D	510 848-9622	25377
The Young Mens Chris Assoc of	8641	D	510 526-2146	25378
The Young Mens Chris Assoc of	8641	D	510 848-6800	25379
The Young Mens Chris Assoc of	8641	D	510 559-2090	25380
Toolworks Inc	8322	B	510 649-1322	24252
Toot Sweets Ltd (PA)	5149	E	510 526-0610	8939
Two Star Dog Inc	5136	E	510 525-1100	8364
United States Dept of Energy	8733	A	510 486-4000	26815
United States Dept of Energy	8731	A	510 486-4936	26626
University California Berkeley	8011	D	510 642-2000	20171
Unycom Inc	8741	D	415 513-0316	27267
Westpost Berkeley LLC	7011	D	510 548-7920	13407
Westward Hospitality MGT	7011	D	510 548-7920	13408

BERMUDA DUNES, CA - Riverside County

Company	SIC	EMP	PHONE	ENTRY #
Bermuda Dunes Country Club	7997	E	760 360-2481	18890
Bermuda Dunes Learning Ctr Inc	8351	E	760 772-7127	24417
Cockrell Electric Inc	1731	D	760 864-6233	2553
Desert Cncpts Ldscpg Maint Inc	0781	C	760 200-9007	761
Earth Systems Southwest (HQ)	8711	D	760 345-1588	25777
Hort Tech Inc	0782	E	760 360-9000	870
KDI Elements	1743	C	760 345-9933	3016
Turf Star Inc	5083	D	760 772-3575	7812
Vantage Plaster & Drywall	1742	C	760 345-3622	2993
Vintage Associates Inc	0782	C	760 772-3673	976

BEVERLY HILLS, CA - Los Angeles County

Company	SIC	EMP	PHONE	ENTRY #
A Sutton Carlos	7381	D	310 286-0010	16534
Academy Foundation (HQ)	7819	E	310 247-3000	18212
Academy Mpic Arts & Sciences (PA)	8621	E	310 247-3000	25112
Active Lawyers Referral Svc	8999	D	310 247-0425	28106
Advance Building Maintenance	7349	B	310 247-0077	14214
Aeroflot Russian Airlines	4512	A	323 272-4861	4777
Agency For Performing Arts Inc (PA)	7389	D	310 557-9049	16975
American Corporation	5015	D	310 274-1800	6794
American Health Connection	7389	B	424 226-0420	16987
American Intl Telephonics LLC	4813	C	800 600-6151	5457
Amtrow Group Inc	8742	D	310 557-0857	27322
Anderson Associates Staffing (PA)	7363	C	323 930-3170	14838
APA Incorporated	8742	C	310 888-4200	27329
Baker Winokur	7389	D	310 248-6169	27733
Beauty Recognized LP	7231	D	310 278-7646	13668
Beck International Inc	1541	B	310 281-2980	1405
Belvedere Hotel Partnership	7011	B	310 551-2888	12434
Belvedere Partnership	7011	B	310 551-2888	12435
Bentley Health Care Inc	8742	D	310 967-3300	27345
Berlitz Languages Inc	7389	E	310 858-8931	17028
Bhrac LLC	7514	D	310 862-1933	17666
Bloom Hergott Diemer Cook LLC	8111	D	310 859-6800	23123
Brillstein Entrmt Partners LLC (PA)	7812	D	310 205-5100	18054
Bwr Public Relations	8743	D	310 248-6100	27736
Calpoint	4813	E	310 274-6600	5569
Canessa Investments N V	6799	D	310 273-8543	12291
Cardivsclr Mdcl Grp of Sthrn	8011	D	310 278-3400	19403
Casden Builders LLC	6512	E	310 274-5553	10966
Casden Company LLC	6552	D	310 274-5553	11957
Casewise Systems Inc (HQ)	5045	D	424 284-4101	7107
Cedars-Sinai Medical Center	8062	C	310 385-3400	21473
Charles & Cynthia Eberly Inc	6513	D	323 937-6468	11114
Citigroup Global Markets Inc	6211	D	310 285-6500	9974
City of Beverly Hills	7521	B	310 285-2552	17716
Colateral Lender Inc	6159	D	310 659-4353	9798
Coldwell Bnkr Residential Brkg	6531	D	310 273-3113	11433
Collective MGT Group LLC	8741	C	323 655-8585	26975
Core Nutrition LLC	5149	D	310 424-5077	8819
Douglas Elliman Real Estate	6531	E	310 595-3888	11477
Duckpunk Productions Inc	7812	D	310 836-3818	18078
E H Summit Inc	7011	D	310 273-0300	12605
Evolve Growth Initiatives LLC	8361	E	424 281-5000	24656
Fillmore Theatrical Services	7929	D	310 867-7000	18466
Financial Group of America	6163	D	310 860-5160	9924
Finn Holding Corporation (PA)	4449	A	310 712-1850	4722
G Katen Partners Ltd Lblty Co	4731	E	424 354-3241	5082
Gersh Agency Inc (PA)	7922	D	310 274-6611	18394
Ggwh LLC	7011	E	310 786-1700	12665
Global Horizons Inc	7361	B	310 234-8475	14662
God Help Films Inc	4899	D	323 556-0699	6075
Gores Group LLC (PA)	6211	D	310 209-3010	10008
Granite Escrow Services	6099	D	310 288-0110	9719
Griffin Slr Management Inc	8741	D	310 270-4031	27046
Hair Fashion Inc	7231	D	310 274-0851	13678
Hilltop Securities Inc	6211	E	800 765-2200	10011
Hilton Worldwide Inc	7011	C	310 415-3340	12726
Honeymoon Real Estate LP	7011	D	310 277-5221	12757
Hong Kong & Shanghai Hotels	7011	D	310 551-2888	12758
Hyatt Vacation Ownership Inc	6531	D	310 285-0990	11578
Insomniac Inc	7929	D	323 874-7020	18475
Interdependent Pictures LLC	7812	D	310 779-2119	18095
Js Tamers Inc	6531	E	323 609-4101	11603

GEOGRAPHIC SECTION

BONITA, CA

	SIC	EMP	PHONE	ENTRY #
Kate Somerville Holdings LLC	5122	D	323 655-4170	8271
Kate Somerville Skincare LLC **(HQ)**	5122	D	323 655-7546	8272
Keller Wllams Rlty Bvrly Hills	6531	D	310 432-5490	11613
Kennedy-Wilson Inc **(PA)**	6531	C	310 887-6400	11614
Kpmg LLP	8721	E	310 273-2770	26384
La Peer Surgery Center LLC	8011	D	310 360-9119	19696
Labelle Fmly Rtreat Orgnzation	8361	D	310 527-1883	24705
Linden Crest Surgery Center	8011	D	310 601-3900	19712
Litewave US LLC	1799	E	888 399-6710	3547
Live Love Laugh Global	8699	D	310 362-1783	25551
Live Nation Entertainment Inc	7389	D	323 462-4785	17298
Live Nation Entertainment Inc **(PA)**	7922	C	310 867-7000	18408
M L Stern & Co LLC **(DH)**	6211	C	323 658-4400	10027
Magic Workforce Solutions LLC	8743	A	310 246-6153	27756
Massachusetts Mutl Lf Insur Co	6311	D	323 951-0131	10212
Mayer Associates	6513	D	310 274-5553	11164
Mediaplatform Inc	7812	D	310 909-8410	18108
Medical Group Bverly Hills Inc **(PA)**	8011	E	310 385-3200	19737
Medical Group Bverly Hills Inc	8011	E	310 247-4646	19738
Merrill Lynch Pierce Fenner	6211	E	310 858-1500	10032
Metro-Gldwyn-Mayer Studios Inc	7812	C	310 449-3620	18111
Metro-Gldwyn-Mayer Studios Inc	7812	C	310 449-3000	18112
Metro-Goldwyn-Mayer Inc **(DH)**	7812	B	310 449-3000	18113
Mob Scene LLC	7311	D	323 648-7200	13887
Montage Hotels & Resorts LLC	7011	B	310 499-4199	13004
Morgan Stanley & Co LLC	6211	D	310 285-4800	10059
Mufg Union Bank Na	6021	D	310 550-6522	9404
N S B N Investments Llc	6799	D	310 273-2501	12328
Nelson Shelton & Associates	6531	C	310 271-2229	11703
Next Management LLC	8742	E	323 782-0038	27567
Nextpoint Inc **(PA)**	4813	D	310 360-5904	5670
Nourmand & Associates	6531	E	310 274-4000	11715
Omninet Twin Towers Gp LLC	6531	E	310 300-4118	11719
Omninet Twin Towers LP	6531	E	310 300-4110	11720
Paradigm A Tlent Literary Agcy **(PA)**	7922	E	310 288-8000	18422
Parkman Agents	6722	E	310 860-7757	12121
Participant Media LLC	7812	D	310 550-5100	18127
Playboy Enterprises Inc **(HQ)**	7812	C	310 424-1800	18130
Porter Ranch Development Co	1531	D	323 655-7330	1382
Premier Exec Solutions Inc	8748	E	310 989-9925	28021
Project Boat Holdings LLC	6719	A	310 712-1850	12085
Protected Outcomes Corporation	7381	D	203 545-9565	16767
Protravel International LLC	4724	D	310 271-9566	4971
Radnet Management Inc	8741	D	323 549-3000	27191
Raffles Lrmitage Beverly Hills	7011	C	310 278-3344	13124
Raines Law Group LLP	8111	E	310 440-4100	23526
Rbc Wealth Management	6211	E	310 273-7600	10072
Regis Corporation	7231	E	310 274-8791	13687
Revel Travel Service Inc	4724	D	310 553-5555	4972
Rodeo Realty Inc **(PA)**	6531	E	818 349-9997	11819
Row Management Ltd Inc	6531	C	310 887-3671	11824
Roxbury Management Company	6531	D	310 350-9164	11825
S J S Link International Inc **(PA)**	5142	E	310 860-7666	8569
Sajahtera Inc	7011	A	310 276-2251	13190
Shapell Industries LLC **(HQ)**	6552	D	323 655-7330	12008
Skidmore Owings & Merrill LLP	8712	C	310 651-9924	26251
Skin Health Experts Medic	8093	D	310 623-6869	22832
Sony Music Entertainment Inc	5099	C	310 272-2555	8141
SOS Security LLC	7381	D	310 859-8248	16828
Star Lax LLC	7514	D	310 642-4500	17693
Starpoint Property MGT LLC	6531	E	310 247-0550	11857
Stockcross Financial Services **(PA)**	6211	E	800 225-6196	10078
Studio 71 LP	7313	C	323 370-1500	13979
Sunrise Senior Living Inc	8051	D	650 326-1108	20957
Sunrise Senior Living Inc	8051	D	310 274-4479	20960
Tabak Steven William M MD	8011	D	310 278-3400	20127
Telestar Consulting Inc	8742	E	310 748-0008	27683
Tower Hematology Oncology Medi	8011	D	310 888-8680	20140
Travel Syndicate	4724	D	818 297-9979	4980
Treepeople Inc	0783	E	818 753-4600	1000
Trendshift LLC	7371	D	866 644-8877	15509
UBS Financial Services Inc	6211	D	310 274-8441	10087
Universal Home Care Inc	8082	C	323 653-9222	22586
Universe Holdings Dev Co LLC	6531	E	310 785-0077	11892
Upload Demo Inc	7389	D	818 983-2395	17576
Warner Films LLC	7812	D	310 601-3184	18202
Weinstein Company LLC	7812	D	424 204-4800	18204
Weintraub Tobin Chediak	8111	D	310 858-7888	23616
Wells Fargo Bank National Assn	6021	C	310 285-5817	9462
West Coast Storm Inc **(PA)**	8744	E	909 890-5700	27802
William Morris Endeavor	7922	B	310 285-9000	18445
William Morris Endeavor Entert **(PA)**	7922	C	310 285-9000	18446
Wilner Klein Siegel	8111	E	310 550-4595	23623
Wilshire West LLC	7542	E	310 828-2910	17867
Zillionaire Empress Danielle B	6722	A	310 461-9923	12132

BIG BEAR CITY, CA - San Bernardino County

	SIC	EMP	PHONE	ENTRY #
Snow Summit Ski Corporation	7999	A	909 585-2517	19285

BIG BEAR LAKE, CA - San Bernardino County

Bear Vly Cmnty Healthcare Dst **(PA)**	8062	C	909 866-6501	21463
Golden State Water Company	4911	E	909 866-4678	6134
Snow Summit Ski Corporation **(PA)**	7011	C	909 866-5766	13272

BIG CREEK, CA - Fresno County

Southern California Edison Co	4911	C	559 893-3611	6212
Southern California Edison Co	4911	C	559 893-2037	6217
Southern California Edison Co	4911	D	559 893-3646	6223

BIG SUR, CA - Monterey County

48123 CA Investors LLC	7011	C	831 667-2331	12363
Golden Living LLC	8082	D	831 624-1875	22444

BIGGS, CA - Butte County

Chuck Jones Flying Service **(PA)**	0721	E	530 868-5798	478
Red Top Rice Growers	0723	E	530 868-5975	578
Sun West Wild Rice Facility	0112	E	530 868-5188	6

BISHOP, CA - Inyo County

Bishop Paiute Gaming Corp	7999	C	760 872-6005	19151
Bishop Waste Disposal Inc	4953	E	760 872-6561	6443
Eastern Sierra Transit Auth	4131	C	760 872-1901	3878
Fedex Freight Corporation	4213	D	760 873-8655	4163
Fedex Ground Package Sys Inc	4213	C	760 873-3133	4178
Hospice of Owens Valley	8082	D	760 872-4663	22477
Northern Inyo Cty Hospital Dst	8062	B	760 873-5811	21764
Owens Valley Inter Agency	8611	E	760 873-2405	25097
SCE Eastern Hydro Division	4911	D	760 873-0767	6205
Southern California Edison Co	4911	C	760 873-0715	6215
Toiyabe Indian Health Prj Inc **(PA)**	8021	D	760 873-8461	20280
Triad Homes Assoc	8711	D	760 873-4273	26104
United Parcel Service Inc OH	4215	C	760 872-7661	4441

BLOOMINGTON, CA - San Bernardino County

Accurate Delivery Systems Inc	4212	D	951 823-8870	3970
Acts For Children **(PA)**	8361	E	909 877-5499	24540
C M C Steel Fabricators Inc	1791	D	909 873-3060	3371
Calmex Engineering Inc	1771	D	909 546-1311	3238
Chiro Inc **(PA)**	5087	D	909 879-1160	7965
Distribution Alternatives Inc	4225	C	909 673-1000	4543
Empire Oil Co	5172	D	909 877-0226	9018
Fedex Ground Package Sys Inc	4213	A	909 879-7180	4181
Flyers Energy LLC	5172	C	909 877-2441	9020
Inland Valley Cnstr Co Inc	1531	D	909 875-2112	1370
J&R Fleet Services LLC	7538	D	909 820-7000	17802
Kinder Mrgan Enrgy Partners LP	4619	E	909 873-1553	4951
Lineage Logistics Holdings LLC	4214	D	909 874-1200	4360
MCM Construction Inc	1622	C	909 875-0533	1897
Revchem Composites Inc **(PA)**	5033	D	909 877-8477	7014
Roberts Lumber Sales Inc	5031	D	909 350-9164	6957
Santana Concrete	1771	D	909 421-2218	3326
Social Science Service Center	8069	D	909 421-7120	22176
Unified Aircraft Services Inc **(PA)**	4783	C	909 877-0535	5205
Union Pacific Railroad Company	4011	D	909 685-2710	3622
UPS Freight Services Inc	4213	D	909 879-7400	4284
Verizon Communications Inc	7389	A	909 421-5053	17588

BLUE JAY, CA - San Bernardino County

Alpine Camp Conference Ctr Inc	7999	D	909 337-6287	19133
Cbsrr Inc	6531	D	909 336-2131	11361

BLUE LAKE, CA - Humboldt County

Blue Lake Casino	7011	D	707 668-5101	12455

BLYTHE, CA - Riverside County

Aztec Harvesting	0761	A	760 922-7348	653
Barnes and Berger	0722	E	760 922-6136	490
Blythe Nursing Care Center	8051	D	760 922-8176	20414
Fisher Ranch LLC	0723	D	760 922-4151	533
Hayday Farms Inc	0139	D	760 922-4713	25
Palo Verde Health Care Dst	8062	C	760 922-4115	21778
Palo Verde Hospital Assn	8621	D	760 922-4115	25151
Palo Verde Irrigation District	4971	D	760 922-3144	6651
Xpo Enterprise Services Inc	4213	D	760 922-8538	4317

BODEGA BAY, CA - Sonoma County

Bodega Harbour Homeowners Assn	8641	D	707 875-3519	25208
NAPA Valley Lodge LP	7011	D	707 875-3525	13013

BONITA, CA - San Diego County

Abington Homes Inc	6531	D	619 208-9486	11273
Child Development Assoc Inc **(PA)**	8351	E	619 427-4411	24429
Crockett & Coinc	7992	D	619 267-1103	18729
John Collins Co Inc	6513	D	818 227-2190	11146
Kaiser Foundation Hospitals	8062	D	619 409-6405	21669

Employment Codes: A=Over 500 employees, B=251-500, C=101-250, D=51-100, E=45-50

2017 Directory of California Wholesalers and Services Companies

© Mergent Inc. 1-800-342-5647

1629

BONITA, CA

	SIC	EMP	PHONE	ENTRY #
Paradise Valley Hospital Inc	8082	D	619 472-7500	22531
Permanente Kaiser Intl	8062	A	619 409-6050	21789

BONSALL, CA - San Diego County

	SIC	EMP	PHONE	ENTRY #
Cunningham Group Inc	8742	D	303 295-1982	27401
Euroamerican Propagators LLC	0181	B	760 731-6029	280

BORON, CA - Kern County

	SIC	EMP	PHONE	ENTRY #
Kjc Operating Company	4911	C	760 762-5562	6143
Rio Tinto Minerals Inc	1241	C	760 762-7121	1026

BORREGO SPRINGS, CA - San Diego County

	SIC	EMP	PHONE	ENTRY #
Borrego Springs Country Club	7997	E	760 767-3289	18897
Rams Hill Country Club	7997	D	760 767-4259	19033

BOULDER CREEK, CA - Santa Cruz County

	SIC	EMP	PHONE	ENTRY #
Easter Seals Inc	7032	D	831 338-3383	13463

BOULEVARD, CA - San Diego County

	SIC	EMP	PHONE	ENTRY #
La Posta Casino	7011	C	619 824-4100	12899

BRADLEY, CA - Monterey County

	SIC	EMP	PHONE	ENTRY #
Mount Hermon Association Inc	7032	D	805 472-9201	13468

BRAWLEY, CA - Imperial County

	SIC	EMP	PHONE	ENTRY #
Afshan Baig MD	8011	E	760 344-6471	19325
Border Valley Trading Ltd	5191	D	760 344-6700	9127
Clinicas De Slud Del Peblo Inc (PA)	8011	D	760 344-9951	19447
Clinicas De Slud Del Peblo Inc	8011	D	760 344-6471	19448
Esparza Enterprises Inc	0762	B	760 344-2031	703
EZ Labor & Harvesting Inc	0761	D	760 344-6693	659
Grimmway Enterprises Inc	7538	A	760 344-0204	17799
Irby Construction Company	1623	D	760 344-4478	1943
Jesus A Nava Farm Labor	0761	D	760 344-8084	669
Kelomar Inc	0161	C	760 344-5253	77
Michael W Morgan	0161	E	760 344-5253	80
Pioneers Mem Healthcare Dst (PA)	8062	A	760 351-3333	21800
Planters Hay Inc	5191	A	760 344-0620	9147
Rothfleisch Ranches Inc	0762	D	760 344-1819	721

BREA, CA - Orange County

	SIC	EMP	PHONE	ENTRY #
Aer Technologies Inc	7699	B	714 871-7357	17956
Air Treatment Corporation (PA)	5075	D	909 869-7975	7733
Albertsons LLC	4225	D	714 990-8200	4520
Allan Automatic Sprinkler Corp	1711	D	714 993-9500	2121
Alta Resources Corp	7389	D	714 672-9700	16983
American Financial Network Inc	6141	D	909 606-3905	9736
Americold Logistics LLC	4222	E	714 993-3533	4486
Apollo Electric	1731	D	714 256-8414	2522
Audiobahn Inc	5065	D	714 988-0400	7526
Bergman Kprs LLC (PA)	1542	C	714 924-7000	1504
Blaine Convention Services Inc	7389	D	714 522-8270	17032
Brookdale Senior Living Inc	8322	C	714 671-7898	23696
Burns & McDonnell Inc	8711	E	714 256-1595	25710
C & L Refrigeration Corp	1711	C	800 901-4822	2171
California Automobile Insur Co	6331	A	714 232-8669	10405
Caremore Medical Group	8011	C	714 256-1345	19408
Cellco Partnership	4812	C	714 256-6015	5314
City of Brea	8744	D	714 990-7650	27778
Cmre Financial Services Inc	7322	B	714 528-3200	14025
CNA Financial Corporation	6411	C	714 255-2200	10672
Community Home Care	8082	C	714 671-6877	22407
Contact Security Inc	7381	C	714 572-6760	16610
Contract Services Group Inc	7349	C	714 582-1800	14261
Core Communications Group LLC	6531	D	714 729-8404	11454
Cosco Fire Protection Inc	1711	C	714 989-1800	2192
Diversfied Cmmnctions Svcs Inc	4813	D	562 696-9660	5592
Edwards Brea 10 West	7832	E	714 672-4136	18320
Emergency Ambulance Service	4119	D	714 990-1331	3787
Energy Berkeley Office US Dept	8733	B	510 486-7089	26757
Evangelical Christian Cr Un	6062	D	714 671-5700	9667
Evangelical Christian Cr Un (PA)	6062	D	714 671-5700	9668
Exmart International Trdg Corp	6211	D	714 993-1139	9995
Extra Express (cerritos) Inc	4731	E	714 985-6000	5074
Fit Electronics Inc (HQ)	8731	D	714 988-9388	26518
Glen Ivy Hot Springs	7299	D	714 990-2090	13763
Griffith Company (PA)	1611	D	714 984-5500	1794
Hardage Group of Companies	7011	D	714 579-3200	12692
Henley Enterprises Inc	7389	A	714 990-1900	17217
Insight Envmtl Engrg Cnstr Inc (PA)	8711	D	714 678-6700	25881
Intercontinental Exchange Inc (HQ)	6231	B	770 857-4700	10109
International Code Council	8621	B	562 699-0541	25140
Isys Solutions Inc	8742	D	714 521-7656	27486
Kaiser Foundation Hospitals	8011	D	714 672-5100	19588
Kehe Distributors LLC	5149	D	714 255-4600	8865
Kindred Healthcare Inc	8051	D	714 529-6842	20698
Kirkhill Aircraft Parts Co (PA)	5088	D	714 223-5400	7996
Kirkhill Aircraft Parts Co	5088	D	714 223-5400	7997
Kprs Construction Services Inc (PA)	1542	D	714 672-0800	1597
Leidos Inc	8731	D	714 257-6400	26550
Leidos Engineering LLC	8711	D	714 257-6400	25934
Louis Wurth and Company (DH)	5072	D	714 529-1771	7692
Mddr Inc	1711	C	714 792-1993	2291
Mercury Casualty Company (HQ)	6331	A	323 937-1060	10439
Mercury Insurance Company	6331	A	714 671-6700	10441
Mercury Insurance Company	6331	A	714 255-5000	10444
Merrill Lynch Pierce Fenner	6221	D	714 257-4400	10106
Natures Best Distribution LLC	5149	C	714 255-4600	8883
Nestle Waters North Amer Inc	5149	D	714 792-2100	8889
New Dream Network LLC (PA)	4813	D	626 644-9466	5668
New York Life Insurance Co	6411	D	714 672-0236	10798
Norcal Inc	1751	C	714 224-3949	3067
Northstar Dem & Remediation LP (DH)	1795	D	714 672-3500	3462
Orora North America	5113	D	714 984-2300	8202
Otb Acquisition LLC	7011	C	520 458-0540	13049
P B C Pavers Inc	1721	D	714 278-0488	2472
Pacific Western Sales	5199	D	714 572-6730	9288
Paglia & Associates Cnstr	1521	D	714 982-5151	1231
Peterson Bros Contruction Inc	1771	A	714 278-0488	3313
Premier Medical Transport Inc	4731	D	888 353-9556	5155
Priority Building Services LLC	7349	B	714 255-2940	14393
Radiometer America Inc (HQ)	5047	C	800 736-0600	7310
Renal Trtmnt Cntrs-Clfrnia Inc	8092	D	714 990-0110	22638
Resmae Financial Corporation	6163	C	714 577-4577	9948
RMA - Ecc A Joint Venture LLC	1542	D	714 985-2888	1650
Sears Roebuck and Co	7699	C	714 256-7328	18011
Seeley Brothers	1751	C	714 224-3949	3087
Solugenix Corporation (PA)	8748	D	866 749-7658	28058
Specialty Risk Services Inc	6411	D	714 674-1000	10874
Springhuse Manor Care Hlth Svc	8361	D	714 671-7898	24818
Strategic Enlace Inc	8742	D	714 256-8648	27671
Sully-Miller Contracting Co (DH)	1611	A	714 578-9600	1869
Sunshine Clearing Corporation	7361	E	714 829-0273	14798
Superior Machining Mfg Co Inc	5084	D	714 529-6000	7893
Systems and Software Entps LLC (HQ)	7371	D	714 854-8600	15488
Teac Aerospace Tech Inc	5065	C	323 837-2700	7646
Team Finish Inc	1771	D	714 671-9190	3341
The Nevell Group Inc (PA)	1542	C	714 579-7501	1691
Tiger Electric Inc (PA)	1731	D	714 529-8061	2773
Travel Store	4724	D	714 529-1947	4978
Travelers Property Cslty Corp	6411	C	714 671-8000	10909
V A Anderson Enterprises Inc	7389	D	714 990-6100	17580
Veterinary Pet Insur Svcs Inc (DH)	6411	D	714 989-0555	10924
Walters Wholesale Electric Co	5063	C	714 784-1900	7483
West Coast Prime Meats LLC	5147	C	714 255-8560	8691
Win-Dor Inc (PA)	1751	C	714 576-2030	3102
Windsor Capital Group Inc	7011	D	714 990-6000	13419
Xdimensional Technologies Inc	7373	D	714 672-8960	16082

BRENTWOOD, CA - Contra Costa County

	SIC	EMP	PHONE	ENTRY #
American Mdsg Specialists Inc	7319	C	925 516-3220	13988
Bay Standard Inc	5085	D	925 634-1181	7924
Bay Standard Manufacturing Inc (PA)	5072	E	925 634-1181	7676
Cellco Partnership	4812	D	925 626-3480	5290
Ellison Framing Inc	1751	C	925 516-9269	3045
Groundworks Inc	1771	D	925 513-0300	3271
Hot Line Construction Inc	1731	D	925 634-9333	2615
New York Life Insurance Co	6311	D	925 809-7020	10213
Nines Restaurant	8742	D	925 516-3413	27569
Pacific Communications Assoc	8748	E	925 634-1203	28015
Padilla Landscape Inc	0782	D	925 513-9353	928
Robert Cecchini Inc	0161	D	925 634-4400	90
Rodda Electric Inc (PA)	1711	D	925 240-6024	2350
T&C Roofing Inc	1761	D	925 513-8463	3217
Thorpe Design Inc	1711	D	925 634-0787	2397
V Development Inc	1522	D	925 634-4890	1349

BRISBANE, CA - San Mateo County

	SIC	EMP	PHONE	ENTRY #
Amen Clinics Inc A Med Corp	8011	E	650 416-7830	19338
Bay Porter Ex Arprt Shuttle	4111	D	415 467-1800	3636
Bi-Rite Restaurant Sup Co Inc	5141	B	415 656-0187	8460
Caredx Inc (PA)	8071	C	415 287-2300	22197
Edward B Ward & Company Inc (DH)	5075	E	415 330-6600	7736
Exel Inc	4731	C	415 531-0596	5067
Expeditors Intl Wash Inc	4731	E	415 657-3600	5068
Fedex Corporation	7389	E	415 657-0403	17168
Forward Air Inc	4731	E	415 570-6040	5079
Frito-Lay North America Inc	5145	D	415 467-1860	8613
FW Spencer & Son Inc	1711	C	415 468-5000	2232
Hitachi America Ltd	5084	D	650 827-6240	7848
Kinder Mrgan Lqds Trminals LLC	4226	D	415 467-8107	4694
Ksf Channel 26	4833	E	415 467-6397	5889
Kuehne + Nagel Inc	4731	E	415 656-4100	5111
Lincoln Television Inc	4833	D	415 468-2626	5895

GEOGRAPHIC SECTION

BURBANK, CA

	SIC	EMP	PHONE	ENTRY #
Mode Media Corporation (PA)	7313	C	650 244-4000	13973
Monster Inc (PA)	5099	B	415 840-2000	8127
Norman S Wright Mech Eqp Corp (PA)	5075	D	415 467-7600	7745
Novitex Entp Solutions Inc	7334	C	415 528-2960	14123
Nsw Real Estate Holdings LLC	7389	D	415 467-7600	17369
Oakville Produce Partners LLC	5148	C	415 647-2991	8757
Pearson English Corporation (HQ)	4813	C	650 246-6000	5684
Pitney Bowes Presort Svcs Inc	7389	D	415 468-1660	17416
PSI Group	7331	C	415 468-1660	14087
Purcell-Murray Company Inc (PA)	5074	D	415 468-6620	7728
Sage Hospitality Resources LLC	7011	D	650 589-1600	13189
Shoppingcom Inc	7374	C	650 616-6500	16185
Tyco Integrated Security LLC	7382	D	650 634-9000	16935
Vox Network Solutions Inc	8748	D	650 989-1000	28095
Xojet Inc (PA)	4581	D	650 594-6300	4949

BROOKS, CA - Yolo County

	SIC	EMP	PHONE	ENTRY #
Cache Creek Casino Resort	7011	A	530 796-3118	12479

BROWNSVILLE, CA - Yuba County

	SIC	EMP	PHONE	ENTRY #
Sutter North Med Foundation	8011	D	530 675-1245	20121

BUELLTON, CA - Santa Barbara County

	SIC	EMP	PHONE	ENTRY #
American Medical Response Inc	4119	C	805 688-6550	3758
Excelta Corporation (PA)	5072	D	805 686-4686	7683
Kang Family Partners LLC	7011	C	805 688-1000	12875

BUENA PARK, CA - Orange County

	SIC	EMP	PHONE	ENTRY #
A J Parent Company Inc (PA)	7389	C	714 521-1100	16991
Abad Foam Inc	5199	E	714 994-2223	9241
Allstate Building Maintenance	7349	D	714 739-8080	14222
Amada America Inc (HQ)	5084	D	714 739-2111	7819
Amada Capital Corporation	7359	D	714 739-2111	14511
American Wht Mssn In Sthrn	8322	D	714 522-4599	23662
Angeles Contractor Inc (PA)	1541	D	714 523-1021	1399
AT&T Services Inc	4813	D	714 992-3359	5550
AT&T Services Inc	4813	C	510 732-0830	5552
Automatic Data Processing Inc	7374	C	714 690-7000	16090
Beach and La Mirada Car Wash	7542	E	714 994-1099	17830
Bitech-Ace A Joint Venture	1771	D	714 521-1477	3234
Borbon Incorporated	1721	D	714 994-0170	2431
Buena Park Medical Group Inc (PA)	8011	E	714 994-5290	19382
Buena Park Police Association	8631	D	714 562-3901	25167
Cal Fresco LLC	5148	C	714 690-7700	8698
Cambium Business Group Inc (PA)	5021	C	714 670-1171	6810
Communications Supply Corp	4899	D	714 670-7711	6066
Continental Exch Solutions Inc (HQ)	7389	C	714 522-7044	17094
Dr Fresh LLC (PA)	5047	D	714 690-1573	7261
Dr Fresh Inc	5047	D	714 690-1573	7262
Edco Disposal Corporation Inc	4953	D	714 522-3577	6479
Fibertron Corporation	5065	D	714 670-7711	7565
Fueling and Service Tech Inc	5084	D	714 523-0194	7845
Hannam Chain USA Inc	6531	D	714 670-0670	11567
Hilton Worldwide Inc	7011	D	714 739-5600	12731
Houdini Inc	4225	C	714 228-4406	4573
Islamic Relief USA	8322	D	714 676-1300	24037
JC Penney Corporation Inc	4225	C	714 523-6558	4581
King Supply Company LLC	1799	C	714 670-8980	3544
Knott Avenue Care Center	8051	C	714 826-2330	20713
Knotts Berry Farm LLC	7011	C	714 995-1111	12891
Korean Community Services Inc	8322	E	714 527-6561	24059
Legacy Farms LLC	5148	C	714 736-1800	8745
McAuley Lcx Corporation	7997	C	714 994-7788	18994
Noritsu America Corporation (HQ)	5043	D	714 521-9040	7037
Oasis Brands Inc	5113	C	540 658-2830	8201
Orora North America	5113	C	714 562-6002	8210
Orora Packaging Solutions (HQ)	5113	C	714 562-6000	8211
Pacific Bulk Trnsp Co Inc	4214	D	714 521-2399	4369
Pacific Chemical Dist Corp (DH)	4226	D	714 521-7161	4699
Partners Information Tech Inc (HQ)	7379	D	714 736-4487	16454
Radisson Suites Hotel Buena Pk	7011	D	714 739-5600	13122
Royal Crest Building Maint	7349	E	714 562-5034	14411
States Logistics Services Inc	4731	C	714 523-1276	5170
States Logistics Services Inc (PA)	4225	C	714 521-6520	4642
Tawa Services Inc (PA)	5149	C	714 521-8899	8936
Team Spirit Realty Inc	6531	E	714 562-0404	11865
Tech Systems Inc	5065	C	714 523-5404	7647
Ted Ford Jones Inc (PA)	7538	C	714 521-3110	17817
Uniwell Corporation	7011	C	714 522-7000	13367
VWR International LLC	5049	E	714 220-2615	7352
Walong Marketing Inc (PA)	5149	C	714 670-8899	8955
Wayne Perry Inc (PA)	1799	C	714 826-0352	3600
West Coast Sand and Gravel Inc (PA)	5032	C	714 522-0282	7001
Yamaha Corporation of America (HQ)	5099	B	714 522-9011	8150

BURBANK, CA - Los Angeles County

	SIC	EMP	PHONE	ENTRY #
24 Hour Fitness Usa Inc	8099	E	818 531-0257	22871
3ality Digital LLC (PA)	7812	D	818 759-5551	18035
ABC Cable Networks Group	7822	C	818 560-4365	18268
ABC Cable Networks Group (DH)	4832	C	818 460-7477	5745
ABC Family Worldwide Inc (HQ)	7812	B	818 560-1000	18036
Access Hollywood	4833	C	818 840-4444	5833
Adcom Interactive Media inc	7379	D	800 296-7104	16314
Adstream North America Inc	7373	C	212 459-0290	15897
Allianz Globl Risks US Insur (DH)	6331	D	818 260-7500	10395
Allianz Underwriters Insur Co	6331	D	818 260-7500	10396
Amberfin Limited	5045	E	818 768-8948	7090
American Multi-Cinema Inc	7832	D	818 953-4020	18294
and Syndicated Productions Inc	7812	D	818 308-5200	18042
Andrews International Inc	7381	C	818 260-9586	16561
Andrews International Inc	7381	C	805 409-4160	16562
Andrews International Inc	7381	C	626 407-2290	16564
Ane Productions Inc	7812	D	818 972-0777	18043
Angeles Los Equestrian Center	7999	C	818 840-9063	19137
Aptiv Digital Inc	7372	D	818 295-6789	15583
Aramark Unf & Career AP LLC	7218	C	818 973-3700	13603
Aramark Unf & Career AP LLC (DH)	7218	C	818 973-3700	13607
Aramark Unf Svcs Midwest LLC	7218	C	800 388-3300	13615
Ardwin	4213	C	818 767-7777	4111
Artesia Healthcare Inc	8051	D	818 843-1771	20383
Atlantic Recording Corporation	7389	B	818 238-6800	17008
Atlas Digital LLC (PA)	7812	D	323 762-2626	18046
Avis Rent A Car System Inc	7514	D	818 566-3001	17665
AWH Burbank Hotel LLC	7011	D	813 843-6000	12408
Belmont Village LP	6513	D	818 972-2405	11095
Bonanza Productions Inc	7929	A	818 954-4212	18460
Borrmann Metal Center (PA)	5051	D	818 846-7171	7362
Boulevard Entertainment Inc	7389	D	818 840-6969	17038
BRC Imagination Arts Inc	7812	D	818 841-8084	18052
Bryant Ranch Prepack	5122	E	818 764-7225	8240
Buena Vista International Inc (HQ)	7822	E	818 560-1000	18271
Buena Vista International Inc (HQ)	7812	B	818 295-5200	18055
Buena Vista Television (DH)	7383	C	818 560-1878	16946
Burbank Dental Laboratory Inc	5047	C	818 841-2256	7248
Burbank Plg & Zoning Div of	8748	E	818 238-5250	27856
Burbank Television Entps LLC	4833	C	818 954-6000	5835
Burbank Water & Power	7389	D	818 238-3706	17043
Bvs Entertainment Inc (DH)	7812	E	818 460-6917	18057
C D Payroll Inc	8721	D	818 848-1562	26304
Callan Management Corporation	7382	D	818 846-2215	16873
Cast & Crew Payroll LLC (HQ)	8721	C	818 848-6022	26307
CBS Interactive Inc	7319	C	818 556-1538	13991
Cellco Partnership	4812	D	818 842-2722	5327
Chase Credit Systems Inc	7371	D	818 762-6262	15080
Check Disc Labs	8742	D	818 847-2255	27380
CIT Bank National Association	6021	D	818 525-3760	9361
Citizens Business Bank	6021	D	818 843-0707	9384
City of Burbank	4931	B	818 238-3550	6284
Clp Resources Inc	7363	D	818 260-9190	14861
Cmp Film & Design Burbank LLC	8743	D	818 729-0800	27742
Corne Land Maint Svc Co Inc	7349	A	818 567-2455	14258
Condusiv Technologies Corp (PA)	7372	C	818 771-1600	15628
Consolidated Elec Distrs Inc	5063	D	626 345-0000	7431
Cookie Jar Entrmt USA Inc	7812	D	818 955-5400	18064
Cooks Warehouse Inc	5023	E	818 556-2740	6856
County of Los Angeles	8322	C	818 557-4164	23858
Credit Management Association (PA)	7322	C	818 972-5300	14030
Cw Network LLC (PA)	4833	D	818 977-2500	5850
Deluxe Entrmt Svcs Group Inc (PA)	7929	D	818 565-3600	18462
Deluxe Laboratories Inc (DH)	7819	A	323 462-6171	18222
Deluxe Media Services	7374	B	818 526-3700	16121
Digital International Corp	7389	D	818 847-1157	17124
Disney Enterprises Inc (HQ)	7812	A	818 560-1000	18074
Disney Enterprises Inc	4833	D	818 569-7500	5852
Disney Enterprises Inc	7812	B	818 560-3692	18075
Disney Incorporated (DH)	7812	C	818 560-1000	18076
Disney Interactive Studios Inc	7371	D	818 553-5000	15144
Disney Interfinance Corp	7822	B	818 560-1000	18272
Disney Regional Entrmt Inc (HQ)	7999	D	818 560-1000	19198
Disney Worldwide Services Inc (DH)	7812	A	818 560-1000	18077
Disneyland International Inc (DH)	7996	D	818 560-1000	18819
Dtecnet Inc	7371	B	208 685-1810	15149
Electrosonic Inc (DH)	8711	D	818 333-3600	25783
Emerson Elementary	8641	D	818 558-5419	25254
Emmis Communications Corp	8742	D	818 238-6705	27423
Emmis Radio LLC	4832	C	818 525-5000	5768
Encompass Dgtal Mdia Group Inc	4833	D	323 344-4500	5853
Entertainment Partners (PA)	8721	B	818 955-6000	26336
Esc Entertainment Inc	7819	D	818 954-1018	18226
Esolar Inc (DH)	1629	D	818 303-9500	2049
Estrella Communications Inc	4833	D	818 260-5700	5859
Executive Fitness Management	7991	E	818 259-6753	18630

Employment Codes: A=Over 500 employees, B=251-500, C=101-250, D=51-100, E=45-50

BURBANK, CA — GEOGRAPHIC SECTION

Company	SIC	EMP	PHONE	ENTRY #
Facey Medical Foundation	8031	C	818 861-7831	20290
Fact Foundation	7389	D	818 729-8105	17157
Final Film	7336	C	323 467-0700	14145
Firemans Fund Insurance Co	6331	C	818 953-6533	10421
Foto-Kem Industries Inc (PA)	7819	A	818 846-3102	18227
Foto-Kem Industries Inc	7819	B	818 846-3102	18228
Frasco Inc (PA)	7381	D	818 848-3888	16647
Freshology Inc	5149	D	818 847-1888	8838
Front Porch Communities & Svcs	8059	D	818 729-8100	21224
Gat Airline Ground Support	4729	B	818 847-9127	5010
Gentle Giant Studios Inc	7389	D	818 504-3555	17184
GL Nemirow Inc	7311	D	818 562-9433	13854
GL Newmirow Inc	7311	D	818 562-9433	13855
Global Entertainment Inds Inc	1799	D	818 567-0000	3525
Guardsmark LLC	7381	C	818 841-0288	16686
Guardsmark LLC	7381	C	818 841-0288	16690
Guardsmark LLC	7381	C	818 841-0288	16698
Healthlink Staffing Inc	7363	D	818 972-2140	14885
Hertz Corporation	7514	E	818 997-0414	17684
Hertz Corporation	7514	E	818 569-6900	17688
Iheartcommunications Inc	4833	D	818 846-0029	5873
IKEA Purchasing Svcs US Inc	8741	B	818 841-3500	27061
Image IV Systems Inc (PA)	5044	D	323 849-3049	7053
International Fmly Entrmt Inc (DH)	4841	D	818 560-1000	6008
Ion Media Networks Inc	4833	E	818 953-7193	5875
J H Maddocks Photography	7384	D	818 842-7150	16952
Jake Hey Incorporated (PA)	7384	D	323 856-5255	16953
Jetblue Airways Corporation	4512	D	718 286-7900	4806
Jim & Doug Carters Automotive	7521	C	818 842-5702	17724
JP Allen Extended Stay	7011	E	818 841-4770	12870
Kan-Di-Ki LLC	8071	A	818 549-1880	22229
Kcetlink (PA)	4833	D	747 201-5000	5879
Kpwr Inc	4832	D	818 953-4200	5798
Krca Television Inc	4833	D	818 563-5722	5887
L B I Holdings I Inc (PA)	4832	D	818 563-5722	5802
Laec Incorporated	0752	D	818 840-9063	642
Lakeside Golf Club	7997	D	818 984-0601	18977
Lawyers Title Company (HQ)	6361	E	818 767-0425	10530
Lbi Media Inc	4832	B	818 729-5316	5804
Le Bleu Chateau Inc	8361	E	818 843-3141	24708
Liberman Broadcasting Inc (PA)	4832	B	818 729-5300	5806
Logix Federal Credit Union (PA)	6061	C	888 718-5328	9610
Louie Almeida & Settler (PA)	8111	D	818 461-9559	23409
M-N-Z Janitorial Services Inc	7349	C	323 851-4115	14345
Machinima Inc	7379	D	323 872-5300	16427
Maverick Records LLC	7389	E	212 275-2000	17317
Mel Bernie and Company Inc	5137	C	818 841-1928	8400
Minneapolis Radio Assets LLC	4832	C	612 617-4000	5810
Mis Sciences Corp	4813	C	818 847-0213	5659
Modern Videofilm (PA)	7819	C	818 840-1700	18235
My Eye Media LLC	7372	C	818 559-7200	15767
NBC Universal Inc	4833	C	818 260-5746	5899
NBC Universal Inc	4833	C	818 840-4395	5900
Nbcuniversal Media LLC	7812	D	818 526-7000	18118
Neurobrands LLC	5149	C	310 393-6444	8890
New Deal Studios Inc	7819	D	310 578-9929	18239
Norco Delivery Service Inc	7389	C	818 558-4810	17364
NW Entertainment Inc (PA)	7812	C	818 295-5000	18123
One K Studios LLC	7336	E	818 531-3800	14157
Outlook Amusements Inc	7379	C	818 433-3800	16450
P Murphy & Associates Inc	7371	C	818 841-2002	15363
Pacific Homes Foundation	8059	D	818 729-8106	21342
Paint Sundries Solutions Inc	5198	D	818 843-2382	9238
Performance Designed Pdts LLC (HQ)	5092	D	323 234-9911	8051
Petrol Advertising Inc	7311	C	323 644-3720	13895
PHF II Burbank LLC	7011	D	818 843-6000	13091
Playboy Entrmt Group Inc (DH)	7812	C	323 276-4000	18131
Point360	7819	D	818 556-5700	18244
Power 106 Radio	4832	D	818 953-4200	5816
Prdctions N Fremantle Amer Inc (DH)	7922	D	818 748-1100	18425
Producer -Writers Guild	6371	D	818 846-1015	10559
Providence Health & Services	8011	D	818 847-4999	19883
Providence Health & Services	8099	C	818 841-0112	23026
Providence Health & Services F	8399	A	818 843-5111	24965
Providence Health System	8062	D	818 843-5111	21822
Providence Health System	6733	D	818 846-8141	12201
Rgis LLC	7389	C	248 651-2511	17452
Roundabout Entertainment Inc	7812	D	818 842-9300	18146
Rudy Carrillo Drywall Inc	1742	D	818 841-9571	2971
Ryan Herco Products Corp (PA)	5074	D	818 841-1141	7730
Sag- Aftra Federal	6061	D	818 562-3400	9622
Sag-Aftra	6371	E	818 954-9400	10562
Sca Enterprises Inc (PA)	7389	D	818 845-7621	17477
Secure Net Protection	7381	E	818 848-4900	16780
Shadkor Inc	7216	D	818 953-4627	13586
Shamrock Plus Inc	6211	E	818 845-4444	10076
Shc Burbank II LLC	7011	C	818 843-6000	13239
Silverado Senior Living Inc	8052	D	818 848-4048	21109
Spire Concessions LLC	7011	D	818 843-6000	13280
SRS Distribution Inc	5033	D	818 840-8851	7019
Starbucks Corporation	8742	D	818 565-3510	27662
Stereo D LLC	7819	B	818 861-3100	18256
Stumbaugh & Associates Inc (PA)	1799	D	818 240-1627	3586
Survival Insurance Inc	6411	D	818 565-1584	10902
Taurus West Inc (DH)	8071	C	818 954-0202	22289
Team Companies Inc (PA)	8721	D	818 558-3261	26450
Technicolor Inc	7384	B	818 260-4577	16959
Technicolor New Media Inc	7812	E	818 480-5100	18167
Technicolor Thomson Group	7819	B	818 260-3600	18264
Terminix Intl Co Ltd Partnr	7342	E	818 972-2037	14191
Tidavater Inc	7389	C	818 848-4151	17531
Time Warner Cable Entps LLC	7812	D	818 972-0808	18168
Time Warner Cable Entps LLC	4841	D	818 953-3283	6030
Touchstone Television Prod LLC (PA)	7812	D	323 671-5116	18169
Trailblazer Technologies	7389	D	818 848-6500	17538
Tri-Tech Restoration Co Inc	1541	D	818 565-3900	1475
Turner Broadcasting System Inc	7812	E	818 977-5452	18173
Turtle Entertainment America	7299	D	818 861-7315	13800
Tyco Integrated Security LLC	7382	C	818 428-6669	16931
Unx Inc A Delaware Corp	7371	C	818 333-3300	15517
Velocity Arospc - Burbank Inc (HQ)	7699	D	818 246-8431	18031
Ver Sales Inc (PA)	5051	D	818 567-3000	7409
Vintage Senior Management Inc	8322	A	818 954-9500	24278
Wad Productions Inc	7812	B	818 260-5673	18188
Walt Disney Company	4833	B	818 295-3134	5925
Walt Disney Company	4833	D	818 560-1268	5926
Walt Disney Company	7929	B	818 567-5590	18504
Walt Disney Company	4832	B	972 448-3143	5830
Walt Disney Company	7996	D	818 553-7333	18837
Walt Disney Company	4833	B	818 460-6655	5927
Walt Disney Company	4833	A	818 560-1000	5928
Walt Disney Company (PA)	4833	D	818 560-1000	5929
Walt Disney Company	4833	D	818 560-1000	5930
Walt Disney Music Company (DH)	6794	D	818 560-1000	12229
Walt Disney Pictures and TV	7829	D	818 560-1000	18292
Walt Disney Records Direct (DH)	7812	D	818 560-1000	18190
Warner Bros Consumer Pdts Inc (DH)	8748	C	818 954-7980	28097
Warner Bros Distributing Inc	8741	C	818 954-6000	27277
Warner Bros Entertainment Inc	7812	C	818 954-1817	18191
Warner Bros Entertainment Inc	7812	B	818 954-7232	18192
Warner Bros Entertainment Inc	7812	C	818 954-3000	18193
Warner Bros Entertainment Inc	7812	C	818 954-5301	18194
Warner Bros Entertainment Inc (HQ)	7812	A	818 954-6000	18195
Warner Bros Entertainment Inc	7389	C	818 954-6901	17607
Warner Bros Entertainment Inc	7812	C	818 954-3000	18196
Warner Bros Entertainment Inc	7812	D	818 954-7065	18197
Warner Bros Entertainment Inc	7812	C	818 954-2181	18198
Warner Bros Entertainment Inc	7812	C	818 954-2187	18199
Warner Bros Entertainment Inc	7812	C	818 954-6000	18200
Warner Bros Intl TV Dist Inc	7812	C	818 954-6000	18201
Warner Bros Records Inc (DH)	7389	C	818 953-3378	17608
Warner Bros Transatlantic Inc (DH)	7822	A	818 954-6000	18285
Warner Bros Transatlantic Inc	7822	B	818 977-6384	18286
Warner Bros Transatlantic Inc	7822	A	818 972-0777	18287
Warner Brothers Studios	5043	D	818 954-5000	7038
Wdpt Film Distribution LLC	5065	C	818 560-1000	7656
Westwind Media Inc	7812	D	818 972-9000	18205
Westwind Studios LLC	7812	E	818 972-9000	18206
William F Kellogg Corporation	5088	D	818 845-7455	8010
Wonderland Music Company Inc	6794	D	818 840-1671	12230
Xerox Corporation	7334	D	818 848-8676	14130
Young Mens Christian (PA)	8641	D	818 845-8551	25439

BURLINGAME, CA - San Mateo County

Company	SIC	EMP	PHONE	ENTRY #
24 Hour Fitness Usa Inc	7991	E	650 343-7922	18593
Abx Engineering Inc	7373	D	650 552-2300	15892
Acumen LLC	7373	C	650 558-8882	15896
Agility Logistics Corp	4731	C	650 645-5800	5018
Airline Coach Service Inc (PA)	4111	E	650 697-7733	3632
Alain Pinel Realtors Inc	6531	D	650 375-1111	11286
Allen Drywall & Associates	1742	D	650 579-0664	2851
Amato Industries Incorporated	4119	D	650 697-2087	3740
American Med	4119	C	650 235-1333	3744
American Medical Response	4119	D	650 235-1333	3755
American Residential Svcs LLC	1711	D	650 652-1050	2135
AMS Relocation Incorporated	4214	D	650 697-3530	4329
Ares Project Management LLC (HQ)	8711	D	650 401-7100	25662
AT&T Services Inc	4813	C	650 579-5266	5545
Burlingame Senior Care LLC	8059	B	650 692-3758	21169
California Teachers Assn (PA)	8621	E	650 697-1400	25125
Carr Mc Clellan Ingersoll Thom (PA)	8111	D	650 342-9600	23144

GEOGRAPHIC SECTION

CALISTOGA, CA

	SIC	EMP	PHONE	ENTRY #
Coldwell Bnkr Residential Brkg	6531	D	650 558-4200	11427
Comcast Corporation	4841	D	650 689-5392	5952
CP Opco LLC	7359	D	650 652-0300	14531
Crystal Springs Golf Partners	7997	E	650 342-4188	18934
Cushman & Wakefield Inc	6531	E	650 347-3700	11462
Disney Construction Inc	1611	D	650 689-5149	1766
Doubletree LLC	7011	C	650 344-5500	12598
Edwards Frank Co (HQ)	5084	D	801 736-8000	7840
El Concilio San Mateo Cnty Inc	8322	E	650 373-1080	23958
Environmental Chemical Corp (PA)	8711	D	650 347-1555	25797
Epitomics Inc (HQ)	8733	D	650 583-6688	26764
Guardsmark LLC	7381	C	650 685-2400	16694
Guardsmark LLC	7381	C	650 652-9130	16697
Hamilton Partners	8742	E	650 347-8800	27457
Hanergy Holding America Inc	4911	B	650 288-3722	6137
Harbor View Hotels Inc	7011	E	650 340-8500	12691
Hilton Worldwide Inc	7011	D	650 342-4600	12728
Host Hotels & Resorts LP	7011	D	650 347-1234	12764
Host Hotels & Resorts LP	7011	D	650 692-9100	12772
Jacobs Consultancy Inc	8748	D	650 579-7722	27957
Jbs International Inc	8733	D	650 373-4900	26776
Jet Airways of India Inc	4512	D	650 762-2345	4805
JS International Shipg Corp (PA)	4731	D	650 697-3963	5107
Kindred Healthcare Operating	8069	B	650 697-1865	22149
Korean Airlines	4512	C	650 375-7123	4811
Ksi Corp	7389	C	650 952-0815	17278
Marriott International Inc	7011	C	650 692-9100	12979
Mid-Peninsula Roofing Inc	1761	D	650 375-7850	3191
Mills-Peninsula Health Svcs (HQ)	8062	A	650 696-5400	21748
Morgan Stanley & Co LLC	6211	D	650 340-6550	10057
Palcare Inc	8351	E	650 340-1289	24496
Parsons Brinckerhoff Inc	8742	D	650 697-1869	27583
Peninsula Assoc For Retarded	8322	D	650 312-0730	24127
Peninsula Humane Soc & Spca	8699	D	650 340-7022	25565
Peninsula Womens Health (PA)	8011	E	650 692-3818	19823
Prime Time Athletic Club Inc	7991	D	650 204-3662	18672
Pro Unlimited Inc	8741	E	650 344-1099	27174
Provident Mrtg Cpitl Assoc Inc	6162	A	650 652-1300	9889
Randstad Professionals Us LP	7361	C	650 343-5111	14744
Robert Meuschke Company Inc	1721	E	650 342-3993	2485
Safway Services LP	5082	D	650 692-9255	7788
Sage Software Inc	7372	C	650 579-3628	15831
San Mateo Healthcare & Wellnes	8051	D	650 692-3758	20892
Senior Assist of Peninsula LLC	8322	D	650 652-9791	24205
Shud Wcv Inc	7216	D	650 697-7380	13587
Sky Chefs Inc	4225	C	650 652-7886	4639
Sunkist Enterprises	5072	D	650 347-3900	7700
Synagro West LLC	8748	D	650 652-6531	28065
Tata Communications Amer Inc	7389	D	650 262-0004	17517
Tenex Greenhouse Ventures LLC	6799	D	650 375-7021	12350
Virgin America Inc (PA)	4512	C	877 359-8474	4839
Walter E McGuire RE Inc	6531	C	650 348-0222	11906
Wedriveu Holdings Inc	7361	D	650 579-5800	14817
Wilco Imports Inc	5199	D	650 204-7800	9313

BURNEY, CA - Shasta County

	SIC	EMP	PHONE	ENTRY #
Dicalite Minerals Corp	7699	D	530 335-5451	17972
Hat Creek Cnstr & Mtls Inc (PA)	1629	E	530 335-5501	2056
Pit River Health Service Inc (PA)	8099	D	530 335-5090	23021
Pit River Tribal Council	8011	D	530 335-3651	19874
Pit River Tribal Council	7999	D	530 335-2334	19260

BUTTONWILLOW, CA - Kern County

	SIC	EMP	PHONE	ENTRY #
Buttonwillow Warehouse Co Inc (HQ)	5191	D	661 764-5234	9130
Choice Hotels Intl Inc	7011	D	661 764-5207	12516
Omni Family Health	8099	D	661 764-5211	23012

BYRON, CA - Contra Costa County

	SIC	EMP	PHONE	ENTRY #
G3 Enterprises Inc	4731	D	209 341-3441	5084
New Discovery Inc	7997	D	925 783-6613	19013
New Discovery Inc	7992	D	925 634-0505	18765
Pacific Coast Ldscp MGT Inc	0781	D	925 513-2310	784
San Luis Dlta-Mendota Wtr Auth	4971	D	209 835-2593	6652
Simoni & Massoni Farms	0115	E	925 634-2304	8

CABAZON, CA - Riverside County

	SIC	EMP	PHONE	ENTRY #
Calvin Klein Inc	7699	E	951 849-9538	17964
Casino Morongo	7996	D	951 849-3080	18812
Casino Morongo Resort Spa	7991	D	951 846-5100	18620

CALABASAS, CA - Los Angeles County

	SIC	EMP	PHONE	ENTRY #
Abbyson Living Corp	5021	B	805 465-5500	6798
Able Cable Inc (PA)	7629	C	818 223-3600	17928
AIA Holdings Inc (PA)	6351	D	818 222-4999	10488
All Motorists Insurance Agency	6411	C	818 880-9070	10585
American Travel Solutions LLC	4724	D	800 243-2724	4956
Apex Development Inc	1522	C	818 887-0400	1291
Arcs Commercial Mortgage Co LP (DH)	6162	C	818 676-3274	9819
Asana Integrated Medical Group	8322	D	888 212-7545	23671
Atlas Database Software Corp (PA)	7371	D	818 340-7080	15040
Avanquest North America Inc (HQ)	7371	D	818 223-8967	15044
Brightview Companies LLC (DH)	1629	C	818 223-8500	2028
Brightview Golf Maint Inc (DH)	1629	D	818 223-8500	2030
Brightview Landscape Dev Inc (DH)	0781	E	818 223-8500	746
Calabasas Country Club	7997	D	818 222-8111	18905
Cartel Marketing Inc	6411	C	818 483-1130	10665
Center For Civic Education (PA)	8733	D	818 591-9321	26750
Coldwell Bnkr Residential Brkg	6531	D	818 222-0023	11432
Countrywide Capital Mkts LLC (DH)	6162	C	818 225-3000	9832
Countrywide Financial Corp (HQ)	6162	A	818 225-3000	9833
Countrywide Securities Corp	6211	B	818 225-3000	9987
Crown Media Holdings Inc	4833	D	818 755-2400	5849
Custom Tours Inc	4729	D	310 274-8819	5007
Davis Research LLC	8732	C	818 591-2408	26654
Dts Inc (PA)	7819	C	818 436-1000	18224
Ellie Mae Inc	7371	B	818 223-2000	15161
Endocrine Sciences Inc	8071	C	818 880-8040	22214
Exterior Solutions Inc	5033	D	310 400-3510	7012
Galaxy Building Systems Inc	7349	C	818 340-6557	14305
Grant & Weber (PA)	7322	D	818 878-7700	14034
Hearthstone Inc	6282	D	818 385-0005	10151
Idrive Inc	7379	D	818 594-5972	16400
Informa Research Services Inc (DH)	8742	C	818 880-8877	27474
Knight-Calabasas LLC (PA)	7997	D	818 222-3200	18966
Lantz Security Systems Inc	7382	C	818 871-0193	16897
Las Virgenes Municipal Wtr Dst	4941	D	818 251-2100	6362
Litigtion Rsrces of America-CA (PA)	7389	C	818 878-9227	17296
M S E Enterprises Inc (PA)	6531	D	818 223-3500	11650
Marcus Millichap Reis Nev Inc	6531	C	650 494-1400	11656
Nailagio	7231	C	818 222-6633	13682
Naked Infusions LLC	5149	D	818 239-9058	8882
New View Landscape Inc	0782	C	818 222-8972	921
Nowher Partners LLC	5149	D	818 857-3366	8894
NTS Technical Systems (PA)	8734	B	818 591-0776	26880
On Assignment Inc (PA)	7363	C	818 878-7900	14920
PNC Realty Investors Inc	8742	D	818 880-3300	27590
Prolifics Inc (DH)	7379	B	212 267-7722	16464
Quantum Solutions Inc	7379	E	818 577-4555	16466
Rainbow Camp Inc	7999	E	310 456-3066	19266
Red Peak Group LLC	8742	D	818 222-7762	27610
Sedgwick Claims MGT Svcs Inc	6411	C	818 591-9444	10868
T M Mian & Associates Inc	7011	B	818 591-2300	13336
Top Seed Tennis Academy Inc	7999	D	818 222-2782	19295
Triad Systems International (PA)	8748	B	818 222-6811	28083
Unifax Insurance Systems Inc	6411	D	818 591-9800	10912
Valleycrest Ldscp Maint Vcc	0781	E	800 466-8510	803
Western General Holding Co (PA)	6331	C	818 880-9070	10481
Western General Insurance Co	6331	C	818 880-9070	10482
Worxsitehr Insur Solutions Inc	6411	D	877 479-3591	10947

CALABASAS HILLS, CA - Los Angeles County

	SIC	EMP	PHONE	ENTRY #
Helmet House Inc (PA)	5136	D	800 421-7247	8345

CALEXICO, CA - Imperial County

	SIC	EMP	PHONE	ENTRY #
Adventures In Hospitality Inc	7997	D	760 356-2806	18842
ARC - Imperial Valley	8093	D	760 768-1944	22658
California Super Market	4225	D	760 357-3065	4530
City of Calexico (PA)	4119	C	760 768-2130	3781
Coppel Corporation	5021	D	760 357-3707	6813
Martech Medical Products Inc	8011	D	215 256-8833	19733
R L Jones-San Diego Inc (PA)	4731	D	760 357-3177	5158
R L Jones-San Diego Inc	4731	D	760 357-0140	5159
Service Container Company LLC	7389	D	310 223-1666	17486
Technicolor HM Entrmt Svcs Inc	7819	B	760 357-3372	18260
U S Xpress Inc	4213	C	760 768-6707	4282

CALIENTE, CA - Kern County

	SIC	EMP	PHONE	ENTRY #
James McCutcheon	1522	E	661 867-1810	1317

CALIFORNIA CITY, CA - Kern County

	SIC	EMP	PHONE	ENTRY #
Corrections Corp America	8744	C	760 373-1764	27782
Silver Saddle Ranch & Club Inc	6552	D	760 373-8617	12011

CALIMESA, CA - Riverside County

	SIC	EMP	PHONE	ENTRY #
Tommy Gun Plastering Inc	1742	D	909 795-9966	2988

CALIPATRIA, CA - Imperial County

	SIC	EMP	PHONE	ENTRY #
Brandt Co Inc	0211	D	760 348-2295	407
Calenergy LLC	1731	B	402 231-1527	2548
Frank Barraza	0761	D	760 348-7363	662
Hudson Ranch Power I LLC	4911	D	858 509-0150	6139

CALISTOGA, CA - Napa County

	SIC	EMP	PHONE	ENTRY #
Calistoga Spa Inc	7991	D	707 942-6269	18618
Enzennauer Vineyard Managment	0762	D	707 433-0532	702

CALISTOGA, CA

Company	SIC	EMP	PHONE	ENTRY #
Madrigal Vineyard Management	7389	E	707 942-8691	17309
Mv Hospitality Inc	7991	E	707 942-6877	18666
Schramsberg Vineyards Company	0172	E	707 942-4558	188
Silver Oak Wine Cellars LP	5182	E	707 857-3562	9109
Spa Partners Inc	7991	E	707 942-5789	18687

CALPELLA, CA - Mendocino County

Company	SIC	EMP	PHONE	ENTRY #
Mendocino Forest Pdts Co LLC	5031	D	707 485-6800	6937
Mendocino Forest Pdts Co LLC	5099	C	707 620-2961	8125

CAMARILLO, CA - Ventura County

Company	SIC	EMP	PHONE	ENTRY #
Aecom C&E Inc	8711	D	805 388-3775	25620
Affiliated Communications Inc	7389	E	805 650-4949	16973
Airport Connection Inc	4111	C	805 389-8196	3633
All Control Cleaning Inc	7349	D	805 987-4210	14219
American Airlines Inc	4581	D	805 988-0407	4901
Anthem Insurance Companies Inc	6324	D	805 557-6655	10258
Applied Engineering MGT Corp	7371	D	805 484-1909	15024
Arconix/Usa Inc	5065	D	805 388-2525	7522
AT&T Corp	4813	D	805 445-6562	5482
Atria Senior Living Group Inc	8361	D	805 482-9771	24557
Automatic Data Processing Inc	7374	D	805 383-8630	16092
Battery-Biz Inc	5045	D	805 437-7777	7099
Bml Industries Inc	5063	D	805 388-6800	7419
Boskovich Farms Inc	0161	B	805 987-1443	42
C & C Boats Inc	4499	E	805 445-9456	4774
Camarillo Healthcare Center	8741	A	805 482-9805	26957
Camarillo Ranch Foundation	7389	D	805 389-8182	17050
Casa Pacifica Centers (PA)	8322	C	805 482-3260	23706
Central Purchasing LLC (PA)	5085	B	805 388-1000	7928
Channel Islands Young Mens Ch	8641	D	805 484-0423	25232
CIT Bank National Association	6021	D	805 465-1053	9360
Coast Farms Inc	0161	D	805 383-0455	53
Coastal Grading and Excavating	1794	E	805 445-6433	3423
Community Memorial Health Sys	8011	D	805 482-1282	19457
County of Ventura	8322	B	805 654-5529	23935
Crown Golf Properties LP	8742	D	909 481-6663	27398
D B Roberts Inc	5065	D	805 388-4482	7551
D P Technology Corp (PA)	7371	D	805 388-6000	15118
Data Exchange Corporation (PA)	5045	D	805 388-1711	7117
Delicate Productions Inc (PA)	7922	D	415 484-1174	18388
Dex Corporation	8711	C	805 388-1711	25769
Dial Security (PA)	7382	C	805 389-6700	16878
Dignity Health	8062	D	805 384-8071	21534
Dignity Health	8062	D	805 389-5800	21540
Edwards Theatres Circuit Inc	7832	D	805 383-8866	18332
Electronic Clearing House Inc (HQ)	7372	D	805 419-8700	15653
Holthouse Carlin Van Trigt LLP	8721	D	805 374-8555	26370
Houweling Nurseries Oxnard Inc	5141	B	805 488-8832	8486
Institute For Applied Behavior	8049	C	805 987-5886	20324
Interface Community (PA)	8322	D	805 485-6114	24031
Jpmorgan Chase Bank Nat Assn	7389	C	805 482-2902	17265
Juvenile Justice Division Cal	8741	B	805 485-7951	27085
Kaiser Foundation Hospitals	8011	A	888 515-3500	19606
Kaiser Foundation Hospitals	6324	D	805 482-0707	10342
Keller Williams	6531	D	805 389-1919	11606
Las Posas Club Inc	7997	D	805 482-1811	18979
Las Posas Country Club	7997	D	805 482-4518	18980
Leisure Village Association	8641	D	805 484-2861	25286
Logix Development Corporation	7371	D	888 505-6449	15283
Market Scan Info Systems Inc (PA)	7371	D	805 823-4258	15290
Meathead Movers Inc	4213	D	805 437-5100	4226
Michael Baker Jr Inc	8711	D	805 383-3373	25964
Mid Coast Builders Supply Inc	1521	C	805 484-3157	1221
Nallatech Inc	5065	D	805 383-8997	7611
New Inspiration Brdcstg Co Inc	4832	A	805 987-0400	5813
Northrop Grumman Systems Corp	7373	D	805 987-9739	16015
Oasis Technology Inc	7371	D	805 445-4833	16021
Odu-Usa Inc (HQ)	5065	D	805 484-0540	7616
Omniupdate Inc	7371	D	805 484-9400	15350
Pacific Earth Resources (PA)	0181	D	805 986-8277	309
People Creating Success Inc	8011	C	805 644-9480	19824
Research Management Cons Inc (PA)	8748	D	805 987-5538	28040
Rincon Pacific LLC	0171	D	805 986-8806	130
Saalex Corp (PA)	8711	C	805 482-1070	26048
Salem Media Group Inc (PA)	4832	D	818 956-4980	5817
Solarworld Americas LLC (DH)	5063	D	503 844-3400	7476
Solimar Farms Inc	0171	D	805 986-8806	134
Spanish Hills Country Club (PA)	7997	C	805 389-1644	19085
Sunrise Senior Living LLC	8051	D	805 388-8086	20982
Techniclor Vdocassette Mfch Inc (DH)	7819	D	805 445-1122	18259
Technicolor HM Entrmt Svcs Inc (DH)	7819	D	805 445-1122	18262
Technicolor Thomson Group	7819	A	805 445-1122	18266
Telecare Corporation	8063	D	805 383-3669	22104
Telecare Las Posadas	8093	D	805 383-3669	22851
Teledyne Scientific Imaging LLC	8731	C	805 373-4979	26620

Company	SIC	EMP	PHONE	ENTRY #
Tommy Bahama Group Inc	7389	C	805 482-8868	17533
Travel Store	4724	D	805 987-3425	4977
Ventura County Fire Department	8641	D	805 389-9710	25388
Verizon Communications Inc	7822	C	805 445-8125	18281
Vitas Healthcare Corporation	8082	D	805 437-2100	22608
Voice Print International Inc (PA)	7374	D	805 389-5200	16210
Wilshire Health and Cmnty Svcs	8361	D	805 484-2777	24858

CAMBRIA, CA - San Luis Obispo County

Company	SIC	EMP	PHONE	ENTRY #
Moonstone Management Corp (PA)	6531	C	805 927-4200	11692
Pacific Cambria Inc	7011	D	805 927-6114	13055

CAMERON PARK, CA - El Dorado County

Company	SIC	EMP	PHONE	ENTRY #
Americas Flood Services Inc	6411	D	916 636-9460	10600
Cameron Park Country Club Inc	7997	D	530 672-9840	18911
CBS Maxpreps Inc	4813	E	530 676-6440	5572
Hemington Landscape Svcs Inc	0782	D	530 677-9290	869
McClone Construction Company	1521	D	703 433-9406	1215

CAMINO, CA - El Dorado County

Company	SIC	EMP	PHONE	ENTRY #
Snowline Hspc Eldorado Cnty	8052	C	530 647-2703	21110

CAMP PENDLETON, CA - San Diego County

Company	SIC	EMP	PHONE	ENTRY #
Lion-Vallen Ltd Partnership	8741	E	760 385-4885	27117
Marine Corps United States	7011	E	760 430-4709	12942
Marine Corps United States	8331	E	760 725-7144	24361
Transitamerica Services Inc	4111	E	760 430-0770	3729

CAMPBELL, CA - Santa Clara County

Company	SIC	EMP	PHONE	ENTRY #
24/7 Customer Inc (PA)	7379	D	650 385-2247	16310
Adorno Construction Inc	1771	D	408 369-8675	3225
Aicent Inc	7379	C	408 324-1316	16319
B C C S Inc (PA)	1542	C	408 379-5500	1495
Barracuda Networks Inc (PA)	7372	C	408 342-5400	15596
Bio-Reference Laboratories Inc	8071	C	408 341-8600	22191
Campbell Hhg Hotel Dev LP	7011	E	408 626-9590	12484
Cape Clear Software Inc	7371	D	408 879-7365	15074
Cdnetworks Inc (DH)	4813	D	408 228-3379	5573
Cem Builders Inc	8711	E	408 395-1490	25731
Century 21 Alpha LLC	6531	D	408 369-2000	11366
Cenzic Inc	5065	E	408 200-0700	7547
Charles Culberson Inc	1742	C	650 335-4730	2876
Comglobal Systems Inc (DH)	7373	D	619 321-6000	15924
Daleys Drywall and Taping Inc	1742	C	408 378-9500	2883
Dentistat Inc	8742	D	408 376-0336	27408
Douglas Ross Construction Inc	1522	D	408 429-7700	1308
Duran Human Capital Partners	7361	E	408 540-0070	14639
Durham School Services L P	4151	D	408 377-6655	3920
Education Program Associates	8399	D	408 374-3720	24918
Farmers Group Inc	6411	E	408 557-1100	10705
Fernandes & Sons Gen Contrs	7363	D	408 626-9090	14878
Groupware Technology Inc (PA)	7373	C	408 540-0090	15955
Hightail Inc (PA)	4813	D	408 879-9118	5629
Howard Fischer Associates Inc	7361	A	408 374-0580	14674
Intrepid Security Solutions	7382	E	855 379-2223	16892
Kaiser Foundation Hospitals	8011	D	408 871-6500	19672
Kindred Healthcare Inc	8099	D	408 871-9860	22989
Knights of Columbus	8641	C	408 371-1531	25277
Largo Concrete Inc	1771	D	408 874-2500	3290
Leidos Engineering LLC	8711	D	408 364-4700	25935
LLP Moss Adams	8721	D	408 369-2400	26400
Martina Landscape Inc	0782	D	408 871-8800	909
Masudas Landscape Services	0781	D	408 379-7100	779
Mblox Incorporated (HQ)	7371	D	408 617-3700	15296
Merrill Gardens LLC	6531	D	408 370-6431	11685
Mission Vlla Alzhmers Rsidence	8361	E	408 559-8301	24738
Mohler Nixon & Williams Accoun (PA)	8721	D	408 369-2400	26411
Monster Mechanical Inc	1711	D	408 727-8362	2296
Movaris Inc	7372	E	408 213-3400	15763
Netnow	4813	B	408 370-0425	5666
Netpolarity Inc	7361	B	408 971-1100	14706
Odyssey Healthcare Inc	8051	D	408 626-4868	20825
On-Site Manager Inc (PA)	7389	E	866 266-7483	17376
Panzura Inc	7373	D	408 457-8504	16027
Rainmaker Systems Inc	8741	C	408 659-1800	27193
Saab Sensis Corporation	7371	D	315 445-0550	15432
Saama Technologies Inc (PA)	7371	C	408 371-1900	15433
San Andreas Regional Center (PA)	8322	C	408 374-9960	24171
Sandis Civil Engineers (PA)	8713	D	408 636-0900	26280
Senior Living Solutions LLC	8052	C	408 385-1835	21106
Signature Building Maint Inc	7349	D	408 377-8066	14430
Silver Creek Home Owners	8741	E	408 559-1977	27211
Skyhigh Networks Inc	7382	D	408 564-0278	16928
Spiraledge Inc (PA)	7372	E	800 691-4065	15843
SR Freeman Inc	1751	D	408 364-2200	3093
Streamray Inc	7929	B	408 745-5449	18500
Subacute Childrens Hosp of Cal	8069	D	408 558-3644	22179

GEOGRAPHIC SECTION — CARLSBAD, CA

Company	SIC	EMP	PHONE	ENTRY #
Telecmmnctons MGT Slutions Inc	1731	D	408 866-5495	2769
TownePlace Suites	7011	D	408 370-4510	13350
Uplift Family Services (PA)	8361	D	408 379-3790	24840
Vencore Inc	7373	D	408 961-3250	16075
Vencore Inc	8748	E	571 313-6000	28088
Vencore Inc	7373	D	619 321-6000	16076
Vencore Svcs & Solutions Inc	7373	E	408 961-3200	16077
Wells Fargo Bank National Assn	6021	E	408 378-8155	9443
West Valley Cnstr Co Inc (PA)	1623	C	408 371-5510	2018
Xcommerce Inc (PA)	7371	E	310 954-8012	15553

CAMPO, CA - San Diego County

Company	SIC	EMP	PHONE	ENTRY #
Campo Band Missions Indians	7993	B	619 938-6000	18802

CANBY, CA - Modoc County

Company	SIC	EMP	PHONE	ENTRY #
Warner Mountain Group Hom	8361	D	530 233-5200	24852

CANOGA PARK, CA - Los Angeles County

Company	SIC	EMP	PHONE	ENTRY #
24 Hour Fitness Usa Inc	7991	D	818 887-2582	18595
A Yafa Pen Company	5112	E	818 704-8888	8158
Aegis Treatment Centers LLC (PA)	8093	D	818 206-0360	22650
American Landscape Inc	0781	C	818 999-2041	738
American Landscape Management (PA)	0781	C	818 999-2041	739
Bay Clubs Inc	7997	D	818 884-5034	18884
Boeing Company	8711	E	818 466-8800	25698
Bubbla Inc	5199	E	818 884-2000	9249
Buyers Consultation Svc Inc (PA)	5065	D	818 341-4820	7539
C P Holiday Manor Inc	8059	D	818 341-9800	21172
Canew Inc	8072	C	818 703-5100	22302
Canoga Park Worksource Center	7361	E	818 596-4448	14620
Catholic Charities of La Inc	8322	E	818 883-6015	23710
Cellco Partnership	4812	D	818 316-0865	5335
Cellco Partnership	4812	D	818 715-9143	5367
Computrition Inc (HQ)	7371	D	818 961-3999	15102
Golden State West Valley	8051	D	818 348-8422	20630
Green Thumb International Inc	5193	D	818 340-6400	9190
Heritage Landscape Inc	0781	C	818 999-2041	772
Hmi Associates Inc	7381	C	818 887-6800	16703
Interamerican Motor Corp (HQ)	5013	C	818 678-6571	6740
Jones & Jones MGT Group Inc	6513	C	818 594-0019	11147
Landcare USA LLC	0782	C	818 346-7552	898
Leisure Care LLC	8052	D	818 713-0900	21089
Mailmark Enterprises LLC	7331	E	818 407-0660	14082
Mark Land Electric Inc	1731	D	818 883-5110	2640
New Start Home Health Care Inc	8322	C	818 665-7898	24102
Northeast Valley Health Corp	8099	C	818 340-3570	23007
One Call Medical Inc	8742	D	818 346-8700	27575
P-Cove Enterprises Inc	7373	D	818 341-1101	16025
Platinum Group Companies Inc (PA)	6719	C	818 721-3800	12084
Richard Huetter Inc	5013	D	818 700-8001	6759
Right Choice In-Home Care Inc	8082	A	818 836-6001	22550
Rte Enterprises Inc	1721	D	818 999-5300	2487
S1 Corporation	7373	C	818 992-3299	16041
Sela Healthcare Inc	8051	B	818 341-9800	20903
Shield Security Inc	7381	C	818 239-5800	16822
Socal Auto Supply Inc	7213	D	302 360-8373	13569
Software Dynamics Incorporated	7373	D	818 992-3299	16055
Southern California Mtl Hdlg	5084	D	818 349-1220	7890
Super Garden Centers Inc	5193	E	818 348-9266	9218
T & T Solutions Inc	7379	D	818 676-1786	16496
T M P Inc	5136	D	818 718-1222	8361
West Valley Jewish Cmnty Ctr	7999	D	818 348-0048	19308
Westwood Insurance Agency (DH)	6411	D	818 990-9715	10938

CANYON COUNTRY, CA - Los Angeles County

Company	SIC	EMP	PHONE	ENTRY #
County of Los Angeles	6371	D	661 298-3406	10549
Design Masonry Inc	1741	D	661 252-2784	2809
Jencor Door and Trim Inc	1751	E	661 251-8161	3058
Northeast Valley Health Corp	8099	D	661 673-8888	23008
Sulphur Springs Union Pta	8641	D	661 252-2725	25353

CANYON LAKE, CA - Riverside County

Company	SIC	EMP	PHONE	ENTRY #
A Caregiver LLC	8082	E	951 676-4190	22317
Canyon Lk Property Owners Assn	8641	C	951 244-6841	25228
Cbabr Inc (PA)	6531	C	951 640-7056	11349
My Choice Inhome Care LLC	8082	D	951 244-8770	22511

CAPISTRANO BEACH, CA - Orange County

Company	SIC	EMP	PHONE	ENTRY #
Capistrano Beach Extended	8051	D	949 496-5786	20435
Golden Living LLC	8051	D	949 496-5786	20616
National Rtrement Partners Inc (PA)	6411	D	949 848-8726	10794
Soto Company Inc	0782	D	949 493-9403	956

CAPITOLA, CA - Santa Cruz County

Company	SIC	EMP	PHONE	ENTRY #
AT&T Corp	4812	D	831 465-6771	5267
Bay Federal Credit Union (PA)	6061	D	831 479-6000	9590
CA Ste Atom Assoc Intr-Ins Bur	7549	D	831 824-9128	17877
Cellco Partnership	4812	D	831 475-3100	5304
Coldwell Bnkr Residential Brkg	6531	D	831 462-9000	11426
Covenant Care LLC	8051	D	831 476-0770	20483
Profile of Santa Cruz	7361	D	831 479-0393	14737

CARLSBAD, CA - San Diego County

Company	SIC	EMP	PHONE	ENTRY #
24 Hour Fitness Usa Inc	7991	D	760 602-5001	18580
3share Acquisition Inc	7371	E	888 505-1625	14990
4g Wireless Inc	4813	D	760 828-2543	5444
Abtech Technologies Inc	7379	D	760 827-5100	16312
Active Motif Inc (PA)	8731	D	760 431-1263	26460
Acutus Medical Inc	8099	D	858 673-1621	22873
Adicio Inc	4813	D	760 602-9502	5454
Advanced Commercial Corporatio	6722	C	760 431-8500	12100
Amgen Distribution Inc	4213	D	760 438-2538	4109
ARC Hosp Portfolio II NTC Trs	7011	E	760 431-9399	12395
Arnel Development Company	1522	D	760 599-6111	1293
Autogenomics Inc	8731	D	760 477-2248	26481
Aviara Fsrc Associates Limited	7011	A	760 603-6800	12406
Aviara Resort Associates (PA)	7011	A	760 448-1234	12407
Bayside Solutions Inc	7363	E	760 448-2970	14845
Beauty Service Inc	7231	E	760 434-4141	13669
Brehm Communities (PA)	1521	D	760 448-2420	1138
Brightview Landscapes LLC	0781	D	760 929-8509	756
Buffini & Company (PA)	8331	C	760 827-2100	24315
Business Intelligence	8742	E	858 452-8200	27362
Buzztime Inc	4833	D	760 476-1976	5836
By Referral Only Inc	8748	D	760 707-1300	27859
Calatlantic Group Inc	1521	C	760 476-0104	1146
Calatlantic Group Inc	1531	D	760 931-4414	1359
California Bistro At Fo	7011	D	760 603-3700	12481
Califrnia Cnema Invstments Inc	7832	C	760 827-6700	18314
Callaway Golf Ball Oprtons Inc	5091	A	760 931-1771	8013
Canon Solutions America Inc	7389	C	760 438-6990	17052
Carlsbad Inn Vactn Condo Ownrs	8641	D	760 434-7542	25229
Carlsbad Municipal Water Dst	4941	E	760 438-2722	6323
Carlsbad Surgery Center LLC	8093	E	760 438-2488	22672
CAV Inc	4119	D	760 729-5199	3780
CDM SMITH INC	8711	D	760 438-7755	25727
Celico Partnership	4812	D	760 720-8400	5306
Celimatics	7373	E	760 692-2424	15917
Chambers Belt Company	5139	D	760 602-9688	8424
Chopra Cntre For Wll-Being LLC	7999	D	760 494-1600	19163
Cierra Wireless	8711	E	760 476-8700	25737
Coast Environmental Inc	7389	D	760 929-9570	17086
Coast Waste Management	4953	C	760 753-9412	6465
Cofa Media Group LLC	4813	C	877 293-2007	5580
Community Interface Services	8322	D	760 729-3866	23775
Continuing Lf Communities LLC (PA)	6411	D	760 704-1000	10679
Corporate Visions Inc	8742	C	760 458-0914	27390
Deepak Chopra LLC	7991	E	760 494-1600	18627
Document Sciences Corporation (DH)	7372	D	760 602-0809	15642
El Camino Rental	7513	D	760 438-7368	17641
Electronic Entrmt Design & RES	8732	D	760 579-7100	26659
Electronic Online Systems Intl	7373	D	760 431-8400	15939
Encina Wastewater Authority	4952	D	760 438-3941	6411
Enviance Inc (HQ)	7371	D	760 496-0200	15168
Federal Express Corporation	7389	C	800 463-3339	17163
Ferguson Salon Management Inc	7231	E	760 434-5008	13675
Fmt Consultants LLC	7379	D	760 930-6400	16371
Four Seasons Resort Aviara	7992	E	760 603-6900	18741
Franconnect LLC	7373	D	760 720-5354	15949
Freedom Mortgage Corporation	6162	D	760 692-3977	9810
Front Porch Communities	8059	D	760 729-4983	21220
Genoptix Inc (DH)	8071	D	760 268-6200	22222
Glenview Assisted Living LLP	8099	E	760 704-6800	22964
Global Domains International	4813	D	760 602-3000	5616
Gordon R Levinson A Prof Corp	8111	D	760 692-2260	23280
Grand Pacific Carlsbad Ht LP	7011	B	760 827-2400	12672
Grand Pacific Resorts Inc	7389	C	760 431-8500	17198
Grand Pacific Resorts Inc (PA)	6531	C	760 431-8500	11559
Grand Pacific Resorts Svcs LP	7011	C	760 431-8500	12673
Hansen Icc LLC	8721	D	760 268-7299	26365
Havas Edge LLC (PA)	7311	C	760 929-1357	13858
Hay House Inc (PA)	5192	D	760 431-7695	9165
Hilton Garden Inns MGT LLC	7011	E	760 476-0800	12708
Ibis Biosciences Inc	8731	D	760 476-3200	26533
Integral Senior Living LLC (PA)	8741	C	760 547-2863	27066
Interior Specialists Inc (HQ)	1752	D	760 929-6700	3120
Interstate Hotels Resorts Inc	8741	D	760 476-0800	27068
Intravas Inc	8742	D	760 650-4040	27484
Ipitek Inc (PA)	1731	E	760 438-1010	2620
Jazzercise Inc (PA)	7991	D	760 476-1750	18647
Jefferson California Congress	8641	D	760 331-5500	25273
Jenny Craig Inc (HQ)	7299	C	760 696-4000	13770
Jenny Craig Wght Loss Ctrs Inc (DH)	7299	C	760 696-4000	13771
Jet Source Inc	4789	D	760 438-1042	5227

Employment Codes: A=Over 500 employees, B=251-500, C=101-250, D=51-100, E=45-50

2017 Directory of California Wholesalers and Services Companies

CARLSBAD, CA

Company	SIC	EMP	PHONE	ENTRY #
Kaiser Foundation Hospitals	8011	C	760 931-4228	19680
Kendal Floral Supply LLC (PA)	5193	D	760 431-4910	9196
Kennedy Masonry Inc	1741	D	760 931-2671	2824
La Costa Limousine (PA)	4119	D	760 438-4455	3811
Lawinfocom Inc	7372	D	760 510-3000	15732
Lc Trs Inc	7011	A	760 438-9111	12911
Legoland California LLC	7996	B	760 918-5346	18824
Lg Display America Inc	5065	E	760 692-0900	7596
Mardx Diagnostics Inc	5047	D	760 929-0500	7275
Marriott	7011	D	760 720-9898	12946
Marriott International Inc	7011	C	760 431-9399	12950
Mc Consultants Inc (PA)	8711	D	760 930-9966	25955
Medsphere Systems Corporation (PA)	8742	D	760 692-3700	27540
Merlin Entertainments	7996	D	877 350-5346	18826
National Assn Mus Mrchants Inc	8611	D	760 438-8001	25095
North Coast Home Care Inc	8082	D	760 260-8700	22514
Ntent Inc	7371	D	760 930-7600	15341
NTN Buzztime Inc (PA)	4833	C	760 438-7400	5903
Optumrx Inc	6324	B	760 804-2399	10363
Ostendo Technologies Inc (PA)	8731	D	760 710-3003	26579
Pacific Bonding Corporation (PA)	7389	C	760 431-9911	17389
Pacific Western Bank	6021	D	760 918-2469	9416
Pavigym America Corp	5023	D	858 414-8624	6879
Petra Risk Solutions	6411	D	800 466-8951	10826
Physical Rehabilitation Netwrk (PA)	8049	D	760 931-8310	20340
Prana Living LLC	5136	D	866 915-6457	8357
Premiere Financial	6282	D	760 518-5034	10174
Prescott Companies	6531	E	760 634-4700	11761
Prescription Solutions	8742	A	760 804-2370	27592
Product Slingshot Inc	7389	D	760 929-9380	17430
Providence Seminars Inc	8742	D	760 827-2100	27600
Pulse-Link Inc	8731	D	760 496-2136	26593
R Q Construction Inc	1541	C	760 477-1199	1459
R Q Construction LLC	1541	C	760 631-7707	1460
Rancho Leonero Resort	7011	E	760 438-2905	13128
Really Likeable People Inc	5139	E	760 431-5577	8444
Relationedge LLC	8711	D	858 227-2955	26038
Rialto Bioenergy Facility LLC	8711	C	760 436-8870	26039
Richard Realty Group Inc	6531	C	760 603-8377	11813
Richardson A Clark	8711	D	760 496-3714	26041
Riolo Transportation Inc	4789	C	760 729-4405	5239
Rockstar San Diego	7374	C	760 929-0700	16179
Rowan Incorporated	1731	D	760 692-0700	2719
Safc Carlsbad Inc	8733	D	760 918-0007	26804
Sambreel Services LLC	7371	D	760 266-5090	15434
San Diego Gas & Electric Co	4939	C	760 438-6200	6306
Sap America Inc	7371	C	760 603-8034	15437
Search Engine Optimization Inc	7389	D	760 929-0039	17482
Securematics Inc	5045	E	408 970-8566	7184
Sethi Management Inc	8741	D	760 692-5288	27209
Sierra Wireless America Inc	4812	D	760 444-5650	5407
Signet Armorlite Inc (DH)	8099	B	760 744-4000	23058
Sonic Boom Wellness Inc	7371	D	760 438-1600	15469
Sound Technologies Inc	5047	D	760 918-9626	7315
Source 44 LLC	8748	C	877 916-6337	28060
South Cone Inc	5139	C	760 431-2300	8446
Southern Cal Prmnnte Med Group	8049	A	619 528-5000	20354
Sunrise Senior Living LLC	8051	D	760 930-0060	20972
Synteracthcr Inc (DH)	8731	B	760 268-8200	26614
Synteracthcr Corporation (HQ)	8731	B	760 268-8200	26615
Synteracthcr Holdings Corp (PA)	8731	B	760 268-8200	26616
Tamarack Bch Condo Owners Assn	8641	E	760 729-3500	25368
Technology Associates EC Inc	8742	D	760 765-5275	27679
Teg Staffing Inc	7363	A	619 584-3444	14956
Tri City Emergency Med Group	8721	E	760 439-1963	26452
Triton Management Services LLC	8741	D	760 431-9911	27259
Two Jinn Inc (PA)	7389	D	760 431-9911	17548
Valley Radiology Consultants (PA)	8071	D	619 797-8248	22295
Vertical Search Works Inc	7311	D	212 967-9502	13936
Villas De Carlsbad Ltd A Cali	8361	D	760 434-7116	24850
Wells Fargo Home Mortgage Inc	6162	B	760 603-7000	9907
West Inn & Suites LLC	7011	D	760 448-4500	13400
Weston Solutions Inc	8731	D	760 795-6900	26638
White Digital Media Inc	5192	D	760 827-7800	9175

CARMEL, CA - Monterey County

Company	SIC	EMP	PHONE	ENTRY #
Alain Pinel Realtors	6531	D	831 622-1040	11279
B S I Holdings Inc	1742	A	831 622-1840	2860
Bayview Properties Inc	7011	D	831 624-1841	12427
Carmel Mission Inn	7011	D	831 624-1841	12490
Carmel Valley Ranch	7011	D	831 625-9500	12491
Carmel Vly Mrtg Borrower LLC	7011	D	831 625-9500	12492
Highlands Inn Investors II LP	7011	B	831 624-3801	12704
Kagan Capital Management Inc	6282	D	831 624-1536	10155
Mission Ranch Inc	7011	E	831 624-6436	12998
Monterey Pacific Inc (PA)	0762	E	831 678-4845	710
Northern CA Cngrgtnl Rtmt	8059	C	831 624-1281	21329
Preserve Golf Club Inc	7992	E	831 620-6871	18771
Quail Lodge Inc	7011	C	831 624-1581	13117
Santa Lucia Preserve Company	7997	C	831 620-6760	19065
Stewardship Company LLC	8741	D	831 620-6700	27231
Tehama Golf Club LLC	7997	D	831 622-2200	19103
Trevi Partners A Calif LP	7011	D	831 624-1841	13357
Wyndham International Inc	7011	C	831 625-9500	13437

CARMEL VALLEY, CA - Monterey County

Company	SIC	EMP	PHONE	ENTRY #
Blue Sky Lodge Motel	7011	D	831 659-2935	12456
Keller Williams Realty	6531	D	831 622-6200	11607

CARMICHAEL, CA - Sacramento County

Company	SIC	EMP	PHONE	ENTRY #
Acct Holdings LLC	7389	A	916 971-1981	16967
AEgis of Carmichael	8361	D	916 972-1313	24543
Atria Senior Living Group Inc	6513	D	916 488-5722	11091
Cal Sierra Construction Inc	1623	D	916 416-7901	1915
Capital Eye Medical Group	8011	D	916 241-9378	19400
Carmichael Care Inc	8051	C	916 483-8103	20439
Carmichael Recreation & Pk Dst	8322	E	916 485-5322	23704
Crestwood Behavioral Hlth Inc	8063	D	916 977-0949	22065
Diez & Leis RE Group Inc	6531	D	916 487-4475	11471
Eskaton (PA)	6512	D	916 334-0296	10980
Eskaton Properties Inc	8322	D	916 334-1072	23962
Eskaton Properties Inc	8051	D	916 974-2060	20549
Eskaton Properties Inc	8051	D	916 331-8513	20550
Eskaton Properties Inc (PA)	8361	D	916 334-0810	24653
Eskaton Properties Inc	8059	D	916 974-2000	21213
Fairwood Associates Apts	6513	D	916 944-0152	11128
H B J Corporation	1742	D	707 333-7066	2907
Helios Healthcare LLC	8051	C	916 482-0465	20662
Horizon West Inc	8051	C	916 488-8601	20674
Laurels Medical Services	4121	C	408 898-6360	3864
Mercy Healthcare Sacramento	8062	C	916 537-5151	21735
Mercy Healthcare Sacramento	8062	C	916 537-5000	21736
Pacific Cities Management Inc (PA)	6531	D	916 348-1188	11723
Quick Quack Car Wash	8741	C	888 772-2792	27187
SSC Carmichael Operating Co LP	8051	C	916 485-4793	20924
Sunbridge Brittany Rehab Centr	8051	C	916 484-1393	20939
Sunrise Senior Living Inc	8051	C	916 485-4500	20965
Walnut Whtney Cnvalescent Hosp	8051	C	916 488-8601	21023
Wenmat Inc	8699	D	916 485-0714	25597

CARPINTERIA, CA - Santa Barbara County

Company	SIC	EMP	PHONE	ENTRY #
Astro Aerospace	8711	C	805 684-6641	25670
Brand Flower Farms Inc (PA)	5193	D	805 684-5531	9179
CP Opco LLC	7359	C	805 566-3566	14530
Dako North America Inc (HQ)	5122	C	805 566-6655	8252
Divecon Services LP	1629	C	805 488-6428	2042
Gallup & Stribling Orchids LLC	0181	E	805 684-1998	283
Hollandia Produce LP	0182	C	805 684-8739	334
Johannes Flowers Inc	0181	C	805 684-5686	293
Myriad Flowers International	0181	D	805 684-8079	304
Ocean Breeze International	0181	D	805 684-1747	306
Plan Member Financial Corp	6282	D	805 684-1199	10172
Procore Technologies Inc	7371	B	866 477-6267	15397
Sunshine Floral Inc	5193	D	805 684-1177	9216
Ucp Work Inc (PA)	8331	C	805 566-9000	24398
Valley Flowers Inc	5193	D	805 684-6651	9224
Westland Orchids Inc	5193	E	805 684-1436	9229

CARSON, CA - Los Angeles County

Company	SIC	EMP	PHONE	ENTRY #
Advanced Cleanup Tech Inc (PA)	8744	C	310 763-1423	27771
Agility Logistics Corp	4731	D	310 507-6700	5017
Alameda Corridor Engrg Team	8711	D	310 816-0460	25645
Alliedbarton Security Svcs LLC	7381	C	310 324-1219	16545
American Guard Services Inc (PA)	7381	B	310 645-6200	16556
Americare Medservices Inc (PA)	4119	C	310 632-1141	3767
Anheuser-Busch LLC	5181	C	310 761-4600	9040
Anschutz So Calif Sports Compl	7941	D	310 630-2000	18536
Apw International Inc	5013	C	310 884-5003	6707
Apw Knox-Seeman Warehouse Inc (HQ)	5013	D	310 604-4373	6708
Ashland Inc	5169	D	310 223-3505	8978
AT&T Corp	4813	C	310 225-3028	5471
Auto Parts Warehouse Inc (PA)	5013	E	800 913-6119	6710
Berkley International LLC	5199	D	310 900-1771	9246
BP West Coast Products LLC	1311	B	310 816-8787	1030
BP West Coast Products LLC	5171	C	310 549-6204	9004
Buswest LLC (HQ)	4141	D	310 984-3900	3891
California Access Scaffold LLC	1799	D	310 324-3388	3505
Calko Transport Company Inc	4214	D	310 816-0602	4333
Carpet Solutions	7217	E	310 886-3800	13592
Carson Operating Company LLC	7011	D	310 830-9200	12495
Carson Senior Assisted Living	8361	D	310 830-4010	24581
Cellco Partnership	4812	D	310 329-9325	5357
Ceva Logistics LLC	4731	B	310 223-6500	5043

	SIC	EMP	PHONE	ENTRY #
Cintas Corporation No 2	7299	D	310 635-8713	13745
Cirrus Enterprises LLC	5162	D	310 204-6159	8967
City Fashion Express Inc	4731	C	310 223-1010	5048
City of Carson	8322	D	310 835-0212	23752
Clay Dunn Enterprises Inc	1711	C	310 549-1698	2182
Color Spot Nurseries Inc	5193	D	310 549-7470	9184
County of Los Angeles	8631	C	310 847-4018	25171
Custom Goods LLC	4225	B	310 241-6700	4538
Defcon Inc	1761	D	310 516-5200	3163
Durham School Services L P	4151	C	310 767-5820	3918
East Crson II Hsing Prtners LP	6531	C	310 522-9606	11488
Epson America Inc	4225	C	562 290-5855	4548
Grand View Geranium Grdns Inc	0181	D	310 217-0490	286
H & C Headwear Inc (PA)	5136	C	310 324-5263	8344
H D Smith LLC	5122	C	310 641-1885	8260
H Rauvel Inc (PA)	4225	D	310 604-0060	4566
Hanjin Transportation Co Ltd	4731	C	310 522-5030	5092
Harry Group Inc	4731	D	310 631-9646	5098
Harvard Grand Inv Inc A Cal	6799	D	310 513-7560	12312
Hellmann Wrldwide Lgistics Inc	4731	E	310 847-4600	5100
Herc Rentals Inc	7514	E	310 233-5000	17678
JB Dental Supply Co Inc (PA)	5047	C	310 202-8855	7271
Kaiser Foundation Hospitals	8093	D	310 513-6707	22757
Kinder Mrgan Enrgy Partners LP	4226	E	310 518-7700	4693
Klx Inc	5088	C	310 604-0228	7998
Kole Imports	5199	D	310 834-0004	9274
Long-Lok Fasteners Corporation	5072	C	310 667-4200	7691
Mainfreight Inc (HQ)	4731	D	310 900-1974	5119
Margate Construction Inc	1623	C	310 830-8610	1965
MB Landscaping & Nursery Inc	5193	D	310 965-1923	9199
Merchants Bank California N A	6021	D	310 549-4350	9400
Multiquip Inc (DH)	5063	D	310 537-3700	7458
Nnr Global Logistics USA Inc	4731	C	310 357-2100	5134
North American Security Inc	7381	D	310 630-4840	16746
North Amrcn SEC Invstgtons Inc	7381	B	323 634-1911	16747
Northrop Grmmn Spce & Mssn Sys	7371	C	310 764-3000	15336
Nova Ortho-Med Inc	5047	D	310 352-3600	7286
Phoenix Engineering Co Inc	7363	D	310 532-1134	14924
Providence Health & Services	8099	D	310 835-6627	23027
Quik Pick Express LLC	4731	D	310 763-3000	5157
Schafer Bros Trnsf Pano Movers (PA)	4225	D	310 835-7231	4638
Scotts Labor Leasing Co Inc	7361	D	310 835-8388	14780
Secrom Inc	8059	E	310 830-4010	21368
Sony Electronics Inc	5064	C	310 835-6121	7512
South Bay Vocational Center	8331	E	310 784-2032	24389
Southwind Foods LLC (PA)	5146	D	323 262-8222	8655
Spectra I California	1731	D	310 835-0808	2737
Ssf Imported Auto Parts LLC	5013	E	562 782-8859	6774
Sunstone Hotel Investors LLC	7011	D	310 830-9200	13320
Swayzers Incorporated	7349	C	323 979-7223	14442
Tabletops Unlimited (PA)	5023	C	310 549-6000	6890
Total Trnsp & Dist Inc	4214	D	310 603-0467	4381
Watson Cogeneration Co Inc	4911	D	310 816-8100	6251

CARUTHERS, CA - Fresno County

	SIC	EMP	PHONE	ENTRY #
Caruthers Raisin Pkg Co Inc (PA)	0723	C	559 864-9448	519
Charanjit Singh Batth	0173	D	559 864-9421	196
Fresno Cnty Supt Schools Cent	4151	D	559 644-1000	3938
H & R Gunlund Ranches Inc	0172	D	559 864-8186	157
Hammer Down Davila Cnstr	1522	D	559 864-2001	1312
Karam Bath	0172	E	559 864-3868	162
Pacific Boring Incorporated	1781	E	559 864-9444	3359

CASPAR, CA - Mendocino County

	SIC	EMP	PHONE	ENTRY #
Caspar Community	8322	E	707 964-4997	23707

CASTRO VALLEY, CA - Alameda County

	SIC	EMP	PHONE	ENTRY #
American Building Service	7349	D	510 483-5120	14228
Baywood Court (PA)	8082	C	510 733-2102	22374
Coldwell Bankers Residential	6531	D	510 583-5400	11419
East Bay Regional Park Dst	7999	D	510 881-1833	19202
Eden Labs Med Group Inc	8011	E	510 537-1234	19511
Eden Township Hospital Dst	8062	A	510 537-1234	21550
Ku Kyoung	8051	C	510 582-2765	20715
Mason-Mcduffie Real Estate Inc	6531	E	510 886-7511	11664
Mekwus Solar Energy	4931	D	510 731-4134	6289
Online Energy LLC	5084	D	510 583-0091	7872
Ras Management Inc (PA)	4225	D	510 727-1800	4628
Redwood Convalescent Hospital	8059	D	510 537-8848	21358
Solar Company Inc	1711	D	510 888-9488	2371
Valley Pinte Nursing Rehab Ctr	8361	E	510 538-8464	24842

CASTROVILLE, CA - Monterey County

	SIC	EMP	PHONE	ENTRY #
Ajax Portable Services	7359	E	831 384-5000	14509
Brady Company/Central Cal	1742	C	831 633-3315	2864
California Artichoke & Vegetab	0723	D	831 633-2144	517
Dorr Distribution Systems	4142	E	831 633-7111	3900
Giannas Baking Company	5149	D	831 633-3700	8841
National Custom Packing Inc	0723	E	831 633-4011	567
Ocean Mist Farming Company (PA)	0161	B	831 633-2144	84
Randazzo Enterprises Inc	1795	D	831 633-4420	3465
USA Waste of California Inc	4212	C	831 384-4860	4081
USA Waste of California Inc	4953	C	831 633-7878	6578
Valley Pride Inc (PA)	0761	B	831 633-5883	687
Vps Companies Inc	5142	E	831 633-4011	8573

CATHEDRAL CITY, CA - Riverside County

	SIC	EMP	PHONE	ENTRY #
American Golf Corporation	7997	D	702 431-2191	18860
Big Lgue Dreams Consulting LLC	7032	C	760 324-5600	13461
Briar Golf LP	7999	D	760 328-6571	19154
Crystal Chrysler Plymouth Dodge	7538	D	760 324-9375	17789
Daniel Robert Knowlton	8111	D	760 265-5293	23195
Desert Princess Home	7997	E	760 322-1655	18939
Desert Prncess Homeowners Assn	8641	D	760 322-0567	25251
Heartland Payment Systems Inc	7389	D	760 324-0133	17212
Resort Parking Services Inc	7521	C	760 328-4041	17741

CAZADERO, CA - Sonoma County

	SIC	EMP	PHONE	ENTRY #
Camp Royaneh Boy Scout	8641	D	707 632-5291	25227

CEDAR GLEN, CA - San Bernardino County

	SIC	EMP	PHONE	ENTRY #
San Bernardino Mtns Wildlife	0279	E	909 226-6189	462

CEDARVILLE, CA - Modoc County

	SIC	EMP	PHONE	ENTRY #
Surprise Valley Hlth Care Dst	8062	D	530 279-6111	21938

CERES, CA - Stanislaus County

	SIC	EMP	PHONE	ENTRY #
Ames Taping Tools	7359	D	209 538-0113	14512
Bet-Nahrain Inc	7389	D	209 538-4111	17030
Chateaux Framing Inc	1751	C	209 537-6799	3035
Dan Avila and Sons	0161	D	209 495-3899	55
Dbi Beverage Inc	5181	D	209 524-2477	9050
Irish Construction	1623	D	209 576-8766	1947
Mark One Corporation	8059	D	209 537-4581	21308
Procter & Gamble Distrg LLC	5169	B	209 538-3987	8998
Ram Mechanical Inc	1711	D	209 531-9155	2338
Stanislaus Recovery Center	8093	D	209 541-2121	22841
Sutter Health	8011	D	209 538-1733	20096
Timmerman Starlite Trckg Inc	4212	D	209 538-1706	4071
United Parcel Service Inc OH	4215	C	800 742-5877	4443
West Coast Grape Farming Inc	0762	A	209 538-3131	733

CERRITOS, CA - Los Angeles County

	SIC	EMP	PHONE	ENTRY #
A & D Hauling Services Inc	4212	D	310 514-8969	3964
Access Info MGT Shred Svcs LLC	8741	D	805 529-6866	26904
Achem Industry America Inc (PA)	5085	E	562 802-0998	7910
All Care Industries Inc	7349	D	562 623-4009	14218
Amkotron Inc	7378	D	562 921-3330	16285
Apex Computer Systems Inc	7378	D	562 926-6820	16286
Astro Realty Inc	6531	D	562 924-3381	11308
Atkinson And Ly Rd & Rm Lw (PA)	8111	C	562 653-3200	23096
Audio Visual Headquarters (DH)	7359	C	310 603-0652	14514
Avalon A Cerritos	8322	E	562 865-9500	23675
Best Label Company Inc (PA)	5084	C	562 926-1452	7824
Bunzl Usa Inc	5113	C	314 997-5959	8186
Cafta	5047	C	562 860-9808	7249
Caremore Health Plan (HQ)	8011	C	562 622-2950	19407
Caremore Medical Management A (HQ)	8741	C	562 741-4300	26958
Cea-Pack Services Inc	4215	C	562 407-0660	4395
Cellco Partnership	4812	C	562 809-5650	5310
College Hospital Inc (PA)	8063	C	562 924-9581	22055
Commercial Carriers Insur Agcy	6331	C	562 404-4900	10411
Complete Office California Inc	5021	C	714 880-1222	6812
Crest Financial Corporation (DH)	6411	C	562 733-6500	10682
Daiohs USA Inc (HQ)	7389	C	562 293-2888	17115
David Levy Co Inc	5065	E	562 404-9998	7552
Firm A Chugh Professional Corp	8111	C	562 229-1220	23239
First Choice Bank (PA)	6022	E	562 345-9092	9495
Global Med Services Inc	8082	A	562 207-6970	22441
Healthview Inc	8361	E	562 468-0136	24689
Hometown Buffet Inc	7299	D	562 402-8307	13764
Iron Mountain Info MGT LLC	4226	D	714 526-0916	4692
Kabafusion LLC	5122	D	562 863-0555	8270
Kaiser Foundation Hospitals	8011	A	800 823-4040	19605
Malaysian Airline System	4729	C	310 539-9288	5011
Management Trust Assn Inc	8742	D	562 926-3372	27521
Marcor Environmental-West	1799	D	562 921-2733	3551
Mark 1 Mortgage Corporation	6162	E	562 924-6173	9872
Memorex Products Inc	5064	C	562 653-2800	7501
Microtek Lab Inc (HQ)	5044	E	310 687-5823	7060
Midway International Inc	5199	E	562 802-0800	9282
Mulhearn	6531	D	562 860-2443	11700
O E C Shipg Los Angeles Inc	4731	E	562 926-7186	5136
Oocl (usa) Inc	4731	D	562 499-2600	5140

CERRITOS, CA

	SIC	EMP	PHONE	ENTRY #
Pioneer Medical Group Inc	8099	D	562 229-0902	23020
Poliseek Ais Insur Sltions Inc	6411	D	866 480-7335	10828
Private Medical-Care Inc	6324	C	562 924-8311	10371
Providence Health & Services	8082	C	562 865-4600	22541
Razor USA LLC (PA)	5091	D	562 345-6000	8027
Robert Half International Inc	7361	C	562 356-1031	14761
Royal Plywood Company LLC (PA)	5031	D	562 404-2989	6959
Secure One Data Solutions LLC	7374	E	562 924-7056	16183
Southern Wine & Spirits Amrca	5182	B	562 926-2000	9113
Temp Unlimited LLC	7363	C	562 860-3340	14958
Tenet Healthsystem Medical	8062	A	562 531-2550	21962
Time Warner Cable Inc	4841	D	562 677-0228	6038
Trinitycare LLC (PA)	8082	E	818 709-4221	22584
United Exchange Corp	5122	C	562 977-4500	8300
United Parcel Service Inc OH	4215	C	562 404-3236	4460
Usaco Service Corp	7629	C	562 483-8747	17948
Wells Fargo Bank National Assn	6021	E	562 924-1616	9460
Young Systems Corporation	5044	E	562 921-2256	7079
Zero Energy Contracting Inc	1711	C	626 701-3180	2423
Zero Energy Contracting Inc	1711	D	626 701-3180	2424

CHATSWORTH, CA - Los Angeles County

	SIC	EMP	PHONE	ENTRY #
101communications Holdings LLC (HQ)	7313	D	818 734-1520	13957
A I T Development Corp	1521	D	818 407-5533	1119
Accunex Inc	1731	E	818 882-5858	2510
Ace Usa Inc	6411	C	818 428-3600	10582
Acme Laundry Products Inc	5023	C	818 341-0700	6840
Adco Container Company	5085	E	818 998-2565	7911
Aderans Hair Goods Inc	5131	D	818 428-1626	8308
Align Aerospace LLC (DH)	5088	C	818 727-7800	7992
All Tmperatures Controlled Inc	1711	D	818 882-1478	2120
Allstate Imaging Inc (PA)	5044	D	818 678-4550	7040
American Industrial Supply	5085	D	818 841-7788	7913
American Technical Svcs Inc	8711	D	818 590-7784	25655
Atlantic Optical Co Inc	5048	D	818 407-1890	7330
Brookdale Senior Living Inc	6411	D	818 718-1547	10649
Cardinal Cartridge Inc	8999	D	818 727-9740	28122
Cbol Corporation	5065	C	818 704-8200	7543
Child Care Resource Center Inc (PA)	8322	C	818 717-1000	23732
Child Care Resource Center Inc	8322	B	661 255-2474	23733
CIT Bank National Association	6021	C	818 885-9065	9346
Comet Electric Inc	1731	C	818 340-0965	2558
Cpcc Inc	8059	C	818 882-3200	21200
Danish Environment Inc	7349	D	818 992-6722	14281
Develop Point Education	7299	E	805 624-6171	13757
Dolphin Imaging Systems LLC	7371	E	818 435-1368	15145
Eisenberg International Corp (PA)	5136	C	818 365-8161	8339
Eurodent Inc	8072	D	818 832-1325	22306
Fromer Inc	1521	D	818 341-3896	1177
Genesis Tech Partners LLC	7699	C	800 950-2647	17975
Golden State Health Ctrs Inc	8059	D	818 882-8233	21253
Goldstar Hlthcr Cntr of Chtswr	8059	D	818 882-8233	21254
Green Scene Landscape Inc	0782	D	818 280-0420	861
Guardian National Inc	7381	E	800 700-1467	16674
Idea Bits LLC	7384	D	818 736-5361	16951
Infinite Computer Group LLC	7378	D	800 922-8075	16299
Joerns LLC (HQ)	5047	C	800 966-6662	7272
Lennox Industries Inc	5075	C	818 739-1616	7743
Logistical Support LLC	5088	C	818 341-3344	8000
Logix Federal Credit Union	6061	D	818 709-3896	9609
Los Angeles County MTA	4111	C	213 922-6308	3659
Marotto Corporation	7349	B	818 775-0320	14350
Minilec Service Inc	7622	E	818 341-1125	17911
Mj Star-Lite Inc	1731	E	818 717-0834	2654
National Mentor Holdings Inc	8361	A	818 366-8389	24743
National Notary Association	8621	C	818 739-4071	25147
Natrol LLC (DH)	5122	C	818 739-6000	8286
Nna Services LLC (PA)	6411	C	818 739-4071	10811
OBryant Electric Inc	1731	C	818 407-1986	2671
Ontic Engineering and Mfg Inc	5088	C	818 678-6555	8001
Pacific Toxicology Labs	8071	D	818 598-3110	22251
Patterson Dental Supply Inc	7371	E	818 435-1368	15371
Pd Liquidation Inc	5199	C	818 772-0100	9290
Piege Co (PA)	5137	D	818 727-9100	8409
Premier America Credit Union (PA)	6062	D	818 772-4000	9678
Primitive Shoes Inc	5139	D	818 639-3690	8443
Printing Technology Inc	5085	D	818 576-9220	7947
PS Development Corporation	1731	D	818 340-0965	2691
R M B Packaging Co Inc	5199	E	818 998-0658	9297
Rancho San Antonio Boys HM Inc (PA)	8361	D	818 882-6400	24778
Red Pointe Roofing LP	1761	D	818 998-3857	3208
Regency Enterprises Inc (PA)	5063	B	818 901-0255	7467
Ricoh Usa Inc	5044	E	818 294-8601	7065
Ronco Inventions LLC (PA)	5023	C	800 486-1806	6884
Rubicon Corporation America	6531	C	818 765-2001	11826
Sage Electric Company	1731	D	818 718-9080	2722

	SIC	EMP	PHONE	ENTRY #
Seven One Inc (PA)	7389	D	818 904-3435	17488
Sexy Hair Concepts	5131	D	800 848-3383	8325
Silver Strand	1751	E	818 701-9707	3092
Southern California Gas Co	4922	B	818 701-2592	6258
Staffchex Inc	7361	A	818 709-6100	14794
Summerville Senior Living Inc	8361	D	818 341-2552	24826
Telesis Community Credit Union (PA)	6061	D	818 885-1226	9631
Time Warner Cable Inc	4841	D	818 700-6126	6044
Trendex Corporation	1542	D	818 407-9600	1694
Tuttle Family Enterprises Inc	7349	B	818 534-2566	14449
United Cp/S Chldrns Fndn La	8361	C	818 998-8755	24839
US Interstate Distrg Inc	4813	C	818 678-4592	5713
Verizon Communications Inc	4813	C	818 388-8549	5724
West Coast Coupon Inc	7319	E	818 341-2400	14014
West-Spec Partners	5085	E	818 725-7000	7959

CHERRY VALLEY, CA - Riverside County

	SIC	EMP	PHONE	ENTRY #
David-Kleis Inc	8051	C	951 845-1166	20512
Little Peoples	8361	D	951 849-1959	24712
Little Peoples World Inc	8361	E	951 845-8367	24713

CHESTER, CA - Plumas County

	SIC	EMP	PHONE	ENTRY #
Chester Public Utility Dst	4939	D	530 258-2171	6300
Collins Pine Company	5031	D	530 258-2111	6917
Seneca Healthcare District	8011	D	530 258-2151	19985
Seneca Healthcare District	8011	D	530 258-1977	19986
Seneca Healthcare District (PA)	8062	C	530 258-2151	21878

CHICO, CA - Butte County

	SIC	EMP	PHONE	ENTRY #
11 Main Inc	4813	C	530 892-9191	5437
4 Seasons Roofing	1761	D	530 865-4998	3135
Addus Healthcare Inc	8082	E	530 566-0405	22334
Adventist Health System/West	8999	D	530 342-4576	28107
Agreserves Inc	0173	D	530 343-5365	194
Ampla Health	8011	D	530 342-4395	19342
ARC of Butte County (PA)	8322	C	530 891-5865	23665
Associated Pension Cons Inc (PA)	6411	D	530 343-4233	10630
AT&T Corp	4812	D	530 891-2025	5262
Auctiva Corporation	8748	D	530 894-7400	27842
B A M I Inc	7991	E	530 343-5678	18605
Baney Corporation	7011	D	530 899-9090	12415
Bank America National Assn	6021	D	530 891-7019	9323
BCM Construction Company Inc	1541	E	530 342-1722	1403
Buildcom Inc	5074	B	800 375-3403	7706
Butte Home Health Inc	8082	C	530 895-0462	22385
Caldwell Ventures LLC	8051	D	530 899-0814	20432
Caminar	8093	D	530 343-4472	22670
Catamount Broadcasting of Chic (PA)	4833	C	530 893-2424	5838
Cellco Partnership	4812	D	530 892-6900	5311
Chico Area Recreation & Pk Dst (PA)	7999	D	530 895-4711	19162
Chico Csu Research Foundation	7389	A	530 898-6811	17071
Chico Electric	1731	D	530 891-1933	2551
Chico Immdate Care Med Ctr Inc (PA)	8011	E	530 891-1676	19428
College Housing Northwest	7021	D	530 345-1393	13450
County of Butte	8093	B	530 891-2850	22693
Cummings-Violich Inc	0762	D	530 894-5494	696
Dfa of California	8699	D	530 345-5077	25525
Digital Path Inc	4813	E	800 676-7284	5591
Enloe Hospt-Phys Thrpy	8062	C	530 891-7300	21561
Enloe Medical Center	8062	D	530 332-6745	21562
Enloe Medical Center	8049	D	530 332-4111	20316
Enloe Medical Center	8011	D	530 332-7522	19515
Enloe Medical Center	8082	B	530 332-6050	22432
Enloe Medical Center	8049	D	530 332-6138	20317
Enloe Medical Center	8062	C	530 332-6400	21563
Enloe Medical Center	8011	D	530 332-6000	19516
Evergreen Healthcare Inc	8051	C	530 342-4885	20561
Far Northern Coordinating Coun	8322	D	530 895-8633	23976
Farmers International Inc	0173	E	530 566-1405	200
Federal Express Corporation	4513	C	800 463-3339	4846
First Rsponder Emrgncy Med Svc	4119	C	530 891-4357	3793
Gas Transmission Systems Inc	8711	C	530 893-6711	25828
Golden Living LLC	8051	D	530 343-6084	20626
Gonzales Enterprises Inc	5136	D	530 343-8725	8343
Graig Hall Service Company	6513	D	530 345-1393	11138
Helios Healthcare LLC	8059	C	530 345-1306	21263
Heritage One Carpentry Inc	5031	C	530 345-6622	6929
Hignell Companies	6513	D	530 345-1965	11141
Hmclause Inc	0181	D	530 713-5838	290
Holdrege Kull Consultimg Engr	8711	D	530 894-2487	25866
Home Health Care Management	8082	D	530 226-0120	22462
Hotel Diamond	7011	E	530 893-3100	12786
Interwest Insurance Svcs Inc	6411	D	530 895-1010	10749
Jeff Stover Inc	7991	D	530 345-9427	18648
Lifetouch Nat Schl Studios Inc	7221	D	530 345-3993	13661
Mangrove Medical Group	8011	E	530 345-0064	19727

GEOGRAPHIC SECTION — CHULA VISTA, CA

Company	SIC	EMP	PHONE	ENTRY #
Mission Linen Supply	7213	E	530 342-4110	13561
Modern Building Inc	1541	E	530 891-4533	1453
Mooney Farms	0723	E	530 899-2661	565
Morrison MGT Specialists Inc	8741	D	530 332-7557	27135
Mountain Mining Incorporated	4953	E	530 342-6059	6507
Nhic Corp	6411	D	530 332-1168	10810
North State Radiology	8011	E	530 898-0504	19778
Northern Vly Indian Hlth Inc	8021	C	530 896-9400	20267
Nph Medical Services	7361	D	530 899-2255	14710
Pacific Gas and Electric Co	4924	C	530 894-4739	6272
Paradise Ambulance Service	4119	D	530 879-5520	3825
Retinal Consultants Inc	8748	D	530 899-2251	28042
Rgis LLC	7389	D	530 898-1015	17456
Rhc Equipment LLC	1542	E	530 892-1918	1649
Riverside Health Care Corp (PA)	8059	E	530 897-5100	21362
Selig Construction Corp	1521	E	530 893-5898	1253
Sierra Landscape & Maint Inc	0781	D	530 895-0263	797
Stansbury Hm Preservation Assn	8412	E	530 895-3848	25050
Sungard Bi-Tech Inc (DH)	7371	E	530 891-5281	15483
Terraces Retirement Community	8361	E	530 894-1010	24834
Travidia Inc (PA)	7372	E	530 343-6400	15863
Tri Counties Bank (HQ)	6029	D	530 898-0300	9562
Unitedhealth Group Inc	6324	B	530 879-8251	10388
Veolia Transportation Svcs Inc	4111	D	530 342-6851	3735
Veterans Health Administration	8011	A	530 879-5000	20207
W K G Company	6531	C	530 345-1393	11903

CHINO, CA - San Bernardino County

Company	SIC	EMP	PHONE	ENTRY #
Acepex Management Corporation	8741	B	909 591-1999	26907
American Beef Packers Inc	0751	C	909 628-4888	635
American Eagle Wheel Corp (PA)	5013	B	909 590-8828	6704
American Financial Network Inc (PA)	6162	C	909 606-3905	9812
Angels In Motion LLC	8082	D	909 590-9102	22365
Applied P & Ch Laboratory Sout	8731	D	909 590-1828	26472
Aspects Furniture Mfg Inc	5021	C	909 606-5806	6804
Baronhr LLC	7361	D	909 517-3800	14613
Canyon Ridge Hospital Inc	8063	C	909 590-3700	22052
Carlisle Construction Mtls Inc	5033	D	909 591-7425	7010
Cellco Partnership	4812	D	909 591-9740	5374
Chino Grading Inc	1794	D	909 364-8667	3422
Chino Medical Group Inc	8011	D	909 591-6446	19436
Chino Rdological Registry Corp	8062	D	909 591-6688	21487
City of Chino	4959	D	909 591-9843	6621
Clima-Tech Inc	7623	D	909 613-5513	17919
Cls Landscape Management Inc	0783	B	909 628-3005	989
Concept Green Enrgy Sltons Inc	7389	A	855 459-6535	17091
Consolidated Plastics Corp (PA)	5162	C	909 393-8222	8968
Correctons Rhbltation Cal Dept	8062	C	909 597-1821	21512
Custom Bilt Holdings LLC	5084	D	909 664-1587	7837
Diamond Power System Corp	5063	E	866 882-8088	7435
DL Long Landscaping Inc	0781	D	909 628-5531	762
Donovan Golf Courses MGT	7992	E	714 528-6400	18736
Duke Pacific Inc	1761	D	909 591-0191	3166
El & El Wood Products Corp (PA)	5031	C	909 591-0339	6921
El Prado Golf Course LP	7992	D	909 597-1751	18738
Elecnor Inc	1711	D	909 993-5470	2216
Farmers Group Inc	6411	D	909 839-2020	10704
Fisher Scientific Company LLC	5049	D	909 393-2100	7342
Flatiron Electric Group Inc	1731	E	714 228-9631	2595
Flatiron West Inc	1622	D	909 597-8413	1890
Generation Construction Inc	1542	C	909 923-2077	1555
Gentek Media Inc	5045	E	909 476-3818	7139
Gilbert Service Corp	4214	C	909 393-7575	4347
Harrington Industrial Plas LLC (HQ)	5074	D	909 597-8641	7722
Inland Empire Utilities Agency (PA)	4941	D	909 993-1600	6356
Interior Experts General Bldrs	1742	D	909 203-4922	2911
J Goodman & Associates	5142	D	310 828-5040	8556
Jose Corona	1521	D	909 606-3168	1198
June A Grothe Construction Inc	1542	D	909 993-9400	1587
Kaiser Foundation Hospitals	6324	D	888 750-0036	10323
Koury Engrg Tstg & Insptn	7389	D	310 851-8685	17277
McKesson Medical-Surgical Inc	5047	D	800 767-6339	7277
Metrocell Construction Inc	1623	E	909 627-1502	1969
Microtel Computer Systems Inc	7379	D	626 839-6038	16434
Mission Linen Supply	7213	B	909 393-5589	13566
Motivational Marketing Inc	7389	B	909 517-2200	17341
Navy Exchange Service Command	4225	C	909 517-2640	4602
Nexgrill Industries Inc	5023	D	908 958-8799	6875
Omnia Italian Design Inc	5021	D	909 393-4400	6827
Paat & Kimmel Development Inc	1542	D	909 315-8074	1624
Prestige Autotech Corporation	5013	E	909 627-6411	6755
Quetico LLC	5199	C	909 628-6200	9296
R & B Reinforcing Steel Corp	1791	C	909 591-1726	3397
RDM Electric Co Inc	1731	D	909 591-0990	2698
Redwood Products Chino Inc	5031	D	909 923-5656	6955
Rocky Packaging Solutions Inc	5199	E	909 591-3331	9300
SA Recycling LLC	4953	D	909 622-3337	6554
Savant Construction Inc	1542	D	909 614-4300	1659
Skate Enterprises Inc	7999	D	562 924-0911	19283
Spanish Trls Girl Scout Cncil	8322	E	909 627-2609	24224
Tactical Lgistic Solutions Inc	4225	D	909 464-2813	4644
Threshold Technologies Inc	4581	D	909 606-1666	4945
Universal Packg Systems Inc	4225	C	909 517-2442	4648
USA Waste of California Inc	4953	D	909 590-1793	6582
Veritas Health Services Inc	8062	A	909 464-8600	22012
Wp Electric Communications Inc	1731	E	909 606-3510	2798
Year Round Landscape Maint Inc	0782	D	909 597-7734	982
Yoshimura Research & Dev Amer	5013	D	909 628-4722	6783

CHINO HILLS, CA - San Bernardino County

Company	SIC	EMP	PHONE	ENTRY #
Bank America National Assn	6021	D	909 393-3002	9332
Bates Sample Case Company Inc	7389	D	951 371-4922	17023
Beachside Realtors	1799	D	909 606-1299	3498
Big Lgue Drams Chino Hills LLC	7941	D	909 287-6900	18539
Boys Republic (PA)	8361	C	909 902-6690	24567
Ch Market Center Inc	6531	D	909 628-9100	11384
CIT Bank National Association	6021	D	909 631-2560	9351
Gateway Fresh LLC	6719	C	951 378-5439	12065
Hobby Lobby Stores Inc	7389	C	909 393-8727	17222
Los Serranos Golf Club	7992	C	909 597-1769	18756
Optima Network Services Inc (DH)	8999	D	305 599-1800	28150
Positive Solution Staffing LLC	7361	C	909 606-7512	14730
Prh Pro Inc	5085	C	714 510-7226	7946
USA Truck Inc	4213	D	909 334-1406	4295
West Hills Golf Associates	7997	E	714 528-6400	19124

CHOWCHILLA, CA - Madera County

Company	SIC	EMP	PHONE	ENTRY #
Agriland Holding Inc	0179	D	559 665-2100	252
Avalon Health Care Inc	8051	D	559 665-4826	20398
Brake Parts Inc LLC	5013	C	559 665-5781	6718
Case Vlott Cattle	0241	E	559 665-7399	420
Chowchilla Mem Hlth Care Dst (PA)	8051	D	559 665-3781	20457
Golden Living LLC	8361	D	559 665-3745	24670
Madera Community Hospital	8062	D	559 665-3768	21721
Madera Disposal Systems Inc (DH)	4953	D	559 665-3099	6497
Richard De Benedetto	0762	D	559 665-1712	718
Richard De Benedetto	0762	D	559 665-1712	719
Seaman Nurseries Inc	0721	D	559 665-1860	483
Triangle T Ranch Inc	0131	D	559 665-2964	15
Vlot Brothers Trucking Co Inc	0241	D	559 665-7399	440

CHUALAR, CA - Monterey County

Company	SIC	EMP	PHONE	ENTRY #
C & G Farms Inc	0161	C	831 679-2978	44
Clinica Salud Del Valle Salns	8011	D	831 679-0138	19445
P & P Agrilabor	7361	D	831 679-2307	14717

CHULA VISTA, CA - San Diego County

Company	SIC	EMP	PHONE	ENTRY #
24 Hour Fitness Usa Inc	7991	D	619 425-6600	18582
Aetna Health California Inc	6324	D	619 656-3104	10252
ARC Starlight Center	8322	D	619 427-7524	23667
At Your Svc Htg & Coolg LLC	1542	D	602 550-6946	1494
Bayview Hospital and Mental	8063	C	619 426-6311	22041
California American Water Co	4941	D	619 656-2400	6316
California Baking Company	5149	B	619 591-8289	8811
Care Plus North of San Diego	7361	D	619 421-0807	14621
CDI Marine Company LLC	8711	D	619 407-4010	25725
Celico Partnership	4812	D	619 409-4600	5315
Celico Partnership	4812	D	619 216-5840	5348
Citibank National Association	6021	D	619 870-0609	9375
Citigroup Inc	6021	D	619 498-3158	9382
City of Chula Vista	7389	C	619 691-5137	17073
Community Health Group	8011	C	619 422-0422	19453
Coronado Financial Corp	6531	E	619 946-1900	11459
Cox Communications Cal LLC	4841	B	619 263-9251	5980
Culinary Hispanic Foods Inc	5149	A	619 955-6101	8827
Dirt Cheap Demolition Inc	1795	E	619 426-9598	3454
Econa Corp	8721	D	619 722-6555	26331
Episcopal Community	8351	D	619 422-1642	24460
Eximex Inc	8732	D	619 585-1327	26661
FJ Willert Contracting Co	1794	D	619 421-1980	3428
Fredericka Manor	8361	D	619 422-9271	24664
Front Porch Communities	8059	D	619 427-2777	21222
George G Sharp Inc	8711	D	619 425-4211	25838
Global Exprnce Specialists Inc	7389	D	619 498-6300	17192
Healthcare MGT Systems Inc (PA)	8051	D	619 521-9641	20659
Heartland Meat Company Inc	5147	D	619 407-3668	8670
Home Carpet Investment (PA)	1752	D	619 262-8040	3117
J C Towing Inc	7549	D	619 429-1492	17885
McMillin RE & Mrtg Co Inc	6531	D	619 422-4500	11670
Metropolitan Area Advisory Com (PA)	8331	D	619 426-3595	24363
Metropolitan Area Advisory Com	8331	D	619 420-8981	24365
Nitai Partners Inc	7371	D	855 879-2847	15333
North Island Hispanic Assn	8699	D	619 545-6156	25561

Employment Codes: A=Over 500 employees, B=251-500, C=101-250, D=51-100, E=45-50

CHULA VISTA, CA

Company	SIC	EMP	PHONE	ENTRY #
Pacific Spanish Network Inc.	4832	D	619 427-6323	5814
Phoenix Intl Holdings Inc.	7389	C	619 207-0871	17411
Plastiflex Company Inc (DH)	7389	C	619 662-8792	17418
Profil Inst For Clncal RES Inc.	8731	C	619 427-1300	26591
Quality Coast Incorporated	7349	C	619 443-9192	14400
Racelegal.Com	8699	E	619 265-8159	25568
San Diego Country Club Inc	7997	D	619 422-8895	19055
San Diego County Adult Support	8322	D	619 476-6300	24173
San Diego Gas & Electric Co	4922	C	800 411-7343	6254
Scripps Health	8011	B	619 862-6600	19970
Scripps Health	8062	A	619 691-7000	21868
Sharp Chula Vista Medical Ctr	8062	A	619 502-5800	21883
Sharp Healthcare	8051	C	858 499-2000	20909
Siemens Government Tech Inc	7699	E	619 656-4740	18015
Silla Automotive LLC	5013	D	619 424-7752	6767
SMK Electronics Corp USA (HQ)	5063	E	619 216-6400	7475
Sonora Trade Company Inc	5199	D	619 878-5848	9305
South Bay Community Services	8322	C	619 420-3620	24219
Sunrise Senior Living LLC	8051	C	619 470-2220	20973
Sweetwater Authority (PA)	4941	C	619 422-8395	6405
Tap Worldwide LLC	7389	D	619 216-1444	17516
Tenet Healthsystem Medical	8063	C	619 426-6310	22110
Three Rvers Prvider Netwrk Inc	7373	D	619 230-0508	16064
Traffic Tech Inc	4731	C	800 396-2531	5174
Traffic Tech Inc (DH)	4731	B	514 343-0044	5175
Trepco Imports & Dist Ltd	5194	E	619 690-7999	9236
United Parcel Service Inc OH	4215	C	714 491-7000	4472
United Sttes Olympic Committee	7941	E	619 656-1500	18565
Veterans Health Administration	8011	B	619 409-1600	20209
Village Club	7999	E	619 425-3333	19303
YMCA of San Diego County	8641	D	619 422-8068	25428

CITRUS HEIGHTS, CA - Sacramento County

Company	SIC	EMP	PHONE	ENTRY #
A Community For Peace	8399	D	916 728-5613	24860
Accountable Health Staff Inc	7363	A	916 286-7667	14830
Always Home Nursing Svc Inc	8082	D	916 989-6420	22354
Anka Behavioral Health Inc	8099	D	916 722-3700	22888
Brookdale Senior Living Inc	7993	C	916 725-7418	18801
Cellco Partnership	4812	D	916 536-0440	5370
Cypress Garden At Citrus Hts	8052	E	916 729-2722	21077
Dignity Health	8011	D	916 536-2420	19504
Farmers Group Inc	6411	D	916 727-4600	10707
Hcr Manorcare Med Svcs Fla LLC	8051	D	916 967-2929	20650
Itc Service Group Inc (PA)	8748	E	877 370-4482	27956
J R Roberts Corp (HQ)	1542	D	916 729-5600	1579
J R Roberts Enterprises Inc	1542	D	916 729-5600	1580
Kings Casino Management Corp	7999	B	916 560-4405	19234
L W Roth Insurance Agency	6411	D	916 721-6273	10763
Lifetouch Inc	7221	D	916 535-7733	13660
Lucky Derby Casino	7999	C	916 727-2727	19242
Paradise Oaks Youth Services	8322	D	916 725-7182	24121
Phoenix Lounge and Casino	7011	D	916 334-4225	13093
Probe Information Services Inc	7381	D	916 676-1826	16764
Rolling Willow LLC	7991	D	916 961-6171	18675
SD Deacon Corp (PA)	1542	D	916 969-0900	1661
Sunrise Food Ministry	8322	D	916 965-5431	24240
Taxresources Inc (PA)	8721	C	877 369-7827	26449
Terra Nova Counseling (PA)	8322	D	916 344-0249	24249
Travelmasters Inc	4724	E	916 722-1648	4981
Zikko Inc	4214	C	916 949-8989	4393

CITY OF INDUSTRY, CA - Los Angeles County

Company	SIC	EMP	PHONE	ENTRY #
Acme Furniture Industry Inc (PA)	5021	D	626 964-3456	6800
Advanced Industrial Cmpt Inc (PA)	5045	D	909 895-8989	7084
Air Tiger Express (usa) Inc	4731	E	626 965-8647	5019
Airgas Safety Inc	5169	D	562 699-5239	8972
Alaska Diesel Electric	7539	C	626 934-6211	17819
Allied Entertainment Group Inc (PA)	7812	B	626 330-0600	18040
America Chung Nam (group) (PA)	5093	C	909 839-8383	8059
America Chung Nam LLC (HQ)	5093	C	909 839-8383	8060
American AC Distrs LLC	1711	D	407 850-0147	2125
American Ace International Co	5141	C	626 937-6116	8455
American Future Tech Corp	5045	C	888 462-3899	7091
American Multi-Cinema Inc	7832	D	626 810-7949	18306
American Paper & Plastics Inc	5113	C	626 444-0000	8184
American Solar Direct Inc	1711	D	626 435-9211	2140
Anning-Johnson Company	1742	E	626 369-7131	2857
Apw Construction Inc	1799	D	626 855-1720	3493
Arakelian Enterprises Inc	4953	D	626 336-3636	6427
Arakelian Enterprises Inc	4953	D	626 336-3636	6429
ARC Document Solutions Inc	7334	C	626 333-7005	14108
Arconic Global Fas & Rings Inc	5085	B	626 968-3831	7915
Boiling Point Rest Sca Inc	7361	B	626 551-5181	14615
California Country Club	7997	D	626 333-4571	18906
California Floral Imports Inc	5023	D	562 696-1039	6852
Carrara Marble Company America (PA)	1743	D	626 961-6010	3007

GEOGRAPHIC SECTION

Company	SIC	EMP	PHONE	ENTRY #
Chefs Warehouse Westcoast LLC (HQ)	5141	D	626 465-4200	8464
China Yngxin Phrmceuticals Inc	5047	A	626 581-9098	7257
CIT Bank National Association	6021	D	626 435-2260	9350
City of Industry Disposal Co	4953	E	626 336-5439	6459
Classic Distrg & Bev Group Inc	5181	B	626 330-8231	9047
Closet World Inc	1751	D	626 855-0846	3036
Commercial Lbr & Pallet Co Inc	5031	C	626 968-0631	6918
Concept Enterprises Inc	5064	D	626 968-8827	7493
County of Los Angeles	8322	C	626 854-4987	23844
Cyberpower Inc	5045	D	626 813-7730	7114
D & D Wholesale Distrs Inc	5148	D	626 333-2111	8711
Dacor Holdings Inc	8734	C	626 626-4461	26841
Dean Socal LLC	5143	C	951 734-3950	8583
Delta Creative Inc	5092	C	800 423-4135	8042
E-Sceptre Inc	8731	D	888 350-8989	26507
Eastern Broadcasting Amer Corp	4841	D	626 581-8899	5997
Eforcity Corp - Nfm	5065	D	626 442-3168	7559
El Encanto Healthcare & Rehab	8051	D	626 336-1274	20529
Elmco/Duddy Inc (HQ)	5074	E	626 333-9942	7708
Essendant Co	5112	C	626 961-0011	8166
Estes Express Lines Inc	4213	D	626 333-9090	4149
Ever Win International Corp	5065	E	626 810-8218	7561
Express Transport Solutions	4214	D	626 961-4800	4345
Federal Express Corporation	4215	C	800 463-3339	4410
Ferguson Enterprises Inc	5074	D	626 965-0724	7712
Fiserv Inc	7374	D	909 595-9074	16129
Foria International Inc (PA)	5136	D	626 912-8836	8341
Fortune Dynamic Inc	5139	D	909 979-8318	8435
Freshpoint Inc	5148	C	626 855-1400	8727
Freshpoint Southern Cal Inc	5148	C	626 855-1400	8729
Frito-Lay North America Inc	5145	B	626 855-1300	8611
Frize Corporation	1541	D	626 369-6088	1424
Furniture America Cal Inc	5021	D	909 718-7276	6815
Gale Lina Inc	5122	D	909 595-8898	8254
GBT Inc	5045	D	626 854-9333	7136
Gels Logistics Inc	4731	D	909 610-2277	5086
Genuine Parts Distributors	5013	D	562 692-9034	6733
Graycon Inc	1711	D	626 961-9640	2239
Halbert Brothers Inc	4214	D	626 913-1800	4349
Haralambos Beverage Company (PA)	5181	C	562 347-4300	9061
Heidi Corporation	1522	D	626 333-6317	1313
Hikvision USA Inc (HQ)	7382	C	909 895-0400	16887
J P Original Corp (PA)	5139	D	626 839-4300	8437
Kaiser Foundation Hospitals	8011	A	562 463-4377	19608
Kellwood Company LLC	5136	C	626 934-4133	8348
Kellwood Company LLC	5137	C	626 934-4155	8391
Klm Management Company	5143	D	626 330-3479	8586
Lasertech Computer Distr Inc	5045	D	626 435-2800	7153
Lee & Ro Inc	8711	E	626 912-3391	25933
Leon Chien Corp	6162	D	626 964-8302	9869
Loretta Lima Trnsp Corp	4213	D	626 330-5517	4213
Los Altos Food Products Inc	5143	D	626 330-6555	8587
MA Laboratories Inc	8731	D	626 820-8988	26563
Magnell Associate Inc (HQ)	5045	C	562 695-8823	7157
Magnell Associate Inc	5045	D	626 271-1580	7158
Majestic Industry Hills LLC	7011	B	626 810-4455	12936
Management Applied Programming (PA)	7374	D	562 463-5000	16156
Markwins Beauty Products Inc	5122	D	909 595-8898	8276
Marquez Brothers Entps Inc	5141	C	626 330-3310	8494
Max Group Corporation (PA)	5045	D	626 935-0050	7160
Mercado Latino Inc (PA)	5141	D	626 333-6862	8501
Micro-Technology Concepts Inc	5045	D	626 839-6800	7163
Mike Campbell & Associates Ltd (PA)	4222	A	626 369-3981	4500
Mohan Dialysis Center Industry	8092	D	626 333-3801	22634
Morrow-Meadows Corporation (PA)	1731	A	858 974-3650	2657
MSI Computer Corp (HQ)	5045	D	626 913-0828	7165
Mtc Worldwide Corp	5045	D	626 839-6800	7166
Mtm & Thomasville Co	1542	D	626 934-1112	1615
Nafta Shoes Inc	7251	D	626 369-9681	13701
Neiman Marcus Group LLC	4225	D	562 463-9333	4603
New Century Media Corp	5099	E	562 695-1000	8130
New Century Science & Tech	5091	D	626 581-5500	8024
Performance Food Group Inc	5149	C	714 535-2111	8906
Performance Sheets LLC	1761	C	626 333-0195	3198
Pilot Inc (PA)	5013	D	800 237-7560	6754
Port Logistics Group Inc	4731	B	626 330-1300	5153
Potter Roemer LLC (PA)	5031	D	626 855-4890	6950
Poundex Associates Corporation (PA)	5021	D	909 444-5874	6830
Private Label Pc LLC	5045	D	626 965-8686	7175
Pruitthealth Corporation	8059	E	626 810-5567	21353
Public Hlth Fndation Entps Inc (PA)	8741	C	562 692-4643	27185
Quest Components Inc	5065	E	626 333-5858	7623
Quinn Company	5084	C	562 463-4000	7878
Quinn Shepherd Machinery	5082	B	562 463-6000	7785
Rongcheng Trading LLC	5147	D	626 338-1090	8683

Mergent email: customerrelations@mergent.com
2017 Directory of California Wholesalers and Services Companies
(P-0000) Products & Services Section entry number
(PA)=Parent Co (HQ)=Headquarters (DH)=Div Headquarters

GEOGRAPHIC SECTION

COLTON, CA

	SIC	EMP	PHONE	ENTRY #
Royal Crown Enterprises Inc (PA)	5149	D	626 854-8080	8915
Rutland Tool & Supply Co (HQ)	5085	C	562 566-5000	7950
Shipbycom LLC	4212	D	626 271-9800	4063
Snap-On Incorporated	5072	D	626 965-0668	7698
Southern California Gas Co	4924	D	213 244-1200	6276
Sweda Company LLC	5094	C	626 357-9999	8101
Tf Courier Inc	4215	D	214 560-9000	4428
TFC Holding Company	6021	D	626 363-9708	9425
Thunder Group Inc (PA)	5023	E	626 935-1605	6892
Time Warner Cable Inc	4841	D	626 705-7482	6046
Toll Global Fwdg Americas	4789	D	626 363-8600	5246
Tq Inc (PA)	7361	D	562 908-9655	14806
U C L Incorporated (PA)	4213	D	323 232-3469	4281
Unical Aviation Inc (PA)	5088	C	626 813-1901	8008
Unical Enterprises Inc	5045	D	626 965-5588	7207
United Pumping Service Inc	4212	D	626 961-9326	4077
US Bankcard Services Inc	7389	D	888 888-8872	17578
Valley Management Services	8741	B	626 333-1243	27272
Valor Communication Inc	5065	D	626 581-8085	7653
W Diamond Supply Co (DH)	5023	D	909 859-8939	6904
Waterhill Ltd	5021	E	626 369-6828	6837
Wsj Worldwide Inc	5013	D	626 961-7380	6782
Yale/Chase Eqp & Svcs Inc (PA)	5084	C	562 463-8000	7907
Zerep Management Corporation	4953	D	626 961-6291	6617
Zmodo Technology Corp Ltd	5065	A	217 903-5673	7664

CLAREMONT, CA - Los Angeles County

	SIC	EMP	PHONE	ENTRY #
Ben Bollinger Productions Inc	7922	D	909 626-3296	18371
CB&i Inc	1791	B	909 962-6400	3375
Citigroup Global Markets Inc	6211	D	909 625-0781	9983
Claremont Star LP	7011	E	909 482-0124	12525
Claremont Tennis Club	7997	C	909 625-9515	18919
Corey Nursery Co Inc (PA)	5193	D	909 621-6886	9185
Epitome Enterprises LLC	7371	D	909 625-4728	15169
Front Porch Communities	8059	C	909 626-1227	21221
HDR Engineering Inc	8711	D	909 626-0967	25858
Kaiser Foundation Hospitals	8062	B	888 750-0036	21675
Keck Graduate Institute (PA)	8733	C	909 621-8000	26780
Lovely Living Homecare	8082	D	909 625-7999	22501
Pacific Unified Pd Inc	7382	D	310 817-3346	16908
Pilgrim Place In Claremont (PA)	8059	C	909 399-5500	21347
Pilgrim Place In Claremont	7231	C	909 621-9581	13685
Pomona College	7929	D	909 607-8650	18487
Pomona College	7331	D	909 621-8000	14086
Pomona Valley Hospital Med Ctr	8062	A	909 865-9104	21803
Pomona Valley Hospital Med Ctr	8049	D	909 621-7956	20342
Pomona Valley Hospital Med Ctr	8062	A	909 865-9977	21804
Rancho Santa Ana Botanic Grdn	8422	D	909 625-8767	25068
Technip Usa Inc	8711	B	909 447-3600	26087
Therapak LLC (HQ)	5047	D	909 267-2000	7318
Tierra Del Sol Foundation	7999	D	909 626-8301	19294
Trinity Youth Services (PA)	8361	D	909 825-5588	24837
Visiting Nurse Associ	8082	D	909 621-3961	22592
Vna Hospice & Pllatve Cre S CA (PA)	8082	C	909 624-3574	22611

CLARKSBURG, CA - Yolo County

	SIC	EMP	PHONE	ENTRY #
Vino Farms Inc	0191	C	916 775-4095	405

CLAYTON, CA - Contra Costa County

	SIC	EMP	PHONE	ENTRY #
American Golf Corporation	7997	D	925 672-9737	18864

CLEARLAKE, CA - Lake County

	SIC	EMP	PHONE	ENTRY #
Adventist Health Clearlake (HQ)	8062	B	707 994-6486	21430
Adventist Health System/West	8011	C	707 995-4888	19321
Adventist Health System/West	8062	B	707 995-4500	21433
Adventist Health System/West	8011	B	707 994-6486	19324
Advtinst Hlth Clearlake Hosp	8062	B	707 994-6486	21435
Vindra Inc	8051	B	707 994-7738	21015
Westamerica Bank	6022	E	707 995-4140	9536

CLEARLAKE OAKS, CA - Lake County

	SIC	EMP	PHONE	ENTRY #
Shannon Ranches Inc	8742	C	707 998-9656	27644

CLOVERDALE, CA - Sonoma County

	SIC	EMP	PHONE	ENTRY #
Ensign Cloverdale LLC	8051	D	707 894-5201	20536
Redwood Credit Union	6141	C	800 479-7928	9762
Star H-R	7361	A	707 894-4404	14797

CLOVIS, CA - Fresno County

	SIC	EMP	PHONE	ENTRY #
Agriculture and Priority Pollu (PA)	8734	E	559 275-2175	26828
AT&T Corp	4813	D	559 294-5431	5503
Been Enterprises	1521	D	559 298-8864	1133
Borunda Private SEC Patrol Inc	7381	E	559 299-2662	16578
Bowie Enterprises	7542	D	559 292-6565	17833
Cellco Partnership	4812	D	559 325-1420	5350
Central Valley Community Bank (HQ)	6712	C	559 323-3384	12040
Central Valley Indian Hlth Inc (PA)	8011	D	559 299-2578	19421
Clovis Custom Drywall Inc	1742	E	559 297-7073	2878
Clovis Unified School District	7911	A	559 327-3900	18362
Community Medical Centers	8062	D	559 324-4000	21502
Death Valley 49ers Inc	8699	D	559 297-5691	25523
Elite Landscaping Inc	0782	C	559 292-7760	847
Floyd Johnston Cnstr Co Inc	1623	D	559 299-7373	1931
Golden Living LLC	8051	D	559 299-2591	20617
Graham Concrete Cnstr Inc	1771	D	559 292-6571	3269
Hodges Electric Inc	1731	E	559 298-5533	2614
John Birdsell Construction Inc	1751	E	559 834-6212	3059
Kaiser Foundation Hospitals	6324	D	559 324-5100	10315
Kings Credit Services	7322	D	559 322-2550	14038
Krazan & Associates (PA)	8748	C	559 348-2200	27968
Ladell Inc	1711	E	559 650-2000	2274
Niacc-Avitech Technologies Inc (PA)	7699	D	559 291-2500	17791
Peachwood Medical Group Clovis	8011	D	559 324-6200	19822
Pk Autobody Inc	7532	D	559 298-9691	17765
Regent Assisted Living Inc	8361	D	559 325-8400	24785
Tri-Star Drywall Lp	1742	D	559 299-9858	2992
Valleywide Construction Inc	1521	C	559 834-6212	1277
Vibra Healthcare LLC	8062	D	559 325-5601	22020
Westech Systems Inc	1731	D	559 298-5237	2793
Willow Creek Hlthcare Ctr LLC	8051	A	559 323-6200	21041
Willow Creek Hlthcare Ctr LLC	8051	D	559 323-6200	21042

COACHELLA, CA - Riverside County

	SIC	EMP	PHONE	ENTRY #
29 Palms Enterprises Corp	7999	A	760 775-5566	19129
Agri-Cal Venture Associates	0762	C	760 398-9520	690
Anthony Vineyards Inc	0762	D	760 391-5400	692
Coachella Valley Water Dst (PA)	4941	C	760 398-2651	6330
Desert Valley Date Inc	0723	E	760 398-0999	524
Downtown Metro	4812	E	760 398-3310	5394
Esparza Enterprises Inc	7361	C	760 398-0349	14654
Naumann/Hobbs Mtl Hdlg Corp II	5082	C	866 266-2244	7778
Primetime International Inc	5148	D	760 399-4166	8763
SA Recycling LLC	4953	D	760 391-5591	6553
Skanska USA Cvil W Cal Dst Inc	1611	B	760 342-8004	1861
Sun and Sands Enterprises LLC (PA)	0161	D	760 399-4278	96
Sun World International Inc	0723	B	760 398-9300	591
Sunline Transit Agency	4119	C	760 972-4059	3849
Valley Pride Inc	0722	D	760 398-1353	503
Woodspur Farming LLC	6289	D	760 398-9464	10199

COALINGA, CA - Fresno County

	SIC	EMP	PHONE	ENTRY #
Califrnia Dept State Hospitals	8063	B	559 935-4300	22046
Coalinga Dstngished Cmnty Care	8051	D	559 935-5939	20462
Coalinga Regional Medical Ctr	8062	C	559 935-6400	21496
Harris Farms Inc	0191	E	559 884-2203	366
Harris Farms Inc	0191	B	559 935-0717	367
Harris Farms Inc	0191	B	559 884-2477	368
Harris Woolf Almonds	0723	C	559 884-1040	545
Leidos Inc	8731	B	559 935-2305	26554
Robert Heely Inc	1623	D	559 935-0570	1989

COARSEGOLD, CA - Madera County

	SIC	EMP	PHONE	ENTRY #
Chukchansi Gold Resort Casino	7011	A	866 794-6946	12519
Wb Electric Inc	1731	D	408 842-7911	2790
Yosemite Lakes Owners Assn	8641	D	559 658-7466	25438

COLMA, CA - San Mateo County

	SIC	EMP	PHONE	ENTRY #
Cypress Funeral Services Inc	7261	C	650 550-8808	13704
Lucky Chances Inc	7999	D	650 758-2237	19241
Precision Auto Detailing LLC	7542	D	650 992-9775	17859

COLTON, CA - San Bernardino County

	SIC	EMP	PHONE	ENTRY #
A-Z Bus Sales Inc (PA)	5012	D	951 781-7188	6657
All Pro Tools Inc	5072	E	888 425-5776	7667
Alma Construction Co Inc	1742	D	909 825-1328	2853
Arrowhead Regional Medical Ctr	8062	A	909 580-1000	21454
Auto Buyline Systems Inc (PA)	7389	E	909 881-7828	17011
Bob Hubbard Horse Trnsp Inc (PA)	4212	E	951 369-3770	3983
Brithinee Electric	5063	D	909 825-7971	7420
C E P	8011	D	909 580-1456	19387
Cardinal Health Inc	5047	D	909 824-1820	7251
CBS Radio Inc	4832	D	909 825-9525	5761
Charter Hospice Inc	8052	D	909 825-2969	21070
Colton Joint Unified Schl Dst	8351	D	909 876-4240	24441
Cornerstone Hospice Cal LLC	8082	D	909 872-8100	22416
County of San Bernardino	8071	D	909 580-1000	22207
Greenpath Recovery West Inc	5093	D	909 954-0686	8072
Inland Eye Inst Med Group Inc (PA)	8011	D	909 825-3425	19569
Inland Family Health Wellness	8062	E	909 475-2300	21611
Kaiser Foundation Hospitals	6733	A	909 427-5521	12186
King Equipment LLC	7359	D	909 986-5300	14554
Medlin Development	0782	E	909 825-5296	910
Pacific Vision Services Inc	8042	D	909 824-6090	20302
Premier Medical Trnsp Inc	4119	D	909 433-3939	3828
Property Insight	6512	C	909 876-6505	11033

COLTON, CA

	SIC	EMP	PHONE	ENTRY #
Reche Canyon Convalescent Ctr	8059	C	909 370-4411	21356
Reche Cyn Rhblitation Hlth Ctr	8051	B	909 370-4411	20866
Republic Services Inc	4953	E	909 370-3377	6537
SA Recycling LLC	4953	D	909 825-1662	6556
Southern Cal Prmnnte Med Group	8011	E	909 370-2501	20030
Superior Masonry Walls Ltd	1741	D	909 370-1800	2836
Valley Ob Gyn Medical Group	8011	E	909 580-6333	20184
Van Dyk Tank Lines Inc	4212	E	951 682-5000	4087
VFW Post 6476	8641	C	909 754-3828	25394
Western Healthcare Management	8051	C	909 824-1530	21032
Westrux International Inc	4731	E	909 825-5121	5190

COLUMBIA, CA - Tuolumne County

	SIC	EMP	PHONE	ENTRY #
Twain Harte Horsemen	8641	D	209 601-5585	25384
Zephyr River Expeditions Inc	7999	D	800 431-3636	19313

COLUSA, CA - Colusa County

	SIC	EMP	PHONE	ENTRY #
Childrens Services	8322	D	530 458-0300	23745
Colusa Cnty Sbstnce Abuse Svcs	8322	D	530 458-0520	23767
Colusa Indian Cmnty Council	8399	A	530 458-6572	24891
Premier Mushrooms LP (PA)	0182	D	530 458-2700	341
Premier Mushrooms LP	0182	C	530 458-2700	342

COMMERCE, CA - Los Angeles County

	SIC	EMP	PHONE	ENTRY #
Acco Engineered Systems Inc	7623	D	323 727-7765	17916
Acco Engineered Systems Inc	7389	E	323 201-0931	16966
Altamed Health Services Corp (PA)	8011	E	323 725-8751	19335
Amec Fstr Whlr Envrnmnt Infrst	8711	E	323 889-5300	25652
American De Rosa Lamparts LLC (PA)	5063	D	323 728-6300	7412
American International Inds (PA)	5122	C	323 728-2999	8228
American Security Force Inc	7381	D	323 722-8585	16559
Arden-Mayfair Inc	4225	E	310 638-2842	4525
Armstrong Logistics LLC	4731	E	323 721-1500	5031
Ashland Inc	5169	D	323 767-1300	8979
Associated Landscape	7389	E	714 558-6100	17005
Ben Myerson Candy Co Inc (PA)	5182	B	323 724-1700	9092
Bnsf Railway Company	4011	B	323 869-3002	3609
California Commerce Club Inc	7011	A	323 721-2100	12482
California Produce Wholsalers	5148	D	562 776-5770	8702
Califrnia Intermodal Assoc Inc (PA)	4213	E	323 562-7788	4124
Cellco Partnership	4812	D	323 725-9750	5388
Cellphone LLC	5065	C	323 727-9131	7546
Ceramic Decorating Company Inc	7389	E	323 268-5135	17064
Challenge Dairy Products Inc	5143	D	323 724-3130	8581
CIT Bank National Association	6021	D	323 838-6881	9372
City of Commerce	7999	D	323 722-4805	19167
Commerce Center Theatres	7832	D	323 722-5577	18318
County of Los Angeles	8399	D	323 869-7063	24906
County of Los Angeles	8322	D	323 889-3405	23826
D J American Supply Inc	5099	C	323 582-2650	8109
Dart International A Corp (HQ)	4214	C	323 264-8746	4340
E & J Gallo Winery	5182	D	323 720-6400	9098
East Los Angeles Community Un (PA)	6153	E	323 721-1655	9781
East Los Angeles Mental Hlth	8093	D	323 725-1337	22725
EDS West LLC	4212	D	323 887-7367	4013
El Guapo Spices Inc (PA)	5149	D	213 312-1300	8832
Elkay Plastics Co Inc (PA)	5113	C	323 727-7073	8189
Enky Health	8093	E	323 725-1337	22728
Ernest Packaging Solutions Inc (PA)	5113	C	800 233-7788	8190
Express Messenger Systems Inc	4215	D	323 725-2100	4401
Farwest Insulation Contracting	1742	E	310 634-2800	2896
Fedex Smartpost Inc	4215	E	323 888-8879	4415
Fox Luggage Inc	5099	D	323 588-1688	8114
Gehr Development Corporation (HQ)	6512	D	323 728-5558	10987
Gibson Overseas Inc	5023	A	323 832-8900	6864
Glamour Industries Co	5122	B	323 728-2999	8255
Gold Coast Ingredients Inc	5149	D	323 724-8935	8844
Grocers Specialty Company (HQ)	5141	E	323 264-5200	8484
Haldeman Inc	5075	D	323 726-7011	7739
Haldeman Inc	1711	E	323 726-7011	2243
Hkf Inc (PA)	5075	D	323 225-1318	7740
Ingenue Inc	0254	D	323 726-8084	459
Innovo Azteca Apparel Inc	5131	D	323 837-3700	8313
Interstate Electric Co Inc (PA)	5046	D	323 724-0420	7219
Interstate Meat & Provision	5142	D	323 838-9400	8554
Ivo Wall Experts Inc	1742	D	323 246-4026	2913
Iworks Us Inc	1791	D	323 278-8363	3384
Jfc International Inc (HQ)	5149	D	323 721-6100	8861
Justman Packaging & Display	5113	D	323 728-8888	8195
Kevala International LLC	5149	E	210 767-3324	8867
LA Impact	7389	D	323 869-6874	17281
Los Angeles County Apprentices	6732	D	323 221-5881	12160
Malibu Design Group	5137	D	323 271-1700	8398
Maravilla Foundation (PA)	8641	D	323 721-4162	25293
Meridian Textiles Inc (PA)	5131	D	323 869-5700	8318
Mexican Amrcn Oprtnty Fndation	8322	D	323 890-1555	24086

	SIC	EMP	PHONE	ENTRY #
Michelson Laboratories Inc (PA)	8734	D	562 928-0553	26866
Miken Sales Inc (PA)	5137	D	323 266-2560	8402
Milspec Industries Inc (DH)	5072	C	213 680-9690	7694
Nora Lighting Inc	5063	D	800 686-6672	7460
Parsec Inc	4789	A	323 268-5011	5234
Penny Lane Centers	8399	C	323 318-9960	24961
Pixior LLC (PA)	7389	D	323 721-2221	17417
Printing Inds Assn Suthern Cal	8611	D	323 728-9500	25099
Progressive Produce Lcc (HQ)	5148	C	323 890-8100	8768
Prudential Overall Supply	7218	D	323 724-4888	13634
Prudential Overall Supply	7218	D	323 722-0636	13638
PWS Holdings LLC	5087	C	323 721-8832	7979
Ramcar Batteries Inc	5013	E	323 726-1212	6757
Reading Entertainment Inc (HQ)	7832	D	213 235-2226	18343
Rolled Steel Products Corp (PA)	5051	D	323 723-8836	7399
Safeway Inc	4225	C	323 889-4240	4635
Samuel Son & Co Inc	5051	E	323 722-0300	7401
Securitas SEC Svcs USA Inc	7381	D	323 832-9074	16805
Seiu United Healthcare Workers	8631	E	323 734-8399	25185
Shason Inc (PA)	5131	D	323 269-6666	8326
Shims Bargain Inc	1541	C	323 726-8800	1463
Starline Tours Hollywood Inc (PA)	7999	D	323 262-1114	19289
Stitches Inc	7389	C	323 622-0175	17505
Sun Coast Merchandise Corp	5099	C	323 720-9700	8142
Telacu Industries Inc (HQ)	6162	E	323 721-1655	9901
Telacu NW Five Inc (PA)	6512	C	323 721-1655	11062
Thyssenkrupp Elevator Corp	7699	E	323 278-9888	18025
Tpg La Commerce LLC	7011	D	401 946-4600	13351
Unified Grocers Inc (PA)	5141	A	323 264-5200	8540
Union Pacific Railroad Company	4011	D	213 446-1900	3624
Uniserve Facilities Svcs Corp (PA)	7349	B	213 533-1000	14451
United Insurance Company	6411	E	323 869-9381	10915
United Parcel Service Inc OH	7389	B	323 837-1220	17557
Univar USA Inc	5169	C	323 727-7005	9001
Veritiv Operating Company	5113	C	323 725-3700	8222
W2005 Wyn Hotels LP	7011	D	323 887-8100	13389
Waste Mgt Collectn & Recycl	4953	E	626 960-7551	6602
Wildcat Retro Brands LLC	5137	E	213 572-0431	8416
Wyndham International Inc	7011	A	323 887-4331	13438
Xpo Cartage Inc (DH)	4212	D	800 837-7584	4095
Zemarc Corporation (PA)	5084	E	323 721-5598	7909

COMPTON, CA - Los Angeles County

	SIC	EMP	PHONE	ENTRY #
Advanced Logistics MGT Inc	4213	E	310 638-0715	4104
All Phase Business Supplies	5112	E	310 631-1900	8159
Apex Logistics Intl Inc	4731	D	310 665-0288	5028
Appliance Recycl Ctrs of Amer	4953	D	310 223-2800	6425
Asbury Environmental Services (PA)	4212	D	310 886-3400	3978
Auto Expressions LLC	5013	D	310 639-0666	6709
Az/CFS West Inc	4213	D	310 898-2090	4676
Beauchamp Distributing Company	5181	D	310 639-5320	9043
Benettis Italia Inc	5021	D	310 537-8036	6806
Blake H Brown Inc (DH)	5084	D	310 764-0110	7826
Bst Enterprises Inc	5013	D	310 638-1222	6719
Cal-State Steel Corporation	1791	C	310 632-2772	3372
CCC Property Holdings LLC	6719	C	310 609-1957	12050
Celebrity Casinos Inc	7011	B	310 631-3838	12506
Cintas Corporation No 3	7218	D	310 725-2850	13623
City of Compton	7999	D	310 635-3484	19168
Color Ad Inc	7311	E	310 632-5500	13824
Colosseum Athletics Corp	5136	D	310 667-8341	8337
Concrete Tie Industries Inc (PA)	5032	D	310 886-1000	6979
Contractors Cargo Company (PA)	4213	D	310 609-1957	4128
Cordelia Lighting Inc	5063	C	310 886-3490	7432
County of Los Angeles	8099	D	310 885-2100	22928
County of Los Angeles	8099	D	310 668-6845	22929
County of Los Angeles	8111	D	310 603-7483	23174
County of Los Angeles	8111	C	310 603-7271	23176
County of Los Angeles	8322	C	310 603-7311	23854
Crew Inc	1794	D	310 608-6860	3425
Damco Distribution Svcs Inc	4225	E	310 661-4600	4539
Demenno Kerdoon	1382	C	310 537-7100	1064
Demenno-Kerdoon	4212	B	310 898-3848	4006
Dependable Aircargo Ex Inc	4731	D	310 537-2000	5056
Dna Specialty Inc	5013	D	310 767-4070	6726
Dnow LP	4226	D	310 900-3900	4684
Dti Inc	4212	D	310 635-9002	4012
Dynamic Medical Systems LLC (HQ)	7352	D	310 928-0251	14474
Element Mtrls Tech HB Inc	8734	D	310 632-8500	26846
Evox Productions LLC (PA)	7371	E	310 605-1400	15177
Florence Filter Corporation	5075	D	310 637-1137	7738
FNS Customs Brokers Inc	4731	E	310 667-4880	5078
General Petroleum Corporation (DH)	5172	C	562 983-7300	9022
Geodis Logistics LLC	4225	D	310 604-8185	4558
Global Mail Inc	7331	C	310 735-0800	14071
Gourmet Foods Inc (PA)	5149	C	310 632-3300	8482

GEOGRAPHIC SECTION

CONCORD, CA

	SIC	EMP	PHONE	ENTRY #
Hydroprocessing Associates LLC	7389	E	310 667-6456	17230
Interstate Foods	5144	C	323 264-4024	8598
JAM Industries Inc	4225	D	310 254-0300	4580
Kawai America Corporation (HQ)	5099	E	310 631-1771	8123
Knight Transportation Inc	4213	C	888 549-7802	4205
LMD Intgrted Lgistics Svcs Inc	4225	D	310 605-5100	4588
Los Angeles County Health Svc	8011	E	310 763-2244	19721
Lynwood Developmental Care	8059	D	310 764-2023	21302
M M Fab Inc	5131	D	310 763-3800	8317
Mitsubishi Warehouse Cal Corp	4225	D	310 886-5500	4600
Nabors Well Services Co	1389	C	310 639-7074	1089
National Retail Trnsp Inc	4213	D	310 605-3777	4233
New Pride Corporation	7534	E	310 631-7000	17780
Newport Apparel Corporation (PA)	5137	D	310 605-1900	8405
Ocean Knight Shipping Inc	4731	C	310 885-3388	5137
Pacific Lighting Manufacturer	5063	D	310 327-7711	7464
Pasha Group	4731	C	310 735-0952	5148
Petrochem Insulation Inc	1742	C	310 638-6663	2954
Pitney Bowes Presort Svcs Inc	7389	D	310 763-4615	17415
Port Logistics Group Inc	4789	C	310 669-2551	5236
Progressive Trnsp Svcs Inc	5085	C	510 268-3776	7948
Purolator International Inc	4731	D	650 871-7075	5156
RPM Mechanical - A Joint Ventr	1711	D	858 565-4131	2352
Sanitation District	4959	D	310 638-1161	6639
Silla Automotive LLC (PA)	5013	C	800 624-1499	6764
Southern California Edison Co	4911	C	310 608-5029	6229
Southern California Gas Co	4923	C	310 605-7800	6261
Star View Chldrn Fmly Srvcs	8322	D	310 868-5379	24234
Stk International Inc	5092	C	310 720-1277	8056
System Solding (usa) Inc	8732	C	310 608-5588	26710
Tap Operating Co LLC	5013	A	310 900-5500	6775
Tap Worldwide LLC (PA)	5013	C	310 900-5500	6776
Transport Express Inc	4214	D	310 898-2000	4382
Uma Enterprises Inc (PA)	5023	D	310 631-1166	6898
United Fabricare Supply Inc (PA)	5087	D	310 886-3790	7984
Universal Mail Delivery Svc	4212	D	310 884-5900	4079
USA Waste of California Inc	4953	D	310 763-8500	6585
Vanguard Lgistics Svcs USA Inc	4225	D	310 637-3700	4654
Viharas Group Inc	6722	D	310 537-6700	12129
Wenzlau Engineering Inc	5065	D	310 604-3400	7657
West Coast Ship Supply	5099	D	562 435-5245	8147
World Wide Technology Inc	5045	E	310 537-8335	7211

CONCORD, CA - Contra Costa County

	SIC	EMP	PHONE	ENTRY #
Admiral Security Services Inc	7382	B	888 471-1128	16860
Agostini and Associates Inc	7363	E	925 691-7300	14834
Albert D Seeno Cnstr Co Inc	1531	D	925 671-7711	1355
Alsco Inc	7213	C	707 751-0652	13518
American Brdge/Fluor Entps Inc	1622	D	510 808-4623	1886
American Med	4119	C	925 602-1300	3741
American Medical Response	4119	C	925 454-6000	3750
American National Red Cross	8322	E	925 603-7400	23659
Anka Behavioral Health Inc (PA)	8093	C	925 825-4700	22657
Apria Healthcare LLC	5047	D	925 827-8800	7239
Aramark Services Inc	7999	C	925 798-3321	19140
Aramark Unf & Career AP LLC	7218	C	925 827-3782	13611
Assetmark Inc (DH)	6282	E	925 521-1040	10119
AT&T Corp	4813	C	925 673-2120	5468
AT&T Corp	4813	D	925 356-6204	5480
AT&T Services Inc	4813	C	925 671-1902	5551
AT&T Services Inc	4813	C	925 671-1059	5554
Athens Insurance Service Inc	6411	C	925 826-1000	10632
Ausenco PSI LLC (HQ)	8711	D	925 939-4420	25674
Bay Area Seating Service Inc	7999	B	925 671-4000	19146
Bay Area/Diablo Petroleum Co	5172	C	925 228-2222	9014
Bay Cities Pav & Grading Inc	1794	C	925 687-6666	3419
Bay Medic Transportation Inc	4119	A	800 689-9511	3770
Brenden Theatre Corporation (PA)	7832	C	925 677-0462	18312
Building Services/System Inc	6512	D	925 688-1234	10964
California Ticketscom Inc	7922	C	925 671-4000	18377
Cantel Medical Corp	1629	D	925 609-6328	2036
Carlton Senior Living Inc	6552	D	925 935-1660	11956
Carone & Company Inc	1794	D	925 602-8800	3421
CB&i Envmtl Infrastructure Inc	8748	C	925 288-9898	27871
CB&i Government Solutions Inc	8711	D	925 288-9898	25723
City of Concord	7922	B	925 692-2400	18383
City of Concord	7992	D	925 686-6262	18722
Clyde Miles Cnstr Co Inc	1521	D	925 427-4473	1156
Coldwell Bnkr Residential Brkg (DH)	6531	D	925 275-3000	11425
Comcast Corporation	1731	B	925 271-9794	2557
Comfort Systems Usa Inc	1711	D	925 827-0578	2187
Compumail Information Svcs Inc	7389	D	925 689-7100	17089
Concord Hotel LLC	7011	D	925 521-3751	12539
Contra Costa Vet Med Emrgcy CL	0742	E	925 798-5830	617
Contra Costa Water District (PA)	4941	C	925 688-8000	6333
Contra Csta Child Care Council (PA)	8399	E	925 676-5442	24902
Contra Csta Child Care Council	8399	D	925 676-5437	24903
County of Contra Costa	7349	D	925 646-5877	14267
County of Contra Costa	8093	E	925 646-5480	22694
Courtyards At Pine Creek Inc	8082	E	925 798-3900	22419
Cowell Homeowners Association (PA)	8641	D	925 825-0250	25244
Customer Loyalty Builders Inc	8742	D	888 478-7787	27403
D A McCosker Construction Co	1611	E	925 686-1958	1761
D C Taylor Co	1761	E	925 603-1100	3159
Delta Personnel Services Inc	7363	D	925 356-3034	14870
Denova Home Sales Inc	6531	D	925 852-0545	11468
Dianne Adair Day Care Centers (PA)	8351	D	925 429-3232	24455
Durham School Services L P	4151	C	925 686-3391	3923
East Bay Connection Inc	4111	E	925 609-1920	3643
Edgewater Plumbing of Benicia	1711	D	707 747-9204	2215
Eichleay Inc (PA)	8711	C	925 689-7000	25782
Electric Tech Construction Inc	1623	D	925 849-5324	1928
Encore Inc	7999	E	925 932-1033	19206
Enterprise Roofing Service Inc	1761	D	925 689-6103	3171
Fidelity Nat HM Warranty Co	6351	C	925 356-0194	10493
First American Title Insur Co	6531	C	925 356-7000	11524
First American Title Insur Co	6361	C	925 798-2800	10526
First Student Inc	4142	D	925 676-1956	3902
Fleetcor Technologies Inc	7389	B	800 877-9019	17171
Frys Electronics Inc	5065	B	925 852-0300	7570
General Electric Company	8711	D	925 602-5950	25834
Gilbane Aecom JV	8744	D	925 946-3100	27791
Gilbane Federal (DH)	8711	C	925 946-3100	25842
Goldman Avram	8741	D	925 275-3000	27042
Gonsalves & Santucci Inc (PA)	1771	E	925 685-6799	3268
Gonsalves & Santucci Inc	1791	C	707 745-5019	3382
Harris & Associates Inc (PA)	8711	C	925 827-4900	25849
High Adrenaline Enterprises	5012	D	925 687-7742	6680
High End Development Inc	1799	D	925 687-2540	3531
Homecare Professionals Inc	8082	D	925 215-1214	22471
Jacobs Engineering Group Inc	8711	D	925 356-3900	25893
James C Jenkins Insur Svc Inc	6411	C	925 798-3334	10751
Janus Corporation (PA)	1799	D	925 969-9200	3534
John Muir Behavioral Hlth Ctr	8063	C	925 674-4100	22075
John Muir Health	8062	A	925 692-5600	21616
John Muir Health	8062	A	925 682-8200	21621
John Muir Physician Network	8062	A	925 682-8200	21624
John Muir Physician Network	8062	A	925 674-2200	21627
Jopari Solutions Inc	7389	D	925 459-5200	17263
Kindred Healthcare Oper Inc	8051	D	925 692-5886	20696
Kissito Health Case Inc	8082	D	925 689-9222	22496
Kyocera Dcment Sltons Amer Inc	5044	D	925 849-3300	7059
Land Home Financial Svcs Inc (PA)	6162	C	925 676-7038	9867
Leisure Planet	7999	C	925 687-4386	19235
Lemore Transportation Inc (PA)	4213	D	925 689-6444	4212
Mike McCall Landscape Inc	0782	C	925 363-8100	912
Mike Roses Auto Body Inc	7532	E	925 686-1739	17762
Montclair Hotels Mb LLC	7011	D	925 687-5500	13005
New Way LLC	8361	D	925 686-1520	24745
Nextel Communications Inc	4812	D	925 682-2355	5404
Office Movers Inc	4214	E	408 254-5010	4368
Pace Inc	1742	D	925 602-0900	2946
Pacific Gas and Electric Co	4911	A	925 676-0948	6175
Pacific Gas and Electric Co	4911	A	925 674-6305	6176
Pacific Service Credit Union (PA)	6062	C	888 858-6878	9677
Pacificdental Benefits Inc (PA)	6324	D	925 363-6000	10368
Parc Management LLC	7999	A	909 691-1364	19257
Patriot Contract Services LLC	4412	B	925 296-2000	4717
Patterson Dental Supply Inc	5047	E	408 773-0776	7298
Peppermill Casinos Inc	7011	C	925 671-7711	13090
Planned Prnthood Shst-Dblo Inc (PA)	8093	E	925 676-0300	22805
Precision Television Inc	7622	E	925 825-5296	17912
Ricoh Usa Inc	5044	E	925 988-4000	7070
Saxco International LLC	5199	C	707 422-9999	9301
Seecon Built Homes Inc	6552	D	925 671-7711	12007
Shaw Group Inc	8734	A	925 288-2011	26887
Shelter Inc	8748	C	925 335-0698	28055
Sierra Bay Contractors Inc	1541	E	925 671-7711	1464
Stonebrook Convalescent Center	8051	E	925 689-7457	20932
Sutter Vsting Nrse Assn Hspice	8082	E	925 677-4250	22577
Swift Worldwide Inc (PA)	4213	C	510 351-7949	4274
Swinerton Builders Inc	1521	E	925 602-6400	1269
Swinerton Incorporated	1522	D	925 689-2336	1342
Telstar Instruments (PA)	1731	C	925 671-2888	2770
Tranquility Incorporated	8059	C	925 825-4280	21392
Travis Credit Union	6061	B	800 877-8328	9634
United Behavioral Health	6324	C	925 246-1343	10385
United Parcel Service Inc OH	4215	C	925 689-6584	4468
URS Group Inc	8711	D	925 446-3800	26124
Valley Relocation and Storage (PA)	4213	E	925 230-2025	4298
Versa Engineering & Tech Inc	8711	D	925 405-4505	26141

CONCORD, CA

Company	SIC	EMP	PHONE	ENTRY #
Vwi Concord LLC	7011	C	925 827-2000	13383
Windsor Convalescent	8051	C	925 689-2266	21045
Youth Homes Incorporated	8361	D	925 933-2627	24859
Zero Waste Solutions Inc	8741	C	925 270-3339	27288
Zwicker & Associates PC	8111	C	925 689-7070	23638

COPPEROPOLIS, CA - Calaveras County

Company	SIC	EMP	PHONE	ENTRY #
Commercial Site Imprvs Inc	1794	E	209 785-1920	3424
Meridian Gold Inc	1041	C	209 785-3222	1023

CORCORAN, CA - Kings County

Company	SIC	EMP	PHONE	ENTRY #
Corcoran District Hospital	8062	D	559 992-3300	21511
Gilkey Farms Inc	0131	D	559 992-2136	11
Hansen Ranches	0191	D	559 992-3111	365
J G Boswell Company	0723	D	559 992-2141	551
J G Boswell Company	0131	B	559 992-5141	13
Jason Proctor Trnsp Co	4119	E	559 992-1767	3806
Vista Verde Farms Inc	0721	D	559 992-3111	487

CORNING, CA - Tehama County

Company	SIC	EMP	PHONE	ENTRY #
Andersncttonwood Disposal Svcs	4212	D	530 824-4700	3977
Omega Waste Management Inc	8742	D	530 824-1890	27573
Rolling Hills Casino	7999	B	530 528-3500	19270

CORONA, CA - Riverside County

Company	SIC	EMP	PHONE	ENTRY #
A M Ortega Construction Inc	1731	D	951 360-1352	2506
ABC School Equipment Inc	5049	D	951 817-2200	7338
Ability Counts Inc (PA)	8331	C	951 734-6595	24302
Acm Technologies Inc (PA)	5044	C	951 738-9898	7039
Advanced Communication Service	7389	C	909 210-9328	16972
Ae & Associates LLC	8748	E	951 278-3477	27810
Agile Sourcing Partners Inc	4939	C	951 279-4154	6299
AK Constructors Inc	1542	E	951 280-0269	1487
All American Asphalt (PA)	1611	D	951 736-7600	1725
All American Asphalt	1611	D	951 736-7617	1726
All American Asphalt	1611	D	951 736-7617	1727
All American Service & Sups	7699	C	951 736-3880	17958
Amec E & C Services Inc	8711	D	951 273-7400	25650
American Electric Supply Inc (PA)	5063	D	951 734-7910	7413
Amerisourcebergen Corporation	5122	C	951 493-2339	8231
Amerisourcebergen Corporation	5122	C	951 371-2000	8233
ARC Fastener Supply & Mfg	5085	D	909 481-8171	7914
Arizona Pipe Line Company	1623	C	951 270-3100	1905
Beador Construction Co Inc	1611	C	951 674-7352	1739
Brookdale Senior Living Inc	8361	C	951 808-9387	24573
C & R Systems Inc (PA)	1731	E	951 270-0255	2544
Calatlantic Group Inc	1521	D	951 898-5500	1147
Cannon Fabrication Inc	1761	C	951 278-1830	3146
Canyon Insulation Inc	1742	C	951 278-9200	2872
Cellco Partnership	4812	C	951 549-6400	5312
Cellco Partnership	4812	C	951 898-0980	5324
Championship Golf Services Inc	7992	D	951 272-4340	18720
Chief Protective Services Inc	7381	D	951 738-0881	16596
Chilis 898 Corona	8741	D	951 734-7275	26964
City of Corona	8743	C	951 279-3647	27741
City of Corona	4939	C	951 736-2266	6301
Combustion Associates Inc	4911	E	951 272-6999	6118
Comcast Corporation	4841	C	951 268-9378	5959
Community Access Network	8322	D	951 279-1333	23768
Community Bank	6022	E	951 808-8940	9488
Compass Bancshares Inc	6021	B	951 279-7071	9390
Core-Mark Interrelated (DH)	5199	D	951 272-4790	9256
Corona Clipper Inc	5072	C	951 737-6515	7680
Couts Heating & Cooling Inc	1711	D	951 278-5560	2194
De La Torre Landscape & Maint	0782	C	951 549-3525	834
Downs Fuel Transport Inc	5172	E	951 256-8286	9016
DR Horton Inc	1531	D	951 272-9000	1363
E P N Inc	7812	E	951 279-8877	18080
Eagle Glen Country Club LLC	7992	D	951 272-4653	18737
Ebs Concrete Inc	1771	E	951 279-6869	3261
Ebs General Engineering Inc	1611	D	951 279-6869	1769
Empire Demolition Inc	1771	D	909 393-8300	3262
Excel Landscape Inc	0782	C	951 735-9650	851
Express Cable Communication	4841	C	951 272-2029	5999
F M Tarbell Co	6531	C	951 280-6040	11507
Fire Sprinkler Systems Inc (PA)	1711	D	951 688-0336	2227
First Student Inc	4173	C	951 736-3234	3958
Fst Sand & Gravel Inc	5032	E	951 277-8440	6984
Fullmer Cattle Nthrn Cal LLC	0212	C	909 597-3274	410
Garys Carpeting Inc	1541	C	951 272-8210	1426
Green River Golf Corporation	7992	D	714 970-8411	18743
H & H Transportation LLC	4213	D	951 271-2700	4193
Halo Unlimted Inc	8099	D	714 692-2270	22966
Hillcrest Contracting Inc	1611	D	951 273-9600	1800
Hoffman Concrete Company Inc	1771	E	951 372-8333	3274
HP Communications Inc	1623	D	951 572-1200	1940
Humble Hustle Incorporated	8742	E	951 444-0263	27468
Hyde & Hyde Inc (PA)	7389	C	951 279-5239	17229
JJ Mac Intyre Co Inc (PA)	7322	C	951 898-4300	14037
K&B Engineering	8711	C	951 808-9501	25913
Kaiser Foundation Hospitals	8711	A	951 270-1220	25914
Kaiser Foundation Hospitals	8099	D	866 984-7483	22983
Kaiser Foundation Hospitals	6733	A	866 984-7483	12188
Kaiser Permenents	8011	A	951 270-1888	19683
Kec Engineering	1611	C	951 734-3010	1808
Kobelco Compressors Amer Inc (HQ)	1623	B	951 739-3030	1957
La Steel Services Inc	1791	E	951 393-2013	3389
Latara Enterprise Inc	8071	D	951 272-9420	22237
Laurence-Hovenier Inc	1751	C	951 736-2990	3063
LDI Mechanical Inc (PA)	1711	D	951 340-9685	2277
Lennar Homes Inc	1531	C	951 739-0267	1376
Lexani Wheel Corporation	5013	C	951 808-4220	6746
Live Media LLC	7929	E	951 279-8877	18477
M E Nollkamper Inc (PA)	8742	E	951 737-9300	27517
Management Trust Assn Inc	6733	D	951 694-1758	12193
Marie Cllender Wholesalers Inc	5142	C	951 737-6760	8560
Marriott International Inc	7011	C	951 371-0107	12967
Med-Link Nursing Services Inc	7361	D	951 279-6333	14702
Minka Lighting Inc (PA)	5063	D	951 735-9220	7456
Mission Ambulance Inc	4119	D	951 272-2300	3819
Monster Energy Company (DH)	5149	C	951 739-6200	8880
More Truck Lines Inc	4212	D	951 371-6673	4042
MS Industrial Shtmtl Inc	1761	C	951 272-6610	3193
National Distribution Services	5099	C	951 739-2400	8129
Pacific Shores Masonry	1741	E	951 371-8550	2831
Pacwest Instrument Labs	7699	D	951 737-0790	17998
Pamco Construction Services	1542	C	951 279-1962	1629
Paramount Bldg Solutions LLC	7349	B	951 272-4001	14381
Peaceful Hearts Home Care Inc	8082	D	951 541-9343	22533
Peoples Choice Staffing Inc	7361	C	951 735-0550	14725
Peppermint Ridge (PA)	8361	D	951 273-7320	24767
Pet Partners Inc (PA)	5199	C	951 279-9888	9292
Ply Gem Pacific Windows Corp	5031	D	951 272-1300	6949
Primary Provider MGT Co Inc (PA)	8741	D	951 280-7700	27172
Pro Building Maintenance Inc	7349	C	951 279-3386	14394
Pro Group Inc	6531	C	951 271-3000	11763
Provident Group Crown Pnte LLC	6513	C	951 737-7482	11190
Quality Wall Systems Inc	1742	D	951 739-4409	2961
R W Lyall & Company Inc (DH)	1382	C	951 270-1500	1067
Ranch House Doors Inc	5031	D	951 278-2884	6954
Reliable Interiors Inc	8741	C	951 371-3390	27197
Remax All Stars Realty	6531	C	951 739-6000	11805
Rosen Electronics LLC	5099	C	951 898-9808	8136
Rugby Laboratories Inc (DH)	5122	D	951 270-1400	8292
Ryland Hmes Inlnd Empire Cstmr	1521	D	951 273-3473	1249
Schaper Construction Inc	1721	D	951 808-1140	2491
Screenworks LLC	7336	D	951 279-8877	14161
Signature Interiors Inc	1521	B	951 340-2200	1260
Smart Energy Solar Inc	1711	C	951 273-9595	2370
So Cal Sandbags Inc	5085	D	951 277-3404	7953
Spectrum Communications Cablin	4899	C	951 371-0549	6090
SSC Construction Inc	8711	D	951 278-1177	26074
Sun Rich Fresh Foods USA Inc (HQ)	0723	D	951 735-3800	589
Superior Construction Inc	1521	D	951 808-8780	1267
Superior Paving Company Inc	1611	D	951 739-9200	1870
T W R Framing	7361	D	951 279-2000	14800
Talco Plastics Inc (PA)	4953	D	951 531-2000	6567
Team Dykspra (PA)	7542	C	951 898-6482	17863
Team West Contracting Corp	1629	D	951 340-3426	2089
Titan Sheet Metal Inc	1761	C	951 372-1362	3221
Total Drywall Inc	1742	E	951 279-0044	2990
Troy Lee Designs (PA)	5091	D	951 371-5219	8032
TWR Enterprises Inc	1751	C	951 279-2000	3098
Uhs-Corona Inc (HQ)	8062	A	951 737-4343	21978
Uhs-Corona Inc	8093	D	951 736-7200	22855
United Transport Service Inc	7389	E	951 258-2262	17566
US Foods Inc	5141	C	951 256-2400	8545
US Foods Inc	5149	C	800 888-3147	8946
US Foods Inc	5149	C	951 582-8500	8947
US Foods Inc	5149	C	951 256-2400	8953
US Green Building Council -	6732	D	818 621-4880	12166
US Home Corporation	1531	E	951 817-3500	1387
US Security Associates Inc	7381	C	951 256-4601	16848
USA Waste of California Inc	4953	D	800 423-9986	6577
Valente Concrete	1771	D	951 279-2221	3346
Veg-Fresh Farms LLC	5148	C	800 422-5535	8784
VIP Transport Inc	4213	E	951 272-3700	4300
Vipstore USA Co	5199	B	626 934-7880	9310
Volt Telecom Group Inc	8748	E	727 571-2268	28093
Volt Telecom Group Inc	8748	C	951 493-8900	28094
Waste MGT of Alameda Cnty	4953	C	909 280-5438	6611
West Hills Construction Inc	1521	E	800 515-5270	1284

GEOGRAPHIC SECTION

COSTA MESA, CA

	SIC	EMP	PHONE	ENTRY #
Western Staffing Solutions LLC	7361	C	951 545-4449	14819
Wurms Janitorial Service Inc	7349	D	951 582-0003	14466
X-Act Finish & Trim Inc	1751	D	951 582-9229	3104

CORONA DEL MAR, CA - Orange County

	SIC	EMP	PHONE	ENTRY #
Balboa Yacht Club	7997	E	949 673-3515	18882
Broker Solutions Inc	6153	B	800 450-2010	9775
CIT Bank National Association	6021	D	949 675-2890	9371
Crown Cove Senior Care Cmnty	8361	D	949 760-2800	24626
Delta Max	7379	E	949 759-8529	16355
First Team RE - Orange Cnty	6531	D	949 759-5747	11531
Pacific Cleaning Service Inc	7349	E	949 829-8790	14376
Service Corp International	6531	D	949 644-2700	11839

CORONADO, CA - San Diego County

	SIC	EMP	PHONE	ENTRY #
51st St & 8th Ave Corp	7011	A	619 424-4000	12365
Affordable Engrg Svcs Inc	8711	D	973 890-8915	25644
City of Coronado	7999	D	619 522-7342	19169
City of Coronado	4931	D	619 522-7380	6285
El Cordova Hotel	7011	D	619 435-4131	12612
Four Sisters Inns	7011	C	619 437-1900	12650
G & K Management Co Inc	6531	E	619 437-1777	11548
Hotel Del Coronado LP	7011	D	619 522-8011	12785
L-O Coronado Hotel Inc	7011	A	619 435-6611	12894
Loews Corporation	8111	B	619 424-4000	23406
Mariner Systems Inc (PA)	7389	E	305 266-7255	17312
Pickford Realty Inc	6531	D	619 435-8722	11751
R3 Strategic Support Group Inc	8742	D	800 418-2040	27608
San Diego Private Bank	6022	E	619 437-1000	9522
Sanspan Corporation	7011	A	619 435-6611	13211
Star & Crescent Boat Company (PA)	4489	E	619 234-4111	4740

CORTE MADERA, CA - Marin County

	SIC	EMP	PHONE	ENTRY #
Aegis Senior Communities LLC	8082	D	415 483-1399	22343
Alain Pinel Realtors Inc	6531	D	415 755-1111	11281
Cellco Partnership	4812	D	415 924-9084	5307
Guarantee Mortgage Corporation	6163	E	415 925-8080	9927
Marin Municipal Water District (PA)	4941	C	415 945-1455	6369
Pottery Barn Inc	5023	D	415 924-1391	6882
Tommy Bahama Group Inc	7389	C	415 737-0400	17534
Western Athletic Clubs LLC	7991	D	415 945-3000	18703

COSTA MESA, CA - Orange County

	SIC	EMP	PHONE	ENTRY #
24 Hour Fitness Usa Inc	8099	E	949 610-0651	22872
24 Hour Fitness Usa Inc	7991	D	949 650-3600	18588
ABC Bus Inc	5012	D	714 444-5888	6658
Accredited Nursing Services	8051	D	714 973-1234	20369
Adopt-A-Highway Maintenance	1611	C	800 200-0003	1723
Advantage Ground Trnsp Corp	4111	D	714 557-2465	3631
Advantage Waypoint LLC	5141	D	717 424-4973	8453
Alfreds Pictures Frames Inc	7389	E	714 434-4838	16978
All-Rite Leasing Company Inc	7349	B	714 530-7074	14220
Altametrics LLC	5045	C	800 676-1281	7088
Amen Clinics Inc A Med Corp (PA)	8071	E	888 564-2700	22189
American Reprographics Co LLC	7334	C	714 751-2680	14104
Americash	6162	E	714 994-7554	9817
Amica Mutual Insurance Company	6331	D	877 972-6422	10401
Andrew L Youngquist Cnstr Inc	1542	D	949 862-5611	1491
Arnel Interior Corp	8741	B	714 481-5100	26926
Arta Western Medical Group	6321	E	949 260-6575	10234
Auto Club Enterprises (PA)	6321	A	714 850-5111	10235
Automobile Club Southern Cal	6411	D	714 885-1343	10636
Automobile Club Southern Cal	7538	A	714 850-5111	17784
Ayres Group (PA)	7011	D	714 540-6060	12409
Balboa Capital Corporation (PA)	6141	D	949 756-0800	9740
Bdo Usa LLP	8721	D	714 957-3200	26296
Benco Dental Supply Co	5047	D	714 424-0977	7244
Benq America Corp (HQ)	5045	D	714 559-4900	7101
Boyd & Associates	7381	C	714 835-5423	16581
Bright Bristol Street LLC	7011	D	714 557-3000	12465
Brookfeld Sthland Holdings LLC	1521	D	714 427-6868	1140
Bureau Veritas North Amer Inc	8748	D	714 431-4100	27857
C2 Imaging (PA)	7334	D	714 668-5955	14115
Caliber Bodyworks Inc	7532	E	714 436-5010	17750
California Pharmacy MGT LLC	7322	D	714 777-3100	14022
California Ticketscom Inc (DH)	7922	D	714 327-5400	18378
Califrnia Dept State Hospitals	8063	A	714 957-5000	22047
Canon Solutions America Inc	5044	D	949 753-4200	7047
Cardflex Inc	7389	D	714 361-1900	17053
Carecredit LLC	7389	C	800 300-3046	17057
Casanova Pndrill Pblicidad Inc (PA)	7311	D	949 474-5001	13823
Cellco Partnership	4812	D	714 427-0733	5296
Center For Better Health and	8099	D	714 751-8110	22913
Central Parking System Inc	7521	D	714 751-2855	17713
Coit Services Inc	7216	E	949 760-0760	13579
Competent Care Inc	8082	D	714 545-4818	22412
Cooksey Toolen Gage Duffy (PA)	8111	D	714 431-1100	23162
Countryside Inn-Corona LP	7011	D	714 549-0300	12543
County of Orange	4581	C	949 252-5006	4913
Creative Design Cons Inc (PA)	7389	C	714 641-4868	17103
Deloitte & Touche LLP	8721	A	714 436-7419	26323
Deloitte Consulting LLP	8742	D	714 436-7100	27407
Developmental Svcs Cal Dept	8331	A	714 957-5151	24335
Donahue Schrber Rlty Group Inc (PA)	6531	D	714 545-1400	11475
Donahue Schrber Rlty Group LP (PA)	6512	D	714 545-1400	10975
Dvs Shoe Co Inc (PA)	5139	D	310 715-8300	8431
Dwiw Inc	0782	E	949 574-7147	846
Edward Straling	1731	E	760 887-3673	2580
Edwards Theatres Circuit Inc	7832	D	714 428-0962	18322
Elite Tek Services Inc	7379	D	714 881-5301	16363
Empire Leasing Inc	1751	D	949 646-7400	3046
Emulex Corporate Services Corp	8741	D	714 662-5600	27015
Ensign Group Inc	8051	D	949 642-0387	20537
Experian Info Solutions Inc (DH)	7323	A	714 830-7000	14059
EZ Lube LLC (PA)	7549	D	714 556-1312	17882
Federal Express Corporation	4513	D	800 463-3339	4849
Food & Agriculture Cal Dept	7999	D	714 751-3247	19215
Food Sales West Inc (PA)	5141	D	714 966-2900	8478
Ford Motor Company	7514	D	949 642-1291	17675
Forma Systems Visuart	8748	D	949 660-1900	27923
Frank Gustafson	5199	D	714 438-1590	9265
Geek Squad Inc	7379	D	714 434-0132	16386
General Electric Capital Corp	6159	C	714 434-4111	9799
Global Business Solutions Inc	7379	B	714 257-1488	16391
Golden Living LLC	8051	D	949 642-0387	20605
Gtt Communications (mp) Inc	4813	D	714 327-2000	5626
Hanford Hotels Inc	7011	D	714 957-6951	12687
Hanley Wood Mkt Intelligence (HQ)	8732	D	714 540-8500	26672
Hanley Wood Mkt Intelligence (PA)	8748	D	714 540-8500	27939
HB Parkco Construction Inc (PA)	1771	B	714 444-1443	3273
Hilton Worldwide Inc	7011	D	714 540-7000	12735
Hoag Family Cancer Institute	8099	A	949 764-7777	22976
Holthouse Carlin Van Trigt LLP	8721	D	714 361-7600	26372
Host Hotels & Resorts LP	7011	D	714 957-1100	12770
HP Inc	7373	C	714 432-6588	15959
Human Options Inc	8322	E	949 757-3635	24014
Independent Options	8322	D	714 434-1175	24024
Industrial Pharmacy MGT LLC	8741	D	949 777-3100	27063
Inhouseit Inc	7378	D	949 660-5655	16300
Insight Investments LLC (HQ)	7377	C	714 939-2300	16284
International Bus Mchs Corp	7379	B	714 327-3501	16408
Jabez Building Services Inc	7349	B	714 776-7705	14329
Janico Building Maintenance	7349	B	714 444-4339	14331
JD Power and Associates (PA)	8732	C	714 621-6200	26679
Juniper Networks Inc	7373	D	949 584-4591	15978
Koce-TV Foundation	4833	C	714 241-4100	5885
Kyocera International Inc	5065	E	714 428-3600	7592
Latham & Watkins LLP	8111	C	714 540-1235	23371
Lawrence B Bonas Company	1721	D	714 668-5250	2462
Lewis Brsbois Bsgard Smith LLP	8111	D	714 545-6015	23389
Livetime Software Inc	7372	E	415 905-4009	15735
Maersk Inc	4731	D	714 428-5500	5118
Manatt Phelps & Phillips LLP	8111	E	714 371-2500	23419
Materials Marketing	8742	D	949 729-9881	27526
Medical Eye Services Inc	6411	D	714 619-4660	10783
Mesa Cnsld Wtr Dst Imprv Corp (PA)	4941	D	949 631-1200	6370
Mesa Verde Country Club	7997	C	714 549-0377	18998
Mesa Verde Partners	7992	D	714 540-7500	18759
Mesa Vrde Cnvalescent Hosp Inc	8051	C	949 548-5584	20789
Michael Maguire & Associates	6411	E	714 435-7500	10786
Morgan Lewis & Bockius LLP	8111	C	949 399-7000	23442
Mt Supply Inc	5085	D	714 434-4748	7942
National Safety Services	8748	E	714 679-9118	27997
Nds Americas Inc (DH)	4841	D	714 434-2100	6009
Newma Garris Gilmo + Partne l	8712	D	949 756-0818	26242
Newport Sbacute Healthcare Ctr	8059	C	949 642-1974	21327
Nissan North America Inc	5012	D	714 433-3700	6691
North American Acceptance Corp	6141	C	714 868-3195	9760
Nwp Services Corporation (HQ)	7372	C	949 253-2500	15782
Olson & Assoc	7379	D	714 878-6649	16442
Orange Cnty Sprntndent Schools	8351	D	949 650-2506	24493
Orange County Plst Co Inc	1742	C	714 957-1971	2944
Ovations Fanfare	8741	D	714 708-1880	27153
Pacific Mercantile Bank (HQ)	6022	E	714 438-2500	9514
Parkco Building Company	1542	D	714 444-1441	1631
Paul Hastings LLP	8111	C	714 668-6200	23495
Payoff Inc	6141	D	949 430-0630	9761
Pcw Contracting Services	1799	D	949 548-9969	3568
PDC Capital Group LLC	6552	D	866 500-8550	12001
Pivot Interiors Inc	1731	D	949 988-5400	2685
Planned Parenthood Federation	8093	D	949 548-8830	22801
Plexicor Inc (PA)	7382	E	714 918-8700	16911

Employment Codes: A=Over 500 employees, B=251-500,
C=101-250, D=51-100, E=45-50

2017 Directory of California
Wholesalers and Services Companies

© Mergent Inc. 1-800-342-5647
1645

COSTA MESA, CA

	SIC	EMP	PHONE	ENTRY #
Pmd Industries Inc	1731	E	949 222-0999	2686
Powerplant Mint Spcialists Inc	1629	E	714 427-6900	2077
Precise Fit Limited One LLC	7361	B	310 824-1800	14731
Profit Recovery Partners LLC	8748	D	949 851-2777	28023
Progress Advocates Group LLC	7299	C	800 279-9319	13789
R S I Insurance Brokers Inc (PA)	6411	E	714 546-6616	10851
Random Holdings Inc	8741	D	949 722-7103	27194
Remax Metro Inc	6531	D	714 557-2544	11807
Restaurant In A Box Llc	7371	E	800 676-1281	15418
Robinson Pharma Inc	5122	C	714 241-0235	8291
Rosanna Inc	7011	C	714 751-5100	13167
Rromeo Corporation	8741	D	714 640-3800	27202
Rutan & Tucker LLP (PA)	8111	C	714 641-5100	23542
Safe Harbor Treatment Cen	8093	E	949 645-1026	22819
Seaview Industries	7389	E	714 957-5073	17484
Sheppard Mullin Richter	8111	D	714 513-5100	23565
Silverado Senior Living Inc	8059	D	949 945-0189	21373
Site Crew Inc	7349	B	714 668-0100	14432
Smith & Sons Investment Co	6531	E	949 646-9648	11847
Snell & Wilmer LLP	8111	D	714 427-7000	23576
Software Management Cons Inc	7371	D	714 662-1841	15464
Solopoint Solutions Inc	8711	D	714 708-3639	26069
South Coast Plaza LLC (PA)	6512	D	714 546-0110	11054
South Coast Plaza LLC	6512	D	714 435-2000	11055
South Coast Repertory Inc	7922	D	714 708-5500	18435
South Coast Westin Hotel Co	7011	D	714 540-2500	13274
Southern California Mar Assn	7538	D	714 850-4004	17815
Sprouts Farmers Market Inc	5141	C	714 751-6399	8527
St Jude Hospital Yorba Linda	8011	D	714 557-6300	20061
Stearns Lending LLC (PA)	6162	B	714 513-7777	9899
Sure Haven	8069	A	949 467-9213	22180
Syspro Impact Software Inc	5045	C	714 437-1000	7199
T Boyer Company	1731	E	949 642-2431	2763
Talon Executive Services Inc	7382	E	714 434-7476	16930
Telecare Corporation	8063	D	714 361-6760	22094
Tk Carsites Inc	7371	E	714 937-1239	15506
Tsi	7349	C	949 515-7800	14448
Ultralink LLC	6311	C	714 427-5500	10227
University California Irvine	8011	E	949 646-2267	20172
US Hotel and Resort MGT Inc	7011	D	949 650-2988	13371
UTC Fire SEC Americas Corp Inc	7371	D	949 737-7800	15519
Valassis Communications Inc	7331	D	714 751-4006	14096
Villa Pacific Contractors Inc	1741	E	714 850-1640	2838
Viva Life Science Inc	5122	D	949 645-6100	8305
Volcom LLC	5136	C	949 646-2175	8365
Volcom LLC (DH)	7389	C	949 646-2175	17600
Waddell & Reed Inc	6211	D	714 437-7510	10097
Warmington Homes (PA)	1531	C	714 434-4435	1390
Warmington Residential Cal Inc	1521	D	714 557-5511	1281
Wcct Global LLC (PA)	8733	D	714 668-1500	26819
Westar Capital Assoc II LLC	6799	A	714 481-5160	12352
Woodruff Spradlin & Smart	8111	D	714 558-7000	23633
Wyndham International Inc	7011	D	714 751-5100	13439

COTATI, CA - Sonoma County

	SIC	EMP	PHONE	ENTRY #
21st Century Health Club (PA)	8093	D	707 795-0400	22647
Mike Brown Electric Co	1731	D	707 792-8100	2653
Stockham Construction Inc	1751	C	707 664-0945	3094
Sutter Health	8011	C	707 586-0440	20081

COTTONWOOD, CA - Shasta County

	SIC	EMP	PHONE	ENTRY #
All Pro Drywall	1742	E	530 722-5182	2850
County of Shasta	8641	D	530 347-6276	25243
Shasta Livestock Auction Yard	5154	D	530 347-3793	8962

COURTLAND, CA - Sacramento County

	SIC	EMP	PHONE	ENTRY #
Delta Breeze Farming Inc	0191	C	916 775-2055	354

COVELO, CA - Mendocino County

	SIC	EMP	PHONE	ENTRY #
Round Valley Indian Health Ctr	8011	D	707 983-6182	19928

COVINA, CA - Los Angeles County

	SIC	EMP	PHONE	ENTRY #
A-1 Event & Party Rentals	7299	D	626 967-0500	13729
Accentcare Home Health Cal Inc	8082	D	626 869-0250	22329
Accu-Count Inventory Svcs Inc	7389	D	805 231-6310	16968
Acf Components & Fasteners Inc	5072	D	949 833-0506	7665
American Multi-Cinema Inc	7832	D	626 974-8624	18297
Assistance League Covina Vly	8399	C	626 966-7550	24874
Baltazar Construction Inc	1771	E	626 339-8620	3229
Bowlmor AMF Corp	7933	D	626 339-1286	18511
Briteworks Inc	7349	D	626 966-7669	14241
Brutoco Engrg & Cnstr Inc	1611	D	909 350-3535	1743
Central Health Plan Cal Inc	8082	A	626 938-7120	22403
Charter Behavioral Health Syst	8063	D	626 966-1632	22053
Citrus Valley Medical Ctr Inc	8062	B	626 858-8515	21489
Citrus Valley Medical Ctr Inc	8062	D	626 331-7331	21491
Citrus Vly Hlth Partners Inc (PA)	8741	A	626 331-7331	26968
Citrus Vly Hlth Partners Inc	8099	A	626 732-3100	22920
Coldwell Banker Town & Country	6531	D	626 966-3688	11418
Covina Bowl Inc	7933	D	626 339-1286	18516
Covina Rehabilitation Center	8051	C	626 967-3874	20504
Cruz Hoffstetter LLC	7389	D	626 915-5621	17108
Cwf Inc	7359	D	626 967-0500	14534
Dynamic Realty Corp	6531	D	626 931-3200	11482
Garcia Asset Management Inc	7349	D	626 289-8755	14307
Golden Empire Mortgage	6162	D	626 967-3236	9847
Grand Auto Care	7538	E	626 331-8390	17797
Hilton Worldwide Inc	7011	D	626 915-3441	12725
Home Capital Group	6162	D	626 331-4213	9856
International Mrtg Corp Assn	6162	D	626 339-9094	9929
John Stewart Company	8111	D	626 967-3734	23327
K-Fed Mutual Holding Company	6712	C	626 339-9663	12043
Keller Williams Realty	6531	D	626 384-2803	11608
Lereta LLC (PA)	6211	B	626 543-1765	10025
Los Angeles Engineering Inc	1795	C	626 869-1400	3459
Magan Medical Clinic Inc (PA)	8011	C	626 331-6411	19725
Masonic Homes of California	8361	D	626 251-2200	24729
Mohan Dialysis Ctr of Covina	8092	C	626 859-2522	22635
Outsource Testing Inc	8748	D	909 592-8898	28013
Rgis LLC	7389	D	626 974-4841	17457
Rowland Convalescent Hosp Inc	8051	C	626 967-2741	20882
San Gabriel Childrens Ctr Inc	8361	C	626 859-2089	24803
Securitas SEC Svcs USA Inc	7381	C	571 321-0913	16789
Staff Today Incorporated	7363	C	800 928-5561	14952
Verizon Communications Inc	1731	D	626 858-1739	2785
Vitas Healthcare Corp Cal	8082	D	626 918-2273	22603
Wood Castle Construction Inc	1521	E	626 966-8600	1286

CRESCENT CITY, CA - Del Norte County

	SIC	EMP	PHONE	ENTRY #
Blake Alexandre	0241	E	707 487-1000	418
County of Del Norte	8399	C	707 464-3191	24904
Elk Valley Casino Inc	7999	C	707 464-1020	19205
Full Spectrum Services Inc	8322	E	707 465-1460	23989
Leavitt Group Enterprises Inc	8741	C	707 465-6508	27109
North Shore Investment Inc	8051	D	707 464-6151	20809
Snoozie Shavings Inc (HQ)	4213	D	707 464-6186	4264
Sutter Coast Hospital (HQ)	8062	C	707 464-8511	21942

CROCKETT, CA - Contra Costa County

	SIC	EMP	PHONE	ENTRY #
Sugar Workers Local 1	8631	B	510 787-1676	25188

CUDAHY, CA - Los Angeles County

	SIC	EMP	PHONE	ENTRY #
County of Los Angeles	8399	C	323 560-5001	24907
General Testing & Insptn Inc	8734	D	323 583-1653	26856
Kaiser Foundation Hospitals	8062	D	323 562-6400	21652
Mistras Group Inc	8711	D	323 583-1653	25969
Southern Cal Prmnnte Med Group	8011	E	323 562-6459	20039

CULVER CITY, CA - Los Angeles County

	SIC	EMP	PHONE	ENTRY #
A-1 Electric Service Co Inc	1731	E	310 204-1077	2507
ACC	0742	D	310 558-6100	610
Anonymous Content LLC (PA)	7812	D	310 558-6000	18044
Automatic Data Processing Inc	7374	D	800 226-5237	16102
Avoca Productions Inc	7812	D	310 244-4000	18048
Bally Total Fitness Corp	7991	D	310 204-2030	18608
Cadforce Inc	7389	A	310 876-1800	17045
California Clinical Trials	6411	C	310 945-1780	10656
Century Wilshire Inc	7011	D	310 558-9400	12507
CIT Bank National Association	6021	D	310 390-7745	9358
CIT Bank National Association	6021	D	310 559-7222	9365
Columbia Pictures Inds Inc (DH)	7812	C	310 244-4000	18063
Common Area Maint Svcs Inc (PA)	7349	D	310 390-3552	14259
Companion Hospice and	8082	D	310 338-1257	22409
Compulaw LLC	7371	E	310 553-3355	15097
Crp Centinela LP	7011	C	901 821-4117	12557
Cuningham Group Arch Inc	8712	E	310 895-2200	26179
D K Fortune & Associates Inc	8059	C	310 391-7266	21205
Didi Hirsch Psychiatric Svc (PA)	8322	D	310 390-6612	23944
Digital Kitchen LLC	7812	E	310 499-9255	18072
Dual Diagnosis Trtmnt Ctr Inc	8093	C	424 207-2220	22724
Esaloncom LLC	7231	D	310 846-9100	13673
Exceptional Chld Foundation (PA)	8331	D	310 204-3300	24338
Exceptional Chld Foundation	8331	D	323 870-2000	24339
Exceptional Chld Foundation	8331	D	310 204-3300	24340
Exodus Recovery Inc (PA)	8093	D	310 945-3350	22729
Exodus Recovery Ctr At Brotman (PA)	8069	D	310 253-9494	22141
Force-Oakleaf LP	7011	D	310 484-7000	12641
G & K Management Co Inc (PA)	6531	D	310 204-2050	11547
Gardner Neurologic Orthopedic	8741	D	310 649-5824	27033
Genex (HQ)	7371	C	424 672-9500	15202
Globecast America Incorporated (HQ)	4841	D	212 373-5140	6004
Goldrich & Kest Industries LLC (PA)	6552	A	310 204-2050	11970
Goldrich and Kest Construction (PA)	6552	D	310 204-2050	11971
Hackett Group Inc	7379	D	310 842-8444	16395

GEOGRAPHIC SECTION

CYPRESS, CA

Company	SIC	EMP	PHONE	ENTRY #
Hellmuth Obata & Kassabaum Inc	8712	E	310 838-9555	26200
Hlw Corp	7542	E	310 838-7100	17843
Hok Group Inc	8712	E	310 838-9555	26207
I Mean It Creative Inc	7311	E	310 287-1000	13861
Investment Tech Group Inc	6211	C	310 216-6777	10017
Jeopardy Productions Inc	7812	C	310 244-8855	18096
Jesse Lee Group Inc	8741	D	510 351-3700	27078
Kaercher Campbell Associate In	6411	C	310 556-1900	10754
Kovel/Fuller LLC	7311	D	310 841-4444	13875
L A Services Inc	1711	D	310 838-0408	2271
Lax Plaza Hotel	7011	C	310 902-2202	12910
Liveoffice LLC	7372	D	877 253-2793	15734
LMS Corporation	7389	E	310 641-4222	17299
M-E Engineers Inc	8711	E	310 842-8700	25945
Maker Studios Inc (HQ)	7929	C	310 606-2182	18481
Marycrest Manor	8059	D	310 838-2778	21310
Max Leather	5199	E	310 841-6990	9279
Mbs Equipment Company (PA)	7819	D	310 558-3100	18234
Midnight Snack LP	8741	E	310 202-1470	27130
Morphosis Architects	8712	D	310 453-2247	26238
Mpc La	7812	D	310 526-5800	18116
Nantmobile LLC	7371	C	310 883-7888	15321
Nantworks LLC (PA)	7373	D	310 405-7539	16001
Nfl Properties LLC	7922	B	310 840-4635	18419
Office of Child Development	8351	D	310 842-4230	24488
Oracle Corporation	7372	D	310 258-7500	15802
Otx Corporation (HQ)	8742	C	310 736-3400	27577
Pacifica Hotel & Conference Ce	7011	C	310 649-1776	13066
Paychex Inc	8721	D	310 338-7900	26419
Permanente Kaiser Intl	8062	A	310 737-4800	21793
Pine Data Processing Inc	7374	D	310 815-5700	16168
Prestige Security Service Inc	7381	B	310 670-5999	16762
Prime Focus North America Inc (DH)	7819	D	323 461-7887	18247
Property Management Assoc Inc (PA)	6531	C	323 295-2000	11772
Psychemedics Corporation	8071	D	310 216-7776	22263
Punch Studio LLC (PA)	5112	C	310 390-9900	8176
Quadra Productions Inc	7812	C	310 244-1234	18137
Quadrix Information Tech Inc	8748	E	424 603-2140	28027
Reliable Health Care Svcs Inc	7363	E	310 397-2229	14935
Rick Solomon Enterprises Inc (PA)	5136	C	310 280-3700	8359
Roe Holdings LLC	7311	D	310 559-9222	13914
Roman Cath Arch of Los Angels	7261	E	310 836-5500	13712
Security Indust Spcialists Inc (PA)	7381	C	310 215-5100	16816
Social Studies School Service	5049	C	310 839-2436	7349
Sony Media Cloud Services	7812	E	310 244-4000	18153
Sony Pictures Entrmt Inc	7929	B	310 840-8000	18497
Sony Pictures Entrmt Inc	7929	B	310 202-1234	18498
Sony Pictures Entrmt Inc (DH)	7812	A	310 244-4000	18154
Sony Pictures Imageworks Inc	7374	D	310 840-8000	16191
Sony Pictures Television Inc (DH)	7812	B	310 244-7625	18156
Southern Cal Hosp At Culver Cy (HQ)	8062	D	310 836-7000	21900
Spectrum MGT Holdg Co LLC	4841	C	310 417-4260	6023
Stan Tashman & Associates Inc	8741	A	310 460-7600	27229
Starwood Hotel	7011	D	310 641-7740	13288
State Farm Mutl Auto Insur Co	6411	D	310 568-5824	10884
State Farm Mutl Auto Insur Co	6411	D	310 568-5200	10890
Steel House Inc	7311	D	310 773-3331	13923
Sunny TV Productions Inc	7812	C	310 840-7440	18163
Syska & Hennessy Engineers Inc	8711	D	310 312-0200	26082
Topson Downs California Inc (PA)	5137	C	310 558-0300	8414
Totallyfreepagingcom Inc	4812	D	310 845-8700	5420
Transwestern Corp Pointe LLC	6531	D	310 642-1001	11880
Tristar Television Music Inc	7922	E	310 244-4000	18441
Triton Media Group LLC	4832	D	661 294-9000	5825
U S Private Protection SEC Inc	7381	C	310 301-0010	16838
United Refrigeration Inc	5078	D	310 204-2500	7761
Venice Family Clinic	8011	D	310 392-8636	20188
Virgin Fish Inc (PA)	4119	C	310 391-6161	3855
West Publishing Corporation	7373	C	424 243-2100	16081
Westside Childrens Center Inc	8351	D	310 846-4100	24533
Woven Digital Inc (PA)	4899	D	310 488-8941	6101
X Prize Foundation Inc	8399	E	310 741-4880	25000
Xap Corporation (PA)	7371	E	310 743-0450	15552
Zb National Association	6021	D	310 258-9300	9466
Zoic Inc	7812	C	310 838-0770	18209

CUPERTINO, CA - Santa Clara County

Company	SIC	EMP	PHONE	ENTRY #
Arcsight LLC	7371	C	408 864-2600	15029
Aspen Ranch LLC	8361	C	435 836-2080	24553
California Dental Arts LLC	8072	D	408 255-1020	22301
Century 21 Champion	6531	E	408 725-4000	11370
Ch Cupertino Owner LLC	7011	D	408 253-8900	12508
Corinthian Intl Prkg Svcs Inc	7299	B	408 867-7275	13750
CRC Health Corporate (DH)	8093	D	408 367-0044	22718
CRC Health Corporation (DH)	8069	D	877 272-8668	22134
Cupertino Dental Group	8021	D	408 446-4353	20251
Cupertino Healthcare	8051	D	408 253-9034	20509
Digital Keystone Inc	7373	E	650 938-7301	15933
Digite Inc	7371	D	408 418-3834	15140
Ecrio Inc	7372	D	408 973-7290	15647
Epairs Inc	7379	D	408 973-8866	16365
Ewing-Foley Inc (PA)	5065	E	408 342-1201	7562
Forge-Vidovich Motel Limited	7011	D	408 996-7700	12642
Forum Healthcare Center	8051	C	650 944-0200	20579
HP Inc	7382	D	408 886-3200	16890
Huawei Enterprise USA Inc	4813	D	408 330-4295	5632
Ice Center Enterprises LLC	7999	D	510 604-8878	19226
Kaiser Foundation Hospitals	6324	D	408 366-4247	10298
Knova Software Inc (HQ)	7372	E	408 863-5800	15725
Lanwave Technology Inc	8711	E	408 253-3311	25932
Marriott International Inc	7011	C	408 252-9100	12970
Panasonic Corp North America	8731	C	408 861-3900	26583
Pleasant View Convalescent Hos	8059	D	408 253-9034	21350
Rancho San Antonio Retirement	8361	B	650 265-2637	24779
Referral Realty Inc	6531	D	408 996-8100	11801
Self-Help For Elderly	8322	E	408 873-1183	24202
Silver Lake Partners II LP	6726	E	408 454-4732	12145
Stevens Creek Quarry Inc (PA)	1611	D	408 253-2512	1865
Sugarcrm Inc (PA)	7371	C	408 454-6900	15482
Sunny Retirement Home	8059	D	408 454-5600	21387
Trend Micro Incorporated	5045	D	408 257-1500	7203
Z & M Assciates Inc	6531	D	408 996-8100	11933
Zend Technologies Usa Inc	7371	D	408 253-8800	15557

CUTLER, CA - Tulare County

Company	SIC	EMP	PHONE	ENTRY #
Penas Disposal Inc	4953	D	559 528-3909	6513
Richard M Gonzalez	7361	D	559 591-2207	14753
Wawona Packing Co LLC	0723	A	559 528-4000	603
Wawona Packing Co LLC	7389	B	559 528-4699	17616

CYPRESS, CA - Orange County

Company	SIC	EMP	PHONE	ENTRY #
American Honda Finance Corp	6141	D	714 816-8110	9738
Apple Eght Hospitality MGT Inc	7011	D	714 827-1010	12392
Asplundh Tree Expert Co	0783	C	714 893-2405	987
B2b Staffing Services Inc	7363	A	714 243-4104	14842
Barcott Frank A SEC Invstgtons	7381	C	714 891-8556	16570
Beacon Health Options Inc	8322	C	714 763-2405	23678
Bravo Tech Inc	4812	E	714 230-8333	5279
Cal Southern United Food	6371	D	714 220-2297	10542
Caliber Capital Group LLC	6282	A	714 507-1998	10125
Cellco Partnership	4812	D	714 899-4690	5364
Christie Dgtal Systems USA Inc (DH)	5043	C	714 527-7056	7030
Clarion Corporation America (DH)	5064	D	310 327-9100	7492
Consolted Med Bo-Analysis Inc (PA)	8071	C	714 657-7369	22202
Cypress Ctr For Fmly Medicine	8011	D	562 799-4801	19483
Cypress Education Foundation	8641	D	714 220-6900	25249
Daiwa Corporation	5091	D	562 375-6800	8015
Dean Goodman Inc	6531	D	714 229-8999	11466
Focus Diagnostics Inc	8071	B	714 220-1900	22216
Focus Technologies Holding Co	8071	B	800 838-4548	22217
Forest Lawn Memorial-Park Assn	6553	D	714 828-3131	12029
Freeway Insurance (PA)	6411	D	714 252-2500	10722
Fujifilm North America Corp	5043	C	714 372-4200	7032
Global Exprnce Specialists Inc	7389	D	562 310-1500	17190
Healthsmart Management Service	6411	D	714 947-8600	10739
Hoyu America Co	5122	D	714 230-3000	8263
Hybrid Promotions LLC (PA)	5136	D	714 952-3866	8347
Irhythm Technologies Inc	8733	C	714 855-4030	26774
J Perez Associates Inc (PA)	1799	D	562 801-5397	3533
Jvc Americas Corp	7622	D	714 527-7500	17909
Legacy Long Distance Intl Inc	4813	D	800 670-0015	5647
Marriott International Inc	7011	C	714 209-6586	12951
Mercury Defense Systems Inc (HQ)	8711	D	714 898-8200	25962
Mitsubishi Electric Us Inc (DH)	5065	C	714 220-2500	7605
Mitsubishi Motors Cr Amer Inc (DH)	6141	B	714 799-4730	9757
Pacific Pioneer Insur Group (PA)	6411	D	714 228-7888	10822
Pacificare Health Systems LLC (HQ)	6324	A	714 952-1121	10367
Pick-A-Part Auto Wrecking	5093	D	559 485-3071	8080
Pilot Painting & Construction	1721	D	714 229-5900	2474
Plumbing Piping & Cnstr Inc	1711	D	714 821-0490	2325
Premier Disp & Exhibits Inc (PA)	7389	D	562 431-2731	17423
Riphagen & Bullerdick Inc	6531	E	714 763-2100	11814
Scientific Applications & RES (PA)	8731	D	714 828-1465	26601
Siemens Product Life Mgmt Sftw	7371	D	714 952-6500	15453
Silliker Labs Group Inc	8734	E	714 226-0000	26889
Spectrum MGT Holdg Co LLC	4841	C	714 657-1040	6019
Spectrum MGT Holdg Co LLC	4841	C	714 657-1060	6024
Sws2 Inc	7361	D	714 821-6699	14799
Uhc of California (DH)	6324	A	714 952-1121	10384
United Chinese American Genera (PA)	6411	E	714 228-7800	10914
Unitedhealth Group Inc	6324	D	952 936-1300	10387
Ushio America Inc (HQ)	5063	D	714 236-8600	7480

Employment Codes: A=Over 500 employees, B=251-500, C=101-250, D=51-100, E=45-50

CYPRESS, CA

	SIC	EMP	PHONE	ENTRY #
Valueoptions of California	6411	C	800 228-1286	10920
Viad Corp	7389	D	562 370-1500	17590
Western Overseas Corporation (PA)	4731	E	562 985-0616	5189
Yamaha Motor Corporation USA (HQ)	5088	B	714 761-7300	8011
Yamaha Motor Corporation USA	5063	B	714 761-7300	7485
Yamaha Motor Corporation USA	5083	B	714 236-9754	7815

DALY CITY, CA - San Mateo County

	SIC	EMP	PHONE	ENTRY #
American General Life Insur	6411	D	650 994-6679	10595
ARC San Francisco	8322	C	650 756-1304	23666
Bdp Bowl Inc	7933	E	650 878-0300	18510
Casbn Investment Inc	6531	D	650 991-2800	11345
Catholic Chrts Cyo Archdiocs	4151	E	650 757-2110	3915
City of Daly City	8711	D	650 991-8064	25738
Equity One Incorporated	6531	D	415 421-5100	11494
Forte Enterprises Inc (PA)	8741	C	650 994-3200	27028
Genesys Telecom Labs (HQ)	7372	B	650 466-1100	15677
Gerson Baker & Associates	6513	D	650 756-0959	11137
Kaiser Foundation Hospitals	6324	D	650 301-5860	10324
Lake Merced Golf & Country CLB	7997	D	650 755-2233	18975
Larry Blair Realtor	6531	D	650 991-5267	11628
Mission Villa LLC	8361	E	650 756-1995	24737
Nurse Providers Inc	7361	A	650 992-8559	14711
Olympic Club	8641	D	415 404-4300	25305
Oracle Systems Corporation	7371	D	650 506-8648	15358
Pacific Gas and Electric Co	4911	C	650 755-1236	6178
Permanente Medical Group Inc	8011	D	650 301-5860	19866
Reneson Hotels Inc (PA)	7011	D	650 449-5353	13144
Rgis LLC	7389	E	650 757-6770	17459
Roman Catholic Archdiocese of	6553	D	650 756-2060	12035
San Mateo Cnty Pub Hlth Clinic	8093	E	650 301-8600	22827
Seton Medical Center (HQ)	8062	A	650 992-4000	21880
Seton Medical Center	8062	D	650 992-4000	21882
Spinecare Medical Group Inc	8011	D	650 985-7500	20051
St Francis Heights Convales	8059	D	650 755-9515	21383
West Lake Touchless Car Wash	7542	E	650 992-5344	17866
Westlake Nail Spa	7991	D	650 994-7777	18706

DANA POINT, CA - Orange County

	SIC	EMP	PHONE	ENTRY #
Altera Real Estate	6531	B	949 547-7351	11295
Cph Monarch Hotel LLC	7011	A	949 234-3200	12551
Doubletree LLC	7011	D	949 661-1100	12600
Monarch Beach Golf Links (HQ)	7992	D	949 240-8247	18762
North American Health Care Inc (PA)	8741	C	949 240-2423	27145
Pangea Corporation	8999	E	949 443-0666	28153
Pop-Tent Inc	7311	D	949 313-7160	13897
Prutel Joint Venture	7011	A	949 240-2000	13112
Ritz-Carlton Hotel Company LLC	7011	B	949 240-5020	13155
Sunrise Senior Living Inc	8051	D	949 234-3000	20958

DANVILLE, CA - Contra Costa County

	SIC	EMP	PHONE	ENTRY #
2 G Fitness LLC	7991	D	925 838-9200	18577
Ameritac Inc (PA)	8744	D	925 743-8398	27774
Architrends Inc	8711	D	925 648-8800	25661
ATI Engineering Services Inc (PA)	8712	D	925 648-8800	26165
Bara Infoware Inc (PA)	8711	E	925 465-5354	25680
Blackhawk Country Club	7997	C	925 736-6500	18895
Braddock & Logan Group II LP	6552	C	925 736-4000	11952
Braddock & Logan Services Inc	1542	C	925 736-4000	1509
Brookfeld Bay Area Hldngs LLC	6552	D	925 743-8000	11954
Crow Canyon Management Corp	7997	E	925 735-5700	18932
Danville Long-Term Care Inc	8051	D	925 837-4566	20510
Danville Village Skilled Nursn	8099	D	925 837-4566	22937
DW Morgan LLC	4731	D	925 460-2700	5062
Empire Realty Associates Inc	6531	D	925 217-5000	11493
Home For Jewish Parents	8322	D	925 964-2062	24008
James E Roberts-Obayashi Corp	1522	D	925 820-0600	1316
Mason-Mcduffie Real Estate Inc	6531	D	925 837-4281	11661
Pacific Union Homes Inc (PA)	6552	D	925 314-3800	11997
Patelco Credit Union	6061	D	925 785-9487	9620
Royal Ridge Frt Cold Stor LLC	5149	D	925 600-0224	8916
Stratcitycom LLC	7372	D	408 858-0006	15849
Sunrise Senior Living LLC	8322	D	925 309-4178	24241
Tenet Healthsystem Medical	8011	B	925 275-8303	20130
Town of Danville	7999	C	925 314-3400	19296

DAVENPORT, CA - Santa Cruz County

	SIC	EMP	PHONE	ENTRY #
Swanton Berry Farms Inc	0191	E	831 425-8919	395

DAVIS, CA - Yolo County

	SIC	EMP	PHONE	ENTRY #
Anderson Farms Inc	0112	D	530 753-5695	3
Bme Cmgi Uc Davis	8731	B	530 754-5488	26490
Brown and Caldwell	8711	D	530 747-0650	25707
Communicare Health Centers	8011	C	530 758-2060	19450
Covenant Care Courtyard LLC	8051	D	530 756-1800	20502
Davis Community Clinic (PA)	8011	D	530 758-2060	19487
Davis Hallmark Partnership	7011	E	530 753-3320	12565
Doug Arnold Real Estate Inc (PA)	6531	E	530 758-3080	11476
HFS North America LLC (PA)	8748	C	530 758-8253	27944
Hmclause Inc	8731	D	530 747-3235	26529
Ikes Landscaping & Maintenance	0782	D	530 758-1698	871
Kaiser Foundation Hospitals	8011	E	530 757-7100	19665
Mariner Health Care Inc	8051	C	530 758-2060	20763
Mec International	8711		415 866-4497	25961
Novozymes Inc (DH)	8732	D	530 757-8100	26697
Novozymes Us Inc	6719	A	530 757-8100	12079
Omni Consulting Group LLP	8742	D	530 750-5199	27574
Pacific Gas and Electric Co	4911	B	530 757-5803	6188
Pacific Retirement Svcs Inc	8361	D	530 753-1450	24760
Schilling Robotics LLC	8711	D	530 753-6718	26056
Sciots Tract Association	8641	D	530 753-5219	25343
Sutter Health	8011	C	530 747-0389	20078
Sutter Health	8011	A	530 757-5111	20084
Sutter Health	8011	B	530 750-5888	20111
Sutter Hlth Scrmnto Sierra Reg	8011	A	530 747-5010	20114
Sutter Hlth Scrmnto Sierra Reg	8062	D	530 756-6440	21948
Travis Credit Union	6061	B	707 449-4000	9632
Ucd Recreation Hall	7999	D	530 752-6071	19299
Ucdavis	7389	D	530 757-3322	17551
Ucde - Center For Human Svcs	8999	E	530 757-8538	28164
University California Davis	8011	C	530 752-2300	20168
West Yost & Associates Inc (PA)	8711	D	530 756-5905	26145
Woodland Healthcare	8062	D	530 756-2364	22034
Yolo Hospice Inc (PA)	8082	D	530 758-5566	22616

DEATH VALLEY, CA - Inyo County

	SIC	EMP	PHONE	ENTRY #
Xanterra Parks & Resorts Inc	7011	C	760 786-2345	13443

DEL MAR, CA - San Diego County

	SIC	EMP	PHONE	ENTRY #
Aecom Energy & Cnstr Inc	1611	B	858 481-9502	1724
Automobile Club Southern Cal	6411	C	858 481-7181	10640
Brookfield Homes of California	1521	E	858 481-8500	1141
Brookfield Homes Pacific Inc (DH)	1521	D	858 481-8500	1142
Crest Beverage Company Inc	5181	C	858 452-2300	9049
Del Mar Thoroughbred Club	7948	B	858 755-1141	18569
Humetrix Inc	8742	E	858 259-8987	27469
JP Morgan Securities LLC	6211	D	310 201-2693	10021
Lee Johnson	8059	C	858 481-4411	21288
Lhoberge Lessee Inc	7011	E	858 259-1515	12919
Liquid Investments Inc (PA)	5181	C	858 509-8510	9069
Mesa Distributing Coinc (HQ)	5181	C	858 452-2300	9074
Spa Gregories LLC	7231	D	858 481-6672	13691
Ws Hdm LLC	7011	D	858 792-5200	13430
Ws Hdm LLC	7011	C	858 792-5200	13431

DEL REY, CA - Fresno County

	SIC	EMP	PHONE	ENTRY #
Chooljian & Sons Inc (PA)	0723	D	559 888-2031	521
Wonderful Citrus Packing LLC	0723	E	661 720-2400	604

DELANO, CA - Kern County

	SIC	EMP	PHONE	ENTRY #
City of Delano	7992	E	661 721-3350	18723
Clinica Sierra Vista	8021	C	661 725-3882	20250
Coronel Construction Inc	1521	D	661 725-4400	1160
County of Kern	8322	D	661 721-5134	23818
Covanta Delano Inc	4911	D	661 792-3067	6121
Delano Dst Sklled Nrsing Fclty	8051	D	661 720-2100	20517
Delano Farms Company	5148	D	661 721-1485	8715
Hronis Inc A California Corp (PA)	0174	D	661 725-2503	219
Innovel Solutions Inc	4731	A	661 725-5910	5105
Jorge Pimental Diaz	0761	C	661 344-5139	671
M Caratan Inc	0172	A	661 725-1777	169
Monarch Nut Company LLC	0723	C	661 725-6458	564
Moyles Health Care Inc	8059	D	661 725-2501	21321
Munger Bros LLC	0179	A	661 721-0390	258
P C A Farm Management LLC	0762	D	661 720-2400	713
Pandol & Sons	0172	E	661 725-3755	175
Proteus Inc	8322	C	661 721-5800	24141
Railex LLC	4731	D	661 370-4300	5160
San-Joaquin Helicopters Inc	8711	D	661 725-2682	26054
Triple R Transportation Inc	4119	D	661 725-6494	3852
Vista Verde Farms	5149	D	661 720-9733	8954
Wonderful Citrus Packing LLC (HQ)	0723	B	661 720-2400	605
Wonderful Company LLC	0174	D	661 720-2400	225

DELHI, CA - Merced County

	SIC	EMP	PHONE	ENTRY #
Califrnia Psychtric Trnsitions	8011	D	209 667-9304	19398
Richard Swanson Inc	0173	D	209 632-3883	209

DENAIR, CA - Stanislaus County

	SIC	EMP	PHONE	ENTRY #
Hamlow Ranches Inc	0175	E	209 632-2873	234
J Crecelius Inc	0191	D	209 883-4826	372
Montpelier Orchards MGT Co Inc	0175	D	209 883-4079	244
Valley Fresh Foods Inc	0252	D	209 669-5510	449

GEOGRAPHIC SECTION

DESERT HOT SPRINGS, CA - Riverside County

Company	SIC	EMP	PHONE	ENTRY #
Desert Springs Hotel	6512	E	760 251-3399	10974
Two Bunch Palms LLC	7011	D	760 329-8791	13362
Whatever It Takes Inc	7011	E	760 329-6000	13409

DIABLO, CA - Contra Costa County

Company	SIC	EMP	PHONE	ENTRY #
Diablo Country Club	7997	D	925 837-4221	18941
Diablo Country Club	7992	E	925 837-9233	18734

DIAMOND BAR, CA - Los Angeles County

Company	SIC	EMP	PHONE	ENTRY #
24-Hour Med Staffing Svcs LLC	7363	C	909 895-8960	14827
Allstate Insurance Company	6331	A	909 612-5504	10397
American Golf Corporation	7997	D	909 861-5757	18863
E-N Realty II	6531	E	909 597-1736	11484
F M Tarbell Co	6531	E	909 861-3100	11511
First Team RE - Orange Cnty	6531	D	909 861-1380	11528
Futurenet Technologies Corp	7371	C	909 396-4000	15199
Graybar Electric Company Inc	5063	C	909 451-4300	7442
Hdl Coren & Cone	8741	D	909 861-4335	27052
Insperity Inc	8742	D	909 569-1000	27479
Joseph Fan	7011	D	909 860-5440	12868
Kaiser Foundation Hospitals	8011	A	800 780-1277	19611
Legally Yours LLC	8111	C	909 396-7200	23382
Liferay Inc (PA)	7373	D	877 543-3729	15985
March International Inc	1629	E	909 821-5128	2065
Mitsuba Corporation	5045	D	909 374-2631	7164
Motech Americas LLC	8731	B	302 451-7500	26571
Novatime Technology Inc (PA)	7361	D	909 895-8100	14709
Oak Creek LP	7011	D	909 860-5440	13031
Point of View Inc	7371	D	909 860-0705	15387
Qtc Management Inc (HQ)	8099	D	909 396-6902	23038
Schneider Electric Usa Inc	5063	D	909 612-5400	7471
Specialty Equipment Mkt Assn (PA)	8611	D	909 396-0289	25105
Tetra Tech Bas Inc (HQ)	8711	D	909 860-7777	26092
Transport Drivers Inc	7363	B	800 497-6345	14961
Travelers Indemnity Company	6411	C	909 612-3000	10907
Walnut Valley Unified Schl Dst	8351	D	909 444-3460	24529

DIAMOND SPRINGS, CA - El Dorado County

Company	SIC	EMP	PHONE	ENTRY #
Cook Cabinets Inc	1751	D	530 621-0851	3039
County of El Dorado	4953	D	530 626-4141	6469
El Dorado County Transit Auth	4111	D	530 642-5383	3644
Johnsen Construction Inc	1771	D	530 642-2123	3282
Snowline Hspice El Dorado Cnty	8399	D	530 621-7820	24979

DINUBA, CA - Tulare County

Company	SIC	EMP	PHONE	ENTRY #
Boss Poultry	0253	E	559 897-7507	450
Calpine Containers Inc	5113	D	559 591-6555	8188
College Operations LLC	8351	E	559 353-0576	24440
Gillette Citrus Company	0723	C	559 626-4236	535
Mikaelian & Sons Inc	0161	C	559 591-6324	81
New Covenant Care of Dinuba	8051	D	559 591-3300	20805
Patterson Dental Supply Inc	5047	D	559 595-1450	7297
S Surabian & Sons	0174	S	559 591-5215	222
Valley Labor Service Inc	7361	D	559 591-5591	14815

DIXON, CA - Solano County

Company	SIC	EMP	PHONE	ENTRY #
Alonzo Farms Inc	0191	D	707 678-5282	344
Baxter Healthcare Corporation	5047	D	503 285-0212	7242
Button Transportation Inc	4213	C	707 678-1983	4123
Cardinal Health Inc	5047	C	530 406-3600	7253
Carlisle Construction Mtls Inc	5033	D	707 678-6900	7011
Century 21 Dstnctive Prpts Inc	6531	D	707 678-9211	11372
First Northern Bank of Dixon (HQ)	6022	D	707 678-4422	9496
First Student Inc	4111	D	707 678-8679	3645
John Stewart Company	6531	D	707 676-5660	11599
Mayoral Bros	0761	B	707 693-9111	674
Recology Inc	4953	D	916 379-3300	6521

DOS PALOS, CA - Merced County

Company	SIC	EMP	PHONE	ENTRY #
Clark Bros Farming Inc	0131	E	209 392-6144	10
Dos Palos Memorial Hosp Inc	8011	D	209 392-6121	19507

DOWNEY, CA - Los Angeles County

Company	SIC	EMP	PHONE	ENTRY #
American Financial Network Inc	6282	B	562 861-1414	10117
Association For Retarded Citzn (PA)	8331	D	562 803-1556	24311
AT&T Corp	4813	D	562 923-3032	5508
Cantamar Property MGT Inc	6531	E	562 862-4470	11340
Cellco Partnership	4812	D	562 401-1045	5346
Central Refill Pharmaceuticals	5122	D	562 401-4214	8250
Century 21 A Better Svc Rlty	6531	D	562 287-0230	11364
City of Downey	7922	D	562 861-8211	18384
Coldwell Bnkr First Class Rlty	6531	D	323 721-7430	11421
Companion Hospice Care LLC	8082	C	562 944-2711	22410
Companion Hospice LLC	8082	C	562 944-2711	22411
Conrad A Cox	8011	E	562 927-0033	19460
County of Los Angeles	8322	C	562 401-9413	23825
County of Los Angeles	8093	A	562 401-7088	22699
County of Los Angeles	8322	B	562 940-2476	23856
County of Los Angeles	8322	C	562 803-6682	23857
Covenant Care California LLC	8051	D	562 923-9301	20485
Downey Community Health Center	8051	C	562 862-6506	20522
Downey Regional Medical	8062	A	562 698-0811	21547
Downey Retirement Ctr	6513	E	562 869-2416	11121
El Camino Children & Fmly Svcs	8322	E	562 364-1258	23956
Ellite Management Inc	8748	D	562 806-2062	27909
Farwest Corrosion Control Co (PA)	1799	D	310 522-9524	3515
Financial Partners Credit Un (PA)	6061	D	562 904-3000	9596
First Family Homes	6531	E	562 862-7373	11525
Healthcare Ctr of Downey LLC	8051	C	562 869-0978	20658
Hilton Worldwide Inc	7011	D	562 861-1900	12730
Intero Real Estate Svcs Inc	6531	D	562 861-7242	11587
Kaiser Foundation Hospitals	8062	B	562 657-9000	21636
Kaiser Foundation Hospitals	8011	A	800 823-4040	19609
Kaiser Foundation Hospitals	8011	A	800 823-4040	19613
Kaiser Foundation Hospitals	6324	A	562 622-4190	10341
Lakewood Park Health Center (PA)	7389	B	562 869-0978	17286
Liberty Ambulance LLC	4119	D	562 741-6210	3814
Liberty Utilities Pk Wtr Corp (DH)	4941	D	562 923-0711	6363
Los Amigos Country Club Inc	7997	D	562 923-9696	18984
Macerich Company	6512	E	562 861-9233	11014
Mental Hlth Cnvlscent Svcs Inc	8051	B	562 869-0978	20788
Mullahey Chevrolet Inc	7532	E	714 871-2545	17763
Nationwide SEC & Bldg Svcs Inc (PA)	7699	D	800 804-0059	17990
Newwest Mortgage Company	6163	D	562 861-8393	9942
Omniteam Inc	5078	C	562 923-9660	7756
Parking Co Amer Universal Inc	7521	D	562 862-2118	17732
Pioneer Medical Group Inc	8011	D	562 862-2775	19872
Presbyterian Intrcmmnty Hosptl	8062	A	562 904-5482	21806
Prestige Too Auto Body Inc	7532	E	310 787-8852	17768
Prudential 24 Hour Real Estate	6531	D	562 861-7257	11773
Ralphs Grocery Company	4225	D	562 633-0830	4622
Ralphs Grocery Company	4225	D	562 869-2042	4625
Rancho Los Amigos Nationa	8322	B	562 401-7111	24144
Rancho Los Amigos Nationa	8322	A	562 401-7111	24145
Rancho Los Amigos Nationa	8322	A	310 940-7266	24146
Rancho Los Amigos Nationa (PA)	8322	A	562 401-7111	24147
Rancho Research Institute	8733	C	562 401-8111	26800
Rockview Dairies Inc (PA)	5149	C	562 927-5511	8913
Santa Paula Water Works Ltd	6719	D	562 923-0711	12089
Sanwa Jutaku Co Ltd	7011	E	562 861-1900	13219
Southern Cal Prmnnte Med Group	8099	A	562 657-2200	23061
Southern California Alcohol An (PA)	8093	D	562 923-4545	22838
Southern California Gas Co	4924	E	562 803-7453	6279
Southland Credit Union	6062	D	562 862-6831	9691
Spectrum MGT Holdg Co LLC	4841	D	562 372-4008	6022
Steve Roberson	6531	D	562 927-2626	11858
Sunbridge Healthcare LLC	8052	C	562 869-2567	21116
Tarsco Inc (DH)	7699	C	562 231-5400	18021
USF Reddaway Inc	4213	A	562 923-0648	4296
Westar Manufacturing Inc	1799	D	562 633-0581	3603
Young Mens Chrstn Assn of La	8322	C	562 862-4201	24295
Young Mens Chrstn Assn of La	8641	D	562 862-4201	25469

DUARTE, CA - Los Angeles County

Company	SIC	EMP	PHONE	ENTRY #
Beckman Research Inst Hope	8733	C	626 359-8111	26738
Begroup	8051	D	626 359-9371	20408
Bershtel Enterprises LLC (PA)	7389	C	626 301-9214	17029
Cal Southern Presbt Homes	8051	D	626 359-8141	20430
Cal Southern Presbt Homes	6513	C	626 357-1632	11109
City Hope National Medical Ctr	8062	A	626 256-4673	21495
City of Hope	8399	C	213 202-5735	24889
ESP Group Ltd	5137	D	626 301-0280	8382
Event Guard Services Inc	7381	D	626 531-6772	16636
General Electric Company	7378	C	626 359-7988	16295
Integrated Mech Systems Inc	1711	E	626 446-1854	2254
Kf Community Care LLC	8059	C	626 357-3207	21279
Maryvale Day Care Center	8351	D	626 357-1514	24481
Monrovia Convalescent Hospital	8059	D	626 359-6618	21318
Royal Terrace Healthcare	8051	D	626 256-4654	20883
Santa Teresita Inc (PA)	8062	C	626 359-3243	21864
United Hauling Corp	7513	D	626 358-9417	17656
Westminster Gardens	8059	D	626 359-2571	21420

DUBLIN, CA - Alameda County

Company	SIC	EMP	PHONE	ENTRY #
4g Wireless Inc	4813	D	925 307-8990	5440
AMS Electric Inc	1731	D	925 961-1600	2520
AT&T Corp	7389	B	925 560-5011	17007
Bay Area News Group E Bay LLC (HQ)	7319	D	925 302-1683	13989
Callidus Software Inc (PA)	7371	D	925 251-2200	15073
Care Options Management Plans	8082	D	925 551-3227	22389
Cellco Partnership	4812	D	925 847-0320	5382
Challenge Dairy Products Inc (HQ)	5143	D	925 828-6160	8582

Employment Codes: A=Over 500 employees, B=251-500, C=101-250, D=51-100, E=45-50

2017 Directory of California Wholesalers and Services Companies

DUBLIN, CA

	SIC	EMP	PHONE	ENTRY #
Corelynx Inc	7371	C	877 267-3599	15109
Corizon Health Inc	8011	C	925 551-6500	19463
Desilva Gates Construction LP (PA)	1611	D	925 361-1380	1765
Develpment Dimensions Intl Inc	8742	B	925 361-4246	27409
Ecorptech LLC	7363	E	408 216-8116	14872
Epicor Software Corporation	7372	C	925 361-9900	15657
Franklin Tmpleton Inv Svcs LLC	6282	C	925 875-2619	10147
Gateway Landscape Cnstr Inc	0782	C	925 875-0000	857
Gettler-Ryan Inc (PA)	1799	C	925 551-7555	3524
Ipac Inc	7389	C	925 556-5530	17251
Joint Labor Mgmt Coop Committe	1731	D	925 828-6322	2628
Lusardi Construction Co	1542	C	925 829-1114	1603
Micro Dental Laboratories (HQ)	8072	C	925 829-3611	22311
New Home Professionals	6531	C	925 556-1555	11705
Pacific Sttes Envmtl Cntrs Inc	1542	E	925 803-4333	1627
Rakon America LLC	5065	A	847 930-5100	7624
Rgis LLC	7389	C	925 829-2875	17453
Rockin Jump Inc	7999	D	925 401-7200	19269
Sanrise Inc	7374	C	925 560-3900	16181
Service King Paint & Body LLC	7532	C	925 829-5571	17771
Sybase 365 LLC	4812	C	925 236-5000	5412
Taleo Corporation	7372	D	925 452-3000	15856
Trevi Partners A Calif LP (HQ)	7011	D	925 828-7750	13356
Water & Sewer Service	1623	D	925 828-8524	2014

DUNCANS MILLS, CA - Sonoma County

	SIC	EMP	PHONE	ENTRY #
Russian River Sportsman Club	7997	D	707 865-9429	19052

DURHAM, CA - Butte County

	SIC	EMP	PHONE	ENTRY #
Chico Produce Inc (PA)	5148	C	530 893-0596	8705
Fedex Ground Package Sys Inc	4213	C	530 534-5924	4177

E RNCHO DMNGZ, CA - Los Angeles County

	SIC	EMP	PHONE	ENTRY #
Dependable Global Express Inc	4731	C	310 537-2000	5057
Murray Plumbing and Htg Corp (PA)	1711	D	310 637-1500	2302

EARLIMART, CA - Tulare County

	SIC	EMP	PHONE	ENTRY #
Vincent V Zaninovich & Sons	0172	D	661 849-2613	193

EARP, CA - San Bernardino County

	SIC	EMP	PHONE	ENTRY #
Colorado River Adventures Inc (PA)	7033	C	760 663-3737	13478

EAST PALO ALTO, CA - Santa Clara County

	SIC	EMP	PHONE	ENTRY #
Burr Pilger Mayer Inc	8721	E	650 855-6800	26303
Cintas Corporation No 3	7218	D	650 589-4300	13627
County of San Mateo	8322	D	650 853-3139	23913
Dla Piper LLP (us)	8111	B	650 833-2000	23219
Dla Piper LLP (us)	8111	B	650 833-2000	23221
Drew Health Foundation	8399	E	650 328-1619	24914
Duff & Phelps LLC	8742	D	650 798-5500	27416
East Palo Alto Hotel Dev Inc	7011	D	650 566-1200	12607
East Palo Alto Y M C A	8641	E	650 328-9622	25252
Four Seasons Hotel Inc	7011	A	650 566-1200	12648
Golf & Tennis Pro Shop Inc	7999	D	650 600-5200	19218
Greenberg Traurig LLP	8111	D	650 328-8500	23290
Hggc LLC (PA)	6799	B	650 321-4910	12314
Howrey LLP	8111	D	650 798-3300	23313
Riley & Powell MD	8011	E	650 328-0511	19920
Ropes & Gray LLP	8111	B	650 617-4000	23540
Roto-Rooter Services Company	7699	D	650 322-2366	18007
South Cnty Cmnty Hlth Ctr Inc (PA)	8099	D	650 330-7407	23060

EASTVALE, CA - Riverside County

	SIC	EMP	PHONE	ENTRY #
Mentor Media (usa) Sup	8741	D	909 930-0800	27126

EDGEWOOD, CA - Siskiyou County

	SIC	EMP	PHONE	ENTRY #
Siskiyou Development Company	7011	D	530 938-2731	13259

EDISON, CA - Kern County

	SIC	EMP	PHONE	ENTRY #
Giumarra Farms Inc	0134	D	661 395-7000	19
Giumarra Vineyards Corporation (PA)	0172	B	661 395-7000	156
Johnston Farms	0134	D	661 366-3201	20
Kirschenman Enterprises Sls LP	7389	B	661 366-5736	17274
Kirschenman Packing Inc	0723	C	661 366-5736	554

EDWARDS, CA - Kern County

	SIC	EMP	PHONE	ENTRY #
Jt3 LLC	8711	A	661 277-4900	25912
US Dept of the Air Force	4899	C	661 277-3030	6097
US Dept of the Air Force	8731	D	661 275-5410	26631

EDWARDS AFB, CA - Kern County

	SIC	EMP	PHONE	ENTRY #
GE Aviation Systems LLC	4581	C	661 277-7308	4920

EL CAJON, CA - San Diego County

	SIC	EMP	PHONE	ENTRY #
16 3 Inc	1761	D	619 588-2000	3134
A Better Solution In Home Care	8082	C	619 447-1528	22315
Aeromedevac Inc	8742	D	619 284-7910	27307
AJM Packaging Corporation	5199	D	619 448-4007	9242
American Residential Svcs LLC	1711	D	858 292-4452	2132
Anthony P Garofalo A Dental	8021	D	619 440-0071	20246
ARC of San Diego	8399	C	619 448-2415	24872
AT&T Corp	4812	D	619 660-0637	5264
Automotive Service Council	8699	D	800 810-4272	25504
California Shtmtl Works Inc	1541	D	619 562-7010	1411
Care With Dignity Healthcare	8051	D	619 447-1020	20437
Cass Construction Inc (PA)	1623	C	619 590-0929	1916
Cellco Partnership	4812	D	619 596-7201	5308
Classic Residential Inc	1521	D	619 818-5793	1155
Coit Clg & Restoration Svcs	7217	A	619 726-4734	13595
Country Hills Health Care Inc	8051	D	619 441-8745	20473
Countywide Mech Systems Inc	1711	C	619 449-9900	2193
Cox Communications Cal LLC	4841	B	619 562-9820	5979
Demko Drywall & Demolition Co	1742	E	619 590-0025	2885
Division 8 Inc	1793	D	619 741-7552	3409
EC Closing Corp	6162	D	800 546-1531	9838
Edwards Theatres Circuit Inc	7832	D	619 660-3460	18323
El Cajon Motors (PA)	7515	D	619 579-8888	17699
El Cajon Plumbing & Htg Sup Co	5075	E	619 449-7300	7737
El Cajon Vly Convalescent Ctr	8051	C	619 440-1211	20528
Eldorado Care Center LP	8051	B	619 440-1211	20531
Eugene N Townsend	7532	D	619 442-8807	17752
Executive Protection Agency K-	7381	E	619 442-5771	16639
F R Ghianni Enterprises Inc	1521	D	619 279-1073	1173
Fox Factory Holding Corp	5013	A	619 768-1800	6732
G M A C-One Source Realty	6531	D	619 405-6231	11550
Gardner Pool Company Inc (PA)	1799	D	619 593-8880	3523
Global Check Service	7389	C	619 449-5150	17188
Granite Hills Healthcare	8051	D	619 440-2036	20636
Grossmont-Cuyamaca Community	8641	D	619 644-7684	25268
Hamann Construction	1541	D	619 440-7424	1435
Helix Water District	4941	D	619 466-0585	6354
Home Guiding Hands Corporation (PA)	8361	B	619 938-2850	24694
Inland Kenworth (us) Inc	5012	E	619 328-1600	6682
Jeffrey Pine Holdings LLC	8051	D	619 442-0544	20691
K T A Construction Inc	1623	E	619 562-9464	1954
Kaiser Foundation Hospitals	8062	E	619 528-5000	21651
Kaiser Foundation Hospitals	8062	E	619 528-5000	21653
Koch-Armstrong General Engrg	8711	D	619 561-2005	25925
La Maestra Family Clinic Inc	8011	D	619 280-1155	19692
Lundstrom & Associates Inc	8711	D	619 641-5900	25943
Madison Care Center LLC	8051	D	619 444-1107	20753
Magnolia Special Care Center	8052	D	619 442-8826	21090
Mc Clintock Enterprises	4141	D	619 579-5300	3894
Nan McKay and Associates Inc	8742	D	619 258-1855	27557
National Public Safety	7381	D	619 401-9431	16742
Neighborhood Healthcare	8011	D	619 440-2751	19768
Newport Diversified Inc	7389	D	619 449-7800	17357
Newport Diversified Inc	7389	C	619 448-3147	17358
Our Lady of Grace P T G	7389	E	619 466-0055	17385
Pacific Production Plumbing (PA)	1711	E	951 509-3100	2315
Paradise Electric Inc	1731	D	619 449-4141	2680
Parkside Special Care Center	8051	D	619 442-7744	20841
Patric Communications Inc (PA)	1731	D	619 579-2898	2681
Plum Healthcare Group LLC	8051	C	619 873-2500	20854
Premier Golf Properties LP	7992	D	619 442-9891	18770
Probuild Company LLC	5031	E	619 440-7711	6951
Prommis Solutions LLC	6211	B	619 590-9200	10071
R D S Unlimited Inc	1751	E	619 443-0221	3077
San Diego Aerospace Museum	8412	D	619 258-1221	25040
San Diego Blood Bank	8099	C	619 441-1804	23047
Schilling Paradise Corp	1623	C	619 449-4141	1994
Seal Electric Inc	1731	C	619 449-7323	2728
Somerset Special Care Center	8052	D	619 442-0245	21111
Southern Cal Prmnnte Med Group	8011	E	619 528-5000	20032
St Madeleine Sophies Center	8331	D	619 442-5129	24392
Steve Duich Inc	1771	E	619 444-6118	3337
Sunfood Corporation	5149	D	619 596-7979	8929
Sunshine Communications Inc	1731	C	619 448-7600	2758
Sycuan Casino	7999	A	619 445-6002	19291
The Pines Ltd	6513	C	619 447-1880	11213
Thomas J Hoban (PA)	6531	D	619 442-1665	11874
Timesharerentorsell Com LLC	7389	E	888 872-2517	17532
Tony Gomez Tree Service	0783	D	619 593-1552	999
University Mechanical & (DH)	1711	D	619 956-2500	2403
USA Waste of California Inc	4953	D	619 596-5117	6581
Victoria Post Acute Care	8059	C	619 440-5005	21410
Walter Anderson Plumbing Inc	1711	C	619 449-7646	2413
Waste Management Cal Inc	4953	D	619 596-5100	6598
Way Cool Homecare Inc	8082	E	619 444-3200	22614
West Coast AC Co Inc	1711	C	619 561-8000	2415
Xl Staffing Inc	7361	C	619 579-0442	14822

EL CENTRO, CA - Imperial County

	SIC	EMP	PHONE	ENTRY #
Accentcare Home Health	8082	E	760 352-4022	22323
All Star Seed (PA)	0723	D	760 482-9400	506

GEOGRAPHIC SECTION

EL SEGUNDO, CA

	SIC	EMP	PHONE	ENTRY #
ARC - Imperial Valley (PA)	8322	D	760 352-0180	23664
Canon Solutions America Inc	7389	D	800 323-4827	17051
Cellco Partnership	4812	D	760 337-5508	5365
City of El Centro	1611	C	760 337-4505	1748
County of Imperial	8099	C	760 482-4441	22926
County of Imperial	8322	D	760 336-3581	23813
County of Imperial	8093	D	760 482-4120	22698
El Centro Regional Medical Ctr (PA)	8062	A	760 339-7100	21553
Employment Dev Cal Dept	7361	E	760 339-2709	14650
Granite Construction Inc	1611	C	760 337-3030	1784
Halliburton Energy Svcs Inc	1389	D	760 353-2710	1079
Harbor Freight Tools Usa Inc	4731	C	760 336-0532	5095
Hay Kuhn Inc	5199	E	760 353-0124	9270
I N C Builders Inc	7363	B	760 352-4200	14886
Imperial County Behavioral HLT	8093	D	760 482-2149	22749
Imperial Irrigation District	4931	D	760 339-9800	6288
Noblesse Oblige Inc	0722	A	760 353-3336	498
Original Sid Blackman Plbg Inc	1711	D	760 352-3632	2314
Schaefer Ambulance Service Inc	4119	E	760 353-3380	3842
Securitas SEC Svcs USA Inc	7381	C	760 353-8177	16792
Simplexgrinnell LP	5063	D	760 336-0109	7474
South Pacific Financial Corp	8742	D	760 353-5185	27658
Southern Building & Con Inc	1771	E	760 337-8932	3333
Time Warner Cable Inc	4841	D	760 335-4800	6051
Valencia Bros Inc	1771	D	760 353-2168	3345
Vib Corp	6022	A	760 352-5000	9534
Wilbur-Ellis Company LLC	5191	D	760 352-2847	9158

EL CERRITO, CA - Contra Costa County

	SIC	EMP	PHONE	ENTRY #
Berkeley Clinic Auxuillary	8699	D	510 525-7844	25506
Mira Vista Golf and Cntry CLB	7997	D	510 233-7550	19001
Office of Special Services	7389	D	510 524-9559	17374
Shields Nursing Centers Inc	8051	D	510 525-3212	20912
West Coast Childrens Center	8011	E	510 269-9030	20233

EL DORADO, CA - El Dorado County

	SIC	EMP	PHONE	ENTRY #
Conforti Plumbing Inc	1711	A	530 622-0202	2188

EL DORADO HILLS, CA - El Dorado County

	SIC	EMP	PHONE	ENTRY #
Action Home Nursing Services	8082	D	530 756-2600	22333
Amdocs Inc	7371	B	916 934-7000	15008
Amdocs Bcs Inc	7371	B	916 934-7000	15009
Bayview Engrg & Cnstr Co Inc	1711	D	916 939-8986	2160
California Physicians Service	6324	D	916 350-7800	10265
Coldwell Bnkr Rsdntial RE Svcs	6531	D	916 933-1155	11439
Comerit Inc	7379	C	888 556-5990	16338
Consensus Orthopedics Inc	5047	D	916 355-7110	7259
Dorado Software Inc	7371	D	916 673-1100	15146
Dst Output California Inc	7378	C	916 939-4617	16291
Frank Gates Service Company	8742	D	916 934-0812	27439
G R Helm Inc	7363	D	916 933-9697	14881
Lyon Realty	6531	D	916 939-5300	11646
Marshall Medical Center	8062	C	916 933-2273	21728
O1 Communications Inc	4813	D	888 444-1111	5671
Patrick K Willis and Co Inc	7389	B	800 398-6480	17405
R Systems Inc (HQ)	7379	C	916 939-9696	16469
Response 1 Medical Staffing	7361	C	916 932-0430	14752
Roebbelen Construction Inc	1542	B	916 939-4000	1654
Roebbelen Contracting Inc	1542	B	916 939-4000	1655
School Innovations Achievement (PA)	7372	D	916 933-2290	15835
Serrano Associates LLC	7997	D	916 933-5005	19072
Serrano Country Club Inc	7997	D	916 933-5005	19073
Sierra Equipment Leasing Inc	7359	E	925 676-7300	14579
Suds Car Wash Inc	7542	E	916 673-6300	17862
Weckworth Construction Co Inc	1731	D	916 939-6636	2791
Wyndgate Technologies	7379	D	916 404-8400	16528
Yamas Controls Group Inc (PA)	5075	E	916 357-6000	7751

EL GRANADA, CA - San Mateo County

	SIC	EMP	PHONE	ENTRY #
Indyne	8621	D	805 606-0664	25138
Range Generation Next LLC	8748	E	310 647-9438	28034

EL MACERO, CA - Yolo County

	SIC	EMP	PHONE	ENTRY #
El Macero Country Club Inc	7997	D	530 753-3363	18946

EL MONTE, CA - Los Angeles County

	SIC	EMP	PHONE	ENTRY #
Access Services	4111	D	213 270-6000	3630
Ahm Gemch Inc	8062	C	626 579-7777	21436
Bangkit (usa) Inc	5112	D	626 672-0888	8160
California Schl Employees Assn	7363	B	626 258-3300	14849
Cathay Bank (HQ)	6022	C	626 279-3698	9479
Center Medical Company	8011	E	626 575-7500	19416
County of Los Angeles	8322	D	626 574-4059	23823
County of Los Angeles	8361	D	626 455-4700	24613
Edwards Theatres Circuit Inc	7832	D	626 580-7660	18334
Eighty One Enterprise Inc	5137	E	626 371-1980	8381
El Monte Community Credit Un	6062	D	626 444-0501	9666
El Monte Convalescent Hospital	8059	D	626 442-1500	21208
Employee Health System Medical	8621	D	866 430-4288	25134
Enki Health and RES Systems	8322	C	626 227-0341	23961
ERs SEC Alarm Systems Inc	5063	D	626 579-2525	7440
Events Bio Services Inc	5099	C	626 350-4490	8113
Exterran Inc	7353	D	626 455-0739	14481
Firefighter Cancer Support Ntw	8322	E	866 994-3276	23979
First Student Inc	4111	D	626 448-9446	3646
Foundation For Early Childhood (PA)	8322	D	626 572-5107	23981
Georgia Atkison Snf LLC	8051	D	626 444-2535	20596
Gibralter Convalescent Hosp	8059	D	626 443-9425	21234
Healthcare Partners LLC	8011	D	626 444-0333	19549
Hope Hse For Mltpl-Handicapped (PA)	8361	D	626 443-1313	24695
K T Lucky Co Inc	5149	D	626 571-7725	8863
Mammoet Western Inc	4213	D	626 444-4942	4215
Neighborhood Legal Svcs LLC	8111	D	626 572-9330	23465
Nestle Waters North Amer Inc	5149	D	626 443-3236	8886
Nijjar Realty Inc (PA)	6531	D	626 575-0691	11707
Optics Laboratory Inc	8071	D	626 350-1926	22249
Pacific Coast Drum Company	5085	D	626 443-3096	7944
Public Hlth Fndation Entps Inc	8099	C	626 856-6618	23037
R and L Lopez Associates Inc (PA)	8711	D	626 336-9655	26028
Ramona Care Center Inc	8051	D	626 442-5721	20862
Rio Hondo Community Dev Corp	8399	D	626 401-2784	24968
S & S Portable Services Inc	7359	D	626 967-9300	14576
S & S Rent-A-Fence Inc	7359	D	818 896-7710	14577
SA Recycling LLC	4953	D	626 444-9530	6552
Sabu Enterprises Inc	8059	E	626 443-1351	21364
San Gabriel Transit Inc (PA)	4111	C	626 258-1310	3709
San Gabriel Valley Water Co (PA)	4941	C	626 448-6183	6395
San Gbriel Vly Cnvlescent Hosp	8063	D	626 401-1557	22090
Tiger Financial Management LLC	6099	D	626 448-2400	9724
Trap	7389	D	626 572-5610	17542
Triple-E Machinery Moving Inc	4213	D	626 444-1137	4280
Turn Around Communications Inc	1623	D	626 443-2400	2004
Vons Companies Inc	4225	D	626 350-8405	4657
Washington Inventory Service	7389	D	626 288-1200	17610
Wells Fargo Bank National Assn	6021	D	626 312-3006	9440
Wells Fargo Bank National Assn	6021	D	626 573-1338	9447
Wgg Enterprises Inc	1742	C	626 442-5493	3001

EL SEGUNDO, CA - Los Angeles County

	SIC	EMP	PHONE	ENTRY #
24hr Homecare LLC	8361	D	310 906-3683	24537
Accenture LLP	8742	B	310 726-2700	27294
Advantage Sales & Mktg Inc	5141	C	310 321-6869	8449
Aerospace Corporation (PA)	8733	A	310 336-5000	26722
After-Party2 Inc	7359	D	310 535-3660	14507
Air Force US Dept of	8733	B	310 336-5000	26729
Air New Zealand Limited	4512	D	310 648-7000	4780
ARC Hospitality Portfolio	7011	E	310 333-0818	12396
Arinwine Arcft Maint Svcs LLC	4581	D	310 338-0063	4902
Asset Athene Management L P (HQ)	8741	D	310 698-4444	26929
BMC Group Inc	8111	D	310 321-5555	23124
Boeing Satellite Systems	5088	C	310 662-9000	7995
Booz Allen Hamilton Inc	8711	C	310 524-1557	25699
BT Americas Inc	5065	D	310 335-2600	7537
BT Americas Inc	5065	D	646 487-7400	7538
California Physicians Service	6324	C	310 744-2668	10266
Cambria Global Tactical Fund 2	6722	D	310 683-5500	12108
Carson Kurtzman Consultants (DH)	8111	C	310 823-9000	23146
Cathay Pacific Airways Limited	4729	D	310 615-1113	5006
Cbre Inc	6531	C	310 363-4900	11355
Century Pk Capitl Partners LLC (PA)	6726	D	310 867-2210	12137
Cetera Financial Group Inc (HQ)	7389	C	800 879-8100	17066
Chipton-Ross Inc (wisconsin)	7361	B	310 414-7800	14624
Citigroup Global Markets Inc	6211	D	310 727-9533	9975
City National Bank	6021	D	310 297-6606	9388
Cls Trnsprttion Los Angeles LLC (HQ)	4119	D	310 414-8189	3782
Conill Advertising Inc	7311	C	424 290-4400	13826
Conill Advertising Inc	7311	D	424 290-4400	13827
Continental 155 5th Corp	6531	E	310 640-1520	11452
Core Nutrition LLC	5149	D	310 640-0500	8820
CSC Consulting Inc	7379	D	310 563-2062	16346
CSRA LLC	7379	E	310 615-0311	16347
David & Goliath LLC	7311	C	310 445-5200	13831
Daz Systems Inc (PA)	7371	D	310 640-1300	15124
Dedicated Media Inc (PA)	7311	D	310 524-9400	13836
Directv Customer Services Inc (DH)	4841	D	310 964-5000	5985
Directv Enterprises LLC	4841	A	310 535-5000	5986
Directv Group Holdings LLC (HQ)	4841	D	310 964-5000	5989
Directv Group Inc (DH)	4841	D	310 964-5000	5990
Directv International Inc (DH)	4841	D	310 964-6460	5991
Diverse Journeys Inc (PA)	8322	D	310 643-7403	23947
Doubletree By Hilton Hotel	7011	D	310 322-0999	12588
Ebsco Industries Inc	5192	D	310 322-5000	9163
Edwards Technologies Inc	1731	D	310 536-7070	2581

Employment Codes: A=Over 500 employees, B=251-500, C=101-250, D=51-100, E=45-50

EL SEGUNDO, CA

Company	SIC	EMP	PHONE	ENTRY #
El Segundo Eductl Foundation	8399	B	310 615-2650	24919
EMC Corporation	7375	E	310 341-1600	16234
Empire Chauffeur Service Ltd	4212	D	310 414-8189	4014
En Pointe Technologies Sls LLC	5045	C	310 337-5200	7126
Ernst & Young LLP	8721	F	310 725-1764	26338
European Hotl Invstrs of CA	7011	E	310 322-0999	12626
Excela Technology Inc	7373	D	310 607-9400	15946
Experian Info Solutions Inc	8742	C	310 343-6700	27428
F&E Aircraft Maintenance (PA)	4581	E	310 338-0063	4918
Fc El Segundo LLC	7011	D	702 439-7945	12632
Federal Express Corporation	7389	B	310 563-4176	17164
Forsythe Solutions Group Inc	7379	D	424 217-6500	16374
Frito-Lay North America Inc	4225	E	310 322-5001	4553
Fujitsu America Inc	7373	D	310 563-7000	15954
Fujitsu Glovia Inc (HQ)	7371	C	310 563-7000	15196
Glovia Inc	7371	C	310 563-7000	15207
Governmentjobscom Inc	7372	D	310 606-6304	15682
Hco Holding I Corporation (HQ)	6719	D	323 583-5000	12068
Healthcare Partners LLC (HQ)	8011	A	310 354-4200	19551
Hilton El Segundo LLC	7011	E	310 726-0100	12705
Hilton Garden Inns MGT LLC	7011	E	310 726-0100	12709
HP Enterprise Services LLC	7374	C	310 331-1074	16142
Ignited LLC (PA)	7311	D	310 773-3100	13863
Infonet Services Corporation	4225	A	310 335-2600	4577
Infonet Services Corporation (DH)	4813	A	310 335-2859	5636
Infrascale Inc	7372	C	310 878-2621	15704
Integrated Data Services Inc (PA)	7371	D	310 647-3439	15241
Integrity Mrtg Solutions Inc	6162	E	310 643-8700	9860
International Rectifier Corp	8721	A	310 726-8000	26378
Internet Brands Inc (PA)	7374	C	310 280-4000	16150
Irise (PA)	7371	D	800 556-0399	15257
Ispace Inc	7379	D	310 563-3800	16414
Jackson Tull Chrtred Engineers	7373	E	310 658-2132	15976
Jalux Americas Inc (HQ)	7359	E	310 524-1000	14552
Japan Airlines Co Ltd	4724	D	310 607-2305	4963
Katch	7311	D	310 219-6200	13873
Kleinpartners Capital Corp	6799	B	310 426-2055	12318
Konami Digital Entrmt Inc	7372	D	310 220-8100	15726
Kyocera International Inc	5043	D	310 647-2805	7036
L E Coppersmith Inc (PA)	4731	D	310 607-8000	5114
L E Coppersmith Inc	4731	D	310 607-8000	5115
Leidos Inc	8731	C	310 524-3134	26552
Liberty Mutual Insurance Co	6331	E	310 316-9428	10432
Login Consulting Services Inc	7379	D	310 607-9091	16426
Los Angeles Lakers Inc	7941	D	310 426-6000	18554
Los Angeles Kings Hockey CLB LP	7941	D	310 535-4502	18556
Manduka LLC (HQ)	5091	E	310 426-1495	8022
Mantech International Corp	7373	C	310 765-9324	15991
Marketwire Inc (DH)	7383	D	310 765-3200	16949
Marriott International Inc	7011	C	310 333-0888	12962
Marriott International Inc	7011	C	310 322-0700	12968
Mattel Inc	7371	D	310 227-8230	15294
Mattel Toy Company	5092	A	310 252-2357	8049
Mission Critical Tech Inc	7371	E	310 246-4455	15307
Mullin TBG Insur Agcy Svcs LLC (DH)	6411	D	310 203-8770	10792
Nagra Usa Inc (HQ)	5084	D	310 335-5225	7866
National Air Cargo Inc	4731	D	310 662-4766	5126
National Planning Corporation	6141	C	800 881-7174	9759
NBC Suite Hotel	7011	D	310 640-3600	13017
Netapp Inc	7373	E	310 426-1700	16008
Nippon Express USA Inc	4731	D	310 535-7200	5132
NRG El Segundo Operations Inc	4911	D	310 615-6344	6155
Oracle Corporation	7372	B	310 343-7405	15803
Orbital Sciences Corporation	8731	B	703 406-5000	26578
Osata Enterprises Inc	5139	D	310 297-1550	8441
Pacific Theaters Inc	7832	D	310 607-0007	18341
Patterson Dental Supply Inc	5047	D	310 426-3100	7295
Peopleware Technical Resources	7361	D	310 640-2406	14726
Performance Team Frt Sys Inc (PA)	4731	C	562 345-2200	5151
Plumb Tech Inc	1711	D	310 322-4925	2323
Primary Color Systems Corp	7335	C	310 841-0250	14132
Prodege LLC (PA)	4813	D	310 294-9599	5687
Professional Janitorial Svc	7349	E	310 410-1452	14395
Prologic Rdmption Slutions Inc (PA)	7389	A	310 322-7774	17434
Prosum Inc (PA)	7374	D	310 404-1545	16172
PWC STRategy& (us) LLC	8742	D	281 685-8325	27602
Radica Enterprises Ltd	5092	D	310 252-2000	8052
Rainier Financial Group LLC	7389	E	310 335-9200	17443
Raytheon Command and Control	5065	E	714 446-3232	7626
Raytheon Company	8711	C	310 647-9438	26035
Renal Treatment Centers Inc (HQ)	8733	D	310 536-2400	26802
Rhythm and Hues Inc (PA)	7812	D	310 448-7500	18144
Rpd Hotels 18 LLC (PA)	7011	A	213 746-1531	13177
Rubicon B Hacienda LLC	7011	B	424 290-5555	13179
Rydek Eletronics LLC	7361	D	310 641-9800	14776
Savvis Communications Corp	7373	D	310 726-1166	16043
SC Harp El Segundo LLC	7011	D	310 322-0999	13223
Scope Seven LLC	5099	D	310 220-3939	8139
Securitas Critical Infrastruct	7381	A	310 426-3300	16783
Singapore Airlines Limited	4512	C	310 647-1922	4820
Softscript Inc	7338	A	310 451-2110	14169
Source Interlink Media LLC	7371	D	310 531-9394	15472
Square Enix Inc	5045	C	310 846-0400	7195
Stampscom Inc (PA)	7331	C	310 482-5800	14091
T G Construction	1522	E	310 321-5900	1343
TBG Insurance Services Corp	6411	D	310 203-8770	10903
Tecolote Research Inc	8742	C	310 640-4700	27680
Telenet Voip Inc	7629	D	310 253-9000	17946
Ten Enthusiast Network LLC (HQ)	5192	C	310 531-9900	9173
Time Warner Cable Entps LLC	4841	A	469 665-7735	6029
Time Warner Cable Inc	4841	D	310 647-3000	6049
Trace3 Inc	8742	D	310 220-0164	27693
Transportation Management LLC	4212	E	310 524-1555	4073
Tri-Star Ccw Management L P	7011	D	310 322-0999	13359
US Dept of the Air Force	7373	C	310 363-1155	16072
Vagabond Inn Corporation (HQ)	7011	D	213 284-7533	13372
Vision Tech Solutions LLC	4813	D	310 656-3100	5727
Vista Investments LLC (PA)	7011	D	213 284-7500	13382
Wash Mltfmily Ldry Systems LLC (PA)	7215	C	310 643-8491	13578
Westport Capital Partners LLC	6799	D	310 294-1234	12334
Whelan Security Co	7381	A	310 343-8628	16852
Wyle Information Systems LLC	7374	C	310 563-6694	16211
Xceed Financial Credit Union (PA)	6061	D	800 932-8222	9648
Your Man Tours Inc (DH)	4725	D	310 649-3820	5004
Your Man Tours Inc	8699	D	513 772-4411	25603

EL SOBRANTE, CA - Contra Costa County

Company	SIC	EMP	PHONE	ENTRY #
D & H Landscaping Inc	0782	D	510 223-6597	830
Greenridge Senior Care	8361	C	510 758-9600	24674
Ppm Real Estate Inc	6531	D	510 758-5636	11758

EL TORO, CA - Orange County

Company	SIC	EMP	PHONE	ENTRY #
Certainteed Gypsum Inc	5031	E	949 282-5300	6913
Cohen Richard Ldscp & Cnstr	0782	E	949 768-0599	827
Frito-Lay North America Inc	5145	D	949 586-4644	8619
Hallmark Rehabilitation GP LLC	8322	A	949 282-5900	24000
Sunset Landscape Maintenance	0782	D	949 455-4636	961

ELK GROVE, CA - Sacramento County

Company	SIC	EMP	PHONE	ENTRY #
Alldata LLC (HQ)	7372	C	916 684-5200	15578
Banner Bank	6021	D	916 685-6546	9338
Bennathon Corp (PA)	1542	E	916 405-2100	1503
Bradshaw Veterinary Clinic	0742	E	916 685-2494	616
Brookdale Senior Living Inc	8052	D	916 683-1881	21067
California Family Health LLC	7991	E	916 685-3355	18617
Cardinal Health Inc	5122	C	916 372-9880	8242
Carlton Senior Living Inc	6531	E	916 714-2404	11343
Comprehensive SEC Svcs Inc (PA)	7381	D	916 683-3605	16608
County of Sacramento	8744	C	916 874-1927	27784
Customcare Home Hlth Svcs Inc	8082	D	916 714-1155	22421
Dominion International Inc	7011	D	916 683-9545	12586
Elk Grove Adult Cmnty Training	8611	D	916 431-3162	25085
Farmers Mrchants Bnk Centl Cal	6022	C	916 394-3200	9494
Future Energy Corporation	8711	D	916 685-4200	25825
Kaiser Foundation Hospitals	6324	C	916 544-6000	10301
Lifestyles Senior Housing Man	8322	D	916 714-3755	24067
Matheson Fast Freight Inc (HQ)	4213	D	916 686-4600	4218
OC Communications Inc	4841	A	916 686-3700	6010
Pacific Excavation Inc	1794	D	916 686-2800	3440
Professional Bureau of Collect	7359	C	916 685-3399	14571
R & A Painting Inc	1721	D	916 688-3955	2479
Rhodes Retail Services Inc	8742	D	916 714-9233	27618
River Oak Center For Children	8049	C	916 226-2800	20350
Sacramento Reg Co Sanit Dist	4952	B	916 875-9000	6415
Sacramento Yolo Cnty Mosquito	4959	D	916 685-1022	6638
Saia Motor Freight Line LLC	4213	E	916 690-8417	4257
Spare-Time Inc	7997	E	916 859-5910	19091
Sutter Health	8011	B	916 691-5900	20089
Sutter Health	8641	B	916 544-5423	25359
Sutter Health	8011	B	916 691-5900	20098
Tim Paxins Pacific Excavation	1794	E	916 686-2800	3445
Valley-HI Country Club	7997	E	916 684-2120	19117
Veterans of Foreign Wars of US	8641	D	916 786-7757	25392
XI Construction Corporation	1521	C	916 282-2900	1287

EMERYVILLE, CA - Alameda County

Company	SIC	EMP	PHONE	ENTRY #
AAA Northern Cal Nev & Utah	6331	B	510 596-3669	10393
Agilysys Inc	5045	E	702 759-4879	7086
Aguatierra Associates Inc (PA)	8744	D	510 450-6000	27772
Alpha-Winfield Contractors Inc	1521	D	510 652-4712	1124
APM Terminals Pacific Ltd	4731	B	510 992-6430	5030
Armstrong Installation Service	1721	D	408 777-1234	2430

GEOGRAPHIC SECTION — ESCONDIDO, CA

Company	SIC	EMP	PHONE	ENTRY #
Behavioral Intervention Assn	7363	E	510 652-7445	14846
Berkeley Research Group LLC **(PA)**	8748	C	510 285-3300	27848
Bishop Barry Howe Haney & Ryde	8111	D	510 596-0888	23116
Broadmoor Hotel	7011	D	415 673-8445	12469
Cep America LLC	8011	D	510 350-2691	19424
Cooper Vali & Associates Inc **(PA)**	8711	D	510 446-8301	25752
Daniel Loria Novartis	8069	C	510 655-8729	22136
E2 Consulting Engineers Inc	8711	B	510 652-1164	25775
Elemental Led Inc	5063	D	877 564-5051	7438
Energy Berkeley Office US Dept	8733	A	510 495-2490	26756
Ernest Gallo Clinic & RES Ctr	8732	C	510 985-3856	26660
Exponential Interactive Inc **(HQ)**	7311	D	510 250-5500	13848
Federal Express Corporation	4212	E	800 463-3339	4017
Fort James Corporation	8741	C	510 594-4900	27027
Giampolini & Co	1721	C	415 673-1236	2449
Gracenote Inc **(HQ)**	7371	C	510 428-7200	15211
Grifols Diagnstc Solutions Inc **(HQ)**	8071	C	323 225-2221	22224
Grill Recording Studio	7389	D	510 531-4351	17201
International Bus Mchs Corp	7371	B	510 652-6700	15250
Leidos Inc	8731	D	510 428-2550	26555
Medeanalytics Inc **(PA)**	8741	D	510 647-1300	27124
Mobitv Inc **(PA)**	4813	D	510 981-1303	5660
Nmi Holdings Inc	6351	D	855 530-6642	10496
Onebody Inc	8082	D	510 285-2000	22521
Pacific Hotel Management LLC	7011	D	510 547-7888	13058
Pixar	7812	A	510 922-3000	18129
Ramboll Environ US Corporation	8748	C	510 655-7400	28032
Ratcliff Architects	8712	D	510 899-6400	26244
Rlj Hgn Emeryville Lessee LP	7041	D	510 658-9300	13497
Rljhgn Emeryville Lessee LP	7011	D	510 658-9300	13163
Santen Incorporated	8733	D	415 268-9100	26806
Seagate Services	7373	D	510 903-7100	16047
Sutter Vsting Nrse Assn Hspice **(HQ)**	8082	E	866 652-9178	22576
The Young Mens Chris Assoc of	8641	D	510 601-8674	25374
Tubemogul Inc **(PA)**	7372	C	510 653-0126	15866
Upek Inc	7373	C	510 868-0800	16071
Wargaming America Inc **(HQ)**	7372	D	510 962-6747	15878
Waze Market Inc **(PA)**	7371	D	510 469-3123	15541
Ziprealty Inc **(DH)**	6531	D	510 735-2600	11935

ENCINITAS, CA - San Diego County

Company	SIC	EMP	PHONE	ENTRY #
Black Box Inc	5136	D	760 804-3300	8334
Broker Solutions Inc	6153	C	760 633-0102	9776
Burtech Pipeline Incorporated	1623	D	760 634-2822	1913
Callcatchers Inc	4813	D	800 477-1477	5568
Cellco Partnership	4812	D	760 642-0430	5323
City of Encinitas	1611	E	760 633-2850	1749
Cloudtrigger Inc	8742	D	858 367-5272	27384
Coldwell Banker	6531	D	760 753-5616	11405
Crown Hardware Inc	5072	C	760 334-0300	7682
Dudek **(PA)**	8711	D	760 942-5147	25773
Five Star Quality Care Inc	8361	E	760 479-1818	24658
Global Understanding Inc	8331	D	760 812-9650	24343
Hcr Manorcare Med Svcs Fla LLC	8051	D	760 944-0331	20654
J Robert Echter	0181	E	760 436-0188	292
JC Resorts LLC	8741	D	760 944-1936	27076
New Earth Enterprises Inc	0782	D	760 942-1298	919
Nixon Inc **(PA)**	5094	C	760 944-0900	8100
North Coast Presbyterian Ch	8351	D	760 753-2535	24486
Olivenhain Municipal Water Dst	4941	D	760 753-6466	6384
Rancho Santa Fe Protective Svc	7381	E	760 433-8887	16770
Recreational Equipment Inc	5046	D	760 479-0128	7225
San Diego Hebrew Homes **(PA)**	8051	C	760 942-2695	20888
Scripps Health	8011	D	760 753-8413	19968
Scripps Health	8011	D	760 479-3900	19971
Scripps Health	8062	D	760 753-6501	21867
Scripps Health	8011	D	760 633-6915	19975
Sethi Management Inc	7011	D	760 652-4010	13234
Silverado Senior Living Inc	8059	D	760 270-9917	21376
So Cal Truck Management	4212	D	858 759-1964	4067
Ycg LLC	8748	D	760 230-8016	28103
YMCA of San Diego County	8641	D	858 292-4034	25417

ENCINO, CA - Los Angeles County

Company	SIC	EMP	PHONE	ENTRY #
A-Able Inc **(PA)**	7342	D	323 658-5779	14170
Actual Reality Pictures Inc	6531	E	818 325-8800	11275
Adept Consumer Testing Inc	8732	D	310 279-4600	26642
Anello SEC & Consulting LLC	8748	E	818 632-3277	27833
Answer Financial Inc **(HQ)**	7389	D	818 644-4000	16994
Automobile Club Southern Cal	8699	E	818 997-6230	25494
Brite Media LLC	7313	E	818 849-3560	13961
Burkshire Has A Way Home Servc	6531	E	818 501-4800	11332
C M A Alliance	6411	D	818 981-0800	10652
Campanile II LP	5149	B	323 939-6813	8812
Cellco Partnership	4812	D	818 990-4610	5340
Childrens Hospital Los Angeles	8071	C	818 728-4930	22199
CIT Bank National Association	6021	D	818 817-5320	9364
Concrete Holding Co Cal Inc	6719	B	818 788-4228	12053
Danerica Enterprises Inc	7299	D	818 201-3300	13754
Elizabeth Glaser Pedia	8099	A	310 231-0400	22954
Encino Center Car Wash Inc	7542	E	818 788-6300	17841
Encino Hospital Medical Center	8062	D	818 995-5000	21559
Encino Trzana Regional Med Ctr	8062	B	818 995-5000	21560
Executive Marketing Firm	8742	E	818 713-1998	27427
First Interstate Security Inc	7381	C	818 995-6664	16642
Global Shield Security Inc	7381	E	818 988-9010	16665
Granville Glendale Inc	8741	D	818 981-1171	27044
Graypay LLC	7372	E	818 387-6735	15683
Heartland Payment Systems Inc	7389	D	818 784-6665	17214
Hemar Rousso & Heald L L P	8111	E	818 501-3800	23306
Holthouse Carlin Van Trigt LLP	8721	D	818 849-3140	26371
Interstate Protective Services	7381	D	818 995-6664	16710
Israel Pops Orchestra	7929	E	818 343-6450	18476
Kramer-Wilson Company Inc **(PA)**	6331	C	818 760-0880	10431
Kravitz Investment Svcs Inc	6282	D	818 995-6100	10158
KSL Media Inc	7319	D	212 468-3395	13999
Life Alert Emergency Response **(PA)**	7382	C	800 247-0000	16899
Lmno Productions Inc	7812	C	818 995-5555	18102
Lodgen Lacher Golditch Sard	8721	E	818 783-0570	26404
Malka Communications Group	4812	E	818 528-6894	5400
Max/Mr Imaging Inc	8071	D	818 382-2220	22241
Menchies Group Inc	5143	D	818 708-0316	8588
Merrill Lynch Pierce Fenner	6211	D	818 528-7809	10031
Merrill Lynch Pierce Fenner	6282	D	818 528-7800	10164
Nations Capital Group LLC	6153	D	818 793-2050	9788
Oracle Systems Corporation	7372	D	818 817-2900	15806
Orthopedic Consultants **(PA)**	8011	D	818 788-7343	19801
Pearlman Borska & Wax LLP **(PA)**	8111	D	818 501-4343	23500
Price Associates	7311	E	818 995-9216	13900
Price Law Group A Prof Corp **(PA)**	8111	C	818 995-4540	23515
Providence Health & Services	8049	D	818 401-4173	20343
Ralphs Grocery Company	4225	C	818 345-6882	4623
Reprints Desk Inc	7375	D	310 477-0354	16257
Republic Indemnity Co Amer **(DH)**	6331	D	818 990-9860	10454
Republic Indemnity Company Cal	6331	D	818 990-9860	10455
Rodeo Realty Inc	6531	D	818 285-3700	11817
Schweizer Rena	6531	D	818 501-7100	11835
Southern Cal Stone Ctr LLC	8011	D	818 784-8975	20045
State Farm Mutl Auto Insur Co	6411	D	818 849-5126	10880
Sunrise Senior Living Inc	8051	E	818 346-9046	20954
Survey Sampling Intl LLC	8732	C	866 872-4006	26709
Umpqua Bank	6021	D	818 385-1362	9426
Uniworld River Cruises Inc	4725	C	818 382-2322	5002
Valuation Concepts LLC	6531	D	818 812-6233	11886
Vitas Healthcare Corp Cal	8082	D	818 760-2273	22606
Wagner Jacobson Brokerage Inc	6531	D	323 872-1636	11904
Working With Autism	8093	D	818 501-4240	22868

ESCALON, CA - San Joaquin County

Company	SIC	EMP	PHONE	ENTRY #
Dan R Costa Inc	0191	C	209 234-2004	353
Noralco Inc	0723	C	209 551-4545	570

ESCONDIDO, CA - San Diego County

Company	SIC	EMP	PHONE	ENTRY #
4g Wireless Inc	4813	D	760 705-7133	5443
A & G Grove Service	0722	D	760 728-5447	488
A K P LLP	8721	D	760 746-1560	26284
American Financial Network Inc	6162	C	760 291-1059	9811
American Pride Gen Engrg Inc	8711	E	760 736-4056	25654
ARS National Services Inc **(PA)**	7322	C	800 456-5053	14017
ARS West LLC	7549	D	760 480-6631	17874
Associate Mechanical Contrs	1711	D	760 294-3517	2154
AT&T Services Inc	4813	D	760 489-3519	5549
AT&T Services Inc	4813	B	760 489-3187	5556
Baker Distributing Company LLC	5078	D	760 708-4201	7753
Bergelectric Corp	1731	A	760 746-1003	2531
Blanchard Training and Dev Inc **(PA)**	8742	C	760 489-5005	27349
Blanchardcoachingcom Inc	8331	B	760 489-5005	24314
Bmt Scientific Marine Svcs Inc **(HQ)**	8711	D	760 737-3505	25696
Cal Southern Presbt Homes	8361	D	760 747-4306	24575
Cal Southern Presbt Homes	8361	D	760 737-5110	24576
Cal Southern Sound Image Inc **(PA)**	1731	D	760 737-3900	2547
California Healthcare	6411	D	760 520-1333	10658
Central State Pre-School	8351	E	760 432-2499	24425
Chicago Title & Escrow	6531	E	760 746-3882	11387
Chicago Title Insurance Co	6361	D	760 546-1000	10507
Choa Hope LLC	7011	E	712 277-4101	12515
Christiansen Amusements Corp	7999	D	760 735-8542	19164
Concrete Concepts Inc	1771	D	760 737-5470	3247
Conrad Acceptance Corporation	6153	D	760 735-5000	9779
Conrad Credit Corporation	7322	D	760 735-5000	14028
Construction Tstg & Engrg Inc **(PA)**	8711	D	760 746-4955	25749
Covenant Care California LLC	8051	E	760 745-1288	20499

Employment Codes: A=Over 500 employees, B=251-500, C=101-250, D=51-100, E=45-50

ESCONDIDO, CA

	SIC	EMP	PHONE	ENTRY #
Davey Tree Surgery Company	0783	D	760 975-0225	992
Echo PCF Communications LLC	8741	D	760 737-3003	27009
Eleven Western Builders Inc	1542	D	760 796-6346	1548
Emeritus Corporation	6513	E	760 741-3055	11124
Ensign Group Inc	8051	D	760 746-0303	20541
Erickson-Hall Construction Co (PA)	1542	D	760 796-7700	1551
Garrick Motors Inc	7538	C	760 489-2656	17793
George Richard	1541	D	619 805-6751	1427
Graybill Medical Group Inc (PA)	8011	C	866 228-2236	19542
Henry Avocado Corporation (PA)	0179	D	760 745-6632	256
Hidden Valley Companies Inc	4731	B	760 466-7100	5101
Hidden Valley Mvg & Stor Inc (PA)	4214	D	602 252-7800	4351
Hmt Electric Inc	1731	D	858 458-9771	2613
In & Out Car Wash Inc	7542	E	619 316-8492	17844
Innovative Drywall Systems Inc	1742	D	760 743-0331	2910
Integrity Hlthcare Sltions Inc	8082	D	760 432-9811	22485
J & P Financial Inc (PA)	6163	E	760 738-9000	9931
Jangho Curtain Wall Americas	8712	D	650 588-9688	26213
JR Filanc Cnstr Co Inc (PA)	1623	D	760 941-7130	1952
Kaiser Foundation Hospitals	8011	A	442 281-5000	19610
Kaiser Foundation Hospitals	8011	D	760 739-3000	19612
Kaiser Foundation Hospitals	8011	E	619 528-5000	19661
Landcare USA LLC	0782	D	760 747-1174	889
Las Villas Del Norte	8051	D	760 741-1047	20720
Learning Services Corporation	8093	E	760 746-3223	22767
Legacy Partners Limited Inc	1611	D	760 747-2711	1815
Life Care Centers America Inc	8051	D	760 741-6109	20727
Lincoln Witt Mercury	7538	D	760 233-3333	17804
Marathon General Inc	1611	D	760 738-9714	1822
Master Design Drywall Inc	1742	D	760 480-9001	2928
Medley Communications Inc	1731	D	760 294-4579	2649
Mek Escondido LLC	8051	D	760 747-0430	20785
Mountain Meadow Mushrooms Inc	0182	D	760 749-1201	338
Mountain Shadows Support Group (PA)	8052	D	760 743-3714	21094
Neighborhood Healthcare (PA)	8011	E	760 520-8372	19766
Neighborhood Healthcare	8011	D	760 737-7896	19767
Neighborhood Healthcare	8011	D	760 737-2000	19769
North County Serenity Hse Inc (PA)	8361	D	760 233-4533	24747
Oj Insulation LP	1742	D	760 839-3200	2941
Pacific Structures Cnstr Inc	1771	E	740 480-4133	3310
Pacific Western Bank	6021	C	760 432-1350	9414
Pacific Western Bank	6021	D	760 432-1100	9418
Pack & Crate Services Inc	4214	E	760 737-6893	4370
Palomar Gem & Mineral Club	7997	D	760 743-0809	19026
Palomar Health	8099	B	858 675-5360	23015
Palomar Health (PA)	8062	C	442 281-5000	21779
Palomar Health	8062	A	760 739-3000	21780
Palomar Health	8742	D	760 739-2243	27581
Par Electrical Contractors Inc	1731	D	760 291-1192	2677
Paray Development Corp	1521	C	760 685-2462	1232
Park Landscape Maintenance	0782	E	760 317-2550	929
Permanente Kaiser Intl	8062	A	760 739-3000	21792
Physical Therapy Hand Ctrs Inc	8049	E	760 233-9655	20341
Pine Tree Lumber Company LP (PA)	5031	D	760 745-0411	6947
Pinery LLC	0811	D	858 675-3575	1012
Polestar Labs Inc	5047	C	760 480-2600	7301
Pro Scape Inc	0782	E	760 480-1544	938
Prowall Lath and Plaster	1742	D	760 480-9001	2959
R A Greene Corporation	1742	D	760 747-0810	2962
Rapid Product Dev Group Inc	8748	C	760 703-5770	28035
Red Hawk Fire & SEC CA Inc	1731	D	760 233-9787	2702
Redwood Elderlink Scph	8361	B	760 480-1030	24780
Rio Vista Ventures LLC (PA)	5141	E	760 480-8502	8514
Rocky Coast Builders Inc	1751	D	760 489-7770	3080
Romero General Cnstr Corp	1611	C	760 489-8412	1853
Saber Plumbing Inc	1711	D	760 480-5716	2356
Salazar Labor Contracting	0761	D	760 746-0805	683
San Diego County Water Auth	4941	D	760 480-1991	6393
San Diego Gas & Electric Co	1731	C	760 432-2508	2724
San Diego Gas & Electric Co	4939	B	760 432-5885	6307
Santa Fe Plaster	1742	D	760 747-9950	2977
Sbrm Inc (PA)	7349	B	760 480-0208	14422
Scripps Health	8011	B	760 737-7373	19976
Service Master Industries Inc	7389	D	760 480-0208	17487
Silverado Senior Living Inc	8059	D	760 456-5137	21375
Sound-Crete Contracting	5082	D	760 291-1240	7791
Southern Cal Prmnnte Med Group	8011	E	760 839-7200	20038
Southland Paving Inc	1771	D	760 747-6895	3334
Southwest General Contrs Inc	5082	E	760 480-8747	7792
Structures West Inc	1771	D	760 737-2349	3338
Sunrize Staging Inc	6531	D	760 743-2043	11861
Surecraft Supply Inc	1751	C	760 737-2120	3096
Sylvester Roofing Company Inc	1761	D	760 743-0048	3216
The For Califo Cente	8412	C	760 839-4138	25052
TNT Grading Inc	1611	D	760 736-4054	1874
Total Source Enviromental Inc	1522	E	619 822-8518	1347
Tpd Dell Dios	8322	E	760 741-2888	24254
Transmrcan Mling Flfilment Inc	7331	D	760 745-5343	14094
Tri-Ad Actuaries Inc	6411	C	760 743-7555	10910
Valle Vsta Cnvlescent Hosp Inc	8059	D	760 745-1288	21407
Veterans Health Administration	8011	B	760 745-2000	20210
Welk Group Inc (PA)	7011	B	760 749-3000	13398
West Escondido Healthcare LLC	8051	D	760 746-0303	21031
Western Rim Constructors Inc	1611	E	760 489-4328	1884
Westmed Ambulance Inc	4119	C	310 219-1779	3859
Wier Construction Corporation	1542	E	760 743-6776	1717
X3 Management Services Inc	8748	D	760 597-9336	28102
YMCA of San Diego County	8641	B	760 745-7490	25419
Zoological Society San Diego	8422	A	760 747-8702	25072
Zymax Envirotechnology Inc	8734	D	760 781-3338	26902

ESPARTO, CA - Yolo County

	SIC	EMP	PHONE	ENTRY #
Granite Construction Inc	1611	D	530 787-2012	1788
R H Phillips Inc (DH)	0172	D	530 757-5557	176

ETIWANDA, CA - San Bernardino County

	SIC	EMP	PHONE	ENTRY #
C M C Steel Fabricators Inc	1791	C	909 899-9993	3370

ETNA, CA - Siskiyou County

	SIC	EMP	PHONE	ENTRY #
Cal North Cellular Inc	4812	E	530 467-6128	5280
Etna Police Activities League	8322	C	530 467-3400	23963

EUREKA, CA - Humboldt County

	SIC	EMP	PHONE	ENTRY #
Cal-North Wireless	4812	D	707 442-8334	5281
Coast Central Credit Union (PA)	6061	D	707 445-8801	9591
Correctons Rhbltation Cal Dept	8322	D	707 445-6520	23788
County of Humboldt	8322	B	707 445-6180	23812
County of Humboldt	8093	C	707 476-4054	22697
E G Ayers Distributing Inc	5141	E	707 445-2077	8476
Eureka Rehab & Wellness Center	8051	D	707 445-3261	20554
Forest Products Distrs Inc	5031	D	707 443-7024	6923
Fred H Lundblade Jr	6512	D	707 442-8049	10985
Ghd Inc	8711	E	707 443-8326	25840
Granada Healthcre & Rehab Cntr	8059	D	707 443-1627	21255
Humboldt Commnty Accss Resrc	8322	D	707 444-9631	24016
Humboldt Senior Resource Ctr (PA)	8322	D	707 443-9747	24017
Humboldt Yacht Club	7997	D	707 443-1469	18961
Keenan & Associates	6411	D	707 268-1616	10757
Kristine Nickel	8082	D	707 443-9332	22498
Laco Associates (PA)	8711	E	707 443-5054	25931
Mission Linen Supply	7213	D	707 443-8681	13557
Pacific Choice Seafood Company	5146	B	707 442-2981	8645
Pacific Gas and Electric Co	4911	D	707 444-0700	6177
Pacific Rehabilitation & Wel	8051	D	707 443-9767	20833
Redwood Coast Regional	8322	E	707 445-0893	24150
RI Eureka LLC	7011	D	707 268-8341	13161
Seaview Hlthcre & Rehab Ctr LL	8361	D	707 443-5668	24806
Securitas SEC Svcs USA Inc	7381	D	707 445-5463	16798
Security Nat Mstr Holdg Co LLC (PA)	6162	C	707 442-2818	9896
Shn Consulting Engin (PA)	8711	D	707 441-8855	26061
Six Rivers National Bank (HQ)	6021	D	707 443-8400	9424
Six Rivers Planned Parenthood	8399	D	707 442-5700	24978
St Joseph Health System	8011	D	707 443-9371	20054
St Joseph Hospital (PA)	8062	D	707 445-8121	21919
St Joseph Hospital	7363	A	707 268-0191	14951
St Joseph Hospital of Eureka	8062	A	707 445-8121	21920
State Compensation Insur Fund	6331	D	707 443-9721	10473
Verizon Wireless Inc	4812	D	707 442-8334	5431
Veterans Health Administration	8011	B	707 442-5335	20208
Wayne Maples Plumbing & Htg	1711	D	707 445-2500	2414

EXETER, CA - Tulare County

	SIC	EMP	PHONE	ENTRY #
Badger Farming Company Inc	0174	D	559 592-5520	214
Best Western International Inc	7011	D	559 592-8118	12439
Bowsmith Inc (PA)	7218	D	559 592-9485	13617
Boys Grls Clubs of Squoias Inc	8322	D	559 592-4074	23691
Earlibest Orange Assn Inc	0722	D	559 592-2124	494
Exeter Packers Inc (PA)	0723	C	559 592-5168	529
Exeter-Ivanhoe Citrus Assn	0723	D	559 592-3141	531
Farmers Insurance Exchange	6411	B	559 594-4149	10713
Frontier California Inc	4813	D	559 592-2100	5612
Griffith Farms	0174	D	559 592-1009	217
Kaweah Dlta Hlth Care Dst Gild	8099	D	559 592-7300	22985
Kaweah Dlta Hlth Care Dst Gild	8011	D	559 592-7128	19684
Randstad North America	7363	B	559 592-6700	14932
Redding Tree Growers Corp	0851	D	559 594-9299	1017
San Joaquin Valley Railroad Co	4011	C	559 592-1857	3616
Sequoia Enterprises Inc	5148	D	559 592-9455	8773
Sun Pacific Farming Coop Inc (PA)	0762	B	559 592-7121	724
Venida Packing Company	4783	C	559 592-2816	5206

GEOGRAPHIC SECTION

FOLSOM, CA

	SIC	EMP	PHONE	ENTRY #

FAIR OAKS, CA - Sacramento County

	SIC	EMP	PHONE	ENTRY #
Burger Rhblitation Systems Inc	8049	D	916 863-5785	20311
Clarklift-West Inc	5084	C	916 381-5674	7835
Coldwell Bnkr Residential Brkg	6531	E	916 966-8200	11430
Eskaton	8082	A	916 536-3750	22433
Eskaton Properties Inc	8051	C	916 965-4663	20551
Lyon Realty	6531	B	916 962-0111	11644
North Ridge Country Club	7997	D	916 967-5716	19016
Wightman Enterprises Inc	7363	D	916 961-2959	14983
William L Lyon & Assoc Inc	6531	D	916 535-0356	11923
Womans Thursday Club Fair Oak	8699	D	916 967-7891	25600

FAIRFAX, CA - Marin County

	SIC	EMP	PHONE	ENTRY #
Meadow Club	7997	D	415 453-3274	18995
Melissa Bradley RE Inc	6531	D	415 485-4300	11677

FAIRFIELD, CA - Solano County

	SIC	EMP	PHONE	ENTRY #
All Day Electric Company Inc	1731	E	707 748-1036	2515
Anheuser-Busch LLC	5084	B	707 429-7595	7820
AT&T Services	4813	B	707 428-2512	5518
B R Funsten & Co	5023	E	707 863-8300	6846
Bay Span Inc	7363	D	707 863-4949	14844
Bay-TEC Engineering (PA)	8711	D	707 252-6575	25681
Blood Centers of Pacific	8099	E	707 428-6001	22899
Brand Services Inc	5082	E	707 603-3400	7763
Calbee North America LLC	5142	E	707 427-2500	8552
Caliber Home Loans Inc	6162	B	707 432-1000	9823
Century 21	6531	E	707 429-2121	11363
Certified Coatings Company	1721	D	707 639-4414	2435
City of Fairfield	6512	C	707 428-7435	10972
Coastal Select Insurance Co	6411	E	707 863-3700	10674
Community Housing Opport	8741	E	707 759-6043	26979
Corey Delta Constructors Inc	1711	D	925 370-9808	2191
County of Solano	8322	D	707 784-8400	23920
County of Solano	8322	D	707 784-7600	23921
County of Solano	8052	D	707 784-2000	21076
Delta One Security Inc	7381	D	707 425-9346	16624
Directv Group Inc	4841	C	707 452-7409	5987
Fairfield Inn Suites By M	7011	D	707 864-6672	12629
Fairfield Nursing & Rehab Ctr	8051	D	707 425-0623	20563
Fairfield-Suisun Sewer Dst	4953	D	707 429-8930	6483
Frank-Lin Distillers Pdts Ltd (PA)	5182	C	408 259-8900	9101
Gaw Van Male Smith Myers	8111	D	707 425-1250	23264
Geovera Specialty Insurance Co	6411	E	707 863-3700	10729
Green Valley Country Club	7997	D	707 864-1101	18957
Guzmans Painting	1721	E	707 428-3727	2453
Hd Supply Construction Supply	5072	D	707 863-8282	7686
J & J Maintenance Inc	7349	C	707 423-7453	14328
Jpmorgan Chase Bank Nat Assn	6035	D	707 864-4700	9572
Kaiser Foundation Hospitals	8011	A	707 427-4000	19614
Kiewit Corporation	1542	D	707 439-7300	1592
Laborers Funds Administrative (PA)	6371	D	707 864-2800	10553
Lanza Vineyards Inc	0172	E	707 864-0730	168
Loyalton At Rancho Solano	8361	D	707 425-3588	24722
Meyer Corporation US	5023	D	707 399-2100	6874
Muehlhan Certifed Coatings Inc	1799	C	707 639-4414	3556
Mv Transportation Inc	4142	D	707 446-5573	3904
New Desserts Inc	5149	D	415 780-6860	8891
Nor-Cal Pipeline Services	7699	D	530 673-3886	17992
Northbay Healthcare Corp (PA)	8062	D	707 646-5000	21761
Northbay Healthcare Group (PA)	8062	A	707 646-5000	21762
Northern CA Retiredd Ofcrs	8361	D	707 432-1200	24748
Northstate Plastering Inc	1771	D	707 207-0950	3304
Pacific Gas and Electric Co	4911	D	415 973-7000	6161
Partnership Health Plan Cal	6324	B	707 863-4100	10369
Permanente Medical Group Inc	8062	E	707 427-4000	21796
Petersen-Dean Inc	1761	E	707 469-7470	3200
Petersen-Dean Commercial Inc	1761	E	707 469-7470	3203
Pfs Investments Inc	6411	C	707 435-9507	10827
Professional Hospital Sup Inc	5047	C	707 720-0164	7306
S & S Tool & Supply Inc (PA)	5085	D	925 335-4000	7951
Schurman Fine Papers (PA)	5113	D	707 425-8006	8215
Service Pro Security Inc	6289	D	707 746-6532	10197
Solano County Mental Health	8322	E	707 428-1131	24216
Solano Family & Chld Council	8351	D	707 863-3950	24516
Solano Garbage Company Inc	4953	D	707 437-8900	6564
Solano Regional Medical Group (PA)	8011	C	707 426-3911	20006
Sutter Regional Med Foundation	8011	B	707 374-6833	20123
Transportation California Dept	1611	C	707 428-2031	1878
Travis Credit Union	6061	D	707 449-4000	9641
Tri-Valley Supply Inc (PA)	5033	D	707 469-7470	7022
Trugreen Limited Partnership	0782	D	707 864-5594	968
Two Jinn Inc	7389	D	707 421-9600	17547
United Parcel Service Inc OH	4215	C	707 864-8200	4444
Valley Inventory Service Inc	7389	D	707 422-6050	17582
Verizon Wireless Inc	4812	D	707 399-0866	5427
West Coast Contractors Inc	1542	C	541 267-7689	1715

FALLBROOK, CA - San Diego County

	SIC	EMP	PHONE	ENTRY #
Armstrong Garden Centers In C	5193	E	760 414-1490	9177
County of San Diego	8322	D	866 262-9881	23897
Edsi	8711	E	760 728-1899	25779
Elston Masonry Inc	1741	D	760 728-3593	2813
Executive Landscape Inc	0782	C	760 731-9036	852
Fallbrook Fire Protection Dst	7389	D	760 723-2010	17160
Fallbrook Public Utility Dst	8111	D	760 728-1125	23236
Fallbrook Sklled Nrsing Fcilty	8051	D	760 728-2330	20565
Garich Inc	7361	B	951 302-4750	14661
Garys Construction Inc	4959	C	760 639-4456	6628
Hamilton Family Ranch	0174	D	760 728-1358	218
Hines Horticulture Inc	5193	B	760 723-1500	9193
Kendall Farms LP	0181	E	760 731-0681	295
Little Sisters Truck Wash Inc (PA)	7542	D	760 731-3170	17853
New Visa Health Services Inc	8059	B	760 723-0053	21324
Olive Hill Greenhouses	0181	D	760 728-4596	308
Pala Band of Mission Indians	7929	C	760 207-2603	18485
Pala Mesa Limited Partnership	7011	C	760 728-5881	13071
Petes Connection Inc	4841	E	760 723-1972	6013
Quality Childrens Services	8351	D	760 723-3228	24506
Rainbow Municipal Water Dst	4941	D	760 728-1178	6388
Scrape Certified Welding Inc	1791	D	760 728-1308	3402
Southwest Construction Co Inc	1771	D	760 728-4460	3335
Straub - Brutoco A Joint Ventr	1531	C	760 414-9000	1385
Sycamore Cc Inc	7997	D	760 451-3700	19102
William C Arterberry	0179	D	760 728-9096	262

FARMINGTON, CA - San Joaquin County

	SIC	EMP	PHONE	ENTRY #
Brightview Tree Company	0811	D	209 886-5511	1010

FELLOWS, CA - Kern County

	SIC	EMP	PHONE	ENTRY #
Aera Energy LLC	1381	E	661 768-3100	1054
Watson ME Inc	1521	D	661 768-1717	1282

FELTON, CA - Santa Cruz County

	SIC	EMP	PHONE	ENTRY #
Cupertino Electric Inc	1731	A	408 808-8260	2567
Granite Construction Inc	1611	D	831 335-3445	1791

FIDDLETOWN, CA - Amador County

	SIC	EMP	PHONE	ENTRY #
Murray Entps Staffing Svcs	7363	D	530 409-5703	14914

FILLMORE, CA - Ventura County

	SIC	EMP	PHONE	ENTRY #
B & R Farm Labor Contractor	7361	C	805 524-1346	14612
Brightview Tree Company	0811	C	805 524-3939	1008
California Watercress Inc (PA)	0161	C	805 524-4808	47
Fillmore Convalescent Ctr LLC	8059	D	805 524-0083	21215
Magana Labor Services	7361	C	805 524-0446	14701
Moon Mountain Farms LLC	0191	E	805 521-1742	384
Pan American Agriculture Corp	0139	D	805 524-1489	30
Wilmay Inc	7389	D	805 524-2603	17628
Wonderful Citrus Packing LLC	0174	D	805 525-3818	224

FIREBAUGH, CA - Fresno County

	SIC	EMP	PHONE	ENTRY #
Britz Fertilizers Inc	5191	E	559 659-2033	9128
Hall Company	0191	D	209 364-0070	363
Hammonds Ranch Inc	0191	D	209 364-6185	364
J & J Farms	0191	D	559 659-1457	370
JR Simplot Company	0711	E	559 659-2033	475
Oxford Farms Inc	0762	D	559 659-3033	712
R & N Packing Co	0723	D	209 364-6101	575
Seasholtz John	0161	C	559 659-3805	95
Thomason Tractor Co California	5083	E	559 659-2039	7811
Tri-State AG Inc	4961	D	209 364-6185	6641
Vaquero Farms Inc	0191	D	559 659-2790	402

FIVE POINTS, CA - Fresno County

	SIC	EMP	PHONE	ENTRY #
ATI Machinery Inc	5083	E	559 884-2471	7799
Britz Fertilizers Inc	5191	D	559 884-2421	9129
Coelho West Custom Farming	0191	D	559 884-2566	351
Crop Production Services Inc	5191	E	559 884-6010	9133
Telesis Onion Co	0723	E	559 884-2441	598

FOLSOM, CA - Sacramento County

	SIC	EMP	PHONE	ENTRY #
24 Hour Fitness Usa Inc	7991	E	916 984-1924	18578
Agreeya Solutions Inc (PA)	8742	D	916 294-0075	27310
Benefit & Risk Management Svcs	6411	C	916 467-1200	10645
Brookdale Senior Living Inc	8051	D	916 983-9300	20428
Burger Physcl Therapy Svcs Inc (HQ)	8049	D	916 983-5900	20308
Burger Physical Therapy	8049	D	916 983-5900	20309
Burger Rhblitation Systems Inc (PA)	8049	D	800 908-8491	20312
Califrnia Ind Sys Oprator Corp	8742	D	916 608-7000	27367
Califrnia Ind Sys Oprator Corp (PA)	4911	B	916 351-4400	6108
Celico Partnership	4812	D	212 395-1000	5293
Celico Partnership	4812	D	916 357-1000	5354
Chicago Title Insurance Co	6361	E	916 985-0300	10505

FOLSOM, CA

Company	SIC	EMP	PHONE	ENTRY #
City of Folsom	7999	D	916 355-7285	19170
Cpg Solutions LLC	8742	E	561 988-8611	27394
Csac Excess Insurance Auth	6411	D	916 850-7300	10684
Denc Services Inc	8331	E	916 351-1720	24334
Dignity Health	8011	C	916 983-7400	19496
Dokken Engineering (PA)	8711	D	916 858-0642	25772
Ea Consulting Inc	7379	E	916 357-6767	16360
Erepublic Inc (PA)	7389	C	916 932-1300	17154
Eurofins Air Toxics Inc	8734	D	916 985-1000	26852
Flt Inc	7538	C	916 355-1500	17790
Folsom Recreation Corp	7933	D	916 983-4411	18518
FPI Management Inc (PA)	6531	E	916 357-5300	11543
Green Acres Nursery & Sup LLC	5083	D	916 782-2273	7802
HDR Engineering Inc	8742	D	916 817-4700	27462
HDR/Cardno Entrix Joint Ventr	8711	D	916 817-4700	25859
Hoshall Corporation	7231	E	916 987-1995	13679
Infinite Technologies Inc (PA)	8711	D	916 987-3261	25875
Kaiser Foundation Hospitals	8011	A	916 986-4178	19617
Kaiser Foundation Hospitals	8011	C	916 817-5200	19671
Kindred Healthcare Operating	8051	C	916 351-9151	20705
Lake Natoma Lodging LP	7011	D	916 351-1500	12902
Liberty American Mortgage Corp (PA)	6163	C	916 780-3000	9933
Liberty Mutual Insurance Co	6331	C	916 294-9518	10434
Lyon Real Estate	6531	D	916 355-7000	11641
Matthew Burns	1542	D	209 676-4940	1610
Maximus Inc	8742	D	916 673-2175	27528
Maximus Inc	8742	E	916 673-4162	27529
Mercury Insurance Company	6331	D	916 353-4859	10442
Mercy Healthcare Sacramento	8062	B	916 983-7400	21738
Meridian Project Systems Inc (HQ)	7372	D	916 294-2000	15749
Morton & Pitalo Inc (PA)	8711	D	916 984-7621	25976
Norcal Gold Inc	6531	E	916 984-8778	11713
Numonyx Inc	5045	A	916 458-3888	7169
Objective Systems Integrators (HQ)	7371	E	916 467-1500	15346
Oncor Insurance Services LLC	6411	D	916 932-3210	10817
Quagga Corporation	1623	D	916 357-5129	1984
Retail Pro International LLC	7371	E	916 605-7200	15419
Rightsourcing Inc (DH)	7363	D	800 660-9544	14937
Safe Credit Union (PA)	6062	C	916 979-7233	9681
Safe Credit Union	6062	C	916 979-7233	9682
Sierra Pacific Mortgage Co Inc (PA)	6162	D	916 932-1700	9898
Spare-Time Inc	7997	D	916 983-9180	19086
Sparta Consulting Inc	7379	B	916 985-0300	16487
Trimark Associates Inc	8748	D	916 357-5970	28084
Vibra Hospital Sacramento LLC	8069	C	916 351-9151	22185
Visio Integ Profe LLC (HQ)	8742	D	916 608-8320	27712
VPD IV IV (PA)	7822	D	916 605-1500	18283

FONTANA, CA - San Bernardino County

Company	SIC	EMP	PHONE	ENTRY #
ABF Freight System Inc	4213	C	909 355-9805	4102
Advanced Environmental Inc	4212	E	909 356-9025	3973
Advanced Network Tech Inc	1623	D	909 428-9030	1901
Advanced Sterlization	4225	D	909 356-6987	4517
American Asphalt South Inc	1611	D	909 427-8276	1729
American Bolt & Screw Mfg Corp (PA)	5072	D	909 390-0522	7669
AMS Paving Inc (PA)	1611	E	909 357-0711	1731
Anfinson Lumber Sales (PA)	5031	D	951 681-4707	6908
Apex Bulk Commodities Inc	6221	C	909 854-9991	10104
Aqua-Serv Engineers Inc (HQ)	5169	D	951 681-9696	8977
Automotive Sup Co Southern Cal (PA)	5013	C	909 428-9072	6711
B&B Industrial Services Inc (PA)	1741	D	909 428-3167	2802
Blue Rose Concrete Contrs Inc	1771	C	909 823-6190	3235
Boyd Flotation Inc	5021	D	909 357-6400	6808
Budway Enterprises Inc (PA)	4213	D	909 463-0500	4120
Burrtec Waste Industries Inc (HQ)	4953	C	909 429-4200	6448
California Speedway Corp	7948	E	909 429-5000	18567
Cattrac Construction Inc	1629	D	909 355-1146	2038
Central Reinforcing Corp	1791	D	909 773-0840	3376
Complete Logistics Company	4212	C	909 427-9951	3998
Conco Pumping	1771	D	909 350-0503	3246
Costco Wholesale Corporation	5199	C	909 823-8270	9257
Cox Automotive Inc	5012	A	404 843-5000	6669
CRST International Inc	4213	C	909 829-1313	4129
D W Powell Construction Inc	1611	E	909 356-8880	1762
Dalton Trucking Inc (PA)	4212	D	909 823-0663	4001
Defenders Trnsp Svcs Inc	4731	E	909 854-7000	5054
Desert Coastal Transport Inc (PA)	4213	D	909 357-3395	4138
Dispatch Trucking Inc (PA)	4731	D	909 355-5531	5059
Elegance Wood Products Inc	5023	D	909 484-7676	6858
Estes Express Lines Inc	4213	D	909 427-9850	4148
Express Contractors Inc	7217	C	951 360-6500	13598
Fedex Freight West Inc	4213	B	909 357-3555	4172
Flash Transport Inc	4213	D	909 829-1369	4184
Fontana Resources At Work	8331	C	909 428-3833	24341
Foundation Pile Inc	1629	D	909 350-1584	2052
Friends Group Express Inc	4213	D	909 346-6814	4186
General Motors LLC	4225	D	951 361-6302	4556
Hanks Inc	4212	D	909 350-8365	4022
Hartman Industries	5051	D	909 428-0114	7374
Hawk Transportation Inc	4213	D	800 709-4295	4195
Hsn LLC	4225	C	909 349-2600	4576
Inland Cc Inc	1771	C	909 355-1318	3275
Inland Empire Utilities Agency	4941	C	909 357-0241	6357
Inland Kenworth (us) Inc (HQ)	5012	C	909 823-9955	6681
Interstate Distributor Co	4213	E	909 349-3400	4198
Ips Inc	7381	E	909 428-2647	16711
James Hardie Building Pdts Inc	5031	C	909 355-6500	6934
Jst Fontana	7361	D	909 854-4062	14690
Kaiser Foundation Hospitals	8011	C	909 355-3800	19592
Kaiser Foundation Hospitals	8011	A	866 205-3595	19616
Kaiser Foundation Hospitals	8011	A	909 427-5000	19652
Kaiser Foundation Hospitals	6324	D	909 427-3910	10340
Kaiser Permanente	8062	C	909 427-3910	21680
Kds Printing and Packaging Inc	7389	E	909 770-5400	17268
Kenco Group Inc	4789	D	909 356-1635	5228
Lemans Corporation	4225	D	909 428-2424	4586
Little Sisters Truck Wash Inc	7542	D	909 549-1862	17852
Los Angeles Truck Centers LLC	5012	C	909 510-4000	6687
Ltl Ex Inc	4731	D	951 255-1222	5116
McCollisters Trnsp Group Inc	4213	D	909 428-5700	4220
McGuire Contracting Inc	1771	D	909 357-1200	3294
Naumann/Hobbs Material	5084	D	909 427-0125	7868
Network Global Logistics LLC	4513	C	888 285-7447	4871
No Shnacks Inc	8741	E	909 293-8747	27143
Norco Ranch Inc (DH)	0252	B	951 737-6735	447
NY Transport Inc	4213	D	909 355-9832	4237
Orwick Fresh Foods Inc	5149	E	909 985-5604	8895
Parkhouse Tire Service Inc	5014	C	909 428-1415	6788
Patrick Industries Inc	5032	C	909 350-4440	6992
Permanente Kaiser Intl	8062	A	909 427-5000	21790
Pointdirect Transport Inc	4731	D	909 371-0837	5152
Rail Delivery Services Inc	4212	D	909 355-4100	4054
Rapid Armada SEC Svcs Rass LLC	7381	E	909 609-4370	16711
Romark Logistics of California	4225	D	909 356-5600	4631
Rush Enterprises Inc	4212	C	800 776-3647	4060
S N S West LLC	4225	D	909 355-8118	4701
San Gabriel Valley Water Co	4941	C	909 822-2201	6396
Schneider National Inc	4213	C	909 574-2165	4262
Sierra Lakes Golf Club	7992	D	909 350-2500	18786
Slater Inc	1629	D	909 822-6800	2086
Soltis Golf Incorporated	1629	D	909 822-7000	2088
Sonsray Machinery LLC	5082	D	909 355-1075	7790
Southern Cal Prmnnte Med Group	8062	E	909 427-5000	21902
Stantru Resources Inc	1541	D	909 587-1441	1466
State Farm Mutl Auto Insur Co	6411	D	909 349-2050	10887
STC Netcom Inc (PA)	1731	D	951 685-8181	2748
Sun Mar Management Services	8741	D	909 822-8066	27236
Tikos Tanks Inc	7692	D	951 757-8014	17955
Tire Centers LLC	5014	C	909 854-1200	6791
Tonys Express Inc (PA)	4213	C	909 427-8700	4278
Tst Inc	4212	D	310 835-0115	4075
Tst Inc	5093	D	909 590-1098	8093
United Facilities Inc	4225	E	951 685-7030	4647
United Family Care Inc	8011	D	909 822-1164	20152
United Family Care Inc (PA)	8011	D	909 874-1679	20153
Uti Integrated Logistics LLC	4226	C	909 427-1939	4706
Utility Trailer Sales of S CA (PA)	5012	D	909 428-8300	6699
Valori Sand & Gravel Company	5032	C	909 350-3000	6999
Verizon Wireless Inc	4812	D	909 355-0725	5429
Vineyard Plastering Inc	1742	E	909 357-3701	2994
Vitco Distributors Inc	5113	D	909 355-1300	8224
Wal-Mart Stores Inc	4225	B	909 349-3600	4658
Werner Enterprises Inc	4213	D	909 823-5803	4302
West Valley Mrf LLC	4953	C	909 899-5501	6613
Weyerhaeuser Company	5031	D	909 877-6100	6970
Windrow Earth Transport Inc	1629	E	909 355-5531	2096
Xpo Enterprise Services Inc	4213	C	951 685-1244	4321

FOOTHILL RANCH, CA - Orange County

Company	SIC	EMP	PHONE	ENTRY #
Arq LLC	8711	D	888 384-0971	25666
Cox Communications Inc	4841	D	949 546-2000	5977
Debisys Inc (PA)	6099	D	949 699-1401	9716
Frontech N Fujitsu Amer Inc (DH)	7373	C	949 855-5500	15950
Guthy-Renker LLC	7389	D	949 454-1400	17205
Hampton Products Intl Corp (PA)	5072	D	949 472-4256	7685
Ibaset Inc	8748	D	949 598-5200	27948
Ibaset Federal Services LLC (PA)	7379	D	949 598-5200	16399
Image Options	7319	D	949 586-7665	13998
Impact Mktg Specialists Inc	7389	E	949 348-2292	17235
Kaiser Foundation Hospitals	8011	A	800 922-2000	19615
Kawasaki Motors Corp USA (HQ)	5012	B	949 837-4683	6686
Loandepotcom LLC (PA)	6162	A	949 474-1322	9870

GEOGRAPHIC SECTION

FREMONT, CA

	SIC	EMP	PHONE	ENTRY #
Nth Degree Inc	7389	E	714 734-4155	17371
Professional Cmnty MGT Cal Inc	6541	D	949 768-7261	11240
Professional Community MGT Cal Inc (PA)	6531	E	800 369-7260	11769
Spectrum Brands Inc	7299	B	949 672-4003	13798
Tri Alpha Energy Inc	8731	D	949 830-2117	26623
Venus Group Inc	5023	D	949 609-1299	6903

FOREST RANCH, CA - Butte County

	SIC	EMP	PHONE	ENTRY #
Sierra Cascade Blueberries	0171	E	530 894-8728	133

FORT BRAGG, CA - Mendocino County

	SIC	EMP	PHONE	ENTRY #
Mendocino Coast Clinics Inc	8093	D	707 964-1251	22773
Mendocino Coast District Hosp (PA)	8062	B	707 961-1234	21733
Mendocino Coast District Hosp	8062	C	707 961-4736	21734
Mendocino Transit Authority	4111	D	707 462-1422	3672
Redwood Coast Seniors Inc	8322	D	707 964-0443	24151
Sherwood Oaks Enterprises	8051	D	707 964-6333	20910
Tradewinds Lodge (PA)	7011	D	707 964-4761	13353
Waste MGT Collectn & Recycl	4953	D	707 462-0210	6605

FORT IRWIN, CA - San Bernardino County

	SIC	EMP	PHONE	ENTRY #
Family Mrale Wlfare Recreation	7997	D	760 380-3493	18948
Iap World Services Inc	8744	B	760 380-6772	27794
Leidos Inc	8731	D	910 574-4597	26559
Northrop Grumman Enterprise Mg	8741	B	760 380-4268	27147
Raytheon Company	7629	D	760 386-2572	17941
Solution One Industries Inc	4225	D	254 702-7329	4640

FORTUNA, CA - Humboldt County

	SIC	EMP	PHONE	ENTRY #
Reaching For Independence Inc	8399	D	707 725-9010	24966
Redwood Memorial Hospital Inc (PA)	8062	C	707 725-7327	21829
St Luke Hlthcr & Rehab Ctr LL	8051	D	707 725-4467	20928

FOSTER CITY, CA - San Mateo County

	SIC	EMP	PHONE	ENTRY #
American Infrastructure Mlp Fu	8748	D	650 854-6000	27829
Amobee (HQ)	7371	D	650 802-8871	15011
Applied Biosystems	8731	A	800 327-3002	26470
Applied Underwriters Inc	6411	E	415 656-5000	10620
Arena Solutions Inc (PA)	7371	D	650 513-3500	15032
Asian Legal Workforce	0761	D	650 703-2190	651
B B & K Fund Services Inc	6211	E	650 571-5800	9961
Bayshore Ambulance Inc (PA)	4119	D	650 525-9700	3771
C S G Consultants Inc (PA)	8711	E	650 522-2525	25713
City of Foster City	7999	B	650 286-3380	19171
Cybersource Corporation (HQ)	7374	C	650 432-7350	16119
Ecker Consumer Recruiting Inc (PA)	8732	E	650 871-6800	26658
Emeter Corporation	7371	C	650 227-7770	15164
Emove Express Company	7374	D	650 377-0913	16124
Entelos Inc	8731	E	650 578-2900	26513
Founders Management II Corp	7011	B	650 570-5700	12644
Global Ground Automation Inc	5084	D	201 293-4900	7846
Guidewire Software (PA)	7372	C	650 357-9100	15686
Hilton Garden In San Mateo	7011	D	650 522-9000	12706
Ic Compliance LLC (PA)	7371	A	650 378-4150	15231
International Bus Mchs Corp	7379	B	800 426-4968	16409
Legacy Prtners Residential Inc (HQ)	8741	C	650 571-2250	27112
Menlo Gateway Inc	6514	D	650 356-2900	11236
Midpen Housing Corporation	6552	B	650 356-2900	11984
Midpen Resident Services Corp	6514	B	650 356-2965	11238
On Link Technologies Inc	7389	D	650 477-5000	17375
Oracle Corporation	7372	B	650 678-3612	15790
Peninsula Jewish Community Ctr	8322	C	650 212-7522	24131
Peter H Mattson & Co Inc	8731	D	650 356-2500	26589
Philips Hlthcare Infrmtics Inc (HQ)	7371	D	650 293-2300	15379
Quinstreet Inc (PA)	7389	E	650 578-7700	17439
Rainbow Networking	7374	D	650 377-0913	16176
Sanzaru Games Inc	7371	D	650 312-1000	15436
Scientific Concepts Inc	7699	B	650 578-1142	18010
Sling Media Inc (HQ)	4812	C	650 293-8000	5408
Sonifi Solutions Inc	4841	C	650 752-1980	6017
Sony Corporation of America	7371	C	650 655-8000	15470
Sony Intrctive Entrmt Amer LLC (DH)	5092	A	650 655-8000	8055
Steelwave Inc (PA)	6552	B	650 571-2200	12013
Steelwave LLC	6552	A	650 571-2200	12014
USB Solarcity Master Tenant	6719	D	650 963-5693	12097
Vb Golf LLC	8741	D	650 573-7888	27274
Visa International Svc Assn (HQ)	7389	B	650 432-3200	17593
Visa USA Inc (HQ)	7389	B	650 432-3200	17594
Wiline Networks Inc (PA)	4813	D	888 494-5463	5733
Zuora Inc	4813	D	650 241-4508	5740

FOUNTAIN VALLEY, CA - Orange County

	SIC	EMP	PHONE	ENTRY #
AMI Electrical & Telecom Inc	1731	D	714 531-0872	2519
B T B Events Inc	8743	D	714 415-3313	27732
Bell Private Security Inc	7381	D	714 964-9381	16574
Boys Girls CLB Huntington Vly (PA)	8322	D	714 531-2582	23689
Brightview Companies LLC	0782	C	714 437-1586	815
Brightview Landscape Dev Inc	1629	B	714 546-7975	2032
Carmel Vlg Rtirement Residence	6513	D	714 962-6661	11112
Ceridian Tax Service Inc	8721	D	714 963-1311	26310
D-Link Systems Incorporated	5045	C	714 885-6000	7116
Fountain Valley Body Works M2	7532	E	714 751-8812	17754
Fountain Valley Regl Hospl	8062	A	714 966-7200	21568
Fountain Valley School Dst	7349	C	714 668-5882	14301
Hcr Manorcare Med Svcs Fla LLC	8051	C	714 241-9800	20649
His Passion Inc	8082	E	800 760-6389	22459
Hobby Shack (PA)	5092	E	714 964-0827	8044
Hyundai Atver Tlmtics Amer Inc	7371	D	949 381-6000	15228
Jmg Security Systems Inc	1731	D	714 545-8882	2625
Longwood Management Corp	8361	D	714 962-6661	24715
Memorial Healthtec Labratories	8731	A	714 962-4677	26567
Metamor Entp Solutions LLC	7379	E	866 565-4746	16432
Mile Square Golf Course	7992	C	714 962-5541	18761
Mitsubishi Materials USA Corp (HQ)	5085	E	714 352-6100	7941
Mobis Parts America LLC	5012	D	786 515-1101	6690
New CAM Commerce Solutions LLC	7389	D	714 241-9241	17353
Norco Hills Car Wash	7542	E	951 279-4398	17857
Noritz America Corporation (HQ)	5075	D	714 433-2905	7744
Nty Franchise Company LLC	0175	D	714 964-3488	246
Orange Cost Cntr For Surg Care	8062	D	714 369-1070	21770
Orange County Sanitation (PA)	4953	B	714 962-2411	6511
Pacific Advnced Civil Engrg Inc (PA)	8711	D	714 481-7300	26002
Pacific Aquascape Inc	1799	D	714 481-7260	3560
Pan-Pacific Mechanical LLC (PA)	1711	C	949 474-9170	2318
Premier Commercial Painting	1721	E	714 546-3692	2475
Rcsn Inc	7361	C	714 965-0244	14745
Restaurant Depot	5141	C	714 378-3535	8513
Restaurant Depot LLC	5142	C	714 378-3535	8566
Richard Brady & Associates Inc	8711	D	657 204-9124	26040
Spec Services Inc	8711	E	714 963-8077	26071
Spec Services Inc (PA)	8711	D	714 963-8077	26072
St Jude Hospital Yorba Linda	8011	C	714 665-1797	20059
Starbucks Corporation	8742	D	714 378-1107	27663
Stephouse Recovery Center	8322	D	714 394-3494	24237
US Investmnt Cmrce Fisheries	5146	D	714 823-5209	8663

FOWLER, CA - Fresno County

	SIC	EMP	PHONE	ENTRY #
Bedrosian Farms Inc	0172	E	559 834-5981	143
Boghosian Raisin Pkg Co Inc	0723	D	559 834-5348	513
Fowler Convalescent Hospital	8059	E	559 834-2542	21216
Fowler Labor Service Inc	7361	B	559 834-3723	14658
Gahvejian Enterprises Inc	5113	E	559 834-5956	8192
Golden Living LLC	8051	D	559 834-2542	20604
Kandarian Agri Enterprises	0172	C	559 834-1501	161
Trius Trucking Inc	4731	B	559 834-4000	5182

FREMONT, CA - Alameda County

	SIC	EMP	PHONE	ENTRY #
24 Hour Fitness Usa Inc	7991	E	510 795-6666	18579
314e Corporation	7371	D	510 371-6736	14988
Abode Services (PA)	8322	D	510 657-7409	23641
Ace Financial Services Inc	6411	D	510 790-4600	10579
Ace USA	6411	D	510 790-4695	10580
Acma Computers Inc	7373	C	214 587-1829	15893
Actelis Networks Inc (PA)	4813	C	510 545-1045	5452
Activ Identity Corporation	7374	D	510 574-0100	16088
Aegis Asssted Living Prpts LLC	8059	E	510 739-1515	21125
Aegis Senior Communities LLC	8082	E	510 739-0909	22344
Aer Electronics Inc (PA)	4953	D	510 300-0500	6422
Agama Solutions Inc	8742	C	510 796-9300	27308
Alameda County Water District (PA)	4941	D	510 668-4200	6310
Alom Technologies Corporation (PA)	7819	D	510 360-3600	18213
Amax Engineering Corporation (PA)	5045	D	510 651-8886	7089
American Bldg Maint Co of Ill	7349	E	510 573-1618	14225
American Dept of Inspections	7389	D	510 683-9360	16986
Anaspec Inc (HQ)	8731	E	800 452-5530	26469
Angioscore Inc	5047	C	510 933-7900	7235
Anka Behavioral Health Inc	8099	D	510 494-1567	22889
Apptivo Inc	7371	D	650 906-1034	15026
Arcsoft Inc (PA)	7371	D	510 440-9901	15030
Asi Computer Technologies Inc (PA)	5045	C	510 226-8000	7094
Asus Computer International	5045	D	510 739-3777	7095
AT&T Services Inc	4813	D	510 791-6605	5548
Atlas Security & Patrol Inc	7381	E	510 791-7380	16565
Aver Construction Inc	1611	D	510 354-2000	1737
Aver Information Inc	5045	E	408 263-3828	7097
Bay Area Intl Translation Svcs	7389	D	510 673-8912	17025
Bayside Interiors Inc (PA)	1742	C	510 580-3950	2861
BFI Waste Systems N Amer Inc	4953	D	510 657-1350	6442
Bigbyte Corporation	7378	D	510 249-1100	16288
Blocka Construction Inc	1711	D	510 657-3686	2168
Brilliant Sftwr Solutions Inc	7373	D	510 742-5120	15910
By-The-Bay Investments Inc	6799	B	510 793-2581	12289
C J Health Services Inc	8051	D	510 793-3000	20428

Employment Codes: A=Over 500 employees, B=251-500, C=101-250, D=51-100, E=45-50

FREMONT, CA — GEOGRAPHIC SECTION

Company	SIC	EMP	PHONE	ENTRY #
Cancer Prevention Inst Cal (PA)	8733	C	510 608-5000	26743
Cellco Partnership	4812	D	510 490-3800	5313
Chrisp Company (PA)	1611	C	510 656-2840	1747
Cintas Corporation No 3	7218	D	510 573-5300	13628
City of Fremont	8412	C	510 791-4196	25010
City of Fremont	8712	C	510 494-4460	26177
Club Sport of Fremont	7389	C	510 226-8500	17083
Coldwell Bnkr Residential Brkg	6531	D	510 608-7600	11437
Concentrix Corporation	7379	D	510 668-3717	16341
Concessionaires Urban Park	7999	D	530 529-1596	19190
Covansys Corporation	7371	D	510 304-3430	15112
Crestwood Behavioral Hlth Inc	8361	C	510 651-1244	24623
Crestwood Behavioral Hlth Inc	8361	C	510 793-8383	24624
D F Rios Construction Inc	1751	D	510 226-7467	3041
Dcm Limited	7379	D	510 494-2321	16350
Dcm Technologies Inc	7371	D	510 791-2182	15125
Del Contes Landscaping Inc	0782	C	510 353-6030	836
Delta America Ltd (HQ)	5065	D	510 668-5100	7554
Delta Products Corporation (DH)	5065	D	510 668-5100	7555
Digital Nirvana Inc	8742	B	510 226-9000	27411
Digitalpersona Inc (HQ)	5065	D	650 474-4000	7556
DMS Facility Services Inc	7349	A	510 656-9400	14283
Droisys Inc	7389	C	408 329-1761	17135
Dryco Construction Inc (PA)	1611	D	510 438-6500	1768
E & E Co Ltd (PA)	5023	C	510 490-9788	6857
E21 Corp	7336	C	510 818-9600	14144
Elliott Laboratories Inc	8071	E	510 440-9500	22213
Etrade Financial Corporation	6282	D	650 331-6435	10137
Eurogentec North America Inc	8748	D	510 791-9560	27918
Everest Consulting Group Inc	7371	D	510 494-8440	15175
Excelfore Corporation	7373	E	510 868-2500	15947
First American Financial Corp	8742	B	510 252-1563	27436
Fortuna Technologies Inc	8748	C	510 687-9797	27924
Foxconn	7389	D	510 226-0822	17172
Fremont Ambltory Srgery Ctr LP	8011	D	510 456-4600	19530
Fremont Bank (HQ)	6022	C	510 505-5226	9499
Fremont Candle Lighters	8699	C	510 796-0595	25531
Fremont Marriott	7011	C	510 413-3700	12652
Fremont Sports Inc	7933	E	510 656-1955	18520
Fremont Unified School Dst	7349	D	510 657-0761	14303
Gammatronic Computer Corporation	5045	D	510 824-6700	7134
Globalways Inc (PA)	7379	D	510 580-1974	16393
Golden N-Life Diamite Intl Inc (PA)	5122	E	510 651-0405	8258
Greenbriar Management Company	6531	D	510 497-8200	11560
Growith Inc	1711	D	805 650-6650	2241
Homelegance Inc	5021	D	510 933-6888	6818
HP Inc	7372	C	650 265-5448	15693
Hyve Solutions Corporation	7374	A	864 349-4415	16143
Infinity Nurses Care Inc	7363	D	510 713-8892	14887
Instant Systems Inc	7372	D	510 657-8100	15705
Intelliswift Software Inc (PA)	7379	C	510 490-9240	16405
ISE Labs Inc	8734	E	510 687-2500	26863
ISE Labs Inc (DH)	8734	C	510 687-2500	26864
Ists Worldwide Inc	7379	C	510 794-1400	16415
John J Maguire DDS	8021	E	213 740-6462	20258
Jonce Thomas Construction Co	1751	E	510 657-7171	3060
Kaiser Foundation Hospitals	8011	B	510 248-3000	19670
Kositch Enterprises Inc	1731	C	510 657-4460	2633
Land Services Landscape Contrs	0782	C	510 656-8101	887
Leisure Sports Inc	7991	C	510 226-8500	18654
Lifestyle Solutions Inc (PA)	5021	E	510 249-9301	6823
Lipman Insur Admnistrators Inc (PA)	6371	D	510 796-4676	10554
Lite-On Sales and Dist Inc	5045	D	510 687-1800	7155
Luxar Tech Inc	4813	C	408 835-2551	5649
Luxera Inc	7349	E	510 456-7690	14344
Magnum Drywall Inc	1742	D	510 979-0420	2925
Mariner Health Care Inc	8051	D	510 792-3743	20758
Marriott International Inc	7011	C	510 413-3700	12958
Med Staffing LLC	7363	E	510 795-0114	14907
Merrill Gardens	6514	D	510 790-1645	11237
Metabyte Inc	7379	D	510 494-9700	16431
Milan Corporation	1761	E	510 656-6400	3192
Milestone Technologies Inc (PA)	7373	C	510 651-2454	15994
Myoscience Inc	8748	E	510 933-1500	27995
Neptune Management Corporation	7261	D	510 797-2269	13708
Net Express	7373	D	510 887-4395	16002
Netversant - Silicon Vly Inc (PA)	1731	C	510 771-1200	2665
New Image Landscape Company	0782	D	510 226-9191	920
Nidek Incorporated	5048	C	510 226-5700	7335
Northland Control Systems Inc (PA)	1731	D	510 403-7600	2669
Novariant Inc (HQ)	8711	D	510 933-4800	25992
OES Equipment LLC (PA)	7359	D	510 284-1900	14562
Omnitrol Networks Inc	7373	E	408 919-1100	16023
On Lok Senior Health Services	6324	E	510 249-2700	10362
Overton Security Services Inc	7382	C	510 791-7380	16907
Pacific Gas and Electric Co	4911	C	510 770-2025	6185
Pacific Royal Group	5199	C	510 200-2993	9287
Page Front Catering	5087	D	408 406-8487	7975
Pape Material Handling Inc	5084	D	510 651-8200	7874
Park Cntl Care Rhblitation Ctr	8361	D	510 797-5300	24765
Penguin Computing Inc (PA)	5045	E	415 954-2800	7173
Permanente Medical Group Inc	8011	D	510 248-3000	19834
Petersen-Dean Inc	1761	C	510 494-9982	3202
Phihong USA Corp (HQ)	5045	D	510 445-0100	7174
Philips & Lite-On Digital (DH)	5049	E	510 824-9690	7346
PJs Lumber Inc	5031	C	510 743-5300	6948
Procera Networks Inc (HQ)	7371	D	510 230-2777	15395
Prudential CA Realty	6531	D	510 487-6088	11774
Psychiatric Solutions Inc	8011	D	510 796-1100	19896
PW Stephens Envmtl Inc	1799	D	510 651-9506	3572
Pyramid Painting Inc	1721	E	650 903-9791	2478
Quadrant Components Inc	5045	D	510 656-9988	7177
Quanta Computer Usa Inc (HQ)	5045	D	510 226-1371	7178
Ravenswood Solutions Inc	7373	D	650 241-3661	16038
Raymond Handling Concepts Corp (PA)	7699	D	510 745-7500	18003
Red Hawk Fire & SEC CA Inc	1731	D	510 438-1300	2699
Remax Active Realty	6531	E	510 505-1660	11804
Retirement Lf Care Communities	8361	D	510 505-0555	24787
RK Electric Inc	1731	C	510 580-2850	2713
Rk Logistics Group Inc	4731	C	408 942-8107	5162
Robert Half International Inc	7361	D	510 744-6486	14758
S & M Moving Systems	4213	D	510 497-2300	4255
San Francisco Bay Area Rapid	4111	B	510 441-2278	3699
San Francisco Herb Natural Fd (PA)	5149	D	510 770-1215	8918
San Jose Arena Management LLC	8741	D	510 623-7200	27204
Sansei Gardens Inc	0782	C	510 226-9191	948
Scholastic Book Fairs Inc	5192	D	510 771-1700	9172
Select Hotels Group LLC	7011	D	510 623-6000	13231
Seneca Family of Agencies	8322	D	510 226-6180	24204
Serrato-Mcdermott Inc	5013	D	510 656-6233	6762
Sigmaways Inc	8742	D	510 573-4208	27404
Soffront Software Inc	7371	D	510 413-9000	15461
Softsol Resources Inc (HQ)	7371	D	510 824-2000	15462
Soleeva Energy Inc	1711	D	408 396-4954	2378
Sonata Software North Amer Inc (HQ)	7371	D	510 791-7220	15468
Spinacom Inc	5045	C	510 270-2669	7193
Sportvision Inc	7812	E	510 736-2925	18158
SRS Consulting Inc	7379	D	510 252-0625	16489
Startup Farms Intl LLC	7371	D	510 440-0110	15477
Strategic Security Services	6289	C	510 623-2355	10198
Sun Innovations Inc	8731	E	510 573-3913	26612
Sunnyvale Fluid Sys Tech Inc	5085	D	510 933-2500	7956
Superior Automatic Sprnklr Co	1711	D	408 946-7272	2392
Sysco San Francisco Inc (HQ)	5141	A	510 226-3000	8535
T-Mobile Usa Inc	4812	C	510 797-8290	5414
Technology Credit Union	6062	D	408 467-2385	9693
Tenergy Corporation	5063	D	510 687-0388	7478
Timbre Technologies Inc	7371	D	510 624-3300	15504
Toyota Logistics Services	7549	C	510 498-7817	17900
Tri-City Health Center (PA)	8011	D	510 770-8040	20143
Triple Play Services Inc (PA)	4731	D	408 748-3929	5179
Tyan Computer Corporation	5045	D	510 651-8868	7206
U-Haul Co of California (DH)	7513	C	800 528-0463	17655
Underwriters Laboratories Inc	8734	B	510 771-1000	26897
United Mfg Assembly Inc	8734	D	510 490-1065	26900
United Parcel Service Inc OH	7389	B	800 742-5877	17563
Unitek Inc	7373	D	510 623-8544	16070
Unitek Information Systems Inc (PA)	7379	D	510 249-1060	16517
US Merchant Systems LLC	5065	D	877 432-8871	7652
Valgenesis Inc	5045	E	510 445-0505	7208
Vasona Management Inc	1521	D	510 413-0091	1279
Verizon Bus Netwrk Svcs Inc	7376	D	510 497-2500	16283
Vertisystem Inc	7373	D	510 794-8099	16078
Via Communications Inc	8731	C	510 687-4650	26636
Via Technologies Inc	5065	D	510 683-3300	7655
Walters & Wolf Glass Company (PA)	1793	C	510 490-1115	3417
Walters & Wolf Interiors (PA)	1751	D	415 243-9400	3100
Washington Hosp Healthcare Sys	8062	A	510 797-3342	22027
Washington Inventory Service	7389	E	510 498-5979	17614
Washington Outpatient	8011	D	510 791-5374	20228
Wells Fargo Bank National Assn	6021	D	510 792-3512	9453
Wells Fargo Bank National Assn	6021	C	415 222-6834	9457
Wells Fargo Bank National Assn	6021	B	510 745-5025	9461
YC Cable Usa Inc (HQ)	7389	D	510 824-2788	17636

FRENCH CAMP, CA - San Joaquin County

Company	SIC	EMP	PHONE	ENTRY #
County of San Joaquin	8322	D	209 468-6966	23907
Fresno Truck Center	5012	C	209 983-2400	6677
Health Plan of San Joaquin	6324	C	209 942-6300	10290
Healthy Beginnings French Camp	8011	D	209 468-6147	19553
Interstate Con Pmpg Co Inc	1771	D	209 983-3092	3277

GEOGRAPHIC SECTION

FRESNO, CA

Company	SIC	EMP	PHONE	ENTRY #
San Joaquin General Hospital	8011	C	209 468-6000	19945
San Joaquin Hospital	8062	A	209 468-6000	21850
Silva Trucking Inc	4212	E	209 982-1114	4066

FRESNO, CA - Fresno County

Company	SIC	EMP	PHONE	ENTRY #
A & A Plastering Co Inc	1742	D	559 439-2500	2843
A Colmenero Plastering Inc	1742	D	559 435-3606	2845
Aaron Dowling Incorporated	8111	D	559 432-4500	23079
ABM Janitorial Services Inc	7349	B	559 276-9096	14202
ABM Jntrial Svcs - Sthwest Inc	7349	D	559 276-9096	14208
Activision Blizzard Inc	4225	C	310 431-4000	4515
Adult Health Center At Sierra	8011	E	559 459-1550	19315
Aecom Global II LLC	8711	C	559 347-5669	25632
Agri Valley Services	8721	D	559 233-5633	26288
Aims Education Foundation	8748	C	559 255-4094	27821
All Commercial Landscape Svc	0782	E	559 453-1670	805
Allen Spees Family Homes	8361	E	559 432-3664	24544
Alliant Educational Foundation	8093	C	559 456-2777	22654
Allied Electric Motor Svc Inc (PA)	5063	D	559 486-4222	7411
Amdal In-Home Care Inc	8059	D	559 227-1701	21134
American All Risk Loss Adm	8742	C	559 277-4960	27318
American Baptist Homes of West	8361	E	559 439-4770	24546
American Fidelity Assurance Co	6411	D	559 230-2107	10592
American Paving Co	1611	E	559 268-9886	1730
Ameripride Services Inc	7218	D	559 266-0627	13601
Anthony Lambe	5013	D	559 268-0709	6705
AON Consulting Inc	6411	D	559 449-7200	10605
Apple Valley Farms Inc	1799	E	559 498-7115	3492
Aramark Unf & Career AP LLC	7213	C	559 291-6631	13536
ARC Fresno/Madera Counties (PA)	8331	D	559 226-6268	24304
Arise LLC	7999	E	559 485-0881	19141
Arise Construction Inc	1711	D	559 449-8989	2149
Art Piccadilly Shaw LLC	7011	D	559 375-7760	12397
Art Piccadilly Shaw LLC	7011	C	559 224-4200	12398
Arthur J Gallagher & Co	6411	D	559 436-0833	10626
Ascension Insurance Inc	6411	C	661 321-3290	10628
Ashwood Construction Inc	1522	E	559 253-7240	1294
AT&T Corp	4812	D	559 353-3999	5263
AT&T Services Inc	4813	B	559 454-3579	5531
AT&T Services Inc	4813	E	800 662-6252	5541
B T & T Travel Inc	4724	D	559 237-9410	4958
Baker Mnock Jensen A Prof Corp	8111	C	559 432-5400	23101
Baloian Packing Co Inc (PA)	0161	D	559 485-9200	38
Baloian Packing Co Inc	0161	D	559 441-7043	39
Bank America National Assn	6021	D	559 445-7731	9320
Bbt Health LLC	8082	D	559 222-0007	22375
Beverly Lving Ctr Cnty Vw Alzh	8059	D	559 275-4785	21157
BFI Waste Services LLC	4953	D	559 275-1551	6439
Bill Nlson Gen Engrg Cnstr Inc	1623	D	559 439-1756	1910
Bio Mdcal Applications Fla Inc	8092	D	559 221-6311	22618
Black & Veatch Corporation	8711	D	913 458-9406	25692
Bowie Enterprises (PA)	7542	D	559 227-6221	17832
Bowie Enterprises	7549	D	559 227-3400	17876
Bradford Messenger Service	7389	D	559 252-0775	17040
Brand Energy Solutions LLC	1799	D	559 444-1970	3500
Brix Group Inc (PA)	5065	D	559 457-4700	7534
Brix Group Inc	5065	D	559 499-1890	7535
Broder Bros Co	5136	D	559 233-9900	8336
Bronco Concrete Inc	1771	D	559 323-5005	3236
Brookdale Lving Cmmunities Inc	6513	D	559 321-8624	11101
BSK Associates	8711	D	559 497-2888	25709
Buckingham Property Management	7299	D	559 322-1105	13739
C&S Wholesale Grocers Inc	5141	B	559 442-4700	8461
Calif Stat Univ Fres Foun (PA)	8699	C	559 278-0850	25510
Calif Stat Univ Fres Foun	8699	C	559 278-0850	25511
California Cancer Asscts	8011	D	559 447-4949	19390
California Eye Institute	8011	D	559 449-5000	19391
California Hlth Collaborative (PA)	7389	D	559 221-6315	17047
California HM For The Aged Inc	8059	C	559 251-8414	21174
California Imaging Inst LLC	8011	D	559 447-4000	19394
Candor-Ags Inc (PA)	0173	D	559 439-2365	195
Cardinal Health Inc	5122	D	559 448-0788	8244
Cardiovascular Consultants Hea	8011	D	559 432-4303	19402
Carrollco Inc	1521	E	559 396-3939	1151
CBS Radio Inc	4832	C	559 490-0106	5757
Cellco Partnership	4812	D	559 454-0803	5295
Cellco Partnership	4812	D	559 451-0556	5309
Central Cal Nikkei Foundation	8322	D	559 237-4006	23725
Central California Blood Ctr	8099	D	559 389-5433	22915
Central California Blood Ctr	8099	D	559 324-1211	22916
Central California Blood Ctr (PA)	8099	D	559 389-5433	22917
Central California Ear Nose	8011	E	559 432-3724	19418
Central California Faculty Med (PA)	8011	D	559 453-5200	19419
Central Freight Lines Inc	4212	D	559 233-5559	3993
Central Valley Cmnty Bancorp (PA)	6022	C	559 298-1775	9482
Central Valley Community Bank	6712	C	559 298-1775	12041
Central Valley Presort Inc	7331	D	559 498-6151	14067
Central Vly Chld Svcs Netwrk	8322	D	559 456-1100	23727
Central Vly Yng MNS Chrn Assoc	8641	E	559 225-9191	25230
Century Adanalian & Vasquez	6531	D	559 244-6000	11382
Champagne Landscape Nurs Inc	0782	D	559 277-8188	823
Charles McMurray Co (PA)	5072	D	559 292-5751	7679
Charlies Enterprises	5148	C	559 445-8600	8704
Cherry Avenue Auction Inc	7389	E	559 266-9856	17070
Chicago Title Company	6361	D	559 451-3700	10503
Citigroup Global Markets Inc	6211	D	559 438-2542	9981
City of Fresno	4581	D	559 621-4500	4906
City of Fresno	4941	C	559 621-5300	6324
City of Fresno	7389	D	559 445-8200	17074
City of Fresno	6726	D	559 621-7080	12138
Clandestine Laboratory Invest	8734	D	760 597-7946	26838
Clay Miranda Trucking Inc	4212	D	559 275-6250	3995
Clinica Sierra Vista	8322	C	559 457-6900	23763
Club One Casino Inc	7999	B	559 497-3000	19185
Comcast Corporation	4841	D	559 389-7251	5960
Comcast Corporation	4841	D	559 718-9917	5962
Community Hospitals Centl Cal	8069	A	559 459-6000	22130
Community Integrated Work Prog	8331	E	559 276-8564	24324
Community Medical Center (PA)	8062	A	559 459-6000	21500
Community Medical Centers	8062	C	559 459-2916	21501
Community Medical Centers	8062	C	559 222-7416	21503
Community Medical Centers	8062	C	559 320-2200	21504
Community Medical Centers	8062	D	559 447-4050	21505
Community Medical Centers	8062	D	559 447-4000	21506
Comprehensive Youth Ser	8322	D	559 229-3561	23784
Congregation of Poor Sisters	8361	D	559 237-3444	24604
Contemporary Services Corp	7381	C	559 225-9325	16611
Copper River Country Club LP (PA)	7997	E	559 434-5200	18925
County of Fresno	8111	D	559 600-3420	23169
County of Fresno	8322	D	559 600-3800	23805
County of Fresno	8322	D	559 600-5127	23806
County of Fresno	8111	D	559 600-3546	23170
County of Fresno	8322	C	559 453-4099	23807
County of Fresno	8093	D	559 600-4600	22695
County of Fresno	8621	D	559 600-3534	25132
County of Fresno	8322	D	559 600-3996	23808
County of Fresno	8699	D	559 600-8135	25519
County of Fresno	8322	C	559 488-3275	23809
Covenant Care California LLC	8051	D	559 251-8463	20493
Crestwood Behavioral Hlth Inc	8063	D	559 445-9094	22062
D E F Express Corporation	4213	D	559 264-0705	4131
Darden Architects Inc	8712	D	559 448-8051	26181
De Benedetto Farms Inc	0173	D	559 276-2400	197
Decipher Inc (HQ)	8732	D	559 436-6940	26655
Deloitte & Touche LLP	8721	D	559 449-6300	26325
Der Mnuel Insur Fincl Svcs Inc	6411	D	559 447-4600	10689
Diamond Intl Investment LLC	7011	D	559 226-2200	12568
Diamond Learning Center Inc	8322	D	559 241-0580	23943
Dibuduo Dfendis Insur Brks LLC (PA)	6411	D	559 432-0222	10690
Diversified Transport Systems	4225	E	559 268-2760	4544
Donaghy Sales Inc	5181	C	559 486-0901	9054
Donahue Schriber Rlty Group LP	6512	D	714 545-1400	10976
Donald P Dick AC Inc (PA)	1711	E	559 255-1644	2207
Douglas L Myovich Trucking Inc	4212	D	559 264-1181	4010
E & S Rsidential Care Svcs LLC	8361	D	559 275-3555	24637
East Bay Clarklift Inc	5084	D	559 268-6621	7839
Edgewood Partners Insur Ctr	6411	D	559 451-3189	10695
Educational Employees Cr Un (PA)	6062	C	559 437-7700	9662
Educational Employees Cr Un	6062	D	559 896-0222	9664
Electric Motor Shop	5063	D	559 233-1153	7436
Electronic Recyclers Intl Inc (PA)	4953	C	800 884-8466	6481
Elim Alzheimers & Rehab	8051	D	559 320-2200	20532
Elitecare Medical Staffing LLC	7361	D	559 438-7700	14646
Energy Experts International	8748	C	559 449-1124	27912
Enterprise Holdings Inc	7514	D	559 261-9221	17670
Environment Control	7349	E	559 456-9791	14291
Exceptnl Prents Unlimited Inc	8322	D	559 229-2000	23964
Express Messenger Systems Inc	4513	C	559 277-4910	4843
Eye Medical Clinic Fresno Inc	8011	D	559 486-5000	19518
Eye Q Vision Care (PA)	8011	C	559 486-2000	19519
F & F Contracting Inc	0761	C	559 276-2418	660
Family Mdcine Rsidency Program	8062	D	559 499-6450	21564
Famous Software LLC (PA)	7371	D	559 438-3600	15180
Fedex Freight West Inc	4213	C	559 266-0732	4171
Ferguson Enterprises Inc	5074	E	559 253-2900	7713
Fig Garden Golf Course Inc	7997	D	559 439-2928	18950
Firemans Fund Insurance Co	6331	C	559 435-5050	10417
Five Star Quality Care Inc	8051	D	559 446-6226	20577
Fort Wash Golf & Cntry CLB	7997	D	559 434-1702	18953
Fort Washington Parent Assoc	8641	D	559 327-6600	25255
Foster Poultry Farms	0254	A	559 265-2000	458

Employment Codes: A=Over 500 employees, B=251-500, C=101-250, D=51-100, E=45-50

2017 Directory of California Wholesalers and Services Companies

© Mergent Inc. 1-800-342-5647

FRESNO, CA

Company	SIC	EMP	PHONE	ENTRY #
Four CS Service Inc	1761	D	559 237-3990	3174
Fowler Packing Company Inc	0723	C	559 834-5911	534
Freshko Produce Services Inc	5148	C	559 497-7000	8725
Fresno AG Hardware Inc	7299	D	559 224-6441	13761
Fresno Airport Hotels LLC	7011	D	559 252-3611	12654
Fresno Auto Dealers Auction	5012	C	559 268-8051	6675
Fresno Beverage Company Inc	5181	C	559 650-1500	9057
Fresno Cmnty Hosp & Med Ctr (HQ)	8062	A	559 459-6000	21572
Fresno Cnty Economic Opportunt	8322	A	559 263-1000	23983
Fresno Cnty Economic Opportunt (PA)	8322	A	559 263-1010	23984
Fresno Cnty Economic Opportunt	7389	B	559 263-1013	17176
Fresno Cnty Economic Opportunt	1742	D	559 485-3733	2899
Fresno County Federal Cr Un (PA)	6061	E	559 252-5000	9602
Fresno County Private Security	7381	D	559 233-9800	16648
Fresno Heart Hospital LLC	8069	B	559 433-8000	22142
Fresno Heritage Partners	8361	E	559 446-6226	24665
Fresno Hotel Partners LP	7011	E	559 224-4040	12655
Fresno Irrigation District	4971	D	559 233-7161	6643
Fresno Metro Flood Ctrl Dst	7389	D	559 456-3292	17177
Fresno Plumbing & Heating Inc (PA)	1711	C	559 294-0200	2230
Fresno Rescue Mission Inc (PA)	8322	E	559 268-0839	23985
Fresno Roofing Co Inc	1761	D	559 255-8377	3175
Fresno Skilled Nursing	8051	D	559 268-5361	20583
Fresno Surgery Center LP (PA)	8062	D	559 431-8000	21573
Fresno Truck Center	5012	C	559 486-4310	6676
Fresno Unified School District	7349	C	559 457-3074	14304
Fresnos Chaffee Zoo Corp	8422	C	559 498-5910	25063
Frito-Lay North America Inc	5145	C	559 226-8153	8612
Frontier California Inc	4812	C	559 224-9222	5397
Ganduglia Trucking	4214	C	559 251-7101	4346
Gateway Auto Sales & Lsg Inc	5012	C	800 921-4336	6678
Geil Enterprises Inc (PA)	7381	C	559 495-3000	16664
Gene A Garcia Construction	1521	E	559 352-6173	1182
General Coatings Corporation	1721	C	559 495-4004	2447
GLad Entertainment Inc (PA)	7999	D	559 292-9000	19217
Glaxosmithkline Consumer	5122	D	559 650-1550	8256
Golden Cross Care II Inc	8051	D	559 268-3023	20602
Golden Living LLC	8051	D	559 237-8377	20603
Golden Living LLC	8051	D	559 275-4785	20607
Golden Living LLC	8059	D	559 486-4433	21246
Golden Living LLC	8051	D	559 227-4807	20619
Golden Living LLC	8051	D	559 227-5383	20621
Golden Living LLC	8059	D	559 227-4063	21248
Golden State Plastering	5032	C	559 439-3920	6986
Graham-Prewett Inc	1542	E	559 291-3741	1556
Granite Construction Company	1611	C	559 441-5700	1783
Granville Homes Inc	1521	C	559 268-2000	1186
Greyhound Lines Inc	4173	C	559 268-1829	3959
Guarantee Real Estate	6531	E	559 650-6030	11565
Guarantee Real Estate Corp	6531	C	559 431-8600	11566
Guardsmark LLC	7381	C	559 243-1217	16689
Harris Construction Co Inc	1542	C	559 251-0301	1563
Health Comp Administrators (PA)	6411	C	559 499-2450	10737
Healthcare California	8082	D	559 243-9990	22454
Healthcare Centre of Fresno	8051	D	559 268-5361	20657
Healthcomp	6411	B	559 499-2450	10738
HI Fresno Hospitality LLC	7011	D	559 233-6650	12702
Hinds Hospice (PA)	8082	D	559 248-8579	22457
Hispanic Business Student Assn	8621	C	209 769-7279	25137
Howe Electric Construction Inc	1731	C	559 255-8992	2616
I Heart Media Inc	4832	C	559 243-4300	5778
Iheartcommunications Inc	4833	D	559 222-4302	5872
Iheartcommunications Inc	4832	D	559 230-4300	5787
Inland Star Dist Ctrs Inc (PA)	4225	D	559 237-2052	4578
Ipsos Public Affairs Inc	8732	C	559 451-2820	26677
J & D Meat Company	5149	D	559 445-1123	8858
J M C International LLC	1542	E	559 256-1300	1578
J M Equipment Company Inc	5082	C	559 233-0187	7776
James G Parker Insurance Assoc (PA)	6411	D	559 222-7722	10752
Jorgensen & Sons Inc (PA)	5099	C	559 268-6241	8122
JR Simplot Company	0211	C	559 439-3900	408
Jra Landscape Inc	0782	D	559 276-1726	882
K W P H Enterprises	4119	B	559 443-5900	3808
Kaiser Foundation Hospitals	6324	C	559 448-4555	10300
Kaiser Foundation Hospitals	8062	A	559 448-4500	21674
Kaiser Foundation Hospitals	8011	A	559 448-4500	19679
Kaiser Radiology	8071	D	559 448-5541	22228
Karsyn Construction Inc	1542	E	559 271-2900	1589
Keisers Holdings LLC	7991	C	559 265-4700	18649
Kenyon Construction Inc	1742	C	559 277-5645	2920
Kertel Communications Inc (HQ)	1731	C	559 432-5800	2631
Kfsn Television LLC	4833	C	559 442-1170	5880
Kftv	4833	D	559 222-2121	5881
Kid Iq 24 Hr Childcare	8351	D	310 492-3037	24471
Kimberlite Corporation (PA)	7382	D	559 264-9730	16895
Kings River Conservation Dst	8999	D	559 237-5567	28140
Kisco Senior Living LLC	8741	D	559 449-8070	27098
Kleinfelder Inc	8711	D	559 486-0750	25922
Kmph Fox 26	4833	C	559 255-2600	5883
Knax Country 98	4832	E	559 490-9800	5796
Kraft Heinz Foods Company	5149	C	559 499-5300	8870
Krm Risk Management Svcs Inc	8741	D	559 277-4800	27103
Kroeker Inc	1795	C	559 237-3764	3458
L A S Transportation Inc	4213	B	559 264-6583	4206
Labor Fnders of The Palm Bches	7363	D	559 221-2023	14895
Lang Richert & Patch	8111	C	559 228-6700	23364
Lassley Enterprises Inc	6513	E	559 226-4300	11153
Leisure Care LLC	8361	C	559 434-1237	24710
Liberty Mutual Insurance Co	6331	C	559 435-2144	10437
Lily Holdings LLC	8051	D	559 222-4807	20736
Linkus Enterprises LLC	1623	C	559 256-6600	1962
Lozano Smith A Prof Corp (PA)	8111	D	559 431-5600	23413
Lyles Mechanical Co	1711	C	559 237-2200	2286
M & L Plumbing Co Inc	1711	E	559 291-5525	2287
Major Transportation Svcs Inc	4213	E	559 485-5949	4214
Manning Gardens Inc	8059	E	559 834-2586	21307
Manning Gardens Care Ctr Inc	8051	D	559 834-2586	20754
McCormick Barstow Shepprd Wayt (PA)	8111	C	559 433-1300	23424
McCutcheon Enterprises Inc	0172	D	559 864-3200	170
McKesson Technologies Inc	7389	C	559 455-4000	17320
Medmark Services Inc	8069	E	559 264-2700	22159
Melos Plst Lthg & Drywall	1742	D	559 237-0028	2930
Mesa Energy Systems Inc	1711	D	559 277-7900	2294
Mikes Vineyard Spray Inc	7342	D	559 269-7109	14190
Millmens Local 1496	8631	E	559 275-8676	25179
Mirabella Farms Inc	0172	D	559 237-4495	171
Mission Linen Supply	7213	D	559 268-0647	13556
Moore Twining Associates Inc (PA)	8734	D	559 268-7021	26871
Morgan Stanley & Co LLC	6211	D	559 431-5900	10052
Morrison MGT Specialists Inc	8099	C	559 459-6449	23002
Muniservices LLC (HQ)	8742	C	800 800-8181	27553
Netafim Irrigation Inc (HQ)	5083	C	559 453-6800	7805
New England Shtmtl Works Inc	8711	C	559 268-7375	25990
New York Life Insurance Co	6411	D	559 447-3900	10808
Newport Television LLC	7922	C	559 761-0243	18418
Nexstar Broadcasting Group Inc	4833	C	559 222-2411	5902
Nia Healthcare Services Inc	8051	D	559 251-1526	20806
Nicole Pttrson Crt Rprting LLC	8111	E	559 400-2407	23469
North Pt Hlth Wellness Ctr LLC	8051	D	559 320-2200	20808
North West Learning Center	8351	E	559 228-3057	24487
Northern Rfrigerated Trnsp Inc	4213	D	559 241-7350	4236
Northwest Medical Group Inc	8011	D	559 271-6302	19784
Northwest Physicians Med Group	8011	D	559 271-6370	19785
Ocb Restaurant Company LLC	7299	D	559 271-1927	13781
Ohanians Drywall Inc	1742	D	559 277-2946	2939
Olam Americas Inc (DH)	0723	A	559 447-1390	572
Omni Womens Hlth Med Group Inc	8011	E	559 441-4271	19794
Organic Pastures Dairy Co LLC	0241	E	559 846-9732	437
Paccar Leasing Corporation	7513	C	559 268-4344	17642
Pacific Gas and Electric Co	4911	B	559 268-2868	6171
Pacific Grain & Foods LLC (PA)	5153	C	559 276-2580	8961
Pacific Trellis Fruit LLC (PA)	5148	D	559 255-5437	8762
Park Inn By Radisson	7011	D	559 226-2200	13075
Park Inn By Readisson Fresno	7011	D	559 226-2200	13076
Patton Sheet Metal Works Inc	1761	E	559 486-5222	3196
Paychex Inc	8721	D	559 432-1100	26417
Pbc Solution One Inc	1799	C	559 348-0019	3567
PDM Steel Service Centers	5051	E	559 442-1410	7389
Penske Truck Leasing Co LP	7513	C	559 486-7000	17648
Permanente Medical Group Inc	8011	A	559 448-4500	19837
Piccadilly Hospitality LLC	7011	E	559 348-5520	13094
Plumbing Limited Inc	1711	E	559 453-0690	2324
Principal Financial Group Inc	6311	C	559 261-2000	10221
Producers Dairy Foods Inc (PA)	5142	C	559 264-6583	8563
Professional Exchange Svc	7389	E	559 229-6249	17432
Protosource Corporation	7374	D	559 490-8600	16173
Prudential Overall Supply	7218	C	559 264-8231	13639
Pv Acquisition Bank	6029	C	559 438-2002	9555
Qc (us) International Inc	8741	D	559 447-1390	27186
Quest Diagnostics Incorporated	8071	C	559 438-2893	22268
Quiring Corporation	1542	D	559 432-2800	1642
Quiring General LLC	1542	E	559 432-2800	1643
R Fellen Inc	8051	D	559 233-6248	20861
Randstad North America Inc	7361	C	559 297-0054	14743
Reading and Beyond	8641	D	559 840-1668	25326
Regent Corp	7299	E	559 226-3850	13790
Renaissance Inc	1742	D	559 320-0048	2965
Rescue Children Inc	8322	E	559 268-1123	24154
Residence Inn By Marriott	7011	D	559 222-8900	13146
Rex More Elec Contrs Engineers	1731	D	559 294-1300	2708

GEOGRAPHIC SECTION

FULLERTON, CA

	SIC	EMP	PHONE	ENTRY #
Rgis LLC	7389	D	559 224-5898	17463
Riverside Nursery & Ldscp Inc	5193	D	559 275-1891	9211
Ron D & Shelley N Horn	0172	E	559 834-2118	181
Royal Express Inc **(PA)**	4214	C	559 272-3500	4373
SA Recycling LLC	4953	D	559 237-6677	6541
Saint Agnes Med Providers Inc	8099	D	559 450-7200	23042
Saint Agnes Medical Center **(HQ)**	8062	A	559 450-3000	21837
Saladinos Inc **(PA)**	5141	C	559 271-3700	8517
San Joaquin Country Club	7997	D	559 439-3483	19058
San Joaquin Figs Inc	0723	E	559 224-4492	582
San Joaquin Valley A P C D	8748	D	559 230-6000	28051
San Joaquin Valley Intergrp	8699	E	559 856-0559	25573
San Joaquin Valley Rehabili **(HQ)**	8093	B	559 436-3600	22826
San Mar Properties Inc **(PA)**	6531	E	559 439-5500	11831
Sante Health System Inc	8011	C	559 228-5400	19963
Scrip Advantage Inc	7389	D	559 320-0052	17481
Sears Roebuck and Co	7699	C	559 244-6214	18013
Securitas SEC Svcs USA Inc	7381	C	559 221-2302	16788
Ser Jobs For Progress Inc San	8322	D	559 452-0881	24209
Servi-Tech Controls Inc **(PA)**	1711	D	559 264-6679	2364
Shaw Hospitality Group Inc	7011	D	559 224-4040	13238
Shaws Strctures Unlimited Inc	1541	E	559 275-3475	1462
Sierra Bancorp	6029	D	559 449-8145	9559
Sierra Pacific Development	6552	D	559 256-1300	12009
Sierra Pacific Ortho	8011	C	559 256-5200	20003
Signature Flight Support Corp	4581	D	559 981-2490	4934
Silla Automotive LLC	5013	D	559 457-0711	6771
Simone Fruit Co Inc	0723	D	559 275-1368	586
Smg Holdings Inc	7389	B	559 445-8100	17493
Spirit of Woman of California	8093	D	559 233-4353	22840
State Compensation Insur Fund	6331	D	559 433-2700	10467
Steven G Fogg MD	8011	D	559 449-5010	20069
Strategic Mechanical Inc	1711	C	559 291-1952	2386
Sunnyside Country Club	7997	D	559 255-8926	19101
Sunrise Senior Living LLC	8051	D	559 325-8170	20979
Swift Transportation Company	4213	D	559 441-0340	4272
T Royal Management **(PA)**	6531	D	559 447-9887	11862
Target Corporation	4226	D	559 431-0104	4705
Terry Tuell Concrete Inc	1771	D	559 431-0812	3342
Teter LLP **(PA)**	8711	E	559 437-0887	26089
Thomas M Obinson Jr	6531	D	559 432-6200	11875
Torres Fence Co Inc	1799	E	559 237-4141	3591
Trinity Home Health Svcs Inc	8082	D	559 450-5112	22583
Turner Security Systems Inc	7381	C	559 486-3466	16836
Tutor Perini/Zachry/Parsons	1629	E	559 385-7025	2093
Twilight Haven	8051	D	559 251-8417	20997
Unifirst Corporation	7218	D	559 233-0400	13647
Union Pacific Railroad Company	4011	C	559 443-2244	3621
Union Pacific Railroad Company	4013	C	559 443-2277	3629
United Crbrl Plsy of Cntrl CA **(PA)**	8322	E	559 221-8272	24270
United States Cold Storage	4222	E	559 237-6145	4505
Univision Radio Inc	4832	E	559 430-8500	5828
Univision Television Group Inc	4833	D	559 222-2121	5921
Uniwell Corporation	6552	D	559 268-1000	12022
Uniwell Fresno Hotel LLC	7011	D	559 268-1000	13368
UPS Ground Freight Inc	4213	D	559 445-9010	4285
Urology Assoc of Cen Cal	8011	D	559 321-2800	20174
US Property Group Inc	6512	E	559 227-1901	11066
USA Waste of California Inc	4953	D	559 834-9151	6583
Utility Trlr Sls of Centl Cal	5084	E	559 237-2001	7899
Valley Fig Growers	0723	E	559 237-3893	600
Valley Floor Maintenance Inc	7349	D	559 495-3083	14461
Valley Healthcare Center LLC	8051	A	559 251-7161	21002
Valley Healthcare Center LLC	8051	D	559 251-7161	21003
Valley Teen Ranch	8361	D	559 437-1144	24843
Van De Pol Enterprises Inc	5172	D	559 860-4100	9032
Veritiv Operating Company	5113	D	559 268-0467	8219
Veterans Health Administration	8062	A	559 225-6100	22019
Veterans Health Administration	8011	A	559 225-6100	20199
Veterans Home Cal - Fresno	8051	D	559 493-4400	21007
Vibra Healthcare LLC	8062	D	559 436-3600	22021
Vision Care Center **(PA)**	8011	D	559 486-2000	20227
Volt Management Corp	7363	C	559 435-1255	14974
Vucovich Inc **(PA)**	5083	D	559 486-8020	7814
W M Lyles Co **(HQ)**	1623	E	951 973-7393	2013
Well Being Group Inc	8082	D	559 432-3737	22615
Wells Fargo Insur Svcs USA Inc	6411	D	559 228-6300	10929
West Air Inc	4513	D	559 454-7843	4878
Western Building Materials Co **(PA)**	1742	D	559 454-8500	2999
Wild Electric Incorporated	1731	D	559 251-7770	2795
Windham At Saint Agnes	6513	D	559 449-8070	11230
Winegard Energy Inc	1742	D	559 441-0243	3002
Winnresidential Ltd Partnr	7513	A	559 435-3434	17658
Wish I Ah Care Center Inc	8051	C	559 855-2211	21059
Wish-Ah Hlthcre & Wellness	8051	D	559 855-2211	21060
Wish-I-Ah Skilled Nursing	8051	C	949 285-8859	21061
Wm B Saleh Co	1721	D	559 275-2046	2504
Wm Michael Stemler Inc	6411	D	559 228-4144	10943
Xpo Enterprise Services Inc	4213	D	559 485-1164	4310
Xpo Logistics Supply Chain Inc	4731	C	559 408-7951	5193
Xtreme Zone Inc	7999	C	559 474-6861	19311
Zumwalt Construction Inc	1542	D	559 252-1000	1721

FRIANT, CA - Fresno County

	SIC	EMP	PHONE	ENTRY #
Table Mountain Casino	7999	A	559 822-2485	19292

FULLERTON, CA - Orange County

	SIC	EMP	PHONE	ENTRY #
A1 Building Management Inc	7349	C	714 447-3800	14198
Alpha Swimming Pool & Spa	7389	D	714 879-4667	16982
Altura Comm Solutions LLC **(DH)**	5065	D	714 948-8400	7517
American Golf Corporation	7992	D	714 672-6800	18713
American Multi-Cinema Inc	7832	E	714 992-6961	18301
AMS American Mech Svcs MD Inc	1711	D	714 888-6820	2143
Anaheim Park Hotel	7011	D	714 992-1700	12388
Anderson Air Conditioning LP	1711	D	714 998-6850	2145
Ans World Service Inc	4789	D	714 441-2400	5214
Arconic Global Fas & Rings Inc	5085	D	714 871-1550	7919
Associated Students Californi	8641	D	657 278-2468	25200
Austin Builders	1521	E	714 879-1100	1131
Bakery Ex Southern Cal LLC	5149	D	714 446-9470	8804
Bon Suisse Inc	8748	D	714 578-0001	27853
Cardservice International	7389	D	714 871-1778	17055
Catalina Enterprise Inc	8748	D	949 637-3091	27867
Cellco Partnership	4812	D	714 449-0715	5380
City of Fullerton	8742	C	714 738-6897	27382
Corecare I I I	8361	C	714 256-8000	24606
Corecare V A Cal Ltd Partnr	8051	D	714 256-1000	20472
County of Orange	8111	E	714 626-3700	23179
Diverse Staffing Inc	7361	A	714 525-8477	14638
Dunlap Property Group Inc	6531	D	714 879-0111	11481
Elliott Auto Supply Co Inc	5013	D	310 527-2500	6729
Excel Construction Svcs Inc **(PA)**	1541	D	714 680-9200	1423
Federal Express Corporation	4513	C	800 463-3339	4859
Florence Crittenton Services	8361	B	714 680-9000	24659
Fullerton College	7538	D	714 732-5453	17792
Fullerton Guest Home Inc	8059	D	714 441-0313	21229
Fullerton Healthcare	8051	C	714 992-5701	20587
Geek Squad Inc	7379	D	800 433-5778	16385
Gordon Lane Convalescent Hosp	8062	D	714 879-7301	21586
Harte Hanks Inc	7374	D	210 829-9000	16138
Harte-Hanks Direct Mail/Califo	7331	D	714 738-5478	14073
Henry Bros Electronics Inc	7373	C	714 525-4350	15958
Hot Dogger Tours Inc	4142	C	714 449-6888	3903
Huoyen International Inc	7011	D	714 635-9000	12805
Jcv Inc	1742	E	714 871-2007	2917
Jdf Construction Inc	1521	E	714 526-1120	1192
John G Shipley	6531	D	714 626-2000	11598
Lare Framing Systems Inc	1751	D	714 630-7686	3062
Loewy Enterprises	5148	D	323 726-3838	8748
Merritt Hospitality LLC	7011	C	714 738-7800	12991
National Technical Systems Inc	8734	D	714 998-4351	26876
Opus Bank	6035	C	714 578-7500	9578
Opus Inspection	7371	D	714 999-6727	15355
Orange Pacific Plumbing Inc	1711	D	714 992-4547	2313
Orora North America	5113	C	714 278-6000	8207
Orora North America	5113	D	714 773-0124	8209
Pacific Couriers Inc	4215	B	714 278-6100	4419
Prestige Sales II LLC	5149	D	714 632-8020	8911
Progressive Floor Covering Inc	1752	D	714 213-8805	3128
Pss World Medical Inc	5047	C	714 449-4000	7308
Quaker Oats Company	4225	E	714 526-8800	4618
Real Estate Image	7331	C	714 502-3900	14088
Romach LLC	5063	D	805 378-1174	7468
Rosary Academy Parent Council	8641	D	714 879-6302	25327
RPM Consolidated Services Inc **(PA)**	4225	D	714 388-3500	4633
RPM Transportation Inc **(HQ)**	4213	D	714 388-3500	4254
Sage Behavior Services Inc	8063	D	714 773-0077	22089
Salon Lujon Inc	7231	C	714 738-1882	13689
Salon Technique	7299	E	714 871-4247	13792
Southern California Edison Co	4911	C	714 870-3225	6220
St Joseph Health System	8062	D	714 992-3000	21917
St Jude Hospital **(DH)**	8062	A	714 871-3280	21925
St Jude Hospital	8062	C	714 578-8500	21926
St Jude Hospital	8011	D	714 992-3057	20058
St Jude Hospital Yorba Linda **(PA)**	8742	D	714 449-4800	27661
Sun Haven Care Inc	8051	D	714 578-2794	20934
Swinford Electric Inc	1731	E	714 578-8888	2762
Tf Courier Inc	4215	D	714 888-1452	4427
Thales-Raytheon Systems Co LLC **(HQ)**	5065	A	714 446-3118	7649
Therapy For Kids Inc	8049	D	714 870-6116	20358
Time Warner Cable Inc	4841	D	714 772-2643	6043

Employment Codes: A=Over 500 employees, B=251-500, C=101-250, D=51-100, E=45-50

FULLERTON, CA

GEOGRAPHIC SECTION

	SIC	EMP	PHONE	ENTRY #
TW Services Inc	4789	B	714 441-2400	5248
UPS Ground Freight Inc	4213	D	866 372-5619	4294
US Foods Inc	5149	C	714 449-9990	8948
Veg-Land Inc	4221	E	714 871-6712	4484
Viele & Sons Inc	5141	D	714 446-1686	8551
Walt Disney Company	7996	D	714 449-6600	18838
Ware Disposal Inc (PA)	4953	D	714 834-0234	6594
Windsor Gardns Healthcare Cntr	8051	C	714 871-6020	21050
Wyndham International Inc	7011	C	714 992-1700	13434
YMCA of North Orange County	8641	D	714 879-9622	25413
Young Mens Chrstn Assn Orange	8641	D	714 879-9622	25473

GALT, CA - Sacramento County

	SIC	EMP	PHONE	ENTRY #
Building Material Distrs Inc (PA)	5031	C	209 745-3001	6911
City of Galt	7999	D	209 366-7180	19172
Concrete North Inc	1771	D	209 745-7400	3249
Dry Creek Lath & Plaster Inc	1742	D	209 367-8607	2887
Eliseo Esparza Delgadillo	0761	E	209 745-3937	658
Golden Living LLC	8082	D	209 745-1537	22442
Gonzales Salvador Labor Contrs	0761	D	209 745-2223	664
Keb Keb Magic Clown	7999	D	916 369-6054	19232
Norogachi Construction Inc/CA	1742	D	916 236-4201	2936
Western Star Nurseries LLC	5193	E	209 744-2552	9228

GARBERVILLE, CA - Humboldt County

	SIC	EMP	PHONE	ENTRY #
Southern Hmbldt Cmnty Dst Hosp	8062	D	707 923-3921	21905

GARDEN GROVE, CA - Orange County

	SIC	EMP	PHONE	ENTRY #
Aaron Thomas Company Inc (PA)	7389	C	714 894-4468	16963
Abbey-Properties LLC (PA)	6512	D	562 435-2100	10953
Act Home Health Inc	8082	D	714 560-0800	22332
AGR Group Inc	8742	A	714 245-7151	27309
Alta Care Center LLC	8059	C	714 530-6322	21132
Ap-Redlands LLC	8742	E	562 435-2100	27328
Audio Visual MGT Solutions	8741	D	714 590-8755	26931
Bank America National Assn	6021	E	714 973-8495	9329
Best Valet Parking Corporation	7299	D	800 708-2538	13738
Boys Grls Clubs Grdn Grove Inc (PA)	8641	D	714 530-0430	25219
Boys Grls Clubs Grdn Grove Inc	8641	D	714 537-8833	25220
Chapman Hbr Skiled Nrsing Care	8051	D	714 971-5517	20455
Community Action Partnershi	8322	D	714 897-6670	23769
Compass Group Usa Inc	7359	D	714 899-2520	14524
Complete Relocation Svcs Inc	4214	D	714 901-7411	4335
Concorde Career Colleges Inc	8062	D	714 620-1000	21510
Consoldted Med Bo-Analysis Inc	8071	D	714 467-0240	22204
Customfab Inc	7389	C	714 891-9119	17111
Elrob Inc	5065	D	714 230-6100	7560
Ferguson Enterprises Inc	5074	D	714 893-1936	7718
G Brothers Construction Inc	1742	E	714 590-3070	2902
Garden Grove Convales	8059	D	714 638-9470	21231
Garden Grove Medical Investors (HQ)	8051	D	714 534-1041	20590
Goodwin Ammonia Company	4225	D	714 894-0531	4563
Hansol Goldpoint LLC	4731	C	714 594-5073	5093
Healthcare System 2000	8011	D	714 899-2000	19552
Hyatt Corporation	7011	B	714 750-1234	12817
Informative Research (PA)	7323	E	714 638-2855	14061
Janitorial Equipment Svcs Inc	7349	D	951 205-8937	14332
Kaiser Foundation Hospitals	8011	D	714 741-3448	19584
Kenneth Corp	8062	A	714 537-5160	21682
Limbach Company LP	1711	C	714 653-7000	2281
M M Direct Marketing Inc	7331	B	714 265-4100	14081
Mastroianni Family Entps Ltd	7299	D	310 952-1700	13775
Mitsubishi Electric Us Inc	5065	D	714 934-5300	7606
Money Mailer LLC (HQ)	7331	C	714 889-3800	14084
OfficeMax Incorporated	4225	C	951 485-9353	4608
Ohi Resort Hotels LLC	7011	D	714 867-5555	13037
Onesource Distributors LLC	5063	D	714 523-1012	7462
Orange County Trnsp Auth	4111	D	714 560-6282	3686
Our Watch	8082	D	714 897-1022	22526
Pacific Exteriors Inc	1742	D	714 265-1998	2948
Pacific Haven Convalescent HM	8059	D	714 534-1942	21341
Pacific Rim Rsrces Search Agcy	7361	C	714 638-0307	14719
Party Pantry Garden Room	7299	E	714 899-0626	13786
Pathfinder Health Inc	8082	D	714 636-5649	22532
Prime Health Care Svcs Grdn Gr	8062	B	714 537-5160	21808
Progressive Power Group Inc	1711	E	714 899-2300	2331
Public Bell Inc	7371	D	818 396-1675	15402
Quail Engineering Inc	1611	E	714 636-0612	1847
RJ Allen Inc	7353	D	714 539-1022	14497
Schlumberger Technology Corp	1389	D	714 379-7332	1095
Sherton Grdn Grove Anheim S Ht	7011	D	714 703-8400	13247
South Coast Logistics	4214	E	714 894-4744	4376
Southern California Edison Co	4911	C	714 636-2166	6231
Southland Industries (PA)	1711	E	800 613-6240	2383
Southland Industries	1711	D	714 901-5800	2384
Spectrum MGT Holdg Co LLC	4841	D	714 903-4000	6025

	SIC	EMP	PHONE	ENTRY #
Stonebridge McWhinney LLC	7011	E	714 703-8800	13306
Teletrac Inc (HQ)	4899	C	714 897-0877	6093
Western Transit Systems Inc	4121	D	949 515-0188	3871

GARDEN VALLEY, CA - El Dorado County

	SIC	EMP	PHONE	ENTRY #
Buckland Vineyard Management (PA)	8741	D	530 333-1534	26949

GARDENA, CA - Los Angeles County

	SIC	EMP	PHONE	ENTRY #
Acme Metals & Steel Supply Inc	5051	D	310 329-2263	7353
Action Force Security	7381	E	310 715-6053	16537
Administrative Svcs Coop LLC	8742	C	310 715-1968	27304
American Residential Svcs LLC	1711	E	310 637-1454	2130
Andrew M Martin Company Inc	7389	D	310 323-2000	16992
Anvil Steel Corporation	1791	D	310 329-5811	3363
Arena Painting Contractors Inc	1721	D	310 316-2446	2429
Avanti Hospitals LLC	8062	C	310 532-4200	21457
Avongard Products USa Ltd	7819	D	310 319-2300	18215
Bank America National Assn	6021	D	800 432-1000	9331
Behavioral Health Services Inc (PA)	8322	E	310 679-9031	23679
Best Contracting Services Inc (PA)	1761	B	310 328-6969	3142
Brightview Landscape Svcs Inc	0781	C	310 327-8700	754
California Supply Inc (PA)	5113	D	310 532-2500	8187
California Waste Services LLC	4953	C	310 538-5998	6450
Canon Bus Solutions-West Inc	5044	B	310 217-3000	7043
Cardinal Trnsp Group Inc	4151	C	310 769-2400	3914
Carroll Shelby Licensing Inc	4225	C	310 914-1843	4531
Ceridian LLC	8721	C	310 719-7400	26309
Charles E Thomas Company Inc (PA)	5084	D	310 323-6730	7833
City of Gardena	4111	D	310 324-1475	3639
Classic Tile & Mosaic Inc (PA)	5032	D	310 538-9605	6978
Claud Townsley Inc	1761	D	310 527-6770	3151
Cleanstreet	4959	C	310 329-3078	6623
CM Laundry LLC	7219	C	310 436-6170	13651
Cns Logistics Inc	4731	D	562 229-1133	5049
Commercial Protective Svcs Inc	7381	D	310 515-5290	16606
Coretco Inc	1623	C	323 770-2920	1923
Counseling and Research Assoc (PA)	8361	C	310 715-2020	24607
CPS Security Solutions Inc (PA)	7381	D	310 818-1030	16614
Cymetrix Corporation	8741	D	424 201-6300	27000
Dependable Auto Shippers Inc	4213	C	310 719-9915	4134
Duggan & Associates Inc	1721	D	323 965-1502	2440
Eagle Security Service Inc	7381	C	310 532-1626	16630
Ecamsecure	5065	E	800 257-5512	7558
El Dorado Enterprises Inc	7011	A	310 719-9800	12613
Esi Publishing Inc	7371	D	310 768-1800	15172
Fedex Freight Corporation	4213	B	310 323-5230	4165
First Student Inc	4151	C	310 715-6122	3932
Gardena Flores Inc	8051	D	310 323-4570	20592
Gardena Hospital LP	8062	A	310 532-4200	21574
Gfk Custom Research LLC	8732	C	310 527-2100	26668
Gina B Ltd Inc	5023	D	310 366-7926	6865
Global Paratransit Inc	4119	B	310 715-7550	3800
Global Stainless Supply	5099	B	310 525-1865	8116
Greater South Bay Area HM Hlth	8082	E	310 329-4835	22448
Guardsmark LLC	7381	D	310 522-9603	16676
Guardsmark LLC	7381	C	310 225-3977	16696
Harbor Distributing LLC	5181	B	310 538-5483	9063
Health Care Investments Inc	8051	D	310 323-3194	20656
Houston Salem Inc	5136	E	310 719-7004	8346
Image First Healthcre Lndry Sp	7218	B	310 819-1463	13631
JH Bryant Jr Inc (PA)	1541	D	310 532-1840	1440
Jk Imaging Ltd	5043	D	310 667-4898	7034
John S Meek Company Inc	1629	D	310 830-6323	2063
Jomar Industries Inc	7389	E	323 770-0505	17261
JS Real Estate Prpts Inc	1791	D	310 856-6868	3385
Kaiser Foundation Hospitals	8011	A	800 780-1230	19618
Kaiser Foundation Hospitals	8062	D	310 517-2956	21656
Kintetsu Intl Ex USA Inc	4724	C	310 525-1650	4965
Knd Development 53 LLC	8069	D	310 323-5330	22150
Landcare USA LLC	0782	D	310 719-1008	892
Landcare USA LLC	0782	C	310 354-1520	895
Legions Protective Svcs LLC	7381	E	310 819-8881	16722
Los Angeles Unified School Dst	7349	D	310 808-1500	14343
M&M Asseet Management Gnl	6513	D	310 769-6669	11162
Magnetika Inc (PA)	5063	D	310 527-8100	7453
Martin Bros/Marcowall Inc (PA)	1742	D	310 532-5335	2926
MGA Healthcare California Inc	7363	D	310 324-5591	14912
MGT Industries Inc	8741	D	310 324-3152	27129
Monark LP	6513	D	310 769-6669	11169
Mufg Union Bank Na	6021	E	310 354-4700	9407
Mutual Propane Inc	5169	E	310 515-0553	8995
Nippon Travel Agency Amer Inc	4724	D	310 768-1817	4969
Nippon Travel Agency PCF Inc (DH)	4724	D	310 768-0017	4970
Normandie Club LP	7999	A	310 352-3486	19251
Northrop Grumman Federal Cr Un (PA)	6061	D	310 808-4000	9617
Nygard Inc	5137	D	310 776-8900	8406

GEOGRAPHIC SECTION

GLENDALE, CA

	SIC	EMP	PHONE	ENTRY #
Pacific Systems Interiors Inc	1742	C	310 436-6820	2950
Phase 1 Tele-Team	7361	E	562 746-8734	14727
Premier Tile & Marble	1743	D	310 516-1712	3022
Ps2 (PA)	1721	D	310 243-2980	2477
Pulp Studio Incorporated (PA)	7336	D	310 815-4999	14160
Quest Discovery Services Inc	7363	D	310 769-5557	14929
R Haupt Roofing Construction	1761	E	310 515-9709	3205
Radford Alexander Corporation	4212	D	310 523-2555	4053
Radiant Services Corp (PA)	7211	C	310 327-6300	13506
Rancho California Landscaping	0782	E	310 768-1680	941
Republic Services Inc	4953	D	310 527-6980	6538
Roadex America Inc	4731	D	310 878-9800	5163
Rotor Exchange	5015	C	310 323-5710	6796
Schumacher Cargo Logistics Inc (PA)	4731	D	310 324-1365	5166
Security America Inc	7381	C	310 532-0121	16815
Silverline Construction Inc	1542	C	310 464-8314	1669
SMS Transportation	8111	D	310 527-9200	23575
Softline Home Fashions Inc	5131	D	310 630-4848	8327
SOS Metals Inc (DH)	5093	C	310 217-8848	8089
South Bay Auto Auction	5012	C	310 719-2000	6694
Southern Cal Maid Svc Crpt Clg	7349	D	310 675-0585	14436
Stefan Merli Plastering Co Inc (PA)	1771	C	310 323-0404	3336
Tireco Inc (PA)	5014	C	310 767-7990	6792
United El Segundo Inc (PA)	5172	C	310 323-3992	9029
United Parcel Service Inc OH	4215	B	310 217-2646	4448
US Foods International LLC	5141	D	310 515-2189	8549
Usfi Inc	5141	D	310 768-1937	8550
Valley of Sun Cosmetics LLC	5122	C	310 327-9062	8302
Vernon Autoparts Inc	7539	D	323 249-7545	17827
Washington Orna Ir Works Inc (PA)	1799	D	310 327-8660	3599
Waste Management Cal Inc	4212	D	562 427-7277	4091
West Coast Maintenance Inc	7349	D	310 324-2511	14465
World Service West	4581	C	310 538-7000	4947
Wragtime Air Freight Inc (PA)	4213	D	800 586-9701	4306
Wsa Group Inc (PA)	7381	E	310 743-3000	16856
XCEL Mechanical Systems Inc	1711	C	310 660-0090	2422
Yrc Inc	4213	D	310 404-2221	4324

GERBER, CA - Tehama County

	SIC	EMP	PHONE	ENTRY #
Haleakala Ranch LLC	0291	E	530 529-6651	466

GEYSERVILLE, CA - Sonoma County

	SIC	EMP	PHONE	ENTRY #
Redwood Empire Vineyard Mgt	0762	D	707 857-3401	717
River Rock Entertainment Auth	7011	A	707 857-2777	13159
Robert Young Family Ltd Partnr	0762	D	707 433-3228	720
Vimark Inc	0762	D	707 857-3588	729
Vinwood Cellars Inc	5182	E	707 857-4011	9115

GILROY, CA - Santa Clara County

	SIC	EMP	PHONE	ENTRY #
Advance Services Inc	7631	A	408 767-2797	17949
Aspen Grove Apartments LLC	6513	D	408 848-6400	11088
Bert E Jessup Transportation	4213	D	408 848-3390	4114
Calvin Klein Inc	7699	E	408 842-9132	17965
Cellco Partnership	4812	A	408 846-5170	5329
Christopher Ranch LLC (PA)	0139	C	408 847-1100	21
Cintas Corporation No 3	7218	C	408 337-2910	13621
Cleaning Services	7217	E	408 778-9251	13594
Communty Slns For Chldrn Fmls (PA)	8322	C	408 779-2113	23780
Countryside Mushrooms Inc	0182	D	408 683-2748	328
Covenant Care California LLC	8051	D	408 842-9311	20497
Daleo Inc	1623	D	408 846-9621	1925
Eagle Ridge Golf Cntry CLB LLC	7997	C	408 846-4531	18942
Faith T & B Plating Inc	7389	D	408 986-1226	17159
Faria Drywall Inc	1742	E	408 847-2058	2895
G B Group Inc (PA)	1522	D	408 848-8118	1311
Gilroy Fitness Inc (PA)	7991	E	408 848-1234	18636
Gilroy Fitness Inc	7991	E	408 848-1234	18637
Gilroy Gardens Family Theme Pk	7996	C	408 840-7100	18822
Headstart Nursery Inc (PA)	5193	D	408 842-3030	9192
Intero Real Estate Services	6531	D	408 848-8400	11585
Learning Services Corporation	8093	E	408 848-4379	22766
Leonard Anthony Valenti Inc	0782	D	408 848-9688	905
Mariner Health Care Inc	8051	C	408 842-9311	20759
Melo Concrete Construction	1771	D	408 842-3484	3295
Noah Concrete Corporation	1771	D	408 842-7211	3302
Odd Fellow-Rebekah Chld HM Cal (PA)	8361	D	408 846-2100	24751
Oj Insulation LP	1742	D	408 842-6315	2940
Olam Spices & Vegetables Inc	5148	D	408 846-3200	8758
PSI Fire	7371	E	408 842-9308	15400
Recology South Valley (HQ)	4953	D	408 842-3358	6530
Renn Transportation Inc	4213	D	408 842-3545	4251
Saint Louise Hospital	8062	B	408 848-2000	21840
See-Grins Inc	0291	D	408 683-4652	473
Syngenta Seeds Inc	5191	E	408 847-4242	9154
Trees Apartments LLC	6513	D	408 848-6400	11216
Uesugi Farms Inc (PA)	0161	D	408 842-1294	101

GLENDALE, CA

	SIC	EMP	PHONE	ENTRY #
Verity Health System Cal Inc	8062	A	408 848-2000	22016

GLEN ELLEN, CA - Sonoma County

	SIC	EMP	PHONE	ENTRY #
Servico Building Maint Co	7349	D	707 935-1224	14428

GLENDALE, CA - Los Angeles County

	SIC	EMP	PHONE	ENTRY #
24 Hour Fitness Usa Inc	7991	D	818 247-4334	18590
A J R Trucking Inc	4212	D	562 989-9555	3967
Abc Inc	4833	B	818 863-7801	5831
Access Integrated Healthcare	8059	D	866 460-7465	21124
Across Services	5045	D	877 922-7677	7081
Adventist Health System/West	8011	C	818 246-5900	19322
Adventist Health System/West	8062	E	818 409-8540	21432
Aerospace Corporation	8733	B	818 952-6075	26725
Amco Foods Inc	8742	B	818 247-4716	27317
American Realty Advisors	6798	D	818 545-1152	12236
American Realty Centre Inc	6531	D	323 666-6111	11298
Amgen Distribution Inc	4213	D	760 989-4424	4110
Arakelyan Aram	6531	E	818 247-0191	11301
ARC Document Solutions Inc	7334	D	818 242-6555	14107
Armenian Amrcn Cuncil On Aging	8322	E	818 241-8690	23669
Arthur J Gallagher & Co	6411	C	818 539-2300	10624
Assign Corporation	7379	E	818 247-7100	16326
AT&T Services Inc	1623	E	818 242-4102	1906
Atkinson-Baker Inc (PA)	7338	C	818 551-7300	14166
Automated Systems America Inc	7699	D	877 500-0002	17963
Avery Corp	8731	C	626 304-2000	26482
Bank America National Assn	6021	A	800 432-1000	9324
Bartholomew Barry & Associates	8111	D	818 543-4000	23107
Begroup (PA)	8059	D	818 638-4563	21149
Buena Ventura Care Center Inc	8059	D	818 247-4476	21168
Cal Southern Presbt Homes (PA)	8051	D	818 247-0420	20429
Cal Southern Presbt Homes	6513	C	818 244-7219	11107
Cal Southern Presbt Homes	6513	C	818 247-0420	11108
California Credit Union (PA)	6062	D	818 291-6700	9657
Califrnia Insur Guarantee Assn	6399	D	818 844-4300	10566
Camble Center	8331	D	818 242-2434	24319
Caroline Promotions Inc	8742	D	877 507-7666	27738
Caspian Commercial Plbg Inc	1711	D	818 649-2500	2176
Cbre Inc	6531	D	818 502-6700	11354
Cellco Partnership	4812	A	818 500-7779	5316
Chandler Convalescent Hospital	8051	D	818 240-1610	20453
Chicago Title and Trust Co	6361	E	818 548-0222	10500
Childrens Hospital Los Angeles	8069	B	323 361-2215	22125
Ciba Insurance Svcs Cal Inc (PA)	6411	E	818 638-8525	10670
Cigna Healthcare Cal Inc (DH)	6324	B	818 500-6262	10272
Cinovation Inc	7812	D	818 246-3160	18061
CIT Bank National Association	6021	D	818 502-8400	9354
City of Glendale	8711	D	818 548-3945	25739
City of Glendale	7941	D	818 548-3950	18542
City of Glendale	4911	B	818 548-3300	6112
City of Glendale	4911	E	818 548-3980	6113
City of Glendale	4941	C	818 548-2011	6325
Coinmach Corporation (PA)	7215	D	818 637-4300	13574
Comprehensive Cmnty Hlth Ctrs	8082	E	818 265-2210	22414
Compspec Inc	8742	D	818 551-4200	27387
Country Villa Service Corp	8051	D	818 246-5516	20477
Countrywide Home Loans Inc	6162	D	818 550-8700	9835
CT Lien Solution	8742	C	818 662-4100	27399
Dish Network Corporation	4841	E	818 334-8740	5993
Disney Interactive Studios Inc	7371	D	818 560-1000	15142
Disney Interactive Studios Inc	7371	D	801 595-1020	15143
Dma Claims Inc (PA)	6411	D	323 342-6800	10691
Dma Claims Inc	6411	C	323 342-6800	10692
Dreamworks Animation LLC	7929	B	818 695-5000	18464
Dwa Holdings LLC (DH)	7812	D	818 695-5000	18079
Dwa Nova LLC	7372	D	818 695-5000	15646
E Z Staffing Inc (PA)	7361	B	818 845-2500	14640
Easter Seals Southern Cal Inc	8399	D	818 551-0128	24916
Elms Sanitarium Inc	8051	D	818 240-6720	20533
Emeritus Corporation	6513	E	818 246-7457	11125
Equity Title Company (DH)	6361	D	818 291-4400	10512
Front Porch Communities (PA)	8059	D	818 729-8100	21219
General Networks Corporation	7379	D	818 249-1962	16389
Ggis Insurance Services Inc	6411	C	818 553-2110	10730
Glendale Adventist Medical Ctr (HQ)	8062	A	818 409-8000	21576
Glendale Associates Ltd	6512	D	818 246-6737	19875
Glendale Eye Medical Group	8011	D	818 956-1010	19536
Glendale Healthcare Center	8051	D	818 246-5516	20600
Glendale Memorial Health Corp	8062	A	818 502-2323	21577
Glenoaks Convalescent Hosp LP	8062	D	818 240-4300	21579
Global Exprnce Specialists Inc	7389	D	818 638-5959	17191
Global Holdings Inc	6719	C	818 905-6000	12066
Goway Travel Inc	4724	D	800 810-3687	4961
Griffith Pk Rhbltation Ctr LLC	8051	D	818 845-8507	20638
Grizzard Cmmncations Group Inc	7331	D	818 543-1315	14072

Employment Codes: A=Over 500 employees, B=251-500, C=101-250, D=51-100, E=45-50

GLENDALE, CA

Company	SIC	EMP	PHONE	ENTRY #
Gsa Design Inc	7389	C	818 241-2558	17202
H L Moe Co Inc (PA)	1711	C	818 572-2100	2242
Health Net Inc	6324	C	818 543-9037	10282
Health Services Advisory Group	8099	D	818 409-9220	22969
Hemodialysis Inc (PA)	8092	E	818 500-8736	22628
Howroyd-Wright Emplymnt Agcy (HQ)	7361	C	818 240-8688	14675
Howroyd-Wright Emplymnt Agcy	7361	C	818 240-8688	14676
Hutchinson & Bloodgood LLP (PA)	8721	D	818 637-5000	26375
Interstate Rhbltation Svcs LLC (PA)	8049	D	818 244-5656	20330
J P Allen Co (PA)	1711	E	818 848-1952	2258
Jimmys Fashions	7389	E	818 790-8932	17259
Johnson & Johnson Pistaccios	0139	E	818 242-7853	28
JP Allen Extended Stay (PA)	7011	D	818 956-0202	12871
Kaiser Foundation Hospitals	8011	A	800 954-8000	19620
Kaiser Foundation Hospitals	8011	A	818 552-3000	19658
Kaza Azteca America Inc	4833	C	818 241-5400	5877
Kradjian Importing Company Inc (PA)	5149	D	818 502-1313	8868
Ksm Healthcare Inc	8051	D	818 242-1183	20714
Leekilpatrick Management Inc	8742	D	818 500-9631	27505
Longwood Management Corp	8059	D	818 246-7174	21296
Los Angeles Federal Credit Un (PA)	6061	D	818 242-8640	9611
Mader News Inc	5192	D	818 551-5000	9168
Mariner Health Care Inc	8051	C	818 246-5677	20764
Mediashift Inc	7313	C	949 407-8488	13972
Modern Videofilm Inc	7819	C	818 637-6800	18236
Mv Transportation Inc	4111	D	818 409-3387	3678
National Teleconsultants Inc (PA)	8711	D	818 265-4400	25987
New York Life Insurance Co	6311	D	818 662-7500	10215
Next Venture Inc	1542	D	818 637-2888	1619
Nurses Tuch HM Hlth Prvder Inc	8082	E	818 500-4877	22516
Oakmont Country Club	7997	C	818 542-4260	19018
Oel/Hhh Inc	8712	C	818 246-6050	26243
Old Republic Title Company	6361	A	818 240-1936	10533
Parexel International Corp	8731	C	818 254-7076	26584
Patterson Ritner Lockwood (PA)	8111	E	818 241-8001	23493
PCL Construction Services Inc	1542	C	818 246-3481	1633
Pegasus Home Health Care A CA	8082	D	818 551-1932	22534
Pegasus Maritime Inc	4731	D	714 728-8565	5149
Pinnacle Electrical Svcs Inc	8748	D	818 241-6009	28018
Pinnacle Networking Svcs Inc	1731	D	818 241-6009	2684
Pkf Certif Pub Accts A Prof (PA)	8721	D	818 630-7630	26423
Primary Critical Care Medical	8011	C	818 847-9950	19877
Principal Financial Group Inc	6311	D	818 243-7141	10220
PS Business Parks (PA)	6798	D	818 244-8080	12268
PS Business Parks LP	6531	D	818 244-8080	11780
PS Partners III Ltd	4225	C	818 244-8080	4616
Public Stor Coml Prpts Group	6512	C	818 244-8080	11034
Public Storage	6798	C	818 244-8080	12269
Public Storage Prpts IV Ltd	4225	C	818 244-8080	4617
Public Storage Prpts Xviii Inc	6719	C	818 244-8080	12086
Ralphs Grocery Company	4225	C	818 549-0035	4619
RES-Care Inc	8052	C	818 637-7727	21099
Rev Enterprises	7381	E	818 551-7111	16772
Rose International Inc	7371	C	636 812-4000	15429
Safeco Insurance Company Amer	6411	C	818 956-4250	10859
Salem Media Group Inc	4832	C	818 956-5254	5818
Scan Health Plan	6324	C	818 550-4900	10375
Sitv Inc	4833	D	323 317-9534	5910
Smg	6512	C	310 432-2893	11049
Sodexo Inc	8742	D	818 952-2201	27656
Software Management Cons Inc (PA)	7379	B	818 240-3177	16484
Spad Holdings LLC	7991	D	818 552-2027	18694
State Compensation Insur Fund	6331	D	213 576-7335	10468
State Compensation Insur Fund	6331	C	323 266-5551	10470
State Compensation Insur Fund	6331	D	888 782-8338	10472
Stations Group LLC	4833	D	818 247-0400	5913
Stewart Title California Inc (DH)	6361	C	818 291-9145	10535
Sunbelt Controls Inc (HQ)	1731	B	818 244-6571	2756
Tacori Enterprises	5094	D	818 863-1536	8102
Tmp Worldwide Advertising & Co	7311	D	818 539-2000	13928
Trading America Corp	8742	E	786 842-7888	27695
Tri-Tech Internet Services Inc	7375	E	818 548-5400	16264
TTT West Coast Inc	7812	D	818 972-0500	18172
Ucc Direct Services Inc	7374	D	818 662-4100	16204
United Merchant Svcs Cal Inc	5044	D	818 246-6767	7075
Universal Studios Inc	7812	D	818 262-4301	18182
Univision Communications Inc	4832	C	818 484-7399	5827
UNUM Life Insurance Co Amer	6411	C	818 291-4739	10917
Usc Verdugo Hills Hospital LLC	8062	A	818 790-7100	22008
Verdugo Hills Hosp Foundation (PA)	8062	B	818 790-7100	22011
Verdugo Hills Urgent Care Mg	8011	D	818 241-4331	20194
Verdugo Mental Health	8093	D	818 244-7257	22861
Viking Equipment Corp	1795	D	818 500-9447	3472
Walt Disney Company	4833	B	818 544-5009	5924
Walt Disney Company	7996	A	818 544-6500	18836
Walt Disney Company	7812	C	818 553-4222	18189
Walt Disney Imagineering (DH)	7819	A	818 544-6500	18267
Wfg National Title Insur Co (PA)	6361	D	818 476-4000	10538
Young Mens Chrstn Assoc Gndl	8641	D	818 484-8256	25476
Ypcom LLC (HQ)	7389	B	818 937-5500	17637

GLENDORA, CA - Los Angeles County

Company	SIC	EMP	PHONE	ENTRY #
Americas Christian Credit Un (PA)	6062	D	626 208-5400	9652
Automobile Club Southern Cal	8699	E	626 963-8531	25497
Building Electronic Contrls Inc (PA)	1731	E	909 305-1600	2541
Care Unlimited Health Systems	8082	D	626 332-3767	22394
Carmen Casa Inc	8059	D	626 852-9477	21179
Community Convalescent Hospita	8051	D	626 963-6091	20467
East Valley Glendora Hosp LP	8062	B	626 335-0231	21549
Foothill Hospital-Morris L Jo (PA)	8062	C	626 857-3145	21567
Glendora Country Club	7997	D	626 335-4051	18955
Harbor Glen Care Center	8051	D	626 963-7531	20644
Homestreet Bank	6022	D	626 339-9663	9502
National Hot Rod Association (PA)	7948	C	626 914-4761	18571
National Link Incorporated	5044	E	909 670-1900	7062
Oakdale Memorial Park (PA)	6553	D	626 335-0281	12034
Right Choice A Health Care	7361	B	626 335-1318	14754
Seidner-Miller Automotive Inc	7538	E	909 394-3500	17813
Time Warner Cable Inc	4841	D	626 857-1075	6034
Ulta Salon Cosmt Fragrance Inc	7231	C	909 592-5393	13694
Verizon Wireless Inc	4812	C	909 592-5211	5426
Vicenti Lloyd & Stutzman	8721	D	626 857-7300	26456
Village Glen Apartments	6513	D	626 963-4575	11222
Zurich Financial Resources (PA)	6531	D	626 963-4398	11936

GOLD RIVER, CA - Sacramento County

Company	SIC	EMP	PHONE	ENTRY #
Ehealthinsurance Services Inc	7371	C	916 608-6101	15156
Eskaton	8052	D	916 852-7900	21082
Hartford Fire Insurance Co	6411	B	916 294-1000	10735
Health Net Inc	6324	B	916 935-3520	10284
Health Net California Inc	6324	C	916 935-1600	10285
Health Net Cmnty Solutions Inc	8011	C	800 675-6110	19545
Performance Tech Partners LLC	7379	C	916 307-5669	16456
Practice Wares Inc	5047	E	916 526-2674	7303
Premier Pools and Spas LP (PA)	1799	C	916 852-0223	3570
Salu Beauty Inc	8621	D	916 475-1400	25154
Spare-Time Inc	7997	E	916 859-5910	19087
Spare-Time Inc	7997	E	916 638-7001	19089
Synergex International Corp	7372	D	916 635-7300	15853
USA Waste of California Inc (HQ)	4953	C	916 387-1400	6576

GOLETA, CA - Santa Barbara County

Company	SIC	EMP	PHONE	ENTRY #
Aecom Global II LLC	8711	D	805 692-0600	25624
Appfolio Inc (PA)	7372	C	805 364-6093	15582
Asplundh Tree Expert Co	0783	D	805 964-9216	984
AT&T Corp	4812	D	805 562-0121	5259
Cathedral Oaks Tennis Swim Ath	7997	D	805 964-7762	18914
Citrix Systems Inc	7371	B	805 690-6400	15086
Community Action Commsn Santa (PA)	8399	E	805 964-8857	24895
Control Point Corporation (PA)	8711	E	805 685-6390	25751
Curvature LLC (HQ)	4813	D	805 964-9975	5586
Devereux Foundation	8399	D	805 968-2525	24913
Devereux Foundation	6733	B	805 968-2525	12173
Eucalyptus Systems Inc	7372	E	805 845-8000	15659
Flir Commercial Systems Inc (HQ)	5065	B	805 690-6685	7566
Gamma PHI Beta Sorority Inc	7041	D	805 968-4221	13492
Givens John	0161	D	805 964-4477	70
Hpt Trs Ihg 2 Inc	7011	D	805 964-6241	12796
Intouch Technologies Inc	7372	D	805 562-8686	15710
Khp III Goleta LLC	7011	D	805 964-6241	12883
Kitson Landscape MGT Inc	0782	D	805 681-9460	884
L-3 Communications Maripro Inc	8711	D	805 683-3881	25930
Las Cumbres Observatory Global	8733	D	805 880-1600	26781
Lastline Inc	7372	C	805 456-7075	15731
Millenium Athletic Club LLc	7991	D	805 562-3845	18661
Raytheon Company	7389	D	805 562-2941	17446
Santa Barbara Airbus	4119	D	805 964-7759	3840
Santa Barbara Trnsp Corp (HQ)	4151	D	805 681-8355	3947
Schulte Ranches	0191	D	805 563-0821	391
Securitas SEC Svcs USA Inc	7381	C	805 967-8987	16797
Sitestuff Yardi Systems I	8742	C	805 966-3666	27648
Southern California Edison Co	4911	D	805 683-5291	6230
Toyon Research Corporation (PA)	8711	C	805 968-6787	26101
United Parcel Service Inc OH	4215	C	805 964-7848	4466
Verizon South Inc	4813	D	805 681-8527	5725
Waterfall Resort	7011	D	805 879-3780	13394

GONZALES, CA - Monterey County

Company	SIC	EMP	PHONE	ENTRY #
Alicia Arroyo Inc	0761	C	831 675-2850	648
Bulmaro Castro Contractors	7361	C	831 675-2927	14617
Ed Silva (PA)	0161	D	831 675-2327	61
George Amaral Ranches Inc	0161	D	831 679-2977	66

GEOGRAPHIC SECTION HAPPY CAMP, CA

	SIC	EMP	PHONE	ENTRY #
Granite Construction Inc	1611	D	831 763-5595	1790
L & J Farms Caraccioli LLC	0191	E	831 675-7901	379
RC Packing LLC	0722	B	831 675-0308	501

GOSHEN, CA - Tulare County

	SIC	EMP	PHONE	ENTRY #
Western Milling LLC (HQ)	5191	C	559 302-1000	9155

GRANADA HILLS, CA - Los Angeles County

	SIC	EMP	PHONE	ENTRY #
Aegis Senior Communities LLC	8082	D	818 363-3373	22348
Atlas Security Inc	7382	E	323 876-1401	16868
Brad Watkins Masonry Inc	1741	D	818 360-3796	2806
Errama Trucking Company Inc	4213	E	818 381-3341	4146
Global Work Group LLC	8742	D	424 220-9994	27449
Jag Framing Inc	1751	E	818 822-7110	3056
James I Miller	0742	E	818 363-7444	620
Kaiser Foundation Hospitals	8011	A	818 832-7200	19619
Longwood Management Corp	8051	D	818 360-1864	20742
Medical Investment Co	8059	C	818 360-1003	21313
Metropolitan Water District	4941	D	818 368-3731	6376
Park Regency Inc	6531	D	818 363-6116	11739
Prellis Group Inc	6531	D	818 363-1717	11760
PS National Inc	7361	B	818 366-1300	14739
San Fernando City of Inc	8093	D	818 832-2400	22823
Siracusa Enterprises Inc	7361	D	818 831-1131	14786
Valley Properties Inc	6512	D	818 360-3430	11067
Wells Fargo Bank National Assn	6021	D	818 673-1857	9449

GRAND TERRACE, CA - San Bernardino County

	SIC	EMP	PHONE	ENTRY #
Grand Terrace Care Center	8051	D	909 825-5221	20634
James McMinn Inc	1611	E	909 514-1231	1804
Keystone NPS LLC (DH)	8399	D	909 633-6354	24934
Peace Officrs For A Grn Envirn	1799	E	909 798-1122	3569
West Coast Arborists Inc	0783	E	909 783-6544	1003

GRANITE BAY, CA - Placer County

	SIC	EMP	PHONE	ENTRY #
Bushnell Gardens	5193	D	916 791-4199	9180
C & C Construction Inc	1542	E	916 434-5280	1516
Eskaton Lodge	8361	C	916 789-0326	24650
Granite Bay Golf Club	7997	C	916 791-5379	18956
Green Valley Security Inc	7381	C	916 797-4058	16666
Paramount Equity Mortgage LLC	6162	D	916 290-9999	9883
United States Pony Clubs	7997	D	916 791-1223	19116
Village At Granite Bay	8361	D	916 789-0326	24848

GRASS VALLEY, CA - Nevada County

	SIC	EMP	PHONE	ENTRY #
Alta Sierra Country Club Inc	7997	E	530 273-2041	18848
AT&T Corp	4813	D	530 274-8255	5481
Beam Vacuums California Inc	1731	E	916 564-3279	2529
Blue Eagle Contracting	4212	D	530 272-0287	3982
Briarpatch Coop Nev Cnty Inc	8699	C	530 272-5333	25508
Byers Enterprises Inc	1761	D	530 272-7777	3145
Durham School Services L P	4151	D	530 273-7282	3922
Eskaton Properties Inc	8361	D	530 265-2699	24651
Evercom Systems Inc	4813	D	530 272-8223	5597
Golden Empire Convalescent Hos	8062	D	530 273-1316	21580
Grass Valley LLC	8361	D	530 272-1055	24673
Hansen Bros Enterprises (PA)	1442	D	530 273-3100	1105
Hills Flat Lumber Co (PA)	1731	D	530 273-6171	2612
Hospice of Foothills (PA)	8082	D	530 272-5739	22476
Meadow View Manor Inc	8051	D	530 272-2273	20781
Networked Insurance Agents LLC	6411	C	800 682-8476	10796
Nevada County Behavioral Hlth	8093	E	530 265-1450	22780
Nevada Irrigation District (PA)	4971	C	530 273-6185	6649
Pacific Gas and Electric Co	4911	C	530 477-3245	6169
Pride Industries	8331	C	530 477-1832	24381
Ray Stone Incorporated	8322	D	530 272-5274	24148
Sierra Nevada Memorial Hm Care	8082	D	530 274-6350	22564
Springhill Manor Rehabilitatio	8059	E	530 273-7247	21380
USA Waste of California Inc	4212	E	530 274-3090	4083
Victor Cmnty Support Svcs Inc	8999	D	530 273-2244	28168

GREENBRAE, CA - Marin County

	SIC	EMP	PHONE	ENTRY #
County of Marin	8093	D	415 448-1500	22704
Marin General Hospital	8062	A	415 925-7000	21724
Northern California Presbyteri	8059	D	415 464-1767	21330
Ocadian Care Centers LLC	8051	D	415 461-9700	20821
Petroleum Sales Inc	1311	D	415 945-1309	1048
Ross Valley Homes Inc	8052	D	415 461-2300	21101

GREENFIELD, CA - Monterey County

	SIC	EMP	PHONE	ENTRY #
Azcona Harvesting LLC	0761	C	831 674-2526	652
Neil Bassetti Farms	0161	E	831 674-2040	83
Southern Mnterey Cnty Mem Hosp	8062	C	831 674-0112	21907
Southern Mntrrey Cnty Lbor Sup	0761	D	831 674-2727	686

GREENVILLE, CA - Plumas County

	SIC	EMP	PHONE	ENTRY #
Indian Valley Health Care Dist	8062	D	530 284-7191	21610

GRIDLEY, CA - Butte County

	SIC	EMP	PHONE	ENTRY #
Evergreen Gridley Health Ctr	8051	D	530 846-6266	20559
Gridley Hlthcare & Wellnss Cen	8051	D	530 846-6266	20637
Gridley Packing Inc	0723	D	530 846-3753	537
Hovlid Skilled Nursing	8051	E	530 846-9065	20679
Orchard Hospital	8062	C	530 846-5671	21773
Wild Goose Storage Inc	4922	D	530 846-7350	6259

GROVELAND, CA - Tuolumne County

	SIC	EMP	PHONE	ENTRY #
Evergreen Dstntion Hldings LLC	7011	D	209 379-2606	12627
Pine Mountain Lake Association	8641	C	209 962-4080	25315
Thousand Trails Inc	7033	E	209 962-0100	13484

GROVER BEACH, CA - San Luis Obispo County

	SIC	EMP	PHONE	ENTRY #
Bill Papich Construction Inc	1629	E	805 489-9420	2026
Papich Construction Co Inc (PA)	1611	D	805 473-3016	1842

GUADALUPE, CA - Santa Barbara County

	SIC	EMP	PHONE	ENTRY #
Ball Horticultural Company	0181	C	805 343-2723	265
Byrd Harvest Inc	0722	B	805 343-1608	491
Community Action Commsn Santa	8399	C	805 343-0615	24893
Freitas Brothers	0161	C	805 343-3134	63

GUERNEVILLE, CA - Sonoma County

	SIC	EMP	PHONE	ENTRY #
Dawn Ranch Lodge & Rd Hse Rest	7011	D	707 869-0656	12566
Russian River Health Center	8011	E	707 869-2849	19929
West County Health Centers Inc	8011	D	707 869-2849	20234

GUSTINE, CA - Merced County

	SIC	EMP	PHONE	ENTRY #
Anderson Nut Company	0723	E	209 854-6820	509

HACIENDA HEIGHTS, CA - Los Angeles County

	SIC	EMP	PHONE	ENTRY #
Berkshire Hattaway Home Servcs	6531	D	626 913-2808	11320
Care Associates Inc	8361	D	626 330-4048	24579
Courtyard By Marriott	7011	D	626 965-1700	12547
CSX Corporation	4011	C	626 336-1377	3612
Good Deal Insurance Services	6411	D	626 275-6795	10731

HALF MOON BAY, CA - San Mateo County

	SIC	EMP	PHONE	ENTRY #
Bay City Flower Co (PA)	0181	D	650 726-5535	268
Bay City Flower Co	0181	C	650 712-8147	269
Bre Diamond Hotel LLC	7011	D	650 712-7000	12463
Coastside Senior Housing Limit	6531	E	415 355-7100	11402
Coldwell Banker	6531	E	650 726-1100	11406
Earthly Delights	7999	D	650 726-7227	19200
Giusti Farms LLC	0161	E	650 726-9221	69
Home Helpers San Mateo County	8082	D	650 532-3122	22463
Iwf Half Moon Bay LP	7011	E	650 726-9000	12860
K N Properties Inc	4493	D	650 726-4479	4770
Lesley Foundation	8748	D	650 726-4888	27974
Ocean Colony Partners LLC	6552	D	650 726-5764	11992
Ocean Links Corporation	7992	D	650 726-1800	18767
Pacifica Hotel Company	7011	E	650 726-9000	13068

HANFORD, CA - Kings County

	SIC	EMP	PHONE	ENTRY #
Adventist Health System/West	8011	D	559 537-0305	19320
Adventist Health System/West	8099	D	559 537-2299	22876
Adventist Health System/West	8099	D	888 443-2273	22877
Adventist Health System/West	8082	C	559 537-2860	22340
Adventist Health System/West	8093	C	559 537-2510	22649
All Health Services Corp (PA)	7361	C	559 583-9101	14603
B & R Tevelde	0241	D	559 583-1277	417
Central Valley General Hosp (HQ)	8062	B	559 583-2100	21475
City Hanford Public Imprv Corp	1623	D	559 585-2550	1920
County of Kings	8322	C	559 582-4316	23820
Danell Custom Harvesting LLC	0722	C	559 582-1251	492
Educational Employees Cr Un	6062	E	559 587-4460	9663
Hacienda Rehabilitation & Heal	8051	C	559 582-9221	20642
Hanford Community Hospital (HQ)	8062	A	559 582-9000	21589
Hanford Joint Un High Schl Dst	8322	D	559 583-5905	24002
High Plains Ranch LLC (PA)	0241	D	559 583-1277	427
Kings Community Action O (PA)	8322	D	559 582-4386	24056
Kings Rehabilitation Center (PA)	8322	D	559 582-9234	24057
Kings View	8093	D	559 582-9307	22762
Lone Oak Farms	0191	E	559 583-1277	381
Marquez Brothers Intl Inc	5141	C	559 584-8000	8496
Mission Medical Entps Inc	8051	C	559 582-2871	20792
Mission Medical Entps Inc	8051	D	559 582-4414	20793
Randstad North America Inc	7363	C	559 582-2700	14931
Smith Residential Care Fcilty (PA)	8082	D	559 584-8451	22566
Texture Specialties Inc	1791	E	559 904-6047	3407
Veterinary Pharmaceuticals Inc	5122	D	559 582-6800	8304
Wilshire Hlth & Cmnty Svcs Inc	8059	D	559 582-4414	21425

HAPPY CAMP, CA - Siskiyou County

	SIC	EMP	PHONE	ENTRY #
Happy Camp Chamber Commerce	8611	E	530 493-2900	25089

HARBOR CITY, CA

	SIC	EMP	PHONE	ENTRY #

HARBOR CITY, CA - Los Angeles County

	SIC	EMP	PHONE	ENTRY #
Bennett Enterprises A CA	0782	D	310 534-3543	813
Del AMO Insurance Services	6411	D	310 534-3444	10687
Kaiser Foundation Hospitals	8011	A	310 325-5111	19653
Permanente Kaiser Intl	8062	A	310 517-2645	21791
R M S Car Movers Corp	4212	E	310 325-2192	4052
Southern Cal Prmnnte Med Group	8011	D	800 780-1230	20024

HAT CREEK, CA - Shasta County

	SIC	EMP	PHONE	ENTRY #
United States Forest Service	0851	E	530 335-4103	1018

HAWAIIAN GARDENS, CA - Los Angeles County

	SIC	EMP	PHONE	ENTRY #
Cypress Garden Villas	6513	D	562 860-9260	11119
Gardens Rgnal Hosp Med Ctr Inc	8062	B	877 877-1104	21575
Hawaiian Gardens Casino (PA)	7999	C	562 860-5887	19220
Hawaiian Gardens Casino	7999	A	562 860-5887	19221
Howard Contracting Inc	1794	D	562 596-2969	3432
Richmond Plastering Inc	1742	E	562 924-4202	2968
Total Building Care Inc	1542	D	562 467-8333	1693

HAWTHORNE, CA - Los Angeles County

	SIC	EMP	PHONE	ENTRY #
2300 West El Secundo LP	6531	D	310 769-6669	11268
7days Inc	5065	C	424 255-5872	7514
American Linehaul Corporation	4213	D	323 418-8900	4107
Argon Enterprises Inc	6531	D	310 349-8777	11305
Axminster Medical Group Inc (PA)	8011	D	310 670-3255	19364
Blue Chip Moving and Stor Inc	4213	D	323 463-6888	4119
Calhot Illinios LLC	7011	C	310 536-9800	12480
Eastbiz Corporation (PA)	7999	D	310 212-7134	19204
Family First Financial Service	8742	D	310 355-1788	27431
Federal Express Corporation	4513	C	800 463-3339	4848
Hawthorne Healthcare	8051	D	310 679-9732	20645
Longwood Management Corp	8051	C	310 679-1461	20741
Los Angeles Guild LLC	8742	D	323 733-5033	27511
Marriott International Inc	7011	C	310 725-9696	12969
Pb Car Movers	7389	D	310 283-2741	17407
Providence Health & Services	8099	D	310 355-0100	23025
Roofing Supply Group LLC	5033	D	424 269-7330	7015
Sandhurst Convales Grp Ltd A	8051	E	310 675-3304	20894
Schnierow Dental Care	8021	E	310 377-6453	20276
Seems Plumbing Co Inc	1711	E	310 297-4969	2363
Servicon Systems Inc	1771	A	310 970-0700	3329
Skyone Federal Credit Union (PA)	6061	D	310 491-7500	9627
South Bay Rgonal Pub Comm Auth	4899	E	310 973-1802	6089
Tech Flex Package	7336	E	323 241-1800	14162
Thinkom Solutions Inc	4899	E	310 317-5486	6095
Tricor America Inc	4731	D	310 676-0800	5177
Trident Labs Inc	8072	C	310 915-9121	22313
Wilshire Hlth & Cmnty Svcs Inc	8059	D	310 679-9732	21424
Windsor Gardens	8051	D	310 675-3304	21048
Xdbs Corporation	8732	D	302 566-3006	26720
Zaharoni Holdings	8741	E	310 297-9722	27287

HAYWARD, CA - Alameda County

	SIC	EMP	PHONE	ENTRY #
24 Hour Fitness Usa Inc	7991	D	510 264-3275	18600
American Asp Repr Rsrfcing Inc (PA)	1611	D	510 723-0280	1728
American Messaging Svcs LLC	4813	D	510 889-2300	5458
American Residential Svcs LLC	1711	D	510 657-7601	2136
American Synergy Asbestos Remo	1799	D	510 444-2333	3489
American Technologies Inc	1799	D	510 429-5000	3490
Ameriflight LLC	4512	D	510 569-6000	4794
Anning-Johnson Company	1742	D	510 670-0100	2856
Aramark Unf & Career AP LLC	7218	D	510 487-1855	13609
Arborwell Inc (PA)	0783	D	510 881-4260	983
ARC of Alameda County	8331	C	510 582-8151	24306
Aurora Algae Inc (PA)	8731	D	510 266-5000	26480
Axis Services Inc	1522	C	510 732-6111	1295
Bassard Convalescent & Med Hm (PA)	8059	D	510 537-6700	21148
Bay Valley Medical Group Inc	8011	D	510 785-5000	19369
Berkeley Farms LLC (HQ)	5143	B	510 265-8600	8578
Bess Testlab Inc	1623	E	408 988-0101	1909
Big Joe California North Inc (PA)	5084	D	510 785-6900	7825
Bigham Taylor Roofing Corp	1761	D	510 886-0197	3144
Blue River Seafood Inc	5146	D	510 300-6800	8629
Boyett Construction Inc (PA)	1742	D	510 264-9100	2863
Brightview Landscape Svcs Inc	0781	E	510 723-0690	748
Brook Furniture Rental Inc	7359	E	510 487-4440	14519
Cafepresscom Inc	8742	D	650 655-3000	27364
California Golden Realty	6531	A	408 822-6000	11339
California Hydronics Corp (PA)	5075	D	510 293-1993	7735
California State University	8741	D	510 885-2700	26955
Casa Sandoval LLC	6513	D	510 727-1700	11113
Casey-Fogli Con Contrs Inc	1771	D	510 887-0837	3239
Cell-Crete Corporation	1771	D	510 471-7257	3240
Centimark Corporation	1761	C	510 614-1140	3148
Chapel of Chimes (DH)	6553	D	510 471-3363	12028
Chipman Corporation	4213	D	510 748-8787	4127
Cintas Corporation No 3	7218	D	510 352-6330	13622
Classic Soft Trim Inc	5199	D	510 782-4911	9255
Cnet Technology Corporation (HQ)	5065	C	408 392-9966	7549
Comcast Corporation	4841	D	510 266-3200	5957
Commercial Rfrgn Spcialist Inc	5078	E	510 784-8990	7754
Community Integrated Work Prog	8331	E	510 487-9768	24325
Controlled Contamination Svcs	7349	D	510 728-1106	14263
Core-Mark International Inc	5149	C	510 487-3000	8824
County of Alameda	1611	B	510 670-5455	1753
County of Alameda	8331	D	510 670-5700	24329
Cox Automotive Inc	5012	B	510 786-4500	6670
Custom Commercial Dry Clrs Inc (PA)	7216	E	510 723-1000	13580
D S P Service Inc	7349	E	510 782-2200	14279
D W Nicholson Corporation (PA)	1711	C	510 887-0900	2199
Dominos Pizza LLC	4225	D	510 489-0333	4545
Double D Transportation Co	4212	D	510 783-2335	4009
Dt Floormasters Inc	1752	D	510 476-1000	3112
Durham School Services L P	4151	C	510 887-6005	3921
E W C H Inc	8051	D	510 783-4811	20523
Eagle Systems Intl Inc	1711	B	510 259-1700	2213
Earle M Jorgensen Company	5051	D	510 487-2700	7368
Early Transportation Services	4213	D	510 324-1119	4144
Eden Area Regnl Occupational P	8331	D	510 293-2900	24336
Eden Housing Inc	1522	D	510 582-1460	1309
Eden Housing Management Inc (PA)	6531	E	510 582-1460	11489
Eden West Rehabilitation	8051	D	510 783-4811	20526
Exel Inc	4225	D	510 784-7360	4550
Fedex Freight Corporation	4213	B	510 895-0440	4166
Felson Companies Inc	6531	D	510 538-1150	11518
Foam Distributors Incorporated	5199	D	510 441-8377	9264
Foster Dairy Farms	5143	E	510 783-1270	8585
Gallo Sales Company Inc (DH)	5182	C	510 476-5000	9103
Gco Inc (PA)	5074	E	510 786-3333	7720
Gel Pak LLC	7336	D	510 576-2220	14147
Glazier Steel Inc	1794	D	510 471-5300	3430
Glen Alpine Building Svcs Inc	7349	D	510 582-7400	14332
H U S D Maintenance Operation	7349	D	510 784-2666	14318
Hayward Area Recreation Pkdist	8041	D	510 881-6700	20295
Hayward Area Recreation Pkdist	7992	E	510 317-2300	18744
Hayward Area Recreation Pkdist	4225	D	510 881-6700	4568
Hayward Police Officers Assn	8631	D	510 293-7207	25172
Hayward Sisters Hospital (HQ)	8062	A	510 264-4000	21592
HEs Transportation Svcs Inc	4212	E	510 783-6100	4024
Hillsdale Group LP	8059	D	510 538-3866	21270
HUG Company	5141	D	510 887-0340	8487
Imp Foods Inc	5146	D	510 429-4600	8634
Interactive Data Corporation	6289	C	510 266-6000	10196
J & M Inc	1623	D	510 782-3434	1949
Jagpreet Enterprises Inc	5149	D	510 336-8376	8860
Jon K Takata Corporation (PA)	8322	D	510 315-5400	24050
Kaiser Foundation Hospitals	6324	D	510 454-1000	10305
Kaiser Foundation Hospitals	8011	A	510 678-4000	19662
Katherine Bousson	7999	D	510 582-1166	19231
Keeco LLC (PA)	5023	D	510 324-8800	6870
Kissito Health Care Inc	8082	D	510 582-8311	22495
Kosan Biosciences Incorporated	8731	D	510 732-8400	26545
Kuehne + Nagel Inc	4225	D	510 785-0555	4584
Kwan Wo Ironworks Inc	1791	C	415 822-9628	3388
L & W Supply Corporation	5032	D	510 429-8003	6990
Lansing Mall Ltd Partnership	6512	E	510 782-3527	11010
LBC Mundial Corporation (HQ)	4513	D	650 873-0750	4867
Leggett & Platt Incorporated	7319	D	510 487-8063	14000
Level 3 Communications Inc	4899	D	510 887-8920	6080
Lifetouch Nat Schl Studios Inc	7221	E	510 293-1818	13662
Marelich Mechanical Co Inc (HQ)	1711	D	510 785-5500	2289
Mariner Health Care Inc	8051	D	510 538-4424	20766
Mariner Health Care Inc	8051	D	510 785-2880	20767
Metric Equipment Sales Inc	5065	D	510 264-0887	7603
Mygrant Glass Company Inc (PA)	5013	E	510 785-4360	6750
Nor-Cal Moving Services (PA)	4214	C	510 371-4942	4366
Northstar Contg Group Inc (DH)	1799	D	510 491-1300	3559
Nova Commercial Company Inc (PA)	7349	D	510 728-7000	14372
Oakhurst Industries Inc	5141	D	510 265-2400	8507
Omnicare Inc	5122	D	510 293-9663	8287
Pacific Cheese Co Inc (PA)	5143	D	510 784-8000	8591
Pacific Gas and Electric Co	4924	B	510 784-3253	6271
PW Stephens Envmtl Inc	4959	D	510 782-9600	6634
R F Macdonald Co (PA)	5084	C	510 784-0110	7880
R2g Enterprises Inc	1761	D	510 489-6218	3206
Restec Contractors Inc	1799	D	510 670-0100	3576
Rjms Corporation (PA)	5084	D	510 675-0500	7883
RJS & Associates Inc	1771	C	510 670-9111	3320
Roadstar Trucking Inc	4213	D	510 487-2404	4253
Rural/Metro Corporation	4119	C	510 266-0885	3835

GEOGRAPHIC SECTION

HOLLISTER, CA

	SIC	EMP	PHONE	ENTRY #
Safeco Door & Hardware Inc	1793	D	510 429-4768	3415
San Francisco Bay Area Rapid	4111	B	510 441-2278	3704
Serpico Landscaping Inc	0782	E	510 293-0341	951
Shaklee Corporation	5122	D	510 887-5000	8294
Siemens Industry Inc	8711	B	510 783-6000	26064
Siemens Industry Inc	5084	C	510 783-6000	7886
Signet Testing Labs Inc **(HQ)**	7389	E	510 887-8484	17489
Solcom Inc	1623	A	510 940-2490	1995
Solcom Group Inc	1623	D	510 940-2490	1996
SOS Security Incorporated	7381	D	510 782-4900	16827
St Francis Extended Care Inc	8059	D	510 785-3630	21382
St Michael Convalescent Hosp	8051	D	510 782-8424	20929
Stonebrae LP	7997	D	510 728-7878	19097
TCI Aluminum/North Inc	5051	D	510 786-3750	7406
Telecare Corporation	8063	C	510 582-7676	22101
Thyssenkrupp Elevator Corp	5084	E	510 476-1900	7897
Tiburcio Vasquez Hlth Ctr Inc	8011	D	510 471-5907	20137
Tps Aviation Inc **(PA)**	5088	D	510 475-1010	8007
Tricor America Inc	4513	C	510 293-3960	4873
Ty Five Star Corporation	8062	D	510 317-7360	21975
Tyco Integrated Security LLC	7382	D	510 785-2912	16936
Ultraex LLC	4215	D	510 723-3760	4432
Ultraex Inc	4215	D	800 882-1000	4433
Underwriters Laboratories Inc	8734	C	408 754-6500	26898
Urban Trading Software Inc	7372	E	877 633-6171	15871
USA Waste of California Inc	4953	D	831 384-5000	6591
Wagan Corporation	5013	E	800 231-5806	6779
Wells Fargo Bank National Assn	6021	D	510 266-0595	9454
Western State Design Inc **(PA)**	5087	D	510 786-9271	7989
Windsor Gardens Healthcare C	8059	D	510 582-4636	21426
Winward International **(PA)**	5193	D	510 487-8686	9230
Xpo Enterprise Services Inc	4213	C	510 785-6920	4320
Yrc Inc	4213	D	510 783-7010	4323

HEALDSBURG, CA - Sonoma County

	SIC	EMP	PHONE	ENTRY #
Alliance Medical Center Inc	8011	D	707 431-8234	19331
Avalon Health Care Inc	8051	D	707 433-4877	20396
Clendenen Vineyard MGT LLC	0172	D	707 473-0881	148
Corporate Soul LLC	7299	B	707 431-7781	13751
E & J Gallo Winery	0172	D	707 431-5400	153
E & M Electric and McHy Inc **(PA)**	5084	E	707 433-5578	7838
Healdsburg Dist Hosp Rehab Svc	6324	D	707 433-9150	10279
Hotel Healdsburg **(PA)**	7011	D	707 431-2800	12788
Klein Foods Inc	0172	D	707 431-1533	164
Madrona Mnr Wine Cntry Inn	7011	D	707 433-4231	12935
Metier Ltd	7379	D	707 546-9300	16433
North Sonoma County Hosp Dst	8062	C	707 431-6500	21760
Salvation Army Residences Inc	8361	D	707 433-3334	24800
Scheid Vineyards Inc	0172	D	707 433-1858	187
Syar Industries Inc	5032	D	707 433-3366	6994
Vino Farms Inc	0762	D	707 433-8241	731

HEBER, CA - Imperial County

	SIC	EMP	PHONE	ENTRY #
Ormat Nevada Inc	4939	E	760 353-8200	6305
Ralph Collazo Packing Inc	7389	D	760 353-0856	17445

HELENDALE, CA - San Bernardino County

	SIC	EMP	PHONE	ENTRY #
Silver Lakes Association	8641	D	760 245-1606	25350

HELM, CA - Fresno County

	SIC	EMP	PHONE	ENTRY #
Terranova Ranch Inc	0191	E	559 866-5644	398
Wilbur-Ellis Company LLC	5191	D	559 866-5667	9156

HEMET, CA - Riverside County

	SIC	EMP	PHONE	ENTRY #
American Medical Response Inc	4119	C	951 658-2826	3756
American Medical Response Inc	4119	C	951 765-3900	3761
Anka Behavioral Health Inc	6411	C	951 929-2744	10604
Bank America National Assn	6021	E	951 929-8614	9330
Brookdale Senior Living Inc	8361	D	951 929-5988	24571
Brookdale Senior Living Inc	8059	D	951 744-9861	21166
Caring Companions Home	8082	D	951 765-1441	22397
Casa-Pacifica Inc	8361	B	951 658-3369	24585
Casa-Pacifica Inc	8361	D	951 766-5116	24587
County of Riverside	8322	D	951 791-3500	23885
Devonshire Care Center LLC	8059	D	951 925-2571	21207
Hcr Manorcare Med Svcs Fla LLC	8051	D	951 925-9171	20651
Hemet Vly Med Center-Education	8062	A	951 652-2811	21599
Horizon Solar Power Inc	1711	D	844 765-2780	2245
Johnre Care LLC	8051	D	951 658-6374	20692
Lake Hemet Municipal Wtr Dst **(PA)**	4941	D	951 927-1816	6361
Meadowbrook Convalescent Hosp	8361	D	951 658-2293	24731
Pama Management Co	8741	E	951 929-0340	27157
Primerica Life Insurance Co	6411	C	951 652-6190	10838
Ramona Community Services Corp **(HQ)**	8082	C	951 658-9288	22546
Ramona Rehabilitation and Post	8051	C	951 652-0011	20863
Roto Rooter Plumbing & Drain S	7699	E	951 658-8541	18006
Spectrum MGT Holdg Co LLC	4841	D	951 260-3143	6020
Sprouts Farmers Market Inc	5141	C	951 766-6746	8523
Sunrise Senior Living LLC	8051	D	951 929-5988	20983
Time Warner Cable Inc	4841	D	951 306-3117	6041
Trilar Management Group	8741	C	951 925-2021	27257
Valley Resource Center For Th **(PA)**	8331	E	951 657-0609	24402
Valley Rsrce Ctr For Retarded	8399	D	951 766-8659	24994
Veterans of Foreign Wars of US	8641	D	951 202-3792	25390

HERCULES, CA - Contra Costa County

	SIC	EMP	PHONE	ENTRY #
Bio RAD Laboratories	8734	D	510 741-1000	26834
Bio-RAD Laboratories Inc	5049	C	510 741-1000	7339
Bio-RAD Laboratories Inc	8731	A	510 232-7000	26487
Hercules Fitness	7991	E	510 724-2900	18641
Mechanics Bank	4225	C	510 741-7545	4597
Security Pacific RE Brkg	6531	D	510 245-9901	11838
Shields Nursing Centers Inc **(PA)**	8051	C	510 724-9911	20911
Unipark LLC	7521	D	510 724-0811	17745
Watkin & Bortolussi Inc	0782	D	415 453-4675	978

HERLONG, CA - Lassen County

	SIC	EMP	PHONE	ENTRY #
Aecom Global II LLC	8711	D	530 827-2406	25631

HERMOSA BEACH, CA - Los Angeles County

	SIC	EMP	PHONE	ENTRY #
24 Hour Fitness Worldwide Inc	7991	E	310 374-4524	18602
All Environmental Inc	8748	C	310 798-4255	27825
AT&T Corp	4812	D	310 303-3888	5261
CIT Bank National Association	6021	D	310 372-8473	9353
Liminex Inc	7371	D	310 963-3031	15275
Marlin Equity Partners LLC **(PA)**	6282	D	310 364-0100	10161
Perverted Jstice Fundation Inc	6732	C	310 910-9380	12163
Southbay Website Design LLC	7374	D	310 370-4043	16192
Sunrise Senior Living LLC	8051	E	310 937-0959	20971

HESPERIA, CA - San Bernardino County

	SIC	EMP	PHONE	ENTRY #
Arizona Pipe Line Company **(PA)**	1623	B	760 244-8212	1904
Ascon Recycling Co	4953	C	760 948-1538	6432
Best Way Disposal Co Inc	4953	D	760 244-9773	6438
Caremark Rx LLC	8011	E	760 948-6606	19405
Celico Partnership	4812	D	760 662-5914	5347
Desert Recycling Inc	4953	E	760 244-3122	6472
Flyers Energy LLC	5171	D	760 949-3356	9006
Foremost Healthcare Centers	6513	D	760 244-5579	11132
Foremost Operations LLC	8361	E	760 244-5579	24661
Hesperia Senior Living LLC	8748	D	760 244-5579	27942
High Dsert Ptent Care Svcs LLC	8011	D	760 956-4150	19558
Lake Arrowhead Cmnty Svcs Dst	8399	E	909 337-6395	24936
Ram-Mar Painting Inc	7699	D	760 949-4844	18002
Total Renal Care Inc	8092	C	760 947-7405	22646
Veolia Transportation Svcs Inc	4111	C	760 947-5719	3733

HICKMAN, CA - Stanislaus County

	SIC	EMP	PHONE	ENTRY #
Dave Wilson Nursery Inc **(PA)**	0181	E	209 874-1821	275
Foster Dairy Farms	7699	C	209 874-9605	17974
Frantz Wholesale Nursery LLC	0181	C	209 874-1459	282

HIDDEN HILLS, CA - Los Angeles County

	SIC	EMP	PHONE	ENTRY #
Cyton Industries Inc	5013	D	818 999-3398	6723

HIDDEN VALLEY LAKE, CA - Lake County

	SIC	EMP	PHONE	ENTRY #
Adventist Health System/West	8011	D	707 987-8344	19319
Hidden Valley Lake Association **(PA)**	8641	D	707 987-3146	25270

HIGHLAND, CA - San Bernardino County

	SIC	EMP	PHONE	ENTRY #
Beaver Medical Group LP **(HQ)**	8011	D	909 425-3321	19372
Cedar Holdings LLC	8051	D	909 862-0611	20442
Century 21 Showcase Inc	6531	D	909 936-9334	11381
County of San Bernardino	8351	E	909 425-0785	24451
East Valley Water District	4941	D	909 889-9501	6344
Immanuel Baptist Cruch	8351	D	909 862-6641	24467
Kcb Towers Inc	1791	D	909 862-0322	3386
Kindred Healthcare Oper Inc	8051	C	909 862-0611	20699
San Manuel Indian Bingo Casino **(PA)**	7999	A	909 864-5050	19275
YMCA of East Valley	8641	E	909 425-9622	25412

HILLSBOROUGH, CA - San Mateo County

	SIC	EMP	PHONE	ENTRY #
Burlingame Country Club	7997	D	650 696-8100	18903
John Plane Construction Inc	1542	C	415 468-0555	1585

HOLLISTER, CA - San Benito County

	SIC	EMP	PHONE	ENTRY #
Alpha Teknova Inc	8731	E	831 637-1100	26465
American Electrical Svcs Inc	1731	C	831 638-1737	2517
American Medical Response Inc	4119	C	831 636-9391	3762
Bhandal Bros Inc	4213	E	831 728-2691	4116
Bhandal Bros Trucking Inc	4213	D	831 728-2691	4117
Chamberlains Children Ctr Inc	8361	D	831 636-2121	24590
Guerra Nut Shelling Company	0723	D	831 637-4471	544
Hollister Process Service	7389	E	831 634-1479	17224
Icu Eyewear Inc	5099	D	510 848-4700	8121
Infinity Staffing Service	7363	B	831 638-0360	14888

HOLLISTER, CA

	SIC	EMP	PHONE	ENTRY #
Mufg Union Bank Na	6021	D	831 638-3350	9412
PSC Industrial Outsourcing LP	4959	D	831 635-0220	6633
R and R Labor Inc	0761	D	831 638-0290	680
San Benito Health Care Dst (PA)	8062	B	831 637-5711	21844
San Benito Htg & Shtmtl Inc	1711	D	831 637-1112	2358
San Juan Oaks LLC	7992	D	831 636-6113	18780
Woltcom Inc	1731	C	831 638-4900	2796

HOLLYWOOD, CA - Los Angeles County

	SIC	EMP	PHONE	ENTRY #
Cellco Partnership	4812	D	323 465-0640	5358
Deep Focus Inc	8742	A	323 790-5340	27405
Loews Hollywood Hotel LLC	7011	B	323 450-2235	12926

HOLT, CA - San Joaquin County

	SIC	EMP	PHONE	ENTRY #
Victoria Island Farms	0191	D	209 465-5609	403

HOLTVILLE, CA - Imperial County

	SIC	EMP	PHONE	ENTRY #
Black Dog Farms of California	0161	C	760 356-2951	40
Five Star Packing LLC	0761	A	760 356-4103	661
Grimmway Farms	0191	D	760 356-2513	362
John Grizzle Farming	0191	E	760 356-4381	375
Ormesa LLC	4911	D	760 356-3020	6160
Sunharbor Management LLC	8361	D	760 356-1262	24829

HOMELAND, CA - Riverside County

	SIC	EMP	PHONE	ENTRY #
Harvest V Citizens Patrol	7381	C	951 926-9763	16701

HOOPA, CA - Humboldt County

	SIC	EMP	PHONE	ENTRY #
Klma W Medical Center	8093	D	530 625-4114	22759

HOPLAND, CA - Mendocino County

	SIC	EMP	PHONE	ENTRY #
Hopland Band Pomo Indians Inc	7999	C	707 744-1395	19223
Hopland Band Pomo Indians Inc (PA)	8699	D	707 472-2100	25542
Shokawah Casino	7011	E	707 744-1395	13249

HORNITOS, CA - Mariposa County

	SIC	EMP	PHONE	ENTRY #
Hornitos Telephone Co	4813	D	608 831-1000	5630

HUGHSON, CA - Stanislaus County

	SIC	EMP	PHONE	ENTRY #
Alderwoods (delaware) Inc	6553	E	209 883-0411	12027
Community Hospice Inc	8052	E	209 578-6380	21073
Douglas & Jayne Starn	0173	D	209 883-4886	198
Duarte Nursery Inc (PA)	0181	E	209 531-0351	279
Grower Direct Nut Company Inc	0723	E	209 883-4890	542
Lakewood Mem Pk Fnrl Svcs Inc	6553	D	209 883-4465	12033
Samaritan Village Inc	8322	C	209 883-3212	24170

HUNTINGTON BEACH, CA - Orange County

	SIC	EMP	PHONE	ENTRY #
2nd Floor Main Street Concepts	6513	E	714 969-9000	11077
A Growing Concern Landscapes	0781	D	714 843-5137	736
AES Huntington Beach LLC	4911	E	714 374-1476	6103
Aire-Rite AC & Rfrgn Inc	1711	E	714 895-2338	2116
Alltek Company U S A Inc	5084	E	714 375-9785	7818
Alzheimers Family Services Ctr	8322	E	714 593-9630	23654
American Golf Corporation	7997	D	714 536-8866	18856
American Golf Corporation	7997	D	714 846-1364	18868
AMG Huntington Beach LLC	8711	E	714 894-9802	25656
Apple One Service Arizona Inc	7361	D	714 848-2610	14608
Applied Computer Solutions (PA)	7371	D	714 861-2200	15023
Aramark Facility Services LLC	7349	E	714 372-0683	14233
AT&T Corp	4813	D	714 965-4685	5461
Bartco Lighting Inc	5063	E	714 230-3200	7417
Beachside Realtors (PA)	6531	E	714 969-6100	11315
Boeing Company	8711	A	714 896-1301	25697
California Closet Co O	1799	C	714 899-4905	3506
Captured Sea Inc	1542	D	714 856-3358	1522
Cellco Partnership	4812	D	714 847-8799	5352
Child Development Incorporated	6531	D	714 842-4064	11388
Childrens Hospital Los Angeles	8021	A	714 841-4990	20249
Coastal Traffic Systems Inc	5063	D	714 641-3744	7428
Coastline Cnstr & Awng Co Inc	1521	D	714 891-9798	1157
Confie Seguros Inc (HQ)	6411	D	714 252-2500	10678
Custom Building Products Inc	1521	E	562 598-8808	1162
Dix Metals Inc	5051	D	714 677-0777	7366
Douglas Fir Holdings LLC	8051	D	714 842-5551	20521
Element Mtrls Tech HB Inc (HQ)	8734	D	714 892-1961	26847
EMC Corporation	7372	E	866 438-3622	15654
First Team RE - Orange Cnty	6531	E	714 965-2244	11533
Forty Four Group LLC	7311	D	949 407-6360	13851
Friedman Professional Mgt Co	8011	D	714 842-1426	19531
Galkos Construction Inc (PA)	7299	D	714 373-8545	13762
GBI Tile & Stone Inc (PA)	5032	E	949 567-1880	6985
Geosyntec Consultants Inc	8641	D	714 969-0800	25259
Goldenwest Ldry & Valet Svcs	7216	D	714 843-0723	13581
Grani Installation Inc (PA)	1542	D	714 898-0441	1557
Harbor Distributing LLC (HQ)	5181	C	714 933-2400	9062
HB Healthcare Associates LLC	8051	D	714 887-0144	20646
Hobbs Herder Advertising	7311	D	800 999-6090	13859
Horsemen Inc	7381	D	714 847-4243	16704
Huntington Bch Cnvlescent Hosp	8051	B	714 847-3515	20680
Huntington Beach Commnty Clinc	8011	C	714 847-4222	19563
I Hot Leads	7374	D	714 960-8028	16144
Icallfirst	4813	D	808 557-9299	5633
Ics Professional Services Inc	1752	C	714 868-3900	3119
Innocean Wrldwide Americas LLC (PA)	7311	D	714 861-5200	13864
K Line America Inc	4412	E	714 861-5000	4716
Kings Seafood Company LLC	5146	D	714 793-1177	8637
Magnet In Sand Inc	7374	C	623 703-5650	16154
Managed Health Network	6324	A	714 934-5519	10357
Marblewest Inc	1743	E	714 847-6472	3018
MCB-Cjs LLC	8742	D	714 230-3600	27531
Medical Diagnostic	8059	D	714 841-2273	21312
Merrill Gardens LLC	6531	B	714 842-6569	11684
Michaelson Connor & Boul (PA)	8742	D	714 846-6099	27549
Mortgage Fax Inc	7323	D	714 899-2656	14063
Nakase Brothers Wholesale Nurs (PA)	5193	D	949 855-4388	9203
Netball America Inc	7389	E	949 307-4455	17352
New Port Orthopedic Institute	8011	D	949 722-5071	19770
No Ordinary Moments Inc	8082	C	714 848-3800	22513
Nuvision Fncl Federal Cr Un (PA)	6062	C	714 375-8000	9675
Orange County Sanitation	4952	C	714 962-2411	6414
Pachinko World Inc	7993	C	714 895-7772	18807
Paragon Partners Ltd (PA)	8748	D	714 379-3376	28016
Pasha Distribution Svcs LLC	4731	D	714 889-2460	5146
Paul Maurer Company	7999	D	714 231-8241	19259
Portermatt Electric Inc	1731	D	714 596-8788	2688
Prime Hlthcare Hntngton Bch	8062	D	714 843-5000	21816
Pyro-Comm Systems Inc (PA)	1731	C	714 902-8000	2692
Quad/Graphics Inc	7819	D	949 930-5400	18248
Quiksilver Inc	5136	C	714 893-5187	8358
R C Hotels Inc	7011	C	714 891-0123	13119
Rainbow Disposal Co Inc (HQ)	4953	C	714 847-3581	6517
Rainbow Transfer Recycling	4953	C	714 847-5818	6518
Ralphs Grocery Company	4225	C	714 377-0024	4627
RC Wendt Painting Inc	1721	C	714 960-2700	2482
Reliable Wholesale Lumber Inc (PA)	5031	D	714 848-8222	6956
Reloaded Games Inc	7372	C	714 333-1420	15827
Ricoh Usa Inc	5044	E	714 396-0568	7066
Russell Fisher Partnership	7542	E	714 842-4453	17861
San Pedro Court House	6531	D	562 519-6023	11832
Sea Breeze Health Care Inc	8051	D	714 847-9671	20900
Shekinah Inc	8111	E	714 475-5460	23560
Sho-Air International Inc (PA)	4731	E	949 476-9111	5168
Skyhill Financial Inc	6531	D	714 657-3938	11845
Southern Cal Prmnnte Med Group	8011	E	714 841-7293	20031
Staff Pro Inc (PA)	7382	A	714 230-7200	16929
Star Real Estate	6531	D	714 500-3300	11855
Thomas Crane and Trckg Co Inc	1629	E	562 592-2837	2090
Tscm Corporation	7349	D	714 841-1988	14447
Two Roads Prof Resources Inc	7363	C	714 901-3804	14966
Unison Electric	1731	E	714 375-5915	2779
United States Technical Svcs	7379	D	714 374-6300	16516
Unitedhealth Group Inc	6324	B	714 969-9050	10386
Waterfront Hotel LLC	7011	B	714 845-8000	13395

HUNTINGTON PARK, CA - Los Angeles County

	SIC	EMP	PHONE	ENTRY #
Aircraft Xray Laboratories Inc	8734	D	323 587-0164	26829
All Care Medical Group Inc	8011	D	408 278-3550	19329
AT&T Corp	4812	D	323 589-7045	5256
Avanti Hospitals LLC	7389	B	323 583-1931	17016
Cellco Partnership	4899	D	323 826-9880	6064
Chhp Holdings II LLC (PA)	8062	D	323 583-1931	21481
Chhp Management LLC	8062	D	323 583-1931	21482
Covenant Care California LLC	8051	C	323 589-5941	20492
D2j Management	7389	D	323 589-1374	17114
Huntington Pk Police League	8322	D	323 584-6254	24018
Living Opportunities MGT Co	6513	C	323 589-5956	11158
Mexican Amrcn Oprtnty Fndation	8351	E	323 588-7320	24483
New Cingular Wireless Svcs Inc	4899	D	323 588-9348	6084
Powerhouse Realty Inc	6531	D	323 562-7777	11757
Prajin 1 Stop Distributors Inc (PA)	5099	E	323 395-5302	8133
Saroyan Lumber Company Inc (PA)	5031	D	800 624-9309	6960
St Francis Medical Ce	8011	D	323 588-8558	20052
Steelwrkers Old Tmers Fndation	8322	E	323 582-6090	24236

HURON, CA - Fresno County

	SIC	EMP	PHONE	ENTRY #
California Valley Land Co Inc (PA)	0721	D	559 945-9292	477
Dick Anderson & Sons Farming	0191	C	559 945-2511	355
Dole Fresh Vegetables Inc	0723	C	559 945-2591	525
Dresick Farms Inc (PA)	0161	E	559 945-2513	60
Royal Packing Dcf	0161	D	559 945-2537	91
West Cotton AG Management Inc	0762	C	559 945-2511	734

GEOGRAPHIC SECTION — IRVINE, CA

IDYLLWILD, CA - Riverside County

Company	SIC	EMP	PHONE	ENTRY #
Guided Discoveries Inc	7032	E	951 659-6062	13464

IMPERIAL, CA - Imperial County

Company	SIC	EMP	PHONE	ENTRY #
County of Imperial	1611	D	760 355-1748	1756
Crop Production Services Inc	5191	D	760 355-1133	9131
Empire Southwest LLC	5082	B	760 545-6200	7768
Imperial Irrigation District (PA)	4911	A	800 303-7756	6140
Imperial Irrigation District	4971	B	760 339-9220	6644
Western Meat Processors Inc	0212	E	760 355-1175	414

IMPERIAL BEACH, CA - San Diego County

Company	SIC	EMP	PHONE	ENTRY #
Boys Girls CLB of Imperl Bch	8641	D	619 424-2266	25217
Intervec Phoenix Travel Club	7997	C	828 728-5287	18963
Jpmorgan Chase Bank Nat Assn	6035	E	619 424-8197	9576
Offshore Service Vessels LLC	4491	D	619 237-1314	4751
Sodexo Operations Inc	7349	C	619 429-5692	14434

INDEPENDENCE, CA - Inyo County

Company	SIC	EMP	PHONE	ENTRY #
County of Inyo	7513	D	760 878-0292	17640
Los Angeles Dept Wtr & Pwr	4941	A	760 878-2156	6366
Sheriffs Offices	8111	D	760 878-0383	23566

INDIAN WELLS, CA - Riverside County

Company	SIC	EMP	PHONE	ENTRY #
Coldwell Bnkr Residential Brkg	6531	D	760 771-5454	11435
Dhccnp	7997	D	760 340-4646	18940
El Dorado Country Club	7997	C	760 346-8081	18945
Hyatt Corporation	7011	B	760 341-1000	12818
Indian Wells Resort Hotel	7011	E	760 345-6466	12836
Iw Golf Club Inc	7997	C	760 345-2561	18964
Lh Indian Wells Operating LLC	7011	C	760 341-2200	12916
Renaissance Hotel Operating Co	7011	A	760 773-4444	13142
Renaissnce Esmralda Resort Spa	7011	A	760 773-4444	13143
Reserve Club	7997	D	760 674-2222	19041
Senior Prdcrs In Rtrmnt TV	7812	D	760 773-9525	18148
Toscana Country Club Inc	7997	D	760 404-1444	19111
Troon Golf LLC	8741	C	760 346-4653	27260
Vintage Club (PA)	7997	E	760 341-1476	19120
Vintage Club Master Assn Inc	8641	D	760 340-0500	25399

INDIO, CA - Riverside County

Company	SIC	EMP	PHONE	ENTRY #
Cabazon Band Mission Indians	7011	A	760 342-5000	12478
Coachella Valley Mosquito Abat	7389	D	760 342-8287	17085
Coachella Vly Rescue Mission	8322	E	760 347-3512	23764
Commercial Lighting Inds Inc	5063	D	800 755-0155	7429
County of Riverside	8011	D	760 863-8283	19481
County of Riverside	8361	D	760 863-7600	24614
County of Riverside	7999	D	760 863-8247	19193
Desert Recreation District (PA)	7999	D	760 347-3484	19195
Drum Security Service Inc	7381	D	818 708-7914	16628
Easia Golf Investment LLC	6799	D	760 775-2000	12300
East Valley Tourist Dev Auth	7999	D	760 342-5000	19203
Elite Anywhere Corp	4731	D	917 860-9247	5065
Fc Landscape Inc	0781	D	760 347-6600	767
Frontier California Inc	4813	D	760 342-0500	5605
Gate City Beverage Distrs	5181	B	760 775-5483	9059
GE Holdings Inc	1751	D	760 343-1299	3050
Granite Construction Company	1611	B	760 775-7500	1779
HMS Agricultural Corporation	6531	D	760 347-2335	11571
Indio Hlthcare Wllness Ctr LLC	8051	D	760 347-6000	20683
JB Finish Inc	1751	D	760 342-6300	3057
John F Kennedy Memorial Hosp	8062	A	760 347-6191	21615
Kaiser Foundation Hospitals	8011	A	866 984-7483	19621
Kirkpatrick Ldscpg Svcs Inc	0782	C	760 347-6926	883
Lb Hills Golf Club LLC	7992	D	760 775-2000	18754
Marthas Village & Kitchen	8322	D	760 347-4741	24077
Oasis Mental Health Trtmnt Ctr	8063	D	760 863-8609	22085
P H B Contracting Inc	1742	D	760 347-7290	2945
Pauley Construction Inc	1623	D	760 347-7608	1978
Plantation Golf Club Inc	7997	D	760 775-3688	19030
Triangle Distributing Co	5181	D	760 347-4052	9089

INGLEWOOD, CA - Los Angeles County

Company	SIC	EMP	PHONE	ENTRY #
Aero Port Services Inc (PA)	7382	D	310 623-8230	16862
After-Party2 Inc (HQ)	7359	C	310 202-0011	14506
Air-Sea Forwarders Inc (PA)	4731	D	310 216-1616	5020
Alamo Rental (us) Inc	7514	D	310 649-2242	17659
American Nursing Home MGT Inc	8748	D	310 672-1012	27830
American Service Industries	7382	D	323 779-4000	16866
Big 5 Sporting Goods Corp	7999	A	323 755-2663	19149
Centinela Skilled Nursing and	8062	D	310 674-3216	21474
Centinela Skild Nrsng & Wllnss	8051	D	310 674-3216	20443
Centinela Valley Care Center	8361	C	310 674-3216	24589
Cfhs Holdings Inc	8062	A	310 673-4660	21478
City of Inglewood	7999	D	310 412-5370	19173
CP Opco LLC (HQ)	7299	A	310 966-4900	13752
Dolphin Hkg Ltd (PA)	5199	D	310 215-3356	9259
Eldorado Community Service Ctr	8011	D	424 227-7971	19513
Forum Enterprises Inc	7929	E	310 330-7300	18467
Gelshmal Enterprises LLC	5043	E	310 672-9090	7033
Gentle Dental Service Corp (HQ)	8021	C	310 765-2400	20255
Holiday Meat & Provision Corp	5147	C	310 674-0541	8672
Inglewood Meadows Kbs LP	6513	D	310 820-4888	11142
Inglewood Unified School Dst	8351	D	310 419-2691	24468
Interdent Inc (HQ)	8021	D	310 765-2400	20256
Interdent Service Corporation (DH)	8021	E	310 765-2400	20257
J Robert Scott Inc (PA)	5131	C	310 659-4910	8314
Kaiser Foundation Hospitals	8011	D	310 419-3303	19677
Motel 6 Operating LP	7011	D	310 419-1234	13010
Msg Networks Inc	7941	D	310 330-7300	18559
Oplv Inc	8051	D	310 672-1012	20827
Prime Healthcare Centinela LLC	8062	A	310 673-4660	21810
Prime International Security	7381	D	310 670-4565	16763
Rainbow Childrens Academy Inc	8351	E	310 672-2400	24507
RHO Chem LLC (DH)	4959	E	323 776-6234	6635
Royal Airline Linen Inc	7211	D	310 677-9885	13507
Sea-Air International Inc	4731	D	310 338-0778	5167
Smith Coleman Inc	6531	E	310 671-8271	11848
UPS Worldwide Logistics Inc	4731	C	310 673-7661	5185
Usas Express International	4731	D	310 645-2313	5186
Watts Health Foundation Inc (HQ)	8052	B	310 424-2220	21119
West Cntinela Vly Care Ctr Inc	8051	D	310 674-3216	21030

INYOKERN, CA - Kern County

Company	SIC	EMP	PHONE	ENTRY #
Global Tech MGT Resources Inc	8621	D	760 377-5522	25135

IONE, CA - Amador County

Company	SIC	EMP	PHONE	ENTRY #
Concessionaires Urban Park	7999	E	209 763-5121	19188
Concessionaires Urban Park	7999	E	209 763-5166	19189
Parks and Recreation Cal Dept	7999	E	209 763-5121	19258

IRVINE, CA - Orange County

Company	SIC	EMP	PHONE	ENTRY #
1105 Media Inc	4899	C	949 265-1520	6059
4g Wireless Inc (PA)	4812	C	949 748-6100	5252
7 Layers Inc	8711	D	949 716-6512	25604
A & H Communications Inc	1623	D	949 250-4555	1900
ABM Electrical & Ltg Solutions (DH)	7349	E	877 546-2937	14199
ABM Facility Services LLC (DH)	8711	C	949 330-1555	25609
ABS Consulting Inc	8711	D	714 734-4242	25610
Absg Consulting Inc	8748	D	714 734-4242	27806
Accurate Background LLC	7375	B	800 784-3911	16215
Ace Parking Management Inc	7521	C	949 727-1470	17709
Action Property Management Inc (PA)	6514	D	949 450-0202	11232
Activision Blizzard Inc	7372	D	949 955-1380	15568
Adams Streeter Civil Engineers	8711	D	949 474-2330	25615
Advantage Sales & Mktg Inc (PA)	5141	C	949 797-2900	8450
Advantage Sales & Mktg LLC (HQ)	5141	C	949 797-2900	8452
Agendia Inc	8093	C	949 540-6300	22651
Agility Holdings Inc (DH)	4731	D	714 617-6300	5016
Ahtna-CDM Smith JV	8711	D	714 824-3471	27820
Aids Svcs Fndation Orange Cnty	8322	D	949 809-5700	23648
Alcone Marketing Group Inc (HQ)	7311	D	949 595-5322	13816
Alecto Healthcare Services LLC (PA)	8062	A	323 938-3161	21442
Aleks Corporation	7372	C	714 245-7191	15575
All Environmental Inc	8748	D	949 752-9300	27824
Allen Matkins Leck Gmble	8111	D	949 553-1313	23087
Allergan Sales LLC (DH)	5122	A	714 246-4500	8227
Alorica Inc (PA)	7389	D	949 527-4600	16981
Alton Irvine Inc	5021	D	949 428-4141	6802
Amec Fstr Whlr Envrnmnt Infrst	8748	D	949 642-0245	27828
American Express Travel	4724	D	949 453-7123	4955
American Funds Service Company	6289	E	949 975-5000	10195
American Golf Corporation	7997	C	949 786-1224	18853
American Interbanc Mrtg LLC	6162	E	714 957-9430	9813
American Liberty Capital Corp	6163	C	949 623-0288	9913
American Medical Tech Inc	5047	D	949 553-0359	7233
Ameripath Mortgage Corporation	6162	D	949 753-9211	9818
Ampronix Inc	5047	D	949 273-8000	7234
Anatec International Inc (HQ)	8711	D	949 498-3350	25657
Ancca International	1742	D	949 553-0084	2855
Anderson & Howard Electric Inc	1731	D	949 250-4555	2521
Andrew Lauren Company Inc	7389	C	949 861-4222	16991
Anheuser-Busch LLC	5181	C	949 263-9270	9041
Antech Diagnostics Inc (HQ)	0742	E	800 745-4725	615
AON Consulting Inc	6411	D	562 345-4600	10609
Applied Geokinetics	8711	D	949 502-5353	25660
Apria Healthcare LLC	7352	B	714 508-3000	14471
Arbitech LLC	5045	D	949 376-6650	7093
ARC Partners Inc	7379	D	703 757-0402	16324
Argent Management Co LLC	6531	D	949 777-4070	11304
Aria Group Incorporated	8711	D	949 475-2915	25664
Arthur J Gallagher & Co	6411	E	949 349-9800	10623
Artistic Maintenance Inc	0782	C	949 733-8690	810

Employment Codes: A=Over 500 employees, B=251-500, C=101-250, D=51-100, E=45-50

IRVINE, CA

GEOGRAPHIC SECTION

Company	SIC	EMP	PHONE	ENTRY #
Ashley Management Group	8742	E	949 754-3120	27333
Asics America Corporation (HQ)	5139	C	949 453-8888	8420
Aspect Software Inc	7372	E	408 595-5002	15585
Assi Security (PA)	1731	D	949 955-0244	2523
AT&T Corp.	4812	D	949 559-1457	5257
AT&T Corp.	4813	D	949 622-8240	5494
Aten Technology Inc	5045	D	949 428-1111	7096
Atkinson Construction Inc	1611	B	303 410-2540	1736
Atria Senior Living Group Inc	8741	D	949 786-5665	26930
Auctioncom Inc	6531	C	800 499-6199	11310
Autobytel Inc (PA)	7375	D	949 225-4500	16218
Autowebcom Inc	7375	B	949 862-1371	16219
Avamar Technologies Inc	7371	D	949 743-5100	15043
Avnet Inc	5065	C	949 789-4100	7528
Ayco Company LP	6282	C	949 955-1544	10121
Banc California National Assn (HQ)	6035	D	877 770-2262	9567
Banc of California Inc (PA)	6021	C	855 361-2262	9319
Bankruptcy MGT Solutions Inc	8111	C	949 222-1212	23104
Bastanchury Waters Company Inc (PA)	5149	C	909 824-2430	8805
BDS Marketing Inc (PA)	7311	C	949 472-6700	13820
Bear Data Solutions Inc	7373	D	949 833-3282	15909
Bear Stearns Companies LLC	6162	A	949 856-8300	9821
Beneficial Administration Co	6411	D	949 756-1000	10644
Bergelectric Corp	1731	D	949 250-7005	2533
Berger Kahn	8111	E	310 821-9000	23111
Berkshire Mortgage Fin Corp	6162	D	949 754-6300	9822
Best Life and Health Insur Co	6311	D	949 253-4080	10202
Bigrentz Inc	7353	D	855 999-5438	14478
Birtcher N Goodman Amer LLC	6531	D	949 407-0100	11324
Black & Veatch Corporation	8711	E	913 458-2000	25693
Black & Veatch Corporation	8711	D	562 345-9332	25694
Blb Resources Inc (PA)	8742	C	949 261-9155	27350
Blizzard Entertainment Inc (HQ)	7372	D	949 955-1380	15602
Bogart Construction Inc	1542	D	949 453-1400	1508
Boost Mobile LLC (PA)	7389	C	949 451-1563	17036
Brady Vorwerck Rydr & Cspno (PA)	8111	D	480 456-9888	23130
Brandrep Inc	8742	E	800 405-7119	27355
Brer Affiliates Inc (DH)	6794	D	949 794-7900	12211
Brinderson LP (HQ)	8711	C	714 466-7100	25703
Brinderson LP	8711	D	714 466-7100	25704
Brinderson & Associates	8711	E	714 466-7100	25705
Broadcom Foundation	8641	D	949 926-9500	25223
Brooker Associates	0783	D	949 559-4877	988
Brookfield Relocation Inc (DH)	6794	D	949 794-7900	12212
Brown and Streza LLP	8742	E	949 453-2900	27361
Bryan Cave LLP	8111	D	949 223-7000	23134
Buchalter Nemer A Prof Corp	8111	D	714 549-5150	23137
Cal Southern Illumination	5063	E	949 622-3000	7422
Cal Southern Presbt Homes	6513	D	949 854-9500	11106
Calatlantic Group Inc (PA)	1531	D	949 789-1600	1357
Calatlantic Group Inc	1522	D	949 789-1600	1300
Calico Building Services Inc	1542	C	949 380-8707	1520
California First National Bank	6029	D	949 255-0500	9546
Calteck USA Inc	7539	E	949 786-4854	17820
Caltrop Corporation	8741	D	949 337-4280	26956
Canon Solutions America Inc	5084	D	800 333-6395	7830
Canon USA Inc	5043	B	949 753-4000	7029
Cape Environmental MGT Inc	8744	B	949 236-3000	27776
Capital Group Companies Inc	6282	D	949 975-5000	10130
Capital Research and MGT Co	6282	D	949 975-5000	10132
Carfinance Capital LLC	6799	A	800 900-5150	12292
Carpenter Fund Manager Gp LLC	6021	C	949 261-8888	9341
Catalina Marketing Corporation	8743	E	949 930-6500	27739
CB&i Envmtl Infrastructure Inc	8748	D	949 261-6441	27868
CB&i Government Solutions Inc	8711	D	949 261-6441	25722
CDM SMITH INC	8711	D	949 752-5452	25726
Cellco Partnership	4812	D	949 286-7000	5299
Centex Homes Inc	1521	C	949 453-0113	1153
Cfp Fire Protection Inc	1711	D	949 338-4280	2178
Cgtech (PA)	7373	E	949 753-1050	15919
Chambers Group Inc	8748	E	949 261-5414	27877
Child Development Incorporated	8351	B	949 854-5060	24432
Cie Digital Labs LLC (PA)	7319	E	949 381-6200	13993
Citigroup Global Markets Inc	6211	D	949 955-7500	9979
Citigroup Inc	6021	D	949 726-5124	9381
City of Irvine	8742	D	949 724-7600	27383
City of Irvine	7999	C	949 724-7740	19174
City of Irvine	8621	D	949 724-7101	25129
City Ventures LLC (PA)	6531	E	949 258-7555	11394
Clark Cnstr Group-California	1541	B	714 754-0764	1415
Clark Cnstr Grup-California LP	1542	B	714 429-9779	1530
Clark/Mccarthy A Joint Venture	1521	A	714 429-9779	1154
Coast To Coast Bus Eqp Inc (PA)	5044	D	949 457-7300	7050
Commerce Velocity LLC	7372	E	949 756-8950	15624
Commonwealth Land Title Co	6361	D	949 460-4500	10510
Compucom Systems Inc	5045	E	949 222-0949	7110
Comwork	7389	E	405 703-8889	17090
Concerto Healthcare Inc	8322	C	949 537-3400	23785
Connect Your Home LLC	1542	D	949 777-0100	1533
Connotate Technologies Inc	7371	E	949 270-1916	15107
Consoldted Fire Protection LLC (HQ)	7389	A	949 727-3277	17092
Consumer Portfolio Svcs Inc	6141	C	949 788-5695	9744
Contec Microelectronics USA	5045	D	949 250-4025	7111
Corelogic Inc	6531	E	714 250-6400	11457
Corner Products Company	5065	D	949 255-3982	7550
Corporate Risk Hldings III Inc	7389	A	949 428-5839	17096
Corvel Corporation (PA)	8741	C	949 851-1473	26984
Corvel Enterprise Comp Inc	6411	D	949 851-1473	10681
Courtney Inc (PA)	1799	D	949 222-2050	3509
Cox Communications Inc	4841	D	949 546-1000	5976
Creative Maintenance Systems	7349	D	949 852-2871	14271
Crescent Staffing Inc (PA)	7371	C	949 724-0304	15114
Critchfeld Mech Inc Sthern Cal	1711	D	949 390-2900	2195
Crowdstrike Holdings Inc	7379	E	949 954-6785	16345
Crowell & Moring LLP	8111	E	949 263-8400	23190
Cushman & Wakefield Cal Inc	6531	E	949 474-4004	11464
Custom Business Solutions Inc (PA)	5044	D	949 380-7674	7051
Customer Srvc Dlvry Pltfrm Crp	7379	E	717 896-8889	16349
Cwpfl Inc	7389	E	714 564-7900	17113
Cybercoders Inc	7361	C	949 885-5151	14635
D P S Inc	1721	D	714 564-7900	2438
D R I Residential Corporation	1761	D	949 266-1950	3160
Database Marketing Group Inc	7331	B	714 727-0800	14068
Davita Inc	8092	B	949 930-4400	22622
Dechert LLP	8111	C	949 442-6000	23201
Decision Toolbox Inc	8748	D	562 377-5600	27895
Delta Galil USA Inc	5137	D	949 296-0380	8377
Dentons US LLP	8111	E	949 732-3700	23206
Developers Surety Indemnity Co (DH)	6351	D	949 263-3300	10491
Dharne & Company	7379	D	949 293-5675	16356
Dkn Hotel LLC (PA)	7011	B	714 427-4320	12579
DOT Leasing Company	5111	C	949 474-1100	8152
Dri Companies (PA)	1761	D	949 266-1900	3165
Duke Energy Corporation	4911	C	949 727-7434	6124
Dzyne Technologies Inc	8711	E	703 291-6663	25774
Edison Capital (DH)	6799	D	909 594-3789	12302
Edwards Lifesciences LLC (HQ)	8011	A	949 250-2500	19512
Edwards Theatres Circuit Inc	7832	D	949 854-8811	18333
Egl Holdco Inc	7372	A	800 678-7423	15650
Ekedal Masonry & Concrete Inc	1741	D	949 720-8011	2812
Elevate Property Services LP	6519	D	562 219-2101	11252
Eleven Agency LLC	7311	E	949 679-1182	13843
Elite Engineering Services Inc	8711	E	949 536-7199	25784
Elite Security Services Inc	7381	B	949 222-2203	16633
Empcc Inc	1721	D	714 564-7900	2441
Enclarity Inc	7374	D	949 614-8110	16125
Eplus Technology Inc	7373	D	949 417-7000	15942
Equinox-76th Street Inc	8049	B	949 975-8400	20318
Equistar Irvine Company LLC	7011	D	949 833-3331	12621
Ernst & Young LLP	8721	B	949 794-2300	26342
Ernst & Young LLP	8721	E	949 838-3300	26344
Esis Inc	6411	D	949 242-6950	10701
Essex Realty Management Inc	6531	D	949 798-8100	11496
European Hotl Invstrs of CA (PA)	6513	E	949 474-7368	11127
Evisions Inc (PA)	7371	D	949 833-1384	15176
Experian Info Solutions Inc	7323	C	949 567-3731	14060
Exult Inc	8742	A	949 856-8800	27430
F M Tarbell Co	6531	D	949 559-8451	11515
Federal Express Corporation	7389	B	800 463-3339	17166
Federal Express Corporation	4512	D	949 862-4500	4803
Fedex Freight Corporation	4213	D	800 706-1687	4169
Festival Fun Parks LLC	7999	D	949 559-8336	19211
Ficcadenti & Waggoner Consul (PA)	8711	C	949 474-0502	25808
Fidelity Nat Title Insur Co (HQ)	6361	C	949 622-4600	10514
Fieldstone Communities Inc	1521	E	949 790-5400	1175
Fieldstone Communities Inc (PA)	1531	E	949 790-5400	1364
Finance America LLC (HQ)	6162	C	949 440-1000	9840
First Amercn Prof RE Svcs Inc (PA)	6531	D	714 250-1400	11521
First Team RE - Orange Cnty (PA)	6531	C	888 236-1943	11532
First Team RE - Orange Cnty	6531	D	949 857-0414	11534
Firstplus Bank	6141	E	949 851-7101	9747
Fisher & Paykel Healthcare Inc	5047	B	949 453-4000	7265
Fisher & Phillips LLP	8111	D	949 851-2424	23244
Flagship Credit Acceptance LLC	7389	C	949 748-7172	17170
Fluor Enterprises Inc	8711	D	949 349-2000	25813
Fnc Inc	7371	D	714 866-1099	15190
Footh The / Easte Trans Corri	1611	D	949 754-3400	1771
Ford Motor Company	8111	B	949 341-5800	23252
Fostering Executive Leadership	8742	D	949 651-6250	27438
Fox Head Inc (PA)	5136	C	408 776-8633	8342

GEOGRAPHIC SECTION — IRVINE, CA

Company	SIC	EMP	PHONE	ENTRY #
Fragomen Del Rey Bernse	8111	D	949 660-3504	23256
Francisco Emilio Assoc Law Off	8111	D	949 474-2222	23258
Frank D Yelian MD PC	8011	E	949 788-1133	19527
Full Circle Wireless Inc	5065	E	949 783-7979	7571
Fuscoe Engineering Inc (PA)	8711	D	949 474-1960	25824
GA Services LLC	7379	E	949 752-6515	16379
Gallup Inc	8742	E	949 474-2700	27445
Gdr Group Inc	7379	D	949 453-8818	16381
Genea Energy Partners Inc	1711	D	714 694-0536	2234
General Electric Capital Corp	6159	C	949 838-3043	9800
General Tool Inc	5085	D	949 261-2322	7933
Genpact Mortgage Services Inc	6162	D	949 417-5131	9844
George Fischer LLC (DH)	5051	D	714 731-8800	7372
Gfk Etilize Inc	8732	D	888 608-1212	26669
Ggec America Inc	5065	D	714 750-2280	7573
Ghost Management Group LLC	7313	C	949 870-1400	13969
Gibson Dunn & Crutcher LLP	8111	C	949 451-3800	23267
Gkk Corporation (PA)	8712	D	949 250-1500	26190
Gkk Works (HQ)	8741	E	949 250-1500	27038
Global Ascent Inc	7389	E	714 930-6860	17187
Global Eagle Entertainment Inc	7812	C	949 608-8700	18089
Global Language Solutions LLC	7389	D	949 798-1400	17194
Glovis America Inc (HQ)	4731	D	714 435-2960	5088
Go2 Systems Inc	7375	D	949 553-0800	16238
Golden Hotels Ltd Partnership	7011	C	949 833-2770	12668
Golden West Partners Inc (PA)	8748	D	949 477-3090	27935
Gordian Medical Inc	5047	B	714 556-0200	7266
Gordon Rees Sclly Mnskhani LLP	8111	D	949 255-6950	23282
Gradient Engineers Inc	8711	D	949 477-0555	25845
Greenberg Traurig LLP	8111	D	949 732-6500	23291
Greystar Management Svcs LP	8741	B	949 705-0010	27045
Grubb Ellis Rlty Investors LLC	6799	B	714 667-8252	12311
Halyard Health Inc	8099	A	800 448-3569	22967
Hardesty LLC (PA)	7361	E	949 407-6625	14668
Harmony Escrow Inc	6531	D	949 474-1134	11569
Harris & Associates Inc	8711	D	949 655-3900	25848
Haskell & White (PA)	8721	D	949 450-6200	26366
Hcp Inc (PA)	6798	D	949 407-0700	12248
HDR Engineering Inc	8711	C	714 730-2300	25854
Healthcare MGT Partners LLC	8741	B	949 263-8620	27053
HEI Irvine LLC	7011	D	949 553-8332	12697
Hensel Phlps Grnte Hngr JV	1542	C	949 852-0111	1570
Heritage Indemnity Company	6331	D	303 987-5500	10428
Hff Inc	6162	D	949 253-8800	9855
Hilton Worldwide Inc	7011	C	949 553-8332	12734
Hireright LLC (HQ)	7375	C	949 428-5800	16243
Hntb Corporation	8711	D	949 460-1700	25864
Hoag Memorial Hospital Presbt	8062	A	949 764-4624	21604
HPM Construction LLC	1542	D	949 474-9170	1574
Huitt - Zollars Inc	8713	E	949 988-5815	26275
Hunsaker & Assoc Irvine Inc (PA)	8711	D	949 583-1010	25870
Huron Development Inc	6799	D	949 863-9789	12315
Hyatt Corporation	7011	B	949 975-1234	12816
Hyland Software Inc	7371	D	949 242-3100	15227
Hyundai ABS Funding LLC	6211	C	949 732-2697	10013
Hyundai Capital America (DH)	6141	D	714 965-3000	9754
Ibi Group (us) Inc (HQ)	8711	E	949 477-5030	25872
Icf Jones & Stokes Inc	8742	D	949 333-6600	27471
Idexx Reference Labs Inc	8071	E	949 477-2840	22225
Ignite Health LLC (PA)	7311	D	949 861-3200	13862
Impac Companies	6719	C	949 475-3933	12070
Impac Mortgage Corp	6162	B	949 475-3600	9859
Impac Mortgage Holdings Inc (PA)	6798	D	949 475-3600	12250
Impac Mortgage Holdings Inc	6798	D	949 475-3781	12251
Impac Secured Assets Corp	6733	D	949 475-3600	12176
Imperial Contracting	1522	D	949 333-6460	1315
Indemnity Company California (DH)	6351	D	949 263-3300	10494
Inductors Inc	5065	E	949 623-2460	7585
Indvls	8742	E	949 339-0575	27473
Ingram Micro Inc (PA)	5045	A	714 566-1000	7145
Insco Insurance Services Inc (HQ)	6411	D	949 797-9243	10743
Insituform Technologies LLC	1623	E	714 724-2324	1942
Integra Lifesciences Corp	8731	C	949 595-8710	26536
Interactive Media Holdings (PA)	7311	D	949 861-8888	13866
Intercntnntal Ht Group Rsurces	7011	D	949 863-1999	12841
Intercontinental Hotels Group	7011	D	949 863-1999	12842
Interior Office Solutions Inc (PA)	7389	E	949 724-9444	17245
International Toy Inc	5092	E	949 333-3777	8045
Interstate Hotels Resorts Inc	8741	C	949 833-9999	27072
Interwall Dev Systems Inc	1742	D	949 553-9102	2912
Intratek Computer Inc	7379	B	949 334-4200	16411
Inventus Power Inc	8322	C	949 553-0097	24036
Ipass Inc	7373	D	650 232-4100	15974
Irvine APT Communities LP (HQ)	6513	C	949 720-5600	11144
Irvine Company LLC	8699	D	949 653-5300	25546
Irvine Company LLC	6552	C	949 720-4400	11974
Irvine Pharmaceutical Svcs Inc (PA)	8734	C	949 951-4425	26862
Irvine Ranch Water District (PA)	4941	C	949 453-5300	6358
Irvine Ranch Water District	4941	C	949 453-5300	6359
Irvine Technology Corporation	8742	B	714 445-2624	27485
Irvine Unified School Distict	4151	D	949 936-5300	3939
Irvine Valencia Growers	0179	D	949 936-8000	257
Isotis Orthobiologics Inc	8731	C	949 595-8710	26540
Ixos Software Inc (PA)	5045	D	949 784-8000	7148
J Baron Inc	6531	D	949 451-1200	11593
Jackson Demarco Tidus Peter (PA)	8111	D	949 752-8585	23324
Jacobs Engineering Group Inc	8711	D	949 224-7585	25890
Jacobs Field Svcs N Amer Inc	1629	C	949 224-7585	2060
Jacobs Project Management Co	8711	D	949 224-7695	25904
Jacobus Consulting Inc	8742	E	949 713-2101	27492
James R Glidewell Dental	8072	A	800 411-9723	22308
Jeff Tracy Inc	1711	E	949 582-0877	2262
Jeffrey Rome & Associates	8712	D	949 760-3929	26214
Jetsuite Inc	4522	C	949 892-4300	4881
JF Shea Construction Inc	1521	D	949 526-8792	1194
Jmac Lending Inc	6141	D	949 390-2688	9755
Jnr Inc	8742	D	949 476-2788	27494
Jones Day Limited Partnership	8111	D	949 851-3939	23331
Jones Lang Lsalle Americas Inc	6282	C	949 296-3600	10154
Jonset Corporation	4959	D	949 551-5151	6630
K Hovnanian Companies Cal Inc (PA)	1521	D	949 222-7700	1200
K&L Gates LLP	8111	E	949 756-0210	23335
Kaiser Foundation Hospitals	8062	C	949 262-5780	21629
Kaiser Foundation Hospitals	6733	B	949 932-5000	12189
Kasdan Smnds Riley Vaughan LLP (PA)	8111	D	949 851-9000	23337
Katten Muchin Rosenman LLP	8111	C	714 386-5708	23338
Keating Dental Arts Inc	8072	C	949 955-2100	22310
Keystone PCF Property MGT Inc (PA)	6531	D	949 833-2600	11617
Kieckhafer Schiffer & Co LLP (PA)	8721	D	949 250-3900	26383
Kilroy Realty LP	6531	C	949 788-1200	11619
Kinetic Systems Inc	1711	E	949 770-7364	2269
Kite Electric Inc	1731	C	949 380-7471	2632
Knobbe Martens Olson Bear LLP (PA)	8111	B	949 760-0404	23358
Koeller Nbker Crlson Hluck LLP (PA)	8111	D	949 864-3400	23359
Koll Company LLC (PA)	1542	D	562 948-5296	1596
Kore1 Inc	7379	D	949 706-6990	16420
Kronos Incorporated	7372	D	800 580-7374	15730
Ksm Marketing Inc	7389	C	949 597-2222	17279
Ktgy Group Inc (PA)	8712	D	949 851-2133	26219
L S A Associates Inc (PA)	8748	D	949 553-0666	27970
La Jolla Group Inc (PA)	7389	D	949 428-2800	17283
La Jolla Group Inc	7389	D	949 428-2800	17284
Landmark Event Staffing	7381	A	714 293-4248	16719
Lawyers Title Insurance Corp	6361	D	949 223-5575	10531
Lba Realty Fund III - III LLC	6798	D	949 833-0400	12255
Lba Realty LLC (PA)	6531	E	949 833-0400	11629
Lba Rlty Fund I-Company IV LLC	6798	D	949 955-9321	12256
Lee & Associates Coml RE Svcs (PA)	6531	E	949 727-1200	11631
Legacy Prtners Coml Capitl Inc	6552	D	949 863-0390	11978
Leighton and Associates Inc (PA)	8748	D	949 250-1421	27973
Liberty Dental Plan Cal Inc	6324	B	949 223-0007	10355
Lifted Research Group Inc (PA)	5136	D	949 581-1144	8350
Lineage Logistics LLC (HQ)	4222	C	800 678-7271	4497
Lineage Logistics Holdings LLC (PA)	4222	D	800 678-7271	4499
Lineage Logistics Holdings LLC	4214	A	909 433-3100	4359
Linksys LLC (HQ)	5065	B	949 270-8500	7600
Live Nation Worldwide Inc	7922	D	949 860-2070	18411
Lizhang Enterprises Corp	6719	E	714 734-6683	12073
LLP Moss Adams	8721	E	949 221-4000	26403
Loan Administration Netwrk Inc	7361	D	949 752-5246	14697
Loangeniecom Inc	6163	D	949 788-6161	9934
Local Corporation (PA)	7311	D	949 784-0800	13876
Logicor	7371	E	949 260-2260	15282
LPA Inc (PA)	8712	D	949 261-1001	26225
M F Commercial Landscape Svcs	0781	D	949 660-8655	777
M F Salta Co Inc (PA)	8742	D	562 421-2512	27518
Magarro Farms	0723	D	949 859-6506	558
Malcolm & Cisneros A Law Corp	8111	C	949 252-1039	23417
Marriott	7011	D	949 380-3000	12947
Marriott International Inc	7011	B	949 724-3606	12957
Maruchan Inc	4225	D	949 789-2300	4594
Mavent Inc	7373	D	949 223-6424	15993
Mazda Research & Dev of N Amer	8711	D	949 852-8898	25953
MBK Real Estate Companies	6531	E	949 789-8300	11668
MBK Real Estate Ltd A Calfor (HQ)	6552	D	949 789-8300	11982
MBK Senior Living LLC (PA)	8322	D	949 242-1400	24078
McDermott Will & Emery LLP Inc	8111	D	949 757-7165	23426
McKinley Equipment Corporation (PA)	5084	E	800 770-6094	7863
Mds Consulting (PA)	8711	D	949 251-8821	25960
Mechanics Bank	6022	B	949 270-9700	9508

Employment Codes: A=Over 500 employees, B=251-500, C=101-250, D=51-100, E=45-50

IRVINE, CA — GEOGRAPHIC SECTION

Company	SIC	EMP	PHONE	ENTRY #
Medata Inc (HQ)	7372	D	714 918-1310	15744
Mercer (us) Inc	8742	D	949 222-1300	27544
Mercury Technology Group Inc	7374	D	949 417-0260	16160
Merit Property Management Inc (HQ)	6531	C	949 448-6000	11679
Merrill Lynch Pierce Fenner	6211	D	949 859-2900	10045
Mesa Energy Systems Inc (HQ)	1711	C	949 460-0460	2293
Mhh Holdings Inc	5149	C	949 651-9903	8876
Michael Madden Co Inc	5113	D	800 834-6248	8198
Microsoft Corporation	7372	C	949 263-3000	15753
Midnite Air Corp (HQ)	4513	D	310 330-2300	4870
Mind Research Institute	8733	C	949 345-8700	26788
Mirion Technologies Gds Inc (HQ)	8734	D	949 419-1000	26868
Mission Energy Holding Company	6719	A	949 752-5588	12075
Mission Hills Mortgage Corp (HQ)	6163	C	714 972-3832	9937
Mobilenet Services Inc (PA)	8711	C	949 951-4444	25972
Mobilityware Inc	7371	D	949 788-9900	15311
Monarch Healthcare A Medical (HQ)	8011	C	949 923-3200	19761
Montage Hotels & Resorts LLC (PA)	6531	A	949 715-5002	11691
Morgan Stanley	6211	D	949 809-1200	10050
Mtc Financial Inc	6733	E	949 252-8300	12195
Murtaugh Myer Nlson Trglia LLP	8111	D	949 794-4000	23460
Mv Transportation Inc	4111	D	949 553-1639	3677
Mve + Partners Inc (PA)	8712	D	949 809-3388	26239
MWH Americas Inc	8711	D	949 328-2400	25981
Nationwide Funding LLC	6159	E	949 679-3600	9802
Neogenomics Inc	8731	B	239 768-0600	26574
Netapp Inc	7373	C	949 754-6600	16003
Network Capital Funding Corp (PA)	6162	B	949 442-0060	9876
Neudesic LLC (PA)	7379	C	949 754-4500	16438
New York Life Insurance Co	6411	D	949 797-2400	10801
Newton Softed Inc	8748	E	949 396-6192	27998
Nexa Technologies Inc (HQ)	7371	D	972 590-8669	15330
Nexgenix Inc (PA)	7371	B	714 665-6240	15331
Nextel Communications Inc	4812	D	949 727-1400	5405
Nihon Kohden America Inc (HQ)	5047	D	949 580-1555	7285
Nikken Global Inc (HQ)	5087	C	949 789-2000	7972
Ninyo & Moore Geotechnical	8748	D	949 753-7070	28001
North Amercn Science Assoc Inc	8734	D	949 951-3110	26879
Nossaman LLP	8111	E	949 833-7800	23475
Nri Secure Technologies Ltd	7379	C	949 537-2957	16441
NRLL LLC	6799	E	949 768-7777	12332
Nrp Holding Co Inc (PA)	6719	C	949 583-1000	12080
Ntrust Infotech Inc	7372	D	562 207-1600	15780
NW Manor Community Partners LP	6552	D	714 662-5565	11990
Ocmbc Inc	6162	C	714 479-0999	9877
Oerlikon USA Inc	7374	D	949 863-1857	16166
One 3 Two Inc	5137	C	949 596-8400	8407
Operation Technology Inc (PA)	7371	D	949 462-0100	15353
Optima Mortgage Corporation	6162	D	714 389-4650	9878
Optumrx Inc (DH)	6324	B	714 825-3600	10364
Oracle Corp	8999	A	650 506-7000	28151
Oracle Systems Corporation	7371	D	949 224-1000	15361
Oracle Systems Corporation	7372	B	949 623-9460	15810
Orange County Produce LLC	0171	D	949 451-0880	125
Orchard Holdings Group Inc	6531	C	949 502-8300	11722
Ortiz Enterprises Incorporated (PA)	1611	D	949 753-1414	1839
OSI Consulting Inc	7379	E	949 724-8300	16449
Owl Education and Training	8331	A	949 797-2000	24375
Pacific City Bank	6029	D	714 263-1800	9554
Pacific Dental Services Inc (PA)	8021	E	714 845-8500	20269
Pacific Pharma Inc	5122	A	714 246-4600	8288
Pacific Premier Bank (HQ)	6531	D	714 431-4000	11729
Pacific Sterling Properties	6512	E	949 222-9911	11030
Pacifica Home Loans Inc	6162	E	949 417-1063	9880
Paciolan Inc	7372	C	949 476-2050	15813
Paramount Equity Mortgage LLC	6162	C	916 290-9999	9882
Passco Companies LLC	6531	D	949 442-1000	11743
Pathway Capital Management LP (PA)	8741	D	949 622-1000	27161
Payne & Fears LLP (PA)	8111	D	949 851-1101	23499
Peoples Choice Home (PA)	6162	D	949 494-6167	9885
Philips Medical Systems Clevel	5047	D	949 699-2300	7300
Physician Weblink of Cal (HQ)	8741	D	949 923-3201	27164
Piercey Management Svcs Inc (PA)	8741	D	949 379-3701	27165
Plaza Home Mortgage Inc	6211	D	714 508-6406	10070
Ponderosa Electric Inc	1731	D	949 253-3100	2687
Post Modern Edit LLC (PA)	7812	D	949 608-8700	18133
Precept Inc (DH)	6411	D	949 955-1430	10831
Premier Office Centers LLC (PA)	7389	E	949 253-4147	17424
Pricewaterhousecoopers LLP	8721	B	949 437-5200	26424
Prime Tech Cabinets Inc	1751	D	714 558-4837	3073
Primecare Quality HM Care Inc	1521	D	949 681-3515	1238
Products & Services Inc	5064	D	949 583-1681	7509
Proove Medical Labs Inc	8071	C	949 427-5303	22261
Proview Advanced Solutions Inc	6411	D	949 752-2484	10841
Prudential Insur Co of Amer	6411	E	949 440-5300	10842
Prudential Overall Supply (PA)	7218	D	949 250-4855	13635
Prudential Overall Supply	7218	D	760 717-6803	13640
Pts Staffing Solutions	8711	C	949 268-4000	26024
Qbe First Insurance Agency Inc	6411	B	949 206-6200	10847
Quadion LLC	6282	A	714 546-0994	10176
Quality Systems Inc (PA)	7372	C	949 255-2600	15823
Quest Group (PA)	5099	D	949 585-0111	8134
Quest Intl Monitor Svc Inc (PA)	7378	D	949 581-9900	16304
Quovera Inc	8748	E	949 224-3825	28030
Racquet Club of Irvine	7997	D	949 786-3000	19032
Railpros Inc (PA)	8711	D	714 734-8765	26031
Railpros Field Services	7389	E	877 315-0513	17442
Ramboll Environ US Corporation	8748	E	949 798-3604	28031
Ramboll Environ US Corporation	8748	D	949 261-5151	28033
Rand Technology LLC (PA)	5065	D	949 255-5700	7625
Ranscapes Inc	7349	E	866 883-9297	14402
Redhill Group Inc	8732	B	949 752-5900	26703
Rels LLC	6531	A	949 214-1000	11803
Renal Treatment Ctrs - Cal Inc	8092	C	949 930-6882	22637
Renovo Solutions LLC	7699	B	714 599-7969	18004
Renwood Realtytrac LLC	6531	D	949 502-8300	11810
Residence Mutual Insurance Co	6331	A	949 724-9402	10456
Resolve Systems LLC (PA)	7371	D	949 325-0120	15415
Resources Connection Inc (PA)	8742	A	714 430-6400	27617
Resources Connection LLC (HQ)	7361	D	714 430-6400	14751
Result Group Inc	7373	D	480 777-7130	16040
Richmond American Homes	1521	E	949 467-2600	1246
Ricoh Usa Inc	5044	D	949 225-2300	7072
RMS Group Inc	1542	D	714 373-4882	1652
Robert Half International Inc	7361	D	949 476-3199	14769
Rockefeller Group Dev Corp	6552	C	949 468-1800	12005
Roland Dga Corporation (HQ)	5045	C	949 727-2100	7180
Rose International Inc	8748	E	636 812-4000	28046
RSM US LLP	8721	A	949 255-6500	26433
Ryland Homes of Texas Inc	1531	E	805 367-3800	1383
S K & A Information Svcs Inc (DH)	8732	D	949 476-2051	26705
S W P T X Inc	1721	C	714 546-7900	2488
Sage Software Holdings Inc (HQ)	7372	B	866 530-7243	15832
San Joaquin Hills Transporttn (PA)	1611	D	949 754-3400	1855
Sand Canyon Corporation (HQ)	6163	D	949 727-9425	9950
Sand Canyon LLC	7992	D	949 551-2560	18781
Savoy Contractors Group Inc	1521	D	949 753-1919	1251
SCC Acquisitions Inc	6552	C	949 777-4000	12006
SD Deacon Corp	1542	D	949 222-9060	1662
Sea Breeze Financial Services (PA)	6162	E	949 223-9700	9895
Sean P OConnor	8111	D	949 851-7323	23548
Second Harvest Food	8322	D	949 653-2900	24197
Secureauth Corporation (PA)	7371	D	949 777-6959	15444
Sedgwick LLP	8111	E	949 852-8200	23552
Sema Construction Inc	1622	D	949 330-4300	1899
Sentinel Monitoring Corp	7382	D	949 453-1550	16925
Sentinel Offender Services LLC (PA)	7382	D	949 453-1550	16926
Seven Resorts Inc (PA)	7999	C	949 588-7100	19280
Sfn Group Inc	7363	D	949 727-8500	14947
Sgii Inc	5122	E	949 521-6161	8293
Shady Canyon Golf Club Inc	7997	C	949 856-7000	19076
Shaw Group Inc	8734	A	949 261-6441	26888
Shimano American Corporation (HQ)	5091	C	949 951-5003	8029
Shimmick Construction Co Inc	1521	A	510 777-5000	1258
Signature Resources Ins/Fncl	6411	D	949 794-0800	10872
Silverado Energy Company	4911	B	949 752-5588	6207
Silverado Senior Living Inc (PA)	8059	D	949 240-7200	21371
Singerlewak LLP	8721	D	949 261-8600	26443
Sitelite Holdings Inc	7379	C	949 265-6200	16479
Smart Energy Systems LLC (PA)	7371	C	909 703-9609	15459
Smart Energy Systems LLC	7371	C	909 703-9609	15460
Smart Systems Technologies (PA)	4911	D	949 367-9375	6209
SMC Networks Inc (HQ)	5045	D	949 679-8000	7187
Smile Brands Group Inc (PA)	8741	D	714 668-1300	27216
Snyder Langston L P	1542	D	949 863-9200	1673
Solutions 2 Go LLC	5092	D	949 825-7700	8053
Sony Electronics Inc	7812	C	714 508-7634	18151
Southern Cal Prmnnte Med Group	8011	D	949 262-5780	20018
Southern California Edison Co	4911	C	949 587-5416	6234
Spad Holdings LLC	7991	D	949 733-0473	18691
Specialty Surgical Centers	8011	E	949 341-3499	20049
Spectrum Hotel Group LLC	7011	D	949 471-8888	13278
Spectrum Hotel Group LLC	7011	D	949 471-8888	13279
Spectrum Information Services (PA)	7331	D	949 752-7070	14090
Sph-Irvine LLC	8011	E	949 833-1432	20050
Sprint Corporation	4812	D	949 748-3353	5410
Ssinfotek Inc	7373	E	949 732-3100	16058
St Andrews Children Center	8351	E	949 651-0198	24518
St Joseph Health System (HQ)	8082	A	949 381-4000	22570
Standard Pacific of Texas Inc	1531	D	949 789-1621	1384

Mergent email: customerrelations@mergent.com
2017 Directory of California Wholesalers and Services Companies
(P-0000) Products & Services Section entry number
(PA)=Parent Co (HQ)=Headquarters (DH)=Div Headquarters

GEOGRAPHIC SECTION
JAMUL, CA

	SIC	EMP	PHONE	ENTRY #
Stantec Arch & Engrg PC	8711	C	949 923-6000	26076
Stantec Architecture Inc	8712	C	949 923-6000	26255
Stantec Consulting Svcs Inc	8713	D	949 474-1000	26281
Stantec Consulting Svcs Inc	8712	C	949 923-6000	26258
Startel Corporation **(PA)**	7371	D	949 863-8700	15476
State Farm Mutl Auto Insur Co	6411	D	309 766-2311	10891
State Group LLC	8742	B	949 612-2879	27666
Stout & Burg Electric Inc	1731	E	714 544-5066	2752
Stratacare Llc	7371	C	949 743-1200	15480
Strategic Financial Group	6411	E	949 622-7200	10899
Strategy Companion Corp	7372	D	714 460-8398	15850
Strategy For Water & Land Reso	8731	E	949 572-3034	26611
Stratham Homes Inc	1522	D	949 833-1554	1341
Strawberry Farms Golf Club LLC	7997	D	949 551-2560	19099
Student Government Associat	4724	C	949 824-5547	4975
Student Works Painting Inc	1721	B	714 564-7900	2496
Success Strategies Inst Inc	8331	D	888 866-3377	24394
Sullivancurtismonroe Insurance **(PA)**	8742	C	800 427-3253	27672
Sun Healthcare Group Inc **(DH)**	8011	B	949 255-7100	20075
Sun Ten Labs Liquidation Co	5149	D	949 587-0509	8926
Sunwest Bank **(DH)**	6022	E	714 730-4441	9527
Synoptek	7379	D	949 241-8600	16494
Sysco Newport Meat Company	5147	C	949 399-4200	8686
Tanaka Farms	5149	D	949 653-2100	8935
Tantra Lake Partners LP	6513	C	949 756-5959	11211
Taylor & Assoc Architects Inc	8712	E	949 574-1325	26261
Tcg Software Services Inc	7371	E	714 665-6200	15494
Team Makena LLC **(PA)**	5047	D	949 474-1753	7316
Team Mobile	4812	C	949 567-6800	5417
Team Post-Op Inc **(DH)**	5047	D	949 253-5500	7317
Ten-X LLC **(PA)**	6531	C	949 859-2777	11868
Testamerica Laboratories Inc	8734	C	949 261-1022	26892
Tetra Tech Inc	8711	D	949 263-0846	26090
Tetra Tech Inc	8711	B	949 809-5000	26091
Teva Pharmaceuticals Usa Inc	5122	C	949 457-2828	8298
Thomas Gallaway Corporation **(PA)**	7371	D	949 716-9500	15501
Thomas P Cox Architects Inc	8712	D	949 862-0270	26262
Tnppm North Stafford LLC	6512	D	949 833-8252	11063
Tonner Hills Hsing Partners LP	1522	E	949 263-8676	1345
Toshiba Amer Bus Solutions Inc **(DH)**	5044	B	949 462-6000	7073
Toshiba Bus Solutions USA Inc **(DH)**	7629	D	949 462-6000	17947
Toshiba Education Center	8732	D	949 583-3000	26713
Toshiba TEC America Retail Inf **(DH)**	5044	E	949 462-2850	7074
Total Renal Care Inc	8092	D	949 930-6882	22644
Trace3 Inc **(PA)**	8742	D	949 333-1801	27694
TRC Solutions Inc **(HQ)**	8748	D	949 753-0101	28082
Tressler LLP	8111	D	949 336-1200	23597
Tri Pointe Homes Inc **(HQ)**	1531	C	949 438-1400	1386
Trimark Raygal Inc	7389	D	949 474-1000	17545
True Air Mechanical Inc	1711	C	949 382-6337	2401
Truesdail Laboratories Inc	8731	E	714 730-6239	26625
Turner Techtronics Inc	7378	C	949 724-1339	16307
TW Security Corp **(DH)**	5045	C	949 932-1000	7205
Tyco Integrated Security LLC	7382	C	714 223-2300	16938
Tyler Palmieri Wiener	8111	D	949 851-9400	23604
Uc Irvine Recreation Center	7997	D	949 824-5346	19115
UFS International LLC	7389	C	714 713-6311	17553
Unisys Corporation	7371	A	949 380-5000	15516
United Agribusiness League **(PA)**	8611	E	949 975-1424	25107
United Cerebral Palsy Assoc	8322	C	949 333-6400	24266
United Infrstrcture Prjcts Inc	8711	D	213 402-1232	26115
United Samples Inc	5122	B	949 251-1768	8301
Universal Card Inc	7389	B	949 861-4000	17568
Universal Care Inc **(PA)**	8093	B	562 424-6200	22858
University Cal Irvine Med Cent	8099	D	714 456-5678	23078
US Best Repair Service Inc	1521	C	888 750-2378	1276
USI South Coast	6411	D	949 790-9200	10919
V G Carelli International Corp	7389	E	310 247-8410	17581
Velocitel Rf Inc	8711	C	949 809-4999	26140
Ventas Inc	6552	D	949 718-4400	12024
Venture Pacific Tools Inc	5072	D	949 475-5505	7702
Verizon Wireless Inc	4812	C	714 730-7790	5428
Victory Foam LLC **(PA)**	5085	D	949 474-0690	7958
Villa Balboa Community Assoc	8641	D	949 450-1515	25397
Vinculums Services Inc	8748	C	949 783-3552	28092
Vintage Design Inc **(PA)**	1752	D	714 974-4822	3132
Vision Solutions Inc **(HQ)**	7371	D	949 253-6500	15528
Vision Solutions Inc	7379	D	949 253-6500	16523
Visioneering Studios Inc	7299	D	949 417-5800	13803
Voit Development Manager Inc	6552	D	949 851-5110	12025
Vpm Management Inc	8741	B	949 863-1500	27276
W Brown & Assc Property & Csu	6411	D	949 851-2060	10926
Walker & Dunlop Inc	6162	C	949 660-1999	9904
Ware Malcomb **(PA)**	8712	D	949 660-9128	26265
Warmington Homes	1531	D	949 679-3100	1391
Warrior Custom Golf Inc **(PA)**	5091	C	949 699-2499	8034
Waste MGT Collectn & Recycl	4953	D	949 451-2600	6606
Wells Fargo Dealer Svcs Inc **(DH)**	6141	B	949 727-1002	9766
West Coast Consulting LLC	7372	D	949 250-4102	15879
Western Alliance Bank	6022	D	949 222-0855	9543
Western Growers Association **(PA)**	8611	C	949 863-1000	25110
Western Medical Management LLC	8741	E	949 260-6575	27279
Western National Contractors	8741	D	949 862-6200	27280
Western National Properties **(PA)**	1522	D	949 862-6200	1351
Western National Securities **(PA)**	6531	C	949 862-6200	11917
Western United Insurance Co	6411	D	800 959-9842	10937
White Nelson & Co Cpas LLP	8721	D	714 978-1300	26457
Whiting-Turner Contracting Co	1542	E	949 863-0800	1716
Wimberly Allison Tong Goo Inc	8712	D	949 574-8500	26269
Wnc & Associates Inc	8748	D	714 662-5565	28100
Wnc Housing LP	6799	E	714 662-5565	12355
Wolf Firm A Law Corporation	8111	D	949 720-9200	23631
Woodbridge Village Association	8641	D	949 786-1800	25403
Wyndham Irvn-Orange Cnty Arprt	8741	D	949 260-6575 (sic) 949 260-6575	27285
Wynne Systems Inc **(DH)**	7371	D	949 224-6300	15549
Xavor Corporation	7379	D	949 529-7372	16530
Your Practice Online LLC	4813	C	877 388-8569	5738
Zippy Usa Inc	5063	D	949 366-9525	7486
Zymo Research Corp	8731	D	949 679-1190	26640

IRWINDALE, CA - Los Angeles County

	SIC	EMP	PHONE	ENTRY #
American Med	4119	B	626 633-4600	3743
Best Overnite Express Inc **(PA)**	4212	D	626 256-6340	3981
Bonneville Steel Inc	1791	D	866 956-8323	3368
Brightview Companies LLC	0781	C	626 574-3940	745
Calibre International LLC **(PA)**	8743	C	626 969-4660	27737
Church & Larsen Inc	1742	C	626 303-8741	2877
Ds Services of America Inc	5149	D	626 472-7201	8830
East San Gbriel Vly Consortium	4119	C	626 960-3964	3785
Eggleston Youth Centers Inc **(PA)**	8322	D	626 480-8107	23955
Essilor Laboratories Amer Inc	5048	C	626 969-6181	7331
Gano Excel (usa) Inc	5149	D	626 338-8081	8840
Gc Services Ltd Partnership	7322	C	626 851-8227	14033
Health Valley Foods Inc	5149	B	626 334-3241	8851
Mariposa Landscapes Inc **(PA)**	0782	D	626 463-2200	908
Mee Industries Inc	0711	D	626 359-4550	476
Metro One Telecom Inc	7311	C	626 337-8100	13886
Mountain Gear Corporation	5136	C	626 261-2488	8353
Neovia Logistics Dist LP	4731	C	626 359-4500	5129
Pacific Wine Distributors Inc	4212	D	626 471-9997	4048
Phfe Wic Program	8322	C	626 856-6650	24135
Pierre Landscape Inc	0781	C	818 373-0023	787
Public Hlth Fndation Entps Inc	8099	C	626 856-6600	23032
SA Recycling LLC	4953	C	626 359-5815	6548
Service Solutions Group LLC	7629	D	626 960-9390	17943
Southern California Edison Co	4911	C	626 543-8081	6211
Southern California Edison Co	4911	C	626 815-7296	6226
Southern California Edison Co	4911	C	626 633-3070	6235
Southern California Edison Co	4911	C	626 814-4212	6237
United Site Services Cal Inc **(PA)**	7359	E	626 462-9110	14587
Western Paving Contractors Inc	1611	D	626 338-7889	1883
Wor International Inc	5136	C	626 812-8888	8366

IVANHOE, CA - Tulare County

	SIC	EMP	PHONE	ENTRY #
Family Healthcare Network	8011	C	559 798-1877	19521
Klink Citrus Association	0723	C	559 798-1881	555

JACKSON, CA - Amador County

	SIC	EMP	PHONE	ENTRY #
Amador Tlmne Cmnty Action Agcy **(PA)**	8399	D	209 296-2785	24864
Amador-Tolumne Cmnty Resources	8399	D	209 223-1485	24866
Apria Healthcare LLC	8099	C	209 223-7727	22891
AT&T Services Inc	4813	D	209 223-0012	5530
Capitol Fitness Network LLC	7991	D	916 928-4999	18619
Citisite Inc	5065	D	209 418-7620	7548
Farms of Amador	8699	D	209 257-0112	25530
Jackson Rancheria Casino & Ht	7999	A	209 223-1677	19229
Sita Ram LLC	7011	D	209 223-0211	13260
Sutter Amador Hospital **(HQ)**	8062	B	209 223-7500	21939
Sutter Health	8011	D	209 223-5445	20087
Sutter Hlth Scrmnto Sierra Reg	8011	A	209 223-7540	20115
Tutera Group Inc	8361	D	209 223-2231	24838

JAMESTOWN, CA - Tuolumne County

	SIC	EMP	PHONE	ENTRY #
Chicken Ranch Bingo & Casino	7999	C	209 984-3000	19161
Diestel Turkey Ranch	0253	C	209 984-0826	451
Sterling Construction	1522	E	209 984-5594	1340

JAMUL, CA - San Diego County

	SIC	EMP	PHONE	ENTRY #
Poltex Company Inc	7371	D	619 669-1846	15391
Steele Canyon Golf Club Corp	7992	D	619 441-6900	18789

JOSHUA TREE, CA

	SIC	EMP	PHONE	ENTRY #
JOSHUA TREE, CA - San Bernardino County				
Hi-Desert Mem Hlth Care Dst (PA)	8062	B	760 366-3711	21602
JULIAN, CA - San Diego County				
Borrego Cmnty Hlth Foundation	8011	A	760 765-1223	19376
YMCA of San Diego County	8641	E	760 765-0642	25423
JURUPA VALLEY, CA - Riverside County				
Pavement Recycling Systems Inc (PA)	5093	C	951 682-1091	8078
KEENE, CA - Kern County				
United Farm Workers America (PA)	8631	C	661 822-5571	25189
KELSEY, CA - El Dorado County				
California Teachers Assn	8621	C	530 622-8013	25124
Lyon Realty	6519	C	530 295-4444	11258
KELSEYVILLE, CA - Lake County				
BT Holdings Inc	0175	E	707 279-4317	229
Ua Local 38 Bonbelsent Tr Fund	7011	B	707 279-4281	13364
KENTFIELD, CA - Marin County				
1125 Sir Francis Drake Bouleva	8069	C	415 456-9680	22112
Ross Hospital	8069	C	415 258-6900	22169
KENWOOD, CA - Sonoma County				
Arthur Kunde & Sons Inc	0762	E	707 833-5501	693
Dirt Farmer & Co Inc	0172	D	707 833-2054	150
Palo Alto Vineyard MGT LLC	0761	D	707 996-7725	677
KERMAN, CA - Fresno County				
Acemi Nursery Inc	0174	D	559 842-7766	212
Hall AG Enterprises Inc	0761	C	559 846-7360	665
Hall Management Corp	8741	A	559 846-7382	27050
Kerman Telephone Co	4813	D	559 846-4868	5643
Kermantelnet Internet Service	4813	D	559 842-2223	5644
KETTLEMAN CITY, CA - Kings County				
Chemical Waste Management Inc	4953	D	559 386-9711	6457
Keenan Farms Inc	0173	D	559 945-1400	203
KEYES, CA - Stanislaus County				
A L Gilbert Company	5153	D	209 537-0766	8959
KING CITY, CA - Monterey County				
Anthony Harvesting Inc	0722	C	831 385-6460	489
L A Hearne Company (PA)	5191	D	831 385-5441	9139
Rava Ranches Inc	0291	E	831 385-3285	471
San Bernabe Vineyards	0172	D	831 385-4897	182
Southern Mnterey Cnty Mem Hosp (PA)	8062	B	831 385-7100	21906
KINGS BEACH, CA - Placer County				
Robert Morken Construction	1521	E	530 386-1512	1248
KINGS CANYON NATIONA, CA - Tulare County				
Montecito Sequoia Inc	7011	D	559 565-3388	13006
KINGSBURG, CA - Fresno County				
Design Machine and Mfg	7699	E	559 897-7374	17971
Enns Packing Company Inc	0175	D	559 897-7700	232
Jeff W Boldt Farms	0175	D	559 897-0859	238
Kingsburg Apple Packers Inc	5148	B	559 897-5132	8743
Kingsburg Apple Partners LP	0175	D	559 897-5132	239
Kingsburg Hospital District Bd	8062	D	559 897-5841	21692
Mike Jensen Farms	0175	D	559 897-4192	243
Peterson Family Inc	0175	D	559 897-5064	247
Sun-Maid Growers California (PA)	5149	A	559 897-6235	8927
Sun-Maid Growers California	5149	B	559 897-8900	8928
Sunbridge Care Entps W Inc	8051	A	559 897-5881	20940
Sunbridge Care Entps W LLC	8051	A	559 897-5881	20941
Van Beurden Insurance Svcs Inc (PA)	6411	A	559 634-7125	10921
Wildwood Express	4213	E	559 805-3237	4303
KIRKWOOD, CA - Alpine County				
Mountain Springs Kirkwood LLC	7011	C	209 258-6000	13011
KNIGHTS LANDING, CA - Yolo County				
Cattail Farms Inc	0112	D	916 207-6580	4
Richter Bros Inc	0161	D	530 735-6721	89
KORBEL, CA - Humboldt County				
Green Diamond Resource Company	0811	D	707 668-4446	1011
LA CANADA, CA - Los Angeles County				
Child Educational Center	8351	D	818 354-3418	24433
Crescenta-Canada YMCA (PA)	8641	C	818 790-0123	25246
Dilbeck Inc (PA)	6531	D	818 790-6774	11472
La Canada Flintridge Cntry CLB	7997	D	818 790-0611	18968
Landmark Entertainment Group	7389	E	818 952-6292	17287
LA CANADA FLINTRIDGE, CA - Los Angeles County				
Allen Lund Company Inc (PA)	4731	E	818 790-8412	5023
Allen Lund Company LLC (HQ)	4731	D	818 790-1110	5024
Caltech Emplyees Federal Cr Un	6062	D	818 952-4444	9658
LA CRESCENTA, CA - Los Angeles County				
Angels of Vly Hospice Care LLC	8082	D	818 542-3070	22366
Century 21 Crest	6531	D	818 248-9100	11371
Dilbeck Inc	6531	D	818 248-2248	11473
EAM Enterprises Inc (PA)	6531	D	818 248-9100	11486
Mariner Health Care Inc	8051	D	818 957-0850	20774
Monarch E & S Insurance Svcs	6411	D	559 226-0200	10789
Neardata Inc	8742	D	818 249-2469	27561
LA HABRA, CA - Orange County				
Albertsons LLC	4225	D	714 578-4670	4519
American First Credit Union (PA)	6061	D	562 691-1112	9588
Applied Language Solutions LLC	7389	C	800 579-5010	16998
Cellco Partnership	4812	D	562 694-8630	5301
City of La Habra	8322	E	562 905-9708	23753
Corner Bakery Store	5149	E	714 459-1420	8825
Haircutters	7241	D	562 690-2217	13699
Infinity Metals Inc	1796	E	562 697-8826	3477
JKB Corporation	1771	E	562 905-3477	3280
JWdangelo Company Inc	5087	E	562 690-1000	7969
Life Care Centers America Inc	8051	D	562 690-0852	20724
Mary and Friends	8361	C	562 691-1575	24725
Peerless Maintenance Service	7349	B	714 871-3380	14385
Seasons	8361	D	562 691-1200	24805
Southwest Inspection and Tstg	7389	D	562 941-2990	17497
Westridge Golf Inc	7992	D	562 690-4200	18798
LA HABRA HEIGHTS, CA - Orange County				
Hacienda Golf Club	7997	D	562 694-1081	18958
R Navarro Landscape Services	0782	D	562 690-6414	940
LA JOLLA, CA - San Diego County				
A Ursgi-Bmdc Joint Venture	8711	D	858 812-9292	25606
Advance Health Solutions LLC	8082	D	858 876-0136	22338
Aegis Software Inc	7319	E	858 551-1652	13987
Altium Inc (HQ)	7371	C	858 864-1661	15005
Altium LLC	7372	D	858 864-1500	15579
Bartell Hotels	7011	D	858 453-5500	12421
Bdo Usa LLP	8721	D	858 404-9200	26294
Bh Partn A Calif Limit Partne	7011	D	858 453-4420	12449
Birch Aquarium At Scripps	8422	E	858 534-4109	25059
Cable Doctors Inc	4841	D	619 595-4650	5938
Cal Southern Presbt Homes	8361	C	858 454-4201	24574
Califrnia Inst For Bmdical RES	8733	C	858 242-1000	26742
Care Health Services of Fla	8082	D	619 692-1020	22388
Chateau La Jolla Inn	6513	E	858 459-4451	11115
Citigroup Global Markets Inc	6211	D	858 456-4900	9980
Cloisters of La Jolla Inc	8051	D	858 459-4361	20460
Covenant Care La Jolla LLC	8051	D	858 453-5810	20503
Cripts Health Care	8011	E	858 554-8646	19482
CSS Holdings Inc	7371	D	866 343-7185	15116
Dealstruck Inc	6153	D	858 218-6703	9780
Destination Residences LLC	7299	B	858 550-1000	13756
Dewhurst & Associates	1521	D	858 456-5345	1167
Enterprise Partners MGT LLC	6799	C	858 731-0300	12306
Fargo Colonial LLC	7011	D	858 454-2181	12631
Front Porch Communities	6513	D	858 454-2151	11134
Gary Mary W Wireless Hlth Inst	8733	E	858 412-8600	26767
Geneohm Sciences Inc	8731	C	201 847-5824	26521
Glaxosmithkline LLC	5122	E	858 260-5900	8257
Guaranteed Rate Inc	6162	C	760 310-6008	9850
Hensel Phelps Construction Co	1542	D	619 544-6828	1569
Hilton Worldwide Inc	7011	E	858 450-4569	12720
Hotel La Jolla	7011	D	858 459-0261	12789
Impact Assessment Inc	8731	D	858 459-0142	26534
Institute For La Jolla	8733	C	858 752-6500	26772
Joshua J Bodenstadt CPA A Prof	8721	E	858 642-5050	26380
La Jolla Bch & Tennis CLB Inc (PA)	7011	D	858 454-7126	12897
La Jolla Bch & Tennis CLB Inc	7011	C	858 459-8271	12898
La Jolla Country Club Inc	7997	C	858 454-9601	18970
La Jolla Cove Hotel & Motel	6513	D	858 459-2621	11151
La Jolla Nurses Home Care	7361	D	858 454-9339	14695
La Jolla Orthopaedic	8011	D	858 657-0055	19690
Lav Hotel Corp	7011	D	858 454-0771	12907
Lavine Lofgren Morris & Enge	8721	C	858 455-1200	26394
Lawrence Family Jewish Commu (PA)	8399	C	858 362-1144	24937
Leidos Inc	7373	B	858 826-6000	15984
Machintel Corporation	7311	D	617 517-3090	13879
Marriott International Inc	7011	B	858 587-1414	12959
Medpharm Communications	8742	D	858 412-6848	27539
Merrill Lynch Pierce Fenner	6211	D	858 456-3600	10046
Mfw Partners	6512	E	858 454-3600	11018
Museum Cntmprary Art San Diego	8412	D	858 454-3541	25028
National Marine Fisheries Svc	8731	C	858 546-7081	26572

GEOGRAPHIC SECTION — LA VERNE, CA

Company	SIC	EMP	PHONE	ENTRY #
Northwestern Mutl Fincl Netwrk (PA)	6211	D	619 234-3111	10066
Professional Health Tech	8011	D	858 449-1599	19879
Robert Half International Inc	7363	D	888 744-9202	14942
Sanford Burnham Prebys Medical (PA)	8733	A	858 795-5000	26805
Scripps Clinic Carmel Valley	8011	B	858 554-8096	19965
Scripps Clinic Medical Group	8011	B	858 554-9606	19966
Scripps Dialasys Inc (PA)	8011	E	619 453-9070	19967
Scripps Health	8062	B	858 455-9100	21869
Scripps Health	8062	C	800 727-4777	21871
Scripps Health	8011	B	858 458-5100	19977
Scripps Health	8011	B	858 626-5200	19978
Scripps Health	8062	C	858 626-6150	21872
Scripps Health	8011	C	858 554-8892	19979
Scripps Health	8011	C	858 554-9489	19980
Scripps Health	8062	C	858 626-4123	21873
Scripps Health	8731	C	858 652-5504	26602
Scripps Memorial Hospitals	8062	A	858 450-4481	21874
Scripps Research Institute (PA)	8733	A	858 784-1000	26807
Sk Sanctuary Day Spa Salon LLC	7991	E	858 459-2400	18682
Synthetic Genomics Inc (DH)	8731	C	858 754-2900	26617
Theat and Arts Found of San Di	8641	C	858 623-3366	25381
Tom Hom Investment Corp	6512	C	858 456-5000	11064
UBS Financial Services Inc	7389	D	858 454-9181	17550
University Cal San Diego	7374	B	858 534-5000	16206
University Cal San Diego	8062	B	858 657-7000	21993
URS Group Inc	8711	D	619 294-9400	26125
Vaco Lajolla LLC	7361	D	858 642-0000	14813
Wells Fargo Bank National Assn	6021	A	858 454-0362	9441
Westmont Living Inc (PA)	8361	C	858 456-1233	24855
Willis Allen Real Estate (PA)	6531	E	858 459-4033	11924
Willis Insurance Svcs Cal Inc	6311	E	858 678-2000	10228
YMCA of San Diego County	8641	C	858 453-3483	25415

LA MESA, CA - San Diego County

Company	SIC	EMP	PHONE	ENTRY #
Abbood Zeyad	8711	E	619 212-2820	25608
Age Advantage HM Care Svcs	8059	D	619 449-5900	21128
Anthonys Fish Grotto	5146	D	619 713-1853	8626
Automobile Club Southern Cal	8699	D	619 464-7001	25503
Bh-SD Opco LLC	8063	C	619 465-4411	22045
Borrego Springs Bank	6029	D	619 668-5159	9545
Brady Company/San Diego Inc	1742	D	619 462-2600	2866
Brady Socal Incorporated	1742	D	619 462-2600	2867
Cal West General Engrg Inc	7359	E	619 469-5811	14521
California Coast Credit Union	6062	D	858 495-1600	9656
Center Glass Co No 3	1793	D	619 469-6181	3408
City of La Mesa	1611	E	619 667-1450	1750
Coldwell Banker	6531	D	619 460-6600	11404
Comprehensive Autism Ctr Inc	8049	D	951 813-4035	20314
Cox Communications Inc	4899	D	619 218-2967	6067
Custom Medical Products Inc	5047	C	619 461-2068	7260
Davis Framing Inc	1751	E	619 463-2394	3043
Excel Home Health Inc	8082	E	619 460-6622	22434
Grossmont Family Medical Group	8011	E	619 644-6500	19543
Grossmont Hospital Corporation (HQ)	8062	A	619 740-6000	21587
Grossmont Hospital Corporation	8062	C	619 667-1900	21588
Grossmont Shopping Center Co	6512	D	619 465-2900	10992
Healthcare Group	8361	C	619 463-0281	24686
Helix Healthcare Inc	8063	B	619 465-4411	22073
Helm Management Co (PA)	6531	E	619 589-6222	11570
Home Instead Senior Care	8082	E	619 460-6222	22467
Kaiser Foundation Hospitals	8011	A	619 528-5000	19622
Kaiser Foundation Hospitals	8062	A	619 528-5000	21662
Kensington Agency Inc	7363	E	619 280-6993	14893
La Mesa Health Care Center	8059	E	619 465-1313	21287
La Mesa Intrnl Mdc Mdcl Gr	8011	E	619 460-4050	19695
La Mesa Lions Club	8641	E	619 469-9988	25279
Life Gnerations Healthcare LLC	8051	C	619 460-2330	20733
Perry & Shaw Inc	8711	E	619 390-6500	26019
Pvcc Inc (PA)	6512	E	619 463-4040	11035
Razavi Corporation	8051	D	619 465-8010	20864
Risk Mngement Strategies Inc	8748	A	619 281-1100	28043
San Diego Mortgage & RE	6531	E	619 334-7779	11830
Scripps Health	8011	D	619 670-5400	19973
Senior Care Inc	8052	C	619 928-5644	21104
Sharp Healthcare	8011	D	619 460-6200	19998
Team Health Holdings Inc	8011	B	619 740-4401	20129
Umpqua Bank	6022	D	619 668-5159	9531
YMCA of San Diego County	8641	D	619 464-1323	25418

LA MIRADA, CA - Los Angeles County

Company	SIC	EMP	PHONE	ENTRY #
Aecom Energy & Cnstr Inc	8711	C	714 228-4300	25622
American Financial Network Inc	8742	C	562 926-2401	27319
American Golf Corporation	7997	D	562 943-7123	18871
B S A Partners	7011	D	714 523-2800	12411
Beaulieu Group LLC	5023	D	714 522-2080	6847
Beven-Herron Inc	1761	C	714 523-5870	3143
Compremex LLC	4215	C	714 739-1348	4396
Dynamex Operations West Inc	4215	E	714 994-1615	4399
E T Horn Company (PA)	5169	C	714 523-8050	8987
Eagle High Reach Equipment LLC	7359	D	619 265-2637	14536
Estes Express Lines Inc	4212	D	714 994-3770	4016
Estes Express Lines Inc	4213	D	714 523-1122	4155
Far East Broadcasting Co Inc	4832	D	562 947-4651	5774
Georgia-Pacific LLC	5093	D	562 926-8888	8070
H&E Equipment Services Inc	7359	C	714 522-6590	14544
Holiday Inn Select	7011	E	714 739-8500	12753
Ideal Equipment Rental Inc	7359	D	714 237-9232	14548
Life Care Centers America Inc	8051	C	562 947-8691	20725
Life Care Centers America Inc	8051	D	562 943-7156	20726
Life Care Centers America Inc	8051	C	562 943-7156	20729
Makita USA Inc (HQ)	5072	C	714 522-8088	7693
Mejico Express Inc (PA)	4513	C	714 690-8300	4868
Mirada Hills Rehabilitation	8059	D	562 947-8691	21316
Nittany Lion Landscaping Inc	0782	D	714 635-1788	924
Northeast Protective Svcs Inc	7381	D	800 577-0899	16749
Penske Leasing	7359	D	714 522-3330	14567
Precision Relocation Inc	7389	D	714 690-9344	17422
Reliance Steel & Aluminum Co	5051	C	714 736-4800	7396
Southern Cal Spcialty Care (DH)	8069	D	562 944-1900	22177
Special Dispatch Cal Inc (PA)	4214	D	602 296-8860	4377
Sunstone Hotel Investors LLC	7011	E	714 739-8500	13318
Tiffany Dale Inc (PA)	5023	C	714 739-2700	6893
Tomarco Contractor Spc Inc (PA)	5072	D	714 523-1771	7701
US Foods Inc	5141	C	714 670-3500	8547
US Foods Inc	5141	C	714 670-3500	8548
US Foods Inc	5149	C	714 670-3500	8951
Vend Catering Supply Inc	5087	D	562 483-7337	7985
Veritiv Operating Company	5113	D	714 690-4000	8220
Wow Party Rental Inc	7359	D	714 367-3380	14592

LA PALMA, CA - Orange County

Company	SIC	EMP	PHONE	ENTRY #
Applecare Medical MGT LLC	8741	C	714 443-4507	26923
Arco Envmtl Remediation LLC	8742	C	714 523-5674	27332
Automatic Data Processing Inc	7374	D	714 994-2000	16098
BP West Coast Products LLC	1311	B	714 670-5400	1032
Honeywell International Inc	7382	C	714 562-8713	16889
Honeywell International Inc	8711	D	714 562-9003	25868
Honeywell International Inc	8741	D	714 562-3114	27054
Idg Usa LLC	5085	C	714 994-6960	7935
Kaiser Foundation Hospitals	8011	E	714 562-3420	19657
La Palma Hospital Medical Ctr	8062	B	714 670-7400	21696
Parsons Corporation	1629	C	714 736-6826	2075
Slade Gorton & Co Inc	5146	C	714 676-4200	8653
Sunrise Senior Living LLC	8361	C	714 739-8111	24832
Tech Knowledge Associates LLC	7699	D	714 735-3810	18022
Travelers Club Luggage Inc	5099	C	714 523-8808	8143
Veritiv Operating Company	5113	B	714 690-6600	8223

LA PUENTE, CA - Los Angeles County

Company	SIC	EMP	PHONE	ENTRY #
Alert Insulation Company Inc	1742	D	626 961-9113	2849
Arrow Disposal Services Inc	4953	E	626 336-2255	6430
Athens Disposal Company Inc (PA)	4953	B	626 336-3636	6433
Cacique Distributors US	5143	C	626 961-3399	8579
Cal-Lift Inc	5084	C	562 566-1400	7829
Deluxe Auto Carriers Inc	4212	D	909 823-1617	4005
Michael McCarthy	7381	E	310 800-5367	16736
Wave Plastic Surgery Ctr Inc	8011	B	626 964-7788	20231

LA QUINTA, CA - Riverside County

Company	SIC	EMP	PHONE	ENTRY #
Captiva Verde Farming Corp	0191	C	760 771-3333	349
Cartwright Termite & Pest Ctrl	7342	D	760 771-6091	14173
Chapman Golf Development LLC	7992	D	760 564-8723	18721
CIT Bank National Association	6021	C	760 771-3498	9348
David Chapman Investments LLC	7992	D	760 564-3355	18733
Deser Sands Unifi Schoo Distr	8351	D	760 777-4200	24454
Imperial Irrigation District	4939	C	760 398-5811	6303
Interiors By Linda	7389	E	760 341-9651	17247
Ksi II Mngement Operations LLC	8741	D	760 564-8000	27104
La Quinta Country Club	7997	D	760 564-4151	18971
Lqr Property LLC	7011	D	760 564-4111	12932
Madison Club Owners Assn	7992	D	760 777-9320	18758
Platinum Landscape Inc	0781	D	760 200-3673	788
Professional Golf MGT LLC	8741	D	760 564-0804	27177
Silver Rock Resort Golf Club	7992	D	760 777-8884	18787
TD Desert Dev Ltd Partnr (HQ)	6552	D	760 777-1001	12018
Tradition Golf Club Associates	7997	D	760 564-3355	19112
Trilogy Golf At La Quinta	7992	D	760 771-0707	18796
Verizon Wireless Inc	4812	D	760 771-5587	5425

LA VERNE, CA - Los Angeles County

Company	SIC	EMP	PHONE	ENTRY #
American Eagle Services Inc	7363	D	574 859-2055	14836
Automobile Club Southern Cal	6411	C	909 392-1444	10637
Brethren Hillcrest Homes	8361	C	909 593-4917	24568

Employment Codes: A=Over 500 employees, B=251-500, C=101-250, D=51-100, E=45-50

LA VERNE, CA

Company	SIC	EMP	PHONE	ENTRY #
David and Margaret Home Inc	8361	C	909 596-5921	24627
Haaker Equipment Company (PA)	5012	D	909 542-0800	6679
Haynes Family Programs Inc	8361	D	909 593-2581	24685
J C French & Company	1721	D	909 596-1423	2455
Mass Electric Construction Co	1731	D	800 933-6322	2642
Metropolitan Water District	4941	B	909 593-7474	6377
Opus Bank	6022	D	909 599-0871	9512
Peter Kiewit Sons Inc	1611	C	909 962-6001	1846
Sierra La Verne Cntry CLB Inc	7997	D	909 596-2100	19078
Steve and Beth Chaput	7349	E	909 596-9994	14439
Tofasco of America Inc (PA)	8741	D	909 392-8282	27253

LADERA RANCH, CA - Orange County

Company	SIC	EMP	PHONE	ENTRY #
AT&T Corp	4813	D	949 364-4052	5478
Jpmorgan Chase Bank Nat Assn	7389	C	949 429-6071	17264
Xqawesome Inc	8331	C	949 929-9622	24407

LAFAYETTE, CA - Contra Costa County

Company	SIC	EMP	PHONE	ENTRY #
Advanced Acoustics	1742	E	925 299-0515	2847
Arthur J Gallagher & Co	6411	E	925 299-1112	10627
Cellco Partnership	4812	D	925 472-0487	5345
Clubsport San Ramon LLC	7991	C	925 283-4000	18621
Futures Explored Inc	8322	D	925 284-3240	23990
Independent Quality Care Inc	8059	D	925 284-5544	21275
Lescure Company Inc	1711	D	925 283-2528	2280
Murphy McKay & Associates Inc	7379	E	925 283-9555	16436
Optimum Solutions Group LLC (HQ)	7372	D	415 954-7100	15787
Prestige Car Wash Lafayette LP	7542	E	925 283-1190	17860
Rate Is Low	6162	E	925 299-9364	9892
Techexcel Inc (PA)	7371	D	925 871-3900	15496

LAGUNA BEACH, CA - Orange County

Company	SIC	EMP	PHONE	ENTRY #
Andersen Hotels Inc	7011	D	949 494-1151	12391
Baja Life Online Partners	7371	E	949 376-4619	15049
C & B Delivery Services	4225	D	909 623-4708	4528
Festival of Arts Laguna Beach	7999	D	949 494-1145	19213
JC Resorts LLC	8741	B	949 376-2779	27075
Laguna Bch Golf Bnglow Vlg LLC	0291	E	949 499-2271	468
Laguna Bch Golf Bnglow Vlg LLC	7992	E	949 499-2271	18752
Laguna Playhouse (PA)	7922	C	949 497-2787	18405
Laguna Woods Village	6531	A	949 597-4267	11625
Landmark Hotels LLC	7011	E	949 640-5040	12904
National Film Laboratories	7819	C	323 466-0281	18238
Pacific Housing Management (PA)	6531	D	714 508-1777	11724
Pauls Tv LLC (PA)	5064	D	949 596-8800	7506
Seaside Laguna Inn & Suites	7011	D	949 494-9717	13229

LAGUNA HILLS, CA - Orange County

Company	SIC	EMP	PHONE	ENTRY #
Altec Products Inc (PA)	7389	D	949 727-1248	16985
AT&T Corp	4812	D	949 581-1600	5269
Automobile Club Southern Cal	8699	E	949 951-1400	25502
Birtcher/Aetna Laguna Hills	6513	D	949 458-2311	11098
California Limousines	4119	D	949 581-7531	3778
Care Plus Home Care Inc	8082	D	949 716-2273	22391
Care Plus Nursing Services Inc	8082	C	949 600-7194	22392
Cirrus Health II LP	8011	D	949 855-0562	19438
CIT Bank National Association	6021	D	949 454-4100	9362
Dva Renal Healthcare Inc	8092	D	949 588-9211	22625
Ephesoft Inc	5045	D	949 335-5335	7128
ESS LLC	1711	D	888 303-6424	2221
Eworkplace Solutions Inc	5045	C	949 583-1646	7130
F M Tarbell Co	6531	D	949 830-6030	11508
Factory R D	5049	D	949 900-3460	7341
Gate Three Healthcare LLC	8361	D	949 770-3348	24667
Hardrock Tile & Marble Inc	1741	D	714 282-1766	2817
Herren Enterprises Inc	4119	D	949 951-1666	3804
Hillview Acres	8361	D	714 694-2828	24692
Hines Nurseries LLC	5193	D	602 254-2831	9194
Investors Mortgage Asset Recov	6162	D	657 859-6200	9862
Jamboree Realty Corp (PA)	6531	C	949 380-0104	11595
Kennedy Pipeline Company	1623	D	949 380-8363	1956
Laguna Hills Hotel Dev Ventr	7011	D	949 586-5000	12900
Laguna Woods Golf Club	7992	E	949 597-4336	18753
Motoir Ltd	4971	C	949 552-6552	6648
Muller Taj LLC	6512	D	949 470-9840	11020
Muller-Ing-Gateway LLC	6512	D	951 687-2900	11021
Nms Data Inc	8748	E	949 472-2700	28002
Nvision Laser Eye Centers	8049	C	949 951-1405	20335
Professional Cmnty MGT Cal Inc	6531	B	949 268-2271	11767
Professional Cmnty MGT Cal Inc	6531	C	949 597-4200	11768
Rye Electric Inc	1731	D	949 441-0545	2720
Saddleback Memorial Med Ctr (HQ)	8062	A	949 837-4500	21836
South County Orthopedic Specia	8011	D	949 586-3200	20012
Spectrum Care Landscpe Mngmnt	0782	B	949 454-6900	959
Sun Coast Gen Insur Agcy Inc	6411	E	949 768-1132	10901
Sunrise Senior Living Inc	8051	D	949 581-6111	20964
Support Associates Inc	8744	C	949 595-4379	27799
Tech Mahindra (americas) Inc	7371	D	949 462-0640	15495
Tom Ray Industries Inc	5023	D	949 380-8333	6894
Varsity Contractors Inc	7349	D	949 586-8283	14462
Villageway Management Inc	6531	D	949 450-1515	11898

LAGUNA NIGUEL, CA - Orange County

Company	SIC	EMP	PHONE	ENTRY #
Aegis Senior Communities LLC	8082	E	949 496-8080	22347
Birtcher Andrson Property Svcs (PA)	6531	D	949 831-0707	11323
Bitfone Corporation (PA)	7371	E	949 234-7000	15055
Cellco Partnership	4812	D	949 831-3955	5376
E Tradeshowgirlscom	7389	D	949 661-4177	17139
Enterprise Rent-A-Car	7514	D	949 373-9350	17673
Exotic Imports Intl Inc	5199	E	949 306-8816	9262
First Team RE - Orange Cnty	6531	D	949 240-7979	11536
Focus 360 Inc	7371	D	949 234-0008	15191
Mission Internal Med Group Inc	8011	D	949 364-3605	19754
Moulton Niguel Water (PA)	4941	D	949 831-2500	6381
Pacific Line Clean-Up Inc	1799	D	949 348-0245	3562
Pacific Monarch Resorts Inc	6531	D	949 228-1396	11726
Rancho Niguel Dental Group	8021	E	949 249-4180	20272
Spearman Clubs Inc (PA)	7999	E	949 496-2070	19286
Unger & Associates Inc	8742	E	949 249-2800	27703

LAGUNA WOODS, CA - Orange County

Company	SIC	EMP	PHONE	ENTRY #
Professional Cmnty MGT Cal Inc	6531	C	949 597-4359	11764
Professional Cmnty MGT Cal Inc	6531	C	949 206-0580	11766
Rainbow Realty Corporation	6531	D	949 770-9626	11784
Withrow Phrm & Hlth Spc Lab	5122	D	323 721-4281	8307

LAKE ARROWHEAD, CA - San Bernardino County

Company	SIC	EMP	PHONE	ENTRY #
Lake Arrwhead Rsort Oprtor Inc (PA)	7011	C	909 744-3012	12901
Mountains Commu	8062	C	909 336-3651	21758
RE Max All Cities Lk Arrowhead	6531	E	909 337-6111	11789

LAKE ELSINORE, CA - Riverside County

Company	SIC	EMP	PHONE	ENTRY #
AAA Restoration Inc	1799	E	951 471-5828	3484
AT&T Corp	4813	D	951 253-3304	5469
AWI Management Corporation	8741	D	951 674-8200	26933
Aztec Engineering Group Inc	8711	D	951 471-6190	25676
Chief Trnsp & Engrg Contrs Inc	1611	D	951 258-6607	1746
County of Riverside	8322	D	951 245-3060	23883
County of Riverside	8322	D	951 245-3100	23884
Division Three Cnstr Svcs	1542	D	951 609-3043	1542
Elsinore Vly Municpl Wtr Dst (PA)	4941	D	951 674-3146	6348
F M Tarbell Co	6531	E	951 471-5333	11502
F M Tarbell Co	6531	E	951 471-5333	11513
Gbc Concrete Masnry Cnstr Inc	1741	C	951 245-2355	2816
Hakes Sash & Door Inc	1751	C	951 674-2414	3052
JD Miller Construction Inc	1721	E	951 471-3513	2458
Perfection Glass Inc	1793	E	951 674-0240	3412
Sci Inc	1771	D	951 245-7511	3327
Volume Services Inc	7999	D	951 245-9995	19307
West Coast Ltg & Enrgy Inc	1731	D	951 296-0680	2792

LAKE FOREST, CA - Orange County

Company	SIC	EMP	PHONE	ENTRY #
24 Hour Fitness Usa Inc	7991	D	949 830-4213	18592
Advanced Protection Inds Inc	7382	E	949 215-8000	16861
AMF Bowling Centers Inc	7933	E	949 770-0055	18509
Apria Healthcare LLC (DH)	5047	B	949 616-2606	7237
Arb Inc (HQ)	1629	C	949 598-9242	2022
Beech Street Corporation (DH)	8741	B	949 672-1000	26941
Bel Esprit Builders Inc	1542	E	949 709-3500	1501
Casa-Pacifica Inc	8361	C	949 586-4466	24586
Cellco Partnership	4812	D	949 472-0700	5334
Chapel Funding Corporation	6162	C	949 580-1800	9829
Commercial Indus Design Co Inc	5045	C	949 273-6199	7109
Digital Networks Group Inc	4899	D	949 428-6333	6069
Environments For Learning Inc (PA)	8351	D	949 855-5630	24459
Extend A Hand Inc	8322	D	949 586-5142	23965
Freedom Village Healthcare Ctr	8741	D	949 472-4733	20581
Golden West Custom WD Shutters	5099	E	949 951-0600	8117
Great Destinations Inc	8742	D	949 667-9401	27455
Gypsum Contractors Inc	1742	E	949 340-9100	2906
Heinaman Contract Glazing Inc (PA)	1799	E	949 587-0266	3530
Horizon Technology	5045	D	949 454-4614	7142
Infor (us) Inc	7372	C	678 319-8000	15699
Inspiria Inc (PA)	8711	D	949 206-0606	25882
Insulectro	5065	D	949 587-3200	7586
Intertek Testing Svcs NA Inc	8734	D	949 448-4100	26860
Intertek Testing Svcs NA Inc	7389	D	949 349-1684	17249
Invensys Processs Systems Inc	7371	C	949 727-3200	15254
Itek Services Inc	7379	D	949 770-4835	16417
Lake Forest LI Master Homeown	8641	D	949 586-0860	25282
Life Care Centers America Inc	8051	C	949 380-9380	20728
Miguelito Manpower Inc	4213	C	323 582-3376	4229
Mike Rovner Construction Inc	8741	C	949 458-1562	27132
Molly Maid	7349	E	949 367-8000	14362

Mergent email: customerrelations@mergent.com
2017 Directory of California Wholesalers and Services Companies
(P-0000) Products & Services Section entry number
(PA)=Parent Co (HQ)=Headquarters (DH)=Div Headquarters

GEOGRAPHIC SECTION

LATHROP, CA

	SIC	EMP	PHONE	ENTRY #
Nakase Brothers Wholesale Nurs	5193	C	949 855-4388	9204
National Crdtors Cnnection Inc	6411	D	949 461-7540	10793
Natures Image Inc	0781	D	949 680-4400	782
Nelson Moving & Storage Inc	4214	E	949 582-0380	4365
Panasonic	5064	C	949 581-0661	7502
Parsons Government Svcs Inc **(HQ)**	8731	D	949 768-8161	26585
Performance Building Services	7349	C	949 364-4364	14388
Primoris Services Corporation	1623	B	949 598-9242	1983
Quantum Technologies Inc	1311	C	949 399-4500	1049
RJP Construction & Painting **(PA)**	1721	D	949 707-5449	2484
Schneider Electric Sftwr LLC **(PA)**	7373	B	949 727-3200	16044
Ses LLC	7371	A	949 727-3200	15450
Streamline Finishes Inc	1542	D	949 600-8964	1678
US Real Estate Services Inc	6531	D	949 598-9920	11893
Vadnais Trenchless Svcs Inc	1623	A	858 550-1460	2008
Validus Group Inc	7361	D	949 457-7606	14814
W B Starr Inc	0782	E	949 770-8835	977
Wonderware Corporation **(HQ)**	5045	B	949 727-3200	7210
Xpo Enterprise Services Inc	4213	D	949 581-9030	4315

LAKE ISABELLA, CA - Kern County

	SIC	EMP	PHONE	ENTRY #
First Transit Inc	4111	D	760 379-1711	3650
Kern River Tours Inc	7999	D	760 379-4616	19233
Kern Valley Hosp Foundation **(PA)**	8062	B	760 379-2681	21683

LAKE VIEW TERRACE, CA - Los Angeles County

	SIC	EMP	PHONE	ENTRY #
Phoenix Houses Los Angeles Inc	8361	D	818 686-3000	24769

LAKEPORT, CA - Lake County

	SIC	EMP	PHONE	ENTRY #
County Lake Health Services	8099	D	707 263-1090	22924
Evergreen At Lakeport LLC **(PA)**	8051	D	707 263-6382	20555
Lake Cnty Trbal Hlth Cnsortium	8021	D	707 263-8382	20261
Sutter Health	8011	C	707 263-6885	20091
Sutter Health	8011	C	707 263-6885	20103
Sutter Lakeside Hospital **(HQ)**	8062	B	707 262-5000	21950
Windflower Holdings LLC	8051	D	707 263-6101	21044
Xpo Enterprise Services Inc	4213	C	916 399-8291	4319

LAKESHORE, CA - Fresno County

	SIC	EMP	PHONE	ENTRY #
China Peak Mountain Resort LLC	7011	D	559 233-2500	12513

LAKESIDE, CA - San Diego County

	SIC	EMP	PHONE	ENTRY #
A M Ortega Construction Inc **(PA)**	1731	C	619 390-1988	2505
Barona Creek Golf Club	7992	D	619 387-7018	18715
Barona Resort & Casino	7011	A	619 443-2300	12416
Buds & Son Trucking Inc	4212	D	619 443-4200	3984
Clauss Construction	1795	D	619 390-4940	3450
Errecas Inc	1794	D	619 390-6400	3427
J P Witherow Roofing Company	1761	D	619 297-4701	3180
Johnson Finch & McClure Cnstr **(PA)**	1799	C	619 938-9727	3539
Lakeside Fire Protection Dst	7389	D	619 390-2350	17285
Marco Crane & Rigging Co	7353	D	619 938-8080	14487
McDonough-Western Rim JV	1629	E	619 749-5339	2066
Minshew Brothers Stl Cnstr Inc	1541	C	619 561-5700	1452
Neighborhood Healthcare	8099	C	619 390-9975	23005
Nicholas Grant Corporation	1611	D	619 390-3900	1834
Rdo Construction Equipment Co	7353	D	619 443-3758	14496
Standard Drywall Inc **(HQ)**	1742	B	619 443-7034	2983
Towne Construction Inc	1742	D	619 390-4557	2991
Turning Point For God	7922	D	619 258-3600	18442
Unyeway Inc	8331	D	619 562-6330	24399
Williams & Sons Masonry Inc	1741	D	619 443-1751	2840

LAKEWOOD, CA - Los Angeles County

	SIC	EMP	PHONE	ENTRY #
Admiral Home Health Inc	8082	D	562 421-0777	22337
American Golf Corporation	7992	E	562 421-0550	18711
Cal Bowl Enterprises LLC	7933	E	562 421-8448	18515
Caremore Medical Group	6321	B	562 622-2900	10238
Center For Dscovery Adolescent	8069	E	562 425-6404	22121
Contractor Warehouse	1542	D	562 633-1428	1534
County of Los Angeles	8322	B	562 497-3500	23829
Discovery Practice Management	8011	E	562 425-6404	19505
Lakewood Cerritos Dental Ctr	8021	D	562 860-0388	20262
Nationwide Theatres Corp	7933	D	562 421-8448	18527
Pacific Theaters Inc	7832	D	562 634-1183	18342
Rainbow Properties Inc	6531	D	323 562-0730	11783
Tarzana Treatment Centers Inc	8093	A	562 428-4111	22847
Tenet Healthsystem Medical	8011	A	562 531-2550	20131
Time Warner Cable Inc	4841	C	424 529-6011	6045
Western States Fire Protection	1711	D	562 731-2961	2418
Young Mens Chrstn Assc Gr L B	8641	C	562 272-4884	25457
Young Mens Chrstn Assc Gr L B	8641	C	562 425-7431	25460

LAMONT, CA - Kern County

	SIC	EMP	PHONE	ENTRY #
Grimmway Enterprises Inc	5148	B	661 845-3758	8738
Maxco Supply Inc	5113	D	559 646-6700	8197

LANCASTER, CA - Los Angeles County

	SIC	EMP	PHONE	ENTRY #
Aerospace Fclities Support LLC	7376	D	661 723-3148	16274
Aids Healthcare Foundation	8011	C	661 723-3244	19326
Allied Risk Management Inc	7381	D	661 305-0455	16542
American Med Rspnse Sthern Cal	4119	A	661 945-9310	3749
Antelope Valley Foundation	8322	E	661 945-7290	23663
Antelope Valley Hospital Aux	8011	D	661 949-1550	19351
Antelope Valley Hospital Aux	8011	B	661 726-6180	19352
Antelope Valley Hospital Aux **(PA)**	8062	A	661 949-5000	21453
Antelope Valley Medical Group	8011	E	661 945-2783	19353
Antelope Vly Retirement HM Inc	8059	B	661 948-7501	21140
Antelope Vly Retirement HM Inc	8059	C	661 949-5524	21141
Antelope Vly Schl Trnsp Agcy	4151	C	661 945-3621	3911
BDR Industries Inc **(PA)**	4841	D	661 940-8554	5935
C D R Enterprises Inc	1742	D	661 940-0344	2869
California Traffic Safety Inst	8748	C	661 940-1907	27864
Cellco Partnership	4812	D	661 726-4762	5386
Counseling and Research Assoc	8361	D	661 726-5500	24608
County of Los Angeles	8322	B	661 940-4181	23824
County of Los Angeles	8322	C	661 723-4051	23827
County of Los Angeles	8322	C	661 948-2320	23831
County of Los Angeles	8011	A	661 948-8581	19470
County of Los Angeles	8711	C	661 723-6088	25755
County of Los Angeles	8093	D	661 524-2005	22703
Daniel O Mongiano MD A PR	8011	E	661 951-9195	19485
Desert Haven Enterprises **(PA)**	0782	A	661 948-8402	838
Desert Haven Enterprises	0782	A	661 948-8402	839
Easter Seals Southern Cal Inc	8399	E	661 723-3414	24917
Esna Corporation	6163	E	661 206-6010	9922
Excel Contractors Inc	1521	D	661 942-6944	1172
Fidelity National Title Co	6361	E	818 881-7800	10515
Five Star Quality Care Inc	8051	C	661 940-0452	20574
Frito-Lay North America Inc	5145	D	661 951-1399	8616
Gene Wheeler Farms Inc	0191	C	661 951-2100	360
Granite Construction Company	1611	C	661 726-4447	1781
Hanes & Associates Inc	1751	E	661 723-0779	3053
Hathaway-Sycamores Chld Fam Sv	8361	B	661 942-5749	24682
High Desert Med Corp A Med Grp **(PA)**	8011	E	661 945-5984	19557
High Desert Phoenix	7999	E	661 547-5630	19222
Iheartcommunications Inc	4832	C	661 942-1268	5784
Kaiser Foundation Hospitals	8062	A	661 726-2500	21632
Kaiser Foundation Hospitals	8062	B	661 949-5000	21644
Kaiser Foundation Hospitals	8011	A	661 951-0070	19624
La County High Desert Hlth Sys	8011	B	661 945-8461	19689
Lancaster Comm Svcs Fndtn	7538	C	661 723-6230	17803
Lancaster Crdlgy Med Group Inc **(PA)**	8011	D	661 726-3058	19698
Lancaster Jethawks	7997	D	661 726-5400	18978
Lantz Security Systems Inc **(PA)**	7381	D	661 949-3565	16721
Lifelong Learning ADM Corp	8741	D	661 272-1225	27116
Mayflower Gardens Health Facil	8051	D	661 943-2832	20779
Metropolitan Dst Private SEC	7381	D	661 942-3999	16735
Michaels Stores Inc	5199	C	661 951-3500	9281
Mission Linen Supply	7213	D	661 948-5051	13563
Nibbelink Masonry Cnstr Corp	1741	D	661 948-7859	2829
North La County Regional Ctr	8748	D	661 945-6761	28004
Opsec Specialized Protection	7381	D	661 942-3999	16754
Penny Lane Centers	8399	C	661 274-0770	24962
Penny Lane Centers	8399	C	818 892-3423	24963
SA Recycling LLC	4953	C	661 723-1383	6555
Sarah Elizabeth Treusdell	8093	E	661 949-0131	22828
Solarcity Corporation	1711	C	888 765-2489	2375
Southland Transit Inc	4111	D	661 726-4225	3722
Spiral Technology Inc	7381	D	661 723-3148	26073
State Preschool	8351	E	661 940-4535	24519
Sygma Network Inc	5149	C	661 723-0405	8932
Taft Electric Company	1731	C	661 729-2581	2767
Tarzana Treatment Centers Inc	8093	C	661 726-2630	22849
Time Warner Inc	4841	D	661 344-1546	6053
United Parcel Service Inc OH	4215	C	800 828-8264	4459
United Way Inc	8399	C	661 874-4288	24991
V Troth Inc	6531	E	661 948-4646	11895
West Antlope Vly Hstorical Soc	8412	D	661 945-5369	25055
Wilshire Insurance Company	6411	E	661 940-7300	10939

LARKSPUR, CA - Marin County

	SIC	EMP	PHONE	ENTRY #
Clarabridge Inc	7379	D	415 721-1300	16335
Courtyard By Marriott	7011	D	415 925-1800	12546
Golden Gate	4785	D	415 455-2000	5208
Hospice By Bay **(PA)**	8082	D	415 927-2273	22473
Lilien LLC **(HQ)**	7373	E	415 389-7500	15987
ONeill Beverages Co LLC **(PA)**	0172	D	844 825-6600	174
Stalker Services Inc	7372	E	415 569-2280	15847
Sysorex USA **(HQ)**	7373	D	415 389-7500	16061

LATHROP, CA - San Joaquin County

	SIC	EMP	PHONE	ENTRY #
Cunha Draying Inc	4213	D	209 858-1400	4130

LATHROP, CA

Company	SIC	EMP	PHONE	ENTRY #
Global Building Services Inc	8999	B	209 858-9501	28131
Home Depot USA Inc	4225	B	209 858-9243	4571
Mid Valley Plastering Inc	1742	B	209 858-9766	2933
Nbccat Corp	7539	D	209 858-0283	17823
Performant Recovery Inc	7322	C	209 858-3500	14041
Silicatec Rentals Inc	7359	E	209 234-1500	14580
Super Store Industries	5149	A	209 858-2010	8930
Swift Transportation Company	4213	D	209 858-1630	4271
UPS Ground Freight Inc	4213	D	209 858-5095	4287

LATON, CA - Fresno County

Company	SIC	EMP	PHONE	ENTRY #
Zonneveld Dairies Inc	0241	D	559 923-4546	442
Zonneveld Farms	0241	D	559 923-4546	443

LAWNDALE, CA - Los Angeles County

Company	SIC	EMP	PHONE	ENTRY #
Advanced Veterinary Care Ctr	0742	D	310 542-8018	613
Alondra Golf Course Inc	7992	D	310 217-9915	18710
Lawndle Hlthcare & Wellnss Cen	8051	D	310 679-3344	20721
McCarthy Framing Construction	1751	D	310 219-3038	3066
Southwestern Orthpd Med Corp	8011	E	562 803-0600	20047
Ultimate Maintenance Svcs Inc	7349	E	310 542-1474	14450

LE GRAND, CA - Merced County

Company	SIC	EMP	PHONE	ENTRY #
J Marchini & Son Inc	0161	C	559 665-9710	75
Martini Inc	0173	E	209 389-4566	207

LEBEC, CA - Kern County

Company	SIC	EMP	PHONE	ENTRY #
Schneider National Inc	4213	C	661 858-1031	4261
Tejon Marketing Company	8742	D	661 248-3000	27681
Tejon Ranch Co (PA)	6531	D	661 248-3000	11866

LEMON GROVE, CA - San Diego County

Company	SIC	EMP	PHONE	ENTRY #
Aztec Landscaping Inc (PA)	0782	C	619 464-3303	811
Developmental Svcs Continuum	8361	D	619 460-7333	24631
Family Hlth Ctrs San Diego Inc	8099	D	619 515-2550	22963
Fred Finch Youth Center	8011	E	619 797-1090	19528
Pacific Sthwest Structures Inc	1771	E	619 469-2323	3308
San Diego Recycling Inc	4953	B	619 287-7555	6559
Thompson Building Mtls Inc	5032	E	619 287-9410	6995

LEMOORE, CA - Kings County

Company	SIC	EMP	PHONE	ENTRY #
Aecom Global II LLC	8711	D	559 998-1820	25633
Boeing Company	7629	E	559 998-8260	17930
Boq	6514	D	619 556-0266	11233
R & D Leasing Inc	7359	D	559 924-1276	14574
Rainbow - Brite Indus Svcs LLC	7349	D	559 925-2580	14401
Santa Rosa Rnchria Gaming Comm	7929	D	559 924-6948	18494
Tachi Palace Hotel & Casino	7011	A	559 924-7751	13339
United States Dept of Navy	8062	A	559 998-4201	21981
United States Dept of Navy	8062	A	559 998-4481	21982
United States Dept of Navy	8062	B	559 998-2894	21985
Wood Bros Inc	1629	B	559 924-7715	2097

LINCOLN, CA - Placer County

Company	SIC	EMP	PHONE	ENTRY #
B Z Plumbing Company Inc	1711	C	916 645-1600	2156
Calhoun Construction Inc	1521	C	916 434-8356	1149
Catta Verdera Country Club	7997	D	916 645-7200	18915
Clubcorp Usa Inc	7992	E	916 434-9100	18726
Crstb Partners LLC	7992	D	916 645-7200	18730
Gdsa-Lincoln Inc (PA)	7629	D	916 645-8961	17935
Gold Hill Grange No 326	8641	D	916 645-3605	25265
Kaiser Foundation Hospitals	8011	A	916 543-5153	19623
Kerry McCaffrey Cnstr Inc	1521	D	916 645-1388	1203
Lincoln Hills Golf Club	7992	E	916 543-9200	18755
Raylee Electric	1731	E	916 408-7556	2696
RE Max Advantage	6531	D	800 247-4200	11788
Rocklin Power Investors LP	4911	D	916 645-3383	6198
Sutter Health	8049	C	916 434-1224	20355
United Auburn Indian Community	7011	A	916 408-7777	13366
Verifone Inc	4225	D	916 408-4900	4655
Weygandt & Associates	7699	D	916 543-0431	18034

LINDEN, CA - San Joaquin County

Company	SIC	EMP	PHONE	ENTRY #
Duarte Nursery Inc	0181	B	209 887-3409	278
Normans Nursery Inc	5193	C	209 887-2033	9206

LINDSAY, CA - Tulare County

Company	SIC	EMP	PHONE	ENTRY #
Cal Citrus Packing Co	0723	D	559 562-2536	516
California Silver-Agriculture	0851	E	559 562-3795	1014
Friant Water Users Association	4941	D	559 562-6305	6349
GTE Corporation	8748	D	559 562-0000	27937
Lindsay Fruit Company LLC	7389	D	559 562-1327	17295
Lo Bue Bros Inc	0723	C	559 562-6367	557
Padilla Farm Labor Inc	0174	C	559 562-1166	221
Ron Faulkner Trucking	4212	E	559 684-8536	4057
Sheldon Ranches	0191	E	559 562-3978	393
Suntreat Pkg Shipg A Ltd Prtnr	4783	C	559 562-4991	5203

LITTLE LAKE, CA - Inyo County

Company	SIC	EMP	PHONE	ENTRY #
Coso Operating Company LLC	4911	D	760 764-1300	6120

LITTLE RIVER, CA - Mendocino County

Company	SIC	EMP	PHONE	ENTRY #
Little River Inn Inc	7011	D	707 937-5942	12924

LITTLEROCK, CA - Los Angeles County

Company	SIC	EMP	PHONE	ENTRY #
Ascon Recycle Company	4953	E	661 533-0154	6431

LIVE OAK, CA - Sutter County

Company	SIC	EMP	PHONE	ENTRY #
Geo Group Inc	8744	E	530 695-1846	27788
Malloy Orchards Inc	0175	C	530 695-1861	241
Micheli Farms Inc	0175	E	530 695-9022	242
Smith Ranch	0175	E	530 695-2521	250

LIVERMORE, CA - Alameda County

Company	SIC	EMP	PHONE	ENTRY #
5 Star Pool Plaster Inc	1541	D	209 599-3111	1395
Access Info MGT Shred Svcs LLC (PA)	7375	E	925 461-5352	16214
Aero Precision Industries LLC	5088	D	925 579-5327	7991
Aeronautical Radio Inc	4812	D	925 294-8400	5253
All-Guard Alarm Systems Inc (PA)	1731	D	510 887-7055	2516
Altamont Infrastructure Co	4911	D	925 245-5500	6107
American Med	4119	C	510 895-7600	3747
Amsnet Inc (PA)	7373	C	925 245-6100	15901
Aqua Gunite Inc	1799	E	408 271-2782	3494
Architectural GL & Alum Co Inc (PA)	5051	C	925 583-2460	7358
Califrnias Gnite Pool Plst Inc	1771	D	925 960-9500	3237
Care Solution Associates LLC	8082	D	925 443-1000	22393
Cattlemens	7299	D	925 447-1224	13743
Cellco Partnership	4812	A	925 245-0494	5287
Central Whl Elec Distrs Inc	5063	D	925 245-9310	7424
Charter Oak Investments Inc	6411	D	925 447-1753	10668
City of Livermore	1629	E	925 960-8100	2041
Clark Pest Ctrl Stockton Inc	7342	D	925 449-6203	14180
CMS Llnl	7819	D	925 422-5584	18219
Cosco Fire Protection Inc	1731	D	925 455-2751	2563
Country Builders Inc	1522	C	925 373-1020	1304
Custom Product Dev Corp	1761	D	925 960-0577	3158
Davey Tree Surgery Company (HQ)	0783	A	925 443-1723	991
Fault Line Plumbing	1711	E	925 443-6450	2224
Fbd Vanguard Construction Inc	8741	C	925 245-1300	27024
Fields Construction Services	7349	B	925 294-8183	14297
For Hospital Committee	8741	A	925 447-7000	27026
Green Ridge Services LLC	4911	D	925 245-5500	6136
GSe Construction Company Inc (PA)	1623	C	925 447-0292	1936
Haskell Company (inc)	1541	C	925 960-1815	1436
High Summit LLC	7539	E	925 605-2900	17822
Hilton Garden Inns MGT LLC	7011	E	925 292-2000	12710
J & M Inc	1623	E	925 724-0300	1950
J Redfern Inc	0782	C	925 371-3300	873
Jacobs Facilities Inc	1542	D	925 423-7564	1581
JF Shea Construction Inc	1521	C	925 245-3660	1197
Jpa Landscape & Cnstr Inc	0782	C	925 960-9602	881
Kenyon Construction Inc	1771	B	925 371-8102	3288
Kier & Wright Civil ENGrs&srvy	8713	E	925 245-8788	26276
Kindred Healthcare Oper Inc	8051	D	925 443-1800	20700
Kinetics Mechanical Svc Inc	1711	D	925 245-6200	2270
Leisure Care LLC	6513	D	925 371-2300	11156
Livermore Area Rcration Pk Dst	7999	C	925 373-5700	19237
Livermore Area Rcration Pk Dst (PA)	7999	B	925 373-5700	19238
Livermore Snior Lving Assoc LP	6719	E	925 371-2300	12072
Livermore Valley Tennis Club	7991	D	925 443-7700	18655
Livermore World Travel Inc	4725	D	925 373-2400	4994
LJ Walch Co Inc	5088	D	925 449-9252	7999
McGrath Rentcorp	7359	D	925 453-3312	14557
McGrath Rentcorp	7359	C	877 221-2813	14558
McGrath Rentcorp (PA)	7359	C	925 609-6200	14559
Mch Electric Inc (PA)	1731	D	209 835-9755	2645
Mike Champlin	1721	B	925 961-1004	2468
Mthuron Inc	1743	C	925 932-4101	3020
National Security Tech LLC	8711	D	925 960-2500	25986
Nestle Waters North Amer Inc	5149	D	925 294-7720	8888
North Valley Construction Inc	1799	D	925 373-1246	3558
Operating Engineers Local Un 3 (PA)	8631	D	925 454-4000	25180
Pacific Gas and Electric Co	4911	C	925 373-2623	6187
Packaging Innovators Corp	5113	D	925 371-2000	8213
Pen-Cal Administrators Inc	8741	D	925 251-3400	27162
Performant Financial Corp (PA)	7375	C	925 960-4800	16252
Performant Recovery Inc (HQ)	7322	C	209 858-3994	14042
Performant Technologies Inc	6282	B	925 960-4800	10171
Permanente Medical Group Inc	8011	A	925 243-2600	19864
Peterson Painting Inc	1721	B	925 455-5864	2473
Pinamar LLC	7359	D	925 243-8979	14569
Pinnacle Telecom Inc	7373	D	916 426-1032	16030
Poppy Ridge Inc	7992	D	925 456-8229	18769
Prevent Life Safety Svcs Inc	7389	E	925 667-2088	17425

GEOGRAPHIC SECTION — LONG BEACH, CA

Company	SIC	EMP	PHONE	ENTRY #
Produce Exchange Incorporated (HQ)	5148	D	925 454-8700	8766
Pta California Cong P A S Elem	8641	E	925 606-4700	25319
Puronics Retail Services Inc	1711	D	925 456-7000	2332
Puronics Water Systems Inc	5074	D	925 456-7000	7729
Roma Food Enterprises Inc	5149	D	800 233-6211	8914
Sidjon Corporation	7011	D	925 606-6135	13253
Sosa Granite & Marble Inc	1743	E	925 373-7675	3025
Standard Register Inc	4226	D	925 449-3700	4703
Tao Mechanical Ltd	1711	E	925 447-5220	2393
Tennyson Electric Inc	1731	E	925 606-1038	2771
Tgcon Inc (HQ)	8711	C	925 449-5764	26094
The National Food Lab LLC	8733	C	925 828-1440	26813
Uncle Credit Union (PA)	6062	D	925 447-5001	9696
Unified Grocers Inc	5141	E	323 264-5200	8543
United States Dept of Energy	8731	A	925 422-1100	26627
US Foods Inc	5141	B	925 606-3525	8546
Valleycare Hospital Corp (DH)	8011	C	925 447-7000	20185
Veolia Transportation Svcs Inc	4111	D	925 455-7500	3736
Veritiv Operating Company	5084	C	925 245-6075	7902
Veterans Health Administration	8011	B	925 447-2560	20214
Waxies Enterprises Inc	5087	E	925 454-2900	7987

LIVINGSTON, CA - Merced County

Company	SIC	EMP	PHONE	ENTRY #
E & J Gallo Winery	0762	D	209 394-6271	697
Foster Poultry Farms (PA)	0254	C	209 394-6914	454
Foster Poultry Farms	5144	E	209 394-7901	8597
Foster Poultry Farms	0254	A	209 394-7901	456
Livingston Community Health	8011	C	209 394-7913	19713
Quail H Farms LLC	0139	A	209 394-8001	31
Yagi Bros Inc	0139	D	209 394-7311	34

LLANO, CA - Los Angeles County

Company	SIC	EMP	PHONE	ENTRY #
Crystal Aire Country Club Golf	7997	E	661 944-2112	18933

LODI, CA - San Joaquin County

Company	SIC	EMP	PHONE	ENTRY #
Alexander Delu	0172	D	209 334-6660	140
Anka Behavioral Health Inc	8099	D	209 982-4697	22887
Bjj Company LLC (PA)	4213	D	209 941-8361	4118
Boething Treeland Farms Inc	0811	C	209 727-3741	1006
California Fruit Exchange LLC (PA)	5148	D	209 365-2340	8701
Clark Pest Ctrl Stockton Inc (PA)	7342	C	209 368-7152	14175
Color Spot Nurseries Inc	0181	D	209 369-3018	274
Crescent Court Nursing Home	8059	E	209 367-7400	21201
Diede Construction Inc	1542	D	209 369-8255	1541
ED Safety Services Inc	1611	C	209 333-0807	1770
Evergreen Company Inc	7389	D	916 257-5994	17155
F & H Construction (PA)	1542	D	209 931-3738	1552
Ford Construction Company Inc	1629	D	209 333-1116	2050
Frank C Alegre Trucking Inc (PA)	4213	C	209 334-2112	4185
Golden Living LLC	8051	D	209 368-0693	20612
Greg H Carpenter Concrete Inc	1771	E	209 367-4224	3270
Gross Convalescent Hospital	8051	E	209 334-3760	20639
Haro & Haro Enterprises Inc	0761	A	209 334-2035	666
J & L Collections Services Inc	7322	D	800 481-6006	14036
J Rivera Associates Inc	8999	D	415 617-5660	28138
John H Kautz Farms	0721	B	209 334-4786	480
Jose Vramontes	0191	E	209 810-5384	376
Lodi Development Inc	6552	E	209 367-7600	11979
Lodi Memorial Hosp Assn Inc	8099	D	209 334-8520	22993
Lodi Memorial Hosp Assn Inc	8099	D	209 339-7441	22994
Lodi Memorial Hosp Assn Inc (PA)	8062	A	209 334-3411	21708
Lodi Memorial Hosp Assn Inc	8062	E	209 339-7583	21709
Lodi Memorial Hosp Assn Inc	8011	D	209 333-3100	19715
Lodi Unified School District	7349	D	209 331-7181	14341
Lodi Unified School District	4151	C	209 331-7169	3943
M & R Co	5148	D	209 941-2631	8749
Mv Transportation Inc	4111	D	209 339-1972	3680
Oak Ridge Winery LLC	0172	E	209 369-4768	173
Odyssey Landscaping Co Inc	1771	D	209 369-6197	3305
Pacific Coast Producers	7389	B	209 365-9982	17391
R DS For Healthcare	8049	E	209 333-2115	20346
Rdr Builders LP	1522	D	209 368-7561	1335
Schryver Med Sls & Mktg LLC	8071	D	303 459-8150	22284
Spare-Time Inc	7933	D	209 371-0241	18529
Sutter Health	8099	D	209 366-2007	23068
T & T Trucking Inc (PA)	4213	C	800 692-3457	4275
Tiger Lines LLC (HQ)	4213	D	209 334-4100	4276
Trinchero Family Estates Inc	7389	C	707 963-5928	17546
Valley Landscaping & Maint Inc	0782	D	209 334-3659	974
Vienna Convalescent Hospital	8059	D	209 368-7141	21411
Vino Farms Inc (PA)	0762	E	209 334-6975	730
Vino Farms LLC	5182	A	209 334-6975	9114
Vpl Inc	4212	D	209 931-2682	4089
Westrec Marina Management Inc	4493	D	209 369-1041	4773
Wine Country Care Center	8051	E	209 334-3760	21056

LOLETA, CA - Humboldt County

Company	SIC	EMP	PHONE	ENTRY #
Bear River Casino	7011	B	707 733-9644	12430

LOMA LINDA, CA - San Bernardino County

Company	SIC	EMP	PHONE	ENTRY #
Brookdale Snior Lving Cmmnties	8059	D	909 796-5421	21167
Chancellor Hlth Care Cal I Inc (PA)	8059	D	909 796-0235	21183
Faculty Physcans Srgeons Llusm	8011	D	909 558-4000	19520
Heritage Health Care Inc	8051	C	909 796-0216	20667
Laren D Tan MD	8011	D	909 558-4444	19700
Linda Loma Univ Hlth Care (HQ)	8062	D	909 558-2806	21706
Linda Loma Univ Hlth Care	8011	C	909 558-2851	19709
Linda Loma Univ Hlth Care (PA)	8011	A	909 558-4985	19710
Linda Loma Univ Hlth Care	8011	C	909 558-2840	19711
Loma Linda - Inland Empire C	8062	C	909 651-5832	21710
Loma Linda University Med Ctr	8062	B	909 558-2100	21711
Loma Linda University Med Ctr (DH)	8062	A	909 558-4000	21712
Loma Linda University Med Ctr	8062	B	909 558-8244	21713
Loma Linda University Med Ctr	8082	C	909 558-2995	22500
Loma Linda University Med Ctr	8062	C	909 796-0167	21715
Mountain View Child Care Inc (PA)	8062	B	909 796-6915	21757
Universal Self Storage	4225	E	951 206-5263	4649
Veterans Health Administration	8011	A	909 825-7084	20215

LOMITA, CA - Los Angeles County

Company	SIC	EMP	PHONE	ENTRY #
City of Lomita	4941	E	310 325-7114	6326
City of Lomita	4941	E	310 325-9830	6327
Industry Events	7993	E	310 834-3422	18804
Kaiser Foundation Hospitals	8011	A	310 325-6542	19625
Kaiser Foundation Hospitals	8093	C	424 251-7000	22752
Lomita Verde Inc	8059	D	310 325-1970	21293
Long Beach Investment Group	6162	E	562 595-7277	9871
Travers Tree Service Inc	0721	E	310 545-5816	486

LOMPOC, CA - Santa Barbara County

Company	SIC	EMP	PHONE	ENTRY #
Aerospace Corporation	8733	D	805 320-9599	26724
Air Force US Dept of	8741	D	805 606-5355	26913
Carnahan Occupational Therapy	8093	E	805 737-1604	22673
Channel Islands Young Mens Ch	8641	D	805 736-3483	25231
Coasthills Credit Union (PA)	6062	B	805 733-7600	9660
Family Service Agency	8322	E	805 735-4376	23971
Ghc of Lompoc LLC	8093	C	805 735-4010	22734
Imerys Minerals California Inc	1481	B	805 736-1221	1113
Imerys Minerals California Inc (DH)	1499	B	805 736-1221	1116
Jay Fisher Farms Inc	0161	E	805 735-1598	76
Kbrwyle Tech Solutions LLC	4899	B	805 734-2982	6078
Lockheed Martin Corporation	4581	D	303 971-4631	4924
Lompoc Valley Medical Center	8011	C	805 735-9229	19717
Lompoc Valley Medical Center (PA)	8062	B	805 737-3300	21716
Lompoc Valley Medical Center	8059	D	805 736-3466	21294
Ocean View Flowers LLC	0181	C	800 736-5608	307
Pacific Cast CLB Vndenburg Afb	8641	D	805 734-4375	25308
Santa Barbara County of	8322	D	805 737-7080	24189
Santa Barbara Farms LLC (PA)	0161	B	805 736-9776	93
Valley Medical Group of Lompoc	8011	D	805 736-1253	20183
Vandenberg Afb Child Care	8351	E	805 606-1555	24528
Velazquez Packing Inc	0761	E	805 735-6477	688

LONE PINE, CA - Inyo County

Company	SIC	EMP	PHONE	ENTRY #
Southern Inyo Healthcare Dst	8051	C	760 876-5501	20922

LONG BARN, CA - Tuolumne County

Company	SIC	EMP	PHONE	ENTRY #
Silicon Valley Monterey Bay Co	7032	D	209 965-3432	13470

LONG BEACH, CA - Los Angeles County

Company	SIC	EMP	PHONE	ENTRY #
1130 W La Palma Ave Inc	8051	D	562 930-0777	20363
4g Wireless Inc	4813	D	562 432-7744	5447
A-Throne Co Inc	7359	D	562 981-1197	14504
Abbey Management Company LLC	6719	D	562 243-2100	12047
Abilty First	8361	D	562 426-6161	24539
Ace Relocation Systems Inc	4212	E	310 632-2000	3971
Acom Solutions Inc (PA)	7373	C	562 424-7899	15894
Advanced Medical MGT Inc	8741	D	562 766-2000	26911
Advertising Consultants Inc (PA)	7319	E	310 233-2750	13986
Aecom Global II LLC	8748	D	310 343-6977	27814
AES Southland LLC	4911	D	562 430-8685	6104
Airflite Inc	4581	D	562 490-6200	4896
Airgas Usa LLC- West Division	5169	A	562 497-1991	8973
Airgas USA LLC	5169	A	562 497-1991	8976
Alamitos-Belmont Rehab Inc	8069	C	562 434-8421	22113
Alltrade Tools LLC	5072	E	310 522-9008	7668
Alpert & Alpert Iron & Met Inc	5051	E	562 624-8833	7354
Als Services Usa Corp	8734	E	562 597-3912	26830
American Corporate SEC Inc (PA)	7381	D	562 216-7440	16553
American Golf Corporation	7997	E	562 494-4424	18858
American Textile Maint Co	7213	C	562 438-7656	13521
American Textile Maint Co	5023	D	562 438-1126	6842
American Textile Maint Co	7213	C	562 424-1607	13523

Employment Codes: A=Over 500 employees, B=251-500, C=101-250, D=51-100, E=45-50

LONG BEACH, CA — GEOGRAPHIC SECTION

Company	SIC	EMP	PHONE	ENTRY #
Amerifleet Transportation Inc	4789	C	562 420-5604	5213
AON Consulting Inc	6411	D	562 496-2888	10616
Apriso Corporation	7373	C	562 951-8000	15903
Aquarium of Pacific	8422	D	562 590-3100	25056
Aquarium of Pacific (PA)	8422	C	562 590-3100	25057
Aramark MGT Svcs Ltd Partnr	7349	E	562 593-2724	14234
Argus Management Company LLC	8744	B	562 491-9673	27775
ASAP Staffing Inc	7361	E	562 499-2120	14609
Associated Students California	8641	B	562 985-4994	25201
Association For Retarded (PA)	8331	C	562 597-7716	24310
Atlantic Express Trnsp	4119	C	562 997-6868	3768
Atlantic Mem Healthcare Assoc (PA)	8051	D	562 424-8101	20388
Auto Insur Spcialists-Long Bch	6411	D	562 496-2888	10634
Bank America National Assn	6021	E	562 624-4330	9325
Beach Cities Eldercare Inc (PA)	8082	D	562 596-4884	22376
Behavioral Health Services Inc	8322	D	562 599-4194	23680
Belmont Athletic Club	7997	D	562 438-3816	18889
Beta Operating Company LLC	1311	B	562 628-1526	1029
Boeing Company	8741	A	562 593-5511	26945
Bowers Companies Inc (HQ)	4119	D	562 988-6460	3776
Bowers Companies Inc	4119	E	562 988-6460	3777
Bragg Investment Company Inc (PA)	7389	A	562 984-2400	17041
Bret Boylan Property Mgt	8741	E	562 437-7886	26947
Brittany House LLC	8361	D	562 421-4717	24569
Brittney House	8082	E	562 421-4717	22382
Brookdale Senior Living Inc	8059	C	714 489-8966	21165
C S I Patrol Services	7381	E	562 981-8988	16588
California Broadcast Ctr LLC	4841	C	310 233-2425	5939
California Charter Inc	4141	C	562 634-7969	3892
California Repertory Company	7922	E	562 985-7891	18375
California Resources Corp	1311	C	562 624-3400	1038
California Traffic Control	7389	D	562 595-7575	17049
Camp Fire USA Long Beach Cncl	8322	E	562 421-2725	23700
Career Transition Center	8331	C	562 570-9675	24320
Careonsite Inc (PA)	8011	E	562 437-0831	19410
Carfax Studios	7299	D	562 377-0223	13742
Carnival Corporation	4724	A	562 901-3232	4960
Catalina Channel Express Inc (HQ)	4489	C	310 519-7971	4732
Catalina Channel Express Inc	4491	C	562 435-8686	4745
Catalina Channel Express Inc	4489	C	562 495-3565	4733
Catholic Hlthcare W Sthern Cal (HQ)	8062	C	562 491-9000	21472
Cdcf III Pacific Catalina	6722	D	562 453-1353	12109
CE Allencompany Inc	1629	E	562 989-6100	2039
Cemak Trucking Inc	4212	D	949 253-2800	3991
Century 21 Beachside	6531	D	562 430-2121	11368
Century 21 Landmark Properties	6531	E	562 422-0911	11378
Charles Drew Univ Mdcine Scnce	8351	C	310 605-0164	24427
Charter Cmmnctons Oprating LLC	4841	B	310 971-4001	5941
Childnet Youth & Fmly Svcs Inc (PA)	8399	C	562 498-5500	24888
Childnet Youth & Fmly Svcs Inc	8361	D	562 492-9983	24593
Childrens Clinic serving Chl	8011	B	562 264-4638	19430
China Shipg N Amer Holdg Ltd	4731	E	562 590-3845	5046
China Shipg N Amer Holdg Ltd	4731	E	562 590-0900	5047
Chlb LLC	8063	D	562 997-2000	22054
Choura Venue Services	7299	D	562 426-0555	13744
Circle Marina Car Wash Inc	7542	E	562 494-4698	17836
CIT Bank National Association	6021	D	562 433-0972	9366
Citadel Security Inc	7381	D	562 248-2300	16597
City of Long Beach	7389	B	562 570-7298	17075
City of Long Beach	7538	C	562 570-2828	17788
City of Long Beach	8111	D	562 570-5423	23152
City of Long Beach	4959	C	562 570-2890	6622
City of Long Beach	4932	C	562 570-2000	6296
City of Long Beach	4581	D	562 570-2600	4907
City of Long Beach	7389	B	562 436-3636	17076
City of Long Beach	8111	D	562 570-6919	23153
City of Long Beach	4941	C	562 570-2390	6328
Cmac Construction Company	1623	D	562 435-5611	1921
Coast Carwash LP	7542	E	562 961-5555	17837
Coastal Alliance Holdings Inc	6531	C	562 370-1000	11401
Coastal Closeouts Inc	7389	D	323 589-7900	17087
Coastal Cmnty Senior Care LLC	8322	C	562 596-4884	23766
Cogent Financial Group	6153	D	562 985-1388	9778
College Park Realty Inc	6531	E	562 982-0300	11442
Comcast Corporation	4841	D	800 240-3640	5967
Community Hospital Long Beach	8062	A	562 494-0600	21499
Compulink Management Ctr Inc	7372	D	562 988-1688	15627
Conservation Corps Long Beach	8331	D	562 986-1249	24326
Consolidated Disposal Svc LLC	4953	D	562 531-2670	6466
Continental Graphics Corp	8711	A	714 503-4200	25750
Corridor Recycling Inc	4953	D	310 835-3849	6468
Cosco Agencies (los Angeles) (DH)	4731	D	213 689-6700	5052
Country Villa Blmnt Hght Hlth	8059	D	562 597-8817	21193
Country Villa Service Corp	8741	D	562 597-8817	26987
County of Los Angeles	4941	C	213 367-3176	6336
County of Los Angeles	8011	C	562 599-9200	19474
Covenant Care California LLC	8051	D	562 426-0394	20486
Covenant Care California LLC	8051	D	562 427-7493	20490
Covenant Industries Inc	7361	D	951 808-3708	14630
Crane Co	5085	C	562 426-2531	7929
Csulb 49er Foundation	8699	A	562 985-5778	25522
Culver City Hsing Partners LP	6513	D	562 257-5100	11118
Daylight Transport LLC (PA)	4213	D	310 507-8200	4132
Demler Armstrong & Rowland LLP	8111	E	562 498-8979	23204
Denso Pdts & Svcs Americas Inc (DH)	5013	C	310 834-6352	6725
Dhs Member Services	8021	D	562 595-5151	20252
Dignity Health	8062	A	562 491-9000	21536
Dignity Health	8322	E	562 494-0576	23945
Douglas W Jackson MD	8011	D	562 424-6666	19508
Dream Home Care Inc	8361	D	562 595-9021	24634
Duthie Electric Service Corp	7629	E	562 790-1772	17933
E2 Managetech Inc (PA)	8711	D	562 740-1060	25776
Edgewater Convalescent Hosp	8051	D	562 434-0974	20527
Edwards Theatres Circuit Inc	7832	D	562 429-3321	18328
Eichleay Engineers Inc Cal	8711	C	562 256-8600	25781
Elements Behavioral Health Inc (HQ)	8093	D	562 741-6470	22727
Elite Craftsman (PA)	7349	C	562 989-3511	14288
Envent Corporation (PA)	8748	D	562 997-9465	27916
Envirobusiness Inc	8999	D	562 481-3365	28129
Epcm Prof Svc Partners LLC	8748	D	562 936-1000	27917
Eric D Feldman MD Inc	8011	E	562 424-6666	19517
Eversoft Inc (PA)	5074	D	562 495-7766	7710
Fabric Barn	5131	C	562 494-3450	8312
Faith Com Inc (PA)	8748	D	562 719-9300	27919
Family Plg Assoc Med Group	7389	D	562 595-5653	17161
Family Plg Assoc Med Group (PA)	8011	D	213 738-7283	19525
Farmers Merchants Bnk Long Bch (HQ)	6022	C	562 437-0011	9492
Federal Express Corporation	4513	C	800 463-3339	4863
Federal Express Corporation	4513	C	562 522-4014	4864
Fire and Police	8611	E	562 961-0066	25086
First Team RE - Orange Cnty	6531	D	562 346-5088	11535
First Transit Inc	4111	D	310 515-8270	3649
Foasberg Laundry & Clrs Inc (PA)	7213	D	562 426-7345	13548
Forest Lawn Memorial-Park Assn	6553	D	562 424-1631	12031
Foss Maritime Company	4412	C	562 435-0171	4715
Free Conferencing Corporation	4813	C	562 437-1411	5603
Fresenius Med Care Long Beach	8092	E	562 432-4444	22627
Glenn E Thomas Company Inc	7538	D	562 426-5111	17796
Gold Tree Inc	8742	D	562 801-0218	27451
Greater Alarm Company Inc (HQ)	1731	C	949 474-0555	2600
Gulfstream Aerospace Corp GA	8711	A	562 420-1818	25846
Harbor Diesel and Eqp Inc	5084	D	562 591-5665	7847
Healthcare Partners LLC	8011	C	562 304-2100	19547
Healthcare Partners LLC	8099	D	562 429-2473	22971
Healthcare Partners LLC	8011	B	562 988-7000	19548
Healthcare Services Group Inc	8999	A	562 494-7939	28133
HEI Long Beach LLC	7011	C	562 983-3400	12698
Hellmann Wrldwide Lgistics Inc	4731	D	310 847-4600	5099
Hillcrest Cnvalescent Hosp Inc	8059	C	323 636-3462	21267
Hlb Funding LLC	7011	C	562 983-3400	12744
Hospitlity Fcsed Solutions Inc	8712	D	562 424-1720	26209
Howard John	7011	C	562 425-4232	12794
Howard CDM	1521	E	562 427-4124	1191
Human Touch LLC	5021	D	562 426-8700	6819
Hutchison Corporation	1542	D	310 763-7991	1575
Hyatt Corporation	7011	B	562 432-0161	12814
ICI Enterprises Inc	8331	D	562 989-7715	24351
Intelsat Corporation	4899	C	310 525-5500	6076
Intercommunity Care Centers	8051	C	562 427-8915	20688
International Garment Finisher	7218	C	562 983-7400	13632
International Trnsp Svc (HQ)	4491	C	562 435-7781	4747
Intertrend Communications Inc	7311	D	562 733-1888	13867
Intex Recreation Corp	5021	D	310 549-1846	6821
Intex Recreation Corp (PA)	5091	D	310 549-5400	8021
Intex Recreation Corp	6512	D	310 549-5400	11006
Iqa Solutions Inc	8711	D	562 420-1000	25886
Irwin Industries Inc (HQ)	1629	A	310 233-3000	2057
Jacobs Civil Inc	8711	A	310 847-2500	25887
Jacobs Engineering Group Inc	8711	A	310 847-2500	25894
Jewish Community Ctr Long Bch	8322	C	562 426-7601	24043
Jfe Shoji Trade America Inc (DH)	5051	D	562 637-3500	7376
Jvckenwood USA Corporation (HQ)	5064	D	310 639-9000	7500
Kaiser Foundation Hospitals	8062	E	310 325-5111	21655
Kazarian/Jewett Inc	1541	E	562 594-5927	1443
Keesal Young Logan A Prof Corp (PA)	8111	D	562 436-2000	23345
Kenny Pabst	6531	D	562 439-2147	11616
Kevcomp Inc	8711	D	562 423-3028	25918
Kindercare Learning Ctrs LLC	8351	D	562 961-8882	24474
Km Industrial Inc	7349	D	562 786-6200	14335
Kpff Inc	8711	D	562 437-9100	25927

Mergent email: customerrelations@mergent.com — 2017 Directory of California Wholesalers and Services Companies — (P-0000) Products & Services Section entry number — (PA)=Parent Co (HQ)=Headquarters (DH)=Div Headquarters

GEOGRAPHIC SECTION

LONG BEACH, CA

Company	SIC	EMP	PHONE	ENTRY #
Ld Products Inc	5045	C	562 986-6940	7154
Life Steps Foundation Inc	8322	D	562 436-0751	24065
Lite Solar Corp	1711	D	562 256-1249	2282
Long Bch Museum Art Foundation	8412	D	562 439-2119	25025
Long Beach Care Center Inc	8051	C	562 426-6141	20740
Long Beach Cmnty Action Partnr	8399	C	562 216-4600	24939
Long Beach Cmnty College Dst	4225	A	562 938-4291	4590
Long Beach Day Nursery	8351	E	562 421-1488	24477
Long Beach Golden Sails Inc	7011	D	562 795-5241	12929
Long Beach Memorial Med Ctr (HQ)	8062	A	562 933-2000	21717
Long Beach Mntl Hlth Srvcs	8011	C	562 218-4001	19718
Long Beach Public Trnsp Co	4111	B	562 591-2301	3656
Long Beach Public Trnsp Co (PA)	4111	B	562 591-8753	3657
Long Beach Public Trnsp Co	4111	B	562 591-8753	3658
Long Beach Unified School Dist	7349	D	562 997-7550	14342
Long Beach Unified School Dst	7361	B	562 491-1281	14698
Long Beach Unified School Dst	4151	D	562 426-6176	3944
Long Beach Unified School Dst	7389	B	562 493-3596	17301
Long Beach Yacht Club	7997	D	562 598-9401	18982
Longwood Management Corp	8059	C	562 432-5751	21301
Loofs Lite A Line	7993	E	562 436-2978	18805
M O Dion & Sons Inc (PA)	5172	D	714 540-5535	9026
M P O Inc (DH)	5122	D	562 628-1007	8275
M4 Wind Services Inc	8999	D	562 981-7797	28143
Macro-Pro Inc (PA)	7389	C	562 595-0900	17306
Maintenance Staff Inc	7349	A	562 493-3982	14348
Mangan Inc (PA)	8711	B	310 835-8080	25950
Maritzcx Research LLC	8732	A	310 525-1300	26686
Marlora Investments LLC	8051	D	562 494-3311	20776
Marriott International Inc	7011	C	562 425-5210	12964
Marriott International Inc	7011	C	562 595-0909	12973
Matrix Environmental Inc	1799	D	562 236-2704	3552
Matrix Industries Inc	1799	B	562 236-2700	3553
Medasend Biomedical Inc (PA)	8099	C	800 200-3581	22997
Memor Ortho Surgic Group A M	8011	D	562 424-6666	19741
Memorial Counseling Assoc Inc	8011	D	562 961-0155	19742
Memorial Psychiatric Hlth Svcs	8011	E	562 494-9243	19743
Memorial Surgical Group	8011	D	562 424-6666	19744
Mental Health Amer Los Angeles	8322	D	562 437-6717	24083
Mercedes-Benz RE	8731	E	310 549-7600	26568
Merritt Hospitality LLC	7011	D	562 983-3400	12990
Metropower Inc	1731	D	562 305-9617	2652
Mida Industries Inc	7349	C	562 616-1020	14359
Milco Constructors Inc	1629	E	562 595-1977	2067
Mistras Group Inc	8711	D	562 597-3932	25968
Moffatt & Nichol	8711	D	562 426-9551	25974
Molina Healthcare Inc (PA)	8011	A	562 435-3666	19759
Molina Healthcare of Californi	6321	A	562 435-3666	10246
Molina Information Systems LLC	8011	A	562 435-3666	19760
Muni-Fed Energy Inc	1711	E	714 321-3346	2300
Museum of Latin American Art	8412	E	562 437-1689	25030
New Directions Inc (PA)	8322	D	310 914-4045	24099
Noble/Utah Long Beach LLC	7011	C	562 436-3000	13025
NRC Environmental Services Inc	4953	D	562 432-1304	6510
Ocean Blue Envmtl Svcs Inc (PA)	4212	D	562 624-4120	4046
Olive Crest	8361	D	562 216-8841	24756
Onewest Bank NA	6035	D	562 433-0971	9577
Oocl (usa) Inc	4731	C	562 499-2600	5139
Opex Communications Inc	4813	E	562 968-5420	5675
Oshyn Inc	7374	D	213 483-1770	16167
Overland Pacific & Cutler (PA)	7389	D	562 429-9391	17386
P2s Engineering Inc	8711	D	562 497-2999	26001
Pacific Care Inc	8082	D	562 494-6500	22528
Pacific Crane Maint Co LP (PA)	7699	D	562 432-8066	17996
Pacific Gtwy Wrkfrce Prtnr Inc	7361	E	562 570-3700	14718
Pacific Maritime Freight Inc	4492	D	562 590-8188	4768
Pacific Occptnal Medicine Svcs	8062	E	562 997-2290	21776
Pacific Palms Healthcare LLC	8082	D	562 433-6791	22530
Pacific Shores Med Group Inc (PA)	8011	D	562 590-0345	19805
Pacific Towboat & Salvage Co	4492	D	562 435-0171	4769
Palm Harbor Residency LP	8059	C	562 595-4551	21343
Palmcrest Grand Care Ctr Inc	8051	D	562 595-4551	20837
Palmcrest Medallion Convalesc	8051	D	562 595-4336	20838
Palp Inc	1611	C	562 599-5841	1841
Parwood Preservation LP	6531	D	562 531-7880	11741
Passport Acceptance Facility	7389	C	562 494-2296	17403
Pbi-Birkenwald Market Eqp Inc (PA)	5046	E	562 595-4785	7223
Pegasus Building Svcs Co Inc (PA)	7349	C	562 961-1998	14387
Penske Truck Leasing Co LP	7513	D	310 327-3116	17647
Perona Langer Beck A Prof Corp	8111	D	562 426-6155	23504
Phillips Steel Company	5051	E	562 435-7571	7392
Pioneer Electronics (usa) Inc (DH)	5064	B	310 952-2000	7507
Pioneer Electronics Service (DH)	5064	C	213 746-6337	7508
Pioneer Medical Group Inc	8011	B	562 597-4181	19873
Platt Security Systems Inc	7381	C	562 986-4484	16759
Polar Air Cargo LP	4512	B	310 568-4551	4818
Polar Tankers Inc (DH)	4424	D	562 388-1400	4720
Porchlight Inc	8059	D	562 989-5100	21351
Port of Long Bch Employees CLB	8631	E	562 590-4102	25181
Pponext Inc	8099	B	888 446-6098	23023
Praxair Inc	5084	D	562 427-0099	7876
Preferred Construction Co Inc	1542	D	714 630-3004	1640
Premier Insite Group Inc	7361	D	562 741-5018	14734
Prindle Decker & Amaro LLP (PA)	8111	D	562 436-3946	23517
Psav Holdings LLC	7359	A	562 366-0138	14572
PSC Industrial Outsourcing LP	4953	D	562 997-6000	6516
Qualfax Inc	7389	D	562 988-1272	17436
Queensbay Hotel LLC	7011	D	562 481-3910	13118
R G Vanderweil Engineers LLP	8711	C	562 256-8623	26029
R L Klein & Associates	7363	D	562 427-5577	14930
Rance King Properties Inc (PA)	6513	C	562 240-1000	11194
Recovery Place Inc	8069	D	954 200-8308	22167
Redbarn Pet Products Inc	5199	C	562 495-7315	9298
Regency Oaks Care Center	8051	D	562 498-3368	20868
Rehabilitation California Dept	8322	E	562 422-8325	24153
Restaurant Depot LLC	5142	D	562 634-6771	8567
Retirement Housing Foundation (PA)	6531	D	562 257-5100	11811
Reynolds Health Industries	8059	D	562 591-7621	21359
RMS Foundation Inc	7011	A	562 435-3511	13164
Ronald J Lemieux Assoc Law Off	8111	D	562 375-0095	23537
Roux Associates Inc	8748	D	562 446-8600	28047
Ruffin Hotel Corp of Cal	7011	D	562 425-5210	13180
Ruth Perkowitz Inc (PA)	8712	C	562 628-8000	26249
Safe Refuge	8361	D	562 987-5722	24794
Save Queen LLC	7011	B	562 435-3511	13221
Scan Health Plan (PA)	6324	D	562 989-5100	10374
Securitas SEC Svcs USA Inc	7381	C	562 427-2737	16808
Sees Candy Shops Incorporated	4226	C	310 559-4911	4702
Senior Care (PA)	6324	A	562 989-5100	10378
Senior Care	6324	D	562 492-9878	10379
Shelton Construction Company	1611	D	714 903-7853	1858
Shield Security Inc	7381	B	562 283-1100	16823
Shimadzu Precision Instrs Inc (DH)	5088	C	562 420-6226	8005
Shipco Transport Inc	4449	D	562 295-2900	4723
Shoreline Holdings Inc (PA)	1731	C	562 498-6444	2733
Signature Flight Support Corp	4581	D	562 997-0700	4937
Smg Holdings Inc	6512	D	562 436-3636	11051
Southern California Edison Co	4911	B	562 491-3803	6240
Spectacor Management Group	6512	D	562 436-3636	11057
Ssa Containers Inc	4491	D	206 623-0304	4758
Ssa Marine Inc	4491	D	562 983-1001	4759
St Mary Medical Center (HQ)	8062	A	562 491-9000	21928
Star Brite Building Maint	7349	B	562 988-2829	14438
State Farm Mutl Auto Insur Co	6411	D	310 632-9810	10886
Sunbridge Harbor View	8051	C	562 989-9907	20942
Sunbridge Healthcare LLC	8052	C	562 981-9392	21115
Sunrise Plumbing & Mech Inc	1711	E	562 424-0332	2390
Synergy Health North Amer Inc	7213	D	562 428-5858	13570
Tarzana Treatment Centers Inc	8093	D	562 218-1868	22848
Telecare Corporation	8063	D	562 630-8672	22098
Telecare Corporation	8063	C	562 634-9534	22099
Telecare La Step Down	8093	E	562 216-4900	22850
Tell Steel Inc	5051	D	562 435-4826	7407
The Designory Inc (HQ)	7336	C	562 624-0200	14163
Tom Dreher Sales Inc	5046	D	562 355-4074	7230
Total Intermodal Services Inc (PA)	4491	E	562 427-6300	4763
Toyota Logistics Services	7549	B	562 437-6767	17899
Tp-Link USA Corporation	5045	D	562 528-7700	7202
Trinity Health Systems	8051	D	562 437-2797	20993
Tristar Insurance Group Inc (PA)	6331	A	562 495-6600	10478
Twining Labs Southern Cal Inc (PA)	8734	D	562 426-3355	26895
Ultimate Construction Inc	1751	C	562 633-3389	3099
Universal Protection Svc LP	7381	A	562 981-5700	16841
USA Waste of California Inc	4953	D	310 830-7100	6584
Vanguard Lgistics Svcs USA Inc (HQ)	4731	A	310 847-3000	5188
Ventura Transfer Company (PA)	4213	D	310 549-1660	4299
Veolia Es Waste-To-Energy Inc	4953	D	562 436-0636	6593
Verizon Communications Inc	4813	C	562 496-0288	5721
Villa De La Mar Inc	8059	E	562 494-5001	21412
Virginia Cntry CLB of Long Bch	7997	C	562 427-0924	19121
Vista Cove Care Center At Long	8051	C	562 426-4461	21017
W A Rasic Cnstr Co Inc (PA)	1623	C	562 928-6111	2012
Walter Voss Cynthia RE Max	6531	E	562 434-5980	11909
Warren E&P Inc	5172	D	562 590-0909	9034
Wells Hse Hspice Fundation Inc	8051	D	714 952-3755	21027
Western Exterminator Company	7342	E	310 835-3513	14195
Weyerhaeuser Company	0811	D	562 983-6709	1013
William H Warden III MD	8011	D	562 424-6666	20240
Windes McClghry Accntancy Corp (PA)	8721	C	562 435-1191	26458
Wm Wireless Inc	4812	E	562 633-9288	5436

LONG BEACH, CA

Name	SIC	EMP	PHONE	ENTRY #
Women Infant & Children	8322	D	562 570-4228	24293
World Trade Ctr Ht Assoc Ltd	7011	D	562 983-3400	13429
Wsc America	4731	C	562 367-4212	5191
Xerox Education Services LLC (DH)	7374	D	310 830-9847	16212
Yhb Long Beach LLC	7011	D	562 597-4401	13445
Young Mens Christian Associat	8641	D	562 624-2376	25455
Young Mens Chrstn Asc Gr L B	8641	B	562 596-3394	25458
Young Mens Chrstn Assc Gr L B	8641	D	562 423-0491	25461
Young Mens Chrstn Assc Gr L B	8641	D	562 423-0491	25462
Young Mens Chrstn Assc Gr L B	8641	D	562 633-0106	25463
Yusen Logistics Americas Inc	4225	C	310 518-3008	4675

LOOMIS, CA - Placer County

Name	SIC	EMP	PHONE	ENTRY #
Abshear Landscape Development	0781	E	916 660-1617	737
Applimotion Inc	5063	D	916 652-3118	7416
Jls Environmental Services Inc	8744	D	916 660-1525	27797
Online Communications Inc	1731	C	916 652-7253	2673
VCA Animal Hospitals Inc	0742	E	916 652-5816	626
Wilkie Masonry Inc	1741	E	916 652-0118	2839

LOS ALAMITOS, CA - Orange County

Name	SIC	EMP	PHONE	ENTRY #
Advantage Plumbing Group Inc	1711	D	714 898-6020	2108
Alamitos Enterprises LLC (PA)	7549	D	562 596-1827	17870
Apfeld & Neal Insurance Svcs	6411	E	714 821-7041	10619
Barrys Security Services Inc	7381	C	562 493-7007	16572
Benchmark Internet Group LLC	7379	D	562 286-6820	16328
Carol Electric Company Inc	1731	D	562 431-1870	2549
College Park Realty Inc (PA)	6531	D	562 594-6753	11441
Dynalectric Company	1731	C	714 236-2242	2578
Friedas Inc	5148	D	714 733-7655	8730
Fruit Guys	5148	D	714 826-2993	8731
General Services Cal Dept	7374	D	562 342-7212	16134
Goodman Group Inc	6531	D	562 596-5561	11558
Katella Properties	8051	C	562 596-5561	20694
Kdc Inc (HQ)	1731	D	714 828-7000	2630
Lakewood South Car Wash LLC	7542	E	562 430-4975	17847
Los Alamitos Medical Ctr Inc (HQ)	8062	A	714 826-6400	21720
Los Almtos Hmodialysis Ctr Inc	8092	D	562 426-6881	22633
Marinow Harry MD Facs Inc	8011	E	562 430-3561	19729
Mda US Systems LLC	8711	C	626 296-1373	25958
Mggb Inc	8711	C	714 226-0520	25963
Millie and Severson Inc	1541	D	562 493-3611	1451
Severson Group Incorporated (PA)	1542	D	562 493-3611	1664
Southland Credit Union (PA)	6062	D	562 862-6831	9690
Sure Forming Systems Inc	1771	E	562 598-6348	3340
Tenet Healthsystem Medical	8011	A	805 546-7698	20132
Thermo Power Industries	1742	D	562 799-0087	2987
Trojan Professional Svcs Inc	7375	D	714 816-7169	16265
US Bank National Association	6162	E	562 795-7520	9902
Utblo Inc	6719	C	562 493-3664	12098

LOS ALAMOS, CA - Santa Barbara County

Name	SIC	EMP	PHONE	ENTRY #
National Maintenance Inc	7349	C	805 680-6779	14365

LOS ALTOS, CA - Santa Clara County

Name	SIC	EMP	PHONE	ENTRY #
Adobe Animal Hospital Inc	0742	D	650 948-9661	611
Alain Pinel Realtors Inc	6531	D	650 941-1111	11288
American Baptist Homes of West	8059	C	650 948-8291	21138
Coldwell Banker Affiliates	6531	D	650 947-7040	11408
Covenant Care California LLC	8051	D	650 941-5255	20501
Elateral Inc	8741	D	650 917-9141	27014
Guardsmark LLC	7381	B	408 241-1493	16682
Guardsmark LLC	7381	C	800 238-5878	16687
Kisco Senior Living LLC	8741	E	650 948-7337	27101
Los Altos Golf and Country CLB	7997	D	650 947-3100	18983
Midpeninsul Rgnl Opn Sp	8999	D	650 691-1200	28148
Mw2 Consulting LLC	8742	D	408 573-6310	27555
Netcube Systems Inc	7372	D	650 862-7858	15771
Netskope Inc	7371	D	800 979-6988	15326
Older Adults Care Management (PA)	8322	D	650 329-1411	24112
Palo Alto Medical Foundation	8011	D	650 254-5200	19815
R J Dailey Construction Co	1521	D	650 948-5196	1241
Robertson Piper Management LLC	8742	C	650 625-8333	27623
State Farm Mutl Auto Insur Co	6411	D	650 694-6767	10883
The David Lcile Pckard Fndtion	8699	D	650 917-7167	25588

LOS ALTOS HILLS, CA - Santa Clara County

Name	SIC	EMP	PHONE	ENTRY #
Footh-De Anza Commun Colleg Di	4832	D	650 949-7260	5776
Idea Travel Company	4724	A	650 948-0207	4962

LOS ANGELES, CA - Los Angeles County

Name	SIC	EMP	PHONE	ENTRY #
120 South Los Angeles Street H	7011	D	213 629-1200	12357
1755 Efm 1 LLC	6531	D	323 231-4174	11267
1st Century Bancshares Inc	6022	D	310 270-9500	9467
24 Hour Fitness Usa Inc	7991	D	310 553-7600	18584
3dna Corp	7371	D	213 394-4623	14989
4g Wireless Inc	4813	D	310 429-9048	5441
4g Wireless Inc	4813	D	323 679-9991	5442
5 Design Inc	8712	D	323 308-3558	26158
550 Flower St Operations LLC	7011	C	213 892-8080	12366
711 Hope LP	7011	C	213 488-3500	12368
800 Degrees LLC	8741	E	310 443-1911	26903
834 W Arrow Highway LP	8052	D	213 355-1024	21065
901 West Olympic Blvd LP	7011	D	347 992-5707	12370
A A A Packing and Shipping Inc	4212	E	626 310-7787	3965
A Community of Friends	6513	D	213 480-0809	11079
A F Gilmore Company	6531	D	323 939-1191	11270
A Filmi Inc	7819	D	213 977-8600	18211
A M S Partnership (PA)	6552	D	310 312-6698	11944
A S E C International Inc	7374	A	803 939-4809	16087
A Touch of Kindness	8322	D	323 997-6500	23639
A World Fit For Kids	8742	C	213 387-7712	27290
A&E Television Networks LLC	4841	C	310 201-6015	5932
AA Autmtive Personnel Svcs Inc	7549	C	310 914-3012	17868
Aaaza Inc	7311	D	213 380-8333	13810
Aab Water Company Inc	4941	D	559 497-2700	6309
ABC Cable Networks Group	4832	C	323 860-5900	5746
Abilityfirst	8322	D	213 748-7309	23640
ABM Distributors Inc	7812	D	310 401-0434	18037
ABM Industries Incorporated	7349	E	323 720-4020	14201
ABM Janitorial Services Inc	6211	A	213 384-0600	9956
Abode Communities	6531	C	213 629-2702	11274
Absolute Towing-Hollenbeck Div	7549	D	323 225-9294	17869
Aca Financial Guaranty Corp	6163	D	323 255-3583	9909
Access To Loans For Learning	6163	E	310 979-4700	9910
Accor Corp	7011	C	310 278-5444	12373
Accurate Courier Services Inc	4212	D	310 481-3937	3969
Accurate Services Inc	6099	D	323 906-1000	9705
Ace Beverage Co	5181	D	323 266-6238	9036
Acetech Construction Inc	8711	E	213 637-4702	25612
Aceteck Roofing Co Inc	1761	D	323 231-6060	3136
Aci International (PA)	5139	D	310 889-3400	8419
Aclu Fndation Southern Cal LLC	8641	D	213 977-9500	25193
ACS Security Industries Inc	7382	D	310 475-9016	16859
Action Property Management Inc	8641	C	800 400-2284	25194
Added Value LLC	8742	C	323 254-4326	27302
Adee Plumbing and Heating Inc (PA)	1711	D	323 296-8787	2106
Adeste Program Company	8351	B	213 251-3551	24413
Adexa Inc (PA)	7372	C	310 642-2100	15570
Adir International LLC	4225	D	213 386-4412	4516
Adir Money Transfer Corp	7299	E	213 639-2195	13730
Adlink Cable Advertising LLC	7311	C	310 477-3994	13812
Admarketing Inc	7311	D	310 203-8400	13813
Admiralty Partners Inc	6799	D	310 471-3772	12281
Advanced Digital Services Inc (PA)	7812	D	323 962-8585	18038
Advantage Produce Inc	5148	E	213 627-2777	8693
Adventist Health System/West	8099	D	323 454-4481	22874
Aecom (PA)	8711	C	213 593-8000	25619
Aecom C&E Inc	8742	C	213 593-8000	27305
Aecom E&C Holdings Inc (DH)	8711	C	213 593-8000	25621
Aecom Global II LLC (HQ)	8711	D	213 593-8000	25626
Aecom Global II LLC	8748	C	213 996-2200	27813
Aecom Services Inc (HQ)	8712	C	213 593-8000	26160
Aecom Technical Services Inc (HQ)	4953	C	213 593-8000	6421
Aecom Usa Inc	8748	C	213 330-7200	27816
Aecom Usa Inc	8748	B	213 593-8000	27818
AEG Global Partnerships LLC	8742	E	213 763-7700	27306
AEG Live LLC (DH)	7922	C	323 930-5700	18367
AEG Management Lacc LLC	8741	C	213 741-1151	26912
Aegis Film Group Inc	7822	D	323 848-7977	18269
Aero-Engines Inc	7699	D	323 663-3961	17957
Aerotransporte De Cargne Union	4512	B	310 649-0069	4778
Aesthetic Maintenance Corp	7349	E	213 353-1525	14216
African American Unity Center	8322	D	323 789-7300	23645
AG Facilities Operations LLC	8059	A	323 651-1808	21126
Agencycom LLC (HQ)	7372	D	415 817-3800	15573
Aids Healthcare Foundation	8011	B	323 662-0492	19327
Aids Project Los Angeles (PA)	8322	D	213 201-1600	23647
Air Lease Corporation (PA)	7359	D	310 553-0555	14508
Aircraft Service Intl Inc	7349	D	310 646-2990	14217
Airgas USA LLC	5169	D	323 568-2244	8975
Airport Century Inn	7011	D	310 649-4000	12376
Airpush Inc	7311	C	877 944-2490	13815
Ajit Healthcare Inc	8741	D	213 484-0510	26914
Akin Gump Strauss	8111	D	310 229-1000	23083
Alameda Produce Market LLC	6531	D	213 221-3400	11290
Alaska Airlines Inc	4512	C	310 342-4401	4782
Alaska Experiment Inc	1731	E	323 904-4680	2512
Alexandria Care Center LLC	8059	C	323 660-1800	21131
All Area Plumbing Inc	1711	C	323 939-9990	2119
Allaquaria LLC	5199	D	310 645-1107	9243
Alldayeveryday Productions LLC	7812	E	323 556-6200	18039

GEOGRAPHIC SECTION

LOS ANGELES, CA

Company	SIC	EMP	PHONE	ENTRY #
Allen Matkins Leck Gmble (PA)	8111	C	213 622-5555	23088
Alliance Ground Intl LLC	4581	D	310 646-2446	4898
Alliancebernstein LP	6282	D	310 286-6000	10111
Allied Protection Services Inc	7381	D	310 330-8314	16541
Allied Refrigeration Inc	5075	D	310 202-2220	7734
Alliedbarton Security Svcs LLC	7381	B	800 418-6423	16550
Allstate Construction Co	1521	D	310 652-6942	1123
Alpha Entrprneur Hlth Fndation	8062	C	323 735-0873	21444
Alsco Inc	7213	C	323 465-5111	13511
Alston & Bird LLP	8111	C	213 626-8830	23089
Alta Healthcare System LLC (HQ)	8399	C	323 267-0477	24863
Alta Hospitals System LLC	8062	C	323 267-0477	21445
Alta Hospitals System LLC (HQ)	8062	C	310 943-4500	21446
Alta Los Angeles Hospitals Inc	8062	C	323 267-0477	21447
Altamed Health Services Corp	8011	D	323 980-4466	19334
Altamed Health Services Corp	8011	D	323 869-5448	19336
Altegra Health	8742	D	310 776-4001	27315
Altoon Partners LLP (PA)	8712	E	213 225-1900	26162
Altour International Inc	4724	C	310 571-6000	4953
Altour International Inc (PA)	4724	C	310 571-6000	4954
Alzheimers Greater Los Angeles	8322	C	323 938-3379	23655
Amada Enterprises Inc	8051	C	323 757-1881	20377
Amanecer Cmnty Counseling Svc	8093	C	213 481-7464	22656
Amcap Fund Inc	6722	B	213 486-9200	12101
American Airlines Inc	4512	C	310 215-7054	4789
American Airlines Inc	4729	C	213 535-6045	5005
American Airlines Inc	4581	B	310 646-0093	4900
American Airlines Inc	4512	C	310 646-3013	4792
American Care Givers Westwood	8322	C	310 208-8005	23656
American Contrs Indemnity Co (HQ)	6399	C	213 330-1309	10565
American Funds Distrs Inc (DH)	6722	C	213 486-9200	12102
American Golf Corporation (PA)	7997	C	310 664-4000	18854
American Golf Corporation	7997	C	310 476-2411	18862
American Heart Association Inc	8399	E	213 291-7000	24868
American Home Assurance Co	6331	B	213 689-3500	10399
American Homeowners & Renters	6531	E	310 913-9263	11296
American Intl Group Inc	6411	B	213 689-3500	10596
American Multi-Cinema Inc	7832	C	310 228-5500	18304
American Mutual Fund Inc	6722	C	213 486-9200	12103
American Professional Security	7381	E	213 487-2100	16558
American Red Cross	8322	C	310 445-9900	23661
American Red Cross La Chapter (PA)	8399	C	310 445-9900	24869
American Reprographics Co LLC	7334	D	213 745-3145	14100
American Textile Maint Co	7213	E	213 749-4433	13520
American Textile Maint Co	7213	C	323 735-1661	13522
Americantours Intl LLC (HQ)	4725	C	310 641-9953	4985
Amgreen Solar and Electrics	1711	E	213 388-5647	2141
Amgreen Solutions Inc	8742	E	213 388-5647	27320
AMS - Exotic LLC	5148	D	213 612-5888	8694
Analytic US Market Neutral Off	6211	D	213 688-3015	9958
Andersen Tax LLC	7291	D	213 593-2300	13719
Anderson Kayne Inv MGT Inc (PA)	8742	D	310 556-2721	27323
Anderson McPharlin Conners LLP (PA)	8111	D	213 688-0080	23092
Angel Care Home Health Inc	8082	E	818 248-8811	22362
Angeles Home Health Care Inc	8082	C	213 487-5131	22363
Angelus Western Ppr Fibers Inc	5093	D	213 623-9221	8062
Annenberg Foundation (PA)	8641	D	310 209-4560	25198
Anschutz Entrmt Group Inc (HQ)	7929	D	213 763-7700	18450
Anschutz Film Group	1742	A	310 887-1000	2858
Ant Farm LLC	7819	C	323 850-0700	18214
AON Consulting Inc	6411	D	818 506-4300	10606
AON Consulting Inc	6411	D	213 630-2900	10608
Apla Health & Wellness	8011	D	213 201-1546	19354
App Wholesale LLC	5149	B	323 980-8315	8796
Apumac LLC	5065	C	888 248-7775	7521
Aramark Facility Services LLC	7349	C	213 740-8968	14232
Aramark Services Inc	7219	C	323 587-7661	13650
Aramark Spt & Entrmt Group LLC	7929	C	213 740-1224	18452
Aramark Unf & Career AP LLC	7218	C	323 266-0555	13605
ARC Mid-Cities Inc	8331	C	310 329-9272	24305
Arclight Cinema Company	7832	C	323 464-1465	18309
Arden Realty Inc (DH)	6512	D	310 966-2600	10960
Arent Fox LLP	8111	C	213 629-7400	23094
Ares Management LP (PA)	6282	D	310 201-4100	10118
Ares Management LLC (HQ)	6799	D	310 201-4100	12283
Ares Management LLC	8741	C	310 201-4100	26925
Aris Vision Ins of C A A Medcl	8011	C	310 914-0150	19355
Armand Hammer Museum	8412	C	310 443-7000	25002
Armanino LLP	8721	C	310 478-4148	26290
Armenian Amrcn Thea Msical Soc	7922	D	323 668-1030	18370
Arnies Supplies Service Ltd	7699	D	323 263-1696	17962
Aroma Spa & Sports LLC	7999	D	213 387-2111	19142
Arthrtis Fundation PCF Reg Inc	8641	E	323 954-5760	25199
Artwear Inc	5136	E	310 217-1393	8333
Arup North America Limited	8711	C	310 578-4182	25668
Arya Group Inc	1521	E	310 446-7000	1130
Arya Ice Cream Distrg Co Inc	5143	D	323 234-2994	8577
Asbestos Instant Response Inc	1799	D	323 733-0508	3495
Ascension Insurance Inc	6411	C	800 537-1777	10629
Asia Pacific Capital	6726	D	213 628-8800	12133
Asian PCF Hlth Care Ventr Inc (PA)	8399	C	323 644-3880	24873
Asian Rehabilitation Svc Inc (PA)	8331	D	213 743-9242	24307
Asian Rehabilitation Svc Inc	8331	D	213 680-3790	24308
Asiana Airlines Inc	4512	C	213 365-2000	4795
Assist 65 Plus	7389	E	323 557-4426	17004
Associated Entrmt Releasing (PA)	7812	E	323 934-7044	18045
Associated Press	7383	D	213 626-1200	16944
Associated Students UCLA (PA)	8399	B	310 825-4321	24877
Associated Students UCLA	8399	C	310 794-0242	24878
Associated Students UCLA	8011	A	310 825-9451	19362
AT&T Corp	4812	D	310 473-3649	5258
AT&T Corp	4813	D	213 787-0055	5487
AT&T Corp	4812	D	310 659-7600	5274
AT&T Corp	4813	D	213 787-0055	5511
AT&T Services Inc	4813	A	213 975-4089	5538
AT&T Services Inc	4813	D	213 741-3111	5546
AT&T Services Inc	4813	B	323 468-6813	5558
Authority Tax Services LLC	7389	D	213 486-5135	17010
Authorized Taxi Cab	7382	D	323 776-5324	16869
Auto Club Enterprises	6321	B	310 914-8500	10236
Automobile Club Southern Cal (PA)	6411	C	213 741-3686	10635
Autry Museum of American West	8412	C	323 667-2000	25004
Avanti Hospitals LLC	7389	A	323 268-5514	17015
Avida Caregivers Inc	8082	C	323 498-1500	22373
Axa Advisors LLC	6282	D	213 251-1600	10120
B F Management	6531	C	323 931-7776	11312
Bachelor Productions Inc	7812	D	310 567-9249	18050
Bain & Company Inc	8742	D	310 229-3000	27337
Baker Keener & Nahra	8111	E	213 241-0900	23097
Baker & Hostetler LLP	8111	D	310 820-8800	23098
Ballard Spahr LLP	8111	D	424 204-4400	23102
Bamko Inc	7312	C	310 470-5859	13950
Bamko LLC	7389	C	310 470-5859	17021
Banamex USA (DH)	6022	C	310 203-3400	9468
Banamex USA	6022	C	800 222-1234	9469
Banamex USA Bancorp (DH)	6712	C	310 203-3400	12039
Banc California National Assn	6022	E	310 286-0710	9470
Bank America National Assn	6021	C	310 384-4562	9328
Bank Leumi USA	6021	C	323 966-4700	9335
Bank of Hope (HQ)	6021	C	213 639-1700	9336
Bank of Tky-Mitsubishi Ufj Ltd	6029	C	213 488-3700	9544
Barclays Capital Inc	6211	C	310 481-4100	9964
Barlow Group (PA)	8069	D	213 250-4200	22115
Barlow Respiratory Hospital (PA)	8069	D	213 250-4200	22116
Barnes & Thornburg LLP	8111	C	310 284-3880	23106
Bbcn Bank	6022	E	213 389-5550	9477
Behringer Harvard Wilshire	7011	D	310 475-8711	12431
Behringer Harvard Wilshire Blv	7011	D	310 475-8711	12432
Beitler & Associates Inc (PA)	6531	E	310 820-2955	11318
Bel-Air Country Club	7997	C	310 472-9563	18888
Belmont Village LP	6513	C	323 874-7711	11097
Beres Consulting	8611	D	310 476-9941	25076
Berg Lacquer Co (PA)	5198	D	323 261-8114	9237
Bergelectric Corp (PA)	1731	C	310 337-1377	2530
Berkeley Research Group LLC	8732	D	310 499-4750	26646
Bestway Recycling Company Inc (PA)	5093	D	323 588-8157	8065
Bet Tzedek	8111	D	323 939-0506	23114
Better Life Produce Inc	5148	E	213 623-0640	8696
Beverly Blvd Leaseco LLC	7011	D	310 278-5444	12445
Beverly Hills Country Club	6552	C	310 836-4400	11949
Beverly Hills Luxury Hotel LLC	7011	B	310 274-9999	12446
Beverly Sunstone Hills LLC	7011	D	310 228-4100	12447
Beverly West Health Care Inc	8051	D	323 938-2451	20412
Beverlywood Realty Inc	6531	E	310 836-8322	11322
Biomat Usa Inc	8099	A	310 772-7777	22894
Biomat Usa Inc (DH)	8099	E	323 225-2221	22895
Bird Mrlla Bxer Wlpert A Prof	8111	D	310 201-2100	23115
Birth Family Services Inc	8322	E	310 323-8181	23686
Blackstone Consulting Inc (PA)	8742	C	310 826-4389	27348
Blair Television Inc	7812	D	714 537-5923	18051
Blakely Skloff Tylor Zfman LLP (PA)	8111	D	310 207-3800	23117
Blank Rome LLP	8111	D	424 239-3400	23119
Blank Rome LLP	8111	D	650 690-9500	23120
Blank Rome LLP	8111	E	310 772-8300	23121
Bloom David Law Offices of	8111	D	323 988-5785	23122
Bls Lmsine Svc Los Angeles Inc (PA)	4119	C	323 644-7166	3775
BLT & Associates Inc	7336	C	323 860-4000	14134
Blue Cross & Blue Shield Mich	6324	C	323 782-3046	10259
Blue Planet International Inc	5137	E	213 742-9999	8370
Blx Group LLC	6282	D	213 612-2400	10123

Employment Codes: A=Over 500 employees, B=251-500, C=101-250, D=51-100, E=45-50

2017 Directory of California Wholesalers and Services Companies

© Mergent Inc. 1-800-342-5647

1683

LOS ANGELES, CA — GEOGRAPHIC SECTION

Company	SIC	EMP	PHONE	ENTRY #
Bonne Bridge Muell Okeef & (PA)	8111	D	213 480-1900	23125
Bonneville International Corp	4832	E	323 634-1800	5750
Bonnie Brae Cnvlscent Hosp Inc (PA)	8059	D	213 483-8144	21158
Booz Allen Hamilton Inc	8742	D	310 297-2100	27352
Booz Allen Hamilton Inc	8742	D	213 620-1900	27354
Borg Produce Inc	0723	C	213 305-6621	514
Boy Scouts of America (PA)	8641	D	213 353-9879	25210
Bradford Building Services	7349	E	323 720-4020	14239
Braille Institute America Inc (PA)	8322	C	323 663-1111	23692
Breitburn Energy Partners I LP	1311	D	213 225-5900	1033
Breitburn GP LLC	1311	A	213 225-5900	1034
Brentwood Bmdical RES Inst Inc	8733	C	310 312-1554	26739
Brentwood Country Club	7997	C	310 451-8011	18900
Brier Oak On Sunset LLC	8059	D	323 663-3951	21163
Brinks Incorporated	7381	C	818 503-8630	16582
Brinks Incorporated	7381	E	323 262-2646	16586
Brisam Lax (de) LLC	7011	D	310 649-5151	12467
Broad Beach Films Inc	7336	C	323 468-5120	14135
Broadreach Capitl Partners LLC	6799	A	310 691-5760	12286
Broadview Inc	8051	E	323 221-9174	20421
Brookfield Dtla Fund Office	6798	D	213 626-3300	12239
Browning Apartments	6513	E	213 252-8847	11104
Buchalter Nemer A Prof Corp (PA)	8111	D	213 891-0700	23136
Buck Consultants LLC	8999	D	310 282-8232	28119
Buckingham Affrdbl Aprtmnts LP	8741	D	424 273-6162	26948
Buena Ventura Care Center Inc (PA)	8051	D	323 268-0106	20424
Bungalow 16 Entertainment LLC	5094	E	310 226-7870	8096
Bunker Hill Club Inc	8641	D	213 620-9662	25224
Burke Williams & Sorensen LLP (PA)	8111	D	213 236-0600	23138
Burlington Convalescent Hosp (PA)	8051	D	213 381-5585	20426
Burlington Convalescent Hosp	8059	D	323 295-7737	21170
Burton-Way House Ltd A CA	7011	D	310 273-2222	12474
Burton-Way House Ltd A CA (PA)	7011	D	310 552-6623	12475
BV General Inc	8059	D	323 651-0043	21171
C M I Management Inc	6513	C	323 465-8044	11105
C P Document Technologies LLC (PA)	5065	D	213 617-4040	7540
C-Air International Inc	4731	C	310 695-3400	5038
CA Safety Compliance Corp	8748	D	213 747-0805	27860
Caffeine Productions	7812	D	323 860-8111	18058
Cal Southern Assn Governments (PA)	8748	C	213 236-1800	27861
California Assn Realtors Inc (PA)	8611	C	213 739-8200	25079
California Club	8641	D	213 622-1391	25225
California Cmnty Foundation (PA)	6732	D	213 413-4130	12155
California Cryobank Inc (PA)	8099	D	310 443-5244	22905
California Endowment (PA)	8399	D	800 449-4149	24882
California Fair Plan Assn	6411	D	213 487-0111	10657
California Mart LLC	6512	D	213 630-3600	10965
California Omicron Chapter	7041	D	310 979-3857	13489
California Rain Company Inc	5137	D	213 624-1771	8372
California State Univ Aux Svcs	8741	A	323 343-2531	26954
California Suncare Inc	5122	D	310 578-4400	8241
California Transit Inc	4111	D	323 234-8750	3637
California United Bank (HQ)	6022	D	213 430-7000	9478
Califrnia Fmly Hlth Cuncil Inc (PA)	8399	D	213 386-5614	24884
Califrnia Hosp Med Ctr Fndtion	8062	A	213 748-2411	21470
Califrnia Scnce Ctr Foundation	8412	B	213 744-2545	25005
Call To Action LLC	6799	D	310 996-7200	12290
Callisonrtkl Inc	8712	C	213 627-7373	26170
Callisonrtkl Inc	8712	D	213 633-6000	26171
Cannon Design Inc	8712	D	310 229-2700	26172
Canon Solutions America Inc	5044	E	213 629-6733	7044
Canon USA Inc	5044	C	323 461-1862	7048
Canon USA Inc	5044	D	213 629-6700	7049
Canton Food Co Inc	5141	D	213 688-7707	8462
Canyon Partners Incorporated (PA)	6211	D	310 272-1000	9968
Cap-Mpt (PA)	6351	C	213 473-8600	10490
Capital Brands LLC	5149	D	310 996-7200	8813
Capital Group Companies Inc	6282	B	310 996-6238	10127
Capital Group Companies Inc (PA)	6282	A	213 486-9200	10128
Capital Guardian Trust Company (HQ)	6733	D	213 486-9200	12169
Capital Research and MGT Co (HQ)	6282	B	213 486-9200	10131
Capnet Financial Services Inc (PA)	6159	D	818 859-8377	9797
Captain Marketing Inc	8742	D	310 402-9709	27369
Cara Communications Corp	7812	E	310 442-5600	18059
Career Group Inc (PA)	7361	D	310 277-8188	14622
Carleton Booker Marketing Inc	8742	D	925 752-1973	27371
Carmichael International Svc (DH)	4731	D	213 353-0800	5040
Carpenters Southwest ADM Corp (PA)	7011	D	213 386-8590	12494
Caruso MGT Ltd A Cal Ltd Prtnr	6531	D	323 900-8100	11344
Casa Dscanso Convalescent Hosp	8744	D	323 225-5991	27777
Catapult Marketing	8742	E	203 682-4000	27374
Cathay Bank	6022	D	213 896-0098	9480
Cathedral Center of St Paul	8699	D	213 482-2040	25514
Catholic Charities of La Inc (PA)	8733	D	213 251-3400	26748
Catholic Charities of La Inc	8322	D	213 251-3400	23711
CB Richard Ellis RE Svcs LLC	6531	D	213 613-3333	11348
CB Richard Ellis Strategic Par	6799	D	213 614-6862	12294
CB Richard Ellis Strtgc Prtnrs	6512	D	213 683-4200	10967
Cbest Inc	8069	D	310 445-2378	22120
Cbre Inc (HQ)	6726	C	310 477-5876	12136
Cbre Inc	6531	D	310 550-2500	11356
Cbre Global Investors LLC (DH)	8742	D	213 683-4200	27375
Cbre Group Inc (PA)	6531	D	213 613-3333	11359
Cbre Services Inc	6531	D	213 613-3333	11360
CBS Broadcasting Inc	4833	D	310 577-3457	5840
CBS Broadcasting Inc	6153	D	310 284-6835	9777
CBS Broadcasting Inc	8711	D	212 975-3240	25724
CBS Corporation	4833	D	323 575-2345	5842
CBS Radio Inc	4832	D	323 525-0980	5760
CBS Radio Inc	4832	D	323 930-1067	5762
CBS Radio Inc	4832	C	323 930-7580	5763
CBS Studios Inc (DH)	7812	B	323 634-3519	18060
CBS Television City	4833	D	323 651-0255	5844
Cdsnet LLC	8748	D	310 981-9500	27872
Cecico Inc	5137	D	323 269-7000	8373
Cecil Hotel Company LLC	7011	D	213 213-7829	12505
Cedars-Sinai Medical Center	8011	C	310 423-3849	19413
Cedars-Sinai Medical Center	8011	A	323 866-8483	19414
Cellco Partnership	4812	C	213 380-2299	5342
Cellco Partnership	4812	D	310 659-0775	5353
Cellco Partnership	4812	D	213 738-9771	5356
Cellular Palace Inc	5065	D	310 278-2007	7545
Cels Enterprises Inc (PA)	5139	D	310 838-0280	8423
Center Thtre Group Los Angeles (PA)	7922	C	213 972-7344	18380
Centurion Security Inc	7381	C	818 755-0202	16593
Century 21 Beverlywood Realty	6531	D	310 836-8321	11369
Century City Primary Care	8011	E	310 553-3189	19423
Century Plaza Garage	7521	C	310 226-7495	17715
Century Properties Owners Assn	6531	E	310 272-8580	11383
Cha Hollywood Medical Ctr LP (PA)	8062	C	213 413-3000	21479
Charles Dunn Co Inc	6531	C	213 481-1800	11385
Charles Dunn RE Svcs Inc (PA)	6531	D	213 270-6200	11386
Chase Care Center Inc	8059	D	323 935-8490	21185
Checkfree Corporation	7373	D	310 954-5600	15920
Chicago Title Company	6361	D	213 488-4375	10502
Childrens Bureau Southern Cal (PA)	8361	C	213 342-0100	24594
Childrens Hospital Los (PA)	8011	C	323 361-2336	19432
Childrens Hospital Los Angeles	8069	C	323 361-2153	22123
Childrens Hospital Los Angeles (PA)	8069	D	323 660-2450	22124
Childrens Hospital Los Angeles	8011	B	323 361-2119	19433
Childrens Hospital Los Angeles	8062	D	323 660-2450	21484
Childrens Hospital Los Angeles	8069	D	323 361-5702	22126
Childrens Inst Los Angeles	8322	A	213 383-2765	23741
Childrens Inst Los Angeles (PA)	8733	D	213 385-5100	26753
Childrens Institute Inc (PA)	8322	D	213 385-5100	23742
China Airlines Ltd (HQ)	4512	C	310 646-4233	4796
Chinese Laundry Inc	5139	E	310 945-3299	8425
Chiquita Brands Intl Inc	5148	D	213 488-0925	8706
Chodorow De Castro West	8111	D	310 478-2541	23149
Christmas Bonus Fund of The PI	6733	D	213 385-6161	12171
Chrome River Technologies Inc	7371	C	323 857-5800	15082
Chsp Trs Los Angeles LLC	7011	D	213 624-0000	12518
Churchill MGT Group Corp	6282	E	877 937-7110	10133
Churchill PCF Asset MGT LLC	6722	C	213 489-3810	12110
Cim Group Inc (PA)	6531	D	323 860-4900	11391
Cinelease Inc (HQ)	7819	C	855 441-5500	18218
Cinnabar	7336	C	818 842-8190	14137
Cinnabar California Inc	7336	D	818 842-8190	14138
CIT Bank NA	6021	D	310 477-0546	9342
CIT Bank National Association	6021	D	310 475-4594	9352
CIT Bank National Association	6021	D	310 826-2741	9356
CIT Bank National Association	6021	D	310 820-9650	9369
Citadel Broadcasting Corp	4832	D	310 840-4900	5764
Citadel Group Solutions LLC	7373	D	213 649-7500	15921
Citigroup Global Markets Inc	6211	C	213 486-8811	9973
Citigroup Inc	6021	D	818 638-5714	9380
City Charter School	4142	D	310 273-2489	3898
City National Bank (DH)	6021	B	310 888-6000	9385
City National SEC Svcs Inc	7381	D	310 641-6666	16598
City of Los Angeles	8711	A	213 978-0259	25740
City of Los Angeles	8111	C	213 978-4049	23154
City of Los Angeles	8412	D	213 473-0800	25011
City of Los Angeles	8712	D	213 485-4282	26178
City of Los Angeles	8699	D	213 202-5500	25518
City of Los Angeles	7349	D	213 847-2799	14247
City of Los Angeles	8111	A	213 978-8100	23155
City of Los Angeles	7032	E	323 467-7193	13462
City of Los Angeles	8322	D	310 204-6707	23754
City of Los Angeles	6371	D	213 978-4551	10548
CJ America Inc (HQ)	5169	C	213 738-1400	8983

GEOGRAPHIC SECTION — LOS ANGELES, CA

Company	SIC	EMP	PHONE	ENTRY #
Classic Protection Inc	7381	E	213 742-1238	16600
Clinic Inc (PA)	8093	D	323 730-1920	22687
Clinica Msr Oscar A Romero (PA)	8011	E	213 989-7700	19442
Clinica Popular Medical Group	8011	E	213 381-7175	19443
Club Assist North America Inc (PA)	6719	D	213 388-4333	12052
Club Assist US LLC	5013	C	213 388-4333	6721
Cmts LLC	8741	C	310 215-0237	26974
Cnc Worldwide Inc	4512	D	310 670-1222	4797
Cnn America Inc	4841	D	323 993-5000	5943
Coast Citrus Distributors	5148	C	213 955-3444	8708
Coast Produce Company (PA)	5148	C	213 955-4900	8710
Cohen Brown MGT Group Inc (PA)	8742	D	310 966-1001	27385
Cohnreznick LLP	8721	E	310 477-3722	26313
Colliers International Greater (HQ)	6531	D	213 627-1214	11444
Collins Avenue LLC	4833	E	323 930-6633	5847
Colony Management Inc	6531	D	310 282-8820	11449
Comcast Cble Cmmunications LLC	4841	E	310 216-3500	5946
Comcast Cble Cmmunications LLC	4841	C	310 216-3686	5949
Comcast Corporation	4841	D	323 993-8000	5971
Command Security Corporation	7381	A	310 981-4530	16604
Commercial Coating Company Inc	1611	D	323 256-1331	1752
Commercial Property Management (PA)	6513	D	213 739-2000	11117
Commodity Forwarders Inc (PA)	4731	D	310 348-8855	5050
Community Care Health Centers	8011	E	323 980-4000	19451
Community Partners	8322	C	323 780-7605	23776
Community Partners (PA)	8399	D	213 346-3200	24900
Community Recovery	8099	E	323 525-0961	22923
Concession Management Svcs Inc	7999	C	310 846-5830	19186
Concord Document Services Inc (PA)	7334	D	213 745-3175	14116
Connexity Inc (HQ)	4813	C	310 571-1235	5581
Constellation Newenergy Inc	4911	D	213 576-6001	6119
Coopertive Amrcn Physcians Inc (PA)	8621	D	213 473-8600	25131
Cordoba Corporation	7373	D	213 895-0224	15925
Cornerstone Research Inc	8732	D	213 553-2500	26652
Corp of Church of Christ Ld St	7641	C	323 268-7281	17951
Corporate Building Svcs Inc	7349	C	213 252-0999	14264
Country Villa East LP	8059	C	323 939-3184	21194
Country Villa Imperial LLC	8051	D	323 666-1544	20476
Country Villa Service Corp	8741	C	323 666-1544	26985
Country Villa Service Corp	8741	C	323 734-1101	26989
Country Villa Service Corp	8741	C	310 574-3733	26990
Country Villa Service Corp	8741	C	323 734-9122	26991
Country Villa Terrace (PA)	8059	D	323 653-3980	21195
Country Villa Terrace	8059	E	323 939-3184	21196
County of Los Angeles	8099	D	213 739-2360	22927
County of Los Angeles	7375	A	213 974-1102	16226
County of Los Angeles	8069	A	213 974-7284	22132
County of Los Angeles	8062	C	310 668-4545	21518
County of Los Angeles	8082	C	323 780-2373	22418
County of Los Angeles	8361	D	323 226-8611	24610
County of Los Angeles	8011	B	323 226-6221	19468
County of Los Angeles	8093	C	323 846-4122	22700
County of Los Angeles	8011	B	213 744-3677	19469
County of Los Angeles	8322	C	818 374-2161	23832
County of Los Angeles	8111	C	323 226-8998	23172
County of Los Angeles	7336	A	213 922-6210	14140
County of Los Angeles	8322	C	213 744-5730	23833
County of Los Angeles	8099	D	213 744-3922	22931
County of Los Angeles	8322	B	323 586-7263	23834
County of Los Angeles	8093	D	323 769-7800	22701
County of Los Angeles	8322	C	213 351-8739	23835
County of Los Angeles	8322	C	323 226-8511	23836
County of Los Angeles	8069	A	323 226-3468	22133
County of Los Angeles	8322	D	213 351-5600	23837
County of Los Angeles	8322	C	213 974-9331	23839
County of Los Angeles	8621	A	213 240-8412	25133
County of Los Angeles	8062	C	323 226-6021	21519
County of Los Angeles	8099	D	213 351-7800	22932
County of Los Angeles	8322	B	213 744-5601	23841
County of Los Angeles	8322	C	323 727-1639	23842
County of Los Angeles	8412	D	323 857-6000	25017
County of Los Angeles	8099	D	213 240-7780	22934
County of Los Angeles	8011	C	323 730-3502	19471
County of Los Angeles	8111	C	213 974-2811	23175
County of Los Angeles	8322	D	323 780-2185	23850
County of Los Angeles	8322	A	213 351-7257	23852
County of Los Angeles	8322	C	323 586-6469	23853
County of Los Angeles	1611	C	626 458-1700	1758
County of Los Angeles	7389	C	323 267-2771	17098
County of Los Angeles	8062	B	213 473-6100	21520
County of Los Angeles	4789	C	213 974-4561	5216
County of Los Angeles	8011	C	323 226-6056	19475
County of Los Angeles	4941	C	213 974-8301	6337
Covenant House California	8361	C	323 461-3131	24616
Covington & Burling LLP	8111	B	424 332-4800	23187
Cox Castle & Nicholson LLP (PA)	8111	C	310 284-2200	23188
CP Opco LLC	7359	C	310 966-4900	14532
Creative Artists Agency LLC (PA)	7922	A	424 288-2000	18386
Creative Channel Services LLC (HQ)	8742	D	310 482-6500	27395
Creative Circle LLC (DH)	7361	C	323 634-0156	14631
Credit Ssse Securities USA LLC	6211	D	213 253-2600	9988
Cremation Spclists Los Angeles	7261	D	323 469-9933	13703
Crenshaw YMCA	8641	D	323 290-9113	25245
Crestline Hotels & Resorts Inc (DH)	7011	C	213 629-1200	12553
Crestline Hotels & Resorts LLC	8741	D	213 624-0000	26997
Crew Creative Advertising LLC	7311	C	310 451-3225	13828
Crime Impact Security Patrol	7381	C	323 296-6406	16616
Crispy Sewing Inc	7389	D	323 262-9639	17106
Crown Building Maintenance Co	7349	E	213 765-7800	14277
Crown Energy Services Inc	7349	A	213 765-7800	14278
Crown Transportation Inc	4119	D	310 737-0888	3784
Crowne Plaza Lax LLC	7011	C	310 258-1321	12556
Crystal Cruises LLC (DH)	4481	C	310 785-9300	4724
Crystal Stairs Inc (PA)	8322	B	323 299-8998	23938
Crystal Valet Parking Inc	7299	D	323 663-7275	13753
Culinary Services America Inc	7363	E	323 965-7582	14868
Culver City Roofing Company	1761	D	323 930-1311	3157
Culver West Health Center LLC	8059	D	310 390-9506	21202
Curatel LLC	4813	B	213 427-7411	5585
Custom Hotel LLC	7011	D	310 645-0400	12558
D Bailey Management Comp	8741	B	213 626-2665	27001
D L Ryan Companies LLC	8743	C	310 442-0400	27744
D3publisher of America Inc	7372	D	310 268-0820	15636
DA Davidson & Co	6211	B	213 620-1850	9991
Dailey & Associates	7311	D	310 360-3100	13830
Daily Journal Corporation	7313	E	213 229-5500	13963
DAndrea Graphic Corportion	7336	D	310 642-0260	14142
Daniel J Edelman Inc	8743	D	323 857-9100	27746
Daniel J Edelman Inc	7313	C	323 857-9100	13966
Danning Gill Damnd Kollitz LLP	8111	D	310 277-0077	23196
Daqri LLC (PA)	7371	D	213 375-8830	15119
Davalan Sales Inc	5148	C	213 623-2500	8712
David E Bland	8111	D	310 552-0130	23198
David Evans Enterprises Inc	8711	A	213 337-3680	25764
Davie Brown Entertainment Inc	7922	D	310 979-1980	18387
Davis Wright Tremaine LLP	8111	D	213 633-6800	23200
Daviselen Advertising Inc (PA)	7311	C	213 688-7000	13832
DDB Worldwide	7311	C	310 907-1500	13834
Dechert LLP	8111	D	213 489-1357	23202
Decron Properties Corp	6531	D	310 363-4887	11467
Decurion Corporation (PA)	7832	D	310 659-9432	18319
Defined Contribution Trust Fun	6733	D	213 385-6161	12172
Deloitte & Touche LLP	8721	A	213 688-0800	26320
Deloitte & Touche LLP	8721	C	213 688-0800	26327
Deloitte Consulting LLP	8748	C	212 489-1600	27896
Delta Air Lines Inc	4731	D	310 646-9614	5055
Delta Air Lines Inc	4512	D	323 417-7374	4798
Delta Floral Distributors Inc	5193	C	323 751-8116	9187
Deluxe Digital Dist Inc	7819	E	818 260-6202	18221
Deluxe Media Services LLC	7812	A	323 462-6171	18070
Dentons US LLP	8111	C	213 623-9300	23210
Dentons US LLP	8111	D	213 688-1000	23211
Dependable Highway Express Inc (PA)	4213	B	323 526-2200	4136
Design Collection Inc	5131	D	323 277-9200	8311
Desmond Mail Delivery Service	4212	D	323 262-1085	4008
Destination Shuttle Svcs LLC	4111	C	310 338-9466	3641
Destinationrx Inc (HQ)	7371	D	800 379-9060	15132
Deutsch La Inc	7311	D	310 862-3000	13837
Deutsche Bank National Tr Co (DH)	6111	D	213 620-8200	9727
Deutsche Bank Tr Co Americas	6021	D	213 620-8200	9395
Dfusion Software Inc	7371	E	323 617-5577	15135
Dianas Mexican Food Pdts Inc	7231	C	323 758-4845	13672
Diba Fashions Inc	7389	D	323 232-3775	17123
Digital Domain 3.0 Inc (PA)	7812	B	310 314-2800	18071
Dignity Health	8062	B	213 484-7111	21532
Dignity Health	8062	A	213 748-2411	21539
Direct Partners Inc (HQ)	7311	D	310 482-4200	13840
Directors Guild America Inc (PA)	7819	C	310 289-2000	18223
Discovery Communications Inc	4899	B	310 975-5906	6071
Diversified RE Packaging Corp	8748	D	310 855-1946	27899
Diversified Transportation LLC	4111	D	310 981-9500	3642
Dla Piper LLP (us)	8111	B	213 330-7700	23218
Dla Piper LLP (us)	8111	C	310 595-3000	23220
Docler Media LLC (DH)	7374	D	424 777-3999	16122
Document Technologies LLC	7389	D	213 892-9000	17131
Doma Laszlo	4215	D	323 478-1313	4397
Domestic Linen Supply Co Inc (HQ)	7213	E	213 749-6300	13547
Donald T Sterling Corporation	7011	D	310 275-5575	12587
Double G Productions Ltd	7929	D	310 479-0978	18463
Doubleline Capital LP	7389	C	213 633-8200	17133

Employment Codes: A=Over 500 employees, B=251-500, C=101-250, D=51-100, E=45-50

LOS ANGELES, CA — GEOGRAPHIC SECTION

Company	SIC	EMP	PHONE	ENTRY #
Doubletwist Inc	7371	C	510 628-0100	15147
Drew Child Dev Corp Inc (PA)	8322	D	323 249-2950	23948
Drinker Biddle & Reath LLP	8111	C	310 229-1282	23227
Drinks Holdings LLC (PA)	5182	D	310 441-8400	9097
Drive Thru Technology Inc	7382	C	323 576-1400	16881
Dsd Trucking Inc (PA)	4581	D	310 338-1210	4914
Dti Services Inc (PA)	7379	D	213 670-1100	16358
Dtt Surveillance Holdings Inc	7382	D	323 576-1400	16882
Dual Diagnosis Trtmnt Ctr Inc	8071	C	424 289-9031	22211
Duff & Phelps LLC	8742	D	213 270-2300	27417
Dya Assoc	6552	D	323 364-4270	11963
Dykema Gossett PLLC	8111	D	213 457-1800	23231
E & C Fashion Inc	7389	B	323 262-0099	17138
E H Summit Inc (PA)	7011	D	310 476-6571	12604
E L Payne Heating Company	1711	E	310 275-5331	2212
E-Times Corporation Ltd	7375	B	213 452-6720	16230
Ea Mobile Inc	4812	B	310 754-7125	5396
Earle M Jorgensen Company	5051	A	323 567-1122	7369
Earth Technology Corp USA	4953	A	213 593-8000	6474
Earthbound Productions LLC	7812	D	504 734-3337	18081
East Los Angeles Doctors	8062	B	323 268-5514	21548
East Los Angeles Employment	7361	E	323 838-5710	14642
Eastside Group Corporation	7381	C	213 368-9777	16631
Ebisu Marketing Corp	8742	D	213 674-2330	27419
Ebm Inc	7349	D	213 365-4905	14286
EC Group Inc (PA)	5021	D	310 815-2700	6814
Economic Dev Corp of La County	8748	E	213 622-4300	27907
Edgemine Inc	5137	C	323 267-8222	8380
Edmonds Record Group	7929	E	323 860-1520	18465
Efilm LLC	7812	C	323 463-7041	18082
Eharmony Inc (PA)	7991	C	424 258-1199	18628
El Al Israel Airlines Ltd	4729	C	323 852-1252	5008
El Pas-Los Angeles Lmsne Ex Inc	4142	E	213 623-2323	3901
Eladh LP	8062	D	323 268-5514	21554
Elite Information Group Inc (DH)	7373	B	323 642-5200	15940
Elvis Schoenberg Production	7922	E	323 344-1745	18389
Emerik Hotel Corp	7011	D	213 748-1291	12618
Emery Smith Laboratories Inc	8734	C	213 745-5333	26849
Emmi Inc	5094	D	213 622-7234	8099
Emp III Inc	6799	D	323 231-4174	12303
Emser International LLC (PA)	5032	C	323 650-2000	6982
End-Time Message & Support	6799	E	323 756-6252	12304
Endurance Specialty Insurance	6411	D	213 270-7700	10700
Englekirk Institutional Inc (PA)	8711	E	323 733-2640	25795
Englekirk Structural Engineers (PA)	8711	D	323 733-6673	25796
Engstrom Lipscomb and Lack A (PA)	8111	D	310 552-3800	23233
Entertainment & Sports Today	4833	D	213 388-9050	5854
Entravsion Communications Corp	4833	D	323 900-6100	5856
Epstein Becker & Green PC	8111	D	310 556-8861	23234
Equator LLC (HQ)	7371	C	310 469-9500	15170
Equicare Medical Supply Inc	8051	D	213 385-1715	20548
Eric Jones Customs Brokerage	4731	E	310 348-3777	5066
Ernst & Young LLP	8721	A	213 977-3200	26337
Espn Inc	4841	B	212 456-7439	5998
Ethiopian World Federation	8399	E	323 844-1826	24920
Evergreen Cleaning Systems Inc	7349	E	213 386-3260	14292
Evolution Holdings LLC (PA)	6719	C	541 826-2113	12060
Evolve Discovery La LLC	8111	D	213 802-1260	23235
Evolve Media LLC (PA)	4813	D	310 449-1890	5600
Evoq Properties Inc	6531	D	213 988-8890	11498
Excellence Ventures Inc	7389	D	323 262-6800	17156
Expeditors Intl Wash Inc	4731	D	310 343-6200	5070
Expeditors Intl Wash Inc	4731	D	310 343-6200	5071
F O C Electronics Corporation	5064	E	213 625-5775	7497
Facter Direct Ltd	7389	C	323 634-1999	17158
Fame Assistance Corporation	8748	D	323 373-7720	27920
Far East Home Care Inc	8082	C	949 673-3100	22437
Far East National Bank (DH)	6021	C	213 687-1300	9397
Farmers Group Inc	6311	D	213 615-2500	10206
Farmers Group Inc	6411	D	818 249-3000	10706
Farmers Insurance Fed Cred UNI (PA)	6061	D	323 209-6000	9595
Farmers Insurance Group (DH)	6411	A	888 327-6335	10714
Farmers Services LLC	6411	A	323 932-3200	10715
Fc Metropolitan Lofts Inc	6552	D	213 488-0010	11968
Fcs Medical Corporation	8031	D	323 317-9200	20291
Federal Deposit Insurance Corp	6399	D	323 545-9260	10569
Federal Express Corporation	4213	D	800 463-3339	4159
Federal Rsrve Bnk San Frncisco	6011	A	213 683-2300	9316
Fedex Office & Print Svcs Inc	7334	E	213 892-1700	14121
Fei Enterprises Inc	1731	E	323 937-0856	2592
Fender Digital LLC	7371	D	480 845-5452	15183
Fidelity Capital Mortgage Brks	6163	E	323 315-1700	9923
Fifth & Sunset Enterprises LLC	7359	D	310 979-0212	14541
Fiji Water Company LLC (HQ)	5149	D	310 966-5700	8836
Film Payroll Services Inc (PA)	8721	D	310 440-9600	26350
Financial Consulting &	8742	C	310 201-2535	27433
Fire Insurance Exchange	6411	A	323 932-3200	10721
First Amrcn Cash Advnce SC LLC	6361	D	213 271-1700	10528
First City Credit Union (PA)	6061	E	213 482-3477	9597
First Entertainment Credit Un (PA)	6061	D	323 851-3673	9598
First Fire Systems Inc	1731	D	310 559-0900	2593
First Legal Support Svcs LLC (PA)	8111	D	213 250-1111	23241
First Regional Bancorp	6022	B	310 552-1776	9497
First Republic Bank	6029	C	213 239-8883	9551
First Republic Bank	6029	D	310 712-1888	9553
Fitzgerald Cantor L P	6211	D	310 282-6500	10001
Five Long Island Properties LL	6512	E	310 772-6306	10982
Five Star Transportation Inc	4729	E	310 348-0820	5009
Floorgate Inc	1752	D	323 478-2000	3114
FM Seoul Bang Song Inc	4832	E	323 525-1650	5775
Focus Psycho Educational	8733	D	323 851-4577	26766
Foley & Lardner LLP	8111	C	213 972-4500	23250
Forest Lawn Memorial-Park Assn	6553	D	323 254-7251	12030
Forever 21 Retail Inc	5137	D	323 343-9368	8384
Fortress Investment Group LLC	6722	D	310 228-3030	12115
Fortuna Enterprises LP	7011	B	310 410-4000	12643
Four Points By Sheraton	7011	B	310 645-4600	12646
Fox Inc (DH)	4833	A	310 369-1000	5862
Fox Animation Studios Inc	7812	B	323 857-8800	18087
Fox Baseball Holdings Inc	7941	A	323 224-1500	18545
Fox Broadcasting Company (DH)	4833	C	310 369-1000	5863
Fox BSB Holdco Inc	7941	A	323 224-1500	18546
Fox Latin American Channel LLC	4841	B	305 774-4167	6000
Fox Networks Group Inc	4841	A	310 369-9369	6001
Fox Rent A Car Inc (PA)	7514	C	310 342-5155	17676
Fox Rothschild LLP	8111	D	213 624-6560	23253
Fox Television Stations LLC (DH)	4833	B	310 584-2000	5864
Fragomen Del Rey Bernse	8111	E	310 820-3322	23255
Frandzel Share Robins Bloom Lc	8111	D	323 852-1000	23259
Fred Leeds Properties	6513	D	310 826-2466	11133
Freeman Freeman & Smiley LLP (PA)	8111	D	310 398-6227	23260
Friends of Angeles Chapter	8699	E	213 387-4287	25533
Friends of The Los Angeles	8399	C	323 653-0440	24922
Front Line MGT Group Inc	8741	D	310 209-3100	27031
Front Porch Communities	8051	C	323 661-1128	20584
Fti Consulting Inc	8711	D	213 689-1200	25820
Fuel TV	4833	D	310 444-8564	5865
Fulbright & Jaworski LLP	8111	C	213 244-9941	23261
Fulwider and Patton LLP	8111	D	310 824-5555	23262
Fund Services Advisors Inc	6282	E	213 612-2196	10149
Futuredontics Inc (PA)	8742	D	310 215-6400	27444
Fx Networks LLC	4841	C	310 369-1000	6002
G J Sullivan Co Inc	6411	D	213 626-1000	10724
G M Floral Company	5193	E	213 489-7055	9189
G4s Secure Solutions (usa)	7381	B	323 938-9100	16651
Gabriella Foundation	7911	D	213 365-2491	18363
Gamefly Inc (PA)	7379	C	310 568-8224	16380
Garco Enterprises Inc	8748	D	323 933-1089	27930
Garda CL West Inc (DH)	7381	B	213 383-3611	16660
Garden Crest Convalesce	8051	C	323 663-8281	20589
Garden Grove Advanced Imaging	8071	D	310 445-2800	22218
Garment Industry Laundry	7218	C	323 752-8335	13630
Gartner Inc	8742	D	310 479-2108	27446
Gary Lask	8011	D	310 825-0631	19533
Gateway Security Inc	7381	A	310 410-0790	16662
Gateway Security Inc	7381	B	310 642-0529	16663
Gateways Hosp Mental Hlth Ctr	8063	C	323 644-2026	22069
Gateways Hosp Mental Hlth Ctr (PA)	8063	C	323 644-2000	22070
Gdf Parent LLC	7389	D	646 262-9635	17183
Gehry Partners LLP	8712	D	310 482-3000	26185
Gelfand Rennert & Feldman LLP (PA)	8721	C	310 553-1707	26352
Gelfand Rennert & Feldman LLP	8721	C	310 553-1707	26353
General Services Cal Dept	8712	D	213 897-3995	26187
General Services Cal Dept	7349	D	213 897-2241	14310
Genesis Healthcare Corporation	8051	D	310 391-8266	20595
Genesis Vocational Specialist	6531	E	213 892-6307	11554
Gentlecare Transport Inc	4119	D	323 662-8777	3798
Genzyme Corporation	8734	D	310 482-5000	26857
George Elkins Mrtg Bnkg Co LP (DH)	6162	D	310 979-5749	9845
Getty Images Inc	7389	D	323 202-4200	17185
Gibbs Giden Locher	8111	D	310 552-3400	23265
Gibson Dunn & Crutcher LLP (PA)	8111	B	213 229-8063	23268
Gibson Dunn & Crutcher LLP	8111	D	310 552-8500	23269
Gilbert Klly Crwley Jnnett LLP (PA)	8111	D	213 615-7000	23271
Gipson Hoffman & Pancione A	8111	D	310 556-4660	23272
Girardi & Keese (PA)	8111	D	213 977-0211	23273
Girardi and Keefe	6512	D	213 489-5330	10988
Girl Scuts Greater Los Angeles (PA)	8641	D	626 677-2200	25263
Giroux Glass Inc (PA)	1793	C	213 747-7406	3410
Giumarra Bros Fruit Co Inc (PA)	5148	D	213 627-2900	8734

GEOGRAPHIC SECTION

LOS ANGELES, CA

	SIC	EMP	PHONE	ENTRY #
Glaser Weil Fink Jacobs (PA)	8111	C	310 553-3000	23274
Global Management Company LLC	8742	D	323 261-8114	27448
Global Staffing Inc	7361	D	303 451-5602	14663
Golden International	6799	A	213 628-1388	12310
Golden State Mutl Lf Insur Co (PA)	6311	D	713 526-4361	10209
Goldman Sachs & Co	6211	C	310 407-5700	10007
Golin/Harris International Inc	8743	D	213 623-4200	27749
Gonzalez Barba Enterprises	4731	E	323 233-7995	5090
Good Samaritan Hospital (PA)	8062	D	213 977-2121	21583
Good Samaritan Hospital Aux	8011	A	213 977-2121	19540
Goodwin Procter LLP	8111	D	213 426-2500	23278
Gordon Edelstein Krepack	8111	E	213 739-7000	23279
Gordon Rees Sclly Mnskhani LLP	8111	E	213 576-5000	23284
Gores Capital Partners LP	7389	D	310 209-3010	17197
Gores Norment Holdings Inc (HQ)	6719	D	310 209-3010	12067
Gorilla Offroad Lights LLC (HQ)	4813	D	310 449-1890	5620
Grand Park Convalescent Hosp	8051	C	213 382-7315	20633
Grand Performances	7389	D	213 687-2190	17199
Grant Thornton LLP	8721	E	213 627-1717	26357
Grant Thornton LLP	8721	E	213 627-1717	26358
Great American Insurance Co	6331	D	323 937-8600	10425
Great American Insurance Co	6331	D	213 430-4300	10426
Greater Los Angeles Agency	8322	D	323 478-8000	23998
Greater Los Angeles Zoo Assn	8399	D	323 644-4200	24924
Green Equity Investors III L P	6211	A	310 954-0444	10009
Green Farms Inc (PA)	5148	D	213 747-4411	8736
Green Glusk Field Clama & Mach	8111	C	310 553-3610	23287
Green Hasson & Janks LLP	8721	C	310 873-1600	26360
Greenberg Traurig LLP	8111	D	310 586-7708	23289
Greenhill & Co Inc	6211	E	310 432-4400	10010
Greenland US Consulting Inc	1531	D	213 362-9300	1366
Greenway Arts Alliance Inc	7922	D	323 655-7679	18395
Greybor Medical Transportation	4119	E	213 250-4444	3801
Greyhound Lines Inc	4173	D	213 629-8400	3960
Grifols Biologicals Inc	4225	B	323 255-2221	4564
Grifols Shared Svcs N Amer Inc (HQ)	5122	C	323 225-2221	8259
Grill On The Alley The Inc	7389	A	323 856-5530	17200
Grosslight Insurance Inc	6411	D	310 473-9611	10732
Gruen Associates	8712	D	323 937-4270	26193
Guardian Eagle Security Inc	7381	B	888 990-0002	16673
Guardian Rehabilitation Hosp	8059	D	323 930-4815	21257
Guardians of The Los Angeles	8051	D	310 479-2468	20640
Guardsmark LLC	7381	C	310 216-9081	16677
Gursey Schneider & Co LLC (PA)	8721	C	310 552-0960	26362
Guru Knits Inc	7389	D	323 235-9424	17204
Gva Enterprises Inc (PA)	8059	D	213 484-0510	21258
Gva Enterprises Inc	8059	D	213 484-0784	21259
H & K Abouaf Corporation	8082	D	310 393-1282	22449
H D S I Managment	6512	E	323 231-1104	10994
H&R Block Inc	7291	D	323 292-8836	13723
H2 Wellness Incorporated	7372	D	310 362-1888	15687
Haight Brown & Bonesteel LLP (PA)	8111	D	213 542-8000	23297
Hall Windsor	8361	D	213 383-1547	24675
Hamburger Home (PA)	8361	D	323 876-0550	24676
Hamburger Home	1521	D	213 637-5000	1188
Hana Financial Inc (PA)	7359	D	213 240-1234	14545
Hancock Pk Rhblitation Ctr LLC	8051	C	323 937-4860	20643
Hanil Development Inc	6553	E	213 387-0111	12032
Hanmi Bank (HQ)	6022	D	213 382-2200	9500
Hannam Chain USA Inc (PA)	5046	C	213 382-2922	7217
Harley Ellis Devereaux Corp	8712	D	213 542-4500	26197
Harris Stockwell (PA)	8111	E	310 277-6669	23301
Harrys Auto Body Inc	7532	D	323 933-4600	17757
Hartford Fire Insurance Co	6411	D	213 452-5179	10736
Harvest Sensations LLC (PA)	5148	E	213 895-6968	8740
Hatch Animation & Prod Studios	7929	D	973 454-8654	18468
Hatchbeauty Products LLC (PA)	5122	D	310 396-7070	8261
Hathaway Resource Center	8322	E	323 837-0838	24003
Hathaway-Sycamores Chld Fam Sv	8361	D	323 257-9600	24681
Hathaway-Sycamores Chld Fam Sv	8361	D	323 733-0322	24683
Hawaiian Airlines Inc	4512	D	310 417-1677	4804
Hazens Investment LLC	7011	B	310 642-1111	12696
Health Link Medi Van	4789	D	310 981-9500	5221
Height Brown and Bonesteel	8111	D	213 241-0900	23305
Herbalife Intl Amer Inc (DH)	5122	B	310 410-9600	8262
Here Films	8748	E	310 806-4288	27941
Here Media Inc (PA)	4813	D	310 943-5858	5628
Hff Inc	6162	D	310 407-2100	9854
Highland Park Skilled Nursing	8051	D	323 254-6125	20671
Hill Farrer & Burrill	8111	D	213 620-0460	23308
Hillcrest Country Club	7997	C	310 553-8911	18960
Hilton Worldwide Inc	7011	C	310 410-4000	12739
Hinerfeld-Ward Inc	1521	D	310 842-7929	1189
Hirsh Inc	1389	E	213 622-9441	1082
Historical Soc Centinela Vly	8412	B	310 649-6272	25022

	SIC	EMP	PHONE	ENTRY #
Hntb Corporation	8711	E	213 403-1000	25862
Hob Entertainment LLC (DH)	7929	C	323 769-4600	18472
Holland & Knight LLP	8111	D	213 896-2500	23309
Holland Flower Market Inc (PA)	5193	D	213 627-9900	9195
Hollywood Community Hospital M	8062	C	323 462-2271	21605
Hollywood Medical Center LP	8062	A	213 413-3000	21606
Hollywood Mental Health Center	8093	D	323 769-6100	22746
Hollywood Standard LLC	7011	C	323 822-3111	12754
Holthouse Carlin Van Trigt LLP (PA)	8721	C	310 477-5551	26373
Homeboy Industries (PA)	8322	B	323 526-1254	24009
Hong Kong & Shanghai Banking	6081	C	213 626-2460	9700
Horizon Media Inc	7319	C	310 282-0909	13996
Hospital Assn Southern Cal (PA)	8399	D	213 347-2002	24928
Hospital Housekeeping	7349	D	323 913-4820	14321
Host Hotels & Resorts LP	7011	D	310 417-3807	12767
Host Hotels & Resorts LP	7011	D	310 216-5858	12774
Host Hotels & Resorts LP	7011	D	310 216-5858	12777
Hotchkis Wiley Capitl MGT LLC (PA)	8741	E	213 430-1000	27056
Hotel Bel-Air	7011	B	310 472-1211	12781
Houlihan Lokey Inc (PA)	6211	B	310 553-8871	10012
House Ear Clinic Inc (PA)	8011	D	213 483-9930	19561
House of Blues Concerts Inc (DH)	7929	C	323 769-4977	18473
Hpt Trs Ihg-2 Inc	7011	C	310 642-7500	12799
Hsbc Business Credit (usa)	6153	D	213 553-8089	9784
Hsbc Finance Corporation	6141	D	213 628-8167	9753
Hubbard Dianetics Foundation	8699	D	323 953-3206	25543
Hudson Pacific Properties Inc (PA)	6798	D	310 445-5700	12249
Humnit Hotel At Lax LLC	7011	D	424 702-1234	12803
Hunton & Williams LLP	8111	D	213 532-2000	23316
Hustle Digital Inc	7389	E	310 882-2680	17228
Hwn Mariposa Associates LLC	1531	D	310 478-8757	1369
Hyatt Corporation	7011	C	323 656-1234	12807
Hyatt Corporation	7011	C	312 746-1234	12809
Hyatt Regency Century Plaza	7011	A	310 228-1234	12830
Hyde Park Convalescent Hosp	8051	E	323 753-1354	20681
Hyperloop One	4789	C	213 800-3270	5222
Hypermedia Systems Inc	7379	D	213 908-2214	16398
Hyrian LLC	7361	C	212 590-2567	14677
I D Property Corporation	6531	C	213 625-0100	11579
Ias Administrations Inc	8399	D	323 953-4900	24929
Ibisworld Inc (DH)	8732	D	800 330-3772	26674
Icon Exposure Inc	7384	D	323 933-1666	16950
IDS Real Estate Group (PA)	6531	D	213 627-9937	11581
Ifncom Inc (PA)	4813	D	213 452-1505	5634
Ignition Creative LLC	7812	D	310 315-6300	18094
Ihg Management (maryland) LLC	7011	D	310 642-7500	12834
Imaging Technologies Group LLC	5112	D	310 638-2500	8169
Imax Corporation	7819	C	310 255-5500	18232
Imperial Capital Group LLC (PA)	6211	D	310 246-3700	10014
Imperial Capital LLC (PA)	6211	D	310 246-3700	10015
Imperial Mridian Companies Inc	7359	D	310 447-3460	14549
Imperial Parking Industries (PA)	7521	D	323 651-5588	17723
Infinity Broadcasting Corp Cal	4832	D	323 936-5784	5788
Infinity Care of East LA	8051	D	323 261-8108	20684
Inland Medical Enterprises	8051	D	323 732-0350	20686
Insignia/Esg Ht Partners Inc (DH)	6512	D	310 765-2600	11005
Institute For Applied Behavior (PA)	8049	C	310 649-0499	20323
Institute For Mltcltrl Cnslng	8748	D	213 381-1239	27951
Integrated Decision Systems	7373	C	310 954-5530	15966
Integrated Trnsp Svcs Inc	4119	D	310 553-6060	3805
Interbake Foods LLC	5149	D	213 484-8161	8854
Intercare Therapy Inc	8049	C	323 866-1880	20327
Interior Office Solutions Inc	7389	E	310 726-9067	17246
Interlink	6159	C	310 734-1499	9801
International Creative Mgt Inc (HQ)	7922	C	310 550-4000	18398
International Creative MGT Inc	7922	C	310 550-4000	18399
International Design Services	8711	D	323 662-3963	25885
International Inst Los Angeles (PA)	8322	D	323 224-3800	24032
International Lease Fin Corp (HQ)	7359	C	310 788-1999	14550
International Marine Pdts Inc (HQ)	5146	D	213 680-0190	8635
International Media Group Inc	4833	D	310 478-1818	5874
International Medical Corps (PA)	8322	D	310 826-7800	24033
Internet Corp For Assigned Nam (PA)	7373	D	310 823-9358	15969
Interstate Hotels Resorts Inc	7011	D	213 617-1133	12849
Interstate Hotels Resorts Inc	7011	B	213 624-1000	12850
Investors Capital MGT Group	8741	C	310 553-5175	27073
Irell & Manella LLP	8111	D	310 277-1010	23318
Irell & Manella LLP	8111	B	213 620-1555	23320
Irp Lax Hotel LLC	7011	D	310 645-4600	12854
Irwin Naturals	5122	D	310 306-3636	8265
ISE Corporation	8731	E	858 413-1720	26539
Israel Discount Bank New York	6022	D	213 861-6440	9504
Italee Optics Inc (PA)	5048	C	213 385-8805	7332
Ivie McNeill Wyatt A Prof Law	8111	E	213 489-0028	23322
Ivy Realty	6531	E	213 386-8888	11592

Employment Codes: A=Over 500 employees, B=251-500, C=101-250, D=51-100, E=45-50

2017 Directory of California Wholesalers and Services Companies

© Mergent Inc. 1-800-342-5647

LOS ANGELES, CA — GEOGRAPHIC SECTION

Company	SIC	EMP	PHONE	ENTRY #
J Alexander Investments Inc (PA)	6726	E	213 687-8400	12141
J C Entertainment Ltg Svcs Inc	7922	D	818 252-7481	18400
J H Synder Co LLC	6531	C	323 857-5546	11594
J Hellman Produce Inc	5148	D	213 627-1093	8741
J M Carden Sprinkler Co Inc	1711	D	323 258-8300	2257
J P H Consulting Inc (PA)	8051	C	323 934-5660	20689
J P H Consulting Inc	8051	C	323 934-5660	20690
J Paul Getty Trust	8732	D	310 440-7325	26678
J2 Cloud Services Inc (HQ)	4822	C	323 860-9200	5743
J2 Global Inc (PA)	4822	D	323 860-9200	5744
Jack Engle & Co (PA)	5093	C	323 589-8111	8074
Jack Nadel Inc (PA)	8742	D	310 815-2600	27489
Jackoway Tyreman Wertheimer Au	8111	D	310 553-0305	23323
Jacobs Engineering Group Inc	8711	C	213 362-4336	25901
Jameson Properties Co Inc	6512	E	213 487-3770	11008
Jarrow Formulas Inc (PA)	5122	D	310 204-6936	8267
Jay Nolan Community Svcs Inc	8331	B	323 937-0094	24354
Jean Mart Inc	5137	D	323 752-7775	8388
Jeffer Mngels Btlr Mtchell LLP (PA)	8111	C	310 203-8080	23325
Jefferies LLC	6211	D	310 445-1199	10018
Jenkins Gales & Martinez Inc	8741	D	310 645-0561	27077
Jetro Cash and Carry Entps LLC	5181	C	323 964-1200	9065
Jewish Cmnty Fndn of (PA)	8641	C	323 761-8700	25274
Jewish Family Svc Los Angeles (PA)	8322	E	323 761-8800	24046
Jewish Family Svc Los Angeles	8322	E	323 937-5900	24048
Jewish Student Union	8322	D	310 229-9006	24049
Jewish Vocational Services (PA)	8331	E	323 761-8888	24356
Jim Henson Company Inc (PA)	7812	D	323 856-6680	18097
Jirbo Inc	7371	D	310 775-8085	15263
Jj Grand Hotel	7011	D	213 383-3000	12866
John Hancock Life Insur Co USA (DH)	7389	A	213 689-0813	17260
John Stewart Company	6531	E	213 787-2700	11600
Johnson Fain Inc	8712	D	323 224-6000	26215
Jonair Services LLC	4522	C	310 529-5482	4882
Jonathan Club (PA)	8641	C	213 624-0881	25275
Jones Day Limited Partnership	7389	D	213 489-3939	17262
Jones Lang La Salle	6798	D	213 239-6000	12253
Julio Gonzalez	8748	D	310 310-4055	27961
Juno Healthcare Registry Inc	7361	D	323 937-7210	14691
Jwmcc Limited Partnership	7011	B	310 277-1234	12873
K A Associates Inc	6211	D	310 556-2721	10022
K B Home Coastal	1531	D	310 231-4000	1371
K&L Gates LLP	8111	E	310 552-5000	23334
Kaa Design Group Inc	8712	D	310 821-1400	26216
Kaiser Foundation Hospitals	8062	D	323 783-4011	21633
Kaiser Foundation Hospitals	8011	A	323 857-2000	19591
Kaiser Foundation Hospitals	6324	D	800 954-8000	10297
Kaiser Foundation Hospitals	6324	D	800 954-8000	10310
Kaiser Foundation Hospitals	6733	E	323 881-5516	12183
Kaiser Foundation Hospitals	8093	C	323 298-3300	22755
Kaiser Foundation Hospitals	8063	C	213 580-7200	22076
Kaiser Foundation Hospitals	8062	A	800 954-8000	21673
Kajima Construction Svcs Inc	1541	E	323 269-0020	1442
Kash Apparel LLC	5137	D	213 747-8885	8389
Katten Muchin Rosenman LLP	8111	D	310 788-4498	23339
Katten Muchin Rosenman LLP	8111	D	310 788-4498	23341
Katz Media Group Inc	8748	D	323 966-5000	27963
Kaufman & Broad San Antonio	6531	D	310 231-4000	11605
Kaufman and Broad Limited	1541	D	310 231-4000	1372
Kava Holdings Inc (PA)	7011	C	310 472-1211	12876
Kaye Scholer LLP	8111	C	310 788-1000	23344
Kayne Anderson Rudni	6722	D	310 229-9260	12118
Kayne Andrson Cpitl Advsors LP	6282	B	800 231-7414	10156
KB Home (PA)	1531	D	310 231-4000	1373
KB Home Grater Los Angeles Inc (HQ)	1521	D	310 231-4000	1202
Keck Hospital of Usc	8011	D	800 872-2273	19685
Kedren Community Hlth Ctr Inc	8322	C	562 335-9601	24053
Kedren Community Hlth Ctr Inc (PA)	8063	B	323 233-0425	22077
Kedren Community Hlth Ctr Inc	8322	C	323 524-0634	24054
Keiro Services	8741	B	213 873-5700	27088
Kelley Drye & Warren LLP	8111	C	310 712-6100	23347
Kelly Slater Wave Company LLC	8732	E	310 202-9283	26680
Kennedy Care Center	8059	D	323 651-0043	21278
Kenneth Brdwick Intr Dsgns Inc	7389	D	310 274-9999	17270
Keolis Transit America Inc (DH)	4119	E	310 981-9500	3809
Kerlan-Jobe Orthopedic Clinic (PA)	8011	D	310 665-7200	19686
Ketchum Inc	8743	D	310 295-3300	27753
Kevin Holubowski LLC	8399	C	310 908-6542	24933
Kf Sunray LLC	8059	C	323 734-2171	21281
Kfco Inc	4212	D	310 441-2483	4035
Kilroy Realty Corporation (PA)	6798	D	310 481-8400	12254
Kindred Healthcare Operating	8062	B	310 642-0325	21690
Kinecta Alternative Fin	7331	D	323 269-3929	14077
Kings Pawnshop	6163	D	213 383-5555	9932
Kingsley Apartments	6513	D	323 666-8862	11148
Kintetsu Enterprises	8741	D	213 687-2000	27096
Kintetsu Enterprises Co Amer	7011	C	213 687-2000	12888
Kirkland & Ellis LLP	8111	C	213 680-7480	23355
KI Cutting Service Inc	7219	C	213 742-9001	13655
Km Fresno Investors LLC	6799	E	323 556-6600	12319
Knet TV	4833	E	323 469-5638	5884
Kommonwealth Inc	5139	E	310 278-7328	8438
Korean Air Lines Co Ltd	4512	C	310 646-4866	4809
Korean Airlines	4512	C	310 417-5294	4810
Korean Airlines Co Ltd	4512	C	310 410-2000	4812
Korean Airlines Co Ltd	4512	D	213 484-1900	4813
Korean Health Education (PA)	8322	D	213 427-4000	24060
Korn/Ferry International (PA)	8742	C	310 552-1834	27501
Kpff Inc	8711	D	310 665-1536	25926
Kpmg LLP	8721	A	212 758-9700	26387
Kst Data Inc	7371	D	213 384-9555	15271
Ktgy Group Inc	8712	E	310 394-2625	26220
L & T Meat Co	5142	C	323 262-2815	8559
L A U S D Program	8361	E	323 962-9560	24703
L and R Auto Parks Inc	7521	C	213 629-3263	17725
L J Trucking USA	4213	C	323 469-9663	4207
L R Investment Company	7521	D	213 627-8211	17726
La Asociacion Nacional Pro Per	8322	B	213 202-5900	24061
La Cienega Associates	6531	D	310 854-0071	11624
La Follette Johnson De Haas (PA)	8111	C	213 426-3600	23361
La Hotel Venture LLC	7011	B	213 617-1133	12896
La Inc Convention Vistors Bur	7389	D	213 236-2301	17282
La Laser Center Pc Cpmc	8011	D	310 446-4400	19691
La Live Properties LLC	7922	E	213 763-7700	18404
LA Metropolitan Medical Ctr	8062	A	323 730-7300	21695
La Radio LLC	4832	E	310 840-4900	5803
La Vida Mltispecialty Med Ctrs	8011	D	213 765-7500	19697
Laaco Ltd (PA)	6519	C	213 622-1254	11257
Lac Basketball Club Inc	7941	E	213 742-7500	18553
Lac Usc Medical Center	8062	C	323 226-7858	21697
Ladas & Parry LLP	8111	E	323 934-2300	23362
Laguna Country Mart Ltd Inc	6512	E	310 826-5635	11009
Lakewood Manor North Inc	8051	D	213 380-9175	20719
Lambda Lambda Sigma LLC	7312	D	310 558-8555	13951
Language Weaver Inc	7371	D	310 437-7300	15272
Larchmont Radiology Med Group	8011	D	213 483-5953	19699
Latham & Watkins LLP (PA)	8111	A	213 485-1234	23369
Latham & Watkins LLP	8111	D	213 891-7108	23370
Latham & Watkins LLP	8111	C	213 891-1200	23373
Lathrop & Gage LLP	8111	D	310 789-4600	23374
Lax Hospitality LP	7011	C	310 670-9000	12908
Lax Hotel Ventures LLC	7011	E	310 645-4600	12909
Lax International Service Ctr	7389	D	310 337-8764	17290
LAX Wheel Refinishing Inc	5013	E	323 269-1484	6745
Lax-C Inc	5141	E	323 343-9000	8490
Ldla Clothing LLC	5137	D	323 312-2805	8394
Lear Capital Inc	6211	D	310 571-0190	10023
Led Global LLC	1711	D	917 921-4315	2278
Legacy Partners Hollywood	6513	D	949 930-7706	11154
Legal Support Network LLC	7389	D	213 975-9850	17291
Legend3d Inc	7812	D	858 793-4420	18099
LEK Consulting LLC	8742	D	310 209-9800	27507
Lendlease US Construction Inc	8741	D	213 430-4660	27113
Lenexa Hotel LP	7011	C	310 475-8711	12915
Lenlyn Limited Which Will Do B (DH)	6099	D	310 417-3432	9721
Leo A Daly Company	8712	D	213 627-9300	26222
Leo A Daly Company	8712	D	213 533-8855	26223
Level Four Business MGT LLC	8748	E	310 914-1600	27975
Levity Entertainment Group LLC	8742	D	310 417-4861	27509
Levy Prmium Fdsrvice Ltd Prtnr	1541	D	213 742-7867	1448
Lewis Brsbois Bsgard Smith LLP	8111	D	213 250-1800	23385
Lewis Brsbois Bsgard Smith LLP (PA)	8111	A	213 250-1800	23387
Lewis P C Jackson	8111	D	213 689-0404	23394
Lgh Digital Media Inc	7822	E	323 469-3986	18276
Libsource LLC	8741	C	323 852-1083	27115
Lieberman RES Worldwide Inc (PA)	8732	C	310 553-7721	26683
Lifetime Entrmt Svcs LLC	4833	E	310 556-7500	5894
Lightcrest LLC	7373	E	888 320-8495	15986
Lighthouse Healthcare Ctr LLC	8051	D	323 564-4461	20735
Linden Center	8063	D	213 251-8226	22080
Liner LLP (PA)	8111	D	310 500-3500	23396
Linquest Corporation (PA)	8711	D	323 924-1600	25937
Little Citizens Schools Inc	8351	D	323 732-1212	24476
Live Nation Entertainment Inc	7389	D	323 468-1160	17297
Live Nation Entertainment Inc	7922	D	213 639-6178	18407
Live Nation Entertainment Inc	7929	D	323 464-1330	18478
Live Nation Worldwide Inc	7922	C	323 966-5066	18410
Livhome Inc (PA)	8322	A	800 807-5854	24069
LLP Locke Lord	8111	D	213 485-1500	23399
LLP Locke Lord	8111	C	310 860-8700	23401

GEOGRAPHIC SECTION — LOS ANGELES, CA

Company	SIC	EMP	PHONE	ENTRY #
LLP Mayer Brown	8111	C	213 229-9500	23403
LLP Moss Adams	8721	C	310 278-5850	26401
LLP Robins Kaplan	8111	D	310 552-0130	23404
Local Initiative Health Author	6324	A	213 694-1250	10356
Lockton Companies Llc-Pacific (HQ)	6411	B	213 689-0500	10766
Loeb & Loeb LLP (PA)	8111	C	310 282-2000	23405
Longwood Management Corp	8059	D	323 735-5146	21295
Longwood Management Corp	8059	D	323 737-7778	21297
Longwood Management Corp	8059	D	213 382-8461	21299
Longwood Management Corp	8051	E	323 933-1560	20745
Longwood Manor	8051	C	323 935-1157	20746
Lookout Productions LLC	7812	E	310 408-5687	18103
Los Angeles 2024	8699	E	310 407-0204	25552
Los Angeles 2024 Exploratory	7997	C	310 407-0539	18985
Los Angeles Airport Peace Offc	8641	B	310 242-5218	25290
Los Angeles Athletic Club Inc	7991	C	213 625-2211	18656
Los Angeles Cardiology Assoc (PA)	8011	D	213 977-0419	19719
Los Angeles Chmber Orchstra	7929	E	213 622-7001	18479
Los Angeles Christn Hlth Ctrs (HQ)	8011	D	213 893-1960	19720
Los Angeles Cnty Dev Svc Fndtn	8099	C	213 383-1300	22995
Los Angeles Cnty Mseum of Art	8412	C	323 857-6000	25026
Los Angeles Convention and Exh	6512	B	213 741-1151	11012
Los Angeles Country Club	7997	C	310 276-6104	18986
Los Angeles County Bar Assn (PA)	8621	D	213 627-2727	25144
Los Angeles County MTA	4111	C	213 922-5887	3660
Los Angeles County MTA	4111	C	213 922-6301	3661
Los Angeles County MTA	4111	B	213 922-6203	3662
Los Angeles County MTA	4111	C	213 922-6202	3663
Los Angeles County MTA (PA)	4111	A	323 466-3876	3664
Los Angeles County MTA	4111	C	213 922-6207	3665
Los Angeles County MTA	4111	B	213 533-1506	3667
Los Angeles County MTA	4111	C	213 922-5012	3668
Los Angeles County MTA	4111	C	213 244-6783	3670
Los Angeles County MTA	4111	C	213 626-4455	3671
Los Angeles Dept Wtr & Pwr (PA)	4941	C	213 367-4043	6367
Los Angeles Dept Wtr & Pwr	4911	D	213 367-4211	6146
Los Angeles Dept Wtr & Pwr	4941	A	213 367-5706	6368
Los Angeles Free Clinic (PA)	8742	D	323 653-8622	27510
Los Angeles Free Clinic	8011	D	323 653-8622	19722
Los Angeles Job Corps	8331	C	213 748-0135	24359
Los Angeles Lgbt Center (PA)	8399	C	323 993-7618	24940
Los Angeles Magazine Inc	5192	D	323 801-0100	9167
Los Angeles Orphans Home Soc (HQ)	8361	C	323 463-2119	24718
Los Angeles Philharmonic Assn (PA)	7929	D	213 972-7300	18480
Los Angeles Police Command	8699	B	877 275-5273	25553
Los Angeles Rubber Company (PA)	5063	C	323 263-4131	7451
Los Angeles Senior Citizen	6513	D	310 271-9670	11161
Los Angeles Unified School Dst	4173	C	323 227-4400	3961
Los Angeles Unified School Dst	7378	D	213 485-3691	16301
Los Angeles Unified School Dst	7374	A	213 847-6911	16153
Los Angeles Unified School Dst	8641	C	323 753-3175	25291
Los Angeles Unified School Dst	8351	D	323 939-7322	24478
Los Angeles Unified School Dst	8322	C	213 739-5600	24071
Los Angeles Unified School Dst	8322	C	310 258-2000	24072
Los Angeles World Airports (PA)	4581	C	310 646-7911	4925
Los Angles Area Chmber Cmmerce	8611	D	213 580-7500	25092
Los Angles Child Gdance Clinic (PA)	8322	C	323 766-2360	24074
Los Angles Clippers Foundation	8742	D	213 742-7555	27512
Los Angles Cnsrvtion Corps Inc (PA)	7363	C	213 362-9000	14901
Los Angles Cnty Employees Assn	8631	D	213 368-8660	25178
Los Angles Trism Convention Bd (PA)	7389	E	213 624-7300	17303
Los Angles Universal Preschool	8351	C	213 416-1200	24479
Lotus Communications Corp (PA)	4832	D	323 512-2225	5808
Lotus Interworks Inc	8742	C	310 442-3330	27513
Louis Luskin & Sons Inc	1711	D	323 938-5142	2283
Lowcom LLC	7311	C	213 408-0080	13878
Lowe Enterprises Inc (PA)	6531	C	310 820-6661	11638
Lowe Enterprises Coml Group	6552	D	310 820-6661	11980
Lowe Enterprises Inc	6552	D	310 820-6661	11981
Loyola Marymount University	4832	C	310 338-2866	5809
Lq Management LLC	7011	D	310 645-2200	12931
Lrn Corporation	8111	D	310 209-5400	23414
Lrw Investments LLC	7521	D	310 337-1944	17729
Lucky Strike Entertainment LLC	5049	D	818 933-3752	7344
Lufthnsa Crgo Aktngesellschaft	4512	D	310 242-2590	4814
Lumina Healthcare LLC (PA)	8082	D	888 958-6462	22502
Lusive Decor	8748	C	323 227-9207	27978
Lynberg & Watkins A Prof Corp (PA)	8111	E	213 624-8700	23415
M & S Acquisition Corporation (PA)	6531	C	213 385-1515	11649
M Arthur Gensler Jr Assoc Inc	8712	C	213 927-3600	26232
M Channel Inc	7313	D	310 231-5124	13971
Macdonald Mott Group Inc	8711	D	323 903-4100	25946
Macerich Company	6512	D	310 474-6255	11013
Macerich Company	6531	D	310 474-5940	11652
Made In USA Foundation Inc	8641	E	310 623-3872	25292
Mafab Inc (PA)	6719	D	714 893-0551	12074
Magma Consulting Group LLC	7379	D	415 315-9364	16428
Magnolia Ventures Ltd	7389	D	213 389-6900	17310
Main Source Group Inc	7349	D	213 387-1001	14346
Management Tech Consulting LLC	8748	D	323 851-5008	27980
Manatt Phelps & Phillips LLP	8111	E	310 312-4249	23418
Manchster Mnor Cnvlescent Hosp	8059	D	323 753-1789	21306
Mandalay Sports Entrmt LLC (PA)	7941	D	323 549-4300	18557
Manning Kass Ellrod Ram Trestr (PA)	8111	C	213 624-6900	23420
Manual Arts Svc Ctr Studnt Bdy	7991	D	323 732-0153	18657
Manufacturers Bank (DH)	6022	C	213 489-6200	9506
Marcum LLP	8721	D	310 432-7400	26407
Marina Auto Body Shop Inc	7532	E	310 822-6615	17760
Mariner Health Care Inc	8051	D	323 665-1185	20762
Marketshare Partners LLC (HQ)	8732	D	310 914-5677	26687
Marland Co LP	0174	E	213 614-6171	220
Marmol Radziner	8712	D	310 826-6222	26234
Marriott International Inc	7011	B	310 337-2800	12952
Marriott International Inc	7011	A	310 641-5700	12954
Marriott International Inc	7011	C	213 284-3862	12978
Marsh Risk & Insurance Svcs (HQ)	6411	A	213 624-5555	10776
Martin AC Partners Inc	8712	D	213 683-1900	26235
Martin Associates Group Inc (PA)	8711	D	213 483-6490	25952
Martin Lther King/Drew Med Ctr	8011	D	310 773-4926	19734
Masa Trucking Co	4214	C	310 329-1567	4361
Massage Place	7299	C	310 204-3004	13774
Matrix Aviation Services Inc	4729	C	310 337-3037	5012
Maui Fresh International LLC	5148	D	213 688-0880	8750
Maxim Healthcare Services Inc	8082	C	323 937-9410	22505
Maxus USA	8999	B	323 202-4650	28146
Mayesh Wholesale Florist Inc (PA)	5193	E	310 342-0980	9198
Mayfair Hotel	7011	D	213 484-9789	12984
McDermott Will & Emery LLP Inc	8111	C	310 277-4110	23425
McGuirewoods LLP	8111	D	310 315-8200	23427
MCI Communications Svcs Inc	4813	B	323 460-5178	5651
MCI Communications Svcs Inc	4813	C	213 625-1005	5652
McKinsey & Company Inc	8742	E	424 249-1000	27533
McKool Smith Hennigan	8111	D	213 694-1200	23428
Med-Life Ambulance Services	4119	D	818 242-1785	3816
Media Link LLC	8748	C	646 722-3632	27985
Media Temple Inc	4813	D	877 578-4000	5653
Mediabrands Worldwide Inc	7319	B	323 370-8000	14001
Medical Management Cons Inc (PA)	7363	E	310 659-3835	14909
Medical Support Services	7363	D	323 860-7994	14910
Mellano & Co (PA)	5193	D	213 622-0796	9200
Memorial Hospital of Gardena	8062	B	323 268-5514	21732
Memory To Go	5045	D	310 446-0111	7162
Mendelsohn/Zien Advg LLC	7311	D	310 444-1990	13885
Mercer (us) Inc	8742	C	213 346-2200	27542
Merchant of Tennis Inc	7389	C	310 855-1946	17327
Merchants Building Maint Co	7349	B	800 560-6700	14357
Mercury Air Cargo Inc (HQ)	4581	C	310 258-6100	4926
Mercury General Corporation (PA)	6331	C	323 937-1060	10440
Mercury Insurance Company (HQ)	6331	C	323 937-1060	10445
Mercury Insurance Services LLC	6331	A	323 937-1060	10448
Mercury Mailing Systems Inc	7331	D	323 730-0307	14083
Merlot Film Productions Inc	7812	C	323 575-2906	18109
Merrill Lynch Pierce Fenner	6211	C	310 407-3900	10040
Metro Service South Inc	7349	D	310 995-8950	14358
Metrolux Theatres	7822	B	310 858-2800	18278
Metropolitan Water District	4941	D	213 217-6000	6371
Metropolitan Water District	4971	A	213 217-6667	6646
Mgh Corporation	8361	E	323 754-1408	24736
Michael A Meczka	8732	D	310 670-4824	26689
Mid Century Insurance Company	6331	C	323 932-7116	10450
Mid Cities Assn Retarded Ctzns (PA)	8331	D	310 537-4510	24366
Mid Wilshire Health Care Ctr	8051	D	213 483-9921	20790
Midnight Mission (PA)	8641	D	213 624-9258	25298
Midnite Air Corp	4513	E	310 330-2300	4869
Midway Rent A Car Inc	7514	D	310 445-4355	17689
Milbank Tweed Hdley McCloy LLP	8111	C	213 892-4000	23432
Millennia Holdings Inc	8742	D	213 252-1230	27550
Millward Brown LLC	8732	D	323 966-5770	26691
Minority Aids Project Inc	8322	D	323 936-4949	24090
Mintie Corporation (PA)	7349	D	323 225-4111	14360
Mission Beverage Co (HQ)	5181	C	323 266-6238	9075
Mitchell Silberberg Knupp LLP (PA)	8111	D	310 312-2000	23437
Mitsui & Co (usa) Inc	5051	D	213 896-1100	7384
Miyako Hotels	7011	D	213 617-2000	13001
Mizuho Corporate Bank Cal (DH)	6022	D	213 612-2848	9509
Mobile Messenger Americas Inc (PA)	7389	D	310 957-3300	17338
Mobilona LLC	6531	E	213 260-3200	11689
Mocean LLC	7374	D	310 481-0808	16164
Modern Alloys Inc	5039	D	714 893-0551	7026
Modern Alloys Inc	6719	D	714 893-0551	12077

Employment Codes: A=Over 500 employees, B=251-500, C=101-250, D=51-100, E=45-50

LOS ANGELES, CA

GEOGRAPHIC SECTION

	SIC	EMP	PHONE	ENTRY #
Modern Button Company of Cal	5131	E	213 747-7431	8319
Monarchy Diamond Inc	1499	B	213 924-1161	1117
Morgan Lewis & Bockius LLP	8111	C	213 612-2500	23444
Morgan Lewis & Bockius LLP	8111	C	213 680-6400	23446
Morgan Services Inc	7213	D	213 485-9666	13567
Morgans Hotel Group MGT LLC	7011	D	323 650-8999	13008
Morris Polich & Purdy LLP (PA)	8111	D	213 891-9100	23447
Morrison & Foerster LLP	8111	D	213 892-5200	23448
Mortgage Capital Assoc Inc	6163	D	310 477-6877	9938
Mortgage Capital Partners Inc	6162	D	310 295-2900	9874
Motion Picture and TV Fund	8062	D	310 231-3000	21754
Motion Theory Inc	7336	C	310 396-9433	14155
Mpower Communications Corp (DH)	4813	D	213 213-3000	5661
MSS Nurses Registry Inc	7363	D	323 467-5717	14913
Mufg Union Bank Na	6021	E	213 972-5500	9402
Mufg Union Bank Na	6021	D	213 312-4500	9405
Muir-Chase Plumbing Co Inc	1711	D	818 500-1940	2298
Mulholland SEC & Patrol Inc	7381	B	818 755-0202	16741
Munger Tolles & Olson LLP	8111	C	213 683-9100	23455
Munger Tolles Olson Foundation (PA)	8111	B	213 683-9100	23456
Murchison & Cumming LLP (PA)	8111	D	213 623-7400	23458
Murphy OBrien Inc	8743	D	310 453-2539	27757
Museum Associates	8412	B	323 857-6172	25027
Museum of Contemporary Art (PA)	8412	C	213 626-6222	25029
Musick Peeler & Garrett LLP (PA)	8111	C	213 629-7600	23461
Mutual Trading Co Inc (PA)	5149	C	213 626-9458	8881
Mv Medical Management	8742	D	323 257-7637	27554
Mystic Inc (PA)	5137	B	213 746-8538	8404
Nadel Inc (PA)	8712	D	310 826-2100	26240
Namecheap Inc	4813	D	310 259-3259	5663
National Cble Cmmnications LLC	7319	D	310 231-0745	14002
National Center For The Pres	8412	B	213 625-0414	25031
National Economic RES Assoc	8748	D	213 346-3000	27996
National Genetics Institute	8071	C	310 996-6610	22246
National Research Group Inc	8732	B	323 817-2000	26693
National Technical Systems Inc	8734	C	310 671-6488	26878
Nationwide Legal LLC (PA)	8111	D	213 249-9999	23463
Nationwide Theatres Corp (HQ)	7833	D	310 657-8420	18361
Natural History Museum of Los	8412	B	213 763-3442	25032
Navigant Consulting Inc	8742	D	213 452-4516	27560
Nb Enterprises & Dist Inc	8741	D	866 216-1515	27138
NBBJ LP	8712	E	213 243-3333	26241
Near N Entrmt Insurances L L C	6411	E	310 556-1900	10795
Nederlander of California Inc	6512	E	323 468-1700	11023
Nestle Waters North Amer Inc	5149	D	213 763-1380	8887
Network Automation Inc	7372	E	213 738-1700	15773
Network Management Group Inc (PA)	8741	C	323 263-2632	27139
Network Physics Inc	7373	D	240 497-3000	16010
New Crew Production Corp	7389	C	323 234-8880	17354
New Dream Network LLC	4813	D	323 375-3842	5669
New Economics For Women (PA)	8322	D	213 483-2060	24100
New Figueroa Hotel Inc	7011	D	213 627-8971	13018
New Global Telecom Inc	7389	D	213 489-3708	17355
New Regency Productions Inc (PA)	7812	D	310 369-8300	18121
New Vista Health Services	8059	C	310 477-5501	21325
New York Life Insurance Co	6411	E	323 782-3000	10807
Newsways Services Inc	5192	C	323 258-6000	9169
Nextel Communications Inc	4812	C	323 290-2400	5403
Ngs Group Inc	5149	D	323 735-1700	8892
Nielsen Company (us) LLC	8732	B	323 817-2000	26694
Nielsen Company (us) LLC	7929	D	323 462-0050	18483
Nixon Peabody LLP	8111	D	213 629-6000	23471
Northrop Grumman Systems Corp	7389	B	310 556-4911	17367
Nossaman LLP (PA)	8111	D	213 612-7800	23473
Notellage Corporation	8059	E	323 257-8151	21332
Now Medical Services Inc	7363	D	310 479-4520	14918
Nowcom Corporation	7379	D	323 938-6449	16440
Nrea-TRC 711 LLC	7011	D	213 486-6500	13030
Nri Usa LLC	4731	D	323 345-6456	5135
Nsbn LLP (PA)	8721	D	310 273-2501	26414
Nu Image Inc (PA)	7829	D	310 388-6900	18288
Nuevo Amnecer Latino Chld Svcs (PA)	8361	D	323 720-9951	24749
Numero Uno Market	6799	D	323 231-9403	12333
Numero Uno Market	6799	D	213 381-1734	12334
O & S Holdings LLC	6552	E	310 207-8600	11991
Oak Paper Products Co Inc (PA)	5113	C	323 268-0507	8200
Oaks Diagnostics Inc (PA)	8011	D	310 855-0035	19787
Oaktree Capital Management LP (HQ)	6282	C	213 830-6300	10167
Oaktree Holdings Inc	6799	A	213 830-6300	12335
Oaktree Real Estate Opportunit	6531	D	213 830-6300	11718
Oaktree Strategic Income LLC	7389	B	213 830-6300	17372
Oakwood Corporate Housing Inc (PA)	7021	D	310 478-1021	13453
Oberman Tivoli Miller Pickert	7373	C	310 440-9600	16022
Oblong Industries Inc (PA)	7371	D	213 683-8863	15347
Ocb Restaurant Company LLC	7299	D	310 216-9208	13782

	SIC	EMP	PHONE	ENTRY #
Ocean Breeze Manufacturing	7389	D	323 586-8760	17373
Ocean Group Inc (PA)	5146	D	213 622-3677	8640
Ocm Real Estate Opportunities	6799	A	213 830-6300	12336
ODonnell & Shaeffer LLP	8111	D	213 627-3769	23476
Ods Technologies LP	4833	C	310 242-9400	5904
Olympia Convalescent Hospital	8059	C	213 487-3000	21335
Olympia Health Care LLC	8062	A	323 938-3161	21769
Olympus Adhc Inc	8351	E	310 572-7272	24490
Omega/Cinema Props Inc	7819	D	323 466-8201	18242
OMelveny & Myers LLP (PA)	8111	A	213 430-6000	23477
OMelveny & Myers LLP	8111	D	310 553-6700	23479
Omni Hotels Corporation	7011	C	213 617-3300	13045
On Central Realty Inc	6531	B	323 543-8500	11721
One Legal Inc	7389	D	213 617-1212	17377
ONeil Data Systems LLC	5084	D	310 448-6400	7871
Onelegacy (PA)	8099	D	213 625-0665	23013
Oneunited Bank	6022	D	323 295-3381	9510
Oneunited Bank	6022	D	323 290-4848	9511
Onsite Consulting LLC	8748	D	323 401-3190	28009
Ore-Cal Corp (PA)	5146	D	213 623-8493	8642
Organic & Sustainable Buty Inc	7231	E	310 815-8201	13683
Organztion Amrcn Kdaly Edctors	8699	E	310 441-3555	25563
Orrick Hrrington Sutcliffe LLP	8111	C	213 629-2020	23485
Orthopaedic Hospital (PA)	8062	C	213 742-1000	21775
Otis Elevator Company	5084	E	323 342-4500	7873
Our Alchemy LLC	7829	D	310 893-6289	18289
Outdoor Systems Advertising	7312	C	323 222-7171	13954
Overseenet (PA)	7311	C	213 408-0080	13893
Oxford Palace	7011	D	213 382-7756	13053
P-Wave Holdings LLC	6799	A	310 209-3010	12337
P8ge Consulting Inc	8748	A	310 666-2301	28014
Pachulski Stang Zehl Jones LLP (PA)	8111	D	310 277-6910	23487
Pacific Asian Consortm Emplymn	8322	D	213 989-3228	24119
Pacific Asian Consortm Emplymn (PA)	8331	D	213 353-3982	24377
Pacific Aviation Corporation (PA)	4581	C	310 646-4015	4927
Pacific Capital Companies LLC	6159	C	800 583-3015	9803
Pacific Concept Laundry Inc	7215	C	323 980-3800	13577
Pacific Equities Captl	6519	C	310 477-5300	11261
Pacific Indemnity Company	6411	B	213 622-2334	10821
Pacific Theaters Inc (PA)	7832	D	310 657-8420	18340
Pacific Theatres Entrmt Corp (HQ)	8742	D	310 657-8420	27580
Pacific Western Bank	6021	E	310 996-9100	9415
Pacifica Hosts Inc	7011	C	310 670-9000	13065
Packard Realty Inc	7011	D	310 649-5151	13070
Packetvideo Corporation	7371	D	310 526-5200	15365
Pamc Ltd	8011	D	323 343-9460	19820
Pamc Ltd (PA)	8062	A	213 624-8411	21782
Panasonic Corp North America	5064	C	323 436-3500	7503
Para Los Ninos	8351	D	213 623-3942	24498
Paracelsus Los Angeles Comm	8062	C	323 267-0477	21784
Paradigm Industries Inc	7389	D	310 965-1900	17394
Paragon Textiles Inc	5137	D	310 323-7500	8408
Paramount Pictures Corporation (HQ)	7812	A	323 956-5000	18125
Paramount Television Service	7812	A	323 956-5000	18126
Paramunt Contrs Developers Inc	6531	E	323 464-7050	11738
Parker Milliken Clark OHar	8111	D	818 784-8087	23490
Parker Stanbury LLP (PA)	8111	D	619 528-1259	23491
Parking Concepts Inc	7521	E	310 208-1611	17733
Parking Concepts Inc	7521	E	213 746-5764	17734
Parking Concepts Inc	7521	E	213 623-2661	17736
Parking Network Inc	1799	C	213 613-1500	3564
Parsec Inc	4789	D	323 276-3116	5235
Parsons Brinckerhoff Inc	8711	E	212 465-5000	26010
Pasadena Model Railroad Club	7997	D	323 222-1718	19028
Passprt Accept Fclty Los Angel	7389	D	323 460-4811	17404
Pathways La (PA)	8322	E	213 427-2700	24126
Paul Hastings LLP (PA)	8111	C	213 683-6000	23496
Payden and Rygel (PA)	6282	D	213 625-1900	10170
Pbms Inc	7349	D	213 386-2552	14383
Pcs Link Inc	8748	B	949 655-5000	28017
Pcs Property Managment LLC	6531	C	310 231-1000	11745
Peach Inc	4215	C	323 654-2333	4420
Pediatric & Family Medical Ctr	8093	C	213 342-3325	22796
Penny Roofing Company	1761	E	323 731-5424	3197
Penske Truck Leasing Co LP	7513	C	213 628-1255	17646
People Assisting Homeless	8322	D	323 644-2216	24132
Performing Arts Center of La C	7922	D	213 972-7211	18423
Permanente Kaiser Intl	8011	A	323 857-2000	19825
Perot Systems Corporation	7376	D	310 342-3200	16281
Pete Helling	7389	D	310 390-2710	17410
Petersen Auto Mseum Foundation	8412	E	323 930-2277	25037
Phelps Group	7311	D	310 752-4400	13896
Phenomenon Mktg & Entrmt Inc (PA)	8742	D	323 648-4035	27589
Philippine Airlines	4512	D	310 646-1981	4816
Philmont Management Inc	1542	D	213 380-0159	1636

GEOGRAPHIC SECTION

LOS ANGELES, CA

Company	SIC	EMP	PHONE	ENTRY #
Phoenix Textile Inc	7389	D	213 239-9640	17412
Pico Cleaner Inc (PA)	7216	D	310 274-2431	13583
Pico Rents Inc	7359	D	310 275-9431	14568
Pillsbury Winthrop Shaw	8111	C	213 488-7100	23508
Pircher Nichols & Meeks (PA)	8111	D	310 201-0132	23512
Pixelmags Inc	7371	D	310 598-7303	15384
Planned Parenthood Los Angeles (PA)	8093	D	213 284-3200	22804
Plasma Collection Centers Inc	8099	C	323 441-7720	23022
Plaza De La Raza Child Develop	8351	D	323 224-1788	24502
Plb Management LLC	6513	E	323 549-5400	11188
PLD Enterprises Inc	5146	D	213 626-4444	8648
Plh Aviation Services Corp	4581	D	310 417-0124	4930
Pmk-Bnc Inc (PA)	8743	D	310 854-0455	27761
Pmk-Bnc Inc	8743	E	310 854-4800	27762
Point360	7819	D	310 481-7000	18243
Point360 (PA)	7819	C	818 565-1400	18245
Polsinelli PC	8111	D	310 556-1801	23514
Portsmouth Square Inc	6552	B	310 889-2500	12003
Post Group Inc (PA)	7819	C	323 462-2300	18246
Pounce Consulting Inc	7379	C	714 774-3500	16459
Precise Air Systems Inc	1711	D	818 240-1737	2327
Premier Healthcare Svcs LLC (PA)	7361	C	626 204-7930	14733
Premiere Valet Service Inc	7521	D	310 652-4647	17739
Prg Parking Century LLC	7521	D	310 642-0947	17740
Prime Administration LLC	6798	A	323 549-7155	12265
Prime Marketing Holdings LLC	7389	D	888 991-6412	17426
Pro-Wash Inc	7211	D	323 756-6000	13505
Professional Cir Staffing Inc (PA)	7361	D	323 930-2333	14735
Professional Produce	5148	D	323 277-1550	8767
Professional Security Cons (PA)	7381	C	310 207-7729	16765
Proland Property Managment LLC (PA)	6531	D	213 738-8175	11770
Promo Shop Inc (PA)	8742	D	208 333-0881	27596
Prosearch Strategies Inc	8732	E	213 355-1260	26699
Proskauer Rose LLP	8111	C	310 557-2900	23520
Prospect Enterprises Inc (PA)	5146	C	213 599-5700	8649
Prospect Medical Holdings Inc (PA)	8011	C	310 943-4500	19882
Protiviti Inc	8742	C	213 327-1400	27599
Providence Health & Services	8099	D	323 298-2530	23029
Pryor Cashman LLP	8111	D	310 556-9608	23521
PS Arts	8748	E	310 586-1017	28026
Psomas (PA)	8713	C	310 954-3700	26279
Public Communications Svcs Inc	4813	C	310 231-1000	5688
Public Counsel	8111	D	213 385-2977	23522
Public Health California Dept	8011	C	213 620-6160	19898
Public Hlth Fndation Entps Inc	8099	C	323 261-6388	23033
Public Hlth Fndation Entps Inc	8641	D	323 263-0262	25324
Public Hlth Fndation Entps Inc	8099	C	323 733-9381	23035
Public Security Inc	7382	E	323 293-9884	16915
Qre Operating LLC	1382	C	213 225-5900	1066
Qualified Bliing Cllctions LLC	7322	C	323 556-3470	14043
Queen of Angels Hollywood Pres	8062	A	213 413-3000	21826
Queenscare Health Centers	8011	D	323 780-4510	19902
Queenscare Health Centers	8011	C	323 644-6180	19903
Quigly-Simpson Heppelwhite Inc	7311	D	818 444-3450	13904
Quinn Emanuel Urquhart (PA)	8111	B	213 443-3000	23525
Qwest Corporation	4813	D	213 612-0193	5689
R & B Realty Group	6513	D	323 851-3450	11191
R & B Realty Group LP	6531	A	310 478-1021	11782
R & R Electric	1731	E	310 785-0288	2693
R F R Corporation	6552	D	800 346-7663	12004
R W Zant Co (PA)	5147	C	323 980-5457	8679
Radar Medical Systems Inc	8999	C	440 337-9521	28159
Radiology Department Cal Hosp	8011	E	213 742-5840	19904
Radix Textile Inc	5131	D	213 623-6006	8322
Radlax Gateway Hotel LLC	7011	B	310 670-9000	13123
Radleys	7812	D	310 765-2223	18138
Radnet Inc (PA)	8071	C	310 445-2800	22269
Raleigh Enterprises Inc	7819	C	323 466-3111	18250
Raleigh Enterprises Inc (PA)	7011	D	310 899-8900	13125
Ralphs Grocery Company	4225	A	310 637-1101	4621
Ramsey-Shilling Residential RE	6531	D	323 851-5512	11786
Randall Mc-Anany Company	1721	D	310 822-3344	2481
Ranker Inc	7311	E	323 782-1448	13905
Rapp Worldwide Inc	7311	D	310 563-7200	13906
Rbb Architects Inc (PA)	8712	D	310 479-1473	26245
Reading International Inc (PA)	7832	D	213 235-2240	18347
Real Estate Law Center PC	6512	D	213 201-6384	11036
Reaume and Associates Inc	8711	D	310 398-5768	26037
Red Hawk Fire & SEC CA Inc (HQ)	1731	D	818 683-1500	2701
Reed Smith LLP	8111	C	213 457-8000	23528
Regent Worldwide Sales LLC	7812	E	310 806-4288	18141
Rehabltion Cntre of Bvrly Hlls	8051	D	323 782-1500	20869
Reliance Media Works Vfx Inc	7819	E	818 557-7333	18251
Reliance Steel & Aluminum Co (PA)	5051	D	213 687-7700	7393
Reliant Immediate Care	8099	D	310 215-6020	23040
Religious Technology Center	6794	D	323 663-3258	12222
Relx Inc	7375	D	213 627-1130	16256
Restaurant Depot LLC	5181	C	323 964-1220	9081
Revenue Frontier LLC	7319	D	310 584-9200	14009
Revolt Media and Tv LLC	4833	C	323 645-3000	5906
Rey-Crest Roofg Waterproofing	1799	D	323 257-9329	3577
Rheumatology Diagnostics Lab	8071	D	310 253-5455	22274
Richard J Metz MD Inc	8011	E	310 553-3189	19918
Richards Watson & Gershon PC (PA)	8111	C	213 626-8484	23532
Richards Group Inc	7311	D	214 891-5700	13912
Ricoh Usa Inc	7334	E	213 489-1700	14125
Riot Games Inc (DH)	7371	A	310 828-7953	15425
Rnc Capital Management LLC	6282	D	310 477-6543	10182
Robert Consl Englekirk Strctrl (PA)	8711	D	323 733-6673	26043
Robert Half International Inc	7361	D	213 270-6731	14756
Robert Kaufman Co Inc	5131	E	310 538-3482	8323
Robincrost Care Corporation	8051	D	323 934-3515	20880
Rocket Smog Inc	7549	D	310 390-7664	17891
Rockport ADM Svcs LLC	8051	D	323 223-3441	20881
Rockport ADM Svcs LLC (PA)	8742	D	323 330-6500	27624
Rodeo Realty Inc	6531	D	310 873-0100	11816
Rogers Poultry Co (PA)	5144	D	323 585-0802	8605
Roland Corporation US (HQ)	5099	C	323 890-3700	8135
Roosevelt Hotel LLC	7011	B	323 466-7000	13165
Rosano Partners	6531	E	213 802-0300	11823
Rostami Nejat Medical Group	8011	D	213 413-2700	19927
Rp Realty Partners LLC	6512	E	310 207-6990	11037
Rubicon Project Inc (PA)	7311	C	310 207-0272	13915
Ruby Creek Resources	8742	E	212 671-0404	27628
Rutherford Co Inc (PA)	1742	D	323 666-5284	2972
S L G G Consulting Group LLC (PA)	8721	C	310 477-3924	26435
S W K Properties LLC (PA)	8741	D	213 383-9204	27203
SA Recycling LLC	4953	D	323 564-5601	6543
Saatchi & Saatchi N Amer Inc	7311	C	310 437-2500	13918
Saban Brands LLC (HQ)	8742	D	310 557-5230	27632
Saban Capital Group Inc	6726	D	310 557-5100	12142
Saban Music Group Inc (PA)	6726	D	310 557-5100	12143
Sac International Steel Inc (PA)	5051	D	323 232-2467	7400
Saehan Bank (PA)	6022	E	213 368-7700	9521
Sag-Aftra	7929	C	323 954-1600	18489
Saint Justin Education Fu	8399	D	323 221-3400	24972
Salt of Earth Productions Inc	7389	D	818 399-1860	17470
Saltzburg Ray & Bergman LLP	8111	C	310 481-6700	23543
Salvation Army	8069	D	323 254-9015	22170
Salvation Army	8322	E	213 484-0772	24167
Salvation Army Residences Inc	8322	D	213 553-3273	24169
Sam Jung USA Inc	5131	D	323 231-0811	8324
San Judas Medical Group Inc	8011	D	213 483-1902	19950
San Vicente Hospital	8062	D	323 930-1040	21856
Santa Mnica Wlshire Imging LLC	8071	E	323 549-3055	22278
Santa Monica Bay Physicians He (PA)	8011	D	310 417-5900	19961
Santa Monica Express Inc	4212	D	310 458-6000	4062
Santee Systems Services II	8322	D	323 445-0044	24196
Santee Systems Services II LL	7991	E	323 445-0044	18680
Sbb Roofing Inc (PA)	1761	D	323 254-2888	3212
SBE Hotel Group LLC	6799	D	323 655-8000	12342
Sbehg 465 S La Cienega LLC	7011	B	310 247-0400	13222
Schaefer Ambulance Service Inc (PA)	4119	C	323 469-1473	3841
Schindler Elevator Corporation	5084	D	310 785-9775	7885
Schirmer Fire Protection Eng	6411	D	213 630-2020	10862
Schmidt Phyllis MD Corporation	8062	A	213 613-1163	21866
Scottel Voice & Data Inc	7629	C	310 737-7300	17942
SDI Media USA Inc (DH)	7819	D	323 602-5455	18252
Sea Win Inc	5146	E	213 688-2899	8652
Seabury & Smith Delaware Inc	6411	D	213 346-5000	10864
Search Agency Inc (PA)	7311	D	310 582-5706	13919
Season Produce Co Inc	5148	B	213 689-0008	8772
Secom International (PA)	7373	D	310 641-1290	16048
Secure Nursing Service Inc	7361	B	213 736-6711	14783
Securitas SEC Svcs USA Inc	7381	A	213 217-7489	16806
Securitas SEC Svcs USA Inc	7381	C	213 580-8825	16807
Securitech Security Services	7382	D	213 387-5050	16920
Securonix Inc	7373	D	310 641-1000	16050
Sedgwick LLP	8111	D	213 426-6900	23551
Seiu Local 2015	8631	B	213 985-0463	25183
Seiu Local 721	8322	D	213 368-8660	24199
Seiu Ultcw	8361	D	213 985-0463	24807
Senior Keiro Health Care	8361	D	323 263-9651	24808
Sequoia Green	7371	D	310 753-0728	15447
Serrano Covalescent Hospital	8051	D	323 465-2106	20904
Service Parking Corporation	7521	D	323 851-2416	17743
ServiceMaster Company LLC	7349	D	760 298-7500	14426
Seven Licensing Company LLC	5137	D	323 881-0308	8411
Seyfarth Shaw LLP	8111	C	213 270-9600	23556
Seyfarth Shaw LLP	8111	C	310 277-7200	23557

Employment Codes: A=Over 500 employees, B=251-500, C=101-250, D=51-100, E=45-50

2017 Directory of California Wholesalers and Services Companies

LOS ANGELES, CA — GEOGRAPHIC SECTION

Company	SIC	EMP	PHONE	ENTRY #
Shadow Animation LLC	7812	E	323 466-7771	18149
Shapiro-Gilman-Shandler Co (PA)	5148	D	213 593-1200	8775
Sharon Care Center LLC	8051	D	323 655-2023	20907
Sharp Guard Services Inc	7381	A	213 739-1900	16819
Shawmut Woodworking & Sup Inc	1542	C	323 602-1000	1665
Shed Media US Inc	7313	D	323 904-4680	13978
Sheppard Mullin Richter (PA)	8111	B	213 620-1780	23561
Sheppard Mullin Richter	8111	D	310 228-3700	23564
Sheraton Corporation	7011	B	310 642-1111	13242
Shields For Families (PA)	8069	D	323 242-5000	22172
Shilpark Paint Corporation (PA)	5198	D	323 732-7093	9239
Shriners Hspitals For Children	8069	B	213 388-3151	22173
Sia Engineering (usa) Inc	8711	D	310 693-7108	26062
Signature Consultants LLC	8748	D	310 229-5731	28056
Silla Automotive LLC	5013	D	323 733-5027	6766
Silv Communication Inc	8748	D	213 381-7999	28057
Silver Cinemas Acquisition Co (PA)	7832	D	310 473-6701	18352
Silver Fredman A Prof Law Corp	8111	E	310 556-2356	23571
Silverado Senior Living Inc	8059	D	323 984-7313	21377
Silvestri Studio Inc	5046	D	323 277-0800	7229
Simpson & Simpson	8741	D	213 736-6664	27212
Sinai Temple	7261	C	323 469-6000	13715
Singerlewak LLP (PA)	8721	C	310 477-3924	26442
Sisters of Nzareth Los Angeles	8361	C	310 839-2361	24813
Sitrick Brincko Group LLC	8742	D	310 788-2850	27649
Six Continents Hotels Inc	7011	D	213 748-1291	13263
Six Point Harness	7819	E	323 462-3344	18253
Skadden Arps Slate Meagher & F	8111	C	213 687-5000	23574
Skanska-Rados A Joint Venture	1611	D	213 978-0600	1862
Skidmore Owings & Merrill LLP	8712	C	213 996-8366	26252
Skilled Healthcare LLC	8051	A	323 663-3951	20918
Skirball Cultural Center	8699	C	310 440-4500	25577
Skyline Healthcare & Wellness	8051	D	323 665-1185	20919
SM 10000 Property LLC	6552	D	305 374-5700	12012
Smart & Final Holdings LLC	5141	A	310 843-1900	8519
Smith-Emery Company (PA)	8742	D	213 745-5312	27653
SMS Transportation Svcs Inc	4111	C	213 489-5617	3718
Smuk Inc	7812	C	323 904-4680	18150
Sobel Ross H Law Offices	8111	E	310 788-8995	23577
Sobol Philip A MD P C Inc	8011	E	310 649-5894	20005
Socie of Saint Vince De PA	8322	C	323 224-6280	24214
Society of St Vincent De Paul (PA)	8699	D	323 224-6214	25582
Solheim Lutheran Home	8361	C	323 257-7518	24815
Solver Inc	5045	E	310 691-5300	7188
Sonicocom Inc	7379	D	213 291-0475	16486
Sony Interactive Entrmt LLC (DH)	7389	D	310 981-1500	17496
Sony Pictures Entrmt Inc	7929	B	310 244-3558	18499
Sony Pictures Studios Inc	7812	B	310 244-4000	18155
South Bay Senior Services Inc	8082	D	310 338-7558	22567
South Bay Vlla Preservation LP	6513	D	310 516-7325	11206
South Baylo University	8093	C	213 387-2414	22835
South Central Family Hlth Ctr	8011	D	323 908-4200	20011
South Central Los (PA)	8399	D	213 744-7000	24980
South China Sheet Metal Inc	1711	D	323 225-1522	2380
South Cntl Heatlh & Rehab Prog	8093	D	323 751-2677	22837
Southern Building Maint Inc	7349	D	213 598-7071	14435
Southern Cal Hlthcare Sys Inc	8062	A	310 943-4500	21899
Southern Cal Pipe Trades ADM (PA)	6733	D	213 385-6161	12203
Southern Cal Prmnnte Med Group	8011	D	323 857-2000	20023
Southern Cal Prmnnte Med Group	8011	D	323 783-5455	20026
Southern Cal Prmnnte Med Group	8011	A	323 783-4893	20029
Southern Cal Rgional Rail Auth (PA)	4111	D	213 452-0200	3721
Southern California Gas Co (DH)	4924	C	213 244-1200	6274
Southern California Gas Tower (PA)	4924	D	213 244-1200	6281
Southwest Airlines Co	4512	D	310 665-5700	4825
Southwest Rgnal Cncil Crpnters (PA)	8631	E	213 385-1457	25187
Sp Plus Corporation	1799	D	213 488-3100	3584
Spanish Brdcstg Sys of Cal	4832	D	310 203-0900	5822
Spark Networks Inc (PA)	7299	D	310 893-0550	13797
Spear Management Company	7381	D	323 963-7515	16829
Special Needs Network	8069	E	323 291-7100	22178
Special Service For Groups Inc (PA)	8331	D	213 368-1888	24391
Special Service For Groups Inc	8399	D	213 620-5713	24982
Spectrum MGT Holdg Co LLC	4841	D	323 657-0899	6021
Sperry Van Ness Intl Corp	6531	D	310 979-0800	11854
Spring Break 83 Production LLC	7812	E	323 871-4466	18159
Sprint Spectrum LP	1731	D	323 473-5454	2740
Sprint Spectrum LP	1731	D	424 372-2500	2741
Sprouts Farmers Market Inc	5141	C	310 500-1192	8524
Spus7 Miami Acc LP	6726	E	213 683-4200	12148
Squire Sanders (us) LLP	8111	D	213 624-2500	23580
Srht Property Mgmt Co	8741	D	213 683-0522	27228
SRK Global Consulting	7379	D	310 295-2524	16488
Ssg Hop Sp	8999	B	323 432-4399	28162
St Annes Maternity Home	8361	C	213 381-2931	24819
St Barnabas Senior Center of L	8322	D	213 388-4444	24227
St Johns Well Child (PA)	8021	D	323 541-1600	20278
St Vincent Medical Center	8062	A	213 484-7111	21930
St Vincent Senior Citizn Nutr (PA)	8621	D	213 484-7775	25158
Standard Chartered Bank	6022	C	626 639-8000	9525
Standard-Southern Corporation	4222	C	213 624-1831	4501
Standard-Southern Corporation	4222	C	213 624-1831	4502
Standard-Southern Corporation	4222	C	213 624-1831	4503
Standardaero Bus AVI Svcs LLC	4581	D	310 568-3700	4939
Starline Tours Hollywood Inc	7999	D	323 463-3333	19288
Starwood Hotels & Resorts	7011	C	310 208-8765	13290
Starwood Hotels & Resorts	7011	C	213 624-1000	13294
Starwood Hotels & Resorts	7011	C	323 798-1300	13302
State Bar of California	8621	B	213 765-1000	25160
State Farm Mutl Auto Insur Co	6411	B	309 766-2311	10879
State Farm Mutl Auto Insur Co	6411	D	323 852-6868	10895
Steiny and Company Inc (PA)	1731	D	626 962-1055	2749
Steiny and Company Inc	1731	D	213 382-2331	2751
Stella Travel Services USA Inc	4724	D	310 535-1000	4974
Steptoe & Johnson LLP	8111	E	213 439-9400	23585
Sterling Westwood Inc	7216	D	310 287-2431	13588
Steve Beattie Inc	1721	D	310 454-1786	2494
Stjohn God Rtirement Care Ctr	8051	C	323 731-0641	20931
Stockbridge/Sbe Holdings LLC	7011	A	323 655-8000	13305
Stone Tree Landscape Corp	0782	E	323 965-0944	960
Stopirsdebtcom Inc	7291	E	323 857-5809	13727
Storybook Productions Inc	7922	D	323 468-5050	18437
Straight Lander Inc	8741	D	323 337-9075	27233
Stroock & Stroock & Lavan LLP	8111	C	310 556-5800	23588
Study US Research Inst Inc	8733	D	213 840-9575	26811
Stv Architects Inc	8712	D	213 482-9444	26260
Success Healthcare 1 LLC (PA)	8082	A	213 989-6100	22574
Suffock Construction Co Inc	1542	D	949 453-9400	1679
Sullivan & Cromwell LLP	8111	D	310 712-6600	23589
Sullivan Gj & Associates Inc (PA)	6411	D	213 626-1000	10900
Sumitomo Mitsui Tr Bnk USA Inc	6022	D	213 955-0800	9526
Sun America Housing Fund	6512	D	310 772-6000	11058
SunAmerica Annuity Lf Asrn Co (DH)	6311	D	310 772-6000	10222
SunAmerica Hsng Fnd 1071	6512	D	310 772-6000	11059
SunAmerica Inc (HQ)	6091	A	310 772-6000	9704
SunAmerica Investments (DH)	8741	D	310 772-6000	27239
SunAmerica Investments Inc	6722	C	310 772-6000	12125
Sunrise Senior Living Inc	8051	D	310 437-7178	20959
Sunset Tower Hotel LLC	7011	D	323 654-7100	13311
Sunstone Hotel Investors Inc	7011	C	310 215-1000	13315
Sunstone Hotel Investors Inc	7011	D	310 649-1400	13317
Sunstone Hotel Properties Inc	7011	D	310 228-4100	13324
Super Center Concepts Inc	7389	C	323 223-3878	17511
Superbalife International LLC	5122	B	310 553-7400	8297
Superior Home Design Inc	5023	D	213 455-8972	6889
Sushi Nozawa LLC	7371	C	310 963-7377	15484
Sutherland Haltcare Solutions	8741	D	310 464-5000	27241
Svi Lax LLC	7011	D	310 281-0300	13329
Swinerton Builders	1542	D	213 896-3400	1682
Swiss Port Corp	8744	B	310 417-0258	27800
Swissport Cargo Services LP	4581	A	310 910-9541	4940
Swissport Usa Inc	4581	B	310 345-1986	4941
Swissport Usa Inc	4581	B	310 910-9560	4944
Swisstex California Inc (PA)	7389	E	310 516-6800	17512
Sycamore Park Care Center LLC	8059	D	323 223-3441	21388
Syconex Corporation	5084	E	213 386-7383	7895
Sydell Hotels LLC	7011	E	213 381-7411	13333
Synermed	8741	D	213 626-4556	27246
T C R Limited Partnership	7514	C	213 645-1881	17694
T C W Realty Fund VI	6798	C	213 683-4200	12275
T Points Inc	7219	D	323 846-9176	13658
TAJ Marketing Llc	8742	E	213 232-0150	27678
Talkmex California Corporation	4813	D	323 479-3279	5707
Tanner Mainstain Blatt & Gly	8721	D	310 446-2700	26448
Tarrant Apparel Group	5137	C	323 780-8250	8413
Tbwa Chiat/Day Inc	7389	C	310 305-5000	17518
Tbwa Worldwide Inc	7311	D	310 305-4400	13927
Tcw Absolute Return Credit LLC	6282	C	213 244-0000	10188
Tcw Funds Management Inc	6211	A	213 244-0000	10081
Tcw Group Inc (HQ)	6022	B	213 244-0000	9529
Tcw Specialized Cash Mgt Ltd	8741	D	213 244-0000	27249
Tcw Value Added Ltd Partnr	6733	D	213 244-0000	12204
Team-One Emplyment Spclsts LLC	7361	A	310 481-4482	14802
Technclor Crative Svcs USA Inc (DH)	7819	B	818 260-3800	18257
Technclor Crative Svcs USA Inc	7819	D	323 467-1244	18258
Technicolor Thomson Group	7819	B	323 817-6600	18263
Telaflora LLC	5193	D	310 231-9199	9220
Tele-Car Couriers Inc	4215	D	877 910-1313	4424
Temple Hospital Corporation	8062	B	213 355-3200	21960
Temple Israel of Hollywood (PA)	7261	D	323 876-8330	13717

Mergent email: customerrelations@mergent.com
2017 Directory of California Wholesalers and Services Companies
(P-0000) Products & Services Section entry number
(PA)=Parent Co (HQ)=Headquarters (DH)=Div Headquarters

GEOGRAPHIC SECTION LOS ANGELES, CA

Company	SIC	EMP	PHONE	ENTRY #
Temple Park Convalescent Hosp	8059	D	213 380-2035	21390
Tenet Health Systems Norris	8069	B	323 865-3000	22181
Tessie Clvland Cmnty Svcs Corp	8322	D	323 586-7333	24250
The Boston Cnsulting Group Inc	8742	D	213 621-2772	27686
The Gray-Line Tours Company	4142	C	323 463-3333	3908
The Music Ctr of La Cty Inc	8399	C	213 972-8007	24985
The Teecor Group Inc	1799	D	213 632-2350	3589
Thermasource LLC	8711	D	530 476-3333	26096
Think Passenger Inc (PA)	7371	D	323 556-5400	15499
Thinkwell Group Inc	7922	D	818 333-3444	18439
Thompson Coburn LLP	8111	B	310 282-2500	23595
Thomson Financial Services	8748	E	213 955-5902	28076
Thoreau Janitorial Svcs Inc	7349	C	310 822-8017	14443
Ticketmob LLC	8741	A	800 927-0939	27251
Time Inc	7313	C	310 268-7200	13982
Time Warner Cable Entps LLC	4841	C	323 993-7076	6028
Time Warner Cable Entps LLC	4833	D	818 972-0328	5915
Time Warner Cable Inc	4841	D	213 599-7968	6037
Time Warner Cable Inc	4841	D	951 682-6180	6039
Time Warner Cable Inc	4841	B	323 993-8000	6048
Tinco Sheet Metal Inc	1761	D	323 263-0511	3220
Tishman Construction Corp Cal	8741	D	213 542-6400	27252
TNT USA Inc	4513	C	310 242-9700	4872
To Celerity Educational Group	8748	D	323 231-7005	28080
Tog Landscaping Inc	0781	C	323 549-3150	801
Tom Malloy Corporation (PA)	5082	E	310 327-5554	7793
Topa Berkeley Ltd	6531	D	310 203-9199	11877
Topa Insurance Company (HQ)	6399	D	310 201-0451	10573
Topa Management Company (PA)	6512	C	310 203-9199	11065
Torres Construction Corp (PA)	1541	C	323 257-7460	1474
Total Professional Network	7361	D	213 382-5550	14805
Towers Watson Pennsylvania Inc	8742	C	310 551-5600	27692
Tpg Reflections II LLC	6513	D	213 613-1900	11215
Tps Parking Management LLC	7521	D	310 846-4747	17744
Trailer Park Inc	7311	D	310 845-8400	13930
Trailer Park Inc (PA)	7311	D	310 845-3000	13931
Trams Inc (DH)	7373	D	310 641-8726	16067
Trans West Investigations Inc	7381	D	213 381-1500	16834
Transamerica Securities Sales	6211	D	213 741-7702	10083
Transmerica Fincl Advisors Inc	6211	C	213 741-7702	10084
Transmrica Occidental Lf Insur (DH)	6311	A	213 742-2111	10225
Travel Store (PA)	4724	D	310 575-5540	4979
Triage Entertainment Inc	7812	D	310 417-4800	18170
Trope and Trope LLP	8111	D	323 879-2726	23598
Troygould PC	8111	D	310 553-4441	23601
Truck Underwriters Association (DH)	8111	D	323 932-3200	23602
Trust Company of West (DH)	6211	A	213 244-0000	10085
Trz Holdings II Inc	6531	B	213 955-7170	11886
Tucker Ellis LLP	8111	D	213 430-3400	23603
Tumbleweed Educational Entps	7999	C	310 444-3232	19298
Turner Broadcasting System Inc	4832	D	310 788-6767	5826
Turner Construction Company	1521	D	213 891-3000	1275
Tustin Hospital and Med Ctr	8062	B	714 619-7700	21974
Twentieth Century Fox (DH)	7822	B	310 369-1000	18279
Twentieth Century Fox Home E (DH)	4833	D	310 369-1000	5919
Twentieth Century Fox In	6531	A	310 369-1000	11888
Twentieth Cntury Fox Film Corp (DH)	7812	D	310 369-1000	18174
Twentieth Cntury Fox Film Corp	7812	D	310 369-2582	18175
Tzippy Care Inc	8059	D	323 737-7778	21397
U S Army Corps of Engineers	8711	D	213 452-3139	26110
U S Army Corps of Engineers	5082	D	213 452-3403	7795
U Turn Seven Corporation	5141	C	323 662-1587	8539
Uaw-Lbor Emplyment Trning Corp	7361	C	323 730-7900	14810
UBS Financial Services Inc	6211	D	213 972-1511	10086
UBS Financial Services Inc	6211	D	310 556-0746	10094
Uc Regents	8011	D	310 301-8777	20150
Ucla Assoc Stdnts Event Servs	7382	E	310 206-0832	16939
Ucla Copy Services	7334	E	310 794-6371	14128
Ucla Faculty Center Assn Inc	8621	D	310 825-0877	25161
Ucla Foundation	6732	B	310 794-3193	12164
Ucla Health System	8011	D	310 825-9111	20151
Ucla Health System Auxiliary	8082	A	310 794-0500	22585
Ucla Marina Center	7999	D	310 825-3671	19300
Ucla SC Theater Film & TV Eqp	7622	D	310 825-6165	17915
Umina Bros Inc (PA)	5148	D	213 622-9206	8782
Unified Grocers Inc	5143	D	323 232-6124	8595
Unified Grocers Inc	5141	C	323 373-1339	8541
Union Bank Foundation (DH)	6022	A	213 236-5000	9532
Union Bank of California	6022	A	213 236-6444	9533
Uniserve Facilities Svcs Corp	7349	A	310 440-6747	14452
Unitas Global LLC (PA)	7374	D	213 785-6200	16205
United Airlines Inc	4512	C	310 342-8086	4830
United Airlines Inc	4512	C	310 646-3107	4832
United Airlines Inc	4512	B	310 258-3319	4834
United Artists Productions Inc	7822	C	310 449-3000	18280
United Convalescent Facilities	8059	D	626 629-6950	21399
United Cp/S Chldrns Fndn La	8322	D	323 737-0303	24269
United Express Messengers Inc	7389	D	310 261-2000	17554
United Fabrics Intl Inc	5131	D	213 749-8200	8329
United Food and Commercial (PA)	8631	D	213 487-7070	25190
United Independent Taxi Co	4121	E	213 385-2227	3870
United Medical Imaging Inc	8011	C	310 943-8400	20155
United Parcel Service Inc OH	4215	C	310 474-0019	4454
United Parcel Service Inc OH	4215	A	323 729-6762	4471
United States Fire Insur Co	6411	D	213 797-3100	10916
United Talent Agency Inc	8742	C	310 385-2800	27704
United Teachers Los Angeles	8631	D	213 487-5560	25191
United Way Inc (PA)	8399	D	213 808-6220	24992
Universal Studios Inc	7812	C	310 235-4749	18183
University Cal Los Angeles	8062	D	310 825-9771	21987
University Cal Los Angeles	8062	A	310 825-0640	21988
University Cal Los Angeles	8062	A	310 825-9111	21991
University Credit Union	6062	C	310 477-6628	9697
University Southern California	8062	D	213 740-9790	22004
University Southern California	8062	A	323 442-8500	22005
University Southern California	8011	D	213 743-5319	20173
University Student Union Inc	7389	C	323 343-2450	17575
URS Group Inc	8711	D	213 996-2200	26121
URS Group Inc	8711	D	213 996-2200	26123
US Army Corps of Engineers	8711	A	213 452-3967	26136
US International Media LLC (PA)	7319	D	310 482-6700	14013
US Metro Group Inc	7349	A	213 382-6435	14460
US Telepacific Corp (HQ)	4813	E	213 213-3000	5714
USA Vily Group	7374	E	323 457-6888	16207
Usc Care Medical Group Inc	8062	D	323 442-5100	22007
Usc Credit Union	6061	D	213 821-7100	9647
Usc Emergency Medicine Assoc	8011	D	323 226-6667	20177
Usc Institute For Neuroimaging	8011	C	323 442-7246	20178
Usc Shoah Fndn Inst For Visual	8699	D	213 740-6001	25594
Usc Surgeons Incorporated	8011	C	323 442-5910	20179
Uscb Inc	7322	D	213 387-6181	14050
Uscb Inc	7322	C	213 985-2111	14051
Vacation and Holiday Benefit F	6733	D	213 385-6161	12207
Valet Parking Svc A Cal Partnr (PA)	7521	A	323 465-5873	17746
Valetor Inc	7216	E	323 654-1271	13589
Valley Couriers Inc (PA)	4212	D	818 591-2212	4086
Vancrest Construction Corp	1542	D	323 256-0011	1710
Vayan Marketing Group LLC	8742	E	310 943-4990	27709
VCA Animal Hospitals Inc (HQ)	0742	C	310 571-6500	628
VCA Antech Inc	0742	C	310 207-0781	629
VCA Inc	0742	C	310 473-2951	630
Veatch Carlson Grogan & Nelson	8111	E	213 381-2861	23605
Vector Security Inc	1731	D	323 224-6700	2784
Vendor Direct Solutions LLC	8741	D	213 362-5622	27275
Verifi Inc	8742	D	323 655-5789	27710
Veritiv Operating Company	5113	C	310 527-3000	8221
Verizon Business Global LLC	4813	D	909 466-5633	5720
Verizon Communications Inc	7389	A	213 330-2556	17589
Verizon Digital Media Svcs Inc	7379	A	310 396-7400	16521
Versa Products Inc (PA)	5021	D	310 353-7100	6835
Veterans Health Administration	8011	A	310 478-3711	20196
Veterans Health Administration	8011	D	213 253-2677	20220
Via Care Cmnty Hlth Ctr Inc	8011	D	323 268-9191	20223
Viacom Consumer Products Inc	6794	E	323 956-5634	12228
Vicar Operating Inc (HQ)	0742	C	310 571-6500	632
VIP Tours of California Inc	4725	D	310 216-7507	5003
Virgil Sntrium Cnvlescent Hosp	8051	D	323 665-5793	21016
Virgin Mobile Usa Inc	4813	C	310 445-7000	5726
Visalus Inc	6411	B	323 801-2400	10925
Viscount Petroleum LLC	5172	E	213 382-1058	9033
Visionaire Group Inc	7311	D	310 823-1800	13937
Visionstar Inc	8742	D	213 387-3700	27713
Vista Anglina Hsing Prtners LP	6531	D	213 482-4718	11900
Vista Del Sol Health Services	8059	D	310 390-9045	21416
Viva Group Inc	6513	D	310 449-6400	11226
Viva Vina Inc	7389	D	323 225-4984	17596
Vivid Entertainment LLC	7812	E	323 845-4557	18187
Vivid Solution	7389	D	310 498-2559	17597
Volume Services Inc	7999	D	323 644-6038	19306
Volunteer Center Los Angeles	8322	E	818 908-5151	24281
Vxi Global Solutions LLC (PA)	7389	A	213 739-4720	17602
W Los Angeles	7011	B	310 208-8765	13385
W P Media Complex	7389	D	310 477-1938	17603
W Scott Bllard Dsign Arch Inc	7389	E	323 386-4740	17604
Walter J Conn & Associates	8712	D	213 683-0500	26264
Warren Drye Kelley	8111	D	310 712-6100	23610
Washington Enterprises 3 LLC	8051	D	323 731-0861	21024
Wasserman Media Group LLC (PA)	8742	C	310 407-0200	27717
Watts Health Foundation Inc	6733	B	323 357-6688	12209
Watts Healthcare Corporation	8011	C	213 241-1780	20229

Employment Codes: A=Over 500 employees, B=251-500, C=101-250, D=51-100, E=45-50

2017 Directory of California Wholesalers and Services Companies

LOS ANGELES, CA

GEOGRAPHIC SECTION

	SIC	EMP	PHONE	ENTRY #
Watts Healthcare Corporation (PA)	8011	C	323 568-3059	20230
Wealth Educators Inc	8741	C	310 623-9145	27278
Wedbush Securities Inc (HQ)	6211	B	213 688-8000	10098
Weingart Center Association	8322	C	213 622-6359	24286
Weitz & Luxenberg PC	8111	D	310 247-0921	23618
Wells Fargo Bank Ltd	6022	D	213 253-6227	9535
Wells Fargo Bank National Assn	6512	C	213 628-2251	11069
West Coast Ambulance Corp	4119	C	310 435-1862	3856
West Corporation	7389	C	310 481-7878	17620
West Oahu Mall Associates	6798	E	310 276-1290	12277
West Side Rehab Corporation	6512	C	323 231-4174	11070
Western Exterminator Company	7342	D	310 274-9244	14194
Westfield LLC (DH)	6512	B	813 926-4600	11072
Westfield America Inc (HQ)	6512	C	310 478-4456	11073
Westfield America Ltd Partnr	6552	C	310 478-4456	12026
Westfield America Ltd Partnr	6512	B	310 277-3898	11074
Westlake Health Care Center	8051	C	805 494-1233	21035
Westlake Services LLC	6159	C	323 692-8800	9808
Weston Bnshf Rchfrt Rublcv & M	8111	C	213 576-1000	23620
Westpoint Marketing Intl Inc	7389	C	323 233-0233	17625
Westside Jewish Cmnty Ctr Inc (PA)	8399	C	323 938-2531	24998
Weststar Cinemas Inc	7832	C	323 461-3331	18354
Westwood Healthcare Center LP	8051	D	310 826-0821	21038
Westwoodone	7922	C	323 904-4660	18443
Wga West Inc	7313	D	323 782-4512	13985
Whb Corporation	7011	A	213 624-1011	13410
White & Case LLP	8111	C	213 687-9655	23621
White Carnival LLC	8741	E	310 914-1600	27283
White Memorial Med Group Inc (PA)	8011	D	323 987-1300	20239
White Memorial Medical Center (HQ)	8062	A	323 268-5000	22031
WI Spa LLC	7991	E	213 487-2700	18707
Wiemar Distributors Inc	5148	D	213 747-7036	8790
Will Perkins Inc	8712	C	213 270-8400	26266
William Morris Endeavor	7922	B	310 285-9000	18444
William Oneil & Co Inc	6211	C	310 448-6800	10103
Williamson Enterprises Inc	7532	C	310 822-6615	17776
Wilmer Cutler Pick Hale Dorr	8111	C	213 443-5300	23622
Wilshire Center Dental Group	8021	E	213 386-3336	20288
Wilshire Consumer Credit	6141	E	323 692-8585	9767
Wilshire Country Club	7997	C	323 934-6050	19126
Wilshire Investments Corp	6531	C	310 207-0704	11928
Wilson Elser Moskowitz	8111	C	213 443-5100	23624
Windsor Grdns Cnvalescent Hosp	8051	C	323 937-5466	21051
Winterthur U S Holdings Inc	6411	C	213 228-0281	10940
Wood Smith Henning Berman LLP (PA)	8111	E	310 481-7600	23632
Woodcraft Rangers	8641	B	213 749-3031	25404
Workmens Auto Insurance Co	6331	D	213 742-8700	10484
World Acceptance Group Corp (PA)	7375	D	800 388-1266	16271
Worldlink LLC (PA)	7389	D	323 866-5900	17632
Worldwide Flight Services Inc	4581	C	310 646-7510	4948
Worldwide Flight Services Inc	4512	C	310 342-7830	4840
Worldwide Holdings Inc (PA)	6411	D	213 236-4500	10946
Worldwide Security Associates (HQ)	7381	B	310 743-3000	16855
Worleyparsons Group Inc	8711	B	610 855-2000	26154
Woundco Holdings Inc	7352	D	310 551-0101	14477
Writers Guild America West Inc	8631	C	323 951-4000	25192
Xenos Fashion Inc	5137	C	323 585-0088	8417
Xpo Enterprise Services Inc	4213	C	213 744-0664	4316
Yeshiva Rau Isacsohn Academy	8351	C	323 549-3170	24535
Yogibotanicals	5149	C	310 275-9891	8958
York Hlthcare Wllness Cntre LP	8051	D	323 254-3407	21063
Young Mens Chrstn Assn of La (PA)	8641	D	213 351-2256	25466
Young Mens Chrstn Assn of La	8641	E	310 216-9036	25467
Young Mens Chrstn Assn of La	8322	C	323 467-4161	24296
Young Mens Chrstn Assn of La	8641	E	213 624-2348	25470
Youngs Market Company LLC	5182	B	213 629-3929	9121
Yucaipa Companies LLC (PA)	8748	C	310 789-7200	28104
Yuen Yee Laundry & Cleaners	7211	C	323 734-7205	13508
Z Valet Inc	7299	C	323 954-3700	13806
Zabin Industries Inc (PA)	5131	C	213 749-1215	8330
Zastrow Construction Inc	1522	C	323 478-1956	1354
Zestfinance Inc	7371	D	323 450-3000	15559
Ziffren B B F G-L S&C Fnd	8111	C	310 552-3388	23637
Zimmer Gunsul	8712	C	213 617-1901	26271
Zubi Advertising Services Inc	7311	C	310 575-4839	13948
Zurich American Insurance Co	6331	D	213 270-0600	10487
Zynx Health Incorporated (DH)	7371	C	310 954-1950	15562

LOS BANOS, CA - Merced County

	SIC	EMP	PHONE	ENTRY #
Al Barcellos Et	0131	E	209 826-2636	9
Bowles Farming Co Inc	0191	E	209 827-3000	347
David Santos Farming	7389	D	209 826-1065	17116
Facilities Operation and Trnsp	4151	D	209 826-1936	3926
Kings View Work Experience Ctr	6321	E	209 826-8118	10243
McElvany Inc	1623	D	209 826-1102	1967
New Bthny Rsdntl CRE&sklld	8361	D	209 827-8933	24744
Para & Palli Inc	8051	D	209 826-0790	20839
Ranchwood Contractors Inc	1542	D	209 826-6200	1645
Sutter Health	8641	C	209 827-4866	25360
Wolfsen Incorporated	0131	C	209 827-7700	17

LOS GATOS, CA - Santa Clara County

	SIC	EMP	PHONE	ENTRY #
Accel Biotech LLC	8711	D	408 354-1700	25611
Alain Pinel Realtors Inc	6531	D	408 358-1111	11283
American Baptist Homes of West	8059	C	408 357-1100	21139
Audrey Adams MD	8011	E	408 354-2114	19363
Auto World Car Wash LLC	7542	A	408 345-6532	17829
Butter Paddle	7389	D	408 395-1678	17044
Calvary Baptist Ch Los Gatos	8351	D	408 356-5126	24422
Caresouth Home Health Svcs LLC	8082	E	408 378-6131	22396
Coldwell Bnkr Rsdential RE LLC	6531	C	408 355-1500	11438
Courtside Tennis Club	7997	D	408 395-4181	18930
Episcopal Senior Communities	8361	C	408 354-0211	24646
Golden Living LLC	8059	C	408 356-8136	21243
Golden Living LLC	8051	C	408 356-9151	20623
Good Samaritan Hospital LP	8062	C	408 354-4111	21585
Infogain Corporation (PA)	7379	C	408 355-6000	16401
Intellicus Tech Pvt Ltd	7373	D	408 213-3314	15967
Joie De Vivre Hospitality LLC	1731	A	408 335-1700	2627
La Rinconada Country Club Inc (PA)	7997	C	408 395-4181	18972
Netline Corporation (PA)	4813	C	408 374-4200	5665
Roku Inc (PA)	4841	B	408 556-9040	6015
SA Photonics Inc	8748	D	408 560-3500	28049
Sanco Pipelines Incorporated	1623	E	408 377-2793	1993
Santa Clara County of	7999	C	408 355-2200	19277
Santa Clara Valley Water	4941	D	408 395-8121	6400
Sierra Nevada Corporation	8711	C	408 395-2004	26066
Sierra Weatherization Co Inc	7311	D	408 354-1900	13921
Society For Info Display	8699	D	408 399-6000	25579
Stratford School Inc	8351	D	408 371-3020	24521
Sutter Health	8641	B	408 523-3900	25361
Tenet Healthsystem Medical	8062	A	408 378-6131	21965
Therapy In Your Home O TP TS	8082	D	408 358-0201	22580
Trevi Partners A Calif LP	7011	D	408 395-7070	13355
Uplift Family Services	8093	C	408 379-3790	22860
Verizon Wireless Inc	4812	C	408 354-6374	5424

LOS OSOS, CA - San Luis Obispo County

	SIC	EMP	PHONE	ENTRY #
California Resources Corp	1311	C	661 763-6107	1036
Cellco Partnership	4812	C	805 596-2300	5294

LOST HILLS, CA - Kern County

	SIC	EMP	PHONE	ENTRY #
Roll Properties Intl Inc	6799	D	661 797-6500	12341
Wonderful Orchards LLC	0173	C	661 797-6400	211

LOTUS, CA - El Dorado County

	SIC	EMP	PHONE	ENTRY #
Adventure Connection Inc	7999	D	530 626-7385	19131

LOWER LAKE, CA - Lake County

	SIC	EMP	PHONE	ENTRY #
Barrick Gold Corporation	1041	D	707 995-6070	1021
Epidenio Construction Inc	1771	E	707 994-5100	3263
Laidlaw International Inc	4151	C	707 994-3384	3941

LOYALTON, CA - Sierra County

	SIC	EMP	PHONE	ENTRY #
Eastern Plumas Health Care	8051	D	530 993-1225	20525

LUCERNE VALLEY, CA - San Bernardino County

	SIC	EMP	PHONE	ENTRY #
Specialty Minerals Inc	1422	C	760 248-5300	1100

LYNWOOD, CA - Los Angeles County

	SIC	EMP	PHONE	ENTRY #
ADM Furniture Inc	5021	D	310 762-2800	6801
Country Villa Service Corp	8051	D	310 537-2500	20479
Kaiser Foundation Hospitals	8011	A	310 604-5700	19627
Legacy Frames	5065	D	310 537-4210	7594
Marlinda Management Inc (PA)	8059	C	310 638-6691	21309
Midas Express Los Angeles Inc	4226	C	310 609-0366	4698
South Cntl Heatlh & Rehab Prog	8093	D	310 667-4070	22836
Southern CA Hlth & Rhbltn Prg	8011	D	310 631-8004	20013
Southern Cal Prmnnte Med Group	8011	D	310 604-5700	20022
St Francis Medical Center	8011	C	310 900-8900	20053
St Francis Medical Center of (PA)	8062	A	310 900-8900	21914
Verity Health System Cal Inc	8062	D	310 900-2000	22017
Verity Health System Cal Inc	8062	A	650 917-4500	22018
Via Trading Corporation	5199	D	877 202-3616	9309

LYTLE CREEK, CA - San Bernardino County

	SIC	EMP	PHONE	ENTRY #
Burlingame Industries Inc	7033	C	909 887-7038	13476

MACDOEL, CA - Siskiyou County

	SIC	EMP	PHONE	ENTRY #
Plant Sciences Inc	5193	E	530 398-4042	9209

MADERA, CA - Madera County

	SIC	EMP	PHONE	ENTRY #
Agri-World Cooperative	0762	E	559 673-1306	691
Avalon Care Ctr - Madera LLC	8051	D	559 673-9278	20392
Comcast Corporation	4841	D	559 474-4194	5961

GEOGRAPHIC SECTION

MARINA DEL REY, CA

	SIC	EMP	PHONE	ENTRY #
Community Action Prtnrshp (PA)	8351	C	559 673-9173	24444
Costa View Farms	0241	E	559 675-3131	421
County of Los Angeles	8322	C	559 675-7739	23861
County of Madera	7549	D	559 675-7811	17880
Deniz Packing Incorporated	0175	E	559 673-0066	231
Eurodrip USA Inc	5083	D	559 674-2670	7801
First Student Inc	4119	C	559 661-7433	3794
Fresno-Madera Federal Land	6111	D	559 674-2437	9731
Golden Living LLC	8059	D	559 673-9278	21247
Iest Family Farms	0241	D	559 674-9417	429
Kronos Foods Corp	5149	D	559 674-4445	8871
Lamanuzzi & Pantaleo LLC (PA)	0172	D	559 432-3170	166
Lion Raisins Inc	0191	C	559 662-8686	380
Madera Cnty Bhvioral Hlth Svcs	8093	C	559 673-3508	22771
Madera Community Hospital	8011	D	559 675-5530	19724
Madera Community Hospital (PA)	8062	A	559 675-5555	21722
Madera Convalescent Hospital (PA)	8051	D	559 673-9228	20752
Madera Private Security Patrol	7381	D	559 662-1546	16730
Mid-Valley Labor Services Inc	7361	B	559 661-6390	14705
Our House Residential Care Ctr	8059	D	559 674-8670	21339
Pediatric Physical Rehab Clnc	8093	E	559 353-6130	22797
Ready Roast Nut Company LLC (PA)	0723	C	559 661-1696	577
Resource Rfrral Child Care Dev	8322	C	559 673-9173	24156
Richard Iest Dairy Inc	0139	C	559 673-2635	32
S & J Ranches LLC	0762	D	559 437-2600	722
Span Construction & Engrg Inc (PA)	1542	C	559 661-1111	1676
Stellar Distributing Inc	5148	C	559 664-8400	8778
Talley Transportation	4212	D	559 673-9013	4070
Turning Point Central Cal Inc	8322	C	559 664-9021	24261
Valley Childrens Healthcare	8011	A	559 353-3000	20180
Valley Childrens Hospital	8011	C	559 353-6425	20181
Valley Childrens Hospital (PA)	8069	A	559 353-3000	22184
Valley Productions Inc	7389	E	559 661-6121	17583

MAGALIA, CA - Butte County

	SIC	EMP	PHONE	ENTRY #
Pacific Gas and Electric Co	4911	D	530 892-4519	6168

MALIBU, CA - Los Angeles County

	SIC	EMP	PHONE	ENTRY #
California Fuji International	7992	E	818 889-6680	18719
County of Los Angeles	8361	D	818 889-0260	24612
County of Los Angeles	8322	C	818 889-1353	23860
Dun & Bradstreet Emerging (DH)	7389	C	310 456-8271	17137
Fitness Ridge Malibu LLC	7011	B	818 874-1300	12637
Grasshopper House LLC	8093	C	310 589-2880	22738
Hrl Laboratories LLC	8733	B	310 317-5000	26769
James H Cowan & Associates Inc	0782	D	310 457-2574	875
Las Vegas Intrntnl Tours	7389	D	310 581-0718	17289
Malibu Conference Center Inc	6512	B	818 889-6440	11015
Marmalade LLC	7389	E	310 317-4242	17313
Mbipch LLC	7011	B	310 456-6444	12985
Parks and Recreation Cal Dept	8412	C	310 456-8432	25036
Phifactor Technologies LLC	8071	D	424 234-9494	22255
Pritchett Rapf and Associates	6531	D	310 456-6771	11762
Sobaliving Llc	8099	E	800 595-3803	23059
Sothebys Intl Rlty Inc	6531	E	310 456-6431	11851
Soulcycle Inc	7991	A	310 973-7685	18683
Tall Pony Productions Inc	7812	C	310 456-7495	18166
Terra Coastal Properties Inc	6531	E	310 457-2534	11869
Westmed Ambulance Inc	4119	C	310 456-3830	3858
Wilshire Boulevard Temple	7032	C	310 457-7861	13474

MAMMOTH LAKES, CA - Mono County

	SIC	EMP	PHONE	ENTRY #
Horizons 4 Condominiums Inc	8641	D	760 934-6779	25271
Mammoth Mountain Lake Corp	7032	B	760 934-2571	13467
Mammoth Mountain Ski Area LLC (HQ)	7011	B	760 934-2571	12938
Neubauer-Jennison Inc	1542	E	760 934-2511	1618
Snowcreek Property Management	6531	B	760 934-3333	11849
Southern Mono Healthcare Dst	8062	B	760 934-3311	21908

MANHATTAN BEACH, CA - Los Angeles County

	SIC	EMP	PHONE	ENTRY #
1334 Partners LP	7997	D	310 546-5656	18839
Adventureplex	7991	E	310 546-7708	18604
Aerospace Corporation	8733	B	310 336-1025	26727
CIT Bank National Association	6021	D	310 727-5660	9349
Comstock Crosser Assoc Dev Inc	6552	E	310 546-5781	11960
Connectx Inc	7379	E	310 702-8686	16342
Dalaklis McKeown Entertainment	7812	D	310 545-0120	18067
Ebc Inc (PA)	1521	D	310 753-6407	1170
Fox US Productions 27 Inc	7822	D	310 656-6100	18274
Frys Electronics Inc	5045	C	310 364-3797	7132
GBS Financial Corp	7389	D	310 937-0073	17182
Guru Denim Inc (DH)	5137	C	323 266-3072	8385
Hmointerfacecom LLC	7371	D	310 251-4861	15220
Host Hotels & Resorts LP	7011	B	310 546-7511	12775
Human Touch Home Health	8082	C	424 247-8165	22479
Indigo Hospitality Management	8742	E	310 787-7795	27472
Jag Professional Services Inc	8748	C	310 945-5648	27958

	SIC	EMP	PHONE	ENTRY #
Kinecta Alternative Fin (PA)	6099	D	310 538-2242	9720
Kinecta Federal Credit Union (PA)	6061	D	310 643-5400	9608
Marvel Studios LLC	7336	D	310 727-2700	14153
Pancreatic Cancr Actn Netwrk I (PA)	8099	D	310 725-0025	23016
Pottery Barn Inc	5023	E	310 545-1906	6881
Providence Health & Services	8011	D	310 545-6627	19886
Puttin On Productions Corp	7812	E	310 546-5544	18136
Re/Max Beach Cities Realty Mar	6531	C	310 376-2225	11793
Scheid Vineyards Inc	0172	C	310 545-4757	185
Sunstone Hotel Properties Inc	7011	D	310 546-7627	13325
Trilogy Squaw Spa LLC	7231	E	310 760-0044	13693
True Religion Sales LLC	5136	B	323 266-3072	8363
Vantage Oncology LLC (HQ)	8011	B	310 335-4000	20187
Western America Properties LLC	6531	E	310 374-4381	11916

MANTECA, CA - San Joaquin County

	SIC	EMP	PHONE	ENTRY #
1st Light Energy Inc (PA)	1799	E	209 824-5500	3483
American Legion Aux	8641	D	209 823-4406	25197
AT&T Corp	4813	D	209 956-8324	5488
B R Funsten & Co	5023	D	209 825-5375	6845
Bay Area Cnstr Framers Inc	1751	C	925 454-8514	3031
Brookdale Senior Living Inc	7538	D	209 823-0164	17787
Cen Cal Plastering Inc	1742	D	209 858-1045	2875
Clearpath Workforce MGT Inc	7363	B	209 239-8700	14854
Compass Bancshares Inc	6021	B	209 239-1381	9392
Cool Roofing Systems Inc (PA)	1761	D	209 825-0818	3155
Delta National Bancorp (PA)	6712	D	209 824-4000	12042
Doctors Hospital Manteca Inc	8069	B	209 823-3111	22138
Ecologic Brands Inc	5199	C	209 239-3600	9260
Ford Motor Company	5013	C	209 824-6600	6731
Frontier California Inc	4813	C	209 239-4128	5609
J M Equipment Company Inc (PA)	7359	C	209 522-3271	14551
Kaiser Foundation Hospitals	8062	A	209 825-3700	21668
Kaiser Manteca Medical Office	8071	C	209 825-3700	22227
Kamps Company	7363	C	209 823-8924	14892
Karma Inc	8051	C	209 239-1222	20693
Merrill Gardens LLC	8361	C	209 823-0164	24734
Palm Haven Nursing & Rehab LLC	8051	C	209 823-2782	20836
Pgande	8611	D	209 942-1745	25098
Propane Transport Service Inc	4212	D	209 823-8005	4049
South San Jquin Irrigation Dst	4971	C	209 249-4600	6654
Stockton Cardiology Medical Gr	8011	C	209 824-1555	20070
Tenet Healthsystem Medical	8062	B	209 823-3111	21963
Transforce Inc	7363	C	209 952-2573	14960
United Parcel Service Inc OH	4513	C	209 944-5932	4876
Valley Oak Dental Group	8021	C	209 823-9341	20282
Valley Oaks Residential	8322	C	209 239-3244	24276
Van Groningen & Sons Inc	0191	C	209 982-5248	401
Villara Corporation	1711	D	209 824-1082	2410

MARCH ARB, CA - Riverside County

	SIC	EMP	PHONE	ENTRY #
Ames Construction inc	1522	B	951 697-9094	1290
Taft Broadcasting Company LLC	7812	D	951 413-2337	18165

MARICOPA, CA - Kern County

	SIC	EMP	PHONE	ENTRY #
Aera Energy LLC	1381	C	661 665-3200	1055
Luis Esparza Services Inc	7361	B	661 766-2344	14699

MARINA, CA - Monterey County

	SIC	EMP	PHONE	ENTRY #
American Medical Response Inc	4119	C	831 718-9555	3760
Child & Youth Services	8351	D	831 583-1050	24428
Monterey Rgional Waste MGT Dst	4953	C	831 384-5313	6506

MARINA DEL REY, CA - Los Angeles County

	SIC	EMP	PHONE	ENTRY #
Al Anwa USA Incorporated	7011	C	310 301-2000	12377
ARINC Incorporated	8711	D	310 301-9040	25665
Berger Kahn (PA)	8111	D	310 578-6800	23110
Calatlantic Group Inc	1521	D	310 821-9843	1148
Can-Do	8322	D	646 228-7049	23701
Cfhs Holdings Inc	8062	A	310 823-8911	21476
Cfhs Holdings Inc	8062	A	310 448-7800	21477
CIT Bank National Association	6021	D	310 577-6142	9368
Diagnostic and Interventio	8011	D	310 574-0400	19495
Enterprise Tech Group Inc	7371	C	972 373-8800	15167
Executive Network Entps Inc (PA)	4119	C	310 447-2759	3790
Fedex Office & Print Svcs Inc	7334	C	310 827-2297	14119
Four Medica Inc	4899	C	310 348-4100	6074
Gebbs Software Intl Inc	7379	C	201 227-0088	16382
Guidance Solutions Inc	7375	E	310 754-4000	16242
Host Hotels & Resorts LP	7011	B	310 301-3000	12776
International Mgt Systems	8748	D	310 822-2022	27954
Laaco Ltd	7997	D	310 823-4567	18973
Liquidate Direct LLC	7373	E	800 750-7617	15988
Marina City Club LP A Cali	6513	C	310 822-0611	11163
Marina Del Rey Hospital	8062	A	310 823-8911	21725
Modern Parking Inc	7521	D	310 821-1081	17730
Ntt Data Inc	7373	C	310 301-7835	16017

MARINA DEL REY, CA

	SIC	EMP	PHONE	ENTRY #
Post Modern Edit LLC	7812	D	310 396-7375	18132
R & B Realty Group	6513	D	310 751-4545	11193
Razorgator Inc (PA)	7999	D	310 481-3400	19268
Regents of Uc	8011	D	310 827-3700	19910
Regional Investment & MGT LLC	1522	E	310 821-1945	1337
Ritz-Carlton Marina Del Rey	7011	D	310 823-1700	13158
Skylar Film Studios LLC	7819	C	424 653-8902	18254
Telesign Holdings Inc	7372	D	310 742-8228	15860
Textplus Inc	4812	D	424 272-0296	5418
Thirdwave Technology Services	7378	E	310 563-2160	16306
Trotta Associates	8732	D	310 306-6866	26715
US Mktg Promotions Agcy Inc	8732	E	310 754-3000	26717
USG Enterprises Inc	4489	D	310 827-2220	4741
Veba Administrators Inc	6411	E	310 577-1444	10922
Vergence Labs Inc	8071	B	650 691-3009	22298
Washington Inn LLC	7011	D	310 821-4455	13393
Yosan University	8049	E	310 301-8115	20361

MARIPOSA, CA - Mariposa County

	SIC	EMP	PHONE	ENTRY #
John C Fremont Healthcare Dst	8062	C	209 966-3631	21614

MARTINEZ, CA - Contra Costa County

	SIC	EMP	PHONE	ENTRY #
Alhambra Convalescent Hosp LLC	8051	D	925 228-2020	20374
Ally Financial Inc	6159	D	925 370-7200	9792
Baja Construction Co Inc (PA)	1791	D	925 229-0732	3364
Bay Area/Diablo Petroleum Co (HQ)	5172	C	925 228-2222	9013
Braddock & Logan Inc	6513	D	925 229-1747	11099
Brightview Landscape Svcs Inc	0781	D	925 957-8831	750
Careonsite Inc	8011	D	562 437-0381	19409
Central Contra Costa Sanit	4952	E	925 228-9500	6410
Cleary Bros Landscape Inc	0782	D	925 335-9335	826
Contra Costa Electric Inc (DH)	1731	B	925 229-4250	2561
County of Contra Costa	8322	C	925 313-4000	23801
County of Contra Costa	1611	D	925 313-2000	1754
County of Contra Costa	7349	D	925 313-7052	14268
County of Contra Costa	8322	D	925 313-1500	23802
County of Contra Costa	8062	D	925 370-5000	21514
Dawson Electric	1731	D	925 723-3535	2573
Dynalectric Company	1731	C	415 487-4700	2579
Dynamic Maintenance Svcs Inc	7349	D	925 228-7434	14284
Engineering/Remdtn Rsrcs Grp (PA)	8748	D	925 839-2200	27914
Gregg Drilling & Testing Inc	1781	D	925 313-8855	3356
Kaiser Foundation Hospitals	6733	C	925 372-1000	12182
Martinez Cert	8699	D	925 228-0911	25555
Mecs Inc	7389	D	925 313-0681	17322
Mobility Plus Trnsp LLC	4111	D	925 957-9841	3674
Muir Senior Care	8322	D	925 228-8383	24092
Nalco Company LLC	5169	D	925 957-9720	8996
National Railroad Pass Corp	4011	A	925 335-5180	3613
Parsons Government Svcs Inc	8711	D	925 313-3217	26015
Permanente Medical Group Inc	8011	D	925 372-1000	19843
Plant Maintenance Inc	7363	C	925 228-3285	14925
Power Engineers Incorporated	8711	D	925 372-9284	26022
R M Harris Company Inc	1622	D	925 335-3000	1898
RE Milano Plumbing Corp	1711	E	925 500-1372	2342
Telfer Oil Company (PA)	1611	D	925 228-1515	1873
Terracare Associates LLC	8742	D	925 374-0060	27684
Waters Moving & Storage Inc	4214	D	925 372-0914	4391
YWCA Contra Costa/Sacramento (PA)	8322	D	925 372-4213	24301

MARYSVILLE, CA - Yuba County

	SIC	EMP	PHONE	ENTRY #
Alliance Wall Systems Inc	1742	E	530 740-7800	2852
Aramark Spt & Entrmt Group LLC	7929	B	530 740-4758	18453
Childrens Protective Services	8322	D	530 749-6311	23744
Comprehensive SEC Svcs Inc	7381	D	530 743-6762	16609
County of Yuba	8322	C	530 749-7550	23936
Frank M Booth Inc (PA)	8711	D	650 871-8292	25818
Fremont Hospital	8062	A	530 751-4000	21570
HB Orchards Co Inc	0175	D	530 743-5121	235
Marysvlle Nrsing Rehab Ctr LLC	8051	D	530 742-7311	20778
Melon Holdings LLC	8051	D	530 742-7311	20787
Pacific Gas and Electric Co	4911	D	530 742-3251	6164
Peach Tree Healthcare	8011	D	530 749-3242	19821
Recology Yuba-Sutter	4953	D	530 743-6933	6533
Rideout Memorial Hospital (HQ)	8062	A	530 749-4416	21831
US Dept of the Air Force	8062	B	530 634-4839	22006

MATHER, CA - Sacramento County

	SIC	EMP	PHONE	ENTRY #
Bloodsource Inc (PA)	8099	B	916 456-1500	22902
Reynen & Bardis Construction (PA)	1521	C	916 366-3665	1244
Sutter Health	8051	D	916 454-8200	20987
Veterans Health Administration	8011	D	916 366-5427	20198
Veterans Health Administration	8011	D	916 843-7000	20213

MAYWOOD, CA - Los Angeles County

	SIC	EMP	PHONE	ENTRY #
Food Express Inc	4212	E	323 589-1417	4019
Jack H Caldwell & Sons Inc	5148	D	323 589-4008	8742
Keeney Truck Lines Inc	4212	E	323 589-3231	4033
Maywood Halthcare Wellness Ctr	8051	E	323 560-0720	20780
R G Canning Enterprises Inc	7389	C	323 560-7469	17440
Tapia Enterprises Inc (PA)	5141	D	323 560-7415	8538

MC FARLAND, CA - Kern County

	SIC	EMP	PHONE	ENTRY #
A G Hacienda Incorporated	4212	B	661 792-2418	3966
Armando Gonzalez Contracting	0761	B	661 792-3785	650
Etchegaray Farms LLC	0214	E	661 393-0920	416
Geo Group Inc	8741	C	661 792-2731	27035
Jakov P Dulcich & Sons	0172	E	661 792-6360	159
LS Farms LLC	0191	B	661 792-3192	382
Renteria Santiago J Farm Labo	7361	C	661 792-0052	14750
Sandrini Farms	0172	E	661 792-3192	183
Wonderful Citrus Packing LLC	0723	E	661 387-1288	607

MC KITTRICK, CA - Kern County

	SIC	EMP	PHONE	ENTRY #
Dwaynes Engineering & Cnstr	1389	D	661 762-7261	1073

MCCLELLAN, CA - Sacramento County

	SIC	EMP	PHONE	ENTRY #
AAR Manufacturing Inc	7629	D	916 830-7011	17926
AAR Manufacturing Inc	7629	D	800 422-2213	17927
Califrnia Shock Truma A Rescue (PA)	4522	D	916 921-4000	4879
Lionsgate Ht & Conference Ctr	7011	D	916 643-6222	12923
Mansion Hospitality Services	8742	D	916 643-6222	27522
McClellan Business Park LLC	8742	D	916 965-7100	27532
McClellan Facilities Svcs LLC	6512	D	916 965-7100	11016
McClellan Hospitality Svcs LLC	7011	D	916 965-7100	12987
Monument Security Inc (PA)	7381	C	916 564-4234	16740
Northern Sheets LLC	7389	D	916 437-2800	17365
Pinnacle Telecom Inc (PA)	7373	E	916 426-1000	16031
Sbm Management Services LP	7349	A	866 855-2211	14420
Sbm Site Services LLC (PA)	7349	D	916 922-7600	14421
Traffic Management Inc	8741	D	916 394-2200	27256
Villara Corporation (PA)	1711	D	916 646-2700	2408
Villara Corporation	1711	D	916 646-2222	2411

MCKINLEYVILLE, CA - Humboldt County

	SIC	EMP	PHONE	ENTRY #
Kernen Construction	1541	D	707 826-8686	1446

MEADOW VISTA, CA - Placer County

	SIC	EMP	PHONE	ENTRY #
Winchester Reo LLC	7997	E	530 878-3000	19127

MECCA, CA - Riverside County

	SIC	EMP	PHONE	ENTRY #
Richard Bagdasarian Inc	0172	D	760 396-2168	177

MENDOCINO, CA - Mendocino County

	SIC	EMP	PHONE	ENTRY #
Big River Ltd-Design	7011	D	707 937-5615	12451
Mendocino Hotel & Resort Corp	7011	D	707 937-0511	12988
Sweetwater Gardens Inc	7991	E	707 937-4140	18697

MENDOTA, CA - Fresno County

	SIC	EMP	PHONE	ENTRY #
S & S Ranch Inc	0721	D	559 655-3491	482
S Stamoules Inc	0723	A	559 655-9777	581

MENIFEE, CA - Riverside County

	SIC	EMP	PHONE	ENTRY #
Bedon Construction Inc	8711	D	951 246-9005	25686
Cellco Partnership	4813	C	951 679-6083	5574
F M Tarbell Co	6531	E	951 301-5932	11509
Mackenzie Landscape A Cal Corp	0782	D	951 679-5477	907
Valley Pacific Concrete Inc	1771	C	951 672-6151	3347

MENLO PARK, CA - San Mateo County

	SIC	EMP	PHONE	ENTRY #
Accel-KKR Company LLC (PA)	7371	D	650 233-9723	14996
Alain Pinel Realtors Inc	6531	D	650 462-1111	11289
Allstate Research and Plg Ctr	6411	D	650 833-6200	10589
Atieva Usa Inc	8711	B	650 802-8181	25672
Atrium Capital Corp	6211	A	650 233-7878	9960
Barclays Capital Inc	6211	D	650 289-6000	9963
Battery Ventures LP	7389	D	650 372-3939	17024
Boardvantage Inc (HQ)	8741	C	650 614-6000	26944
Bodega Bay Associates	7011	D	650 330-8888	12457
Boys & Girls CLB of Peninsula	7997	D	650 322-6255	18898
Cal Care Inc	8742	C	650 325-8600	27365
Caprion Proteomics USA LLC	8733	E	650 470-2300	26745
Carr & Ferrell	8111	D	650 812-3400	23142
Carr & Ferrell LLP (PA)	8111	D	650 812-3400	23143
Cataphora Inc (PA)	7371	D	650 622-9840	15077
Citigroup Global Markets Inc	6211	C	650 926-7600	9984
Cornerstone Research Inc (PA)	8748	D	650 853-1660	27889
Critchfield Mechanical Inc	1711	B	650 321-7801	2196
Endovascular Technologies Inc	8731	D	650 325-1600	26511
Exponent Inc (PA)	8711	C	650 326-9400	25805
Facebook Inc	7375	A	650 543-4800	16236
First Republic Bank	6029	D	650 233-8880	9550
Gachina Landscape MGT Inc	0782	B	650 853-0400	855
Geological Survey US Dept	8731	D	650 329-5229	26527
Grid Dynamics Intl Inc (PA)	7379	E	650 523-5000	16394
Henry J Kaiser Fmly Foundation (PA)	6732	D	650 854-9400	12157

GEOGRAPHIC SECTION — MILPITAS, CA

Company	SIC	EMP	PHONE	ENTRY #
Hewlett Wlliam Flora Fndation	8699	D	650 234-4500	25541
Intuit Inc	7372	C	650 944-6000	15715
Kilpatrick Twnsend Stckton LLP	8111	C	650 326-2595	23350
Kohlberg Kravis Roberts Co LP	6799	D	650 233-6560	12320
Kranz & Assoc Holdings LLC	8721	D	650 854-4400	26391
Latham & Watkins LLP	8111	C	650 328-4600	23365
Lifemoves (PA)	8322	E	650 685-5880	24066
Lovazzano Mechanical Inc	1711	D	650 367-6216	2284
Lucile Salter Packard Chil	8069	C	650 724-0503	22154
Mc Graw Commercial Insur Svc (PA)	6411	D	650 780-4800	10781
Menlo Med Clinic A Med Corp	8011	C	650 498-6500	19746
Merrill Lynch Pierce Fenner	6211	C	650 473-7888	10030
Merrill Lynch Pierce Fenner	6211	C	650 473-7888	10037
Morningside Corecare Assoc LP	8051	C	650 854-5600	20798
Novo Construction Inc (PA)	1542	D	650 701-1500	1621
Nuance Communications Inc	7371	C	650 847-0000	15344
Oak Hill Capital Partners LP	8082	A	650 234-0500	22518
OMelveny & Myers LLP	8111	C	650 473-2600	23480
Orrick Hrrington Sutcliffe LLP	8111	C	650 614-7454	23483
Orrick Hrrington Sutcliffe LLP	8111	C	650 614-7400	23484
Pall Fortebio Corp	8731	D	650 322-1360	26580
Pan-Pacific Mechanical LLC	1711	B	650 561-8810	2319
Peninsula Family Service	8322	C	650 325-8719	24128
Personalis Inc	8731	D	650 752-1300	26588
Protiviti Inc (HQ)	8742	C	650 234-6000	27598
Robert Half International Inc (PA)	7363	C	650 234-6000	14940
Robert Half International Inc	7361	C	650 234-6000	14766
Robert Half International Inc	7361	C	650 234-6000	14767
Robert Half International Inc	7361	C	650 234-6000	14768
Rosewood Hotels & Resorts LLC	7011	B	650 561-1500	13170
S R I C B I	8748	D	650 859-4865	28048
Sequoia Capital Operations LLC	6799	D	650 854-3927	12343
Sharon Crest Apts	6513	E	650 854-5130	11201
Silver Lake Partners LP (PA)	6726	C	650 233-8120	12144
Space Systems/Loral LLC	4225	C	650 852-4000	4641
SRI International (PA)	8733	A	650 859-2000	26809
Stanford Park Hotel	7011	C	650 322-1234	13286
Strategic Bus Insights Inc (PA)	8742	C	650 859-4600	27670
Veterans Health Administration	8011	A	650 614-9997	20216
Vitesse LLC	7374	A	650 543-4400	16208
Western Allied Mechanical Inc	1711	C	650 326-8290	2417
Winston & Strawn LLP	8111	B	650 858-6500	23630

MENTONE, CA - San Bernardino County

Company	SIC	EMP	PHONE	ENTRY #
International Paving Svcs Inc	1611	D	909 794-2101	1801
Nice Avenue LLC	8051	D	909 794-1189	20807

MERCED, CA - Merced County

Company	SIC	EMP	PHONE	ENTRY #
Avalon Care Center - Merced Fr	8051	D	209 722-6231	20390
Avalon Care Cntr Merced Hy	8051	D	209 384-8839	20391
Bear Creek Manor	6513	E	209 723-4674	11093
Bloodsource Inc	8099	D	209 724-0428	22903
Central Valley Concrete Inc	5032	D	209 383-7292	6977
Central Valley Concrete Inc (PA)	4212	C	209 723-8846	3994
CF Merced La Sierra LLC	8051	A	209 723-4224	20446
Country Villa Service Corp	8322	D	209 723-2911	23791
County of Merced	1611	E	209 826-2253	1759
County of Merced	8331	C	209 724-2000	24330
Culver-Melin Enterprises	1741	D	209 726-9182	2808
Dedicated Management Group LLC	7389	C	209 385-0694	17117
Educational Employees Cr Un	6062	E	209 726-7421	9665
Fuentes Farms Ag Inc	7361	B	209 722-7201	14659
Golden Living LLC	8059	D	209 722-6231	21249
Golden Valley Health Centers (PA)	8093	C	209 383-1848	22735
Golden Valley Health Centers	8093	D	209 383-5871	22736
Golden Valley Health Centers	8011	C	209 723-7441	19539
Guardco Security Services	7381	C	209 723-4273	16672
Harbor Freight Tools Usa Inc	4789	D	209 386-0829	5219
Holiday Inn Express Merced	7011	D	209 383-0333	12749
Madera Convalescent Hospital	8063	D	209 723-8814	22081
Madera Convalescent Hospital	8059	C	209 723-2911	21303
Mater Misericordiae Hospital (PA)	8062	A	209 564-5000	21730
McLane/Pacific Inc	5141	B	209 725-2500	8499
Merced Irrigation District (PA)	4911	E	209 722-5761	6147
Merced Irrigation District	4971	C	209 722-2719	6645
Merced School Employees F C U (PA)	6061	D	209 383-5550	9612
Merced Transportation Company	4151	D	209 384-2575	3945
Mercy HM Svcs A Cal Ltd Partnr	8011	B	209 564-4200	19748
Mercy Medical Center Nampa	8062	C	209 485-1380	21743
Mobley Enterprises Inc	7349	D	209 726-9185	14361
N & S Tractor Co (PA)	7699	D	209 383-5888	17989
Paul Pietrzyk	1742	E	209 726-5034	2953
Promesa Behavioral Health	8361	D	209 725-3114	24774
Sintex Security Services Inc	8999	D	510 208-0474	28161
Travis Credit Union	6061	B	209 723-0732	9638
Via Adventures Inc (PA)	4142	E	209 384-1315	3910

Company	SIC	EMP	PHONE	ENTRY #
WLMD (PA)	1799	C	209 723-9120	3605

MERIDIAN, CA - Sutter County

Company	SIC	EMP	PHONE	ENTRY #
Colusa Produce Corporation	5149	D	530 696-0121	8816

MIDDLETOWN, CA - Lake County

Company	SIC	EMP	PHONE	ENTRY #
Cpn Wild Horse Geothermal LLC	4911	B	707 431-6229	6122
Gr Hardester LLC	6798	C	707 987-2325	12247
Heart Consciousness Church (PA)	7041	C	707 987-2477	13493
Northern California Power Agcy	4911	D	707 987-2381	6153

MILL VALLEY, CA - Marin County

Company	SIC	EMP	PHONE	ENTRY #
Adventres Rlling Cross-Country	7032	C	415 332-5075	13457
City of Mill Valley	7999	E	415 383-1370	19175
City of Mill Valley	1611	D	415 383-4033	1751
First Marin Realty Inc	6531	D	415 383-9393	11526
Haggin Marketing Inc (PA)	7311	C	415 289-1110	13857
Kabler Construction Svcs Inc	8742	E	415 888-8812	27497
Kaiser Foundation Hospitals	8011	A	415 444-2000	19626
Marin Horizon School Inc	8351	E	415 388-8408	24480
Melissa Bradley RE Inc	6531	D	415 388-5113	11672
Rabin Worldwide Inc	7389	D	415 522-5700	17441
Redwood Trust Inc (PA)	6798	D	415 389-7373	12272
Sequoia Residential Funding	6153	D	415 389-7373	9789
Telecommunictns Cmmnctns Srvcs	4899	E	415 869-9000	6092
The Redwoods A Cmnty Seniors	8361	C	415 383-2741	24835
Unified Teldata Inc	5065	D	415 888-8940	7651
Van Acker Cnstr Assoc Inc	1521	D	415 383-5589	1278
Wisdom University	8699	D	415 259-7122	25599

MILLBRAE, CA - San Mateo County

Company	SIC	EMP	PHONE	ENTRY #
A & C Health Care Services Inc	8011	C	650 689-5784	19314
El Rancho Motel Inc	7011	C	650 588-8500	12614
Hillsdale Group LP	8059	E	650 742-9150	21269
Magnolia of Millbrae Inc	8361	D	650 697-7700	24723
Millbrae Racquet Club	7997	D	650 583-4345	19000
Millbrae Serra Sanitarium	8059	C	650 697-8386	21315
Millbrae Wcp Hotel II LLC	7011	E	650 443-5500	12997
Starwood Hotels & Resorts	7011	D	650 692-6363	13296
Trans World Maintenance Inc	1721	D	650 455-2450	2498
Western Host Inc (DH)	7011	E	650 692-3500	13402

MILPITAS, CA - Santa Clara County

Company	SIC	EMP	PHONE	ENTRY #
3k Technologies LLC	7373	C	408 716-5900	15889
Abbyy USA Software House Inc (PA)	7371	C	408 457-9777	14994
Abzooba Inc	7371	C	650 453-8760	14995
Advantech Corporation (HQ)	5045	C	408 519-3800	7085
Aerohive Networks Inc (PA)	7373	C	408 510-6100	15899
Alhambra/Sierra Springs	5149	D	408 727-0677	8793
American Golf Corporation	7997	E	408 262-8813	18865
Anjaneyap Inc	8742	C	408 922-9690	27325
Appfabrix Software Inc	7371	C	408 834-4435	15021
Array Networks Inc (PA)	4813	C	408 240-8700	5459
Aryaka Networks Inc	8743	C	408 273-8420	27730
At Road Inc (HQ)	7373	B	510 668-1638	15905
Automatic Data Processing Inc	7374	C	408 876-6600	16097
B H R Operations LLC	7011	C	408 321-9500	12410
B T Mancini Co Inc (PA)	1752	D	408 942-7900	3106
Bizcom Electronics Inc (HQ)	5045	C	408 262-7877	7102
Bottomley Distributing Co Inc	5181	C	408 945-0660	9044
Boys & Girls Club Silicon Vly	8322	D	408 957-9685	23688
Bright Horizons Chld Ctrs LLC	8351	C	408 853-2196	24418
Browning-Ferris Industries Inc	4953	C	408 262-1401	6446
California Wireless Solutions	4812	C	408 771-1249	5282
Celico Partnership	4812	C	408 263-1960	5333
Cetecom Inc (DH)	8748	C	408 586-6200	27875
Clark Pest Ctrl Stockton Inc	7342	C	408 945-3600	14181
Clement Support Services Inc	5051	C	408 227-1171	7364
Command Security Corporation	7381	C	510 623-2355	16603
Composite Software LLC (HQ)	7372	C	800 553-6387	15625
Coyote Creek Consulting Inc	7379	C	408 383-9200	16344
Creative Labs Inc (DH)	5045	C	408 428-6600	7112
Custom Drywall Inc	1742	C	408 263-1616	2881
Daylight Foods Inc	5148	C	408 284-7300	8713
Devcon Construction Inc (PA)	1541	B	408 942-8200	1418
Enquero Inc	7373	D	408 406-3203	15941
Fieldserver Technologies	4932	E	408 262-2299	6297
Fireeye Inc (PA)	7372	C	408 321-6300	15665
First Call Nursing Svcs Inc	7361	C	408 262-1533	14656
Frontrange Holding Inc	7372	C	408 601-2800	15672
Frontrange Solutions Inc (HQ)	8742	C	408 601-2800	27442
General Dynmics Mssion Systems	5045	C	954 846-3400	7137
H V Welker Co Inc	1752	D	408 263-4400	3115
Haworth Inc	5021	C	408 262-6400	6817
Hilton Worldwide Inc	7011	D	408 942-0400	12716
Homefrst Svcs Santa Clara Cnty	8322	C	408 539-2100	24011
HP Inc	4225	A	650 857-1501	4575

Employment Codes: A=Over 500 employees, B=251-500, C=101-250, D=51-100, E=45-50

MILPITAS, CA

GEOGRAPHIC SECTION

	SIC	EMP	PHONE	ENTRY #
Humane Society Silicon Valley	0752	D	408 262-2133	641
Idc Technologies Inc	7361	C	408 376-0212	14678
Interntional Disposal Corp Cal	4953	D	408 945-2802	6491
Iron Mountain Fulfillment (HQ)	7331	E	408 945-1600	14075
Jag Software Inc	5045	D	408 262-0572	7149
Kaiser Foundation Hospitals	8011	E	408 945-2900	19667
Knights of Columbus	8699	D	408 262-6609	25547
Lightwaves 2020 Inc	8731	E	408 503-8888	26561
Lite-On Inc (HQ)	5065	E	408 946-4873	7601
Loomis Armored Us Inc	7381	D	408 273-1101	16725
Macronix America Inc (HQ)	5065	D	408 262-8887	7602
Marketshare Inc (PA)	7312	D	408 262-0677	13952
Mega Professional Intl	7371	D	408 946-1500	15297
Messagesolution Inc	7374	D	408 383-0100	16161
Moschip Semiconductor Tech USA	5065	C	408 737-7141	7609
Nanolab Technologies Inc (PA)	8734	D	408 433-3320	26873
Nanosys Inc	8733	C	408 240-6700	26790
New Solar Incorporated	8741	D	888 886-0103	27141
Nikewoman	5139	E	408 942-6457	8440
NTS It Care Inc	7371	C	408 480-4083	15343
Ohana Partners Inc (PA)	7359	D	408 856-3232	14563
Oracle America Inc	7379	B	408 635-3072	16446
Pacific Gas and Electric Co	4911	D	408 945-6215	6190
Permanente Medical Group Inc	8011	D	408 945-2900	19846
Preston Pipelines Inc (PA)	1623	C	408 262-1418	1981
Preston Pipelines Inc A Cal	1623	B	408 262-6989	1982
Promise Technology Inc	5045	D	408 228-1400	7176
Prudential Overall Supply	7218	D	408 719-0886	13637
R S Software India Limited	7379	D	408 382-1200	16468
Reading Partners	8322	D	408 945-5720	24149
Saint-Joseph Home Health	8099	E	408 244-5488	23043
Sandisk Corporation	8742	C	408 801-1000	27635
Sankara Eye Foundation USA	8699	E	408 456-0555	25574
SJ Distributors Inc (PA)	5142	E	888 988-2328	8570
Spidercloud Wireless Inc	4813	D	408 567-9165	5703
Ss8 Networks Inc (PA)	4899	C	408 894-8400	6091
Stellartech Research Corp (PA)	8731	D	408 331-3134	26610
Tcg Builders Inc	1542	E	408 321-6450	1688
Technical Temps Inc	7361	D	408 956-8256	14803
Union Pacific Railroad Company	4011	E	510 874-1174	3626
Universal Site Services Inc	7349	C	408 295-9688	14459
Varian Medical Systems Inc	5047	C	408 321-9400	7324
Vitas Healthcare Corp Cal	8082	D	408 964-6800	22600
Winmax Systems Corporation	7371	C	408 894-9000	15545
Xcerra Corporation	5065	C	408 635-4300	7661
Xl Construction Corporation (PA)	1542	C	408 240-6000	1720
Zl Technologies Inc	5045	D	408 240-8989	7214

MIRA LOMA, CA - Riverside County

	SIC	EMP	PHONE	ENTRY #
Act Fulfillment Inc	4225	C	909 930-9083	4514
Adesa Corporation LLC	5012	E	951 361-9400	6661
Big League Dreams Jurupa LLC	7941	D	951 685-6900	18538
C P S Express (HQ)	4212	D	951 685-1041	3988
Cellco Partnership	4812	D	951 361-1850	5297
Ceva Logistics US Inc	4226	E	951 332-3202	4679
Complete Food Service Inc	5149	D	951 685-8490	8817
CR England Inc	4212	D	909 946-1555	4000
DSC Logistics Inc	4212	D	909 605-7233	4011
Galleano Enterprises Inc	0172	D	951 685-5376	154
Geodis Logistics LLC	4225	D	951 571-2481	4561
Hino Motors Mfg USA Inc	5013	C	951 727-0286	6738
Home Depot USA Inc	4225	C	951 361-1235	4569
Kmart Corporation	4225	B	951 727-3200	4583
Le Vecke Corporation (PA)	5181	D	951 681-8600	9068
Lineage Logistics LLC	4222	E	951 360-7970	4498
Meiko America Inc	4225	D	951 360-0281	4598
Olivet International Inc (PA)	5099	D	951 681-8888	8131
Riverside Medical Clinic	8011	D	951 360-5260	19921
RSI Professional Cab Solutions	1751	C	909 614-2900	3082
S P Richards Company	5112	D	951 681-3114	8180
Southwest Material Hdlg Inc (PA)	5084	C	951 727-0477	7892
Swift Transportation Company	4213	D	951 360-0130	4273
Time and Alarm Systems (PA)	1731	D	951 685-1761	2774
Total Trnsp Logistics Inc	4213	D	951 360-9521	4279
Triways Inc	4214	D	951 361-4840	4384
United Parcel Service Inc OH	7389	B	951 749-3400	17562
UPS Ground Freight Inc	4213	D	951 361-1300	4288
UPS Supply Chain Solutions Gen	4215	C	951 749-3134	4480
W W Grainger Inc	5087	C	951 727-2300	7986
Wal-Mart Stores Inc	4225	B	951 681-7256	4661

MIRAMONTE, CA - Fresno County

	SIC	EMP	PHONE	ENTRY #
Hume Lake Christian Camps Inc	7032	D	559 305-7770	13466

MISSION HILLS, CA - Los Angeles County

	SIC	EMP	PHONE	ENTRY #
Ararat Home of Los Angeles	8059	C	818 837-1800	21142
Best Friends Animal Society	8699	B	818 643-3989	25507
Clean King Laundry Systems Inc	7215	E	818 363-5500	13573
Ecola Services Inc	7342	D	818 920-7301	14185
El Nido Family Centers (PA)	8322	D	818 830-3646	23959
Facey Medical Foundation (PA)	8099	C	818 365-9531	22957
Facey Medical Foundation	8099	C	818 365-5677	22958
Greater Valley Medical Group (PA)	8093	D	818 838-4500	22740
Hemodialysis Inc	8092	D	818 365-6961	22629
Jade Inc	1742	D	818 365-7137	2916
Kaiser Foundation Hospitals	6324	D	888 778-5000	10308
Laboratory Corp Amer Holdings	8071	D	818 361-7089	22231
Los Angeles Unified School Dst	8331	C	818 365-9645	24360
National Business Group Inc (PA)	7353	D	818 221-6000	14489
National Cnstr Rentals Inc (HQ)	7353	D	818 221-6000	14490
Prescott Communications Inc	8748	C	818 898-2352	28022
Providence Health & Services	8021	D	818 898-4445	20271
Providence Health & Svcs - Ore	8062	B	818 365-8051	21820
Providence Health System	8011	A	818 898-4530	19889
Providence Health System	8062	A	818 898-4561	21821
Providence Holy Cross (PA)	8062	D	818 365-8051	21824

MISSION VIEJO, CA - Orange County

	SIC	EMP	PHONE	ENTRY #
Associated Realtors	6531	D	949 813-1888	11307
Auxiliary of Mission	8062	D	949 364-1400	21456
Auxilio Inc (PA)	7334	C	949 614-0700	14113
Auxilio Solutions Inc	7334	C	949 614-0700	14114
Black Dot Wireless LLC	4812	D	949 502-3800	5278
Centex Homes Inc	1521	C	949 453-0113	1152
CIT Bank NA	6021	D	949 598-9621	9343
CIT Bank National Association	6021	D	949 347-7014	9363
Claim Jumper Restaurant	1542	C	949 461-7170	1528
Coldwell Banker Residential RE (DH)	6531	B	949 367-1800	11416
Community Orthopedic Medical	8011	D	949 348-4000	19458
Cs Concrete Solutions Inc	1771	D	949 285-3122	3251
Edwards Theatres Circuit Inc	7832	D	949 582-4078	18324
Ensign Services Inc	8051	D	949 487-9500	20545
Ensign Southland LLC	8051	C	949 487-9500	20546
Fitness International LLC	7991	E	949 421-6082	18633
Foundstone Inc	7372	D	949 297-5600	15671
Global Exchange Marketing Inc	7389	D	949 367-0388	17189
Golda & I Chocolatiers Inc	5149	D	949 660-9581	8846
Greenleaf Paper Products	5113	D	949 348-0048	8194
Home Instead Senior Care	8082	E	949 347-6767	22470
James Hardie Building Pdts Inc (DH)	5031	C	949 348-1800	6933
Jewish Home For The Aged of or	8361	D	949 364-0010	24698
Kaiser Foundation Hospitals	6324	D	888 988-2800	10309
Lake Mission Viejo Association	8641	D	949 770-1313	25283
Lauras House	8322	D	949 361-3775	24064
Law Enforcement Officers Inc	7382	C	855 477-3536	16898
Mimg Medical Management LLC	8741	D	949 282-1600	27133
Mission Hosp Regional Med Ctr (PA)	8062	A	949 364-1400	21749
Mission Internal Med Group Inc	8011	D	949 364-3570	19752
Mission Internal Med Group Inc	8011	C	949 364-6559	19753
Mission Viejo Country Club	7997	C	949 582-1550	19003
Olympus America Inc	5047	C	949 466-3548	7288
Omnitek Information Systems	7371	D	949 581-5895	15349
Orange County Royale Convlscnt	8059	D	949 458-6346	21336
Philip DAmato Racing LLC	7948	D	949 830-7027	18573
Planned Prnthood Mar Monte Inc	8093	E	949 768-3643	22808
Prestige Auto Collision Inc	7532	D	949 470-6031	17767
Quest Diagnostics Incorporated	8071	B	949 728-4235	22267
Rock Canyon Healthcare Inc	8059	B	949 487-9500	21363
Saddleback Vly	7997	D	949 586-1234	19053
South Coast Childrens Soc Inc	8322	B	714 966-8650	24221
Southern Cal Prmnnte Med Group	8099	A	949 376-8619	23062
St Jude Hospital Yorba Linda	8011	E	949 365-2492	20060
Standardbearer Insur Co Ltd	8051	B	949 487-9500	20930
Sunrise Senior Living LLC	8051	D	949 582-2010	20970
Swiss RE America Holding Corp	6311	E	858 485-5018	10223
Trendsettah Usa Inc	5099	D	888 775-4881	8145
Vintage Senior Living Corp	6513	D	949 364-6210	11224
Vocational Visions	8331	C	949 837-7280	24404
Wakunaga of America Co Ltd (HQ)	5122	D	949 855-2776	8306
Western Youth Services	8322	D	949 595-8610	24289
Young Mens Chrstn Assn Orange	8641	D	949 859-9622	25474

MODESTO, CA - Stanislaus County

	SIC	EMP	PHONE	ENTRY #
Acme Construction Company Inc	1541	D	209 523-2674	1396
Addus Healthcare Inc	7361	D	209 526-8451	14602
Aderholt Specialty Company Inc	1742	D	209 526-2000	2846
American Alliance Always Avail	7699	E	209 948-9220	17959
Aramark Unf & Career AP LLC	7218	D	209 368-9785	13602
Arcadia Health Services Inc	8082	D	209 572-7650	22370
AT&T Services Inc	4813	D	209 578-7161	5529
Avalon Care Ctr - Modesto LLC	8051	D	209 529-0516	20393
Avalon Health Care Inc	8051	D	209 526-1775	20395

	SIC	EMP	PHONE	ENTRY #
Basic Resources Inc **(PA)**	1611	E	209 521-9771	1738
Bethel Retirement Community	8059	D	209 577-1901	21156
Beyer Park Villas LLC	8361	D	209 236-1900	24565
BJs Restaurants Inc	5094	A	209 526-8850	8095
Blue Diamond Growers	0723	C	209 545-6221	512
Brenden Theatre Corporation	7832	D	209 491-7770	18311
C & S Draperies Inc	7217	C	209 466-5371	13591
C L Bryant Inc	5171	C	209 566-5000	9005
California Forensic Med Group	8011	C	209 525-5670	19393
Capax Management and Services	6411	D	209 526-3110	10662
Cellco Partnership	4812	D	209 543-6500	5355
Center For Human Services **(PA)**	8322	D	209 526-1476	23722
Central Valley Autism Project	8322	D	209 521-4791	23726
Central Vly Specialty Hosp Inc	8051	D	209 248-7700	20445
Chadlor Enterprises Inc	8051	C	209 577-1001	20452
Charles Fenley Enterprises	7542	E	209 523-2832	17835
Childrens Crisis Cntr Stanisls	8322	D	209 577-4413	23739
Clark Pest Ctrl Stockton Inc	7342	D	209 524-6384	14176
Co Team Staffing	7363	D	209 578-4286	14862
Comcast Corporation	4841	D	209 222-3656	5955
Community Hospice Inc **(PA)**	8052	D	209 578-6300	21072
County of Stanislaus	4959	D	209 525-4130	6625
County of Stanislaus	8062	A	209 525-7000	21525
County of Stanislaus	8322	D	209 558-8828	23923
County of Stanislaus	8322	C	209 567-4120	23924
County of Stanislaus	8322	D	209 558-7377	23925
County of Stanislaus	8322	D	209 558-9675	23926
County of Stanislaus	8399	D	209 525-6225	24911
County of Stanislaus	8093	D	209 525-7423	22713
County of Stanislaus	8322	D	209 558-2500	23927
County of Stanislaus	8331	D	209 558-2100	24333
Covenant Care California LLC	8059	C	209 521-2094	21198
CP Opco LLC	7359	D	209 524-1966	14528
Crestwood Behavioral Hlth Inc	8063	D	209 526-8050	22059
Curtis Legal Group A Professi	8111	E	209 521-1800	23192
D A Wood Construction Inc	8711	D	209 491-4970	25762
D C Vient Inc **(PA)**	1721	D	209 578-1224	2437
De Hart Plumbing Htg & A Inc	1711	E	209 523-4578	2204
Del Rio Golf & Country Club	7997	C	209 341-2414	18937
Delta Blood Bank	8099	D	209 943-3830	22938
Delta Brands Inc	5181	D	209 522-9044	9053
Directline Technologies Inc	8732	D	209 491-2020	26656
DOT Foods Inc	5141	C	209 581-9090	8474
Doubletree LLC	7011	B	209 526-6000	12596
Eastside Management Co Inc	0762	C	209 578-9852	699
Ed Rocha Livestock Trnsp Inc	4213	D	209 538-1302	4145
Enviro Tech Chemical Svcs Inc **(PA)**	5169	D	209 581-9576	8988
Fig Holdings LLC	8051	D	209 524-4817	20570
Focus Up LLC	7991	E	209 545-9055	18635
Foster Dairy Farms **(PA)**	0241	A	209 576-3400	424
G C H Insurance Group	6411	E	209 526-3110	10723
G3 Enterprises Inc **(PA)**	4731	C	209 341-7515	5083
G3 Enterprises Inc	4731	C	209 341-4045	5085
General Petroleum Corporation	5171	D	209 537-1056	9007
Golden Living LLC	8059	D	209 529-0516	21241
Golden Living LLC	8051	D	209 548-0318	20622
Golden Valley Health Centers	8011	D	209 556-5040	19538
Graham Packaging Company LP	5199	D	209 572-5187	9268
Grand Events Inc	7359	E	209 569-0399	14543
Grover Landscape Services Inc	0181	D	209 545-4401	287
Hamilton and Dillon Elc Inc	1731	D	209 529-6292	2605
Hi-TEC Sports Usa Inc **(DH)**	5139	D	209 545-1111	8436
Hmclause Inc **(DH)**	0181	C	530 747-3700	289
Holt of California	5084	D	209 623-1149	7849
House of Prayer	6732	E	916 410-3349	12158
Howard Training Center **(PA)**	8331	E	209 538-2431	24350
Kaiser Foundation Hospitals	8011	A	209 735-5000	19628
Kaiser Foundation Hospitals	8011	A	209 735-5000	19630
Kaiser Foundation Hospitals	6324	D	855 268-4096	10329
Kaiser Foundation Hospitals	6324	D	209 557-1000	10348
Khatri Inc	7011	E	209 576-1481	12881
Kissito Health Case Inc	8051	C	209 524-4817	20710
Kiwanis International Inc	8641	D	209 578-1448	25276
McClatchy Newspapers Inc	7389	B	209 238-4636	17319
McHenry Bowl Inc	7933	E	209 571-2695	18526
McHenry Medical Group Inc	8011	D	209 577-3388	19735
Medamerica Billing Svcs Inc **(HQ)**	8721	D	209 491-7710	26409
Medex Pratice Solutions Inc	8721	D	209 845-1346	26410
Melvin T Wheeler & Sons	0723	D	209 526-9770	562
Mocse Federal Credit Union	6061	D	209 572-3600	9615
Modesto Court Room Inc	7997	E	209 577-1060	19004
Modesto Hospitality Lessee LLC	7011	D	209 526-6000	13002
Modesto Industrial Elec Co Inc **(PA)**	1731	C	209 495-1597	2656
Modesto Irrigation District	4911	B	209 526-7563	6149
Modesto Irrigation District **(PA)**	4911	C	209 526-7337	6150
Modesto Irrigation District	4911	B	209 526-7373	6151
Modesto Wstewater Trtmnt Plant	4953	D	209 577-5300	6504
Muscolino Inventory Svc Inc	7389	E	209 576-8469	17344
Mve Inc **(PA)**	8711	D	209 526-4214	25978
Nasco Healthcare Inc	5191	D	209 545-1600	9145
Ontel Security Services Inc	7382	D	209 521-0200	16906
Pacific Gas and Electric Co	4911	E	209 576-6636	6179
Paratransit Incorporated	4119	C	209 522-2300	3827
Pegasus Risk Management Inc **(PA)**	6411	D	209 574-2800	10824
Pepsi-Cola Metro Btlg Co Inc	4225	D	209 557-5100	4612
Permanente Medical Group Inc	8011	D	209 735-5000	19868
Provident Care Inc	8082	C	209 526-5160	22542
Radnet Management Inc	8741	D	209 524-6800	27190
Rangel Drywall Inc	1742	E	209 525-9490	2963
Regent Assisted Living Inc	0781	D	209 491-0800	792
Riverside Health Care Corp	8059	D	209 523-5667	21361
Salon-Salon	7231	D	209 571-3500	13690
Satellite Healthcare Inc	8092	D	209 578-0691	22640
Sawyers Heating & AC	1711	D	209 416-7700	2359
Scotts Plant Service Co	0782	D	209 545-0903	949
Seca Eqp Removal & Dismantle	1795	E	209 543-1600	3466
Silla Automotive LLC	5013	D	209 577-5089	6770
Solecon Industrial Contrs Inc	1711	D	209 572-7390	2377
Sportsmen of Stanislaus Inc	7991	D	209 578-5801	18696
Squab Producers Calif Inc	5144	D	209 537-4744	8606
Stanislaus County Police	8322	D	209 529-9121	24232
Stanislaus Farm Supply Company **(PA)**	5191	D	860 678-5160	9153
Stanislaus Surgical Hosp LLC **(PA)**	8062	D	209 572-2700	21936
Stellar Group Incorporated	5078	D	209 549-0899	7760
Sterling Mktg & Fincl Corp	8742	E	209 593-1140	27669
Stone Real Estate Inc **(PA)**	6531	D	209 847-1230	11859
Storer Transportation Service **(PA)**	4141	B	209 521-8250	3896
Sutter Central Vly Hospitals **(HQ)**	8062	C	209 526-4500	21941
Sutter Central Vly Hospitals	4522	E	209 526-4500	4888
Sutter Gould Med Foundation **(PA)**	8011	E	209 948-5940	20077
Sutter Health	8011	C	209 524-1211	20094
Sutter Health	8011	B	209 522-0146	20097
Sysco Central California Inc	5141	D	209 527-7700	8530
T-Mobile Usa Inc	4812	D	209 529-0539	5415
Tcb Industrial Inc **(PA)**	1541	D	209 571-0569	1472
Tennis Pro Shop	7991	E	209 529-2446	18698
Thompson Hysell Engineers	8711	D	209 521-8986	26098
Tyco Integrated Security LLC	7382	D	209 574-2704	16937
United Sttes Intrmdal Svcs LLC	4731	D	209 341-4045	5183
US Foods Inc	5149	C	209 522-2662	8949
Valley Mtn Regional Ctr Inc	8361	D	209 529-2626	24841
Vinson Chase Inc	6531	D	209 577-4747	11899
Wells Fargo Bank National Assn	6021	D	209 578-6810	9434
Wondertreats Inc	5199	B	209 521-8881	9314
Woodside Group Inc	6162	E	209 579-2030	9908
Yosemite Meat Company Inc	4222	D	209 524-5117	4511
Young Mens Chrstn Assn Stanis	8641	D	209 578-9622	25475

MOFFETT FIELD, CA - Santa Clara County

	SIC	EMP	PHONE	ENTRY #
Millennium Engrg Integration	8711	D	703 413-7750	25966

MOJAVE, CA - Kern County

	SIC	EMP	PHONE	ENTRY #
Golden Queen Mining Co LLC	1041	D	661 824-4300	1022

MONROVIA, CA - Los Angeles County

	SIC	EMP	PHONE	ENTRY #
Adams & Barnes Inc	6531	E	626 358-1858	11276
Alakor Healthcare LLC	8062	C	626 408-9800	21441
Arch Bay Holdings LLC	6719	D	949 679-2400	12049
Brookdale Senior Living Inc	6513	D	626 301-0204	11103
California Business Bureau Inc **(PA)**	7322	C	626 303-1515	14021
California Cancer Specialists **(PA)**	8621	E	626 775-3200	25120
Converse Consultants Inc **(HQ)**	7389	E	626 930-1200	17095
Country Villa Service Corp	8741	C	626 358-4547	26988
Federal Deposit Insurance Corp	6399	D	626 359-7152	10567
Garden View Inc	0781	E	626 303-4043	768
Genzyme Corporation	8071	D	800 255-1616	22223
H C Olsen Cnstr Co Inc	1541	D	626 359-8900	1433
Harris Corporation	8711	B	626 584-4527	25850
Kentmaster Mfg Co Inc **(PA)**	5084	E	626 359-8888	7854
Krikorian Premiere Theatre LLC	1542	D	626 305-7469	1598
Linear Industries Ltd **(PA)**	5085	D	626 303-1130	7939
M T M & M Inc	7353	D	626 445-2922	14486
Monrovia Health Center	8011	D	626 256-1600	19762
MWH Americas Inc	8734	C	626 386-1100	26872
Parasoft Corporation **(PA)**	5045	E	626 305-0041	7171
Sage Hospitality Resources LLC	7011	D	626 357-5211	13188
Santa Anita Family Young	8331	D	626 359-9244	24386
SM Broadway Corp	6798	D	626 301-1198	12273
Southern California Edison Co	4911	D	626 303-8480	6213
St Baldricks Foundation Inc **(PA)**	8621	D	626 792-8247	25157
Visionfund International	7389	D	626 303-8811	17595

Employment Codes: A=Over 500 employees, B=251-500, C=101-250, D=51-100, E=45-50

2017 Directory of California Wholesalers and Services Companies

MONROVIA, CA

	SIC	EMP	PHONE	ENTRY #
Vivopools Inc	7389	D	818 952-2121	17598
Vivopools LLC	7389	D	888 702-8486	17599
World Class Distribution Inc	4225	B	909 574-4140	4673
World Vision International (HQ)	8699	C	626 303-8811	25601
Xerox Corporation	5044	C	626 294-3754	7077
Yang Ming America Corporation	4731	D	626 782-9797	5195

MONTCLAIR, CA - San Bernardino County

	SIC	EMP	PHONE	ENTRY #
Acepex Management Corporation (PA)	8744	C	909 625-6900	27770
Aragon Construction Inc	1542	D	909 621-2200	1492
Bally Total Fitness Corp	7991	E	909 625-2411	18612
Community Convalescent Center	8051	D	909 621-4751	20466
Converse Inc	5139	C	909 625-6655	8427
Cramer Painting Inc	1721	E	909 397-5770	2436
E M S Trading Inc	5139	C	909 581-7800	8432
Foundation For Dance Education	7922	D	909 482-1590	18393
Jeff Kerber Pool Plst Inc	1799	B	909 465-0677	3537
Medicrest of California 1	8051	D	909 626-1294	20784
Mission Drive-In Theatre Co	7833	C	909 465-9219	18360
Omnitrans	4111	C	909 379-7100	3685
Oparc (PA)	8331	E	909 982-4090	24373
Prime Healthcare Svcs III LLC (HQ)	8062	D	909 625-5411	21814
Silla Automotive LLC	5013	C	909 624-2801	6769
US Skillserve Inc	8051	C	909 621-4751	21000

MONTE SERENO, CA - Santa Clara County

	SIC	EMP	PHONE	ENTRY #
Oracle Systems Corporation	7371	D	650 506-4060	15359

MONTEBELLO, CA - Los Angeles County

	SIC	EMP	PHONE	ENTRY #
Advanced Data Transcribing Ctr	7374	D	626 571-1570	16089
Allied Building Products Corp	5031	D	323 721-9011	6905
American Multi-Cinema Inc	7832	E	323 722-4583	18307
AMF Bowling Centers Inc	7933	E	323 728-9161	18507
Bally Total Fitness Corp	7991	E	323 722-0994	18613
Beverly Community Hosp Assn	8062	B	323 889-2452	21464
Beverly Community Hosp Assn (PA)	8062	C	323 726-1222	21465
Beverly Community Hosp Assn	8062	A	323 725-1519	21466
California Creations Inc	5021	C	323 722-9832	6809
Delancey Street Foundation	4225	E	323 890-9339	4541
Eastwestproto Inc	4119	C	888 535-5728	3786
Epsilon Electronics Inc	5064	C	323 722-3333	7496
Express Services Inc	7363	A	323 832-9405	14876
Healthcare Partners LLC	8011	D	323 720-1144	19550
Honolulu Freight Service (PA)	4731	E	323 887-6777	5102
Hubbard Iron Doors Inc	5051	E	323 724-6500	7375
Kaiser Foundation Hospitals	8011	A	800 780-1277	19633
Katzkin Leather Inc (PA)	5199	C	323 725-1243	9273
L&T Staffing Inc	7363	B	323 727-9056	14894
Lockheed Martin Government Ser	7379	D	323 721-6979	16424
Marquez Brothers Intl Inc	5141	D	323 722-8103	8495
Mexican Amrcn Oprtnty Fndation (PA)	8322	D	323 890-9600	24085
Modern Concepts Medical Group	8011	D	323 728-6070	19757
Montebello School Transportion	4151	D	323 887-7900	3946
Montebello Transit	4111	C	323 887-4600	3675
Montebello Unified School Dst	7349	D	323 887-2140	14363
Old Dominion Freight Line Inc	4213	D	323 725-3400	4240
Orora North America	5113	C	323 832-2000	8205
Paladin Eastside Services Inc	8361	D	323 890-0180	24761
Rio Hndo Sbcute Nrsing Ctr LLC	8051	C	323 838-5915	20872
SA Recycling LLC	4953	C	323 723-8327	6549
Star Scrap Metal Company Inc	5093	D	562 921-5045	8091
Volum Staffing Inc	7361	B	310 499-4902	14816
Worldwide Intgrted Rsurces Inc	5087	D	323 838-8938	7990

MONTEREY, CA - Monterey County

	SIC	EMP	PHONE	ENTRY #
1000 Aguajito Op Co LLC	7011	D	831 373-6141	12356
Advantacare Health Inc (PA)	7352	D	831 373-1111	14468
Aramark Spt & Entrmt Group LLC	7929	C	831 648-9809	18454
AT&T Corp	4812	D	831 642-0100	5276
AT&T Services Inc	4813	D	831 394-2690	5527
AT&T Services Inc	4813	D	831 649-2029	5534
Ave Maria Convalescent Hosp	8051	D	831 373-1216	20400
Bayview Properties Inc	7011	D	831 655-7650	12426
Bayview Properties Inc (PA)	8741	D	831 394-3321	26939
California Capital Insur Co (PA)	6331	C	831 233-5500	10406
Casa Munras Hotel LLC	7011	E	831 375-2411	12497
Cellco Partnership	4812	D	831 644-0858	5288
Central Coast Cmnty Hlth Care	8059	C	831 372-6668	21182
Central Coast Cmnty Hlth Care	8099	B	831 648-4200	22919
Central Coast Vna & Hospice (PA)	8082	C	831 372-6668	22401
Classic Park Lane Partnership	6513	D	831 373-0101	11116
Classic Riverdale Inc	7011	D	831 373-0101	12527
Classic Rsdence Mgt Ltd Partnr	7011	D	831 373-0101	12528
Coastal Hotel Group Inc	7011	D	831 646-8900	12531
Coastal Hotel Group Inc	7011	D	831 373-5700	12532
Coastal Hotel Group Inc	7011	E	831 373-8000	12533
Comcast Corporation	4841	D	831 657-6095	5972
Community Hospital Foundation (PA)	8741	A	831 625-4830	26978
Credit Interlink America	7323	E	831 655-7890	14056
Custom House Hotel LP	7011	D	831 649-4511	12559
Cypress Hlthcare Partners LLC (PA)	8011	E	831 649-1000	19484
Data Recognition Corporation	8748	E	831 393-0700	27893
Del Mar French Laundry	7211	E	831 375-9597	13502
DMC Construction Incorporated	1542	D	831 656-1600	1543
Entravsion Communications Corp	4833	E	831 333-9736	5855
Federal Express Corporation	4513	D	800 463-3339	4851
Granite Construction Inc	1611	D	831 657-1700	1786
Healthcare Pathways Management	8082	D	831 373-1111	22455
Hospital of Community (HQ)	8069	A	831 624-5311	22146
Hyatt Corporation	7011	B	831 372-1234	12815
Hyatt Hotels Corporation	7011	B	831 372-1234	12825
Intercntnntal Clement Monterey	7011	E	831 375-4500	12838
Low Ball & Lynch A Prof Corp	8111	E	831 655-8822	23410
Mangold Property Management	6531	D	831 372-1338	11654
Michael Bruington	1521	B	831 663-1772	1220
Monterey Bay Aqar Foundation (PA)	8422	C	831 648-4800	25067
Monterey Credit Union (PA)	6062	D	831 647-1000	9673
Monterey Dental Group	8021	D	831 373-3068	20265
Monterey Inst of Intl Studies	8733	C	831 647-4100	26789
Monterey Peninsula Dntl Group	8021	D	831 373-3068	20266
Monterey Peninsula Hospital	8062	E	831 373-0924	21752
Monterey Pines Sklld Nursg Fac	8051	D	831 373-3716	20797
Monterey Plaza Ht Ltd Partnr	7011	B	800 334-3999	13007
National Parking Corporation	4959	C	831 646-0426	6631
Northwest Correctnl Med Grp	8093	E	831 649-8994	22782
Ocean Park Hotels Inc	7011	C	831 373-6141	13034
Old Fishermans Grotto	6552	D	831 375-4604	11993
P Monterey LP	8361	D	831 250-6159	24758
Pacific Gas and Electric Co	4911	E	831 648-3231	6184
Pater Digintas Inc	8051	D	831 624-1875	20845
Portfolio Hotels & Resorts LLC	7011	D	831 375-2411	13105
Pro Act LLC	5148	D	831 655-4250	8764
Procall Solutions Inc	7389	C	800 733-9675	17429
Product Development Corp (PA)	7389	C	831 333-1100	17429
Robert Half International Inc	7361	D	831 241-9042	14759
Salinas Valley Memorial Hlthca	8011	B	831 884-5048	19935
San Carlos Associates Ltd	7011	C	831 649-4234	13194
Sequoia Insurance Company (HQ)	6331	B	831 655-9612	10459
Southwest Correctional Medical	8093	D	831 641-3298	22839
Stocker & Allaire Inc	1521	E	831 375-1890	1264
Sunrise Senior Living Inc	8051	D	831 643-2400	20966
Tele-Interpreters LLC	7389	B	800 811-7881	17524
Triad Broadcasting Company (PA)	4832	C	831 655-6350	5824
United Parcel Service Inc OH	4215	C	831 757-6294	4462
United States Dept of Navy	8731	D	831 656-4613	26629
Visiting Nurse Association	8082	D	831 385-1014	22593
Windsor Monterey Care Ctr LLC	8059	D	831 373-2731	21427
Zhg Inc	7011	D	831 394-3321	13447

MONTEREY PARK, CA - Los Angeles County

	SIC	EMP	PHONE	ENTRY #
Ahmc Garfield Medical Ctr LP	8051	C	626 573-2222	20371
American Multi-Cinema Inc	7832	D	626 407-0240	18296
American Reprographics Co LLC	7334	D	626 289-5021	14102
Arroyo Developmental Services	8322	D	626 307-2240	23670
Care 1st Health Plan (PA)	8099	C	323 889-6638	22909
Childrens Law Center Cal (PA)	8111	D	323 980-8700	23148
City of Monterey Park	7999	D	626 307-1388	19176
County of Los Angeles	8322	C	323 265-1804	23830
East West Bank	6036	D	626 280-1688	9584
F & A Federal Credit Union	6061	D	323 268-1226	9594
Guard-Systems Inc	7381	B	323 881-6711	16670
Guard-Systems Inc	7381	B	323 881-6715	16671
Heritage Manor Inc	8051	D	626 573-3141	20668
JC Foodservice Inc (PA)	5046	D	626 299-3800	7220
Lincoln Plaza Hotel Inc	7011	D	626 571-8818	12922
Merchants Building Maint Co (PA)	7349	C	323 881-6701	14354
Merchants Building Maint Co	7349	C	323 881-8902	14356
Monterey Park Hospital	8062	C	626 570-9000	21751
Monterey Pk Convalescent Hosp	8059	D	626 280-0280	21319
Ntt Data Inc	7373	D	213 228-2500	16016
Roque Development and Inv Inc	8711	D	626 427-9077	26044
Southern California Gas Co	8741	B	213 244-1200	27225
Southern California Gas Co	4923	C	213 244-1200	6266
State Compensation Insur Fund	6331	C	323 266-5000	10477
Synermed	8011	C	216 406-2845	20126
Syntelesys Inc	7622	E	323 859-2160	17914
United Parcel Service Inc OH	7389	A	626 280-8012	17560
Uti Leak Seekers	1623	D	323 724-0081	2007
Wah Hung Intl McHy Inc	5012	D	323 263-3513	6700

MONTROSE, CA - Los Angeles County

	SIC	EMP	PHONE	ENTRY #
Golden Living LLC	8059	D	818 249-3925	21239
Great Wstn Cnvlescent Hosp Inc	8059	C	818 248-6856	21256

	SIC	EMP	PHONE	ENTRY #
Sara Enterprises Inc (HQ)	4724	D	818 553-3200	4973
Senior Care Inc	8052	C	818 275-9717	21105

MOORPARK, CA - Ventura County

	SIC	EMP	PHONE	ENTRY #
Alliance Envmtl Group Inc	8999	D	805 378-6590	28111
Cardservice International Inc (HQ)	7389	B	805 648-1425	17056
Cimatron Gibbs LLC	7371	D	805 523-0004	15085
City of Moorpark	8322	D	805 517-6261	23755
Dbi Services Inc	1623	D	805 523-7114	1926
Donovan Bros Golf LLC	7992	D	805 531-9300	18735
Dynalectric Company	1731	C	805 517-1253	2576
EBM Janitorial Services Inc	7349	D	805 523-3700	14287
Fiserv Inc	7374	D	805 532-9100	16132
Gemmm Corp	6531	D	805 267-2700	11551
Kretek International Inc (PA)	5194	D	805 531-8888	9234
Lane Stuart Company LLC	6531	D	805 553-9562	11626
Malibu Canyon Ldscp & Maint	0781	D	805 523-2676	778
Muranaka Farm	0161	C	805 529-0201	82
Ned L Webster Concrete Cnstr	1771	D	805 529-4900	3300
Pacific Rim Realty Group	6531	E	805 553-9562	11730
Pennymac Financial Svcs Inc	6162	A	818 224-7442	9884
Pindler & Pindler Inc (PA)	5131	D	805 531-9090	8321
Prudential Overall Supply	7218	D	805 529-0833	13641
Raycon Environmental Cnstr	1799	E	805 955-0900	3575
Wall Systems Inc	1742	D	805 523-9091	2996
Xp Systems Corporation (HQ)	7373	C	805 532-9100	16083

MORAGA, CA - Contra Costa County

	SIC	EMP	PHONE	ENTRY #
Engineered Forest Products LLC	6799	D	925 376-0881	12305
Moraga Cntry CLB Hmowners Assn	7997	D	925 376-2200	19008
Pioneer Health Care Services	8741	C	925 631-9100	27166
Sunrise Senior Living Inc	8051	D	510 531-7190	20950

MORENO VALLEY, CA - Riverside County

	SIC	EMP	PHONE	ENTRY #
Atsugi Kokusai Kanko USA Inc	7997	D	951 924-4444	18879
Bluegill Technologies LLC	7382	D	877 765-2770	16871
Community Health Systems Inc	8011	C	951 571-2300	19454
Consoldted Med Bo-Analysis Inc	8071	D	951 243-2600	22205
County of Riverside	8011	D	951 486-4000	19478
County of Riverside	8011	B	951 486-4000	19480
Friends For Life	8699	D	951 601-6722	25532
Integrted Care Communities Inc	8051	E	951 243-3837	20687
Kaiser Foundation Hospitals	6733	E	951 601-6174	12184
Kaiser Foundation Hospitals	8011	B	951 243-0811	19676
Lowes Home Centers LLC	4225	C	951 601-2230	4592
National Lgal Studies Inst Inc	7389	E	951 653-4240	17348
Parenthood of Planned	8093	D	951 222-3101	22793
Plaza Hand Carwash Inc	7542	E	951 697-4420	17858
Ritchie Plumbing Inc	1711	C	949 709-7575	2348
Time Warner Cable Inc	4841	D	951 571-8738	6052
Walgreen Arizona Drug Co	4225	D	928 526-1400	4663
Washington Inventory Service	7389	D	951 653-1472	17609
Waste MGT Collectn & Recycl	4953	C	951 242-0421	6601
Waste MGT Collectn & Recycl	4953	D	909 242-0421	6607

MORGAN HILL, CA - Santa Clara County

	SIC	EMP	PHONE	ENTRY #
Aragen Bioscience Inc	8731	E	408 779-1700	26475
Cal Color Growers LLC	5193	D	408 778-0835	9181
City of Morgan Hill	8748	D	408 776-7333	27880
Cloverleaf Construction Co	1751	B	408 776-3122	3037
Coast Distribution System Inc (DH)	5013	D	408 782-6686	6722
Covenant Care LLC	8051	D	408 779-7347	20484
Coyote Creek Golf Club	7992	D	408 463-1400	18728
Del Monaco Specialty Foods Inc	5141	D	408 500-4100	8473
George Chiala Farms Inc	0161	C	408 778-0562	67
Hillview Convalescent Hospital	8051	E	408 779-3633	20672
Institute LLC	7992	E	408 782-7101	18749
Irish Construction	1623	D	408 612-8440	1946
K R Anderson Inc (PA)	5169	D	408 825-1800	8991
Kawahara Nursery Inc	0181	D	408 779-2400	294
Lusamerica Foods Inc (PA)	5146	D	408 294-6622	8639
Medallion Landscape MGT Inc (PA)	0781	D	408 782-7500	780
Micro-Mechanics Inc	5065	E	408 779-2927	7604
Monterey Mushrooms Inc	0182	B	408 779-4191	335
Monument Construction Inc	0782	D	408 778-1350	915
Pacific States Industries Inc	5031	D	408 779-7354	6945
Prism Electronics Corp (PA)	5065	E	408 778-7050	7621
Psynergy Programs Inc	8361	D	408 776-0422	24775
Reinhardt Roofing Inc	1761	D	510 713-7014	3209
Resonate Inc (PA)	7371	C	408 545-5500	15416
Royal Oaks Enterprises Inc	0182	E	408 779-2362	343
Sakata Seed America Inc (HQ)	5191	D	408 778-7758	9149
Santa Clara County of	8361	D	408 201-7600	24804
South County Housing Corp (PA)	6531	E	510 582-1460	11852
Town Cats Morgan Hill Rescue	0752	E	408 779-5761	646
Youngs Market Company LLC	5182	D	408 782-3121	9119

MORRO BAY, CA - San Luis Obispo County

	SIC	EMP	PHONE	ENTRY #
Compass Health Inc	8059	C	805 772-7372	21190
Mission Linen Supply	7213	E	805 772-4451	13553
Morro Bay Public Works	1611	D	805 772-6261	1829
Smile Housing Corporation	8093	D	805 772-6066	22833

MOSS BEACH, CA - San Mateo County

	SIC	EMP	PHONE	ENTRY #
Friends Fitzgerald Mar Reserve	8399	D	650 728-3584	24921
Seton Medical Center	8062	C	650 728-5521	21881

MOSS LANDING, CA - Monterey County

	SIC	EMP	PHONE	ENTRY #
Capurro Marketing LLC	5148	D	831 728-1767	8703
Dobler & Sons LLC	0161	B	831 724-6727	58
Dynegy Marketing & Trade LLC	4911	D	831 633-6700	6125
Dynegy Moss Landing LLC	4911	D	831 633-6618	6126
Monterey Bay Aquarium RES Inst	8731	C	831 775-1700	26570
Moss Landing Marine Labs	8071	C	831 771-4400	22243

MOUNT HERMON, CA - Santa Cruz County

	SIC	EMP	PHONE	ENTRY #
Mount Hermon Association Inc (PA)	7032	D	831 335-4466	13469

MOUNT SHASTA, CA - Siskiyou County

	SIC	EMP	PHONE	ENTRY #
County of Siskiyou	8093	D	530 918-7200	22712
Mercy HM Svcs A Cal Ltd Partnr	8062	B	530 926-6111	21741
Siskiyou Lake Golf Resort Inc	7992	D	530 926-3030	18788
Siskiyou Opportunity Center (PA)	8331	D	530 926-4698	24387

MOUNTAIN PASS, CA - San Bernardino County

	SIC	EMP	PHONE	ENTRY #
Chevron Mining Inc	1221	B	760 856-7625	1024

MOUNTAIN VIEW, CA - Santa Clara County

	SIC	EMP	PHONE	ENTRY #
24 Hour Fitness Usa Inc	7991	E	650 941-2268	18598
Achievo Corporation (PA)	7371	D	925 498-8864	14998
Addepar Inc (PA)	7371	D	855 692-3337	15000
Advance Staffing Inc	7363	D	408 205-6154	14831
Agilepoint Inc	7372	C	650 968-6789	15574
American Century Inv MGT Inc	6282	D	650 965-8300	10116
Artificial Solutions Inc	7371	D	650 943-2325	15034
Assure Consulting Inc	8748	D	650 966-1967	27837
AT&T Corp	4813	D	415 276-0039	5510
AT&T Services Inc	4813	D	650 960-2255	5537
Atrenta Inc (HQ)	7371	D	408 453-3333	15042
Auto-Chlor System LLC	7359	D	650 967-3085	14515
Axcient Inc (PA)	7371	D	650 314-7300	15047
Balboa Enterprises Inc	8051	C	650 961-6161	20404
Bdna Corporation (PA)	7372	D	650 625-9530	15597
Bella Terra Technologies Inc	4899	D	650 316-6660	6060
Bops Inc	7372	D	650 254-2800	15605
Branderscom Inc (PA)	5199	D	650 292-2752	9247
CA Ste Atom Assoc Intr-Ins Bur	6411	D	650 623-3200	10653
Camino Real Group LLC	7011	E	650 964-1700	12483
Carrier Iq Inc (HQ)	7371	D	650 625-5400	15076
Channel Intelligence Inc (DH)	4813	D	321 939-5600	5575
Churchill Downs Incorporated	7948	A	502 638-3879	18568
Clearwell Systems Inc	7372	C	877 253-2793	15622
Coherent Inc	8732	D	408 764-4000	26650
Complete Genomics Inc	8733	B	650 943-2800	26754
Computer History Museum	8412	D	650 810-1010	25012
Covenant Care California LLC	8062	D	650 964-0543	21526
Cumulus Networks Inc (PA)	7372	C	650 383-6700	15633
Deutsche Telekom Inc	8748	D	650 335-4100	27898
Devcxom Inc	4813	E	650 390-6553	5589
Dg Architects Inc (PA)	8712	D	650 943-1660	26183
Drchronocom Inc	7371	E	650 600-2079	15148
Egnyte Inc (PA)	7371	C	650 968-4018	15155
Ehealth Inc (PA)	6411	D	650 584-2700	10698
Ehealthinsurance Services Inc (HQ)	6411	D	650 584-2700	10699
El Camino Hospital	8322	C	650 988-7444	23957
El Camino Hospital	8092	D	650 940-7310	22626
El Camino Hospital	8069	C	650 988-4825	22140
El Camino Hospital Auxiliary	8082	A	650 940-7214	22430
El Camino Surgery Center LLC	8062	C	650 961-1200	21552
Fenwick & West LLP (PA)	8111	B	650 988-8500	23237
First Technology Federal Cr Un (PA)	6061	D	855 855-8805	9600
Fusionops Inc	7371	C	408 524-2222	15198
General Dynamics Advanced Info	8711	A	650 966-2000	25831
Gigya Inc	7372	C	650 353-7230	15679
Google Fiber Inc	4813	D	650 253-0000	5617
Google Inc (HQ)	4813	D	650 253-0000	5618
Google Inc	7375	D	650 253-7323	16239
Google International LLC (DH)	4813	D	650 253-0000	5619
Google Payment Corp	7389	E	650 253-0000	17195
Group Avantica Inc	7371	B	650 248-9678	15215
Healthpocket Inc	6321	D	800 984-8015	10240
Hytrust Inc (PA)	7372	D	650 681-8100	15695
Iap World Services Inc	8744	D	650 604-0451	27793
Intellisync Corporation (HQ)	7371	D	650 625-2185	15246

MOUNTAIN VIEW, CA

Company	SIC	EMP	PHONE	ENTRY #
Intermedia Holdings Inc (PA)	7379	D	650 641-4000	16407
Intuit Inc (PA)	7372	D	650 944-6000	15711
Intuit Inc	7372	D	650 944-6000	15712
Intuit Inc	7372	C	650 944-6000	15713
Jacobs Technology Inc	1629	C	650 604-3784	2061
Jacobs Technology Inc	8711	E	650 604-5946	25906
Kaiser Foundation Hospitals	8062	D	650 903-3000	21647
Kaiser Med Clinic	8011	C	650 903-2103	19681
Khan Academy Inc	7372	D	650 336-5426	15722
Kindred Healthcare Oper Inc	8062	D	650 962-6000	21686
Kosmix Corporation	4813	D	605 938-2300	5645
Linkedin Corporation (PA)	7375	C	650 687-3600	16249
Lozeno Inc	7542	C	650 941-0590	17854
Meebo Inc (PA)	4813	D	650 253-0000	5654
Microsoft Corporation	4813	D	650 964-7200	5658
Mindsource Inc	7371	D	650 314-6400	15304
Mobileiron Inc (PA)	7372	C	650 919-8100	15760
Mojo Networks Inc (PA)	7382	D	650 961-1111	16901
Moog Inc	8711	D	650 210-9000	25975
Mozilla Corporation (HQ)	7373	B	650 903-0800	15998
Mp Shoreline Assoc Ltd Partnr	6513	E	650 966-1327	11172
Nagra Usa Inc	5084	D	310 335-5225	7865
Nebula Inc	8731	D	650 539-9900	26573
Neuropace Inc	8731	D	650 237-2700	26575
Northrop Grumman Systems Corp	7373	C	650 604-6056	16014
Northrop Grumman Systems Corp	7371	C	650 604-5381	15339
Odesk Corporation	7361	E	650 853-4100	14714
OGrady Paving Inc	1611	C	650 966-1926	1837
Palo Alto Medical Foundation	8011	D	650 934-3565	19813
Palo Alto Medical Foundation	8011	D	408 739-6000	19819
Peel Technologies Inc	5045	D	650 204-7977	7172
Perkstreet Financial Inc	8742	E	978 801-1177	27586
Polaris Building Maintenance	7349	D	650 964-9400	14391
Polaris Wireless Inc	7371	E	408 492-8900	15389
Project Consulting Specialists	8748	E	650 265-2400	28024
Quintiles Pacific Incorporated (DH)	8732	E	650 567-2000	26700
Quctient Technology Inc (PA)	7319	C	650 605-4600	14008
Quova Inc	8748	D	650 965-2898	28028
Recreational Equipment Inc	5046	C	650 969-1938	7224
Recis Labs Inc	7371	D	415 930-9666	15412
Rhythmone LLC	7371	D	650 961-9024	15421
Samsung Electronics Amer Inc	8742	A	650 210-1000	27634
Samsung Research America Inc (DH)	8731	E	408 544-5700	26597
Sectek Inc	7382	D	650 604-1785	16918
Sequoia Retail Systems Inc (DH)	7371	E	650 237-9000	15448
Service By Medallion	7349	B	650 625-1010	14425
Seti Institute	8733	C	650 961-6633	26808
Siemens AG	8711	D	650 969-9112	26063
Siemens Med Solutions USA Inc	5047	B	650 694-5747	7314
Silicon Vly Cmnty Foundation	8641	C	650 450-5400	25349
Soaprojects Inc (PA)	8742	E	650 960-9900	27655
Soasta Inc	7379	D	650 210-4941	16482
Spotcues Inc	5045	A	408 435-2700	7194
Stewart Painting Inc	1721	D	650 968-3706	2495
Symantec Corporation	7372	B	650 527-8000	15852
Synopsys Inc (PA)	7371	B	650 584-5000	15486
Tabula Inc	5065	D	408 986-9140	7644
Takara Bio Usa Inc	8731	C	650 237-5700	26618
Thoits Insurance Service Inc	6411	D	408 792-5400	10904
Thomson Reuters (legal) Inc	8748	D	650 210-1900	28077
Tidebreak Inc	5045	D	650 289-9869	7200
Tintri Inc	7375	C	650 810-8200	16263
Travelzoo Usa Inc	7313	D	650 316-6956	13983
Trialpay Inc (PA)	7379	D	650 318-0000	16511
Twilio Inc	7371	B	877 889-4546	15512
Upwork Inc	7361	B	650 316-7500	14812
Upwork Inc (PA)	7311	D	650 316-7500	13933
Varmour Networks Inc	7371	E	650 564-5100	15521
Vendavo Inc (HQ)	7372	C	650 960-4300	15874
Verifaya Corporation	7372	C	408 566-0220	15875
Veritas Technologies LLC (HQ)	7371	C	650 933-1000	15524
Veritas US Inc (PA)	7371	C	650 933-1000	15525
Villa Siena	8059	D	650 961-6484	21413
Vimo Inc	8748	D	650 618-4600	28091
Wso2 Inc (PA)	7371	D	650 745-4499	15548
Xad Inc	8742	C	650 386-6867	27725
YMCA of Silicon Valley	8641	B	650 969-9622	25433
Zeeaero Inc	8711	D	650 964-4570	26157
Zelos Consulting LLC	8748	E	650 968-2881	28105
Zonare Medical Systems Inc (HQ)	8733	D	650 230-2800	26827

MURPHYS, CA - Calaveras County

Company	SIC	EMP	PHONE	ENTRY #
Kautz Vineyards Inc (PA)	0172	D	209 728-1251	163

MURRIETA, CA - Riverside County

Company	SIC	EMP	PHONE	ENTRY #
Alta Loma Assisted Living LLC	8322	D	909 481-2600	23653
Bear Creek Golf Club Inc	7997	D	951 677-8621	18886
Bear Creek Partners LLC	7997	D	951 677-8621	18887
Bowlmor AMF Corp	7933	E	951 698-2202	18514
Cell Site Management Group LLC	4812	E	800 906-9778	5283
Community Health Network LLC	8082	D	951 265-8281	22406
Cumming Corporation	8742	D	951 200-7860	27400
Elite Enfrcment SEC Sltons Inc	7381	E	866 354-8308	16632
F M Tarbell Co	6531	D	951 677-3565	11503
Faith Quality Auto Body Inc	7532	D	951 698-8215	17753
First American Card Service	7389	E	951 677-8720	17169
Golden Living LLC	8322	D	951 600-4640	23996
Harbor Freight Tools Usa Inc	4731	D	951 304-2714	5097
Heliopower (PA)	1711	D	951 677-7755	2244
Jpi Development Group Inc	1711	D	951 973-7680	2263
Medley Communications Inc (PA)	1731	C	951 245-5200	2650
Monique Suraci	7991	D	951 677-8111	18663
Mulligan Ltd A Cal Ltd Partnr	7996	D	951 696-9696	18828
National Bus Invstigations Inc	7389	D	951 677-3500	17347
National Mentor Holdings Inc	8361	B	951 677-1453	24742
Oak Grove Inst Foundation Inc (PA)	8011	D	951 677-5599	19786
Ptac Rail Ranch Elem School	8641	D	951 696-1404	25323
Rancho Physical Therapy Inc (PA)	8049	D	951 696-9353	20348
Reading International Inc	7832	E	951 696-7045	18344
S I J Inc	1751	E	951 304-9444	3083
Sanborn Theatres Inc	7832	D	909 296-9728	18351
Scga Golf Course MGT Inc	7992	D	951 677-7446	18784
SI Inc	1751	E	951 304-9444	3089
Skywest Airlines Inc	4512	D	951 600-9181	4822
Southwest Healthcare Sys Aux	8062	E	800 404-6627	21909
Southwest Healthcare Sys Aux (HQ)	8062	B	951 696-6000	21910
Temecula Valley Drywall Inc	1742	D	951 600-1742	2986
Tvdcc EC Murrieta	8011	D	951 566-5229	20145
Twin Advantage Inc	6531	D	951 445-4200	11889
Utah Pacific Construction Co	1623	D	951 677-9876	2006
Your Way Fumigation Inc	7342	D	951 699-9116	14197

NAPA, CA - Napa County

Company	SIC	EMP	PHONE	ENTRY #
Back Street Fitness Inc	7991	E	707 254-7200	18606
Barrel Ten Quarter Circle Inc	5182	B	707 265-4000	9090
Bell Products Inc	1711	D	707 255-1811	2162
Blacktalon Enterprises Inc	7381	D	707 256-1810	16576
California Odd Fellows (PA)	6513	D	707 257-7885	11110
California Odd Fellows	6513	D	707 257-7885	11111
Califrnia Dept State Hospitals	8063	A	707 253-5000	22048
Carneros Inn LLC	7011	B	707 299-4880	12493
Cello & Maudru Cnstr Co Inc	1542	E	707 257-0454	1523
Chardonnay/ Club Shakespeare	7997	D	707 257-1900	18916
City of NAPA	4131	E	707 255-7631	3876
Coldwell Banker	6531	D	707 257-7673	11407
Collabria Care	8082	D	707 258-9080	22405
Comcast Corporation	4841	D	707 266-7012	5963
Copia The American C	8412	D	707 259-1600	25013
Corizon Health Inc	8011	D	707 253-4384	19462
County of NAPA	8322	D	707 253-4625	23868
County of NAPA	8322	E	707 253-4361	23869
County of NAPA	8093	D	707 253-4461	22706
CP Opco LLC	7359	D	707 253-2332	14526
Dickenson Peatman & Fogarty A (PA)	8111	E	707 252-7122	23212
Doctors Company	8011	D	707 226-0289	19506
Doctors Company Insurance Svcs	6351	B	707 226-0100	10492
Doctors Management Company (HQ)	6411	C	707 226-0100	10693
DOD Constructors A JV	1629	D	707 265-1100	2043
DOD Fueling Constructors A JV	1629	D	707 265-1100	2044
DOD Marine Constructors A JV	1629	D	707 265-1100	2045
Dolce International / NAPA LLC	7011	B	707 257-0200	12583
Domaine Carneros Ltd	0172	D	707 257-0101	151
Folio Wine Company LLC	5182	D	707 256-2757	9100
GD Nielson Construction Inc	1623	D	707 253-8774	1932
Golden Living LLC	8059	D	707 255-6060	21240
Guardsmark LLC	7381	C	415 898-9022	16684
Guardsmark LLC	7381	C	415 898-9020	16691
Hilton Worldwide Inc	7011	D	707 253-9540	12721
Hired Hands Inc	7361	D	707 226-6400	14671
JD Wesson & Associates Inc	7389	D	707 255-8667	17256
Kaiser Foundation Hospitals	6733	C	707 258-2500	12185
La Tavola LLC (PA)	7213	D	707 257-3358	13550
Lamson Investment Corp	6799	D	707 257-7461	12321
Melissa Bradley RE Inc	6531	D	707 258-3900	11673
Meritage Resort and Spa	7991	B	707 259-0633	18660
NAPA Ambulance Service Inc	4119	D	707 224-3123	3821
NAPA Golf Associates LLC	7997	D	707 257-1900	19010
NAPA Nursing Center Inc	8051	D	707 257-0931	20803
NAPA Sanitation District	4952	E	707 254-9231	6412
NAPA Sunrise Rotary Club Inc	8641	D	707 257-9564	25302
NAPA Valley Country Club	7997	D	707 252-1111	19011
NAPA Valley PSI Inc	8331	D	707 255-0177	24367

GEOGRAPHIC SECTION

NEWPORT BEACH, CA

	SIC	EMP	PHONE	ENTRY #
NAPA Valley Wine Train Inc (HQ)	7999	C	707 253-2160	19250
Napastyle Inc (PA)	7313	D	707 251-5100	13974
North Bay Developmental (PA)	8331	D	707 256-1224	24370
Nova Brink A Joint Venture	1629	C	707 265-1100	2071
Nova Group Inc	1623	C	707 257-3200	1972
Nova Group Inc	1629	C	707 265-1100	2072
Nova Grp Inc -Obayashi Corp A	1623	E	707 265-1116	1973
Nova Lane Constructors A JV	1629	C	707 265-1100	2073
Nova-Cpf Inc	1623	C	707 257-3200	1974
Ole Health	8011	E	707 254-1770	19791
On The Move	8399	D	707 251-9432	24950
Peck & Hiller Company	1771	D	707 258-8800	3311
Permanente Kaiser Intl	8049	D	707 258-4541	20338
Pina Vineyard Management LLC	0762	E	707 944-2229	716
Piners Nursing Home Inc	8051	D	707 224-7925	20847
Queen of Valley Medical Center (DH)	8062	A	707 252-4411	21827
Regulus Group LLC (DH)	7374	D	707 259-7100	16177
Retreat & Conference Center	7299	E	707 252-3810	13791
San Francisco City & County	8322	D	415 753-4439	24181
Seguin Mreau NAPA Coperage Inc	5085	D	707 252-3408	7952
Sheehan Construction Inc	1521	B	707 603-2610	1257
Silverado Country CLB & Resort	7997	B	707 257-0200	19081
Silverado Rsort Svcs Group LLC	7011	B	707 257-0200	13256
Sisters of St Joseph Orange	8082	C	707 257-4124	22565
Stagecoach Vineyards	0172	D	707 255-5459	189
Star H-R	7361	A	707 265-9911	14796
Sunstone Hotel Investors Inc	7011	D	707 253-8600	13314
Tahoe Lake Partners LLC	6552	D	707 255-9890	12017
Tailored Living Choices LLC	1799	D	707 259-0526	3587
Travis Credit Union	6061	B	800 877-8328	9635
United Parcel Service Inc OH	4215	C	707 224-1205	4446
US Advisor LLC	6798	D	707 253-9953	12276
Verasa Management LLC	7011	D	707 257-1800	13378
Vin Lux LLC	4214	E	707 265-4100	4389
Vino Farms Inc	0191	C	707 258-2729	404
Walsh Vineyards Management Inc	6531	D	707 255-1650	11905
Wells Fargo Bank National Assn	6021	D	707 259-5552	9438
Winiarski Management Inc	5182	D	707 944-2020	9116

NATIONAL CITY, CA - San Diego County

	SIC	EMP	PHONE	ENTRY #
Bally Total Fitness Corp	7991	E	619 474-6392	18614
Castle Manor Inc	8059	D	619 791-7900	21181
Centro De Salud De La	8322	D	619 477-0165	23729
Ehmcke Sheet Metal Corp	1761	D	619 477-6484	3168
Framing Associates Inc	7389	C	619 336-9991	17173
Greenwalds Autobody Frameworks (PA)	7532	E	619 477-2600	17756
Hardisty Construction Administ	1542	D	619 245-6828	1561
Harvest Meat Company Inc (HQ)	5147	D	619 477-0185	8669
Horizons Adult Day Health Care	8099	D	619 474-1822	22977
Hyperbaric MGT Systems Inc	8011	C	619 336-2022	19566
Imaginative Horizons Inc	8051	D	619 477-1176	20682
Maniflo Money Exchange Inc (PA)	6099	E	619 434-7200	9722
McKinley Plaza LLC	8741	D	619 405-6307	27122
Motivational Systems Inc (PA)	7336	D	619 474-8246	14156
National City Floor Covering	1752	D	619 477-7000	3127
Nms Management Inc	7349	C	619 425-0440	14370
Operation Samahan Inc	8748	D	619 477-4451	28011
Oxyheal Medical Systems Inc	7699	C	619 336-2022	17994
Paradise Valley Hospital (PA)	8062	A	619 470-4100	21785
Paradise Vly Hlth Care Ctr Inc	8051	D	619 470-6700	20840
Plaza Manor Preservation LP	6531	A	619 475-2125	11755
Probuild Company LLC	5031	E	619 425-6660	6952
San Diego-Imperial	8322	D	619 336-6600	24178
Sand Dollar Holdings Inc (PA)	5147	D	619 477-0185	8684
Six Continents Hotels Inc	7011	D	619 474-2800	13268
South Bay Sand Blasting and Ta	7699	D	619 238-8338	18016
St Pauls Episcopal Home Inc	8361	D	619 232-2996	24822
Superior Marine Solutions LLC	7699	D	619 773-7800	18019
Sureride Charter Inc	4142	C	619 336-9200	3907
US Foods Inc	5149	C	619 474-6525	8952
Westair Gases & Equipment Inc	5084	D	619 474-0079	7905
Windsor Healthcare Management	8051	D	619 474-6741	21052

NEEDLES, CA - San Bernardino County

	SIC	EMP	PHONE	ENTRY #
Colorado River Medical Center	8011	D	760 326-4531	19449
Havasu Landing Casino (PA)	7011	D	760 858-5380	12693

NEVADA CITY, CA - Nevada County

	SIC	EMP	PHONE	ENTRY #
Milhous Childrens Services Inc	8052	C	530 265-9057	21093
Milhous Feed	5191	C	530 292-3242	9144
Northern Queen Inc	7011	D	530 265-4492	13027
Patrick Dean Bryan	1799	D	530 273-5484	3566
Robinson & Sons	0212	D	530 265-5844	412
Tri Counties Bank	6029	D	530 478-6001	9563

NEWARK, CA - Alameda County

	SIC	EMP	PHONE	ENTRY #
Advanced Cell Diagnostics Inc (HQ)	8731	D	510 576-8800	26462
Alliance Bay Funding Inc	6531	D	510 742-6600	11291
Apn Software Services Inc (PA)	7379	D	510 623-5050	16322
Bay Advanced Technologies LLC	5084	D	510 857-0900	7822
Bioclinca (PA)	8731	C	415 817-8900	26488
D&A Enterprises Inc	5141	B	510 445-1600	8472
Elitegroup Cmpt Systems Inc	5045	C	510 794-2952	7123
Energy Experts International	8748	C	510 574-1822	27913
Fitness 2000 Inc	7991	E	510 791-2481	18632
Hardage Investments Inc	6512	E	510 795-1200	10997
Infosys Limited	7371	D	510 742-3000	15234
Innovated Packaging Company	7389	C	510 713-3560	17240
Integrated Pkg & Crating Svcs	4783	E	510 494-1622	5201
Itrenew Inc (PA)	4953	E	510 795-1591	6492
Javelin Logistics Corporation (PA)	4214	E	510 477-6911	4354
Kutir Corporation	7373	D	510 402-4526	15982
Lancashire Group Incorporated	8742	B	510 792-9384	27504
Marriott International Inc	7011	D	510 657-4600	12972
Membrane Technology & RES Inc (PA)	8731	D	650 328-2228	26566
Mickwee Group Inc	7389	D	510 651-5527	17335
Mshift Inc	7371	E	408 437-2740	15317
National Distribution Agcy Inc (HQ)	4225	D	510 487-6226	4601
Nefab Packaging West LLC	7389	E	408 678-2516	17350
Newark Courtyard By Marriott	7011	D	510 792-5200	13020
Nordstrom Inc	4225	C	510 794-5440	4606
Oak Harbor Freight Lines Inc	4213	C	510 608-8841	4238
Oatey Supply Chain Svcs Inc	5074	E	510 797-4677	7726
Palo Alto Egg and Food Svc Co	5141	E	510 456-2420	8508
Perlegen Sciences Inc	8731	C	650 625-4500	26587
Risk Management Solutions Inc (DH)	6794	D	510 505-2500	12223
Roseryan Inc	8721	E	510 456-3056	26431
Special Dispatch Cal Inc	4213	E	510 713-0300	4265
Stomper Co Inc	1795	D	510 574-0570	3469
Tegile Systems Inc	8731	D	510 791-7900	26619
Triple Ring Technologies Inc	8742	E	510 592-3000	27700
University Healthcare Alliance	8082	D	510 974-8281	22587
Valassis Direct Mail Inc	7331	C	510 505-6500	14097
Vm Services Inc (DH)	7371	E	510 744-3720	15531
Worldpac Inc (DH)	5013	C	510 742-8900	6781
Xtraplus Corporation	5045	D	510 897-1890	7212
Zenith Infotech Limited	7373	D	510 687-1943	16085
Zws/ABS Joint Venture LLC	7349	D	510 461-1433	14467

NEWBERRY SPRINGS, CA - San Bernardino County

	SIC	EMP	PHONE	ENTRY #
Southern California Gas Co	4923	D	800 427-0018	6267

NEWBURY PARK, CA - Ventura County

	SIC	EMP	PHONE	ENTRY #
Alliedbarton Security Svcs LLC	7381	C	805 480-3563	16547
Anthem Inc	6321	C	805 557-6655	10232
Area Housing Authority (PA)	6531	E	805 480-9991	11303
BMW of North America LLC	5013	D	909 975-7355	6715
Carnegie Agency Inc	6411	E	805 445-1470	10664
Compulink Business Systems Inc	7372	E	805 446-2050	15626
Conejo Pacific Technologies	1541	D	805 498-5315	1416
Designworks/Usa Inc (HQ)	8711	D	805 499-9590	25767
Giant Bicycle Inc (DH)	5091	D	805 267-4600	8020
Hawaiian Hotels & Resorts Inc	7011	D	805 480-0052	12694
Hearst Communications Inc	4841	B	805 375-3121	6005
Isolutecom Inc (PA)	7372	E	805 498-6259	15718
Mary Hlth SCK Cnvlscnt &NRsng	8051	A	805 498-3644	20777
McKesson Medical-Surgical Inc	5047	D	805 375-8800	7278
Time Warner Cable Inc	4841	D	805 214-1353	6033
United Parcel Service Inc OH	4215	C	805 375-1832	4470
United Payment Services Inc	7389	B	866 886-4833	17565

NEWHALL, CA - Los Angeles County

	SIC	EMP	PHONE	ENTRY #
Calex Engineering Inc	1794	D	661 254-1866	3420
Hollenbeck Palms	8361	C	323 263-6195	24693
N V Landscape Inc	0782	D	661 286-8888	917
Santa Clarita Athletic Club	7991	D	661 255-3365	18679
Valencia Health Care Inc	8059	D	661 254-2425	21406

NEWMAN, CA - Stanislaus County

	SIC	EMP	PHONE	ENTRY #
Avalon Care Ctr - Newman LLC	8051	D	209 862-2862	20394
Cerutti Bros Inc	0161	D	209 862-2249	49
Dimare Enterprises Inc (PA)	0161	D	209 827-2900	57
Golden Living LLC	8051	D	209 862-2862	20627
Precision Inspection Co Inc (PA)	7389	D	209 862-9511	17421

NEWPORT BEACH, CA - Orange County

	SIC	EMP	PHONE	ENTRY #
Absolute Return Portfolio	6722	A	800 800-7646	12099
Accentcare Home Health Cal Inc	8082	D	949 250-0133	22330
Alamo Rental (us) Inc	7514	E	949 852-0403	17660
Alliance Healthcare Svcs Inc (PA)	8071	C	949 242-5300	22188
Alliant Insurance Services Inc (PA)	6411	C	949 756-0271	10586
Allianz Globl Invstors Amer LP	6282	C	949 219-2200	10113
Allianz Globl Invstors Amer LP (HQ)	6282	C	949 219-2200	10114
Allied Lube Texas LP (PA)	7549	D	949 486-4008	17872

NEWPORT BEACH, CA — GEOGRAPHIC SECTION

Company	SIC	EMP	PHONE	ENTRY #
Ambassador Gaming Inc.	7999	C	714 969-8730	19134
Andersonpenna Partners Inc	8742	D	949 428-1500	27324
AON Hewitt LLC	8742		949 725-4500	27327
Applebee Leasing Inc.	7389	D	818 612-6218	16997
Avalon At Newport LLC	8361	D	949 631-3555	24561
Baid Vivek	4813		888 550-8553	5564
Balboa Bay Club Inc (HQ)	7997	B	949 645-5000	18881
Barcelo Enterprises Inc	0181	D	760 728-3444	267
Bassenian/Lagoni Architects	8712	D	949 553-9100	26168
Beacon Accunting Resources LLC	8742	E	949 981-5946	27341
Beacon Healthcare Services	8063	D	949 650-9750	22042
Beacon Resources LLC	8742	E	949 955-1773	27342
Ben Bennett (PA)	8059	C	949 209-9712	21151
Big Canyon Country Club	7997	C	949 706-5260	18891
Bremer & Whyte LLP (PA)	8111	E	949 221-1000	23132
Buchanan Fund I LLC	6799	D	949 721-1414	12288
Buchanan Street Partners LP	6531	D	949 721-1414	11331
C B Coast Newport Properties	6531	D	949 644-1600	11334
Call & Jensen APC	8111	E	949 717-3000	23141
Canadian Imperial Bank	6021	D	949 759-4718	9340
Capital Pacific Holdings	1531	E	951 279-2447	1360
Cbre Global Investors LLC	8742	E	949 725-8500	27376
Centurion Security Services	7381	D	949 474-0444	16594
Childrens Hospital Orange Cnty	8351	A	949 631-2062	24438
Citivest Inc.	6531	D	949 474-0440	11393
Citizens Business Bank	6022	D	949 440-5200	9485
Clean Energy	4924	A	949 437-1000	6268
Clean Energy Fuels Corp (PA)	4924	C	949 437-1000	6269
Core Realty Holdings LLC (PA)	6798	D	949 863-1031	12241
Core Realty Holdings MGT Inc	6531	D	949 863-1031	11455
Dans Landscape Service Inc	0782	D	714 241-9591	832
Dansk Enterprises Inc	7381	D	714 751-0347	16622
Donald Lucky LLC	8741	D	949 752-0647	27007
Downtown SD Ventures LLC	7999	D	619 231-9200	19199
Dpr Construction Inc	1542	E	949 955-3771	1546
Dream Home Estates Inc	6531	D	949 415-4646	11480
Duxford Financial Inc	6162	E	949 471-2010	9837
Dyntek Inc (PA)	7379	C	949 271-6700	16359
Edwards Theatres Circuit Inc (DH)	7832	C	949 640-4600	18327
Emery Financial Inc (PA)	6163	D	949 219-0640	9921
Entrepreneurial Capital Corp	6512	C	949 809-3900	10979
ESA P Prtfolio Oper Lessee LLC	7011	E	949 851-2711	12623
Executive Express Inc (PA)	4215	D	949 852-0450	4400
Fallon Land Company Inc	5051	E	213 880-1279	7370
Festival Fun Parks LLC	7999	D	954 921-1411	19208
Festival Fun Parks LLC	7996	E	949 261-0404	18821
Fidelity National Fincl Inc.	6411	D	949 622-5000	10717
Five Star Quality Care Inc	8051	C	949 642-8044	20571
Frandeli Group LLC (PA)	6794	D	714 450-7660	12216
Ghc of Lakeview Terrace LLC	8051	D	714 241-5600	20598
Global Risk MGT Solutions LLC	7375	C	949 759-8500	16237
Guardsmark LLC	7381	C	949 757-4693	16681
Harbor Health Systems LLC	8099	C	949 273-7020	22968
Healthcare Cost Solutions Inc.	8721	C	949 721-2795	26367
Healthsmart Pacific Inc (PA)	8062	A	562 595-1911	21598
Hoag Memorial Hospital Presbt (PA)	8062	A	949 764-4624	21603
Host Hotels & Resorts LP	7011	E	949 640-4000	12762
Host Hotels & Resorts LP	7011	E	949 854-4500	12771
Houalla Enterprises Ltd	1542	D	949 515-4350	1573
Hyatt Corporation	7011	B	949 729-1234	12819
International Bay Clubs LLC (PA)	7997	C	949 645-5000	18962
Internet Booking Agencycom Inc.	7361	B	949 673-7707	14686
Interstate Hotels Resorts Inc	8741	D	949 783-2500	27067
Irell & Manella LLP	8111	D	949 760-0991	23319
Iron Mountain Incorporated	4226	D	562 345-6900	4691
Irvine Eastgate Office II LLC	6798	A	949 720-2000	12252
James R Glidewell Dental (PA)	8072	E	949 440-2600	22309
JP Morgan Securities LLC	6211	D	949 467-3900	10020
Jwc Construction Inc	1522	E	949 252-2107	1319
Koll Investment Management	6282	D	949 833-3030	10157
Koll Management Services Inc	6531	A	949 833-3030	11622
Kollwood Golf Operating LP	7992	B	949 833-3025	18751
La Habra Villa	8361	D	714 529-1697	24704
Labmed Partners	8742	E	949 242-9925	27503
Lbs Financial Credit Union	6111	D	714 893-5111	9733
Lee Hong Degerman Kang	8111	D	949 250-9954	23379
Lee & Associates Realty Group	6531	E	949 724-1000	11632
Leisure Care Inc	6513	D	949 645-6833	11155
Lennar Partners of Los Angeles (PA)	7389	E	949 885-8500	17294
Lionakis	8711	C	949 955-1919	25938
LLP Locke Lord	8111	D	949 423-2100	23400
Lyon Promenade LLC	1531	E	949 252-9101	1378
M Arthur Gensler Jr Assoc Inc.	8712	D	949 863-9434	26233
Marriotts Newport Coast Villa	7011	D	949 464-6000	12982
Mbit Wireless Inc	4812	C	949 205-4559	5401
McCarthy Bldg Companies Inc.	1542	B	949 851-8383	1611
McCarthy Bldg Companies Inc.	1542	D	949 851-8383	1612
Merrill Lynch Pierce Fenner	6211	C	949 467-3760	10035
Mesa Management Inc.	6531	D	949 851-0995	11687
Message Broadcastcom LLC	7389	E	949 428-3111	17332
Mf Services Company LLC (HQ)	8742	D	949 474-5800	27548
Mig Management Services LLC	8741	D	949 474-5800	27131
Montrenes Financial Svcs Inc	7323	D	562 795-0450	14062
Morgan Stanley	6282	D	949 760-2440	10165
Mscsoftware Corporation (DH)	7372	C	714 540-8900	15764
Mscsoftware Corporation	7373	C	714 540-8900	15999
Multipoint Wireless LLC	8711	E	714 262-4172	25977
Nadavon Capital Partners LLC	6719	C	714 427-1000	12078
National Liquidators	5091	E	949 631-6715	8023
National Therapeutic Svcs Inc (PA)	8093	D	949 650-4334	22778
Newmark & Company RE Inc	6531	D	949 608-2000	11706
Newmeyer & Dillion LLP (PA)	8111	E	949 854-7000	23467
Newport Beach Country Club Inc	7997	D	949 644-9550	19014
Newport Beach Medspa	8011	D	949 631-2800	19771
Newport Beach Orthopedic Inst.	8011	D	949 722-7038	19772
Newport Beach Surgery Ctr LLC	8011	D	949 631-0988	19773
Newport Diagnostic Center Inc (PA)	8071	D	949 760-3025	22247
Newport Fmly Mdcne/A Med Group	8011	D	949 644-1025	19774
Newport Harbor Radiology Assoc.	8011	D	949 721-8191	19775
Olen Commercial Realty Corp	6512	B	949 644-6536	11027
Olen Residential Realty Corp (HQ)	1522	D	949 644-6536	1329
OMelveny & Myers LLP	8111	C	949 760-9600	23478
On Call Employee Solutions Inc	7363	D	949 955-4994	14921
Outside Lines Inc	0781	E	714 637-4747	783
Pacific Bay Properties	1521	E	949 440-7200	1229
Pacific Club (PA)	7997	D	949 955-1123	19023
Pacific Communities Bldr Inc	6552	D	949 660-8988	11996
Pacific Hotel Management Inc.	7011	D	949 608-1091	13061
Pacific Investment MGT Co LLC (DH)	6282	C	949 720-6000	10168
Pacific Life & Annuity Company	6311	A	949 219-3011	10218
Pacific Monarch Resorts Inc (PA)	6531	D	949 609-2400	11728
Palace Entertainment Inc (DH)	7999	E	949 261-0404	19256
Panattoni Development Co Inc (PA)	6531	B	916 381-1561	11735
Park Newport Ltd (PA)	6513	D	949 644-1900	11184
Payment Resources Intl	7389	E	949 729-1400	17406
Pimco Funds Distribution Co	6722	B	949 720-4761	12122
Pyramid Peak Corporation	6799	C	949 769-8600	12338
Qw Media International LLC	7313	C	949 200-4616	13977
R Mc Closkey Insurance Agency	6411	C	949 223-8100	10850
Rcg International	8748	B	714 956-7027	28036
REO World Inc	6722	C	949 478-8000	12123
Research Affiliates Capital LP	6282	D	949 325-8700	10180
Research Affiliates LLC	6282	D	949 325-8700	10181
Riverside Research Institute	8733	E	949 631-0107	26803
Roth Capital Partners LLC (PA)	6211	D	800 678-9147	10075
Scicon Technologies Corp	8711	B	949 252-1341	26058
Secova Inc	8742	C	714 384-0530	27638
Secova Eservices Inc (HQ)	8742	D	714 384-0655	27639
Signature Services	6512	D	949 851-9391	11048
Sleepy Giant Entertainment Inc	7371	C	949 464-7986	15458
Sleepy Giant Entertainment Inc	7929	D	714 460-4113	18495
Squar Milner Peterson Miran (PA)	8721	C	949 222-2999	26446
SSC Newport Beach Oper Co LP	8051	D	949 642-8044	20925
Stradling Yocca Carlson & Raut (PA)	8111	C	949 725-4000	23586
Sunstone Hotel Investors Inc	7011	B	949 476-2001	13316
Synnexxus LLC	8111	E	714 933-4500	23591
T-Force Inc (PA)	8748	D	949 208-1527	28067
Thrifty Rent-A-Car System Inc	7514	E	949 757-0659	17696
Toni & Guy Hairdressing (PA)	7231	C	949 721-1666	13692
Tribeworx LLC	7372	D	800 949-3432	15864
Twenty4seven Hotels Corp	8741	C	949 734-6400	27261
Tz Holdings LP	7372	A	949 719-2200	15868
UBS Financial Services Inc	6211	D	949 760-5308	10090
Uka LLC	7011	E	949 610-8000	13365
Umpqua Bank	6029	D	949 474-1020	9564
United Cpitl Fncl Advisers LLC	6282	D	949 999-8500	10190
US Healthcare Partners Inc	8059	C	949 261-5000	21404
US Lines LLC (HQ)	8611	D	714 751-3333	25108
Ventage Senior Housing	8361	E	949 631-3555	24845
Vital Express Inc	4789	C	330 777-5450	5250
Voit Real Estate Services Lp	6531	C	949 644-8648	11902
Whitaker Welness Institute In	8011	C	949 851-1550	20238
William Lyon Homes (PA)	1531	C	949 833-3600	1393
Wright Finley & Zak LLP	8111	C	949 477-5050	23634
Young Mens Chrstn Assn Orange	8641	D	949 642-9990	25472

NEWPORT COAST, CA - Orange County

Company	SIC	EMP	PHONE	ENTRY #
Pricemetrix Usa Inc	7374	E	714 357-6192	16171
Resort At Pelican Hill LLC	7011	C	949 467-6800	13150

NICASIO, CA - Marin County

Company	SIC	EMP	PHONE	ENTRY #
Lucasfilm Ltd LLC	7812	C	415 662-1800	18105

NIPOMO, CA - San Luis Obispo County

Company	SIC	EMP	PHONE	ENTRY #
American Golf Corporation	7997	D	805 343-1214	18855
Clearwater Nursery Inc	5193	E	805 929-3241	9183
Community Health Centers (PA)	8011	E	805 929-3211	19452
Integrity Management Svcs Inc	7349	C	805 238-0905	14326

NIPTON, CA - San Bernardino County

Company	SIC	EMP	PHONE	ENTRY #
Primm Valley Golf Club	7992	D	702 679-5509	18772

NORCO, CA - Riverside County

Company	SIC	EMP	PHONE	ENTRY #
Anna Corporation	1721	E	951 736-6037	2427
Cal West Underground Inc	1629	D	951 371-6775	2035
Cal-West Nurseries Inc	0782	C	951 270-0667	819
Car Spa Inc	7549	E	951 279-1422	17878
County of Riverside	8322	E	951 272-5400	23881
CSRA LLC	7371	D	951 898-3015	15115
CSRA System and Solutions LLC	7379	E	951 735-3300	16348
F J Hoover Plumbing Inc	1711	D	951 360-8262	2222
Guy Yocom Construction Inc (PA)	1771	D	951 284-3456	3272
Hampton Inn Norco Corona North	7011	D	951 279-1111	12684
Hci Inc (HQ)	1623	B	951 520-4202	1937
Industrial Masonry Inc	1741	D	951 284-0251	2819
Janus Corporation	1799	E	951 479-0700	3535
Lombardy Holdings Inc (PA)	1623	C	951 808-4550	1964
Luberski Inc	5144	D	951 271-3866	8600
Norco Fire Department	6371	A	951 737-8097	10558
North Orange Coast Pntg Inc	1721	D	951 279-2694	2471
Royal West Drywall Inc	1742	D	951 271-4600	2970

NORDEN, CA - Nevada County

Company	SIC	EMP	PHONE	ENTRY #
Sugar Bowl Corporation	7999	D	530 426-9000	19290

NORTH FORK, CA - Madera County

Company	SIC	EMP	PHONE	ENTRY #
Mono Nation	8322	D	559 877-2450	24091

NORTH HIGHLANDS, CA - Sacramento County

Company	SIC	EMP	PHONE	ENTRY #
AAA Drain Patrol	1711	E	916 348-3098	2104
Amerifleet Transportation Inc	4789	D	916 331-2355	5212
Capital City Drywall Inc	1742	D	916 331-9200	2873
Eagle Lath & Plaster Inc	1542	D	916 925-1435	1547
Energetic Pntg & Drywall Inc (PA)	1742	C	916 488-8455	2893
Heritage 1 Window and Building	5031	C	916 481-5030	6928
Heritage Interests LLC (PA)	1751	D	916 481-5030	3054
Heritage One Door and Building	5031	D	916 481-5030	6930
Homeq Servicing Corporation (DH)	6162	A	916 339-6192	9857
Kenyon Construction Inc	1742	D	916 514-9502	2921
Lund Construction Co	8711	D	916 344-5800	25942
Lund Equipment LP	1611	E	916 344-5800	1816
Martins Achievement Place	8361	D	916 338-1001	24724
MCM Construction Inc (PA)	1622	D	916 334-1221	1896
Mission Courier Inc	7389	D	916 484-1992	17337
Pacific Coast Supply LLC	5031	C	916 481-2220	6943
Pacific Coast Supply LLC (HQ)	5031	C	916 971-2301	6944
Paladin Prtction Spcalists Inc	7382	C	916 331-3175	16910
Paragon Coml Bldg Maint Inc	7349	D	916 334-8801	14380
Pride Industries	8331	D	916 334-5415	24382
Recycling Industries Inc	4953	D	916 452-3961	6534
Rick H Hitch Plastering Inc	1742	C	916 334-3591	2969
Security Contractor Svcs Inc (PA)	5039	C	916 338-4200	7027
U S Army Corps of Engineers	8711	D	916 925-7001	26112

NORTH HILLS, CA - Los Angeles County

Company	SIC	EMP	PHONE	ENTRY #
Brentwood Cmmncations Intl Inc	7812	E	818 333-3680	18053
Dynamo Aviation Inc	4581	D	818 785-9561	4915
Living Colors Inc	1721	D	818 893-5068	2463
New Horizons Worldwide Inc	8082	A	818 894-9301	22512
Penny Lane Centers (PA)	8399	B	818 892-3423	24952
Penny Lane Centers	8399	C	818 892-3423	24953
Penny Lane Centers	8399	C	818 892-3423	24954
Penny Lane Centers	8399	C	818 892-3423	24956
Penny Lane Centers	8399	C	818 894-9162	24957
Penny Lane Centers	8399	C	818 892-1112	24958
Penny Lane Centers	8399	C	818 892-3423	24959
Plummer Vlg Preservation LP	6513	E	818 891-0646	11189
Prn Ambulance LLC	4119	B	818 810-3600	3830
Veterans Health Administration	8011	C	818 895-9311	20204
Veterans Health Administration	8011	A	818 891-7711	20206
Veterans Health Administration	8011	C	818 895-9449	20217
Walker & Zanger Inc (PA)	5032	D	818 280-8300	7000

NORTH HOLLYWOOD, CA - Los Angeles County

Company	SIC	EMP	PHONE	ENTRY #
1658 Camden LLC	6513	E	818 769-1944	11076
51 Minds Entertainment LLC	7929	D	323 466-9200	18449
Academy TV Arts & Sciences	8621	D	818 754-2800	25113
Albany Inventory Services	7389	E	818 505-8138	16976
Alpha Systems Fire Protection	5099	E	323 227-0700	8104
Ambulnz Health LLC	7375	D	310 968-3999	16217
American Solar Solution Inc	1521	D	877 946-8855	1126
Andy Gump Inc	7359	D	818 255-0650	14513
Arriaga Usa Inc	1743	D	818 982-9559	3005
AT&T Corp	4813	D	818 506-9118	5495
Bento Box Entertainment LLC	7929	B	818 333-7900	18458
Blufocus Inc	7371	E	818 294-7695	15060
Break Floor Productions LLC	7922	E	212 247-7277	18373
Cats USA Inc	7342	D	818 506-1000	14174
CB Associates Inc	7322	E	818 284-3699	14023
Center For Autism Related Svcs	8748	D	323 850-7177	27873
Century National Properties (PA)	6512	D	818 760-0880	10969
Century Theatres Inc	7833	D	818 508-1943	18358
Chapman/Leonard Studio Eqp Inc (PA)	7819	C	323 877-5309	18217
Circulating Air Inc (PA)	1711	D	818 764-0530	2180
Clairmont Camera Inc (PA)	7359	D	818 761-4440	14523
Coastal Tile Inc	1743	D	818 988-6134	3009
Coldwater Care Center LLC	8051	D	818 766-6105	20464
Cri-Help Inc (PA)	8361	D	818 985-8323	24625
Education Management Corp	8741	B	818 487-0201	27012
Emergency Technologies Inc	5063	E	818 765-4421	7439
Eqal Inc	7311	C	818 276-6300	13846
ESP Computer Services Inc (PA)	7374	D	818 487-4500	16127
Four Seasons Healthcare	8051	D	818 985-1814	20580
Golden Care Inc	8059	D	818 763-6275	21236
Hillsdale Group LP	8059	D	818 623-2170	21268
Hollywood Health System Inc	8082	D	323 662-3731	22460
Hollywood Spa Inc	7991	E	323 464-0445	18642
Horizon Actuarial Services LLC	8742	D	818 691-2000	27466
Insurance Auto Auctions Inc	5012	D	818 487-2222	6683
Intrepid Healthcare Svcs Inc (HQ)	8011	C	888 447-2362	19572
Jackson Shrub Supply Inc	7819	D	818 982-0100	18233
Japanese Assistance Netwrk Inc	7389	B	818 505-6080	17255
JC Party Rentals Inc	7359	D	818 765-4819	14553
Jessica Cosmetics Intl Inc	5122	D	818 759-1050	8268
Jewish Family Svc Los Angeles	8322	D	818 984-0276	24047
Kaiser Foundation Hospitals	8011	A	888 778-5000	19629
Kaiser Foundation Hospitals	8062	D	818 503-7082	21670
L A Family Housing Corp	8361	D	818 503-3908	24702
M Gaw Inc	1799	D	818 503-7997	3548
Mariner Health Care Inc	8051	D	818 985-5990	20773
Mark Herzog & Company Inc	7812	D	818 762-4640	18106
Messenger Express (PA)	4215	C	213 614-0475	4417
Midway Rent A Car Inc	7515	C	818 985-9770	17703
Mikado Hotels Inc	7011	E	818 763-9141	12994
Mindring Productions LLC	7812	E	323 466-9200	18114
Morigon Technologies LLC	5047	E	818 764-8880	7283
O P I Products Inc (DH)	5087	B	818 759-8688	7974
On-Scene Security Services Inc	7381	E	661 263-2343	16753
Pie Town Productions Inc	7812	C	818 255-9300	18128
Pierce Brothers (DH)	7261	D	818 763-9121	13710
Protection Specialists	7381	B	818 503-1306	16768
Rio Vista Development Company (PA)	7011	D	818 980-8000	13152
Rodin & Co Inc	1721	D	818 358-3427	2486
Sada Systems Inc	7379	D	818 766-2400	16473
Silla Automotive LLC	5013	D	818 902-0334	6763
Silverscreen Healthcare Inc	8051	D	818 763-8247	20917
SLC Operating Ltd Partnership	7299	B	818 980-1212	13795
Southern Cal Prmnnte Med Group	8011	D	888 778-5000	20025
Southern California Golf Assn (PA)	8611	D	818 980-3630	25104
Stark Services	7374	D	818 985-2003	16193
Student Trnsp Amer Inc	4142	B	818 982-1663	3906
Toner Supply USA Inc	5045	E	818 504-6540	7201
Trinity Health Systems	8059	D	818 983-0103	21393
Universal Studios Inc (DH)	7812	C	818 777-1000	18180
Universal Studios Inc	7812	D	818 753-0000	18184
Valley Community Healthcare	8011	D	818 763-8836	20182
Valley Wholesale Supply Corp (PA)	5023	D	818 769-5656	6901
Village Family Services (PA)	8093	D	818 755-8786	22862
Volunteers of Amer Los Angeles	8322	E	818 506-0597	24282
Western Costume Leasing	7299	D	818 760-0900	13805
Western General Agency Inc	6411	D	818 766-6500	10936
Western Magnesite Inc	1799	E	818 255-1150	3604
Woods Maintenance Services Inc	1799	C	818 764-2515	3606
Young Mens Chrstn Assn of La	8351	D	818 763-5126	24536

NORTH PALM SPRINGS, CA - Riverside County

Company	SIC	EMP	PHONE	ENTRY #
Lloyd Pest Control Co	7342	D	951 232-9687	14187

NORTHRIDGE, CA - Los Angeles County

Company	SIC	EMP	PHONE	ENTRY #
1-800-4-insure Insurance Svcs	6411	C	818 701-3733	10574
3m/Pharmaceuticals	1741	D	818 341-1300	2801
Alliant Tchsystems Oprtons LLC	8731	B	818 887-8195	26464
Apex Group	8741	D	818 885-0513	26922
Arete Associates (PA)	8731	C	818 885-2200	26477

NORTHRIDGE, CA

	SIC	EMP	PHONE	ENTRY #
Assisted Home Recovery Inc (PA)	7361	C	818 894-8117	14610
Automobile Club Southern Cal	8699	D	818 993-1616	25499
Bellis Steel Company Inc (PA)	1791	C	818 886-5601	3366
Child and Family Guidance Ctr (PA)	8093	C	818 739-5140	22682
Child and Family Guidance Ctr	8093	E	818 830-0200	22683
Contemporary Services Corp (PA)	7361	C	818 885-5150	14628
Elite & Associates	1761	D	805 582-0353	3169
Eminence Home Health Care Inc	8082	E	818 830-7113	22431
Extreme Telecom Inc	4813	C	818 902-4821	5602
Facey Medical Foundation	8099	E	818 734-3600	22962
First Nationwide Mortgage Corp	6163	C	818 209-3134	9926
Freshlunches Inc	8322	E	310 478-5705	23982
Friends of Family	8322	E	818 988-4430	23987
Holman Family Counseling Inc (PA)	8049	D	818 704-1444	20320
Ikano Communications Inc (PA)	7374	D	801 924-0900	16145
Lakeside Systems Inc	8741	A	866 654-3471	27108
Lansing Mall Ltd Partnership	6512	D	818 885-9700	11011
M K H Inc	7542	D	818 882-9274	17855
Mikuni American Corporation (HQ)	5013	D	310 676-0522	6749
Move Inc	6531	C	818 701-0012	11695
MSC Chatsworth	5099	C	818 718-7696	8128
National Center On Deafness	8322	D	818 677-2054	24094
Northwest Excavating Inc	7353	D	818 349-5861	14492
Omega Security Services & Cons	7381	D	818 831-1100	16752
Pacific Theaters	7829	D	818 501-5121	18290
PHI Delta Theta Inc	7041	E	818 885-9940	13496
Pinnacle Estate Properties (PA)	6531	C	818 993-4707	11752
Porter Valley Country Club	7997	D	818 360-1071	19031
Production Special Events Svcs	7922	D	818 831-5326	18427
Progressive Health Care System	8011	D	818 707-9603	19880
Prudential California Realty	6531	E	818 993-8900	11775
Quality Speaks LLC	7375	C	818 264-4400	16254
Rashman Corporation	5087	C	818 993-3030	7980
Regal Medical Group Inc (PA)	8621	C	818 654-3400	25153
Rodeo Realty Inc	6531	D	818 349-9997	11820
Ryder Integrated Logistics Inc	7513	E	818 701-9332	17650
San Frnndo Vly Intrfith Cuncil	8399	C	818 885-5220	24976
Scl Company Inc	7539	C	818 993-4758	17826
Securitas SEC Svcs USA Inc	7381	C	818 891-0458	16812
Shapell Industries LLC	1521	E	818 366-1132	1254
Social Vocational Services Inc	8093	D	818 831-1321	22834
Southern California Mtl Hdlg	5084	C	805 650-6000	7889
Spad Holdings LLC	7991	D	818 772-8900	18693
Sunrise Senior Living LLC	8051	D	818 886-1616	20969
Telecom Evolutions LLC	7389	E	818 264-4400	17525
Teutonic Holdings LLC	7375	C	818 264-4400	16262
Tri - Star Win Coverings Inc	5023	E	818 718-3188	6896
University Student Union of CA	8641	B	818 677-2251	25386
Valley Hospital Medical Center (HQ)	8062	B	818 885-8500	22009
Village At Northridge	8361	C	818 514-4497	24849
Washington Inventory Service	7389	D	818 407-2680	17615
Working Solutions Inc	8611	E	818 366-5009	25111
World Private Security Inc	7381	C	818 894-1800	16854

NORWALK, CA - Los Angeles County

	SIC	EMP	PHONE	ENTRY #
American Multi-Cinema Inc	7832	E	562 864-6206	18303
Aquirecorps Norwalk Auto Auctn	5012	C	562 864-7464	6665
Avanti Hospitals LLC	8062	A	562 868-3751	21458
Bally Total Fitness Corp (HQ)	7991	C	562 484-2000	18607
County of Los Angeles	7374	A	562 462-2094	16113
County of Los Angeles	8322	C	562 807-7860	23851
El Clasificado (PA)	7313	D	323 837-4095	13968
Elena Villa Healthcare Center	8059	C	562 868-0591	21209
Faro Services Inc	4225	C	562 483-7799	4552
Front Porch Communities & Svcs	8059	C	562 868-9761	21226
Granville Hotel Corp	7011	C	562 863-5555	12675
Joes Sweeping Inc	1799	C	562 929-4344	3538
Jwch Institute Inc	8733	D	562 281-0306	26779
Kaiser Foundation Hospitals	8011	A	562 807-6100	19631
Kerber Bros Inc	1799	C	562 921-3447	3543
Life Care Centers America Inc	8051	D	562 921-6624	20731
Lj Distributors Inc	5148	D	562 229-7660	8747
Mulhearn Realtors Inc	6531	D	562 462-1055	11701
Norwalk Community Hospital	8062	A	562 863-4763	21765
Norwalk Meadows Nursing Ctr LP	8051	C	562 864-2541	20811
Norwalk Transit System	4111	D	562 929-5550	3684
Seepeedee Inc	8062	D	562 868-3751	21876
Tap Ram Reinforcing Inc	1791	D	562 484-0859	3406
Tvb (usa) Inc (DH)	4841	E	562 345-9871	6055
Weber Distribution Warehouses	4225	E	562 404-9996	4668
West Central Produce Inc	5148	B	213 629-3600	8788

NOVATO, CA - Marin County

	SIC	EMP	PHONE	ENTRY #
Activision Blizzard Inc	7372	E	415 881-9100	15566
Arntz Builders Inc	1541	E	415 382-1188	1401
Atria Senior Living Group Inc	8361	E	415 892-0944	24559
Automatic Data Processing Inc	7374	C	415 899-7300	16096
Bank of Marin Bancorp (PA)	6022	C	415 763-4520	9472
Bear Flag Marketing Corp	8082	C	415 899-8466	22377
Birkenstock Usa Lp (DH)	5139	D	415 884-3200	8421
Braden Partners LP A Calif (DH)	8082	D	415 893-1518	22379
Brayton Purcell APC	8111	C	415 898-1555	23131
Buck Inst For RES On Aging (PA)	8733	D	415 209-2000	26740
Charming Trim & Packaging	5131	A	415 302-7021	8309
Comet Building Maintenance Inc	0781	D	415 383-1035	760
County of Marin	7374	D	415 499-7060	16114
Drivesavers Inc	7375	D	415 382-2000	16229
EDG Interior Arch & Design Inc	7389	D	415 454-2277	17144
Firemans Fund Insurance Co (HQ)	6331	A	415 899-2000	10416
Indian Valley Golf Club Inc	7992	E	415 897-1118	18748
Interntnl Prnsrance Assoc LLC	6411	E	415 223-5548	10747
Jaylaneentertainment Corp	7313	D	707 820-2773	13970
Johann B Garovi	1622	E	415 898-1801	1894
Kaiser Foundation Hospitals	8062	E	415 899-7400	21660
King Security Services Inc	7381	A	415 556-5464	16717
L & L Logic and Logistics LP	5139	E	707 795-2475	8439
Marin Airporter Inc	4131	D	415 884-2878	3882
Marin Country Club Inc	7997	D	415 382-6700	18991
Marin County Sart Program	8063	D	415 892-1628	22082
Marin Humane Society	8699	D	415 883-4621	25554
Melissa Bradley RE Inc	6531	E	415 209-1000	11676
Navitas LLC	5149	C	415 883-8116	8884
North Marin Water District (PA)	4941	E	415 897-4133	6382
Novato Fire Protection Dist	7389	D	415 878-2690	17368
Novato Healthcare Center LLC	8051	C	415 897-6161	20812
Pacific Inptient Med Group Inc	8011	D	415 485-8824	19804
Permanente Medical Group Inc	8011	D	415 209-2444	19855
Permanente Medical Group Inc	8011	D	415 899-7400	19857
Radiant Logic Inc (PA)	7371	D	415 209-6800	15405
Raptor Pharmaceutical Corp (PA)	8733	D	415 408-6200	26801
Rosenthal & Company LLC	8742	E	415 884-1100	27625
Scene7 Inc	7371	E	415 506-6000	15443
Stonetree Golf LLC	7992	E	415 209-6744	18791
Sutter Health	8099	D	415 897-8495	23071
Sutter West Bay Hospitals (HQ)	8062	B	415 209-1300	21956
Tennis Everyone Incorporated	7997	E	415 897-2185	19104
Thompson Builders Corporation	1522	C	415 456-8972	1344
Visual Concepts Entertainment	7371	D	415 479-3634	15529
W Bradley Electric Inc (PA)	1731	E	415 898-1400	2787
Young Mens Christian Assoc SF	8641	D	415 883-9622	25454

OAK HILLS, CA - San Bernardino County

	SIC	EMP	PHONE	ENTRY #
Double Eagle Trnsp Corp	4213	C	760 956-3770	4140
Little Sisters Truck Wash Inc	7542	D	760 947-4448	17850
M & R Wood Products Inc	1521	E	909 460-1865	1207

OAK VIEW, CA - Ventura County

	SIC	EMP	PHONE	ENTRY #
Casablanca Alzheimers Resid	8361	D	805 649-5143	24588

OAKDALE, CA - Stanislaus County

	SIC	EMP	PHONE	ENTRY #
Alldrin Brothers Inc	0723	E	855 667-4231	507
Amerine Systems Incorporated	0781	E	209 847-5968	740
Central Valley AG Grinding	1629	D	209 544-9246	2040
Damrell Nelson Schrimp Pall	8111	E	209 848-3500	23194
Gcu Trucking Inc	4213	D	209 845-2117	4188
Gilton Resource Recovery	4953	C	209 527-3781	6487
Gilton Solid Waste MGT Inc	4953	D	209 527-3781	6488
Mozingo Construction Inc	1794	E	209 848-0160	3439
Oak Valley Hospital District (HQ)	8062	B	209 847-3011	21766
Oakdale Golf and Country Club	7997	D	209 847-2984	19017
Oakdale Irrgtion Dst Fing Corp	4941	D	209 847-0341	6383
Phase 3 Inc	4581	E	209 848-0290	4928
Remediation Constructors Inc	1611	D	209 847-9186	1850
Ross F Carroll Inc	8711	E	209 848-5959	26045

OAKHURST, CA - Madera County

	SIC	EMP	PHONE	ENTRY #
Associated Koi Clubs America	7997	D	949 650-5225	18878
Kaiser Foundation Hospitals	6324	D	559 658-8388	10318
Oakhurst Skilled Nursing Welln	8051	D	559 683-2244	20816
Sierra Masonic Association	8641	D	559 683-7713	25348
Sierra Tel Cmmunications Group	4813	D	559 683-7717	5698
Sierra Tel Cmmunications Group (PA)	4813	D	559 683-4611	5699
Sierra Telephone Company Inc	4813	C	559 683-4611	5700
State Farm Mutl Auto Insur Co	6411	D	559 683-3467	10892

OAKLAND, CA - Alameda County

	SIC	EMP	PHONE	ENTRY #
A T Associates Inc	8059	D	510 261-8564	21122
ABF Freight System Inc	4213	D	510 533-8575	4099
ABM Facility Services Inc (HQ)	7349	D	510 251-0381	14200
Abrams Kazan McClain	8111	C	510 465-7728	23080
Absg Consulting Inc	8748	E	510 508-6289	27805
Aecom C&E Inc	8748	D	510 622-6600	27811
Aecom Global II LLC	8711	D	510 874-3000	25625

GEOGRAPHIC SECTION — OAKLAND, CA

Company	SIC	EMP	PHONE	ENTRY #
Aecom Technical Services Inc	8748	D	510 285-2010	27815
Aecom Technical Services Inc	8711	C	510 834-4304	25637
Alameda Cnty Cmnty Fd Bnk Inc	8322	D	510 635-3663	23649
Alameda County	8322	A	510 383-1556	23650
Alameda County Employees Retir	6371	D	510 628-3000	10539
Alameda-Contra Costa Trnst Dst (PA)	4111	D	510 891-4777	3634
Alameda-Contra Costa Trnst Dst	4173	C	510 577-8816	3954
Alaska Airlines Inc	4512	D	510 577-5813	4784
All Axis Enterprise Inc	1521	D	510 451-1200	1122
Allied Fire Protection	1711	D	510 533-5516	2122
Allied Information & Services	6411	D	510 769-9648	10588
Altenheim Inc	6513	D	510 530-4013	11083
Amec Fstr Whlr Envrnmnt Infrst	8711	C	510 663-4100	25651
American Automobile Asscctn	8699	C	510 350-2042	25489
American Baptist Homes of West	8361	C	510 654-7172	24547
American National Red Cross	8099	C	510 594-5100	22885
Aperian Global Inc (PA)	8742	D	415 749-2920	27330
Aramark Unf & Career AP LLC	7218	C	510 835-9285	13604
Asian Community Mental Hlth Bd	8093	D	510 625-1650	22661
Asian Health Services	8011	D	510 986-0601	19358
Asian Health Services (PA)	8011	D	510 986-6800	19359
Associated Internal Medicine (PA)	8011	D	510 465-6700	19360
Athletics Investment Group LLC (PA)	7941	C	510 638-4900	18537
Atrium Hotels LP	7011	B	510 658-9300	12400
Autumn LP	7389	D	415 277-1245	17013
B&C Transit Inc (PA)	8711	D	510 483-3560	25677
Balfour Beatty Cnstr LLC	1542	C	510 903-2060	1496
Bay Alarm Company	8732	D	510 452-3211	26645
Bay Area Community Svcs Inc (PA)	8322	E	510 613-0330	23676
Belcampo Group Inc	0279	D	510 250-7810	461
Berry & Berry Law Firm	8111	D	510 250-0200	23112
Bonita House Inc	8322	D	510 923-0180	23687
Boornazian Jensen & Garthe A	8111	D	510 834-4350	23126
Brightcurrent (PA)	8742	D	877 896-3306	27357
Brightsource Energy Inc (PA)	1629	D	510 550-8161	2027
Brilliance Investment LLC	7011	D	510 568-1880	12466
Brita Products Company	5074	D	510 271-7000	7705
Broadway Mech - Contrs Inc	1711	D	510 746-4000	2170
Brown & Toland Medical Group (PA)	8011	C	415 972-4162	19380
Building Services Maint Inc	4213	C	510 636-1224	4121
Burnham Brown A Prof Corp	8111	C	510 444-6800	23139
C/O Uc San Francisco (PA)	8741	C	858 534-7323	26951
Calidad Industries Inc	8331	D	510 534-6666	24316
California Cereal Products Inc (PA)	5153	D	510 452-4500	8960
California Child Care Resourc	8322	E	510 658-0381	23698
California Motorcycle Club	7997	D	510 534-6222	18908
California Nurses Association (PA)	8621	C	510 273-2200	25122
California Waste Solutions Inc	4953	D	408 292-0830	6451
Califrnia Hlth Care Foundation (PA)	8399	D	510 891-3963	24885
Califrnia-Nevada Methdst Homes	8059	D	510 835-5511	21176
Carpenter Funds	6733	D	510 633-0333	12170
Cartridge Family Inc	5112	C	510 658-0400	8162
Cass Inc (PA)	5093	D	510 893-6476	8066
Catholic Charities of The Dioc (PA)	8322	D	510 768-3100	23714
Cellco Partnership	4812	D	510 267-0731	5349
Center For Elders Independence	6324	C	510 433-1150	10269
Center To Promote Healthcare A (PA)	8099	E	510 834-1300	22914
Central Parking Corporation	7521	D	510 832-7227	17712
Cgi Technologies Solutions Inc	7379	D	510 238-5300	16334
Ch2m Hill Inc	8711	C	510 604-4144	25734
Chapel of Chimes	7261	D	510 654-1288	13702
Charles Pankow Bldrs Ltd A Cal	1542	B	510 893-5170	1526
Childrens Hosp Oklnd Res Inst	8733	D	510 450-7600	26752
Childrens Hospotal & Research (PA)	8062	A	510 428-3000	21485
Christian Church Homes	6531	C	510 893-2998	11390
Cim/Oakland City Center LLC	7011	D	510 451-4000	12521
City of Oakland	8322	B	510 238-6796	23756
City of Oakland	7999	E	510 238-3494	19177
City of Oakland	7999	E	510 268-9000	19178
Civicorps	4953	C	510 992-7800	6463
Claremont Country Club	7997	D	510 653-6789	18918
Claremont House Incorporated	8361	D	510 658-9266	24600
Clorox Services Company (HQ)	8741	D	510 271-7000	26973
Cohen Ventures Inc (PA)	8748	D	510 482-4420	27884
College Track	8742	C	510 834-3295	27386
Colony Strwood Homes Partnr LP	1521	A	510 250-2200	1158
Computer Sciences Corporation	7379	D	510 645-3000	16340
Condon-Johnson & Assoc Inc (PA)	1771	E	510 636-2100	3250
Consolidated Cleaning Services	7349	D	510 663-2585	14260
County of Alameda	8742	D	510 272-6442	27391
Covenant Care California LLC	8051	D	510 261-2628	20489
Creative Energy Foods Inc	5149	D	510 638-8668	8826
Crucible	8322	D	510 444-0919	23937
Cw Healthcare Inc	7363	E	510 636-9000	14869
Dealey Renton and Associates	6411	D	510 465-3090	10686
Delivery Solutions Inc	4212	D	925 819-1289	4004
Deloitte Consulting LLP	8742	D	510 251-4400	27406
Destiny Arts Center	7999	E	510 597-1619	19197
District Council DC (PA)	8322	D	510 638-7600	23946
Donahue Gallager Woods LLP (PA)	8111	D	415 381-4161	23224
Dorado Network Systems Corp	7372	C	650 227-7300	15644
Dreyers Grand Ice Cream Hold (DH)	5143	C	510 652-8187	8584
East Bay Asian Local Dev Corp	6513	D	510 267-1917	11123
East Bay Asian Youth Center	8322	E	510 533-1092	23949
East Bay Btncal Zoological Soc	7999	D	510 632-9525	19201
East Bay Community Foundation	8399	D	510 836-3223	24915
East Bay Foundation Grad Med	8099	D	510 437-4197	22950
East Bay Municipl Utility Distr (PA)	4941	A	866 403-2683	6343
East Bay Municipl Utility Distr	4953	C	866 403-2683	6475
East Bay Municipl Utility Distr	6371	C	510 287-0760	10551
EBSC LP	8011	D	510 547-2244	19510
Education For Change	8741	C	510 879-3140	27011
Elliott and Elliott Co	1761	D	510 444-7270	3170
Environmental Health Hazard	8734	D	510 622-3200	26851
Episcopal Senior Communities	8361	C	510 835-4700	24645
F H One Inc	6552	D	510 832-3240	11966
Fair Trade USA	8733	C	510 663-5260	26765
Family Bridges Inc	8322	D	510 839-2270	23967
Federal Express Corporation	4513	D	800 463-3339	4852
Federal Express Corporation	4513	D	510 465-5209	4853
Federal Express Corporation	4215	B	510 382-2344	4412
Fidelity Roof Company	1761	D	510 547-6330	3172
First Place For Youth (PA)	8322	E	510 272-0979	23980
First Transit Inc	4151	D	510 535-9192	3937
First Transit Inc	4111	D	510 437-8990	3652
Fitzgrald Abbott Beardsley LLP	8111	D	510 451-3300	23245
Fruitvale Long Term Care LLC	8051	D	510 261-5613	20586
Future State	7379	D	925 956-4200	16378
General Services Cal Dept	8712	D	510 622-3101	26186
George E Masker Inc	1721	D	510 568-1206	2448
Geosyntec Consultants Inc	8711	E	510 836-3034	25839
Give Something Back Inc (PA)	5112	D	510 635-5500	8168
Global Health Fellows Program	8699	D	510 285-5660	25535
Golden State Warriors LLC	7941	D	510 986-2200	18547
Grubb Co Inc	6531	D	510 339-0400	11563
GSC Logistics Inc (PA)	4214	D	510 844-3700	4348
Gt Nexus Inc (DH)	4813	D	510 808-2222	5622
Guardsmark LLC	7381	C	510 562-7606	16685
Hanna Brophy Mac Lean Mc Ale (PA)	8111	E	510 839-1180	23298
Hans Technologies Inc	1629	D	510 464-8018	2055
Hapag-Lloyd (america) LLC	4731	E	510 251-8405	5094
Health Care Workers Union (PA)	6512	D	510 251-1250	11000
Health Net Inc	6324	B	510 465-9600	10283
HealthSouth Corporation	8069	D	510 547-2244	22143
Herc Rentals Inc	7514	C	510 633-2040	17682
High Street Hand Car Wash Inc	7549	D	510 536-4333	17883
Highcom Security Services	7381	D	510 893-7600	16702
Hilton Worldwide Inc	7011	C	510 635-5000	12719
Hntb-Gerwick JV	8712	D	510 839-8972	26205
Homewood Suites Management LLC	7011	E	510 663-2700	12756
Horizon Beverage Company	5181	D	510 465-2212	9064
Horizon Beverage Company LP	5149	D	510 465-2212	8853
Hospice & Home Health of E Bay	8082	D	510 632-4390	22472
IAC Search & Media Inc (HQ)	7375	C	510 985-7400	16244
Imperial Parking (us) LLC	7521	E	510 382-2144	17722
Intelliguard Security Services	7381	D	510 547-7656	16706
Interactive Solutions Inc (HQ)	7372	D	510 214-9002	15708
Itron Inc	1731	A	510 844-2800	2621
Jacobs Project Management Co	8742	D	510 457-2436	27491
Jetblue Airways Corporation	4512	D	510 381-1369	4807
Jt2 Integrated Resources (PA)	8741	D	925 556-7012	27084
K G O T V News Bureau	4832	D	510 451-4772	5790
Kaiser Foundation Hospital	8082	E	510 752-6295	22488
Kaiser Foundation Hospitals	8011	D	510 752-1000	19585
Kaiser Foundation Hospitals (HQ)	8062	C	510 271-6611	21637
Kaiser Foundation Hospitals	8062	D	510 752-1000	21638
Kaiser Foundation Hospitals	6324	D	510 752-7864	10299
Kaiser Foundation Hospitals	8011	D	510 987-1000	19666
Kaiser Foundation Hospitals	8062	B	510 891-3400	21664
Kaiser Foundation Hospitals	6324	D	510 251-0121	10332
Kaiser Fundation Hlth Plan (PA)	6324	D	510 271-5800	10351
Kaiser Fundation Hlth Plan Inc	6324	D	510 752-7644	10352
Kaiser Fundation Hlth Plan Inc	6324	D	510 987-2255	10354
Kaiser Group Holdings Inc	8711	D	510 419-6000	25915
Kaiser Hlth Plan Asset MGT Inc	8741	E	510 271-7100	27087
Kaiserair Inc (PA)	5172	C	510 569-9622	9025
Kapstone Container Corporation	5113	D	510 569-2616	8196
Katten Muchin Rosenman LLP	8111	C	415 360-5444	23340
Kerna Inc	8748	C	510 891-0446	27964
Kemeera Incorporated	5045	D	510 281-9000	7152

Employment Codes: A=Over 500 employees, B=251-500, C=101-250, D=51-100, E=45-50

2017 Directory of California Wholesalers and Services Companies

© Mergent Inc. 1-800-342-5647

OAKLAND, CA

GEOGRAPHIC SECTION

	SIC	EMP	PHONE	ENTRY #
Kids Overcoming LLC	8082	D	415 748-8052	22492
Kiewit Infrastructure West Co	1611	D	510 452-1400	1809
Ktgy Group Inc	8712	E	510 463-2097	26218
Ktvu Partnership Inc	4833	C	510 834-1212	5890
La Clinica De La Raza Inc	8021	B	510 535-4700	20259
La Clinica De La Raza Inc	8093	D	510 535-6200	22764
Lake Merritt Hotel Associates	1522	E	510 832-2300	1323
Landmark Event Staffing	7363	A	510 632-9000	14897
Lange Trucking Inc (PA)	4213	D	510 836-1105	4209
Lapham Company Inc	6531	D	510 531-6000	11627
Laughlin Falbo Levy Moresi LLP (PA)	8111	D	510 628-0496	23375
Lazar Landscape Design & Cnstr	0782	D	510 444-5195	904
Lehar Sales Co	5144	D	510 465-3255	8599
Leidos Inc	8731	E	408 364-4700	26557
Lincoln Child Center	8699	C	510 531-3111	25550
Lincoln Child Center Inc (PA)	8093	D	510 273-4700	22768
Lion Creek Senior Housing Part	6531	D	510 878-9120	11634
LN Curtis and Sons Inc	5087	D	510 839-5111	7970
Lucid Design Group Inc	7373	C	510 907-0400	15990
M Arthur Gensler Jr Assoc Inc	8712	C	510 625-7400	26231
Macdonald-Bedford LLC	8742	D	510 436-4020	27519
Magnetic Imaging Affiliates	8071	D	510 204-1820	22240
Mariner Health Care Inc	8051	D	510 261-5200	20771
Marriott Foundation For People	8331	D	510 834-4700	24362
Marriott Hotels & Resorts	7011	D	510 451-4000	12949
Mason-Mcduffie Real Estate Inc	6531	D	510 834-2010	11665
Matson Navigation Company Inc (HQ)	4424	C	510 628-4000	4718
Mbh Enterprises Inc	5045	D	510 302-6680	7161
McGuire and Hester (PA)	1623	C	510 632-7676	1968
Medical Insurance Exchange Cal	6411	D	510 596-4935	10784
Meditab Software Inc	7372	C	510 632-2021	15746
Mercy Retirement and Care Ctr	8361	C	510 534-8540	24732
Merrill Lynch Pierce Fenner	6221	D	510 208-3800	10107
Meyers Nave Riback Silver & (PA)	8111	D	510 351-4300	23431
Michael Baker Intl Inc	8711	C	510 879-0950	25965
Miller Milling Company Inc	0723	E	510 536-9555	563
Moc Products Company Inc	7549	D	510 635-1230	17888
Monarch Place Piedmont LLC	8361	C	510 658-9266	24739
Monterey Mechanical Co (PA)	1629	E	510 632-3173	2069
Monument Security Inc	7381	D	510 430-3540	16738
Morgan Stanley & Co LLC	6211	D	510 839-8080	10056
Mufg Union Bank Na	6021	D	510 891-2495	9410
Multivision Inc (DH)	7389	D	510 740-5600	17343
Museum of Childrens Art	7999	E	510 465-8770	19249
Nancy Smith Construction Inc	1522	E	510 923-1671	1326
National Rental (us) Inc	7514	D	510 877-4507	17690
Native American Health Ctr Inc (PA)	8011	D	510 535-4400	19764
Navis Corporation	4491	B	510 267-5000	4750
Navis Holdings LLC	7371	D	510 267-5000	15322
Noble Tower Preservation LP	6531	D	510 444-5228	11712
North Star Emergency Svcs Inc	4119	D	510 452-3400	3822
Northgate Ter Cmnty Partner LP	6531	D	510 465-9346	11714
Nt Sunset Inc	8733	E	510 420-3772	26791
O C Jones & Sons Inc	8748	D	510 663-6911	28006
Oakland Healthcare & Wellness	8051	C	323 330-6572	20817
Oakland Mrtime Spport Svcs Inc	4493	E	510 868-1005	4771
Oakland Museum of California	8412	D	510 318-8519	25034
Oakland Private Industry Counc	8331	D	510 768-4400	24372
Oakland Public Education Fund	6732	D	510 221-6968	12161
Oakland Unified School Dst	7349	C	510 535-2717	14373
Ocadian Care Centers LLC	8051	D	510 832-3222	20820
Opterra Energy Services Inc (DH)	8711	D	844 678-3772	25998
Otis Elevator Intl Inc	1796	C	510 874-5129	3479
Pacific Gas and Electric Co	4911	D	510 450-5744	6165
Pacific Union Residential Brkg	6531	D	510 339-6460	11733
Paradigm Staffing Solutions	7361	E	510 663-7860	14720
Paramount Theatre of Arts Inc	6512	C	510 893-2300	11031
Parent Child Development Ctr (PA)	8351	E	510 452-0492	24499
Park Plaza Hotel	7011	E	510 635-5300	13077
Pasta Shop (PA)	5149	D	510 250-6005	8898
Paylocity Holding Corporation	7372	B	847 956-4850	15816
Peralta Service Corporation	8331	D	510 535-5027	24379
Permanente Federation LLC	8742	D	510 625-6920	27587
Permanente Medical Group Inc (DH)	8099	B	866 858-2226	23019
Permanente Medical Group Inc	8011	B	510 752-1000	19844
Permanente Medical Group Inc	8011	B	510 752-1190	19845
Phillips & Assoc Law Offs PC	8111	D	510 464-8040	23506
Playworks	8641	E	510 893-4180	25316
Playworks Education Energized (PA)	7999	D	510 893-4180	19261
Porrey Pines Bank Inc	6021	B	510 899-7500	9421
Port Dept City of Oakland (PA)	4491	B	510 627-1100	4753
Port Dept City of Oakland	4581	C	510 563-3300	4931
Prevention Institute	8742	D	510 444-4133	27593
Proactive Bus Solutions Inc	8741	D	510 302-0120	27176
Protean Health Services Inc	8059	D	510 536-6512	21352

	SIC	EMP	PHONE	ENTRY #
Providence Health & Svcs - Ore	8062	B	510 444-0839	21819
Public Health Institute (PA)	8733	D	510 285-5500	26798
Ramsell Public Health Rx LLC	6411	D	510 587-2600	10853
Rcc Facility Incorporated	8059	D	510 658-2041	21355
Rdp Acquisition Company	8732	B	510 652-8187	26702
Reading Partners (PA)	8699	B	510 444-9800	25569
Regents of The University Cal	8062	A	619 543-3713	21830
Regional Center of E Bay Inc (PA)	8322	C	510 383-1200	24152
Reliant Travel LLC	4173	D	847 509-0097	3962
Restaurant Depot LLC	5142	C	510 628-0600	8565
Ricoh Usa Inc	7334	E	510 839-6399	14126
Rmt Landscape Contractors Inc	0782	E	510 568-3208	946
Robert Half MGT Resources	8742	E	510 271-0910	27622
Rory V Parker	7381	C	510 595-5543	16775
Salestar LLC (PA)	5045	D	510 637-4700	7182
San Francisco Bay Area Rapid	4111	E	510 464-6000	3700
San Francisco Bay Area Rapid	4111	D	510 834-1297	3701
San Francisco Bay Area Rapid	4111	E	510 464-6126	3702
San Francisco Bay Area Rapid (PA)	4111	B	510 464-6000	3705
San Francisco Bay Area Rapid	4111	D	510 286-2893	3706
San Francisco Bay Area Rapid	4111	D	510 464-7000	3707
San Francisco Bay Area Rapid	4111	E	510 464-6000	3708
Schnitzer Steel Industries Inc	5051	D	510 444-3919	7402
Securitas SEC Svcs USA Inc	7381	C	925 746-0552	16803
Security Central Inc	7699	D	510 652-2477	18014
Sedgwick Claims MGT Svcs Inc	6411	C	510 302-3000	10869
SEIU Local 1021	0761	C	510 350-9811	685
Seiu United Healthcare Workers (PA)	8631	C	510 251-1250	25184
Shimmick Construction Co Inc (PA)	1629	D	510 777-5000	2083
Sierra Club (PA)	8641	C	415 977-5500	25347
Silverado Contractors Inc (PA)	1795	C	510 658-9960	3468
Simpson Gumpertz & Heger Inc	8711	C	510 835-0705	26068
Society of St Vincent (PA)	8699	D	510 638-7600	25581
Solar Millennium LLC	1629	D	510 524-4517	2087
Southwest Airlines Co	4512	C	510 563-1000	4823
Southwest Airlines Co	4512	C	510 563-1234	4826
Spectrum Credit Union	6061	D	510 251-6000	9628
SSC Oakland Excell Oper Co LP	8051	D	510 261-5200	20926
Standard Iron & Metals Co	5093	E	510 535-0222	8090
State Compensation Insur Fund	6331	C	510 577-3000	10463
Sterling Hsa Inc	7389	E	800 617-4729	17504
Stuart Lovett	8011	D	510 444-0790	20073
Sungevity Inc (PA)	1711	D	510 496-5500	2388
Sunrise Senior Living LLC	8051	D	303 410-0500	20976
Sutta Company Incorporated (PA)	5093	E	510 873-8777	8092
Sutter Health	8011	A	510 547-2244	20093
Sutter Health	8071	B	510 869-8777	22287
Swissport Fueling Inc	5172	D	510 562-1701	9027
T25cl Entertainment LLC	7812	C	951 308-2040	18164
Ted Jacob Engrg Group Inc (PA)	8711	D	510 763-4880	26088
Telecare Corporation	8063	C	510 261-9191	22100
Telecare Corporation	8063	D	510 535-5115	22109
Telecom Inc	7389	D	510 873-8283	17526
Thomson Rters Tax Accnting Inc	7291	D	510 452-6900	13728
Tree Sculpture Group	0782	D	510 562-4000	964
Tuolumne Me-Wuk Tribal Council	8641	C	707 319-3472	25383
Turner Construction Company	1542	E	510 267-8100	1700
URS Group Inc	8711	C	510 893-3600	26119
URS-Gei Joint Venture	8711	E	510 874-3051	26133
Veterans Health Administration	8011	B	510 267-7820	20202
W S B & Associates Inc	7381	D	510 444-6266	16850
Wallis Fashions Inc	7389	C	510 763-8018	17606
Waste MGT of Alameda Cnty (HQ)	4953	A	510 613-8710	6609
Waterfront Plaza Hotel LLC	7011	D	510 836-3800	13396
Waypoint Real Estate Group LLC	6531	D	510 250-2200	11912
Wells & Bennett Realtors (PA)	6531	D	510 531-7000	11914
Wells Fargo Bank National Assn	6021	D	510 530-3095	9459
Wendel Rosen Black & Dean LLP (PA)	8111	D	510 834-6600	23619
West Oakland Health Council (PA)	8093	C	510 465-1800	22865
Westcoast Childrens Clinic	8093	C	510 269-9030	22866
Wested	8733	D	510 302-4200	26820
Willow Tree Nursing Center	8059	D	510 261-2628	21422
Wipfli LLP	8742	D	510 768-0066	27722
Workers Compensation (PA)	6331	C	415 777-0777	10483
Wulfsberg Reese Colving and	8111	D	510 835-9100	23635
Xantrion Incorporated	7379	E	510 272-4701	16529
YMCA of East Bay	8641	D	510 654-9622	25407
Youth Uprising	7363	D	510 777-9909	14986

OAKLEY, CA - Contra Costa County

	SIC	EMP	PHONE	ENTRY #
Coldwell Banker Amaral & Assoc	6531	D	925 439-7400	11409
Contra Costa Water District	4941	D	925 625-6534	6334
Foundation Constructors Inc (PA)	1629	D	925 754-6633	2051
Semafone	7389	D	925 855-7400	17485

GEOGRAPHIC SECTION
ONTARIO, CA

	SIC	EMP	PHONE	ENTRY #

OCCIDENTAL, CA - Sonoma County
Alliance Rdwods Cnfrnce Grunds	7032	D	707 874-3507	13459
Westminster Woods Camp & Confe	7032	E	707 874-2426	13473

OCEANO, CA - San Luis Obispo County
Phelan & Taylor Produce Co	0723	C	805 489-2413	574

OCEANSIDE, CA - San Diego County
Aegis Asssted Living Prpts LLC	8361	D	760 806-3600	24542
Allied Swiss Limited	6512	C	760 941-1702	10956
American Golf Corporation	7997	D	760 757-2100	18866
AT&T Services	4813	C	760 722-7261	5521
Automation Engrg Systems Inc	7373	D	858 967-8650	15907
Bergensons Property Svcs Inc	7349	A	760 631-5111	14237
Business and Support Services	8021	B	760 725-5187	20247
Business and Support Services	8351	E	760 725-2817	24420
Campbell Certified Inc	1791	E	760 842-5226	3374
Cardinal Point Captains Inc	7363	D	760 438-7361	14851
Cinemastar Luxury Theaters	7832	B	760 945-2500	18317
CK Enterprises Inc	7389	D	760 967-8863	17082
Cox Automotive Inc	5012	B	760 754-3600	6672
Cox California Telcom LLC	4813	C	760 966-0447	5583
E R I T Inc (PA)	8361	D	760 433-6024	24638
E R I T Inc	8361	C	760 721-1706	24639
El Camino Rental	7359	E	760 722-7368	14537
Future Energy Corporation	1742	E	760 477-9700	2901
Gfp Oceanside Block 21 LLC	7011	D	760 722-1003	12664
Go-Staff Inc	7361	A	760 730-8520	14664
Goodwill Inds San Diego Cnty	8699	A	760 806-7670	25537
Impact Solutions LLC	7361	E	760 231-0450	14681
Infrastructure Engrg Corp	8711	E	760 529-0795	25877
La Cantina Doors Inc	5039	C	888 221-0141	7025
Labor Ready Southwest Inc	7363	E	760 433-4980	14896
Laconstructora Co Inc	1521	E	760 439-7686	1204
Marine Corps United States	8069	A	760 725-1304	22157
McAlister Institute For Treat	8093	C	760 726-4451	22772
Mellano & Co	5193	C	760 433-9550	9201
Merrill Gardens LLC	6531	D	760 414-9880	11686
Mission Linen Supply	7213	C	760 757-9099	13552
Mold Testing and Inspection	7389	E	760 643-1834	17340
Monterey Financial Svcs Inc (PA)	6141	C	760 639-3500	9758
Nitto Denko Technical Corp	8732	D	760 435-7011	26696
North Coast Surgery Center	8093	D	760 940-0997	22781
North County Transit District (PA)	4111	D	760 966-6500	3683
Ocean Holiday LP	7011	D	760 231-7000	13033
Oceans Eleven Casino	7999	B	760 439-6988	19254
Oceanside Lifeguards	7999	E	760 435-4500	19255
OConnell Landscape Maint Inc	0782	E	760 630-4963	926
Onesource Distributors LLC (DH)	5063	D	760 966-4500	7461
Pacific Marine Credit Union (PA)	6061	C	760 430-7511	9619
Pardee Tree Nursery	5193	D	760 630-5400	9208
Pendleton Farms	0171	C	760 754-2359	126
Pepperjam LLC	7371	C	760 585-7150	15373
Primeco Painting & Cnstr	1721	D	760 967-8278	2476
R & R Production	8049	C	760 754-9020	20345
Rancho Del Oro Ldscp Maint Inc	0781	C	760 726-0215	791
Rocket Farms Inc	0139	D	760 439-6515	33
San Diego Coastl Med Group Inc	8099	C	760 901-5259	23048
Scripps Health	8011	D	760 901-5070	19972
Scripps Health	8011	B	760 901-5200	19981
Service Corp International	6553	D	760 754-6600	12038
Sharp Healthcare	8011	B	760 901-5100	19995
Sol Transportation Inc	4119	A	310 800-8069	3846
Spectrum Construction Inc	1542	E	760 631-3450	1677
Sundance Natural Foods Company	0179	E	760 945-9898	261
Superior Support Services Inc	8741	B	559 458-0507	27240
Tri City Orthopedic Sgy & Mdcl	8011	E	760 724-9000	20142
Tri-City Hospital District (PA)	8062	A	760 724-8411	21972
United Services Auto Assn	6331	A	760 757-1340	10479
Waste Management Cal Inc	4953	D	760 439-2824	6600
World Mark of Oceanside	7011	D	760 721-0890	13428
YMCA of San Diego County	8641	D	760 754-6042	25414
YMCA of San Diego County	8641	D	760 758-0808	25426
YMCA of San Diego County	8641	D	760 757-8270	25427

OJAI, CA - Ventura County
ARC of Ventura County Inc	8093	D	805 650-8611	22659
Gables of Ojai LLC	6513	D	805 646-1446	11136
Hotrollergirl Productions	7941	D	530 521-2745	18549
Krishnmrti Foundation of Amer (PA)	6732	E	805 646-2726	12159
Mf Daily Oxnard Ranch Partnr	7992	E	805 646-5633	18760
Ojai Raptor Center	0752	D	805 649-6884	643
Ojai Valley Community Hospital	8062	C	805 646-1401	21768
Ojai Valley Inn Golf Course	7011	A	805 646-2420	13038
Ovis Llc	7011	A	805 646-5511	13052
Wilde & Guernsey Inc	6531	D	805 646-7288	11921

OLIVEHURST, CA - Yuba County
Ampla Health	8011	D	530 743-4614	19343
Lindhurst Dental Clinic	8021	E	530 743-4614	20263
Naumes Inc	0181	E	530 743-2055	305
Nordic Industries Inc	1629	D	530 742-7124	2070
Shoei Foods USA Inc	5141	D	530 742-7866	8518

OLYMPIC VALLEY, CA - Placer County
Bruce Olson Construction Inc	1521	C	530 581-1087	1143
Cncml A California Ltd Partnr	7011	D	530 583-1578	12530
Squaw Valley Development Co (HQ)	7011	C	530 583-6985	13283
Squaw Valley Ski Corporation (DH)	7011	C	530 583-6985	13284

ONTARIO, CA - San Bernardino County
3M Company	4225	C	909 974-3004	4512
Accentcare Home Health Cal Inc	8082	D	909 605-7000	22326
ACI Construction Company Inc	8711	E	909 391-4477	25613
Aecom Technical Services Inc	8711	D	909 554-5000	25638
AEG Ontario Arena LLC	7941	D	909 244-5500	18533
Air Control Systems Inc	1711	E	714 572-6880	2111
Aircraft Service International	4581	D	909 937-3210	4893
Aircraft Service Intl Inc	4581	D	909 937-3998	4894
Aircraft Service Intl Inc	4581	D	909 937-3210	4895
Alaska Airlines Inc	4512	D	800 426-0333	4781
AMC Entertainment Inc	7832	E	909 476-1288	18293
American Fidelity Assurance Co	6411	D	909 941-1175	10591
Americold Logistics LLC	4222	E	909 390-4950	4487
Ameriwest Industries Inc	5072	E	909 390-1898	7671
Aryzta LLC	5149	C	909 472-3500	8798
AT&T Corp	4812	C	909 930-6508	5255
Automotive Tstg & Dev Svcs Inc (PA)	7549	C	909 390-1100	17875
Avis Rent A Car System Inc	7514	D	909 974-2192	17662
Baxter Healthcare Corporation	5047	C	303 222-6837	7241
Beauty 21 Cosmetics Inc	5122	D	909 945-2220	8236
Bella Vista Healthcare Center	8051	D	909 985-2731	20409
Bernards Bros Inc	1542	C	909 941-5225	1505
Biagi Bros Inc	4225	D	909 390-6910	4527
Bio-Med Services Inc	8099	D	909 235-4400	22893
Blumenthal Distributing Inc (PA)	5021	D	909 930-2000	6807
Boshart Automotive Tstg Svcs	7389	D	909 466-1602	17037
BP Industries Incorporated	5023	D	909 481-0227	6848
Broker Solutions Inc	8742	C	909 458-0718	27359
C E B M Inc	7349	C	909 475-4440	14242
Calico Brands	5199	E	909 930-5000	9250
Canon Solutions America Inc	8742	D	909 390-7400	27368
Cardinal Health Inc	5047	D	909 605-0900	7254
CAT Logistics Inc	4225	D	909 390-1920	4534
Cbre Inc	6531	D	909 418-2000	11358
Celestica LLC	5065	B	909 418-6986	7544
Centimark Corporation	1541	E	909 652-9200	1412
Chino Valley Sawdust Inc	4953	C	909 947-5983	6458
Chino-Pacific Warehouse Corp (PA)	4225	D	909 545-8100	4535
Cintas Corporation No 3	7213	C	909 930-9096	13544
Cintas Corporation No 3	7218	C	909 390-4912	13625
Citizens Business Bank (HQ)	6022	C	909 980-4030	9484
Coastal Pacific Fd Distrs Inc	5141	C	909 947-2066	8467
Coldwell Bnkr Frst Prmier Rlty	6531	D	909 395-5400	11422
Comcast Corporation	4841	D	909 390-4777	5969
Comfort Systems Usa Inc	1711	D	909 390-6677	2186
Compass Home Inc	5023	D	909 605-9899	6853
Concord Foods Inc (PA)	5141	D	909 975-2000	8468
Converse Inc	5139	D	909 974-5695	8429
Corporate Resource Services	7361	D	909 230-4510	14629
Country Inn &SUite By Carlson	7011	E	909 937-6000	12541
CU Direct Corporation (PA)	7371	C	909 481-2300	15117
Customized Dist Svcs Inc	8742	D	909 947-0084	27404
Damao Luggage Intl Inc	5099	A	909 923-6531	8110
David Evans and Associates Inc	8711	E	909 481-5750	25763
Dejuno Corporation	5199	D	909 230-6744	9258
Dennis Foland Inc	5099	D	909 390-9900	8112
Dependable Highway Express Inc	4213	D	909 923-0065	4135
Directv LLC	4841	D	909 509-4790	5984
Dlt Growers Inc	0181	E	909 947-8198	276
Dominos Pizza LLC	4226	C	909 390-1990	4685
Doubletree LLC	7011	B	909 605-4222	12591
Dpi Specialty Foods West Inc (DH)	5141	D	909 975-1019	8475
Edc Service Corporation (del)	6099	D	909 390-4747	9717
Electrolux Home Products Inc	5064	D	909 605-9448	7495
Exel Inc	4225	D	623 907-2338	4551
Ez-Flo International Inc (PA)	5074	C	909 947-5256	7711
F M Tarbell Co	6531	D	951 270-1022	11516
F R T International Inc	4731	C	909 390-4892	5075
Federal Express Corporation	7389	B	800 463-3339	17037
Federal Express Corporation	4513	D	909 390-3237	4858
Fortune Avenue Foods Inc	5141	D	909 930-5989	8480
Foster Enterprises	5144	D	909 947-6207	8596

Employment Codes: A=Over 500 employees, B=251-500, C=101-250, D=51-100, E=45-50

ONTARIO, CA

Company	SIC	EMP	PHONE	ENTRY #
Frontier California Inc	4813	D	951 461-7713	5610
Fuji Natural Foods Inc (HQ)	0182	D	909 947-1008	330
Fullmer Construction	1541	C	909 947-9467	1425
Genco Distribution System Inc	4225	E	909 605-9210	4554
Gold Star Foods Inc	5142	C	909 843-9600	8553
Goplus Corp	7375	D	909 483-1220	16240
Greatwide Logistics Svcs LLC	4731	E	877 379-6394	5091
Gregg Electric Inc	1731	C	909 983-1794	2601
Grove Lumber & Bldg Sups Inc (PA)	5031	C	909 947-0277	6925
Guard-Systems Inc	7381	B	909 947-5400	16669
Hci Systems Inc (PA)	1731	E	909 628-7773	2609
HHS Communications Inc	1731	D	909 230-5170	2610
Hilton Worldwide Inc	7011	C	909 980-3420	12722
Hilton Worldwide Inc	7011	C	909 980-4001	12732
HMC Group (PA)	8712	C	909 989-9979	26202
HMC Group	8712	D	909 980-8058	26203
Hospital Business Services Inc	7389	C	909 235-4400	17226
Hub Construction Spc Inc	5082	E	909 947-4669	7775
Hub Group Trucking Inc	4212	C	951 693-9813	4026
Iapmo Research and Testing Inc (PA)	8611	D	909 472-4100	25090
Impact Logistics	7361	E	909 937-9035	14680
In-Roads Creative Programs	8322	B	909 947-9142	24020
Industrial Labor MGT Group Inc	7361	C	323 582-4100	14684
Inland Christian Home Inc	8051	C	909 395-9322	20685
Inland Empire Chapter-Assn of	8699	D	512 478-9000	25544
Innovel Solutions Inc	4731	E	909 605-1400	5106
Intercontinental Hotels Group	7011	C	909 930-5555	12846
Island Hospitality MGT LLC	7011	E	909 937-6788	12858
Jack Jones Trucking Inc	4214	C	909 456-2500	4352
Jacobs Engineering Group Inc	8711	E	909 974-2700	25897
Jeeva Corporation	1731	E	909 238-4073	2623
Jett Pro Line Maintenance Inc (PA)	4581	D	909 944-7035	4922
K A R Construction Inc	1771	D	909 988-5054	3287
Kaiser Foundation Hospitals	8011	A	909 724-5000	19632
Kaiser Foundation Hospitals	6324	D	888 750-0036	10319
Kaman Industrial Tech Corp	5085	E	909 390-7919	7937
Kenco Group Inc	4789	D	909 483-1199	5229
Kf Ontario Healthcare LLC	8059	E	909 984-6713	21280
Kindred Healthcare Oper Inc	8062	B	909 391-0333	21689
Kmart Corporation	4225	B	909 390-4515	4582
Lanting Hay Dealer Inc	5191	D	909 563-5601	9142
Las Vegas / LA Express Inc (PA)	4213	C	909 972-3100	4210
Lee & Assoc Comm Real Est Svcs	6531	E	909 989-7771	11630
Liberty Hardware Mfg Corp	5072	C	909 605-2300	7690
Liberty Mutual Insurance Co	6331	E	909 476-6688	10435
Main Street Fibers Inc	4953	E	909 986-6310	6499
Marriott International Inc	7011	C	909 937-6788	12965
Mazar Corp	7381	C	909 292-8269	16733
Menifee Lakes Country Club	7997	D	951 672-4824	18996
Merchant of Tennis Inc	7389	A	909 923-3388	17328
Michael Baker Intl Inc	8748	E	909 974-4900	27988
Mills Corporation	6512	A	909 484-8300	11019
Mission Landscape Service	0782	E	909 947-7290	913
Mondelez Global LLC	5149	E	909 605-0140	8879
NAFTA Distributors	5141	E	909 605-7515	8504
National Distribution Centers	7319	D	909 390-5696	14003
National Employee Benefits LLC	8742	C	877 778-8330	27558
National General Insurance Co	6331	D	909 944-8085	10451
Nationwide Trans Inc (PA)	4731	D	909 355-3211	5127
Nordstrom Inc	4225	B	909 390-1040	4605
North American Med MGT Cal Inc (DH)	8741	D	909 605-8012	27146
Ontario Convention Center Corp	7389	C	909 937-3000	17378
Ontario Health Educatn Co Inc	8082	E	951 817-8553	22522
Ontario Montclar Sch Dist Food	8099	C	909 930-6360	23014
Ontario Refrigeration Svc Inc (PA)	1711	D	909 984-2771	2311
Optec Displays Inc	5046	D	626 369-7188	7222
Oregon PCF Bldg Pdts Maple Inc	5031	D	909 627-4043	6942
Otto International Inc (PA)	5136	E	909 937-1998	8356
Owens & Minor Inc	5047	A	909 944-2100	7292
Pacific Rebar Inc	1791	D	909 984-7199	3394
Penske Logistics LLC	4213	D	800 529-6531	4243
Pentel of America Ltd	5112	E	909 975-2200	8174
Performance Food Group Inc	5149	C	909 673-1780	8905
Premiere Rack Solutions Inc	5021	D	909 605-6300	6831
Prime Halthcare Foundation Inc	8011	A	909 235-4400	19878
Prize Proz	8742	E	909 509-8600	27595
Pro-Med Hlth Care Admnistrator	8741	D	909 932-1045	27175
Providian Staffing Corporation	7363	A	909 456-7529	14928
R & B Wholesale Distrs Inc (PA)	5064	E	909 230-5400	7510
Rancho Pacific Electric Inc	1731	E	909 476-1022	2695
Raymond Handling Solutions Inc	5084	C	909 930-9399	7882
Redlands Employment Services	7361	B	951 688-0083	14748
Ridgeside Construction Inc	1521	D	909 218-7593	1247
Rockland Intl Trading Inc	5139	D	909 923-8061	8445
Romeo & Layla Warehousing Inc	4225	D	909 947-9055	4632
Ruuhwa Dann and Associates Inc	5045	E	909 467-4800	7181
San Dimas Luggage Company	5099	D	909 510-8820	8138
Scandia Recreation Centers	7993	D	909 390-3092	18809
Sears Roebuck and Co	7699	C	909 390-4210	18012
Securitas SEC Svcs USA Inc	7381	D	909 974-3160	16793
Securitas Security Svcs USA	7381	B	909 974-3160	16814
Sega Entertainment USA Inc	7993	D	909 987-4263	18810
Sigmanet Inc (HQ)	5045	C	909 230-7500	7186
Smg Food and Beverage LLC (PA)	7389	D	909 937-3000	17492
Solar Link International Inc	5085	C	909 605-7789	7954
Southtown Industrial Park	6512	E	909 947-3768	11056
Synnex Corporation	4225	D	909 923-8900	4643
Taylored Services Holdings LLC	4731	C	909 628-5200	5173
Tcm Group LLC	8741	D	909 527-8580	27247
Technicolor HM Entrmt Svcs Inc	7819	B	909 974-2016	18261
Technicolor Thomson Group	7819	B	909 974-2222	18265
Test-Rite Products Corp (DH)	5023	D	909 605-9899	6891
Texas Home Health America LP (PA)	8049	D	972 201-3800	20357
Todays Vi LLC	7011	D	909 980-2200	13348
Toyo Tire USA Corp	5014	E	562 431-6502	6793
Transport Drivers Inc	7363	D	909 937-3312	14962
Turbine Repair Services LLC (PA)	7699	D	909 947-2256	18026
Ua Galaxy Los Cerritos	7832	D	562 865-6499	18353
Uline Inc	5113	D	909 605-7090	8217
Ultra Solutions LLC	5047	E	909 628-1778	7323
Unifirst Corporation	7218	C	909 390-8670	13646
United Parcel Service Inc OH	7389	A	909 974-7250	17558
United Parcel Service Inc OH	4513	C	909 974-7190	4877
United Parcel Service Inc OH	4215	D	909 974-7000	4475
United Road Towing Inc	7549	C	909 923-6100	17901
United Road Towing Inc	7549	D	702 649-5711	17904
URS Group Inc	8711	D	909 980-4000	26122
US Merchants Fincl Group Inc	7389	C	909 923-3388	17579
UST Development Inc	4812	C	626 205-1123	5422
Verizon New York Inc	5065	D	909 481-7897	7654
Vertex Coatings Inc	1721	D	909 923-5795	2501
Vitran Logistics Inc	4225	D	909 972-3100	4656
Wells Frgo Insur Svcs Minn Inc	6411	C	909 481-3802	10935
Xpo Logistics Supply Chain Inc	4731	C	909 390-9799	5192
Xpo Logistics Supply Chain Inc	4731	C	909 975-6300	5194
Yuneec USA Inc	5065	D	855 284-8888	7662

ORANGE, CA - Orange County

Company	SIC	EMP	PHONE	ENTRY #
ABF Freight System Inc	4213	E	714 974-2485	4100
Adair Enterprises	7922	D	714 998-5551	18365
Aecom Usa Inc	8748	D	714 567-2501	27819
Aerospace Corporation	8733	B	714 248-1194	26723
Alan Smith Pool Plastering Inc	1742	E	714 628-9494	2848
Alignment Health Plan	6324	D	323 728-7232	10255
All Seasons Framing Corp	1751	E	714 634-2324	3028
All-Pro Remodeling	1522	E	714 288-1314	1289
Alliance Funding Group	6159	D	714 940-0653	9791
Alliedbarton Security Svcs LLC	7381	C	626 213-3100	16543
Alliedbarton Security Svcs LLC	7382	C	714 260-0805	16865
Alta Home Care Inc	7361	E	714 744-8191	14605
American Advisors Group (PA)	6282	E	866 948-0003	10115
American Contractors Inc	1711	D	714 282-5700	2126
American Multi-Cinema Inc	7832	A	714 769-4288	18300
American Residential Svcs LLC	1711	D	714 634-1826	2137
American Technologies Inc (PA)	1521	C	714 283-9990	1127
Ameripride Services Inc	7213	E	714 385-8911	13528
Ameriquest Capital Corporation (PA)	6163	B	714 564-0600	9915
Amerisourcebergen Corporation	5122	A	714 385-4000	8230
Amerisourcebergen Corporation	8741	C	610 727-7000	26919
Amerisourcebergen Corporation	8741	C	714 704-4407	26920
Anaheim Ca LLC	7011	D	714 634-4500	12386
Angelica Textile Services Inc	7213	E	714 998-6109	13532
Arbormed Inc (PA)	8099	C	714 689-1500	22892
Architects Orange	8712	E	714 639-9860	26164
Ashunya Inc	7371	E	714 385-1900	15037
Avanti Agency Corporation	7389	B	714 935-0900	17014
B C Rentals Inc	5084	D	714 974-1190	7821
Baghouse Parts & Services Inc	1541	C	800 584-4720	1402
Bapko Metal Inc	1791	D	714 639-9380	3365
Begroup	8051	D	714 282-1409	20407
Beks Acquisition Inc	1781	E	714 744-2990	3353
Bergen Brunswig Drug Company	5122	A	714 385-4000	8237
Bernel Inc	1711	C	714 778-6070	2164
Boyle Engineering Corporation (HQ)	8711	D	949 476-3300	25700
Boyle Engineering Corporation	8711	D	714 543-5274	25701
Cal/Pac Paintings & Coatings	1721	D	714 628-1515	2434
Calnev Pipe Line LLC	8711	C	714 560-4400	25715
Cashcall Inc	6141	A	949 752-4600	9742
Cellco Partnership	4812	D	714 921-5130	5289
Cellco Partnership	4812	D	714 564-0050	5302
Center For Indvdual and Fam Th	8322	D	714 558-9266	23723

ORANGEVALE, CA

Company	SIC	EMP	PHONE	ENTRY #
Chapman Global Medical Center	8062	B	714 633-0011	21480
Chapman University	7389	C	714 997-6821	17068
Chc Consulting LLC	8748	B	949 250-0004	27878
Childrens Healthcare Cal	8011	A	714 997-3000	19431
Childrens Healthcare Cal (PA)	8069	A	714 997-3000	22122
Childrens Hospital Orange Cnty (PA)	8069	D	714 997-3000	22127
Childrens Hospital Orange Cnty	8069	A	949 365-2416	22128
Choc Health Alliance	6324	D	714 565-5100	10270
Choic Admini Insur Servi	6411	B	714 542-4200	10669
Cik Power Distributors LLC	8741	D	714 938-0297	26965
Citigroup Inc	6162	C	714 938-0748	9831
City of Orange	8322	D	714 744-7264	23757
City of Orange	7999	E	714 744-7272	19179
Cleveland Marble LP	1741	E	714 998-3280	2807
Cleveland Wrecking Company	1795	C	510 568-2626	3451
Cleveland Wrecking Company (DH)	1795	D	626 967-4287	3452
Cmf Inc	1761	D	714 637-2409	3152
Coastal Building Services Inc	7349	B	714 775-2855	14256
Cobb Waterblasting Inc	7349	D	714 769-2622	14257
Colonial Home Care Svcs Inc	7361	C	714 289-7220	14627
Companion Home Hlth & Hospice	8082	D	714 560-8177	22408
Comppartners Inc	8082	D	949 253-3111	22413
Conexis Bneft Admnistrators LP (HQ)	6411	D	714 835-5006	10677
County of Orange	8322	D	714 935-7411	23873
County of Orange	8322	D	714 704-8000	23874
County of Orange	8322	D	714 935-6435	23876
County Whl Elc Co Los Angeles	5063	D	714 633-3801	7433
Cruz Modular Inc (PA)	4214	D	714 283-2890	4338
De Par Inc	8734	D	714 771-6900	26842
Destination Science LLC	8748	C	714 289-9100	27897
Disneyland International (DH)	7011	D	714 490-3004	12576
Doctors of Affiliated	8741	D	714 539-3100	27006
Dynamic Auto Images Inc	7542	D	714 981-4367	17840
Elliott Auto Supply Co Inc	5013	E	800 278-6394	6728
Emergency Medicine Specialist	8062	D	714 543-8911	21558
Enterprise Rent-A-Car (DH)	7515	D	657 221-4400	17700
Ergs Aim Hotel Realty LLC	7011	D	714 938-1111	12622
Es Engineering Inc	8711	D	714 919-6500	25803
ESA P Prtfolio Oper Lessee LLC	7011	D	714 639-8608	12624
Fedex Freight Corporation	4231	E	714 637-9346	4710
Field Data Services	8748	D	714 997-4498	27922
Finjan Inc	7371	C	408 452-9700	15186
Ford Plastering Inc	1771	B	714 921-0624	3264
Frick Paper Company	5113	C	323 726-8200	8191
Garda CL West Inc	7381	D	714 771-6010	16658
Geek Squad Inc	7379	D	714 938-0380	16388
General Coatings Corporation	1721	C	858 587-1277	2445
General Underground	1711	C	714 632-8646	2236
Hill Brothers Chemical Company (PA)	5169	C	714 998-8800	8990
Hilton Suites Inc	7011	C	714 938-1111	12712
Holmes & Narver Inc (HQ)	8711	C	714 567-2400	25867
Honeywell International Inc	5063	E	714 283-0110	7445
Interior Electric Incorporated	1731	D	714 771-9098	2619
Jack P Selman	8712	D	714 639-9860	26212
Jezowski & Markel Contrs Inc	1771	C	714 978-2222	3279
John Jory Corporation (PA)	1742	B	714 279-7901	2918
K & S Air Conditioning Inc	1711	C	714 685-0077	2265
K T W Productions Inc	5023	A	714 685-0428	6869
Kaiser Foundation Hospitals	6324	D	714 748-7622	10335
Kaiser Foundation Hospitals	6324	D	888 988-2800	10349
Kings Seafood Company LLC	5146	D	714 771-6655	8638
Larkin Leasing Inc	1623	D	714 528-3232	1959
Leonard Chaidez Inc	0783	D	714 279-8173	994
Liberty Mutual Insurance Co	6331	C	714 937-1400	10436
Lres Corporation (PA)	6531	C	714 520-5737	11639
Lucky Strike Entertainment LLC	7933	D	248 374-3420	18525
M S International Inc (PA)	5032	B	714 685-7500	6991
Madden Corporation	7389	D	714 922-1670	17308
Main Street Specialty Surgery	8062	C	714 704-1900	21723
Maintech Incorporated	7371	C	714 921-8000	15288
Mark 1 Mortgage Corporation (PA)	6163	E	714 752-5700	9936
Marne Construction Inc	1771	D	714 935-0995	3293
Martin Integrated Systems	1742	D	714 998-9100	2927
Matrix Service Inc	1623	C	714 289-4419	1966
MB Coatings Inc	7389	D	714 625-2118	17318
McClier Corporation	8712	B	714 835-8923	26237
Medical Specialties Managers	8742	C	714 571-5000	27538
Meyer Coatings Inc	1721	E	714 467-4600	2466
Miller Environmental Inc	1795	C	714 385-0099	3460
Mx Courier Systems Inc	7389	E	714 288-8622	17346
Nestle Waters North Amer Inc	5149	C	714 532-6220	8885
Nexinfo Solutions Inc	5045	E	714 368-1452	7167
Omega Insurance Services	6411	E	714 973-0311	10816
Omnigen	1521	E	714 288-0077	1228
Optisource Technologies Inc	7334	E	714 288-0825	14124
Orange Children & Parents	8351	D	714 639-4000	24492
Orange Coast Masonry Acquisit	1741	D	714 538-4386	2830
Orange County Association (PA)	8093	D	714 547-7559	22786
Orange County Health Auth	8621	B	714 246-8500	25148
Orange County Trnsp Auth (PA)	4111	B	714 636-7433	3687
Orange County Trnsp Auth	4111	A	714 999-1726	3688
Orange Healthcare & Wellness	8051	C	714 633-3568	20828
Outfront Media Inc	7312	B	657 221-2760	13955
P & D Consultants Inc (HQ)	8711	E	714 835-4447	26000
P H S Management Group (PA)	8742	E	714 547-7551	27578
Padilla Construction Company	1742	C	714 685-8500	2952
Parsons Brinckerhoff Inc	8711	D	714 973-4880	26009
Pentron Clinical Tech LLC	8071	D	203 265-7397	22254
Platinum Strands Salon	7231	D	714 532-2633	13686
Prospect Medical Systems Inc (HQ)	8741	C	714 667-8156	27180
Providence Speech Hearing Ctr	8093	E	714 639-4990	22812
Ralis Services Corp	7389	C	844 347-2547	17444
Raymond Group (PA)	8741	D	714 771-7670	27195
Red Hawk Fire & SEC CA Inc	1731	C	714 685-8100	2700
Rick Hamm Construction Inc	1611	D	714 532-0815	1851
Rika Corporation	1791	D	949 830-9050	3399
RJ Noble Company (PA)	1611	D	714 637-1550	1852
Robert Half International Inc	7361	D	714 450-9838	14760
Roger L Crumley MD Inc	8011	E	714 456-5750	19926
Roth Staffing Companies LP (PA)	7363	E	714 939-8600	14944
SA Recycling LLC (PA)	5093	C	714 632-2000	8082
Sanders & Wohrman Corporation	1721	D	714 919-0446	2489
Sas Institute Inc	7372	D	949 250-9999	15834
Schryver Med Sls & Mktg LLC	8071	D	303 459-8160	22283
Sedgwick Claims Mgt Svcs	6411	D	714 245-7800	10865
Sendgrid Inc	7374	D	888 985-7363	16184
Sfpp LP (PA)	4613	C	714 560-4400	4950
Shade Structures Inc	1799	B	714 427-6981	3581
Signature Flooring Inc	1752	D	714 558-9200	3130
Solari Enterprises Inc	6512	D	714 282-2520	11052
Southern Counties Oil Co (PA)	5171	D	714 744-7140	9009
St Joseph Hospital of Orange (DH)	8062	A	714 633-9111	21921
St Joseph Hospital of Orange	8062	A	714 771-8037	21922
St Joseph Prof Svcs Entps Inc	8111	D	714 347-7500	23581
States Drawer Box Spc LLC	5031	D	714 744-4247	6963
Steger Inc	1721	E	714 974-4383	2493
Td Service Company	7389	C	714 543-8372	17519
TD Service Financial Corp (PA)	7322	C	714 543-8372	14048
Tiller Constructors Partnr Inc	1542	D	714 771-1692	1692
Transportation Chrtr Svcs Inc	4142	E	714 396-0346	3909
United Spectrum Inc	1799	E	714 283-1010	3594
Universal Cylinder Exch Inc	8999	D	714 744-1036	28165
University California Irvine	8011	A	714 456-6170	20169
University California Irvine	8062	A	714 456-6011	22002
University California Irvine	8062	A	714 456-5558	22003
URS Group Inc	8711	D	714 835-6886	26129
Valley Couriers Inc	4212	D	714 541-0111	4085
Valori Sand & Gravel Company (PA)	5032	D	714 637-0104	6998
Van Grow Jack S MD	8011	D	714 564-3300	20186
Vandorpe Chou Associates Inc	8711	E	714 978-9780	26137
VCA Code Group	8711	D	714 363-4700	26138
Village Nurseries Whl LLC (PA)	5193	E	714 279-3100	9225
Volt Information Sciences Inc	4931	C	714 921-8000	6295
Volt Management Corp	7363	B	714 921-7460	14971
Volt Management Corp	7363	C	714 921-8800	14975
W Corporation	8748	D	949 861-2927	28096
Walsrwth Frnklin Bevins McCall (PA)	8111	D	714 634-2522	23609
Waste Mgt Collectn & Recycl (HQ)	4953	E	714 282-0200	6603
West Coast Firestopping Inc	1799	D	714 935-1104	3602
West Corporation	7389	C	949 294-2801	17621
Western Dental Services Inc (PA)	8021	B	714 480-3000	20287
Western Pacific Distrg LLC	5032	D	714 974-6837	7002
Westpac Materials LLC	5032	D	714 974-6837	7003
Word & Brown Insurance	8741	C	714 567-4398	27284
Xpo Enterprise Services Inc	4213	D	714 282-7717	4313
Young Mens Christn Assn Orange	8641	D	714 771-1287	25456
Zettler Components Inc (PA)	5065	C	714 939-6699	7663

ORANGE COVE, CA - Fresno County

Company	SIC	EMP	PHONE	ENTRY #
Booth Ranches LLC	0291	D	559 626-4472	464
Cecelia Packing Corporation	0723	C	559 626-5000	520
Nnncc Ranch	7389	C	559 626-4890	17362
United Health Ctrs San Joaquin	8093	D	559 626-4031	22857

ORANGEVALE, CA - Sacramento County

Company	SIC	EMP	PHONE	ENTRY #
Fountainwood Residential Care	8361	D	916 988-2200	24662
MA Steiner Construction Inc	1541	D	916 988-6300	1449
Security On-Site Services Inc	7382	D	916 988-6500	16922
Summerville At Hazel Creek LLC	8361	A	916 988-7901	24824

ORINDA, CA — GEOGRAPHIC SECTION

	SIC	EMP	PHONE	ENTRY #
ORINDA, CA - Contra Costa County				
Action Technologies Inc	7372	D	510 638-8300	15565
Agemark Corporation (PA)	8051	D	925 257-4671	20370
First Republic Bank	6029	C	925 254-8993	9552
Flexera Software LLC	7371	E	847 466-4000	15187
Mason-Mcduffie Real Estate Inc	6531	D	925 254-0440	11662
Miramnte High Schl Parents CLB	8399	E	925 280-3965	24942
Orinda Convalescent Hospital	8059	D	925 254-6500	21338
Orinda Country Club	7997	D	925 254-4313	19022
Security Officers & Investigat	7381	D	817 386-6947	16817
ORLAND, CA - Glenn County				
Glenn County Office Education	8351	D	530 865-1145	24465
Golden State Bridge Inc	1611	D	530 865-8400	1775
Lassen Land Co	0762	E	530 865-7676	706
Omega Walnut Inc	8322	E	530 865-0136	24114
OROSI, CA - Tulare County				
Abe-El Produce	0161	B	559 528-3030	35
Mountain View AG Services Inc	0761	A	559 528-6004	675
OROVILLE, CA - Butte County				
1000 Executive Parkway LLC	8051	D	530 533-7335	20362
Artists of River Town	8621	E	530 534-7690	25117
Bird Street Media Project	4832	E	530 534-1200	5749
Butte County Office Education	8699	B	530 532-5786	25509
Complete Equipment Repair	7699	D	530 589-1187	17969
County of Butte	8322	C	530 538-7661	23794
County of Butte	8322	C	530 538-7721	23795
County of Butte	8322	A	530 538-7572	23797
County of Butte	8322	D	530 538-6802	23798
County of Butte	8322	A	530 538-7711	23799
Evergreen At Oroville LLC	8051	D	530 533-7335	20557
Lake Oroville Country Retirem	8361	D	530 533-7857	24706
Mooretown Rancheria	7993	B	530 533-3885	18806
Mooretown Rancheria (PA)	7999	E	530 533-3625	19247
Orohealth Corporation	8011	A	530 534-9183	19799
Oroville Hospital (PA)	8062	A	530 533-8500	21774
Oroville Hospital	8049	D	530 533-8700	20336
Oroville Internal Meds Group	8011	E	530 538-3171	19800
Peter J Wolk MD	8011	E	530 534-6517	19870
Recology Inc	4953	D	530 533-5868	6523
Shadowbrook Health Care Inc	8051	C	530 534-1353	20906
The For Work Training Center	8331	E	530 534-1112	24395
Tyme Maidu Tribe-Berry Creek	7011	A	530 538-4560	13363
Youth For Change	8322	D	530 538-8347	24300
OXNARD, CA - Ventura County				
Apria Healthcare LLC	7352	D	805 278-6700	14469
Aptos Berry Farms Inc	0171	D	831 726-3256	103
Ava Enterprises Inc	5064	E	805 988-0192	7491
Ayala Drywall	1742	E	805 487-3392	2859
Best Western Oxnard Inn	7011	E	805 483-9581	12440
Blois Construction Inc	1623	C	805 485-0011	1911
BMW of North America LLC	5013	E	805 271-2400	6716
BMW of North America LLC	5013	E	805 271-2400	6717
Boskovich Farms Inc (PA)	0723	C	805 487-2299	515
Boyd & Associates	7381	D	805 988-8298	16579
California Resources Prod Corp	1311	D	805 483-8017	1040
Channel Islnds Vgtble Frms Inc (PA)	0182	D	805 984-1910	327
Chicago Title Insurance Co	6361	D	805 656-1300	10506
Child Development Resources of (PA)	8322	D	805 485-7878	23736
Chiquita Fresh North Amer LLC	0179	B	954 924-5642	253
City Impact Inc	8322	D	805 983-3636	23749
City of Oxnard	8322	D	805 385-8019	23758
City of Oxnard	4941	D	805 385-8136	6329
City of Oxnard	7996	D	805 385-7950	18814
City of Oxnard	7992	D	805 983-4653	18724
Clifton Tatum Center	8361	D	805 652-5727	24602
Clinicas Del Camino Real Inc	8093	D	805 487-5351	22688
Coalition For Family Harmony	8322	D	805 983-6014	23765
Community Memorial Health Sys	8011	D	805 981-3770	19456
Conroy Farms Inc	0171	B	805 061-0537	108
County of Ventura	8322	C	805 385-8654	23933
County of Ventura	8351	E	805 240-2701	24453
Covenant Care California LLC	8051	C	805 488-3696	20491
Dataprose Inc	7374	D	805 278-7431	16120
Deardorff-Jackson Co	5148	E	805 487-7801	8714
Dignity Health	8062	A	805 988-2500	21541
Dw Berry Farms LLC	0191	B	805 795-8403	357
Engility LLC	8711	D	805 383-7551	25789
Epic Production Tech US Inc	7359	D	805 278-2400	14539
Etchandy Farms LLC	0171	D	805 983-4700	110
Fame Systems Inc	7349	E	805 485-0808	14296
Family Circle Inc	8322	E	805 385-4180	23968
Federal Express Corporation	4513	D	800 463-3339	4860
Fresh Venture Farms LLC	0161	D	805 754-4449	65
G P M M Money Centers Inc	6099	E	619 288-7607	9718
Gama Berry Farms LLC	0171	D	805 483-1000	113
Geek Squad Inc	7379	D	805 278-9555	16384
Gibbs International Inc (PA)	7538	C	805 485-0551	17795
Gill Transport LLC	4213	B	805 240-1979	4189
Gills Onions LLC	0161	D	805 240-1983	68
Glenwood Corporation	8059	D	805 983-0305	21235
Gmh Inc	7623	E	805 485-1410	17921
Golden Living LLC	8051	D	805 983-0305	20611
Grolink Plant Company Inc (PA)	5193	C	805 984-7958	9191
GTE Corporation	7361	A	805 988-5760	14667
H & F Grain Farms LLC	8748	D	805 754-4449	27938
Helman Group Ltd (PA)	5064	D	805 487-7772	7499
High Tide and Green Grass Inc	7992	D	805 981-8722	18747
ICI Services Corporation	8711	B	805 988-3210	25873
Insurance Services Amercn LLC	6411	D	805 981-2220	10744
Irwin Industries Inc	1629	C	805 874-3050	2058
Iwamoto & Gean Farm	0161	B	805 659-4568	74
Joyous Management Inc	7011	D	805 278-2200	12869
Js Hospitality Group LLC	7011	D	805 988-3600	12872
Jsl Technologies Inc	8711	A	805 985-7700	25911
Kaiser Foundation Hospitals	8011	A	888 515-3500	19634
Kaiser Foundation Hospitals	8011	A	805 988-6300	19636
Kindred Healthcare Oper Inc	8059	D	805 487-7840	21283
Koxr Spanish Radio	4832	E	805 487-0444	5797
L J T Flowers Inc	5191	C	805 488-0879	9140
Las Islas Family Med Group PC	8011	D	805 385-8662	19701
Marathon Land Inc (PA)	0181	C	805 488-3585	300
Mariz Berry Farms	0171	D	805 981-9908	121
Maxim Healthcare Services Inc	8999	A	805 278-4593	28145
Merrill Lynch Pierce Fenner	6211	C	800 964-5182	10036
Mission Linen Supply	7213	D	805 485-6794	13558
Mission Produce Inc	5148	D	805 981-3650	8751
New York Life Insurance Co	6411	E	805 656-4598	10806
Nordman Cormany Hair & Compton	8111	C	805 485-1000	23472
Oceanview Produce Company	0161	D	805 488-6401	85
Olde Thompson Inc	5023	C	805 983-0388	6877
Oxnard City Corps	8331	D	805 385-8081	24376
Oxnard Manor LP	8051	D	805 983-0324	20831
Oxnard Perfrmn Arts & Convtn	7389	E	805 486-2424	17387
Pacific Building Maint Inc (PA)	7349	D	805 642-0214	14375
Pacific Coast Produce Inc	5148	D	805 240-3385	8760
Pacific Labor Services Inc	7021	E	805 488-4625	13454
Pleasant Valley Flowers Inc	0182	B	805 986-2776	340
Pyramid Flowers Inc	0181	E	805 382-8070	312
Quinn Company	5082	D	805 485-2171	7782
Quinn Group Inc	5083	D	805 485-2171	7806
Ramco Enterprises LP	0723	A	805 486-9328	576
Recp Cy Oxnard LLC	7011	D	805 604-7527	13131
Recp RI Oxnard LLC	7011	C	805 278-2200	13132
Republic Services Inc	4953	D	805 385-8060	6539
Rescue Mission Alliance (PA)	8699	D	805 487-1234	25570
Rescue Mission Alliance	8099	D	805 201-4341	23041
River Ridge Farms Inc	0181	D	805 647-6880	314
River Ridge Golf Club	7997	D	805 981-8724	19044
Rm Esop Inc	5083	E	805 483-5331	7808
Safeguard Business Systems Inc	5112	D	805 486-9769	8181
San Miguel Produce Inc	0161	C	805 488-6461	92
Santa Paula Berry Farms LLC	0171	E	805 981-1469	132
Saticoy Lemon Association	0723	C	805 654-6543	584
Scarborough Farms Inc	0161	C	805 483-9113	94
Scorpion Athc Booster CLB Inc	8641	E	805 482-2005	25344
Sea View Medical Group Inc	8099	D	805 373-5781	23056
Seaboard Produce Distrs Inc	5083	D	805 981-8001	7810
Seminis Inc (HQ)	8731	B	805 485-7317	26604
Seminis Vegetable Seeds Inc (HQ)	5191	A	855 733-3834	9151
State Compensation Insur Fund	6321	B	888 782-8338	10249
Sunrise Ranch	0181	D	805 488-0813	321
Sunshine Floral LLC	5193	D	805 982-8822	9217
Superior Berry Farms LLC	0171	D	805 483-1000	135
Supermedia Sales Inc	7319	D	805 278-3400	14011
Synectic Solutions Inc (PA)	7379	D	805 483-4800	16491
Sysco Ventura Inc	5141	B	805 205-7000	8537
Systems Application & Tech Inc	8711	D	805 487-7373	26083
T M Mian & Associates Inc	7011	D	805 983-8600	13337
Tanimura & Antle Inc	4225	D	805 483-2358	4645
Topstar Floral Inc	0181	E	805 984-7972	323
Toro Enterprises Inc	1611	D	805 483-4515	1875
Tradewind Seafood Inc	5146	D	805 483-8555	8658
Tri County Regional Center	8049	D	805 485-3177	20359
Venco Western Inc (PA)	0782	C	805 981-2400	975
Ventura Cnty Council On Aging	8322	D	805 986-1424	24277
Veterans Health Administration	8011	B	805 983-6384	20211
Volt Management Corp	7363	C	805 485-0506	14979

GEOGRAPHIC SECTION

PALM SPRINGS, CA

	SIC	EMP	PHONE	ENTRY #
West Flower Growers Inc	0181	D	805 488-0814	326
Western Precooling Systems	7359	D	805 486-6371	14591
Windsor Capital Group Inc	7011	D	805 988-0627	13414
Wonderful Citrus Packing LLC	0723	D	805 988-1456	608
Workrite Uniform Company Inc (HQ)	7218	B	805 483-0175	13649

PACHECO, CA - Contra Costa County

	SIC	EMP	PHONE	ENTRY #
Bay Alarm Company (PA)	1731	D	925 935-1100	2528
Cherne Contracting Corporation	1799	C	952 944-4300	3507
Hertz Corporation	7514	D	925 680-0316	17686
Pleasant Hl Byshore Dspsal Inc	4953	C	925 685-4711	6514
Universal Bldg Svcs & Sup Co	7349	C	925 934-5533	14456
Yellow Cab Company	4121	E	925 779-9292	3873

PACIFIC GROVE, CA - Monterey County

	SIC	EMP	PHONE	ENTRY #
Aramark Services Inc	7929	C	831 372-8016	18451
California American Water Co	4941	D	831 373-3051	6315
Episcopal Senior Communities	8361	D	831 373-3111	24647
Gateway Ctr of Monterey Cnty (PA)	8361	D	831 372-8002	24668
K&M Construction	1522	D	831 643-2819	1320
Mission Linen Supply	7213	D	831 375-2491	13562
Pacific Grove Aslmar Oper Corp	7011	C	831 372-8016	13056
Pacific Grove Cnvalescnet Hosp	8059	D	831 375-2695	21340

PACIFIC HOUSE, CA - El Dorado County

	SIC	EMP	PHONE	ENTRY #
Sacramento Municpl Utility Dst	4911	D	530 644-2013	6204

PACIFIC PALISADES, CA - Los Angeles County

	SIC	EMP	PHONE	ENTRY #
Bel-Air Bay Club Ltd	8641	C	310 230-4700	25207
Fusionzone Automotive Inc	7379	E	888 576-1136	16377
Lighthouse Capital Funding	6799	E	310 230-8335	12322
Palisades Optimist Foundation	8641	D	310 454-4111	25310
Santa Monica Bay Physcians	8011	C	310 459-2363	19960
Snap Inc	7372	A	310 745-0632	15839
State Farm Mutl Auto Insur Co	6411	D	310 454-0349	10894

PACIFICA, CA - San Mateo County

	SIC	EMP	PHONE	ENTRY #
Cal-Pacific Construction Inc	1542	E	650 557-1238	1519
City of Pacifica-Vallemar	8351	D	650 738-7466	24439
Little Giant Bldg Maint Inc	7349	C	415 508-0282	14340
Ortega Elementary Pto	8641	D	650 738-6670	25307
Pacific Engineering Builders	1542	D	650 557-1238	1626
Pacifica Care Center	8051	D	650 355-5622	20834
Pacifica Linda Mar Inc	8051	D	650 359-4800	20835

PACOIMA, CA - Los Angeles County

	SIC	EMP	PHONE	ENTRY #
Brewster Marble Co Inc	1743	E	818 834-2195	3006
County of Los Angeles	8011	C	818 896-1903	19473
CPI Luxury Group	5094	D	818 249-9888	8097
Energy Club Inc	5145	D	818 834-8222	8610
Global Bakeries Inc	5149	D	818 896-0525	8842
Gonzalez Management Co Inc	8741	D	818 485-0596	27043
Hathaway-Sycamores Chld Fam Sv	8361	D	818 897-1766	24680
Hillview Mental Health Center	8063	D	818 363-7813	22074
Looney Bins Inc (PA)	4953	D	818 485-8200	6494
Moc Products Company Inc (PA)	5169	D	818 794-3500	8994
Northeast Valley Health Corp	8011	D	818 896-0531	19781
Phillips Plywood Co Inc	5031	D	818 897-7736	6946
Purchasing 411 Inc	5087	D	818 717-9980	7976
Scenic Route Inc	1799	E	818 896-6006	3578
Wetzel & Sons Moving and Stor	4214	D	818 890-0992	4392
Xpo Enterprise Services Inc	4213	C	818 890-2095	4312

PALA, CA - San Diego County

	SIC	EMP	PHONE	ENTRY #
Pala Casino Spa & Resort	7991	A	760 510-5100	18667

PALM DESERT, CA - Riverside County

	SIC	EMP	PHONE	ENTRY #
Alliedbarton Security Svcs LLC	7381	C	760 568-5550	16551
Ambiente Enterprises Inc	8082	C	760 674-1905	22357
American Golf Corporation	7997	E	760 568-9311	18870
Atria Senior Living Group Inc	8361	D	760 341-0890	24560
Bank America National Assn	8741	D	760 636-7500	26935
Bighorn Golf Club	7997	D	760 773-2468	18893
Boys Grls CLB Dsert Hot Sprng	8322	D	760 329-1312	23690
CJ Construction & Dev Inc	1522	D	760 247-6868	1301
Coachella Valley Water Dst	4941	D	760 398-2651	6331
Coachella Valley Water Dst	4941	D	760 398-2651	6332
Coldwell Bnkr Residential Brkg	6531	D	760 776-9898	11434
Cora Constructors Inc	8711	E	760 674-3201	25753
Cove Electric Inc	1731	D	760 568-9924	2564
Danny Mahagna Shapprie	7929	E	760 341-5070	18461
Desert Falls Country Club Inc	7997	D	760 340-5646	18938
Desert Resort Management	6531	D	760 831-0172	11469
Desert Services Inc	7381	D	760 837-2000	16625
Desert Television LLC	4833	D	760 343-5700	5851
Desert Willow Golf Resort Inc	7999	C	760 346-0015	19196
Desertarc (PA)	8322	C	760 346-1611	23941
Destination Resort MGT Inc	7011	E	760 346-4647	12567
Dlo Enterprises Inc	7381	D	760 346-8033	16627
Emerald Brook LLC	7033	E	760 345-4770	13481
Enterprise Rent-A-Car	7514	D	760 772-0281	17671
Family YMCA of Desert	8322	D	760 423-5860	23975
First Team RE - Orange Cnty	6531	D	760 340-9911	11527
Gary Cardiff Enterprises Inc	4119	D	760 568-1403	3797
Guardsmark LLC	7381	D	760 328-8320	16693
Host Hotels & Resorts LP	7011	D	760 341-2211	12766
Jacobsson Engrg Cnstr Inc	1611	D	760 345-8700	1803
Jones John	1761	D	760 275-4168	3182
Journal Broadcast Group Inc	4833	D	760 568-3636	5876
Kaiser Foundation Hospitals	8011	A	800 777-1256	19635
Kaiser Foundation Hospitals	8011	A	866 984-7483	19638
Kaiser Foundation Hospitals	6324	D	760 360-1475	10343
Lakes Country Club Assn Inc (PA)	7997	C	760 568-4321	18976
Leighton Group Inc	8621	C	760 776-4192	25142
Living Desert	8422	C	760 346-5694	25064
Marrakesh Golf Shop	7997	D	760 568-2688	18992
Marrakesh Management Corp	6531	E	760 568-2688	11658
Marriott International Inc	7011	D	760 776-0050	12961
Medical Technologies Intl	7381	E	760 837-4778	26565
Oasis Palm Dsert Hmowners Assn	7997	D	760 345-5661	19019
Odyssey Healthcare Inc	8059	E	760 674-0066	21334
Oj Insulation LP	1742	D	760 200-4343	2942
Olive Crest	8361	D	760 341-8507	24754
Palm Desert Greens Association	8641	D	760 346-8005	25311
Palm Dsert Rcrtl Fclities Corp	7997	D	760 346-0015	19025
Paul Williams Tile Co Inc	1743	D	760 772-7440	3021
Quarry At La Quinta Inc (PA)	7992	D	760 777-1100	18774
Renova Energy Corp	1711	E	760 568-3413	2346
Securitas SEC Svcs USA Inc	7381	C	760 779-0728	16801
Shamrock-Hostmark Palm Desrt	7011	D	760 340-6600	13237
Spectrum MGT Holdg Co LLC	4841	D	760 340-2225	6026
Stearns Lending LLC	6141	D	760 776-5555	9764
Sun City Palm Dsert Cmnty Assn (PA)	8641	D	760 200-2100	25354
Sunrise Desert Partners	6552	D	760 404-1280	12016
Sunrise Senior Living Inc	8051	D	760 340-5999	20948
Sunrise Senior Living LLC	8051	D	760 346-5420	20985
Toscana Homes LP	1522	E	760 772-7227	1346
Toscana Land LLC	6552	D	760 772-7200	12019
United Brothers Concrete Inc	1771	C	760 346-1013	3343
Universal Services America LP	8999	A	760 200-2865	28166
Visitng Nurse Assn Inlnd CNT	8082	C	760 346-3982	22597
Watermark Rtrment Cmmnties Inc	8051	D	760 346-5420	21026
West Coast Turf (PA)	0181	E	760 340-7300	325
West Ville Palm Desert	6512	E	760 346-2121	11071
Westin Desert Willow	7011	D	760 636-7003	13404

PALM SPRINGS, CA - Riverside County

	SIC	EMP	PHONE	ENTRY #
A & A Home Care Services	8082	D	760 416-6769	22314
A A A Five Star Adventures	7997	E	760 320-1500	18841
Ace Parking Management Inc	8741	B	760 320-8974	26906
Agua Caliente Development Auth	6531	D	760 699-6800	11278
Agua Clnte Band Chilla Indians (PA)	8699	C	760 699-6800	25485
Agua Clnte Band Chilla Indians	7011	A	800 854-1279	12375
Alta Home Care Inc	8082	C	760 778-3443	22353
American Airlines Inc	4512	D	760 778-2878	4790
American Med	4119	D	760 883-5000	3745
American Medical Response Inc	4119	D	760 322-4134	3759
Angel View Inc	8361	E	760 322-2440	24549
Auto Knight Motor Club Inc	8699	D	760 969-4300	25493
California Nursing and Rehab	8051	D	760 325-2937	20434
Cardinal Health Inc	5047	D	951 360-2199	7252
Casa Real Estate Ltd Partnr	7011	D	760 320-4117	12498
City of Palm Springs	4581	D	760 318-3800	4909
Cnrc LLC	8051	D	760 325-2937	20461
Coldwell Bnkr Residential Brkg	6531	D	760 325-4500	11429
County of Riverside Department	8099	D	760 320-1048	22935
Crestline Hotels & Resorts LLC	7011	C	760 322-6000	12554
Desert Aids Project (PA)	8322	D	760 323-2118	23940
Desert Air Conditioning Inc	1761	E	760 323-3383	3164
Desert Arts Center	8412	D	760 323-7973	25019
Desert Medical Group Inc (PA)	8011	C	760 323-8657	19490
Desert Medical Group Inc	8011	C	760 323-8657	19491
Desert Regional Med Ctr Inc (HQ)	8062	A	760 323-6374	21529
Desert Regional Med Ctr Inc	8069	D	760 323-6640	22137
Desert Water Agency Fing Corp	4941	D	760 323-4971	6340
Ensign Palm I LLC	8051	D	760 323-2638	20544
Federal Express Corporation	4512	C	800 463-3339	4802
First Student Inc	4151	D	760 320-4659	3929
Five Star Quality Care Inc	8741	D	760 327-8541	27025
HHC Trs Portsmouth LLC	7011	D	760 322-6000	12700
Highland Hospitality Corp	7011	D	760 322-6000	12703
Hilton Resort Palm Springs	7389	C	760 320-6868	17219
Hyatt Hotels Management Corp	7011	D	760 322-9000	12828
Interstate Hotels Resorts Inc	8741	C	760 322-7000	27069

Employment Codes: A=Over 500 employees, B=251-500, C=101-250, D=51-100, E=45-50

PALM SPRINGS, CA

Company	SIC	EMP	PHONE	ENTRY #
Jack Parker Corp	7011	C	760 770-5000	12862
Joseph Dipuzo	7212	E	760 325-1200	13509
Kaiser Foundation Hospitals	6324	C	866 370-1942	10336
Kittridge Hotels & Resorts LLC	7011	D	760 325-9676	12889
M C Builder Corp	1721	E	760 323-8010	2464
Mahler Enterprises Inc	7363	B	760 537-7690	14903
Mesquite Golf & Country Club	7999	D	760 323-9377	19245
Morrison MGT Specialists Inc	8741	D	760 323-6296	27134
Mount San Jcnto Winter Pk Corp	7999	D	760 325-1449	19248
Palm Canyon Resort & Spa	7991	D	760 866-1800	18668
Palm Springs Art Museum Inc	8412	D	760 322-4800	25035
Palm Springs Disposal Services	4953	D	760 327-1351	6512
R P S Resort Corp	7011	C	760 327-8311	13120
Rbd Hotel Palm Springs LLC	7011	D	760 322-1383	13130
Remington Hotel Corporation	7011	D	760 322-6000	13138
Riviera Reincarnate LLC	7011	D	760 327-8311	13160
S S W Mechanical Cnstr Inc	1711	D	760 327-1481	2355
Seven Lakes Hm Assn Cntry CLB	7997	E	760 328-2695	19074
Smg Holdings Inc	8742	D	760 325-6611	27652
Smoke Tree Inc	7011	D	760 327-1221	13271
Spa Resort Casino (PA)	7011	D	760 883-1000	13276
Spa Resort Casino	7011	A	760 883-1034	13277
Springs Ambulance Service Inc	4119	D	760 883-5000	3847
Sunrise Senior Living LLC	8051	D	760 322-3444	20980
Temalpakh Inc	1542	D	760 770-5778	1690
United Airlines Inc	4512	C	760 778-5690	4836
United Parcel Service Inc OH	4215	B	760 325-1762	4436
VCA Animal Hospitals Inc	0742	C	760 778-9999	627
Walters Family Partnership	7011	C	760 320-6868	13391
Wyndham International Inc	7011	C	760 322-6000	13435
Wyndham Resort Dev Corp	7389	C	760 864-8726	17633

PALMDALE, CA - Los Angeles County

Company	SIC	EMP	PHONE	ENTRY #
Aecom Technology Corporation	8712	C	661 266-0802	26161
Antelope Valley Mall	6512	D	661 266-9150	10959
Cellco Partnership	4812	D	661 274-2112	5351
Child and Family Guidance Ctr	8093	D	661 265-8627	22681
Child Care Resource Center Inc	8322	E	661 723-3246	23734
City of Palmdale	7349	C	661 267-5338	14248
Colsa Corporation	8731	C	661 273-3859	26498
County of Los Angeles	1611	C	661 947-7173	1757
Csi Electrical Contractors Inc	1731	D	661 723-0869	2565
Delta Scientific Corporation (PA)	7382	C	661 575-1100	16877
Forest City Rental Prpts Corp	6512	D	661 266-9150	10983
Jacobs Engineering Group Inc	8711	D	661 275-5685	25891
Lancaster Community Hospital	8082	B	661 947-3300	22499
Lou Bozigian	6531	C	661 948-4737	11637
Palmdale Center For Pain MGT	8011	E	661 267-6876	19809
Palmdale Regional Medical Ctr	8011	A	661 382-5000	19810
Palmdale Resort Inc	7011	E	661 267-8055	13072
Palmdale Water District	4941	D	661 947-4111	6387
Palmdale Womans Club	7299	D	661 266-3008	13784
Passport To Learning Inc	5047	D	661 538-9200	7294
Penny Lane Centers	8399	C	818 892-3423	24960
People Creating Success Inc	8322	D	661 225-9700	24133
Primerica Life Insurance Co	6411	C	661 947-9070	10837
Spectrum MGT Holdg Co LLC	4841	C	661 947-3130	6018
Sunstone Hotel Investors LLC	7011	C	661 267-6587	13319
Tarzana Treatment Centers Inc	8093	C	818 654-3815	22845
Universal Pain MGT Med Corp (PA)	8741	E	661 267-6876	27266
Waste Management Cal Inc	4953	D	661 947-7197	6599
Xi Enterprise Inc	7991	D	661 266-3200	18708

PALO ALTO, CA - Santa Clara County

Company	SIC	EMP	PHONE	ENTRY #
4290 El Camino Properties LP	7011	C	650 857-0787	12362
Actian Corporation (PA)	7373	D	650 587-5500	15895
Adaptive Insights Inc (PA)	7372	C	800 303-6346	15569
Affymax Research Institute	8733	E	650 812-8700	26728
Alain Pinel Realtors Inc	6531	D	650 323-1111	11287
Alfatech Cambridge Group GP	8741	D	650 543-3030	26915
Ariba Inc (DH)	7372	C	650 849-4000	15584
Baker & McKenzie LLP	8111	D	650 856-2400	23100
Beauty Bazar Inc	7231	D	650 326-8522	13667
Beneficent Technology Inc	7389	E	650 644-3400	17027
Billcom Inc	7372	D	650 353-3301	15599
Bml Works Na LLC	8741	D	650 268-8305	26943
Broadrach Cpitl Prtners Fund I	6722	A	650 331-2500	12107
Broadreach Capitl Partners LLC (PA)	6211	D	650 331-2500	9966
Business Objects Inc (HQ)	5045	D	650 849-4000	7104
Cambridge Design Partnr Inc	8711	D	650 387-7812	25716
Capiot Software Inc	7379	D	650 766-2469	16332
Capital Asset Exch & Trdg LLC	5084	D	650 326-3313	7831
Cardic Arithmias	8011	E	650 617-8100	19401
Cc-Palo Alto Inc	8052	C	650 853-5000	21069
Cellco Partnership	4812	D	650 323-6127	5381
Channing House	8059	D	650 327-0950	21184
City of Palo Alto	7389	D	650 329-2598	17077
Cloudera Inc (PA)	7371	C	650 644-3900	15092
Community Housing Inc	8361	E	650 328-3300	24603
Cooley Godward Kronish LLP	8111	D	650 842-7201	23163
Cooley LLP (PA)	8111	B	650 843-5000	23165
Cooley LLP	8111	C	650 843-5124	23166
Covenant Care California LLC	8051	D	415 327-0511	20487
Danger Inc	4813	C	650 323-9700	5587
Datasafe Inc	4226	E	650 875-3800	4683
Declara Inc	7379	D	650 800-7695	16352
Dentons US LLP	8111	D	650 798-0300	23205
Digicash Incorporated	7371	E	650 321-0300	15137
Document Technologies LLC	7389	D	650 485-2705	17132
E3 Healthcare Management LLC	8741	D	650 324-0100	27008
Electric Power RES Inst Inc (PA)	8731	A	650 855-2000	26510
Episolutions Inc	8711	C	650 855-8900	25798
Ernst & Young LLP	8721	C	650 496-1600	26340
Essex Management Corporation	6798	C	650 494-3700	12244
Ferrado Garden Court LLC	7011	D	650 543-2224	12634
Fiorano Software Inc	7372	D	650 326-1136	15664
Foley & Lardner LLP	8111	C	650 856-3700	23248
Foster Moore Inc	7361	D	650 819-3042	14657
Garden Court Hotel	7011	D	650 322-9000	12658
Gibson Dunn & Crutcher LLP	8111	D	650 849-5300	23266
Gordon Betty Moore Foundation	8641	D	650 213-3000	25267
Gordon E Btty I More Foundation	8748	D	650 213-3000	27936
Gstc LLC	8742	D	650 773-7700	27456
H & Q Asia Pacific Ltd	6282	D	650 838-8088	10150
Harris Mycfo Inc	8742	D	480 348-7725	27458
Haynes and Boone LLP	8111	D	650 687-8800	23304
Hewlett Packard	7371	A	650 857-1501	15219
Hewlett Packard Enterprise Co (PA)	7372	C	650 857-5817	15691
Houzz Inc (PA)	7371	D	650 326-3000	15223
HP Inc	8731	C	650 857-4946	26532
HP Inc	7378	C	650 857-1501	16298
HP Inc	7372	C	650 617-3330	15694
Hyatt Hotels Management Corp	7011	B	650 352-1234	12829
Ideo LP	7389	C	650 289-3400	17231
Ideo LP (PA)	7336	C	650 289-3400	14149
Inapp	7389	D	650 424-0496	17236
Instart Logic Inc	7371	D	888 418-5044	15239
Intapp Inc (PA)	7372	D	650 852-0400	15706
Integral Development Corp (PA)	7372	D	650 424-4500	15707
Integrien Corporation	7371	E	323 810-6870	15243
Intellectsoft LLC	7371	C	650 300-4335	15245
Jewish Family and Chld Svcs	8322	B	650 688-3030	24045
Jive Software Inc (PA)	7372	C	650 319-1920	15720
Jones Day Limited Partnership	8111	D	650 320-8412	23330
Kawela One LLC	8111	D	650 843-5000	23342
Kaye Scholer LLP	8111	C	650 319-4500	23343
Kingsoft Office Software Inc	7371	A	408 806-0998	15268
Kirkland & Ellis LLP	8111	A	650 852-9131	23353
Leland Stanford Junior Univ	8732	C	650 723-6254	26681
Leland Stanford Junior Univ	8099	C	650 723-5548	22992
Leland Stanford Junior Univ	8062	E	650 723-2997	21699
Leland Stanford Junior Univ	8732	B	650 723-7546	26682
Leland Stanford Junior Univ	8062	C	650 725-2377	21700
Leland Stanford Junior Univ	8062	A	650 723-4000	21701
Leland Stanford Junior Univ	8011	D	650 725-4416	19704
Leland Stanford Junior Univ	8069	C	650 497-8000	22151
Leland Stanford Junior Univ	8062	A	650 725-4617	21702
Leland Stanford Junior Univ	8733	D	650 723-4733	26785
LLP Mayer Brown	8111	A	650 331-2000	23402
Lockheed Martin Corporation	8731	A	650 424-2000	26562
Lowenstein Sandler LLP	8111	D	650 433-5800	23412
Lucile Packard Childrens Hosp	8069	D	650 736-4089	22153
Lucile Salter Packard Chil (PA)	8069	C	650 736-7398	22155
Lucile Salter Packard Chil	8999	B	650 736-4030	28142
Lytton Gardens Inc (PA)	8051	C	650 328-3300	20749
Lytton Gardens Inc	8051	C	650 328-3300	20750
Lytton Gardens Inc	8051	C	650 321-0400	20751
Magnus Tech Solutions Inc	7371	D	650 320-0073	15287
Marcus & Millichap Capitl Corp	6531	C	650 494-1400	11655
Mc Graw Insurance Services Co	6411	D	650 780-4800	10782
McKinsey & Company Inc	8742	C	650 494-6262	27535
Medallia Inc (PA)	7372	C	650 321-3000	15743
Menlo Charity Horse Show Inc	7999	C	650 858-0202	19244
Mercury Interactive LLC (HQ)	7372	B	650 857-1501	15748
Merrill Lynch Pierce Fenner	6211	D	650 842-2440	10033
Metricstream Inc (PA)	7372	C	650 620-2900	15750
Metricus Inc	7389	D	650 328-2500	17334
Morgan Lewis & Bockius LLP	8111	D	650 843-4000	23441
Morgan Lewis & Bockius LLP	8111	C	650 858-2400	23443
Morrison & Foerster LLP	8111	B	650 813-5600	23452
Nest Labs Inc (DH)	5065	D	650 331-1127	7612

Name	SIC	EMP	PHONE	ENTRY #
News Distribution Network Inc	7372	D	773 426-5938	15776
Northwest Vntr Partners VII LP	6799	D	650 321-8000	12330
Norwest Venture Partners VI LP	6799	D	650 289-2243	12331
Npario Inc	7371	D	650 461-9696	15340
Oak Creek Apartments	6513	E	650 327-1600	11177
Odyssey Telecorp Inc	4813	C	650 470-7550	5672
Ofjcc	8322	E	650 223-8600	24111
Ooma Inc	4813	D	650 566-6600	5674
Oshman Family Jewish Cmnty Ctr	8322	C	650 223-8700	24118
Pacific Hotel Dev Ventr LP	7011	C	650 347-8260	13057
Pacific Hotel Management LLC	7011	B	650 328-2800	13060
Pacific Specialty Insurance Co	6411	E	650 780-4800	10823
Pacific States Investors	6719	C	650 326-0990	12082
Packard Childrens Hlth Aliance	8011	D	650 723-0439	19806
Packard Medical Group Inc	8011	D	650 724-3637	19807
Pahc Apartments Inc	6513	E	650 321-9709	11182
Palantir Technologies Inc (PA)	7371	C	650 815-0200	15367
Palantir Usg Inc	7371	C	650 815-0240	15368
Palmetto Hospitality	7011	D	650 843-0795	13073
Palo Alto Commons	8361	D	650 494-0760	24764
Palo Alto Family Y M C A	8641	E	650 856-9622	25312
Palo Alto Hills Golf An	7299	D	650 948-1800	13785
Palo Alto Medical Clinic	8011	E	650 321-4121	19812
Palo Alto Medical Foundation (HQ)	8011	A	650 321-4121	19814
Palo Alto Medical Foundation	8731	E	650 826-8120	26581
Palo Alto Research Center Inc	8731	C	650 812-4000	26582
Palo Alto Vterans Inst For RES	8733	C	650 858-3970	26793
Paloras Corporation	8742	D	650 440-7663	27582
Parkwest Apartments	6513	E	650 856-0930	11186
Paul Hastings LLP	8111	C	650 320-1800	23498
Paycycle Inc	4813	D	866 729-2925	5681
Perkins Coie LLP	8111	D	415 725-1313	23501
Pillsbury Winthrop Shaw	8111	D	650 233-4500	23511
Pivotal Software Inc (DH)	7371	D	650 846-1600	15382
Precision Ideo Inc	7389	B	650 688-3400	17420
Primerica Life Insurance Co	6411	D	650 323-2554	10836
Quora Inc	7375	E	650 485-2464	16255
Quovera Inc (PA)	8748	D	650 691-0114	28029
R H O Capital Partners Inc	6799	E	650 463-0300	12339
Remitware Payments Inc	7311	C	650 843-9192	13911
Robert Bosch Healthcare	7371	C	650 690-9100	15426
Robert Half International Inc	7361	C	650 812-9790	14772
Sap Labs LLC	7371	C	650 849-4129	15438
Sap Labs LLC (DH)	7371	B	650 849-4000	15439
Sharethis Inc (PA)	7311	E	650 641-0191	13920
Shopping Center Mgt Corp	6512	D	650 617-8234	11045
Sidley Austin LLP	8111	D	650 565-7000	23569
Simpson Thacher & Bartlett LLP	8111	C	650 251-5000	23573
Skoll Foundation	8699	E	650 331-1031	25578
Skype Inc	4813	D	650 493-7900	5702
Sourcebits Inc	7371	C	650 433-7920	15473
Stanford Federal Credit Union (PA)	6061	C	650 725-1000	9629
Stanford Fmly Prctc-Blake Wilb	8011	D	650 723-6963	20064
Stanford Health Care	8062	A	650 736-7844	21934
Stanford Hospital and Clinics	8062	A	650 213-8360	21935
Suning Cmmerce R D Ctr USA Inc	8732	D	650 834-9800	26708
Sutter Health	8641	C	650 853-2975	25356
Sutter Health	8011	C	650 853-2904	20104
Swaminatha Mahadevan MD	8011	D	650 723-6576	20125
Tcmi Inc (PA)	6799	E	650 614-8200	12349
Tcv Management 2004 LLC	8741	E	650 614-6200	27248
Technology Credit Union	6062	D	650 326-6445	9695
Teris-Bay Area LLC	8111	D	650 213-9922	23592
Tibco Finance Technology Inc	7373	B	650 461-3000	16065
Tibco Software Inc (PA)	7371	D	650 846-1000	15503
Total Quality Maintenance Inc	7349	C	650 846-4700	14445
Veterans Health Administration	8011	A	650 493-5000	20201
Vinson & Elkins LLP	8111	C	650 617-8400	23606
Vm Ware	7371	D	650 424-8193	15532
Vmware Inc	7371	D	650 427-2100	15533
Vmware Inc (DH)	7371	D	650 427-5000	15534
Vmware Inc	7371	D	650 812-8200	15535
Vmware Inc	7371	D	650 812-8200	15536
Watercourse Way	7299	C	650 462-2000	13804
Willow Garage Inc	8731	D	650 322-2584	26639
Wilson Sonsini Goodrich & Rosa (PA)	8111	A	650 493-9300	23626
Xcelmobility Inc	7372	D	650 632-4210	15883

PALO CEDRO, CA - Shasta County

Name	SIC	EMP	PHONE	ENTRY #
Rotary International	8641	D	530 547-5272	25328

PALOS VERDES ESTATES, CA - Los Angeles County

Name	SIC	EMP	PHONE	ENTRY #
Palos Verdes Beach & Athc CLB	7997	D	310 375-8777	19027
Plantasia Inc	0782	D	310 375-0387	936

PALOS VERDES PENINSU, CA - Los Angeles County

Name	SIC	EMP	PHONE	ENTRY #
County of Los Angeles	8062	B	310 222-2401	21517

PANORAMA CITY, CA - Los Angeles County

Name	SIC	EMP	PHONE	ENTRY #
AT&T Corp	4813	D	818 920-1216	5513
Cellco Partnership	4812	D	818 920-4848	5319
Creative Technology Group Inc (HQ)	7389	D	818 779-2400	17104
Deanco Healthcare LLC	8063	A	818 787-2222	22067
E2 Corp	7373	D	818 904-5660	15937
Ensign Group Inc	8051	C	818 893-6385	20538
Golden Living LLC	8059	D	818 893-6385	21238
Import Collection (PA)	5199	D	818 782-3060	9271
Kaiser Foundation Hospitals	8062	A	818 375-2000	21641
Kaiser Foundation Hospitals	6324	D	818 375-2028	10306
Panorama Community Hospital	8062	E	818 787-2222	21783
Panorama Madows Nursing Ctr LP	8059	D	818 894-5707	21344
Qmadix Inc	5065	D	818 988-4300	7622
Southern Cal Prmnnte Med Group	8011	D	800 272-3500	20019

PARADISE, CA - Butte County

Name	SIC	EMP	PHONE	ENTRY #
Butte Primary Care Med Group	8011	D	530 877-0762	19385
C A C H Inc	8051	C	530 877-9316	20427
California Vocations Inc	8059	C	530 877-0937	21175
County of Butte	8322	B	530 872-6328	23796
Family Resource Center	8322	E	530 872-4015	23970
Feather River Hospital (PA)	8062	A	530 877-9361	21565
Feather River Hospital	8062	A	530 872-3378	21566
Feather River Hospital	5047	C	530 876-7216	7264
Maqui Holdings LLC	8051	D	530 877-9316	20755
Sunbridge Paradise Rhblttn Ctr	8051	D	530 872-3200	20944
Tegtmeier Associates Inc	6512	C	530 872-7700	11061
USA Waste of California Inc	4953	C	530 877-2777	6586
Youth For Change (PA)	8322	C	530 877-1965	24299

PARAMOUNT, CA - Los Angeles County

Name	SIC	EMP	PHONE	ENTRY #
Advanced Industrial Svcs Inc	1721	D	562 940-8305	2426
Aramark Unf & Career AP LLC	7213	D	323 774-4216	13534
Braun Linen Service Inc (PA)	7213	C	909 623-2678	13539
Calmet Inc (PA)	4953	C	323 721-8120	6453
Calmet Inc	4212	C	562 869-0901	3990
Calmet Services Inc	4953	D	562 259-1239	6454
Carber Holdings Inc	8748	D	562 531-2400	27866
Cfr Rinken LLC	4731	C	310 223-0474	5044
Cort Business Services Corp	7359	C	562 582-1515	14525
Direct Way Personnel	7361	C	562 531-8808	14637
Don Brandel Plumbing Inc	1711	E	562 408-0400	2206
Fortress Resources LLC (PA)	7538	C	562 633-9951	17791
Gdm Concepts	5046	E	562 633-0195	7215
Goldenpark LLC	7011	D	562 863-5555	12669
LMS Intellibound Inc	4225	A	562 602-2217	4589
MB Herzog Electric Inc	1731	D	562 531-2002	2644
Modern Dev Co A Ltd Partnr	7389	D	949 646-6400	17339
Mountain Valley Express Co Inc	4731	C	562 630-5500	5125
Mv Transportation Inc	4111	D	562 790-8642	3682
Paramount Convalescent Group	8059	D	562 634-6895	21345
Paramunt Madows Nursing Ctr LP	8741	D	562 531-0990	27158
Promise Hosp E Los Angeles LP	8062	C	323 261-0432	21817
Reliable Energy Management Inc	1711	D	562 984-5511	2345
Schaefer Mary-Judith	1799	D	562 634-3164	3579
Telecare Corporation	8063	C	562 633-5111	22107
Total-Western Inc (HQ)	1389	E	562 220-1450	1097
Triage Partners LLC	7379	D	562 634-0058	16510
Vernon Security Inc	7382	C	562 790-8993	16942

PARKER DAM, CA - San Bernardino County

Name	SIC	EMP	PHONE	ENTRY #
Black Meadow Landing	7011	D	760 663-4901	12453
Metropolitan Water District	4941	C	760 663-4911	6375

PARLIER, CA - Fresno County

Name	SIC	EMP	PHONE	ENTRY #
Kozuki Farming Inc	0175	D	559 646-2652	240
United Health Ctrs San Joaquin (PA)	8093	D	559 646-6618	22856

PASADENA, CA - Los Angeles County

Name	SIC	EMP	PHONE	ENTRY #
24 Hour Fitness Usa Inc	7991	D	626 795-7121	18585
3M Cogent Inc (HQ)	7373	D	626 325-9600	15890
A P H Technological Consulting	8711	E	626 796-0331	25605
Aah Hudson LP	6513	A	626 794-9179	11080
Ab/SW 70 S Lake Owner LLC	6519	E	650 571-2200	11248
Access Pacific Inc	1542	D	626 792-0616	1483
Accredited Nursing Services	8051	D	626 573-1234	20368
Algos Inc A Medical Corp (PA)	8093	D	626 696-1400	22653
Altria Group Distribution Co	5159	C	804 274-2000	8963
Altria Group Distribution Co	5194	D	626 792-2900	9231
American Multi-Cinema Inc	7832	E	626 585-8900	18302
American Union Fincl Svcs Inc	6141	C	714 619-2520	9739
Amstar/Davidson Robles LLC	7011	D	626 577-1000	12385
An Companion Hospice	8082	D	877 303-0692	22361

PASADENA, CA — GEOGRAPHIC SECTION

Company	SIC	EMP	PHONE	ENTRY #
Annandale Golf Club	7997	C	626 796-6125	18874
AON Consulting Inc	6411	D	626 683-5200	10617
Are- Maryland No 31 LLC	6512	E	626 578-0777	10961
Arpom Inc	8051	D	626 798-6777	20381
Arroyo Seco Medical Group (PA)	8011	D	626 795-7556	19357
Art & Logic Inc	7373	D	818 500-1933	15904
AT&T Corp	4813	D	626 396-0100	5472
Atk Space Systems Inc	8731	D	626 351-0205	26479
Aurora Las Encinas LLC	8063	C	626 356-2500	22040
Ayzenberg Group Inc	7311	D	626 584-4070	13818
B Jacqueline and Assoc Inc	7371	B	626 844-1400	15048
Boston Brick & Stone Inc	1741	E	626 269-2622	2805
Brighton Convalescent Center	8059	D	626 798-9124	21164
Brookfield Dtla Fund Office	7011	D	626 792-2727	12471
C W Driver Incorporated (PA)	1542	D	626 351-8800	1517
California Convalescent Hosptl	8051	D	626 793-5114	20433
California Credits Group LLC	7389	E	626 584-9800	17046
California Institute Tech (PA)	8733	A	626 395-6811	26741
California Institute Tech	8731	C	626 395-8700	26491
California Linen Services Inc	7213	D	626 564-4576	13541
Carnegie Institution Wash	8733	D	626 577-1122	26746
Casecentral Inc (HQ)	7389	D	415 989-2300	17058
Cellco Partnership	4812	D	626 395-0956	5330
Century 21 Golden Realty	6531	E	626 204-2400	11375
Charles Pankow Bldrs Ltd A Cal (PA)	1542	E	626 304-1190	1525
CIT Bank NA (HQ)	6021	D	626 535-4300	9344
City of Pasadena	7349	D	626 744-4311	14249
City of Pasadena	4939	D	626 405-4409	6302
City of Pasadena	7992	D	626 543-4708	18725
Citywide Limo Services Inc	4121	C	424 335-9818	3863
Cogent Systems Incorporated (DH)	8731	D	626 325-9600	26497
Community Bank (PA)	6022	E	626 577-1700	9487
Community Hlth Alance Pasadena (PA)	8062	D	626 398-6300	21497
Congress Med Surgery Ctr LLC	8011	D	626 396-8100	19459
Corporate Driver Services Inc	7363	C	626 791-9020	14865
County of Los Angeles	8322	D	626 356-5281	23821
County of Los Angeles	8099	D	626 229-3825	22930
County of Los Angeles	8322	D	626 356-5281	23855
Cpo Commerce LLC	5072	D	626 585-3600	7681
D & C Care Center Inc	8059	D	626 798-1175	21204
Dallas Union Hotel Inc	6798	C	626 356-1000	12242
David Ross Inc	8051	D	323 684-7673	20511
Dilbeck Inc	6531	D	626 584-0101	11474
Disc Marketing In Flight Div	7389	D	626 795-9510	17126
Diversified Health Svcs Del	8361	E	626 798-6753	24632
Dy-Dee Service Pasadena Inc	7219	D	626 792-6183	13652
Dydee Service of Pasedena	7219	D	626 240-0115	13653
E Z Data Inc (HQ)	7371	D	626 585-3505	15152
East West Bank (HQ)	6022	B	626 768-6000	9489
Econnections Inc	8741	C	626 307-6200	27010
Electric Svc & Sup Co Pasadena	1731	D	626 795-8641	2584
Emmis Communications Corp	4832	C	626 484-4440	5767
Employee Benefits Security ADM	6371	D	626 229-1000	10552
Energy Innovations Inc	8731	D	626 585-6900	26512
Everbridge Inc	4899	C	818 230-9700	6073
Fed Air Security Corporation	7382	D	626 535-2200	16884
Financial Healthcare Services	8742	E	626 356-7950	27435
Forza Silicon Corporation	8711	D	626 796-1182	25817
Founders Healthcare LLC	8082	D	626 683-5401	22440
Front Porch Communities & Svcs	8361	C	626 796-8162	24666
Full Spectrum Lending Inc (DH)	6162	D	626 584-2220	9843
Garda CL West Inc	7381	D	800 883-8305	16661
Gates of Spain Wibel	7231	E	626 441-3078	13677
Gem Transitional Care Center	8051	D	626 737-0560	20594
Glenn Building Services Inc	7349	D	626 398-8000	14313
Golden Cross Care Inc	8059	D	626 791-1948	21237
Golds Gym International Inc	7991	D	626 304-1133	18638
Gonzalez/Goodale Architects	8712	D	626 568-1428	26191
Good Works LLC	8082	D	626 584-8130	22446
Gourmets Fresh Pasta	5149	D	626 798-0841	8849
Grandcare Health Services LLC (PA)	8082	C	866 554-2447	22447
Green Dot Corporation (PA)	6141	D	626 765-2000	9750
Greensoft Technology Inc	7374	C	323 254-5961	16137
Gs1 Group Inc	7381	D	626 844-4377	16667
Gsg Associates Inc	8741	D	626 585-1808	27049
Guidance Software Inc (PA)	7372	C	626 229-9191	15685
Hahn & Hahn LLP	8111	D	626 796-9123	23296
Hathaway-Sycamores Chld Fam Sv (PA)	8361	D	626 844-1677	24684
HDR Architecture Inc	8711	D	626 584-1700	25852
HDR Engineering Inc	8742	D	626 584-1700	27460
Hertz Claim Management Corp	7514	D	626 296-4760	17683
Hillsides	8361	B	323 254-2274	24691
Hilton Worldwide Inc	7011	D	626 577-1600	12723
Holmes Body Shop Inc (PA)	7532	D	626 795-6447	17758
Holthouse Carlin Van Trigt LLP	8721	D	626 243-5100	26369
Home Care of America Inc	8082	D	626 309-7696	22461
Hunt Ortmann Palffy Nieves	8111	E	626 440-5200	23314
Hunter Mc Clellan Inc	8712	D	626 397-2700	26210
Huntington Ambltry Surg Ctr	8011	E	626 229-8999	19562
Huntington Care LLC	8082	B	877 405-6990	22480
Huntington Hospital	8062	C	626 397-5000	21608
Huntington Med Res Institutes	8733	D	626 397-5804	26770
Huntington Otpent Surgery Ctr	8011	D	626 535-2434	19564
Huntington Reprodctve Ctr Inc (PA)	8011	E	626 440-9161	19565
Idealab Holdings LLC (PA)	6799	A	626 585-6900	12316
Imagescan Inc	7374	D	626 844-2050	16146
Integro USA Inc	6411	E	626 795-9000	10745
Inter-Con Investigators Inc	7381	D	626 535-2200	16707
Inter-Con Security Systems Inc (PA)	7381	C	626 535-2200	16708
Interntional Un Oper Engineers	8631	D	626 792-2519	25176
Interprsnal Dvlpmntal Fclttors	8322	D	626 793-8967	24035
Ironwrker Emplyees Beneft Corp	6733	D	626 792-7337	12179
Jacobs Engineering Company	8711	A	626 449-2171	25888
Jacobs Engineering Group Inc (PA)	8711	B	626 578-3500	25895
Jacobs Engineering Group Inc	1629	B	626 578-3500	2059
Jacobs Engineering Inc (HQ)	8711	D	626 578-3500	25902
Jacobs International Ltd Inc	8711	B	626 578-3500	25903
Jpmorgan Chase Bank Nat Assn	6035	D	626 795-5177	9573
Kaiser Foundation Hospitals	6324	E	626 405-5000	10295
Kaiser Foundation Hospitals	8011	E	626 583-2200	19663
Kaiser Foundation Hospitals	8062	B	626 440-5659	21672
Kids Klub Care Centers Inc (PA)	8351	D	626 795-2501	24472
Kidspace A Prticipatory Museum	8412	D	626 449-9144	25023
Kinemetrics Inc (DH)	8711	D	626 795-2220	25920
La Restaurant Management Inc	8741	D	626 792-0405	27106
Land Design Consultants Inc	8748	D	626 578-7000	27971
Langham Hotels Pacific Corp	7011	D	617 451-1900	12905
Law School Financial Inc	6111	C	626 243-1800	9732
Lender Processing Services Inc	7374	D	626 808-9000	16152
Linden Optometry A Prof Corp	8042	D	323 681-5678	20300
Los Angeles Cnty Emp Retiremnt (PA)	6371	C	626 564-6000	10555
Madison Radiology Med Group	8071	D	626 793-8189	22239
Marianne Frostig Center (PA)	8621	E	626 791-1255	25145
Maxim Planning Group	8748	D	818 425-4343	27983
Mda US Systems LLC (HQ)	8711	D	626 296-1373	25956
Mda US Systems Inc	8711	D	626 296-1373	25957
Merrill Lynch Pierce Fenner	6221	D	626 844-8500	10108
Mhh Holdings Inc	5149	D	626 744-9370	8877
Monte Vista Grove Homes	8361	D	626 796-6135	24740
Morgan Stanley	6211	D	626 405-9313	10048
Msj Healthcare LLC	8082	E	818 244-8446	22510
Msla Management LLC	8748	C	626 824-6020	27994
MWH Americas Inc	8711	D	626 796-9141	25982
Myers Capital Partners LLC	6211	E	626 568-1398	10063
Myinternetservicescom LLC	4813	D	213 256-0575	5662
Najarian Furniture Company Inc	5021	D	626 839-8700	6826
Norton Simon Museum	8412	D	626 449-6840	25033
Nrt Commercial Utah LLC	6531	D	626 449-5222	11716
Odona Central Security Inc	7381	C	323 728-8818	16751
Old Republic Construction Prog	6411	D	626 683-5200	10814
Openx Technologies Inc (DH)	7311	C	855 673-6948	13891
Operating Engineers Funds Inc (PA)	6733	D	626 792-8900	12197
Pacific Program/Design Managem	8741	D	626 440-2000	27154
Pacifica Services Inc	8711	D	626 405-0131	26007
Pardee Homes (DH)	6552	D	310 955-3100	11999
Park Marino Convalescent Ctr	8059	D	626 463-4105	21346
Parsons Constructors Inc	8741	A	626 440-2000	27159
Parsons Corporation (PA)	1629	A	626 440-2000	2074
Parsons Engrg Science Inc (DH)	8711	B	626 440-2000	26013
Parsons Government Svcs Inc (HQ)	8711	D	626 440-2000	26014
Parsons Gvrnment Svcs Intl Inc	1542	B	626 440-6000	1632
Parsons Project Services Inc	1541	C	626 440-4000	1457
Parsons Technical Services Inc	8711	D	626 440-3998	26016
Parsons Wtr Infrastructure Inc	8711	A	626 440-7000	26017
Pasadena Baking Co	5149	E	626 796-5093	8897
Pasadena Billing Associates	8721	D	626 795-6596	26416
Pasadena Center Operating Co	7389	C	626 795-9311	17402
Pasadena Child Dev Assoc Inc	8093	D	626 793-7350	22794
Pasadena Child Development Ass	8322	D	626 793-7350	24123
Pasadena Cyto Pathology Lab	8071	B	626 397-8616	22252
Pasadena Hospital Assn Ltd (PA)	8062	A	626 397-5000	21787
Pasadena Hospital Assn Ltd	8051	D	626 397-3322	20843
Pasadena Hotel Dev Ventr LP	7011	D	626 449-4000	13078
Pasadena Humane Society	8699	D	626 792-7151	25564
Pasadena Madows Nursing Ctr LP	8051	D	626 796-1103	20844
Pasadena Rbles Acquisition LLC	7011	D	626 577-1000	13079
Permits Today LLC	7389	D	626 585-2931	17409
Pgs Subsidiary II Company	8711	C	626 440-2000	26020
Physician Assoc San Gabriel	6324	C	626 817-8300	10370
PNC Realty Investors Inc	6021	D	626 432-4500	9419

Mergent email: customerrelations@mergent.com
2017 Directory of California Wholesalers and Services Companies
(P-0000) Products & Services Section entry number
(PA)=Parent Co (HQ)=Headquarters (DH)=Div Headquarters

GEOGRAPHIC SECTION

PETALUMA, CA

	SIC	EMP	PHONE	ENTRY #
PNC Realty Investors Inc	6021	D	626 351-2211	9420
Pollard Crnert Crwford Stevens	8111	E	626 793-4440	23513
Prima Royale Enterprises Ltd	5139	D	626 960-8388	8442
Principles Inc (PA)	8093	D	323 681-2575	22810
Ptsi Managed Services Inc	8711	D	626 440-3118	26025
Ralphs Grocery Company	4225	D	626 793-7480	4626
Raytheon Company	7629	D	626 304-1007	17940
Real Property Systems Inc	6531	C	760 243-1143	11797
Regency Park Senior Living Inc	8361	D	626 396-4911	24781
Regency Park Senior Living Inc	6531	D	626 578-0460	11802
Restaurant Depot LLC	5142	C	626 744-0204	8564
Robert C Hamilton	8361	D	626 794-4103	24790
Robert Half International Inc	7361	D	626 463-2037	14770
Roisman Leon D DMD Inc	8021	D	626 795-6855	20273
Rose Bowl Aquatics Center	7997	D	626 564-0330	19047
Rosemary Childrens Services (PA)	8361	C	626 844-3033	24791
Rt Pasad Hotel Partners LP	7011	D	626 403-7600	13178
Sabal Financial Group LP	8742	D	626 351-6859	27631
Saiful/Bouquet Con Stru Eng (PA)	8711	D	626 304-2616	26049
Sedgwick Claims MGT Svcs Inc	6411	D	626 568-1415	10866
Seville Construction Svcs Inc	8742	D	626 204-0800	27643
Sierra Lobo Inc	8711	D	626 510-6340	26065
Sigma Investment Holdings LLC	1629	E	626 398-3098	2084
Slch Inc (PA)	8051	E	626 798-0558	20920
Smith Brothers Restaurant Inc	8741	D	626 577-2400	27218
Snap Technologies Inc	8742	D	626 585-6900	27654
Southern Cal Prmnnte Med Group (PA)	6324	D	626 405-5704	10382
Special Events Staffing	7361	A	626 296-6771	14793
Swca Incorporated	8748	D	626 240-0587	28064
Symtech Industries Inc (PA)	8741	D	626 683-7555	27244
Symtech Industries Inc	8741	C	626 683-7555	27245
Synopsys Inc	7372	D	626 795-9101	15854
Tetra Tech Executive Svcs Inc	7361	C	626 470-2400	14804
Tetra Tech Nus Inc	8748	D	412 921-7090	28075
Tetra Tech Technical Services	8711	D	626 351-4664	26093
Ticor Title Insurance Company (DH)	6361	C	616 302-3121	10537
Tokio Marine Management Inc	6411	D	626 568-7600	10906
Trinus Corporation	7371	E	818 246-1143	15510
Ttg Engineers (PA)	8711	C	626 463-2800	26107
Two Palms Nursing Center	8059	D	323 681-4615	21394
Two Palms Nursing Center Inc (PA)	8059	D	626 798-8991	21395
Two Palms Nursing Center Inc	8059	D	626 796-1103	21396
UBS Financial Services Inc	6211	E	626 449-1501	10092
Unified Valet Parking Inc	7299	D	818 822-5807	13801
Union Station Homeless Svcs	8322	D	626 240-4550	24265
United Agencies Inc (PA)	6411	D	626 564-2670	10913
United Couriers Inc (DH)	4512	C	213 383-3611	4838
Unity SEC & Protective Svc	7381	D	323 695-7234	16839
Universal Accounts Inc	7322	D	626 356-7900	14049
Valley Hunt Club	8641	D	626 793-7134	25387
Verdugo Hlls Vsting Nurse Assn	8082	C	949 263-4704	22588
Vincent Hayley Enterprises	8059	D	626 398-8182	21414
Voch Inc	8059	D	626 798-1111	21418
Wells Fargo Bank National Assn	6021	E	626 685-9900	9444
Wescom Central Credit Union (PA)	6062	B	888 493-7266	9699
Western Asset Management Co (HQ)	6282	E	626 844-9265	10193
Western Asset Mrtg Capitl Corp	6798	A	626 844-9400	12279
Zenith Health Care	6531	D	626 578-0460	11934

PASO ROBLES, CA - San Luis Obispo County

	SIC	EMP	PHONE	ENTRY #
Ameripride Services Inc	7213	D	805 239-9449	13524
AT&T Services Inc	4813	C	805 237-9503	5533
Cellco Partnership	4812	D	805 237-8200	5321
County of Los Angeles	8322	C	805 237-3110	23840
Dave Spurr Excavating Inc	1794	E	805 238-0834	3426
Emeritus Corporation	6513	E	805 239-1313	11126
Fairgrounds	7922	D	805 239-0655	18392
Iqms (PA)	7371	C	805 227-1122	15255
JIT Corporation	5065	D	805 238-5000	7589
Mge Underground Inc	1623	D	805 238-3510	1970
Michael Dusi Trucking Inc	4214	D	805 237-9499	4362
Omega 2 Alpha Services LLC	8742	D	805 610-2249	27572
Paso Robles Inn LLC	7011	D	805 238-2660	13080
Paso Robles Tank (PA)	1791	D	805 227-1641	3395
Pearce Services LLC	1623	E	805 237-7480	1980
RE Max Parkside Real Estate	6531	D	805 239-3310	11790
Special Service Contrs Inc	1799	D	805 227-1081	3585
Treasury Wine Estates Americas	0172	C	805 237-6000	190
Union Pacific Railroad Company	4011	D	805 286-5851	3620
Villa Paseo Senior Residences	6513	D	805 227-4588	11220
Western Pacific Packaging Inc	7389	D	805 239-1188	17623

PATTERSON, CA - Stanislaus County

	SIC	EMP	PHONE	ENTRY #
Del Puerto Health Care Dst	8011	D	209 892-9100	19488
Designed MBL Systems Inds Inc	1542	C	209 892-6298	1539
Diablo Grande Ltd Partnership	6552	D	209 892-7421	11962
Lucich Santos Farms	0191	C	209 892-6500	383
Thorkelson Ranches	0161	C	209 892-9111	100
Traina Dried Fruit Inc	5149	C	209 892-5472	8940

PATTON, CA - San Bernardino County

	SIC	EMP	PHONE	ENTRY #
Califrnia Dept State Hospitals	8063	A	909 425-7000	22049

PAUMA VALLEY, CA - San Diego County

	SIC	EMP	PHONE	ENTRY #
Pauma Band of Mission Indians	7011	B	760 742-2177	13082
Pauma Valley Country Club	7997	D	760 742-1230	19029
T - Y Nursery Inc	5193	C	760 742-2151	9219

PEBBLE BEACH, CA - Monterey County

	SIC	EMP	PHONE	ENTRY #
California Golf Association	7997	D	831 625-4653	18907
Czech Commerce Ltd	5169	D	831 649-4633	8985
I Cypress Company	7011	D	831 647-7500	12832
Lone Cypress Company LLC	7011	A	831 624-3811	12928
Lone Cypress Company LLC	7997	D	831 625-8507	18981
Monterey Peninsula Country CLB	7997	C	831 373-1556	19007
Pebble Bch Resrt Co DBA Lone C (PA)	7011	D	831 647-7500	13085
Pebble Beach Co A Ltd Partnr (PA)	7011	D	831 647-7500	13086
Poppy Hills Inc	7992	D	831 625-1513	18768

PENN VALLEY, CA - Nevada County

	SIC	EMP	PHONE	ENTRY #
Lake Wildwood Association	8641	C	530 432-1152	25285

PENRYN, CA - Placer County

	SIC	EMP	PHONE	ENTRY #
Sinclair Concrete	1771	D	916 663-0303	3331

PERRIS, CA - Riverside County

	SIC	EMP	PHONE	ENTRY #
4g Wireless Inc	4813	D	951 210-7980	5445
American Airlines Group Inc	4512	A	310 251-9184	4793
Basic Occpational Training Ctr	8399	C	951 657-8028	24879
Big Lgue Dreams Consulting LLC	7941	D	619 846-8855	18540
Brightview Landscapes	0781	C	951 657-4603	755
Building Material Distrs Inc	5031	C	951 341-0708	6912
County of Riverside	8322	D	951 443-2262	23882
Eastern Municipal Water Dst (PA)	4941	B	951 928-3777	6345
Global PET Inc	5093	C	951 657-5466	8071
Griswold Industries	5085	D	951 657-1718	7934
Herca Telecomm Services Inc	5082	C	951 940-5941	7771
Integrity Rebar Placers	1791	C	951 696-6843	3383
Jeff Carpenter Inc	1794	D	951 657-5115	3434
Kindred Healthcare Inc	8062	D	951 436-3535	21684
Mamco Inc (PA)	1611	D	951 776-9300	1819
Pacific Hydrotech Corporation	8711	D	951 943-8803	26005
Pacific Restoration Group Inc	0781	E	951 940-6069	785
Peed Equipment Company	7353	E	951 657-0900	14494
Silver Creek Industries Inc	1542	C	951 943-5393	1668
Solar Service Center Inc (PA)	1711	D	888 760-7652	2374
Southwest Hospital Dev Group	8062	C	951 943-4555	21911
SR Bray LLC	7359	E	951 436-2920	14581
Student Trnsp Amer Inc	4151	D	951 940-0300	3950
Transdev Services Inc	4119	C	951 943-1371	3850
Village Nurseries Whl LLC	5193	B	951 657-3940	9227

PESCADERO, CA - San Mateo County

	SIC	EMP	PHONE	ENTRY #
Joie De Vivre Hospitality LLC	8741	D	650 879-1100	27083
King-Reynolds Ventures LLC	7389	D	650 879-2136	17273
Pescadero Conservation Aliance	8641	E	650 879-1441	25313

PETALUMA, CA - Sonoma County

	SIC	EMP	PHONE	ENTRY #
AB Closing Corporation	7361	C	707 766-1777	14596
Accentcare Inc	8082	D	707 792-2211	22320
American Insurance Company Inc	6331	A	415 899-2000	10400
Amos of America Inc	7379	C	899 415-2000	16320
Associated Indemnity Corp	6311	A	415 899-2000	10200
Bay Area Envmtl Res Inst	8731	D	707 938-9387	26484
Boys & Girls Clubs of Marin A	8399	D	707 769-5322	24881
Club One At Petaluma	7997	D	707 766-8080	18922
County Engineers Assn Cal	8711	D	707 762-3492	25754
Crocodile Bay Lodge	7021	C	707 559-7990	13451
Daymen US Inc	5043	D	707 827-4053	7031
Dun-Rite Maintenance Inc	7217	D	707 765-2434	13597
Evergreen At Petaluma LLC	8051	D	707 763-6887	20558
Exchange Bank	6022	D	707 762-5555	9491
Federal Express Corporation	4513	D	800 463-3339	4844
Fedex Freight West Inc	4213	E	707 778-3191	4173
First California Mrtg Co II	6162	D	415 209-0910	9841
Goebel Mechanical Inc	1541	D	707 778-2340	1431
Golden Living LLC	8051	D	707 763-4109	20610
Incom Mechanical Inc	1711	D	707 586-0511	2249
Kaiser Foundation Hospitals	8062	E	707 765-3900	21659
Legacy Marketing Group (PA)	8742	D	707 778-8638	27506
Lok Petaluma Marina Ht Co LLC	7011	D	707 283-2888	12927
Marketlive Inc	7374	D	707 780-1600	16158
McEvoy of Marin LLC	5199	D	707 778-2307	9280
Midstate Construction Corp	1521	D	707 763-3200	1222

Employment Codes: A=Over 500 employees, B=251-500, C=101-250, D=51-100, E=45-50

2017 Directory of California Wholesalers and Services Companies

© Mergent Inc. 1-800-342-5647

PETALUMA, CA

	SIC	EMP	PHONE	ENTRY #
Molecular Bioproducts Inc	5049	C	707 762-6689	7345
Morris Distributing Inc	5181	D	707 769-7294	9076
National Surety Corporation	6351	A	415 899-2000	10495
NMN Construction Inc	1771	D	707 763-6981	3301
North Bay Construction Inc	1611	D	707 283-0093	1835
North Bay Drywall & Plst Inc	1742	C	707 763-6819	2937
Oak Knoll Convalescent Center	8051	D	707 778-8686	20813
Pacific Gas and Electric Co	4911	E	707 765-5118	6170
Permanente Medical Group Inc	8011	D	707 765-3900	19861
Petaluma Health Center Inc	8011	D	707 559-7500	19869
Petaluma Jint Un High Schl Dst	6531	D	707 778-4677	11746
Photo TLC Inc	7384	C	415 462-0010	16954
Point Reyes Bird Observatory	8699	D	415 868-0371	25567
Point Reyes Bird Observatory	8733	D	707 781-2555	26795
Praetorian USA	7299	D	707 780-8020	13788
Pure Luxury Limousine Service	4119	C	800 626-5466	3831
Redwood Building Maint Co	7349	D	707 782-9100	14404
Reichardt Duck Farm Inc	0259	D	707 762-6314	460
Rooster Run Golf Club Inc	7992	E	707 778-1211	18778
San Francisco Reinsurance Co	6321	D	415 899-2000	10247
San Frncsco North/Petaluma KOA	7033	C	707 763-1492	13482
Securitas SEC Svcs USA Inc	7381	C	707 586-1393	16796
Sequoia Senior Solutions Inc	8322	C	707 763-6600	24208
Sonoma Cnty Ind Living Skills	8361	C	707 765-8444	24816
Sonoma Technology Inc	8748	D	707 665-9900	28059
Spring Hill Jersey Cheese Inc	5143	D	707 762-3446	8592
Srm Alliance Hospital Services (PA)	8062	B	707 778-1111	21912
St Joseph Health System	8062	E	707 778-2505	21918
Sunrise Farms LLC	5144	D	707 778-6450	8607
Sunrise of Petaluma	8361	D	707 776-2885	24831
Sunrise Senior Living Inc	8051	D	707 776-2885	20951
Sunset Aviation LLC (PA)	4522	C	707 775-2786	4887
Team Ghilotti Inc	1611	E	707 763-8700	1872
Transportation California Dept	1611	C	707 762-6641	1876
United Cmps Cnfrences Retreats (PA)	7032	E	707 762-3220	13472
United Parcel Service Inc OH	4215	C	650 952-5200	4465
Wells Fargo Insur Svcs USA Inc	6411	A	707 769-2900	10928

PETROLIA, CA - Humboldt County

	SIC	EMP	PHONE	ENTRY #
Gold Rush Coffee	5149	E	707 629-3460	8845

PICO RIVERA, CA - Los Angeles County

	SIC	EMP	PHONE	ENTRY #
ABF Freight System Inc	4213	E	323 773-2580	4098
Altamed Health Services Corp	8099	D	562 949-8717	22882
Amini Innovation Corp	5021	C	562 222-2500	6803
AP Express LLC	4731	D	562 236-2250	5027
AP Express International LLC	4789	D	562 236-2250	5215
Aurora World Inc	5092	C	562 205-1222	8036
California Hispanic Com	8069	C	562 942-9625	22118
Cellco Partnership	4812	D	562 942-8527	5389
Century 21 Excellence	6531	E	562 948-4553	11373
Chalmers Corporation	1541	D	562 948-4850	1413
Clarklift Los Angeles Inc	5084	C	562 949-1006	7834
Daniels Western Mt Packers Inc	5147	D	562 948-2254	8667
Fedex Office & Print Svcs Inc	4215	D	562 942-1953	4414
Grm Information MGT Services	8741	D	562 373-9000	27047
Grm Information MGT Svcs Inc	8741	D	562 373-9000	27048
Herb Thyme Farm Inc	0139	D	603 542-3690	26
Howards Appliances Inc	4225	D	626 288-4010	4574
Ionics Altrpure Wtr Crparation	5149	D	562 948-2188	8856
Jjj Floor Covering Inc (PA)	1752	D	562 692-9008	3123
Krikorian Premiere Theatre LLC	7922	D	562 205-3456	18403
L I Metal Systems	1761	E	562 948-5950	3183
Level 9 Security Services	7381	D	562 949-7180	16723
Los Angeles Unified School Dst	7389	D	562 654-9007	17302
Lucky Installations	1761	D	562 948-5950	3187
Manhole Adjusting Contrs Inc	1611	E	323 725-1387	1821
Mariner Health Care Inc	8051	D	562 942-7019	20768
Monterey Pnnsula Hrtclture Inc	0139	C	310 884-5911	29
Noble Rents Inc	7353	D	855 767-4424	14491
Pacific Logistics Corp (PA)	4731	C	562 478-4700	5142
Partschannel Inc	5013	C	562 654-3400	6752
Plaza De La Raza Child Develop (PA)	8351	D	562 776-1301	24504
Public Hlth Fndation Entps Inc	8099	D	562 801-2323	23034
Rivera Sanitarium Inc	8051	D	562 949-2591	20874
Riviera Nursing & Conva	8051	D	562 806-2576	20879
Rocket Farms Herbs Inc	0191	B	562 205-1900	389
Rolo Transportation Company	4212	D	562 463-1440	4056
Romans Transportation Inc	4225	D	562 463-1433	4630
Santa Teresa Conv Hospital	8062	D	562 948-1961	21863
Sectran Security Incorporated (PA)	7381	D	562 948-1446	16779
Three Sons Inc	5147	D	562 801-4100	8687
Unisource Solutions Inc (PA)	5021	C	562 654-3500	6833
United Pacific Waste	4953	D	562 699-7600	6572
United Rentals North Amer Inc	7359	C	562 695-0748	14586
UPS Ground Freight Inc	4213	D	562 801-1300	4292
Wm Recycle America LLC	4953	D	562 948-3888	6615
Your Executive Solutions	7361	A	562 388-4150	14824

PIEDMONT, CA - Alameda County

	SIC	EMP	PHONE	ENTRY #
Kinemed Inc	8731	D	510 655-6525	26543
Linda Beach Coop Pre-School	8351	E	510 547-4432	24475
Piedmont Cncil Boy Scouts Amer	8641	D	510 547-4493	25314

PINE GROVE, CA - Amador County

	SIC	EMP	PHONE	ENTRY #
Volcano Communications Company (PA)	4813	D	209 296-7502	5728
Volcano Vision Inc	4841	C	209 296-2288	6057

PINECREST, CA - Tuolumne County

	SIC	EMP	PHONE	ENTRY #
Dodge Ridge Corporation	7011	B	209 536-5300	12582

PINOLE, CA - Contra Costa County

	SIC	EMP	PHONE	ENTRY #
Geek Squad Inc	7379	D	800 433-5778	16383
Kaiser Foundation Hospitals	8011	A	510 243-4000	19637
Pathway To Choices Inc	8322	D	510 724-9044	24125
Pinole Assisted Living Cmnty	8059	D	510 758-1122	21348
Pinole Senior Center	8322	D	510 724-9800	24136
State Farm Mutl Auto Insur Co	6411	D	510 222-1102	10897

PIONEER, CA - Amador County

	SIC	EMP	PHONE	ENTRY #
Pacific Gas and Electric Co	4911	D	209 295-2651	6191

PIRU, CA - Ventura County

	SIC	EMP	PHONE	ENTRY #
La Verne Nursery Inc	0181	D	805 521-0111	299

PISMO BEACH, CA - San Luis Obispo County

	SIC	EMP	PHONE	ENTRY #
Castlblack Pismo Bch Owner LLC	7011	E	805 773-6020	12499
Castleblack Owner Holdings LLC	8741	E	805 773-6020	26962
Pacific Gas and Electric Co	4911	D	805 773-6109	6182
Pismo Beach Athletic Club	7991	E	805 773-3011	18670
Pismo Coast Village Inc	7011	D	805 773-5649	13101
T I C Hotels Inc	7011	D	805 773-4671	13335

PITTSBURG, CA - Contra Costa County

	SIC	EMP	PHONE	ENTRY #
A T Associates Inc (PA)	8059	D	925 808-6540	21123
Allied Food Distributors Inc	5149	D	925 432-1625	8794
Angelica Corporation	7213	C	925 473-2520	13531
Aquamatic Fire Protection Inc (PA)	7389	E	925 753-0420	16999
Arb Inc	4225	E	925 432-3649	4524
Comcast Corporation	4841	D	925 432-0500	5968
Concord Iron Works Inc	1791	D	925 432-0136	3380
First Baptist Head Start	8351	D	925 473-2000	24463
Harbor Freight Tools Usa Inc	4789	D	925 757-8435	5220
Hydrochem LLC	7349	D	925 432-1749	14323
La Clinica De La Raza Inc	8021	B	925 431-1250	20260
Lincoln Child Center Inc	8361	D	925 521-1270	24711
McCampbell Analytical Inc	8734	D	925 252-9262	26865
Pittsburg Care Center Ltd	8051	D	925 432-3831	20848
Pittsburg Pre-School & C	8351	D	925 439-2061	24501
Pittsburg Skilled Nursing	8051	D	925 808-6540	20849
Redwood Painting Co Inc	1721	C	925 432-4500	2483
SSC Pittsburg Operating Co LP	8059	A	925 427-4444	21381
State Preschool	8351	D	925 473-4380	24520

PLACENTIA, CA - Orange County

	SIC	EMP	PHONE	ENTRY #
Alta Vista Country Club LLC	7997	D	714 524-1591	18849
Bejac Corporation (PA)	5084	D	714 528-6224	7823
Car Wash of America	7542	E	714 528-0833	17834
Customline Professional	7336	D	714 996-1333	14141
Elljay Acoustics Inc	1742	B	714 961-1173	2892
Facility Solutions Group Inc	5063	E	714 993-3966	7441
GD Heil Inc	1795	C	714 687-9100	3455
Gsf Enterprises Inc	1542	D	714 524-9500	1559
Interface Rehab Inc	8049	A	714 646-8300	20328
Kana Pipeline Inc	1623	D	714 986-1400	1955
Linda Placentia-Yorba	4225	D	714 985-8775	4587
Linda Yorba Water District (PA)	4941	D	714 701-3000	6364
Micon Construction Cal Inc	1542	D	714 666-0203	1613
Osscim Inc	1761	E	714 680-0015	3195
Residence Inn By Marriott	7011	D	714 996-0555	13149
SGF Produce Holding Corp	5148	B	714 630-2170	8774
So California Ventures Ltd	1542	D	714 524-0021	1674
Spad Holdings LLC	7991	E	714 993-6003	18690
Sunrise Growers Inc (HQ)	5148	D	714 630-2170	8781
Tenet Healthsystem Medical	8069	D	714 993-2000	22182
Total Woman	7991	D	714 993-6003	18700

PLACERVILLE, CA - El Dorado County

	SIC	EMP	PHONE	ENTRY #
Centene Corporation	6324	D	530 626-5773	10268
Consortm On Reachng Excellnce	8748	E	510 540-4200	27887
County of El Dorado	8063	D	530 621-6210	22056
County of El Dorado	7349	D	530 621-5845	14269
County of El Dorado	8322	D	530 642-7130	23804
El Dorado Irrigation District	4941	B	530 622-4513	6346
El Dorado Savings Bank (PA)	6035	D	530 622-1492	9570

PLEASANTON, CA

	SIC	EMP	PHONE	ENTRY #
El Dorado Wtr & Shower Svc Inc	4941	E	530 622-8995	6347
ERA Realty Center	6531	D	530 295-2900	11495
Gladiolus Holdings LLC	8051	D	530 622-3400	20599
Gold Country Health Center Inc (PA)	8399	C	530 621-1100	24923
Hangtown Knnel CLB Plcrvlle CA	0752	D	530 622-4867	640
Harmony Home Health LLC	8082	D	916 933-9777	22450
Help At Home Inc	8322	D	916 933-9050	24004
Innovative Education MGT Inc	8741	D	530 295-3566	27065
Marshall Medical Center (PA)	8062	A	530 622-1441	21729
Marshall Medical Center	8011	D	530 626-2920	19732
Mother Lode Rehabilit	8361	C	530 622-4848	24741
NPS Marketing	8742	B	916 941-5510	27571
Placervlle Pnes Cnvlscent Hosp	8059	C	530 622-3400	21349
Quality In-Hmecare Specialists	8082	D	530 303-3477	22544
Shingle Sprng Trbal Gming Auth	7999	A	530 677-7000	19282
Summitview Child Treatment	8322	D	530 621-9800	24238
Summitview Child Treatment Ctr	8361	E	530 644-2412	24827
USDA Forest Service	0851	D	530 626-1546	1019
W F Hayward Co	1742	D	530 303-3030	2995
Western Slope Health Center	8051	D	530 622-6842	21033

PLAYA DEL REY, CA - Los Angeles County

	SIC	EMP	PHONE	ENTRY #
Automate Parking Inc	7521	D	310 674-3396	17711
Los Angeles Dept Wtr & Pwr	4939	D	310 524-8500	6304
Lpl Financial Holdings Inc	6282	B	310 823-4999	10160
Parking Concepts Inc	7521	D	310 322-5008	17737

PLAYA VISTA, CA - Los Angeles County

	SIC	EMP	PHONE	ENTRY #
72andsunny LLC	7311	C	310 215-9009	13808
Belkin International Inc (PA)	5065	B	310 751-5100	7533
Chownow Inc	7372	D	888 707-2469	15619
Convertro Inc	7371	E	800 797-0176	15108
Fullscreen Inc (HQ)	7311	D	310 202-3333	13852
Gehry Technologies Inc (HQ)	7371	D	310 862-1200	15201
Lee Burkhart Liu Inc (PA)	8712	D	310 829-2249	26221
Linksys LLC	5065	D	310 751-5100	7599
Lowermybills Inc (HQ)	7375	D	310 348-6800	16251
Luxury Link LLC	7011	E	310 215-8060	12933
Microsoft Corporation	7372	D	213 806-7300	15754
Pop Media Networks LLC (DH)	7929	D	323 856-4000	18488

PLEASANT GROVE, CA - Sutter County

	SIC	EMP	PHONE	ENTRY #
Holt of California (HQ)	5082	C	916 991-8200	7772
Sysco Sacramento Inc	5141	B	916 275-2714	8533
Withrow Cattle	0241	D	916 780-0364	441

PLEASANT HILL, CA - Contra Costa County

	SIC	EMP	PHONE	ENTRY #
Accentcare Home Health Cal Inc	8082	D	925 356-6066	22324
Aegis Senior Communities LLC	8082	D	925 588-7030	22345
Ahtna Environmental Inc	8999	D	907 433-0729	28110
Ascendantfx Capital USA Inc	6099	D	201 633-4667	9707
Assetmark Capital Corp	6211	D	925 521-1040	9959
AT&T Corp	4813	D	925 603-9476	5462
Brighter Beginnings (PA)	8322	E	510 903-7503	23695
Carlton Senior Living	8082	D	925 935-1001	22398
CDM Field Services Inc	7335	C	936 537-7786	14131
Contra Costa Country Club	7997	D	925 798-7135	18924
Courtyard Management Corp	7011	E	925 691-1444	12549
Crestwood Behavioral Hlth Inc	8063	D	925 938-8050	22066
Diablo Vly College Foundation (PA)	7389	D	925 685-1230	17122
Dreamctchers Empwerment Netwrk	8361	D	925 935-6630	24635
Geico Corporation	6411	D	415 330-9999	10726
Helios Healthcare LLC	8051	C	925 935-6630	20664
John Muir Health	8062	A	925 952-2887	21617
John Muir Physician Network	8062	A	925 685-0843	21623
Mark Scott Construction Inc (PA)	1542	E	925 944-0502	1608
Marriott International Inc	7011	C	925 689-1010	12976
Professional Healthcare At HM	8082	D	925 363-7876	22539
Quest Diagnostics Incorporated	8071	B	925 687-2514	22266
Solo W-2 Inc	8742	C	925 680-0200	27657
The Young Mens Chris Assoc of	8641	D	925 687-8900	25373
Tmg Financial	8742	D	925 989-7180	27688

PLEASANTON, CA - Alameda County

	SIC	EMP	PHONE	ENTRY #
1st United Services Credit Un (PA)	6062	D	800 649-0193	9649
ABM Janitorial Services Inc	7349	B	925 924-0270	14203
Acosta Inc	5141	D	925 600-3500	8447
Advantage Sales & Marketing	5141	C	925 463-5600	8448
Advantage Sales & Mktg LLC	5141	D	925 463-5600	8451
Aegis Enterprises Inc	1711	D	925 417-5550	2109
Alain Pinel Realtors Inc	6531	D	925 251-1111	11285
Alameda County AG Fair Assn	7999	D	925 426-7600	19132
American Baptist Homes of West (PA)	8059	D	925 924-7100	21137
American Property Management	7011	C	925 463-8000	12383
Anixter Inc	5063	E	925 469-8500	7415
AOC Technologies Inc	5051	B	925 875-0808	7357
Ata Retail Services LLC (PA)	5199	D	925 621-4700	9245
Automatic Data Processing Inc	7374	D	925 251-5300	16099
Axis Community Health Inc	8093	D	925 462-1755	22662
Better Living Brands LLC	7389	E	888 723-3929	17031
Black Tie Transportation LLC	4119	C	925 847-0747	3774
Blackhawk Network Inc (HQ)	6099	A	925 226-9990	9710
Blackhawk Network Holdings Inc (PA)	6099	B	925 226-9990	9711
Blackrock Logistics Inc	4731	E	925 523-3878	5034
Bricsnet FM America Inc	7379	D	202 756-1840	16331
Brightview Landscape Svcs Inc	0781	B	925 373-9500	753
Buxton Consulting	8748	D	925 467-0700	27858
C & C Security Patrol Inc	7381	D	925 227-1400	16587
C S G Consultants Inc	8711	E	925 931-0370	25712
Calatlantic Group Inc	1531	E	925 847-8700	1358
Califrnia Yuth Soccer Assn Inc	8699	D	925 426-5437	25512
Can-AM Plumbing Inc	1711	C	925 846-1833	2175
Capincrouse LLP	8721	D	925 201-1187	26306
Castlewood Country Club	7997	D	925 846-2871	18913
Ce2 Kleinfelder JV	8711	D	925 463-7301	25729
Center Cnslng Edctn & Crisis	8322	D	925 462-1755	23721
Citimortgage Inc	6211	E	925 730-3800	9986
CJ Model Home Maintenance Inc	7349	D	925 485-3280	14252
Clarity Medical Systems Inc	5047	D	925 463-7984	7258
Clorox Services Company	8741	D	925 425-6748	26972
Co-Sales Company	5141	D	925 327-7322	8465
Comcast Corporation	4841	D	925 249-2060	5951
Commerce West Insurance Co	6141	D	925 730-6400	9743
Construction Testing Services (PA)	8734	D	925 462-5151	26839
Conti Life Comm Plea LLC	7389	D	925 227-6800	17093
Convergint Technologies LLC	7382	E	510 300-2800	16875
Cornerstone Affiliates Inc	8322	A	925 924-7100	23787
Cpu Technology Inc	8731	D	925 398-7659	26501
Crossmark Incorporated	5141	B	925 463-3555	8471
D+H USA Corporation	7372	B	925 463-8356	15635
Dahlin Group Inc (PA)	8712	D	925 251-7200	26180
Dan Lofgren	7349	D	925 846-6632	14280
Deloitte & Touche LLP	8721	C	415 782-4020	26326
Deploy Hr Inc	7361	D	925 426-1010	14636
Diamond Concessions LLC	8742	D	925 226-2889	27410
Dimension Data North Amer Inc	7373	D	925 226-8378	15934
Documentum Inc	7372	A	925 600-6800	15643
Dublin San Ramon Services Dist	4941	D	925 846-4565	6341
E-Loan Inc (DH)	6163	D	925 847-6200	9920
Elavon Inc	7375	B	925 734-8939	16233
Ellie Mae Inc (PA)	7371	C	925 227-7000	15160
EMC Corporation	5045	D	925 948-9000	7124
Ernst & Young LLP	8721	D	925 734-6388	26348
Excel Building Services LLC	7349	A	650 755-0900	14293
Farmers Group Inc	6311	B	925 847-3100	10207
Federal Express Corporation	7389	D	800 463-3339	17165
Forsys Inc	7379	D	844 409-0510	16373
Gatan Inc (HQ)	8711	D	925 463-0200	25829
Geniuscom Incorporated	7379	D	650 931-1382	16390
Glass Pak Inc	4783	D	707 207-0400	5200
Global Cellular Inc	5065	D	925 469-9039	7574
Gtt Communications (mp) Inc (DH)	4813	C	925 201-2500	5627
Guardian Computer Support	7378	D	925 251-8800	16297
Guardsmark LLC	7381	B	925 484-4412	16678
Hatch Mott Macdonald Group Inc	8711	D	925 469-8010	25851
Hitachi High Tech Amer Inc	5065	D	925 218-2800	7578
Jpmorgan Xign Corporation	8721	D	925 469-9446	26381
Kaiser Foundation Hospitals	8062	B	925 598-2799	21645
Kaiser Foundation Hospitals	8062	B	925 847-5000	21649
Kaiser Fundation Hlth Plan Inc	6324	D	510 271-5800	10353
Kiewit Infrastructure West Co	1611	D	925 462-1088	1810
Kleinfelder Inc	8711	D	925 484-1700	25923
Kraft Heinz Foods Company	5149	B	925 469-0057	8869
Legacy Vulcan Corp	1442	D	925 373-1802	1108
Leisure Sports Inc	6719	B	925 942-6311	12071
Leisure Sports Inc	7999	B	925 934-4050	19236
Mackay Smps Civil Engineers Inc (PA)	8711	D	925 416-1790	25949
Market Smart Inc	5141	D	925 846-6237	8493
Mason-Mcduffie Real Estate Inc	6531	D	925 734-5000	11666
McM Partners Inc	6531	D	925 463-9500	11669
Meadowbrook Meat Company Inc	5142	D	252 985-7200	8561
Megapath Cloud Company LLC (PA)	4813	D	925 201-2500	5655
North American Title Co Inc	6361	D	925 399-3000	10532
Oc IV A California LP	7538	E	925 734-5800	17808
On-Time AC & Htg Inc (PA)	1711	C	925 444-4444	2310
Optimum Design Associates Inc (PA)	8711	D	925 401-2004	25999
Oracle Corporation	7372	B	877 767-2253	15799
Oracle Systems Corporation	7372	B	925 694-3000	15809
Patelco Credit Union (PA)	6061	C	800 358-8228	9621
Pinnacle Document Systems (PA)	5044	D	925 417-8400	7063
Pleasant Canyon Hotel Inc	7011	E	925 847-0535	13103
Pleasanton Unified School Dst	7336	B	925 426-5500	14159

Employment Codes: A=Over 500 employees, B=251-500, C=101-250, D=51-100, E=45-50

PLEASANTON, CA

Company	SIC	EMP	PHONE	ENTRY #
Plex Systems Inc	7374	C	248 391-8001	16170
Ponderosa Homes Inc	6552	D	925 460-8900	12002
Product Quality Partners Inc	7379	D	925 484-6491	16463
Prolifics Testing Inc	7371	D	925 485-9535	15398
Protection One Inc	7382	E	925 251-9088	16914
Psinapse Technology Ltd	7361	D	925 225-0400	14740
Pulte Home Corporation	1521	D	925 249-3200	1239
Pyramid Advisors LLC	7011	D	925 847-6000	13114
Quality Auto Craft Inc	7538	A	925 426-0120	17812
Raico Inc	7371	C	925 271-5555	15406
Ray A Morgan Company	7371	D	925 400-4160	15409
Roche Molecular Systems Inc (DH)	8731	B	925 730-8000	26596
Rs Calibration Services Inc	7699	E	925 462-4217	18008
Ruby Hill Golf Club LLC	7997	D	925 417-5840	19051
Sabah International Inc (PA)	1731	D	925 734-5750	2721
Schneider Electric Usa Inc	5063	D	925 462-0986	7470
Servicemax Inc (PA)	7371	D	925 965-7859	15449
Sheraton Corporation	7011	B	925 463-3330	13245
Shooter & Butts Inc	0781	E	925 460-5155	796
Signature Properties Inc	6552	D	925 463-1122	12010
Silicon Valley Bank	6021	D	408 654-7730	9422
Simbol Inc (PA)	8731	D	925 226-7400	26607
Simpson Strong-Tie Intl Inc	5051	D	925 560-9000	7403
Six Continents Hotels Inc	7011	D	925 847-6000	13266
Smartzip Analytics Inc	6531	D	925 218-1900	11846
Spacetone Acoustics Inc	1742	E	925 931-0749	2981
Specialty Risk Services Inc	6411	C	877 809-9478	10875
State Compensation Insur Fund	6331	C	925 523-5000	10475
State Compensation Insur Fund	6331	C	888 782-8338	10476
Steelwedge Software Inc (PA)	7372	D	925 460-1700	15848
Sunbelt Controls Inc	7623	E	925 660-3900	17924
Telecom Technology Svcs Inc	8748	C	925 224-7812	28070
Terminix Intl Co Ltd Partnr	7342	D	925 460-5063	14193
The For Hospital Committee (DH)	8062	B	925 847-3000	21966
Toll Brothers Inc	1521	D	925 855-0260	1273
Toolwire Inc	7371	D	925 227-8500	15507
Total Renal Care Inc	8092	E	925 737-0120	22643
Transbay Fire Protection Inc (PA)	1796	E	925 846-9484	3481
Trevi Partners A Calif LP (PA)	7011	C	925 225-4000	13358
Unisource Packaging Inc	5113	C	925 227-6000	8218
Veeva Systems Inc (PA)	7372	C	925 452-6500	15872
Verizon Wireless Inc	4812	C	925 224-9868	5432
Wells Fargo Bank National Assn	6021	D	925 463-1983	9450
West Valley Engineering Inc	7361	D	925 416-9707	14818
Workday Inc (PA)	7371	D	925 951-9000	15547
Youngs Market Company LLC	5182	B	510 475-2200	9120
Zantaz Inc (DH)	7371	D	925 598-3000	15556
Zenith Insurance Company	6311	D	925 460-0600	10229

PLS VRDS PNSL, CA - Los Angeles County

Company	SIC	EMP	PHONE	ENTRY #
Aichinger International Inc	5012	D	310 375-1533	6663
Episcopal Communities & Servic	8051	D	310 544-2204	20547

PLYMOUTH, CA - Amador County

Company	SIC	EMP	PHONE	ENTRY #
Borjon Iscander	0761	C	209 245-6289	654

POINT ARENA, CA - Mendocino County

Company	SIC	EMP	PHONE	ENTRY #
Manchester Band Pomo Indians	8322	D	707 882-2788	24076

POINT REYES STATION, CA - Marin County

Company	SIC	EMP	PHONE	ENTRY #
Pacific Slope Tree Coop Inc	0783	E	415 663-1300	996

POMONA, CA - Los Angeles County

Company	SIC	EMP	PHONE	ENTRY #
American National Red Cross	8099	A	909 859-7006	22886
Angelica Textile Services Inc	7213	D	909 623-5135	13533
Anka Behavioral Health Inc	8011	C	909 622-8217	19350
Behavioral Health Services Inc	8322	D	909 865-2336	23681
Braun Linen Service Inc	7211	D	909 623-2678	13501
Casa Colin Comprehensive	8093	C	909 596-7733	22674
Casa Colina Inc (PA)	8322	B	909 596-7733	23705
Casa Colina Hospital and Cente (HQ)	8062	B	909 596-7733	21471
Central Reference Lab Inc (PA)	8071	D	909 861-6966	22198
Centrescapes Inc	0782	D	909 392-3303	822
Chino Valley Healthcare Center	8051	D	909 628-1245	20456
Circle Wood Services Inc	8741	D	909 784-0733	26966
City of Pomona	8399	B	909 397-5506	24890
City of Pomona	4953	C	909 620-2361	6460
Coan Construction Co Inc	1771	D	909 868-6812	3243
Continental Agency Inc (PA)	4731	D	909 595-8884	5051
Coptic Clinics	8011	D	562 900-2692	19461
Country Oaks Partners LLC	8051	D	909 622-1067	20475
County of Los Angeles	8322	C	909 620-3189	23822
County of Los Angeles	8111	D	909 620-3330	23173
County of Los Angeles	7992	D	909 629-1166	18727
County of Los Angeles	8322	D	909 469-4500	23846
Dedicated Fleet Systems Inc (PA)	4212	D	909 590-8209	4002
DJ Scheffler Inc (PA)	1741	E	909 595-2924	2811
F & B Inc	7692	E	909 203-8436	17953
Fairplex Child Development Ctr	8351	D	909 623-3899	24461
Fairplex Enterprises Inc	7999	D	909 623-3111	19207
FBC Industries (PA)	6552	D	909 627-6131	11967
Ferguson Enterprises Inc	5074	C	909 364-8700	7714
Ferguson Fire Fabrication Inc (DH)	5074	D	909 517-3085	7719
Frank S Smith Masonry Inc	1741	D	909 468-0525	2815
Furniture Trnsp Systems	4731	D	909 869-1200	5081
Henkels & McCoy Inc	1623	D	925 493-7800	1938
Howard Roofing Company Inc	1761	D	909 622-5598	3179
Hsbc Finance Corporation	6141	A	909 623-3355	9752
Inland Valley Partners LLC	8049	C	909 623-7100	20322
Inter-Valley Health Plan Inc	6324	D	909 623-6333	10292
K K W Trucking Inc (PA)	4213	C	909 869-1200	4201
Keith T Kusunis MD	8093	D	909 469-9494	22758
Landmark Medical Services Inc	8063	D	909 593-2585	22079
Latara Enterprise Inc (PA)	8071	C	909 623-9301	22234
LDI Transportation Inc	4214	D	909 620-7001	4356
Lexmar Distribution Inc	4214	D	909 620-7001	4358
Longwood Management Corp	6513	D	818 884-7100	11160
Los Angeles County Fair Assn (PA)	7999	D	909 623-3111	19240
Master Disposal Co	4953	E	626 444-6789	6502
Merchants Building Maint Co	7349	C	909 622-8260	14355
MJB Partners LLC	8051	D	909 623-2481	20794
Murcor Inc	6531	D	909 623-4001	11702
New York Life Insurance Co	6411	D	909 902-1027	10803
Nmc Group Inc	5085	D	909 451-2290	7943
NW Packaging LLC (PA)	5199	D	909 706-3627	9283
Pomona Housing Partners LP	6531	E	909 622-1010	11756
Pomona Valley Hospital Med Ctr (PA)	8062	A	909 865-9500	21802
Pomona Valley Hospital Med Ctr	8069	C	909 865-9700	22161
Prototypes Centers For Innov	8322	D	909 624-1233	24142
Rwp Transfer Inc	5099	E	909 868-6882	8137
San Gabriel/Pomona Valleys	8322	B	909 620-7722	24186
Schaefer Ambulance Service Inc	4119	D	626 333-4533	3843
Second Image National LLC	7335	D	909 445-8080	14133
Securitas SEC Svcs USA Inc	7381	C	909 865-4356	16804
Southern California Edison Co	4911	D	909 469-0251	6227
Spectra Company	1741	C	909 599-0760	2835
Spiniello Companies	1623	D	909 629-1000	1999
Starwood Hotels & Resorts	7011	C	909 622-2220	13303
Sunbridge Braswell Entps Inc	8051	E	909 622-1069	20937
Sunbridge Braswell Entps Inc	8051	C	909 628-6024	20938
T McGee Electric Inc	1731	D	909 591-6461	2764
Tri City Mental Health Center	8093	D	909 784-3200	22853
Trinity Health Systems	8051	E	949 623-2481	20995
Ultimate Removal Inc	1795	D	909 524-0800	3471
Valley Nurses	8049	D	714 549-2512	20360
W Why W Enterprises Inc	4214	D	626 969-4292	4390
Whitefield Medical Lab Inc (PA)	8071	E	909 625-2114	22299
Yamamoto of Orient Inc (HQ)	5149	C	909 594-7356	8957

PORT HUENEME, CA - Ventura County

Company	SIC	EMP	PHONE	ENTRY #
Advantedge Technology Inc	8711	D	805 488-0405	25618
Alion Science and Tech Corp	8711	D	805 488-8761	25648
Cecos	8711	E	805 982-5400	25730
Interntional Longshore Whse Un	7361	D	805 488-2944	14687
Nasdaq Information Tech Ctr	7374	D	805 982-2707	16165
Oxnard Beach Hotel LP	7011	E	805 488-6455	13054
Pride Industries	1522	C	805 985-8481	1332
United States Dept of Navy	8011	A	805 982-6392	20159
United States Dept of Navy	8011	A	805 982-6370	20161
Waggoners Trucking	4213	D	800 999-9097	4301

PORTER RANCH, CA - Los Angeles County

Company	SIC	EMP	PHONE	ENTRY #
Coast To Coast Realty	6531	D	818 360-2609	11400

PORTERVILLE, CA - Tulare County

Company	SIC	EMP	PHONE	ENTRY #
Baird-Neece Packing Corp	0723	C	559 784-3393	510
Bank of Sierra (HQ)	6022	C	559 782-4300	9474
Developmental Svcs Cal Dept	8051	A	559 782-2222	20519
E M Tharp Inc (PA)	5012	D	559 782-5800	6674
Exeter Packers Inc	0723	C	559 784-8820	530
Foster Farms LLC	0252	B	559 793-5501	445
Gaithers Family Home	8059	E	559 781-0301	21230
Good Shepherd Lutheran Hm of W (PA)	8361	D	559 791-2000	24672
Mitch Brown Construction Inc	1629	D	559 781-6389	2068
Moyles Central Vly Hlth Care	8051	D	559 782-1509	20802
Nuvi Global	5047	A	559 306-2646	7287
Pro Document Solutions Inc	5112	D	559 719-1281	8175
R & G Enterprises	0722	C	559 781-1351	500
Raul Acevedo	0783	E	559 791-1304	997
River Island Country Club Inc	7997	D	559 781-2917	19043
Salvador Martinez	0761	C	559 781-5150	684
Sierra Valley Rehab Center	8059	C	559 784-7375	21370
Sierra View Local Hospital Dst (PA)	8011	C	559 784-1110	20004

GEOGRAPHIC SECTION

RANCHO CORDOVA, CA

Company	SIC	EMP	PHONE	ENTRY #
Sierra View Local Hospital Dst	8062	B	559 781-7877	21892
Sun Villa Inc	8051	C	559 784-6644	20936
Tharp Truck Rental Inc (PA)	7699	D	559 782-5800	18024
Tule River Indian Hlth Ctr Inc	8093	D	559 784-2316	22854
Wal-Mart Stores Inc	4225	B	559 783-1109	4662
Wescordon Incorporated (PA)	8051	D	559 784-8371	21028

PORTOLA, CA - Plumas County

Company	SIC	EMP	PHONE	ENTRY #
Eastern Plumas Health Care (PA)	8099	C	530 832-4277	22952

PORTOLA VALLEY, CA - San Mateo County

Company	SIC	EMP	PHONE	ENTRY #
Boething Treeland Farms Inc	0811	A	650 851-4770	1004
Intuit Inc	7372	D	650 944-2840	15714
McClenahan Pest Control Inc	7342	E	650 326-8781	14189
Norse Corp	7382	D	650 513-2881	16905
Pointspeed Inc	7379	D	650 638-3720	16458
SP McClenahan Co	0783	D	650 326-8781	998

PORTOLA VALLY, CA - San Mateo County

Company	SIC	EMP	PHONE	ENTRY #
Semans Communications (PA)	1731	D	650 529-9984	2729

POTRERO, CA - San Diego County

Company	SIC	EMP	PHONE	ENTRY #
Rancho De Sus Ninos Inc	8361	D	619 661-9232	24777

POTTER VALLEY, CA - Mendocino County

Company	SIC	EMP	PHONE	ENTRY #
McFadden Farm	0112	E	707 743-1122	5

POWAY, CA - San Diego County

Company	SIC	EMP	PHONE	ENTRY #
American Golf Corporation	7997	E	760 737-9762	18859
Arch Health Partners Inc (HQ)	8742	C	858 675-3100	27331
Bay City Equipment Inds Inc	5063	D	619 938-8200	7418
Benchmark Landscape Inc	0782	E	858 513-7190	812
Braswells Villa Monte Vista	8059	E	858 487-6242	21160
Brieck Restoration Inc	1521	E	858 679-9928	1139
Centre Care Management Co LLC	8011	D	858 613-6255	19422
Climatec LLC	1731	E	858 391-7000	2552
Community Dev Inst Head Start	8351	D	858 668-2985	24446
Concrete Images International	1771	D	858 676-1253	3248
Corodata Corporation (PA)	4226	D	858 748-1100	4681
Corovan Corporation (PA)	4214	C	858 762-8100	4336
Corovan Moving & Storage Co (HQ)	4214	D	858 748-1100	4337
D and D Concrete Cnstr Inc	1771	D	619 518-9737	3252
Decision Sciences Intl Corp	5065	D	858 602-1600	7553
Decision Sciences Intl Corp	7371	D	858 571-1900	15128
Eappraiseit LLC (PA)	6531	C	800 281-6200	11487
Electronic Control Systems LLC	1731	E	858 513-1911	2587
Ems Construction Inc	1542	D	858 679-8292	1549
First American Appraisal Svcs (HQ)	6531	C	619 938-7078	11522
Geico General Insurance Co	6411	B	858 848-8200	10728
Generation Contracting & Emerg	1521	E	858 679-9928	1183
Gould Electric Inc	1731	C	858 486-1727	2599
Honeywell International Inc	8711	D	858 679-4140	25869
Ickler Electric Corporation	1731	E	858 486-1585	2617
Intelligent Automation Corp	8711	E	858 679-4140	25883
Kiewit Corporation	1542	D	858 208-4285	1593
Kiewit Infrastructure West Co	1622	D	360 693-1478	1895
Kiewit Infrastructure West Co	1611	D	858 486-3410	1812
Law Offices of Thomas W	8111	C	858 883-2000	23378
Lorber Greenfield & Polito LLP (PA)	8111	E	858 486-6757	23408
Maderas Golf Club	7997	D	858 451-8100	18988
Palomar Health	8062	B	858 613-4000	21781
Palomar Health	8072	B	858 613-4000	22312
Picture It On Canvas Inc	7384	D	858 679-1200	16955
Pkl Services Inc	7699	C	858 679-1755	18000
Pomerado Operations LLC	8051	D	858 487-6242	20857
Prestige Concrete	1771	D	858 679-2772	3315
Quality Reinforcing Inc	1791	C	858 748-8400	3396
Rax Inc	5091	E	858 715-2500	8026
Rutledge Claims Management Inc	7322	D	858 888-2000	14045
San Diego Bay Area Elc Inc	1731	D	858 748-2060	2723
Stoneridge Country Club	7997	D	858 487-2117	19098
Sysco San Diego Inc	5141	B	858 513-7300	8534
T G T Enterprises Inc	7331	C	858 413-0300	14092
Tekworks Inc (PA)	7389	C	858 668-1705	17522
Wr Chavez Construction Inc	1542	D	858 375-2100	1719

QUAIL VALLEY, CA - Riverside County

Company	SIC	EMP	PHONE	ENTRY #
Francois Annanie	7349	E	619 846-3438	14302

QUINCY, CA - Plumas County

Company	SIC	EMP	PHONE	ENTRY #
Artimisa & Co	8711	D	530 283-3700	25667
CF Quincy LLC	8051	D	530 283-2110	20447
Plumas District Hospital (PA)	8062	C	530 283-2121	21801
Plumas District Hospital	8011	D	530 283-0650	19876
Plumas Rural Services	8322	D	530 283-2725	24138
Sierra Cscade Fmly Opprtnities (PA)	8351	D	530 283-1242	24515

RAMONA, CA - San Diego County

Company	SIC	EMP	PHONE	ENTRY #
Burch Construction Company Inc	1542	E	760 788-9370	1514
Casa De Las Campanas Inc	8361	C	760 789-4746	24583
Famous Ramona Water Inc	5149	E	760 789-0174	8835
Prudential California Realty	6531	D	858 487-3520	11778
San Diego Country Estates Assn	8641	C	760 789-3788	25332
Spe Go Holdings Inc	7997	E	858 638-0672	19092
Triton Logistics Corporation	4731	D	619 822-8832	5181
United Power Contractors Inc	1623	D	760 735-8028	2005

RANCHO CORDOVA, CA - Sacramento County

Company	SIC	EMP	PHONE	ENTRY #
A B C D Associates	8051	C	916 363-4843	20366
Accentcare HM Hlth Scrmnto Inc	8082	D	916 852-5888	22322
Ad Land Venture LP	0782	D	916 853-9015	804
AmeriGas Propane LP	5172	C	916 852-7400	9012
AT&T Services Inc	4813	C	916 638-6096	5540
Austin Security Patrol Inc	7381	D	916 631-9877	16566
Bergelectric Corp	1731	D	916 636-1880	2532
Bissell Brothers Janitorial	7349	D	916 635-1852	14238
Capital Engineering Cons (PA)	8711	D	916 851-3500	25717
Child Support Svcs Cal Dept (DH)	8322	C	916 464-5000	23737
Cisco Webex LLC	4813	E	916 861-3135	5576
Clark Pest Ctrl Stockton Inc	7342	C	916 635-7770	14182
Cldwll/Vrsar A Brown Jint Vntr	8711	C	916 444-0123	25746
Courtyard Management Corp	7011	E	916 638-3800	12550
Dignity Health	8062	C	916 861-1100	21531
Dignity Health	8011	C	916 851-2153	19497
Dignity Health Med Foundation	8099	A	916 379-2840	22942
Dignity Health Med Foundation (PA)	8099	A	916 379-2840	22944
Ducks Unlimited Inc	0971	E	916 852-2000	1020
Eyefinity Inc	7371	D	877 481-4455	15179
Federal HM Ln Bnk San Frncisco	6141	C	916 851-6900	9746
Firemans Fund Insurance Co	6331	C	916 852-4500	10418
Firemans Fund Insurance Co	6331	C	949 255-1981	10420
Franklin Tmpleton Inv Svcs LLC	6282	C	650 312-2000	10146
Franklin Tmpleton Inv Svcs LLC (DH)	6211	A	916 463-1500	10003
Gei Consultants Inc	8744	D	916 631-4500	27786
General Electric Capital Corp	6153	D	916 286-8020	9783
General Pool & Spa Supply Inc (PA)	5091	D	916 853-2401	8019
Health Net Federal Svcs LLC (DH)	6324	A	916 935-5000	10288
Heritage Community Credit Un	6061	E	916 364-1700	9605
Home Instead Senior Care	8082	D	916 920-2273	22465
HP Enterprise Services LLC	7374	A	916 636-1000	16140
Infor (us) Inc	7372	C	916 921-0883	15700
Infor Public Sector Inc (DH)	7372	C	916 921-0883	15701
Kaiser Foundation Hospitals	8062	C	916 631-3088	21658
Keenan & Associates	6411	D	916 858-2981	10758
Kleinfelder Inc	8711	C	916 366-1701	25924
Kls Air Express Inc (PA)	4731	D	916 373-3353	5108
Landcare USA LLC	0782	D	916 635-0936	896
Lennar Homes Inc	1531	C	916 517-4950	1375
LLP Moss Adams	8721	D	916 503-8100	26396
Lyle Company	8748	D	916 266-7000	27979
Maximus Inc	8082	C	916 364-6610	22506
Mercy Healthcare Sacramento (HQ)	8062	B	916 379-2871	21737
Mercy Healthcare Sacramento	4225	B	916 851-3800	4599
Mercy Methodist Hospital	8062	A	916 379-2996	21745
Michael Baker Intl Inc	8748	D	916 361-8384	27986
Mitchell Jones Concrete Inc	1771	C	916 638-6870	3297
Nec Corporation of America	7371	D	916 636-5740	15324
Nehemiah Construction Inc	1611	E	707 746-6815	1833
Nevada Republic Electric N Inc	1731	C	916 294-0140	2666
Nightingale Vantagemed Corp (HQ)	7372	D	916 638-4744	15778
North State Elec Contrs Inc	1731	D	916 572-0571	2668
Pacific Coast Companies Inc	7389	C	916 631-6500	17390
Paramount Equity Mortgage LLC	6162	C	916 290-9999	9881
Permanente Medical Group Inc	8011	C	916 631-3000	19865
Pick Pull Auto Dismantling Inc (HQ)	5093	E	916 689-2000	8079
Presidio Hotel Group LLC	7011	D	916 631-7500	13110
Progressive West Insurance Co	6411	B	916 864-6000	10840
Rci Electric Inc	1731	D	916 858-8000	2697
Ricoh Usa Inc	7371	A	916 638-3333	15422
River City Auto Recovery Inc	7389	D	916 851-1100	17465
Robert Half International Inc	7361	D	916 852-1705	14763
Ron Nurss Inc	1771	D	916 631-9761	3323
Russell Mechanical Inc	1711	D	916 635-2522	2354
Scott Silva Concrete Inc	1771	D	916 859-0593	3328
Select Hotels Group LLC	7011	E	916 638-4141	13232
Sierra PCF HM & Comfort Inc	5075	D	916 638-0543	7746
Superior Vision Services Inc (PA)	6324	B	916 859-6218	10383
Technology Services Cal Dept	7374	E	916 464-3747	16198
Tetra Tech Ec Inc	8748	A	916 852-8300	28074
True North Ar LLC	7361	A	916 369-9850	14809
Two Rivers Demolition Inc	1795	D	916 638-6775	3470
Urata & Sons Cement Inc	1771	D	916 638-5364	3344

Employment Codes: A=Over 500 employees, B=251-500, C=101-250, D=51-100, E=45-50

RANCHO CORDOVA, CA

	SIC	EMP	PHONE	ENTRY #
Varis LLC	8742	D	916 294-0860	27708
Verizon Bus Netwrk Svcs Inc	4813	C	916 779-5600	5715
Vision Service Plan (PA)	6324	A	916 851-5000	10390
Vsp Holding Company Inc	6324	D	916 851-5000	10391
Wells Fargo Coml Dist Fin LLC	6153	D	916 636-2020	9790
Wells Fargo Insur Svcs USA Inc	6411	C	916 589-8000	10931
Wells Fargo Insurance Svcs Inc	6411	D	916 231-3400	10934
Western Alliance Bank	6022	D	916 851-6800	9540
William E Heinselman	8711	E	916 920-0220	26149
Wireless Store Inc	4899	D	916 206-3600	6100

RANCHO CUCAMONGA, CA - San Bernardino County

	SIC	EMP	PHONE	ENTRY #
24 Hour Fitness Usa Inc	7991	D	909 944-1000	18586
AB Health Inc	6411	E	949 464-4300	10577
ABM Janitorial Services Inc	7349	C	909 987-3700	14205
ABM Office Solutions Inc	5021	D	909 527-8145	6799
Agent Franchise LLC	6321	D	949 930-5025	10231
Allmark Inc (PA)	6531	D	909 989-7556	11294
Aloft Ontario-Rancho Cucamonga	7011	D	909 484-2018	12381
American Med	4119	C	909 948-1714	3746
Apex Staffing Service	7363	E	909 941-0267	14839
Artic Mechanical Inc (PA)	1711	D	909 980-2539	2152
Assistance League Foothill Com	8399	D	909 987-2813	24875
AT&T Corp	4813	D	909 646-9644	5467
Automatic Data Processing Inc	7374	D	909 477-4266	16091
Automobile Club Southern Cal	6411	C	909 980-0233	10639
Bowlmor AMF Corp	7933	E	909 945-9392	18513
Bradshaw International Inc (PA)	5023	B	909 476-3884	6849
Branlyn Prominence Inc (PA)	8082	D	909 476-9030	22380
C A Hofmann Construction Inc	1742	E	909 484-5888	2868
C W Construction Inc	1751	D	909 989-9099	3034
California Empire Bancorp Inc	6162	E	909 484-7988	9824
Ccna Vons Athletes For Life	8699	D	805 453-2499	25515
CDM Constructors Inc	1623	D	909 579-3500	1918
Cellco Partnership	4812	C	909 899-8910	5377
Century 21 Home Realtors	6531	D	909 980-8000	11377
Cerenzia Foods Inc	5141	D	909 989-4000	8463
Childrens Btq At Stevens Hope	5137	C	909 256-0100	8374
CMC Fontana Steel	1791	B	909 899-9993	3377
CMC Rebar	1791	B	909 899-9993	3378
Collection Technology Inc	7322	D	800 743-4284	14027
Corvel Corporation	6411	C	209 257-3700	10680
County of San Bernardino	8322	D	909 945-4000	23893
CU Cooperative Systems Inc (PA)	6099	B	909 948-2500	9715
Cucamonga Valley Water Dst	4941	D	909 987-2591	6339
Davis Brothers Framing Inc	1751	C	909 944-4899	3042
Deardens	4225	E	909 942-4599	4540
Diplomatic Security Svcs LLC	7381	E	909 463-8409	16626
Empire Estates Inc	6531	D	909 980-3100	11492
Etiwanda Historical Society	8412	D	909 899-8432	25020
Evolution Fresh Inc (HQ)	5148	D	909 478-0895	8722
Excellnce of Inland Empire Inc	6531	C	909 758-4311	11500
Falken Tire Holdings Inc	5014	C	800 723-2553	6784
Farmers Insurance Exchange	6411	A	909 758-7060	10711
Fox Transportation Inc (PA)	8748	C	909 291-4646	27925
Friends of Bear Gulch	8699	D	909 989-9396	25534
Gamut Construction Company Inc	1521	D	909 948-0500	1181
General Coatings Corporation	1721	C	909 204-4150	2444
General Motors LLC	4225	D	800 521-7300	4555
Gentex Corporation	8731	D	909 481-7667	26526
Giti Tire (usa) Ltd (DH)	5014	D	909 527-8800	6785
Harrison Iyke	7382	D	909 463-8409	16886
Hibshman Trading Corporation	5137	D	909 581-1800	8387
Hoffman Southwest Corp	7699	D	909 397-0567	17980
Honeyville Inc	4221	D	909 980-9500	4482
Hubzone-Cw Driver Joint Ventr	7389	D	909 484-0933	17227
In-Roads Creative Programs	8322	B	909 989-9944	24019
Inland Empire Health Plan (PA)	6321	A	909 890-2000	10241
Inland Empire Real Estate	6531	E	909 944-2070	11583
Inland Empire Utilities Agency	4941	D	909 993-1755	6355
Iron Mountain Incorporated	4226	D	909 484-4333	4690
J B Hunt Transport Inc	4213	C	909 466-5361	4199
JB Upland Ltd Liability Co	8742	E	909 944-5456	27493
Jones/Covey Group Incorporated	1799	D	888 972-7581	3540
Just Mortgage Inc	6162	C	562 908-5000	9865
Kaiser Foundation Hospitals	8011	A	888 750-0036	19598
Katella Property Solutions Inc	1521	E	909 896-4489	1201
Kings Seafood Company LLC	5146	D	909 803-1280	8636
Knd Development 55 LLC	8062	D	909 581-6400	21693
L & R Distributors Inc	5131	B	909 980-3807	8315
Ledesma & Meyer Cnstr Co Inc	1542	D	909 297-1100	1600
Ledesma & Meyer Dev Inc	8741	D	909 476-0590	27111
Lewis Family Playhouse	8699	D	909 477-2775	25549
Lexxiom Inc	8741	B	909 481-2536	27114
M & G Jewelers Inc	7631	D	909 989-2929	17950
Majesty One Properties Inc	6531	C	909 980-8000	11653
McGuire Talent Inc	7922	D	909 527-7006	18414
Meadowbrook Meat Company Inc	5147	C	909 484-6100	8676
Miracle Home Health Agency	8082	E	562 653-0668	22508
Monoprice Inc	5099	C	909 989-6887	8126
National Cmnty Renaissance Cal (PA)	6552	D	909 483-2444	11987
National Community Renaissance (PA)	7041	D	909 483-2444	13494
National Mentor Inc	8331	D	909 483-2505	24368
Network Intgrtion Partners Inc	7373	D	909 919-2800	16009
Newco Distributors Inc	5191	D	909 291-2240	9146
Nongshim America Inc (HQ)	5141	D	909 481-3698	8506
NRG California South LP	4911	D	909 899-7241	6154
Pacific Cycle Inc	4225	E	909 481-5613	4609
Pacific West Corporation (PA)	7379	D	515 270-8181	16451
Par Electrical Contractors Inc	1731	C	909 854-2880	2678
Paradise Building Services	7349	C	909 399-0707	14379
Penwal Industries Inc	1542	D	909 466-1555	1634
Perris Valley Cmnty Hosp LLC	8062	C	909 581-6400	21797
Priority One Med Trnspt Inc (PA)	4119	D	909 948-4400	3829
Professnal Elec Cnstr Svcs Inc	1731	D	909 373-4100	2690
Promed Hlth Care Admnistrators	8011	D	909 932-1045	19881
Provident Savings Bank	6162	E	909 484-6286	9890
Puratos Corporation	4221	D	909 484-1312	4483
R M A Group Inc (PA)	8711	D	909 980-6096	26030
Rancho Ccamonga Cmnty Hosp LLC	8062	C	909 581-6400	21828
Recreational Equipment Inc	5046	C	909 646-8360	7226
Red Hill Country Club	7997	D	909 982-1358	19038
Replanet LLC	4953	D	909 980-1203	6536
Rwc Enterprises Inc	8711	E	909 373-4100	26046
Ryder Truck Rental Inc	7513	D	909 980-5084	17653
SA Recycling LLC	4953	D	909 899-1767	6550
San Antonio Community Hospital	8062	E	909 948-8000	21843
Scheu Manufacturing Co	0175	D	909 981-5343	249
Schwarz Paper Company LLC	5113	D	909 476-2457	8216
Sheraton Corporation	7011	B	909 204-6100	13244
Sherman Security	7381	C	909 941-4167	16820
Shii LLC	6531	E	909 354-8000	11844
Southwire Company LLC	5063	C	909 989-2888	7477
Starwood Hotels & Resorts	7011	C	909 484-2018	13289
Steno Employment Services Inc	7363	A	909 476-1404	14953
Sumitomo Rubber North Amer Inc (HQ)	5014	D	909 466-1116	6790
Sunrise Senior Living Inc	8051	D	909 941-3001	20947
Superior Elec Mech & Plbg Inc	1731	B	909 357-9400	2760
Supershuttle International Inc	4111	C	909 944-2606	3724
TMT Industries Inc	4213	D	909 770-8514	4277
Treeline and Associates	8742	D	909 476-2757	27697
TRL Systems Incorporated	1731	D	909 390-8392	2776
US Tournament Golf Ltd Lblty	8742	E	909 987-6695	27705
Vavrinek Trine Day and Co LLP (PA)	8721	C	909 466-4410	26455
Vocational Imprv Program Inc (PA)	8331	D	909 483-5924	24403
Weber Distribution Warehouses	4225	E	909 481-1600	4666
West End Yung MNS Christn Assn	8641	D	909 477-2780	25402

RANCHO DOMINGUEZ, CA - Los Angeles County

	SIC	EMP	PHONE	ENTRY #
Alg Worldwide Logistics LLC	4731	E	800 932-3383	5022
Allied High Tech Products Inc	5085	D	310 635-2466	7912
Calpipe Industries Inc	5051	C	562 803-4388	7363
Cds Moving Equipment Inc (PA)	5084	D	310 631-1100	7832
Dhx-Dependable Hawaiian Ex Inc (PA)	4731	C	310 537-2000	5058
Eco Flow Transportation LLC	4731	D	310 816-0260	5064
Iap West Inc	5013	D	310 667-9720	6739
Kw International Inc	4731	D	310 747-1380	5112
Kw International Inc	4731	B	213 703-6914	5113
Mariak Industries Inc	5023	B	310 661-4400	6873
Mover Services Inc	4214	D	310 868-5143	4363
Neway Packaging Corp (PA)	5113	D	602 454-9000	8199
Nippon Ex Nec Lgstics Amer Inc	4212	D	310 604-6100	4044
Samsung Electronics Amer Inc	5064	D	310 537-7000	7511
Seeds of Change Inc	5191	D	310 764-7700	9150
Union Supply Group Inc (PA)	5141	C	310 603-8899	8544
Westcoast Warehousing LLC	4225	E	310 537-9958	4669

RANCHO MIRAGE, CA - Riverside County

	SIC	EMP	PHONE	ENTRY #
Agua Clnte Band Chilla Indians	7011	A	760 321-2000	12374
Annenberg Foundation Trust (PA)	6733	D	760 202-2222	12168
Betty Ford Center (HQ)	8069	C	760 773-4100	22117
Blx Group Inc	0181	D	760 776-6622	270
Brookdale Senior Living Inc	6513	D	760 340-5999	11102
Brookdale Senior Living Inc	8361	D	760 346-7772	24572
Cellco Partnership	4812	D	760 568-5542	5332
Charlie W Shaeffer Jr MD	8011	D	760 346-0642	19427
Childrens Museum of Desert	8412	E	760 321-0602	25008
Club of Sunrise Country	7997	D	760 328-6549	18921
Community Blood Bank Inc	8099	D	760 773-4190	22922
Desert Cardiology Consultants	8011	D	760 346-0642	19489
Desert Orthopdc Center A Mdcl (PA)	8011	D	760 568-2684	19492
Eisenhower Medical Center (PA)	8062	A	760 340-3911	21551

GEOGRAPHIC SECTION

REDDING, CA

Company	SIC	EMP	PHONE	ENTRY #
Janet K Hartzler MD	8011	D	760 340-3937	19574
Mission Hills Country Club	7997	C	760 324-9400	19002
Morningside Community Assn	8641	D	760 328-3323	25301
Omni Hotels Corporation	7011	B	760 568-2727	13042
Outpatnt Eye Srgry Ctr of Dsrt	8011	E	760 340-3937	19802
Protect-For-Less Security Svcs	7382	E	760 343-1192	16913
Ritz-Carlton Hotel Company LLC	7011	B	760 321-8282	13154
Ritz-Carlton Hotel Company LLC	7011	B	760 321-8282	13157
Sedona Surgical Center Inc	8011	E	760 413-8056	19984
Spa Cas Palmas	7991	E	760 836-3106	18684
Springs Club Inc	7997	D	760 328-0254	19094
Starwood Hotels & Resorts	7011	A	760 328-5955	13297
Thunderbird Country Club	7997	D	760 328-2161	19108
Windermere Real Estate East	6531	D	760 568-2568	11929

RANCHO MURIETA, CA - Sacramento County

Company	SIC	EMP	PHONE	ENTRY #
Empire Golf Inc (PA)	7992	D	916 314-3150	18739
Energy Store of California Inc	1711	D	916 825-8751	2219
Rancho Murieta Country Club	7997	D	916 354-2400	19035
Whiting Construction Inc	1771	D	916 354-2756	3351

RANCHO PALOS VERDES, CA - Los Angeles County

Company	SIC	EMP	PHONE	ENTRY #
American Golf Corporation	7997	D	310 377-7370	18867
Artists Studio Gallery	7999	D	424 206-9902	19144
Bally Total Fitness Corp	7991	E	310 732-2100	18609
Belmont Village LP	6513	D	310 377-9977	11096
CIT Bank National Association	6021	D	310 265-1656	9373
Inman Spinosa & Buchan Inc	6531	D	310 519-1080	11584
Long Point Development LLC	7011	A	310 265-2800	12930
Los Verdes MNS Golf Cntry CLB	7992	D	310 377-7370	18757
Re/Max Plos Vrdes Rlty / Exces	6531	E	310 541-5224	11795
Wells Fargo Bank National Assn	6021	D	310 831-0632	9448

RANCHO SANTA FE, CA - San Diego County

Company	SIC	EMP	PHONE	ENTRY #
A W Properties West LLC	1521	D	858 832-1462	1121
Bridges Club At Rancho SA	8641	C	858 759-7200	25222
Clubcorp Usa Inc	7997	C	858 756-2471	18923
Crosby National Golf Club LLC	7997	D	858 756-6310	18931
Del Mar Country Club Inc	7997	D	858 759-5500	18935
Fairbanks Ranch Cntry CLB Inc	7997	C	858 259-8811	18947
Farms Golf Club Inc	7997	D	858 756-5585	18949
HCC Investors LLC	7997	C	858 759-7200	18959
Helen Woodward Animal Center (PA)	8699	D	858 756-4117	25540
Huntington Hotel Company	7011	B	858 756-1131	12804
Merrill Lynch Pierce Fenner	6211	E	858 381-8112	10044
Rancho Santa Fe Association A	7997	C	858 756-1182	19036
Rancho Valencia Resort	7011	B	858 756-1123	13129
Willis Allen Real Estate	6531	E	858 756-2444	11925

RANCHO SANTA MARGARI, CA - Orange County

Company	SIC	EMP	PHONE	ENTRY #
Aliso Mechanical Incorporated	1711	C	949 544-1601	2118
Foundation 9 Entertainment Inc (PA)	7372	C	949 698-1500	15670
Jct Company LLC	1711	E	949 589-2021	2261
Safe Harbor Intl Relief	8399	E	949 858-6786	24971
Wendt Landscape Services Inc	0782	E	949 589-8680	979

RCHO STA MARG, CA - Orange County

Company	SIC	EMP	PHONE	ENTRY #
C-21 Super Stars	6531	D	949 389-1600	11336
Capital Invstmnts Vntures Corp (PA)	8621	C	949 858-0647	25127
Fakouri Electrical Engrg Inc	7378	D	949 888-2400	16293
Hackney Electric Inc (PA)	1731	D	949 264-4000	2604
Jipc Management Inc	8741	A	949 916-2000	27080
Kisco Senior Living LLC	8741	E	949 888-2250	27099
Lucas and Mercier Cnstr Inc	1751	C	949 589-4480	3065
Mission Viejo Pateadores Inc	7941	E	949 350-5590	18558
Padi Americas Inc	8621	C	949 858-7234	25149
Padi Worldwide Corp (HQ)	8621	C	949 858-7234	25150
Park Landscape Maintenance (PA)	0782	B	949 546-8300	930
Park West Rescom Inc	0782	C	949 546-8300	931
Prudential California Realty	6531	A	949 888-2300	11776
Santa Margarita Water District (PA)	4941	C	949 459-6400	6401
Santa Margarita Water District	4941	C	949 459-6400	6402

RED BLUFF, CA - Tehama County

Company	SIC	EMP	PHONE	ENTRY #
Bio Industries Inc	0711	E	530 529-3290	474
Brentwood Skill Nursng & Rehab	8059	D	530 527-2046	21161
Business Connections	7361	D	530 527-6229	14618
Concessionaires Urban Park (PA)	7999	B	530 529-1512	19187
County of Tehama	8322	C	530 527-5631	23928
County of Tehama	8322	C	530 527-4052	23929
Lassen Hse Assisted Living LLC	8361	E	530 529-2900	24707
Lassen Medical Group Inc (PA)	8011	E	530 527-0414	19702
Northern Vly Indian Hlth Inc	8021	D	530 529-2567	20268
St Elizabeth Community Hosp (HQ)	8062	A	530 529-7760	21913
United Sttes Bowl Congress Inc	8699	D	530 527-9049	25593
Wal-Mart Stores Inc	4225	A	530 529-0916	4660

REDDING, CA - Shasta County

Company	SIC	EMP	PHONE	ENTRY #
Addus Healthcare Inc	8049	D	530 247-0858	20304
Airgas Inc	5169	B	530 241-1544	8970
Ameripride Services Inc	7213	E	530 242-0564	13525
Aramark Unf & Career AP LLC	7218	E	530 241-6433	13606
Best Western Hilltop Inn	7011	E	530 221-6100	12437
Big Lgue Dreams Consulting LLC	7997	C	530 223-1177	18892
California Oregon Broadcasting (HQ)	4833	D	530 243-7777	5837
California Physicians Service	6324	D	530 351-6115	10264
Califrnia Physcn Reimbursement	6411	D	530 241-0473	10659
Cardinal Health Inc	5122	B	530 225-8735	8245
Care Options Management Plans (PA)	8082	D	530 242-8580	22390
CB C&C Properties/Comm Di Inc	6531	D	530 221-7551	11347
Cellco Partnership	4812	D	530 223-0420	5362
Ch2m Hill Inc	8711	C	530 243-5832	25732
Charter Cmmnctons Oprating LLC	4841	E	530 241-7352	5942
Class Act Hair & Nail Salon	7231	D	530 223-3442	13670
Copper Ridge Care Center	8051	C	530 222-2273	20471
County of Shasta	6371	D	530 225-5000	10550
County of Shasta	8322	D	530 225-5554	23918
County of Shasta	8111	D	530 245-6300	23183
County of Shasta	8351	E	530 225-2999	24452
Crestwood Behavioral Hlth Inc	8361	D	530 221-0976	24620
David Civalier MD Inc	8011	E	530 244-4034	19486
Dignity Health	8011	C	530 225-6345	19499
Donor Network West	8099	D	510 418-0336	22948
Far Northern Coordinating Coun (PA)	8322	D	530 222-4791	23977
Federal Express Corporation	4513	C	800 463-3339	4854
Fedex Ground Package Sys Inc	4213	E	530 247-0935	4174
Foothill Distributing Co Inc	5181	C	530 243-3932	9056
Forestry and Fire Protection	0851	C	530 225-2418	1015
Golden Living LLC	8059	D	530 241-6756	21245
Hfrm II Inc (PA)	6512	B	530 242-2010	11001
Hoopa Modular Building Entp	1531	D	530 244-2421	1368
Interim Assisted Care of Nort	8082	D	530 722-1530	22487
James D Tate MD	8011	D	530 225-8710	19573
JF Shea Construction Inc	1521	D	530 246-4292	1193
Kindred Nursing Centers W LLC	8051	C	530 243-6317	20708
Lassen Canyon Nursery Inc (PA)	0171	D	530 223-1075	120
MD Imaging Inc A Prof Med Corp	8011	D	530 243-1249	19736
Medical Home Specialists Inc	7363	D	530 226-5577	14908
Mercy Foundation North	8099	D	530 247-3424	22999
Mercy HM Svcs A Cal Ltd Partnr (HQ)	8062	A	530 225-6000	21740
Mercy HM Svcs A Cal Ltd Partnr	8011	B	530 225-6000	19747
Mercy HM Svcs A Cal Ltd Partnr	8082	D	530 245-4070	22507
Meyers Earthwork Inc	1794	D	530 365-8858	3437
Mission Provider Services Inc	8059	D	530 222-5633	21317
Muse Concrete Contractors Inc	1611	D	530 226-5151	1830
North State Security Inc	7381	D	530 243-0295	16748
Northern California Hlth Care	8082	D	530 223-2332	22515
Northern California Rehab	8062	D	530 246-9000	21763
Northern Valley Catholic Socia	8322	C	530 241-0552	24108
Northstar Senior Living Inc	8741	A	530 242-8300	27148
Oakdale Heights MGT Corp (PA)	6513	B	530 222-6797	11178
Ocadian Care Centers LLC	8051	D	530 246-9000	20818
Owens Health Care	8082	C	530 246-1075	22527
Pacific Gas and Electric Co	4911	C	530 365-7672	6173
Patients Hospital	8062	D	530 225-8700	21788
Peerless Building Maint Inc	7349	D	530 222-6369	14384
Peloria Bridge Bay LLC	7011	D	530 275-3021	13088
Pre-Employcom	7381	D	800 300-1821	16760
Prime Healthcare Services	8062	D	530 244-5400	21811
Prime Healthcare Servs Sh	8062	D	530 244-5458	21812
Redding Aero Enterprises Inc	4111	D	530 224-2300	3691
Redding Bank of Commerce (HQ)	6029	D	530 224-7355	9556
Redding Drywall Systems Inc	1742	E	530 222-8767	2964
Redding Family Medicine Assoc	8011	E	530 244-4907	19907
Redding Lumber Transport Inc	4214	D	530 241-8193	4372
Redding Pathologists Lab (PA)	8011	D	530 225-8050	19908
Redding Pathologists Lab	8071	D	530 225-8050	22270
Redding Rancheria (PA)	7011	D	530 225-8979	13136
Redding Rancheria	8099	D	530 224-2700	23039
Riverview Golf and Country CLB	7997	D	530 224-2254	19045
RI Redding LLC	7011	D	530 221-8700	13162
Roy E Ladd Inc	1611	D	530 241-6102	1854
Sac River Outfitters	7999	D	530 275-3500	19273
Securitas SEC Svcs USA Inc	7381	D	530 245-0256	16791
Set Free Services Inc	8742	D	530 243-3373	27642
Sfn Group Inc	7363	D	530 222-3434	14948
Shasta Convalescent Center	8059	D	530 222-3634	21369
Shasta County Head Start Child (PA)	8351	E	530 241-1036	24514
Shasta Lake Resorts LP	7999	D	209 785-3300	19281
Shasta Medical Associates	8011	D	530 243-3231	20001
Sierra Oaks Senior Living	8361	D	530 241-5100	24810
Slideco Recreation Inc	7996	D	530 246-9550	18835

Employment Codes: A=Over 500 employees, B=251-500, C=101-250, D=51-100, E=45-50

REDDING, CA

Company	SIC	EMP	PHONE	ENTRY #
State Compensation Insur Fund	6331	C	888 782-8338	10465
Steve Manning Construction Inc	1611	D	530 222-0810	1864
Tenet Healthsystem Medical	8082	C	530 222-1992	22579
Tenet Healthsystem Medical	8322	C	530 246-9000	24247
Thom Sharon & G Enterprises	8082	E	530 226-8350	22581
Tierra Oaks Golf Club Inc	7997	D	530 275-0795	19110
Transportation California Dept	0782	C	530 225-3349	963
Turtle Bay Exploration Park	8412	E	530 243-4282	25053
Utility Tree Service Inc (DH)	0783	C	530 226-0330	1001
VCA Inc	0742	D	530 224-2200	631
Veterans Affairs Cal Dept	8051	C	530 224-3300	21006
Veterans Health Administration	8011	B	530 226-7555	20200
Veterans of Foreign Wars of US	8641	D	530 241-9168	25393
Vibra Healthcare LLC	8051	D	530 246-9000	21008
Willow Sprngs Alzhmrs Spcl Cr	8361	E	530 242-0654	24857
Win River Hotel Corporation	7011	E	530 226-5111	13412
Win-River Resort & Casino	7999	B	530 243-3377	19309
Windsor Redding Care Ctr LLC	8051	D	530 246-2586	21053
Yaley Enterprises Inc	5099	E	530 365-5252	8149
Youth For Change	8322	D	530 605-1520	24298

REDLANDS, CA - San Bernardino County

Company	SIC	EMP	PHONE	ENTRY #
ABI Attorneys Service Inc (PA)	7334	D	909 793-0613	14098
AG Redlands LLC	8059	C	909 793-2678	21127
American Baptist Homes of West	6513	D	909 335-3077	11084
American Baptist Homes of West	8059	D	909 793-1233	21136
American Med	4119	C	909 793-7676	3742
Angels Everyday Inc	8082	D	909 793-7788	22364
Ash Holdings LLC	8051	D	909 793-2609	20384
Assistance League of Redlands	8399	C	909 792-2675	24876
Beaver Medical Clinic Inc (PA)	8011	C	909 793-3311	19371
Becton Dickinson and Company	5047	D	909 748-7300	7243
Bon Appetit Management Co	8742	C	909 748-8970	27351
Braswell Col Care Redlands CA	8059	C	909 792-6050	21159
Citigroup Inc	6021	D	909 335-0547	9379
City of Redlands	4953	E	909 798-7525	6461
Clear View Treatment Center	8093	D	909 794-6688	22686
Coldwell Banker RE Corp	6531	E	909 792-4147	11414
Contain-A-Way Inc	4953	B	909 796-2960	6467
Countryside Inn-Corona LP	8741	D	909 335-9024	26992
County of San Bernardino	8412	D	909 307-2669	25018
David Ollis Landscape Dev Inc	0782	E	909 307-1911	833
DSC Logistics Inc	4213	D	909 363-4354	4142
Edco Health Info Solution	7389	D	909 793-0613	17143
Enerpath Services Inc	1731	D	909 335-1699	2589
Epic Management LP (PA)	8741	C	909 799-1818	27017
Farmers Insurance	6411	D	909 801-3300	10710
First American Title Insur Co	6361	C	909 889-0311	10522
Geodis Logistics LLC	4225	D	909 801-3145	4559
Haralambos Beverage Company	5181	C	909 307-1777	9060
Harvest Facility Holdings LP	6513	D	909 793-8691	11139
Hobby Lobby Stores Inc	6794	C	909 307-0135	12217
Hr Mission Commons Fc 5183	8361	D	909 793-8691	24696
Hydro Tek Systems Inc	5087	D	909 799-9222	7968
Inland Hlth Org of So Cal (HQ)	8011	E	909 335-7171	19570
Jonbec Care Incorporated (PA)	8052	D	909 798-4003	21085
Kaiser Foundation Hospitals	8011	D	888 750-0036	19593
Kuehne + Nagel Inc	4225	D	909 574-2300	4585
L Lyon Distributing Inc	7389	E	909 798-7129	17280
Larry Jacinto Construction Inc	1611	D	909 794-2151	1814
Lois Lauer Realty	6531	C	909 748-7000	11635
Loma Linda University	8049	D	909 558-4934	20331
Loma Linda University	8011	D	909 558-6422	19716
Loma Linda University Med Ctr	8062	B	909 558-9275	21714
Loma Linda Vet Association For	8641	D	909 583-6250	25288
M Block & Sons Inc	4225	C	909 335-6684	4593
Mountain West Financial Inc (PA)	6162	B	909 793-1500	9875
Option One Home Med Eqp Inc	7352	D	909 478-5413	14475
P & R Paper Supply Co Inc (PA)	5113	D	909 389-1811	8212
Pacific Maintenance Svcs Inc	7349	C	909 793-7111	14377
Performance Team Frt Sys Inc	7389	C	801 301-1732	17408
Plum Healthcare Group LLC	7389	D	909 793-2609	17419
Prime-Line Products Company (PA)	5072	B	909 887-8118	7695
Pro-Craft Construction Inc	1711	D	909 389-7990	2329
R J M Construction Inc	1542	E	909 794-8853	1644
Redlands Cmnty Hosp Foundation	8059	C	909 793-5585	21357
Redlands Community Hospital (PA)	8069	D	909 335-5500	22168
Redlands Country Club	7997	D	909 793-2661	19039
Redlands Foothill Groves	0723	E	909 793-2164	579
Redlands Ford Inc	7532	D	909 793-3211	17770
RHS Corp	8741	A	909 335-5500	27201
Silverscreen Healthcare Inc	8059	D	909 793-1382	21378
Soren McAdam Christianson LLP	8721	D	909 798-2222	26445
Southern California Gas Co	4924	B	909 335-7802	6275
Study Tapes	7812	D	909 792-0111	18162
Tarbell Financial Corporation	6531	D	909 335-0750	11864
United Road Towing Inc	7549	D	909 798-4863	17902
Unlimited Frontiers Inc	8059	D	909 793-0142	21402
West Dermatology Med MGT Inc	6324	C	909 793-3000	10392
Westcor Construction of Cal	1521	C	909 796-8900	1285
YMCA of East Valley (PA)	8641	C	909 798-9622	25410

REDONDO BEACH, CA - Los Angeles County

Company	SIC	EMP	PHONE	ENTRY #
4g Wireless Inc	4813	D	310 376-2299	5446
Aamcom LLC	4813	E	310 318-8100	5450
Aerospace Corporation	8733	D	310 374-8866	26726
AES Corporation	6531	D	310 318-7510	11277
Beach Cities Health District	8399	C	310 318-7939	24880
Beachsports Inc	7032	E	310 372-2202	13460
Bicara Ltd (PA)	5147	B	310 316-6222	8664
Brownstone Companies Inc	5065	A	310 297-3600	7536
Corporate Production Designs	7812	E	310 937-9663	18065
Craft Resources Inc	7363	C	310 937-3744	14867
D & W LLC	7011	D	310 345-0075	12562
Fire Safe Systems Inc	8711	D	310 542-0585	25809
Hpt Trs Ihg-2 Inc	7011	B	310 318-8888	12800
K & P Janitorial Services	7349	D	310 540-8878	14333
Leidos Inc	8731	D	310 791-9671	26549
Leight Sales Co Inc	5072	D	310 223-1000	7689
Map Cargo Global Logistics (PA)	4731	D	310 297-8300	5120
Max Sommers Real Estate	6531	D	310 560-1499	11667
Muscle Improvement Inc	7991	D	310 374-5522	18664
New-Jack Industries Inc	7381	B	310 297-3605	16745
Northrop Grmmn Spce & Mssn Sys	8748	C	855 737-8364	28005
Portofino Hotel Partners LP	7011	C	310 379-8481	13106
Reign Accessories Inc	8741	E	310 297-6400	27196
Scat Enterprises Inc	5013	D	310 370-5501	6761
Silverado Senior Living Inc	8051	D	424 257-6418	20916
Social Vocational Services Inc	8322	D	310 793-9600	24213
Sport Center Fitness Inc	7991	D	310 376-9443	18695
Stevens Global Logistics Inc (PA)	4731	D	310 216-5645	5171
Studio 13	7311	E	310 837-8107	13924
Transportation Concept Inc	4111	D	323 268-2202	3730
Westwind Engineering Inc	8711	D	310 831-3454	26146

REDWOOD CITY, CA - San Mateo County

Company	SIC	EMP	PHONE	ENTRY #
ABC Bus Inc	5012	D	650 368-3364	6659
ABS-Cbn International (DH)	4841	C	800 527-2820	5933
Accor Bus & Leisure N Amer Inc	7011	C	650 598-9000	12372
Acxiom Corporation	7375	D	650 356-3400	16216
Adaptive Spectrum and Signal A	4813	D	650 264-2667	5453
Anomali Incorporated	7371	D	408 800-4050	15017
Aricent Inc (DH)	7371	C	650 632-4310	15033
AT&T Corp	4813	D	650 780-1005	5491
AT&T Corp	4813	D	800 222-0300	5509
Automatic Data Processing Inc	7374	C	800 225-5237	16095
Badgeville Inc	7372	E	650 323-6668	15594
Bay Brokerage Inc	5141	E	650 413-1721	8458
Bkf Engineers (PA)	8711	D	650 482-6300	25691
Bluevine	6153	D	888 452-7805	9774
Bnbuilders	1611	D	650 227-1957	1742
Box Inc (PA)	7372	C	877 729-4269	15607
Broadvision Inc (PA)	7372	D	650 331-1000	15610
Broadway By Bay	7922	C	650 579-5565	18374
Brookdale Lving Cmmunities Inc	8051	D	650 366-3900	20422
C3 Inc	7372	C	650 503-2200	15611
Cake Corporation	7371	D	650 215-7777	15071
Cardiodx Inc	8071	C	650 475-2788	22196
Cavaya Inc	7373	E	831 338-1008	15916
Child Care Coordinating Counsi	8322	E	650 517-1400	23731
Clp Resources Inc	7363	C	650 261-2100	14858
Community Gatepath	8322	C	650 259-8500	23773
Coretechs Staffing Inc	7371	D	650 363-7960	15110
County of San Mateo	8322	C	650 599-7336	23910
County of San Mateo	8741	C	650 363-4915	26994
County of San Mateo	8741	E	650 363-4343	26995
County of San Mateo	8741	D	650 363-4321	26996
County of San Mateo	8999	C	650 363-4548	28125
County of San Mateo	8322	D	650 363-1910	23914
County of San Mateo	7033	D	650 363-4020	13479
County of San Mateo	8322	C	650 312-8803	23917
Covington & Burling LLP	8111	C	650 632-4700	23185
Crystal Dynamics Inc	7372	D	650 421-7600	15632
Dealix Corporation	5012	D	650 599-5500	6673
Delphix Corp (PA)	7372	E	650 494-1645	15637
Des Architects + Engineers Inc	8712	D	650 364-6453	26182
Digital Insight Corporation (HQ)	7375	C	818 879-1010	16228
Diva Systems Corporation	4841	C	650 779-3000	5996
Dpr Construction Inc (PA)	1541	B	650 474-1450	1421
Dpr Construction A Gen Partnr	1541	A	650 474-1450	1422
E A Com Inc	7371	C	650 628-1500	15151
Electronic Arts Inc (PA)	7372	B	650 628-1500	15652

GEOGRAPHIC SECTION

RICHMOND, CA

	SIC	EMP	PHONE	ENTRY #
Equilar Inc	7389	C	650 241-6600	17153
Equinix Inc (PA)	4813	C	650 598-6000	5596
Equinix (us) Enterprises Inc	4899	D	650 598-6363	6072
Ernst & Young LLP	8721	C	650 802-4500	26346
Evernote Corporation (PA)	4813	C	650 216-7700	5599
Fish & Richardson PC	8111	D	650 839-5070	23242
French Redwood Inc	7011	D	650 598-9000	12653
Genomic Health Inc (PA)	8071	D	650 556-9300	22220
Genomic Health Inc	8071	A	650 556-9300	22221
Gic Real Estate Inc (HQ)	6799	D	650 593-3122	12309
Global Meddata Inc	8099	D	650 369-9734	22965
Goodhire Llc	7374	E	650 618-9910	16135
Goodwill Inds San Frncisco Inc	8331	D	650 556-9709	24346
Grail Inc	8731	E	858 766-1512	26528
Granite Rock Co	1611	B	650 869-3370	1793
Green Again Ldscpg & Con Inc	0782	D	650 368-9304	860
Gunderson Dettmer Stough Ville (PA)	8111	C	650 321-2400	23294
Heartflow Inc	7373	C	650 241-1221	15957
Heartland Payment Systems Inc	7389	C	650 678-2824	17211
I2c Inc	5045	B	650 480-5222	7143
Imperva Inc (PA)	7371	C	650 345-9000	15233
Impossible Foods Inc	5141	C	650 461-4385	8488
Inflection LLC	7374	E	650 618-9910	16147
Informatica LLC (HQ)	7372	C	650 385-5000	15702
Ipass Inc (PA)	4813	D	650 232-4100	5640
Isheriff Inc	7371	D	650 412-4300	15260
Itco Solutions Inc	7379	B	650 367-0514	16416
Itson Inc	5065	D	650 517-2780	7588
Kainos Home & Training Ctr	8322	E	650 361-1355	24052
Kaiser Foundation Hospitals	8011	A	650 299-2000	19655
Kaspick & Co LLC (HQ)	8742	E	650 585-4100	27498
Keenan & Associates	6411	D	650 306-0616	10755
Liveops Inc (PA)	7363	C	650 453-2700	14900
Livescribe Inc	5045	C	510 777-0071	7156
Lucky Pacific LLC	8742	E	650 330-0263	27514
Lydia C Gonzalez	8322	E	650 299-4707	24075
Managed Network Services LLC	7374	B	650 232-4287	16155
Multiven Inc	7379	E	408 828-2715	16435
N F L Alumni	8699	C	650 366-3659	25556
N Model Inc (PA)	7371	C	650 610-4600	15320
Nominum Inc (PA)	7371	E	650 381-6000	15335
Openwave Mobility Inc	7372	D	650 480-7200	15785
Optimus Ventures LLC	5065	C	888 881-5969	7617
Oracle America Inc	5045	D	800 633-0584	7170
Oracle Corporation (PA)	7372	A	650 506-7000	15805
Oracle Systems Corporation	7372	B	650 506-0300	15807
Oracle Systems Corporation (HQ)	7372	A	650 506-7000	15808
Oracle Usa Inc	7372	A	650 506-7000	15811
Origin Systems Inc	7371	E	650 628-1500	15362
Paxata Inc	7372	D	650 542-7897	15815
Permanente Kaiser Intl	8011	C	650 299-3888	19826
Permanente Medical Group Inc	8011	A	650 299-2000	19835
Permanente Medical Group Inc	8011	D	650 299-2015	19849
Permanente Medical Group Inc	8011	D	650 598-2852	19851
Provident Credit Union (PA)	6062	C	650 508-0300	9679
Pubmatic Inc (PA)	7311	D	650 351-9162	13902
Qualys Inc (PA)	7371	C	650 801-6100	15404
Quinn Emanuel Urquhart	8111	E	650 801-5000	23524
Reach Fitness Club	7991	E	650 327-3224	18673
Reliable International Svcs	7349	C	760 772-1377	14405
Reltio Inc	7371	C	855 360-3282	15413
Reputationcom Inc (PA)	7382	D	650 381-3056	16916
Reynolds Cleaning Services Inc	7349	C	650 599-0202	14407
Robert Bosch Start-Up Platf	7371	E	248 876-6430	15427
Rocket Fuel Inc (PA)	7311	C	650 595-1300	13913
Ropers Majeski Kohn Bentley (PA)	8111	C	650 364-8200	23538
Rudolph and Sletten Inc (HQ)	1542	D	650 216-3600	1656
Ruiz Janitorial Co Inc	7349	E	650 361-1303	14414
S J Amoroso Cnstr Co Inc (PA)	1542	B	650 654-1900	1657
Saba Software Inc (HQ)	7372	C	650 581-2500	15830
San Mateo Credit Union (PA)	6062	D	650 363-1725	9686
Satmetrix Systems Inc (PA)	7371	D	650 227-8300	15441
Seiler LLP (PA)	8721	C	650 365-4646	26438
Selligent Inc (HQ)	7373	C	650 421-4200	16051
Senior Companions At Home	8322	E	650 364-1265	24206
Sequoia Adrc LP	8322	E	650 364-5504	24207
Sequoia Health Services (HQ)	8062	D	650 369-5811	21879
Shopkick Inc	7371	E	650 763-8727	15452
Shutterfly Inc (PA)	7384	C	650 610-5200	16957
Silicon Valley Clean Water	4952	D	650 591-7121	6416
Skire Inc	7371	E	650 289-2600	15457
Supportcom Inc (PA)	7374	C	650 556-9440	16195
Talend Inc (HQ)	7373	C	650 539-3200	16063
Telecare Corporation	8063	C	650 367-1890	22105
Tradebeam Inc	7379	D	650 653-4800	16509
Trilliant Networks Inc (PA)	7389	D	650 204-5050	17543
Trion Worlds Inc (PA)	7372	D	650 631-9800	15865
Truebeck Construction (PA)	1542	D	650 227-1957	1697
Turn Inc (PA)	7319	C	650 353-4399	14012
Verinata Health Inc	8731	D	650 632-1680	26634
Verity Health System Cal Inc	8062	B	310 900-8900	22013
Verity Health System Cal Inc	8062	D	650 551-6507	22015
Verity Health System Cal Inc	8999	A	650 551-6700	28167
Vindicia Inc	7372	D	650 264-4700	15877
Vodafone Americas Inc (HQ)	4812	D	650 832-6600	5435
W Bradley Electric Inc	1731	E	650 701-1502	2786
W L Butler Construction Inc (PA)	1542	E	650 361-1270	1711
Water Heaters Only Inc	5064	D	650 368-9998	7513
Weil Gotshal & Manges LLP	8111	D	650 802-3000	23613
Western Athletic Clubs Inc	7991	C	650 593-1112	18705
WL Butler Inc	1522	E	650 361-1270	1352
Yodlee Inc (HQ)	8742	C	650 980-3600	27726
Yume Inc	7311	C	650 591-1400	13945
Zb Rehab Staffing Inc	7363	D	650 396-2207	14987
Zyme Solutions Inc (PA)	7375	D	650 585-2258	16273

REDWOOD VALLEY, CA - Mendocino County

	SIC	EMP	PHONE	ENTRY #
Consolidated Tribal Health Prj	8093	D	707 485-5115	22691
Redwood Valley Industrial Park	4225	D	707 485-8766	4629

REEDLEY, CA - Fresno County

	SIC	EMP	PHONE	ENTRY #
Adventist Health System/West	8099	C	559 638-8155	22878
Adventist Health System/West	8011	A	559 637-2384	19323
Adventist Med Center-Reedley	8062	A	559 638-8155	21434
Cal Packing & Storage LP	4222	C	559 638-2929	4489
Community Youth Ministries	8322	C	559 638-6585	23779
Golden Living LLC	8051	C	559 638-3577	20620
Ito Packing Co Inc	0723	C	559 638-2531	550
Moonlight Packing Corporation (PA)	5148	C	559 638-7799	8753
Moya Luna Farm Labor Services	0761	C	559 638-9498	676
Paragon Health & Rehab CT	8093	E	559 638-3578	22790
Rio Vista Ventures LLC	5141	C	559 897-6730	8515
Sierra View Homes	8051	C	559 637-2256	20915
The Central Valley Trnsp Auth	4111	D	559 305-7037	3728
Trinity Fruit Packing Company	0723	C	559 743-3913	599
Youngstown Grape Distrs Inc	0723	C	916 635-2200	609

RESEDA, CA - Los Angeles County

	SIC	EMP	PHONE	ENTRY #
Advanced Bioservices LLC (PA)	8741	D	818 342-0100	26910
Alumatec Inc	1381	D	818 609-7460	1056
Auto Body Management Inc	7532	C	818 888-7654	17748
Chase Group Llc	8742	D	818 708-3533	27378
G & K Management Co Inc	6531	D	818 705-8834	11549
Honda R&D Americas Inc	8732	E	818 345-7922	26673
Longwood Management Corp	8062	D	818 881-7414	21718
Los Angles Jewish HM For Aging (PA)	8051	B	818 774-3000	20747
Los Angles Jewish HM For Aging	8051	B	818 774-3000	20748
Mid Vlley Racquetball Athc CLB	7997	C	818 705-6500	18999
Permanente Kaiser Intl	8011	C	818 705-5500	19833
Spa Dreams	7991	C	818 298-1120	18685
Statewide Enterprises Inc	6513	C	818 709-4434	11207
Verizon Communications Inc	7389	A	818 438-1104	17587
West Valley Family YMCA	8351	C	818 774-2840	24531
Woodland Care Center LLC	8059	C	818 881-4540	21429

RIALTO, CA - San Bernardino County

	SIC	EMP	PHONE	ENTRY #
B & B Plastics Recyclers Inc (PA)	5093	D	909 829-3606	8063
Burlingame Industries Inc (PA)	7033	D	909 355-7000	13475
Caremark Rx Inc	8011	D	909 822-1164	19404
Clem-Trans Inc	4212	E	909 877-4450	3996
Crestview Cnvalescent Hosp Inc	8051	C	909 877-1361	20507
Eze Trucking LLC (DH)	4213	D	909 770-8800	4156
Filter Recycling Services Inc (PA)	4953	D	909 873-4141	6484
Geodis Logistics LLC	4225	D	909 240-6298	4560
Mercy Air Tri-County LLC	4522	D	909 829-1051	4885
Molina Healthcare Inc	8011	C	909 546-7116	19758
Ptr Group Inc	8741	E	951 965-1822	27184
Robert Clapper Cnstr Svcs Inc	1542	D	909 829-3688	1653
Sierra Lathing Company Inc	1742	C	909 421-0211	2979
Simple Luxuries LLC	1771	E	310 627-6514	3330
So-Cal Strl Stl Fbrication Inc	1791	C	909 877-1299	3403
State Pipe & Supply Inc	1623	E	909 356-5670	2001
State Pipe & Supply Inc (DH)	5051	D	909 877-9999	7405
Sudhakar Company International	1611	D	909 879-2933	1867
Vance Corporation	1611	E	909 355-4333	1881
Vista Cove Care Ctr - Rialto	8051	C	909 877-1361	21018

RICHGROVE, CA - Tulare County

	SIC	EMP	PHONE	ENTRY #
Vincent B Zaninovich Sons Inc	0172	C	661 720-9031	192

RICHMOND, CA - Contra Costa County

	SIC	EMP	PHONE	ENTRY #
Alsco Inc	7213	D	510 237-9634	13510

RICHMOND, CA

	SIC	EMP	PHONE	ENTRY #
Alta Vista Solutions	8711	C	510 594-0510	25649
Alten Construction Inc	1542	D	510 234-4200	1489
Ameripride Services Inc	7213	E	800 748-6178	13529
Aquatic Science Center	8731	E	510 746-7334	26474
AT&T Corp	4813	D	510 965-9714	5507
Bay Area Beverage Co	5182	C	510 965-6120	9091
Bay Area Distributing Coinc	5181	E	510 232-8554	9042
Bay City Mechanical Inc	1711	C	510 233-7000	2159
Ben Myerson Candy Co Inc	5182	D	510 236-2233	9093
BP West Coast Products LLC	1311	B	510 231-4724	1031
Brand Services LLC	1799	D	510 231-9640	3501
Brookside Community Health Ctr	8011	E	510 215-5001	19379
C Overaa & Co	1541	B	510 234-0926	1409
C Overaa & Co/Bayview	1541	D	510 234-0926	1410
Cardinal Health Inc	5122	D	510 232-2030	8243
Century Theatres Inc	7833	D	510 758-9626	18357
Chevron Energy Technology Co (HQ)	8711	D	510 242-5059	25736
Chevron Investor Inc	8741	D	510 242-3000	26963
City of Richmond	7999	D	510 620-6788	19180
Connexsys Engineering Inc	8711	D	510 243-2050	25748
Contra Costa ARC	8361	D	510 233-7303	24605
Dahl-Beck Electric Co	5063	D	510 237-2325	7434
Department Health Care Svcs	8071	D	510 412-3700	22208
East Bay Municipl Utility Distr	4941	C	866 403-2683	6342
Ecology Control Industries	4959	C	510 235-1393	6626
First Student Inc	4131	C	510 237-6677	3879
First Student Inc	4151	C	510 237-6365	3934
Foss Maritime Company	4412	C	510 307-4271	4714
Gardeners Guild Inc	0782	C	415 457-0400	856
Hartmann Studios Incorporated	7389	C	510 232-5060	17209
Hotel Mac Restaurant Inc	7011	E	510 233-0576	12790
Hydrox Properties Xii LLC	6512	D	510 262-7200	11003
Inter-Rail Trnspt Nshville LLC	4789	D	510 231-2744	5223
International Delicacies	5149	E	510 669-2444	8855
Kaiser Foundation Hospitals	8011	B	510 307-1500	19590
Levin-Richmond Terminal Corp	4491	D	510 232-4422	4748
Loomis Armored Us LLC	7381	D	510 233-1055	16726
Macdonald Housing Partners LP	6531	E	510 620-0865	11651
New Ngc Inc	5093	E	510 234-6745	8077
Oliver & Company Inc	1542	D	510 412-9090	1623
Pacific Hotel Management LLC	7011	C	510 262-0700	13059
Palecek Imports Inc (PA)	5021	C	510 236-7730	6829
Permanente Medical Group Inc	8011	D	510 231-5406	19850
Public Health California Dept	8011	C	510 412-1502	19900
Richmond Country Club	7997	D	510 231-2241	19042
Richmond Rescue Mission (PA)	8322	D	510 215-4555	24158
Richmond Sanitary Service Inc (HQ)	4959	C	510 262-7100	6636
Richmond Wholesale Meat Co	5147	D	510 233-5111	8681
Rubicon Enterprises Inc	7349	C	510 235-1516	14412
Rubicon Programs Incorporated (PA)	7349	C	510 235-1516	14413
S P R E Inc	6531	D	510 222-8340	11829
San Francisco Bay Area Rapid	4111	D	510 233-6848	3703
San Francisco Bay Area Rapid	4789	D	510 233-7444	5241
Sims Group USA Corporation (DH)	5093	D	510 412-5300	8086
Sims Group USA Corporation	5093	D	510 236-0606	8087
Sunpower Corporation Systems (DH)	1711	D	510 260-8200	2389
T F Louderback Inc (PA)	5181	C	510 965-6120	9087
United Parcel Service Inc OH	4215	C	510 262-2338	4438
Universal Bldg Svcs & Sup Co (PA)	7349	C	510 527-1078	14455
Vicor Inc	7373	D	510 621-2000	16079
West Countra Costa Youth Svcs (PA)	8322	D	510 412-5647	24287
West County Resource Recovery	4953	E	510 231-4200	6612
Wr Forde Associates	1611	D	415 924-3072	1885
YMCA of East Bay	8641	B	510 412-5647	25408
YMCA of East Bay	8641	C	510 222-9622	25409

RIDGECREST, CA - Kern County

	SIC	EMP	PHONE	ENTRY #
Altaone Federal Credit Union (PA)	6061	C	760 371-7000	9587
Community Action Partnr Kern	8399	C	760 371-1469	24899
Desert Area Resources Training	8399	D	760 375-8494	24912
Drummond Medical Group Inc	8011	D	760 446-4571	19509
Golden Living LLC	8082	D	760 446-3591	22445
Great Western Hotels Corp	7011	E	760 446-6543	12676
Jacobs Technology Inc	8711	D	760 446-7084	25905
Jacobs Technology Inc	8711	C	760 446-1549	25907
Kern River Adventures	4489	C	760 376-3648	4738
L-3 Communications Corporation	7373	D	760 375-0390	15983
Leidos Inc	7374	B	858 826-7670	16151
Lockheed Martin Corporation	8711	C	760 446-1700	25941
Navy Exchange Service Command	7041	D	760 939-8681	13495
Naws Children Center	8351	D	760 939-2653	24485
New Directions Tech Inc (PA)	7373	D	760 384-2444	16011
Pre Con Industries Inc	1742	D	760 499-6176	2956
Ridgecrest Healthcare Inc (PA)	8051	D	323 344-0601	20871
Ridgecrest Regional Hospital	8062	B	760 446-3551	21832

RIO LINDA, CA - Sacramento County

	SIC	EMP	PHONE	ENTRY #
KRC Builders Incorporated	1751	D	916 417-1200	3061
Marques Pipeline Inc	8711	E	916 923-3434	25951
U S Army Corps of Engineers	8711	D	916 649-0133	26111

RIO VISTA, CA - Solano County

	SIC	EMP	PHONE	ENTRY #
California Vegetable Spc Inc	0161	D	707 374-2111	46
James M Stewart Inc	0139	D	707 374-6369	27
Lindsay Transportation	5084	C	707 374-6800	7855
Paul Graham Drilling & Svc Co	1381	C	707 374-5123	1061
Trilogy Rio Vista	1541	D	707 374-1100	1476

RIPON, CA - San Joaquin County

	SIC	EMP	PHONE	ENTRY #
Brocchini Farms Inc	0172	E	209 599-4229	144
Cheema Freightlines LLC	4213	D	209 599-0777	4126
Fishers Nursery	5193	D	209 599-3412	9188
Gico Management	5145	D	209 599-7131	8621
Jim Aartman Inc (PA)	4212	D	209 599-5066	4030
Lassen Canyon Nursery Inc	0171	D	209 599-7777	119
Nulaid Foods Inc (PA)	5144	D	209 599-2121	8602
Nushake Inc	1761	D	209 239-8616	3194
V&V Farm Labor Contractor	0191	E	209 599-4834	400

RIVERBANK, CA - Stanislaus County

	SIC	EMP	PHONE	ENTRY #
Eco2 Plastics Inc	4953	C	209 863-6200	6476
Econtactlive Inc	7389	D	209 863-8547	17141
LMC West Inc	5084	E	209 869-0144	7856
Valley West Health Care Inc	8051	D	209 869-2569	21005

RIVERDALE, CA - Fresno County

	SIC	EMP	PHONE	ENTRY #
Ayala Corporation	7361	C	559 867-5700	14611
Linda Terra Farms (PA)	0213	C	559 867-3473	415
Maddox Dairy LLC	0241	D	559 867-3545	431
Maddox Dairy A Ltd Partnership (PA)	0241	D	559 867-3545	432
Maddox Dairy A Ltd Partnership	0241	D	559 867-4457	433
Maddox Dairy A Ltd Partnership	0241	D	559 866-5624	434
Terra Linda Farms 1	0191	E	559 867-3400	397

RIVERSIDE, CA - Riverside County

	SIC	EMP	PHONE	ENTRY #
20/20 Plumbing & Heating Inc	1711	C	951 396-2020	2098
A F V W Health Center	8051	C	951 697-2025	20367
A-Check America Inc (PA)	7323	C	951 750-1501	14053
A-Check America Inc	7323	C	800 872-2677	14054
Abbey Partner VI	6531	E	951 785-8800	11272
Ace Cash Express Inc	6099	C	951 509-3506	9706
Adkison Engineers Inc	8711	D	951 688-0241	25616
Adventist Media Center Inc	7922	C	805 955-7777	18366
Air Force Village West Inc	8051	B	951 697-2000	20372
Albert A Webb Associates (PA)	8711	D	951 686-1070	25646
Allied Steel Co Inc	1791	D	951 241-7000	3361
Alliedbarton Security Svcs LLC	7381	C	951 801-7300	16544
Alta Interiors Inc	1742	D	951 784-1400	2854
Alta Vista Healthcare and Well	8011	C	951 688-8200	19333
Altura Credit Union (PA)	6062	D	888 883-7228	9651
Always There Live In Care LLC	8082	C	888 606-8880	22355
American Dntl Partners of Cal	8021	C	951 689-5031	20244
American Medical Response (DH)	4119	C	951 782-5200	3754
American Medical Rspnse AmbInc	4119	A	303 495-1217	3765
American Reprographics Co LLC	7334	C	951 686-0530	14105
American Residential Svcs LLC	1711	D	951 341-9371	2134
Anheuser-Busch LLC	5181	C	951 782-3935	9039
AON Consulting Inc	6411	D	562 345-4900	10610
Apria Healthcare LLC	8082	D	951 320-1100	22367
Arakelian Enterprises Inc	4953	B	951 342-3300	6428
Aramark Unf & Career AP LLC	7218	D	909 888-4272	13612
Asplundh Tree Expert Co	0783	C	951 352-3144	985
AT&T Corp	4813	D	951 275-8801	5476
Automobile Club Southern Cal	8699	D	951 684-4250	25501
Azteca Landscape	0781	D	951 369-9210	741
B & B Nurseries Inc	5193	C	951 352-8383	9178
Babcock Laboratories Inc	8734	D	951 653-3351	26832
Banquet Facilities	7299	E	951 360-2081	13736
Barrys Security Services Inc (PA)	7381	C	951 789-7575	16571
Bedrock Company	1771	B	951 273-1931	3231
Behavioral Health Resources	8063	C	951 275-8400	22044
Bens Asphalt & Maint Co Inc	1611	E	951 248-1103	1741
Best Best & Krieger LLP (PA)	8111	C	951 686-1450	23113
Bio-Mdcal Applications Cal Inc	8092	D	951 343-7700	22621
Blazing Industrial Steel Inc	1791	C	951 360-8340	3367
Bledsoe Masonry Inc	1741	D	951 360-6140	2804
Blue Banner Company Inc (PA)	0723	E	951 682-6183	511
Bright Expectations	8082	D	951 360-2070	22381
Broker Solutions Inc	7389	D	951 637-2300	17042
Bx Construction LLC	1521	D	951 509-9412	1144
California Citrus Cooperative	0174	D	951 683-4045	216
Canyon Crest Country Club Inc	7997	D	951 274-7900	18912
Carolyn E Wylie Center	8351	D	951 683-5193	24424

GEOGRAPHIC SECTION

RIVERSIDE, CA

	SIC	EMP	PHONE	ENTRY #
Cellco Partnership	4812	D	951 697-3035	5291
Champion Electric Inc	1731	D	951 276-9619	2550
Champion Lumber Co	5031	D	951 684-5670	6915
Childrens Therapeutic Community	8361	D	951 789-4410	24597
Citibank N A	6021	C	800 627-3999	9377
City National Bank	6021	E	951 276-8800	9386
City of Riverside	7389	D	951 346-4700	17078
Clpf - Sycamore	6531	D	212 883-2500	11399
Combine Residential Cnstr	8748	D	951 360-1260	27885
Community Care Rehab Ctr LLC	8051	C	951 680-6500	20465
Community Med Group of Rvrside	8011	C	951 274-3414	19455
Complete Coach Works	7549	B	951 682-2557	17879
Corona - College Heights Ora	0723	B	951 359-6451	522
County of Riverside	8111	C	951 955-6000	23180
County of Riverside	8011	D	951 955-0840	19477
County of Riverside	8399	B	951 358-5306	24909
County of Riverside	8011	D	951 358-5600	19479
County of Riverside	8322	D	951 275-8783	23887
County of Riverside	8322	D	951 697-4699	23888
County of Riverside	7379	E	951 486-7700	16343
County of Riverside	8322	A	951 955-0905	23889
County of Riverside	8322	D	951 358-4415	23890
County of Riverside	1521	B	951 955-4800	1161
County of Riverside	8331	D	951 955-3100	24331
Cox Automotive Inc	5012	D	951 689-6000	6671
Cross Country Healthcare Inc	7361	D	951 786-7683	14632
Cypress Gardens Convalescent H	8059	C	951 688-3643	21203
Del Mar Plastering Inc	1742	D	951 343-5955	2884
Del Rey Lathing Inc	1791	C	951 683-1177	3381
Delta Kappa Gamma Society	8641	E	951 686-8630	25250
Diaz Construction Company Inc	1771	B	951 352-9960	3257
Digiquest Corp	5045	E	951 776-4344	7120
Dmcg Inc (PA)	7389	E	951 683-9685	17128
Dynamic Plumbing Commercial	1711	D	951 343-1200	2210
Dynamic Plumbing Systems Inc	1711	B	951 343-1200	2211
Edwards Theatres Circuit Inc	7832	D	951 361-1917	18321
Elias Elliott Lampasi Fehn (PA)	8021	D	951 689-5031	20253
Empire Company LLC	5031	E	951 742-5273	6922
Encore Senior Living III LLC	8361	E	951 360-1616	24643
Entrepreneurial Hospitality	7389	C	951 346-4700	17151
Erlanger Distribution Ctr Inc	5199	E	951 784-5147	9261
Etairos Consulting	7379	E	844 219-7027	16367
Far West Electric Inc	1731	D	909 684-8661	2591
Farmer Boy Foods Inc (PA)	6794	D	951 275-9900	12215
Fata Travel	8711	E	951 328-0200	25806
Fencecorp Inc	1799	D	951 686-3170	3516
Fenceworks Inc (PA)	1799	C	951 788-5620	3518
Festival Fun Parks LLC	7996	D	951 785-3000	18820
First American Financial Corp	6361	B	909 376-4247	10516
Foundation Building Mtls LLC	5051	E	951 300-2650	7371
FS Commercial Landscape Inc (PA)	0782	D	951 360-7070	854
G4s Secure Solutions (usa)	7381	B	951 341-3000	16652
Ghossain & Truelock Entps Inc	7349	E	951 781-9345	14311
Gless Ranch Inc (PA)	0762	E	951 780-8458	705
Gonzales Painting Corp	1721	D	951 214-6400	2451
Guardsmark LLC	7381	B	909 989-5345	16699
Haider Spine Ctr Med Group Inc	8011	E	951 413-0200	19544
Hal Hays Construction Inc (PA)	1541	C	951 369-1008	1434
Hamblins Bdy Pnt Frame Sp Inc	7538	D	951 689-8440	17800
Herman Weissker Inc (HQ)	1623	B	951 826-8800	1939
High-Light Electric Inc	1731	D	951 352-9646	2611
Honeyflower Holdings LLC	8051	C	951 351-2800	20673
Hy-Tech Tile Inc	1752	C	951 788-0550	3118
Hyatt Corporation	7011	B	909 240-9526	12810
Iheartcommunications Inc	4832	D	951 684-1992	5780
Index Fresh Inc (PA)	0723	D	909 877-0999	549
Interntnal Communications Corp	7373	E	951 934-0531	15970
J Ginger Masonry LP (PA)	1741	D	951 688-5050	2820
J M J Enterprises Intl	8621	D	951 343-2323	25141
J M V B Inc	1721	D	714 288-9797	2456
Jaguar Computer Systems Inc	5045	E	951 273-7950	7150
John L Ginger Masonry Inc	1741	D	951 688-5050	2823
Johnson Machinery Co (PA)	5082	C	951 686-4560	7777
Kadena Pacific Inc	1542	E	951 990-7865	1588
Kaiser Foundation Hospitals	8011	A	951 248-4000	19639
Kaiser Foundation Hospitals	8011	A	866 984-7483	19640
Kaiser Foundation Hospitals	8011	A	951 247-3183	19674
Keenan & Associates	6411	D	951 788-0330	10759
Kindred Healthcare Operating	8059	D	951 688-8200	21284
Kleinfelder Inc	8748	D	951 801-3681	27965
Knollwood Psychiatric and Chem	8063	D	951 275-8400	22078
Kretschmar & Smith Inc	1741	E	951 361-1405	2825
Lennox Industries Inc	5075	C	951 241-8966	7742
Liberty Landscaping Inc	0782	D	951 683-2999	906
M & M Interiors Inc	1542	C	951 279-9535	1604

	SIC	EMP	PHONE	ENTRY #
M & M Plumbing Inc	1711	D	951 354-5388	2288
Magnolia Rhblttion Nursing Ctr	8059	C	951 688-4321	21305
Main Electric Supply Co	5063	D	951 784-2900	7455
Masonry Group Nevada Inc	1741	D	951 509-5300	2827
McKesson Corporation	5122	D	951 686-3575	8278
Meadowbrook Meat Company Inc	4213	C	951 686-1200	4221
Mef Realty LLC	6531	D	951 687-2900	11671
Metropolitan Water District	4941	E	951 688-5672	6373
Metropolitan Water District	4941	D	951 780-1511	6379
Mgb Construction Inc	1611	C	951 342-0303	1826
ML Electricworks Inc	1731	D	951 687-5078	2655
Moduslink Corporation	7372	C	951 571-8300	15762
Mount Rbdoux Convalescent Hosp	8051	C	951 681-2200	20799
National Paving Company Inc	1611	D	951 369-1332	1832
Neal Trucking Inc	4212	D	951 685-5048	4043
New York Life Insurance Co	6311	D	951 354-2094	10216
Officeworks Inc	7361	D	951 784-2534	14715
Olive Grove Retirement Resort	6513	D	951 687-2241	11181
Onrad Inc	8741	D	800 848-5876	27150
Orangetree Convalescent Hosp	8062	C	951 785-6060	21772
Pacific Monarch Resorts Inc	6531	C	951 905-5377	11727
Pacific Tank Lines Inc	4923	C	951 680-1900	6260
Parkview Cmnty Hosp Med Ctr	8062	A	951 354-7404	21786
Paul Kittle	8742	E	951 684-0918	27585
Paychex Inc	8721	E	951 682-6100	26420
Peggs Company Inc (PA)	7699	D	253 584-9548	17999
Pepsi-Cola Metro Btlg Co Inc	5149	B	909 885-0741	8900
Pepsi-Cola Metro Btlg Co Inc	5078	B	951 697-3200	7757
Permanente Kaiser Intl	8399	C	951 662-8194	24964
Permanente Kaiser Intl	8082	C	951 358-2600	22536
Perry Coast Construction Inc	1542	C	951 774-0677	1635
Pinnacle Rvrside Hspitality LP	7011	C	951 784-8000	13099
Plan-It Life Inc	8322	D	951 742-7561	24137
Ppc Enterprises Inc	1711	D	951 354-5402	2326
Precise Distribution Inc	4225	E	951 367-1037	4615
Prestige Gunite California Inc	1771	E	909 276-9096	3316
Provident Savings Bank (HQ)	6035	D	951 782-6177	9581
Provident Savings Bank	6035	D	951 686-6060	9582
Providnt Svngs Bank Chrtble FN	6022	D	951 686-6060	9517
Prudential Overall Supply	7218	C	951 687-0440	13636
Psychiatric Solutions Inc	8011	C	951 789-4405	19897
R&S Carpet Services Inc	5023	D	909 740-6645	6883
Ralphs Grocery Company	4225	D	310 884-9000	4620
Rancho Jurupa Park	7999	E	951 684-7032	19267
Rcr Plumbing and Mech Inc (PA)	1711	C	951 371-5000	2341
Rdo Construction Equipment Co	5082	C	951 778-3700	7786
Real Estate California Dept	6531	D	951 715-0130	11796
Realty One Group Inc	6531	C	951 565-8105	11800
Recycler Core Company Inc	5013	D	951 276-1687	6758
Regional Connector Constrs	1521	D	951 368-6400	1243
Reid & Helly	8111	D	951 682-1771	23531
Rhf Plymouth Tower	8361	D	951 248-6455	24788
Richard Finn	8011	D	951 274-3506	19917
Rls Electrical Contrs Inc	1731	E	951 688-8049	2711
River Side Cmnty Hosp Fd Svcs	8062	D	951 788-3121	21833
Riverside Care Inc	8051	C	951 683-7111	20875
Riverside Cmnty Hlth Systems (DH)	8062	D	951 788-3000	21834
Riverside Dialysis Center	8092	E	951 682-2700	22639
Riverside Equities LLC	8051	D	951 688-2222	20876
Riverside Healthcare System LP	8062	A	951 788-3000	21835
Riverside Medical Clinic Inc	8011	B	951 683-6370	19922
Riverside Medical Clinic Inc (PA)	8011	B	951 683-6370	19923
Riverside Sanitarium LLC	8051	D	951 684-7701	20878
Riverside Scrap Ir & Met Corp (PA)	5093	E	951 686-2120	8081
Riverside Transit Agency (PA)	4111	B	951 565-5000	3692
Robert Half International Inc	7361	D	951 779-9081	14762
Roberts & Associates Inc	8082	D	951 727-4357	22551
Rogan Building Services Inc	7349	D	951 248-1261	14409
Roy E Whitehead Inc	1751	D	951 682-1490	3081
S R S M Inc	5023	C	310 952-9000	6885
Secure Transportation Company	4119	D	951 737-7300	3844
Security California Bancorp	6712	D	951 368-2265	12045
Skanska USA Civil West Rocky M (DH)	1629	D	970 565-8000	2085
Skanska USA Cvil W Cal Dst Inc (DH)	1611	A	951 684-5360	1860
Sky Scan Satelite Systems	4841	D	909 322-1393	6016
South Coast Concrete Cnstr	1771	E	951 351-7777	3332
Southern California Fleet Svc	7538	E	951 272-8655	17814
Southern Wine & Spirits Amrca	5182	D	951 274-2420	9110
Spectra Premium (usa) Corp	5013	D	951 653-0640	6772
Sprin Nonpr Consu Credi Manag	7299	B	951 684-3168	13799
State Compensation Insur Fund	6331	C	888 782-8338	10474
Stronghold Engineering Inc (PA)	1611	D	951 684-9303	1866
Sun Mar Management Services	8051	D	951 687-3842	20935
Sunrise Senior Living LLC	8051	D	951 785-1200	20986
Sunstone Hotel Management Inc	7011	D	951 784-8000	13322

Employment Codes: A=Over 500 employees, B=251-500,
C=101-250, D=51-100, E=45-50

2017 Directory of California
Wholesalers and Services Companies

© Mergent Inc. 1-800-342-5647

1727

RIVERSIDE, CA

	SIC	EMP	PHONE	ENTRY #
Sysco Riverside Inc	5141	B	951 601-5300	8532
T C H P Inc	8059	D	951 687-7330	21389
T S J Elec Communications Inc	1731	D	951 785-0921	2765
Team Truck Dismantling Inc	5015	D	951 685-6744	6797
Thompson & Colegate LLP	8111	E	951 682-5550	23594
Ticor Title Company California	6361	D	951 509-0211	10536
Toad 1350	4832	E	951 369-1350	5823
Tony R Crisalli Inc	7353	E	951 727-0110	14500
Top Priority Couriers Inc (PA)	4215	D	951 781-1000	4429
Trugreen Limited Partnership	0782	E	951 683-0144	969
Tyco Integrated Security LLC	7382	D	951 787-0420	16932
UBS Financial Services Inc	7389	E	951 684-6300	17549
Ucr Botany and Plant Sciences	6732	D	951 827-5133	12165
Unique Carpets Ltd	5023	E	951 352-8125	6899
United Service Tech Inc	7699	D	714 224-1406	18029
USA Fact Inc (PA)	8742	D	951 656-7800	27706
USDA Forest Service	8731	D	951 680-1560	26632
Van Daele Development Corp	1531	C	951 354-6800	1388
Venvest Ballard Inc	1711	D	951 276-9744	2407
Verizon Business Global LLC	4841	D	951 653-4482	6056
Veterinary Service Inc	5047	D	951 328-4900	7325
Villa Health Care Center Inc	8051	E	951 689-5788	21010
Visitng Nurse Assn Inlnd CNT (PA)	8082	A	951 413-1200	22596
Vista Behavioral Health Inc	8063	D	800 992-0901	22111
Vista Pacifica Enterprises Inc (PA)	8051	C	951 682-4833	21020
Vista Pacifica Enterprises Inc	8059	C	951 682-4867	21417
Vitas Healthcare Corp Cal (DH)	8082	B	305 374-4143	22599
Vitas Healthcare Corp Cal	8082	C	909 386-6000	22605
Volt Management Corp	7363	D	951 789-8133	14977
Waterman Convalescent Hospital	8069	C	951 681-2200	22186
West Coast Drywall & Co Inc	1742	B	951 778-3592	2998
West Coast Interiors Inc	1721	A	951 778-3592	2502
West Riverside Veterinary Hosp	0742	E	951 686-2242	633
West States Skanska Inc	1623	C	970 565-4903	2017
Westcoe Realtors Inc	6531	D	951 784-2500	11915
Western Dental Services Inc	8021	E	951 643-6104	20284
Wilmon Corporation	8051	D	951 685-7474	21043
Windsor Capital Group Inc	7011	D	951 276-1200	13424
Z-Best Concrete Inc	1771	D	951 774-1870	3352

RLLNG HLS EST, CA - Los Angeles County

	SIC	EMP	PHONE	ENTRY #
Citigroup Global Markets Inc	6211	D	310 544-3600	9982
Cox California Telcom LLC	4813	D	310 377-1800	5582
Das Global Capital Corp	8732	D	702 967-1688	26653
Dincloud Inc	7372	D	424 286-2300	15639
Dinco Inc (HQ)	5045	C	424 331-1200	7121
Metropolitan Water District	4971	A	310 832-6106	6647
Regal Cinemas Inc	7832	D	310 544-3042	18349
Rolling Hlls Esttes Tennis CLB	7999	E	310 541-4585	19271
Seatech Consulting Group Inc	7379	E	310 356-6828	16476
Spalding Srgcl Ctr of Bvrly Hl	8011	C	310 385-7755	20048
Sqa Services Inc	8742	B	310 544-6888	27660

ROCKLIN, CA - Placer County

	SIC	EMP	PHONE	ENTRY #
American Hlthcare ADM Svcs Inc	8099	B	916 773-7227	22883
Brower Mechanical Inc	7623	D	530 749-0808	17917
Builders & Tradesmens	6411	D	916 772-9200	10651
Builders & Tradesmens Insur	6311	D	916 772-9200	10203
Business Index Group Inc	8732	E	916 577-1010	26647
Casa De Santa Fe of Rocklin	8059	D	916 435-8800	21180
Cellco Partnership	4812	C	916 408-7958	5326
Cha-Dor Realty	5031	D	916 624-0627	6914
Clearcaptions LLC	4813	E	866 868-8695	5578
Data Control Corporation	7373	D	916 774-4000	15927
Ecorp Consulting Inc (PA)	8742	D	916 782-9100	27420
Educational Media Foundation (PA)	4832	C	916 251-1600	5766
Eyecenter Optometric Inc	8042	E	916 624-2020	20299
Federal Express Corporation	4512	C	800 463-3339	4801
Financial Pacific Insur Agcy	6411	C	916 630-5000	10719
Financial Pacific Insurance Co	6411	C	916 630-5000	10720
First Technology Federal Cr Un	6061	C	855 855-8805	9601
Habitat Rstration Sciences Inc	0782	E	916 408-2990	866
Horizon West Healthcare Inc (HQ)	8051	D	916 624-6230	20676
Jemtown Inc	7542	E	916 315-0555	17845
Jkf Auto Service Inc	7542	D	916 315-0555	17846
JR Perce Plbg Inc Sacramento	1711	C	916 434-9554	2264
Kniesels Auto Collision Center	5013	E	916 315-8888	6744
L&H Airco LLC	1711	D	916 677-1000	2273
La Voie & Sons Construction	8741	E	916 408-6900	27107
Oracle Corporation	7372	D	916 435-8342	15798
Oracle Corporation	7372	D	916 315-3500	15804
Pacific Secured Equities Inc (PA)	8742	D	916 677-2500	27579
Progress Rail Services Corp	4789	D	916 645-6006	5238
Quality Telecom Consultants (PA)	1623	D	916 315-0500	1985
Road Safety Inc	7389	D	916 543-4600	17466
SE Scher Corporation	7361	B	916 632-1363	14782

	SIC	EMP	PHONE	ENTRY #
Sierra View Landscape Inc	0782	E	916 408-2990	954
SMA Solar Technology Amer LLC (HQ)	5065	C	916 625-0870	7635
Sonoran Roofing Inc (PA)	1761	D	916 624-1080	3213
Stantec Consulting Svcs Inc	8712	D	916 773-8100	26257
Star Inc	8322	C	916 632-8407	24233
Strikes Unlimited Inc	7933	D	916 626-3600	18531
Sunrise Senior Living LLC	8051	D	916 632-3003	20984
Surveillance Systems	5065	E	800 508-6981	7643
Trane US Inc	5075	D	916 577-1100	7748
United Natural Foods Inc	5149	D	916 625-4100	8944
United Natural Foods West Inc (HQ)	5149	B	401 528-8634	8945
Wpcs Intrntional-Suisun Cy Inc	1731	D	916 624-1300	2799
Zentek Corporation	7371	D	916 749-3610	15558

ROHNERT PARK, CA - Sonoma County

	SIC	EMP	PHONE	ENTRY #
24 Hour Fitness Usa Inc	8099	E	707 536-0048	22870
Animal Care Center	0742	C	707 584-4343	614
Artizen Incorporated	7371	C	650 261-9400	15035
Calif Institute Human Ser	8742	D	707 664-2416	27366
Catati Rohnert Park Inc	7389	E	707 792-4531	17060
Codding Construction Co	1542	E	707 795-3550	1532
Cve Nb Contracting Group Inc	8744	D	707 584-1900	27785
Doubletree LLC	7011	C	707 584-5466	12599
Federted Indans Grton Rncheria	7011	C	707 588-7100	12633
Herc Rentals Inc	7514	D	707 586-4444	17677
Kaiser Foundation Hospitals	6324	C	707 206-3000	10330
Kisco Senior Living LLC	8741	D	707 585-1800	27100
Lemo USA Inc	5065	D	707 206-3700	7595
Merrill Gardens LLC	6531	C	707 585-7878	11682
North Bay Eye Assoc A Med Corp	8011	D	707 206-0849	19776
OHagin Manufacturing LLC	1711	E	707 872-3620	2308
OHagins Inc	1711	D	707 303-3660	2309
Pace Supply Corp (PA)	5074	D	707 303-0320	7727
Red Condor Inc	7371	D	707 569-7419	15411
Soligent Distribution LLC (HQ)	5065	D	707 992-3100	7637
State Farm Fire and Cslty Co	6411	B	707 588-6011	10878

ROMOLAND, CA - Riverside County

	SIC	EMP	PHONE	ENTRY #
Southern California Gas Co	4924	D	213 244-1200	6277

ROSAMOND, CA - Kern County

	SIC	EMP	PHONE	ENTRY #
Catalina Solar Lessee LLC	4911	A	888 903-6926	6111
Tapia Farms	0191	E	661 256-4401	396

ROSEMEAD, CA - Los Angeles County

	SIC	EMP	PHONE	ENTRY #
Anka Behavioral Health Inc	8999	D	626 573-5902	28113
Cathay Bank	6091	C	626 452-1582	9702
Chinese Youth Arts	8699	D	323 985-4699	25516
Cox Automotive Inc	5012	C	626 573-8001	6668
Del Mar Convalescent Hospital	8062	D	626 288-8353	21528
Doubletree Hotel	7011	D	323 722-8800	12589
Durham School Services L P	4151	C	626 573-3769	3924
Edison International (PA)	4911	D	626 302-2222	6130
Edison Mssion Midwest Holdings	4911	A	626 302-2222	6131
Ensign Group Inc	8051	D	626 287-0438	20542
Ensign Group Inc	8051	D	626 607-2400	20543
Herald Christian Health Center (PA)	8011	D	626 286-8700	19555
Irish Communication Company (DH)	1623	D	626 288-6170	1944
Irish Construction (HQ)	1623	C	626 288-8530	1945
Landcare USA LLC	0782	D	310 354-1520	893
Longwood Management Corp	8051	D	626 280-2293	20743
Longwood Management Corp	8051	C	626 280-4820	20744
Los Angeles Orphan Asylum Inc	8361	C	323 283-9311	24717
Maryvale	8361	D	626 280-6510	24726
Monterey Healthcare & Wellness	8051	D	626 280-3220	20796
Psychiatric Solutions Inc	8093	C	626 286-1191	22813
SM Uni Inc	5146	E	213 626-2557	8654
Southern California Edison Co (HQ)	4911	A	626 302-1212	6210
Southern California Edison Co	4911	C	626 302-5101	6218
Southern California Edison Co	4911	C	626 302-1212	6222
Southern California Edison Co	4911	D	714 895-0488	6228
Southern California Edison Co	4911	C	626 302-0530	6242
Success Healthcare 1 LLC	8011	C	626 288-1160	20074
Sun Mar Management Services	8741	D	626 288-8353	27237
Sunny Cal Adhc Inc	8322	D	626 307-7772	24239

ROSEVILLE, CA - Placer County

	SIC	EMP	PHONE	ENTRY #
10up LLC	7373	D	888 571-7130	15888
A & M Gyms LLC	7991	D	916 788-4241	18603
Aardvark Staffing Inc	7363	E	916 774-7115	14829
Abso	7361	C	800 943-2589	14597
Adventist Health System/West (PA)	8062	B	916 781-2000	21431
American Pacific Mortgage Corp (PA)	6162	C	916 960-1325	9815
Bianchi Plumbing Co Inc	1711	C	916 772-7364	2166
Cal Consolidated Communications	4813	D	916 786-6141	5566
California State Automobile	6331	E	916 472-2701	10409
California Sun Centers Inc	7299	D	916 789-9767	13740

GEOGRAPHIC SECTION — SACRAMENTO, CA

Company	SIC	EMP	PHONE	ENTRY #
Caranythingcom Inc	8742	D	916 781-4344	27370
Cellco Partnership	4812	D	916 786-6151	5298
Century 21 Haley & Associates	6531	D	916 782-1500	11376
Century Theatres Inc	7833	D	916 797-3466	18356
Chicago Title Insurance Co	6361	B	916 783-7195	10508
Claims Management Inc	6411	C	916 631-1250	10671
Clark & Sullivan Builders Inc	1542	C	916 338-7707	1529
CLC Incorporated (PA)	7361	E	916 789-7600	14626
Clearcapitalcom Inc	6531	D	530 582-5011	11398
Clp Resources Inc	7363	D	916 788-0300	14857
Cokeva Inc	7378	C	916 462-6001	16289
Coldwell Banker RE Corp	6531	E	408 981-7200	11413
Crocus Holdings LLC	8051	D	916 782-1238	20508
D Augustine & Associates	7311	D	916 774-9600	13829
Denios Roseville Farmers	5191	C	916 782-2704	9135
Dignity Health Med Foundation	8099	D	916 787-0404	22943
Directapps Inc (PA)	7379	C	916 787-2200	16357
Dwayne Nash Industries Inc	1761	C	916 253-1900	3167
Enterprise Rent-A-Car Compan (DH)	7515	E	916 787-4500	17701
Erickson Construction LP	1751	C	916 774-1100	3048
Erickson Framing AZ LLC	1751	C	916 774-1100	3049
Ernst & Young LLP	8721	C	916 218-1900	26347
Eskaton Properties Inc	8361	D	916 334-0810	24652
Esl Technologies Inc	7378	B	916 677-4500	16292
Federal Deposit Insurance Corp	6399	C	916 789-8580	10570
Flexcare LLC	7363	A	866 543-3589	14879
Flintco Pacific Inc	8711	D	916 757-1000	25810
Fmr LLC	6282	D	916 784-3649	10142
Fraternal Order Eagles 1582	6512	C	916 782-2694	10984
Genuent Usa LLC	7371	C	916 772-3700	15203
Golden State Collision Centers	7532	C	916 772-1666	17755
Horizon West Healthcare Inc	8069	C	916 782-1238	22145
Hotel Contracting Services Inc	7011	D	916 865-4204	12784
Huppe Landscape Company Inc (HQ)	0781	D	916 784-7666	773
Ibs Enterprise Usa Inc (HQ)	7371	C	916 542-2820	15230
Industrial Container Services	5085	D	916 781-2775	7936
Intech Mechanical Company Inc	1711	D	916 797-4900	2252
Intech Mechanical Company LLC	1711	D	916 797-4900	2253
Intercare Holdings Insur Svcs	6411	B	916 677-2500	10746
Jbwo Inc	8741	E	916 239-7013	27074
Kaiser Foundation Hospitals	8062	C	916 746-3937	21630
Kaiser Foundation Hospitals	8011	D	916 784-4000	19656
Kaiser Foundation Hospitals	6324	D	916 784-4050	10317
Kaiser Foundation Hospitals	6324	D	916 784-4190	10347
Kaiser Foundation Hospitals	8011	D	916 784-4000	19678
Kellogg Sales Company	5149	E	916 787-0414	8866
Lancaster Burns Cnstr Inc	1742	C	916 624-8404	2923
Lyon Realty	6531	D	916 784-1500	11642
Lyon Realty	6531	D	916 787-7700	11645
Med-Data Incorporated	8721	D	916 771-1362	26408
Neptune Management Corporation	7261	D	916 771-5300	13709
New York Life Insurance Co	6411	D	916 774-6200	10804
Nortech Waste LLC	4953	C	916 645-5230	6509
Northern California Power Agcy (PA)	4911	D	916 781-3636	6152
Olivieri Enterprises LP	1751	C	916 791-7857	3068
Palms Assistd Lvng & Mmry Cre	8361	D	916 786-7200	24763
Parchment Inc	7389	D	480 719-1646	17395
Patterson Dental Supply Inc	5047	C	916 780-5100	7296
Permanente Medical Group Inc	8011	D	916 784-4000	19858
Pinnacle Builders Inc	1521	B	916 372-5000	1236
Polycomp Administrative Svcs	6411	E	916 773-3480	10829
Precision Framing Inc	1751	B	916 791-7464	3072
Premiere Agency of California	6411	D	916 784-1008	10834
Pride Industries (PA)	4226	C	916 788-2100	4700
Production Framing Inc	1751	D	916 978-2843	3074
Production Framing Systems Inc (PA)	1751	C	916 978-2888	3075
Project Go Incorporated	1799	E	916 782-3443	3571
Psomas	8711	C	916 788-8122	26023
Reeve-Knight Construction Inc	1542	C	916 786-5112	1648
River Rock Equipment LLC	6719	C	916 791-1609	12087
Roseville Sportworld Inc	7999	D	916 783-8550	19272
Roseville Towne Place Suites	7011	D	916 782-2232	13169
Safe Credit Union	6163	E	916 979-7233	9949
Sierra Care Rehabilitation Ctr	8051	D	916 782-3188	20913
Sierra Hills Care Center Inc	8052	D	916 782-7007	21108
Sierra View Country Club	7997	D	916 782-3741	19079
Sign of Dove	6513	D	916 786-3277	11203
South Coast Medical Center (PA)	8062	A	949 364-1770	21898
Spare-Time Inc	7997	D	916 782-2600	19088
Specialty Steel Service Co Inc (HQ)	5051	D	916 771-4737	7404
Sun City Rsvlle Cmnty Assn Inc (PA)	7992	C	916 774-3880	18792
Sunrise Retirement Villa	6513	D	916 786-3277	11210
Sutter Health	8011	D	916 797-4725	20080
Sutter Health	8099	C	916 797-4715	23069
Sutter Health	8011	D	916 784-2277	20105
Sutter Health	8051	D	916 797-4700	20988
Sutter Hlth Scrmnto Sierra Reg	8062	A	916 781-1000	21949
Sutter Roseville Medical Ctr	8062	A	916 781-1000	21952
Sutter Rsvlle Med Ctr Fndation	8062	A	916 781-1000	21953
T-Mobile Usa Inc	4812	C	916 786-3339	5413
Tasq Technology Inc	6099	B	916 632-7600	9723
Tech-Ed Networks Inc	7379	C	916 784-2005	16502
Teleplan Service Solutions Inc	7378	C	916 677-4619	16305
Ufcw Employers Benefit Plan (PA)	6733	C	925 746-7530	12206
Union Pacific Corporation	4011	A	916 789-5311	3619
Union Pacific Railroad Company	4011	D	916 789-5930	3623
Union Pacific Railroad Company	4011	D	916 789-6055	3625
United Building Maintenance	7349	C	916 772-8101	14453
United States Info Systems Inc	1731	D	845 353-9224	2780
USA Multifamily Management	6531	C	916 773-6060	11894
USA Properties Fund Inc (PA)	6552	D	916 773-6060	12023
Verizon Wireless Inc	4812	D	916 784-6886	5430
Vexilium Inc	4911	C	916 218-3815	6250
Volt Management Corp	7363	D	916 923-0454	14976
Walt Disney Company	4832	D	916 780-1470	5829
Waterhouse Management Corp	6515	C	916 772-4918	11246
Wells Fargo Bank National Assn	6021	B	916 724-2982	9442
Wells Fargo Bank National Assn	6021	B	916 774-2249	9446
Wells Fargo Home Mortgage Inc	6162	E	916 782-2221	9906
Westmont Living Inc	8361	B	916 786-3277	24854
Westower Communications Inc	8999	D	916 783-6400	28169

ROYAL OAKS, CA - Santa Cruz County

Company	SIC	EMP	PHONE	ENTRY #
Cal Southern Seafood Inc	5146	D	805 698-8262	8630
Falcon Trading Company (PA)	5149	C	831 786-7000	8834
Faurot Ranch	0161	E	831 722-1346	62
Gino Rinaldi Inc	1743	D	831 761-0195	3014
Kelvin Hildebrand Inc	4212	E	831 768-9104	4034
Monterey Mushrooms Inc	0182	A	831 728-8300	337

RUTHERFORD, CA - Napa County

Company	SIC	EMP	PHONE	ENTRY #
Amer Zoetrope Research LLC	8732	C	707 963-9230	26643
Terre Du Soleil Ltd	7011	B	707 963-1211	13341
Vyborny Vineyard Management	0762	D	707 944-9135	732

SACRAMENTO, CA - Sacramento County

Company	SIC	EMP	PHONE	ENTRY #
15th & L Investors LLC	7011	D	916 267-6805	12359
A Meissners Hhld & Indus Svc	5084	D	916 920-2121	7816
A Teichert & Son Inc (HQ)	5032	C	916 484-3011	6971
A1 Protective Services Inc	7381	D	916 421-3000	16535
AAA Signs Inc	7534	D	916 568-3456	17779
Abacus Service Corporation	7371	B	916 288-8948	14993
ABC Security Service Inc	7381	C	916 442-7001	16536
ABF Freight System Inc	4213	D	916 428-3531	4101
Accenture LLP	8742	C	916 557-2200	27300
Access Dental Plan (PA)	8021	D	916 922-5000	20242
Ace High Entertainnment LLC	7941	E	916 243-5515	18532
Ace Parking Management Inc	8741	B	916 498-9852	26905
Adesa Corporation LLC	5012	C	916 388-8899	6660
Administrative Systems Inc	7389	D	916 563-1121	16971
Advanced HM Hlth & Hospice Inc	8021	D	916 978-0744	20243
Advanced Health Home Inc	8082	D	916 978-0744	22339
Aecom Global II LLC	8711	B	916 679-2000	25627
Aecom Global II LLC	8748	D	916 679-8700	27812
Aecom Technology Corporation	8711	D	916 414-5800	25639
After Market Group Inc (HQ)	5047	D	916 361-1687	7232
Agamerica Fcb (PA)	6111	D	651 282-8800	9726
Air Systems Sacramento Inc	1711	C	916 368-0336	2114
Airco Mechanical Inc	1711	C	916 381-4523	2115
All West Coachlines Inc	4142	C	916 423-4000	3897
Alliedbarton Security Svcs LLC	7381	C	916 489-8280	16546
Alsco Inc	7213	C	916 454-5545	13519
Alston Construction Co Inc (PA)	1541	D	916 340-2400	1398
Amador Stage Lines Inc	4141	D	916 444-7880	3890
American Building Supply Inc (PA)	5031	B	916 503-4100	6906
American Dream	1521	D	916 613-4917	1125
American Institute Research	8733	B	916 286-8800	26734
American Medical Response	4119	B	916 563-0600	3751
American Patriot Security	7381	D	916 706-2449	16557
American Reprographics Co LLC	7334	D	916 443-1322	14101
American Water Works Co Inc	4941	D	916 568-4236	6312
Amerisourcebergen Corporation	5122	C	916 830-4500	8232
Anova Architects Inc	8712	E	530 626-1810	26163
AON Consulting Inc	6411	D	800 558-0655	10607
Apple Hospitality Reit Inc	7011	D	916 568-5400	12393
Applewood Care Center	8051	E	916 446-2506	20379
Appliance Distribution Inc	5064	D	916 497-0274	7490
Apria Healthcare LLC	5047	D	530 677-2713	7238
Aramark Unf & Career AP LLC	7218	B	916 286-4100	13608
Aramark Uniform Services	7218	C	916 286-4100	13616
Arden Hills Country Club Inc	7997	D	916 482-6111	18877

Employment Codes: A=Over 500 employees, B=251-500, C=101-250, D=51-100, E=45-50

SACRAMENTO, CA — GEOGRAPHIC SECTION

Company	SIC	EMP	PHONE	ENTRY #
Arraycon LLC (PA)	1711	E	916 925-0201	2150
Arreolas Complete Ldscp Svc	0782	E	916 387-6777	809
Asbury Pk Nrsing Rhblttion Ctr	8059	C	916 649-2000	21146
Asian Community Center of Sac	8361	C	916 393-9020	24552
AT&T Corp	4813	B	916 830-5000	5502
AT&T Services	4813	C	916 972-2248	5517
AT&T Services	4813	C	916 972-2423	5522
AT&T Services Inc	4813	D	916 453-6267	5553
Atkinson Youth Services Inc	8322	D	916 927-1863	23674
Atlas Disposal Industries LLC	4953	D	916 455-2800	6434
Atlaz Inc	7371	D	415 671-6142	15041
Atrium Hotels LP	7011	C	916 446-0100	12401
Atrium Hotels LP	7011	C	916 446-0100	12402
Auburn Constructors Inc	1629	D	916 924-0344	2023
Avis Rent A Car System Inc	7514	C	916 922-5601	17664
Awm LLC	5031	D	916 381-4200	6909
B & G Delivery System Inc	4212	C	916 921-4401	3980
B B & T Management Corp	5031	D	916 428-8060	6910
Baco Realty Corporation	7381	C	916 974-9898	16567
Bank America National Assn	8741	C	916 326-3161	26936
Banner Bank	6035	D	916 648-2100	9568
Barnum & Celillo Electric Inc (PA)	1731	E	916 564-9976	2527
Bayer Protective Services Inc	7382	C	916 486-5800	16870
Benetech Inc (PA)	8742	D	916 484-6811	27344
Benetech Inc	6411	E	916 484-6811	10646
Bickmore and Associates Inc (DH)	6411	D	916 244-1100	10648
Biz Vision Inc	8742	D	916 792-2124	27347
Blackstone Consulting Inc	8748	C	916 383-8060	27850
Bloodsource Inc	8099	E	916 488-1701	22904
Bmi Imaging Systems Inc	5044	D	916 924-6666	7042
Bradford & Barthel LLP (PA)	8111	E	916 569-0790	23129
Briarwood Health Care Inc	8059	E	916 383-2741	21162
Brightview Landscape Svcs Inc	0781	D	916 381-1121	752
Brinckerhoff Parsons Group LLC	8742	D	916 567-2500	27358
Brinks Incorporated	7381	C	916 452-5279	16584
Brunswick Corner Partnership	6531	E	916 649-7500	11330
Burgett Incorporated	5099	D	916 567-9999	8107
Buzz Oates Management Services	6531	E	916 381-3843	11333
C & S Wholesale Grocers Inc	4225	B	916 383-5275	4529
C A H H S	8611	D	916 552-7507	25078
C H W Mercy Healthcare	8062	A	916 453-4545	21467
C H W Mercy Healthcare	8062	A	916 423-3000	21468
Cal Fed Investments Inc	6726	D	916 614-2440	12135
California American Water Co	4941	E	916 568-4216	6318
California Association O (PA)	8621	C	916 443-7401	25119
California Chamber Commerce (PA)	8611	D	916 444-6670	25081
California Community Colleges	8331	C	916 445-8752	24317
California Dental Association (PA)	8621	C	916 443-0505	25121
California Govrnmnt Opr Agncy	6371	A	800 228-5453	10544
California Medical Association (PA)	8011	D	916 444-5532	19396
California Pavement Maint Inc	1611	C	916 381-8033	1745
California Public Emplyees Ret	6371	C	916 795-3000	10545
California Public Emplyees Ret (DH)	6371	C	916 795-3000	10546
California Rural Indian Health	8399	D	916 437-0104	24883
Califrnia High Speed Rail Auth	4011	D	916 324-1541	3611
Califrnia Hlth Humn Srvcs Agcy	7374	B	916 739-7640	16106
Califrnia State Employees Assn (PA)	8631	D	916 444-8134	25170
Calstars	8721	E	916 445-0211	26305
Capital Athletic Club Inc	7299	D	916 442-3927	13741
Capital Commercial Flrg Inc	1752	E	916 569-1960	3108
Capital Public Radio Inc	4832	E	916 278-8900	5753
Capitol Casino	7999	C	916 446-0700	19158
Capitol Corporate Services	8732	E	916 444-6787	26648
Capitol Regency LLC	7011	B	916 443-1234	12487
Careability Health Svcs Corp	8082	D	916 479-8554	22395
Carescope LLC	8322	D	916 780-1384	23703
Carlton Senior Living Inc	8361	D	916 971-4800	24580
Carrier Corporation	7623	E	916 928-9500	17918
Carson Frank Ldscp & Maint Inc	0782	C	916 856-5400	821
Carter & Burgess Inc	8711	E	916 929-3323	25721
Case Dealer Holding Co LLC	5082	C	916 649-0096	7766
Cathedral Pioneer Church Homes (PA)	8051	D	916 442-4906	20441
CB&i Envmtl Infrastructure Inc	8748	D	916 928-3300	27869
Cbre Inc	6531	D	916 446-6800	11350
CBS Radio	4832	D	916 923-6800	5756
Cellco Partnership	4812	D	916 331-6833	5331
Cellco Partnership	4812	D	916 419-6200	5343
Center For Aids Research	8011	C	916 443-3299	19415
Central Anesthesia Service	8011	D	916 481-6800	19417
Central Freight Lines Inc	4231	D	800 782-5036	4709
Central Parking System Inc	7521	D	916 441-1074	17714
Cessna Aircraft Company	4581	D	916 929-5656	4905
Ceva Freight LLC	4731	C	916 379-6000	5042
Ch2m Hill Inc	8712	E	916 920-0300	26174
Ch2m Hill Inc	8711	A	916 920-0300	25733
Ch2m Hill Constructors Inc	1623	B	916 920-0212	1919
Channel 40 Inc	4833	C	916 454-4422	5845
Chem Quip Inc	5091	C	916 923-5091	8014
Chemical Dependency Recovery	5169	E	916 482-1132	8982
Childrens Law Center Cal	8111	D	916 520-2000	23147
Childrens Recvg Hm Sacramento	8361	C	916 482-2370	24596
Choice Medical Group Inc	8093	D	916 483-2885	22685
Cim/J Street Ht Sacramento Inc	7011	B	916 447-1700	12520
Cintas Corporation No 3	7218	C	916 419-8519	13624
Citigroup Global Markets Inc	6211	E	916 567-2056	9976
Clark Pest Ctrl Stockton Inc	7342	D	916 723-3390	14178
Coldwell Banker	6531	D	916 447-5900	11403
Colliers Intl Prperty Cons Inc	6531	D	916 929-5999	11446
Columbia Woodlake LLC	7011	D	206 728-9063	12534
Comcast Corporation	4841	D	916 459-2964	5950
Comcast Corporation	4841	D	916 520-6813	5965
Comcast Corporation	1731	B	916 830-6790	2556
Cook Realty Inc	6531	C	916 451-6702	11453
Cooperative Personnel Services (PA)	8742	D	916 263-3600	27389
Corporation of The President	8331	D	916 482-1480	24328
Corporation Service Company	7349	D	302 636-5400	14265
Correctons Rhbltation Cal Dept	7374	C	916 358-2319	16111
County of Sacramento	7376	D	916 874-7752	16277
County of Sacramento	8051	D	916 875-0900	20481
County of Sacramento	1622	B	916 875-2711	1888
County of Sacramento	7349	D	916 874-0746	14270
County of Sacramento	8111	D	916 874-5411	23181
County of Sacramento	7996	D	916 363-8383	18816
County of Sacramento	8322	D	916 875-4467	23891
Covenant Care California LLC	8051	D	916 391-6011	20494
Craig and Hamilton Meat Co	5147	D	916 419-5500	8666
Creative Design Interiors Inc (PA)	1752	D	916 641-1121	3109
Crestwood Behavioral Hlth Inc	8063	D	916 452-1431	22060
Crocker Art Museum Association	8699	D	916 808-7000	25521
Crossroads Facility Svcs Inc	7349	D	916 568-5230	14272
Crown Building Maintenance Co	7349	A	916 920-9556	14273
Cuneo Black Ward Missler A Law	8111	E	916 363-6822	23191
Cusa AWC LLC	4111	D	916 423-4000	3640
Cy Sac Operator LLC	7011	D	916 455-6800	12561
D & J Plumbing Inc	1711	D	916 922-4888	2198
D7 Roofing Services Inc	1761	D	916 447-2175	3161
Dal Cais Inc	1542	D	916 381-8080	1535
Dave Gross Enterprises Inc	1799	D	916 388-2000	3511
DC Transport Inc	4213	D	916 438-0888	4133
Dealertrack Collte Manag Servi	7379	C	916 368-5300	16351
Del Paso Country Club	7997	D	916 489-3681	18936
Delegata Corporation	7373	D	916 609-5400	15930
Delta Dental of California	6324	A	916 853-7373	10278
Delta Stewardship Council	8741	D	916 445-5511	27002
Dentists Insurance Company (HQ)	6411	C	916 443-4567	10688
Desert View Power Inc	4911	D	916 596-2500	6123
Desilva Gates Construction LP	1611	D	916 386-9708	1764
Develop Disabilities Svc Org	8322	E	916 973-1953	23942
Diablo Valley Masonry Inc	1741	E	916 438-0607	2810
Dialysis Clinic Inc	8092	E	916 453-0803	22624
Diepenbrock Elkin LLP	8111	D	916 492-5000	23213
Dignity Health	8011	D	916 667-0000	19498
Dignity Health	8011	C	916 423-5940	19503
Dimare Fresh	5148	B	916 921-6302	8716
Disability Rights California (PA)	8111	D	916 488-9950	23216
Dish Network Corporation	4841	D	916 381-5084	5995
Dominguez Landscape Svcs Inc	0782	D	916 381-8855	843
Domus Construction & Design	1521	E	916 381-7500	1168
Dongalen Enterprises Inc (PA)	5162	E	916 422-3110	8969
Doubletree LLC	7011	B	916 929-8855	12594
Doumit Communication Inc	1611	D	916 362-3519	1767
Downey Brand LLP (PA)	8111	C	916 444-1000	23225
Dpr Construction Inc	1542	B	916 568-3434	1534
Dreyer Bbich Bccola Cllham LLP	8111	D	916 379-3500	23226
Drywall Works Inc	1742	D	916 383-6667	2888
Easter Seal Soc Superior Cal (PA)	8099	D	916 485-6711	22951
Easun Inc	7011	C	916 929-8855	12608
Eclipse Solutions Inc	7379	D	916 565-8090	16361
Edaw Inc	0781	D	916 414-5800	765
Edco Health Info Solution	7389	E	909 793-0613	17142
Edward E Straine CPA	8721	D	916 646-6464	26333
Ehealthwirecom Inc	8099	D	916 924-8092	22953
Elegant Surfaces	5032	D	209 823-9388	6981
Elica Health Centers	8011	D	916 454-2345	19514
Elite Power Inc	1731	D	916 739-1580	2588
Elizabethan Inn Associates LP	7011	D	916 448-1300	12615
Elk Grove Unified School Dst	4151	C	916 686-7733	3925
Els Investments	0781	C	916 388-0308	766
Employment Dev Cal Dept	7361	A	916 654-7867	14649
Employment Development Dept	7361	D	916 653-2065	14651

GEOGRAPHIC SECTION

SACRAMENTO, CA

Company	SIC	EMP	PHONE	ENTRY #
Energy Salvage Inc	8741	E	916 737-8640	27016
Entercom Communications Corp	4832	C	916 766-5000	5769
Entercom Communications Corp	4832	C	916 334-7777	5771
Enterprise Rent-A-Car Compan	7514	D	916 576-3164	17674
Entravsion Communications Corp	4832	E	916 646-4000	5772
Entravsion Communications Corp	4833	D	916 648-6029	5857
Environmental Protection Agcy	4959	D	916 324-7572	6627
Environmental Systems Research	5045	D	916 448-2412	7127
Eskaton Properties Inc	8051	C	916 393-2550	20552
Essendant Co	5112	C	916 344-6707	8167
Essex Property Trust Inc	6798	D	916 381-0345	12245
Ethan Conrad Properties Inc	6512	D	916 779-1000	10981
Eugene Burger Management Corp	8741	E	916 443-6637	27018
Excel Managed Care Disa	8742	D	916 944-7185	27426
Executive Office State of CA	8731	D	916 322-2318	26515
Express Messenger Systems Inc	4215	D	916 921-6016	4407
Fdx Advisors Inc	6282	D	916 920-5293	10138
Federal Express Corporation	4513	D	916 361-5500	4861
Federico Beauty Institute	7231	E	916 929-4242	13674
Fidelity National Title Co Cal	6411	D	916 646-9993	10718
First Responder Ems Inc	4119	C	916 381-3780	3792
Firstline Trnsp SEC Inc	7381	C	916 456-5166	16643
Fischer Tile and Marble Inc	1743	C	916 452-1426	3013
Fni International Inc	6799	C	916 643-1400	12307
Frys Electronics Inc	8748	B	916 286-5800	27926
Fusion Real Estate Network Inc	6531	D	916 448-3174	11546
G&K Services Inc	7218	C	916 381-5500	13629
Gat Airline Ground Support	4581	B	916 923-2349	4919
Gccfc 2005-Gg5 Y St Ltd Partnr	7011	D	916 455-6800	12660
Geico Corporation	6411	C	707 448-7172	10727
General Prod A Cal Ltd Partnr (PA)	5148	C	916 441-6431	8733
General Services Cal Dept	7349	C	916 845-4942	14308
General Services Cal Dept	8711	B	916 657-9960	25835
General Services Cal Dept	8711	D	916 657-9903	25836
General Services Cal Dept	7349	A	916 445-4566	14309
Girl Scouts Heart Central Cal	8641	C	916 452-9181	25260
Gold Country Management Inc	6531	D	916 929-3003	11556
Gold Star Insulation Inc	1742	E	916 928-1100	2904
Golden 1 Credit Union (PA)	6062	B	916 732-2900	9669
Golden Pond LP	8361	E	916 369-8967	24671
Goodwill Industries of Sacrame	8699	E	916 331-0237	25538
Gordon & Schwenkmeyer Inc	7389	D	916 569-1740	17196
Gordon Rees Scully Mnskhani LLP	8111	D	916 830-6900	23281
Granite Construction Company	1629	D	916 855-4400	2054
Granite Construction Inc	1611	D	916 855-4495	1787
Greater Sacramento Sur	8093	D	916 929-7229	22739
Growing Company Inc	0782	D	916 379-9088	863
Guardian Environmental Inc (PA)	1799	D	916 641-5695	3527
Guardsmark LLC	7381	C	209 575-4972	16683
Gudgel Roofing Inc	1761	E	916 387-6900	3177
Guild Mortgage Company	6163	E	916 486-6257	9928
H & D Electric	1731	B	916 332-0794	2602
H C C S Inc	8051	D	916 454-5752	20641
Halstead Partnership	6512	D	916 830-8000	10996
Hammel Green & Abrahamson Inc	8712	D	916 787-5100	26194
Hank Fisher Properties Inc	8361	C	916 447-4444	24677
Hank Fisher Properties Inc	8059	D	916 921-1970	21260
Hanson Bridgett LLP	8111	E	916 442-3333	23299
Harold E Nutter Inc	1731	E	916 334-4343	2607
Harris & Sloan Consulting	8748	D	916 921-2800	27940
HDR Engineering Inc	8711	D	916 564-4214	25857
Health By Design	8082	E	916 974-3322	22451
HealthSouth Corporation	8093	D	916 929-9431	22744
Heartland Payment Systems Inc	7389	D	916 844-9548	17216
Helping Hearts Foundation Inc	8361	D	916 368-7200	24690
Hendrickson Trucking Inc	4213	B	916 387-9614	4196
Henwood Energy Services Inc (DH)	8711	C	916 955-6031	25861
Herc Rentals Inc	7514	D	916 448-2228	17679
Heritage Community Credit Un (PA)	6061	E	916 364-1700	9604
Hilary A Brodie MD PHD	8011	D	916 734-3744	19559
Holiday Inn Northeast	7011	C	916 338-5800	12751
Horizon Government Svcs Inc	7361	D	916 760-7913	14673
Horizon West Inc	8051	D	916 331-4590	20675
Howe Community Center	7999	E	916 927-3802	19225
HP Inc	7373	C	916 449-9553	15960
Hub Intrntional Insur Svcs Inc	6411	D	916 974-7800	10741
Hunt Convenience Stores LLC	8741	E	916 383-4868	27059
Hurley Construction Inc	1522	D	916 446-7599	1314
Hussmann Services Corporation	7623	C	916 920-4993	17922
Huttig Building Products Inc	5031	D	916 383-3721	6932
Hylton Security Inc	7381	D	916 442-1000	16705
Icf Jones & Stokes Inc (DH)	8748	C	916 737-3000	27949
Iheartcommunications Inc	4832	C	916 929-5325	5783
Iheartcommunications Inc	4832	D	916 929-5325	5785
Inland Business Machines Inc (DH)	7699	D	916 928-0770	17985
Innovative Maint Solutions Inc	1711	C	916 568-1400	2251
Internal Mdcine Rsdncy Affairs	8621	D	916 734-7080	25139
Interntional Un Oper Engineers (PA)	8631	D	916 444-6880	25177
Interstate Fuel Systems Inc	5172	D	916 457-6572	9023
Interstate Hotels Resorts Inc	7011	C	916 922-4700	12853
Interwest Insurance Svcs Inc (PA)	6411	C	916 488-3100	10748
Iron Mechanical Inc	1711	D	916 341-3530	2255
Iron Mntin/Pacific Rec MGT Inc	4226	D	916 924-1558	4688
Iunlimited Incorporated	7381	D	916 218-6198	16713
J and J Wall Baking Co Inc	5142	D	916 381-1410	8555
J B Company	1542	D	916 929-3003	1577
Jackson Construction (PA)	1541	E	916 381-8113	1439
Jacobs Engineering Group Inc	8711	E	916 273-5500	25898
Jacobs Engineering Group Inc	8711	D	916 929-9323	25899
Jarka Enterprises Inc	1799	D	916 491-6180	3536
Jensen Enterprises Inc	5039	D	916 992-8301	7024
Jerry S Powell MD	8011	D	916 734-5959	19575
Jetro Cash and Carry Entps LLC	5141	D	916 492-2305	8489
JJR Enterprises Inc (PA)	7629	D	916 363-2666	17936
Jma Investments Ltd	0782	D	916 685-1355	880
John F Otto Inc	1542	D	916 441-6870	1583
John Jackson Masonry	1741	D	916 381-8021	2822
Judianne Chew Lcsw	8093	D	916 734-6629	22750
Juniper Networks Inc	7373	D	916 503-1518	15979
Justice California Department	8748	A	916 324-5039	27962
Kaiser Foundation Hospitals	8062	D	916 973-5000	21646
Kaiser Foundation Hospitals	8011	A	916 688-2000	19669
Kaiser Foundation Hospitals	8062	C	916 525-6300	21676
Kindred Healthcare Oper Inc	8051	D	916 454-5752	20697
Kindred Healthcare Oper Inc	8059	D	916 457-6521	21282
Kings Arena Ltd Partnership	7941	D	916 928-0000	18552
Kojenov Arkadi Nilovich	4731	E	916 718-1790	5109
Kpmg LLP	8721	C	916 448-4700	26388
Kronick Moskovitz Tiedemann (PA)	8111	C	916 321-4500	23360
Kvie Inc (PA)	4833	D	916 929-5843	5891
Kxtv Inc (HQ)	4833	C	916 441-2345	5893
La Familia Counseling Center	8322	D	916 452-3601	24062
Landmark Healthcare Svcs Inc (PA)	8041	C	800 638-4557	20297
Lawnman II Inc	0782	D	916 739-1420	903
Lawson Mechanical Contractors (PA)	1711	D	916 381-6704	2275
LDI Mechanical Inc	1711	E	916 361-3925	2276
League of California Cities (PA)	8743	D	916 341-0140	27754
Leo A Daly Company	8712	D	916 564-3259	26224
Lewis-Goetz and Company Inc	5085	D	916 366-9340	7938
Lexisnexis Courtlink Inc	8621	C	425 974-5000	25143
Liberty Mutual Insurance Co	6331	B	916 564-1792	10438
Lionakis (PA)	8711	C	916 558-1901	25939
Loomis Armored Us LLC	7381	D	916 441-1091	16728
Lpa Insurance Agency Inc	7372	D	916 286-7850	15736
Lpas Inc	8712	D	916 443-0335	26227
Lukenbill Enterprises	4512	D	916 454-2400	4815
Lumens (PA)	5063	D	916 444-5585	7452
Luppen and Hawley Inc	1711	C	916 456-7831	2285
Lupton Excavation Inc	1794	D	916 387-1104	3436
Lyon Realty	6531	D	916 481-3840	11643
Lyon Realty (PA)	6531	D	916 574-6800	11647
M K S Construction Inc	1521	D	916 446-2521	1208
Macdonald Mott LLC	8711	D	916 399-0580	25948
Macias Gini & OConnell LLP (PA)	8721	D	916 928-4600	26405
Macys Inc	4226	D	916 373-0333	4697
Mariner Health Care Inc	8051	C	916 422-4825	20760
Mariner Health Care Inc	8051	C	916 481-5500	20775
Mark Diversified Inc	1542	E	916 923-6275	1607
Mark H Leibenhaut MD	8011	E	916 454-6600	19731
Mark III Construction Inc	1731	D	916 381-8080	2639
Markstein Bev Co Sacramento	5181	C	916 920-3911	9070
Marticus Electric Inc	1731	D	916 368-2186	2641
Martin Brothers Construction (PA)	1611	D	916 381-0911	1823
Matheny Sars Linkert Jaime LLP	8111	D	916 978-3434	23421
Matheson Fast Freight Inc	4213	D	209 342-0184	4217
Matheson Postal Services Inc	4212	A	916 685-2330	4038
Matheson Trucking Inc (PA)	4213	D	916 685-2330	4219
May-Han Electric Inc	1731	D	916 929-0150	2643
McClatchy Company	8999	A	916 321-1941	28147
McKinley Park Care Center	8062	D	916 452-3592	21731
McWong Envrmtl & Enrgy Group	8748	E	916 371-8000	27984
Medstar Inc	4119	D	916 669-0550	3818
Mek Norwood Pines LLC	8051	D	916 922-7177	20786
Mercy Healthcare Sacramento	8071	D	916 453-4453	22242
Mercy HM Svcs A Cal Ltd Partnr	8062	D	916 453-4545	21742
Mercy Housing California Xxvi	6531	D	916 414-4400	11678
Mercy Methodist Hospital (PA)	8062	D	916 423-6063	21744
Mercy Methodist Hospital	8011	E	916 681-1600	19749
Metagenics	5122	D	800 692-9400	8284
Mexican Amrcn Alcoholism Progr (PA)	8322	D	916 394-2320	24084

Employment Codes: A=Over 500 employees, B=251-500, C=101-250, D=51-100, E=45-50

2017 Directory of California Wholesalers and Services Companies

© Mergent Inc. 1-800-342-5647

1731

SACRAMENTO, CA — GEOGRAPHIC SECTION

Company	SIC	EMP	PHONE	ENTRY #
Mission Linen Supply	7213	C	916 423-3179	13554
Mission Linen Supply	7213	E	916 423-3135	13564
Morgan Stanley & Co LLC	6211	D	916 444-8041	10051
Morton Golf LLC	7992	D	916 481-4653	18763
Mueller Pet Medical Center	0742	E	916 428-9202	622
MWH Americas Inc	8711	B	916 924-8844	25983
Myers & Sons Construction LP	1611	C	916 283-9950	1831
National Security Industries	7382	B	916 779-0640	16902
Nationwide Legal LLC	8111	D	916 443-4400	23462
Nehemiah Progressive Housing D	6552	D	916 231-1999	11988
New West Partitions	1742	D	916 456-8365	2935
Nissan North America Inc	4225	D	916 920-4712	4604
Northern California Cardiology (PA)	8011	E	916 733-1788	19783
Northern California Inalliance (PA)	8331	D	916 381-1300	24371
Northwest Staffing Resources	7361	A	916 960-2668	14708
Nutricion Fundamental Inc	8049	C	916 922-0150	20334
Nv5 Inc (DH)	8711	D	916 641-9100	25994
Nv5 Inc	8711	D	916 641-9100	25996
Oates Buzz Enterprises	6512	D	916 381-3600	11026
Office Depot Inc	5112	D	916 927-0171	8172
Office of The Legislative Coun	4812	B	916 341-8708	5406
Office of The Legislative Coun	8748	A	916 445-3796	28008
Ogilvy Pub Rltons Wrldwide Inc	8743	D	916 231-7700	27759
Oleander Holdings LLC	8051	D	916 331-4590	20826
Oregon PCF Bldg Pdts Calif Inc	5031	D	916 381-8051	6941
Original Petes Pizza Inc	6794	E	916 442-6770	12220
Orrick Hrrington Sutcliffe LLP	8111	D	916 447-9200	23486
Owen & Company	6411	D	916 993-2700	10819
Owen Dunn Insurance Services	6411	D	916 443-0200	10820
Pacific Civil & Strl Cons LLC	8711	E	916 421-1000	26004
Pacific Coast Trnsp Svcs Inc	4789	E	916 266-5300	5233
Pacific Fresh Sea Food Company (HQ)	5142	C	916 419-5500	8562
Pacific Frnsic Psychlogy Assoc	8093	D	925 253-3111	22789
Pacific Gas and Electric Co	4911	D	916 386-5204	6183
Pacific Legal Foundation (PA)	8111	E	916 419-7111	23488
Pacific Sea Food Co Inc	5146	D	916 419-5500	8646
Pacific West Lath & Plaster	1742	E	916 329-9028	2951
Pacifica Host Inc	7011	E	916 444-8000	13064
Pape Machinery Inc	5082	D	916 922-7181	7779
Paramount Bldg Solutions LLC	1542	B	916 564-4102	1630
Parasec Incorporated (PA)	8111	E	916 576-7000	23489
Paratransit Incorporated (PA)	4119	D	916 429-2009	3826
Parc Specialty Contractors	1799	D	916 992-5405	3563
Parker Landscape Dev Inc	0781	E	916 383-4071	786
Patricks Construction Clean-Up	1629	D	916 452-5495	2076
Pd Hotel Associates LLC	7011	C	916 922-2020	13083
PDQ Automatic Transm Parts Inc	5013	D	916 870-6543	6753
Permanente Kaiser Intl	8011	D	916 979-3531	19829
Permanente Medical Group Inc	8011	D	916 688-2055	19838
Personlzed Hmcare Hmmaker Agcy	8082	D	916 979-4975	22537
Pinelands Preservation Inc	0782	D	609 703-0359	935
Pinsetters Inc	7933	D	916 488-7545	18528
Pioneer Towers Rhf Partners LP	6513	E	916 443-6548	11187
Planet Technologies Inc	7373	D	631 269-6140	16033
Planned Parenthood Federation	8093	D	916 446-5247	22803
Poolmaster Inc	5091	E	916 567-9800	8025
Pricewaterhousecoopers LLP	8721	D	916 930-8100	26427
Pride Industries	8999	D	916 649-9499	28156
Primrose Alzheimers Living	8361	D	916 392-3510	24773
Procida Landscape Inc	0782	E	916 387-5296	939
Professnl Ldscp Solutions Inc	0781	E	916 424-3815	790
Protege Builders Inc	1751	E	916 825-8478	3076
Prs/Roebbelen JV	1542	E	916 641-0324	1641
Psychiatric Solutions Inc	8011	D	916 288-0300	19894
Psychiatric Solutions Inc	8011	D	916 489-3336	19895
Public Consulting Group Inc	8742	D	916 565-8090	27601
Public Employees Retirement	6371	B	916 795-3400	10560
Public Employees Retirement	6371	D	916 326-3065	10561
Public Health Institute	8099	C	916 285-1231	23031
Pulmonary Medicine Assoc	8011	D	916 733-5040	19901
Quality Group Homes Inc	1521	C	916 930-0066	1240
Quest Media & Supplies Inc (PA)	7373	D	916 338-7070	16037
Ragingwire Data Centers Inc (DH)	7376	B	916 286-3000	16282
Ram Commercial Enterprises Inc	6531	E	916 429-1205	11785
Rcb Corporation (PA)	6022	D	916 567-2600	9519
Rdo Vermeer LLC	5082	D	916 643-0999	7787
Reach Removal Inc	1761	D	916 447-9679	3207
Reading International Inc	7832	D	916 442-0985	18346
Recp/Wndsor Scramento Ventr LP	7011	D	916 455-6800	13133
Regal Cinemas Inc	7832	D	916 419-0205	18348
Remax Gold	6531	E	916 609-2800	11806
Republic Electric Inc	1731	B	916 294-0140	2704
Republic Electric West Inc	1731	B	916 294-0140	2705
Rescue Concrete Inc	1771	D	916 852-2400	3318
Research of America	7374	C	916 443-4722	16178
Retinal Consultants Inc (PA)	8011	D	916 454-4861	19914
Rex Moore Group Inc	1731	B	916 372-1300	2706
Rex More Elec Contrs Engineers (PA)	1731	B	916 372-1300	2707
Rex More Elec Contrs Engineers	1731	B	510 785-1300	2709
Rgis LLC	7389	D	916 387-9692	17451
River City Bank (HQ)	6022	D	916 567-2600	9520
River Oak Center For Children (PA)	8063	C	916 609-5100	22088
River Oak Center For Children	8059	D	916 550-5600	21360
Riverside Health Care Corp	8051	D	916 446-2506	20877
Rose & Kindel Grayling	8399	C	916 441-1034	24970
Royal Plywood Company LLC	5031	D	916 386-9873	6958
Runyon Saltzman Einhorn Inc	7311	D	916 446-9900	13916
S L H C C Inc	8051	E	916 457-6521	20884
Saccani Distributing Company	5181	D	916 441-0213	9083
Sacramento Area Sewer District (PA)	4953	B	916 876-6000	6558
Sacramento Childrens Home	8361	D	916 927-5059	24792
Sacramento Childrens Home (PA)	8361	C	916 452-3981	24793
Sacramento Chinese Community S	8322	C	916 442-4228	24163
Sacramento County Off Educatn	8322	D	916 875-0312	24164
Sacramento County Water Agency	4941	D	916 874-6851	6389
Sacramento Credit Union (PA)	6062	D	916 444-6070	9680
Sacramento Cy Unified Schl Dst (PA)	8641	B	916 643-7400	25330
Sacramento Ear Nose & Throat (PA)	8011	D	916 736-3399	19930
Sacramento Employement & Train	8331	C	916 263-3800	24383
Sacramento Employement & Train (PA)	8331	C	916 263-3800	24384
Sacramento Harness Association	7948	D	916 239-4040	18574
Sacramento Heart and Cardiovas (PA)	8011	B	916 830-2000	19931
Sacramento Hotel Partners LLC	7011	B	916 326-5000	13185
Sacramento Loaves & Fishes (PA)	8322	D	916 446-0874	24165
Sacramento Municpl Utility Dst	4911	A	916 452-3211	6200
Sacramento Municpl Utility Dst	4911	A	916 452-3211	6201
Sacramento Municpl Utility Dst	7539	A	916 452-3211	17824
Sacramento Municpl Utility Dst	4911	B	916 732-5155	6202
Sacramento Municpl Utility Dst	4911	B	916 732-5616	6203
Sacramento Operating Co LP	8051	D	916 422-4825	20886
Sacramento Reg Co Sanit Dist (PA)	4959	C	916 876-6000	6637
Sacramento Regional Trnst Dist (PA)	4111	A	916 726-2877	3694
Sacramento Suburban Water Dst	4941	D	916 972-7171	6390
Sacramento Suburban Water Dst	4941	D	916 972-7171	6391
Sacramento Theatrical Ltg Ltd	7922	D	916 447-3258	18430
Sacramento Zoological Society	8422	E	916 808-5888	25069
Sacramnto Forty Niner Trvl Plz	7011	C	916 927-4774	13186
Sacramnto Hsing Rdvlpment Agcy	6411	D	916 440-1376	10858
Sacramnto Ntiv Amercn Hlth Ctr	8011	C	916 341-0575	19932
Sacromento Eductn Readng Lions	8641	E	916 228-2219	25331
Safelite Fulfillment Inc	7536	D	916 442-4715	17782
Saia Inc	4213	C	916 483-8331	4256
Saint Claires Nursing Center	8051	D	916 392-4440	20887
Salvation Army	8399	D	916 563-3700	24973
Sandwich Spot (PA)	7011	D	916 492-2613	13210
Scandia Sports Inc	7999	E	916 331-5757	19279
Schetter Electric Inc (PA)	1731	B	916 446-2521	2727
Schools Financial Credit Union (PA)	6062	C	916 569-5400	9688
Scott A Porter Prof Corp	8111	D	916 929-1481	23547
Securitas SEC Svcs USA Inc	7381	C	916 564-2009	16787
Securitas SEC Svcs USA Inc	7381	C	916 569-4500	16799
Sedgwick Claims MGT Svcs Inc	6411	D	916 568-7394	10870
Service Partners Supply LLC (DH)	5033	D	916 379-2290	7018
Shaw Envmtl & Infrastructure	8711	A	916 928-3300	26060
Sheraton Corporation	7011	B	916 447-1700	13243
Shermn-Lehr Cstm Tile Wrks Inc	1743	D	916 386-0417	3024
Shri Laxmi Naryan Hsptlty Grp	7011	D	916 922-8041	13251
Shri Sidhi Vinayaka Hotel Inc	7011	C	855 922-5252	13252
Shriners Hspitals For Children	8069	B	916 453-2050	22174
Shriners Hspitals For Children	8069	B	916 453-2000	22175
Sierra Bookkeeping & Tax Svc	8721	D	916 349-7610	26440
Sierra Forever Families	8322	D	916 368-5114	24210
Sierra Waste Transport Inc	4789	E	916 386-9937	5243
Silla Automotive LLC	5013	D	916 929-2646	6765
Simas Floor Co Inc (PA)	1752	C	916 452-4933	3131
Sitoa	4121	D	916 444-0008	3869
Six Flags Entertainment Corp	7996	B	916 924-3747	18834
Sky Park Gardens Assisted	8361	B	916 422-5650	24814
Skyles Insurance Agency	6411	E	916 361-9585	10873
Smart Management & Companies	8741	B	916 392-3000	27215
Southgate Recreation & Pk Dst	8322	E	916 421-7275	24223
Spare-Time Inc	7997	D	916 649-0909	19090
Spectrum Services Group Inc	8748	D	916 760-7913	28062
Spencer Building Maintenance	7349	B	916 922-1900	14437
Ssmb Pacific Holding Co Inc	5012	D	916 371-3372	6697
St Vincent De Paul Society	8322	D	916 485-3482	24230
Stafford-King-Wiese Architects	8712	E	916 930-5900	26254
Stanford Youth Solutions (PA)	8399	D	916 344-0199	24983
Starwest Botanicals Inc (PA)	5149	D	916 638-8100	8923
Starwood Hotels & Resorts	7011	C	916 447-1700	13291

GEOGRAPHIC SECTION

SALINAS, CA

	SIC	EMP	PHONE	ENTRY #
State Compensation Insur Fund	6331	B	916 924-5100	10471
Stericycle Comm Solutions Inc	7389	D	888 370-6711	17502
Stradling Yocca Carlson & Raut	8111	C	916 449-2350	23587
Stratgies To Empwer People Inc (PA)	8052	D	916 679-1527	21113
Stucco Works Inc	1742	B	916 383-6699	2984
Students of Associated	8351	D	916 278-6216	24522
Summit Funding Inc (PA)	6162	E	916 571-3000	9900
Sunrise Senior Living LLC	8051	E	916 486-0200	20974
Supershuttle International Inc	4111	D	916 648-2500	3725
Support For Home Inc	1521	E	530 792-8484	1268
Surety West Logistics Inc	4731	D	800 761-2551	5172
Surgical Care Affiliate	8721	E	916 529-4590	26447
Surgical Staff Inc	7363	C	916 444-4424	14954
Sutherland Asbill Brennan LLP	8111	D	916 241-0500	23590
Sutter Club Inc	8641	D	916 442-0456	25355
Sutter Connect LLC (HQ)	8742	A	916 854-6600	27674
Sutter Health	8011	B	916 733-1025	20079
Sutter Health	8011	C	916 733-9588	20082
Sutter Health	8011	E	916 455-8137	20090
Sutter Health	8099	C	916 566-4819	23070
Sutter Health	8011	C	916 646-8300	20092
Sutter Health (PA)	8062	A	916 733-8800	21945
Sutter Health	8093	C	916 733-8133	22843
Sutter Health	8011	E	916 451-3344	20106
Sutter Health	8011	B	916 453-5955	20107
Sutter Health	8011	C	916 262-9456	20112
Sutter Health	8641	D	916 551-9550	25364
Sutter Health At Work	8011	D	916 565-8607	20113
Sutter Hlth Rhabilitation Svcs	8322	D	916 733-3040	24244
Sutter Hlth Scrmnto Sierra Reg	8099	A	916 733-7080	23072
Sutter Hlth Scrmnto Sierra Reg (HQ)	8062	B	916 733-8800	21947
Sutter Hlth Scrmnto Sierra Reg	8322	D	916 446-3100	24245
Sutter Hlth Scrmnto Sierra Reg	8099	A	916 733-3095	23073
Sutter Medical Foundation	8049	A	916 924-7764	20356
Swinerton Builders Hc	1542	C	916 383-4825	1683
System Integrators Inc (HQ)	7373	C	916 830-2400	16062
T M Cobb Company	5031	C	916 381-7330	6964
Tammi R James MD	8011	E	916 383-6783	20128
Technology Services Cal Dept (DH)	7379	C	916 319-9223	16504
Tele-Direct Communications	7389	C	916 348-2170	17523
Terkensha Associates Inc	8322	C	916 922-9868	24248
Terracina Meadows Apts	6513	E	916 419-0925	11212
Tf Courier Inc	4215	D	916 379-0708	4425
The For Sacramento Society	8699	D	916 383-7387	25589
Tierra Del Oro Girl Scout Cnsl	8641	D	916 452-9174	25382
Timber Works Construction Inc	1521	C	916 786-6666	1272
Tlcs Inc	8322	D	916 441-0123	24251
Tradewinds Partnership	7011	D	916 333-5239	13354
Training Toward Self Reliance	8322	E	916 442-8877	24256
Transition Connection	7389	D	916 481-3470	17541
Travis Credit Union	6061	B	916 443-1446	9637
Tri-Ed Distribution Inc	5063	D	916 563-7560	7479
Tricorp Construction Inc (PA)	1542	D	916 979-8010	1695
Trinity Fresh Distribution LLC	5149	D	916 714-7368	8941
Trinity Technology Group Inc	7373	D	916 779-0201	16068
Turner Construction Company	1542	D	916 444-4421	1699
Turner Construction Company	1542	D	916 444-4421	1703
Tyco Integrated Security LLC	7382	D	916 565-2061	16934
U C Med Humn Rsrces Aplcat Svc	8062	D	916 734-5916	21976
Uc Davis Health System (PA)	8011	D	916 734-1005	20148
Uc Davis Hlth Systm Fclts Dsgn	8011	E	916 734-6570	20149
Ucd Mc Home Care Services	8741	C	916 734-2458	27262
Unifirst Corporation	7213	E	916 929-3766	13571
Unilab Corporation	8071	C	916 927-9900	22291
United Airlines Inc	4729	C	916 877-3002	5013
United Parcel Service Inc OH	4215	D	916 373-4089	4447
United Parcel Service Inc OH	4215	C	916 857-0311	4479
United States Dept of Army	8711	B	916 557-5100	26116
Universal Limousine & Trnsp Co	4119	D	916 361-5466	3853
Universal Network Dev Corp (PA)	8748	C	916 475-1200	28086
University California Davis	8062	A	916 734-2011	21998
University California Davis	8011	E	916 734-2846	20167
University California Davis	8062	A	916 734-3141	21999
University California Davis	8062	A	916 734-2011	22000
University California Davis	8062	A	916 734-5113	22001
Univision Communications Inc	4833	D	916 927-2041	5920
Uplift Family Services	8322	D	916 366-6820	24272
URS Group Inc	8711	D	916 679-2000	26127
URS Group Inc	8711	C	916 929-2346	26130
US Army Corps of Engineers	8711	D	916 557-7490	26135
US Loan Auditors LLC	8721	D	916 248-8625	26454
USA Valet Parking LLC	7299	E	916 792-1055	13802
USA Waste of California Inc	4953	D	916 379-0500	6575
USA Waste of California Inc	4212	C	916 379-2611	4080
V S N F Inc	8051	D	916 452-6631	21001

	SIC	EMP	PHONE	ENTRY #
Valley Can	8399	E	916 273-4890	24993
Valley Communications Inc (PA)	1731	D	916 349-7300	2781
Valley Health Care Systems Inc	8322	C	916 669-0508	24274
Vanir Construction MGT Inc (PA)	8741	D	916 444-3700	27273
Vasko Electric Inc	1731	D	916 568-7700	2782
Verizon Bus Netwrk Svcs Inc	4813	C	916 569-5999	5717
Verizon Communications Inc	4813	D	916 568-0440	5723
Veterans Affairs Cal Dept	8748	B	916 653-2535	28090
Village Nurseries Whl LLC	5193	B	916 993-2292	9226
Villara Corporation	1711	D	916 364-9370	2409
Visions Unlimited (PA)	8093	D	916 394-0800	22863
Vitas Healthcare Corp Cal	8082	D	916 925-7010	22601
Volunteers of America Greater	8322	B	916 265-3400	24284
W H C Inc	8051	D	916 927-9300	21022
Washington Inventory Service	7389	C	916 485-3427	17612
Water Resources Cal Dept	7375	E	916 324-3812	16268
Watson Contractors Inc	1541	D	916 481-6293	1478
Wdc Explrtion Wells Holdg Corp	1623	C	916 419-6043	2016
WEAVE Incorporated (PA)	7363	D	916 448-2321	14981
Weintraub Tobin Chediak (PA)	8111	E	916 558-6000	23617
Wellhead Electric Company Inc	4911	E	916 447-5171	6252
Wells Fargo Bank National Assn	6021	E	916 440-4570	9451
Wellspace Health (PA)	8093	D	916 325-5556	22864
Western Dental Services Inc	8021	E	916 509-3350	20285
Western Health Advantage	6321	D	916 567-1950	10250
Western Repacking Lllp	7389	D	916 688-8443	17624
Western States Fire Protection	1711	D	916 924-1631	2419
Western States Info Netwrk Inc	8733	D	916 263-1180	26824
Whgca LLC	7011	D	916 922-4700	13411
William L Lyon & Assoc Inc	6531	D	916 447-7878	11922
Wilmor & Sons Plumbing & Cnstr	1711	D	916 381-9114	2420
Winter Care Center Sacramento	8051	C	916 922-8855	21058
Wmk Sacramento LLC	7011	C	916 929-8855	13426
Wood Rodgers Inc (PA)	8711	D	916 341-7760	26152
Xerox Corporation	5044	D	916 444-8100	7076
Xpo Enterprise Services Inc	4213	C	916 399-8291	4314
Yrc Inc	4213	D	916 371-4555	4325
Zimmerman Roofing Inc	1761	D	916 454-3667	3224
Zoel Holding Company Inc	7361	D	916 646-3100	14826

SAINT HELENA, CA - Napa County

	SIC	EMP	PHONE	ENTRY #
Burr Pilger Mayer Inc	8721	D	707 968-5207	26300
Chappellet Vineyard	0172	E	707 286-4219	145
E & J Gallo Winery	8748	E	707 967-9284	27900
Hall Wines LLC	5182	E	707 967-2626	9105
Jack Neal & Son Inc	0172	C	707 963-7303	158
Mitchell Vineyards LLC	0762	D	707 963-7050	709
Nissen Vineyard Services Inc	0762	D	707 963-3480	711
Penterman Farming Co Inc	0762	D	707 967-9977	714
Rios Farming Company LLC	0172	C	707 965-2587	179
Silverado Orchards (PA)	6513	D	707 963-1461	11204
St Helena Hospital (PA)	8062	A	707 963-1882	21915
T and M Agricultural Svcs LLC	0762	D	707 963-3330	725
Taylor Bailey Inc	1542	D	707 967-8090	1686

SALIDA, CA - Stanislaus County

	SIC	EMP	PHONE	ENTRY #
Western Drywall Inc	1742	D	209 847-6401	3000

SALINAS, CA - Monterey County

	SIC	EMP	PHONE	ENTRY #
Adobe Packing Company (PA)	0723	C	831 753-6195	504
American Farms LLC	0161	D	831 424-1815	37
Americold Logistics LLC	4222	E	831 424-1537	4485
Ameripride Services Inc	7213	E	800 882-5326	13530
AON Consulting Inc	6411	D	408 288-8000	10615
BFI Waste Systems N Amer Inc	4953	D	831 775-3850	6441
Blazer Wilkinson LP	0171	B	831 455-3700	105
California Forensic Med Group	8011	D	831 755-3886	19392
Carmel Valley Packing Inc	0723	D	831 771-8860	518
Central Coast Cooling LLC	4222	D	831 422-7265	4490
Central Coast Vna & Hospice	8082	D	831 758-8243	22402
Christensen & Giannini LLC	0161	D	831 449-2494	50
Church Brothers LLC (PA)	0161	D	831 796-1000	52
City of Salinas	7349	D	831 758-7233	14250
Coast Building Products	1742	E	831 757-1089	2879
Color Spot Nurseries Inc	0181	B	831 444-0523	273
Community Catalysts California	8641	E	831 769-0934	25240
Corral De Tierra Country Club	7997	D	831 484-1325	18927
Corral Del Tierra	7997	D	831 372-6244	18928
County of Monterey	7389	D	831 755-4944	17100
County of Monterey	7389	D	831 755-5027	17101
County of Monterey	8399	E	831 755-4500	24908
County of Monterey	8062	A	831 755-4201	21521
County of Monterey	8011	E	831 769-8800	19476
County of Monterey	8699	B	831 755-3700	25520
County of Monterey	8322	A	831 755-8500	23867
County of Monterey	8744	C	831 755-3782	27783

Employment Codes: A=Over 500 employees, B=251-500, C=101-250, D=51-100, E=45-50

SALINAS, CA

	SIC	EMP	PHONE	ENTRY #
County of Monterey	1611	B	831 755-4800	1760
County of Monterey	8062	A	831 647-7611	21522
Cowles California Media Co	4833	D	831 422-3500	5848
Crop Production Services Inc	5191	D	831 757-5391	9134
DArrigo Broscoof California (PA)	0161	E	831 455-4500	56
Dassels Petroleum Inc	5172	D	831 636-5100	9015
Elioco Produce Inc	0761	C	831 424-5450	657
Ferguson Enterprises Inc	5074	D	831 373-5578	7717
Foothill Estates Inc	6552	B	831 422-7819	11969
Fresh Leaf Farms LLC (HQ)	0161	E	831 422-7405	64
Gold Valley Properties	8111	D	831 424-1414	23277
Growers Company Inc	7361	D	831 424-3850	14666
Growers Express LLC (PA)	5148	D	831 757-9951	8739
Growers Street Cooling LLC	0723	D	831 424-2929	543
Growers Transplanting Inc (HQ)	0182	D	831 449-3440	332
Guardsmark LLC	7381	C	831 769-8981	16692
Hearst Television Inc	4833	D	831 424-1414	5868
Helios Healthcare LLC	8051	C	831 449-1515	20663
Henry Hibino Farms	0161	D	831 757-3081	73
Higard Farms LLC	0191	D	831 753-5982	369
Hilltown Packing Co Inc	0723	B	831 784-1931	548
Hope Services	8331	D	831 455-4940	24348
Interim Inc	8999	C	831 754-3838	28136
J Waters Inc	7381	E	831 424-1946	16714
Jensco Inc	1731	E	831 422-7819	2624
Jlg Harvesting Inc	0723	C	831 422-7871	552
Kindred Healthcare Oper Inc	8051	C	831 424-8072	20702
Kion News Talk 1460	4832	E	831 633-1460	5794
M V Transportation	4789	C	831 373-1395	5230
Mann Packing Co Inc (PA)	0723	E	831 422-7405	559
Matsui Nursery Inc (PA)	0181	D	831 422-6433	302
Mission Linen Supply	7213	D	831 424-1707	13555
Mission Linen Supply	7218	C	831 424-1753	13633
Monterey County Office Educatn	8732	C	831 755-0324	26692
Monterey-Salinas Transit Corp	4131	C	831 754-2804	3883
Mufg Union Bank Na	6021	E	831 449-7251	9409
Natividad Hospital Inc	8062	A	831 755-4111	21759
Newstar Fresh Foods LLC	0723	C	831 758-7800	568
Newstar Fresh Foods LLC (PA)	0723	C	831 758-7800	569
Nunes Company Inc (PA)	5148	E	831 751-7510	8756
Nunes Cooling Inc	0723	C	831 751-7510	571
Odd Fellow-Rebekah Chld HM Cal	8361	E	831 775-0348	24752
Old Republic Title Company	6361	E	831 757-8051	10534
Organicgirl LLC	5148	A	831 758-7800	8759
Pacific Intl Vgetable Mktg Inc (PA)	5148	D	831 422-3745	8761
Pemer Packing Co Inc	7361	D	831 758-8586	14723
Porter Construction Co Inc	1521	C	831 455-3020	1237
Pre Con Industries Inc	8741	E	805 345-3147	27169
Premium Packing Inc	0722	C	831 443-6855	499
Quality Plumbing Associates	1711	D	831 775-0655	2333
Quinn Group Inc	5082	A	831 758-8461	7784
Quinn Lift Inc	5084	C	831 758-4086	7879
R H Framing Incorporated	1751	C	831 759-8860	3078
Rabobank National Association	6022	A	831 422-6642	9518
Rancho Salinas Packing Inc	0761	C	831 758-3624	682
Red Blossom Sales Inc	0191	A	831 751-9169	388
Reegs Inc	1522	E	831 455-7931	1336
River Ranch Fresh Foods LLC (HQ)	5148	B	831 758-1390	8769
Rm Esop Inc	5199	D	831 783-3140	9299
Rocket Farms Inc (PA)	0181	C	831 442-2400	315
S&P Global Inc	6282	C	831 393-6044	10183
Salinas Med Mngt Srvcs Org Inc	8099	D	831 751-7070	23044
Salinas Valley Memorial Hlthca	8011	B	831 759-3236	19934
Salinas Valley Memorial Hlthca	8322	B	831 759-1995	24166
Salinas Valley Memorial Hlthca (PA)	8062	B	831 757-4333	21841
Salinas Valley Memorial Hlthca	8011	B	831 755-7880	19936
San Vincente Labor LLC	5148	C	831 755-0955	8771
Scheid Vineyards Cal Inc	0172	D	831 385-4801	184
Scheid Vineyards Inc (PA)	0172	D	310 301-1555	186
Securitas SEC Svcs USA Inc	7381	C	831 444-9607	16802
Seed Dynamics Inc	0723	D	831 424-1177	585
Sysco San Francisco Inc	5141	C	831 771-5000	8536
Tanimura Antle Fresh Foods Inc (PA)	0161	D	831 455-2950	97
Tanimura Brothers	6211	D	831 424-0841	10080
Taylor Farms California Inc (HQ)	0723	E	831 754-0471	596
Taylor Fresh Foods Inc (PA)	0723	E	831 676-9023	597
The Housing Authority of	7021	D	831 449-7268	13456
Universal Services America LP	7389	A	831 751-3230	17572
UPS Ground Freight Inc	4213	D	831 751-0262	4291
USA Waste of California Inc	4953	C	831 754-2500	6587
Vals Plumbing and Heating Inc	1711	D	831 424-1633	2406
Vegetable Growers Supply Co (PA)	5199	E	831 759-4600	9308
Villa Serra Corporation	6513	D	831 754-5532	11221
Western Dental Services Inc	8021	E	831 998-9427	20286
Whole Leaf Co LLC	5148	D	831 755-2057	8789
Wilbur-Ellis Company LLC	5191	D	831 422-6473	9159
Windsor Convalescent	8051	C	831 424-0687	21046
Windsor Rdge Rhblttion Ctr LLC	8093	D	831 449-1515	22867
Windsor Skyline Care Ctr LLC	8051	D	831 449-5496	21054
Xpo Enterprise Services Inc	4213	D	831 758-8874	4311

SAN ANDREAS, CA - Calaveras County

	SIC	EMP	PHONE	ENTRY #
Avalon Health Care Inc	8051	C	209 754-3823	20397
Calaveras County Water Dst	4941	D	209 754-3543	6313
County of Calaveras	8322	D	209 754-6402	23800
Dignity Health	8011	D	209 754-3521	19502
Mark Twain Medical Center (HQ)	8062	D	209 754-3521	21726
Mark Twain Medical Center	8062	B	209 754-1487	21727
Resource Connection of Amador (PA)	8399	D	209 754-3114	24967
Rite of Pass Athletic Trng Ctr	8361	C	209 736-4500	24789

SAN ARDO, CA - Monterey County

	SIC	EMP	PHONE	ENTRY #
PSC Industrial Outsourcing LP	4212	D	831 627-2595	4050

SAN BERNARDINO, CA - San Bernardino County

	SIC	EMP	PHONE	ENTRY #
Alliance Fc	8699	E	909 784-0005	25487
Allied Building Products Corp	5039	E	909 796-6926	7023
American Force Private SEC Inc	7381	D	909 384-9820	16555
Arrowhead Central Credit Union (PA)	6061	B	866 212-4333	9589
Arrowhead Convalescent Home	8051	D	909 886-4731	20382
Assistance Leag San Bernardino	6732	D	909 885-2045	12153
Assoc For Retarded Citizens	8331	D	909 884-6484	24309
AT&T Corp	4813	D	909 381-7729	5505
Aviation & Defense Inc	4581	C	909 382-3487	4903
Baron Pool Plst Sthern Cal Inc	1799	D	909 792-8891	3496
Bear Trucking Inc	4214	D	909 799-1616	4330
Blood Bank of San Bernardino A (PA)	8099	C	909 885-6503	22897
Bnsf Railway Company	4011	D	909 386-4002	3607
Brennan Electric Inc	1731	C	909 772-2263	2538
Brickley Construction Co Inc	1799	C	909 888-2010	3502
Budget Electrical Contrs Inc	1731	C	909 381-2646	2540
California Title Co Nthrn Cal	6361	C	909 825-8800	10498
Care Tech Inc	8051	D	909 882-2965	20436
Caston Inc	1742	C	909 381-1619	2874
Cellco Partnership	4812	D	909 381-0576	5369
Community Hosp San Bernardino (HQ)	8062	B	909 887-6333	21498
Cornerstone Medical Group	8041	E	909 890-4353	20294
Correctons Rhbltation Cal Dept	8322	D	909 806-3516	23789
County of San Bernardino	8322	D	909 891-3300	23892
County of San Bernardino	8351	D	909 387-5455	24449
County of San Bernardino	8351	D	909 387-2363	24450
County of San Bernardino	8361	D	909 387-0535	24615
County of San Bernardino	8721	C	909 386-8818	26317
D M Electric Inc	1731	D	909 888-8639	2570
Daart Engineering Company Inc	1711	D	909 888-8696	2201
Del Rosa Villa Inc	8051	D	909 885-3261	20516
Destine One Wholesale Inc	5112	C	951 202-3545	8163
Dish Network Corporation	4841	D	909 381-4767	5992
DSC Logistics Inc	4731	B	540 377-2302	5060
Eagle Systems Inc	4213	D	909 386-4343	4143
Early Learning Art-Tech Group	8699	E	866 491-2432	25526
Empire Disposal LLC	4953	E	909 797-9125	6482
Far West Inc	8051	D	909 884-4781	20568
Fedex Freight Corporation	4213	C	909 887-3970	4162
First Hotels International Inc	7011	C	909 884-9364	12636
First Student Inc	4151	D	909 383-1640	3928
First Student Inc	4151	D	909 383-7104	3931
Fischer Inc	1711	D	909 881-2910	2228
Garda CL West Inc	7381	E	909 574-2676	16659
Gate City Beverage Distrs (PA)	5181	B	909 799-0281	9058
Gerdau Reinforcing Steel	1541	D	909 713-1130	1429
Gresham Savage Nolan & Tilden (PA)	8111	D	619 794-0050	23293
Help For The Hurting Inc	8322	D	909 796-4222	24005
Hillcrest Care Inc	8059	D	909 882-2965	21266
Hub Construction Spc Inc (PA)	7359	E	909 235-4100	14547
Inland Bhavioral Hlth Svcs Inc (PA)	8099	D	909 881-6146	22981
Inland Cnties Regional Ctr Inc (PA)	8741	C	909 890-3000	27064
Inland Empire Health Plan	6324	B	866 228-4347	10291
Inland Empre 66ers Bsebll CLB	7941	C	909 888-9922	18550
Iron Workers Local 433	6733	E	909 884-5500	12178
J G Golfing Enterprises Inc	7992	E	909 885-2414	18750
Jenco Productions Inc	7389	C	909 381-9453	17257
Job Options Incorporated	7219	A	909 890-4612	13654
Kaiser Foundation Hospitals	8011	E	909 886-6711	19664
Kaiser Foundation Hospitals	6324	D	888 750-0036	10322
Kindred Healthcare Inc	8099	C	909 887-6391	22990
Konica Minolta Business Soluti	5044	D	909 824-2000	7058
L & L Nursery Supply Inc (PA)	5191	C	909 591-0461	9138
Legacy Vulcan Corp	1442	E	909 875-1150	1106
Lewis Brsbois Bsgard Smith LLP	8111	D	909 387-1130	23391
Llu Advntist Hlth Sciences Ctr	8011	D	909 558-4386	19714

GEOGRAPHIC SECTION

SAN DIEGO, CA

	SIC	EMP	PHONE	ENTRY #
Lucky Farms Inc	0161	D	909 799-6688	79
Marna Health Services Inc	8099	D	909 882-2965	22996
Matich Corporation **(PA)**	1611	D	909 382-7400	1824
Maxim Healthcare Services Inc	7363	B	951 684-4148	14904
McLane/Southern California Inc	5141	B	909 887-7500	8500
Metropolitan Automotive Whse **(PA)**	5013	D	909 885-2886	6748
Metropolitan Water District	4941	E	909 890-3776	6372
Michael Grove	7299	E	909 883-5398	13777
Michael P Byko DDS A Prof Corp **(PA)**	8021	D	909 888-7817	20264
Midnight Auto Recycling LLC	5093	D	909 884-5308	8076
National Construction & Maint	1542	E	909 888-7042	1617
National Technical Systems Inc	8734	C	909 382-2360	26875
Northrop Grmmn Spce & Mssn Sys	7373	C	909 382-6800	16013
Northrop Grmmn Spce & Mssn Sys	8731	C	909 382-6800	26577
Nursefinders LLC	7361	C	909 890-2286	14712
Omnitrans	8361	B	909 383-1680	24757
On Trac Overhead Door Co Inc	1751	E	909 799-8555	3069
Ortiz Asphalt Paving Inc	1611	E	951 966-7060	1838
Pacific Airworks Group LLC	8711	D	909 815-7012	26003
Parsons Brinckerhoff Inc	8711	D	909 888-1106	26012
Pathway Inc	8322	D	909 890-1070	24124
Planned Parenthood	8093	D	909 890-5511	22800
Plott Management Co	8051	D	909 803-0288	20851
Renzenberger Inc	7514	C	909 888-8858	17692
Robert Ballard Rehab Hospital **(HQ)**	8049	D	909 473-1200	20351
Roofing Wholesale Co Inc	5033	D	909 825-8440	7017
Rudolph Foods Company Inc	5141	D	909 383-7463	8516
Sac Health System **(PA)**	8021	D	909 382-7100	20274
Safety Security Patrol LLC	7381	D	909 888-7778	16778
Salvation Army	8093	D	909 889-9604	22822
San Bernardino California City	8711	D	909 384-5111	26052
San Bernardino City Unf School	7349	C	909 388-6100	14416
San Bernardino City Unf School	8351	C	909 388-6307	24509
San Bernardino City Unf School	8099	C	909 881-8000	23045
San Bernardino Hilton **(HQ)**	7011	C	909 889-0133	13193
San Bernardino Med Group Inc **(PA)**	8011	C	909 883-8611	19938
San Bernardino Symphony Assn	7929	D	909 381-5388	18490
San Brnrdino Pub Emplyees Assn	8631	E	909 386-1260	25182
Soffietti Co	5072	D	909 907-2277	7699
Southern California Gas Co	4923	C	909 335-7941	6265
Sprint Communications Co LP	4813	D	909 382-6030	5705
Terminix Intl Co Ltd Partnr	7342	E	909 332-2479	14192
Time Warner Cable Inc	4841	D	909 918-6972	6036
United Medical Management Inc	8059	C	909 886-5291	21401
Universal	7349	D	909 882-5337	14454
Vibra Hosp San Bernardino LLC	8062	D	909 473-1233	22023
Vna Hospice & Pllatve Cre S CA	8069	D	909 384-0737	22610
Vocational Imprv Program Inc	5047	D	909 478-7537	7327
Waterman Convalescent Hospital **(PA)**	8051	D	909 882-1215	21025
Westside Counseling Center	8069	D	909 881-2425	22187
YMCA of East Valley	8641	E	909 881-9622	25411

SAN BRUNO, CA - San Mateo County

	SIC	EMP	PHONE	ENTRY #
Artichoke Joes Inc	7999	B	650 589-8812	19143
Cbr Systems Inc **(HQ)**	8099	D	650 635-1420	22912
Emlab P&K LLC **(DH)**	8734	D	650 829-5800	26850
Intake Initiatives Inc	5122	D	800 788-9637	8264
Kaiser Foundation Hospitals	6324	D	650 742-2100	10326
Kaiser Foundation Hospitals	6324	D	650 742-2000	10350
Ksi Corp **(PA)**	4731	D	650 952-0815	5110
La Petite Baleen Inc	7991	D	650 588-7665	18653
Medical Couriers Inc	4215	D	650 872-1144	4416
Permanente Medical Group Inc	8011	D	650 742-2100	19839
Premier Source LLC	8733	D	415 349-2010	26796
Provident Funding Assoc LP **(PA)**	6162	E	650 652-1300	9888
Qumu Inc	7372	D	650 396-8530	15824
Responsys Inc **(DH)**	7371	C	650 745-1700	15417
Skypark Inc	7299	D	650 875-6655	13794
Spiritual Direction	8322	E	650 952-9456	24225
Staffing Specialists Intl	8082	E	650 737-0777	22573
United Airlines Inc	4512	C	650 634-2468	4829
Vantagepoint Management Inc **(PA)**	6799	D	650 866-3100	12351
Vantagepoint Venture Partners	6722	D	650 866-3100	12128

SAN CARLOS, CA - San Mateo County

	SIC	EMP	PHONE	ENTRY #
A G Paceman Inc	6519	D	650 592-7282	11247
Browning-Ferris Inds Cal Inc	4953	D	650 637-1411	6445
Califrnia Dsster Med Svcs Assn	8099	C	408 970-9202	22908
Check Point Software Tech Inc **(HQ)**	7372	C	800 429-4391	15618
Coldwell Banker	6411	D	650 596-5400	10675
D & J Tile Company Inc	1743	D	650 632-4000	3010
Duckys of San Carlos Inc	7542	E	650 637-1301	17839
Emagined Security Inc	7382	E	415 944-2977	16883
George P Johnson Company	5199	C	650 226-0600	9267
Inside Source Inc **(PA)**	5021	D	650 508-9101	6820
Ira Services Inc	6733	C	650 593-2221	12177

	SIC	EMP	PHONE	ENTRY #
ISS Facility Services Inc	7349	B	650 593-9774	14327
Judy Spiegel	6531	D	650 596-5400	11604
Lifestreet Corporation	5199	C	650 508-2220	9276
Marklogic Corporation **(PA)**	7371	C	650 655-2300	15292
Maxx Metals Inc	5051	D	650 654-1500	7383
Morrow-Meadows Corporation	1731	C	510 562-1980	2658
Natera Inc	8071	C	650 249-9090	22245
Peninsula Crrdor Jint Pwers Bd	4111	C	650 508-6200	3690
Peninsula Custom Homes Inc	1521	D	650 574-0241	1233
Professional Insur Assoc Inc **(PA)**	6411	D	650 592-7333	10839
Recology San Mateo County	4953	D	650 595-3900	6528
Rountree Plumbing and Htg Inc	1711	D	650 298-0300	2351
Rovi Corporation **(PA)**	7372	C	408 562-8400	15829
San Mateo County Transit Dst **(PA)**	4111	C	650 508-6200	3711
San Mateo County Transit Dst	4173	C	650 508-6412	3963
Sb Group Us Inc	6282	D	650 562-8110	10184
Starvista	8322	C	650 591-9623	24235
Teradata Corporation	7371	C	650 232-4400	15498
Thrifty Rent-A-Car System Inc	7514	E	650 737-8084	17697
Transiris Corporation	8742	D	650 303-3495	27696
Universal General Builders	8711	C	650 591-3104	26118
Walgreens Home Care Inc	8082	C	650 551-7020	22613
Wells Fargo Insur Svcs USA Inc	6411	C	650 413-4499	10932

SAN CLEMENTE, CA - Orange County

	SIC	EMP	PHONE	ENTRY #
Advanced Mp Technology Inc **(PA)**	5065	C	949 492-6589	7515
American Corrective Counseling	8322	B	949 369-6210	23657
Asociacon De Bomberos Del Esta	8611	D	949 355-4249	25075
Bernus Landscape Inc	1629	B	714 557-7910	2025
Brad Rambo & Associates Inc **(PA)**	5136	D	949 366-9911	8335
Cameron Health Inc	5047	D	949 940-4000	7250
Cellco Partnership	4812	D	949 488-9990	5387
Dealersocket Inc **(PA)**	7371	D	949 900-0300	15126
Dual Diagnosis Trtmnt Ctr Inc **(PA)**	8093	D	949 276-5553	22723
Evolution Hospitality LLC **(PA)**	8741	C	949 498-2056	27020
Evr Lending Inc	6531	D	949 492-4868	11499
F M Tarbell Co	6531	D	949 366-8810	11512
Garwood Laboratories Inc	8734	D	562 949-2727	26854
GCI Construction Inc	1611	E	714 957-0233	1772
HCA Inc	8062	C	949 496-1122	21595
Heritage Golf Group Inc	7992	C	949 369-6226	18745
International Speedway Inc	7941	D	949 492-9933	18551
Internet Marketing Assn Inc	8742	D	949 443-9300	27482
Julius Steve Construction Inc	1541	E	949 369-7820	1441
Keenan & Associates	6411	D	949 940-1760	10761
Kinnser Software Inc	7371	D	949 478-0890	15269
Mark R Eggen Construction Inc	1521	E	949 661-2674	1213
Matsushita International Corp **(PA)**	6799	D	949 498-1000	12324
Mega Mail Mall Inc	6512	E	888 998-6245	11017
Pacific Golf & Country Club	7997	D	949 498-6604	19024
Partner Hero Inc	7389	E	888 968-2767	17398
Regenesis Bioremediation Pdts **(PA)**	8748	E	949 366-8000	28039
Sambazon Inc **(PA)**	5148	D	877 726-2296	8770
San Clemente Medical Ctr LLC	8062	B	949 496-1122	21845
San Clemente Villas By Sea	8361	D	949 489-3400	24801
San Diego Gas & Electric Co	4931	E	949 361-8090	6293
Southern California Edison Co	4911	A	949 368-2881	6221
Speedy Locksmith	7699	D	760 439-5000	18018
Transpacific Management Svc	6531	D	949 248-2822	11878

SAN DIEGO, CA - San Diego County

	SIC	EMP	PHONE	ENTRY #
15th Island LLC	6531	D	619 321-1111	11266
1835 Columbia Street LP	7011	D	619 564-3993	12360
21st Century Insurance Company	6411	D	858 637-9070	10576
24 Hour Fitness Usa Inc	7991	E	619 294-2424	18594
24 Hour Fitness Usa Inc	7991	E	858 538-4400	18599
5th Avenue Partners LLC	7011	B	619 515-3000	12367
600b Ag-Lo Owner L P	6531	D	619 234-7036	11269
6th & Island Investments	6282	D	619 236-0624	10110
8110 Aero Holding LLC	7011	C	858 277-8888	12369
A C Rentals LLC	1711	E	858 271-8571	2102
A Caos Medical Corporation	8082	D	800 362-2731	22316
A J Esprit	7011	E	619 223-8171	12371
A O Reed & Co	1711	B	858 565-4131	2103
A-Star Staffing Inc	7361	C	619 574-7600	14595
AAR Parts Trading Inc	4225	D	858 627-6029	4513
Aat Sorrento Pointe LLC	6798	D	858 350-2600	12232
Aat Torrey Reserve 6 LLC	6512	D	858 350-2600	10952
Aba Holdings LLC	6719	C	858 565-4131	12046
Abe Entercom Holdings LLC	4832	D	619 291-9797	5747
ABM Parking Services **(PA)**	7521	D	619 235-4000	17708
Acadia Pharmaceuticals Inc **(PA)**	8733	C	858 558-2871	26721
Accentcare Inc	8082	A	858 576-7410	22321
Accentcare Home Health Cal Inc	8082	C	858 576-7410	22328
Accenture Federal Services LLC	8742	C	619 574-2400	27293
Access Control Centres Inc	4841	D	858 455-1500	5934

Employment Codes: A=Over 500 employees, B=251-500, C=101-250, D=51-100, E=45-50

2017 Directory of California Wholesalers and Services Companies

© Mergent Inc. 1-800-342-5647

SAN DIEGO, CA — GEOGRAPHIC SECTION

Company	SIC	EMP	PHONE	ENTRY #
Access Nurses Inc	7361	D	858 458-4400	14599
Accriva Dgnostics Holdings Inc (PA)	6719	B	858 263-2300	12048
Accumen Inc (PA)	8082	D	858 777-8160	22331
Ace Parking Management Inc (PA)	7521	E	619 233-6624	17710
Ace Relocation Systems Inc (PA)	4213	D	858 677-5500	4103
Ace Usa Inc	6411	C	619 563-2400	10583
Achates Power Inc	8731	C	858 535-9920	26459
Activcare Living Inc (PA)	8741	C	858 565-4424	26908
Adesa Corporation LLC	5012	C	619 661-5565	6662
Administrative Services SD	4121	E	619 398-2314	3862
Adminstrtive Office of US Crts	8322	C	619 557-6650	23644
Adroit Energy Inc	1711	D	858 483-3568	2107
Advanced Rehabilitation Tech	5047	D	858 621-5959	7231
Advanced Rsrvation Systems Inc	7379	D	858 300-8600	16316
Advanced Test Equipment Corp	7359	D	858 558-6500	14505
Aecom Global II LLC	8711	D	619 241-4568	25634
Aerospace Corporation	8711	D	619 491-3557	25641
Affinity Auto Programs Inc	7389	C	858 643-9324	16974
Affinity Development Group Inc	8699	C	858 643-9324	25484
Affymetrix Inc	8731	C	858 642-2058	26463
Age Concerns Inc	8322	D	619 544-1622	23646
Aggressive Action Security	7381	E	858 829-2516	16538
Ahern Agribusiness Inc	5191	D	619 661-9450	9124
AIG Direct Insurance Svcs Inc	6411	B	858 309-3000	10584
Airgas Inc	5169	C	858 279-8200	8971
Airgas USA LLC	5169	D	858 279-8200	8974
Akela Pharma Inc	8733	E	512 391-3525	26731
Alaska Airlines Inc	4512	E	619 238-2042	4783
Aldridge Pite LLP	8111	D	858 750-7700	23085
All Star Glass Inc (PA)	7536	E	619 275-3343	17781
All Star Maintenance Inc	1799	D	858 259-0900	3487
All Stars	1799	B	858 259-0900	3488
All Valley Home Hlth Care Inc	8099	D	619 276-8001	22881
Allegis Residential Svcs Inc	8741	D	858 430-5700	26917
Allen Lee Rose Inc	7361	E	858 587-3100	14604
Alliant Insurance Services Inc	6411	D	619 238-1828	10587
Allied Gardens Towing Inc (HQ)	7549	D	619 563-4060	17871
Alliedbarton Security Svcs LLC	7381	B	858 874-8200	16549
Allstar Commercial Cleaning	7349	E	858 715-0500	14221
Alpha Mechanical Inc	1711	C	858 278-3500	2123
Alpha Mechanical Inc (PA)	1711	C	858 278-3500	2124
Alsco Inc	7213	C	619 234-7291	13513
Alta-Dena Certified Dairy LLC	5143	D	858 292-6930	8576
Alvizia Landscape Co LLC	0782	C	619 661-6557	806
America West Airlines Inc	4512	E	619 231-7340	4785
American Assets Trust Inc (PA)	6798	D	858 350-2600	12233
American Freightways LP	4213	D	866 326-5902	4106
American Gen Lf Accident Insur	6411	D	619 299-5213	10593
American Institute of Aeronaut	8733	D	619 545-3736	26733
American Internet Mortgage Inc	6162	C	619 610-9900	9814
American Intl Group Inc	6411	D	619 682-4058	10597
American Medical Response Inc	4119	C	858 492-3500	3757
American Multi-Cinema Inc	7832	E	619 296-0370	18295
American Multi-Cinema Inc	7832	D	619 296-2737	18305
American National Red Cross	8322	D	858 309-1200	23660
American Nwland Communities LP (PA)	6552	E	858 455-7503	11947
American Prprty-Mnagement Corp	7011	C	619 232-3121	12384
American Red Cross San Diego (PA)	8399	D	858 309-1200	24870
American Residential Svcs LLC	1711	D	858 457-5547	2129
American Residential Svcs LLC	1711	D	858 677-5445	2131
American Residential Svcs LLC	1711	D	858 277-2606	2139
American Spclty Hlth Group Inc (HQ)	8082	B	858 754-2000	22360
American Specialty Health Inc (PA)	6411	D	858 754-2000	10598
American Sunrise Inc	7371	D	858 610-4766	15010
American Technologies Inc	8748	D	858 530-2400	27831
Amn Healthcare Inc (HQ)	8011	C	858 792-0711	19341
Amn Healthcare Services Inc	8049	A	858 792-0711	20306
Amn Healthcare Services Inc (PA)	7363	C	866 871-8519	14837
Amsec LLC	8731	B	858 522-6319	26467
Anaptysbio Inc	8731	E	858 362-6295	26468
Anchor General Insurance Agcy	6411	C	858 527-3600	10602
Andrew and Williamson Sales Co (PA)	5148	D	619 661-6000	8695
Andrew M Golden MD	8011	D	619 528-5342	19347
Anesthesia Svc Med Group Inc	8011	E	858 277-4767	19349
Anixter Inc	5087	D	858 505-1950	7960
Anixter International Inc	5087	B	858 571-6571	7961
Anixter International Inc	5087	D	858 974-6714	7962
Anthem Insurance Companies Inc	6324	D	858 571-8136	10256
Anthony Robbins & Associates	6794	D	858 535-9900	12210
Antimite Associates Inc	7342	C	619 231-2900	14172
APAC Customer Services Inc	7389	A	619 298-7103	16995
Apex Mechanical Systems Inc	1711	D	858 536-8700	2146
Applied Molecular Evolution (HQ)	8731	E	858 597-4990	26471
Apria Healthcare LLC	7352	D	858 653-6800	14470
Aramark Unf & Career AP LLC	7213	E	858 550-1131	13537
ARC of San Diego (PA)	8399	C	619 685-1175	24871
Archer Western Contractors LLC	1611	D	858 715-7200	1734
Argon St Inc A Boeing Company	8711	D	312 544-2537	25663
Armanino LLP	8721	D	858 794-9401	26289
Armed Forces Officials Assn	8621	E	858 672-1438	25116
Arrowhead Gen Insur Agcy Inc (DH)	6331	C	619 881-8600	10402
Arrowhead Management Company (DH)	6411	D	800 669-1889	10621
Ashford Trs Nickel LLC	8741	D	619 260-0111	26928
ASI Hastings Inc	1711	C	858 590-9300	2153
Asset Marketing Systems Insu	8742	D	888 303-8755	27334
Associated Research Svcs Inc	8748	D	858 551-0008	27836
Associated Students San Diego (PA)	8699	A	619 594-0234	25492
Associated Third Pty Admnstrtors	6371	C	619 358-8140	10540
At Your Home Familycare	7299	C	858 625-0406	13734
AT&T Corp	4813	D	858 693-0815	5489
AT&T Services Inc	4813	C	619 515-5100	5525
AT&T Services Inc	4813	C	858 886-2762	5535
AT&T Services Inc	4813	B	858 495-3907	5555
AT&T Services Inc	4813	C	858 268-6751	5557
Ata Engineering Inc (PA)	8711	D	858 480-2000	25671
Atk Space Systems Inc	8733	D	858 621-5700	26737
Atkins North America Inc	8711	D	858 874-1810	25673
Atlas Construction Supply Inc (PA)	5032	D	858 277-2100	6973
Atlas General Insur Svcs LLC	6411	C	858 529-6700	10633
Audatex North America Inc (DH)	7372	C	858 946-1900	15588
Aurora Behavioral Health Care	8063	C	858 487-3200	22039
Aurora Healthcare Inc	8062	E	858 487-3200	21455
Ausgar Technologies Inc	8711	C	855 428-7427	25675
Austin Veum Rbbins Prtners Inc (PA)	8712	D	619 231-1960	26166
Automatic Data Processing Inc	7374	D	619 293-4800	16103
AV Courtyard SD Spectrum	7011	D	858 573-0700	12405
Avia Tech LLC	7311	D	858 777-5000	13817
Aviva Systems Biology Corp	8731	D	858 552-6979	26483
Avnet Inc	5065	B	858 385-7500	7531
Awarepoint Corporation (PA)	7371	D	858 345-5000	15046
Axa Advisors LLC	6311	D	619 239-0018	10201
Axa Equitable Life Insur Co	6411	D	858 552-1234	10641
Aya Healthcare Inc	7363	B	858 458-4410	14841
Bae Systems Inc	7389	A	619 788-5000	17019
Bae Systems Maritime Engineeri	8711	D	619 238-1000	25679
Baechler Investigative Svcs	7381	D	619 464-5600	16568
Bahia Sternwheelers Inc	4489	E	858 539-7720	4730
Baja Metal Shredder LLC	5093	D	847 622-9898	8064
Bakbone Software Inc (DH)	7371	D	858 450-9009	15050
Baker & Taylor LLC	5192	C	858 457-2500	9161
Bald Eagle Security Svcs Inc	7381	D	619 230-0022	16569
Ballard Spahr LLP	8111	D	619 696-9200	23103
Bally Total Fitness Corp	7991	E	858 831-0773	18610
Banner Bank	6021	E	619 243-7900	9339
Barney & Barney Inc (DH)	6411	C	800 321-4696	10642
Barnhart-Balfour Beatty Inc (DH)	1542	D	858 635-7400	1498
Bartell Hotels	7011	C	619 224-3411	12417
Bartell Hotels	7011	D	619 222-6440	12418
Bartell Hotels	7011	E	858 581-3500	12419
Bartell Hotels	7011	E	619 222-0561	12420
Basile Construction Inc	1623	E	858 278-2739	1908
Bay Area Credit Service LLC	6062	B	858 653-3824	9653
Bay City Television Inc (PA)	4833	C	858 279-6666	5834
Bay Club Hotel and Marina A C	7011	D	619 222-0314	12424
Bay Rosie Hotel LLP	7011	B	619 276-4010	12425
Bear Data Solutions Inc	7373	C	858 824-2920	15908
Being Fit Inc	7991	D	858 483-9294	18616
Bella Limousines	4119	E	619 302-4062	3772
Belmont Village LP	8059	D	858 486-5020	21150
Belville Enterprises Inc	8011	D	858 652-6960	19373
Ben F Smith Inc	1771	C	858 271-4320	3232
Berkshire Hathaway Homestates	6411	D	619 686-8424	10647
Bernardo Hts Healthcare Inc	8059	D	858 673-0101	21153
Beston Development	7011	D	619 232-6315	12444
Bh Partn A Calif Limit Partne (PA)	7011	B	858 539-7635	12448
Bill Howe Plumbing Inc	1711	D	800 245-5469	2167
Binding Site Inc	5047	B	858 453-9177	7245
Biocept Inc	8071	B	858 320-8200	22192
Biomedicure LLC	8731	D	858 586-1888	26489
Bionano Genomics Inc (PA)	8071	D	858 888-7600	22194
Biosite Inc	5047	B	510 683-9063	7246
Biotheranostics Inc (DH)	8071	D	858 678-0940	22195
Bit Medtech LLC	8711	D	858 613-1200	25689
Blackstone Consulting Inc	8745	C	619 293-0043	27849
Blue Box Opco LLC (PA)	5092	D	800 840-4916	8039
BMC Software Inc	7372	D	713 918-8800	15604
Bmr 21 Erie St LLC	6531	D	858 485-9840	11327
Bofi Federal Bank (HQ)	6141	D	858 350-6200	9741
Bonded Inc	7217	B	858 576-8400	13590
Booz Allen Hamilton Inc	8742	D	619 725-6500	27353

GEOGRAPHIC SECTION

SAN DIEGO, CA

	SIC	EMP	PHONE	ENTRY #
Boykin Mgt Co Ltd Lblty Co	7011	E	619 299-6633	12459
Boykin Mgt Co Ltd Lblty Co	7011	C	619 298-8281	12461
Brady Gce II	8711	D	858 496-0500	25702
Brady-Fortitude	1542	D	858 496-0500	1510
Braemar Partnership	7011	B	858 539-8600	12462
Brandes Inv Partners Inc (PA)	6282	C	858 755-0239	10124
Brightcloud Inc	7382	C	858 652-4803	16872
Brighton Gardens Inc	8051	D	858 259-2222	20417
Brighton Health Alliance (PA)	8051	D	619 461-0376	20418
Brighton Place San Diego	8051	D	619 263-2166	20420
Brightscope Inc	7372	D	858 452-7500	15609
Brightview Landscape Dev Inc	1629	B	858 458-9900	2031
Brightview Landscape Svcs Inc	0781	C	858 458-1900	749
Brinks Incorporated	7381	C	619 263-6615	16583
Bristol Hotel	7011	D	619 232-6141	12468
Broadcast Co of Americas LLC (PA)	4832	E	858 453-0658	5752
Broadway Typewriter Co Inc	5045	D	619 645-0253	7103
Brokerage Lgstics Slutions Inc	4731	D	619 671-0276	5036
Brown and Caldwell	8711	D	858 514-8822	25708
Buck Consultants LLC	8999	D	619 725-1769	28120
Business and Support Services	7999	A	858 577-4786	19155
Butterwick Dr Kimberly Jane MD	8011	D	858 657-1002	19386
Bw-Budget-Sda LLC	7514	E	619 542-8686	17667
Bycor General Contractors Inc	1542	D	858 587-1901	1515
Byrom-Davey Inc	1629	B	858 513-7199	2033
C N L Hotel Del Partners LP	7011	A	619 522-8299	12477
Ca Inc	7372	C	631 342-6000	15613
Cableconn Industries Inc	5063	D	858 571-7111	7421
Cabrillo Gen Insur Agcy Inc	6411	D	858 244-0550	10654
Caci Inc - Federal	7373	E	619 881-6000	15911
Cal Pinnacle Mltary Cmmunities	8741	D	619 764-5087	26952
Calderon Building Maintenance	7349	D	619 269-5940	14243
California American Water Co (HQ)	4941	C	619 409-7703	6314
California Building Maint	7349	E	858 451-9111	14244
California Club Lucky Lady	7999	E	619 287-6690	19157
California Coast Credit Union (PA)	6062	D	858 495-1600	9654
California Coast Credit Union	6062	C	858 495-1600	9655
California Comfort Systems USA	1711	B	858 564-1100	2172
California Forensic Med Group	8099	D	858 694-4690	22906
California Home Care Inc	8082	B	619 521-5858	22386
California Marine Cleaning Inc (PA)	4953	C	619 231-8788	6449
California Title Company	6361	D	619 516-5227	10499
Califrnia Rgional Intranet Inc	4813	D	858 974-5080	5567
Calworks Partnr Conference	6732	E	858 292-2900	12156
Canji Inc	8733	C	858 597-0177	26744
Capital Plus Financial Corp	6162	E	619 744-1900	9826
Captiva Software Corporation (DH)	7373	D	858 320-1000	15914
Cardinal Health 200 LLC	5047	C	951 686-8900	7255
Cardium Biologics Inc	8731	E	858 436-1000	26492
Care Medical Trnsp Inc	7363	C	858 653-4520	14852
Carefusion Solutions LLC (DH)	5047	A	858 617-2100	7256
Carrier Johnson (PA)	8712	D	619 236-9462	26173
Casa De Las Campanas Inc (PA)	8361	C	858 451-9152	24584
Casas - Comprehensive	8699	D	858 292-2900	25513
Casas International Brkg Inc (PA)	4225	C	619 661-6162	4532
Caster Family Enterprises Inc	6799	C	619 287-8893	12293
Castle Access Inc (PA)	4813	D	858 836-0200	5571
Catalina Slar Lssee Holdco LLC	4911	D	888 903-6926	6109
Catalina Solar 2 LLC	4911	A	888 903-6926	6110
Catholic Charities Diocese San	8322	C	619 286-1100	23708
Catholic Charities Diocese San	8322	E	619 287-9454	23709
CB&i Envmtl Infrastructure Inc	8748	B	619 239-1690	27870
Cbre Inc	6531	C	858 546-4600	11357
CBS Radio Inc	4832	D	858 560-1037	5758
Celgene Corporation	8731	D	858 558-7500	26494
Celgene Corporation	5122	C	858 677-0034	8249
Cellco Partnership	4812	D	619 209-5818	5317
Cellco Partnership	4812	D	858 625-7751	5318
Cellco Partnership	4812	D	858 614-0011	5373
Cellco Partnership	4822	C	858 618-2100	5742
Cement Cutting Inc	1771	D	619 296-9592	3241
Center For Autsm Rsrch Evltn	8093	C	858 444-8823	22676
Center For Sustainable Energy	8748	D	858 244-1177	27874
Central Garden & Pet Company	5199	D	858 695-0743	9252
Century 21 Able Inc	6531	D	858 450-2100	11365
Century Contract Services Inc	7349	C	858 672-4118	14246
Certified Air Conditioning Inc	1711	D	858 292-5740	2177
Chaduxtt JV	8711	D	619 525-7188	25735
Chadwick Center For Children &	8011	E	858 966-5814	19425
Champion Signs Incorporated	7336	E	858 751-2900	14136
Chargers Football Company LLC (PA)	7941	C	619 280-2121	18541
Charles Schwab Corporation	6211	E	858 523-2454	9971
Chicago Title Company	6361	C	619 230-6340	10501
Chief San Diego Hotel LLC	7011	D	619 239-2400	12512
Children of Rainbow Inc (PA)	8351	D	619 615-0652	24435

	SIC	EMP	PHONE	ENTRY #
Children of The Rainbow Head	8351	C	619 266-7311	24436
Childrens Angelcare Aid Intl	8322	C	619 795-6234	23738
Childrens Assoc Medical Group	8011	E	858 576-1700	19429
Childrens Specialist of San D (PA)	8011	B	858 576-1700	19435
Christian and Wakefield (PA)	6531	D	619 236-1555	11389
Chromalloy San Diego Corp	7699	C	858 877-2800	17966
CIC Research Inc	8732	D	858 637-4000	26649
Cielo Azul Inc	0782	C	858 565-8344	824
Cintas Corporation No 3	7218	C	619 239-1001	13620
Cintiva Financial Corporation	6163	D	858 226-0955	9917
Citigroup Global Markets Inc	6211	D	858 597-7777	9977
City Leasing & Rentals	7515	C	619 276-6171	17698
City National Bank	6021	D	619 645-6100	9387
City of San Diego	8748	E	619 533-3012	27881
City of San Diego	8069	D	619 533-6518	22129
City of San Diego	8711	C	858 627-3210	25742
Citywide Plumbing Heating	1711	D	619 231-2022	2181
Clairemont Healthcare	8051	D	858 278-4750	20459
Clark Enterprises Inc	6531	C	858 320-3900	11395
Clean Enviroment	7349	C	619 521-0543	14253
Clearbalance Holdings LLC	6719	E	858 535-0870	12051
Clinapps Inc	7371	D	858 866-0228	15090
Clinicomp International Inc (PA)	7373	D	858 546-8202	15922
Closingcorp Inc	7379	D	858 551-1500	16336
CNA Surety Corporation	6411	D	619 682-3550	10673
Coast Citrus Distributors (PA)	5148	C	619 661-7950	8707
Coastal Transport Co Inc	4212	D	619 584-1055	3997
Coffman Specialties Inc (PA)	1771	C	858 536-3100	3245
Colliers Intl Prperty Cons Inc	6531	E	858 455-1515	11445
Collwood Ter Stellar Care Inc	8059	D	619 287-2920	21188
Colrich Communities Inc	6552	E	858 350-7672	11959
Colsa Corporation	7371	C	619 260-1100	15095
Colt Services Inc	7217	C	858 271-9988	13596
Commercial Finance & L	6029	D	858 866-8525	9547
Communction Wirg Spcalists Inc	1731	D	858 278-4545	2559
Community Clinics Hlth Netwrk	8621	E	619 542-4300	25130
Competitive Edge RES Comm Inc	8732	D	619 702-2372	26651
Competitor Group Events Inc	8743	E	858 450-6510	27743
Comprehensive Enviro	8711	E	619 294-9400	25747
Comps Inc	7375	C	858 658-0576	16223
Computer Proc Unlimited Inc	7371	C	858 530-0875	15098
Compuware Corporation	7371	D	858 824-5200	15104
Conam Management Corporation (PA)	6531	C	858 614-7200	11451
Concerro Inc (DH)	7371	E	858 882-8500	15106
Considine & Considine An Acco	8721	D	619 231-1977	26315
Consolidated Elec Distrs Inc	5063	C	858 268-1020	7430
Contrlled Cntmination Svcs LLC	7349	C	858 457-3157	14262
Cooley LLP	8111	C	858 550-6000	23167
Copley Press Inc	7372	C	619 718-5200	15629
Coram Alternate Site Svcs Inc	8082	C	858 576-6969	22415
Corinthian Title Company Inc	6361	D	619 299-4800	10511
Correctional Services Corp	8744	D	858 866-9816	27780
Corrections Corp America	8744	C	619 661-9119	27781
Cortel Inc	4812	D	650 703-7217	5390
Cosco Fire Protection Inc	7389	D	858 444-2000	17097
Costar Group Inc	6531	C	858 458-4900	11460
County of San Diego	8322	D	619 694-5141	23896
County of San Diego	8322	D	858 495-5537	23898
County of San Diego	8322	D	619 515-8202	23899
County of San Diego	8111	D	619 531-4040	23182
County of San Diego	8322	D	619 692-8202	23900
County of San Diego	8748	D	619 236-2191	27891
County of San Diego	8063	B	619 692-8200	22057
County of San Diego	8322	D	619 563-2765	23902
County of San Diego	8099	D	619 531-4521	22936
County of San Diego	8322	D	619 236-8725	23903
County of San Diego Dept Chil	8322	B	619 578-6660	23904
Courier Leasing Inc	7382	A	619 275-7000	16876
Courtyard By Marriott	7011	D	619 291-5720	12544
Covance Inc	8731	D	858 352-2300	26500
Covario Inc (PA)	8742	D	858 397-1500	27392
Cox Communications Inc	4841	D	858 715-4500	5974
Cox Communications Cal LLC	4841	B	619 262-1122	5981
CP Opco LLC	7359	D	858 496-9700	14527
Crash Inc Short Term I	8093	E	619 282-7274	22716
Creative Nail Design Inc	7231	C	760 599-2900	13671
Credit Solutions Corp	6141	C	858 650-0812	9745
Crestline Funding Corporation	6162	D	949 863-8600	9836
Cricket Communications LLC (DH)	4812	D	858 882-6000	5391
Cricket Indiana Property Co	4812	D	858 587-2648	5392
Crown Building Maintenance Co	7349	B	858 560-5785	14276
Crown Plaza SD	7011	D	619 297-1101	12555
Csi Financial Services LLC	8741	E	858 200-9200	26999
CSRA LLC	7376	A	619 225-2600	16278
Ctk Biotech Inc	8731	E	858 487-8698	26502

Employment Codes: A=Over 500 employees, B=251-500, C=101-250, D=51-100, E=45-50

2017 Directory of California Wholesalers and Services Companies

© Mergent Inc. 1-800-342-5647

SAN DIEGO, CA — GEOGRAPHIC SECTION

Company	SIC	EMP	PHONE	ENTRY #
Cubic Corporation	7373	A	858 277-6780	15926
Cubic Global Defense Inc (HQ)	7629	E	858 277-6780	17932
Cusa Gcbs LLC	4725	D	619 266-7365	4993
Cuso Financial Services LP	6282	D	800 686-4724	10135
Customzed Svcs Admnstrtors Inc	6411	C	858 810-2000	10685
Cutting Edge Drywall Inc	1742	E	858 408-0870	2882
D & K Engineering	8711	A	858 451-8999	25761
Dart Neuroscience LLC	8731	C	858 736-3060	26503
Davenport Development Corp	1752	E	858 300-3333	3110
Daw Industries Inc	5099	E	858 622-4955	8111
Daybreak Game Company LLC	7371	B	858 239-0500	15123
Daymark Realty Advisors Inc	6531	B	714 975-2999	11465
DCS Corporation	8711	C	619 278-3600	25765
De Anza Land & Leisure Corp	7833	E	619 423-2727	18359
Defenseweb Technologies Inc	7379	D	858 272-8505	16353
Dehart Inc	1799	D	858 695-0882	3512
Delimex Holdings Inc	6719	A	619 210-2700	12058
Dell Software Inc	7371	D	858 450-7153	15129
Deloitte & Touche LLP	8721	C	619 232-6500	26321
Delta Dental of California	6324	B	619 683-2549	10276
Delta-T Group Inc	8082	A	619 543-0556	22422
Dentons US LLP	8111	C	619 595-5400	23207
Dentons US LLP	8111	B	619 236-1414	23208
Diamondrock San Dego Tnant LLC	7011	D	619 239-4500	12570
Dietz Glmor Chazen A Prof Corp (PA)	8111	D	858 565-0269	23214
Digitalmojo Inc	8742	E	800 346-7147	27412
Dimension Development Two LLC	7011	D	619 233-8408	12571
Dimension Development Two LLC	7011	D	858 485-9250	12572
Distinctive Concrete Inc	1771	E	858 277-9707	3258
Divx Corporation (HQ)	5065	D	858 882-0700	7557
Dla Piper LLP (us)	8111	C	619 699-2700	23222
Dla Piper LLP (us)	8111	C	858 677-1400	23223
DMS Facility Services LLC	8711	C	858 560-4191	25771
Dollar Thrifty Auto Group Inc	7514	A	619 298-7635	17669
Donahue Schriber Rlty Group LP	6512	D	858 793-5757	10978
Doubletree LLC	7011	C	858 485-4145	12590
Doubletree LLC	7011	B	619 297-5466	12597
Downtown San Diego Partnr Inc	8611	D	619 234-8900	25083
Dpr Construction	1541	B	858 646-0757	1419
DR Systems Inc	8071	C	858 625-3344	22210
Drain Patrol	1711	D	858 560-1137	2209
Dreamscape Ldscp & Maint Inc	0781	E	619 583-4439	763
Drx LLC	8099	D	888 315-1519	22949
Duckor Spradling Metzger	8111	D	619 209-3000	23230
Dynalectric Company	1731	B	858 712-4700	2577
Dyncorp	7373	C	619 522-2222	15936
Eagle Estates Inc	6531	B	858 484-3829	11485
Ealliant LLC	8748	E	619 255-9344	27903
Eastern Goldfields Inc	8742	E	619 497-2555	27418
Eastrdge Prsonnel of Las Vegas (PA)	7361	E	619 260-2000	14644
Ebuys Inc	5139	C	858 547-7545	8434
Edaw Inc	0781	D	619 233-1454	764
Edf Msschstts Spnsor Mmber LLC	4911	A	888 903-6926	6127
Edf Renewable Energy Inc (PA)	4911	C	858 521-3300	6128
Edf Renewable Energy Inc	8721	C	760 329-1437	26332
Edf Renewable Services Inc (HQ)	7539	C	858 521-3575	17821
Edf Rnwable Asset Holdings Inc	4911	A	888 903-6926	6129
Edgewave Inc	7372	D	858 676-2277	15648
Edmin Open Systems Inc (PA)	7379	D	858 712-9341	16362
Education Management Corp	8741	C	858 810-0215	27013
Educational Funding Co LLC	6111	D	858 350-1313	9729
Edwards Theatres Circuit Inc	7832	D	858 635-7716	18325
Einstein Industries Inc	7371	C	858 459-1182	15157
Elavon Inc	7375	A	954 776-7990	16232
Electra Owners Assoc	8611	C	619 236-3310	25084
Elite Maintenance Services Inc	7349	D	619 516-7000	14289
Elite Show Services Inc	7381	A	619 574-1589	16634
Embassy Suites Management LLC	7011	C	858 453-0400	12617
Emcor Fclities Svcs N Amer Inc	1711	C	858 712-4700	2217
Emerald Connect LLC (HQ)	7374	D	800 233-2834	16123
Emerald Textiles LLC	7211	B	619 690-7353	13503
Emeritus Corporation	8052	E	858 292-8044	21078
Employment & Community Options	8331	C	858 565-9870	24337
Encore Capital Group Inc (PA)	6153	C	877 445-4581	9782
Encore Semi Inc	8711	C	858 225-4993	25786
Engility Corporation	8711	C	703 708-1400	25788
Engility LLC	8711	C	858 552-9500	25790
Enginring Sftwr Sys Sltons Inc (PA)	8711	D	619 338-0380	25794
Enterprise Rent-A-Car	7514	D	619 297-0311	17672
Envoy Air Inc	4512	B	619 231-5452	4799
Envoy Air Inc	4581	E	619 260-9069	4916
Epicenter Live Inc	7922	C	424 235-4835	18391
Epicor Software Corporation	7372	D	858 352-1600	15658
Eplica Inc (PA)	7363	D	619 260-2000	14874
Epsilon Mission Solutions Inc	8711	D	619 702-1700	25799
Epsilon Systems Solutions Inc	8711	C	619 702-1700	25800
Epsilon Systems Solutions Inc (PA)	8711	D	619 702-1700	25801
Equitable Variable Lf Insur Co	6311	D	619 239-0018	10205
Ernst & Young LLP	8721	C	858 535-7200	26343
Escalate Inc (DH)	7371	B	858 457-3888	15171
Eset LLC (HQ)	5045	C	619 876-5400	7129
Esquire Landscape Inc	0782	E	858 530-2949	850
Evergreen Distributors Inc (PA)	0181	E	858 481-0622	281
EW Scripps Company	4833	C	619 237-1010	5860
Exp US Services Inc	8711	D	858 597-0555	25804
Expeditors Intl Wash Inc	4731	C	619 710-1900	5072
Exprescom LLC	5065	D	619 271-0531	7564
EZ Acceptance Inc	7359	C	858 278-8351	14540
Fairfield Development Inc (PA)	1522	C	858 457-2123	1310
Faith Jones & Associates Inc (PA)	8082	D	619 297-9601	22436
Falconwood Inc	7378	D	619 297-9080	16294
Family Hlth Ctrs San Diego Inc	8011	D	619 515-2526	19522
Family Hlth Ctrs San Diego Inc	8011	D	619 515-2435	19523
Family Hlth Ctrs San Diego Inc	8021	D	619 515-2300	20254
Family Hlth Ctrs San Diego Inc (PA)	8093	D	619 515-2303	22730
Farmers Insurance Exchange	6411	C	858 677-1100	10712
Fas Holdings Inc	6211	C	619 702-9600	9998
Federal Express Corporation	4513	C	800 463-3339	4845
Federal Express Corporation	4731	C	619 688-9203	5076
Fedex Freight Corporation	4213	D	619 710-0268	4164
Fedex Ground Package Sys Inc	4215	C	619 661-1051	4413
Fedex Ground Package Sys Inc	4513	C	800 463-3339	4865
Fenton Scripps Landing LLC	6513	D	858 586-0206	11130
Ferguson Enterprises Inc	5074	C	619 515-0300	7715
Ferring Research Institute Inc	8731	C	858 657-1400	26517
Festival Funparks LLC	7999	E	858 560-4213	19212
Fibrwrap Construction LP (HQ)	1796	D	909 390-4363	3475
Fieldstone Communities Inc	1521	E	858 546-8081	1174
Fieno Inc	0723	C	760 352-2996	532
Figi Acquisition Company LLC	5199	C	800 678-3444	9263
Firemans Fund Insurance Co	6331	C	858 492-3019	10419
First Allied Facilities Corp	6211	D	619 702-9600	9999
First Allied Securities Inc (PA)	6211	D	619 702-9600	10000
First American Title Insur Co	6361	C	619 238-1776	10521
First National Bank	6021	C	760 602-5518	9398
First National Bank (PA)	6733	D	619 233-5588	12174
Firstat Nursing Services Inc	8082	C	619 220-7600	22438
Fish & Richardson PC	8111	C	858 678-5070	23243
Fitness International LLC	7991	E	858 550-5912	18634
Five Star Quality Care Inc	8051	B	858 673-6300	20576
Focuspoint International	7381	B	415 446-9418	16644
Foley & Lardner LLP	8111	D	858 847-6700	23251
Forward Slope Incorporated	8711	D	619 299-4400	25816
Foshay Electric Coinc	1731	D	858 277-7676	2596
Foster Wheeler Energy Svcs Inc	1796	E	800 500-1993	3476
Fragomen Del Rey Bernse	8111	D	858 793-1600	23254
Frank Sciarrino Marble G	5032	D	858 695-8030	6983
Front Porch Communities & Svcs	8059	B	858 274-4110	21223
Fuji Food Products Inc	5149	C	619 268-3118	8839
G & L Penasquitos Inc	8322	D	858 538-0802	23992
G Instruments	7389	D	858 231-5156	17179
G2 Software Systems Inc	8711	D	619 222-8025	25826
G4s Secure Solutions (usa)	7381	C	619 295-2394	16650
G5 Global Partners Ix LLC	7011	D	619 291-6500	12656
G7 Productivity Systems	7372	D	858 675-1095	15673
Gafcon Inc (PA)	8741	D	858 875-0010	27032
Garich Inc (PA)	7361	B	858 453-1331	14660
Garrad Hassan America Inc (DH)	8711	D	858 836-3370	25827
Gary R Edwards Inc	7389	C	619 299-8700	17181
Gaslamp Hotel Management Inc	7011	D	619 234-0977	12659
Gen-Probe Incorporated (HQ)	8731	C	858 410-8000	26520
General Atomics (HQ)	8731	A	858 455-2810	26523
General Atomics	8731	D	858 676-7100	26524
General Atomics	8731	B	858 455-4000	26525
General Coatings Corporation (PA)	1721	C	858 587-1277	2446
General Dynamics Corporation	8711	D	619 544-3400	25832
General Dynamics Info Tech Inc	8711	E	619 881-8989	25833
Genesis Healthcare Partners PC	8093	D	619 230-0400	22733
Genomedx Biosciences Corp	8071	D	888 975-4540	22219
Gentry Associates LLC	7011	C	619 296-0551	12662
Geocon Consultants Inc (PA)	8748	D	858 558-6900	27931
Geocon Incorporated	8711	D	858 558-6900	25837
George G Sharp Inc	4225	C	619 575-0511	4562
Gerdau Reinforcing Steel (DH)	1541	E	858 737-7700	1428
Gerwend Enterprises Inc	8744	E	619 254-5018	27790
Girl Scts Sn Diego-Imprl Cncl (PA)	8641	D	619 610-0751	25262
Gkk Corporation	8712	D	619 398-0215	26189
Glenn A Rick Engrg & Dev Co (PA)	8711	C	619 291-0708	25843
Global Dev Strategies Inc	7699	D	858 408-1173	17976
Gmg Stone Inc	1743	E	619 258-6899	3015

GEOGRAPHIC SECTION   SAN DIEGO, CA

	SIC	EMP	PHONE	ENTRY #
GMI Building Services Inc	7349	C	858 279-6262	14316
Gms Janitorial Services Inc	7349	D	858 569-6009	14317
Gnf	8733	D	858 812-1976	26768
Go-Staff Inc (PA)	7363	D	858 292-8562	14883
Goal Financial LLC	6162	C	858 731-9000	9846
Goforth & Marti (PA)	5021	D	951 684-0870	6816
Gold Coast Design Inc	1721	D	619 574-0111	2450
Golden Eagle Insurance Corp (DH)	6331	C	619 744-6000	10424
Golden Hour Data Systems Inc	4731	C	858 768-2500	5089
Goodwill Inds San Diego Cnty	8331	D	619 955-5626	24345
Gordon Rees Scully Mnskhani LLP	8111	D	619 696-6700	23285
Gordon Rees Scully Mnskhani LLP	8111	D	415 986-5900	23286
Grand Del Mar Resort LP	7011	A	858 314-2000	12671
Grant Thornton LLP	8721	C	858 704-8000	26359
Gray Systems Inc	7378	E	619 285-5848	16296
Graybar Electric Company Inc	5063	D	858 549-9017	7443
Great Western Wind Energy LLC	4911	D	888 903-6926	6135
Greater San Diego AC Co Inc	1711	D	619 469-7818	2240
Green Farms Inc	5148	C	858 831-7701	8735
Group 3 Technologies	7622	D	858 874-3081	17908
GS Levine Insurance Svcs Inc	6411	D	858 481-8692	10733
Guard Management Inc	7381	A	858 279-8282	16668
Guardsmark LLC	7381	C	858 499-0025	16688
Guild Mortgage Company (PA)	6162	C	800 283-8823	9852
H & R Accounts Inc	7371	D	619 819-8844	15218
H - Investment Company	5031	D	650 872-0500	6926
H C T Inc	7011	B	619 224-1234	12681
Hampstead Lafayette Hotel LLC	7011	E	619 296-2101	12683
Handlery Hotels Inc	7011	C	415 781-4550	12686
Hansen Quality Loan Svcs Inc	6531	C	858 909-4300	11568
Harbor View Hotel Ventures LLC	7011	D	619 239-6800	12690
Harmonium Inc (PA)	8351	C	858 684-3080	24466
Harmonium Inc	7032	A	858 271-4000	13465
Harper Construction Co Inc (PA)	1542	C	619 233-7900	1562
Harper Mechanical Contrs LLC	5046	D	619 543-1296	7218
Harte-Hanks Mkt Intelligence (PA)	7374	C	858 450-1667	16139
Harvey	1542	C	858 769-4000	1564
Havas Formula LLC	8743	D	619 234-0345	27750
Hawthorne Machinery Co (PA)	7353	C	858 674-7000	14484
Hawthorne Machinery Co (HQ)	7353	C	858 674-7000	14485
Hawthorne Machinery Co	7538	D	858 674-7000	17801
Hawthorne Machinery Co	5082	D	858 974-6800	7770
Hazard Construction Company	1622	D	858 587-3600	1893
HDR Engineering Inc	8711	D	619 231-4865	25855
HDR Engineering Inc	8742	E	858 712-8400	27459
HDR Environmental Ope	8712	D	858 712-8400	26198
Health Source Staffing Inc	8082	D	619 220-8044	22453
Healthline Systems LLC (HQ)	7372	D	858 673-1700	15688
Healthright 360	8093	C	213 216-0484	22742
Healthstream Inc	7372	C	800 733-8737	15689
HEI Mission Valley LP	7011	C	619 299-2729	12699
Hensel Phelps Construction Co	1542	D	858 266-7979	1567
Herring Broadcasting Company	4833	E	858 270-6900	5869
Herring Networks Inc	4833	C	858 270-6900	5870
HG Fenton Company	6513	D	619 400-0120	11140
Hhlp San Diego Lessee LLC	7011	D	619 446-3000	12701
Higgs Fletcher & Mack Llp	8111	D	619 236-1551	23307
High Ridge Wind LLC	4911	A	888 903-6926	6138
Hilton Worldwide Inc	7011	B	619 276-4010	12717
Hilton Worldwide Inc	7011	D	858 431-2116	12736
Historical Properties Inc (PA)	7011	D	619 230-8417	12743
Hitachi Data Systems Corp	5045	C	858 537-3000	7140
HLT Operate Dtwc LLC	7011	C	619 297-5466	12745
Hob Entertainment LLC	7929	C	619 299-2583	18471
Holiday Inn Rncho Bernardo LLC	7011	D	858 485-6530	12752
Home Instead Senior Care	8082	D	858 277-3722	22464
Hornblower Yachts Inc	4489	C	619 686-8700	4736
Hornblower Yachts Inc	8742	C	619 234-8687	27467
Host Hotels & Resorts Inc	7011	C	619 232-1234	12761
Host Hotels & Resorts LP	7011	D	619 692-3800	12763
Host Hotels & Resorts LP	7011	D	619 291-2900	12768
Host International Inc	7011	C	619 231-5100	12779
Hotel Circle Inn & Suites	7011	E	619 851-6800	12782
Hotel Circle Property LLC	7011	B	619 291-7131	12783
Hotel Managers Group Llc	8741	C	858 673-1534	27057
HP Enterprise Services LLC	7374	B	619 817-3851	16141
HP Inc	5065	B	858 655-4100	7581
Hronopoulos	8741	E	619 237-6161	27058
Hst Lessee Boston LLC	7011	D	619 692-2255	12802
Hst Lessee San Diego LP	6531	A	619 291-2900	11575
Huntleigh USA Corporation	4581	D	619 231-8111	4921
Hyatt Corporation	7011	C	619 849-1234	12822
Hyatt Hotels Management Corp	7011	B	858 552-1234	12827
Iboss Inc	7371	D	877 742-6832	15229
Icw Group Holdings Inc (PA)	6331	D	858 350-2400	10429
Icw Valencia LLC	6512	D	858 350-2600	11004
ID Analytics LLC	7382	C	858 312-6200	16891
Idun Pharmaceuticals Inc	8733	E	858 622-3000	26771
Igo Medical Group A Med Corp (PA)	8011	D	858 455-7520	19567
Iheartcommunications Inc	4832	B	858 522-5547	5781
Iheartcommunications Inc	4832	D	858 292-2000	5782
Iheartcommunications Inc	4832	D	858 565-6006	5786
Imageware Systems Inc (PA)	7372	D	858 673-8600	15697
Imaging Hlthcare Spcalists LLC	8734	D	619 229-2299	26859
IMS Recycling Services Inc (PA)	5093	D	619 231-2521	8073
Independa Inc	7373	E	800 815-7829	15965
Indus Technology Inc	8711	C	619 299-2555	25874
Indyme Solutions LLC	8999	E	858 268-0717	28135
Information Systems Labs Inc (PA)	8711	E	858 535-9680	25876
Ingenium Technologies Corp	8711	D	858 227-4422	25878
Innovasystems Intl LLC	7371	D	619 955-5890	15236
Innovasystems Intl LLC (PA)	7371	C	619 756-6500	15237
Innovtive Emplyee Slutions Inc	8721	A	858 715-5100	26377
Insurance Company of West (HQ)	6331	D	858 350-2400	10430
Integral Senior Living LLC	0291	D	858 484-3801	467
Integrits Corporation (PA)	7379	E	858 300-1600	16403
Integrity Hlthcare Sltions Inc (PA)	8082	E	858 576-9501	22484
Inter Con Security Inc	8742	E	619 523-0291	27480
Interactivate Inc	7379	D	619 814-1999	16406
Intercntnntal Ht Group Rsurces	7011	D	619 727-4000	12839
Interlab Inc	5049	E	619 302-3095	7343
International Industrial Park	6726	D	858 623-9000	12140
Interntional Pet Sups Dist Inc	5199	D	858 453-7845	9272
Interntnal Rscue Committee Inc	8322	D	619 641-7510	24034
Interstate Btry San Diego Inc	5013	E	858 790-8244	6741
Interstate Electronics Corp	7373	D	858 552-9500	15971
Intuit Inc	7372	B	858 215-8000	15716
Ips Group Inc (PA)	4899	D	858 404-6067	6077
Iq Pipeline LLC	7363	D	858 483-7400	14890
Iq4bis Software Incorporated	5045	D	858 565-4238	7147
Isaac Fair Corporation	7371	D	858 369-8000	15258
Iserve Residential Lending LLC	6162	D	858 486-4169	9863
J D L Motor Express	4212	D	619 232-6136	4028
J Gelt Corporation	8322	E	619 424-8181	24038
J W Floor Covering Inc (PA)	1752	C	858 536-8565	3122
J5th LLC	7011	D	619 487-1200	12861
Ja Automation & Control LLC	5084	D	619 661-2591	7853
Jackson & Blanc	1711	C	858 831-7900	2260
Jacobs Center For Nghbrhood (PA)	8742	C	619 527-6161	27490
Jacobs Cshman San Diego Fd Bnk	8322	E	619 527-1419	24039
Jacobs Engineering Group Inc	8711	D	619 795-8872	25896
Jaycor Inc	8733	B	858 720-4000	26775
Jaynes Corporation California	1542	C	619 233-4081	1582
JB Hunt Transport Svcs Inc	4789	A	619 230-0054	5226
JC Resorts Inn	7011	C	858 487-0700	12863
Jck Hotels LLC	7011	D	858 635-5566	12864
Jensen Meat Company Inc	5147	C	619 754-6450	8673
Jetblue Airways Corporation	4512	C	619 725-0807	4808
Jetmore Wind LLC	4911	A	888 903-6926	6141
JM Driver LLC	7371	D	858 663-6226	15264
Joe Canpagna	6531	D	619 222-0555	11597
Jones Day Limited Partnership	8111	D	858 314-1200	23309
Jones Sign Co Inc	5046	D	858 569-1400	7221
Jpmorgan Chase Bank Nat Assn	7389	C	858 605-3300	17266
Jr Construction Inc	1542	D	858 505-4760	1586
Juan Lopez	1521	D	619 428-3138	1199
June Group LLC	7363	D	858 450-4290	14891
K Love (kiqv)	4832	D	619 235-0600	5791
K Tech Security & Protect Svc	7381	E	619 858-5832	16715
Ka Management Inc	8741	D	858 404-6080	27086
Kaiser Foundation Hospitals	6733	D	619 662-5107	12180
Kaiser Foundation Hospitals	8011	D	619 542-7210	19581
Kaiser Foundation Hospitals	6733	D	619 528-7100	12181
Kaiser Foundation Hospitals	8062	D	619 528-2583	21640
Kaiser Foundation Hospitals	6324	D	619 528-5000	10303
Kaiser Foundation Hospitals	6324	D	619 528-5000	10304
Kaiser Foundation Hospitals	8011	A	858 847-3500	19641
Kaiser Foundation Hospitals	8011	E	858 502-1350	19642
Kaiser Foundation Hospitals	8093	C	858 573-0090	22753
Kaiser Foundation Hospitals	8011	E	858 573-0299	19660
Kaiser Foundation Hospitals	8062	E	619 641-4663	21661
Kalpana LLC	7011	D	619 543-9000	12874
Kbm Fclity Sltons Holdings LLC	7349	B	858 467-0202	14334
Kearny Villa Hotel Venture LLC	7011	D	858 573-0700	12877
Kesari Hospitality LLC	7011	E	619 298-1291	12879
Kforce Inc	7361	D	858 550-1645	14693
Khp II San Diego Hotel LLC	7011	D	619 515-3000	12882
Kidder Mathews LLC	6531	C	858 509-1200	11618
Kifrn Smooth Jazz 981 Inc	4832	D	619 297-3698	5793
Kimball Tirey & St John LLP (PA)	8111	D	619 234-1690	23351

Employment Codes: A=Over 500 employees, B=251-500, C=101-250, D=51-100, E=45-50

2017 Directory of California Wholesalers and Services Companies

© Mergent Inc. 1-800-342-5647

SAN DIEGO, CA

GEOGRAPHIC SECTION

Company	SIC	EMP	PHONE	ENTRY #
Kimley-Horn and Associates Inc	8711	D	619 234-9411	25919
Kinder Mrgan Lqds Trminals LLC	4226	D	619 283-6511	4695
Kindred Healthcare Inc	8082	D	858 380-4491	22494
Kindred Healthcare Inc	8062	B	619 546-9653	21685
Kindred Healthcare Oper Inc	8069	C	502 596-7300	22148
Kindred Hospital San Diego	8093	D	619 543-4500	22760
Kineticom Inc (PA)	7361	D	619 330-3100	14694
Kintera Inc (HQ)	7372	D	858 795-3000	15723
Kleinfelder Inc (HQ)	8711	C	619 831-4600	25921
Kleinfelder Associates	8748	A	619 831-4600	27966
Knox Attorney Service Inc (PA)	7334	D	619 233-9700	14122
Koam Engineering Systems Inc	7373	C	858 292-0922	15980
Kobey Corporation Inc (PA)	7389	D	619 523-2700	17275
Kone Inc	7699	B	858 578-5100	17987
Kpmg LLP	8721	C	858 750-7100	26385
Kratos Public Safety & Securit (HQ)	7382	D	858 812-7300	16896
Kratos Tech Trning Sltions Inc (HQ)	7372	D	858 812-7300	15729
Kros-Wise	8748	D	619 223-1980	27969
Kscf 1037 FM	4832	D	858 560-1037	5800
Kswb Inc	4833	D	858 492-9269	5888
Kyocera International Inc (HQ)	5043	D	858 576-2600	7035
Kyriba Corp (HQ)	8742	E	858 210-3560	27502
L & W Supply Corporation	5032	E	858 627-0811	6989
L A Swikard Inc	0782	C	858 408-3700	885
L C C H Associates Inc	8059	E	858 565-4424	21286
L-3 Communications Corporation	4899	D	858 623-6513	6079
La Jolla Pharmaceutical Co (PA)	8731	D	858 207-4264	26547
La Jolla Village Towers 500	8051	D	858 646-7700	20716
La Maestra Family Clinic Inc	8011	D	619 280-4213	19693
La Maestra Family Clinic Inc	8011	D	619 501-1235	19694
La Maestra Family Clinic Inc (PA)	8322	C	619 584-1612	24063
La Puerta	8641	E	619 696-3466	25280
Laboratory Specialty Gases	5169	C	619 234-6060	8992
Landcare USA LLC	0782	D	858 252-0658	894
Landcare USA LLC	0782	C	858 453-1755	897
Largo Concrete Inc	1521	C	619 356-2142	1205
Latham & Watkins LLP	8111	D	619 236-1234	23367
Lawyers Title Company	6361	D	858 650-3900	10529
Laz Parking Ltd	7521	A	858 587-8888	17727
Lbf Travel Inc	4724	B	858 429-7599	4967
Ledcor CMI Inc	1541	A	602 595-3017	1447
Ledcor Management Services Inc	8741	D	858 527-6400	27110
Ledcor Technical Services Inc	1731	D	858 527-6400	2636
Legacy Vulcan Corp	1442	D	858 547-9459	1107
Legal Recovery Law Offices Inc	8111	D	619 275-4001	23380
Leidos Inc	7379	B	858 826-5552	16422
Leidos Inc	7389	C	858 535-4499	17293
Leidos Inc	8731	D	858 826-6616	26553
Leidos Inc	8731	D	858 826-6000	26556
Leidos Inc	8731	C	858 826-7129	26558
Leidos Engineering LLC	8711	D	858 826-6000	25936
Leidos Engrg & Sciences LLC	8731	D	619 542-3130	26560
Lenore John & Co (PA)	5149	C	619 232-6136	8875
Leonards Carpet Service Inc	1771	E	858 453-9525	3291
Lewis Brsbois Bsgard Smith LLP	8111	D	619 233-1006	23388
Lg Elctrnics Mbilecomm USA Inc (DH)	5065	D	858 635-5300	7598
Lge Electrical Sales Inc	5063	B	408 379-8568	7450
Liberty Station Hhg Hotel LP	7011	D	619 221-1900	12920
Liberty Station Hhg Hotel LP	7011	E	619 222-0500	12921
Life Cycle Engineering Inc	7349	D	619 785-5990	14339
Lifetouch Portrait Studios Inc	7221	E	858 693-9197	13664
Lightbridge Hospice LLC	8069	D	858 458-2992	22152
Lincoln Mariners Assoc Ltd	6513	D	619 225-1473	11157
Linda Vista Manor Inc	8051	C	858 278-8121	20737
Lindbergh Parking Inc	7521	C	619 291-1508	17728
Liva Distributors Inc (HQ)	5141	D	619 423-9997	8492
LLP Moss Adams	8721	D	858 627-1400	26402
Local Media of America LLC	4832	D	858 888-7000	5807
Locator Services Inc	7381	C	619 229-6100	16724
Lockheed Martin Corporation	7371	C	858 740-5100	15279
Lockheed Martin Orincon	7371	D	858 455-5530	15280
Lockheed Martin Orincon Corp (HQ)	7371	C	858 455-5530	15281
Lockton Companies Llc-Pacific	6411	C	858 587-3100	10767
Lodge At Torrey Pines Partners	7011	B	858 550-3908	12925
Loma Riviera Community Assn	8641	D	619 224-1313	25289
Loomis Armored Us LLC	7381	C	619 232-5106	16727
Lpl Holdings Inc (HQ)	6211	D	858 450-9606	10026
Luth Research Inc (PA)	8732	B	619 234-5884	26685
Lynup Corporation	8742	D	619 427-4610	27516
Mabie Marketing Group Inc	7389	C	858 279-5585	17305
Magnesite Specialties Inc	1752	E	858 578-4186	3125
Magnus Security	7381	E	619 546-7789	16731
Management Trust Assn Inc	6733	D	858 547-4373	12192
Manas Hospitality LLC	7011	E	619 298-1291	12939
Manchester Grand Resorts LP	7011	A	619 232-1234	12940
Mantech International Corp	7373	C	858 492-9938	15992
Mantech Systems Engrg Corp	8748	D	858 292-9000	27981
Marika Group Inc	5137	D	858 537-5300	8399
Marine Band San Diego	7929	E	619 524-1754	18482
Marriott International Inc	7011	C	858 523-1700	12953
Marriott International Inc	7011	D	619 831-0225	12956
Marriott International Inc	7011	D	858 587-1770	12960
Marriott International Inc	7011	D	858 278-2100	12963
Marriott International Inc	7011	D	619 831-0224	12981
Marsh & McLennan Agency LLC	6411	C	858 457-3414	10775
Martinez Farms Inc	0181	B	619 661-6571	301
Mason-West Inc	5084	E	619 226-8253	7859
Mbp Land LLC	7011	D	619 291-5720	12986
McAfee Inc	7372	D	858 967-2342	15740
McKinnon Publishing Company	4833	A	858 571-5151	5897
McKowskis Maint Systems Inc	7349	C	619 269-4600	14352
McMillin Communities Inc (PA)	6799	D	619 561-5275	12325
McMillin Companies LLC (PA)	6799	D	619 477-4117	12326
McMillin Construction Svcs LP	1521	E	619 477-4170	1217
McMillin Management Svcs LP (HQ)	6722	C	619 477-4117	12119
Md7 LLC (PA)	7389	D	858 799-7850	17321
Mea Digital Worx LLC	7311	D	619 238-8923	13883
Media All Stars Inc	7389	D	858 300-9600	17323
Medical Management Cons Inc	8742	A	858 587-0609	27536
Medical Transcription Billing	7372	A	800 869-3700	15745
Medimpact Hlthcare Systems Inc (HQ)	8621	A	858 566-2727	25146
Medimpact Holdings Inc (PA)	6799	A	858 790-6646	12327
Meeting Services Inc	7359	D	858 348-0100	14560
Mental Health Systems Inc (PA)	8093	D	858 573-2600	22774
Mercury Insurance Company	6331	C	858 694-4100	10446
Meridian Rack & Pinion Inc	5013	C	858 587-8777	6747
Merit Technologies LLC	8742	D	858 623-9800	27546
Merrill Gardens LLC	6531	C	619 961-4990	11683
Merrill Lynch Pierce Fenner	6211	C	619 699-3700	10038
Merritt Hawkins & Assoc LLC (HQ)	7363	C	858 792-0711	14911
Merry X-Ray Chemical Corp (PA)	5047	C	858 565-4472	7280
Merry X-Ray Corporation	5047	B	858 565-4472	7281
Message Center Communication	7389	E	858 974-7419	17333
Messenger Express	4215	D	858 550-1400	4418
Metron Incorporated	8742	E	858 792-8904	27547
Metropolitan Area Advisory Com	8331	B	619 255-7284	24364
MHS Customer Service Inc	7361	D	858 695-2151	14704
Michael Baker Intl Inc	8748	D	858 453-3602	27987
Microconstants Inc	8748	E	858 652-4600	27989
Microsoft Corporation	7372	D	619 849-5872	15751
Midland Credit Management Inc	6153	A	877 240-2377	9786
Millennium Health LLC (PA)	8734	C	877 451-3534	26867
Milo Wind Project LLC	4911	D	888 903-6926	6148
Mintz Levin Cohn Ferris GL	8111	C	858 314-1500	23436
Miramar Ford Truck Sales Inc	5012	D	858 450-0707	6689
Miramar Transportation Inc	4731	D	858 693-0071	5124
Mirnavseh Inc	7371	D	858 335-2470	15306
Miro Technologies Inc	7373	C	858 677-2100	15995
Mirum Inc	7336	D	619 237-5552	14154
Mission Federal Services LLC (PA)	6061	C	800 500-6328	9614
Mission Hills Healthcare Inc	8051	D	619 297-4086	20791
Mission Valley Ht Operator Inc	7011	D	619 291-5720	13000
Mission Valley Hts Surgery Ctr	8011	D	619 291-3737	19756
Mitchell International Inc (HQ)	7371	C	858 368-7000	15308
Mitek Systems Inc (PA)	7372	D	858 309-1700	15759
Mlim Holdings LLC	6719	A	619 299-3131	12076
Mogl Loyalty Services Inc	7299	D	858 436-7036	13778
Molecular Bioproducts Inc (DH)	4953	C	858 453-7551	6505
Molina Healthcare Inc	8099	C	858 614-1580	23001
Monte Vista Retirement Lodge	6513	D	619 465-1331	11171
Mopar Enterprises	7331	D	858 492-1123	14085
Morgan Stanley	6211	E	858 597-7777	10049
Morgan Stanley & Co LLC	6211	D	619 236-1331	10054
Morrison & Foerster LLP	8111	D	858 720-5100	23449
Mosaic	8741	D	858 397-2261	27137
Motorola Mobility LLC	5065	C	858 455-1500	7610
Mpci Holdings Inc (PA)	5147	D	619 294-2222	8677
Mr Copy Inc (DH)	5044	D	858 573-6300	7061
Mrp Real Estate Services Inc	6163	E	858 362-6005	9940
Mscsoftware Corporation	7372	D	858 546-4414	15765
Mufg Union Bank Na	6021	D	619 230-4666	9406
Mufg Union Bank Na	6021	D	619 533-7612	9413
Multimodal Esquer Inc	4213	D	619 710-0477	4232
Murray Plumbing and Htg Corp	1711	B	858 952-8795	2301
Musicmatch Inc	7372	D	858 485-4300	15766
My Office Inc	1799	D	858 549-6700	3557
Narven Enterprises Inc (PA)	7011	D	619 239-2261	13014
Narven Enterprises Inc	7011	D	619 232-2261	13015
National Air Inc	1711	D	619 299-2500	2304
National Railroad Pass Corp	4011	C	619 239-9989	3614

GEOGRAPHIC SECTION   SAN DIEGO, CA

	SIC	EMP	PHONE	ENTRY #
Nationl Medcl Assn Comp Health	8093	D	619 231-9300	22779
Naval Coating Inc	1721	C	619 234-8366	2469
Naval Fac Eng Cmmd SW Wrkng CA	8711	D	619 532-1158	25988
Neighborhood House Association (PA)	8322	B	858 715-2642	24095
Neighborhood House Association	8322	E	619 527-1287	24096
Neighborhood House Association	8322	D	619 263-7761	24097
Neil Dymott Frank McFall	8111	C	619 238-1712	23466
Nek Services Inc	8711	D	858 277-8760	25989
Nestwise LLC	7389	A	855 444-6378	17351
Networkfleet Inc	7371	B	858 450-3245	15327
New Bi US Gaming LLC	7372	E	858 592-2472	15774
New Day Staffing Inc	7363	C	619 481-5400	14916
New Way Landscape & Tree Svcs	0782	C	858 505-8300	922
New York Life Insurance Co	6411	C	858 623-8600	10805
Newland Group Inc (PA)	6552	E	858 455-7503	11989
Newland Real Estate Group LLC (HQ)	6282	D	858 455-7503	10166
Nex Coronado Nab	8742	E	619 522-7403	27565
Next Image Medical Inc (PA)	8742	D	858 847-9185	27566
Nextivity Inc	5065	D	858 485-9442	7613
Nielsen Claritas Inc	7371	B	858 622-0800	15332
Nielsen Company (us) LLC	8732	C	858 677-9542	26695
Nine-Twenty Inc	6531	D	619 497-4900	11708
Ninyo & Moore Geotechnical (PA)	8748	B	858 576-1000	28000
Nnj Services Inc	6531	C	858 550-7900	11711
Noble Amrcas Enrgy Sltions LLC (HQ)	4931	C	877 273-6772	6290
Noiro West LLC	7011	D	619 819-6620	13026
Norman Industrial Mtls Inc	5051	E	858 277-8200	7387
North Island Financial Cr Un (PA)	6062	B	858 656-6525	9674
Northrop Grmmn Spce & Mssn Sys	8731	A	858 592-3000	26576
Northrop Grmmn Spce & Mssn Sys	7371	C	858 514-9000	15337
Northrop Grumman Systems Corp	7371	B	858 514-0400	15338
Northwest Circuits Corp	8711	D	619 661-1701	25991
Novaeon Inc	8322	D	858 503-1588	24109
Nphase LLC	4899	D	312 577-1650	6085
Ntrepid Corporation	8741	D	800 921-2414	27149
Nu Flow America Inc (PA)	1711	D	619 275-9130	2306
Nurlogic Design Inc (DH)	7373	D	858 455-7570	16018
Nursefinders Inc (PA)	7363	E	800 445-0459	14919
Nursefinders LLC (HQ)	7361	C	858 314-7427	14713
Nv5 Inc	8711	D	858 385-0500	25995
Oasis Repower LLC	4911	A	888 903-6926	6158
Odyssey Healthcare Inc	8082	D	858 565-2499	22519
Old Globe Theatre	7922	B	619 234-5623	18420
Old Town Fmly Hospitality Corp	7011	C	619 246-8010	13039
Old Town Trlley Turs San Diego	4725	C	619 298-8687	4997
Olivermcmillan LLC (PA)	6552	D	619 321-1111	11994
Omni Hotels Corporation	7011	B	619 231-6664	13043
Oracle Corporation	7372	C	858 587-5374	15794
Overseas Service Corporation	8999	C	858 408-0751	28152
P C Vericare	8049	C	858 454-3610	20337
P J J Enterprises Inc	7359	D	619 232-6136	14564
Pacific Ambulance Inc	4119	B	949 470-2355	3824
Pacific Building Group	1742	C	858 552-0600	2947
Pacific Building Group (PA)	1542	C	858 552-0600	1625
Pacific Event Productions Inc (PA)	7389	D	858 458-9908	17392
Pacific Gas Turbine Center LLC	7699	C	858 877-2910	17997
Pacific Marine Development	8711	E	858 674-6642	26006
Pacific Medical Buildings LP	6531	B	858 794-1900	11725
Pacific Rim Mech Contrs Inc (PA)	1711	B	858 974-6500	2317
Pacific Western Bank	6021	A	858 436-3500	9417
Pacifica Companies LLC (PA)	6798	D	619 296-9000	12264
Pacifica Health and Medical	7299	C	619 688-1848	13783
Pacifica Hotel Company	7011	D	619 221-8000	13067
Pacifica Katie Avenue LLC	8732	D	619 296-9000	26698
Pacifica San Jose LP	7011	D	619 296-9000	13069
Pacira Pharmaceuticals Inc	5122	B	858 625-2424	8289
Packaging Manufacturing Inc	5199	C	619 498-9199	9289
Packard Hospitality Group LLC	8741	C	858 277-4305	27156
Packetvideo Corporation (DH)	7371	D	858 731-5300	15366
Padres LP	7941	A	619 795-5000	18560
Pan Pcfic Htels Rsrts Amer Inc	7011	B	619 239-4500	13074
Pan-Pacific Mechanical LLC	1711	A	858 764-2464	2320
Panasonic Corp North America	5064	D	619 661-1134	7505
Paradigm Information Services	8999	D	858 693-6115	28154
Pardee Homes	6552	E	858 259-6390	11998
Parenthood of Planned (PA)	8093	D	619 881-4500	22791
Parma Management Co Inc	6531	E	858 457-4999	11740
Parpro Holdings Co Ltd	6719	C	619 498-9004	12083
Parsons Airgas Inc	5084	C	858 278-2050	7875
Patenaude & Felix A Prof Corp (PA)	8111	D	702 952-2031	23492
Patientsafe Solutions Inc (PA)	7371	D	858 746-3100	15370
Paul Hastings LLP	8111	C	858 458-3000	23494
Paxvax Inc	8731	E	858 450-9595	26586
Paychex Inc	8721	C	858 547-2920	26418
Paychex Benefit Tech Inc	4813	C	800 322-7292	5680
Payrollingcom Corp	8721	E	858 866-2626	26421
Pbp Hotel LLC	6552	D	619 881-6900	12000
PCI Collections Inc	7322	B	619 595-3114	14040
Pegasus Building Svcs Co Inc	7349	C	858 457-8201	14386
Pentair Technical Products	5199	C	858 740-2400	9291
Perfect Bar LLC	5149	D	866 628-8548	8904
Permanente Kaiser Intl	8099	D	619 641-4300	23018
Petco Animal Supplies Inc (DH)	0752	B	858 453-7845	644
Petti Kohn Ingrassia & L PR Co	8111	D	310 649-5772	23505
Phamatech Incorporated	8734	D	858 643-5555	26882
Pharmatek Laboratories Inc	8734	D	858 805-6383	26883
Phone Ware Inc	7389	B	858 530-8550	17413
Physician Management Group Inc	8741	D	858 309-6300	27163
Pickford Realty Inc	6531	D	858 793-6106	11749
Pickford Realty Inc	6531	D	619 294-3113	11750
Pinnacle 1617 LLC	7011	E	619 239-9600	13097
Pinnacle Hotels Usa Inc	7011	D	858 974-8201	13098
Piveg Inc	5141	D	858 436-3070	8511
Pivot Technology Solutions Ltd	7379	A	647 788-2034	16457
Planned Parenthood Federation	8093	D	619 262-3941	22802
Plaza Home Mortgage Inc (PA)	6162	B	858 346-1200	9886
Point Loma Convalescent Hosp	8051	C	619 224-4141	20855
Point Loma Rhblitation Ctr LLC	8051	C	619 224-4141	20856
Polexis Inc	7371	D	858 812-7300	15390
Poor Sisters of Nazareth of SA	8361	D	619 563-0480	24770
Pre Con Industries Inc	1742	D	805 928-3397	2955
Precision Toxicology LLC	8071	D	858 274-4813	22258
Preferred Care West Inc	8051	C	619 291-5270	20858
Preferred Employers Insur Co	6411	D	619 688-3900	10832
Preferred Hlthcare Rgistry Inc	7363	C	800 462-1896	14926
Preferred Valet Parking LLC	7521	E	619 233-7275	17738
Premier Dealer Services Inc	6411	D	858 810-1700	10833
Premier Healthcare Svcs LLC	7361	C	619 491-0300	14732
Premier Hlthcare Solutions Inc	8741	B	858 569-8629	27170
Premier Management Company	8082	D	619 582-5168	22538
Pricewaterhousecoopers LLP	8721	B	858 677-2400	26426
Pro Specialties Group Inc	5199	D	858 541-1100	9294
Professional Maint Systems Inc	7349	A	619 276-1150	14396
Progenity Inc (PA)	8071	C	855 293-2639	22260
Project Concern International (PA)	8611	C	858 279-9690	25100
Project Design Consultants	8748	C	619 235-6471	28025
Project Management Institute	8741	D	760 458-6198	27178
Propulsion Controls Engrg (PA)	7699	D	619 235-0961	18001
Protec Association Services (PA)	7349	C	858 569-1080	14397
Psychiatric Ctrs At San Diego (PA)	8011	D	619 528-4600	19893
Ptac Carmel Valley Mid School	8641	D	858 481-8221	25322
Qualcomm Innovation Center Inc (HQ)	7372	D	858 587-1121	15822
Qualcomm International Inc (HQ)	6794	A	858 587-1121	12221
Quality Claims Management Corp	6411	D	619 450-8600	10849
Quality Loan Service Corp	6733	B	619 645-7711	12202
Quality Plus Auto Parts Inc	5013	E	619 424-9991	6756
Quantum Properties LP	8062	B	619 582-3800	21825
Quartus Engineering Inc (PA)	8711	D	858 875-6000	26027
R & V Management Corporation	8741	D	619 429-3305	27189
Rady Childrens Hosp & Hlth Ctr (PA)	8069	A	858 576-1700	22163
Rady Chld Hospital-San Diego	8069	A	858 966-6795	22164
Rady Chld Hospital-San Diego (PA)	8069	A	858 576-1700	22165
Rady Chld Hospital-San Diego	8741	A	858 966-5833	27192
Rady Chld Hospital-San Diego	8069	E	858 576-5803	22166
Rady Chld Physcn MGT Svcs Inc	8011	C	619 262-3415	19906
Rancho Bernardo Golf Club	7997	D	858 487-1134	19034
Rancho Bernardo Partners Ltd	7011	D	858 451-6600	13127
Randstad Technologies LP	7379	D	619 798-7300	16470
Raphaels Party Rentals Inc (PA)	7359	C	858 441-1692	14575
Raytheon Company	8711	C	858 455-9741	26034
RB Anglers Club	7997	D	858 487-6484	19037
Reading International Inc	7832	D	858 207-2606	18345
Real Time Logic Inc	7373	D	858 812-7300	16039
Realtor Sfr Green	6531	E	858 488-4090	11799
Realty Income Corporation (PA)	6798	D	858 284-5000	12271
Recon Environmental Inc (PA)	8748	D	520 325-9977	28037
Red Door Interactive Inc (PA)	7311	D	619 398-2676	13909
Redhorse Corporation (PA)	8742	D	619 241-4609	27611
Redwood Bridge Club	7997	D	619 296-4274	19040
Redwood Healthcare Staffing	7363	D	619 238-4180	14934
Regency Hill Associates	6513	D	619 281-5200	11195
Relational Investors LLC	6282	D	858 704-3333	10179
Remax Ranch Beach	6531	E	858 391-5800	11809
Renovate America Inc	7371	D	858 605-5333	15414
Renty LLC	4119	E	858 560-0066	3832
REO Vista Healthcare Center	8051	D	619 475-2211	20870
Reputation Impression LLC	8742	D	858 633-4500	27613
Residence Inn By Marriott	7011	D	858 673-1900	13148
Residntial Alzheimers Care Inc	8741	D	858 565-4424	27198
Resort Procomm Inc	8742	D	858 866-6280	27616

Employment Codes: A=Over 500 employees, B=251-500, C=101-250, D=51-100, E=45-50

SAN DIEGO, CA — GEOGRAPHIC SECTION

Company	SIC	EMP	PHONE	ENTRY #
Resource Management Group Inc (PA)	8748	E	858 677-0884	28041
Rett Inc	7338	D	619 231-0403	14167
Reuben H Fleet Science Center	8412	D	619 238-1233	25038
Reyes Holdings LLC	6211	B	858 452-2300	10074
Rgis LLC	7389	D	858 653-0355	17450
Rgis LLC	7389	D	619 624-9882	17454
Rhino Building Services Inc	7349	C	858 455-1440	14408
Richard Heath & Associates Inc	8742	D	858 514-4025	27619
Riosoft Holdings Inc	7371	E	858 529-5005	15424
Rjc Architects Inc	8712	D	619 239-9292	26247
Robbins Geller Rudman Dowd LLP (PA)	8111	B	619 231-1058	23533
Robinsn Clgne Rsn Shpr Dvs Inc	8111	D	619 338-4060	23534
Rock Cancer CARE Inc	8322	C	888 251-0620	24160
Romeo Cecylia K Beauty Salon	7231	E	858 946-0179	13688
Roosevelt Wind Holdings LLC	4911	A	888 903-6926	6199
Rore Inc (PA)	1541	D	858 404-7393	1461
Rose Ox Inc (DH)	7338	D	619 239-4111	14168
Royal Hospitality Incorporated	7011	D	858 278-0800	13172
Rp Scs Wsd Hotel LLC	7011	D	619 398-3020	13173
RPC Old Town Avenue Owner LLC	7011	D	619 299-7400	13175
RPC Old Town Jefferson	7011	D	619 725-4221	13176
RR Donnelley & Sons Company	7389	D	858 693-6662	17469
RR Donnelley & Sons Company	5111	C	619 527-4600	8154
Rural/Metro San Diego Inc	4119	D	619 280-6060	3837
Rx Pro Health LLC	7363	A	858 369-4050	14945
S & L Specialty Contracting	1742	E	619 264-3771	2973
SA Recycling LLC	4953	D	619 238-6740	6542
SA Recycling LLC	4953	D	714 632-2000	6557
Sackett National Holdings Inc	8742	D	866 834-6242	27633
Saddle Creek Corporation	4225	C	619 229-2200	4634
Sadie Rose Baking Co	5149	D	858 831-0290	8917
Salvation Army	8361	D	858 279-1100	24797
Salvation Army	8361	D	858 279-1100	24798
Salvation Army	7991	D	619 269-1404	18677
San Dego Cnty Rgnal Arprt Auth (PA)	4581	C	619 400-2400	4932
San Dego Cnvntion Ctr Corp Inc (PA)	6512	D	619 525-5000	11038
San Dego Soc of Ntural History	8412	D	619 232-3821	25039
San Dego State Univ Foundation	8322	D	888 999-6897	24172
San Dego State Univ Foundation	4832	D	619 594-1515	5819
San Diego Arcft Carier Museum	8412	C	619 544-9600	25041
San Diego Blood Bank (PA)	8099	D	619 296-6393	23046
San Diego Center For Children (PA)	8059	D	858 277-9550	21365
San Diego Community Hsing Corp	8748	C	619 527-4633	28050
San Diego County Credit Union	6062	C	858 453-2112	9683
San Diego County Employees Ret	6411	D	619 515-6800	10860
San Diego County Water Auth (PA)	4941	D	858 522-6600	6392
San Diego Creative Community S	8322	E	619 250-3394	24174
San Diego Data Proc Corp Inc	7374	C	858 581-9600	16180
San Diego Family Care (PA)	8011	D	858 279-0925	19939
San Diego Family Housing LLC	8699	B	858 874-8100	25571
San Diego Farah Partners	7011	E	619 239-2261	13195
San Diego Gas & Electric Co (DH)	4931	C	619 696-2000	6292
San Diego Gas & Electric Co	4939	C	619 699-1018	6308
San Diego Hbr Excursions Inc	1629	D	619 234-4111	2081
San Diego Homecare	8082	C	858 457-1520	22553
San Diego Hospice	8082	A	619 688-1600	22554
San Diego Hotel Cir Owner LLC	7011	D	619 881-6900	13196
San Diego Hotel Company LLC	7011	C	619 696-0234	13197
San Diego Hotel Lease LLC	7011	D	619 446-3000	13198
San Diego Imaging - Chula Vist (PA)	8071	E	858 565-0950	22275
San Diego Land Systems	0781	E	858 558-0542	794
San Diego Lesbian Gay Bisexu	8322	E	619 692-2077	24175
San Diego Med Svcs Entp LLC	4119	B	619 280-6060	3838
San Diego Messenger Inc	4215	E	858 514-8866	4422
San Diego Metro Trnst Sys	4111	A	619 231-1466	3695
San Diego Metropolitan Cr Un (PA)	6062	D	619 297-4835	9684
San Diego Museum of Art	8412	D	619 696-1971	25042
San Diego Opera Association (PA)	7922	E	619 232-7636	18431
San Diego Orthopaedic Associat	8011	D	619 299-8500	19940
San Diego Paradise Pt Resort	7011	B	858 274-4630	13199
San Diego Rescue Mission Inc (PA)	8399	D	619 819-1880	24974
San Diego Sheraton Corporation	7011	A	619 291-6400	13200
San Diego State University	4832	D	619 265-6438	5820
San Diego Symphony Orchestra	7929	C	619 235-0800	18491
San Diego Testing Engineers	8711	D	858 715-5800	26053
San Diego Theatres Inc	6512	C	619 615-4000	11039
San Diego Tourism Authority (PA)	7389	D	619 232-3101	17471
San Diego Transit Corporation (PA)	4111	A	619 238-0100	3696
San Diego Transit Corporation	4111	B	619 238-0100	3697
San Diego Trolley Inc	4111	B	619 595-4933	3698
San Diego Unified Port Dst	4491	C	619 686-6585	4756
San Diego Unified Port Dst (PA)	4491	B	619 686-6200	4757
San Diego Unified Port Dst	5088	C	619 683-8966	8004
San Diego Unified School Dst	7349	A	858 627-7130	14417
San Diego Urban League Inc	8641	D	619 266-6247	25333
San Diego Youth Services Inc (PA)	8322	D	619 221-8600	24176
San Diego-Imperial Counties De (PA)	8322	B	858 576-2996	24179
San Miguel Hospital Assn	8062	C	619 297-2251	21852
Santaluz Club Inc	7997	C	858 759-3120	19067
Saturn Electric Inc	1731	E	858 271-4100	2726
SC Wright Construction Inc	8711	B	619 698-6909	26055
Scalematrix Holdings Inc	7379	D	888 349-9994	16474
Schmidt Fire Protection Co Inc	1711	D	858 279-6122	2360
Schryver Med Sls & Mktg LLC	8071	D	303 459-8160	22282
Science Applications Intl Corp	7379	D	703 676-4300	16475
Science Applications Intl Corp	7373	A	858 826-3061	16045
Science Applications Intl Corp	7373	A	858 826-6000	16046
Scripps Clinic	8011	C	858 794-1250	19964
Scripps Clinic Foundation	8741	D	858 554-9000	27207
Scripps Health	8011	D	858 622-9076	19969
Scripps Health	8051	D	619 294-8111	20897
Scripps Health	8641	D	858 678-6966	25345
Scripps Health	8051	C	858 657-4218	20898
Scripps Health	8093	D	858 271-9770	22829
Scripps Health	8099	B	619 245-2350	23055
Scripps Health	8049	C	858 554-4100	20352
Scripps Health (PA)	8051	D	858 678-7000	20899
Scripps Health	8011	D	858 292-4211	19974
Scripps Health	8062	B	619 294-8111	21870
Scripps Health	8082	B	858 764-3000	22557
Scripps Health	8011	D	858 784-5888	19982
Scripps Health	8093	C	858 794-0160	22830
Scripps Mercy Hospital	8062	D	619 294-8111	21875
Scst Inc (PA)	8734	D	619 280-4321	26885
SD Sports MDCne&fmly Hlth Cntr	8011	D	619 229-3910	19983
SD Stadium Hotel LLC	7011	D	858 278-9300	13225
SE San Diego Hotel LLC	7011	D	619 515-3000	13226
SE Scher Corporation	7361	B	858 546-8300	14781
Sea World LLC	7996	A	619 226-3842	18832
Seacoast Commerce Bank (PA)	6029	D	858 432-7000	9558
Sealaska Envmtl Svcs LLC	8748	D	619 564-8329	28053
Search Optics LLC (PA)	8742	D	858 678-0707	27637
Sears Home Imprv Pdts Inc	1521	D	858 790-7721	1252
Secure Transportation Co Inc	4789	D	858 790-3958	5242
Securitas Critical Infrastruct	7381	A	858 560-0448	16781
Securitas SEC Svcs USA Inc	7381	C	619 641-0049	16794
Security On-Demand Inc	7373	E	858 563-5655	16049
Seltzer Caplan McMahon (PA)	8111	D	619 685-3003	23554
Semantic Research Inc (PA)	7373	D	619 222-4050	16052
Sempra Energy (PA)	4932	A	619 696-2000	6298
Sempra Energy Global Entps	4924	A	619 696-2000	6273
Sempra Energy International (HQ)	4911	A	619 696-2000	6206
Sempra US Gas & Power LLC (HQ)	4922	D	877 736-7721	6255
Senior Care Inc	8052	C	619 817-8855	21103
Senomyx Inc	8731	B	858 646-8300	26605
Sentek Consulting Inc	7379	C	619 543-9550	16478
Sequenom Inc (HQ)	8731	B	858 202-9000	26606
Sequenom Center For Molecular	8071	B	858 202-9051	22285
Serco Inc	8711	C	858 569-8979	26059
Servi-Tek Inc	7349	B	858 638-7735	14424
Seven Seas Associates LLC	7011	C	619 291-1300	13235
Shake Smart Inc	7384	C	661 993-7383	16956
Sharp Chula Vista Medical Ctr	8062	D	858 499-5150	21884
Sharp Community Medical Group	8621	C	858 499-4525	25156
Sharp Health Plan	6324	D	858 499-8300	10380
Sharp Healthcare	8011	D	619 398-2988	19990
Sharp Healthcare	8011	D	858 621-4090	19991
Sharp Healthcare	8011	C	858 939-5434	19992
Sharp Healthcare (PA)	8062	A	858 499-4000	21885
Sharp Healthcare	8051	C	619 446-1575	20908
Sharp Healthcare	8011	D	619 688-3543	19993
Sharp Healthcare	8011	D	858 653-6100	19994
Sharp Healthcare	8062	C	858 627-5152	21886
Sharp Healthcare	8082	D	858 541-4850	22561
Sharp Healthcare	8011	D	858 616-8411	19996
Sharp Healthcare	8062	D	858 621-4010	21888
Sharp Healthcare	8011	D	800 827-4277	19997
Sharp Healthcare	8082	D	858 541-4896	22562
Sharp Healthcare	8011	D	858 616-8200	19999
Sharp Mary Birch H	8062	D	858 939-3400	21889
Sharp Memorial Hospital (HQ)	8062	A	858 939-3636	21890
Sharp Memorial Hospital	8063	D	858 278-4110	22091
Shea Family Care Mission Hlth	8093	D	619 297-4484	22831
Shelter Pointe LLC	4493	C	619 221-8000	4772
Sheppard Mullin Richter	8111	B	619 338-6500	23562
Sheraton Htl San Diego Msn Vly	8742	D	619 321-4602	27645
Sherwood Mechanical Inc	1711	D	858 679-3000	2366
Shoreline Land Care Inc	0782	D	858 560-8555	953
Show Call Productions Inc	7922	B	619 602-0656	18434
Siemens Industry Inc	5084	D	858 693-8711	7887

GEOGRAPHIC SECTION

SAN DIEGO, CA

Company	SIC	EMP	PHONE	ENTRY #
Signal Pharmaceuticals LLC	5122	C	858 795-4700	8295
Silicon Space Inc	7371	D	858 751-0200	15456
Simpson Delmore and Greene LLP (PA)	8111	E	619 515-1194	23572
Sinclair Companies	7011	C	619 238-1818	13258
Six Continents Hotels Inc	7011	D	619 232-3861	13265
Six Continents Hotels Inc	7011	D	619 795-4000	13267
Skygroup Investments LLC	7999	D	619 432-4359	19284
Skylight Halthcare Systems Inc	8742	D	858 523-3700	27650
Slate Creek Wind Project LLC	4911	A	888 903-6926	6208
Smartdrive Systems Inc	5099	B	866 933-9930	8140
Socal Services Inc	7361	C	858 453-1331	14791
Socal Sportsnet LLC	7929	A	619 795-5000	18496
Social Advocates For Youth	8322	C	858 974-3603	24211
Social Advocates For Youth	8322	C	619 283-9624	24212
Softhq	7379	E	858 658-9200	16483
Soleil Communications LLC	8732	D	619 624-2888	26707
Solimar Systems Inc (PA)	7371	D	619 849-2800	15466
Solomon Ward Sdnwurm Smith LLP	8111	D	619 231-0303	23578
Solpac Inc	1542	C	619 296-6247	1675
Solpac Construction Inc	8741	C	619 296-6247	27224
Sony Intrctive Entrmt Amer LLC	5092	C	858 824-5501	8054
Sorrento Therapeutics Inc (PA)	8731	D	858 210-3700	26608
Souldriver Lessee Inc	7011	D	619 819-9500	13273
Southbay Sndblst & Tank Clg	7699	D	619 238-8338	18017
Southern Cal Prmnnte Med Group	6324	D	858 974-1000	10381
Southern Cal Prmnnte Med Group	8011	D	619 528-5000	20021
Southern Cal Prmnnte Med Group	8011	E	619 516-6000	20037
Southern Cal Prmnnte Med Group	8011	D	619 528-5000	20042
Southern California Car Transf	4789	D	858 586-0006	5244
Southern California Physicia	8741	D	858 824-7000	27226
Southern Wine & Spirits Amrca	5182	C	858 537-3912	9111
Southland Electric Inc (PA)	1731	D	858 634-5050	2735
Southland Technology Inc	5045	D	858 694-0932	7190
Southwest Airlines Co	4512	B	619 231-7345	4824
Southwestern Artists Assn	8412	E	619 232-3522	25049
Southwestern Yacht Club Inc	7997	E	619 222-0438	19084
Sovereign Capitl MGT Group Inc	6531	A	619 294-8989	11853
Specialty Textile Services LLC	5131	E	619 476-8750	8328
Spectrum Prof Staffing Inc	7363	C	800 644-1150	14950
Spinning Spur Wind Three LLC	4911	A	858 521-3319	6243
Spreadtrum Cmmncations USA Inc	8731	D	858 546-0895	26609
St Pauls Episcopal Home Inc	8361	D	619 239-8687	24820
St Pauls Episcopal Home Inc	8361	D	619 239-2097	24821
St Vincent De Paul Vlg Inc	8699	C	619 233-8500	25586
Staccato Communications Inc	7389	D	858 812-0981	17498
Staff Pro Inc	7381	E	619 544-1774	16831
Stanley M Kirkpatrick MD	8011	E	858 966-5855	20065
Starwood Hotels & Resorts	7011	E	619 239-2200	13301
Starwood Hotels & Resorts	7011	E	619 239-9600	13304
State Compensation Insur Fund	6331	B	888 782-8338	10466
Station Venture Operations LP	4833	D	619 578-0233	5912
Steren Electronics Intl LLC (PA)	5065	D	800 266-3333	7639
Stewart Enterprises Inc	7261	E	858 453-2121	13716
Strata Information Group Inc	7379	D	619 296-0170	16490
Strategic Data Systems	7373	D	619 546-7200	16060
Strategic Property Management	6531	D	619 295-2211	11860
Structure Cnstr & Dev Inc	1521	D	619 846-2555	1265
Stu Segall Productions Inc	7812	C	858 974-4988	18161
Student Movers Inc	4214	D	303 296-0600	4379
Stx Wireless Operations LLC	4812	A	858 882-6000	5411
Suja Life LLC	5149	C	855 879-7852	8924
Sullinovo	4959	C	619 260-1432	6640
Sullivan Moving & Storage (PA)	4213	E	858 874-2600	4268
Sun Pharmaceuticals Inc	8731	C	858 380-8865	26613
Sunbelt Towing Inc (PA)	7549	E	619 297-8697	17895
Sundance Financial Inc	6552	E	619 298-9877	12015
Sunstone Hotel Investors Inc	7011	E	619 239-6171	13313
Sunstone Top Gun LLC	7011	D	858 453-0400	13328
Superior Envmtl Svcs Inc	7349	E	619 462-7079	14441
Superior Mobile Medics Inc	8099	D	619 299-3926	23066
Superior Ready Mix Concrete LP	1611	E	619 265-0955	1871
Supreme Court United States	8322	C	619 557-7149	24242
Survivalcave Inc	5149	E	800 719-7650	8931
Swinerton Bldrs Pacific R	1542	D	619 954-8011	1681
Swinerton Builders	1541	E	858 622-4040	1469
Swvp Del Mar Hotel LLC	7011	C	858 481-5900	13331
Symitar Systems Inc	7371	D	619 542-6700	15485
Synergy Health Ast LLC (DH)	8742	D	858 586-1166	27677
Sysintelli Inc	7371	C	858 271-1600	15487
Syzygy Technologies Inc	8711	D	619 297-0970	26084
T B Penick & Sons Inc (PA)	1541	D	858 558-1800	1470
T I C Hotels Inc	7011	D	619 238-7577	13334
T-12 Three LLC	7011	B	619 702-3000	13338
Tachyon Inc	4813	E	858 882-8108	5706
Tactical Engrg & Analis Inc (PA)	7379	D	858 573-9869	16498
Takeda California Inc	8733	C	858 622-8528	26812
Tangoe Inc	7372	D	858 452-6800	15858
Tapestry Solutions Inc (HQ)	7371	D	858 503-1990	15490
Targetsolutions Inc (HQ)	8748	D	858 592-6880	28068
Tax Compliance Inc	7371	D	858 547-4100	15493
Tcp Global Corporation (PA)	5198	D	858 909-2110	9240
Tealium Inc	7374	C	858 779-1344	16197
Tegp Inc	7363	A	619 584-3408	14957
Telecare Corporation	8063	D	619 275-8000	22097
Telecare Corporation	8063	D	619 692-8225	22103
Telisimo International Corp	4813	B	619 325-1593	5708
Teris LLC	7374	E	619 231-3282	16201
Terra Vista Management Inc	6531	C	858 581-4200	11870
Tesi Investment Company LLC	7371	D	619 224-3254	13342
Tetra Tech Inc	8742	D	619 525-7188	27685
Tetra Tech Ec Inc	8748	D	619 234-8690	28073
Tf Courier Inc	4215	D	858 271-0021	4426
Therastaff Inc	7363	C	858 569-7555	14959
Thorsnes Bartolotta & McGuire	8111	D	619 236-9363	23596
Thurston Martin H DDS Ms	8021	E	858 676-5010	20279
Tiburon Inc	7373	D	858 799-7000	16066
Tic Hotels Inc	7011	E	619 238-7577	13344
Tic World-Wide Corp	7011	D	619 233-7500	13345
Tillster Inc (PA)	7379	D	858 784-0800	16508
Time Warner Cable Inc	4841	D	619 346-4573	6031
Time Warner Cable Inc	4841	B	858 695-3220	6040
Time Warner Cable Inc	4841	D	619 684-6106	6042
Time Warner Cable Inc	4841	B	858 695-3110	6050
Tomatoes Extraordinaire Inc	5149	C	619 295-3172	8937
Tommy Bahama Group Inc	7389	C	619 651-2200	17535
Top of Market	8741	D	619 234-4867	27254
Torrey Pines Bank (HQ)	6022	C	858 523-4600	9530
Torrey Pines Institute For MO	8733	D	858 455-3803	26814
Toward Maximum Independence (PA)	8322	C	858 467-0600	24253
Toyota Logistics Services	7549	D	619 531-0157	17897
Trandes Corp	8711	C	619 398-0464	26102
Trans-Pak Incorporated	4214	D	858 292-9094	5204
Transwest San Diego LLC	4214	B	858 450-0707	4383
Treefrog Developments Inc	5099	D	619 324-7755	8144
Trellisware Technologies Inc	4812	D	858 753-1600	5421
Trendsource	8732	C	619 718-7467	26714
Trex Partners LLC	6719	C	858 646-5300	12096
Tri-Union Seafoods LLC (DH)	5146	D	858 558-9662	8660
Trigild International Inc	7011	D	619 291-6500	13360
Trilink Biotechnologies Inc	8731	D	858 546-0004	26624
Trilogy Financial Services Inc	7389	E	858 755-6696	17544
Triton Structural Concrete Inc	1542	C	858 866-2450	1696
Troutman Sanders LLP	8111	D	858 509-6000	23599
Tru Green Landcare Inc	0782	B	602 276-4311	967
Tum Yeto Inc	5091	E	619 232-7523	8033
Turelk Inc	1542	D	858 633-8085	1698
Turner Construction Company	1542	D	858 320-4040	1702
Turning Pt Rvnue Cycle Sltions	7363	E	800 360-2300	14965
Tuv Sud America Inc	8734	D	858 546-3999	26894
Twin Oaks Power LP (HQ)	4911	D	619 696-2034	6248
Tyco Integrated Security LLC	7382	C	561 988-3600	16933
Tyler Bluff Wind Project LLC	4911	A	888 903-6926	6249
Ucsd Healthcare	8099	D	858 657-7105	23076
Underground Elephant Inc	7311	D	800 466-4178	13932
Unifirst Corporation	7218	C	619 263-6116	13645
Union Pan Asian Communities (PA)	8322	D	619 232-6454	24264
United Airlines Inc	4512	C	619 692-3310	4833
United Behavioral Health	8741	D	619 641-6800	27263
United Cerebral Palsy Assn San (PA)	8699	E	858 495-3155	25592
United Development Group Inc	6552	D	858 244-0900	12021
United Parcel Service Inc OH	4215	C	858 455-8800	4455
United Parcel Service Inc OH	4215	C	909 279-5111	4457
United States Dept of Navy	7363	D	619 524-1069	14967
United States Dept of Navy	8011	A	619 532-6397	20156
United States Dept of Navy	8011	A	619 532-8953	20157
United States Dept of Navy	8011	B	619 556-8210	20158
United States Dept of Navy	8711	C	619 532-2317	26117
United States Dept of Navy	8062	A	619 532-6400	21984
United States Dept of Navy	8731	E	619 532-1897	26628
United States Dept of Navy	8011	D	619 532-7400	20160
United States Dept of Navy	8011	D	619 767-6592	20162
United Svcs Amer Federal Cr Un (PA)	6061	D	858 831-8100	9646
Univers of Calif San Diego Hs	8062	A	619 543-3713	21986
University Cal San Diego	8062	A	619 543-6654	21992
Univision Television Group Inc	4833	E	858 576-1919	5923
UPS Store Inc (HQ)	7389	D	858 455-8800	17577
Upwind Blade Solutions Inc	7699	D	866 927-3142	18030
Urban Corps of San Diego	8331	C	619 235-6884	24400
US Bank National Association	6021	D	619 744-2140	9427
US Grant Hotel Ventures LLC	7011	D	619 744-2007	13370

Employment Codes: A=Over 500 employees, B=251-500, C=101-250, D=51-100, E=45-50

2017 Directory of California Wholesalers and Services Companies

© Mergent Inc. 1-800-342-5647

SAN DIEGO, CA

	SIC	EMP	PHONE	ENTRY #
Valley Ho Hotels Inc	7011	D	619 297-2231	13374
Vanguard Resources Corp	8744	D	858 336-7147	27801
Vanpike Inc (PA)	7363	D	858 453-1331	14968
Vector Resources Inc	8711	E	858 546-1014	26139
Verance Corporation	8732	D	858 202-2800	26718
Vertex Phrmctcals San Dego LLC (HQ)	8731	C	858 404-6600	26635
Veterans Health Administration	8021	B	858 552-7525	20283
Veterans Health Administration	8011	B	619 400-5000	20205
Veterans Medical Research Fund	8733	C	858 642-3080	26817
Viacyte Inc	8733	B	858 455-3708	26818
Vibra Healthcare LLC	8062	C	619 260-8300	22022
Vibra Hospital San Diego LLC	8062	C	619 260-8300	22024
Vietnam Veterans of San Diego (PA)	8641	D	619 497-0142	25395
Vietnms-Mrcan Yuth Alance Corp	8641	E	619 320-8292	25396
Villa Rancho Brno Hlth Cr LLC	8051	C	858 672-3900	21011
Vista Hill Foundation (PA)	8621	E	585 514-5100	25163
Vistage International Inc (PA)	8742	C	858 523-6800	27714
Vitas Healthcare Corp Cal	8082	D	619 680-4400	22607
Vitro LLC	7311	D	619 234-0408	13938
Vitrorobertson LLC	7311	D	619 234-0408	13939
Volt Management Corp	7363	C	858 576-3140	14972
Volt Management Corp	7363	D	858 578-0920	14973
Volume Services Inc	7999	D	619 525-5800	19304
VT Milcom Inc	8711	C	619 424-9024	26142
W-Emerald LLC	7011	D	619 239-4500	13387
Walter N Coffman Inc	1742	D	619 266-2642	2997
Wamc Company Inc (PA)	6513	D	858 454-2753	11227
Washington Inventory Service (DH)	7389	C	858 565-8111	17611
Washington Inventory Service	7389	D	619 461-8198	17613
Water Resources Control Bd Cal	8611	D	619 521-3010	25109
Watermark Rtrment Cmmnties Inc	6531	D	858 597-8000	11910
Wawanesa General Insurance Co	6331	B	619 285-6020	10480
Webb Sunrise Inc	5199	E	619 220-7050	9312
Weber Distribution Warehouses	4225	E	619 423-8770	4667
Welk Group Inc	8732	B	619 516-7800	26719
Wells Fargo Bank National Assn	6021	D	858 622-6958	9436
Wells Fargo Bank National Assn	6021	C	858 646-0550	9437
Wermers Multi-Family Corp (PA)	1522	D	858 535-1475	1350
West Coast Arborists Inc	1521	C	858 566-4204	1283
Westair Gases & Equipment Inc (PA)	5084	E	866 937-8247	7906
Westcore Delta LLC	6799	D	858 625-4100	12353
Western Pump Inc (PA)	7699	D	619 239-9988	18033
Westgroup Kona Kai LLC	7997	D	619 221-8000	19125
Westgroup San Diego Associates	7011	B	858 274-4630	13403
Wheatland Wind Project LLC	4911	A	888 903-6926	6253
Whiskey Girl	8741	D	619 236-1616	27282
Whittier Inst For Diabetes	8733	B	877 944-8843	26825
William Brammer	5148	C	858 756-3088	8791
Willmark Cmmnties Univ Vlg Inc (PA)	6513	D	858 271-0582	11228
Wilmark Management Services (PA)	6531	D	858 271-0583	11927
Wilson Sonsini Goodrich & Rosa	8111	C	858 350-2300	23625
Wilson Turner Kosmo LLP	8111	C	619 236-9600	23628
Win Time Ltd (PA)	7011	C	858 695-2300	13413
Wind River Systems Inc	8711	B	858 824-3100	26150
Window Factory Inc	1751	E	858 689-9737	3103
Wingert Grebing Brubaker & Jus	8111	D	619 232-8151	23629
Wirtz Qulty Installations Inc	1741	D	858 569-3816	2842
Wirtz Tile & Stone Inc	1752	D	858 569-3816	3133
Wis International	7389	D	858 565-8111	17631
Wmbe Payrolling Inc	7361	D	858 810-3000	14820
Wmk Office San Diego LLC (PA)	5021	D	858 569-4700	6839
Woodfin Suite Hotels LLC	7011	A	858 314-7910	13427
Wordsmart Corporation	7372	D	858 565-8068	15881
Wright Broadband Group Inc	8748	D	858 362-0380	28101
Wtw Delaware Holdings LLC	8742	D	858 523-5500	27724
Ww San Diego Harbor Island LLC	7011	C	619 291-6700	13433
Wyndham International Inc	7011	D	619 239-4500	13436
Xpo Enterprise Services Inc	4213	E	858 569-8921	4308
YMCA of San Diego County (PA)	8641	D	619 292-9622	25416
YMCA of San Diego County	8641	D	619 281-8313	25420
YMCA of San Diego County	8641	D	619 226-8888	25421
YMCA of San Diego County	8641	C	619 521-3055	25422
YMCA of San Diego County	8641	D	619 298-3576	25424
YMCA Youth & Family Services	8641	D	619 543-9850	25436
YWCA of San Diego County (PA)	8641	D	619 239-0355	25479
Z57 Inc (DH)	7311	D	858 623-5577	13946
Zb National Association	6021	E	858 793-7400	9465
Zeetogroup LLC	7311	D	888 771-9194	13947
Zenith Insurance Company	6331	D	619 299-6252	10486
Zmicro Inc (PA)	7373	D	858 831-7000	16086
Zoological Society San Diego (PA)	8422	A	619 231-1515	25071
Zoological Society San Diego	8422	A	619 744-3325	25073
Zs Associates Inc	8742	D	858 677-2200	27728

SAN DIMAS, CA - Los Angeles County

	SIC	EMP	PHONE	ENTRY #
AON Consulting Inc	6411	D	800 815-1823	10613
Associations of United Nurses (PA)	8631	D	909 599-8622	25166
Automatic Data Processing Inc	7374	C	909 592-6411	16094
Automatic Data Processing Inc	7374	C	800 225-5237	16100
Christian Community Credit Un (PA)	6062	D	626 915-7551	9659
Eastbrook Construction Inc	1742	D	909 394-4994	2890
Festival Fun Parks LLC	5091	A	909 802-2200	8018
Golden State Water Company (HQ)	4941	C	909 394-3600	6351
Golden State Water Company	4941	C	909 394-3600	6352
I P S Services Inc	8093	D	909 305-0250	22748
Imobile LLC	4813	B	909 599-8822	5635
Kaiser Foundation Hospitals	8062	C	909 394-2530	21639
L Barrios & Associates Inc	0782	E	626 960-2934	886
Legal Solutions Holdings Inc	8111	C	800 244-3495	23381
Magan Medical Clinic Inc	8011	D	909 592-9712	19726
McKinley Childrens Center Inc (PA)	8361	D	909 599-1227	24730
McKinley Home Foundation	8399	D	909 599-1227	24941
ML Prior Inc	8111	D	626 653-5160	23438
National Credit Industries Inc	6163	D	626 967-4355	9941
New York Life Insurance Co	6411	D	909 305-6500	10809
Pacific W Space Cmmnctions Inc	1623	D	909 592-4321	1977
Prime Healthcare-San Dimas LLC	8062	B	909 599-6811	21815
San Dimas Golf Inc	7997	D	909 599-8486	19056
San Dimas Retirement Center (PA)	6513	D	909 599-8441	11199
Second Image National LLC (PA)	8111	C	800 229-7477	23549
Southern Cal Prmnnte Med Group	8011	E	909 394-2505	20043
Southern California Edison Co	4911	C	909 592-3757	6238
Southern California Gas Co	4922	A	909 305-8297	6257
Star Electric	1731	D	626 422-9227	2747
Wyndham Resort Dev Corp	7389	D	909 484-8500	17634

SAN FERNANDO, CA - Los Angeles County

	SIC	EMP	PHONE	ENTRY #
All State Association Inc	4212	C	877 425-2558	3976
Bank America National Assn	6021	D	818 898-3033	9326
Brightview Landscape Dev Inc	0782	D	818 838-4700	816
Cacho Landscape Maintenance Co	0782	E	818 365-0773	818
County of Los Angeles	8011	C	818 837-6969	19466
First Student Inc	4151	C	818 896-0333	3936
Frontier California Inc	4813	C	818 365-0542	5608
Industrial Stitchtech Inc	7389	D	818 361-6319	17237
Jme Inc (PA)	5063	D	201 896-8600	7447
Masterserv Inc	1711	E	818 356-4602	2290
Mv Transportation Inc	4111	D	323 666-0856	3676
Northeast Valley Health Corp (PA)	8322	D	818 898-1388	24107
Northeast Valley Health Corp	8011	D	818 365-8086	19780
Pepsi-Cola Metro Btlg Co Inc	5149	D	818 898-3829	8902
Prg (california) Inc	7812	E	818 252-2600	18135
Prg Lighting	7359	E	818 252-1268	14570
Stan Winston Inc	7819	D	818 782-0870	18255
Tyan Inc	7381	D	818 785-5831	16837
Universal Mail Delivery Svc (PA)	4212	D	818 997-7531	4078
Wild Side West (PA)	7336	D	818 837-5000	14165

SAN FRANCISCO, CA - San Francisco County

	SIC	EMP	PHONE	ENTRY #
1life Healthcare Inc	8099	D	415 644-5265	22869
3vr Security Inc	7382	D	415 513-4577	16858
425 North Point Street LLC	7011	D	800 648-4626	12361
42nd Street Moon	7929	E	415 255-8207	18448
495 Geary LLC	7011	C	415 775-4700	12364
A Ruiz Cnstr Co & Assoc Inc	1542	D	415 647-4010	1480
A Smwm California Corporation	8712	D	415 546-0400	26159
A T Kearney Inc	8742	D	415 490-4000	27289
ABB Enterprise Software Inc	7372	C	415 527-2850	15563
ABC Cable Networks Group	4833	C	415 954-7911	5832
Abingdon Rough Riders Tou	8699	D	415 566-9796	25483
ABS Capital Partners III LP	8742	D	415 617-2800	27291
Absolutelynew Inc	8742	D	415 865-6200	27292
Accenture LLP	8742	B	415 537-5000	27297
Access Public Relations LLC	8743	D	415 904-7070	27729
Accountants 4 Contract	8721	D	415 781-8644	26287
Ace Usa Inc	6411	C	415 547-4400	10581
Addiction RES & Trtmnt Inc	8093	D	415 928-7800	22648
Adg Corporation	6799	E	415 864-4090	12280
Adivo Associates LLC	8742	D	415 992-1449	27303
Adobe Systems Incorporated	7372	A	415 832-2000	15571
Adolph Gasser Inc (PA)	5043	D	415 495-3852	7028
Adroll Inc (PA)	7311	C	877 723-7655	13814
Advanced Discovery Inc	8111	C	866 342-3282	23082
Advantis Global Inc (PA)	7379	C	415 395-4444	16317
Advent Software Inc (HQ)	7371	C	415 543-7696	15003
Advisory Board Company	8082	D	415 671-7750	22342
Aecom Global II LLC	8711	C	415 774-2700	25629
Aecom Global II LLC	8711	C	415 774-2700	25636
Aecom Technology Corporation	8711	C	415 908-6135	25640
Aetna Health California Inc	6324	D	415 645-8200	10251
Affiliated Engineers Inc	8711	E	415 764-3700	25642
Affiliated Engineers W Inc (HQ)	8711	D	925 933-8400	25643

GEOGRAPHIC SECTION

SAN FRANCISCO, CA

Company	SIC	EMP	PHONE	ENTRY #
Affirm Inc	6153	C	415 984-0490	9768
Aimia Proprietary Loyalty	8742	D	415 398-3534	27311
Aimia Proprietary Loyalty	8742	D	415 844-2200	27312
Air France (air Nationale)	4512	C	415 877-0179	4779
Airbnb Inc (PA)	7041	A	415 800-5959	13486
Akin Gump Strauss	8111	C	415 765-9500	23084
Akqa Inc (HQ)	8742	B	415 645-9400	27313
Alain Pinel Realtors Inc	6531	C	415 814-6690	11280
Alcatraz Cruises LLC	4725	C	415 981-7625	4984
Alegrecare Inc	7389	B	415 974-3530	16977
Aliphcom (PA)	5065	C	415 230-7600	7516
All Hallows Preservation LP	6513	A	415 285-3909	11082
Allen Matkins Leck Gmble	8111	D	415 837-1515	23086
Allianz Globl Investors US LLC	6282	D	415 954-5400	10112
Allied Medical Service of Cal	4119	E	415 931-1400	3739
Almavia of San Francisco	8051	D	415 337-1339	20376
Alsco Inc	7213	D	415 648-9266	13514
Alta Equipment Leasing Company	7359	D	415 875-1000	14510
Altschool Inc	7371	C	415 255-9766	15006
Alvarez & Marsal Holdings LLC	8742	C	415 490-2300	27316
Amber Holding Inc	7371	A	415 765-6500	15007
AMD Trading Company Inc	5199	C	415 391-0601	9244
American Academy of Opthalmlgy (PA)	8621	C	415 561-8500	25114
American Bldg Maint Co-West (HQ)	7349	C	415 733-4000	14226
American Building Maint Co NY	7349	A	415 733-4000	14227
American Carequest Inc	8082	D	415 752-9100	22358
American Commercial SEC Svcs	7381	C	415 856-1020	16552
American Conservatory	7922	D	415 749-2228	18368
American Conservatory	7922	D	415 749-2228	18369
American Conservatory Theater	7299	C	415 439-2379	13731
American Gen Lf Insur Co Del	6411	B	415 836-2700	10594
American Legal Copy-Or LLC	7334	D	415 777-4449	14099
American Marketing Systems Inc	6531	D	800 747-7784	11297
American Medical Response	4119	A	415 922-9400	3752
American Multi-Cinema Inc	7832	E	415 674-4630	18298
American National Red Cross	8322	C	415 427-8134	23658
Ammunition LLC	8742	D	415 632-1170	27321
Amoeba Music Inc	7389	D	415 831-1200	16989
Amplify Education Inc	7371	D	562 209-7875	15013
Anaplan Inc (PA)	7379	C	415 742-8199	16321
Andatha International Inc (PA)	8111	D	415 398-8600	23091
Anderson Rowe & Buckley Inc	1711	D	415 282-1625	2144
Animoto LLC	7371	C	415 987-3139	15014
Annie App Inc (PA)	7371	D	844 277-2664	15016
Annuzzi Concrete Service Inc	1611	E	415 468-2795	1732
Anvil Builders Inc	1611	D	415 397-4925	1733
AON Benfield Fac Inc	6321	C	415 486-6900	10233
AON Consulting Inc	6411	D	800 283-1667	10612
AON Consulting Inc	6411	C	415 486-6226	10614
AON Consulting & Insur Svcs	6411	D	415 486-7500	10618
Appdirect Inc (PA)	7372	D	415 852-3924	15580
Appdynamics Inc (PA)	7371	C	415 442-8400	15019
Apperience Corporation	7371	D	415 813-2995	15020
Appirio Inc (PA)	7371	C	415 663-4433	15022
Appsflyer Ltd	7313	D	415 636-9430	13958
Appster Inc	7371	D	415 926-2741	15025
Apteligent Inc	7371	D	415 371-1402	15027
AR Preservation LP	6513	D	415 776-2151	11086
Aramark Unf & Career AP LLC	7213	C	415 244-8332	13538
Arb Inc	1623	E	415 206-1015	1903
ARC Document Solutions Inc	7334	E	415 495-8700	14110
Arctouch LLC	7371	C	415 944-2000	15031
Arlene Keller MD	8011	E	415 923-3598	19356
Arnold & Porter PC	8111	B	415 434-1600	23095
Arnold Palmer Golf MGT LLC	8741	C	415 561-4670	26927
Arroyo & Coates Inc	6531	D	415 445-7800	11306
Arthur J Gallagher & Co	6411	C	415 546-9300	10625
Arup North America Limited (DH)	8711	C	415 957-9445	25669
Ascendify Corporation	7371	E	415 528-5503	15036
Asia Foundation (PA)	6732	D	415 982-4640	12152
Asian Art Museum Found San Fra	8412	C	415 581-3701	25003
Aspen Apts I	6513	D	415 673-5879	11087
Aspiranet	8361	A	415 759-3690	24554
Aspiriant LLC	7389	E	415 371-7800	17003
Assocted Third Pty Admnstrtors	6371	C	415 777-3707	10541
Astoria Software	7371	D	415 956-3917	15038
AT&T Corp	4813	D	415 970-8520	5463
AT&T Corp	4813	A	415 442-2600	5465
AT&T Corp	8743	C	415 442-5900	27731
AT&T Services	4813	C	415 774-1957	5520
AT&T Services Inc	4813	C	415 545-9051	5528
AT&T Services Inc	4813	B	415 394-3000	5547
Atel Capital Group (PA)	6159	D	415 989-8800	9794
Athenahealth Inc	7372	C	415 416-3500	15586
Atkins North America Inc	8748	E	916 325-8500	27841
Atlassian Inc (DH)	7372	C	415 701-1110	15587
Augmedix Inc	7389	D	954 903-4993	17009
Autodesk Inc	7372	D	415 356-0700	15589
Automattic Inc	4813	D	650 388-0901	5562
Avalon Golden Gate LLC	8361	D	415 664-6264	24562
Avolent Inc	7372	D	415 553-6400	15592
Axa Advisors LLC	6726	D	415 276-2100	12134
Ayoob & Peery Plumbing Co Inc	1711	D	415 550-0975	2155
B F C Inc	1731	C	415 495-3085	2525
Ba Leasing & Capital Corp (DH)	7359	C	415 765-1804	14516
Baart Behavioral Hlth Svcs Inc	8093	D	415 928-7800	22663
Baart Behavioral Hlth Svcs Inc (PA)	8093	D	415 552-7914	22664
Baart Community Healthcare	8093	D	415 928-7800	22665
Babcock & Brown Holdings Inc (HQ)	6211	C	415 512-1515	9962
Babcock & Brown Latin America	6159	D	415 512-1515	9795
Babycenter LLC (DH)	7299	D	415 537-0900	13735
Bain & Company Inc	8742	C	415 627-1000	27338
Baker & McKenzie LLP	8111	C	415 576-3000	23099
Baker Places Inc	8093	C	415 503-3137	22666
Banc America Lsg & Capitl LLC (DH)	6159	C	415 765-7349	9796
Bank America National Assn	6021	E	800 432-1000	9321
Bank America National Assn	6021	C	415 913-5891	9322
Bank America National Assn	8732	C	415 913-3438	26644
Bank of Orient (HQ)	6022	D	415 338-0668	9473
BANK OF THE WEST (HQ)	6022	A	415 765-4800	9476
Bankamerica Financial Inc	6153	A	415 622-3521	9772
Bar Architects	8712	C	415 293-5700	26167
Bar Asscation of San Francisco (PA)	8621	B	415 982-1600	25118
Barclays Globl Investors Funds	6722	E	415 597-2000	12104
Barger & Wolen LLP	8111	E	415 434-2800	23105
Bartko Zankel Tarrant & Mil	8111	E	415 956-1900	23108
Bauers Intelligent Trnsp Inc (PA)	4119	C	415 522-1212	3769
Bay Area Video Coalition Inc	7819	D	415 861-3282	18216
Bay Bread LLC	5149	D	415 440-0356	8806
Bay Club Golden Gateway Inc	7997	E	415 616-8800	18883
Bay Clubs Inc (HQ)	7991	D	415 781-1874	18615
Bay Grove Capital Group LLC (PA)	6722	E	415 229-7953	12105
Bay West Shwplace Invstors LLC (PA)	6512	E	415 490-5800	10962
Bayer Healthcare LLC	8731	B	415 437-5800	26485
Bayorg	8422	D	415 623-5300	25058
Bayspring Medical Group A Pro	8011	E	415 674-2600	19370
Bayview Hunters Point Y M C A	8641	D	415 822-7728	25205
Bayview Preservation LP	6513	A	415 285-7344	11092
Bbam Arcft Holdings 137 Labuan	7359	D	415 267-1600	14518
Bbam US LP	6211	D	415 267-1600	9965
BBDO Worldwide Inc	7311	D	415 808-6200	13819
Bcci Construction Company (PA)	1542	C	415 817-5100	1499
Bdo Usa LLP	8721	C	415 397-7900	26293
Bear Data Solutions Inc	5045	D	415 788-1501	7100
Beats Music LLC	7372	D	415 590-5104	15598
Bechtel Capital MGT Corp	8741	A	415 768-1234	26940
Bechtel Corporation (HQ)	8711	A	415 768-1234	25682
Bechtel Energy Corporation	8711	A	415 768-1234	25683
Bechtel Enterprises Holdings (HQ)	8711	A	415 768-1234	25684
Bechtel Entps Holdings Inc	1542	B	415 768-6745	1500
Bechtel Group Inc (PA)	8711	A	415 768-1234	25685
Beresford Corp	0174	C	415 981-7386	215
Beresford Corporation	7011	D	415 673-9900	12436
Best Western Hotel Tomo	7011	E	415 921-4000	12438
Bikrams Yoga College of India	7999	E	415 346-2480	19150
Birst Inc (PA)	7371	C	415 766-4800	15054
Bite Communications LLC (HQ)	8742	D	415 365-0222	27346
Black Bear Security Services	7381	C	415 559-5159	16575
Blackrock Global Investors	6282	A	415 670-2000	10122
Blackrock Holdco 2 Inc	6531	D	415 678-2000	11325
Blackrock Instnl Tr Nat Assn (HQ)	6722	A	415 597-2000	12106
Blackstone Technology Group (PA)	8748	D	415 837-1400	27851
Bleacher Report Inc	7374	D	415 777-5505	16104
Bleacher Report Inc	7822	C	415 777-5505	18270
Blood Centers of Pacific (PA)	8099	C	415 567-6400	22898
Bloomberg LP	7383	D	415 912-2960	16945
Blue and Gold Fleet	4489	D	415 705-8200	4731
Blue Bus Tours LLC	7999	D	415 353-5310	19153
Bmr Apps Inc	7379	D	954 651-1412	16330
BNP Paribas Asset MGT Inc	6082	D	415 772-1300	9701
Bohemian Club (PA)	8641	D	415 885-2440	25209
Boku Inc (PA)	7371	D	415 375-3160	15061
Bonhams Bttrflds Actneers Corp (DH)	7389	C	415 861-7500	17034
Bonhams Corporation	7389	C	415 861-7500	17035
Bonneville International Corp	4832	E	415 777-0965	5751
Boston Properties Ltd Partnr	6552	D	415 772-0500	11951
Bracket Global LLC	7371	C	415 293-1340	15063
Brandnet Inc	8748	D	415 216-4152	27854
Bre/Japantown Owner LLC	7011	D	415 922-3200	12464
Brickwalk Systems Integration	8742	D	800 495-5779	27356

SAN FRANCISCO, CA — GEOGRAPHIC SECTION

Company	SIC	EMP	PHONE	ENTRY #
Bridge Housing Acquisition	6512	D	415 989-1111	10963
Bridge Housing Corporation (PA)	6552	D	415 989-1111	11953
Brience Inc (DH)	7371	D	415 974-5300	15064
Brighterion Inc	7371	D	415 986-5600	15066
Brightroll Inc (HQ)	7311	C	415 677-9222	13821
Brite Media Group LLC	7313	C	877 479-7777	13960
Broadmoor Hotel (PA)	6513	D	415 776-7034	11100
Broadmoor Hotel	7011	D	415 673-2511	12470
Broadreach Capitl Partners LLC	6799	A	415 354-4640	12287
Brown & Toland Medical Group	8011	C	415 923-3015	19381
Browsercam	7375	D	415 378-6936	16221
Bryan Cave LLP	8111	E	415 675-3400	23133
Bserv Inc (PA)	6099	A	415 277-9900	9712
Btig LLC (PA)	6211	D	415 248-2200	9967
Build Group Inc	1542	D	415 777-4070	1513
Burr Pilger Mayer Inc (PA)	8721	C	415 421-5757	26301
Business For Social Responsibi (PA)	8611	E	415 984-3200	25077
Business Services Network	7331	D	415 282-8161	14066
Bynd LLC	7371	D	415 944-2293	15070
CA Ste Atom Assoc Intr-Ins Bur	6331	A	415 565-2012	10403
Cahill Contractors Inc (PA)	1542	C	415 986-0600	1518
Cai International Inc (PA)	7359	D	415 788-0100	14520
Cal-Steam Supply	5074	D	415 861-3071	7707
California Academy Sciences (PA)	8422	A	415 379-8000	25060
California Club of CA	8641	D	415 474-3516	25226
California Pacific CA	8011	E	415 345-0940	19397
California Pacific Medical Ctr	8062	D	415 600-1378	21469
California Physicians Service (PA)	6324	A	415 229-5000	10263
California Shellfish Co Inc	5146	B	707 542-9490	8631
Callan Associates Inc (PA)	6282	C	415 974-5060	10126
Canon Solutions America Inc	5044	D	415 743-7300	7046
Canterbury Hotel Corp	7011	C	415 474-1452	12486
Capcom Entertainment Inc	5092	C	650 350-6500	8040
Capcom U S A Inc (HQ)	5092	C	650 350-6500	8041
Capital Group Companies Inc	6282	B	213 486-1698	10129
Capstar San Francisco Co LLC	7011	C	415 937-6084	12488
Carbonfive Incorporated	7371	D	415 546-0500	15075
Caritas Management Corporation	6531	D	415 647-7191	11341
Carlton Hotel Properties LP	7011	D	415 673-0242	12489
Carroll Burdick Mc Donough LLP (PA)	8111	C	415 989-5900	23145
Casey Securities Inc (PA)	6211	D	415 544-5030	9969
Cassidy Trly Prop MGT Sn Frncs	6531	D	415 781-8100	11346
Castlight Health Inc	7374	B	415 829-1400	16107
Catholic Chrts Cyo Archdiocs	8322	D	415 743-0017	23715
Catholic Chrts Cyo Archdiocs	8322	D	415 405-2000	23716
Catholic Chrts Cyo Archdiocs	8322	D	415 334-5550	23717
Catholic Chrts Cyo Archdiocs (PA)	8322	D	415 972-1200	23718
Catholic Chrts Cyo Archdiocs	8322	D	415 553-8700	23719
Cb-1 Hotel	7011	D	415 633-3838	12503
Cbre Group Inc	6512	C	415 772-0123	10968
CBS Broadcasting Inc	4833	B	415 765-0928	5839
CBS Broadcasting Inc	4832	C	415 765-4097	5754
CBS Corporation	4832	C	415 765-4000	5755
CBS Interactive Inc (DH)	7319	A	415 344-2000	13992
CBS Radio Inc	4832	C	415 765-4097	5759
Cdc San Francisco LLC	7011	D	415 616-6512	12504
Celerity Consulting Group Inc (PA)	7374	D	415 986-8850	16109
Cellco Partnership	4812	D	415 402-0640	5336
Cellco Partnership	4812	D	415 695-8400	5360
Cellco Partnership	4812	D	415 351-1700	5371
Central Gardens Inc	8051	C	415 567-2967	20444
Centro Inc	7373	C	415 788-6190	15918
Certain Inc (PA)	7371	D	415 353-5330	15079
Cesar Chavez Student Center	6512	C	415 338-7362	10970
Cesars Productions	7389	E	415 821-1156	17065
Chandler Chicco Agency LLC (DH)	8743	D	415 643-1101	27740
Changeorg	7375	D	415 817-1840	16222
Charles Schwab Corporation (PA)	6211	D	415 667-7000	9970
Charolais Care V Inc	8082	D	415 921-5038	22404
Chesapeake Lodging Trust	7011	D	415 296-2900	12511
Chikpea Inc	8748	E	888 342-3828	27879
Childrens Creativity Museum	8412	D	415 820-3320	25007
Childrens Day School	8351	E	415 861-5432	24437
Chinese Cnsld Benevolent Assn	8641	D	415 982-6000	25238
Chinese Hospital Association (PA)	8062	B	415 982-2400	21486
Chirag Hospitality Inc	7011	D	415 922-0244	12514
Chong Partners Architecher Inc	8712	C	613 995-8210	26176
Chronicle Broadcasting Co	4833	B	415 561-8000	5846
Chsp Trs Fisherman Wharf LLC	7011	D	415 563-1234	12517
Cie Games LLC	7371	E	415 800-6100	15083
Cigna Healthcare Cal Inc	6324	D	415 374-2500	10271
Citco Fund Svcs San Francisco	6282	D	415 228-0390	10134
Citibank National Association	6021	C	415 431-6940	9374
Citibank N A	6035	C	415 627-6000	9569
Citigroup Inc	6211	D	415 617-8524	9985
Citiscape Prprty MGT Group LLC	6531	D	415 674-1440	11392
City & County of San Francisco	8322	C	415 553-1706	23747
City & County of San Francisco	7922	D	415 621-6600	18381
City & County of San Francisco	7922	D	415 621-6600	18382
City & County of San Francisco	8412	D	415 581-3500	25009
City & County of San Francisco	8062	A	415 206-8000	21492
City & County of San Francisco	8621	D	415 557-4713	25128
City & County of San Francisco	8062	A	415 759-2300	21493
City & County of San Francisco	8111	C	415 554-4700	23150
City & County of San Francisco	8111	C	415 553-1752	23151
City & County of San Francisco	8322	D	415 753-7561	23748
City & County of San Francisco	8741	D	415 554-4799	26969
City Impact	8699	E	415 292-1770	25517
Clara	5045	D	415 342-9740	7108
Clean-A-Rama Maintenance Co	7349	D	415 495-5298	14254
Clearesult Consulting Inc	8748	D	415 848-1250	27882
Clearslide Inc (PA)	7372	D	877 360-3366	15621
Click Labs Inc	7371	A	415 658-5227	15088
Clickability Inc	7371	E	415 200-0410	15089
Climate Corporation (HQ)	0762	D	415 363-0500	695
Cloud4wi Inc	7371	D	415 852-3900	15091
Cloudflare Inc (PA)	7382	D	650 319-8930	16874
Cloudmark Inc (PA)	7371	D	415 946-3800	15093
Cloudpassage Inc	7371	D	800 215-7404	15094
Clp Resources Inc	7363	E	415 508-0910	14855
Club Quarters San Francisco	7041	D	415 268-3606	13491
Clune Construction Company LP	1542	C	415 395-7245	1531
Clyde & Co US LLP	8111	D	415 365-9800	23157
Cnet Networks Inc	7373	D	415 344-2000	15923
CNX Media Inc	7812	D	415 229-8300	18062
Coblentz Patch Duffy Bass LLP	8111	D	510 655-4598	23158
Coldwell Bnkr Residential Brkg	6531	D	415 447-8800	11428
Collabrus Inc	8721	C	415 288-1826	26314
Collier Warehouse Inc	5031	E	415 920-9720	6916
Colliers International	6531	D	415 788-3100	11443
Comca Sport Net Bay Area	4841	C	415 896-2557	5944
Comcast Cble Cmmunications LLC	4841	C	415 715-0524	5947
Comcast Corporation	4841	D	415 665-5507	5953
Comcast Corporation	4841	D	415 255-5644	5958
Comcast Corporation	7313	D	415 835-5700	13962
Comcast Spotlight Inc	7311	D	415 675-2300	13825
Comfort California Inc	7011	E	415 928-5000	12535
Commune Hotels and Resorts LLC (PA)	7011	D	415 248-5930	12538
Compass Family Services	8351	D	415 644-0504	24447
Compass Family Services	8351	D	415 644-0504	24448
Compass Family Services	8322	D	415 644-0504	23781
Compass Family Services	8322	D	415 644-0504	23782
Compass Family Services	8322	D	415 644-0504	23783
Computer Resources Group Inc	7371	C	415 398-3535	15099
Conrad Imports Inc	5023	D	415 626-3303	6854
Conservation Liquidation	8999	D	415 676-5000	28124
Consumer Credit Counseling Svc (PA)	7299	D	415 788-0288	13749
Converse Inc	5139	C	415 433-1174	8426
Convoy Inc	7378	E	415 403-2770	16290
Cooley LLP	8111	D	415 693-2000	23164
Cooper White & Cooper LLP (PA)	8111	C	415 433-1900	23168
Corelogic	6531	E	714 250-6400	11456
Cornerstone Cnsulting Tech Inc	8748	D	415 705-7800	27888
Cornerstone Hotel Management (DH)	8741	D	415 397-5572	26983
Cornerstone Research Inc	8748	A	415 229-8100	27890
Corporate Security Service Inc	7381	D	415 626-9271	16612
Corportion of Fine Arts Mseums	8412	C	415 750-3600	25014
Corportion of Fine Arts Mseums	8412	C	415 750-3600	25015
Corportion of Fine Arts Mseums (PA)	8412	C	415 750-3600	25016
Corwe Horwath	8721	D	415 576-1100	26316
Costless Maintenance Svcs Co	7349	D	415 550-8819	14266
Coverity LLC (HQ)	7371	D	415 321-5200	15113
Covington & Burling LLP	8111	D	415 591-6000	23186
Craftworks Rest Breweries Inc	7389	A	415 292-5800	17102
Crane Acquisition Inc	7342	D	415 922-1666	14184
Credit Suisse (usa) Inc	6211	D	415 249-2100	9989
Credit Suisse (usa) Inc	6211	E	415 678-3940	9990
Credo Mobile Inc	4813	D	415 369-2000	5584
Creedence Lessee LLC	7011	D	415 561-1100	12552
Crestline Hotels & Resorts LLC	8741	C	415 775-7555	26998
Cross Link Inc	4492	D	415 495-3191	4766
Crowdflower Inc	7374	D	415 471-1920	16118
Crowell & Moring LLP	8111	D	415 986-2800	23189
Crown Building Maintenance Co	7349	B	303 680-3713	14275
Crunch LLC	7991	A	415 495-1939	18624
Cumulus Media Inc	4899	C	415 835-8120	6068
Cupertino Electric Inc	1731	D	415 970-3400	2569
Current Tv LLC	7389	C	415 995-8328	17110
Cusa FI LLC	4142	C	415 642-9400	3899
Cushman & Wakefield Cal Inc (DH)	6531	C	408 275-6730	11463

GEOGRAPHIC SECTION

SAN FRANCISCO, CA

	SIC	EMP	PHONE	ENTRY #
Cutler Group LP	7389	E	415 645-6745	17112
Cvpartners Inc **(HQ)**	7361	C	415 543-8600	14634
Cybernet Entertainment LLC	7812	C	415 865-0230	18066
Cypress Security LLC **(PA)**	7381	D	415 240-4494	16618
Daniel J Edelman Inc	8743	D	415 222-9944	27745
Dannis Wlver Klley A Prof Corp **(PA)**	8111	D	415 543-4111	23197
Databricks Inc	7371	D	415 494-7672	15121
Datameer Inc **(PA)**	7371	D	650 286-9100	15122
Davis Wright Tremaine LLP	8111	D	415 276-6500	23199
Davis Ziff Publishing Inc	4813	C	415 551-4800	5588
DDB Worldwide	7311	D	415 732-3600	13835
Decarta Inc	7371	D	408 294-8400	15127
Dechert LLP	8111	E	415 262-4500	23203
Degenkolb Engineers **(PA)**	8711	D	415 392-6952	25766
Delancey Street Foundation	4212	B	415 512-5110	4003
Delancey Street Foundation **(PA)**	8361	B	415 957-9800	24629
Delivery Agent Inc **(PA)**	7319	D	415 696-5800	13994
Deloitte & Touche LLP	8721	B	415 783-4000	26322
Deloitte Tax LLP	8721	B	415 783-4000	26328
Delta Dental of California **(PA)**	6324	B	415 972-8300	10277
Demand Chain Inc	5045	C	800 466-3786	7119
Demandbase Inc **(PA)**	7372	C	415 683-2660	15638
Demandforce Inc	7371	C	415 904-8080	15130
Dena Corp	7371	D	415 375-3170	15131
Dentons US LLP	8111	E	415 882-5000	23209
Deutsche Bank Tr Co Americas	6211	C	415 617-4200	9992
Deutsche Inv MGT Americas Inc	6282	E	415 648-9408	10136
Dewolf Realty Co Inc	8741	D	415 221-2032	27004
Dhap Digital Inc	7371	D	415 962-4900	15136
Dhl Express (usa) Inc	4513	D	415 826-7338	4842
Dietrich Post Co Inc	5112	D	510 596-0080	8164
Digital Realty Trust Inc **(PA)**	6798	C	415 738-6500	12243
Digitalthink Inc **(DH)**	8742	E	415 625-4000	27413
Dignity Health **(PA)**	8062	C	415 438-5500	21537
Dignity Health	8062	B	415 438-5500	21538
Directorate of Mwr Fmd Usag	8741	D	210 466-1376	27005
Discount Builders Supply	5031	C	415 285-2800	6920
Doctor On Demand Inc	7372	D	415 935-4447	15641
Document Technologies LLC	7389	D	415 495-4100	17130
Docusign Inc **(PA)**	7373	E	415 489-4940	15935
Dodge & Cox	6722	D	415 981-1710	12112
Dolby Labs Licensing Corp	6794	C	415 558-0200	12214
Doremus & Company	7311	E	415 398-5699	13841
Double Dutch Inc	7372	C	800 748-9024	15645
Dpk Consulting	8742	D	415 495-7772	27414
Dppm Inc	6531	D	415 695-7707	11479
Drinker Biddle & Reath LLP	8111	D	415 591-7500	23228
Ds Services of America Inc	5149	E	415 282-1060	8828
Duane Morris LLP	8111	D	415 957-3000	23229
Duff & Phelps LLC	7389	D	415 693-5300	17136
Dun & Bradstreet Inc	7323	D	415 343-6540	14057
E M Electric Co	5013	C	415 315-3300	6727
Earls Organic	5149	C	415 824-7419	8831
East West Bank	6022	C	415 391-8912	9490
Eastrdge Prsonnel of Las Vegas	7361	D	415 248-2567	14643
Eco Bay Services Inc	8748	C	415 643-7777	27905
Ecology and Environment Inc	8748	D	510 893-6700	27906
Edaw Inc **(HQ)**	6552	D	415 955-2800	11964
Edgewood Ctr For Childrens	8322	C	415 865-3000	23954
Edgewood Ctr For Childrens **(PA)**	8361	D	415 681-3211	24640
Edgewood Partners Insur Ctr	6411	D	415 356-3900	10696
Edgewood Partners Insur Ctr **(PA)**	6411	D	415 356-3900	10697
Efinance Corporation	7389	E	866 433-6878	17145
Eileen Nottoli	8111	D	415 837-1515	23232
Eis Group Inc	7372	C	415 402-2622	15651
Eisneramper LLP	8721	D	415 974-6000	26335
Eleven Inc	7311	C	415 707-1111	13842
Elizabeth Larson	6531	D	415 409-7300	11490
Ellation Inc	7371	D	415 796-3560	15159
Embarcadero Inn Associates	7011	C	415 495-2100	12616
Embassador Private Securities	6211	D	415 822-8811	9993
EMC Corporation	5045	E	650 871-1970	7125
Emergent Ventures Intl Inc	8748	D	415 655-6617	27911
Emmett A Larkin Company Inc **(PA)**	6211	D	415 986-2332	9994
Emotiv Systems Inc	7993	E	415 503-3601	18803
Encore Capital LP	6722	D	415 676-4200	12113
Energy Livermore Off US Dept	8733	A	415 648-3878	26762
Enertis Solar Inc	8711	E	415 400-5271	25787
Engine Yard Inc	7371	D	866 518-9273	15165
Entercom Communications Corp	4832	C	610 660-5610	5770
Environ Hardwood Floors	1752	D	415 487-0200	3113
Environmental Science Assoc **(PA)**	8731	D	415 896-5900	26514
Envivio Inc **(DH)**	4813	D	650 243-2700	5595
Episcopal Senior Communities	8361	C	415 776-0500	24649
Epocrates Inc **(HQ)**	8099	D	650 227-1700	22955

	SIC	EMP	PHONE	ENTRY #
Equal Access International	1731	D	415 561-4884	2590
Equinox-76th Street Inc	7991	D	415 398-0747	18629
Equity Firm Golden Gate Capitl	7379	D	415 983-2703	16366
Ernst & Young LLP	8721	D	415 894-8000	26339
Ernst & Young LLP	8721	A	415 894-8000	26349
Esurance Inc	6411	C	415 875-4500	10702
Euro Rscg San Francisco LLC	7331	E	415 345-7700	14069
Eventbrite Inc **(PA)**	8741	D	888 541-9753	27019
Everest Wtrprfing Rstrtion Inc	7299	D	415 282-9800	13758
Evidera Archimedes Inc	6411	D	415 490-0400	10703
Evolent Health Inc	8099	B	571 389-6000	22956
Execushield Inc	7381	D	415 508-0825	16638
Executives Outlet Inc	7991	C	415 433-6044	18631
Exigen (usa) Inc **(PA)**	7371	B	415 402-2600	15178
Exploratorium **(PA)**	8412	D	415 528-4462	25021
Express Messenger Systems Inc	4215	D	415 495-7300	4408
Fairmont Hotel Partners LLC **(DH)**	8741	A	415 772-5000	27022
Family Svc Agcy San Francisco **(PA)**	7363	D	415 474-7310	14877
Farallon Capital MGT LLC **(PA)**	6722	E	415 421-2132	12114
Fastly Inc	7371	C	415 488-6329	15181
Fcb Worldwide Inc	7311	A	415 820-8545	13849
Fcb Worldwide Inc	7311	C	415 820-8000	13850
Federal Deposit Insurance Corp	6399	C	415 546-0160	10568
Federal Express Corporation	4513	C	800 463-3339	4862
Federal Hm Ln Bnk San Frncisco **(PA)**	6111	D	415 616-1000	9730
Federal Insurance Company	6411	C	415 273-6300	10716
Federal Rsrve Bnk San Frncisco **(HQ)**	6011	A	415 974-2000	9315
Fenton Communications Inc	8743	E	415 255-1946	27747
Fenwick & West LLP	8111	B	415 875-2300	23238
Ffl Partners LLC **(PA)**	6726	E	415 402-2100	12139
Fillmore Marketplace LP	6531	E	415 921-6514	11519
Financialforcecom Inc **(DH)**	7371	D	866 743-2220	15185
Fine Line Group Inc	1542	E	415 777-4010	1553
First Databank Inc	7374	D	650 588-5454	16128
First Republic Bank	6029	A	415 392-1400	9548
First Republic Bank	6029	C	415 392-1400	9549
First Republic Bank **(PA)**	6022	B	415 392-1400	9498
First Student Inc	4151	B	415 647-9012	3933
Fitstar Inc	7372	D	415 409-8348	15666
Fleischman Field Research Inc	8732	C	415 398-4140	26662
Fleishman-Hillard Inc	8743	E	415 318-4000	27748
Fliesler Dubb Myer Lovejoy LLP	8111	D	415 362-3800	23246
Flite Inc	7379	D	415 992-5870	16370
Florence Villa Hotel	7011	C	415 397-7700	12639
Florence Villa Hotel LLC	7011	C	415 397-7700	12640
Fluid Inc	7371	D	415 263-7700	15189
Flurish Inc	6141	D	855 253-6387	9748
Fluxx Labs Inc	7299	E	855 358-9946	13759
Flynn Properties Inc	6531	D	415 835-0225	11541
Foley & Lardner LLP	8111	D	415 434-4484	23249
Foodbuzz Inc	7379	D	415 321-1200	16372
Forex Capital Markets LLC	6211	D	415 834-4874	10002
Forgerock Inc **(PA)**	7372	D	415 599-1100	15668
Fort Mason Center	8999	D	415 345-7500	28130
Fortress Investment Group LLC	6722	D	415 284-7400	12116
Forward Management LLC	6282	D	415 869-6300	10143
Four Seasons Hotel Inc	7011	A	415 633-3441	12647
France Telecom RES & Dev LLC	8732	D	415 284-9765	26663
Franciscan Lines Inc	4119	D	415 642-9400	3796
Francisco Partners LP **(HQ)**	7373	C	415 418-2900	15948
Francisco Partners MGT LP **(PA)**	6799	E	415 418-2900	12308
Frank Rimerman & Co LLP	8721	D	415 439-1144	26351
Frankly Co	7371	D	415 861-9797	15193
Frederick Labs LLC	8742	C	646 738-8303	27440
Frederick Meiswinkel Inc	1742	C	415 550-0400	2898
Free Stream Media Corp	5199	D	415 889-6404	9266
Fremont Group LLC **(PA)**	6282	D	415 284-8880	10148
Fremont Mutual Funds Inc	6211	D	800 548-4539	10004
Fremont Properties Inc	6512	D	415 284-8500	10986
Fremont Realty Capital LP	6519	D	415 284-8665	11255
Fritz Companies Inc **(HQ)**	4731	C	650 635-2693	5080
Frog Design Inc **(DH)**	7336	C	415 442-4804	14146
Fti Consulting Inc	8748	D	415 283-4200	27927
Fujitsu America Inc	7373	D	408 992-3561	15953
Fundbox Inc	8742	D	415 509-1343	27443
Funding Circle Usa Inc	6141	D	855 385-5356	9749
Fuse Project LLC	8748	D	415 908-1492	27928
Fusionstorm **(PA)**	7379	D	415 623-2626	16376
G2 Direct and Digital	7371	E	415 421-1000	15200
G4s Secure Solutions (usa)	7381	C	415 591-0780	16653
Galleria Park Associates LLC	7011	D	415 781-3060	12657
Gastroenterology Division	8011	E	415 206-8823	19534
Gcl Solar Energy Inc	1711	D	415 362-2601	2233
Geary Darling Lessee Inc	7011	C	415 292-0100	12661
Gensler Arch Design & Plg PC	8712	B	415 433-3700	26188

Employment Codes: A=Over 500 employees, B=251-500, C=101-250, D=51-100, E=45-50

2017 Directory of California Wholesalers and Services Companies

© Mergent Inc. 1-800-342-5647

SAN FRANCISCO, CA — GEOGRAPHIC SECTION

Company	SIC	EMP	PHONE	ENTRY #
Genstar Capital LP	6211	A	415 834-2350	10005
Geo Reentry Inc	8744	D	415 346-9769	27789
German Motors Corporation	7538	D	415 551-2639	17794
Gfk Custom Research LLC	8732	D	415 398-2812	26667
Giant Creative Strategy Llc	7311	C	415 655-5200	13853
Gibson Dunn & Crutcher LLP	8111	C	415 393-8200	23270
Giga Omni Media Inc	7383	D	415 974-6355	16947
Glass Lewis & Co LLC (HQ)	8732	D	415 678-4110	26670
Global Data Publications Inc	7379	B	415 800-0336	16392
Global Innovation Partners LLC	7389	D	650 233-3600	17193
Global USA Green Card	8111	D	415 915-4151	23276
Globant LLC	7371	D	877 798-8104	15206
Glu Mobile Inc (PA)	7371	C	415 800-6100	15208
Gmg Janitorial Inc	7349	C	415 642-2100	14315
Golden Bear Rest Assn LLC	8611	E	415 227-8660	25088
Golden Gate Brdg Hwy & Transpo (PA)	4785	C	415 921-5858	5209
Golden Gate Capital MGT II LLC	8741	D	415 983-2700	27041
Golden Gate Capitol	8748	D	415 983-2700	27934
Golden Gate Nat Prks Cnsrvancy (PA)	8999	D	415 561-3000	28132
Golden Gate Regional Ctr Inc (PA)	8322	E	415 546-9222	23994
Golden Gate Scnic Stmship Corp	4489	E	415 901-5249	4735
Golden Living LLC	8051	D	415 563-0565	20608
Goldman Sachs & Co	6211	C	415 393-7500	10006
Goodby Silverstein Partners Inc (HQ)	7311	C	415 392-0669	13856
Goodwill Industrs of San Franc	8331	D	415 354-8570	24347
Gordon Rees Scully Mnskhani LLP (PA)	8111	E	415 986-5900	23283
Gould Evans P C	8712	D	415 503-1411	26192
Grand Central Communications	4813	C	415 344-3200	5621
Grand View Research Inc	8742	E	415 349-0058	27453
Granite Solutions Groupe Inc	7361	D	415 963-3999	14665
Grant Thornton LLP	8721	D	415 986-3900	26355
Gree International Inc	7371	C	415 409-5159	15213
Greenberg Traurig LLP	8111	D	415 655-1300	23288
Greene Rdvsky Maloney Share LP	8111	E	415 981-1400	23292
Greentree Property MGT Inc	6512	E	415 347-8600	10991
Groundwork Open Source Inc	7375	D	415 992-4500	16241
Guardsmark LLC	7381	E	415 956-6070	16680
Guidebook Inc	7371	D	650 319-7233	15217
H & R Block Inc	8111	E	415 441-2666	23295
Habenicht & Howlett A Corp	1793	D	415 824-7040	3411
Hagen Streiff Newton & Oshiro	8721	E	415 982-4704	26363
Hal-Mar-Jac Enterprises	7381	C	415 467-1470	16700
Hamilton Families	8322	D	415 409-2100	24001
Handlery Hotels Inc	7011	D	415 781-7800	12685
Hands-On Mobile Americas Inc (PA)	7373	E	415 580-6400	15956
Hanson Bridgett LLP (PA)	8111	B	415 543-2055	23300
Harley Ellis Devereaux Corp	8712	D	510 268-3800	26196
Harrison Drywall Inc	1742	D	415 821-9584	2908
Hart Howerton Ltd (PA)	0781	D	415 439-2200	771
Hartford Casualty Insurance Co	6331	A	415 836-4800	10427
Hassard Bonnington LLP (PA)	8111	D	415 288-9800	23303
Hathaway Dinwiddie Cnstr Co	1542	B	415 986-2718	1565
Hathaway Dinwiddie Cnstr Group (PA)	1542	D	415 352-1501	1566
HDR Architecture Inc	8711	D	415 546-4242	25853
HDR Engineering Inc	8742	D	415 546-4200	27461
Healy & Co	8999	D	925 543-5700	28134
Hearsay Social Inc (PA)	7372	D	888 990-3777	15690
Hearst Communications Inc	4833	B	415 441-4444	5867
Heartland Payment Systems Inc	7389	D	415 518-4810	17725
Hebrew Home For Aged Disabled	8051	A	415 334-2500	20661
Heffernan Insurance Brokers	6411	E	415 398-7733	10740
Heidrick & Struggles Intl Inc	7361	D	415 981-2854	14670
Hellman & Friedman Capital IV	6799	E	415 788-5111	12313
Hellmuth Obata & Kassabaum Inc (DH)	8712	C	415 243-0555	26199
Henry Broadcasting Co	4832	E	415 285-1133	5777
Herrero Builders Incorporated (PA)	1541	C	415 824-7675	1437
Highmark Capital Management	6282	D	800 582-4734	10152
Hill & Knowlton Strategies LLC	8743	D	415 281-7120	27751
Hilton Worldwide Inc	7011	B	415 771-1400	12718
Hilton Worldwide Inc	7011	B	415 392-8000	12724
Hilton Worldwide Inc	7011	D	415 771-1400	12738
Hines Gs Properties Inc	6552	E	415 982-6200	11973
Hinttech Inc	8748	C	415 874-3200	27945
Hks Architects Inc	8712	E	415 356-3800	26201
Hlm Venture Partners II LP	6282	D	415 814-6110	10153
Hntb Corporation	8712	D	415 963-6700	26204
Hok Group Inc	8712	D	415 243-0555	26206
Holland & Knight LLP	8111	E	415 743-6900	23310
Holzmueller Corporation	7359	D	415 826-8383	14546
Homebridge Inc	8322	B	415 255-2079	24010
Homeless Prenatal Program	8322	E	415 546-6756	24012
Homestar Systems Inc	7379	D	415 694-6000	16397
Honeybook Inc	7371	D	770 403-9234	15221
Hood & Strong LLP (PA)	8721	E	415 781-0793	26374
Hornberger Worstell Assoc Inc	8712	E	415 391-1080	26208
Hornblower Yachts LLC (PA)	4489	C	415 788-8866	4737
Host Hotels & Resorts Inc	7011	D	415 775-7555	12760
Host Hotels & Resorts LP	7011	D	415 896-1600	12769
Hotel Nikko San Francisco Inc	7011	B	415 394-1111	12791
Hotel Tonight Inc	7011	D	800 208-2949	12792
Hotel Whitcomb	7011	D	415 626-8000	12793
Hotpads Com	7299	D	563 289-7368	13766
Hotwire Inc	4813	C	415 645-7350	5631
House of Air LLC	7999	D	415 345-9675	19224
Howard Hughes Medical Inst	8731	C	415 476-9668	26531
Htec Groupinc	7371	D	650 949-4880	15225
Humanitycom Inc	7371	E	415 230-0108	15226
Hunton & Williams LLP	8111	E	415 975-3700	23315
Huntsman Architectural Group (PA)	8712	D	415 394-1212	26211
Huskies Lessee LLC	7011	B	415 392-7755	12806
Hvsf Transition LLC	7311	D	415 477-1999	13860
Hyatt Corporation	7011	B	415 848-6050	12811
Hyatt Corporation	7011	A	415 788-1234	12812
Hyatt Corporation	7011	A	415 788-1234	12821
Ic BP III Holdings Xii LLC	6531	D	415 549-5054	11580
Ic BP III Holdings Xv LLC	6519	C	415 273-4250	11256
Ideo LP	7389	D	415 615-5000	17232
Ifwe Inc (PA)	7372	C	415 946-1850	15696
Igate Corporation	7361	B	415 836-8800	14679
Iheartcommunications Inc	4832	B	415 975-5555	5779
Ihms (sf) LLC	7011	B	415 781-5555	12835
Ima Europe Mwr Single Fund	8741	D	210 466-1376	27062
Imperial Parking (us) LLC	7521	A	415 495-3909	17718
Indus Light & Magic (vanco) LL	7699	C	415 292-4671	17984
Information Resources Inc	7372	E	415 227-4500	15703
Infotech Global Services	8742	D	415 986-5400	27475
Ingenio Inc	4813	C	415 248-4000	5637
Ingenio Inc	7389	D	415 992-8220	17238
Inkling Systems Inc	8742	D	415 975-4420	27476
Inner Circle Entertainment	5145	C	415 693-0777	8622
Inner City Broadcasting Corp	4832	E	415 284-1029	5789
Innotas	8742	D	415 263-9800	27477
Inside Track Inc	8748	B	415 243-4440	27950
Insideview Technologies Inc	5045	C	415 728-9309	7146
Insikt Inc	7389	D	415 391-2431	17242
Institute For Health & Healing	8049	E	415 600-3503	20326
Institute For One World Health	7991	D	650 392-2510	18646
Institute On Aging	8322	C	415 600-2690	24028
Institute On Aging (PA)	8322	D	415 750-4101	24029
Insurance Services Office Inc	7375	B	415 874-4361	16245
Integrated Clg Solutions Inc	7349	E	415 821-6757	14325
Intercntnntal Ht Group Rsrces	7011	B	415 771-9000	12840
Intercontinental Hotels Group	7011	C	415 626-6103	12843
Intercontinental Hotels Group	7011	C	415 398-8900	12844
Intercontinental Hotels Group	7011	D	415 409-4600	12845
Intercontinental Hotels Group	7011	B	415 616-6500	12847
International Bus Mchs Corp	5044	C	415 545-4747	7055
Internet Archive	7375	C	415 561-6767	16246
Interstate Hotels Resorts Inc	7011	C	415 362-5500	12848
Invitae Corporation (PA)	8734	D	415 374-7782	26861
Invuity Inc	5047	C	415 665-2100	7270
ISO Services Inc	8999	A	415 434-4599	28137
Isyndicate Inc	7375	D	415 896-1900	16247
Ita Group Inc	8742	C	415 277-3200	27487
Itseez Inc	7371	D	832 781-7169	15261
Ixonos USA Limited	7373	A	949 278-1354	15975
J Walter Thompson USA LLC	7311	D	415 268-5555	13870
Jack I Kaiser	8641	D	415 833-8152	25272
Japanese Cmnty Youth Council (PA)	8399	D	415 202-7905	24930
Jeffer Mngels Btlr Mtchell LLP	8111	D	415 398-8080	23326
Jelani House Inc	8322	E	415 822-5977	24042
Jetro Cash and Carry Entps LLC	5147	D	415 920-2888	8674
Jewis Vocational & Counseling	8331	D	415 391-3600	24355
Jewish Community Fedrtn San Fr (PA)	8399	D	415 777-0411	24931
Jewish Family and Chld Svcs (PA)	8322	D	415 449-1200	24044
Jewish Senior Living Group	6513	D	415 562-2600	11145
Jh Capital Partners LP	6799	E	415 364-0300	12317
Jill Taylor Macari	8748	D	781 315-2597	27959
Jillians San Francisco CA	7389	D	415 369-6100	17258
Jim Couch	4813	D	415 381-2800	5642
Jmp Securities LLC (DH)	6211	D	415 835-8900	10019
Jn Projects Inc	7299	D	415 766-0273	13772
John Stewart Company (PA)	6531	D	213 833-1860	11601
Joie De Vivre Hospitality LLC (PA)	8741	D	415 835-0300	27081
Joie De Vivre Hospitality LLC	8741	D	415 986-2000	27082
Jones Lang Lasalle Inc	6531	C	415 395-4900	11602
K&L Gates LLP	8111	D	415 882-8200	23333
K&L Gates LLP	8111	D	415 249-1000	23336
Kabam Inc (PA)	7371	E	415 391-0817	15265
Kaiser Foundation Hospitals	6324	D	415 833-2616	10294

GEOGRAPHIC SECTION

SAN FRANCISCO, CA

	SIC	EMP	PHONE	ENTRY #
Kaiser Foundation Hospitals	8011	A	415 833-2000	19586
Kaiser Foundation Hospitals	6733	A	415 833-2000	12187
Kaiser Med Security Services	7381	D	415 833-3683	16716
Kallidus Inc	7371	D	877 554-2176	15266
Kane & Finkel LLC	7311	D	415 777-4990	13872
Kcbs News Radio 74	4832	D	415 765-4112	5792
Keker and Van Nest LLP	8111	C	415 391-5400	23346
Kendo Brands Inc	8741	C	415 284-3700	27090
Kennedy/Jenks Consultants Inc (PA)	8711	D	415 243-2150	25917
Kenshoo Inc	8742	C	877 536-7462	27499
Ketchum Incorporated	8743	D	415 984-6100	27752
Kfi	8741	E	415 956-9812	27092
Kgo Television Inc	4833	C	415 954-7777	5882
Kid Stock Inc	7922	D	415 753-3737	18402
Kilroy Realty LP	6531	D	415 243-8803	11620
Kimpton Hotel & Rest Group LLC	7011	A	415 885-2500	12884
Kimpton Hotel & Rest Group LLC (HQ)	8741	D	415 397-5572	27093
Kimpton Hotel & Rest Group LLC	7011	C	415 561-1100	12885
Kimpton Hotel & Rest Group LLC	8741	E	415 394-0500	27094
Kimpton Hotel & Rest Group LLC	8741	D	415 292-0100	27095
Kindred Healthcare Oper Inc	8051	D	415 922-5085	20703
Kindred Healthcare Oper Inc	8062	C	415 566-1200	21688
Kindred Nursing Centers W LLC	8093	C	415 673-8405	22761
King & Spalding LLP	8111	B	415 318-1200	23352
Kinsale Holdings Inc	5122	C	415 400-2600	8273
Kipp Foundation	8399	C	415 399-1556	24935
Kirkland & Ellis LLP	8111	C	415 439-1400	23354
Kisco Senior Living LLC	8741	D	415 664-6264	27097
Kixeye Inc (PA)	5092	C	415 956-3413	8048
Klingbeil Company	6552	D	415 398-0106	11977
KMD Architects (PA)	8712	C	415 398-5191	26217
Kms Fishermans Wharf LP	7011	C	415 561-1100	12890
Kpff Inc	8711	E	415 989-1004	25928
Kpisoft Inc	7372	D	415 439-5228	15727
Kpmg LLP	8721	E	415 963-5100	26386
Kqed Inc (PA)	4833	B	415 864-2000	5886
Kraft & Kennedy Inc	7373	D	415 956-4000	15981
L-O Soma Hotel Inc	7011	B	415 974-6400	12895
La Salle Apartments	6513	D	415 647-0607	11152
Landor Associates Intl Ltd (DH)	7336	C	415 365-1700	14150
Lateral Designs Inc	7336	D	415 847-6618	14151
Latham & Watkins LLP	8111	C	415 391-0600	23372
Launch Media Inc (HQ)	4813	C	310 593-6152	5646
Lawson Roofing Co Inc	1761	D	415 285-1661	3184
Leemah Electronics Inc	4911	C	415 394-1288	6144
Leerink Partners LLC	6211	D	800 778-1164	10024
Legend Merchant Group Inc	7389	E	415 957-9555	17292
Lendingclub Corporation (PA)	6153	D	415 632-5600	9785
Lesconcierges Inc (PA)	7363	D	415 905-6088	14899
Levin and Simes	8111	E	415 426-3000	23384
Lewis & Taylor LLC	7349	C	415 781-3496	14338
Lewis Brsbois Bsgard Smith LLP	8111	C	415 362-2580	23390
Lewis P C Jackson	8111	E	415 394-9400	23393
Lewis PR Inc (PA)	8743	D	415 432-2400	27755
Liberty Mutual Insurance Co	6331	C	415 957-1175	10433
Licensale Inc	6794	D	604 681-6888	12219
Lieff Cabraser Heimann & (PA)	8111	C	415 788-0245	23395
Liffey Thames Group LLC	7379	C	415 392-2900	16423
Lightbend Inc	7371	D	877 989-7372	15274
Linden Research Inc (PA)	7371	C	415 243-9000	15276
Lithium Technologies Inc (PA)	7372	D	510 653-6800	15733
Little Sisters of Poor	8361	C	415 751-6510	24714
Littler Mendelson PC (PA)	8111	B	415 433-1940	23397
Live Nation Merchandise Inc (HQ)	5199	E	415 247-7400	9277
Live Nation Worldwide	7922	D	415 371-5500	18409
Livefyre Inc (PA)	7371	C	415 800-0900	15277
Livevox Inc (PA)	8748	C	415 671-6000	27976
LLP Locke Lord	8111	C	415 318-8800	23398
LLP Moss Adams	8721	C	415 956-1500	26399
Lockheed Martin Corporation	8711	C	415 402-0406	25940
Lockton Companies Llc-Pacific	6411	C	415 568-4000	10765
Long & Levit LLP	8111	E	415 777-2222	23407
Low Ball & Lynch A Prof Corp (PA)	8111	D	415 981-6630	23411
Loyal3 Holdings Inc	7389	D	415 981-0700	17304
Lucasfilm Ltd LLC (HQ)	7812	C	415 623-1000	18104
Lumetra Healthcare Solutions	8748	E	415 677-2000	27977
Luxor Cabs Inc	4121	D	415 282-4141	3865
Lyft Inc	4119	C	415 230-2905	3815
Lynch Gilardi & Grummer LLP	8111	E	415 397-2800	23416
M & H Realty Partners LP	6799	D	415 693-9000	12323
M Arthur Gensler Jr Assoc Inc (PA)	8712	B	415 433-3700	26230
M T C Holdings (DH)	4491	E	912 651-4000	4749
M+w US Inc	8711	E	415 621-1199	25944
Macarthur Transit Community	1521	C	415 989-1111	1209
Macquire Arcft Lsg Svcs US Inc	7359	D	415 829-6500	14556
Malcolm Drilling Company Inc (PA)	1799	C	415 901-4400	3550
Marcum LLP	8721	E	415 543-6900	26406
Marcus Mllchap RE Inv Svcs Inc	6531	E	415 391-9220	11657
Mariadb Usa Inc	5045	D	847 562-9000	7159
Marin Software Incorporated (PA)	7374	C	415 399-2580	16157
Marines Memorial Association	8641	C	415 673-6672	25294
Maritime Hotel Associates LP	7011	C	415 563-0800	12943
Mark Hopkins IHC	7011	B	415 616-6991	12944
Marketwatch Inc (DH)	7383	D	415 439-6400	16948
Markmonitor Holdings Inc	7371	B	415 278-8400	15293
Markmonitor Inc (DH)	7379	D	415 278-8400	16429
Maroevich OShea & Coghlan	6411	D	415 957-0600	10771
Marriot Courtyard	7011	E	415 775-1103	12945
Marriott International Inc	7011	D	415 947-0700	12955
Marriott International Inc	7011	D	415 989-3500	12971
Marriott International Inc (PA)	7011	D	415 929-2030	12977
Mars & Co Consulting LLC	8742	C	415 288-6970	27525
Marsh & McLennan Agency LLC	6411	D	415 243-4160	10773
Marsh USA Inc	6411	D	415 743-8000	10777
Martin Media Inc (PA)	7311	E	415 913-7446	13880
Mason Street Opco LLC	7011	A	415 772-5000	12983
Masonic Homes of California (PA)	8361	B	415 776-7000	24727
Massdrop Inc	8748	D	415 340-2999	27982
Maverick Hotel Partners LLC	8741	B	415 655-9526	27121
Maxson Young Assoc Inc	6411	C	415 228-6400	10779
Maynard Cooper & Gale PC	8111	C	415 704-7433	23422
Mazzetti Inc (PA)	8711	C	415 362-3266	25954
McCann World Group Inc (PA)	7311	D	415 262-5500	13881
McCann-Erickson Corporation (HQ)	7312	C	415 348-5600	13882
McCann-Erickson Usa Inc	8732	C	415 262-5600	26688
McKesson Corporation (PA)	5122	A	415 983-8300	8281
McKinsey & Company Inc	8742	B	415 981-0250	27534
McMillan Bros Electric Inc	1731	C	415 826-5100	2646
McMillan Data Cmmnications Inc	1731	C	415 826-5100	2647
MD P Foundation Inc	8322	C	415 552-0240	24079
Meals On Whels San Frncsco Inc	8322	E	415 920-1111	24082
Meany Wilson L P	6552	E	415 905-5300	11983
Medidata Solutions Inc	8733	C	415 295-4300	26786
Medrio Inc	7372	D	415 963-3700	15747
Mellon Capital Management Corp (HQ)	6282	D	415 905-5448	10162
Meltwater News US Inc (DH)	8742	C	415 829-5900	27541
Meraki Inc	7371	C	415 632-5800	15300
Mercer (us) Inc	8742	C	415 743-8700	27543
Mercer Health & Benefits LLC	8742	C	415 743-8751	27545
Merchant Services Inc (PA)	7374	B	817 725-0900	16159
Mercy Hsing California Xxxiv	6513	D	415 503-0816	11167
Meridian Industrial Trust	6798	D	415 281-3900	12261
Meridian Management Group	6513	C	415 434-9700	11168
Meritage Group LP	8741	A	415 399-5330	27127
Merlin Securities LLC	6211	C	415 848-0269	10029
Merrill Lynch Pierce Fenner	6211	C	415 955-3700	10039
Merrill Lynch Pierce Fenner	6211	E	415 274-7000	10043
Metromile Inc (PA)	6331	C	888 244-1702	10449
Metropolitan Club	8641	D	415 673-0600	25297
Metropolitan Elec Cnstr Inc	1731	C	415 642-3000	2651
Metropolitan Life Insur Co	6411	B	415 536-1065	10785
Metropolitan Trnsp Comm (PA)	4111	C	510 817-5700	3673
Mg Restaurants Inc	8741	C	415 296-8222	27128
Mhm Services Inc	8093	C	415 416-6992	22776
Micro Holding Corp	7374	A	415 788-5111	16162
Microsoft Corporation	7372	D	415 972-6400	15755
Midokura USA Inc	7371	E	888 512-0460	15303
Mile Post Properties LLC	7011	D	415 673-4711	12995
Millbrae Wcp Hotel I LLC	7011	A	415 397-7000	12996
Millennium Partners Sports C	7991	B	415 243-0492	18662
Milliman Inc	8999	D	415 403-1333	28149
Minami Tamaki LLP	8111	E	415 788-9000	23435
Mindfull Body	7999	D	415 931-2639	19246
Mindjet LLC (HQ)	7372	B	415 229-4344	15758
Minimalisms Inc	7389	D	415 309-3108	17336
Mission Neighborhood Hlth Ctr (PA)	8011	C	415 552-3870	19755
Mission Stuart Ht Partners LLC	7011	D	415 278-7400	12999
Mitchell Engineering	1794	E	415 227-1040	3438
Mixpanel Inc	7371	D	415 528-2827	15309
Mizuho Securities USA Inc	6211	D	415 268-5500	10047
Mma Renewable Ventures LLC	5074	C	415 229-8817	7725
Mobpartner Inc	7312	D	415 813-1202	13953
Mobsoc Media LLC	7372	D	415 974-5429	15761
Mocana Corporation	7374	D	415 617-0055	16163
Moffitt H C Hospital	8062	D	415 476-1000	21765
Monitise Americas Inc	7371	D	415 526-7000	15313
Monitor Company Group GP LLC	8742	C	415 932-5300	27552
Monroe Residence Club	6513	D	415 771-9119	11170
Moov Corporation	7371	C	877 666-8932	15316
Morgan Lewis & Bockius LLP	8111	A	415 393-2000	23440

Employment Codes: A=Over 500 employees, B=251-500, C=101-250, D=51-100, E=45-50

2017 Directory of California Wholesalers and Services Companies

SAN FRANCISCO, CA

GEOGRAPHIC SECTION

	SIC	EMP	PHONE	ENTRY #
Morgan Lewis & Bockius LLP	8111	B	415 442-1000	23445
Morgan Stanley & Co LLC	6211	B	415 693-6000	10061
Morgans Hotel Group MGT LLC	7011	C	415 775-4700	13009
Morrison & Foerster LLP (PA)	8111	B	415 268-7000	23450
Morrison & Foerster LLP	8111	C	415 268-7178	23451
Morrison & Foerster LLP	8111	E	925 295-3300	23453
Mufg Union Bank Na (DH)	6021	A	212 782-6800	9401
Mulesoft Inc (PA)	7371	C	415 229-2009	15318
Munger Tolles Olson Foundation	8111	E	415 512-4000	23457
Murphy (PA)	8111	D	415 788-1900	23459
Music Hall LLC	7922	E	415 885-0750	18416
MWH Americas Inc	8711	D	415 430-1800	25984
Mypointscom LLC (HQ)	7311	D	415 615-1100	13888
N A Citibank	6153	D	415 627-6000	9787
National Assn Ltr Carriers	8699	B	415 362-0214	25558
National Council Negro Women	8699	D	415 564-4153	25559
NBC Universal Inc	4832	C	415 995-6800	5811
Ncc Group Inc (HQ)	7379	C	415 268-9300	16437
Ncircle Network Security Inc (DH)	7371	D	415 625-5900	15323
Netfortris Corporation	4899	C	888 469-5100	6083
Netsource Inc	7361	D	415 831-3681	14707
Network Affiliates Inc	6211	D	415 291-2914	10064
Nevin Levy LLP A Partnership	6531	D	415 800-5770	11704
New Civic Company Ltd	6799	C	415 986-1668	12329
New Paradigm Productions Inc (PA)	7812	D	415 924-8000	18120
New Relic Inc (PA)	7372	C	650 777-7600	15775
New York Life Insurance Co	6411	E	415 393-6060	10802
Nexant Inc (PA)	8748	D	415 369-1000	27999
Nextdoorcom Inc	8399	D	415 236-0000	24948
Nibbi Bros Associates Inc	1522	C	415 863-1820	1327
Nicolaides Fink Tho	8111	D	415 745-3778	23468
Nielsen Mobile (DH)	7389	D	917 435-9301	17360
Ninth House Inc	8331	E	612 339-0927	24369
Nitro Software Inc	7372	D	415 632-4894	15779
Nixon Peabody LLP	8111	C	415 984-8200	23470
No More Dirt Inc	5087	C	415 821-6757	7973
Nob Hill Properties Inc	7011	B	415 474-5400	13023
Nomura Securities Intl Inc	6211	D	415 445-3831	10065
Norcal Mutual Insurance Co (PA)	6411	B	415 397-9703	10812
Norcal Painters Inc	1721	C	415 566-6800	2470
Northern California Institute	8399	B	415 750-6954	24949
Northern California Presbyteri	6513	C	415 673-2352	11175
Northern California Presbyteri	8051	C	415 922-9700	20810
Nossaman LLP	8111	E	415 398-3600	23474
Novo Construction Inc	1542	D	650 701-1500	1622
Novogradac and Co LLP	8721	E	415 356-8000	26413
NRG Energy Inc	4911	D	415 255-8105	6156
Nuna Incorporated	7371	D	650 390-7745	15345
Obscura Digital Incorporated	7313	D	415 227-9979	13975
Ocean Park Health Center	8011	E	415 753-8100	19788
Odc	7911	D	415 863-9834	18364
Okabe International Inc (PA)	4725	E	415 921-0808	4996
Okta Inc (PA)	7371	C	415 494-8029	15348
Olympic Club	7997	D	415 676-1412	19020
Olympic Club (PA)	8641	C	415 345-5100	25304
OMelveny & Myers LLP	8111	C	415 984-8700	23481
Omni Hotels Corporation	7011	B	415 677-9494	13044
On Lok Inc	8011	D	415 292-8888	19795
On Lok Senior Health Services (PA)	6324	A	415 292-8888	10361
On24 Inc (PA)	4813	C	877 202-9599	5673
One Embarcadero Center Venture	6798	C	415 772-0700	12263
One Medical Group Inc (PA)	8011	D	415 578-3100	19796
One Medical Group Inc	8011	D	415 529-4522	19797
One Medical Group Inc	8011	D	415 291-0480	19798
One Nob Hill Associates LLC	7011	D	415 392-3434	13046
One Workplace L Ferrari LLC	5021	E	415 357-2200	6828
One Workplace L Ferrari LLC	8744	D	415 357-2200	27798
Open Harbor Inc	8742	D	650 413-4200	27576
Opentable Inc (HQ)	7389	C	415 344-4200	17379
Opentv Inc (DH)	7372	C	415 962-5000	15784
Opower Inc	7372	D	415 848-4700	15786
Optimizely Inc (PA)	7371	B	415 376-4598	15354
Oracle Corporation	7372	C	415 402-7200	15797
Orange Silicon Valley	8748	D	415 243-1500	28012
Orchard International Group (PA)	7011	D	415 362-8878	13048
Organic Inc (HQ)	7379	D	415 581-5300	16448
Organic Holdings Inc	7311	B	415 581-5300	13892
Orrick Hrrington Sutcliffe LLP (PA)	8111	C	415 773-5700	23482
Osterhout Group Inc	7389	E	415 644-4000	17384
Otis Elevator Company	1796	C	415 546-0880	3478
Oum & Co LLP (PA)	8721	C	415 434-3744	26415
Outcast Agency LLC	8743	C	415 392-8282	27760
Pac-12 Enteprises LLC	7313	C	415 580-4200	13976
Pacific Bell Telephone Company (HQ)	4813	A	415 542-9000	5677
Pacific Eagle Holdings Corp	6512	D	415 398-2473	11029

	SIC	EMP	PHONE	ENTRY #
Pacific Energy Fuels Company	4924	A	415 973-8200	6270
Pacific Eye Associated Inc	8011	D	415 923-3007	19803
Pacific Gas and Electric Co (HQ)	4911	D	415 973-7000	6162
Pacific Gas and Electric Co	4911	D	415 973-0778	6174
Pacific Gas and Electric Co	4911	B	415 695-3513	6189
Pacific Gas and Electric Co	4911	D	415 973-8089	6194
Pacific Growth Equities LLC	6211	D	415 274-6800	10067
Pacific Metro LLC (PA)	5199	B	408 201-5000	9286
Pacific Park Management (PA)	7521	D	415 434-4400	17731
Pacific Structures Inc	1771	C	415 367-9399	3309
Pacific Union Club	8641	D	415 775-1234	25309
Pacific Union Co	6531	D	415 474-6600	11731
Pacific Union RE Group (DH)	6531	D	415 929-7100	11732
Paganini Electric Corporation	1731	C	415 575-3900	2676
Pagerduty Inc	4899	D	650 989-2965	6086
Palomino Db Inc	7379	D	775 572-8854	16453
Paragon Real Estate Group	6531	C	415 738-7000	11736
Paragon Real Estate Group	6531	D	415 292-2384	11737
Pariveda Solutions Inc	7373	C	415 946-6100	16028
Parkmerced Investors LLC	7359	E	877 243-5544	14566
Parkside Lending LLC	6211	D	415 771-3700	10068
Parsons Brinckerhoff Inc	8711	D	415 243-4600	26011
Parthenon DCS Holdings LLC	8741	A	925 960-4800	27160
Pattern Energy Group LP (PA)	4911	D	415 283-4000	6195
Paul Hastings LLP	8111	D	415 856-7000	23497
Pax Labs Inc	0132	D	510 828-8174	18
Pepsi-Cola Metro Btlg Co Inc	5149	D	415 206-7400	8903
Pereira & ODell LLC (PA)	7311	D	415 284-9916	13894
Perkins Coie LLP	8111	C	415 344-7000	23503
Permanente Medical Group Inc	8011	D	415 833-2000	19841
Permanente Medical Group Inc	8011	D	415 833-2000	19859
Pets Unlimited	8699	D	415 563-6700	25566
PG&e Capital LLC	8742	C	415 321-4600	27588
PG&e Corporation (PA)	4931	C	415 973-1000	6291
Phacil Inc	7371	A	415 901-1600	15378
PHF Ruby LLC	7011	C	415 885-4700	13092
Philharmonia Baroque Orchestra	7929	D	415 252-1288	18486
Philippine Airlines Inc	4512	C	415 217-3100	4817
Philotic Inc	7371	D	510 730-1740	15380
Pier 39 Limited Partnership (PA)	6512	D	415 705-5500	11032
Pillsbury Winthrop Shaw	8111	D	415 983-1000	23507
Pillsbury Winthrop Shaw	8111	D	415 983-1075	23510
Pine & Powell Partners LLC	7011	D	415 989-3500	13096
Pinterest Inc	7319	B	415 400-4645	14006
Pinterest Inc (PA)	7375	C	650 561-5407	16253
Pioneer Square Hotel Company	7011	E	415 346-2323	13100
Planet Labs Inc	7374	C	415 829-3313	16169
Planetout Inc (HQ)	4813	E	415 834-6500	5685
Plangrid Inc	7372	D	415 349-7440	15817
Playwrights Foundation Inc	7922	D	415 626-2176	18424
Plivo Inc	4813	D	415 758-3659	5686
Polaris Research & Development	8748	D	415 777-3229	28019
Pomeroy Rcrtion Rhbltation Ctr (PA)	8322	C	415 665-4100	24139
Post Street Renaissance	7011	B	415 563-0303	13109
Postmates Inc (PA)	4789	B	800 882-6106	5237
Powerreviews Oc LLC	7371	D	415 315-9208	15392
Practice Fusion Inc (PA)	7371	C	415 346-7700	15393
Praetorian Group	7379	E	415 962-8310	16460
Presidio Surgerycenter	8062	D	415 346-1218	21807
Presidio Wealth Management LLC	6282	E	415 449-2500	10175
Pricewaterhousecoopers LLP	8721	E	415 498-5000	26428
Primitive Logic Inc	7373	C	415 391-8080	16034
Prn LLC (HQ)	7371	D	415 805-2525	15394
Professional Technical SEC Svcs	7381	B	415 243-2100	16766
Progress Foundation	8641	D	415 553-3100	25317
Progress Glass Co Inc (PA)	1793	C	415 824-7040	3413
Project Frog Inc	1522	D	415 814-8500	1333
Project Open Hand (PA)	8322	D	415 292-3400	24140
Prologis Inc (PA)	6798	D	415 394-9000	12266
Prologis LP (HQ)	6798	B	415 394-9000	12267
Prophet Brand Strategy (PA)	8742	E	415 677-0909	27597
Prosper Marketplace Inc (PA)	6163	D	415 593-5400	9946
Prudential California Realty	6531	D	415 664-9400	11777
Prudential Insur Co of Amer	6411	D	415 398-7310	10843
Prudential Insur Co of Amer	6411	D	415 486-3050	10845
Prudential Realty Corp	6531	D	415 566-9800	11779
Public Policy Institute Cal (PA)	8611	D	415 291-4400	25101
Publicis & Hal Riney (HQ)	7311	C	415 981-0950	13901
PWC STRategy& (us) LLC	8742	C	415 391-1900	27603
Quality Planning Corporation	8742	D	415 369-0707	27606
Quantcast Corporation (PA)	7319	C	415 738-4755	14007
Questus Inc (PA)	7374	E	415 677-5700	16175
Quicksilver Delivery Inc	7389	D	415 431-1600	17437
Quinn Emanuel Urquhart	8111	E	415 875-6600	23523
Quri Inc	8732	E	888 886-8423	26701

GEOGRAPHIC SECTION

SAN FRANCISCO, CA

	SIC	EMP	PHONE	ENTRY #
R S Investments LLC	6282	D	415 591-2700	10177
Radisson Ht Fishermans Wharf	7011	D	415 392-6700	13121
Radiumone Inc (PA)	8743	D	415 418-2840	27765
Rai Care Ctrs Nthrn Cal II LLC	8092	E	415 206-9775	22636
Rainbow Wtrprofing Restoration	1799	C	415 641-1578	3574
Randstad North America Inc	7363	C	415 397-3384	14933
Ranger Pipelines Incorporated	1623	C	415 822-3700	1987
RCM Capital Management LLC (DH)	6211	B	415 954-5400	10073
RCM Capital Management LLC	6282	C	415 364-2327	10178
RE Barren Ridge 1 LLC	4911	C	415 675-1500	6197
RE La Mesa LLC	1629	D	415 675-1500	2078
RE Mohican LLC	1629	D	415 675-1500	2079
RE Santa Clara LLC	1629	D	415 675-1500	2080
Real Branding LLC	7311	E	415 522-1516	13908
Rec Center	5091	C	415 831-6818	8028
Recology Cleanscapes	7349	C	415 626-5685	14403
Recology Inc (PA)	4953	D	415 875-1000	6519
Recology Inc	4953	D	415 330-1300	6520
Recology Inc	4953	D	415 970-1582	6522
Recology Inc	4953	C	415 330-1400	6524
Recology San Francisco	4953	D	415 468-1752	6527
Recurrent Energy (HQ)	1711	D	415 956-3168	2343
Recurrent Enrgy Dev Hldngs LLC (DH)	6799	C	415 675-1500	12340
Recurve Inc	7623	D	510 540-4860	17923
Red Sky Interactive	7311	C	415 430-3200	13910
Reed Smith LLP	8111	C	415 659-5964	23527
Reed Smith LLP	8111	D	415 543-8700	23529
Reed Smith LLP	8111	D	415 543-8700	23530
Regents of The Univ of Cal	8063	D	415 476-9000	22086
Regents of The Univ of Cal	7389	D	510 987-0700	17448
Reliable Caregivers Inc	8082	D	415 436-0100	22547
Reneson Hotels Inc	7011	C	415 621-7001	13145
Rentjuice Corporation	4813	D	415 376-0369	5691
Republic Indemnity Co Amer	6331	D	415 981-3200	10453
Respond 2 LLC	7812	D	415 398-4200	18143
Restaurant Depot LLC	5181	C	415 920-2888	9080
Retailnext Inc	8732	C	408 298-2585	26704
Rex Rising L P	7011	D	415 273-9790	13151
Rfj Corporation	1742	D	415 824-6890	2966
Rhythmone LLC (HQ)	4813	D	415 655-1450	5692
Richard J Mendoza Inc	6331	D	415 644-0180	10457
Richmond Area Mlt-Services Inc	8049	D	415 668-5998	20349
Richmond Area Mlt-Services Inc	8093	D	415 392-4453	22814
Richmond Area Mlt-Services Inc	8093	D	415 800-0699	22815
Richmond Area Mlt-Services Inc	8093	D	415 800-0699	22816
Richmond Area Mlt-Services Inc	8093	D	415 689-5662	22817
Richmond Area Mlt-Services Inc (PA)	8063	D	415 668-5955	22087
Richmond Dst Neighborhood Ctr	8322	D	415 750-8554	24157
Ricoh Usa Inc	5044	C	415 733-5600	7064
Ricoh Usa Inc	5044	C	415 392-6850	7068
Rim Architects California Inc	8712	D	415 247-0400	26246
Ritz-Carlton Hotel Company LLC	7011	B	415 781-9000	13153
Ritz-Carlton Hotel Company LLC	7011	B	415 773-6168	13156
Riviera Partners LLC (PA)	8742	C	877 748-4372	27620
RMR Construction Company	1542	C	415 647-0884	1651
Robert Half International Inc	7361	D	415 434-2429	14757
Robert Half International Inc	7361	D	415 434-1909	14765
Rockyou Inc (PA)	7375	D	415 580-6400	16259
Rogers Joseph ODonnell A Pro (PA)	8111	D	415 956-2828	23536
Room & Board Inc	6513	C	415 252-9280	11198
Ropes & Gray LLP	8111	B	415 315-6300	23539
Rosendin Electric Inc	1731	A	415 495-9300	2717
Rosendin Electric Inc	1731	A	415 495-9300	2718
Rp/Kinetic Parc 55 Owner LLC	7011	B	415 392-8000	13174
Rpx Corporation (PA)	6794	D	866 779-7641	12224
Rs Investment Management LP (PA)	6722	C	415 591-2700	12124
RSM US LLP	8721	D	415 848-5300	26432
Ruth Barajas	8322	E	415 977-6949	24162
Ryder Truck Rental Inc	7513	C	415 285-0756	17651
S F Auto Parts Whse Inc	5013	D	415 255-0115	6760
Saarman Construction Ltd	1522	C	415 749-2700	1338
Saint Francis Memorial Hosp (HQ)	8062	A	415 353-6000	21838
Salesforcecom (PA)	7372	A	415 901-7000	15833
Salesforcecom Foundation	4813	C	800 667-6389	5695
Salesian Boys and Girls Club	7997	D	415 397-3068	19054
Salt Lake Hotel Associates LP (PA)	7011	C	415 397-5572	13192
Salvation Army	8361	D	415 643-8000	24799
Salvation Army Glden State Div (PA)	8322	D	415 553-3500	24168
San Francisco City & County	8322	D	415 695-5660	24180
San Francisco City & County	8062	A	415 557-3013	21846
San Francisco Aids Foundation (PA)	8322	D	415 487-3000	24182
San Francisco Ballet Assn	7922	D	415 865-2000	18432
San Francisco City & County	8322	D	415 356-2700	24183
San Francisco City & County	8322	D	415 356-2700	24184
San Francisco City & County	7539	C	415 550-4600	17825
San Francisco City Clinic	8093	D	415 487-5500	22825
San Francisco Federal Cr Un (PA)	6062	D	415 775-5377	9685
San Francisco Fertility Ctrs	8011	D	415 834-3000	19942
San Francisco Food Bank	8322	D	415 286-3614	24185
San Francisco Foundation	7389	D	415 733-8500	17472
San Francisco Health Authority (PA)	8621	D	415 615-4407	25155
San Francisco Hotel Associates	7011	D	415 392-4666	13201
San Francisco Hotel Group LLC	7011	C	415 276-9888	13202
San Francisco Ladies Protecti	8361	D	415 931-3136	24802
San Francisco Medical Group	8011	D	415 221-0665	19943
San Francisco Meritime N H P	8412	D	415 561-7000	25043
San Francisco Museum Modrn Art (PA)	8412	D	415 357-4035	25044
San Francisco Opera Assn	7922	A	415 861-4008	18433
San Francisco Radio Assets LLC (DH)	4832	C	415 216-1300	5821
San Francisco Symphony Inc (PA)	7929	C	415 552-8000	18492
San Francisco Tennis Club	7991	D	415 777-9000	18678
San Francisco Travel Assn	7389	D	415 974-6900	17473
San Francisco Zoological Soc	7999	C	415 753-7080	19274
San Frncsco Conservation Corps	8099	B	415 928-7417	23049
San Frncsco Econ Oprtnty Cncil	8399	D	415 749-3798	24975
Sauce Labs Inc	7373	D	415 946-1117	16042
SC Hotel Partners LLC	7011	D	415 775-5000	13224
Schwartz Msl LLC	8743	D	415 817-2500	27767
SCM Advisors LLC	6282	D	415 486-6500	10185
Scott Street Senior Housing Co	8052	C	415 345-5083	21102
Scribd Inc	7375	D	415 896-9890	16261
Securitas SEC Svcs USA Inc	7381	C	510 568-6818	16790
Sedgwick LLP (PA)	8111	C	415 781-7900	23550
Sedgwick LLP	8111	D	415 537-3000	23553
Sega of America Inc	5045	C	415 701-6000	7185
Selectquote Insurance Services (PA)	6411	C	415 543-7338	10871
Self-Help For Elderly	8322	D	415 391-3843	24200
Self-Help For Elderly (PA)	8322	D	415 677-7600	24201
Sendme Inc	4813	D	415 978-9504	5697
Sentient Technologies USA LLC	7371	E	415 422-9886	15446
Servicesource Intl Inc (PA)	8742	C	415 901-6030	27641
Severson & Werson A Prof Corp	8111	D	415 283-4911	23555
Seyfarth Shaw LLP	8111	D	415 397-2823	23558
Sfd Partners LLC	7011	B	415 392-7755	13236
Sfi 2365 Iron Point LLC	6512	E	415 395-9701	11042
Sfi Carlsbad LLC	6512	E	415 395-9701	11043
Sfi Pleasanton LLC	6799	E	415 395-0960	12344
Sfo Airporter Inc	4111	D	415 495-3909	3716
Sfusd Building Ground	7349	D	415 695-5508	14429
Sfusd Jrotc Brigade	7371	D	415 242-2546	15451
Sharper Future	8011	D	415 297-6767	20000
Shartsis Friese LLP	8111	C	415 421-6500	23559
Shea Labagh Dobberstein Cpa (PA)	8721	E	415 731-0100	26439
Sheedy Drayage Co (PA)	7353	D	415 648-7171	14498
Shell Vacations LLC	8741	D	415 441-7100	27210
Shenyang Zhong Yi Tin-Plating	6512	C	415 788-2280	11044
Sheppard Mullin Richter	8111	D	415 434-9100	23563
Sheraton Corporation	7011	B	415 362-5500	13241
Shift Technologies Inc	5012	C	415 800-2038	6693
Shinazy Enterprises Inc	7532	E	415 673-4700	17772
Shook Hardy & Bacon LLP	8111	D	415 544-1900	23567
Shorenstein Company LLC	6512	E	415 772-8209	11046
Shorenstein Properties LLC (PA)	6512	C	415 772-7000	11047
Shoreview Preservation LP	6513	D	415 647-6922	11202
Sideman & Bancroft LLP	8111	D	415 392-1960	23568
Sidley Austin LLP	8111	D	415 772-1200	23570
Signaldemand Inc	7371	E	415 356-0800	15454
Signature Consultants LLC	8999	C	415 544-7510	28160
Silver Lake Partners II LP	6726	C	415 293-4355	12146
Simpson Gumpertz & Heger Inc	8711	D	415 495-3700	26067
Situs Holdings LLC	6799	B	415 374-2820	12345
Skidmore Owings & Merrill LLP	8712	C	415 981-1555	26250
Skyblue Sewing Manufacturing	7389	E	415 777-9978	17491
Skyline Coml Interiors Inc (PA)	1542	D	415 908-1020	1672
Slack Technologies Inc	7372	A	415 373-8825	15837
Smartrecruiters Inc	7361	D	415 508-3755	14789
Smg Holdings Inc	6512	D	650 738-8737	11050
Smith-Emery San Francisco Inc	7389	D	415 642-7326	17494
Smithgroupjjr Inc	8712	C	313 442-8351	26253
Soc/General Services/Bpm	8741	D	415 703-5341	27220
Social Finance Inc	6163	D	415 697-2078	9952
Socialize Inc	7372	E	415 529-4019	15841
Society For San Francisco	8699	C	415 554-3000	25580
Sodexo Management Inc	8741	D	925 325-9657	27221
Soiree Valet Parking Service	7299	C	415 284-9700	13796
Sol Republic Inc	5065	D	877 400-0310	7636
Solution Set LLC	7311	C	415 367-6300	13922
Soma Surgicenter	8011	E	415 641-6889	20007
Sony Electronics Inc	7812	B	415 833-4796	18152
South of Market Child Care	8351	D	415 820-3500	24517

Employment Codes: A=Over 500 employees, B=251-500, C=101-250, D=51-100, E=45-50

2017 Directory of California Wholesalers and Services Companies

© Mergent Inc. 1-800-342-5647

SAN FRANCISCO, CA — GEOGRAPHIC SECTION

Company	SIC	EMP	PHONE	ENTRY #
Southbourne Inc	7011	C	415 781-5555	13275
Southern Pacific Trnsp	4011	D	415 541-2589	3618
Spectrum Sttlment Recovery LLC	8742	E	415 392-5900	27659
Spigit Inc	5045	C	855 774-4480	7192
Splunk Inc (PA)	7372	C	415 848-8400	15844
Sports Basement	5091	D	408 732-0300	8031
Sprig Electric Co	1731	D	415 947-0138	2738
Spus7 235 Pine LP	6726	D	231 683-4200	12147
Square Inc (PA)	7372	E	415 375-3176	15845
Squaretrade Inc (PA)	6411	C	415 541-1000	10876
Squire Patton Boggs (us) LLP	8111	C	415 954-0334	23579
St Anthony Foundation (PA)	8322	E	415 241-2600	24226
St Francis Yacht Club	7997	C	415 563-6363	19095
St Lukes Hospital (HQ)	8062	A	415 600-3959	21927
St Marys Med Ctr Foundation	8062	A	415 668-1000	21929
Stadtner Co Inc	1731	E	415 752-2850	2746
Standard Pacific Capital LLC	6211	E	415 352-7100	10077
Standard Poors Fincl Svcs LLC	6282	C	415 371-5000	10186
Stanford Hotels Corporation	7011	E	415 398-3333	13285
Stantec Arch & Engrg PC	8711	C	415 882-9500	26075
Stantec Architecture Inc	8711	C	415 882-9500	26077
Stantec Consulting Svcs Inc	8711	C	415 882-9500	26078
Starbucks Corporation	8742	C	415 537-7170	27665
Starr Investment Holdings LLC	6726	D	415 216-4000	12149
Starwood Hotels & Resorts	7011	C	415 777-5300	13293
Starwood Hotels & Resorts	7011	C	415 284-4049	13298
Starwood Hotels & Resorts	7011	C	415 512-1111	13299
Starwood Hotels & Resorts	7011	C	415 284-4000	13300
State Bar of California	8621	B	415 538-2000	25159
State Compensation Insur Fund (PA)	6331	C	888 782-8338	10460
Steele Cis Inc	8111	B	415 692-5000	23582
Steele International Inc (PA)	7381	C	415 781-4300	16832
Steelriver Infrastructure Fund (HQ)	4924	C	415 848-5448	6282
Steelriver Infrastructure Part (PA)	6719	C	415 512-1515	12092
Stein & Lubin LLP	8111	E	415 981-0550	23583
Steinhart & Falconer LLP	8111	D	415 836-2500	23584
Sterling Consulting Group LLC	8742	D	415 248-7900	27668
Steve Silver Productions Inc	7922	D	415 421-4284	18436
Stone & Youngberg LLC (PA)	6211	C	415 445-2300	10079
Strevus Inc	7372	D	415 704-8182	15851
Stripe Payments Company	7389	D	888 963-8955	17507
Stubhub Inc (HQ)	7374	D	415 222-8400	16194
Successor To San Francisco	8748	D	415 749-2400	28063
Sunday Bazaar Inc	5023	E	415 621-0764	6888
Sunrise Senior Living Inc	8051	C	415 664-6264	20962
Sunset Scavenger Company	4953	B	415 330-1300	6566
Surplus Line Association Cal	8611	D	415 434-4900	25106
Sutter Bay Hospitals (HQ)	8062	A	415 600-6000	21940
Sutter Health	8742	D	415 600-3311	27675
Sutter Health	8011	B	415 345-0100	20085
Sutter Health	8011	C	415 731-6300	20086
Sutter Health	8011	C	415 600-0110	20088
Sutter Health	8711	C	415 600-1020	26081
Sutter Health	8741	C	415 600-4280	27242
Sutter Health	8011	C	415 647-8600	20108
Sutter Vsting Nrse Assn Hspice	8082	B	415 600-6200	22575
Swander Pace Capital LLC	8742	A	415 477-8500	27676
Swinerton Builders (HQ)	1541	C	415 421-2980	1468
Swinerton Incorporated (PA)	1542	C	415 421-2980	1684
Switchfly Inc (PA)	5045	C	415 541-9100	7198
Synergy Labs	7379	E	415 291-8080	16492
Sypartners LLC (HQ)	8748	D	415 536-6600	28066
T Y Lin International (HQ)	8711	C	415 291-3700	26085
T-Mobile Usa Inc	4812	C	415 440-5370	5416
Tacit Knowledge Inc	7379	C	415 694-4322	16497
Tactical Telesolutions Inc	7389	C	415 788-8808	17514
Talentburst Inc	7389	C	415 813-4011	17515
Talix Inc	7372	C	415 281-3100	15857
Taos Mountain Inc	7363	D	888 826-7686	14955
Tapjoy Inc (PA)	7311	D	415 766-6900	13926
Tariff Building Associates LP (PA)	6512	E	415 397-5572	11060
Taulia Inc (PA)	7371	D	415 376-8280	15491
Techsoup Global	8641	C	415 633-9325	25369
Tegsco LLC	7549	C	415 865-8200	17896
Telegraph Hill Partners Invest	8742	E	415 765-6980	27682
Telmate LLC	7389	C	415 300-4314	17527
Tenderloin Housing Clinic Inc	8099	C	415 771-2427	23074
Textainer Equipment Mgt US Ltd (DH)	7359	C	415 434-0551	14582
Textainer Group Holdings Ltd (HQ)	8741	C	415 434-0551	27250
Textaner Eqp Income Fund II LP	7359	C	415 434-0551	14583
The Charles Schwab Trust Co (HQ)	6733	E	415 371-0518	12205
Thermasource LLC (PA)	8711	D	707 523-2960	26095
Third & Mission Associates LLC	6531	E	415 341-8457	11873
Thismoment Inc	7371	C	415 200-4730	15500
Thomas Weisel Partners LLC (DH)	6211	B	415 364-2500	10082
Thompson/Brooks Inc	1521	E	415 581-2600	1271
Thomson Reuters (legal) Inc	8748	D	415 344-6000	28078
Thomson Reuters (markets) LLC	7389	D	415 677-2500	17530
Thornton Tomasetti Inc	8711	D	415 365-6900	26099
Thousandeyes Inc	7372	D	415 513-4526	15861
Ticketweb LLC	7999	C	415 901-0210	19293
Tides Inc (PA)	8399	D	415 561-6400	24986
Tides Center	7011	D	415 359-9401	13346
Tides Center	8399	D	415 673-0234	24987
Tides Network	8399	D	415 561-6400	24988
Time Inc	7313	D	415 982-5000	13981
Tm Financial Forensics LLC (PA)	8748	E	415 692-6350	28079
Todays Hotel Corporation (PA)	7011	D	415 441-4000	13347
Tomahawk Acquisition LLC	6726	A	415 765-6500	12151
Toolworks Inc (PA)	8331	E	415 733-0990	24396
Topdown Consulting Inc	8742	D	888 644-8445	27690
Topica Inc	4813	D	415 344-0800	5710
Towers Watson & Co	8742	C	415 733-4100	27691
Towns End Studios LLC	7371	C	415 802-7936	15508
Tradeshift Holdings Inc (HQ)	6719	D	800 381-3585	12094
Transamerica Cbo I Inc	6282	D	415 983-4000	10189
Transamerica Intl Holdings	6719	D	415 983-4000	12095
TransMontaigne PDT Svcs LLC	4789	D	415 576-2000	5247
Travana Inc	4724	D	415 919-4140	4976
Treadwell & Rollo Inc (DH)	8711	E	415 955-9040	26103
Triage Consulting Group (PA)	8742	B	415 512-9400	27698
Trifacta Inc	7374	D	415 429-7570	16202
Trinity Capital Corporation (DH)	6159	D	415 956-5174	9806
Triton Cont Intl Inc N Amer (DH)	7353	C	415 956-6311	14501
Troutman Sanders LLP	8111	D	415 477-5700	23600
True Ultimate Standards	7379	D	415 520-3400	16513
Truecar Inc	4813	C	415 821-8270	5711
Trulia Inc (HQ)	7374	B	415 648-4358	16203
Truste	4813	D	415 520-3490	5712
Turk & Eddy Associates LP	6513	D	415 474-6524	11218
Turner Construction Company	1542	D	415 705-8900	1701
Turner Duckworth LLC	7336	D	415 675-7777	14164
Tutor Perini Corporation	1542	C	415 638-6941	1706
Twilio Inc (PA)	7372	D	415 390-2337	15867
Twitter Inc (PA)	7375	C	415 222-9670	16266
TY Lin International Group (PA)	8711	C	415 291-3700	26108
U C S F School of Dentistry	8021	E	415 476-5609	20281
U C San Francisco Gynecology	8011	B	415 885-7788	20147
Uber Technologies Inc (DH)	7372	D	415 986-2715	15869
Ubi Soft Entertainment	7929	C	415 547-4000	18501
Ubisoft Holdings Inc (DH)	7371	C	415 547-4000	15514
UBS Financial Services Inc	6211	C	415 954-6700	10088
UBS Financial Services Inc	6211	C	415 398-6400	10091
UBS Financial Services Inc	6211	C	415 398-6400	10093
UBS Securities LLC	6211	C	415 352-5650	10095
Ucsf Aids Health Project	8322	D	415 476-3902	24263
United Behavioral Health (HQ)	8741	C	415 547-1403	27264
United Biosource LLC	0762	C	415 293-1340	727
United California Glass & Door	7699	D	415 824-8500	18028
United Parcel Service Inc OH	4215	D	415 252-4564	4451
United Way of Bay Area (PA)	8322	C	415 808-4300	24271
Unity Software Inc	7372	C	415 848-2533	15870
Universal Protection Svc LP	7381	C	415 759-5056	16844
University Cal San Francisco	8733	D	415 476-9000	26816
University Cal San Francisco	8062	C	415 476-1000	21994
University Cal San Francisco	8062	A	415 476-1000	21995
University Cal San Francisco	8062	A	415 476-7000	21996
University Cal San Francisco	8721	C	415 476-2075	26453
University Cal San Francisco	8011	D	415 353-3155	20164
University Cal San Francisco	8062	B	415 567-6600	21997
University Cal San Francisco	8011	C	415 353-2573	20165
University Cal San Francisco	8011	C	415 476-6880	20166
University of San Francisco	7389	C	415 502-8600	17573
University of San Francisco	7389	D	415 422-2028	17574
Univision Television Group Inc	4833	D	415 538-8000	5922
UPS Supply Chain Solutions Inc	4225	E	415 775-6644	4652
URS Group Inc	8711	D	415 896-5858	26120
URS Group Inc	8711	B	415 896-5858	26131
URS Holdings Inc (DH)	8711	B	415 774-2700	26132
Urs/Contrack-Pacer Forge JV	1629	C	415 774-2700	2094
Usag Ansbach Financial MGT Div	8741	D	210 466-1376	27268
Usag Rheinland Pfalz Fincl MGT	8741	D	210 466-1376	27269
Usag Vicenza Italy Dmwr F M D	8741	D	210 466-1376	27270
Usag Wiesbaden Fincl MGT Div	8741	D	210 466-1376	27271
Van Ness Hotel Inc	7011	D	415 673-4711	13375
Vegiworks Inc	5148	D	415 643-8686	8785
Velti Inc (PA)	7372	D	415 362-2077	15873
Venables/Bell & Partners LLC	7311	C	415 288-3300	13935
Vendini Inc (PA)	7371	D	415 693-9611	15522
Veritable Vegetable Inc	5148	D	415 641-3500	8786

GEOGRAPHIC SECTION

SAN JOSE, CA

	SIC	EMP	PHONE	ENTRY #
Veritiv Operating Company	5111	D	415 586-9160	8156
Verizon Business Global LLC	4813	D	415 606-3621	5718
Verticalresponse	8742	C	415 905-6880	27711
Vestek Systems Inc (DH)	7375	D	415 344-6000	16267
Veterans Health Administration	8011	D	415 750-2009	20203
Viking Asset Management LLC	6282	A	415 981-6500	10191
Vinson & Elkins LLP	8111	C	415 979-6900	23607
Vintrust Inc	4226	E	877 846-8787	4707
Viscira LLC	5045	D	415 848-8010	7209
Vista Equity Partners Fund Vi-	6722	A	415 765-6500	12130
Vladigor Investment Inc	7542	D	415 558-9274	17865
Volume Services Inc	7999	D	415 972-1500	19305
Vungle Inc	7311	C	415 800-1400	13940
W Hotel	7011	E	415 777-5300	13384
W R Hambrecht Co Inc (PA)	6211	D	415 551-8600	10096
W S B & Associates Inc (PA)	7381	D	415 864-3510	16851
Wachovia A Division Wells F	6021	A	415 571-2832	9428
Waiters On Wheels Inc (PA)	4212	C	415 452-6600	4090
Walkme Inc	7371	D	855 492-5563	15538
Walkup Mldia Klly Schoenberger	8111	E	415 981-7210	23608
Walt Disney Family Museum	8412	D	415 345-6800	25054
Walter E McGuire RE (PA)	6531	E	415 929-1500	11907
Walter E McGuire RE Inc	6531	E	415 296-0123	11908
Wartnick Chaber Harowitz	8111	D	415 986-5566	23611
Warwick California Corporation	7011	D	415 992-3809	13392
Watchit Media Inc	7812	C	702 740-1700	18203
Web Spiders Inc	7371	D	415 230-2202	15542
Weber Shandwick	8743	D	415 262-5600	27768
Webpass Inc	4813	D	415 233-4100	5731
Weisscomm Group Ltd (PA)	8748	D	415 362-5018	28098
Weisscomm Group Ltd	8742	D	415 362-5018	27718
Wells Fargo & Company (PA)	6021	B	866 249-3302	9429
Wells Fargo & Company	6029	C	801 246-1774	9565
Wells Fargo Advisors LLC	6211	D	415 291-1200	10099
Wells Fargo Bank National Assn (DH)	6021	A	415 396-7392	9431
Wells Fargo Bank National Assn	6021	E	415 396-6267	9432
Wells Fargo Bank National Assn	6021	D	415 396-6161	9433
Wells Fargo Bank National Assn	6021	B	415 777-9497	9445
Wells Fargo Bank National Assn	6021	A	415 394-4021	9456
Wells Fargo Bank National Assn	6021	C	415 222-1360	9458
Wells Fargo Intl Bond CIT	6722	C	415 396-4943	12131
Wells Fargo Securities LLC	6211	D	415 645-0800	10102
Wentworth Hauser & Violich Inc	6282	D	415 981-6911	10192
Wested (PA)	8733	C	415 565-3000	26822
Wested	8733	D	415 565-3000	26823
Western Alliance Bank	6022	E	415 230-4834	9538
Western Athletic Clubs Inc (DH)	7991	E	415 781-1874	18702
Western Messenger Service Inc	4212	C	415 487-4229	4094
Westside Lodge	8399	E	415 864-1515	24999
Weststar Marine Services Inc.	4499	C	415 495-3191	4776
Wetherby Asset Management	6282	D	415 399-9159	10194
Wfc Holdings Corp (HQ)	6021	E	415 396-7392	9464
Wideorbit Inc (PA)	7371	D	415 675-6700	15544
Wikia Inc	7375	D	415 762-0780	16269
Wikimedia Foundation Inc	8699	D	415 839-6885	25598
Wilbur-Ellis Company LLC (HQ)	5191	A	415 772-4000	9157
Wildenradt-Mcmurray Inc	5072	D	510 835-5500	7704
Will Perkins Inc	8712	D	415 896-0800	26267
Wilson Sonsini Goodrich & Rosa	8111	D	415 947-2000	23627
Wingz Inc	4813	E	415 420-2222	5734
Winkler Advertising Inc	7311	D	415 957-0242	13942
Winston Retail Solutions LLC (PA)	8742	E	415 558-9000	27721
Wise Commerce Inc	7371	D	855 469-4737	15546
Woodruff-Sawyer & Co (PA)	6411	C	415 391-2141	10945
Workforcelogic	7361	D	707 939-4300	14821
Wrns Studio	8712	D	415 489-2268	26270
Wsp USA Corp	8711	D	415 398-3833	26155
Wu Yee Childrens Services	8351	D	415 677-0100	24534
Wu Yee Childrens Services	8999	D	415 677-0100	28171
Xamarin Inc (PA)	7371	C	855 926-2746	15551
Xoom Corporation (DH)	6099	D	415 777-4800	9725
Yammer Inc	7379	C	415 796-7401	16532
Yellow Cab Cooperative Inc	4121	D	415 333-3333	3875
Yelp Inc (PA)	7375	D	415 908-3801	16272
Yhb San Francisco LLC.	7011	D	415 421-7500	13446
Yosemite Foundation	8641	D	415 434-1782	25437
Young & Rubicam Inc	7311	D	415 882-0600	13944
Young & Rubicam Inc	8743	D	415 591-4000	27769
Young Brdcstg of San Francisco	4833	C	415 441-4444	5931
Young Dowlin L	0174	E	760 397-4104	226
Young Electric Co	1731	C	415 648-3355	2800
Young Mens Christian Assnsf	8641	D	415 447-9602	25440
Young Mens Christian Assnsf	8641	D	415 447-9605	25441
Young Mens Christian Assnsf	8641	D	415 447-9645	25442
Young Mens Christian Assnsf	8641	D	415 752-0790	25444

	SIC	EMP	PHONE	ENTRY #
Young Mens Christian Assnsf	8641	D	415 421-5721	25445
Young Mens Christian Assoc SF	8641	D	415 831-4093	25448
Young Mens Christian Assoc SF (PA)	8641	E	415 777-9622	25450
Young Mens Christian Assoc SF	8641	D	415 666-9622	25451
Young Mens Christian Assoc SF	8641	D	415 957-9622	25452
Young Mens Christian Assoc SF	8641	D	415 885-0460	25453
Yourpeople Inc	6411	A	415 798-9086	10948
Zelle Hofmann Voelbel Masn LLP	8111	E	415 693-0700	23636
Zendesk Inc (PA)	7372	C	415 418-7506	15884
Zephyr Health Inc	7374	D	415 529-7649	16213
Zignal Labs Inc	7371	D	415 683-7871	15560
Zinio Systems Inc	7372	D	415 494-2700	15885
Zoe Holding Company Inc	8999	C	415 421-4900	28172
Zoosk Inc	4813	D	415 728-9543	5739
Zurich American Insurance Co	6411	D	415 538-7100	10949
Zvents Inc	7311	E	408 376-7346	13949
Zynga Inc (PA)	7372	C	855 449-9642	15886
Airport Commisions	4581	A	650 821-5000	4897
Alliance Ground Intl LLC	4581	D	650 821-0855	4899
American Airlines Inc	4512	B	650 877-6000	4788
Imperial Parking (us) LLC	7521	D	650 877-0430	17720
Sfo Shuttle Bus Inc	4111	C	650 877-0430	3717
Signature Flight Support Corp	4581	D	650 877-6800	4935
Singapore Airlines Cargo Pte	4512	C	650 876-7363	4819
Swissport Usa Inc	4581	C	650 821-6220	4942
Swissport Usa Inc	4581	C	571 214-7068	4943
Thrifty Car Rental	7514	C	415 788-8111	17695
United Airlines Inc	4512	C	650 634-4209	4827
United Airlines Inc	4512	C	650 634-7800	4831
United Airlines Inc	4512	C	650 634-4469	4835
United Airlines Inc	4512	C	650 634-2772	4837

SAN GABRIEL, CA - Los Angeles County

	SIC	EMP	PHONE	ENTRY #
Alderwood Inc	8059	D	626 289-4439	21130
Cal Southern Services	7213	D	626 281-5942	13540
Facey Medical Foundation	8099	D	626 576-0800	22961
Fernview Convalescent Hospital	8051	D	626 285-3131	20569
Hilton Worldwide Inc	7011	C	626 270-2700	12733
Information & Referral Fed Los	7299	D	626 350-1841	13768
Life Care Centers of America	8051	D	626 289-5365	20732
Longwood Management Corp	8059	D	626 289-3763	21300
Normans Nursery Inc (PA)	5193	E	626 289-9795	9205
Park Cleaners Inc (PA)	7213	D	626 281-5942	13568
Pine Grove Healthcare	8051	D	626 285-3131	20846
San Gabriel Ambulatory Sugery	8011	A	626 300-5300	19944
San Gabriel Country Club	7997	D	626 287-9671	19057
San Gabriel Nursery and Flor (PA)	0181	D	626 286-0787	317
San Gbriel Vly Med Ctr Fndtion	8062	A	626 289-5454	21847
San Marino Manor	8059	E	626 446-5263	21366
Temple City Youth Dev Fund	8641	D	626 548-5085	25371

SAN GERONIMO, CA - Marin County

	SIC	EMP	PHONE	ENTRY #
National Golf Properties Inc	7997	D	415 488-4030	19012

SAN JACINTO, CA - Riverside County

	SIC	EMP	PHONE	ENTRY #
AT&T Corp	4813	D	951 654-2081	5484
Healthcare MGT Systems Inc	8051	D	951 654-9347	20660
Millenia Development	1521	E	951 660-5691	1224
Physicians For Healthy Hospita	8062	C	951 652-2811	21799
Riverside-San Bernardino	8011	D	951 654-0803	19924
San Jacinto Unified School	6519	D	951 654-7769	11264
Soboba Band Luiseno Indians	7389	A	951 665-1000	17495
Valley Wide Recreation Pk Dst (PA)	7999	D	951 654-1505	19302

SAN JOSE, CA - Santa Clara County

	SIC	EMP	PHONE	ENTRY #
2wire Inc (DH)	4813	C	678 473-2907	5438
4 CS Council	8351	C	408 487-0747	24408
40 Hrs Inc	7361	A	408 414-0158	14593
4d Inc	7371	C	408 557-4600	14991
8x8 Inc (PA)	4813	C	408 727-1885	5449
A & A Mechanical Contractors	1711	D	408 225-1321	2099
A A A Furnace AC Co	1711	D	408 293-4717	2101
A C Freight Systems Inc (PA)	4213	D	408 392-8900	4096
A Is For Apple Inc	8049	D	877 991-0009	20303
A10 Networks Inc (PA)	7373	C	408 325-8668	15891
Abbott Stringham Lynch Acctg	8721	D	408 377-8700	26286
ABF Freight System Inc	4213	E	408 435-8550	4097
Able Exterminators Inc	7342	D	408 251-6500	14171
Accenture LLP	8742	D	408 817-2100	27298
Accenture LLP	8742	D	650 213-2000	27299
Acer America Corporation (DH)	7379	D	408 533-7700	16313
Achiever Christian Pre-Schl E	8351	E	408 264-2345	24410
Acme Building Maintenance Co	7349	D	408 526-5939	14212
Acronics Systems Inc	8711	C	408 432-0888	25614
Action Day Nrseries Prmry Plus	8351	E	408 266-8952	24412
Adminstrtive Office of US Crts	8322	D	408 535-5200	23643
Adobe Systems Incorporated (PA)	7372	A	408 536-6000	15572

Employment Codes: A=Over 500 employees, B=251-500, C=101-250, D=51-100, E=45-50

2017 Directory of California Wholesalers and Services Companies

© Mergent Inc. 1-800-342-5647

SAN JOSE, CA — GEOGRAPHIC SECTION

Company	SIC	EMP	PHONE	ENTRY #
Advanced Discovery Inc	7379	D	408 294-0091	16315
Advantage Logistics Inc	4731	C	408 943-6300	5015
Advantel Incorporated (PA)	7629	D	408 954-5100	17929
Advent Group Ministries Inc	8361	D	408 281-0708	24541
Aecom Usa Inc	8748	C	408 392-0670	27817
Aerospace & Marine Intl	8999	E	408 360-0440	28108
Air Systems Inc	1711	D	408 280-1666	2113
Airdrome Orchards Inc (PA)	0174	E	408 297-6461	213
Airgas USA LLC	5084	D	408 998-6380	7817
Al - Amir Group Llc	4911	D	408 505-9458	6105
Alfa Tech Cnslting Engners Inc (PA)	8711	D	408 487-1200	25647
All Fab Prcsion Sheetmetal Inc	1761	D	408 279-1099	3138
Alliance Credit Union (PA)	6062	D	408 445-3386	9650
Alliedbarton Security Svcs LLC	7381	B	408 954-8274	16548
Almaden Golf & Country Club	7997	D	408 323-4812	18846
Almaden Valley Athletic Club	7997	D	408 445-4900	18847
Alsco Inc	7213	C	408 279-2345	13517
American Airlines Inc	4512	A	408 291-3800	4787
American Cancer Soc Cal Div	8399	E	408 265-5535	24867
American Funding	6163	D	408 269-4238	9912
American Metal & Iron Inc	5093	D	408 452-0777	8061
American Residential Svcs LLC	1711	B	650 856-1612	2133
American Residential Svcs LLC	7699	D	408 435-3810	17960
Amtel Inc	8748	E	408 615-0522	27832
AON Consulting Inc	8742	D	408 321-2500	27326
Aopen America Incorporated	5045	D	408 586-1200	7092
Apigee Corporation	7373	B	408 343-7300	15902
Appcelerator Inc (HQ)	7371	E	650 200-4255	15018
Apria Healthcare LLC	7352	D	408 383-4400	14472
Apttus Corporation	7379	D	650 722-1619	16323
Apx Inc (PA)	8748	D	408 899-3300	27834
Aqualine Piping Inc	1711	D	408 745-7100	2148
Aquantia Corp (PA)	7389	D	408 228-8300	17000
Aquinas Corporation	8051	C	408 248-7100	20380
Aragon Commercial Ldscpg Inc	0782	C	408 998-0600	808
Aramark Unf & Career AP LLC	7213	D	408 243-9824	13535
Arcadia Management Service Co	6531	E	408 266-4440	11302
Ariosa Diagnostics Inc	8731	C	408 229-7500	26478
Asian Amercn Recovery Svcs Inc	8069	C	408 271-3900	22114
Associated Students Cdc	8351	A	408 924-6988	24415
AT&T Corp	8999	D	408 729-8400	28118
AT&T Corp	4813	D	408 871-3870	5493
AT&T Services Inc	4813	D	408 973-7504	5560
Ati Inc	7379	E	408 942-1780	16327
Atkinson & Mullen Travel Inc	4724	B	408 452-0202	4957
Atria Senior Living Group Inc	6513	D	408 266-1660	11090
Avnet Inc	5065	D	408 501-3925	7530
Axolotl Inc	7372	E	408 920-0800	15593
Bad Boys Bail Bonds Inc (PA)	7389	D	408 298-3333	17018
Bae Systems Land Armaments LP	8711	A	408 289-0111	25678
Barbaccia Properties	6515	D	408 225-1010	11244
Bay Area Surgical MGT LLC	8011	E	408 297-3432	19366
Baynote Inc	7375	D	866 921-0919	16220
Baysand Inc	5065	D	408 960-8263	7532
Bdo Usa LLP	8721	D	408 278-0220	26295
Bea Systems Inc (HQ)	7371	A	650 506-7000	15051
Beacon Roofing Supply Inc	5033	D	408 293-5947	7007
Belmont Bruns Construction Inc	1542	D	408 977-1708	1502
Big Bulb Ideas Inc	7371	E	408 888-2346	15053
Biggs Cardosa Associates Inc (PA)	8711	D	408 296-5515	25688
Bill Brown Construction Co	1522	D	408 297-3738	1296
Bill Brown Construction Co	1521	D	408 297-3738	1134
Bizmatics Inc (PA)	7372	E	408 873-3030	15600
Bkf Engineers	8711	B	408 467-9100	25690
Blach Construction Company (PA)	1541	D	408 244-7100	1406
Blackarrow Inc (HQ)	7371	D	408 642-6400	15056
Blossom Valley Cnstr Inc	0782	D	408 993-0766	814
Brandvia Alliance Inc	5199	D	408 955-0500	9248
Breakout Prison Outreach	8322	D	408 702-2405	23694
Brilliant General Maintinc	7349	C	408 287-6708	14240
Brinks Incorporated	7381	C	408 436-7717	16585
Bristlecone Incorporated	7371	A	650 386-4000	15067
Brocade Cmmnctions Systems Inc	8748	D	408 333-4300	27855
Brookdale Lving Cmmunities Inc	8361	C	408 445-7770	24570
Buckles-Smith Electric Company (PA)	5084	D	408 280-7777	7828
Burr Pilger Mayer Inc	8721	E	408 961-6355	26302
C & O Painting Inc	1721	E	408 279-8011	2432
C H Reynolds Electric Inc	1731	D	408 436-9280	2545
C R S Drywall Inc	1742	D	408 998-4360	2870
C W Driver Incorporated	1521	D	650 308-4001	1145
Caden TV	7622	E	408 275-1908	17907
Cadence Design Systems Inc (PA)	7372	A	408 943-1234	15614
Cadent Inc	7373	C	408 470-1000	15912
California Drywall Co (PA)	1742	C	408 292-7500	2871
California Schl Employees Assn (PA)	8631	C	408 473-1000	25169
California United Mech Inc (PA)	1711	B	408 232-9000	2174
California Waste Solutions Inc (PA)	4953	D	510 832-8111	6452
California Water Service Co (HQ)	4941	C	408 367-8200	6319
Cambium Networks Inc	4899	C	847 640-3809	6062
Careage Inc	8051	E	408 238-9751	20438
Carlton Senior Living Inc	6411	D	408 972-1400	10663
Casavina Foundation Corp	8051	C	408 238-9751	20440
Catholic Charities	8011	E	408 468-0100	19412
Catholic Charities of Santa CL (PA)	8322	C	408 468-0100	23712
Cavendish Kinetics Inc	5065	C	408 240-7370	7542
Cbre Inc	6162	D	408 453-7400	9827
Cbsj Financial Corporation	7322	D	408 792-4600	14024
Ccintegration Inc	8731	E	408 228-1314	26493
Center For Employment Training (PA)	8331	D	408 287-7924	24321
Central Valley Clinic Inc	8093	E	408 885-5400	22677
Ch2m Hill Inc	8712	D	408 436-4936	26175
Challenger Schools	8351	E	408 266-7073	24426
Chelbay Schuler & Chelbay (PA)	6371	D	408 288-4400	10547
Chester C Lehmann Co Inc (PA)	5063	D	408 293-5818	7426
Child Development Incorporated (PA)	8351	E	408 556-7300	24431
Christian Counseling Centers	8011	D	408 559-1115	19437
Cintas Corporation No 2	7218	D	408 292-6700	13618
Ciphermax Inc (PA)	8742	D	408 382-6500	27381
Cisco Ironport Systems LLC (HQ)	7372	B	650 989-6500	15620
City II Enterprises Inc	0782	E	408 275-1200	825
City of San Jose	7389	B	408 277-5277	17079
City of San Jose	8422	D	408 794-6400	25061
City of San Jose	4581	B	408 392-3600	4910
City of San Jose	7011	C	408 226-6765	12523
Ckl Construction Inc	1522	B	408 244-7042	1302
Clarion Hotel San Jose Airport	7011	D	408 453-5340	12526
Clark Richardson and Biskup	8711	D	408 931-6030	25745
Classic Custom Vacations Inc	4725	C	800 221-3949	4989
Classic Parking Inc	7521	B	408 278-1444	17717
Classic Vacations LLC	4725	C	800 221-3949	4990
Cloudike Inc	7379	D	609 910-0911	16337
Coassure Inc	8748	C	408 244-0400	27883
Coast Insulation Contrs Inc (DH)	1742	C	386 304-2222	2880
Coldwell Banker Prof Group	6531	D	408 383-1044	11411
Coldwell Banker Real Estate	6531	D	408 491-1600	11415
Colliers Parrish Intl Inc	6531	D	408 282-3800	11447
Comcast Corporation	4841	D	408 216-2878	5966
Command Security Corporation	7381	D	650 574-0911	16605
Common Ground Ldscp MGT Inc	0782	E	408 278-9847	828
Commonwealth Central Credit Un (PA)	6062	D	408 531-3100	9661
Computer Task Group Inc	7371	C	408 573-6070	15100
Computer Task Group Inc	7371	B	800 992-5350	15101
Corventis Inc (PA)	7375	D	408 790-9300	16225
Creative Security Company Inc	7381	B	408 295-2600	16615
Crestwood Behavioral Hlth Inc	8361	D	408 275-1067	24621
Cse Holdings Inc (DH)	5087	D	408 436-1907	7966
Cupertino Electric Inc (PA)	1731	B	408 808-8000	2568
Cws Utility Services Corp	8999	B	408 367-8200	28126
Cypress Security LLC	7381	B	408 217-6063	16619
Dapcon Inc	1721	B	408 573-7200	2439
De Mattei Construction Inc	1521	D	408 295-7516	1164
Della Maggiore Tile Inc	1743	D	408 286-3991	3011
Deloitte & Touche LLP	8721	B	408 704-4000	26324
Deloitte Tax LLP	8721	B	408 704-4000	26329
Dga Services Inc (PA)	4214	D	408 232-4800	4341
DH Smith Company Inc	1742	D	408 532-7617	2886
Diablo Landscape Inc	0782	D	408 487-9620	840
Digex Inc	4813	E	408 468-5000	5590
Dinyari Construction Inc	1522	E	408 289-5401	1307
Doubletree LLC	7011	B	408 453-4000	12592
Doudell Trucking Company (PA)	4213	D	408 263-7300	4141
Dpr Construction Inc	1541	E	408 370-2322	1420
Dt Research Inc (PA)	8731	D	408 934-6220	26506
Dtex Systems Inc	7371	E	408 418-3786	15150
Durham School Services	8999	D	408 448-0740	28128
Echelon Security Inc	8748	D	408 436-8844	27904
Econosoft Inc	7371	D	408 324-1203	15154
Edgewater Networks Inc	4813	D	408 351-7200	5594
Ees Residential Group Homes	8361	D	408 265-8780	24641
Efuel LLC	5172	D	408 280-5235	9017
Eileen Shi	8742	D	866 777-6104	27421
Ek Health Services Inc	8742	C	408 973-0888	27422
El Camino Hospital	8071	C	650 940-7000	22212
Elastica Inc	7371	D	925 699-6714	15158
Emor Consulting Inc	8733	D	408 505-0453	26755
Empress Care Center	8059	D	408 287-0616	21211
Emulex Communications Corp	7372	E	408 434-6064	15656
Encore Software Services Inc	7379	D	408 573-7337	16364
Energy Livermore Off US Dept	8733	B	408 267-1413	26763
Ensighten Inc (HQ)	8742	D	650 249-4712	27424

GEOGRAPHIC SECTION

SAN JOSE, CA

	SIC	EMP	PHONE	ENTRY #
Epicentro Advertising Mktg Svc	7311	E	408 453-0353	13845
Epson Portland Inc	7373	E	408 678-0100	15943
Eric Stark Interiors Inc	1742	D	408 441-6136	2894
Ericsson Inc	7373	A	408 750-5000	15944
Ericsson Inc	7373	A	408 597-3600	15945
Ernest E Pestana Inc	1623	D	408 432-8110	1929
Ernst & Young LLP	8721	A	408 947-5500	26341
Estes Express Lines Inc	4213	E	408 286-3894	4150
Etrigue Corp	7371	E	408 490-2900	15174
European Paving Designs Inc	1721	D	408 283-5230	2442
Exis Inc	5065	E	408 944-4600	7563
F-Secure Inc	5045	E	408 938-6700	7131
Facility Masters Inc (PA)	7349	C	408 436-9090	14295
Fair Isaac Corporation (PA)	7372	C	408 535-1500	15661
Family and Children Services	8748	D	408 292-9353	27921
Far Western Graphics Inc	7334	D	408 481-9777	14117
Fcs Software Solutions Limited	7371	D	408 324-1203	15182
Federal Express Corporation	4215	A	800 463-3339	4411
Fedex Ground Package Sys Inc	4213	B	408 943-9960	4180
Fertility & Reproductive	8011	D	408 358-2500	19526
First Alarm SEC & Patrol Inc (HQ)	7381	C	831 685-1110	16641
Flexera Software LLC	7371	D	408 642-3700	15188
Flextronics Logistics USA Inc	4783	A	408 576-7000	5199
Fluor Enterprises Inc	8711	D	408 256-0853	25812
Fluor Facility & Plant Svcs	7349	C	408 256-1333	14299
Forescout Technologies Inc (PA)	7371	D	408 213-3191	15192
Foundtion For Hispanic Educatn (PA)	8641	C	408 585-5022	25256
Fourth Street Bowl	7933	E	408 453-5555	18519
FPI Management Inc	8741	E	408 267-3952	27029
Freescale Semiconductor Inc	5065	C	408 518-5500	7568
Frontiir Corporation	4813	C	510 996-2071	5613
Fujitsu America Inc	7373	D	408 746-8419	15952
Fusionone Inc	7371	D	408 282-1200	15197
Future Paging & Cellular Inc	4812	C	408 238-8833	5398
Gaia Interactive Inc	4813	C	408 573-8800	5615
Galli Produce Company	5148	D	408 436-6100	8732
Garden City Inc	7999	A	408 244-3333	19216
Gardner Family Care Corp	8093	C	408 935-3906	22731
Gardner Family Hlth Netwrk Inc (PA)	8093	E	408 918-2682	22732
Gda Technologies Inc (HQ)	8711	D	408 753-1191	25830
GE Ionics Inc	5074	D	408 360-5900	7721
Geek Squad Inc	7379	D	408 297-2520	16387
Geico Corporation	6411	C	408 286-4342	10725
General George W Sliney Basha	8641	D	408 296-3423	25258
George M Robinson & Co (PA)	1711	D	510 632-7017	2238
Giarretto Institute	8322	E	408 453-7616	23993
Gilbane Building Company	8741	D	408 660-4400	27037
Glenrock Group	7992	D	408 323-9900	18742
Global Eqp Svcs & Mfg Inc	5046	C	408 441-0682	7216
Global Industry Analysts Inc	8732	A	408 528-9966	26671
Global Infotech Corporation	8748	A	408 567-0600	27933
Globallogic Inc (PA)	7371	E	408 273-8900	15205
Golden Living LLC	8051	C	408 923-7232	20618
Golden Living LLC	8361	E	408 255-5555	24669
Good Samaritan Hospital LP (DH)	8062	A	408 559-2011	21584
Goodwill of Silicon Valley (PA)	7363	D	408 998-5774	14884
Graham Contractors Inc	1611	D	408 293-9516	1776
Grand Intelligence LLC	7371	E	408 954-7368	15212
Grant Thornton LLP	8721	E	408 275-9000	26356
Green Valley Corporation (PA)	1542	E	408 287-0246	1558
Greenbriar Homes Communities	1531	D	510 497-8200	1365
Greenwaste Recovery Inc	4953	E	408 283-4804	6489
Greenwaste Recovery Inc (PA)	4953	D	408 283-4800	6490
Greystone Plastering Inc	1742	D	408 298-5934	2905
H M H Engineers	8711	D	408 487-2200	25847
Hacienda Involved Parent Staff	8641	D	408 535-6259	25269
Harding Mktg Cmmunications Inc (PA)	7336	E	408 345-4545	14148
Hayes Mansion Conference Ctr	7011	C	408 226-3200	12695
HCA Inc	8062	D	408 729-2801	21593
Hd Supply Construction Supply	5072	E	408 428-2000	7687
Health & Rehabilitation Center	8051	E	408 377-9275	20655
Health Trust (PA)	8621	D	408 513-8700	25136
Healthright 360	8093	C	408 934-1110	22741
Heavenly Construction Inc	1799	D	408 723-4954	3529
Hensel Phelps Construction Co	1542	C	408 452-1800	1568
Heritage Bank of Commerce (HQ)	6022	D	408 947-6900	9501
Herman Health Care Center	8051	C	408 269-0701	20669
Herman Sanitarium	8051	C	408 269-0701	20670
Hetrosys LLC	8748	D	408 270-0240	27943
Home Depot USA Inc	4225	A	408 971-4890	4570
Home Port Inc	6514	E	408 377-4134	11235
Homeguard Incorporated (PA)	7342	D	408 993-1900	14186
Hope Services (PA)	8331	E	408 284-2850	24349
Hopkins & Carley A Law Corp (PA)	8111	D	408 286-9800	23312
Host International Inc	7011	C	408 294-1702	12778
Hsbc Finance Corporation	6141	C	408 796-3600	9751
Hyatt Corporation	7011	B	408 453-3006	12820
Hyatt Equities LLC	7011	B	408 993-1234	12824
Ice Delivery Systems Inc	4212	C	408 640-4625	4027
Icom Mechanical Inc	1711	C	408 292-4968	2248
Ics Integrated Comm Systems	1731	D	408 491-6000	2618
Imerys Filtration Minerals Inc (DH)	1499	D	805 562-0200	1115
Immersion Medical Inc	8111	D	408 467-1900	23317
Incline Incorporated	7361	C	408 454-1140	14682
Indosys Corporation	7361	C	408 705-1953	14683
Inspira Inc	7371	E	408 247-9500	15238
Integra Telecom Inc	7389	D	408 758-7700	17243
Interface Masters Tech Inc	8748	E	408 441-9341	27952
International Bus Mchs Corp	7371	A	408 463-2000	15248
International Bus Mchs Corp	5044	C	408 452-4800	7056
International Bus Mchs Corp	8731	B	408 927-1080	26538
Intero Real Estate Svcs Inc	6531	C	408 574-5000	11589
Intero Real Estate Svcs Inc	6531	E	408 558-3600	11590
Invesmart Inc	6411	D	408 961-2800	10750
Iscs Inc	7371	C	408 362-3000	15259
Ixsystems Inc	7372	D	408 943-4100	15719
J & J Air Conditioning Inc	1711	D	408 920-0662	2256
J T R Company Inc	4225	E	408 293-3272	4579
Jacobs Engineering Group Inc	8711	D	408 995-3257	25900
Jade Global Inc	7373	D	408 899-7200	15977
Jan Marini Skin Research Inc	5122	D	408 620-3600	8266
Jass & Associates Inc	7379	B	408 436-1624	16418
Jensen Corp Landscape Contr	0782	C	408 446-4881	876
Jensen Corporate Holdings Inc (PA)	0782	C	408 446-1118	877
Jensen Landscape Services Inc	0782	C	408 446-1118	878
Jeppesen Dataplan Inc	7375	D	408 961-2825	16248
JF Shea Construction Inc	1521	B	408 225-1475	1196
John A Maida Enterprises	5112	D	408 254-3100	8170
Johns Dog Food Distributing	5149	D	408 275-1943	8862
Josephines Prof Staffing (PA)	7361	C	408 943-0111	14689
Kaiser Foundation Hospitals	8082	A	408 361-2100	22489
Kaiser Foundation Hospitals	8062	B	408 972-6010	21642
Kaiser Foundation Hospitals	8011	A	408 972-7000	19594
Kaiser Foundation Hospitals	8011	A	408 972-3000	19675
Kaiser Foundation Hospitals	6324	D	408 972-3376	10346
Kaiser Foundation Hospitals	8062	C	408 972-6700	21671
Keenan & Associates	6411	C	408 441-0754	10760
Kidango Inc	8099	C	408 297-9044	22986
Kinder Mrgan Lqds Trminals LLC	4226	C	408 435-7399	4696
Kindred Healthcare Inc	8052	C	408 297-2078	21088
Kranem Corporation	7372	C	650 319-6743	15728
Krty Ltd A Cal Ltd Partnr	4832	E	408 293-8030	5799
Kusumoto Farms	0171	D	408 927-8348	116
Landcare USA LLC	0782	C	408 727-4099	899
Landmark Protection Inc	5136	C	408 293-6300	8349
Lark Avenue Car Wash	7542	D	408 371-2565	17848
Lavante Inc	8721	E	408 754-0505	26393
Le Technology Inc	5065	C	310 845-5838	7593
Lee Bros Foodservices Inc (PA)	5141	D	408 275-0700	8491
Leed International LLC	8748	E	650 861-7883	27972
Legacy Transportation Svcs Inc (PA)	4214	E	408 294-9800	4357
Lg Display America Inc (HQ)	5065	D	408 350-0190	7597
Liberty Healthcare of Oklahoma	8051	D	408 532-7677	20723
Lightbeam Power Company Gridle	1623	D	800 696-7114	1960
Lightbeam Pwr Gridley Main LLC	1623	D	800 696-7114	1961
Lincoln Glen Manor	8059	C	408 267-1492	21291
Liveworld Inc (PA)	4813	D	408 564-6286	5648
Logitech Ice At San Jose	7999	E	408 279-6000	19239
Loglogic Inc	7371	D	408 215-5900	15284
Loring Ward Advisor Services	6282	D	408 260-3109	10159
LPA Inc	8712	D	408 780-7200	26226
Lumenis Inc (HQ)	5047	C	408 764-3000	7274
Lwi Financial Inc	8741	E	408 260-3100	27119
Lwi Financial Inc	8742	E	408 217-8886	27515
Lynx Software Technologies Inc (PA)	7372	C	408 979-3900	15737
M Arthur Gensler Jr Assoc Inc	8712	E	408 885-8100	26228
M Arthur Gensler Jr Assoc Inc	8712	C	408 858-8100	26229
M K Technical Services Inc	7363	E	408 528-0401	14902
Macdonald Mott LLC	8711	D	408 321-5900	25947
Magma Design Automation Inc (HQ)	7371	B	408 565-7500	15286
MAI Construction Inc	1521	E	408 434-9800	1211
Mapr Technologies Inc (PA)	7371	D	408 428-9472	15289
Mariner Health Care Inc	8051	D	408 298-3950	20761
Mariner Health Care Inc	8051	E	408 377-9275	20770
Marquez Brothers Advg Agcy	7389	D	408 926-2700	17314
Marsh USA Inc	6411	D	408 467-5600	10778
Mass Precision Inc	7532	D	408 451-0929	17761
Mavenir Intl Holdings Inc	7371	D	408 855-2900	15295
McManis Faulkner A Prof Corp	8111	E	408 279-8700	23429
ME Fox & Company Inc	5181	D	408 435-8510	9073

SAN JOSE, CA — GEOGRAPHIC SECTION

Company	SIC	EMP	PHONE	ENTRY #
Meals On Wheels-The Health Tr	8322	E	408 961-9870	24081
Megapath Group Inc (HQ)	4813	C	408 952-6400	5656
Megapath Group Inc	4813	C	408 324-1353	5657
Meriwest Credit Union (PA)	6061	C	408 363-3200	9613
Merrill Lynch Pierce Fenner	6211	E	408 283-3000	10041
MGM Drywall Inc	1742	D	408 292-4085	2931
Mike Rovner Construction Inc	1521	C	408 453-4061	1223
Mission Truck Sales	7515	D	408 436-2920	17704
Mobica US Inc	7373	A	650 450-6654	15996
Mobilygen Corporation	5065	D	408 601-1000	7608
Momentum For Mental Health	8399	D	408 261-7777	24943
Montavista Software LLC (HQ)	7371	D	408 572-8000	15314
Monterey Bay Masonry Inc	1741	E	408 289-8295	2828
Morgan Stanley & Co LLC	6211	E	408 947-2200	10058
Mt Eden Nursery Co Inc (PA)	6519	E	408 213-5777	11259
Mv Transportation Inc	8322	C	408 292-3600	24093
N A Aricent Inc	7371	E	408 324-1800	15319
Nagarro Inc (PA)	7373	D	408 436-6170	16000
Navisite LLC	4813	E	408 965-9000	5664
ND Systems Inc	7319	D	408 776-0085	14004
Nds Surgical Imaging LLC	5047	C	408 776-0085	7284
Neals Janitorial Service	7349	E	408 271-9944	14367
Netapp Inc	7373	C	408 822-3803	16007
Netcontinuum Inc	7382	D	408 961-5600	16904
Netronix Integration Inc	1731	C	408 573-1444	2664
New Age Electric Inc	1731	D	408 279-8787	2667
New York Life Insurance Co	6411	D	408 392-9782	10799
Nexsentio	7349	E	408 392-9249	14368
Nexsentio Inc	7349	E	408 392-9249	14369
Next Door Sltons To Dom Vlence	8399	D	408 279-2962	24947
Nor-Cal Moving Services	4214	D	408 954-1175	4367
Normandin Auto Brokers	5012	C	408 266-2824	6692
Normandins	7538	C	877 330-0391	17807
Northbound LLC	8742	C	408 245-6500	27570
Northrop Grmmn Spce & Mssn Sys (HQ)	7373	A	703 280-2900	16012
Northwest Landscape Maint Co	0782	E	408 298-6489	925
Nsg Technology Inc (DH)	7629	C	408 547-8700	17938
Nth Connect Telecom Inc	7389	D	408 922-0800	17370
Nu Horizons Electronics Corp	5065	E	408 946-4154	7614
Nutanix Inc (PA)	7373	A	408 216-8360	16019
Nuvoton Technology Corp Amer	5065	D	408 544-1718	7615
O C McDonald Co Inc	1711	C	408 295-2182	2307
Ocadian Care Centers LLC	8051	E	408 295-2665	20823
OConnor Hospital (PA)	8062	A	408 947-2500	21767
OConnor Hospital	8011	D	408 947-2990	19789
Oconnor Hospital Radiology	8011	D	408 947-2992	19790
Olympus America Inc	5047	B	408 935-5000	7289
Oocl (usa) Inc	4731	D	408 576-6543	5138
Opera San Jose Inc	7922	D	408 437-4450	18421
Operating Engineers Local Un 3	6061	D	408 995-5095	9618
Operatix Inc	7389	D	408 332-5796	17380
Oracle Corporation	7372	B	408 276-3822	15793
Oracle Corporation	7372	B	408 390-8623	15796
Oracle Corporation	7372	B	925 694-6258	15800
Orchard Supply Company LLC	5099	D	408 269-1550	8132
Outreach & Escort Inc (PA)	4111	D	408 436-2865	3689
Pacific Groservice Inc	5194	D	408 727-4826	9235
Pacific West Security Inc	7382	D	801 748-1034	16909
Packet Design Inc	7371	D	408 490-1000	15364
Pan American Body Shop Inc	7532	D	408 289-8745	17764
Panasonic Corp North America	5064	D	201 348-7000	7504
Parsons Corporation	1611	D	626 440-2000	1843
Pathway Society	8093	E	408 244-1834	22795
Paypal Inc (HQ)	4813	C	877 981-2163	5682
Pds Tech Inc	7361	A	408 916-4848	14721
Penske Automotive Group Inc	7513	E	408 293-7688	17645
Permanente Medical Group Inc	8011	D	408 972-6883	19842
Pernixdata Inc	7371	D	408 724-8413	15375
Petalon Landscape MGT Inc	0782	D	408 453-3998	934
Phase 3 Communications Inc	7373	D	408 946-9011	16029
Phoenix RE Investment Co	6531	D	408 213-8600	11747
Physical Rehabilitation Netwrk	8049	E	408 570-0510	20339
Piedmont Transfer & Storage	4213	E	408 288-5600	4244
Pivot Systems Inc	7371	C	408 435-1000	15381
Pixim Inc	7373	D	650 934-0550	16032
Planned Prnthood Mar Monte Inc	8093	C	408 287-7529	22806
Planned Prnthood Mar Monte Inc (PA)	8093	D	408 287-7532	22807
Platinum Facilities Services	7349	D	408 998-9004	14390
Platinum Roofing Inc	1761	D	408 280-5028	3204
Playmar Inc	5032	D	408 324-1930	6993
Plaza Home Mortgage Inc	6211	D	408 573-7880	10069
Plda Inc	6519	D	408 273-4528	11263
Plum Healthcare Group LLC	8051	D	408 998-8447	20852
Polaris Networks Incorporated	7371	D	408 625-7273	15388
Polycom Inc (PA)	8741	C	408 586-6000	27168
Pragiti Inc	8748	D	408 891-7423	28020
Pricewaterhousecoopers LLP	8721	A	408 817-3700	26425
Principal Financial Group Inc	6311	D	408 273-7500	10219
Prolinx Services Inc	7361	D	408 689-5777	14738
Propel Software Corporation	7379	C	408 571-6300	16465
Pta California Congress of Par	8641	E	408 928-7900	25321
Ptc Inc	7371	E	408 434-8500	15401
Pulse Secure LLC (HQ)	7371	D	408 372-9600	15403
Qal Affiliate Inc	6531	E	408 238-5111	11781
Qct LLC	7373	A	510 270-6111	16035
Quail Hill Investments Inc	6798	C	408 978-9000	12270
Quantum Secure Inc	7373	D	408 453-1008	16036
Quantumscape Corporation	8742	D	408 452-2051	27607
Quest Dgnstics Clncal Labs Inc	8071	B	408 975-1015	22264
R E Cuddie Co	1752	D	408 998-1250	3129
R L Safety Inc	8322	E	408 557-0887	24143
R W Garcia Co Inc (PA)	5145	C	408 275-1597	8625
R-Bros Painting Inc	1721	E	408 291-6820	2480
Race Street Foods Inc (PA)	5144	C	408 294-6161	8603
Radonich Corp	1731	D	408 275-8888	2694
Ranch Golf Club	7992	D	408 270-0557	18775
Rando AAA Hvac Inc	1711	E	408 293-4717	2339
Rawitser Golf Shop Mike	7992	E	408 441-4653	18776
Red Oak Technologies Inc	7379	D	408 200-3500	16471
Red Road Sobriety House	7021	E	408 512-8474	13455
Reliable Concepts Corporation	0781	D	408 271-6655	793
Responselink LLC	8011	D	650 864-9801	19912
Responselogix Inc	8741	C	408 220-6505	27199
Restaurant Depot LLC	5142	C	408 344-0107	8568
Retailnext Inc (PA)	7371	D	408 884-2162	15420
RFI Enterprises Inc (PA)	1731	D	408 298-5400	2710
Rgis LLC	7389	D	408 243-9141	17462
Robert Half International Inc	7361	D	408 961-2975	14755
Robert Half International Inc	7363	D	408 293-8611	14941
Robinson and Wood Inc	8111	D	408 298-7120	23535
Ron Filice Enterprises Inc	6411	E	408 294-0477	10857
Rosendin Electric Inc (PA)	1731	A	408 286-2800	2715
Rosendin Electric Inc	1731	A	408 321-2200	2716
Rosetta LLC	8742	C	408 275-7117	27626
Rossi Hamerslough Reishchl &	8111	D	408 244-4570	23541
Rovi Corporation	7371	D	408 445-8100	15430
Royal Coach Tours (PA)	4111	D	408 279-4801	3693
Royalty Tours	4725	E	408 279-4801	4999
RSM US LLP	8721	D	408 572-4440	26434
Rural/Metro Corporation	4119	C	888 876-0740	3836
S J General Building Maint	7349	D	408 392-0800	14415
Salas OBrien Engineers Inc (PA)	8711	E	408 282-1500	26050
Samsung SDS America Inc	7371	D	408 638-8800	15435
Samsung Semiconductor Inc (DH)	5065	C	408 544-4000	7630
San Jose Airport Garden Hotel	7011	D	408 793-3300	13203
San Jose Airport Hotel LLC	7011	C	408 793-3939	13204
San Jose Chld Discovery Museum	8412	D	408 298-5437	25045
San Jose Conservation Corps	8331	C	408 283-7171	24385
San Jose Country Club	7997	D	408 258-3636	19059
San Jose Fairmont Lessee LLC	7011	B	408 998-1900	13205
San Jose Foothill Family Comm	8011	C	408 729-4290	19946
San Jose Jet Center Inc	4581	E	408 297-7552	4933
San Jose Medical Clinic Inc (PA)	8011	D	408 278-3000	19947
San Jose Medical Clinic Inc	8011	B	408 278-3000	19948
San Jose Museum of Art Assn	8412	E	408 271-6840	25046
San Jose Redevelopment Agency	8748	C	408 535-8500	28052
San Jose Sharks LLC	7941	C	408 287-6655	18563
San Jose Silicon Valley Cham	8611	D	408 291-5250	25102
San Jose State University	8011	E	408 924-1000	19949
San Jose Surgical Supply Inc (PA)	5047	D	408 293-9033	7312
San Jose Water Company (HQ)	4941	C	408 288-5314	6397
San Jose Water Company	4941	C	408 298-0364	6398
San Joses Healthcare & Well	8051	C	408 295-2665	20889
Santa Clara County of	8322	D	408 435-2000	24192
Santa Clara Cnty Fderal Cr Un (PA)	6061	D	408 282-0700	9623
Santa Clara County of	8111	A	408 792-2704	23545
Santa Clara County of	8721	C	408 885-7200	26436
Santa Clara County of	7349	E	408 993-4700	14418
Santa Clara County of	8062	E	408 885-6818	21859
Santa Clara County of	7322	D	408 282-3200	14046
Santa Clara County of	8322	C	408 435-2111	24193
Santa Clara County of	8011	D	408 792-5680	19954
Santa Clara County of	8721	C	408 885-7354	26437
Santa Clara Valley Corporation	7349	D	408 947-1100	14419
Santa Clara Valley Medical Ctr	8011	B	408 885-6300	19955
Santa Clara Valley Medical Ctr	8011	D	408 792-5586	19956
Santa Clara Valley Medical Ctr	8099	A	408 885-5730	23054
Santa Clara Valley Medical Ctr (PA)	8062	B	408 885-5000	21860
Santa Clara Valley Trnsp Auth	4131	B	408 321-5555	3885
Santa Clara Valley Water (PA)	4941	C	408 265-2600	6399

GEOGRAPHIC SECTION

SAN JUAN CAPISTRANO, CA

	SIC	EMP	PHONE	ENTRY #
Santa Teresa Golf Club	7992	D	408 225-2650	18783
Santana Row Hotel Partners LP	7011	C	408 551-0010	13218
Saratoga Capital Inc	7011	D	408 286-1000	13220
Sarpa-Feldman Enterprises Inc	7389	D	408 982-1790	17476
Satellite Healthcare Inc (PA)	8092	D	650 404-3600	22641
Satellite Healthcare Inc	8092	D	408 258-8720	22642
SCC ESA Dept of Risk Mgmt	6411	D	408 441-4207	10861
Schaper Construction Inc (PA)	1721	D	408 437-0337	2490
Schurman Fine Papers	7389	C	408 971-8843	17479
Schwager Davis Inc	1629	C	408 281-9300	2082
SE Scher Corporation	7363	A	408 844-0772	14946
Second Harvest Food Bank (PA)	8322	E	408 266-8866	24198
Semiconductor Eqp & Mtls Intl (PA)	8611	C	408 943-6900	25103
Service Workers Local 715 (PA)	8631	D	408 678-3300	25186
SGS Accutest Inc	8734	D	408 588-0200	26886
Sharks Sports & Entrmt LLC	7941	A	408 287-7070	18564
Sierra Lumber Co	1751	C	408 286-7071	3090
Sigma Networks Inc	4813	C	408 876-4002	5701
Significant Cleaning Svcs LLC	7349	C	408 559-5959	14431
Silicon Valley Hwang LLC	7011	C	408 452-0200	13255
Silicon Valley Mechanical Inc	1711	D	408 943-0380	2367
Silicon Vly Educatn Foundation	8399	A	408 790-9400	24977
Silicon Vly SEC & Patrol Inc (PA)	7381	C	408 267-1539	16825
Siliconware Usa Inc (HQ)	5065	E	408 573-5500	7633
Silver Creek Vly Cntry CLB Inc	7997	C	408 239-5775	19080
Silver Spring Networks Inc (PA)	4899	B	669 770-4000	6088
SIM Investment Corporation	7991	D	408 445-3310	18681
Sims Group USA Corporation	5093	D	408 494-4242	8085
Sj Hotel Manager LLC	8741	D	401 946-4600	27214
Sjsu Foundation	8699	D	408 924-1410	25576
SJW Corp (PA)	4941	B	408 279-7800	6403
Sk Hynix America Inc (HQ)	5065	D	408 232-8000	7634
Sk Hynix Memory Solutions Inc	7379	D	408 514-3500	16480
Slakey Brothers Inc	5075	E	408 494-0460	7747
Smashon Inc	7379	E	855 762-7466	16481
SMC Corporation of America	5084	E	408 943-9600	7888
Somansa Technologies Inc	5045	D	408 297-1234	7189
Sonics Inc (PA)	7373	C	408 457-2800	16056
Sourcewise	8322	D	408 350-3200	24217
South Bay Airport Shuttle	4111	D	408 225-4444	3720
South Bay Regl Public Safety T	8331	E	408 270-6494	24388
South Bay Senior Solutions Inc	8082	D	408 370-6360	22568
South Valley Plumbing Inc	1711	C	408 265-5566	2382
Southern Wine & Spirits Amrca	5182	D	408 750-3540	9112
Sprig Electric Co (PA)	1731	D	408 298-3134	2739
SSC San Jose Operating Co LP	8051	D	408 249-0344	20927
STA Clara Valley Medical Ctr	8011	E	408 885-2334	20062
Staffing Solutions Inc	7361	D	408 980-9000	14795
Stanford Health Care	8062	A	408 426-4900	21932
Starlight Management Group	7011	D	408 334-7456	13287
State Compensation Insur Fund	6331	C	888 782-8338	10464
Steinberg Architects (PA)	8712	D	408 295-5446	26259
Structural Integrity Assoc Inc (PA)	8711	D	408 978-8200	26079
Student Trnsp Amer Inc	4119	D	408 998-8275	3848
Student Un San Jose State Univ	8699	D	408 924-6405	25587
Suddath Relo Sys of No CA	4213	D	408 288-3030	4267
Sumitomo Electric Device Innov	5065	D	408 232-9500	7641
Summit Hr Worldwide Inc	8742	D	408 884-7100	27673
Sunrise Senior Living Inc	8051	D	408 223-1312	20963
Sunrun Installation Svcs Inc	1711	A	408 746-3062	2391
Super Talent Technology Corp	5045	A	408 957-8133	7196
Supertex Inc	8734	E	408 222-8880	26891
Syniverse Technologies LLC	7379	C	408 324-1830	16493
Systech Integrators Inc	7379	C	408 441-2700	16495
Talent Space Inc	7361	D	408 330-1900	14801
Tamtron Corporation (DH)	7371	D	408 323-3303	15489
Taos Mountain LLC (PA)	7379	B	408 324-2800	16500
Team San Jose	7389	A	408 295-9600	17520
Tech Museum of Innovation (PA)	8412	C	408 795-6116	25051
Techaisle LLC	8732	E	408 253-4416	26711
Technology Credit Union	6062	D	408 467-2382	9692
Technology Credit Union (PA)	6062	C	408 451-9111	9694
Ted Cooper/Cooper Industries	0782	E	408 358-3060	962
Telemundo of Northern Cal	4833	D	408 432-6221	5914
Terry Meyer	6531	D	408 723-3300	11871
Thermo Fisher Scientific	5049	D	408 894-9835	7350
Thomas Mark & Company Inc (PA)	8711	E	408 453-5373	26097
Threatmetrix Inc	7379	C	408 200-5700	16506
Tim Brown	6531	D	408 717-2575	11876
Topbuild Services Group Corp	1799	D	408 882-0411	3590
Total Defense Inc	7372	D	408 598-4299	15862
Tradecom Med Transcription Inc	5047	C	408 225-9200	7321
Traditions Golf LLC	7992	D	408 323-5200	18795
Trans-Pak Incorporated (PA)	7389	D	408 254-0500	17539
Trim Tech Industries Inc	5031	E	408 573-4514	6966
Tsmc North America (HQ)	8742	C	408 382-8000	27702
Tumi Inc	5099	D	408 244-6512	8146
TV 36	4833	E	408 953-3636	5918
TWC Aviation LLC	4522	E	408 286-3832	4890
U S Perma Inc	1743	E	408 436-0600	3027
Ubiquiti Networks Inc (PA)	7373	D	408 942-3085	16069
Udp USA	7382	D	408 519-5774	16940
Ultimo Software Solutions Inc	7371	C	408 943-1490	15515
Underwriters Laboratories Inc	8734	B	248 427-5300	26896
Underwriters Laboratories Inc	8734	D	408 493-9910	26899
Unifirst Corporation	7218	D	408 297-8101	13648
Unilab Corporation	8071	B	408 927-8331	22293
Unish Corporation	7379	E	408 708-9300	16515
United Administrative Services	6371	C	408 288-4400	10563
United Airlines Inc	4512	C	408 294-4028	4828
United Parcel Service Inc OH	4215	B	408 291-2942	4450
United Site Services Cal Inc	7359	C	408 295-2263	14588
United Temp Services Inc	7361	D	408 472-4309	14811
Univar USA Inc	5169	D	408 435-8649	9002
Universal Bldg Svcs & Sup Co	7349	C	408 995-5111	14457
Universal Services America LP	7382	A	408 993-1965	16941
URS Group Inc	8711	D	408 297-9585	26128
User Zoom Inc	7373	D	408 533-8619	16073
Valin Corporation (PA)	5084	D	408 730-9850	7900
Valley US Inc	7389	D	408 260-7342	16519
Ventrum LLC	7379	D	510 304-0852	16520
Veolia Transportation Svcs Inc	4111	C	408 277-3661	3732
Vera Bradley Inc	7389	D	408 615-8370	17585
Verity Health System Cal Inc	8062	C	408 947-2762	22014
Verizon Bus Netwrk Svcs Inc	4813	D	408 975-2244	5716
Viaworld Advanced Products	5072	C	408 597-7051	7703
Victor Corsiglia MD	8011	D	408 278-3210	20224
Vidhwan Inc	7371	C	408 521-0167	15527
Villages Golf and Country Club	7997	D	408 274-4400	19119
Virident Systems Inc	8731	C	408 573-5000	26637
Virtual Instruments Corp	7379	C	408 579-4000	16522
Vitron Electronic Services Inc	5063	D	408 251-1600	7481
Vivente 1 Inc	6514	D	408 279-2706	11242
Vivente 2 Inc	6514	D	408 279-2706	11243
Vn Home Health Care LP	8082	D	408 998-0550	22609
Vormetric Inc (HQ)	7379	D	408 433-6000	16524
Vss Monitoring Inc	4813	C	408 585-6800	5729
Vta Telephone Information	4813	D	408 321-7127	5730
Waste Connections Cal Inc (PA)	4953	C	408 282-4400	6596
Watson Carton	8399	D	408 979-9618	24996
Wells Fargo Bank National Assn	6021	E	408 998-3714	9435
West Coast Legal Service Inc	7389	E	408 938-6520	17619
West Hotel Partners LP	7011	E	408 947-4450	13399
West San Crlos Ht Partners LLC	7011	D	408 998-0400	13401
Western Alliance Bank	6022	D	408 423-8500	9537
Western Alliance Bank	6022	D	408 423-8500	9539
Western Alliance Bank	6022	D	408 282-1670	9541
Western Alliance Bank	6022	D	408 423-8500	9542
Wfg National Title Insur Co	6541	D	408 560-3000	11943
Willow Glen Hsing Partners LP	6531	E	408 267-7252	11926
Willow Glen Villa A	6513	D	408 266-1660	11229
Winbond Electronics Corp Amer (HQ)	5065	D	408 943-6666	7659
Winchester Mystery House LLC	7999	D	408 247-2000	19310
Womans Alliance Woma	8322	D	408 279-2962	24292
WW Grainger Inc	5063	C	408 432-8200	7484
Wyndham International Inc	7011	C	408 451-3050	13441
Xactly Corporation (PA)	7371	C	408 977-3132	15550
Xerox Corporation	7378	C	408 953-2700	16309
Xo Communications LLC	4813	D	408 817-2800	5735
Xpo Enterprise Services Inc	4213	D	408 435-3876	4309
Yang C Park	7361	C	408 260-8066	14823
YMCA of Silicon Valley	8641	B	650 493-9622	25431
YMCA of Silicon Valley	8641	C	408 298-1717	25432
YMCA of Silicon Valley	8641	C	408 226-9622	25434
YMCA of The Mid-Peninsula Inc	8641	B	650 493-9622	25435
Yosh Enterprises Inc	7381	E	408 287-4411	16857
Young Womens Christian Associ	8641	C	408 295-4011	25477
Zanker Road Resource MGT Ltd	4953	D	408 457-1189	6616
Zenith Talent Corporation	7361	C	844 467-2300	14825
Ziontech Solutions Inc	7379	D	408 434-6001	16533
Zscaler Inc	7371	A	408 533-0288	15561

SAN JUAN BAUTISTA, CA - San Benito County

	SIC	EMP	PHONE	ENTRY #
Anthony Botelho	0175	D	831 623-4228	227
Christopher Ranch LLC	0161	D	831 636-8722	51
Earthbound Farm LLC (DH)	0723	A	831 623-7880	527
Seminis Inc	8731	C	831 623-4554	26603

SAN JUAN CAPISTRANO, CA - Orange County

	SIC	EMP	PHONE	ENTRY #
Action Sports Retailer	7389	D	949 226-5744	16969
Atria Senior Living Group Inc	8361	C	949 661-1220	24558

SAN JUAN CAPISTRANO, CA

	SIC	EMP	PHONE	ENTRY #
Birtcher Andrson Investors LLC	6799	E	949 545-0526	12285
Carparts Technologies	7372	C	949 488-8860	15615
Celera Corporation (HQ)	8733	C	510 749-4200	26749
Coastal Mirage Landscapes	0781	D	949 496-7070	759
Cox Communications Inc	4841	C	949 240-1212	5975
Emerald Expositions LLC (HQ)	7389	A	949 226-5700	17150
Ip Access International	7379	E	949 655-1000	16412
Kaiser Foundation Hospitals	6324	D	888 988-2800	10339
Marbella Country Club	7997	C	949 248-3700	18989
Marbella Golf & Country Club	7997	C	949 248-3700	18990
Medusind Solutions Inc	7389	A	949 240-8895	17324
Merit Integrated Logistics LLC	4731	A	949 481-0685	5122
Nichols Inst Reference Labs (DH)	8071	A	949 728-4000	22248
PRC Builders Inc	1522	D	949 529-7011	1331
Premier Silica LLC	1446	D	949 728-0171	1110
San Juan Golf Inc	7992	E	949 493-1167	18779
Solag Inc	4953	D	949 728-1206	6563
Southern Cal Prmnnte Med Group	8011	E	949 234-2139	20034
Sunrise Senior Living Inc	8051	D	949 248-8855	20956
Technicon Design Corporation	7389	C	949 218-1300	17521

SAN LEANDRO, CA - Alameda County

	SIC	EMP	PHONE	ENTRY #
A-Para Transit Corp	4119	C	510 732-9400	3738
Aa/Acme Locksmiths Inc	1731	D	510 483-6584	2508
Acco Engineered Systems Inc	1711	C	510 346-4300	2105
Advantage Medical Group Inc	8011	D	510 614-3700	19317
Alameda County Industries Inc	4953	E	510 357-7282	6423
Alco Iron & Metal Co (PA)	5093	D	510 562-1107	8058
Alemeda County Industries LLC	4953	D	510 357-7282	6424
American College Phlebology	8621	A	510 346-6800	25115
Apple Inns Inc	7011	E	510 895-1311	12394
Apria Healthcare LLC	8082	D	510 346-4000	22368
Aryzta LLC	5149	D	214 630-8292	8799
Aryzta LLC	5149	D	704 357-0369	8800
Aviation Port Services LLc	4491	D	510 636-8790	4743
Avis Rent A Car System Inc	7514	C	510 562-8828	17663
Bae Sys Sierra Detroit Allison (DH)	7538	D	510 635-8991	17785
Bay Area Installations Inc (PA)	1799	D	510 895-8196	3497
Bluewater Envmtl Svcs Inc	1799	D	510 346-8800	3499
Carlton Senior Living	6531	D	510 636-0660	11342
Cinemark 16 Bayfair	7832	D	510 276-9684	18316
Cintas Corporation No 3	7299	E	510 562-6330	13746
Cnh Industrial America LLC	5082	C	510 351-2015	7767
Coast Counties Truck & Eqp Co	5012	D	510 568-6933	6667
Community MBL Diagnostics LLC	8071	D	925 516-6851	22201
County of Alameda	8322	D	510 618-3452	23793
County of Alameda	8011	C	510 481-4141	19464
Crossroad Services Inc	7389	B	510 895-5055	17107
Cummins Pacific LLC	5084	B	510 351-6101	7836
Datapark Inc	7373	D	510 483-7275	15929
Davis Street Community Center (PA)	8322	D	510 347-4620	23939
Dependable Highway Express Inc	4225	E	510 357-2223	4542
Dependable Highway Express Inc	4213	D	510 357-2223	4137
Dunbar Armored Inc	7381	D	510 569-7400	16629
East Bay Innovations	7389	D	510 618-1580	17140
Engility LLC	8711	D	510 357-4610	25791
Estes Express Lines Inc	4213	D	510 635-0165	4151
Federal Express Corporation	4513	C	510 347-2430	4850
Fedex Freight West Inc	4213	D	650 244-9522	4170
Fidelity Home Energy Inc (PA)	1711	D	858 220-7784	2226
Frank Ghiglione Inc (PA)	4212	D	510 483-7000	4020
Frank Ghiglione Inc	4212	D	510 483-2063	4021
Galena Equipment Rental LLC	7353	E	510 638-8100	14482
H A Bowen Electric Inc	1731	D	510 483-0500	2603
Hilton Garden Inn	7011	D	510 346-5533	12707
Home Instead Senior Care	8082	D	510 686-9940	22469
Independent Electric Sup Inc (DH)	5063	C	520 908-7900	7446
J R Pierce Plumbing Company	1711	D	510 483-5473	2259
Johnson Western Gunite Company (PA)	1771	D	510 568-8112	3283
K/P LLC	7331	E	510 614-7800	14076
Kaimanu Outrigger Canoe Club	7999	D	510 895-0435	19230
Kaiser Foundation Hospitals	8011	A	510 454-1000	19644
Kaiser Foundation Hospitals	8069	B	510 481-8575	22147
Karcher Environmental Inc	1799	D	510 297-0180	3542
Kindred Healthcare Oper Inc	8062	B	510 357-8300	21687
Kissito Health Case Inc	8082	D	510 357-4015	22497
KMA Emergency Services Inc	4119	D	510 614-1420	3810
Koffler Elec Mech Apprts Repai	5063	D	510 567-0630	7449
Kp LLC	7331	C	510 346-0729	14078
Kp LLC	7331	C	510 614-7800	14079
L-3 Applied Technologies Inc	8731	D	510 577-7100	26546
Laboratory Corp Amer Holdings	8071	D	510 635-4555	22233
Macro-Pro Inc	7389	D	510 483-2679	17307
Marymount Villa LLC	8052	D	510 895-5007	21091
Monarch Bay Golf Resort	7997	D	510 895-2162	19005
Mv Transportation Inc	4119	C	510 351-1603	3820

GEOGRAPHIC SECTION

	SIC	EMP	PHONE	ENTRY #
N V Heathorn Inc	1711	D	510 569-9100	2303
Nan Fang Dist Group Inc	5084	D	510 297-5382	7867
Osisoft LLC (PA)	7372	D	510 297-5800	15812
Pacific Coast Container Inc (PA)	4789	C	510 346-6100	5232
Penhall Company	1795	D	510 357-8810	3463
Permanente Kaiser Intl	8011	C	510 454-1000	19830
Permanente Medical Group Inc	8011	D	510 454-1000	19852
Peterson Machinery Co	7629	A	541 302-9199	17939
Providnce All STS Subacute LLC	8051	D	510 481-3200	20859
Pyro Spectaculars Inc	7999	E	510 632-4516	19264
Ransome Company	1542	D	510 686-9900	1646
Robert C Davis MD	8011	E	510 893-2820	19925
Roofing Constructors Inc	1761	C	415 648-6472	3210
Royal Ambulance Inc	4119	C	510 568-6161	3834
Royal Investigation Patrol Inc	7381	C	510 352-6800	16776
Saia Motor Freight Line Inc	4213	D	510 347-6890	4259
San Francisco-Bay Cncl Bsa	8641	D	510 577-9000	25334
San Leandro Healthcare Center	8051	D	510 357-4015	20890
San Leandro Hospital LP	8062	B	510 357-6500	21851
San Leandro Surgery Center Lt	8011	D	510 276-2800	19951
Schryver Med Sls & Mktg LLC	8071	D	303 371-0073	22281
Service Lathing Company	1742	E	510 483-9732	2978
Silman Venture Corporation (PA)	1541	D	510 347-4800	1465
Ssmb Pacific Holding Co Inc (PA)	5012	D	510 836-6100	6695
St Francis Electric Inc	1731	C	510 639-0639	2744
St Francis Electric LLC	1731	D	510 750-8271	2745
State Roofing Systems Inc	1761	D	510 317-1477	3214
Stepping Stn Grwth Ctr Fr Chld	8331	D	510 568-3331	24393
Subacute Trtmnt Adolescnt Reha (PA)	8051	D	510 352-9020	20933
Sunbridge Healthcare LLC	8052	D	510 352-2211	21117
Sutter Vsting Nrse Assn Hspice	8051	D	510 618-5277	20989
Telecare Corporation	8063	D	510 895-5502	22095
Telecare Corporation	8063	D	510 352-9690	22102
Thyssenkrupp Elevator Corp	5084	D	510 476-1900	7896
Trinet Group Inc (PA)	7361	C	510 352-5000	14808
Trinet Hr Corporation	8742	A	972 789-3900	27699
TRM Corporation (PA)	1743	D	510 895-2700	3026
True Wrld Fods San Frncsco LLC	5146	D	510 352-8140	8662
Unec Solutions Inc	7379	D	510 851-2808	16514
Unity Courier Service Inc	7389	D	510 568-8890	17567
UPS Expedited Mail Svcs Inc	7331	E	510 297-4600	14095
Vanguard Legato A Cal Corp	5021	D	510 351-3333	6834
Vasona Management Inc	6513	B	510 352-8728	11219
Waste MGT of Alameda Cnty	4953	D	510 638-2303	6610
Webers Quality Meats Inc	5147	D	510 635-9892	8690
Westates Mechanical Corp Inc	1711	D	510 635-9830	2416
Westmed Ambulance	4119	D	510 401-5420	3857
Wild Karma Inc	8051	C	510 639-9088	21040

SAN LORENZO, CA - Alameda County

	SIC	EMP	PHONE	ENTRY #
Aecom Global II LLC	8711	D	510 258-0152	25630
Directv Group Inc	4841	D	510 481-1324	5988
Hillshire Brands Company	5147	B	510 276-1300	8671
Oakland Pallet Company Inc (PA)	5031	C	510 278-1291	6940
Scyence Inc	0782	D	510 481-8614	950
Too Good Gourmet Inc	5149	D	510 317-8150	8938
Wells Fargo Bank National Assn	6021	E	510 276-0875	9452

SAN LUIS OBISPO, CA - San Luis Obispo County

	SIC	EMP	PHONE	ENTRY #
American West	4213	E	805 926-2800	4108
American West Worldwide Ex Inc (PA)	4214	D	800 788-4534	4328
Amir Ahmad MD	8011	D	805 545-8100	19340
Amk Foodservices Inc	5141	C	805 544-7600	8456
Associated Students Inc (PA)	8322	D	805 756-1281	23673
Associated Students Inc	8999	C	805 756-1281	28116
Aviation Consultants Inc (PA)	8741	D	805 548-1300	26932
Bank of Sierra	6021	D	805 541-0400	9337
Bayshore Healthcare Inc	8051	C	805 544-5100	20406
Blood Systems Inc	8099	D	805 543-1077	22900
Blood Systems Inc	8099	D	831 751-1993	22901
Boeing Company	4581	D	805 606-6340	4904
Cal Poly Corporation	7021	D	805 756-1587	13449
Cal Poly Corporation	8741	C	805 756-1131	26953
Cannon Corporation (PA)	8713	D	805 544-7407	26273
Cellco Partnership	4812	D	805 549-6260	5383
Community Action Partnership (PA)	8322	D	805 544-4355	23770
Compass Health Inc	8059	D	805 543-0210	21189
Correctons Rhbltation Cal Dept	8093	A	805 547-7900	22692
County of San Luis Obispo	8062	B	805 781-4800	21523
County of San Luis Obispo	8322	C	805 781-5437	23908
County of San Luis Obispo	8093	C	805 781-4700	22709
County of San Luis Obispo	8322	B	805 781-1864	23909
County of San Luis Obispo	8711	C	805 781-5258	25758
Courtyard By Marriott	7011	D	805 786-4200	12545
Drug & Alcohol Services of	8093	D	805 781-4275	22721
Experts Exchange LLC	7379	D	805 787-0603	16369

GEOGRAPHIC SECTION

SAN MATEO, CA

	SIC	EMP	PHONE	ENTRY #
Family Care Network Inc (PA)	8351	D	805 503-6240	24462
First American Title Insur Co	6361	E	805 543-8900	10523
French Hosp Med Ctr Foundation (HQ)	8062	B	805 543-5353	21571
Glenn Burdette Phillips Bryson	8721	D	805 544-1441	26354
GTE Corporation	4813	C	805 441-4001	5623
Harvest Management Sub LLC	8361	A	805 543-0187	24679
High Road Sports	8742	D	805 545-7940	27464
Kci Environmental Inc	8999	E	805 543-3311	28139
Kennedy Club Fitness	7991	D	805 781-3488	18650
King Ventures	6552	C	805 544-4444	11976
Ksby Communications Inc	7812	C	805 541-6666	18098
Leidos Inc	8731	D	805 546-0307	26548
Level Studios Inc (DH)	8742	C	805 781-0546	27508
Lindamood-Bell Lrng Processes (PA)	8093	C	805 541-3836	22769
Meathead Movers Inc	4213	A	805 541-4285	4224
Meathead Movers Inc (PA)	4213	D	805 544-6328	4225
Merrill Lynch Pierce Fenner	6211	E	661 802-0764	10034
Mindbody Inc (PA)	7372	C	877 755-4279	15757
Morris Grritano Insur Agcy Inc	6411	E	805 543-6887	10791
Mufg Union Bank Na	6021	D	805 541-6100	9411
National Assn Ltr Carriers	8699	B	805 543-7329	25557
Nipomo Dial A Ride	4131	D	805 929-2881	3884
Ocean View Manor LP	6519	C	805 781-3088	11260
Oddworld Inhabitants Inc	7372	D	805 503-3000	15783
Pain Management Specialists PC	8011	E	805 544-7246	19808
Pathpoint	8331	D	805 782-8890	24378
Pickford Realty Inc	6531	D	805 782-6000	11748
Q S San Luis Obispo LP	7011	E	805 541-5001	13116
Quest Transportation Inc	8743	D	805 545-8400	27764
Rec Solar Commercial Corp	1623	C	844 732-7652	1988
Rew Inc	6324	D	805 541-1308	10372
Rosetta LLC	8742	C	347 332-7659	27627
Rrm Design Group (PA)	8712	D	805 439-0442	26248
San Luis Ambulance Service Inc	4119	C	805 543-2626	3839
San Luis Obispo Golf	7997	D	805 543-3400	19060
Sealant Systems International	5014	C	805 489-0490	6789
Sesloc Federal Credit Union (PA)	6061	D	805 543-1816	9626
Sierra Vista Hospital Inc (HQ)	8062	A	805 546-7600	21893
Snapnrack Inc	5074	A	877 732-2860	7731
Specialty Construction Inc	1731	C	805 543-1706	2736
SRI International	8733	D	805 542-9330	26810
Sunrun Installation Svcs Inc (HQ)	1731	D	805 528-9705	2757
Sycamore Mineral Spring Resort	7011	D	805 595-7302	13332
Thoma Electric Inc	1731	C	805 543-3850	2772
Transitions - Mental Hlth Assn (PA)	8322	D	805 540-6500	24257
Trust Automation Inc	8711	D	805 544-0761	26105
United Cerebral Palsy Assoc of	8399	D	805 543-2039	24990
United Parcel Service Inc OH	4215	C	801 973-3400	4464
Veterans Health Administration	8011	A	805 543-1233	20197
Villa La Esperanza LP	1531	D	805 781-3088	1389
Village Pacific Mgt Group	8051	D	805 543-2350	21012
Village Pacific Mgt Group (PA)	8051	D	805 543-2300	21013
Wells Fargo Bank National Assn	6021	D	805 541-0143	9455

SAN MARCOS, CA - San Diego County

	SIC	EMP	PHONE	ENTRY #
American Concrete	1771	D	760 471-9907	3226
American Homes Trust	6798	D	619 694-7821	12235
Americare Hlth Retirement Inc	6512	D	760 744-4484	10958
Associated Students Inc	7041	E	760 750-4990	13487
AT&T Corp	4813	D	760 752-3273	5486
Birth Choice of San Marco	8322	D	760 744-1313	23685
Black & Veatch-Balfour Beatty	8711	D	760 510-7715	25695
Casa De Amparo (PA)	8361	D	760 754-5500	24582
Cellco Partnership	4812	D	760 738-0088	5303
Chateau Lake San Marcos Homeow	8641	D	760 471-0083	25237
Citizens Development Corp (PA)	7997	D	760 744-0120	18917
Control Air Conditioning Corp	7623	C	760 744-2727	17920
Corkys Pest Control Inc	7342	C	760 432-8801	14183
David Shaposhnick Inc	1711	D	760 758-6090	2202
Diamond Environmental Svcs LP	7359	D	760 744-7191	14535
Doose Landscape Incorporated	0782	D	760 591-4500	844
Edco Waste & Recycl Svcs Inc (HQ)	4953	D	760 744-2700	6480
Edwards Theatres Circuit Inc	7832	D	760 471-3734	18329
Fresh Origins LLC	0139	D	760 801-1087	22
Global World Group	4499	D	760 744-4800	4775
Golden Door Properties LLC	7011	C	760 744-5777	12667
Hokto Kinoko Company (HQ)	0182	C	760 774-8453	333
Hollandia Dairy Inc (PA)	0241	C	760 744-3222	428
Home Improvement Company Inc	1799	E	760 744-4840	3532
Hunter Industries Incorporated (PA)	5087	C	800 383-4747	7967
Iron Law Inc (PA)	8111	E	844 476-6529	23321
Kaiser Foundation Hospitals	8062	A	760 591-4276	21628
Kindred Healthcare Oper Inc	8051	C	760 471-2986	20701
KRC Equipment LLC	5083	D	760 744-1036	7803
La Provence Inc	5149	E	760 736-3299	8873
M Bar C Construction Inc	1791	D	760 744-4131	3391
Markstein Beverage Co	5181	C	760 744-9100	9071
Naumann/Hobbs Material	5084	C	858 207-2800	7869
North County Health Prj Inc (PA)	8011	D	760 736-6755	19777
Orora North America	5113	D	760 510-7170	8203
Orora North America	5113	D	760 510-7000	8208
Paramount Trnsp Systems Inc (PA)	4731	E	760 510-7979	5145
Plant Source Inc	0181	D	760 743-7743	310
Plum Healthcare Group LLC (PA)	8051	D	760 471-0388	20853
Primary Care Assod Med Group (PA)	8741	D	760 471-7505	27171
Rancho Physical Therapy Inc	8049	C	760 752-1011	20347
Rehab West Inc	6411	E	619 518-3710	10855
Rose Thompson Company	0181	D	760 736-6020	316
San Diego-Imperial	8322	D	760 736-1200	24177
San Marcos Caterers Inc	7011	D	760 744-0120	13206
San Marcos Country Club	7299	E	760 744-9385	13793
San Marcos Operating Co LP	8051	D	760 471-2986	20891
San Marcos Unified School Dst	8351	D	760 752-1252	24510
Shasta Landscaping Inc	0782	D	760 744-6551	952
Southern Contracting Company	1731	C	760 744-0760	2734
Tel Tech Plus Inc	1731	E	760 510-1323	2768
Ulta Salon Cosmt Fragrance Inc	7231	C	760 744-0853	13697
Unified Food Ingredients Inc	5149	C	760 744-7225	8942
United Parcel Service Inc OH	4215	C	760 752-7809	4445
Village Square Nursing Center	8051	C	760 471-2986	21014
Welk Resort Group Inc (PA)	6531	E	760 652-4913	11913

SAN MARINO, CA - Los Angeles County

	SIC	EMP	PHONE	ENTRY #
Accentcare Home Health Cal Inc	8082	E	626 568-9478	22327
CIT Bank National Association	6021	D	323 767-1180	9347
Tricor Entertainment Inc	7812	D	626 282-5184	18171

SAN MARTIN, CA - Santa Clara County

	SIC	EMP	PHONE	ENTRY #
Cordevalle Golf Club LLC	7997	C	408 695-4500	18926

SAN MATEO, CA - San Mateo County

	SIC	EMP	PHONE	ENTRY #
AAA Travel	6331	E	650 572-5600	10394
Aauw Action Fund Inc	8699	D	650 574-9160	25482
Abd Insurance & Fincl Svcs Inc (PA)	6411	C	650 488-8565	10578
Aceva Technologies Inc	7323	C	650 227-5500	14055
Adaptv Inc (DH)	5045	D	650 286-4420	7082
Addus Healthcare Inc	8082	B	650 638-7943	22335
Alain Pinel Realtors Inc	6531	D	650 548-1111	11282
Alfresco Software Inc (PA)	7372	D	888 317-3395	15576
Alienvault LLC (PA)	7372	D	650 713-3333	15577
Allegis Group Inc	7363	C	650 425-6950	14835
Allen Lund Company LLC	4731	D	650 358-9454	5025
Alliance Hospital Services	8082	E	650 697-6900	22350
American Institute Research	8733	D	650 843-8100	26735
Andreini & Company (PA)	6411	D	650 573-1111	10603
Apttus Corporation	7371	C	650 445-7700	15028
Archives Management Corp (PA)	8741	C	650 544-2200	26924
Athoc Inc	7371	D	650 685-3000	15039
Atrium Plaza LLC	7011	C	650 653-6000	12404
Barrett Business Services Inc	8741	A	650 653-7588	26937
Bay Area Senior Services Inc	8322	D	650 579-5500	23677
Bay Meadows Racing Association	7948	D	650 573-4500	18566
Belectric Inc (HQ)	1629	D	510 896-3940	2024
Bertram Capital Management LLC	6799	C	650 358-5000	12284
Big Oak Hardwood Floor Co Inc	1752	D	650 591-8651	3107
Borland Software Corporation	7372	D	650 286-1900	15606
Brightedge Technologies Inc (PA)	7371	D	800 578-8023	15065
Bunchball Inc	7371	D	408 215-2924	15069
C9 Edge Inc	5045	D	650 561-7855	7105
CA Ste Atom Assoc Intr-Ins Bur	6331	D	650 572-5600	10404
California Casualty Mgt Co (PA)	6331	C	650 574-4000	10407
California Envmtl Hlth Assn	8748	D	650 363-4726	27863
Califrnia CPA Edcatn Fundation	8621	D	800 922-5272	25126
Califrnia Cslty Indemnity Exch (PA)	6331	C	650 574-4000	10410
Camico Mutual Insurance Co (PA)	6411	C	650 378-6874	10660
Childcare Careers LLC	7363	A	650 372-0211	14853
Cir	8731	C	650 574-6900	26496
City of San Mateo	7349	D	650 522-7300	14251
Clarizen Inc	8741	D	866 502-9813	26971
Coldwell Bnkr Residential Brkg	6531	D	650 558-6800	11423
County of San Mateo	8322	C	650 312-5327	23911
County of San Mateo	8322	B	650 312-8887	23912
County of San Mateo	8093	D	650 312-8710	22710
County of San Mateo	8322	D	650 312-8803	23916
Coupa Software Incorporated (PA)	7372	D	650 931-3200	15631
Daniel J Edelman Inc	7313	D	650 762-2800	13965
David D Bohannon Organization (PA)	6512	D	650 345-8222	10973
Device Anywhere	7371	D	650 655-6400	15133
Digimarc Corporation	7373	C	888 300-9114	15932
Drawbridge Inc	8742	D	650 513-2323	27415
Duckys Car Wash Inc	7542	D	650 375-8100	17838
Ero-Tech Corp	7822	D	415 468-5600	18273

SAN MATEO, CA

Company	SIC	EMP	PHONE	ENTRY #
Essex Property Trust Inc (PA)	6798	C	650 655-7800	12246
Essex Queen Anne LLC	6519	A	650 849-1600	11253
Fhar Fmly Hsing Adult Rsources	8322	D	650 573-3341	23978
Fifty Peninsula Partners	6513	D	650 344-8200	11131
First Student Inc	4151	D	650 685-8245	3927
Franklin Advisers Inc	6282	A	650 312-2000	10144
Franklin Resources Inc (PA)	6722	C	650 312-2000	12117
Franklin Templeton Instnl LLC (HQ)	6091	D	650 312-2000	9703
Franklin Templeton Svcs LLC	6282	D	650 312-3000	10145
Freecom Financial Network LLC (PA)	7299	D	650 393-6619	13760
Funny or Die Inc	7379	E	650 461-3929	16375
Gazillion Inc (PA)	7372	C	650 393-6500	15675
Glenborough LLC (PA)	6531	D	650 343-9300	11555
Golden Gate Regional Ctr Inc	8322	D	650 574-9232	23995
Greenplum Inc	7374	C	650 286-8023	16136
Guavus Inc (PA)	7372	C	650 243-3400	15684
Inclin Inc	8731	D	650 961-3422	26535
Infogroup Inc	7331	C	650 389-0700	14074
Instill Corporation	7371	C	650 645-2600	15240
Institute For Humn Social Dev (PA)	8351	D	650 871-5613	24469
Intelpeer Cloud Cmmnctions LLC	4813	C	650 525-9200	5639
Ip International Inc	7379	E	650 403-7800	16413
Isearch Media LLC	7311	D	415 358-0882	13868
Island Hospitality MGT LLC	7011	D	650 574-4700	12856
IXL Learning Inc	8351	C	650 357-6976	24470
Jobvite Inc	8742	C	650 376-7200	27495
John Gore Organization Inc	7922	C	650 340-0469	18401
Judy Madrigal & Associates Inc	8011	A	650 873-3444	19578
Kaiser Foundation Hospitals	8011	A	650 358-7000	19643
Kurt Meiswinkel Inc	1742	E	650 344-7200	2922
La Joie Jerry	8741	E	650 375-1808	27105
Lattice Engines Inc (PA)	7379	D	877 460-0010	16421
Lisi Inc (PA)	6411	D	650 348-4131	10764
Logictier Inc	7379	C	650 235-6600	16425
Lolapps Inc	7371	C	415 243-0749	15285
Marketo Inc (HQ)	7371	C	650 376-2300	15291
Meta Company	7371	D	844 638-2266	15301
Movoto LLC	6531	D	888 766-8686	11698
National Fncl Srvcs Cnsrtm LLC	8742	C	650 572-2872	27559
NC Interactive LLC	7372	C	650 393-2200	15769
Netsuite Inc (PA)	7372	C	650 627-1000	15772
New York Life Insurance Co	6411	B	650 571-1220	10797
Nlyte Software Americas Ltd (DH)	7371	D	650 561-8200	15334
Nursing & Rehab At Home	8082	A	650 286-4272	22517
Oracle Systems Corporation	7371	C	650 506-6780	15360
Peninsula Community Foundation	6732	D	650 358-9369	12162
Peninsula Family Service (PA)	8322	D	650 403-4300	24129
People Science Inc	7361	E	888 924-1004	14724
Perficient Inc	7371	C	877 654-0033	15374
Permanente Medical Group Inc	8011	D	650 358-7000	19867
Personlized Buty Discovery Inc	7231	C	888 769-4526	13684
Playphone Inc (PA)	7371	C	408 261-6200	15386
Prometheus RE Group Inc (PA)	6531	C	650 931-3400	11771
Quickhealth Inc	8741	D	650 286-1986	27188
Raiser Senior Services LLC	8361	D	650 342-4106	24776
Rapid Solutions Consulting LLC	7371	E	801 755-7828	15408
Research Libraries Group Inc	7375	C	650 288-1288	16258
Robert Half International Inc	7363	E	650 574-8200	14943
San Mateo Cnty Expo Fair Assn	7999	E	650 574-3247	19276
San Mateo County Community	4833	D	650 574-6586	5909
San Mateo Credit Union	6062	D	650 363-1725	9687
Scott Place Associates	6531	D	650 345-8222	11836
Securitas SEC Svcs USA Inc	7382	D	650 358-1556	16919
Sequoia Bnefits Insur Svcs LLC	8742	D	650 369-0200	27640
Signalfx Inc	7374	E	888 958-5950	16186
Sigos LLC (HQ)	7374	C	650 376-3033	16187
Sociable Labs Inc	7374	E	415 225-8740	16189
Solarcity Corporation (PA)	1711	A	650 638-1028	2376
Sonim Technologies Inc (PA)	4812	D	650 378-8100	5409
State Farm Mutl Auto Insur Co	6411	D	650 345-3571	10889
Strands Inc A Delaware Corp	7371	E	541 753-4426	15478
Strands Labs Inc	7371	E	415 398-4333	15479
Sunrise Senior Living Inc	8051	D	650 558-8555	20952
Sutter Health	8011	C	650 262-4262	20099
Tano Capital LLC	6799	E	650 212-0330	12347
Telesys Software	7371	E	650 522-9922	15497
Templeton Franklin Intl Tr	6722	E	650 312-2000	12126
Tokio Marine Management Inc	6411	C	650 295-1180	10905
Total Airport Services Inc	4581	D	650 358-0144	4946
Tunari Corp Inc	7371	D	650 249-6740	15511
Veterinary Surgical Associates	8011	A	650 696-8196	20222
Visa International Svc Assn	7389	B	650 432-3579	17592
Wageworks Inc (PA)	8742	C	650 577-5200	27716
Westlake Development Group LLC (PA)	6512	D	650 579-1010	11075
Westlake Realty Group Inc (PA)	6531	D	650 579-1010	11918
Womencom Networks Inc	7375	C	650 378-6500	16270
Yellow A Cab	4121	E	650 344-2060	3872
Young Mens Christian Assoc SF	8641	C	650 286-9622	25449
Zs Associates Inc	7389	D	650 762-7800	17639

SAN PABLO, CA - Contra Costa County

Company	SIC	EMP	PHONE	ENTRY #
Doctors Medical Center LLC (HQ)	8062	D	510 970-5000	21545
Durkee Drayage Company	4214	D	510 970-7550	4343
Fred Finch Youth Center	8361	D	510 439-3130	24663
Grancare LLC	8051	B	510 232-5945	20632
Lytton Rancheria	7999	A	510 215-7888	19243
Making Waves Education Program (PA)	6733	C	510 237-3434	12190
Mariner Health Care Inc	8741	D	510 232-5945	27120
Norrise Institute of Training	8322	D	510 229-6545	24105
Promab Biotechnologies Inc	8731	D	510 860-4615	26592
San Pblo Hlthcare Wellness Ctr	8099	C	510 235-3720	23051

SAN PEDRO, CA - Los Angeles County

Company	SIC	EMP	PHONE	ENTRY #
Advanced Quality Logistics LLC	4731	C	310 221-6651	5014
Advent Resources Inc	7371	C	310 241-1500	15002
APL Logistics Ltd	4412	C	310 548-8700	4713
APM Terminals Pacific LLC	4731	E	310 221-4000	5029
APM Terminals Pacific LLC (DH)	4491	C	704 571-2768	4742
AT&T Corp	4813	D	310 547-0400	5473
Beach Cities Invest & Protctn	7381	B	310 322-4724	16573
Boys and Girls Clubs of The La (PA)	8641	D	310 833-1322	25213
Boys and Girls Clubs of The La	8641	D	310 833-1322	25214
Bridges At Sn Pdro Pnnsla Hspt	8093	D	310 514-5359	22669
California Untd Terminals Inc	4491	E	310 521-5000	4744
City of Los Angeles	4491	C	310 732-7681	4746
Gs Brothers Inc (PA)	0782	C	310 833-1369	864
Healthview Inc (PA)	8361	D	310 547-3341	24688
Little Sisters The Poor of La	8051	D	310 548-0625	20738
Los Defensores Inc	7311	E	310 519-4050	13877
Meristar San Pedro Hilton LLC	7011	D	310 514-3344	12989
Neptune Management Corporation	7261	D	310 832-6923	13707
Nhca Inc	7011	D	310 519-8200	13022
Nippon Express USA Inc	4731	C	310 532-6300	5131
Performance Team Frt Sys Inc	4225	C	310 241-4100	4614
Ports America Group	4731	C	310 241-1742	5154
Procel Temporary Services Inc	7363	B	310 372-0560	14927
Proficient LLC	7011	E	310 519-8200	13111
Providence Health & Services	8071	D	310 831-0371	22262
Providence Health & Services	8011	D	310 831-9482	19887
Providence Health & Services S	8062	D	310 832-3311	21818
San Pedro Convalescent Home	8051	D	310 519-0359	20893
San Pedro Peninsula Hospital (PA)	8062	A	310 832-3311	21853
San Pedro Peninsula Hospital	8062	D	310 514-5270	21854
Seacrest Convalescent Hosp Inc	8051	D	310 833-3526	20901
So Cal Ship Services	4489	C	310 519-8411	4739
Ssa Pacific Inc	4491	E	310 833-9606	4761
Tri-Marine Fish Company LLC	5146	D	310 547-1144	8659
Tri-State Employment Svc Inc	7361	B	310 521-9616	14807
Trimarine Fishing MGT LLC	8741	E	310 547-1144	27258
Walker Advertising Inc	7311	C	310 519-4050	13941
Y & S Enterprises Inc (PA)	7532	E	310 548-1120	17777
Yusen Terminals Inc (DH)	4491	D	310 548-8000	4765

SAN QUENTIN, CA - Marin County

Company	SIC	EMP	PHONE	ENTRY #
Distillery Inc	7372	D	415 505-5446	15640

SAN RAFAEL, CA - Marin County

Company	SIC	EMP	PHONE	ENTRY #
Aldersly Retirement Center	6513	D	415 453-9271	11081
Arcadia Health Care Inc	8082	C	415 472-2273	22369
Arcadia Services Inc	7363	D	248 352-7530	14840
AT&T Corp	4812	D	415 721-1470	5265
Autodesk Inc (PA)	7372	E	415 507-5000	15590
Autodesk Inc	7372	C	415 507-5000	15591
Bank of Marin	6022	D	415 472-2265	9471
Bernard Osher Marin Jewish Com	8322	C	415 444-8000	23682
Bradley Melissa Real Estate	6531	D	415 459-1010	11328
Buckelew Programs (PA)	8322	D	415 457-6964	23697
Cal-Coast Healthcare Inc	8051	D	415 479-5149	20431
Casa Allegra Community Svcs	8742	D	415 499-1116	27373
Catholic Chrts Cyo Archdiocs	8322	B	415 507-2000	23720
Cellco Partnership	4812	D	415 258-8404	5341
Cellmark Inc (DH)	5099	D	415 927-1700	8108
Center Point Inc (PA)	8322	C	415 492-4444	23724
Central Payment Co LLC	7389	D	415 462-8335	17061
CF San Rafael LLC	8051	D	415 479-5161	20448
Clp Resources Inc	7363	E	415 446-7000	14859
Comcast California Ix Inc	4841	D	215 286-3345	5945
Comcast E San Fernando Vly LP	4899	D	415 233-8328	6065
Community Action Marin	8093	C	415 459-6330	22689
County of Marin	8322	B	415 499-6970	23863
County of Marin	8711	C	415 499-7877	25757
De Mello Roofing Inc	1761	D	415 456-0741	3162

GEOGRAPHIC SECTION

SAN RAMON, CA

	SIC	EMP	PHONE	ENTRY #
Dutra Dredging Company (HQ)	1629	D	415 721-2131	2046
Dutra Group (PA)	1629	D	415 258-6876	2047
Dutra Manson JV	1629	D	415 258-6876	2048
Eah Inc (PA)	6514	D	415 258-1800	11234
Enterprise Events Group Inc	8742	C	415 499-4444	27425
Fair Isaac International Corp (HQ)	7372	A	415 446-6000	15662
Family Svcs Agcy Marin Cnty (PA)	8322	D	415 491-5700	23974
Frank Howard Allen Fincl Corp	6531	D	415 456-3000	11544
Ghilotti Bros Inc	1611	B	415 454-7011	1773
Gilardi & Co LLC	8741	D	415 461-0410	27036
Golden Gate Bridge High	4785	A	415 457-3110	5210
Guide Dogs For Blind Inc (PA)	0752	C	415 499-4000	639
Herbs Pool Service Inc	7389	D	415 479-4040	17218
Hilton Worldwide Inc	7011	D	415 499-9222	12737
Icf Consulting Group Inc	8742	A	703 934-3000	27470
Independent Quality Care Inc	8059	D	415 479-1230	21273
Innovative Sleep Centers Inc	8011	D	415 927-4990	19571
Interactive Medical Specialist	7363	D	415 472-4204	14889
Jacksons Hardware Inc	5072	D	415 454-3740	7688
Jerry Thompson & Sons Pntg Inc	1721	C	415 454-1500	2460
Kaiser Foundation Hospitals	8011	A	415 444-2000	19589
Kaiser Foundation Hospitals	6324	D	415 444-3522	10311
Kindred Nursing Centers W LLC	8051	D	415 456-7170	20707
Kisco Senior Living LLC	6513	C	415 491-1935	11149
Knight-Calabasas LLC	7997	D	415 453-4940	18967
Managed Health Network (DH)	6324	B	415 460-8168	10358
Managed Health Network	6324	A	510 620-6143	10359
Marin Community Clinic	8011	D	415 448-1500	19728
Marin Sanitary Service Inc	4953	D	415 456-2601	6501
Mariner Health Care Inc	8051	D	415 479-3610	20769
McG Services Corporation	7363	E	415 721-1444	14905
Mhn Government Services Inc	8322	C	916 294-4941	24087
Mhn Services	6324	A	415 460-8300	10360
Michael B Mayock Inc	1742	D	415 456-9306	2932
Mighty Leaf Tea	5149	D	415 491-2650	8878
Mill Valley Refuse Service Inc	4953	D	415 457-2287	6503
Millsap Degnan & Assoc Inc	1522	D	415 472-4244	1325
Mountain Play Association	7922	E	415 383-1100	18415
Northgate Care Center	8059	D	415 479-1230	21331
Ocadian Care Centers LLC	8051	D	415 479-8282	20822
Pasha Group (PA)	4731	B	415 927-6400	5147
Penske Automotive Group Inc	7513	E	415 492-1922	17644
Permanente Medical Group Inc	8011	D	415 444-2000	19853
Pf West LLC	7991	C	415 479-9600	18669
Phoenix American Incorporated (PA)	4841	D	415 485-4500	6014
Powerhouse Building Inc	1771	D	415 446-0188	3314
Quaker Pet Group Inc	5199	D	415 721-7400	9295
R C Roberts & Co (PA)	6515	C	415 456-8600	11245
Rafael Convalescent Hospital	8059	D	415 479-3450	21354
Redhill Towing & Autobody	7549	D	415 456-8943	17890
Redhorse Constructors Inc	1521	D	415 492-2020	1242
Richard Shames MD	8011	D	415 388-0456	19919
Rotary Club San Rafael Fund	7997	D	415 457-4284	19048
San Rafael Rock Quarry Inc (HQ)	1429	D	415 459-7740	1102
Sisters of Nazareth	8059	D	415 479-8282	21379
Starwood Hotels & Resorts	7011	C	415 479-8800	13295
Urban Bros Painting Inc	1721	D	415 485-1130	2500
Valentine Corporation	1799	E	415 453-3732	3595
Villa Marin Homeowners Assn	8641	C	415 499-8711	25398
Warren Security Systems Inc	7382	E	415 456-7034	16943
Whitegold Solutions Inc	7379	E	415 456-4493	16525
Young Mens Christian Assnsf	8641	C	415 459-9622	25443
Young Mens Christian Assnsf	8641	B	415 492-9622	25446

SAN RAMON, CA - Contra Costa County

	SIC	EMP	PHONE	ENTRY #
24 Hour Fitness Usa Inc (HQ)	7991	C	925 543-3100	18583
24 Hour Fitness Usa Inc	7991	D	916 722-7588	18589
24 Hour Fitness Worldwide Inc (PA)	7991	D	925 543-3100	18601
A D Bilich Inc	6162	E	925 820-5557	9809
A S A P Professional Services	7361	D	800 303-2727	14594
Accela Inc (PA)	7372	D	925 659-3200	15564
Accelon Inc	7361	E	925 216-5735	14598
Accountnow Inc	8742	D	925 498-1800	27301
Aetna Health California Inc (DH)	6324	C	925 543-9000	10253
Alexander Properties Company	6512	D	925 866-0100	10954
AMP Technologies LLC (PA)	7371	C	877 442-2824	15012
AMR Appraisals Inc	6531	D	925 400-6066	11299
Annabel Investment Company	6552	D	925 866-0100	11948
Armanino LLP (PA)	8721	C	925 790-2600	26291
Arrand Properties LLC	1521	E	925 289-1032	1129
AT&T Corp	8748	B	925 823-6949	27838
AT&T Corp	4812	D	925 327-7100	5273
AT&T Corp	4813	D	415 394-3000	5496
AT&T Corp	4813	D	925 275-8048	5500
AT&T Corp	4813	A	925 823-5388	5501
AT&T Corp	4813	A	925 823-9700	5514
AT&T Services	4813	C	925 901-9318	5515
AT&T Services	4813	D	925 831-4443	5519
AT&T Services	4813	C	415 823-0993	5524
AT&T Services Inc	4813	A	925 823-1443	5539
Bara Construction Services	1531	E	925 790-0130	1356
Bay Area Techworkers	7361	B	925 359-2200	14614
Bentley Company	8711	B	925 543-3500	25687
Blackhawk Information Services	7371	E	925 244-6701	15057
Bridges At Gale Ranch LLC	7997	D	925 735-4253	18901
Cabinda Gulf Oil Co Inc	1311	B	925 842-1000	1035
Carlson Barbee & Gibson Inc	8711	C	925 866-0322	25719
Castro Valley Health Inc	8082	C	510 690-1930	22399
Cellco Partnership	4812	D	925 743-9327	5338
Chase Home Finance	6162	C	925 277-3700	9830
Chevron Investor Inc (HQ)	6799	B	925 842-1000	12296
Chevron USA Inc	1311	D	925 842-0855	1042
Clubsport San Ramon LLC (PA)	7991	C	925 735-1182	18622
Cmg Financial Services	7389	D	925 983-3073	17084
Cmg Mortgage Inc (PA)	6163	B	619 554-1327	9918
Concessionaires Urban Park	7999	D	530 529-1513	19191
Digicentury Corporation	7371	D	408 213-0146	15138
Donor Network West (PA)	8099	C	925 480-3100	22947
Enpower Management Corp	4911	E	925 244-1100	6132
Express System Intermodal Inc	4731	C	801 302-6625	5073
Expressworks International LLC (PA)	8742	D	925 244-0900	27429
Ferreira Service Inc (PA)	1711	D	925 831-9330	2225
Five9 Inc (PA)	7372	C	925 201-2000	15667
G4s Secure Solutions (usa)	7381	C	925 543-0008	16655
General Electric Company	7372	C	925 242-6200	15676
Gorilla Tech Americas Inc	8742	C	925 365-1161	27452
Greystone Homes Inc	1521	C	925 242-0811	1187
Hill Physicians Med Group Inc (PA)	8011	B	800 445-5747	19560
Homegaincom Inc	6531	D	888 542-0800	11572
Hyatt Corporation	7011	D	925 743-1882	12813
Independent Quality Care Inc (PA)	8059	D	925 855-0881	21274
International Bus Mchs Corp	8742	D	925 277-5000	27481
Interntnal Ch of Frsqare Gospl	6022	D	925 964-9044	9503
Iron Horse Insurance Co	1311	A	925 842-1000	1045
Jaroth Inc	1731	D	925 553-3650	2622
Kaiser Foundation Hospitals	8011	A	925 244-7600	19645
KB Home South Bay Inc	1522	D	925 983-2500	1321
Kindercare Education LLC	8351	D	925 824-0267	24473
Legacy Mech & Enrgy Svcs Inc	1711	D	925 820-6938	2279
Lindquist LLP (PA)	8721	C	925 277-9100	26395
Logistic Air Inc	4522	E	925 465-0400	4883
Lucile Salter Packard Chil	8011	D	925 277-7550	19723
Marriott International Inc	7011	C	925 866-1228	12980
Mortgage X L	6211	E	925 830-8951	10062
Mountain Retreat Incorporated	6552	D	925 838-7780	11986
Mt View Apartments LLC	6513	D	925 866-8429	11173
Native Sons Landscaping Inc	0782	E	925 837-8175	918
Netpace Inc	7371	D	925 543-7760	15325
New York Life Insurance Co	6311	D	415 999-9576	10217
Old Republic HM Protection Inc	6411	B	925 866-1500	10815
One Planet Ops Inc (PA)	7311	C	925 983-3400	13890
Pacifica Reflections	1531	E	925 275-9800	1381
Parkway Apartments LLC	6513	E	925 866-8429	11185
Pinnacle Funding Group Inc	6163	E	925 552-5302	9944
Planetpro Inc (PA)	7361	D	925 277-0727	14728
Plus Group Inc	7361	B	925 831-8551	14729
Primed MGT Consulting Svcs Inc	8741	B	925 327-6710	27173
Procter & Gamble Distrg LLC	5169	B	925 867-4900	8999
Protiviti Inc	8721	D	415 402-3663	26429
Quicksort Inc (PA)	7389	D	925 820-8272	17438
R R Donnelley & Sons Company	5112	D	925 901-5300	8177
Reproductive Science Center	8011	D	925 867-1800	19911
Rfxcel Corporation	5045	D	925 824-0300	7179
Robert Half International Inc	7361	C	925 913-1000	14773
Rose International	8748	C	636 812-4000	28045
RW Lynch Co Inc (PA)	7311	C	925 837-3877	13917
Safe Security Inc	7382	B	925 830-4777	16917
Samsung	5063	A	925 380-6523	7469
San Ramon Regional Med Ctr Inc	8062	A	925 275-0634	21855
Sansa Technology LLC	8731	E	866 204-3710	26599
Seacastle Inc	7359	D	925 480-3000	14578
Security Alarm Fing Entps Inc	7382	D	925 830-4777	16921
Shapell Inc	7992	E	925 735-4253	18785
Simonich Corporation (HQ)	6163	D	925 830-1500	9951
Sirva Inc	4213	C	925 824-3109	4263
Splash Swim School Inc	7999	E	925 838-7946	19287
Spruce Technology Inc	7371	D	925 415-8160	15475
Summerhill Construction Co	1521	E	925 244-7520	1266
Toyota Motor Credit Corp	6141	D	925 830-8200	9765
Tracy Trujillo MD	8011	E	925 838-6511	20141
United Parcel Service Inc OH	4215	C	800 833-9943	4476

Employment Codes: A=Over 500 employees, B=251-500, C=101-250, D=51-100, E=45-50

SAN RAMON, CA

	SIC	EMP	PHONE	ENTRY #
Universal Protection Svc LP	7381	D	805 496-4401	16840
V A Anderson Enterprises Inc	7334	C	925 866-6150	14129
Warmington Homes	1531	C	925 866-6700	1392
Webly Systems Inc	7389	E	888 444-6400	17617
Wurldtech Security Tech Ltd	5065	D	604 669-6674	7660

SAN SIMEON, CA - San Luis Obispo County

	SIC	EMP	PHONE	ENTRY #
Cavalier Inn Incorporated	7011	D	805 927-6444	12501

SAN YSIDRO, CA - San Diego County

	SIC	EMP	PHONE	ENTRY #
Centro De Salud De La (PA)	8093	D	619 428-4463	22680

SANGER, CA - Fresno County

	SIC	EMP	PHONE	ENTRY #
Chooljian Bros Packing Co Inc	5149	E	559 875-5501	8814
Farmex Land Management Inc	7389	C	559 875-7181	17162
Gerawan Farming Partners Inc	0721	B	559 787-8780	479
Golden Living LLC	8059	E	559 875-6501	21250
Gongs Market of Sanger Inc (PA)	6512	E	559 875-5576	10990
J M Telford Farms	0191	E	559 875-4955	373
Rick Berry Inc	1743	E	559 875-1460	3023
Suma Fruit Intl USA Inc	0723	E	559 875-5000	587
Virginia Sarabian	0175	E	559 493-2900	251

SANTA ANA, CA - Orange County

	SIC	EMP	PHONE	ENTRY #
2100 Trust LLC (PA)	6733	C	877 469-7344	12167
5 Diamond Protection Inc	6512	D	949 466-1367	10951
A White and Yellow Cab Inc	4121	C	714 258-1000	3861
Accent Service Company Inc	7349	D	714 557-2837	14210
Adtek Engineering Service	8711	D	800 451-0782	25617
Advanced Clnroom McRclean Corp	7349	C	714 751-1152	14215
Aecom Global II LLC	8711	B	714 835-6886	25628
Affiliated Funding Corporation	6163	D	714 619-3100	9911
Ag/LPC Griffin Towers LP	6799	E	714 662-5902	12282
Alan B Whitson Company Inc	8742	A	949 955-1200	27314
Aldoc Inc	1711	D	714 836-8477	2117
Allied Anesthesia Med Group	8011	D	951 830-9816	19332
Allied Building Products Corp	5033	D	714 647-9792	7005
Alzheimers Care Since 1983	8082	E	714 641-0959	22356
AM Products Inc	5051	E	714 662-4454	7355
America West Airlines Inc	4512	D	949 852-5451	4786
American Airlines Inc	4512	C	949 852-5470	4791
American Concrete Cutting Inc	1795	D	714 547-7181	3447
American Express Travel	6153	D	714 547-7116	9769
American Leak Detection Inc	1711	E	714 836-8477	2128
American National Red Cross	8699	E	714 481-5300	25491
American Transport Inc	6162	D	714 567-8000	9816
American-1 Airtight SEC Co	7381	E	714 799-0605	16500
Aramark Unf & Career AP LLC	7218	C	714 545-4877	13610
Architectural Coatings Inc	1721	E	714 701-1360	2428
Assurant Inc	6411	B	714 571-3900	10631
B-Per Electronic Inc	4812	C	626 912-0600	5277
Banc of California Inc	6021	A	714 569-0451	9317
Barry McPherson Inc	6411	C	425 343-5000	10643
Beacon Sales Acquisition Inc	5033	C	714 288-1974	7008
Behr Process Sales Company	8743	C	714 545-7101	27734
Blower-Dempsay Corporation (PA)	5111	D	714 481-3800	8151
Boys Town California Inc	8641	D	714 558-0303	25221
Brethren Inc	5099	E	714 836-4800	8106
Brightview Landscape Svcs Inc	0781	E	714 546-7843	751
C V Productions Inc	4841	D	714 352-4446	5937
California Anesthesia Asso Med	8011	D	800 888-2186	19389
Calvalry Church Santa Ana Inc	8351	D	714 973-4800	24423
Capario Inc	6411	E	949 553-1974	10661
Carrasco Heleo	7349	D	714 639-1759	14245
Cellco Partnership	4812	D	714 775-0600	5384
Celmol Inc	5199	D	714 259-1000	9251
Certified Trnsp Svcs Inc	4151	D	714 835-8676	3916
Chamson Management Inc	7011	D	714 751-2400	12510
Charles W Bowers Museum Corp	8412	D	714 567-3600	25006
Chroma Systems	7217	C	714 557-8480	13593
Clear World Communications	4813	B	714 445-3900	5577
Clinica Medica Familiar	8011	D	714 541-0870	19441
Collectors Universe Inc (PA)	7699	D	949 567-1234	17968
Colton Real Estate Group (PA)	6519	D	949 475-4200	11250
Community Service Programs Inc (PA)	8322	D	714 492-1010	23777
Compwest Insurance Company	6331	D	714 641-9500	10412
Continental Currency Svcs Inc (HQ)	6099	E	714 569-0300	9713
Continental Currency Svcs Inc (PA)	6099	D	714 569-0300	9714
Contractors Flrg Svc Cal Inc	5023	C	714 556-6100	6855
County of Orange	8071	E	714 834-8385	22206
County of Orange	4953	B	714 834-4000	6470
County of Orange	8651	E	714 547-7500	25480
County of Orange	8322	D	714 834-8899	23875
County of Orange	8052	A	714 834-6021	21075
Cove Builders Inc	1522	E	714 436-2973	1305
Covenant Care California LLC	8051	D	714 554-9700	20500
CP Opco LLC	7359	D	714 540-6111	14533

	SIC	EMP	PHONE	ENTRY #
CRC Health Corporate	8093	D	714 542-3581	22717
Crown Building Maintenance Co	7349	E	714 434-9494	14274
D+h USA Corporation	7372	C	714 427-1000	15634
Data Trace Info Svcs LLC (HQ)	8999	D	714 250-6700	28127
Debtmerica LLC	7299	D	714 389-4200	13755
Dekra-Lite Industries Inc	7389	D	714 436-0705	17119
Deutsche Bank National Tr Co	6111	E	714 247-6000	9728
Dgwb Inc	7311	D	714 881-2300	13838
Dgwb Ventures LLC	7311	D	714 881-2308	13839
Discovery Scnce Ctr Ornge Cnty	7996	C	714 913-5010	18817
Dish Network Corporation	4841	E	714 424-0503	5994
Doubletree LLC	7011	D	714 825-3333	12595
Duplo USA Corporation (PA)	5044	D	949 752-8222	7052
Durham School Services L P	4173	C	714 542-8989	3957
East Katella Partnership	7011	E	714 978-8088	12606
Edison Mission Energy (DH)	4931	D	714 513-8000	6286
Edwards Theatres Circuit Inc	7832	D	714 557-5701	18326
Elite Nursing Services Inc	7361	E	949 475-0700	14645
Empire Building Services Inc	7349	D	714 836-7700	14290
Ephonamationcom Inc	7389	C	714 560-1000	17152
Experian Corporation	7323	A	714 830-7000	14058
F M Tarbell Co (HQ)	6531	C	714 972-0988	11506
F M Tarbell Co	6531	C	714 639-0677	11514
F R A L P	7261	D	714 633-1442	13706
Family Assessment Cnslng Edctn	8322	E	714 547-7345	23966
Financial Statement Svcs Inc (PA)	7331	D	714 436-3326	14070
First American Financial Corp (PA)	6361	C	714 250-3000	10517
First American Mortgage Svcs	6361	B	714 250-4210	10518
First American Title Company	6361	C	505 881-3300	10519
First American Title Insur Co (HQ)	6361	C	800 854-3643	10520
First American Title Insur Co	6361	C	714 800-3000	10524
First American Title Insur Co	6361	A	714 250-4000	10527
First American Trust Company (HQ)	6282	D	714 560-7856	10140
First Student Inc	4131	D	714 850-7578	3880
Fishel Company	1623	D	714 668-9268	1930
Freedom Cmmnctns Holdings Inc (DH)	6719	C	714 796-7000	12062
Freedom Colorado Info Inc	4813	B	719 632-5511	5604
French Park Care Center	8051	C	714 973-1656	20582
Fresh Grill LLC	5149	D	714 444-2126	8837
G W Maintenance Inc (PA)	5085	D	714 541-2211	7932
Gamboa Service Inc	7349	D	714 966-5325	14306
General Procurement Inc (PA)	5045	E	949 679-7960	7138
Goglanian Bakeries Inc (HQ)	5149	B	714 549-1524	8843
Goodwill Inds Orange Cnty Cal	8699	C	714 754-7808	25536
Gps Painting Wallcovering Inc	1721	C	714 730-8904	2452
Grants Landscape Services Inc	0782	D	714 444-1903	859
Guardsmark LLC (DH)	7381	C	714 619-9700	16679
Hardy & Harper Inc	1611	E	714 444-1851	1798
Hart King Coldren A Prof Corp	8111	D	714 432-8700	23302
Harveys Industries Inc	5137	D	714 277-4700	8386
Health Resources Corp	8062	B	714 754-5454	21596
Healthcare Partners LLC	8099	E	714 964-6229	22972
Hirsch Electronics LLC	5065	D	949 250-8888	7577
Hntb Corporation	8711	D	714 460-1600	25863
Hntb Gerwick Water Solutions	8711	D	714 460-1600	25865
Hollins Schechter A Prof Corp	8111	D	714 558-9119	23311
Honeywell International Inc	5075	C	714 796-7500	7741
Hospice Touch Inc	8082	D	310 574-5750	22478
Iaccess Technologies Inc	8711	D	714 922-9158	25871
Innovative Cnstr Solutions	8744	D	714 893-6366	27796
Integrus LLC	5044	D	714 547-9500	7054
Intergro Rehab Service	8049	D	714 901-4200	20329
IPC (usa) Inc (HQ)	5172	D	949 648-5600	9024
Jhc Investment Inc	7011	D	714 751-2400	12865
John M Frank Construction Inc	1542	D	714 210-3600	1584
Johnson La Follette	8111	D	714 558-7008	23328
Joint Corp	8041	D	714 294-2846	20296
Kaiser Foundation Hospitals	8011	A	714 223-2606	19646
Kaiser Foundation Hospitals	6324	D	888 988-2800	10321
Kaiser Foundation Hospitals	8062	E	714 967-4700	21679
Klein-Testan-Brundo	8111	E	714 245-8888	23357
Kpc Healthcare Inc	8062	C	714 800-1919	21694
Kya Services LLC	1752	D	714 659-6476	3124
La Boxing Franchise Corp	6794	B	714 668-0911	12218
Landcare USA LLC	0782	D	949 559-7771	888
Landcare USA LLC	0781	D	714 245-1465	776
Landmark Services Inc	7349	D	714 547-6308	14336
Latham & Watkins LLP	8111	B	714 755-8288	23366
Lenox Financial Mortgage Corp	6162	C	949 428-5100	9868
Lisi Inc	6399	D	714 460-5153	10572
Lloyd Pest Control Co	7342	E	714 979-6021	14188
M & A Mortgage Inc	6163	D	714 560-1970	9935
Macro-Z-Technology Company (PA)	1611	D	714 564-1130	1818
Madison Materials	4953	D	714 664-0159	6498
Main Electric Supply Co (PA)	5063	D	949 833-3052	7454

GEOGRAPHIC SECTION

SANTA BARBARA, CA

	SIC	EMP	PHONE	ENTRY #
Managed Homecare Inc	8082	E	951 341-0782	22503
Marketlinx Inc	7372	E	714 250-6751	15739
Marriott International Inc	7011	C	714 545-5261	12975
Medical Network Inc	8741	D	949 863-0022	27125
Melmet Steven J Law Ofc	8111	D	949 263-1000	23430
Merchants Building Maint Co	7349	B	714 973-9272	14353
Metropro Road Services Inc (PA)	7549	D	714 556-7600	17887
Midori Landscape Inc	0782	D	714 751-8792	911
Mission Ldscp Companies Inc	0782	C	714 545-9962	914
Moms Orange County	8082	E	714 972-2610	22509
Moore Law Group A Prof Corp	8111	D	714 431-2000	23439
Morgan Stanley & Co LLC	6211	D	714 836-5181	10053
Morrison Landscaping Inc	5052	E	714 571-0455	7410
Mpl Enterprises Inc	0782	D	714 545-1717	916
Newmark & Company RE Inc	8742	E	714 667-8252	27564
Newport Beach Fbo LLC	7363	D	949 851-0049	14917
Nieves Landscape Inc	0782	C	714 835-7332	923
North River Ranch LLC	0171	D	714 556-6244	124
Northgate Gonzalez Inc	7389	C	714 957-2529	17366
Nova Plumbing Inc	1711	C	714 556-6682	2305
NRG Power Inc	1731	D	714 424-6484	2670
Ntrust Infotech Private Ltd	7371	C	562 207-1610	15342
Oc Engineering	8711	D	714 667-3212	25997
Oc Lighthouse Construction	1522	E	949 797-0151	1328
OC Special Events SEC Inc	7381	C	714 541-4111	16750
Odyssey Healthcare Inc	8051	D	714 245-7420	20824
Olive Crest (PA)	8361	B	714 543-5437	24755
Optima Tax Relief LLC	7291	D	714 361-4636	13726
Orange Cast Title Southern Cal (PA)	7389	D	714 558-2836	17381
Orange County Cncl Bsa (PA)	8641	D	714 546-4990	25306
Orange County Employees Retir	6722	C	714 558-6200	12120
Orange County Global Med Ctr	8062	D	714 953-3500	21771
Orange County Head Start (PA)	8351	D	714 241-8920	24494
Orange County Internet Xchange	4813	C	714 450-7109	5676
Orange County Royale Convlscnt (PA)	8059	B	714 546-6450	21337
Orange County Services Inc	1711	E	714 541-9753	2312
Orange Countys Credit Union (PA)	6062	C	714 755-5900	9676
Orange Courier Inc	7389	B	714 384-3600	17382
Orangewood Chld Foundation	8699	D	714 480-2300	25562
Orchid MPS	5047	D	714 549-9203	7290
P J Video Services Inc	7812	D	714 705-6088	18124
Pacific Eastern Intl Pdts	5199	D	714 538-3434	9285
Pacific Foods & Dist Inc	5149	D	714 547-0787	8896
Pacific Rim Contractors Inc	1742	D	714 641-7380	2949
Pacific Rim Mech Contrs Inc	1711	D	714 285-2600	2316
Pacific Symphony	7929	D	714 876-2301	18484
Pacific Union Financial LLC	6282	C	714 918-0799	10169
Pacifica Hiorange LP	7011	D	714 556-3838	13063
Pacificare Dental	6324	C	661 631-8613	10365
Pacificare Health Plan Admin (DH)	6324	D	714 825-5200	10366
Parking Concepts Inc	7389	C	949 752-5558	17396
Parking Concepts Inc	7389	D	714 836-6009	17397
Partners Capital Group Inc	7389	C	949 916-3900	17399
Patrol Masters Inc	7381	C	714 426-2526	16756
Pds Tech Inc	7361	C	214 647-9600	14722
Perennial Engrg & Cnstr Inc	1521	B	714 771-2103	1234
Phoenix House Orange County	8361	D	714 939-9373	24768
Pipe Restoration Inc	1711	E	714 564-7600	2322
Platinum Equity Partners Inc	7532	C	714 444-3100	17766
Ponderosa Builders Inc	7349	A	714 434-9494	14392
Pps Parking Inc	7299	A	949 223-8707	13787
Professional Coin Grading Svc	7389	D	949 567-1246	17431
Prospect Medical Group Inc (HQ)	8741	B	714 796-5900	27179
Psomas	8713	C	714 751-7373	26277
Q S H Properties Inc	7011	B	714 957-9200	13115
R A F LP	7261	D	714 633-1442	13711
Ralph D Mitzel Inc	7353	D	714 554-4745	14495
Reed Thomas Company Inc	1794	D	714 558-7691	3441
Reputation Management Cons Inc	8742	D	949 682-7906	27614
Rgis LLC	7389	C	714 541-1431	17458
Rice Drywall Inc	1742	D	714 543-5400	2967
S E O P Inc	8742	C	949 682-7906	27630
S W K Properties LLC	7011	D	714 481-6300	13184
SA Recycling LLC	4953	D	714 667-7898	6545
Sager Electrical Supply Co Inc	5065	C	714 962-8666	7629
Santa Ana City of	7361	E	714 565-2600	14778
Santa Ana Country Club	7997	D	714 556-3000	19061
Santa Ana Police Officers Assn	8641	A	714 836-1211	25337
Santa Ana Radiology Center	8011	D	714 835-6055	19953
Santa Ana Unified School Dst	8099	D	714 431-1900	23052
Satellite Management Co (PA)	6531	C	714 558-2411	11834
Schaefer Ambulance Service Inc	7352	E	714 545-8486	14476
Schoolsfirst Federal Credit Un (PA)	6061	B	714 258-4000	9625
Scottish American Insurance (PA)	6411	D	714 550-5050	10863
Script To Screen Inc	7812	D	714 558-3287	18147
Service First Contrs Netwrk	1542	E	714 573-2200	1663
ServiceMaster Company LLC	7349	C	714 245-1465	14427
Shield Security Inc (DH)	7381	B	714 210-1501	16821
Silverwood Landscape Cnstr Inc	0782	C	714 427-6134	955
Simons Wholesale Bakery Inc	5149	E	714 259-0855	8921
Skeffington Enterprises Inc	6719	D	714 540-1700	12090
South Coast Fencing Center	1799	D	714 549-2946	3583
South Coast Stone Paving	1611	D	714 835-0258	1863
Southern Cal Blldog Rescue Inc	8699	E	714 547-5725	25585
Southern Cal Prmnnte Med Group	8011	D	714 967-4760	20036
Southern Cal Spcialty Care Inc	8062	D	714 564-7800	21904
Southern California Edison Co	4911	C	714 973-5481	6224
Southern California Edison Co	4911	C	714 973-5574	6232
Southwest Express LLC	4212	D	949 474-5038	4068
Southwest Landscape Inc	0782	D	714 545-1084	957
St Joseph Heritage Med Group (PA)	8011	C	714 633-1011	20055
State Compensation Insur Fund	6331	B	714 565-5000	10461
Sterling Plumbing Inc	1711	D	714 641-5480	2385
Sukut Construction LLC	1611	D	714 540-5351	1868
Sukut Construction Inc (PA)	1794	D	714 540-5351	3443
Sun Electric LP	1731	D	714 210-3744	2755
Sundance Construction Inc	1751	C	714 437-0802	3095
Systems Paving Inc (PA)	1741	D	714 957-5776	2837
T-Mobile Usa Inc	7629	C	626 261-7359	17945
Taber Company Inc	5031	D	714 543-7100	6965
Tait Environmental Svcs Inc (PA)	1799	D	714 560-8200	3588
Tang E TSE Inc	7379	E	714 957-4000	16499
Tarbell Financial Corporation (PA)	6163	D	714 972-0988	9955
Tc3 Health Inc (DH)	8748	D	949 943-8700	28069
Technology Resource Center Inc	7379	D	714 542-1004	16503
Tecta America Southern Cal (HQ)	1761	E	714 973-6233	3218
Templo Calvario Cmnty Dev Corp	8399	D	714 543-3711	24984
Ten The Enthusiast Network LLC	5192	C	714 709-9021	9174
Tenet Healthsystem Medical	8062	A	714 966-8191	21961
Terra Pacific Landscape (PA)	0781	D	714 567-0177	800
Toms Truck Center Inc	7513	C	714 835-1978	17654
Town & Country Manor of The Ch	8051	C	714 547-7581	20992
Towne Inc	7331	D	714 540-3095	14093
Transit Air Cargo Inc	4731	D	714 571-0393	5176
Trilogy Realty Group Inc	6531	D	937 206-0725	11882
Tristar Risk Management	6411	D	714 543-0700	10911
Union Environmental Inc	1799	E	714 550-0005	3593
United Petrochemicals Inc	5169	D	949 629-8736	9000
Universal Building Maint LLC	7349	A	714 619-9700	14458
Universal Protection Svc LP (HQ)	7381	A	714 619-9700	16843
Universal Services America LP (PA)	7381	A	714 619-9700	16845
University California Irvine	8011	D	714 480-2443	20170
URS-Weston Joint Venture	8711	E	714 433-7710	26134
USA Waste of California Inc	4953	D	714 637-3010	6590
Utility Systems Science (PA)	7371	D	714 542-1004	15520
Vietnamese Cmnty Orange Cnty (PA)	8399	D	714 558-6009	24995
Visiting Nrse Assn Orange Cnty (PA)	8082	D	949 263-4700	22591
Voice Cnty Amer & Lrng For Lf	8641	D	714 546-8558	25400
Volunteers of America	8322	A	714 426-9834	24283
Waste MGT Collectn Recycl Inc	7353	B	714 637-3010	14502
Wells Fargo Bank National Assn	6021	E	714 571-2200	9463
West Coast Aviation Svcs LLC (PA)	8742	E	949 852-8340	27719
Western Medical Center Aux (HQ)	8062	C	714 835-3555	22030
White Cap Construction Supply	5031	A	949 794-5300	7797
William Hzmlhlch Archtects Inc	8712	D	949 250-0607	26268
Windsor Capital Group Inc	7011	D	714 241-3800	13423
Wm Vandergeest Landscape Care	0782	D	714 545-8432	980
Womens Law Center	8322	E	714 667-1038	24294
Xerox Corporation	5044	B	714 565-1100	7078

SANTA BARBARA, CA - Santa Barbara County

	SIC	EMP	PHONE	ENTRY #
1260 Bb Property LLC	7011	B	805 969-2261	12358
Advanced Dental Imaging LLC	8072	E	805 687-5571	22300
Agilysys Inc	7373	C	805 692-6339	15900
Air Pollution Control District	8748	D	805 961-8800	27822
American Baptist Homes of West	6513	E	805 687-1571	11085
American Indian Health & Svcs	8099	E	805 681-7356	22884
Applied Research Assoc Inc	8731	D	805 662-4810	26473
Arcana Corporation	7389	E	805 882-1305	17001
Bartlett Pringle & Wolf LLP	8721	E	805 564-2103	26292
Bcra Resort Services Inc	7011	C	805 571-3176	12428
Beach Motel Partners Ltd	7011	B	800 755-0222	12429
BFI Waste Systems N Amer Inc	4953	D	805 965-5248	6440
Birnam Wood Golf Club	7997	D	805 969-2223	18894
Brightview Golf Maint Inc	1629	E	805 968-6400	2029
Brown & Brown Inc	6411	D	805 965-0071	10650
Butler International Inc (PA)	7363	A	805 882-2200	14847
Butler Service Group Inc (HQ)	7363	D	201 891-5312	14848
Caesar and Seider Insur Svcs (PA)	6411	D	805 682-2571	10655
California Convalescent Hosp	8059	D	805 682-1355	21173
Cancer Foundation Trtmnt Ctr	8011	D	805 682-7300	19399

Employment Codes: A=Over 500 employees, B=251-500, C=101-250, D=51-100, E=45-50

2017 Directory of California Wholesalers and Services Companies

© Mergent Inc. 1-800-342-5647

1763

SANTA BARBARA, CA

Company	SIC	EMP	PHONE	ENTRY #
Cellco Partnership	4812	D	805 569-2525	5378
Channel Islands Young Mens Ch	8641	C	805 687-7727	25233
Channel Islands Young Mens Ch	8641	D	805 969-3288	25234
Chicago Title Insurance Co (HQ)	6361	C	805 565-6900	10509
Child Abuse Lstening Mediation	8322	E	805 965-2376	23730
Cicileo Landscapes	0781	E	805 967-3939	758
Cliff View Terrace Inc	8361	D	805 682-7443	24601
Coldwell Banker Premier Prpts	6531	D	805 565-2200	11410
Commission Junction Inc (DH)	7371	D	805 730-8000	15096
Compass Health Inc	8051	A	805 687-6651	20469
Cottage Care Center	8062	D	805 682-7111	21513
County of Santa Barbara Alcoho	8093	D	805 681-4093	22711
Covenant Care California LLC	8051	C	805 964-4871	20495
Cox Communications Inc	4841	D	805 681-6600	5978
CP Opco LLC	7359	D	805 563-3800	14529
Dennis Allen Associates (PA)	1521	D	805 884-8777	1165
Due West LLC	7011	D	805 884-0300	12603
El Capitan Ranch LLC	7033	D	805 685-3887	13480
Employbridge LLC (HQ)	7363	C	805 882-2200	14873
Encina Pepper Tree Joint Ventr (PA)	7011	E	805 687-5511	12619
Encina Pepper Tree Joint Ventr	7011	E	805 682-7277	12620
Evangelical Covenant Church	8361	C	805 687-0701	24655
Evans Hardy & Young Inc	7311	E	805 963-5841	13847
Family Svc Agcy Santa Barbara	8322	D	805 965-1001	23973
Fastclick Inc	7319	D	805 689-9839	13995
Fess Prker-Red Lion Gen Partnr	7011	B	805 564-4333	12635
First American Financial Corp	6282	B	805 969-6883	10139
Frank Schipper Construction Co	1542	E	805 963-4359	1554
Freeman Investments Inc	7533	D	805 687-4327	17778
Front Prch Cmmunities/Services	8059	D	805 687-0793	21227
Goleta Valley Cottage Hospital	8062	B	805 681-6468	21581
Granite Construction Company	1622	C	805 964-9951	1892
Green Hills Software Inc (PA)	5013	C	805 965-6044	6735
H D G Associates	7011	D	805 963-0744	12682
Help Unlmted Personnel Svc Inc	8082	C	805 962-4646	22456
Helping Hands Sanctuary of Ida	8051	D	805 687-6651	20665
Hillside House Inc	8052	D	805 687-4818	21084
Hilton Worldwide Inc	7011	B	805 564-4333	12715
Hub Intrntional Insur Svcs Inc	6411	D	805 682-2571	10742
International Alliance Thea	8631	D	805 898-0442	25173
Interstate Hotels Resorts Inc	8741	D	805 966-2285	27071
JM Roofing Company Inc	1761	D	805 966-3696	3181
John Kenney Construction Inc	1771	D	805 884-1579	3281
Jordanos Inc (PA)	5181	C	805 964-0611	9066
Kenneth P Slaught Inc	6531	E	805 962-8989	11615
La Cumbre Country Club	7997	D	805 687-2421	18969
Lacolina Jr High CA Congress O	8641	D	805 967-4506	25281
Leidos Inc	8731	D	805 563-9597	26551
Logicmonitor Inc	7375	D	805 617-3884	16250
Los Prietos Boys Camp	8361	D	805 692-1750	24721
Marborg Industries (PA)	4953	C	805 963-1852	6500
Master Clean USA Inc	7349	E	805 681-0950	14351
Meathead Movers Inc	4213	D	805 966-6328	4227
Mentor Worldwide LLC	5047	B	805 681-6000	7279
Mercer Advisors Inc (PA)	6282	D	805 565-1681	10163
Mercer Global Securities LLC	6211	D	805 565-1681	10028
Mission Linen Supply	7213	E	805 962-7687	13560
Mission Security and Patrol	7381	D	805 899-3039	16737
MNS Engineers Inc (PA)	8711	D	805 692-6921	25971
Modular Systems Inc	6531	D	805 963-9350	11690
Montecito Country Club Inc	7997	D	805 969-0800	19006
Montecito Fire Protection Dst	8641	E	805 969-7762	25299
Montecito Retirement Assn	8051	B	805 969-8011	20795
Mufg Union Bank Na	6021	D	805 965-5091	9403
Mullen & Henzell LLP	8111	E	805 966-1501	23454
National Security Tech LLC	7381	A	805 681-2488	16743
Nevins-Adams Properties Inc (PA)	6512	C	805 963-2884	11024
New York Life Insurance Co	6311	D	805 898-7625	10214
Nhr Newco Holdings LLC (PA)	5045	B	800 230-6638	7168
Pacifica Hotel Company (HQ)	6531	E	805 957-0095	11734
Parenthood of Planned (PA)	8093	D	805 963-2445	22792
People Creating Success Inc	8322	D	805 692-5290	24134
Peoplefluent Inc	7371	D	805 730-1450	15372
Pitts & Bachmann Realtors Inc	6531	D	805 963-1391	11753
Price Postel and Parma LLP	8111	D	805 962-0011	23516
Qad Inc (PA)	7372	C	805 566-6000	15821
Real Time Staffing Services	7361	D	805 882-2200	14747
Rightscale Inc	7371	C	805 500-4164	15423
Roman Cath Arch of Los Angeles	7261	A	805 687-5451	13713
Ronald L Wolfe & Assoc Inc	6531	E	805 964-6770	11822
S B C Senior Care Inc	8082	D	805 560-6995	22552
San Marcos Kids Helpng Kids FN	8641	C	800 659-6411	25335
San Ysidro Bb Property LLC	7011	C	805 969-5046	13209
Sansum Clinic	8011	D	805 681-7700	19952
Sansum Clinic	8082	E	805 682-6507	22556
Santa Barbara Athletic CLB Inc	7997	D	805 966-6147	19062
Santa Barbara City of	7389	C	805 564-5485	17474
Santa Barbara Cottage Hospital (PA)	8062	A	805 682-7111	21857
Santa Barbara County of	8322	B	805 882-3700	24187
Santa Barbara County of	8099	D	805 681-5100	23053
Santa Barbara County of	8322	C	805 884-1600	24190
Santa Barbara County of	8322	C	866 901-3212	24191
Santa Barbara Fabricare Inc	7216	E	805 963-6677	13585
Santa Barbara Metro Trnst Dst (PA)	4111	C	805 963-3364	3713
Santa Barbara Museum	8412	D	805 682-4711	25047
Santa Barbara Museum of Art (PA)	8412	D	805 963-4364	25048
Santa Barbara PC Users Group	7389	E	805 964-5411	17475
Santa Barbara San Luis Obispo	6321	D	800 421-2560	10248
Santa Barbra Cttge Hsptl	8071	D	805 569-7367	22276
Santa Barbra Cttge Hsptl	8071	A	805 569-7224	22277
Santa Brbara Zlgcal Foundation	8422	C	805 962-1673	25070
Select Temporaries LLC (DH)	7361	D	805 882-2200	14784
Smith Broadcasting Group Inc (PA)	8741	D	805 965-0400	27217
Smith Broadcasting Group Inc	4833	D	805 882-3933	5911
Specialty Team Plastering Inc	1742	C	805 966-3858	2982
Stantec Consulting Svcs Inc	8713	D	805 963-9532	26282
Stewart Information Svcs Corp	6541	D	805 899-7700	11940
Sutter Health	8011	B	805 966-1600	20100
Tempest Telecom Solutions LLC (PA)	8748	D	805 879-4800	28071
The Valley Club of Montecito	7997	E	805 969-2215	19105
Tnci Operating Company LLC (HQ)	4813	D	800 800-8400	5709
Towbes Group Inc (PA)	6552	B	805 962-2121	12020
Town & Country Event Rentals	7389	B	805 770-5729	17536
Tri-Counties Association F (PA)	8322	D	805 962-7881	24259
Tropicana Gardens Holdings LLC	7011	E	805 968-4319	13361
Trueblue Inc	7363	E	805 963-5370	14964
Ucp Work Inc	8699	C	805 962-6699	25591
United Paradyne Corporation	8741	D	805 734-2359	27265
United Seal Coating Slurryseal	1542	D	805 563-4922	1708
United States Marines Youth Fd	8641	D	805 967-7990	25385
Upham Hotel	7011	D	805 962-0058	13369
URS Group Inc	8711	D	805 964-6010	26126
Valencia Tree Landscape	0781	E	805 965-4244	802
Vetronix Sales Corporation	5013	D	805 966-2000	6778
Visiting Care & Companions Inc	8082	D	805 690-6202	22590
Visiting Nurse & Hospice Care (PA)	8621	D	805 965-5555	25162
W J Griffin Inc	0181	C	805 683-5639	324
Wayne R Kidder	8011	D	805 967-6993	20232
Yardi Systems Inc (PA)	7371	B	805 699-2040	15555

SANTA CLARA, CA - Santa Clara County

Company	SIC	EMP	PHONE	ENTRY #
Abacus Business Solutions Inc	7379	D	408 200-0977	16311
Accel North America Inc	5045	C	408 514-5199	7080
Access Intelligence LLC	8732	D	650 384-4300	26641
Adesto Technologies Corp	8731	D	408 400-0578	26461
Aeris Communications Inc	4813	D	408 557-1900	5455
Aerohive Networks Inc	7373	B	408 988-9918	15898
Alliance Roofing Company Inc (PA)	1761	E	800 579-2595	3139
American Labor Pool Inc	7361	E	408 496-9950	14606
American Reprographics Co LLC	7334	D	408 295-5770	14103
Anderson PCF Engrg Cnstr Inc	1629	D	408 970-9900	2021
Applied Materials Inc	1522	D	408 727-5555	1292
Applied Materials Inc	4225	D	408 727-5555	4523
Aramark Spt & Entrmt Group LLC	7929	D	408 748-7030	18455
Arrow Electronics Inc	5065	C	631 847-2918	7523
Asiainfo-Linkage Inc	4813	A	408 970-9788	5460
AT&T Corp	4813	D	408 980-2004	5506
Atac (PA)	7373	D	408 736-2822	15906
B A Technolinks Corporation	8742	D	408 940-5921	27336
Backweb Technologies Inc	5045	E	408 933-1700	7098
Bandai Namco Entrmt Amer Inc	5092	C	408 235-2000	8038
Bay Counties Waste Svcs Inc	4953	D	408 565-9900	6436
Bill Wilson Center (PA)	8322	C	408 243-0222	23684
Biltmore Hotel	7011	C	408 988-8411	12452
Burdick Painting	1799	D	408 567-1330	3503
Bytemobile Inc (DH)	4899	D	408 327-7700	6061
Ca Inc	7372	C	800 225-5224	15612
California Eastern Labs Inc (PA)	5065	D	408 919-2500	7541
Calsoft Labs Inc (HQ)	7373	B	408 755-3001	15913
Cedar Fair LP	7996	C	408 988-1776	18813
Centrify Corporation	7371	B	669 444-5200	15078
Cerium Systems Inc	7379	D	408 623-0787	16333
Church of Scientology	8322	C	650 969-5262	23746
Church of Vly Rtrment Hmes Inc	8361	D	408 241-7750	24599
Cignex Datamatics Inc (PA)	7371	C	408 327-9900	15084
Cisco Webex LLC (HQ)	7389	A	408 435-7000	17072
Citrix Systems Inc	7371	D	408 790-8000	15087
City of Santa Clara	1799	D	408 615-3770	3508
City of Santa Clara	4911	E	408 615-2300	6116
City of Santa Clara	4911	C	408 615-2046	6117
Coast Personnel Services Inc (PA)	7363	A	408 653-2100	14863

SANTA CLARA, CA

Company	SIC	EMP	PHONE	ENTRY #
Coastal Paving Incorporated	1771	D	408 988-5559	3244
Community Home Partners LLC	8052	D	408 985-5252	21071
Complete Millwork Services Inc	5031	D	408 567-9664	6919
Covenant Care California LLC	8051	D	408 248-3736	20488
Cybercsi Inc	5045	D	408 727-2900	7113
Cyphort Inc	5045	E	408 841-4665	7115
Dan Connolly Inc	7381	D	408 241-0910	16621
Data Domain LLC (DH)	7373	C	408 980-4800	15928
Datastax Inc (PA)	8748	D	650 389-6000	27894
Decathlon Club Inc	7991	D	408 738-2582	18626
Dewmobile USA Inc	7371	E	408 550-2818	15134
Dimension Data Cloud Solutions (DH)	7371	D	408 567-2000	15141
Dolan Concrete Construction	1771	D	408 869-3250	3259
Drain Doctor	1711	E	408 970-3800	2208
Drobo Inc	5045	D	408 454-4200	7122
E2c Inc	8748	E	408 327-5700	27901
Eag Holdings LLC	8748	A	408 530-3500	27902
Eag Inc (PA)	8734	C	408 454-4600	26845
Elcor Electric Inc	1731	C	408 986-1320	2582
Electric USA	1731	E	800 921-1151	2585
Emagia Corporation	7389	E	408 654-6575	17149
Embrane Inc	7371	E	408 550-2700	15163
EMC Corporation	7372	C	408 566-2000	15655
Encore Trucking Inc	4212	D	408 330-7600	4015
Enterprise Solutions Inc	8748	C	408 727-3627	27915
Environmental Systems Inc (PA)	1711	D	408 980-1711	2220
Evans Analytical Group LLC (HQ)	8734	C	408 454-4600	26853
Everett Basham	4813	D	408 261-3000	5598
Fast Pro Inc	5013	D	408 566-0200	6730
Fedex Freight Corporation	4212	E	408 988-2111	4018
Filemaker Inc (HQ)	7372	C	408 987-7000	15663
Firm A Chugh Professional Corp	8111	E	408 970-0100	23240
Flair Building Services	7349	D	408 987-4040	14298
Forest Park Cabana Club	7997	E	408 244-1884	18952
Forty Niners Football Co LLC	7941	D	408 562-4949	18544
Fragomen Del Rey Bernse	8111	D	408 919-0600	23257
Frontech N Fujitsu Amer Inc	7371	D	408 982-3697	15195
Frost & Sullivan	8732	D	650 475-4500	26666
Futurewei Technologies Inc	4813	C	469 277-5700	5614
Gigamon Inc (PA)	7372	C	408 831-4000	15678
Globalfoundries Americas Inc (DH)	5065	D	408 462-3900	7575
Granite Construction Company	1611	C	408 327-7000	1782
Gridiron Systems Inc	7371	C	201 502-0512	15214
Hathaway Dinwiddie Cnstr Co	6512	D	415 986-2718	10998
Hathaway Dinwiddie Cnstr Group	6512	D	408 988-4200	10999
Hcl Finance Inc (PA)	6162	D	408 845-9035	9853
Hertz Corporation	7514	D	408 450-6025	17685
Hitachi Data Systems Corp (DH)	5045	B	408 970-1000	7141
Honeywell International Inc	5065	D	408 986-8200	7580
Hortonworks Inc	7372	C	408 916-4121	15692
Host Hotels & Resorts LP	7011	D	408 988-1500	12765
Hostmark Investors Ltd Partnr	8741	C	408 330-0001	27055
Hpt Trs Ihg-2 Inc	7011	D	408 241-9305	12797
Hudson Tchmart Cmmerce Ctr LLC	6512	D	408 451-4440	11002
Hyatt Regency Santa Clara	7011	D	408 200-1234	12831
Immigration Voice	6733	D	408 204-2200	12175
Impec Group Inc	7349	C	408 330-9350	14324
In Home Health Inc	8082	D	408 986-8160	22481
Infoblox Inc (PA)	7374	C	408 986-4000	16148
Innova Solutions Inc	7379	C	408 889-2020	16402
Innovative Silicon Inc	7389	D	408 572-8700	17241
Intel Media Inc	4841	B	408 765-0063	6007
Intellipro Group Inc	7379	B	408 200-9891	16404
International Bus Mchs Corp	7371	A	408 850-8999	15249
International SEC Svcs Inc	7381	D	925 634-1935	16709
Intervision Systems Tech Inc (PA)	7373	E	408 980-8550	15972
Ip Infusion Inc (HQ)	7373	D	408 400-1900	15973
Irdeto Usa Inc (DH)	7371	D	760 268-7299	15256
Ironclad Security Services Inc	7381	D	408 773-2800	16712
J & J Acoustics Inc	1742	C	408 275-9255	2914
Jamcracker Inc	4813	E	408 496-5500	5641
Jiangsu Juwang Info Tech Co	7371	D	510 967-3729	15262
Joseph J Albanese Inc	1771	A	408 727-5700	3284
Kaiser Foundation Hospitals	8062	A	408 851-1000	21678
Kana Software Inc (HQ)	7372	D	650 614-8300	15721
Kazeon Systems Inc	7371	D	650 641-8100	15267
Keypoint Credit Union (PA)	6062	C	408 731-4100	9670
Keypoint Credit Union	6062	D	408 562-7011	9671
Kno Inc	7372	D	408 844-8120	15724
Laxmi Group Inc	7371	D	408 329-7733	15273
Legrande Affaire Inc	4119	D	408 988-4884	3813
Lockheed Martin Corporation	7373	A	408 734-4980	15989
Lombardo Diamnd Core Drlg Inc	1771	D	408 727-7922	3292
Marianis Inn & Restaurant	7011	C	408 243-0312	12941
Matomy USA Inc	4813	C	408 400-2401	5650
Maxonic Inc	7379	D	408 777-6825	16430
McAfee Inc (HQ)	7372	A	408 346-3832	15741
McAfee Security LLC	7372	A	866 622-3911	15742
Mera Software Services Inc	7371	D	650 703-7226	15299
Microsoft Corporation	7372	D	408 987-9608	15756
Mission Trail Wste Systems Inc	4212	D	408 727-5365	4041
Mobileum Inc (PA)	4899	D	408 844-6600	6082
Move Inc (HQ)	6531	B	408 558-7100	11696
Moving Solutions Inc	4214	C	408 920-0110	4364
Msr Hotels & Resorts Inc	7011	D	408 496-6400	13012
National Instruments Corp	7372	B	408 610-6800	15768
National Rental (us) Inc	7514	D	408 492-0501	17691
Net Optics Inc	7372	D	408 737-7777	15770
Net4site Inc	8742	B	408 427-3004	27562
Netbase Solutions Inc (PA)	8742	D	650 810-2100	27563
Nexenta Systems Inc	7372	C	408 791-3341	15777
Ni Ki Cruz LLC	7389	D	408 332-7616	17359
Norland Group	7379	C	408 855-8255	16439
O2 Micro Inc	7373	D	408 987-5920	16020
Onebill Software Inc	7371	D	844 462-7638	15351
Ontario Airport Hotel Corp	7011	C	408 562-6709	13047
Ooyala Inc (DH)	7371	C	650 961-3400	15352
Opallios Inc	8748	E	408 769-4594	28010
Optmial Hospice Foundation	8082	D	408 207-9222	22525
Oracle America Inc	7371	C	408 276-4300	15356
Oracle America Inc	7371	C	408 276-3331	15357
Oracle Corporation	7372	B	408 421-2890	15791
Oracle Corporation	7372	B	408 276-5552	15792
Oracle Corporation	7372	B	650 506-9864	15795
Owens Corning Sales LLC	5033	B	408 235-1351	7013
Pactron	7379	B	408 329-5500	16452
PDM Steel Service Centers	5051	D	408 988-3000	7388
Permanente Kaiser Intl	8011	E	408 236-6400	19831
Persistent Systems Inc (HQ)	7371	D	408 216-7010	15376
Plaza Suites	7011	D	408 748-9800	13102
Plumgrid Inc	7372	D	408 800-7586	15818
Posh Bagel Inc (PA)	5149	C	408 980-8451	8909
Posh Bakery Inc	5149	C	408 980-8451	8910
Priority Dispatch Service Inc	4215	D	408 400-3860	4421
Processweaver Inc	7371	D	888 932-8373	15396
Pyramid Building Maint Corp (PA)	7349	A	408 727-9393	14398
Q Analysts LLC (PA)	8742	D	408 907-8500	27604
Quality Investment Santa Clara	7374	D	408 844-6000	16174
Radiabeam Technologies LLC	8733	E	310 822-5845	26799
Recology Los Altos	4953	D	650 961-8044	6525
Recology South Bay	4953	D	408 725-4020	6529
Redwood Electric Group Inc (PA)	1731	A	707 451-7348	2703
Renesas Electronics Amer Inc (DH)	5065	B	408 588-6000	7627
Renesas Technology America Inc	5065	C	408 588-6000	7628
Restivo Enterprises	4119	C	408 988-4884	3833
Rivio Inc	4813	E	408 653-4400	5693
Robert A Bothman Inc (PA)	1771	C	408 279-2277	3322
Rocket Ems Inc	1731	C	408 727-3700	2714
Royal Glass Company Inc	1793	D	408 969-0444	3414
Rsa Security LLC	7371	C	650 529-9992	15431
San Francisco Forty Niners	6719	C	408 562-4949	12088
San Francisco Forty Niners (PA)	7941	C	408 562-4949	18562
San Jose Bluprt Svc & Sup Co (PA)	7334	D	408 295-5770	14127
San Jose Construction Co Inc (PA)	1542	D	408 986-8711	1658
Sandcraft Inc	8731	D	925 253-8311	26598
Santa Clara Tenant Corp	7011	D	408 496-6400	13212
Santa Clara Vngard Booster CLB	8641	E	408 727-5532	25338
Santa Clara Womens Club	7997	D	408 246-8000	19064
Sat Corporation (DH)	7371	D	402 208-9200	15440
Savvis Communications Corp	7375	C	408 884-6269	16260
Serrano Electric Inc	1731	E	408 986-1570	2730
Sezzo Labs Inc	7373	E	408 562-0081	16053
Sharedata Inc	7372	D	408 490-2500	15836
Silicon Valley Bank (HQ)	6029	A	408 654-7400	9561
Silicon Vly McRelectronics Inc (PA)	5065	E	408 844-7100	7632
Siliconexpert Technologies	7374	E	408 330-7575	16188
Simco Electronics (PA)	8734	D	408 734-9750	26890
Soft Machines Inc	7373	D	408 969-0215	16054
Software Ag Inc	7372	C	408 490-5300	15300
Solidcore Systems Inc (DH)	7371	D	408 387-8400	15465
Solix Technologies Inc (PA)	7371	C	408 654-6400	15467
Sonicwall LLC (DH)	7373	C	800 509-1265	16057
Soundhound Inc (PA)	7371	D	408 441-3200	15471
South Bay Historical RR Soc	8699	E	408 243-3969	25584
Spec Personnel LLC	7361	C	408 727-8000	14792
Special Home Needs	8052	D	408 985-8666	21112
Sra Oss Inc	7372	C	408 855-8200	15846
Stmicroelectronics Inc	5065	D	408 452-8585	7640
Stone Publishing Inc (PA)	8741	D	408 450-7910	27232
Sunset Building Maintance Inc	7349	E	408 727-3408	14440

Employment Codes: A=Over 500 employees, B=251-500, C=101-250, D=51-100, E=45-50

2017 Directory of California Wholesalers and Services Companies

© Mergent Inc. 1-800-342-5647

SANTA CLARA, CA

Company	SIC	EMP	PHONE	ENTRY #
Sutter Health	8011	B	408 524-5952	20083
Sutter Health	8011	C	408 241-3801	20110
Svb Financial Group **(PA)**	6022	D	408 654-7400	9528
Tata America Intl Corp	7379	D	408 569-5845	16501
Tavant Technologies Inc **(PA)**	7371	C	408 519-5400	15492
Teen Challenge Norwestcal Nev	8322	D	408 703-2001	24246
Tekever Corporation	7372	D	408 730-2617	15859
Tensilica Inc **(HQ)**	6794	D	408 986-8000	12225
Thermal Mechanical Inc	1711	D	408 988-8744	2395
Three Way Inc	4214	C	408 748-6902	4380
Tiger Analytics LLC	8732	D	408 508-4430	26712
TLC of Bay Area Inc	8051	D	408 988-7667	20990
Trianz **(HQ)**	7379	C	408 387-5800	16512
Turnstone Systems Inc	6531	D	408 907-1400	11887
United Marble & Granite Inc	5032	D	408 347-3300	6997
Valley Process Systems Inc	1711	D	408 261-1277	2405
Valley Water Proofing Inc	1799	D	408 985-7701	3597
Verint Americas Inc	7371	D	408 830-5400	15523
Vertical Communications Inc **(PA)**	7372	D	408 404-1600	15876
Webyog Inc	7371	C	408 512-1434	15543
Wescon Technology Inc	7373	C	408 727-8818	16080
Western Athletic Clubs Inc	7991	D	408 738-2582	18704
Whatsapp Inc	4899	D	650 336-3079	6099
Whitehat Security Inc	7379	D	408 343-8300	16526
Wincere Inc	7379	C	408 841-4355	16527
Worldwide Ground Transportatio	4119	D	408 727-0000	3860
Xyka Inc	7371	E	408 340-1923	15554
Yahoo Inc	4813	C	408 349-5080	5737
Yellow Cab Company Penninsula	4121	D	408 739-1234	3874
Yes Videocom Inc **(PA)**	7812	D	408 907-7600	18207
YMCA of Silicon Valley **(PA)**	8641	D	408 351-6400	25430

SANTA CLARITA, CA - Los Angeles County

Company	SIC	EMP	PHONE	ENTRY #
American Health Services LLC	8011	C	661 254-6630	19339
American Postal Workers Union	8631	D	661 775-8174	25165
Applied Companies Inc **(PA)**	8711	D	661 257-0090	25659
AT&T Corp	4813	D	661 297-1720	5474
Broadspire Inc	4813	D	213 785-8043	5565
Canon Recruiting Group LLC	7363	B	661 252-7400	14850
Cellco Partnership	4812	C	661 296-7585	5325
CMA Baking Co	5149	D	661 775-0854	8815
Curtiss-Wright Controls	8711	C	661 257-4430	25759
Curtiss-Wright Controls **(DH)**	8711	D	661 702-1494	25760
De Oliviera Concrete Inc	1771	E	661 252-7522	3254
Facey Medical Foundation	8099	D	661 250-5225	22959
Facey Medical Foundation	8099	D	661 513-2100	22960
Friendly Valley Recrtl Assn	8322	E	661 252-3223	23986
Gierahn Dry Wall Inc	1742	E	661 257-7900	2903
Golden Crust Bakeries Inc	5149	D	661 294-9750	8847
Henry Mayo Newhall Mem Hosp	8099	B	661 253-8227	22974
Hobby Lobby Stores Inc	7389	C	661 513-0005	17223
Honda Performance Dev Inc	7549	D	661 294-7300	17884
Hope of Valley Mission	8093	E	661 673-5951	22747
Internet Security Systems Inc	7371	C	661 296-5752	15253
Kaiser Foundation Hospitals	8011	A	888 778-5000	19647
Kaiser Foundation Hospitals	8093	D	661 222-2000	22754
Kaiser Foundation Hospitals	8011	D	661 222-2323	19673
Los Angeles Resdntl Cmmnty Fdn	8361	D	661 296-8636	24719
Los Angeles Residential Comm F	8361	D	661 296-8636	24720
Marathon Industries Inc	5012	C	661 286-1520	6688
Midwest Enviromental Control	8731	E	661 255-0722	26569
Mountasia Family Fun Center	7996	D	661 253-4386	18827
Mufg Union Bank Na	6021	D	661 799-8529	9408
National Technical Systems Inc	8734	D	661 259-8184	26877
Oceanside Hlthcare Stffing Inc	8099	C	213 503-5649	23011
Paul Mitchell John Systems **(PA)**	5122	C	661 298-0400	8290
Petersen-Dean Inc	1761	D	661 254-3322	3199
Princess Cruise Lines Ltd **(HQ)**	4481	A	661 753-0000	4725
Princess Cruise Lines Ltd	4481	A	661 753-2291	4726
Providence Health & Services	8999	A	661 257-9999	28157
Robinson Ranch Golf LLC	7992	C	818 885-0599	18777
S C Security Inc	7381	E	661 251-6999	16777
Santa Clarita City of	4131	B	661 294-1287	3886
Santa Clarita City of	7999	D	661 284-1423	19278
Santa Clarita Concrete	1771	E	661 252-2012	3325
Santa Clarita Health Care Assn **(PA)**	8741	D	661 253-8000	27205
Santa Clarita Interiors Inc	1791	D	661 253-0861	3400
Santa Clarita Valley Bldrs Inc	1751	D	661 295-6722	3086
Santa Clarita Vlly Cmmtt Aging	8322	D	661 259-9444	24194
Saugus Union School District	4151	D	661 298-3240	3949
Sheldon Mechanical Corporation	1711	D	661 286-1361	2365
Southern Cal Prmnnte Med Group	8062	D	661 290-3100	21901
Southern Cal Prmnnte Med Group	8011	E	661 222-2150	20041
Storer Transportation Service	4789	C	661 288-0400	5245
Trio Consulting LLC	8699	C	818 309-7919	25590
United Westlabs Inc	8071	D	661 254-0801	22294
Universal Wood Moulding Inc **(PA)**	5023	E	661 362-6262	6900
USA Waste of California Inc	4953	D	661 259-2398	6589

SANTA CRUZ, CA - Santa Cruz County

Company	SIC	EMP	PHONE	ENTRY #
(a) Tool Shed Inc **(PA)**	7359	D	831 477-7133	14503
7th Avenue Center LLC	8063	D	831 476-1700	22036
Alliance Member Services Inc	8699	D	831 459-0980	25488
American Medical Response	4119	D	831 423-7030	3753
Associated Pathology Med Group	8011	D	831 462-7625	19361
AT&T Corp	4812	D	831 457-8255	5271
Benchmark-Tech Corporation	7389	C	831 475-5600	17026
Bontadelli Inc	5148	D	831 423-8572	8697
California Certified Organic	8611	D	831 421-2263	25080
Camp Recovery Centers LLP	8093	D	831 438-1868	22671
Canyon View Capital Inc	6798	D	831 480-6335	12240
Capitola Care Center Inc	8059	D	831 477-0329	21178
Cellco Partnership	4812	C	831 421-0753	5368
Chaminade Ltd	7389	C	831 475-5600	17067
Coldwell Bnkr Residential Brkg	6531	D	831 420-2628	11436
Comcast Corporation	4841	D	831 316-9258	5964
Cruz Veterinary Hospital	0742	D	831 475-5400	618
Derijan Associates Inc **(PA)**	8741	C	831 423-4111	27003
Dignity Health	8011	A	831 462-7700	19501
Dignity Health Med Foundation	8099	D	831 475-8330	22941
Dominican Hospital Foundation	8361	C	831 457-7057	24633
Dominican Hospital Foundation **(HQ)**	8062	C	831 462-7700	21546
Dominican Oaks Corporation	6513	D	831 462-6257	11120
Ecology Action of Santa Cruz	8731	C	831 426-5925	26508
First American Title Insur Co	6361	D	831 426-6500	10525
Friends Santa Cruz State Parks	8641	D	831 429-1840	25257
Front St Inc	8059	D	831 420-0120	21228
Geo H Wilson Inc	1711	D	831 423-9522	2237
His Manna Inc	8742	D	831 423-5515	27465
Housing Athrty of The Cnty of	6531	D	831 454-9455	11574
Janus of Santa Cruz	8322	D	831 462-1060	24041
Lho Santa Cruz One Lesse Inc	7011	C	831 475-5600	12918
Lifespan Inc	8399	D	831 469-4900	24938
Lockheed Martin Corporation	7389	D	831 425-6375	17300
Mariner Health Care Inc	8051	D	831 475-6323	20765
Mercy Medical Group Inc	8641	C	831 475-1111	25296
Moose International Inc	8641	D	831 438-1817	25300
Nicholas B Macy Dvm	0742	D	831 475-5400	624
Palo Alto Med Fndtion STA Cruz	8011	A	831 458-5670	19811
Performance Food Group Inc	5141	C	831 462-4400	8509
Pfyffer Associates Inc	0161	E	831 423-8572	88
Regent Assisted Living Inc	8361	D	831 459-8400	24784
Rope Partner Inc	5085	D	831 460-9448	7949
Santa Cruz Biotechnology Inc	8731	D	831 457-3800	26600
Santa Cruz County of	7374	D	831 454-2030	16182
Santa Cruz County Symphony	7929	E	831 462-0553	18493
Santa Cruz Hotel Associates	7011	C	831 426-4330	13213
Santa Cruz Medical Foundation **(HQ)**	8011	D	831 458-5537	19959
Santa Cruz Metro Trnst Dst	4131	D	831 469-1954	3888
Santa Cruz Seaside Company **(PA)**	7996	B	831 423-5590	18830
Santa Cruz Seaside Company	7011	A	831 427-3400	13214
Santa Cruz Westside Elc Inc	1731	D	831 469-8888	2725
Smartrevenuecom Inc	8732	D	203 733-9156	26706
Stagnaro Brothers Seafood Inc	5146	D	831 423-1188	8656
Stearns Lending LLC	6163	D	831 471-1977	9953
Sutter Health	8641	D	831 458-6310	25357
Sutter Health	8062	E	831 477-3600	21946
Sutter Health	8641	C	831 458-5500	25362
Sutter Maternity & Surgery Ctr	8062	C	831 477-2200	21951
United Natural Foods Inc	5149	D	831 462-5870	8943
United Parcel Service Inc OH	4215	C	831 425-1054	4474
Univ of CA	8732	D	831 459-5041	26716
Visiting Nurse Association of **(DH)**	8082	D	831 477-2600	22595
Well Within Spa	1799	D	831 458-9355	3601
Western Med Assoc Med Group **(PA)**	8011	D	831 475-1111	20237

SANTA FE SPRINGS, CA - Los Angeles County

Company	SIC	EMP	PHONE	ENTRY #
All-City Management Svcs Inc	8748	A	310 202-8284	27826
Alliedbarton Security Svcs LLC	7382	B	562 906-4800	16863
Alpha Shirt Company	5136	D	562 802-9919	8331
American Rlction Logistics Inc	4214	D	562 229-3600	4327
Askew Industrial Corporation **(PA)**	5085	E	323 727-7772	7923
B & E Convalescent Center Inc **(PA)**	8059	D	562 923-9449	21147
Barr Engineering Inc	1711	D	562 944-1722	2158
Bekins Moving Solutions Inc **(PA)**	4214	D	714 736-6100	4331
Brenntag Pacific Inc **(DH)**	5169	D	562 903-9626	8981
Brsc Inc	5072	C	310 549-9180	7677
Brunton Enterprises Inc	1791	D	562 945-0013	3369
Cadnchev Inc	5015	D	562 944-6422	6795
California Lab Sciences LLC	8734	B	562 758-6900	26836
Central Garden & Pet Company	5199	C	562 926-5252	9253
Coa Inc **(PA)**	5021	C	562 944-7899	6811

GEOGRAPHIC SECTION — SANTA MARIA, CA

Company	SIC	EMP	PHONE	ENTRY #
Coast Alum & Architectural Inc (PA)	5051	C	562 946-6061	7365
Coast Iron & Steel Co	1791	E	562 946-4421	3379
Commodity Distribution Service	8748	E	562 777-9969	27886
County of Los Angeles	8322	B	562 903-5000	23828
Crescent Healthcare Inc (DH)	8082	C	714 520-6300	22420
Crown Fence Co	1799	D	562 864-5177	3510
Csi Electrical Contractors Inc (PA)	1731	C	562 946-0700	2566
Custom Companies Inc	4731	D	310 672-8800	5053
Cypress Security LLC	7381	D	562 222-4197	16620
D&D Equipment Rental LLC	7353	E	562 595-4555	14479
Dynamic Worldwide West Inc	4731	D	310 357-2460	5063
El Monte Rents Inc (PA)	7519	D	972 562-1900	17706
Electric Sales Unlimited	5063	E	562 463-8300	7437
Ellison Machinery Co (DH)	5084	D	562 949-8311	7841
Ethosenergy Field Services LLC (DH)	1389	D	310 639-3523	1075
Federal Express Corporation	4513	D	800 463-3339	4856
Field Foundation	1389	E	562 921-3567	1076
Galleher Corporation (PA)	5023	C	562 944-8885	6862
Georgia-Pacific LLC	5113	B	562 861-6226	8193
Goodrich Corporation	7699	D	562 944-4441	17977
Griffith Company	1611	D	562 929-1128	1796
Hadco Metal Trading Co LLC	5051	D	562 404-4040	7373
Haringa Inc (PA)	7389	D	800 499-9991	17207
Harris L Woods Elec Contr	1731	D	562 945-8751	2608
Hillshire Brands Company	5149	E	562 903-9260	8852
Holbrook Construction Inc	1542	D	714 523-1150	1572
Horner-Galleher Holding Co (PA)	5023	C	562 944-8885	6867
Igt Global Solutions Corp	7999	D	562 946-9922	19228
Interntnl Win Treatments Inc (PA)	5023	D	562 236-2120	6868
Janus Et Cie (PA)	5021	E	310 601-2958	6822
Jvc Americas Corp	7622	D	562 463-8110	17910
Kbl Group International Ltd	5137	E	562 699-9995	8390
Kelly Pipe Co LLC (DH)	5051	D	562 868-0456	7379
Kemp Bros Construction Inc	1541	E	562 236-5000	1444
Key Air Cnditioning Contrs Inc	1711	D	562 941-2233	2267
Kiewit Corporation	1542	D	907 222-9350	1594
Kiewit Infrastructure West Co	1611	C	562 946-1816	1811
Kloeckner Metals Corporation	5051	D	562 906-2020	7380
Kloeckner Metals Corporation	5051	D	562 906-2020	7381
L Tech Network Services Inc	1731	D	562 222-1121	2634
LA Specialty Produce Co (PA)	5148	B	562 741-2200	8744
Lakin Tire West Incorporated (PA)	5014	D	562 802-2752	6787
Larsen Supply Co (PA)	5074	D	562 698-0731	7723
Masonry Concepts Inc	1741	D	562 802-3700	2826
Material Handling Supply Inc (HQ)	5084	D	562 921-7715	7860
Matt Construction Corporation	8742	C	562 903-2277	27527
Matt-Colombo A Joint Venture	1542	D	562 903-2277	1609
Maxon Lift Corporation	5084	C	562 464-0099	7861
McKesson Corporation	5122	C	562 463-2100	8279
McMurray Stern Inc	5021	E	562 623-3000	6824
MCP Industries Inc	5169	D	562 944-5511	8993
Memo Scaffolding Inc	1799	D	562 404-8600	3554
Mias Fashion Mfg Co Inc	5137	B	562 906-1060	8401
Millennia Stainless Inc	5085	D	562 946-3545	7940
Monument Security Inc	7381	D	562 944-2666	16739
Morrison Concrete Inc	1771	E	562 802-1450	3299
Murata Rockey Landscaping	0781	D	562 921-3210	781
Nelson & Associates Inc	5063	D	562 921-4423	7459
New Cingular Wireless Svcs Inc	4812	D	562 941-6422	5402
Newport Diversified Inc	7389	C	562 921-4359	17356
Ninos Latino Unidos FSA	8361	D	562 801-5454	24746
Norman International Inc	5023	D	562 946-0420	6876
Northstar Contg Group Inc	1795	C	714 639-7600	3461
Oil Well Service Company (PA)	1389	C	562 612-0600	1090
Pacific Clinics	8093	D	562 942-8256	22787
Pacific Clinics	8093	D	562 949-8455	22788
Partitions Installation Inc	1799	D	562 207-9868	3565
Penny Lane Centers	8399	C	562 903-4135	24955
Performance Team Frt Sys Inc	4225	D	562 741-1300	4613
Pro-Tech Design & Mfg Inc	7389	D	562 207-1680	17427
Production Delivery Svcs Inc	4213	D	562 777-0060	4246
Raymond Handling Solutions Inc (DH)	5084	C	562 944-8067	7881
Rebar Engineering Inc	1791	C	562 946-2461	3398
Reliance Steel & Aluminum Co	5051	D	562 695-0467	7395
Reliance Steel & Aluminum Co	5051	D	562 777-9672	7398
Rentokil North America Inc	5191	D	562 802-2238	9148
Royal Paper Corp	5113	D	562 903-9030	8214
Ryder Truck Rental Inc	7513	D	562 921-0033	17652
S E Pipe Line Construction Co	1623	D	562 868-9771	1991
Scorpio Enterprises	1711	D	562 946-9464	2361
Sequel Contractors Inc	1611	E	562 802-7227	1857
Sfadia Inc	1731	E	323 622-1930	2732
Shoring Engineers	1799	D	562 944-9331	3582
Simplexgrinnell LP	7382	C	562 405-3817	16927
Sohnen Enterprises Inc (PA)	7622	E	562 903-4957	17913
Solaris Paper Inc	5093	C	562 376-9717	8088
Southeast Area Social Services	8322	E	562 946-2237	24222
Southern California Edison Co	4911	D	562 903-3191	6239
Spicers Paper Inc (HQ)	5111	C	562 698-1199	8155
State Farm Mutl Auto Insur Co	6411	E	562 903-2800	10881
Strand Energy Company	1311	B	562 944-9580	1051
Swann Communications USA Inc	5045	D	562 777-2551	7197
Talley Inc (PA)	5065	C	562 906-8000	7645
Think Together	7991	A	562 236-3835	18699
Trail Lines Inc	4212	D	562 758-6980	4072
Tri-West Ltd (PA)	5023	D	562 692-9166	6897
Triangle Distributing Co (PA)	5181	C	562 699-3424	9088
Troyer Contracting Company Inc	1799	D	562 944-6452	3592
Twin Med LLC (PA)	5047	C	323 582-9900	7322
Ugm Citatah Inc (PA)	5032	C	562 921-9549	6996
Ultradot Media	7313	D	562 906-0737	13984
Universal Asphalt Co Inc	1611	E	562 941-0201	1879
Valverde Construction Inc	1623	E	562 906-1826	2010
Valvoline International Inc	7549	E	562 906-6200	17905
Van King & Storage Inc (PA)	4212	D	562 921-0555	4088
Van King & Storage Inc	4225	E	562 921-0555	4653
Van Torrance & Storage Company (PA)	4214	D	562 567-2100	4387
Warren Distributing Inc (PA)	5013	D	562 789-3360	6780
Western Allied Service Company	7623	B	562 941-3243	17925
Western Exterminator Company	7342	C	562 802-2238	14196
Whittier Equipment Rentals	1623	D	562 863-0641	2019
Wilsonart LLC	4225	D	562 921-7426	4671
Wismettac Asian Foods Inc (DH)	5149	C	562 802-1900	8956
Xpo Enterprise Services Inc	4213	C	562 946-8331	4322
Xtra Department Inc	8741	D	562 462-3800	27286

SANTA MARIA, CA - Santa Barbara County

Company	SIC	EMP	PHONE	ENTRY #
Aardex Inc	1542	D	805 928-7600	1481
Agro-Jal Farms Inc	0723	D	805 928-2682	505
Ais Construction Company	1542	D	805 928-9467	1486
Babe Farms	0191	C	805 928-3728	346
Big F Company Inc	5191	D	805 928-2333	9126
Boca Mesa Incorporated	8748	D	805 934-9470	27852
Brannon	1541	C	805 621-5000	1408
Buona Terra Farming Co Inc	8741	D	805 614-9229	26950
Caci Nss Inc	5045	C	703 841-7800	7106
Cal Gran Theatres LLC	7832	E	805 934-1582	18313
Cardenas Bros Farming Company	0171	D	805 928-1559	106
Central Coast Distributing LLC	5181	D	805 922-2108	9046
Central Coast Pub Safety Inc	7381	D	805 556-4450	16592
Certified Frt Logistics Inc (PA)	4213	C	805 925-9900	4125
CJJ Farming Inc	0171	E	805 739-1723	107
Community Action Commsn Santa	8399	D	805 614-0786	24894
Community Action Commsn Santa	8399	D	805 922-2243	24896
Country Oaks Care Center Inc	8051	D	805 922-6657	20474
Crop Production Services Inc	5191	D	805 922-5848	9132
Darensberries LLC	0171	C	805 937-8000	109
Diani Building Corp (PA)	1542	D	805 925-9533	1540
Dignity Health	8062	B	805 739-3000	21533
Dignity Health	8082	D	805 739-3830	22424
Dignity Health	8051	C	805 739-3650	20520
Dignity Health	8093	A	805 739-3100	22720
Eagle Resources Inc	7361	D	805 922-0000	14641
Edwards Theatres Circuit Inc	7832	D	805 347-1164	18336
Employment Dev Cal Dept	7361	D	805 614-1550	14648
Ensign Group Inc	8361	D	805 925-8713	24644
Express Messenger Systems Inc	4215	D	800 488-2829	4405
Festival Fun Parks LLC	7999	C	805 922-1574	19209
First Transit	4111	D	805 925-5254	3648
Foothill Packing Inc	5141	B	805 925-7500	8479
Freshway Farms LLC	0171	C	805 349-7170	112
Frey Farming & Tpsry Vineyards	0762	D	805 937-1542	704
Frontier California Inc	4813	D	805 925-0000	5606
Fusion Contact Centers LLC	7389	C	805 922-2108	17178
Glad-A-Way Gardens Inc (PA)	0181	D	805 938-0569	284
Good Samaritan Shelter	8322	D	805 346-8185	23997
Greka Inc	1241	D	805 347-8700	1025
H & R Block Inc	7291	D	805 349-9266	13721
Hardy Diagnostics (PA)	5047	D	805 346-2766	7267
Hunter Realty Inc	6531	D	805 346-8688	11577
Hvi Cat Canyon Inc	1389	D	805 621-5800	1084
KG Berry Farms LLC	0191	C	805 680-6715	377
Kimberly Care Center Inc	8051	D	805 925-8877	20695
La Palma Farms Inc	5191	D	805 928-2333	9141
Lacuesta Farming Inc	0171	D	805 349-1940	117
Larrabee Brothrs Distribtng Co	5181	D	805 922-2108	9067
Laurel Labor Services Inc	7361	D	805 928-0113	14696
Los Dos Valles Harvstg & Pkg	0722	C	805 739-1688	497
Meathead Movers	4213	D	805 349-8000	4223
Mendoza Farms Inc	0171	E	805 352-1070	122
Merrill Gardens LLC	8059	D	805 310-4102	21314

Employment Codes: A=Over 500 employees, B=251-500, C=101-250, D=51-100, E=45-50

SANTA MARIA, CA

Company	SIC	EMP	PHONE	ENTRY #
Mesa Vineyard Management Inc	0762	D	805 925-7200	707
Mission Linen Supply	7213	D	805 922-3579	13565
Nursecore Management Svcs	8361	D	805 938-7660	24750
Oilfield Envmtl Compliance Inc	8734	D	805 922-4772	26881
PC Mechanical Inc	1389	E	805 925-2888	1092
Pre Con Industries Inc	1751	D	805 345-3147	3071
Premier Drywall	1742	D	805 928-3397	2957
Primus Group Inc (PA)	8742	E	805 922-0055	27594
Quinn Company	5082	D	805 925-8611	7783
Ramco Enterprises LP	7361	A	805 922-9888	14741
Rancho Laguna Farms Inc	0191	D	805 925-7805	387
Red Blossom Sales Inc	0171	B	805 349-9404	127
Reiter Affl Companies LLC	0171	D	805 925-8577	128
RMR Inc (PA)	1771	D	805 928-4013	3321
Safari Harvstg & Farming LLC	0191	B	805 925-2600	390
Santa Barbara County of	8322	C	805 614-1550	24188
Santa Barbara County of	8111	E	805 346-7540	23544
Santa Barbara Trnsp Corp	4151	D	805 928-0402	3948
Santa Barbra Cttge Hsptl	8062	C	805 346-7135	21858
Santa Maria Airport Regency	7011	D	805 928-8000	13215
Santa Maria Hotel Corp	7011	B	805 928-6000	13216
Santa Maria Valley YMCA	8641	C	805 937-8521	25339
Segura Enterprises Inc	7382	D	805 349-0550	16924
Shepard Eye Center	8011	E	805 925-2637	20002
Skylstad-Schoelen Co Inc	7349	D	805 349-0503	14433
Smith Packing Inc	5199	C	805 343-0329	9304
Spiess Construction Co Inc	1623	D	805 937-5859	1998
Sturgeon Son Grading & Pav Inc	8711	D	805 938-0618	26080
Teixeira Farms Inc	0161	D	805 928-3801	98
Tetra Tech Inc	8748	D	805 739-2600	28072
Transitions - Mental Hlth Assn	8093	C	805 614-4940	22852
Tri Valley Vegetable Harvstg	0722	D	805 928-2727	502
Tri-Counties Association F	8399	D	805 922-4640	24989
Union Asphalt Inc	4212	D	805 922-3551	4076
United Parcel Service Inc OH	4215	C	805 922-7851	4467
Valley Garbage Rubbish Co Inc	4953	D	805 614-1131	6592
Verizon Wireless Inc	4812	D	805 928-7433	5423
Vtc Enterprises (PA)	8331	D	805 928-5000	24405
White Hills Vineyard Ranc	0762	D	805 934-1986	735

SANTA MONICA, CA - Los Angeles County

Company	SIC	EMP	PHONE	ENTRY #
180la LLC	7311	C	310 382-1400	13807
24 Hour Fitness Usa Inc	7991	D	310 450-4464	18591
525 Studios Inc	7819	D	310 525-1234	18210
Activision Blizzard Inc	7371	C	310 581-4700	14999
Activision Blizzard Inc (PA)	7372	B	310 255-2000	15567
Adconion Media Inc (PA)	7311	D	310 382-5521	13811
Advanced Medical Reviews Inc	7363	D	310 575-0900	14832
Air Force US Dept of	8733	B	310 393-0411	26730
Alisam Oxnard Operating	6512	C	310 877-7179	10955
American Retirement Corp	8361	D	310 399-3227	24548
Apex Machine Works Inc	8711	D	310 393-5987	25658
ARC	7334	C	310 575-5759	14106
Arizona and 21st Corp	8059	D	310 829-5377	21144
Artisan Pictures Inc	5099	C	310 449-9200	8105
Attendant Care Referrals Inc	8082	D	310 399-2904	22372
Beach Club	7997	D	310 395-3254	18885
Beachbody LLC (PA)	7313	D	310 883-9000	13959
Berkeley E Convalescent Hosp	8059	C	310 829-5377	21152
Blue Devils Lessee LLC	7011	C	310 399-9344	12454
Box Bros Corp	7389	E	310 394-8660	17039
Boys Grls CLB Snta Monica Inc	8641	B	310 361-8500	25218
Bryan Cave LLP	8111	C	310 576-2100	23135
Businesscom Inc	8742	D	310 586-4000	27363
By The Blue Sea LLC	7011	B	310 458-0030	12476
C/O Uc San Francisco	8011	D	310 794-1841	19388
Caliber Bodyworks Inc	7532	D	310 392-7662	17749
Callfire Inc	7371	D	213 221-2289	15072
Callison LLC	8712	C	310 394-8460	26169
Campus Explorer Inc	4813	D	310 574-2243	5570
Capital Oversight Inc	8748	B	310 453-8000	27865
Carat Usa Inc	7319	C	310 255-1000	13990
Casestack Inc (PA)	4731	D	310 473-8885	5041
Cedar Management LLC	6531	D	310 396-3100	11362
Century Finance Incorporated	6162	D	310 281-3081	9828
Childrens Hospital Los Angeles	8011	D	310 820-8608	19434
CIT Bank National Association	6021	D	310 394-1640	9355
CIT Bank National Association	6021	D	310 452-3802	9357
CIT Bank National Association	6021	D	310 399-9262	9359
CIT Bank National Association	6021	D	310 829-4477	9370
City of Santa Monica	4131	B	310 451-5444	3877
Clare Foundation Inc (PA)	8322	D	310 314-6200	23761
Clare Foundation Inc	8322	D	310 314-6200	23762
Clearlake Capital Group LP (PA)	6799	B	310 400-8800	12297
Coastal Health Care Inc	8051	D	310 828-5596	20463
Colfin Esh Funding LLC	6722	B	310 282-8820	12111
Colony Capital LLC (PA)	6799	D	310 282-8820	12298
Company 3 Inc	7819	D	310 255-6600	18220
Converse Inc	5139	D	310 451-0314	8428
Cornerstone Ondemand Inc (PA)	7372	C	310 752-0200	15630
County of Los Angeles	8322	D	310 266-3711	23849
Creating Arts Company	7922	E	310 804-0223	18385
Cwgp Limited Partnership	7011	D	310 395-9700	12560
Cypress Creek Holdings LLC	1711	D	310 581-6299	2197
David King Convalescent Hosp	8059	D	310 451-9706	21206
Dcp Rights LLC	7812	E	310 255-4600	18068
Deckers Outdoor Corporation	5139	D	310 395-1120	8430
Demand Media Inc (PA)	7313	C	310 656-6253	13967
Disability Group Inc	8111	B	310 829-5100	23215
Dlr Group Inc of California (HQ)	8712	D	310 828-0040	26184
Douglas Emmett Realty Fund 199	6531	D	310 255-7700	11478
Dtrs Santa Monica LLC	7011	B	310 458-6700	12602
Ecompanies LLC	4813	E	310 586-4000	5593
Edmunds Holding Company (PA)	7375	D	310 309-6300	16231
Edward Thomas Hospitality Corp	7011	B	310 458-0030	12611
Ellie Fashion Group Inc	7389	D	818 355-3812	17147
Emperors Clg Trdtnl Orntl Mdc	8049	D	310 453-8383	20315
Entravsion Communications Corp (PA)	4833	C	310 447-3870	5858
Epochcom LLC	7374	C	310 664-5700	16126
Et Whitehall Seascape LLC	7011	B	310 581-5533	12625
Executive Network Entps Inc	4119	D	310 457-8822	3789
Fairmont Hotel Partners LLC	7011	B	310 319-3122	12630
Focus Features LLC	7812	C	424 214-6360	18086
Friends of Max Rose LLC	7812	D	424 901-1260	18088
Futuris Global Holdings LLC (HQ)	6719	C	510 771-2333	12063
Game Show Network LLC (DH)	4841	C	310 255-6800	6003
Genius Products Inc	5099	D	310 453-1222	8115
Georgian Hotel	7011	D	310 395-9945	12663
Global-Dining Inc California	8741	D	310 576-9922	27040
Good Shepherd Health Care Ce	8051	D	310 451-4809	20631
GTE Corporation	7389	D	310 315-7597	17203
GTE Corporation	4813	D	310 319-6148	5625
Gumbiner & Savett Inc	6512	D	310 828-9798	10993
Guthy-Renker LLC (PA)	5099	D	760 773-9022	8118
Guthy-Renker LLC	5099	D	310 581-6250	8119
Hammel Green & Abrahamson Inc	8712	D	310 557-7600	26195
HBO Indpendent Productions Inc (DH)	7812	D	310 382-3000	18091
Hirsch Bedner Associates (PA)	7389	D	310 829-9087	17220
Hirsch/Bedner Intl Inc (PA)	7389	D	310 829-9087	17221
Home Box Office Inc	4841	D	310 382-3000	6006
HP Inc	7371	D	310 255-3000	15224
Hulu LLC (PA)	4833	D	310 571-4700	5871
I PCA L P	7011	C	310 395-3332	12833
Ilanguagecom Inc	7389	E	310 899-6800	17233
Imagestat Corporation	5045	C	310 392-1100	7144
Innovative Artists Talent Agny (PA)	7922	D	310 656-0400	18397
Interactive Data Corporation	7371	D	310 664-2500	15247
Jackson National Life Insur Co	6311	D	310 899-7900	10210
Jakks Sales Corporation	5092	E	424 268-9444	8046
John M Adams Jr MD	8011	D	310 829-2663	19576
John Wayne Institute For Ctr	8733	D	310 449-5253	26777
Jonathan Club	7997	C	310 393-9245	18965
Jurlique Hlistic Skin Care Inc	7231	B	310 899-1923	13680
Jurlique Hlistic Skin Care Inc (PA)	7231	E	914 998-8800	13681
K-Micro Inc	5045	D	310 442-3200	7151
Kcrw Foundation Inc	8399	D	310 450-5183	24932
Kite Pharma Inc (PA)	8731	D	310 824-9999	26544
Koi Design LLC	5137	D	310 828-0055	8392
Kor Hotel Groups Inc	8741	D	310 309-8066	27102
Les Kelley Family Health Ctr	8011	D	310 319-4700	19706
Ling-Su Chinn Inc	5137	D	310 396-1102	8396
Lions Gate Entertainment Inc (HQ)	7812	D	310 449-9200	18100
Lions Gate Films Inc	7812	C	310 449-9200	18101
Lionsgate Productions	7822	D	310 255-3937	18277
Lubert-Dler Mnagement-West Inc	6798	D	310 496-4130	12257
M&C Hotel Interests Inc	7011	D	310 399-9344	12934
Macerich Company (PA)	6798	D	310 394-6000	12258
Maguire Properties Twr 17 LLC	6798	D	310 857-1100	12259
MBK Real Estate Ltd A Califor	6513	E	310 399-3227	11166
Media Vntures Entrmt Group LLC	7812	E	310 260-3171	18107
Medicl Imgng Ctr of Southrn CA	8011	D	310 829-9788	19739
Mens Apparel Guild In Cal Inc	8611	D	310 857-7500	25093
Mercury Insurance Company	6331	D	310 451-4943	10443
Method Studios LLC	7812	D	310 434-6500	18110
Milken Family Foundation	8322	C	310 570-4800	24089
Milken Institute	8733	D	310 570-4600	26787
Miller & Associates LLP	8111	D	310 315-1100	23434
Millward Brown LLC	8732	E	310 309-3352	26690
Miramax Film Ny LLC	7812	D	310 409-4321	18115
Morgan Stanley & Co LLC	6211	D	310 319-5200	10060
Morley Construction Company (HQ)	1771	D	310 399-1600	3298

GEOGRAPHIC SECTION   SANTA ROSA, CA

	SIC	EMP	PHONE	ENTRY #
MSC Service Co	8721	D	310 399-1600	26412
National Apartment Flooring	1752	D	800 773-6904	3126
Natural Rsrces Def Council Inc	8641	D	310 434-2300	25303
Nms Properties Inc	6531	D	310 475-7600	11710
Ocean Avenue LLC	7011	B	310 576-7777	13032
Ocean Park Community Center	8748	D	310 828-6717	28007
Ocean Park Community Center	8322	D	310 450-0650	24110
Ogilvy & Mather Worldwide Inc	7311	D	310 280-2200	13889
Palisades Media Group Inc (PA)	7319	D	310 564-5400	14005
Pandora Media Inc	4832	B	424 653-6803	5815
Partos Company	7389	D	310 458-7800	17401
Patientpop Inc	7372	D	310 260-3968	15814
Perkins Coie LLP	8111	D	310 788-9900	23502
Perr & Knight Inc (PA)	6411	D	310 230-9339	10825
Pk Nevada LLC	6531	E	310 255-0025	11754
Platinum Clg Indianapolis LLC	7349	B	310 584-8000	14389
Playhaven LLC	7371	D	310 308-9668	15385
Playtika Santa Monica LLC	7993	C	310 622-7380	18808
Porter Crispin & LLC Bogusky	7311	D	305 859-2070	13898
Postaer Rubin and Associates (PA)	7311	D	310 394-4000	13899
Provident Financial Management	8741	D	310 282-0477	27183
Purelife LLC	5047	D	877 777-3303	7309
Red Bull Distribution Co Inc (HQ)	5149	D	916 515-3501	8912
Reel Fx Inc	7812	E	310 264-6440	18140
Reilly Worldwide Inc	7812	E	310 449-4065	18142
Rick Weiss New Hope Apartments	6513	E	310 395-1026	11197
Right At Home	8082	D	310 313-0600	22549
Rock Paper Scissors LLC	7812	E	310 586-0600	18145
Roscoe Real Estate Ltd Partnr	7011	D	310 260-7500	13168
S F Broadcasting of Wisconsin	4833	C	310 586-2410	5907
Saint Jhns Hlth Ctr Foundation	8011	C	310 315-6111	19933
Saint Jhns Hlth Ctr Foundation	8351	D	310 829-8921	24508
Saint Jhns Hlth Ctr Foundation	8062	E	310 829-8970	21839
Santa Monica Amusements LLC	7996	B	310 451-9641	18831
Santa Monica Bay Womens Club	8699	E	310 395-1308	25575
Santa Monica City of	8351	D	310 399-5865	24512
Santa Monica City of	4111	B	310 451-5444	3714
Santa Monica City of	6512	D	310 458-8551	11040
Santa Monica Family YMCA	8641	D	310 451-7387	25341
Santa Monica Hsr Ltd Partnr	7011	D	310 395-3332	13217
Santa Monica Orthopedic	8011	D	310 315-2018	19962
Santa Monica Seafood Company	5146	B	310 393-5244	8651
Scope Industries (PA)	4953	D	310 458-1574	6562
Screen Gems-EMI Music Inc	7389	E	310 586-2700	17480
Seaside Hotel Lessee Inc	7389	D	310 260-7500	17483
Second Street Corporation	7011	D	310 394-5454	13230
Shore Hotel	7011	B	310 458-1515	13250
Six Per Cent Management	8741	D	310 399-2611	27213
Society6 LLC	7374	E	310 394-6400	16190
SOS Security Incorporated	7381	C	310 392-9600	16826
St Johns Health Center	8099	D	310 829-5511	23063
Stephen B Meisel MD PC	8011	E	310 828-8843	20067
Stephen B Meisel MD A Med Corp (HQ)	8011	D	310 828-8843	20068
Summit Entertainment LLC (DH)	7829	E	310 309-8400	18291
Taskus Inc	7374	A	888 400-8275	16196
Taslimi Construction Co Inc	1542	D	310 447-3000	1685
Tennenbaum Capitl Partners LLC (PA)	6726	D	310 396-5451	12150
Tennis Channel Inc (HQ)	7922	D	310 392-1920	18438
Threshold Digital Research Lab	8742	E	310 452-8885	27687
Tigertext Inc	7379	E	310 401-1820	16507
Tonopah Solar Energy LLC	1711	D	310 315-2200	2399
Truecar Inc (PA)	5012	E	800 200-2000	6698
Ucla Health System	7389	D	310 393-5153	17552
Ucla Healthcare	8062	D	310 319-4560	21977
Universal City Studios Inc	7812	D	310 865-5000	18176
Universal Mus Investments Inc (HQ)	7389	D	818 577-4700	17569
Universal Music Enterprises	6794	D	310 865-7857	12226
Universal Music Group Inc (HQ)	7389	D	310 865-4000	17570
Universal Music Group Inc	7929	D	310 865-4000	18502
University Cal Los Angeles	8062	A	310 319-4000	21990
US Credit Bancorp Inc	6162	D	310 829-2112	9903
US Small Cpitl Value Portfolio	6722	D	310 395-8005	12127
Van Etten Suzumoto Becket LLP	8742	D	310 315-8284	27707
Venice Family Clinic	8011	C	310 392-8636	20190
Viacom Networks	7822	A	310 453-4826	18282
Vista Del Mar Child Fmly Svcs	8361	B	310 836-1223	24851
Watt Investment Partners LLC	6531	D	310 450-3802	11911
Watt Properties Inc (PA)	6512	D	310 314-2430	11068
Weintraub Tobin Chediak	8111	E	310 393-9500	23615
Wells Fargo Capital Fin Inc (DH)	7389	C	310 453-7300	17618
Wells Fargo Capital Fin LLC (DH)	6159	D	310 453-7300	9807
William Warren Group Inc (PA)	7513	D	310 451-2130	17657
Wilshire Animal Hospital	0742	E	310 828-4587	634
Wilshire Associates Inc (PA)	8742	C	310 451-3051	27720
Windsor Capital Group Inc	7011	D	310 566-1100	13415
Windsor Capital Group Inc	7011	D	310 566-1100	13416
Windsor Capital Group Inc	7011	D	209 577-3825	13417
Windsor Capital Group Inc	7011	D	209 577-3825	13418
Windsor Capital Group Inc	7011	D	310 566-1100	13421
Windsor Capital Group Inc	7011	D	310 566-1100	13422
Yoga Works Inc (PA)	7991	E	310 664-6470	18709

SANTA PAULA, CA - Ventura County

	SIC	EMP	PHONE	ENTRY #
Calavo Growers Inc (PA)	5148	C	805 525-1245	8699
Calavo Growers Inc	4783	D	805 525-5511	5197
California Resources Corp	1311	C	310 208-8800	1039
Coastal Harvesting Inc	0761	B	805 525-6250	655
Do Rights Plant Growers	0181	D	805 525-2155	277
Fenceworks Inc	1799	D	661 265-0082	3519
Hayward Baker Inc	1799	D	805 933-1331	3528
Jj Valencia Harvesting Inc	0722	D	805 525-8467	495
Knights of Columbus	8641	C	805 525-7810	25278
Limoneira Company (PA)	0723	C	805 525-5541	556
Marin Labor Services	0761	C	805 525-7730	673
Raycon Construction Inc	1741	E	805 525-5256	2833
Rey Con Construction Inc	1771	C	805 525-8134	3319
Santa Clara Vly Job Career Ctr	7361	D	805 933-8300	14779
Saticoy Lemon Association (PA)	0723	D	805 654-6500	583
Time Warner Cable Inc	4841	C	888 892-2253	6032
Ventura County Medical Center	8011	D	805 933-8600	20191
Vista Cove Care Center	8059	D	805 525-7134	21415

SANTA ROSA, CA - Sonoma County

	SIC	EMP	PHONE	ENTRY #
Advanced Surgery Institute LLC	8011	C	707 528-6331	19316
Airport Club	7997	C	707 528-2582	18844
Alain Pinel Realtors Inc	6531	D	707 636-3800	11284
Allied Building Products Corp	5033	E	707 584-7599	7006
Allison Dowdy	6531	D	707 303-3472	11293
Alsco Inc	7213	D	707 523-3311	13516
Amaturo Sonoma Media Group LLC	4832	D	707 543-0126	5748
American Agcredit Flca (PA)	6159	D	707 545-1200	9793
American Automobile	6331	C	707 566-4000	10398
American Med Resp Amblnc Svc	4119	D	707 536-0400	3748
Americas Home Loans Inc	6163	E	707 577-7464	9914
Apria Healthcare LLC	7352	D	707 543-0979	14473
Argonaut Constructors	1611	C	707 542-4862	1735
Ashley Ltc Inc	8051	D	707 528-2100	20385
At Home Nursing	8082	D	707 546-8773	22371
AT&T Corp	4812	D	707 591-9500	5266
AT&T Services Inc	4813	C	707 545-5000	5544
Atech Logistics Inc	4731	C	707 526-1910	5032
Atech Warehousing & Dist Inc (PA)	4213	D	707 526-1910	4113
Aurora Behavioral Health	8063	D	707 800-7700	22038
B&M Racing & Prfmce Pdts Inc (PA)	5013	C	707 544-4761	6712
Bavarian Lion Company Cal (PA)	7011	D	707 545-8530	12423
Boys & Girls Clubs Cent Sonoma	8641	C	707 528-7977	25212
Bridger Commercial Funding LLC	6163	E	707 953-7475	9916
Burbank Housing Dev Corp	6552	D	707 526-9782	11955
Burr Pilger Mayer Inc	8721	D	707 544-4078	26299
California American Water Co	4941	E	707 542-1717	6317
California Human Dev Corp (PA)	8331	C	707 523-1155	24318
Canine Cmpnons For Indpendence (PA)	0752	D	707 577-1700	637
Carlilemacy Inc	8711	D	707 542-6451	25718
Cellco Partnership	4812	D	707 525-5010	5379
Century 21 Les Ryan Realty	6531	D	707 577-7777	11379
Childrens Vlg of Sonoma Cnty	8361	E	707 566-7044	24598
City Towel & Dust Service Inc	7213	D	707 542-0391	13546
Clp Resources Inc	7363	E	707 569-0200	14856
Community Action Partnership O	8399	C	707 544-0120	24897
Community Chld Cre Cncl Sonoma (PA)	8351	C	707 522-1413	24445
County of Sonoma	8063	C	707 565-4850	22058
County of Sonoma	7374	C	707 527-2911	16115
County of Sonoma	8111	C	707 565-2209	23184
County of Sonoma	8322	C	707 527-2641	23922
County of Sonoma	7374	C	707 527-2911	16116
CPI International (PA)	5049	E	707 525-5788	7340
Creekside Cnvalescent Hosp Inc	8051	C	707 544-7750	20505
Creekside Rehab and Behavioral	8051	C	707 524-7030	20506
Dennett Tile & Stone Inc	1743	E	707 541-3700	3012
Deposition Sciences Inc	8731	C	707 573-6700	26504
Devincenzi Concrete Cnstr	1771	E	707 568-4370	3256
Direct Flow Medical Inc (PA)	8099	C	707 576-0420	22945
Drug Abuse Alternatives Center	8093	D	707 571-2233	22722
Dura Metrics Inc (PA)	8072	D	707 546-5138	22305
Ensign Group Inc	8051	C	707 525-1250	20540
Epic Ventures Inc (PA)	5182	E	831 219-9100	9099
Episcopal Senior Communities	8361	B	707 538-8400	24648
Exchange Bank (HQ)	6036	C	707 524-3000	9585
Exchange Bank	6021	C	707 524-3399	9396
F Korbel & Bros	4581	C	707 525-1875	4917
Famand Inc	1711	D	707 255-9295	2223

Employment Codes: A=Over 500 employees, B=251-500, C=101-250, D=51-100, E=45-50

SANTA ROSA, CA

Company	SIC	EMP	PHONE	ENTRY #
Finley Swim Center	7999	E	707 543-3760	19214
Flyers Energy LLC	5172	D	707 546-0766	9021
Fountain Grove Golf & Athc CLB	7992	D	707 521-3207	18740
Fountaingrove Inn LLC	7011	D	707 578-6101	12645
Frank Howard Allen Fincl Corp	6531	D	707 523-3000	11545
Gallaher Construction Inc	1521	E	707 535-3200	1180
Ghd Inc	8711	D	707 523-1010	25841
Ghilotti Construction Co Inc **(PA)**	1629	C	707 585-1221	2053
Golden Living LLC	8051	D	707 546-0471	20613
Heartland Payment Systems Inc	7389	D	707 338-0510	17213
Hired Hand	8082	C	707 575-4700	22458
Independent Quality Care Inc	8059	D	707 578-3226	21276
Individuals Now	8322	D	707 544-3299	24025
Inoxpa USA Inc	5084	B	707 585-3900	7851
Integra Telecom Inc	7389	D	707 284-4000	17244
J W Leavy Inc	1742	E	707 579-3805	2915
Jackson Family Wines Inc	5182	C	415 819-0301	9107
Jlp Landscape Contracting	0782	E	707 526-6285	879
Joe Lunardi Electric Inc	1731	D	707 823-2129	2626
Johnson Controls Inc	8711	D	707 546-3042	25910
K G Walters Cnstr Co Inc	1629	D	707 527-9968	2064
Kaiser Foundation Hospitals	8011	A	707 393-4000	19582
Kaiser Foundation Hospitals	6324	D	707 571-3835	10327
Kaiser Foundation Hospitals	6324	D	707 393-4033	10328
Kaiser Permanente	8011	E	707 393-4000	19682
Keith Development Corporation	6552	D	707 528-8703	11975
Klh Consulting Inc	8748	D	707 575-9986	27967
La Tortilla Factory Inc **(PA)**	5149	B	707 586-4000	8874
Laidlaw International Inc	4151	C	707 545-8064	3940
Lanahan & Reilley LLP **(PA)**	8111	D	415 856-4700	23363
Landesign Cnstr & Maint Inc	0782	D	707 578-2657	901
Luther Burbank Mem Foundation	7922	D	707 546-3600	18412
Luther Burbank Savings Corp **(HQ)**	6036	E	707 578-9216	9586
Manor Bell L P	1531	D	707 526-9782	1379
Mark E Jacobson M D	8011	D	707 571-4022	19730
Mayacama Golf Club LLC	7997	C	707 569-2915	18993
Melissa Bradley RE Inc	6531	C	707 536-0888	11674
Merritt Hospitality LLC	7011	C	707 523-7555	12992
Mhm Services Inc	8093	C	707 623-9080	22777
Mission Car Wash	7542	E	707 537-2040	17856
Murphy-True Inc	1542	C	707 576-7337	1616
Neese Inc	4121	E	707 544-4444	3866
Noble Aew Vineyard Creek LLC	7011	D	707 284-1234	13024
North American Cinemas Inc	7832	B	707 571-1412	18339
Northwest Insurance Agency	6411	D	707 573-1300	10813
Oakmont Golf Club Inc **(PA)**	7992	D	707 538-2454	18766
Occidental Cnty Sanitation Dst	4952	C	707 547-1900	6413
Optima Building Services Maint	7349	D	707 586-6640	14374
Orenda Center	8399	D	707 565-7450	24951
Pacific Gas and Electric Co	4911	C	800 756-7243	6167
Pepsi-Cola Metro Btlg Co Inc	5149	D	707 535-4500	8899
Permanente Medical Group Inc	8011	D	707 393-4000	19840
Primrose Alzheimers Living **(PA)**	8361	E	707 568-4355	24771
Primrose Alzheimers Living	8361	E	707 578-8360	24772
Pw Jade LLC	8082	D	707 843-5192	22543
Realogy Holdings Corp	6531	B	707 284-1111	11798
Redwood Credit Union **(PA)**	6141	C	707 545-4000	9763
Redwood Empir	4953	D	707 586-5533	6535
Redwood Regional Medical Group	8071	E	707 546-4062	22271
Redwood Regional Medical Group **(PA)**	8071	D	707 525-4080	22272
Redwood Toxicology Lab Inc	8071	C	707 577-7958	22273
Retirement Project-Oakmont	6513	D	707 538-1914	11196
Roman Cthlic Bshp of Snta Rosa	8399	C	707 528-8712	24969
Saint Joseph Home Care Network	8361	D	707 206-9124	24795
Santa Rosa City of	8111	D	707 543-3040	23546
Santa Rosa & Sonoma Co Real Es	6531	E	707 524-1124	11833
Santa Rosa Community Hlth Ctrs **(PA)**	8322	D	707 547-2222	24195
Santa Rosa Dental Group	8021	D	707 545-0944	20275
Santa Rosa Golf & Country Club	7997	D	707 546-3485	19066
Santa Rosa Memorial Hospital **(DH)**	8062	A	707 546-3210	21861
Santa Rosa Memorial Hospital	8051	D	707 542-2771	20896
Santa Rosa Radiology Med Group **(PA)**	8071	E	707 546-4062	22279
Santa Rosa Surgery Center LP	8062	D	707 578-4100	21862
Security One Inc	7381	D	800 778-3017	16818
Simplexgrinnell LP	1711	D	707 578-3212	2369
Sonoma County Airport Express	4111	D	707 837-8700	3719
Sonoma County Humane Society	0752	E	707 542-0882	645
Sonoma County Indian Health PR **(PA)**	8011	C	707 521-4545	20008
Sonoma County Water Agency	4941	D	707 526-5370	6404
Sonoma Grapevines Inc **(PA)**	5193	D	707 542-5521	9213
Sonoma Vly Cnty Sanitation Dst	4952	C	707 547-1900	6417
Sotoyome Medical Building LLC	6512	D	707 525-4000	11053
Ss Skikos Incorporated	4214	D	707 575-3000	4378
Steven N Ledson	1521	D	707 537-3810	1263
Summit Electric Inc	1731	E	707 542-4773	2753
Summit Technology Group Inc	1731	E	707 542-4773	2754
Sunrise Senior Living Inc	8051	E	707 575-7503	20967
Sutter Health	8099	B	707 526-1800	23067
Sutter Health	8011	C	707 545-2255	20102
Sutter Health	8641	C	707 523-7253	25363
Sutter Med Group of Redwoods	8011	D	707 546-2788	20117
United Parcel Service Inc OH	7389	A	678 339-3171	17556
UPS Ground Freight Inc	4213	D	707 526-1910	4289
Venture Design Services Inc	7389	D	707 524-8368	17584
Veolia Transportation Svcs Inc	4111	C	707 585-7516	3737
Verihealth Inc	4119	C	707 303-8000	3854
Veterans Health Administration	8011	B	707 570-3800	20212
Victor Treatment Centers Inc	8361	C	707 576-0171	24847
Vintners Inn	7011	D	707 575-7350	13380
Warrack Corporation	8062	B	707 523-7271	22026
Windsor Redwoods LP	7389	D	707 526-1020	17629
Winzler & Kelly	8711	D	707 523-1010	26151
Woodmont Real Estate Svcs LP	8999	B	707 569-0582	28170
Xpo Enterprise Services Inc	4213	D	707 584-0211	4318
Y W C A of Sonoma County	8641	E	707 546-9922	25406
Youngs Market Company LLC	5182	D	707 584-5170	9122

SANTA ROSA VALLEY, CA - Ventura County

Company	SIC	EMP	PHONE	ENTRY #
Tucker Electric Corporation	1731	E	818 426-7645	2777

SANTA YNEZ, CA - Santa Barbara County

Company	SIC	EMP	PHONE	ENTRY #
Channel Islands Young Mens Ch	8641	D	805 686-2037	25236
Chumash Casino Resort	7999	A	805 688-7997	19165
Chumash Casino Resort **(PA)**	7999	D	805 686-0855	19166

SANTEE, CA - San Diego County

Company	SIC	EMP	PHONE	ENTRY #
A & D Fire Protection Inc	1711	D	619 258-7697	2100
AT&T Corp	4813	D	619 448-1798	5464
Aztec Sheet Metal Inc	1761	D	619 937-0005	3140
C & M Transfer San Diego Inc	4212	D	619 562-6111	3987
Catania Hijar Corporation	1623	C	800 400-3401	1917
Challenger Sheet Metal Inc	1761	D	619 596-8040	3149
Edgemoor Hospital	8069	B	619 956-2880	22139
International Thermoproducts	5084	E	619 562-7001	7852
J Vitale Landscape & Maint	0782	D	619 938-2435	874
Life Gnerations Healthcare LLC	8059	D	619 449-5555	21290
Pacific Western Bank	6022	D	619 562-6400	9515
Padre Dam Municipal Water Dst **(PA)**	4941	D	619 258-4617	6386
R & R Mechanical Contrs Inc	1711	D	619 449-9900	2334
Ra Hughes Enterprises In	1711	E	619 390-4880	2337
Scantibodies Clinical Lab Inc	8071	E	866 249-1212	22280
T C Construction Company Inc	1623	C	619 448-4560	2002
Tarpy Heating and Air	1711	E	619 820-4580	2394
Torres General Inc	1521	D	619 448-8900	1274
Tower Glass Inc	1793	D	619 596-6199	3416
Ty Investment Inc	7997	D	619 448-4242	19114
YMCA of San Diego County	8641	D	619 449-9622	25425

SARATOGA, CA - Santa Clara County

Company	SIC	EMP	PHONE	ENTRY #
Action Day Nrseries Prmry Plus	8351	D	408 370-0350	24411
G T Technology Inc	8748	E	408 257-5245	27929
Intero Real Estate Svcs Inc	6531	D	408 741-1600	11586
Montalvo Association	8422	D	408 961-5800	25066
Odd Fellows Home California	8361	B	408 741-7100	24753
Our Lady of Fatima Villa Inc	8051	D	408 741-2950	20830
Preston Wynne Spa Inc	7991	D	408 741-1750	18671
Progressive Sub-Acute Care	8069	C	408 378-8875	22162
Saratoga Court Inc	6514	D	408 866-1392	11241
YMCA of Silicon Valley	8699	C	408 370-1877	25602

SAUGUS, CA - Los Angeles County

Company	SIC	EMP	PHONE	ENTRY #
Desert Star Co	5169	E	661 259-5848	8986
Mountasia of Santa Clarita	7299	D	661 253-4386	13779
Pleasantview Industries Inc	8093	D	661 296-6700	22809

SAUSALITO, CA - Marin County

Company	SIC	EMP	PHONE	ENTRY #
Active Wellness LLC	8741	A	415 331-1600	26909
Aperio Group LLC	7389	D	415 339-4300	16996
Bay Equity LLC **(PA)**	6162	D	415 632-5150	9820
Butler Shine Stern Prtners LLC	7311	C	415 331-6049	13822
Casa Madrona Hotel and Spa LLC	7011	C	415 332-0502	12496
Cavallo Point LLC **(PA)**	7011	D	415 339-4700	12502
Coastal International Inc **(PA)**	7389	D	415 339-1700	17088
Comcast Corporation	4841	D	415 367-4153	5956
County of Marin	8322	B	415 332-6158	23862
Gate Five Group LLC	5023	E	415 339-9500	6863
Marine Mammal Center **(PA)**	0742	E	415 289-0430	621
Naturebridge	8699	D	415 332-5771	25560
Qlm Consulting Inc	8742	E	415 331-9292	27605
Swa Group **(PA)**	0781	D	415 332-5100	799
U S Army Corps of Engineers	8711	A	415 289-3067	26113
Ubics Inc	7371	C	415 289-1400	15513

	SIC	EMP	PHONE	ENTRY #
Wested	8733	D	415 289-2300	26821

SCOTTS VALLEY, CA - Santa Cruz County

	SIC	EMP	PHONE	ENTRY #
Ava The Rabbit Haven Inc	8748	D	831 600-7479	27843
Bellavista Landscape Svcs Inc	0781	D	831 461-1761	743
Bfp Fire Protection Inc	1711	D	831 461-1100	2165
Hospice Caring Project of Sant	8082	D	831 430-3000	22474
Inn At Scotts Valley LLC	7011	D	831 440-1000	12837
Market Motive	8742	C	831 706-2369	27523
MBK Real Estate Ltd A Calfor	6513	D	831 438-7533	11165
Roi Communications Inc (PA)	8748	D	831 430-0170	28044
Scotts Montessori Valley Inc	8351	E	831 439-9313	24513
Zero Motorcycles Inc	5012	D	831 438-3500	6701

SEAL BEACH, CA - Orange County

	SIC	EMP	PHONE	ENTRY #
Autism Partnership Inc	8742	D	562 431-9293	27335
Bakercorp (HQ)	7359	C	562 430-6262	14517
Bixby Ranch Co A California LP	6552	D	562 596-4425	11950
Califrn/Nvada Developments LLC	6519	C	714 677-5721	11249
Country Villa Service Corp	8322	D	562 598-2477	23790
Countryside Inn-Corona LP	8741	E	562 596-8330	26993
Encore Aerospace LLC	1799	D	562 344-1700	3513
Farmers Merchants Bnk Long Bch	6022	C	562 430-4724	9493
First Team RE - Orange Cnty	6531	C	562 596-9911	11530
Golden Living LLC	8059	D	562 598-2477	21244
Golden Rain Foundation	8011	D	562 493-9581	19537
Kendrick Construction Services	1541	D	562 546-0200	1445
National Product Services LLC	8743	E	562 594-8206	27758
Olson Company LLC (PA)	1521	D	562 596-4770	1227
Olson Urban Housing LLC	6552	D	562 596-4770	11995
P2f Holdings	5199	D	562 296-1055	9284
Saga Seal Co Ltd	7011	D	562 493-7501	13187
Samedan Oil Corporation	1311	B	661 319-5038	1050
String Path Medcl Corp	7549	E	562 799-8900	17894
Sunrise Senior Living Inc	8051	D	562 594-5788	20953
Tenet Healthsystem Medical	8011	D	562 493-9581	20133
Tyr Sport Inc	5137	D	562 430-1380	8415
UBS Financial Services Inc	6211	D	562 495-5500	10089
Wells Fargo Advisors LLC	6211	E	562 594-1220	10100
Williams and Williams Homecare	7363	D	562 597-1006	14984

SEASIDE, CA - Monterey County

	SIC	EMP	PHONE	ENTRY #
Atrium Hotels LP	7011	C	831 393-1115	12403
Bsl Golf Corp	7992	C	831 899-7271	18718
County Monterey Social Svcs	8322	D	831 899-8001	23792
Morale Welfare Recreation Fund	8399	C	831 242-6631	24944
Sodexo Operations LLC	8741	D	831 582-3838	27223

SEBASTOPOL, CA - Sonoma County

	SIC	EMP	PHONE	ENTRY #
Apple Vly Cnvalescent Hosp Inc	8051	C	707 823-7675	20378
Big O Tires LLC (DH)	5013	D	707 829-9864	6714
Camp Recovery Centers LP	8069	A	707 823-3385	22119
County of Sonoma	8062	C	707 823-8511	21524
Hermitage Health Care	8069	D	707 823-1238	22144
Seaver International	7379	C	707 291-4929	16477
Sebastopol Rifle & Pistol Club	7997	D	707 824-0184	19070
Sonoma West Medical Center	8011	D	707 823-8511	20009
Sonoma West Medical Center	8062	C	707 823-8511	21896

SELMA, CA - Fresno County

	SIC	EMP	PHONE	ENTRY #
Adventist Health System/West	8011	C	559 891-2611	19318
Bethel Lutheran Home Inc	8059	D	559 896-4900	21155
Circle K Ranch	0172	D	559 834-1571	146
Clarence Unruh Farms Inc	0175	D	559 896-9499	230
Jane McClurg	0172	D	559 834-3080	160
Kaiser Foundation Hospitals	6324	D	559 898-6000	10334
Robert Alves Farms Inc	0172	D	559 896-3309	180
Selma Community Hospital Inc	8062	B	559 891-1000	21877
Selma Portuguese Azorian Assn	8322	E	559 896-2508	24203
Serimian M S D L Ranch	0191	E	559 896-1517	392
Westar Transport	4212	D	559 834-3551	4093

SHAFTER, CA - Kern County

	SIC	EMP	PHONE	ENTRY #
Baker Hughes Incorporated	1389	D	661 831-7686	1068
Bakersfield Pipe and Sup Inc (PA)	5051	D	661 589-9141	7360
Cummings Vacuum Service Inc	1389	D	661 746-1786	1072
Delmart Farms Inc	0172	D	661 746-2148	149
Farm Pump & Irrigation Co Inc (PA)	5084	D	661 589-6901	7843
Grimmway Enterprises Inc	0723	D	661 393-3320	538
Grimmway Enterprises Inc	0191	B	661 399-0844	361
Lufkin Industries LLC	5084	D	661 746-0030	7857
Standard Industries Inc	5033	D	661 387-1110	7021
Tryad Service Corporation	1389	D	661 391-1524	1099
Varner Family Ltd Partnership (PA)	6733	D	661 399-1163	12208
Vignolo Farms Inc	0131	C	661 391-0682	16
Wonderful Orchards LLC (PA)	0173	C	661 399-4456	210

SHELL BEACH, CA - San Luis Obispo County

	SIC	EMP	PHONE	ENTRY #
Dolphin Bay Ht & Residence Inc	7011	D	805 773-4300	12584

SHERMAN OAKS, CA - Los Angeles County

	SIC	EMP	PHONE	ENTRY #
Adhei Enterprises Inc	7349	E	818 788-7680	14213
Ansira Partners Inc	7389	D	818 461-6100	16993
Arclight Cinema Company	7832	E	818 501-0753	18308
Avad LLC (PA)	5065	C	818 742-4800	7527
Azubu North America Inc	5092	E	310 759-9529	8037
Barazani Outdoors Inc	0781	D	818 701-6977	742
Baseline Consulting Group Inc	8742	D	818 906-7638	27339
Beating Wall Street Inc (PA)	8742	C	818 332-9696	27343
Blue Chip Inventory Service	7389	D	818 461-1765	17033
Body Conqueror Inc	8093	C	310 651-0387	22668
Bright Pharmaceutical Services	5122	B	818 981-9100	8239
California Strl Concepts Inc	1542	D	661 257-6903	1521
Cameron Pace Group LLC	7922	D	818 565-0005	18379
Care Inc	8052	E	818 232-7940	21068
Cherokee Inc (PA)	6794	D	818 908-9868	12213
Coldwell Banker RE Corp	6531	D	818 995-2424	11412
Compuware Corporation	7371	D	818 380-3019	15103
Crowe Horwath LLP	8721	C	818 501-5200	26319
Dynamic Home Care Service Inc (PA)	8082	D	818 981-4446	22428
Fedelity National Title Co Org	6361	D	818 758-6849	10513
Filmquest Pictures Corporation	7812	C	818 905-1006	18085
Frank N Magid Associates Inc	8732	D	818 263-3300	26664
Frank N Magid Associates Inc	8732	D	818 263-3300	26665
Golden State Health Ctrs Inc (PA)	8051	D	818 385-3200	20629
Golden State Health Ctrs Inc	8059	D	818 783-4969	21252
Help Group West (PA)	8093	D	818 781-0360	22745
Highpoint Productions Inc	7812	C	818 728-7600	18093
Ideal Living Management LLC	8741	D	818 217-2000	27060
Investors MGT Tr RE Group Inc (PA)	6513	E	818 784-4700	11143
Lucky Strike Entertainment LLC	7933	C	818 933-0872	18523
Malka Communications Group Inc	8999	D	818 990-0278	28144
Mega Appraisers Inc	7389	E	818 246-7370	17325
Metro Home Loan Inc	6162	D	818 461-9840	9873
Moss & Company Inc (PA)	6531	D	310 453-0911	11693
Motion Picture Assn Amer Inc	8611	D	818 995-6600	25094
Nexcare Collaborative (PA)	8322	E	818 907-0322	24103
Organic Affinity LLC	5065	D	801 870-7433	7618
P& JP Brokerage LLC	4731	E	310 801-9707	5141
Pk Management LLC	8741	B	818 808-0600	27167
Premiere Radio Network Inc (DH)	7922	C	818 377-5300	18426
Prime Healthcare Svcs II LLC	8062	B	818 981-7111	21813
Project Six	7389	D	818 781-0360	17433
Prospect Mortgage LLC (PA)	6163	A	818 981-0606	9945
Prudential Insur Co of Amer	6411	E	818 990-2122	10844
Rodeo Realty Inc	6531	D	818 986-7300	11815
Royal Specialty Undwrt Inc	6331	D	818 922-6700	10458
Sedgwick Claims MGT Svcs Inc	6411	D	818 782-8820	10867
Seymour Gale & Associates	5137	E	213 622-5361	8412
Sherman Oaks Health System	8062	D	818 981-7111	21891
Silicon Valley Bank	6021	D	818 382-2600	9423
Spark Unlimited Inc	7371	E	818 788-1005	15474
Sunrise Delivery Service Inc	4215	D	323 464-5121	4423
Tharpe & Howell (PA)	8111	D	714 437-4900	23593
Thoughtful Media Group Inc	7313	D	818 465-7500	13980
Top Notch Security	7381	E	818 528-2875	16833
Unlimited Security Specialist	7381	E	877 310-4877	16846
Vubiquity Inc	7822	C	818 526-5000	18284
Vubiquity Holdings Inc (PA)	4841	D	818 526-5000	6058
Wells Fargo Insur Svcs USA Inc	6411	C	818 464-9300	10930
WERM Investments LLC	7929	E	213 627-8070	18505
Xsolla (usa) Inc	4813	D	818 435-6613	5736

SHERWOOD FOREST, CA - Los Angeles County

	SIC	EMP	PHONE	ENTRY #
Slade Industrial Landscape Inc	0781	D	818 885-1916	798

SHINGLE SPRINGS, CA - El Dorado County

	SIC	EMP	PHONE	ENTRY #
County of El Dorado	8322	C	530 621-5625	23803
Foothill Duplicate Bridge Club	7997	E	530 677-3771	18951
Salutary Sports Clubs Inc	7991	E	530 677-5705	18676
Straight Line Roofing & Cnstr	1761	E	530 672-9995	3215

SIGNAL HILL, CA - Los Angeles County

	SIC	EMP	PHONE	ENTRY #
2h Construction Inc	1541	D	562 490-2897	1394
Ajr Trucking Inc	4212	D	562 989-9555	3975
American Tile Brick Veneer Inc	1743	D	562 595-9293	3004
Edco Disposal Corporation Inc (PA)	4953	D	619 287-7555	6478
Edge Systems LLC	5047	D	562 597-0102	7263
Fenderscape Inc	0782	D	562 988-2228	853
First American Team Realty Inc (PA)	6531	C	562 427-7765	11523
Gem Mobile Treatment Svcs Inc (DH)	4959	D	562 436-2999	6629
Goldsmith Construction Co Inc	1771	E	562 595-5975	3267
Gregg Drilling & Testing Inc (PA)	1799	D	562 427-6899	3526

SIGNAL HILL, CA

GEOGRAPHIC SECTION

Company	SIC	EMP	PHONE	ENTRY #
Independent Physician MGT LLC	8011	D	562 981-9500	19568
Intertek USA Inc	7389	E	562 494-4999	17250
Liftech Elevator Services Inc	8999	D	562 997-3639	28141
Lovco Construction Inc	1794	C	562 595-1601	3435
MD Care Inc	6321	D	562 344-3400	10245
Optmial Hospice Foundation	8052	D	562 494-7687	21096
Radnet Inc	8011	E	562 216-5137	19905
SCCH Inc (PA)	8741	D	562 494-5188	27206
Traffic Management Inc (PA)	7389	C	562 595-4278	17537
Viking Office Products Inc (HQ)	5112	B	562 490-1000	8183
Walters Wholesale Electric Co (HQ)	5063	D	562 988-3100	7482
Wannajob Inc	7363	D	562 426-5272	14980

SILVERADO, CA - Orange County

Company	SIC	EMP	PHONE	ENTRY #
Inside Outdoors Foundation	8322	C	714 708-3885	24027

SIMI VALLEY, CA - Ventura County

Company	SIC	EMP	PHONE	ENTRY #
Aerovironment Inc	8611	C	805 581-2187	25074
American GNC Corporation	8711	E	805 582-0582	25653
American Golf Corporation	7997	D	805 522-0803	18872
American Golf Corporation	7992	D	805 527-9663	18712
American Technologies Inc	1521	E	818 700-5060	1128
American Vision Windows Inc	7699	C	805 582-1833	17961
Anjana Software Solutions Inc	7371	D	805 583-0121	15015
ARC Industries	8361	D	805 520-0399	24550
Arconic Global Fas & Rings Inc (HQ)	5085	C	310 530-2220	7918
AT&T Corp	4812	D	805 583-9483	5268
Avaya Inc	4813	D	805 581-6119	5563
B & M Contractors Inc	1771	D	805 581-5480	3228
Bank America National Assn	6153	D	805 520-5100	9771
Bestitcom Inc (PA)	7379	D	602 667-5613	16329
Big Sky Country Club LLC	7992	D	805 522-4653	18716
Boys & Girls Club Simi Vly Inc	8641	E	805 527-4437	25211
Cardservice International Inc	7389	A	800 217-4622	17054
Cellco Partnership	4812	D	805 955-9035	5366
CFS Tax Software	7372	D	805 522-1157	15617
Chase Group Llc	8742	D	805 522-9155	27379
CM Concrete Inc	1771	C	805 520-8100	3242
Cobalt Construction Company	1522	D	805 577-6222	1303
Collectech Systems Inc (DH)	7322	C	818 597-7500	14026
Computerized Management	7363	D	805 522-5999	14864
Computerized Mgt Svcs Inc	8741	D	805 522-5940	26980
Crunch Fitness	7991	D	805 522-5454	18625
Edwards Theatres Circuit Inc	7832	D	805 526-4329	18335
Encore Repair Services Inc	7629	D	805 584-6599	17934
Engility LLC	8711	A	703 664-6274	25792
Expert Building Maint LLC	7349	D	805 520-1580	14294
Facey Medical Foundation	8031	C	805 206-2000	20289
First & La Realty Corp (PA)	6531	D	805 581-0021	11520
Foreign Trade Corporation (PA)	5065	D	805 823-8400	7567
Genesis Home Health Inc	7363	E	805 520-7100	14882
GI Industries	4953	D	805 522-2150	6486
Golden State Water Company	4941	E	805 583-6400	6353
Harold Jones Landscape Inc	0781	E	805 582-7443	770
Hewitt and Canfield Cnstr Inc	1751	D	805 522-4426	3055
Home Instead Senior Care	8082	C	805 577-0926	22466
Johnson Controls Inc	5065	D	805 522-5555	7590
Kaiser Foundation Hospitals	6324	D	888 515-3500	10338
Kidney Center Inc	8092	C	805 433-7777	22632
Landcare USA LLC	0782	C	805 520-9394	890
LBC Inc	1761	D	805 581-1068	3185
Mortgage Corp America Inc	6163	D	805 582-2220	9939
Nfp Property & Casualty Svcs	8742	E	805 579-1900	27568
North Star Building Maint Inc	7349	D	805 518-0417	14371
Official Police Garage Assn of	4492	A	805 624-0572	4767
Pars Publishing Corp	7336	D	818 280-0540	14158
Posada Royale Hotel & Suites	7011	E	805 584-6300	13108
PW Gillibrand Co Inc	1446	D	805 526-2195	1111
Q L P Inc	5063	D	805 579-0440	7466
Rand Medical Billing Inc	8721	D	805 578-8300	26430
Revolution Eyewear Inc	5048	E	818 989-2020	7337
S E C C Corporation	8711	D	805 578-3596	26047
SA Recycling LLC	4953	D	805 483-0512	6544
Sdj General Partnership	6512	D	805 582-3200	11041
Second Opinion Med Grp Inc	6324	D	805 496-4315	10377
Shopper Inc	5046	B	805 527-6700	7228
Sierra Vista Family Medical	8099	D	805 582-4000	23057
Simi Radiology & Imaging	8742	D	805 522-5978	27647
Simi Vly Hosp & Hlth Care Svcs (HQ)	8049	D	805 955-6000	20353
Simi West Inc	7011	D	805 583-2000	13257
Smart Living Company (PA)	5199	E	805 578-5500	9303
Specialized Landscape MGT Svcs	0782	D	805 520-7590	958
Sunrise Senior Living Inc	8051	D	805 584-8881	20949
Time Warner Inc	4841	D	805 431-4467	6054
Troop Real Estate Inc (PA)	6531	D	805 581-3200	11885
United Parcel Service Inc OH	7389	B	866 553-1069	17564
Vickie Lobello	8699	D	805 750-2327	25595
Vintage Senior Housing LLC	6513	B	805 583-3500	11223
Wsm Investments LLC	6794	D	818 332-4600	12231
Xavient Info Systems Inc	7372	A	805 955-4111	15882
Young Mens Christian Asso	7999	D	805 583-5338	19312

SMITH RIVER, CA - Del Norte County

Company	SIC	EMP	PHONE	ENTRY #
Smith River Lucky 7 Casino	7011	D	707 487-7777	13270

SNELLING, CA - Merced County

Company	SIC	EMP	PHONE	ENTRY #
JS Homen Trucking Inc	4212	D	209 723-9559	4032

SODA SPRINGS, CA - Nevada County

Company	SIC	EMP	PHONE	ENTRY #
Boreal Ridge Corporation	7011	C	530 426-1012	12458
Royal Gorge Nordic Ski Resort (PA)	7011	C	530 426-3871	13171

SOLANA BEACH, CA - San Diego County

Company	SIC	EMP	PHONE	ENTRY #
All-Pro Bail Bonds Inc (PA)	7389	D	858 481-1200	16979
American Golf Corporation	7997	C	858 755-6768	18851
Bridge Medical Inc	5122	D	858 350-0100	8238
Cambridge Home Loans Inc FN	6162	D	858 481-2929	9825
Child Development Center	8351	E	858 794-7160	24430
Daley & Heft Attorneys	8111	E	858 755-5666	23193
Daviselen Advertising Inc	7311	D	858 847-0789	13833
Healthfusion Holdings Inc (HQ)	6719	D	858 523-2120	12069
International Network Corp	7371	E	858 794-2610	15251
Jacobs Engineering Group Inc	8711	A	858 793-0461	25892
Mellmo Inc (DH)	7371	D	858 847-3272	15298
Merlin Global Services LLC	4522	C	904 305-9559	4886
Onehealth Solutions Inc	7379	D	858 947-6333	16444
Probuild Company LLC	5031	D	858 755-0246	6953
Senior Resource Group LLC	6513	E	858 519-0890	11200
Sprouts Farmers Market Inc	5141	C	858 350-7900	8525
Srg Management LLC	8741	C	858 792-9300	27227
Steelpoint Capital Partners LP	6282	D	858 764-8700	10187
Warren Auto De Mexico LLC	5199	D	858 794-7947	9311

SOLEDAD, CA - Monterey County

Company	SIC	EMP	PHONE	ENTRY #
Braga Fresh Family Farms Inc	0161	B	831 675-2154	43
Costa Sons	0161	E	831 678-0799	54
Dole Fresh Vegetables Inc	0723	C	831 678-5030	526
Estancia Estates	6552	D	707 431-1975	11965
Kvl Holdings Inc (PA)	0172	B	831 678-2132	165
Robertas Labor Contracting	7361	B	831 678-8176	14775
Sandoval Brothers Inc	7361	D	831 678-1465	14777
Soledad Cmnty Hlth Care Dst	8051	D	831 678-2462	20921
Valley Farm Management Inc	0762	D	831 678-1592	728
Vasquez Brothers Inc	0723	D	831 678-8894	601

SOLVANG, CA - Santa Barbara County

Company	SIC	EMP	PHONE	ENTRY #
Alisal Properties (PA)	7032	C	805 688-6411	13458
MWH Americas Inc	8711	D	805 683-2409	25979
National Hospitality LLC	7011	D	805 688-8000	13016
Pacific Western Bank	6035	C	805 688-6644	9580
Santa Ynez Valley Cottage Hosp	8062	D	805 688-6431	21865

SOMIS, CA - Ventura County

Company	SIC	EMP	PHONE	ENTRY #
Saticoy Country Club	7997	D	805 647-1153	19069

SONOMA, CA - Sonoma County

Company	SIC	EMP	PHONE	ENTRY #
Appellation Tours Inc	4725	E	707 938-9390	4986
Artisan Bakers	5149	D	707 939-1765	8797
Clarbec Inc	0172	E	707 996-4012	147
Credit Bureau NAPA County Inc	7322	C	707 940-3000	14029
Diageo North America Inc	5182	D	707 939-6200	9095
Emeritus Corporation	8052	D	707 996-7101	21079
Enterprise Vineyards	0762	E	707 996-6513	701
Freixenet Usa Inc	5182	D	707 996-7256	9102
Golden Living LLC	8051	D	707 938-1096	20625
Grega Brooke Sra	6531	E	707 938-3362	11561
John Benward Company Inc	1611	E	707 996-7809	1805
Marriott International Inc	7011	C	707 935-6600	12974
Merrill Gardens LLC	8361	E	707 996-7101	24733
North Counties Drywall Inc	1742	E	707 996-0198	2938
Renaissance Hotel Holdings Inc	7011	B	707 935-6600	13141
Smisc Holdings	7948	E	707 938-8448	18575
Sonoma Valley Health Care Dst (PA)	8062	B	707 935-5000	21895
Sonoma Valley Womans Club	8641	E	707 938-8313	25351
Speedway Sonoma LLC	7948	D	707 938-8448	18576
Swiss Hotel Group Inc	7011	D	707 938-2884	13330
V Sangiacomo & Sons	0172	C	707 938-5503	191
Vintage Senior Management Inc	6513	A	707 595-0009	11225
Workforce Logic LLC	8742	A	866 296-3343	27723

SONORA, CA - Tuolumne County

Company	SIC	EMP	PHONE	ENTRY #
Adventist Health System/West	8099	D	209 536-5700	22879
Aladdin Sonora Motor Inn	7011	E	209 533-4971	12378
Amador Tlmne Cmnty Action Agcy	8399	E	209 533-1397	24865

GEOGRAPHIC SECTION

SOUTH SAN FRANCISCO, CA

Company	SIC	EMP	PHONE	ENTRY #
Avalon Health Care Inc	8051	D	209 533-2500	20399
County of Tuolumne	7374	B	209 533-5561	16117
County of Tuolumne	8322	C	209 533-5711	23930
Diestel Turkey Ranch (PA)	0253	D	209 532-4950	452
Front Porch Inc (PA)	7371	D	209 288-5500	15194
Golden Living LLC	8059	C	209 533-2500	21242
Jk Consultants	8748	E	209 532-7772	27960
Kingsview Corp	8093	D	209 533-6245	22763
Sonora Regional Medical Center (HQ)	8062	A	209 532-5000	21897
Sonora Retirement Center Inc	8361	E	209 588-0373	24817
Tuolumne Utilities District	4941	D	209 532-5536	6406
Visiting Nurse Association of	8082	D	209 736-2338	22594
Watch Resources Inc (PA)	8322	E	209 533-0510	24285

SOQUEL, CA - Santa Cruz County

Company	SIC	EMP	PHONE	ENTRY #
Balance4kids	8641	D	831 464-8669	25204
Bask Jewelry Inc	5094	D	831 479-8849	8094
Bay Photo Inc	7221	C	831 475-6090	13659
Federal Express Corporation	4215	D	800 463-3339	4409
Sutter Health	8641	B	831 458-6272	25358
Trailer Park Inc	7033	C	831 462-3271	13485

SOUTH EL MONTE, CA - Los Angeles County

Company	SIC	EMP	PHONE	ENTRY #
Ahmc Healthcare Inc	8062	B	626 579-7777	21439
American Wrecking Inc	1795	D	626 350-8303	3448
Bali Construction Inc	1623	D	626 442-8003	1907
Commonwealth International	7381	D	626 279-9201	16607
Fresh Air Environmental Svcs	1799	D	323 913-1965	3522
Halcore Group Inc	4119	D	626 575-0880	3802
Ideal Transit Inc	4111	E	626 448-2690	3655
Jetworld Inc	5012	C	626 448-0150	6685
Leader Industries Inc	4119	D	626 575-0880	3812
Lincoln Trainin	8331	D	626 442-0621	24358
Out of Shell LLC	1541	D	626 401-1923	1456
Ted Levine Drum Co (PA)	7699	D	626 579-1084	18023

SOUTH GATE, CA - Los Angeles County

Company	SIC	EMP	PHONE	ENTRY #
AT&T Corp	4813	D	323 568-2006	5477
Castle Dental	8021	E	323 567-1227	20248
Century 21 A Better Svc Rlty	6411	D	562 806-1000	10666
County of Los Angeles	8099	D	562 861-0316	22933
Daily Saw Service	5085	D	323 564-1791	7930
Dickson Testing Co Inc (DH)	8734	D	562 862-8378	26843
Eppink of California Inc	1751	E	562 633-1275	3047
Far West Inc	8051	D	323 564-7761	20567
Interior Rmoval Specialist Inc	1795	C	323 357-6900	3457
Koos Manufacturing Inc	7389	A	323 249-1000	17276
Meribear Productions Inc	7389	D	323 588-7421	17330
Pan Pacific Petroleum Co Inc (PA)	4213	D	562 928-0100	4242
Privilege International Inc	5021	D	323 585-0777	6832
Pws Inc (HQ)	5087	D	323 721-8832	7978
Quality Carriers Inc	4213	D	800 282-2031	4248
Rick Studer	4213	E	323 357-1720	4252
Samuel J Piazza & Son Inc (PA)	4214	D	323 357-1999	4374
Scott Jacks DDS Inc	8021	C	323 564-2444	20277
United Pacific Services Inc	0782	E	562 691-4600	973

SOUTH LAKE TAHOE, CA - El Dorado County

Company	SIC	EMP	PHONE	ENTRY #
Algonquin Power and Utilities	1731	B	530 543-5288	2514
Barton Hospital	8062	A	530 543-5685	21462
Barton Memorial Hospital	8361	B	530 543-5581	24563
Belmont Corporation	7011	D	530 542-1101	12433
California Land Mgt Svcs Corp	7033	E	530 544-5994	13477
California Tahoe Conservancy	8999	D	530 542-5580	28121
City of South Lake Tahoe	7999	D	530 542-6056	19181
Healthcare Barton System (PA)	8062	A	530 541-3420	21597
Healthcare Barton System	8059	E	530 543-5685	21262
Hilton Worldwide Inc	7011	C	530 543-2126	12727
Hilton Worldwide Inc	7011	E	530 541-6122	12742
Lake Tahoe Secret Witness	7381	D	530 541-6800	16718
Liberty Utlties Clpeco Elc LLC	4911	B	530 543-5288	6145
Marriott Grand Residence	7011	B	530 542-8400	12948
Roppongi-Tahoe Lp A Californi	7011	D	530 544-5400	13166
Saa Sierra Programs LLC	8641	D	530 541-1244	25329
Soroptomist Intl Tahoe Sierra	8699	D	530 573-1657	25583
South Tahoe Public Utility Dst	4952	C	530 544-6474	6418
South Tahoe Refuse Co	4953	D	530 541-5105	6565
Tahoe Beach & Ski Club	7011	D	530 541-6220	13340
Tahoe Seasons Resort Time Inte	6531	C	530 541-6700	11863
United Parcel Service Inc OH	7389	B	800 742-5877	17559

SOUTH PASADENA, CA - Los Angeles County

Company	SIC	EMP	PHONE	ENTRY #
Anderson Burton Construction	1542	D	626 441-2464	1490
Cccc Growth Fund LLC	6799	D	626 441-8770	12295
City of Hope	8011	C	626 396-2900	19440
Collins Cllins Muir Stwart LLP	8111	E	626 243-1100	23159
Hospice Cheers	8082	D	626 799-2727	22475
Michael G Fortaanasce Phys	8049	D	323 254-6000	20332
Omni Ventures Group Llc	6719	D	510 384-1033	12081
Stargate Films Inc	7812	D	626 403-8403	18160
Total Education Solutions Inc (PA)	8748	E	323 341-5580	28081
Young Mens Chrstn Assn of La	8641	D	626 799-9119	25465
Young Mens Chrstn Assn of La	8641	D	323 682-2147	25471

SOUTH SAN FRANCISCO, CA - San Mateo County

Company	SIC	EMP	PHONE	ENTRY #
Abp Liquidating Corp	5148	E	650 871-7689	8692
Aeroground Inc (DH)	4581	A	650 266-6965	4891
Ageis Living	8999	D	650 952-6100	28109
Air Serv Corporation	4581	B	650 872-5400	4892
American Etc Inc	7211	B	650 873-5353	13499
Andrighetto Produce Inc	1799	D	650 588-0930	3491
Antonelli & Sons Fish & Plty	5146	D	650 952-7413	8627
Apria Healthcare LLC	5047	D	650 588-9744	7236
Aramark Unf & Career AP LLC	7218	D	650 244-9332	13614
Ashbury Market Inc	5149	D	650 952-8889	8802
Automatic Data Processing Inc	7374	E	650 829-6900	16093
Avis Budget Group Inc	7514	D	650 616-0150	17661
Balliet Bros Construction Corp	1542	E	650 871-9000	1497
California Golf CLB San Frncsco	7997	D	650 588-9021	18910
Centra Freight Services Inc (PA)	4783	D	650 873-8147	5198
Cintas Corporation No 3	7218	D	650 278-4004	13626
Coast Citrus Distributors	5148	D	650 588-0707	8709
Collabnet Inc (PA)	7372	D	650 228-2500	15623
Comfort Suites	7011	D	650 589-7100	12537
Comparenetworks Inc (PA)	8731	D	650 873-9031	26499
Cooper & Jackson Inc	8734	C	408 437-2750	26840
Core-Mark International Inc (HQ)	5141	D	650 589-9445	8469
Core-Mark Midcontinent Inc (DH)	5194	D	650 589-9445	9233
Covenant Aviation Security LLC	7381	A	650 219-3473	16613
Datasafe Inc (PA)	4226	E	650 875-3800	4682
Dbi Beverage San Francisco	5181	C	415 643-9900	9051
Decker Elc Co Inc Elec Contrs	1731	D	650 635-1390	2574
Discharge Resource Group	7363	C	650 877-8111	14871
Djont/Cmb Ssf	7011	D	650 589-3400	12578
Double Day Office Services Inc	4214	E	650 872-6600	4342
Elan Drug Delivery Inc	8731	D	770 531-8100	26509
Elevate Expo Inc	7389	E	415 625-2821	17146
Exelixis Inc	8731	D	650 837-7000	26516
Expeditors Intl Wash Inc	4731	C	919 489-7431	5069
Formation Brands LLC	5023	D	650 238-1009	6861
Freeman Expositions Inc	7389	D	650 871-1597	17175
Geodis Wilson Usa Inc	4731	C	650 692-9850	5087
Grosvenor Properties Ltd	7011	C	650 873-3200	12679
Hertz Corporation	7514	C	650 624-6391	17687
Hilton Worldwide Inc	7011	D	650 589-3400	12741
Hoem & Associates Inc	1752	D	650 871-5194	3116
Imperial Parking (us) LLC	7521	D	650 871-5423	17719
Inter-City Cleaners	7216	D	650 875-9200	13582
Italfoods Inc	5149	D	650 873-2640	8857
Jacobs Farm/Del Cabo Inc	0191	D	650 827-1133	374
Janssen Alzheimer Immunothera	8731	D	650 794-2500	26541
JMB Construction Inc	1623	D	650 267-5300	1951
Kaiser Foundation Hospitals	8011	A	650 742-2000	19668
L B C Holdings U S A Corp (PA)	4724	C	650 873-0750	4966
Larkspur Hsptality Dev MGT LLC	7011	D	650 871-1515	12906
Latino Commission	8093	E	650 244-0304	22765
Legalmatchcom	8111	E	415 946-0800	23383
Mad Dog Express Inc (PA)	4212	D	650 588-1900	4037
Master Roofing Systems Inc	1761	D	415 407-4450	3189
Matagrano Inc	5181	C	650 829-4829	9072
McKesson Corporation	5122	D	650 952-8400	8277
Medical Care Professionals	8051	D	650 583-9898	20783
Medical Linen Services Inc	7213	D	650 873-1221	13551
Moodys Wall St Analytics Inc	7371	E	650 266-9660	15315
Panalpina Inc	4731	E	650 873-1390	5143
Parts Warehouse Distrs Inc	5013	D	650 616-4988	6751
Pathways Home Health	8099	E	650 634-0133	23017
Peeters Transportation Co	4214	D	800 356-5877	4371
Peking Handicraft Inc (PA)	5023	C	650 871-3788	6880
Peninou French Ldry & Clrs Inc (PA)	7219	D	800 392-2532	13656
Peninsula Family Service	8322	D	650 952-6848	24130
Peninsula Pthlogists Med Group	8071	D	650 616-2940	22253
Permanente Medical Group Inc	8011	A	650 827-6495	19848
Pribuss Engineering Inc	1711	D	650 588-0447	2328
Prothena Biosciences Inc	8733	E	650 837-8550	26797
Quality Conservation Svcs Inc	8999	D	650 266-9490	28158
Quality Systems Installations	1799	D	650 875-9000	3573
Raven Biotechnologies Inc	8731	D	650 624-2600	26594
San Mateo County Transit Dst	4111	B	650 588-2400	3712
San Mateo Health Commission	8099	C	650 616-0050	23050
Schenker Inc	4731	D	650 745-3000	5165
Seafus Corporation	7349	E	415 584-6100	14423
Sfo Airporter Inc (PA)	4111	D	650 246-2775	3715

Employment Codes: A=Over 500 employees, B=251-500, C=101-250, D=51-100, E=45-50

SOUTH SAN FRANCISCO, CA

	SIC	EMP	PHONE	ENTRY #
Silk Botanica Inc	5193	D	415 594-0888	9212
Society of St Vincent De Paul	8322	D	650 589-9039	24215
Ssf Imported Auto Parts LLC (PA)	5013	D	800 203-9287	6773
Starlink Freight Sys Sfo Inc (PA)	4731	E	650 589-2575	5169
Steven Engineering Inc	5085	D	650 588-9200	7955
Successfactors Inc (DH)	7371	C	800 845-0395	15481
Terravia Holdings Inc (PA)	8731	D	650 780-4777	26622
Thermo Fisher Scientific Inc	5049	D	650 876-1949	7351
Tosoh Bioscience Inc	5047	D	650 615-4970	7320
Tricor International	4731	D	650 877-3678	5178
Trinity Building Services	7349	B	650 873-2121	14446
U-2 Home Entertainment Inc	5065	E	650 871-8118	7650
United Parcel Service Inc	4215	C	650 737-3737	4435
UPS Supply Chain Solutions Inc	4225	C	650 875-8300	4650
UPS Supply Chain Solutions Inc	4225	C	650 635-2678	4651
Uti United States Inc	4731	D	650 588-9477	5187
Veracyte Inc	8071	C	650 243-6300	22297
Yrc Worldwide Inc	4213	D	650 952-1112	4326

SPRING VALLEY, CA - San Diego County

	SIC	EMP	PHONE	ENTRY #
B-Spring Valley LLC	8051	D	619 797-3991	20402
Brighton Place East Inc	8051	D	619 461-3222	20419
Brightview Landscapes LLC	0781	D	619 644-8584	757
Burns and Sons Trucking Inc	4212	D	619 460-5394	3985
Casper Company	1795	D	619 589-6001	3449
Commercial Indus Roofg Co Inc	1761	D	619 465-3737	3153
County of San Diego	8322	D	619 479-1832	23901
Covenant Rtirement Communities	8059	C	619 479-4790	21199
Evangelical Covenant Church	8361	D	619 931-1114	24654
Family Hlth Ctrs San Diego Inc	8011	D	619 515-2555	19524
Greenbrier Lawn Tree Exprt Co	0782	D	619 469-8720	862
Hugo Alonso Inc	1541	E	619 660-5395	1438
Irish Construction	1623	D	619 713-1991	1948
J&M Keystone Inc	7217	D	619 466-9876	13599
Kim Wilson	8082	D	619 741-1548	22493
Layfield USA Corporation (DH)	1799	D	619 562-1200	3546
Mt Miquel Covenant Village	8059	C	619 479-4790	21323
Otay Water District	4941	C	619 670-2222	6385
Pnc Inc	5147	C	619 713-2278	8678
Robinson Company Contrs Inc	1711	D	619 697-6040	2349
Roofing Wholesale Co Inc	5033	E	619 287-7600	7016
Socal Coatings Inc	1721	E	619 660-5395	2492
Treebeard Landscape Inc	0782	D	619 697-8302	965

STANFORD, CA - Santa Clara County

	SIC	EMP	PHONE	ENTRY #
Associated Students Stanford (PA)	8641	D	650 723-4331	25202
Carnegie Institution Wash	8733	C	650 319-8904	26747
General Electric Company	4911	C	650 725-0516	6133
Howard Hughes Medical Inst	8731	D	650 725-8252	26530
Imperial Parking (us) LLC	7521	E	650 724-4309	17721
Leland Stanford Junior Univ	4832	D	650 725-4868	5805
Leland Stanford Junior Univ	8011	D	650 723-7863	19703
Leland Stanford Junior Univ	8641	C	650 723-2021	25287
Leland Stanford Junior Univ	8733	D	650 723-4150	26782
Leland Stanford Junior Univ	1731	D	650 723-9633	2637
Leland Stanford Junior Univ	8733	D	650 723-0107	26783
Leland Stanford Junior Univ	8733	C	650 724-8899	26784
Leland Stanford Junior Univ	8062	A	650 725-2386	21703
Leland Stanford Junior Univ	8062	A	650 725-6127	21704
Leland Stanford Junior Univ	8011	D	650 723-0821	19705
Leland Stanford Junior Univ	8062	A	650 723-4000	21705
Lucile Salter Packard Chil	8069	D	650 723-5791	22156
Palo Alto Community Child Care	8351	D	650 855-9828	24497
Stanford	8011	D	650 799-3773	20063
Stanford Health Care	8062	A	650 723-4000	21931
Stanford Health Care (HQ)	8062	A	650 723-4000	21933
Stanford Management Company	8741	D	650 721-2200	27230
Stanford Univ Med Ctr Aux	8322	B	650 723-6636	24231

STANTON, CA - Orange County

	SIC	EMP	PHONE	ENTRY #
California Friends Homes	8361	B	714 530-9100	24577
Denver D Darling Inc	1541	D	714 761-8299	1417
Great Scott Tree Service Inc (PA)	0783	E	714 826-1750	993
Haulaway Storage Cntrs Inc	4225	A	800 826-9040	4567
Johnson & Turner Painting Co	1721	E	714 828-8282	2461
Muth Development Co Inc	6512	D	714 527-2239	11022
USS Cal Builders Inc	1542	C	714 828-4882	1709

STEVENSON RANCH, CA - Los Angeles County

	SIC	EMP	PHONE	ENTRY #
AT&T Corp	4813	D	661 799-0800	5475
Century Bankcard Services	7389	D	818 700-3100	17063
Global Building Services Inc (PA)	7349	A	661 288-5733	14314
King Monster Inc	6531	D	661 253-3000	11621
Mventix Inc	7389	B	661 263-1768	17345

STEVINSON, CA - Merced County

	SIC	EMP	PHONE	ENTRY #
Frank J Gomes Dairy A Califo	0241	D	209 669-7978	425
James J Stevinson A Corp (PA)	0241	E	209 632-1681	430
Stevinson Ranch-Savannah GP	7992	D	209 668-8200	18790

STOCKTON, CA - San Joaquin County

	SIC	EMP	PHONE	ENTRY #
3900 West Lane Bowl Inc	7933	E	209 466-6100	18506
A G Spanos Management Inc	6531	E	209 478-7954	11271
ABM Janitorial Services Inc	7349	C	209 983-3923	14206
AC Square Inc	8748	C	650 293-2730	27807
Ace Tomato Company Inc	0161	D	209 982-0734	36
American Automobile Assctn	8699	E	209 952-4100	25490
American Building Supply Inc	5031	D	209 941-8852	6907
American Cstm Private SEC Inc	7381	D	209 369-1200	16554
American Golf Corporation	7997	E	209 477-4653	18861
Ameripride Services Inc	7213	E	209 982-0020	13527
Aryzta LLC	5149	E	209 462-3601	8801
Ashley Lane Cherry Orchards LP	0175	E	209 546-0426	228
Associated Students Univ PCF	8641	D	209 946-2233	25203
AT&T Corp	4813	D	209 954-1033	5485
Auto Town Inc	7538	D	209 473-2513	17783
Bank of Stockton (HQ)	6022	C	209 929-1600	9475
Best Western Royal Host Inn	7011	D	209 810-2619	12441
Boboli International LLC (PA)	5149	D	209 473-3507	8809
Bockmon & Woody Elc Co Inc	1731	D	209 464-2615	2535
Boretech Resrce Recovry Engine	5084	E	209 373-2588	7827
Borgens & Borgens Inc	7381	D	209 547-2980	16577
Brightview Companies LLC	0781	C	209 993-9277	744
Brock G and L Cnstr Co Inc	1623	E	209 931-3626	1912
Brookside Country Club	7997	D	209 956-6200	18902
Burlingame Industries Inc	5033	D	209 464-9001	7009
Calcedar Export Inc	5112	C	209 944-5800	8161
California Guard Inc	7381	D	209 465-8420	16589
California Materials Inc	4212	D	209 472-7422	3989
California Security Cons	7381	D	209 465-8420	16591
California Water Service Co	4941	D	209 547-7900	6321
Caraustar Industries Inc	4953	C	209 476-7155	6455
Caremark Rx LLC	8011	E	209 957-7050	19406
Cargill Incorporated	8741	D	209 982-4632	26959
Castlehill Properties Inc (PA)	7011	D	209 472-9800	12500
Chicago Title Insurance Co	6541	D	209 952-5500	11937
Childrens Home of Stockton	8361	D	209 466-0853	24595
Citadel Broadcasting Corp	4832	C	209 766-5103	5765
Clark Pest Ctrl Stockton Inc	7342	D	209 474-3204	14179
Coastal Pacific Fd Distrs Inc (PA)	5141	C	909 947-2066	8466
Collins Electrical Company Inc (PA)	1731	C	209 466-3691	2554
Comcast Corporation	4841	D	209 955-6521	5970
Comfort Air Inc	1711	D	209 466-4601	2185
Communication Svc For Deaf Inc	8399	E	209 475-5000	24892
Community Medical Centers Inc	8062	D	209 944-4700	21507
Community Medical Centers Inc (PA)	8093	D	209 373-2800	22690
Compass Bancshares Inc	6021	B	209 473-6925	9393
Compass Bancshares Inc	6021	B	209 939-3288	9394
County of San Joaquin	8322	B	209 468-2601	23905
County of San Joaquin	8399	D	209 468-3021	24910
County of San Joaquin	8093	B	209 468-8750	22708
County of San Joaquin	8322	A	209 468-4100	23906
County of San Joaquin	8331	C	209 468-3500	24332
Covenant Care California LLC	8059	C	209 477-5252	21197
Covey Auto Express Inc (PA)	7549	C	253 826-0461	17881
D S S Company	1623	E	209 948-0302	1924
Dameron Hospital Association (PA)	8062	A	209 944-5550	21527
Dbi Beverage San Joaquin	5181	D	209 948-9400	9052
Delta Blood Bank (HQ)	8099	D	800 244-6794	22939
Delta Hawkeye Security Inc	7381	D	209 957-3333	16623
Dfa of California	7389	D	209 465-2289	17121
Dignity Health	8071	C	209 467-6430	22209
Dignity Health	8082	E	209 943-4663	22426
Dorfman-Pacific Co (PA)	5136	D	209 982-1400	8338
Dreamctchers Empwerment Netwrk	8361	D	209 477-4817	24636
Dynamex Inc	4215	D	209 464-7008	4398
E D D 2100	6321	D	209 941-6501	10239
E J Williams Property MGT	6513	D	209 473-4022	11122
Ecs Refining LLC	4953	D	209 774-5000	6477
Embarcadero Homes Association	8641	D	209 951-4420	25253
Employment Training Academy	8699	D	209 475-1529	25528
Estes Express Lines Inc	4213	D	209 982-1841	4153
Exel N Amercn Logistics Inc	4222	D	209 942-0102	4493
Exel N Amercn Logistics Inc	4222	D	209 932-2400	4494
Express Messenger Systems Inc	4215	D	209 234-8255	4403
Family Resource & Referral Ctr	8322	D	209 948-1553	23969
Farmington Fresh Sales LLC (PA)	0175	D	209 983-9700	233
Federal Express Corporation	4513	E	800 463-3339	4855
Fedex Freight Corporation	4213	D	209 466-7726	4168
First Student Inc	4151	C	209 466-7737	3930
Five Star Quality Care Inc	8082	E	209 951-6500	22439
Five Star Quality Care Inc	8051	C	209 466-2066	20572
Franke Con J Electric Inc	1731	D	209 462-0717	2597

GEOGRAPHIC SECTION

SUISUN CITY, CA

Name	SIC	EMP	PHONE	ENTRY #
Friends Outside	8322	C	209 955-0701	23988
Frontier Land Companies	1521	E	209 957-8112	1178
Fsq Rio Las Palmas Business Tr	6513	D	209 957-4711	11135
Fuel Delivery Services Inc	4213	D	209 751-2185	4187
Golden Living LLC	8051	D	707 546-0471	20606
Golden Living LLC	8051	D	209 466-3522	20624
Golden State Lumber Inc	5031	C	209 234-7700	6924
Greyhound Lines Inc	4513	E	209 466-3568	4866
Groupe Development Associates	6552	D	209 473-6000	11972
Grupe Company (PA)	6531	D	209 473-6000	11564
Grupe Dev Companynorthern Cal	1531	D	209 473-6000	1367
Grupe Properties Co	4225	E	209 956-7885	4565
H and H Drug Stores Inc	5099	D	209 931-5200	8120
Heritage Land Company Inc	0181	E	209 444-1700	288
Holistic Approach Inc	7361	D	209 956-7050	14672
Holt of California	5082	C	209 462-3660	7774
Hospice of San Joaquin	8051	D	209 957-3888	20678
Hospitality Solutions LLC	7011	E	209 474-3301	12759
Hub Group Trucking Inc	4212	D	209 943-6975	4025
Human Services Projects Inc	8361	C	209 951-9625	24697
In Shape Management Company	7991	B	209 472-2231	18643
In-Shape Health Clubs (PA)	7991	E	209 472-2231	18644
Inreach Internet LLC (HQ)	4813	D	888 467-3224	5638
International Longshoremens	8631	D	209 464-1827	25175
Interstate Truck Center LLC (PA)	5012	D	209 944-5821	6684
Its Technologies Logistics LLC	4789	C	209 460-6023	5225
J & P Solari	0175	D	209 931-1765	237
John Aguilar & Company Inc	4212	D	209 546-0171	4031
Jpmorgan Chase & Co	6035	A	209 460-2888	9571
Kaiser Foundation Hospitals	8062	C	209 476-3101	21677
Kimberlite Corporation	7382	D	209 948-2551	16894
Kindred Nursing Centers W LLC	8051	C	209 957-4539	20709
Kxtv Inc	4833	D	209 463-8471	5892
Lafaltte Rhbilitation Care Ctr	8051	E	209 466-2066	20718
Lincoln School Bus Trnsp	4131	D	209 953-8596	3881
Lithia Motors Inc	7538	E	209 956-1930	17805
LLP Moss Adams	8721	E	209 955-6100	26398
Lowes Home Centers LLC	4225	D	209 513-9560	4591
M & M Stone Inc	6531	D	209 478-1791	11648
Marchbrook Building Co	1521	D	209 473-6084	1212
Mariner Health Care Inc	8051	C	209 466-2066	20772
Mark Scott Construction Inc	1522	E	209 982-0502	1324
Martin-Brower Company LLC	5141	D	209 466-2980	8497
Maxim Crane Works LP	7353	C	209 464-7635	14488
Meadowood Hlth Rehabilitation	8051	B	209 956-3444	20782
Melissa & Doug LLC	7389	D	209 830-7900	17326
Mg Computers Inc	7378	D	831 970-3231	16302
Mid State Steel Erection (PA)	1791	D	209 464-9497	3393
Midstate Barrier Inc	1611	D	209 944-9565	1827
Mike Campbell & Associates Ltd	4212	B	209 234-7920	4039
Morada Produce Company LP	0723	A	209 546-0426	566
Mountain Valley Express Co Inc (PA)	4213	D	209 823-2168	4231
Mv Transportation Inc	4111	D	209 547-7879	3679
New Stockton Poultry Inc	5144	E	209 466-1952	8601
OConner Woods A California	6513	D	209 956-3400	11179
OConnor Woods Housing Corp	6513	D	209 956-3400	11180
Pacific Coast Services Inc	8082	C	209 956-2532	22529
Pacific Gas and Electric Co	4911	D	209 942-1787	6180
Pacific Metro Electric Inc	1731	D	209 939-3222	2674
Pacific State Bancorp	6035	D	209 870-3214	9579
PDM Steel Service Centers (HQ)	5051	D	209 943-0555	7390
PDM Steel Service Centers	5051	D	209 234-0548	7391
Pearl Crop Inc (PA)	0723	D	209 808-7575	573
Permanente Medical Group Inc	8011	D	209 476-3737	19856
Permanente Medical Group Inc	8011	E	209 476-2000	19862
Pinasco Plumbing & Heating Inc	1711	D	209 463-7793	2321
Platinum Home Mortgage Corp	6282	D	209 955-2200	10173
Recreational Equipment Inc	5046	C	209 957-9479	7227
Reeve Trucking Company Inc (PA)	4213	D	209 948-4061	4249
Reliance Intermodal Inc	5141	D	209 946-0200	8512
Retirement Housing Foundation	6531	D	209 466-4341	11812
Sahargun Plumbing Inc	1711	D	209 474-2611	2357
Salvation Army	8093	D	209 466-3871	22821
Sam Freitas Trucking Inc	4212	D	209 474-0294	4061
San Joaquin Beverage Inc	5181	D	209 320-2400	9084
San Joaquin Regional Trnst Dst	4111	C	209 948-5566	3710
Scan-Vino LLC (PA)	4213	D	209 931-3570	4260
Schuff Steel Company	1791	C	209 938-0869	3401
Securitas SEC Svcs USA Inc	7381	C	209 943-1401	16786
Sierra Health Services LLC	8721	E	209 956-7715	26441
Southwest Traders Incorporated	5141	D	209 462-1607	8520
St Joseph Community Home Care	8082	D	209 478-9547	22569
St Joseph Surgery Center LP	8011	D	209 467-6316	20056
St Josephs Med Ctr Stockton	8062	A	209 943-2000	21923
St Josephs Medical Center	8062	C	209 943-2000	21924
Standard Industries Inc	5033	E	209 242-5000	7020
State Compensation Insur Fund	6331	C	888 782-8338	10469
Stockton Cardiology Medical Gr (PA)	8011	D	209 754-1012	20071
Stockton Congregational Home	8361	D	209 466-4341	24823
Stockton Edson Healthcare Corp	8059	D	209 948-8762	21385
Stockton Orthpd Med Group Inc	8011	E	209 948-1641	20072
Stockton Port District	4491	D	209 946-0246	4762
Stockton Unlimited Company	7389	D	209 464-2200	17506
Storer Transportation	4111	D	209 644-5100	3723
Strocal Inc (PA)	1791	B	209 948-4646	3404
Sugar Transport of The NW	4212	D	209 931-3587	4069
Sunbridge Healthcare LLC	8051	D	209 477-4817	20943
Sygma Network Inc	5141	C	209 932-5300	8529
Table Community Foudation	8641	D	209 951-1753	25366
Thompson & Rich Crane Service	7389	E	209 465-3161	17529
Unified Grocers Inc	5141	C	209 931-1990	8542
Unifirst Corporation	7218	E	209 941-8364	13644
United Cerebral Palsy Assoc (PA)	8322	C	209 956-0290	24267
United Cerebral Palsy Associat	8069	C	209 956-0295	22183
United Parcel Service Inc OH	4215	C	209 463-1971	4449
United Rentals North Amer Inc	7359	C	209 948-9500	14585
University of Pacific	7999	A	209 946-2030	19301
US Security Associates Inc	7381	C	209 476-7062	16847
USA Waste of California Inc	4212	E	209 946-5721	4082
USG Interiors LLC	5031	D	209 466-4636	6967
Valley Mtn Regional Ctr Inc (PA)	8322	C	209 473-0951	24275
Valley Wholesale Drug Co LLC	5122	D	209 466-0131	8303
Van De Pol Enterprises Inc (PA)	5172	D	209 944-9115	9031
Village West Yacht Club	7997	D	209 478-8992	19118
Volt Management Corp	7363	C	209 952-5627	14978
Westland Hotel Corporation	7011	E	209 931-3131	13406
Whispering Hope Care Center	8051	D	209 473-3004	21039
Williams Tank Lines (PA)	4213	D	209 944-5613	4304
Wm Michael Stemler Inc (PA)	6411	C	209 948-8483	10942
World Class Distribution Inc	4225	B	909 574-4140	4672
Xpo Enterprise Services Inc	4213	D	209 983-8285	4307
YMCA of San Joaquin County	8641	D	209 472-9622	25429
Yuen SOO Benevolent Assn	8641	D	209 464-3048	25478
Zeiter Eye Medical Group Inc (PA)	8011	D	209 366-0446	20241

STRATFORD, CA - Kings County

Name	SIC	EMP	PHONE	ENTRY #
Crisp Warehouse Inc	0723	D	559 947-9221	523
Stone Land Company (PA)	0131	D	559 947-3185	14

STRATHMORE, CA - Tulare County

Name	SIC	EMP	PHONE	ENTRY #
Golden Valley Citrus Inc	0723	D	559 568-1768	536
Lopez Harvesting	0722	D	559 568-2553	496

STUDIO CITY, CA - Los Angeles County

Name	SIC	EMP	PHONE	ENTRY #
American Private Duty Inc	8082	D	818 386-6358	22359
Blayne Pacelli	6531	D	310 383-6281	11326
CBS Broadcasting Inc	4833	B	818 655-2000	5841
Cellco Partnership	4812	D	818 980-4200	5344
Commercial Prgrm Systems Inc (PA)	7379	C	818 308-8560	16339
Crown Media Holdings Inc (HQ)	4841	D	888 390-7474	5982
Crown Media United States LLC (DH)	4841	D	818 755-2400	5983
Dino Bones Productions Inc	7812	D	818 827-5100	18073
Dpr Holdings LLC	6719	E	323 761-9829	12059
Enrichment Eductl Experiences	8351	D	818 989-7509	24458
Everett Mall 01 LLC	6519	E	818 505-6777	11254
Fort Hill Construction (PA)	1521	D	323 656-7425	1176
Gavin De Becker & Associates	8742	C	818 760-4213	27447
High Technology Video Inc	7819	D	323 969-8822	18230
Jpmorgan Chase Bank Nat Assn	6035	E	818 763-7343	9574
Longwood Management Corp	8059	D	818 980-8200	21298
Motion Pcture Hlth Wlfare Fund	6371	D	818 769-0007	10556
Motion Picture Industry Plans	6371	D	818 769-0007	10557
Music Collective LLC	7819	E	818 508-3303	18237
Northridge 07 A LLC	6512	E	818 505-6777	11025
Radford Studio Center Inc	7922	B	818 655-5000	18428
Ranch Hand Entertainment Inc	7812	D	612 396-2632	18139
Rodeo Realty Inc	6531	D	818 308-8273	11818
Sportsmens Lodge Hotel LLC	7011	C	818 769-7441	13281
Sunrise Senior Living LLC	8051	D	818 505-8484	20978
Universal Studios Inc	7812	C	818 777-2351	18185
Wurzel Landscape Maintenance	0782	E	818 762-8653	981

SUISUN CITY, CA - Solano County

Name	SIC	EMP	PHONE	ENTRY #
Cement Mason Health & Welfare	8399	D	707 864-3300	24887
E B Stone & Son Inc	5191	D	707 249-4699	9136
Redevelopment Agency of The Ci	8748	D	707 421-7309	28038
Villara Corporation	1761	E	707 863-8222	3222
Walker Communications Inc	1731	D	707 421-1300	2788
Westamerica Bancorporation	6029	C	707 863-6029	9566
Wpcs International Inc (PA)	4899	D	707 421-1300	6102

Employment Codes: A=Over 500 employees, B=251-500, C=101-250, D=51-100, E=45-50

2017 Directory of California Wholesalers and Services Companies

SUN CITY, CA — GEOGRAPHIC SECTION

SUN CITY, CA - Riverside County

Company	SIC	EMP	PHONE	ENTRY #
Cambrian Homecare Inc	8082	C	951 301-4300	22387
Case Shella Management Service	8741	C	951 723-8460	26961
Compass Bancshares Inc	6021	B	951 672-4829	9391
Ennis Inc	5112	E	951 928-1125	8165
In-Roads Creative Programs	8322	D	951 672-1800	24021
Physicians For Healthy Hospita	8062	B	951 679-8888	21798
Sun City Rhf Housing Inc	8361	D	951 679-2391	24828
United Parcel Service Inc OH	4513	C	951 928-5221	4875

SUN VALLEY, CA - Los Angeles County

Company	SIC	EMP	PHONE	ENTRY #
Aadlen Brothers Auto Wrecking (PA)	5093	D	323 875-1400	8057
Alcorn Fence Company (PA)	1799	D	818 983-0650	3486
Arakelian Enterprises Inc	4953	D	818 768-0689	6426
Arcadia Transit Inc	4111	E	818 252-0630	3635
Browning-Ferris Industries Inc	4953	C	818 790-5410	6447
Ceramic Tile Art Inc	1743	D	818 767-9088	3008
Coast To Coast Water Damage	7349	E	818 255-3323	14255
Crown Disposal Company Inc	4953	C	818 767-0675	6471
Daybreak Care Center (PA)	8361	D	818 504-6154	24628
Dazian LLC	5131	D	818 287-3800	8310
Estes Express Lines Inc	4213	D	818 504-4155	4152
Express Messenger Systems Inc	4215	D	818 504-9043	4402
Express Messenger Systems Inc	4215	D	818 504-9043	4406
Fathers of St Charles	6513	C	818 768-6500	11129
Federal Express Corporation	4512	C	800 463-3339	4800
Fedex Freight Corporation	4213	D	818 899-1141	4167
Fedex Ground Package Sys Inc	4213	D	818 767-7650	4183
Firstmed Ambulance Svcs Inc	4119	D	800 608-0311	3795
Gilbert Barco	7389	D	323 232-7672	17186
Hawker Pacific Aerospace	7699	B	818 765-6201	17978
Hope of Valley Rescue Mission	8322	D	818 392-0020	24013
JP Motorsports Inc	4119	D	818 381-8313	3807
LA Hydro-Jet Rooter Svc Inc	7699	D	818 768-4225	17988
Landco	0782	D	818 612-0118	900
Light & Sound Design Inc	7922	D	818 260-6260	18406
Los Angeles County MTA	4111	B	213 922-6215	3666
Los Angeles Dept Wtr & Pwr	4941	A	213 367-1342	6365
Mission Valley Bancorp	6712	D	818 394-2300	12044
Mountain View Child Care Inc	8351	C	818 252-5863	24484
Nicola International Inc	5149	C	818 767-1133	8893
Norman Industrial Mtls Inc (PA)	5051	C	818 729-3333	7386
Northeast Valley Health Corp	8099	C	818 432-4400	23009
Pacific Pavingstone Inc	1771	C	818 244-4000	3307
Pacifica of Valley Corporation	8062	A	818 767-3310	21777
PBM Maintenance Corp	7349	B	818 771-1100	14382
Pena Grading & Demolition Inc	1611	E	818 768-5202	1845
Penske Truck Rental Inc	7513	C	818 718-2536	17649
PRI Medical Technologies Inc (DH)	5047	D	818 394-2800	7304
Pro Ponds West Inc	0781	D	818 244-4000	789
Quixote Studios LLC	7519	E	818 252-7722	17707
Rawlings Mechanical Corp (PA)	1711	D	323 875-2040	2340
Recology Los Angeles	4953	B	415 875-1140	6526
Refrigeration Hdwr Sup Corp	5078	E	818 768-3636	7758
Reliable Carriers Inc	4213	E	818 252-6400	4250
REM Optical Company Inc	5049	D	818 504-3950	7348
Rose Brand Wipers Inc	7922	D	818 505-6290	18429
SA Recycling LLC	4953	D	323 875-2520	6546
San Gabriel Transit Inc	4121	D	818 771-0374	3868
Serra Community Med Clinic Inc	8011	D	818 768-8882	19988
Serra Medical Clinic Inc	8011	D	818 768-3000	19989
Smg Stone Company Inc	1741	D	818 767-0000	2834
Sugar Foods Corporation	7389	C	818 768-7900	17508
Sugar Foods Corporation	7389	D	818 768-7900	17509
Svd Inc	5143	D	818 504-1775	8594
Title Records Inc	6541	D	818 767-9610	11942
Walgreens Home Care Inc	8082	D	818 351-3000	22612
Waste Management Cal Inc (HQ)	4953	C	877 836-6526	6597
Wet (PA)	7389	C	818 769-6200	17626

SUNLAND, CA - Los Angeles County

Company	SIC	EMP	PHONE	ENTRY #
Brightview Tree Company	0811	C	661 305-3312	1007
New Vista Health Services	8059	C	818 352-1421	21326
P R N Convalescent Hospital	8051	D	818 352-3158	20832
Shadow Hlls Cnvlscent Hosp Inc	8051	D	818 352-4438	20905
Tierra Del Sol Foundation (PA)	8361	D	818 352-1419	24836
Wimer Construction	1542	E	818 848-0400	1718

SUNNYVALE, CA - Santa Clara County

Company	SIC	EMP	PHONE	ENTRY #
Access Systems Americas Inc	7371	A	408 400-3000	14997
Agiliance Inc	7379	E	408 200-0400	16318
Airmagnet Inc	5045	D	408 400-0200	7087
Alphavista Services Inc	8049	D	408 331-2181	20305
Alvarion Inc (HQ)	5065	E	650 314-2500	7518
Amazon Lab126	8731	A	206 266-1000	26466
Applied Weather Technology Inc	8999	C	408 731-8600	28114
Ase (us) Inc (HQ)	5065	D	408 636-9500	7525
AT&T Corp	8999	D	650 960-2313	28117
Avenuesocial Inc	7371	C	510 275-4485	15045
Backproject Corporation	5047	D	408 730-1111	7240
Banyan Solutions Inc	7363	D	650 766-9338	14843
Belmont Village LP	6513	D	408 720-8498	11094
Bioimagene Inc	8071	E	408 207-4200	22193
Blakely Skloff Tylor Zfman LLP	8111	C	408 720-8300	23118
Blue Coat Systems LLC (DH)	7372	B	408 220-2200	15603
Broadsoft Contact Center Inc	7371	E	408 338-0900	15068
Cashedge Inc	7389	D	408 541-3900	17059
Chelsio Communications Inc	7371	C	408 962-3600	15081
City of Sunnyvale	7041	D	408 730-7451	13490
City of Sunnyvale	7389	D	408 730-7510	17800
City of Sunnyvale Nova	7361	D	408 730-7232	14625
Clover Network Inc	4813	D	650 210-7888	5579
Compvue Inc	7371	D	408 892-9909	15105
Comtel Systems Technology	1731	D	408 543-5600	2560
Convalescent Management Svcs	8051	C	408 745-1168	20470
De Anza Square Shopping Center	1531	D	408 738-4444	1361
Display Works LLC	7389	D	408 746-9654	17127
E-Infochips Inc	7371	C	408 496-1882	15153
Egain Corporation (PA)	7372	C	408 636-4500	15649
Estuate Inc	7371	D	408 400-0680	15173
Exablox Corporation	7375	D	408 773-8477	16235
Executive Inn Inc	7011	D	408 245-5330	12628
Federal Express Corporation	4513	C	800 463-3339	4847
Financial Engines Inc (PA)	8742	C	408 498-6000	27434
Fiserv Inc	7374	D	408 242-3011	16131
Fortinet Inc (PA)	7372	C	408 235-7700	15669
Fujitsu America Inc (DH)	7373	B	408 746-6000	15951
Fujitsu Computer Pdts Amer Inc (HQ)	5045	B	408 746-6000	7133
Fujitsu Electronics Amer Inc (DH)	8711	D	408 737-5600	25823
Fujitsu Laboratories Amer Inc (DH)	8731	D	408 530-4500	26519
Ghc of Sunnyvale LLC	8059	D	408 738-4880	21233
Giva Inc	7371	D	408 260-9000	15204
Good Technology Corporation (HQ)	7371	C	408 212-7500	15210
Good Technology Software Inc	7372	A	408 212-7500	15681
Goodman Usa Inc	8011	D	408 329-5400	19541
Hcl America Inc (HQ)	7376	D	408 733-0480	16280
Hcr Manorcare Med Svcs Fla LLC	8051	D	408 735-7200	20652
Headstrong Corporation	7379	D	408 732-8700	16396
Honeywell International Inc	5065	E	408 962-2000	7579
Horizon Technologies Inc	7371	C	408 733-1530	15222
Hpt Trs Ihg-2 Inc	7011	E	408 745-1515	12801
Idec Corporation (HQ)	5065	D	408 747-0550	7584
Illumio Inc	7371	C	669 800-5000	15232
Indium Software Inc	7372	C	408 501-8844	15698
Inko Industrial Corporation	7374	D	408 830-1040	16149
Innopath Software Inc (PA)	7371	C	408 962-9200	15235
Interwoven Inc (HQ)	7372	B	312 580-9100	15709
Ipolipo Inc	7372	D	408 916-5290	15717
Island Hospitality MGT LLC	7011	E	408 720-1000	12855
Island Hospitality MGT LLC	7011	D	408 720-8893	12857
Joie De Vivre Hospitality Inc	7011	D	408 738-0500	12867
Kaiser Foundation Hospitals	8011	A	408 851-1000	19649
Level 10 Construction LP	1542	C	408 747-5000	1601
Luxn Inc	4899	D	408 213-7437	6081
MDE Electric Company Inc	1731	E	408 738-8600	2648
Microsoft Corporation	7372	C	650 693-1009	15752
Mlslistings Inc	8742	D	408 874-0200	27551
Moreno & Associates Inc	7349	D	408 924-0353	14364
Mp Morse Court Associates	6514	D	408 734-9442	11239
Netapp Inc	7373	C	408 822-3402	16004
Netapp Inc	7373	D	408 419-5301	16006
Nuance Communications Inc	7372	C	408 245-5358	15781
Opal Soft Inc	7379	D	408 267-2211	16445
Oracle Corporation	7372	B	650 607-5402	15789
Osram Opto Semiconductors Inc	5065	D	408 588-3800	7619
Osram Opto Semiconductors Inc (HQ)	5065	E	408 588-3800	7620
Palo Alto Medical Foundation	8011	C	408 730-4321	19816
Palo Alto Medical Foundation	8011	D	408 730-4391	19817
Palo Alto Medical Foundation	8011	D	408 524-5900	19818
Panasas Inc (PA)	7371	C	408 215-6800	15369
Pareto Networks Inc	4813	C	877 727-8020	5679
Parkinsons Institute	8733	D	800 786-2958	26794
Pivotcloud Inc	7371	C	408 475-6090	15383
Polyvore Inc	5199	D	650 968-1195	9293
Positea Inv & Pub Relations	8743	E	408 736-1120	27763
Proofpoint Inc (PA)	7371	C	408 517-4710	15399
Qubera Solutions Inc	7379	E	650 294-4460	16467
Real-Time Innovations Inc	7371	D	408 990-7400	15410
Redseal Inc	7372	D	408 641-2200	15826
Ruckus Wireless Inc (HQ)	4813	C	650 265-4200	5694
S R H H Inc	7011	E	408 247-0800	13183

	SIC	EMP	PHONE	ENTRY #
SC Builders Inc (PA)	1542	D	408 328-0688	1660
Screen Spe Usa LLC (DH)	5065	C	408 523-9140	7631
Selvi-Vidovich LP	7011	D	408 720-8500	13233
Sendmail Inc (HQ)	4813	D	510 594-5400	5696
Sensity Systems Inc (PA)	8748	D	408 774-9492	28054
Silicon Valley Bank	6029	D	415 610-4855	9560
Software AG Usa Inc	7371	C	703 860-5050	15463
Star One Credit Union (PA)	6061	D	408 543-5202	9630
Sunnyside Gardens	8361	D	408 730-4070	24830
Sunnyvale Healthcare Center	8051	D	408 245-8070	20946
Sunnyvale Sof-X Owner L P	7011	E	408 542-8264	13310
Sunrise Senior Living LLC	8051	D	408 749-8600	20975
Sutter Health	8011	C	408 733-4380	20101
Synplicity Inc (HQ)	7372	C	408 215-6000	15855
Teraburst Networks Inc	4899	E	408 400-4100	6094
Texas Instruments Sunnyvale	7389	E	408 541-9900	17528
Thomson Reuters Corporation	7371	E	408 524-4628	15502
Toyota-Sunnyvale Inc (PA)	7538	D	408 245-6640	17818
Tri-Power Group Inc	4899	C	925 583-8200	6096
Tusa Inc (PA)	7378	C	888 848-3749	16308
UPS Ground Freight Inc	4213	D	408 400-0595	4290
US Interactive Corp Delaware	7311	C	408 863-7500	13934
Verizon Business Global LLC	4813	E	408 222-2300	5719
W L Hickey Sons Inc	1711	C	408 736-4938	2412
W2005 New Cntury Ht Prtflio LP	7011	D	408 745-6000	13388
Waste Connections Cal Inc	4953	C	408 752-8530	6595
West Valley Engineering Inc (PA)	7363	D	408 735-1420	14982
Westak International Sales Inc (HQ)	5065	D	408 734-8686	7658
Wm ONeill Lath and Plst Corp	1522	E	408 329-1413	1353
Xad Inc	7311	B	415 480-6366	13943
Xoriant Corporation (PA)	7379	C	408 743-4427	16531
Yahoo Inc (PA)	7373	C	408 349-3300	16084
Zspace Inc	5063	C	408 498-4050	7487
Zyrion Inc	7372	C	408 524-7424	15887

SUNOL, CA - Alameda County

	SIC	EMP	PHONE	ENTRY #
Brightview Tree Company	0811	D	925 862-2485	1009
Save Our Sunol	8641	D	925 862-2263	25342
Shimmick Construction Co Inc	1521	C	925 862-1901	1259
Sunol Vly Golf & Recreation Co	7992	C	925 862-2404	18793

SUSANVILLE, CA - Lassen County

	SIC	EMP	PHONE	ENTRY #
AT&T Corp	4812	D	530 251-0666	5275
Banner Health	8062	C	530 251-3147	21460
Banner Lassen Medical Center	8062	C	530 252-2000	21461
Diamond Mountain Casino	7011	D	530 252-1100	12569
Honey Lake Hospice Inc	5047	C	530 257-3137	7268
Millers Custom Work Inc	1611	D	530 257-4207	1828
Northeastern Rur Hlth Clinics (PA)	8011	D	530 251-5000	19782
Sierra-Cascade Nursery Inc (PA)	0181	B	530 254-6867	319

SUTTER CREEK, CA - Amador County

	SIC	EMP	PHONE	ENTRY #
Amador Water Agency	4941	D	209 223-3018	6311
American Legion Ambulance Svc	8641	D	209 223-2963	25196
Resource Connection of Amador	8322	D	209 223-7685	24155

SYLMAR, CA - Los Angeles County

	SIC	EMP	PHONE	ENTRY #
A A Gonzalez Inc	1742	D	818 367-2242	2844
Allied Beverage LLC	5078	B	818 493-6400	7752
Allied Beverages Incorporated (PA)	5181	B	818 493-6400	9038
American Residential Svcs LLC	1711	D	818 833-6677	2138
Ansett Arcft Spares & Svcs Inc (PA)	5088	D	818 362-1100	7993
Aramark Unf & Career AP LLC	7218	D	818 364-8272	13613
Astoria Convalescent Hospital	8051	C	818 367-5881	20386
AWI Acquisition Company (PA)	5072	D	818 364-2333	7674
BCI Coca-Cola Btlg Los Angeles	5149	D	818 362-4307	8807
Becho Inc	1611	D	818 362-8391	1740
Canyon Properties III LLC	8059	D	818 890-0430	21177
Childrens Hunger Fund (PA)	8322	D	818 979-7100	23740
County of Los Angeles	8062	C	818 364-1555	21516
County of Los Angeles	8361	D	818 896-0571	24609
County of Los Angeles	8361	D	818 364-2011	24611
Desert Mechanical Inc	1711	A	702 873-7333	2205
Fisk Electric Company	1731	C	818 884-1166	2594
Foothill Waste Reclamation Inc	4953	D	818 897-5099	6485
G and E Healthcare Svcs LLC	8051	D	818 367-5881	20588
Garda CL Technical Svcs Inc	7381	D	818 362-7011	16657
Golden State Health Ctrs Inc	8063	D	818 834-5082	22071
Hollywood Rntals Prod Svcs LLC (PA)	7819	D	818 407-7800	18231
Lopez Canyon Landfill	4953	D	818 834-5122	6495
Merle Norman Cosmetics Inc	5122	D	818 362-3235	8282
Morrison MGT Specialists Inc	8741	D	818 364-4219	27136
Mountain View Cnvalescent Hosp	8051	E	818 367-1033	20800
Oak Springs Nursery Inc	4971	D	818 367-5832	6650
Olive View-Ucla Medical Center (PA)	8011	D	818 364-1555	19792
Olive View/Ucla Education &	8733	D	818 364-3434	26792
Pearson Dental Supplies Inc (PA)	5047	C	818 362-2600	7299

	SIC	EMP	PHONE	ENTRY #
Quality Long Term Care Nev Inc	8051	D	818 361-0191	20860
Quinn Company	5082	D	818 767-7171	7780
Security Paving Company Inc	1611	D	818 362-9200	1856
Sigue Corporation (PA)	7389	D	818 837-5939	17490
Superior Gunite (PA)	1771	C	818 896-9199	3339
Sylmar Hlth Rehabilitation Ctr	8063	C	818 834-5082	22093
Tony Marquez Pool Plst Inc	1742	D	818 767-5177	2989
Tri-Signal Integration Inc (PA)	1731	D	818 566-8558	2775
Tutor Perini Corporation (PA)	1542	D	818 362-8391	1704
Tutor Perini Corporation	1542	A	818 362-8391	1705
Tutor-Saliba Corporation (HQ)	1542	D	818 362-8391	1707
United Cerebral Palsy	8059	D	818 364-5911	21398
United Parcel Service Inc	4215	D	800 742-5877	4434
University Cal Los Angeles	8062	A	818 364-1555	21989
Wildlife Waystation	0279	E	818 899-5201	463
Winning Performance Pdts Inc	7389	D	818 367-1041	17630

TAFT, CA - Kern County

	SIC	EMP	PHONE	ENTRY #
Adventist Health System/West	8099	D	661 763-5131	22875
Braun Electric Company Inc	1731	C	661 763-1531	2537
County of Kern	8322	D	661 763-1535	23817
County of Kern	7999	E	661 763-4246	19192
Gene Watson Construction A CA	1389	A	661 763-5254	1077
General Production Svc Cal Inc	1623	C	661 765-5330	1933
Geo Group Inc	8744	B	661 765-2510	27787
Jerry Melton & Sons Cnstr	1389	D	661 765-5546	1085
Mashburn Trnsp Svcs Inc	4213	C	661 765-5724	4216
Physicians Automated Lab Inc	8734	D	661 765-4522	26884
Taft College Children Center	8351	E	661 763-7850	24524
Taft Production Company	1241	D	661 765-7194	1027
Watkins Construction Co Inc	1623	D	661 765-5395	2015
West Side District Hospital	8062	C	805 763-4211	22029

TAHOE CITY, CA - Placer County

	SIC	EMP	PHONE	ENTRY #
Bruce Olson Construction Inc	1522	D	530 581-1087	1299
Granlibakken Management Co Ltd	7011	D	800 543-3221	12674
John Brink General Contractor	1611	E	530 583-2005	1806
Pepper Tree Inn	7011	D	530 583-3711	13089
Sunnyside Resort	7011	D	530 583-7200	13309

TARZANA, CA - Los Angeles County

	SIC	EMP	PHONE	ENTRY #
Advanced Medical Placement	8399	C	818 996-9812	24861
AMI-Hti Tarzana Encino Joint V	8062	A	818 881-0800	21449
Amisub of California Inc (DH)	8062	A	818 881-0800	21451
Atlas Textile Co Inc	5023	D	818 881-8862	6844
Attorney Recovery Systems Inc (PA)	7322	D	818 774-1420	14018
Blue Sky Services Inc	4731	D	818 609-8779	5035
Braemar Country Club Inc	7997	C	323 873-6880	18899
El Caballero Country Club	7997	C	818 654-3000	18944
Global Futures Exch & Trdg Co	6221	D	818 996-0401	10105
Guardnow Inc (PA)	7381	E	877 482-7366	16675
Institute For Applied Behavior	8049	D	818 881-1933	20325
JB Partners Group Inc	6531	D	818 668-8201	11596
M P M & Associates Inc	1542	D	818 708-9676	1605
National Organization of	8099	C	800 489-0210	23003
Providence Health & Services	8099	D	818 881-0800	23024
Providence Health & Services	8011	D	818 344-3143	19884
Providence Tarzana Medical Ctr	8011	A	818 881-0800	19892
Shapp International Trdg Inc	5031	C	818 348-3000	6961
Sinanian Development Inc	1542	D	818 996-9666	1671
Tarzana Treatment Centers Inc (PA)	8093	C	818 996-1051	22846
Wasserman Comden & Casselman (PA)	8111	C	323 872-0995	23612
Zohar Construction Inc	1521	D	818 609-7473	1288

TECATE, CA - San Diego County

	SIC	EMP	PHONE	ENTRY #
Temarry Recycling Inc	4953	D	619 270-9453	6569

TEHACHAPI, CA - Kern County

	SIC	EMP	PHONE	ENTRY #
Bear Valley Springs Assn	8641	C	661 821-5537	25206
Benz Sanitation Inc (PA)	4953	D	661 822-5273	6437
Galice Inc	7389	D	323 731-8200	17180
Loves Travel Stops	4724	C	661 823-1484	4968
Selecta Products Inc (PA)	5063	D	661 823-7050	7472
Tehachapi Recycling Center	4953	D	661 822-6421	6568
Tehachapi Vly Hosp Hlthcre Dis (PA)	8062	D	661 823-3000	21959
Worldwind Services LLC	1731	D	661 822-4877	2797

TEMECULA, CA - Riverside County

	SIC	EMP	PHONE	ENTRY #
Altaf Zahid Engineering Svcs	7389	E	760 481-9072	16984
Bank America National Assn	6021	D	951 676-4114	9334
Bbk Performance Inc	5013	D	951 296-1771	6713
Calavo Growers Inc	5148	E	951 676-7331	8700
Cellco Partnership	4812	D	951 296-9495	5285
Charles Schwab Corporation	7389	D	951 587-2840	17069
County of Riverside	8322	D	951 600-6500	23886
Cutting Edge Staffing Inc	7361	D	951 587-0550	14633
Eco Farm Field Inc	0762	D	951 676-4047	700

TEMECULA, CA

	SIC	EMP	PHONE	ENTRY #
Eco Farms Avocados Inc (PA)	0723	D	951 694-3013	528
Eco Farms Sales Inc (PA)	5148	E	951 694-3013	8721
Edwards Theatres Circuit Inc	7832	D	951 296-0144	18331
F M Tarbell Co	6531	C	951 303-0307	11510
Fairway Independent Mrtg Corp	6211	D	951 676-0527	9997
Fff Enterprises Inc (PA)	5122	C	951 296-2500	8253
Four Star Private Patrol Inc	7381	D	951 695-4245	16645
Guaranteed Rate Inc	6162	D	949 430-0809	9851
Homeland Security Services Inc	7382	B	714 956-2200	16888
Inland Erosion Control Svcs	1794	D	951 301-8334	3433
Inland Valley Business and Com	8699	D	951 378-5316	25545
Irri-Scape Construction Inc	0782	D	951 694-6936	872
Kaiser Foundation Hospitals	6324	D	866 984-7483	10307
Kelly Moses Floors	1743	E	951 296-5147	3017
Kenedco Inc	7389	D	951 699-9339	17269
Lewis Brsbois Bsgard Smith LLP	8111	D	951 252-6150	23386
Maneri Traffic Control Inc	1611	D	951 695-5104	1820
MBK Senior Living LLC	8059	D	951 506-5555	21311
McCusker Enterprises Inc	8351	D	951 676-5445	24482
McMillan Farm Management	8741	C	951 676-2045	27123
McMillin Communities Inc	1521	A	951 506-3303	1216
Miles Construction Group Inc	1541	C	951 260-2504	1450
Neighborhood Healthcare	8099	D	951 225-6400	23004
Oreq Corporation	8741	E	951 296-5076	27152
Partners In Leadership Interme (PA)	8742	D	951 506-6878	27584
Pechanga Development Corp	7011	A	951 695-4655	13087
Phs / Mwa (HQ)	4581	E	950 695-1008	4929
Ponte Vineyard Inn	7011	D	951 587-6688	13104
Primerica Financial Svcs Inc	6411	D	951 695-4325	10835
Professional Hospital Sup Inc (HQ)	5047	E	951 699-5000	7305
Pslq Inc	1522	D	951 795-4260	1334
Raintree Systems Inc	7371	D	951 252-9400	15407
Rancho California Water Dst (PA)	1623	C	951 296-6900	1986
Rancho West Landscape	0782	D	951 301-3979	942
Rancon Real Estate Corporation (PA)	6531	D	951 677-1800	11787
Rbf Consulting	8711	D	951 676-8042	26036
Responsible Med Solutions Corp	8011	D	951 308-0024	19913
Richard Burns MD	8011	D	951 296-9300	19916
RR Donnelley & Sons Company	5112	D	951 296-2890	8178
Sears Roebuck and Co	7549	D	951 719-3528	17892
Securitas SEC Svcs USA Inc	7381	D	951 676-3954	16800
Sft Realty Galway Downs LLC	6531	D	951 232-1880	11840
Sierra Pacific Farms Inc (PA)	0762	C	951 699-9980	723
Solex Contracting Inc	1623	D	951 308-1706	1997
Southwest Traders Incorporated (PA)	5141	C	951 699-7800	8521
T B Penick & Sons Inc	1521	C	951 719-1492	1270
Talentscale LLC	8711	D	951 744-0053	26086
Temecula Vly Unified Schl Dst	4151	C	951 695-7110	3951
Temecula Vly Unified Schl Dst	8641	C	951 302-5140	25370
Time Warner Cable Inc	4841	D	951 587-8660	6035
Walz Group LLC (HQ)	7371	C	951 491-6800	15539
Wholesale Air-Time Inc	4813	E	951 693-1880	5732
Windsor Capital Group Inc	7011	D	951 676-5656	13420

TEMPLE CITY, CA - Los Angeles County

	SIC	EMP	PHONE	ENTRY #
Community Care Adhc Inc	8322	D	626 614-8999	23772
Exquisite Dental Technology	8071	D	626 237-0107	22215
Fran-Jom Inc	8059	D	626 443-3028	21217
Golden State Health Ctrs Inc	8059	D	626 579-0310	21251
Santa Anita Convalescent Hospi	8059	C	626 579-0310	21367
Temple Garden Homes Inc	8361	E	626 286-6408	24833
Western Tear-Off & Disposal	1761	D	626 443-9984	3223

TEMPLETON, CA - San Luis Obispo County

	SIC	EMP	PHONE	ENTRY #
Austin Construction	1521	E	805 610-0622	1132
Compass Health Inc	8051	D	805 434-3035	20468
Grants Custom Cabinets	1521	C	805 466-9680	1185
Mesa Vineyard Management Inc (PA)	0762	D	805 434-4100	708
Pacific Gas and Electric Co	4911	D	805 434-4418	6193
Twin Cities Community Hosp Inc	8011	B	805 434-3500	20146
Wilshire Health and Cmnty Svcs	8059	D	805 434-3035	21423

TERRA BELLA, CA - Tulare County

	SIC	EMP	PHONE	ENTRY #
Setton Pstchio Terra Bella Inc (HQ)	5149	D	559 535-6050	8920

THERMAL, CA - Riverside County

	SIC	EMP	PHONE	ENTRY #
Drake Larson Ranchs	0172	C	760 399-5494	152
Golden Acres Farms	0161	E	760 399-1923	71
Gomez Farm Labor Contg Inc	0761	D	760 399-1994	663
Interntnl Pvment Slutions Inc	1771	D	909 794-2101	3276
James Fedor Masonry Inc	1741	D	760 772-3036	2821
Nissho of California Inc	0175	B	760 727-9719	245
North Shore Greenhouses Inc	0182	D	760 397-0400	339
Red Earth Casino	7011	D	760 395-1200	13134
Thermal Club	7997	C	760 674-0088	19107
Torres-Martinez	7011	C	760 395-1200	13349
West Coast Aggregate Supply	1442	E	760 342-7598	1109

THOUSAND OAKS, CA - Ventura County

	SIC	EMP	PHONE	ENTRY #
A P R Inc	7363	C	805 379-3400	14828
American Golf Corporation	7997	D	805 495-5407	18852
American Services and Products	7349	D	805 375-2858	14229
Amgen Pharmaceuticals Inc	8733	A	805 447-1000	26736
Atria Senior Living Inc	8361	D	805 370-5400	24556
Bead Society	8699	C	805 495-2550	25505
Bob Dillon Construction Inc	1751	C	805 495-2607	3033
Bright Horizons Chld Ctrs LLC	8351	D	805 447-6793	24419
California Kidney Med Group	8011	D	805 497-7775	19395
Calleguas Municipal Water Dict	4941	D	805 526-9323	6322
Cellco Partnership	4812	D	805 376-8917	5292
Change Healthcare Inc	7374	D	805 777-7773	16110
Cigna Healthcare Cal Inc	6324	D	805 230-8300	10273
CIT Bank NA	6021	D	805 379-5520	9345
Citigroup Inc	6021	D	805 557-0930	9378
Conejo Valley Unified Schl Dst	8641	C	805 492-3531	25241
Countrywide Home Loans Inc (DH)	6162	A	818 225-3000	9834
Durham School Services L P	4151	D	805 495-8338	3919
Edo LLC	8711	D	914 641-2000	25778
Enhanced Landscape MGT Inc	0782	C	805 557-2737	849
Fedex Office & Print Svcs Inc	7334	E	805 379-1552	14118
Five Star Quality Care Inc	8051	C	805 492-2444	20575
Floyd Skeren & Kelly LLP (PA)	8111	D	818 206-9222	23247
Gemmm Corp (PA)	6531	D	805 496-0555	11553
Kaiser Foundation Hospitals	8011	A	888 515-3500	19648
Kaiser Foundation Hospitals	8011	A	888 515-3500	19650
Kaiser Foundation Hospitals	6324	A	888 515-3500	10345
Kevin Persons Inc	0781	E	805 371-8746	775
Los Robles Bank	6022	D	805 373-6763	9505
Management Trust Assn Inc	6733	C	805 496-5514	12191
Meathead Movers	4213	D	805 496-1416	4222
Miramed Global Services Inc	8748	A	805 277-1017	27991
Musclebound Inc	7991	B	805 496-9331	18665
Mv Transportation Inc	4111	D	805 557-7372	3681
National Real Estate Solutions	7349	D	805 496-1084	14366
Permanente Kaiser Intl	8011	B	805 374-7433	19828
R T Framing Corporation	1751	D	805 496-3985	3079
S A Cali-U Acoustics Inc	1742	D	805 376-9300	2974
Sherwood Country Club	7997	C	805 496-3036	19077
Southern Cal Orthpd Inst LP	8011	D	805 497-7015	20014
Southern California Edison Co	4911	D	818 999-1880	6225
Star of California	8099	D	805 379-1401	23064
Tecom Industries Incorporated	5065	C	818 341-4010	7648
Teledyne Scientfic Imaging LLC (HQ)	8731	C	805 373-4545	26621
Thousand Oaks Surgical Hosp LP	8062	E	805 777-7750	21967
Ventu Park LLC	7011	D	805 716-4200	13376
Ventura County Office Educatn	8641	D	805 495-7037	25389
Young Mens Christian Asso	8641	E	805 523-7613	25447
Zs Associates Inc	8742	D	805 413-5900	27727

THOUSAND PALMS, CA - Riverside County

	SIC	EMP	PHONE	ENTRY #
CBS Corporation	4833	D	760 343-5700	5843
Club At Shnndoah Sprng Vlg Inc	7997	E	760 343-3497	18920
Gulf- California Broadcast Co	4833	C	760 773-0342	5866
Kincaid Industries Inc	1711	D	760 343-5457	2268
Little Sisters Truck Wash Inc	7542	D	760 343-3448	17849
Readylink Healthcare	7361	D	760 343-7000	14746
San Val Corp (PA)	0781	B	760 346-3999	795
Sunline Transit Agency (PA)	4131	C	760 343-3456	3889
Vorwaller & Brooks Inc	7389	D	760 262-6300	17601

TIPTON, CA - Tulare County

	SIC	EMP	PHONE	ENTRY #
Bosman Dairy	0241	C	559 752-1012	419
Mendes Calf Ranch	0211	D	559 688-4708	409
Sunkist Growers Inc	0723	C	909 983-9811	592
Sunkist Growers Inc	0723	C	559 752-4256	593

TOLLHOUSE, CA - Fresno County

	SIC	EMP	PHONE	ENTRY #
Duleys Landscape Inc	0782	E	559 855-5090	845

TOLUCA LAKE, CA - Los Angeles County

	SIC	EMP	PHONE	ENTRY #
James B Branch Inc (PA)	4214	E	818 765-3521	4353
Wells Fargo Bank National Assn	6021	E	818 766-7172	9430

TOPANGA, CA - Los Angeles County

	SIC	EMP	PHONE	ENTRY #
Rock-It Cargo USA LLC	4731	D	310 455-1900	5164

TOPAZ, CA - Mono County

	SIC	EMP	PHONE	ENTRY #
Northern Mono Chamber Commerce	8611	E	530 208-6078	25096

TORRANCE, CA - Los Angeles County

	SIC	EMP	PHONE	ENTRY #
A L S Industries Inc (PA)	5092	E	310 532-9262	8035
Act 1 Group Inc	7361	D	310 532-1529	14600
Act 1 Group Inc (PA)	7361	D	310 532-1529	14601
Active Storage Inc	7389	E	818 709-1133	16970
Adia LLC	8082	D	310 370-0555	22336

GEOGRAPHIC SECTION — TORRANCE, CA

Company	SIC	EMP	PHONE	ENTRY #
Aestiva Software Inc	7371	E	310 697-0338	15004
Ait Worldwide Logistics Inc	4731	D	310 538-4383	5021
All In One Inc	8741	D	310 538-3374	26916
All South Bay Central Office	8699	D	310 618-1180	25486
Allied Digital Services LLC (HQ)	7376	C	310 431-2375	16275
Alpine Electronics America Inc	5064	C	310 783-7391	7488
Alpine Electronics America Inc (HQ)	5064	C	310 326-8000	7489
Alpine Village	6512	C	310 327-4384	10957
American Datamed (PA)	7299	D	949 250-4000	13732
American Honda Finance Corp (DH)	6141	C	310 972-2239	9737
American Honda Motor Co Inc (HQ)	5012	A	310 783-2000	6664
American Multi-Cinema Inc	7832	C	310 326-5011	18299
Arconic Global Fas & Rings Inc	5085	C	310 784-0700	7916
Arconic Global Fas & Rings Inc	5085	B	310 530-2220	7917
Arconic Global Fas & Rings Inc	5085	E	310 530-2220	7920
Arconic Global Fas & Rings Inc	5085	A	310 530-2220	7921
Automobile Club Southern Cal	8699	D	310 325-3111	25495
Bankcard Services (PA)	7389	C	213 365-1122	17022
Bayco Financial Corporation (PA)	6531	D	310 378-8181	11314
Binex Line Corp (PA)	4731	E	310 416-8600	5033
Bio-Diagnostics Laboratories (PA)	8071	C	818 780-3300	22190
Biofusion LLC	8011	D	310 803-8100	19374
Bioscreen Testing Services Inc (PA)	8734	D	602 277-1154	26835
Bitas	8051	D	310 324-2273	20413
Bowman and Brooke LLP	8111	D	310 768-3068	23128
BQE Software Inc	7372	D	310 602-4020	15608
Breast Diagnostic Center	8011	E	310 517-4709	19377
Breville Usa Inc	5023	E	310 755-3000	6850
Burdette De Cock Inc	8082	C	310 542-0563	22384
C H Robinson Intl Inc	4731	D	310 763-6080	5037
California Mfg Tech Consulting	8711	D	310 263-3060	25714
CCH Incorporated	7374	B	310 800-9800	16108
Cellco Partnership	4812	D	310 891-6991	5286
Century 21 Amber Realty Inc	6531	D	310 625-4363	11367
Century 21 Exclusive Realtors	6531	E	310 373-5252	11374
Ceva Freight LLC	4513	C	310 972-5500	4841
CH Robinson Freight Svcs Ltd	4731	E	310 515-7755	5045
Charles M Kamiya and Sons Inc	6411	D	310 781-2066	10667
Childrens Hospital Los Angeles	8093	C	310 303-3890	22684
Childrens Institute Inc	8322	D	310 783-4677	23743
Choura Events	7359	C	310 320-6200	14522
Citigroup Global Markets Inc	6211	E	310 540-9511	9978
City of Torrance	7999	D	310 781-6901	19182
Compex Legal Services Inc (PA)	8111	C	310 782-1801	23161
Continental Dntl Ceramics Inc	8072	E	310 618-8821	22303
County of Los Angeles	8011	D	310 222-4220	19467
County of Los Angeles	5122	D	310 222-2357	8251
County of Los Angeles	8111	D	310 222-3552	23177
Credit Card Services Inc (PA)	7389	D	213 365-1122	17105
Crenshaw Bowling	7933	E	310 326-5120	18517
Ctc Group Inc (PA)	6719	C	310 540-0500	12055
Del AMO Construction	1542	D	310 378-6203	1538
Del AMO Diagnostic Center	8093	E	310 316-2424	22719
Del AMO Grdns Cnvlscnt Hosp &	8051	D	310 378-4233	20513
Del AMO Hospital Inc	8063	D	310 530-1151	22068
Delta Computer Consulting	7379	C	310 541-9440	16354
Dfs Group LP	8721	D	310 783-6600	26330
Dicaperl Corporation (DH)	1499	D	610 667-6640	1114
Docmagic Inc	7389	D	800 649-1362	17129
Dreamgear LLC	5092	D	310 222-5522	8043
DTM Services Inc (PA)	4731	D	310 521-1200	5061
Earlwood LLC	8051	D	310 371-1228	20524
Easy Ride Transportation	4789	D	424 999-8830	5217
Electronic Data Care Inc	7373	D	310 791-2600	15938
Emax Laboratories Inc	8734	E	310 618-8889	26848
Express Imaging Services Inc	4226	D	888 846-8804	4686
First Evang Lutheran Ch & Schl	8351	D	310 320-9920	24464
Fns Inc (PA)	4731	D	661 615-2300	5077
Freedom Staff Leasing Inc	7363	B	310 834-6621	14880
Friction Materials LLC	8711	C	248 362-3600	25819
Frito-Lay North America Inc	8741	C	310 224-5600	27030
Fujitsu Ten Corp of America	5064	C	310 327-2151	7498
G & H Dental Arts Inc (PA)	8072	D	310 214-8007	22307
Gable House Inc	7933	D	310 378-2265	18521
Gerber Ambulance Company Inc	4119	C	310 542-6464	3799
Geri Care Inc	8051	D	310 320-0961	20597
Geri-Care II Inc	8059	D	310 328-0812	21232
Global Accents Inc	5023	D	310 639-2600	6866
Golden Arrow Construction Inc	1521	D	310 523-9056	1184
Good Sports Plus Ltd	7371	B	310 671-4400	15209
Goodridge Usa Inc (DH)	5013	D	310 533-1924	6734
Harbor Building Services	7349	D	310 320-2966	14319
Harbor Developmental Disabilit	8399	C	310 540-1711	24926
Harbor-Cla Med Ctr Dept Srgery	8062	D	310 222-2700	21590
Harbor-Ucla Med Foundation Inc (PA)	8741	D	310 222-5015	27051
Harbor-Ucla Medical Center	8062	A	310 222-2345	21591
Herbalife Ltd Inc	5169	B	310 410-9600	8989
Holiday Inn Hotel Torrance	7011	C	310 781-9100	12750
Hpt Trs Ihg 2 Inc	7011	C	310 781-9100	12795
Human Potential Cons LLC	8744	D	310 756-1560	27792
Hunt Enterprises Inc	6531	C	310 325-1496	11576
I C Class Components Corp (PA)	5065	D	310 539-5500	7583
Imperial Cfs Inc	4226	E	310 768-8188	4687
Industrial Parts Depot LLC (HQ)	5084	D	310 530-1900	7850
Janet Hilton	6411	D	310 851-7200	10753
Jessie Lord Bakery LLC	5142	D	310 328-7738	8557
Jtb Americas Ltd (HQ)	4724	E	310 303-3750	4964
Kaiser Foundation Hospitals	6324	D	800 780-1230	10337
Keenan & Associates (PA)	6411	B	310 212-3344	10756
Keller Williams Realty	6531	B	310 375-3511	11609
Kingdom Express Inc	4214	D	310 258-0900	4355
Kintetsu Enterprises Co Amer (HQ)	7011	C	310 782-9300	12887
Kubota Tractor Corporation (DH)	5083	C	310 370-3370	7804
Laboratory Corp Amer Holdings	8071	D	818 908-3600	22232
Lifecare Systems Inc	8051	C	310 540-7676	20734
Little Company Mary Hospital	8062	A	310 540-7676	21707
Lomita Logistics LLC	7331	C	310 784-8485	14080
Longwood Management Inc	8361	D	310 370-5828	24716
Los Angeles Bio Med RES Inst	8732	E	310 222-3604	26684
Lucky Strike Entertainment LLC	7933	D	310 802-7010	18524
Mainline Equipment Inc	7629	D	800 444-2288	17937
Makkunis Inc	5099	D	310 328-1999	8124
Mariner Health Care Inc	8051	D	310 371-4628	20757
Maritzcx Research LLC	4725	D	310 783-4300	4995
Mayekawa USA Inc	5078	C	310 618-3170	7755
Metroplex Theatres LLC	7832	A	310 856-1270	18338
Mighty Enterprises Inc	5084	D	310 516-7478	7864
Milestone Hospice	8099	C	310 782-1177	23000
MIS International Inc	4212	C	310 320-4546	4040
Mishima Foods USA Inc (PA)	5141	D	310 787-1533	8503
Never Ignore Kids Education	8399	D	310 984-6847	24945
Nippon Express USA Inc	4731	E	310 532-6300	5130
Nissin Intl Trnspt USA Inc (HQ)	4731	E	310 222-8500	5133
Organic Inc	7379	D	310 543-4600	16447
Oriental Motor U S A Corp (HQ)	5063	D	310 715-3300	7463
Pacific Echo Inc	5091	D	310 539-1822	7945
Pacific Home Works Inc	1799	D	310 781-3012	3561
Panalpina Inc	4731	C	310 819-4060	5144
Partner Assessment Corporation (PA)	8711	C	800 419-4923	26018
Pediatric Therapy Network	8093	D	310 328-0275	22798
Pentel of America Ltd (HQ)	5112	C	310 320-3831	8173
Performance Team Frt Sys Inc	4731	B	562 345-2200	5150
Physical Optics Corporation (PA)	8731	D	310 320-3088	26590
Pioneer Theatres Inc	7389	C	310 532-8183	17414
Polypeptide Laboratories Inc (DH)	8071	D	310 782-3569	22257
Praxair Distribution Inc	4925	D	310 371-1254	6283
Providence Health & Services	8082	C	310 370-5895	22540
Providence Health & Services	8099	C	310 540-1334	23028
Providence Health & Services	8093	D	310 792-3440	22811
Providence Health & Services	8049	D	310 618-8217	20344
Providence Health & Services	8011	D	310 792-5050	19885
Providence Health & Services	8099	D	310 937-1980	23030
Providence Health & Services	8011	D	310 793-4263	19888
Providence Health System	8011	A	310 376-9474	19890
Providence Health System	6733	C	310 543-5900	12198
Providence Health System	8011	D	310 540-7676	19891
Providence Health System	6733	C	310 370-5895	12199
Providence Health System	6733	C	310 378-8587	12200
Providence Health System	8062	B	310 530-3800	21823
Providence Little Co of Mary (DH)	8741	C	310 540-7676	27181
Providence Little Co of Mary	8741	D	310 303-6970	27182
PS Environmental Svcs Inc	7389	D	310 373-6259	17435
Pt Gaming LLC	7011	D	323 260-5060	13113
Pta California Congress of Par	8641	D	310 328-3100	25320
Public Hlth Fndation Entps Inc	8641	D	310 320-5215	25325
Quality Production Svcs Inc	1742	D	310 406-3350	2960
R C I Enterprises Inc	5049	E	310 370-5900	7347
Resource Collection Inc	7349	A	310 219-3272	14406
Restaurant Depot LLC	5181	C	310 516-7400	9079
Riad Aoumie MD	8011	D	310 373-6864	19915
Rmi International Inc	7381	D	310 781-6768	16774
Robert Half International Inc	7361	D	310 719-1400	14771
Roy Jorgensen Associates Inc	7349	D	310 468-2478	14410
RR Donnelley & Sons Company	7331	D	310 784-8485	14089
Ryans Express Trnsp Svcs Inc (PA)	4725	D	702 795-7021	5000
Saatchi & Saatchi North Amer	7319	B	310 214-6000	14010
Sakura Finetek USA Inc (HQ)	5047	C	310 972-7800	7311
Salson Logistics Inc	4789	C	310 328-6906	5240
San Pedro Peninsula Hospital	8082	C	310 370-5895	22555
Sanyo Denki America Inc (HQ)	5045	D	310 783-5400	7183

Employment Codes: A=Over 500 employees, B=251-500, C=101-250, D=51-100, E=45-50

2017 Directory of California Wholesalers and Services Companies

TORRANCE, CA

Company	SIC	EMP	PHONE	ENTRY #
Securitas Critical Infrastruct	7381	A	310 817-2177	16782
Securitas SEC Svcs USA Inc	7381	C	310 787-0747	16810
Shimadzu Precision Instrs Inc	5047	D	310 217-8855	7313
Silicon Prime Technologies Inc	7371	E	310 279-0222	15455
Simplehuman LLC **(PA)**	5023	D	310 436-2250	6886
Six Continents Hotels Inc	7011	D	310 371-8525	13261
Six Continents Hotels Inc	7011	D	310 781-9100	13264
Smart Choice Investments Inc	7361	D	310 944-6985	14788
Sonic Industries Inc	8711	C	310 532-8382	26070
Sonsray Machinery LLC **(HQ)**	7353	C	323 319-1900	14499
South Bay Family Medical Group	8011	D	310 378-2234	20010
Space Age Metal Products Inc	5045	C	310 539-5500	7191
Special Service For Groups Inc	8399	D	310 323-6887	24981
Stanley R Klein MD Facs Inc	8011	E	310 373-6864	20066
Star View Adolescent Center	8063	C	310 373-4556	22092
Sumitomo Elc USA Holdings Inc	8741	D	310 792-6016	27234
Sun Chlorella USA Inc	5149	D	310 891-0600	8925
Sunnyside Rhbltition Nrsing Ctr	8051	C	310 320-4130	20945
Supershuttle Los Angeles Inc	4111	C	310 222-5500	3726
Supershuttle Orange County	4111	B	310 222-5500	3727
Sweis Inc **(PA)**	5087	D	310 375-0558	7983
System One Holdings LLC	7389	D	310 483-7800	17513
Taisei Construction Corp **(HQ)**	1541	D	714 886-1530	1471
Time Warner Cable Inc	4812	C	714 709-3617	5419
Timeshare Relief Inc	6541	C	310 755-6434	11941
Topwin Corporation **(PA)**	5136	D	310 325-2255	8362
Toro Nursery Inc	5193	D	310 715-1982	9221
Torrance Care Center West Inc	8051	C	310 370-4561	20991
Torrance Health Assn Inc **(PA)**	8062	A	310 325-9110	21968
Torrance Hospital IPA	8062	E	310 784-0800	21969
Torrance Memorial Medical Ctr **(HQ)**	8062	A	310 325-9110	21970
Torrance Surgery Center LP	8011	A	310 784-5880	20138
Torrence Family Practice	8011	D	310 542-0455	20139
Tower Energy Group **(PA)**	5172	C	310 538-8000	9028
Toyota Logistics Services **(DH)**	7549	C	310 618-5009	17898
Toyota Motor Sales USA Inc **(DH)**	6159	B	310 468-4003	9804
Toyota Motor Sales USA Inc	6159	B	310 468-7626	9805
Trans-Pak Incorporated	7389	C	310 618-6937	17540
Trendnet Inc **(PA)**	5045	E	310 961-5500	7204
Unified Inv Programs Inc **(PA)**	8099	E	310 782-1878	23077
Unify Financial Federal Cr Un **(PA)**	6061	D	310 536-5000	9645
United Parcel Service Inc OH	4215	D	800 742-5877	4439
UPS Supply Chain Solutions Inc	4731	C	310 404-2719	5184
Vector Resources Inc **(PA)**	1731	C	310 436-1000	2783
Virco Inc **(HQ)**	5021	D	310 533-0474	6836
Vitas Healthcare Corp Cal	8082	D	310 324-2273	22604
Volt Management Corp	7363	C	310 316-8523	14970
Windsor Gardens	8051	D	562 422-9219	21047
Xld Group LLC	7011	D	310 316-3636	13444

TRABUCO CANYON, CA - Orange County

Company	SIC	EMP	PHONE	ENTRY #
Coto De Caza Golf Club Inc	7941	C	949 766-7886	18543
Coto De Caza Golf Racquet CLB	7997	C	949 858-4100	18929
Davlor Company	1542	D	949 244-9748	1537

TRACY, CA - San Joaquin County

Company	SIC	EMP	PHONE	ENTRY #
American Engrg Contrs Inc	1731	C	209 229-1591	2518
Arconic Global Fas & Rings Inc	5072	D	209 839-3005	7672
Arnaudo Bros Transport Inc **(PA)**	0191	D	209 835-0406	345
Bossard North America Inc	5085	D	562 906-2003	7927
Brookdale Senior Living Inc	8082	C	209 839-6623	22383
Cascade Logistics LLC	4225	D	209 832-4205	4533
D and S Landscaping Inc	0782	C	925 455-4630	831
DSC Logistics Inc	4225	D	209 833-0200	4546
Ed Thoming & Sons Inc	0173	D	209 835-2792	199
Es3 LLC	4225	E	209 832-4205	4549
Faith Enterprises Inc	8051	E	209 835-6034	20564
Glassfab Tempering Services **(PA)**	8748	D	209 229-1060	27932
Green Valley Trnsp Corp	4213	E	209 836-5192	4192
Home Depot USA Inc	4225	D	209 835-5133	4572
Imobile LLC	4812	B	209 833-6757	5399
In-Shape Health Clubs LLC	7991	C	209 836-2504	18645
Jesse Lee Group Inc	8741	D	209 832-2273	27079
Kaiser Foundation Hospitals	8011	A	209 839-3200	19596
Kaiser Foundation Hospitals	6324	D	209 832-6339	10344
Mch Electric Inc	7299	D	209 835-9755	13776
McLane Company Inc	5141	D	209 221-7500	8498
Myra Investment and Dev Corp	6798	D	209 834-2343	12262
Owens & Minor Inc	5047	D	209 833-4600	7293
Pacific Medical Inc **(PA)**	7389	D	800 726-9180	17393
Petz Enterprises Inc **(PA)**	7371	D	209 835-1360	15377
Safeway Inc	4225	B	209 833-4700	4636
Tracy Dlta Solid Waste Mgt Inc	4953	D	209 835-0601	6570
Tracy Interfaith Ministries	8322	D	209 836-5424	24255
Tracy Sutter Community Hosp	8062	B	209 835-1500	21971
United Facilities Inc	4225	E	209 839-8051	4646

Company	SIC	EMP	PHONE	ENTRY #
United States Cold Storage Inc	4222	E	209 835-2653	4508
We Care Day Care & Pre School	8351	D	209 832-4072	24530
Yrc Inc	4789	C	209 833-1300	5251

TRANQUILLITY, CA - Fresno County

Company	SIC	EMP	PHONE	ENTRY #
Don Gragnani Farms	0191	D	559 693-4352	356

TRAVER, CA - Tulare County

Company	SIC	EMP	PHONE	ENTRY #
Foster Poultry Farms	5191	A	559 457-6509	9137

TRAVIS AFB, CA - Solano County

Company	SIC	EMP	PHONE	ENTRY #
US Airforce Band of Golden W	7929	E	707 424-2263	18503

TRINIDAD, CA - Humboldt County

Company	SIC	EMP	PHONE	ENTRY #
Cher-Ae Heights Indian Cmnty	7999	C	707 677-3611	19160

TRUCKEE, CA - Nevada County

Company	SIC	EMP	PHONE	ENTRY #
Clearcapitalcom Inc	6531	C	530 550-2500	11397
Hyatt Corporation	7011	B	530 562-3900	12808
Lahontan Golf Club	7997	C	530 550-2400	18974
Tahoe Donner Association	8641	C	530 587-9437	25367
Tahoe Donner Golf Course Inc	7992	D	530 587-9455	18794
Tahoe Forest Hospital District	8062	C	530 582-3277	21957
Tahoe Forest Hospital District **(PA)**	8062	B	530 587-6011	21958
Tahoe-Truckee Sanitation Agcy	4952	C	530 587-2525	6419
Trimont Land Company **(HQ)**	6531	B	530 562-2252	11883
Truckee Dnner Rcreation Pk Dst	7999	C	530 582-7720	19297
Truckee Donner Pub Utility Dst	4911	D	530 587-3896	6246
Western Nevada Supply Co	5099	C	530 582-5009	8148

TUJUNGA, CA - Los Angeles County

Company	SIC	EMP	PHONE	ENTRY #
Crescenta-Canada YMCA	8641	E	818 352-3255	25247
Dynasty Farms Inc **(PA)**	5148	D	831 755-1398	8720
Oakview Convalescent Hospital	8059	E	818 352-4426	21333
Sun Mar Management Services	8741	D	818 352-1454	27238

TULARE, CA - Tulare County

Company	SIC	EMP	PHONE	ENTRY #
Altura Centers For Health	8011	D	559 686-9097	19337
Amdal In-Home Care Inc **(PA)**	8059	E	559 686-6611	21133
Central California Tr	8733	D	559 686-4973	26751
City of Tulare	4953	D	559 684-4200	6462
Curti Family Inc	0241	D	559 688-8323	422
Curtimade Dairy Inc	0241	E	559 688-8323	423
Dan Freitas Electric	1731	D	559 686-9572	2572
Darrell L Green Inc	4214	D	559 688-0686	4339
Faulkner Trucking Inc	4213	D	559 684-9298	4158
Goodwill Inds S Centl Cal	8093	D	559 366-1030	22737
Hillman Holdings LLC **(PA)**	0723	B	559 685-6100	546
Kings County Truck Lines **(HQ)**	4213	C	559 686-2857	4203
Kloeckner Metals Corporation	5051	D	559 688-7980	7382
Klx Inc	4213	D	559 684-1037	4204
Knight Transportation Inc	4212	C	559 685-9838	4036
M & T Calf Ranch	0212	D	559 686-7663	411
Mj Brothers Trucking	4213	E	559 686-4413	4230
Moyles Central Vly Hlth Care **(PA)**	8051	C	559 688-0288	20801
Moyles Health Care Inc	8059	D	559 686-1601	21320
Nielsens Creamery **(PA)**	0241	E	559 686-4744	436
Porterville Sheltered Workshop	5047	D	559 684-9168	7302
SA Recycling LLC	4953	D	559 688-0271	6547
Southern California Edison Co	4911	D	559 685-3742	6214
Tulare Local Health Care Dst	8062	A	559 685-3462	21973
Tulare Nrsing Rhbliation Hosp	8051	C	559 686-8581	20996
Tulare Youth Service Bureau **(PA)**	8322	E	559 685-8547	24260
Turnupseed Electric Service	1731	D	559 686-1541	2778
United States Cold Storage Inc	4222	E	559 686-1110	4507
Vander Weerd General Cnstr	1794	D	559 688-1099	3446

TULELAKE, CA - Siskiyou County

Company	SIC	EMP	PHONE	ENTRY #
Lava Beds National Monuments	8699	E	530 667-2282	25548

TUOLUMNE, CA - Tuolumne County

Company	SIC	EMP	PHONE	ENTRY #
Black Oak Casino	7999	D	209 928-9300	19152
Silver Spur Christian Camp	7032	D	209 928-4248	13471
Tuolumne City Inv Grp II LP	6513	E	209 928-1567	11217
Tuolumne Me-Wuk Indian	8011	D	209 928-5400	20144

TURLOCK, CA - Stanislaus County

Company	SIC	EMP	PHONE	ENTRY #
American Medical Response Inc	4119	C	209 567-4030	3764
Aspiranet	8361	D	209 669-2582	24555
Aspiranet	8322	D	209 667-0327	23672
Associated Feed & Supply Co **(PA)**	5191	C	209 667-2708	9125
Cellco Partnership	4812	C	209 668-9579	5337
Central California Faculty Med	8099	B	209 620-6937	22918
Central Valley Cheese Inc	5143	D	209 664-1080	8580
Covenant Care California LLC	8051	D	209 632-3821	20496
Covenant Rtirement Communities	8361	C	209 632-9976	24617
Creative Alternatives	8361	C	209 668-9361	24618
Crimetek Security	7381	B	209 668-6208	16617
Emanuel Medical Center Inc	8062	C	209 667-5600	21555

GEOGRAPHIC SECTION

UNION CITY, CA

	SIC	EMP	PHONE	ENTRY #
Emanuel Medical Center Inc (DH)	8062	A	209 667-4200	21556
Emanuel Medical Center Inc	8062	C	209 664-2520	21557
Foster Poultry Farms	0254	E	209 668-5922	457
Freshpoint Central California	5148	C	209 216-0200	8728
Gemperle Enterprises	0252	D	209 667-2651	446
Humphrey Plumbing Inc	1711	D	209 634-4626	2247
Indian River Transport Co	4213	B	209 664-0456	4197
Joe L Coelho Inc	4213	E	209 667-2676	4200
LJC Construction Inc	1761	D	209 668-2700	3186
Machado & Sons Cnstr Inc	1521	E	209 632-5260	1210
Mickey Wall Painting Inc	1721	E	209 669-0557	2467
Northern Rfrigerated Trnsp Inc (PA)	4213	C	209 664-3800	4235
Poppy State Express Inc (PA)	4213	D	209 664-3950	4245
Ruan	4212	A	209 634-4928	4059
Select Harvest Usa LLC	5159	C	209 668-2471	8965
Sodexo Management Inc	8741	D	209 667-3634	27222
Ssi-Turlock Dairy Division	5143	C	209 668-2100	8593
Swanson Farms	0253	D	209 667-2002	453
Sward Trucking Inc	4213	E	209 847-4210	4270
Thorsens Inc	1761	D	209 524-5296	3219
Turlock Dairy & Rfrgn Inc	5083	D	209 667-6455	7813
Turlock Irrigation District (PA)	4911	B	209 883-8222	6247
Turlock Irrigation District	4971	B	209 883-8300	6655
Ulta Salon Cosmt Fragrance Inc	7231	C	209 664-1725	13696
Valley Fresh Foods Inc	0252	D	209 669-5600	448
Volk Enterprises Inc	5084	D	209 632-3826	7903
Winton Ireland Strom & Green (PA)	6411	D	209 667-0995	10941
Yosemite Farm Credit Aca (PA)	6111	D	209 667-2366	9735

TUSTIN, CA - Orange County

	SIC	EMP	PHONE	ENTRY #
AB Cellular Holding LLC	4813	A	562 468-6846	5451
Absolute Exhibits Inc (PA)	7389	D	714 685-2800	16965
AJ Kirkwood & Associates Inc	1731	D	714 505-1977	2511
Alexanders Mobility Services	4789	D	714 731-1658	5211
All Care Services Inc	8322	D	714 669-1148	23651
All Counties Courier Inc	4215	C	949 224-0900	4394
Ansar Gallery	5141	D	949 220-0000	8457
AT&T Corp	4813	D	714 258-8290	5466
Autocrib Inc	7389	C	714 274-0400	17012
Avid Bioservices Inc	5122	D	714 508-6100	8234
Briggs Electric Inc (PA)	1731	D	714 544-2500	2539
Broker Solutions Inc (PA)	8742	A	800 450-2010	27360
Cellco Partnership	4812	C	714 258-8870	5339
Cellco Partnership	4812	D	714 669-3500	5385
Centrl Territrl Salvation Army	8322	D	714 832-7100	23728
Corland Companies (PA)	8741	E	714 573-7780	26982
Cosmopro West Inc	8082	E	714 258-8301	22417
Crown Golf Properties LP	8742	C	714 730-1611	27397
Day Star Fixtures	1751	E	714 838-4613	3044
Exodus Wireless Corp	4813	D	714 665-6500	5601
First Team RE - Orange Cnty	6531	C	714 544-5456	11537
Foundation Building Mtls LLC (PA)	1742	D	714 380-3127	2897
Hanford Hotels LLC	7011	C	714 210-0400	12688
HealthSouth Corporation	8093	C	714 832-9200	22743
Heritage Construction	1611	D	714 573-2223	1799
Hmwc Cpas & Business Advisors	8721	D	714 505-9000	26368
Hotel Adventures LLC	7011	D	714 730-7717	12780
House of Seven Gables Re (PA)	6531	D	714 731-3777	11538
I L S West Inc	8721	E	714 507-7530	26376
Innovative Medical Solutions	7699	D	714 505-7070	17986
Innovative Surgical Products	5047	D	714 836-4474	7269
Innovtive Scntfic Slutions Inc	7361	C	714 508-8620	14685
Integrium LLC (PA)	8731	D	714 541-5591	26537
Internet Blueprint Inc	7371	E	714 673-6000	15252
Kaiser Foundation Hospitals	8011	A	888 988-2800	19651
Key Inn Ltd	7011	D	714 832-3220	12880
Kinship Center	8322	D	714 979-2365	24058
Ledra Brands Inc	5023	D	714 259-9959	6871
Logomark Inc	5199	C	714 675-6100	9278
M & S Trading Inc	5136	D	714 241-7190	8352
Management Trust Assn Inc (PA)	6733	D	714 285-2626	12194
Memorialcare Med Foundation (PA)	8641	D	714 389-5353	25295
Mobile Line Cmmunications Corp	5065	D	877 247-2544	7607
Nmn Constr Solana Generating	1542	E	714 389-2104	1620
Oracle Corporation	7372	D	713 654-0919	15788
Orange County Dept Education	8741	A	714 730-7301	27151
Pacificore Construction Inc	1542	E	657 859-4500	1628
Portellus Inc	7372	D	949 250-9600	15820
Pramira Inc	7379	D	800 678-1169	16461
R Ranch Market	0291	A	714 573-1182	470
Rainbow Home Care Services	8082	D	714 544-8070	22545
RES-Care Inc	8082	D	800 707-8781	22548
RJN Investigations Inc	7381	D	951 686-7638	16773
Sanyo Foods Corp America	7997	C	714 730-1611	19068
Schick Moving & Storage Co (PA)	4214	D	714 731-5500	4375
Schoolsfirst Federal Credit Un	6029	B	714 258-4000	9557
Silverado Senior Living Inc	8361	D	657 888-5752	24811
Southern Cal Prmnnte Med Group	8011	D	714 734-4500	20028
Starwood Hotels & Resorts	7011	D	714 258-4575	13292
Steadfast Management Co Inc	6513	B	714 542-2229	11208
Sterling Collision Center LLC (PA)	7532	D	714 259-1111	17775
Superior Sod I LP	0181	C	909 923-5068	322
Swh Mimis Cafe LLC	5147	D	714 544-5522	8685
Toshiba Amer Med Systems Inc (DH)	5047	B	714 730-5000	7319
Transpacific Management Svc	6531	D	714 285-2626	11879
Trinity Brdcstg Netwrk Inc	4833	D	714 832-2950	5916
Trinity Christian Center of SA (PA)	4833	D	714 665-3619	5917
Tustin Care Center Corp	8052	D	714 832-6780	21118
Western Med Rhblttion Assoc LP	8322	D	714 832-9200	24288
Wood Gutmann Bogart Insur Brkg	6411	D	714 505-7000	10944
Woodbridge Glass Inc	1793	C	714 838-4444	3418
Youngs Holdings Inc (PA)	5182	D	714 368-4615	9117
Youngs Market Company LLC (HQ)	5182	B	714 368-4615	9118

TWENTYNINE PALMS, CA - San Bernardino County

	SIC	EMP	PHONE	ENTRY #
Business and Support Services	7997	D	760 830-6873	18904
United States Dept of Navy	8062	B	760 830-2190	21983

TWIN BRIDGES, CA - El Dorado County

	SIC	EMP	PHONE	ENTRY #
Barton Memorial Hospital	8011	D	530 659-7434	19365
Healthcare Barton System	7389	C	530 543-5575	17210
Sierra At Taho Ski Resorts	7011	E	530 659-7519	13254

UKIAH, CA - Mendocino County

	SIC	EMP	PHONE	ENTRY #
Berryman Health Inc	8059	D	707 462-8864	21154
County of Mendocino	4581	D	707 463-4363	4912
County of Mendocino	8322	B	707 463-2437	23864
County of Mendocino	4959	D	707 463-4363	6624
County of Mendocino	8093	C	707 463-4396	22705
Fedex Ground Package Sys Inc	4213	D	707 485-8638	4176
Ford Street Project Inc	8361	E	707 462-1934	24660
Granite Construction Inc	1611	D	707 467-4100	1789
Hildreth Farm Incorporated	0175	D	707 462-0648	236
Horizon West Healthcare Inc	8051	D	707 462-1436	20677
Lake County Home Loans	6162	E	707 462-4000	9866
Mendocino Cmnty Hlth Clnic Inc (PA)	8011	C	707 468-1010	19745
Mendocino Forest Pdts Co LLC	5031	D	707 468-1431	6936
Pacific Gas and Electric Co	4911	D	707 468-3954	6181
Redwood Empire Packing Inc	0723	C	707 462-5521	580
Redwood Health Club (PA)	7991	D	707 468-0441	18674
Redwood Regional Medical Group	8011	D	707 463-3636	19909
Savings Bank Mendocino County (PA)	6022	C	707 462-6613	9523
Ukiah Adventist Hospital (PA)	8062	B	707 463-7346	21979
Ukiah Adventist Hospital	8062	C	707 462-3111	21980
Ukiah SC Transportation	4151	D	707 463-5234	3952
United Parcel Service Inc OH	4215	C	707 468-5481	4461
Valley View Skiled Nursing Ctr	8051	D	707 462-1436	21004
Waste MGT Collectn & Recycl	4953	D	707 462-0210	6608

UNION CITY, CA - Alameda County

	SIC	EMP	PHONE	ENTRY #
AAA Restaurant Fire Ctrl Inc	7389	D	510 786-9555	16962
Anixter Inc	5063	D	510 477-2400	7414
Basquez Tiburcio Health Center	8093	C	510 471-5907	22667
Best Contracting Services Inc	1761	D	510 886-7240	3141
Buffalo Distribution	5139	E	510 475-9810	8422
Cellco Partnership	4812	D	510 324-5740	5361
Child Family & Cmnty Svcs Inc	8351	D	510 796-9512	24434
China Japan Global Inc (PA)	6211	D	510 441-2993	9972
Coinmach Corporation	7215	C	510 429-0900	13575
Corinthian Realty LLC	6531	D	510 487-8653	11458
Dust Networks Inc	4812	D	510 400-2900	5395
Excel Moving Services	4214	D	800 392-3596	4344
Finezi Inc	7361	D	510 790-4768	14655
Freshpoint Inc	5148	C	510 476-5900	8726
Genesis Logistics Inc	4225	D	510 476-0790	4557
Graybar Electric Company Inc	5063	D	925 557-3000	7444
Intero Real Estate Svcs Inc	6531	D	510 489-8989	11581
Interstate Hotels Resorts Inc	7011	C	510 489-2200	12852
Kaiser Foundation Hospitals	6324	D	510 675-5777	10293
Kaiser Foundation Hospitals	8011	A	510 675-4010	19597
Kaiser Foundation Hospitals	6324	D	510 675-2170	10325
Masonic Homes of California	8361	B	510 441-3700	24728
Mercado Latino Inc	5141	E	510 475-5500	8502
Mission Linen Supply	7213	C	510 429-7305	13559
Oracle Corporation	7372	B	510 471-6971	15801
Orora North America	5113	D	510 487-1211	8204
Permanente Medical Group Inc	8011	D	510 675-4010	19863
Purebeauty Inc	5087	D	510 487-7950	7977
Reliance Steel & Aluminum Co	5051	D	510 476-4400	7394
Rki Instruments Inc (PA)	5084	D	510 441-5656	7884
Specialized Laundry Svcs Inc	7219	E	510 487-8297	13657
Tiburcio Vasquez Hlth Ctr Inc (PA)	8011	D	510 471-5880	20136
Tri-City Economic Dev Corp	4953	D	510 489-8030	6571

Employment Codes: A=Over 500 employees, B=251-500, C=101-250, D=51-100, E=45-50

UNION CITY, CA

	SIC	EMP	PHONE	ENTRY #
Union Sanitary District	4952	C	510 477-7500	6420
United States Cold Storage Inc	4222	E	510 489-8300	4506
United States Pipe Fndry LLC	4619	C	510 441-5810	4952

UNIVERSAL CITY, CA - Los Angeles County

	SIC	EMP	PHONE	ENTRY #
Amblin/Reliance Holding Co LLC	7812		818 733-6272	18041
Hilton Los Angles Universal Cy	7011	B	818 506-2500	12711
Hilton Universal Hotel	7011	D	818 506-2500	12713
Latham & Watkins LLP	8111	B	818 753-5000	23368
Lh Universal Operating LLC	7011	D	818 980-1212	12917
NBC Studios Inc (DH)	7922	C	818 777-1000	18417
NBC Subsidiary (knbc-Tv) LLC	4833	D	818 684-5746	5898
NBC Universal Inc (HQ)	7812	E	818 777-1000	18117
Nbcuniversal Media LLC	4832	D	818 777-1000	5812
Shen Zhen New World II LLC	7011	D	818 980-1212	13240
Sprint Communications Co LP	4813	E	818 755-7100	5704
Sun Hill Properties Inc (HQ)	7011	B	818 506-2500	13308
Universal City Studios LLC	7812	D	818 777-1000	18177
Universal Music Group Inc	7389	E	818 286-4000	17571
Universal Stdios HM Entrmt LLC	7812	A	818 777-1000	18178
Universal Stdios Licensing Inc	6794	C	818 762-6284	12227
Universal Studios Inc	7812	B	818 622-4455	18179
Universal Studios Inc	7812	C	818 777-1000	18181

UPLAND, CA - San Bernardino County

	SIC	EMP	PHONE	ENTRY #
Allied Prof Nursing Care	8082	D	909 949-1066	22352
Apex Parks Group LLC	7999	D	909 981-5251	19138
Azalea & Rose Co	0181	E	909 949-2442	264
B & L Consulting LLC	8748	D	682 238-6994	27845
Bms Parent Inc (PA)	8721	D	909 981-2341	26297
Bni Enterprises Inc	8743	A	909 305-1818	27735
C P Construction Co Inc	1623	E	909 981-1091	1914
California Ldscp & Design Inc	0782	C	909 949-1601	820
California Skateparks	7389	D	909 949-1601	17048
Camstar International Inc	5072	D	909 931-2540	7678
Cascade Drilling LP	1781	C	909 946-1605	3354
F M Tarbell Co	6531	D	909 982-8881	11517
Firstsrvice Rsidential Cal Inc (DH)	6531	D	909 981-4131	11539
Golden Eagle Moving Svcs Inc	4213	D	909 946-7655	4190
Hamilton Brwart Insur Agcy LLC	6411	D	909 920-3250	10734
Hardcore Skateparks Inc	7996	C	909 949-1601	18823
Holliday Rock Co Inc (PA)	5032	D	909 982-1553	6988
Inland Empire Therapy Provider (PA)	8049	D	909 985-7905	20321
Inland Valley Drug & Alcohol (PA)	8322	D	909 932-1069	24026
Inland-Metro Services Inc	7389	D	909 373-6810	17239
JAS Pacific	8711	C	909 605-7777	25908
Kanopy Insurance Center LLC	6399	D	877 513-2434	10571
Largo Concrete Inc	1771	C	909 981-7844	3289
Lewis Companies (PA)	1531	C	909 985-0971	1377
Lifetouch Nat Schl Studios Inc	7221	E	909 985-3532	13663
Loma Sola House	8059	E	909 931-7534	21292
Mgr Services Inc	6531	D	909 981-4466	11688
Mladen Buntich Cnstr Co Inc	1623	D	909 920-9977	1971
Mountain View Physical Therapy	8049	D	909 949-6235	20333
Nationwide Guard Services Inc	7381	D	909 608-1112	16744
Park Place Ford LLC	7538	D	909 946-5555	17809
Perry Floor Systems Inc	1771	D	909 949-1211	3312
Petes Connection Inc	4841	D	909 373-6414	6012
Re/Max LLC	6531	E	303 770-5531	11792
Rgis LLC	7389	C	909 605-1893	17464
San Antonio Community Hospital (PA)	8062	A	909 985-2811	21842
Sela Healthcare Inc (PA)	8051	C	909 985-1981	20902
Serec Entertainment LLC	5072	E	626 893-0600	7696
Shield Security Inc	7381	B	909 920-1173	16824
Sneary Construction Inc	1742	E	909 982-1833	2980
Starbucks Corporation	8742	D	626 203-1862	27664
United Van Lines Agent	4213	E	909 946-7655	4283
Upland Community Care Inc	8059	D	909 985-1903	21403
Vci Construction LLC (HQ)	1623	D	909 946-0905	2011
Vincent Lozano Investigations	7381	E	909 949-0179	16849
Walton Electric Corporation	1731	D	909 981-5051	2789
West End Yung MNS Christn Assn	8641	D	909 946-6120	25401

UPPER LAKE, CA - Lake County

	SIC	EMP	PHONE	ENTRY #
Running Creek Casino	7011	C	707 275-9209	13181

VACAVILLE, CA - Solano County

	SIC	EMP	PHONE	ENTRY #
AFA Constrctn Grp/Cal Inc JV	1542	D	707 446-7996	1484
Albertsons LLC	4225	B	707 446-5922	4521
Allied Framers Inc	1751	B	707 452-7050	3030
Blue Mountain Cnstr Svcs Inc	1711	B	707 820-2323	2169
BMC Stock Holdings Inc	1751	B	707 301-4475	3032
Brenden Theatre Corporation	7832	B	707 469-0180	18310
Citadel Roofing & Solar	1761	C	707 446-5500	3150
City of Vacaville	8322	D	707 449-6122	23759
City of Vacaville	8711	B	707 449-5170	25743
Clark Pest Ctrl Stockton Inc	7342	E	707 446-9748	14177
Contemprary Hstrical Vhcl Assn	8641	D	707 448-7266	25242
County of Solano	4941	D	707 451-6090	6338
General Electric Company	1731	D	707 469-8346	2598
International Brthrhd of Elctr (PA)	8631	D	707 452-2700	25174
Kaiser Foundation Hospitals	8011	A	707 624-4000	19595
Kaiser Foundation Hospitals	6324	E	707 624-4000	10313
Kuic Inc	4832	D	707 446-0200	5801
M&G Duravent Inc	4225	B	800 835-4429	4594
Mariani Packing Co Inc (PA)	0723	D	707 452-2800	561
Mark Garcia	7349	D	707 446-4529	14349
Master Drywall Inc	1742	C	707 448-8659	2929
Maximum Fitness LLC	7991	E	707 447-0606	18659
Mental Health California Dept	8063	B	707 449-6504	22084
Merrill Gardens LLC	6531	D	707 447-7496	11680
Navy Federal Credit Union	6061	D	888 842-6328	9616
No Barriers	8322	D	707 451-1947	24104
North Bay Distribution Inc	5136	D	707 450-1219	8354
North Bay Distribution Inc (PA)	5136	D	707 452-9984	8355
Par Electrical Contractors Inc	1731	D	707 693-1237	2679
Permanente Kaiser Intl	8062	B	707 453-5197	21794
Planned Prnthod Shst-Dblo Inc	8011	D	707 317-2111	19875
Pyramid Building Maint Corp	7349	C	707 454-2020	14399
Recology Vacaville Solano	4953	D	707 448-2945	6531
Solano Irrigation District	4971	D	707 448-6847	6653
Stars Recreation Center LP	7933	E	707 455-7827	18530
Sutter Regional Med Foundation	8011	A	707 454-5800	20124
Taylor Structures Inc	1542	D	707 499-6870	1687
Transpac Inc	5023	C	707 452-0600	6895
Travis Credit Union (PA)	6061	B	707 449-4000	9636
Travis Credit Union	6061	B	707 449-4000	9640
Travis Credit Union	6061	B	707 449-4000	9643
Vacavlle Cnvalescent Rehab Ctr	8059	C	707 449-8000	21405
Valyria LLC	5023	D	707 452-0600	6902
Winsor House Compalessant	8051	D	707 448-6458	21057

VALENCIA, CA - Los Angeles County

	SIC	EMP	PHONE	ENTRY #
AAA Elctrcal Cmmunications Inc (PA)	1731	C	800 892-4784	2509
Adept Fasteners Inc (PA)	5072	D	661 257-6600	7666
Advantage Media Services Inc	4225	B	661 705-7588	4518
Advantage Media Services Inc (PA)	4783	D	661 775-0611	5196
Ai Inc/CSC Grou	7381	D	661 775-8400	16539
Amerisourcebergen Corporation	5122	C	661 257-6400	8229
Andrews International Inc (PA)	7381	A	661 775-8400	16563
Atk Audiotek	1731	C	661 705-3700	2524
Balboa Water Group LLC	8748	D	661 678-5109	27846
C A Rasmussen Inc (PA)	1629	E	661 367-9040	2034
Cardinal Health Inc	5122	C	661 295-6100	8247
CC Wellness LLC (HQ)	5122	D	661 295-1700	8248
Cellco Partnership	4812	D	661 286-2399	5363
Cintas Corporation No 3	7213	D	661 310-7400	13545
Circle W Enterprises Inc	5063	E	661 257-2400	7427
Cns Industries Inc	5169	E	661 775-8877	8984
Deluxe Entrmt Svcs Group Inc	7812	C	661 702-5000	18069
Dimension Data (DH)	4899	C	661 257-1500	6070
Discoverready LLC	8111	D	661 284-6401	23217
Efs West	8711	E	661 705-8200	25780
Encore Media Services Inc	7819	D	661 705-1323	18225
Falcon Aerospace Holdings LLC	8741	A	661 775-7200	27023
Fidelity Security Services Inc	7381	C	661 295-5007	16640
Flair Cleaners Inc	7699	D	661 753-9900	17973
Flight Line Products LLC	1799	B	661 775-8366	3520
Fpk Security Inc	7381	B	661 792-9091	16646
Gothic Landscaping Inc	0781	D	661 257-5085	769
Gothic Landscaping Inc (PA)	0782	C	661 257-1266	858
Harbor Freight Tools Usa Inc	4731	C	661 799-4907	5096
Henry Mayo Newhall Hospital (PA)	8062	D	661 253-8000	21600
Henry Mayo Newhall Mem Hlth	8062	A	661 253-8000	21601
Henry Mayo Newhall Mem Hosp	8011	D	661 253-8112	19554
Heritage Golf Group Inc	7992	D	661 254-4401	18746
Hoffman Texas Inc	7699	E	661 257-9200	17981
Hrd Aero Systems Inc	7699	D	661 295-0670	17982
Hrd Aero Systems Inc (PA)	7699	D	661 295-0670	17983
Hyatt Hotels Management Corp	7011	C	661 799-1234	12826
Hypercel Corporation	5065	E	661 310-1000	7582
Ice Station Valencia L L C	7999	D	661 775-8686	19227
Iron Mountain Incorporated	4226	D	661 775-9008	4689
JT Wimsatt Contg Co Inc (PA)	1771	D	661 775-8090	3285
Jyg Concrete Construction Inc	1771	C	661 607-0337	3286
Klm Orthotic Laboratories Inc	5047	D	661 295-2600	7273
Krg Technologies Inc	7371	B	661 257-9967	15270
Landscape Development Inc (PA)	0782	B	661 295-1970	902
Luminous Consumer Services Inc	6531	D	661 993-1475	11640
Magic Mountain LLC	7922	B	661 255-4100	18413
Mannkind Corporation (PA)	8731	C	661 775-5300	26564
Market Tech Media Corporation	7336	D	661 257-4745	14152
Mercury Insurance Company	6331	D	661 291-6470	10447

	SIC	EMP	PHONE	ENTRY #
N Qiagen Amercn Holdings Inc (HQ)	5122	C	661 702-3000	8285
Nutec Enterprises Inc	6531	D	661 287-3200	11717
Oakridge Landscape Inc (PA)	0721	D	661 295-7228	481
Ocean Park Hotels Inc	7011	D	661 284-3200	13035
Ocean Park Hotels Mmex LLC	7011	E	661 284-2101	13036
Pacific Coast Mines Inc	1474	C	661 287-5400	1112
Princess Cruise Lines Ltd	4481	A	661 753-0000	4727
Princess Cruise Lines Ltd	4481	A	661 753-0000	4728
Princess Cruise Lines Ltd	4481	A	661 753-0000	4729
Princess Cruises and Tours Inc (HQ)	7999	A	206 336-6000	19262
Providence Health & Services	5047	D	661 294-1030	7307
Pyramid Enterprises Inc (PA)	7999	D	661 702-1420	19263
Quest Dgnstics Clncal Labs Inc	8071	B	661 964-6582	22265
Rgis LLC	7389	D	661 702-8987	17455
Samrod Corporation	8711	D	661 945-3602	26051
Santa Clarita Medical Group	8011	E	661 255-6802	19957
Scicon Technologies Corp (PA)	8711	E	661 295-8630	26057
Scorpion Design LLC	8742	C	661 702-0100	27636
Southern California Gas Co	4924	A	800 427-2200	6280
Spad Holdings LLC	7991	D	661 286-0229	18689
Specialty Laboratories Inc (DH)	8071	A	661 799-6543	22286
Sprouts Farmers Market Inc	5141	C	661 414-1109	8522
Star Nail Products Inc	5122	C	661 257-3376	8296
Star Nail Products Inc	5087	C	661 257-7827	7982
Stellar Microelectronics Inc	5065	C	661 775-3500	7638
Summer Systems Inc	1542	C	661 257-4419	1680
Sunkist Growers Inc (PA)	5148	C	818 986-4800	8780
Sunrise Senior Living Inc	8051	D	661 253-3551	20961
Sunshine Day Camp Inc	8351	D	661 254-6855	24523
Trianim Health Services Inc	8099	D	818 362-6882	23075
Ultraviolet Devices Inc	5075	D	661 295-8140	7750
US Healthworks Inc (HQ)	8011	D	800 720-2432	20176
Veolia Transportation Svcs Inc	4111	C	661 294-2541	3734
Vista Valencia Group Inc	6531	E	661 255-4600	11901
Way Forward Technology Inc	7371	E	661 286-2769	15540
Wesco Aircraft Hardware Corp (HQ)	5088	B	661 775-7200	8009
Weslar Inc	1751	D	661 702-1362	3101
William S Hart Pony & Softball	8748	D	661 254-9780	28099
Young Mens Chrstn Assn of La	8641	C	661 253-3593	25468

VALLEJO, CA - Solano County

	SIC	EMP	PHONE	ENTRY #
Blu Homes Inc	1521	C	415 625-0809	1135
Blu Homes Inc	1521	B	707 674-5368	1136
City of Vallejo	7996	D	707 644-4000	18815
Commonwealth Hotels LLC	8741	C	707 644-1200	26976
Crestwood Behavioral Hlth Inc	8361	C	707 552-0215	24622
Crestwood Behavioral Hlth Inc	8063	D	707 558-1777	22063
Crestwood Behavioral Hlth Inc	8063	D	707 552-0215	22064
CSRA LLC	7376	D	703 876-1026	16279
Emeritus Corporation	8052	E	707 552-3336	21080
Empres Financial Services LLC	8051	D	707 643-2793	20535
Execusheld Prtection Group LLC	7381	D	707 439-6351	16637
Ghiringhlli Spcialty Foods Inc	1541	D	707 561-7670	1430
Greater Vallejo Recreation Dst	7999	C	707 648-4600	19219
H & R Block Inc	7291	D	707 643-1856	13722
Helios Healthcare LLC	8059	D	707 644-7401	21264
J B Laquindanum & Associates	7291	E	707 648-0501	13724
James-Timec International	1629	E	707 642-2222	2062
Jeffco Painting & Coating Inc	1721	D	707 562-1900	2459
Kaiser Foundation Hospitals	6324	D	707 645-2720	10296
Kaiser Foundation Hospitals	8062	A	707 651-1000	21666
La Clinica De La Raza Inc	8011	B	707 556-8100	19688
M F Maher Inc	1611	D	707 552-2774	1817
Medic Ambulance Service Inc (PA)	4119	C	707 644-1761	3817
Merrill Gardens LLC	6531	D	707 553-2698	11681
Michaels Trnsp Svc Inc	4141	D	707 647-6013	3895
Milestones Adult Dev Ctr	8322	D	707 644-0464	24088
Milestones of Development Inc	8052	D	707 644-0496	21092
Park Management Corp	7996	C	707 643-6722	18829
Permanente Medical Group Inc	8011	D	707 765-3930	19836
R & R Maher Cnstr Co Inc	1611	D	707 552-0330	1848
Recology Vallejo	4953	C	707 552-3110	6532
San Pablo Lodge 43	8641	D	707 642-1391	25336
Six Flags Entertainment Corp	7996	C	707 644-4000	18833
Steiny and Company Inc	1731	D	707 552-6900	2750
Sutter Regional Med Foundation	8641	C	707 551-3616	25365
Sutter Solano Medical Center (HQ)	8062	A	707 554-4444	21954
Syar Industries Inc	1422	D	707 643-3261	1101
Teamross Inc	7538	C	707 643-9000	17816
Timec Acquisitions Inc (HQ)	1629	A	707 642-2222	2091
Timec Companies Inc (DH)	1629	B	707 642-2222	2092
Total Renal Care Inc	8092	A	707 556-3637	22645
Travis Credit Union	6061	B	800 877-8328	9633
United Parcel Service Inc OH	4215	C	707 252-4560	4452
Valle Sanit and Flood Contr Di	8748	D	707 644-8949	28087
Veterans Health Administration	8011	B	707 562-8200	20195

VALLEY CENTER, CA - San Diego County

	SIC	EMP	PHONE	ENTRY #
Indian Health Council	8611	D	760 749-1410	25091
San Psqual Band Mssion Indians	7011	B	760 291-5500	13207
San Psqual Csino Dev Group Inc	7011	E	760 291-5500	13208
Survival Systems Intl Inc (PA)	7699	D	760 749-6800	18020
Valley Center Municipal	4941	D	760 735-4500	6407

VALLEY SPRINGS, CA - Calaveras County

	SIC	EMP	PHONE	ENTRY #
Bolin Builders Inc	1521	E	209 772-9721	1137

VALLEY VILLAGE, CA - Los Angeles County

	SIC	EMP	PHONE	ENTRY #
Apparel Concepts Intl Inc	5136	A	626 233-9198	8332
Executive Financial HM Ln Corp	6162	E	818 285-5626	9839
Imperial Project Inc	7929	D	310 671-3263	18474

VAN NUYS, CA - Los Angeles County

	SIC	EMP	PHONE	ENTRY #
1370 Realty Corp	6531	C	818 817-0092	11265
14545 Friar LLC	6512	D	818 817-0082	10950
16700 Roscoe Associates LLC	7997	D	818 989-2300	18840
Accentcare Home Health Cal Inc	8082	E	818 528-8855	22325
AG Air Conditioning & Htg Inc	1711	E	818 988-5388	2110
Airespring Inc	4813	D	818 786-8990	5456
All Valley Washer Service Inc	7215	D	818 787-1100	13572
Allen Medical Group Inc	8011	E	818 698-8444	19330
Alta Healthcare System LLC	8399	C	818 787-1511	24862
Alta Hollywood Community Hsptl	8063	C	818 787-1511	22037
American Merchant Center Inc	6153	D	818 947-1700	9770
American Prof Ambulance Corp	4119	C	818 996-2200	3766
American Unique Staff Provider	7361	E	818 908-9051	14607
Apprentice & Journeymen Traini	1711	D	818 464-4579	2147
Apprentice & Journeymen Trn Tr	8331	D	323 636-9871	24303
Apu Inc (PA)	5013	C	661 948-2880	6706
ARC Document Solutions Inc	7334	C	818 908-0222	14111
Arrow Tools Fas & Saw Inc	5072	E	818 780-1464	7673
AT&T Corp	4813	D	818 374-6458	5490
AT&T Corp	4813	D	818 373-6896	5492
AT&T Corp	8748	D	818 997-5998	27839
Baby Dica Inc	7812	C	818 988-0671	18049
Barazani Pave Stone Inc	1741	C	818 701-6977	2803
Bauer Hockey Inc	5091	B	818 782-6445	8012
Berkley Vly Cnvlscent Hosp Inc	8051	C	818 786-0020	20411
Bunim-Murray Productions	7812	C	818 756-5100	18056
C B B Z S Inc	1721	D	818 908-1900	2433
California Contrs Sups Inc	5082	D	818 785-8823	7764
California Survey Res Svcs	7374	C	818 780-2777	16105
Carlisle Research Corporation	7373	C	818 785-8677	15915
Cbre Inc	6531	C	818 907-4600	11353
Century-National Insurance Co (HQ)	6311	B	818 760-0880	10204
City of Los Angeles	8711	A	818 756-8022	25741
City of Los Angeles	4911	D	818 902-3000	6115
City of Los Angeles	4581	D	818 908-5950	4908
Clay Lacy Aviation Inc (PA)	4581	D	818 989-2900	4911
Command International SEC Svcs	7381	D	818 997-1666	16601
County of Los Angeles	8322	C	818 362-6437	23843
County of Los Angeles	8322	D	818 374-2000	23847
County of Los Angeles	8111	D	818 374-2406	23178
Courtyard Plaza	8051	E	818 780-5005	20482
Dee Sign Co	7389	D	818 904-3400	17118
Dfs Flooring Inc (PA)	1752	D	818 374-5200	3111
Ds Services of America Inc	5149	D	818 787-9397	8829
Dsg Associates Inc	8732	E	714 835-3020	26657
E & S International Entps Inc (PA)	5064	C	818 702-2207	7494
Ea Environmental Construction	1742	D	818 785-0956	2889
Easton Hockey Inc (DH)	5091	B	818 782-6445	8016
Electro Rent Corporation (PA)	7359	C	818 786-2525	14538
Elite Aviation LLC	4522	E	818 988-5387	4880
Energy Enterprises USA Inc	1711	D	424 339-0005	2218
ET Security Inc	7381	C	818 988-9617	16635
Exandal Corporation	5141	C	818 905-9497	8477
Factory 2-U Import Export Inc	5137	D	323 587-9900	8383
Ferguson Enterprises Inc	5074	E	818 786-9720	7716
Financial Information Network	7371	C	818 782-0331	15184
Five Star Quality Care Inc	8051	D	818 997-1841	20573
Fusefx Inc	7819	C	661 644-0783	18229
George M Rajacich MD PC	8011	D	818 787-2020	19535
Golden Living LLC	8082	D	805 494-4949	22443
Grand Valley Health Care Ctr	8051	D	818 786-3470	20635
Grht Inc	5199	D	323 873-6393	9269
Grobstein Horwath & Co	8721	D	818 501-5200	26361
Health Advocates LLC	8399	B	818 995-9500	24927
Health Entps Lf Long Plan	8082	B	818 654-0330	22457
Helinet Aviation Services LLC (PA)	7812	D	818 902-0229	18092
Hemacare Corporation (PA)	8099	C	818 986-3883	22973
Icon Media Direct Inc (PA)	7319	D	818 995-6400	13997
Incare Dme	8099	D	818 582-1016	22980
Interviewing Service Amer Inc (PA)	8732	A	818 989-1044	26675

Employment Codes: A=Over 500 employees, B=251-500, C=101-250, D=51-100, E=45-50

VAN NUYS, CA

Company	SIC	EMP	PHONE	ENTRY #
Kay Automotive Distrs Inc (PA)	5013	E	818 781-6850	6743
Kdk Management Inc	5149	D	818 786-1700	8864
Khorrami Shawn Law Office	8111		818 947-5111	23348
L A Party Rents Inc	7359	D	818 989-4300	14555
Lees Maintenance Service Inc	7349	B	818 988-6644	14337
Leigh Jerry California Inc (PA)	5137	C	818 909-6200	8395
Longwood Management Corp	6513	E	818 781-6348	11159
Los Angeles Police Credit Un (PA)	6062	E	818 787-6520	9672
Los Angeles Unified School Dst	8093	B	818 997-2640	22770
M Network Television Inc	4833	D	818 756-5150	5896
Maguire Aviation Group LLC	4522	E	818 989-2300	4884
ME and ME Inc	7363	D	818 891-0197	14906
Memeged Tevuot Shemesh (PA)	1711	C	866 575-1211	2292
Merabi & Sons LLC	6798	D	818 817-0006	12260
Mercury Messenger Service Inc	7389	E	818 989-3115	17329
Mesa Energy Systems Inc	1711	C	818 756-0500	2295
MGA Entertainment Inc (PA)	5092	B	818 894-2525	8050
Momentous Insurance Brkg Inc	6411	D	818 933-2700	10788
Moreno-Menco Pacific JV	1542	E	760 747-4405	1614
Moulton Logistics Management (PA)	7389	D	818 997-1800	17342
Mp Aero LLC	1799	D	818 901-9828	3555
Nat Sim Corp	5112	D	818 705-3131	8171
National Commercial Services	7322	D	818 701-4400	14039
Nep Group Inc	7812	D	412 423-1354	18119
Network Medical Management Inc	8741	C	818 370-9125	27140
Normand/Wlshire Rtrment Ht Inc	6513	E	818 373-5429	11174
North La County Regional Ctr (PA)	8748	B	818 778-1900	28003
One Generation (PA)	8322	C	818 708-6625	24115
Parkwood Landscape Maint Inc	0782	B	818 988-9677	932
Pride Collision Centers Inc (PA)	7532	D	818 909-0660	17769
Primex Clinical Labs Inc (PA)	8071	C	818 779-0496	22259
Prudential Insur Co of Amer	6411	D	818 901-0028	10846
Ptsa 31st Dst Creative Kids	8351	C	818 996-2668	24505
Regency Fire Protection Inc	1711	D	818 982-0126	2344
Reliable Gardens Inc	0782	D	818 904-9801	943
Restaurant Depot LLC	5181	C	818 376-7687	9082
Richmond American Homes	1521	E	818 908-3267	1245
Rite Way Enterprises	4731	E	818 376-6960	5161
Rotorcraft Support Inc	5088	D	818 997-8060	8003
S D Property Management Inc	6531	D	323 658-7990	11828
S G D Enterprises	0782	E	818 782-3455	947
San Fernando Valley Community (PA)	8093	D	818 901-4830	22824
Shalev Senior Living	8361	D	818 780-4808	24809
Sharf Woodward & Associates	7361	D	818 989-2200	14785
Signature Flight Support Corp	4581	D	818 464-9500	4936
Six Continents Hotels Inc	7011	D	818 989-5010	13262
SMA Builders Inc	1521	E	818 994-8306	1262
Southern Cal Orthpd Inst LP	8011	C	818 901-6600	20015
Southern Cal Orthpd Inst LP (PA)	8011	C	818 901-6600	20017
Sport Chalet LLC	5091	D	818 781-4000	8030
Sylmark Inc (PA)	8741	B	818 217-2000	27243
T & R Painting Construction	1721	C	818 779-3800	2497
Town & Country Event Rentals (PA)	7359	B	818 908-4211	14584
Transtar Industries Inc	5013	E	818 785-2000	6777
Triton Consolidated Industries	4731	C	323 852-0370	5180
TWC Aviation LLC	4522	E	888 923-1001	4889
United Parcel Service Inc OH	4215	C	404 828-6000	4456
United Road Towing Inc	7549	D	818 782-1996	17903
Valley Clark Plbg & Htg Co Inc (PA)	1711	E	818 782-1047	2404
Valley Presbyterian Hospital	8062	A	818 782-6600	22010
Van Nuys Care Center Inc	8059	D	818 343-0700	21409
Weinstein Construction Corp	1542	E	818 782-4000	1714
Wolfe Trucking Inc	4213	C	818 376-6960	4305
Woodley Lakes Golf Course	7992	D	818 780-6886	18800
Young Mens Chrstn Assn of La	8641	E	818 989-3800	25464

VANDENBERG AFB, CA - Santa Barbara County

Company	SIC	EMP	PHONE	ENTRY #
Aecom Global II LLC	8711	D	805 260-8440	25635
Indyne Inc	8744	A	805 606-7225	27795
Range Generation Next LLC	8711	D	310 647-9438	26033
Securitas Critical Infrastruct	7381	A	805 685-1100	16784

VENICE, CA - Los Angeles County

Company	SIC	EMP	PHONE	ENTRY #
Globalex Corporation (PA)	7372	D	310 593-4833	15680
Host Hotels & Resorts LP	7011	D	310 823-1700	12773
Intrinsik Envmtl Sciences Inc	8748	D	310 392-6462	27955
Ketchum Sheppard Inc	8742	E	310 584-8300	27500
Kiosked	7379	D	310 392-2470	16419
Los Angeles County MTA	4111	C	310 392-8636	3669
Mad Dogg Athletics Inc (PA)	5137	C	310 823-7008	8397
Outrigger Hotels Hawaii	7011	D	310 301-2000	13050
Parking Concepts Inc	7521	D	310 821-1081	17735
Power Studios Inc	7812	C	310 314-2800	18134
Safetypark Corporation	7521	C	310 399-1499	17742
Snap Inc (PA)	7372	D	310 399-3339	15840
Southern California Gas Co	4922	D	310 823-7945	6256
St Joseph Center	8322	D	310 396-6468	24228
Trg Inc	6531	D	310 396-6750	11881
Venice Family Clinic (PA)	8011	D	310 664-7703	20189
Zefr Inc	7812	C	310 392-3555	18208

VENTURA, CA - Ventura County

Company	SIC	EMP	PHONE	ENTRY #
A M Ortega Construction Inc	1521	D	951 360-1352	1120
Agi Holding Corp (PA)	7997	C	805 667-4100	18843
Alsco Inc	7213	D	805 650-6578	13512
American Landscape Management	0782	E	805 647-5077	807
Arb Inc	1623	E	805 643-4188	1902
ARC of Ventura County Inc	8093	C	805 644-0880	22660
Asplundh Tree Expert Co	0783	D	805 641-0528	986
Automobile Club Southern Cal	8699	D	805 644-7171	25496
Bentley-Simonson Inc	1311	D	805 650-2794	1028
Beverly Health Care Corp (PA)	8741	E	805 642-1736	26942
Boyd & Associates (PA)	7381	C	818 752-1888	16580
Bsia Natural Resources Co	1389	D	805 650-2794	1070
Buenaventura Medical Group (PA)	8011	D	805 477-6000	19383
Buenaventura Medical Group	8011	D	805 477-6220	19384
C D Lyon Construction Inc (PA)	8711	D	805 653-0173	25711
C J Vandergeest Ldscp Care Inc	0782	D	805 650-0726	817
California Forensic Med Group	8099	D	805 654-3343	22907
Catholic Charities of Santa CL	8322	D	805 643-4694	23713
Cellco Partnership	4812	D	805 650-0410	5320
Central Courier LLC	4212	D	805 654-1145	3992
Channel Islands Young Mens Ch	8641	C	805 484-0423	25235
Clocktower Inn	7011	D	805 652-0141	12529
Coastal View Halthcare Ctr LLC	8059	D	805 642-4101	21187
Community Mem HSP/Sn Benua	8062	D	805 652-5072	21508
Community Memorial Health Sys	8062	D	805 658-5800	21509
Convenience Management Group	8741	D	805 644-6784	26981
Cornell Corrections Cal Inc (DH)	8322	D	805 644-8700	23786
County of Ventura	8322	C	805 654-2561	23931
County of Ventura	8322	C	805 654-3456	23932
County of Ventura	8721	C	805 654-3152	26318
County of Ventura	8322	A	805 652-6000	23934
D S R Inc	7699	D	805 275-0039	17970
Dcor LLC (PA)	1382	D	805 535-2000	1062
Dcor LLC	1382	D	805 576-1200	1063
Del Mar Seafoods Inc	5146	C	805 850-0421	8632
Dialysis Centers Ventura Cnty	8092	D	805 658-9211	22623
E & M Concrete Construction	1771	D	805 658-2888	3260
E J Harrison & Sons Inc	4953	C	805 647-1414	6473
E&S Financial Group Inc	6163	D	805 644-1621	9919
Evans/Sipes Inc (PA)	6531	C	805 644-1242	11497
Fedex Office & Print Svcs Inc	7334	D	805 339-2000	14120
Florida Beauty Flora Inc	7231	B	805 642-1633	13676
Fpl LLC	7011	D	805 643-6144	12651
Fugro West Inc (DH)	8711	D	805 650-7000	25822
Golden Living LLC	8051	D	805 642-1736	20615
GPA Technologies Inc	8711	D	805 643-7878	25844
Hailwood Inc	6512	D	805 487-4981	10995
Harbor Island Hotel Group LP	7011	D	805 658-1212	12689
Inter Act Pmti Inc (PA)	8711	D	805 658-5600	25884
J L S Concrete Pumping Inc	1771	D	805 643-0766	3278
Jensen Design & Survey Inc	8711	E	805 654-6977	25909
Kaiser Foundation Hospitals	6324	D	888 515-3500	10320
Kingledon Inc	7011	D	805 643-6000	12886
Kkzz 1590	4832	E	805 289-1400	5795
L A Fitness Intl LLC	7991	D	805 289-9907	18652
Livingston Mem Vna Hlth Corp	8741	D	805 642-0239	27118
M C M Harvesters Inc	7361	B	805 659-6833	14700
Nabors Well Services Co	1389	D	805 641-0390	1087
Northstar Duplicators	7819	D	805 984-3888	18240
Offshore Crane & Service Co (PA)	7353	D	805 648-3348	14493
Oilfield Electric Company	1731	D	805 648-3131	2672
Ojai Ambulance Inc	4119	E	805 653-9111	3823
Ost Trucks and Cranes Inc	7389	D	805 643-9963	17383
Pacific Diagnostic Labs LLC	8071	D	805 653-5443	22250
Pier Pont Hotel LP	7011	E	805 643-6144	13095
Plowboy Landscapes Inc	0782	D	805 643-4966	937
Ralphs Grocery Company	4225	D	805 650-0239	4624
Registration Ctrl Systems Inc (PA)	7389	D	805 654-0171	17449
Rgis LLC	7389	D	805 644-0454	17461
Sam Hill & Sons Inc	1623	E	805 620-0828	1992
Saticoy Lemon Association	0174	D	805 654-6500	223
Scan Health Plan	6324	C	805 658-0365	10376
Securitas SEC Svcs USA Inc	7381	D	805 650-6285	16785
Sigma Services Inc (PA)	1542	D	805 642-8377	1667
Simplexgrinnell LP	1711	D	805 642-0366	2368
Snapdragon Place 1 LP	6513	D	805 659-3791	11205
SRS Protection Inc	7381	D	805 744-7122	16830
Star of California (PA)	8099	C	805 644-7823	23065
Stewart Information Svcs Corp	6541	D	805 677-6915	11939
Taft Electric Company (PA)	1731	C	805 642-0121	2766

GEOGRAPHIC SECTION — VISALIA, CA

Company	SIC	EMP	PHONE	ENTRY #
Tidwell Excav Acquisition Inc	1794	D	805 647-4707	3444
Trade Desk Inc (PA)	7311	D	805 585-3434	13929
United Parcel Service Inc OH	4215	C	805 656-3442	4477
US Data Management LLC (PA)	7379	D	888 231-0816	16518
Ventura County Credit Union (PA)	6062	D	805 477-4000	9698
Ventura County Lemon Coops	0723	D	805 385-3345	602
Ventura County Medical Center (PA)	8011	C	805 652-6000	20192
Ventura County Medical Center	8011	C	805 652-6201	20193
Ventura Hsptality Partners LLC	7011	C	805 648-2100	13377
Ventura Streets Dept	1521	D	805 652-4515	1280
Veternary Med Srgcal Group Inc	7363	D	805 339-2290	14969
Victoria Care Center	8051	D	805 642-1736	21009
Vista Steel Co Inc	1629	E	805 653-1189	2095
West Coast Arborists Inc	0783	C	805 671-5092	1002
West Ventura Family Care Ctr	8011	D	805 641-5620	20236
Willow Farms LLC	0191	D	805 647-0720	406

VERNON, CA - Los Angeles County

Company	SIC	EMP	PHONE	ENTRY #
Adir International LLC	1541	C	213 639-7716	1397
Americold Logistics LLC	4222	D	323 581-0025	4488
Bcbg Max Azria Group LLC	5137	E	213 624-2224	8367
Bcbg Max Azria Group LLC	5137	D	323 589-2224	8368
Bcbg Max Azria Group LLC (PA)	5137	A	323 589-2224	8369
Bnsf Railway Company	4011	D	323 267-4133	3610
Bobco Metals LLC	5051	E	213 748-5171	7361
City Fibers Inc (PA)	5093	D	323 583-1013	8069
City Fibers Inc	4225	D	323 583-1013	4536
City of Los Angeles	4173	D	213 485-4981	3956
Claudia Richard Inc	5137	D	323 264-3915	8375
Comak Trading Inc A Cal Corp	5137	D	323 261-3404	8376
Completely Fresh Foods Inc	5149	C	323 722-9136	8818
Core-Mark International Inc	5149	C	323 583-6531	8822
DOT-Line Transportation Inc	4213	D	877 900-7768	4139
Douglas Steel Supply Inc (PA)	5051	D	323 587-7676	7367
Dutch LLC	5137	E	323 277-3900	8378
Dutch LLC (HQ)	5137	D	323 277-3900	8379
Fedex Freight Corporation	4213	D	323 269-9800	4160
Flowserve Corporation	5084	B	323 584-1890	7844
Goldberg and Solovy Foods Inc	5141	B	323 581-6161	8481
Golden West Trading Inc	5147	B	323 581-3663	8668
Greatwide Logistics Svcs LLC	4213	D	323 268-7100	4191
H & N Foods International Inc (HQ)	5146	C	323 586-9300	8633
Jordana Cosmetics Corporation	5122	C	323 585-4859	8269
Joseph T Ryerson & Son Inc	5051	B	323 267-6000	7378
Kellytoy Worldwide Inc	5092	D	323 923-1300	8047
Kenan Advantage Group Inc	4213	D	323 582-3778	4202
Kim Chong	7389	D	323 581-4700	17272
Lafayette Textile Inds LLC	5131	D	323 264-2212	8316
Los Angeles Junction Rlwy Co	4013	E	323 277-2004	3628
Los Angeles Regional Food Bank	8322	C	323 234-3030	24070
Macsei Industries Corporation	5147	D	323 233-7864	8675
Martys Cutting Inc	7389	D	323 582-5758	17315
Mola Inc	5137	C	323 582-0088	8403
Morgan Fabrics Corporation (PA)	5131	D	323 583-9981	8320
Natures Produce Company	5148	C	323 235-4343	8754
Ocean Queen 87 Inc	5146	E	323 585-1200	8641
Orient Fisheries Inc	5146	D	323 588-4185	8643
Ozoo Inc	7389	C	323 585-4383	17388
Pacific American Fish Co Inc (PA)	5146	D	323 319-1551	8644
Rancho Foods Inc	5147	D	323 585-0503	8680
Randall Foods Inc	5144	D	323 587-2383	8604
Red Chamber Co (PA)	5146	D	323 234-9000	8650
Reliance Steel & Aluminum Co	5051	C	323 583-6111	7397
Rite-Way Meat Packers Inc	5147	D	323 826-2144	8682
Robin K	5137	D	323 235-5152	8410
Rose & Shore Inc	7389	B	323 826-2144	17468
Saia Motor Freight Line LLC	4213	D	323 277-2880	4258
Shims Bargain Inc (PA)	5199	D	323 881-0099	9302
Soex West Usa LLC	5136	B	323 264-8300	8360
Soofer Co Inc	5149	C	323 234-6666	8922
Spilo Worldwide Inc	5087	B	213 687-8600	7981
Stone Blue Inc	7218	D	323 277-0008	13643
Tadin Inc	5149	D	213 406-8880	8933
Tama Trading Company	5149	D	213 748-8262	8934
True Wrld Fods Los Angeles LLC	5146	D	323 846-3300	8661
United Parcel Service Inc OH	4513	B	323 260-8957	4874
US Growers Cold Storage Inc (PA)	4222	C	323 583-3163	4509
US Growers Cold Storage Inc	4222	D	323 583-3163	4510
V & L Produce Inc	5148	D	323 589-3125	8783
Vernon Central Warehouse Inc	4214	C	323 234-2200	4388
Vernon Truck Wash Inc	7542	D	323 267-0706	17864
Wayne Provision Co (PA)	5147	D	323 277-5888	8689
West Pico Foods Inc	5142	D	323 586-9050	8575
Williams Service Corporation (PA)	4226	E	323 234-3453	4708
Wm Healthcare Solutions Inc	4953	D	713 328-7350	6614
World Variety Produce Inc	5148	B	323 588-0151	8792

Company	SIC	EMP	PHONE	ENTRY #
Young Bae Fashions Inc	5137	D	323 583-8684	8418

VICTOR, CA - San Joaquin County

Company	SIC	EMP	PHONE	ENTRY #
Victor Treatment Centers Inc	8361	C	209 340-7900	24846

VICTORVILLE, CA - San Bernardino County

Company	SIC	EMP	PHONE	ENTRY #
Branlyn Prominence Inc	8322	C	760 843-5655	23693
Cemex Cnstr Mtls PCF LLC	5032	C	760 381-7600	6976
Charter Cmmnctons Oprating LLC	4841	C	760 452-8609	5940
County of San Bernardino	8322	C	760 843-5100	23894
Desert Valley Hospital Inc (HQ)	8062	C	760 241-8000	21530
Desert Valley Med Group Inc	8011	D	760 241-2474	19493
Desert Valley Med Group Inc (PA)	8011	B	760 241-8000	19494
Desert View Funeral Home	7261	E	760 244-0007	13705
E & T Foods Inc	0291	B	760 843-7730	465
Green Tree Capital LP	7011	C	760 245-3461	12677
Hartwick & Hand Inc (PA)	4212	D	760 245-1666	4023
Heritage Medical Group	8099	C	760 956-1286	22975
In Shape Health Club	8099	E	760 381-1200	22979
Innovative Bus Partnerships	8059	E	760 243-2229	21277
Jamboor Medical Corporation	8092	D	760 241-8063	22631
Kaiser Foundation Hospitals	6324	D	888 750-0036	10302
Keller Williams Realty	6531	D	760 951-5242	11610
Kindred Healthcare Inc	8052	C	760 241-7044	21087
Knolls Convalescent Hospital (PA)	8051	C	760 245-5361	20711
Knolls Convalescent Hospital	8051	D	760 245-6477	20712
Knolls West Enterprise	8361	C	760 245-0107	24701
Knolls West Post Acute LLC	8059	C	760 245-5361	21285
L & S Investment Co Inc	7011	D	760 245-3461	12893
Landforce Express Corporation	4213	C	760 843-7839	4208
Leading Edge Aviation Servs	4581	A	760 246-1651	4923
Lee-Victorville Hotel Corp	7011	C	760 245-3461	12913
Odyssey Healthcare Inc	8082	D	760 241-7044	22520
Pacific Arspc Rsurces Tech LLC	7699	D	760 530-1767	17995
Peoples Care Inc	8082	C	760 962-1900	22555
Psomas	8713	E	760 843-5700	26278
Securitas SEC Svcs USA Inc	7381	C	760 245-1915	16811
Sonshine Collision Services	7532	D	760 243-3185	17773
Sonshine North Autobody	7532	D	760 245-3183	17774
Southern California AVI LLC	4581	C	760 523-5057	4938
Southern California Edison Co	4911	C	760 951-3242	6241
Spring Valley Lake Country CLB	7997	D	760 245-5356	19093
Spring Valley Post Acute LLC	8051	C	760 245-6477	20923
Sterling-Ase Ltd Partnership	6513	C	760 951-9507	11209
Stress Relief Services	7011	D	760 241-7472	13307
Telecare Corporation	8063	D	760 245-8837	22096
United California Realty Inc	6531	D	760 949-4040	11891
United Parcel Service Inc	7389	A	760 241-5540	17555
United Parcel Service Inc OH	4215	C	619 443-3266	4463
Valley Bulk Inc	4213	D	760 843-0574	4297
Verizon Communications Inc	4813	C	760 245-0409	5722
Victor Vly Hosp Acqisition Inc	6324	D	760 245-8691	10389
Victorvlle Trsure Holdings LLC	7011	D	760 245-6565	13379
Visitng Nurse Assn Inlnd CNT	8082	D	760 962-1966	22598

VILLA PARK, CA - Orange County

Company	SIC	EMP	PHONE	ENTRY #
Melissa Sweitzer PHD Inc	8063	D	714 974-8727	22083
School Portraits By Kranz	7221	D	714 545-1775	13665
Tropical Plaza Nursery Inc	0782	D	714 998-4100	966

VINA, CA - Tehama County

Company	SIC	EMP	PHONE	ENTRY #
Andersen & Sons Shelling Inc	0723	D	530 839-2236	508

VISALIA, CA - Tulare County

Company	SIC	EMP	PHONE	ENTRY #
Agsource Services LLC	0761	E	559 735-9700	647
Allen Development Partners LLC (PA)	6552	D	559 732-5425	11945
American Incorporated	1711	B	559 651-1776	2127
Bacci Glinn Physcl Therapy Inc	8049	E	559 733-2478	20307
Bank America National Assn	6021	E	800 432-1000	9327
Beethoven Holdings Inc	6531	C	559 733-4100	11317
Bethesda Lthran Cmmunities Inc	8361	D	559 636-6300	24564
Bowie Enterprises	7542	D	559 732-2988	17831
California Coml Solar Inc	1711	D	559 667-9200	2173
Central Valley Community Bank	6022	D	559 625-8733	9483
Central Vly Regional Ctr Inc	8093	D	559 738-2200	22678
Chicago Title Company	6361	D	559 733-3814	10504
Cigna Healthcare Cal Inc	6324	B	559 738-2000	10274
Citizen Potawatomi Nation	6021	D	559 635-1039	9383
City of Visalia	7389	D	559 713-4000	17081
Comcast Cble Cmmunications LLC	4841	D	559 253-4050	5948
CSC Consulting Inc	8748	C	559 739-8180	27892
Dae-IL Usa Inc	5013	D	559 651-5170	6724
Delta Nrsing Rhbilitation Hosp	8051	D	559 625-4003	20518
Donald Lawrence Fulbright Co	1531	D	559 625-0762	1362
E & M AG Svc Inc A Cal Corp	0762	E	559 627-2724	698
Family Services	8699	E	559 741-7310	25529
Family Services Tulare County	8322	D	559 732-1970	23972

Employment Codes: A=Over 500 employees, B=251-500, C=101-250, D=51-100, E=45-50

VISALIA, CA

	SIC	EMP	PHONE	ENTRY #
Far West Inc	8051	D	559 627-1241	20566
Far West Inc	8059	C	559 733-0901	21214
Federal Express Corporation	4513	D	800 463-3339	4857
Financial Credit Network Inc (PA)	7322	E	559 733-7550	14032
Frito-Lay North America Inc	5145	D	559 651-1334	8620
GAF Holdings Inc	6719	B	559 734-3333	12064
Grosvenor Visalia Associates	7011	D	559 651-5000	12680
Heilind Electronics Inc	5065	D	559 651-0168	7576
J & S Farm	0191	D	559 308-0294	371
J A Contracting Inc	0761	B	559 733-4865	667
Jacobs Tree Specialist Inc	0761	E	559 639-7138	668
Kaweah Dlta Hlth Care Dst Gild	8099	C	559 624-3100	22984
Kaweah Dlta Hlth Care Dst Gild (PA)	8062	A	559 624-2000	21681
Keller Williams Realty Inc	6531	D	559 636-1235	11611
Kern 2008 Cmnty Partners LP	1522	D	559 651-3559	1322
Kreger Inc	0761	A	559 884-2585	672
L E Cooke Co	0181	C	559 732-9146	298
Lamp Liter Associates	7011	D	559 733-4328	12903
Michael SD Nagatini	8011	D	559 738-7502	19751
Mitchell Buckman Inc (PA)	6411	D	559 733-1181	10787
Morgan Kleppe & Nash	6411	D	559 732-3436	10790
Moyles Health Care Inc	8059	D	559 732-2244	21322
Orange Belt Stages (PA)	4142	D	559 733-4408	3905
Original Mowbrays Tree Svc Inc	0783	C	559 798-0530	995
Phillips Farms	0175	E	559 798-1871	248
Quad Knopf Inc (PA)	8711	E	559 733-0440	26026
Quail Park	8052	D	559 624-3500	21097
Red One - PSI Joint Ventr LLC	1542	E	559 772-8264	1647
Robert Quintero Labor Contg	7361	D	559 732-6954	14774
Self Help Enterprises (PA)	8641	D	559 651-1000	25346
Sequoia Beverage	5181	C	559 651-2444	9085
Sequoia Regional Cancer Center	8069	D	559 624-3000	22171
State Farm Fire and Cslty Co	6411	D	559 625-4330	10877
Tim Hofer Inc	7349	C	559 732-6676	14444
Todd Plumbing Inc	1711	C	559 651-5820	2398
Tucoemas Federal Credit Union	6061	D	559 429-7094	9644
Tulare Cnty Chld Care Home Edu	8351	D	559 651-0247	24527
Tulare Cty Trng Ctr Hndcpd	8331	E	559 651-3683	24397
Turning Point Central Cal Inc	8322	E	559 627-1490	24262
United Parcel Service Inc OH	4215	C	559 651-0995	4458
United Parcel Service Inc OH	4215	D	559 651-7690	4473
USA Waste of California Inc	4953	D	559 741-1766	6574
USA Waste of California Inc	4953	D	559 834-4070	6588
Visalia Country Club	7997	D	559 734-3733	19122
Visalia Medical Clinic Inc (PA)	8011	C	559 733-5222	20226
Visalia Unified School Dst	8322	D	559 730-7871	24279
Viscamar LLC	7011	D	559 636-1111	13381
Welcome Group Management LLC	7011	D	310 378-6666	13397
Westgate Gardens Care Center	8051	C	559 733-0901	21034
Wonderful Citrus Packing LLC	0723	D	559 798-3100	606

VISTA, CA - San Diego County

	SIC	EMP	PHONE	ENTRY #
Access Biologicals LLC	5122	D	760 597-9749	8225
Aciontalk International Inc	8748	B	619 393-1710	27809
All-Pro Bail Bonds Inc	7389	D	760 941-4100	16980
Altman Specialty Plants Inc (PA)	5193	A	760 744-8191	9176
American Faucet Coatings Corp	5023	E	760 598-5895	6841
Apical Industries Inc	5088	D	760 724-5300	7994
ARS American Residential (HQ)	1711	E	760 941-7000	2151
Bachem Americas Inc	5169	D	760 597-8820	8980
Baked In Sun	5149	D	760 591-9045	8803
Bent Tree Nursing Center Inc	8051	D	760 945-3033	20410
Caldwell Banker Inc	6531	D	760 941-6888	11337
Cassidy Medical Group Inc (PA)	8011	E	760 630-5487	19411
City of Vista	7999	D	760 940-9283	19183
Cols Inc	4119	C	714 720-6100	3783
Demaria Landtech Inc	0782	E	858 481-5500	837
Deployment Solutions LLC	1731	E	317 281-9682	2575
Drug Enforcement ADM	8734	D	760 597-7955	26844
Ellison Biner	7389	D	760 598-6500	17148
Excel Mdular Scaffold Lsg Corp	1799	A	760 598-0050	3514
Experienced Home Care Registry	8082	D	760 724-0880	22435
Festival Fun Parks LLC	7999	D	760 945-9474	19210
Frito-Lay North America Inc	5145	D	760 727-6022	8618
Habitat Rstration Sciences Inc (PA)	0782	D	760 479-4210	865
Harbor Freight Tools Usa Inc	4789	D	760 631-0347	5218
Harmatz Entertainment Corp	7933	E	760 941-1032	18522
Heaviland Enterprises Inc	0782	D	760 598-7065	868
HMS Construction Inc (PA)	1781	D	760 727-9808	3357
I Pwlc Inc	0781	D	760 630-0231	774
Industrial Coml Systems Inc	1711	D	760 300-4094	2250
Jeld-Wen Inc	5031	B	760 597-4201	6935
Jwc Construction Inc (PA)	1522	E	760 727-2494	1318
Kids First Foundation	8361	C	760 631-7550	24699
Kids First Foundation	8361	D	760 631-7550	24700
Krikorian Premiere Theatre LLC	7832	C	760 945-7469	18337
Lee-Mar Aquarium & Pet Sups	5199	D	760 727-1300	9275
Life Care Centers America Inc	8059	C	760 724-8222	21289
Mc Painting (PA)	1721	E	760 599-8000	2465
McCain Inc (PA)	5084	C	760 727-8100	7862
Minegar Contracting Inc	1771	E	760 598-5001	3296
Neal Electric Corp (HQ)	1731	D	858 513-2525	2663
Neostyle Eyewear Corporation	5048	C	760 305-4004	7334
New Haven Youth Fmly Svcs Inc	8322	C	760 630-4060	24101
Novo Engineering Inc (PA)	8711	D	760 598-6686	25993
Orion Construction Corporation	1623	D	760 597-9660	1975
Pac West Land Care Inc	0782	C	760 630-0231	927
Pave-Tech Inc	1611	E	760 727-8700	1844
Pleasant Care of Vista	8051	C	760 945-3033	20850
Plug Connection LLC	0181	D	760 631-0992	311
Ponto Nursery Inc	5193	D	760 724-6003	9210
Production Plus Plumbing Inc	1711	C	760 597-0235	2330
Prudential Overall Supply Inc	7218	D	760 727-7163	13642
Rancho Vista Health Center	8052	C	760 941-1480	21098
Regency Centers LP	8051	A	760 724-9795	20867
Rescom Services Inc	0782	D	760 930-3900	944
Sharp Healthcare	8062	D	760 806-5600	21887
Sherpaul Corporation	8082	D	760 639-6472	22563
Sierra Pacific West Inc	1542	D	760 599-0755	1666
Spa Havens LP	7991	D	760 945-2055	18686
Tri-City Home Care Services	8082	D	760 940-5800	22582
Unite Eurotherapy Inc	5122	D	760 585-1800	8299
United Floral Exchange Inc	5193	D	760 597-1940	9222
US Foods Inc	5199	B	760 599-6200	9307
USA Bouquet LLC	5193	D	800 878-9909	9223
Vadnais Trenchless Svcs Inc	1623	D	858 550-1460	2009
Vista Care Group LLC (PA)	8322	D	760 295-3900	24280
Vista Community Clinic (PA)	8031	B	760 631-5000	20292
Vista Community Clinic	8031	E	760 631-5030	20293
Vista Irrigation District	4971	D	760 597-3100	6656
Vista Knoll Inc	8051	D	760 630-2273	21019
Vista Valley Country Club	7997	D	760 758-5275	19123
Vista Woods Health Assoc LLC	8051	C	760 630-2273	21021
Western Concrete Pumping Inc (PA)	1771	D	760 598-7855	3350
Winners Only Inc	5021	C	760 599-0300	6838

WALNUT, CA - Los Angeles County

	SIC	EMP	PHONE	ENTRY #
A-1 Delivery Co	4212	D	909 444-1220	3968
Able Hands Inc	8082	D	626 965-2233	22318
Adesso Inc	5045	C	909 839-2929	7083
Amerifreight Inc	4225	A	909 839-2600	4522
Bulk Transportation (PA)	4213	D	909 594-2855	4122
Caliber Bodyworks Inc	7532	E	909 598-1111	17751
Capacity LLC	4226	C	732 745-7770	4678
Clarion Construction Inc	1541	E	909 598-4060	1414
Dura Freight Inc	4225	C	909 444-1025	4547
East Lion Corporation	5139	E	626 912-1818	8433
Emeritus Corporation	8052	D	909 544-4871	21081
Fiserv Inc	7374	D	909 598-8700	16130
Fiserv Inc	7374	D	909 595-9074	16133
I3pl LLC	4731	D	909 839-2600	5103
JF Shea Construction Inc	1521	D	909 594-0998	1195
Kelly Paper Company (HQ)	5111	E	909 859-8200	8153
Los Angeles Royal Vista Golf C	7997	D	909 595-7471	18987
M & R Joint Venture Electrical	1731	D	909 598-7700	2638
Nestle Dreyers Ice Cream Co	5143	D	909 595-0677	8589
Oparc	8322	D	909 598-8055	24116
Ronsin Photocopy Inc (PA)	7389	D	909 594-5995	17467
Secured Shuttle Service Inc	4119	D	909 594-9054	3845
Shea Homes Arizona Ltd Partnr	6531	D	909 594-9500	11841
Shea Homes At Montage LLC	1521	D	909 594-9500	1255
Shea Homes Lmtd Partnership A (HQ)	1521	E	909 594-9500	1256
Shea Homes Vantis LLC	1522	D	909 594-9500	1339
Sysco Los Angeles Inc	5141	A	909 595-9595	8531
United Riggers & Erectors Inc (PA)	1796	D	909 978-0400	3482
Vistancia Marketing LLC	8742	D	909 594-9500	27715
Walnut Valley Unified School	8699	D	909 444-3415	25596
Walnut Valley Water District	4941	D	909 595-7554	6408

WALNUT CREEK, CA - Contra Costa County

	SIC	EMP	PHONE	ENTRY #
24 Hour Fitness Usa Inc	7991	D	925 930-7900	18597
A F Evans Company Inc	7389	D	925 937-1700	16960
Accenture LLP	8742	D	925 974-5220	27295
Advanced Software Design Inc	7371	D	925 975-0691	15001
Alliedbarton Security Svcs LLC	7382	B	510 839-4041	16864
American Automobile	6411	D	925 279-2300	10590
Amerit Fleet Solutions Inc (PA)	7549	C	877 512-6374	17873
Anderson & Martella Inc	1796	E	925 934-3831	3473
Anesthesia Business Cons Inc	8011	D	925 951-1366	19348
Appery LLC	7372	D	925 602-5504	15581
Arch Mortgage Insurance Co	6351	D	800 909-4264	10489
Archer Norris A Prof Law Corp (PA)	8111	C	925 930-6600	23093

GEOGRAPHIC SECTION — WATSONVILLE, CA

Company	SIC	EMP	PHONE	ENTRY #
Argonaut Kensington Associates	8322	D	925 943-1121	23668
Ascend Learning LLC	8748	A	925 300-3203	27835
Ascent Services Group Inc	7379	B	925 627-4900	16325
AT&T Services	4813	B	925 943-4383	5523
Atria Senior Living Group Inc	6513	D	925 938-6611	11089
Axiom Global Technologies Inc	8748	C	925 393-5800	27844
Barcelon Associates MGT Corp	6531	D	925 627-7000	11313
Bay Imaging Cons Med Group Inc (PA)	8011	D	925 296-7150	19367
Bay Medical Management LLC	8011	D	925 296-7150	19368
BDS Plumbing Inc	1711	D	925 939-1004	2161
Bentley Systems Incorporated	7371	D	925 933-2525	15052
Berding & Weil LLP (PA)	8111	D	925 838-2090	23109
Bowles & Verna	8111	E	925 935-3300	23127
Bpg Storage Solutions Inc	8741	D	562 467-2000	26946
Brosamer & Wall LLC	6531	E	925 932-7900	11329
Brown and Caldwell (PA)	8711	C	925 937-9010	25706
C C Connection Inc	6531	C	925 937-0100	11335
C T Corporation System	8111	D	925 287-9801	23140
California Physicians Service	6324	C	925 927-7419	10262
California State Automobile (HQ)	6331	A	925 287-7600	10408
Carollo Engineers Inc	8742	D	925 932-1710	27372
Carollo Engineers PC (PA)	8711	D	925 932-1710	25720
Caswell Bay Inc	8082	D	925 933-8181	22400
CDM SMITH INC	8711	D	617 452-6000	25728
Century Vision Developers Inc	1542	E	925 682-4830	1524
Colliers Parrish Intl Inc	6531	D	925 279-1050	11448
Comerica Bank	6021	D	925 941-1900	9389
Computer Sciences Corporation	7376	C	702 558-8092	16276
Csaa Insurance Exchange (PA)	6411	C	800 922-8228	10683
Cytosport Holdings Inc	6719	C	707 751-3942	12056
Davidon Five Star Corp	6799	D	925 945-8000	12299
Diablo Realty Inc	6531	E	925 933-9300	11470
Engineered Soil Repairs Inc	1741	D	408 297-2150	2814
Erm-West Inc (DH)	8711	D	925 946-0455	25802
Exadel Inc (PA)	7372	D	925 363-9510	15660
Factory Mutual Insurance Co	6331	C	925 934-2200	10413
Fehr & Peers (PA)	8711	D	925 937-3200	25807
Friends Abroad	8611	D	925 939-9420	25087
Fugro Consultants Inc	8711	E	925 256-6070	25821
Galloway Lucchese Everson	8111	E	925 930-9090	23263
Glaspy & Glaspy A Prof Corp	8111	E	408 279-8844	23275
Golden Rain Foundation (PA)	6531	D	925 988-7700	11557
Golden Rain Foundation	8641	B	925 988-7800	25266
Gwf Power Systems LP	4931	C	925 933-7000	6287
Hagen Streiff Newton Oshiro	8721	D	925 941-1050	26364
Harvest Technical Service Inc	7361	C	925 937-4874	14669
Hcr Manorcare Med Svcs Fla LLC	8051	D	925 274-1325	20647
Hcr Manorcare Med Svcs Fla LLC	8051	C	925 975-5000	20653
HDR Engineering Inc	8711	D	925 974-2500	25856
Identity Theft Recovery & Moni	7299	D	888 269-2314	13767
Interstate Hotels Resorts Inc	8741	C	925 934-2500	27070
Izt Mortgage Inc (PA)	6163	E	925 946-1858	9930
John Muir Health (PA)	8062	A	925 939-3000	21618
John Muir Health	8062	E	925 947-5300	21619
John Muir Health	8062	D	925 939-3000	21620
John Muir Physician Network	8062	A	925 952-2701	21622
John Muir Physician Network	8062	B	925 939-3000	21625
John Muir Physician Network (PA)	8062	A	925 296-9700	21626
Kaiser Foundation Hospitals	8062	D	925 906-2380	21634
Kaiser Foundation Hospitals	8093	A	925 295-4145	22751
Kaiser Foundation Hospitals	8011	A	925 295-4000	19654
Kaiser Foundation Hospitals	8062	A	925 906-2000	21648
Kaiser Foundation Hospitals	6324	D	925 926-3000	10314
Kelleyamerit Holdings Inc	8741	A	877 512-6374	27089
Kilpatrick Twnsend Stckton LLP	8111	C	925 472-5000	23349
Kimco Staffing Services Inc	8099	E	925 256-3132	22987
Kolonaki (PA)	5137	E	415 554-8000	8393
Kpmg LLP	8721	E	925 946-1300	26389
Kropa Realty	6531	E	925 937-4040	11623
Leisure Sports Inc	7011	B	925 938-3058	12914
Lindsay Wildlife Museum	8412	D	925 935-1978	25024
Malikco LLC	7372	E	925 974-3555	15738
Marsh & McLennan Agency LLC	6411	A	510 273-8888	10774
Mason-Mcduffie Real Estate Inc	6531	D	925 932-1000	11660
Mc Namara Dodge Ney Beatt (PA)	8111	D	925 939-5330	23423
Mechanics Bank (DH)	6022	C	800 797-6324	9507
Merrill Lynch Pierce Fenner	6211	D	925 945-4800	10042
Miller Starr & Regalia A Pro (PA)	8111	D	925 935-9400	23433
Moffatt & Nichol	8711	E	925 944-5411	25973
Mp Tice Oaks Associates A CA	6531	D	650 356-2976	11699
Muir Labs	8071	B	925 947-3335	22244
Muir Orthopedic Specialists	8011	C	925 939-8585	19763
MWH Americas Inc	8711	C	925 627-4500	25980
New Covenant Care Cal Inc	8051	D	925 930-7733	20804
Newport Group Inc (PA)	8741	C	925 328-4540	27142
Northern Cal Ret Clks-Emp Fund	6733	C	925 746-7530	12196
Ocadian Care Centers LLC	8051	D	925 939-5820	20819
Olympic Investors Ltd	7997	D	925 322-8996	19021
Pacific Coast Bankers Bank	6022	D	415 399-1900	9513
Pacific Ygnacio Corporation	6519	D	925 939-3275	11262
Permanente Medical Group Inc	8011	D	925 906-2000	19854
Portal Insurance Agency Inc	6411	B	925 937-8787	10830
Qwest Corporation	4813	D	925 974-4908	5690
Ricoh Usa Inc	5044	C	925 938-2049	7071
Robert Half International Inc	7361	D	925 930-7766	14764
RPM Mortgage Inc	6162	D	925 627-7100	9894
RR Donnelley & Sons Company	4011	E	925 951-1320	3615
Savvius Inc (PA)	7371	D	925 937-3200	15442
SEC Pac Inc	6531	D	925 938-9200	11837
Sequoia Surgical Center LP	8011	D	925 935-6700	19987
Signature Painting & Cnstr Inc	1611	E	925 287-0444	1859
Stantec Architecture Inc	8712	D	925 941-1400	26256
Steele International Inc	8742	E	415 781-4300	27667
Sunrise Senior Living LLC	8051	D	925 932-3500	20968
Thomas Wirig Doll & Co Cpas	8721	D	925 939-2500	26451
Tony La Russas Animal RES Fnd	0742	D	925 256-1273	625
Travelers Property Cslty Corp	6411	B	925 945-4000	10908
Treasure Island Yacht Club	7997	D	925 939-0230	19113
Vitas Healthcare Corp Cal	8082	D	925 930-9373	22602
Vodafone Americas Inc	4812	D	925 210-3812	5434
Waste Mgt Collectn & Recycl	4212	C	925 935-8900	4092
Wells Fargo Bank National Assn	6021	D	925 746-3718	9439
Wells Fargo Home Mortgage Inc	6162	C	925 288-7100	9905
Wells Fargo Insur Svcs USA Inc	6411	D	925 988-1700	10933
West Unfied Cmrnnctons Svcs Inc	7389	D	925 988-7112	17622
William Lettis & Associates	8733	D	713 369-5400	26826
Windsor Capital Group Inc	7011	D	925 934-2000	13425
XI Specialty Insurance Corp	6351	D	925 942-6142	10497
Yapstone Inc (PA)	7389	C	866 289-5977	17635
Yupana LLC	8711	E	925 482-0657	26156
ZMC Hotels LLC	7011	D	925 933-4000	13448

WALNUT GROVE, CA - Sacramento County

Company	SIC	EMP	PHONE	ENTRY #
Ryde Hotel LLC	7011	E	916 776-1318	13182

WASCO, CA - Kern County

Company	SIC	EMP	PHONE	ENTRY #
Community Action Partnr Kern	8351	C	661 758-0129	24442
Community Support Options Inc	8322	C	661 758-5331	23778
Darr & Pitcairn AG Inc	0722	E	661 758-5156	493
Demler Egg Ranch	0252	E	661 758-4577	444
R Mora Farm Labor	0761	E	661 746-2858	681
South Valley Almond Co LLC	5159	E	661 391-9000	8966

WATERFORD, CA - Stanislaus County

Company	SIC	EMP	PHONE	ENTRY #
Foster Poultry Farms	0254	E	209 394-7901	455
Frazier Nut Farms Inc	0173	E	209 522-1406	201
Stanislaus Consol Fire Prot	7389	E	209 549-8404	17500

WATSONVILLE, CA - Santa Cruz County

Company	SIC	EMP	PHONE	ENTRY #
3-Way Farms (PA)	0181	E	831 722-0748	263
Amar Transportation Inc (PA)	4213	C	831 728-8209	4105
Ameri-Kleen	7349	B	831 722-8888	14223
California Pajarosa	0181	D	831 722-6374	271
California Pajarosa Floral	5193	C	831 722-6374	9182
Camflor Inc	0181	C	831 726-1330	272
CB North LLC	0191	A	831 786-1642	350
Cellco Partnership	4812	D	831 786-0267	5300
CF Watsonville LLC	8051	D	831 724-7505	20449
CF Watsonville East LLC	8051	D	310 574-3733	20450
CF Watsonville West LLC	8051	D	831 724-7505	20451
Community Action Brd of Snt Cr	8641	E	831 724-0206	25239
Couch Distributing Company Inc	5181	C	831 724-0649	9048
Driscoll Strawberry Assoc Inc (PA)	5148	D	831 424-0506	8718
E K T Farms	0191	E	831 724-0832	358
Elkhorn Berry Farms LLC	0191	E	831 728-2472	359
Elyxir Distributing LLC	5181	C	831 761-6400	9055
Encompass Community Services	8322	B	831 724-3885	23960
Fedex Ground Package Sys Inc	4213	D	831 786-0751	4182
Field Fresh Farms LLC	5148	E	831 722-1402	8724
Fitz Fresh Inc	0182	E	831 763-4440	329
G I L C Inc	1521	E	831 724-1011	1179
Granit-Bayashi 2 A Joint Ventr	1623	D	831 724-1011	1935
Granite Construction Company (HQ)	1611	C	831 724-1011	1777
Granite Construction Inc (PA)	1611	C	831 724-1011	1785
Granite Rock Co (PA)	1442	B	831 768-2000	1103
Guy George	0171	E	831 728-2410	114
International Almond Exchange	0173	E	831 728-4534	202
Jacobs Farm/Del Cabo Inc	4212	E	831 460-3500	4029
Kitayama Bros Inc	0181	E	831 722-2912	296
Kitayama Brothers Inc	0181	D	831 722-8118	297
Maggiora Brosdrilling Inc (PA)	1781	E	831 724-1338	3358
Marty Franich Leasing Co	7515	E	831 722-2463	17702

WATSONVILLE, CA

	SIC	EMP	PHONE	ENTRY #
Miguel Ramos	0291	D	831 761-9941	469
Monte Vsta Mem Schlrshp Assoc	8748	E	831 722-8178	27992
Monterey Bay Acadamy Laundry	7211	D	831 728-1481	13504
Monterey Bay Bouquet Acquisit	5193	C	831 786-2700	9202
Monterey Mushrooms Inc (PA)	0182	E	831 763-5300	336
Morgan Farm LLC	0171	D	831 726-5120	123
Oceanside Laundry LLC	7215	D	831 722-4358	13576
Optics East Inc (PA)	5048	C	831 763-6931	7336
Pajaro Valley Greenhouses (PA)	5193	D	831 722-2773	9207
Pajaro Valley Prevntn & Studen	8322	D	831 728-6445	24120
Pt Logistics Inc	4212	E	831 728-4535	4051
Ramco Enterprises LP	7361	A	831 722-3370	14742
Reiter Affl Companies LLC	0171	D	831 786-4244	129
Rio Mesa Farms LLC	0171	D	831 728-1965	131
Salud Para La Gente	8011	C	831 728-0222	19937
Santa Cruz County of	8011	E	831 763-8400	19958
Santa Cruz Metro	4131	B	831 426-6080	3887
Suncrest Nurseries Inc	5193	D	831 728-2595	9214
Superior Foods Inc	5142	D	831 728-3691	8571
Sweetbrier Development	0212	E	831 722-5577	413
T T Miyasaka Inc	0171	B	831 722-3871	136
Uyeda Farm	0171	E	831 722-6345	137
Uyematsu Inc	0171	D	831 724-2200	138
Vps Companies Inc (PA)	5142	D	831 724-7551	8572
Waste Mgt Collectn & Recycl	4953	D	831 768-9505	6604
Watsonville Coast Produce Inc	5148	C	831 722-3851	8787
Watsonville Community Hospital	8062	A	831 724-4741	22028
West Coast Hospitals Inc	8059	D	831 722-3581	21419

WEAVERVILLE, CA - Trinity County

	SIC	EMP	PHONE	ENTRY #
Mountain Comm Hlth Cre Dist	8062	C	530 623-5541	21755
Mountain Comm Hlth Cre Dist (PA)	8062	C	530 623-5541	21756
United Parcel Service Inc OH	4215	C	530 623-3938	4437

WEED, CA - Siskiyou County

	SIC	EMP	PHONE	ENTRY #
Lassen Canyon Nursery Inc	0171	D	530 938-4720	118
Personnel Preference Inc	7363	C	530 938-3909	14922

WEST COVINA, CA - Los Angeles County

	SIC	EMP	PHONE	ENTRY #
Assisted Home Recovery Inc	8999	D	626 915-5595	28115
Big Lgue Dreams Consulting LLC	1542	D	626 839-1100	1506
BKK Corporation (PA)	4953	D	626 965-0911	6444
Bowlmor AMF Corp	7933	D	626 960-3636	18512
Certified Nursing Registry Inc	7361	C	626 912-1877	14623
Citrus Valley Hospice	8051	D	626 859-2263	20458
Citrus Valley Medical Ctr Inc (PA)	8062	A	626 962-4011	21488
Citrus Valley Medical Ctr Inc	8062	A	626 963-8411	21490
Citrus Vly Hlth Partners Inc	8011	B	626 962-4011	19439
Clara Baldwin Stocker Home	8059	E	626 962-7151	21186
Combined Management Svcs Inc	6411	C	626 856-2263	10676
Concorde Battery Corporation	4225	C	626 962-4006	4537
Doctors Hospital W Covina Inc	8062	C	626 338-8481	21544
East Valley Cmnty Hlth Ctr Inc (PA)	8093	D	626 919-3402	22726
Eastland Tower Partnership	6519	E	626 858-2000	11251
First Financial Credit Union (PA)	6061	D	626 814-4611	9599
Foothill Transit Service Corp (PA)	4111	D	626 967-3147	3653
Futuro Infantil Hispano Ffa	8322	E	626 339-1824	23991
Golden Living LLC	8051	D	626 962-3368	20614
Harris & Ruth Painting Contg (PA)	1721	D	626 960-4004	2454
In Home Health Inc	8082	D	419 254-7841	22482
Jpmorgan Chase Bank Nat Assn	6035	D	626 919-3129	9575
Kaiser Foundation Hospitals	8062	E	866 319-4269	21654
Kent Daniels & Associates Inc	7361	C	626 859-5018	14692
Lead Staffing Corporation	7363	D	800 928-5561	14898
Master Lightning SEC Solutions	7381	D	310 419-2915	16732
Matrix Group International Inc	1521	D	626 960-6205	1214
Paul Calvo and Company	6531	E	626 814-8000	11744
Permanente Kaiser Intl	8011	C	626 960-4844	19832
Premier Auto W Covina LLC	7538	D	626 858-7202	17811
Queen of Valley Hospital	8621	A	626 962-4011	25152
Regent Assisted Living Inc	8361	D	626 332-3344	24782
Reynolds Buick/GMC Trucks	7515	D	626 966-4461	17705
RM Galicia Inc	7322	C	626 813-6200	14044
Solugenix Corporation	7379	D	866 749-7658	16485
South Hills Country Club	7997	D	626 339-1231	19083
Southern Cal Prmnnte Med Group	8011	D	626 960-4844	20027
Southern Cal Spcialty Care Inc	8062	D	626 339-5451	21903
Think Together	8351	A	626 373-2311	24525
Universal Bank (PA)	6035	D	626 854-2818	9583
West Covina Medical Clinic Inc (PA)	8011	C	626 960-8614	20235
Wicoro Inc (HQ)	8059	E	626 962-4489	21421

WEST HILLS, CA - Los Angeles County

	SIC	EMP	PHONE	ENTRY #
Care 4 U LLC	8322	D	818 593-7911	23702
Damon Electrical	1731	D	818 426-3450	2571
Dlh Davinci LLC	8072	D	818 703-5100	22304
HCA Inc	8062	C	818 676-4000	21594
Intelex Systems Inc	7371	D	818 518-1100	15244
Unilab Corporation (HQ)	8071	B	818 737-6000	22292

WEST HOLLYWOOD, CA - Los Angeles County

	SIC	EMP	PHONE	ENTRY #
19 Entertainment Worldwide LLC	7929	D	310 777-1940	18447
24 Hour Fitness Usa Inc	7991	E	310 652-7440	18587
4g Wireless Inc	4813	D	310 310-7998	5448
Aries Filterworks	5085	E	323 262-1600	7922
AT&T Corp	4812	D	323 874-7000	5272
Atlas Entertainment Inc	7812	E	310 786-4900	18047
Black & White TV Inc	7622	D	310 855-1040	17906
Cellco Partnership	4812	D	323 603-0369	5359
Chamber Maid Lessee Inc	7011	D	310 657-7400	12509
Coldwer Banker Previews	6531	C	310 278-9470	11440
Cpe Hr Inc	8742	D	310 270-9800	27393
Cpe Peo Inc	7363	D	310 385-1000	14866
Crunch LLC	7991	D	323 654-4550	18623
Endemol	7922	D	310 860-9914	18390
Engage Bdr Inc	7311	E	310 954-0751	13844
Graphic Orb Inc	8742	D	310 967-2350	27454
Harpo	7922	D	312 633-1000	18396
Harpo Productions Inc	7812	C	312 633-1000	18090
Hmbl LLC	7011	D	323 656-8090	12746
Hob Entertainment LLC	7929	C	323 848-5100	18470
Iw Group (PA)	7311	D	310 289-5500	13869
Jack Morton Worldwide Inc	7311	D	310 967-2400	13871
Le Montrose Hotel	7011	D	310 855-1115	12912
Lexington Group International (PA)	8051	D	310 385-1071	20722
Modani Los Angeles LLC	5021	E	310 652-2323	6825
Modern Hr Inc	7291	B	310 270-9800	13725
N Compass International	8742	D	323 785-1700	27556
Ols Hotels & Resorts LP	7011	D	310 855-1115	13040
Outrigger Hotels Hawaii	7011	D	323 491-9015	13051
Own LLC	4841	D	323 602-5500	6011
Quixote Mm LLC	7819	E	323 851-5030	18249
Quixote Studios LLC (PA)	7359	D	323 851-5030	14573
Rogers & Cowan (HQ)	8743	D	310 854-8100	27766
S&F Management Company Inc (PA)	8051	D	310 385-1090	20885
Snf Management	8741	D	310 385-1090	27219
Suissa Miller Advertising LLC	7311	D	310 392-9666	13925
Super Photo Laboratory Inc	7384	D	323 512-0247	16958
Ticketmaster Entertainment LLC	7922	A	800 653-8000	18440
US Control Group Inc	8322	D	888 500-7090	24273
Valadon Hotel LLC	7011	D	310 854-1114	13373
W-Bel Age LLC	7011	D	310 854-1111	13386
White Rabbit Partners Inc	8361	C	310 975-1450	24856

WEST SACRAMENTO, CA - Yolo County

	SIC	EMP	PHONE	ENTRY #
A Csg-Nova Joint Venture	1611	D	916 371-7303	1722
ABM Janitorial Services Inc	7349	B	916 374-1739	14204
AEP Span Inc	1761	D	916 372-0933	3137
Ahtna Government Services Corp	1542	D	916 372-2000	1485
Allen L Bender Inc	1542	C	916 372-2190	1488
American Metals Corporation (HQ)	5051	C	916 371-7700	7356
AT&T Services Inc	4813	D	916 376-2006	5561
Aus Decking Inc	1771	D	916 373-5320	3227
Big City Access Inc (PA)	5082	D	916 374-4090	7762
Blazona Concrete Cnstr Inc	1542	D	916 375-8337	1507
Brown Construction Inc	1522	D	916 374-8616	1298
Burger Rhblitation Systems Inc	8049	D	916 617-2400	20310
Bytheways Manufacturing Inc	5023	B	916 453-1212	6851
Califor State Teach Retire Sys (DH)	6371	C	800 228-5453	10543
California Chamber Commerce	8611	D	916 928-2124	25082
California Correctnl Peace Ofc (PA)	8631	D	916 372-6060	25168
California School Boards Assn	8611	D	916 371-4691	25123
California Sierra Express Inc	4731	C	916 375-7070	5039
Capay Incorporated (PA)	0161	D	916 303-7145	48
Capital Beverage Company (PA)	5181	C	916 371-8164	9045
Cardinal Health Inc	5122	C	916 372-9880	8246
Cgi Technologies Solutions Inc	8731	E	916 281-3200	26495
Cirks Construction Inc	1542	D	916 362-5460	1527
Collins Electrical Company Inc	1731	C	209 466-3691	2555
Core-Mark International Inc	5149	C	916 927-0795	8823
Creative Living Options Inc	8361	D	916 372-2102	24619
Dbi Beverage Sacramento (HQ)	5182	C	916 373-5700	9094
Dennis Blazona Construction	1771	D	916 375-8337	3255
Dependable Highway Express Inc	4212	D	916 374-0782	4007
Devine & Son Trucking Co Inc (PA)	4449	C	559 486-7440	4721
Frito-Lay North America Inc	5145	C	916 372-5400	8614
Holt of California	5082	C	916 373-4100	7773
Idexx Reference Labs Inc	8071	D	916 372-4200	22226
Jacmar Ddc LLC	5149	D	916 372-9795	8859
McKesson Corporation	5122	C	916 372-3655	8280
Miyamoto International Inc (PA)	8711	D	916 373-1995	25970
Mounting Systems Inc	1711	B	916 374-8872	2297
Nor-Cal Beverage Co Inc (PA)	5181	B	916 372-0600	9077

Mergent email: customerrelations@mergent.com
2017 Directory of California Wholesalers and Services Companies
(P-0000) Products & Services Section entry number
(PA)=Parent Co (HQ)=Headquarters (DH)=Div Headquarters

GEOGRAPHIC SECTION

WHITTIER, CA

	SIC	EMP	PHONE	ENTRY #
Nor-Cal Produce Inc	5148	C	916 373-0830	8755
Oak Harbor Freight Lines Inc	4213	D	916 371-3960	4239
Occupnl Urgnt Care Hlth Syst	8099	B	916 374-4600	23010
Pacific Gas and Electric Co	4911	C	916 375-5005	6163
Parts	7513	D	916 371-3115	17643
PC World Corp **(PA)**	4813	C	240 855-8988	5683
Phillips Pet Food and Supplies **(PA)**	5149	D	916 373-7300	8907
Pitco Foods	5141	D	916 372-7772	8510
Quad/Graphics Inc	7311	D	916 371-9500	13903
Ramos Oil Co Inc **(PA)**	5171	D	916 371-2570	9008
Redstone Print & Mail Inc	8742	D	916 318-6450	27612
River Bend Nursing Home Inc	8051	D	916 371-1890	20873
River Cy Geoprofessionals Inc	8711	D	916 372-1434	26042
Rural Cmnty Assistance Corp **(PA)**	8322	D	916 447-2854	24161
Sacramento River Cats Baseball	7941	E	916 376-4700	18561
Sacramento Television Stns Inc **(DH)**	4833	C	916 374-1452	5908
Sacramento-Yolo Port District	4491	C	916 371-8000	4755
Safeway Inc	4225	C	916 373-3900	4637
Serving Seniors LLC	8082	D	916 372-9640	22560
Siemens Industry Inc	7629	D	916 371-2600	17944
Singley Enterprises **(PA)**	5031	E	916 427-4573	6962
Ssa Pacific Inc	4491	D	916 374-1866	4760
Testamerica Laboratories Inc	8734	D	916 373-5600	26893
Tonys Fine Foods **(HQ)**	5147	B	916 374-4000	8688
Tricor America Inc	4215	C	916 371-1704	4431
Triton Tower Inc **(PA)**	1623	D	916 375-8546	2003
U S Army Corps of Engineers	8711	D	916 557-7491	26109
United Parcel Service Inc OH	4215	C	916 373-4076	4442
UPS Ground Freight Inc	4213	D	916 371-9101	4293
Valley Toxicology Service Inc	8071	D	916 371-5440	22296
Vss International Inc **(HQ)**	1611	D	916 373-1500	1882
Wallace-Kuhl Investments LLC **(PA)**	8711	D	916 372-1434	26144
Walton Engineering Inc	1799	D	916 372-1888	3598
Xyratex Technology Ltd	5045	E	916 375-8181	7213
Youngs Market Company LLC	5182	E	916 617-4402	9123

WESTLAKE VILLAGE, CA - Ventura County

	SIC	EMP	PHONE	ENTRY #
5 Nine Group Inc	7371	C	805 880-2948	14992
Adelson Testan Brundo Novel **(PA)**	8111	E	805 367-5663	23081
Allen Construction Inc	1751	D	818 879-5334	3029
Allied Interstate Inc **(DH)**	7322	D	818 575-5400	14016
Alston & Bird LLP	8111	B	202 239-3673	23090
Anthem Insurance Companies Inc	6324	D	805 557-6655	10257
AP Global Inc	5065	D	818 707-3167	7520
Appraiser Loft LLC	6531	E	858 832-8334	11300
Bankcard USA Merchant Srvc	5044	D	818 597-7000	7041
Baxter Healthcare Corporation	5122	A	805 372-3000	8235
Blue Cross of California **(DH)**	6324	C	805 557-6050	10260
Burton-Way House Ltd A CA	7011	B	805 214-8075	12473
California Coml Inv Group Inc	8748	E	805 495-8400	27862
CIT Bank National Association	6021	D	805 496-4034	9367
Citibank N A	6021	D	805 497-7361	9376
Conversant LLC **(HQ)**	7375	C	818 575-4500	16224
Cornerstone Healthcare Inc	8052	C	805 777-1133	21074
Country Floral Supply Inc **(PA)**	5193	D	805 520-8026	9186
Dennis M McCoy & Sons Inc **(PA)**	1611	E	818 874-3872	1763
Digital Insight Corporation	7375	C	818 879-1010	16227
Dole Food Company Inc **(HQ)**	0179	C	818 874-4000	254
Dole Fresh Fruit Company **(DH)**	5148	B	818 874-4000	8717
Dole Holding Company LLC	0179	A	818 879-6600	255
Ernst & Young LLP	8721	C	805 778-7000	26345
Fdsi Logistics Inc	8742	E	818 971-3300	27432
Four Seasons Westlake	7011	D	818 575-3000	12649
Frontier California Inc	5065	A	805 372-6000	7569
Frontier California Inc	4813	D	805 372-6000	5611
G4s Secure Solutions (usa)	7381	C	818 889-1113	16656
Gemmm Corp	6531	D	818 522-0740	11552
Hanover Builders Inc	1731	E	818 706-2279	2606
Hyatt Corporation	7011	C	805 557-1234	12823
Integrated Dynmc Solutions Inc	7371	E	818 879-8797	15242
Intellirisk Management Corp	7322	E	818 575-5400	14035
International Advisors LLC	8748	D	497 961-7988	27953
Ipayment Holdings Inc **(HQ)**	7389	D	310 436-5294	17252
Jackie Hoofring	7361	E	818 961-7272	14688
Jri Inc	5065	E	818 706-2424	7591
Lantz Security Systems Inc	7381	B	805 496-5775	16720
Mediaplex Inc **(DH)**	7311	D	818 575-4036	13884
Microfinancial Incorporated	7359	C	805 367-8900	14561
Move Co	6531	C	805 557-2300	11697
Move Sales Inc **(DH)**	7299	D	805 557-2300	13780
Mws Precision Wire Inds Inc	5051	D	818 991-8553	7385
National Builder Services Inc	7363	D	714 634-7800	14915
North Ranch Country Club	7997	C	818 889-3531	19015
Northstar Media Packg Svcs LLC	7819	D	805 650-0990	18241
Ownit Mortgage Solutions Inc	6162	B	513 872-6922	9879
Pacific Compensation Insur Co	6331	C	818 575-8500	10452
Pds Tech Inc	7379	A	805 418-9862	16455
Pleasant Holidays LLC **(HQ)**	4725	B	818 991-3390	4998
Premium Rock Drywall Inc	1742	D	818 676-3350	2958
Pyj V A California Ltd Partnr	7992	D	805 495-8437	18773
Registry Monitoring Ins Srvcs	6411	D	818 933-6350	10854
Remax Olson	6531	D	805 267-4929	11808
Sdg Enterprises	1711	D	805 777-7978	2362
Securitas SEC Svcs USA Inc	7381	B	818 706-4909	16795
Securitas SEC Svcs USA Inc	7381	C	818 706-6800	16813
Select Home Care	8082	C	805 777-3855	22558
Sky Court USA Inc	7011	C	805 497-9991	13269
Southern Cal Orthpd Inst LP	8011	D	818 901-6600	20016
Spad Holdings LLC	7991	D	805 496-9978	18688
Sunrise Senior Living LLC	8051	D	805 557-1100	20977
Triplecurve LLC	8742	D	855 874-2878	27701
Troop Real Estate Inc	6531	D	805 402-3028	11884
United Cp/S Chldrns Fndn La	8322	E	805 494-1141	24268
United Parcel Service Inc OH	7389	A	818 735-0945	17561
University Cal Los Angeles	8011	E	805 494-6920	20163
Velocity Commercial Capitl LLC	6531	E	818 532-3700	11897
Verizon Communications Inc	7389	C	805 390-5417	17586
Warner Pacific Insur Svcs Inc **(PA)**	6411	C	408 298-4049	10927
Westlake Village Inn	7011	C	805 496-1667	13405
Westminster Presbyterian Ch	8351	E	818 889-1491	24532
WF Cinema Holdings LP	7832	C	805 379-8966	18355
Young Estates	6531	D	805 446-1800	11931
Young Realtors	6531	D	805 497-0947	11932

WESTMINSTER, CA - Orange County

	SIC	EMP	PHONE	ENTRY #
Abrazar Inc	8322	D	714 893-3581	23642
Anderson News LLC	5192	D	714 892-7766	9160
B & E Farms Inc	0171	E	714 893-8166	104
Consoldted Med Bo-Analysis Inc	8071	D	714 657-7389	22203
County of Orange	8322	D	714 896-7188	23870
County of Orange	8322	D	714 896-7500	23872
Edco Drywall Inc	1742	E	714 799-9886	2891
Extended Care Hosp Westminster	8051	C	714 891-2769	20562
Helping Hands Sanctuary of Ida	8051	D	714 892-6686	20666
Kindred Hospital-Westminster	8062	B	714 372-3014	21691
Lbs Financial Credit Union **(PA)**	6111	C	714 893-5111	9734
Maxwell Petersen Associates	8742	D	714 230-3150	27530
National Fail Safe Inc	1731	E	562 493-5447	2661
Orange County One Stop Center	7361	D	714 241-4900	14716
Pyramid Logistics Services Inc **(PA)**	4213	D	714 903-2600	4247
Snowbounders Ski Club	7997	D	714 892-4897	19082
South West Sun Solar Inc	5074	E	714 582-3909	7732
Southern California Edison Co	4911	C	714 934-0838	6216
Southern California Edison Co	4911	D	714 895-0420	6233
Southern California Edison Co	4911	C	714 895-0163	6236
Thompson Family Farms LLC	0191	E	714 848-7536	399
Vina Holdings Inc	8082	D	714 622-5334	22589
Westminster Housing Partenrs	6531	E	714 891-3000	11919
Westview Services Inc	8331	D	714 418-2090	24406

WHEATLAND, CA - Yuba County

	SIC	EMP	PHONE	ENTRY #
Bear River Veterinary Clinic	0752	D	530 633-2957	636
Wheatland School District	6531	D	530 633-3135	11920

WHITEWATER, CA - Riverside County

	SIC	EMP	PHONE	ENTRY #
Painted Hills Power	1611	E	760 406-1771	1840

WHITTIER, CA - Los Angeles County

	SIC	EMP	PHONE	ENTRY #
24 Hour Fitness Usa Inc	7991	D	562 943-3771	18596
Ahmc Whittier Hosp Med Ctr LP	8062	A	562 945-3561	21440
Aids Healthcare Foundation	8011	B	562 693-2654	19328
Assocted Reproduction Svcs Inc	7334	C	562 696-1981	14112
Beachside Realtors	6531	D	562 947-7834	11316
Bright Health Physicians **(PA)**	8011	D	562 947-8478	19378
Caldwell Realty	6531	D	562 907-5655	11338
California Med Response Inc	4119	D	562 968-1818	3779
Capc Inc	8399	C	562 693-8826	24886
Cellco Partnership	4812	D	562 789-0911	5372
Cintas Corporation No 3	7213	D	562 692-8741	13543
City of Whittier	8322	D	562 567-9446	23760
Complete Landscape Care Inc	0782	D	562 946-4441	829
County of Los Angeles	8322	D	562 908-3119	23838
County of Los Angeles	4151	D	562 945-2581	3917
Credit Union Southern Cal **(PA)**	6061	D	562 698-8326	9592
Cypress College Foundation	8641	D	714 484-7128	25248
Del Rio Health Care Inc	8051	D	562 947-5221	20514
Ensign Group Inc	8051	D	562 947-7817	20539
Fedex Freight Corporation	4231	B	800 288-0743	4711
Freedom Painting Inc	1721	E	562 696-0785	2443
Friendly Hills Country Club	7997	C	562 698-0331	18954
Ghg Properties LLC	7011	D	562 945-8511	12666
Gourmet India Food Company LLC	5149	D	562 698-9763	8848
Grand Supercenter Inc	5141	D	562 318-3451	8483

WHITTIER, CA

	SIC	EMP	PHONE	ENTRY #
Greenleaf Hotel Inc	7011	C	562 945-8511	12678
Helpline Youth Counseling (PA)	8322	E	562 273-0722	24007
In2vision Programs LLC	8322	C	562 789-8888	24022
Inclusion Services LLC	8322	C	562 945-2000	24023
Intercommunity Child	8322	D	562 692-0383	24030
Intercommunity Dialysis Svcs	8092	E	562 696-1841	22630
Interhealth Corporation (PA)	8062	A	562 698-0811	21613
Interhealth Services Inc (HQ)	8082	D	562 698-0811	22486
International Home Mortgage	6162	D	562 945-7753	9861
J P Carroll Co Inc	1721	D	323 660-9230	2457
John Shannon Mc Gee Co Inc	5063	D	562 789-1777	7448
Kaiser Foundation Hospitals	8062	E	562 907-3510	21667
League of Wmen Voters Whittier	8651	E	562 947-5818	25481
Longwood Management Corp	8062	D	562 693-5240	21719
Mac Pro Inc	7299	D	562 623-4300	13773
Magnell Associate Inc	4225	C	626 271-1420	4595
Mercedes Diaz Homes Inc	1521	D	562 698-7479	1218
Merrill Gardens LLC	8361	D	562 693-0505	24735
NLc Enterprises Incorporated	7389	E	562 693-3590	17361
Oltmans Construction Co (PA)	1541	D	562 948-4242	1454
Oltmans Investment Company	6512	E	562 948-4242	11028
Orchard - Post Acute Care Ctr	8051	A	562 693-7701	20829
Peoples Care Inc	8351	C	562 320-0174	24500
Pep Boys Manny Moe Jack of Cal	7538	E	562 908-4400	17810
Plaza De La Raza Child Develop	8351	D	562 695-1070	24503
Presbyterian Intrcmmnty Hosptl (PA)	8062	A	562 698-0811	21805
Rio Hondo Education Consortium	8322	C	562 945-0150	24159
Rose Hills Company (HQ)	6553	A	562 699-0921	12036
Rose Hills Holdings Corp (PA)	6553	B	562 699-0921	12037
Rose Hills Mortuary Inc	7261	D	562 699-0921	13714
S CA University Hlth Sciences	8041	E	562 947-8755	20298
Sanitation District	4953	D	562 699-5204	6560
Sanitation Districts	4953	A	562 908-4288	6561
Southern California Gas Co	4923	D	562 803-3341	6264
Southern California Mtl Hdlg (DH)	5084	C	562 949-1006	7891
Southern Fresh Prod Provs Inc	5148	C	562 236-2784	8776
Southern Fresh Produce Inc	5148	C	562 236-2784	8777
Summerville Senior Living Inc	8361	D	562 943-3724	24825
Transportation California Dept	1611	C	562 692-0823	1877
Whittier Hospital Med Ctr Inc	8062	C	562 945-3561	22032
Whole Child	8322	D	562 692-0383	24290

WILDOMAR, CA - Riverside County

	SIC	EMP	PHONE	ENTRY #
Asr Constructors Inc	1542	B	951 779-6580	1493
Classic Installs Inc	1796	D	951 678-9906	3474
Diverscape Inc	0782	D	951 245-1686	841
Inland Vly Rgional Med Ctr Inc (HQ)	8062	E	951 677-1111	21612
Kaiser Foundation Hospitals	8062	E	951 353-2000	21650
Kilcrew Productions	7389	D	619 564-2080	17271
Lake Elsinore Unified Schl Dst	4151	D	951 253-7830	3942
S Taylor Construction Inc	1521	C	310 291-4505	1250
Solar Service Center Inc	1711	D	951 928-3300	2373
Sunpro Solar Inc	1796	D	951 678-7733	3480

WILLIAMS, CA - Colusa County

	SIC	EMP	PHONE	ENTRY #
ACC-Gwg LLC	8748	D	530 473-2827	27808
Elvira Sandoval	7361	C	530 473-5718	14647
La Grande Farm	0161	D	530 473-5923	78
Valley West Health Care Inc (PA)	8059	D	530 473-5321	21408

WILLITS, CA - Mendocino County

	SIC	EMP	PHONE	ENTRY #
Adventist Health System/West	8082	C	707 459-1818	22341
Brooktrails Lodge LLC	7011	D	707 459-1596	12472
Ensign Willits LLC	8059	D	707 459-5592	21212
Sherwood Valley Rancheria	7011	D	707 459-7330	13248
Shusters Transportation Inc	4212	D	707 459-4131	4064
Willits Hospital Inc	8062	B	707 459-6801	22033
Willits Seniors Inc	8322	D	707 459-6826	24291

WILLOW CREEK, CA - Humboldt County

	SIC	EMP	PHONE	ENTRY #
Northcoast Childrens Services	8322	D	530 629-2283	24106

WILLOWS, CA - Glenn County

	SIC	EMP	PHONE	ENTRY #
County of Glenn	8099	D	530 934-6582	22925
County of Glenn	1611	C	530 934-6530	1755
County of Glenn	8322	D	530 934-6453	23810
County of Glenn	8322	C	530 934-6514	23811
County of Glenn	8093	D	530 934-6582	22696
Glenn Cnty Humn Resource Agcy	8331	C	530 934-6510	24342
Glenn Medical Center Inc	8062	D	530 934-4681	21578
Kumar Hotels Inc	7011	D	530 934-8900	12892
Paul P Ortner DDS	7011	D	530 934-4603	13081
Sunbridge Healthcare LLC	8052	D	530 934-2834	21114

WILMINGTON, CA - Los Angeles County

	SIC	EMP	PHONE	ENTRY #
Ajc Sandblasting Inc	1799	D	562 436-3606	3485
American Integrated Svcs Inc (PA)	8744	E	310 522-1168	27773
Ampam Parks Mechanical Inc	1711	A	310 835-1532	2142
Banc of California Inc	6021	A	310 835-9826	9318
Boys and Girls Clubs of The La	8641	E	310 833-1322	25215
California Cartage Company LLC	4226	D	562 590-8591	4677
City of Los Angeles	4911	A	310 522-1750	6114
City of Los Angeles	4173	B	310 732-3550	3955
Conglobal Industries LLC	4226	D	310 518-2850	4680
County of Los Angeles	8011	D	310 518-8800	19472
Estes Express Lines Inc	4213	D	310 549-7306	4154
Fast Lane Transportation Inc (PA)	4213	D	562 435-3000	4157
Harbor Industrial Services	7353	D	310 522-1193	14483
Konoike-Pacific California Inc (HQ)	4222	D	310 518-1000	4496
Los Angeles Unified School Dst	8322	C	310 518-1128	24073
Marine Technical Services Inc	7389	D	310 549-8030	17311
Pacific Sea Food Co Inc	5146	E	310 835-4343	8647
Pasha Stevedoring Terminals LP	4491	E	310 233-2006	4752
Pasha Stevedoring Terminals LP	4424	D	415 927-6353	4719
Potential Industries Inc (PA)	4953	C	310 807-4466	6515
Praxair Inc	5169	D	562 983-2100	8997
Public Hlth Fndation Entps Inc	8099	D	310 518-2835	23036
South Bay Ctr For Counseling	8322	D	310 414-2090	24220
Star Fisheries	5146	D	310 549-4992	8657
Sun Pacific Trucking Inc	4213	D	310 830-4528	4269
Trapac LLC (HQ)	4491	E	310 513-1572	4764
Wwl Vehicle Svcs Americas Inc	4225	C	310 835-8806	4674

WINCHESTER, CA - Riverside County

	SIC	EMP	PHONE	ENTRY #
Help Hospitalized Veterans II	8322	D	951 926-4500	24006
Metropolitan Water District	4941	D	951 926-7095	6378
Metropolitan Water District	4941	D	951 926-1501	6380
Mind Dragon Inc	8748	E	877 367-6060	27990
Skywest Airlines Inc	4512	D	951 926-9511	4821

WINDSOR, CA - Sonoma County

	SIC	EMP	PHONE	ENTRY #
Arete Associates	8731	D	818 885-2200	26476
Bacchus Vineyard MGT LLC	8741	D	707 837-8304	26934
Engineering & Tstg Svcs Corp	8711	B	707 838-1113	25793
Fedex Ground Package Sys Inc	4213	C	707 836-9890	4179
Happy Pet Co	0742	E	707 586-8660	619
Landcare USA LLC	0782	D	707 836-1460	891
North Bay Construction Inc	1771	E	707 836-8500	3303
Petersen Builders Inc	1521	D	707 838-3035	1235
Richards Grove Saralees Vinyrd	0172	D	707 837-9200	178
Robert A Hall	7363	D	707 837-8564	14939
Selex Inc	1799	D	707 836-8836	3580
Shook & Waller Cnstr Inc	1751	B	707 578-3933	3088
Windsor Golf Club Inc	7992	D	707 838-7888	18799

WINNETKA, CA - Los Angeles County

	SIC	EMP	PHONE	ENTRY #
Clayton Place Associates Inc	6531	D	818 702-0115	11396
Memon Aamir	7381	E	818 339-8810	16734

WINTERHAVEN, CA - Imperial County

	SIC	EMP	PHONE	ENTRY #
Indian Health Service	8062	D	760 572-0217	21609
Quechan Indian Tribe	7999	B	760 572-2413	19265

WINTERS, CA - Yolo County

	SIC	EMP	PHONE	ENTRY #
Andres Bermudez	0761	D	530 795-1000	649
Button & Turkovich	0191	D	530 795-2090	348
Mariani Nut Company	0723	D	530 662-3311	560
Mariani Nut Company Inc (PA)	0173	D	530 795-3311	204
Mariani Nut Company Inc	0173	D	530 795-1272	205
Mariani Nut Company Inc	0173	D	530 795-2225	206
Ramos Orchards	0173	D	530 795-4748	208
Terra Firma Farm Corp	0161	E	530 795-2473	99

WINTON, CA - Merced County

	SIC	EMP	PHONE	ENTRY #
Central Valley Oprtnty Ctr Inc (PA)	8331	D	209 357-0062	24322
P H Ranch Inc	0241	E	209 358-5111	438

WOODBRIDGE, CA - San Joaquin County

	SIC	EMP	PHONE	ENTRY #
The Woodbridge Golf Cntry CLB	7997	D	209 369-2371	19106

WOODLAKE, CA - Tulare County

	SIC	EMP	PHONE	ENTRY #
Gold Coast Farms LLC	0181	E	559 564-6316	285
Pete Santellan	0761	C	559 564-3748	678

WOODLAND, CA - Yolo County

	SIC	EMP	PHONE	ENTRY #
Alcohol DRG Program Yolo Cnty	8093	E	530 666-8650	22652
Apria Healthcare LLC	8099	D	530 669-6441	22890
AT&T Corp	4812	D	530 661-7724	5270
Broward Builders Inc	1542	D	530 406-1815	1511
Butterfield Electric Inc	1731	C	530 666-2116	2542
Butterfield Electric Inc (PA)	1731	D	530 666-2116	2543
Calgene LLC	0161	C	530 753-6313	45
Campos Dmetrio Frm Labor Contr	7361	D	530 662-4143	14619
City of Woodland	7999	C	530 661-5878	19184
City of Woodland	8744	C	530 661-5962	27779

GEOGRAPHIC SECTION

WOODLAND HILLS, CA

	SIC	EMP	PHONE	ENTRY #
City of Woodland	8711	D	530 661-5961	25744
County of Yolo	8093	D	530 666-8630	22715
CPI Econco Division (DH)	7629	D	530 662-7553	17931
Dignity Health	8011	C	530 666-8828	19500
E & E Co Ltd	1521	A	530 669-5991	1169
Half Moon Fruit & Produce Co (PA)	0161	E	530 662-1727	72
Home Instead Senior Care	8082	E	707 678-2005	22468
Interpac Technologies Inc	7389	D	530 662-6363	17248
Joe Heidrick Enterprises Inc	0115	E	530 662-2339	7
Joe Muller and Sons	0111	D	530 662-0105	1
Liberty Packing Company LLC (PA)	5148	C	209 826-7100	8746
Lions Club House	8322	E	530 661-3104	24068
Mann Lake Ltd	5191	E	530 662-4061	9143
Mendocino Railway	4731	C	530 666-9646	5121
Monsanto Company	5148	B	530 669-6224	8752
North American Health Care	8741	D	530 662-9193	27144
Nugget Market Inc	4225	C	530 662-5479	4607
Oscar Valero	0191	E	530 668-4342	385
Palm Grdns Rsdntial Care Fclty	8361	E	530 661-0574	24762
Payne Brothers Ranches	0161	E	530 662-2354	87
S P Richards Company	5112	C	916 564-5891	8179
Seminis Vegetable Seeds Inc	5191	E	530 669-6903	9152
Sierra Entertainment	4011	E	530 666-9646	3617
St Johns Retirement Village (PA)	8059	D	530 662-9674	21384
St Johns Retirement Village	8062	D	530 662-9674	21916
Sunfoods LLC (HQ)	5141	D	530 661-0578	8528
Sutter Health	8322	B	530 406-5600	24243
Sutter Health	8011	D	530 406-5600	20095
Sutter Hlth Scrmnto Sierra Reg	8011	A	530 406-5616	20116
Target Corporation	4226	B	530 666-3705	4704
Tc Property Mgt A Californi	6799	D	530 666-5799	12348
Travis Credit Union	6061	B	800 877-8328	9642
United Health Systems Inc	8051	C	530 662-9161	20999
Walgreen Co	4225	D	530 406-7700	4664
Woodland Healthcare	8062	C	530 668-2600	22035
Woodland Jint Unified Schl Dst	4151	E	530 662-0201	3953
Woodland Residential Services	6513	D	530 419-0059	11231
Woodland Sklled Nursing Fclty	8051	D	530 668-1190	21062
Woodland Swim Team Bosters CLB	8641	D	530 662-9783	25405

WOODLAND HILLS, CA - Los Angeles County

	SIC	EMP	PHONE	ENTRY #
21st Century Insurance Company (DH)	6411	A	877 310-5687	10575
21st Century Lf & Hlth Co Inc (PA)	6321	D	818 887-4436	10230
7410 Woodman Avenue LLC	6513	D	805 496-4336	11078
8020 Consulting LLC	8748	E	818 523-3201	27804
Advanced Critical Care Emerge	0742	D	818 887-2262	612
All Action Security Inc	7381	E	800 482-7371	16540
Alliant Asset MGT Co LLC (PA)	6531	D	818 668-2805	11292
Allied Industries Inc (PA)	8748	C	818 781-2490	27827
Amwins Insurance Brkg Cal LLC (HQ)	6411	D	818 772-1774	10601
Andwin Corporation (PA)	5113	D	818 999-2828	8185
AON Consulting Inc	6411	D	562 345-4700	10611
Arrow Electronics Inc	5065	D	818 932-1022	7524
Assertive Security Services &	7382	A	818 888-2405	16867
Associated Foreign Exch Inc (HQ)	6099	D	888 307-2339	9708
Assocted Fgn Exch Holdings Inc (PA)	6099	D	818 386-2702	9709
Automatic Data Processing Inc	7374	C	661 631-1456	16101
Automobile Club Southern Cal	8699	E	818 883-2660	25500
Avnet Inc	5065	D	818 594-8310	7529
B C Life & Health Insurance Co	6321	D	818 703-2345	10237
B Riley Financial Inc (PA)	7389	C	818 884-3737	17017
Bank America National Assn	6021	D	818 577-2000	9333
Benefitvision Inc	8331	D	818 348-3100	24313
Blackline Inc	7371	B	818 223-9008	15058
Blackline Systems Inc (PA)	7372	C	818 746-4700	15601
Blh Construction Company	1522	C	818 905-3837	1297
Boething Treeland Farms Inc (PA)	0811	D	818 883-1222	1005
Brenner Info Tech Staffing Inc	7361	E	818 705-7500	14616
Caine & Weiner Company Inc (PA)	7322	B	818 226-6000	14020
California Physicians Service	6324	B	818 598-8000	10267
California Preferred Bldrs Inc	1521	E	818 402-3345	1150
Canoga Hotel Corporation	7011	C	818 595-1000	12485
Center For Autism & (PA)	8049	C	818 345-2345	20313
Centrelink Insur & Fincl Svcs	7389	D	818 587-2001	17062
Chameleon Group Inc	7381	C	818 734-8448	16595
Child Development Institute	8322	D	818 888-4559	23735
Classmates Media Corporation	7299	B	818 287-3600	13747
Cohnreznick LLP	8721	D	818 205-2600	26312
Conduit Lngage Specialists Inc	7299	D	859 299-3178	13748
Corptax	7371	D	818 316-2400	15111
Courtyard Management Corp	7011	D	818 999-2200	12548
Creative Events Enterprises	8742	C	818 610-7000	27396
Custom Design Co Inc	1521	E	818 507-5959	1163
Dassault Systemes Americas	7371	C	818 999-2500	15120
Digital Communications Network (PA)	4812	D	818 227-3333	5393
Dunn & Berger Inc	8082	B	818 986-1234	22427

	SIC	EMP	PHONE	ENTRY #
Environmental Construction Inc	1542	D	818 449-8920	1550
Ev Ray Inc	5023	E	818 346-5381	6859
Factory Mutual Insurance Co	6331	D	818 227-2200	10414
Farmers Group Inc (HQ)	6331	A	323 932-3200	10415
Farmers Group Inc	6411	D	888 327-6335	10708
Farmers Group Inc	6411	A	805 583-7400	10709
Farmers Insurance Exchange (PA)	6311	A	323 932-3200	10208
Film Roman Llc	7812	C	818 748-4000	18083
Film Roman LLC	7812	C	818 748-4000	18084
Firstfed Financial Corp	6021	A	562 618-0573	9399
Fountain Court Essex	6531	E	818 227-2100	11542
Goetzman Group Inc (PA)	8742	D	818 595-1112	27450
Greystar Management Svcs LP	6531	A	818 596-2180	11562
Guarachi Wine Partners Inc	5182	D	818 225-5100	9104
Harris Direct	7389	D	818 357-2040	17208
Health Net Inc	6324	D	818 676-5603	10280
Health Net Inc (HQ)	6324	C	818 676-6000	10281
Health Net California Inc (DH)	6324	C	818 676-6775	10286
Health Net Community Solutions	6324	D	818 676-6000	10287
Health Net Life Insurance Co	6324	B	800 865-6288	10289
Hilton Woodland Hills & Towers	7011	B	818 595-1000	12714
HP Inc	7373	C	818 227-5033	15961
Hsbc Finance Corporation	6162	D	818 999-9175	9858
Image Entertainment Inc (HQ)	7822	D	818 407-9100	18275
Infinite Home Health Inc	8082	D	818 888-7772	22483
Innovative Merch Solutions LLC	8742	C	818 936-7800	27478
Inter/Media Time Buying Corp (PA)	7311	E	818 995-1455	13865
Interquantum LLC	6211	E	818 455-4434	10016
Intuit Inc	8721	D	818 436-7800	26379
Invitation Homes	6512	D	805 372-2900	11007
John Alden Life Insurance Co	6311	D	818 595-7600	10211
Joseph C Sansone Company (PA)	8111	D	818 226-3400	23332
Kaiser Foundation Hospitals	8062	A	818 719-2000	21631
Kaiser Foundation Hospitals	8062	D	818 592-3100	21657
Kaiser Foundation Hospitals	6324	D	888 515-3500	10316
Kellogg Andlson Accntancy Corp (PA)	8721	D	818 971-5100	26382
Kern Organization Inc	7311	D	818 703-8775	13874
Kpmg LLP	8721	D	818 227-6900	26390
Law Offices Berglund & Johnson (PA)	8111	D	951 276-4783	23377
Lewis Marenstein Wicke Sherwin	8111	E	818 703-6000	23392
Lifecare Assurance Company	6321	C	818 887-4436	10244
LLP Moss Adams	8721	D	818 577-1822	26397
Markel Corp	6411	B	818 595-0600	10769
Markel West Inc	6411	E	818 595-0600	10770
Marriott International Inc	7011	D	818 887-4800	12966
Mediscan Diagnostic Svcs LLC	8099	D	818 758-4224	22998
Medpoint Management Inc	8011	E	818 702-0100	19740
Motion Picture and TV Fund (PA)	8062	A	818 876-1777	21753
Netapp Inc	7373	C	818 227-5025	16005
Netzero Inc (DH)	7371	C	805 418-2000	15328
Neversoft Entertainment Inc	7371	C	818 610-4100	15329
New Mediscan II LLC	8099	D	818 662-0105	23006
Nmms Twin Peaks LLC	6531	D	818 710-6100	11709
Novastar Post Inc	7812	D	323 467-5020	18122
Omnikron Systems Inc	7379	D	818 591-7890	16443
Pacific Lodge Youth Services	8361	D	818 347-1577	24759
Pacific Protection Services	7381	C	818 313-9369	16755
Panavision Inc (PA)	7359	B	818 316-1000	14565
Physicians Choice LLC	8721	D	818 340-9988	26422
Pinnacle Contracting Corp	1542	E	818 888-6548	1637
Pro-Tek Consulting (PA)	7379	C	805 807-5571	16462
Prober & Raphael A Law Corp	8111	D	818 227-0100	23519
Pta CA Congress of Parents	8641	E	818 340-6700	25318
Qualified Benefits Inc	6411	E	818 594-4900	10848
R & B Realty Group	6513	D	818 710-5400	11192
Ramkade Insurance Services	6411	D	818 444-1340	10852
Reachlocal Inc (HQ)	7311	C	818 274-0260	13907
Real Software Systems LLC (PA)	7372	E	818 313-8000	15825
Realty Alliance Inc	6163	D	818 610-0080	9947
Ricoh Usa Inc	5044	D	213 629-1838	7067
Ricoh Usa Inc	5044	E	818 703-0265	7069
Robany Inc	8742	D	818 721-2150	27621
Rodeo Realty Inc	6531	D	818 999-2030	11821
Russon Financial Services Inc	8742	D	818 999-2800	27629
Santa Mnica Mntins Trls Cncil	8641	D	818 222-4531	25340
Scherzer International Corp (PA)	7389	D	818 227-2770	17478
Singerlewak LLP	8721	D	818 999-3924	26444
Solar Energy LLC	1711	D	818 449-5816	2372
Southern Cal Prmnnte Med Group	8011	E	818 592-3038	20040
Spad Holdings LLC	7991	D	818 710-7606	18692
Splash Entertainment LLC	7812	D	818 999-0062	18157
State Farm Mutl Auto Insur Co	6411	D	818 887-1060	10893
Top Tier Consulting	8742	D	818 338-2121	27689
Topanga Villas Company	6513	D	818 884-8017	11214
Tr Warner Center LP	7011	B	818 887-4800	13352

Employment Codes: A=Over 500 employees, B=251-500, C=101-250, D=51-100, E=45-50

2017 Directory of California Wholesalers and Services Companies

© Mergent Inc. 1-800-342-5647

WOODLAND HILLS, CA

	SIC	EMP	PHONE	ENTRY #
Truck Underwriters Association	6311	A	323 932-3200	10226
Ullmen Associates LLC	8748	D	310 444-3915	28085
United Cp/S Chldrns Fndn La	8059	D	818 782-2211	21400
United Ribbon Company Inc	5112	D	818 716-1515	8182
Universal Protection Svc LP	7381	D	818 227-1240	16842
USI of Southern California Ins	6411	E	818 251-3000	10918
Venbrook Insurance Svcs LLC **(PA)**	6411	D	818 598-8900	10923
Viking River Cruises Inc **(HQ)**	4724	D	818 227-1234	4982
W M Klorman Construction Corp	1542	D	818 591-5969	1712
Wells Fargo Advisors LLC	6211	D	818 226-2222	10101
West Valley Area Squad Club	8399	C	818 888-0980	24997
Willits Perpetual LLC	7389	D	818 668-6800	17627
Zenith Insurance Company **(DH)**	6331	B	818 713-1000	10485

WOODSIDE, CA - San Mateo County

	SIC	EMP	PHONE	ENTRY #
Filoli Center	8422	D	650 364-8300	25062
Skyline Consulting Group	8742	C	650 529-3455	27651

WRIGHTWOOD, CA - San Bernardino County

	SIC	EMP	PHONE	ENTRY #
MHRP Resort Inc	7011	D	760 249-5808	12993
Mountain High Resort Assoc LLC	6531	A	760 249-5808	11694

YERMO, CA - San Bernardino County

	SIC	EMP	PHONE	ENTRY #
AT&T Corp	4813	D	909 381-7378	5504

YORBA LINDA, CA - Orange County

	SIC	EMP	PHONE	ENTRY #
Alliance Rvrside Hsptality LLC	7011	E	949 229-3168	12380
American Golf Corporation	7997	D	714 779-2461	18857
Black Gold Golf Club	7992	D	714 961-0060	18717
Brewsters Automotive Inc	7538	D	714 528-4683	17786
Carefusion Corporation	8099	D	800 231-2466	22911
Coldwell Bnkr Residential Brkg	6531	E	714 832-0020	11431
Dsh West Inc	7336	D	714 692-8777	14143
Eastern Star Homes California **(PA)**	8322	D	714 986-2380	23953
First Team RE - Orange Cnty	6531	D	714 223-2143	11529
Food Management Associates Inc	8742	E	714 694-2828	27437
Homes By Shabbir Kazi	1521	E	714 524-4131	1190
Hulk Construction	1795	D	714 701-9458	3456
IMG **(PA)**	7389	E	714 974-1700	17234
Kaiser Foundation Hospitals	8011	E	714 685-3520	19659
Loma Vista Nursery	5193	D	714 779-5583	9197
Mesa Contracting Corporation	1611	C	714 974-7300	1825
Metropolitan Water District	4941	D	714 528-7231	6374
Nasser Company Inc **(PA)**	5141	D	714 279-2100	8505
Professnal Rgistry Netwrk Corp	7361	C	714 394-4071	14736
Reeves Tractor Service Inc	1611	D	714 692-4020	1849
Robert Moreno Insurance Svcs	6411	C	714 525-5168	10856
Southern Cal Prmnnte Med Group	8011	E	714 685-3520	20035
Sprouts Farmers Market Inc	5141	C	714 572-3535	8526
St Jude Heritage Medical Group	8011	D	714 528-4211	20057
Stanton Holdings Americas	7389	E	714 689-9551	17501
Ta-Kai Home Care Inc	8082	D	714 393-4586	22578
V-Tek Systems Corporation	7373	D	909 396-5355	16074
Vident	5047	D	714 221-6700	7326
Yamazen Inc	5084	D	800 882-8558	7908
Yorba Properties Corp	6531	D	714 777-5112	11930

YOSEMITE NTPK, CA - Mariposa County

	SIC	EMP	PHONE	ENTRY #
DNC Prks Rsrts At Yosemite Inc	7011	A	209 372-1001	12581

YOUNTVILLE, CA - Napa County

	SIC	EMP	PHONE	ENTRY #
Bazan Mario AG Services & Vine	0172	D	707 945-0718	142
Remington Ldging Hsptality LLC	7011	A	877 932-5333	13139
Villagio Inn & Spa LLC	7991	C	707 944-8877	18701
Vintners Golf Club	7992	E	707 944-1992	18797

YREKA, CA - Siskiyou County

	SIC	EMP	PHONE	ENTRY #
Belcampo Butchery	7299	E	530 842-5200	13737
County of Siskiyou	8322	D	530 841-2700	23919

	SIC	EMP	PHONE	ENTRY #
R C O Reforesting Inc	0851	E	530 842-7647	1016
Scott Valley Bank **(HQ)**	6022	D	530 623-2732	9524
Siskiyou Hospital Inc	8062	B	530 842-4121	21894
Siskiyou Opportunity Center	7361	D	530 842-4110	14787
Southern Oregon Goodwill Inds	8331	D	530 842-6627	24390
Stidham Trucking Inc	4213	C	530 842-4161	4266

YUBA CITY, CA - Sutter County

	SIC	EMP	PHONE	ENTRY #
Alta Cal Regional Ctr Inc	8322	B	530 674-3070	23652
Ampla Health **(PA)**	8021	C	530 674-4261	20245
AT&T Corp	4813	D	530 822-2700	5483
Bi-County Ambulance Service	4119	D	530 674-2780	3773
Bianchi Ag Services Inc	0762	D	530 923-7675	694
Butte-Yb-Stter Wtr Qlty Cltion	4221	D	530 673-5131	4481
Carl J Woods Construction Inc	1629	E	530 674-7877	2037
Cellco Partnership	4812	D	530 674-8007	5375
County of Sutter	8093	C	530 822-7250	22714
E Center	8351	C	530 634-1200	24457
Easter Seal Soc Superior Cal	8322	D	530 673-4585	23950
Express Personnel Services	7363	D	530 671-9202	14875
Freemont Rideout Health Group	8011	D	530 751-4000	19529
Freemont Rideout Health Group	8062	E	530 749-4386	21569
Gene M Accito	0139	D	530 674-3179	24
Golden 1 Credit Union	6061	B	877 465-3361	9603
Hilbers Inc	1542	D	530 673-2947	1571
Lamon Construction Company Inc	1542	E	530 671-1370	1599
New Legend Inc	4213	C	530 674-3100	4234
Northgate Terrace Apts	6513	D	530 671-2026	11176
R B Spencer Inc	1711	D	530 674-8307	2336
Sears Roebuck and Co	7549	D	530 751-4628	17893
Sierra Central Credit Union **(PA)**	6062	D	530 671-3009	9689
Sierra Gold Nurseries Inc	0181	D	530 674-1145	318
Sutter Health	8011	C	530 749-3585	20109
Sutter N Med Group A Prof Corp **(PA)**	8011	D	530 749-3661	20118
Sutter North Med Foundation **(PA)**	8011	D	530 741-1300	20119
Sutter North Med Foundation	8011	D	530 749-3635	20120
Sutter North Med Foundation	8011	D	530 749-3450	20122
Sutter Surgical Hospital N Vly	8062	C	530 749-5700	21955
Thiara Sukhwant	0721	E	530 673-1581	485
Tri County Respite Care Svc	8322	D	530 755-3500	24258
Trueblue Inc	7363	C	530 755-3291	14963
United Com Serve	8051	D	530 790-3000	20998
United Landscape Resource Inc	0782	D	530 671-1029	972
Valley Aggregate Transport Inc	4212	D	530 821-2600	4084
Yuba City Nursing & Rehab LLC	8051	D	530 671-0550	21064
Yuba City Racquet Club Inc	7997	D	530 673-6900	19128

YUCAIPA, CA - San Bernardino County

	SIC	EMP	PHONE	ENTRY #
Avenue H LLC	8051	D	909 795-2476	20401
B B G Management Group **(PA)**	5145	E	909 797-9581	8609
Braswells Yucaipa Valley C	8051	D	909 795-2476	20415
Kad Paving Company	1611	D	909 790-3366	1807
Veterans of Foreign Wars of US	8641	D	909 797-1898	25391
Winegardner Masonry Inc	1741	C	909 795-9711	2841
Yucaipa Valley Water District **(PA)**	4941	D	909 797-5117	6409

YUCCA VALLEY, CA - San Bernardino County

	SIC	EMP	PHONE	ENTRY #
A & W Maintenance	1521	D	310 619-8694	1118
A-1 Elite Painting Inc	1721	E	760 365-6702	2425
Catalyst Development Corp	7372	D	760 228-9653	15616
County of San Bernardino	8322	D	760 228-5234	23895
Desert Manor Care Center LP	8361	D	760 365-0717	24630
National Vision Inc	8042	D	760 365-7350	20301
Yucca Valley Fire Protection	7389	E	760 365-3335	17638